BECKETT®

THE #1 AUTHORITY ON COLLECTIBLES

FOOTBALL PRICE GUIDE

NUMBER 36

THE HOBBY'S MOST RELIABLE AND RELIED UPON SOURCE™

Founder: Dr. James Beckett III
Edited by the staff of Beckett Football

Prices in this guide reflect current retail rates determined just prior to printing. They do not reflect for-sale prices by the author, publisher, distributors, advertisers, or any card dealers associated with this guide. Every effort has been made to eliminate errors. Readers are invited to write us noting any errors which may be researched and corrected in subsequent printings. The publisher will not be held responsible for losses which may occur in the sale or purchase of cards because of information contained herein.

BECKETT is a registered trademark of BECKETT MEDIA LLC, DALLAS, TEXAS
Manufactured in the United States of America | Published by Beckett Media LLC

Beckett Media LLC
4635 McEwen Dr., Dallas, TX 75244
(972) 991-6657 • www.beckett.com

First Printing
ISBN: 978-1-936681-27-3

COVER PHOTO: GETTY IMAGES

CONTENTS

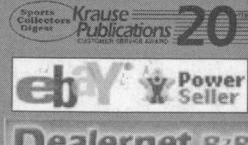

HOW TO USE AND CONDITION GUIDE

HOW TO USE

Every year this book gets bigger and better with all the new sets coming out and this edition has been enhanced and expanded from the previous volume with new releases, updated prices, and additions to older listings. The Beckett Guide has been successful where other attempts have failed because it is complete, current, and valid. The prices were added to the card lists just prior to printing and reflect not the author's opinions or desires but the going retail prices for each card, based on the marketplace (sports memorabilia conventions and shows, sports card shops, on-line computer trading, auction results, and other firsthand reports of realized prices).

To facilitate proper use of this book, please read the complete introductory section before going to the pricing pages, especially the sections on grading and card conditions.

ADVERTISING

Within this Price Guide you will find advertisements for sports memorabilia material, mail order, and retail sports collectibles establishments. All advertisements were accepted in good faith based on the reputation of the advertiser; however neither the author, the publisher, the distributors, nor the other advertisers in this Price Guide accept any responsibility for any particular advertiser not complying with the terms of his or her ad.

HOW TO COLLECT

PRESERVING YOUR CARDS

Cards are fragile so they must be handled properly in order to retain their value. Careless handling can easily result in damaged cards and lower values. Although there are many collectors who use boxes to store their cards, plastic sheets or single card sleeves and plastic holders are the preferred methods for storing cards. Most card shops and websites (such as Beckett.com), and virtually all card shows, will have these plastic storage materials available for you.

COLLECTING VS. INVESTING

Collecting individual players and complete sets are popular methods for both investment and speculation. There is obviously no guarantee in this book, or anywhere else for that matter, that cards will outperform the stock market or other investment alternatives in the future. After all, football cards do not pay quarterly dividends and cards are not nearly as liquid as stocks or bonds. Nevertheless, investors have sometimes experienced favorable long-term trends in past performance of hot sports collectibles and certain cards have outperformed many traditional investments in some years. Many hobbyists maintain that the best investment is and always will be the building of a collection and the more you learn about your collection and the hobby the better you're likely to make decisions. We're not providing investment tips, but simple information about the current value of football cards. It's up to you to use that information to your best advantage.

UNDERSTANDING CARD VALUES

Why are some cards more valuable than others? Obviously, the economic laws of supply and demand are applicable to card collecting just as they are to any other field where a commodity is bought, sold or traded in a free, unregulated market.

Supply (the number of cards available on the market) is often less than the total number of cards originally produced since attrition tends to diminish that original quantity. Each year a percentage of cards is typically thrown away, destroyed or otherwise lost to collectors. This percentage is much, much smaller today than it was in the past because more and more people have become increasingly aware of the value of cards.

Demand is never equal for all sets so price correlations can be complicated. The demand for a card is influenced by many factors including: (1) the age of the card; (2) the attributes attached to it like autographs or memorabilia; (3) the player(s) portrayed; (4) the attractiveness and popularity of the set; and (5) the physical condition of the card. In general, (1) the older the card, (2) the fewer cards printed, (3) the more famous, popular and talented the player, (4) the more attractive and popular the set, and (5) the better the condition of the card, the higher the value of the card will be. While those guidelines help to establish the value of a card, the countless exceptions and peculiarities make any simple, direct mathematical formula to determine card values impossible.

SET PRICES

A somewhat paradoxical situation exists in the price of a complete set vs. the combined cost of the individual cards in the set. In nearly every case, the sum of the prices for the individual cards is higher than the typical selling price for a complete set. This is prevalent especially in the cards of the past few years. The reasons for this apparent anomaly stem from the habits of collectors and from the carrying costs to dealers. Many collectors pick up only stars, superstars and particular teams. As a result, the dealer is left with a shortage of certain player cards and an abundance of others. He therefore incurs an expense in "carrying" these remainder cards in stock which discourages him from selling them at the same discount a bulk, or "set" sale might afford.

GRADING YOUR CARDS

Each hobby has its own grading terminology and collectors of sports cards are no exception. The one invariable criterion for determining the value of a card is its condition: the better the condition of the card, the more valuable it is. Card grading, however, is subjective. Individual card dealers and collectors often differ in the strictness of their grading, but the stated condition of a card should be determined without regard to whether it is being bought or sold. In the past fifteen years professional third party card grading services (like PSA, SGC, and BGS) have become a staple of the industry and are a valuable resource for collectors and dealers. Their grading scales, standards and terminology are used industry-wide and help to facilitate trade particularly when a transaction occurs by mail.

CENTERING

Current centering terminology typically uses numbers representing the percentage of border on either side of the main design. Obviously, centering is diminished in importance for borderless cards such as Stadium Club. A slightly off-center card (60/40) is one that upon close inspection is found to have one border bigger than the opposite border. This slight degree was once offensive to only purists, but now some hobbyists try to avoid cards that are anything but perfectly centered. Off-Center (70/30) cards have one border that is more than twice as wide as the opposite border. Badly Off-Center (80/20 or worse) and miscut cards have virtually no border on one side of the card which severely lowers the card's value.

CORNER WEAR

Corner wear is the most scrutinized grading criteria in the hobby. These are the major categories of corner wear:

Corner with a slight touch of wear: The corner still is sharp, but there is a slight touch of wear showing. On a dark-bordered card, this

shows as a dot of white.

Fuzzy corner: The corner still comes to a point, but the point has just begun to fray. A slightly "dinged" corner is considered the same as a fuzzy corner.

Slightly rounded corner: The fraying of the corner has increased to where there is only a hint of a point. Mild layering may be evident. A "dinged" corner is considered the same as a slightly rounded corner.

Rounded corner: The point is completely gone. Some layering is noticeable.

CREASES

A third common defect is creasing. The degree of creasing in a card is difficult to show in a drawing or picture but will greatly affect the card's value. Any creasing on the average modern era card will render it nearly worthless but three typical categories of severity found on some rare and vintage cards are:

Light Crease: a crease that is barely noticeable upon close inspection. In fact, when cards are in plastic sheets or holders, a light crease may not be seen. A light crease on the front is much more serious than a light crease on the card back only.

Medium Crease: A medium crease is fairly noticeable, but does not overly detract from the appearance of the card. It is an obvious crease, but not one that breaks the picture surface of the card.

Heavy Crease: A heavy crease is one that has torn or broken through the card's picture surface, e.g., puts a tear in the photo surface.

ALTERATIONS

Trimming: This occurs when someone alters the card in order (1) to shave off edge wear, (2) to improve the sharpness of the corners, or (3) to improve centering - obviously their objective is to falsely increase the perceived value of the card to an unsuspecting buyer. The shrinkage usually is evident only if the trimmed card is compared to an adjacent full-sized card or if the trimmed card is measured.

Retouched Borders: This occurs when the borders (especially on those cards with dark borders) are touched up on the edges and corners with magic marker or crayons of appropriate color in order to make the card appear to be Mint.

MISCELLANEOUS FLAWS

There are a number of minor flaws that, depending on severity, may lower a card's condition by one to four grades: bubbles (lumps in surface), gum and wax stains, diamond cutting (slanted borders), notching, off-centered backs, paper wrinkles, scratched-off cartoons or puzzles on back, rubber band marks, scratches, surface impressions and warping. The following are common serious flaws that, depending on severity, lower a card's condition at least four grades and often render it no better than Good: chemical or sun fading, erasure marks, mildew, miscutting (severe off-centering), holes, bleached or retouched borders, tape marks, tears, trimming, water or coffee stains and writing.

CONDITION GUIDE

Gem Mint (Gem Mt) - A card with no flaws or wear even under magnification. This grade is usually reserved for a card certified by a third party grading company.

Mint (Mt): A card with no noticeable flaws or wear. The card has four square corners, 60/40 or better centering from top to bottom and from left to right, original gloss, smooth edges and original color borders. A Mint card does not have distracting print spots, color or focus imperfections.

Near Mint-Mint (NrMt-Mt): A card with one minor flaw. Any one of the following would lower a Mint card to Near Mint-Mint: one corner with a slight touch of wear, barely noticeable print spots, color or focus imperfections. The card must have 60/40 or better centering in both directions, original gloss, smooth edges and original color borders.

Near Mint (NrMt): A card with one minor flaw. Any one of the following would lower a Mint card to Near Mint: one fuzzy corner or two to four corners with slight touches of wear, 70/30 to 60/40 centering, slightly rough edges, minor print spots, color or focus imperfections. The card must have original gloss and original color borders.

Excellent-Mint (ExMt): A card with two or three fuzzy, but not rounded, corners and centering no worse than 80/20. The card may have no more than two of the following: slightly rough edges, very slightly discolored borders, minor print spots, color or focus imperfections. The card must have original gloss.

Excellent (EX): A card with four fuzzy but not rounded corners and centering no worse than 80/20. The card may have a small amount of original gloss lost, rough edges, slightly discolored borders and minor print spots, color or focus imperfections.

Very Good (VG): A card that has been handled but not abused: slightly rounded corners with slight layering, slight notching on edges, a significant amount of gloss lost from the surface but no scuffing and moderate discoloration of borders. The card may have a few light creases.

Good (G), Fair (F), Poor (P): A well-worn, mishandled or abused card: badly rounded and layered corners, scuffing, most or all original gloss missing, seriously discolored borders, moderate or heavy creases, and one or more serious flaws. Good, Fair and Poor cards generally are used only as fillers.

SELLING YOUR CARDS

Just about every collector sells cards or will sell cards eventually. Someday you may be interested in selling your duplicates or maybe even your whole collection. You may sell to other collectors, friends or dealers. You may even sell cards you purchased from a certain dealer back to that same dealer. In any event, it helps to know some of the mechanics of the typical transaction between buyer and seller. Dealers will buy cards in order to resell them to other collectors who are interested in the cards. Dealers will always pay a higher percentage for items that (in their opinion) can be resold quickly, and a much lower percentage for those items that are perceived as having low demand and hence are slow moving. In either case, dealers must buy at a price that allows for the expense of doing business and a margin for profit.

If you have cards for sale, the best advice we can give is that you get several offers for your cards - either from card shops or at a card show - and take the best offer, all things considered. Note, the "best" offer may not be the one for the highest amount. And remember, if a dealer really wants your cards, he won't let you get away without making his best competitive offer. Another alternative is to place your cards in an auction as one or several lots.

Many people think nothing of going into a department store and paying $15 for an item of clothing for which the store paid $5. But if you were selling your $15 card to a dealer and he offered you $5 for it, you might think his mark-up unreasonable. To complete the analogy: most department stores (and card dealers) that consistently pay $10 for $15 items eventually go out of business. An exception is when the dealer has lined up a willing buyer for the item(s) you are attempting to sell, or if the cards are so Hot that it's likely he'll have to hold the cards for only a short period of time. In those cases, an offer of up to 75 percent of book value still will allow the dealer to make a reasonable profit considering the short time he will need to hold the merchandise. In general, however, most cards and collections will bring offers in the range of 25 to 50 percent of retail price. Also consider that most material from the past 20 to 30 years is plentiful. If that's what you're selling, don't be surprised if your best offer is well below that range.

ACKNOWLEDGEMENTS

A great deal of diligence, hard work, and dedicated effort went into this, our 36th Edition. The high standards to which we hold ourselves, however, could not have been met without the expert input and generous amount of time contributed by many people. Our sincere thanks are extended to each and every one of you.

Each year we refine the process of developing the most accurate and up-to-date information for this book. Thanks again to all of the contributors nationwide (listed below) as well as our staff here in Dallas.

A special thank you goes to the following contributors who made an extraordinary contribution to this year's book:

Pat Blandford, A.J. Firestone, Mike Hattley, Carl Lamendola, Steve Liskey, Morgan Moore, Jayson Morand, Mike Mosier, and Steve Taft.

At the risk of inadvertently overlooking or omitting the many other key contributors over the years, we would like to individually thank A & J Cards, Jonathan Abraham, Action Sports Cards, Jerry Adamic, Mehdi and Danny Alaei, Aliso Hills Stamp and Coin, Rich Altman, Neil Armstrong, Mike Aronstein, Chris Bak, Tom Barborich, Red Barnes, Bob Bawiel, William E. Baxendale, Dean Bedell, Jerry Bell, Patrick Benes, Bubba Bennett, Chuck Bennett, Carl Berg, Eric Berger, Kevin Bergson, Skip Bertman, Brian L. Bigelow, Lance Billingsley, David Bitar, Mike Blaisdell, Pat Blandford, Jeff Blatt, Mike Bonner, Bill Bossert, Terry Boyd, John Bradley (JOGO), Virgil Burns, Dave Byer, Mike Caffey, David Carenbauer, Dale Carlson, Bud Carter, Sally Carves, Ric Changdie, Dwight Chapin, Don Chubey, Howard Churchill, Ralph Ciarlo, Orr Cihlar, Mike Clark, Craig Coddling, Jon Cohen, Joe Colabella, Collector's Edge, Matt Collett, George Courter, Taylor Crane, Scott Crump, Jim Curie, Alan Custer, Paul Czuchna, Joe Davey, Steve Davidow, Samuel Davis, Tony Wayne Davis, Robert Der, Bill and Diane Dodge, Cliff Dolgins, Rick Donohoo, Patrick Dorsey, Vic Dougan, John Douglas, Joseph Drelich, John Durkos, Al Durso, E&R Galleries, Buck Easley, Ed Emmitt, The End Zone, Joe Ercole, Darrell Ereth, Doak Ewing, Rodney Faciane, Bob Farmer, Terry Faulkner, A.J. Firestone, Fleischman and Walsh, Fleer, Flickball, Gervise Ford, Craig Frank, Mark Franke, Ron Frasier, Steve Freedman, Tom Freeman, Richard Freiburghouse, Craig Friedemann, Larry and Jeff Fritsch, Brian Froehlich, Chris Gala, Mike Gallella, Steven Galletta, Tony Galovich, Gerry Gartland (The Gallagher Archives), Tom Giacchino, Dick Gilkeson, Michael R. Gionet, David Giove, Steve Glass, Steve Gold (AU Sports), Todd Goldenberg, Jeff Goldstein, Mike and Howard Gordon, Gregg Gornes, George Grauer, Joseph Griffin, Bob Grissett, Robert G. Gross, Hall's Nostalgia, Steve Hart, Michael Hattley, Rod Heffern, Kevin Heffner, Dennis Heitland, Jon Helfenstein, Jerry and Etta Hersh, Mike Hersh, Clay Hill, Gary Hlady, Geof Hollenbeck, Russ Hoover, Neil Hoppenworth, Nelson Hu, Don Hurry, John Inouye, Terrell Irwin, Barry Isak, Jeff Issler, Robert R. Jackson, Joe and Mike Jardina, Dan Jaskula, Terry Johnson, Craig Jones, Stewart Jones, Larry Jordon, Jeff Juhnke, Chuck Juliana, Loyd Jungling, Ed Kabala, Wayne Kleman, Andrew Kaiser, Jay and Mary Kasper, Frank and Rose Katen, Jack Kemps, Rick Keplinger, John Kilian, Ron Klassnik, Steve Kluback, Albert Klumpp, Don Knutsen, Raymond Kong, Bob and Bryan Kornfield, Terry Kreider, George Kruk, Thomas Kunnecke, Carl Lamendola, Dan Lavin, Scott Lawson, Walter Ledzki, Marc Lefkowitz, Tom Leon, Irv Lerner, Ed Lim, Lew Lipset, Frank Lopez, Neil Lopez, Joe Lucia, Frank Lucito, Kevin Lynch, Bud Lyle, Jim Macie, Gary Madrack, Paul Marchant, Adam Martin, Chris Martin (Chris Martin Enterprises), Alex McCollum, Bob McDonald, Michael McDonald, Steve McHenry, Mike McKee, Carlos Medina, Fernando Mercado, Joe Merkel, Chris Merrill, Blake Meyer, Lee Milazzo, Wayne Miller, Dick Millerd, Pat Mills, Ron Moermond, Morgan Moore, John Morales, Rev. Michael Moran, Jayson Morand, Michael Moretto, Brian Morris, Rusty Morse, Kyle Morton, Mike and Cindy Mosier, Dick Mueller, Roger Neufeldt, NFL Properties, Don Niemi, Raymond Ng, Steve Novella, Larry Nyeste, Mike O'Brien, Richard Ochoa, John O'Hara, Glenn Olsen, Mike Orth, Pacific Trading Cards, Andrew Pak, Chris Park, Clay Pasternack, Paul and Judy's, John Peavy, Mark Perna, Michael Perrotta, Steve Peters, Ira Petsrillo, Tom Pfirrmann, Playoff Corp, Arto Poladian, Steve Poland, Jack Pollard, Chris Pomerleau, Jeff Porter, Press Pass, Jeff Prillaman, Jonathan Pullano, Loran Pulver, Pat Quinn, Don and Tom Ras, Phil Regli, Owen Ricker, Gavin Riley, Carson Ritchey, Evelyn Roberts, Jim Roberts, Jeff Rogers, Mark Rose, Greg Rosen, Chip Rosenberg, Rotman Productions, Blake and Sheldon Rudman, John Rumierz, George Rusnak, Terry Ryan, Terry Sack, SAGE, Joe Sak, Barry Sanders, John Sandstrom, Kevin Savage, Nathan Schank, Mike Schechter (MSA), R.J. Schulhof, Perry Schwartzberg, Patrick W. Scoggin, Dan Scolman, Rick Scruggs, Burns Searfoss, Eric Shillito, Shinder's Cards, Bob Singer, Sam Sliheet, John Smith, Keith Smith, Rick Smith, Gerry Sobie, Don Spagnolo, John Spalding, John Spano, Carl Specht, Nigel Spill, Sportcards Etc., Vic Stanley, Bill Steinberg, Cary Stephenson, Murvin Sterling Dan Stickney, Jack Stowe, Del Stracke, Richard Strobino, Kevin Struss, Bob Swick, Steve Taft, George Tahinos, Richard Tattoli, Paul S. Taylor, Lee Temanson, Jeff Thomas, Rodney Thomas, Tatoo Thomas, TK Legacy, Bud Tompkins, Steve Tormollen, Topps, Greg Tranter, John Tumazos, Upper Deck, U-Trading Cards (Mike Livingston), Eric Valkys, Wayne Varner, Kevin M. VanderKelen, Rob Veres, Bill Vizas, Tom Wall, Mike Wasserman, Keith Watson, Mark Watson, Brian Wentz, Dale Wesolewski, Bill Wesslund, Mike Wheat, Joe White, Rick Wilson, John Wirtanen, Wizards of the Coast, Jay Wolt, Paul Wright, Darryl Yee, Sheraton Yee, Kit Young, Eugene Zalewski, Robert Zanze, Steve Zeller, Dean Zindler, and Tim Zwick.

Every year we make active solicitations for expert input. We are particularly appreciative of the help (however extensive or cursory) provided for this volume. We receive many inquiries, comments and questions regarding material within this book. In fact, each and every one is read and digested. Time constraints, however, prevent us from personally replying. But keep sharing your knowledge. Even though we cannot respond to each letter, you are making significant contributions to the hobby through your interest and comments.

The effort to continually refine and improve our books also involves a growing number of people and types of expertise on our home team. Our company boasts a substantial Sports Data Publishing team, which strengthens our ability to provide comprehensive analysis of the marketplace.

Our price guide team played a major part in compiling this year's book through dedicated efforts to compile the most complete and accurate checklists and pricing data available. The majority of additions, corrections, and changes to this edition were made by Beckett football senior market analyst Justin Grunert and information analyst Jeff Camay. Their efforts were ably assisted by Brian Fleischer (department manager) and the rest of the price guide team: Matt Bible, Eric Norton, Sam Zimmer, Steve Dalton, and Kristian Redulla. Finally, Surajpal Singh Bisht and Hemant Tiwari were responsible for layout of the book. The reason this book looks as good as it does is due to their hard work and expertise.

In the years since this guide debuted, Beckett Media has grown beyond any rational expectation. Many talented and hardworking individuals have been instrumental in this growth and success. Our whole team is to be congratulated for what we have accomplished.

1994 A1 Masters of the Grill

Sponsored by A.1. Steak Sauce, this 28-card standard-size set is actually a recipe card set. Inside gold and black borders, the fronts display a football player wearing his team's jersey, an apron, a hat with A.1. on it, and holding either A.1. steak sauce or barbeque utensils. The player's facsimile autograph appears in one of the upper corners, with player's name and team name immediately below. The backs present a picture of a prepared dish as well as recipe instructions for its preparing the food. The cards are unnumbered and checklisted below in alphabetical order.

COMPLETE SET (28)	10.00	25.00
1 Harris Barton	.40	1.00
2 Jerome Bettis	1.25	3.00
3 Ray Childress	.40	1.00
4 Eugene Chung	.30	.75
5 Jamie Dukes	.30	.75
6 Steve Emtman	.30	.75
7 Burt Grossman	.30	.75
8 Courtney Hall	.30	.75
9 Ken Harvey	.40	1.00
10 Chris Hinton	.30	.75
11 Kent Hull	.30	.75
12 Keith Jackson	.50	1.25
13 Rickey Jackson	.40	1.00
14 Cortez Kennedy	.50	1.25
15 Tim Krumrie	.30	.75
16 Jeff Lageman	.30	.75
17 Greg Lloyd	.50	1.25
18 Howie Long	.60	1.50
19 Hardy Nickerson	.40	1.00
20 Bart Oates	.30	.75
21 Ken Ruettgers	.30	.75
22 Dan Saleaumua	.30	.75
23 Alonzo Spellman	.40	1.00
24 Eric Swann	.50	1.25
25 Pat Swilling	.40	1.00
26 Tommy Vardell	.40	1.00
27 Erik Williams	.40	1.00
28 Gary Zimmerman	.30	.75

1995 Absolute Previews

10 Jeff Blake	1.50	4.00

1995 Absolute

This 200-card standard-size set was released both through hobby and retail packaging. The hobby product was called Absolute while the retail product was titled Prime. The hobby boxes contained 24 packs per box with eight cards per pack. Cards 179-200 are dedicated to a draft pick subset. These "Absolute" draft pick cards are easy to differentiate from the regular cards as the words "Draft Picks" are emblazoned in large letters at the bottom of the card. In between the words "Draft Picks", the player is identified in white lettering against a black background. The "Prime" cards features full-bleed photos. The player is identified in the upper right corner and the words "Prime Playoff" are in the lower left corner. Against a yellowish background, the backs feature a player photo, some information as well as seasonal and career stats. Two special cards of both Tony Boselli and Kerry Collins were also inserted into both types of packs. Boselli cards were DP1G for the gold version and DP1S for the silver and Collins cards were DP2G for the gold and DP2S for the silver. Rookie Cards include Jeff Blake, Ki-Jana Carter, Kerry Collins, Joey Galloway, Napoleon Kaufman, Steve McNair, Rashaan Salaam, J.J. Stokes, Michael Westbrook and Tyrone Wheatley.

COMPLETE SET (200)	7.50	20.00
1 John Elway	.75	2.00
2 Reggie White	.15	.40
3 Errict Rhett	.07	.20
4 Deion Sanders	.20	.50
5 Rocket Ismail	.07	.20
6 Jerome Bettis	.15	.40
7 Randall Cunningham	.15	.40
8 Mario Bates	.07	.20
9 Dave Brown	.07	.20
10 Stan Humphries	.07	.20
11 Drew Bledsoe	.25	.60
12 Neil O'Donnell	.07	.20
13 Dan Marino	.75	2.00
14 Larry Centers	.07	.20
15 Craig Heyward	.07	.20
16 Bruce Smith	.15	.40
17 Erik Kramer	.02	.10
18 Jeff Blake RC	.40	1.00
19 Vinny Testaverde	.07	.20
20 Barry Sanders	.60	1.50
21 Boomer Esiason	.07	.20
22 Emmitt Smith	.60	1.50
23 Warren Moon	.07	.20
24 Junior Seau	.15	.40
25 Heath Shuler	.07	.20
26 Jackie Harris	.02	.10
27 Terance Mathis	.07	.20
28 Raymont Harris	.02	.10
29 Jim Kelly	.15	.40
30 Dan Wilkinson	.07	.20
31 Herman Moore	.15	.40
32 Shannon Sharpe	.07	.20
33 Antonio Langham	.02	.10
34 Charles Haley	.07	.20
35 Brett Favre	.75	2.00
36 Marshall Faulk	.50	1.25
37 Neil Smith	.07	.20
38 Harvey Williams	.02	.10
39 Johnny Bailey	.02	.10
40 O.J. McDuffie	.15	.40
41 David Palmer	.07	.20
42 Willie McGinest	.07	.20
43 Quinn Early	.07	.20
44 Johnny Johnson	.02	.10
45 Derek Brown TE	.02	.10
46 Charlie Garner	.15	.40
47 Byron Bam Morris	.02	.10
48 Natrone Means	.07	.20
49 Ken Norton Jr	.07	.20
50 Troy Aikman	.40	1.00
51 Reggie Brooks	.07	.20
52 Trent Dilfer	.15	.40
53 Cortez Kennedy	.07	.20
54 Chuck Levy	.02	.10
55 Jeff George	.07	.20
56 Steve Young	.30	.75
57 Lewis Tillman	.02	.10
58 Carl Pickens	.07	.20
59 Brett Perriman	.07	.20
60 Jay Novacek	.07	.20
61 Greg Hill	.07	.20
62 James Jett	.07	.20
63 Terry Kirby	.07	.20
64 Qadry Ismail	.07	.20
65 Ben Coates	.07	.20
66 Kevin Greene	.07	.20
67 Bryant Young	.07	.20
68 Brian Mitchell	.02	.10
69 Steve Walsh	.02	.10
70 Darnay Scott	.07	.20
71 Daryl Johnston	.07	.20
72 Glyn Milburn	.02	.10
73 Tim Brown	.15	.40
74 Isaac Bruce	.30	.75
75 Bernie Parmalee	.07	.20
76 Terry Allen	.07	.20
77 Jim Everett	.02	.10
78 Thomas Lewis	.07	.20
79 Vaughn Hebron	.02	.10
80 Rod Woodson	.07	.20
81 Rick Mirer	.07	.20
82 Dana Stubblefield	.07	.20
83 Bert Emanuel	.15	.40
84 Andre Reed	.07	.20
85 Jeff Graham	.02	.10
86 Johnnie Morton	.07	.20
87 LeShon Johnson	.07	.20
88 Michael Irvin	.15	.40
89 Derrick Alexander WR	.15	.40
90 Lake Dawson	.07	.20
91 Cody Carlson	.02	.10
92 Chris Warren	.07	.20
93 William Floyd	.07	.20
94 Charles Johnson	.07	.20
95 Roosevelt Potts	.02	.10
96 Cris Carter	.15	.40
97 Aaron Glenn	.02	.10
98 Curtis Conway	.15	.40
99 Kevin Williams WR	.07	.20
100 Jerry Rice	.40	1.00
101 Frank Reich	.02	.10
102 Harold Green	.02	.10
103 Russell Copeland	.02	.10
104 Rob Moore	.07	.20
105 Edgar Bennett	.07	.20
106 Darren Carrington	.02	.10
107 Tommy Maddox	.15	.40
108 Dave Meggett	.02	.10
109 Fred Barnett	.07	.20
110 Mark Seay	.07	.20
111 Gus Frerotte	.07	.20
112 Brent Jones	.02	.10
113 Chris Miller	.02	.10
114 Cedric Tillman	.02	.10
115 Mark Ingram	.02	.10
116 Eric Turner	.02	.10
117 Mark Carrier WR	.07	.20
118 Garrison Hearst	.15	.40
119 Craig Erickson	.02	.10
120 Derek Russell	.02	.10
121 Mike Sherrard	.02	.10
122 Horace Copeland	.02	.10
123 Jack Trudeau	.02	.10
124 Leroy Hoard	.02	.10
125 Gary Brown	.02	.10
126 Mel Gray	.02	.10
127 Steve Beuerlein	.07	.20
128 Marcus Allen	.15	.40
129 Irving Fryar	.07	.20
130 Marion Butts	.02	.10
131 Ricky Watters	.07	.20
132 Tony Martin	.07	.20
133 Lawrence Dawsey	.02	.10
134 Ronnie Harmon	.02	.10
135 Herschel Walker	.07	.20
136 Michael Haynes	.07	.20
137 Eric Green	.02	.10
138 Steve Bono	.07	.20
139 Jamir Miller	.02	.10
140 Rod Smith DB	.07	.20
141 Andre Rison	.07	.20
142 Eric Metcalf	.07	.20
143 Michael Timpson	.02	.10
144 Cornelius Bennett	.07	.20
145 Sean Dawkins	.07	.20
146 Scott Mitchell	.07	.20
147 Ray Childress	.02	.10
148 Jim Harbaugh	.07	.20
149 Reggie Cobb	.02	.10
150 Willie Roaf	.02	.10
151 Stevie Anderson	.02	.10
152 Barry Foster	.07	.20
153 Joe Montana	.75	2.00
154 David Klingler	.07	.20
155 Chris Chandler	.07	.20
156 Carnell Lake	.02	.10
157 Calvin Williams	.07	.20
158 Kenneth Davis	.02	.10
159 Tydus Winans	.02	.10
160 Sam Adams	.02	.10
161 Ronald Moore	.02	.10
162 Vincent Brisby	.02	.10
163 Alvin Harper	.02	.10
164 Jake Reed	.07	.20
165 Jeff Hostetler	.07	.20
166 Mark Brunell	.25	.60
167 Leonard Russell	.02	.10
168 Greg Truitt	.02	.10
169 Pete Metzelaars	.02	.10
170 Dave Krieg	.02	.10
171 Lorenzo White	.02	.10
172 Robert Brooks	.15	.40
173 Willie Davis	.07	.20
174 Irving Spikes	.07	.20
175 Rodney Hampton	.07	.20
176 Erric Pegram	.07	.20
177 Brian Blades	.07	.20
178 Shawn Jefferson	.02	.10
179 Tyrone Poole RC	.15	.40
180 Rob Johnson RC	.60	1.50
181 Ki-Jana Carter RC	.15	.40
182 Steve McNair RC	2.00	5.00
183 Michael Westbrook RC	.15	.40
184 Kerry Collins RC	1.25	3.00
185 Kevin Carter RC	.15	.40
186 Tony Boselli RC	.15	.40
187 Joey Galloway RC	.75	2.00
188 Kyle Brady RC	.15	.40
189 J.J. Stokes RC	.15	.40
190 Warren Sapp RC	1.00	2.50
191 Tyrone Wheatley RC	.60	1.50
192 Napoleon Kaufman RC	.75	2.00
193 James O. Stewart RC	.60	1.50
194 Rashaan Salaam RC	.07	.20
195 Ray Zellars RC	.07	.20
196 Todd Collins RC	.07	.20
197 Sherman Williams RC	.02	.10
198 Frank Sanders RC	.15	.40
199 Terrell Fletcher RC	.02	.10
200 Chad May RC	.02	.10
DP1G Tony Boselli Draft Gold	1.50	3.00
DP1S Tony Boselli Draft Silver	.75	2.00
DP2G Kerry Collins Draft Gold	2.00	5.00
DP2S Kerry Collins Draft Silver	2.00	5.00

1995 Absolute Die Cut Helmets

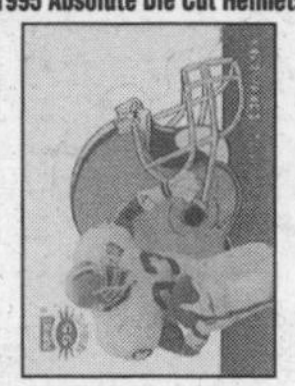

This 30 card set was inserted only in "Absolute" packs at a rate of one in 25. Leading NFL players are featured in this set. These are acetate cards with a die-cut outline of a NFL helmet. The player is featured on the left of the card. The "Playoff Absolute" logo is imprinted in gold in the upper left corner. The cards are numbered on the back with a "HDC" prefix.

COMPLETE SET (30)	50.00	120.00
STATED ODDS 1:25 ABSOLUTE		
1 Garrison Hearst	1.50	4.00
2 Jim Kelly	1.50	4.00
3 Jeff Blake	4.00	10.00
4 Emmitt Smith	6.00	15.00
5 John Elway	8.00	20.00
6 Brett Favre	6.00	15.00
7 Marshall Faulk	5.00	12.00
8 Marcus Allen	1.50	4.00
9 Jerome Bettis	1.50	4.00
10 Dan Marino	8.00	20.00
11 Cris Carter	1.50	4.00
12 Drew Bledsoe	2.50	6.00
13 Jim Everett	.40	1.00
14 Rodney Hampton	.75	2.00
15 Natrone Means	.75	2.00
16 Steve Young	3.00	8.00
17 Rick Mirer	.75	2.00
18 Errict Rhett	.75	2.00
19 Heath Shuler	.75	2.00
20 Lewis Tillman	.40	1.00
21 Barry Sanders	6.00	15.00
22 Leroy Hoard	.40	1.00
23 Rod Woodson	.75	2.00
24 Gary Brown	.40	1.00
25 Terance Mathis	.75	2.00
26 Frank Reich Panthers	.40	1.00
27 Steve Beuerlein Jaguars	.75	2.00
28 Rocket Ismail	.75	2.00
29 Johnny Johnson	.40	1.00
30 Charlie Garner	1.50	4.00

1995 Absolute/Prime Pigskin Previews

This 12-card standard-size set includes a section made with real leather. This set was issued in both 'Absolute" packs (cards 1-6) and "Prime" packs (cards 7-12).

COMPLETE SET (12)	40.00	100.00
COMP.SERIES 1 (6)	20.00	50.00
COMP.SERIES 2 (6)	20.00	50.00
1-6 STATED ODDS 1:145 ABSOLUTE		
7-12 STATED ODDS 1:145 PRIME		
1 Emmitt Smith	8.00	20.00
2 Steve Young	5.00	12.00
3 Barry Sanders	8.00	20.00
4 Deion Sanders	3.00	8.00
5 Cris Carter	2.50	6.00
6 Errict Rhett	1.25	3.00
7 Dan Marino	8.00	20.00
8 Marshall Faulk	8.00	20.00
9 Natrone Means	1.25	3.00
10 Tim Brown	2.50	6.00
11 Drew Bledsoe	4.00	10.00
12 Marcus Allen	2.50	6.00

1995 Absolute Quad Series

This 50-card standard-size set features only players in the base Playoff "Absolute" set. All cards have 4 players pictured on them. Most cards have a common theme which is usually either they play the same position or play for the same team. This set was randomly inserted into hobby packs. Each card has two photos on each side. The cards are numbered with a "Q" prefix.

COMPLETE SET (50)	125.00	300.00
STATED ODDS 1:25 ABSOLUTE		
Q1 Mont/Mar/You/Elw	25.00	60.00
Q2 Aik/Fav/Bled/Mirer	15.00	40.00
Q3 Trent Dilfer	5.00	12.00
Heath Shuler		
Mark Brunell		
Jeff Blake		
Q4 Randall Cunningham	2.00	5.00
Warren Moon		
Jim Kelly		
Boomer Esiason		
Q5 Jeff George	3.00	8.00
Dave Brown		
Stan Humphries		
Jim Everett		
Q6 Smith/Sand/Faulk/Rhet	15.00	40.00
Q7 Marcus Allen	5.00	12.00
Ricky Watters		
William Floyd		
Natrone Means		
Q8 Garrison Hearst	3.00	8.00
Jerome Bettis		
Lewis Tillman		
Gary Brown		
Q9 Irvin/Rice/Brow/Cart	15.00	30.00
Q10 Pete Metzelaars	3.00	8.00
Byron Bam Morris		
Ben Coates		
Andre Rison		
Q11 Whit/Smit/Sand/Seau	6.00	15.00
Q12 Rob Moore	3.00	8.00
Larry Centers		
Jamir Miller		
Chuck Levy		
Q13 Craig Heyward UER	3.00	8.00
Terance Mathis		
Bert Emanuel		
Eric Metcalf		
Q14 Kenneth Davis	3.00	8.00
Andre Reed		
Russell Copeland		
Cornelius Bennett		
Q15 Frank Reich	5.00	12.00
Jack Trudeau		
Mark Carrier WR		
Tyrone Poole		
Q16 Jeff Graham	3.00	8.00
Curtis Conway		
Erik Kramer		
Steve Walsh		
Q17 Carl Pickens	3.00	8.00
Darnay Scott		
Harold Green		
David Klingler		
Q18 Vinny Testaverde	2.00	5.00
Derrick Alexander WR		
Leroy Hoard		
Lorenzo White		
Q19 Charles Haley	3.00	8.00
Kevin Williams WR		
Daryl Johnston		
Jay Novacek		
Q20 Glyn Milburn	2.00	5.00
Leonard Russell		
Derek Russell		
Shannon Sharpe		
Q21 Scott Mitchell	3.00	8.00
Brett Perriman		
Herman Moore		
Johnnie Morton		
Q22 Edgar Bennett	3.00	8.00
LeShon Johnson		
Robert Brooks		
Mark Ingram		
Q23 Cody Carlson	2.00	5.00
Mel Gray		
Chris Chandler		
Ray Childress		
Q24 Craig Erickson	3.00	8.00
Jim Harbaugh		
Roosevelt Potts		
Sean Dawkins		
Q25 Steve Beuerlein	5.00	12.00
Rob Johnson		
Cedric Tillman		
Reggie Cobb		
Q26 Greg Hill	3.00	8.00
Willie Davis		
Lake Dawson		
Steve Bono		
Q27 Harvey Williams	2.00	5.00
Jeff Hostetler		
James Jett		
Rocket Ismail		
Q28 Bernie Parmalee	2.00	5.00
Irving Spikes		
Terry Kirby		
Irving Fryar		
Q29 Terry Allen	3.00	8.00
David Palmer		
Qadry Ismail		
Jake Reed		
Q30 Marion Butts	2.00	5.00
Vincent Brisby		
Dave Meggett		
Willie McGinest		
Q31 Willie Roaf	2.00	5.00
Mario Bates		
Quinn Early		
Michael Haynes		
Q32 Herschel Walker	2.00	5.00
Mike Sherrard		
Derek Brown TE		
Thomas Lewis		
Q33 Stevie Anderson	3.00	8.00
Aaron Glenn		
Johnny Johnson		
Ron Moore		
Q34 Calvin Williams	5.00	12.00
Fred Barnett		
Vaughn Hebron		
Charlie Garner		
Q35 Charles Johnson	3.00	8.00
Neil O'Donnell		
Rod Woodson		
Erric Pegram		
Q36 Ronnie Harmon	2.00	5.00
Shawn Jefferson		
Tony Martin		
Mark Seay		
Q37 Brent Jones	3.00	8.00
Dana Stubblefield		
Bryant Young		
Ken Norton		
Q38 Chris Warren	3.00	8.00
Cortez Kennedy		
Sam Adams		
Brian Blades		
Q39 Tommy Maddox	5.00	12.00
Chris Miller		
Johnny Bailey		
Isaac Bruce		
Q40 Lawrence Dawsey	2.00	5.00
Alvin Harper		
Jackie Harris		
Horace Copeland		
Q41 Gus Frerotte	3.00	8.00
Brian Mitchell		
Reggie Brooks		
Tydus Winans		
Q42 McNa/Coll/Coll/May	6.00	15.00
Q43 Ki-Jana Carter	5.00	12.00
Tyrone Wheatley		
Napoleon Kaufman		
Rashaan Salaam		
Q44 Terrell Fletcher	3.00	8.00
Sherman Williams		
Ray Zellars		
James O.Stewart		
Q45 Michael Westbrook	3.00	8.00
Joey Galloway		
J.J. Stokes		
Frank Sanders		
Q46 Kevin Carter	5.00	12.00
Tony Boselli		
Warren Sapp		
Kyle Brady		
Q47 Greg Truitt	2.00	5.00
Dan Wilkinson		
Eric Turner		
Antonio Langham		
Q48 Carnell Lake	3.00	8.00
Neil Smith		
Rod Smith DB		
Kevin Greene		
Q49 O.J. McDuffie	3.00	8.00
Darren Carrington		
Michael Timpson		
Raymont Harris		
Q50 Rodney Hampton	2.00	5.00
Dave Krieg		
Barry Foster		
Eric Green		

1995 Absolute Unsung Heroes

This 28-card standard-size set was randomly inserted in both "Absolute" and "Prime" packs. This set features players who do not garner heavy publicity. The set is checklisted in alphabetical order by team. Cards were available in both gold and silver foils, with gold inserted into "Absolute" packs and silver inserted into "Prime" packs.

COMPLETE SET (28)	5.00	12.00
*GOLD/SILVER: SAME VALUE		
GOLD ODDS 1:13 ABSOLUTE		
SILVER ODDS 1:13 PRIME		
1 Garth Jax	.20	.50
2 Craig Heyward	.30	.75
3 Steve Tasker	.30	.75
4 Raymont Harris	.20	.50
5 Jeff Blake	.50	1.25
6 Bob Dahl	.20	.50
7 Jason Garrett	.40	1.00
8 Gary Zimmerman	.20	.50
9 Tom Beer	.20	.50
10 John Jurkovic	.20	.50
11 Spencer Tillman	.20	.50
12 Devon McDonald	.20	.50
13 John Alt	.20	.50
14 Steve Wisniewski	.20	.50
15 Tim Bowens	.20	.50
16 Amp Lee	.20	.50
17 Todd Rucci	.20	.50
18 Tyrone Hughes	.30	.75
19 Michael Strahan	.60	1.50
20 Brad Baxter	.20	.50
21 Mark Bavaro	.20	.50
22 Yancey Thigpen	.60	1.50
23 Courtney Hall	.20	.50
24 Eric Davis	.20	.50
25 Rufus Porter	.20	.50
26 Jackie Slater	.30	.75
27 Courtney Hawkins	.30	.75
28 Gus Frerotte	.30	.75

1996 Absolute Samples

These promo cards were issued to preview the 1996 Playoff Absolute release. Each is very similar to its base brand card in design, except for the word "sample" where the card number otherwise would be.

COMPLETE SET (4)	3.00	8.00
1 Zack Crockett	.50	1.25
2 Terrell Davis	2.00	5.00
3 Rashaan Salaam	.60	1.50
4 Tamarick Vanover	.50	1.25

1996 Absolute

The 1996 Playoff Absolute set was issued in one series totalling 200 cards. The 6-card packs retailed for $3.75 each. Within every pack is five cards and an additional inner pack, featuring one collectible card. This concept from Playoff created three levels of color coded insertion ratios for the base cards: red, white and blue. The red level (1-100) are the most frequently inserted cards. The white level cards (101-150) appear in white inner packs which are found inside the Absolute pack. With one card per pack, the white packs appear approximately 18 per box. The blue level cards (151-200) are the hardest to find and also contain one card per pack. Approximately six packs per box will contain a blue pack, in place of the white pack. Rookie Cards in this set include Tim Biakabutuka, Terry Glenn, Eddie George, Keshawn Johnson, Leeland McElroy, Eric Moulds and Lawrence Phillips.

COMPLETE SET (200)	25.00	60.00
COMP.RED SET (100)	6.00	15.00
1 Jim Kelly	.25	.60
2 Michael Irvin	.25	.60
3 Jim Harbaugh	.10	.30
4 Warren Moon	.10	.30
5 Rick Mirer	.10	.30
6 Drew Bledsoe	.40	1.00
7 Steve Young	.50	1.25
8 Junior Seau	.25	.60
9 Sherman Williams	.05	.15
10 Jay Novacek	.05	.15
11 Bill Brooks	.05	.15
12 Steve Bono	.05	.15
13 Leroy Hoard	.05	.15
14 Willie Jackson	.10	.30
15 Irving Fryar	.10	.30
16 Tony McGee	.05	.15
17 Neil O'Donnell	.10	.30
18 Fred Barnett	.05	.15
19 Erric Pegram	.05	.15
20 Derrick Moore	.05	.15
21 Johnnie Morton	.10	.30
22 James Jett	.10	.30
23 Tim Brown	.25	.60
24 Kevin Miniefield	.05	.15
25 Jim McMahon	.10	.30
26 Brian Blades	.05	.15
27 Henry Ellard	.05	.15
28 Calvin Williams	.05	.15
29 Chris Chandler	.10	.30
30 Rod Woodson	.10	.30
31 Ronnie Harmon	.05	.15
32 Brent Jones	.05	.15
33 Qadry Ismail	.10	.30
34 Steve Tasker	.05	.15
35 Eric Green	.05	.15
36 Brian Mitchell	.05	.15
37 Herschel Walker	.10	.30
38 Sean Dawkins	.05	.15
39 Bryce Paup	.05	.15
40 Dorsey Levens	.25	.60
41 Andre Rison	.10	.30
42 Lamont Warren	.05	.15
43 Earnest Byner	.05	.15
44 Bobby Engram RC	.25	.60
45 Simeon Rice RC	.60	1.50
46 Michael Jackson	.10	.30
47 Marvin Harrison RC	1.50	4.00
48 Thurman Thomas	.25	.60
49 Charles Haley	.10	.30
50 Rob Moore	.10	.30
51 Bryan Cox	.05	.15
52 Horace Copeland	.05	.15
53 Rodney Peete	.05	.15
54 Jeff Graham	.05	.15
55 Charles Johnson	.05	.15
56 Natrone Means	.10	.30
57 Terrell Fletcher	.05	.15
58 Eric Bieniemy	.05	.15
59 Karim Abdul-Jabbar RC	.25	.60
60 Quinn Early	.05	.15
61 Mark Bruener	.05	.15
62 Shawn Jefferson	.05	.15
63 Vinny Testaverde	.10	.30
64 Derrick Mayes RC	.25	.60
65 Mario Bates	.10	.30
66 J.J. Birden	.05	.15
67 Eddie Kennison RC	.25	.60
68 Steve Walsh	.05	.15
69 Mark Chmura	.10	.30
70 Mike Sherrard	.05	.15
71 Boomer Esiason	.10	.30
72 Alex Van Dyke RC	.10	.30
73 Jake Reed	.10	.30
74 Jackie Harris	.05	.15
75 Mark Rypien	.05	.15
76 Chris Calloway	.05	.15
77 Amani Toomer RC	.60	1.50
78 Terrell Davis	1.25	3.00
79 Rocket Ismail	.05	.15
80 Derek Loville	.05	.15
81 Ben Coates	.10	.30
82 Kyle Brady	.05	.15
83 Willie Green	.05	.15
84 Randall Cunningham	.25	.60
85 Amp Lee	.05	.15
86 Bert Emanuel	.10	.30
87 Jason Dunn RC	.10	.30
88 Michael Haynes	.05	.15
89 Robert Green	.05	.15
90 Willie Davis	.05	.15
91 O.J. McDuffie	.10	.30
92 Harold Green	.05	.15
93 Ken Dilger	.10	.30
94 Brett Perriman	.05	.15
95 Eric Zeier	.05	.15
96 Jerome Bettis	.25	.60
97 Rickey Dudley RC	.25	.60
98 Darnay Scott	.10	.30
99 Mark Brunell	.40	1.00
100 Christian Fauria	.05	.15
101 Jeff Blake	.60	1.50
102 Troy Aikman	1.50	4.00
103 John Elway	3.00	8.00
104 Barry Sanders	2.50	6.00
105 Curtis Conway	.60	1.50
106 Wayne Chrebet	.75	2.00
107 Lake Dawson	.30	.75
108 Jerry Rice	1.50	4.00
109 Kevin Williams	.08	.25
110 Zack Crockett	.08	.25
111 Vincent Brisby	.08	.25
112 Rodney Thomas	.08	.25
113 Rodney Hampton	.30	.75
114 Adrian Murrell	.10	.30
115 Bruce Smith	.60	1.50
116 Napoleon Kaufman	.60	1.50
117 Byron Bam Morris	.08	.25
118 Anthony Miller	.30	.75
119 Aaron Hayden RC	.30	.75
120 Joey Galloway	.25	.60
121 Trent Dilfer	.30	.75
122 Stoney Case	.08	.25
123 Tamarick Vanover	.10	.30
124 Eric Metcalf	.30	.75
125 Marcus Allen	.60	1.50
126 James O. Stewart	.30	.75
127 Charlie Garner	.30	.75
128 Yancey Thigpen	.30	.75
129 William Floyd	.30	.75
130 Terry Allen	.30	.75
131 Robert Smith	.30	.75
132 Todd Kinchen	.08	.25
133 Gus Frerotte	.30	.75
134 Frank Sanders	.30	.75
135 Scott Mitchell	.30	.75
136 Greg Hill	.30	.75
137 Edgar Bennett	.30	.75
138 Alvin Harper	.08	.25
139 Reggie White	.60	1.50
140 Craig Heyward	.08	.25
141 Todd Collins	.30	.75
142 Ernie Mills	.08	.25
143 Keyshawn Johnson RC	1.00	2.50
144 Mark Carrier WR	.08	.25
145 Robert Brooks	.60	1.50
146 Bernie Parmalee	.08	.25
147 Carl Pickens	.30	.75
148 Kevin Hardy RC	.60	1.50
149 Jonathan Ogden RC	1.25	3.00
150 Lawrence Phillips RC	.60	1.50
151 Emmitt Smith	4.00	10.00
152 Brett Favre	5.00	12.00
153 Dan Marino	5.00	12.00
154 Jim Everett	.25	.60
155 Dave Brown	.50	1.25
156 Jeff Hostetler	.50	1.25
157 Heath Shuler	.50	1.25
158 Daryl Johnston	.50	1.25
159 Terance Mathis	.50	1.25
160 Curtis Martin	2.00	5.00
161 Ray Zellars	.25	.60
162 Ricky Watters	.50	1.25
163 Chris Warren	.50	1.25
164 Larry Centers	.50	1.25
165 Steve McNair	2.00	5.00
166 Terry Kirby	.50	1.25
167 Rob Johnson	1.00	2.50
168 Dave Meggett	.25	.60
169 Antonio Freeman	.25	.60
170 Marshall Faulk	1.50	4.00
171 Andre Hastings	.05	.15
172 Stan Humphries	.50	1.25
173 Errict Rhett	.50	1.25
174 Michael Westbrook	1.00	2.50
175 Deion Sanders	1.50	4.00
176 Jeff George	.50	1.25
177 Cris Carter	1.00	2.50
178 Chris Sanders	.50	1.25
179 Ki-Jana Carter	.50	1.25
180 Kordell Stewart	1.00	2.50
181 Isaac Bruce	1.00	2.50
182 Terry Glenn RC	2.00	5.00
183 Garrison Hearst	.50	1.25
184 Erik Kramer	.25	.60
185 Leeland McElroy RC	.50	1.25
186 Rashaan Salaam	.50	1.25
187 Kimble Anders	.25	.60
188 Chad May	.25	.60
189 Tony Martin	.50	1.25
190 J.J. Stokes	1.00	2.50
191 Darick Holmes	.25	.60
192 Eric Moulds RC	2.50	6.00
193 Shannon Sharpe	.50	1.25
194 Tim Biakabutuka RC	1.00	2.50
195 Eddie George RC	2.50	6.00
196 Mike Alstott RC	2.00	5.00
197 Kerry Collins	1.00	2.50
198 Harvey Williams	.25	.60
199 Herman Moore	.50	1.25
200 Tyrone Wheatley	.50	1.25

1996 Absolute Metal XL

Series one cards were randomly inserted into Absolute packs at a rate of one in 96-blue packs, while series two card were random inserts in Prime packs. A metal coin commemorating each player's team was inset in the standard-size cards. Each is numbered with an "XL" prefix.

COMPLETE SET (36)	125.00	300.00
COMP.SERIES 1 SET (18)	75.00	200.00
COMP.SERIES 2 SET (18)	40.00	100.00
1-18: STATED ODDS 1:96 ABSOLUTE PACKS		
19-36: STATED ODDS 1:80 PRIME PACKS		
1 Troy Aikman	5.00	12.00
2 Emmitt Smith	12.50	30.00
3 Barry Sanders	8.00	20.00
4 Brett Favre	15.00	40.00
5 Dan Marino	15.00	40.00
6 Jerry Rice	5.00	12.00
7 Marshall Faulk	5.00	12.00
8 Curtis Martin	6.00	15.00
9 Rashaan Salaam	1.50	4.00
10 Harvey Williams	.75	2.00
11 Ricky Watters	1.50	4.00
12 Yancey Thigpen	1.00	2.50
13 Chris Warren	1.50	4.00
14 Errict Rhett	1.50	4.00
15 Terry Allen	1.00	2.50
16 Robert Brooks	2.00	5.00
17 Anthony Miller	1.00	2.50
18 Erik Kramer	.75	2.00
19 Michael Irvin	.75	2.00
20 John Elway	10.00	25.00
21 Jim Harbaugh	.40	1.00
22 Steve Young	1.50	4.00
23 Deion Sanders	5.00	12.00
24 Terrell Davis	4.00	10.00
25 Reggie White	2.00	5.00
26 Herman Moore	1.50	4.00
27 Rodney Hampton	1.00	2.50
28 Cris Carter	3.00	8.00
29 Isaac Bruce	3.00	8.00
30 Kordell Stewart	3.00	8.00
31 Brett Perriman	.20	.50
32 Joey Galloway	.75	2.00
33 Drew Bledsoe	1.25	3.00
34 J.J. Stokes	3.00	8.00
35 Napoleon Kaufman	2.00	5.00
36 Tim Brown	.75	2.00

1996 Absolute Quad Series

Randomly inserted in packs at a rate of one in 24 red packs, this 35-card set features popular players from each team. There are also some rookie-only quad cards. Cards 1-30 are sequenced in alphabetical team order while cards 31-35 are the rookie only quads.

COMPLETE SET (35)	200.00	400.00
STATED ODDS 1:24		
1 F.Sndrs	4.00	10.00
Cse		
Hearst		
Moore		
2 Birden	2.50	6.00
Emanl		
J.Grge		
Heyw.		
3 T.Collins	6.00	15.00
Brooks		
Kelly		
Paup		
4 K.Collins	6.00	15.00
Carr		
Grn		
D.Mre		
5 Cnwy	4.00	10.00
Green		
Kramer		
Minie.		
6 J.Blake	6.00	15.00
Bien		
Green		
McGee		
7 Zeier	2.50	6.00
Byner		
Jackson		
Rison		
8 D.Sand	7.50	20.00
Irvin		
Nova		
K.Will		
9 T.Davis	15.00	40.00
Elway		
Mill		
Sharpe		
10 H.Mre	4.00	10.00
Mitch.		
Mrtn		
Perr.		
11 Freeman	10.00	25.00
Ben		
Chmu		
White		
12 McNair	6.00	15.00
CSand		
Thom		
Chan		
13 Crckt	4.00	10.00
Dwkns		
Dilger		
Harb.		
14 Brunell	10.00	25.00
Jack		
John		
Stew		
15 Allen	6.00	15.00
And		
Daws		
Vanover		
16 Green	4.00	10.00
Kirby		
McDuf.		
Prmlee		
17 Carter	4.00	10.00
Moon		
Smith		
May		
18 Bledsoe	10.00	25.00
Bris		
Coat		
Megg		
19 M.Bts	2.50	6.00
Evrtt		
Hynes		
Zell.		
20 Whtly	4.00	10.00
D.Brwn		
Callwy		
Hamp.		
21 Brady	7.50	20.00
Chrebet		
Murr		
O'Don.		

22 N.Kauf. 6.00 15.00
T.Brwn
Host.
R.Ism.
23 Grnr 4.00 10.00
Peete
Wtters
C.Will.
24 K.Stewart 6.00 15.00
Hast
Mill
Wood
25 Fltchr 6.00 15.00
Hrmon
Hyden
Seau
26 S.Young 12.50 30.00
Floyd
Lov
Stoke
27 Galloway 6.00 15.00
Blad
Faur
Mirer
28 Bruce 6.00 15.00
Kinch
Walsh
Ryp.
29 Dilfer 4.00 10.00
H.Cope.
Hrper
J.Hrrs
30 Westbrook 6.00 15.00
Ell
Frer
Shuler
31 K.Johns. 8.00 20.00
Hard
S.Ric
Ogd.
32 Phillips 7.50 20.00
T.Biak
Glenn
Dud.
33 E.Grge 12.50 30.00
M.Harr
Mlds
Kenn
34 Mayes 6.00 15.00
AbJab
VanDy
Engr.
35 Alstott 6.00 15.00
McElr
JDunn
Toom

1996 Absolute Unsung Heroes

Randomly inserted in Absolute or Prime packs at a rate of one in 24 red packs, this 30-card standard-size set is a special insert honoring players chosen by the fans and teammates. One player from each NFC team is featured in Absolute packs while the AFC players were honored in the Prime packs. These cards are sequenced in alpahabetical order. Full 30-card sets were also given out at the actual banquet in early 1997.

COMPLETE SET (30) 10.00 25.00
COMP.SERIES 1 SET (15) 4.00 10.00
COMP.SERIES 2 SET (15) 6.00 15.00
1-15 ODDS 1:24 ABSOLUTE PACKS
16-30 ODDS 1:24 PRIME PACKS
1 Bill Bates 1.00 2.50
2 Jeff Brady .30 .75
3 Ray Brown .30 .75
4 Isaac Bruce 1.00 2.50
5 Larry Centers .50 1.25
6 Mark Chmura .50 1.25
7 Keith Elias .30 .75
8 Robert Green .30 .75
9 Andy Harmon .30 .75
10 Rodney Holman .30 .75
11 Derek Loville .30 .75
12 J.J. McCleskey .30 .75
13 Sam Mills .50 1.25
14 Hardy Nickerson .50 1.25
15 Jessie Tuggle .30 .75
16 Eric Bieniemy .30 .75
17 Blaine Bishop .30 .75
18 Mark Brunell 1.00 2.50
19 Wayne Chrebet 1.00 2.50
20 Vince Evans .30 .75
21 Sam Gash .30 .75
22 Tim Grunhard .30 .75
23 Jim Harbaugh .50 1.25
24 Dwayne Harper .30 .75
25 Bernie Parmalee .30 .75
26 Reggie Rivers .30 .75
27 Eugene Robinson .50 1.25
28 Kordell Stewart 1.00 2.50
29 Steve Tasker 1.00 2.50
30 Bennie Thompson .30 .75

1996 Absolute Xtreme Team

Randomly inserted in packs at a rate of one in 24 white packs, this 30-card standard-size set features some of Football's best players. The cards are issued on clear-plastic which have been foil-enhanced. The cards are numbered with an "TX" prefix.

COMPLETE SET (30) 150.00 300.00
STATED ODDS 1:24
1 Troy Aikman 5.00 12.00
2 Emmitt Smith 12.50 30.00
3 Jerry Rice 5.00 12.00
4 Dan Marino 15.00 40.00
5 Brett Favre 10.00 25.00
6 Barry Sanders 8.00 20.00
7 Michael Irvin 2.00 5.00
8 John Elway 10.00 25.00
9 Joey Galloway 1.00 2.50
10 Steve Young 2.00 5.00
11 Deion Sanders 5.00 12.00
12 Terrell Davis 4.00 10.00
13 Herman Moore 1.00 2.50
14 Reggie White 2.00 5.00
15 Cris Carter 2.00 5.00
16 Rodney Hampton 1.00 2.50
17 Isaac Bruce 2.00 5.00
18 Brett Perriman .50 1.25
19 Curtis Conway 2.00 5.00
20 Scott Mitchell 1.00 2.50
21 Rashaan Salaam 1.00 2.50
22 Robert Brooks 2.00 5.00
23 Marshall Faulk 5.00 12.00
24 Curtis Martin 6.00 15.00
25 Harvey Williams .50 1.25
26 Yancey Thigpen 1.00 2.50
27 Chris Warren 1.00 2.50
28 Errict Rhett 1.00 2.50
29 Terry Allen 1.00 2.50
30 Carl Pickens 1.00 2.50

1997 Absolute

The 1997 Playoff Absolute set was issued together as three series totaling 200 cards. The first 100-cards (green bordered) were the easiest to pull with the second 50 (blue bordered) slightly tougher and the final 50 (red bordered) the most difficult to pull. Several insert sets were included with the product which was packaged five-cards and one Chip Shot per pack with 24-packs per box.

COMPLETE SET (200) 30.00 80.00
COMP.GREEN SET (100) 10.00 25.00
1 Marcus Allen .20 .50
2 Eric Bieniemy .07 .20
3 Jason Dunn .07 .20
4 Jim Harbaugh .10 .30
5 Michael Westbrook .10 .30
6 Tiki Barber RC 1.50 4.00
7 Frank Reich .07 .20
8 Irving Fryar .10 .30
9 Courtney Hawkins .07 .20
10 Eric Zeier .10 .30
11 Kent Graham .07 .20
12 Trent Dilfer .20 .50
13 Neil O'Donnell .10 .30
14 Reidel Anthony RC .20 .50
15 Jeff Hostetler .07 .20
16 Lawrence Phillips .07 .20
17 Dave Brown .07 .20
18 Mike Tomczak .07 .20
19 Jake Reed .10 .30
20 Anthony Miller .07 .20
21 Eric Metcalf .10 .30
22 Sedrick Shaw RC .10 .30
23 Anthony Johnson .07 .20
24 Mario Bates .07 .20
25 Dorsey Levens .20 .50
26 Stan Humphries .10 .30
27 Ben Coates .10 .30
28 Tyrone Wheatley .10 .30
29 Adrian Murrell .10 .30
30 William Henderson .10 .30
31 Warrick Dunn RC .75 2.00
32 LeShon Johnson .07 .20
33 James O.Stewart .10 .30
34 Edgar Bennett .10 .30
35 Raymont Harris .07 .20
36 LeRoy Butler .07 .20
37 Darren Woodson .07 .20
38 Darnell Autry RC .10 .30
39 Johnnie Morton .10 .30
40 William Floyd .10 .30
41 Terrell Fletcher .07 .20
42 Leonard Russell .07 .20
43 Henry Ellard .07 .20
44 Terrell Owens .20 .50
45 John Friesz .07 .20
46 Antowain Smith RC .60 1.50
47 Charles Johnson .10 .30
48 Rickey Dudley .10 .30
49 Lake Dawson .07 .20
50 Bert Emanuel .10 .30
51 Zach Thomas .20 .50
52 Earnest Byner .07 .20
53 Yatil Green RC .10 .30
54 Chris Spielman .07 .20
55 Muhsin Muhammad .10 .30
56 Bobby Engram .10 .30
57 Eric Bjornson .07 .20
58 Willie Green .07 .20
59 Derrick Mayes .10 .30
60 Chris Sanders .07 .20
61 Jimmy Smith .10 .30
62 Tony Gonzalez RC 1.00 2.50
63 Rich Gannon .20 .50
64 Stanley Pritchett .07 .20
65 Brad Johnson .20 .50
66 Rodney Peete .07 .20
67 Sam Gash .07 .20
68 Chris Calloway .07 .20
69 Chris T. Jones .07 .20
70 Will Blackwell RC .10 .30
71 Mark Bruener .07 .20
72 Terry Kirby .10 .30
73 Brian Blades .07 .20
74 Craig Heyward .07 .20
75 Jamie Asher .07 .20
76 Terance Mathis .10 .30
77 Troy Davis RC .10 .30
78 Bruce Smith .10 .30
79 Simeon Rice .10 .30
80 Fred Barnett .07 .20
81 Tim Brown .20 .50
82 James Jett .10 .30
83 Mark Carrier WR .07 .20
84 Shawn Jefferson .07 .20
85 Ken Dilger .07 .20
86 Rae Carruth RC .07 .20
87 Keenan McCardell .10 .30
88 Michael Irvin .20 .50
89 Mark Chmura .10 .30
90 Derrick Alexander WR .10 .30
91 Andre Reed .10 .30
92 Ed McCaffrey .10 .30
93 Erik Kramer .07 .20
94 Albert Connell RC .20 .50
95 Frank Wycheck .07 .20
96 Zack Crockett .07 .20
97 Jim Everett .07 .20
98 Michael Haynes .07 .20
99 Jeff Graham .07 .20
100 Brent Jones .10 .30
101 Troy Aikman 1.25 3.00
102 Byron Hanspard RC .10 .30
103 Robert Brooks .50 1.25
104 Karim Abdul-Jabbar .50 1.25
105 Drew Bledsoe .60 1.50
106 Napoleon Kaufman .50 1.25
107 Steve Young .75 2.00
108 Leeland McElroy .07 .20
109 Jamal Anderson .20 .50
110 David LaFleur RC .20 .50
111 Vinny Testaverde .30 .75
112 Eric Moulds .50 1.25
113 Tim Biakabutuka .50 1.25
114 Rick Mirer .20 .50
115 Jeff Blake .50 1.25
116 Jim Schwantz RC .20 .50
117 Herman Moore .30 .75
118 Ike Hilliard RC 1.00 2.50
119 Reggie White .50 1.25
120 Steve McNair .75 2.00
121 Marshall Faulk .75 2.00
122 Natrone Means .30 .75
123 Greg Hill .30 .75
124 O.J. McDuffie .30 .75
125 Robert Smith .30 .75
126 Bryant Westbrook RC .50 1.25
127 Ray Zellars .20 .50
128 Rodney Hampton .30 .75
129 Wayne Chrebet .20 .50
130 Desmond Howard .30 .75
131 Ty Detmer .30 .75
132 Erric Pegram .20 .50
133 Yancey Thigpen .30 .75
134 Danny Wuerffel RC .20 .50
135 Charlie Jones .20 .50
136 Chris Warren .30 .75
137 Isaac Bruce .50 1.25
138 Errict Rhett .30 .75
139 Gus Frerotte .50 1.25
140 Frank Sanders .30 .75
141 Todd Collins .30 .75
142 Jake Plummer RC 5.00 12.00
143 Darnay Scott .30 .75
144 Rashaan Salaam .50 1.25
145 Terrell Davis .75 2.00
146 Scott Mitchell .30 .75
147 Junior Seau .50 1.25
148 Warren Moon .30 .75
149 Wesley Walls .20 .50
150 Daryl Johnston .30 .75
151 Brett Favre 5.00 12.00
152 Emmitt Smith 4.00 10.00
153 Dan Marino 5.00 12.00
154 Larry Centers .50 1.25
155 Michael Jackson .50 1.25
156 Kerry Collins .20 .50
157 Curtis Conway .50 1.25
158 Peter Boulware RC .75 2.00
159 Carl Pickens .50 1.25
160 Shannon Sharpe .50 1.25
161 Brett Perriman .30 .75
162 Eddie George .75 2.00
163 Mark Brunell 1.60 1.00
164 Tamarick Vanover .50 1.25
165 Cris Carter .75 2.00
166 Corey Dillon RC 6.00 15.00
167 Curtis Martin 1.50 4.00
168 Amani Toomer .50 1.25
169 Jeff George .50 1.25
170 Kordell Stewart .75 2.00
171 Garrison Hearst .50 1.25
172 Tony Banks .50 1.25
173 Mike Alstott .75 2.00
174 Jim Druckenmiller RC .10 .30
175 Chris Chandler .50 1.25
176 Byron Bam Morris .30 .75
177 Billy Joe Hobert .50 1.25
178 Ernie Mills .30 .75
179 Ki-Jana Carter .30 .75
180 Deion Sanders .75 2.00
181 Ricky Watters .50 1.25
182 Shawn Springs RC .75 2.00
183 Barry Sanders 4.00 10.00
184 Antonio Freeman .75 2.00
185 Marvin Harrison .75 2.00
186 Elvis Grbac .50 1.25
187 Terry Glenn .75 2.00
188 Willie Roaf .30 .75
189 Keyshawn Johnson .75 2.00
190 Orlando Pace RC .75 2.00
191 Jerome Bettis .75 2.00
192 Tony Martin .50 1.25
193 Jerry Rice 2.50 6.00
194 Joey Galloway .50 1.25
195 Terry Allen .75 2.00
196 Eddie Kennison .50 1.25
197 Thurman Thomas .75 2.00
198 Darrell Russell RC .30 .75
199 Rob Moore .50 1.25
200 John Elway 5.00 12.00

1997 Absolute Bronze Redemption

COMP.BRONZE SET (200) 100.00 200.00
*BRONZE 1-100: .6X TO 1.5X HI COL.
*BRONZE 101-150: .6X TO 1.5X HI COL.
*BRONZE 151-200: .5X TO 1X HI COL.
BRONZE REDEMPTION SET ODDS 1:1440
COMP.GOLD SET (200) 150.00 400.00
*GOLD 1-100: 1.2X TO 3X HI COL.
*GOLD 101-150: 1.2X TO 3X HI COL.
*GOLD 151-200: .8X TO 2X HI COL.
GOLD REDEMPTION SET ODDS 1:2880
COMP.SILVER SET (200) 150.00 300.00
*SILVER 1-100: 1X TO 2.5X HI COL.
*SILVER 101-150: 1X TO 2.5X HI COL.
*SILVER 151-200: .6X TO 1.5X HI COL.
SILVER REDEMPTION SET ODDS 1:1920
FOIL SET AVAILABLE VIA MAIL REDEMPTION

1997 Absolute Chip Shots Black

COMPLETE SET (200) 60.00 150.00
EACH PRINTED IN BLUE, BLACK, AND RED
*RED CHIP: .4X TO 1X BLACK
ONE PER PACK
1 Marcus Allen .60 1.50
2 Eric Bieniemy .15 .40
3 Jason Dunn .15 .40
4 Jim Harbaugh .30 .75
5 Michael Westbrook .30 .75
6 Tiki Barber 2.00 5.00
7 Frank Reich .15 .40
8 Irving Fryar .30 .75
9 Courtney Hawkins .15 .40
10 Eric Zeier .30 .75
11 Kent Graham .15 .40
12 Trent Dilfer .60 1.50
13 Neil O'Donnell .30 .75
14 Reidel Anthony .30 .75
15 Jeff Hostetler .15 .40
16 Lawrence Phillips .15 .40
17 Dave Brown .15 .40
18 Mike Tomczak .15 .40
19 Jake Reed .30 .75
20 Anthony Miller .15 .40
21 Eric Metcalf .30 .75
22 Sedrick Shaw .30 .75
23 Anthony Johnson .15 .40
24 Mario Bates .15 .40
25 Dorsey Levens .60 1.50
26 Stan Humphries .30 .75
27 Ben Coates .30 .75
28 Tyrone Wheatley .30 .75
29 Adrian Murrell .30 .75
30 William Henderson .30 .75
31 Warrick Dunn 1.00 2.50
32 LeShon Johnson .15 .40
33 James O.Stewart .30 .75
34 Edgar Bennett .30 .75
35 Raymont Harris .15 .40
36 LeRoy Butler .15 .40
37 Darren Woodson .15 .40
38 Darnell Autry .15 .40
39 Johnnie Morton .30 .75
40 William Floyd .15 .40
41 Terrell Fletcher .15 .40
42 Leonard Russell .15 .40
43 Henry Ellard .15 .40
44 Terrell Owens .60 1.50
45 John Friesz .15 .40
46 Antowain Smith .60 1.50
47 Charles Johnson .30 .75
48 Rickey Dudley .30 .75
49 Lake Dawson .15 .40
50 Bert Emanuel .30 .75
51 Zach Thomas .60 1.50
52 Earnest Byner .15 .40
53 Yatil Green .30 .75
54 Chris Spielman .15 .40
55 Muhsin Muhammad .30 .75
56 Bobby Engram .30 .75
57 Eric Bjornson .15 .40
58 Willie Green .15 .40
59 Derrick Mayes .30 .75
60 Chris Sanders .15 .40
61 Jimmy Smith .30 .75
62 Tony Gonzalez 1.25 3.00
63 Rich Gannon .60 1.50
64 Stanley Pritchett .15 .40
65 Brad Johnson .60 1.50
66 Rodney Peete .15 .40
67 Sam Gash .15 .40
68 Chris Calloway .15 .40
69 Chris T. Jones .15 .40
70 Will Blackwell .15 .40
71 Mark Bruener .15 .40
72 Terry Kirby .30 .75
73 Brian Blades .15 .40
74 Craig Heyward .15 .40
75 Jamie Asher .15 .40
76 Terance Mathis .30 .75
77 Troy Davis .30 .75
78 Bruce Smith .30 .75
79 Simeon Rice .30 .75
80 Fred Barnett .15 .40
81 Tim Brown .60 1.50
82 James Jett .30 .75
83 Mark Carrier WR .15 .40
84 Shawn Jefferson .15 .40
85 Ken Dilger .15 .40
86 Rae Carruth .15 .40
87 Keenan McCardell .30 .75
88 Michael Irvin .60 1.50
89 Mark Chmura .30 .75
90 Derrick Alexander WR .30 .75
91 Andre Reed .30 .75
92 Ed McCaffrey .30 .75
93 Erik Kramer .15 .40
94 Albert Connell .15 .40
95 Frank Wycheck .15 .40
96 Zack Crockett .15 .40
97 Jim Everett .15 .40
98 Michael Haynes .15 .40
99 Jeff Graham .15 .40
100 Brent Jones .15 .40
101 Troy Aikman 2.00 5.00
102 Byron Hanspard .30 .75
103 Robert Brooks .30 .75
104 Karim Abdul-Jabbar .60 1.50
105 Drew Bledsoe 1.25 3.00
106 Napoleon Kaufman .60 1.50
107 Steve Young 1.50 4.00
108 Leeland McElroy .15 .40
109 Jamal Anderson .60 1.50
110 David LaFleur .15 .40
111 Vinny Testaverde .30 .75
112 Eric Moulds .60 1.50
113 Tim Biakabutuka .30 .75
114 Rick Mirer .15 .40
115 Jeff Blake .30 .75
116 Jim Schwantz .15 .40
117 Herman Moore .30 .75
118 Ike Hilliard .60 1.50
119 Reggie White .60 1.50
120 Steve McNair 1.00 2.50
121 Marshall Faulk .75 2.00
122 Natrone Means .30 .75
123 Greg Hill .15 .40
124 O.J. McDuffie .30 .75
125 Robert Smith .30 .75
126 Bryant Westbrook .15 .40
127 Ray Zellars .15 .40
128 Rodney Hampton .30 .75
129 Wayne Chrebet .60 1.50
130 Desmond Howard .30 .75
131 Ty Detmer .30 .75
132 Erric Pegram .15 .40
133 Yancey Thigpen .30 .75
134 Danny Wuerffel .60 1.50
135 Charlie Jones .30 .75
136 Chris Warren .30 .75
137 Isaac Bruce .60 1.50
138 Errict Rhett .15 .40
139 Gus Frerotte .15 .40
140 Frank Sanders .15 .40
141 Todd Collins .15 .40
142 Jake Plummer 1.50 4.00
143 Darnay Scott .30 .75
144 Rashaan Salaam .15 .40
145 Terrell Davis 1.00 2.50
146 Scott Mitchell .30 .75
147 Junior Seau .60 1.50
148 Warren Moon .60 1.50
149 Wesley Walls .30 .75
150 Daryl Johnston .30 .75
151 Brett Favre 4.00 10.00
152 Emmitt Smith 3.00 8.00
153 Dan Marino 4.00 10.00
154 Larry Centers .30 .75
155 Michael Jackson .30 .75
156 Kerry Collins .60 1.50
157 Curtis Conway .30 .75
158 Peter Boulware .60 1.50
159 Carl Pickens .30 .75
160 Shannon Sharpe .30 .75
161 Brett Perriman .15 .40
162 Eddie George .60 1.50
163 Mark Brunell 1.25 3.00
164 Tamarick Vanover .30 .75
165 Cris Carter .60 1.50
166 Corey Dillon 2.00 5.00
167 Curtis Martin 1.00 2.50
168 Amani Toomer .30 .75
169 Jeff George .30 .75
170 Kordell Stewart .60 1.50
171 Garrison Hearst .30 .75
172 Tony Banks .60 1.50
173 Mike Alstott .60 1.50
174 Jim Druckenmiller .30 .75
175 Chris Chandler .30 .75
176 Byron Bam Morris .15 .40
177 Billy Joe Hobert .30 .75
178 Ernie Mills .15 .40
179 Ki-Jana Carter .15 .40
180 Deion Sanders .60 1.50
181 Ricky Watters .30 .75
182 Shawn Springs .15 .40
183 Barry Sanders 3.00 8.00
184 Antonio Freeman .60 1.50
185 Marvin Harrison .60 1.50
186 Elvis Grbac .30 .75
187 Terry Glenn .60 1.50
188 Willie Roaf .15 .40
189 Keyshawn Johnson .60 1.50
190 Orlando Pace .60 1.50
191 Jerome Bettis .60 1.50
192 Tony Martin .30 .75
193 Jerry Rice 2.00 5.00
194 Joey Galloway .30 .75
195 Terry Allen .60 1.50
196 Eddie Kennison .30 .75
197 Thurman Thomas .60 1.50
198 Darrell Russell .15 .40
199 Rob Moore .30 .75
200 John Elway 4.00 10.00
S162 Eddie George Sample .40 1.00

1997 Absolute Honors

Randomly inserted in packs at a rate of one in 7200, these felt-like cards feature the latest honorees in this continuation set from the 1996 Prime and Contenders sets.

STATED ODDS 1:7200
PH7 Jerry Rice 30.00 80.00
PH8 Reggie White 20.00 50.00
PH9 John Elway 50.00 120.00

1997 Absolute Leather Quads

This set of 18-cards features four players per card on leather stock. Each was randomly inserted at the rate of 1:144 in 1997 Playoff Absolute packs. A Gold parallel set was also produced and issued via a redemption card in packs for a complete set. Each of these cards features a gold foil star on the front to differentiate it.

COMPLETE SET (18) 200.00 400.00
STATED ODDS 1:144
*GOLD CARDS: 1.2X TO 3X BASIC INSERTS
GOLD REDEMPTION SET ODDS 1:28,800
1 Smith/Marino/Rice/Favre 30.00 80.00
2 George/Martin/Sanders/Davis 12.50 30.00
3 Moore/Stewart/Grbac/Warren 5.00 12.00
4 McEloy/Aikman/Thomas/Carter 10.00 25.00
5 Harb/Jackson/Bled/Anderson 6.00 15.00
6 Elway/White/Moon/Owens 15.00 40.00
7 Salaam/Collins/Sharpe/Watters 5.00 12.00
8 Centers/bates/Moulds/Brunell 5.00 12.00
9 Bettis/Pickens/Brooks/Abdul 5.00 12.00
10 George/Martin/Young/Biaka 7.50 20.00
11 Glenn/Blake/Alstott/Conway 5.00 12.00
12 Mirer/Johnson/Freeman/Gallo 5.00 12.00
13 McNair/Faulk/Smith/Bruce 6.00 15.00
14 Testav/Hampt/Deion/Banks 5.00 12.00
15 Chand/Thomas/Harrison/Phillips 5.00 12.00
16 Hill/Frot/Kaut/Keyshawn 5.00 12.00
17 Allen/Kenn/Rhett/Mitchell 3.00 8.00
18 Dunn/Druck/pace/Russell 7.50 20.00

1997 Absolute Pennants

COMPLETE SET (192) 150.00 300.00
COMMON CARD (1-192) .30 .75
SEMISTARS .60 1.50
UNLISTED STARS 1.25 3.00
ONE PER BOX
*GOLD REDEMPTION : .5X TO 1.2X BASIC INSERT
GOLD REDEMPTION SET ODDS 1:14,400
6 Tiki Barber 4.00 10.00
31 Warrick Dunn 2.00 5.00
62 Tony Gonzalez 2.50 6.00
81 Jerry Rice 4.00 10.00
101 Troy Aikman 4.00 10.00
105 Drew Bledsoe 2.50 6.00
107 Steve Young 3.00 8.00
120 Steve McNair 2.00 5.00
121 Marshall Faulk 1.50 4.00
142 Jake Plummer 3.00 8.00
145 Terrell Davis 2.00 5.00
151 Brett Favre 8.00 20.00
152 Emmitt Smith 6.00 15.00
153 Dan Marino 8.00 20.00
163 Mark Brunell 2.50 6.00
166 Corey Dillon 4.00 10.00
167 Curtis Martin 2.00 5.00
183 Barry Sanders 6.00 15.00
187 John Elway 8.00 20.00

1997 Absolute Pennant Autographs

Randomly inserted at the rate of one per box, this "chip-topper" set is very similar to the Pennant Insert set except for the gold foil stamping on the side of the pennant and an autograph of one of the seven players in the set. The autographs are signed in gold ink across the photo of the player and many times onto the pennant material as well. Some cards have been found in unsigned form as well.

RANDOMLY INSERTED BOX TOPPER
A1 Kordell Stewart 12.00 30.00
A2 Eddie George 15.00 40.00
A3 Karim Abdul-Jabbar 10.00 25.00
A4 Mike Alstott 15.00 40.00
A5 Terry Glenn 12.00 30.00
A6 Napoleon Kaufman 10.00 25.00
A7 Terry Allen 10.00 25.00
A8 Tim Brown 25.00 50.00
A6U Napoleon Kaufman Unsigned 5.00 12.00

1997 Absolute Reflex

Randomly inserted in packs at a rate of one in 288, this set features the same 200-players as the base set, but with different card numbers and design. The card backs have full-bleed glossy player photos and no text.

COMMON CARD (1-200) 3.00 8.00
SEMISTARS 5.00 12.00
UNLISTED STARS 8.00 20.00
STATED ODDS 1:288
1 Brett Favre 30.00 80.00
7 Drew Bledsoe 10.00 25.00
8 Curtis Martin 10.00 25.00
16 Mark Brunell 10.00 25.00
19 John Elway 30.00 80.00
20 Terrell Davis 10.00 25.00
23 Steve Young 10.00 25.00
25 Jerry Rice 15.00 40.00
26 Troy Aikman 15.00 40.00
28 Emmitt Smith 25.00 60.00
50 Marshall Faulk 10.00 25.00
57 Dan Marino 30.00 80.00
61 Steve McNair 10.00 25.00
88 Barry Sanders 25.00 60.00
116 Terrell Owens 10.00 25.00
149 Corey Dillon 25.00 60.00
163 Jake Plummer 20.00 50.00

1997 Absolute Unsung Heroes

Randomly inserted in packs at the rate of one in 12, this 30 card set highlights players that are not found very often in the spotlight. The players in the set were selected by fan ballots inserted in 1996 Playoff Prime packs. Zach Thomas highlights a set full of unheralded hard workers. The cards were released again in factory set form at the February 28, 1997 Unsung Heroes Banquet.

COMPLETE SET (30) 10.00 25.00
STATED ODDS 1:12
1 Larry Centers .60 1.50
2 Jessie Tuggle .40 1.00
3 Stevon Moore .40 1.00
4 Mark Pike .40 1.00
5 Anthony Johnson .60 1.50
6 Anthony Carter RB .40 1.00
7 Eric Bieniemy .40 1.00
8 Jim Schwantz .40 1.00
9 Tyrone Braxton .40 1.00
10 Bennie Blades .40 1.00
11 Don Beebe .40 1.00
12 Barron Wortham .40 1.00
13 Jason Belser .40 1.00
14 Mickey Washington .40 1.00
15 Dave Szott .40 1.00
16 Zach Thomas .75 2.00
17 Chris Walsh .40 1.00
18 Sam Gash .40 1.00
19 Willie Roaf .40 1.00
20 Charles Way .60 1.50
21 Wayne Chrebet .75 2.00
22 Russell Maryland .40 1.00
23 Michael Zordich .40 1.00
24 Tim Lester .40 1.00
25 Harold Green .40 1.00
26 Rodney Harrison .75 2.00
27 Gary Plummer .40 1.00
28 Winston Moss .40 1.00
29 Robb Thomas .40 1.00
30 Darrick Brownlow .40 1.00

1998 Absolute Hobby

The 1998 Playoff Absolute set consists of 200 standard size cards issued in three card packs printed on 42 pt. brushed silver foil. Each card included a plastic player image laminated between the card's front and back.

COMPLETE SET (200) 40.00 100.00
1 John Elway 4.00 10.00
2 Marcus Nash RC .60 1.50
3 Brian Griese RC 2.50 6.00
4 Terrell Davis 1.00 2.50
5 Rod Smith WR .60 1.50
6 Shannon Sharpe .60 1.50
7 Ed McCaffrey .60 1.50
8 Brett Favre 4.00 10.00
9 Dorsey Levens 1.00 2.50
10 Derrick Mayes .60 1.50
11 Antonio Freeman 1.00 2.50
12 Robert Brooks .60 1.50
13 Mark Chmura .60 1.50
14 Reggie White 1.00 2.50
15 Kordell Stewart 1.00 2.50
16 Hines Ward RC 6.00 12.00
17 Jerome Bettis 1.00 2.50
18 Charles Johnson .40 1.00
19 Courtney Hawkins .40 1.00
20 Will Blackwell .40 1.00
21 Mark Bruener .40 1.00
22 Steve Young 1.50 4.00
23 Jim Druckenmiller .40 1.00
24 Garrison Hearst 1.00 2.50
25 R.W. McQuarters RC 1.00 2.50
26 Marc Edwards .40 1.00
27 Irv Smith .40 1.00
28 Jerry Rice 2.00 5.00
29 Terrell Owens 1.00 2.50
30 J.J. Stokes .60 1.50
31 Elvis Grbac .60 1.50
32 Rashaan Shehee RC 1.00 2.50
33 Donnell Bennett .40 1.00
34 Kimble Anders .60 1.50
35 Ted Popson .40 1.00
36 Derrick Alexander WR .60 1.50
37 Tony Gonzalez 1.00 2.50
38 Andre Rison .60 1.50
39 Brad Johnson 1.00 2.50
40 Randy Moss RC 6.00 15.00
41 Robert Smith 1.00 2.50
42 Leroy Hoard .40 1.00
43 Cris Carter 1.00 2.50
44 Jake Reed .60 1.50
45 Drew Bledsoe 1.50 4.00
46 Tony Simmons RC 1.00 2.50
47 Chris Floyd RC .60 1.50
48 Robert Edwards RC 1.00 2.50
49 Shawn Jefferson .40 1.00
50 Ben Coates .60 1.50
51 Terry Glenn 1.00 2.50
52 Trent Dilfer 1.00 2.50
53 Jacquez Green RC 1.00 2.50
54 Warrick Dunn 1.00 2.50
55 Mike Alstott 1.00 2.50
56 Reidel Anthony .60 1.50
57 Bert Emanuel .60 1.50
58 Warren Sapp .60 1.50
59 Charlie Batch RC 1.25 3.00
60 Germane Crowell RC 1.00 2.50
61 Scott Mitchell .60 1.50
62 Barry Sanders 3.00 8.00
63 Tommy Vardell .40 1.00
64 Herman Moore .60 1.50
65 Johnnie Morton .60 1.50
66 Mark Brunell 1.00 2.50
67 Jonathan Quinn RC 1.25 3.00
68 Fred Taylor RC 2.00 5.00
69 James Stewart .60 1.50
70 Jimmy Smith .60 1.50
71 Damon Jones .40 1.00
72 Keenan McCardell .60 1.50
73 Dan Marino 4.00 10.00
74 Larry Shannon RC .60 1.50
75 John Avery RC 1.00 2.50
76 Troy Drayton .40 1.00
77 Stanley Pritchett .40 1.00
78 Karim Abdul-Jabbar 1.00 2.50
79 O.J. McDuffie .60 1.50
80 Yatil Green .40 1.00
81 Danny Kanell .60 1.50
82 Tiki Barber 1.00 2.50
83 Tyrone Wheatley .60 1.50
84 Charles Way .40 1.00
85 Gary Brown .40 1.00
86 Brian Alford RC .60 1.50
87 Joe Jurevicius RC 1.25 3.00
88 Ike Hilliard .60 1.50
89 Troy Aikman 2.00 5.00
90 Deion Sanders 1.00 2.50
91 Emmitt Smith 3.00 8.00
92 Chris Warren .60 1.50
93 Daryl Johnston .60 1.50
94 Michael Irvin 1.00 2.50
95 David LaFleur .40 1.00
96 Kevin Dyson RC 1.25 3.00
97 Steve McNair 1.00 2.50
98 Eddie George 1.00 2.50
99 Yancey Thigpen .40 1.00
100 Frank Wycheck .40 1.00
101 Glenn Foley .60 1.50
102 Vinny Testaverde .60 1.50
103 Keyshawn Johnson 1.00 2.50
104 Curtis Martin 1.00 2.50
105 Keith Byars .40 1.00
106 Scott Frost RC .60 1.50
107 Wayne Chrebet 1.00 2.50
108 Warren Moon 1.00 2.50
109 Ahman Green RC 3.00 8.00
110 Steve Broussard .40 1.00
111 Ricky Watters .60 1.50
112 Joey Galloway .60 1.50
113 Mike Pritchard .40 1.00
114 Brian Blades .40 1.00
115 Gus Frerotte .40 1.00
116 Skip Hicks RC 1.00 2.50
117 Terry Allen 1.00 2.50
118 Michael Westbrook .60 1.50
119 Jamie Asher .40 1.00
120 Leslie Shepherd .40 1.00
121 Jeff Blake .60 1.50
122 Corey Dillon 1.00 2.50
123 Carl Pickens .60 1.50
124 Tony McGee .40 1.00
125 Darnay Scott .60 1.50
126 Kerry Collins .60 1.50
127 Fred Lane .40 1.00
128 William Floyd .40 1.00
129 Rae Carruth .40 1.00
130 Wesley Walls .60 1.50
131 Muhsin Muhammad .60 1.50
132 Jake Plummer 1.00 2.50
133 Adrian Murrell .60 1.50
134 Michael Pittman RC 2.00 4.00
135 Larry Centers .40 1.00
136 Frank Sanders .60 1.50
137 Rob Moore .60 1.50
138 Andre Wadsworth RC 1.00 2.50
139 Mario Bates .60 1.50
140 Chris Chandler .60 1.50
141 Byron Hanspard .40 1.00
142 Jamal Anderson 1.00 2.50
143 Terance Mathis .60 1.50
144 O.J. Santiago .40 1.00
145 Tony Martin .60 1.50
146 Jammi German RC .60 1.50
147 Jim Harbaugh .60 1.50
148 Errict Rhett .60 1.50
149 Michael Jackson .40 1.00
150 Pat Johnson RC 1.00 2.50
151 Eric Green .40 1.00
152 Doug Flutie 1.00 2.50
153 Rob Johnson .60 1.50
154 Antowain Smith 1.00 2.50
155 Bruce Smith .60 1.50
156 Eric Moulds 1.00 2.50
157 Andre Reed .60 1.50
158 Erik Kramer .40 1.00
159 Darnell Autry .40 1.00
160 Edgar Bennett .40 1.00
161 Curtis Enis RC .60 1.50
162 Curtis Conway .60 1.50
163 E.G. Green RC 1.00 2.50
164 Jerome Pathon RC 1.25 3.00
165 Peyton Manning RC 12.00 30.00
166 Marshall Faulk 1.25 3.00
167 Zack Crockett .40 1.00
168 Ken Dilger .40 1.00
169 Marvin Harrison 1.00 2.50
170 Danny Wuerffel .60 1.50
171 Lamar Smith .60 1.50
172 Ray Zellars .40 1.00
173 Qadry Ismail .60 1.50
174 Sean Dawkins .40 1.00
175 Andre Hastings .40 1.00
176 Jeff George .60 1.50
177 Charles Woodson RC 3.00 8.00
178 Napoleon Kaufman 1.00 2.50
179 Jon Ritchie RC 1.00 2.50
180 Desmond Howard .60 1.50
181 Tim Brown 1.00 2.50
182 James Jett .60 1.50
183 Rickey Dudley .40 1.00
184 Bobby Hoying .60 1.50
185 Rodney Peete .40 1.00
186 Charlie Garner .60 1.50
187 Irving Fryar .60 1.50
188 Chris T. Jones .40 1.00
189 Jason Dunn .40 1.00
190 Tony Banks .60 1.50
191 Robert Holcombe RC 1.00 2.50
192 Craig Heyward .40 1.00
193 Isaac Bruce 1.00 2.50
194 Az-Zahir Hakim RC 1.25 3.00
195 Eddie Kennison .60 1.50
196 Mikhael Ricks RC 1.00 2.50
197 Ryan Leaf RC 1.25 3.00
198 Natrone Means .60 1.50
199 Junior Seau 1.00 2.50
200 Freddie Jones .40 1.00

1998 Absolute Hobby Gold

*GOLD STARS: 10X TO 25X HI COL.
*GOLD RCs: 5X TO 10X
STATED PRINT RUN 25 SERIAL #'d SETS

1998 Absolute Hobby Silver

COMPLETE SET (200) 200.00 400.00
*STARS: 1.25X TO 2.5X BASIC CARDS
*RC'S: .75X TO 1.5X BASIC CARDS
STATED ODDS 1:3 HOBBY

1998 Absolute Retail

COMP.RETAIL SET (200) 40.00 80.00
*RETAIL CARDS: .25X TO .5X HOBBY

1998 Absolute Retail Green

COMPLETE SET (200) 75.00 150.00
*GREEN STARS: 1.2X TO 3X RETAIL
*GREEN RCs: .6X TO 1.5X RETAIL
RANDOM INSERTS IN RETAIL PACKS

1998 Absolute Retail Red

COMPLETE SET (200) 125.00 250.00
*RED RETAIL STARS: 1.2X TO 3X BASIC RETAIL
*RED RETAIL RC'S: .8X TO 2X BASIC RETAIL
RED RETAIL STATED ODDS 1:3 RETAIL

1998 Absolute 7-Eleven

*STARS: 1.2X TO 3X BASIC RETAIL
*ROOKIES: .4X TO 1X BASIC RETAIL

1998 Absolute Checklists

The 1998 Playoff Absolute Checklist set consists of 30 cards and is an insert to the 1998 Playoff Absolute base set. The cards are randomly inserted in packs at a rate of one in 19. The fronts carry a speckled holographic foil with holographic foil stamping and feature 30 NFL home stadiums with a star player from each team.

COMPLETE SET (30) 125.00 250.00
STATED ODDS 1:19
*SILVER DIE CUTS: .3X TO .6X BASIC INSERTS
SILVER DIE CUT STATED ODDS 1:25 RETAIL
1 Jake Plummer 3.00 8.00
2 Jamal Anderson 3.00 8.00
3 Jim Harbaugh 2.00 5.00
4 Rob Johnson 2.00 5.00
5 Fred Lane 1.25 3.00
6 Curtis Enis .75 2.00
7 Corey Dillon 3.00 8.00
8 Troy Aikman 6.00 15.00
9 Terrell Davis 3.00 8.00
10 Barry Sanders 10.00 25.00
11 Brett Favre 12.50 30.00
12 Peyton Manning 15.00 40.00
13 Mark Brunell 3.00 8.00
14 Elvis Grbac 2.00 5.00
15 Dan Marino 10.00 25.00
16 Cris Carter 3.00 8.00
17 Drew Bledsoe 5.00 12.00
18 Ray Zellars 1.25 3.00
19 Charles Way 1.25 3.00
20 Curtis Martin 3.00 8.00
21 Napoleon Kaufman 3.00 8.00
22 Irving Fryar 2.00 5.00
23 Kordell Stewart 3.00 8.00
24 Tony Banks 2.00 5.00
25 Ryan Leaf 1.50 4.00
26 Jerry Rice 6.00 15.00
27 Warren Moon 3.00 8.00
28 Warrick Dunn 3.00 8.00
29 Eddie George 3.00 8.00
30 Terry Allen 3.00 8.00

1998 Absolute Draft Picks

The 1998 Playoff Absolute Draft Picks set consists of 36 cards and is an insert to the 1998 Playoff Absolute base set. The cards are randomly inserted in packs at a rate of one in 10. The fronts feature full bleed action photos of 36 NFL top picks on gold etched foil with silver foil stamping.

COMPLETE SET (36) 75.00 150.00
STATED ODDS 1:10
*BRONZE: .4X TO 1X BASIC GOLD
BRONZE BONUS PACKS 1:4 BOXES
*SILVER DIE CUT: .3X TO .6X GOLD
SILVER DIE CUT STATED ODDS 1:13 RETAIL
*BLUE DIE CUT: .4X TO 1X GOLD
BLUE DIE CUT INSERTED IN SPECIAL RETAIL
1 Peyton Manning 15.00 40.00
2 Ryan Leaf 1.50 4.00
3 Andre Wadsworth 1.25 3.00
4 Charles Woodson 4.00 10.00
5 Curtis Enis .75 2.00
6 Fred Taylor 2.50 6.00
7 Kevin Dyson 1.50 4.00
8 Robert Edwards 1.25 3.00
9 Randy Moss 10.00 25.00
10 R.W. McQuarters 1.25 3.00
11 John Avery 1.25 3.00
12 Marcus Nash .75 2.00
13 Jerome Pathon 1.50 4.00
14 Jacquez Green 1.25 3.00
15 Robert Holcombe 1.25 3.00
16 Pat Johnson 1.25 3.00
17 Germane Crowell 1.25 3.00
18 Tony Simmons 1.25 3.00
19 Joe Jurevicius 1.50 4.00
20 Mikhael Ricks 1.25 3.00
21 Charlie Batch 1.50 4.00
22 Jon Ritchie 1.25 3.00
23 Scott Frost .75 2.00
24 Skip Hicks 1.25 3.00
25 Brian Alford .75 2.00
26 E.G. Green 1.25 3.00
27 Jammi German .75 2.00
28 Ahman Green 4.00 10.00
29 Chris Floyd .75 2.00
30 Larry Shannon .75 2.00
31 Jonathan Quinn 1.50 4.00
32 Rashaan Shehee 1.25 3.00
33 Brian Griese 3.00 8.00
34 Hines Ward 6.00 15.00
35 Michael Pittman 2.00 5.00
36 Az-Zahir Hakim 1.50 4.00

1998 Absolute Honors

The 1998 Playoff Absolute Honors set consists of 3 cards and is an insert to the 1998 Playoff Absolute base set. The cards are randomly inserted in packs at a rate of one in 3,970. The fronts offer a die-cut Playoff logo printed in black over holographic foil. The set is a continuation of the highly successful insert set that honors three of the NFL's best.

COMPLETE SET (3) 60.00 150.00
STATED ODDS 1:3970
PH13 John Elway 30.00 80.00
PH14 Jerome Bettis 12.50 30.00
PH15 Steve Young 20.00 50.00

1998 Absolute Dan Marino Milestones Autographs

The 1998 Playoff Absolute Marino Milestones set consisted of 15 cards distributed in three different 1998 Playoff products (5-cards per release):1:321 Prestige, 1:397 Absolute, 1:385 Momentum. The cards offer authentic Dan Marino autographs commemorating records set by the NFL great.

COMMON CARD (1-15) 50.00 120.00
1-5: STATED ODDS 1:321 PRESTIGE
6-10: STATED ODDS 1:397 ABSOLUTE
11-15: STATED ODDS 1:385 MOMENTUM

1998 Absolute Platinum Quads

The 1998 Playoff Absolute Platinum Quads set consists of 18 cards and is an insert to the 1998 Playoff Absolute base set. The cards are randomly inserted in packs at a rate of one 73. The foiled cards with "sunburst" etching highlights 4 NFL players with 2 on the front and 2 on the back.

COMPLETE SET (18) 200.00 500.00
STATED ODDS 1:73
1 Favre/Elway/Sanders/Dunn 30.00 80.00
2 Marino/Davis/Kauf/Bott 20.00 50.00
3 Rice/Johnson/Faulk/Smith 12.50 30.00
4 Aikman/Moore/Chmura/Frer 15.00 40.00
5 Young/Alst/Barber/Keysh 10.00 25.00
6 Stewart/Brooks/Abdul/Sharpe 10.00 25.00
7 Brunell/Levens/Pckns/Moore 10.00 25.00
8 Bledsoe/Galloway/Brown/Lane 12.50 40.00

9 George/Johnson/Fryar/Rison 10.00 25.00
10 Plummer/Free/McNair/Moon 10.00 25.00
11 Emmitt/Carter/Seau/Kanell 25.00 60.00
12 Dillon/Reed/Martin/Hoying 10.00 25.00
13 Deion/Druck/Anthony/Allen 10.00 25.00
14 Smith/Walls/Bruce/Glenn 10.00 25.00
15 Batch/Frost/Quinn/Griese 10.00 25.00
16 Dyson/Moss/Nash/Pathon 25.00 50.00
17 Enis/Taylor/Edwards/Avery 10.00 25.00
18 Mann/Leaf/Wads/Woodson 25.00 60.00

1998 Absolute Red Zone

The 1998 Playoff Absolute Red Zone set consists of 26 cards and is an insert to the 1998 Playoff Absolute base set. The cards are randomly inserted in packs at a rate of one in 19. The fronts are printed on silver mirror board with red foil stamping and feature players with outstanding stats within the football "red zone."

COMPLETE SET (26) 100.00 200.00
STATED ODDS 1:19
*DIE CUTS: .3X TO .6X BASIC INSERTS
DIE CUT STATED ODDS 1:25 RETAIL
1 Terrell Davis 2.50 6.00
2 Jerome Bettis 2.50 6.00
3 Mike Alstott 2.50 6.00
4 Brett Favre 10.00 25.00
5 Mark Brunell 2.50 6.00
6 Jeff George 1.50 4.00
7 John Elway 10.00 25.00
8 Troy Aikman 5.00 12.00
9 Steve Young 4.00 10.00
10 Kordell Stewart 2.50 6.00
11 Drew Bledsoe 4.00 10.00
12 James Jett 1.50 4.00
13 Dan Marino 10.00 25.00
14 Brad Johnson 2.50 6.00
15 Jake Plummer 2.50 6.00
16 Karim Abdul-Jabbar 2.50 6.00
17 Eddie George 2.50 6.00
18 Warrick Dunn 2.50 6.00
19 Cris Carter 2.50 6.00
20 Barry Sanders 8.00 20.00
21 Corey Dillon 2.50 6.00
22 Steve McNair 2.50 6.00
23 Herman Moore 1.50 4.00
24 Antonio Freeman 2.50 6.00
25 Dorsey Levens 2.50 6.00
26 James Stewart 1.50 4.00

1998 Absolute Shields

The 1998 Playoff Absolute Shield set consists of 20 cards. The cards were randomly inserted in packs at a rate of 1:37 hobby or 1:49 retail. The fronts feature 20 of the NFL's brightest players on a die cut design featuring embossed football textured paper with foil stamping. The retail version included an extra die cut portion on one of the card's corners.

COMP.HOBBY SET (20) 125.00 250.00
STATED ODDS 1:37
*RETAIL DIE CUT CORNER: .25X TO .6X HOBBY
RETAIL DIE CUT CORNER ODDS 1:49 RETAIL
1 Terrell Davis 3.00 8.00
2 Corey Dillon 3.00 8.00
3 Dorsey Levens 2.50 6.00
4 Brett Favre 12.50 30.00
5 Warrick Dunn 3.00 8.00
6 Jerome Bettis 3.00 8.00
7 John Elway 12.50 30.00
8 Troy Aikman 6.00 15.00
9 Mark Brunell 3.00 8.00
10 Kordell Stewart 2.50 6.00
11 Eddie George 3.00 8.00
12 Jerry Rice 6.00 15.00
13 Dan Marino 12.50 30.00
14 Emmitt Smith 10.00 25.00
15 Napoleon Kaufman 2.50 6.00
16 Ryan Leaf 2.50 6.00
17 Curtis Martin 3.00 8.00
18 Peyton Manning 20.00 50.00
19 Cris Carter 3.00 8.00
20 Barry Sanders 10.00 25.00

1998 Absolute Statistically Speaking

The 1998 Playoff Absolute Statistically Speaking set consists of 18 cards and is an insert to the 1998 Playoff Absolute base set. The cards are randomly inserted in packs at a rate of one in 55. The fronts carry a brushed foil with black foil stamping and feature individual statistics of the spotlighted player.

COMPLETE SET (18) 100.00 200.00
STATED ODDS 1:55
*DIE CUTS: .3X TO .6X BASIC INSERTS
DIE CUT STATED ODDS 1:73 RETAIL
1 Jerry Rice 6.00 15.00
2 Barry Sanders 10.00 25.00
3 Deion Sanders 3.00 8.00
4 Brett Favre 12.50 30.00
5 Curtis Martin 3.00 8.00
6 Warrick Dunn 3.00 8.00
7 John Elway 12.50 30.00
8 Steve Young 5.00 12.00
9 Cris Carter 3.00 8.00
10 Kordell Stewart 3.00 8.00
11 Terrell Davis 3.00 8.00
12 Irving Fryar 2.00 5.00
13 Dan Marino 12.50 30.00
14 Tim Brown 3.00 8.00
15 Jerome Bettis 3.00 8.00
16 Troy Aikman 6.00 15.00
17 Napoleon Kaufman 3.00 8.00
18 Emmitt Smith 10.00 25.00

1998 Absolute Tandems

Randomly inserted in retail packs only at the rate of one in 97, this six-card retail only insert set features color action photos of two players pictured on one card, Only one side of the card was printed with micro-etch technology, but each player can be found in both versions on his side of the card.

COMPLETE SET (6) 60.00 120.00
EACH PLAYER HAS BOTH VERSIONS
STATED ODDS 1:97 RETAIL
1A T.Davis ME 6.00 15.00
C.Enis
1B T.Davis 6.00 15.00
C.Enis ME
2A J.Elway ME 20.00 50.00
R.Leaf
2B J.Elway 20.00 50.00
R.Leaf ME
3A B.Favre ME 25.00 60.00
P.Manning
3B B.Favre 25.00 60.00
P.Manning ME
4A R.Moss ME 25.00 50.00
J.Rice
4B R.Moss 25.00 50.00
J.Rice ME
5A B.Sanders ME 10.00 25.00
F.Taylor
5B B.Sanders 10.00 25.00
F.Taylor ME
6A D.Sanders ME 6.00 15.00
C.Woodson
6B D.Sanders 6.00 15.00
C Woodson ME

1999 Absolute EXP

Released as a 200-card set, 1999 Playoff Absolute EXP is comprised of 160 regular player cards and 40 draft pick cards printed on 20-point stock enhanced with foil stamping. EXP was packaged in eight card packs.

COMPLETE SET (200) 25.00 50.00
1 Tim Couch RC .25 .60
2 Donovan McNabb RC 1.25 3.00
3 Akili Smith RC .20 .50
4 Edgerrin James RC .30 .75
5 Ricky Williams RC .30 .75
6 Torry Holt RC .40 1.00
7 Champ Bailey RC .40 1.00
8 David Boston RC .20 .50
9 Chris Claiborne RC .20 .50
10 Chris McAlister RC .20 .50
11 Daunte Culpepper RC .30 .75
12 Cade McNown RC .20 .50
13 Troy Edwards RC .20 .50
14 Kevin Johnson RC .25 .60
15 James Johnson RC .20 .50
16 Rob Konrad RC .20 .50
17 Jim Kleinsasser RC .30 .75
18 Kevin Faulk RC .20 .50
19 Joe Montgomery RC .20 .50
20 Shaun King RC .20 .50
21 Peerless Price RC .20 .50
22 Mike Cloud RC .20 .50
23 Jermaine Fazande RC .20 .50
24 D'Wayne Bates RC .20 .50
25 Brock Huard RC .20 .50
26 Marty Booker RC .20 .50
27 Karsten Bailey RC .20 .50
28 Shawn Bryson RC .20 .50
29 Jeff Paulk RC .20 .50
30 Sedrick Irvin RC .20 .50
31 Craig Yeast RC .20 .50
32 Joe Germaine RC .25 .60
33 Dameane Douglas RC .20 .50
34 Brandon Stokley RC .25 .60
35 Larry Parker RC .25 .60
36 Wane McGarity RC .20 .50
37 Na Brown RC .20 .50
38 Cecil Collins RC .20 .50
39 Darrin Chiaverini RC .20 .50
40 Madre Hill RC .20 .50
41 Adrian Murrell .20 .50
42 Jake Plummer .20 .50
43 Frank Sanders .20 .50
44 Rob Moore .20 .50
45 Andre Wadsworth .20 .50
46 Simeon Rice .20 .50
47 Eric Swann .20 .50
48 Terance Mathis .20 .50
49 Tim Dwight .25 .60
50 Jamal Anderson .25 .60
51 Chris Chandler .25 .60
52 Chris Calloway .20 .50
53 O.J. Santiago .20 .50
54 Jermaine Lewis .20 .50
55 Priest Holmes .20 .50
56 Scott Mitchell .20 .50
57 Tony Banks .25 .60
58 Rod Woodson .30 .75
59 Andre Reed .30 .75
60 Thurman Thomas .25 .60
61 Bruce Smith .25 .60
62 Rob Johnson .25 .60
63 Eric Moulds .20 .50
64 Doug Flutie .30 .75
65 Antowain Smith .20 .50
66 Tim Biakabutuka .25 .60
67 Muhsin Muhammad .20 .50
68 Steve Beuerlein .25 .60
69 Bobby Engram .20 .50
70 Curtis Conway .25 .60
71 Curtis Enis .20 .50
72 Edgar Bennett .25 .60
73 Jeff Blake .25 .60
74 Darnay Scott .20 .50
75 Carl Pickens .25 .60
76 Corey Dillon .20 .50
77 Ty Detmer .20 .50
78 Leslie Shepherd .20 .50
79 Sedrick Shaw .20 .50
80 Rocket Ismail .25 .60
81 Emmitt Smith .50 1.25
82 Michael Irvin .30 .75
83 Troy Aikman .40 1.00
84 Deion Sanders .25 .60
85 Darren Woodson .25 .60
86 Chris Warren .25 .60
87 John Elway .50 1.25
88 Brian Griese .20 .50
89 Shannon Sharpe .25 .60
90 Terrell Davis .25 .60
91 Bubby Brister .20 .50
92 Ed McCaffrey .25 .60
93 Rod Smith .25 .60
94 Germane Crowell .20 .50
95 Johnnie Morton .25 .60
96 Barry Sanders .50 1.25
97 Herman Moore .25 .60
98 Charlie Batch .20 .50
99 Mark Chmura .20 .50
100 Derrick Mayes .20 .50
101 Dorsey Levens .25 .60
102 Brett Favre .60 1.50
103 Antonio Freeman .25 .60
104 Robert Brooks .25 .60
105 Desmond Howard .25 .60
106 Jerome Pathon .20 .50
107 Marvin Harrison .25 .60
108 Peyton Manning 1.00 2.50
109 E.G. Green .20 .50
110 Tavian Banks .20 .50
111 Keenan McCardell .25 .60
112 Jimmy Smith .25 .60
113 Mark Brunell .25 .60
114 Fred Taylor .20 .50
115 Byron Bam Morris .20 .50
116 Andre Rison .25 .60
117 Elvis Grbac .20 .50
118 Warren Moon .30 .75
119 Tony Gonzalez .25 .60
120 Derrick Alexander WR .20 .50
121 Rashaan Shehee .20 .50
122 Zach Thomas .25 .60
123 Oronde Gadsden .20 .50
124 Dan Marino .60 1.50
125 Karim Abdul-Jabbar .20 .50
126 O.J. McDuffie .25 .60
127 Jake Reed .25 .60
128 John Randle .30 .75
129 Randy Moss .25 .60
130 Cris Carter .30 .75
131 Randall Cunningham .25 .60
132 Robert Smith .20 .50
133 Terry Glenn .25 .60
134 Ben Coates .25 .60
135 Drew Bledsoe .25 .60
136 Ty Law .30 .75
137 Tony Simmons .20 .50
138 Eddie Kennison .25 .60
139 Cam Cleeland .20 .50
140 Ike Hilliard .20 .50
141 Joe Jurevicius .20 .50
142 Gary Brown .20 .50
143 Kerry Collins .20 .50
144 Tiki Barber .25 .60
145 Jason Sehorn .25 .60
146 Dedric Ward .20 .50
147 Vinny Testaverde .20 .50
148 Wayne Chrebet .20 .50
149 Curtis Martin .25 .60
150 Keyshawn Johnson .25 .60
151 James Jett .20 .50
152 Napoleon Kaufman .20 .50
153 Tim Brown .30 .75
154 Charles Woodson .30 .75
155 Rickey Dudley .20 .50
156 Charles Johnson .20 .50
157 Duce Staley .20 .50
158 Chris Fuamatu-Ma'afala .20 .50
159 Jerome Bettis .30 .75
160 Kordell Stewart .20 .50
161 Levon Kirkland .20 .50
162 Hines Ward .25 .60
163 Mikhael Ricks .20 .50
164 Natrone Means .25 .60
165 Ryan Leaf .25 .60
166 Jim Harbaugh .25 .60
167 Junior Seau .25 .60
168 Steve Young .40 1.00
169 J.J. Stokes .20 .50
170 Terrell Owens .25 .60
171 Jerry Rice .75 2.00
172 Garrison Hearst .20 .50
173 Ricky Watters .25 .60
174 Jon Kitna .20 .50
175 Joey Galloway .25 .60
176 Ahman Green .25 .60
177 Isaac Bruce .30 .75
178 Marshall Faulk .25 .60
179 Trent Green .20 .50
180 Amp Lee .20 .50
181 Greg Hill .20 .50
182 Warren Sapp .25 .60
183 Hardy Nickerson .20 .50
184 Trent Dilfer .20 .50
185 Reidel Anthony .20 .50
186 Jacquez Green .20 .50
187 Warrick Dunn .20 .50
188 Mike Alstott .20 .50
189 Kevin Dyson .20 .50
190 Eddie George .25 .60
191 Yancey Thigpen .20 .50
192 Steve McNair .25 .60
193 Chris Sanders .20 .50
194 Frank Wycheck .25 .60
195 Darrell Green .30 .75
196 Stephen Alexander .20 .50
197 Albert Connell .20 .50
198 Michael Westbrook .20 .50
199 Brad Johnson .25 .60
200 Skip Hicks .20 .50

1999 Absolute EXP Tools of the Trade

*DEF.PLAYER: 1.5X TO 4X BASIC CARDS
DEFENSIVE STATED PRINT RUN 1000
*RECEIVERS: 2X TO 5X BASIC CARDS
RECEIVER STATED PRINT RUN 750
*RUNNING BACKS: 2.5X TO 6X BASIC CARDS
RUNNING BACK PRINT RUN 500
*QUARTERBACKS: 4X TO 10X BASIC CARDS
QUARTERBACK PRINT RUN 250

1999 Absolute EXP Terrell Davis Salute

Randomly inserted in packs, this 5-card set pays tribute to Terrell Davis and his to date career achievements. This set was release across Playoff brands, and EXP contains numbers TD6-TD10. Card backs carry a "TD" prefix.

COMPLETE SET (5) 15.00 40.00
COMMON CARD (TD6-TD10) 4.00 10.00
STATED ODDS 1:289

1999 Absolute EXP Terrell Davis Salute Autographs

Randomly seeded in packs, this 5-card set parallels the base Terrell Davis Salute set with and autographed version. Each card is sequentially numbered to 150.

COMMON AUTO/150 20.00 50.00
AUTO STATED PRINT RUN 150

1999 Absolute EXP Extreme Team

Randomly seeded in packs at the rate of one in 25, this 36-card set features team leaders on a holographic foil card with enhanced foil stamping. Card backs carry an "ET" prefix.

COMPLETE SET (36) 60.00 120.00
STATED ODDS 1:25
ET1 Steve Young 2.00 5.00
ET2 Fred Taylor 1.00 2.50
ET3 Kordell Stewart 1.00 2.50
ET4 Emmitt Smith 2.50 6.00
ET5 Barry Sanders 2.50 6.00
ET6 Jerry Rice 4.00 10.00
ET7 Jake Plummer 1.00 2.50
ET8 Eric Moulds 1.00 2.50
ET9 Randy Moss 1.25 3.00
ET10 Steve McNair 1.25 3.00
ET11 Curtis Martin 1.25 3.00
ET12 Dan Marino 3.00 8.00
ET13 Peyton Manning 5.00 12.00
ET14 Jon Kitna 1.00 2.50
ET15 Napoleon Kaufman 1.00 2.50
ET16 Eddie George 1.25 3.00
ET17 Brett Favre 3.00 8.00
ET18 Marshall Faulk 1.25 3.00
ET19 John Elway 2.50 6.00
ET20 Corey Dillon 1.00 2.50
ET21 Terrell Davis 1.25 3.00
ET22 Randall Cunningham 1.25 3.00
ET23 Mark Brunell 1.25 3.00
ET24 Tim Brown 1.50 4.00
ET25 Drew Bledsoe 1.25 3.00
ET26 Jerome Bettis 1.50 4.00
ET27 Charlie Batch 1.00 2.50
ET28 Jamal Anderson 1.25 3.00
ET29 Mike Alstott 1.00 2.50
ET30 Troy Aikman 2.00 5.00
ET31 Dorsey Levens 1.25 3.00
ET32 Joey Galloway 1.25 3.00
ET33 Skip Hicks 1.00 2.50
ET34 Terrell Owens 1.25 3.00
ET35 Keyshawn Johnson 1.25 3.00
ET36 Doug Flutie 1.50 4.00

1999 Absolute EXP Heroes

Randomly inserted in packs at the rate of one in 25, this 24-card set consisits of 24 NFL superstars that are highlighted on die-cut mirror board with silver borders, toil stamping, and micro-etching. Card backs carry an "HE" prefix.

COMPLETE SET (24) 30.00 60.00
STATED ODDS 1:25
HE1 Terrell Owens .75 2.00
HE2 Troy Aikman 1.25 3.00
HE3 Cris Carter 1.00 2.50
HE4 Brett Favre 2.00 5.00
HE5 Jamal Anderson .75 2.00
HE6 Doug Flutie 1.00 2.50
HE7 John Elway 1.50 4.00
HE8 Steve Young 1.25 3.00
HE9 Jerome Bettis 1.00 2.50
HE10 Emmitt Smith 1.50 4.00
HE11 Drew Bledsoe .75 2.00
HE12 Fred Taylor .60 1.50
HE13 Dan Marino 2.00 5.00
HE14 Antonio Freeman .75 2.00
HE15 Mark Brunell .75 2.00
HE16 Jake Plummer .60 1.50
HE17 Warrick Dunn .60 1.50
HE18 Peyton Manning 3.00 8.00
HE19 Randy Moss .75 2.00
HE20 Barry Sanders 1.50 4.00
HE21 Keyshawn Johnson .75 2.00
HE22 Eddie George .75 2.00
HE23 Terrell Davis .75 2.00
HE24 Jerry Rice 2.50 6.00

1999 Absolute EXP Rookie Reflex

Randomly inserted in packs at the rate of one in 49, this 18-card set features top rookies on mirror board stock with holographic foil stamping and micro-etching. Card backs carry an "RR" prefix.

COMPLETE SET (18) 25.00 60.00
STATED ODDS 1:49
RR1 Peerless Price .75 2.00
RR2 Daunte Culpepper 1.25 3.00
RR3 Joe Montgomery .75 2.00
RR4 David Boston .75 2.00
RR5 Shaun King .75 2.00
RR6 Champ Bailey 1.50 4.00
RR7 Rob Konrad .50 1.25
RR8 Torry Holt 1.50 4.00
RR9 Kevin Faulk .75 2.00
RR10 Ricky Williams 1.25 3.00
RR11 James Johnson .75 2.00
RR12 Edgerrin James 1.25 3.00
RR13 Kevin Johnson 1.00 2.50
RR14 Akili Smith .75 2.00
RR15 Troy Edwards .75 2.00
RR16 Donovan McNabb 2.50 6.00
RR17 Cade McNown .75 2.00
RR18 Tim Couch 1.00 2.50

1999 Absolute EXP Rookies Inserts

Randomly inserted in packs at one in 13, this green bordered 36 card base set features the hottest rookies from the NFL on holographic foil with blue foil stamping and micro-etching. These cards have a prefix of "AR".

COMPLETE SET (36) 10.00 25.00
STATED ODDS 1:13
AR1 Champ Bailey .50 1.25
AR2 Karsten Bailey .25 .60
AR3 D'Wayne Bates .25 .60
AR4 Marty Booker .25 .60
AR5 David Boston .25 .60
AR6 Shawn Bryson .25 .60
AR7 Chris Claiborne .25 .60
AR8 Mike Cloud .25 .60
AR9 Cecil Collins .25 .60
AR10 Tim Couch .30 .75
AR11 Daunte Culpepper .40 1.00
AR12 Dameane Douglas .25 .60
AR13 Troy Edwards .25 .60
AR14 Kevin Faulk .25 .60
AR15 Jermaine Fazande .25 .60
AR16 Joe Germaine .30 .75
AR17 Torry Holt .50 1.25
AR18 Brock Huard .25 .60
AR19 Edgerrin James .40 1.00
AR20 James Johnson .25 .60
AR21 Kevin Johnson .30 .75
AR22 Shaun King .25 .60
AR23 Jim Kleinsasser .40 1.00
AR24 Rob Konrad .25 .60
AR25 Chris McAlister .25 .60
AR26 Travis McGriff .25 .60
AR27 Donovan McNabb .75 2.00
AR28 Cade McNown .25 .60
AR29 Joe Montgomery .25 .60
AR30 Larry Parker .30 .75
AR31 Jeff Paulk .25 .60
AR32 Peerless Price .25 .60
AR33 Akili Smith .25 .60
AR34 Brandon Stokley .30 .75
AR35 Ricky Williams .40 1.00
AR36 Craig Yeast .25 .60

1999 Absolute EXP Barry Sanders Commemorative

Randomly inserted in packs at the rate of one in 289, this 5-card set pays tribute to Barry Sanders and his NFL career achievements. This set was distributed across other Playoff Products with EXP containing numbers 2-6.

COMPLETE SET (5) 30.00 60.00
COMMON CARD (RR2-RR6) 6.00 15.00
STATED ODDS 1:289

1999 Absolute EXP Team Jersey Tandems

Randomly seeded in packs at the rate of one in 97, this 31-card set features two swatches, one home and one away, from a replica (not game used) jersey on the card front. Card backs carry a "TJ" prefix.

STATED ODDS 1:97
TJ1 J.Plummer/D.Boston 4.00 10.00
TJ2 T.Aikman/E.Smith 10.00 25.00
TJ3 S.Hicks/B.Johnson 5.00 12.00
TJ4 J.Montgomery/Hilliard 4.00 10.00
TJ5 C.Johnson/D.McNabb 12.00 30.00
TJ6 R.Moss/C.Carter 6.00 15.00
TJ7 W.Dunn/M.Alstott 4.00 10.00
TJ8 B.Sanders/C.Batch 10.00 25.00
TJ9 A.Freeman/B.Favre 12.00 30.00
TJ10 C.Enis/C.McNown 4.00 10.00
TJ11 Biakabut/Muhammad 5.00 12.00
TJ12 Kennison/R.Williams 6.00 15.00
TJ13 S.Young/J.Rice 15.00 40.00
TJ14 M.Faulk/T.Holt 8.00 20.00
TJ15 J.Anderson/Chandler 5.00 12.00
TJ16 D.Marino/McDuffie 12.00 30.00
TJ17 D.Bledsoe/T.Glenn 5.00 12.00
TJ18 E.Moulds/D.Flutie 6.00 15.00
TJ19 P.Manning/E.James 20.00 50.00
TJ20 K.Johnson/W.Chrebet 5.00 12.00
TJ21 K.Stewart/J.Bettis 6.00 15.00
TJ22 M.Brunell/F.Taylor 5.00 12.00
TJ23 T.Couch/K.Johnson 5.00 12.00
TJ24 C.Pickens/A.Smith 5.00 12.00
TJ25 J.Lewis/T.Banks 5.00 12.00
TJ26 E.George/S.McNair 5.00 12.00
TJ27 N.Kaufman/T.Brown 6.00 15.00
TJ28 J.Elway/T.Davis 10.00 25.00
TJ29 J.Kitna/J.Galloway 5.00 12.00
TJ30 A.Rison/E.Grbac 5.00 12.00
TJ31 N.Means/M.Ricks 5.00 12.00

1999 Absolute SSD

The 1999 Playoff Absolute SSD base set contains 200-cards. The base card design showcases the featured player printed on a animation cell within a card stock frame printed with foil stamping on a solid background color. Cards #1-110 and #161-200 can be found in five different colored borders: Blue, Green, Orange, Purple, and Red. The Purple and Orange borderd cards are the most difficult to find.

COMPLETE SET (200) 125.00 250.00
1 Rob Moore .40 1.00
2 Frank Sanders .40 1.00
3 Jake Plummer .40 1.00
4 Adrian Murrell .40 1.00
5 Chris Chandler .50 1.25
6 Jamal Anderson .50 1.25
7 Tim Dwight .50 1.25
8 Terance Mathis .40 1.00
9 Priest Holmes .40 1.00
10 Jermaine Lewis .40 1.00
11 Antowain Smith .40 1.00
12 Doug Flutie .60 1.50
13 Eric Moulds .40 1.00
14 Muhsin Muhammad .40 1.00
15 Tim Biakabutuka .50 1.25
16 Curtis Enis .40 1.00
17 Curtis Conway .50 1.25
18 Bobby Engram .40 1.00
19 Corey Dillon .40 1.00
20 Carl Pickens .50 1.25
21 Darnay Scott .40 1.00
22 Sedrick Shaw .40 1.00
23 Leslie Shepherd .40 1.00
24 Ty Detmer .40 1.00
25 Deion Sanders .50 1.25
26 Troy Aikman .75 2.00
27 Michael Irvin .60 1.50
28 Emmitt Smith 1.00 2.50
29 Rocket Ismail .50 1.25
30 Rod Smith WR .50 1.25
31 Ed McCaffrey .50 1.25
32 Bubby Brister .40 1.00
33 Terrell Davis .50 1.25
34 Shannon Sharpe .50 1.25
35 Brian Griese .40 1.00
36 John Elway 1.00 2.50
37 Charlie Batch .40 1.00
38 Herman Moore .50 1.25
39 Barry Sanders 1.00 2.50
40 Johnnie Morton .50 1.25
41 Antonio Freeman .50 1.25
42 Brett Favre 1.25 3.00
43 Dorsey Levens .50 1.25
44 Derrick Mayes .40 1.00
45 Mark Chmura .40 1.00
46 Peyton Manning 2.00 5.00
47 Marvin Harrison .50 1.25
48 Jerome Pathon .40 1.00
49 Fred Taylor .40 1.00
50 Mark Brunell .50 1.25
51 Jimmy Smith .50 1.25
52 Keenan McCardell .50 1.25
53 Elvis Grbac .40 1.00
54 Andre Rison .50 1.25
55 Byron Bam Morris .40 1.00
56 O.J. McDuffie .50 1.25
57 Karim Abdul-Jabbar .40 1.00
58 Dan Marino 1.25 3.00
59 Oronde Gadsden .40 1.00
60 Robert Smith .40 1.00
61 Randall Cunningham .50 1.25
62 Cris Carter .60 1.50
63 Randy Moss .50 1.25
64 Drew Bledsoe .50 1.25
65 Ben Coates .50 1.25
66 Terry Glenn .50 1.25
67 Cam Cleeland .40 1.00
68 Eddie Kennison .50 1.25
69 Kerry Collins .40 1.00
70 Gary Brown .40 1.00
71 Joe Jurevicius .40 1.00
72 Ike Hilliard .40 1.00
73 Keyshawn Johnson .50 1.25
74 Curtis Martin .50 1.25
75 Wayne Chrebet .40 1.00
76 Tim Brown .60 1.50
77 Napoleon Kaufman .40 1.00
78 James Jett .40 1.00
79 Duce Staley .40 1.00
80 Charles Johnson .40 1.00
81 Kordell Stewart .40 1.00
82 Jerome Bettis .60 1.50
83 Chris Fuamatu-Ma'afala .40 1.00
84 Jim Harbaugh .50 1.25
85 Ryan Leaf .50 1.25
86 Natrone Means .50 1.25
87 Mikhael Ricks .40 1.00
88 Garrison Hearst .40 1.00
89 Jerry Rice 1.50 4.00
90 Terrell Owens .50 1.25
91 J.J. Stokes .40 1.00
92 Steve Young .75 2.00
93 Joey Galloway .50 1.25
94 Jon Kitna .40 1.00
95 Ricky Watters .50 1.25
96 Trent Green .40 1.00
97 Marshall Faulk .50 1.25
98 Isaac Bruce .60 1.50
99 Mike Alstott .40 1.00
100 Warrick Dunn .40 1.00
101 Jacquez Green .40 1.00
102 Reidel Anthony .40 1.00
103 Trent Dilfer .40 1.00
104 Steve McNair .50 1.25
105 Yancey Thigpen .40 1.00
106 Eddie George .50 1.25
107 Kevin Dyson .40 1.00
108 Skip Hicks .40 1.00
109 Brad Johnson .50 1.25
110 Michael Westbrook .40 1.00
111 Thurman Thomas CA 1.50 4.00
112 Andre Reed CA 2.00 5.00
113 Emmitt Smith CA 3.00 8.00
114 Troy Aikman CA 2.50 6.00
115 Deion Sanders CA 1.50 4.00
116 John Elway CA 3.00 8.00
117 Terrell Davis CA 1.50 4.00
118 Barry Sanders CA 3.00 8.00
119 Brett Favre CA 4.00 10.00
120 Warren Moon CA 2.00 5.00
121 Dan Marino CA 4.00 10.00
122 Cris Carter CA 2.00 5.00
124 Tim Brown CA 2.00 5.00
125 Jerome Bettis CA 2.00 5.00
126 Junior Seau CA 1.50 4.00
127 Jerry Rice CA 5.00 12.00
127 Vinny Testaverde CA 1.25 3.00
128 Steve Young CA 2.50 6.00
129 Eddie George CA 1.50 4.00
130 Cardinals CL 1.25 3.00
131 Falcons CL 1.25 3.00
132 Ravens CL 1.50 4.00
133 Bills CL 2.00 5.00
134 Panthers CL 1.25 3.00
135 Bears CL 1.50 4.00
136 Bengals CL 1.25 3.00
137 Browns CL 1.50 4.00
138 Cowboys CL 3.00 8.00
139 Broncos CL 3.00 8.00
140 Lions CL 3.00 8.00
141 Packers CL 3.00 8.00
142 Colts CL 3.00 8.00
143 Jaguars CL 1.50 4.00
144 Chiefs CL 1.25 3.00
145 Dolphins CL 1.25 3.00
146 Vikings CL 1.50 4.00
147 Patriots CL 1.25 3.00
148 Saints CL 1.50 4.00
149 Giants CL 1.25 3.00
150 Jets CL 1.50 4.00
151 Raiders CL 2.00 5.00
152 Eagles CL 2.00 5.00
153 Steelers CL 2.00 5.00
154 Chargers CL 2.00 5.00
155 49ers CL 3.00 8.00
156 Seahawks CL 1.25 3.00
157 Rams CL 1.50 4.00
158 Buccaneers CL 1.25 3.00
159 Titans CL 1.50 4.00
160 Redskins CL 2.00 5.00
161 Tim Couch RC .50 1.25
162 Donovan McNabb RC 3.00 8.00
163 Akili Smith RC .40 1.00
164 Edgerrin James RC .60 1.50
165 Ricky Williams RC .60 1.50
166 Torry Holt RC .75 2.00
167 Champ Bailey RC .75 2.00
168 David Boston RC .40 1.00
169 Chris Claiborne RC .40 1.00
170 Chris McAlister RC .40 1.00
171 Daunte Culpepper RC .60 1.50
172 Cade McNown RC .40 1.00
173 Troy Edwards RC .40 1.00
174 Kevin Johnson RC .50 1.25
175 James Johnson RC .40 1.00
176 Rob Konrad RC .40 1.00
177 Jim Kleinsasser RC .60 1.50
178 Kevin Faulk RC .40 1.00
179 Joe Montgomery RC .40 1.00
180 Shaun King RC .40 1.00
181 Peerless Price RC .40 1.00
182 Mike Cloud RC .40 1.00
183 Jermaine Fazande RC .40 1.00
184 D'Wayne Bates RC .40 1.00
185 Brock Huard RC .40 1.00
186 Marty Booker RC .40 1.00
187 Karsten Bailey RC .40 1.00
188 Shawn Bryson RC .40 1.00
189 Jeff Paulk RC .40 1.00
190 Sedrick Irvin RC .40 1.00
191 Craig Yeast RC .40 1.00
192 Joe Germaine RC .50 1.25
193 Dameane Douglas RC .40 1.00
194 Brandon Stokley RC .50 1.25
195 Larry Parker RC .50 1.25
196 Wane McGarity RC .40 1.00
197 Na Brown RC .40 1.00
198 Cecil Collins RC .40 1.00
199 Darrin Chiaverini RC .40 1.00
200 Madre Hill RC .40 1.00

1999 Absolute SSD Coaches Collection Gold

*VETS 1-110: 6X TO 15X BASIC CARDS
*CANTON ABS 111-129: 2.5X TO 6X
*TEAM CLs 130-160: 2X TO 5X
*ROOKIES 161-200: 6X TO 15X
GOLD PRINT RUN 25 SER. #'d SETS

1999 Absolute SSD Coaches Collection Silver

*VETS 1-110: 1.5X TO 4X BASIC CARDS
*CANTON ABS 111-129: .6X TO 1.5X
*TEAM CLs 130-160: .6X TO 1.5X
*SILVER ROOKIES: 1.5X TO 4X
SILVER PRINT RUN 500 SER.#'d SETS

1999 Absolute SSD Green

GREEN BORDER: .4X TO 1X BASIC CARDS

1999 Absolute SSD Honors Gold

*GOLD VETS/25: 8X TO 20X BASIC CARDS
*GOLD ROOK/25: 5X TO 12X BASIC CARDS
GOLD PRINT RUN 25 SER.#'d SETS

1999 Absolute SSD Honors Red

*RED/200: 2X TO 5X BASIC CARDS
RED PRINT RUN 200 SER.#'d SETS

1999 Absolute SSD Honors Silver

*SILVER/100: 3X TO 8X BASIC CARDS
SILVER STATED PRINT RUN 100 SER.#'d SETS

1999 Absolute SSD Orange

*ORANGE: 2.5X TO 6X BASIC CARDS

1999 Absolute SSD Purple

*PURPLE BORDER: .6X TO 1.5X BASIC CARDS

1999 Absolute SSD Red

*RED BORDER: .4X TO 1X BASIC CARDS

1999 Absolute SSD Boss Hogs Autographs

Randomly inserted in packs (1:217), this set contains the autographs of such players as Peyton Manning and Barry Sanders on genuine football leather with a print run of 400 autographed cards per player. Ricky Williams was scheduled to sign card #1 but, according to spokesmen for Playoff Inc., never did sign cards for the set. His redemption cards were exchanged for a variety of other signed cards.

STATED PRINT RUN 400 SER.#'d SETS
BH2 Terrell Davis 12.50 30.00
BH3 Mike Alstott 12.50 30.00
BH4 Jake Plummer 12.50 30.00
BH5 Vinny Testaverde 12.50 30.00
BH6 Cris Carter 15.00 40.00
BH7 Peyton Manning 40.00 100.00
BH8 Natrone Means 12.50 30.00
BH9 Eddie George 12.50 30.00
BH10 Barry Sanders 50.00 120.00

1999 Absolute SSD Force

Randomly inserted in packs (1:19), this 36 card set of star players is featured on mirror board with gold foil stamping. Cards are designated with the prefix 'AF'.

COMPLETE SET (36) 75.00 150.00
STATED ODDS 1:19
AF1 Steve Young 2.50 6.00
AF2 Fred Taylor 1.25 3.00
AF3 Kordell Stewart 1.25 3.00
AF4 Emmitt Smith 3.00 8.00
AF5 Barry Sanders 3.00 8.00
AF6 Jerry Rice 5.00 12.00
AF7 Jake Plummer 1.25 3.00
AF8 Eric Moulds 1.25 3.00
AF9 Randy Moss 1.50 4.00
AF10 Steve McNair 1.50 4.00
AF11 Curtis Martin 1.50 4.00
AF12 Dan Marino 4.00 10.00
AF13 Peyton Manning 6.00 15.00
AF14 Jon Kitna 1.25 3.00
AF15 Napoleon Kaufman 1.25 3.00
AF16 Keyshawn Johnson 1.50 4.00
AF17 Eddie George 1.50 4.00
AF18 Antonio Freeman 1.50 4.00
AF19 Doug Flutie 2.00 5.00
AF20 Brett Favre 4.00 10.00
AF21 Marshall Faulk 1.50 4.00
AF22 John Elway 3.00 8.00
AF23 Warrick Dunn 1.25 3.00
AF24 Corey Dillon 1.25 3.00
AF25 Terrell Davis 1.50 4.00
AF26 Randall Cunningham 1.50 4.00
AF27 Cris Carter 2.00 5.00
AF28 Mark Brunell 1.50 4.00
AF29 Tim Brown 2.00 5.00
AF30 Drew Bledsoe 1.50 4.00
AF31 Jerome Bettis 2.00 5.00
AF32 Charlie Batch 1.25 3.00
AF33 Jamal Anderson 1.50 4.00
AF34 Mike Alstott 1.25 3.00
AF35 Troy Aikman 2.50 6.00
AF36 Terrell Owens 1.50 4.00

1999 Absolute SSD Heroes

Randomly inserted in packs (1:19), set consisits of 24 NFL superstars that are highlighted on die-cut mirror board with red foil stamping and micro-etching.

COMPLETE SET (24) 60.00 120.00
STATED ODDS 1:19
*JUMBOS: .3X TO .8X BASIC INSERTS
JUMBOS ONE PER HOBBY BOX
*RED/100: 1.5X TO 4X BASIC INSERTS
HE1 Terrell Owens 1.25 3.00
HE2 Troy Aikman 2.00 5.00
HE3 Cris Carter 1.50 4.00
HE4 Brett Favre 3.00 8.00
HE5 Jamal Anderson 1.25 3.00
HE6 Doug Flutie 1.50 4.00
HE7 John Elway 2.50 6.00
HE8 Steve Young 2.00 5.00
HE9 Jerome Bettis 1.50 4.00
HE10 Emmitt Smith 2.50 6.00
HE11 Drew Bledsoe 1.25 3.00
HE12 Fred Taylor 1.00 2.50
HE13 Dan Marino 3.00 8.00
HE14 Antonio Freeman 1.25 3.00
HE15 Mark Brunell 1.25 3.00
HE16 Jake Plummer 1.00 2.50
HE17 Warrick Dunn 1.00 2.50
HE18 Peyton Manning 5.00 12.00
HE19 Randy Moss 1.25 3.00
HE20 Barry Sanders 2.50 6.00
HE21 Keyshawn Johnson 1.25 3.00
HE22 Eddie George 1.25 3.00
HE23 Terrell Davis 1.25 3.00
HE24 Jerry Rice 4.00 10.00

1999 Absolute SSD Rookie Roundup

Randomly inserted in packs, this 18-card set features the top rookies in the NFL on mirror board card stock with foil stamping and micro-etching printing. The cards have an "RR" prefix and were divided into First Rounders (1:46 packs) and Second Rounders (labeled as "2" below; 1:69 packs).

COMPLETE SET (18) 25.00 60.00
1ST ROUNDER STATED ODDS 1:46
2ND ROUNDER STATED ODDS 1:69
RR1 Peerless Price 2 1.00 2.50
RR2 Daunte Culpepper 1.50 4.00
RR3 Joe Montgomery 2 1.00 2.50
RR4 David Boston 1.00 2.50
RR5 Shaun King 2 1.00 2.50
RR6 Champ Bailey 2.00 5.00
RR7 Rob Konrad 2 1.00 2.50
RR8 Torry Holt 2.00 5.00
RR9 Kevin Faulk 2 1.00 2.50
RR10 Ricky Williams 1.50 4.00
RR11 James Johnson 2 1.00 2.50
RR12 Edgerrin James 1.50 4.00
RR13 Kevin Johnson 2 1.25 3.00
RR14 Akili Smith 1.00 2.50
RR15 Troy Edwards 1.00 2.50
RR16 Donovan McNabb 3.00 8.00
RR17 Cade McNown 1.00 2.50
RR18 Tim Couch 1.25 3.00

1999 Absolute SSD Rookies Inserts

Randomly inserted in packs (1:10), this blue bordered 36 card base set features the hottest rookies from the NFL on holographic foil with blue foil stamping and micro-etching. These cards have a prefix of "AR".

COMPLETE SET (36) 40.00 80.00
STATED ODDS 1:10
*RED/100: 2X TO 5X BASIC INSERTS
AR1 Champ Bailey 1.00 2.50
AR2 Karsten Bailey .50 1.25
AR3 D'Wayne Bates .50 1.25
AR4 Marty Booker .50 1.25
AR5 David Boston .50 1.25
AR6 Shawn Bryson .50 1.25
AR7 Chris Claiborne .50 1.25
AR8 Mike Cloud .50 1.25
AR9 Cecil Collins .50 1.25
AR10 Tim Couch .60 1.50
AR11 Daunte Culpepper .75 2.00
AR12 Dameane Douglas .50 1.25
AR13 Troy Edwards .50 1.25
AR14 Kevin Faulk .50 1.25
AR15 Jermaine Fazande .50 1.25
AR16 Joe Germaine .60 1.50
AR17 Torry Holt 1.00 2.50
AR18 Brock Huard .50 1.25
AR19 Edgerrin James .75 2.00
AR20 James Johnson .50 1.25
AR21 Kevin Johnson .60 1.50
AR22 Shaun King .50 1.25
AR23 Jim Kleinsasser .75 2.00
AR24 Rob Konrad .50 1.25
AR25 Chris McAlister .50 1.25
AR26 Travis McGriff .50 1.25
AR27 Donovan McNabb 3.00 8.00
AR28 Cade McNown .50 1.25
AR29 Joe Montgomery .50 1.25
AR30 Larry Parker .60 1.50
AR31 Jeff Paulk .50 1.25
AR32 Peerless Price .50 1.25
AR33 Akili Smith .50 1.25
AR34 Brandon Stokley .60 1.50
AR35 Ricky Williams .75 2.00
AR36 Craig Yeast .50 1.25

1999 Absolute SSD Team Jersey Quad

Randomly inserted in packs (1:73), this set features an authentic replica jersey (not game used) swatch and four superstars from each of the 31 NFL teams on foil board with micro-etching. These cards have a prefix of "TQ". Some cards were issued via mail redemptions.

STATED ODDS 1:73
TQ1 Boston/Murr/Plum/Sand 5.00 12.00
TQ2 Aikm/Irvin/Deion/Smith 12.00 30.00
TQ3 Bailey/Hick/Johns/West 8.00 20.00
TQ4 Brown/Coll/Hilliard/Mont. 5.00 12.00
TQ5 Brown/John/McNa/Stal 12.00 30.00
TQ6 Carter/Cunn/Moss/Smith 15.00 40.00
TQ7 Alstott/Anth/Dilfer/Dunn 5.00 12.00
TQ8 Batch/Moore/Mort/Sand 12.00 30.00
TQ9 Chmura/Favre/Free/Lev 15.00 40.00
TQ10 Conw/Eng/Enis/McNown 6.00 15.00
TQ11 Beuerlein/Biak/Muh/Walls 6.00 15.00
TQ12 Williams/Cleel/Kenn/Roaf 6.00 15.00
TQ13 Hearst/Owe/Rice/Young 20.00 50.00
TQ14 Bruce/Faulk/Green/Holt 8.00 20.00
TQ15 And/Chan/Dwight/Mathis 6.00 15.00
TQ16 Jabbar/Coll/Marino/McDu 15.00 40.00
TQ17 Bled/Coat/Faulk/Glenn 6.00 15.00
TQ18 Flutie/Moulds/Price/Smith 8.00 20.00
TQ19 Harr/James/Mann/Path 25.00 60.00
TQ20 Chreb/Johns/Mart/Test 6.00 15.00
TQ21 Bettis/Edw/Stew/Ward 8.00 20.00
TQ22 Brun/McCar/Smith/Tayl 6.00 15.00
TQ23 Couch/John/Shaw/Shep 6.00 15.00
TQ24 Dillon/Pick/Scott/Smith 6.00 15.00
TQ25 Banks/Holm/Lewis/McAl 6.00 15.00
TQ26 Dyson/Geor/McNair/Thig 6.00 15.00
TQ27 Brown/Jett/Kauf/Wood 8.00 20.00
TQ28 Davis/Elway/McCa/Smith 12.00 30.00
TQ29 Gallo/Green/Kitna/Watt 6.00 15.00
TQ30 Cloud/Grbac/Morris/Rison 6.00 15.00
TQ31 Leaf/Means/Ricks/Seau 6.00 15.00

2000 Absolute

Released as a 250-card set, Playoff Absolute features 150 veteran cards and 100 rookie cards sequentially numbered to 3000. Base cards feature player action photos and holographic foil stamping. Absolute was packaged in 20-pack boxes with packs containing six cards and carried a suggested retail price of $3.99.

COMPLETE SET (250) 125.00 250.00
COMP.SET w/o SP's (150) 7.50 20.00
151-250 ROOKIE PRINT RUN 3000
1 Frank Sanders .20 .50
2 Rob Moore .20 .50
3 Jake Plummer .20 .50
4 David Boston .20 .50
5 Chris Chandler .25 .60
6 Tim Dwight .25 .60
7 Terance Mathis .20 .50
8 Jamal Anderson .25 .60
9 Priest Holmes .20 .50
10 Tony Banks .20 .50
11 Jermaine Lewis .20 .50
12 Qadry Ismail .20 .50
13 Brandon Stokley .20 .50
14 Shannon Sharpe .25 .60
15 Trent Dilfer .20 .50
16 Eric Moulds .20 .50
17 Doug Flutie .25 .60
18 Antowain Smith .25 .60
19 Jonathan Linton .20 .50
20 Peerless Price .25 .60
21 Rob Johnson .25 .60
22 Muhsin Muhammad .20 .50
23 Wesley Walls .20 .50
24 Tim Biakabutuka .25 .60
25 Steve Beuerlein .25 .60
26 Patrick Jeffers .20 .50
27 Natrone Means .25 .60
28 Curtis Enis .20 .50
29 Bobby Engram .20 .50
30 Marcus Robinson .25 .60
31 Marty Booker .20 .50
32 Cade McNown .20 .50
33 Darnay Scott .25 .60
34 Carl Pickens .25 .60
35 Corey Dillon .20 .50
36 Akili Smith .20 .50
37 Michael Basnight .20 .50
38 Karim Abdul-Jabbar .20 .50
39 Tim Couch .25 .60
40 Kevin Johnson .20 .50
41 Darrin Chiaverini .20 .50
42 Errict Rhett .25 .60
43 Emmitt Smith .50 1.25
44 Michael Irvin .30 .75
45 Rocket Ismail .25 .60
46 Troy Aikman .40 1.00
47 Jason Tucker .20 .50
48 Randall Cunningham .25 .60
49 Joey Galloway .25 .60
50 Ed McCaffrey .25 .60
51 Rod Smith .25 .60
52 Brian Griese .20 .50
53 John Elway .50 1.25
54 Terrell Davis .25 .60
55 Olandis Gary .25 .60
56 Johnnie Morton .25 .60
57 Charlie Batch .20 .50
58 Barry Sanders .50 1.25
59 Germane Crowell .20 .50
60 Herman Moore .20 .50
61 James Stewart .20 .50

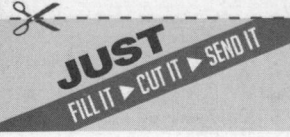

62 Corey Bradford .20 .50
63 Dorsey Levens .25 .60
64 Antonio Freeman .25 .60
65 Brett Favre .60 1.50
66 Bill Schroeder .25 .60
67 Marvin Harrison .25 .60
68 Peyton Manning .75 2.00
69 Terrence Wilkins .20 .50
70 Edgerrin James .25 .60
71 Keenan McCardell .25 .60
72 Mark Brunell .25 .60
73 Fred Taylor .20 .50
74 Jimmy Smith .25 .60
75 Elvis Grbac .20 .50
76 Tony Gonzalez .25 .60
77 Donnell Bennett .20 .50
78 Warren Moon .30 .75
79 Kimble Anders .20 .50
80 Dan Marino .60 1.50
81 O.J. McDuffie .25 .60
82 Tony Martin .25 .60
83 James Johnson .20 .50
84 Thurman Thomas .25 .60
85 Randy Moss .25 .60
86 Cris Carter .30 .75
87 Robert Smith .20 .50
88 Daunte Culpepper .25 .60
89 Terry Glenn .25 .60
90 Drew Bledsoe .25 .60
91 Kevin Faulk .20 .50
92 Ricky Williams .25 .60
93 Jeff Blake .25 .60
94 Jake Reed .25 .60
95 Amani Toomer .20 .50
96 Kerry Collins .20 .50
97 Tiki Barber .25 .60
98 Ike Hilliard .20 .50
99 Curtis Martin .25 .60
100 Vinny Testaverde .20 .50
101 Wayne Chrebet .20 .50
102 Ray Lucas .20 .50
103 Tyrone Wheatley .20 .50
104 Napoleon Kaufman .25 .60
105 Tim Brown .30 .75
106 Rich Gannon .25 .60
107 Duce Staley .20 .50
108 Donovan McNabb .25 .60
109 Kordell Stewart .20 .50
110 Jerome Bettis .30 .75
111 Troy Edwards .20 .50
112 Junior Seau .25 .60
113 Jim Harbaugh .25 .60
114 Ryan Leaf .25 .60
115 Jermaine Fazande .20 .50
116 Curtis Conway .25 .60
117 Terrell Owens .25 .60
118 Charlie Garner .25 .60
119 Jerry Rice .75 2.00
120 Steve Young .40 1.00
121 Jeff Garcia .20 .50
122 Derrick Mayes .20 .50
123 Ricky Watters .25 .60
124 Jon Kitna .20 .50
125 Sean Dawkins .20 .50
126 Az-Zahir Hakim .20 .50
127 Isaac Bruce .30 .75
128 Marshall Faulk .25 .60
129 Trent Green .20 .50
130 Kurt Warner .50 1.25
131 Torry Holt .25 .60
132 Jacquez Green .20 .50
133 Warren Sapp .25 .60
134 Mike Alstott .25 .60
135 Warrick Dunn .20 .50
136 Shaun King .20 .50
137 Keyshawn Johnson .25 .60
138 Eddie George .25 .60
139 Yancey Thigpen .20 .50
140 Steve McNair .25 .60
141 Kevin Dyson .25 .60
142 Frank Wycheck .25 .60
143 Jevon Kearse .20 .50
144 Stephen Davis .20 .50
145 Brad Johnson .25 .60
146 Michael Westbrook .20 .50
147 Albert Connell .20 .50
148 Bruce Smith .25 .60
149 Jeff George .25 .60
150 Deion Sanders .25 .60
151 Peter Warrick RC .75 2.00
152 Courtney Brown RC 1.00 2.50
153 Plaxico Burress RC 1.00 2.50
154 Corey Simon RC 1.00 2.50
155 Thomas Jones RC 1.00 2.50
156 Travis Taylor RC .75 2.00
157 Shaun Alexander RC 1.25 3.00
158 Chris Redman RC .75 2.00
159 Chad Pennington RC 1.00 2.50
160 Jamal Lewis RC 1.25 3.00
161 Brian Urlacher RC 4.00 10.00
162 Bubba Franks RC .75 2.00
163 Dez White RC .75 2.00
164 Ahmed Plummer RC .75 2.00
165 Ron Dayne RC 1.25 3.00
166 Shaun Ellis RC 1.00 2.50
167 Sylvester Morris RC .75 2.00
168 Deltha O'Neal RC .75 2.00
169 R.Jay Soward RC .75 2.00
170 Sherrod Gideon RC .75 2.00
171 John Abraham RC 1.25 3.00
172 Travis Prentice RC .75 2.00
173 Darrell Jackson RC .75 2.00
174 Giovanni Carmazzi RC .75 2.00
175 Anthony Lucas RC .75 2.00
176 Danny Farmer RC .75 2.00
177 Dennis Northcutt RC .75 2.00
178 Troy Walters RC .75 2.00
179 Laveranues Coles RC 1.00 2.50
180 Kwame Cavil RC .75 2.00
181 Tee Martin RC .75 2.00
182 J.R. Redmond RC .75 2.00
183 Tim Rattay RC 1.00 2.50
184 Jerry Porter RC 1.25 3.00
185 Sebastian Janikowski RC 1.25 3.00
186 Michael Wiley RC .75 2.00
187 Reuben Droughns RC .75 2.00
188 Trung Canidate RC .75 2.00
189 Shyrone Stith RC .75 2.00
190 Ian Gold RC .75 2.00
191 Hank Poteat RC .75 2.00
192 Darren Howard RC .75 2.00
193 Rob Morris RC 1.00 2.50
194 Marc Bulger RC 1.00 2.50
195 Tom Brady RC 125.00 250.00
196 Doug Johnson RC .75 2.00
197 Todd Husak RC .75 2.00
198 Gari Scott RC .75 2.00
199 Erron Kinney RC .75 2.00
200 Nate Webster RC .75 2.00
201 Anthony Becht RC .75 2.00
202 Sammy Morris RC .75 2.00
203 Rondell Mealey RC .75 2.00
204 Doug Chapman RC .75 2.00
205 Rogers Beckett RC .75 2.00
206 Ron Dugans RC .75 2.00
207 Deon Dyer RC .75 2.00
208 Marcus Knight RC .75 2.00
209 Thomas Hamner RC .75 2.00
210 Joe Hamilton RC .75 2.00
211 Todd Pinkston RC .75 2.00
212 Chris Cole RC 1.00 2.50
213 Ron Dixon RC .75 2.00
214 JaJuan Dawson RC .75 2.00
215 Terrelle Smith RC .75 2.00
216 Curtis Keaton RC .75 2.00
217 Keith Bulluck RC 1.00 2.50
218 John Engelberger RC .75 2.00
219 Raynoch Thompson RC .75 2.00
220 Cornelius Griffin RC .75 2.00
221 William Bartee RC .75 2.00
222 Fred Robbins RC .75 2.00
223 Dwayne Goodrich RC .75 2.00
224 Deon Grant RC .75 2.00
225 Jacoby Shepherd RC .75 2.00
226 Ben Kelly RC .75 2.00
227 Corey Moore RC .75 2.00
228 Aaron Shea RC 1.00 2.50
229 Trevor Gaylor RC .75 2.00
230 Frank Moreau RC .75 2.00
231 Avion Black RC .75 2.00
232 Paul Smith RC .75 2.00
233 Dante Hall RC .75 2.00
234 Muneer Moore RC .75 2.00
235 James Whalen RC .75 2.00
236 Chad Morton RC 1.00 2.50
237 Frank Murphy RC .75 2.00
238 Mareno Philyaw RC .75 2.00
239 James Williams RC .75 2.00
240 Mike Anderson RC .75 2.00
241 Jarious Jackson RC 1.00 2.50
242 Demario Brown RC .75 2.00
243 Chris Coleman RC .75 2.00
244 Rashard Anderson RC .75 2.00
245 John Jones RC .75 2.00
246 Erik Flowers RC .75 2.00
247 JaJuan Seider RC .75 2.00
248 Leon Murray RC .75 2.00
249 Bashir Yamini RC .75 2.00
250 Na'il Diggs RC .75 2.00

2000 Absolute Coaches Honors

*VETS 1-150: 2X TO 5X BASIC CARDS
*ROOKIE 151-250: .5X TO 1.2X BASIC CARDS
STATED PRINT RUN 300 SER.#'d SETS
47 Jason Tucker 1.00 2.50
195 Tom Brady 125.00 200.00

2000 Absolute Boss Hogg Autographs

Randomly inserted in packs at the rate of one in 298 hobby or 1:447 retail, this set features authentic player autographs across a full color action photo. A total of 200 cards were signed by each player. Several players were issued in redemption format with an expiration date of 9/30/2001.
AUTO/200 ODDS 1:298 HOB, 1:447 RET
STATED PRINT RUN 200 SETS
BH1 Eric Moulds 8.00 20.00
BH2 Cade McNown 8.00 20.00
BH3 Tim Couch 10.00 25.00
BH4 Terrell Davis 10.00 25.00
BH5 Barry Sanders 50.00 100.00
BH6 Peyton Manning 50.00 100.00
BH7 Edgerrin James 10.00 25.00
BH8 Marvin Harrison 10.00 25.00
BH9 Mark Brunell 10.00 25.00
BH11 Dan Marino 50.00 120.00
BH12 Cris Carter 12.00 30.00
BH13 Drew Bledsoe 10.00 25.00
BH14 Ricky Williams 10.00 25.00
BH16 Kurt Warner 20.00 40.00
BH17 Isaac Bruce 12.00 30.00
BH18 Eddie George 10.00 25.00
BH19 Steve McNair 10.00 25.00
BH20 Brad Johnson 10.00 25.00

2000 Absolute Canton Absolutes

Randomly inserted in packs at the rate of one in 39, this 30-card set features favorites for the hall of fame on a die cut foil-board card stock. Player action photos are framed by a black circle on this gold foil card.
COMPLETE SET (30) 50.00 100.00
STATED ODDS 1:39
CA1 Tim Couch .75 2.00
CA2 Emmitt Smith 1.50 4.00
CA3 Troy Aikman 1.25 3.00
CA4 John Elway 1.50 4.00
CA5 Terrell Davis .75 2.00
CA6 Barry Sanders 1.50 4.00
CA7 Brett Favre 2.00 5.00
CA8 Peyton Manning 2.50 6.00
CA9 Edgerrin James .75 2.00
CA10 Mark Brunell .75 2.00
CA11 Dan Marino 2.00 5.00
CA12 Randy Moss .75 2.00
CA13 Drew Bledsoe .75 2.00
CA14 Jerry Rice 2.50 6.00
CA15 Steve Young 1.25 3.00
CA16 Kurt Warner 1.50 4.00
CA17 Eddie George .75 2.00
CA18 Deion Sanders .75 2.00
CA19 Antonio Freeman .75 2.00
CA20 Warren Moon 1.00 2.50
CA21 Cris Carter 1.00 2.50
CA22 Randall Cunningham .75 2.00
CA23 Curtis Martin .75 2.00
CA24 Tim Brown 1.00 2.50
CA25 Marshall Faulk .75 2.00
CA26 Michael Irvin 1.00 2.50
CA27 Thurman Thomas .75 2.00
CA28 Vinny Testaverde .60 1.50
CA29 Ricky Watters .75 2.00
CA30 Jeff George .75 2.00

2000 Absolute Extreme Team

Randomly inserted in packs at the rate of 1:18 hobby packs or 1:27 retail, this 40-card set features top NFL players on a metalized film board with gold foil highlights. Player photos are set agains a multicolored rainbow background.
COMPLETE SET (40) 60.00 150.00
STATED ODDS 1:18 HOB, 1:27 RET
XT1 Jake Plummer .75 2.00
XT2 Tim Couch 1.00 2.50
XT3 Terrell Davis 1.00 2.50
XT4 Brett Favre 2.50 6.00
XT5 Peyton Manning 3.00 8.00
XT6 Edgerrin James 1.00 2.50
XT7 Mark Brunell 1.00 2.50
XT8 Fred Taylor .75 2.00
XT9 Randy Moss 1.00 2.50
XT10 Drew Bledsoe 1.00 2.50
XT11 Ricky Williams 1.00 2.50
XT12 Kurt Warner 2.00 5.00
XT13 Eddie George 1.00 2.50
XT14 Cade McNown .75 2.00
XT15 Kevin Johnson .75 2.00
XT16 Joey Galloway 1.00 2.50
XT17 Olandis Gary 1.00 2.50
XT18 Dorsey Levens 1.00 2.50
XT19 Marvin Harrison 1.00 2.50
XT20 Daunte Culpepper 1.00 2.50
XT21 Duce Staley .75 2.00
XT22 Donovan McNabb 1.00 2.50
XT23 Marshall Faulk 1.00 2.50
XT24 Shaun King .75 2.00
XT25 Keyshawn Johnson 1.00 2.50
XT26 Steve McNair 1.00 2.50
XT27 Stephen Davis .75 2.00
XT28 Brad Johnson 1.00 2.50
XT29 Akili Smith .75 2.00
XT30 Brian Griese .75 2.00
XT31 Emmitt Smith 2.00 5.00
XT32 Isaac Bruce 1.25 3.00
XT33 Peter Warrick .75 2.00
XT34 Jamal Lewis 1.00 2.50
XT35 Thomas Jones 1.00 2.50
XT36 Plaxico Burress 1.00 2.50
XT37 Travis Taylor .75 2.00
XT38 Ron Dayne 1.25 3.00
XT39 Chad Pennington .75 2.00
XT40 Shaun Alexander 1.00 2.50

2000 Absolute Ground Hoggs Shoe

Randomly inserted in Hobby packs at the rate of one in 188, this 30-card set features player action photography on the left, a team logo in the center, and circular swatches of game worn shoes on the right. Each card is serial numbered as listed below.
STATED ODDS 1:188 HOBBY
FIRST 25 SER.#'D SETS SIGNED
GH1 Jake Plummer/110* 5.00 12.00
GH1AU Jake Plummer AU/25* 40.00 80.00
GH2 Muhsin Muhammad/75 6.00 15.00
GH3 Emmitt Smith/135 12.00 30.00
GH4 Ricky Watters/135 6.00 15.00
GH5 Terrell Davis/135 6.00 15.00
GH6 Brett Favre/135 15.00 40.00
GH7 Dorsey Levens/135 6.00 15.00
GH8 Antonio Freeman/135 6.00 15.00
GH9 Edgerrin James/110* 6.00 15.00
GH9AU Edgerrin James AU/25* 50.00 100.00
GH10 Marvin Harrison/135 6.00 15.00
GH11 Mark Brunell/135 6.00 15.00
GH12 Fred Taylor/135 5.00 12.00
GH13 Jimmy Smith/135 6.00 15.00
GH14 James Johnson/135 5.00 12.00
GH15 Dan Marino/135 15.00 40.00
GH16 Jon Kitna/135 5.00 12.00
GH17 Ricky Williams/100* 6.00 15.00
GH17AU Ricky Williams AU/25* 40.00 80.00
GH18 Curtis Martin/135 6.00 15.00
GH19 Wayne Chrebet/135 5.00 12.00
GH20 Steve Young/135 10.00 25.00
GH21 Junior Seau/135 6.00 15.00
GH22 Kurt Warner/110* 12.00 30.00
GH22AU Kurt Warner AU/25* 50.00 100.00
GH23 Marshall Faulk/135 6.00 15.00
GH24 Eddie George/135 6.00 15.00
GH25 Steve McNair/135 6.00 15.00
GH26 Joey Galloway/135 6.00 15.00
GH27 Jerry Rice/135 20.00 50.00
GH28 Jevon Kearse/135 5.00 12.00
GH29 Stephen Davis/135 5.00 12.00
GH30 Albert Connell/135 5.00 12.00

2000 Absolute Leather and Laces

Randomly inserted in packs, this set features triangular swatches of game used footballs. Each card contains the date of the game the football was used in, the final score, and was sequentially numbered to either 175 or 350
*COMBO/20: 1X TO 2.5X BASIC INS/350
*COMBO/10: 1.2X TO 3X BASIC INS/175
COMBOS PRINT RUN 10-20
AC83 Albert Connell/175 2.00 5.00
AF86A Antonio Freeman/350 2.00 5.00
AF86B Antonio Freeman/175 2.50 6.00
AS11 Akili Smith/350 1.50 4.00
AS23 Antowain Smith/350 2.00 5.00
BC85 Ben Coates/175 2.00 5.00
BE81 Bobby Engram/175 2.00 5.00
BF4A Brett Favre/350 5.00 12.00
BF4B Brett Favre/175 6.00 15.00
BJ14 Brad Johnson/175 2.50 6.00
BM74 Bruce Matthews/175 2.00 5.00
BS20 Barry Sanders/350 4.00 10.00
BS78 Bruce Smith/350 2.00 5.00
CC80 Cris Carter/175 3.00 8.00
CC80 Curtis Conway/175 2.50 6.00
CD28 Corey Dillon/350 1.50 4.00
CE44 Curtis Enis/350 1.50 4.00
CG25 Charlie Garner/350 2.00 5.00
CM28 Curtis Martin/175 2.50 6.00
CP81 Carl Pickens/175 2.50 6.00
DB89 David Boston/350 1.50 4.00
DC84 Darrin Chiaverini/175 2.00 5.00
DD11 Drew Bledsoe/350 2.00 5.00
DH11 Damon Huard/175 2.00 5.00
DL25A Dorsey Levens/350 2.00 5.00
DL25B Dorsey Levens/175 2.50 6.00
DM5 Donovan McNabb/350 2.00 5.00
DM13 Dan Marino/350 5.00 12.00
DM87 Derrick Mayes/175 2.00 5.00
DS21 Deion Sanders/175 2.50 6.00
DS22 Duce Staley/350 1.50 4.00
DS86 Darnay Scott/175 2.50 6.00
EG27A Eddie George/350 2.00 5.00
EG27B Eddie George/175 2.50 6.00
EJ32 Edgerrin James/175 2.50 6.00
EM80 Eric Moulds/350 1.50 4.00
EM87 Ed McCaffrey/175 2.50 6.00
ER23 Errict Rhett/175 2.50 6.00
ES22 Emmitt Smith/175 5.00 12.00
FS81 Frank Sanders/350 1.50 4.00
FT28A Fred Taylor/350 1.50 4.00
FT28B Fred Taylor/175 2.00 5.00
FW89 Frank Wycheck/175 2.50 6.00
HM84 Herman Moore/175 2.00 5.00
HW86 Hines Ward/175 2.50 6.00
IB80 Isaac Bruce/350 2.50 6.00
JB18 Jeff Blake/175 2.50 6.00
JB36 Jerome Bettis/350 8.00 20.00
JE7 John Elway/175 5.00 12.00
JG5 Jeff Garcia/350 1.50 4.00
JG87 Jammi German/175 2.00 5.00
JH4 Jim Harbaugh/175 2.50 6.00
JJ32 James Johnson/350 1.50 4.00
JK90A Jevon Kearse/350 1.50 4.00
JK90B Jevon Kearse/175 2.00 5.00
JL84 Jermaine Lewis/175 2.00 5.00
JM87 Johnnie Morton/175 2.50 6.00
JP16 Jake Plummer/350 1.50 4.00
JR80A Jerry Rice/350 6.00 15.00
JR80B Jerry Rice/175 8.00 20.00
JS33 James Stewart/350 1.50 4.00
JS55 Junior Seau/175 2.50 6.00
JS82 Jimmy Smith/350 2.00 5.00
JS83 J.J. Stokes/175 2.50 6.00
KD87 Kevin Dyson/175 2.50 6.00
KJ19 Keyshawn Johnson/175 2.50 6.00
KJ85 Kevin Johnson/350 1.50 4.00
KM87 Keenan McCardell/350 2.00 5.00
KS10 Kordell Stewart/350 1.50 4.00
KW13A Kurt Warner/350 4.00 10.00
KW13B Kurt Warner/175 10.00 25.00
LK99 Levon Kirkland/175 2.00 5.00
MA40 Mike Alstott/350 1.50 4.00
MB8A Mark Brunell/350 2.00 5.00
MB8B Mark Brunell/175 2.50 6.00
MB35 Michael Basnight/175 2.00 5.00
MF28A Marshall Faulk/175 2.50 6.00
MF28B Marshall Faulk/175 2.50 6.00
MH88 Marvin Harrison/175 2.50 6.00
MM87 Muhsin Muhammad/350 1.50 4.00
MW82 Michael Westbrook/175 2.00 5.00
NK26 Napoleon Kaufman/175 2.50 6.00
NM20 Natrone Means/175 2.50 6.00
NO14 Neil O'Donnell/175 2.00 5.00
OG86 Oronde Gadsden/175 2.50 6.00
OM81 O.J. McDuffie/175 2.50 6.00
PH33 Priest Holmes/175 2.00 5.00
PM18 Peyton Manning/350 6.00 15.00
PP81 Peerless Price/175 2.50 6.00
PW80 Peter Warrick/350 1.50 4.00
QI87 Qadry Ismail/175 2.00 5.00
RA85 Reidel Anthony/175 2.00 5.00
RC7 Randall Cunningham/175 2.50 6.00
RD27 Ron Dayne/350 2.50 6.00
RD83 Rickey Dudley/175 2.00 5.00
RG12 Rich Gannon/175 2.50 6.00
RI81 Rocket Ismail/175 2.50 6.00
RJ11 Rob Johnson/175 2.50 6.00
RM84 Randy Moss/175 2.50 6.00
RS26 Robert Smith/175 2.00 5.00
RS80 Rod Smith/175 2.50 6.00
RW34 Ricky Williams/350 2.00 5.00
RW92 Reggie White/350 4.00 10.00
SD48 Stephen Davis/175 2.00 5.00
SM9A Steve McNair/350 2.00 5.00
SM9B Steve McNair/175 2.50 6.00
SM29 Sam Madison/175 2.00 5.00
SY8 Steve Young/350 3.00 8.00
TA8 Troy Aikman/175 4.00 10.00
TB21 Tim Biakabutuka/350 2.00 5.00
TB81 Tim Brown/350 2.50 6.00
TC2 Tim Couch/350 2.00 5.00
TD7 Trent Dilfer/175 2.00 5.00
TD30 Terrell Davis/175 2.50 6.00
TD83 Tim Dwight/350 2.00 5.00
TE81 Troy Edwards/350 1.50 4.00
TG88 Terry Glenn/175 2.50 6.00
TH88 Torry Holt/175 2.50 6.00
TM80 Tony Martin/175 2.50 6.00
TM81 Terance Mathis/175 2.00 5.00
TO81A Terrell Owens/175 2.50 6.00
TO81B Terrell Owens/175 2.50 6.00
TT34 Thurman Thomas/350 2.00 5.00
TW47 Tyrone Wheatley/175 2.00 5.00
VT16 Vinny Testaverde/175 2.00 5.00
WC80 Wayne Chrebet/175 2.00 5.00
WD28 Warrick Dunn/350 1.50 4.00
WS99 Warren Sapp/350 2.00 5.00
YT82 Yancey Thigpen/175 2.00 5.00
ZT54 Zach Thomas/175 2.50 6.00

2000 Absolute Playoff Fever

Randomly inserted in retail packs at the rate of one in 47, this 40-card set features top NFL players.
1 Jake Plummer .75 2.00
2 Emmitt Smith 2.00 5.00
3 Troy Aikman 1.50 4.00
4 John Elway 2.00 5.00
5 Terrell Davis 1.00 2.50
6 Charlie Batch .75 2.00
7 Barry Sanders 2.00 5.00
8 Brett Favre 2.50 6.00
9 Peyton Manning 3.00 8.00
10 Edgerrin James 1.00 2.50
11 Mark Brunell 1.00 2.50
12 Fred Taylor .75 2.00
13 Dan Marino 2.50 6.00
14 Randy Moss 1.00 2.50
15 Drew Bledsoe 1.00 2.50
16 Jerry Rice 3.00 8.00
17 Steve Young 1.50 4.00
18 Kurt Warner 2.00 5.00
19 Eddie George 1.00 2.50
20 Eric Moulds .75 2.00
21 Doug Flutie 1.00 2.50
22 Dorsey Levens 1.00 2.50
23 Antonio Freeman 1.00 2.50
24 Marvin Harrison 1.00 2.50
25 Cris Carter 1.25 3.00
26 Curtis Martin 1.00 2.50
27 Marshall Faulk 1.00 2.50
28 Torry Holt 1.00 2.50
29 Keyshawn Johnson 1.00 2.50
30 Mike Alstott .75 2.00
31 Shaun King .75 2.00
32 Steve McNair 1.00 2.50
33 Stephen Davis .75 2.00
34 Brad Johnson 1.00 2.50
35 Ed McCaffrey 1.00 2.50
36 Germane Crowell .75 2.00
37 James Stewart .75 2.00
38 Jimmy Smith 1.00 2.50
39 Isaac Bruce 1.25 3.00
40 Michael Westbrook .75 2.00

2000 Absolute Rookie Reflex

Randomly inserted in packs at the rate of one in 10 hobby or 1:15 retail, this 30-card set features top rated rookies from the 2000 NFL Draft. Each card is printed on holographic foil board and contains player action shots.
COMPLETE SET (30) 25.00 60.00
STATED ODDS 1:10 HOB, 1:15 RET
*GOLD/100: 2X TO 5X BASIC INSERTS
GOLD STATED PRINT RUN 100 SER.#'d SETS
RR1 Peter Warrick .50 1.25
RR2 Jamal Lewis .75 2.00
RR3 Thomas Jones .60 1.50
RR4 Plaxico Burress .60 1.50
RR5 Travis Taylor .50 1.25
RR6 Ron Dayne .75 2.00
RR7 Bubba Franks .50 1.25
RR8 Chad Pennington .60 1.50
RR9 Shaun Alexander .75 2.00
RR10 Sylvester Morris .50 1.25
RR11 R.Jay Soward .50 1.25
RR12 Trung Canidate .50 1.25
RR13 Dennis Northcutt .50 1.25
RR14 Todd Pinkston .50 1.25
RR15 Jerry Porter .75 2.00
RR16 Travis Prentice .50 1.25
RR17 Giovanni Carmazzi .50 1.25
RR18 Ron Dugans .50 1.25
RR19 Erron Kinney .50 1.25
RR20 Dez White .50 1.25
RR21 Chris Cole .60 1.50
RR22 Doug Chapman .50 1.25
RR23 Chris Redman .50 1.25
RR24 J.R. Redmond .50 1.25
RR25 Laveranues Coles .60 1.50
RR26 JaJuan Dawson .50 1.25
RR27 Darrell Jackson .50 1.25
RR28 Reuben Droughns .50 1.25
RR29 Curtis Keaton .50 1.25
RR30 Gari Scott .50 1.25

2000 Absolute Tag Team Quads

Randomly inserted in packs at the rate of one in 79, this 31-card set features four players from each of the NFL's teams on one card. Two players appear on each side and are separated by a centered team logo outlined in silver foil.
COMPLETE SET (31) 125.00 250.00
STATED ODDS 1:79
TTQ1 Jake Plummer 3.00 8.00
David Boston
Thomas Jones
Frank Sanders
TTQ2 Jamal Anderson 3.00 8.00
Tim Dwight
Chris Chandler
Terance Mathis
TTQ3 Tony Banks 2.50 6.00
Travis Taylor
Shannon Sharpe
Jamal Lewis
TTQ4 Rob Johnson 3.00 8.00
Eric Moulds
Antowain Smith
Peerless Price
TTQ5 Steve Beuerlein 3.00 8.00
Tim Biakabutuka
Patrick Jeffers
Muhsin Muhammad
TTQ6 Curtis Enis 3.00 8.00
Cade McNown
Marcus Robinson
Dez White
TTQ7 Corey Dillon 2.50 6.00
Akili Smith
Peter Warrick
Ron Dugans
TTQ8 Tim Couch 3.00 8.00
Errict Rhett
Kevin Johnson
Courtney Brown
TTQ9 Rocket Ismail 6.00 15.00
Emmitt Smith
Troy Aikman
Joey Galloway
TTQ10 Terrell Davis 3.00 8.00
Ed McCaffrey
Olandis Gary
Brian Griese
TTQ11 James Stewart 2.50 6.00
Charlie Batch
Herman Moore
Germane Crowell
TTQ12 Brett Favre 8.00 20.00
Bubba Franks
Dorsey Levens
Antonio Freeman
TTQ13 Peyton Manning 10.00 25.00
Marvin Harrison
Edgerrin James
Terrence Wilkins
TTQ14 Keenan McCardell 3.00 8.00
Mark Brunell
Jimmy Smith
Fred Taylor
TTQ15 Elvis Grbac 3.00 8.00
Sylvester Morris
Tony Gonzalez
Derrick Alexander WR
TTQ16 James Johnson 3.00 8.00
O.J. McDuffie
Tony Martin
Damon Huard
TTQ17 Randy Moss 4.00 10.00
Robert Smith
Cris Carter
Daunte Culpepper
TTQ18 Drew Bledsoe 3.00 8.00
Kevin Faulk
J.R. Redmond
Terry Glenn
TTQ19 Sherrod Gideon 3.00 8.00
Jeff Blake
Ricky Williams
Jake Reed
TTQ20 Kerry Collins 4.00 10.00
Amani Toomer
Ron Dayne
Ike Hilliard
TTQ21 Curtis Martin 2.00 5.00
Chad Pennington
Vinny Testaverde
Wayne Chrebet
TTQ22 Tim Brown 4.00 10.00
Napoleon Kaufman
Rich Gannon
Tyrone Wheatley
TTQ23 Donovan McNabb 3.00 8.00
Corey Simon
Todd Pinkston
Duce Staley
TTQ24 Plaxico Burress 4.00 10.00
Troy Edwards
Kordell Stewart
Jerome Bettis
TTQ25 Jim Harbaugh 3.00 8.00
Junior Seau
Curtis Conway
Jermaine Fazande
TTQ26 Charlie Garner 10.00 25.00
Jerry Rice
Terrell Owens
Steve Young
TTQ27 Derrick Mayes 4.00 10.00
Shaun Alexander
Ricky Watters
Jon Kitna
TTQ28 Kurt Warner 6.00 15.00
Torry Holt
Isaac Bruce
Marshall Faulk
TTQ29 Warrick Dunn 3.00 8.00
Keyshawn Johnson
Shaun King
Mike Alstott
TTQ30 Kevin Dyson 3.00 8.00
Eddie George
Steve McNair
Jevon Kearse
TTQ31 Albert Connell 3.00 8.00
Brad Johnson
Michael Westbrook
Stephen Davis

2000 Absolute Tag Team Tandems

Randomly inserted in Retail packs at the rate of one in 71, this 62-card set pairs lethal combinations from all NFL teams.
COMPLETE SET (62) 75.00 150.00
STATED ODDS 1:71 RETAIL
1 J.Plummer 1.25 3.00
D.Boston
2 T.Jones 1.00 2.50
F.Sanders
3 J.Anderson 1.50 4.00
T.Dwight
4 C.Chandler 1.50 4.00
T.Mathis
5 T.Banks 1.25 3.00
T.Taylor
6 S.Sharpe 1.25 3.00
J.Lewis
7 E.Moulds 1.50 4.00
R.Johnson
8 An.Smith 1.50 4.00
P.Price
9 S.Beuerlein 1.50 4.00
T.Biakabutuka
10 P.Jeffers 1.25 3.00
M.Muhammad
11 C.McNown 1.25 3.00
C.Enis
12 M.Robinson 1.50 4.00
D.White
13 C.Dillon 1.25 3.00
Ak.Smith
14 P.Warrick 1.25 3.00
R.Dugans
15 T.Couch 1.50 4.00
E.Rhett
16 Kv.Johnson 1.50 4.00
C.Brown
17 E.Smith 3.00 8.00
R.Ismail
18 T.Aikman 2.50 6.00
J.Galloway
19 T.Davis 1.50 4.00
E.McCaffrey
20 B.Griese 1.50 4.00
O.Gary
21 C.Batch 1.25 3.00
J.Stewart
22 G.Crowell 1.25 3.00
H.Moore
23 B.Favre 4.00 10.00
B.Franks
24 D.Levens 1.50 4.00
A.Freeman
25 P.Manning 5.00 12.00
M.Harrison
26 E.James 1.50 4.00
T.Wilkins
27 M.Brunell 1.50 4.00
K.McCardell
28 F.Taylor 1.50 4.00
J.Smith
29 E.Grbac 1.25 3.00
Syl.Morris
30 T.Gonzalez 1.50 4.00
D.Alexander
31 J.Johnson 1.50 4.00
O.McDuffie
32 T.Martin 1.25 3.00
D.Huard
33 R.Moss 1.50 4.00
R.Smith
34 C.Carter 2.00 5.00
D.Culpepper
35 D.Bledsoe 1.50 4.00
K.Faulk
36 T.Glenn 1.50 4.00
J.Redmond
37 R.Williams 1.50 4.00
S.Gideon
38 J.Blake 1.50 4.00
J.Reed
39 A.Toomer 1.25 3.00
K.Collins
40 R.Dayne 2.00 5.00
I.Hilliard
41 C.Martin 1.50 4.00
W.Chrebet
42 C.Pennington 1.00 2.50
V.Testaverde
43 T.Brown 2.00 5.00
N.Kaufman
44 R.Gannon 1.50 4.00
T.Wheatley
45 D.McNabb 1.50 4.00
C.Simon
46 T.Pinkston 1.25 3.00
D.Staley
47 P.Burress 1.50 4.00
T.Edwards
48 J.Bettis 2.00 5.00
K.Stewart
49 J.Seau 1.50 4.00
J.Harbaugh
50 J.Fazande 1.50 4.00
C.Conway
51 J.Rice 5.00 12.00
C.Garner
52 S.Young 2.50 6.00
T.Owens
53 S.Alexander 1.25 3.00
D.Mayes
54 R.Watters 1.50 4.00
J.Kitna
55 K.Warner 3.00 8.00
T.Holt
56 M.Faulk 2.00 5.00
I.Bruce
57 Ky.Johnson 1.50 4.00
W.Dunn
58 S.King 1.25 3.00
M.Alstott
59 E.George 1.50 4.00
K.Dyson
60 S.McNair 1.50 4.00
J.Kearse
61 B.Johnson 1.50 4.00
A.Connell
62 S.Davis 1.25 3.00
M.Westbrook

2000 Absolute Tools of the Trade

Randomly inserted in packs, this 60-card set is divided up into three tiers. Card numbers 1-20, Quarterbacks, are sequentially numbered to 2000. Card numbers 21-40, Running Backs, are sequentially numbered to 1500, and card numbers 41-60, Wide Receivers, are sequentially numbered to 1000.
TT1-TT20 PRINT RUN 2000
TT21-TT40 PRINT RUN 1500
TT41-TT60 PRINT RUN 1000
*1-20 DIE CUT/25: 4X TO 10X BASIC INSERTS
1-20 DIE CUT PRINT RUN 25
*21-40 DIE CUT/50: 2.5X TO 6X BASIC INSERTS
21-40 DIE CUT PRINT RUN 50
*41-60 DIE CUT/100: 1.2X TO 3X BASIC INSERTS
41-60 DIE CUT PRINT RUN 100
TT1 Jake Plummer .75 2.00
TT2 Tim Couch 1.00 2.50
TT3 Troy Aikman 1.50 4.00
TT4 John Elway 2.00 5.00
TT5 Charlie Batch .75 2.00
TT6 Brett Favre 2.50 6.00
TT7 Peyton Manning 3.00 8.00
TT8 Mark Brunell 1.00 2.50
TT9 Dan Marino 2.50 6.00
TT10 Drew Bledsoe 1.00 2.50
TT11 Steve Young 1.50 4.00
TT12 Kurt Warner 2.00 5.00
TT13 Cade McNown .75 2.00
TT14 Daunte Culpepper 1.00 2.50
TT15 Donovan McNabb 1.00 2.50
TT16 Jon Kitna .75 2.00
TT17 Steve McNair 1.00 2.50
TT18 Brad Johnson 1.00 2.50
TT19 Akili Smith .75 2.00
TT20 Chad Pennington 1.00 2.50
TT21 Emmitt Smith 2.00 5.00
TT22 Terrell Davis 1.00 2.50
TT23 Barry Sanders 2.00 5.00
TT24 Edgerrin James 1.00 2.50
TT25 Fred Taylor .75 2.00
TT26 Ricky Williams 1.00 2.50
TT27 Eddie George 1.00 2.50
TT28 Jamal Anderson 1.00 2.50
TT29 Corey Dillon .75 2.00
TT30 Dorsey Levens 1.00 2.50
TT31 Robert Smith .75 2.00
TT32 Curtis Martin 1.00 2.50
TT33 Jerome Bettis 1.25 3.00
TT34 Marshall Faulk 1.00 2.50
TT35 Stephen Davis .75 2.00
TT36 Jamal Lewis 1.25 3.00
TT37 Thomas Jones 1.00 2.50
TT38 Ron Dayne 1.25 3.00
TT39 Shaun Alexander 1.25 3.00
TT40 Trung Canidate .75 2.00
TT41 Randy Moss 1.25 3.00
TT42 Jerry Rice 4.00 10.00
TT43 Eric Moulds 1.00 2.50
TT44 Kevin Johnson 1.00 2.50
TT45 Joey Galloway 1.25 3.00
TT46 Antonio Freeman 1.25 3.00
TT47 Marvin Harrison 1.25 3.00
TT48 Cris Carter 1.50 4.00
TT49 Tim Brown 1.50 4.00
TT50 Terrell Owens 1.25 3.00
TT51 Keyshawn Johnson 1.25 3.00
TT52 Muhsin Muhammad 1.00 2.50
TT53 Patrick Jeffers 1.00 2.50
TT54 Marcus Robinson 1.25 3.00
TT55 Jimmy Smith 1.25 3.00
TT56 Amani Toomer 1.00 2.50
TT57 Isaac Bruce 1.50 4.00
TT58 Peter Warrick 1.00 2.50
TT59 Plaxico Burress 1.25 3.00
TT60 Travis Taylor 1.00 2.50

2001 Absolute Memorabilia

In July of 2001 Playoff Inc. released its Playoff Absolute Memorabilia product. Its hobby release was packed in boxes of 18 6-card packs along with a signed mini-helmet. The cardfronts featured a foilboard design. The set consisted of 185-cards with 85 of those being short printed rookies. Cards numbered 101-150 were Rookie Premieres that were serial numbered to 1750. Cards that were numbered 151-185 are Rookie Premiere Materials serial numbered to 850, with the first 25 of each card autographed. The Rookie Premiere Materials also had an authentic event-used football swatch.
COMP.SET w/o SP's (100) 12.50 30.00
151-185 RPM PRINT RUN 850
1 David Boston .30 .75
2 Jake Plummer .30 .75
3 Thomas Jones .30 .75
4 Jamal Anderson .40 1.00
5 Chris Redman .50 1.25
6 Jamal Lewis .50 1.25
7 Qadry Ismail .30 .75
8 Ray Lewis .50 1.25
9 Shannon Sharpe .40 1.00
10 Travis Taylor .30 .75
11 Trent Dilfer .30 .75
12 Elvis Grbac .40 1.00
13 Eric Moulds .30 .75
14 Rob Johnson .40 1.00
15 Muhsin Muhammad .30 .75
16 Brian Urlacher .60 1.50
17 Cade McNown .40 1.00
18 Marcus Robinson .40 1.00
19 Akili Smith .30 .75
20 Corey Dillon .30 .75
21 Peter Warrick .30 .75
22 Courtney Brown .30 .75
23 Tim Couch .30 .75
24 Emmitt Smith .75 2.00
25 Troy Aikman .60 1.50
26 Brian Griese .30 .75
27 Ed McCaffrey .40 1.00
28 John Elway .75 2.00
29 Mike Anderson .30 .75
30 Rod Smith .40 1.00
31 Terrell Davis .40 1.00
32 Barry Sanders .75 2.00
33 James Stewart .30 .75
34 Ahman Green .40 1.00
35 Antonio Freeman .50 1.25
36 Brett Favre 1.00 2.50
37 Edgerrin James .40 1.00
38 Marvin Harrison .40 1.00
39 Peyton Manning 1.25 3.00
40 Fred Taylor .30 .75
41 Jimmy Smith .40 1.00
42 Keenan McCardell .40 1.00
43 Mark Brunell .40 1.00
44 Sylvester Morris .30 .75
45 Tony Gonzalez .40 1.00
46 Dan Marino 1.00 2.50
47 Jay Fiedler .40 1.00
48 Lamar Smith .40 1.00
49 Cris Carter .50 1.25
50 Daunte Culpepper .40 1.00
51 Randy Moss .40 1.00
52 Drew Bledsoe .40 1.00
53 Terry Glenn .40 1.00
54 Aaron Brooks .30 .75
55 Joe Horn .30 .75
56 Ricky Williams .40 1.00
57 Amani Toomer .30 .75
58 Ike Hilliard .30 .75
59 Kerry Collins .30 .75
60 Ron Dayne .40 1.00
61 Tiki Barber .40 1.00
62 Chad Pennington .30 .75
63 Curtis Martin .40 1.00
64 Laveranues Coles .40 1.00
65 Vinny Testaverde .30 .75
66 Wayne Chrebet .30 .75
67 Charles Woodson .50 1.25
68 Rich Gannon .40 1.00
69 Tim Brown .50 1.25
70 Tyrone Wheatley .40 1.00
71 Corey Simon .30 .75
72 Donovan McNabb .40 1.00
73 Duce Staley .30 .75
74 Jerome Bettis .50 1.25
75 Plaxico Burress .30 .75
76 Doug Flutie .40 1.00
77 Junior Seau .40 1.00
78 Charlie Garner .40 1.00
79 Jeff Garcia .30 .75
80 Jerry Rice 1.00 2.50
81 Steve Young .60 1.50
82 Terrell Owens .40 1.00
83 Darrell Jackson .40 1.00
84 Ricky Watters .40 1.00
85 Shaun Alexander .30 .75
86 Isaac Bruce .50 1.25
87 Kurt Warner .75 2.00
88 Marshall Faulk .40 1.00
89 Torry Holt .40 1.00
90 Brad Johnson .40 1.00
91 Keyshawn Johnson .40 1.00
92 Mike Alstott .30 .75
93 Shaun King .30 .75
94 Warren Sapp .40 1.00
95 Warrick Dunn .30 .75
96 Eddie George .50 1.25
97 Jevon Kearse .30 .75
98 Steve McNair .40 1.00
99 Jeff George .40 1.00
100 Stephen Davis .30 .75
101 Jason McKinley RC 1.25 3.00
102 Bobby Newcombe RC 1.50 4.00
103 Cedrick Wilson RC 1.50 4.00
104 Ken-Yon Rambo RC 1.25 3.00
105 Kevin Kasper RC 1.25 3.00
106 Jamal Reynolds RC 1.25 3.00
107 Scotty Anderson RC 1.25 3.00
108 T.J. Houshmandzadeh RC 1.50 4.00
109 Chris Taylor RC 1.25 3.00
110 Vinny Sutherland RC 1.25 3.00
111 Jabari Holloway RC 1.25 3.00
112 Shad Meier RC 1.25 3.00
113 Correll Buckhalter RC 1.25 3.00
114 Dan Alexander RC 1.50 4.00
115 David Allen RC 1.25 3.00
116 LaMont Jordan RC 2.00 5.00
117 Nate Clements RC 1.50 4.00
118 Reggie White RC 1.25 3.00
119 Javon Green RC 1.25 3.00
120 Shaun Rogers RC 2.00 5.00
121 Heath Evans RC 1.50 4.00
122 Moran Norris RC 1.25 3.00
123 Ben Leard RC 1.25 3.00
124 David Rivers RC 1.25 3.00
125 A.J. Feeley RC 1.50 4.00
126 Boo Williams RC 1.25 3.00
127 Ronney Daniels RC 1.25 3.00
128 Alge Crumpler RC 2.00 5.00
129 Todd Heap RC 1.50 4.00
130 Tim Hasselbeck RC 1.50 4.00
131 Josh Booty RC 1.50 4.00
132 Jamie Winborn RC 1.50 4.00
133 Brian Allen RC 1.25 3.00
134 Sedrick Hodge RC 1.25 3.00
135 Tommy Polley RC 1.25 3.00
136 Torrance Marshall RC 1.25 3.00
137 Damione Lewis RC 1.50 4.00
138 Marcus Stroud RC 1.50 4.00
139 Aaron Schobel RC 2.00 5.00
140 DeLawrence Grant RC 1.25 3.00
141 Fred Smoot RC 1.50 4.00
142 Jamar Fletcher RC 1.25 3.00
143 Ken Lucas RC 1.50 4.00
144 Will Allen RC 2.00 5.00
145 Adam Archuleta RC 1.50 4.00
146 Derrick Gibson RC 1.25 3.00
147 Jarrod Cooper RC 1.50 4.00
148 Eddie Berlin RC 1.25 3.00
149 Steve Smith RC 4.00 10.00
150 Willie Middlebrooks RC 1.50 4.00
151 Michael Vick RPM RC 12.00 30.00
152 Drew Brees RPM RC 25.00 50.00
153 Chris Weinke RPM RC 3.00 8.00
154 M.Tuiasosopo RPM RC 3.00 8.00
155 Mike McMahon RPM RC 3.00 8.00
156 Deuce McAllister RPM RC 4.00 10.00
157 Leonard Davis RPM RC 4.00 10.00
158 L.Tomlinson RPM RC 10.00 25.00
159 A.Thomas RPM RC 5.00 12.00
160 Travis Henry RPM RC 3.00 8.00
161 James Jackson RPM RC 2.50 6.00
162 Michael Bennett RPM RC 3.00 8.00
163 Kevan Barlow RPM RC 3.00 8.00
164 Travis Minor RPM RC 3.00 8.00
165 David Terrell RPM RC 3.00 8.00
166 Santana Moss RPM RC 4.00 10.00
167 Rod Gardner RPM RC 3.00 8.00
168 Quincy Morgan RPM RC 3.00 8.00
169 Freddie Mitchell RPM RC 2.50 6.00
170 Reggie Wayne RPM RC 5.00 12.00
171 Koren Robinson RPM RC 3.00 8.00
172 Chad Johnson RPM RC 4.00 10.00
173 Chris Chambers RPM RC 2.50 6.00
174 Josh Heupel RPM RC 4.00 10.00
175 Andre Carter RPM RC 3.00 8.00
176 Justin Smith RPM RC 5.00 12.00
177 R.Seymour RPM RC 4.00 10.00
178 Dan Morgan RPM RC 3.00 8.00
179 Gerard Warren RPM RC 3.00 8.00
180 R.Ferguson RPM RC 4.00 10.00
181 Sage Rosenfels RPM RC 3.00 8.00
182 Rudi Johnson RPM RC 4.00 10.00
183 Snoop Minnis RPM RC 2.50 6.00
184 Jesse Palmer RPM RC 3.00 8.00
185 Quincy Carter RPM RC 3.00 8.00

2001 Absolute Memorabilia Rookie Premiere Materials Autographs

Randomly inserted in packs of 2001 Playoff Absolute Memorabilia, this 25-card set was the same as the Rookie Premiere Materials from the base set, with the exception of adding a signed silver sticker. These cards were the first 25 serial numbered cards from the base Rookie Premiere Materials cards.

FIRST 25 SER.#'d RPM's SIGNED
151 Michael Vick 40.00 100.00
152 Drew Brees 200.00 400.00
153 Chris Weinke 20.00 50.00
155 Mike McMahon 20.00 50.00
156 Deuce McAllister 25.00 60.00
158 LaDainian Tomlinson 125.00 250.00
159 Anthony Thomas 15.00 40.00
160 Travis Henry 20.00 50.00
162 Michael Bennett 20.00 50.00
163 Kevan Barlow 20.00 50.00
164 Travis Minor 20.00 50.00
165 David Terrell 20.00 50.00
166 Santana Moss 25.00 60.00
168 Quincy Morgan 20.00 50.00
169 Freddie Mitchell 15.00 40.00
170 Reggie Wayne 30.00 80.00
171 Koren Robinson 20.00 50.00
172 Chad Johnson 25.00 60.00
173 Chris Chambers 15.00 40.00
176 Justin Smith 30.00 80.00
180 Robert Ferguson 25.00 60.00
182 Rudi Johnson 25.00 60.00
183 Snoop Minnis 15.00 40.00
184 Jesse Palmer 20.00 50.00

2001 Absolute Memorabilia Spectrum

UNPRICED 1-100 VET PRINT RUN 10
*ROOKIES 101-150: 1.2X TO 3X BASIC CARDS
*RPM ROOKIES 151-185: .8X TO 2X
101-185 ROOKIE PRINT RUN 25

2001 Absolute Memorabilia Ground Hoggs Shoe

Randomly inserted in packs of 2001 Playoff Absolute Memorabilia, this 50-card set featured a piece of a game-used shoe from one of the NFL's top turf-churners. These cards were serial numbered to 125 and the first 25 of each card were stamped with a holofoil label "Boss Hoggs." Some cards in the Boss Hoggs version were also signed.

GROUND HOGG PRINT RUN 125 SER.#'d SETS
GH1 Amani Toomer 3.00 8.00
GH2 Antonio Freeman 5.00 12.00
GH3 Brett Favre 10.00 25.00
GH4 Bruce Matthews 3.00 8.00
GH5 Chad Pennington 3.00 8.00
GH6 Champ Bailey 4.00 10.00
GH7 Charles Woodson 5.00 12.00
GH8 Charlie Batch 3.00 8.00
GH9 Chris Samuels 3.00 8.00
GH10 Cris Carter 5.00 12.00
GH11 Curtis Martin 4.00 10.00
GH12 Dan Marino 15.00 40.00
GH13 Darrell Green 5.00 12.00
GH14 Darren Woodson 4.00 10.00
GH15 Daunte Culpepper 4.00 10.00
GH16 Deion Sanders 4.00 10.00
GH17 Derrick Mason 3.00 8.00
GH18 Eddie George 5.00 12.00
GH19 Edgerrin James 4.00 10.00
GH20 Emmitt Smith 8.00 20.00
GH21 Frank Wycheck 3.00 8.00
GH22 Fred Taylor 3.00 8.00
GH23 Ike Hilliard 3.00 8.00
GH24 Isaac Bruce 5.00 12.00
GH25 Jeff George 4.00 10.00
GH26 Jerry Rice 10.00 25.00
GH27 Jessie Armstead 3.00 8.00
GH28 Jevon Kearse 3.00 8.00
GH29 Jimmy Smith 4.00 10.00
GH30 Keyshawn Johnson 4.00 10.00
GH31 Lamar Smith 4.00 10.00
GH32 Laveranues Coles 4.00 10.00
GH33 Mark Brunell 4.00 10.00
GH34 Marshall Faulk 4.00 10.00
GH35 Marvin Harrison 4.00 10.00
GH36 Peerless Price 3.00 8.00
GH37 Peyton Manning 12.00 30.00
GH38 Rocket Ismail 4.00 10.00
GH39 Robert Smith 3.00 8.00
GH40 Ron Dayne 4.00 10.00
GH41 Stephen Davis 3.00 8.00
GH42 Terrell Owens 4.00 10.00
GH43 Terry Glenn 4.00 10.00
GH44 Tyrone Wheatley 4.00 10.00
GH45 Vinny Testaverde 3.00 8.00
GH46 Warren Moon 5.00 12.00
GH47 Warren Sapp 4.00 10.00
GH48 Wayne Chrebet 3.00 8.00
GH49 Willie McGinest 3.00 8.00
GH50 Zach Thomas 4.00 10.00

2001 Absolute Memorabilia Boss Hoggs Shoe

*UNSIGNED BOSS/25: .6X TO 1.5X GROUND
GH12 Dan Marino AU 150.00 300.00
GH19 Edgerrin James AU 25.00 60.00
GH20 Emmitt Smith AU 150.00 300.00
GH24 Isaac Bruce AU 30.00 80.00
GH26 Jerry Rice AU 125.00 250.00
GH29 Jimmy Smith AU 25.00 60.00
GH34 Marshall Faulk AU 25.00 60.00
GH35 Marvin Harrison AU 25.00 60.00

2001 Absolute Memorabilia Leather and Laces

Randomly inserted in packs of 2001 Playoff Absolute Memorabilia, these 50 cards featured a piece of a game-used football, and some featured the football along with some pieces of the football's laces. The stated print runs for cards 1-16 were 825, cards 17-34 were numbered to 550, and cards numbered 35-50 were serial numbered to 275. Some of these cards also featured autographed versions.

LL1-LL16 PRINT RUN 825
LL17-LL34 PRINT RUN 550
LL35-LL50 PRINT RUN 275
*COMBOS: .8X TO 2X BASIC INSERTS
LL1-LL16 COMBOS PRINT RUN 75
LL17-LL34 COMBOS PRINT RUN 50
LL35-LL50 COMBOS PRINT RUN 25
LL1 David Boston 2.00 5.00
LL2 Thomas Jones 2.00 5.00
LL3 Akili Smith 2.00 5.00
LL4 Cris Carter 3.00 8.00
LL5 Tiki Barber 2.50 6.00
LL6 Jevon Kearse 2.00 5.00
LL7 Jamal Anderson 2.50 6.00
LL8 Corey Simon 2.00 5.00
LL9 Deion Sanders 2.50 6.00
LL10 Stephen Davis 2.00 5.00
LL11 Peter Warrick 2.00 5.00
LL12 Kerry Collins 2.00 5.00
LL13 Bruce Smith 2.50 6.00
LL14 Jake Plummer 2.00 5.00
LL15 Darren Woodson 2.50 6.00
LL16 Steve McNair 2.50 6.00
LL17 Brian Urlacher 5.00 12.00
LL18 Cade McNown 3.00 8.00
LL19 Marcus Robinson 3.00 8.00
LL20 Corey Dillon 2.50 6.00
LL21 Emmitt Smith 6.00 15.00
LL22 Brett Favre 8.00 20.00
LL23 Peyton Manning 10.00 25.00
LL24 Fred Taylor 2.50 6.00
LL25 Mark Brunell 3.00 8.00
LL26 Dan Marino 8.00 20.00
LL27 Daunte Culpepper 3.00 8.00
LL28 Randy Moss 3.00 8.00
LL29 Drew Bledsoe 3.00 8.00
LL30 Ron Dayne 3.00 8.00
LL31 Donovan McNabb 3.00 8.00
LL32 Jerome Bettis 8.00 20.00
LL33 Jerry Rice 8.00 20.00
LL34 Eddie George 4.00 10.00
LL35 Isaac Bruce 5.00 12.00
LL36 Ray Lewis 5.00 12.00
LL37 Tim Couch 3.00 8.00
LL38 Eric Moulds 3.00 8.00
LL39 Doug Flutie 4.00 10.00
LL40 Edgerrin James 4.00 10.00
LL41 Curtis Martin 4.00 10.00
LL42 Wayne Chrebet 3.00 8.00
LL43 Jamal Lewis 5.00 12.00
LL44 Kurt Warner 8.00 20.00
LL45 Barry Sanders 8.00 20.00
LL46 Marvin Harrison 4.00 10.00
LL47 Ricky Williams 4.00 10.00
LL48 Jimmy Smith 4.00 10.00
LL49 Tim Brown 5.00 12.00
LL50 Troy Aikman 6.00 15.00

2001 Absolute Memorabilia Leather and Laces Autographs

Randomly inserted in packs of 2001 Playoff Absolute Memorabilia, these 10 cards featured a piece of a game-used football, and some featured the football along with some pieces of the football's laces. The stated print run was 25 serial numbered sets. These were the autographed version.

PLAYERS SIGNED FIRST 25 OF PRINT RUN
LL10 Stephen Davis 12.00 30.00
LL20 Corey Dillon 12.00 30.00
LL26 Dan Marino 100.00 200.00
LL27 Daunte Culpepper 15.00 40.00
LL40 Edgerrin James 15.00 40.00
LL44 Kurt Warner 30.00 80.00
LL45 Barry Sanders 75.00 150.00
LL46 Marvin Harrison 15.00 40.00
LL47 Ricky Williams 15.00 40.00
LL49 Tim Brown 20.00 50.00

2001 Absolute Memorabilia Mini Helmet Autographs

These were Riddell replica mini helmets that were signed and individually packaged inside of the 2001 Playoff Absolute Memorabilia hobby boxes. The helmets had a sticker of authenticity on them from Playoff Inc. Please note the number of autographs for each individual player varies and is listed below. Some of the autographs were available on a chrome Riddell mini helmet which has the steel facemask. Helmets serial numbered under 26 are not priced due to scarcity.

ONE PER SEALED BOX
1 Troy Aikman/86 60.00 120.00
2 Troy Aikman CHR/24 90.00 150.00
3 Will Allen/252 10.00 25.00
4 Alex Bannister/250 10.00 25.00
5 Kevan Barlow/226 12.00 30.00
7 Michael Bennett/251 12.00 30.00
8 Cliff Branch/554 12.00 30.00
10 Drew Brees/273 100.00 200.00
11 Drew Brees CHR/24 200.00 400.00
12 Willie Brown/1005 12.00 30.00
13 Quincy Carter/236 15.00 40.00
15 Chris Chambers/242 15.00 40.00
18 Randall Cunningham/70 20.00 40.00
19 Trent Dilfer SB/100 25.00 50.00
20 John Elway/40 125.00 250.00
21 Robert Ferguson/226 12.00 30.00
22 Robert Ferguson CHR/24 30.00 60.00
23 Chuck Foreman/600 12.00 30.00
24 Rich Gannon/1033 12.00 30.00
25 Jeff Garcia/1000 12.00 30.00
26 Rod Gardner/226 12.00 30.00
27 Kevin Greene/474 12.00 30.00
29 John Hannah/500 12.00 30.00
30 Todd Heap/225 15.00 40.00
31 Todd Heap CHR/24 40.00 80.00
32 Travis Henry/225 15.00 40.00
33 Travis Henry CHR/24 30.00 60.00
34 James Jackson/238 10.00 25.00
36 Chad Johnson/249 20.00 50.00
37 Rob Johnson/501 10.00 25.00
38 Rudi Johnson/238 15.00 40.00
40 Charlie Joiner/511 12.00 30.00
40 Gerard Warren/250 12.00 30.00
41 LaMont Jordan/237 15.00 40.00
42 Jevon Kearse/40 30.00 60.00
43 Jim Kelly/20 90.00 150.00
44 Bob Lilly/600 15.00 40.00
45 Peyton Manning/287 90.00 150.00
46 Dan Marino/80 100.00 200.00
47 Harvey Martin/250 50.00 100.00
48 Deuce McAllister/224 15.00 40.00
49 Deuce McAllister CHR/24 40.00 80.00
50 Mike McMahon/289 10.00 25.00
52 Donovan McNabb/58 40.00 80.00
53 Cade McNown/1024 10.00 20.00
54 Snoop Minnis/225 10.00 25.00
55 Snoop Minnis CHR/24 30.00 60.00
56 Travis Minor/250 12.00 30.00
57 Freddie Mitchell/217 12.00 30.00
58 Freddie Mitchell CHR/24 30.00 60.00
59 Quincy Morgan/238 12.00 30.00
61 Santana Moss/238 15.00 40.00
62 Jesse Palmer/250 10.00 25.00
63 Drew Pearson/600 15.00 40.00
64 Jake Plummer/1003 12.00 30.00
66 Ken-Yon Rambo/226 10.00 25.00
67 Ken-Yon Rambo CHR/24 30.00 60.00
68 Koren Robinson/227 10.00 25.00
69 Koren Robinson CHR/23 30.00 60.00
70 Sage Rosenfels/250 10.00 25.00
71 Barry Sanders/20 100.00 175.00
72 Richard Seymour/228 15.00 40.00
73 Richard Seymour CHR/22 40.00 80.00
74 Justin Smith/239 15.00 40.00
76 Charlie Taylor/485 12.00 30.00
77 Anthony Thomas/238 15.00 40.00
79 LaDainian Tomlinson/226 40.00 80.00
80 LaD.Tomlinson CHR/24 75.00 150.00
81 Michael Vick/226 50.00 80.00
82 Michael Vick CHR/24 90.00 150.00
83 Kurt Warner/119 50.00 120.00
85 Reggie Wayne/232 15.00 40.00
87 Chris Weinke/226 12.00 30.00
88 Chris Weinke CHR/24 40.00 80.00
89 Ricky Williams/1046 15.00 40.00
90 Steve Young/20 90.00 150.00

2001 Absolute Memorabilia Tools of the Trade

Tools of the Trade were randomly inserted into packs of 2001 Playoff Absolute Memorabilia. There were 4 types of swatch that could be had in this set, and please note below which swatch could be found on each player. The swatches included player used: gloves, face-masks, pants, and jerseys. Each card was serial numbered to the type of memorabilia that was on the card: jerseys were numbered to 300, gloves were numbered to 50, face-masks were numbered to 125, and pants were numbered to 100. There was also an autographed version which was parallel to this set. The autographs were the first 25 serial numbered cards of the sequence.

TT1-TT19 JERSEY PRINT RUN 300
TT20-TT30 GLOVE PRINT RUN 50
TT31-TT40 FACEMASK PRINT RUN 125
TT41-TT50 PANTS PRINT RUN 100
TT1 Antonio Freeman JSY 6.00 15.00
TT2 Barry Sanders JSY/275* 12.00 30.00
TT3 Brett Favre JSY 12.00 30.00
TT4 Brian Griese JSY 4.00 10.00
TT5 Donovan McNabb JSY 5.00 12.00
TT6 Daunte Culpepper JSY 5.00 12.00
TT7 Drew Bledsoe JSY/275* 5.00 12.00
TT8 Emmitt Smith JSY 10.00 25.00
TT9 Jamal Lewis JSY 6.00 15.00
TT10 Jimmy Smith JSY 5.00 12.00
TT11 Edgerrin James JSY/275* 5.00 12.00
TT12 Mike Anderson JSY/275* 4.00 10.00
TT13 Peyton Manning JSY 15.00 40.00
TT14 Randy Moss JSY 5.00 12.00
TT15 Rich Gannon JSY 5.00 12.00
TT16 Ricky Williams JSY/275* 5.00 12.00
TT17 Steve McNair JSY 5.00 12.00
TT18 Terrell Owens JSY 5.00 12.00
TT19 Ricky Watters JSY 5.00 12.00
TT20 Warren Sapp JSY 5.00 12.00
TT21 Champ Bailey GLV 10.00 25.00
TT22 Courtney Brown GLV 8.00 20.00
TT23 Deion Sanders GLV 10.00 25.00
TT24 Derrick Mason GLV 8.00 20.00
TT25 Eddie George GLV 12.00 30.00
TT26 Jevon Kearse GLV 8.00 20.00
TT27 Keyshawn Johnson GLV 10.00 25.00
TT28 Ron Dayne GLV 10.00 25.00
TT29 Terry Glenn GLV 10.00 25.00
TT30 Wayne Chrebet GLV 8.00 20.00
TT31 Curtis Martin FM 8.00 20.00
TT32 Corey Dillon FM 6.00 15.00
TT33 Cris Carter FM 10.00 25.00
TT34 Junior Seau FM 8.00 20.00
TT35 Jerome Bettis FM 10.00 25.00
TT36 Warrick Dunn FM 6.00 15.00
TT37 Eric Moulds FM 6.00 15.00
TT38 Stephen Davis FM 6.00 15.00
TT39 Steve Young FM 12.00 30.00
TT40 Troy Aikman FM/100* 12.00 30.00
TT41 Dan Marino Pants/75* 15.00 40.00
TT42 Isaac Bruce Pants 8.00 20.00
TT43 Jerry Rice Pants 15.00 40.00
TT44 John Elway Pants/75* 12.00 30.00
TT45 Kurt Warner Pants/75* 12.00 30.00
TT46 Mark Brunell Pants 6.00 15.00
TT47 Marshall Faulk Pants/75* 6.00 15.00
TT48 Terrell Davis Pants 6.00 15.00
TT49 Tim Couch Pants 5.00 12.00
TT50 Torry Holt Pants 6.00 15.00

2001 Absolute Memorabilia Tools of the Trade Autographs

Tools of the Trade Autographs were randomly inserted into packs of 2001 Absolute Memorabilia. There were 3 types of swatches that could be had in this set: face masks, pants, and jerseys. The autographed versions were the first 25-serial numbered cards of the sequence. Please note below that only 10 cards from the Tools of the Trade set were available in autographed form.

FIRST 25 CARDS OF PRINT RUN SIGNED
TT2 Barry Sanders JSY 100.00 200.00
TT7 Drew Bledsoe JSY 40.00 80.00
TT11 Edgerrin James JSY 40.00 80.00
TT12 Mike Anderson JSY 30.00 60.00
TT16 Ricky Williams JSY 40.00 80.00
TT40 Troy Aikman FM 75.00 150.00
TT41 Dan Marino Pants 125.00 250.00
TT44 John Elway Pants 75.00 150.00
TT45 Kurt Warner Pants 40.00 80.00
TT47 Marshall Faulk Pants 40.00 80.00

2001 Absolute Memorabilia Chicago Collection

NOT PRICED DUE TO SCARCITY

2002 Absolute Memorabilia

Released in October 2002, this 232-card base set includes 150 veterans, 50 rookies, and 32 Rookie Premiere Materials cards that feature one swatch each of event-used footballs and jerseys. The rookie cards are sequentially numbered to 1500 and Rookie Premiere Materials cards are serial #'d 825. Each full box contains two mini-boxes of 9 packs. Each pack contains 6 cards. In addition, each full sealed box contains one Signing Bonus plaque.

COMP.SET w/o SP's (150) 12.50 30.00
151-200 ROOKIE PRINT RUN 1500
201-232 RPM PRINT RUN 825
1 Aaron Brooks .25 .60
2 Ahman Green .30 .75
3 Alge Crumpler .30 .75
4 Amani Toomer .25 .60
5 Andre Carter .25 .60
6 Anthony Thomas .30 .75
7 Antonio Freeman .40 1.00
8 Antowain Smith .30 .75
9 Az-Zahir Hakim .25 .60
10 Bill Schroeder .25 .60
11 Brad Johnson .30 .75
12 Brett Favre .75 2.00
13 Brian Griese .25 .60
14 Brian Urlacher .40 1.00
15 Chad Johnson .25 .60
16 Chad Pennington .25 .60
17 Champ Bailey .30 .75
18 Charles Woodson .40 1.00
19 Charlie Batch .25 .60
20 Charlie Garner .30 .75
21 Chris Chambers .25 .60
22 Chris Redman .25 .60
23 Chris Weinke .25 .60
24 Corey Dillon .25 .60
25 Correll Buckhalter .25 .60
26 Cris Carter .40 1.00
27 Curtis Martin .30 .75
28 Darnay Scott .30 .75
29 Darrell Jackson .30 .75
30 Daunte Culpepper .30 .75
31 David Boston .25 .60
32 David Terrell .25 .60
33 Derrick Alexander .25 .60
34 Derrick Mason .25 .60
35 Deuce McAllister .30 .75
36 Dominic Rhodes .25 .60
37 Donald Hayes .25 .60
38 Donovan McNabb .30 .75
39 Doug Flutie .30 .75
40 Drew Bledsoe .30 .75
41 Drew Brees .75 2.00
42 Duce Staley .25 .60
43 Ed McCaffrey .30 .75
44 Eddie George .30 .75
45 Edgerrin James .30 .75
46 Elvis Joseph .25 .60
47 Emmitt Smith .60 1.50
48 Eric Moulds .25 .60
49 Frank Sanders .25 .60
50 Fred Taylor .25 .60
51 Freddie Mitchell .25 .60
52 Garrison Hearst .25 .60
53 Gerard Warren .25 .60
54 Germane Crowell .25 .60
55 Isaac Bruce .40 1.00
56 Jake Plummer .25 .60
57 Jamal Anderson .30 .75
58 Jamal Lewis .30 .75
59 James Allen .25 .60
60 James Jackson .25 .60
61 James Stewart .25 .60
62 Jason Brookins .25 .60
63 Jay Fiedler .30 .75
64 Jeff Garcia .25 .60
65 Jerome Bettis .40 1.00
66 Jerry Rice .75 2.00
67 Jevon Kearse .25 .60
68 Jim Miller .25 .60
69 Jimmy Smith .30 .75
70 Joe Horn .25 .60
71 Joey Galloway .30 .75
72 Jon Kitna .25 .60
73 Junior Seau .30 .75
74 Keenan McCardell .30 .75
75 Kendrell Bell .25 .60
76 Kerry Collins .25 .60
77 Kevan Barlow .25 .60
78 Kevin Dyson .30 .75
79 Kevin Johnson .25 .60
80 Kevin Kasper .25 .60
81 Keyshawn Johnson .30 .75
82 Kordell Stewart .25 .60
83 Koren Robinson .25 .60
84 Kurt Warner .30 .75
85 LaDainian Tomlinson .40 1.00
86 Lamar Smith .25 .60
87 Laveranues Coles .30 .75
88 MarTay Jenkins .25 .60
89 Mark Brunell .30 .75
90 Marshall Faulk .30 .75
91 Marty Booker .25 .60
92 Marvin Harrison .30 .75
93 Snoop Minnis .25 .60
94 Michael Bennett .25 .60
95 Michael Strahan .30 .75
96 Michael Vick .30 .75
97 Mike Alstott .25 .60
98 Mike Anderson .25 .60
99 Mike McMahon .25 .60
100 Muhsin Muhammad .25 .60
101 Nate Clements .25 .60
102 Oronde Gadsden .25 .60
103 Peter Warrick .25 .60
104 Peyton Manning 1.00 2.50
105 Plaxico Burress .25 .60
106 Priest Holmes .25 .60
107 Quincy Carter .25 .60
108 Quincy Morgan .25 .60
109 Rocket Ismail .30 .75
110 Randy Moss .30 .75
111 Ray Lewis .40 1.00
112 Reggie Wayne .30 .75
113 Rich Gannon .30 .75
114 Rickey Dudley .25 .60
115 Ricky Watters .30 .75
116 Ricky Williams .30 .75
117 Rod Gardner .25 .60
118 Rod Smith .30 .75
119 Robert Ferguson .30 .75
120 Santana Moss .30 .75
121 Shaun Alexander .25 .60
122 Stephen Davis .25 .60
123 Steve McNair .30 .75
124 Steve Smith .40 1.00
125 Terrell Davis .30 .75
126 Terrell Owens .30 .75
127 Terry Glenn .30 .75
128 Thomas Jones .25 .60
129 Tiki Barber .30 .75
130 Tim Brown .40 1.00
131 Tim Couch .25 .60
132 Todd Heap .25 .60
133 Todd Pinkston .25 .60
134 Tom Brady 2.00 5.00
135 Tony Boselli .30 .75
136 Tony Gonzalez .30 .75
137 Torry Holt .30 .75
138 Travis Henry .25 .60
139 Travis Taylor .25 .60
140 Trent Dilfer .25 .60
141 Trent Green .25 .60
142 Troy Brown .25 .60
143 Troy Hambrick .25 .60
144 Trung Canidate .25 .60
145 Vinny Testaverde .25 .60
146 Warren Sapp .30 .75
147 Warrick Dunn .25 .60
148 Wayne Chrebet .25 .60
149 Wesley Walls .30 .75
150 Zach Thomas .30 .75
151 Quentin Jammer RC 2.00 5.00
152 Randy Fasani RC 1.25 3.00
153 Kurt Kittner RC 1.25 3.00
154 Chad Hutchinson RC 1.25 3.00
155 Major Applewhite RC 2.00 5.00
156 Wes Pate RC 1.25 3.00
157 J.T. O'Sullivan RC 1.50 4.00
158 Ryan Denney RC 1.25 3.00
159 Ronald Curry RC 1.25 3.00
160 Lamar Gordon RC 1.50 4.00
161 Brian Westbrook RC 2.50 6.00
162 Jonathan Wells RC 1.50 4.00
163 Ricky Williams RC 1.50 4.00
164 Verron Haynes RC 1.25 3.00
165 Josh Scobey RC 1.50 4.00
166 Larry Ned RC 1.25 3.00
167 Adrian Peterson RC 1.50 4.00
168 Chester Taylor RC 2.00 5.00
169 Luke Staley RC 1.25 3.00
170 Damien Anderson RC 1.25 3.00
171 Lee Mays RC 1.25 3.00
172 Deion Branch RC 2.00 5.00
173 Terry Charles RC 1.25 3.00
174 Woody Dantzler RC 1.50 4.00
175 Jason McAddley RC 1.50 4.00
176 Kelly Campbell RC 1.50 4.00
177 Freddie Milons RC 1.25 3.00
178 Kahlil Hill RC 1.25 3.00
179 Brian Poli-Dixon RC 1.25 3.00
180 Mike Echols RC 1.25 3.00
181 Pete Rebstock RC 1.25 3.00
182 Dwight Freeney RC 2.50 6.00
183 Bryan Thomas RC 1.25 3.00
184 Charles Grant RC 2.00 5.00
185 Kalimba Edwards RC 1.50 4.00
186 Ryan Sims RC 2.00 5.00
187 John Henderson RC 1.50 4.00
188 Wendell Bryant RC 1.25 3.00
189 Albert Haynesworth RC 2.00 5.00
190 Larry Tripplett RC 1.25 3.00
191 Phillip Buchanon RC 2.00 5.00
192 Lito Sheppard RC 2.00 5.00
193 Mike Rumph RC 1.25 3.00
194 Levar Fisher RC 1.25 3.00
195 Ed Reed RC 8.00 20.00
196 Rocky Calmus RC 1.50 4.00
197 Michael Lewis RC 1.50 4.00
198 Napoleon Harris RC 1.50 4.00
199 Robert Thomas RC 1.25 3.00
200 Anthony Weaver RC 1.25 3.00
201 Ladell Betts RPM RC 3.00 8.00
202 Antonio Bryant RPM RC 3.00 8.00
203 Reche Caldwell RPM RC 2.50 6.00
204 David Carr RPM RC 2.00 5.00
206 Tim Carter RPM RC 2.50 6.00
206 Eric Crouch RPM RC 3.00 8.00
207 Rohan Davey RPM RC 3.00 8.00
208 Andre Davis RPM RC 2.00 5.00
209 T.J. Duckett RPM RC 2.00 5.00
210 DeShaun Foster RPM RC 3.00 8.00
211 Jabar Gaffney RPM RC 2.00 5.00
212 Daniel Graham RPM RC 2.50 6.00
213 William Green RPM RC 2.50 6.00
214 Joey Harrington RPM RC 2.00 5.00
215 David Garrard RPM RC 2.50 6.00
216 Ron Johnson RPM RC 2.50 6.00
217 Ashley Lelie RPM RC 2.00 5.00
218 Josh McCown RPM RC 3.00 8.00
219 Maurice Morris RPM RC 2.50 6.00
220 Julius Peppers RPM RC 5.00 12.00
221 Clinton Portis RPM RC 3.00 8.00
222 Patrick Ramsey RPM RC 2.50 6.00
223 Antwaan Randle El RPM RC 2.50 6.00
224 Josh Reed RPM RC 2.50 6.00
225 Cliff Russell RPM RC 2.00 5.00
226 Jeremy Shockey RPM RC 3.00 8.00
227 Donte Stallworth RPM RC 3.00 8.00
228 Travis Stephens RPM RC 2.00 5.00
229 Javon Walker RPM RC 3.00 8.00
230 Marquise Walker RPM RC 2.00 5.00
231 Roy Williams RPM RC 2.00 5.00
232 Mike Williams RPM RC 2.00 5.00

2002 Absolute Memorabilia Spectrum

*1-150 VETS/100: 3X TO 8X BASIC CARDS
1-150 VET PRINT RUN 100
*151-200 ROOKIES/50: 1.5X TO 4X
151-200 ROOKIE PRINT RUN 50
*201-232 RPM ROOKIE/25: 1.5X TO 4X
201-232 ROOKIE RPM PRINT RUN 25

2002 Absolute Memorabilia Absolutely Ink

This set features authentic player autographs applied with a holofoil sticker. Each card was sequentially numbered to 30. Cards #AI20, 34, 35, and 38 were not released.

STATED PRINT RUN 30 SER.#'d SETS
AI1 Randy Moss 50.00 120.00
AI2 Brett Favre 125.00 250.00
AI3 Dan Marino 100.00 200.00
AI4 Tim Brown 20.00 50.00
AI5 Todd Heap 12.00 30.00
AI6 Correll Buckhalter 12.00 30.00
AI7 Mike McMahon 12.00 30.00
AI8 John Riggins 20.00 50.00
AI9 Aaron Brooks 12.00 30.00
AI10 David Terrell 12.00 30.00
AI11 Ray Lewis 50.00 100.00
AI12 Torry Holt 15.00 40.00
AI13 Stephen Davis 12.00 30.00
AI14 Mike Anderson 12.00 30.00
AI15 Jimmy Smith 15.00 40.00
AI16 Troy Aikman 50.00 100.00
AI17 Josh Heupel 15.00 40.00
AI18 Marcus Robinson 15.00 40.00
AI19 Kurt Warner 15.00 40.00
AI21 LaMont Jordan 15.00 40.00
AI22 Peter Warrick 12.00 30.00
AI23 Santana Moss 15.00 40.00
AI24 Terrell Owens 15.00 40.00
AI25 Koren Robinson 12.00 30.00
AI26 Quincy Carter 12.00 30.00
AI27 Jamal Lewis 15.00 40.00
AI28 Ronnie Lott 20.00 50.00
AI29 Eric Moulds 12.00 30.00
AI30 Cade McNown 15.00 40.00
AI31 Isaac Bruce 20.00 50.00
AI32 Jesse Palmer 12.00 30.00
AI33 Travis Minor 12.00 30.00
AI36 Damione Lewis 12.00 30.00
AI37 Daunte Culpepper 15.00 40.00
AI39 Phil Simms 20.00 50.00
AI40 Deuce McAllister 15.00 40.00
AI41 Will Allen 12.00 30.00
AI42 Mark Brunell 15.00 40.00
AI43 Edgerrin James 15.00 40.00
AI44 Steve Young 40.00 80.00
AI45 Chris Weinke 12.00 30.00
AI46 Emmitt Smith 125.00 250.00
AI47 Sage Rosenfels 15.00 40.00
AI48 Kevan Barlow 12.00 30.00
AI49 Marshall Faulk 15.00 40.00
AI50 Thurman Thomas 15.00 40.00

2002 Absolute Memorabilia Boss Hoggs Shoe

This 15-card set features a swatch of game-worn shoe on each card and is sequentially numbered to 125.

STATED PRINT RUN 125 SER.#'d SETS
GH1 Edgerrin James 3.00 8.00
GH2 Eddie George 3.00 8.00
GH3 Curtis Martin 3.00 8.00
GH4 Stephen Davis 2.50 6.00
GH5 Lamar Smith 2.50 6.00
GH6 Emmitt Smith 6.00 15.00
GH7 Troy Aikman 5.00 12.00
GH8 Dan Marino 8.00 20.00
GH9 Drew Bledsoe 3.00 8.00
GH10 Zach Thomas 3.00 8.00
GH11 Michael Strahan 3.00 8.00
GH12 Troy Brown 2.50 6.00
GH13 Derrick Mason 2.50 6.00
GH14 Terrell Owens 3.00 8.00
GH15 Isaac Bruce 4.00 10.00

2002 Absolute Memorabilia Ground Hoggs

This 15-card insert is inserted in packs at a rate of 1:17, and features the NFL's top players. There is also a gold parallel which was inserted at a rate of 1:85.

COMPLETE SET (15) 10.00 25.00
STATED ODDS 1:17
*GOLD: 1X TO 2.5X BASIC INSERTS
GOLD STATED ODDS 1:85
GH1 Edgerrin James 1.00 2.50
GH2 Eddie George 1.00 2.50
GH3 Curtis Martin 1.00 2.50
GH4 Stephen Davis .75 2.00
GH5 Lamar Smith .75 2.00
GH6 Emmitt Smith 2.00 5.00
GH7 Troy Aikman 1.50 4.00
GH8 Dan Marino 2.50 6.00
GH9 Drew Bledsoe 1.00 2.50
GH10 Zach Thomas 1.00 2.50
GH11 Michael Strahan 1.00 2.50
GH12 Troy Brown .75 2.00
GH13 Derrick Mason .75 2.00
GH14 Terrell Owens 1.00 2.50
GH15 Isaac Bruce 1.25 3.00

2002 Absolute Memorabilia Leather and Laces

This 50-card insert displays one swatch from a game-used football. A Combos parallel was created with the addition of a piece from the laces of a game-used football with each of those cards serial numbered of 25 (#LL1-LL25) or 50 (#LL26-LL50). The basic insert cards #LL1-LL25 are serial numbered to 250 with #LL26-LL50 numbered to 500.

LL1-LL25 PRINT RUN 250
LL26-LL50 PRINT RUN 500
*COMBO/25: 2X TO 5X INSERT/250
*COMBO/50: 1.5X TO 4X INSERT/500
LL1 Kurt Warner 4.00 10.00
LL2 Rod Smith 4.00 10.00
LL3 Curtis Martin 4.00 10.00
LL4 Ahman Green 4.00 10.00
LL5 Daunte Culpepper 4.00 10.00
LL6 David Boston 3.00 8.00
LL7 Brian Urlacher 5.00 12.00
LL8 Dominic Rhodes 3.00 8.00
LL9 Doug Flutie 4.00 10.00
LL10 Kordell Stewart 3.00 8.00
LL11 Antowain Smith 4.00 10.00
LL12 Torry Holt 4.00 10.00
LL13 Eric Moulds 3.00 8.00
LL14 Marvin Harrison 4.00 10.00
LL15 Troy Brown 3.00 8.00
LL16 Garrison Hearst 3.00 8.00
LL17 Mike Anderson 3.00 8.00
LL18 Priest Holmes 3.00 8.00
LL19 David Terrell 3.00 8.00
LL20 Peyton Manning 12.00 30.00
LL21 Isaac Bruce 5.00 12.00
LL22 Randy Moss 4.00 10.00
LL23 Kerry Collins 3.00 8.00
LL24 Shaun Alexander 3.00 8.00
LL25 Terrell Davis 4.00 10.00
LL26 Anthony Thomas 3.00 8.00
LL27 Keyshawn Johnson 3.00 8.00
LL28 Quincy Carter 2.50 6.00
LL29 Rich Gannon 3.00 8.00
LL30 Tom Brady 20.00 50.00
LL31 Aaron Brooks 2.50 6.00
LL32 Tim Brown 4.00 10.00
LL33 Chris Chambers 2.50 6.00
LL34 Stephen Davis 2.50 6.00
LL35 Cris Carter 4.00 10.00
LL36 Brett Favre 8.00 20.00
LL37 Eddie George 3.00 8.00
LL38 Travis Henry 2.50 6.00
LL39 Jerry Rice 8.00 20.00
LL40 Correll Buckhalter 2.50 6.00
LL41 Jeff Garcia 2.50 6.00
LL42 Emmitt Smith 6.00 15.00
LL43 Steve McNair 3.00 8.00
LL44 LaDainian Tomlinson 4.00 10.00
LL45 Ricky Williams 3.00 8.00
LL46 Brian Griese 2.50 6.00
LL47 Terrell Owens 3.00 8.00
LL48 Marshall Faulk 3.00 8.00
LL49 Jake Plummer 2.50 6.00
LL50 Donovan McNabb 3.00 8.00

2002 Absolute Memorabilia Signing Bonus

Inserted one per sealed full box, this plaque like item features a jersey material background, a base card, and a signed sticker. Each item is serial #'d to varying quantities.

SER.#'d 5-400: ONE PER BOX
SERIAL #'d UNDER 25 NOT PRICED
4 Jamal Anderson/125 20.00 50.00
5 Mike Anderson/50 20.00 50.00
6 Mike Anderson/150 15.00 40.00
7 Kevan Barlow/100 15.00 40.00
8 Kevan Barlow/300 12.00 30.00
9 Charlie Batch/150 15.00 40.00
10 Charlie Batch/250 12.00 30.00
11 Michael Bennett/50 20.00 50.00
13 Drew Bledsoe/50 50.00 100.00
14 Drew Bledsoe/100 20.00 50.00
15 David Boston/50 20.00 50.00
16 Drew Brees/200 40.00 80.00
17 Drew Brees/400 40.00 80.00
20 Aaron Brooks/100 15.00 40.00
21 Aaron Brooks/200 12.00 30.00
22 Tim Brown/50 50.00 100.00
23 Tim Brown/300 30.00 60.00
25 Isaac Bruce/175 20.00 50.00
26 Isaac Bruce/300 20.00 50.00
28 Mark Brunell/150 20.00 50.00
29 Mark Brunell/350 15.00 40.00
30 Correll Buckhalter/150 15.00 40.00
31 Correll Buckhalter/350 12.00 30.00
32 Cris Carter/50 60.00 120.00
33 Cris Carter/100 25.00 60.00
35 Quincy Carter/250 12.00 30.00
36 Quincy Carter/350 12.00 30.00
38 Chris Chambers/125 15.00 40.00
39 Laveranues Coles/100 20.00 50.00
40 Kerry Collins/200 12.00 30.00
41 Kerry Collins/380 12.00 30.00
43 Daunte Culpepper/100 20.00 50.00
45 Stephen Davis/75 15.00 40.00
46 Stephen Davis/400 12.00 30.00
47 Terrell Davis/50 50.00 120.00
48 Terrell Davis/150 20.00 50.00
50 Corey Dillon/100 15.00 40.00
53 Marshall Faulk/50 25.00 60.00
54 Marshall Faulk/300 15.00 40.00
56 Brett Favre/75 125.00 250.00
57 Robert Ferguson/150 20.00 50.00
58 Robert Ferguson/250 15.00 40.00
60 Jeff Garcia/40 20.00 50.00
61 Rod Gardner/50 20.00 50.00
62 Tony Gonzalez/50 25.00 60.00
63 Tony Gonzalez/150 20.00 50.00
65 Ahman Green/100 20.00 50.00
67 Brian Griese/25 25.00 60.00
68 Brian Griese/175 12.00 30.00
69 Marvin Harrison/50 60.00 100.00
70 Marvin Harrison/150 20.00 50.00
71 Todd Heap/150 15.00 40.00
72 Todd Heap/400 12.00 30.00
73 Torry Holt/100 20.00 50.00
74 Torry Holt/300 15.00 40.00
75 James Jackson/150 15.00 40.00
76 James Jackson/300 12.00 30.00
79 Edgerrin James/150 20.00 50.00
80 Edgerrin James/250 15.00 40.00
81 Chad Johnson/100 15.00 40.00
82 Chad Johnson/250 12.00 30.00
83 Jamal Lewis/100 20.00 50.00
84 Ray Lewis/150 50.00 120.00
85 Ray Lewis/350 60.00 120.00
86 Jamal Lewis/400 15.00 40.00
89 Deuce McAllister/200 15.00 40.00
90 Deuce McAllister/400 15.00 40.00
91 Mike McMahon/150 15.00 40.00
92 Mike McMahon/300 12.00 30.00
93 Quincy Morgan/200 12.00 30.00
94 Quincy Morgan/400 12.00 30.00
95 Santana Moss/200 15.00 40.00
96 Santana Moss/400 15.00 40.00
97 Eric Moulds/125 15.00 40.00
98 Eric Moulds/300 12.00 30.00
100 Terrell Owens/25 50.00 100.00
101 Terrell Owens/75 40.00 80.00
102 Chad Pennington/100 15.00 40.00
103 Chad Pennington/200 12.00 30.00
104 Jake Plummer/100 15.00 40.00
105 Jerry Rice/125 75.00 150.00
107 Junior Seau/25 60.00 120.00
108 Junior Seau/100 30.00 60.00
111 Emmitt Smith/75 150.00 300.00
112 Emmitt Smith/150 125.00 250.00
113 Jimmy Smith/300 15.00 40.00
114 Jimmy Smith/400 15.00 40.00
116 Michael Strahan/90 50.00 80.00
117 David Terrell/200 12.00 30.00
118 David Terrell/400 12.00 30.00
119 Vinny Testaverde/25 25.00 60.00
120 Vinny Testaverde/75 15.00 40.00
122 Anthony Thomas/50 25.00 60.00
123 Anthony Thomas/150 20.00 50.00
124 Brian Urlacher/50 60.00 120.00
125 Brian Urlacher/200 75.00 150.00
126 Michael Vick/75 60.00 100.00
128 Kurt Warner/100 40.00 100.00
129 Kurt Warner/250 30.00 60.00
130 Peter Warrick/150 15.00 40.00
131 Peter Warrick/350 12.00 30.00
132 Ricky Watters/50 25.00 60.00
133 Ricky Watters/200 15.00 40.00
134 Reggie Wayne/75 20.00 50.00
135 Reggie Wayne/200 15.00 40.00
137 Chris Weinke/200 12.00 30.00
138 Chris Weinke/300 12.00 30.00
140 Ricky Williams/75 20.00 50.00

2002 Absolute Memorabilia Tools of the Trade

This 50-card insert is inserted in packs at a rate of 1:17, and features players who have the tools to win. There is also a gold parallel version that was inserted at a rate of 1:85.

STATED ODDS 1:17
*GOLD: .8X TO 2X BASIC INSERTS
GOLD STATED ODDS 1:85
TT1 Emmitt Smith 2.50 6.00
TT2 Brett Favre 3.00 8.00
TT3 Donovan McNabb 1.25 3.00
TT4 Brian Griese 1.00 2.50
TT5 Peyton Manning 4.00 10.00
TT6 Kurt Warner 1.25 3.00
TT7 Dan Marino 3.00 8.00
TT8 Shaun Alexander 1.00 2.50
TT9 Anthony Thomas 1.25 3.00
TT10 Troy Aikman 2.00 5.00
TT11 Barry Sanders 2.50 6.00
TT12 Mike Anderson 1.00 2.50
TT13 Jerry Rice 3.00 8.00
TT14 Daunte Culpepper 1.25 3.00
TT15 Chris Chambers 1.00 2.50
TT16 Marshall Faulk 1.25 3.00
TT17 Doug Flutie 1.25 3.00
TT18 Travis Henry 1.00 2.50
TT19 LaDainian Tomlinson 1.50 4.00
TT20 Eddie George 1.25 3.00
TT21 Aaron Brooks 1.00 2.50
TT22 Chris Weinke 1.00 2.50
TT23 Ricky Williams 1.25 3.00
TT24 Jerome Bettis 1.50 4.00
TT25 Ahman Green 1.25 3.00
TT26 Steve Young 2.00 5.00
TT27 Zach Thomas 1.25 3.00
TT28 Randy Moss 1.25 3.00
TT29 Quincy Carter 1.00 2.50
TT30 Jeff Garcia 1.00 2.50
TT31 Tim Brown 1.50 4.00
TT32 Jimmy Smith 1.25 3.00
TT33 Torry Holt 1.25 3.00
TT34 Todd Pinkston 1.00 2.50
TT35 Eric Moulds 1.00 2.50
TT36 Marvin Harrison 1.25 3.00
TT37 Derrick Mason 1.00 2.50
TT38 Troy Brown 1.00 2.50
TT39 Marty Booker 1.00 2.50
TT40 Wayne Chrebet 1.00 2.50
TT41 Darrell Green 1.50 4.00
TT42 Charles Woodson 1.50 4.00
TT43 Bruce Matthews 1.00 2.50
TT44 Tim Couch 1.00 2.50
TT45 Mark Brunell 1.25 3.00
TT46 Hines Ward 1.25 3.00
TT47 Corey Dillon 1.00 2.50
TT48 Edgerrin James 1.25 3.00
TT49 John Elway 2.50 6.00
TT50 Frank Wycheck 1.00 2.50

2002 Absolute Memorabilia Tools of the Trade Materials

This 50-card insert includes swatches of game-used memorabilia. Jersey cards are sequentially numbered to 150, glove cards to 50, and FaceMask cards to 300.

TT1-TT30 JSY PRINT RUN 150
TT31-TT42 PRINT RUN 50 SER.#'d SETS
TT43-TT50 FACE MASK PRINT RUN 300
TT1 Emmitt Smith JSY 10.00 25.00
TT2 Brett Favre JSY 12.00 30.00
TT3 Donovan McNabb JSY 5.00 12.00
TT4 Brian Griese JSY 4.00 10.00
TT5 Peyton Manning JSY 15.00 40.00
TT6 Kurt Warner JSY 5.00 12.00
TT7 Dan Marino JSY 12.00 30.00
TT8 Shaun Alexander JSY 4.00 10.00
TT9 Anthony Thomas JSY 5.00 12.00
TT10 Troy Aikman JSY 8.00 20.00
TT11 Barry Sanders JSY 10.00 25.00
TT12 Mike Anderson JSY 4.00 10.00
TT13 Jerry Rice JSY 12.00 30.00
TT14 Daunte Culpepper JSY 5.00 12.00
TT15 Chris Chambers JSY 4.00 10.00
TT16 Marshall Faulk JSY 5.00 12.00
TT17 Doug Flutie JSY 5.00 12.00
TT18 Travis Henry JSY 4.00 10.00
TT19 LaDainian Tomlinson JSY 6.00 15.00
TT20 Eddie George JSY 5.00 12.00
TT21 Aaron Brooks JSY 4.00 10.00
TT22 Chris Weinke JSY 4.00 10.00
TT23 Ricky Williams JSY 5.00 12.00
TT24 Jerome Bettis JSY 6.00 15.00
TT25 Ahman Green JSY 5.00 12.00
TT26 Steve Young JSY 8.00 20.00
TT27 Zach Thomas JSY 5.00 12.00
TT28 Randy Moss JSY 5.00 12.00
TT29 Quincy Carter JSY 4.00 10.00
TT30 Jeff Garcia JSY 4.00 10.00
TT31 Tim Brown GLV 8.00 20.00
TT32 Jimmy Smith GLV 6.00 15.00
TT33 Torry Holt GLV 6.00 15.00
TT34 Todd Pinkston GLV 5.00 12.00
TT35 Eric Moulds GLV 5.00 12.00
TT36 Marvin Harrison GLV 6.00 15.00
TT37 Derrick Mason GLV 5.00 12.00
TT38 Troy Brown GLV 5.00 12.00
TT39 Marty Booker GLV 5.00 12.00
TT40 Wayne Chrebet GLV 5.00 12.00
TT41 Darrell Green GLV 8.00 20.00
TT42 Charles Woodson GLV 8.00 20.00
TT43 Bruce Matthews FM 3.00 8.00
TT44 Tim Couch FM 3.00 8.00
TT45 Mark Brunell FM 4.00 10.00
TT46 Hines Ward FM 5.00 12.00
TT47 Corey Dillon FM 3.00 8.00
TT48 Edgerrin James FM 4.00 10.00
TT49 John Elway FM 8.00 20.00
TT50 Frank Wycheck FM 3.00 8.00

2003 Absolute Memorabilia Samples

*VETS 1-100: .8X TO 2X BASIC CARDS
*ROOKIE 101-150: .2X TO .5X BASIC CARD

2003 Absolute Memorabilia

Released in August of 2003, this set consists of 180 cards, including 100 veterans, 50 rookies serial numbered to 1100, and 30 rookies serial numbered to 750 that contain an event used jersey and football swatch. Each full box contained two min-boxes of nine packs, each with six cards.

COMP.SET w/o SP's (100) 10.00 25.00
1 Jamal Lewis .40 1.00
2 Ray Lewis .50 1.25
3 Todd Heap .30 .75
4 Drew Bledsoe .40 1.00
5 Travis Henry .30 .75
6 Peerless Price .30 .75
7 Corey Dillon .30 .75
8 Chad Johnson .30 .75
9 Tim Couch .30 .75
10 William Green .30 .75
11 Andre Davis .30 .75
12 Brian Griese .30 .75
13 Ashley Lelie .30 .75
14 Clinton Portis .30 .75
15 Rod Smith .40 1.00
16 David Carr .30 .75
17 Corey Bradford .30 .75
18 Jonathan Wells .30 .75
19 Peyton Manning 1.25 3.00
20 Edgerrin James .40 1.00
21 Marvin Harrison .40 1.00
22 Mark Brunell .40 1.00
23 Fred Taylor .30 .75
24 Jimmy Smith .40 1.00
25 Trent Green .30 .75
26 Priest Holmes .30 .75
27 Tony Gonzalez .40 1.00
28 Jay Fiedler .30 .75
29 Ricky Williams .40 1.00
30 Chris Chambers .30 .75
31 Zach Thomas .40 1.00
32 Tom Brady 2.00 5.00
33 Troy Brown .30 .75
34 Antowain Smith .40 1.00
35 Chad Pennington .30 .75
36 Curtis Martin .40 1.00
37 Laveranues Coles .30 .75
38 Rich Gannon .40 1.00
39 Charlie Garner .40 1.00
40 Jerry Rice 1.00 2.50
41 Tim Brown .50 1.25
42 Tommy Maddox .30 .75
43 Jerome Bettis .50 1.25
44 Plaxico Burress .30 .75
45 Hines Ward .40 1.00

46 Drew Brees .50 1.25
47 LaDainian Tomlinson .50 1.25
48 Junior Seau .40 1.00
49 Steve McNair .40 1.00
50 Eddie George .40 1.00
51 Jevon Kearse .30 .75
52 Jake Plummer .30 .75
53 David Boston .30 .75
54 Marcel Shipp .30 .75
55 Michael Vick .40 1.00
56 T.J. Duckett .30 .75
57 Warrick Dunn .30 .75
58 Muhsin Muhammad .30 .75
59 Julius Peppers .50 1.25
60 Steve Smith .50 1.25
61 Anthony Thomas .40 1.00
62 Brian Urlacher .50 1.25
63 Marty Booker .30 .75
64 Antonio Bryant .30 .75
65 Chad Hutchinson .30 .75
66 Roy Williams .30 .75
67 Emmitt Smith .75 2.00
68 Joey Harrington .30 .75
69 James Stewart .30 .75
70 Az-Zahir Hakim .30 .75
71 Brett Favre 1.00 2.50
72 Ahman Green .40 1.00
73 Donald Driver .40 1.00
74 Daunte Culpepper .40 1.00
75 Randy Moss .40 1.00
76 Michael Bennett .30 .75
77 Aaron Brooks .30 .75
78 Deuce McAllister .40 1.00
79 Donte Stallworth .30 .75
80 Tiki Barber .40 1.00
81 Kerry Collins .30 .75
82 Jeremy Shockey .30 .75
83 Donovan McNabb .40 1.00
84 Duce Staley .30 .75
85 Antonio Freeman .40 1.00
86 Jeff Garcia .30 .75
87 Terrell Owens .40 1.00
88 Garrison Hearst .30 .75
89 Matt Hasselbeck .30 .75
90 Koren Robinson .40 1.00
91 Shaun Alexander .30 .75
92 Kurt Warner .40 1.00
93 Marshall Faulk .40 1.00
94 Isaac Bruce .50 1.25
95 Brad Johnson .40 1.00
96 Keyshawn Johnson .50 1.25
97 Warren Sapp .40 1.00
98 Patrick Ramsey .40 1.00
99 Rod Gardner .30 .75
100 Stephen Davis .30 .75
101 Jason Gesser RC 2.00 5.00
102 Brandon Lloyd RC 2.50 6.00
103 Ken Dorsey RC 2.00 5.00
104 Avon Cobourne RC 1.50 4.00
105 Cecil Sapp RC 1.50 4.00
106 Derek Watson RC 1.50 4.00
107 Dwone Hicks RC 1.50 4.00
108 Earnest Graham RC 2.50 6.00
109 LaBrandon Toefield RC 1.50 4.00
110 Quentin Griffin RC 2.00 5.00
111 Sultan McCullough RC 1.50 4.00
112 Lee Suggs RC 1.50 4.00
113 Talman Gardner RC 1.50 4.00
114 Arnaz Battle RC 2.50 6.00
115 Billy McMullen RC 1.50 4.00
116 Doug Gabriel RC 2.00 5.00
117 Justin Gage RC 2.00 5.00
118 Kareem Kelly RC 1.50 4.00
119 Paul Arnold RC 1.50 4.00
120 Sam Aiken RC 2.00 5.00
121 Shaun McDonald RC 2.00 5.00
122 Terrence Edwards 1.50 4.00
123 Walter Young RC 1.50 4.00
124 Ryan Hoag RC 1.50 4.00
125 Jason Witten RC 6.00 15.00
126 Bennie Joppru RC 1.50 4.00
127 George Wrighster RC 1.50 4.00
128 L.J. Smith RC 2.50 6.00
129 Robert Johnson RC 1.50 4.00
130 Chris Kelsay RC 2.00 5.00
131 Cory Redding RC 2.00 5.00
132 DeWayne White RC 1.50 4.00
133 Kenny Peterson RC 2.00 5.00
134 Jerome McDougle RC 1.50 4.00
135 Michael Haynes RC 1.50 4.00
136 Jimmy Kennedy RC 2.00 5.00
137 Kevin Williams RC 2.50 6.00
138 Johnathan Sullivan RC 1.50 4.00
139 Rien Long RC 1.50 4.00
140 Ty Warren RC 2.00 5.00
141 William Joseph RC 1.50 4.00
142 E.J. Henderson RC 2.00 5.00
143 Boss Bailey RC 2.00 5.00
144 Dennis Weathersby RC 1.50 4.00
145 Chris Simms RC 1.50 4.00
146 Rashean Mathis RC 1.50 4.00
147 Charles Rogers RC 2.00 5.00
148 Andre Woolfolk RC 1.50 4.00
149 Troy Polamalu RC 12.00 30.00
150 Mike Doss RC 2.50 6.00
151 Carson Palmer RPM RC 5.00 12.00
152 Byron Leftwich RPM RC 3.00 8.00
153 Kyle Boller RPM RC 2.50 6.00
154 Rex Grossman RPM RC 3.00 8.00
155 Dave Ragone RPM RC 2.50 6.00
156 Kliff Kingsbury RPM RC 4.00 10.00
157 Seneca Wallace RPM RC 3.00 8.00
158 Larry Johnson RPM RC 3.00 8.00
159 Willis McGahee RPM RC 3.00 8.00
160 Justin Fargas RPM RC 4.00 10.00
161 Onterrio Smith RPM RC 2.50 6.00
162 Chris Brown RPM RC 2.50 6.00
163 Musa Smith RPM RC 2.50 6.00
164 Artose Pinner RPM RC 2.50 6.00
165 Andre Johnson RPM RC 6.00 15.00
166 Kelley Washington RPM RC 2.50 6.00
167 Taylor Jacobs RPM RC 2.50 6.00
168 Bryant Johnson RPM RC 4.00 10.00
169 Tyrone Calico RPM RC 2.50 6.00
170 Anquan Boldin RPM RC 4.00 10.00
171 Bethel Johnson RPM RC 2.50 6.00
172 Nate Burleson RPM RC 3.00 8.00
173 Kevin Curtis RPM RC 2.50 6.00
174 Dallas Clark RPM RC 4.00 10.00
175 Teyo Johnson RPM RC 3.00 8.00
176 Terrell Suggs RPM RC 3.00 8.00
177 DeWayne Robertson RPM RC 3.00 8.00
178 Brian St.Pierre RPM RC 2.50 6.00
179 Terence Newman RPM RC 4.00 10.00
180 Marcus Trufant RPM RC 3.00 8.00

2003 Absolute Memorabilia Spectrum

*VETS 1-100: 2.5X TO 6X BASIC CARDS
1-100 PRINT RUN 150 SER.#'d SETS
*ROOKIES 101-150: 1X TO 2.5X
101-150 PRINT RUN 100 SER.#'d SETS
*RPM 151-180: 1X TO 2.5X
151-180 RPM PRINT RUN 25 SER.#'d SETS
149 Troy Polamalu 50.00 100.00

2003 Absolute Memorabilia Absolute Patches

Randomly inserted into packs, this set features oversize game worn jersey patch swatches, with each card serial numbered to 25.
STATED PRINT RUN 25 SER. #'d SETS
AP1 Brett Favre 30.00 80.00
AP2 Brian Urlacher 15.00 40.00
AP3 Clinton Portis 10.00 25.00
AP4 David Carr 10.00 25.00
AP5 Deuce McAllister 12.00 30.00
AP6 Donovan McNabb 12.00 30.00
AP7 Drew Bledsoe 12.00 30.00
AP8 Edgerrin James 12.00 30.00
AP9 Emmitt Smith 25.00 60.00
AP10 Priest Holmes 10.00 25.00
AP11 Jeremy Shockey 10.00 25.00
AP12 Jerry Rice 30.00 80.00
AP13 Joey Harrington 10.00 25.00
AP14 Kurt Warner 12.00 30.00
AP15 LaDainian Tomlinson 15.00 40.00
AP16 Marshall Faulk 12.00 30.00
AP17 Michael Vick 12.00 30.00
AP18 Peyton Manning 40.00 100.00
AP19 Randy Moss 12.00 30.00
AP20 Steve McNair 12.00 30.00

2003 Absolute Memorabilia Absolutely Ink

Randomly inserted into packs, this set features authentic player autographs on a silver foil sticker. Each card is serial numbered to 25. Please note that cards 2, 5, and 20 were issued in packs as exchange cards.
STATED PRINT RUN 25 SERIAL #'d SETS
AI1 Marty Booker 15.00 40.00
AI2 Ahman Green 20.00 50.00
AI4 Deion Branch 15.00 40.00
AI6 Ed McCaffrey 20.00 50.00
AI7 Eric Moulds 15.00 40.00
AI8 Garrison Hearst 15.00 40.00
AI9 Jeff Garcia 15.00 40.00
AI10 Joe Horn 15.00 40.00
AI11 Jimmy Smith 20.00 50.00
AI12 Kurt Warner 20.00 50.00
AI13 Michael Vick 50.00 100.00
AI14 Patrick Ramsey 20.00 50.00
AI15 Randy Moss 60.00 120.00
AI16 Ricky Williams 20.00 50.00
AI17 Rod Smith 20.00 50.00
AI18 Tim Brown 25.00 60.00
AI19 Tom Brady 175.00 300.00
AI20 Zach Thomas 20.00 50.00

2003 Absolute Memorabilia Boss Hoggs Shoe

Randomly inserted into packs, this set features swatches of game worn shoes. Each card is serial numbered to 125.
STATED PRINT RUN 125 SERIAL #'d SETS
BH1 Amani Toomer 4.00 10.00
BH2 Chad Pennington 4.00 10.00
BH3 Curtis Martin 5.00 12.00
BH4 Daunte Culpepper 5.00 12.00
BH5 Eddie George 5.00 12.00
BH6 Edgerrin James 5.00 12.00
BH7 Emmitt Smith 10.00 25.00
BH8 Fred Taylor 4.00 10.00
BH9 Jerry Rice 12.00 30.00
BH10 Keyshawn Johnson 6.00 15.00
BH11 Marvin Harrison 5.00 12.00
BH12 Peyton Manning 15.00 40.00
BH13 Rich Gannon 5.00 12.00
BH14 Steve McNair 5.00 12.00
BH15 Terrell Owens 5.00 12.00

2003 Absolute Memorabilia Boss Hoggs Shoe Autographs

BH2 Chad Pennington 20.00 50.00
BH5 Eddie George 25.00 60.00
BH9 Jerry Rice 60.00 120.00
BH11 Marvin Harrison 25.00 60.00
BH13 Rich Gannon 25.00 60.00
BH14 Steve McNair 25.00 60.00
BH15 Terrell Owens 25.00 60.00

2003 Absolute Memorabilia Canton Absolutes Jersey

Randomly inserted into packs, this set features swatches of game worn jersey. Each card is serial numbered to 150.
STATED PRINT RUN 150 SER. #'d SETS
1 Ahman Green 3.00 8.00
2 Anthony Thomas 3.00 8.00
3 Brett Favre 8.00 20.00
4 Chris Chambers 2.50 6.00
5 Clinton Portis 2.50 6.00
6 Curtis Martin 3.00 8.00
7 Daunte Culpepper 3.00 8.00
8 David Carr 2.50 6.00
9 Donovan McNabb 3.00 8.00
10 Donte Stallworth 2.50 6.00
11 Drew Brees 4.00 10.00
12 Eddie George 3.00 8.00
13 Edgerrin James 3.00 8.00
14 Emmitt Smith 6.00 15.00
15 Garrison Hearst 2.50 6.00
16 Isaac Bruce 4.00 10.00
17 Jamal Lewis 3.00 8.00
18 Jeff Garcia 2.50 6.00
19 Jeremy Shockey 2.50 6.00
20 Jerry Rice 8.00 20.00
21 Jevon Kearse 2.50 6.00
22 Jimmy Smith 3.00 8.00
23 Joey Harrington 2.50 6.00
24 Julius Peppers 4.00 10.00
25 Junior Seau 3.00 8.00
26 Keyshawn Johnson 4.00 10.00
27 Kurt Warner 3.00 8.00
28 LaDainian Tomlinson 4.00 10.00
29 Marshall Faulk 3.00 8.00
30 Marvin Harrison 3.00 8.00
31 Michael Bennett 2.50 6.00
32 Michael Vick 3.00 8.00
33 Mike Alstott 2.50 6.00
34 Peyton Manning 10.00 25.00
35 Priest Holmes 2.50 6.00
36 Randy Moss 3.00 8.00
37 Ray Lewis 4.00 10.00
38 Rich Gannon 3.00 8.00
39 Ricky Williams 3.00 8.00
40 Rod Smith 3.00 8.00
41 Roy Williams 2.50 6.00
42 Shaun Alexander 2.50 6.00
43 Stephen Davis 2.50 6.00
44 Steve McNair 3.00 8.00
45 Terrell Owens 3.00 8.00
46 Tim Brown 4.00 10.00
47 T.J. Duckett 2.50 6.00
48 Tom Brady 15.00 40.00
49 Travis Henry 2.50 6.00
50 Zach Thomas 3.00 8.00

2003 Absolute Memorabilia Canton Absolutes Jersey Autographs

16 Isaac Bruce/25* 25.00 60.00
17 Jamal Lewis/25* 20.00 50.00
18 Jeff Garcia/25*
27 Kurt Warner/50* 40.00 80.00
32 Michael Vick/25* 30.00 80.00

2003 Absolute Memorabilia Glass Plaques

Included one per sealed box, this set features etched glass plaques. Each plaque is serial numbered and may feature a memorabilia swatch, an autograph, or a combination of the two.
ONE PER SEALED BOX
SERIAL #'d UNDER 15 NOT PRICED
1 Shaun Alexander AU/50 20.00 50.00
2 Shaun Alexander JSY/250 10.00 25.00
3 Shaun Alexander JSY-JSY/100 12.00 30.00
4 Mike Alstott AU/25 25.00 60.00
6 Mike Alstott JSY/200 10.00 25.00
7 Michael Bennett AU/50 20.00 50.00
8 Michael Bennett JSY/250 10.00 25.00
10 Jerome Bettis JSY/150 15.00 40.00
11 Jerome Bettis JSY-JSY/50 20.00 50.00
13 Drew Bledsoe JSY/50 15.00 40.00
14 Drew Bledsoe JSY-JSY/25 20.00 50.00
15 David Boston JSY/150 10.00 25.00
16 David Boston JSY-Pants/50 12.00 30.00
18 Terry Bradshaw JSY/250 20.00 60.00
19 Terry Bradshaw JSY-JSY/75 25.00 60.00
21 Tom Brady JSY/150 60.00 150.00
22 Tom Brady JSY-JSY/75 80.00 200.00
23 Drew Brees JSY/150 15.00 40.00
24 Aaron Brooks JSY/150 10.00 25.00
25 Tim Brown AU/25 40.00 100.00
27 Tim Brown JSY/150 15.00 40.00
28 Tim Brown JSY-JSY/75 20.00 50.00
29 Tim Brown Shoes/125 15.00 40.00
30 Isaac Bruce AU/50 30.00 80.00
31 Isaac Bruce JSY/150 15.00 40.00
32 Isaac Bruce JSY-Pants/75 20.00 50.00
33 Mark Brunell JSY/150 12.00 30.00
34 Mark Brunell JSY-Pants/100 15.00 40.00
35 Mark Brunell Shoes/150 12.00 30.00
36 Plaxico Burress JSY/150 10.00 25.00
38 David Carr JSY/150 10.00 25.00
39 Chris Chambers AU/50 20.00 50.00
41 Chris Chambers JSY/200 10.00 25.00
42 Chris Chambers JSY-JSY/50 12.00 30.00
43 Laveranues Coles AU/50 20.00 50.00
44 Laveranues Coles JSY/150 10.00 25.00
45 Laveranues Coles JSY-JSY/50 12.00 30.00
46 Tim Couch JSY/200 10.00 25.00
47 Tim Couch JSY-Pants/75 12.00 30.00
48 Daunte Culpepper JSY/200 12.00 30.00
49 Daunte Culpepper JSY-Shoes/50 15.00 40.00
51 Eric Dickerson JSY/250 12.00 30.00
52 Eric Dickerson JSY-JSY/100 15.00 40.00
53 Corey Dillon JSY/150 10.00 25.00
54 Corey Dillon JSY-GLV/100 12.00 30.00
56 John Elway JSY/250 25.00 60.00
57 John Elway JSY-JSY/75 30.00 80.00
58 John Elway Pants/200 25.00 60.00
59 Marshall Faulk JSY/250 12.00 30.00
60 Marshall Faulk JSY-Pants/150 12.00 30.00
61 Marshall Faulk Shoes/15
63 Brett Favre JSY/200 30.00 80.00
64 Brett Favre JSY-Shoes/75 40.00 100.00
65 Rich Gannon AU/50 25.00 60.00
66 Rich Gannon JSY/150 12.00 30.00
67 Rich Gannon JSY-Shoes/125 12.00 30.00
68 Jeff Garcia AU/50 20.00 50.00
70 Jeff Garcia JSY/200 10.00 25.00
71 Jeff Garcia JSY-JSY/50 12.00 30.00
72 Jeff Garcia Shoes/125 10.00 25.00
73 Rod Gardner AU/25 25.00 60.00
74 Rod Gardner JSY/200 10.00 25.00
76 Eddie George JSY/150 12.00 30.00
77 Eddie George JSY-GLV/75 15.00 40.00
78 Eddie George Shoes/25 20.00 50.00
79 Ahman Green AU/25 30.00 80.00
81 Ahman Green JSY/150 12.00 30.00
82 Ahman Green JSY-JSY/50 15.00 40.00
83 Brian Griese JSY/150 10.00 25.00
84 Brian Griese JSY-JSY/75 12.00 30.00
85 Joey Harrington AU/25 25.00 60.00
86 Joey Harrington JSY/250 10.00 25.00
87 Marvin Harrison AU/25 30.00 80.00
88 Marvin Harrison JSY/150 12.00 30.00
89 Marvin Harrison JSY-Shoes/50 15.00 40.00
90 Garrison Hearst AU/50 20.00 50.00
91 Garrison Hearst JSY/150 10.00 25.00
92 Travis Henry JSY/200 10.00 25.00
94 Priest Holmes JSY/250 10.00 25.00
95 Priest Holmes JSY-JSY/50 12.00 30.00
96 Torry Holt AU/50 25.00 60.00
97 Torry Holt JSY/150 12.00 30.00
98 Torry Holt JSY-Pants/50 15.00 40.00
99 Edgerrin James JSY/200 12.00 30.00
100 Edgerrin James JSY-JSY/50 15.00 40.00
101 Edgerrin James Shoes/25 20.00 50.00
102 Andre Johnson AU/200 25.00 60.00
103 Keyshawn Johnson GLV/75 20.00 50.00
104 Keyshawn Johnson JSY/150 15.00 40.00
105 Key.Johnson JSY-JSY/100 20.00 50.00
106 Larry Johnson AU/200 12.00 30.00
107 Jevon Kearse JSY/200 10.00 25.00
108 Jevon Kearse JSY-JSY/100 12.00 30.00
109 Jevon Kearse Shoes/100 12.00 30.00
110 Byron Leftwich AU/200 12.00 30.00
111 Jamal Lewis AU/25 30.00 80.00
113 Jamal Lewis JSY/250 12.00 30.00
114 Peyton Manning JSY/250 40.00 100.00
115 P.Manning JSY-Shoes/50 50.00 120.00
116 Curtis Martin JSY/150 12.00 30.00
117 Curtis Martin JSY-Pants/100 15.00 40.00
118 Derrick Mason AU/25 25.00 60.00
120 Derrick Mason JSY/100 12.00 30.00
121 Derrick Mason JSY-Shoes/75 12.00 30.00
123 Deuce McAllister JSY/50 15.00 40.00
124 Ed McCaffrey AU/25 30.00 80.00
126 Ed McCaffrey JSY/150 12.00 30.00
127 Donovan McNabb JSY/250 12.00 30.00
128 D.McNabb JSY-JSY/100 15.00 40.00
130 Steve McNair JSY/200 12.00 30.00
131 Steve McNair JSY-Shoes/125 12.00 30.00
132 Randy Moss AU/50 25.00 60.00
134 Randy Moss JSY/250 12.00 30.00
135 Randy Moss JSY-JSY/75 15.00 40.00
136 Eric Moulds AU/25 25.00 60.00
138 Eric Moulds JSY/150 10.00 25.00
139 Terrell Owens AU/50 25.00 60.00
140 Terrell Owens JSY/250 12.00 30.00
141 Terrell Owens JSY-JSY/50 15.00 40.00
142 Terrell Owens Shoes/15 20.00 50.00
143 Carson Palmer AU/150 20.00 50.00
144 Chad Pennington AU/25 25.00 60.00
145 Chad Pennington Shoes/50 12.00 30.00
147 Clinton Portis JSY/250 10.00 25.00
148 Clinton Portis JSY-JSY/75 12.00 30.00
150 Jerry Rice JSY/150 30.00 80.00
151 Jerry Rice JSY-JSY/50 40.00 100.00
152 Warren Sapp JSY/150 12.00 30.00
153 Warren Sapp JSY-Shoes/150 12.00 30.00
154 Junior Seau JSY/150 12.00 30.00
155 Junior Seau JSY-JSY/50 15.00 40.00
156 Jeremy Shockey JSY/100 12.00 30.00
157 Jeremy Shockey JSY-JSY/50 12.00 30.00
158 Emmitt Smith JSY/250 25.00 60.00
159 E.Smith JSY-Shoe/50 30.00 80.00
160 Emmitt Smith Shoes/125 25.00 60.00
161 Jimmy Smith AU/50 25.00 60.00
163 Jimmy Smith JSY/150 12.00 30.00
164 Jimmy Smith JSY-Shoes/75 15.00 40.00
165 Rod Smith AU/50 25.00 60.00
166 Rod Smith JSY/200 12.00 30.00
167 Rod Smith JSY-Pants/75 15.00 40.00
168 Fred Taylor JSY/200 10.00 25.00
169 Fred Taylor JSY-Shoes/50 12.00 30.00
170 Anthony Thomas AU/25 30.00 80.00
171 Anthony Thomas JSY/200 12.00 30.00
172 Zach Thomas JSY/100 15.00 40.00
173 Zach Thomas Shoes/200 12.00 30.00
174 LaDainian Tomlinson AU/25 75.00 150.00
176 LaDainian Tomlinson JSY/250 15.00 40.00
177 LaDainian Tomlinson JSY-JSY/50 20.00 50.00
178 Brian Urlacher AU/25 75.00 150.00
180 Brian Urlacher JSY/200 15.00 40.00
181 Brian Urlacher JSY-GLV/100 20.00 50.00
182 Michael Vick AU/15 40.00 100.00
184 Michael Vick JSY/200 12.00 30.00
185 Hines Ward AU/50 25.00 60.00
186 Hines Ward JSY/150 12.00 30.00
187 Kurt Warner AU/200 50.00 100.00
188 Kurt Warner JSY AU/200 50.00 100.00
189 Kurt Warner JSY/250 12.00 30.00
190 Kurt Warner JSY-Shoe/125 12.00 30.00
191 Kurt Warner Pants/150 12.00 30.00
192 Ricky Williams JSY/150 12.00 30.00
193 Roy Williams JSY/250 10.00 25.00
194 Charles Woodson JSY/200 25.00 50.00
195 C.Woodson JSY-GLV/100 30.00 60.00

2003 Absolute Memorabilia Gridiron Force

RANDOM INSERTS IN RETAIL PACKS
GF1 A.J. Feeley 2.50 6.00
GF2 Amani Toomer 2.50 6.00
GF3 Brian Griese 2.50 6.00
GF4 Charles Woodson 4.00 10.00
GF5 Corey Dillon 2.50 6.00
GF6 Cory Schlesinger 2.50 6.00
GF7 Darren Woodson 3.00 8.00
GF8 David Boston 2.50 6.00
GF9 Derrick Mason 2.50 6.00
GF10 Duce Staley 2.50 6.00
GF11 Eric Moulds 2.50 6.00
GF12 Fred Taylor 2.50 6.00
GF13 Jake Plummer 2.50 6.00
GF14 Jerome Bettis 4.00 10.00
GF15 Donald Driver 3.00 8.00
GF16 Josh Reed 2.50 6.00
GF17 Kerry Collins 2.50 6.00
GF18 Kevin Johnson 2.50 6.00
GF19 Kordell Stewart 2.50 6.00
GF20 Koren Robinson 3.00 8.00
GF21 Muhsin Muhammed 2.50 6.00
GF22 Peerless Price 2.50 6.00
GF23 Peter Warrick 2.50 6.00
GF24 Randy McMichael 2.50 6.00
GF25 Rod Gardner 2.50 6.00
GF26 Ron Dayne 3.00 8.00
GF27 Santana Moss 3.00 8.00
GF28 Terry Glenn 3.00 8.00

2003 Absolute Memorabilia Leather and Laces

Randomly inserted into packs, this set features swatches of game used football. Cards 1-20 are serial numbered to 500, and cards 21-40 are serial numbered to 250. A Combos holofoil parallel also exists with the first 20 cards numbered to 50, and the remaining cards numbered to 25.
LL1-LL20 PRINT RUN 500 SER.#'d SETS
LL21-LL40 PRINT RUN 250 SER.#'d SETS
*LL1-LL20 COMBOS/50: 1X TO 2.5X
LL1-LL20 COMBOS PRINT RUN 50 SETS
*LL21-LL40 COMBOS/25: 1X TO 2.5X
LL21-LL40 COMBOS PRINT RUN 25 SETS
LL1 Drew Brees 3.00 8.00
LL2 Jeremy Shockey 2.00 5.00
LL3 Antonio Bryant 2.00 5.00
LL4 Marc Bulger 2.00 5.00
LL5 Shaun Alexander 2.00 5.00
LL6 Koren Robinson 2.50 6.00
LL7 Jerry Porter 2.50 6.00
LL8 Joey Harrington 2.00 5.00
LL9 Kevan Barlow 2.00 5.00
LL10 Kurt Warner 2.50 6.00
LL11 Deuce McAllister 2.50 6.00
LL12 Eddie George 2.50 6.00
LL13 Donovan McNabb 2.50 6.00
LL14 Hines Ward 2.50 6.00
LL15 Michael Bennett 2.00 5.00
LL16 Steve McNair 2.50 6.00
LL17 Randy Moss 2.50 6.00
LL18 Mike Alstott 2.00 5.00
LL19 Curtis Martin 2.50 6.00
LL20 Ray Lewis 3.00 8.00
LL21 LaDainian Tomlinson 4.00 10.00
LL22 Marcel Shipp 2.50 6.00
LL23 Emmitt Smith 6.00 15.00
LL24 Marshall Faulk 3.00 8.00
LL25 Rich Gannon 3.00 8.00
LL26 Jerry Rice 8.00 20.00
LL27 Jeff Garcia 2.50 6.00
LL28 Priest Holmes 2.50 6.00
LL29 Michael Vick 3.00 8.00
LL30 Ahman Green 3.00 8.00
LL31 Brett Favre 8.00 20.00
LL32 Peyton Manning 10.00 25.00
LL33 Marvin Harrison 3.00 8.00
LL34 Travis Henry 2.50 6.00
LL35 Peerless Price 2.50 6.00
LL36 Rod Gardner 2.50 6.00
LL37 Terrell Owens 3.00 8.00
LL38 Charlie Garner 3.00 8.00
LL39 Daunte Culpepper 3.00 8.00
LL40 Anthony Thomas 3.00 8.00

2003 Absolute Memorabilia Pro Bowl Souvenirs

Randomly inserted into packs, this set features game worn jersey swatches. Each card is serial numbered to various quantities. A gold parallel also exists, with each card serial numbered to 25.
*GOLD/25: 1X TO 2.5X PRO BOWL/400-600
*GOLD/25: .8X TO 2X PRO BOWL/250-300
GOLD PRINT RUN 25 SER.#'d SETS
PB1 Eddie George/400 3.00 8.00
PB2 Edgerrin James/300 4.00 10.00
PB3 Tim Brown/600 4.00 10.00
PB4 Tom Brady/600 15.00 40.00
PB5 Jeff Garcia/600 2.50 6.00
PB6 Daunte Culpepper/300 4.00 10.00
PB7 Drew Bledsoe/600 3.00 8.00
PB8 Peyton Manning/250 12.00 30.00
PB9 Mark Brunell/400 3.00 8.00
PB10 Kevin Hardy/600 2.50 6.00
PB11 Jimmy Smith/250 4.00 10.00
PB12 Harvey Martin/500 3.00 8.00
PB13 John Elway/250 8.00 20.00
PB14 Terry Bradshaw/250 6.00 15.00
PB15 Richard Dent/600 3.00 8.00

2003 Absolute Memorabilia Pro Bowl Souvenirs Gold Autographs

AUTO STATED PRINT RUN 15-25
PB13 John Elway/15 75.00 150.00
PB14 Terry Bradshaw/15 75.00 150.00
PB15 Richard Dent/25 25.00 50.00

2003 Absolute Memorabilia Quad Series

Inserted into packs at a rate of 1:9, this set features four players with a holofoil background.
STATED ODDS 1:9
QS1 Bleds/Henry/Reed/Moulds 2.00 5.00
QS2 Couch/Green/Davis/Morgan 1.50 4.00
QS3 Plumm/Portis/R.Smith/Lelie 2.00 5.00
QS4 Carr/Wells/Gaff/Bradford 1.50 4.00
QS5 Mann/James/Mung/Harr 6.00 15.00
QS6 Brun/Garr/Taylor/J.Smith 2.00 5.00
QS7 Fied/Will/Cham/Z.Thomas 2.00 5.00
QS8 Brdy/A.Smith/T.Brwn/Brnch 10.00 25.00
QS9 Penn/Mart/Jordan/Moss 2.00 5.00
QS10 Gannon/Garn/Rice/Brown 5.00 12.00
QS11 Madd/Randl El/Burr/Ward 2.00 5.00
QS12 Brees/Toml/Jamm/Boston 2.50 6.00
QS13 McN/George/Mas/Kearse 2.00 5.00
QS14 Vick/Dunn/Duckett/Price 2.00 5.00
QS15 Stew/A.Thomas/Terr/Urlach 2.50 6.00
QS16 Hutch/Glenn/Bryant/Ro.Will 2.00 5.00
QS17 Harr/Stew/Hakim/Schroed 1.50 4.00
QS18 Favre/Green/Driver/Walker 5.00 12.00
QS19 Culp/Benn/Moss/Chamb 2.00 5.00
QS20 Brook/McAll/Stall/Horn 2.00 5.00
QS21 Coll/BarB/Toom/Strahan 2.00 5.00
QS22 McNabb/Feel/Stal/Thrash 2.00 5.00
QS23 Garcia/Hearst/Barl/Owens 2.00 5.00
QS24 Hass/Alex/Robins/Jackson 2.00 5.00
QS25 Warner/Faulk/Bruce/Holt 2.50 6.00
QS26 B.John/Alst/K.John/Sapp 2.50 6.00
QS27 Rams/Coles/Gard/Bailey 2.00 5.00
QS28 Palm/Left/Gross/Simms 2.00 5.00
QS29 L.Joh/L.Sug/C.Bro/M.Smi 1.25 3.00
QS30 A.John/Jaco/Rog/Wash 2.50 6.00

2004 Absolute Memorabilia

Absolute Memorabilia initially released in mid-August 2004. The base set consists of 150-veterans serial numbered of 1150, 50-rookies numbered of 750 and 33-rookie jersey cards numbered of 750. Hobby boxes contained 6-packs of 4-cards and carried an S.R.P. of $40 per pack. Two parallel sets and a variety of inserts can be found seeded in hobby and retail packs highlighted by the Signature Materials and Signature Spectrum autographs and Tools of the Trade Material inserts.
COMP.SET w/o SP's (150) 40.00 80.00
151-233 PRINT RUN 750 SER.#'d SETS
UNPRICED SPECTRUM PLATINUM #'d TO 1
1 Anquan Boldin .75 2.00
2 Emmitt Smith 2.00 5.00
3 Josh McCown 1.00 2.50
4 Marcel Shipp .75 2.00
5 Michael Vick 1.00 2.50
6 Peerless Price .75 2.00
7 T.J. Duckett .75 2.00
8 Warrick Dunn .75 2.00
9 Jamal Lewis 1.00 2.50
10 Kyle Boller .75 2.00
11 Ray Lewis 1.25 3.00
12 Terrell Suggs .75 2.00
13 Drew Bledsoe 1.00 2.50
14 Eric Moulds .75 2.00
15 Josh Reed .75 2.00
16 Travis Henry .75 2.00
17 DeShaun Foster 1.00 2.50
18 Jake Delhomme .75 2.00
19 Julius Peppers 1.00 2.50
20 Muhsin Muhammad .75 2.00
21 Stephen Davis .75 2.00
22 Steve Smith 1.25 3.00
23 Anthony Thomas 1.00 2.50
24 Brian Urlacher 1.25 3.00
25 Marty Booker .75 2.00
26 Rex Grossman .75 2.00
27 Carson Palmer 1.00 2.50
28 Chad Johnson .75 2.00
29 Corey Dillon .75 2.00
30 Peter Warrick .75 2.00
31 Rudi Johnson .75 2.00
32 Andre Davis .75 2.00
33 Dennis Northcutt .75 2.00
34 Lee Suggs 1.00 2.50
35 Tim Couch 1.00 2.50
36 Jeff Garcia .75 2.00
37 William Green .75 2.00
38 Antonio Bryant 1.00 2.50
39 Quincy Carter .75 2.00
40 Roy Williams S .75 2.00
41 Terence Newman 1.00 2.50
42 Keyshawn Johnson 1.00 2.50
43 Garrison Hearst .75 2.00
44 Champ Bailey 1.00 2.50
45 Ashley Lelie .75 2.00
46 Jake Plummer .75 2.00
47 Rod Smith 1.00 2.50
48 Shannon Sharpe 1.00 2.50
49 Charles Rogers .75 2.00
50 Joey Harrington .75 2.00
51 Ahman Green 1.00 2.50
52 Brett Favre 2.50 6.00
53 Donald Driver 1.00 2.50
54 Javon Walker .75 2.00
55 Robert Ferguson .75 2.00
56 Andre Johnson 1.00 2.50
57 David Carr .75 2.00
58 Domanick Davis .75 2.00
59 Edgerrin James 1.00 2.50
60 Marvin Harrison 1.00 2.50
61 Peyton Manning 3.00 8.00
62 Reggie Wayne 1.00 2.50
63 Byron Leftwich .75 2.00
64 Fred Taylor .75 2.00
65 Jimmy Smith 1.00 2.50
66 Dante Hall .75 2.00
67 Priest Holmes .75 2.00
68 Tony Gonzalez 1.00 2.50
69 Trent Green .75 2.00
70 Chris Chambers .75 2.00
71 Jay Fiedler .75 2.00
72 David Boston .75 2.00
73 Ricky Williams 1.00 2.50
74 Zach Thomas 1.00 2.50
75 Daunte Culpepper 1.00 2.50
76 Michael Bennett .75 2.00
77 Moe Williams .75 2.00
78 Randy Moss 1.00 2.50
79 David Givens .75 2.00
80 Deion Branch .75 2.00
81 Kevin Faulk .75 2.00
82 Richard Seymour .75 2.00
83 Tom Brady 5.00 12.00
84 Troy Brown .75 2.00
85 Ty Law 1.25 3.00
86 Aaron Brooks .75 2.00
87 Deuce McAllister 1.00 2.50
88 Donte Stallworth .75 2.00
89 Joe Horn .75 2.00
90 Amani Toomer .75 2.00
91 Jeremy Shockey .75 2.00
92 Kerry Collins .75 2.00
93 Michael Strahan 1.00 2.50
94 Tiki Barber 1.00 2.50
95 Chad Pennington .75 2.00
96 Curtis Martin 1.00 2.50
97 Santana Moss 1.00 2.50
98 Wayne Chrebet .75 2.00
99 Justin McCareins .75 2.00
100 Charles Woodson 1.25 3.00
101 Jerry Porter .75 2.00
102 Jerry Rice 2.50 6.00
103 Rich Gannon 1.00 2.50
104 Tim Brown 1.25 3.00
105 Warren Sapp 1.00 2.50
106 A.J. Feeley .75 2.00
107 Brian Westbrook .75 2.00
108 Correll Buckhalter .75 2.00
109 Donovan McNabb 1.00 2.50
110 Freddie Mitchell .75 2.00
111 Terrell Owens 1.00 2.50
112 Jevon Kearse .75 2.00
113 Todd Pinkston .75 2.00
114 Antwaan Randle El .75 2.00
115 Hines Ward 1.00 2.50
116 Jerome Bettis 1.25 3.00
117 Kendrell Bell .75 2.00
118 Plaxico Burress .75 2.00
119 Tommy Maddox .75 2.00
120 Duce Staley .75 2.00
121 Drew Brees 1.25 3.00
122 LaDainian Tomlinson 1.25 3.00
123 Kevan Barlow .75 2.00
124 Tai Streets .75 2.00
125 Tim Rattay .75 2.00
126 Darrell Jackson 1.00 2.50
127 Koren Robinson .75 2.00
128 Matt Hasselbeck .75 2.00
129 Shaun Alexander .75 2.00
130 Isaac Bruce 1.25 3.00
131 Kurt Warner 1.00 2.50
132 Marc Bulger .75 2.00
133 Marshall Faulk 1.00 2.50
134 Torry Holt 1.00 2.50
135 Derrick Brooks .75 2.00
136 Keenan McCardell .75 2.00
137 Mike Alstott .75 2.00
138 Thomas Jones .75 2.00
139 Charlie Garner 1.00 2.50
140 Derrick Mason .75 2.00
141 Drew Bennett 1.00 2.50
142 Eddie George 1.00 2.50
143 Keith Bulluck .75 2.00
144 Steve McNair 1.00 2.50
145 LaVar Arrington .75 2.00
146 Laveranues Coles .75 2.00
147 Patrick Ramsey 1.00 2.50
148 Rod Gardner .75 2.00
149 Clinton Portis .75 2.00
150 Mark Brunell 1.00 2.50
151 Craig Krenzel AU RC 4.00 10.00
152 Andy Hall AU RC 4.00 10.00
153 Josh Harris RC 1.50 4.00
154 Jim Sorgi AU RC 5.00 12.00
155 Jeff Smoker AU RC 5.00 12.00
156 John Navarre AU RC 4.00 10.00
157 Jared Lorenzen AU RC 5.00 12.00
158 Cody Pickett AU RC 4.00 10.00
159 Casey Bramlet RC 1.50 4.00
160 Matt Mauck AU RC 4.00 10.00
161 B.J. Symons AU RC 4.00 10.00
162 Bradlee Van Pelt RC 2.00 5.00
163 Ryan Dinwiddie RC 1.50 4.00
164 Michael Turner RC 1.50 4.00
165 Drew Henson RC 1.50 4.00
166 Troy Fleming RC 1.50 4.00
167 Adimchinobe Echemandu RC 2.00 5.00
168 Quincy Wilson RC 1.50 4.00
169 Derrick Ward RC 2.50 6.00
170 Bruce Perry RC 1.50 4.00
171 Brandon Miree RC 1.50 4.00
172 Jarrett Payton AU RC 5.00 12.00
173 Ran Carthon RC 1.50 4.00
174 Carlos Francis AU RC 4.00 10.00
175 Samie Parker RC 1.50 4.00
176 Jerricho Cotchery RC 2.00 5.00
177 Ernest Wilford RC 2.00 5.00
178 Johnnie Morant RC 1.50 4.00
179 Maurice Mann AU RC 4.00 10.00
180 D.J. Hackett RC 1.50 4.00
181 Drew Carter RC 2.00 5.00
182 P.K. Sam RC 1.50 4.00
183 Jamaar Taylor RC 1.50 4.00
184 Ryan Krause RC 1.50 4.00
185 Triandos Luke RC 1.50 4.00
186 Jeris McIntyre RC 1.50 4.00
187 Clarence Moore AU RC 4.00 10.00
188 Mark Jones RC 1.50 4.00
189 Sloan Thomas AU RC 5.00 12.00
190 Sean Taylor RC 10.00 25.00
191 Derek Abney RC 1.50 4.00
192 Jonathan Vilma RC 2.00 5.00
193 Tommie Harris RC 2.00 5.00
194 D.J. Williams RC 2.50 6.00
195 Will Smith RC 2.00 5.00
196 Kenechi Udeze RC 2.00 5.00
197 Vince Wilfork RC 2.50 6.00
198 Ahmad Carroll RC 1.50 4.00
199 Jason Babin RC 2.50 6.00
200 Chris Gamble RC 1.50 4.00
201 Larry Fitzgerald RPM RC 8.00 20.00
202 DeAngelo Hall RPM RC 3.00 8.00
203 Matt Schaub RPM RC 2.00 5.00
204 Michael Jenkins RPM AU RC 6.00 15.00
205 Devard Darling RPM AU RC 6.00 15.00
206 J.P. Losman RPM RC 2.00 5.00
207 Lee Evans RPM RC 3.00 8.00
208 Keary Colbert RPM AU RC 6.00 15.00
209 Bernard Berrian RPM AU RC 6.00 15.00
210 Chris Perry RPM RC 2.00 5.00
211 Kellen Winslow RPM RC 2.00 5.00
212 Luke McCown RPM RC 2.00 5.00
213 Julius Jones RPM RC 2.00 5.00
214 Darius Watts RPM RC 2.00 5.00
215 Tatum Bell RPM AU RC 6.00 15.00
216 Kevin Jones RPM RC 2.50 6.00
217 Roy Williams RPM RC 2.00 5.00
218 Dunta Robinson RPM RC 2.00 5.00
219 Greg Jones RPM AU RC 6.00 15.00
220 Reggie Williams RPM RC 2.00 5.00
221 Mewelde Moore RPM RC 2.50 6.00
222 Ben Watson RPM RC 2.50 6.00
223 Cedric Cobbs RPM RC 2.00 5.00
224 Dev Henderson RPM AU RC 6.00 15.00
225 Eli Manning RPM RC 15.00 40.00
226 Robert Gallery RPM RC 2.50 6.00
227 Roethlisberger RPM RC 12.00 30.00
228 Philip Rivers RPM RC 10.00 25.00
229 Derrick Hamilton RPM RC 2.00 5.00
230 Rashaun Woods RPM RC 2.00 5.00
231 Steven Jackson RPM RC 3.00 8.00
232 Michael Clayton RPM RC 2.50 6.00
233 Ben Troupe RPM RC 2.00 5.00

2004 Absolute Memorabilia Retail

*RETAIL VETS: .1X TO .3X HOBBY
RETAIL CARDS NOT SERIAL NUMBERED

2004 Absolute Memorabilia Spectrum

*VETS 1-150: 1X TO 2.5X BASIC CARD
*ROOKIES 151-200: .6X TO 1.5X BASIC RCs
*ROOKIES 151-200: .25X TO .6X AUTO RCs
1-200 PRINT RUN 100 SER.#'d SETS
*ROOKIES 201-233: .6X TO 1.5X BASIC RCs
*ROOKIES 201-233: .4X TO 1X AUTO RCs
201-233 RPM PRINT RUN 75 SER.#'d SETS
UNPRICED SPECTRUM PLATINUM #'d TO 1

2004 Absolute Memorabilia Absolute Patches

STATED PRINT RUN 25 SER.#'d SETS
UNPRICED SPECTRUM #'d TO 1 SET
AP1 Anquan Boldin 5.00 12.00
AP2 Barry Sanders 12.00 30.00
AP3 Brett Favre 15.00 40.00
AP4 Brian Urlacher 8.00 20.00
AP5 Chad Pennington 5.00 12.00
AP6 Clinton Portis 5.00 12.00
AP7 Dan Marino 15.00 40.00
AP8 Daunte Culpepper 6.00 15.00
AP9 David Carr 5.00 12.00
AP10 Deuce McAllister 6.00 15.00
AP11 Donovan McNabb 6.00 15.00
AP12 Drew Bledsoe 6.00 15.00
AP13 Edgerrin James 6.00 15.00
AP14 Emmitt Smith 12.00 30.00
AP15 Jeremy Shockey 5.00 12.00
AP16 Jerry Rice 15.00 40.00
AP17 John Elway 12.00 30.00
AP18 Joey Harrington 5.00 12.00
AP19 LaDainian Tomlinson 8.00 20.00
AP20 Michael Vick 6.00 15.00
AP21 Peyton Manning 20.00 50.00
AP22 Priest Holmes 5.00 12.00
AP23 Randy Moss 6.00 15.00
AP24 Ricky Williams 6.00 15.00
AP25 Tom Brady 50.00 100.00

2004 Absolute Memorabilia Boss Hoggs

COMPLETE SET (25) 20.00 50.00
STATED PRINT RUN 1000 SER.#'d SETS
BH1 Amani Toomer .75 2.00
BH2 Brett Favre 2.50 6.00
BH3 Charles Woodson 1.25 3.00
BH4 Curtis Martin 1.00 2.50
BH5 Eddie George 1.00 2.50
BH6 Edgerrin James 1.00 2.50
BH7 Emmitt Smith 2.00 5.00
BH8 Jeff Garcia .75 2.00
BH9 Jerry Rice 2.50 6.00
BH10 Jevon Kearse .75 2.00
BH11 Jimmy Smith 1.00 2.50
BH12 Keith Bulluck .75 2.00
BH13 Kurt Warner 1.00 2.50
BH14 Laveranues Coles .75 2.00
BH15 Mark Brunell 1.00 2.50
BH16 Marshall Faulk 1.00 2.50
BH17 Marvin Harrison 1.00 2.50
BH18 Michael Strahan 1.00 2.50
BH19 Michael Vick 1.00 2.50
BH20 Peyton Manning 3.00 8.00
BH21 Rich Gannon 1.00 2.50
BH22 Samari Rolle .75 2.00
BH23 Steve McNair 1.00 2.50
BH24 Tim Brown 1.25 3.00
BH25 Wayne Chrebet .75 2.00

2004 Absolute Memorabilia Boss Hoggs Material

STATED PRINT RUN 125 SER.#'d SETS
UNPRICED PRIME SPECTRUM #'d TO 1 SET
BH1 Amani Toomer 2.00 5.00
BH2 Brett Favre 6.00 15.00
BH3 Charles Woodson 3.00 8.00
BH4 Curtis Martin 2.50 6.00
BH5 Eddie George 2.50 6.00
BH6 Edgerrin James 2.50 6.00
BH7 Emmitt Smith 5.00 12.00
BH8 Jeff Garcia 2.00 5.00
BH9 Jerry Rice 6.00 15.00
BH10 Jevon Kearse 2.00 5.00
BH11 Jimmy Smith 2.50 6.00
BH12 Keith Bulluck 2.00 5.00
BH13 Kurt Warner 2.50 6.00
BH14 Laveranues Coles 2.00 5.00
BH15 Mark Brunell 2.50 6.00
BH16 Marshall Faulk 2.50 6.00
BH17 Marvin Harrison 2.50 6.00
BH18 Michael Strahan 2.50 6.00
BH19 Michael Vick 2.50 6.00
BH20 Peyton Manning 8.00 20.00
BH21 Rich Gannon 2.50 6.00
BH22 Samari Rolle 2.00 5.00
BH23 Steve McNair 2.50 6.00
BH24 Tim Brown 3.00 8.00
BH25 Wayne Chrebet 2.00 5.00

2004 Absolute Memorabilia Canton Absolutes Jersey Bronze

BRONZE PRINT RUN 100 SER.#'d SETS
*GOLD/25: .8X TO 2X BRONZE
GOLD PRINT RUN 25 SER.#'d SETS
*SILVER/50: .5X TO 1.2X BRONZE
SILVER PRINT RUN 50 SER.#'d SETS
UNPRICED PLATINUM PRINT RUN 1 SET
CA1 Barry Sanders 5.00 12.00
CA2 Brett Favre 6.00 15.00
CA3 Brian Urlacher 3.00 8.00
CA4 Clinton Portis 2.00 5.00
CA5 Dan Marino 6.00 15.00
CA6 Daunte Culpepper 2.50 6.00
CA7 Deuce McAllister 2.50 6.00
CA8 Donovan McNabb 2.50 6.00
CA9 Earl Campbell 3.00 8.00
CA10 Edgerrin James 2.50 6.00
CA11 Emmitt Smith 5.00 12.00
CA12 Jerry Rice 6.00 15.00
CA13 Jim Kelly 3.00 8.00
CA14 John Elway 5.00 12.00
CA15 LaDainian Tomlinson 3.00 8.00
CA16 Marshall Faulk 2.50 6.00
CA17 Marcus Allen 3.00 8.00
CA18 Michael Vick 2.50 6.00
CA19 Peyton Manning 8.00 20.00
CA20 Priest Holmes 2.00 5.00
CA21 Randy Moss 2.50 6.00
CA22 Ricky Williams 2.50 6.00
CA23 Steve McNair 2.50 6.00
CA24 Tom Brady 12.00 30.00
CA25 Warren Moon 3.00 8.00

2004 Absolute Memorabilia Fans of the Game

COMPLETE SET (4) 3.00 8.00
STATED ODDS 1:12 HOB, 1:24 RET
FG1 Erik Estrada .75 2.00
FG3 Chris Berman 1.00 2.50
FG4 Rich Eisen .75 2.00
FG5 John Clayton .75 2.00

2004 Absolute Memorabilia Fans of the Game Autographs

GOLD/SILVER: SAME PRICE
GOLD/300 INSERTED IN HOBBY PACKS
SILVER INSERTED IN RETAIL PACKS
FG1A Erik Estrada/300 12.50 30.00
FG1B Erik Estrada 12.50 30.00
FG3A Chris Berman/300 15.00 40.00
FG3B Chris Berman 15.00 40.00
FG4A Rich Eisen/300 12.50 30.00
FG4B Rich Eisen 12.50 30.00
FG5A John Clayton/300 7.50 20.00
FG5B John Clayton 7.50 20.00

2004 Absolute Memorabilia Gridiron Force

COMPLETE SET (25) 20.00 50.00
STATED PRINT RUN 1000 SER.#'d SETS
GF1 Aaron Brooks .75 2.00
GF2 Anquan Boldin .75 2.00
GF3 Brian Urlacher 1.25 3.00
GF4 Byron Leftwich .75 2.00
GF5 Chad Johnson .75 2.00
GF6 Chad Pennington .75 2.00
GF7 Clinton Portis .75 2.00
GF8 Daunte Culpepper 1.00 2.50
GF9 David Carr .75 2.00
GF10 Deuce McAllister 1.00 2.50
GF11 Donovan McNabb 1.00 2.50
GF12 Edgerrin James 1.00 2.50
GF13 Emmitt Smith 2.00 5.00
GF14 Jamal Lewis 1.00 2.50
GF15 Jeff Garcia .75 2.00
GF16 Jeremy Shockey .75 2.00
GF17 Joey Harrington .75 2.00
GF18 Koren Robinson .75 2.00
GF19 LaDainian Tomlinson 1.25 3.00
GF20 Plaxico Burress .75 2.00
GF21 Priest Holmes .75 2.00
GF22 Ricky Williams 1.00 2.50
GF23 Shaun Alexander .75 2.00
GF24 Terrell Owens 1.00 2.50
GF25 Tom Brady 5.00 12.00

2004 Absolute Memorabilia Gridiron Force Jersey Bronze

BRONZE PRINT RUN 100 SER.#'d SETS
*GOLD/25: .8X TO 2X BRONZE
GOLD PRINT RUN 25 SER.#'d SETS
*SILVER/50: .5X TO 1.2X BRONZE
SILVER PRINT RUN 50 SER.#'d SETS
UNPRICED PLATINUM PRINT RUN 10 SET
GF1 Aaron Brooks 2.00 5.00
GF2 Anquan Boldin 2.00 5.00
GF3 Brian Urlacher 3.00 8.00
GF4 Byron Leftwich 2.00 5.00
GF5 Chad Johnson 2.00 5.00
GF6 Chad Pennington 2.00 5.00
GF7 Clinton Portis 2.00 5.00
GF8 Daunte Culpepper 2.50 6.00
GF9 David Carr 2.00 5.00
GF10 Deuce McAllister 2.50 6.00
GF11 Donovan McNabb 2.50 6.00
GF12 Edgerrin James 2.50 6.00
GF13 Emmitt Smith 5.00 12.00
GF14 Jamal Lewis 2.50 6.00
GF15 Jeff Garcia 2.00 5.00
GF16 Jeremy Shockey 2.00 5.00
GF17 Joey Harrington 2.00 5.00
GF18 Koren Robinson 2.00 5.00
GF19 LaDainian Tomlinson 3.00 8.00
GF20 Plaxico Burress 2.00 5.00
GF21 Priest Holmes 2.00 5.00
GF22 Ricky Williams 2.50 6.00
GF23 Shaun Alexander 2.00 5.00

Card	Low	High
GF24 Terrell Owens	2.50	6.00
GF25 Tom Brady	12.00	30.00

2004 Absolute Memorabilia Ground Hoggs Shoe

STATED PRINT RUN 125 SER.#'d SETS

Card	Low	High
GH1 Amani Toomer	4.00	10.00
GH2 Brett Favre	12.00	30.00
GH3 Curtis Martin	5.00	12.00
GH4 Derrick Brooks	4.00	10.00
GH5 Derrick Mason	4.00	10.00
GH6 Dexter Coakley	4.00	10.00
GH7 Eddie George	5.00	12.00
GH8 Edgerrin James	5.00	12.00
GH9 Emmitt Smith	10.00	25.00
GH10 Jason Taylor	5.00	12.00
GH11 Jerry Rice	12.00	30.00
GH12 Jevon Kearse	4.00	10.00
GH13 Joey Galloway	5.00	12.00
GH14 Junior Seau	6.00	15.00
GH15 Keyshawn Johnson	5.00	12.00
GH16 Kurt Warner	5.00	12.00
GH17 Laveranues Coles	4.00	10.00
GH18 Marvin Harrison	5.00	12.00
GH19 Patrick Surtain	4.00	10.00
GH20 Peyton Manning	15.00	40.00
GH21 Rich Gannon	5.00	12.00
GH22 Samari Rolle	4.00	10.00
GH23 Steve McNair	5.00	12.00
GH24 Terry Glenn	5.00	12.00
GH25 Wayne Chrebet	4.00	10.00

2004 Absolute Memorabilia Leather and Laces

STATED PRINT RUN 250 SER.#'d SETS
*COMBOS/25: 1.2X TO 3X BASIC JSY

Card	Low	High
LL1 Ahman Green	4.00	10.00
LL2 Anquan Boldin	3.00	8.00
LL3 Brett Favre	10.00	25.00
LL4 Chad Johnson	3.00	8.00
LL5 Chad Pennington	3.00	8.00
LL6 Curtis Martin	4.00	10.00
LL7 Daunte Culpepper	4.00	10.00
LL8 Donovan McNabb	4.00	10.00
LL9 Emmitt Smith	8.00	20.00
LL10 Jake Delhomme	3.00	8.00
LL11 Jamal Lewis	4.00	10.00
LL12 Kevan Barlow	3.00	8.00
LL13 Koren Robinson	3.00	8.00
LL14 Marc Bulger	3.00	8.00
LL15 Marshall Faulk	4.00	10.00
LL16 Matt Hasselbeck	3.00	8.00
LL17 Randy Moss	4.00	10.00
LL18 Ricky Williams	4.00	10.00
LL19 Rudi Johnson	3.00	8.00
LL20 Shaun Alexander	3.00	8.00
LL21 Stephen Davis	3.00	8.00
LL22 Steve McNair	4.00	10.00
LL23 Steve Smith	5.00	12.00
LL24 Terrell Owens	4.00	10.00
LL25 Torry Holt	4.00	10.00

2004 Absolute Memorabilia Marks of Fame

Card	Low	High
COMPLETE SET (25)	25.00	60.00
STATED PRINT RUN 1000 SER.#'d SETS		
MOF1 Aaron Brooks	.75	2.00
MOF2 Anquan Boldin	.75	2.00
MOF3 Brett Favre	2.50	6.00
MOF4 Brian Urlacher	1.25	3.00
MOF5 Chad Pennington	.75	2.00
MOF6 Clinton Portis	.75	2.00
MOF7 Daunte Culpepper	1.00	2.50
MOF8 David Carr	.75	2.00
MOF9 Deuce McAllister	1.00	2.50
MOF10 Donovan McNabb	1.00	2.50
MOF11 Emmitt Smith	2.00	5.00
MOF12 Jamal Lewis	1.00	2.50
MOF13 Jeremy Shockey	.75	2.00
MOF14 Jerry Rice	2.50	6.00
MOF15 Joey Harrington	.75	2.00
MOF16 LaDainian Tomlinson	1.25	3.00
MOF17 Marvin Harrison	1.00	2.50
MOF18 Michael Vick	1.00	2.50
MOF19 Peyton Manning	3.00	8.00
MOF20 Priest Holmes	.75	2.00
MOF21 Ricky Williams	1.00	2.50
MOF22 Steve McNair	1.00	2.50
MOF23 Terrell Owens	1.00	2.50
MOF24 Tom Brady	5.00	12.00
MOF25 Torry Holt	1.00	2.50

2004 Absolute Memorabilia Marks of Fame Material

STATED PRINT RUN 75 SER.#'d SETS
UNPRICED PRIME SPECTRUM 1 SET

Card	Low	High
MOF1 Aaron Brooks	4.00	10.00
MOF2 Anquan Boldin	4.00	10.00
MOF3 Brett Favre	12.00	30.00
MOF4 Brian Urlacher	6.00	15.00
MOF5 Chad Pennington	4.00	10.00
MOF6 Clinton Portis	4.00	10.00
MOF7 Daunte Culpepper	5.00	12.00
MOF8 David Carr	4.00	10.00
MOF9 Deuce McAllister	5.00	12.00
MOF10 Donovan McNabb	5.00	12.00
MOF11 Emmitt Smith	10.00	25.00
MOF12 Jamal Lewis	5.00	12.00
MOF13 Jeremy Shockey	4.00	10.00
MOF14 Jerry Rice	8.00	20.00
MOF15 Joey Harrington	4.00	10.00
MOF16 LaDainian Tomlinson	6.00	15.00
MOF17 Marvin Harrison	5.00	12.00
MOF18 Michael Vick	5.00	12.00
MOF19 Peyton Manning	15.00	40.00
MOF20 Priest Holmes	4.00	10.00
MOF21 Ricky Williams	5.00	12.00
MOF22 Steve McNair	5.00	12.00
MOF23 Terrell Owens	5.00	12.00
MOF24 Tom Brady	25.00	60.00
MOF25 Torry Holt	5.00	12.00

2004 Absolute Memorabilia Marks of Fame Material Prime

*UNSIGNED PRIME: .6X TO 1.5X BASIC INSERTS
PRIME PRINT RUN 25 SER.#'d SETS

Card	Low	High
MOF1 Aaron Brooks AU	15.00	40.00
MOF2 Anquan Boldin AU	15.00	40.00
MOF3 Brett Favre AU	150.00	250.00
MOF5 Chad Pennington AU	15.00	40.00
MOF6 Clinton Portis AU	15.00	40.00
MOF8 David Carr AU	15.00	40.00
MOF14 Jerry Rice AU	125.00	200.00
MOF15 Joey Harrington AU	15.00	40.00
MOF16 LaDainian Tomlinson AU	40.00	100.00
MOF19 Peyton Manning AU	60.00	150.00
MOF22 Steve McNair AU	30.00	80.00

2004 Absolute Memorabilia Signature Material

STATED PRINT RUN 19-300
UNPRICED PRIME PRINT RUN 5 SETS
UNPRICED SPECTRUM PRINT RUN 1 SET

Card	Low	High
SM1 Ahman Green/194	15.00	40.00
SM2 Antwaan Randle El/119	12.00	30.00
SM3 Chris Chambers/94	12.00	30.00
SM4 Deuce McAllister/94	10.00	25.00
SM5 Joe Horn/94	12.00	30.00
SM6 Roy Williams S/194	10.00	25.00
SM7 Shaun Alexander/144	12.00	30.00
SM8 Stephen Davis/144	12.00	30.00
SM9 Tom Brady/194	125.00	250.00
SM10 Joe Namath/94	40.00	100.00
SM11 Terry Bradshaw/19	60.00	120.00
SM12 Jim Kelly/19	40.00	80.00
SM13 Cedric Cobbs/300	8.00	20.00
SM14 Chris Perry/280	8.00	20.00
SM15 Devery Henderson/280	8.00	20.00
SM16 Julius Jones/300	8.00	20.00
SM17 Keary Colbert/300	8.00	20.00
SM18 Kevin Jones/280	10.00	25.00
SM19 Lee Evans/300	12.00	30.00
SM20 Matt Schaub/280	8.00	20.00
SM21 Michael Clayton/300	10.00	25.00
SM22 Philip Rivers/300	25.00	60.00
SM23 Reggie Williams/280	8.00	20.00
SM24 Steven Jackson/280	12.00	30.00
SM25 Tatum Bell/300	8.00	20.00

2004 Absolute Memorabilia Signature Spectrum

RANDOM INSERTS IN PACKS

Card	Low	High
3 Josh McCown/300	8.00	20.00
10 Kyle Boller/225	6.00	15.00
18 Jake Delhomme/150	6.00	15.00
21 Stephen Davis/50	8.00	20.00
22 Steve Smith/300	12.00	30.00
31 Rudi Johnson/300	6.00	15.00
58 Domanick Davis/300	6.00	15.00
60 Marvin Harrison/25	12.00	30.00
65 Jimmy Smith/125	8.00	20.00
83 Tom Brady/50	150.00	250.00
89 Joe Horn/50	8.00	20.00
93 Michael Strahan/25	12.00	30.00
117 Kendrell Bell/25	10.00	25.00
128 Matt Hasselbeck/125	6.00	15.00
134 Torry Holt/50	10.00	25.00
140 Derrick Mason/125	6.00	15.00
146 Laveranues Coles/25	10.00	25.00
153 Josh Harris/50	8.00	20.00
164 Michael Turner/50	8.00	20.00
165 Drew Henson/300	6.00	15.00
168 Quincy Wilson/50	8.00	20.00
175 Samie Parker/50	8.00	20.00
176 Jerricho Cotchery/50	10.00	25.00
177 Ernest Wilford/50	10.00	25.00
178 Johnnie Morant/75	8.00	20.00
180 D.J. Hackett/50	8.00	20.00
182 P.K. Sam/50	8.00	20.00
192 Jonathan Vilma/50	10.00	25.00
194 D.J. Williams/25		
195 Will Smith/25	12.00	30.00
196 Kenechi Udeze/25	12.00	30.00
197 Vince Wilfork/25	15.00	40.00
198 Ahmad Carroll/25	10.00	25.00

2004 Absolute Memorabilia Team Quads

STATED PRINT RUN 250 SER.#'d SETS
UNPRICED SPECTRUM PRINT RUN 5 SETS

Card	Low	High
TQ1 Bold/Emmitt/McCow/Shipp	4.00	10.00
TQ2 Lewis/Lewis/Suggs/Boller	2.50	6.00
TQ3 Bleds/Moulds/Henry/Reed	2.00	5.00
TQ4 Thom/Urlach/Gross/Terrell	2.50	6.00
TQ5 Portis/Smith/Plummer/Lelie	2.00	5.00
TQ6 Favre/Green/Walker/Driver	5.00	12.00
TQ7 James/Mann/Harris/Wayne	6.00	15.00
TQ8 Holmes/Green/Gonz/Hall	2.00	5.00
TQ9 Chamb/Ri.Will/Thom/Taylor	2.00	5.00
TQ10 Shockey/Collins/Strah/Barb	2.00	5.00
TQ11 Penn/Martin/Moss/Abra.	2.00	5.00
TQ12 Rice/Brown/Gan/Woodson	5.00	12.00
TQ13 Ward/Bettis/Ran.El/Burress	2.50	6.00
TQ14 Warner/Faulk/Bulger/Holt	2.00	5.00
TQ15 Geor/McNair/Kearse/Mason	2.00	5.00

2004 Absolute Memorabilia Team Quads Material

STATED PRINT RUN 50 SER.#'d SETS
UNPRICED PRIME PRINT RUN 5 SETS
UNPRICED SPECTRUM PRINT RUN 1 SETS

Card	Low	High
TQ1 Bold/Emmitt/McCow/Shipp	25.00	60.00
TQ2 Lewis/Lewis/Suggs/Boller	12.00	30.00
TQ3 Bleds/Moulds/Henry/Reed	10.00	25.00
TQ4 Thom/Urlach/Gross/Terrell	12.00	30.00
TQ5 Portis/Smith/Plummer/Lelie	10.00	25.00
TQ6 Favre/Green/Walker/Driver	25.00	60.00
TQ7 James/Mann/Harris/Wayne	15.00	40.00
TQ8 Holmes/Green/Gonz/Hall	10.00	25.00
TQ9 Chamb/Ri.Will/Thom/Taylor	10.00	25.00
TQ10 Shockey/Collins/Strah/Barb	10.00	25.00
TQ11 Penn/Martin/Moss/Abra.	10.00	25.00
TQ12 Rice/Brown/Gan/Woodson	25.00	60.00
TQ13 Ward/Bettis/Ran.El/Burress	12.00	30.00
TQ14 Warner/Faulk/Bulger/Holt	10.00	25.00
TQ15 Geor/McNair/Kearse/Mason	10.00	25.00

2004 Absolute Memorabilia Team Tandems

Card	Low	High
COMPLETE SET (25)	25.00	60.00
STATED PRINT RUN 1000 SER.#'d SETS		
*SPECTRUM/25: 2X TO 5X TANDEM/1000		
SPECTRUM PRINT RUN 25 SER.#'d SETS		
TAN1 A.Boldin/E.Smith	2.00	5.00
TAN2 M.Vick/P.Price	1.00	2.50
TAN3 J.Lewis/R.Lewis	1.25	3.00
TAN4 S.Davis/J.Peppers	1.00	2.50
TAN5 B.Urlacher/A.Thomas	1.25	3.00
TAN6 C.Portis/Ro.Smith	1.00	2.50
TAN7 C.Rogers/J.Harrington	.75	2.00
TAN8 A.Green/B.Favre	2.50	6.00
TAN9 A.Johnson/D.Carr	1.00	2.50
TAN10 E.James/P.Manning	3.00	8.00
TAN11 B.Leftwich/F.Taylor	.75	2.00
TAN12 P.Holmes/T.Green	.75	2.00
TAN13 C.Chambers/Ri.Williams	1.00	2.50
TAN14 D.Culpepper/R.Moss	1.00	2.50
TAN15 T.Brady/Tr.Brown	5.00	12.00
TAN16 A.Brooks/D.McAllister	1.00	2.50
TAN17 J.Shockey/K.Collins	.75	2.00
TAN18 C.Pennington/C.Martin	1.00	2.50
TAN19 J.Rice/T.Brown	2.50	6.00
TAN20 D.McNabb/C.Buckhalter	1.00	2.50
TAN21 D.Brees/L.Tomlinson	1.25	3.00
TAN22 Hasselbeck/Alexander	.75	2.00
TAN23 K.Warner/M.Faulk	1.00	2.50
TAN24 E.George/S.McNair	1.00	2.50
TAN25 P.Ramsey/L.Coles	1.00	2.50

2004 Absolute Memorabilia Team Tandems Material

STATED PRINT RUN 125 SER.#'d SETS
*PRIME/25: 1X TO 2.5X TANDEM JSY/125
PRIME PRINT RUN 25 SER.#'d SETS
UNPRICED SPECTRUM PRINT RUN 1 SET

Card	Low	High
TT1 A.Boldin/E.Smith	8.00	20.00
TT2 M.Vick/P.Price	4.00	10.00
TT3 J.Lewis/R.Lewis	5.00	12.00
TT4 S.Davis/J.Peppers	4.00	10.00
TT5 B.Urlacher/A.Thomas	5.00	12.00
TT6 C.Portis/Ro.Smith	4.00	10.00
TT7 C.Rogers/J.Harrington	3.00	8.00
TT8 A.Green/B.Favre	10.00	25.00
TT9 A.Johnson/D.Carr	4.00	10.00
TT10 E.James/P.Manning	12.00	30.00
TT11 B.Leftwich/F.Taylor	3.00	8.00
TT12 P.Holmes/T.Green	3.00	8.00
TT13 C.Chambers/Ri.Williams	4.00	10.00
TT14 D.Culpepper/R.Moss	4.00	10.00
TT15 T.Brady/Tr.Brown	20.00	60.00
TT16 A.Brooks/D.McAllister	4.00	10.00
TT17 J.Shockey/K.Collins	3.00	8.00
TT18 C.Pennington/C.Martin	4.00	10.00
TT19 J.Rice/T.Brown	10.00	25.00
TT20 D.McNabb/C.Buckhalter	4.00	10.00
TT21 D.Brees/L.Tomlinson	5.00	12.00
TT22 Hasselbeck/Alexander	3.00	8.00
TT23 K.Warner/M.Faulk	4.00	10.00
TT24 E.George/S.McNair	4.00	10.00
TT25 P.Ramsey/L.Coles	4.00	10.00

2004 Absolute Memorabilia Team Trios

STATED PRINT RUN 500 SER.#'d SETS
UNPRICED SPECTRUM PRINT RUN 10 SETS

Card	Low	High
TTR1 Boldin/Emmitt/McCown	3.00	8.00
TTR2 Vick/Price/Duckett	1.50	4.00
TTR3 J.Lewis/R.Lewis/Suggs	2.00	5.00
TTR4 Bledsoe/Moulds/Henry	1.50	4.00
TTR5 Thom/Urlacher/Grossman	2.00	5.00
TTR6 C.Johnson/Dillon/Warrick	1.25	3.00
TTR7 Carter/Williams/Newman	1.50	4.00
TTR8 Portis/Ro.Smith/Plummer	1.50	4.00
TTR9 Rogers/Harrington/Stewart	1.25	3.00
TTR10 Green/Favre/Walker	4.00	10.00
TTR11 James/Manning/Harrison	5.00	12.00
TTR12 Leftwich/Taylor/J.Smith	1.50	4.00
TTR13 Holmes/Green/Gonzalez	1.50	4.00
TTR14 Chamb/Ri.Williams/Thomas	1.50	4.00
TTR15 Culpepp/R.Moss/Bennett	1.50	4.00
TTR16 Brooks/McAllister/Horn	1.50	4.00
TTR17 Shockey/Collins/Strahan	1.50	4.00
TTR18 Penning/Martin/S.Moss	1.50	4.00
TTR19 Rice/Brown/Gannon	4.00	10.00
TTR20 Ward/Bettis/Randle El	2.00	5.00
TTR21 Brees/Tomlinson/Flutie	2.00	5.00
TTR22 Hasselbeck/Alex/Robinson	1.25	3.00
TTR23 Warner/Faulk/Bulger	1.50	4.00
TTR24 George/McNair/Kearse	1.50	4.00
TTR25 Coles/Ramsey/Arrington	1.50	4.00

2004 Absolute Memorabilia Team Trios Material

STATED PRINT RUN 100 SER.#'d SETS
UNPRICED PRIME PRINT RUN 10 SETS
UNPRICED SPECTRUM PRINT RUN 1 SETS

Card	Low	High
TTR1 Boldin/Emmitt/McCown	10.00	25.00
TTR2 Vick/Price/Duckett	5.00	12.00
TTR3 J.Lewis/R.Lewis/Suggs	6.00	15.00
TTR4 Bledsoe/Moulds/Henry	5.00	12.00
TTR5 Thom/Urlacher/Grossman	6.00	15.00
TTR6 C.Johnson/Dillon/Warrick	4.00	10.00
TTR7 Carter/Williams/Newman	5.00	12.00
TTR8 Portis/Ro.Smith/Plummer	5.00	12.00
TTR9 Rogers/Harrington/Stewart	4.00	10.00
TTR10 Green/Favre/Walker	10.00	25.00
TTR11 James/Manning/Harrison	15.00	40.00
TTR12 Leftwich/Taylor/J.Smith	5.00	12.00
TTR13 Holmes/Green/Gonzalez	5.00	12.00
TTR14 Chamb/Ri.Williams/Thomas	5.00	12.00
TTR15 Culpep/R.Moss/Bennett	5.00	12.00
TTR16 Brooks/McAllister/Horn	5.00	12.00
TTR17 Shockey/Collins/Strahan	5.00	12.00
TTR18 Penning/Martin/S.Moss	5.00	12.00
TTR19 Rice/Brown/Gannon	12.00	30.00
TTR20 Ward/Bettis/Randle El	6.00	15.00
TTR21 Brees/Tomlinson/Flutie	6.00	15.00
TTR22 Hasselbeck/Alex/Robinson	4.00	10.00
TTR23 Warner/Faulk/Bulger	5.00	12.00
TTR24 George/McNair/Kearse	5.00	12.00
TTR25 Coles/Ramsey/Arrington	5.00	12.00

2004 Absolute Memorabilia Tools of the Trade

STATED PRINT RUN 250 SER.#'d SETS
UNPRICED SPECTRUM PRINT RUN 10 SETS

Card	Low	High
TT1 Aaron Brooks	1.25	3.00
TT2 Ahman Green	1.50	4.00
TT3 Andre Johnson	1.50	4.00
TT4 Anquan Boldin	1.25	3.00
TT5 Anthony Thomas	1.50	4.00
TT6 Antwaan Randle El	1.25	3.00
TT7 Ashley Lelie	1.25	3.00
TT8 Brad Johnson	1.50	4.00
TT9 Brett Favre	4.00	10.00
TT10 Brian Urlacher	2.00	5.00
TT11 Byron Leftwich	1.25	3.00
TT12 Chad Johnson	1.25	3.00
TT13 Chad Pennington	1.25	3.00
TT14 Charles Rogers	1.25	3.00
TT15 Charles Woodson	2.00	5.00
TT16 Chris Chambers	1.25	3.00
TT17 Clinton Portis	1.25	3.00
TT18 Corey Dillon	1.25	3.00
TT19 Curtis Martin	1.50	4.00
TT20 Dante Hall	1.25	3.00
TT21 Daunte Culpepper	1.50	4.00
TT22 David Boston	1.25	3.00
TT23 David Carr	1.25	3.00
TT24 Deuce McAllister	1.50	4.00
TT25 Donovan McNabb	1.50	4.00
TT26 Donte Stallworth	1.25	3.00
TT27 Drew Bledsoe	1.50	4.00
TT28 Eddie George	1.50	4.00
TT29 Edgerrin James	1.50	4.00
TT30 Emmitt Smith	3.00	8.00
TT31 Eric Moulds	1.25	3.00
TT32 Fred Taylor	1.25	3.00
TT33 Hines Ward	1.50	4.00
TT34 Isaac Bruce	2.00	5.00
TT35 Jake Plummer	1.25	3.00
TT36 Jamal Lewis	1.50	4.00
TT37 Javon Walker	1.25	3.00
TT38 Jeff Garcia	1.25	3.00
TT39 Jeremy Shockey	1.25	3.00
TT40 Jerome Bettis	2.00	5.00
TT41 Jerry Rice	4.00	10.00
TT42 Jevon Kearse	1.25	3.00
TT43 Joey Harrington	1.25	3.00
TT44 Josh McCown	1.50	4.00
TT45 Julius Peppers	1.50	4.00
TT46 Kendrell Bell	1.25	3.00
TT47 Kerry Collins	1.25	3.00
TT48 Keyshawn Johnson	1.50	4.00
TT49 Koren Robinson	1.25	3.00
TT50 Kurt Warner	1.50	4.00
TT51 Kyle Boller	1.25	3.00
TT52 LaDainian Tomlinson	2.00	5.00
TT53 LaVar Arrington	1.25	3.00
TT54 Laveranues Coles	1.25	3.00
TT55 Marc Bulger	1.25	3.00
TT56 Marcel Shipp	1.25	3.00
TT57 Mark Brunell	1.50	4.00
TT58 Marshall Faulk	1.50	4.00
TT59 Marvin Harrison	1.50	4.00
TT60 Matt Hasselbeck	1.25	3.00
TT61 Michael Bennett	1.25	3.00
TT62 Michael Strahan	1.50	4.00
TT63 Michael Vick	1.50	4.00
TT64 Patrick Ramsey	1.50	4.00
TT65 Peerless Price	1.25	3.00
TT66 Peter Warrick	1.25	3.00
TT67 Peyton Manning	5.00	12.00
TT68 Plaxico Burress	1.25	3.00
TT69 Priest Holmes	1.25	3.00
TT70 Quincy Carter	1.25	3.00
TT71 Randy Moss	1.50	4.00
TT72 Ray Lewis	2.00	5.00
TT73 Reggie Wayne	1.50	4.00
TT74 Rex Grossman	1.25	3.00
TT75 Rich Gannon	1.50	4.00
TT76 Ricky Williams	1.50	4.00
TT77 Rod Smith	1.50	4.00
TT78 Roy Williams S	1.25	3.00
TT79 Santana Moss	1.50	4.00
TT80 Shaun Alexander	1.25	3.00
TT81 Stephen Davis	1.25	3.00
TT82 T.J. Duckett	1.25	3.00
TT83 Terence Newman	1.50	4.00
TT84 Terrell Owens	1.50	4.00
TT85 Terrell Suggs	1.25	3.00
TT86 Tiki Barber	1.50	4.00
TT87 Tim Brown	2.00	5.00
TT88 Tom Brady	8.00	20.00
TT89 Tony Gonzalez	1.50	4.00
TT90 Torry Holt	1.50	4.00
TT91 Travis Henry	1.25	3.00
TT92 Trent Green	1.25	3.00
TT93 Warrick Dunn	1.25	3.00
TT94 Zach Thomas	1.50	4.00
TT95 Barry Sanders	4.00	10.00
TT96 Dan Marino	5.00	12.00
TT97 Deion Sanders	2.00	5.00
TT98 Joe Montana	10.00	25.00
TT99 John Elway	4.00	10.00
TT100 Warren Moon	2.00	5.00

2004 Absolute Memorabilia Tools of the Trade Material Jersey

JERSEY PRINT RUN 100 SER.#'d SETS
UNPRICED PRIME SPEC.PRINT RUN 1 SET
UNPRICED SPECTRUM PRINT RUN 10 SETS

Card	Low	High
TT1 Aaron Brooks	2.00	5.00
TT2 Ahman Green	2.50	6.00
TT3 Andre Johnson	2.50	6.00
TT4 Anquan Boldin	2.00	5.00
TT5 Anthony Thomas	2.50	6.00
TT6 Antwaan Randle El	2.00	5.00
TT7 Ashley Lelie	2.00	5.00
TT8 Brad Johnson	2.50	6.00
TT9 Brett Favre	6.00	15.00
TT10 Brian Urlacher	3.00	8.00
TT11 Byron Leftwich/50*	3.00	8.00
TT11A Byron Leftwich AU/50*	10.00	25.00
TT12 Chad Johnson AU	10.00	25.00
TT13 Chad Pennington	2.00	5.00
TT14 Charles Rogers	2.00	5.00
TT15 Charles Woodson	3.00	8.00
TT16 Chris Chambers AU	10.00	25.00
TT17 Clinton Portis	3.00	8.00
TT18 Corey Dillon	2.00	5.00
TT19 Curtis Martin	2.50	6.00
TT20 Dante Hall	2.00	5.00
TT21 Daunte Culpepper	2.50	6.00
TT22 David Boston	2.00	5.00
TT23 David Carr/75*	2.00	5.00
TT23A David Carr AU/25*	12.00	30.00
TT24 Deuce McAllister	2.50	6.00
TT25 Donovan McNabb	2.50	6.00
TT26 Donte Stallworth	2.00	5.00
TT27 Drew Bledsoe	2.50	6.00
TT28 Eddie George	2.50	6.00
TT29 Edgerrin James	2.50	6.00
TT30 Emmitt Smith	5.00	12.00
TT31 Eric Moulds	2.00	5.00
TT32 Fred Taylor	2.00	5.00
TT33 Hines Ward AU	30.00	60.00
TT34 Isaac Bruce	3.00	8.00
TT35 Jake Plummer	2.00	5.00
TT36 Jamal Lewis	2.50	6.00
TT37 Javon Walker	2.00	5.00
TT38 Jeff Garcia	2.00	5.00
TT39 Jeremy Shockey	2.00	5.00
TT40 Jerome Bettis	3.00	8.00
TT41 Jerry Rice	6.00	15.00
TT42 Jevon Kearse	2.00	5.00
TT43 Joey Harrington	2.00	5.00
TT44 Josh McCown	2.50	6.00
TT45 Julius Peppers	2.50	6.00
TT46 Kendrell Bell	2.00	5.00
TT47 Kerry Collins	2.00	5.00
TT48 Keyshawn Johnson	2.50	6.00
TT49 Koren Robinson	2.00	5.00
TT50 Kurt Warner	2.50	6.00
TT51 Kyle Boller AU	10.00	25.00
TT52 LaDainian Tomlinson	3.00	8.00
TT53 LaVar Arrington	2.00	5.00
TT54 Laveranues Coles	2.00	5.00
TT55 Marc Bulger	2.00	5.00
TT56 Marcel Shipp	2.00	5.00
TT57 Mark Brunell	2.50	6.00
TT58 Marshall Faulk	2.50	6.00
TT59 Marvin Harrison	2.50	6.00
TT60 Matt Hasselbeck AU	10.00	25.00
TT61 Michael Bennett	2.00	5.00
TT62 Michael Strahan	2.50	6.00
TT63 Michael Vick	2.50	6.00
TT64 Patrick Ramsey	2.50	6.00
TT65 Peerless Price	2.00	5.00
TT66 Peter Warrick	2.00	5.00
TT67 Peyton Manning	8.00	20.00
TT68 Plaxico Burress	2.00	5.00
TT69 Priest Holmes	2.00	5.00
TT70 Quincy Carter	2.00	5.00
TT71 Randy Moss	2.50	6.00
TT72 Ray Lewis	3.00	8.00
TT73 Reggie Wayne	2.50	6.00
TT74 Rex Grossman AU	10.00	25.00
TT75 Rich Gannon	2.50	6.00
TT76 Ricky Williams	2.50	6.00
TT77 Rod Smith	2.50	6.00
TT78 Roy Williams S AU	10.00	25.00
TT79 Santana Moss	2.50	6.00
TT80 Shaun Alexander/50*	2.50	6.00
TT80A Shaun Alexander AU/50*	10.00	25.00
TT81 Stephen Davis	2.00	5.00
TT82 T.J. Duckett	2.00	5.00
TT83 Terence Newman	2.50	6.00
TT84 Terrell Owens	2.50	6.00
TT85 Terrell Suggs	2.00	5.00
TT86 Tiki Barber	2.50	6.00
TT87 Tim Brown	3.00	8.00
TT88 Tom Brady	12.00	30.00
TT89 Tony Gonzalez	2.50	6.00
TT90 Torry Holt/50*	3.00	8.00
TT90A Torry Holt AU/50*		
TT91 Travis Henry	2.00	5.00
TT92 Trent Green/25*	3.00	8.00
TT92A Trent Green AU/75*	10.00	25.00
TT93 Warrick Dunn	2.00	5.00
TT94 Zach Thomas	2.50	6.00
TT95 Barry Sanders	5.00	12.00
TT96 Dan Marino	6.00	15.00
TT97 Deion Sanders	10.00	25.00
TT98 Joe Montana/50*	25.00	60.00
TT98A Joe Montana AU/50*	100.00	175.00
TT99 John Elway	5.00	12.00
TT100 Warren Moon/50*	6.00	15.00
TT100A Warren Moon AU/50*	15.00	40.00

2004 Absolute Memorabilia Tools of the Trade Material Jersey Prime

Card	Low	High
*UNSIGNED PRIME: .8X TO 2X BASIC JSY		
COMMON AUTO	20.00	50.00
AUTO SEMISTARS	25.00	60.00
AUTO UNL.STARS	30.00	80.00
PRIME PRINT RUN 25 SER.#'d SETS		
TT25 Donovan McNabb AU	25.00	60.00
TT41 Jerry Rice AU	125.00	250.00
TT63 Michael Vick AU	60.00	100.00
TT67 Peyton Manning AU	75.00	150.00
TT88 Tom Brady AU	150.00	300.00
TT95 Barry Sanders AU	100.00	200.00
TT96 Dan Marino AU	125.00	250.00
TT97 Deion Sanders AU	60.00	120.00
TT98 Joe Montana AU	125.00	250.00
TT99 John Elway AU	100.00	200.00

2004 Absolute Memorabilia Tools of the Trade Material Combos

*UNSIGNED COMBO: .5X TO 1.2X BASIC JSY
STATED PRINT RUN 75 SER.#'d SETS
UNPRICED PRIME PRINT RUN 10 SETS

Card	Low	High
TT13 Pennington Jsy-Pnt/50	2.50	6.00
TT13A Pennington Jsy-Pnt AU/25	10.00	25.00
TT20 Dante Hall Jsy-Pants AU	10.00	25.00
TT23 David Carr Jsy-Jsy/50	2.50	6.00
TT23A D.Carr Jsy-Jsy AU/25	10.00	25.00
TT27 Drew Bledsoe Jsy-Jsy/25	4.00	10.00
TT27A Bledsoe Jsy-Jsy AU/50	12.00	30.00
TT28 E.George Jsy-Pants/50	3.00	8.00
TT28A E.George Jsy-Pnt AU/25	12.00	30.00
TT44 J.McCown Jsy-Pnt AU	12.00	30.00
TT48 Key.Jhnsn Jsy-Shoe AU	12.00	30.00
TT79 San.Moss Jsy-Pants AU	12.00	30.00
TT86 Tiki Barber Jsy-Pants AU	12.00	30.00
TT90A T.Holt Jsy-Pnts AU/50*	12.00	30.00
TT98 Montana Jsy-Shoe/50	12.00	30.00
TT98A Montana J-Sh AU/25	125.00	225.00

2004 Absolute Memorabilia Tools of the Trade Material Quads

*UNSIGNED QUADS: 1.5X TO 4X SINGLE JSYs
STATED PRINT RUN 25 SER.#'d SETS
UNPRICED PRIME PRINT RUN 1 SET

Card	Low	High
TT44 J.McCown J-J-P-F AU	20.00	50.00
TT79 San.Moss J-P-F-H AU	25.00	60.00
TT90 Torry Holt J-P-F-H	25.00	60.00
TT96 Dan Marino J-J-P-S AU	100.00	200.00

2004 Absolute Memorabilia Tools of the Trade Material Trios

*TRIOS: .8X TO 2X SINGLE JSY 100
*TRIOS: .6X TO 1.5X SINGLE JSY 50
STATED PRINT RUN 50 SER.#'d SETS
UNPRICED PRIME PRINT RUN 5 SET

2005 Absolute Memorabilia

This 234-card set was released in August, 2005. The set was issued in four-card hobby packs with an $40 SRP which also came four packs to a box. Cards numbered 1-150 feature veteran players in team alphabetical order while cards numbered 151-234 all feature rookies. In that rookie groups cards numbered 151-205 are printed to a stated print run of 999 serial numbered sets and cards numbered 206-234 (which included a player-worn swatch) were issued to a stated print run of 750 serial numbered sets. A way to differentiate the hobby cards from the retail version is that the hobby cards were printed on holofoil stock.

151-205 PRINT RUN 999 SER.#'d SETS
206-234 PRINT RUN 750 SER.#'d SETS
UNPRICED PLATINUM PRINT RUN 1 SET
HOBBY PRINTED ON HOLOFOIL STOCK

Card	Low	High
1 Anquan Boldin	.75	2.00
2 Kurt Warner	1.00	2.50
3 Josh McCown	1.00	2.50
4 Larry Fitzgerald	1.25	3.00
5 Alge Crumpler	1.00	2.50
6 Michael Vick	1.00	2.50
7 Peerless Price	.75	2.00
8 T.J. Duckett	.75	2.00
9 Warrick Dunn	.75	2.00
10 Deion Sanders	1.00	2.50
11 Derrick Mason	.75	2.00
12 Ed Reed	1.00	2.50
13 Jamal Lewis	1.00	2.50
14 Kyle Boller	.75	2.00
15 Ray Lewis	1.25	3.00
16 Todd Heap	.75	2.00
17 Eric Moulds	.75	2.00
18 J.P. Losman	.75	2.00
19 Lee Evans	1.00	2.50
20 Travis Henry	.75	2.00
21 Willis McGahee	.75	2.00
22 DeShaun Foster	1.00	2.50
23 Jake Delhomme	.75	2.00
24 Julius Peppers	1.00	2.50
25 Keary Colbert	.75	2.00
26 Stephen Davis	.75	2.00
27 Steve Smith	1.25	3.00
28 Brian Urlacher	1.25	3.00
29 Muhsin Muhammad	.75	2.00
30 Thomas Jones	.75	2.00
31 Rex Grossman	.75	2.00
32 Carson Palmer	1.00	2.50
33 Chad Johnson	.75	2.00
34 Peter Warrick	.75	2.00
35 Rudi Johnson	.75	2.00
36 T.J. Houshmandzadeh	.75	2.00
37 Antonio Bryant	.75	2.00
38 Dennis Northcutt	.75	2.00
39 Trent Dilfer	.75	2.00
40 Kellen Winslow	.75	2.00
41 Lee Suggs	.75	2.00
42 Reuben Droughns	.75	2.00
43 Drew Bledsoe	1.00	2.50
44 Jason Witten	1.00	2.50
45 Julius Jones	.75	2.00
46 Keyshawn Johnson	1.00	2.50
47 Terence Newman	.75	2.00
48 Roy Williams S	.75	2.00
49 Jake Plummer	.75	2.00
50 Rod Smith	1.00	2.50
51 Ashley Lelie	.75	2.00
52 Tatum Bell	.75	2.00
53 Charles Rogers	.75	2.00
54 Joey Harrington	.75	2.00
55 Kevin Jones	.75	2.00
56 Roy Williams WR	.75	2.00
57 Ahman Green	1.00	2.50
58 Brett Favre	2.50	6.00
59 Donald Driver	1.00	2.50
60 Javon Walker	.75	2.00
61 Andre Johnson	1.00	2.50
62 David Carr	.75	2.00
63 Domanick Davis	.75	2.00
64 Brandon Stokley	.75	2.00
65 Dallas Clark	.75	2.00
66 Edgerrin James	1.00	2.50
67 Marvin Harrison	1.00	2.50
68 Peyton Manning	3.00	8.00
69 Reggie Wayne	1.00	2.50
70 Reggie Williams	.75	2.00
71 Byron Leftwich	.75	2.00
72 Fred Taylor	.75	2.00
73 Jimmy Smith	1.00	2.50
74 Priest Holmes	.75	2.00
75 Tony Gonzalez	1.00	2.50
76 Dante Hall	.75	2.00
77 Trent Green	.75	2.00
78 Eddie Kennison	.75	2.00
79 A.J. Feeley	.75	2.00
80 Chris Chambers	.75	2.00
81 Zach Thomas	1.00	2.50
82 Junior Seau	1.00	2.50
83 Marty Booker	.75	2.00
84 Daunte Culpepper	1.00	2.50
85 Nate Burleson	.75	2.00
86 Michael Bennett	.75	2.00
87 Onterrio Smith	.75	2.00
88 Corey Dillon	.75	2.00
89 Deion Branch	.75	2.00
90 Tom Brady	5.00	12.00
91 Troy Brown	.75	2.00
92 Tedy Bruschi	1.00	2.50
93 Aaron Brooks	.75	2.00
94 Donte Stallworth	.75	2.00
95 Joe Horn	.75	2.00
96 Deuce McAllister	1.00	2.50
97 Amani Toomer	.75	2.00
98 Plaxico Burress	.75	2.00
99 Jeremy Shockey	.75	2.00
100 Eli Manning	2.00	5.00
101 Tiki Barber	1.00	2.50
102 Chad Pennington	.75	2.00
103 Laveranues Coles	.75	2.00
104 Curtis Martin	1.00	2.50
105 Justin McCareins	.75	2.00
106 Wayne Chrebet	.75	2.00
107 Jerry Porter	.75	2.00
108 LaMont Jordan	1.00	2.50
109 Randy Moss	1.00	2.50
110 Kerry Collins	.75	2.00
111 Charles Woodson	1.25	3.00
112 Brian Westbrook	.75	2.00
113 Donovan McNabb	1.00	2.50
114 Jevon Kearse	.75	2.00
115 Terrell Owens	1.00	2.50
116 Ben Roethlisberger	2.00	5.00
117 Hines Ward	1.00	2.50
118 Duce Staley	.75	2.00
119 Jerome Bettis	1.25	3.00
120 Antonio Gates	1.25	3.00
121 Eric Parker	.75	2.00
122 Keenan McCardell	1.00	2.50
123 Drew Brees	1.25	3.00
124 LaDainian Tomlinson	1.25	3.00
125 Brandon Lloyd	.75	2.00
126 Kevan Barlow	.75	2.00
127 Tim Rattay	.75	2.00
128 Koren Robinson	.75	2.00
129 Darrell Jackson	.75	2.00
130 Jerry Rice	2.50	6.00
131 Matt Hasselbeck	.75	2.00
132 Shaun Alexander	.75	2.00
133 Isaac Bruce	1.25	3.00
134 Marc Bulger	.75	2.00
135 Marshall Faulk	1.00	2.50
136 Steven Jackson	.75	2.00
137 Torry Holt	1.00	2.50
138 Brian Griese	.75	2.00
139 Michael Clayton	.75	2.00
140 Michael Pittman	.75	2.00
141 Mike Alstott	.75	2.00
142 Chris Brown	.75	2.00
143 Drew Bennett	1.00	2.50
144 Steve McNair	1.00	2.50
145 Clinton Portis	.75	2.00
146 LaVar Arrington	.75	2.00
147 Santana Moss	1.00	2.50
148 Patrick Ramsey	1.00	2.50
149 Rod Gardner	.75	2.00
150 Sean Taylor	1.25	3.00
151 DeMarcus Ware RC	5.00	12.00
152 Shawne Merriman RC	2.50	6.00
153 Thomas Davis RC	1.50	4.00
154 Derrick Johnson RC	2.00	5.00
155 Travis Johnson RC	1.50	4.00
156 David Pollack RC	1.50	4.00
157 Erasmus James RC	1.50	4.00
158 Marcus Spears RC	1.50	4.00
159 Fabian Washington RC	1.50	4.00
160 Marlin Jackson RC	1.50	4.00
161 Cedric Benson RC	1.50	4.00
162 Matt Roth RC	1.50	4.00
163 Dan Cody RC	1.50	4.00
164 Bryant McFadden RC	2.00	5.00
165 Chris Henry RC	2.00	5.00
166 Brandon Jones RC	2.00	5.00
167 Marion Barber RC	1.50	4.00
168 Brandon Jacobs RC	2.00	5.00
169 Jerome Mathis RC	2.50	6.00
170 Craphonso Thorpe RC	1.50	4.00
171 Alvin Pearman RC	1.50	4.00
172 Darren Sproles RC	2.50	6.00
173 Fred Gibson RC	1.50	4.00
174 Roydell Williams RC	2.00	5.00
175 Airese Currie RC	1.50	4.00
176 Damien Nash RC	2.00	5.00
177 Dan Orlovsky RC	1.50	4.00
178 Adrian McPherson RC	1.50	4.00
179 Larry Brackins RC	1.50	4.00
180 Aaron Rodgers RC	30.00	60.00
181 Cedric Houston RC	2.50	6.00
182 Mike Williams	2.00	5.00
183 Heath Miller RC	3.00	8.00
184 Dante Ridgeway RC	1.50	4.00
185 Craig Bragg RC	1.50	4.00
186 Deandra Cobb RC	1.50	4.00
187 Derek Anderson RC	2.00	5.00
188 Paris Warren RC	2.00	5.00
189 David Greene RC	1.50	4.00
190 Lionel Gates RC	1.50	4.00
191 Anthony Davis RC	1.50	4.00
192 Noah Herron RC	1.50	4.00
193 Ryan Fitzpatrick RC	2.50	6.00
194 J.R. Russell RC	1.50	4.00
195 Jason White RC	2.50	6.00
196 Kay-Jay Harris RC	1.50	4.00
197 Steve Savoy RC	1.50	4.00
198 T.A. McLendon RC	1.50	4.00
199 Taylor Stubblefield RC	1.50	4.00
200 Josh Davis RC	1.50	4.00
201 Shaun Cody RC	2.00	5.00
202 Rasheed Marshall RC	2.00	5.00
203 Chad Owens RC	1.50	4.00
204 Tab Perry RC	1.50	4.00
205 James Kilian RC	1.50	4.00
206 Adam Jones RPM RC	2.50	6.00
207 Alex Smith QB RPM RC	10.00	25.00
208 Antrel Rolle RPM RC	4.00	10.00
209 Andrew Walter RPM RC	2.50	6.00
210 Braylon Edwards RPM RC	2.50	6.00
211 Cadillac Williams RPM RC	2.50	6.00
212 Carlos Rogers RPM RC	4.00	10.00
213 Charlie Frye RPM RC	2.50	6.00
214 Ciatrick Fason RPM RC	2.50	6.00
215 Courtney Roby RPM RC	2.50	6.00
216 Eric Shelton RPM RC	2.50	6.00
217 Frank Gore RPM RC	5.00	12.00
218 J.J. Arrington RPM RC	3.00	8.00
219 Kyle Orton RPM RC	2.50	6.00
220 Jason Campbell RPM RC	2.50	6.00
221 Mark Bradley RPM RC	2.50	6.00
222 Mark Clayton RPM RC	2.50	6.00
223 Matt Jones RPM RC	2.50	6.00
224 Maurice Clarett RPM	2.50	6.00
225 Reggie Brown RPM RC	2.50	6.00
226 Ronnie Brown RPM RC	3.00	8.00
227 Roddy White RPM RC	4.00	10.00
228 Ryan Moats RPM RC	2.50	6.00
229 Roscoe Parrish RPM RC	2.50	6.00
230 Stefan LeFors RPM RC	2.50	6.00
231 Terrence Murphy RPM RC	2.50	6.00
232 Troy Williamson RPM RC	2.50	6.00
233 Vernand Morency RPM RC	2.50	6.00
234 Vincent Jackson RPM RC	4.00	10.00

2005 Absolute Memorabilia Retail

Card	Low	High
COMPLETE SET (150)	15.00	30.00

*VETERANS: .1X TO .25X BASIC CARDS
*ROOKIES 151-205: .2X TO .5X BASIC CARDS
RETAIL PRINTED ON WHITE STOCK

2005 Absolute Memorabilia Spectrum Black Retail

*VETERANS: 1X TO 2.5X BASIC CARDS
*ROOKIES: .6X TO 1.5X BASIC CARDS
BLACK STATED ODDS 1:12 RETAIL

2005 Absolute Memorabilia Spectrum Blue Retail

*VETERANS: .8X TO 2X BASIC CARDS
*ROOKIES: .5X TO 1.2X BASIC CARDS
BLUE STATED ODDS 1:8 RETAIL
*RPM ROOKIES: .5X TO 1.2X BASIC CARDS
RPM PRINT RUN 75 SER.#'d SETS

2005 Absolute Memorabilia Spectrum Gold

*VETS: 2.5X TO 6X BASIC CARDS
*ROOKIES: 1X TO 2.5X BASIC CARDS
STATED PRINT RUN 25 SER.#'d SETS

2005 Absolute Memorabilia Spectrum Platinum

UNPRICED PLATINUM SER.#'d OF 1

2005 Absolute Memorabilia Spectrum Red Retail

*VETERANS: .8X TO 2X BASIC CARDS
*ROOKIES: .5X TO 1.2X BASIC CARDS
RED STATED ODDS 1:8 RETAIL

2005 Absolute Memorabilia Spectrum Silver

*VETERANS: 1.2X TO 3X BASIC CARDS
*ROOKIES: .8X TO 2X BASIC CARDS
STATED PRINT RUN 100 SER.#'d SETS

2005 Absolute Memorabilia Absolute Heroes Silver

SILVER PRINT RUN 250 SER.#'d SETS
*GOLD/150: .5X TO 1.2X SILVER
*SPECTRUM/25: 1.2X TO 3X SILVER

Card	Low	High
AH1 Bo Jackson	4.00	10.00
AH2 Brian Urlacher	2.50	6.00
AH3 Brian Westbrook	1.50	4.00
AH4 Dan Marino	5.00	12.00
AH5 Domanick Davis	1.50	4.00
AH6 Donovan McNabb	2.00	5.00
AH7 Edgerrin James	2.00	5.00
AH8 Hines Ward	2.00	5.00
AH9 Jake Delhomme	1.50	4.00
AH10 Jamal Lewis	2.00	5.00
AH11 Jeremy Shockey	1.50	4.00
AH12 Jerry Rice	5.00	12.00
AH13 Joe Montana	10.00	25.00
AH14 LaDainian Tomlinson	2.50	6.00
AH15 Larry Fitzgerald	2.50	6.00
AH16 Marvin Harrison	2.00	5.00
AH17 Matt Hasselbeck	1.50	4.00
AH18 Michael Clayton	1.50	4.00
AH19 Michael Irvin	3.00	8.00
AH20 Roy Williams S	1.50	4.00
AH21 Steve Young	4.00	10.00
AH22 Steven Jackson	1.50	4.00
AH23 Terrell Davis	2.50	6.00
AH24 Troy Aikman	4.00	10.00
AH25 Walter Payton	8.00	20.00

2005 Absolute Memorabilia Absolute Heroes Material

STATED PRINT RUN 150 SER.#'d SETS
*PRIME/25: 1X TO 2.5X BASIC JSY/150
PRIME PRINT RUN 25 SER.#'d SETS
UNPRICED SPECTRUM PRINT RUN 1 SET

Card	Low	High
AH1 Bo Jackson	4.00	10.00
AH2 Brian Urlacher	3.00	8.00
AH3 Brian Westbrook	2.00	5.00
AH4 Dan Marino	6.00	15.00
AH5 Domanick Davis	2.00	5.00
AH6 Donovan McNabb	2.50	6.00
AH7 Edgerrin James	2.50	6.00
AH8 Hines Ward	2.50	6.00
AH9 Jake Delhomme	2.00	5.00
AH10 Jamal Lewis	2.50	6.00
AH11 Jeremy Shockey	2.00	5.00
AH12 Jerry Rice	6.00	15.00
AH13 Joe Montana	10.00	25.00
AH14 LaDainian Tomlinson	3.00	8.00
AH15 Larry Fitzgerald	3.00	8.00
AH16 Marvin Harrison	2.50	6.00
AH17 Matt Hasselbeck	2.00	5.00
AH18 Michael Clayton	2.00	5.00
AH19 Michael Irvin	3.00	8.00
AH20 Roy Williams S	2.00	5.00
AH21 Steve Young	4.00	10.00
AH22 Steven Jackson	2.00	5.00
AH23 Terrell Davis	2.50	6.00
AH24 Troy Aikman	4.00	10.00
AH25 Walter Payton	8.00	20.00

2005 Absolute Memorabilia Absolute Patches

STATED PRINT RUN 25 SER.#'d SETS
UNPRICED SPECTRUM PRINT RUN 1

Card	Low	High
1 Barry Sanders	20.00	50.00
2 Ben Roethlisberger	20.00	50.00
3 Bo Jackson	15.00	40.00
4 Brett Favre	25.00	60.00
5 Brian Urlacher	12.00	30.00
6 Chad Pennington	8.00	20.00
7 Dan Marino	25.00	60.00
8 Donovan McNabb	10.00	25.00
9 Edgerrin James	10.00	25.00
10 Eli Manning	20.00	50.00
11 Jerry Rice	25.00	60.00
12 Joe Montana	40.00	100.00
13 John Elway	20.00	50.00
14 Julius Jones	8.00	20.00
15 Kevin Jones	8.00	20.00
16 LaDainian Tomlinson	12.00	30.00
17 Michael Irvin	12.00	30.00
18 Peyton Manning	30.00	80.00
19 Priest Holmes	8.00	20.00
20 Randy Moss	10.00	25.00
21 Steve Young	15.00	40.00
22 Terrell Davis	10.00	25.00
23 Tom Brady	50.00	125.00
24 Troy Aikman	15.00	40.00
25 Walter Payton	30.00	80.00

2005 Absolute Memorabilia Canton Absolutes Silver

SILVER PRINT RUN 250 SER.#'d SETS
*GOLD/150: .5X TO 1.2X SILVER
*SPECTRUM/25: 1.2X TO 3X SILVER

Card	Low	High
1 Chad Pennington	.75	2.00
2 Curtis Martin	1.00	2.50
3 Dan Marino	2.50	6.00
4 David Carr	.75	2.00
5 Deion Sanders	1.00	2.50
6 Donovan McNabb	1.00	2.50
7 Drew Bledsoe	1.00	2.50
8 Earl Campbell	1.25	3.00
9 Eli Manning	2.00	5.00
10 Jerry Rice	2.50	6.00
11 Joe Montana	4.00	10.00
12 Joe Namath	2.00	5.00
13 John Elway	2.00	5.00
14 Junior Seau	1.00	2.50
15 Marvin Harrison	1.00	2.50
16 Michael Irvin	1.25	3.00
17 Michael Vick	1.00	2.50
18 Peyton Manning	3.00	8.00
19 Priest Holmes	.75	2.00
20 Randy Moss	1.00	2.50
21 Ray Lewis	1.25	3.00
22 Steve McNair	1.00	2.50
23 Steve Young	1.50	4.00
24 Troy Aikman	1.50	4.00
25 Walter Payton	3.00	8.00

2005 Absolute Memorabilia Canton Absolutes Jersey Bronze

BRONZE PRINT RUN 150 SER.#'d SETS
*PRIME/25: .8X TO 2X BASIC JSY/150
UNPRICED SPECTRUM PRINT RUN 1

Card	Low	High
1 Chad Pennington	2.50	6.00
2 Curtis Martin	3.00	8.00
3 Dan Marino	10.00	25.00
4 David Carr	2.50	6.00
5 Deion Sanders	3.00	8.00
6 Donovan McNabb	3.00	8.00
7 Drew Bledsoe	3.00	8.00
8 Earl Campbell	5.00	12.00
9 Eli Manning	6.00	15.00
10 Jerry Rice	8.00	20.00
11 Joe Montana	15.00	40.00
12 Joe Namath	8.00	20.00
13 John Elway	8.00	20.00
14 Junior Seau	3.00	8.00
15 Marvin Harrison	3.00	8.00
16 Michael Irvin	4.00	10.00
17 Michael Vick	3.00	8.00
18 Peyton Manning	10.00	25.00

19 Priest Holmes 2.50 6.00
20 Randy Moss 3.00 8.00
21 Ray Lewis 4.00 10.00
22 Steve McNair 3.00 8.00
23 Steve Young 6.00 15.00
24 Troy Aikman 6.00 15.00
25 Walter Payton 12.00 30.00

2005 Absolute Memorabilia Leather

LEATHER PRINT RUN 250 SER.#'d SETS
*LACES/25: .8X TO 2X LEATHER/250
RANDOM INSERTS IN RETAIL PACKS
1 LaDainian Tomlinson 4.00 10.00
2 Rod Smith 3.00 8.00
3 Tim Brown 4.00 10.00
4 Jerry Porter 2.50 6.00
5 Tiki Barber 3.00 8.00
6 Amani Toomer 2.50 6.00
7 Eric Moulds 2.50 6.00
8 Michael Vick 3.00 8.00
9 Josh McCown 3.00 8.00
10 Anquan Boldin 2.50 6.00
11 Shaun Alexander 2.50 6.00
12 Darrell Jackson 2.50 6.00
13 Terrell Owens 3.00 8.00
14 Brian Urlacher 4.00 10.00
15 Zach Thomas 3.00 8.00
16 Chris Chambers 2.50 6.00
17 Keyshawn Johnson 3.00 8.00
18 Chad Johnson 2.50 6.00
19 Corey Dillon 2.50 6.00
20 Peyton Manning 10.00 25.00
21 Marvin Harrison 3.00 8.00
22 LaVar Arrington 2.50 6.00
23 Tom Brady 15.00 40.00
24 Priest Holmes 2.50 6.00
25 Trent Green 2.50 6.00
26 Tony Gonzalez 3.00 8.00
27 Jerry Rice 8.00 20.00
28 Donovan McNabb 3.00 8.00
29 Torry Holt 3.00 8.00
30 Kurt Warner 3.00 8.00
31 Aaron Brooks 2.50 6.00
32 Deuce McAllister 3.00 8.00
33 Joe Horn 2.50 6.00
34 Reggie Wayne 3.00 8.00
35 Charles Woodson 4.00 10.00
36 Curtis Martin 3.00 8.00
37 Duce Staley 2.50 6.00
38 Daunte Culpepper 3.00 8.00
39 Ray Lewis 4.00 10.00
40 Drew Brees 4.00 10.00
41 Larry Fitzgerald 4.00 10.00
42 Hines Ward 3.00 8.00
43 Steve McNair 3.00 8.00
44 Marshall Faulk 3.00 8.00
45 Isaac Bruce 4.00 10.00
46 Freddie Mitchell 2.50 6.00
47 Travis Henry 2.50 6.00
48 Muhsin Muhammad 2.50 6.00
49 Jimmy Smith 3.00 8.00
50 Jerome Bettis 6.00 15.00

2005 Absolute Memorabilia Marks of Fame Silver

SILVER PRINT RUN 250 SER.#'d SETS
*GOLD/150: .5X TO 1.2X SILVER/250
*SPECTRUM/25: 1.2X TO 3X SILVER/250
1 Antonio Gates 2.50 6.00
2 Ben Roethlisberger 4.00 10.00
3 Brian Westbrook 1.50 4.00
4 Chad Johnson 1.50 4.00
5 Domanick Davis 1.50 4.00
6 Hines Ward 2.00 5.00
7 Rudi Johnson 1.50 4.00
8 Chris Brown 1.50 4.00
9 Tatum Bell 1.50 4.00
10 Michael Vick 2.00 5.00
11 Tom Brady 10.00 25.00
12 Willis McGahee 1.50 4.00
13 Ickey Woods 2.00 5.00
14 Earl Campbell 3.00 8.00
15 Joe Namath 5.00 12.00
16 Alex Smith QB 3.00 8.00
17 Troy Williamson .75 2.00
18 Ronnie Brown 1.00 2.50
19 Cadillac Williams .75 2.00
20 J.J. Arrington 1.00 2.50
21 Jason Campbell .75 2.00
22 Mark Clayton .75 2.00
23 Reggie Brown .75 2.00
24 Roscoe Parrish .75 2.00
25 Roddy White 1.25 3.00

2005 Absolute Memorabilia Marks of Fame Material Prime

PRIME PRINT RUN 25 SER.#'d SETS
*BASIC JSY/150: .15X TO .4X PRIME/25
UNPRICED SPECTRUM PRINT RUN 1 SET
1 Antonio Gates 10.00 25.00
2 Ben Roethlisberger 15.00 40.00
3 Brian Westbrook 6.00 15.00
4 Chad Johnson 6.00 15.00
5 Domanick Davis 6.00 15.00
6 Hines Ward 8.00 20.00
7 Rudi Johnson 6.00 15.00
8 Chris Brown 6.00 15.00
9 Tatum Bell 6.00 15.00
10 Michael Vick 8.00 20.00
11 Tom Brady 40.00 100.00
12 Willis McGahee 6.00 15.00
13 Ickey Woods 8.00 20.00
14 Earl Campbell 12.00 30.00
15 Joe Namath 12.00 30.00
16 Alex Smith QB 20.00 50.00
17 Troy Williamson 5.00 12.00
18 Ronnie Brown 6.00 15.00
19 Cadillac Williams 5.00 12.00
20 J.J. Arrington 6.00 15.00
21 Jason Campbell 5.00 12.00
22 Mark Clayton 5.00 12.00
23 Reggie Brown 5.00 12.00
24 Roscoe Parrish 5.00 12.00
25 Roddy White 8.00 20.00

2005 Absolute Memorabilia Marks of Fame Material Autographs

STATED PRINT RUN 15-300
*PRIME/25: .6X TO 1.5X BASE AU/150-300
*PRIME/25: .5X TO 1.2X BASE AU/50-100
PRIME PRINT RUN 10-25
UNPRICED PRIME SPECT.PRINT RUN 1
1 Antonio Gates/300 10.00 25.00
2 Ben Roethlisberger/50 75.00 150.00
3 Brian Westbrook/200 8.00 20.00
4 Chad Johnson/150 8.00 20.00
5 Domanick Davis/300 8.00 20.00
6 Hines Ward/150 30.00 80.00
7 Rudi Johnson/250 8.00 20.00
8 Chris Brown/250 8.00 20.00
9 Tatum Bell/300 8.00 20.00
10 Michael Vick/100 15.00 40.00
11 Tom Brady/15 150.00 300.00
12 Willis McGahee/100 8.00 20.00
13 Ickey Woods/300 8.00 20.00
14 Earl Campbell/100 15.00 40.00
15 Joe Namath/150 30.00 80.00
16 Alex Smith QB/150 20.00 50.00
17 Troy Williamson/250 6.00 15.00
18 Ronnie Brown/300 8.00 20.00
19 Cadillac Williams/300 6.00 15.00
20 J.J. Arrington/300 8.00 20.00
21 Jason Campbell/300 6.00 15.00
22 Mark Clayton/300 6.00 15.00
23 Reggie Brown/200 6.00 15.00
24 Roscoe Parrish/200 6.00 15.00
25 Roddy White/200 10.00 25.00

2005 Absolute Memorabilia National Treasures Jerseys

STATED PRINT RUN 50 SER.#'d SETS
*PRIME/25: .6X TO 1.5X BASIC JSY/50
UNPRICED SPECT.PRINT RUN 10
1 Montana/Brady/Aikman 25.00 50.00
2 Young/Vick/McNabb 10.00 25.00
3 B.Sanders/Tomlin/K.Jones 12.00 30.00
4 Marino/Manning/Manning 20.00 50.00
5 Culpepper/McNair/Leftwich 6.00 15.00
6 Allen/Holmes/James 8.00 20.00
7 Bo/J.Lewis/Ru.Jhnsn 10.00 25.00
8 Dickerson/Faulk/S.Jcksn 6.00 15.00
9 Campbell/George/Davis 8.00 20.00
10 Elway/Favre/Brady 15.00 40.00
11 Rice/Harrison/Holt 15.00 40.00
12 Irvin/R.Moss/T.Owens 10.00 25.00
13 Namath/Penning/Roethls 15.00 40.00
14 Green/Bulger/Hasselbeck 5.00 12.00
15 J.Wlkr/Ro.Will.WR/Mi.Clytn 5.00 12.00
16 Ward/Ch.John/A.John 6.00 15.00
17 Green/Alexander/McAllister 6.00 15.00
18 Dorsett/J.Jones/C.Martin 8.00 20.00
19 Carr/Palmer/Boller 6.00 15.00
20 Plummer/Delhomme/Brees 8.00 20.00
21 R.Lewis/Urlach/Arring 8.00 20.00
22 Dillon/McGahee/Westbrook 5.00 12.00
23 Riggins/Davis/Portis 6.00 15.00
24 J.Brown/Payton/B.Sanders 20.00 50.00
25 Deion/Ro.Will.S/Newman 12.00 30.00
26 Montana/Rice/Young 25.00 60.00
27 Aikman/Dorsett/Irvin 10.00 25.00
28 Vick/McNabb/Culpepper 6.00 15.00
29 Elway/Marino/Roethlis 15.00 40.00
30 Namath/Favre/Manning 20.00 50.00

2005 Absolute Memorabilia Rookie Jerseys

STATED ODDS 1:8 SPECIAL RETAIL
1 Ronnie Brown 2.00 5.00
2 Troy Williamson 1.50 4.00
3 Carlos Rogers 2.50 6.00
4 Matt Jones 1.50 4.00
5 Jason Campbell 1.50 4.00
6 Roddy White 2.50 6.00
7 Terrence Murphy 1.50 4.00
8 Vincent Jackson 2.50 6.00
9 Charlie Frye 1.50 4.00
10 Ciatrick Fason 1.50 4.00

2005 Absolute Memorabilia Rookie Premiere Materials Oversize

*SINGLES: .6X TO 1.5X BASIC CARDS
STATED PRINT RUN 50 SER.#'d SETS

2005 Absolute Memorabilia Rookie Premiere Materials Triple Spectrum

*TRIPLE/75: 1X TO 2.5X BASIC RPM RC

2005 Absolute Memorabilia Rookie Reflex Jersey Autographs

STATED PRINT RUN 100 SER.#'d ETS
1 Alex Smith QB 30.00 80.00
2 Braylon Edwards 10.00 25.00
3 Cadillac Williams 10.00 25.00
4 Charlie Frye 10.00 25.00
5 Ciatrick Fason 10.00 25.00
6 Courtney Roby 10.00 25.00
7 Frank Gore 20.00 50.00
8 Jason Campbell 10.00 25.00
9 Kyle Orton 10.00 25.00
10 Mark Bradley 10.00 25.00
11 Mark Clayton 10.00 25.00
12 Matt Jones 10.00 25.00
13 Reggie Brown 10.00 25.00
14 Roddy White 15.00 40.00
15 Ronnie Brown 12.00 30.00
16 Roscoe Parrish 10.00 25.00
17 Stefan LeFors 10.00 25.00
18 Terrence Murphy 10.00 25.00
19 Troy Williamson 10.00 25.00
20 Vincent Jackson 15.00 40.00

2005 Absolute Memorabilia Rookie Reflex Oversized Jersey

STATED PRINT RUN 25 SER.#'d SETS
*PRIME/10: .6X TO 1.5X BASIC INSERTS
1 Alex Smith QB 20.00 50.00
2 Braylon Edwards 5.00 12.00
3 Cadillac Williams 5.00 12.00
4 Charlie Frye 5.00 12.00
5 Ciatrick Fason 5.00 12.00
6 Courtney Roby 5.00 12.00
7 Frank Gore 10.00 25.00
8 Jason Campbell 5.00 12.00
9 Kyle Orton 5.00 12.00
10 Mark Bradley 5.00 12.00
11 Mark Clayton 5.00 12.00
12 Matt Jones 5.00 12.00
13 Reggie Brown 5.00 12.00
14 Roddy White 8.00 20.00
15 Ronnie Brown 6.00 15.00
16 Roscoe Parrish 5.00 12.00
17 Stefan LeFors 5.00 12.00
18 Terrence Murphy 5.00 12.00
19 Troy Williamson 5.00 12.00
20 Vincent Jackson 8.00 20.00

2005 Absolute Memorabilia Spectrum Silver Autographs

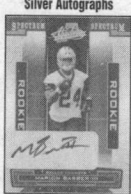

STATED PRINT RUN 15-249
UNPRICED PLATINUM PRINT RUN 1 SET
5 Alge Crumpler/99 6.00 15.00
10 Deion Sanders/35 50.00 80.00
11 Derrick Mason/125 6.00 15.00
18 J.P. Losman/99 8.00 20.00
25 Keary Colbert/99 6.00 15.00
43 Drew Bledsoe/35 20.00 40.00
47 Terence Newman/149 8.00 20.00
85 Nate Burleson/75 10.00 25.00
93 Aaron Brooks/75 8.00 20.00
95 Joe Horn/100 8.00 20.00
152 Shawne Merriman/249 8.00 20.00
154 Derrick Johnson/249 10.00 25.00
155 Travis Johnson/249 6.00 15.00
156 David Pollack/249 8.00 20.00
157 Erasmus James/249 10.00 25.00
161 Cedric Benson/99 15.00 40.00
162 Matt Roth/75 10.00 25.00
163 Dan Cody/99 8.00 20.00
164 Bryant McFadden/99 10.00 25.00
165 Chris Henry/99 8.00 20.00
167 Marion Barber/249 8.00 20.00
169 Jerome Mathis/249 6.00 15.00
170 Craphonso Thorpe/249 8.00 20.00
172 Darren Sproles/249 12.00 30.00
173 Fred Gibson/249 8.00 20.00
174 Roydell Williams/249 10.00 25.00
178 Adrian McPherson/199* 6.00 15.00
180 Aaron Rodgers/249 250.00 350.00
181 Cedric Houston/249 10.00 25.00
182 Mike Williams/150 10.00 25.00
183 Heath Miller/249 6.00 15.00
184 Dante Ridgeway/150 6.00 15.00
185 Craig Bragg/150 8.00 20.00
186 Deandra Cobb/99 8.00 20.00
187 Derek Anderson/150 8.00 20.00
188 Paris Warren/249 6.00 15.00
189 David Greene/249 8.00 20.00
190 Lionel Gates/249 8.00 20.00
191 Anthony Davis/249 6.00 15.00
193 Ryan Fitzpatrick/249 8.00 20.00
194 J.R. Russell/249 6.00 15.00
195 Jason White/249 8.00 20.00

2005 Absolute Memorabilia Spectrum Gold Autographs

*GOLD/25-100: .5X TO 1.2X SILVER AU
GOLD STATED PRINT RUN 10-100
CARDS SER.#'d UNDER 25 NOT PRICED
180 Aaron Rodgers/100 250.00 400.00

2005 Absolute Memorabilia Star Gazing Jersey Prime

STATED PRINT RUN 150 SER.#'d SETS
1 Larry Fitzgerald 3.00 8.00
2 Michael Vick AU 10.00 25.00
3 Warrick Dunn 2.00 5.00
4 Willis McGahee AU 8.00 20.00
5 Brian Urlacher AU 25.00 60.00
6 Carson Palmer 2.50 6.00
7 Chad Johnson AU 8.00 20.00
8 Julius Jones AU 8.00 20.00
9 Troy Aikman 4.00 10.00
10 Michael Irvin 3.00 8.00
11 Jake Plummer 2.00 5.00
12 Tatum Bell 2.00 5.00
13 Barry Sanders 5.00 12.00
14 Roy Williams WR AU 8.00 20.00
15 Kevin Jones 2.00 5.00
16 Ahman Green 2.50 6.00
17 Brett Favre 6.00 15.00
18 Andre Johnson AU 15.00 40.00
19 Domanick Davis AU 8.00 20.00
20 Edgerrin James 2.50 6.00
21 Marvin Harrison 2.50 6.00
22 Peyton Manning 8.00 20.00
23 Reggie Wayne AU 10.00 25.00
24 Byron Leftwich 2.00 5.00
25 Priest Holmes 2.00 5.00
26 Dan Marino 6.00 15.00
27 Nate Burleson 2.00 5.00
28 Randy Moss 2.50 6.00
29 Corey Dillon 2.00 5.00
30 Tom Brady 25.00 50.00
31 Eli Manning 5.00 12.00
32 Curtis Martin 2.50 6.00
33 Chad Pennington 2.00 5.00
34 Donovan McNabb 2.50 6.00
35 Terrell Owens 2.50 6.00
36 Ben Roethlisberger 5.00 12.00
37 Hines Ward AU 10.00 25.00
38 Antonio Gates AU 12.00 30.00
39 LaDainian Tomlinson 3.00 8.00
40 Joe Montana 10.00 25.00
41 Jerry Rice 6.00 15.00
42 Matt Hasselbeck 2.00 5.00
43 Shaun Alexander 2.00 5.00
44 Steven Jackson AU 8.00 20.00
45 Torry Holt 2.50 6.00
46 Michael Clayton AU 8.00 20.00
47 Chris Brown AU 8.00 20.00
48 Steve McNair 2.50 6.00
49 Clinton Portis 2.00 5.00
50 LaVar Arrington 2.00 5.00

2005 Absolute Memorabilia Star Gazing Jersey Oversized

OVERSIZED PRINT RUN 25 SER.#'d SETS
UNPRICED OS PRIME PRINT RUN 10
1 Larry Fitzgerald 8.00 20.00
2 Michael Vick 6.00 15.00
3 Warrick Dunn 5.00 12.00
4 Willis McGahee 5.00 12.00
5 Brian Urlacher 8.00 20.00
6 Carson Palmer 6.00 15.00
7 Chad Johnson 5.00 12.00
8 Julius Jones 5.00 12.00
9 Troy Aikman 10.00 25.00
10 Michael Irvin 8.00 20.00
11 Jake Plummer 5.00 12.00
12 Tatum Bell 5.00 12.00
13 Barry Sanders 12.00 30.00
14 Roy Williams WR 5.00 12.00
15 Kevin Jones 5.00 12.00
16 Ahman Green 6.00 15.00
17 Brett Favre 15.00 40.00
18 Andre Johnson 6.00 15.00
19 Domanick Davis 5.00 12.00
20 Edgerrin James 6.00 15.00
21 Marvin Harrison 6.00 15.00
22 Peyton Manning 20.00 50.00
23 Reggie Wayne 6.00 15.00
24 Byron Leftwich 5.00 12.00
25 Priest Holmes 5.00 12.00
26 Dan Marino 15.00 40.00
27 Nate Burleson 5.00 12.00
28 Randy Moss 6.00 15.00
29 Corey Dillon 5.00 12.00
30 Tom Brady 60.00 120.00
31 Eli Manning 12.00 30.00
32 Curtis Martin 6.00 15.00
33 Chad Pennington 5.00 12.00
34 Donovan McNabb 6.00 15.00
35 Terrell Owens 6.00 15.00
36 Ben Roethlisberger 12.00 30.00
37 Hines Ward 6.00 15.00
38 Antonio Gates 8.00 20.00
39 LaDainian Tomlinson 8.00 20.00
40 Joe Montana 25.00 60.00
41 Jerry Rice 15.00 40.00
42 Matt Hasselbeck 5.00 12.00
43 Shaun Alexander 5.00 12.00
44 Steven Jackson 5.00 12.00
45 Torry Holt 6.00 15.00
46 Michael Clayton 5.00 12.00
47 Chris Brown 5.00 12.00
48 Steve McNair 6.00 15.00
49 Clinton Portis 5.00 12.00
50 LaVar Arrington 5.00 12.00

2005 Absolute Memorabilia Team Tandems

STATED PRINT RUN 250 SER.#'d SETS
*SPECTRUM/150: .5X TO 1.2X BASIC INSERTS
1 A.Boldin/L.Fitzgerald 2.50 6.00
2 M.Vick/T.J.Duckett 2.00 5.00
3 J.Lewis/R.Lewis 2.50 6.00
4 W.McGahee/D.Bledsoe 2.00 5.00
5 J.Delhomme/J.Peppers 2.00 5.00
6 B.Urlacher/T.Jones 2.50 6.00
7 C.Palmer/C.Johnson 2.00 5.00
8 J.Jones/R.Williams S 1.50 4.00
9 J.Harrington/K.Jones 1.50 4.00
10 B.Favre/J.Walker 5.00 12.00
11 D.Carr/D.Davis 1.50 4.00
12 P.Manning/E.James 6.00 15.00
13 B.Leftwich/F.Taylor 1.50 4.00
14 P.Holmes/T.Gonzalez 2.00 5.00
15 D.Culpepper/R.Moss 2.00 5.00
16 T.Brady/C.Dillon 10.00 25.00
17 E.Manning/J.Shockey 4.00 10.00
18 C.Pennington/C.Martin 2.00 5.00
19 D.McNabb/T.Owens 2.00 5.00
20 D.Roethlisberger/H.Ward 4.00 10.00
21 L.Tomlinson/A.Gates 2.50 6.00
22 J.Rice/K.Barlow 5.00 12.00
23 M.Hasselbeck/S.Alexander 1.50 4.00
24 M.Alstott/M.Clayton 1.50 4.00
25 C.Portis/L.Arrington 1.50 4.00

2005 Absolute Memorabilia Team Tandems Material

STATED PRINT RUN 150 SER.#'d SETS
*PRIME/25: .8X TO 2X DUAL JSY/150
UNPRICED SPECTRUM PRINT RUN 1 SET
1 A.Boldin/L.Fitzgerald 4.00 10.00
2 M.Vick/T.J.Duckett 3.00 8.00
3 J.Lewis/R.Lewis 4.00 10.00
4 W.McGahee/D.Bledsoe 3.00 8.00
5 J.Delhomme/J.Peppers 3.00 8.00
6 B.Urlacher/T.Jones 4.00 10.00
7 C.Palmer/C.Johnson 3.00 8.00
8 J.Jones/R.Williams S 2.50 6.00
9 J.Harrington/K.Jones 2.50 6.00
10 B.Favre/J.Walker 12.00 30.00
11 D.Carr/D.Davis 2.50 6.00
12 P.Manning/E.James 10.00 25.00
13 B.Leftwich/F.Taylor 2.50 6.00
14 P.Holmes/T.Gonzalez 3.00 8.00
15 D.Culpepper/R.Moss 3.00 8.00
16 T.Brady/C.Dillon 15.00 40.00
17 E.Manning/J.Shockey 6.00 15.00
18 C.Pennington/C.Martin 3.00 8.00
19 D.McNabb/T.Owens 3.00 8.00
20 B.Roethlisberger/H.Ward 6.00 15.00
21 L.Tomlinson/A.Gates 4.00 10.00
22 J.Rice/K.Barlow 8.00 20.00
23 M.Hasselbeck/S.Alexander 2.50 6.00
24 M.Alstott/M.Clayton 2.50 6.00
25 C.Portis/L.Arrington 2.50 6.00

2005 Absolute Memorabilia Team Trios

STATED PRINT RUN 150 SER.#'d SETS
*SPECTRUM/100: .5X TO 1.2X BASIC INSERT
1 Boldin/Fitzgerald/McCown 3.00 8.00
2 Vick/Duckett/Dunn 2.50 6.00
3 Urlacher/Jones/Grossman 3.00 8.00
4 Carr/Davis/Johnson 2.50 6.00
5 Manning/James/Harrison 8.00 20.00
6 Leftwich/Taylor/Smith 2.50 6.00
7 Culpepper/Moss/Bennett 2.50 6.00
8 Brooks/McAllister/Stallworth 2.50 6.00
9 Eli/Shockey/Strahan 5.00 12.00
10 Pennington/Martin/Moss 2.50 6.00
11 McNabb/Owens/Westbrook 2.50 6.00
12 Roethlisberger/Ward/Staley 5.00 12.00
13 Gates/Tomlinson/Brees 3.00 8.00
14 Hasselbck/Alxandr/Jcksn 2.00 5.00
15 Portis/Arrington/Ramsey 2.50 6.00

2005 Absolute Memorabilia Team Trios Material

STATED PRINT RUN 100 SER.#'d SETS
UNPRICED PRIME PRINT RUN 10
UNPRICED SPECTRUM PRINT RUN 1
1 Boldin/Fitzgerald/McCown 5.00 12.00
2 Vick/Duckett/Dunn 4.00 10.00
3 Urlacher/Jones/Grossman 5.00 12.00
4 Carr/Davis/Johnson 4.00 10.00
5 Manning/James/Harrison 12.00 30.00
6 Leftwich/Taylor/Smith 4.00 10.00
7 Culpepper/Moss/Bennett 4.00 10.00
8 Brooks/McAllister/Stallworth 4.00 10.00
9 Eli/Shockey/Strahan 8.00 20.00
10 Pennington/Martin/Moss 4.00 10.00
11 McNabb/Owens/Westbrook 4.00 10.00
12 Roethlisberger/Ward/Staley 8.00 20.00
13 Gates/Tomlinson/Brees 5.00 12.00
14 Hasselbck/Alxndr/Jcksn 3.00 8.00
15 Portis/Arrington/Ramsey 4.00 10.00

2005 Absolute Memorabilia Team Quads

STATED PRINT RUN 100 SER.#'d SETS
*SPECTRUM/25: .8X TO 2X BASIC INSERT
1 McGhee/Bldsoe/Evns/Mlds 3.00 8.00
2 Delhomme/Pprs/Fstr/Dvis 3.00 8.00
3 Jns/Wilms S/Jhnsn/Nwmn 3.00 8.00
4 Fvre/Green/Wlkr/Ferguson 8.00 20.00
5 Lftwch/Taylr/Smth/Willms 3.00 8.00
6 Brady/Dillon/Law/Johnson 15.00 40.00
7 Eli/Shockey/Strahan/Tiki 6.00 15.00
8 McNbb/TO/Wstbrook/Krse 3.00 8.00
9 Ben/Ward/Staley/Bettis 8.00 20.00
10 Bulger/Holt/Jackson/Faulk 3.00 8.00

2005 Absolute Memorabilia Team Quads Material

STATED PRINT RUN 50 SER.#'d SETS
UNPRICED PRIME PRINT RUN 5
UNPRICED SPECTRUM PRINT RUN 1
1 McGah/Bldsoe/Evns/Mlds 8.00 20.00
2 Delhme/Pepp/Fost/S.Davis 8.00 20.00
3 Jns/R.Will./Keysh/Newmn 8.00 20.00
4 Favre/Green/Wlkr/Frgusn 25.00 60.00
5 Left/Taylr/J.Smth/Re.Will 8.00 20.00
6 Brady/Dillon/Law/Be.Jhn 25.00 60.00
7 Eli/Shockey/Strahan/Tiki 15.00 40.00
8 McNbb/TO/Wstbrk/Krse 8.00 20.00
9 Ben/Ward/Staley/Bettis 15.00 40.00
10 Bulger/Holt/Jackson/Faulk 8.00 20.00

2005 Absolute Memorabilia Tools of the Trade Red

RED PRINT RUN 250 SER.#'d SETS
*BLACK/100: .6X TO 1.5X RED/250
UNPRICED BLACK SPECT.PRINT RUN 10
*BLUE/150: .5X TO 1.2X RED/250
*BLUE SPECT/25: 1X TO 2.5X RED/250
*RED SPECT/50: .8X TO 2X RED/250
1 Aaron Brooks 1.50 4.00
2 Ahman Green 2.00 5.00
3 Amani Toomer 1.50 4.00
4 Andre Johnson 2.00 5.00
5 Anquan Boldin 1.50 4.00
6 Antwaan Randle El 1.50 4.00
7 Ashley Lelie 1.50 4.00
8 Ben Roethlisberger 4.00 10.00
9 Brett Favre 5.00 12.00
10 Brian Urlacher 2.50 6.00
11 Brian Westbrook 1.50 4.00
12 Byron Leftwich 1.50 4.00
13 Carson Palmer 2.00 5.00
14 Chad Johnson 1.50 4.00
15 Chad Pennington 1.50 4.00
16 Chris Brown 1.50 4.00
17 Chris Chambers 1.50 4.00
18 Clinton Portis 1.50 4.00
19 Corey Dillon 1.50 4.00
20 Curtis Martin 2.00 5.00
21 Dan Marino 5.00 12.00
22 Darrell Jackson 1.50 4.00
23 Daunte Culpepper 2.00 5.00
24 David Carr 1.50 4.00
25 Deuce McAllister 2.00 5.00
26 Domanick Davis 1.50 4.00
27 Donovan McNabb 2.00 5.00
28 Drew Bledsoe 2.00 5.00
29 Duce Staley 1.50 4.00
30 Earl Campbell 2.50 6.00
31 Edgerrin James 2.00 5.00
32 Eli Manning 4.00 10.00
33 Fred Taylor 1.50 4.00
34 Hines Ward 2.00 5.00
35 Ickey Woods 1.50 4.00
36 Jake Delhomme 1.50 4.00
37 Jake Plummer 1.50 4.00
38 Jamal Lewis 2.00 5.00
39 Javon Walker 1.50 4.00
40 Jeremy Shockey 1.50 4.00
41 Jerry Porter 1.50 4.00
42 Jerry Rice 5.00 12.00
43 Jevon Kearse 1.50 4.00
44 Jimmy Smith 2.00 5.00
45 Joe Montana 8.00 20.00
46 Joey Harrington 1.50 4.00
47 John Elway 4.00 10.00
48 Julius Jones 1.50 4.00
49 Julius Peppers 2.00 5.00
50 Kevin Jones 1.50 4.00
51 Keyshawn Johnson 2.00 5.00
52 Kyle Boller 1.50 4.00
53 LaDainian Tomlinson 2.50 6.00
54 Larry Fitzgerald 2.50 6.00
55 LaVar Arrington 1.50 4.00
56 Laveranues Coles 1.50 4.00
57 Lee Evans 2.00 5.00
58 Lee Suggs 1.50 4.00
59 Marc Bulger 1.50 4.00
60 Marcus Allen 2.50 6.00
61 Marshall Faulk 2.00 5.00
62 Marvin Harrison 2.00 5.00
63 Matt Hasselbeck 1.50 4.00
64 Michael Clayton 1.50 4.00
65 Michael Irvin 2.50 6.00
66 Michael Strahan 2.00 5.00
67 Michael Vick 2.00 5.00
68 Mike Alstott 1.50 4.00
69 Patrick Ramsey 2.00 5.00
70 Peter Warrick 1.50 4.00
71 Peyton Manning 6.00 15.00
72 Priest Holmes 1.50 4.00
73 Randy Moss 2.00 5.00
74 Ray Lewis 2.50 6.00
75 Reggie Wayne 2.00 5.00
76 Rex Grossman 1.50 4.00
77 Roy Williams S 1.50 4.00
78 Roy Williams WR 1.50 4.00
79 Rudi Johnson 1.50 4.00
80 Santana Moss 2.00 5.00
81 Shaun Alexander 1.50 4.00
82 Stephen Davis 1.50 4.00
83 Steve McNair 2.00 5.00
84 Steve Smith 2.50 6.00
85 Steve Young 3.00 8.00
86 Steven Jackson 1.50 4.00
87 T.J. Duckett 1.50 4.00
88 Terrell Davis 2.00 5.00
89 Terrell Owens 2.00 5.00
90 Thomas Jones 1.50 4.00
91 Tiki Barber 2.00 5.00
92 Todd Heap 1.50 4.00
93 Tom Brady 10.00 25.00
94 Tony Gonzalez 2.00 5.00
95 Trent Green 1.50 4.00
96 Troy Aikman 3.00 8.00
97 Walter Payton 6.00 15.00
98 Warrick Dunn 1.50 4.00
99 Willis McGahee 1.50 4.00
100 Zach Thomas 2.00 5.00

2005 Absolute Memorabilia Tools of the Trade Material Black

*BLACK UNSIGNED: .8X TO 2X RED
BLACK PRINT RUN 25 SER.#'d SETS
UNPRICED BLACK SPECT.PRINT RUN 1
1 Aaron Brooks AU 12.00 30.00
9 Brett Favre AU 150.00 300.00
12 Byron Leftwich AU 12.00 30.00
15 Chad Pennington AU 12.00 30.00
17 Chris Chambers AU 12.00 30.00
18 Clinton Portis AU 12.00 30.00
19 Corey Dillon AU 12.00 30.00
21 Dan Marino AU 125.00 250.00
24 David Carr AU 12.00 30.00
25 Deuce McAllister AU 15.00 40.00
30 Earl Campbell AU 20.00 50.00
32 Eli Manning AU 90.00 150.00
42 Jerry Rice AU 125.00 250.00
43 Jevon Kearse AU 12.00 30.00
45 Joe Montana AU 125.00 250.00
47 John Elway AU 100.00 200.00
52 Kyle Boller AU 12.00 30.00
56 Laveranues Coles AU 12.00 30.00
62 Marvin Harrison AU 15.00 40.00
63 Matt Hasselbeck AU 12.00 30.00
64 Michael Clayton AU 12.00 30.00
65 Michael Irvin AU 20.00 50.00
69 Patrick Ramsey AU 15.00 40.00
71 Peyton Manning AU 100.00 200.00
72 Priest Holmes AU 12.00 30.00
84 Steve Smith AU 20.00 50.00
85 Steve Young AU 60.00 120.00
88 Terrell Davis AU 15.00 40.00
95 Trent Green AU 12.00 30.00
96 Troy Aikman AU 50.00 100.00

2005 Absolute Memorabilia Tools of the Trade Material Blue

*BLUE UNSIGNED: .5X TO 1.2X RED JSYs
BLUE PRINT RUN 50 SER.#'d SETS
UNPRICED BLUE SPECTRUM PRINT RUN 5
1 Aaron Brooks AU 10.00 25.00
12 Byron Leftwich AU 10.00 25.00
13 Carson Palmer AU 20.00 50.00
15 Chad Pennington AU 10.00 25.00
17 Chris Chambers AU 10.00 25.00
18 Clinton Portis AU 10.00 25.00
24 David Carr AU 10.00 25.00
25 Deuce McAllister AU 12.00 30.00
30 Earl Campbell AU 15.00 40.00
32 Eli Manning AU 75.00 125.00
36 Jake Delhomme AU 10.00 25.00
43 Jevon Kearse AU 10.00 25.00
44 Jimmy Smith AU 12.00 30.00
45 Joe Montana AU 75.00 150.00
46 Joey Harrington AU 10.00 25.00
47 John Elway AU 75.00 150.00
48 Julius Jones AU 10.00 25.00
52 Kyle Boller AU 10.00 25.00
56 Laveranues Coles AU 10.00 25.00
57 Lee Evans AU 12.00 30.00
63 Matt Hasselbeck AU 10.00 25.00
64 Michael Clayton AU 10.00 25.00
65 Michael Irvin AU 15.00 40.00
72 Priest Holmes AU 10.00 25.00
76 Rex Grossman AU 10.00 25.00
77 Roy Williams S AU 10.00 25.00
84 Steve Smith AU 15.00 40.00
85 Steve Young AU 40.00 80.00
91 Tiki Barber AU 25.00 50.00
92 Todd Heap AU 10.00 25.00

2005 Absolute Memorabilia Tools of the Trade Material Red

RED PRINT RUN 100 SER.#'d SETS
UNPRICED RED SPECT.PRINT RUN 10
1 Aaron Brooks AU 8.00 20.00
2 Ahman Green AU 10.00 25.00
3 Amani Toomer 2.50 6.00
4 Andre Johnson 3.00 8.00
5 Anquan Boldin AU 8.00 20.00
6 Antwaan Randle El 2.50 6.00
7 Ashley Lelie 2.50 6.00
8 Ben Roethlisberger 6.00 15.00
9 Brett Favre 8.00 20.00
10 Brian Urlacher 4.00 10.00
11 Brian Westbrook 2.50 6.00
12 Byron Leftwich 2.50 6.00
13 Carson Palmer 3.00 8.00
14 Chad Johnson 2.50 6.00
15 Chad Pennington 2.50 6.00
16 Chris Brown 2.50 6.00
18 Clinton Portis 2.50 6.00
19 Corey Dillon 2.50 6.00
20 Curtis Martin 3.00 8.00
21 Dan Marino 15.00 40.00
22 Darrell Jackson 2.50 6.00
23 Daunte Culpepper 3.00 8.00
24 David Carr 2.50 6.00
25 Deuce McAllister 3.00 8.00
26 Domanick Davis 2.50 6.00
27 Donovan McNabb 3.00 8.00
28 Drew Bledsoe 3.00 8.00
29 Duce Staley 2.50 6.00
30 Earl Campbell 4.00 10.00
31 Edgerrin James 3.00 8.00
32 Eli Manning AU 60.00 100.00
33 Fred Taylor 2.50 6.00
34 Hines Ward 3.00 8.00
35 Ickey Woods 2.50 6.00
36 Jake Delhomme AU 8.00 20.00
37 Jake Plummer 2.50 6.00
38 Jamal Lewis 3.00 8.00
39 Javon Walker 2.50 6.00
40 Jeremy Shockey 2.50 6.00
41 Jerry Porter 2.50 6.00
42 Jerry Rice 8.00 20.00
43 Jevon Kearse AU 8.00 20.00
44 Jimmy Smith AU 10.00 25.00
45 Joe Montana AU 75.00 150.00
46 Joey Harrington 2.50 6.00
47 John Elway AU 75.00 150.00
48 Julius Jones 2.50 6.00
49 Julius Peppers 3.00 8.00
50 Kevin Jones 2.50 6.00
51 Keyshawn Johnson AU 10.00 25.00
52 Kyle Boller AU 8.00 20.00
53 LaDainian Tomlinson 4.00 10.00
54 Larry Fitzgerald 4.00 10.00
55 LaVar Arrington 2.50 6.00
57 Lee Evans AU 10.00 25.00
58 Lee Suggs 2.50 6.00
59 Marc Bulger 2.50 6.00
60 Marcus Allen 4.00 10.00
61 Marshall Faulk 3.00 8.00
62 Marvin Harrison 3.00 8.00
63 Matt Hasselbeck AU 20.00 40.00
64 Michael Clayton AU 8.00 20.00
65 Michael Irvin AU 20.00 40.00
66 Michael Strahan 3.00 8.00
67 Michael Vick 3.00 8.00
68 Mike Alstott 2.50 6.00
69 Patrick Ramsey AU 10.00 25.00
70 Peter Warrick 2.50 6.00
71 Peyton Manning 10.00 25.00
72 Priest Holmes 2.50 6.00
73 Randy Moss 3.00 8.00
74 Ray Lewis 4.00 10.00
75 Reggie Wayne 3.00 8.00
76 Rex Grossman AU 8.00 20.00
77 Roy Williams S AU 8.00 20.00
78 Roy Williams WR 2.50 6.00
79 Rudi Johnson 2.50 6.00
80 Santana Moss 3.00 8.00
81 Shaun Alexander 2.50 6.00
82 Stephen Davis 2.50 6.00
83 Steve McNair 3.00 8.00
84 Steve Smith AU 12.00 30.00
85 Steve Young 6.00 15.00
86 Steven Jackson AU 8.00 20.00
87 T.J. Duckett 2.50 6.00
88 Terrell Davis 3.00 8.00
89 Terrell Owens 3.00 8.00
90 Thomas Jones 2.50 6.00
91 Tiki Barber AU 12.00 30.00
92 Todd Heap AU 8.00 20.00
93 Tom Brady 15.00 40.00
94 Tony Gonzalez 3.00 8.00
95 Trent Green AU 8.00 20.00
96 Troy Aikman 6.00 15.00
97 Walter Payton 15.00 40.00
98 Warrick Dunn 2.50 6.00
99 Willis McGahee 2.50 6.00
100 Zach Thomas 3.00 8.00

2005 Absolute Memorabilia Tools of the Trade Material Double Red

RED PRINT RUN 100 SER.#'d SETS
*BLACK/25: .6X TO 1.5X RED/100
*BLUE/50: .5X TO 1.2X RED/100
*QUAD RED/25: 1X TO 2.5X DBL RED
UNPRICED QUAD BLACK PRINT RUN 1
UNPRICED QUAD BLUE PRINT RUN 5
*TRIPLE RED/50: .6X TO 1.5X DBL RED
UNPRICED TRIPLE BLACK PRINT RUN 5
UNPRICED BLUE PRINT RUN 10
1 Aaron Brooks 5.00 12.00
2 Ahman Green 6.00 15.00
3 Amani Toomer 5.00 12.00
4 Andre Johnson 6.00 15.00
5 Anquan Boldin 5.00 12.00
7 Ashley Lelie 5.00 12.00
9 Brett Favre 15.00 40.00
10 Brian Urlacher 8.00 20.00
12 Byron Leftwich 5.00 12.00
15 Chad Pennington 5.00 12.00
19 Corey Dillon 5.00 12.00
20 Curtis Martin 6.00 15.00
21 Dan Marino 15.00 40.00
23 Daunte Culpepper 6.00 15.00
24 David Carr 5.00 12.00
26 Domanick Davis 5.00 12.00
27 Donovan McNabb 6.00 15.00
30 Earl Campbell 8.00 20.00
31 Edgerrin James 6.00 15.00
34 Hines Ward 6.00 15.00
36 Jake Delhomme 5.00 12.00
37 Jake Plummer 5.00 12.00
38 Jamal Lewis 6.00 15.00
42 Jerry Rice 10.00 25.00
43 Jevon Kearse 5.00 12.00
45 Joe Montana 25.00 60.00
46 Joey Harrington 5.00 12.00
47 John Elway 12.00 30.00
51 Keyshawn Johnson 6.00 15.00
59 Marc Bulger 5.00 12.00
60 Marcus Allen 8.00 20.00
61 Marshall Faulk 6.00 15.00
63 Matt Hasselbeck 5.00 12.00
66 Michael Strahan 6.00 15.00
67 Michael Vick 6.00 15.00
68 Mike Alstott 5.00 12.00
70 Peter Warrick 5.00 12.00
72 Priest Holmes 5.00 12.00
73 Randy Moss 6.00 15.00
80 Santana Moss 6.00 15.00
81 Shaun Alexander 5.00 12.00
83 Steve McNair 6.00 15.00
84 Steve Smith 8.00 20.00
85 Steve Young 10.00 25.00
88 Terrell Davis 6.00 15.00
91 Tiki Barber 6.00 15.00
94 Tony Gonzalez 6.00 15.00
96 Troy Aikman 10.00 25.00
97 Walter Payton 20.00 50.00
100 Zach Thomas 6.00 15.00

2006 Absolute Memorabilia

This 281-card set was released in August, 2006. The set was issued in the hobby in four-card packs, with an $40 SRP, which came 4 packs to a box. Cards numbered 1-150 feature veterans in alphabetical team order based on where the player played in 2005 while 151-281 feature 2006 rookies. The rookies are broken down into three subsets: Cards numbered 151-220 are issued to a stated print run of 999 serial numbered sets, cards numbered 221-250 are signed by the player and those cards have a stated print run of 349 serial numbered cards (unless specifically noted in our checklist) and cards numbered 251-281 have a player-worn uniform swatch and those cards are issued to a stated print run of 849 serial numbered sets.

151-220 PRINT RUN 999 SER.#'d SETS
221-250 PRINT RUN 349 UNLESS NOTED
251-281 PRINT RUN 849 SER.#'d SETS
HOBBY PRINTED ON HOLOFOIL STOCK
1 Anquan Boldin .75 2.00
2 J.J. Arrington .75 2.00
3 Kurt Warner 1.00 2.50
4 Larry Fitzgerald 1.00 2.50
5 Marcel Shipp .75 2.00
6 Alge Crumpler 1.00 2.50
7 Michael Jenkins .75 2.00
8 Michael Vick 1.00 2.50
9 T.J. Duckett .75 2.00
10 Warrick Dunn .75 2.00
11 Derrick Mason .75 2.00
12 Jamal Lewis 1.00 2.50
13 Kyle Boller .75 2.00
14 Mark Clayton .75 2.00
15 Ray Lewis 1.25 3.00
16 Todd Heap .75 2.00
17 Eric Moulds .75 2.00
18 J.P. Losman 1.00 2.50
19 Josh Reed .75 2.00
20 Lee Evans 1.00 2.50
21 Willis McGahee .75 2.00
22 DeShaun Foster 1.00 2.50
23 Jake Delhomme .75 2.00
24 Julius Peppers 1.00 2.50
25 Keary Colbert .75 2.00
26 Stephen Davis .75 2.00
27 Steve Smith 1.25 3.00
28 Brian Urlacher 1.25 3.00
29 Cedric Benson .75 2.00
30 Rex Grossman .75 2.00
31 Thomas Jones .75 2.00
32 Muhsin Muhammad .75 2.00
33 Carson Palmer 1.00 2.50
34 Chad Johnson .75 2.00
35 Rudi Johnson .75 2.00
36 T.J. Houshmandzadeh .75 2.00
37 Charlie Frye 1.00 2.50
38 Dennis Northcutt .75 2.00
39 Reuben Droughns 1.00 2.50
40 Braylon Edwards .75 2.00
41 Drew Bledsoe 1.00 2.50
42 Jason Witten 1.00 2.50
43 Julius Jones .75 2.00
44 Keyshawn Johnson 1.00 2.50
45 Roy Williams S .75 2.00
46 Terry Glenn 1.00 2.50
47 Ashley Lelie .75 2.00
48 Jake Plummer .75 2.00
49 Rod Smith 1.00 2.50
50 Tatum Bell .75 2.00
51 Mike Anderson .75 2.00
52 Joey Harrington .75 2.00
53 Kevin Jones .75 2.00
54 Mike Williams .75 2.00
55 Roy Williams WR .75 2.00
56 Marcus Pollard .75 2.00
57 Aaron Rodgers 3.00 8.00
58 Brett Favre 2.50 6.00
59 Donald Driver 1.00 2.50
60 Javon Walker 1.00 2.50
61 Samkon Gado .75 2.00
62 Bubba Franks .75 2.00
63 Andre Johnson 1.00 2.50
64 Corey Bradford .75 2.00
65 David Carr .75 2.00
66 Domanick Davis .75 2.00
67 Jabar Gaffney .75 2.00
68 Edgerrin James 1.00 2.50
69 Dallas Clark .75 2.00
70 Marvin Harrison 1.00 2.50
71 Peyton Manning 3.00 8.00
72 Reggie Wayne 1.00 2.50
73 Brandon Stokley .75 2.00
74 Byron Leftwich .75 2.00
75 Fred Taylor .75 2.00
76 Jimmy Smith 1.00 2.50
77 Matt Jones .75 2.00
78 Ernest Wilford .75 2.00
79 Larry Johnson .75 2.00
80 Tony Gonzalez 1.00 2.50
81 Trent Green .75 2.00
82 Eddie Kennison .75 2.00
83 Dante Hall .75 2.00
84 Chris Chambers .75 2.00
85 Randy McMichael .75 2.00
86 Terrell Owens 1.00 2.50
87 Ronnie Brown 1.00 2.50
88 Zach Thomas 1.00 2.50
89 Marty Booker .75 2.00
90 Daunte Culpepper 1.00 2.50
91 Mewelde Moore .75 2.00
92 Nate Burleson .75 2.00
93 Troy Williamson .75 2.00
94 Corey Dillon .75 2.00
95 David Givens 1.00 2.50
96 Deion Branch .75 2.00
97 Tedy Bruschi 1.00 2.50
98 Tom Brady 4.00 10.00
99 Aaron Brooks .75 2.00
100 Deuce McAllister 1.00 2.50
101 Donte Stallworth .75 2.00
102 Joe Horn .75 2.00
103 Eli Manning 1.00 2.50
104 Jeremy Shockey .75 2.00
105 Plaxico Burress .75 2.00
106 Tiki Barber 1.00 2.50
107 Chad Pennington .75 2.00
108 Curtis Martin 1.00 2.50
109 Laveranues Coles .75 2.00
110 Justin McCareins .75 2.00
111 Kerry Collins .75 2.00
112 LaMont Jordan 1.00 2.50
113 Randy Moss 1.00 2.50
114 Jerry Porter .75 2.00
115 Brian Westbrook .75 2.00
116 Donovan McNabb 1.00 2.50
117 Reggie Brown .75 2.00
118 Ryan Moats .75 2.00
119 Antwaan Randle El .75 2.00
120 Ben Roethlisberger 1.50 4.00
121 Willie Parker 1.00 2.50
122 Hines Ward 1.00 2.50
123 Antonio Gates 1.25 3.00
124 Drew Brees 1.25 3.00
125 Keenan McCardell 1.00 2.50
126 LaDainian Tomlinson 1.25 3.00
127 Alex Smith QB 1.00 2.50
128 Brandon Lloyd .75 2.00
129 Frank Gore 1.00 2.50
130 Kevan Barlow .75 2.00
131 Darrell Jackson 1.00 2.50
132 Joe Jurevicius .75 2.00
133 Matt Hasselbeck .75 2.00
134 Shaun Alexander .75 2.00
135 Isaac Bruce 1.25 3.00
136 Marc Bulger .75 2.00
137 Steven Jackson .75 2.00
138 Torry Holt 1.00 2.50
139 Cadillac Williams 1.00 2.50
140 Chris Simms .75 2.00
141 Joey Galloway 1.00 2.50
142 Michael Clayton .75 2.00
143 Chris Brown .75 2.00
144 Drew Bennett 1.00 2.50
145 Steve McNair 1.00 2.50
146 Tyrone Calico .75 2.00
147 Clinton Portis .75 2.00
148 LaVar Arrington .75 2.00
149 Mark Brunell 1.00 2.50
150 Santana Moss 1.00 2.50
151 Greg Jennings RC 2.50 6.00
152 Joseph Addai RC 1.50 4.00
153 Erik Meyer RC 1.50 4.00
154 Drew Olson RC 1.50 4.00
155 Darrell Hackney RC 2.00 5.00
156 Paul Pinegar RC 1.50 4.00
157 Brandon Kirsch RC 2.00 5.00
158 Andre Hall RC 2.00 5.00
159 Taurean Henderson RC 1.50 4.00
160 Derrick Ross RC 2.00 5.00
161 Mike Bell RC 1.50 4.00
162 Wendell Mathis RC 2.00 5.00
163 Gerald Riggs RC 2.00 5.00
164 John David Washington RC 1.50 4.00
165 Devin Aromashodu RC 1.50 4.00
166 Ben Obomanu RC 2.00 5.00
167 David Anderson RC 2.00 5.00
168 Marques Colston RC 2.50 6.00
169 Kevin McMahan RC 2.00 5.00
170 Miles Austin RC 2.00 5.00
171 Martin Nance RC 1.50 4.00

172 Greg Lee RC 1.50 4.00
173 Hank Baskett RC 1.50 4.00
174 Anthony Mix RC 2.00 5.00
175 D'Brickashaw Ferguson RC 1.50 4.00
176 Kamerion Wimbley RC 2.00 5.00
177 Tamba Hali RC 2.50 6.00
178 Mathias Kiwanuka RC 2.50 6.00
179 Brodrick Bunkley RC 2.00 5.00
180 John McCargo RC 1.50 4.00
181 Claude Wroten RC 1.50 4.00
182 Gabe Watson RC 1.50 4.00
183 D'Qwell Jackson RC 1.50 4.00
184 Abdul Hodge RC 1.50 4.00
185 Ernie Sims RC 1.50 4.00
186 Chad Greenway RC 2.50 6.00
187 Bobby Carpenter RC 1.50 4.00
188 Manny Lawson RC 2.00 5.00
189 DeMeco Ryans RC 2.00 5.00
190 Rocky McIntosh RC 1.50 4.00
191 Thomas Howard RC 1.50 4.00
192 Jon Alston RC 1.50 4.00
193 A.J. Nicholson RC 1.50 4.00
194 Tye Hill RC 1.50 4.00
195 Antonio Cromartie RC 2.00 5.00
196 Johnathan Joseph RC 2.00 5.00
197 Kelly Jennings RC 2.00 5.00
198 Jimmy Williams RC 1.50 4.00
199 Ashton Youboty RC 1.50 4.00
200 Alan Zemaitis RC 1.50 4.00
201 Anwar Phillips RC 2.00 5.00
202 Jason Allen RC 2.00 5.00
203 Cedric Griffin RC 2.00 5.00
204 Ko Simpson RC 2.00 5.00
205 Pat Watkins RC 2.00 5.00
206 Donte Whitner RC 2.00 5.00
207 Bernard Pollard RC 2.00 5.00
208 Darnell Bing RC 2.00 5.00
209 De'Arrius Howard RC 2.50 6.00
210 Ethan Kilmer RC 2.00 5.00
211 Bennie Brazell RC 2.00 5.00
212 Haloti Ngata RC 2.00 5.00
213 Jeremy Bloom RC 1.50 4.00
214 Jay Cutler RC 2.00 5.00
215 Marcus Vick RC 1.50 4.00
216 Roman Harper RC 2.00 5.00
217 Anthony Smith RC 2.50 6.00
218 Daniel Bullocks RC 1.50 4.00
219 Eric Smith RC 2.00 5.00
220 Dusty Dvoracek RC 2.50 6.00
221 Brodie Croyle AU RC 4.00 10.00
222 Ingle Martin AU RC 5.00 12.00
223 Reggie McNeal AU RC 4.00 10.00
224 Bruce Gradkowski AU RC 5.00 12.00
225 D.J. Shockley AU RC 5.00 12.00
226 P.J. Daniels AU RC 4.00 10.00
227 Marques Hagans AU RC 4.00 10.00
228 Jerome Harrison RC 3.00 8.00
229 Wali Lundy AU RC 4.00 10.00
230 Cedric Humes AU RC 4.00 10.00
231 Quinton Ganther AU RC 4.00 10.00
232 Garrett Mills AU RC 5.00 12.00
233 Anthony Fasano AU RC 4.00 10.00
234 Tony Scheffler AU RC 6.00 15.00
235 Leonard Pope AU RC 6.00 15.00
236 David Thomas AU RC 4.00 10.00
237 Dominique Byrd AU RC 4.00 10.00
238 Jai Lewis AU/299 RC 5.00 12.00
239 Devin Hester AU RC 8.00 20.00
240 Willie Reid AU RC 5.00 12.00
241 Brad Smith AU RC 5.00 12.00
242 Cory Rodgers AU RC 4.00 10.00
243 Skyler Green AU RC 4.00 10.00
244 Domenik Hixon AU RC 6.00 15.00
245 Mike Hass AU RC 4.00 10.00
246 Jonathan Orr AU/299 RC 5.00 12.00
247 Delanie Walker AU/299 RC 8.00 20.00
248 Adam Jennings AU/299 RC 5.00 12.00
249 Jeff Webb AU/299 RC 5.00 12.00
250 Todd Watkins AU RC 4.00 10.00
251 Chad Jackson RPM RC 2.50 6.00
252 Laurence Maroney RPM RC 2.50 6.00
253 Tarvaris Jackson RPM RC 2.50 6.00
254 Michael Huff RPM RC 3.00 8.00
255 Mario Williams RPM RC 4.00 10.00
256 Marcedes Lewis RPM RC 2.50 6.00
257 Maurice Drew RPM RC 4.00 10.00
258 Vince Young RPM RC 2.50 6.00
259 LenDale White RPM RC 2.50 6.00
260 Reggie Bush RPM RC 4.00 10.00
261 Matt Leinart RPM RC 2.50 6.00
262 Michael Robinson RPM RC 2.50 6.00
263 Vernon Davis RPM RC 3.00 8.00
264 Brandon Williams RPM RC 2.50 6.00
265 Derek Hagan RPM RC 3.00 8.00
266 Jason Avant RPM RC 2.50 6.00
267 Brandon Marshall RPM RC 5.00 12.00
268 Omar Jacobs RPM RC 2.50 6.00
269 Santonio Holmes RPM RC 3.00 8.00
270 Jerious Norwood RPM RC 2.50 6.00
271 Demetrius Williams RPM RC 2.50 6.00
272 Sinorice Moss RPM RC 2.50 6.00
273 Leon Washington RPM RC 2.50 6.00
274 Kellen Clemens RPM RC 2.50 6.00
275 A.J. Hawk RPM RC 3.00 8.00
276 Maurice Stovall RPM RC 2.50 6.00
277 DeAngelo Williams RPM RC 3.00 8.00
278 Charlie Whitehurst RPM RC 2.50 6.00
279 Travis Wilson RPM RC 2.50 6.00
280 Joe Klopfenstein RPM RC 2.50 6.00
281 Brian Calhoun RPM RC 2.50 6.00

2006 Absolute Memorabilia Retail

COMPLETE SET (150) 10.00 25.00
*SINGLES: .1X TO .25X BASIC CARDS
RETAIL PRINTED ON WHITE STOCK

2006 Absolute Memorabilia Spectrum Silver Retail

*VETS 1-150: 1X TO 2.5X BASIC CARDS
*ROOKIES 151-220: .6X TO 1.5X
RANDOM INSERTS IN RETAIL PACKS
STATED PRINT RUN 100 SER.#'d SETS

2006 Absolute Memorabilia Spectrum Blue Retail

*VETS 1-150: .8X TO 2X BASIC CARDS
*ROOKIES 151-220: .5X TO 1.2X
RANDOM INSERTS IN RETAIL PACKS
STATED PRINT RUN 250 SER.#'d SETS

2006 Absolute Memorabilia Spectrum Gold

*VETS 1-150: 2X TO 5X BASIC CARDS
*ROOKIES 151-220: 1.2X TO 3X
STATED PRINT RUN 25 SER.#'d SETS

2006 Absolute Memorabilia Spectrum Platinum

UNPRICED PLATINUM PRINT RUN 1

2006 Absolute Memorabilia Spectrum Red Retail

*VETS 1-150: .6X TO 1.5X BASIC CARDS
*ROOKIES 151-220: .4X TO 1X BASIC CARDS
RANDOM INSERTS IN RETAIL PACKS

2006 Absolute Memorabilia Spectrum Silver

*VETS 1-150: 1X TO 2.5X BASIC CARDS
*ROOKIES 151-220: .6X TO 1.5X
STATED PRINT RUN 100 SER.#'d SETS

2006 Absolute Memorabilia Absolute Heroes Silver

SILVER PRINT RUN 250 SER.#'d SETS
*GOLD/100: .5X TO 1.2X SILVER/250
*SPECTRUM/25: 1X TO 2.5X SILVER/250
1 Larry Fitzgerald 1.50 4.00
2 Michael Vick 1.50 4.00
3 Willis McGahee 1.25 3.00
4 Steve Smith 2.00 5.00
5 Carson Palmer 1.50 4.00
6 Julius Jones 1.25 3.00
7 Samkon Gado 1.25 3.00
8 Peyton Manning 5.00 12.00
9 Jimmy Smith 1.50 4.00
10 Larry Johnson 1.25 3.00
11 Ronnie Brown 1.50 4.00
12 Tom Brady 6.00 15.00
13 Eli Manning 1.50 4.00
14 Curtis Martin 1.50 4.00
15 Randy Moss 1.50 4.00
16 Donovan McNabb 1.50 4.00
17 Ben Roethlisberger 2.50 6.00
18 LaDainian Tomlinson 2.00 5.00
19 Alex Smith QB 1.50 4.00
20 Shaun Alexander 1.25 3.00
21 Steven Jackson 1.25 3.00
22 Cadillac Williams 1.50 4.00
23 Chris Brown 1.25 3.00
24 Clinton Portis 1.25 3.00
25 Marvin Harrison 1.50 4.00

2006 Absolute Memorabilia Absolute Heroes Material Autographs

STATED PRINT RUN 14-100
*PRIME/50: .5X TO 1.2X AUTO/100
*PRIME/50: .4X TO 1X AUTO/25
*PRIME/25: .6X TO 1.5X AUTO/100
*PRIME/25: .5X TO 1.2X AUTO/50
*PRIME/14-15: .5X TO 1.2X AUTO/25
UNPRICED PRIME SPECTRUM #'d TO 1
1 Larry Fitzgerald/100 25.00 50.00
2 Michael Vick/25 30.00 60.00
3 Willis McGahee/100 10.00 25.00
4 Steve Smith/100 15.00 40.00
6 Julius Jones/25 12.00 30.00
7 Samkon Gado/100 10.00 25.00
8 Peyton Manning/25 90.00 150.00
9 Jimmy Smith/14 12.00 30.00
10 Larry Johnson/100 15.00 40.00
11 Ronnie Brown/100 15.00 40.00
13 Eli Manning/25 60.00 120.00
16 Donovan McNabb/25 15.00 40.00
17 Ben Roethlisberger/25 90.00 150.00
18 LaDainian Tomlinson/25 30.00 60.00
19 Alex Smith QB/50 25.00 50.00
20 Shaun Alexander/25 12.00 30.00
21 Steven Jackson/100 15.00 40.00
22 Cadillac Williams/100 12.00 30.00
23 Chris Brown/25 12.00 30.00
24 Clinton Portis/25 12.00 30.00
25 Marvin Harrison/25 15.00 40.00

2006 Absolute Memorabilia Absolute Heroes Materials

STATED PRINT RUN 150 SER.#'d SETS
*PRIME/40-50: .6X TO 1.5X BASIC JERSEYS
*PRIME/25-30: .8X TO 2X BASIC JERSEYS
UNPRICED PRIME SPECTRUM #'d TO 1
1 Larry Fitzgerald 3.00 8.00
2 Michael Vick 3.00 8.00
3 Willis McGahee 2.50 6.00
4 Steve Smith 4.00 10.00
5 Carson Palmer 3.00 8.00
6 Julius Jones 2.50 6.00
7 Samkon Gado 2.50 6.00
8 Peyton Manning 10.00 25.00
9 Jimmy Smith 3.00 8.00
10 Larry Johnson 2.50 6.00
11 Ronnie Brown 3.00 8.00
12 Tom Brady 12.00 30.00
13 Eli Manning 3.00 8.00
14 Curtis Martin 3.00 8.00
15 Randy Moss 3.00 8.00
16 Donovan McNabb 3.00 8.00
17 Ben Roethlisberger 5.00 12.00
18 LaDainian Tomlinson 4.00 10.00
19 Alex Smith QB 3.00 8.00
20 Shaun Alexander 2.50 6.00
21 Steven Jackson 2.50 6.00
22 Cadillac Williams 3.00 8.00
23 Chris Brown 2.50 6.00
24 Clinton Portis 2.50 6.00
25 Marvin Harrison 3.00 8.00

2006 Absolute Memorabilia Absolute Patches Prime

STATED PRINT RUN 15-25
UNPRICED SPECTRUM PRINT RUN 1
1 Larry Fitzgerald 15.00 40.00
2 Michael Vick/15 20.00 50.00
3 Willis McGahee 12.00 30.00
4 Steve Smith 20.00 50.00
5 Carson Palmer 10.00 25.00
6 Julius Jones 12.00 30.00
7 Samkon Gado 12.00 30.00
8 Peyton Manning 50.00 120.00
9 Jimmy Smith 15.00 40.00
10 Larry Johnson 12.00 30.00
11 Ronnie Brown 15.00 40.00
12 Tom Brady 60.00 150.00
13 Eli Manning 15.00 40.00
14 Curtis Martin 15.00 40.00
15 Randy Moss 15.00 40.00
16 Donovan McNabb 15.00 40.00
17 Ben Roethlisberger/15 30.00 80.00
18 LaDainian Tomlinson 20.00 50.00
19 Alex Smith QB 15.00 40.00
20 Shaun Alexander 12.00 30.00
21 Steven Jackson 12.00 30.00
22 Cadillac Williams 15.00 40.00
23 Chris Brown 12.00 30.00
24 Clinton Portis 12.00 30.00
25 Marvin Harrison 15.00 40.00
26 Antonio Gates 20.00 50.00
27 Rudi Johnson 12.00 30.00
28 Tiki Barber 15.00 40.00
29 Domanick Davis 12.00 30.00
30 Anquan Boldin 12.00 30.00
31 Torry Holt 15.00 40.00
32 Warrick Dunn 12.00 30.00
33 Zach Thomas 15.00 40.00
34 Chad Johnson 12.00 30.00
35 Brian Urlacher 20.00 50.00
36 Trent Green 12.00 30.00
37 Santana Moss 15.00 40.00
38 Corey Dillon 12.00 30.00

2006 Absolute Memorabilia Canton Absolutes Silver

SILVER PRINT RUN 250 SER.#'d SETS
*GOLD/100: 2.5X TO 1.2X BASIC INSERTS
*SPECTRUM/25: 1X TO 2.5X BASIC INSERTS
1 Derrick Thomas 4.00 10.00
2 Reggie White 3.00 8.00
3 Walter Payton 6.00 15.00
4 Troy Aikman 3.00 8.00
5 Brett Favre 4.00 10.00
6 Shaun Alexander 1.25 3.00
7 Peyton Manning 5.00 12.00
8 Jerome Bettis 2.00 5.00
9 Tom Brady 6.00 15.00
10 Marshall Faulk 1.50 4.00
11 LaDainian Tomlinson 2.00 5.00
12 Jerry Rice 4.00 10.00
13 Ben Roethlisberger 2.50 6.00
14 Corey Dillon 1.25 3.00
15 Curtis Martin 1.50 4.00
16 Dan Marino 5.00 12.00
17 Eric Dickerson 2.00 5.00
18 Marcus Allen 2.00 5.00
19 Marvin Harrison 1.50 4.00
20 Donovan McNabb 1.50 4.00
21 Edgerrin James 1.50 4.00
22 Eli Manning 1.50 4.00
23 Isaac Bruce 2.00 5.00
24 Jeremy Shockey 1.25 3.00
25 John Elway 4.00 10.00

2006 Absolute Memorabilia Canton Absolutes Materials

STATED PRINT RUN 150 SER.#'d SETS
*PRIME/25: .8X TO 2X BASIC JERSEYS
UNPRICED SPECTRUM PRINT RUN 1
1 Derrick Thomas 15.00 30.00
2 Reggie White 8.00 20.00
3 Walter Payton 12.50 30.00
4 Troy Aikman 8.00 20.00
5 Brett Favre 8.00 20.00
6 Shaun Alexander 5.00 12.00
7 Peyton Manning 6.00 15.00
8 Jerome Bettis/57 6.00 15.00
9 Tom Brady 6.00 15.00
10 Marshall Faulk 3.00 8.00
11 LaDainian Tomlinson 4.00 10.00
12 Jerry Rice 6.00 15.00
13 Ben Roethlisberger 8.00 20.00
14 Corey Dillon 3.00 8.00
15 Curtis Martin 4.00 10.00
16 Dan Marino 12.50 30.00
17 Eric Dickerson 4.00 10.00
18 Marcus Allen 4.00 10.00
19 Marvin Harrison 4.00 10.00
20 Donovan McNabb 4.00 10.00
21 Edgerrin James 4.00 10.00
22 Eli Manning 6.00 15.00
23 Isaac Bruce 4.00 10.00
24 Jeremy Shockey 4.00 10.00
25 John Elway 8.00 20.00

2006 Absolute Memorabilia Canton Absolutes Spectrum Autographs

SERIAL #'d UNDER 25 NOT PRICED
7 Peyton Manning/25 60.00 100.00
21 Edgerrin James/50 12.50 30.00

2006 Absolute Memorabilia Marks of Fame Silver

SILVER PRINT RUN 250 SER.#'d SETS
*GOLD/100: .5X TO 1.2X SILVER
*SPECTRUM/25: 1X TO 2.5X SILVER
1 Barry Sanders 4.00 10.00
2 Boomer Esiason 2.00 5.00
3 Dan Marino 5.00 12.00
4 Eric Dickerson 2.00 5.00
5 Joe Montana 5.00 12.00
6 John Elway 4.00 10.00
7 John Riggins 2.00 5.00
8 Marcus Allen 2.00 5.00
9 Steve Largent 2.00 5.00
10 Terrell Davis 1.50 4.00
11 Troy Aikman 3.00 8.00
12 Warren Moon 2.00 5.00
13 Ben Roethlisberger 2.50 6.00
14 Brett Favre 4.00 10.00
15 Carson Palmer 1.50 4.00
16 Eli Manning 1.50 4.00
17 LaDainian Tomlinson 2.00 5.00
18 Michael Vick 1.50 4.00
19 Peyton Manning 5.00 12.00
20 Cadillac Williams 1.50 4.00
21 Larry Johnson 1.25 3.00
22 Shaun Alexander 1.25 3.00
23 Chad Johnson 1.25 3.00
24 Clinton Portis 1.25 3.00
25 Steve Smith 2.00 5.00
26 Vince Young .75 2.00
27 Matt Leinart .75 2.00
28 Kellen Clemens .75 2.00
29 Tarvaris Jackson .75 2.00
30 Omar Jacobs .75 2.00
31 Reggie Bush 1.25 3.00
32 Laurence Maroney .75 2.00
33 DeAngelo Williams 1.00 2.50
34 LenDale White .75 2.00
35 Maurice Drew 1.25 3.00
36 Brian Calhoun .75 2.00
37 Vernon Davis 1.00 2.50
38 Santonio Holmes 1.00 2.50
39 Chad Jackson .75 2.00
40 Sinorice Moss .75 2.00
41 Travis Wilson .75 2.00
42 Derek Hagan 1.00 2.50
43 Michael Robinson .75 2.00
44 Demetrius Williams .75 2.00
45 Mario Williams 1.25 3.00
46 A.J. Hawk 1.00 2.50
47 Michael Huff 1.00 2.50
48 Charlie Whitehurst .75 2.00
49 Brandon Marshall 1.50 4.00
50 Leon Washington .75 2.00

2006 Absolute Memorabilia Marks of Fame Material Autographs

BASE AUTO PRINT RUN 50-100
1 Barry Sanders/50 75.00 135.00
2 Boomer Esiason/50 12.00 30.00
3 Dan Marino/75 75.00 150.00
4 Eric Dickerson/75 12.00 30.00
5 Joe Montana/25 100.00 175.00
6 John Elway/50 75.00 150.00
7 John Riggins/30 20.00 40.00
8 Marcus Allen/75 12.00 30.00
9 Steve Largent/50 20.00 40.00
10 Terrell Davis/75 12.00 30.00
11 Troy Aikman/50 50.00 80.00
12 Warren Moon/50 20.00 40.00
13 Ben Roethlisberger/75 60.00 100.00
14 Brett Favre/75 100.00 200.00
15 Carson Palmer/75 12.00 30.00
16 Eli Manning/75 35.00 60.00
17 LaDainian Tomlinson/75 25.00 60.00
18 Michael Vick/75 20.00 50.00
19 Peyton Manning/75 60.00 120.00
20 Cadillac Williams/100 12.00 30.00
21 Larry Johnson/100 12.00 30.00
22 Shaun Alexander/100 12.00 30.00
23 Chad Johnson/100 12.00 30.00
25 Steve Smith/100 15.00 40.00
26 Vince Young/50 12.00 30.00
27 Matt Leinart/50 12.00 30.00
28 Kellen Clemens/100 12.00 30.00
29 Tarvaris Jackson/100 12.00 30.00
30 Omar Jacobs/100 8.00 20.00
31 Reggie Bush/50 6.00 15.00
32 Laurence Maroney/50 10.00 25.00
33 DeAngelo Williams/50 15.00 40.00
34 LenDale White/50 12.00 30.00
35 Maurice Drew/100 20.00 50.00
36 Brian Calhoun/50 8.00 20.00
37 Vernon Davis/50 12.00 30.00
38 Santonio Holmes/50 12.00 30.00
39 Chad Jackson/100 8.00 20.00
40 Sinorice Moss/50 10.00 25.00
41 Travis Wilson/100 8.00 20.00
42 Derek Hagan/100 8.00 20.00
43 Michael Robinson/100 8.00 20.00
44 Demetrius Williams/100 8.00 20.00
45 Mario Williams/100 12.00 30.00
46 A.J. Hawk/50 15.00 40.00
47 Michael Huff/100 8.00 20.00
48 Charlie Whitehurst/50 10.00 25.00
49 Brandon Marshall/50 12.00 30.00
50 Leon Washington/100 10.00 25.00

2006 Absolute Memorabilia Marks of Fame Material Autographs Prime

*PRIME/25: .6X TO 1.5X JSY AU/75-100
*PRIME/25: .5X TO 1.2X JSY AU/50
*PRIME/25: .4X TO 1X JSY AU/25-30
STATED PRINT RUN 10-25
1 Barry Sanders 100.00 175.00
3 Dan Marino 100.00 200.00
5 Joe Montana 100.00 175.00
6 John Elway 100.00 175.00
13 Ben Roethlisberger 75.00 150.00
14 Brett Favre 125.00 250.00
17 LaDainian Tomlinson 30.00 80.00
19 Peyton Manning 90.00 150.00
26 Vince Young 25.00 60.00
31 Reggie Bush 8.00 20.00

2006 Absolute Memorabilia Marks of Fame Materials

VET PRINT RUN 150 SER.#'d SETS
ROOKIE PRINT RUN 200 SER.#'d SETS
*PRIME/50: .6X TO 1.5X BASIC JERSEYS
*PRIME/25-30: .8X TO 2X BASIC JERSEYS
UNPRICED SPECTRUM PRINT RUN 1
1 Barry Sanders 8.00 20.00
2 Boomer Esiason 4.00 10.00
3 Dan Marino 12.50 30.00
4 Eric Dickerson 4.00 10.00
5 Joe Montana 12.50 30.00
6 John Elway 8.00 20.00
7 John Riggins 4.00 10.00
8 Marcus Allen 4.00 10.00
9 Steve Largent 4.00 10.00
10 Terrell Davis 4.00 10.00
11 Troy Aikman 8.00 20.00
12 Warren Moon 4.00 10.00
13 Ben Roethlisberger 8.00 20.00
14 Brett Favre 8.00 20.00
15 Carson Palmer 5.00 12.00
16 Eli Manning 6.00 15.00
17 LaDainian Tomlinson 4.00 10.00
18 Michael Vick 4.00 10.00
19 Peyton Manning 6.00 15.00
20 Cadillac Williams 3.00 8.00
21 Larry Johnson 4.00 10.00
22 Shaun Alexander 5.00 12.00
23 Chad Johnson 3.00 8.00
24 Clinton Portis 4.00 10.00
25 Steve Smith 4.00 10.00
26 Vince Young 8.00 20.00
27 Matt Leinart 5.00 12.00
28 Kellen Clemens 5.00 12.00
29 Tarvaris Jackson 4.00 10.00
30 Omar Jacobs 4.00 10.00
31 Reggie Bush 4.00 10.00
32 Laurence Maroney 5.00 12.00
33 DeAngelo Williams 6.00 15.00
34 LenDale White 4.00 10.00
35 Maurice Drew 5.00 12.00
36 Brian Calhoun 4.00 10.00
37 Vernon Davis 5.00 12.00
38 Santonio Holmes 5.00 12.00
39 Chad Jackson 3.00 8.00
40 Sinorice Moss 3.00 8.00
41 Travis Wilson 3.00 8.00
42 Derek Hagan 3.00 8.00
43 Michael Robinson 3.00 8.00
44 Demetrius Williams 3.00 8.00
45 Mario Williams 4.00 10.00
46 A.J. Hawk 6.00 15.00
47 Michael Huff 4.00 10.00
48 Charlie Whitehurst 4.00 10.00
49 Brandon Marshall 4.00 10.00
50 Leon Washington 3.00 8.00

2006 Absolute Memorabilia NFL Icons Materials

STATED PRINT RUN 50 SER.#'d SETS
*PRIME/25: .6X TO 1.5X BASIC JERSEYS
UNPRICED SPECTRUM PRINT RUN 5-10
1 John Elway 12.50 30.00
2 Troy Aikman 12.50 30.00
3 Dan Marino 20.00 50.00
4 Walter Payton 20.00 50.00
5 Joe Montana 20.00 50.00
6 Barry Sanders 12.50 30.00
7 Peyton Manning 10.00 25.00
8 Tom Brady 10.00 25.00
9 LaDainian Tomlinson 6.00 15.00
10 Shaun Alexander 8.00 20.00
11 Michael Vick 6.00 15.00
12 Willis McGahee 6.00 15.00
13 Chad Johnson 5.00 12.00
14 Julius Jones 6.00 15.00
15 Kevin Jones 6.00 15.00
16 Brett Favre 12.50 30.00
17 Andre Johnson 5.00 12.00
18 Jimmy Smith 5.00 12.00
19 Larry Johnson 6.00 15.00
20 Chris Chambers 5.00 12.00
21 Daunte Culpepper 6.00 15.00
22 Clinton Portis 6.00 15.00
23 Eli Manning 10.00 25.00
24 Chad Pennington 5.00 12.00
25 Randy Moss 6.00 15.00
26 Donovan McNabb 6.00 15.00
27 Ben Roethlisberger 15.00 40.00
28 Alex Smith QB 6.00 15.00
29 Torry Holt 6.00 15.00
30 Steve McNair 6.00 15.00
31 Jerome Bettis 8.00 20.00
32 Marvin Harrison 6.00 15.00
33 Tiki Barber 6.00 15.00
34 Hines Ward 6.00 15.00
35 Tony Gonzalez 6.00 15.00
36 Carson Palmer 8.00 20.00
37 Jake Delhomme 5.00 12.00
38 Brian Urlacher 6.00 15.00

2006 Absolute Memorabilia Rookie Jerseys

INSERTED IN SPECIAL RETAIL PACKS
1TE A.J. Hawk 3.00 8.00
2TE Brandon Marshall 5.00 12.00
3TE Brandon Williams 2.50 6.00
4TE Brian Calhoun 2.50 6.00
5TE Chad Jackson 2.50 6.00
6TE Charlie Whitehurst 2.50 6.00
7TE DeAngelo Williams 3.00 8.00
8TE Demetrius Williams 2.50 6.00
9TE Derek Hagan 3.00 8.00
10TE Jason Avant 2.50 6.00
11TE Jerious Norwood 2.50 6.00
12TE Joe Klopfenstein 2.50 6.00
13TE Kellen Clemens 2.50 6.00
14TE Laurence Maroney 2.50 6.00
15TE LenDale White 2.50 6.00
16TE Leon Washington 2.50 6.00
17TE Marcedes Lewis 2.50 6.00
18TE Mario Williams 4.00 10.00
19TE Matt Leinart 2.50 6.00
20TE Maurice Drew 4.00 10.00
21TE Maurice Stovall 2.50 6.00
22TE Michael Huff 3.00 8.00
23TE Michael Robinson 2.50 6.00
24TE Omar Jacobs 2.50 6.00
25TE Reggie Bush 4.00 10.00
26TE Santonio Holmes 3.00 8.00
27TE Sinorice Moss 2.50 6.00
28TE Tarvaris Jackson 2.50 6.00
29TE Travis Wilson 2.50 6.00
30TE Vernon Davis 3.00 8.00
31TE Vince Young 2.50 6.00

2006 Absolute Memorabilia Rookie Premiere Materials Autographs

STATED PRINT RUN 100 SER.#'d SETS
*SPECTRUM/50: .6X TO 1.5X BASIC AU/100
251 Chad Jackson 8.00 20.00
252 Laurence Maroney 8.00 20.00
253 Tarvaris Jackson 8.00 20.00
254 Michael Huff 10.00 25.00
255 Mario Williams 12.00 30.00
256 Marcedes Lewis 8.00 20.00
257 Maurice Drew 12.00 30.00
258 Vince Young 8.00 20.00
259 LenDale White 8.00 20.00
260 Reggie Bush 12.00 30.00
261 Matt Leinart 8.00 20.00
262 Michael Robinson 8.00 20.00
263 Vernon Davis 10.00 25.00
264 Brandon Williams 8.00 20.00
265 Derek Hagan 10.00 25.00
266 Jason Avant 8.00 20.00
267 Brandon Marshall 15.00 40.00
268 Omar Jacobs 8.00 20.00
269 Santonio Holmes 10.00 25.00
270 Jerious Norwood 8.00 20.00
271 Demetrius Williams 8.00 20.00
272 Sinorice Moss 8.00 20.00
273 Leon Washington 8.00 20.00
274 Kellen Clemens 8.00 20.00
275 A.J. Hawk 10.00 25.00
276 Maurice Stovall 8.00 20.00
277 DeAngelo Williams 10.00 25.00
278 Charlie Whitehurst 8.00 20.00
279 Travis Wilson 8.00 20.00
280 Joe Klopfenstein 8.00 20.00
281 Brian Calhoun 8.00 20.00

2006 Absolute Memorabilia Rookie Premiere Materials Oversize

*SINGLES: .6X TO 1.5X BASIC CARDS
STATED PRINT RUN 50 SER.#'d SETS
UNPRICED SPECTRUM PRIME PRINT RUN 10

2006 Absolute Memorabilia Rookie Premiere Materials Spectrum Prime

*SINGLES: .5X TO 1.2X BASIC CARDS
STATED PRINT RUN 100 SER.#'d SETS

2006 Absolute Memorabilia Spectrum Gold Autographs

*GOLD/50: .5X TO 1.2X SILVER AUTOS
*GOLD/25: .6X TO 1.5X SILVER AUTOS
SERIAL #'d UNDER 25 NOT PRICED
152 Joseph Addai/50 20.00 50.00
214 Jay Cutler/50 12.00 30.00

2006 Absolute Memorabilia Spectrum Silver Autographs

SERIAL #'d UNDER 25 NOT PRICED
UNPRICED PLATINUM PRINT RUN 1
6 Alge Crumpler/100 5.00 12.00
14 Mark Clayton/100 6.00 15.00
20 Lee Evans/100 5.00 12.00
27 Steve Smith/25 15.00 40.00
35 Rudi Johnson/92 6.00 15.00
36 T.J. Houshmandzadeh/100 6.00 15.00
50 Tatum Bell/100 6.00 15.00
61 Samkon Gado/100 8.00 20.00
66 Domanick Davis/30 6.00 15.00
69 Dallas Clark/100 6.00 15.00
79 Larry Johnson/25 15.00 40.00
96 Deion Branch/100 6.00 15.00
97 Tedy Bruschi/100 20.00 50.00
112 LaMont Jordan/100 6.00 15.00
117 Reggie Brown/100 8.00 20.00
121 Willie Parker/100 20.00 40.00
123 Antonio Gates/100 8.00 20.00
131 Darrell Jackson/100 6.00 15.00
144 Drew Bennett/67 6.00 15.00
151 Greg Jennings/125 6.00 15.00
152 Joseph Addai/125 15.00 40.00
153 Erik Meyer/100 6.00 15.00
154 Drew Olson/76 8.00 20.00
155 Darrell Hackney/70 8.00 20.00
156 Paul Pinegar/100 6.00 15.00
157 Brandon Kirsch/100 8.00 20.00
158 Andre Hall/100 10.00 25.00
159 Taurean Henderson/100 8.00 20.00
160 Derrick Ross/100 6.00 15.00
161 Mike Bell/100 10.00 25.00
162 Wendell Mathis/100 6.00 15.00
163 Gerald Riggs/50 10.00 25.00
165 Devin Aromashodu/100 8.00 20.00
166 Ben Obomanu/100 6.00 15.00
167 David Anderson/100 6.00 15.00
169 Kevin McMahan/100 6.00 15.00
170 Miles Austin/76 5.00 12.00
171 Martin Nance/100 6.00 15.00
172 Greg Lee/100 6.00 15.00
173 Hank Baskett/76 8.00 20.00
174 Anthony Mix/100 6.00 15.00
175 D'Brickashaw Ferguson/150 8.00 20.00
176 Kamerion Wimbley/150 8.00 20.00
177 Tamba Hali/150 8.00 20.00
178 Mathias Kiwanuka/150 10.00 25.00
179 Brodrick Bunkley/150 8.00 20.00
180 John McCargo/150 6.00 15.00
181 Claude Wroten/100 4.00 10.00
182 Gabe Watson/100 6.00 15.00
183 D'Qwell Jackson/100 6.00 15.00
184 Abdul Hodge/100 8.00 20.00
185 Ernie Sims/150
186 Chad Greenway/150 8.00 20.00
187 Bobby Carpenter/150 8.00 20.00
188 Manny Lawson/150 8.00 20.00
189 DeMeco Ryans/100 10.00 25.00
190 Rocky McIntosh/100 8.00 20.00
191 Thomas Howard/100 8.00 20.00
192 Jon Alston/100 8.00 20.00
193 A.J. Nicholson/100 4.00 10.00
194 Tye Hill/150 8.00 20.00
195 Antonio Cromartie/150 8.00 20.00
196 Johnathan Joseph/150 6.00 15.00
197 Kelly Jennings/150 8.00 20.00
198 Jimmy Williams/100 8.00 20.00
199 Ashton Youboty/100 8.00 20.00
200 Alan Zemaitis/100 8.00 20.00
201 Anwar Phillips/50 8.00 20.00
202 Jason Allen/150 8.00 20.00
203 Cedric Griffin/100 6.00 15.00
204 Ko Simpson/100 6.00 15.00
205 Pat Watkins/100 8.00 20.00
206 Donte Whitner/150 8.00 20.00
207 Bernard Pollard/100 6.00 15.00
208 Darnell Bing/100 8.00 20.00
209 De'Arrius Howard/100 8.00 20.00
210 Ethan Kilmer/100 8.00 20.00
211 Bennie Brazell/100 6.00 15.00
212 Haloti Ngata/150 8.00 20.00
213 Jeremy Bloom/100 8.00 20.00
214 Jay Cutler/125 10.00 25.00

2006 Absolute Memorabilia Star Gazing Materials

STATED PRINT RUN 100 SER.#'d SETS
*PRIME/50: .5X TO 1.2X BASIC JERSEYS
*PRIME OVERSIZED/25: .8X TO 2X BASIC JSYs
UNPRICED OVERSIZED SPECTRUM #'d TO 1
1 Chad Jackson 3.00 8.00
2 Laurence Maroney 3.00 8.00
3 Tarvaris Jackson 3.00 8.00
4 Michael Huff 4.00 10.00
5 Mario Williams 5.00 12.00
6 Marcedes Lewis 3.00 8.00
7 Maurice Drew 5.00 12.00
8 Vince Young 3.00 8.00
9 LenDale White 3.00 8.00
10 Reggie Bush 5.00 12.00
11 Matt Leinart 3.00 8.00
12 Michael Robinson 3.00 8.00
13 Vernon Davis 4.00 10.00
14 Brandon Williams 3.00 8.00
15 Derek Hagan 4.00 10.00
16 Jason Avant 3.00 8.00
17 Brandon Marshall 6.00 15.00
18 Omar Jacobs 3.00 8.00
19 Santonio Holmes 4.00 10.00
20 Jerious Norwood 3.00 8.00
21 Demetrius Williams 3.00 8.00
22 Sinorice Moss 3.00 8.00
23 Leon Washington 3.00 8.00
24 Kellen Clemens 3.00 8.00
25 A.J. Hawk 4.00 10.00
26 Maurice Stovall 3.00 8.00
27 DeAngelo Williams 4.00 10.00
28 Charlie Whitehurst 3.00 8.00
29 Travis Wilson 3.00 8.00
30 Joe Klopfenstein 3.00 8.00
31 Brian Calhoun 3.00 8.00

2006 Absolute Memorabilia Team Quads Silver

STATED PRINT RUN 100 SER.#'d SETS
*SPECTRUM: .6X TO 1.5X BASIC INSERTS
SPECTRUM PRINT RUN 25 SER.#'d SETS
1 Lsmn/McGhe/Mlds/Evans 2.50 6.00
2 Palmr/Rudi/Chad/Housh 2.50 6.00
3 Bldsoe/Jnes/Key.Jhn/R.Will 2.50 6.00
4 Favre/Rodgers/Driver/Green 8.00 20.00
5 Manning/Hrrisn/Jmes/Wayne 8.00 20.00
6 Brady/Dillon/Givens/Branch 10.00 25.00
7 Eli/Barber/Burress/Shockey 2.50 6.00
8 Roeth/Ward/Randle El/Parker 4.00 10.00
9 Brees/Tomlin/Gates/McCard 3.00 8.00
10 Bulger/Jackson/Holt/Bruce 3.00 8.00

2006 Absolute Memorabilia Team Quads Materials

STATED PRINT RUN 50 SER.#'d SETS
UNPRICED PRIME PRINT RUN 5
UNPRICED PRIME SPECTRUM PRINT RUN 1
1 Lsmn/McGhe/Mlds/Evns 12.00 30.00
2 Plmr/Rudi/Chad/Housh 12.00 30.00
3 Bldse/Jnes/Key.Jhn/R.Will. 12.00 30.00
4 Favre/Rodgers/Driver/Green 40.00 80.00
5 Manning/Hrrisn/James/Wyne 20.00 50.00
6 Brady/Dillon/Givens/Branch/29 20.00 50.00
7 Eli/Barber/Burress/Shockey 15.00 40.00
8 Roeth/Ward/Randle El/Parker 25.00 60.00
9 Brees/Tomlin/Gates/McCard 15.00 40.00
10 Bulger/Jackson/Holt/Bruce 12.00 30.00

2006 Absolute Memorabilia Team Tandems Silver

STATED PRINT RUN 250 SER.#'d SETS
*SPECTRUM: .5X TO 1.2X BASIC INSERTS
SPECTRUM PRINT RUN 100 SER.#'d SETS
1 M.Vick/W.Dunn 1.50 4.00
2 J.Losman/W.McGahee 1.50 4.00
3 J.Delhomme/S.Smith 2.00 5.00
4 C.Palmer/C.Johnson 1.50 4.00
5 D.Bledsoe/J.Jones 1.50 4.00
6 J.Plummer/T.Bell 1.25 3.00
7 J.Harrington/K.Jones 1.25 3.00
8 P.Manning/M.Harrison 5.00 12.00
9 B.Leftwich/J.Smith 1.50 4.00
10 T.Green/L.Johnson 1.25 3.00
11 C.Chambers/R.Brown 1.50 4.00
12 T.Brady/C.Dillon 6.00 15.00
13 E.Manning/T.Barber 1.50 4.00
14 C.Pennington/C.Martin 1.50 4.00
15 K.Collins/R.Moss 1.50 4.00
16 D.McNabb/B.Westbrook 1.50 4.00
17 Roethlisberger/H.Ward 2.50 6.00
18 D.Brees/L.Tomlinson 2.00 5.00
19 Hasselbeck/Alexander 1.25 3.00
20 S.Jackson/T.Holt 1.50 4.00
21 C.Williams/M.Clayton 1.50 4.00
22 S.McNair/D.Bennett 1.50 4.00
23 C.Portis/S.Moss 1.50 4.00
24 L.Fitzgerald/A.Boldin 1.50 4.00
25 T.Jones/C.Benson 1.25 3.00

2006 Absolute Memorabilia Team Tandems Materials

STATED PRINT RUN 55-100 SER.#'d SETS
*PRIME: .6X TO 1.5X BASIC JSY/100
*PRIME: .5X TO 1.2X BASIC JSY/50-75
PRIME PRINT RUN 25 SER.#'d SETS
UNPRICED PRIME SPECTRUM PRINT RUN 1
1 M.Vick/W.Dunn/100 5.00 12.00
2 J.Losman/W.McGahee/100 5.00 12.00
3 J.Delhomme/S.Smith/100 6.00 15.00
4 C.Palmer/C.Johnson/100 5.00 12.00
5 D.Bledsoe/J.Jones/75 6.00 15.00
6 J.Plummer/T.Bell/70 5.00 12.00
7 J.Harrington/K.Jones/55 5.00 12.00
8 P.Manning/M.Harrison/100 15.00 40.00
9 B.Leftwich/J.Smith/100 5.00 12.00
10 T.Green/L.Johnson/100 4.00 10.00
11 C.Chambers/R.Brown/100 5.00 12.00
12 T.Brady/C.Dillon/100 20.00 50.00
13 E.Manning/T.Barber/100 5.00 12.00
14 C.Pennington/C.Martin/75 6.00 15.00
15 K.Collins/R.Moss/100 5.00 12.00
16 D.McNabb/B.Westbrook/90 5.00 12.00
17 Roethlisberger/Ward/100 8.00 20.00
18 D.Brees/L.Tomlinson/100 6.00 15.00
19 M.Hasselbeck/S.Alexander/100 4.00 10.00
20 S.Jackson/T.Holt/100 5.00 12.00
21 C.Williams/M.Clayton/75 6.00 15.00
22 S.McNair/D.Bennett/50 6.00 15.00
23 C.Portis/S.Moss/100 5.00 12.00
24 L.Fitzgerald/A.Boldin/100 5.00 12.00
25 T.Jones/C.Benson/75 5.00 12.00

2006 Absolute Memorabilia Team Trios Silver

STATED PRINT RUN 200 SER.#'d SETS
*SPECTRUM: .5X TO 1.2X BASIC INSERTS
SPECTRUM PRINT RUN 50 SER.#'d SETS
1 Delhomme/Smith/Foster 2.50 6.00
2 Palmer/Johnson/Johnson 2.00 5.00
3 Bledsoe/Johnson/Jones 2.00 5.00
4 Manning/Harrison/James 6.00 15.00
5 Leftwich/Smith/Taylor 2.00 5.00
6 Green/Gonzalez/Johnson 2.00 5.00
7 Chambers/Brown/Thomas 2.00 5.00
8 Brady/Branch/Dillon 8.00 20.00
9 Manning/Burress/Barber 2.00 5.00
10 Pennington/Coles/Martin 2.00 5.00
11 Roethl/Ward/Parker 3.00 8.00
12 Brees/Gates/Tomlinson 2.50 6.00
13 Hsslbck/Jcksn/Alxnder 2.00 5.00
14 Bulger/Holt/Jackson 2.00 5.00
15 Vick/Crumpler/Dunn 2.00 5.00

2006 Absolute Memorabilia Team Trios Materials

STATED PRINT RUN 80-100
*PRIME/15: .6X TO 1.5X TRIO/80-100
UNPRICED PRIME SPECTRUM PRINT RUN 1
1 Delhomme/Smith/Foster 6.00 15.00
2 Palmer/Johnson/Johnson 5.00 12.00
3 Bledsoe/Johnson/Jones 5.00 12.00
4 Manning/Harrison/James 15.00 40.00
5 Leftwich/Smith/Taylor 5.00 12.00
6 Green/Gonzalez/Johnson 5.00 12.00
7 Chambers/Brown/Thomas 5.00 12.00
8 Brady/Branch/Dillon 20.00 50.00
9 Manning/Burress/Barber 5.00 12.00
10 Pennington/Coles/Martin 5.00 12.00
11 Roeth/Ward/Parker 8.00 20.00
12 Brees/Gates/Tomlinson 6.00 15.00
13 Hsslbck/Jcksn/Alxnder 5.00 12.00
14 Bulger/Holt/Jackson/80 5.00 12.00
15 Vick/Crumpler/Dunn 5.00 12.00

2006 Absolute Memorabilia Tools of the Trade Red

RED PRINT RUN 100 SER.#'d SETS
*BLACK: .5X TO 1.2X RED INSERTS
BLACK PRINT RUN 50 SER.#'d SETS
UNPRICED BLACK SPECTRUM PRINT RUN 5
*BLUE: .4X TO 1X RED INSERTS
BLUE PRINT RUN 75 SER.#'d SETS
UNPRICED BLUE SPECTRUM PRINT RUN 10
*RED SPECTRUM: .8X TO 2X RED INSERTS
RED SPECT.PRINT RUN 25 SER.#'d SETS
1 Aaron Brooks 1.50 4.00
2 Aaron Rodgers 6.00 15.00
3 Ahman Green 2.00 5.00
4 Alex Smith QB 2.00 5.00
5 Alge Crumpler 2.00 5.00
6 Amani Toomer 1.50 4.00
7 Andre Johnson 2.00 5.00
8 Anquan Boldin 1.50 4.00
9 Antonio Bryant 1.50 4.00
10 Antonio Gates 2.50 6.00
11 Antwaan Randle El 1.50 4.00
12 Ashley Lelie 1.50 4.00
13 Barry Sanders 5.00 12.00
14 Ben Roethlisberger 3.00 8.00
15 Bernard Berrian 1.50 4.00
16 Bethel Johnson 1.50 4.00
17 Boomer Esiason 2.50 6.00
18 Brandon Stokley 1.50 4.00
19 Brad Johnson 2.00 5.00
20 Brandon Lloyd 1.50 4.00
21 Brett Favre 5.00 12.00
22 Brian Urlacher 2.50 6.00
23 Brian Westbrook 1.50 4.00
24 Byron Leftwich 1.50 4.00
25 Cadillac Williams 2.00 5.00
26 Carson Palmer 2.00 5.00
27 Cedric Benson 1.50 4.00
28 Chad Johnson 1.50 4.00
29 Chad Pennington 1.50 4.00
30 Chris Chambers 1.50 4.00
31 Charles Rogers 2.00 5.00
32 Chris Brown 1.50 4.00
33 Clinton Portis 1.50 4.00
34 Corey Dillon 1.50 4.00
35 Curtis Martin 2.00 5.00
36 Dallas Clark 1.50 4.00
37 Dan Marino 6.00 15.00
38 Dante Hall 1.50 4.00
39 Daunte Culpepper 2.00 5.00
40 Darrell Jackson 2.00 5.00
41 David Carr 1.50 4.00
42 Derrick Brooks 1.50 4.00
43 David Givens 2.00 5.00
44 Deion Sanders 2.50 6.00
45 Derrick Mason 1.50 4.00
46 DeShaun Foster 1.50 4.00
47 Deuce McAllister 2.00 5.00
48 Domanick Davis 1.50 4.00
49 Donovan McNabb 2.00 5.00
50 Donte Stallworth 1.50 4.00
51 Drew Bennett 2.00 5.00
52 Drew Bledsoe 2.00 5.00
53 Drew Brees 2.50 6.00
54 Duce Staley 1.50 4.00
55 Edgerrin James 2.00 5.00
56 Eli Manning 2.00 5.00
57 Eric Dickerson 2.50 6.00
58 Eric Moulds 1.50 4.00
59 Fred Taylor 1.50 4.00
60 Herschel Walker 3.00 8.00
61 Hines Ward 2.00 5.00
62 Isaac Bruce 2.00 5.00
63 Ickey Woods 2.00 5.00
64 Jeff Garcia 1.50 4.00
65 J.P. Losman 1.50 4.00
66 Jabar Gaffney 1.50 4.00
67 Julius Jones 2.00 5.00
68 Jake Delhomme 1.50 4.00
69 Jake Plummer 1.50 4.00
70 Jamal Lewis 2.00 5.00
71 Jason Campbell 2.00 5.00
72 Jason Taylor 1.50 4.00
73 Javon Walker 2.00 5.00
74 Jeremy Shockey 1.50 4.00
75 Jerome Bettis 2.50 6.00
76 Jerry Rice 6.00 15.00
77 Jevon Kearse 1.50 4.00
78 Jimmy Smith 1.50 4.00
79 Joe Montana 10.00 25.00
80 Joey Harrington 1.50 4.00
81 John Elway 5.00 12.00
82 Kevin Jones 1.50 4.00
83 Junior Seau 2.50 6.00
84 Julius Peppers 2.00 5.00
85 Keenan McCardell 2.00 5.00
86 Keyshawn Johnson 2.00 5.00
87 LaDainian Tomlinson 2.50 6.00
88 LaMont Jordan 2.00 5.00
89 Larry Fitzgerald 2.00 5.00
90 LaVar Arrington 1.50 4.00
91 Laveranues Coles 1.50 4.00
92 Lee Evans 2.00 5.00
93 Marcel Shipp 1.50 4.00
94 Marc Bulger 1.50 4.00
95 Marcus Allen 3.00 8.00
96 Mark Brunell 2.00 5.00
97 Marshall Faulk 2.00 5.00
98 Marvin Harrison 2.00 5.00
99 Matt Hasselbeck 1.50 4.00
100 Matt Jones 1.50 4.00
101 Michael Bennett 1.50 4.00
102 Michael Clayton 1.50 4.00
103 Michael Pittman 1.50 4.00
104 Michael Strahan 2.00 5.00
105 Michael Vick 2.00 5.00
106 Muhsin Muhammad 1.50 4.00
107 Peyton Manning 6.00 15.00
108 Priest Holmes 1.50 4.00
109 Randy Moss 2.00 5.00
110 Ray Lewis 2.50 6.00
111 Reggie Brown 1.50 4.00
112 Reggie Wayne 2.00 5.00
113 Reggie White 4.00 10.00
114 Rex Grossman 1.50 4.00
115 Richard Seymour 1.50 4.00
116 Derrick Thomas 4.00 10.00
117 Rod Smith 2.00 5.00
118 Ronnie Brown 2.00 5.00
119 Roy Williams S 1.50 4.00
120 Rudi Johnson 1.50 4.00
121 Samkon Gado 1.50 4.00
122 Santana Moss 2.00 5.00
123 Shaun Alexander 1.50 4.00
124 Stephen Davis 1.50 4.00
125 Steve McNair 2.00 5.00
126 Steve Smith 2.50 6.00
127 Steve Young 4.00 10.00
128 Steven Jackson 1.50 4.00
129 T.J. Houshmandzadeh 1.50 4.00
130 Tatum Bell 1.50 4.00
131 Terrell Davis 2.50 6.00
132 Terrell Owens 2.00 5.00
133 Terry Glenn 2.00 5.00
134 Thomas Jones 1.50 4.00
135 Tiki Barber 2.00 5.00
136 Todd Heap 1.50 4.00
137 Tom Brady 8.00 20.00
138 Tony Gonzalez 2.00 5.00
139 Torry Holt 2.00 5.00
140 Trent Green 1.50 4.00
141 Troy Aikman 4.00 10.00
142 Troy Williamson 1.50 4.00
143 Tyrone Calico 1.50 4.00
144 Walter Payton 6.00 15.00
145 Warren Moon 3.00 8.00
146 Warren Sapp 2.00 5.00
147 Warrick Dunn 2.00 5.00
148 Willie Parker 2.00 5.00

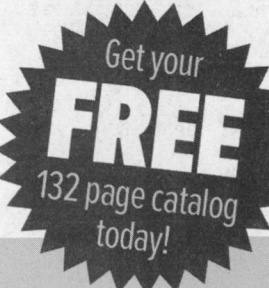

149 Willis McGahee 1.50 4.00
150 Zach Thomas 2.00 5.00

2006 Absolute Memorabilia Tools of the Trade Material Black Spectrum

*BLACK SPECTRUM/35-50: .5X TO 1.2X RED MATERIALS
SERIAL #'d UNDER 25 NOT PRICED
UNPRICED BLACK OVERSIZED PRINT RUN 1
14 Ben Roethlisberger/38 15.00 40.00

2006 Absolute Memorabilia Tools of the Trade Material Blue

*BLUE: .5X TO 1.2X RED MATERIALS
SERIAL #'d UNDER 25 NOT PRICED
UNPRICED BLUE OVERSIZED PRINT RUN 2-5
14 Ben Roethlisberger 12.50 30.00

2006 Absolute Memorabilia Tools of the Trade Material Red

RED STATED PRINT RUN 5-100
1 Aaron Brooks 2.50 6.00
2 Aaron Rodgers 20.00 40.00
3 Ahman Green 3.00 8.00
4 Alex Smith QB 3.00 8.00
5 Alge Crumpler 3.00 8.00
6 Amani Toomer/75 2.50 6.00
7 Andre Johnson 3.00 8.00
8 Anquan Boldin 2.50 6.00
10 Antonio Gates 4.00 10.00
11 Antwaan Randle El 2.50 6.00
12 Ashley Lelie 2.50 6.00
13 Barry Sanders 8.00 20.00
14 Ben Roethlisberger/28 20.00 50.00
15 Bernard Berrian 2.50 6.00
17 Boomer Esiason 4.00 10.00
19 Brad Johnson 3.00 8.00
20 Brandon Lloyd/37 4.00 10.00
21 Brett Favre 8.00 20.00
22 Brian Urlacher 4.00 10.00
23 Brian Westbrook 2.50 6.00
24 Byron Leftwich 2.50 6.00
25 Cadillac Williams 3.00 8.00
26 Carson Palmer 3.00 8.00
27 Cedric Benson 2.50 6.00
28 Chad Johnson 2.50 6.00
29 Chad Pennington 2.50 6.00
30 Chris Chambers 2.50 6.00
31 Charles Rogers 3.00 8.00
32 Chris Brown 2.50 6.00
33 Clinton Portis 2.50 6.00
34 Corey Dillon 2.50 6.00
35 Curtis Martin 3.00 8.00
36 Dallas Clark/75 2.50 6.00
37 Dan Marino 12.50 30.00
38 Dante Hall 2.50 6.00
39 Daunte Culpepper 3.00 8.00
41 David Carr 2.50 6.00
43 David Givens 3.00 8.00
44 Deion Sanders 3.00 8.00
47 Deuce McAllister 3.00 8.00
48 Domanick Davis 2.50 6.00
49 Donovan McNabb 3.00 8.00
50 Donte Stallworth 2.50 6.00
51 Drew Bennett 3.00 8.00
52 Drew Bledsoe 3.00 8.00
53 Drew Brees 4.00 10.00
54 Duce Staley 2.50 6.00
55 Edgerrin James 3.00 8.00
56 Eli Manning 3.00 8.00
57 Eric Dickerson 4.00 10.00
58 Eric Moulds 2.50 6.00
59 Fred Taylor 2.50 6.00
60 Herschel Walker 5.00 12.00
61 Hines Ward 3.00 8.00
62 Isaac Bruce 4.00 10.00
63 Ickey Woods 3.00 8.00
64 Jeff Garcia 2.50 6.00
65 J.P. Losman 3.00 8.00
67 Julius Jones 2.50 6.00
68 Jake Delhomme/82 2.50 6.00
69 Jake Plummer 2.50 6.00
70 Jamal Lewis 3.00 8.00
71 Jason Campbell 2.50 6.00
73 Javon Walker/42 4.00 10.00
74 Jeremy Shockey 2.50 6.00
76 Jerry Rice 10.00 25.00
78 Jimmy Smith 3.00 8.00
79 Joe Montana 15.00 40.00
80 Joey Harrington 2.50 6.00
81 John Elway 8.00 20.00
82 Kevin Jones 2.50 6.00
83 Junior Seau 4.00 10.00
84 Julius Peppers/22
85 Keenan McCardell 3.00 8.00
87 LaDainian Tomlinson 4.00 10.00
88 LaMont Jordan 3.00 8.00
89 Larry Fitzgerald 3.00 8.00
90 LaVar Arrington 2.50 6.00
91 Laveranues Coles 2.50 6.00
92 Lee Evans 3.00 8.00
93 Marcel Shipp/75 2.50 6.00
94 Marc Bulger 2.50 6.00
95 Marcus Allen 5.00 12.00
96 Mark Brunell 3.00 8.00
97 Marshall Faulk 3.00 8.00
98 Marvin Harrison 3.00 8.00
99 Matt Hasselbeck 2.50 6.00
100 Matt Jones 2.50 6.00
102 Michael Clayton 2.50 6.00
103 Michael Pittman 2.50 6.00
104 Michael Strahan 3.00 8.00
105 Michael Vick 3.00 8.00
106 Muhsin Muhammad 2.50 6.00
107 Peyton Manning 10.00 25.00
108 Priest Holmes 2.50 6.00
109 Randy Moss 3.00 8.00
110 Ray Lewis 4.00 10.00
111 Reggie Brown 2.50 6.00
112 Reggie Wayne 3.00 8.00
113 Reggie White 8.00 20.00
114 Rex Grossman 2.50 6.00
115 Richard Seymour 2.50 6.00
116 Derrick Thomas 12.00 30.00
117 Rod Smith 3.00 8.00
118 Ronnie Brown 3.00 8.00
119 Roy Williams S/77 2.50 6.00
120 Rudi Johnson 2.50 6.00
121 Samkon Gado 2.50 6.00
122 Santana Moss 3.00 8.00
123 Shaun Alexander 2.50 6.00
124 Stephen Davis 2.50 6.00
125 Steve McNair 3.00 8.00
127 Steve Young 6.00 15.00
128 Steven Jackson 2.50 6.00
129 T.J. Houshmandzadeh 2.50 6.00
130 Tatum Bell 2.50 6.00
131 Terrell Davis 3.00 8.00
132 Terrell Owens 3.00 8.00
134 Thomas Jones 2.50 6.00
135 Tiki Barber 3.00 8.00
136 Todd Heap 2.50 6.00
137 Tom Brady 12.00 30.00
138 Tony Gonzalez 3.00 8.00
139 Torry Holt 3.00 8.00
140 Trent Green 2.50 6.00
141 Troy Aikman/75 6.00 15.00
142 Troy Williamson 2.50 6.00
144 Walter Payton/75 10.00 25.00
145 Warren Moon/75 5.00 12.00
146 Warren Sapp 3.00 8.00
147 Warrick Dunn/68 4.00 10.00
148 Willie Parker 3.00 8.00
149 Willis McGahee 2.50 6.00
150 Zach Thomas 3.00 8.00

2006 Absolute Memorabilia Tools of the Trade Material Red Oversize

*RED OVER: .8X TO 2X RED MATERIAL
SERIAL #'d UNDER 25 NOT PRICED
14 Ben Roethlisberger/25 30.00 80.00
144 Walter Payton/26 30.00 80.00

2006 Absolute Memorabilia Tools of the Trade Material Double Black Spectrum

*DBLE BLK/15-25: .8X TO 2X RED/68-100
*DBLE BLK/15-25: .6X TO 1.5X RED/28-42
SERIAL #'d UNDER 25 NOT PRICED

2006 Absolute Memorabilia Tools of the Trade Material Double Blue

*DOUB.BLUE: .6X TO 1.5X RED MATERIAL
SERIAL #'d UNDER 25 NOT PRICED

2006 Absolute Memorabilia Tools of the Trade Material Double Red

*DOUB.RED/72-100: .5X TO 1.2X RED MAT.
*DOUB.RED/35-67: .6X TO 1.5X RED MAT.
*DOUB.RED/25-26: .8X TO 2X RED MAT.
SERIAL #'d UNDER 25 NOT PRICED

2006 Absolute Memorabilia Tools of the Trade Material Quad Red

*QUAD RED/25: 1X TO 2.5X RED MATERIAL
SERIAL #'d UNDER 25 NOT PRICED
UNPRICED BLACK PRINT RUN 1
UNPRICED BLUE PRINT RUN 3-10

2006 Absolute Memorabilia Tools of the Trade Material Triple Blue

*TRIP.BLUE/25: .8X TO 2X RED MATERIAL
SERIAL #'d UNDER 25 NOT PRICED

2006 Absolute Memorabilia Tools of the Trade Material Triple Red

*TRIP.RED/50: .6X TO 1.5X RED MATERIAL
*TRIP.RED/25-36: .8X TO 2X RED MATERIAL
UNPRICED BLACK PRINT RUN 1-5
SER.#'d UNDER 25 NOT PRICED

2006 Absolute Memorabilia War Room Materials

STATED PRINT RUN 100 SER.#'d SETS
*PRIME/50: .6X TO 1.5X BASIC JERSEYS
*OVERSIZED/25: 1X TO 2.5X BASIC JERSEYS
UNPRICED OVER.SPECTRUM PRINT RUN 10
1 Chad Jackson 3.00 8.00
2 Laurence Maroney 3.00 8.00
3 Tarvaris Jackson 3.00 8.00
4 Michael Huff 4.00 10.00
5 Mario Williams 5.00 12.00
6 Marcedes Lewis 3.00 8.00
7 Maurice Drew 5.00 12.00
8 Vince Young 3.00 8.00
9 LenDale White 3.00 8.00
10 Reggie Bush 5.00 12.00
11 Matt Leinart 3.00 8.00
12 Michael Robinson 3.00 8.00
13 Vernon Davis 4.00 10.00
14 Brandon Williams 3.00 8.00
15 Derek Hagan 4.00 10.00
16 Jason Avant 3.00 8.00
17 Brandon Marshall 6.00 15.00
18 Omar Jacobs 3.00 8.00
19 Santonio Holmes 4.00 10.00
20 Jerious Norwood 3.00 8.00
21 Demetrius Williams 3.00 8.00
22 Sinorice Moss 3.00 8.00
23 Leon Washington 3.00 8.00
24 Kellen Clemens 3.00 8.00
25 A.J. Hawk 4.00 10.00
26 Maurice Stovall 3.00 8.00
27 DeAngelo Williams 4.00 10.00
28 Charlie Whitehurst 3.00 8.00
29 Travis Wilson 3.00 8.00
30 Joe Klopfenstein 3.00 8.00
31 Brian Calhoun 3.00 8.00

2007 Absolute Memorabilia

This 284-card set was released in September, 2007. The set was issued into the hobby in five-card packs, with a $40 SRP, which came six packs to a box. Cards numbered 1-150 feature veterans in team alphabetical order by division while cards numbered 151-284 feature 2007 NFL rookies. The Rookie Cards are broken down thusly: Cards numbered 151-200 were issued to a stated print run of 699 serial numbered sets, cards numbered 201-250 were signed by the player and were issued to a stated print run of 349 serial numbered sets and cards numbered 251-284 had player-worn swatches and were issued to a stated print run of 849 serial numbered sets.

ROOKIE PRINT RUN 699 SER.#'d SETS
AU ROOKIE PRINT RUN 349 SER.#'d SETS
RPM ROOKIE PRINT RUN 849 SER.#'d SETS
UNPRICED SPECTRUM PLATINUM #'d TO 1
1 Tony Romo 1.50 4.00
2 Julius Jones .75 2.00
3 Terry Glenn 1.00 2.50
4 Terrell Owens 1.00 2.50
5 Marion Barber 1.00 2.50
6 Reuben Droughns 1.00 2.50
7 Eli Manning 1.00 2.50
8 Plaxico Burress .75 2.00
9 Jeremy Shockey .75 2.00
10 Brandon Jacobs .75 2.00
11 Donovan McNabb 1.00 2.50
12 Brian Westbrook .75 2.00
13 Reggie Brown .75 2.00
14 Hank Baskett 1.00 2.50
15 Jason Campbell .75 2.00
16 Clinton Portis .75 2.00
17 Santana Moss 1.00 2.50
18 Ladell Betts .75 2.00
19 Brandon Lloyd .75 2.00
20 Chris Cooley .75 2.00
21 Rex Grossman .75 2.00
22 Cedric Benson .75 2.00
23 Muhsin Muhammad .75 2.00
24 Bernard Berrian .75 2.00
25 Devin Hester 1.00 2.50
26 Brian Urlacher 1.25 3.00
27 Jon Kitna .75 2.00
28 Kevin Jones .75 2.00
29 Roy Williams .75 2.00
30 Mike Furrey 1.00 2.50
31 Ernie Sims .75 2.00
32 Tatum Bell .75 2.00
33 Brett Favre 2.50 6.00
34 Vernand Morency 1.00 2.50
35 Donald Driver 1.00 2.50
36 Greg Jennings .75 2.00
37 AJ Hawk .75 2.00
38 Tarvaris Jackson .75 2.00
39 Chester Taylor .75 2.00
40 Troy Williamson .75 2.00
41 Mewelde Moore .75 2.00
42 Michael Vick 1.00 2.50
43 Warrick Dunn .75 2.00
44 Joe Horn .75 2.00
45 Alge Crumpler 1.00 2.50
46 Jerious Norwood .75 2.00
47 Jake Delhomme .75 2.00
48 DeShaun Foster 1.00 2.50
49 Steve Smith 1.00 2.50
50 DeAngelo Williams .75 2.00
51 Drew Brees 1.25 3.00
52 Deuce McAllister 1.00 2.50
53 Marques Colston .75 2.00
54 Devery Henderson .75 2.00
55 Reggie Bush .75 2.00
56 Jeff Garcia .75 2.00
57 Cadillac Williams 1.00 2.50
58 Joey Galloway 1.00 2.50
59 Michael Clayton .75 2.00
60 Matt Leinart .75 2.00
61 Edgerrin James 1.00 2.50
62 Anquan Boldin .75 2.00
63 Larry Fitzgerald 1.00 2.50
64 Marc Bulger .75 2.00
65 Steven Jackson .75 2.00
66 Torry Holt 1.00 2.50
67 Isaac Bruce 1.25 3.00
68 Randy McMichael .75 2.00
69 Drew Bennett .75 2.00
70 Alex Smith 1.00 2.50
71 Frank Gore 1.00 2.50
72 Darrell Jackson .75 2.00
73 Ashley Lelie 1.00 2.50
74 Vernon Davis .75 2.00
75 Matt Hasselbeck .75 2.00
76 Shaun Alexander .75 2.00
77 Deion Branch .75 2.00
78 J.P. Losman .75 2.00
79 Lee Evans 1.00 2.50
80 Josh Reed .75 2.00
81 Daunte Culpepper 1.00 2.50
82 Ronnie Brown .75 2.00
83 Chris Chambers .75 2.00
84 Marty Booker .75 2.00
85 Zach Thomas 1.00 2.50
86 Tom Brady 4.00 10.00
87 Laurence Maroney 1.00 2.50
88 Randy Moss 1.00 2.50
89 Chad Jackson .75 2.00
90 Ben Watson .75 2.00
91 Donte' Stallworth 1.00 2.50
92 Chad Pennington .75 2.00
93 Thomas Jones .75 2.00
94 Laveranues Coles .75 2.00
95 Jerricho Cotchery .75 2.00
96 Leon Washington .75 2.00
97 Steve McNair 1.00 2.50
98 Willis McGahee .75 2.00
99 Derrick Mason .75 2.00
100 Demetrius Williams .75 2.00
101 Mark Clayton .75 2.00
102 Carson Palmer 1.00 2.50
103 Rudi Johnson .75 2.00
104 Chad Johnson .75 2.00
105 T.J. Houshmandzadeh .75 2.00
106 Charlie Frye 1.00 2.50
107 Braylon Edwards .75 2.00
108 Travis Wilson .75 2.00
109 Kellen Winslow .75 2.00
110 Jamal Lewis 1.00 2.50
111 Ben Roethlisberger 1.25 3.00
112 Willie Parker 1.00 2.50
113 Hines Ward 1.00 2.50
114 Santonio Holmes .75 2.00
115 Ahman Green 1.00 2.50
116 Andre Johnson 1.00 2.50
117 Matt Schaub .75 2.00
118 DeMeco Ryans 1.00 2.50
119 Owen Daniels .75 2.00
120 Peyton Manning 3.00 8.00
121 Joseph Addai .75 2.00
122 Marvin Harrison 1.00 2.50
123 Reggie Wayne 1.00 2.50
124 Dallas Clark 1.00 2.50
125 Byron Leftwich .75 2.00
126 Fred Taylor .75 2.00
127 Matt Jones 1.00 2.50
128 Reggie Williams 1.00 2.50
129 Marcedes Lewis .75 2.00
130 Maurice Jones-Drew .75 2.00
131 Vince Young .75 2.00
132 LenDale White 1.00 2.50
133 Brandon Jones .75 2.00
134 Jay Cutler .75 2.00
135 Travis Henry 1.00 2.50
136 Javon Walker 1.00 2.50
137 Rod Smith 1.00 2.50
138 Mike Bell 1.00 2.50
139 Brandon Marshall 1.00 2.50
140 Larry Johnson .75 2.00
141 Eddie Kennison .75 2.00
142 Tony Gonzalez 1.00 2.50
143 Brodie Croyle 1.00 2.50
144 LaMont Jordan 1.00 2.50
145 Ronald Curry .75 2.00
146 Philip Rivers 1.25 3.00
147 LaDainian Tomlinson 1.25 3.00
148 Vincent Jackson .75 2.00
149 Michael Turner .75 2.00
150 Antonio Gates 1.25 3.00
151 A.J. Davis RC 3.00 8.00
152 Aaron Rouse RC 3.00 8.00
153 Ahmad Bradshaw RC 5.00 12.00
154 Alonzo Coleman RC 4.00 10.00
155 Anthony Spencer RC 4.00 10.00
156 Brandon Siler RC 3.00 8.00
157 Buster Davis RC 4.00 10.00
158 Chris Houston RC 3.00 8.00
159 Dallas Baker RC 3.00 8.00
160 Dan Bazuin RC 4.00 10.00
161 Danny Ware RC 5.00 12.00
162 David Ball RC 3.00 8.00
163 David Irons RC 3.00 8.00
164 D'Juan Woods RC 3.00 8.00
165 Earl Everett RC 3.00 8.00
166 Eric Frampton RC 4.00 10.00
167 Eric Weddle RC 4.00 10.00
168 Eric Wright RC 3.00 8.00
169 Fred Bennett RC 3.00 8.00
170 Gary Russell RC 4.00 10.00
171 H.B. Blades RC 3.00 8.00
172 Jarrett Hicks RC 4.00 10.00
173 Jarvis Moss RC 3.00 8.00
174 Jason Snelling RC 3.00 8.00
175 Jerard Rabb RC 4.00 10.00
176 Jemalle Cornelius RC 4.00 10.00
177 Tyler Thigpen RC 5.00 12.00
178 Jon Beason RC 3.00 8.00
179 Jonathan Wade RC 3.00 8.00
180 Jordan Kent RC 4.00 10.00
181 Josh Gattis RC 3.00 8.00
182 Kenneth Darby RC 3.00 8.00
183 DeMarcus Tank Tyler RC 3.00 8.00
184 Levi Brown RC 3.00 8.00
185 Marcus McCauley RC 3.00 8.00
186 Tim Shaw RC 4.00 10.00
187 Michael Okwo RC 4.00 10.00
188 Mike Walker RC 5.00 12.00
189 Nate Ilaoa RC 4.00 10.00
190 Reggie Ball RC 4.00 10.00
191 Rhema McKnight RC 3.00 8.00
192 Zak DeOssie RC 4.00 10.00
193 Rufus Alexander RC 3.00 8.00
194 Ryan McBean RC 5.00 12.00
195 Ryne Robinson RC 4.00 10.00
196 Selvin Young RC 3.00 8.00
197 Steve Breaston RC 3.00 8.00
198 Stewart Bradley RC 3.00 8.00
199 Thomas Clayton RC 4.00 10.00
200 Tim Crowder RC 4.00 10.00
201 Aaron Ross AU RC 4.00 10.00
202 Adam Carriker AU RC 4.00 10.00
204 Amobi Okoye AU RC 5.00 12.00
205 Aundrae Allison AU RC 4.00 10.00
206 Ben Patrick AU RC 5.00 12.00
207 Brandon Meriweather AU RC 5.00 12.00
208 Chansi Stuckey AU RC 5.00 12.00
210 Chris Davis AU RC 4.00 10.00
211 Chris Leak AU RC 4.00 10.00
212 Courtney Taylor AU RC 4.00 10.00
214 Darius Walker AU RC 4.00 10.00
215 Darrelle Revis AU RC 5.00 12.00
216 David Clowney AU RC 4.00 10.00
217 David Harris AU RC 4.00 10.00
218 Daymeion Hughes AU RC 4.00 10.00
219 DeShawn Wynn AU RC 4.00 10.00
220 Dwayne Wright AU RC 4.00 10.00
221 Ikaika Alama-Francis AU RC 6.00 15.00
222 Isaiah Stanback AU RC 4.00 10.00
223 Jacoby Jones AU RC 4.00 10.00
224 Jamaal Anderson AU RC 5.00 12.00
225 James Jones AU RC 4.00 10.00
226 Jared Zabransky AU RC 4.00 10.00
227 Jeff Rowe AU RC 4.00 10.00
228 Joel Filani AU RC 4.00 10.00
229 Jordan Palmer AU RC 5.00 12.00
230 Josh Wilson AU RC 5.00 12.00
231 Kenny Scott AU RC 4.00 10.00
232 Kolby Smith AU RC 4.00 10.00
233 LaMarr Woodley AU RC 15.00 25.00
234 LaRon Landry AU RC 6.00 15.00
235 Laurent Robinson AU RC 6.00 15.00
236 Lawrence Timmons AU RC 6.00 15.00
237 Leon Hall AU RC 4.00 10.00
238 Matt Spaeth AU RC 6.00 15.00
239 Michael Griffin AU RC 4.00 10.00
240 Paul Posluszny AU RC 4.00 10.00
241 Quentin Moses AU RC 4.00 10.00
242 Ray McDonald AU RC 5.00 12.00
243 Reggie Nelson AU RC 4.00 10.00
244 Ronnie McGill AU RC 5.00 12.00
245 Sabby Piscitelli AU RC 4.00 10.00
246 Scott Chandler AU RC 6.00 15.00
247 Toby Korrodi AU RC 5.00 12.00
248 Tyler Palko AU RC 6.00 15.00
249 Victor Abiamiri AU RC 4.00 10.00
250 Zach Miller AU RC 4.00 10.00
251 JaMarcus Russell RPM RC 2.50 6.00
252 Calvin Johnson RPM RC 8.00 20.00
253 Joe Thomas RPM RC 4.00 10.00
254 Gaines Adams RPM RC 3.00 8.00
255 Greg Olsen RPM RC 4.00 10.00
256 Adrian Peterson RPM RC 8.00 20.00
257 Ted Ginn RPM RC 3.00 8.00
258 Patrick Willis RPM RC 4.00 10.00
259 Marshawn Lynch RPM RC 5.00 12.00
260 Brady Quinn RPM RC 2.50 6.00
261 Dwayne Bowe RPM RC 2.50 6.00
262 Robert Meachem RPM RC 3.00 8.00
263 Anthony Gonzalez RPM RC 2.50 6.00
264 Kevin Kolb RPM RC 3.00 8.00
265 John Beck RPM RC 2.50 6.00
266 Drew Stanton RPM RC 2.50 6.00
267 Sidney Rice RPM RC 3.00 8.00
268 Dwayne Jarrett RPM RC 3.00 8.00
269 Kenny Irons RPM RC 2.50 6.00
270 Chris Henry RPM RC 2.50 6.00
271 Steve Smith RPM RC 2.50 6.00
272 Brian Leonard RPM RC 2.50 6.00
273 Brandon Jackson RPM RC 2.50 6.00
274 Lorenzo Booker RPM RC 3.00 8.00
275 Yamon Figurs RPM RC 2.50 6.00
276 Jason Hill RPM RC 2.50 6.00
277 Paul Williams RPM RC 2.50 6.00
278 Tony Hunt RPM RC 2.50 6.00
279 Trent Edwards RPM RC 2.50 6.00
280 Garrett Wolfe RPM RC 2.50 6.00
281 Johnnie Lee Higgins RPM RC 2.50 6.00
282 Michael Bush RPM RC 2.50 6.00
283 Antonio Pittman RPM RC 2.50 6.00
284 Troy Smith RPM RC 2.50 6.00

2007 Absolute Memorabilia Retail

*VET 1-150: .1X TO .25X BASIC CARDS
*ROOKIES 151-200: .4X TO 1X BASIC CARDS
ROOKIES PRINT RUN 699 SER.#'d SETS

2007 Absolute Memorabilia Rookie Premiere Materials AFC/NFC

*SINGLES: .6X TO 1.5X BASE RPM RCs
AFC/NFC PRINT RUN 50 SER.#'d SETS
*PRIME/10: 1.5X TO 4X BASE RPM RCs
SPECTRUM PRIME PRINT RUN 10 SER.#'d SETS

2007 Absolute Memorabilia Rookie Premiere Materials Oversize

*SINGLES: .8X TO 2X BASE RPM RCs
OVERSIZE PRINT RUN 50 SER.#'d SETS
*SPECT/10: 1.5X TO 4X BASE RPM RCs
SPECTRUM PRINT RUN 10 SER.#'d SETS

2007 Absolute Memorabilia Rookie Premiere Materials Spectrum Prime

*SINGLES: .6X TO 1.5X BASE RPM RCs
STATED PRINT RUN 100 SER.#'d SETS

2007 Absolute Memorabilia Spectrum Silver Retail

*VETS 1-150: 1X TO 2.5X BASIC CARDS
*ROOKIES 151-200: .6X TO 1.5X BASIC RC/699
*ROOKIES 201-250: .4X TO 1X SPECT.SILVER
STATED PRINT RUN 100 SER.#'d SETS

2007 Absolute Memorabilia Spectrum Blue Retail

*VETS 1-150: .8X TO 2X BASIC CARDS
*ROOKIES 151-200: .5X TO 1.2X BASIC CARDS
*ROOKIES 201-250: .3X TO .8X SPECT.SILVER
BLUE PRINT RUN 250 SER.#'d SETS

2007 Absolute Memorabilia Spectrum Gold

*VETS 1-150: 2X TO 5X BASIC CARDS
*ROOKIES 151-200: 1.2X TO 3X BASIC RC/699
*ROOKIES 201-250: .8X TO 2X SPECT.SILVER
STATED PRINT RUN 25 SER.#'d SETS

2007 Absolute Memorabilia Spectrum Red Retail

*VETS 1-150: .6X TO 1.5X BASIC CARDS
*ROOKIES 151-200: .4X TO 1X BASIC RC/699
*ROOKIES 201-250: .25X TO .6X SPECT.SILVER
RANDOM INSERTS IN RETAIL PACKS

2007 Absolute Memorabilia Spectrum Silver

*VETERANS 1-150: 1X TO 2.5X BASIC CARDS
*ROOKIES 151-200: .5X TO 1.2X RC/699
COMMON ROOKIE 201-250 4.00 10.00
ROOKIE SEMISTARS 201-250 5.00 12.00
ROOKIE UNL.STARS 201-250 6.00 15.00
STATED PRINT RUN 100 SER.#'d SETS
225 James Jones 4.00 10.00
226 Jared Zabransky 4.00 10.00
234 LaRon Landry 6.00 15.00
236 Lawrence Timmons 6.00 15.00
240 Paul Posluszny 4.00 10.00

2007 Absolute Memorabilia Absolute Heroes

STATED PRINT RUN 100 SER.#'d SETS
*GOLD/50: .5X TO 1.2X BASIC INSERTS
GOLD PRINT RUN 50 SER.#'d SETS
*SPECTRUM/25: .8X TO 2X BASIC INSERTS
SPECTRUM PRINT RUN 25 SER.#'d SETS
1 Laurence Maroney 1.00 2.50
2 Leon Washington .75 2.00
3 Maurice Jones-Drew .75 2.00
4 Mike Bell 1.00 2.50
5 A.J. Hawk .75 2.00
6 Andre Johnson 1.00 2.50
7 Anquan Boldin .75 2.00
8 Antonio Gates 1.25 3.00
9 Bernard Berrian .75 2.00
10 Brandon Jacobs .75 2.00
11 Brandon Marshall 1.00 2.50
12 Chester Taylor .75 2.00
13 Demetrius Williams .75 2.00
14 Joseph Addai .75 2.00
15 Matt Leinart .75 2.00
16 Philip Rivers 1.25 3.00
17 Tony Romo 1.50 4.00
18 Frank Gore 1.00 2.50
19 Marion Barber 1.00 2.50
20 Fred Taylor .75 2.00
21 Larry Fitzgerald 1.50 4.00
22 Michael Vick 1.00 2.50
23 Reggie Wayne 1.00 2.50
24 Reggie Bush .75 2.00
25 Vince Young .75 2.00

2007 Absolute Memorabilia Absolute Heroes Materials

STATED PRINT RUN 40-200
*PRIME/50: .6X TO 1.5X BASIC JSY/108-200
PRIME PRINT RUN 7-50
UNPRICED PRIME SPECTRUM PRINT RUN 1
1 Laurence Maroney 2.50 6.00
2 Leon Washington 2.00 5.00
3 Maurice Jones-Drew 2.00 5.00
4 Mike Bell 2.50 6.00
5 A.J. Hawk/190 2.00 5.00
6 Andre Johnson 2.50 6.00
7 Anquan Boldin 2.00 5.00
8 Antonio Gates 3.00 8.00
9 Bernard Berrian 2.00 5.00
10 Brandon Jacobs/190 2.00 5.00
11 Brandon Marshall 2.50 6.00
12 Chester Taylor 2.00 5.00
13 Demetrius Williams/40 2.50 6.00
14 Joseph Addai 2.00 5.00
15 Matt Leinart 2.00 5.00
16 Philip Rivers 3.00 8.00
17 Tony Romo 4.00 10.00
18 Frank Gore 2.50 6.00
19 Marion Barber 2.50 6.00
20 Fred Taylor 2.00 5.00
23 Reggie Wayne 2.50 6.00
24 Reggie Bush 2.00 5.00
25 Vince Young/108 2.00 5.00

2007 Absolute Memorabilia Absolute Heroes Materials Autographs

AUTO STATED PRINT RUN 30-50
UNPRICED PRIME SPECTRUM PRINT RUN 1
3 Maurice Jones-Drew 20.00 40.00
4 Mike Bell 10.00 25.00
6 Andre Johnson 10.00 25.00
7 Anquan Boldin 10.00 25.00
8 Antonio Gates 20.00 40.00
9 Bernard Berrian 10.00 25.00
10 Brandon Jacobs 10.00 25.00
11 Brandon Marshall 10.00 25.00
12 Chester Taylor 10.00 25.00
13 Demetrius Williams 10.00 25.00
14 Joseph Addai 20.00 50.00
15 Matt Leinart/30 15.00 40.00
16 Philip Rivers/30 20.00 40.00
17 Tony Romo/30 75.00 150.00
18 Frank Gore 20.00 40.00
19 Marion Barber 20.00 40.00
20 Fred Taylor 10.00 25.00
21 Larry Fitzgerald/30 25.00 50.00
23 Reggie Wayne 12.00 30.00
24 Reggie Bush/30 30.00 60.00
25 Vince Young/30 20.00 50.00

2007 Absolute Memorabilia Absolute Heroes Materials Autographs Prime

*PRIME/25: .6X TO 1.2X BASIC AUTO/30-50
PRIME PRINT RUN 15-25
1 Laurence Maroney
5 A.J. Hawk 25.00 50.00
16 Philip Rivers/15 30.00 60.00
22 Michael Vick 40.00 80.00

2007 Absolute Memorabilia Absolute Patches Prime

STATED PRINT RUN 5-25
UNPRICED SPECTRUM PRINT RUN 1
SERIAL #'d UNDER 15 NOT PRICED
1 Chad Johnson 15.00 40.00
2 Barry Sanders 50.00 120.00
3 Dan Marino 60.00 150.00
4 Joe Montana 100.00 250.00
5 Walter Payton 60.00 150.00
6 Antonio Gates 25.00 60.00
8 Vince Young/15 15.00 40.00
9 Brett Favre 50.00 125.00
10 Brian Urlacher 25.00 60.00
11 Donovan McNabb 20.00 50.00
12 LaDainian Tomlinson 25.00 60.00
13 Larry Johnson 15.00 40.00
14 Peyton Manning 60.00 150.00
15 Steve Smith 20.00 50.00
16 Marvin Harrison 20.00 50.00
17 Torry Holt 20.00 50.00
18 Carson Palmer 20.00 50.00
19 Steven Jackson 15.00 40.00
20 Terrell Owens/24 20.00 50.00

2007 Absolute Memorabilia Canton Absolutes

GOLD PRINT RUN 100 SER.#'d SETS
*GOLD/50: .5X TO 1.2X BASIC INSERTS
GOLD PRINT RUN 50 SER.#'d SETS
*SPECTRUM/25: .8X TO 2X BASIC INSERTS
SPECTRUM PRINT RUN 25 SER.#'d SETS
1 Chad Johnson .75 2.00
2 Bo Jackson 1.50 4.00
3 Reggie Bush .75 2.00
4 Vince Young .75 2.00
5 Ben Roethlisberger 1.25 3.00
6 Brett Favre 2.50 6.00
7 Brian Urlacher 1.25 3.00
8 Corey Dillon .75 2.00
9 Curtis Martin 1.00 2.50
10 Donovan McNabb 1.00 2.50
11 Drew Brees 1.25 3.00
12 Eli Manning 1.00 2.50
13 Hines Ward 1.00 2.50
14 LaDainian Tomlinson 1.25 3.00
15 Larry Johnson .75 2.00
16 Peyton Manning 3.00 8.00
17 Steve Smith 1.00 2.50
18 Marvin Harrison 1.00 2.50
19 Steve McNair 1.00 2.50
20 Torry Holt 1.00 2.50
21 Deuce McAllister 1.00 2.50
22 Roy Williams WR .75 2.00
23 Rudi Johnson .75 2.00
24 Steven Jackson .75 2.00
25 Shaun Alexander .75 2.00

2007 Absolute Memorabilia Canton Absolutes Materials

STATED PRINT RUN 25-200
*PRIME/25: .8X TO 2X BASIC JSY/122-200
*PRIME/25: .5X TO 1.2X BASIC JSY/25
PRIME PRINT RUN 25 SER.#'d SETS
UNPRICED PRIME SPECTRUM PRINT RUN 1
1 Chad Johnson 2.00 5.00
2 Bo Jackson/183 4.00 10.00
3 Reggie Bush 2.00 5.00
4 Vince Young 2.00 5.00
5 Ben Roethlisberger/25 6.00 15.00
6 Brett Favre 6.00 15.00
7 Brian Urlacher 3.00 8.00
8 Corey Dillon 2.00 5.00
9 Curtis Martin 2.50 6.00
10 Donovan McNabb 2.50 6.00
11 Drew Brees 3.00 8.00
12 Eli Manning 2.50 6.00
13 Hines Ward 2.50 6.00
14 LaDainian Tomlinson 3.00 8.00
15 Larry Johnson 2.00 5.00
16 Peyton Manning/122 8.00 20.00
17 Steve Smith 2.50 6.00
18 Marvin Harrison 2.50 6.00
19 Steve McNair 2.50 6.00
20 Torry Holt 2.50 6.00
21 Deuce McAllister 2.50 6.00
22 Roy Williams WR 2.00 5.00
23 Rudi Johnson 2.00 5.00
24 Steven Jackson 2.00 5.00
25 Shaun Alexander 2.00 5.00

2007 Absolute Memorabilia Canton Absolutes Autographs

STATED PRINT RUN 10-27
2 Bo Jackson/25 30.00 60.00
15 Larry Johnson/27 20.00 40.00
24 Steven Jackson/25 20.00 40.00

2007 Absolute Memorabilia College Materials

STATED PRINT RUN 100 SER.#'d SETS
*SPECT.PRIME/10: 2X TO 4X BASIC JSY/100
SPECTRUM PRIME PRINT RUN 5-10
1 Frank Gore 3.00 8.00
2 Robert Meachem 3.00 8.00
3 Dwayne Jarrett 3.00 8.00
4 Steve Smith 2.50 6.00
5 Adrian Peterson 8.00 20.00
6 Brady Quinn 2.50 6.00
7 JaMarcus Russell 2.50 6.00
8 Peyton Manning 10.00 25.00
9 Vince Young 2.50 6.00
10 Reggie Bush 2.50 6.00

2007 Absolute Memorabilia College Materials Autographs

STATED PRINT RUN 25 SER.#'d SETS
UNPRICED SPECTRUM PRIME PRINT RUN 1-5
1 Frank Gore 25.00 50.00
2 Robert Meachem 25.00 50.00
3 Dwayne Jarrett 25.00 50.00
4 Steve Smith 15.00 40.00
5 Adrian Peterson 100.00 200.00
6 Brady Quinn 12.00 30.00
7 JaMarcus Russell 30.00 80.00
8 Peyton Manning 100.00 200.00
9 Vince Young 40.00 100.00
10 Reggie Bush 50.00 120.00

2007 Absolute Memorabilia Marks of Fame

STATED PRINT RUN 100 SER.#'d SETS
*GOLD/50: .5X TO 1.2X BASIC INSERTS
GOLD PRINT RUN 50 SER.#'d SETS
*SPECTRUM/25: .8X TO 2X BASIC INSERTS
SPECTRUM PRINT RUN 25 SER.#'d SETS
1 Jerious Norwood .75 2.00
2 LenDale White 1.00 2.50
3 Brian Westbrook .75 2.00
4 Cadillac Williams 1.00 2.50
5 Cedric Benson .75 2.00
6 DeAngelo Williams .75 2.00
7 DeMeco Ryans 1.00 2.50
8 Devin Hester 1.00 2.50
9 Jay Cutler .75 2.00
10 Marques Colston .75 2.00
11 Rex Grossman .75 2.00
12 Shawne Merriman .75 2.00
13 Vernon Davis .75 2.00
14 Willie Parker 1.00 2.50
15 Santonio Holmes .75 2.00
16 Larry Johnson .75 2.00
17 Ted Ginn Jr. 1.00 2.50
18 Joe Thomas 1.25 3.00
19 Brady Quinn .75 2.00
20 Brandon Jackson .75 2.00
21 Tony Hunt .75 2.00
22 Steve Smith .75 2.00
23 Dwayne Jarrett 1.00 2.50
24 Drew Stanton .75 2.00
25 Antonio Pittman .75 2.00
26 Dwayne Bowe .75 2.00
27 Anthony Gonzalez .75 2.00
28 Lorenzo Booker 1.00 2.50
29 Chris Henry .75 2.00
30 Gaines Adams 1.00 2.50
31 Kevin Kolb 1.00 2.50
32 John Beck .75 2.00
33 Brian Leonard .75 2.00
34 Adrian Peterson 2.50 6.00
35 Greg Olsen 1.25 3.00
36 JaMarcus Russell .75 2.00
37 Garrett Wolfe .75 2.00
38 Yamon Figurs .75 2.00
39 Sidney Rice 1.00 2.50
40 Trent Edwards .75 2.00
41 Michael Bush .75 2.00
42 Patrick Willis 1.25 3.00
43 Kenny Irons .75 2.00
44 Calvin Johnson 2.50 6.00
45 Paul Williams .75 2.00
46 Robert Meachem 1.00 2.50
47 Jason Hill .75 2.00
48 Marshawn Lynch 1.50 4.00
49 Johnnie Lee Higgins .75 2.00
50 Troy Smith .75 2.00

2007 Absolute Memorabilia Marks of Fame Materials

STATED PRINT RUN 100-200
*PRIME/50: .6X TO 1.5X BASIC JSY/100-200
PRIME PRINT RUN 50 SER.#'d SETS
UNPRICED SPECTRUM PRINT RUN 1
1 Jerious Norwood 2.00 5.00
2 LenDale White 2.50 6.00
3 Brian Westbrook/100 2.00 5.00
4 Cadillac Williams 2.50 6.00
5 Cedric Benson 2.00 5.00
6 DeAngelo Williams 2.00 5.00
7 DeMeco Ryans 2.50 6.00
8 Devin Hester 2.50 6.00
9 Jay Cutler 2.00 5.00
10 Marques Colston 2.00 5.00
11 Rex Grossman 2.00 5.00
12 Shawne Merriman 2.00 5.00
13 Vernon Davis 2.00 5.00
14 Willie Parker 2.50 6.00
15 Santonio Holmes 2.00 5.00
16 Larry Johnson 2.00 5.00
17 Ted Ginn Jr. 2.50 6.00
18 Joe Thomas 3.00 8.00
19 Brady Quinn 2.00 5.00
20 Brandon Jackson 2.00 5.00
21 Tony Hunt 2.00 5.00
22 Steve Smith 2.00 5.00
23 Dwayne Jarrett 2.50 6.00
24 Drew Stanton 2.00 5.00
25 Antonio Pittman 2.00 5.00
26 Dwayne Bowe 2.00 5.00
27 Anthony Gonzalez 2.00 5.00
28 Lorenzo Booker 2.50 6.00
29 Chris Henry 2.00 5.00
30 Gaines Adams 2.50 6.00
31 Kevin Kolb 2.50 6.00
32 John Beck 2.00 5.00
33 Brian Leonard 2.00 5.00
34 Adrian Peterson 6.00 15.00
35 Greg Olsen 3.00 8.00
36 JaMarcus Russell 2.00 5.00
37 Garrett Wolfe 2.00 5.00
38 Yamon Figurs 2.00 5.00
39 Sidney Rice 2.50 6.00
40 Trent Edwards 2.00 5.00
41 Michael Bush 2.00 5.00
42 Patrick Willis 3.00 8.00
43 Kenny Irons 2.00 5.00
44 Calvin Johnson 6.00 15.00
45 Paul Williams 2.00 5.00
46 Robert Meachem 2.50 6.00
47 Jason Hill 2.00 5.00
48 Marshawn Lynch 4.00 10.00
49 Johnnie Lee Higgins 2.00 5.00
50 Troy Smith 2.00 5.00

2007 Absolute Memorabilia Marks of Fame Materials Autographs

STATED PRINT RUN 30-50
*PRIME/25: .6X TO 1.2X BASIC JSY AU
PRIME PRINT RUN 25 SER.#'d SETS
UNPRICED PRIME SPECT.PRINT RUN 1
1 Jerious Norwood 12.00 30.00
2 LenDale White 12.00 30.00
4 Cadillac Williams 15.00 40.00
5 Cedric Benson 12.00 30.00
6 DeAngelo Williams 10.00 25.00
7 DeMeco Ryans 10.00 25.00
8 Devin Hester/30 25.00 50.00
9 Jay Cutler/30 8.00 20.00
10 Marques Colston 12.00 30.00
11 Rex Grossman 12.00 30.00
13 Vernon Davis 10.00 25.00
14 Willie Parker 15.00 40.00
15 Santonio Holmes 12.00 30.00
16 Larry Johnson 15.00 40.00
17 Ted Ginn Jr. 15.00 40.00
18 Joe Thomas 12.00 30.00
19 Brady Quinn/30 12.00 30.00
20 Brandon Jackson 15.00 40.00
21 Tony Hunt 12.00 30.00
22 Steve Smith 12.00 30.00
23 Dwayne Jarrett 12.00 30.00
24 Drew Stanton 15.00 40.00
25 Antonio Pittman 10.00 25.00
26 Dwayne Bowe 20.00 50.00
27 Anthony Gonzalez 20.00 50.00
28 Lorenzo Booker 10.00 25.00
29 Chris Henry 12.00 30.00
30 Gaines Adams 10.00 25.00
31 Kevin Kolb 12.00 30.00
32 John Beck 12.00 30.00
33 Brian Leonard 12.00 30.00
34 Adrian Peterson/30 125.00 250.00
35 Greg Olsen 15.00 40.00
36 JaMarcus Russell/30 20.00 50.00
37 Garrett Wolfe 12.00 30.00
38 Yamon Figurs 12.00 30.00
39 Sidney Rice 6.00 15.00
40 Trent Edwards 12.00 30.00
41 Michael Bush 12.00 30.00
42 Patrick Willis 12.00 30.00
43 Kenny Irons 12.00 30.00
44 Calvin Johnson/30 50.00 100.00
45 Paul Williams 12.00 30.00
46 Robert Meachem 12.00 30.00
47 Jason Hill 12.00 30.00
48 Marshawn Lynch 15.00 40.00
49 Johnnie Lee Higgins 10.00 25.00
50 Troy Smith 12.00 30.00

2007 Absolute Memorabilia NFL Icons

STATED PRINT RUN 100 SER.#'d SETS
*SPECT/25 .8X TO 2X BASIC INSERTS
SPECTRUM PRINT RUN 25 SER.#'d SETS
1 Barry Sanders 6.00 15.00
2 Bo Jackson 5.00 12.00
3 Bob Griese 4.00 10.00
4 Dan Marino 8.00 20.00
5 Dick Butkus 5.00 12.00
6 Eric Dickerson 3.00 8.00
7 Franco Harris 4.00 10.00
8 Michael Irvin 4.00 10.00
9 Fred Biletnikoff 4.00 10.00
10 Jack Lambert 4.00 10.00
11 James Lofton 2.50 6.00
12 Jerry Rice 8.00 20.00
13 Jim Kelly 4.00 10.00
14 Jim Otto 2.50 6.00
15 Joe Greene 4.00 10.00
16 Joe Montana 12.00 30.00
17 John Hannah 2.50 6.00
18 John Riggins 3.00 8.00
19 Ken Stabler 5.00 12.00
20 Larry Little 2.50 6.00
21 Paul Hornung 4.00 10.00
22 Paul Krause 2.50 6.00
23 Paul Warfield 3.00 8.00
24 Rosey Brown 2.50 6.00
25 Ron Mix 2.50 6.00
26 Steve Young 5.00 12.00
27 Thurman Thomas 3.00 8.00
28 Tony Dorsett 4.00 10.00
29 Walter Payton 8.00 20.00
30 Y.A. Tittle 4.00 10.00

2007 Absolute Memorabilia NFL Icons Materials

STATED PRINT RUN 3-50
*PRIME/20-25: 1X TO 2.5X BASIC JSY/30-50
*PRIME/10: 1.5X TO 4X BASIC JSY/30-50
PRIME PRINT RUN 4-25
*PRIME SPECT/10: 1.5X TO 4X JSY/30-50
PRIME SPECTRUM PRINT RUN 5-10
1 Barry Sanders 10.00 25.00
2 Bo Jackson 8.00 20.00
3 Bob Griese 6.00 15.00
4 Dan Marino 12.00 30.00
5 Dick Butkus 8.00 20.00
6 Eric Dickerson 5.00 12.00
7 Franco Harris 6.00 15.00
8 Michael Irvin 6.00 15.00
9 Fred Biletnikoff 6.00 15.00
10 Jack Lambert 6.00 15.00
11 James Lofton 4.00 10.00
12 Jerry Rice 12.00 30.00
13 Jim Kelly 6.00 15.00
14 Jim Otto 4.00 10.00
15 Joe Greene 6.00 15.00
16 Joe Montana 20.00 50.00
17 John Hannah 4.00 10.00
18 John Riggins 5.00 12.00
20 Larry Little 4.00 10.00
21 Paul Hornung 6.00 15.00
22 Paul Krause/35 4.00 10.00
23 Paul Warfield 5.00 12.00
24 Rosey Brown 4.00 10.00
25 Ron Mix 4.00 10.00
26 Steve Young 8.00 20.00
27 Thurman Thomas 5.00 12.00
28 Tony Dorsett 6.00 15.00
29 Walter Payton 12.00 30.00
30 Y.A. Tittle 6.00 15.00

2007 Absolute Memorabilia Rookie Jersey Collection

RANDOM INSERTS IN RETAIL PACKS
1 Ted Ginn Jr. 3.00 8.00
2 Joe Thomas 4.00 10.00
3 Brady Quinn 2.50 6.00
4 Brandon Jackson 2.50 6.00
5 Tony Hunt 2.50 6.00
6 Steve Smith 2.50 6.00
7 Dwayne Jarrett 3.00 8.00
8 Drew Stanton 2.50 6.00
9 Antonio Pittman 2.50 6.00
10 Dwayne Bowe 2.50 6.00

PRISTINE
AUCTION
PRISTINEAUCTION.com
DAILY AUCTIONS &
10-MINUTE AUCTIONS
with
NO RESERVES
AUTOGRAPHS • SPORTS CARDS • COLLECTIBLES

GIZMO'S SPORTSCARDS
IS BUYING!
(815) 540-5206
Don't want to wait 45 days to receive your check/cash? Gizmo's Sportscards will pay you today!
WWW.GIZMOSSPORTSCARDS.COM
WE BUY WHAT OTHERS WON'T!
(815) 540-5206
TURN YOUR CARDS INTO CASH
Buying Store Close-outs, Junkwax, basement & closet hordes
as well as Vintage Products!
• All Tobacco Cards, including T3, Turkey Reds, T202 Triple Folders, T204 Ramlyns, T205 Gold Borders and T206 White Borders
• All 19th Century cards, including Allen & Ginters and Old Judge
• All Goudeys, including 1933, 1934 and 1938 Heads-Up
• 1933 Goudey Sports King
• 1933 Delongs
• 1934-36 Diamond Stars
• 1935 National Chicle Football
• 1939, 1940 and 1941 Play Balls
• 1911 M116 Sporting Life
• All early 1900's Caramel Cards, including American Caramel, Standard Caramel and Philadelphia Caramel
• All exhibit cards 1921-1938, including Exhibit Supply Co. Four-On-Ones
• 1932 U.S. Caramel
• 1933 Buttercreams
• 1933 George C. Millers
• 1933, 1934 & 1936 Canadia Goudeys
• 1934-36 Batter-Ups
• 1947 Bond Bread
• 1948-49 Leaf
• All commons pre-1969 all sports
• All Topps cards 1951-1975, including sets & superstars
• All Bowman cards 1948-1955, including sets & superstars
• 1953 Glendale Meats
• 1954 Dan-Dee Potato Chips
• 1954 Red Heart Dog Food
• 1954 Wilson Weiners
• 1953, 1954 and 1955 Stahl Meyer Meats
• Complete football and hockey sets before 1970
• All quality memorabilia
P.O. BOX 134 • DAVIS JUNCTION • ILLINOIS 61020
(815) 540-5206
RICK (GIZMO) GIDDINGS • PIRATE8@AOL.COM
Member of NSCC Board of Directors

EVERY WEDNESDAY 3PM TO 9PM & EVERY SATURDAY 9AM TO 5PM
#1 COLLECTIBLE SHOW IN THE USA
FRANK & SON
COLLECTIBLE SHOW
www.frankandsonshow.com
OVER 200 DEALERS!
FREE ADMISSION & PARKING!
VALLEY BLVD
19649 SAN JOSE AVE.
WALNUT DR. NORTH
FAIRWAY
10
605
57
60

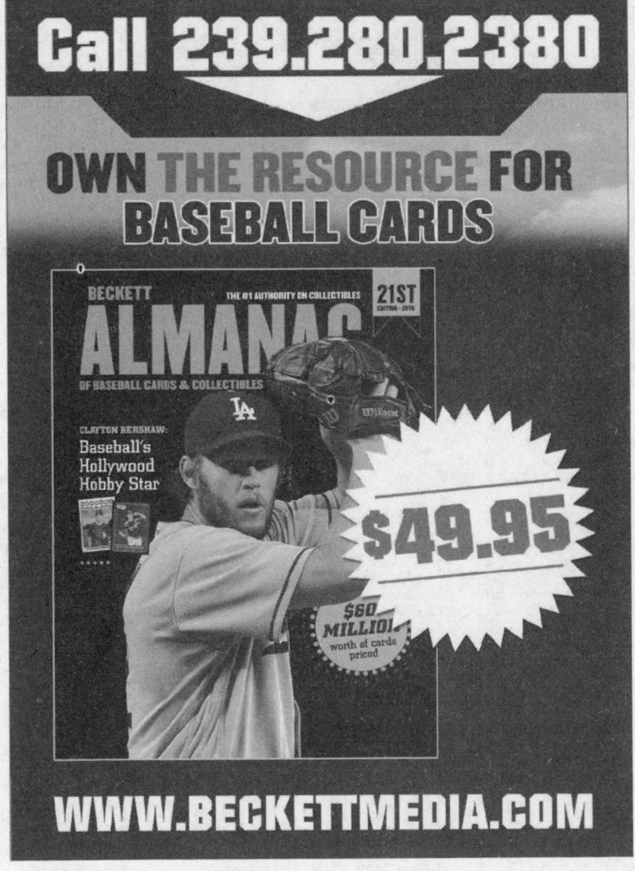

Call 239.280.2380
OWN THE RESOURCE FOR BASEBALL CARDS
BECKETT
THE #1 AUTHORITY ON COLLECTIBLES
21ST
ALMANAC
OF BASEBALL CARDS & COLLECTIBLES
CLAYTON KERSHAW:
Baseball's Hollywood Hobby Star
$49.95
worth of cards priced
WWW.BECKETTMEDIA.COM

11 Anthony Gonzalez 2.50 6.00
12 Lorenzo Booker 3.00 8.00
13 Chris Henry 2.50 6.00
14 Gaines Adams 3.00 8.00
15 Kevin Kolb 3.00 8.00
16 John Beck 2.50 6.00
17 Brian Leonard 2.50 6.00
18 Adrian Peterson 8.00 20.00
19 Greg Olsen 4.00 10.00
20 JaMarcus Russell 2.50 6.00
21 Garrett Wolfe 2.50 6.00
22 Yamon Figurs 2.50 6.00
23 Sidney Rice 3.00 8.00
24 Trent Edwards 2.50 6.00
25 Michael Bush 2.50 6.00
26 Patrick Willis 4.00 10.00
27 Kenny Irons 2.50 6.00
28 Calvin Johnson 8.00 20.00
29 Paul Williams 2.50 6.00
30 Robert Meachem 3.00 8.00
31 Jason Hill 2.50 6.00
32 Marshawn Lynch 5.00 12.00
33 Johnnie Lee Higgins 2.50 6.00
34 Troy Smith 2.50 6.00

2007 Absolute Memorabilia Rookie Premiere Materials Autographs

STATED PRINT RUN 100 SER.#'d SETS
*AFC/NFC/25: .6X TO 1.5X BASIC AU/100
AFC/NFC PRINT RUN 25 SER.#'d SETS
UNPRICED AFC/NFC SPECT.#'d TO 5
*EMBOSSED/25: .5X TO 1.2X BASIC AU/100
EMBOSSED HOLOGRAM PRINT RUN 25
UNPRICED EMBOSSED HOLO.PRIME #'d TO 10
*SPEC.PLAT/50: .5X TO 1.2X BASIC AU/100
SPECTRUM PLATINUM PRINT RUN 50 SER.#'d SETS
251 JaMarcus Russell 8.00 20.00
252 Calvin Johnson 50.00 100.00
253 Joe Thomas 12.00 30.00
254 Gaines Adams 10.00 25.00
255 Greg Olsen 12.00 30.00
256 Adrian Peterson 100.00 200.00
257 Ted Ginn 10.00 25.00
258 Patrick Willis 12.00 30.00
259 Marshawn Lynch 25.00 60.00
260 Brady Quinn 8.00 20.00
261 Dwayne Bowe 8.00 20.00
262 Robert Meachem 10.00 25.00
263 Anthony Gonzalez 8.00 20.00
264 Kevin Kolb 10.00 25.00
265 John Beck 8.00 20.00
266 Drew Stanton 8.00 20.00
267 Sidney Rice 10.00 25.00
268 Dwayne Jarrett 10.00 25.00
269 Kenny Irons 8.00 20.00
270 Chris Henry 8.00 20.00
271 Steve Smith 8.00 20.00
272 Brian Leonard 8.00 20.00
273 Brandon Jackson 8.00 20.00
274 Lorenzo Booker 10.00 25.00
275 Yamon Figurs 8.00 20.00
276 Jason Hill 8.00 20.00
277 Paul Williams 8.00 20.00
278 Tony Hunt 8.00 20.00
279 Trent Edwards 8.00 20.00
280 Garrett Wolfe 8.00 20.00
281 Johnnie Lee Higgins 8.00 20.00
282 Michael Bush 8.00 20.00
283 Antonio Pittman 8.00 20.00
284 Troy Smith 8.00 20.00

2007 Absolute Memorabilia Spectrum Silver Autographs

STATED PRINT RUN 25-100 SER.#'d SETS
UNPRICED PLATINUM PRINT RUN 1
53 Marques Colston/100 10.00 25.00
54 Devery Henderson/100 5.00 12.00
140 Larry Johnson/100 12.50 30.00
148 Vincent Jackson/100 5.00 12.00
151 A.J. Davis/50 6.00 15.00
152 Aaron Rouse/50 6.00 15.00
153 Ahmad Bradshaw/50 10.00 25.00
155 Anthony Spencer/50 8.00 20.00
156 Brandon Siler/25 8.00 20.00
158 Chris Houston/50 6.00 15.00
159 Dallas Baker/50 6.00 15.00
160 Dan Bazuin/50 8.00 20.00
161 Danny Ware/56 10.00 25.00
163 David Irons/25 8.00 20.00
165 Earl Everett/25 8.00 20.00
166 Eric Frampton/50 8.00 20.00
169 Fred Bennett/25 8.00 20.00
171 H.B. Blades/25 8.00 20.00
172 Jarrett Hicks/25 10.00 25.00
174 Jason Snelling/50 6.00 15.00
178 Jon Beason/50 6.00 15.00
179 Jonathan Wade/25 8.00 20.00
180 Jordan Kent/50 8.00 20.00
181 Josh Gattis/25 8.00 20.00
182 Kenneth Darby/50 6.00 15.00
184 Levi Brown/25 8.00 20.00
185 Marcus McCauley/25 8.00 20.00
186 Tim Shaw/25 10.00 25.00
187 Michael Okwo/25 10.00 25.00
188 Mike Walker/50 10.00 25.00
189 Nate Ilaoa/50 8.00 20.00
190 Reggie Ball/25 10.00 25.00
191 Rhema McKnight/25 8.00 20.00
193 Rufus Alexander/30 6.00 15.00
194 Ryan McBean/25 12.00 30.00
195 Ryne Robinson/50 8.00 20.00
196 Selvin Young/25 8.00 20.00
197 Steve Breaston/50 6.00 15.00
198 Stewart Bradley/25 8.00 20.00
200 Tim Crowder/50 8.00 20.00

2007 Absolute Memorabilia Spectrum Gold Autographs

SERIAL #'d UNDER 25 NOT PRICED
10 Brandon Jacobs/27 10.00 25.00
53 Marques Colston/50 12.50 30.00
54 Devery Henderson/50 6.00 15.00
55 Reggie Bush/25 40.00 100.00
98 Willis McGahee/50 10.00 25.00
118 DeMeco Ryans/50 6.00 15.00
130 Maurice Jones-Drew/25
140 Larry Johnson/50 15.00 40.00
148 Vincent Jackson/50 6.00 15.00
153 Ahmad Bradshaw/25 12.00 30.00
155 Anthony Spencer/25 10.00 25.00
158 Chris Houston/25 8.00 20.00
159 Dallas Baker/25 8.00 20.00
160 Dan Bazuin/25 10.00 25.00
161 Danny Ware/25 12.00 30.00
174 Jason Snelling/25 8.00 20.00
178 Jon Beason/25 8.00 20.00
180 Jordan Kent/25 10.00 25.00
182 Kenneth Darby/25 8.00 20.00
188 Mike Walker/25 12.00 30.00
189 Nate Ilaoa/25 10.00 25.00
193 Rufus Alexander/25 8.00 20.00
195 Ryne Robinson/25 10.00 25.00
197 Steve Breaston/25 8.00 20.00
200 Tim Crowder/25 10.00 25.00

2007 Absolute Memorabilia Star Gazing

STATED PRINT RUN 100 SER.#'d SETS
*SPECTRUM/25: .8X TO 2X BASIC INSERTS
SPECTRUM PRINT RUN 25 SER.#'d SETS
UNPRICED AUTO PRINT RUN 5
UNPRICED MATERIAL AU PRINT RUN 5
1 Troy Smith .75 2.00
2 Dwayne Jarrett 1.00 2.50
3 Ted Ginn Jr. 1.00 2.50
4 John Beck .75 2.00
5 Lorenzo Booker 1.00 2.50
6 Antonio Pittman .75 2.00
7 Robert Meachem 1.00 2.50
8 Dwayne Bowe .75 2.00
9 Anthony Gonzalez .75 2.00
10 JaMarcus Russell .75 2.00
11 Greg Olsen 1.25 3.00
12 Michael Bush .75 2.00
13 Johnnie Lee Higgins .75 2.00
14 Kevin Kolb 1.00 2.50
15 Tony Hunt .75 2.00
16 Patrick Willis 1.25 3.00
17 Jason Hill .75 2.00
18 Gaines Adams 1.00 2.50
19 Trent Edwards .75 2.00
20 Marshawn Lynch 1.50 4.00
21 Chris Henry .75 2.00
22 Paul Williams .75 2.00
23 Sidney Rice 1.00 2.50
24 Adrian Peterson 2.50 6.00
25 Drew Stanton .75 2.00
26 Calvin Johnson 2.50 6.00
27 Yamon Figurs .75 2.00
28 Brian Leonard .75 2.00
29 Garrett Wolfe .75 2.00
30 Kenny Irons .75 2.00
31 Joe Thomas 1.25 3.00
32 Brady Quinn .75 2.00
33 Brandon Jackson .75 2.00
34 Steve Smith .75 2.00

2007 Absolute Memorabilia Star Gazing Materials

STATED PRINT RUN 100 SER.#'d SETS
*PRIME/50: .5X TO 1.2X BASIC JSY/100
PRIME PRINT RUN 50 SER.#'d SETS
*OVERSIZE/25: .8X TO 2X BASIC JSY/100
OVERSIZE PRINT RUN 25 SER.#'d SETS
*OVER.SPECT/10: 1.2X TO 3X BASIC JSY/100
OVERSIZE SPECTRUM PRINT RUN 10
1 Troy Smith 2.00 5.00
2 Dwayne Jarrett 2.50 6.00
3 Ted Ginn Jr. 2.50 6.00
4 John Beck 2.00 5.00
5 Lorenzo Booker 2.50 6.00
6 Antonio Pittman 2.00 5.00
7 Robert Meachem 2.50 6.00
8 Dwayne Bowe 2.00 5.00
9 Anthony Gonzalez 2.00 5.00
10 JaMarcus Russell 2.00 5.00
11 Greg Olsen 3.00 8.00
12 Michael Bush 2.00 5.00
13 Johnnie Lee Higgins 2.00 5.00
14 Kevin Kolb 2.50 6.00
15 Tony Hunt 2.00 5.00
16 Patrick Willis 3.00 8.00
17 Jason Hill 2.00 5.00
18 Gaines Adams 2.50 6.00
19 Trent Edwards 2.00 5.00
20 Marshawn Lynch 4.00 10.00
21 Chris Henry 2.00 5.00
22 Paul Williams 2.00 5.00
23 Sidney Rice 2.50 6.00
24 Adrian Peterson 6.00 15.00
25 Drew Stanton 2.00 5.00
26 Calvin Johnson 6.00 15.00
27 Yamon Figurs 2.00 5.00
28 Brian Leonard 2.00 5.00
29 Garrett Wolfe 2.00 5.00
30 Kenny Irons 2.00 5.00
31 Joe Thomas 3.00 8.00
32 Brady Quinn 2.00 5.00
33 Brandon Jackson 2.00 5.00
34 Steve Smith 2.00 5.00

2007 Absolute Memorabilia Team Quads

STATED PRINT RUN 100 SER.#'d SETS
*SPECTRUM/25: .6X TO 1.5X BASIC INSERTS
SPECTRUM PRINT RUN 25 SER.#'d SETS
1 Bold/Lein/Fitz/James 1.50 4.00
2 Muham/Grssmn/Brrn/Bnsn 1.25 3.00
3 Plmr/Chad/Rudi/Housh 1.50 4.00
4 Romo/TO/Jones/Glenn 2.50 6.00
5 Hrrisn/Mann/Wyne/Addai 5.00 12.00
6 McAll/Brees/Bush/Clstn 2.00 5.00
7 Burr/Eli/Shock/Jacobs 1.50 4.00
8 West/McNbb/Buckh/Brwn 1.50 4.00
9 Tmlin/Rivrs/Gates/McCard 2.00 5.00
10 Bruce/Jcksn/Holt/Bulger 2.00 5.00

2007 Absolute Memorabilia Team Quads Materials

STATED PRINT RUN 50 SER.#'d SETS
*PRIME/10: 1X TO 2.5X BASIC JSY/50
PRIME PRINT RUN 10 SER.#'d SETS
UNPRICED SPECTRUM PRINT RUN 1
1 Bold/Lein/Fitz/James 5.00 12.00
2 Muham/Grssmn/Brrn/Bnsn 4.00 10.00
3 Plmr/Chad/Rudi/Housh 5.00 12.00
4 Romo/TO/Jones/Glenn 8.00 20.00
5 Hrrisn/Mann/Wyne/Addai 15.00 40.00
6 McAll/Brees/Bush/Clstn 6.00 15.00
7 Burr/Eli/Shock/Jacobs 5.00 12.00
8 West/McNbb/Buckh/Brwn 5.00 12.00
9 Tmlin/Rivrs/Gates/McCard 6.00 15.00
10 Bruce/Jcksn/Holt/Bulger 6.00 15.00

2007 Absolute Memorabilia Team Tandems

STATED PRINT RUN 100 SER.#'d SETS
*SPECTRUM: .5X TO 1.2X BASIC INSERTS
SPECTRUM PRINT RUN 50 SER.#'d SETS
1 A.Boldin/L.Fitzgerald 1.50 4.00
2 W.Dunn/A.Crumpler 1.50 4.00
3 J.Losman/L.Evans 1.50 4.00
4 J.Delhomme/S.Smith 1.50 4.00
5 M.Muhammad/B.Berrian 1.25 3.00
6 C.Palmer/C.Johnson 1.50 4.00
7 B.Edwards/K.Winslow 1.25 3.00
8 T.Romo/T.Owens 2.50 6.00
9 B.Favre/D.Driver 4.00 10.00
10 M.Harrison/R.Wayne 1.50 4.00
11 F.Taylor/Jones-Drew 1.25 3.00
12 L.Johnson/T.Gonzalez 1.50 4.00
13 C.Chambers/R.Brown 1.25 3.00
14 T.Brady/L.Maroney 6.00 15.00
15 D.McAllister/R.Bush 1.50 4.00
16 P.Burress/J.Shockey 1.25 3.00
17 L.Coles/J.Cotchery 1.25 3.00
18 B.Westbrook/C.Buckhalter 1.25 3.00
19 H.Ward/W.Parker 1.50 4.00
20 L.Tomlinson/A.Gates 2.00 5.00
21 A.Smith QB/F.Gore 1.50 4.00
22 S.Alexander/D.Branch 1.25 3.00
23 I.Bruce/T.Holt 2.00 5.00
24 C.Portis/Sa.Moss 1.50 4.00
25 C.Williams/M.Alstott 1.50 4.00

2007 Absolute Memorabilia Team Tandems Materials

STATED PRINT RUN 100 SER.#'d SETS
*PRIME/25: .6X TO 1.5X BASIC JSY/100
PRIME PRINT RUN 25 SER.#'d SETS
UNPRICED PRIME SPECTRUM PRINT RUN 1
1 A.Boldin/L.Fitzgerald 2.50 6.00
2 W.Dunn/A.Crumpler 2.50 6.00
3 J.Losman/L.Evans 2.50 6.00
4 J.Delhomme/S.Smith 2.50 6.00
5 M.Muhammad/B.Berrian 2.00 5.00
6 C.Palmer/C.Johnson 2.50 6.00
7 B.Edwards/K.Winslow 2.00 5.00
8 T.Romo/T.Owens 4.00 10.00
9 B.Favre/D.Driver 6.00 15.00
10 M.Harrison/R.Wayne 2.50 6.00
11 F.Taylor/Jones-Drew 2.00 5.00
12 L.Johnson/T.Gonzalez 2.50 6.00
13 C.Chambers/R.Brown 2.00 5.00
14 T.Brady/L.Maroney 10.00 25.00
15 D.McAllister/R.Bush 2.50 6.00
16 P.Burress/J.Shockey 2.00 5.00
17 L.Coles/J.Cotchery 2.00 5.00
18 B.Westbrook/C.Buckhalter 2.00 5.00
19 H.Ward/W.Parker 2.50 6.00
20 L.Tomlinson/A.Gates 3.00 8.00
21 A.Smith QB/F.Gore 2.50 6.00
22 S.Alexander/D.Branch 2.00 5.00
23 I.Bruce/T.Holt 3.00 8.00
24 C.Portis/Sa.Moss 2.50 6.00
25 C.Williams/M.Alstott 2.50 6.00

2007 Absolute Memorabilia Team Trios

STATED PRINT RUN 100 SER.#'d SETS
*SPECTRUM/50: .6X TO 1.2X BASIC INSERTS
SPECTRUM PRINT RUN 50 SER.#'d SETS
1 Boldin/Leinart/Fitz 1.50 4.00
2 Muham/Grssmn/Berrian 1.25 3.00
3 Palmer/Chad/Rudi 1.50 4.00
4 Romo/TO/J.Jones 2.50 6.00
5 Harrison/Mann/Wayne 5.00 12.00
6 Taylor/Left/Jones-Drew 1.25 3.00
7 LJ/Gonzalez/Kennison 1.50 4.00
8 McAllis/Brees/Bush 2.00 5.00
9 Burress/Eli/Shockey 1.50 4.00
10 Wstbrk/McNabb/Buck. 1.50 4.00
11 Ward/Roeth/Parker 2.00 5.00
12 Tomlin/Rivers/Gates 2.00 5.00
13 Smith QB/Gore/Davis 1.50 4.00
14 Alexan/Hassel/Branch 1.25 3.00
15 Bruce/Jackson/Holt 2.00 5.00

2007 Absolute Memorabilia Team Trios Materials

STATED PRINT RUN 100 SER.#'d SETS
*PRIME/25: .6X TO 1.5X BASIC JSY/100
PRIME PRINT RUN 25 SER.#'d SETS
UNPRICED PRIME SPECTRUM PRINT RUN 1
1 Boldin/Leinart/Fitz 3.00 8.00
2 Muham/Grssmn/Berrian 2.50 6.00
3 Palmer/Chad/Rudi 3.00 8.00
4 Romo/TO/J.Jones 5.00 12.00
5 Harrison/Mann/Wayne 10.00 25.00
6 Taylor/Left/Jones-Drew 2.50 6.00
7 LJ/Gonzalez/Kennison 3.00 8.00
8 McAllis/Brees/Bush 4.00 10.00
9 Burress/Eli/Shockey 3.00 8.00
10 Wstbrk/McNabb/Buck. 3.00 8.00
11 Ward/Roeth/Parker 4.00 10.00
12 Tomlin/Rivers/Gates 4.00 10.00
13 Smith QB/Gore/Davis 3.00 8.00
14 Alexan/Hassel/Branch 2.50 6.00
15 Bruce/Jackson/Holt 4.00 10.00

2007 Absolute Memorabilia Tools of the Trade Red

RED PRINT RUN 100 SER.#'d SETS
*BLUE/75: .4X TO 1X RED/100
BLUE PRINT RUN 75 SER.#'d SETS
*BLACK/50: .5X TO 1.2X RED/100
BLACK PRINT RUN 50 SER.#'d SETS
*RED SPECT/25: .8X TO 2X RED/100
RED SPECTRUM PRINT RUN 25 SER.#'d SETS
*BLUE SPECT/10: 1.2X TO 3X RED/100
BLUE SPECTRUM PRINT RUN 10 SER.#'d SETS
UNPRICED BLACK SPECTRUM PRINT RUN 5
1 Aaron Rodgers 6.00 15.00
2 Ahman Green 2.00 5.00
3 A.J. Hawk 1.50 4.00
4 Alex Smith QB 2.00 5.00
5 Alge Crumpler 2.00 5.00
6 Amani Toomer 1.50 4.00
7 Andre Johnson 2.00 5.00
8 Anquan Boldin 1.50 4.00
9 Anthony Fasano 1.50 4.00
10 Antonio Gates 2.50 6.00
11 John Hannah 1.50 4.00
12 Ben Roethlisberger 2.50 6.00
13 Ben Watson 1.50 4.00
14 Bernard Berrian 1.50 4.00
15 Bobby Carpenter 1.50 4.00
16 Brad Smith 1.50 4.00
17 Brandon Jacobs 1.50 4.00
18 Brandon Jones 1.50 4.00
19 Brandon Marshall 2.00 5.00
20 Brandon Stokley 1.50 4.00
21 Braylon Edwards 1.50 4.00
22 Brett Favre 5.00 12.00
23 Brian Urlacher 2.50 6.00
24 Brian Westbrook 1.50 4.00
25 Brodie Croyle 2.00 5.00
26 Bruce Gradkowski 1.50 4.00
27 Bubba Franks 1.50 4.00
28 Bryant Young 1.50 4.00
29 Byron Leftwich 1.50 4.00
30 Cadillac Williams 2.00 5.00
31 Carson Palmer 2.00 5.00
32 Cedric Benson 1.50 4.00
33 Chad Johnson 1.50 4.00
34 Chad Lewis 1.50 4.00
35 Chad Pennington 1.50 4.00
36 Champ Bailey 2.00 5.00
37 Charlie Frye 2.00 5.00
38 Chester Taylor 1.50 4.00
39 Chris Brown 1.50 4.00
40 Chris Chambers 1.50 4.00
41 Chris Henry 1.50 4.00
42 Chris Simms 1.50 4.00
43 Clinton Portis 1.50 4.00
44 Correll Buckhalter 1.50 4.00
45 Curtis Martin 2.00 5.00
46 D'Brickashaw Ferguson 1.50 4.00
47 Dallas Clark 2.00 5.00
48 Darrell Jackson 1.50 4.00
49 Daunte Culpepper 2.00 5.00
50 DeAngelo Williams 1.50 4.00
51 Deion Branch 1.50 4.00
52 Demetrius Williams 1.50 4.00
53 Derrick Mason 1.50 4.00
54 DeShaun Foster 2.00 5.00
55 Deuce McAllister 2.00 5.00
56 Devin Hester 2.00 5.00
57 Donald Driver 2.00 5.00
58 Donovan McNabb 2.00 5.00
59 Drew Brees 2.50 6.00
60 Eddie Kennison 1.50 4.00
61 Edgerrin James 2.00 5.00
62 Eli Manning 2.00 5.00
63 Frank Gore 2.00 5.00
64 Fred Taylor 1.50 4.00
65 Greg Lewis 1.50 4.00
66 Hank Baskett 2.00 5.00
67 Heath Miller 1.50 4.00
68 Hines Ward 2.00 5.00
69 Isaac Bruce 2.50 6.00
70 J.P. Losman 1.50 4.00
71 Jason Campbell 1.50 4.00
72 Jason Taylor 2.00 5.00
73 Jason Witten 2.00 5.00
74 Jay Cutler 1.50 4.00
75 Jeremy Shockey 1.50 4.00
76 Jerious Norwood 1.50 4.00
77 Jerome Harrison 1.50 4.00
78 Jerricho Cotchery 1.50 4.00
79 Jevon Kearse 1.50 4.00
80 Joe Klopfenstein 1.50 4.00
81 Joey Galloway 2.00 5.00
82 Jon Kitna 1.50 4.00
83 Joseph Addai 1.50 4.00
84 Josh Reed 1.50 4.00
85 Julius Jones 1.50 4.00
86 Julius Peppers 2.00 5.00
87 Keary Colbert 1.50 4.00
88 Keenan McCardell 1.50 4.00
89 Kellen Winslow Jr. 1.50 4.00
90 Kevin Jones 1.50 4.00
91 Keyshawn Johnson 2.00 5.00
92 LaDainian Tomlinson 2.50 6.00
93 Larry Fitzgerald 2.00 5.00
94 Larry Johnson 1.50 4.00
95 Laurence Maroney 2.00 5.00
96 Laveranues Coles 1.50 4.00
97 Lee Evans 2.00 5.00
98 Leon Washington 1.50 4.00
99 Marc Bulger 1.50 4.00
100 Mario Williams 2.00 5.00
101 Marion Barber 2.00 5.00
102 Mark Clayton 1.50 4.00
103 Marvin Harrison 2.00 5.00
104 Mathias Kiwanuka 1.50 4.00
105 Matt Hasselbeck 1.50 4.00
106 Matt Jones 2.00 5.00
107 Matt Leinart 1.50 4.00
108 Maurice Jones-Drew 1.50 4.00
109 Michael Clayton 1.50 4.00
110 Michael Robinson 2.00 5.00
111 Michael Strahan 4.00 10.00
112 Michael Vick 2.00 5.00
113 Muhsin Muhammad 1.50 4.00
114 Nick Barnett 1.50 4.00
115 Peyton Manning 6.00 15.00
116 Philip Rivers 2.50 6.00
117 Plaxico Burress 1.50 4.00
118 Randy Moss 2.00 5.00
119 Reggie Brown 1.50 4.00
120 Reggie Bush 1.50 4.00
121 Reggie Wayne 2.00 5.00
122 Reggie Williams 2.00 5.00
123 Robert Ferguson 1.50 4.00
124 Ronnie Brown 1.50 4.00
125 Roy Williams S 1.50 4.00
126 Roy Williams WR 1.50 4.00
127 Rudi Johnson 1.50 4.00
128 Santana Moss 2.00 5.00
129 Shaun Alexander 1.50 4.00
130 Steve McNair 2.00 5.00
131 Steve Smith 2.00 5.00
132 Steven Jackson 1.50 4.00
133 T.J. Houshmandzadeh 1.50 4.00
134 Terence Newman 1.50 4.00
135 Terrell Owens 2.00 5.00
136 Terry Glenn 2.00 5.00
137 Todd Heap 1.50 4.00
138 Tony Gonzalez 2.00 5.00
139 Torry Holt 2.00 5.00
140 Trent Green 1.50 4.00
141 Troy Polamalu 2.50 6.00
142 Vernon Davis 1.50 4.00
143 Vince Young 1.50 4.00
144 Warrick Dunn 1.50 4.00
145 Willie Parker 2.00 5.00
146 Barry Sanders 6.00 15.00
147 Dan Marino 8.00 20.00
148 Joe Montana 12.00 30.00
149 Steve Largent 4.00 10.00
150 Walter Payton 8.00 20.00

2007 Absolute Memorabilia Tools of the Trade Material Red Oversize

STATED PRINT RUN 7-50
UNPRICED BLUE OVERSIZE PRINT RUN 1-5
22 Brett Favre 12.00 30.00
74 Jay Cutler 4.00 10.00
83 Joseph Addai 4.00 10.00
92 LaDainian Tomlinson 6.00 15.00
107 Matt Leinart 4.00 10.00
115 Peyton Manning 15.00 40.00
120 Reggie Bush/25 5.00 12.00
143 Vince Young 4.00 10.00
146 Barry Sanders 15.00 40.00
147 Dan Marino 20.00 50.00
148 Joe Montana 30.00 80.00
149 Steve Largent 10.00 25.00
150 Walter Payton 12.00 30.00

2007 Absolute Memorabilia Tools of the Trade Material Black Spectrum

COMMON CARD/40-50 3.00 8.00
SEMISTARS/40-50 4.00 10.00
UNL.STARS/40-50 5.00 12.00
COMMON CARD/15-25 4.00 10.00
SEMISTARS/15-25 4.00 12.00
STATED PRINT RUN 4-50
*DBL BLK SPC/25: 1X TO 2.5X BLK SPCT/40-50
*DBLE BLK/25: .8X TO 2X BLK SPEC/15-25
*DBLE BLK/15-20: 1.2X TO 3X BLK SPEC/40-50
UNPRICED BLACK OVER.SPECT.PRINT RUN 1
12 Ben Roethlisberger 5.00 12.00
22 Brett Favre 10.00 25.00
74 Jay Cutler/45 3.00 8.00
83 Joseph Addai 3.00 8.00
92 LaDainian Tomlinson 5.00 12.00
107 Matt Leinart/25 4.00 10.00
115 Peyton Manning 12.00 30.00
120 Reggie Bush 3.00 8.00
143 Vince Young 3.00 8.00
146 Barry Sanders 12.00 30.00
147 Dan Marino 12.00 30.00
148 Joe Montana 25.00 60.00
149 Steve Largent 8.00 20.00
150 Walter Payton 15.00 40.00

2007 Absolute Memorabilia Tools of the Trade Material Quad Red

STATED PRINT RUN 25 SER.#'d SETS
*BLUE/10: .8X TO 2X RED/25
BLUE PRINT RUN 2-10
UNPRICED BLACK SPECTRUM PRINT RUN 1
6 Amani Toomer 8.00 20.00
8 Anquan Boldin 8.00 20.00
23 Brian Urlacher 12.00 30.00
29 Byron Leftwich 8.00 20.00
30 Cadillac Williams 10.00 25.00
32 Cedric Benson 8.00 20.00
33 Chad Johnson 8.00 20.00
35 Chad Pennington 8.00 20.00
45 Curtis Martin 10.00 25.00
53 Derrick Mason 8.00 20.00
58 Donovan McNabb 10.00 25.00
69 Isaac Bruce 12.00 30.00
72 Jason Taylor 10.00 25.00
93 Larry Fitzgerald 10.00 25.00
96 Laveranues Coles 8.00 20.00
97 Lee Evans 10.00 25.00
103 Marvin Harrison/24 10.00 25.00
111 Michael Strahan 10.00 25.00
112 Michael Vick 10.00 25.00
115 Peyton Manning 30.00 80.00
139 Torry Holt 10.00 25.00
147 Dan Marino 50.00 125.00
149 Steve Largent 20.00 50.00

2007 Absolute Memorabilia Tools of the Trade Material Triple Red

STATED PRINT RUN 13-50
*BLUE/15-25: .8X TO 2X RED/35-50
BLUE PRINT RUN 9-25
UNPRICED BLACK SPECTRUM PRINT RUN 5
6 Amani Toomer 4.00 10.00
7 Andre Johnson 5.00 12.00
8 Anquan Boldin 4.00 10.00
22 Brett Favre 12.00 30.00
23 Brian Urlacher 6.00 15.00
29 Byron Leftwich 4.00 10.00
30 Cadillac Williams/35 5.00 12.00
31 Carson Palmer 5.00 12.00
33 Chad Johnson 4.00 10.00
35 Chad Pennington 4.00 10.00
36 Champ Bailey/40 5.00 12.00
40 Chris Chambers 4.00 10.00
43 Clinton Portis 4.00 10.00
45 Curtis Martin 5.00 12.00
48 Darrell Jackson 4.00 10.00
49 Daunte Culpepper 5.00 12.00
53 Derrick Mason 4.00 10.00
55 Deuce McAllister 5.00 12.00
58 Donovan McNabb 5.00 12.00
60 Eddie Kennison 4.00 10.00
61 Edgerrin James 5.00 12.00
62 Eli Manning 5.00 12.00
68 Hines Ward 10.00 25.00
69 Isaac Bruce 6.00 15.00
75 Jeremy Shockey 4.00 10.00
79 Jevon Kearse 4.00 10.00
81 Joey Galloway 5.00 12.00
92 LaDainian Tomlinson 6.00 15.00
93 Larry Fitzgerald 5.00 12.00
96 Laveranues Coles 4.00 10.00
99 Marc Bulger 4.00 10.00
103 Marvin Harrison/35 5.00 12.00
105 Matt Hasselbeck 4.00 10.00
111 Michael Strahan 5.00 12.00
112 Michael Vick 5.00 12.00
115 Peyton Manning 15.00 40.00
125 Roy Williams 4.00 10.00
129 Shaun Alexander 4.00 10.00
130 Steve McNair 5.00 12.00
131 Steve Smith 5.00 12.00
136 Terry Glenn 5.00 12.00
137 Todd Heap 4.00 10.00
138 Tony Gonzalez 5.00 12.00
139 Torry Holt 5.00 12.00
140 Trent Green 4.00 10.00
144 Warrick Dunn 4.00 10.00
147 Dan Marino 20.00 50.00
148 Joe Montana 30.00 80.00
149 Steve Largent 10.00 25.00

2007 Absolute Memorabilia War Room

STATED PRINT RUN 100 SER.#'d SETS
*SPECTRUM/25: .8X TO 2X BASIC INSERTS
SPECTRUM PRINT RUN 25 SER.#'d SETS
UNPRICED AUTO PRINT RUN 5
UNPRICED MATERIAL AU PRINT RUN 5
1 Ted Ginn Jr. 1.25 3.00
2 Joe Thomas 1.50 4.00
3 Brady Quinn 1.00 2.50
4 Brandon Jackson 1.00 2.50
5 Tony Hunt 1.00 2.50
6 Steve Smith 1.00 2.50
7 Dwayne Jarrett 1.25 3.00
8 Drew Stanton 1.00 2.50
9 Antonio Pittman 1.00 2.50
10 Dwayne Bowe 1.00 2.50
11 Anthony Gonzalez 1.00 2.50
12 Lorenzo Booker 1.25 3.00
13 Chris Henry 1.00 2.50
14 Gaines Adams 1.25 3.00
15 Kevin Kolb 1.25 3.00
16 John Beck 1.00 2.50
17 Brian Leonard 1.00 2.50
18 Adrian Peterson 3.00 8.00
19 Greg Olsen 1.50 4.00
20 JaMarcus Russell 1.00 2.50
21 Garrett Wolfe 1.00 2.50
22 Yamon Figurs 1.00 2.50
23 Sidney Rice 1.25 3.00
24 Trent Edwards 1.00 2.50
25 Michael Bush 1.00 2.50
26 Patrick Willis 1.50 4.00
27 Kenny Irons 1.00 2.50
28 Calvin Johnson 3.00 8.00
29 Paul Williams 1.00 2.50
30 Robert Meachem 1.25 3.00
31 Jason Hill 1.00 2.50
32 Marshawn Lynch 2.00 5.00
33 Johnnie Lee Higgins 1.00 2.50
34 Troy Smith 1.00 2.50

2007 Absolute Memorabilia War Room Materials

STATED PRINT RUN 100 SER.#'d SETS
*PRIME/50: .6X TO 1.5X BASIC JSY/100
PRIME PRINT RUN 50 SER.#'d SETS
*OVERSIZE/25: 1X TO 2.5X BASIC JSY/100
OVERSIZE PRINT RUN 25 SER.#'d SETS
*OVER.SPECT/10: 1.5X TO 4X BASIC JSY/100
OVERSIZE SPECTRUM PRINT RUN 10
1 Ted Ginn Jr. 2.50 6.00
2 Joe Thomas 3.00 8.00
3 Brady Quinn 2.00 5.00
4 Brandon Jackson 2.00 5.00
5 Tony Hunt 2.00 5.00
6 Steve Smith 2.00 5.00
7 Dwayne Jarrett 2.50 6.00
8 Drew Stanton 2.00 5.00
9 Antonio Pittman 2.00 5.00
10 Dwayne Bowe 2.00 5.00
11 Anthony Gonzalez 2.00 5.00
12 Lorenzo Booker 2.50 6.00
13 Chris Henry 2.00 5.00
14 Gaines Adams 2.50 6.00
15 Kevin Kolb 2.50 6.00
16 John Beck 2.00 5.00
17 Brian Leonard 2.00 5.00
18 Adrian Peterson 6.00 15.00
19 Greg Olsen 3.00 8.00
20 JaMarcus Russell 2.00 5.00
21 Garrett Wolfe 2.00 5.00
22 Yamon Figurs 2.00 5.00
23 Sidney Rice 2.50 6.00
24 Trent Edwards 2.00 5.00
25 Michael Bush 2.00 5.00
26 Patrick Willis 3.00 8.00
27 Kenny Irons 2.00 5.00
28 Calvin Johnson 6.00 15.00
29 Paul Williams 2.00 5.00
30 Robert Meachem 2.50 6.00
31 Jason Hill 2.00 5.00
32 Marshawn Lynch 4.00 10.00
33 Johnnie Lee Higgins 2.00 5.00
34 Troy Smith 2.00 5.00

2008 Absolute Memorabilia

This set was released on September 3, 2008. The base set consists of 284 cards. Cards #1-150 feature veterans, while cards #151-250 consist of rookies serial numbered to 799 with some autographed rookie cards serial numbered to 99. Finally, cards #251-284 are autographed rookie jerseys serial numbered of 299.

ROOKIE PRINT RUN 799 SER.#'d SETS
AU ROOKIE PRINT RUN 99 SER.#'d SETS
JSY AU ROOKIE PRINT RUN 299 SER.#'d SETS
1 Anquan Boldin .40 1.00
2 Edgerrin James .50 1.25
3 Kurt Warner .50 1.25
4 Larry Fitzgerald .50 1.25
5 Matt Leinart .40 1.00
6 Jerious Norwood .40 1.00
7 Roddy White .40 1.00
8 Michael Turner .40 1.00
9 Joey Harrington .40 1.00
10 Steve McNair .50 1.25
11 Willis McGahee .40 1.00
12 Derrick Mason .40 1.00
13 Yamon Figurs .40 1.00
14 Ray Lewis .60 1.50
15 Trent Edwards .40 1.00
16 Marshawn Lynch .50 1.25
17 Fred Jackson RC 1.25 3.00
18 Lee Evans .50 1.25
19 Josh Reed .40 1.00
20 Jake Delhomme .40 1.00
21 DeAngelo Williams .40 1.00
22 Steve Smith .50 1.25
23 Jon Beason .40 1.00
24 Rex Grossman .40 1.00
25 Adrian Peterson .40 1.00
26 Greg Olsen .50 1.25
27 Devin Hester .50 1.25
28 Brian Urlacher .60 1.50
29 Carson Palmer .50 1.25
30 Chad Johnson .40 1.00
31 Rudi Johnson .40 1.00
32 T.J. Houshmandzadeh .40 1.00
33 Kenny Watson .40 1.00
34 Derek Anderson .40 1.00
35 Jamal Lewis .50 1.25
36 Braylon Edwards .40 1.00
37 Kellen Winslow .40 1.00
38 Josh Cribbs .40 1.00
39 Tony Romo .50 1.25
40 Terrell Owens .50 1.25
41 Jason Witten .50 1.25
42 Marion Barber .40 1.00
43 DeMarcus Ware .50 1.25
44 Jay Cutler .40 1.00
45 Brandon Marshall .50 1.25
46 Selvin Young .40 1.00
47 Brandon Stokley .40 1.00
48 Tony Scheffler .40 1.00
49 Jon Kitna .40 1.00
50 Tatum Bell .40 1.00
51 Roy Williams WR .40 1.00
52 Calvin Johnson .60 1.50
53 Shaun McDonald .40 1.00
54 Aaron Rodgers 1.25 3.00
55 Greg Jennings .40 1.00
56 Donald Driver .50 1.25
57 James Jones .40 1.00
58 Ryan Grant .50 1.25
59 Matt Schaub .40 1.00
60 Ahman Green .50 1.25
61 Andre Johnson .50 1.25
62 Kevin Walter .50 1.25
63 Owen Daniels .40 1.00
64 Peyton Manning 1.50 4.00
65 Reggie Wayne .50 1.25
66 Marvin Harrison .50 1.25
67 Joseph Addai .40 1.00
68 Anthony Gonzalez .40 1.00
69 David Garrard .40 1.00
70 Fred Taylor .40 1.00
71 Maurice Jones-Drew .40 1.00
72 Jerry Porter .40 1.00
73 Reggie Williams .50 1.25
74 Brodie Croyle .50 1.25
75 Tony Gonzalez .50 1.25
76 Larry Johnson .40 1.00
77 Kolby Smith .40 1.00
78 Dwayne Bowe .50 1.25
79 John Beck .40 1.00
80 Ted Ginn .40 1.00
81 Ernest Wilford .40 1.00
82 Ronnie Brown .40 1.00
83 Tarvaris Jackson .40 1.00
84 Adrian Peterson .60 1.50
85 Chester Taylor .40 1.00
86 Bernard Berrian .40 1.00
87 Tom Brady 2.00 5.00
88 Laurence Maroney .50 1.25
89 Randy Moss .50 1.25
90 Wes Welker .50 1.25
91 Drew Brees .60 1.50
92 Deuce McAllister .50 1.25
93 Marques Colston .40 1.00
94 Reggie Bush .40 1.00
95 Devery Henderson .40 1.00
96 Eli Manning .50 1.25
97 Brandon Jacobs .40 1.00
98 Derrick Ward .40 1.00
99 Plaxico Burress .40 1.00
100 Steve Smith .50 1.25
101 Kellen Clemens .40 1.00
102 Thomas Jones .40 1.00
103 Laveranues Coles .40 1.00
104 Jerricho Cotchery .40 1.00
105 JaMarcus Russell .40 1.00
106 Justin Fargas .40 1.00
107 Michael Bush .40 1.00
108 Javon Walker .50 1.25
109 Zach Miller .40 1.00
110 Donovan McNabb .50 1.25
111 Brian Westbrook .40 1.00
112 Kevin Curtis .40 1.00
113 Reggie Brown .40 1.00
114 Ben Roethlisberger .60 1.50
115 Willie Parker .50 1.25
116 Santonio Holmes .40 1.00
117 Hines Ward .50 1.25
118 Philip Rivers .60 1.50
119 LaDainian Tomlinson .60 1.50
120 Antonio Gates .50 1.25
121 Vincent Jackson .40 1.00
122 Alex Smith .50 1.25
123 Frank Gore .50 1.25
124 Vernon Davis .40 1.00
125 Isaac Bruce .60 1.50
126 Arnaz Battle .40 1.00
127 Matt Hasselbeck .40 1.00
128 Lofa Tatupu .40 1.00
129 Deion Branch .40 1.00
130 Nate Burleson .40 1.00
131 Julius Jones .40 1.00
132 Marc Bulger .40 1.00
133 Steven Jackson .40 1.00
134 Torry Holt .50 1.25
135 Randy McMichael .40 1.00
136 Jeff Garcia .40 1.00
137 Cadillac Williams .50 1.25
138 Warrick Dunn .40 1.00
139 Joey Galloway .50 1.25
140 Michael Clayton .40 1.00
141 Vince Young .40 1.00
142 LenDale White .40 1.00
143 Alge Crumpler .40 1.00
144 Justin Gage .40 1.00
145 Roydell Williams .40 1.00
146 Jason Campbell .40 1.00
147 Clinton Portis .40 1.00
148 Chris Cooley .40 1.00
149 Santana Moss .40 1.00
150 Ladell Betts .40 1.00
151 Adrian Arrington AU RC 4.00 10.00
152 Alex Brink RC 2.00 5.00
153 Ali Highsmith RC 1.50 4.00
154 Allen Patrick AU RC 4.00 10.00
155 Andre Woodson AU RC 4.00 10.00
156 Anthony Alridge RC 1.50 4.00
157 Antoine Cason AU RC 5.00 12.00
158 Aqib Talib AU RC 6.00 15.00
159 Arman Shields RC 2.00 5.00
160 Brad Cottam AU RC 4.00 10.00
161 Brandon Flowers AU RC 5.00 12.00
162 Calais Campbell RC 2.00 5.00
163 Caleb Campbell RC 2.50 6.00
164 Chauncey Washington AU RC 5.00 12.00
165 Chevis Jackson RC 1.50 4.00
166 Chris Long AU RC 5.00 12.00
167 Colt Brennan AU RC 5.00 12.00
168 Cory Boyd AU RC 4.00 10.00
169 Craig Steltz RC 1.50 4.00
170 Curtis Lofton AU RC 5.00 12.00
171 Dan Connor AU RC 4.00 10.00
172 Dantrell Savage RC 2.00 5.00
173 Darius Reynaud RC 1.50 4.00
174 Darrell Strong RC 2.00 5.00
175 Davone Bess RC 2.00 5.00
176 Dennis Dixon AU RC 4.00 10.00
177 Derrick Harvey AU RC 4.00 10.00
178 DJ Hall RC 1.50 4.00
179 D.Rodgers-Cromartie AU RC 5.00 12.00
180 Erik Ainge AU RC 4.00 10.00
181 Erin Henderson RC 2.00 5.00
182 Ernie Wheelwright RC 2.00 5.00
183 Fred Davis AU RC 4.00 10.00
184 Joe Jon Finley RC 1.50 4.00
185 Jacob Hester AU RC 4.00 10.00
186 Jacob Tamme AU RC 5.00 12.00
187 Jalen Parmele RC 2.00 5.00
188 Jamar Adams RC 1.50 4.00
189 Jason Rivers RC 1.50 4.00
190 Jaymar Johnson RC 1.50 4.00
191 Jed Collins RC 2.00 5.00
192 Jermichael Finley AU RC 10.00 20.00
193 Jerod Mayo AU RC 6.00 15.00
194 John Carlson AU RC 4.00 10.00
195 Jonathan Hefney RC 1.50 4.00
196 Jordon Dizon AU RC 4.00 10.00
197 Josh Johnson AU RC 4.00 10.00
198 Josh Morgan AU RC 4.00 10.00
199 Justin Forsett AU RC 5.00 12.00
200 Justin Harper RC 1.50 4.00
201 Kalvin McRae RC 1.50 4.00
202 Keenan Burton AU RC 4.00 10.00
203 Keith Rivers AU RC 4.00 10.00
204 Kellen Davis RC 1.50 4.00
205 Kenneth Moore RC 1.50 4.00
206 Kenny Phillips AU RC 4.00 10.00
207 Kentwan Balmer AU RC 4.00 10.00
208 Kevin Robinson AU RC 4.00 10.00
209 Lavelle Hawkins AU RC 5.00 12.00
210 Lawrence Jackson AU RC 4.00 10.00
211 Leodis McKelvin AU RC 5.00 12.00
212 Marcus Henry RC 1.50 4.00
213 Marcus Monk RC 2.00 5.00
214 Marcus Smith AU RC 5.00 12.00
215 Marcus Thomas AU RC 5.00 12.00
216 Mark Bradford RC 1.50 4.00
217 Martellus Bennett AU RC 5.00 12.00
218 Martin Rucker AU RC 4.00 10.00
219 Matt Flynn AU RC 4.00 10.00
220 Mike Jenkins AU RC 4.00 10.00
221 Mike Hart AU RC 4.00 10.00
222 Owen Schmitt RC 1.50 4.00
223 Pat Sims RC 2.00 5.00
224 Paul Hubbard AU/91 RC 4.00 10.00
225 Paul Smith RC 1.50 4.00
226 Peyton Hillis RC 2.50 6.00
227 Phillip Merling RC 1.50 4.00
228 Pierre Garcon RC 3.00 8.00
229 Quentin Groves RC 2.00 5.00
230 Reggie Smith RC 1.50 4.00
231 Robert Killebrew RC 2.00 5.00
232 Ryan Grice-Mullen RC 1.50 4.00
233 Ryan Torain AU RC 5.00 12.00
234 Adarius Bowman RC 2.00 5.00
235 Sam Keller RC 1.50 4.00
236 Sedrick Ellis AU RC 4.00 10.00
237 Shawn Crable RC 1.50 4.00
238 Simeon Castille RC 1.50 4.00
239 Tashard Choice AU RC 4.00 10.00
240 Terrell Thomas RC 1.50 4.00
241 Dorien Bryant RC 2.00 5.00
242 Thomas Brown AU RC 4.00 10.00
243 Tim Hightower AU RC 5.00 12.00
244 Tracy Porter RC 2.00 5.00
245 Vernon Gholston AU RC 4.00 10.00
246 Bernard Morris RC 2.00 5.00
247 Will Franklin 5.00 12.00
248 Xavier Adibi RC 1.50 4.00
249 Xavier Omon RC 1.50 4.00
250 Zackary Bowman RC 2.00 5.00
251 Chad Henne RPM AU RC 5.00 12.00
252 Dustin Keller RPM AU RC 5.00 12.00
253 J.Stewart RPM AU RC 6.00 15.00
254 Steve Slaton RPM AU RC 4.00 10.00
255 Earl Bennett RPM AU RC 6.00 15.00
256 Brian Brohm RPM AU RC 4.00 10.00
257 Jamaal Charles RPM AU RC 8.00 20.00
258 M.Manningham RPM AU RC 4.00 10.00
259 Felix Jones RPM AU RC 4.00 10.00
260 DeS.Jackson RPM AU RC 8.00 20.00
261 Kevin O'Connell RPM AU RC 4.00 10.00
262 Kevin Smith RPM AU RC 4.00 10.00
263 Jerome Simpson RPM AU RC 5.00 12.00
264 D.McFadden RPM AU RC 4.00 10.00
265 Harry Douglas RPM AU RC 5.00 12.00
266 J.D.Booty RPM AU RC 4.00 10.00
267 R.Mendenhall RPM AU RC 4.00 10.00
268 Malcolm Kelly RPM AU RC 4.00 10.00
269 Matt Ryan RPM AU RC 30.00 80.00
270 Joe Flacco RPM AU RC 8.00 20.00
271 Early Doucet RPM AU RC 4.00 10.00
272 Andre Caldwell RPM AU RC 4.00 10.00
273 James Hardy RPM AU RC 4.00 10.00
274 Jordy Nelson RPM AU RC 20.00 40.00
275 G.Dorsey RPM AU RC EXCH 4.00 10.00
276 Chris Johnson RPM AU RC 5.00 12.00
277 Eddie Royal RPM AU RC 4.00 10.00
278 Matt Forte RPM AU RC 12.00 30.00
279 Ray Rice RPM AU RC 4.00 10.00
280 Devin Thomas RPM AU RC 4.00 10.00
281 Limas Sweed RPM AU RC 4.00 10.00
282 Dexter Jackson RPM AU RC 6.00 15.00
283 Donnie Avery RPM AU RC 5.00 12.00
284 Jake Long RPM AU RC 6.00 15.00

2008 Absolute Memorabilia Retail

*VETS 1-150: .2X TO .5X BASIC CARDS
*ROOKIES 151-250: .4X TO 1X BASIC CARDS
ROOKIES PRINT RUN 799 SER.#'d SETS
PRINTED ON WHITE CARD STOCK
101B Brett Favre 10.00 25.00

2008 Absolute Memorabilia Spectrum Blue Retail

*VETS 1-150: 1.2X TO 3X BASIC CARDS
*ROOKIES: .4X TO 1X SILVER SPECTRUM
RETAIL PACK INSERT PRINT RUN 250

2008 Absolute Memorabilia Spectrum Gold

*VETS 1-150: 3X TO 8X BASIC CARDS
*ROOKIES: 1X TO 2.5X SILVER SPECTRUM
STATED PRINT RUN 25 SER.#'d SETS

2008 Absolute Memorabilia Spectrum Platinum

UNPRICED PLATINUM PRINT RUN 1

2008 Absolute Memorabilia Spectrum Red Retail

*VETS 1-150: 1X TO 2.5X BASIC CARDS
*ROOKIES: .3X TO .8X SILVER SPECTRUM
RANDOM INSERTS IN RETAIL PACKS

2008 Absolute Memorabilia Spectrum Silver

*VETS 1-150: 1.2X TO 3X BASIC CARDS
COMMON ROOKIE 2.00 5.00
ROOKIE SEMISTARS 2.50 6.00
ROOKIE UNL.STARS 3.00 8.00
STATED PRINT RUN 100 SER.#'d SETS
166 Chris Long 2.50 6.00
167 Colt Brennan 2.50 6.00
175 Davone Bess 2.50 6.00
176 Dennis Dixon 2.00 5.00
180 Erik Ainge 2.00 5.00
185 Jacob Hester 2.00 5.00
193 Jerod Mayo 3.00 8.00
219 Matt Flynn 2.00 5.00
220 Mike Jenkins 2.00 5.00
221 Mike Hart 2.00 5.00
222 Owen Schmitt 2.00 5.00
226 Peyton Hillis 3.00 8.00
243 Tim Hightower 2.50 6.00
245 Vernon Gholston 2.00 5.00

2008 Absolute Memorabilia Spectrum Silver Retail

*VETERANS 1-150: 1.5X TO 4X BASIC CARDS
*ROOKIES: .5X TO 1.2X SILVER SPECTRUM
RETAIL PACK INSERT PRINT RUN 100

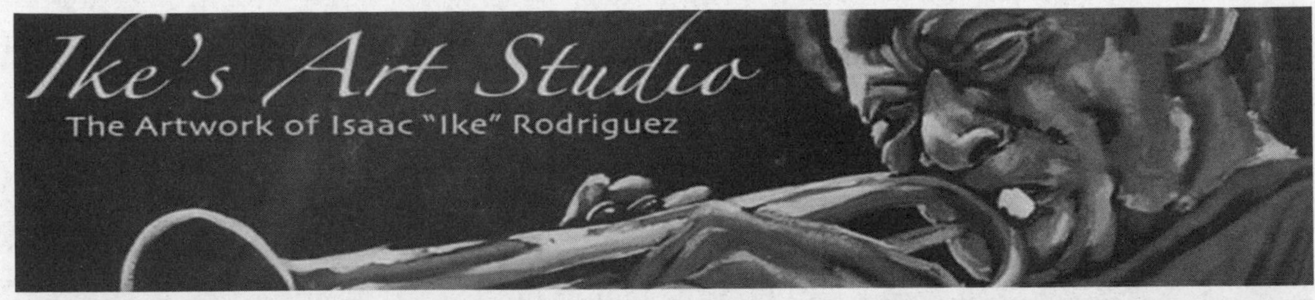

TEXAS ARTIST ISAAC "IKE" RODRIGUEZ

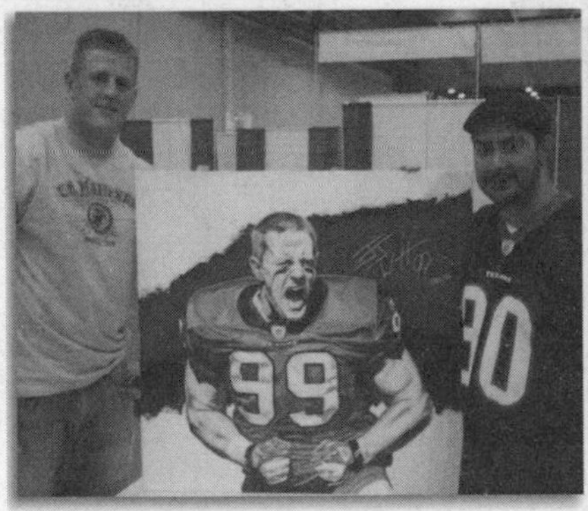

IKE AND JJ WATT @ TRISTAR 2012

IKE AND HACKSAW

"**Painting is what I love to do.** I enjoy getting to capture what and how I see the world through my paintings. And I am truly grateful for everyone who has allowed me to do that." **Ike**

Here at Ike's Art Studio we have available original paintings, high quality, limited-edition and autographed prints, canvas Giclées. We are also available for personal commissions as well. Follow and contact us!

www.ikesartstudio.com

Email: ike@ikesartstudio.com

IG: @izack1976

Twitter: @IkeRodriguez

Facebook: @ikesartstudio

2008 Absolute Memorabilia Absolute Heroes

STATED PRINT RUN 250 SER.#'d SETS
*SPECTRUM/25: 1X TO 2.5X BASIC INSERTS
SPECTRUM PRINT RUN 25 SER.#'d SETS
1 Donovan McNabb .75 2.00
2 Vince Young .60 1.50
3 Antonio Gates .75 2.00
4 Cadillac Williams .75 2.00
5 Philip Rivers 1.00 2.50
6 Kevin Curtis .60 1.50
7 Andre Johnson .75 2.00
8 LaDainian Tomlinson 1.00 2.50
9 Deuce McAllister .75 2.00
10 Marc Bulger .60 1.50
11 Ben Roethlisberger 1.00 2.50
12 Marvin Harrison .75 2.00
13 Eli Manning .75 2.00
14 Derrick Mason .60 1.50
15 Lee Evans .75 2.00
16 Fred Taylor .60 1.50
17 Terrell Owens .75 2.00
18 Roy Williams WR .60 1.50
19 Jon Kitna .60 1.50
20 Amani Toomer .60 1.50
21 Thomas Jones .60 1.50
22 Michael Clayton .60 1.50
23 Frank Gore .75 2.00
24 Peyton Manning 2.50 6.00
25 Devin Hester .75 2.00
26 Ronnie Brown .60 1.50
27 Steve Smith .75 2.00
28 Deion Branch .60 1.50
29 Hines Ward .75 2.00
30 Zach Miller .60 1.50

2008 Absolute Memorabilia Absolute Heroes Autographs Spectrum

STATED PRINT RUN 10-25
SERIAL #'d UNDER 25 NOT PRICED
30 Zach Miller/25 8.00 20.00

2008 Absolute Memorabilia Absolute Heroes Materials

RETAIL PACK INSERT PRINT RUN 130-200
1 Donovan McNabb 2.00 5.00
2 Vince Young 1.50 4.00
5 Philip Rivers 2.50 6.00
7 Andre Johnson 2.00 5.00
9 Deuce McAllister 2.00 5.00
10 Marc Bulger 1.50 4.00
11 Ben Roethlisberger 2.50 6.00
13 Eli Manning 2.00 5.00
14 Derrick Mason 1.50 4.00
18 Roy Williams WR 1.50 4.00
20 Amani Toomer 1.50 4.00
22 Michael Clayton 1.50 4.00
25 Devin Hester 2.00 5.00
26 Ronnie Brown 1.50 4.00
27 Steve Smith 2.00 5.00
28 Deion Branch/130 1.50 4.00
29 Hines Ward 2.00 5.00

2008 Absolute Memorabilia Absolute Heroes Materials Prime

PRIME PRINT RUN 50 SER.#'d SETS
UNPRICED SPECTRUM PRIME PRINT RUN 1
1 Donovan McNabb 3.00 8.00
3 Antonio Gates 3.00 8.00
4 Cadillac Williams 3.00 8.00
5 Philip Rivers 4.00 10.00
6 Kevin Curtis 2.50 6.00
7 Andre Johnson 3.00 8.00
8 LaDainian Tomlinson 4.00 10.00
9 Deuce McAllister 3.00 8.00
10 Marc Bulger 2.50 6.00
11 Ben Roethlisberger 4.00 10.00
12 Marvin Harrison 3.00 8.00
13 Eli Manning 3.00 8.00
14 Derrick Mason 2.50 6.00
15 Lee Evans 3.00 8.00
16 Fred Taylor 2.50 6.00
17 Terrell Owens 3.00 8.00
18 Roy Williams WR 2.50 6.00
19 Jon Kitna 2.50 6.00
20 Amani Toomer 2.50 6.00
21 Thomas Jones 2.50 6.00
22 Michael Clayton 2.50 6.00
23 Frank Gore 3.00 8.00
26 Ronnie Brown 2.50 6.00
27 Steve Smith 3.00 8.00
28 Deion Branch 2.50 6.00
29 Hines Ward 3.00 8.00

2008 Absolute Memorabilia Absolute Heroes Materials Autographs

STATED PRINT RUN 10-25
UNPRICED PRIME PRINT RUN 5-15
UNPRICED SPECTRUM PRIME PRINT RUN 1
SERIAL #'d UNDER 20 NOT PRICED
9 Deuce McAllister/25 10.00 25.00
18 Roy Williams WR/20 8.00 20.00

2008 Absolute Memorabilia Absolute Patches Prime

STATED PRINT RUN 5-25
UNPRICED SPECTRUM PRIME PRINT RUN 1
1 Tom Brady 80.00 200.00
2 Tony Romo/20 20.00 50.00
5 Eli Manning 20.00 50.00
7 LaDainian Tomlinson 25.00 60.00
8 Adrian Peterson 40.00 100.00
9 Brian Westbrook 15.00 40.00
10 Willie Parker 20.00 50.00
11 Marshawn Lynch 20.00 50.00
12 Joseph Addai 15.00 40.00
13 Ryan Grant 20.00 50.00
15 Randy Moss 20.00 50.00
16 Chad Johnson 15.00 40.00
17 Terrell Owens 20.00 50.00
18 Torry Holt 20.00 50.00
19 Greg Jennings 15.00 40.00
20 Tony Gonzalez 20.00 50.00

2008 Absolute Memorabilia Canton Absolutes

STATED PRINT RUN 250 SER.#'d SETS
*SPECTRUM/25: 1X TO 2.5X BASIC INSERTS
SPECTRUM PRINT RUN 25 SER.#'d SETS
1 Emmitt Smith 2.00 5.00
2 Brett Favre 2.50 6.00
3 Brian Westbrook .75 2.00
4 Chad Johnson .75 2.00
5 Peyton Manning 3.00 8.00
6 Tom Brady 4.00 10.00
7 Eli Manning 1.00 2.50
8 Terrell Owens 1.00 2.50
9 Randy Moss 1.00 2.50
10 LaDainian Tomlinson 1.25 3.00
11 Edgerrin James 1.00 2.50
12 Tony Gonzalez 1.00 2.50
13 Steve Smith 1.00 2.50
14 Hines Ward 1.00 2.50
15 Steve McNair 1.00 2.50
16 Warrick Dunn .75 2.00
17 Isaac Bruce 1.25 3.00
18 Marvin Harrison 1.00 2.50
19 Shaun Alexander .75 2.00
20 Torry Holt 1.00 2.50
21 Joey Galloway 1.00 2.50
22 Donovan McNabb 1.00 2.50
23 Tim Brown 1.25 3.00
24 Andre Reed 1.00 2.50
25 Tiki Barber 1.00 2.50
26 Phil Simms 1.00 2.50
27 Michael Strahan 1.00 2.50
28 Jerry Rice 2.50 6.00
29 Michael Irvin 1.25 3.00
30 Darrell Green 1.00 2.50

2008 Absolute Memorabilia Canton Absolutes Autographs Spectrum

UNPRICED AUTO PRINT RUN 10

2008 Absolute Memorabilia Canton Absolutes Materials Autographs

STATED PRINT RUN 5-25
UNPRICED PRIME PRINT RUN 5-20
UNPRICED SPECTRUM PRIME PRINT RUN 1-15
SERIAL #'d UNDER 25 NOT PRICED
30 Darrell Green/25 30.00 60.00

2008 Absolute Memorabilia Canton Absolutes Materials Prime

STATED PRINT RUN 12-25
UNPRICED SPECTRUM PRIME PRINT RUN 1
1 Emmitt Smith 10.00 25.00
3 Brian Westbrook 4.00 10.00
4 Chad Johnson 4.00 10.00
5 Peyton Manning/12 20.00 50.00
6 Tom Brady 20.00 50.00
7 Eli Manning 5.00 12.00
8 Terrell Owens 5.00 12.00
9 Randy Moss 5.00 12.00
10 LaDainian Tomlinson 6.00 15.00
11 Edgerrin James 5.00 12.00
12 Tony Gonzalez 5.00 12.00
13 Steve Smith 5.00 12.00
14 Hines Ward 5.00 12.00
15 Steve McNair 5.00 12.00
16 Warrick Dunn 4.00 10.00
17 Isaac Bruce 6.00 15.00
18 Marvin Harrison 5.00 12.00
19 Shaun Alexander 4.00 10.00
20 Torry Holt 5.00 12.00
21 Joey Galloway 5.00 12.00
22 Donovan McNabb 5.00 12.00
23 Tim Brown 6.00 15.00
24 Andre Reed 5.00 12.00
25 Tiki Barber 5.00 12.00
27 Michael Strahan 5.00 12.00
28 Jerry Rice 12.00 30.00
29 Michael Irvin 6.00 15.00

2008 Absolute Memorabilia College Materials

STATED PRINT RUN 35-100
UNPRICED SPECTRUM PRIME PRINT RUN 1-10
1 Allen Patrick 3.00 8.00
2 Brian Brohm/35 4.00 10.00
3 Chad Henne 4.00 10.00
4 Chris Long 4.00 10.00
5 Dan Connor 3.00 8.00
6 Early Doucet 3.00 8.00
7 Fred Davis 3.00 8.00
8 John David Booty 3.00 8.00
9 Glenn Dorsey 3.00 8.00
10 Keith Rivers 3.00 8.00
11 Kenny Phillips 3.00 8.00
12 Limas Sweed 3.00 8.00
13 Mike Hart 3.00 8.00
14 Brandon Flowers 4.00 10.00
15 Darren McFadden 3.00 8.00
16 Jamaal Charles 5.00 12.00
17 Malcolm Kelly 3.00 8.00
18 Terrell Thomas 3.00 8.00
19 Colt Brennan 4.00 10.00
20 Aqib Talib 5.00 12.00

2008 Absolute Memorabilia College Materials Autographs

STATED PRINT RUN 25 SER.#'d SETS
UNPRICED SPECTRUM PRIME PRINT RUN 5
1 Allen Patrick 10.00 25.00
2 Brian Brohm 6.00 15.00
3 Chad Henne 8.00 20.00
4 Chris Long 8.00 20.00
5 Dan Connor 6.00 15.00
6 Early Doucet 6.00 15.00
7 Fred Davis 6.00 15.00
8 John David Booty 6.00 15.00
9 Glenn Dorsey No AU 4.00 10.00
10 Keith Rivers 6.00 15.00
11 Kenny Phillips 6.00 15.00
12 Limas Sweed 6.00 15.00
13 Mike Hart 15.00 40.00
14 Brandon Flowers 8.00 20.00
15 Darren McFadden 6.00 15.00
16 Jamaal Charles 10.00 25.00
17 Malcolm Kelly 6.00 15.00
18 Terrell Thomas 6.00 15.00
19 Colt Brennan 8.00 20.00
20 Aqib Talib 10.00 25.00

2008 Absolute Memorabilia Gridiron Force

STATED PRINT RUN 250 SER.#'d SETS
*SPECTRUM/25: 1X TO 2.5X BASIC INSERTS
SPECTRUM PRINT RUN 25 SER.#'d SETS
1 Brandon Jacobs .60 1.50
2 Brandon Marshall .75 2.00
3 Braylon Edwards .60 1.50
4 Chris Cooley .60 1.50
5 Dallas Clark .60 1.50
6 DeAngelo Williams .60 1.50
7 DeMeco Ryans .75 2.00
8 Devin Hester .75 2.00
9 Donald Driver .75 2.00
10 Greg Jennings .60 1.50
11 Jason Witten .75 2.00
12 Marion Barber .60 1.50
13 Marshawn Lynch .75 2.00
14 Patrick Willis .75 2.00
15 Roddy White .60 1.50
16 T.J. Houshmandzadeh .60 1.50
17 Vincent Jackson .60 1.50
18 Wes Welker .75 2.00
19 Chester Taylor .60 1.50
20 LaMont Jordan .75 2.00
21 Marques Colston .60 1.50
22 Steven Jackson .60 1.50
23 Willis McGahee .60 1.50
24 Rudi Johnson .60 1.50
25 Jerricho Cotchery .60 1.50
26 LaRon Landry .75 2.00
27 Drew Brees 1.00 2.50
28 Greg Lewis .60 1.50
29 Larry Johnson .60 1.50
30 Clinton Portis .60 1.50
31 Laurence Maroney .75 2.00
32 Joseph Addai .60 1.50
33 Shaun Alexander .60 1.50
34 Reggie Bush .60 1.50
35 Larry Fitzgerald .75 2.00
36 Torry Holt .75 2.00
37 Matt Hasselbeck .60 1.50
38 Plaxico Burress .60 1.50
39 Joey Galloway .75 2.00
40 Santonio Holmes .60 1.50
41 Reggie Wayne .75 2.00
42 Willie Parker .75 2.00
43 Tony Romo .75 2.00
44 Eli Manning .75 2.00
45 Carson Palmer .75 2.00
46 Cedric Benson .60 1.50
47 Shawne Merriman .60 1.50
48 Vernon Davis .60 1.50
49 Maurice Jones-Drew .60 1.50
50 Adrian Peterson 1.00 2.50

2008 Absolute Memorabilia Gridiron Force Autographs Spectrum

STATED PRINT RUN 5-25
SERIAL #'d UNDER 25 NOT PRICED
7 DeMeco Ryans 8.00 20.00
15 Roddy White 6.00 15.00
17 Vincent Jackson 6.00 15.00
19 Chester Taylor 6.00 15.00
20 LaMont Jordan 8.00 20.00
21 Marques Colston 6.00 15.00
24 Rudi Johnson 6.00 15.00
25 Jerricho Cotchery 6.00 15.00
26 LaRon Landry 8.00 20.00
29 Larry Johnson 6.00 15.00
40 Santonio Holmes 6.00 15.00
46 Cedric Benson 6.00 15.00

2008 Absolute Memorabilia Gridiron Force Material Autographs

STATED PRINT RUN 10-25
1 Brandon Jacobs/15 8.00 20.00
5 Dallas Clark/25 8.00 20.00
6 DeAngelo Williams/25 8.00 20.00
7 DeMeco Ryans/25 10.00 25.00
13 Marshawn Lynch/25 10.00 25.00
14 Patrick Willis/25 10.00 25.00
17 Vincent Jackson/25 8.00 20.00
19 Chester Taylor/25 8.00 20.00
20 LaMont Jordan/25 10.00 25.00
21 Marques Colston/25 12.00 30.00
24 Rudi Johnson/20 8.00 20.00
25 Jerricho Cotchery/20 8.00 20.00
26 LaRon Landry/25 10.00 25.00
29 Larry Johnson/25 8.00 20.00
34 Reggie Bush/15 25.00 50.00
40 Santonio Holmes/25 15.00 40.00
46 Cedric Benson/25 8.00 20.00
48 Vernon Davis/20 8.00 20.00
49 Maurice Jones-Drew/25 8.00 20.00

2008 Absolute Memorabilia Gridiron Force Material Autographs Prime

PRIME PRINT RUN 5-25
*JER.NUM/15-25: .4X TO 1X PRIME/15-25
JERSEY NUMBER PRINT RUN 5-25
*POSITION/25: .4X TO 1X PRIME/15-25
POSITION AU PRINT RUN 1-25
10 Greg Jennings/15 8.00 20.00
11 Jason Witten/20 15.00 40.00
12 Marion Barber/20 25.00 50.00
13 Marshawn Lynch/20 10.00 25.00
14 Patrick Willis/25 10.00 25.00
15 Roddy White/20 8.00 20.00
17 Vincent Jackson/20 8.00 20.00
18 Wes Welker/15 30.00 60.00
19 Chester Taylor/15 8.00 20.00
20 LaMont Jordan/25 10.00 25.00
21 Marques Colston/25 12.00 30.00
24 Rudi Johnson/15 8.00 20.00
25 Jerricho Cotchery/15 8.00 20.00
26 LaRon Landry/25 10.00 25.00
29 Larry Johnson/25 8.00 20.00
32 Joseph Addai/15 8.00 20.00
40 Santonio Holmes/20 15.00 40.00
46 Cedric Benson/20 8.00 20.00
48 Vernon Davis/15 8.00 20.00
49 Maurice Jones-Drew/20 8.00 20.00

2008 Absolute Memorabilia Gridiron Force Material Prime Position

STATED PRINT RUN 25 SER.#'d SETS
*JER.NUM/15-25: .4X TO 1X POSITION/25
JERSEY NUMBER PRINT RUN 15-25
*PRIME/50: .3X TO .8X POSITION/25
*PRIME/25-35: .4X TO 1X POSITION/25
PRIME PRINT RUN 3-50
1 Brandon Jacobs 5.00 12.00
2 Brandon Marshall 6.00 15.00
3 Braylon Edwards 5.00 12.00
4 Chris Cooley 5.00 12.00
5 Dallas Clark 5.00 12.00
8 Devin Hester 10.00 25.00
9 Donald Driver 6.00 15.00
10 Greg Jennings 5.00 12.00
11 Jason Witten 8.00 20.00
12 Marion Barber 5.00 12.00
13 Marshawn Lynch 6.00 15.00
14 Patrick Willis 6.00 15.00
15 Roddy White 5.00 12.00
16 T.J. Houshmandzadeh 5.00 12.00
17 Vincent Jackson 5.00 12.00
18 Wes Welker 6.00 15.00
19 Chester Taylor 5.00 12.00
20 LaMont Jordan 6.00 15.00
21 Marques Colston 5.00 12.00
22 Steven Jackson 5.00 12.00
23 Willis McGahee 5.00 12.00
24 Rudi Johnson 5.00 12.00
25 Jerricho Cotchery 5.00 12.00
26 LaRon Landry 6.00 15.00
27 Drew Brees 8.00 20.00
28 Greg Lewis 5.00 12.00
29 Larry Johnson 5.00 12.00
30 Clinton Portis 5.00 12.00
31 Laurence Maroney 6.00 15.00
32 Joseph Addai 5.00 12.00
33 Shaun Alexander 5.00 12.00
34 Reggie Bush 5.00 12.00
36 Torry Holt 6.00 15.00
37 Matt Hasselbeck 5.00 12.00
38 Plaxico Burress 5.00 12.00
39 Joey Galloway 6.00 15.00
40 Santonio Holmes 5.00 12.00
41 Reggie Wayne 6.00 15.00
42 Willie Parker 6.00 15.00
43 Tony Romo 6.00 15.00
44 Eli Manning 6.00 15.00
45 Carson Palmer 6.00 15.00
46 Cedric Benson 5.00 12.00
47 Shawne Merriman 5.00 12.00
48 Vernon Davis 5.00 12.00
49 Maurice Jones-Drew 5.00 12.00
50 Adrian Peterson 15.00 40.00

2008 Absolute Memorabilia Marks of Fame

STATED PRINT RUN 250 SER.#'d SETS
*SPECTRUM/25: 1X TO 2.5X BASIC INSERTS
SPECTRUM PRINT RUN 25 SER.#'d SETS
1 Adrian Peterson 1.50 4.00
2 Anthony Gonzalez 1.00 2.50
3 Brian Westbrook 1.00 2.50
4 Calvin Johnson 1.50 4.00
5 Chris Henry RB 1.25 3.00
6 Earnest Graham 1.00 2.50
7 Frank Gore 1.25 3.00
8 James Jones 1.00 2.50
9 Jerious Norwood 1.00 2.50
10 Justin Fargas 1.00 2.50
11 Kenny Watson 1.00 2.50
12 Kevin Curtis 1.00 2.50
13 Kolby Smith 1.00 2.50
14 Patrick Crayton 1.25 3.00
15 Ryan Grant 1.25 3.00
16 Selvin Young 1.00 2.50
17 Sidney Rice 1.00 2.50
18 Trent Edwards 1.00 2.50
19 Garrett Wolfe 1.25 3.00
20 Anquan Boldin 1.00 2.50
21 Kellen Winslow 1.00 2.50
22 Steve Smith USC 1.25 3.00
23 David Garrard 1.00 2.50
24 Derek Anderson 1.00 2.50
25 Matt Schaub 1.00 2.50
26 Dwayne Bowe 1.25 3.00
27 Kurt Warner 1.25 3.00
28 Brandon Marshall 1.25 3.00
29 Eli Manning 1.25 3.00
30 Jamal Lewis 1.25 3.00
31 LenDale White 1.00 2.50
32 Jay Cutler 1.00 2.50
33 Jason Witten 1.25 3.00
34 Derrick Ward 1.00 2.50
35 Jason Campbell 1.00 2.50
36 Mike Furrey 1.25 3.00
37 Randy Moss 1.25 3.00
38 Santana Moss 1.00 2.50
39 Justin Gage 1.00 2.50
40 Wes Welker 1.25 3.00

2008 Absolute Memorabilia Marks of Fame Autographs Spectrum

STATED PRINT RUN 10-25
9 Jerious Norwood 6.00 15.00
10 Justin Fargas 6.00 15.00
11 Kenny Watson 6.00 15.00
13 Kolby Smith 6.00 15.00
18 Trent Edwards 6.00 15.00
34 Derrick Ward 6.00 15.00
36 Mike Furrey 8.00 20.00

2008 Absolute Memorabilia Marks of Fame Materials

RETAIL PACK INSERT PRINT RUN 15-200
2 Anthony Gonzalez 2.50 6.00
3 Brian Westbrook/135 2.50 6.00
4 Calvin Johnson 4.00 10.00
8 James Jones 2.50 6.00
9 Jerious Norwood 2.50 6.00
10 Justin Fargas 2.50 6.00
14 Patrick Crayton 3.00 8.00
17 Sidney Rice 2.50 6.00
20 Anquan Boldin 2.50 6.00
21 Kellen Winslow 2.50 6.00
22 Steve Smith USC 3.00 8.00
27 Kurt Warner/15 6.00 15.00
29 Eli Manning 3.00 8.00
32 Jay Cutler/75 3.00 8.00
34 Derrick Ward 2.50 6.00
35 Jason Campbell 2.50 6.00
36 Mike Furrey/100 3.00 8.00

2008 Absolute Memorabilia Marks of Fame Materials Prime

PRIME PRINT RUN 1-50
UNPRICED SPECTRUM PRIME PRINT RUN 1
SERIAL #'d UNDER 25 NOT PRICED
1 Adrian Peterson 5.00 12.00
2 Anthony Gonzalez 3.00 8.00
3 Brian Westbrook 3.00 8.00
4 Calvin Johnson 5.00 12.00
7 Frank Gore 4.00 10.00
8 James Jones 3.00 8.00
10 Justin Fargas 3.00 8.00
12 Kevin Curtis 3.00 8.00
14 Patrick Crayton 4.00 10.00
15 Ryan Grant 4.00 10.00
17 Sidney Rice 3.00 8.00
21 Kellen Winslow/45 3.00 8.00
22 Steve Smith USC 4.00 10.00
23 David Garrard 3.00 8.00
24 Derek Anderson 3.00 8.00
26 Dwayne Bowe 4.00 10.00
27 Kurt Warner 4.00 10.00
28 Brandon Marshall 4.00 10.00
29 Eli Manning 4.00 10.00
30 Jamal Lewis 4.00 10.00
31 LenDale White 3.00 8.00
33 Jason Witten 4.00 10.00
34 Derrick Ward 3.00 8.00
35 Jason Campbell/40 3.00 8.00
37 Randy Moss 4.00 10.00
38 Santana Moss 3.00 8.00

2008 Absolute Memorabilia Marks of Fame Materials Autographs

AUTO PRINT RUN 10-100
*PRIME/25: .5X TO 1.2X BASIC AU/100
PRIME PRINT RUN 5-25
UNPRICED SPECTRUM PRIME AU PRINT RUN 1
SERIAL #'d UNDER 15 NOT PRICED
2 Anthony Gonzalez/25 8.00 20.00
3 Brian Westbrook/15 8.00 20.00
4 Calvin Johnson/15 40.00 80.00
7 Frank Gore/15 10.00 25.00
9 Jerious Norwood/25 8.00 20.00
10 Justin Fargas/15 8.00 20.00
14 Patrick Crayton/100 8.00 20.00
17 Sidney Rice/35 8.00 20.00
34 Derrick Ward/25 8.00 20.00
36 Mike Furrey/50 8.00 20.00

2008 Absolute Memorabilia NFL Icons

STATED PRINT RUN 250 SER.#'d SETS
*SPECTRUM/25: 1X TO 2.5X BASIC INSERTS
SPECTRUM PRINT RUN 25 SER.#'d SETS
1 Emmitt Smith 2.00 5.00
2 Brett Favre 2.50 6.00
3 Alan Page .75 2.00
4 Billy Sims 1.00 2.50
5 Troy Aikman 1.50 4.00
6 Dan Fouts 1.00 2.50
7 Chuck Foreman .75 2.00
8 Earl Campbell 1.25 3.00
9 Jim Brown 1.50 4.00
10 Jim McMahon 1.25 3.00
11 Joe Klecko .75 2.00
12 John Elway 2.00 5.00
13 Lawrence Taylor 1.25 3.00
14 Mike Singletary 1.25 3.00
15 Reggie White 1.25 3.00
16 Ronnie Lott 1.00 2.50
17 Roger Staubach 1.50 4.00
18 John Stallworth 1.00 2.50
19 Charlie Joiner .75 2.00
20 Jack Youngblood .75 2.00
21 Phil Simms 1.00 2.50
22 Andre Reed 1.00 2.50
23 Darrell Green 1.00 2.50
24 Tiki Barber 1.00 2.50
25 Ted Hendricks .75 2.00
26 Warren Moon 1.25 3.00
27 Gale Sayers 1.25 3.00
28 LaDainian Tomlinson 1.25 3.00
29 Peyton Manning 3.00 8.00
30 Tom Brady 4.00 10.00

2008 Absolute Memorabilia NFL Icons Materials

STATED PRINT RUN 50 SER.#'d SETS
UNPRICED SPECTRUM PRIME PRINT RUN 1-10
3 Alan Page 5.00 12.00
4 Billy Sims 6.00 15.00
5 Troy Aikman 10.00 25.00
7 Chuck Foreman 5.00 12.00
8 Earl Campbell 8.00 20.00
10 Jim McMahon 8.00 20.00
11 Joe Klecko 5.00 12.00
12 John Elway 12.00 30.00
13 Lawrence Taylor 8.00 20.00
14 Mike Singletary 8.00 20.00
15 Reggie White 10.00 25.00
16 Ronnie Lott 6.00 15.00
17 Roger Staubach 10.00 25.00
18 John Stallworth 6.00 15.00
19 Charlie Joiner 5.00 12.00
20 Jack Youngblood 5.00 12.00
21 Phil Simms 6.00 15.00
23 Darrell Green 6.00 15.00
24 Tiki Barber 6.00 15.00
25 Ted Hendricks 5.00 12.00
26 Warren Moon 8.00 20.00

2008 Absolute Memorabilia NFL Icons Materials Prime

PRIME PRINT RUN 2-25
1 Emmitt Smith 15.00 40.00
3 Alan Page 6.00 15.00
4 Billy Sims 8.00 20.00
7 Chuck Foreman 6.00 15.00
8 Earl Campbell 10.00 25.00
10 Jim McMahon 10.00 25.00
11 Joe Klecko 6.00 15.00
15 Reggie White 12.00 30.00
16 Ronnie Lott 8.00 20.00
17 Roger Staubach 12.00 30.00
18 John Stallworth 8.00 20.00
22 Andre Reed 8.00 20.00
24 Tiki Barber 8.00 20.00
28 LaDainian Tomlinson 10.00 25.00
29 Peyton Manning 25.00 60.00
30 Tom Brady 30.00 80.00

2008 Absolute Memorabilia NFL Icons Materials AFC/NFC

STATED PRINT RUN 25
UNPRICED PRIME PRINT RUN 2-10
UNPRICED SPECTRUM PRIME PRINT RUN 1-5
3 Alan Page 6.00 15.00
4 Billy Sims 8.00 20.00
5 Troy Aikman 12.00 30.00
7 Chuck Foreman 6.00 15.00
8 Earl Campbell 10.00 25.00
9 Jim Brown 12.00 30.00
10 Jim McMahon 10.00 25.00
11 Joe Klecko 6.00 15.00
12 John Elway 15.00 40.00
13 Lawrence Taylor 10.00 25.00
14 Mike Singletary 10.00 25.00
15 Reggie White 10.00 25.00
16 Ronnie Lott 8.00 20.00
17 Roger Staubach 12.00 30.00
18 John Stallworth 8.00 20.00
20 Jack Youngblood 6.00 15.00
21 Phil Simms 8.00 20.00
23 Darrell Green 8.00 20.00
24 Tiki Barber 8.00 20.00
25 Ted Hendricks 6.00 15.00
26 Warren Moon 10.00 25.00
27 Gale Sayers 10.00 25.00

2008 Absolute Memorabilia Rookie Jersey Collection

ONE PER BLASTER RETAIL BOX
1 Brian Brohm 1.50 4.00
2 Chris Johnson 2.00 5.00
3 Darren McFadden 1.50 4.00
4 Devin Thomas 1.50 4.00
5 Donnie Avery 2.00 5.00
6 Earl Bennett 2.50 6.00
7 Eddie Royal 1.50 4.00
8 Harry Douglas 2.00 5.00
9 Jamaal Charles 2.50 6.00
10 Jerome Simpson 2.00 5.00
11 John David Booty 1.50 4.00
12 Jordy Nelson 5.00 12.00
13 Kevin Smith 1.50 4.00
14 Malcolm Kelly 1.50 4.00
15 Matt Forte 2.50 6.00
16 Rashard Mendenhall 1.50 4.00
17 Steve Slaton 1.50 4.00
18 Glenn Dorsey 1.50 4.00
19 Ray Rice 1.50 4.00
20 Matt Ryan 5.00 12.00
21 Mario Manningham 1.50 4.00
22 Limas Sweed 1.50 4.00
23 Kevin O'Connell 1.50 4.00
24 Jonathan Stewart 2.50 6.00
25 Joe Flacco 3.00 8.00
26 James Hardy 1.50 4.00
27 Jake Long 2.50 6.00
28 Felix Jones 1.50 4.00
29 Early Doucet 1.50 4.00
30 Dustin Keller 2.00 5.00
31 Dexter Jackson 2.50 6.00
32 DeSean Jackson 3.00 8.00
33 Chad Henne 2.00 5.00
34 Andre Caldwell 1.50 4.00

2008 Absolute Memorabilia Rookie Premiere Materials AFC/NFC

AFC/NFC PRINT RUN 199
*AFC/NFC SPECT.PRIME/25: .8X TO 2X
AFC/NFC SPECT.PRIME PRINT RUN 25
*NFL/199: .4X TO 1X AFC/NFC/199
NFL PRINT RUN 199
*NFL SPECT.PRIME/100: .5X TO 1.2X
NFL SPECT.PRIME PRINT RUN 100
*OVERSIZE/100: .5X TO 1.2X AFC/NFC/199
OVERSIZE PRINT RUN 100 SER.#'d SETS
UNPRICED OVER.SPECT.PRIME PRINT RUN 10
*JSY NUMBER/100: .5X TO 1.2X AFC/NFC/199
JERSEY NUMBER PRINT RUN 100
UNPRICED JSY NUMB.PRIME PRINT RUN 10
251 Chad Henne 2.00 5.00
252 Dustin Keller 2.00 5.00
253 Jonathan Stewart 2.50 6.00
254 Steve Slaton 1.50 4.00
255 Earl Bennett 2.50 6.00
256 Brian Brohm 1.50 4.00
257 Jamaal Charles 2.50 6.00
258 Mario Manningham 1.50 4.00
259 Felix Jones 1.50 4.00
260 DeSean Jackson 3.00 8.00
261 Kevin O'Connell 1.50 4.00
262 Kevin Smith 1.50 4.00
263 Jerome Simpson 2.00 5.00
264 Darren McFadden 1.50 4.00
265 Harry Douglas 2.00 5.00
266 John David Booty 1.50 4.00
267 Rashard Mendenhall 1.50 4.00
268 Malcolm Kelly 1.50 4.00
269 Matt Ryan 5.00 12.00
270 Joe Flacco 3.00 8.00
271 Early Doucet 1.50 4.00
272 Andre Caldwell 1.50 4.00
273 James Hardy 1.50 4.00
274 Jordy Nelson 5.00 12.00
275 Glenn Dorsey 1.50 4.00
276 Chris Johnson 2.00 5.00
277 Eddie Royal 1.50 4.00
278 Matt Forte 2.50 6.00
279 Ray Rice 1.50 4.00
280 Devin Thomas 1.50 4.00
281 Limas Sweed 1.50 4.00
282 Dexter Jackson 2.50 6.00
283 Donnie Avery 2.00 5.00
284 Jake Long 2.50 6.00

2008 Absolute Memorabilia Rookie Premiere Materials Autographs AFC/NFC

STATED PRINT RUN 25 SER.#'d SETS
*EMB.HOLO/31-35: .3X TO .8X AFC/NFC/25
*EMB.HOLO.PRM/15: .5X TO 1.2X AFC/NFC/25
251 Chad Henne 8.00 20.00
252 Dustin Keller 8.00 20.00
253 Jonathan Stewart 10.00 25.00
254 Steve Slaton 6.00 15.00
255 Earl Bennett 10.00 25.00
256 Brian Brohm 6.00 15.00
257 Jamaal Charles 10.00 25.00
258 Mario Manningham 6.00 15.00
259 Felix Jones 6.00 15.00
260 DeSean Jackson 12.00 30.00
261 Kevin O'Connell 6.00 15.00
262 Kevin Smith 6.00 15.00
263 Jerome Simpson 8.00 20.00
264 Darren McFadden 6.00 15.00
265 Harry Douglas 8.00 20.00
266 John David Booty 6.00 15.00
267 Rashard Mendenhall 6.00 15.00
268 Malcolm Kelly 6.00 15.00
269 Matt Ryan 60.00 120.00
270 Joe Flacco 12.00 30.00
271 Early Doucet 6.00 15.00
272 Andre Caldwell 6.00 15.00
273 James Hardy 6.00 15.00
274 Jordy Nelson 25.00 50.00
275 Glenn Dorsey No AU 6.00 15.00
276 Chris Johnson 8.00 20.00
277 Eddie Royal 6.00 15.00
278 Matt Forte 20.00 50.00
279 Ray Rice 6.00 15.00
280 Devin Thomas 6.00 15.00
281 Limas Sweed 6.00 15.00
282 Dexter Jackson 10.00 25.00
283 Donnie Avery 8.00 20.00
284 Jake Long 10.00 25.00

2008 Absolute Memorabilia Spectrum Gold Autographs

GOLD AUTO PRINT RUN 25 SER.#'d SETS
UNPRICED PLATINUM AU PRINT RUN 1
151 Adrian Arrington 5.00 12.00
154 Allen Patrick 5.00 12.00
155 Andre Woodson 5.00 12.00
157 Antoine Cason 6.00 15.00
158 Aqib Talib 8.00 20.00
160 Brad Cottam 5.00 12.00
161 Brandon Flowers 6.00 15.00
164 Chauncey Washington 6.00 15.00
166 Chris Long 6.00 15.00
167 Colt Brennan 6.00 15.00
168 Cory Boyd 5.00 12.00
170 Curtis Lofton 6.00 15.00
171 Dan Connor 5.00 12.00
176 Dennis Dixon 12.00 30.00
177 Derrick Harvey 5.00 12.00
179 Dominique Rodgers-Cromartie 6.00 15.00
180 Erik Ainge 5.00 12.00
183 Fred Davis 5.00 12.00
185 Jacob Hester 5.00 12.00
186 Jacob Tamme 6.00 15.00
192 Jermichael Finley 15.00 40.00
193 Jerod Mayo 8.00 20.00
194 John Carlson 5.00 12.00
196 Jordon Dizon 5.00 12.00
197 Josh Johnson 5.00 12.00
198 Josh Morgan 5.00 12.00
199 Justin Forsett 6.00 15.00
202 Keenan Burton 5.00 12.00
203 Keith Rivers 5.00 12.00
206 Kenny Phillips 5.00 12.00
207 Kentwan Balmer 5.00 12.00
208 Kevin Robinson 5.00 12.00
209 Lavelle Hawkins 6.00 15.00
210 Lawrence Jackson 5.00 12.00
211 Leodis McKelvin 6.00 15.00
214 Marcus Smith 6.00 15.00
215 Marcus Thomas 6.00 15.00
217 Martellus Bennett 6.00 15.00
218 Martin Rucker 5.00 12.00
219 Matt Flynn 5.00 12.00
220 Mike Jenkins 5.00 12.00
221 Mike Hart 5.00 12.00
233 Ryan Torain 6.00 15.00
236 Sedrick Ellis 5.00 12.00
239 Tashard Choice 5.00 12.00
242 Thomas Brown 5.00 12.00
243 Tim Hightower 20.00 50.00
245 Vernon Gholston 5.00 12.00
247 Will Franklin 6.00 15.00

2008 Absolute Memorabilia Star Gazing Materials

RETAIL PACK INSERT PRINT RUN 250
*PRIME/50: .6X TO 1.5X BASIC JSY/250
PRIME PRINT RUN 50 SER.#'d SETS
*OVER.JER.NUM/25: .8X TO 2X JSY/250
OVERSIZE JER NUM PRINT RUN 25
UNPRICED OVER.JER# PRIME PRINT RUN 10
OVERSIZED PRIME PRINT RUN 25
*OVER.PRIME/25: 1X TO 2.5X JSY/250
UNPRICED OVER.SPECT.PRIME PRINT RUN 10
1 Brian Brohm 1.50 4.00
2 Chris Johnson 2.00 5.00
3 Darren McFadden 1.50 4.00
4 Devin Thomas 1.50 4.00
5 Donnie Avery 2.00 5.00
6 Earl Bennett 2.50 6.00
7 Eddie Royal 1.50 4.00
8 Harry Douglas 2.00 5.00
9 Jamaal Charles 2.50 6.00
10 Jerome Simpson 2.00 5.00
11 John David Booty 1.50 4.00
12 Jordy Nelson 5.00 12.00
13 Kevin Smith 1.50 4.00
14 Malcolm Kelly 1.50 4.00
15 Matt Forte 2.50 6.00
16 Rashard Mendenhall 1.50 4.00
17 Steve Slaton 1.50 4.00
18 Glenn Dorsey 1.50 4.00
19 Ray Rice 1.50 4.00
20 Matt Ryan 5.00 12.00
21 Mario Manningham 1.50 4.00
22 Limas Sweed 1.50 4.00
23 Kevin O'Connell 1.50 4.00
24 Jonathan Stewart 2.50 6.00
25 Joe Flacco 3.00 8.00
26 James Hardy 1.50 4.00
27 Jake Long 2.50 6.00
28 Felix Jones 1.50 4.00
29 Early Doucet 1.50 4.00
30 Dustin Keller 2.00 5.00
31 Dexter Jackson 2.50 6.00
32 DeSean Jackson 3.00 8.00
33 Chad Henne 2.00 5.00
34 Andre Caldwell 1.50 4.00

2008 Absolute Memorabilia Star Gazing Materials Autographs

STATED PRINT RUN 25 SER.#'d SETS
*PRIME/25: .5X TO 1.2X BASIC AU/25
PRIME PRINT RUN 25 SER.#'d SETS
1 Brian Brohm 5.00 12.00
2 Chris Johnson 6.00 15.00
3 Darren McFadden 5.00 12.00
4 Devin Thomas 5.00 12.00
5 Donnie Avery 6.00 15.00
6 Earl Bennett 8.00 20.00
7 Eddie Royal 5.00 12.00
8 Harry Douglas 6.00 15.00
9 Jamaal Charles 8.00 20.00
10 Jerome Simpson 6.00 15.00
11 John David Booty 5.00 12.00
12 Jordy Nelson 25.00 50.00
13 Kevin Smith 5.00 12.00
14 Malcolm Kelly 5.00 12.00
15 Matt Forte 8.00 20.00
16 Rashard Mendenhall 5.00 12.00
17 Steve Slaton 5.00 12.00
18 Glenn Dorsey EXCH 20.00
19 Ray Rice 5.00 12.00
20 Matt Ryan 15.00 40.00
21 Mario Manningham 5.00 12.00
22 Limas Sweed 5.00 12.00
23 Kevin O'Connell 5.00 12.00
24 Jonathan Stewart 8.00 20.00
25 Joe Flacco 10.00 25.00
26 James Hardy 5.00 12.00
27 Jake Long 8.00 20.00
28 Felix Jones 5.00 12.00
29 Early Doucet 5.00 12.00
30 Dustin Keller 6.00 15.00
31 Dexter Jackson 8.00 20.00
32 DeSean Jackson 10.00 25.00
33 Chad Henne 6.00 15.00
34 Andre Caldwell 5.00 12.00

2008 Absolute Memorabilia Team Quads Materials Die Cut

STATED PRINT RUN 100 SER.#'d SETS
*PRIME/25: .6X TO 1.5X BASIC QUAD/100
SPECTRUM PRIME PRINT RUN 25 SER.#'d SETS
1 Romo/TO/Witten/Barber 15.00 40.00
2 Edwrd/Lynch/Evans/Reed 8.00 20.00
3 McNbb/Wstbrk/Crtis/Bckhltr 8.00 20.00
4 Eli/Burress/Jacobs/Shockey 8.00 20.00
5 Brees/Colston/McAllister/Bush 12.00 30.00
6 Rodgers/Jenn/Driver/Grant 15.00 40.00
7 Roeth/Ward/Parker/Holmes 15.00 40.00
8 Mann/Wayne/Harrison/Addai 12.00 30.00
9 Ander/Edwrds/Winslw/Lwis 8.00 20.00
10 Rivers/Tomlin/Gates/Jcksn 10.00 25.00
11 Smith QB/Gore/Davis/Willis 8.00 20.00
12 Leinart/Boldin/James/Fitz 8.00 20.00
13 Campbll/Portis/Cooley/Moss 6.00 15.00
14 Schaub/Jhnsn/Ryans/Will 8.00 20.00
15 Hassel/Alex/Branch/Brlesn 6.00 15.00
16 McGhee/Clytn/Lewis/Sggs 10.00 25.00
17 Young/Whit/Gage/McCare 6.00 15.00
18 Garcia/Gallo/Will/Clayton 8.00 20.00
20 Kitna/Will.WR/Jhnsn/Frrey 10.00 25.00

2008 Absolute Memorabilia Team Tandems Materials

STATED PRINT RUN 100 SER.#'d SETS
*SPECT.PRIME/25: .8X TO 2X BASIC TANDEM
SPECTRUM PRIME PRINT RUN 25 SER.#'d SETS
1 T.Brady/R.Moss 15.00 40.00
2 C.Palmer/C.Johnson 4.00 10.00
3 P.Rivers/L.Tomlinson 5.00 12.00
4 E.Manning/P.Burress 4.00 10.00
5 D.Brees/M.Colston 5.00 12.00
6 D.Anderson/B.Edwards 3.00 8.00
7 A.Rodgers/G.Jennings 10.00 25.00
8 T.Romo/T.Owens 4.00 10.00
9 P.Manning/R.Wayne 12.00 30.00
10 B.Roethlisberger/S.Holmes 8.00 20.00

2008 Absolute Memorabilia Team Trios Materials NFL

NFL TRIO PRINT RUN 100
*NFL SPECT.PRIME/25: .8X TO 2X BASIC TRIO
NFL SPECTRUM PRIME PRINT RUN 25
*AFC/NFC/50: .5X TO 1.2X BASIC TRIO
AFC/NFC PRINT RUN 50
*AFC/NFC SPECT.PRIME/25: .8X TO 2X
AFC/NFC SPECT.PRIME PRINT RUN 25
1 Roethlisberger/Holmes/Parker 8.00 20.00
2 Brady/Moss/Welker 15.00 40.00
3 Manning/Wayne/Addai 10.00 25.00
4 Palmer/Johnson/Houshmandzadeh 6.00 15.00
5 Romo/Owens/Witten 12.00 30.00
6 Jennings/Driver/Grant 8.00 20.00
7 Rivers/Tomlinson/Gates 8.00 20.00
8 Manning/Burress/Jacobs 8.00 20.00
9 Brees/Colston/Bush 6.00 15.00
10 Anderson/Edwards/Winslow 5.00 12.00
11 Garrard/Taylor/Jones-Drew 5.00 12.00
12 Edwards/Lynch/Evans 6.00 15.00
14 Gonzalez/Johnson/Bowe 6.00 15.00
15 Coles/Jones/Cotchery 5.00 12.00
16 Bulger/Holt/Jackson 6.00 15.00
17 Delhomme/Smith/Williams 5.00 12.00
18 Jackson/Peterson/Taylor 10.00 25.00
19 McNabb/Westbrook/Curtis 6.00 15.00
20 Leinart/Fitzgerald/Boldin 5.00 12.00

2008 Absolute Memorabilia Tools of the Trade Red Spectrum

RED PRINT RUN 100 SER.#'d SETS
*BLUE/50: .5X TO 1.2X RED/100
BLUE PRINT RUN 50 SER.#'d SETS
*GREEN/25: 1X TO 2.5X RED/100
GREEN PRINT RUN 25 SER.#'d SETS
*BLACK/10: 1.5X TO 4X RED/100
BLACK PRINT RUN 10 SER.#'d SETS
1 Emmitt Smith 2.50 6.00
2 Brett Favre 2.50 6.00
3 Carson Palmer 1.00 2.50
4 Chad Johnson .75 2.00
5 Cedric Benson .75 2.00
6 Larry Fitzgerald 1.00 2.50
7 Peyton Manning 3.00 8.00
8 Torry Holt 1.00 2.50
9 Tony Romo 1.00 2.50
10 Marvin Harrison 1.00 2.50
11 Eli Manning 1.00 2.50
12 Marion Barber .75 2.00
13 Michael Strahan 1.00 2.50
14 LaDainian Tomlinson 1.25 3.00
15 Tom Brady 4.00 10.00
16 Jerry Rice 3.00 8.00
17 Michael Irvin 1.50 4.00
18 Earl Campbell 1.50 4.00
19 John Elway 2.50 6.00
20 Mike Singletary 1.50 4.00
21 Reggie White 1.50 4.00
22 Roger Staubach 2.00 5.00
23 Phil Simms 1.25 3.00
24 Tiki Barber 1.00 2.50
25 Warren Moon 1.50 4.00
26 Tim Brown 1.50 4.00
27 Reggie Wayne 1.00 2.50
28 Ben Roethlisberger 1.25 3.00
29 Ryan Grant 1.00 2.50
30 Anquan Boldin .75 2.00
31 Greg Jennings .75 2.00
32 Brian Westbrook .75 2.00
33 Antonio Gates 1.00 2.50
34 David Garrard .75 2.00
35 Mike Furrey 1.00 2.50
36 Donovan McNabb 1.00 2.50
37 Philip Rivers 1.25 3.00
38 Marques Colston .75 2.00
39 Braylon Edwards .75 2.00
40 Plaxico Burress .75 2.00
41 T.J. Houshmandzadeh .75 2.00
42 Terrell Owens 1.00 2.50
43 Brandon Jacobs .75 2.00
44 Drew Brees 1.25 3.00
45 Derek Anderson .75 2.00
46 Kellen Winslow .75 2.00
47 Fred Taylor .75 2.00
48 Marshawn Lynch 1.00 2.50
49 Brandon Marshall 1.00 2.50
50 Dwayne Bowe 1.00 2.50
51 Larry Johnson .75 2.00
52 Adrian Peterson 1.25 3.00
53 Calvin Johnson 1.25 3.00
54 Brian Urlacher 1.25 3.00
55 Tony Gonzalez 1.00 2.50
56 Joey Galloway 1.00 2.50
57 Maurice Jones-Drew .75 2.00
58 Jake Delhomme .75 2.00
59 Steve Smith 1.00 2.50
60 Ray Lewis 1.25 3.00
61 Steven Jackson .75 2.00
62 Matt Hasselbeck .75 2.00
63 Clinton Portis .75 2.00
64 Frank Gore 1.00 2.50
65 Jeremy Shockey .75 2.00
66 Aaron Rodgers 2.50 6.00
67 Earnest Graham .75 2.00
68 LaRon Landry 1.00 2.50
69 Jason Witten 1.00 2.50
70 Santana Moss .75 2.00
71 Matt Schaub .75 2.00
72 Trent Edwards .75 2.00
73 Jerricho Cotchery .75 2.00
74 Kevin Curtis .75 2.00
75 Jamal Lewis 1.00 2.50

2008 Absolute Memorabilia Tools of the Trade Material Black Spectrum

BLACK SPECTRUM PRINT RUN 10-50
1 Emmitt Smith 12.00 30.00
2 Brett Favre 12.00 30.00
3 Carson Palmer 5.00 12.00
4 Chad Johnson 4.00 10.00
5 Cedric Benson 4.00 10.00

8 Torry Holt 5.00 12.00
9 Tony Romo 5.00 12.00
10 Marvin Harrison 5.00 12.00
11 Eli Manning 5.00 12.00
12 Marion Barber 4.00 10.00
13 Michael Strahan 5.00 12.00
14 LaDainian Tomlinson 6.00 15.00
15 Tom Brady 20.00 50.00
16 Jerry Rice 20.00 50.00
17 Michael Irvin/25 10.00 25.00
20 Mike Singletary 8.00 20.00
21 Reggie White 10.00 25.00
23 Phil Simms 6.00 15.00
24 Tiki Barber 5.00 12.00
27 Reggie Wayne 5.00 12.00
28 Ben Roethlisberger 6.00 15.00
29 Ryan Grant 5.00 12.00
32 Brian Westbrook 4.00 10.00
33 Antonio Gates 5.00 12.00
34 David Garrard 4.00 10.00
37 Philip Rivers 6.00 15.00
38 Marques Colston 4.00 10.00
39 Braylon Edwards 4.00 10.00
40 Plaxico Burress 4.00 10.00
41 T.J. Houshmandzadeh 4.00 10.00
42 Terrell Owens 5.00 12.00
43 Brandon Jacobs 4.00 10.00
44 Drew Brees 6.00 15.00
46 Kellen Winslow 4.00 10.00
47 Fred Taylor 4.00 10.00
48 Marshawn Lynch 5.00 12.00
49 Brandon Marshall 5.00 12.00
50 Dwayne Bowe 5.00 12.00
51 Larry Johnson 4.00 10.00
52 Adrian Peterson 6.00 15.00
53 Calvin Johnson 6.00 15.00
54 Brian Urlacher 6.00 15.00
55 Tony Gonzalez 5.00 12.00
56 Joey Galloway 5.00 12.00
57 Maurice Jones-Drew/20 5.00 12.00
58 Jake Delhomme 4.00 10.00
59 Steve Smith 5.00 12.00
60 Ray Lewis 6.00 15.00
61 Steven Jackson 4.00 10.00
62 Matt Hasselbeck 4.00 10.00
63 Clinton Portis 4.00 10.00
64 Frank Gore 5.00 12.00
65 Jeremy Shockey 4.00 10.00
66 Aaron Rodgers 12.00 30.00
69 Jason Witten 5.00 12.00
70 Santana Moss 4.00 10.00
73 Jerricho Cotchery 4.00 10.00
75 Jamal Lewis 5.00 12.00

2008 Absolute Memorabilia Tools of the Trade Material Red

STATED PRINT RUN 100 SER.#'d SETS
2 Brett Favre 10.00 25.00
3 Carson Palmer 4.00 10.00
5 Cedric Benson 3.00 8.00
6 Larry Fitzgerald 4.00 10.00
7 Peyton Manning/45 15.00 40.00
8 Torry Holt 4.00 10.00
9 Tony Romo 4.00 10.00
11 Eli Manning 4.00 10.00
12 Marion Barber 3.00 8.00
13 Michael Strahan 4.00 10.00
16 Jerry Rice 12.00 30.00
18 Earl Campbell/50 8.00 20.00
19 John Elway 10.00 25.00
20 Mike Singletary 6.00 15.00
21 Reggie White 8.00 20.00
22 Roger Staubach 10.00 25.00
23 Phil Simms 5.00 12.00
24 Tiki Barber 4.00 10.00
25 Warren Moon 6.00 15.00
26 Tim Brown 6.00 15.00
28 Ben Roethlisberger 5.00 12.00
29 Ryan Grant/90 4.00 10.00
30 Anquan Boldin 3.00 8.00
32 Brian Westbrook 3.00 8.00
34 David Garrard/99 3.00 8.00
35 Mike Furrey 4.00 10.00
36 Donovan McNabb 4.00 10.00
37 Philip Rivers 5.00 12.00
38 Marques Colston 3.00 8.00
40 Plaxico Burress 3.00 8.00
43 Brandon Jacobs 3.00 8.00
44 Drew Brees 5.00 12.00
46 Kellen Winslow 3.00 8.00
48 Marshawn Lynch 4.00 10.00
50 Dwayne Bowe/55 5.00 12.00
51 Larry Johnson 3.00 8.00
53 Calvin Johnson 5.00 12.00
54 Brian Urlacher 5.00 12.00
55 Tony Gonzalez 4.00 10.00
57 Maurice Jones-Drew 3.00 8.00
59 Steve Smith 4.00 10.00
60 Ray Lewis 5.00 12.00
61 Steven Jackson 3.00 8.00
62 Matt Hasselbeck 3.00 8.00
63 Clinton Portis 3.00 8.00
65 Jeremy Shockey 3.00 8.00
66 Aaron Rodgers 10.00 25.00
68 LaRon Landry 4.00 10.00
70 Santana Moss 3.00 8.00
71 Matt Schaub 3.00 8.00
73 Jerricho Cotchery 3.00 8.00

2008 Absolute Memorabilia Tools of the Trade Material Oversize Red

STATED PRINT RUN 50 SER.#'d SETS
UNPRICED OVERSIZE BLACK PRINT RUN 1-10
UNPRICED OVER.BLACK SPECT.PRINT RUN 1-5
UNPRICED TEAM LOGO GRN PRINT RUN 1-10
UNPRICED TEAM LOGO BLK PRINT RUN 1-10
1 Emmitt Smith 12.00 30.00
2 Brett Favre 12.00 30.00
3 Carson Palmer 5.00 12.00
5 Cedric Benson 4.00 10.00
6 Larry Fitzgerald/40 5.00 12.00
7 Peyton Manning 15.00 40.00
8 Torry Holt 5.00 12.00
9 Tony Romo 5.00 12.00
11 Eli Manning 5.00 12.00
13 Michael Strahan 5.00 12.00
16 Jerry Rice/25 20.00 50.00
18 Earl Campbell 8.00 20.00
19 John Elway 12.00 30.00
21 Reggie White/20 12.00 30.00
22 Roger Staubach 12.00 30.00
23 Phil Simms 6.00 15.00
24 Tiki Barber/40 5.00 12.00
26 Tim Brown/45 8.00 20.00
27 Reggie Wayne 5.00 12.00
30 Anquan Boldin 4.00 10.00
32 Brian Westbrook 4.00 10.00
35 Mike Furrey/15 6.00 15.00
36 Donovan McNabb 5.00 12.00
37 Philip Rivers/15 8.00 20.00
38 Marques Colston/15 5.00 12.00
40 Plaxico Burress/15 5.00 12.00
43 Brandon Jacobs 4.00 10.00
44 Drew Brees 6.00 15.00
46 Kellen Winslow 4.00 10.00
48 Marshawn Lynch 5.00 12.00
51 Larry Johnson 4.00 10.00
53 Calvin Johnson 6.00 15.00
54 Brian Urlacher 6.00 15.00
55 Tony Gonzalez/25 6.00 15.00
57 Maurice Jones-Drew/25 5.00 12.00
59 Steve Smith/20 6.00 15.00
60 Ray Lewis/40 6.00 15.00
61 Steven Jackson/25 5.00 12.00
62 Matt Hasselbeck 4.00 10.00
63 Clinton Portis 4.00 10.00
65 Jeremy Shockey 4.00 10.00
66 Aaron Rodgers 12.00 30.00
73 Jerricho Cotchery 4.00 10.00

2008 Absolute Memorabilia Tools of the Trade Material Oversize Jersey Number Blue

*JER# BLU/15-25: .5X TO 1.2X OVR.RED/40-50
*JER# BLUE/15-25: .4X TO 1X OVER.RED/15-25
JSY NUMBER BLUE PRINT RUN 5-25
UNPRICED JER NUM BLACK PRINT RUN 1-10
39 Braylon Edwards 5.00 12.00

2008 Absolute Memorabilia Tools of the Trade Double Material Black Spectrum

BLACK SPECTRUM PRINT RUN 4-50
1 Emmitt Smith 15.00 40.00
3 Carson Palmer/18 8.00 20.00
4 Chad Johnson 5.00 12.00
5 Cedric Benson 5.00 12.00
8 Torry Holt 6.00 15.00
10 Marvin Harrison 6.00 15.00
12 Marion Barber 5.00 12.00
13 Michael Strahan/25 8.00 20.00
14 LaDainian Tomlinson 8.00 20.00
15 Tom Brady 25.00 60.00
16 Jerry Rice 15.00 40.00
18 Earl Campbell 8.00 20.00
20 Mike Singletary/40 8.00 20.00
21 Reggie White 8.00 20.00
24 Tiki Barber 6.00 15.00
29 Ryan Grant/30 8.00 20.00
30 Anquan Boldin 5.00 12.00
32 Brian Westbrook 5.00 12.00
35 Mike Furrey 6.00 15.00
37 Philip Rivers 8.00 20.00
38 Marques Colston 5.00 12.00
40 Plaxico Burress 5.00 12.00
41 T.J. Houshmandzadeh 5.00 12.00
42 Terrell Owens 6.00 15.00
46 Kellen Winslow 5.00 12.00
48 Marshawn Lynch 6.00 15.00
50 Dwayne Bowe 6.00 15.00
51 Larry Johnson 5.00 12.00
53 Calvin Johnson/25 10.00 25.00
54 Brian Urlacher 8.00 20.00
55 Tony Gonzalez 6.00 15.00
56 Joey Galloway 6.00 15.00
57 Maurice Jones-Drew 5.00 12.00
58 Jake Delhomme 5.00 12.00
61 Steven Jackson 5.00 12.00
62 Matt Hasselbeck 5.00 12.00
63 Clinton Portis 5.00 12.00
65 Jeremy Shockey 5.00 12.00
68 LaRon Landry 6.00 15.00
69 Jason Witten 6.00 15.00
70 Santana Moss 5.00 12.00
72 Trent Edwards 5.00 12.00
73 Jerricho Cotchery 5.00 12.00
74 Kevin Curtis 5.00 12.00

2008 Absolute Memorabilia Tools of the Trade Double Material Blue

*DOUBLE BLUE/100: .5X TO 1.2X RED/100
*DOUBLE BLUE/30-42: .6X TO 1.5X RED/100
*DOUBLE BLUE/18: .8X TO 2X RED/100
RETAIL PACK INSERT PRINT RUN 9-100

2008 Absolute Memorabilia Tools of the Trade Double Material Autographs Black Spectrum

STATED PRINT RUN 1-25
SERIAL #'d UNDER 15 NOT PRICED
4 Chad Johnson/15 10.00 25.00
5 Cedric Benson/25 10.00 25.00
17 Michael Irvin/25 25.00 60.00
20 Mike Singletary/25 25.00 60.00
26 Tim Brown/25 25.00 60.00
31 Greg Jennings/25 10.00 25.00
35 Mike Furrey/25 12.00 30.00
38 Marques Colston/25 10.00 25.00
48 Marshawn Lynch/25 12.00 30.00
51 Larry Johnson/25 10.00 25.00
57 Maurice Jones-Drew/25 10.00 25.00
59 Steve Smith/25 12.00 30.00
61 Steven Jackson/25 10.00 25.00
68 LaRon Landry/25 12.00 30.00
69 Jason Witten/15 30.00 60.00
72 Trent Edwards/25 10.00 25.00
73 Jerricho Cotchery/25 10.00 25.00

2008 Absolute Memorabilia Tools of the Trade Triple Material Autographs Green

GREEN PRINT RUN 5-25
UNPRICED BLACK SPECT.PRINT RUN 1-10
22 Roger Staubach/25 40.00 80.00
68 LaRon Landry/25 12.00 30.00

2008 Absolute Memorabilia Tools of the Trade Triple Material Black Spectrum

STATED PRINT RUN 5-50
1 Emmitt Smith 20.00 50.00
3 Carson Palmer 8.00 20.00
13 Michael Strahan 10.00 25.00
16 Jerry Rice 15.00 40.00
21 Reggie White 15.00 40.00
54 Brian Urlacher 10.00 25.00
57 Maurice Jones-Drew 6.00 15.00
63 Clinton Portis 6.00 15.00
68 LaRon Landry 8.00 20.00

2008 Absolute Memorabilia War Room

STATED PRINT RUN 250 SER.#'d SETS
*SPECTRUM/25: 1X TO 2.5X BASIC INSERTS
SPECTRUM PRINT RUN 25 SER.#'d SETS
1 Andre Caldwell .60 1.50
2 Brian Brohm .60 1.50
3 Chad Henne .75 2.00
4 Chris Johnson .75 2.00
5 Darren McFadden .60 1.50
6 DeSean Jackson 1.25 3.00
7 Devin Thomas .60 1.50
8 Dexter Jackson 1.00 2.50
9 Donnie Avery .75 2.00
10 Dustin Keller .75 2.00
11 Earl Bennett 1.00 2.50
12 Early Doucet .60 1.50
13 Eddie Royal .60 1.50
14 Felix Jones .60 1.50
15 Harry Douglas .75 2.00
16 Jake Long 1.00 2.50
17 Jamaal Charles 1.00 2.50
18 James Hardy .60 1.50
19 Jerome Simpson .75 2.00
20 Joe Flacco 1.25 3.00
21 John David Booty .60 1.50
22 Jonathan Stewart 1.00 2.50
23 Jordy Nelson 2.00 5.00
24 Kevin O'Connell .60 1.50
25 Kevin Smith .60 1.50
26 Limas Sweed .60 1.50
27 Malcolm Kelly .60 1.50
28 Mario Manningham .60 1.50
29 Matt Forte 1.00 2.50
30 Matt Ryan 2.00 5.00
31 Rashard Mendenhall .60 1.50
32 Ray Rice .60 1.50
33 Steve Slaton .60 1.50
34 Glenn Dorsey .60 1.50

2008 Absolute Memorabilia War Room Materials

RETAIL PACK INSERT PRINT RUN 250
*PRIME/50: .8X TO 2X BASIC JSY/250
PRIME PRINT RUN 50
*OVER.JER NUM/25: 1X TO 2.5X BASIC JSY/250
OVERSIZE JSY NUMBER PRINT RUN 25
UNPRICED OVER.JER# PRIME PRINT RUN 3-10
*OVER.PRIME/25: 1X TO 2.5X BASIC JSY/250
OVERSIZE PRIME PRINT RUN 5-25
UNPRICED OVER.SPECT.PRIME PRINT RUN 3-10
1 Andre Caldwell 1.50 4.00
2 Brian Brohm 1.50 4.00
3 Chad Henne 2.00 5.00
4 Chris Johnson 2.00 5.00
5 Darren McFadden 1.50 4.00
6 DeSean Jackson 3.00 8.00
7 Devin Thomas 1.50 4.00
8 Dexter Jackson 2.50 6.00
9 Donnie Avery 2.00 5.00
10 Dustin Keller 2.00 5.00
11 Earl Bennett 2.50 6.00
12 Early Doucet 1.50 4.00
13 Eddie Royal 1.50 4.00
14 Felix Jones 1.50 4.00
15 Harry Douglas 2.00 5.00
16 Jake Long 2.50 6.00
17 Jamaal Charles 2.50 6.00
18 James Hardy 1.50 4.00
19 Jerome Simpson 2.00 5.00
20 Joe Flacco 3.00 8.00
21 John David Booty 1.50 4.00
22 Jonathan Stewart 2.50 6.00
23 Jordy Nelson 5.00 12.00
24 Kevin O'Connell 1.50 4.00
25 Kevin Smith 1.50 4.00
26 Limas Sweed 1.50 4.00
27 Malcolm Kelly 1.50 4.00
28 Mario Manningham 1.50 4.00
29 Matt Forte 2.50 6.00
30 Matt Ryan 5.00 12.00
31 Rashard Mendenhall 1.50 4.00
32 Ray Rice 1.50 4.00
33 Steve Slaton 1.50 4.00
34 Glenn Dorsey 1.50 4.00

2008 Absolute Memorabilia War Room Materials Autographs

JSY AU PRINT RUN 25 SER.#'d SETS
*PRIME/25: .5X TO 1.2X BASIC JSY AU
PRIME PRINT RUN 25 SER.#'d SETS
1 Andre Caldwell 5.00 12.00
2 Brian Brohm 5.00 12.00
3 Chad Henne 6.00 15.00
4 Chris Johnson 6.00 15.00
5 Darren McFadden 5.00 12.00
6 DeSean Jackson 10.00 25.00
7 Devin Thomas 5.00 12.00
8 Dexter Jackson 8.00 20.00
9 Donnie Avery 6.00 15.00
10 Dustin Keller 6.00 15.00
11 Earl Bennett 8.00 20.00
12 Early Doucet 5.00 12.00
13 Eddie Royal 5.00 12.00
14 Felix Jones 5.00 12.00
15 Harry Douglas 6.00 15.00
16 Jake Long 8.00 20.00
17 Jamaal Charles 8.00 20.00
18 James Hardy 5.00 12.00
19 Jerome Simpson 6.00 15.00
20 Joe Flacco 10.00 25.00
21 John David Booty 5.00 12.00
22 Jonathan Stewart 8.00 20.00
23 Jordy Nelson 25.00 50.00
24 Kevin O'Connell 5.00 12.00
25 Kevin Smith 5.00 12.00
26 Limas Sweed 5.00 12.00
27 Malcolm Kelly 5.00 12.00
28 Mario Manningham 5.00 12.00
29 Matt Forte 8.00 20.00
30 Matt Ryan 15.00 40.00
31 Rashard Mendenhall 5.00 12.00
32 Ray Rice 5.00 12.00
33 Steve Slaton 5.00 12.00
34 Glenn Dorsey EXCH

2009 Absolute Memorabilia

AUTO ROOKIE PRINT RUN 99-149
RPM AUTO PRINT RUN 149-299
1 Kurt Warner .40 1.00
2 Larry Fitzgerald .40 1.00
3 Tim Hightower .30 .75
4 Matt Ryan .40 1.00
5 Michael Turner .30 .75
6 Roddy White .30 .75
7 Derrick Mason .30 .75
8 Joe Flacco .40 1.00
9 Willis McGahee .30 .75
10 Lee Evans .40 1.00
11 James Hardy .40 1.00
12 Terrell Owens .40 1.00
13 DeAngelo Williams .30 .75
14 Jake Delhomme .30 .75
15 Jonathan Stewart .30 .75
16 Steve Smith .40 1.00
17 Greg Olsen .40 1.00
18 Jay Cutler .30 .75
19 Matt Forte .30 .75
20 Carson Palmer .40 1.00
21 Cedric Benson .30 .75
22 Chad Ochocinco .30 .75
23 Brady Quinn .30 .75
24 Braylon Edwards .30 .75
25 Jamal Lewis .40 1.00
26 Marion Barber .40 1.00
27 Tashard Choice .30 .75
28 Tony Romo .40 1.00
29 Brandon Marshall .40 1.00
30 Correll Buckhalter .30 .75
31 Kyle Orton .30 .75
32 Calvin Johnson .50 1.25
33 Daunte Culpepper .40 1.00
34 Kevin Smith .30 .75
35 Aaron Rodgers 1.00 2.50
36 Greg Jennings .30 .75
37 Ryan Grant .40 1.00
38 Andre Johnson .40 1.00
39 Matt Schaub .30 .75
40 Steve Slaton .30 .75
41 Anthony Gonzalez .30 .75
42 Joseph Addai .30 .75
43 Peyton Manning 1.25 3.00
44 Reggie Wayne .40 1.00
45 David Garrard .30 .75
46 Maurice Jones-Drew .30 .75
47 Marcedes Lewis .30 .75
48 Dwayne Bowe .40 1.00
49 Jamaal Charles .40 1.00
50 Matt Cassel .30 .75
51 Tony Gonzalez .40 1.00
52 Chad Pennington .30 .75
53 Ted Ginn .30 .75
54 Ronnie Brown .30 .75
55 Adrian Peterson .50 1.25
56 Bernard Berrian .30 .75
57 Visanthe Shiancoe .40 1.00
58 Laurence Maroney .40 1.00
59 Tom Brady 1.50 4.00
60 Wes Welker .40 1.00
61 Randy Moss .40 1.00
62 Drew Brees .50 1.25
63 Jeremy Shockey .30 .75
64 Reggie Bush .30 .75
65 Eli Manning .40 1.00
66 Brandon Jacobs .30 .75
67 Kevin Boss .30 .75
68 Thomas Jones .30 .75
69 Jerricho Cotchery .30 .75
70 Leon Washington .30 .75
71 Darren McFadden .50 1.25
72 JaMarcus Russell .30 .75
73 Justin Fargas .30 .75
74 Brian Westbrook .30 .75
75 Kevin Curtis .30 .75
76 Donovan McNabb .40 1.00
77 Ben Roethlisberger .50 1.25
78 Santonio Holmes .30 .75
79 Rashard Mendenhall .30 .75
80 Philip Rivers .50 1.25
81 LaDainian Tomlinson .50 1.25
82 Darren Sproles .40 1.00
83 Frank Gore .40 1.00
84 Josh Morgan .30 .75
85 Vernon Davis .30 .75
86 Matt Hasselbeck .30 .75
87 T.J. Houshmandzadeh .30 .75
88 John Carlson .40 1.00
89 Marc Bulger .30 .75
90 Steven Jackson .30 .75
91 Donnie Avery .30 .75
92 Antonio Bryant .30 .75
93 Derrick Ward .30 .75
94 Kellen Winslow Jr. .30 .75
95 Chris Johnson .30 .75
96 Brandon Jones .30 .75
97 Justin Gage .30 .75
98 Chris Cooley .30 .75
99 Clinton Portis .30 .75
100 Jason Campbell .30 .75
101 Aaron Maybin RC 1.50 4.00
102 Aaron Kelly AU/149 RC 4.00 10.00
103 Aaron Brown RC 1.50 4.00
104 Alphonso Smith RC 1.25 3.00
105 Andre Smith RC 1.25 3.00
106 Anthony Hill RC 1.25 3.00
107 Arian Foster RC 3.00 8.00
108 Asher Allen RC 1.25 3.00
109 Austin Collie AU/149 RC 4.00 10.00
110 B.J. Raji AU/99 RC 5.00 12.00
111 Bernard Scott RC 2.00 5.00
112 Bradley Fletcher RC 1.25 3.00
113 Brandon Tate AU/149 RC 5.00 12.00
114 Brandon Gibson AU/149 RC 5.00 12.00
115 Brian Orakpo AU/99 RC 5.00 12.00
116 Brian Cushing AU/99 RC 4.00 10.00
117 Brian Hartline RC 2.00 5.00
118 Brooks Foster AU/149 RC 4.00 10.00
119 Cameron Morrah AU/149 RC 4.00 10.00
120 Cedric Peerman AU/99 RC 4.00 10.00
121 Chase Coffman AU/149 RC 4.00 10.00
122 Chris Ogbonnaya RC 1.50 4.00
123 Chris Owens RC 1.25 3.00
124 Clay Matthews AU/99 RC 30.00 80.00
125 Clint Sintim AU/99 RC 4.00 10.00
126 Cody Brown RC 1.25 3.00
127 Connor Barwin RC 1.50 4.00
128 C.Ingram AU/149 RC 4.00 10.00
129 Curtis Painter RC 1.25 3.00
130 Darcel McBath RC 1.25 3.00
131 Darius Butler RC 1.50 4.00
132 David Johnson RC 1.50 4.00
133 David Veikune RC 1.50 4.00
134 DeAndre Levy RC 1.50 4.00
135 D.Byrd AU/149 RC 5.00 12.00
136 Devin Moore AU/99 RC 4.00 10.00
137 Davon Drew RC 1.25 3.00
138 D.Edison AU/149 RC 4.00 10.00
139 Eddie Williams RC 1.50 4.00
140 Eugene Monroe RC 1.25 3.00
141 Evander Hood RC 2.00 5.00
142 Everette Brown AU/149 RC 4.00 10.00
143 Gartrell Johnson RC 1.25 3.00
144 Hunter Cantwell AU/149 RC 4.00 10.00
145 Jairus Byrd RC 2.00 5.00
146 J.Laurinaitis AU/149 RC 4.00 10.00
147 James Casey AU/149 RC 5.00 12.00
148 James Davis RC 1.25 3.00
149 Jared Cook AU/149 RC 5.00 12.00
150 Jarett Dillard AU/149 RC 4.00 10.00
151 Jason Williams RC 1.50 4.00
152 Javarris Williams RC 1.50 4.00
153 Jeremy Childs RC 1.25 3.00
154 Jerraud Powers RC 1.25 3.00
155 John Phillips RC 2.00 5.00
156 Johnny Knox AU/149 RC 5.00 12.00
157 Kaluka Maiava RC 1.25 3.00
158 Keith Null RC 1.50 4.00
159 Kenny McKinley AU/149 RC 4.00 10.00
160 Kevin Ogletree AU/149 RC 5.00 12.00
161 Kory Sheets RC 1.50 4.00
162 Lardarius Webb RC 2.00 5.00
163 Larry English AU/99 RC 5.00 12.00
164 Louis Murphy AU/149 RC 4.00 10.00
165 Louis Delmas RC 1.50 4.00
166 Malcolm Jenkins AU/149 RC 4.00 10.00
167 Manuel Johnson RC 1.25 3.00
168 Marko Mitchell RC 1.25 3.00
169 Bear Pascoe RC 1.50 4.00
170 Michael Mitchell RC 1.25 3.00
171 Michael Oher RC 2.00 5.00
172 Mike Teel RC 1.25 3.00
173 Mike Goodson AU/149 RC 5.00 12.00
174 Nathan Brown AU/149 RC 5.00 12.00
175 P.J. Hill AU/149 RC 4.00 10.00
176 Patrick Chung RC 1.25 3.00
177 Peria Jerry RC 1.25 3.00
178 Quan Cosby AU/149 RC 4.00 10.00
179 Quinn Johnson AU/149 RC 4.00 10.00
180 Quinten Lawrence RC 1.25 3.00
181 R.Jennings AU/149 RC 5.00 12.00
182 Rashad Johnson RC 1.25 3.00
183 Rey Maualuga AU/99 RC 6.00 15.00
184 Richard Quinn RC 1.50 4.00
185 Robert Ayers RC 1.25 3.00
186 Ron Brace RC 1.50 4.00
187 Ryan Mouton RC 1.25 3.00
188 Sammie Stroughter RC 1.25 3.00
189 Sean Smith RC 1.25 3.00
190 Shawn Nelson No AU/149 RC 2.50 6.00
191 Sherrod Martin RC 1.25 3.00
192 Tiquan Underwood RC 1.25 3.00
193 Tom Brandstater RC 1.50 4.00
194 Tony Fiammetta AU/149 RC 4.00 10.00
195 Travis Beckum AU/149 RC 4.00 10.00
196 Tyrell Sutton RC 1.25 3.00
197 Tyrone McKenzie RC 1.50 4.00
198 Darius Passmore RC 1.25 3.00
199 Vontae Davis AU/149 RC 4.00 10.00
200 William Moore RC 1.25 3.00
201 M.Stafford RPM AU/299 RC 30.00 80.00
202 Jason Smith RPM AU/199 RC 4.00 10.00
203 Ty.Jackson RPM AU/149 RC 4.00 10.00
204 Aaron Curry RPM AU/299 RC 6.00 15.00
205 M.Sanchez RPM AU/299 RC 4.00 10.00
206 Heyward-By RPM AU/199 RC 6.00 15.00
207 M.Crabtree RPM AU/299 RC 6.00 15.00
208 K.Moreno RPM AU/249 RC 4.00 10.00
209 J.Freeman RPM AU/199 RC 4.00 10.00
210 J.Maclin RPM AU/199 RC 5.00 12.00
211 Pettigrew RPM AU/299 RC 4.00 10.00
212 P.Harvin RPM AU/299 RC 4.00 10.00
213 D.Brown RPM AU/199 RC 8.00 20.00
214 Nicks RPM AU/199 RC EXCH 5.00 12.00
215 Kenny Britt RPM AU/299 RC 6.00 15.00
216 Chris Wells RPM AU/249 RC 4.00 10.00
217 B.Robiskie RPM AU/299 RC 4.00 10.00
218 Pat White RPM AU/149 RC 5.00 12.00
219 Massaquoi RPM AU/149 RC 4.00 10.00
220 L.McCoy RPM AU/199 RC 15.00 40.00
221 S.Greene RPM AU/299 RC 4.00 10.00
222 G.Coffee RPM AU/299 RC 4.00 10.00
223 D.Williams RPM AU/199 RC 4.00 10.00
224 J.Ringer RPM AU/299 RC 4.00 10.00
225 M.Wallace RPM AU/299 RC 6.00 15.00
226 R.Barden RPM AU/149 RC 4.00 10.00
227 P.Turner RPM AU/299 RC 4.00 10.00
228 Deon Butler RPM AU/299 RC 4.00 10.00
229 Juaquin Iglesias RPM AU/149 RC 4.00 10.00
230 McGee RPM AU/149 RC 4.00 10.00
231 Mike Thomas RPM AU/149 RC 4.00 10.00
232 Andre Brown RPM AU/249 RC 5.00 12.00
233 Rhett Bomar RPM AU/199 RC 4.00 10.00
234 Nate Davis RPM AU/199 RC 4.00 10.00

2009 Absolute Memorabilia Retail

*VETS 1-100: .25X TO .6X BASIC CARDS
*ROOKIES 101-200: .4X TO 1X BASIC CARDS
ROOKIE STATED PRINT RUN 499

2009 Absolute Memorabilia Spectrum Black Retail

*1-100 VETS/50: 2X TO 5X BASIC CARDS
*1-200 ROOK/50: .25X TO .6X SPECT.SILVER
RETAIL PACK INSERT PRINT RUN 50

2009 Absolute Memorabilia Spectrum Blue Retail

*VETS/75: 1.5X TO 4X BASIC CARDS
RETAIL PACK INSERT PRINT RUN 75

2009 Absolute Memorabilia Spectrum Red Retail

*VETS 1-100: 1X TO 2.5X BASIC CARDS
RANDOM INSERTS IN RETAIL PACKS

2009 Absolute Memorabilia Spectrum Silver

*VETS 1-100: 3X TO 8X BASIC CARDS
COMMON ROOKIE (101-200) 3.00 8.00
ROOKIE SEMISTARS 4.00 10.00
ROOKIE UNL.STARS 5.00 12.00
STATED PRINT RUN 25 SER.#'d SETS
110 B.J. Raji 4.00 10.00
115 Brian Orakpo 4.00 10.00
116 Brian Cushing 3.00 8.00
124 Clay Matthews 12.00 30.00
141 Evander Hood 5.00 12.00
146 James Laurinaitis 3.00 8.00
156 Johnny Knox 4.00 10.00
183 Rey Maualuga 5.00 12.00
185 Robert Ayers 3.00 8.00

2009 Absolute Memorabilia Absolute Heroes

RANDOM INSERTS IN RETAIL PACKS
*SPECTRUM/25: 1.2X TO 3X BASIC INSERTS
1 Andre Johnson .60 1.50
2 Anthony Gonzalez .50 1.25
3 Antonio Bryant .50 1.25
4 Brandon Marshall .60 1.50
5 Brandon Jacobs .50 1.25
6 Braylon Edwards .50 1.25
7 Brian Urlacher .75 2.00
8 Brian Westbrook .50 1.25
9 Dallas Clark .50 1.25
10 David Garrard .50 1.25
11 Derrick Mason .50 1.25
12 Jerricho Cotchery .50 1.25
13 Kerry Collins .50 1.25
14 Kurt Warner .60 1.50
15 Lee Evans .60 1.50
16 Marc Bulger .50 1.25
17 Matt Schaub .50 1.25
18 Philip Rivers .75 2.00
19 Ricky Williams .60 1.50
20 Santonio Holmes .50 1.25
21 Steve Breaston .60 1.50
22 Steve Smith .60 1.50
23 Tom Brady 2.50 6.00
24 Tony Romo .60 1.50
25 Vince Young .50 1.25

2009 Absolute Memorabilia Absolute Heroes Materials Spectrum Prime

STATED PRINT RUN 50 SER.#'d SETS
1 Andre Johnson 3.00 8.00
2 Anthony Gonzalez 2.50 6.00
5 Brandon Jacobs 2.50 6.00
6 Braylon Edwards 2.50 6.00
7 Brian Urlacher 4.00 10.00
8 Brian Westbrook 2.50 6.00
9 Dallas Clark 2.50 6.00
10 David Garrard 2.50 6.00
11 Derrick Mason 2.50 6.00
12 Jerricho Cotchery 2.50 6.00
15 Lee Evans 3.00 8.00
16 Marc Bulger 2.50 6.00
18 Philip Rivers 4.00 10.00
19 Ricky Williams 3.00 8.00
20 Santonio Holmes 2.50 6.00
22 Steve Smith 3.00 8.00
23 Tom Brady 12.00 30.00
24 Tony Romo 3.00 8.00
25 Vince Young 2.50 6.00

2009 Absolute Memorabilia Absolute Heroes Materials Autographs

STATED PRINT RUN 2-25
SERIAL #'d UNDER 15 NOT PRICED
4 Brandon Marshall/25 10.00 25.00
6 Braylon Edwards/15 8.00 20.00
9 Dallas Clark/25 8.00 20.00
20 Santonio Holmes/20 8.00 20.00

2009 Absolute Memorabilia Absolute Patches Spectrum Prime

STATED PRINT RUN 10-25
SERIAL #'d UNDER 15 NOT PRICED
1 Adrian Peterson/21 20.00 50.00
2 Andre Johnson/25 15.00 40.00
3 Brandon Jacobs/25 12.00 30.00
4 Brian Urlacher/15 20.00 50.00
5 Brian Westbrook/25 12.00 30.00
6 Calvin Johnson/25 25.00 60.00
7 Carson Palmer/25 15.00 40.00
8 Chad Ochocinco/25 12.00 30.00
9 Clinton Portis/25 12.00 30.00
10 DeAngelo Williams/25 12.00 30.00
12 Dwayne Bowe/25 15.00 40.00
13 Eli Manning/25 15.00 40.00
14 Frank Gore/25 15.00 40.00
15 Greg Jennings/25 12.00 30.00
16 Joseph Addai/25 15.00 40.00
17 Larry Fitzgerald/25 15.00 40.00
18 Lee Evans/25 15.00 40.00
19 Michael Turner/24 12.00 30.00
21 Philip Rivers/25 20.00 50.00
22 Ray Lewis/25 25.00 60.00
23 Reggie Wayne/25 15.00 40.00
24 Santonio Holmes/25 12.00 30.00
25 Steven Jackson/25 12.00 30.00

2009 Absolute Memorabilia Canton Absolutes

RANDOM INSERTS IN RETAIL PACKS
*SPECTRUM/25: 1.2X TO 3X BASIC INSERTS
1 Kurt Warner .60 1.50
2 Peyton Manning 2.00 5.00
3 Eli Manning .60 1.50
4 Ben Roethlisberger .75 2.00
5 Tom Brady 2.50 6.00
6 Andre Johnson .60 1.50
7 Steve Smith .60 1.50
8 Randy Moss .60 1.50
9 Hines Ward .60 1.50
10 Jason Witten .60 1.50
11 Chad Ochocinco .50 1.25
12 Brian Westbrook .50 1.25
13 Donovan McNabb .60 1.50
14 LaDainian Tomlinson .75 2.00
15 Adrian Peterson .75 2.00
16 Clinton Portis .50 1.25
17 Tony Romo .60 1.50
18 Maurice Jones-Drew .50 1.25
19 Greg Jennings .50 1.25
20 Tony Gonzalez .60 1.50
21 Larry Fitzgerald .60 1.50
22 Reggie Wayne .60 1.50
23 Brandon Jacobs .50 1.25
24 Terrell Owens .60 1.50
25 Fred Taylor .50 1.25

2009 Absolute Memorabilia Canton Absolutes Materials Spectrum Prime

STATED PRINT RUN 10-50
SERIAL #'d UNDER 15 NOT PRICED
3 Eli Manning/50 3.00 8.00
4 Ben Roethlisberger/50 4.00 10.00
5 Tom Brady/50 12.00 30.00
6 Andre Johnson/50 3.00 8.00
7 Steve Smith/50 3.00 8.00
9 Hines Ward/50 3.00 8.00
10 Jason Witten/50 3.00 8.00
11 Chad Ochocinco/50 2.50 6.00
12 Brian Westbrook/50 2.50 6.00
13 Donovan McNabb/15 5.00 12.00
14 LaDainian Tomlinson/50 4.00 10.00
15 Adrian Peterson/50 4.00 10.00
16 Clinton Portis/50 2.50 6.00
17 Tony Romo/50 3.00 8.00
18 Maurice Jones-Drew/50 2.50 6.00
19 Greg Jennings/50 2.50 6.00
20 Tony Gonzalez/50 3.00 8.00
22 Reggie Wayne/25 4.00 10.00
23 Brandon Jacobs/50 2.50 6.00

2009 Absolute Memorabilia Canton Absolutes Materials Autographs

STATED PRINT RUN 1-25
SERIAL #'d UNDER 15 NOT PRICED
10 Jason Witten/15 20.00 40.00
19 Greg Jennings/20 8.00 20.00
25 Fred Taylor/25 8.00 20.00

2009 Absolute Memorabilia College Materials

STATED PRINT RUN 10-100
1 Brian Orakpo/100 2.50 6.00
2 Brandon Tate/50 3.00 8.00
3 Brian Cushing/75 2.00 5.00
4 Chase Coffman/100 2.00 5.00
5 Chris Wells/75 2.00 5.00
6 Derrick Williams/15 4.00 10.00
8 Graham Harrell/25 3.00 8.00
9 James Laurinaitis/25 3.00 8.00
10 Jeremy Maclin/100 2.50 6.00
11 Josh Freeman/100 2.00 5.00
13 Kenny McKinley/100 2.00 5.00
14 LeSean McCoy/50 6.00 15.00
15 Brandon Gibson/100 2.50 6.00
16 Mark Sanchez/25 3.00 8.00
18 Rey Maualuga/25 5.00 12.00
19 Tyson Jackson/100 2.00 5.00
20 Mohamed Massaquoi/100 2.00 5.00

2009 Absolute Memorabilia College Materials Autographs

STATED PRINT RUN 5-25
SERIAL #'d UNDER 15 NOT PRICED
1 Brian Orakpo/25 6.00 15.00
3 Brian Cushing/25 5.00 12.00
4 Chase Coffman/25 8.00 20.00
5 Chris Wells/25 5.00 12.00
10 Jeremy Maclin/25 6.00 15.00
11 Josh Freeman/25 5.00 12.00
13 Kenny McKinley/25 5.00 12.00
15 Brandon Gibson/25 6.00 15.00
19 Tyson Jackson/25 5.00 12.00
20 Mohamed Massaquoi/25 10.00 25.00

2009 Absolute Memorabilia Gridiron Force

RANDOM INSERTS IN RETAIL PACKS
*SPECTRUM/25: 1.2X TO 3X BASIC INSERTS
1 Aaron Rodgers 1.50 4.00
2 Antonio Gates .60 1.50
3 Calvin Johnson .75 2.00
4 Cedric Benson .50 1.25
5 Clinton Portis .50 1.25
6 Donald Driver .60 1.50
7 Drew Brees .75 2.00
8 Felix Jones .50 1.25
9 Jamal Lewis .60 1.50
10 Jason Campbell .50 1.25
11 Justin Fargas .50 1.25
12 Justin McCareins .50 1.25
13 Kellen Winslow Jr. .50 1.25
14 Kevin Curtis .50 1.25
15 Laveranues Coles .50 1.25
16 Marques Colston .50 1.25
17 Matt Leinart .50 1.25
18 Peyton Manning 2.00 5.00
19 Ray Lewis 1.00 2.50
20 Reggie Wayne .60 1.50
21 Santana Moss .60 1.50
22 Todd Heap .50 1.25
23 Trent Edwards .50 1.25
24 Vernon Davis .50 1.25
25 Vincent Jackson .50 1.25

2009 Absolute Memorabilia Gridiron Force Material Prime Jersey Number

STATED PRINT RUN 25 SER.#'d SETS
1 Aaron Rodgers 12.00 30.00
2 Antonio Gates 5.00 12.00
3 Calvin Johnson 6.00 15.00
5 Clinton Portis 4.00 10.00
6 Donald Driver 5.00 12.00
8 Felix Jones 4.00 10.00
9 Jamal Lewis 5.00 12.00
10 Jason Campbell 4.00 10.00
11 Justin Fargas 4.00 10.00
12 Justin McCareins 4.00 10.00
14 Kevin Curtis 4.00 10.00
16 Marques Colston 4.00 10.00
18 Peyton Manning 15.00 40.00
19 Ray Lewis 8.00 20.00
20 Reggie Wayne 5.00 12.00
21 Santana Moss 5.00 12.00
22 Todd Heap 4.00 10.00
23 Trent Edwards 4.00 10.00
24 Vernon Davis 4.00 10.00
25 Vincent Jackson 4.00 10.00

2009 Absolute Memorabilia Gridiron Force Material Autographs

STATED PRINT RUN 1-50
*JSY #/25-50: .4X TO 1X BASIC JSY AU
*PRIME/25: .6X TO 1.5X BASIC JSY AU/50
*PRIME JSY #/25: .6X TO 1.5X BASIC JSY AU/50
SERIAL #'d UNDER 15 NOT PRICED
14 Kevin Curtis/25 8.00 20.00
16 Marques Colston/50 6.00 15.00
17 Matt Leinart/25 8.00 20.00
25 Vincent Jackson/25 8.00 20.00

2009 Absolute Memorabilia Ground Hoggs

RANDOM INSERTS IN RETAIL PACKS
*SPECTRUM/25: 1.2X TO 3X BASIC INSERTS
1 Adrian Peterson .75 2.00
2 Brandon Jacobs .50 1.25
3 Brian Westbrook .50 1.25
4 Chris Johnson .50 1.25
5 Clinton Portis .50 1.25
6 DeAngelo Williams .50 1.25
7 Derrick Ward .50 1.25
8 Frank Gore .60 1.50
9 Joseph Addai .50 1.25
10 LaDainian Tomlinson .75 2.00
11 Laurence Maroney .60 1.50
12 LenDale White .50 1.25
13 Marion Barber .60 1.50
14 Marshawn Lynch .60 1.50
15 Matt Forte .50 1.25
16 Maurice Jones-Drew .50 1.25
17 Michael Turner .50 1.25
18 Reggie Bush .50 1.25
19 Ronnie Brown .50 1.25
20 Ryan Grant .60 1.50
21 Steve Slaton .50 1.25
22 Steven Jackson .50 1.25
23 Thomas Jones .50 1.25
24 Willie Parker .50 1.25
25 Willis McGahee .50 1.25

2009 Absolute Memorabilia Ground Hoggs Materials Jersey Number

STATED PRINT RUN 25 SER.#'d SETS
1 Adrian Peterson 6.00 15.00
2 Brandon Jacobs 4.00 10.00
3 Brian Westbrook 4.00 10.00
4 Chris Johnson 4.00 10.00
5 Clinton Portis 4.00 10.00
6 DeAngelo Williams 4.00 10.00
8 Frank Gore 5.00 12.00
9 Joseph Addai 4.00 10.00
10 LaDainian Tomlinson 6.00 15.00
11 Laurence Maroney 5.00 12.00
12 LenDale White 4.00 10.00
13 Marion Barber 5.00 12.00
14 Marshawn Lynch 5.00 12.00
16 Maurice Jones-Drew 4.00 10.00
17 Michael Turner 4.00 10.00
18 Reggie Bush 4.00 10.00
19 Ronnie Brown 4.00 10.00
20 Ryan Grant 5.00 12.00
21 Steve Slaton 4.00 10.00
22 Steven Jackson 4.00 10.00
23 Thomas Jones 4.00 10.00
24 Willie Parker 4.00 10.00
25 Willis McGahee 4.00 10.00

2009 Absolute Memorabilia Ground Hoggs Materials Autographs

STATED PRINT RUN 2-25
*JSY #/25: .4X TO 1X BASIC JSY AU
SERIAL #'d UNDER 15 NOT PRICED
21 Steve Slaton/25 8.00 20.00

2009 Absolute Memorabilia Marks of Fame

RANDOM INSERTS IN RETAIL PACKS
*SPECTRUM/25: 1.2X TO 3X BASIC INSERTS
1 Anquan Boldin .50 1.25
2 Bernard Berrian .50 1.25
3 Chris Cooley .50 1.25
4 DeSean Jackson .60 1.50
5 Devin Hester .60 1.50
6 Dwayne Bowe .60 1.50
7 Earnest Graham .50 1.25
8 Eddie Royal .50 1.25
9 Heath Miller .50 1.25
10 Jake Delhomme .50 1.25
11 Jay Cutler .50 1.25
12 Joe Flacco .60 1.50
13 John Carlson .60 1.50
14 Larry Fitzgerald .60 1.50
15 Larry Johnson .50 1.25
16 Leon Washington .50 1.25
17 Mark Clayton .50 1.25
18 Matt Hasselbeck .50 1.25
19 Matt Ryan .60 1.50
20 Owen Daniels .50 1.25
21 Roddy White .50 1.25
22 Selvin Young .50 1.25
23 T.J. Houshmandzadeh .50 1.25
24 Wes Welker .60 1.50
25 Zach Miller .50 1.25

2009 Absolute Memorabilia Marks of Fame Materials Spectrum Prime

STATED PRINT RUN 4-50
SERIAL #'d UNDER 15 NOT PRICED
1 Anquan Boldin/50 3.00 8.00
2 Bernard Berrian/50 3.00 8.00
3 Chris Cooley/50 3.00 8.00
5 Devin Hester/49 4.00 10.00
6 Dwayne Bowe/50 4.00 10.00
7 Earnest Graham/50 3.00 8.00
10 Jake Delhomme/30 4.00 10.00
14 Larry Fitzgerald/44 4.00 10.00
15 Larry Johnson/50 3.00 8.00
17 Mark Clayton/50 3.00 8.00
18 Matt Hasselbeck/50 3.00 8.00
19 Matt Ryan/50 4.00 10.00
21 Roddy White/50 3.00 8.00
22 Selvin Young/50 3.00 8.00
24 Wes Welker/50 4.00 10.00
25 Zach Miller/50 3.00 8.00

2009 Absolute Memorabilia Marks of Fame Materials Autographs

STATED PRINT RUN 10-50
*PRIME/25: .6X TO 1.5X BASIC JSY AU/50
2 Bernard Berrian/15 8.00 20.00
15 Larry Johnson/50 6.00 15.00
25 Zach Miller/20 8.00 20.00

2009 Absolute Memorabilia NFL Icons

RANDOM INSERTS IN RETAIL PACKS
*SPECTRUM/25: 1.2X TO 3X BASIC INSERTS
1 Bart Starr 1.25 3.00
2 Andre Johnson .60 1.50
3 Ben Roethlisberger .75 2.00
4 Brian Westbrook .50 1.25
5 Dan Marino 1.50 4.00
6 Deion Sanders .60 1.50
7 Donovan McNabb .60 1.50
8 Eli Manning .60 1.50
9 Emmitt Smith 1.25 3.00
10 Frank Gifford .75 2.00
11 Jason Witten .60 1.50
12 John Elway 1.25 3.00
13 LaDainian Tomlinson .75 2.00
14 Lance Alworth .60 1.50
15 Maurice Jones-Drew .50 1.25
16 Peyton Manning 2.00 5.00
17 Randy Moss .60 1.50
18 Steve Smith .60 1.50
19 Tom Brady 2.50 6.00
20 Tony Gonzalez .60 1.50

2009 Absolute Memorabilia NFL Icons Materials Spectrum Prime

STATED PRINT RUN 25 SER.#'d SETS
1 Bart Starr 20.00 50.00
2 Andre Johnson 5.00 12.00
3 Ben Roethlisberger 6.00 15.00
4 Brian Westbrook 4.00 10.00
5 Dan Marino 25.00 60.00
6 Deion Sanders 10.00 25.00
7 Donovan McNabb 5.00 12.00
8 Eli Manning 5.00 12.00
9 Emmitt Smith 20.00 50.00
10 Frank Gifford 12.00 30.00
11 Jason Witten 5.00 12.00
12 John Elway 20.00 50.00
13 LaDainian Tomlinson 6.00 15.00
14 Lance Alworth 10.00 25.00
15 Maurice Jones-Drew 4.00 10.00
16 Peyton Manning 15.00 40.00
18 Steve Smith 5.00 12.00
19 Tom Brady 20.00 50.00
20 Tony Gonzalez 5.00 12.00

2009 Absolute Memorabilia NFL Icons Materials Autographs

STATED PRINT RUN 1-25
1 Bart Starr/25 90.00 150.00
5 Dan Marino/15 100.00 200.00
6 Deion Sanders/15 40.00 80.00
9 Emmitt Smith/25 75.00 150.00
10 Frank Gifford/25 25.00 50.00
12 John Elway/25 75.00 150.00
14 Lance Alworth/25 30.00 60.00

2009 Absolute Memorabilia Rookie Jersey Collection

ONE PER BLASTER RETAIL BOX
1 Chris Wells 1.50 4.00
2 Kenny Britt 2.50 6.00
3 Hakeem Nicks 2.00 5.00
4 Donald Brown 1.50 4.00
5 Percy Harvin 1.50 4.00

6 Brandon Pettigrew 1.50 4.00
7 Jeremy Maclin 2.00 5.00
8 Josh Freeman 1.50 4.00
9 Knowshon Moreno 1.50 4.00
10 Michael Crabtree 2.50 6.00
11 Darrius Heyward-Bey 2.50 6.00
12 Mark Sanchez 1.50 4.00
13 Aaron Curry 2.50 6.00
14 Tyson Jackson 1.50 4.00
15 Jason Smith 1.50 4.00
16 Matthew Stafford 8.00 20.00
17 Javon Ringer 1.50 4.00
18 Nate Davis 1.50 4.00
19 Rhett Bomar 1.50 4.00
20 Andre Brown 2.00 5.00
21 Mike Thomas 1.50 4.00
22 Stephen McGee 1.50 4.00
23 Juaquin Iglesias 1.50 4.00
24 Deon Butler 1.50 4.00
25 Patrick Turner 1.50 4.00
26 Ramses Barden 1.50 4.00
27 Mike Wallace 2.50 6.00
28 Brian Robiskie 1.50 4.00
29 Derrick Williams 1.50 4.00
30 Glen Coffee 1.50 4.00
31 Shonn Greene 1.50 4.00
32 LeSean McCoy 4.00 10.00
33 Mohamed Massaquoi 1.50 4.00
34 Pat White 2.00 5.00

2009 Absolute Memorabilia Rookie Premiere Materials AFC/NFC

STATED PRINT RUN 99 SER.#'d SETS
*AFC/NFC SPEC.PRM/25: .8X TO 2X
*NFL SPECT.PRIME/50: .6X TO 1.5X BASIC JSY
*OVER.JSY.#/99: .5X TO 1.2X BASIC JSY
*OVER.JSY.# PRM/10: 1.5X TO 4X BASIC JSY
*OVER.SPEC.PRM/25: 1X TO 2.5X
201 Matthew Stafford 8.00 20.00
202 Jason Smith 1.50 4.00
203 Tyson Jackson 1.50 4.00
204 Aaron Curry 2.50 6.00
205 Mark Sanchez 1.50 4.00
206 Darrius Heyward-Bey 2.50 6.00
207 Michael Crabtree 2.50 6.00
208 Knowshon Moreno 1.50 4.00
209 Josh Freeman 1.50 4.00
210 Jeremy Maclin 2.00 5.00
211 Brandon Pettigrew 1.50 4.00
212 Percy Harvin 1.50 4.00
213 Donald Brown 1.50 4.00
214 Hakeem Nicks 2.00 5.00
215 Kenny Britt 2.50 6.00
216 Chris Wells 1.50 4.00
217 Brian Robiskie 1.50 4.00
218 Pat White 2.00 5.00
219 Mohamed Massaquoi 1.50 4.00
220 LeSean McCoy 4.00 10.00
221 Shonn Greene 1.50 4.00
222 Glen Coffee 1.50 4.00
223 Derrick Williams 1.50 4.00
224 Javon Ringer 1.50 4.00
225 Mike Wallace 2.50 6.00
226 Ramses Barden 1.50 4.00
227 Patrick Turner 1.50 4.00
228 Deon Butler 1.50 4.00
229 Juaquin Iglesias 1.50 4.00
230 Stephen McGee 1.50 4.00
231 Mike Thomas 1.50 4.00
232 Andre Brown 2.00 5.00
233 Rhett Bomar 1.50 4.00
234 Nate Davis 1.50 4.00

2009 Absolute Memorabilia Rookie Premiere Materials Autographs AFC/NFC

*AFC/NFC/25: .5X TO 1.2X BASIC RPM RC
STATED PRINT RUN 25 SER.#'d SETS
201 Matthew Stafford 60.00 150.00
205 Mark Sanchez 6.00 15.00
207 Michael Crabtree 10.00 25.00

2009 Absolute Memorabilia Spectrum Gold Autographs

STATED PRINT RUN 9-100
SERIAL #'d UNDER 23 NOT PRICED
4 Matt Ryan/25 25.00 60.00
11 James Hardy/100 6.00 15.00
27 Tashard Choice/23 6.00 15.00
34 Kevin Smith/30 6.00 15.00
40 Steve Slaton/25 6.00 15.00
49 Jamaal Charles/75 6.00 15.00
79 Rashard Mendenhall/100 5.00 12.00
84 Josh Morgan/100 5.00 12.00
91 Donnie Avery/100 5.00 12.00
93 Derrick Ward/25 6.00 15.00

2009 Absolute Memorabilia Spectrum Platinum Autographs

STATED PRINT RUN 1-25
SERIAL #'d UNDER 15 NOT PRICED
3 Tim Hightower/25 6.00 15.00
11 James Hardy/25 8.00 20.00
21 Cedric Benson/25 6.00 15.00
49 Jamaal Charles/25 8.00 20.00
53 Ted Ginn/15 6.00 15.00
79 Rashard Mendenhall/25 6.00 15.00
84 Josh Morgan/25 6.00 15.00
91 Donnie Avery/25 6.00 15.00

2009 Absolute Memorabilia Star Gazing

RANDOM INSERTS IN RETAIL PACKS
*SPECTRUM/25: 1.2X TO 3X BASIC INSERTS
1 Ramses Barden .50 1.25
2 Mike Wallace .75 2.00
3 Darrius Heyward-Bey .75 2.00
4 Derrick Williams .50 1.25
5 Glen Coffee .50 1.25
6 Shonn Greene .50 1.25
7 LeSean McCoy 1.25 3.00
8 Mohamed Massaquoi .50 1.25
9 Pat White .60 1.50
10 Brian Robiskie .50 1.25
11 Patrick Turner .50 1.25
12 Deon Butler .50 1.25
13 Juaquin Iglesias .50 1.25
14 Stephen McGee .50 1.25
15 Mike Thomas .50 1.25
16 Andre Brown .60 1.50
17 Rhett Bomar .50 1.25
18 Nate Davis .50 1.25
19 Javon Ringer .50 1.25
20 Matthew Stafford 2.50 6.00
21 Jason Smith .50 1.25
22 Tyson Jackson .50 1.25
23 Aaron Curry .75 2.00
24 Mark Sanchez .50 1.25
25 Chris Wells .50 1.25
26 Kenny Britt .75 2.00
27 Hakeem Nicks .60 1.50
28 Donald Brown .50 1.25
29 Percy Harvin .50 1.25
30 Brandon Pettigrew .50 1.25
31 Jeremy Maclin .60 1.50
32 Josh Freeman .50 1.25
33 Knowshon Moreno .50 1.25
34 Michael Crabtree .75 2.00

2009 Absolute Memorabilia Star Gazing Materials

RETAIL INSERT PRINT RUN 250
*OVR.JER.# PRM/25: 1X TO 2.5X BASIC JSY
*OVER.PRIME/25: 1X TO 2.5X BASIC JSY
*PRIME/50: .6X TO 1.5X BASIC JSY
1 Ramses Barden 1.50 4.00
2 Mike Wallace 2.50 6.00
3 Darrius Heyward-Bey 2.50 6.00
4 Derrick Williams 1.50 4.00
5 Glen Coffee 1.50 4.00
6 Shonn Greene 1.50 4.00
7 LeSean McCoy 4.00 10.00
8 Mohamed Massaquoi 1.50 4.00
9 Pat White 2.00 5.00
10 Brian Robiskie 1.50 4.00
11 Patrick Turner 1.50 4.00
12 Deon Butler 1.50 4.00
13 Juaquin Iglesias 1.50 4.00
14 Stephen McGee 1.50 4.00
15 Mike Thomas 1.50 4.00
16 Andre Brown 2.00 5.00
17 Rhett Bomar 1.50 4.00
18 Nate Davis 1.50 4.00
19 Javon Ringer 1.50 4.00
20 Matthew Stafford 6.00 15.00
21 Jason Smith 1.50 4.00
22 Tyson Jackson 1.50 4.00
23 Aaron Curry 2.50 6.00
24 Mark Sanchez 1.50 4.00
25 Chris Wells 1.50 4.00
26 Kenny Britt 2.50 6.00
27 Hakeem Nicks 2.00 5.00
28 Donald Brown 1.50 4.00
29 Percy Harvin 1.50 4.00
30 Brandon Pettigrew 1.50 4.00
31 Jeremy Maclin 2.00 5.00
32 Josh Freeman 1.50 4.00
33 Knowshon Moreno 1.50 4.00
34 Michael Crabtree 2.50 6.00

2009 Absolute Memorabilia Star Gazing Materials Autographs

STATED PRINT RUN 25 SER.#'d SETS
1 Ramses Barden 5.00 12.00
2 Mike Wallace 8.00 20.00
3 Darrius Heyward-Bey 8.00 20.00
4 Derrick Williams 5.00 12.00
5 Glen Coffee 5.00 12.00
6 Shonn Greene 5.00 12.00
7 LeSean McCoy 20.00 50.00
8 Mohamed Massaquoi 5.00 12.00
10 Brian Robiskie 5.00 12.00
11 Patrick Turner 5.00 12.00
12 Deon Butler 5.00 12.00
15 Mike Thomas 5.00 12.00
16 Andre Brown 6.00 15.00
17 Rhett Bomar 5.00 12.00
18 Nate Davis 5.00 12.00
19 Javon Ringer 5.00 12.00
20 Matthew Stafford 30.00 80.00
21 Jason Smith 5.00 12.00
22 Tyson Jackson 5.00 12.00
23 Aaron Curry 8.00 20.00
24 Mark Sanchez 5.00 12.00
25 Chris Wells 5.00 12.00
27 Hakeem Nicks 6.00 15.00
28 Donald Brown 5.00 12.00
29 Percy Harvin 5.00 12.00
30 Brandon Pettigrew 5.00 12.00
31 Jeremy Maclin 6.00 15.00
32 Josh Freeman 5.00 12.00
33 Knowshon Moreno 5.00 12.00
34 Michael Crabtree 8.00 20.00

2009 Absolute Memorabilia Team Quads Materials Die Cut

QUAD JERSEY PRINT RUN 10-100
*QUAD PRIM/25: .8X TO 2X BASIC QUAD/100
*QUAD PRIM/25: .6X TO 1.5X QUAD/40-49
*QUAD PRIM/25: .5X TO 1.2X BASIC QUAD/25
2 Lynch/Evns/Owns/Edw/100 5.00 12.00
5 Ryn/Trnr/Wht/Nrwd/49 6.00 15.00
7 Wittn/Brbr/Nwmn/Rmo/100 5.00 12.00
8 Wstbrk/McNb/Crts/Brwn/100 5.00 12.00
9 Ross/Jcbs/Eli/Moss/100 8.00 20.00
10 Ferg/Ctch/Vlma/Jnes/100 4.00 10.00
11 Rdgrs/Drvr/Jen/Grnt/100 12.00 30.00
12 Will/Delh/Smth/Muh/100 5.00 12.00
13 Mrny/Mss/Brdy/Welk/100 20.00 50.00
15 Msn/Clytn/Lwis/McG/100 6.00 15.00
16 Cly/Prts/Cmpbll/Moss/100 5.00 12.00
17 Hndrsn/Brs/Clstn/Bush/100 6.00 15.00
18 Rthlis/Wrd/Hlms/Prkr/25 10.00 25.00
20 Jns/Jhnsn/Gge/Whte/40 5.00 12.00

2009 Absolute Memorabilia Team Tandems Materials

STATED PRINT RUN 50 SER.#'d SETS
*PRIME/25: .6X TO 1.5X BASIC DUAL/50
1 Evans/Owens 5.00 12.00
2 Newman/Witten 5.00 12.00
3 Wayne/Addai 4.00 10.00
4 Turner/R.White 4.00 10.00
5 Urlacher/Hester 6.00 15.00
6 Portis/Cooley 4.00 10.00
7 Stokley/Marshall 5.00 12.00
8 Bowe/Gonzalez 5.00 12.00
9 Driver/Jennings 5.00 12.00
10 Palmer/Ochocinco 5.00 12.00

2009 Absolute Memorabilia Team Trios Materials NFL

STATED PRINT RUN 4-50
*PRIME/15-25: .6X TO 1.5X BASIC TRIO/40-50
1 Urlacher/Hester/Olsen 6.00 15.00
2 Palmr/Ocho/Coles/40 5.00 12.00
3 Evans/Lynch/Owens 5.00 12.00
4 Gates/Tomlnsn/Rivers 6.00 15.00
5 Addai/P.Mann/Wayne 4.00 10.00
6 Witten/Barber/Romo 5.00 12.00
7 Ryan/Turner/R.White 5.00 12.00
8 Ross/Jacobs/E.Mann 5.00 12.00
9 Wstbrk/McNbb/Lewis 5.00 12.00
10 Ctchry/Wshngtn/Jnes 4.00 10.00
11 Driver/Jennings/Grant 5.00 12.00
12 D.Will/Muha/S.Smith 5.00 12.00
13 Marony/Moss/Welker 5.00 12.00
14 Mason/Clytn/McGahee 4.00 10.00
15 Cooley/Portis/S.Moss 5.00 12.00
16 Brees/Colston/Bush 6.00 15.00
17 Ward/Holmes/Parker 6.00 15.00
18 A.Jhnsn/Schb/Slatn 5.00 12.00
19 B.Jnes/Gage /L.White 4.00 10.00
20 Petrsn/Berrian/Taylor 6.00 15.00

2009 Absolute Memorabilia Tools of the Trade Material Red

RETAIL RED PRINT RUN 250
1 Adrian Peterson 3.00 8.00
2 Adrian Wilson 2.00 5.00
3 Alan Faneca 2.00 5.00
4 Albert Haynesworth 2.00 5.00
5 Andre Johnson 2.50 6.00
6 Anquan Boldin 2.00 5.00
7 Chris Cooley 3.00 8.00
8 DeMarcus Ware 3.00 8.00
9 Drew Brees 3.00 8.00
10 Dwight Freeney 2.00 5.00
11 Eli Manning 2.50 6.00
12 James Farrior 2.00 5.00
13 James Harrison 3.00 8.00
14 Jared Allen 2.00 5.00
15 Jay Cutler 2.00 5.00
16 Jon Beason 2.00 5.00
17 Julius Peppers 2.50 6.00
18 Kurt Warner 2.50 6.00
19 Lance Briggs 2.50 6.00
20 Larry Fitzgerald 2.50 6.00
21 Le'Ron McClain 2.50 6.00
22 Mario Williams 2.50 6.00
23 Michael Turner 2.00 5.00
24 Mike Sellers 2.00 5.00
25 Patrick Willis 2.50 6.00
26 Peyton Manning 8.00 20.00
27 Ray Lewis 4.00 10.00
28 Reggie Wayne 2.50 6.00
29 Robert Mathis 2.00 5.00
30 Roddy White 2.00 5.00
31 Ronnie Brown 2.00 5.00
32 Steve Smith 2.50 6.00
33 Terrell Suggs 2.00 5.00
34 Thomas Jones 2.00 5.00
35 Tony Gonzalez 2.50 6.00
36 Troy Polamalu 3.00 8.00
37 Wes Welker 2.50 6.00

2009 Absolute Memorabilia Tools of the Trade Material Black Spectrum

STATED PRINT RUN 4-50
SERIAL #'d UNDER 15 NOT PRICED
1 Adrian Peterson/38 6.00 15.00
2 Adrian Wilson/50 4.00 10.00
3 Alan Faneca/50 4.00 10.00
4 Albert Haynesworth/50 4.00 10.00
5 Andre Johnson/50 5.00 12.00
6 Anquan Boldin/34 4.00 10.00
7 Chris Cooley/30 6.00 15.00
8 DeMarcus Ware/50 6.00 15.00
9 Drew Brees/39 6.00 15.00
10 Dwight Freeney/50 4.00 10.00
11 Eli Manning/25 6.00 15.00
12 James Farrior/28 5.00 12.00
13 James Harrison/36 10.00 25.00
14 Jared Allen/50 4.00 10.00
15 Jay Cutler/30 4.00 10.00
16 Jon Beason/50 4.00 10.00
17 Julius Peppers/50 5.00 12.00
18 Kurt Warner/25 6.00 15.00
19 Lance Briggs/27 6.00 15.00
20 Larry Fitzgerald/25 6.00 15.00
21 Le'Ron McClain/29 6.00 15.00
22 Mario Williams/50 5.00 12.00
23 Michael Turner/24 5.00 12.00
24 Mike Sellers/30 4.00 10.00
25 Patrick Willis/50 5.00 12.00
26 Peyton Manning/50 15.00 40.00
27 Ray Lewis/50 8.00 20.00
28 Reggie Wayne/50 5.00 12.00
29 Robert Mathis/25 5.00 12.00
30 Roddy White/40 4.00 10.00
31 Ronnie Brown/50 4.00 10.00
32 Steve Smith/50 5.00 12.00
33 Terrell Suggs/50 4.00 10.00
34 Thomas Jones/40 4.00 10.00
35 Tony Gonzalez/50 5.00 12.00
36 Troy Polamalu/25 8.00 20.00
37 Wes Welker/49 5.00 12.00
40 Deion Sanders/15 10.00 25.00
43 LaDainian Tomlinson/50 6.00 15.00
44 Willis McGahee/15 5.00 12.00
45 Dwayne Bowe/50 5.00 12.00
46 Braylon Edwards/50 4.00 10.00
47 Brian Urlacher/50 6.00 15.00
49 Cadillac Williams/50 5.00 12.00
50 Carson Palmer/25 6.00 15.00
51 Chad Ochocinco/50 4.00 10.00
52 Tony Romo/25 6.00 15.00
53 Ricky Williams/50 5.00 12.00
55 Maurice Jones-Drew/50 4.00 10.00
56 Marion Barber/25 6.00 15.00
57 Lee Evans/50 5.00 12.00
58 Clinton Portis/25 5.00 12.00
59 Joseph Addai/25 5.00 12.00
60 Jason Campbell/50 4.00 10.00
61 JaMarcus Russell/25 5.00 12.00
63 Hines Ward/50 5.00 12.00
64 Frank Gore/25 6.00 15.00
65 Ed Reed/19 6.00 15.00

2009 Absolute Memorabilia Tools of the Trade Material Oversize Black Spectrum

STATED PRINT RUN 1-50
SERIAL #'d UNDER 15 NOT PRICED

2009 Absolute Memorabilia Tools of the Trade Material Oversize Jersey Number Black

STATED PRINT RUN 1-30
SERIAL #'d UNDER 15 NOT PRICED
1 Adrian Peterson/15 15.00 40.00
13 James Harrison/15 25.00 60.00
36 Troy Polamalu/15 15.00 40.00

2009 Absolute Memorabilia Tools of the Trade Double Material Black Spectrum

STATED PRINT RUN 10-50
SERIAL #'d UNDER 15 NOT PRICED
1 Adrian Peterson/50 8.00 20.00
2 Adrian Wilson/50 5.00 12.00
3 Alan Faneca/50 5.00 12.00
4 Albert Haynesworth/50 5.00 12.00
5 Andre Johnson/50 6.00 15.00
6 Anquan Boldin/50 3.00 8.00
7 Chris Cooley/50 8.00 20.00
8 DeMarcus Ware/50 8.00 20.00
9 Drew Brees/25 10.00 25.00
10 Dwight Freeney/50 5.00 12.00
11 Eli Manning/50 6.00 15.00
12 James Farrior/50 5.00 12.00
13 James Harrison/50 12.00 30.00
14 Jared Allen/50 5.00 12.00
15 Jay Cutler/50 5.00 12.00
16 Jon Beason/50 5.00 12.00
17 Julius Peppers/50 6.00 15.00
18 Kurt Warner/50 6.00 15.00
19 Lance Briggs/50 6.00 15.00
20 Larry Fitzgerald/50 6.00 15.00
21 Le'Ron McClain/50 6.00 15.00
22 Mario Williams/50 6.00 15.00
23 Michael Turner/50 5.00 12.00
24 Mike Sellers/50 5.00 12.00
25 Patrick Willis/50 6.00 15.00
26 Peyton Manning/25 25.00 60.00
27 Ray Lewis/15 15.00 40.00
28 Reggie Wayne/48 6.00 15.00
29 Robert Mathis/50 5.00 12.00
30 Roddy White/50 5.00 12.00
31 Ronnie Brown/50 5.00 12.00
32 Steve Smith/50 6.00 15.00
33 Terrell Suggs/50 5.00 12.00
34 Thomas Jones/50 5.00 12.00
35 Tony Gonzalez/45 6.00 15.00
36 Troy Polamalu/50 8.00 20.00
37 Wes Welker/50 6.00 15.00
39 Dan Marino/40 15.00 40.00
40 Deion Sanders/30 6.00 15.00
41 Emmitt Smith/50 12.00 30.00
43 LaDainian Tomlinson/50 8.00 20.00
44 Willis McGahee/50 5.00 12.00
45 Dwayne Bowe/50 6.00 15.00
47 Brian Urlacher/50 8.00 20.00
49 Cadillac Williams/50 6.00 15.00
50 Carson Palmer/50 6.00 15.00
51 Chad Ochocinco/35 5.00 12.00
53 Ricky Williams/50 6.00 15.00
55 Maurice Jones-Drew/50 5.00 12.00
56 Marion Barber/25 8.00 20.00
57 Lee Evans/50 6.00 15.00
58 Clinton Portis/50 5.00 12.00
59 Joseph Addai/50 5.00 12.00
60 Jason Campbell/50 5.00 12.00
61 JaMarcus Russell/50 5.00 12.00
62 Jake Delhomme/50 5.00 12.00
63 Hines Ward/50 6.00 15.00
64 Frank Gore/25 8.00 20.00
65 Ed Reed/50 6.00 15.00

2009 Absolute Memorabilia Tools of the Trade Triple Material Black Spectrum

STATED PRINT RUN 2-50
SERIAL #'d UNDER 15 NOT PRICED
5 Andre Johnson/20 8.00 20.00
35 Tony Gonzalez/50 6.00 15.00
39 Dan Marino/15 30.00 80.00
47 Brian Urlacher/50 8.00 20.00
50 Carson Palmer/50 6.00 15.00
53 Ricky Williams/50 6.00 15.00
57 Lee Evans/45 6.00 15.00
58 Clinton Portis/25 6.00 15.00
63 Hines Ward/50 6.00 15.00

2009 Absolute Memorabilia War Room

*SPECTRUM/25: 1.2X TO 3X BASIC INSERTS
1 Mike Wallace .75 2.00
2 Derrick Williams .50 1.25
3 Shonn Greene .50 1.25
4 Mohamed Massaquoi .50 1.25
5 Brian Robiskie .50 1.25
6 Deon Butler .50 1.25
7 Stephen McGee .50 1.25
8 Andre Brown .60 1.50
9 Nate Davis .50 1.25
10 Matthew Stafford 2.50 6.00
11 Tyson Jackson .50 1.25
12 Mark Sanchez .50 1.25
13 Kenny Britt .75 2.00
14 Donald Brown .50 1.25
15 Brandon Pettigrew .50 1.25
16 Josh Freeman .50 1.25
17 Michael Crabtree .75 2.00
18 Darrius Heyward-Bey .75 2.00
19 Knowshon Moreno .50 1.25
20 Jeremy Maclin .60 1.50
21 Percy Harvin .50 1.25
22 Hakeem Nicks .60 1.50
23 Chris Wells .50 1.25
24 Aaron Curry .75 2.00
25 Jason Smith .50 1.25
26 Javon Ringer .50 1.25
27 Rhett Bomar .50 1.25
28 Mike Thomas .50 1.25
29 Juaquin Iglesias .50 1.25
30 Patrick Turner .50 1.25
31 Pat White .60 1.50
32 LeSean McCoy 1.25 3.00
33 Glen Coffee .50 1.25
34 Ramses Barden .50 1.25

2009 Absolute Memorabilia War Room Materials

RETAIL PACK INSERT PRINT RUN 250
*OVR.JER.# PRM/25: 1X TO 2.5X BASIC JSY
*OVER.PRIME/25: 1X TO 2.5X BASIC JSY
*PRIME/50: .6X TO 1.5X BASIC JSY
1 Mike Wallace 2.50 6.00
2 Derrick Williams 1.50 4.00
3 Shonn Greene 1.50 4.00
4 Mohamed Massaquoi 1.50 4.00
5 Brian Robiskie 1.50 4.00
6 Deon Butler 1.50 4.00
7 Stephen McGee 1.50 4.00
8 Andre Brown 2.00 5.00
9 Nate Davis 1.50 4.00
10 Matthew Stafford 8.00 20.00
11 Tyson Jackson 1.50 4.00
12 Mark Sanchez 1.50 4.00
13 Kenny Britt 2.50 6.00
14 Donald Brown 1.50 4.00
15 Brandon Pettigrew 1.50 4.00
16 Josh Freeman 1.50 4.00
17 Michael Crabtree 2.50 6.00
18 Darrius Heyward-Bey 2.50 6.00
19 Knowshon Moreno 1.50 4.00
20 Jeremy Maclin 2.00 5.00
21 Percy Harvin 1.50 4.00
22 Hakeem Nicks 2.00 5.00
23 Chris Wells 1.50 4.00
24 Aaron Curry 2.50 6.00
25 Jason Smith 1.50 4.00
26 Javon Ringer 1.50 4.00
27 Rhett Bomar 1.50 4.00
28 Mike Thomas 1.50 4.00
29 Juaquin Iglesias 1.50 4.00
30 Patrick Turner 1.50 4.00
31 Pat White 2.00 5.00
32 LeSean McCoy 4.00 10.00
33 Glen Coffee 1.50 4.00
34 Ramses Barden 1.50 4.00

2009 Absolute Memorabilia War Room Materials Autographs

STATED PRINT RUN 25 SER.#'d SETS
1 Mike Wallace 8.00 20.00
2 Derrick Williams 5.00 12.00
3 Shonn Greene 5.00 12.00
4 Mohamed Massaquoi 5.00 12.00
5 Brian Robiskie 5.00 12.00
6 Deon Butler 5.00 12.00
7 Stephen McGee 5.00 12.00
8 Andre Brown 6.00 15.00
9 Nate Davis 5.00 12.00
10 Matthew Stafford 50.00 120.00
11 Tyson Jackson 5.00 12.00
12 Mark Sanchez 5.00 12.00
14 Donald Brown 5.00 12.00
15 Brandon Pettigrew 5.00 12.00
16 Josh Freeman 5.00 12.00
17 Michael Crabtree 8.00 20.00
18 Darrius Heyward-Bey 8.00 20.00
19 Knowshon Moreno 5.00 12.00
20 Jeremy Maclin 6.00 15.00
21 Percy Harvin 5.00 12.00
22 Hakeem Nicks 6.00 15.00
23 Chris Wells 5.00 12.00
24 Aaron Curry 8.00 20.00
25 Jason Smith 5.00 12.00
26 Javon Ringer 5.00 12.00
27 Rhett Bomar 5.00 12.00
28 Mike Thomas 5.00 12.00
30 Patrick Turner 5.00 12.00
32 LeSean McCoy 20.00 50.00
33 Glen Coffee 5.00 12.00
34 Ramses Barden 5.00 12.00

2010 Absolute Memorabilia

101-200 ROOKIE PRINT RUN 299
201-235 RPM AU PRINT RUN 299
EXCH EXPIRATION: 4/13/2012
1 Chris Wells .30 .75
2 Larry Fitzgerald .40 1.00
3 Matt Leinart .30 .75
4 Matt Ryan .40 1.00
5 Michael Turner .30 .75
6 Roddy White .30 .75
7 Anquan Boldin .30 .75
8 Joe Flacco .40 1.00
9 Ray Rice .30 .75
10 Lee Evans .40 1.00
11 Marshawn Lynch .40 1.00
12 Ryan Fitzpatrick .30 .75
13 DeAngelo Williams .30 .75
14 Matt Moore .30 .75
15 Steve Smith .40 1.00
16 Devin Hester .40 1.00
17 Jay Cutler .30 .75
18 Matt Forte .30 .75
19 Carson Palmer .40 1.00
20 Cedric Benson .30 .75
21 Chad Ochocinco .30 .75
22 Jake Delhomme .30 .75
23 Josh Cribbs .30 .75
24 Mohamed Massaquoi .40 1.00
25 Felix Jones .30 .75
26 Jason Witten .40 1.00
27 Miles Austin .30 .75
28 Tony Romo .40 1.00
29 Eddie Royal .30 .75
30 Knowshon Moreno .30 .75
31 Kyle Orton .30 .75
32 Calvin Johnson .50 1.25
33 Matthew Stafford .40 1.00
34 Nate Burleson .30 .75
35 Aaron Rodgers 1.00 2.50
36 Donald Driver .40 1.00
37 Ryan Grant .40 1.00
38 Andre Johnson .40 1.00
39 Matt Schaub .30 .75
40 Owen Daniels .30 .75
41 Dallas Clark .30 .75
42 Joseph Addai .30 .75
43 Peyton Manning 1.25 3.00
44 Reggie Wayne .40 1.00
45 David Garrard .30 .75
46 Maurice Jones-Drew .30 .75
47 Mike Sims-Walker .30 .75
48 Dwayne Bowe .40 1.00
49 Jamaal Charles .40 1.00
50 Matt Cassel .30 .75
51 Brandon Marshall .40 1.00
52 Chad Henne .40 1.00
53 Ronnie Brown .30 .75
54 Adrian Peterson .50 1.25
55 Brett Favre 1.00 2.50
56 Sidney Rice .30 .75
57 Randy Moss .40 1.00
58 Tom Brady 1.25 3.00
59 Wes Welker .40 1.00
60 Drew Brees .50 1.25
61 Marques Colston .30 .75
62 Pierre Thomas .30 .75
63 Brandon Jacobs .30 .75
64 Eli Manning .40 1.00
65 Steve Smith USC .30 .75
66 Braylon Edwards .30 .75
67 LaDainian Tomlinson .50 1.25
68 Mark Sanchez .30 .75
69 Shonn Greene .30 .75
70 Darren McFadden .30 .75
71 Jason Campbell .30 .75
72 Louis Murphy .30 .75
73 DeSean Jackson .40 1.00
74 Kevin Kolb .30 .75
75 LeSean McCoy .50 1.25
76 Ben Roethlisberger .50 1.25
77 Hines Ward .40 1.00
78 Rashard Mendenhall .30 .75
79 Antonio Gates .40 1.00
80 Darren Sproles .40 1.00
81 Philip Rivers .50 1.25
82 Vincent Jackson .30 .75
83 Frank Gore .40 1.00
84 Michael Crabtree .30 .75
85 Vernon Davis .30 .75
86 Julius Jones .30 .75
87 Matt Hasselbeck .30 .75
88 T.J. Houshmandzadeh .30 .75
89 Donnie Avery .30 .75
90 James Laurinaitis .40 1.00
91 Steven Jackson .30 .75
92 Cadillac Williams .30 .75
93 Josh Freeman .40 1.00
94 Kellen Winslow Jr. .30 .75
95 Chris Johnson .30 .75
96 Kenny Britt .30 .75
97 Vince Young .30 .75
90 Chris Cooley .30 .75
99 Clinton Portis .30 .75
100 Donovan McNabb .40 1.00
101 Aaron Hernandez RC 2.00 5.00
102 Amari Spievey RC 2.00 5.00
103 Victor Cruz RC 4.00 10.00
104 Anthony Davis RC 2.50 6.00
105 Anthony Dixon RC 2.00 5.00
106 Anthony McCoy RC 2.00 5.00
107 Antonio Brown RC 15.00 40.00
108 Blair White RC 2.00 5.00
109 Brandon Ghee RC 2.00 5.00
110 Brandon Graham RC 2.50 6.00
111 Brandon Spikes RC 2.00 5.00
112 Brian Price RC 2.00 5.00
113 Bryan Bulaga RC 2.00 5.00
114 Carlos Dunlap RC 2.00 5.00
115 Carlton Mitchell RC 2.00 5.00
116 Chad Jones RC 2.00 5.00
117 Charles Scott RC 2.00 5.00
118 Chris Cook RC 2.00 5.00
119 Chris McGaha RC 2.00 5.00
120 Corey Wootton RC 2.00 5.00
121 Dan LeFevour RC 2.00 5.00
122 Dan Williams RC 2.00 5.00
123 Daryl Washington RC 2.00 5.00
124 David Gettis RC 2.00 5.00
125 David Reed RC 2.00 5.00
126 Deji Karim RC 2.50 6.00
127 Dennis Pitta RC 2.00 5.00
128 Derrick Morgan RC 2.00 5.00
129 Devin McCourty RC 2.50 6.00
130 Dezmon Briscoe RC 2.00 5.00
131 Dominique Franks RC 2.00 5.00
132 Donald Butler RC 2.00 5.00
133 Earl Thomas RC 5.00 12.00
134 Ed Dickson RC 2.00 5.00
135 Everson Griffen RC 2.00 5.00
136 Freddie Barnes RC 2.00 5.00
137 Garrett Graham RC 2.00 5.00
138 Jacoby Ford RC 2.00 5.00
139 James Starks RC 2.50 6.00
140 Jared Odrick RC 2.50 6.00
141 Jarrett Brown RC 2.00 5.00
142 Jason Pierre-Paul RC 3.00 8.00
143 Jason Worilds RC 2.00 5.00
144 Javier Arenas RC 2.00 5.00
145 Jeremy Williams RC 2.00 5.00
146 Jermaine Cunningham RC 2.00 5.00
147 Jerome Murphy RC 2.50 6.00
148 Jerry Hughes RC 2.00 5.00
149 Jevan Snead RC 2.00 5.00
150 Jimmy Graham RC 5.00 12.00
151 Joe Haden RC 3.00 8.00
152 Joe Webb RC 2.00 5.00
153 John Conner RC 2.00 5.00
154 John Skelton RC 3.00 8.00
155 Joique Bell RC 2.00 5.00
156 Jonathan Crompton RC 2.00 5.00
157 Kareem Jackson RC 2.00 5.00
158 Kerry Meier RC 2.50 6.00
159 Koa Misi RC 2.50 6.00
160 Kyle Williams RC 3.00 8.00
161 Kyle Wilson RC 2.00 5.00
162 Lamarr Houston RC 2.50 6.00
163 LeGarrette Blount RC 4.00 10.00
164 Levi Brown RC 2.00 5.00
165 Linval Joseph RC 2.00 5.00
166 Lonyae Miller RC 2.50 6.00
167 Major Wright RC 2.00 5.00
168 Marc Mariani RC 3.00 8.00
169 Maurkice Pouncey RC 2.50 6.00
170 Mike Iupati RC 3.00 8.00
171 Mike Neal RC 3.00 8.00
172 Morgan Burnett RC 2.50 6.00
173 Myron Lewis RC 2.50 6.00
174 Nate Allen RC 3.00 8.00
175 NaVorro Bowman RC 4.00 10.00
176 Pat Angerer RC 2.00 5.00
177 Patrick Robinson RC 2.50 6.00
178 Perrish Cox RC 2.50 6.00
179 Ricky Sapp RC 2.00 5.00
180 Riley Cooper RC 2.00 5.00
181 Russell Okung RC 2.00 5.00
182 Rusty Smith RC 3.00 8.00
183 Sean Canfield RC 2.00 5.00
184 Sean Lee RC 4.00 10.00
185 Sean Weatherspoon RC 2.00 5.00
186 Sergio Kindle RC 2.00 5.00
187 Seyi Ajirotutu RC 2.00 5.00
188 Shay Hodge RC 2.00 5.00
189 T.J. Ward RC 3.00 8.00
190 Taylor Mays RC 2.00 5.00
191 Terrence Austin RC 2.50 6.00
192 Terrence Cody RC 2.00 5.00
193 Timothy Toone RC 2.50 6.00
194 Tony Moeaki RC 2.50 6.00
195 Tony Pike RC 2.00 5.00
196 Torell Troup RC 2.00 5.00
197 Trent Williams RC 2.50 6.00
198 Trindon Holliday RC 6.00 15.00
199 Tyson Alualu RC 2.00 5.00
200 Zac Robinson RC 2.50 6.00
201 S.Bradford RPM AU RC 5.00 12.00
202 J.Clausen RPM AU RC 4.00 10.00
203 Colt McCoy RPM AU RC 5.00 12.00
204 Tim Tebow RPM AU RC 25.00 60.00
205 A.Edwards RPM AU RC 5.00 12.00
206 C.J. Spiller RPM AU RC 4.00 10.00
207 Jahvid Best RPM AU RC 4.00 10.00
208 J.Dwyer RPM AU RC 4.00 10.00
209 R.Mathews RPM AU RC 4.00 10.00
210 J.McKnight RPM AU RC 4.00 10.00
211 M.Hardesty RPM AU RC 4.00 10.00
212 Toby Gerhart RPM AU RC 4.00 10.00
213 Ben Tate RPM AU RC 4.00 10.00
214 D.McCluster RPM AU RC 5.00 12.00
215 Dez Bryant RPM AU RC 15.00 40.00
216 Golden Tate RPM AU RC 5.00 12.00
217 Arrelious Benn RPM AU RC 4.00 10.00
218 Brandon LaFell RPM AU RC 6.00 15.00
219 D.Thomas RPM AU RC 12.00 30.00
220 Damian Williams RPM AU RC 4.00 10.00
221 Eric Decker RPM AU RC 5.00 12.00
222 Jordan Shipley RPM AU RC 4.00 10.00
223 Mardy Gilyard RPM AU RC 4.00 10.00
224 Mike Williams RPM AU RC 4.00 10.00
225 Andre Roberts RPM AU RC 5.00 12.00
226 J.Gresham RPM AU RC 4.00 10.00
227 R.Gronkowski RPM AU RC 30.00 60.00
228 N.Suh RPM AU RC 8.00 20.00
229 Gerald McCoy RPM AU RC 4.00 10.00
230 Rolando McClain RPM AU RC 4.00 10.00
231 Eric Berry RPM AU RC 6.00 15.00
232 E.Sanders RPM AU RC 6.00 15.00
233 Marcus Easley RPM AU RC 4.00 10.00
234 Taylor Price RPM AU RC 4.00 10.00
235 Mike Kafka RPM AU RC 5.00 12.00

2010 Absolute Memorabilia Retail

COMP.SET w/o RC's (100) 10.00 20.00
*VETS 1-100: .25X TO .6X BASIC CARDS
*ROOKIES 101-200: .4X TO 1X BASIC CARDS
101-200 ROOKIE PRINT RUN 299

2010 Absolute Memorabilia Rookie Premiere Materials Autographs AFC/NFC

*AFC/NFC/25: .5X TO 1.2X BASIC RPM AU RC
AFC/NFC STATED PRINT RUN 25
EXCH EXPIRATION: 4/13/2012
201 Sam Bradford 6.00 15.00
204 Tim Tebow 40.00 100.00
215 Dez Bryant 20.00 50.00
227 Rob Gronkowski 50.00 100.00

2010 Absolute Memorabilia Spectrum Blue Retail

*VETS 1-100: 2X TO 5X BASIC CARDS
*ROOKIES 101-200: .5X TO 1.2X BASIC CARDS
STATED PRINT RUN 75 SER.#'d SETS

2010 Absolute Memorabilia Spectrum Red Retail

*VETS 1-100: 1.2X TO 3X BASIC CARDS
*ROOKIES 101-200: .3X TO .8X BASIC CARDS
RANDOM INSERT IN RETAIL PACKS

2010 Absolute Memorabilia Spectrum Silver

*VETS 1-100: 2X TO 5X BASIC CARDS
*ROOKIES 101-200: .5X TO 1.2X BASIC CARDS
STATED PRINT RUN 50 SER.#'d SETS
169 Maurkice Pouncey 3.00 8.00

2010 Absolute Memorabilia Spectrum Silver Retail

*1-100 VETS/50: 2X TO 5X BASIC CARDS
*101-200 ROOKIES/50: .5X TO 1.2X BASIC RC
STATED PRINT RUN 50 SER.#'d SETS

2010 Absolute Memorabilia Absolute Heroes

*SPECTRUM/50: 1X TO 2.5X BASIC INSERTS
1 Andre Johnson 1.00 2.50
2 Braylon Edwards .75 2.00
3 Carson Palmer 1.00 2.50
4 Devin Hester 1.00 2.50
5 Eli Manning 1.00 2.50
6 Greg Jennings .75 2.00
7 Hines Ward 1.00 2.50
8 Jeremy Maclin .75 2.00
9 T.J. Houshmandzadeh .75 2.00
10 Jerricho Cotchery .75 2.00
11 Joe Flacco 1.00 2.50
12 Johnny Knox .75 2.00
13 Kyle Orton .75 2.00
14 Larry Fitzgerald 1.00 2.50
15 Marques Colston .75 2.00
16 Matt Hasselbeck .75 2.00
17 Matt Ryan 1.00 2.50
18 Matt Schaub .75 2.00
19 Pierre Garcon 1.00 2.50
20 Randy Moss 1.00 2.50
21 Roddy White .75 2.00
22 Steve Smith 1.00 2.50
23 Steve Smith USC .75 2.00
24 Kenny Britt .75 2.00
25 Tony Romo 1.00 2.50

2010 Absolute Memorabilia Absolute Heroes Materials Spectrum Prime

STATED PRINT RUN 10-50
1 Andre Johnson/50 4.00 10.00
2 Braylon Edwards/50 3.00 8.00
3 Carson Palmer/50 4.00 10.00
4 Devin Hester/50 4.00 10.00
6 Greg Jennings/50 3.00 8.00
7 Hines Ward/50 4.00 10.00
8 Jeremy Maclin/50 3.00 8.00
10 Jerricho Cotchery/50 3.00 8.00
11 Joe Flacco/50 4.00 10.00
12 Johnny Knox/50 3.00 8.00
13 Kyle Orton/50 3.00 8.00
14 Larry Fitzgerald/25 5.00 12.00
15 Marques Colston/50 3.00 8.00
16 Matt Hasselbeck/50 3.00 8.00
17 Matt Ryan/50 4.00 10.00
20 Randy Moss/50 4.00 10.00
21 Roddy White/50 3.00 8.00
22 Steve Smith/50 4.00 10.00
23 Steve Smith USC/50 3.00 8.00
24 Kenny Britt/50 3.00 8.00
25 Tony Romo/50 4.00 10.00

2010 Absolute Memorabilia Absolute Heroes Materials Autographs

STATED PRINT RUN 5-15
2 Braylon Edwards/15 10.00 25.00
11 Joe Flacco/15 25.00 50.00
13 Kyle Orton/15 15.00 40.00
21 Roddy White/15 10.00 25.00
24 Kenny Britt/15 10.00 25.00
25 Tony Romo/15 25.00 60.00

2010 Absolute Memorabilia Absolute Patches Spectrum Prime

STATED PRINT RUN 20-25
1 Adrian Peterson/25 25.00 60.00
2 Ahmad Bradshaw/25 15.00 40.00
3 Antonio Gates/25 20.00 50.00
4 Vincent Jackson/25 15.00 40.00
5 Calvin Johnson/25 25.00 60.00
6 Chad Ochocinco/25 15.00 40.00
7 Chris Johnson/20 15.00 40.00
8 Clinton Portis/25 15.00 40.00
9 Darren McFadden/25 15.00 40.00
10 Darren Sproles/25 20.00 50.00
11 DeAngelo Williams/25 15.00 40.00
12 DeMarcus Ware/25 20.00 50.00
13 Devery Henderson/25 15.00 40.00
14 Donald Driver/25 20.00 50.00
15 Dustin Keller/25 15.00 40.00
16 Dwayne Bowe/20 20.00 50.00
17 Felix Jones/25 15.00 40.00
18 Frank Gore/25 20.00 50.00
19 Greg Olsen/25 20.00 50.00
20 Hines Ward/25 20.00 50.00
21 Jeremy Maclin/25 15.00 40.00
22 Jerricho Cotchery/25 15.00 40.00
23 Jonathan Stewart/25 15.00 40.00
24 Johnny Knox/25 15.00 40.00
25 Kenny Britt/25 15.00 40.00
26 Ladell Betts/25 15.00 40.00
27 Marion Barber/25 12.00 30.00
28 Marques Colston/25 15.00 40.00
29 Maurice Jones-Drew/25 15.00 40.00
30 Reggie Bush/25 15.00 40.00
31 Ronnie Brown/25 15.00 40.00
32 Santana Moss/25 20.00 50.00
33 Steve Smith/25 20.00 50.00
34 Steven Jackson/25 15.00 40.00
35 Tom Brady/25 60.00 120.00
36 Troy Polamalu/25 50.00 100.00
37 Vince Young/25 15.00 40.00
38 Visanthe Shiancoe/25 20.00 50.00
39 Wes Welker/25 20.00 50.00
40 Willis McGahee/25 15.00 40.00

2010 Absolute Memorabilia Canton Absolutes

*SPECTRUM/50: 1X TO 2.5X BASIC INSERTS
1 Bart Starr 2.00 5.00
2 Bob Hayes 1.25 3.00
3 Bruce Smith 1.00 2.50
4 Dan Marino 2.50 6.00
5 Deacon Jones 1.00 2.50
6 Derrick Thomas 1.25 3.00
7 Don Maynard 1.00 2.50
8 Earl Campbell 1.25 3.00
9 Emmitt Smith 2.00 5.00
10 Gale Sayers 1.25 3.00
11 Henry Jordan .75 2.00
12 Howie Long 1.25 3.00
13 Jerry Rice 2.00 5.00
14 Joe Greene 1.25 3.00
15 Joe Montana 4.00 10.00
16 Joe Namath 1.50 4.00
17 John Elway 2.00 5.00
18 John Randle 1.00 2.50
19 Rod Woodson 1.00 2.50
20 Terry Bradshaw 1.50 4.00
21 Thurman Thomas 1.00 2.50
22 Tony Dorsett 1.25 3.00
23 Troy Aikman 1.50 4.00
24 Walter Payton 2.50 6.00
25 Warren Moon 1.25 3.00

2010 Absolute Memorabilia Canton Absolutes Materials Spectrum Prime

STATED PRINT RUN 4-50
2 Bob Hayes/50 8.00 20.00
3 Bruce Smith/50 6.00 15.00
4 Dan Marino/50 15.00 40.00
7 Don Maynard/50 6.00 15.00
9 Emmitt Smith/50 12.00 30.00
10 Gale Sayers/50 8.00 20.00
11 Henry Jordan/50 6.00 15.00
12 Howie Long/50 10.00 25.00
13 Jerry Rice/50 12.00 30.00
15 Joe Montana/25 30.00 80.00
16 Joe Namath/25 12.00 30.00
18 John Randle/50 6.00 15.00
19 Rod Woodson/20 8.00 20.00
20 Terry Bradshaw/50 10.00 25.00
22 Tony Dorsett/50 8.00 20.00
23 Troy Aikman/20 12.00 30.00
24 Walter Payton/25 20.00 50.00

2010 Absolute Memorabilia Canton Absolutes Materials Autographs

STATED PRINT RUN 10-50
*SPECT.PRIM/15: .5X TO 1.2X JSY AU/20-50
1 Bart Starr/25 60.00 120.00
3 Bruce Smith/25 25.00 50.00
5 Deacon Jones/50 15.00 40.00
7 Don Maynard/25 12.00 30.00
8 Earl Campbell/40 20.00 50.00
9 Emmitt Smith/25 100.00 175.00
12 Howie Long/50 25.00 60.00
13 Jerry Rice/15 100.00 200.00
14 Joe Greene/50 20.00 50.00
15 Joe Montana/15 100.00 200.00
16 Joe Namath/25 40.00 80.00
17 John Elway/20 100.00 200.00
18 John Randle/25 15.00 40.00
19 Rod Woodson/35 30.00 60.00
20 Terry Bradshaw/25 50.00 100.00
21 Thurman Thomas/25 15.00 40.00
22 Tony Dorsett/25 20.00 50.00
25 Warren Moon/50 20.00 50.00

2010 Absolute Memorabilia Gridiron Force

*SPECTRUM/50: 1X TO 2.5X BASIC INSERTS
1 Ben Roethlisberger 1.25 3.00
2 Bernard Berrian .75 2.00
3 Brandon Jacobs .75 2.00
4 Chad Ochocinco .75 2.00
5 Darrelle Revis .75 2.00
6 Darren McFadden .75 2.00
7 Donald Driver 1.00 2.50
8 Dustin Keller .75 2.00
9 Dwayne Bowe 1.00 2.50
10 Greg Olsen 1.00 2.50
11 Heath Miller .75 2.00
12 Jason Witten 1.00 2.50
13 Jay Cutler .75 2.00
14 Kevin Boss .75 2.00
15 Ladell Betts .75 2.00
16 Lee Evans 1.00 2.50
17 Patrick Willis 1.00 2.50
18 Philip Rivers 1.25 3.00
19 Rashard Mendenhall .75 2.00
20 Ray Lewis 1.25 3.00
21 Reggie Wayne 1.00 2.50
22 Santana Moss 1.00 2.50
23 Troy Polamalu 1.25 3.00

24 Vincent Jackson .75 2.00
25 Wes Welker 1.00 2.50

2010 Absolute Memorabilia Gridiron Force Material Prime Jersey Number

STATED PRINT RUN 25-50
1 Ben Roethlisberger/50 8.00 20.00
2 Bernard Berrian/50 4.00 10.00
3 Brandon Jacobs/50 4.00 10.00
4 Chad Ochocinco/50 4.00 10.00
5 Darrelle Revis/50 4.00 10.00
6 Darren McFadden/50 4.00 10.00
7 Donald Driver/50 5.00 12.00
8 Dustin Keller/50 4.00 10.00
9 Dwayne Bowe/50 5.00 12.00
10 Greg Olsen/50 5.00 12.00
11 Heath Miller/25 5.00 12.00
12 Jason Witten/50 5.00 12.00
13 Jay Cutler/25 5.00 12.00
14 Kevin Boss/50 4.00 10.00
15 Ladell Betts/50 4.00 10.00
16 Lee Evans/50 5.00 12.00
17 Patrick Willis/50 5.00 12.00
18 Philip Rivers/50 6.00 15.00
19 Rashard Mendenhall/50 4.00 10.00
20 Ray Lewis/50 8.00 20.00
22 Santana Moss/50 5.00 12.00
23 Troy Polamalu/50 12.00 30.00
24 Vincent Jackson/50 4.00 10.00
25 Wes Welker/50 5.00 12.00

2010 Absolute Memorabilia Ground Hoggs

*SPECTRUM/50: 1X TO 2.5X BASIC INSERTS
1 Adrian Peterson 1.25 3.00
2 Chris Wells .75 2.00
3 Cadillac Williams .75 2.00
4 Chris Johnson .75 2.00
5 Clinton Portis .75 2.00
6 Darren Sproles 1.00 2.50
7 DeAngelo Williams .75 2.00
8 Felix Jones .75 2.00
9 Frank Gore 1.00 2.50
10 Jamaal Charles 1.00 2.50
11 Jonathan Stewart .75 2.00
12 Joseph Addai .75 2.00
13 Knowshon Moreno .75 2.00
14 Laurence Maroney .75 2.00
15 Matt Forte .75 2.00
16 Maurice Jones-Drew .75 2.00
17 Michael Turner .75 2.00
18 Pierre Thomas .75 2.00
19 Ray Rice .75 2.00
20 Reggie Bush .75 2.00
21 Ricky Williams 1.00 2.50
22 Ronnie Brown .75 2.00
23 Ryan Grant 1.00 2.50
24 Shonn Greene .75 2.00
25 Steven Jackson .75 2.00

2010 Absolute Memorabilia Ground Hoggs Materials Jersey Number

STATED PRINT RUN 20-50
1 Adrian Peterson/50 10.00 25.00
2 Chris Wells/50 3.00 8.00
3 Cadillac Williams/50 3.00 8.00
4 Chris Johnson/50 3.00 8.00
5 Clinton Portis/50 3.00 8.00
6 Darren Sproles/50 4.00 10.00
7 DeAngelo Williams/45 3.00 8.00
8 Felix Jones/50 3.00 8.00
9 Frank Gore/50 4.00 10.00
10 Jamaal Charles/50 4.00 10.00
11 Jonathan Stewart/50 3.00 8.00
12 Joseph Addai/50 3.00 8.00
13 Knowshon Moreno/50 3.00 8.00
14 Laurence Maroney/50 3.00 8.00
15 Matt Forte/50 3.00 8.00
16 Maurice Jones-Drew/50 3.00 8.00
19 Ray Rice/50 3.00 8.00
20 Reggie Bush/50 3.00 8.00
21 Ricky Williams/50 4.00 10.00
22 Ronnie Brown/50 3.00 8.00
24 Shonn Greene/20 4.00 10.00
25 Steven Jackson/50 3.00 8.00

2010 Absolute Memorabilia Marks of Fame

*SPECTRUM/50: 1X TO 2.5X BASIC INSERTS
1 Aaron Rodgers 2.50 6.00
2 Antonio Gates 1.00 2.50
3 Brent Celek .75 2.00
4 Brett Favre 2.50 6.00
5 Calvin Johnson 1.25 3.00
6 Chris Cooley .75 2.00
7 Dallas Clark .75 2.00
8 DeSean Jackson 1.00 2.50
9 Devery Henderson .75 2.00
10 Drew Brees 1.25 3.00
11 Josh Cribbs .75 2.00
12 LeSean McCoy 1.25 3.00
13 Mark Sanchez .75 2.00
14 Matthew Stafford 1.00 2.50
15 Michael Crabtree .75 2.00
16 Miles Austin .75 2.00
17 Percy Harvin .75 2.00
18 Peyton Manning 3.00 8.00
19 Sidney Rice .75 2.00
20 Tom Brady 3.00 8.00
21 Tony Gonzalez 1.00 2.50
22 Vernon Davis .75 2.00
23 Vince Young .75 2.00
24 Visanthe Shiancoe 1.00 2.50
25 Willis McGahee .75 2.00

2010 Absolute Memorabilia Marks of Fame Materials Spectrum Prime

STATED PRINT RUN 15-50
2 Antonio Gates/50 5.00 12.00
3 Brent Celek/50 5.00 12.00
4 Brett Favre/15 40.00 80.00
5 Calvin Johnson/50 6.00 15.00
6 Chris Cooley/50 4.00 10.00
7 Dallas Clark/50 4.00 10.00
9 Devery Henderson/50 4.00 10.00
10 Drew Brees/35 6.00 15.00
12 LeSean McCoy/50 6.00 15.00
13 Mark Sanchez/50 4.00 10.00
14 Matthew Stafford/50 5.00 12.00
17 Percy Harvin/50 4.00 10.00
18 Peyton Manning/50 15.00 40.00
19 Sidney Rice/50 6.00 15.00
20 Tom Brady/50 15.00 40.00
21 Tony Gonzalez/50 5.00 12.00
22 Vernon Davis/50 4.00 10.00
23 Vince Young/50 4.00 10.00
24 Visanthe Shiancoe/50 5.00 12.00
25 Willis McGahee/50 4.00 10.00

2010 Absolute Memorabilia Marks of Fame Materials Autographs

STATED PRINT RUN 1-15
2 Antonio Gates/15 15.00 40.00
3 Brent Celek/15 12.00 30.00
9 Devery Henderson/15 10.00 25.00
10 Drew Brees/15 60.00 120.00
11 Josh Cribbs/15 15.00 40.00
13 Mark Sanchez/15 30.00 60.00
14 Matthew Stafford/15 30.00 80.00
18 Peyton Manning/15 75.00 150.00
19 Sidney Rice/15 10.00 25.00
22 Vernon Davis/15 10.00 25.00

2010 Absolute Memorabilia NFL Icons

*SPECTRUM/50: 1X TO 2.5X BASIC INSERTS
1 Art Monk 1.25 3.00
2 Bernie Kosar 1.00 2.50
3 Bo Jackson 1.50 4.00
4 Boomer Esiason 1.00 2.50
5 Brent Jones .75 2.00
6 Cris Carter 1.25 3.00
7 Curtis Martin 1.00 2.50
8 D.D. Lewis .75 2.00
9 Deion Sanders 1.00 2.50
10 Ed Too Tall Jones .75 2.00
11 Eddie George 1.00 2.50
12 Fran Tarkenton 1.25 3.00
13 Harvey Martin .75 2.00
15 Jim Kelly 1.25 3.00
16 Joe Montana 4.00 10.00
17 Junior Seau 1.00 2.50
18 Ken Stabler 1.25 3.00
19 L.C. Greenwood .75 2.00
20 Priest Holmes .75 2.00
21 Randall Cunningham 1.00 2.50
22 Raymond Berry 1.00 2.50
23 Rod Smith .75 2.00
24 Roger Craig 1.00 2.50
25 Ronnie Lott 1.00 2.50
26 Steve Largent 1.25 3.00
27 Steve Young 1.50 4.00
28 Terrell Davis 1.00 2.50
29 Todd Christensen .75 2.00
30 Tom Rathman .75 2.00

2010 Absolute Memorabilia NFL Icons Materials Spectrum Prime

STATED PRINT RUN 10-50
1 Art Monk/14 25.00 50.00
2 Bernie Kosar/50 6.00 15.00
3 Bo Jackson/50 10.00 25.00
4 Boomer Esiason/50 6.00 15.00
5 Brent Jones/50 5.00 12.00
6 Cris Carter/50 8.00 20.00
7 Curtis Martin/50 6.00 15.00
8 D.D. Lewis/50 5.00 12.00
9 Deion Sanders/50 6.00 15.00
10 Ed Too Tall Jones/50 5.00 12.00
11 Eddie George/50 6.00 15.00
13 Harvey Martin/25 8.00 20.00
15 Jim Kelly/50 8.00 20.00
16 Joe Montana/25 30.00 80.00
17 Junior Seau/50 6.00 15.00
18 Ken Stabler/50 8.00 20.00
20 Priest Holmes/50 5.00 12.00
22 Raymond Berry/50 6.00 15.00
23 Rod Smith/50 5.00 12.00
24 Roger Craig/50 6.00 15.00
26 Steve Largent/50 8.00 20.00
27 Steve Young/50 10.00 25.00
28 Terrell Davis/50 6.00 15.00
29 Todd Christensen/50 5.00 12.00
30 Tom Rathman/50 5.00 12.00

2010 Absolute Memorabilia NFL Icons Materials Autographs

STATED PRINT RUN 10-50
*SPECT.PRIM/15: .5X TO 1.2X JSY AU/15-50
1 Art Monk/15 75.00 125.00
2 Bernie Kosar/25 15.00 40.00
3 Bo Jackson/25 50.00 100.00
5 Brent Jones/25 15.00 40.00
8 D.D. Lewis/25 12.00 30.00
9 Deion Sanders/25 30.00 60.00
10 Ed Too Tall Jones/25 15.00 40.00
12 Fran Tarkenton/45 20.00 50.00
15 Jim Kelly/25 30.00 60.00
16 Joe Montana/15 100.00 200.00
18 Ken Stabler/50 15.00 40.00
19 L.C. Greenwood/20 20.00 50.00
20 Priest Holmes/25 12.00 30.00
21 Randall Cunningham/50 20.00 50.00
22 Raymond Berry/50 12.00 30.00
23 Rod Smith/25 15.00 40.00
24 Roger Craig/50 10.00 25.00
25 Ronnie Lott/50 15.00 40.00
26 Steve Largent/50 20.00 50.00
27 Steve Young/25 40.00 80.00
28 Terrell Davis/25 20.00 50.00
29 Todd Christensen/25 12.00 30.00
30 Tom Rathman/25 12.00 30.00

2010 Absolute Memorabilia Rookie Jersey Collection

ONE PER BLASTER RETAIL BOX
1 Andre Roberts 2.00 5.00
2 Armanti Edwards 2.00 5.00
3 Arrelious Benn 1.50 4.00
4 Ben Tate 1.50 4.00
5 Brandon LaFell 2.50 6.00
6 C.J. Spiller 1.50 4.00
7 Colt McCoy 2.00 5.00
8 Damian Williams 1.50 4.00
9 Demaryius Thomas 4.00 10.00
10 Dexter McCluster 2.00 5.00
11 Dez Bryant 6.00 15.00
12 Emmanuel Sanders 2.50 6.00
13 Eric Berry 2.50 6.00
14 Eric Decker 2.00 5.00
15 Gerald McCoy 1.50 4.00
16 Golden Tate 2.00 5.00
17 Jahvid Best 1.50 4.00
18 Jermaine Gresham 1.50 4.00
19 Jimmy Clausen 1.50 4.00
20 Joe McKnight 1.50 4.00
21 Jonathan Dwyer 1.50 4.00
22 Jordan Shipley 1.50 4.00
23 Marcus Easley 1.50 4.00
24 Mardy Gilyard 1.50 4.00
25 Mike Kafka 2.00 5.00
26 Mike Williams 1.50 4.00
27 Montario Hardesty 1.50 4.00
28 Ndamukong Suh 3.00 8.00
29 Rob Gronkowski 5.00 12.00
30 Rolando McClain 1.50 4.00
31 Ryan Mathews 1.50 4.00
32 Sam Bradford 2.00 5.00
33 Taylor Price 1.50 4.00
34 Tim Tebow 5.00 12.00
35 Toby Gerhart 1.50 4.00

2010 Absolute Memorabilia Rookie Premiere Materials AFC/NFC

AFC/NFC PRINT RUN 99 SER.#'d SETS
*AFC/NFC SPECTRUM PRIME/25: .8X TO 2X
*NFL SPECTRUM PRIME/50: .6X TO 1.5X
*OVER.JERSEY NUMBER/50: .6X TO 1.5X
*OVER.JSY NUMBER PRIME/10: 1.5X TO 4X
*OVER.SPECTRUM PRIME/25: 1X TO 2.5X
201 Sam Bradford 2.00 5.00
202 Jimmy Clausen 1.50 4.00
203 Colt McCoy 2.00 5.00
204 Tim Tebow 5.00 12.00
205 Armanti Edwards 2.00 5.00
206 C.J. Spiller 1.50 4.00
207 Jahvid Best 1.50 4.00
208 Jonathan Dwyer 1.50 4.00
209 Ryan Mathews 1.50 4.00
210 Joe McKnight 1.50 4.00
211 Montario Hardesty 1.50 4.00
212 Toby Gerhart 1.50 4.00
213 Ben Tate 1.50 4.00
214 Dexter McCluster 2.00 5.00
215 Dez Bryant 4.00 10.00
216 Golden Tate 2.00 5.00
217 Arrelious Benn 1.50 4.00
218 Brandon LaFell 2.50 6.00
219 Demaryius Thomas 4.00 10.00
220 Damian Williams 1.50 4.00
221 Eric Decker 2.00 5.00
222 Jordan Shipley 1.50 4.00
223 Mardy Gilyard 1.50 4.00
224 Mike Williams 1.50 4.00
225 Andre Roberts 2.00 6.00
226 Jermaine Gresham 1.50 4.00
227 Rob Gronkowski 5.00 12.00
228 Ndamukong Suh 3.00 8.00
229 Gerald McCoy 1.50 4.00
230 Rolando McClain 1.50 4.00
231 Eric Berry 2.50 6.00
232 Emmanuel Sanders 2.50 6.00
233 Marcus Easley 1.50 4.00
234 Taylor Price 1.50 4.00
235 Mike Kafka 2.00 5.00

2010 Absolute Memorabilia Spectrum Gold Autographs

1-100 VETERAN PRINT RUN 5-50
101-200 ROOKIE PRINT RUN 99-299
10 Lee Evans/25 8.00 20.00
72 Louis Murphy/50 5.00 12.00
74 Kevin Kolb/25 10.00 25.00
100 Donovan McNabb/15 25.00 50.00
101 Aaron Hernandez/199 8.00 20.00
106 Anthony McCoy/99 4.00 10.00
107 Antonio Brown/99 30.00 80.00
108 Blair White/99 4.00 10.00
110 Brandon Graham/299 4.00 10.00
111 Brandon Spikes/199 3.00 8.00
113 Bryan Bulaga/199 3.00 8.00
114 Carlos Dunlap/199 3.00 8.00
115 Carlton Mitchell/199 3.00 8.00
116 Chad Jones/141 3.00 8.00
117 Charles Scott/299 3.00 8.00
120 Corey Wootton/99 4.00 10.00
121 Dan LeFevour/149 3.00 8.00
124 David Gettis/99 4.00 10.00
128 Derrick Morgan/99 4.00 10.00
129 Devin McCourty/199 4.00 10.00
130 Dezmon Briscoe/99 4.00 10.00
131 Dominique Franks/299 3.00 8.00
133 Earl Thomas/99 10.00 25.00
134 Ed Dickson/199 3.00 8.00
135 Everson Griffen/199 3.00 8.00
136 Freddie Barnes/299 3.00 8.00
137 Garrett Graham/99 4.00 10.00
138 Jacoby Ford/199 3.00 8.00
139 James Starks/99 5.00 12.00
141 Jarrett Brown/99 4.00 10.00
142 Jason Pierre-Paul/199 5.00 12.00
143 Jason Worilds/199 3.00 8.00
145 Jeremy Williams/99 4.00 10.00
148 Jerry Hughes/199 3.00 8.00
149 Jevan Snead/201 3.00 8.00
150 Jimmy Graham/299 15.00 30.00
151 Joe Haden/199 5.00 12.00
154 John Skelton/299 5.00 12.00
155 Joique Bell/199 3.00 8.00
156 Jonathan Crompton/299 3.00 8.00
172 Morgan Burnett/199 4.00 10.00
177 Patrick Robinson/199 4.00 10.00
178 Perrish Cox/199 4.00 10.00
179 Ricky Sapp/299 3.00 8.00
180 Riley Cooper/299 3.00 8.00
183 Sean Canfield/99 4.00 10.00
184 Sean Lee/199 6.00 15.00
185 Sean Weatherspoon/99 4.00 10.00
188 Shay Hodge/299 3.00 8.00
190 Taylor Mays/199 3.00 8.00
195 Tony Pike/99 4.00 10.00
200 Zac Robinson/199 4.00 10.00

2010 Absolute Memorabilia Spectrum Platinum Autographs

1-100 VETERAN PRINT RUN 1-25
101-200 ROOKIE PRINT RUN 19-25
31 Kyle Orton/25 10.00 25.00
48 Dwayne Bowe/25 8.00 20.00
72 Louis Murphy/25 6.00 15.00
96 Kenny Britt/25 6.00 15.00
101 Aaron Hernandez/25 15.00 40.00
105 Anthony Dixon/25 6.00 15.00
106 Anthony McCoy/25 6.00 15.00
107 Antonio Brown/25 50.00 120.00
108 Blair White/25 6.00 15.00
110 Brandon Graham/25 8.00 20.00
111 Brandon Spikes/25 6.00 15.00
113 Bryan Bulaga/25 6.00 15.00
114 Carlos Dunlap/25 6.00 15.00
115 Carlton Mitchell/25 6.00 15.00
116 Chad Jones/25 6.00 15.00
117 Charles Scott/25 6.00 15.00
118 Chris Cook/19 6.00 15.00
120 Corey Wootton/25 6.00 15.00
121 Dan LeFevour/25 6.00 15.00
124 David Gettis/25 6.00 15.00
128 Derrick Morgan/25 6.00 15.00
129 Devin McCourty/25 8.00 20.00
130 Dezmon Briscoe/25 6.00 15.00
133 Earl Thomas/25 15.00 40.00
134 Ed Dickson/25 6.00 15.00
135 Everson Griffen/25 6.00 15.00
136 Freddie Barnes/25 6.00 15.00
137 Garrett Graham/25 6.00 15.00
138 Jacoby Ford/25 6.00 15.00
139 James Starks/25 8.00 20.00
141 Jarrett Brown/25 6.00 15.00
142 Jason Pierre-Paul/25 10.00 25.00
143 Jason Worilds/25 6.00 15.00
145 Jeremy Williams/25 6.00 15.00
148 Jerry Hughes/25 6.00 15.00
149 Jevan Snead/25 6.00 15.00
150 Jimmy Graham/25 30.00 60.00
151 Joe Haden/25 10.00 25.00
154 John Skelton/25 8.00 20.00
155 Joique Bell/25 6.00 15.00
156 Jonathan Crompton/25 6.00 15.00
157 Kareem Jackson/25 6.00 15.00
166 Lonyae Miller/25 8.00 20.00
172 Morgan Burnett/25 8.00 20.00
177 Patrick Robinson/25 8.00 20.00
178 Perrish Cox/25 8.00 20.00
179 Ricky Sapp/25 6.00 15.00
180 Riley Cooper/25 6.00 15.00
183 Sean Canfield/25 6.00 15.00
184 Sean Lee/25 12.00 30.00
185 Sean Weatherspoon/25 6.00 15.00
187 Seyi Ajirotutu/25 6.00 15.00
188 Shay Hodge/25 6.00 15.00
190 Taylor Mays/25 6.00 15.00
195 Tony Pike/25 6.00 15.00
200 Zac Robinson/25 8.00 20.00

2010 Absolute Memorabilia Star Gazing

*SPECTRUM/50: 1X TO 2.5X BASIC INSERTS
1 Tim Tebow 1.50 4.00
2 Sam Bradford .60 1.50
3 Brandon LaFell .75 2.00
4 Colt McCoy .60 1.50
5 Demaryius Thomas 1.25 3.00
6 Dez Bryant 1.25 3.00
7 Eric Berry .75 2.00
8 Gerald McCoy .50 1.25
9 Jahvid Best .50 1.25
10 Jimmy Clausen .50 1.25
11 Jonathan Dwyer .50 1.25
12 Marcus Easley .50 1.25
13 Mike Kafka .60 1.50
14 Montario Hardesty .50 1.25
15 Armanti Edwards .60 1.50
16 C.J. Spiller .50 1.25
17 Damian Williams .50 1.25
18 Emmanuel Sanders .75 2.00
19 Toby Gerhart .50 1.25
20 Dexter McCluster .60 1.50
21 Arrelious Benn .50 1.25
22 Jordan Shipley .50 1.25
23 Mardy Gilyard .50 1.25
24 Andre Roberts .60 1.50
25 Jermaine Gresham .50 1.25
26 Ndamukong Suh 1.00 2.50
27 Taylor Price .50 1.25
28 Rob Gronkowski 1.50 4.00
29 Rolando McClain .50 1.25
30 Mike Williams .50 1.25
31 Ryan Mathews .50 1.25
32 Joe McKnight .50 1.25
33 Ben Tate .50 1.25
34 Eric Decker .60 1.50
35 Golden Tate .60 1.50

2010 Absolute Memorabilia Star Gazing Materials

STATED PRINT RUN 250 SER.#'d SETS
*OVER.JSY NUMBER/10: 1X TO 2.5X
*OVER.JSY NMBR PRIME/25: 1X TO 2.5X
*OVER.SPECTRUM PRIME/15: 1X TO 2.5X
*PRIME/50: .6X TO 1.5X BASIC JSY/250
1 Tim Tebow 5.00 12.00
2 Sam Bradford 2.00 5.00
3 Brandon LaFell 2.50 6.00
4 Colt McCoy 2.00 5.00
5 Demaryius Thomas 4.00 10.00
6 Dez Bryant 4.00 10.00
7 Eric Berry 2.50 6.00
8 Gerald McCoy 1.50 4.00
9 Jahvid Best 1.50 4.00
10 Jimmy Clausen 1.50 4.00
11 Jonathan Dwyer 1.50 4.00
12 Marcus Easley 1.50 4.00
13 Mike Kafka 2.00 5.00
14 Montario Hardesty 1.50 4.00
15 Armanti Edwards 2.00 5.00
16 C.J. Spiller 1.50 4.00
17 Damian Williams 1.50 4.00
18 Emmanuel Sanders 2.50 6.00
19 Toby Gerhart 1.50 4.00
20 Dexter McCluster 2.00 5.00
21 Arrelious Benn 1.50 4.00
22 Jordan Shipley 1.50 4.00
23 Mardy Gilyard 1.50 4.00
24 Andre Roberts 2.00 5.00
25 Jermaine Gresham 1.50 4.00
26 Ndamukong Suh 3.00 8.00
27 Taylor Price 1.50 4.00
28 Rob Gronkowski 5.00 12.00
29 Rolando McClain 1.50 4.00
30 Mike Williams 1.50 4.00
31 Ryan Mathews 1.50 4.00
32 Joe McKnight 1.50 4.00
33 Ben Tate 1.50 4.00
34 Eric Decker 2.00 5.00
35 Golden Tate 2.00 5.00

2010 Absolute Memorabilia Star Gazing Materials Autographs

STATED PRINT RUN 25 SER.#'d SETS
EXCH EXPIRATION: 4/13/2012
1 Tim Tebow 30.00 80.00
2 Sam Bradford 6.00 15.00
3 Brandon LaFell 8.00 20.00
4 Colt McCoy 6.00 15.00
5 Demaryius Thomas 12.00 30.00
6 Dez Bryant 25.00 60.00
7 Eric Berry 8.00 20.00
8 Gerald McCoy 5.00 12.00
9 Jahvid Best 5.00 12.00
10 Jimmy Clausen 5.00 12.00
11 Jonathan Dwyer 5.00 12.00
12 Marcus Easley 5.00 12.00
13 Mike Kafka 6.00 15.00
14 Montario Hardesty 5.00 12.00
15 Armanti Edwards 6.00 15.00
16 C.J. Spiller 5.00 12.00
17 Damian Williams 5.00 12.00
18 Emmanuel Sanders 8.00 20.00
19 Toby Gerhart 5.00 12.00
20 Dexter McCluster 6.00 15.00
21 Arrelious Benn 5.00 12.00
22 Jordan Shipley 5.00 12.00
23 Mardy Gilyard 5.00 12.00
24 Andre Roberts 6.00 15.00
25 Jermaine Gresham 5.00 12.00
26 Ndamukong Suh 15.00 40.00
27 Taylor Price 5.00 12.00
28 Rob Gronkowski 25.00 60.00
29 Rolando McClain 5.00 12.00
30 Mike Williams 5.00 12.00
31 Ryan Mathews 5.00 12.00
32 Joe McKnight 5.00 12.00
33 Ben Tate 5.00 12.00
34 Eric Decker 6.00 15.00
35 Golden Tate 6.00 15.00

2010 Absolute Memorabilia Team Quads Materials Die Cut Spectrum Prime

SPECTRUM PRIME PRINT RUN 15-25
*QUAD MAT/50: .25X TO .6X PRIME/15-25
1 Rice/Shnc/Ptrsn/Fvre/25 30.00 80.00
3 Brees/Clstn/Bsh/Hndrsn/25 12.00 30.00
5 Jones/Austin/Witten/Romo/15 15.00 40.00
6 Eli/Jacobs/Brdshw/Smith/25 12.00 30.00
7 Pola/Roeth/Ward/Miller/25 15.00 40.00
8 Cutler/Forte/Olsen/Knox/25 10.00 25.00
10 Young/Johnson/Britt/Gage/25 12.00 30.00

2010 Absolute Memorabilia Team Tandems Materials Spectrum Prime

SPECTRUM PRIME PRINT RUN 15-25
*TAND.MAT/85-100: .25X TO .6X PRIME/15-25
*TANDEM MAT/30: .3X TO .8X PRIME/15-25
1 F.Jones/J.Witten/25 10.00 25.00
2 D.Sproles/A.Gates/25 8.00 20.00
3 W.Welker/R.Moss/25 8.00 20.00
4 D.Brees/M.Colston/25 8.00 20.00
5 G.Jennings/R.Grant/25 6.00 15.00
6 Jacobs/Bradshaw/25 8.00 20.00
7 Garrard/Jones-Drew/25 6.00 15.00
8 S.Moss/L.Betts/25 6.00 15.00
9 S.Rice/V.Shiancoe/25 8.00 20.00
10 R.White/M.Turner/15 6.00 15.00
11 L.Fitzgerald/C.Wells/25 8.00 20.00
12 Palmer/Ochocinco/25 8.00 20.00
13 V.Young/K.Britt/25 6.00 15.00
14 M.Schaub/A.Johnson/15 6.00 15.00
16 Mendenhall/Polamalu/25 12.00 30.00
17 Stafford/C.Johnson/25 8.00 20.00
18 D.Williams/S.Smith/25 6.00 15.00
19 F.Gore/M.Crabtree/25 8.00 20.00
20 McFadd/Janikow/25 6.00 15.00

2010 Absolute Memorabilia Team Trios Materials NFL

STATED PRINT RUN 75 SER.#'d SETS
3 Peterson/Rice/Harvin 12.00 30.00
4 Witten/Ware/Jones 8.00 20.00
5 Portis/Moss/Betts 5.00 12.00
8 Rice/McGahee/Mason 5.00 12.00
9 Bradshaw/Jacbs/Eli 8.00 20.00
10 Forte/Urlacher/Olsen 8.00 20.00
11 Keller/Cotchery/Greene 5.00 12.00
13 Welker/Brady/Moss 10.00 25.00
14 Leinart/Fitzgerald/Wells 6.00 15.00
15 Young/Britt/Johnson 6.00 15.00
16 Gates/Sproles/Rivers 6.00 15.00
19 Brees/Colston/Bush 8.00 20.00
20 McFad/Mrphy/Janikw 6.00 15.00

2010 Absolute Memorabilia Team Trios Materials NFL Spectrum Prime

PRIME STATED PRINT RUN 5-25
1 Williams/Smith/Stewart/25 8.00 20.00
2 Ward/Polamalu/Menden/25 15.00 40.00
3 Peterson/Rice/Harvin/25 20.00 50.00
4 Witten/Ware/Jones/25 12.00 30.00
5 Portis/Moss/Betts/25 8.00 20.00
7 Gore/Davis/Crabtree/25 10.00 25.00
8 Rice/McGahee/Mason/25 8.00 20.00
9 Bradshaw/Jacobs/Eli/25 12.00 30.00
10 Forte/Urlacher/Olsen/25 12.00 30.00
11 Keller/Cotchery/Greene/25 8.00 20.00
13 Welker/Brady/Moss/25 15.00 40.00
15 Young/Britt/Johnson/25 10.00 25.00
16 Gates/Sproles/Rivers/25 10.00 25.00
19 Brees/Colston/Bush/25 12.00 30.00
20 McFad/Murphy/Janikw/25 10.00 25.00

2010 Absolute Memorabilia Tools of the Trade Material Red

RETAIL INSERT PRINT RUN 35-250
1 Curtis Martin/168 4.00 10.00
3 Eddie George/250 4.00 10.00
4 Jim Kelly/250 6.00 15.00
5 Marion Barber/225 3.00 8.00
6 Dan Marino/250 10.00 25.00
7 Josh Freeman/250 3.00 8.00
8 Tony Romo/100 3.00 8.00
9 Steve Young/250 6.00 15.00
10 Peyton Manning/75 12.00 30.00
11 Reggie Bush/250 2.50 6.00
12 Brett Favre/100 8.00 20.00
13 Rod Smith/50 5.00 12.00
14 Andre Johnson/70 4.00 10.00
15 Steve Largent/250 5.00 12.00
16 Troy Aikman/250 6.00 15.00
17 Randall Cunningham/250 4.00 10.00
18 Larry Fitzgerald/250 3.00 8.00
19 LeSean McCoy/60 5.00 12.00
20 Brian Urlacher/100 4.00 10.00
21 Terrell Davis/250 3.00 8.00
22 Hines Ward/250 3.00 8.00
23 Reggie Wayne/199 3.00 8.00
24 Chris Wells/60 3.00 8.00
25 Jeremy Maclin/35 4.00 10.00
26 Darren McFadden/250 2.50 6.00
27 Matthew Stafford/250 3.00 8.00
28 Warren Moon/250 5.00 12.00
29 Emmitt Smith/250 8.00 20.00
30 Clinton Portis/250 2.50 6.00
31 Terry Bradshaw/250 6.00 15.00
32 Eli Manning/100 3.00 8.00
33 Carson Palmer/250 3.00 8.00
34 Don Maynard/250 4.00 10.00
35 Cadillac Williams/215 2.50 6.00
36 Derrick Thomas/250 10.00 25.00
37 Tom Brady/100 10.00 25.00
38 John Elway/250 8.00 20.00
39 Junior Seau/250 3.00 8.00
40 Mark Sanchez/100 2.50 6.00
41 Bart Starr/250 8.00 20.00
42 Earl Campbell/250 5.00 12.00
43 Frank Gore/200 3.00 8.00
44 Steven Jackson/95 2.50 6.00
45 L.C. Greenwood/100 3.00 8.00
46 Todd Heap/145 2.50 6.00
47 Vince Young/250 2.50 6.00
48 Tony Dorsett/250 5.00 12.00
49 Jerry Rice/250 8.00 20.00
50 Ricky Williams/250 3.00 8.00

2010 Absolute Memorabilia Tools of the Trade Material Black Spectrum

STATED PRINT RUN 1-50
1 Curtis Martin/50 6.00 15.00
2 Deion Sanders/40 6.00 15.00
3 Eddie George/50 6.00 15.00
4 Jim Kelly/50 12.00 30.00
5 Marion Barber/50 5.00 12.00
6 Dan Marino/50 15.00 40.00
9 Steve Young/50 10.00 25.00
10 Peyton Manning/25 20.00 50.00
11 Reggie Bush/50 4.00 10.00
12 Brett Favre/25 15.00 40.00
13 Rod Smith/50 4.00 10.00
14 Andre Johnson/50 5.00 12.00
15 Steve Largent/50 8.00 20.00
16 Troy Aikman/25 12.00 30.00
18 Larry Fitzgerald/25 6.00 15.00
19 LeSean McCoy/50 6.00 15.00
20 Brian Urlacher/50 6.00 15.00
21 Terrell Davis/50 5.00 12.00
22 Hines Ward/50 5.00 12.00
24 Chris Wells/50 4.00 10.00
25 Jeremy Maclin/50 4.00 10.00
26 Darren McFadden/50 4.00 10.00
27 Matthew Stafford/50 5.00 12.00
29 Emmitt Smith/50 12.00 30.00
30 Clinton Portis/50 4.00 10.00
31 Terry Bradshaw/40 10.00 25.00
32 Eli Manning/25 6.00 15.00
33 Carson Palmer/17 6.00 15.00
34 Don Maynard/25 8.00 20.00
35 Cadillac Williams/50 4.00 10.00
37 Tom Brady/50 15.00 40.00
39 Junior Seau/50 5.00 12.00
40 Mark Sanchez/15 5.00 12.00
41 Bart Starr/25 15.00 40.00
43 Frank Gore/45 5.00 12.00
44 Steven Jackson/35 4.00 10.00
45 L.C. Greenwood/50 5.00 12.00
46 Todd Heap/50 4.00 10.00
47 Vince Young/50 4.00 10.00
48 Tony Dorsett/50 8.00 20.00
49 Jerry Rice/50 12.00 30.00
50 Ricky Williams/50 5.00 12.00

2010 Absolute Memorabilia Tools of the Trade Material Oversize Black Spectrum

STATED PRINT RUN 1-50
4 Jim Kelly/39 15.00 40.00
5 Marion Barber/50 6.00 15.00
11 Reggie Bush/35 5.00 12.00
21 Terrell Davis/30 6.00 15.00
22 Hines Ward/25 15.00 40.00
26 Darren McFadden/20 6.00 15.00
30 Clinton Portis/50 5.00 12.00
35 Cadillac Williams/15 6.00 15.00
37 Tom Brady/50 30.00 80.00
43 Frank Gore/50 6.00 15.00
46 Todd Heap/50 5.00 12.00
47 Vince Young/50 5.00 12.00
50 Ricky Williams/22 8.00 20.00

2010 Absolute Memorabilia Tools of the Trade Material Oversize Jersey Number Black

STATED PRINT RUN 1-25
1 Curtis Martin/19 12.00 30.00
2 Deion Sanders/21 12.00 30.00
3 Eddie George/24 12.00 30.00
5 Marion Barber/25 10.00 25.00
30 Clinton Portis/25 8.00 20.00
31 Terry Bradshaw/18 20.00 50.00
37 Tom Brady/25 25.00 60.00
47 Vince Young/25 8.00 20.00
50 Ricky Williams/25 10.00 25.00

2010 Absolute Memorabilia Tools of the Trade Double Material Black Spectrum

STATED PRINT RUN 1-50
1 Curtis Martin/50 8.00 20.00
2 Deion Sanders/50 8.00 20.00
3 Eddie George/50 8.00 20.00
4 Jim Kelly/50 10.00 25.00
6 Dan Marino/50 20.00 50.00
7 Josh Freeman/18 8.00 20.00
8 Tony Romo/50 6.00 15.00
9 Steve Young/50 12.00 30.00
11 Reggie Bush/50 5.00 12.00
12 Brett Favre/25 20.00 50.00
15 Steve Largent/50 10.00 25.00
16 Troy Aikman/17 15.00 40.00
18 Larry Fitzgerald/30 6.00 15.00
19 LeSean McCoy/50 8.00 20.00
20 Brian Urlacher/50 8.00 20.00
21 Terrell Davis/50 8.00 20.00
22 Hines Ward/50 6.00 15.00
24 Chris Wells/50 5.00 12.00
26 Darren McFadden/50 5.00 12.00
28 Warren Moon/40 10.00 25.00
29 Emmitt Smith/50 15.00 40.00
30 Clinton Portis/50 5.00 12.00
31 Terry Bradshaw/50 12.00 30.00
35 Cadillac Williams/40 5.00 12.00
37 Tom Brady/50 20.00 50.00
39 Junior Seau/50 6.00 15.00
40 Mark Sanchez/30 5.00 12.00
44 Steven Jackson/50 5.00 12.00
45 L.C. Greenwood/30 6.00 15.00
47 Vince Young/50 5.00 12.00
50 Ricky Williams/50 6.00 15.00

2010 Absolute Memorabilia Tools of the Trade Triple Material Black Spectrum

STATED PRINT RUN 1-50
1 Curtis Martin/50 8.00 20.00
3 Eddie George/50 8.00 20.00
6 Dan Marino/50 20.00 50.00
15 Steve Largent/35 10.00 25.00
21 Terrell Davis/25 10.00 25.00
29 Emmitt Smith/30 15.00 40.00
31 Terry Bradshaw/50 12.00 30.00
33 Carson Palmer/50 6.00 15.00
35 Cadillac Williams/45 5.00 12.00
37 Tom Brady/38 20.00 50.00
45 L.C. Greenwood/49 6.00 15.00
50 Ricky Williams/50 6.00 15.00

2010 Absolute Memorabilia War Room

*SPECTRUM/50: 1X TO 2.5X BASIC INSERTS
1 Jordan Shipley .50 1.25
2 Andre Roberts .60 1.50
3 Ndamukong Suh 1.00 2.50
4 Rob Gronkowski 1.50 4.00
5 Mike Williams .50 1.25
6 Joe McKnight .50 1.25
7 Eric Decker .60 1.50
8 Golden Tate .60 1.50
9 Arrelious Benn .50 1.25
10 Toby Gerhart .50 1.25
11 Damian Williams .50 1.25
12 Armanti Edwards .60 1.50
13 Mike Kafka .60 1.50
14 Jonathan Dwyer .50 1.25
15 Jahvid Best .50 1.25
16 Eric Berry .75 2.00
17 Demaryius Thomas 1.25 3.00
18 Tim Tebow 1.50 4.00
19 Dez Bryant 1.25 3.00
20 Montario Hardesty .50 1.25
21 Taylor Price .50 1.25
22 Mardy Gilyard .50 1.25
23 Emmanuel Sanders .75 2.00
24 Brandon LaFell .75 2.00
25 Gerald McCoy .50 1.25
26 Colt McCoy .60 1.50
27 Ryan Mathews .50 1.25
28 Rolando McClain .50 1.25
29 Dexter McCluster .60 1.50
30 Marcus Easley .50 1.25
31 C.J. Spiller .50 1.25
32 Jermaine Gresham .50 1.25
33 Ben Tate .50 1.25
34 Jimmy Clausen .50 1.25
35 Sam Bradford .60 1.50

2010 Absolute Memorabilia War Room Materials

STATED PRINT RUN 250 SER.#'d SETS
*OVER.JSY NUMBER/10: 1X TO 2.5X
*OVER.JSY NMBR PRIME/15: 1X TO 2.5X
*PRIME/50: .6X TO 1.5X BASIC JSY/250
1 Jordan Shipley 1.50 4.00
2 Andre Roberts 2.00 5.00
3 Ndamukong Suh 3.00 8.00
4 Rob Gronkowski 5.00 12.00
5 Mike Williams 1.50 4.00
6 Joe McKnight 1.50 4.00
7 Eric Decker 2.00 5.00
8 Golden Tate 2.00 5.00
9 Arrelious Benn 1.50 4.00
10 Toby Gerhart 1.50 4.00
11 Damian Williams 1.50 4.00
12 Armanti Edwards 2.00 5.00
13 Mike Kafka 2.00 5.00
14 Jonathan Dwyer 1.50 4.00
15 Jahvid Best 1.50 4.00
16 Eric Berry 2.50 6.00
17 Demaryius Thomas 4.00 10.00
18 Tim Tebow 5.00 12.00
19 Dez Bryant 4.00 10.00
20 Montario Hardesty 1.50 4.00
21 Taylor Price 1.50 4.00
22 Mardy Gilyard 1.50 4.00
23 Emmanuel Sanders 2.50 6.00
24 Brandon LaFell 2.50 6.00
25 Gerald McCoy 1.50 4.00
26 Colt McCoy 2.00 5.00
27 Ryan Mathews 1.50 4.00
28 Rolando McClain 1.50 4.00
29 Dexter McCluster 2.00 5.00
30 Marcus Easley 1.50 4.00
31 C.J. Spiller 1.50 4.00
32 Jermaine Gresham 1.50 4.00
33 Ben Tate 1.50 4.00
34 Jimmy Clausen 1.50 4.00
35 Sam Bradford 2.00 5.00

2010 Absolute Memorabilia War Room Materials Autographs

*WAR ROOM: .4X TO 1X STAR GAZING
STATED PRINT RUN 25 SER.#'d SETS
EXCH EXPIRATION: 4/13/2012

2011 Absolute Memorabilia

101-200 ROOKIE PRINT RUN 399
201-236 RPM AU PRINT RUN 199-299
EXCH EXPIRATION: 4/26/2013
1 Larry Fitzgerald .40 1.00
2 Steve Breaston .30 .75
3 Tim Hightower .30 .75
4 Matt Ryan .40 1.00
5 Michael Turner .30 .75
6 Roddy White .30 .75
7 Tony Gonzalez .40 1.00
8 Anquan Boldin .30 .75
9 Joe Flacco .40 1.00
10 Ray Lewis .50 1.25
11 Ray Rice .30 .75
12 C.J. Spiller .30 .75
13 Fred Jackson .30 .75
14 Ryan Fitzpatrick .30 .75
15 DeAngelo Williams .30 .75
16 Jonathan Stewart .30 .75
17 Steve Smith .40 1.00
18 Brian Urlacher .50 1.25
19 Jay Cutler .30 .75
20 Julius Peppers .40 1.00
21 Matt Forte .30 .75
22 Carson Palmer .40 1.00
23 Cedric Benson .30 .75
24 Chad Ochocinco .30 .75
25 Terrell Owens .40 1.00
26 Colt McCoy .30 .75
27 Peyton Hillis .30 .75
28 DeMarcus Ware .40 1.00
29 Dez Bryant .50 1.25
30 Jason Witten .40 1.00
31 Tony Romo .40 1.00
32 Brandon Lloyd .30 .75
33 Knowshon Moreno .30 .75
34 Tim Tebow .50 1.25
35 Calvin Johnson .50 1.25
36 Matthew Stafford .40 1.00
37 Ndamukong Suh .40 1.00
38 Aaron Rodgers .75 2.00
39 Greg Jennings .30 .75
40 Jermichael Finley .30 .75
41 Andre Johnson .40 1.00
42 Arian Foster .30 .75
43 Matt Schaub .30 .75
44 Dallas Clark .30 .75
45 Peyton Manning 1.00 2.50
46 Reggie Wayne .40 1.00
47 David Garrard .30 .75
48 Maurice Jones-Drew .30 .75
49 Dwayne Bowe .40 1.00
50 Jamaal Charles .40 1.00
51 Matt Cassel .30 .75
52 Brandon Marshall .40 1.00
53 Ronnie Brown .40 1.00
54 Adrian Peterson .50 1.25
55 Percy Harvin .30 .75
56 Sidney Rice .30 .75
57 BenJarvus Green-Ellis .30 .75
58 Tom Brady 1.25 3.00
59 Wes Welker .40 1.00
60 Drew Brees .50 1.25
61 Marques Colston .30 .75
62 Reggie Bush .30 .75
63 Ahmad Bradshaw .30 .75
64 Brandon Jacobs .30 .75
65 Eli Manning .40 1.00
66 Hakeem Nicks .30 .75
67 Braylon Edwards .30 .75
68 LaDainian Tomlinson .50 1.25
69 Mark Sanchez .30 .75
70 Darren McFadden .30 .75
71 Jason Campbell .30 .75
72 DeSean Jackson .40 1.00
73 Jeremy Maclin .30 .75
74 LeSean McCoy .50 1.25
75 Michael Vick .40 1.00
76 Ben Roethlisberger .50 1.25
77 Hines Ward .40 1.00
78 Mike Wallace .30 .75
79 Rashard Mendenhall .30 .75
80 Troy Polamalu .50 1.25
81 Antonio Gates .30 .75
82 Philip Rivers .50 1.25
83 Ryan Mathews .40 1.00
84 Frank Gore .40 1.00
85 Michael Crabtree .30 .75
86 Patrick Willis .40 1.00
87 Vernon Davis .30 .75
88 Marshawn Lynch .40 1.00
89 Matt Hasselbeck .30 .75
90 James Laurinaitis .30 .75
91 Sam Bradford .30 .75
92 Steven Jackson .30 .75
93 Josh Freeman .40 1.00
94 Kellen Winslow Jr. .30 .75
95 LeGarrette Blount .40 1.00
96 Chris Johnson .30 .75
97 Kenny Britt .30 .75
98 Donovan McNabb .40 1.00
99 Ryan Torain .30 .75
100 Santana Moss .40 1.00
101 Aldrick Robinson RC 2.00 5.00
102 Cecil Shorts RC 1.50 4.00
103 David Ausberry RC 1.50 4.00
104 DeMarco Sampson RC 1.50 4.00
105 Denarius Moore RC 1.50 4.00
106 Dwayne Harris RC 1.50 4.00
107 Greg Salas RC 1.50 4.00
108 Jeremy Kerley RC 2.50 6.00
109 Kealoha Pilares RC 1.50 4.00
110 Kris Durham RC 1.50 4.00
111 Niles Paul RC 1.50 4.00
112 Ronald Johnson RC 1.50 4.00
113 Ryan Whalen RC 1.50 4.00
114 Scotty McKnight RC 1.50 4.00
115 Stephen Burton RC 1.50 4.00
116 Tandon Doss RC 1.50 4.00
117 D.J. Williams RC 1.50 4.00
118 Daniel Hardy RC 2.00 5.00
119 Jordan Cameron RC 2.00 5.00
120 Julius Thomas RC 2.00 5.00
121 Lance Kendricks RC 1.50 4.00
122 Lee Smith RC 2.00 5.00
123 Luke Stocker RC 1.50 4.00
124 Richard Gordon RC 1.50 4.00
125 Robert Housler RC 1.50 4.00
126 Virgil Green RC 1.50 4.00
127 Allen Bradford RC 1.50 4.00
128 Anthony Allen RC 1.50 4.00
129 Baron Batch RC 2.00 5.00
130 Da'Rel Scott RC 1.50 4.00
131 Dion Lewis RC 2.00 5.00
132 Evan Royster RC 1.50 4.00
133 Jacquizz Rodgers RC 1.50 4.00
134 Jay Finley RC 2.00 5.00
135 Johnny White RC 1.50 4.00
136 Roy Helu RC 1.50 4.00
137 Greg McElroy RC 2.50 6.00
138 Nathan Enderle RC 1.50 4.00
139 Ricky Stanzi RC 1.50 4.00
140 T.J. Yates RC 1.50 4.00
141 Terrelle Pryor RC 2.50 6.00
142 Tyrod Taylor RC 3.00 8.00
143 Aaron Williams RC 1.50 4.00
144 Brandon Harris RC 1.50 4.00
145 Jimmy Smith RC 1.50 4.00
146 Marcus Gilchrist RC 1.50 4.00
147 Patrick Peterson RC 3.00 8.00
148 Prince Amukamara RC 1.50 4.00
149 Ras-I Dowling RC 1.50 4.00
150 Adrian Clayborn RC 1.50 4.00
151 Aldon Smith RC 1.50 4.00
152 Brooks Reed RC 2.00 5.00
153 Cameron Heyward RC 2.00 5.00
154 Cameron Jordan RC 2.00 5.00
155 Da'Quan Bowers RC 1.50 4.00
156 J.J. Watt RC 8.00 20.00
157 Jabaal Sheard RC 1.50 4.00
158 Muhammad Wilkerson RC 1.50 4.00
159 Robert Quinn RC 1.50 4.00
160 Akeem Ayers RC 1.50 4.00
161 Bruce Carter RC 1.50 4.00
162 Jonas Mouton RC 2.00 5.00
163 Ryan Kerrigan RC 2.00 5.00
164 Corey Liuget RC 1.50 4.00
165 Jarvis Jenkins RC 1.50 4.00
166 Marvin Austin RC 1.50 4.00
167 Nick Fairley RC 1.50 4.00
168 Phil Taylor RC 1.50 4.00
169 Stephen Paea RC 1.50 4.00
170 Jaiquawn Jarrett RC 1.50 4.00
171 Rahim Moore RC 1.50 4.00
172 Mike Pouncey RC 2.50 6.00
173 Rodney Hudson RC 1.50 4.00
174 Stefen Wisniewski RC 2.50 6.00
175 Danny Watkins RC 1.50 4.00
176 James Carpenter RC 2.00 5.00
177 Orlando Franklin RC 2.00 5.00
178 Anthony Castonzo RC 1.50 4.00
179 Derek Sherrod RC 1.50 4.00
180 Gabe Carimi RC 2.00 5.00
181 Marcus Gilbert RC 2.50 6.00
182 Nate Solder RC 1.50 4.00
183 Tyron Smith RC 2.00 5.00
184 Ahmad Black RC 2.00 5.00
185 Greg Jones RC 2.00 5.00
186 Marcus Cannon RC 1.50 4.00
187 Chris Culliver RC 1.50 4.00

188 Owen Marecic RC 1.50 4.00
189 DeMarcus Van Dyke RC 2.00 5.00
190 Dontay Moch RC 1.50 4.00
191 Quinton Carter RC 1.50 4.00
192 Stanley Havili RC 1.50 4.00
193 Jurrell Casey RC 1.50 4.00
194 Justin Houston RC 2.00 5.00
195 Kelvin Sheppard RC 1.50 4.00
196 Martez Wilson RC 1.50 4.00
197 Mason Foster RC 1.50 4.00
198 Nate Irving RC 2.00 5.00
199 Tyler Sash RC 1.50 4.00
200 Terrell McClain RC 2.00 5.00
201 A.Dalton RPM AU/299 RC 8.00 20.00
202 C.Newton RPM AU/199 RC 50.00 100.00
203 A.Green RPM AU/194 RC 30.00 60.00
204 T.Jones RPM AU/299 RC 4.00 10.00
205 D.Murray RPM AU/299 RC 8.00 20.00
206 T.Smith RPM AU/299 RC 4.00 10.00
207 R.Mallett RPM AU/199 RC 4.00 10.00
208 S.Ridley RPM AU/299 RC 4.00 10.00
209 A.Pettis RPM AU/299 RC 4.00 10.00
210 S.Vereen RPM AU/299 RC 5.00 12.00
211 T.Young RPM AU/299 RC 4.00 10.00
212 M.Leshoure RPM AU/299 RC 8.00 20.00
213 C.Ponder RPM AU/199 RC 4.00 10.00
214 J.Todman RPM AU/298 RC 4.00 10.00
215 V.Brown RPM AU/299 RC 4.00 10.00
216 Von Miller RPM AU/299 RC 20.00 50.00
217 K.Rudolph RPM AU/299 RC 4.00 10.00
218 Baldwin RPM AU/299 RC 4.00 10.00
219 J.Locker RPM AU/199 RC 4.00 10.00
220 J.Harper RPM AU/299 RC 4.00 10.00
221 M.Ingram RPM AU/199 RC 6.00 15.00
222 Hankerson RPM AU/299 RC 4.00 10.00
223 J.Jernigan RPM AU/299 RC 4.00 10.00
224 D.Carter RPM AU/299 RC 4.00 10.00
225 B.Gabbert RPM AU/199 RC 4.00 10.00
226 J.Jones RPM AU/299 RC 30.00 60.00
227 Dareus RPM AU/299 RC EX
228 R.Williams RPM AU/299 RC 4.00 10.00
229 C.Gates RPM AU/299 RC 4.00 10.00
230 Thomas RPM AU/299 RC 4.00 10.00
231 G.Little RPM AU/299 RC 5.00 12.00
232 Kaepernick RPM AU/299 RC 20.00 40.00
233 A.Green RPM AU/299 RC 4.00 10.00
234 R.Cobb RPM AU/299 RC 6.00 15.00
235 B.Powell RPM AU/299 RC 5.00 12.00
236 K.Hunter RPM AU/299 RC 8.00 20.00

2011 Absolute Memorabilia Retail

COMPLETE SET (200) 10.00 25.00
*1-100 VETS: .25X TO .6X BASIC CARDS
*101-200 ROOKIES: .4X TO 1X BASIC CARDS

2011 Absolute Memorabilia Rookie Premiere Materials Autographs AFC/NFC

*AFC/NFC/49: .5X TO 1.2X BASIC RPM AU RC
STATED PRINT RUN 49 SER.#'d SETS
201 Andy Dalton 25.00 60.00
202 Cam Newton 50.00 120.00

2011 Absolute Memorabilia Rookie Premiere Materials Autographs AFC/NFC Spectrum Prime

*AFC/NFC PRIME/25: .6X TO 1.5X RPM AU RC
STATED PRINT RUN 25 SER.#'d SETS
201 Andy Dalton 30.00 80.00
202 Cam Newton 100.00 200.00

2011 Absolute Memorabilia Rookie Premiere Materials Autographs NFL Spectrum Prime

*NFL PRIME/25: .6X TO 1.5X RPM AU RC
STATED PRINT RUN 25 SER.#'d SETS
201 Andy Dalton 12.00 30.00
202 Cam Newton 100.00 200.00

2011 Absolute Memorabilia Rookie Premiere Materials Autographs Oversize

*OVER.AU/18-25: .6X TO 1.5X RPM AU RC
STATED PRINT RUN 18-25
202 Cam Newton/25 75.00 150.00

2011 Absolute Memorabilia Spectrum Black Retail

*1-100 VETS/25: 3X TO 8X BASIC CARDS
*101-200 ROOKIES/25: 1X TO 2.5X
STATED PRINT RUN 25 SER.#'d SETS

2011 Absolute Memorabilia Spectrum Blue Retail

*1-100 VETS/100: 1.5X TO 4X BASIC CARDS
*101-200 ROOKIES/100: .5X TO 1.2X
RETAIL BLUE PRINT RUN 100 SER.#'d SETS

2011 Absolute Memorabilia Spectrum Gold

*1-100 VETS/25: 3X TO 8X BASIC CARDS
*101-200 ROOKIES/25: 1X TO 2.5X
STATED PRINT RUN 25 SER.#'d SETS

2011 Absolute Memorabilia Spectrum Red Retail

*1-100 VETS: 1.2X TO 3X BASIC CARDS
*101-200 ROOKIES: .4X TO 1X BASIC CARDS
RANDOM INSERTS IN RETAIL PACKS

2011 Absolute Memorabilia Spectrum Silver

*1-100 VETS/50: 2X TO 5X BASIC CARDS
*101-200 ROOKIES/50: .6X TO 1.5X
STATED PRINT RUN 50 SER.#'d SETS

2011 Absolute Memorabilia Absolute Heroes

RANDOM INSERTS IN PACKS
*SPECTRUM/100: .8X TO 2X BASIC INSERTS
1 Calvin Johnson 1.25 3.00
2 Kellen Winslow Jr. .75 2.00
3 Joe Flacco 1.00 2.50
4 Bo Scaife .75 2.00
5 Antonio Gates .75 2.00
6 Reggie Wayne 1.00 2.50
7 Mark Sanchez .75 2.00
8 Jeremy Maclin .75 2.00
9 Danny Amendola 1.00 2.50
10 Aaron Rodgers 2.00 5.00
11 DeSean Jackson 1.00 2.50
12 Mike Wallace .75 2.00
13 Dallas Clark .75 2.00
14 Wes Welker 1.00 2.50
15 Santonio Holmes .75 2.00
16 Brandon Lloyd .75 2.00
17 Randy Moss 1.00 2.50
18 Visanthe Shiancoe 1.00 2.50
19 Peyton Manning 2.50 6.00
20 Chris Cooley .75 2.00
21 Tom Brady 3.00 8.00
22 Drew Brees 1.25 3.00
23 Percy Harvin .75 2.00
24 Matt Cassel .75 2.00
25 Hines Ward 1.00 2.50

2011 Absolute Memorabilia Absolute Heroes Materials Autographs

STATED PRINT RUN 5-25
5 Antonio Gates
10 Aaron Rodgers 175.00 300.00
11 DeSean Jackson 12.00 30.00
15 Santonio Holmes 10.00 25.00
20 Chris Cooley 10.00 25.00

2011 Absolute Memorabilia Absolute Heroes Materials Spectrum Prime

STATED PRINT RUN 5-50
1 Calvin Johnson/25 6.00 15.00
2 Kellen Winslow Jr./25 4.00 10.00
3 Joe Flacco/25 5.00 12.00
5 Antonio Gates/50 3.00 8.00
7 Mark Sanchez/25 4.00 10.00
8 Jeremy Maclin/25 4.00 10.00
10 Aaron Rodgers/25 12.00 30.00
11 DeSean Jackson/25 5.00 12.00
12 Mike Wallace/25 4.00 10.00
13 Dallas Clark/25 4.00 10.00
14 Wes Welker/25 5.00 12.00
15 Santonio Holmes/25 4.00 10.00
16 Brandon Lloyd/25 4.00 10.00
18 Visanthe Shiancoe/25 5.00 12.00
20 Chris Cooley/25 4.00 10.00
24 Matt Cassel/25 4.00 10.00
25 Hines Ward/25 5.00 12.00

2011 Absolute Memorabilia Absolute Patches Spectrum Prime

STATED PRINT RUN 5-25
2 Ahmad Bradshaw/25 15.00 40.00
4 Antonio Gates/25 15.00 40.00
17 James Harrison/25 20.00 50.00
22 Michael Turner/25 15.00 40.00
35 Terrell Suggs/25 20.00 50.00

2011 Absolute Memorabilia Canton Absolutes

*SPECTRUM/100: .8X TO 2X BASIC INSERTS
1 Drew Brees 1.25 3.00
2 Ed Reed 1.00 2.50
3 Adam Vinatieri .75 2.00
4 Troy Polamalu 1.25 3.00
5 Charles Woodson 1.25 3.00
6 Brian Urlacher 1.25 3.00
7 Ray Lewis 1.25 3.00
8 LaDainian Tomlinson 1.25 3.00
9 Tom Brady 3.00 8.00
10 Peyton Manning 2.50 6.00
11 Randy Moss 1.00 2.50
12 Terrell Owens 1.00 2.50
13 Tony Gonzalez 1.00 2.50
14 Champ Bailey 1.00 2.50
15 Brett Favre 2.50 6.00
16 Curtis Martin 1.00 2.50
17 Michael Strahan 1.00 2.50
18 Warren Sapp 1.00 2.50
19 Junior Seau 1.00 2.50
20 Andre Reed 1.00 2.50
21 Cris Carter 1.25 3.00
22 Jerome Bettis 1.25 3.00
23 Shannon Sharpe 1.00 2.50
24 Deion Sanders 1.00 2.50
25 Marshall Faulk 1.00 2.50

2011 Absolute Memorabilia Canton Absolutes Materials Autographs

STATED PRINT RUN 5-25
15 Brett Favre/25 100.00 200.00
18 Warren Sapp/25 20.00 50.00
19 Junior Seau/25 40.00 80.00
20 Andre Reed/25 15.00 40.00
22 Jerome Bettis/25 40.00 80.00
23 Shannon Sharpe/25
25 Marshall Faulk/25 30.00 60.00

2011 Absolute Memorabilia Canton Absolutes Materials Spectrum Prime

STATED PRINT RUN 5-25
2 Ed Reed/25 6.00 15.00
4 Troy Polamalu/25 6.00 15.00
7 Ray Lewis/25 6.00 15.00
13 Tony Gonzalez/25 5.00 12.00
16 Curtis Martin/25 5.00 12.00
18 Warren Sapp/25 5.00 12.00
19 Junior Seau/25 5.00 12.00
21 Cris Carter/25 6.00 15.00
22 Jerome Bettis/25 12.00 30.00
23 Shannon Sharpe/25 6.00 15.00
25 Marshall Faulk/25 6.00 15.00

2011 Absolute Memorabilia Gridiron Force

*SPECTRUM/100: .8X TO 2X BASIC INSERTS
1 Asante Samuel .75 2.00
2 Barrett Ruud .75 2.00
3 Brian Urlacher 1.25 3.00
4 Chad Greenway 1.00 2.50
5 Charles Woodson 1.25 3.00
6 Clay Matthews 1.25 3.00
7 Darrelle Revis .75 2.00
8 David Harris .75 2.00
9 DeAngelo Hall .75 2.00
10 DeMarcus Ware 1.00 2.50
11 Dhani Jones .75 2.00
12 Dwight Freeney .75 2.00
13 Ed Reed 1.00 2.50
14 James Harrison 1.00 2.50
15 James Laurinaitis .75 2.00
16 Jared Allen .75 2.00
17 Jerod Mayo .75 2.00
18 Jon Beason .75 2.00
19 London Fletcher 1.00 2.50
20 Nnamdi Asomugha .75 2.00
21 Patrick Willis 1.00 2.50
22 Stephen Tulloch .75 2.00
23 Tamba Hali .75 2.00
24 Terrell Suggs .75 2.00
25 Troy Polamalu 1.25 3.00

2011 Absolute Memorabilia Gridiron Force Materials Prime Jersey Number

STATED PRINT RUN 25 SER.#'d SETS
1 Asante Samuel 5.00 12.00
2 Barrett Ruud 5.00 12.00
3 Brian Urlacher 8.00 20.00
4 Chad Greenway 6.00 15.00
6 Clay Matthews 8.00 20.00
7 Darrelle Revis 5.00 12.00
8 David Harris 5.00 12.00
9 DeAngelo Hall 5.00 12.00
10 DeMarcus Ware 8.00 20.00
12 Dwight Freeney 5.00 12.00
13 Ed Reed 6.00 15.00
14 James Harrison 8.00 20.00
15 James Laurinaitis 5.00 12.00
16 Jared Allen 8.00 20.00
18 Jon Beason 5.00 12.00
19 London Fletcher 6.00 15.00
20 Nnamdi Asomugha 5.00 12.00
21 Patrick Willis 6.00 15.00
22 Stephen Tulloch 5.00 12.00
23 Tamba Hali 5.00 12.00
24 Terrell Suggs 5.00 12.00
25 Troy Polamalu 8.00 20.00

2011 Absolute Memorabilia Ground Hoggs

*SPECTRUM/100: .8X TO 2X BASIC INSERTS
1 Rashard Mendenhall .75 2.00
2 Ryan Grant .75 2.00
3 Jonathan Stewart .75 2.00
4 LeSean McCoy 1.25 3.00
5 Darren McFadden .75 2.00
6 Danny Woodhead 1.00 2.50
7 Knowshon Moreno .75 2.00
8 Jahvid Best .75 2.00
9 Ryan Mathews 1.00 2.50
10 Ahmad Bradshaw .75 2.00
11 Ray Rice .75 2.00
12 Tashard Choice .75 2.00
13 C.J. Spiller .75 2.00
14 Jamaal Charles 1.00 2.50
15 Michael Turner .75 2.00
16 Frank Gore 1.00 2.50
17 Ronnie Brown 1.00 2.50
18 Maurice Jones-Drew .75 2.00
19 Matt Forte .75 2.00
20 Adrian Peterson 1.25 3.00
21 Cedric Benson .75 2.00
22 Chris Johnson .75 2.00
23 LaDainian Tomlinson 1.25 3.00
24 Steven Jackson .75 2.00
25 Arian Foster .75 2.00

2011 Absolute Memorabilia Ground Hoggs Materials Prime Jersey Number

STATED PRINT RUN 1-25
3 Jonathan Stewart/25 5.00 12.00
4 LeSean McCoy/25 8.00 20.00
6 Danny Woodhead/25 6.00 15.00
7 Knowshon Moreno/25 5.00 12.00
8 Jahvid Best/25 5.00 12.00
9 Ryan Mathews/25 6.00 15.00
10 Ahmad Bradshaw/25 5.00 12.00
11 Ray Rice/25 5.00 12.00
12 Tashard Choice/25 5.00 12.00
13 C.J. Spiller/25 5.00 12.00
14 Jamaal Charles/25 6.00 15.00
15 Michael Turner/25 5.00 12.00
18 Maurice Jones-Drew/25 5.00 12.00
19 Matt Forte/25 5.00 12.00
21 Cedric Benson/25 5.00 12.00
22 Chris Johnson/25 5.00 12.00

2011 Absolute Memorabilia Marks of Fame

*SPECTRUM/100: .8X TO 2X BASIC INSERTS
1 Vernon Davis .75 2.00
2 Andre Johnson 1.00 2.50
3 Ben Roethlisberger 1.25 3.00
4 Carson Palmer 1.00 2.50
5 Matt Ryan 1.00 2.50
6 Lee Evans 1.00 2.50
7 Donald Driver 1.00 2.50
8 David Garrard .75 2.00
9 Miles Austin .75 2.00
10 Philip Rivers 1.25 3.00
11 Roddy White .75 2.00
12 Matt Schaub .75 2.00
13 Josh Freeman 1.00 2.50
14 Eli Manning 1.00 2.50
15 Chad Ochocinco .75 2.00
16 Jay Cutler .75 2.00
17 Anquan Boldin .75 2.00
18 Marques Colston .75 2.00
19 Donovan McNabb 1.00 2.50
20 Dwayne Bowe 1.00 2.50
21 Dez Bryant 1.25 3.00
22 Tim Tebow 1.25 3.00
23 Michael Vick 1.00 2.50
24 Greg Jennings .75 2.00
25 Sam Bradford .75 2.00

2011 Absolute Memorabilia Marks of Fame Materials Autographs

STATED PRINT RUN 10-25
1 Vernon Davis/25 10.00 25.00
2 Andre Johnson/25 15.00 40.00
3 Ben Roethlisberger/25 50.00 100.00
8 David Garrard/25 12.00 30.00
9 Miles Austin/25 10.00 25.00
17 Anquan Boldin/25 10.00 25.00
25 Sam Bradford/25 10.00 25.00

2011 Absolute Memorabilia Marks of Fame Materials Spectrum Prime

1 Vernon Davis/25 4.00 10.00
3 Ben Roethlisberger/25 6.00 15.00
6 Lee Evans/25 5.00 12.00
9 Miles Austin/25 4.00 10.00
10 Philip Rivers/25 6.00 15.00
11 Roddy White/25 4.00 10.00
14 Eli Manning/25 5.00 12.00
16 Jay Cutler/25 4.00 10.00
18 Marques Colston/25 4.00 10.00
19 Donovan McNabb/25 5.00 12.00
20 Dwayne Bowe/25 5.00 12.00
22 Tim Tebow/25 6.00 15.00
23 Michael Vick/25 5.00 12.00
25 Sam Bradford/25 4.00 10.00

2011 Absolute Memorabilia NFL Icons

*SPECTRUM/100: .8X TO 2X BASIC INSERTS
1 Jerry Rice 3.00 8.00
2 Jack Lambert 1.50 4.00
3 Jim Plunkett 1.25 3.00
4 Frank Gifford 1.25 3.00
5 Lee Roy Selmon 1.00 2.50
6 Mark Duper 1.00 2.50
7 Ronnie Lott 1.25 3.00
8 Doug Flutie 1.25 3.00
9 Steve Largent 1.50 4.00
10 Thurman Thomas 1.25 3.00
11 Phil Simms 1.25 3.00
12 Fran Tarkenton 1.50 4.00
13 Daryle Lamonica 1.00 2.50
14 Joe Montana 4.00 10.00
15 Tony Dorsett 1.50 4.00
16 Rod Woodson 1.50 4.00
17 Eric Dickerson 1.25 3.00
18 Reggie White 1.50 4.00
19 Marcus Allen 1.50 4.00
20 Dick Butkus 2.00 5.00
21 Bart Starr 2.50 6.00
22 Franco Harris 1.50 4.00
23 Terry Bradshaw 2.00 5.00
24 Walter Payton 3.00 8.00
25 Derrick Thomas 1.25 3.00
26 Terrell Davis 1.25 3.00
27 Steve Young 2.00 5.00
28 Warren Moon 1.50 4.00
29 Howie Long 1.50 4.00
30 Michael Strahan 1.25 3.00

2011 Absolute Memorabilia NFL Icons Materials Autographs

STATED PRINT RUN 5-25
1 Jerry Rice/25 100.00 175.00
2 Jack Lambert/25 30.00 60.00
3 Jim Plunkett/25 15.00 40.00
5 Lee Roy Selmon/25
6 Mark Duper/25 15.00 40.00
7 Ronnie Lott/25 30.00 60.00
8 Doug Flutie/25 15.00 40.00
9 Steve Largent/25 20.00 50.00
10 Thurman Thomas/25 20.00 40.00
11 Phil Simms/25 20.00 50.00
12 Fran Tarkenton/25 20.00 50.00
13 Daryle Lamonica/25 12.00 30.00
16 Rod Woodson/25 40.00 80.00
19 Marcus Allen/25 30.00 60.00
20 Dick Butkus/25 40.00 80.00
21 Bart Starr/25 40.00 100.00
22 Franco Harris/25 30.00 60.00
23 Terry Bradshaw/25 50.00 100.00
27 Steve Young/25 40.00 80.00
28 Warren Moon/25 20.00 50.00
29 Howie Long/25 40.00 80.00

2011 Absolute Memorabilia NFL Icons Materials Spectrum Prime

STATED PRINT RUN 5-25
1 Jerry Rice/25 15.00 40.00
2 Jack Lambert/25 10.00 25.00
3 Jim Plunkett/25 8.00 20.00
5 Lee Roy Selmon/25 6.00 15.00
6 Mark Duper/25 6.00 15.00
8 Doug Flutie/25 8.00 20.00
9 Steve Largent/25 10.00 25.00
10 Thurman Thomas/25 8.00 20.00
11 Phil Simms/25 8.00 20.00
12 Fran Tarkenton/25 10.00 25.00
15 Tony Dorsett/25 10.00 25.00
16 Rod Woodson/25 10.00 25.00
20 Dick Butkus/25 12.00 30.00
21 Bart Starr/25 15.00 40.00
22 Franco Harris/25 10.00 25.00
23 Terry Bradshaw/25 12.00 30.00
24 Walter Payton/25 25.00 60.00
25 Derrick Thomas/25 125.00 200.00
26 Terrell Davis/25 8.00 20.00
27 Steve Young/25 12.00 30.00
28 Warren Moon/25 10.00 25.00

2011 Absolute Memorabilia Rookie Jersey Collection

1 A.J. Green 4.00 10.00
2 Alex Green 1.50 4.00
3 Andy Dalton 3.00 8.00
4 Austin Pettis 1.50 4.00
5 Bilal Powell 2.50 6.00
6 Blaine Gabbert 1.50 4.00
7 Cam Newton 8.00 20.00
8 Christian Ponder 1.50 4.00
9 Clyde Gates 1.50 4.00
10 Colin Kaepernick 2.50 6.00
11 Daniel Thomas 1.50 4.00
12 Delone Carter 1.50 4.00
13 DeMarco Murray 3.00 8.00
14 Greg Little 2.00 5.00
15 Jake Locker 1.50 4.00
16 Jamie Harper 1.50 4.00
17 Jerrel Jernigan 1.50 4.00
18 Jonathan Baldwin 1.50 4.00
19 Jordan Todman 1.50 4.00
20 Julio Jones 4.00 10.00
21 Kendall Hunter 1.50 4.00
22 Kyle Rudolph 1.50 4.00
23 Leonard Hankerson 1.50 4.00
24 Marcell Dareus 1.50 4.00
25 Mark Ingram 2.50 6.00
26 Mikel Leshoure 1.50 4.00
27 Randall Cobb 2.50 6.00
28 Ryan Mallett 1.50 4.00
29 Ryan Williams 1.50 4.00
30 Shane Vereen 2.00 5.00
31 Stevan Ridley 1.50 4.00
32 Taiwan Jones 1.50 4.00
33 Titus Young 1.50 4.00
34 Torrey Smith 1.50 4.00
35 Vincent Brown 1.50 4.00
36 Von Miller 2.50 6.00

2011 Absolute Memorabilia Rookie Premiere Materials AFC/NFC

AFC/NFC PRINT RUN 99 SER.#'d SETS
*AFC/NFC SPECT.PRIME/25: .6X TO 1.5X
*NFL SPECTRUM PRIME/50: .5X TO 1.2X
*OVERSIZE JSY NUMBER/50: .6X TO 1.5X
*OVER.JSY NUMBER PRIME/10: 1.2X TO 3X
*OVER.SPECTRUM PRIME/25: .8X TO 2X
201 Andy Dalton 4.00 10.00
202 Cam Newton 10.00 25.00
203 A.J. Green 5.00 12.00
204 Taiwan Jones 2.00 5.00
205 DeMarco Murray 4.00 10.00
206 Torrey Smith 2.00 5.00
207 Ryan Mallett 2.00 5.00
208 Stevan Ridley 2.00 5.00
209 Austin Pettis 2.00 5.00
210 Shane Vereen 2.50 6.00
211 Titus Young 2.00 5.00
212 Mikel Leshoure 2.00 5.00
213 Christian Ponder 2.00 5.00
214 Jordan Todman 2.00 5.00
215 Vincent Brown 2.00 5.00
216 Von Miller 3.00 8.00
217 Kyle Rudolph 2.00 5.00
218 Jonathan Baldwin 2.00 5.00
219 Jake Locker 2.00 5.00
220 Jamie Harper 2.00 5.00
221 Mark Ingram 3.00 8.00
222 Leonard Hankerson 2.00 5.00
223 Jerrel Jernigan 2.00 5.00
224 Delone Carter 2.00 5.00
225 Blaine Gabbert 2.00 5.00
226 Julio Jones 6.00 15.00
227 Marcell Dareus 2.00 5.00
228 Ryan Williams 2.00 6.00
229 Clyde Gates 2.00 5.00
230 Daniel Thomas 2.00 5.00
231 Greg Little 2.50 6.00
232 Colin Kaepernick 3.00 8.00
233 Alex Green 2.00 5.00
234 Randall Cobb 3.00 8.00
235 Bilal Powell 2.50 6.00
236 Kendall Hunter 2.00 5.00

2011 Absolute Memorabilia Spectrum Gold Autographs

VETERAN STATED PRINT RUN 5-50
ROOKIE STATED PRINT RUN 99-299
*PLAT.ROOK/25: .8X TO 2X GLD AU/99-299
EXCH EXPIRATION: 4/26/2013
6 Roddy White/25 6.00 15.00
9 Joe Flacco/25 20.00 40.00
11 Ray Rice/25
12 C.J. Spiller/50 5.00 12.00
15 DeAngelo Williams/25 6.00 15.00
16 Jonathan Stewart/25 6.00 15.00
21 Matt Forte/25 10.00 25.00
26 Colt McCoy/50 5.00 12.00
27 Peyton Hillis/50 8.00 20.00
29 Dez Bryant/25 20.00 40.00
30 Jason Witten/25 15.00 30.00
32 Brandon Lloyd/25 6.00 15.00
39 Greg Jennings/50 10.00 25.00
42 Arian Foster/50 10.00 25.00
43 Matt Schaub/25
45 Peyton Manning/18 60.00 120.00
46 Reggie Wayne/25 8.00 20.00
47 David Garrard/25 6.00 15.00
49 Dwayne Bowe/25
50 Jamaal Charles/25 8.00 20.00
51 Matt Cassel/25 6.00 15.00
55 Percy Harvin/25 10.00 25.00
56 Sidney Rice/50 5.00 12.00
57 BenJarvus Green-Ellis/50 5.00 12.00
61 Marques Colston/25 10.00 25.00
63 Ahmad Bradshaw/25 6.00 15.00
65 Eli Manning/25 30.00 60.00
66 Hakeem Nicks/25 6.00 15.00
70 Darren McFadden/25 6.00 15.00
73 Jeremy Maclin/25 6.00 15.00
74 LeSean McCoy/25 10.00 25.00
75 Michael Vick/15 30.00 80.00
79 Rashard Mendenhall/25
81 Antonio Gates/25 10.00 25.00
83 Ryan Mathews/25 10.00 25.00
86 Patrick Willis/25 10.00 25.00
90 James Laurinaitis/50 5.00 12.00
93 Josh Freeman/25 8.00 20.00
97 Kenny Britt/25
99 Ryan Torain/50 6.00 15.00
101 Aldrick Robinson/299 5.00 12.00
102 Cecil Shorts/299 3.00 8.00
105 Denarius Moore/299 3.00 8.00
106 Dwayne Harris/299 3.00 8.00
107 Greg Salas/299 3.00 8.00
108 Jeremy Kerley/299 5.00 12.00
109 Kealoha Pilares/299 3.00 8.00
110 Kris Durham/299 3.00 8.00
111 Niles Paul/299 3.00 8.00
112 Ronald Johnson/299 3.00 8.00
113 Ryan Whalen/299 3.00 8.00
114 Scotty McKnight/299 3.00 8.00
115 Stephen Burton/299 4.00 10.00
116 Tandon Doss/299 3.00 8.00
117 D.J. Williams/299 3.00 8.00
119 Jordan Cameron/299 4.00 10.00
120 Julius Thomas/299 4.00 10.00
121 Lance Kendricks/299 3.00 8.00
123 Luke Stocker/299 3.00 8.00
125 Robert Housler/299 3.00 8.00
127 Allen Bradford/299 3.00 8.00
128 Anthony Allen/299 3.00 8.00
130 Da'Rel Scott/299 3.00 8.00
131 Dion Lewis/299 4.00 10.00
132 Evan Royster/299 3.00 8.00
133 Jacquizz Rodgers/299 3.00 8.00
135 Johnny White/299 3.00 8.00
136 Roy Helu/299 3.00 8.00
137 Greg McElroy/299 5.00 12.00
138 Nathan Enderle/299 3.00 8.00
139 Ricky Stanzi/299 3.00 8.00
140 T.J. Yates/299 3.00 8.00
141 Terrelle Pryor/299 5.00 12.00
142 Tyrod Taylor/299 12.00 30.00
143 Aaron Williams/99 4.00 10.00
144 Brandon Harris/299 3.00 8.00
145 Jimmy Smith/299 3.00 8.00
148 Prince Amukamara/299 6.00 15.00
150 Adrian Clayborn/299 6.00 15.00
151 Aldon Smith/299 12.00 30.00
153 Cameron Heyward/299 4.00 10.00
154 Cameron Jordan/299 4.00 10.00
155 Da'Quan Bowers/299 3.00 8.00
156 J.J. Watt/299 50.00 80.00
160 Akeem Ayers/299 3.00 8.00
163 Ryan Kerrigan/299 6.00 15.00
164 Corey Liuget/299 3.00 8.00
168 Phil Taylor/299 3.00 8.00
169 Stephen Paea/299 3.00 8.00
171 Rahim Moore/299 3.00 8.00
178 Anthony Castonzo/299 3.00 8.00
183 Tyron Smith/299 4.00 10.00
184 Ahmad Black/299 4.00 10.00
185 Greg Jones/299 4.00 10.00
186 Marcus Cannon/299 3.00 8.00
188 Owen Marecic/299 EXCH 3.00 8.00
191 Quinton Carter/299 3.00 8.00
192 Stanley Havili/299 3.00 8.00
194 Justin Houston/299 4.00 10.00
196 Martez Wilson/299 3.00 8.00
199 Tyler Sash/299 3.00 8.00

2011 Absolute Memorabilia Star Gazing

*SPECTRUM/50: 1X TO 2.5X BASIC INSERTS
1 Randall Cobb .75 2.00
2 Andy Dalton 1.00 2.50
3 Marcell Dareus .50 1.25
4 Jamie Harper .50 1.25
5 Delone Carter .50 1.25
6 Blaine Gabbert .50 1.25
7 Vincent Brown .50 1.25
8 Kyle Rudolph .50 1.25
9 Shane Vereen .60 1.50
10 Leonard Hankerson .50 1.25
11 Austin Pettis .50 1.25
12 Cam Newton 2.50 6.00
13 Clyde Gates .50 1.25
14 A.J. Green 1.25 3.00
15 Alex Green .50 1.25
16 Daniel Thomas .50 1.25
17 Mikel Leshoure .50 1.25
18 Stevan Ridley .50 1.25
19 Von Miller .75 2.00
20 Greg Little .60 1.50
21 Julio Jones 1.50 4.00
22 Taiwan Jones .50 1.25
23 Jonathan Baldwin .50 1.25
24 Ryan Williams .50 1.25
25 Ryan Mallett .50 1.25
26 Mark Ingram .75 2.00
27 Jerrel Jernigan .50 1.25
28 Jake Locker .50 1.25
29 Jordan Todman .50 1.25
30 Christian Ponder .50 1.25
31 Bilal Powell .60 1.50
32 Colin Kaepernick .75 2.00
33 Torrey Smith .50 1.25
34 Kendall Hunter .50 1.25
35 DeMarco Murray 1.00 2.50
36 Titus Young .50 1.25

2011 Absolute Memorabilia Star Gazing Materials

*OVER.JSY NUM/10: 1X TO 2.5X BSC JSY
*OVER.JSY NUM PRIME/25: .8X TO 2X
*OVER.SPECTRUM PRIME/15: 1.2X TO 3X
*PRIME/50: .6X TO 1.5X BASIC JSY
1 Randall Cobb 2.50 6.00
2 Andy Dalton 3.00 8.00
3 Marcell Dareus 1.50 4.00
4 Jamie Harper 1.50 4.00
5 Delone Carter 1.50 4.00
6 Blaine Gabbert 1.50 4.00
7 Vincent Brown 1.50 4.00
8 Kyle Rudolph 1.50 4.00
9 Shane Vereen 2.00 5.00
10 Leonard Hankerson 1.50 4.00
11 Austin Pettis 1.50 4.00
12 Cam Newton 8.00 20.00
13 Clyde Gates 1.50 4.00
14 A.J. Green 4.00 10.00
15 Alex Green 1.50 4.00
16 Daniel Thomas 1.50 4.00
17 Mikel Leshoure 1.50 4.00
18 Stevan Ridley 1.50 4.00
19 Von Miller 2.50 6.00
20 Greg Little 2.00 5.00
21 Julio Jones 5.00 12.00
22 Taiwan Jones 1.50 4.00
23 Jonathan Baldwin 1.50 4.00
24 Ryan Williams 1.50 4.00
25 Ryan Mallett 1.50 4.00
26 Mark Ingram 2.50 6.00
27 Jerrel Jernigan 1.50 4.00
28 Jake Locker 1.50 4.00
29 Jordan Todman 1.50 4.00
30 Christian Ponder 1.50 4.00
31 Bilal Powell 2.00 5.00
32 Colin Kaepernick 2.50 6.00
33 Torrey Smith 1.50 4.00
34 Kendall Hunter 1.50 4.00
35 DeMarco Murray 3.00 8.00
36 Titus Young 1.50 4.00

2011 Absolute Memorabilia Star Gazing Materials Autographs

STATED PRINT RUN 49 SER.#'d SETS
*PRIME AU/25: .5X TO 1.2X JSY AU/49
EXCH EXPIRATION: 4/26/2013
1 Randall Cobb 8.00 20.00
2 Andy Dalton 10.00 25.00
3 Marcell Dareus 5.00 12.00
4 Jamie Harper 5.00 12.00
5 Delone Carter 5.00 12.00
6 Blaine Gabbert 5.00 12.00
7 Vincent Brown 5.00 12.00
8 Kyle Rudolph 5.00 12.00
9 Shane Vereen 6.00 15.00
10 Leonard Hankerson 5.00 12.00
11 Austin Pettis 5.00 12.00
12 Cam Newton 50.00 120.00
13 Clyde Gates 5.00 12.00
14 A.J. Green 20.00 50.00
15 Alex Green 5.00 12.00
16 Daniel Thomas 5.00 12.00
17 Mikel Leshoure 5.00 12.00
18 Stevan Ridley 5.00 12.00
19 Von Miller 12.00 30.00
20 Greg Little 6.00 15.00
21 Julio Jones 20.00 50.00
22 Taiwan Jones 5.00 12.00
23 Jonathan Baldwin 5.00 12.00
24 Ryan Williams 5.00 12.00
25 Ryan Mallett 5.00 12.00
26 Mark Ingram 8.00 20.00
27 Jerrel Jernigan 5.00 12.00
28 Jake Locker 5.00 12.00
29 Jordan Todman 5.00 12.00
30 Christian Ponder 5.00 12.00
31 Bilal Powell 6.00 15.00
32 Colin Kaepernick 8.00 20.00
33 Torrey Smith 5.00 12.00
34 Kendall Hunter 5.00 12.00
35 DeMarco Murray 10.00 25.00
36 Titus Young 5.00 12.00

2011 Absolute Memorabilia Team Quads Materials Die Cut

STATED PRINT RUN 25-50
*PRIME/20-25: .6X TO 1.5X BASIC QUAD/50
1 Hester/Cutler/Knox/Forte/50 8.00 20.00
2 Jones/Witten/Choice/Austin/50 8.00 20.00
3 Clark/Mann/Garcon/Wayne/50 12.00 30.00
4 Brdshw/Jacbs/Eli/Smith/25 10.00 25.00
5 Gates/Floyd/Rivers/Jacksn/50 10.00 25.00
6 Ryan/Gonz/White/Turner/50 8.00 20.00
7 Boldin/Flacco/Lewis/Rice/50 12.00 30.00
8 Spiller/Jacksn/Evans/Fitzp/50 12.00 30.00
9 Johnsn/Fostr/Schaub/Daniels/25 10.00 25.00
10 Marshl/Henne/Will/Hartline/50 8.00 20.00

2011 Absolute Memorabilia Team Tandems Materials

*PRIME/25 .6X TO 1.5X BASIC DUAL/50
1 E.Reed/R.Lewis 10.00 25.00
2 C.Spiller/F.Jackson 8.00 20.00
3 F.Jones/M.Austin 4.00 10.00
4 B.Lloyd/E.Royal 4.00 10.00
5 C.Johnson/N.Suh 6.00 15.00
6 D.Clark/R.Wayne 5.00 12.00
7 D.Bowe/J.Charles 5.00 12.00
8 T.Brady/W.Welker 15.00 40.00
9 Henderson/M.Colston 4.00 10.00
10 S.Bradford/S.Jackson 4.00 10.00
11 J.Clausen/S.Smith 5.00 12.00
12 B.Urlacher/J.Cutler 6.00 15.00
13 C.Palmer/J.Shipley 5.00 12.00
14 D.Bryant/T.Romo 6.00 15.00
15 T.Tebow/K.Moreno 6.00 15.00
16 M.Stafford/J.Best 5.00 12.00
17 A.Hawk/C.Matthews 10.00 25.00
18 D.Garrard/Jones-Drew 4.00 10.00
19 B.Berrian/V.Shiancoe 5.00 12.00
20 D.Brees/P.Thomas 6.00 15.00
21 S.Greene/D.Keller 5.00 12.00
22 McFadden/J.Campbell 4.00 10.00
23 L.McCoy/B.Celek 6.00 15.00
24 H.Ward/M.Wallace 5.00 12.00
25 R.Mathews/M.Floyd 5.00 12.00
26 D.Hall/L.Landry 5.00 12.00
27 Bradshaw/B.Jacobs 4.00 10.00
28 A.Gates/P.Rivers 6.00 15.00
29 A.Johnson/Schaub/25 5.00 12.00
30 J.Cribbs/P.Hillis 4.00 10.00

2011 Absolute Memorabilia Team Trios Materials NFL

STATED PRINT RUN 25-75
*PRIME/25: .8X TO 2X BASIC TRIPLE/75
1 Turner/White/Gonzalez 5.00 12.00
2 Williams/Smith/Stewart 5.00 12.00
3 Benson/Palmer/Shipley 5.00 12.00
4 Bowe/Cassel/Charles 5.00 12.00
5 Peterson/Harvin/Shiancoe 8.00 20.00
7 Jackson/Vick/Maclin 10.00 25.00
8 Gore/Crabtree/Davis 6.00 15.00
9 Cooley/Landry/Moss 6.00 15.00
10 Graham/Freeman/Winslow 5.00 12.00

2011 Absolute Memorabilia Tools of the Trade Material Red

STATED PRINT RUN 25-250
1 Bernard Berrian/99 3.00 8.00
2 Braylon Edwards/250 2.50 6.00
3 Jabar Gaffney/250 2.50 6.00
4 Fred Jackson/199 6.00 15.00
5 Vincent Jackson/250 2.50 6.00
6 Peyton Manning/25 15.00 40.00
7 Willis McGahee/250 2.50 6.00
8 Jordan Shipley/250 2.50 6.00
9 Darren Sproles/250 3.00 8.00
10 Chad Henne/250 3.00 8.00
11 Sam Hurd/250 2.50 6.00
12 Santana Moss/250 3.00 8.00
13 Cedric Benson/250 2.50 6.00
14 Jason Campbell/250 2.50 6.00
15 Michael Crabtree/250 2.50 6.00
16 Pierre Garcon/250 3.00 8.00
17 Lee Evans/250 3.00 8.00
20 Devery Henderson/250 2.50 6.00
21 Cortland Finnegan/250 3.00 8.00
22 Reggie Bush/250 2.50 6.00
23 Heath Miller/250 2.50 6.00
24 Eddie Royal/250 2.50 6.00
25 Beanie Wells/99 3.00 8.00
26 Felix Jones/250 2.50 6.00
27 Kyle Orton/250 2.50 6.00
28 Malcom Floyd/250 2.50 6.00
30 Marion Barber/250 2.50 6.00
31 Shonn Greene/250 2.50 6.00
32 Devin Hester/250 3.00 8.00
33 Brandon Jacobs/49 3.00 8.00
34 Dustin Keller/199 3.00 8.00
35 Sidney Rice/250 2.50 6.00
36 Johnny Knox/250 2.50 6.00
37 Brent Celek/250 2.50 6.00
38 Todd Heap/250 2.50 6.00
39 Tony Romo/250 3.00 8.00
40 Nate Washington/250 2.50 6.00
41 Matt Hasselbeck/250 2.50 6.00
42 Matthew Stafford/250 3.00 8.00
43 Larry Fitzgerald/250 3.00 8.00
44 Brian Urlacher/250 4.00 10.00
45 Kevin Boss/250 2.50 6.00
46 Kevin Kolb/250 2.50 6.00
47 Cadillac Williams/250 2.50 6.00
48 DeAngelo Williams/99 3.00 8.00
49 Roy Williams WR/250 2.50 6.00
50 Ryan Fitzpatrick/250 2.50 6.00

2011 Absolute Memorabilia Tools of the Trade Material Black Spectrum

STATED PRINT RUN 5-25
5 Vincent Jackson/25 5.00 12.00
7 Willis McGahee/25 5.00 12.00
8 Jordan Shipley/25 5.00 12.00
9 Darren Sproles/25 6.00 15.00
10 Chad Henne/25 6.00 15.00
11 Sam Hurd/25 5.00 12.00
12 Santana Moss/25 6.00 15.00
13 Cedric Benson/25 5.00 12.00
14 Jason Campbell/25 5.00 12.00
16 Pierre Garcon/25 6.00 15.00
17 Lee Evans/25 6.00 15.00
18 Greg Olsen/25 6.00 15.00
19 Hakeem Nicks/25 5.00 12.00
21 Cortland Finnegan/50 6.00 15.00
23 Heath Miller/25 5.00 12.00
24 Eddie Royal/25 5.00 12.00
26 Felix Jones/25 5.00 12.00
27 Kyle Orton/25 5.00 12.00
28 Malcom Floyd/25 5.00 12.00
29 Steve Smith/25 6.00 15.00
30 Marion Barber/25 5.00 12.00
32 Devin Hester/25 6.00 15.00
36 Johnny Knox/25 5.00 12.00
38 Todd Heap/25 5.00 12.00
39 Tony Romo/25 6.00 15.00
40 Nate Washington/25 5.00 12.00
41 Matt Hasselbeck/25 5.00 12.00
42 Matthew Stafford/25 6.00 15.00
43 Larry Fitzgerald/25 6.00 15.00
44 Brian Urlacher/25 8.00 20.00
45 Kevin Boss/25 5.00 12.00
49 Roy Williams WR/25 5.00 12.00
50 Ryan Fitzpatrick/25 5.00 12.00

2011 Absolute Memorabilia Tools of the Trade Double Material Black Spectrum

STATED PRINT RUN 1-25
21 Cortland Finnegan/25 6.00 15.00
30 Marion Barber/25 5.00 12.00
40 Nate Washington/25 5.00 12.00

2011 Absolute Memorabilia Tools of the Trade Triple Material Black Spectrum

STATED PRINT RUN 1-25

2011 Absolute Memorabilia Tools of the Trade Material Autographs Black Spectrum

STATED PRINT RUN 1-25
2 Braylon Edwards/25 10.00 25.00
5 Vincent Jackson/25 10.00 25.00

2011 Absolute Memorabilia War Room

*WAR ROOM: .4X TO 1X STAR GAZING
*WR SPECTRUM/50: 1X TO 2.5X STAR GAZING

2011 Absolute Memorabilia War Room Materials

*WAR ROOM: .4X TO 1X STAR GAZING JSY
*JSY NUMBER/10: 1X TO 2.5X BASIC JSY
*JSY NUMBER PRIME/10: 1.2X TO 3X JSY
*PRIME/50: .6X TO 1.5X STAR GAZING JSY

2011 Absolute Memorabilia War Room Materials Autographs

*WAR ROOM/49: .4X TO 1X STAR GAZING AU/49
WAR ROOM PRINT RUN 49 SER.#'d SETS
*PRIME/25: .5X TO 1.2X JSY AU/49

2012 Absolute

101-200 ROOKIE PRINT RUN 399
201-235 ROOKIE JSY AU PRINT RUN 299
1 Cam Newton .50 1.25
2 Steve Smith .40 1.00
3 DeAngelo Williams .30 .75
4 Joe Flacco .40 1.00
5 Anquan Boldin .30 .75
6 Ray Rice .30 .75
7 Ray Lewis .50 1.25
8 Andy Dalton .40 1.00
9 A.J. Green .50 1.25
10 BenJarvus Green-Ellis .40 1.00
11 Greg Little .30 .75
12 Josh Cribbs .30 .75
13 Ben Roethlisberger .50 1.25
14 Rashard Mendenhall .30 .75
15 Mike Wallace .30 .75
16 Andre Johnson .40 1.00
17 Arian Foster .40 1.00
18 Matt Schaub .30 .75
19 Austin Collie .30 .75
20 Reggie Wayne .40 1.00
21 Donald Brown .30 .75
22 Blaine Gabbert .30 .75
23 Maurice Jones-Drew .30 .75
24 Mike Thomas .40 1.00
25 Jake Locker .50 1.25
26 Kenny Britt .30 .75
27 Chris Johnson .30 .75
28 Ryan Fitzpatrick .30 .75
29 Steve Johnson .40 1.00
30 Fred Jackson .40 1.00
31 Reggie Bush .30 .75
32 Daniel Thomas .30 .75
33 Davone Bess .30 .75
34 Tom Brady 1.25 3.00
35 Rob Gronkowski .50 1.25
36 Wes Welker .40 1.00
37 Aaron Hernandez .40 1.00
38 Mark Sanchez .30 .75
39 Shonn Greene .30 .75
40 Tim Tebow .50 1.25
41 Santonio Holmes .30 .75
42 Peyton Manning 1.00 2.50
43 Willis McGahee .30 .75
44 Demaryius Thomas .50 1.25
45 Matthew Stafford .40 1.00
46 Calvin Johnson .50 1.25
47 Ndamukong Suh .40 1.00
48 Aaron Rodgers .75 2.00
49 Greg Jennings .30 .75
50 Jordy Nelson .40 1.00
51 Jay Cutler .30 .75
52 Matt Forte .30 .75
53 Brandon Marshall .40 1.00
54 Larry Fitzgerald .40 1.00
55 Kevin Kolb .30 .75
56 Beanie Wells .30 .75
57 Matt Ryan .40 1.00
58 Michael Turner .30 .75
59 Roddy White .30 .75
60 Adrian Peterson .50 1.25
61 Percy Harvin .30 .75
62 Christian Ponder .30 .75
63 Drew Brees .50 1.25
64 Darren Sproles .40 1.00
65 Marques Colston .30 .75
66 Eli Manning .40 1.00
67 Hakeem Nicks .30 .75
68 Ahmad Bradshaw .30 .75
69 Carson Palmer .40 1.00
70 Darren McFadden .30 .75
71 Darrius Heyward-Bey .30 .75
72 Michael Vick .40 1.00
73 LeSean McCoy .50 1.25
74 DeSean Jackson .40 1.00
75 Jeremy Maclin .30 .75
76 Philip Rivers .50 1.25
77 Antonio Gates .40 1.00
78 Ryan Mathews .40 1.00
79 Alex Smith .40 1.00
80 Frank Gore .40 1.00
81 Vernon Davis .30 .75
82 Tony Romo .40 1.00
83 DeMarco Murray .40 1.00
84 Dez Bryant .50 1.25
85 Jason Witten .40 1.00
86 Sidney Rice .30 .75
87 Golden Tate .30 .75
88 Marshawn Lynch .40 1.00
89 LeGarrette Blount .40 1.00
90 Josh Freeman .40 1.00
91 Vincent Jackson .30 .75
92 Dallas Clark .30 .75
93 Pierre Garcon .40 1.00
94 Santana Moss .40 1.00

95 Roy Helu .30 .75
96 Dwayne Bowe .40 1.00
97 Jamaal Charles .40 1.00
98 Matt Cassel .30 .75
99 Sam Bradford .30 .75
100 Steven Jackson .30 .75
101 Matt Kalil RC 1.50 4.00
102 Adrien Robinson RC 1.50 4.00
103 Alfred Morris RC 1.50 4.00
104 B.J. Coleman RC 1.50 4.00
105 B.J. Cunningham RC 1.50 4.00
106 Brad Smelley RC 2.00 5.00
107 Brandon Boykin RC 2.00 5.00
108 Brandon Hardin RC 2.00 5.00
109 Brandon Taylor RC 1.50 4.00
110 Bruce Irvin RC 2.00 5.00
111 Bryce Brown RC 1.50 4.00
112 Casey Hayward RC 1.50 4.00
113 Chandler Harnish RC 1.50 4.00
114 Chandler Jones RC 1.50 4.00
115 Charles Mitchell RC 2.00 5.00
116 Chris Rainey RC 1.50 4.00
117 Christian Thompson RC 2.50 6.00
118 Cordy Glenn RC 2.00 5.00
119 Coty Sensabaugh RC 2.00 5.00
120 Courtney Upshaw RC 2.00 5.00
121 Cyrus Gray RC 1.50 4.00
122 Dan Herron RC 1.50 4.00
123 Danny Coale RC 1.50 4.00
124 David DeCastro RC 1.50 4.00
125 Demario Davis RC 1.50 4.00
126 Derek Wolfe RC 2.00 5.00
127 Devon Still RC 2.00 5.00
128 Devon Wylie RC 1.50 4.00
129 Dontari Poe RC 1.50 4.00
130 Dre Kirkpatrick RC 1.50 4.00
131 Bill Bentley RC 2.00 5.00
132 Emmanuel Acho RC 1.50 4.00
133 Evan Rodriguez RC 2.00 5.00
134 Fletcher Cox RC 2.50 6.00
135 Frank Alexander RC 1.50 4.00
136 George Iloka RC 1.50 4.00
137 Josh Gordon RC 4.00 10.00
138 Harrison Smith RC 1.50 4.00
139 Isaiah Frey RC 1.50 4.00
140 Jake Bequette RC 2.50 6.00
141 Jamell Fleming RC 1.50 4.00
142 James Hanna RC 1.50 4.00
143 James-Michael Johnson RC 2.00 5.00
144 Janoris Jenkins RC 2.00 5.00
145 Jared Crick RC 1.50 4.00
146 Jaye Howard RC 2.00 5.00
147 Jayron Hosley RC 2.50 6.00
148 Josh Bush RC 1.50 4.00
149 Josh Robinson RC 2.50 6.00
150 Juron Criner RC 1.50 4.00
151 Keenan Robinson RC 2.00 5.00
152 Kendall Reyes RC 1.50 4.00
153 Keshawn Martin RC 2.00 5.00
154 Kevin Zeitler RC 1.50 4.00
155 Kirk Cousins RC 6.00 15.00
156 Kyle Wilber RC 2.50 6.00
157 Ladarius Green RC 1.50 4.00
158 LaVon Brazill RC 2.50 6.00
159 Lavonte David RC 2.50 6.00
160 Luke Kuechly RC 4.00 10.00
161 Mark Barron RC 1.50 4.00
162 Jorvorskie Lane RC 2.00 5.00
163 Marvin Jones RC 1.50 4.00
164 Marvin McNutt RC 1.50 4.00
165 Matt Johnson RC 2.50 6.00
166 Melvin Ingram RC 1.50 4.00
167 Michael Brockers RC 1.50 4.00
168 Michael Smith RC 2.00 5.00
169 Mike Harris RC 1.50 4.00
170 Mike Martin RC 2.00 5.00
171 Miles Burris RC 2.50 6.00
172 Morris Claiborne RC 1.50 4.00
173 Nick Perry RC 2.00 5.00
174 Nigel Bradham RC 2.00 5.00
175 Olivier Vernon RC 2.50 6.00
176 Orson Charles RC 1.50 4.00
177 Quinton Coples RC 1.50 4.00
178 Riley Reiff RC 1.50 4.00
179 Rishard Matthews RC 1.50 4.00
180 Ron Brooks RC 2.50 6.00
181 Ronnell Lewis RC 1.50 4.00
182 Ryan Lindley RC 1.50 4.00
183 Sean Spence RC 2.00 5.00
184 Shea McClellin RC 2.00 5.00
185 Stephon Gilmore RC 2.00 5.00
186 Tavon Wilson RC 2.00 5.00
187 Terrance Ganaway RC 2.00 5.00
188 Tommy Streeter RC 1.50 4.00
189 Travis Benjamin RC 1.50 4.00
190 Trent Robinson RC 2.00 5.00
191 Trumaine Johnson RC 1.50 4.00
192 Tyrone Crawford RC 1.50 4.00
193 Vick Ballard RC 2.00 5.00
194 Vinny Curry RC 2.00 5.00
195 Whitney Mercilus RC 1.50 4.00
196 Winston Guy Jr. RC 1.50 4.00
197 Zach Brown RC 1.50 4.00
198 Andre Branch RC 1.50 4.00
199 Case Keenum RC 3.00 8.00
200 Kellen Moore RC 2.00 5.00
201 A.J. Jenkins JSY AU RC 4.00 10.00
202 Alshon Jeffery JSY AU RC 8.00 20.00
203 Andrew Luck JSY AU RC 100.00 200.00
204 Bernard Pierce JSY AU RC 4.00 10.00
205 Brandon Weeden JSY AU RC 4.00 10.00
206 Brian Quick JSY AU RC 4.00 10.00
207 Brock Osweiler JSY AU RC 4.00 10.00
208 Chris Givens JSY AU RC 4.00 10.00
209 Coby Fleener JSY AU RC 4.00 10.00
210 David Wilson JSY AU RC 4.00 10.00
211 DeVier Posey JSY AU RC 4.00 10.00
212 Doug Martin JSY AU RC 6.00 15.00
213 Dwayne Allen JSY AU RC 4.00 10.00
214 Isaiah Pead JSY AU RC 4.00 10.00
215 Jarius Wright JSY AU RC 4.00 10.00
216 Joe Adams JSY AU RC 4.00 10.00
217 Justin Blackmon JSY AU RC 4.00 10.00
218 Kendall Wright JSY AU RC 4.00 10.00
219 Lamar Miller JSY AU RC 6.00 15.00
220 LaMichael James JSY AU RC 4.00 10.00
221 Michael Egnew JSY AU RC 4.00 10.00
222 Michael Floyd JSY AU RC 4.00 10.00
223 Mohamed Sanu JSY AU RC 6.00 15.00
224 Nick Foles JSY AU RC 25.00 50.00
225 Nick Toon JSY AU RC 4.00 10.00
226 Robert Griffin III JSY AU RC 5.00 12.00
227 Robert Turbin JSY AU RC 4.00 10.00
228 Ronnie Hillman JSY AU RC 4.00 10.00
229 Rueben Randle JSY AU RC 4.00 10.00
230 Russell Wilson JSY AU RC 60.00 125.00
231 Ryan Broyles JSY AU RC 4.00 10.00
232 Ryan Tannehill JSY AU RC 6.00 15.00
233 Stephen Hill JSY AU RC 4.00 10.00
234 T.J. Graham JSY AU RC 4.00 10.00
235 Trent Richardson JSY AU RC 4.00 10.00

2012 Absolute Retail

*1-100 VETS: .25X TO .6X HOBBY
*101-200 ROOKIES: .4X TO 1X HOBBY
PRINTED ON WHITE CARD STOCK

2012 Absolute Spectrum Black Retail

*VETS/25: 3X TO 8X BASIC CARDS
*ROOKIES/25: 1X TO 2.5X BASIC CARDS

2012 Absolute Spectrum Blue Retail

*VETS/100: 1.5X TO 4X BASIC CARDS
*ROOKIES/100: .5X TO 1.2X BASIC CARDS

2012 Absolute Spectrum Gold

*VETS/25: 3X TO 8X BASIC CARDS
*ROOKIES/25: 1X TO 2.5X BASIC CARDS

2012 Absolute Spectrum Red Retail

*VETS: 1.2X TO 3X BASIC CARDS
*ROOKIES: .4X TO 1X BASIC CARDS
RANDOM INSERTS IN RETAIL PACKS

2012 Absolute Spectrum Silver

*VETS/50: 2X TO 5X BASIC CARDS
*ROOKIES/50: .6X TO 1.5X BASIC CARDS

2012 Absolute Absolute Heroes Materials Autographs

2 Anquan Boldin/25 8.00 20.00

2012 Absolute Absolute Heroes Materials Spectrum Prime

2 Dez Bryant/49 6.00 15.00
3 Tony Romo/49 5.00 12.00
8 Jamaal Charles/49 5.00 12.00
11 Marques Colston/49 4.00 10.00
12 Hakeem Nicks/49 4.00 10.00
13 Darren McFadden/25 5.00 12.00
14 DeSean Jackson/49 5.00 12.00
15 Jeremy Maclin/15 5.00 12.00
19 Roddy White/49 4.00 10.00

2012 Absolute Gridiron Force

*SPECTRUM/100: .8X TO 2X BASIC INSERTS
1 Julius Peppers 1.00 2.50
2 Brian Cushing .75 2.00
3 James Harrison 1.00 2.50
4 Troy Polamalu 1.25 3.00
5 J.J. Watt 1.25 3.00
6 Paul Posluszny .75 2.00
7 Mario Williams .75 2.00
8 Jerod Mayo .75 2.00
9 David Harris .75 2.00
10 Von Miller 1.00 2.50
11 Champ Bailey 1.00 2.50
12 Tamba Hali .75 2.00
13 Lance Briggs 1.00 2.50
14 Charles Woodson 1.25 3.00
15 Clay Matthews 1.25 3.00
16 Jared Allen .75 2.00
17 Jon Beason .75 2.00
18 DeMarcus Ware 1.25 3.00
19 Sean Lee 1.25 3.00
20 Jason Pierre-Paul .75 2.00
21 Nnamdi Asomugha .75 2.00
22 Brian Orakpo 1.00 2.50
23 London Fletcher 1.00 2.50
24 Patrick Willis 1.00 2.50
25 James Laurinaitis .75 2.00

2012 Absolute Gridiron Force Materials Autographs

2 Brian Cushing/25 10.00 25.00
7 Mario Williams/20 12.00 30.00
8 Jerod Mayo/25 10.00 25.00
10 Von Miller/25 12.00 30.00
19 Sean Lee/25 15.00 40.00
22 Brian Orakpo/25 12.00 30.00
23 London Fletcher/25 25.00 50.00
25 James Laurinaitis/25 10.00 25.00

2012 Absolute Ground Hoggs

*SPECTRUM/100: .8X TO 2X BASIC INSERTS
1 Ray Rice .75 2.00
2 Rashard Mendenhall .75 2.00
3 Arian Foster 1.00 2.50
4 Donald Brown .75 2.00
5 Fred Jackson 1.00 2.50
6 Reggie Bush .75 2.00
7 Jamaal Charles 1.00 2.50
8 Darren McFadden .75 2.00
9 Ryan Mathews 1.00 2.50
10 Matt Forte .75 2.00
11 James Starks .75 2.00
12 Adrian Peterson 1.25 3.00
13 Michael Turner .75 2.00
14 DeAngelo Williams .75 2.00
15 Darren Sproles 1.00 2.50
16 LeGarrette Blount 1.00 2.50
17 DeMarco Murray 1.00 2.50
18 Ahmad Bradshaw .75 2.00
19 LeSean McCoy 1.25 3.00
20 Roy Helu .75 2.00
21 Beanie Wells .75 2.00
22 Frank Gore 1.00 2.50
23 Marshawn Lynch 1.00 2.50
24 Steven Jackson .75 2.00
25 Shonn Greene .75 2.00

2012 Absolute Ground Hoggs Materials Autographs

3 Arian Foster/25 25.00 50.00
25 Shonn Greene/25 8.00 20.00

2012 Absolute Hall Worthy

RANDOM INSERTS IN RETAIL PACKS
*SPECTRUM/100: .8X TO 2X BASIC INSERTS
1 Charles Woodson 1.25 3.00
2 Antonio Gates 1.00 2.50
3 LaDainian Tomlinson 1.25 3.00
4 Drew Brees 1.25 3.00
5 Ed Reed 1.00 2.50
6 Brian Urlacher 1.25 3.00
7 Tom Brady 3.00 8.00
8 Peyton Manning 2.50 6.00
9 Randy Moss 1.00 2.50
10 Tony Gonzalez 1.00 2.50
11 Champ Bailey 1.00 2.50
12 Santana Moss 1.00 2.50
13 Kurt Warner 1.00 2.50
14 Warrick Dunn .75 2.00
15 Keyshawn Johnson 1.00 2.50
16 Cris Carter 1.25 3.00
17 Curtis Martin 1.00 2.50
18 Jerome Bettis 1.25 3.00
19 Andre Reed 1.00 2.50
20 Tim Brown 1.25 3.00
21 Terrell Davis 1.00 2.50
22 Eddie George 1.00 2.50
23 Tiki Barber 1.00 2.50
24 Troy Polamalu 1.25 3.00
25 John Elway 2.00 5.00

2012 Absolute Hall Worthy Materials Autographs

17 Curtis Martin/25 12.00 30.00
22 Eddie George/25 30.00 60.00
23 Tiki Barber/20

2012 Absolute Marks of Fame

RANDOM INSERTS IN RETAIL PACKS
*SPECTRUM/100: .8X TO 2X BASIC INSERTS
1 Malcom Floyd .75 2.00
2 Arian Foster 1.00 2.50
3 Beanie Wells .75 2.00
4 Brent Celek .75 2.00
5 DeMarco Murray 1.00 2.50
6 Drew Brees 1.25 3.00
7 Greg Jennings .75 2.00
8 Jay Cutler .75 2.00
9 Larry Fitzgerald 1.00 2.50
10 Marcedes Lewis .75 2.00
11 Mark Sanchez .75 2.00
12 Matt Forte .75 2.00
13 Matt Ryan 1.00 2.50
14 Matt Schaub .75 2.00
15 Michael Crabtree .75 2.00
16 Michael Vick 1.00 2.50
17 Miles Austin .75 2.00
18 Philip Rivers 1.25 3.00
19 Rashard Mendenhall .75 2.00
20 Reggie Wayne 1.00 2.50
21 Ryan Mathews 1.00 2.50
22 Shonn Greene .75 2.00
23 Steve Johnson 1.00 2.50
24 Steven Jackson .75 2.00
25 Vernon Davis .75 2.00

2012 Absolute Marks of Fame Materials Autographs

EXCH EXPIRATION: 6/12/2014
1 Malcom Floyd/25 10.00 25.00
2 Arian Foster/25 25.00 50.00
8 Jay Cutler/25 15.00 40.00
9 Larry Fitzgerald/25 12.00 30.00
13 Matt Ryan/25 12.00 30.00
15 Michael Crabtree/25 10.00 25.00
16 Michael Vick/25 12.00 30.00
22 Shonn Greene/25 EXCH 10.00 25.00
23 Steve Johnson/25 10.00 25.00

2012 Absolute NFL Icons Autographs

EXCH EXPIRATION: 6/12/2014
1 Alan Page/25 15.00 40.00
2 Archie Manning/25 12.00 30.00
3 Barry Sanders/25 60.00 120.00
4 Bart Starr/25 50.00 100.00
5 Bo Jackson/25 40.00 80.00
6 Boomer Esiason/25 12.00 30.00
7 Brett Favre/25 75.00 150.00
8 Cris Carter/10
9 Dan Marino/25 75.00 150.00
10 Deion Sanders/25 30.00 60.00
11 Dick Butkus/25 20.00 50.00
12 Doug Flutie/25 12.00 30.00
13 Ed Too Tall Jones/25 10.00 25.00
14 Emmitt Smith/25 75.00 150.00
15 Eric Dickerson/20 15.00 40.00
16 Gale Sayers/25 EXCH 15.00 40.00
17 Howie Long/25 15.00 40.00
18 Jack Lambert/25 30.00 60.00
19 Jerome Bettis/25 50.00 100.00
20 Jim McMahon/25 12.00 30.00
21 Jim Plunkett/25 12.00 30.00
22 Joe Montana/25 60.00 120.00
23 Joe Namath/25 60.00 120.00
24 John Elway/10
25 Lance Alworth/25 25.00 50.00
26 Marcus Allen/25 15.00 40.00
27 Michael Strahan/10
28 Phil Simms/25 12.00 30.00
29 Shannon Sharpe/10
30 Warren Moon/25 15.00 40.00

2012 Absolute NFL Icons Materials Autographs

EXCH EXPIRATION: 6/12/2014
5 Corey Dillon/49 EXCH 10.00 25.00
6 Jim Brown/49 EXCH 30.00 60.00
7 Roger Staubach/25 50.00 100.00
8 Tony Dorsett/25 30.00 60.00
12 Randall Cunningham/49 15.00 40.00
13 Jerry Rice/25 90.00 150.00
14 Steve Young/25 30.00 80.00
15 Marshall Faulk/25 15.00 40.00

2012 Absolute NFL Icons Materials Autographs Prime

5 Corey Dillon/25
8 Tony Dorsett/25 30.00 60.00
11 Marcus Allen/25 20.00 40.00
15 Marshall Faulk/25 20.00 40.00

2012 Absolute NFL Icons Materials Spectrum Prime

2 Curtis Martin/49 6.00 15.00
4 Walter Payton/49 25.00 50.00
5 Corey Dillon/49 6.00 15.00
8 Tony Dorsett/49 8.00 20.00
11 Marcus Allen/49 8.00 20.00
13 Jerry Rice/49 12.00 30.00
15 Marshall Faulk/49 6.00 15.00

2012 Absolute Rookie Jersey Collection

RANDOM INSERTS IN RETAIL PACKS
1 A.J. Jenkins 1.50 4.00
2 Alshon Jeffery 3.00 8.00
3 Andrew Luck 12.00 30.00
4 Bernard Pierce 1.50 4.00
5 Brandon Weeden 1.50 4.00
6 Brian Quick 1.50 4.00
7 Brock Osweiler 1.50 4.00
8 Chris Givens 1.50 4.00
9 Coby Fleener 1.50 4.00
10 David Wilson 1.50 4.00
11 DeVier Posey 1.50 4.00
12 Doug Martin 2.50 6.00
13 Isaiah Pead 1.50 4.00
14 Jarius Wright 1.50 4.00
15 Joe Adams 1.50 4.00
16 Justin Blackmon 1.50 4.00
17 Kendall Wright 1.50 4.00
18 Lamar Miller 2.50 6.00
19 LaMichael James 1.50 4.00
20 Michael Floyd 1.50 4.00
21 Mohamed Sanu 2.50 6.00
22 Nick Foles 4.00 10.00
23 Nick Toon 1.50 4.00
24 Robert Griffin III 2.00 5.00
25 Rueben Randle 1.50 4.00
26 Russell Wilson 10.00 25.00
27 Ryan Broyles 1.50 4.00
28 Ryan Tannehill 2.50 6.00
29 Stephen Hill 1.50 4.00
30 Trent Richardson 1.50 4.00

2012 Absolute Rookie Premiere Materials NFL Prime

*AFC/NFC/99: .3X TO .8X NFL PRIME
*AFC/NFC PRIME/25: .5X TO 1.2X NFL PRIME
*OVERSIZE JSY NUM/99: .3X TO .8X NFL PRIME
*OVERSIZE JSY NUM/50: .4X TO 1X NFL PRIME
*OVERSIZE JSY NUM/25: .5X TO 1.2X NFL PRIME
*OVERSIZE JSY NUM PRIME/25: .5X TO 1.2X
*OVERSIZE JSY NUM PRIME/10: .8X TO 2X
*OVERSIZE PRIME/25: .5X TO 1.2X NFL PRIME
201 A.J. Jenkins 2.50 6.00
202 Alshon Jeffery 5.00 12.00
203 Andrew Luck 20.00 50.00
204 Bernard Pierce 2.50 6.00
205 Brandon Weeden 2.50 6.00
206 Brian Quick 2.50 6.00
207 Brock Osweiler 2.50 6.00
208 Chris Givens 2.50 6.00
209 Coby Fleener 2.50 6.00
210 David Wilson 2.50 6.00
211 DeVier Posey 2.50 6.00
212 Doug Martin 4.00 10.00
213 Dwayne Allen 2.50 6.00
214 Isaiah Pead 2.50 6.00
215 Jarius Wright 2.50 6.00
216 Joe Adams 2.50 6.00
217 Justin Blackmon 2.50 6.00
218 Kendall Wright 2.50 6.00
219 Lamar Miller 4.00 10.00
220 LaMichael James 2.50 6.00
221 Michael Egnew 2.50 6.00
222 Michael Floyd 2.50 6.00
223 Mohamed Sanu 4.00 10.00
224 Nick Foles 6.00 15.00
225 Nick Toon 2.50 6.00
226 Robert Griffin III 3.00 8.00
227 Robert Turbin 2.50 6.00
228 Ronnie Hillman 2.50 6.00
229 Rueben Randle 2.50 6.00
230 Russell Wilson 12.00 30.00
231 Ryan Broyles 2.50 6.00
232 Ryan Tannehill 4.00 10.00
233 Stephen Hill 2.50 6.00
234 T.J. Graham 2.50 6.00
235 Trent Richardson 2.50 6.00

2012 Absolute Rookie Premiere Materials Autographs AFC/NFC

*AFC/NFC/49: .5X TO 1.2X BASIC RPM AU RC
203 Andrew Luck 125.00 250.00
224 Nick Foles 30.00 60.00
226 Robert Griffin III 6.00 15.00
230 Russell Wilson 100.00 175.00

2012 Absolute Rookie Premiere Materials Autographs AFC/NFC Prime

*AFC/NFC PRIME/25: .6X TO 1.5X RPM AU RC
203 Andrew Luck 150.00 300.00
224 Nick Foles 30.00 80.00
226 Robert Griffin III 8.00 20.00
230 Russell Wilson 125.00 250.00

2012 Absolute Rookie Premiere Materials Autographs NFL Prime

*NFL PRIME/25: .6X TO 1.5X BASIC RPM AU RC
203 Andrew Luck 150.00 300.00
224 Nick Foles 30.00 80.00
226 Robert Griffin III 8.00 20.00
230 Russell Wilson 125.00 200.00

2012 Absolute Rookie Premiere Materials Autographs Oversize

*OVERSIZE/25: .6X TO 1.5X BASIC RPM AU RC
203 Andrew Luck 200.00 350.00
224 Nick Foles 30.00 80.00
226 Robert Griffin III 8.00 20.00
230 Russell Wilson 125.00 200.00

2012 Absolute Spectrum Gold Autographs

EXCH EXPIRATION: 6/12/2014
*PLAT.VET/25: .5X TO 1.2X GOLD AU/49-75
*PLAT.ROOKIE/25: .8X TO 2X GOLD AU/199-299
1 Cam Newton/25 30.00 60.00
3 DeAngelo Williams/75 6.00 15.00
4 Joe Flacco/75 15.00 40.00
5 Anquan Boldin/75 6.00 15.00
8 Andy Dalton/75 8.00 20.00
9 A.J. Green/75 12.00 30.00
10 BenJarvus Green-Ellis/75 10.00 25.00
11 Greg Little/75 6.00 15.00
12 Josh Cribbs/75 6.00 15.00
13 Ben Roethlisberger/75 30.00 60.00
14 Rashard Mendenhall/75 6.00 15.00
15 Mike Wallace/25
18 Matt Schaub/75 6.00 15.00
20 Reggie Wayne/75 8.00 20.00
22 Blaine Gabbert/75 6.00 15.00
25 Jake Locker/25 12.00 30.00
26 Kenny Britt/25 8.00 20.00
28 Ryan Fitzpatrick/75 6.00 15.00
29 Steve Johnson/75 8.00 20.00
30 Fred Jackson/75 8.00 20.00
32 Daniel Thomas/75 6.00 15.00
35 Rob Gronkowski/75 20.00 40.00
37 Aaron Hernandez/25 12.00 30.00
40 Tim Tebow/25 EXCH 30.00 50.00
41 Santonio Holmes/75 6.00 15.00
42 Peyton Manning/49 100.00 175.00
43 Willis McGahee/25 8.00 20.00
45 Matthew Stafford/49 15.00 30.00
48 Aaron Rodgers/25 125.00 200.00
49 Greg Jennings/75 6.00 15.00
50 Jordy Nelson/75 10.00 25.00
52 Matt Forte/75 6.00 15.00
55 Kevin Kolb/75 6.00 15.00
56 Beanie Wells/49 6.00 15.00
57 Matt Ryan/49 15.00 40.00
58 Michael Turner/75 6.00 15.00
59 Roddy White/75 6.00 15.00
61 Percy Harvin/75 6.00 15.00
62 Christian Ponder/75 6.00 15.00
63 Drew Brees/49 30.00 60.00
64 Darren Sproles/49 8.00 20.00
66 Eli Manning/49 30.00 60.00
68 Ahmad Bradshaw/75 6.00 15.00
71 Darrius Heyward-Bey/75 6.00 15.00
73 LeSean McCoy/75 10.00 25.00
77 Antonio Gates/75 8.00 20.00
79 Alex Smith/75 10.00 25.00
82 Tony Romo/49 20.00 40.00
83 DeMarco Murray/25 10.00 25.00
85 Jason Witten/75 12.00 30.00
86 Sidney Rice/25 8.00 20.00
88 Marshawn Lynch/75 25.00 50.00
89 LeGarrette Blount/75 8.00 20.00
91 Vincent Jackson/75 6.00 15.00
92 Dallas Clark/49 6.00 15.00
93 Pierre Garcon/75 8.00 20.00
94 Santana Moss/75 8.00 20.00
95 Roy Helu/75 6.00 15.00
98 Matt Cassel/75 6.00 15.00
99 Sam Bradford/75 6.00 15.00
101 Matt Kalil/299 EXCH 3.00 8.00
102 Adrien Robinson/299 3.00 8.00
103 Alfred Morris/299 3.00 8.00
104 B.J. Coleman/299 3.00 8.00
105 B.J. Cunningham/299 3.00 8.00
108 Brandon Hardin/299 4.00 10.00
109 Brandon Taylor/299 3.00 8.00
110 Bruce Irvin/299 4.00 10.00
111 Bryce Brown/299 3.00 8.00
112 Casey Hayward/299 3.00 8.00
113 Chandler Harnish/299 3.00 8.00
114 Chandler Jones/299 3.00 8.00
116 Chris Rainey/299 3.00 8.00
119 Coty Sensabaugh/299 4.00 10.00
120 Courtney Upshaw/299 4.00 10.00
121 Cyrus Gray/299 3.00 8.00
122 Dan Herron/299 3.00 8.00
123 Danny Coale/299 3.00 8.00
124 David DeCastro/299 3.00 8.00
125 Demario Davis/299 3.00 8.00
127 Devon Still/299 4.00 10.00
128 Devon Wylie/299 3.00 8.00
129 Dontari Poe/299 3.00 8.00
130 Dre Kirkpatrick/299 3.00 8.00
131 Bill Bentley/299 4.00 10.00
134 Fletcher Cox/299 5.00 12.00
136 George Iloka/299 3.00 8.00
137 Josh Gordon/299 8.00 20.00
138 Harrison Smith/299 6.00 15.00
141 Jamell Fleming/299 3.00 8.00
142 James Hanna/299 3.00 8.00
144 Janoris Jenkins/299 4.00 10.00
145 Jared Crick/299 EXCH 3.00 8.00
149 Josh Robinson/299 5.00 12.00
150 Juron Criner/299 3.00 8.00
152 Kendall Reyes/299 3.00 8.00
153 Keshawn Martin/299 4.00 10.00
154 Kevin Zeitler/299 3.00 8.00
155 Kirk Cousins/299 15.00 30.00
157 Ladarius Green/299 3.00 8.00
158 LaVon Brazill/299 5.00 12.00
159 Lavonte David/299 5.00 12.00
160 Luke Kuechly/299 8.00 20.00
161 Mark Barron/299 3.00 8.00
163 Marvin Jones/299 3.00 8.00
164 Marvin McNutt/299 3.00 8.00
166 Melvin Ingram/299 3.00 8.00
167 Michael Brockers/299 3.00 8.00
168 Michael Smith/299 EXCH 4.00 10.00
170 Mike Martin/299 4.00 10.00
172 Morris Claiborne/199 3.00 8.00
173 Nick Perry/299 EXCH 4.00 10.00
175 Olivier Vernon/299 5.00 12.00
176 Orson Charles/299 3.00 8.00
177 Quinton Coples/299 3.00 8.00
178 Riley Reiff/299 3.00 8.00
179 Rishard Matthews/299 3.00 8.00
181 Ronnell Lewis/299 3.00 8.00
182 Ryan Lindley/299 3.00 8.00
183 Sean Spence/299 4.00 10.00
184 Shea McClellin/299 4.00 10.00
185 Stephon Gilmore/299 4.00 10.00
186 Tavon Wilson/299 4.00 10.00
187 Terrance Ganaway/299 4.00 10.00
188 Tommy Streeter/299 3.00 8.00
189 Travis Benjamin/299 3.00 8.00
191 Trumaine Johnson/299 3.00 8.00
192 Tyrone Crawford/299 3.00 8.00
193 Vick Ballard/299 4.00 10.00
194 Vinny Curry/299 4.00 10.00
195 Whitney Mercilus/299 3.00 8.00
197 Zach Brown/299 3.00 8.00
198 Andre Branch/299 3.00 8.00
199 Case Keenum/299 6.00 15.00
200 Kellen Moore/299 4.00 10.00

2012 Absolute Star Gazing Materials

*PRIME/49: .6X TO 1.5X BASIC JSY
1 Robert Griffin III 2.00 5.00
2 A.J. Jenkins 1.50 4.00
3 Alshon Jeffery 3.00 8.00
4 Andrew Luck 12.00 30.00
5 Bernard Pierce 1.50 4.00
6 Brandon Weeden 1.50 4.00
7 Brian Quick 1.50 4.00
8 Brock Osweiler 1.50 4.00
9 Chris Givens 1.50 4.00
10 Coby Fleener 1.50 4.00
12 DeVier Posey 1.50 4.00
13 Doug Martin 2.50 6.00
14 Dwayne Allen 1.50 4.00
15 Isaiah Pead 1.50 4.00
16 Jarius Wright 1.50 4.00
17 Joe Adams 1.50 4.00
18 Justin Blackmon 1.50 4.00
19 Kendall Wright 1.50 4.00
20 Lamar Miller 2.50 6.00
21 LaMichael James 1.50 4.00
22 Michael Egnew 1.50 4.00
23 Michael Floyd 1.50 4.00
24 Mohamed Sanu 2.50 6.00
25 Nick Foles 4.00 10.00
26 Nick Toon 1.50 4.00
27 Robert Turbin 1.50 4.00
28 Ronnie Hillman 1.50 4.00
30 Russell Wilson 8.00 20.00
31 Ryan Broyles 1.50 4.00
32 Ryan Tannehill 2.50 6.00
33 Stephen Hill 1.50 4.00
34 T.J. Graham 1.50 4.00
35 Trent Richardson 1.50 4.00

2012 Absolute Star Gazing Materials Autographs

*PRIME/25: .5X TO 1.2X BASIC JSY AU/49
1 Robert Griffin III 6.00 15.00
2 A.J. Jenkins 5.00 12.00
3 Alshon Jeffery 10.00 25.00
4 Andrew Luck 100.00 200.00
5 Bernard Pierce 5.00 12.00
6 Brandon Weeden 5.00 12.00
7 Brian Quick 5.00 12.00
8 Brock Osweiler 5.00 12.00
9 Chris Givens 5.00 12.00
10 Coby Fleener 5.00 12.00
11 David Wilson 5.00 12.00
12 DeVier Posey 5.00 12.00
13 Doug Martin 8.00 20.00
14 Dwayne Allen 5.00 12.00
15 Isaiah Pead 5.00 12.00
16 Jarius Wright 5.00 12.00
17 Joe Adams 5.00 12.00
18 Justin Blackmon 5.00 12.00
19 Kendall Wright 5.00 12.00
20 Lamar Miller 8.00 20.00
21 LaMichael James 5.00 12.00
22 Michael Egnew 5.00 12.00
23 Michael Floyd 5.00 12.00
24 Mohamed Sanu 8.00 20.00
25 Nick Foles 30.00 60.00
26 Nick Toon 5.00 12.00
27 Robert Turbin 5.00 12.00
28 Ronnie Hillman 5.00 12.00
29 Rueben Randle 5.00 12.00
30 Russell Wilson EXCH 60.00 120.00
31 Ryan Broyles 5.00 12.00
32 Ryan Tannehill 8.00 20.00
33 Stephen Hill 5.00 12.00
34 T.J. Graham 5.00 12.00
35 Trent Richardson 5.00 12.00

2012 Absolute Team Quads Materials Die Cut

2 Bryant/Witten/Austin/Romo/50 20.00 40.00

2012 Absolute Team Quads Materials Die Cut Spectrum Prime

2 Bryant/Witten/Austin/Romo/25
3 Bradshaw/Rolle/Manning/Nicks/25 25.00 50.00
10 Bowe/Charles/Cassel/Hali/15 12.00 30.00

2012 Absolute Team Tandems Materials

*PRIME/25: .6X TO 1.5X TANDEM JSY/50
*PRIME/25: .5X TO 1.2X TANDEM JSY/15-25
1 M.Ryan/R.White/50 5.00 12.00
3 H.Ngata/T.Suggs/20 10.00 25.00
4 D.Williams/S.Smith/25 6.00 15.00
7 D.Murray/F.Jones/25 6.00 15.00
8 D.Bryant/T.Romo/50 6.00 15.00
9 J.Elway/T.Davis/50 12.00 30.00
10 C.Johnson/M.Stafford/25 8.00 20.00
11 A.Rodgers/D.Driver/15
14 D.Bowe/J.Charles/25 6.00 15.00
15 T.Brady/W.Welker/50 12.00 30.00
16 D.Brees/M.Colston/50 6.00 15.00
17 E.Manning/H.Nicks/50 8.00 20.00
18 K.Johnson/W.Chrebet/50 6.00 15.00
19 D.Jackson/J.Maclin/50 5.00 12.00
21 P.Rivers/R.Mathews/50 6.00 15.00
24 L.Fletcher/S.Moss/50 6.00 15.00
25 B.Wells/L.Fitzgerald/50 5.00 12.00
26 M.Turner/T.Gonzalez/20 6.00 15.00
27 J.Gresham/J.Shipley/50 4.00 10.00
29 S.Bradford/S.Jackson/50 4.00 10.00
30 C.Johnson/M.Griffin/50 4.00 10.00

2012 Absolute Team Trios Materials

*PRIME/24-25: .6X TO 1.5X TRIO/49-75
2 Bryant/Austin/Romo/75 8.00 20.00
6 Brees/Colston/Thomas/75 8.00 20.00
7 Bradshaw/Manning/Nicks/50 10.00 25.00
8 Maclin/McCoy/Vick/49 8.00 20.00
10 Floyd/Rivers/Mathews/75 8.00 20.00

2012 Absolute Tools of the Trade Double Material Black

1 Antonio Gates/25 5.00 12.00
4 Haloti Ngata/25 4.00 10.00
5 Ray Lewis/50 5.00 12.00
6 Terrell Suggs/50 3.00 8.00
10 Devin Hester/20 5.00 12.00
11 Lance Briggs/25 5.00 12.00
13 Jordan Shipley/50 3.00 8.00
14 Jermaine Gresham/25 4.00 10.00
16 Miles Austin/50 3.00 8.00
17 Felix Jones/50 3.00 8.00
18 Jay Ratliff/50 4.00 10.00
19 Jason Witten/50 4.00 10.00
20 Jamaal Charles/50 4.00 10.00
22 Matt Cassel/50 3.00 8.00
23 Dwayne Bowe/25 5.00 12.00
27 Marques Colston/50 3.00 8.00
28 Devery Henderson/50 3.00 8.00
29 Hakeem Nicks/50 3.00 8.00
31 DeSean Jackson/50 4.00 10.00
32 Jeremy Maclin/50 3.00 8.00

2012 Absolute Tools of the Trade Double Material Black Prime

2 Tony Gonzalez/25 5.00 12.00
9 Jon Beason/15 4.00 10.00
16 Miles Austin/25 4.00 10.00
17 Felix Jones/25 4.00 10.00
19 Jason Witten/25 5.00 12.00
20 Jamaal Charles/25 5.00 12.00
27 Marques Colston/25 4.00 10.00
28 Devery Henderson/25 4.00 10.00
29 Hakeem Nicks/25 4.00 10.00
32 Jeremy Maclin/15 4.00 10.00
35 Chris Johnson/25 4.00 10.00

2012 Absolute Tools of the Trade Double Material Autographs Black

13 Jordan Shipley/20
14 Jermaine Gresham/25
16 Miles Austin/25 12.00 30.00
17 Felix Jones/25 8.00 20.00
22 Matt Cassel/25 8.00 20.00
27 Marques Colston/25 8.00 20.00
28 Devery Henderson/25 8.00 20.00
31 DeSean Jackson/25 10.00 25.00
32 Jeremy Maclin/25 8.00 20.00

2012 Absolute Tools of the Trade Material Black Prime

1 Antonio Gates/25 5.00 12.00
4 Tony Gonzalez/25 5.00 12.00
12 Jon Beason/25 4.00 10.00
18 DeMarcus Ware/20 6.00 15.00
19 Dez Bryant/50 6.00 15.00
20 Miles Austin/50 5.00 12.00
22 Felix Jones/50 3.00 8.00
23 Tony Romo/50 4.00 10.00
26 Jamaal Charles/50 4.00 10.00
31 Roman Harper/50 3.00 8.00
32 Marques Colston/50 3.00 8.00
33 Devery Henderson/50 3.00 8.00
34 Antrel Rolle/50 3.00 8.00
35 Hakeem Nicks/50 3.00 8.00
36 Darrelle Revis/25 4.00 10.00
37 DeSean Jackson/25 5.00 12.00
38 Jeremy Maclin/15 4.00 10.00
41 Heath Miller/25 4.00 10.00
46 Chris Johnson/50 3.00 8.00
47 Michael Griffin/25 4.00 10.00
49 London Fletcher/50 6.00 15.00
50 Brian Orakpo/50 5.00 12.00

2012 Absolute Tools of the Trade Material Autographs Black Prime

12 Jon Beason/25 10.00 25.00
14 Devin Hester/20 12.00 30.00
18 DeMarcus Ware/20 25.00 50.00
19 Dez Bryant/25 15.00 40.00
22 Felix Jones/25 10.00 25.00
33 Devery Henderson/25 EXCH 10.00 25.00
41 Heath Miller/25 10.00 25.00
49 London Fletcher/25 25.00 50.00
50 Brian Orakpo/25 12.00 30.00

2012 Absolute War Room Materials

*WAR ROOM: .4X TO 1X STAR GAZING JSY
*WR PRIME/49: .6X TO 1.5X STAR GAZING

2012 Absolute War Room Materials Autographs

*WAR ROOM/49: .4X TO 1X STAR GAZING/49
*PRIME/25: .5X TO 1.2X BASIC JSY AU/49

2013 Absolute

*ROOKIE/99: .5X TO 1.2X ROOKIE/199
1-200 ROOKIE PRINT RUN 99-499
EXCH EXPIRATION: 5/1/2015
1 Carson Palmer .30 .75
2 Larry Fitzgerald .30 .75
3 Rashard Mendenhall .25 .60
4 Matt Ryan .30 .75
5 Julio Jones .40 1.00
6 Steven Jackson .25 .60
7 Tony Gonzalez .30 .75
8 Joe Flacco .30 .75
9 Torrey Smith .25 .60
10 Jacoby Jones .25 .60
11 Ray Rice .25 .60
12 Fred Jackson .30 .75
13 Steve Johnson .30 .75
14 C.J. Spiller .25 .60
15 Cam Newton .40 1.00
16 Steve Smith .30 .75
17 Jonathan Stewart .25 .60
18 Jay Cutler .25 .60
19 Brandon Marshall .30 .75
20 Matt Forte .25 .60
21 Andy Dalton .30 .75
22 A.J. Green .40 1.00
23 BenJarvus Green-Ellis .30 .75
24 Brandon Weeden .25 .60
25 Josh Gordon .25 .60
26 Trent Richardson .25 .60
27 Tony Romo .30 .75
28 Dez Bryant .40 1.00
29 DeMarco Murray .30 .75
30 Jason Witten .30 .75
31 Peyton Manning .75 2.00
32 Wes Welker .30 .75
33 Demaryius Thomas .30 .75
34 Matthew Stafford .30 .75
35 Calvin Johnson .40 1.00
36 Reggie Bush .25 .60
37 Aaron Rodgers .60 1.50
38 Jordy Nelson .30 .75
39 James Jones .25 .60
40 Matt Schaub .25 .60
41 Andre Johnson .25 .60
42 Arian Foster .30 .75
43 Andrew Luck .60 1.50
44 Reggie Wayne .30 .75
45 Ahmad Bradshaw .25 .60
46 Blaine Gabbert .25 .60
47 Justin Blackmon .25 .60
48 Maurice Jones-Drew .25 .60
49 Alex Smith .30 .75
50 Dwayne Bowe .30 .75
51 Jamaal Charles .30 .75
52 Ryan Tannehill .30 .75
53 Mike Wallace .25 .60
54 Lamar Miller .25 .60
55 Christian Ponder .25 .60
56 Greg Jennings .25 .60
57 Adrian Peterson .40 1.00
58 Tom Brady 1.00 2.50
59 Danny Amendola .30 .75
60 Rob Gronkowski .40 1.00
61 Drew Brees .40 1.00
62 Marques Colston .25 .60
63 Mark Ingram .30 .75
64 Eli Manning .30 .75
65 Hakeem Nicks .25 .60
66 David Wilson .25 .60
67 Mark Sanchez .25 .60
68 Santonio Holmes .25 .60
69 Chris Ivory .30 .75
70 Matt Flynn .25 .60
71 Denarius Moore .25 .60
72 Darren McFadden .30 .75
73 Michael Vick .30 .75
74 Jeremy Maclin .25 .60
75 LeSean McCoy .40 1.00
76 Ben Roethlisberger .40 1.00
77 Antonio Brown .40 1.00
78 Troy Polamalu .40 1.00
79 Philip Rivers .40 1.00
80 Antonio Gates .30 .75
81 Ryan Mathews .30 .75
82 Colin Kaepernick .30 .75
83 Anquan Boldin .25 .60
84 Frank Gore .30 .75
85 Vernon Davis .25 .60
86 Russell Wilson .75 2.00
87 Percy Harvin .25 .60
88 Marshawn Lynch .30 .75
89 Sam Bradford .25 .60
90 Chris Givens .25 .60
91 Jared Cook .25 .60
92 Josh Freeman .30 .75
93 Vincent Jackson .25 .60
94 Doug Martin .30 .75
95 Jake Locker .30 .75
96 Kenny Britt .25 .60
97 Chris Johnson .25 .60
98 Robert Griffin III .25 .60
99 Pierre Garcon .30 .75
100 Alfred Morris .25 .60
101A Aaron Dobson/199 RC 1.00 2.50
102 Aaron Mellette/499 RC .75 2.00
103A Ace Sanders/499 RC .75 2.00
104 Alec Ogletree/499 RC .75 2.00
105 Alex Okafor/499 RC .75 2.00
106A Andre Ellington/199 RC 1.00 2.50
107 Arthur Brown/499 RC .75 2.00
108A Barkevious Mingo/499 RC .75 2.00
109 Bjoern Werner/499 RC .75 2.00
110 Brice Butler/499 RC .75 2.00
111 Chris Gragg/499 RC .75 2.00
112 Chris Harper/499 RC .75 2.00
113A Christine Michael/199 RC 1.00 2.50
114 Cornellius Carradine/499 RC .75 2.00
115 Conner Vernon/499 RC .75 2.00
116A Cordarrelle Patterson/199 RC 1.00 2.50
117 Corey Fuller/499 RC .75 2.00
118 Damontre Moore/499 RC .75 2.00
119 Jeff Tuel/499 RC .75 2.00
120 Darius Slay/499 RC .75 2.00
121 Datone Jones/499 RC .75 2.00
122A DeAndre Hopkins/199 RC 2.50 6.00
123A Dee Milliner/499 RC .75 2.00
124A Denard Robinson/199 RC 1.00 2.50
125 Dennis Johnson/499 RC .75 2.00
126 Desmond Trufant/499 RC .75 2.00
127A Dion Jordan/199 RC 1.00 2.50
128 Dion Sims/499 RC .75 2.00
129A Eddie Lacy/199 RC 1.00 2.50
130A EJ Manuel/199 RC 1.00 2.50
131A Dustin Hopkins/499 RC .75 2.00
131B Charles Hawkins/99 RC 1.25 3.00
132 Eric Reid/499 RC 1.00 2.50
133 Ezekiel Ansah/499 RC .75 2.00
134A Gavin Escobar/199 RC 1.00 2.50
135A Geno Smith/199 RC 1.00 2.50
136A Giovani Bernard/199 RC 1.00 2.50
137 Jamar Taylor/499 RC .75 2.00
138A Jarvis Jones/499 RC .75 2.00
139 Earl Wolff/499 RC 1.25 3.00
140 Jawan Jamison/499 RC .75 2.00
141 Johnathan Cyprien/499 RC .75 2.00
142A Johnathan Franklin/199 RC 1.00 2.50
143 Johnthan Banks/499 RC .75 2.00
144 Jordan Poyer/499 RC .75 2.00
145A Jordan Reed/199 RC 1.50 4.00
146A Joseph Randle/199 RC 1.00 2.50
147A Josh Boyce/499 RC .75 2.00
148A Justin Hunter/199 RC 1.00 2.50
149A Keenan Allen/199 RC 2.00 5.00
150A Kenjon Barner/499 RC .75 2.00
151A Kenny Stills/199 RC 1.00 2.50
152 Kenny Vaccaro/499 RC .75 2.00
153 Kerwynn Williams/499 RC .75 2.00
154 Kevin Minter/499 RC .75 2.00
155A Knile Davis/199 RC 1.00 2.50
156A Landry Jones/199 RC 1.00 2.50
157A Le'Veon Bell/199 RC 3.00 8.00
158 Jon Bostic/499 RC .75 2.00
159A Manti Te'o/199 RC 1.25 3.00
160 Justin Brown/499 RC 1.25 3.00
161A Marcus Lattimore/199 RC 1.00 2.50
162 Margus Hunt/499 RC .75 2.00
163A Markus Wheaton/199 RC 1.00 2.50
164 Marquess Wilson/499 RC 1.25 3.00
165A Marquise Goodwin/199 RC 1.00 2.50
166A Matt Barkley/199 RC 1.00 2.50
167 Matt Elam/499 RC .75 2.00
168 Matt Scott/499 RC .75 2.00
169A Mike Gillislee/199 RC 1.00 2.50
170A Mike Glennon/199 RC 1.00 2.50
171A Montee Ball/199 RC 1.00 2.50
172 Nick Kasa/499 RC .75 2.00
173 Onterio McCalebb/499 RC 1.00 2.50
174 Phillip Thomas/499 RC .75 2.00
175A Quinton Patton/199 RC 1.00 2.50
176A Rex Burkhead/499 RC 1.00 2.50
177A Robert Woods/199 RC 1.50 4.00
178 Rodney Smith/499 RC .75 2.00
179A Ryan Nassib/199 RC 1.00 2.50
180 Ryan Otten/499 RC .75 2.00
181 Latavius Murray/499 RC 1.00 2.50
182 Sam Montgomery/499 RC .75 2.00
183 Robert Alford/499 RC .75 2.00
184 Alan Bonner/499 RC .75 2.00
185 Kenbrell Thompkins/499 RC 1.25 3.00
186A Stedman Bailey/199 RC 1.00 2.50
187A Stepfan Taylor/199 RC 1.00 2.50
188 Tavarres King/499 RC .75 2.00
189A Tavon Austin/199 RC 1.25 3.00
190A Terrance Williams/199 RC 1.00 2.50
191 Theo Riddick/499 RC .75 2.00
192 Travis Kelce/499 RC 2.00 5.00
193 Tyler Bray/499 RC .75 2.00
194A Tyler Eifert/199 RC 1.00 2.50
195A Tyler Wilson/199 RC 1.00 2.50
196A Tyrann Mathieu/499 RC 1.25 3.00
197A Vance McDonald/199 RC 1.25 3.00
198 Xavier Rhodes/499 RC .75 2.00
199A Zac Dysert/499 RC .75 2.00
200A Zach Ertz/199 RC 2.00 5.00
201 Aaron Dobson JSY AU 3.00 8.00
202 Andre Ellington JSY AU 3.00 8.00
203 Christine Michael JSY AU 3.00 8.00
204 Cordarrelle Patterson JSY AU 3.00 8.00
205 DeAndre Hopkins JSY AU 8.00 20.00
206 Denard Robinson JSY AU 3.00 8.00
207 Dion Jordan JSY AU 3.00 8.00
208 Eddie Lacy JSY AU 3.00 8.00
209 EJ Manuel JSY AU 3.00 8.00
210 Gavin Escobar JSY AU 3.00 8.00
211 Geno Smith JSY AU 3.00 8.00
212 Giovani Bernard JSY AU 3.00 8.00
213 Johnathan Franklin JSY AU 3.00 8.00
214 Jordan Reed JSY AU 5.00 12.00
215 Joseph Randle JSY AU 3.00 8.00
216 Justin Hunter JSY AU 3.00 8.00
217 Keenan Allen JSY AU 6.00 15.00
218 Kenny Stills JSY AU 3.00 8.00
219 Knile Davis JSY AU 3.00 8.00
220 Landry Jones JSY AU 3.00 8.00
221 Le'Veon Bell JSY AU 10.00 25.00
222 Manti Te'o JSY AU 4.00 10.00
223 Marcus Lattimore JSY AU 3.00 8.00
224 Markus Wheaton JSY AU 3.00 8.00
225 Marquise Goodwin JSY AU 3.00 8.00
226 Matt Barkley JSY AU 3.00 8.00
227 Mike Gillislee JSY AU 3.00 8.00
228 Mike Glennon JSY AU 3.00 8.00
229 Montee Ball JSY AU 3.00 8.00
230 Quinton Patton JSY AU 3.00 8.00
231 Robert Woods JSY AU 5.00 12.00
232 Ryan Nassib JSY AU 6.00 15.00
233 Stedman Bailey JSY AU 3.00 8.00
234 Stepfan Taylor JSY AU 3.00 8.00
235 Tavon Austin JSY AU 4.00 10.00
236 Terrance Williams JSY AU 3.00 8.00
237 Tyler Eifert JSY AU 3.00 8.00
238 Tyler Wilson JSY AU 3.00 8.00
239 Vance McDonald JSY AU 4.00 10.00
240 Zach Ertz JSY AU 6.00 15.00

2013 Absolute Spectrum Black

*1-100 VETS/49: 2.5X TO 6X BASIC CARDS
*101-200 ROOKIE/49: .8X TO 2X BASIC RC/499
*101-200 ROOKIE/49: .6X TO 1.5X BASIC RC/199
*101-200 ROOKIE/49: .5X TO 1.2X ROOKIE/99

2013 Absolute Spectrum Blue Retail

*1-100 VETS: 2X TO 5X BASIC CARDS
*101-200 ROOKIE: .6X TO 1.5X BASIC RC/499
*101-200 ROOKIE: .5X TO 1.2X BASIC RC/199
*101-200 ROOKIE: .4X TO 1X ROOKIE/99
STATED ODDS 1:8 WAL-MART PACKS

2013 Absolute Spectrum Blue Autographs
*BLUE/30: .8X TO 2X SILVER/299-499
*BLUE/30: .5X TO 1.2X SILVER/99

2013 Absolute Spectrum Gold
*1-100 VETS/25: 4X TO 10X BASIC CARDS
*101-200 ROOKIE/25: 1.2X TO 3X BASIC RC/499
*101-200 ROOKIE/25: 1X TO 2.5X BASIC RC/199
*101-200 ROOKIE/25: .8X TO 2X ROOKIE/99

2013 Absolute Spectrum Gold Autographs
*GOLD/25: .8X TO 2X SILVER/299-499
*GOLD/25: .5X TO 1.2X SILVER/99
106 Andre Ellington 8.00 20.00
126 Desmond Trufant 4.00 10.00
138 Jarvis Jones 4.00 10.00
143 Johnthan Banks 4.00 10.00
150 Kenjon Barner 4.00 10.00
171 Montee Ball 4.00 10.00
195 Tyler Wilson 4.00 10.00

2013 Absolute Spectrum Red Retail
*1-100 VETS: 1.5X TO 4X BASIC CARDS
*101-200 ROOKIE: .5X TO 1.2X BASIC RC/499
*101-200 ROOKIE: .4X TO 1X BASIC RC/199
*101-200 ROOKIE: .3X TO .8X ROOKIE/99

2013 Absolute Spectrum Red Autographs
*RED/30: .8X TO 2X SILVER/299-499
*RED/30: .5X TO 1.2X SILVER/99

2013 Absolute Spectrum Silver
*1-100 VETS/99: 2X TO 5X BASIC CARDS
*101-200 ROOKIE/99: .6X TO 1.5X BASIC RC/499
*101-200 ROOKIE/99: .5X TO 1.2X BASIC RC/199
*101-200 ROOKIE/99: .4X TO 1X ROOKIE/99

2013 Absolute Spectrum Silver Autographs
101 Aaron Dobson/99 3.00 8.00
102 Aaron Mellette/499 2.00 5.00
103 Ace Sanders/299 4.00 10.00
105 Alex Okafor/499 2.00 5.00
107 Arthur Brown/299 2.00 5.00
109 Bjoern Werner/499 2.00 5.00
110 Brice Butler/499 4.00 10.00
111 Chris Gragg/299 2.50 6.00
112 Chris Harper/499 2.00 5.00
113 Christine Michael/99 3.00 8.00
114 Cornellius Carradine/499 2.00 5.00
115 Conner Vernon/499 2.00 5.00
116 Cordarrelle Patterson/99 3.00 8.00
117 Corey Fuller/399 2.00 5.00
118 Damontre Moore/299 2.00 5.00
119 Jeff Tuel/499 8.00 20.00
120 Darius Slay/499 2.00 5.00
122 DeAndre Hopkins/99 8.00 20.00
125 Dennis Johnson/499 2.00 5.00
127 Dion Jordan/99 3.00 8.00
129 Eddie Lacy/99 3.00 8.00
130 EJ Manuel/99 3.00 8.00
131 Dustin Hopkins/399 2.00 5.00
133 Ezekiel Ansah/299 2.00 5.00
134 Gavin Escobar/99 3.00 8.00
137 Jamar Taylor/499 2.00 5.00
139 Earl Wolff/499 3.00 8.00
140 Jawan Jamison/499 2.00 5.00
141 Johnathan Cyprien/499 2.00 5.00
142 Johnathan Franklin/99 3.00 8.00
145 Jordan Reed/499 6.00 15.00
146 Joseph Randle/99 3.00 8.00
147 Josh Boyce/299 2.00 5.00
149 Keenan Allen/99 6.00 15.00
151 Kenny Stills/99 3.00 8.00
152 Kenny Vaccaro/299 2.00 5.00
153 Kerwynn Williams/299 EXCH 2.00 5.00
155 Knile Davis/99 3.00 8.00
156 Landry Jones/99 3.00 8.00
157 Le'Veon Bell/99 15.00 40.00
158 Jon Bostic/499 6.00 15.00
159 Manti Te'o/99 4.00 10.00
160 Justin Brown/499 3.00 8.00
161 Marcus Lattimore/99 3.00 8.00
162 Margus Hunt/299 2.00 5.00
163 Markus Wheaton/99 3.00 8.00
164 Marquess Wilson/299 3.00 8.00
165 Marquise Goodwin/99 3.00 8.00
166 Matt Barkley/99 8.00 20.00
167 Matt Elam/299 2.00 5.00
168 Matt Scott/299 2.00 5.00
169 Mike Gillislee/99 3.00 8.00
170 Mike Glennon/99 3.00 8.00
172 Nick Kasa/299 2.00 5.00
173 Onterio McCalebb/299 2.50 6.00
175 Quinton Patton/99 3.00 8.00
176 Rex Burkhead/299 2.50 6.00
177 Robert Woods/99 5.00 12.00
178 Rodney Smith/299 2.00 5.00
179 Ryan Nassib/99 3.00 8.00
180 Ryan Otten/499 2.00 5.00
181 Latavius Murray/499 8.00 20.00
183 Robert Alford/499 2.00 5.00
184 Alan Bonner/499 2.00 5.00
185 Kenbrell Thompkins/499 3.00 8.00
187 Stepfan Taylor/99 3.00 8.00
188 Tavarres King/499 2.00 5.00
190 Terrance Williams/99 3.00 8.00
191 Theo Riddick/499 2.00 5.00
193 Tyler Bray/499 2.00 5.00
196 Tyrann Mathieu/299 8.00 20.00
197 Vance McDonald/99 4.00 10.00
198 Xavier Rhodes/299 2.00 5.00
199 Zac Dysert/299 2.00 5.00
200 Zach Ertz/99 6.00 15.00

2013 Absolute Absolute Ink Spectrum Silver
STATED PRINT RUN 25 SER.#'d SETS
*BASE AU/49-99: .3X TO .8X SILVER AU/25
3 Alex Smith 30.00 60.00
5 Alshon Jeffery 12.00 30.00
6 Andrew Hawkins 6.00 15.00
7 Andrew Luck 40.00 100.00
11 Brandon Pettigrew 6.00 15.00
12 Bryce Brown 8.00 20.00
15 Chris Givens 6.00 15.00
16 Chris Ivory 8.00 20.00
17 Clay Matthews 30.00 60.00
18 Colin Kaepernick 8.00 20.00
19 David Wilson 6.00 15.00
20 Demaryius Thomas 8.00 20.00
21 Doug Martin 8.00 20.00
22 Golden Tate 6.00 15.00
23 Jacquizz Rodgers 8.00 20.00
24 Jay Cutler 6.00 15.00
25 Jeremy Maclin 6.00 15.00
27 Leonard Hankerson 6.00 15.00
28 Luke Kuechly 12.00 30.00
29 Mark Ingram 8.00 20.00
33 Maurice Jones-Drew 6.00 15.00
34 Michael Vick 12.00 30.00
35 Patrick Peterson 6.00 15.00
38 Randall Cobb 10.00 25.00
39 Rashard Mendenhall 6.00 15.00
41 Robert Griffin III 6.00 15.00
43 Ryan Broyles 8.00 20.00
44 Ryan Mathews 8.00 20.00
45 Ryan Tannehill 15.00 40.00
46 T.Y. Hilton 8.00 20.00
50 Von Miller 10.00 25.00

2013 Absolute Hogg Heaven
STATED ODDS 1:1 HOB, 1:8 RET
*BOSS HOGG/99: .8X TO 2X BASIC INSERTS
1 Larry Fitzgerald .75 2.00
2 Matt Ryan .75 2.00
3 Julio Jones 1.00 2.50
4 Joe Flacco .75 2.00
5 Ray Rice .60 1.50
6 C.J. Spiller .60 1.50
7 Cam Newton 1.00 2.50
8 Jay Cutler .60 1.50
9 Brandon Marshall .75 2.00
10 A.J. Green 1.00 2.50
11 Trent Richardson .60 1.50
12 Tony Romo .75 2.00
13 Dez Bryant 1.00 2.50
14 Peyton Manning 2.00 5.00
15 Wes Welker .75 2.00
16 Sam Bradford .60 1.50
17 Matthew Stafford .75 2.00
18 Calvin Johnson 1.00 2.50
19 Aaron Rodgers 1.50 4.00
20 Jordy Nelson .75 2.00
21 Andre Johnson .60 1.50
22 Arian Foster .75 2.00
23 Andrew Luck 1.50 4.00
24 Reggie Wayne .75 2.00
25 Justin Blackmon .60 1.50
26 Maurice Jones-Drew .60 1.50
27 Jamaal Charles .75 2.00
28 Ryan Tannehill .75 2.00
29 Mike Wallace .60 1.50
30 Greg Jennings .60 1.50
31 Adrian Peterson 1.00 2.50
32 Tom Brady 2.50 6.00
33 Danny Amendola .75 2.00
34 Doug Martin .75 2.00
35 Drew Brees 1.00 2.50
36 Eli Manning .75 2.00
37 Chris Johnson .60 1.50
38 Chris Ivory .75 2.00
39 Darren McFadden .75 2.00
40 Michael Vick .75 2.00
41 LeSean McCoy 1.00 2.50
42 Ben Roethlisberger 1.00 2.50
43 Antonio Brown 1.00 2.50
44 Philip Rivers 1.00 2.50
45 Antonio Gates .75 2.00
46 Colin Kaepernick .75 2.00
47 Anquan Boldin .60 1.50
48 Russell Wilson 2.00 5.00
49 Percy Harvin .60 1.50
50 Alfred Morris .60 1.50
51 Robert Griffin III .60 1.50
52 Terrance Williams .50 1.25
53 Tavon Austin .60 1.50
54 Stepfan Taylor .50 1.25
55 Stedman Bailey .50 1.25
56 Ryan Nassib .50 1.25
57 Aaron Dobson .50 1.25
58 Andre Ellington .50 1.25
59 Tyler Eifert .50 1.25
60 Christine Michael .50 1.25
61 Cordarrelle Patterson .50 1.25
62 DeAndre Hopkins 1.25 3.00
63 Tyler Wilson .50 1.25
64 Denard Robinson .50 1.25
65 Dion Jordan .50 1.25
66 Eddie Lacy .50 1.25
67 EJ Manuel .50 1.25
68 Gavin Escobar .50 1.25
69 Geno Smith .50 1.25
70 Giovani Bernard .50 1.25
71 Johnathan Franklin .50 1.25
72 Tyrann Mathieu .75 2.00
73 Joseph Randle .50 1.25
74 Justin Hunter .50 1.25
75 Keenan Allen 1.00 2.50
76 Kenjon Barner .50 1.25
77 Kenny Stills .50 1.25
78 Knile Davis .50 1.25
79 Landry Jones .50 1.25
80 Le'Veon Bell 1.50 4.00
81 Manti Te'o .60 1.50
82 Marcus Lattimore .50 1.25
83 Markus Wheaton .50 1.25
84 Marquise Goodwin .50 1.25
85 Matt Barkley .50 1.25
86 Mike Gillislee .50 1.25
87 Mike Glennon .50 1.25
88 Montee Ball .50 1.25
89 Quinton Patton .50 1.25
90 Robert Woods .75 2.00

2013 Absolute Leather and Laces Football
*SHOES/25: .4X TO 1X FOOTBALL/25
1 Aaron Dobson 3.00 8.00
2 Andre Ellington 3.00 8.00
3 Christine Michael 3.00 8.00
4 Cordarrelle Patterson 3.00 8.00
5 DeAndre Hopkins 8.00 20.00
6 Denard Robinson 3.00 8.00
7 Dion Jordan 3.00 8.00
8 Eddie Lacy 3.00 8.00
9 EJ Manuel 3.00 8.00
10 Gavin Escobar 3.00 8.00
11 Geno Smith 3.00 8.00
12 Giovani Bernard 3.00 8.00
13 Johnathan Franklin 3.00 8.00
14 Jordan Reed 5.00 12.00
15 Joseph Randle 3.00 8.00
16 Justin Hunter 3.00 8.00
17 Keenan Allen 6.00 15.00
18 Kenny Stills 3.00 8.00
19 Knile Davis 3.00 8.00
20 Landry Jones 3.00 8.00
21 Le'Veon Bell 10.00 25.00
22 Manti Te'o 4.00 10.00
23 Marcus Lattimore 3.00 8.00
24 Markus Wheaton 3.00 8.00
25 Marquise Goodwin 3.00 8.00
26 Matt Barkley 3.00 8.00
27 Mike Gillislee 3.00 8.00
28 Mike Glennon 3.00 8.00
29 Montee Ball 3.00 8.00
30 Quinton Patton 3.00 8.00
31 Robert Woods 5.00 12.00
32 Ryan Nassib 3.00 8.00
33 Stedman Bailey 3.00 8.00
34 Stepfan Taylor 3.00 8.00
35 Tavon Austin 4.00 10.00
36 Terrance Williams 3.00 8.00
37 Tyler Eifert 3.00 8.00
38 Tyler Wilson 3.00 8.00
39 Vance McDonald 4.00 10.00
40 Zach Ertz 6.00 15.00

2013 Absolute Patches Team Logos
1 A.J. Green/25 20.00 50.00
2 Adrian Peterson/25 75.00 150.00
3 Alfred Morris/25 12.00 30.00
4 Andrew Luck/25
5 Andy Dalton/25 20.00 50.00
6 Antonio Gates/25
7 Arian Foster/25
9 C.J. Spiller/25 12.00 30.00
12 Cameron Wake/25
13 Champ Bailey/25 15.00 40.00
14 Chris Johnson/25 12.00 30.00
15 Colin Kaepernick/25 15.00 40.00
16 Dez Bryant/25 20.00 50.00
17 Doug Martin/25 15.00 40.00
18 Drew Brees/25 40.00 80.00
19 Haloti Ngata /25 20.00 50.00
20 Jamaal Charles/25
21 Jason Witten/25 15.00 40.00
22 Jimmy Graham/25 20.00 50.00
23 Joe Flacco/25 15.00 40.00
24 Kam Chancellor/25 25.00 60.00
25 Lardarius Webb/25
26 Larry Fitzgerald/25 15.00 40.00
27 Matt Schaub/25 12.00 30.00
30 Philip Rivers/20
31 Ray Rice/25
32 Reggie Wayne/25 15.00 40.00
34 Russell Wilson/25 30.00 80.00
35 Ryan Tannehill/25
36 Sam Bradford/25 12.00 30.00
37 Torrey Smith/25 12.00 30.00
38 Trent Richardson/25
39 Terrell Suggs/25 12.00 30.00
40 Von Miller/25 15.00 40.00

2013 Absolute Plates and Patches Autographs
1 Golden Tate/25 25.00 50.00
3 Jared Allen/25 25.00 50.00
5 Jay Cutler/25 25.00 50.00
6 Nate Washington/25 8.00 20.00
7 Ryan Tannehill/25 15.00 40.00
9 Greg Olsen/25 10.00 25.00
10 Dexter McCluster/25 8.00 20.00
12 Darren McFadden/25 20.00 40.00
13 Demaryius Thomas/25 12.00 30.00
14 Justin Blackmon/25 8.00 20.00
15 Kyle Rudolph/25 8.00 20.00
17 Maurice Jones-Drew/25 8.00 20.00
18 Robert Griffin III/25 8.00 20.00
19 Ryan Mathews/25 10.00 25.00
21 Kenny Britt/25
22 Michael Crabtree/25 15.00 30.00
23 Michael Vick/25 20.00 40.00
26 Jake Plummer/25 15.00 30.00
29 Amani Toomer/25 8.00 20.00
30 Keyshawn Johnson/25
31 LaDainian Tomlinson/25 15.00 30.00
33 Bill Romanowski/25 30.00 60.00
34 Bruce Smith/25 30.00 60.00
36 Ronde Barber/25 20.00 40.00
37 Shaun Alexander/25 15.00 30.00
38 Fred Taylor/25 15.00 30.00
39 Ted Hendricks/25 20.00 40.00
40 Steve Largent/20 25.00 50.00

2013 Absolute Retail
*1-100 VETS: .3X TO .8X HOBBY
*101-200 ROOKIE/499: .4X TO 1X RC/499
*101-200 ROOKIE/199: .4X TO 1X RC/199
*101-200 ROOK/99: .4X TO 1X HOBBY/99
1-200 ROOKIE PRINT RUN 99-499
RETAIL PRINTED ON WHITE STOCK

2013 Absolute Rookie Jersey Collection
STATED ODDS 1:8 WAL-MART PACKS
1 Aaron Dobson 1.50 4.00
2 Andre Ellington 1.50 4.00
3 Christine Michael 1.50 4.00
4 Cordarrelle Patterson 1.50 4.00
5 DeAndre Hopkins 4.00 10.00
6 Denard Robinson 1.50 4.00
7 Dion Jordan 1.50 4.00
8 Eddie Lacy 1.50 4.00
9 EJ Manuel 1.50 4.00
10 Gavin Escobar 1.50 4.00
11 Geno Smith 1.50 4.00
12 Giovani Bernard 1.50 4.00
13 Johnathan Franklin 1.50 4.00
14 Jordan Reed 2.50 6.00
15 Joseph Randle 1.50 4.00
16 Justin Hunter 1.50 4.00
17 Keenan Allen 3.00 8.00
18 Kenny Stills 1.50 4.00
19 Knile Davis 1.50 4.00
20 Landry Jones 1.50 4.00
21 Le'Veon Bell 5.00 12.00
22 Manti Te'o 2.00 5.00
23 Marcus Lattimore 1.50 4.00
24 Markus Wheaton 1.50 4.00
25 Marquise Goodwin 1.50 4.00
26 Matt Barkley 1.50 4.00
27 Mike Gillislee 1.50 4.00
28 Mike Glennon 1.50 4.00
29 Montee Ball 1.50 4.00
30 Quinton Patton 1.50 4.00
31 Robert Woods 2.50 6.00
32 Ryan Nassib 1.50 4.00
33 Stedman Bailey 1.50 4.00
34 Stepfan Taylor 1.50 4.00
35 Tavon Austin 2.00 5.00
36 Terrance Williams 1.50 4.00
37 Tyler Eifert 1.50 4.00
38 Tyler Wilson 1.50 4.00
39 Vance McDonald 2.00 5.00
40 Zach Ertz 3.00 8.00

2013 Absolute Rookie Premiere Materials AFC/NFC
*AFC/NFC PRIME/25: .6X TO 1.5X BASIC JSY/99
*NAMEPLATE/25: .8X TO 2X BASIC JSY/99
*NFL/99: .4X TO 1X BASIC JSY/99
*NFL PRIME/25: .6X TO 1.5X BASIC JSY/99
*NUMBERS/10: 1X TO 2.5X BASIC JSY/99
*OVERSIZE/99: .4X TO 1X BASIC JSY/99
*OVER.JSY NUMBER/99: .4X TO 1X JSY/99
*OVER.JSY NUM.PRIME/25: .6X TO 1.5X JSY/99
*OVER.PRIME/25: .6X TO 1.5X JSY/99
201 Aaron Dobson 1.50 4.00
202 Andre Ellington 1.50 4.00
203 Christine Michael 1.50 4.00
204 Cordarrelle Patterson 1.50 4.00
205 DeAndre Hopkins 4.00 10.00
206 Denard Robinson 1.50 4.00
207 Dion Jordan 1.50 4.00
208 Eddie Lacy 1.50 4.00
210 Gavin Escobar 1.50 4.00
211 Geno Smith 1.50 4.00
212 Giovani Bernard 1.50 4.00
213 Johnathan Franklin 1.50 4.00
214 Jordan Reed 2.50 6.00
215 Joseph Randle 1.50 4.00
216 Justin Hunter 1.50 4.00
217 Keenan Allen 3.00 8.00
218 Kenny Stills 1.50 4.00
219 Knile Davis 1.50 4.00
220 Landry Jones 1.50 4.00
221 Le'Veon Bell 5.00 12.00
222 Manti Te'o 2.00 5.00
223 Marcus Lattimore 1.50 4.00
224 Markus Wheaton 1.50 4.00
225 Marquise Goodwin 1.50 4.00
226 Matt Barkley 1.50 4.00
227 Mike Gillislee 1.50 4.00
228 Mike Glennon 1.50 4.00
229 Montee Ball 1.50 4.00
230 Quinton Patton 1.50 4.00
231 Robert Woods 2.50 6.00
232 Ryan Nassib 1.50 4.00
233 Stedman Bailey 1.50 4.00
234 Stepfan Taylor 1.50 4.00
235 Tavon Austin 2.00 5.00
236 Terrance Williams 1.50 4.00
237 Tyler Eifert 1.50 4.00
238 Tyler Wilson 1.50 4.00
239 Vance McDonald 2.00 5.00
240 Zach Ertz 3.00 8.00

2013 Absolute Rookie Premiere Materials Autographs AFC/NFC
*AFC/NFC/99: .4X TO 1X BASE JSY AU/299
*AFC/NFC PRM/49: .6X TO 1.5X BASE JSY AU/299
*NFL PRIME/49: .6X TO 1.5X BASE JSY AU/299
*OVERSIZE/25: .6X TO 1.5X BASE JSY AU/299
*OVER.JSY NUM/99: .4X TO 1X JSY AU/299
*OVR.JSY# PRM/25: .8X TO 2X JSY AU/299
*OVER.PRIME/49: .6X TO 1.5X JSY AU/299

2013 Absolute Rookie Roundup Jerseys
RANDOM INSERTS IN WAL-MART PACKS
1 Cordarrelle Patterson 1.25 3.00
2 DeAndre Hopkins 3.00 8.00
3 Denard Robinson 1.25 3.00
4 Eddie Lacy 1.25 3.00
5 EJ Manuel 1.25 3.00
6 Geno Smith 1.25 3.00
7 Giovani Bernard 1.25 3.00
8 Keenan Allen 2.50 6.00
9 Le'Veon Bell 4.00 10.00
10 Manti Te'o 1.50 4.00
11 Matt Barkley 1.25 3.00
12 Mike Glennon 1.25 3.00
13 Montee Ball 1.25 3.00
14 Quinton Patton 1.25 3.00
15 Robert Woods 2.00 5.00
16 Stepfan Taylor 1.25 3.00
17 Tavon Austin 1.50 4.00
18 Terrance Williams 1.25 3.00
19 Tyler Eifert 1.25 3.00
20 Tyler Wilson 1.25 3.00

2013 Absolute Team Quads Materials
*PRIME/18-25: .8X TO 2X BASIC QUAD/99
1 Wht/Ryn/Gnz/Jns/25 10.00 25.00
3 Jhnsn/Spl/Jcksn/Drs/99 6.00 15.00
4 Will/Nwtn/Smth/Stw/99 8.00 20.00
5 Ork/Fltch/Krgn/Hall/99 8.00 20.00
6 Hstr/Ctlr/Pprs/Brggs/25 8.00 20.00
7 Grn/Dltn/Grn-Es/Krkp/99 8.00 20.00
8 Jcksn/Lttl/Hde/Rchrd/99 5.00 12.00
9 Astn/Rmo/Wttn/Mrry/99 6.00 15.00
10 Bly/Hllmn/Mler/Tme/99 6.00 15.00
11 Blck/Gbb/Jns-D/Lws/99 5.00 12.00
12 Poe/Hli/Jhnsn/Brry/99 8.00 20.00
13 Egnw/Tnhl/Thms/Wk/99 6.00 15.00
14 Rdlp/Pndr/Ptrs/Grnw/99 8.00 20.00
15 Clstn/Brs/Thms/Grhm/99 10.00 25.00
16 Jcksn/Vck/McCy/Clk/99 10.00 25.00
17 Flyd/Rvrs/Mthw/Gts/99 8.00 20.00
18 Tte/Trbn/Mllr/Rice/99 8.00 20.00
19 Brtt/Grffn/Jhnsn/Wrt/99 5.00 12.00
20 Dvi/Mrgn/Hnkr/Mss/99 6.00 15.00

2013 Absolute Team Trios Materials Prime
*BASE TRIO/49-99: .25X TO .6X PRIME/15-25
1 Rice/Flacco/Smith/25 10.00 25.00
2 Dltn/Green/Grshm/25 12.00 30.00
3 Grdn/Wden/Rchrds/25 8.00 20.00
4 Schb/Fostr/Jhnson/15 10.00 25.00
5 Luck/Fleener/Hilton/25 15.00 40.00
6 Blckm/Jnes-D/Lwis/25 8.00 20.00
7 Britt/Jhnsn/Wshng/25 8.00 20.00
8 Jhnsn/Spllr/Jckson/25 10.00 25.00
9 Hrtlne/Tanne/Millr/25 10.00 25.00
10 Mann/Thmas/Dckr/25 30.00 80.00
11 Bowe/Charls/McCls/25 10.00 25.00
12 Mchem/Rivrs/Mthws/25 12.00 30.00
13 Mrshall/Cutler/Forte/25 12.00 30.00
14 Ptrsn/Pondr/Gerhart/25 15.00 40.00
15 Jones/Ryan/White/25 12.00 30.00
16 Stewrt/Newtn/Olsen/25 12.00 30.00
17 Sprles/Brees/Grahm/25 12.00 30.00
18 Jcksn/Frman/Wilms/25 10.00 25.00
19 Bryant/Romo/Murray/25 12.00 30.00
20 Nicks/Eli/Tuck/25 10.00 25.00
21 Jcksn/McCy/Mclin/25 12.00 30.00
22 Garcn/RGIII/Morris/25 10.00 25.00
23 Crabtr/Kprnck/Dvis/25 10.00 25.00
24 Tate/Irvin/Rice/25 8.00 20.00
25 Ware/Lee/Claiborne/25 12.00 30.00
26 Ngata/Webb/Suggs/25 8.00 20.00
27 Hall/Fltchr/Kerrigan/25 10.00 25.00
28 Jones/Bell/Wheatn/25 15.00 40.00
29 Manl/Gdwin/Woods/25 12.00 30.00
30 Escbr/Rndle/Willms/25 5.00 12.00

2013 Absolute Tools of the Trade Material Autographs Face Mask
4 Darrell Green/25
11 Jim Kelly/25 30.00 60.00
13 Joe Montana/25
15 LaDainian Tomlinson/25
20 Jamal Lewis/99 8.00 20.00

2013 Absolute Tools of the Trade Material Autographs Gloves
1 Charles Woodson/25 75.00 125.00
2 Eddie George/25 40.00 80.00

2013 Absolute Tools of the Trade Material Autographs Helmet
1 Darrell Green/25 40.00 80.00
2 Jerome Bettis/25 30.00 120.00
3 Marcus Allen/25 20.00 50.00
5 Phil Simms/25 15.00 40.00
6 Priest Holmes/25 12.00 30.00
7 Ron Jaworski/25 15.00 40.00
8 Warrick Dunn/25 20.00 50.00
10 Edgerrin James/25 15.00 40.00

2013 Absolute Tools of the Trade Material Autographs Shoes
3 Curtis Martin/25 15.00 40.00
5 Eddie George/25 30.00 60.00
6 Edgerrin James/25 15.00 40.00
9 Marcus Allen/20 20.00 50.00
10 Marshall Faulk/25 15.00 40.00

2013 Absolute Tools of the Trade Rookie Material Autographs Prime
1 Aaron Dobson 25.00 50.00
2 Andre Ellington 5.00 12.00
3 Christine Michael 5.00 12.00
4 Cordarrelle Patterson 5.00 12.00
5 DeAndre Hopkins 12.00 30.00
6 Denard Robinson 5.00 12.00
7 Dion Jordan 5.00 12.00
8 Eddie Lacy 5.00 12.00
9 EJ Manuel 20.00 50.00
10 Gavin Escobar 5.00 12.00
11 Geno Smith 5.00 12.00
12 Giovani Bernard 5.00 12.00
13 Johnathan Franklin 5.00 12.00
14 Jordan Reed 8.00 20.00
15 Joseph Randle 5.00 12.00
16 Justin Hunter 5.00 12.00
17 Keenan Allen 10.00 25.00
18 Kenny Stills 5.00 12.00
19 Knile Davis 5.00 12.00
20 Landry Jones 5.00 12.00
21 Le'Veon Bell 20.00 50.00
22 Manti Te'o 6.00 15.00
23 Marcus Lattimore 5.00 12.00
24 Markus Wheaton 5.00 12.00
25 Marquise Goodwin 5.00 12.00
26 Matt Barkley 5.00 12.00
27 Mike Gillislee 5.00 12.00
28 Mike Glennon 5.00 12.00
29 Montee Ball 5.00 12.00
30 Quinton Patton 5.00 12.00
31 Robert Woods 8.00 20.00
32 Ryan Nassib 10.00 25.00
33 Stedman Bailey 5.00 12.00
34 Stepfan Taylor 5.00 12.00
35 Tavon Austin 6.00 15.00
36 Terrance Williams 5.00 12.00
37 Tyler Eifert 5.00 12.00
38 Tyler Wilson 5.00 12.00
39 Vance McDonald 6.00 15.00
40 Zach Ertz 10.00 25.00

2013 Absolute War Room Draft Day Tickets Autographs
EXCH EXPIRATION: 5/1/2015
1 Aaron Dobson 6.00 15.00
2 Andre Ellington 6.00 15.00
3 Christine Michael
4 Cordarrelle Patterson
5 DeAndre Hopkins 15.00 40.00
6 Denard Robinson 6.00 15.00
7 Dion Jordan 6.00 15.00
8 Eddie Lacy 6.00 15.00
9 EJ Manuel 6.00 15.00
10 Gavin Escobar 6.00 15.00
11 Geno Smith EXCH 6.00 15.00
12 Giovani Bernard EXCH 6.00 15.00
13 Johnathan Franklin EXCH 6.00 15.00
14 Jordan Reed EXCH 8.00 20.00
15 Joseph Randle EXCH 6.00 15.00
16 Justin Hunter
17 Keenan Allen 12.00 30.00
18 Kenny Stills
19 Knile Davis
20 Landry Jones
21 Le'Veon Bell EXCH 20.00 50.00
22 Manti Te'o 8.00 20.00
23 Marcus Lattimore 6.00 15.00
24 Markus Wheaton
25 Marquise Goodwin 6.00 15.00
26 Matt Barkley 6.00 15.00
27 Mike Gillislee 6.00 15.00
28 Mike Glennon 6.00 15.00
29 Montee Ball EXCH 6.00 15.00
30 Quinton Patton 6.00 15.00
31 Robert Woods EXCH 10.00 25.00
32 Ryan Nassib 12.00 30.00
33 Stedman Bailey 6.00 15.00
34 Stepfan Taylor 6.00 15.00
35 Tavon Austin 8.00 20.00
36 Terrance Williams 6.00 15.00
37 Tyler Eifert 6.00 15.00
38 Tyler Wilson 6.00 15.00
39 Vance McDonald 8.00 20.00
40 Zach Ertz 12.00 30.00

2014 Absolute
151-200 ROOKIE AU PRINT RUN 199
201-240 ROOKIE JSY AU PRINT RUN 10-99
1 Demaryius Thomas .30 .75
2 Reggie Bush .25 .60
3 Eric Decker .25 .60
4 Steve Smith .30 .75
5 A.J. Green .40 1.00
6 Jimmy Graham .40 1.00
7 Anquan Boldin .25 .60
8 LeSean McCoy .40 1.00
9 Cam Newton .40 1.00
10 Michael Crabtree .25 .60
11 DeSean Jackson .30 .75
12 Reggie Wayne .30 .75
13 Geno Smith .25 .60
14 Steven Jackson .25 .60
15 Aaron Rodgers .75 2.00
16 Antonio Brown .40 1.00
17 Joe Flacco .30 .75
18 Le'Veon Bell .30 .75
19 Carson Palmer .30 .75
20 Dexter McCluster .30 .75
21 Michael Floyd .25 .60
22 Richard Sherman .40 1.00
23 Giovani Bernard .25 .60
24 Tavon Austin .25 .60
25 Adrian Peterson .40 1.00
26 Jordy Nelson .30 .75
27 Arian Foster .30 .75
28 Luke Kuechly .30 .75
29 Charles Woodson .40 1.00
30 Mike Wallace .25 .60
31 Dez Bryant .40 1.00
32 Rob Gronkowski .40 1.00
33 Greg Jennings .25 .60
34 Toby Gerhart .25 .60
35 Justin Forsett .30 .75
36 Josh McCown .25 .60
37 Ben Roethlisberger .40 1.00
38 Marcedes Lewis .25 .60
39 Chris Ivory .30 .75
40 Montee Ball .25 .60
41 Doug Martin .30 .75
42 Robert Griffin III .25 .60
43 Hakeem Nicks .25 .60
44 Tom Brady 1.00 2.50
45 Alex Smith .30 .75
46 Julio Jones .40 1.00
47 Ben Tate .25 .60
48 Marques Colston .25 .60
49 Colin Kaepernick .30 .75
50 Nick Foles .30 .75
51 Drew Brees .40 1.00
52 Russell Wilson .60 1.50
53 J.J. Watt .40 1.00
54 Tony Romo .30 .75
55 Alfred Morris .25 .60
56 Austin Davis .30 .75
57 Bernard Pierce .25 .60
58 Marshawn Lynch .30 .75
59 Cordarrelle Patterson .25 .60
60 Patrick Peterson .25 .60
61 Dwayne Bowe .30 .75
62 Ryan Mathews .30 .75
63 Jake Locker .30 .75
64 Victor Cruz .30 .75
65 Alshon Jeffery .30 .75
66 Keenan Allen .30 .75
67 Brandon Marshall .25 .60
68 Matt Ryan .30 .75
69 Darrelle Revis .25 .60
70 Percy Harvin .25 .60
71 Eddie Lacy .25 .60
72 Ryan Tannehill .30 .75
73 Jamaal Charles .30 .75
74 Vincent Jackson .25 .60
75 Andrew Hawkins .25 .60
76 Kendall Wright .25 .60
77 Brian Hoyer .25 .60
78 Darren McFadden .25 .60
79 DeAngelo Williams .25 .60
80 Peyton Manning .75 2.00
81 EJ Manuel .25 .60
82 Sam Bradford .25 .60
83 Jay Cutler .25 .60
84 Zac Stacy .25 .60
85 Andrew Luck .50 1.25
86 Knowshon Moreno .25 .60
87 C.J. Spiller .25 .60
88 Matthew Stafford .30 .75
89 DeMarco Murray .30 .75
90 Philip Rivers .40 1.00
91 Eli Manning .30 .75
92 Steve Johnson .30 .75
93 Jeremy Maclin .25 .60
94 Andre Johnson .30 .75
95 Andy Dalton .30 .75
96 Larry Fitzgerald .30 .75
97 Calvin Johnson .40 1.00
98 Maurice Jones-Drew .25 .60
99 DeMarcus Ware .30 .75
100 Rashad Jennings .25 .60
101 Aaron Donald RC 1.25 3.00
102 Juwan Thompson RC .75 2.00
103 Alfred Blue RC .50 1.25
104 Taylor Gabriel RC .60 1.50
105 Cyril Richardson RC .50 1.25
106 Corey Washington RC .75 2.00
107 Dargueze Dennard RC .60 1.50
108 David Yankey RC .50 1.25
109 Dee Ford RC .50 1.25
110 Senorise Perry RC .60 1.50
111 Deone Bucannon RC .50 1.25
112 Dominique Easley RC .50 1.25
113 Ed Reynolds RC .50 1.25
114 Trey Burton RC .50 1.25
115 Orleans Darkwa RC .75 2.00
116 Christian Kirksey RC .50 1.25
117 Justin Gilbert RC .50 1.25
118 Jimmie Ward RC .60 1.50
119 Jordan Lynch RC .60 1.50
120 Ryan Grant RC .50 1.25
121 Kony Ealy RC .60 1.50
122 Kyle Van Noy RC .60 1.50
123 Zack Martin RC .60 1.50
124 Lamarcus Joyner RC .60 1.50
125 Trey Watts RC .50 1.25
126 Marcus Roberson RC .60 1.50
127 Marcus Smith RC .50 1.25
128 Jeremiah Attaochu RC .50 1.25
129 Ra'Shede Hageman RC .50 1.25
130 Scott Crichton RC .50 1.25
131 Bene Benwikere RC .50 1.25
132 Stephon Tuitt RC .75 2.00
133 Cody Parkey RC .60 1.50
134 Travis Swanson RC .50 1.25
135 Trent Murphy RC .50 1.25
136 Trevor Reilly RC .50 1.25
137 E.J. Gaines RC .50 1.25
138 T.J. Carrie RC .60 1.50
139 Ryan Hewitt RC .50 1.25
140 Zach Mettenberger RC .50 1.25
141 Tre Mason RC .50 1.25
142 Kelvin Benjamin RC .75 2.00
143 Jadeveon Clowney RC .60 1.50
144 Mike Evans RC 1.25 3.00
145 Sammy Watkins RC .75 2.00
146 Bishop Sankey RC .50 1.25
147 Derek Carr RC 3.00 8.00
148 Teddy Bridgewater RC .75 2.00
149 Blake Bortles RC .60 1.50
150 Johnny Manziel RC .75 2.00
151 Allen Hurns AU RC 3.00 8.00
152 Bruce Ellington AU RC 2.50 6.00
153 C.J. Fiedorowicz AU RC 2.50 6.00
154 C.J. Mosley AU RC 3.00 8.00
155 Philly Brown AU RC 3.00 8.00
156 Devin Street AU RC 2.50 6.00
157 Isaiah Crowell AU RC 3.00 8.00
158 James White AU RC 5.00 12.00
159 Jeff Janis AU RC 5.00 12.00
160 Jerick McKinnon AU RC 3.00 8.00
161 John Brown AU RC 4.00 10.00
162 Josh Huff AU RC 3.00 8.00
163 Kyle Fuller AU RC 2.50 6.00
164 Silas Redd AU RC 3.00 8.00
165 Lorenzo Taliaferro AU RC 2.50 6.00
166 Marion Grice AU RC 2.50 6.00
167 Martavis Bryant AU RC 3.00 8.00
168 Damien Williams AU RC 2.50 6.00
169 Michael Campanaro AU RC 2.50 6.00
170 Michael Sam AU RC 2.50 6.00
171 Pierre Desir AU RC 2.50 6.00
172 Preston Brown AU RC 2.50 6.00
173 Branden Oliver AU RC 4.00 10.00
174 Jace Amaro AU RC 2.50 6.00
175 Richard Rodgers AU RC 4.00 10.00
176 Robert Herron AU RC 2.50 6.00
177 Ryan Shazier AU RC 4.00 10.00
178 Solomon Patton AU RC 3.00 8.00
179 Tevin Reese AU RC 2.50 6.00
180 Troy Niklas AU RC 2.50 6.00
181 Ja'Wuan James AU RC 2.50 6.00
182 Ahmad Dixon AU RC 2.50 6.00
183 Anthony Barr AU RC 2.50 6.00
184 Antonio Andrews AU RC 2.50 6.00
186 Asa Watson AU RC 2.50 6.00
187 Bradley Roby AU RC 2.50 6.00
188 Brandon Coleman AU RC 2.50 6.00
189 Crockett Gillmore AU RC 3.00 8.00
190 Rashad Ross AU RC 2.50 6.00
191 Ha Ha Clinton-Dix AU RC 3.00 8.00
192 Telvin Smith AU RC 2.50 6.00
193 Jason Verrett AU RC 2.50 6.00
194 Keith Wenning AU RC 3.00 8.00
195 Taylor Lewan AU RC 2.50 6.00
196 Greg Robinson AU RC 2.50 6.00
197 Timmy Jernigan AU RC 2.50 6.00
198 Calvin Pryor AU RC 2.50 6.00
199 Chris Borland AU RC 2.50 6.00
200 Jake Matthews AU RC 2.50 6.00
201 Aaron Murray JSY AU/99 RC 4.00 10.00
202 A.J. McCarron JSY AU/99 RC 4.00 10.00
203 Allen Robinson JSY AU/99 RC 6.00 15.00
204 Andre Williams JSY AU/99 RC 4.00 10.00
205 Austin Seferian-Jenkins JSY AU/99 RC 4.00 10.00
206 Bishop Sankey JSY AU/99 4.00 10.00
207 Blake Bortles JSY AU/99 5.00 12.00
208 Brandin Cooks JSY AU/99 RC 6.00 15.00
209 Carlos Hyde JSY AU/99 RC 5.00 12.00
210 Charles Sims JSY AU/99 RC 4.00 10.00
211 Cody Latimer JSY AU/99 RC 5.00 12.00
212 Davante Adams JSY AU/99 RC 6.00 15.00
213 D.Thomas JSY AU/99 RC 4.00 10.00
214 Derek Carr JSY AU/99 30.00 60.00
215 Devonta Freeman JSY AU/99 RC 6.00 15.00
216 Donte Moncrief JSY AU/99 RC 4.00 10.00
217 Dri Archer JSY AU/99 RC 4.00 10.00
218 Eric Ebron JSY AU/99 5.00 12.00
219 Jace Amaro JSY AU/10
220 Jadeveon Clowney JSY AU/99
221 Jarvis Landry JSY AU/99 RC 8.00 20.00
222 Jeremy Hill JSY AU/99 5.00 12.00
223 J.Garoppolo JSY AU/99 RC 40.00 80.00
224 Johnny Manziel JSY AU/99 6.00 15.00
225 Jordan Matthews JSY AU/99 RC 6.00 15.00
226 Ka'Deem Carey JSY AU/99 4.00 10.00
227 Kelvin Benjamin JSY AU/99 6.00 15.00
228 Khalil Mack JSY AU/99 RC 15.00 40.00
229 Logan Thomas JSY AU/99 RC 4.00 10.00
230 Marqise Lee JSY AU/99 RC 5.00 12.00
232 Mike Evans JSY AU/99 10.00 25.00
233 O.Beckham JSY AU/99 RC 40.00 80.00
234 Paul Richardson JSY AU/99 RC
235 Sammy Watkins JSY AU/99 6.00 15.00
236 Tajh Boyd JSY AU/99 RC 4.00 10.00
237 T.Bridgewater JSY AU/99 6.00 15.00
238 Terrance West JSY AU/99 RC 4.00 10.00
239 Tom Savage JSY AU/99 RC 4.00 10.00
240 Tre Mason JSY AU/99 4.00 10.00

2014 Absolute 20th Anniversary Silver
*GOLD RETAIL/20: .4X TO 1X HOBBY
1 LeSean McCoy 4.00 10.00
2 EJ Manuel 2.50 6.00
3 Russell Wilson 8.00 20.00
4 Aaron Murray 2.00 5.00
5 Dez Bryant 4.00 10.00
6 Dri Archer 2.00 5.00
7 Reggie Wayne 3.00 8.00
8 Logan Thomas 2.00 5.00
9 Rob Gronkowski 4.00 10.00
10 Nick Foles 3.00 8.00
11 James White 4.00 10.00
12 C.J. Spiller 2.50 6.00
13 Marshawn Lynch 3.00 8.00
14 A.J. McCarron 2.00 5.00
15 Tony Romo 3.00 8.00
16 Eric Ebron 2.50 6.00
17 Andrew Luck 5.00 12.00
18 Marqise Lee 2.50 6.00
19 Tom Brady 12.00 30.00
20 Jace Amaro 2.00 5.00
21 Antonio Brown 4.00 10.00
22 Cam Newton 4.00 10.00
23 Tavon Austin 2.50 6.00
24 Allen Robinson 3.00 8.00
25 Demaryius Thomas 3.00 8.00
26 Jadeveon Clowney 2.50 6.00
27 Toby Gerhart 2.50 6.00
28 Mike Evans 5.00 12.00
29 Jimmy Graham 4.00 10.00
30 Allen Hurns 2.50 6.00
31 Ben Roethlisberger 4.00 10.00
32 DeAngelo Williams 2.50 6.00
33 Sam Bradford 2.50 6.00
34 Bishop Sankey 2.00 5.00
35 Peyton Manning 15.00 40.00
36 Jarvis Landry 4.00 10.00
37 Marcedes Lewis 2.50 6.00
38 Odell Beckham Jr. 5.00 12.00
39 Drew Brees 4.00 10.00
40 Carson Palmer 3.00 8.00
41 Keenan Allen 3.00 8.00
42 Brandon Marshall 2.50 6.00
43 Doug Martin 3.00 8.00
44 Blake Bortles 2.50 6.00
45 Matthew Stafford 3.00 8.00
46 Jeremy Hill 2.50 6.00
47 Alex Smith 3.00 8.00
48 Paul Richardson 2.50 6.00
49 Victor Cruz 3.00 8.00
50 Patrick Peterson 2.50 6.00
51 Philip Rivers 4.00 10.00
52 Jay Cutler 2.50 6.00
53 Vincent Jackson 2.50 6.00
54 Brandin Cooks 3.00 8.00
55 Calvin Johnson 4.00 10.00
56 Jimmy Garoppolo 15.00 40.00
57 Jamaal Charles 3.00 8.00
58 Sammy Watkins 3.00 8.00
59 Eli Manning 3.00 8.00
60 Larry Fitzgerald 3.00 8.00
61 Anquan Boldin 2.50 6.00
62 A.J. Green 4.00 10.00
63 Dexter McCluster 3.00 8.00
64 Carlos Hyde 2.50 6.00
65 Aaron Rodgers 8.00 20.00
67 Mike Wallace 2.50 6.00
68 Branden Oliver 3.00 8.00
69 Julio Jones 4.00 10.00
70 Eric Decker 2.50 6.00
71 Michael Crabtree 2.50 6.00
72 Andy Dalton 3.00 8.00
73 Jake Locker 3.00 8.00
74 De'Anthony Thomas 2.50 6.00
75 Eddie Lacy 2.50 6.00
76 Jordan Matthews 3.00 8.00
77 Ryan Tannehill 3.00 8.00
78 Teddy Bridgewater 3.00 8.00
79 Geno Smith 2.50 6.00
80 Matt Ryan 3.00 8.00
81 Colin Kaepernick 3.00 8.00
82 Ben Tate 2.50 6.00
83 Robert Griffin III 2.50 6.00
84 Derek Carr 12.00 30.00
85 Arian Foster 3.00 8.00
86 Ka'Deem Carey 2.00 5.00
87 Adrian Peterson 4.00 10.00
88 Terrance West 2.00 5.00
89 Darren McFadden 2.50 6.00
90 Steve Smith 3.00 8.00
91 Richard Sherman 15.00 40.00
92 Brian Hoyer 2.50 6.00
93 Alfred Morris 2.50 6.00
94 Donte Moncrief 2.00 5.00
95 Andre Johnson 3.00 8.00
96 Kelvin Benjamin 3.00 8.00
97 Cordarrelle Patterson 2.50 6.00
98 Tre Mason 2.00 5.00
99 Maurice Jones-Drew 2.50 6.00
100 Joe Flacco 3.00 8.00

2014 Absolute Retail
*1-100 VETS: .3X TO .8X BASIC CARDS
*101-150 ROOKIES: .2X TO .5X BASIC RC
*151-200 ROOKIE AU: .3X TO .8X BASE AU/199

2014 Absolute Retail Blue
*1-100 VETS: 1X TO 2.5X BASIC CARDS
*101-150 ROOKIES: .6X TO 1.5X BASIC RC
RANDOM INSERTS IN RETAIL JUMBO

2014 Absolute Retail Red
*1-100 VETS: .6X TO 1.5X BASIC CARDS
*101-150 ROOKIES: .4X TO 1X BASIC RC
1-200 ONE PER RETAIL RACK PACK
*ROOKIE AU/25: .8X TO 2X BASIC AU RC

2014 Absolute Rookie Premiere Materials Autographs Jersey Ball
*JSY/BALL/20: .6X TO 1.5X BASE JSY AU/99
224 Johnny Manziel
233 Odell Beckham Jr. 90.00 150.00
235 Sammy Watkins 10.00 25.00

2014 Absolute Retail Black
*1-100 VETS/49: 2.5X TO 6X BASIC CARDS
*101-150 ROOKIES/49: 1.2X TO 3X BASIC RC

2014 Absolute Spectrum Gold
*1-100 VETS/25: 4X TO 10X BASIC CARDS
*101-150 ROOKIES/25: 2X TO 5X BASIC RC
*151-200 ROOK.AU/25: .8X TO 2X AU/199

2014 Absolute Spectrum Purple
*1-100 VETS/20: 4X TO 10X BASIC CARDS
*101-150 ROOKIES/20: 2X TO 5X BASIC RC
*151-200 ROOK.AU/20: .8X TO 2X AU/199

2014 Absolute Spectrum Silver
*1-100 VETS/99: 2X TO 5X BASIC CARDS
*101-150 ROOKIES/99: 1X TO 2.5X BASIC RC
*151-200 ROOK.AU/99: .5X TO 1.2X AU/199

2014 Absolute Absolute Ink
*INK: .3X TO .8X SILVER INK/50
40 Joe Montana 75.00 150.00

2014 Absolute Absolute Ink Spectrum Silver
1 Torrey Smith/50 4.00 10.00
2 Len Dawson/50 10.00 25.00
3 Jim Kiick/75 6.00 15.00
4 Brandon Flowers/75 4.00 10.00
5 Dwayne Allen/75 4.00 10.00
6 Carl Eller/50 6.00 15.00
7 Julius Thomas/75 4.00 10.00
8 Bo Jackson/25 40.00 80.00
9 Markus Wheaton/75 4.00 10.00
10 Robert Mathis/50 4.00 10.00
11 Jerome Bettis/50 20.00 50.00
13 John Taylor/75 6.00 15.00
14 Barkevious Mingo/75 4.00 10.00
16 Larry Csonka/15
17 Kenbrell Thompkins/75 4.00 10.00
18 Brett Favre/15 100.00 200.00
19 Von Miller/50 10.00 25.00
20 Jerry Rice/15 75.00 150.00
21 James Laurinaitis/50 5.00 12.00
22 Raymond Berry/25 12.00 30.00
23 Prince Amukamara/75 4.00 10.00
24 Danny Amendola/50 5.00 12.00
25 Dennis Pitta/50 4.00 10.00
26 Ozzie Newsome/50
27 Bruce Smith/25 12.00 30.00
28 Manti Te'o/50 5.00 12.00
29 C.J. Spiller/50 4.00 10.00
30 Justin Hunter/50 4.00 10.00
32 Steve Largent/25 15.00 40.00
33 T.Y. Hilton/50 5.00 12.00
34 Doug Martin/50 5.00 12.00
35 Lenny Moore /50 6.00 15.00
36 Thurman Thomas/25 12.00 30.00
37 Paul Posluszny/75 6.00 15.00
40 Joe Montana/15 100.00 200.00
41 Malcolm Smith/50 10.00 25.00
44 Gavin Escobar/75 4.00 10.00
45 Christine Michael/75 4.00 10.00
47 Sean Lee/75 5.00 12.00
48 Franco Harris/50 15.00 40.00
49 Rob Gronkowski/50 15.00 40.00
51 Terrance Williams/50 4.00 10.00
52 Terrell Davis/50 15.00 40.00
53 Tyrann Mathieu/75 5.00 12.00
54 Jamal Lewis/50 8.00 20.00
55 Billy Howton/75 6.00 15.00
57 Stedman Bailey/75 4.00 10.00
58 Frank Gifford/15 25.00 60.00
59 Vincent Jackson/50 4.00 10.00
60 John Elway/15 50.00 100.00
61 Aaron Dobson/50 4.00 10.00
62 Tony Dorsett/15 25.00 60.00
64 Jarrett Boykin/75 4.00 10.00
65 Joseph Fauria/75 4.00 10.00
66 Fred Biletnikoff/50 20.00 40.00
67 Timothy Wright/75 4.00 10.00
68 Gale Sayers/50 20.00 50.00
69 Giovani Bernard/50 4.00 10.00
70 Kellen Winslow/50 8.00 20.00

71 Dwayne Harris/75 4.00 10.00
72 Warren Moon/50 20.00 40.00
73 Adrian Clayborn/99 4.00 10.00
74 Jeremy Kerley/75 4.00 10.00
75 Da'Rick Rogers/75 4.00 10.00
76 Bob Lilly/50 8.00 20.00
77 Trent Dilfer/50 10.00 25.00
78 Jackie Slater/50 4.00 10.00
79 DeAndre Hopkins/50 5.00 12.00
80 Kurt Warner/15 30.00 60.00
81 Harry Douglas/75 4.00 10.00
84 Jimmy Smith/75 4.00 10.00
85 Chuck Foreman/50 6.00 15.00
86 Paul Hornung/50 10.00 25.00
87 Zach Ertz/75 5.00 12.00
88 Jackie Smith/50 8.00 20.00
89 Luke Kuechly/50 10.00 25.00
90 LaDainian Tomlinson/50 15.00 40.00
91 Janoris Jenkins/75 4.00 10.00
92 Forrest Gregg/25 10.00 25.00
94 Tom Rathman/50 6.00 15.00
95 Joseph Randle/75 4.00 10.00
96 Mike Singletary/50
98 Jan Stenerud/50 6.00 15.00
99 Michael Floyd/50 4.00 10.00
100 Lance Alworth/15 30.00 60.00

2014 Absolute Hogg Heaven

*GOLD/99: .75X TO 2X BASIC INSERTS
*ANNI./20: 1.5X TO 4X BASIC INSERTS
1 Philip Rivers 1.00 2.50
2 Terrance West .50 1.25
3 Larry Fitzgerald .75 2.00
4 Aaron Murray .50 1.25
5 Ben Tate .60 1.50
6 Charles Sims .50 1.25
7 Arian Foster .75 2.00
8 Eric Ebron .60 1.50
9 Jimmy Graham 1.00 2.50
10 Khalil Mack 2.00 5.00
11 Michael Crabtree .60 1.50
12 Tom Savage .50 1.25
13 Matt Ryan .75 2.00
14 A.J. McCarron .50 1.25
15 Dez Bryant 1.00 2.50
16 Cody Latimer .60 1.50
17 Andre Johnson .75 2.00
18 Drew Brees 1.00 2.50
19 Jadeveon Clowney .60 1.50
20 Logan Thomas .50 1.25
21 Colin Kaepernick .75 2.00
22 Tre Mason .50 1.25
23 Joe Flacco .75 2.00
24 Allen Robinson .75 2.00
25 Tony Romo .75 2.00
26 Connor Shaw .50 1.25
27 Andrew Luck 1.25 3.00
28 Jarvis Landry 1.00 2.50
29 Eli Manning .75 2.00
30 Marqise Lee .60 1.50
31 Russell Wilson 1.50 4.00
32 James White 1.00 2.50
33 C.J. Spiller .60 1.50
34 Andre Williams .50 1.25
35 Demaryius Thomas .75 2.00
36 Davante Adams .75 2.00
37 Toby Gerhart .60 1.50
38 Jeremy Hill .60 1.50
39 Geno Smith .60 1.50
40 Mike Evans 1.25 3.00
41 Marshawn Lynch .75 2.00
42 Jace Amaro .50 1.25
43 Cam Newton 1.00 2.50
44 Austin Seferian-Jenkins .50 1.25
45 Peyton Manning 4.00 10.00
46 De'Anthony Thomas .50 1.25
47 Jimmy Garoppolo 4.00 10.00
48 Jamaal Charles .60 1.50
49 Darren McFadden .60 1.50
50 Odell Beckham Jr. 1.25 3.00
51 Tavon Austin .60 1.50
52 Allen Hurns .60 1.50
53 Brandon Marshall .60 1.50
54 Bishop Sankey .50 1.25
55 Matthew Stafford .75 2.00
56 Derek Carr 3.00 8.00
57 Mike Wallace .60 1.50
58 Johnny Manziel .75 2.00
59 Maurice Jones-Drew .60 1.50
60 Paul Richardson .60 1.50
61 Doug Martin .75 2.00
62 Jason Verrett .50 1.25
63 Jay Cutler .60 1.50
64 Blake Bortles .60 1.50
65 Calvin Johnson 1.00 2.50
66 Devonta Freeman .75 2.00
67 Adrian Peterson 1.00 2.50
68 Jordan Matthews .75 2.00
69 Sammy Watkins .75 2.00
70 LeSean McCoy 1.00 2.50
71 Jake Locker .75 2.00
72 John Brown .75 2.00
73 A.J. Green 1.00 2.50
74 Brandin Cooks .75 2.00
75 Aaron Rodgers 3.00 8.00
76 Donte Moncrief .50 1.25
77 Rob Gronkowski 1.00 2.50
78 Ka'Deem Carey .50 1.25
79 Antonio Brown 1.00 2.50
80 Justin Gilbert .50 1.25
81 Robert Griffin III .60 1.50
82 Isaiah Crowell .60 1.50
83 Andy Dalton .75 2.00
84 Carlos Hyde .60 1.50
85 Eddie Lacy .60 1.50
86 Dri Archer .50 1.25
87 Tom Brady 3.00 8.00
88 Kelvin Benjamin .75 2.00
89 Ben Roethlisberger 1.00 2.50
90 Teddy Bridgewater .75 2.00

2014 Absolute Leather and Laces Football

*PURPLE/20: .6X TO 1.5X LEATHER/38-43
LLAM A.J. McCarron/41 3.00 8.00
LLAMU Aaron Murray/38 3.00 8.00
LLAR Allen Robinson/43 5.00 12.00
LLASJ Austin Seferian-Jenkins/43 3.00 8.00
LLAW Andre Williams/41 3.00 8.00
LLBB Blake Bortles/43 4.00 10.00
LLBC Brandin Cooks/40 5.00 12.00
LLBS Bishop Sankey/42 3.00 8.00
LLCH Carlos Hyde/39 4.00 10.00
LLCL Cody Latimer/43 4.00 10.00
LLCS Charles Sims/43 3.00 8.00
LLDA Davante Adams/38 5.00 12.00
LLDA Dri Archer/42 3.00 8.00
LLDC Derek Carr/43 8.00 20.00
LLDF Devonta Freeman/42 5.00 12.00
LLDM Donte Moncrief/42 3.00 8.00
LLDT De'Anthony Thomas/41 3.00 8.00
LLEE Eric Ebron/39 4.00 10.00
LLJC Jadeveon Clowney/42 4.00 10.00
LLJG Jimmy Garoppolo/43 25.00 60.00
LLJH Jeremy Hill/41 4.00 10.00
LLJL Jarvis Landry/43 8.00 20.00
LLJM Johnny Manziel/39 5.00 12.00
LLJMA Jordan Matthews/39 5.00 12.00
LLKB Kelvin Benjamin/43 6.00 15.00
LLKC Ka'Deem Carey/42 3.00 8.00
LLKM Khalil Mack/39 12.00 30.00
LLLT Logan Thomas/43 3.00 8.00
LLME Mike Evans/43 8.00 20.00
LLML Marqise Lee/41 4.00 10.00
LLOB Odell Beckham Jr./43 8.00 20.00
LLSW Sammy Watkins/41 5.00 12.00
LLTB Tajh Boyd/43 3.00 8.00
LLTBR Teddy Bridgewater/40 5.00 12.00
LLTM Tre Mason/38 3.00 8.00
LLTS Tom Savage/42 3.00 8.00
LLTW Terrance West/43 3.00 8.00

2014 Absolute Quads

BICG Brs/Ingrm/Clstn/Grhm 2.50 6.00
BNRM Brs/Nwtn/Ryn/McCwn 2.50 6.00
BREG Brdy/Rdly/Edlmn/Grnkwski 6.00 15.00
BTMS Brdy/Tnnhill/Mnl/Smth 6.00 15.00
CFMJ Ctlr/Frte/Mrshll/Jffry 2.00 5.00
CMBM Chrls/McFddn/Bll/Mthws 2.00 5.00
DBGG Dltn/Brnrd/Grn/Grshm 2.50 6.00
FFJH Ftzptrck/Fstr/Jhnsn/Hpkns 2.00 5.00
FRGG Fstr/Rchrdsn/Grhm/Grne 2.00 5.00
GMJG Grffn/Mrrs/Jcksn/Grcn 2.00 5.00
KGCD Kprnck/Gre/Crbtre/Dvs 2.00 5.00
LRWN Lck/Rchrdsn/Wyne/Ncks 3.00 8.00
MBTT Mnng/Bll/Thms/Thms 5.00 12.00
MMMJ McCy/Mrrs/Mrry/Jnngs 2.50 6.00
PFLB Ptrsn/Frte/Lcy/Bsh 2.50 6.00
RBBM Rthlsbrgr/Bll/Brwn/Mllr 5.00 12.00
RFDH Rthlsbrgr/Flcco/Dltn/Hyr 2.50 6.00
RGMF Rmo/Grffn/Mnng/Fles 2.00 5.00
RJJW Ryn/Jcksn/Jnes/Whte 2.50 6.00
RLNC Rdgrs/Lcy/Nlsn/Cbb 5.00 12.00
RMBW Rmo/Mrry/Brynt/Wttn 5.00 12.00
RSCC Rdgrs/Stffrd/Ctlr/Cssl 5.00 12.00
SJRV Sylli/Jcksn/Rdly/Vrn 2.00 5.00
TMWH Tnnhll/Mrno/Wllce/Hrtlne 2.00 5.00
WKPB Wlsn/Kprnck/Plmr/Brdfrd 4.00 10.00

2014 Absolute Quads Rookies

BCGW Brtls/Crr/Grpplo/Wst 4.00 10.00
BECA Brdgwtr/Ebrn/Cry/Adms .75 2.00
BECF Bnjmn/Evns/Cks/Frmn 1.25 3.00
BLRH Brtls/Lee/Rbnsn/Hrns .75 2.00
BPSB Brdgwtr/Pryr/Smth/Brwn .75 2.00
BTSF Brdgwtr/Thms/Svge/Frmn .75 2.00
CBSM Clwny/Brtls/Snky/Mncrf .60 1.50
CMGB Clwny/Mck/Glbrt/Brr 2.00 5.00
CMMT Crr/Mck/Mrry/Thms 3.00 8.00
EBML Evns/Bckhm/Mtthws/Lndry 5.00 12.00
ESAN Ebrn/SfrnJnkns/Amro/Nkls .60 1.50
GTSM Grpplo/Thms/Svge/Mrry 4.00 10.00
HLRW Hyde/Ltmr/Rbnsn/Whte 1.00 2.50
MBBC Mnzl/Brtls/Brdgwtr/Crr 3.00 8.00
MGSW Mnzl/Glbrt/Shw/Wst .75 2.00
MKMR McCrrn/Kndjo/Msn/Rbnsn .60 1.50
MWAF Msn/Wst/Archr/Frmn .75 2.00
SHSH Snky/Hyde/Sms/Hll .60 1.50
THMR Thms/Hyde/Msn/Rchrdsn .60 1.50
WBBS Wtkns/Bnjmn/Brynt/Strt .75 2.00
WEBC Wtkns/Evns/Bckhm/Cks 5.00 12.00
WEBH Wtkns/Ebrn/Bnjmn/Hrns .75 2.00
WLGA Wtkns/Lndry/Grpplo/Amro 4.00 10.00

2014 Absolute Rookie Jersey Collection

*PURPLE/20: .8X TO 2X BASIC JSY
RJAM A.J. McCarron 1.50 4.00
RJAMU Aaron Murray 1.50 4.00
RJAR Allen Robinson 2.50 6.00
RJASJ Austin Seferian-Jenkins 1.50 4.00
RJAW Andre Williams 1.50 4.00
RJBB Blake Bortles 2.00 5.00
RJBC Brandin Cooks 2.50 6.00
RJBS Bishop Sankey 1.50 4.00
RJCH Carlos Hyde 2.00 5.00
RJCL Cody Latimer 2.00 5.00
RJCS Charles Sims 1.50 4.00
RJDA Davante Adams 2.50 6.00
RJDA Dri Archer 1.50 4.00
RJDC Derek Carr 5.00 12.00
RJDF Devonta Freeman 2.50 6.00
RJDM Donte Moncrief 1.50 4.00
RJDT De'Anthony Thomas 1.50 4.00
RJEE Eric Ebron 2.00 5.00
RJJC Jadeveon Clowney 2.00 5.00
RJJG Jimmy Garoppolo 12.00 30.00
RJJH Jeremy Hill 2.00 5.00
RJJL Jarvis Landry 3.00 8.00
RJJM Johnny Manziel 2.50 6.00
RJJMA Jordan Matthews 2.50 6.00
RJKB Kelvin Benjamin 2.50 6.00
RJKC Ka'Deem Carey 1.50 4.00
RJKM Khalil Mack 6.00 15.00
RJLT Logan Thomas 1.50 4.00
RJME Mike Evans 4.00 10.00
RJML Marqise Lee 2.00 5.00
RJOB Odell Beckham Jr. 10.00 25.00
RJPR Paul Richardson 2.00 5.00
RJSW Sammy Watkins 2.50 6.00
RJTB Tajh Boyd 1.50 4.00
RJTBR Teddy Bridgewater 2.50 6.00
RJTM Tre Mason 1.50 4.00
RJTS Tom Savage 1.50 4.00
RJTW Terrance West 1.50 4.00

2014 Absolute Rookie Jersey Quad

*JSY-BALL/149: .6X TO 1.5X JSY QUAD/249
*JSY-BLL-GLV/99: .8X TO 2X JSY QUAD/249
*JUMBO PATCH/15: 1.2X TO 3X JSY QUAD/249
RJAM A.J. McCarron 1.25 3.00
RJAR Allen Robinson 2.00 5.00
RJAW Andre Williams 1.25 3.00
RJBB Blake Bortles 1.50 4.00
RJBC Brandin Cooks 2.00 5.00
RJBS Bishop Sankey 1.25 3.00
RJCH Carlos Hyde 1.50 4.00
RJCL Cody Latimer 1.50 4.00
RJCS Charles Sims 1.25 3.00
RJDA Davante Adams 2.00 5.00
RJDA Dri Archer 1.25 3.00
RJDC Derek Carr 4.00 10.00
RJDF Devonta Freeman 2.00 5.00
RJDM Donte Moncrief 1.25 3.00
RJDT De'Anthony Thomas 1.25 3.00
RJEE Eric Ebron 1.50 4.00
RJJC Jadeveon Clowney 1.50 4.00
RJJG Jimmy Garoppolo 10.00 25.00
RJJH Jeremy Hill 1.50 4.00
RJJL Jarvis Landry 2.50 6.00
RJJM Johnny Manziel 2.00 5.00
RJKB Kelvin Benjamin 2.00 5.00
RJKC Ka'Deem Carey 1.25 3.00
RJKM Khalil Mack 5.00 12.00
RJLT Logan Thomas 1.25 3.00
RJME Mike Evans 3.00 8.00
RJML Marqise Lee 1.50 4.00
RJOB Odell Beckham Jr. 3.00 8.00
RJPR Paul Richardson 1.50 4.00
RJSW Sammy Watkins 2.00 5.00
RJTB Tajh Boyd 1.25 3.00
RJTM Tre Mason 1.25 3.00
RJTS Tom Savage 1.25 3.00
RJTW Terrance West 1.25 3.00
RJAMU Aaron Murray 1.25 3.00
RJASJ Austin Seferian-Jenkins 1.25 3.00
RJJMA Jordan Matthews 2.00 5.00
RJTBR Teddy Bridgewater 2.00 5.00

2014 Absolute Tools of the Trade

*ANNI./20: .75X TO 2X TOOLS JSY/149-249
*ANNI./20: .6X TO 1.5X TOOLS JSY/49-99
*ANNI./20: .4X TO 1X TOOLS JSY/25
*PRIME/20: .75X TO 2X TOOLS JSY/149-249
*PRIME/20: .6X TO 1.5X TOOLS JSY/49-99
*PRIME/20: .4X TO 1X TOOLS JSY/25
TTAD Andy Dalton/249 2.50 6.00
TTAJ Andre Johnson/99 3.00 8.00
TTCK Colin Kaepernick/249 5.00 12.00
TTCP Cordarrelle Patterson/249 2.00 5.00
TTDB Dez Bryant/49 5.00 12.00
TTDB Dwayne Bowe/249 2.50 6.00
TTDM DeMarco Murray/249 6.00 15.00
TTDMA Dan Marino/110 10.00 25.00
TTDMC Darren McFadden/249 2.00 5.00
TTDS Deion Sanders/25 10.00 25.00
TTDT Demaryius Thomas/249 2.50 6.00
TTDW DeAngelo Williams/149 2.00 5.00
TTEJ EJ Manuel/249 2.00 5.00
TTEM Eli Manning/249 2.50 6.00
TTES C.J. Spiller/249 2.00 5.00
TTFJ Fred Jackson/249 2.50 6.00
TTJC Jamaal Charles/149 2.50 6.00
TTJCA Jordan Cameron/249 2.00 5.00
TTJCU Jay Cutler/249 2.00 5.00
TTJF Joe Flacco/249 3.00 8.00
TTJL Jake Locker/149 2.50 6.00
TTJM Jeremy Maclin/99 2.50 6.00
TTJW Jason Witten/25 5.00 12.00
TTKS Kenny Stills/199 2.00 5.00
TTKW Kendall Wright/249 2.00 5.00
TTLF Larry Fitzgerald/249 2.50 6.00
TTLMC LeSean McCoy/149 3.00 8.00
TTLMI Lamar Miller/249 2.00 5.00
TTMB Montee Ball/249 2.00 5.00
TTMG Marquise Goodwin/249 2.00 5.00
TTMR Matt Ryan/249 2.50 6.00
TTMS Mohamed Sanu/249 2.00 5.00
TTMW Mike Wallace/249 2.00 5.00
TTNF Nick Foles/149 2.50 6.00
TTNW Nate Washington/249 2.00 5.00
TTPP Paul Posluszny/149 2.00 5.00
TTPR Philip Rivers/249 3.00 8.00
TTRWA Reggie Wayne/99 3.00 8.00
TTRWO Robert Woods/249 2.50 6.00
TTSG Shonn Greene/249 2.00 5.00
TTSS Steve Smith/249 2.50 6.00
TTTA Troy Aikman/149 6.00 15.00
TTTDA Terrell Davis/99 1.50 4.00
TTTDO Tony Dorsett/149 5.00 12.00
TTTHA Tamba Hali/249 2.00 5.00
TTTHI T.Y. Hilton/249 2.50 6.00
TTTRI Trent Richardson/249 2.00 5.00
TTTRO Tony Romo/249 2.50 6.00
TTTS Torrey Smith/249 2.00 5.00
TTVM Von Miller/249 2.50 6.00
TTWP Walter Payton/149 10.00 25.00
TTWW Wes Welker/99 3.00 8.00

2014 Absolute Tools of the Trade Complete Rookies

*GOLD/99: .5X TO 1.2X JSY/149-249
*GOLD/49: .6X TO 1.5X JSY/149-249
*GOLD/49: .5X TO 1.2X JSY/99
*PRIME/15: 1X TO 2.5X JSY/149-249
*PRIME/15: .75X TO 2X JSY/99
*PURPLE/20: 1X TO 2.5X JSY/149-249
*PURPLE/20: .75X TO 2X JSY/99
*SILVER/15-25: 1X TO 2.5X JSY/149-249
*SILVER/15-25: .75X TO 2X JSY/99
CRAM A.J. McCarron/249 2.50 6.00
CRAR Allen Robinson/249 4.00 10.00
CRAW Andre Williams/249 2.50 6.00
CRBB Blake Bortles/249 3.00 8.00
CRBC Brandin Cooks/249 4.00 10.00
CRBS Bishop Sankey/249 2.50 6.00
CRCH Carlos Hyde/249 3.00 8.00
CRCL Cody Latimer/249 3.00 8.00
CRCS Charles Sims/199 2.50 6.00
CRDA Davante Adams/249 4.00 10.00
CRDA Dri Archer/249 2.50 6.00
CRDC Derek Carr/249 8.00 20.00
CRDF Devonta Freeman/249 4.00 10.00
CRDM Donte Moncrief/149 2.50 6.00
CRDT De'Anthony Thomas/249 2.50 6.00
CREE Eric Ebron/249 3.00 8.00
CRJC Jadeveon Clowney/249 3.00 8.00
CRJG Jimmy Garoppolo/249 20.00 50.00
CRJH Jeremy Hill/249 3.00 8.00
CRJL Jarvis Landry/99 8.00 20.00
CRJM Johnny Manziel/249 4.00 10.00
CRKB Kelvin Benjamin/249 8.00 20.00
CRKC Ka'Deem Carey/249 2.50 6.00
CRKM Khalil Mack/249 10.00 25.00
CRLT Logan Thomas/249 2.50 6.00
CRME Mike Evans/149 6.00 15.00
CRML Marqise Lee/199 3.00 8.00
CROB Odell Beckham Jr./199 6.00 15.00
CRSW Sammy Watkins/199 4.00 10.00
CRTB Tajh Boyd/249 2.50 6.00
CRTM Tre Mason/249 2.50 6.00
CRTS Tom Savage/249 2.50 6.00
CRTW Terrance West/199 2.50 6.00
CRAMU Aaron Murray/249 2.50 6.00
CRASJ Austin Seferian-Jenkins/199 2.50 6.00
CRJMA Jordan Matthews/249 4.00 10.00
CRTBR Teddy Bridgewater/249 4.00 10.00

2014 Absolute Tools of the Trade Eight Player

*GOLD/99: .5X TO 1.2X JSY/249
*SILVER/25: .75X TO 2X JSY/249
*PURPLE/20: .75X TO 2X JSY/249
*PRIME/15: .75X TO 2X JSY/15
BMMBMHSC Brgwtr/McCrn Mry/Byd/Msn/Snky/Hll/Cry 10.00 25.00
FCSMSCRM Frmn/Cry/Svge Msn/Sms/Cks/Rchsn/Mncrf 5.00 12.00
MBBGMCTS Mnzl/Brtls/Brgwtr Grplo/Mry/Crr/Thms/Svge 25.00 60.00
MMMCLHEB McCrn/Mry/Mcrf Clwny/Ldry/Hll/Evns/Bkhm 8.00 20.00
RLHEBWBM Rbsn/Lee/Hrns/Evns/Bjmn Wtkns/Bkhm/Mthws 10.00 25.00
WSHFHCWM Wlms/Snky Hyde/Frmn/Hll/Cry/Wst/Msn 5.00 12.00

2014 Absolute Tools of the Trade Jumbo Jerseys

*PURPLE/20: 1.2X TO 3X JSY/154-249
*PURPLE/20: .75X TO 2X JSY/49
*PRIME/15: 1.2X TO 3X JSY/154-249
*PRIME/15: .6X TO 1.5X JSY/30
TTJAD Andy Dalton/30 5.00 12.00
TTJAH Allen Hurns/2
TTJAL Andrew Luck/30 8.00 20.00
TTJBB Blake Bortles/249 1.25 3.00
TTJCK Colin Kaepernick/249 2.50 6.00
TTJJD Jadeveon Clowney/249 1.25 3.00
TTJJM Johnny Manziel/249 1.50 4.00
TTJJW Jason Witten/46 4.00 10.00
TTJKB Kelvin Benjamin/249 1.50 4.00
TTJKC Ka'Deem Carey/249 1.00 2.50
TTJME Mike Evans/249 2.50 6.00
TTJNF Nick Foles/49 4.00 10.00
TTJOB Odell Beckham Jr./249 6.00 15.00
TTJPM Peyton Manning/154 20.00 40.00
TTJSW Sammy Watkins/249 1.50 4.00
TTJTB Teddy Bridgewater/249 1.50 4.00
TTJTR Tony Romo/249 2.50 6.00

2014 Absolute Tools of the Trade Quad Jersey

*PRIME/15: .75X TO 2X JSY/125-249
*PRIME/15: .6X TO 1.5X JSY/60-99
*PRIME/15: .5X TO 1.2X JSY/49
*PRIME/15: .4X TO 1X JSY/20
*PURPLE/20: .75X TO 2X JSY/125-249
*PURPLE/20: .6X TO 1.5X JSY/60-99
*PURPLE/20: .5X TO 1.2X JSY/49
*GOLD/75-99: .5X TO 1.2X JSY/125-249
*GOLD/35: .6X TO 1.5X JSY/125-249
*GOLD/25: .5X TO 1.2X JSY/125-249
*GOLD/25: .5X TO 1.2X JSY/49
*GOLD/25: .6X TO 1.5X JSY/60-99
*SILVER/15-25: .75X TO 2X JSY/125-249
*SILVER/15-25: .6X TO 1.5X JSY/60-99
*SILVER/15-25: .5X TO 1.2X JSY/49
1 A.J. Green/99 6.00 15.00
2 C.J. Spiller/149 3.00 8.00
3 Wes Welker/149 4.00 10.00
4 Demaryius Thomas/149 8.00 20.00
5 Peyton Manning/199 25.00 50.00
6 Jamaal Charles/99 5.00 12.00
7 Tony Romo/249 4.00 10.00
8 Dez Bryant/20 10.00 25.00
9 Jason Witten/49 6.00 15.00
10 Joe Flacco/249 4.00 10.00
11 Torrey Smith/199 3.00 8.00
12 Shonn Greene/249 3.00 8.00
13 Steve Smith/125 4.00 10.00
14 Andy Dalton/99 5.00 12.00
15 Alshon Jeffery/249 4.00 10.00
16 Jay Cutler/125 3.00 8.00
17 Calvin Johnson/49 8.00 20.00
18 Cam Newton/75 6.00 15.00
19 Carson Palmer/60 5.00 12.00
20 Colin Kaepernick/249 4.00 10.00

2014 Absolute Tools of the Trade Rookie Helmets

*ANNI/20: .6X TO 1.5X HELMET/99
HAM A.J. McCarron 2.00 5.00
HAR Allen Robinson 3.00 8.00
HAW Andre Williams 2.00 5.00
HBB Blake Bortles 2.50 6.00
HBC Brandin Cooks 3.00 8.00
HBS Bishop Sankey 2.00 5.00
HCH Carlos Hyde 2.50 6.00
HCL Cody Latimer 2.50 6.00
HCS Charles Sims 2.00 5.00
HDA Davante Adams 3.00 8.00
HDA Dri Archer 2.00 5.00
HDC Derek Carr 10.00 25.00
HDF Devonta Freeman 3.00 8.00
HDM Donte Moncrief 2.00 5.00
HDT De'Anthony Thomas 2.00 5.00
HEE Eric Ebron 2.50 6.00
HJC Jadeveon Clowney 2.50 6.00
HJG Jimmy Garoppolo 15.00 40.00
HJH Jeremy Hill 2.50 6.00
HJL Jarvis Landry 4.00 10.00
HJM Johnny Manziel 3.00 8.00
HKB Kelvin Benjamin 3.00 8.00
HKC Ka'Deem Carey 2.00 5.00
HME Logan Thomas 2.00 5.00
HML Khalil Mack 8.00 20.00
HOB Mike Evans 5.00 12.00
HPR Odell Beckham Jr. 10.00 25.00
HSW Sammy Watkins 3.00 8.00
HTB Tajh Boyd 2.00 5.00
HTM Tre Mason 2.00 5.00
HTS Tom Savage 2.00 5.00
HTW Terrance West 2.00 5.00
HAMU Aaron Murray 2.00 5.00
HASJ Austin Seferian-Jenkins 2.00 5.00
HJMA Jordan Matthews 3.00 8.00
HTBR Teddy Bridgewater 3.00 8.00

2014 Absolute Tools of the Trade Rookie Quad Jersey

*GOLD/99: .5X TO 1.2X JSY/149-249
*GOLD/49: .6X TO 1.5X JSY/149-249
*GOLD/49: .5X TO 1.2X JSY/99
*SILVER/25: .75X TO 2X JSY/149-249
*SILVER/25: .6X TO 1.5X JSY/99
*JSY-BALL/149: .6X TO 1.5X JSY QUAD/14-9249
*JSY-BLL-GLV/99: .8X TO 2X JSY QUAD/149-249
*JSY-BLL-GLV-SHE/20: 1.2X TO 3X JSY QUAD/149-249
QAM A.J. McCarron/249 1.25 3.00
QAMU Aaron Murray/249 1.25 3.00
QAR Allen Robinson/249 2.00 5.00
QAW Andre Williams/249 1.25 3.00
QBB Blake Bortles/249 1.50 4.00
QBC Brandin Cooks/249 2.00 5.00
QBS Bishop Sankey/249 1.25 3.00
QCH Carlos Hyde/249 1.50 4.00
QCL Cody Latimer/249 1.50 4.00
QCS Charles Sims/249 1.25 3.00
QDA Davante Adams/249 2.00 5.00
QDA Dri Archer/249 1.25 3.00
QDC Derek Carr/249 8.00 20.00
QDF Devonta Freeman/249 2.00 5.00
QDM Donte Moncrief/249 1.25 3.00
QDT De'Anthony Thomas/249 1.25 3.00
QEE Eric Ebron/249 1.50 4.00
QJC Jadeveon Clowney/249 1.50 4.00
QJG Jimmy Garoppolo/249 10.00 25.00
QJH Jeremy Hill/249 1.50 4.00
QJL Jarvis Landry/249 2.50 6.00
QJM Johnny Manziel/249 2.00 5.00
QJMA Jordan Matthews/249 2.00 5.00
QKB Kelvin Benjamin/249 2.00 5.00
QKC Ka'Deem Carey/249 1.25 3.00
QLT Lorenzo Taliaferro/99 1.50 4.00
QME Mike Evans/149 3.00 8.00
QML Marqise Lee/249 1.50 4.00
QOB Odell Beckham Jr./249 8.00 20.00
QPR Paul Richardson/249 1.50 4.00
QSW Sammy Watkins/149 2.00 5.00
QTB Teddy Bridgewater/249 2.00 5.00
QTM Tre Mason/249 1.25 3.00
QTS Tom Savage/249 1.25 3.00
QTW Terrance West/249 1.25 3.00

2014 Absolute Tools of the Trade Rookie Quad Jersey Purple

*PURPLE/20: .75X TO 2X JSY/149-249
*PURPLE/20: .6X TO 1.5X JSY/99
QOB Odell Beckham Jr. 25.00 60.00

2014 Absolute Tools of the Trade Rookie Quad Jersey Prime

*PRIME/15: .75X TO 2X JSY/149-249
*PRIME/15: .6X TO 1.5X JSY/99
QOB Odell Beckham Jr. 15.00 40.00

2014 Absolute Tools of the Trade Rookie Signatures

TTRSAH Allen Hurns 5.00 12.00
TTRSAM A.J. McCarron 4.00 10.00
TTRSAMU Aaron Murray 4.00 10.00
TTRSAR Allen Robinson 6.00 15.00
TTRSAS Austin Seferian-Jenkins 4.00 10.00
TTRSAW Andre Williams 4.00 10.00
TTRSBB Blake Bortles 5.00 12.00
TTRSBC Brandin Cooks 6.00 15.00
TTRSBS Bishop Sankey 4.00 10.00
TTRSCH Carlos Hyde 5.00 12.00
TTRSCL Cody Latimer 5.00 12.00
TTRSDA1 Davante Adams 6.00 15.00
TTRSDA2 Dri Archer 4.00 10.00
TTRSDC Derek Carr 40.00 80.00
TTRSDF Devonta Freeman 6.00 15.00
TTRSDM Donte Moncrief 4.00 10.00
TTRSDT De'Anthony Thomas 4.00 10.00
TTRSEE Eric Ebron 5.00 12.00
TTRSJC Jadeveon Clowney
TTRSJG Jimmy Garoppolo 50.00 100.00
TTRSJH Jeremy Hill 5.00 12.00
TTRSJL Jarvis Landry 8.00 20.00
TTRSJM Johnny Manziel 6.00 15.00
TTRSJMA Jordan Matthews 6.00 15.00
TTRSKB Kelvin Benjamin 6.00 15.00
TTRSKC Ka'Deem Carey 4.00 10.00
TTRSKM Khalil Mack
TTRSLT Logan Thomas 4.00 10.00
TTRSLT Lorenzo Taliaferro 4.00 10.00
TTRSME Mike Evans 10.00 25.00
TTRSML Marqise Lee 5.00 12.00
TTRSOB Odell Beckham Jr. 40.00 80.00
TTRSPR Paul Richardson 8.00 20.00
TTRSSW Sammy Watkins 6.00 15.00
TTRSTB Tajh Boyd 4.00 10.00
TTRSTBR Teddy Bridgewater 6.00 15.00
TTRSTM Tre Mason
TTRSTS Tom Savage 4.00 10.00
TTRSTW Terrance West 4.00 10.00

2014 Absolute Tools of the Trade Signatures

*PURPLE/20: .4X TO 1X JSY AU/25
TTSAB Anquan Boldin/25
TTSAD Andy Dalton/25
TTSADO Aaron Dobson/25
TTSAE Andre Ellington/00 3.00 8.00
TTSAG Antonio Gates/25 5.00 12.00
TTSAJ Alshon Jeffery/25 6.00 15.00
TTSAL Andrew Luck/20 75.00 150.00
TTSAM Alfred Morris/25
TTSBH Brian Hartline/99
TTSBR Ben Roethlisberger/20 40.00 80.00
TTSCC Charles Clay/25 5.00 12.00
TTSCP Carson Palmer/25
TTSCS C.J. Spiller/25 5.00 12.00
TTSCW Cameron Wake/25 30.00 60.00
TTSDB Dwayne Bowe/25 6.00 15.00
TTSDBR Drew Brees/20
TTSDH Dan Hampton/25 15.00 40.00
TTSDM Doug Martin/25 6.00 15.00
TTSDT Demaryius Thomas/25 8.00 20.00
TTSDW DeMarcus Ware/25 25.00 50.00
TTSDWO Danny Woodhead/25 20.00 40.00
TTSED Eric Decker/25 5.00 12.00
TTSFJ Fred Jackson/25
TTSJC Jordan Cameron/25
TTSJF Joe Flacco/20 20.00 40.00
TTSJN Jordy Nelson/25 20.00 40.00
TTSJR Joseph Randle/25 5.00 12.00
TTSJRE Jordan Reed/25
TTSKA Keenan Allen/25
TTSKAL Kiko Alonso/25 5.00 12.00
TTSKC Kam Chancellor/25
TTSKD Knile Davis/25 5.00 12.00
TTSMR Matt Ryan/20
TTSMS Matthew Stafford/20 25.00 50.00
TTSMT Manti Te'o/25 6.00 15.00
TTSNF Nick Foles/25 6.00 15.00
TTSPM Peyton Manning/18
TTSPP Paul Posluszny/25
TTSRB Reggie Bush/25 5.00 12.00
TTSRG Rob Gronkowski/25 20.00 40.00
TTSRN Ryan Nassib/25 6.00 15.00
TTSRW Reggie Wayne/25 10.00 25.00
TTSTA Tavon Austin/25 5.00 12.00
TTSTD Terrell Davis/25 15.00 30.00
TTSTDO Tony Dorsett/20 40.00 80.00
TTSTH T.Y. Hilton/25 6.00 15.00
TTSTR Tony Romo/20 40.00 80.00
TTSTS Torrey Smith/25 5.00 12.00
TTSTW Terrance Williams/25 5.00 12.00
TTSVM Von Miller/25 6.00 15.00
TTSZE Zach Ertz/25
TTSZS Zac Stacy/25

2014 Absolute Tools of the Trade Six Player Spectrum Silver

*BASE CARD/149: .3X TO .8X SILVER/25
*GOLD/99: .25X TO .6X SILVER/25
*PURPLE/20: .4X TO 1X SILVER/25
BEMCMB Brdg/Evn/Mnz/Clwn/Mk/Brt 15.00 40.00
EMBBCL Evn/Mtw/Bnj/Bck/Cks/Lndr 10.00 25.00
MBCBGS Mnz/Brt/Crr/Brdg/GrpL/Svg 30.00 80.00
WRLHAL Wtk/Rbn/Lee/Hrn/Arc/Ltm 6.00 15.00
WSHFHM Wlm/Snk/Hyd/Frm/Hll/Msn 6.00 15.00

2016 Absolute

1 Marcus Mariota .40 1.00
2 DeMarco Murray .30 .75
3 Dorial Green-Beckham .25 .60
4 Blake Bortles .25 .60
5 Chris Ivory .30 .75
6 T.J. Yeldon .25 .60
7 Allen Robinson .30 .75
8 Andrew Luck .50 1.25
9 Frank Gore .30 .75
10 T.Y. Hilton .30 .75
11 Brock Osweiler .25 .60
12 Lamar Miller .25 .60
13 DeAndre Hopkins .30 .75
14 J.J. Watt .40 1.00
15 Ben Roethlisberger .40 1.00
16 Le'Veon Bell .30 .75
17 Antonio Brown .40 1.00
18 Robert Griffin III .25 .60
19 Duke Johnson .25 .60
20 Gary Barnidge .25 .60
21 Andy Dalton .30 .75
22 Jeremy Hill .25 .60
23 A.J. Green .40 1.00
24 Joe Flacco .30 .75
25 Justin Forsett .30 .75
26 Steve Smith Sr. .30 .75
27 Philip Rivers .40 1.00
28 Melvin Gordon .30 .75
29 Travis Benjamin .25 .60
30 Derek Carr .40 1.00
31 Amari Cooper .40 1.00
32 Khalil Mack .40 1.00
33 Alex Smith .30 .75
34 Jamaal Charles .30 .75
35 Jeremy Maclin .25 .60
36 C.J. Anderson .30 .75
37 Demaryius Thomas .30 .75
38 Von Miller .30 .75
39 Ryan Fitzpatrick .25 .60
40 Matt Forte .25 .60
41 Brandon Marshall .25 .60
42 Tom Brady 1.00 2.50
43 Dion Lewis .25 .60
44 Rob Gronkowski .40 1.00
45 Ryan Tannehill .30 .75
46 Jay Ajayi .30 .75
47 Jarvis Landry .30 .75
48 Tyrod Taylor .30 .75
49 LeSean McCoy .40 1.00
50 Sammy Watkins .40 1.00
51 Jameis Winston .40 1.00
52 Doug Martin .30 .75
53 Mike Evans .30 .75
54 Drew Brees .40 1.00
55 Mark Ingram .30 .75
56 Brandin Cooks .30 .75
57 Cam Newton .40 1.00
58 Jonathan Stewart .25 .60
59 Greg Olsen .30 .75
60 Luke Kuechly .30 .75
61 Matt Ryan .30 .75
62 Devonta Freeman .30 .75
63 Julio Jones .40 1.00
64 Teddy Bridgewater .30 .75
65 Adrian Peterson .40 1.00
66 Stefon Diggs .30 .75
67 Aaron Rodgers .75 2.00
68 Eddie Lacy .25 .60
69 Jordy Nelson .30 .75
70 Clay Matthews .40 1.00
71 Matthew Stafford .30 .75
72 Ameer Abdullah .25 .60
73 Ezekiel Ansah .25 .60
74 Jay Cutler .25 .60
75 Jeremy Langford .30 .75
76 Alshon Jeffery .30 .75
77 Russell Wilson .50 1.25
78 Thomas Rawls .25 .60
79 Richard Sherman .40 1.00
80 Colin Kaepernick .30 .75
81 Carlos Hyde .25 .60
82 Torrey Smith .25 .60
83 Case Keenum .30 .75
84 Todd Gurley .40 1.00
85 Tavon Austin .25 .60
86 Carson Palmer .30 .75
87 David Johnson .40 1.00
88 Larry Fitzgerald .30 .75
89 Kirk Cousins .40 1.00
90 Matt Jones .30 .75
91 Jordan Reed .25 .60
92 Sam Bradford .25 .60
93 Ryan Mathews .30 .75
94 Zach Ertz .30 .75
95 Eli Manning .30 .75
96 Odell Beckham Jr. .40 1.00
97 Victor Cruz .30 .75
98 Tony Romo .30 .75
99 Dez Bryant .40 1.00
100 Jason Witten .30 .75
101 Jim Kelly .75 2.00
102 Bruce Smith .60 1.50
103 Dan Marino 1.50 4.00
104 Bob Griese .75 2.00
105 Doug Flutie .60 1.50
106 Joe Namath 1.00 2.50
107 Curtis Martin .60 1.50
108 John Elway 1.25 3.00
109 Terrell Davis .60 1.50
110 Marcus Allen .60 1.50
111 Fred Biletnikoff .75 2.00
112 Tim Brown .75 2.00
113 Bo Jackson 1.00 2.50
114 LaDainian Tomlinson .60 1.50
115 Ed Reed .60 1.50
116 Michael Irvin .75 2.00
117 Paul Warfield .60 1.50
118 Terry Bradshaw 1.00 2.50
119 Marshawn Lynch .60 1.50
120 Warren Moon .75 2.00
121 Earl Campbell .75 2.00
122 Peyton Manning 1.50 4.00
123 Marvin Harrison .60 1.50
124 Fred Taylor .50 1.25
125 Eddie George .60 1.50
126 Troy Aikman 1.00 2.50
127 Emmitt Smith 1.25 3.00
128 Roger Staubach 1.00 2.50
129 Boomer Esiason .60 1.50
130 Fran Tarkenton .75 2.00
131 Randall Cunningham .60 1.50
132 John Riggins .60 1.50
133 Darrell Green .60 1.50
134 Kurt Warner .60 1.50
135 Marshall Faulk .60 1.50
136 Eric Dickerson .60 1.50
137 Joe Montana 2.00 5.00
138 Jerry Rice 1.25 3.00
139 Steve Young 1.00 2.50
140 Steve Largent .75 2.00
141 Brian Urlacher .75 2.00
142 Jim McMahon .60 1.50
143 Barry Sanders 1.25 3.00
144 Brett Favre 1.50 4.00
145 Don Majkowski .60 1.50
146 Carl Eller .50 1.25
147 Warrick Dunn .50 1.25
148 Kevin Greene .75 2.00
149 Archie Manning .60 1.50
150 Derrick Brooks .50 1.25
151 Brandon Allen RC .60 1.50
152 Brandon Doughty RC .60 1.50
153 Jake Rudock RC .60 1.50
154 Jeff Driskel RC .60 1.50
155 Nate Sudfeld RC .60 1.50
156 Daniel Lasco RC .60 1.50
157 Jacoby Brissett RC .75 2.00
158 Keith Marshall RC .60 1.50
159 Kelvin Taylor RC .60 1.50
160 Tyreek Hill RC 2.50 6.00
161 Austin Hooper RC .60 1.50
162 Nick Vannett RC .60 1.50
163 Jerell Adams RC .60 1.50
164 Tyler Higbee RC .60 1.50
165 Rico Gathers RC .60 1.50
166 Aaron Burbridge RC .60 1.50
167 Charone Peake RC .60 1.50
168 Cody Core RC .60 1.50
169 Daniel Braverman RC .60 1.50
170 Demarcus Ayers RC .60 1.50
171 Jordan Payton RC .60 1.50
172 Kenny Lawler RC 1.00 2.50
173 Kolby Listenbee RC .60 1.50
174 Rashard Higgins RC .60 1.50
175 Tajae Sharpe RC .75 2.00
176 Thomas Duarte RC .60 1.50
177 Derek Watt RC 1.00 2.50
178 Jakeem Grant RC .60 1.50
179 Mike Thomas RC 1.00 2.50
180 Devin Lucien RC .75 2.00
181 Devin Fuller RC .75 2.00
182 Artie Burns RC .75 2.00
183 Eli Apple RC .75 2.00
184 Jalen Ramsey RC 1.00 2.50
185 Vernon Hargreaves III RC 1.00 2.50
186 William Jackson III RC .75 2.00
187 DeForest Buckner RC .60 1.50
188 Shaq Lawson RC .60 1.50
189 Keanu Neal RC .60 1.50
190 Karl Joseph RC .60 1.50
191 Kenny Clark RC .60 1.50
192 Robert Nkemdiche RC .75 2.00
193 Sheldon Rankins RC .75 2.00
194 Vernon Butler RC .60 1.50
195 Darron Lee RC .60 1.50
196 Leonard Floyd RC .75 2.00
197 Jaylon Smith RC .60 1.50
198 Myles Jack RC .75 2.00
199 Jihad Ward RC .60 1.50
200 Malcolm Mitchell RC .60 1.50
201 Jared Goff JSY AU/199 RC 50.00 100.00
202 Carson Wentz JSY AU/199 RC 75.00 150.00
203 Joey Bosa JSY AU/199 RC 8.00 20.00
204 Ezekiel Elliott JSY AU/199 RC EXCH 75.00 150.00
205 Corey Coleman JSY AU/199 RC EXCH 6.00 15.00
206 Will Fuller JSY AU/499 RC 5.00 12.00
207 Josh Doctson JSY AU/499 RC 4.00 10.00
208 Laquon Treadwell JSY AU/199 RC EXCH 5.00 12.00
209 Paxton Lynch JSY AU/199 RC 4.00 10.00
210 Hunter Henry JSY AU/499 RC 4.00 10.00
211 Sterling Shepard JSY AU/499 RC 4.00 10.00
212 Derrick Henry JSY AU/199 RC 10.00 25.00
213 Michael Thomas JSY AU/499 RC 6.00 15.00
214 Christian Hackenberg JSY AU/199 RC EXCH 4.00 10.00
215 Kenyan Drake JSY AU/499 RC 5.00 12.00
216 Braxton Miller JSY AU/199 RC 4.00 10.00
217 Leonte Carroo JSY AU/499 RC 3.00 8.00
218 C.J. Prosise JSY AU/499 RC 3.00 8.00
219 DeAndre Washington JSY AU/499 RC 3.00 8.00
220 Cody Kessler JSY AU/499 RC 3.00 8.00
221 Tyler Boyd JSY AU/499 RC 4.00 10.00
222 Connor Cook JSY AU/499 RC 4.00 10.00
223 Chris Moore JSY AU/499 RC 4.00 10.00
224 Ricardo Louis JSY AU/499 RC EXCH 3.00 8.00
225 Pharoh Cooper JSY AU/499 RC 3.00 8.00
226 Tyler Ervin JSY AU/499 RC 3.00 8.00
227 Demarcus Robinson JSY AU/499 RC 3.00 8.00
228 Kenneth Dixon JSY AU/499 RC EXCH 3.00 8.00
229 Dak Prescott JSY AU/499 RC 30.00 60.00
230 Devontae Booker JSY AU/499 RC 4.00 10.00
231 Cardale Jones JSY AU/499 RC 3.00 8.00
232 Paul Perkins JSY AU/499 RC 3.00 8.00
233 Jordan Howard JSY AU/499 RC 8.00 20.00
234 Wendell Smallwood JSY AU/499 RC 3.00 8.00
236 Kevin Hogan JSY AU/499 RC EXCH 4.00 10.00
237 Alex Collins JSY AU/499 RC EXCH 4.00 10.00
238 Keenan Reynolds JSY AU/499 RC 4.00 10.00
239 Trevor Davis JSY AU/499 RC 3.00 8.00
240 Moritz Bohringer JSY AU/499 RC 3.00 8.00

2016 Absolute Spectrum Blue

*1-150 VETS: 1.5X TO 4X BASIC CARDS
*151-200 ROOKIES: .8X TO 2X BASIC RC

2016 Absolute Spectrum Green

*1-150 VETS/25: 4X TO 10X BASIC CARDS
*151-200 ROOKIES/25: 2X TO 5X BASIC RC

2016 Absolute Spectrum Red

*1-150 VETS/100: 2X TO 5X BASIC CARDS
*151-200 ROOKIES/100: 1X TO 2.5X BASIC RC

2016 Absolute Absolute Heroes Autographs

4 Derek Carr/50 20.00 50.00
7 Jim McMahon/25 12.00 30.00
9 Don Majkowski/50 6.00 15.00
11 DeMarcus Ware/25 12.00 30.00
17 Andy Dalton/25 8.00 20.00
19 Derrick Brooks/50 5.00 12.00
20 Kirk Cousins/36 12.00 30.00
21 Patrick Peterson/25 6.00 15.00
23 Justin Forsett/50 6.00 15.00
25 Greg Olsen/15 10.00 25.00

2016 Absolute Absolute Heroes Autographs Numbers

1 Dez Bryant/88 EXCH 20.00 50.00
2 Danny Woodhead/39 6.00 15.00
8 Darrelle Revis/24 12.00 30.00
11 DeMarcus Ware/94 5.00 12.00
12 Bo Jackson/34 40.00 80.00
14 Clay Matthews/52 15.00 40.00
15 Randall Cobb/18
19 Derrick Brooks/55 5.00 12.00
21 Patrick Peterson/21 6.00 15.00
23 Justin Forsett/29 6.00 15.00
24 Hines Ward/86 20.00 50.00
25 Greg Olsen/88 5.00 12.00

2016 Absolute Absolutely Ink

*GOLD/25: .6X TO 1.5X BASIC AU/99
*GOLD/25: .5X TO 1.2X BASIC AU/50-65
*GOLD/25: .4X TO 1X BASIC AU/25
*GOLD/25: .3X TO .8X BASIC AU/15
1 Doug Flutie/25
2 Brian Bosworth/25 20.00 40.00
3 Christian Hackenberg/99 4.00 10.00
4 Nick Vannett/99 4.00 10.00
5 C.J. Prosise/99 4.00 10.00
6 Dorial Green-Beckham/99 4.00 10.00
7 Paxton Lynch/15 8.00 20.00
8 Karlos Williams/99 4.00 10.00
9 Derrick Henry/15 20.00 50.00
10 Leonte Carroo/99 4.00 10.00
12 Melvin Gordon/50 6.00 15.00
13 Sterling Shepard/99 5.00 12.00
14 Pharoh Cooper/99 4.00 10.00
15 Joey Bosa/99 8.00 20.00
16 David Johnson/99 10.00 25.00
19 Laquon Treadwell/99 EXCH 5.00 12.00
20 Matt Jones/99 5.00 12.00
21 Corey Coleman/99 EXCH 6.00 15.00
22 Jeremy Langford/99 5.00 12.00
24 Tyler Eifert/50 6.00 15.00
25 Reggie Ragland/99 4.00 10.00
27 Brock Osweiler/50 5.00 12.00
28 William Jackson III/99 5.00 12.00
30 Jared Goff/15 50.00 100.00
32 Charcandrick West/99 4.00 10.00
33 Jacoby Brissett/99 5.00 12.00
34 Brandon Doughty/99 4.00 10.00
35 Myles Jack/99 5.00 12.00
37 Ricardo Louis/99 4.00 10.00
38 Golden Tate III/63 5.00 12.00
39 Zach Ertz/99 5.00 12.00
40 Josh Doctson/99 5.00 12.00
41 Devontae Booker/99 5.00 12.00
42 Carson Wentz/15 80.00 200.00
44 Will Fuller/99 6.00 15.00
45 Doug Baldwin/65 6.00 15.00
46 Dak Prescott/99 EXCH 30.00 80.00
47 Allen Hurns/99 4.00 10.00
48 Charles Haley/99 6.00 15.00
49 Phil McConkey/99 5.00 12.00

2016 Absolute Absolutely Ink Numbers

2 Brian Bosworth/55 20.00 40.00
4 Nick Vannett/81 4.00 10.00
5 C.J. Prosise/22 6.00 15.00
6 Dorial Green-Beckham/17 6.00 15.00
8 Karlos Williams/29 5.00 12.00
9 Derrick Henry/24 15.00 40.00
10 Leonte Carroo/88 4.00 10.00
12 Melvin Gordon/28 6.00 15.00
15 Joey Bosa/97 8.00 20.00
16 David Johnson/31 8.00 20.00
20 Matt Jones/31 6.00 15.00
22 Jeremy Langford/33 6.00 15.00
24 Tyler Eifert/85 5.00 12.00
25 Reggie Ragland/19 6.00 15.00
27 Brock Osweiler/17 6.00 15.00
28 William Jackson III/22 8.00 20.00
29 Amari Cooper/89 EXCH 25.00 50.00
30 Jared Goff/16 40.00 100.00
31 Thomas Rawls/34 5.00 12.00
32 Charcandrick West/35 5.00 12.00
35 Myles Jack/44 6.00 15.00
36 Earl Thomas III/29 6.00 15.00
37 Ricardo Louis/80 4.00 10.00
38 Golden Tate III/20 6.00 15.00
39 Zach Ertz/86 5.00 12.00
40 Josh Doctson/18 8.00 20.00
41 Devontae Booker/20 8.00 20.00
44 Will Fuller/15 12.00 30.00
45 Doug Baldwin/89 12.00 30.00
47 Allen Hurns/88 4.00 10.00
48 Charles Haley/94 6.00 15.00
49 Phil McConkey/80 5.00 12.00

2016 Absolute Air Raid Materials

1 Drew Brees/25 6.00 15.00
2 Jameis Winston/199 3.00 8.00
3 Jay Cutler/199 2.00 5.00
4 Matt Ryan/100 3.00 8.00
5 Alex Smith/150 2.50 6.00
6 Marcus Mariota/199 3.00 8.00
7 Eli Manning/50 4.00 10.00
8 Derek Carr/199 3.00 8.00
9 Matthew Stafford/100 3.00 8.00
10 Carson Palmer/186 2.50 6.00
11 Blake Bortles/199 2.00 5.00
12 Philip Rivers/50 5.00 12.00
13 Sam Bradford/199 2.00 5.00
14 Andrew Luck/50 6.00 15.00
15 Teddy Bridgewater/199 2.50 6.00
16 Joe Flacco/100 3.00 8.00
17 Andy Dalton/199 2.50 6.00
18 Ryan Tannehill/199 2.50 6.00
19 Kirk Cousins/199 3.00 8.00
20 Colin Kaepernick/199 2.50 6.00

2016 Absolute Canton Absolute Jerseys

*PRME/25: .6X TO 1.5X BASIC JSY/99
*PRME/15: .8X TO 2X BASIC JSY/99
*PRME/15: .6X TO 1.5X BASIC JSY/50
1 Aaron Rodgers/25 12.00 30.00
2 Adrian Peterson/75 4.00 10.00
3 Allen Robinson/99 3.00 8.00
4 Julio Jones/99 4.00 10.00
5 Amari Cooper/99 4.00 10.00
6 Andrew Luck/50 6.00 15.00
7 Antonio Gates/99 2.50 6.00
8 Brian Urlacher/50 5.00 12.00
9 Demaryius Thomas/99 3.00 8.00
10 DeMarcus Ware/50 4.00 10.00
11 Drew Brees/25 6.00 15.00
12 Jameis Winston/99 3.00 8.00
13 Jason Witten/20 6.00 15.00
14 Ben Roethlisberger/15 8.00 20.00
15 Odell Beckham Jr./99 3.00 8.00
16 Peyton Manning/25 12.00 30.00
17 Russell Wilson/25 8.00 20.00
18 Cam Newton/25 6.00 15.00
19 Todd Gurley/99 3.00 8.00
20 Tom Brady/25 15.00 40.00

2016 Absolute Catching Fire Jerseys

1 Amari Cooper/199 3.00 8.00
2 Jordan Reed/100 2.50 6.00
3 Demaryius Thomas/100 3.00 8.00
4 Antonio Brown/25 6.00 15.00
5 Jarvis Landry/150 2.50 6.00
6 Sammy Watkins /199 3.00 8.00
7 Eric Decker/100 2.50 6.00
8 Kevin White/199 2.00 5.00
9 Sammie Coates/199 2.00 5.00
10 Tyler Eifert/150 2.50 6.00
11 Larry Fitzgerald/100 3.00 8.00
12 Julio Jones/50 5.00 12.00
13 Odell Beckham Jr./199 3.00 8.00

14 Stefon Diggs/199 2.50 6.00
15 Allen Robinson/199 2.50 6.00
16 Tyler Lockett/199 2.50 6.00
17 Dorial Green-Beckham/199 2.00 5.00
18 A.J. Green/135 3.00 8.00
19 T.Y. Hilton/100 3.00 8.00
20 Devin Funchess/199 2.00 5.00

2016 Absolute Glass

1 Marcus Mariota EXCH 60.00 120.00
2 Blake Bortles EXCH 12.00 30.00
3 Andrew Luck EXCH 50.00 100.00
4 J.J. Watt EXCH 30.00 60.00
5 Ben Roethlisberger EXCH 75.00 150.00
6 Antonio Brown EXCH 50.00 100.00
7 A.J. Green EXCH 20.00 50.00
8 Joe Flacco EXCH 15.00 40.00
9 Philip Rivers EXCH 20.00 50.00
10 Derek Carr EXCH 60.00 125.00
11 Amari Cooper EXCH 20.00 50.00
12 Von Miller EXCH 15.00 40.00
13 Tom Brady EXCH 50.00 125.00
14 Rob Gronkowski EXCH 40.00 100.00
15 Jameis Winston EXCH 20.00 50.00
16 Drew Brees EXCH
17 Cam Newton EXCH 20.00 50.00
18 Julio Jones EXCH 20.00 50.00
19 Adrian Peterson EXCH 40.00 100.00
20 Aaron Rodgers EXCH 60.00 120.00
21 Matthew Stafford EXCH 15.00 40.00
22 Russell Wilson EXCH 60.00 120.00
23 Richard Sherman EXCH 60.00 120.00
24 Todd Gurley EXCH 40.00 80.00
25 Carson Palmer EXCH 15.00 40.00
26 Larry Fitzgerald EXCH 15.00 40.00
27 Odell Beckham Jr. EXCH 20.00 50.00
28 Tony Romo EXCH 15.00 40.00
29 Jason Witten EXCH 40.00 80.00
30 Jim Kelly EXCH 20.00 50.00
31 Dan Marino EXCH 75.00 150.00
32 Joe Namath EXCH 60.00 120.00
33 John Elway EXCH 30.00 80.00
34 Bo Jackson EXCH 25.00 60.00
35 Terry Bradshaw EXCH 60.00 125.00
36 Earl Campbell EXCH 20.00 50.00
37 Peyton Manning EXCH 60.00 120.00
38 Troy Aikman EXCH
39 Emmitt Smith EXCH 30.00 80.00
40 Roger Staubach EXCH 25.00 60.00
41 Joe Montana EXCH 60.00 125.00
42 Jerry Rice EXCH 50.00 100.00
43 Steve Young EXCH
44 Barry Sanders EXCH 50.00 100.00
45 Brett Favre EXCH
46 Jared Goff EXCH 30.00 80.00
47 Carson Wentz EXCH 60.00 125.00
48 Ezekiel Elliott EXCH 100.00 200.00
49 Derrick Henry EXCH 15.00 40.00
50 Paxton Lynch EXCH

2016 Absolute Ground Hoggs Jerseys

1 Eddie Lacy/50 3.00 8.00
2 Adrian Peterson/25 6.00 15.00
3 Jeremy Hill/199 2.00 5.00
4 Matt Jones/199 2.50 6.00
5 Devonta Freeman/199 2.50 6.00
6 Darren McFadden/40 3.00 8.00
7 T.J. Yeldon/199 2.00 5.00
8 Melvin Gordon/199 2.50 6.00
9 LeSean McCoy/50 5.00 12.00
10 Duke Johnson/187 2.00 5.00
11 Ryan Mathews/100 3.00 8.00
12 Doug Martin/199 2.50 6.00
13 Ameer Abdullah/199 2.00 5.00
14 David Johnson/199 3.00 8.00
15 Mark Ingram/50 4.00 10.00
16 Jamaal Charles/50 4.00 10.00
17 Todd Gurley/199 3.00 8.00
18 Carlos Hyde/199 2.00 5.00
19 Buck Allen/199 2.00 5.00
20 Jeremy Langford/199 2.50 6.00

2016 Absolute Hall of Fame Jersey Autographs

1 Joe Namath/25 40.00 100.00
2 Earl Campbell/50 15.00 40.00
3 Steve Largent/50 15.00 40.00
4 Brett Favre/25 125.00 250.00
5 Jim Kelly/30 25.00 50.00
6 Jerome Bettis/50 25.00 50.00
7 Steve Young/25 25.00 50.00
8 Gale Sayers/75 12.00 30.00
9 Barry Sanders/25 75.00 150.00
10 Marvin Harrison/25 EXCH 15.00 40.00
11 Marshall Faulk/25 30.00 60.00
12 Dan Hampton/25 25.00 50.00
13 Eric Dickerson/99 30.00 60.00
14 Jerry Rice/25 75.00 150.00
15 Charles Haley/99 30.00 60.00
16 Troy Aikman/25 40.00 80.00
17 Rod Woodson/99 10.00 25.00
18 Dan Marino/25 75.00 150.00
20 Paul Warfield/99 10.00 25.00

2016 Absolute Head to Toe Materials

1 Edgerrin James/50 3.00 8.00
2 Reggie White/45 15.00 40.00
3 Junior Seau/30 10.00 25.00
4 Marshall Faulk/99 2.50 6.00
5 T.J. Yeldon/50 2.50 6.00
6 Tom Brady/65 15.00 40.00
7 Jarvis Landry/28 3.00 8.00
8 Kelvin Benjamin/27 3.00 8.00
10 Curtis Martin/45 3.00 8.00

2016 Absolute Historical Dual Jerseys

1 E.Reed/R.Lewis/99 6.00 15.00
2 J.Kelly/T.Thomas/25 6.00 15.00
3 T.Brady/R.Grnkwski/25 12.00 30.00
4 R.Staubach/B.Lilly/25
5 R.Smith/J.Elway/50 8.00 20.00
6 B.Favre/A.Green/99 8.00 20.00
7 P.Manning/M.Harrison/99 8.00 20.00
8 B.Jackson/M.Allen/99 10.00 25.00
9 B.Griese/L.Csonka/50 5.00 12.00
10 T.Brdshw/J.Stllwrth/25 10.00 25.00
11 S.Young/J.Rice/99 6.00 15.00
12 K.Warner/M.Faulk/99 3.00 8.00
13 R.White/E.Jones/25 5.00 12.00
14 J.Montana/R.Craig/85 12.00 30.00
15 J.Thsmn/J.Riggins/99 4.00 10.00

2016 Absolute Historical Triple Jerseys

1 Klly/Yng/Akmn 10.00 25.00
2 Mntna/Fvre/Elwy 20.00 50.00
3 Mnng/Mrno/Moon 30.00 60.00
4 Sndrs/Grge/Mrtn 15.00 40.00
5 Rice/Crtr/Lrgnt 12.00 30.00
6 Whte/Grne/Hmptn 6.00 15.00
7 Cmpbll/Rggns/Jcksn 10.00 25.00
8 Flk/Alln/Thms 6.00 15.00
9 Dwsn/Grse/Stbch 25.00 50.00
10 Syrs/Drstt/Hrrs 8.00 20.00

2016 Absolute Iconic Ink

2 Antonio Brown/50 30.00 60.00
3 Dan Hampton/100 4.00 10.00
4 Alex Smith/50 12.00 30.00
5 Jordy Nelson/75 10.00 25.00
6 Paul Hornung/100 10.00 25.00
7 Antonio Gates/25 6.00 15.00
8 Tyler Eifert/100 5.00 12.00
9 Matt Forte/50 5.00 12.00
11 Ben Roethlisberger/25 50.00 100.00
12 Travis Kelce/199 8.00 20.00
13 John Brown/199 4.00 10.00
14 Paul Warfield/100 5.00 12.00
16 Charlie Joiner/199 3.00 8.00
17 Matt Ryan/15 15.00 40.00
18 John Hannah/199 3.00 8.00
19 Allen Robinson/199 4.00 10.00
20 James Lofton/74 5.00 12.00
21 Terrell Davis/25 15.00 40.00
22 Mike Evans/150 4.00 10.00
23 Ickey Woods/199 3.00 8.00
24 Steve Smith Sr./25 8.00 20.00
25 Troy Brown/199 3.00 8.00
26 J.J. Watt/25 EXCH 30.00 60.00
27 Bob Lilly/100 5.00 12.00
28 Ozzie Newsome/100 5.00 12.00
29 Walt Garrison/199 10.00 25.00
30 Carl Eller/199 3.00 8.00

2016 Absolute Iconic Ink Dual

2 E.Dckrsn/T.Gurley/35 75.00 150.00
3 T.Thomas/A.Reed/50 20.00 50.00
4 V.Miller/D.Ware/25
7 E.Campbell/W.Moon/25 30.00 60.00
8 D.Carr/A.Cooper/25 60.00 120.00
9 F.Taylor/T.Yeldon/50 8.00 20.00

2016 Absolute Iconic Ink Triple

1 Hmptn/Sngltry/Dent 75.00 150.00
2 White/Jones/Lilly 40.00 80.00
3 Moon/Cnnghm/Brdgwtr
4 Mjkwski/Fvre/Rdgrs 175.00 350.00
5 Stbch/Akmn/Romo 150.00 250.00

2016 Absolute Jerseys

*PATCH/25: .6X TO 1.5X BASIC JSY/99
1 Blake Bortles/99 2.50 6.00
2 Darren McFadden/99 2.50 6.00
3 Demaryius Thomas/50 4.00 10.00
4 Karlos Williams/99 2.50 6.00
5 Devin Funchess/99 2.50 6.00
6 Jeremy Langford/99 3.00 8.00
7 Jeremy Hill/99 2.50 6.00
8 Duke Johnson/50 3.00 8.00
9 Terrance Williams/25 4.00 10.00
10 Ameer Abdullah/99 2.50 6.00
11 T.Y. Hilton/50 4.00 10.00
12 T.J. Yeldon/99 2.50 6.00
13 Brandin Cooks/25 5.00 12.00
14 Khalil Mack/50 5.00 12.00
15 Andy Dalton/25 5.00 12.00
16 Melvin Gordon/99 3.00 8.00
17 Carlos Hyde/99 2.50 6.00
18 Tyler Lockett/99 3.00 8.00
19 Von Miller/40 8.00 20.00
20 Jordan Reed/99 2.50 6.00

2016 Absolute Leather and Laces Materials

1 Jameis Winston 5.00 12.00
2 Marcus Mariota 10.00 25.00
3 Tyler Lockett 4.00 10.00
4 Amari Cooper 5.00 12.00
5 Devin Funchess 3.00 8.00
6 Melvin Gordon 4.00 10.00
7 Ameer Abdullah 3.00 8.00
8 Todd Gurley 5.00 12.00
9 Tom Brady 25.00 50.00
10 Dorial Green-Beckham 3.00 8.00

2016 Absolute Marks of Fame Autographs

2 Jerome Bettis/15 30.00 60.00
3 Randy White/75 5.00 12.00
5 Dan Hampton/50 5.00 12.00
13 Ronnie Lott/15 10.00 25.00
14 Fran Tarkenton/25 15.00 40.00
15 Lawrence Taylor/15 30.00 60.00
22 Ozzie Newsome/45 6.00 15.00
23 Len Dawson/25 10.00 25.00
24 Steve Largent/25 10.00 25.00

2016 Absolute Marks of Fame Autographs Numbers

1 Peyton Manning/18 60.00 125.00
2 Jerome Bettis/36 30.00 60.00
3 Randy White/54 10.00 25.00
5 Dan Hampton/99 4.00 10.00
6 Andre Reed/83 5.00 12.00
7 Tim Brown/81 10.00 25.00
12 Marshall Faulk/28 8.00 20.00
13 Ronnie Lott/42 12.00 30.00
15 Lawrence Taylor/56 15.00 40.00
16 Barry Sanders/20
19 Gale Sayers/40 25.00 50.00
21 Bruce Smith/78 10.00 25.00
22 Ozzie Newsome/82 5.00 12.00
23 Len Dawson/16 12.00 30.00
24 Steve Largent/80 6.00 15.00

2016 Absolute NFL Lifestyle Jerseys

1 Charles Woodson 4.00 10.00
2 Charles Woodson 4.00 10.00
3 Charles Woodson 4.00 10.00
4 Charles Woodson 4.00 10.00
5 Charles Woodson 4.00 10.00
6 Charles Woodson 4.00 10.00
7 Charles Woodson 4.00 10.00
8 Eric Decker 2.50 6.00
9 Eric Decker 2.50 6.00
10 Eric Decker 2.50 6.00
11 Eric Decker 2.50 6.00
12 Eric Decker 2.50 6.00
13 Eric Decker 2.50 6.00

2016 Absolute Red Zone

1 Aaron Rodgers 2.00 5.00
2 Adrian Peterson 1.00 2.50
3 A.J. Green 1.00 2.50
4 Allen Robinson .75 2.00
5 Antonio Brown 1.00 2.50
6 Blake Bortles .60 1.50
7 Brandon Marshall .60 1.50
8 Cam Newton 1.00 2.50
9 Carson Palmer .75 2.00
10 DeAndre Hopkins .75 2.00
11 DeAngelo Williams .60 1.50
12 Devonta Freeman .75 2.00
13 Eli Manning .75 2.00
14 Gary Barnidge .60 1.50
15 Greg Olsen .75 2.00
16 Jason Witten .75 2.00
17 Jeremy Hill .60 1.50
18 Jordan Reed .60 1.50
19 Julio Jones 1.00 2.50
20 Odell Beckham Jr. 1.00 2.50
21 Rob Gronkowski 1.00 2.50
22 Russell Wilson 1.25 3.00
23 Todd Gurley 1.00 2.50
24 Tom Brady 2.50 6.00
25 David Johnson 1.00 2.50

2016 Absolute Rook Ink Silver

*GOLD/25: .8X TO 2X BASIC AU/150-399
*GOLD/25: .6X TO 1.5X BASIC AU/70-100
*BLUE: .4X TO 1X BASIC AU/150-399
*BLUE: .3X TO .8X BASIC AU/70-100
*RED: .4X TO 1X BASIC AU/150-399
*RED: .3X TO .8X BASIC AU/70-100
1 KeiVarae Russell/100 3.00 8.00
2 Brandon Allen/150 2.50 6.00
3 Keith Marshall/399 2.50 6.00
4 Andrew Billings/399 3.00 8.00
5 A'Shawn Robinson/200 2.50 6.00
6 Austin Hooper/250 2.50 6.00
7 Austin Johnson/399 2.50 6.00
8 Brandon Doughty/250 2.50 6.00
9 Moritz Bohringer/199 2.50 6.00
10 William Jackson III/150 3.00 8.00
13 DeForest Buckner/100 3.00 8.00
14 Demarcus Ayers/399 2.50 6.00
15 Demarcus Robinson/250 2.50 6.00
16 DeAndre Washington/100 3.00 8.00
17 Eli Apple/150 3.00 8.00
18 Emmanuel Ogbah/399 3.00 8.00
19 Vernon Butler/399 2.50 6.00
20 Jake Rudock/250 2.50 6.00
21 Jarran Reed/150 2.50 6.00
22 Jaylon Smith/250 2.50 6.00
23 Jeff Driskel/150 2.50 6.00
24 Jerell Adams/150 2.50 6.00
25 Glenn Gronkowski/250 2.50 6.00
26 Tajae Sharpe/250 3.00 8.00
27 Jordan Payton/399 2.50 6.00
28 Kamalei Correa/399 2.50 6.00
29 Karl Joseph/399 2.50 6.00
30 Jacoby Brissett/150 3.00 8.00
31 Kendall Fuller/250 3.00 8.00
32 Kenny Clark/399 2.50 6.00
33 Kevin Dodd/250 2.50 6.00
34 Cody Core/399 2.50 6.00
35 Malcolm Mitchell/250 2.50 6.00
36 Mackensie Alexander/100 3.00 8.00
37 Maliek Collins/399 2.50 6.00
38 Myles Jack/100 4.00 10.00
39 Nick Vannett/250 2.50 6.00
41 Reggie Ragland/250 2.50 6.00
42 Robert Nkemdiche/250 3.00 8.00
43 Nate Sudfeld/399 2.50 6.00
45 Sheldon Rankins/399 3.00 8.00
46 Keanu Neal/399 2.50 6.00
47 Rashard Higgins/250 2.50 6.00
48 Vernon Hargreaves III/70 5.00 12.00
49 Vonn Bell/250 3.00 8.00
50 Kenny Lawler/299 4.00 10.00

2016 Absolute Rookie Force Jerseys

1 Alex Collins/199 1.50 4.00
2 Braxton Miller/199 1.25 3.00
3 C.J. Prosise/50 1.25 3.00
4 Cardale Jones/50 1.25 3.00
5 Carson Wentz/25 12.00 30.00
6 Chris Moore/199 1.50 4.00
7 Christian Hackenberg/99 1.25 3.00
8 Cody Kessler/99 1.25 3.00
9 Connor Cook/99 1.50 4.00
10 Corey Coleman/50 2.00 5.00
11 Dak Prescott/99 10.00 25.00
12 Demarcus Robinson/199 1.25 3.00
13 Derrick Henry/50 3.00 8.00
14 Devontae Booker/99 1.50 4.00
15 Ezekiel Elliott/50 15.00 40.00
16 Hunter Henry/99 1.50 4.00
17 DeAndre Washington/199 1.25 3.00
18 Jared Goff/50 8.00 20.00
19 Joey Bosa/50 2.50 6.00
20 Jonathan Williams/199 1.50 4.00
21 Jordan Howard/199 3.00 8.00
22 Josh Doctson/50 1.50 4.00
23 Keenan Reynolds/199 1.50 4.00
24 Kenneth Dixon/99 1.25 3.00
25 Kenyan Drake/199 2.00 5.00
26 Kevin Hogan/99 1.50 4.00
27 Laquon Treadwell/55 1.50 4.00
28 Leonte Carroo/199 1.25 3.00
29 Moritz Bohringer/199 1.25 3.00
30 Michael Thomas/99 2.50 6.00
31 Paul Perkins/99 1.25 3.00
32 Paxton Lynch/50 1.25 3.00
33 Pharoh Cooper/199 1.25 3.00
34 Ricardo Louis/199 1.25 3.00
35 Sterling Shepard/199 1.50 4.00
36 Trevor Davis/199 1.25 3.00
37 Tyler Boyd/99 1.50 4.00
38 Tyler Ervin/199 1.25 3.00
39 Wendell Smallwood/199 1.25 3.00
40 Will Fuller/99 2.00 5.00

2016 Absolute Rookie Jerseys

1 Jared Goff 10.00 25.00
2 Carson Wentz 15.00 40.00
3 Paxton Lynch 1.50 4.00
4 Christian Hackenberg 1.50 4.00
5 Cody Kessler 1.50 4.00
6 Connor Cook 2.00 5.00
7 Dak Prescott 8.00 20.00
8 Cardale Jones 1.50 4.00
9 Kevin Hogan 2.00 5.00
10 DeAndre Washington 1.50 4.00
11 Joey Bosa 3.00 8.00
12 Corey Coleman 2.50 6.00
13 Josh Doctson 2.00 5.00
14 Will Fuller 2.50 6.00
15 Laquon Treadwell 2.00 5.00
16 Sterling Shepard 2.00 5.00
17 Michael Thomas 3.00 8.00
18 Tyler Boyd 2.00 5.00
19 Braxton Miller 1.50 4.00
20 Leonte Carroo 1.50 4.00
21 Chris Moore 2.00 5.00
22 Moritz Bohringer 1.50 4.00
23 Ricardo Louis 1.50 4.00
24 Pharoh Cooper 1.50 4.00
25 Demarcus Robinson 1.50 4.00
26 Trevor Davis 1.50 4.00
27 Hunter Henry 2.00 5.00
28 Ezekiel Elliott 8.00 20.00
29 Derrick Henry 4.00 10.00
30 Kenyan Drake 2.50 6.00
31 C.J. Prosise 1.50 4.00
32 Tyler Ervin 1.50 4.00
33 Kenneth Dixon 1.50 4.00
34 Devontae Booker 2.00 5.00
35 Paul Perkins 1.50 4.00
36 Jordan Howard 4.00 10.00
37 Wendell Smallwood 1.50 4.00
38 Jonathan Williams 2.00 5.00
39 Alex Collins 2.00 5.00
40 Keenan Reynolds 2.00 5.00

2016 Absolute Rookie Roundup

1 Carson Wentz 5.00 12.00
2 Jared Goff 3.00 8.00
3 Paxton Lynch .50 1.25
4 Connor Cook .60 1.50
5 Christian Hackenberg .50 1.25
6 Ezekiel Elliott 2.50 6.00
7 Derrick Henry 1.25 3.00
8 Devontae Booker .60 1.50
9 Kenneth Dixon .50 1.25
10 Alex Collins .60 1.50
11 Laquon Treadwell .60 1.50
12 Corey Coleman .75 2.00
13 Braxton Miller .50 1.25
14 Josh Doctson .60 1.50
15 Will Fuller .75 2.00
16 Tyler Boyd .60 1.50
17 Sterling Shepard .60 1.50
18 Joey Bosa 1.00 2.50
19 Jalen Ramsey .75 2.00
20 Myles Jack .60 1.50

2016 Absolute Team Quads Jerseys

1 Csns/Jns/Crwdr/Reed/50 5.00 12.00
2 Mrta/Wrght/Wlkr/GrnBckhm/50 5.00 12.00
3 Evns/Wnstn/SfrnJnkns/Mrtn/50 5.00 12.00
4 Lcktt/Thms/Chnclr/Wlsn/20 15.00 40.00
5 Gts/Wdhd/Grdn/Rvrs/15 8.00 20.00
6 Brwn/Rthlsbrgr/Ksl/Whtn/15 8.00 20.00
7 Brdfrd/Mthws/Aghlr/Mtthws/50 4.00 10.00
8 Cks/Brs/Ingrm/Snd/15 8.00 20.00
9 Ptrsn/Brdgwtr/Smth/Dggs/15 8.00 20.00
10 Wke/Tnnhll/Lndry/Ajyi/25 5.00 12.00
11 Ryn/Jns/Frmn/Clmn/25 6.00 15.00
12 Yldn/Thms/Rbnsn/Brtls/25 4.00 10.00
13 Lck/Mncrf/Drstt/Hltn/15
14 Rdgrs/Mtthws/Jns/Lcy/15
15 Mllr/Wre/Thms/Andrsn/15 6.00 15.00

2016 Absolute Team Tandems Jerseys

*PRIME/25: .8X TO 2X BASIC JSY/149
*PRIME/15-20: 1X TO 2.5X BASIC JSY/149
1 B.Marshall/E.Decker/149 2.00 5.00
2 B.Perriman/B.Allen/149 2.00 5.00
3 L.McCoy/S.Watkins /149 3.00 8.00
4 D.Funchess/K.Benjamin/149 2.50 6.00
5 J.Langford/K.White/149 2.50 6.00
6 A.Abdullah/E.Ebron/149 2.00 5.00
7 R.Cobb/C.Matthews/50 5.00 12.00
8 C.Hyde/C.Kpmck/149 2.50 6.00
9 A.Luck/T.Hilton/50 6.00 15.00
10 A.Robinson/T.Yeldon/149 2.50 6.00
11 D.Parker/J.Landry/149 2.50 6.00
12 T.Brdgwtr/S.Diggs/75 3.00 8.00
13 B.Cooks/W.Snead/149 2.50 6.00
14 O.Bckhm/E.Manning/50 5.00 12.00
15 D.Carr/A.Cooper/149 3.00 8.00
16 J.Matthews/N.Agholor/149 2.50 6.00
17 M.Wheaton/S.Coates/149 2.00 5.00
18 R.Wilson/T.Lockett/25 8.00 20.00
19 J.Winston/A.SfrnJnkns/149 3.00 8.00
20 M.Mariota/D.GrnBckhm/149 3.00 8.00
21 J.Crowder/M.Jones/149 2.50 6.00
22 D.Johnson/M.Floyd/149 3.00 8.00
23 M.Ryan/J.Jones/149 3.00 8.00
24 A.Green/A.Dalton/149 3.00 8.00
25 C.Newton/J.Stewart/50 5.00 12.00

2016 Absolute Team Trios Jerseys

1 Rmo/Brynt/Wttn/25 6.00 15.00
2 Nwtn/Stwrt/Bnjmn/50 5.00 12.00
3 Rdgrs/Lcy/Jnes/20 15.00 40.00
4 Brtls/Rbnsn/Yldn/99 3.00 8.00
5 Smth/Klce/Chrls/50 5.00 12.00
6 Tnnhll/Lndry/Prkr/99 3.00 8.00
7 Brdgwtr/Ptrsn/Dggs/50 5.00 12.00
8 Cks/Ingrm/Brees/50 5.00 12.00
9 Bckhm/Mnng/Wllms/99 4.00 10.00
10 Dltn/Grn/Eifrt/99 4.00 10.00
11 Brdfrd/Mtthws/Mthws/99 3.00 8.00
12 Rthlsbrgr/Brwn/Bll/15 30.00 60.00
13 Gts/Rvrs/Grdn/99 4.00 10.00
14 Wlsn/Thms/Chnclr/50 12.00 30.00
15 Mrta/GrnBckhm/Wlkr/99 4.00 10.00

2016 Absolute Tools of the Trade Dual Materials

*PRIME/25: .6X TO 1.5X BASIC JSY/99
*PRIME/25: .5X TO 1.2X BASIC JSY/50
*PRIME/15: .8X TO 2X BASIC JSY/15
*PRIME/15: .5X TO 1.2X BASIC JSY/25
1 Carson Palmer/99 3.00 8.00
2 David Johnson/99 4.00 10.00
3 Barry Sanders/75 12.00 30.00
4 Sam Bradford/50 3.00 8.00
5 Ed Reed/75 3.00 8.00
6 Jamison Crowder/75 2.50 6.00
7 Sammy Watkins /99 4.00 10.00
8 Eric Decker/99 2.50 6.00
9 Earl Thomas III/99 3.00 8.00
10 Julius Thomas/99 2.50 6.00
11 Mike Singletary/25 6.00 15.00
12 Andre Ellington/99 2.50 6.00
13 Rod Woodson/99 3.00 8.00
14 Ronnie Hillman/99 2.50 6.00
15 Peyton Manning/75 8.00 20.00
16 Joe Montana/75 10.00 25.00
17 Sebastian Janikowski/99 2.50 6.00
18 Larry Fitzgerald/99 3.00 8.00
19 Michael Floyd/99 2.50 6.00
20 Warrick Dunn/99 2.50 6.00
21 DeMarcus Ware/99 3.00 8.00
22 Melvin Gordon/99 3.00 8.00
23 Tyler Lockett/99 3.00 8.00
24 Earl Campbell/25 6.00 15.00
25 Brian Urlacher/99 4.00 10.00
26 Ronnie Lott/75 3.00 8.00
27 Randall Cunningham/99 3.00 8.00
28 Bruce Smith/25 5.00 12.00
29 Tony Dorsett/25 12.00 30.00
30 Brandin Cooks/99 3.00 8.00
31 T.J. Yeldon/99 2.50 6.00
32 Jameis Winston/99 4.00 10.00
33 John Elway/15 12.00 30.00
34 Odell Beckham Jr./99 4.00 10.00
35 Marcus Mariota/99 4.00 10.00
36 LeSean McCoy/99 4.00 10.00
37 Jeremy Langford/99 3.00 8.00
38 Troy Aikman/50 6.00 15.00
39 Allen Robinson/99 3.00 8.00
40 Amari Cooper/99 4.00 10.00
41 Ameer Abdullah/99 2.50 6.00
42 Marcus Allen/99 3.00 8.00
43 Russell Wilson/70 6.00 15.00
44 Todd Gurley/99 4.00 10.00
45 Ryan Tannehill/75 3.00 8.00
46 Devin Funchess/99 2.50 6.00
47 Eli Manning/15 6.00 15.00
48 Terrell Davis/15 6.00 15.00
49 Steve Young/15 10.00 25.00
50 Blake Bortles/90 2.50 6.00

2016 Absolute Tools of the Trade Dual Materials Autographs

2 David Johnson/50 15.00 40.00
8 Eric Decker/25
11 Mike Singletary/20 12.00 30.00
20 Warrick Dunn/29 20.00 40.00
21 DeMarcus Ware/30 15.00 40.00
25 Brian Urlacher/25 25.00 60.00
26 Ronnie Lott/30 15.00 40.00
29 Tony Dorsett/15 25.00 50.00
30 Brandin Cooks/50 8.00 20.00
31 T.J. Yeldon/50 6.00 15.00
35 Marcus Mariota/50 25.00 50.00
37 Jeremy Langford/50 8.00 20.00
41 Ameer Abdullah/50 6.00 15.00
47 Eli Manning/15 30.00 60.00
48 Terrell Davis/15 25.00 50.00
49 Steve Young/15

2016 Absolute Tools of the Trade Triple Materials

1 Dan Marino/75 8.00 20.00
2 Amari Cooper/75 4.00 10.00
3 Kelvin Benjamin/99 3.00 8.00
4 Brett Favre/50 10.00 25.00
5 Sammy Watkins /15 8.00 20.00
6 Teddy Bridgewater/99 3.00 8.00
7 Khalil Mack/25 6.00 15.00
8 Michael Strahan/35 4.00 10.00
9 Ricky Williams/25 5.00 12.00
10 Carlos Hyde/99 2.50 6.00
11 Jameis Winston/99 4.00 10.00
12 Marcus Mariota/99 4.00 10.00
13 Jarvis Landry/99 3.00 8.00
14 Antonio Brown/50 10.00 25.00
15 Derek Carr/99 4.00 10.00
16 Devonta Freeman/75 3.00 8.00
17 Jerry Rice/25 10.00 25.00
18 Blake Bortles/99 2.50 6.00
19 Todd Gurley/99 4.00 10.00
20 Jordan Matthews/99 3.00 8.00
21 Tyler Lockett/99 3.00 8.00
22 Mike Evans/50 4.00 10.00
23 T.J. Yeldon/99 2.50 6.00
24 Kevin White/99 2.50 6.00
25 Dorial Green-Beckham/25 4.00 10.00
26 Alshon Jeffery/20 5.00 12.00
27 Matt Jones/50 4.00 10.00
28 Tom Brady/25 15.00 40.00
29 Phillip Dorsett/75 2.50 6.00
30 Le'Veon Bell/25 10.00 25.00

2016 Absolute Tools of the Trade Triple Materials Autographs

3 Kelvin Benjamin/50 10.00 25.00
6 Teddy Bridgewater/45 20.00 40.00
9 Ricky Williams/25 15.00 40.00
14 Antonio Brown/25 75.00 150.00
18 Blake Bortles/25 12.00 30.00

2016 Absolute Unsung Heroes Die Cut

*RETAIL: .25X TO .6X BASIC INSERTS
1 John Kuhn .60 1.50
2 Cole Beasley 1.00 2.50
3 Delanie Walker .60 1.50
4 Delvin Breaux .75 2.00
5 Danny Woodhead .75 2.00
6 Adam Vinatieri .75 2.00
7 Darren Sproles .75 2.00
8 Sebastian Janikowski .60 1.50
9 Chad Greenway .60 1.50
10 Rob Ninkovich .60 1.50
11 Brett Keisel .60 1.50
12 Nick Mangold .60 1.50
13 Joe Thomas .60 1.50
14 Ezekiel Ansah .60 1.50
15 Kyle Long .60 1.50
16 Tyrann Mathieu .75 2.00
17 Eric Berry .75 2.00
18 Mike Tolbert .60 1.50
19 Michael Bennett .60 1.50
20 Dwayne Harris .60 1.50

2016 Absolute Xtreme Team Die Cut

1 Tom Brady 2.50 6.00
2 Todd Gurley 1.00 2.50
3 Russell Wilson 1.25 3.00
4 Rob Gronkowski 1.00 2.50
5 Richard Sherman 1.00 2.50
6 Peyton Manning 2.00 5.00
7 Odell Beckham Jr. 1.00 2.50
8 Marcus Mariota 1.00 2.50
9 Luke Kuechly .75 2.00
10 Le'Veon Bell .75 2.00
11 Khalil Mack 1.00 2.50
12 J.J. Watt 1.00 2.50
13 Jason Witten .75 2.00
14 Jameis Winston 1.00 2.50
15 Emmitt Smith 1.50 4.00
16 Aaron Rodgers 2.00 5.00
17 DeMarco Murray .75 2.00
18 Clay Matthews 1.00 2.50
19 Cam Newton 1.00 2.50
20 Antonio Brown 1.00 2.50
21 Jerry Rice 1.50 4.00
22 Andrew Luck 1.25 3.00
23 Amari Cooper 1.00 2.50
24 Adrian Peterson 1.00 2.50
25 Bo Jackson 1.25 3.00

2017 Absolute

1 Julius Peppers .30 .75
2 T.Y. Hilton .30 .75
3 Jared Goff .40 1.00
4 Alex Smith .30 .75
5 Dak Prescott .40 1.00
6 Tyrod Taylor .30 .75
7 Terrelle Pryor .25 .60
8 Josh McCown .25 .60
9 Clay Matthews .30 .75
10 Kenny Britt .25 .60
11 Drew Brees .40 1.00
12 Blake Bortles .25 .60
13 Todd Gurley II .40 1.00
14 Tyreek Hill .40 1.00
15 Ezekiel Elliott .50 1.25
16 LeSean McCoy .40 1.00
17 Jordan Reed .25 .60
18 Matt Forte .25 .60
19 Randall Cobb .30 .75
20 Isaiah Crowell .25 .60
21 Adrian Peterson .40 1.00
22 Allen Hurns .25 .60
23 Robert Woods .30 .75
24 Travis Kelce .40 1.00
25 Dez Bryant .40 1.00
26 Sammy Watkins .40 1.00
27 Mike Glennon .30 .75
28 Quincy Enunwa .25 .60
29 Sam Bradford .25 .60
30 Ben Roethlisberger .40 1.00
31 Michael Thomas .40 1.00
32 Allen Robinson .30 .75
33 Brian Hoyer .25 .60
34 Philip Rivers .40 1.00
35 Eli Manning .30 .75
36 Ryan Tannehill .30 .75
37 Jordan Howard .40 1.00
38 Joe Flacco .30 .75
39 Latavius Murray .25 .60
40 Le'Veon Bell .30 .75
41 Jameis Winston .30 .75
42 Marcus Mariota .40 1.00
43 Pierre Garcon .30 .75
44 Melvin Gordon .30 .75
45 Brandon Marshall .25 .60
46 Jay Ajayi .30 .75
47 Jeremy Langford .30 .75
48 Mike Wallace .25 .60
49 Stefon Diggs .30 .75
50 Antonio Brown .40 1.00
51 DeSean Jackson .30 .75
52 DeMarco Murray .30 .75
53 Carlos Hyde .25 .60
54 Antonio Gates .25 .60
55 Odell Beckham Jr. .40 1.00
56 Jarvis Landry .30 .75
57 Matthew Stafford .30 .75
58 Danny Woodhead .30 .75
59 Matt Ryan .30 .75
60 Lamar Miller .25 .60
61 Mike Evans .30 .75
62 Delanie Walker .25 .60
63 Russell Wilson .50 1.25
64 Joey Bosa .40 1.00
65 Carson Wentz .50 1.25
66 Tom Brady 1.00 2.50
67 Golden Tate III .25 .60
68 Andy Dalton .30 .75
69 Julio Jones .40 1.00
70 DeAndre Hopkins .30 .75
71 Carson Palmer .30 .75
72 Trevor Siemian .25 .60
73 Eddie Lacy .25 .60
74 Derek Carr .40 1.00
75 Jordan Matthews .25 .60
76 Rob Gronkowski .40 1.00
77 Marvin Jones Jr. .25 .60
78 Jeremy Hill .25 .60
79 Devonta Freeman .30 .75
80 J.J. Watt .40 1.00
81 Larry Fitzgerald .30 .75
82 Emmanuel Sanders .40 1.00
83 Doug Baldwin .30 .75
84 Amari Cooper .40 1.00
85 Alshon Jeffery .30 .75
86 Julian Edelman .40 1.00
87 Aaron Rodgers .75 2.00
88 A.J. Green .40 1.00
89 Cam Newton .40 1.00
90 Andrew Luck .50 1.25
91 David Johnson .40 1.00
92 Demaryius Thomas .30 .75
93 Richard Sherman .40 1.00
94 Marshawn Lynch .30 .75
95 Kirk Cousins .40 1.00
96 Brandin Cooks .30 .75
97 Jordy Nelson .30 .75
98 Corey Coleman .25 .60
99 Greg Olsen .30 .75
100 Frank Gore .30 .75
101 Troy Aikman 1.00 2.50
102 Randy Moss .60 1.50
103 Michael Strahan .60 1.50
104 Earl Campbell .75 2.00
105 Joe Montana 2.00 5.00
106 Ed Reed .60 1.50
107 Jerry Rice 1.25 3.00
108 Kevin Greene .60 1.50
109 Joe Namath 1.00 2.50
110 Eddie George .60 1.50
111 Marvin Harrison .60 1.50
112 Lawrence Taylor .75 2.00
113 Tony Dorsett .75 2.00
114 Johnny Unitas 1.25 3.00
115 Brett Favre 1.50 4.00
116 Bo Jackson 1.00 2.50
117 Jim Thorpe 1.00 2.50
118 Franco Harris .75 2.00
119 Barry Sanders 1.25 3.00
120 Ken Stabler .75 2.00
121 Marshall Faulk .60 1.50
122 Tim Brown .75 2.00
123 Jerome Bettis .75 2.00
124 Dan Fouts .60 1.50
125 Emmitt Smith 1.25 3.00
126 Joe Greene .75 2.00
127 Peyton Manning 1.50 4.00
128 Terrell Davis .60 1.50
129 Deion Sanders .60 1.50
130 Marcus Allen .60 1.50
131 Steve Young 1.00 2.50
132 Warren Moon .75 2.00
133 Calvin Johnson .75 2.00
134 Ray Lewis .75 2.00
135 Terry Bradshaw 1.25 3.00
136 Curtis Martin .60 1.50
137 Michael Irvin .75 2.00
138 Eric Dickerson .75 2.00
139 Roger Staubach 1.00 2.50
140 Bob Griese .75 2.00
141 Brian Urlacher .75 2.00
142 LaDainian Tomlinson .60 1.50
143 Kurt Warner .60 1.50
144 Jim Kelly .75 2.00
145 John Elway 1.25 3.00
146 John Stallworth .60 1.50
147 Dan Marino 1.50 4.00
148 Bruce Smith .60 1.50
149 John Riggins .60 1.50
150 Walter Payton 1.50 4.00
151 Brian Hill RC .60 1.50
152 Jarrad Davis RC .75 2.00
153 DeAngelo Yancey RC .60 1.50
154 Tre'Davious White RC .60 1.50
155 Bucky Hodges RC .60 1.50
156 Gerald Everett RC .60 1.50
157 Michael Roberts RC 1.00 2.50
158 Myles Garrett RC 2.00 5.00
159 Chad Hansen RC .60 1.50
160 Derek Barnett RC .75 2.00
161 Shelton Gibson RC .60 1.50
162 Charles Harris RC .60 1.50
163 Trent Taylor RC .75 2.00
164 Taco Charlton RC .60 1.50
165 Matt Breida RC 1.00 2.50
166 Adam Shaheen RC .60 1.50
167 Josh Malone RC .60 1.50
168 Solomon Thomas RC .60 1.50
169 Jake Butt RC .75 2.00
170 Malik Hooker RC .60 1.50
171 Rodney Adams RC .60 1.50
172 Gareon Conley RC .60 1.50
173 T.J. Logan RC 1.00 2.50
174 David Njoku RC .75 2.00
175 Sam Rogers RC .60 1.50
176 Chad Williams RC .60 1.50
177 Donnel Pumphrey RC .75 2.00
178 Jamal Adams RC .60 1.50
179 George Kittle RC .60 1.50
180 Marlon Humphrey RC .60 1.50
181 Isaiah McKenzie RC .60 1.50
182 Jabrill Peppers RC 1.00 2.50
183 Aaron Jones RC 1.50 4.00
184 T.J. Watt RC 2.00 5.00
185 Robert Davis RC .60 1.50
186 Jonnu Smith RC .60 1.50
187 Ryan Switzer RC .75 2.00
188 Marshon Lattimore RC .75 2.00
189 Jordan Leggett RC .60 1.50
190 Jonathan Allen RC .75 2.00
191 Eric Saubert RC .60 1.50
192 Takkarist McKinley RC .60 1.50
193 Elijah McGuire RC .60 1.50
194 Reuben Foster RC .60 1.50
195 Brad Kaaya RC .60 1.50
196 Tarik Cohen RC 1.25 3.00
197 Jehu Chesson RC .75 2.00
198 Haason Reddick RC .60 1.50
199 Jeremy Sprinkle RC .60 1.50
200 Adoree' Jackson RC .75 2.00
201 O.J. Howard JSY AU/299 RC 4.00 10.00
202 Mack Hollins JSY AU/399 RC 3.00 8.00
203 Dalvin Cook JSY AU/149 RC 25.00 50.00
204 Wayne Gallman JSY AU/399 RC 4.00 10.00
205 Alvin Kamara JSY AU/299 RC 25.00 50.00
206 Carlos Henderson JSY AU/299 RC 3.00 8.00
207 Mitchell Trubisky JSY AU/149 RC 40.00 80.00
208 D'Onta Foreman JSY AU/299 RC 4.00 10.00
209 Christian McCaffrey JSY AU/149 RC 30.00 60.00
210 Amara Darboh JSY AU/299 RC 3.00 8.00
211 Evan Engram JSY AU/299 RC 4.00 10.00
212 Joe Williams JSY AU/299 RC 3.00 8.00
213 Joe Mixon JSY AU/399 RC 6.00 15.00
214 Marlon Mack JSY AU/399 RC 5.00 12.00
215 Cooper Kupp JSY AU/299 RC 5.00 12.00
216 Chris Godwin JSY AU/299 RC 4.00 10.00
217 Leonard Fournette JSY AU/149 RC 12.00 30.00
218 Kenny Golladay JSY AU/399 RC 5.00 12.00
219 John Ross III JSY AU/199 RC 5.00 12.00
220 Dede Westbrook JSY AU/299 RC 3.00 8.00
221 Zay Jones JSY AU/299 RC 4.00 10.00
222 Jamaal Williams JSY AU/399 RC 3.00 8.00
223 DeShone Kizer JSY AU/149 RC 4.00 10.00
224 Jeremy McNichols JSY AU/399 RC 3.00 8.00
225 Taywan Taylor JSY AU/399 RC 3.00 8.00
226 Kareem Hunt JSY AU/299 RC 8.00 20.00
227 Corey Davis JSY AU/199 RC 6.00 15.00
228 C.J. Beathard JSY AU/299 RC 3.00 8.00
229 Patrick Mahomes II JSY AU/149 RC 200.00 400.00
230 Samaje Perine JSY AU/299 RC 3.00 8.00
231 Curtis Samuel JSY AU/299 RC 4.00 10.00
232 R. Joshua Dobbs JSY AU/399 RC 4.00 10.00
233 JuJu Smith-Schuster JSY AU/199 RC 15.00 40.00
234 Nathan Peterman JSY AU/299 RC 4.00 10.00
235 ArDarius Stewart JSY AU/299 RC 3.00 8.00
236 Davis Webb JSY AU/299 RC 3.00 8.00
237 Mike Williams JSY AU/149 RC 6.00 15.00
238 James Conner JSY AU/299 RC EXCH 6.00 15.00
239 Deshaun Watson JSY AU/149 RC 50.00 100.00
240 Josh Reynolds JSY AU/399 RC 3.00 8.00
241 Evan Engram JSY AU/25 10.00 25.00
242 Samaje Perine JSY AU/25
243 Dalvin Cook JSY AU/25
244 Alvin Kamara JSY AU/25 30.00 80.00
245 Mitchell Trubisky JSY AU/25
246 Carlos Henderson JSY AU/25
247 Mike Williams JSY AU/25
248 Davis Webb JSY AU/25
249 Patrick Mahomes II JSY AU/25 500.00 800.00
250 James Conner JSY AU/25 EXCH 15.00 40.00
251 Zay Jones JSY AU/25 10.00 25.00
252 Joe Williams JSY AU/25
253 DeShone Kizer JSY AU/25 8.00 20.00
254 Cooper Kupp JSY AU/25 12.00 30.00
255 Leonard Fournette JSY AU/25 25.00 60.00
256 Chris Godwin JSY AU/25 10.00 25.00
257 Christian McCaffrey JSY AU/25
258 D'Onta Foreman JSY AU/25 10.00 25.00
259 Deshaun Watson JSY AU/25
260 Amara Darboh JSY AU/25
261 Curtis Samuel JSY AU/25 10.00 25.00
262 Nathan Peterman JSY AU/25 10.00 25.00
263 JuJu Smith-Schuster JSY AU/25 20.00 50.00
264 ArDarius Stewart JSY AU/25
265 Corey Davis JSY AU/25 12.00 30.00
266 Kareem Hunt JSY AU/25 20.00 50.00
267 John Ross III JSY AU/25 10.00 25.00
268 C.J. Beathard JSY AU/25 8.00 20.00
269 O.J. Howard JSY AU/25 10.00 25.00
270 Dede Westbrook JSY AU/25 8.00 20.00

2017 Absolute Rookie Premiere Materials Autographs Spectrum

*SPECTRUM/99: .6X TO 1.5X BASIC JSY AU/299-399
*SPECTRUM/99: .5X TO 1.2X BASIC JSY AU/149-199
239 Deshaun Watson JSY AU/99 60.00 125.00

2017 Absolute Spectrum Blue

*1-100 VETS: 1.5X TO 4X BASIC CARDS
*101-150 RET: 1.2X TO 3X BASIC CARDS
*151-200 ROOKIES: .8X TO 2X BASIC RC

2017 Absolute Spectrum Green

*1-100 VETS/25: 4X TO 10X BASIC CARDS
*101-150 RET/25: 3X TO 8X BASIC CARDS
*151-200 ROOKIES/25: 2X TO 5X BASIC RC

2017 Absolute Spectrum Red

*1-100 VETS/100: 2X TO 5X BASIC CARDS
*101-150 RET/100: 1.5X TO 4X BASIC CARDS
*151-200 ROOKIES/100: 1X TO 2.5X BASIC RC

2017 Absolute Absolute Heroes Autographs

*GOLD/25: .6X TO 1.5X BASIC AU/72-99
*NUMBER/80-93: .4X TO 1X BASIC AU/72-99
*NUMBER/41-50: .5X TO 1.2X BASIC AU/72-99
*NUMBER/25-28: .6X TO 1.5X BASIC AU/72-99
*NUMBER/25-28: .4X TO 1X BASIC AU/25
*NUMBER/20-24: .8X TO 2X BASIC AU/72-99
1 Kabeer Gbaja-Biamila/99 10.00 25.00
2 Rocky Bleier/72 10.00 25.00
3 Lenny Moore/99 3.00 8.00
4 Mike Vrabel/99 3.00 8.00
5 Chris Spielman/99 8.00 20.00
7 Eddie George/25 15.00 40.00
8 Steve Atwater/99 8.00 20.00
9 Gilbert Brown/99 6.00 15.00
10 Tom Matte/99 3.00 8.00
11 Kevin Mawae/99 3.00 8.00
12 Paul Krause/99 3.00 8.00
13 Cliff Branch/99 3.00 8.00
14 Phil McConkey/99 4.00 10.00
15 Darren Woodson/99 4.00 10.00
16 Ron Jaworski/99 4.00 10.00
17 Fred Biletnikoff/25 8.00 20.00
18 Steve Tasker/99 3.00 8.00
19 Jim Zorn/99 3.00 8.00
20 Torry Holt/99 4.00 10.00
21 Reggie Wayne/25
22 Mark Gastineau/99 3.00 8.00
24 Randall Cunningham/49 20.00 40.00
25 Dwight Clark/99 8.00 20.00

2017 Absolute Absolute Ink

*GOLD/25: .6X TO 1.5X BASIC AU/99
*GOLD/25: .5X TO 1.2X BASIC AU/49
*NUMBER/80-93: .4X TO 1X BASIC AU/99
*NUMBER/40: .5X TO 1.2X BASIC AU/99
*NUMBER/26-34: .6X TO 1.5X BASIC AU/99
*NUMBER/15-22: .8X TO 2X BASIC AU/99
*NUMBER/15-22: .5X TO 1.2X BASIC AU/25
1 Bill Parcells/49 6.00 15.00
2 Chris Spielman/99 8.00 20.00
4 Corey Coleman/99 3.00 8.00
6 Kenneth Dixon/99 3.00 8.00
7 Bashaud Breeland/99 10.00 25.00
8 Henry Ellard/99 3.00 8.00
9 Andre Reed/99 4.00 10.00
10 Delvin Breaux/99 8.00 20.00
12 Kabeer Gbaja-Biamila/99 10.00 25.00
13 Torry Holt/99 4.00 10.00
14 Gilbert Brown/99 6.00 15.00
15 Jack Ham/99 10.00 25.00
16 Adam Thielen/99 15.00 40.00
17 Derrick Henry/25 6.00 15.00
18 Mark Gastineau/99 3.00 8.00
19 Allen Hurns/99 3.00 8.00
20 Earl Campbell/99 15.00 40.00
21 Mark Brunell/99 4.00 10.00
22 Roberto Aguayo/99 3.00 8.00
23 Ray Guy/99 3.00 8.00
24 Michael Thomas/99 5.00 12.00
25 Dwight Clark/99 8.00 20.00
26 Jacoby Brissett/99 3.00 8.00
27 Travis Benjamin/99 3.00 8.00
28 Phil McConkey/99 4.00 10.00
29 James Lofton/99 4.00 10.00
30 Laquon Treadwell/99 3.00 8.00
32 Robby Anderson/99 3.00 8.00
33 Kevin Mawae/99 3.00 8.00
34 DeAndre Washington/99 3.00 8.00
35 Malcolm Mitchell/99 4.00 10.00
36 Tyler Boyd/99 3.00 8.00
37 Jim Zorn/99 3.00 8.00
38 Jerick McKinnon/99 3.00 8.00
39 Tajae Sharpe/99 3.00 8.00
40 Rishard Matthews/99 3.00 8.00
41 Rayfield Wright/99 6.00 15.00
42 Steve Tasker/99 3.00 8.00
43 Quincy Enunwa/99 3.00 8.00
44 Y.A. Tittle/99 5.00 12.00
45 Mike Vrabel/99 3.00 8.00
46 Will Fuller V/99 3.00 8.00
47 Robert Kelley/99 3.00 8.00
48 Mohamed Sanu/99 3.00 8.00

2017 Absolute Air Raid Materials

*PRIME/25: .8X TO 2X BASIC JSY/175
1 Cam Newton 3.00 8.00
2 Russell Wilson 4.00 10.00
3 Cody Kessler 2.00 5.00
4 Steve Young 4.00 10.00
5 Drew Brees 3.00 8.00
6 Tom Savage 2.00 5.00
7 Jameis Winston 2.50 6.00
8 Jim Kelly 3.00 8.00
9 Andrew Luck 4.00 10.00
10 Marcus Mariota 3.00 8.00
11 Carson Wentz 4.00 10.00
12 Ryan Tannehill 2.50 6.00
13 Dak Prescott 3.00 8.00
14 Terry Bradshaw 5.00 12.00
15 Jacoby Brissett 2.00 5.00
16 Tony Romo 2.50 6.00
17 Jared Goff 3.00 8.00
18 Jimmy Garoppolo 4.00 10.00
19 Blake Bortles 2.00 5.00
20 Paxton Lynch 2.00 5.00

2017 Absolute Canton Absolutes Jerseys

*PRIME/25: .6X TO 1.5X BASIC JSY/99
1 Larry Fitzgerald/99 3.00 8.00
2 Champ Bailey/99 3.00 8.00
3 Antonio Gates/99 2.50 6.00
4 J.J. Watt/49 5.00 12.00
5 Julio Jones/99 4.00 10.00
6 Drew Brees/49 5.00 12.00
7 Eli Manning/49 4.00 10.00
8 Ray Lewis/49 5.00 12.00
9 Aaron Rodgers/49 10.00 25.00
10 Brian Urlacher/49 5.00 12.00
11 Jason Witten/49 4.00 10.00
12 Ed Reed/99 3.00 8.00
13 Antonio Brown/49 5.00 12.00
14 Peyton Manning/49 10.00 25.00
15 Richard Sherman/99 4.00 10.00
16 Tom Brady/49 15.00 40.00
17 Ben Roethlisberger/99 4.00 10.00
18 Randy Moss/49 4.00 10.00
19 Adrian Peterson/99 4.00 10.00
20 Jeff Saturday/99 2.50 6.00

2017 Absolute Catching Fire Jerseys

*PRIME/25: .8X TO 2X BASIC JSY/175
1 Malcolm Mitchell 2.50 6.00
2 Allen Robinson 2.50 6.00
3 Stefon Diggs 2.50 6.00
4 Corey Coleman 2.00 5.00
5 T.Y. Hilton 2.50 6.00
6 DeAndre Hopkins 2.50 6.00
7 Tyler Boyd 2.00 5.00
8 Jordan Matthews 2.00 5.00
9 Will Fuller V 2.00 5.00
10 Kelvin Benjamin 2.50 6.00
11 Michael Thomas 3.00 8.00
12 Amari Cooper 3.00 8.00

13 Sterling Shepard 2.50 6.00
14 Davante Adams 2.50 6.00
15 Tajae Sharpe 2.00 5.00
16 Jarvis Landry 2.50 6.00
17 Tyreek Hill 3.00 8.00
18 Josh Doctson 2.00 5.00
19 Odell Beckham Jr. 3.00 8.00
20 Laquon Treadwell 2.00 5.00

2017 Absolute Fantasy Flashbacks

*RETAIL: .25X TO .6X BASIC INSERTS
1 Jim Brown 1.25 3.00
2 Jerry Rice 1.50 4.00
3 Jamaal Charles .75 2.00
4 Doug Martin .75 2.00
5 Gale Sayers 1.00 2.50
6 Barry Sanders 1.50 4.00
7 Adrian Peterson 1.00 2.50
8 Fred Taylor .75 2.00
9 Y.A. Tittle 1.00 2.50
10 Paul Hornung 1.00 2.50

2017 Absolute Ground Hoggs Jerseys

*PRIME/25: .8X TO 2X BASIC JSY/175
1 Devontae Booker 2.00 5.00
2 Ty Montgomery 2.00 5.00
3 Duke Johnson 2.00 5.00
4 Jay Ajayi 2.50 6.00
5 C.J. Prosise 2.00 5.00
6 Jeremy Langford 2.50 6.00
7 David Johnson 3.00 8.00
8 Melvin Gordon 2.50 6.00
9 Derrick Henry 2.50 6.00
10 Tevin Coleman 2.50 6.00
11 Doug Martin 2.50 6.00
12 Wendell Smallwood 2.00 5.00
13 Ezekiel Elliott 4.00 10.00
14 Jeremy Hill 2.00 5.00
15 Carlos Hyde 2.00 5.00
16 Jordan Howard 3.00 8.00
17 DeAndre Washington 2.00 5.00
18 T.J. Yeldon 2.00 5.00
19 Devonta Freeman 2.50 6.00
20 Todd Gurley II 3.00 8.00

2017 Absolute Hall of Fame Jersey Autographs

*PRIME/25: .6X TO 1.5X BASIC JSY AU/99
*PRIME/25: .5X TO 1.2X BASIC JSY AU/35-49
3 Kurt Warner/35 40.00 80.00
4 Larry Csonka/35 15.00 40.00
5 Jerome Bettis/25 30.00 60.00
6 Curtis Martin/25 8.00 20.00
7 Eric Dickerson/49 25.00 50.00
8 Franco Harris/49 12.00 30.00
9 Terrell Davis/49 12.00 30.00
10 Bob Griese/49 12.00 30.00
11 Thurman Thomas/49 12.00 30.00
12 Ronnie Lott/49 25.00 50.00
13 Len Dawson/49 8.00 20.00
14 Earl Campbell/25 20.00 50.00
15 Fran Tarkenton/99 15.00 40.00
16 Rod Woodson/99 12.00 30.00
17 Bob Lilly/99 8.00 20.00
18 Ken Stabler/49 15.00 40.00
19 Paul Hornung/99 6.00 15.00
20 Charles Haley/99 10.00 25.00

2017 Absolute Head to Toe Materials

1 Corey Davis 4.00 10.00
2 Patrick Mahomes II 30.00 80.00
3 John Ross III 3.00 8.00
4 Leonard Fournette 8.00 20.00
5 Christian McCaffrey 6.00 15.00
6 DeShone Kizer 2.50 6.00
7 Dalvin Cook 6.00 15.00
8 Mitchell Trubisky 12.00 30.00
9 Mike Williams 4.00 10.00
10 Deshaun Watson 15.00 40.00

2017 Absolute Historical Dual Jerseys

1 D.Clark/J.Rice/99 6.00 15.00
2 B.Jackson/M.Allen/49 6.00 15.00
3 T.Bradshaw/F.Harris/49 8.00 20.00
4 J.Elway/D.Marino/49 10.00 25.00
5 J.Montana/S.Young/49 12.00 30.00
6 J.Theismann/J.Riggins/49 5.00 12.00
7 D.Brooks/W.Sapp/49 4.00 10.00
8 J.Unitas/R.Berry/99 6.00 15.00
9 G.Sayers/J.Brown/75 12.00 30.00
10 B.Lilly/E.Jones/99 6.00 15.00
11 S.Sharpe/B.Favre/49 10.00 25.00
12 E.Campbell/W.Moon/49 5.00 12.00
13 E.James/P.Manning/49 10.00 25.00
14 E.Dickerson/J.Bettis/49 5.00 12.00
15 B.Griese/D.Marino/99 8.00 20.00

2017 Absolute Historical Triple Jerseys

1 Elway/Favre/Marino/99 10.00 25.00
2 Elway/Smith/Davis/49 10.00 25.00
3 Marino/Kelly/Theismann/49 12.00 30.00
4 Keisel/Ward/Bettis/99 8.00 20.00
5 Wilcox/Hendricks/Eller/99 3.00 8.00
6 Reed/Sanders/Lewis/99 10.00 25.00
7 Dickerson/Payton/Martin/49 12.00 30.00
8 McMahon/Singletary/Payton/99 15.00 40.00
9 Montana/Namath/Staubach/99 12.00 30.00
10 Staubach/Romo/Aikman/99 12.00 30.00
11 Riggins/Sanders/Harris/49 10.00 25.00
12 Favre/Cunningham/Moon/99 10.00 25.00
13 Moss/Welker/Brady/49 15.00 40.00
14 Rice/Montana/Young/99 12.00 30.00
15 Sanders/Bailey/Woodson/49 12.00 30.00

2017 Absolute Hurdles

*RETAIL: .25X TO .6X BASIC INSERTS
1 Eddie Lacy .60 1.50
2 LeSean McCoy 1.00 2.50
3 Ryan Mathews .75 2.00
4 David Johnson 1.00 2.50
5 Ezekiel Elliott 1.25 3.00
6 Drew Brees 1.00 2.50
7 Eric Ebron .60 1.50
8 Todd Gurley II 1.00 2.50
9 Jimmy Graham 1.00 2.50
10 Jesse James .60 1.50
11 Doug Martin .75 2.00
12 Ezekiel Elliott 1.25 3.00
13 Thomas Rawls .60 1.50
14 Theo Riddick .60 1.50
15 David Johnson 1.00 2.50
16 Ezekiel Elliott 1.25 3.00
17 Eric Ebron .60 1.50
18 Eric Ebron .60 1.50
19 Travis Kelce 1.00 2.50
20 Ezekiel Elliott 1.25 3.00

2017 Absolute Iconic Ink

2 Mark Gastineau/99 3.00 8.00
3 Jason Witten/25
4 Tedy Bruschi/49 15.00 40.00
5 Ron Jaworski/99 4.00 10.00
6 Corey Coleman/99 3.00 8.00
7 Neil Smith/99 3.00 8.00
8 Michael Thomas/99 5.00 12.00
10 Will Fuller V/99 3.00 8.00
11 Larry Csonka/25 12.00 30.00
12 Jerick McKinnon/99 3.00 8.00
13 Randall Cunningham/49 20.00 40.00
14 Mohamed Sanu/99 3.00 8.00
15 Rod Smith/49 8.00 20.00
16 Tajae Sharpe/99 3.00 8.00
17 Chris Spielman/99 8.00 20.00
18 DeAndre Washington/99 3.00 8.00
20 Tyreek Hill/99 12.00 30.00
21 Eddie George/25 15.00 40.00
22 Earl Campbell/49 25.00 50.00
23 Jack Ham/49 12.00 30.00
24 Laquon Treadwell/99 3.00 8.00
25 Tyler Boyd/99 3.00 8.00
26 Gilbert Brown/99 6.00 15.00
27 Priest Holmes/99 3.00 8.00
28 Y.A. Tittle/99 5.00 12.00
30 Henry Ellard/99 3.00 8.00

2017 Absolute Iconic Ink Dual

2 J.Ross III/J.Mixon/49 10.00 25.00
5 D.Webb/E.Engram/49 6.00 15.00
6 J.Conner/J.Smith-Schuster/49 15.00 40.00
7 C.Godwin/O.Howard/49 6.00 15.00
8 C.Davis/T.Taylor/49 8.00 20.00

2017 Absolute Iconic Ink Triple

1 Webb/Engram/Gallman/49 8.00 20.00
2 Dobbs/Conner/Smith-Schuster/49 25.00 60.00
3 Godwin/McNichols/Howard/49 8.00 20.00

2017 Absolute Jerseys

*PRIME/25: .6X TO 1.5X BASIC JSY/99
1 Michael Thomas 4.00 10.00
2 Carson Wentz 5.00 12.00
3 Paxton Lynch 2.50 6.00
4 Jared Goff 4.00 10.00
5 Corey Coleman 2.50 6.00
6 Jordan Howard 4.00 10.00
7 David Johnson 4.00 10.00
8 Amari Cooper 4.00 10.00
9 Jameis Winston 3.00 8.00
10 Dak Prescott 4.00 10.00
11 Ezekiel Elliott 5.00 12.00
12 Jay Ajayi 3.00 8.00
13 Russell Wilson 5.00 12.00
14 Marcus Mariota 4.00 10.00
15 Todd Gurley II 4.00 10.00
16 Andrew Luck 5.00 12.00
17 Odell Beckham Jr. 4.00 10.00
18 Derrick Henry 3.00 8.00
19 Brandin Cooks 3.00 8.00
20 Melvin Gordon 3.00 8.00

2017 Absolute Jumbo Cleats

1 Connor Cook/28 6.00 15.00
2 Jared Goff/29 30.00 60.00
3 Jordan Howard/28
4 Carson Wentz/28 40.00 80.00
5 Michael Thomas/28 20.00 40.00
6 Cody Kessler/24 8.00 20.00
7 Sterling Shepard/28 15.00 40.00
8 Dak Prescott/24
10 Derrick Henry/28 8.00 20.00
11 Hunter Henry/28 12.00 30.00
12 Joey Bosa/26 10.00 25.00
13 Laquon Treadwell/22 25.00 50.00
14 C.J. Prosise/30 25.00 50.00
15 Paxton Lynch/30 6.00 15.00
16 Corey Coleman/28 12.00 30.00
19 Will Fuller V/28 12.00 30.00
20 Ezekiel Elliott/28 40.00 80.00

2017 Absolute Kickoff

*RETAIL: .25X TO .6X BASIC INSERTS
1 Tom Brady 2.50 6.00
2 Dan Marino 2.00 5.00
3 Peyton Manning 2.00 5.00
4 Matt Ryan .75 2.00
5 Kurt Warner .75 2.00
6 Phil Simms .75 2.00
7 Drew Brees 1.00 2.50
8 Troy Aikman 1.25 3.00
9 Eddie George .75 2.00
10 Curtis Martin .75 2.00
11 Eric Dickerson 1.00 2.50
12 Adrian Peterson 1.00 2.50
13 Billy Sims .75 2.00
14 Michael Irvin 1.00 2.50
15 Thurman Thomas .75 2.00
16 Jim Brown 1.25 3.00
17 Tony Dorsett 1.00 2.50
18 Philip Rivers 1.00 2.50
19 Joe Flacco .75 2.00
20 Colin Kaepernick .75 2.00

2017 Absolute Marks of Fame

1 Floyd Little/99 6.00 15.00
2 Earl Campbell/49 12.00 30.00
3 Bob Lilly/99 6.00 15.00
5 Paul Warfield/49 5.00 12.00
7 Chris Doleman/99 3.00 8.00
8 Larry Csonka/25 12.00 30.00
9 Charley Trippi/99 3.00 8.00
10 Raymond Berry/49 5.00 12.00
11 Ray Guy/99 3.00 8.00
12 Jack Ham/49 12.00 30.00
13 Andre Reed/99 4.00 10.00
15 Jim Otto/99 3.00 8.00
17 Willie Roaf/99 3.00 8.00
18 Curtis Martin/25 6.00 15.00
19 Y.A. Tittle/99 5.00 12.00
20 Len Dawson/49 10.00 25.00
21 Fred Dean/99 5.00 12.00
22 Rod Woodson/49 8.00 20.00
23 Paul Hornung/49 6.00 15.00
25 Charles Haley/99 5.00 12.00

2017 Absolute Rookie Force Materials

*PRIME/25: .8X TO 2X BASIC JSY/175
*BLUE: .3X TO .8X BASIC JSY/175
*RED: .3X TO .8X BASIC JSY/175
1 JuJu Smith-Schuster 4.00 10.00
2 Joe Mixon 4.00 10.00
3 Mike Williams 2.50 6.00
4 Leonard Fournette 5.00 12.00
5 Zay Jones 2.00 5.00
6 O.J. Howard 2.00 5.00
7 Taywan Taylor 1.50 4.00
8 Alvin Kamara 4.00 10.00
9 Patrick Mahomes II 15.00 40.00
10 Christian McCaffrey 5.00 12.00
11 Nathan Peterman 2.00 5.00
12 Marlon Mack 2.50 6.00
13 James Conner 3.00 8.00
14 Kenny Golladay 2.50 6.00
15 Jamaal Williams 1.50 4.00
16 Mack Hollins 1.50 4.00
17 Kareem Hunt 3.00 8.00
18 Carlos Henderson 1.50 4.00
19 Samaje Perine 1.50 4.00
20 Amara Darboh 1.50 4.00
21 ArDarius Stewart 1.50 4.00
22 Cooper Kupp 2.50 6.00
23 Deshaun Watson 6.00 15.00
24 John Ross III 2.00 5.00
25 DeShone Kizer 1.50 4.00
26 Dalvin Cook 5.00 12.00
27 Corey Davis 2.50 6.00
28 Mitchell Trubisky 5.00 12.00
29 Curtis Samuel 2.00 5.00
30 Evan Engram 2.00 5.00
31 Davis Webb 1.50 4.00
32 Chris Godwin 2.00 5.00
33 Josh Reynolds 1.50 4.00
34 Dede Westbrook 1.50 4.00
35 Jeremy McNichols 1.50 4.00
36 Wayne Gallman 2.00 5.00
37 C.J. Beathard 1.50 4.00
38 D'Onta Foreman 2.00 5.00
39 R. Joshua Dobbs 2.00 5.00
40 Joe Williams 1.50 4.00

2017 Absolute Rookie Reflex Signatures

*GOLD/25: .8X TO 2X BASIC AU/325-400
*GOLD/25: .6X TO 1.5X BASIC AU/100
1 Malik Hooker/325 2.50 6.00
2 Aaron Jones/325 6.00 15.00
3 Adoree' Jackson/325 3.00 8.00
4 Brian Hill/400 2.50 6.00
5 Mitchell Trubisky/100 40.00 80.00
6 Charles Harris/400 2.50 6.00
7 Mike Williams/100 5.00 12.00
8 Carl Lawson/400 2.50 6.00
9 Cooper Kupp/100 5.00 12.00
10 DeMarcus Walker/400 2.50 6.00
11 Chad Kelly/400 2.50 6.00
12 Jordan Willis/325 2.50 6.00
13 Jake Butt/400 3.00 8.00
14 Raekwon McMillan/400 2.50 6.00
15 Deshaun Watson/100 50.00 100.00
16 Jamal Adams/325 2.50 6.00
17 Christian McCaffrey/100 15.00 40.00
18 Josh Malone/400 2.50 6.00
19 Isaiah Ford/400 2.50 6.00
20 T.J. Watt/400 8.00 20.00
21 Marshon Lattimore/325 3.00 8.00
22 Donnel Pumphrey/325 3.00 8.00
23 Travis Rudolph/400 2.50 6.00
24 Tre'Davious White/400 2.50 6.00
25 Leonard Fournette/100 25.00 50.00
26 Artavis Scott/325 2.50 6.00
27 Dalvin Cook/100 25.00 50.00
28 Jonathan Allen/325 3.00 8.00
29 Corey Clement/400 3.00 8.00
30 Jordan Leggett/400 2.50 6.00
31 Elijah Hood/325 2.50 6.00
32 Elijah Qualls/400 2.50 6.00
33 Ryan Switzer/400 3.00 8.00
34 Tim Williams/400 3.00 8.00
35 Patrick Mahomes II/100 200.00 400.00
36 Matthew Dayes/400 2.50 6.00
37 Corey Davis/100 5.00 12.00
38 Jarrad Davis/325 3.00 8.00
39 DeAngelo Yancey/325 2.50 6.00
40 David Njoku/325 3.00 8.00
41 KD Cannon/400 2.50 6.00
42 Caleb Brantley/325 2.50 6.00
43 Shelton Gibson/400 2.50 6.00
44 Chad Hansen/325 2.50 6.00
45 DeShone Kizer/100 3.00 8.00
46 Solomon Thomas/325 2.50 6.00
47 John Ross III/100 4.00 10.00
48 Cameron Sutton/400 2.50 6.00
49 Quincy Wilson/400 2.50 6.00
50 Haason Reddick/325 2.50 6.00

2017 Absolute Rookie Roundup

*RETAIL: .25X TO .6X BASIC INSERTS
1 Joe Williams .50 1.25
2 D'Onta Foreman .60 1.50
3 Mitchell Trubisky 2.50 6.00
4 Dalvin Cook 1.25 3.00
5 Jeremy McNichols .50 1.25
6 Josh Reynolds .50 1.25
7 Deshaun Watson 3.00 8.00
8 ArDarius Stewart .50 1.25
9 Davis Webb .50 1.25
10 Curtis Samuel .60 1.50
11 Amara Darboh .50 1.25
12 Carlos Henderson .50 1.25
13 Alvin Kamara 2.00 5.00
14 O.J. Howard .60 1.50
15 Jamaal Williams .50 1.25
16 James Conner 1.00 2.50
17 Mike Williams .75 2.00
18 JuJu Smith-Schuster 1.25 3.00
19 Nathan Peterman .60 1.50
20 Patrick Mahomes II 12.00 30.00
21 John Ross III .60 1.50
22 Cooper Kupp .75 2.00
23 Chris Godwin .60 1.50
24 Evan Engram .60 1.50
25 R. Joshua Dobbs .60 1.50
26 C.J. Beathard .50 1.25
27 Corey Davis .75 2.00
28 DeShone Kizer .50 1.25
29 Wayne Gallman .60 1.50
30 Dede Westbrook .50 1.25
31 Leonard Fournette 1.50 4.00
32 Joe Mixon 1.00 2.50
33 Marlon Mack .75 2.00
34 Christian McCaffrey 1.25 3.00
35 Samaje Perine .50 1.25
36 Kareem Hunt 1.00 2.50
37 Taywan Taylor .50 1.25
38 Zay Jones .60 1.50
39 Mack Hollins .50 1.25
40 Kenny Golladay .75 2.00

2017 Absolute Team Tandem Jerseys

*PRIME/25: .6X TO 1.5X BASIC JSY/99
1 J.Goff/T.Gurley II 4.00 10.00
2 C.Coleman/C.Kessler 2.50 6.00
3 J.Hill/G.Bernard 2.50 6.00
4 D.Hopkins/T.Savage 3.00 8.00
5 J.Langford/J.Howard 4.00 10.00
6 T.Coleman/D.Freeman 3.00 8.00
7 D.Henry/M.Mariota 4.00 10.00
8 A.Robinson/B.Bortles 3.00 8.00
9 D.Brees/M.Thomas 4.00 10.00
10 D.Prescott/E.Elliott 6.00 15.00
11 T.Eifert/T.Boyd 3.00 8.00
12 D.Adams/T.Montgomery 3.00 8.00
13 S.Shepard/O.Beckham Jr. 4.00 10.00
14 J.Winston/M.Evans 3.00 8.00
15 K.Allen/M.Gordon 3.00 8.00
16 L.McCoy/T.Taylor 4.00 10.00
17 C.Newton/K.Benjamin 4.00 10.00
18 C.Wentz/J.Matthews 5.00 12.00
19 R.Wilson/C.Prosise 5.00 12.00
20 C.Sims/D.Martin 3.00 8.00

2017 Absolute Tools of the Trade Dual Materials

*PRIME/25: .6X TO 1.5X BASIC JSY/99
*PRIME/15: .5X TO 1.2X BASIC JSY/30
1 Dak Prescott/99 4.00 10.00
2 Devonta Freeman/99 3.00 8.00
3 Joey Bosa/99 4.00 10.00
4 Doug Martin/99 3.00 8.00
5 Todd Gurley II/99 4.00 10.00
6 Matt Ryan/30 6.00 15.00
7 Hunter Henry/99 2.50 6.00
8 Devontae Booker/99 2.50 6.00
9 Joe Montana/49 20.00 40.00
10 Khalil Mack/99 4.00 10.00
11 Derrick Henry/99 3.00 8.00
12 Eddie Lacy/49 3.00 8.00
13 Jordan Howard/99 4.00 10.00
14 Ed Reed/99 3.00 8.00
15 Will Fuller V/99 2.50 6.00
16 Peyton Manning/99 8.00 20.00
17 Blake Bortles/99 2.50 6.00
18 Jameis Winston/99 3.00 8.00
19 Brett Favre/99 8.00 20.00
20 Laquon Treadwell/99 2.50 6.00
21 Ezekiel Elliott/99 5.00 12.00
22 Dan Marino/25 25.00 50.00
23 Michael Thomas/99 4.00 10.00
24 Jim Thorpe/25
25 Jordan Matthews/99 2.50 6.00
26 Tom Brady/49 40.00 80.00
27 Davante Adams/99 3.00 8.00
28 Jeremy Hill/99 2.50 6.00
29 Kurt Warner/99 3.00 8.00
30 Tyler Boyd/99 2.50 6.00
31 Jared Goff/99 4.00 10.00
32 DeAndre Hopkins/49 4.00 10.00
33 Paxton Lynch/99 2.50 6.00
34 Keenan Allen/99 3.00 8.00
35 Cameron Wake/99 2.50 6.00
36 Walter Payton/49 25.00 50.00
37 David Johnson/99 4.00 10.00
38 Jimmy Garoppolo/99 5.00 12.00
39 Carson Wentz/99 5.00 12.00
40 Wendell Smallwood/99 2.50 6.00
41 Boomer Esiason/99 3.00 8.00
42 DeVante Parker/99 3.00 8.00
43 Sterling Shepard/49 4.00 10.00
44 Mark Brunell/99 3.00 8.00
45 Brandin Cooks/99 3.00 8.00
46 Rich Gannon/99 2.50 6.00
47 DeAndre Washington/99 2.50 6.00
48 Josh Doctson/99 2.50 6.00
49 Corey Coleman/99 2.50 6.00
50 Derek Carr/99 4.00 10.00

2017 Absolute Tools of the Trade Five Materials

1 Amari Cooper 10.00 25.00
2 Marcus Mariota 10.00 25.00
3 Rich Gannon 6.00 15.00
4 Stefon Diggs 8.00 20.00
5 Ty Montgomery 6.00 15.00

2017 Absolute Tools of the Trade Quad Materials

1 Paxton Lynch 3.00 8.00
2 Dak Prescott 5.00 12.00
3 Todd Gurley II 5.00 12.00
4 Eddie George 4.00 10.00
5 Jared Goff 5.00 12.00
6 Antonio Brown 5.00 12.00
7 Jordan Howard 5.00 12.00
8 Carson Wentz 6.00 15.00
9 Michael Thomas 5.00 12.00
10 Corey Coleman 3.00 8.00
11 Sterling Shepard 4.00 10.00
12 Derrick Henry 4.00 10.00
13 Will Fuller V 3.00 8.00
14 Ezekiel Elliott 6.00 15.00
15 Joey Bosa 5.00 12.00

2017 Absolute Tools of the Trade Triple Material Autographs

2 DeAndre Washington/49 5.00 12.00
4 Jeremy Hill/49 5.00 12.00
6 Rod Woodson/15
7 Wendell Smallwood/49 5.00 12.00
9 Devonta Freeman/49 6.00 15.00
10 Cody Kessler/49 5.00 12.00
11 Jay Ajayi
12 Devontae Booker/49 5.00 12.00
13 Kelvin Benjamin
14 Jimmy Garoppolo/49 30.00 60.00
15 Laquon Treadwell/49 5.00 12.00
16 Brandin Cooks/49
18 C.J. Prosise
19 Eddie Lacy/49 5.00 12.00
23 Mike Evans/49 6.00 15.00
24 Josh Doctson/49 5.00 12.00
25 Tyler Boyd/49 5.00 12.00
26 Hunter Henry/49 5.00 12.00
27 Derek Carr/25 30.00 60.00
28 Carlos Hyde/49 5.00 12.00
30 David Johnson/25 25.00 50.00

2017 Absolute Tools of the Trade Triple Materials

*PRIME/25: .6X TO 1.5X BASIC JSY/99
1 Jarvis Landry/99 3.00 8.00
2 DeAndre Washington/99 2.50 6.00
3 Jordan Reed/99 2.50 6.00
4 Jeremy Hill/99 2.50 6.00
5 Khalil Mack/99 4.00 10.00
6 Rod Woodson/15 10.00 25.00
7 Wendell Smallwood/99 2.50 6.00
8 Blake Bortles/99 2.50 6.00
9 Devonta Freeman/99 3.00 8.00
10 Cody Kessler/99 2.50 6.00
11 Jay Ajayi/99 3.00 8.00
12 Devontae Booker/99 2.50 6.00
13 Kelvin Benjamin/99 3.00 8.00
14 Jimmy Garoppolo/99 5.00 12.00
15 Laquon Treadwell/99 2.50 6.00
16 Brandin Cooks/99 3.00 8.00
18 C.J. Prosise/99 2.50 6.00
19 Eddie Lacy/99 2.50 6.00
20 Davante Adams/99 3.00 8.00
21 Jerry Rice/99 10.00 25.00
22 Jameis Winston/99 3.00 8.00
23 Mike Evans/99 3.00 8.00
24 Josh Doctson/99 2.50 6.00
25 Tyler Boyd/99 2.50 6.00
26 Hunter Henry/99 2.50 6.00
27 Derek Carr/99 4.00 10.00
28 Carlos Hyde/99 2.50 6.00
29 Jadeveon Clowney/99 2.50 6.00
30 David Johnson/99 4.00 10.00

2017 Absolute Unsung Heroes

*RETAIL: .25X TO .6X BASIC INSERTS
1 Ken Anderson .60 1.50
2 Johnny Hekker .60 1.50
3 Matthew Slater .60 1.50
4 Steve Tasker .60 1.50
5 Aaron Ripkowski 1.00 2.50
6 Erik Walden .60 1.50
7 Markus Golden .60 1.50
8 Bill Bates .60 1.50
9 Danielle Hunter .60 1.50
10 Damon Harrison .60 1.50

2018 Absolute

1 Sam Bradford .25 .60
2 David Johnson .40 1.00
3 Larry Fitzgerald .30 .75
4 Matt Ryan .30 .75
5 Devonta Freeman .30 .75
6 Julio Jones .40 1.00
7 Joe Flacco .30 .75
8 Alex Collins .25 .60
9 Terrell Suggs .25 .60
10 A.J. McCarron .25 .60
11 LeSean McCoy .40 1.00
12 Zay Jones .25 .60
13 Cam Newton .40 1.00
14 Christian McCaffrey .40 1.00
15 Greg Olsen .30 .75
16 Mitchell Trubisky .40 1.00
17 Jordan Howard .40 1.00
18 Allen Robinson .30 .75
19 Andy Dalton .30 .75
20 A.J. Green .40 1.00
21 Joe Mixon .30 .75
22 Tyrod Taylor .30 .75
23 Josh Gordon .25 .60
24 Jarvis Landry .30 .75
25 Dak Prescott .40 1.00
26 Allen Hurns .25 .60
27 Ezekiel Elliott .50 1.25
28 Sean Lee .30 .75
29 Case Keenum .30 .75
30 Demaryius Thomas .30 .75
31 Von Miller .30 .75
32 Matthew Stafford .30 .75
33 Marvin Jones Jr. .25 .60
34 Golden Tate III .25 .60
35 Aaron Rodgers .75 2.00
36 Davante Adams .30 .75
37 Clay Matthews .30 .75
38 Jimmy Graham .40 1.00
39 Deshaun Watson .50 1.25
40 DeAndre Hopkins .30 .75
41 J.J. Watt .40 1.00
42 Jacoby Brissett .25 .60
43 Andrew Luck .50 1.25
44 T.Y. Hilton .30 .75
45 Marlon Mack .25 .60
46 Blake Bortles .25 .60
47 Leonard Fournette .40 1.00
48 Jalen Ramsey .30 .75
49 Patrick Mahomes II 1.00 2.50
50 Tyreek Hill .40 1.00
51 Kareem Hunt .30 .75
52 Jared Goff .40 1.00
53 Todd Gurley II .40 1.00
54 Aaron Donald .40 1.00
55 Philip Rivers .40 1.00
56 Melvin Gordon .30 .75
57 Keenan Allen .30 .75
58 Ryan Tannehill .30 .75
59 Cameron Wake .25 .60
60 DeVante Parker .30 .75
61 Kirk Cousins .40 1.00
62 Dalvin Cook .30 .75
63 Adam Thielen .40 1.00
64 Tom Brady 1.00 2.50
65 Rob Gronkowski .40 1.00
66 Chris Hogan .25 .60
67 James White .30 .75
68 Drew Brees .40 1.00
69 Alvin Kamara .30 .75
70 Marshon Lattimore .25 .60
71 Eli Manning .30 .75
72 Jonathan Stewart .25 .60
73 Odell Beckham Jr. .40 1.00
74 Teddy Bridgewater .30 .75
75 Robby Anderson .25 .60
76 Bilal Powell .25 .60
77 Derek Carr .40 1.00
78 Marshawn Lynch .30 .75
79 Khalil Mack .40 1.00
80 Carson Wentz .50 1.25
81 Alshon Jeffery .30 .75
82 Jay Ajayi .30 .75
83 Ben Roethlisberger .40 1.00
84 Le'Veon Bell .30 .75
85 Antonio Brown .40 1.00
86 Jimmy Garoppolo .50 1.25
87 Jerick McKinnon .25 .60
88 Richard Sherman .40 1.00
89 Russell Wilson .50 1.25
90 Doug Baldwin .30 .75
91 Bobby Wagner .25 .60
92 Jameis Winston .30 .75
93 Mike Evans .30 .75
94 DeSean Jackson .30 .75
95 Marcus Mariota .40 1.00
96 Derrick Henry .40 1.00
97 Rishard Matthews .25 .60
98 Alex Smith .30 .75
99 Chris Thompson .25 .60
100 Josh Norman .25 .60
101 Alex McGough RC .75 2.00
102 Cedrick Wilson Jr. RC .60 1.50
103 Danny Etling RC .75 2.00
104 Terrell Edmunds RC 2.00 5.00
105 Durham Smythe RC .60 1.50
106 Equanimeous St. Brown RC 1.00 2.50
107 Trey Quinn RC .60 1.50
108 Simmie Cobbs Jr. RC 1.00 2.50
109 Derrick Nnadi RC .60 1.50
110 Chukwuma Okorafor RC .60 1.50
111 Dalton Schultz RC .75 2.00
112 Connor Williams RC 1.25 3.00
113 Logan Woodside RC 1.00 2.50
114 Boston Scott RC .75 2.00
115 Javon Wims RC .60 1.50
116 Jordan Wilkins RC .75 2.00
117 Dylan Cantrell RC .60 1.50
118 Jordan Whitehead RC .60 1.50
119 Fred Warner RC .60 1.50
120 Kyzir White RC 1.00 2.50
121 Ray-Ray McCloud RC .60 1.50
122 Tanner Lee RC .75 2.00
123 Trenton Cannon RC .75 2.00
124 Mark Andrews RC 1.00 2.50
125 Armani Watts RC .60 1.50
126 Denzel Ward RC 1.50 4.00
127 Ryan Izzo RC .60 1.50
128 Kemoko Turay RC .75 2.00
129 Justin Jackson RC .75 2.00
130 David Williams RC .75 2.00
131 Bo Scarbrough RC .75 2.00
132 Ian Thomas RC .60 1.50
133 Jaylen Samuels RC .75 2.00
134 Marcus Davenport RC 1.25 3.00
135 Austin Proehl RC .60 1.50
136 Roquan Smith RC 2.00 5.00
137 Josh Sweat RC .75 2.00
138 Vita Vea RC 1.00 2.50
139 Richie James RC .60 1.50
140 Justin Reid RC .60 1.50
141 Tremaine Edmunds RC 1.25 3.00
142 Auden Tate RC .60 1.50
143 Kurt Benkert RC .75 2.00
144 Jester Weah RC .60 1.50
145 Daron Payne RC 1.00 2.50
146 Isaiah Oliver RC .60 1.50
147 Quenton Nelson RC 1.00 2.50
148 Marcell Ateman RC .75 2.00
149 Harold Landry RC .60 1.50
150 Antonio Callaway RC .75 2.00
151 Sam Darnold JSY AU/100 RC 40.00 80.00
152 Josh Rosen JSY AU/365 RC 25.00 50.00
153 Baker Mayfield JSY AU/399 RC 75.00 150.00
154 Josh Allen JSY AU/365 RC 30.00 60.00
155 Mason Rudolph JSY AU/399 RC 8.00 20.00
156 Saquon Barkley JSY AU/399 RC 75.00 150.00
157 Derrius Guice JSY AU/100 RC 8.00 20.00
158 Nick Chubb JSY AU/399 RC 10.00 25.00
159 Sony Michel JSY AU/399 RC 10.00 25.00
160 Ronald Jones II JSY AU/399 RC 3.00 8.00
161 Calvin Ridley JSY AU/100 RC 10.00 25.00
162 Courtland Sutton JSY AU/399 RC 5.00 12.00
163 Christian Kirk JSY AU/100 RC 6.00 15.00
164 Anthony Miller JSY AU/399 RC 5.00 12.00
166 D.J. Moore JSY AU/399 RC 6.00 15.00
167 Lamar Jackson JSY AU/75 RC 40.00 80.00
168 Rashaad Penny JSY AU/399 RC EXCH 5.00 12.00
169 Bradley Chubb JSY AU/199 RC 6.00 15.00
170 Kerryon Johnson JSY AU/399 RC 5.00 12.00
171 Dante Pettis JSY AU/399 RC 5.00 12.00
172 James Washington JSY AU/399 RC 6.00 15.00
173 Royce Freeman JSY AU/199 RC 5.00 12.00
174 Michael Gallup JSY AU/399 RC 6.00 15.00
175 Tre'Quan Smith JSY AU/399 RC 5.00 12.00
176 Keke Coutee JSY AU/399 RC 4.00 10.00
177 Nyheim Hines JSY AU/399 RC 4.00 10.00
178 Kyle Lauletta JSY AU/199 RC 6.00 15.00
179 Mark Walton JSY AU/399 RC 4.00 10.00
180 Kalen Ballage JSY AU/399 RC 4.00 10.00
181 Jaleel Scott JSY AU/399 RC 3.00 8.00
182 J'Mon Moore JSY AU/399 RC 3.00 8.00
183 Daurice Fountain JSY AU/399 RC 4.00 10.00
184 Mike White JSY AU/399 RC 4.00 10.00
185 Jaylen Samuels JSY AU/399 RC 4.00 10.00
186 Marquez Valdes-Scantling JSY AU/299 RC 4.00 10.00
187 Mike Gesicki JSY AU/399 RC 4.00 10.00
188 DaeSean Hamilton JSY AU/399 RC 4.00 10.00
189 Hayden Hurst JSY AU/399 RC 4.00 10.00
190 Ito Smith JSY AU/399 RC 4.00 10.00

2018 Absolute Rookie Premiere Material Autographs Quad

*QUAD/25: .8X TO 2X BASIC JSY AU/299-399
*QUAD/25: .6X TO 1.5X BASIC JSY AU/100-199
153 Baker Mayfield 125.00 250.00
156 Saquon Barkley 100.00 200.00

2018 Absolute Rookie Premiere Material Autographs Spectrum

*SPECTRUM/99: .5X TO 1.2X BASIC JSY AU/299-399
*SPECTRUM/49: .6X TO 1.5X BASIC JSY AU/299-399
*SPECTRUM/49: .5X TO 1.2X BASIC JSY AU/100-199
153 Baker Mayfield/99 100.00 200.00
156 Saquon Barkley/99 75.00 150.00

2018 Absolute Spectrum Blue

*VETS: 1.5X TO 4X BASIC CARDS
*ROOKIES: .6X TO 1.5X BASIC CARDS

2018 Absolute Spectrum Gold

*VETS: 1.5X TO 4X BASIC CARDS
*ROOKIES: 1X TO 2.5X BASIC CARDS

2018 Absolute Spectrum Green

*VETS: 4X TO 10X BASIC CARDS
*ROOKIES: 1.5X TO 4X BASIC CARDS

2018 Absolute Spectrum Orange

*VETS: 2X TO 5X BASIC CARDS
*ROOKIES: .8X TO 2X BASIC CARDS

2018 Absolute Spectrum Red

*VETS/100: 2.5X TO 6X BASIC CARDS
*ROOKIES/100: 1.2X TO 3X BASIC RC

2018 Absolute Absolute Heroes Memorabilia

*PRIME/25: .8X TO 2X BASIC JSY/199
*PRIME/25: .6X TO 1.5X BASIC JSY/99
1 Aaron Rodgers/199 6.00 15.00
2 A.J. Green/199 3.00 8.00
3 Alvin Kamara/199 2.50 6.00
4 Deshaun Watson/199 4.00 10.00
5 Dalvin Cook/199 2.50 6.00
6 Von Miller/199 2.50 6.00
7 Antonio Brown/199 3.00 8.00
8 Khalil Mack/199 3.00 8.00
9 Odell Beckham Jr./99 4.00 10.00
10 Eric Berry/199 2.50 6.00
11 Rob Gronkowski/199 3.00 8.00
12 Russell Wilson/199 4.00 10.00
13 Matthew Stafford/199 2.50 6.00
14 Mike Evans/199 2.50 6.00
15 Jared Goff/199 3.00 8.00
16 Stefon Diggs/199 2.50 6.00
17 Devonta Freeman/199 2.50 6.00
18 T.Y. Hilton/199 2.50 6.00
19 Keenan Allen/199 2.50 6.00
20 Dak Prescott/199 3.00 8.00
21 Doug Baldwin/199 2.50 6.00
22 Joey Bosa/199 3.00 8.00
23 Carson Wentz/199 4.00 10.00
24 Luke Kuechly/199 2.50 6.00
25 Kareem Hunt/199 2.50 6.00

2018 Absolute Boss Hoggs Autographs

*BLUE: .6X TO 1.5X BASIC AU
1 J.D. McKissic 2.50 6.00
2 Keelan Cole 2.50 6.00
3 Corey Davis 3.00 8.00
4 Simmie Cobbs Jr. 4.00 10.00
5 Jordan Lasley 2.50 6.00
6 D.J. Moore 5.00 12.00
7 Marshall Faulk 10.00 25.00
8 O.J. Howard 2.50 6.00
9 Adam Thielen 8.00 20.00
10 Deshaun Watson 40.00 80.00
11 Jake Wieneke 3.00 8.00
12 Dallas Goedert 3.00 8.00
13 Kerryon Johnson 4.00 10.00
14 Ronald Jones II 2.50 6.00
15 Marshawn Lynch 15.00 40.00
16 Brent Jones 2.50 6.00
17 Sterling Shepard 3.00 8.00
18 Justin Watson 3.00 8.00
19 Alvin Kamara 8.00 20.00
20 Alex Collins 2.50 6.00
21 Jordan Thomas 3.00 8.00

2018 Absolute Canton Absolutes Jerseys

*PRIME/25: .8X TO 2X BASIC JSY/199
*PRIME/25: .6X TO 1.5X BASIC JSY/99
1 Joe Namath/199 4.00 10.00
2 Kurt Warner/199 2.50 6.00
3 Jim Kelly/199 3.00 8.00
4 Troy Aikman/199 4.00 10.00
5 John Elway/199 5.00 12.00
6 Warren Moon/199 3.00 8.00
7 Steve Largent/99 4.00 10.00
8 Joe Montana/99 10.00 25.00
9 John Riggins/199 2.50 6.00
10 Dan Marino/199 6.00 15.00
11 Tim Brown/199 3.00 8.00
12 Brian Dawkins/199 3.00 8.00
13 Jerry Rice/99 6.00 15.00
14 LaDainian Tomlinson/199 2.50 6.00
15 Steve Young/199 4.00 10.00
16 Ed Reed/199 2.50 6.00
17 Terrell Davis/199 2.50 6.00
18 Fran Tarkenton/199 3.00 8.00
19 Earl Campbell/199 3.00 8.00
20 Rod Woodson/199 3.00 8.00

2018 Absolute Cleat Combos

2 D.Prescott/E.Elliott/15 40.00 80.00
4 J.Howard/M.Trubisky/30 6.00 15.00
5 J.Mixon/J.Ross III/30 5.00 12.00
6 P.Lynch/D.Booker/49 3.00 8.00
7 D.Watson/W.Fuller V/49 6.00 15.00
8 D.Westbrook/L.Fournette/99 4.00 10.00
9 K.Hunt/P.Mahomes II/99 10.00 25.00
10 J.Goff/C.Kupp/15 8.00 20.00
11 A.Kamara/M.Thomas/49 5.00 12.00
12 E.Engram/W.Gallman/99 2.50 6.00
13 C.Wentz/M.Hollins/15 12.00 30.00
14 J.Smith-Schuster/R.Dobbs/99 4.00 10.00
15 H.Henry/J.Bosa/80 4.00 10.00
16 O.Howard/C.Godwin/99 2.50 6.00
17 C.Davis/D.Henry/58 5.00 12.00
18 J.Doctson/S.Perine/60 3.00 8.00
19 C.Coleman/R.Louis/25 4.00 10.00

2018 Absolute Covering Ground

*GOLD: .6X TO 1.5X BASIC INSERTS
1 Antonio Brown 1.00 2.50
2 Ezekiel Elliott 1.25 3.00
3 Odell Beckham Jr. 1.00 2.50
4 Le'Veon Bell .75 2.00
5 Todd Gurley II 1.00 2.50
6 Julio Jones 1.00 2.50
7 A.J. Green 1.00 2.50
8 Alvin Kamara .75 2.00
9 Tyreek Hill 1.00 2.50
10 Christian McCaffrey 1.00 2.50
11 Keenan Allen .75 2.00
12 Kareem Hunt .75 2.00
13 Alshon Jeffery .75 2.00
14 David Johnson 1.00 2.50
15 Brandin Cooks .75 2.00
16 Devonta Freeman .75 2.00
17 DeAndre Hopkins .75 2.00
18 LeSean McCoy 1.00 2.50
19 T.Y. Hilton .75 2.00
20 Jordan Howard 1.00 2.50

2018 Absolute Head to Toe Materials

1 Alvin Kamara/99 8.00 20.00
2 Ezekiel Elliott/85 12.00 30.00
3 ArDarius Stewart/99 4.00 10.00
4 Blake Bortles/15 8.00 20.00
5 Braxton Miller/55 5.00 12.00
6 Carson Wentz/55 10.00 25.00
7 Amara Darboh/99 4.00 10.00
8 C.J. Beathard/99 4.00 10.00
9 Carlos Henderson/40 5.00 12.00
10 Christian McCaffrey/47 8.00 20.00
11 Connor Cook/62 6.00 15.00
12 Corey Coleman/36 5.00 12.00
13 D'Onta Foreman/70 4.00 10.00
14 Davis Webb/99 4.00 10.00
15 Dede Westbrook/93 4.00 10.00
16 Evan Engram/99 4.00 10.00
17 Jamaal Williams/99 4.00 10.00
18 James Conner/99 6.00 15.00
19 Jared Goff/50 8.00 20.00
20 Joe Mixon/99 5.00 12.00

2018 Absolute Iconic Ink

1 Bert Jones 3.00 8.00
2 Lynn Dickey 10.00 25.00
3 Rod Smith 6.00 15.00
4 Ottis Anderson 3.00 8.00
5 Joe Klecko 3.00 8.00
6 Tom Brady 600.00 1000.00
7 Chris Doleman 3.00 8.00
8 Mark Gastineau 3.00 8.00
9 Steve McMichael 3.00 8.00
10 Curley Culp 4.00 10.00
11 Charlie Joiner 3.00 8.00
12 Pepper Johnson 3.00 8.00
13 Marshall Faulk 12.00 30.00
14 George Rogers 4.00 10.00
15 Tony Romo 25.00 50.00
16 Tom Rathman 3.00 8.00
17 Ken Anderson 3.00 8.00
18 Terry Bradshaw 40.00 80.00
19 Steve Young 15.00 40.00
20 Peyton Manning 60.00 125.00
21 Dan Marino 60.00 125.00

2018 Absolute Introductions

*GOLD: .6X TO 1.5X BASIC INSERTS
1 Sam Darnold 4.00 10.00
2 Josh Rosen 2.00 5.00
3 Baker Mayfield 6.00 15.00
4 Josh Allen 2.50 6.00
5 Mason Rudolph 1.50 4.00
6 Saquon Barkley 5.00 12.00
7 Derrius Guice 1.25 3.00
8 Nick Chubb 2.00 5.00
9 Sony Michel 2.00 5.00
10 Ronald Jones II .60 1.50
11 Calvin Ridley 1.50 4.00
12 Courtland Sutton 1.00 2.50
13 Mike White .75 2.00
14 Anthony Miller 1.00 2.50
15 D.J. Chark .75 2.00
16 D.J. Moore 1.25 3.00
17 Jaylen Samuels .75 2.00
18 Bradley Chubb 1.00 2.50
19 James Washington 1.25 3.00
20 Kerryon Johnson 1.00 2.50

2018 Absolute Late Game Heroics

*GOLD: .6X TO 1.5X BASIC INSERTS
1 Jeff Garcia .60 1.50
2 Matthew Stafford .75 2.00
3 Stefon Diggs .75 2.00
4 Derek Carr 1.00 2.50
5 Jameis Winston .75 2.00
6 Andrew Luck 1.25 3.00
7 Nick Foles .75 2.00
8 Blake Bortles .60 1.50
9 Tom Brady 2.50 6.00
10 Cam Newton 1.00 2.50
11 Drew Brees 1.00 2.50
12 Ben Roethlisberger 1.00 2.50
13 Marcus Mariota 1.00 2.50
14 Philip Rivers 1.00 2.50
15 Dak Prescott 1.00 2.50
16 James White .75 2.00
17 Davante Adams .75 2.00
18 Tyler Boyd .60 1.50
19 Russell Wilson 1.25 3.00
20 Ryan Tannehill .75 2.00

2018 Absolute One Two Punch

*GOLD: .6X TO 1.5X BASIC INSERTS
1 R.Gronkowski/T.Brady 2.50 6.00
2 E.Elliott/D.Prescott 1.25 3.00
3 L.Bell/B.Roethlisberger 1.00 2.50
4 L.Fitzgerald/D.Johnson 1.00 2.50
5 J.Jones/M.Ryan 1.00 2.50
6 C.McCaffrey/C.Newton 1.00 2.50
7 J.Howard/M.Trubisky 1.00 2.50
8 A.Green/A.Dalton 1.00 2.50
9 A.Rodgers/D.Adams 2.00 5.00
10 D.Hopkins/D.Watson 1.25 3.00
11 A.Kamara/D.Brees 1.00 2.50
12 O.Beckham Jr./E.Manning 1.00 2.50
13 A.Cooper/D.Carr 1.00 2.50
14 A.Jeffery/C.Wentz 1.25 3.00
15 K.Allen/P.Rivers 1.00 2.50
16 J.Garoppolo/M.Goodwin 1.25 3.00
17 D.Baldwin/R.Wilson 1.25 3.00
18 T.Gurley II/J.Goff 1.00 2.50
19 J.Winston/M.Evans .75 2.00
20 D.Henry/M.Mariota 1.00 2.50

2018 Absolute Panoramic Materials Prime

*PATCH/25: .6X TO 1.5X BASIC JSY/65-99
1 Kareem Hunt/99 3.00 8.00
2 Alvin Kamara/99 3.00 8.00
3 Tyreek Hill/49 5.00 12.00
4 Tevin Coleman/99 2.50 6.00
5 Travis Kelce/22 8.00 20.00
6 Davante Adams/99 3.00 8.00
7 Ezekiel Elliott/99 5.00 12.00
8 Melvin Gordon/99 3.00 8.00
9 Nelson Agholor/99 2.50 6.00
10 Patrick Peterson/65 3.00 8.00
11 DeAndre Hopkins/99 3.00 8.00
12 Aaron Jones/49 4.00 10.00
13 Devin Funchess/99 2.50 6.00
14 Antonio Brown/99 4.00 10.00
15 Rob Gronkowski/99 4.00 10.00
16 Russell Wilson/99 5.00 12.00
17 Todd Gurley II/30 6.00 15.00
18 Julio Jones/20 8.00 20.00
19 Marcus Mariota/99 4.00 10.00
20 LeSean McCoy/99 4.00 10.00

2018 Absolute Revolutionaries

*GOLD: .6X TO 1.5X BASIC INSERTS
1 Eric Dickerson 1.00 2.50
2 Jonathan Ogden .75 2.00
3 Brian Urlacher 1.00 2.50
4 Ozzie Newsome .75 2.00
5 Troy Aikman 1.25 3.00
6 John Elway 1.50 4.00
7 Barry Sanders 1.50 4.00
8 Brett Favre 2.00 5.00
9 Peyton Manning 2.00 5.00
10 Howie Long 1.00 2.50
11 Dan Marino 2.00 5.00
12 Randy Moss .75 2.00
13 Joe Namath 1.25 3.00
14 Brian Dawkins 1.00 2.50
15 Jerome Bettis 1.00 2.50
16 LaDainian Tomlinson .75 2.00
17 Steve Young 1.25 3.00
18 Charley Taylor .60 1.50
19 Warren Sapp .75 2.00
20 Tony Gonzalez .75 2.00

2018 Absolute Rookie Dual Memorabilia

1 Baker Mayfield 6.00 15.00
2 Josh Rosen 6.00 15.00
3 Nick Chubb 5.00 12.00
4 Sam Darnold 6.00 15.00
5 Josh Allen 5.00 12.00
6 Mason Rudolph 4.00 10.00
7 Saquon Barkley 8.00 20.00
8 Derrius Guice 3.00 8.00
9 Ronald Jones II 3.00 8.00
10 Calvin Ridley 3.00 8.00
11 Sony Michel 3.00 8.00
12 Bradley Chubb 2.50 6.00
13 Christian Kirk 2.50 6.00
14 Courtland Sutton 2.50 6.00
15 James Washington 3.00 8.00
16 Lamar Jackson 6.00 15.00
17 D.J. Moore 3.00 8.00
18 Kyle Lauletta 2.50 6.00
19 Dante Pettis 2.50 6.00
20 Rashaad Penny 2.50 6.00

2018 Absolute Rookie Force Materials

1 James Washington 3.00 8.00
2 Rashaad Penny 2.50 6.00
3 Dante Pettis 2.50 6.00
4 Kerryon Johnson 2.50 6.00
5 Ito Smith 2.00 5.00
6 Royce Freeman 2.00 5.00
7 Sam Darnold 6.00 15.00
8 Josh Rosen 6.00 15.00
9 Baker Mayfield 6.00 15.00
10 Bradley Chubb 2.50 6.00
11 Josh Allen 5.00 12.00
12 Mason Rudolph 4.00 10.00

13 Saquon Barkley 8.00 20.00
14 Derrius Guice 3.00 8.00
15 Nick Chubb 5.00 12.00
16 Sony Michel 3.00 8.00
17 Ronald Jones II 3.00 8.00
18 Calvin Ridley 3.00 8.00
19 Courtland Sutton 2.50 6.00
20 Christian Kirk 2.50 6.00
21 Anthony Miller 2.50 6.00
22 D.J. Chark 2.00 5.00
23 D.J. Moore 3.00 8.00
24 Lamar Jackson 6.00 15.00
25 Mike Gesicki 2.00 5.00
26 Kyle Lauletta 2.50 6.00
27 Mike White 2.00 5.00
28 Kalen Ballage 2.00 5.00
29 Mark Walton 2.00 5.00
30 Hayden Hurst 2.00 5.00

2018 Absolute Rookie Force Signatures

4 Kerryon Johnson 5.00 12.00
6 Sam Darnold 50.00 100.00
7 Courtland Sutton 5.00 12.00
8 Josh Rosen 15.00 40.00
9 Baker Mayfield 125.00 250.00
11 Josh Allen 25.00 50.00
12 Mason Rudolph 12.00 30.00
13 Saquon Barkley 60.00 125.00
14 Daurice Fountain 4.00 10.00
15 D.J. Moore 6.00 15.00
21 Anthony Miller 5.00 12.00
26 Ito Smith 4.00 10.00
28 Tre'Quan Smith 5.00 12.00
29 Mark Walton 4.00 10.00

2018 Absolute Signature Standouts

*BLUE: .6X TO 1.5X BASIC AU
1 John Kelly 3.00 8.00
2 J'Mon Moore 2.50 6.00
3 Marcell Ateman 3.00 8.00
4 Kenneth Dixon 2.50 6.00
5 Kalen Ballage 3.00 8.00
6 Jordan Poyer 2.50 6.00
7 Vernon Hargreaves III 2.50 6.00
8 J.D. McKissic 2.50 6.00
9 Geronimo Allison 2.50 6.00
10 Rashaan Evans 4.00 10.00
11 DeMarcus Walker 2.50 6.00
12 Carl Lawson 2.50 6.00
13 Blake Martinez 2.50 6.00
14 Michael Gallup 5.00 12.00
15 Nyheim Hines 3.00 8.00
16 Roquan Smith 8.00 20.00
17 Taywan Taylor 2.50 6.00
18 Adam Humphries 2.50 6.00
19 Wayne Gallman 2.50 6.00
20 Ito Smith 3.00 8.00
21 James Washington 5.00 12.00
22 Marcus Davenport 5.00 12.00
23 Kyle Allen 3.00 8.00
24 Richie James 2.50 6.00
25 Mike Hughes 4.00 10.00
26 Josh Adams 5.00 12.00
27 Bo Scarbrough 3.00 8.00
28 Luke Falk 3.00 8.00
29 Kyle Lauletta 4.00 10.00
30 Dante Pettis 4.00 10.00

2018 Absolute Tools of the Trade Dual Material Autographs

1 Nelson Agholor/60 5.00 12.00
2 Sterling Shepard/60 6.00 15.00
3 Ezekiel Elliott/60 50.00 100.00
4 JuJu Smith-Schuster/60 12.00 30.00
5 Corey Coleman/99 4.00 10.00
6 Joe Mixon/60 6.00 15.00
7 Jared Goff/25 40.00 80.00
8 Tevin Coleman/60 5.00 12.00
9 David Johnson/25 10.00 25.00
10 D'Onta Foreman/50 5.00 12.00
11 Mike Williams/35 5.00 12.00
12 Dede Westbrook/50 5.00 12.00
13 Giovani Bernard/30 6.00 15.00
14 Curtis Samuel/50
15 Tyler Lockett/30 8.00 20.00
16 Alvin Kamara/99 15.00 40.00
17 Marqise Lee/30 6.00 15.00
18 O.J. Howard/50 5.00 12.00
20 Wayne Gallman/99 4.00 10.00
21 ArDarius Stewart/99 4.00 10.00
23 Jamaal Williams/99 4.00 10.00
24 DeAndre Washington/99 4.00 10.00
26 Marlon Mack/99 4.00 10.00
27 Mitchell Trubisky/25
28 Deshaun Watson/25 60.00 125.00
29 Dak Prescott/25 40.00 80.00
30 Leonard Fournette/25 12.00 30.00
31 Derrick Henry
32 Patrick Mahomes II/25 100.00 200.00
33 Stefon Diggs
34 Joe Montana/10
35 Russell Wilson/15 40.00 80.00
36 Andrew Luck/15
37 Tom Brady/10

2018 Absolute Tools of the Trade Five Materials

*PRIME/15: .6X TO 1.5X BASIC JSY/60
1 Carson Wentz 10.00 25.00
2 Andrew Luck
3 Russell Wilson
4 Marcus Mariota 6.00 15.00
5 Jameis Winston 5.00 12.00

2018 Absolute Tools of the Trade Quad Materials

*PRIME/25: .5X TO 1.2X BASIC JSY/20
*PRIME/25: .4X TO 1X BASIC JSY/25
*PRIME/15: .5X TO 1.2X BASIC JSY/25
1 Dak Prescott/25 8.00 20.00
2 Joe Mixon/60 5.00 12.00
3 John Ross III/60 5.00 12.00
4 Jordan Howard/60 6.00 15.00
5 Christian McCaffrey/60 6.00 15.00
6 Devonta Freeman/60 5.00 12.00
7 David Johnson/60 6.00 15.00
8 Leonard Fournette/60 6.00 15.00
9 Russell Wilson/25 10.00 25.00
10 Kareem Hunt/60 5.00 12.00
11 Jared Goff/60 6.00 15.00
12 DeVante Parker/60 5.00 12.00
13 Stefon Diggs/60 5.00 12.00
14 Alvin Kamara/60 5.00 12.00
15 Amari Cooper/60 6.00 15.00

2018 Absolute Tools of the Trade Triple Material Autographs

1 Alvin Kamara/50 20.00 50.00
2 O.J. Howard/99 4.00 10.00
3 Sterling Shepard/65 6.00 15.00
4 JuJu Smith-Schuster/50 12.00 30.00
5 Ezekiel Elliott/50 50.00 100.00
6 ArDarius Stewart/50 5.00 12.00
7 Corey Coleman/99 4.00 10.00
8 D'Onta Foreman/50 5.00 12.00
9 Marlon Mack/50 5.00 12.00
10 Joe Mixon/50 6.00 15.00
11 Samaje Perine
12 Jared Goff/50 30.00 60.00
13 DeAndre Washington
14 Nelson Agholor/99 4.00 10.00
15 Dede Westbrook/35 5.00 12.00
16 Tevin Coleman/50 5.00 12.00
17 Patrick Mahomes II/35 75.00 150.00
18 David Johnson/35 8.00 20.00
19 Marqise Lee/35 5.00 12.00
20 Tyler Lockett/35 6.00 15.00
21 Deshaun Watson/20
22 Joe Montana/20 60.00 125.00
23 Andrew Luck/20
24 Leonard Fournette/20 15.00 40.00
25 Russell Wilson/20 40.00 80.00
26 Marcus Mariota/30 15.00 40.00

2018 Absolute Tools of the Trade Triple Materials

1 Alvin Kamara/75 3.00 8.00
2 O.J. Howard/75 2.50 6.00
3 Sterling Shepard/75 3.00 8.00
4 JuJu Smith-Schuster/75 4.00 10.00
5 Ezekiel Elliott/75 5.00 12.00
6 ArDarius Stewart/75 2.50 6.00
7 Corey Coleman/75 2.50 6.00
8 D'Onta Foreman/75 2.50 6.00
9 Marlon Mack/75 2.50 6.00
10 Joe Mixon/75 3.00 8.00
11 Samaje Perine/75 2.50 6.00
12 Jared Goff/75 4.00 10.00
13 DeAndre Washington/75 2.50 6.00
14 Nelson Agholor/75 2.50 6.00
15 Dede Westbrook/75 2.50 6.00
16 Tevin Coleman/75 2.50 6.00
17 Patrick Mahomes II/75 10.00 25.00
18 David Johnson/75 4.00 10.00
19 Marqise Lee/75 2.50 6.00
20 Tyler Lockett/75 3.00 8.00
21 Deshaun Watson/75 5.00 12.00
22 Joe Montana/10
23 Andrew Luck/10
24 Leonard Fournette/75 4.00 10.00
25 Russell Wilson/15 10.00 25.00
26 Marcus Mariota/75 4.00 10.00
27 Dak Prescott/25 6.00 15.00
28 Stefon Diggs/75 3.00 8.00
29 Kenyan Drake/75 2.50 6.00
30 Tyler Eifert/75 3.00 8.00

1989 Action Packed Prototypes

These two prototype cards were issued before the 1989 Test issue was released to show the style of Action Packed cards. The cards were folded by hand when they were made, which is why there is no seam on the back of the card as is typical of other Action Packed cards. The standard-size cards feature on the fronts embossed color photos bordered in gold. The horizontally oriented backs have a mugshot, biography, statistics, and an "Action Note" in the form of a caption to the action shot on the front. The primary stylistic difference between these prototype cards and the test set issued later that year is the location of the card number.
72 Freeman McNeil 8.00 20.00
101 Phil Simms 12.00 30.00

1989 Action Packed Test

The 1989 Action Packed Football Test set contains 30 standard-size cards. The cards have rounded corners and gold borders. The fronts have "raised" color action shots, and the horizontally-oriented backs feature mug shots and complete stats. The set, which includes ten players each from the Chicago Bears, New York Giants, and Washington Redskins, was packaged in six-card poly packs. Those cards were not packaged very well; many cards come creased or bent out of packs, and a typical box will yield quite a few duplicates. Although this is considered to be a limited test issue, the test apparently was successful as there were reports that more than 4300 cases were produced of these cards. Factory sets packaged in small dull-gold colored boxes were also available on a limited basis. The cards are copyrighted by Hi-Pro Marketing of Northbrook, Illinois and the packs are labeled "Action Packed." On the card back of number 6 Dan Hampton it lists his uniform number as 95 which is actually Richard Dent's number; Hampton wears 99 for the Bears. The cards are numbered in alphabetical order within teams, Chicago Bears (1-10), New York Giants (11-20), and Washington Redskins (21-30). Since this set was a test issue, the cards of Dave Meggett and Mark Rypien are not considered true Rookie Cards.

COMPLETE SET (30) 6.00 15.00
1 Neal Anderson .25 .60
2 Trace Armstrong .15 .40
3 Kevin Butler .15 .40
4 Richard Dent .25 .60
5 Dennis Gentry .15 .40
6 Dan Hampton UER .25 .60
7 Jay Hilgenberg .15 .40
8 Thomas Sanders .15 .40
9 Mike Singletary .30 .75
10 Mike Tomczak .25 .60
11 Raul Allegre .15 .40
12 Ottis Anderson .25 .60
13 Mark Bavaro .25 .60
14 Terry Kinard .15 .40
15 Lionel Manuel .15 .40
16 Leonard Marshall .25 .60
17 Dave Meggett .30 .75
18 Joe Morris .25 .60
19 Phil Simms .60 1.50
20 Lawrence Taylor .30 .75
21 Kelvin Bryant .15 .40
22 Darrell Green .25 .60
23 Dexter Manley .15 .40
24 Charles Mann .15 .40
25 Wilber Marshall .15 .40
26 Art Monk .30 .75
27 Jamie Morris .15 .40
28 Tracy Rocker .15 .40
29 Mark Rypien UER .25 .60
30 Ricky Sanders .25 .60

1990 Action Packed

This 280-card standard-size set was issued in two skip-numbered series. The cards are the same style as previous year's "test" issue. The set is organized numerically in alphabetical order within team and teams themselves are in alphabetical order by city. For cards numbered 3, 26, 193 and 222, the action note on the card back does not correspond with the picture on the front. Later in the year Action Packed released these cards in the form of pre-packed ten-card complete team sets. The only Rookie Card of any note is Ken Harvey. A special Braille-backed card of Jim Plunkett was released in both 281-card factory sets and as a random insert in wax packs.

COMPLETE SET (280) 8.00 20.00
COMP.FACT.SET (281) 10.00 25.00
1 Aundray Bruce UER .04 .10
2 Scott Case .04 .10
3 Tony Casillas .04 .10
4 Shawn Collins .04 .10
5 Marcus Cotton .04 .10
6 Bill Fralic .04 .10
7 Tim Green RC .04 .10
8 Chris Miller .20 .50
9 Deion Sanders .50 1.25
10 John Settle .04 .10
11 Cornelius Bennett .08 .25
12 Shane Conlan .04 .10
13 Kent Hull .04 .10
14 Jim Kelly .20 .50
15 Mark Kelso .04 .10
16 Scott Norwood .04 .10
17 Andre Reed .20 .50
18 Fred Smerlas .04 .10
19 Bruce Smith .20 .50
20 Thurman Thomas .20 .50
21 Neal Anderson UER .08 .25
22 Kevin Butler .04 .10
23 Richard Dent .08 .25
24 Dennis Gentry .04 .10
25 Dan Hampton .08 .25
26 Jay Hilgenberg .04 .10
27 Steve McMichael .08 .25
28 Brad Muster .04 .10
29 Mike Singletary .08 .25
30 Mike Tomczak .08 .25
31 James Brooks .08 .25
32 Rickey Dixon RC .04 .10
33 Boomer Esiason .08 .25
34 David Fulcher .04 .10
35 Rodney Holman .04 .10
36 Tim Krumrie .04 .10
37 Tim McGee .04 .10
38 Anthony Munoz UER .08 .25
39 Reggie Williams .04 .10
40 Ickey Woods .04 .10
41 Thane Gash RC .04 .10
42 Mike Johnson .04 .10
43 Bernie Kosar .08 .25
44 Reggie Langhorne .04 .10
45 Clay Matthews .08 .25
46 Eric Metcalf .20 .50
47 Frank Minnifield .04 .10
48 Ozzie Newsome .08 .25
49 Webster Slaughter .08 .25
50 Felix Wright .04 .10
51 Troy Aikman .75 2.00
52 James Dixon .04 .10
53 Michael Irvin .20 .50
54 Jim Jeffcoat .04 .10
55 Ed Too Tall Jones .08 .25
56 Eugene Lockhart .04 .10
57 Danny Noonan .04 .10
58 Paul Palmer .04 .10
59 Everson Walls .04 .10
60 Steve Walsh .08 .25
61 Steve Atwater .04 .10
62 Tyrone Braxton .04 .10
63 John Elway 1.25 3.00
64 Bobby Humphrey .04 .10
65 Mark Jackson .04 .10
66 Vance Johnson .04 .10
67 Greg Kragen .04 .10
68 Karl Mecklenburg .04 .10
69 Dennis Smith .08 .25
70 David Treadwell .04 .10
71 Jim Arnold .04 .10
72 Jerry Ball .04 .10
73 Bennie Blades .04 .10
74 Mel Gray .08 .25
75 Richard Johnson .04 .10
76 Eddie Murray .04 .10
77 Rodney Peete UER .08 .25
78 Barry Sanders 1.25 3.00
79 Chris Spielman .20 .50
80 Walter Stanley .04 .10
81 Dave Brown DB .04 .10
82 Brent Fullwood .04 .10
83 Tim Harris .04 .10
84 Johnny Holland .04 .10
85 Don Majkowski .04 .10
86 Tony Mandarich .04 .10
87 Mark Murphy .04 .10
88 Brian Noble UER .04 .10
89 Ken Ruettgers .04 .10
90 Sterling Sharpe UER .20 .50
91 Ray Childress .04 .10
92 Ernest Givins .08 .25
93 Alonzo Highsmith .04 .10
94 Drew Hill .04 .10
95 Bruce Matthews .08 .25
96 Bubba McDowell .04 .10
97 Warren Moon .20 .50
98 Mike Munchak .08 .25
99 Allen Pinkett .04 .10
100 Mike Rozier .04 .10
101 Albert Bentley .04 .10
102 Duane Bickett .04 .10
103 Bill Brooks .04 .10
104 Chris Chandler .20 .50
105 Ray Donaldson .04 .10
106 Chris Hinton .04 .10
107 Andre Rison .20 .50
108 Keith Taylor .04 .10
109 Clarence Verdin .04 .10
110 Fredd Young .04 .10
111 Deron Cherry .04 .10
112 Steve DeBerg .04 .10
113 Dino Hackett .04 .10
114 Albert Lewis .04 .10
115 Nick Lowery .04 .10
116 Christian Okoye .04 .10
117 Stephone Paige .04 .10
118 Kevin Ross .04 .10
119 Derrick Thomas .20 .50
120 Mike Webster .08 .25
121 Marcus Allen .20 .50
122 Eddie Anderson RC .04 .10
123 Steve Beuerlein .08 .25
124 Tim Brown .20 .50
125 Mervyn Fernandez .04 .10
126 Willie Gault .08 .25
127 Bob Golic .04 .10
128 Bo Jackson UER .25 .60
129 Howie Long .20 .50
130 Greg Townsend .04 .10
131 Flipper Anderson .04 .10
132 Greg Bell .04 .10
133 Robert Delpino .04 .10
134 Henry Ellard .08 .25
135 Jim Everett .08 .25
136 Jerry Gray .04 .10
137 Kevin Greene .08 .25
138 Tom Newberry .04 .10
139 Jackie Slater .04 .10
140 Doug Smith .04 .10
141 Mark Clayton .08 .25
142 Jeff Cross .04 .10
143 Mark Duper .08 .25
144 Ferrell Edmunds .04 .10
145 Jim C.Jensen .04 .10
146 Dan Marino 1.25 3.00
147 John Offerdahl .04 .10
148 Louis Oliver .04 .10
149 Reggie Roby .04 .10
150 Sammie Smith .04 .10
151 Joey Browner .04 .10
152 Anthony Carter .08 .25
153 Chris Doleman .04 .10
154 Steve Jordan .04 .10
155 Carl Lee .04 .10
156 Randall McDaniel .08 .25
157 Keith Millard .04 .10
158 Herschel Walker .08 .25
159 Wade Wilson .08 .25
160 Gary Zimmerman .07 .20
161 Hart Lee Dykes .04 .10
162 Irving Fryar .20 .50
163 Steve Grogan .08 .25
164 Maurice Hurst RC .04 .10
165 Fred Marion .04 .10
166 Stanley Morgan .04 .10
167 Robert Perryman .04 .10
168 John Stephens UER .04 .10
169 Andre Tippett .04 .10
170 Brent Williams .04 .10
171 John Fourcade .04 .10
172 Bobby Hebert .04 .10
173 Dalton Hilliard .04 .10
174 Rickey Jackson .08 .25
175 Vaughan Johnson .04 .10
176 Eric Martin .04 .10
177 Robert Massey .04 .10
178 Rueben Mayes UER .04 .10
179 Sam Mills .08 .25
180 Pat Swilling .08 .25
181 Ottis Anderson .08 .25
182 Carl Banks .04 .10
183 Mark Bavaro .04 .10
184 Mark Collins .04 .10
185 Leonard Marshall .04 .10
186 Dave Meggett .08 .25
187 Gary Reasons .04 .10
188 Phil Simms .20 .50
189 Lawrence Taylor .20 .50
190 Odessa Turner RC .04 .10
191 Kyle Clifton .04 .10
192 James Hasty .04 .10
193 Johnny Hector .04 .10
194 Jeff Lageman .04 .10
195 Pat Leahy .04 .10
196 Erik McMillan .04 .10
197 Ken O'Brien .04 .10
198 Mickey Shuler .04 .10
199 Al Toon .08 .25
200 Jo Jo Townsell .04 .10
201 Eric Allen UER .04 .10
202 Jerome Brown .04 .10
203 Keith Byars UER .04 .10
204 Cris Carter .50 1.25
205 Wes Hopkins .04 .10
206 Keith Jackson UER .08 .25
207 Seth Joyner .08 .25
208 Mike Quick .04 .10
209 Andre Waters .04 .10
210 Reggie White .20 .50
211 Rich Camarillo .04 .10
212 Roy Green .04 .10
213 Ken Harvey RC .20 .50
214 Gary Hogeboom .04 .10
215 Tim McDonald .04 .10
216 Stump Mitchell .04 .10
217 Luis Sharpe .04 .10
218 Vai Sikahema .04 .10
219 J.T. Smith .04 .10
220 Ron Wolfley .04 .10
221 Gary Anderson K .04 .10
222 Bubby Brister UER .04 .10
223 Merril Hoge .04 .10
224 Tunch Ilkin .04 .10
225 Louis Lipps .08 .25
226 David Little .04 .10
227 Greg Lloyd .20 .50
228 Dwayne Woodruff .04 .10
229 Rod Woodson .20 .50
230 Tim Worley .04 .10
231 Marion Butts .08 .25
232 Gill Byrd .04 .10
233 Burt Grossman .04 .10
234 Jim McMahon .08 .25
235 Anthony Miller UER .20 .50
236 Leslie O'Neal UER .08 .25
237 Gary Plummer .04 .10
238 Billy Ray Smith .04 .10
239 Tim Spencer .04 .10
240 Lee Williams .04 .10
241 Mike Cofer .04 .10
242 Roger Craig .08 .25
243 Charles Haley .08 .25
244 Ronnie Lott .08 .25
245 Guy McIntyre .04 .10
246 Joe Montana 1.25 3.00
247 Tom Rathman .04 .10
248 Jerry Rice .75 2.00
249 John Taylor .20 .50
250 Michael Walter .04 .10
251 Brian Blades .08 .25
252 Jacob Green .04 .10
253 Dave Krieg .08 .25
254 Steve Largent .20 .50
255 Joe Nash .04 .10
256 Rufus Porter .04 .10
257 Eugene Robinson .04 .10
258 Paul Skansi RC .04 .10
259 Curt Warner UER .04 .10
260 John L.Williams .04 .10
261 Mark Carrier WR .20 .50
262 Reuben Davis .04 .10
263 Harry Hamilton .04 .10
264 Bruce Hill .04 .10
265 Donald Igwebuike .04 .10
266 Eugene Marve .04 .10
267 Kevin Murphy .04 .10
268 Mark Robinson .04 .10
269 Lars Tate .04 .10
270 Vinny Testaverde .08 .25
271 Gary Clark .20 .50
272 Monte Coleman .04 .10
273 Darrell Green .08 .25
274 Charles Mann UER .04 .10
275 Wilber Marshall .04 .10
276 Art Monk .08 .25
277 Gerald Riggs .04 .10
278 Mark Rypien .08 .25
279 Ricky Sanders .04 .10
280 Alvin Walton .04 .10
NNO Jim Plunkett BR 2.00 4.00

1990 Action Packed Rookie Update

This 84-card standard-size set was issued to feature most of the rookies who made an impact in the 1990 season that Action Packed did not issue in their regular set. The first 64 cards in the set are 1990 rookies while the last 20 cards are either players who were traded during the off-season or players such as Randall Cunningham who were not included in the regular set. Rookie Cards include Fred Barnett, Reggie Cobb, Barry Foster, Jeff George, Eric Green, Rodney Hampton, Johnny Johnson, Cortez Kennedy, Scott Mitchell, Rob Moore, Junior Seau, Shannon Sharpe, Emmitt Smith, Chris Warren and Calvin Williams. The set was released through both the Action Packed dealer network and via traditional retail outlets and was available both in wax packs and as collated factory sets.

COMPLETE SET (84) 10.00 25.00
COMP.FACT.SET (84) 12.50 30.00
1 Jeff George RC .75 2.00
2 Richmond Webb RC .05 .15
3 James Williams DB RC .05 .15
4 Tony Bennett RC .08 .25
5 Darrell Thompson RC .05 .15
6 Steve Broussard RC .05 .15
7 Rodney Hampton RC .20 .50
8 Rob Moore RC .60 1.50
9 Alton Montgomery RC .05 .15
10 LeRoy Butler RC .20 .50
11 Anthony Johnson RC .20 .50
12 Scott Mitchell RC .20 .50
13 Mike Fox RC .05 .15
14 Robert Blackmon RC .05 .15
15 Blair Thomas RC .05 .15
16 Tony Stargell RC .05 .15
17 Peter Tom Willis RC .05 .15
18 Harold Green RC .08 .25
19 Bernard Clark .05 .15
20 Aaron Wallace RC .05 .15
21 Dennis Brown RC .05 .15
22 Johnny Johnson RC .08 .25
23 Chris Calloway RC .05 .15
24 Walter Wilson .05 .15
25 Dexter Carter RC .05 .15
26 Percy Snow RC .05 .15
27 Johnny Bailey RC .05 .15
28 Mike Bellamy RC .05 .15
29 Ben Smith RC .05 .15
30 Mark Carrier RC DB UER .20 .50
31 James Francis RC .05 .15
32 Lamar Lathon RC .08 .25
33 Bern Brostek RC .05 .15
34 Emmitt Smith RC 6.00 15.00
35 Andre Collins UER RC .05 .15
36 Alexander Wright RC .05 .15
37 Fred Barnett RC .20 .50
38 Junior Seau RC 1.50 4.00
39 Cortez Kennedy RC .40 1.00
40 Terry Wooden RC .05 .15
41 Eric Davis RC .08 .25
42 Fred Washington RC .05 .15
43 Reggie Cobb RC .05 .15
44 Andre Ware RC .08 .25
45 Anthony Smith RC .05 .15
46 Shannon Sharpe RC 3.00 8.00
47 Harlon Barnett RC .05 .15
48 Greg McMurtry RC .05 .15
49 Stacey Simmons RC .05 .15
50 Calvin Williams RC .08 .25
51 Anthony Thompson RC .05 .15
52 Ricky Proehl RC .20 .50
53 Tony Jones WR RC .05 .15
54 Ray Agnew RC .05 .15
55 Tommy Hodson RC .05 .15
56 Ron Cox RC .05 .15
57 Leroy Hoard RC .20 .50
58 Eric Green UER RC .08 .25
59 Barry Foster RC .08 .25
60 Keith McCants RC .05 .15
61 Oliver Barnett RC .05 .15
62 Chris Warren RC .20 .50
63 Pat Terrell RC .05 .15
64 Renaldo Turnbull RC .05 .15
65 Chris Chandler .20 .50
66 Everson Walls .05 .15
67 Alonzo Highsmith .05 .15
68 Gary Anderson RB .05 .15
69 Fred Smerlas .05 .15
70 Jim McMahon .08 .25
71 Curt Warner .05 .15
72 Stanley Morgan .05 .15
73 Dave Waymer .05 .15
74 Billy Joe Tolliver .05 .15
75 Tony Eason .05 .15
76 Max Montoya .05 .15
77 Greg Bell .05 .15
78 Dennis McKinnon .05 .15
79 Raymond Clayborn .05 .15
80 Broderick Thomas .05 .15
81 Timm Rosenbach .05 .15
82 Tim McKyer .05 .15
83 Andre Rison .20 .50
84 Randall Cunningham .20 .50

1991 Action Packed

This 280-card, standard-size set features action photos on the front that are framed in gold along the left side and on the bottom of the card. The cards are arranged by team. Complete factory sets also included an exclusive subset of 8 Braille cards; card numbers 281-288 which feature the category leaders of the AFC and NFC. They have the same front design as the regular issue, but different borderless embossed color player photos and horizontally oriented backs written in Braille. Two logo cards and an unnumbered checklist card complete the set. There are no key Rookie Cards in this set. Two prototype cards were issued as well and priced below. Each contains the word "prototype" stamped on the card back and neither is considered part of the complete set. We've assigned card numbers to these two for ease in cataloging.

COMPLETE SET (280) 6.00 15.00
COMP.FACT.SET (291) 10.00 25.00
1 Steve Broussard .02 .10
2 Scott Case .02 .10
3 Brian Jordan FAPC .07 .20
4 Darion Conner .02 .10
5 Tim Green .02 .10
6 Chris Miller .07 .20
7 Andre Rison .07 .20
8 Mike Rozier .02 .10
9 Deion Sanders .30 .75
10 Jessie Tuggle .02 .10
11 Leonard Smith .02 .10
12 Shane Conlan .02 .10
13 Kent Hull .02 .10
14 Keith McKeller .02 .10
15 James Lofton .07 .20
16 Andre Reed .07 .20
17 Bruce Smith .15 .40
18 Darryl Talley .02 .10
19 Steve Tasker .07 .20
20 Thurman Thomas .15 .40
21 Neal Anderson .07 .20
22 Trace Armstrong .02 .10
23 Mark Bortz .02 .10
24 Mark Carrier DB .07 .20
25 Wendell Davis FAPC .02 .10
26 Richard Dent .07 .20
27 Jim Harbaugh .15 .40
28 Jay Hilgenberg .02 .10
29 Brad Muster .02 .10
30 Mike Singletary .07 .20
31 Harold Green .02 .10
32 James Brooks .02 .10
33 Eddie Brown .02 .10
34 Boomer Esiason .07 .20
35 James Francis .02 .10
36 David Fulcher .02 .10
37 Rodney Holman .02 .10
38 Tim McGee .02 .10
39 Anthony Munoz .07 .20
40 Ickey Woods .02 .10
41 Rob Burnett RC .07 .20
42 Thane Gash .02 .10
43 Mike Johnson .02 .10
44 Brian Brennan .02 .10
45 Reggie Langhorne .02 .10
46 Kevin Mack .02 .10
47 Clay Matthews .07 .20
48 Eric Metcalf .07 .20
49 Anthony Pleasant .02 .10
50 Ozzie Newsome .07 .20
51 Troy Aikman .50 1.25
52 Issiac Holt .02 .10
53 Michael Irvin .15 .40
54 Jimmie Jones .02 .10
55 Eugene Lockhart .02 .10
56 Kelvin Martin .02 .10
57 Ken Norton Jr. .07 .20
58 Jay Novacek FAPC .15 .40
59 Emmitt Smith 1.50 4.00
60 Daniel Stubbs .02 .10
61 Steve Atwater .02 .10
62 Michael Brooks .02 .10
63 John Elway .75 2.00
64 Simon Fletcher .02 .10
65 Bobby Humphrey .02 .10
66 Mark Jackson .02 .10
67 Vance Johnson .02 .10
68 Karl Mecklenburg .02 .10
69 Dennis Smith .02 .10
70 Greg Kragen .02 .10
71 Jerry Ball .02 .10
72 Lomas Brown .02 .10
73 Robert Clark .02 .10
74 Michael Cofer .02 .10
75 Mel Gray .02 .10
76 Richard Johnson .02 .10
77 Rodney Peete .07 .20
78 Barry Sanders .75 2.00
79 Chris Spielman .07 .20
80 Andre Ware .07 .20
81 Matt Brock RC .02 .10
82 LeRoy Butler .07 .20
83 Tim Harris .02 .10
84 Perry Kemp .02 .10
85 Don Majkowski .02 .10
86 Mark Murphy .02 .10
87 Brian Noble .02 .10
88 Sterling Sharpe .15 .40
89 Darrell Thompson .02 .10
90 Ed West .02 .10
91 Ray Childress .02 .10
92 Ernest Givins .07 .20
93 Drew Hill .02 .10
94 Haywood Jeffires FAPC .07 .20
95 Richard Johnson CB RC .02 .10
96 Sean Jones .07 .20
97 Bruce Matthews .07 .20
98 Warren Moon .15 .40
99 Mike Munchak .07 .20
100 Lorenzo White .02 .10
101 Albert Bentley .02 .10
102 Duane Bickett .02 .10
103 Bill Brooks .02 .10
104 Jeff George .15 .40
105 Jon Hand .02 .10
106 Jeff Herrod .02 .10
107 Jessie Hester .02 .10
108 Mike Prior UER .02 .10
109 Rohn Stark .02 .10
110 Clarence Verdin .02 .10
111 Steve DeBerg .02 .10
112 Dan Saleaumua .02 .10
113 Albert Lewis .02 .10
114 Nick Lowery .02 .10
115 Christian Okoye .02 .10
116 Stephone Paige .02 .10
117 Kevin Ross .02 .10
118 Dino Hackett .02 .10
119 Derrick Thomas UER .15 .40
120 Barry Word UER .02 .10
121 Marcus Allen .15 .40
122 Mervyn Fernandez UER .02 .10
123 Willie Gault .02 .10
124 Bo Jackson .20 .50
125 Terry McDaniel .02 .10
126 Don Mosebar .02 .10
127 Jay Schroeder .02 .10
128 Greg Townsend UER .02 .10
129 Aaron Wallace .02 .10
130 Steve Wisniewski .02 .10
131 Flipper Anderson .02 .10
132 Henry Ellard .07 .20
133 Jim Everett .07 .20
134 Cleveland Gary .02 .10
135 Jerry Gray .02 .10
136 Kevin Greene .07 .20
137 Buford McGee .02 .10
138 Vince Newsome .02 .10
139 Jackie Slater .02 .10
140 Frank Stams .02 .10
141 Jeff Cross .02 .10
142 Mark Duper .07 .20
143 Ferrell Edmunds .02 .10
144 Dan Marino .75 2.00
145 Louis Oliver .02 .10
146 John Offerdahl .02 .10
147 Tony Paige .02 .10
148 Sammie Smith .02 .10
149 Richmond Webb .02 .10
150 Jarvis Williams .02 .10
151 Joey Browner .02 .10
152 Anthony Carter .07 .20
153 Chris Doleman .02 .10
154 Hassan Jones .02 .10
155 Steve Jordan .02 .10
156 Carl Lee .02 .10
157 Randall McDaniel .05 .15
158 Mike Merriweather .02 .10
159 Herschel Walker .07 .20
160 Wade Wilson .07 .20
161 Ray Agnew .02 .10
162 Bruce Armstrong .02 .10
163 Marv Cook FAPC .02 .10
164 Hart Lee Dykes .02 .10
165 Irving Fryar .07 .20
166 Tommy Hodson .02 .10
167 Ronnie Lippett .02 .10
168 Fred Marion .02 .10
169 John Stephens .02 .10
170 Brent Williams .02 .10
171A Morten Andersen ERR .02 .10
171B Morten Andersen COR .02 .10
172A Gene Atkins ERR .02 .10
172B Gene Atkins COR .02 .10
173A Craig Heyward ERR .07 .20
173B Craig Heyward COR .07 .20
174A Rickey Jackson ERR .02 .10
174B Rickey Jackson COR .02 .10
175A Vaughan Johnson ERR .02 .10
175B Vaughan Johnson COR .02 .10
176A Eric Martin ERR .02 .10
176B Eric Martin COR .02 .10
177A Rueben Mayes ERR .02 .10
177B Rueben Mayes COR .02 .10
178A Pat Swilling ERR .07 .20
178B Pat Swilling COR .07 .20
179A Renaldo Turnbull ERR .07 .20
179B Renaldo Turnbull COR .07 .20
180A Steve Walsh ERR .02 .10
180B Steve Walsh COR .02 .10
181 Ottis Anderson .07 .20
182 Rodney Hampton .15 .40
183 Jeff Hostetler FAPC .15 .40
184 Pepper Johnson .02 .10
185 Sean Landeta .02 .10
186 Dave Meggett .07 .20
187 Bart Oates .02 .10
188 Phil Simms .15 .40
189 Lawrence Taylor .15 .40
190 Reyna Thompson .02 .10
191 Brad Baxter FAPC .02 .10
192 Dennis Byrd .02 .10
193 Kyle Clifton .02 .10
194 James Hasty .02 .10
195 Pat Leahy .02 .10
196 Erik McMillan .02 .10
197 Rob Moore .15 .40
198 Ken O'Brien .02 .10
199 Mark Boyer .02 .10
200 Al Toon .07 .20
201 Fred Barnett .15 .40
202 Jerome Brown .02 .10
203 Keith Byars .02 .10
204 Randall Cunningham .15 .40
205 Wes Hopkins .02 .10
206 Keith Jackson .07 .20
207 Seth Joyner .07 .20
208 Heath Sherman .02 .10
209 Reggie White .15 .40
210 Calvin Williams .07 .20
211 Roy Green .02 .10
212 Ken Harvey UER .07 .20
213 Luis Sharpe .02 .10
214 Ernie Jones .02 .10
215 Tim McDonald .02 .10
216 Freddie Joe Nunn .02 .10
217 Ricky Proehl .02 .10
218 Timm Rosenbach .02 .10
219 Anthony Thompson .02 .10
220 Lonnie Young .02 .10
221 Gary Anderson K .02 .10
222 Bubby Brister .02 .10
223 Eric Green .02 .10
224 Merril Hoge .02 .10
225 Carnell Lake .02 .10
226 Louis Lipps .02 .10
227 David Little .02 .10
228 Greg Lloyd .15 .40
229 Gerald Williams .02 .10
230 Rod Woodson .15 .40
231 Marion Butts .02 .10
232 Gill Byrd .02 .10
233 Burt Grossman .02 .10
234 Courtney Hall .02 .10
235 Ronnie Harmon .02 .10
236 Anthony Miller .07 .20
237 Leslie O'Neal .07 .20
238 Junior Seau .15 .40
239 Billy Joe Tolliver .02 .10
240 Lee Williams .02 .10
241 Dexter Carter .02 .10
242 Kevin Fagan .02 .10
243 Charles Haley .07 .20
244 Brent Jones .15 .40
245 Ronnie Lott .07 .20
246 Guy McIntyre .02 .10
247 Joe Montana .75 2.00
248 Jerry Rice .50 1.25
249 John Taylor .07 .20
250 Roger Craig .07 .20
251 Brian Blades .07 .20
252 Derrick Fenner FAPC .02 .10
253 Nesby Glasgow UER .02 .10
254 Jacob Green .02 .10
255 Tommy Kane .02 .10
256 Dave Krieg .07 .20
257 Rufus Porter .02 .10
258 Eugene Robinson .02 .10
259 Cortez Kennedy .15 .40
260 John L. Williams .02 .10
261 Gary Anderson RB .02 .10
262 Mark Carrier WR .15 .40
263 Steve Christie .02 .10
264 Reggie Cobb .02 .10
265 Paul Gruber .02 .10
266 Wayne Haddix .02 .10
267 Bruce Hill .02 .10
268 Keith McCants .02 .10
269 Vinny Testaverde .07 .20
270 Broderick Thomas .02 .10
271 Earnest Byner .02 .10
272 Gary Clark .15 .40
273 Darrell Green .02 .10
274 Jim Lachey .02 .10
275 Chip Lohmiller .02 .10
276 Charles Mann .02 .10
277 Wilber Marshall .02 .10
278 Art Monk .07 .20
279 Mark Rypien .07 .20
280 Alvin Walton .02 .10
281 Randall Cunningham BR .15 .40
282 Warren Moon BR .15 .40
283 Barry Sanders BR 1.25 3.00
284 Thurman Thomas BR .15 .40
285 Jerry Rice BR .60 1.50
286 Haywood Jeffires BR .02 .10
287 Charles Haley BR .02 .10
288 Derrick Thomas BR .15 .40
289 NFC Logo Card .02 .10
290 AFC Logo Card .02 .10
P1 Randall Cunningham Proto. 1.50 4.00
P2 Emmitt Smith Prototype 6.00 15.00
NNO R.Cunningham 18K/26 100.00 200.00
NNO Checklist Card .07 .20

1991 Action Packed 24K Gold

This 42-card standard-size set consists of 24K gold-stamped superstar cards that were randomly inserted in foil packs. The fronts of these cards feature borderless embossed color player photos, with gold indicia bordered in black. The team logo appears in the lower right corner. In a horizontal format, the gold-bordered backs have color head shots, biographical information, statistics, and an "Action Note" in the form of a caption to the action shot on the card front. The cards are numbered on the back. The set numbering follows an alphabetical team order.

COMPLETE SET (42) 75.00 200.00
1G Andre Rison 2.50 6.00
2G Deion Sanders 4.00 10.00
3G Andre Reed 3.00 8.00
4G Bruce Smith 3.00 8.00
5G Thurman Thomas 3.00 8.00
6G Neal Anderson 2.50 6.00
7G Mark Carrier DB 2.00 5.00
8G Mike Singletary 3.00 8.00
9G Boomer Esiason 2.50 6.00
10G James Francis 2.00 5.00
11G Anthony Munoz 2.50 6.00
12G Troy Aikman 6.00 15.00
13G Emmitt Smith 15.00 40.00
14G John Elway 10.00 25.00
15G Bobby Humphrey 2.00 5.00
16G Barry Sanders 10.00 25.00
17G Don Majkowski 2.00 5.00
18G Sterling Sharpe 2.50 6.00
19G Warren Moon 3.00 8.00
20G Jeff George 2.50 6.00
21G Christian Okoye 2.50 6.00
22G Derrick Thomas 3.00 8.00
23G Barry Word 2.00 5.00
24G Marcus Allen 3.00 8.00
25G Bo Jackson 6.00 15.00
26G Jim Everett 2.50 6.00
27G Cleveland Gary 2.00 5.00
28G Dan Marino 10.00 25.00
29G Herschel Walker 3.00 8.00
30G Ottis Anderson 2.50 6.00
31G Rodney Hampton 2.50 6.00
32G Dave Meggett 2.00 5.00
33G Marion Butts 2.00 5.00
34G Randall Cunningham 3.00 8.00
35G Reggie White 3.00 8.00
36G Jerry Rice 8.00 20.00
37G Eric Green 2.00 5.00
38G Charles Haley 2.50 6.00
39G Ronnie Lott 3.00 8.00
40G Joe Montana 15.00 40.00
41G Vinny Testaverde 2.50 6.00
42G Gary Clark 2.50 6.00

1991 Action Packed Rookie Update

This 84-card standard-size set contains 74 Rookie Cards (including 26 first round draft picks) plus ten traded and update cards. The front design consists of embossed color player photos. Designated rookies have an embossed red helmet with a white "R". The gold indicia and logo are bordered in red instead of black as on the regular set. In red print, the horizontally oriented backs have the player's college regular season and career statistics. An Emmitt Smith rookie prototype card was included as a bonus with each case of 1991 Action Packed Rookie Update foil or sets ordered. Rookie Cards in this set include Bryan Cox, Ricky Ervins, Brett Favre, Alvin Harper, Randal Hill, Herman Moore, Russell Maryland, Erric Pegram, Mike Pritchard, Leonard Russell, Ricky Watters, and Harvey Williams.

COMPLETE SET (84) 7.50 20.00
COMP.FACT.SET (84) 10.00 25.00
1 Herman Moore RC .08 .25
2 Eric Turner RC .02 .10
3 Mike Croel RC .01 .05
4 Alfred Williams RC .01 .05
5 Stanley Richard RC .01 .05
6 Russell Maryland RC .08 .25
7 Pat Harlow RC .01 .05
8 Alvin Harper RC .08 .25
9 Mike Pritchard RC .02 .10
10 Leonard Russell RC .08 .25
11 Jarrod Bunch RC .01 .05
12 Dan McGwire RC .01 .05
13 Bobby Wilson RC .01 .05
14 Vinnie Clark RC .01 .05
15 Kelvin Pritchett RC .02 .10
16 Harvey Williams RC .08 .25
17 Stan Thomas .01 .05
18 Todd Marinovich RC .01 .05
19 Antone Davis RC .01 .05
20 Greg Lewis RC .01 .05
21 Brett Favre RC 6.00 15.00
22 Wesley Carroll RC .01 .05
23 Ed McCaffrey RC 1.25 3.00
24 Reggie Barrett .01 .05

25 Chris Zorich RC .08 .25
26 Kenny Walker RC .01 .05
27 Aaron Craver RC .01 .05
28 Browning Nagle RC .01 .05
29 Nick Bell RC .01 .05
30 Anthony Morgan RC .01 .05
31 Jesse Campbell RC .01 .05
32 Eric Bieniemy RC .01 .05
33 Ricky Ervins UER RC .02 .10
34 Kanavis McGhee RC .01 .05
35 Shawn Moore RC .01 .05
36 Todd Lyght RC .01 .05
37 Eric Swann RC .08 .25
38 Henry Jones RC .02 .10
39 Ted Washington RC .01 .05
40 Charles McRae RC .01 .05
41 Randal Hill RC .02 .10
42 Huey Richardson RC .01 .05
43 Roman Phifer RC .01 .05
44 Ricky Watters RC .75 2.00
45 Esera Tuaolo RC .01 .05
46 Michael Jackson WR RC .08 .25
47 Shawn Jefferson RC .02 .10
48 Tim Barnett RC .01 .05
49 Chuck Webb RC .01 .05
50 Moe Gardner RC .01 .05
51 Mo Lewis RC .02 .10
52 Mike Dumas RC .01 .05
53 Jon Vaughn RC .01 .05
54 Jerome Henderson RC .01 .05
55 Harry Colon RC .01 .05
56 David Daniels RC .01 .05
57 Phil Hansen RC .01 .05
58 Ernie Mills RC .02 .10
59 John Kasay RC .02 .10
60 Darren Lewis RC .01 .05
61 James Joseph RC .01 .05
62 Robert Wilson RC .01 .05
63 Lawrence Dawsey RC .02 .10
64 Mike Jones DE RC .01 .05
65 Dave McCloughan .01 .05
66 Erric Pegram RC .08 .25
67 Aeneas Williams RC .50 1.25
68 Reggie Johnson RC .01 .05
69 Todd Scott RC .01 .05
70 James Jones RC .01 .05
71 Lamar Rogers RC .01 .05
72 Darryll Lewis RC .02 .10
73 Bryan Cox RC .08 .25
74 Leroy Thompson RC .01 .05
75 Mark Higgs RC .01 .05
76 John Friesz .08 .25
77 Tim McKyer .01 .05
78 Roger Craig .02 .10
79 Ronnie Lott .02 .10
80 Steve Young .40 1.00
81 Percy Snow .01 .05
82 Cornelius Bennett .02 .10
83 Johnny Johnson .01 .05
84 Blair Thomas .01 .05

1991 Action Packed Rookie Update 24K Gold

This 26-card standard-size set was issued in honor of the first round draft picks. These special cards are identified by "24K" stamped on the card front, and they were randomly inserted in 1991 Rookie Update foil packs. Like the other Rookie Update cards, the fronts have borderless embossed color player photos, with gold indicia and logo bordered in red. In a horizontal format, the backs have the player's collegiate regular season and career statistics in red print. The set numbering order is according to NFL draft order.

COMPLETE SET (26) 150.00 300.00
1G Russell Maryland 7.50 15.00
2G Eric Turner 10.00 20.00
3G Mike Croel 5.00 10.00
4G Todd Lyght 5.00 10.00
5G Eric Swann 10.00 20.00
6G Charles McRae 5.00 10.00
7G Antone Davis 5.00 10.00
8G Stanley Richard 7.50 15.00
9G Herman Moore 10.00 20.00
10G Pat Harlow 5.00 10.00
11G Alvin Harper 10.00 20.00
12G Mike Pritchard 10.00 20.00
13G Leonard Russell 10.00 20.00
14G Huey Richardson 5.00 10.00
15G Dan McGwire 7.50 15.00
16G Bobby Wilson 5.00 10.00
17G Alfred Williams 5.00 10.00
18G Vinnie Clark 5.00 10.00
19G Kelvin Pritchett 7.50 15.00
20G Harvey Williams 10.00 20.00
21G Stan Thomas 5.00 10.00
22G Randal Hill 5.00 10.00
23G Todd Marinovich 7.50 15.00
24G Ted Washington 5.00 10.00
25G Henry Jones 5.00 10.00
26G Jarrod Bunch 5.00 10.00

1991 Action Packed NFLPA Awards

This 16-card standard-size set was produced by Action Packed to honor the athletes who earned various awards in the 1990 NFL season. There were 5,000 sets issued each in their own attractive solid black box; these boxes were individually numbered on the back. The box has the inscription NFLPA/MDA Awards Dinner March 12, 1991 on it. The cards are in the 1991 Action Packed design with a raised, 3-D like photo on the front and a hockey-stick like frame going down the left side of the card and on the bottom identifying the player. The card backs feature a portrait of the player along with biographical information and statistical information where applicable. The cards feature the now-traditional Action Packed rounded corners.

COMPLETE SET (16) 7.50 20.00
1 Jim Lachey .50 1.25
2 Anthony Munoz .75 2.00
3 Bruce Smith .75 2.00
4 Reggie White 1.25 3.00
5 Charles Haley .50 1.25
6 Derrick Thomas 1.25 3.00
7 Albert Lewis .50 1.25
8 Mark Carrier DB .50 1.25
9 Reyna Thompson .50 1.25
10 Steve Tasker .75 2.00
11 James Francis .50 1.25
12 Mark Carrier DB .75 2.00
13 Johnny Johnson .50 1.25
14 Eric Green .50 1.25
15 Warren Moon 1.25 3.00
16 Randall Cunningham 1.25 3.00

1991 Action Packed Whizzer White Award

At the silver anniversary NFLPA/Mackey Awards banquet in Chicago (June 23, 1991), Action Packed presented this 25-card commemorative standard-size set in honor of the 25 winners of the Justice Byron "Whizzer" White Humanitarian Award from 1967-91. Reportedly 3,500 sets were distributed at the dinner and another 5,000 numbered boxed sets were produced for sale into the hobby. The front design features a color embossed action photo, with indicia in silver and the award year inscribed on a silver helmet. The backs have a color head shot, biographical information, career statistics, and a tribute to the player's professional career and community contributions. The card numbering follows chronologically the order in which the award was won, 1967 through 1991, inclusive.

COMPLETE SET (25) 8.00 20.00
1 Bart Starr 2.00 5.00
2 Willie Davis .30 .75
3 Ed Meador .20 .50
4 Gale Sayers 1.00 2.50
5 Kermit Alexander .20 .50
6 Roy May .20 .50
7 Andy Russell .20 .50
8 Floyd Little .20 .50
9 Rocky Bleier .50 1.25
10 Jim Hart .20 .50
11 Lyle Alzado .30 .75
12 Archie Manning .50 1.25
13 Roger Staubach 2.00 5.00
14 Gene Upshaw .30 .75
15 Ken Houston .20 .50
16 Franco Harris .80 2.00
17 Doug Dieken .20 .50
18 Rolf Benirschke .20 .50
19 Reggie Williams .20 .50
20 Nat Moore .20 .50
21 George Martin .20 .50
22 Deron Cherry .20 .50
23 Mike Singletary .50 1.25
24 Ozzie Newsome .30 .75
25 Mike Kenn .20 .50

1991 Action Packed Withdrawals

These cards apparently were withdrawn prior to the release of the 1991 Action Packed issue due to the dispute between the NFL Player's Association and NFL Properties. Each card appears to be a standard 1991 Action Packed card, but none were ever included in packs.

14 Jim Kelly 100.00 250.00
44 Bernie Kosar 50.00 125.00
199 Blair Thomas 50.00 125.00
213 Johnny Johnson 50.00 125.00

1992 Action Packed Prototypes

The 1992 Action Packed Prototype set contains three standard-size cards. The card design is very similar to the 1992 Action Packed regular issue cards. The cards were first distributed at the Super Bowl Show in Minneapolis in January, 1992. The cards are overstamped "Prototype" on the back. The Barry Sanders card seems to be a little more difficult to find than the other two cards.

92A Thurman Thomas .60 1.50
92N Emmitt Smith 4.00 10.00
92P Barry Sanders 4.00 10.00

1992 Action Packed

The 1992 Action Packed football set contains 280 standard-size cards. Cards were issued six per pack. The fronts feature borderless embossed color player photos, accented by either gold and aqua (NFC) or gold and red (AFC) border stripes running down either the left or right side of the card face. The team helmet appears in the lower left or right corner, with the player's name and position printed at the card bottom. The horizontally oriented backs carry biography, player profile, a color head shot, and an "Action Note" in the form of an extended caption to the photo on the front. The cards are numbered on the back and checklisted below alphabetically according to teams. There are no key Rookie Cards in this set. To show support for their injured teammate, a special "thumbs up" logo with Mike Utley's number 60 was placed on the back of all Detroit Lions' cards. The factory set closes with a Braille subset (281-288) and Logo cards (289-290). The inside lid of the factory set box has the set checklist printed on it. The eight Braille cards, available in foil packs as well as factory sets, feature category leaders by division. Action Packed also made 26 18K solid gold Tiffany-designed cards of Action Packed Player of the Year Barry Sanders. Certificates for a chance to win these cards were randomly inserted in the regular series foil packs. Action Packed also produced a 288-card "Mint" parallel version of the regular set. The Mint cards were pacakged seperately in boxes of twenty-four six-card packs.

COMPLETE SET (280) 10.00 25.00
COMP.FACT.SET (292) 12.50 30.00
1 Steve Broussard .05 .15
2 Michael Haynes .08 .25
3 Tim McKyer .05 .15
4 Chris Miller .08 .25
5 Andre Rison .08 .25
6 Jessie Tuggle .05 .15
7 Mike Pritchard .05 .15
8 Moe Gardner .05 .15
9 Brian Jordan .08 .25
10 Mike Kenn and .05 .15
11 Steve Tasker .08 .25
12 Cornelius Bennett .08 .25
13 Shane Conlan .05 .15
14 Darryl Talley .05 .15
15 Thurman Thomas .20 .50
16 James Lofton .08 .25
17 Don Beebe .05 .15
18 Jim Ritcher .05 .15
19 Keith McKeller .05 .15
20 Nate Odomes .05 .15
21 Mark Carrier DB .05 .15
22 Wendell Davis .05 .15
23 Richard Dent .08 .25
24 Jim Harbaugh .20 .50
25 Jay Hilgenberg .05 .15
26 Steve McMichael .08 .25
27 Tom Waddle .05 .15
28 Neal Anderson .05 .15
29 Brad Muster .05 .15
30 Shaun Gayle .05 .15
31 Jim Breech .05 .15
32 James Brooks .05 .15
33 James Francis .05 .15
34 David Fulcher .05 .15
35 Harold Green .05 .15
36 Rodney Holman .05 .15
37 Anthony Munoz .08 .25
38 Tim Krumrie .05 .15
39 Tim McGee .05 .15
40 Eddie Brown .05 .15
41 Kevin Mack .05 .15
42 James Jones DT .05 .15
43 Vince Newsome .05 .15
44 Ed King .05 .15
45 Eric Metcalf .08 .25
46 Leroy Hoard .08 .25
47 Stephen Braggs .05 .15
48 Clay Matthews .08 .25
49 David Brandon RC .05 .15
50 Rob Burnett .05 .15
51 Larry Brown DB .05 .15
52 Alvin Harper .08 .25
53 Michael Irvin .20 .50
54 Ken Norton Jr. .08 .25
55 Jay Novacek .08 .25
56 Emmitt Smith 1.50 4.00
57 Tony Tolbert .05 .15
58 Nate Newton .08 .25
59 Steve Beuerlein .08 .25
60 Tony Casillas .05 .15
61 Steve Atwater .05 .15
62 Mike Croel .05 .15
63 Gaston Green .05 .15
64 Mark Jackson .05 .15
65 Greg Kragen .05 .15
66 Karl Mecklenburg .05 .15
67 Dennis Smith .05 .15
68 Steve Sewell .05 .15
69 John Elway 1.25 3.00
70 Simon Fletcher .05 .15
71 Mel Gray .05 .15
72 Barry Sanders 1.25 3.00
73 Jerry Ball .05 .15
74 Bennie Blades .05 .15
75 Lomas Brown .05 .15
76 Erik Kramer .08 .25
77 Chris Spielman .08 .25
78 Ray Crockett .05 .15
79 Willie Green .05 .15
80 Rodney Peete .08 .25
81 Sterling Sharpe .20 .50
82 Tony Bennett .05 .15
83 Chuck Cecil .05 .15
84 Perry Kemp .05 .15
85 Brian Noble .05 .15
86 Darrell Thompson .05 .15
87 Mike Tomczak .05 .15
88 Vince Workman .05 .15
89 Esera Tuaolo .05 .15
90 Mark Murphy .05 .15
91 William Fuller .08 .25
92 Ernest Givins .08 .25
93 Drew Hill .05 .15
94 Al Smith .05 .15
95 Ray Childress .05 .15
96 Haywood Jeffires .08 .25
97 Cris Dishman .05 .15
98 Warren Moon .20 .50
99 Lamar Lathon .05 .15
100 Mike Munchak and .08 .25
101 Bill Brooks .05 .15
102 Duane Bickett .05 .15
103 Eugene Daniel .05 .15
104 Jeff Herrod .05 .15
105 Jessie Hester .05 .15
106 Donnell Thompson .05 .15
107 Anthony Johnson .08 .25
108 Jon Hand .05 .15
109 Rohn Stark .05 .15
110 Clarence Verdin .05 .15
111 Derrick Thomas .20 .50
112 Steve DeBerg .05 .15
113 Deron Cherry .05 .15
114 Chris Martin .05 .15
115 Christian Okoye .05 .15
116 Dan Saleaumua .05 .15
117 Neil Smith .20 .50
118 Barry Word .05 .15
119 Tim Barnett .05 .15
120 Albert Lewis .05 .15
121 Ronnie Lott .08 .25
122 Marcus Allen .20 .50
123 Todd Marinovich .05 .15
124 Nick Bell .05 .15
125 Tim Brown .20 .50
126 Ethan Horton .05 .15
127 Greg Townsend .05 .15
128 Jeff Gossett and .05 .15
129 Scott Davis .05 .15
130 Steve Wisniewski and .05 .15
131 Kevin Greene .08 .25
132 Roman Phifer .05 .15
133 Tony Zendejas .05 .15
134 Pat Terrell .05 .15
135 Flipper Anderson .05 .15
136 Robert Delpino .05 .15
137 Jim Everett .08 .25
138 Larry Kelm .05 .15
139 Todd Lyght .05 .15
140 Henry Ellard .08 .25
141 Mark Clayton .08 .25
142 Jeff Cross .05 .15
143 Mark Duper .05 .15
144 John Offerdahl .05 .15
145 Louis Oliver .05 .15
146 Pete Stoyanovich .05 .15
147 Richmond Webb .05 .15
148 Mark Higgs .05 .15
149 Tony Paige .05 .15
150 Bryan Cox .08 .25
151 Anthony Carter .08 .25
152 Cris Carter .40 1.00
153 Rich Gannon .20 .50
154 Steve Jordan .05 .15
155 Mike Merriweather .05 .15
156 Henry Thomas .05 .15
157 Herschel Walker .08 .25
158 Randall McDaniel .05 .15
159 Terry Allen .20 .50
160 Joey Browner .05 .15
161 Leonard Russell .08 .25
162 Bruce Armstrong .05 .15
163 Vincent Brown .05 .15
164 Hugh Millen .05 .15
165 Andre Tippett .05 .15
166 Jon Vaughn .05 .15
167 Pat Harlow .05 .15
168 Marv Cook .05 .15
169 Irving Fryar .08 .25
170 Maurice Hurst .05 .15
171 Pat Swilling .08 .25
172 Vince Buck .05 .15
173 Rickey Jackson .05 .15
174 Sam Mills .05 .15
175 Bobby Hebert .05 .15
176 Vaughan Johnson .05 .15
177 Floyd Turner .05 .15
178 Fred McAfee RC .05 .15
179 Morten Andersen .05 .15
180 Eric Martin .05 .15
181 Rodney Hampton .20 .50
182 Pepper Johnson .05 .15
183 Leonard Marshall .05 .15
184 Stephen Baker .05 .15
185 Mark Ingram .05 .15
186 Dave Meggett .08 .25
187 Bart Oates .05 .15
188 Mark Collins .05 .15
189 Myron Guyton .05 .15
190 Jeff Hostetler .08 .25
191 Jeff Lageman .05 .15
192 Brad Baxter .05 .15
193 Mo Lewis .05 .15
194 Chris Burkett .05 .15
195 James Hasty .05 .15
196 Rob Moore .08 .25
197 Kyle Clifton .05 .15
198 Terance Mathis .08 .25
199 Marvin Washington .05 .15
200 Lonnie Young .05 .15
201 Reggie White .20 .50
202 Eric Allen .05 .15
203 Fred Barnett .08 .25
204 Keith Byars .05 .15
205 Seth Joyner .08 .25
206 Clyde Simmons .05 .15
207 Jerome Brown .05 .15
208 Wes Hopkins .05 .15
209 Keith Jackson .08 .25
210 Calvin Williams .08 .25
211 Aeneas Williams .08 .25
212 Ken Harvey .05 .15
213 Ernie Jones .05 .15
214 Freddie Joe Nunn .05 .15
215 Rich Camarillo .05 .15
216 Johnny Johnson .05 .15
217 Tim McDonald .05 .15
218 Eric Swann .08 .25
219 Eric Hill .05 .15
220 Anthony Thompson .05 .15
221 Hardy Nickerson .20 .50
222 Barry Foster .08 .25
223 Louis Lipps .05 .15
224 Greg Lloyd .08 .25
225 Neil O'Donnell .20 .50
226 Jerrol Williams .05 .15
227 Eric Green .05 .15
228 Rod Woodson .20 .50
229 Carnell Lake .05 .15
230 Dwight Stone .05 .15
231 Marion Butts .05 .15
232 John Friesz .08 .25
233 Burt Grossman .05 .15
234 Ronnie Harmon .05 .15
235 Gill Byrd .05 .15
236 Rod Bernstine .05 .15
237 Courtney Hall .05 .15
238 Nate Lewis .05 .15
239 Joe Phillips .05 .15
240 Henry Rolling .05 .15
241 Keith Henderson .05 .15
242 Guy McIntyre .05 .15
243 Bill Romanowski .05 .15
244 Don Griffin .05 .15
245 Dexter Carter .05 .15
246 Charles Haley .08 .25
247 Brent Jones .08 .25
248 John Taylor .08 .25
249 Steve Young .60 1.50
250 Larry Roberts .05 .15
251 Brian Blades .08 .25
252 Jacob Green .05 .15
253 John Kasay .05 .15
254 Cortez Kennedy .08 .25
255 Rufus Porter .05 .15
256 John L. Williams .05 .15
257 Tommy Kane .05 .15
258 Eugene Robinson .05 .15
259 Terry Wooden .05 .15
260 Chris Warren .20 .50
261 Lawrence Dawsey .05 .15
262 Mark Carrier WR .08 .25
263 Keith McCants .05 .15
264 Jesse Solomon .05 .15
265 Vinny Testaverde .08 .25
266 Ricky Reynolds .05 .15
267 Broderick Thomas .05 .15
268 Gary Anderson RB .05 .15
269 Reggie Cobb .05 .15
270 Tony Covington .05 .15
271 Darrell Green .05 .15
272 Charles Mann .05 .15
273 Wilber Marshall .05 .15
274 Gary Clark .20 .50
275 Chip Lohmiller .05 .15
276 Earnest Byner .05 .15
277 Jim Lachey .05 .15
278 Art Monk .08 .25
279 Mark Rypien .05 .15
280 Mark Schlereth RC .05 .15
281 Mark Rypien BR .08 .25
282 Warren Moon BR .20 .50
283 Emmitt Smith BR .75 2.00
284 Thurman Thomas BR .20 .50
285 Michael Irvin BR .20 .50
286 Haywood Jeffires BR .08 .25
287 Pat Swilling BR .08 .25
288 Ronnie Lott BR .20 .50
289 NFC Logo .05 .15
290 AFC Logo .05 .15
43G Barry Sanders 24K Gold 6.00 15.00
44G Barry Sanders 24K Gold 6.00 15.00
NNO Barry Sanders 18K 250.00 400.00

1992 Action Packed Mint Parallel

COMPLETE SET (288) 1000.00 2500.00
*MINT CARDS: 30X TO 80X BASIC CARDS
43G Barry Sanders Promo 25.00 50.00

1992 Action Packed 24K Gold

This 42-card standard-size set consists of 24K gold-stamped cards that were randomly inserted in foil packs. Barry Sanders (card number 13G) autographed 1,000 of his cards. The set numbering follows alphabetical order of team names. The fronts feature borderless embossed color player photos with gold indicia. The horizontally oriented backs have a mugshot, biography, statistics, and an "Action Note" in the form of a caption to the action shot on the front. The style of the cards is very similar to that of the 1992 Action Packed regular issue cards.

COMPLETE SET (42) 150.00 400.00
RANDOM INSERTS IN FOIL PACKS
1G Michael Haynes 4.00 10.00
2G Chris Miller 4.00 10.00
3G Andre Rison 5.00 12.00
4G Cornelius Bennett 4.00 10.00
5G James Lofton 4.00 10.00
6G Thurman Thomas 5.00 12.00
7G Neal Anderson 3.00 8.00
8G Michael Irvin 5.00 12.00
9G Emmitt Smith 25.00 50.00
10G Mike Croel 3.00 8.00
11G John Elway 20.00 50.00
12G Gaston Green 3.00 8.00
13G Barry Sanders 20.00 50.00
14G Sterling Sharpe 5.00 12.00
15G Ernest Givins 3.00 8.00
16G Drew Hill 4.00 10.00
17G Haywood Jeffires 4.00 10.00
18G Warren Moon 5.00 12.00
19G Christian Okoye 4.00 10.00
20G Derrick Thomas 5.00 12.00
21G Ronnie Lott 4.00 10.00
22G Todd Marinovich 3.00 8.00
23G Henry Ellard 4.00 10.00
24G Mark Clayton 4.00 10.00
25G Herschel Walker 4.00 10.00
26G Irving Fryar 4.00 10.00
27G Leonard Russell 4.00 10.00
28G Pat Swilling 4.00 10.00
29G Rodney Hampton 4.00 10.00
30G Rob Moore 4.00 10.00
31G Seth Joyner 3.00 8.00
32G Reggie White 5.00 12.00
33G Eric Green 4.00 10.00
34G Rod Woodson 5.00 12.00
35G Marion Butts 3.00 8.00
36G Charles Haley 4.00 10.00
37G John Taylor 4.00 10.00
38G Steve Young 10.00 25.00
39G Earnest Byner 4.00 10.00
40G Gary Clark 5.00 12.00
41G Art Monk 4.00 10.00
42G Mark Rypien 4.00 10.00
13GAU B.Sanders AU/1000 50.00 120.00

1992 Action Packed Rookie Update

This 84-card standard-size set features 25 first round draft choices pictured in their NFL uniforms and some of the league's outstanding veteran players. Cards were issued in six-card packs. Action Packed guaranteed one 1st round draft pick in each seven-card foil pack. The foil packs also included randomly inserted 24K gold cards of the quarterbacks and 1st round draft choices as well as a special "Neon Deion Sanders" card featuring neon fluorescent orange and numbered "84N". No factory sets were made. The fronts feature full-bleed embossed color player photos that are edged on one side by black and gold foil stripes. The player's name and position are gold-foil stamped at the bottom alongside a representation of the team helmet. The horizontal backs display a color head shot, biography, statistics, and career summary. A black stripe at the bottom carries the card number and an autograph slot. Players aligned with both NFL Properties and the NFL Players Association appear together in this set. Rookie Cards in this set include Edgar Bennett, Terrell Buckley, Marco Coleman,Quentin Coryatt, Steve Emtman, Sean Gilbert, Johnny Mitchell and Carl Pickens. Action Packed also produced a 24K Gold "Mint" rookie/update set. The 24K gold "Mint' cards were sold in separately issued six-card packs, with seven packs to a box. Each of the 250 "Mint" cards of each player were individually numbered (1/250, 2/250, etc.).

COMPLETE SET (84) 5.00 12.00
1 Steve Emtman RC .05 .15
2 Quentin Coryatt RC .05 .15
3 Sean Gilbert RC .08 .25
4 John Fina RC .05 .15
5 Alonzo Spellman RC .08 .25
6 Amp Lee RC .05 .15
7 Robert Porcher RC .20 .50
8 Jason Hanson RC .08 .25
9 Ty Detmer .20 .50
10 Ray Roberts RC .05 .15
11 Bob Whitfield RC .05 .15
12 Greg Skrepenak RC .05 .15
13 Vaughn Dunbar RC .05 .15
14 Siran Stacy RC .05 .15
15 Mark D'Onofrio RC .05 .15
16 Tony Sacca RC .05 .15
17 Dana Hall RC .05 .15
18 Courtney Hawkins RC .08 .25
19 Shane Collins RC .05 .15
20 Tony Smith RC .05 .15
21 Rod Smith DB RC .05 .15
22 Troy Auzenne RC .05 .15
23 David Klingler RC .05 .15
24 Darryl Williams RC .05 .15
25 Carl Pickens RC .20 .50
26 Ricardo McDonald RC .05 .15
27 Tommy Vardell RC .05 .15
28 Kevin Smith RC .05 .15
29 Rodney Culver RC .05 .15
30 Jimmy Smith RC 2.00 5.00
31 Robert Jones RC .05 .15
32 Tommy Maddox RC 1.25 3.00
33 Shane Dronett RC .05 .15
34 Terrell Buckley RC .05 .15
35 Santana Dotson RC .08 .25
36 Edgar Bennett RC .20 .50
37 Ashley Ambrose RC .20 .50
38 Dale Carter RC .08 .25
39 Chester McGlockton RC .08 .25
40 Steve Israel RC .05 .15
41 Marc Boutte RC .05 .15
42 Marco Coleman RC .05 .15
43 Troy Vincent RC .05 .15
44 Mark Wheeler RC .05 .15
45 Darren Perry RC .05 .15
46 Eugene Chung RC .05 .15
47 Derek Brown TE RC .05 .15
48 Phillippi Sparks RC .05 .15
49 Johnny Mitchell RC .05 .15
50 Kurt Barber RC .05 .15
51 Leon Searcy RC .05 .15
52 Chris Mims RC .05 .15
53 Keith Jackson .08 .25
54 Charles Haley .08 .25
55 Dave Krieg .08 .25
56 Dan McGwire UER .05 .15
57 Phil Simms .08 .25
58 Bobby Humphrey .05 .15
59 Jerry Rice 1.00 2.50
60 Joe Montana 1.50 4.00
61 Junior Seau .20 .50
62 Leslie O'Neal .08 .25
63 Anthony Miller .08 .25
64 Timm Rosenbach .05 .15
65 Herschel Walker .08 .25
66 Randal Hill .05 .15
67 Randall Cunningham .20 .50
68 Al Toon .08 .25
69 Browning Nagle .05 .15
70 Lawrence Taylor .20 .50
71 Dan Marino 1.50 4.00
72 Eric Dickerson .08 .25
73 Harvey Williams .20 .50
74 Jeff George .20 .50
75 Russell Maryland .05 .15
76 Troy Aikman .75 2.00
77 Michael Dean Perry .08 .25
78 Bernie Kosar .08 .25
79 Boomer Esiason .08 .25
80 Mike Singletary .08 .25
81 Bruce Smith .20 .50
82 Andre Reed .08 .25
83 Jim Kelly .20 .50
84 Deion Sanders .40 1.00
84N Deion Sanders Neon 4.00 10.00

1992 Action Packed Rookie Update Mint Parallel

COMPLETE SET (84) 600.00 1500.00
*MINT CARDS: 30X TO 80X BASIC CARDS

1992 Action Packed Rookie Update 24K Gold

The players selected by Action Packed for this 35-card 24K Gold set include eight NFL quarterbacks (26-33) and first round draft picks in the regular Rookie/Update set. These rounded-corner cards were randomly inserted into packs and have a similar design to the basic cards. The words, "24 KARAT GOLD" are on front.

COMPLETE SET (35) 200.00 400.00
RANDOM INSERTS IN FOIL PACKS
1G Steve Emtman 5.00 12.00
2G Quentin Coryatt 5.00 12.00
3G Sean Gilbert 5.00 12.00
4G Terrell Buckley 5.00 12.00
5G David Klingler 6.00 15.00
6G Troy Vincent 6.00 15.00
7G Tommy Vardell 5.00 12.00
8G Leon Searcy 2.50 6.00
9G Marco Coleman 5.00 12.00
10G Eugene Chung 2.50 6.00
11G Derek Brown TE 5.00 12.00
12G Johnny Mitchell 6.00 15.00
13G Chester McGlockton 6.00 15.00
14G Kevin Smith DB 5.00 12.00
15G Dana Hall 5.00 12.00
16G Tony Smith RB 2.50 6.00
17G Dale Carter 5.00 12.00
18G Vaughn Dunbar 5.00 12.00
19G Alonzo Spellman 6.00 15.00
20G Chris Mims 6.00 15.00
21G Robert Jones 5.00 12.00
22G Tommy Maddox 10.00 25.00
23G Robert Porcher 5.00 12.00
24G John Fina 2.50 6.00
25G Darryl Williams 2.50 6.00
26G Jim Kelly 6.00 15.00
27G Randall Cunningham 6.00 15.00
28G Dan Marino 25.00 60.00
29G Troy Aikman 20.00 40.00
30G Boomer Esiason 5.00 12.00
31G Bernie Kosar 5.00 12.00
32G Jeff George 6.00 15.00
33G Phil Simms 5.00 12.00
34G Ray Roberts 2.50 6.00
35G Bob Whitfield 2.50 6.00

1992 Action Packed Mackey Award

Only 2,000 numbered sets of these three 24K gold standard-size cards were produced for the attendees at the 1992 NFLPA Mackey Awards Banquet.

COMPLETE SET (3) 30.00 75.00
92W Reggie White 10.00 25.00
HOF John Mackey 6.00 15.00
HUD Jack Kemp 16.00 40.00

1992 Action Packed NFLPA/MDA Award 24K

This 16-card, 24K gold standard-size set was produced by Action Packed to honor NFL Players of the Year for the 1991 season. Cards come packed in an attractive black box imprinted on front with NFLPA/MDA Awards Dinner, March 5, 1992. Only 1,000 sets were produced, and banquet attendees each received a set stamped "Banquet Edition." Card fronts feature a raised-print player photo and team helmet. The Action Packed logo appears in the upper left corner of red cards (AFC) and in the upper right on blue cards (NFC). Players' names appear at the lower right or left of each card offsetting the logo. Handsomely designed with 24K gold borders and lettering, horizontally designed backs feature biographical and statistical information and a head shot of each player within a 24K gold box. Featuring the traditional rounded corners, cards are numbered in the lower left corner.

COMPLETE SET (16) 60.00 120.00
1 Steve Wisniewski 2.00 5.00
2 Jim Lachey 2.00 5.00
3 Reggie White 6.00 12.00
4 William Fuller 2.00 5.00
5 Derrick Thomas 4.00 8.00
6 Pat Swilling 2.00 5.00
7 Darrell Green 4.00 8.00
8 Ronnie Lott 6.00 12.00
9 Steve Tasker 4.00 8.00
10 Mel Gray 2.00 5.00
11 Aeneas Williams 2.00 5.00
12 Mike Croel 2.00 5.00
13 Leonard Russell 2.00 5.00
14 Lawrence Dawsey 2.00 5.00
15 Barry Sanders 16.00 40.00
16 Thurman Thomas 6.00 12.00

1993 Action Packed Troy Aikman Promos

This two-card standard-size set honors Cowboys' quarterback, Troy Aikman. The fronts feature borderless embossed color player photos, accented by a gold border stripe running down either the right or left side of the card face. The stripe is printed with the player's name in large white block letters. The horizontal backs display a color cut-out image from the waist up of Aikman against a green football field background. The player's name and team name are printed in red above biographical information, statistics, and career highlights. Sponsor logos appear in the green margin at the bottom. The phrase "1993 Prototype" are printed in gray across the text. The cards were produced on a prototype sheet which included eleven different Aikmans, TA1 through TA11; however only TA2 and TA3 were formally released.

COMMON CARD (TA2-TA3) 4.00 10.00

1993 Action Packed Emmitt Smith Promos

This five-card standard-size set was issued to promote the 1993 Action Packed All-Madden Team set. The fronts feature borderless embossed color player photos, accented by gold and aqua border stripes running down the right side of the card face. The All-Madden Team logo appears in the upper left corner, with the team helmet, player's name, and position printed at the card bottom. Between aqua border stripes, the horizontal backs carry player profile, a color headshot, and a diagram of a football play. The word "Prototype" is printed across the text. Two of these cards (ES1 and ES4) were given out at the 1993 Super Bowl Card Show. The ES5 card was a give-away to members of the Tuff Stuff Buyers Club.

COMPLETE SET (5) 14.00 35.00
COMMON CARD (ES1-ES5) 2.00 5.00
ES2 Emmitt Smith 4.00 10.00
ES3 Emmitt Smith 4.00 10.00
ES5 Emmitt Smith 3.20 8.00

1993 Action Packed Prototypes

These six standard-size cards were issued to show the design of the 1993 Action Packed regular series. The fronts feature the traditional full-bleed embossed color player photos. The player's last name is printed vertically in gold-foil block lettering running down one of the sides. On a green football field design, the horizontal backs carry biography, 1992 season and career statistics, and an "Action Note". The disclaimer "1993 Prototype" is printed diagonally across the back. A black stripe edged by gold foil has an autograph space and the card number.

COMPLETE SET (6) 12.00 30.00
FB1 Emmitt Smith 4.00 10.00
FB2 Thurman Thomas 1.20 3.00
FB3 Steve Young 1.60 4.00
FB4 Barry Sanders 4.00 10.00
FB5 Barry Foster .60 1.50
FB6 Warren Moon 1.20 3.00

1993 Action Packed

The 1993 Action Packed football set consists of 222 standard-size cards. A 60-card Rookie Update series begins at card number 163, where the first series leaves off. It features players selected in the early rounds of the NFL draft wearing their NFL uniforms. The fronts feature an embossed color player cut-out against a full-bleed background that consists of a tilted colored panel bordered on two sides by foil. Depending on the round the player was drafted, the foil varies from gold (first round, 163-192); to silver (second round, 193-210); to bronze (third round, 211-215). Players drafted after the third round have their panels bordered in a non-foil sky blue color (cards 217-222). The horizontal backs carry a color close-up photo, '92 college season and NCAA career statistics, biography and college career highlights.

COMPLETE SET (222) 20.00 50.00
COMP.SERIES 1 (162) 10.00 25.00
COMP.SERIES 2 (60) 10.00 25.00
1 Michael Haynes .10 .30
2 Chris Miller .10 .30
3 Andre Rison .10 .30
4 Jim Kelly .25 .60
5 Andre Reed .10 .30
6 Thurman Thomas .25 .60
7 Jim Harbaugh .25 .60
8 Harold Green .05 .15
9 David Klingler .05 .15
10 Bernie Kosar .10 .30
11 Troy Aikman .75 2.00
12 Michael Irvin .25 .60
13 Emmitt Smith 1.25 3.00
14 John Elway 1.25 3.00
15 Barry Sanders 1.25 3.00
16 Brett Favre 1.50 4.00
17 Sterling Sharpe .25 .60
18 Ernest Givins .10 .30
19 Haywood Jeffires .10 .30
20 Warren Moon .25 .60
21 Lorenzo White .05 .15
22 Jeff George .25 .60
23 Joe Montana 1.25 3.00
24 Jim Everett .10 .30
25 Cleveland Gary .05 .15
26 Dan Marino 1.25 3.00
27 Terry Allen .25 .60
28 Rodney Hampton .10 .30
29 Phil Simms .10 .30
30 Fred Barnett .10 .30
31 Randall Cunningham .25 .60
32 Gary Clark .10 .30
33 Barry Foster .10 .30
34 Neil O'Donnell .25 .60
35 Stan Humphries .10 .30
36 Anthony Miller .10 .30
37 Jerry Rice 1.00 2.50
38 Ricky Watters .25 .60
39 Steve Young .60 1.50
40 Chris Warren .10 .30
41 Reggie Cobb .05 .15
42 Mark Rypien .05 .15
43 Deion Sanders .50 1.25
44 Henry Jones .05 .15
45 Bruce Smith .25 .60
46 Richard Dent .10 .30
47 Tommy Vardell .05 .15
48 Charles Haley .10 .30
49 Ken Norton Jr. .10 .30
50 Jay Novacek .10 .30
51 Simon Fletcher .05 .15
52 Pat Swilling .05 .15
53 Tony Bennett .05 .15
54 Reggie White .25 .60
55 Ray Childress .05 .15
56 Quentin Coryatt .10 .30
57 Steve Emtman .05 .15
58 Derrick Thomas .25 .60
59 James Lofton .10 .30
60 Marco Coleman .05 .15
61 Bryan Cox .05 .15
62 Troy Vincent .05 .15
63 Chris Doleman .05 .15
64 Audray McMillian .05 .15
65 Vaughn Dunbar .05 .15
66 Rickey Jackson .05 .15
67 Lawrence Taylor .25 .60
68 Ronnie Lott .10 .30
69 Rob Moore .10 .30
70 Browning Nagle .05 .15
71 Eric Allen .05 .15
72 Tim Harris .05 .15
73 Clyde Simmons .05 .15
74 Steve Beuerlein .10 .30
75 Randal Hill .05 .15
76 Darren Perry .05 .15
77 Rod Woodson .25 .60
78 Marion Butts .05 .15
79 Chris Mims .05 .15
80 Junior Seau .25 .60
81 Cortez Kennedy .10 .30
82 Santana Dotson .10 .30
83 Earnest Byner .05 .15
84 Charles Mann .05 .15
85 Pierce Holt .05 .15
86 Mike Pritchard .10 .30
87 Cornelius Bennett .10 .30
88 Neal Anderson .05 .15
89 Carl Pickens .10 .30
90 Eric Metcalf .10 .30
91 Michael Dean Perry .10 .30
92 Alvin Harper .10 .30
93 Robert Jones .05 .15
94 Steve Atwater .05 .15
95 Rod Bernstine .05 .15
96 Herman Moore .25 .60
97 Chris Spielman .10 .30
98 Terrell Buckley .05 .15
99 Dale Carter .05 .15
100 Terry McDaniel .05 .15
101 Tim Brown .25 .60
102 Gaston Green .05 .15
103 Howie Long .25 .60
104 Todd Marinovich .05 .15
105 Anthony Smith .05 .15
106 Flipper Anderson .05 .15
107 Henry Ellard .10 .30
108 Mark Higgs .05 .15
109 Keith Jackson .10 .30
110 Irving Fryar .10 .30
111 Cris Carter .25 .60
112 Leonard Russell .10 .30
113 Wayne Martin .05 .15
114 Mark Jackson .05 .15
115 Dave Meggett .05 .15
116 Brad Baxter .05 .15
117 Boomer Esiason .10 .30
118 Johnny Johnson .05 .15
119 Seth Joyner .05 .15
120 Kevin Greene .10 .30
121 Greg Lloyd .10 .30
122 Brent Jones .10 .30
123 Amp Lee .05 .15
124 Tim McDonald .05 .15
125 Darrell Green .05 .15
126 Art Monk .10 .30
127 Tony Smith RB .05 .15
128 Bill Brooks .05 .15
129 Kenneth Davis .05 .15
130 Donnell Woolford .05 .15
131 Derrick Fenner .05 .15
132 Michael Jackson .10 .30
133 Mark Clayton .05 .15
134 Al Smith .05 .15
135 Curtis Duncan .05 .15
136 Rodney Culver .05 .15
137 Harvey Williams .10 .30
138 Neil Smith .25 .60
139 Marcus Allen .25 .60
140 Eric Dickerson .10 .30
141 Sean Gilbert .10 .30
142 Shane Conlan .05 .15
143 Todd Scott .05 .15
144 Vincent Brown .05 .15
145 Andre Tippett .05 .15
146 Jon Vaughn .05 .15
147 Marv Cook .05 .15
148 Morten Andersen .05 .15
149 Sam Mills .05 .15
150 Mark Collins .05 .15
151 Heath Sherman .05 .15
152 Johnny Bailey .05 .15
153 Eric Green .05 .15
154 Ronnie Harmon .05 .15
155 Gill Byrd .05 .15
156 Leslie O'Neal .10 .30
157 Rufus Porter .05 .15
158 Eugene Robinson .05 .15
159 Broderick Thomas .05 .15
160 Lawrence Dawsey .05 .15
161 Anthony Munoz .10 .30
162 Wilber Marshall .05 .15
163 Drew Bledsoe RC 2.50 6.00
164 Rick Mirer RC .25 .60
165 Garrison Hearst RC .75 2.00
166 Marvin Jones RC .05 .15
167 John Copeland RC .10 .30
168 Eric Curry RC .05 .15
169 Curtis Conway RC .50 1.25
170 Willie Roaf RC .40 1.00
171 Lincoln Kennedy RC .05 .15
172 Jerome Bettis RC 4.00 8.00
173 Dan Williams RC .05 .15
174 Patrick Bates RC .05 .15
175 Brad Hopkins RC .05 .15
176 Steve Everitt RC .05 .15
177 Wayne Simmons RC .05 .15
178 Tom Carter RC .10 .30
179 Ernest Dye RC .05 .15
180 Lester Holmes .05 .15
181 Irv Smith RC .05 .15
182 Robert Smith RC 1.25 3.00
183 Darrien Gordon RC .05 .15
184 Deon Figures RC .05 .15
185 Leonard Renfro RC .05 .15
186 O.J.McDuffie RC .25 .60
187 Dana Stubblefield RC .25 .60
188 Todd Kelly RC .05 .15
189 Thomas Smith RC .10 .30
190 George Teague RC .10 .30
191 Wilber Marshall .05 .15
192 Reggie White .25 .60
193 Carlton Gray RC .05 .15
194 Chris Slade RC .10 .30
195 Ben Coleman RC .05 .15
196 Ryan McNeil RC .25 .60
197 Demetrius DuBose RC .05 .15
198 Coleman Rudolph RC .05 .15
199 Tony McGee RC .10 .30
200 Troy Drayton RC .10 .30
201 Natrone Means RC .25 .60
202 Glyn Milburn RC .25 .60
203 Chad Brown RC LB .10 .30
204 Reggie Brooks RC .10 .30
205 Kevin Williams RC WR .25 .60
206 Micheal Barrow RC .25 .60
207 Roosevelt Potts RC .05 .15
208 Victor Bailey RC .05 .15
209 Qadry Ismail RC .25 .60
210 Vincent Brisby RC .25 .60
211 Billy Joe Hobert RC .25 .60
212 Lamar Thomas RC .05 .15
213 Jason Elam RC .25 .60
214 Andre Hastings RC .10 .30
215 Terry Kirby RC .25 .60
216 Joe Montana 1.25 3.00
217 Derrick Lassic RC .05 .15
218 Mark Brunell RC 1.50 4.00
219 Vaughn Hebron RC .05 .15
220 Troy Brown RC 6.00 15.00
221 Derek Brown RBK RC .05 .15
222 Rocket Ismail .10 .30

1993 Action Packed 24K Gold

Randomly inserted throughout first series foil packs, this 72-card standard-size set features 24K versions of the Quarterback Club (1-18), Moving Targets (19-30), 1000

Yard Rushers (31-42) and Rookies (43-72). In design, the backs and fronts of these cards are identical to the regular series; their fronts are easily distinguished by the 24K notation beneath the Action Packed logo. The cards are numbered on the back with a "G" suffix.
RANDOM INS.IN BOTH SERIES PACKS
1G Troy Aikman 10.00 25.00
2G Randall Cunningham 6.00 15.00
3G John Elway 20.00 50.00
4G Jim Everett 5.00 12.00
5G Brett Favre 20.00 50.00
6G Jim Harbaugh 6.00 15.00
7G Jeff Hostetler 5.00 12.00
8G Jim Kelly 6.00 15.00
9G David Klingler 5.00 12.00
10G Bernie Kosar 5.00 12.00
11G Dan Marino 20.00 50.00
12G Chris Miller 5.00 12.00
13G Boomer Esiason 5.00 12.00
14G Warren Moon 6.00 15.00
15G Neil O'Donnell 6.00 15.00
16G Mark Rypien 5.00 12.00
17G Phil Simms 5.00 12.00
18G Steve Young 8.00 20.00
19G Fred Barnett 5.00 12.00
20G Gary Clark 5.00 12.00
21G Mark Clayton 5.00 12.00
22G Ernest Givins 5.00 12.00
23G Michael Haynes 3.00 8.00
24G Michael Irvin 6.00 15.00
25G Haywood Jeffires 3.00 8.00
26G Anthony Miller 5.00 12.00
27G Andre Reed 6.00 15.00
28G Jerry Rice 15.00 40.00
29G Andre Rison 6.00 15.00
30G Sterling Sharpe 6.00 15.00
31G Terry Allen 6.00 15.00
32G Reggie Cobb 3.00 8.00
33G Barry Foster 5.00 12.00
34G Cleveland Gary 3.00 8.00
35G Harold Green 3.00 8.00
36G Rodney Hampton 5.00 12.00
37G Barry Sanders 15.00 40.00
38G Emmitt Smith 20.00 50.00
39G Thurman Thomas 6.00 15.00
40G Chris Warren 6.00 15.00
41G Ricky Watters 6.00 15.00
42G Lorenzo White 3.00 8.00
43G Drew Bledsoe 8.00 20.00
44G Rick Mirer 6.00 15.00
45G Garrison Hearst 6.00 15.00
46G Marvin Jones 3.00 8.00
47G John Copeland 5.00 12.00
48G Eric Curry 5.00 12.00
49G Curtis Conway 6.00 15.00
50G Willie Roaf 10.00 25.00
51G Lincoln Kennedy 3.00 8.00
52G Jerome Bettis 15.00 30.00
53G Dan Williams 3.00 8.00
54G Patrick Bates 3.00 8.00
55G Brad Hopkins 3.00 8.00
56G Steve Everitt 5.00 12.00
57G Wayne Simmons 5.00 12.00
58G Tom Carter 5.00 12.00
59G Ernest Dye 3.00 8.00
60G Lester Holmes 3.00 8.00
61G Irv Smith 5.00 12.00
62G Robert Smith 6.00 15.00
63G Darrien Gordon 3.00 8.00
64G Deon Figures 3.00 8.00
65G Leonard Renfro 3.00 8.00
66G O.J.McDuffie 6.00 15.00
67G Dana Stubblefield 5.00 12.00
68G Todd Kelly 3.00 8.00
69G Thomas Smith 5.00 12.00
70G George Teague 5.00 12.00
71G Wilber Marshall 3.00 8.00
72G Reggie White 6.00 15.00

1993 Action Packed Mint Parallel

*MINT CARDS: 30X TO 80X BASIC CARDS
STATED PRINT RUN 500 SER.#'d SETS

1993 Action Packed Moving Targets

This 12-card standard-size set was randomly inserted in first series packs. A black stripe carrying an autograph slot and the card number (with a "MT" prefix) round out the back.
COMPLETE SET (12) 5.00 10.00
MT1 Fred Barnett .20 .50
MT2 Gary Clark .20 .50
MT3 Mark Clayton .08 .25
MT4 Ernest Givins .20 .50
MT5 Michael Haynes .20 .50
MT6 Michael Irvin .40 1.00
MT7 Haywood Jeffires .20 .50
MT8 Anthony Miller .20 .50
MT9 Andre Reed .20 .50
MT10 Jerry Rice 2.00 4.00
MT11 Andre Rison .20 .50
MT12 Sterling Sharpe .40 1.00

1993 Action Packed Quarterback Club

This 18-card set was randomly inserted in first series packs. The Quarterback Club cards were also done in braille; these cards have a "B" prefix after the number, and some were donated to over 400 schools for the blind. Finally, certificates for Mint versions (which are totally 24K gold leaf) of these cards were randomly packed in hobby boxes. Five hundred of each card were produced and individually numbered. Complete sheets were also available as a pack redemption offer. The uncut sheets are worth the same as the complete sets.
COMPLETE SET (18) 8.00 20.00
*BRAILLE: 1.2X TO 3X BASIC INSERTS
*MINT CARDS: 25X to 60X BASIC INSERTS
QB1 Troy Aikman 1.25 2.50
QB2 Randall Cunningham .30 .75
QB3 John Elway 2.00 4.00
QB4 Jim Everett .15 .40
QB5 Brett Favre 2.50 5.00
QB6 Jim Harbaugh .30 .75
QB7 Jeff Hostetler .15 .40
QB8 Jim Kelly .30 .75
QB9 David Klingler .07 .20
QB10 Bernie Kosar .15 .40
QB11 Dan Marino 2.00 4.00
QB12 Chris Miller .15 .40
QB13 Boomer Esiason .15 .40
QB14 Warren Moon .30 .75
QB15 Neil O'Donnell .30 .75
QB16 Mark Rypien .07 .20
QB17 Phil Simms .15 .40
QB18 Steve Young 1.00 2.00

1993 Action Packed Rookie Update Previews

These three standard-size cards preview the design of the 1993 Action Packed Rookies set. Card numbers 1-3 represent quarterbacks taken in the first three rounds of various NFL drafts. The fronts feature a color player cut-out against a full-bleed background that consists of a tilted colored panel bordered on two sides by foil. Depending on the round the player was drafted, the foil varies from gold (first round) to silver (second round) and then to bronze (third round). The horizontal backs carry a color close-up photo, '92 and career passing statistics, biography, and an "Action Note" that describes the game situation portrayed by the front picture before summarizing the player's performance. The set was issued as a special chiptopper in first series hobby boxes. The cards are numbered on the back with an "RU" prefix.
COMPLETE SET (3) 2.40 6.00
RU1 Troy Aikman 1.50 2.00
RU2 Brett Favre 1.50 4.00
RU3 Neil O'Donnell .40 1.00

1993 Action Packed Rushers

Featuring outstanding running backs, this 12-card set was randomly inserted in first series packs. The fronts display full-bleed, embossed color action photos, with a special "1000 Yard Rushers" logo in one of the lower corners. The player's last name is gold-foil stamped in block lettering and runs parallel to the side of the card. On a background consisting of an oil painting of a runner breaking through the line, the horizontal backs carry a color head shot and statistics on all-time single-season rushing leaders for the player's team. A black stripe at the bottom with a white slot for autograph rounds out the back. The cards are numbered on the back with an "RB" prefix.
COMPLETE SET (12) 6.00 12.00
RB1 Terry Allen .30 .75
RB2 Reggie Cobb .07 .20
RB3 Barry Foster .15 .40
RB4 Cleveland Gary .07 .20
RB5 Harold Green .07 .20
RB6 Rodney Hampton .15 .40
RB7 Barry Sanders 1.50 4.00
RB8 Emmitt Smith 1.50 4.00
RB9 Thurman Thomas .30 .75
RB10 Chris Warren .15 .40
RB11 Ricky Watters .30 .75
RB12 Lorenzo White .07 .20

1993 Action Packed Emmitt Smith Mint Collection

This 2-card set was issued in honor of Emmitt Smith's 1993 season MVP performance. Each card is essentially a 24K Gold serial numbered parallel to his base card and Rusher insert card. The set was issued in a black factory box with each set serial numbered of 1486.
COMPLETE SET (2) 60.00 150.00
13 Emmitt Smith 30.00 75.00
RB8 Emmitt Smith 30.00 75.00

1993 Action Packed NFLPA Awards

Held on March 4, 1993 in Washington, D.C., and sponsored by Action Packed, the 20th annual NFLPA banquet honored outstanding professional football players from the 1992 season. The set was produced to benefit the District of Columbia's Special Olympics. Reportedly less than 2,000 sets were produced. This 17-card standard-size set features the players selected as the best at their position by their peers and was issued in a special black box. The fronts feature an embossed action player photo overlapping a black-bordered gold stripe. The backs have a player photo and the award recipient's statistics.
COMPLETE SET (17) 20.00 50.00
1 Randall McDaniel 1.20 3.00
2 Bruce Matthews 1.20 3.00
3 Richmond Webb 1.20 3.00
4 Cortez Kennedy 1.60 4.00
5 Clyde Simmons 1.20 3.00
6 Wilber Marshall 1.20 3.00
7 Junior Seau 2.00 5.00
8 Henry Jones 1.20 3.00
9 Audray McMillian 1.20 3.00
10 Mel Gray 1.20 3.00
11 Steve Tasker 1.60 4.00
12 Marco Coleman 1.20 3.00
13 Santana Dotson 1.20 3.00
14 Vaughn Dunbar 1.20 3.00
15 Carl Pickens 2.00 5.00
16 Barry Foster 1.20 3.00
17 Steve Young 6.00 15.00

1994 Action Packed Prototypes

The 1994 Action Packed Prototype set consists of standard-size cards with rounded corners. An 11-card set (without Barry Foster) was distributed in a black cardboard display frame which held three cards horizontally down the middle and four cards vertically on either side. The display frame is packaged with a black cardboard sleeve with the gold-stamped Action Packed logo and lettering. The prototypes were made available to dealers. The cards were also given out at the Super Bowl XXVIII card show. The set includes: one regular issue 1994 Action Packed card; one "Quarterback Challenge" subset card; one "Catching the Fire" subset card that honors NFL's best receivers; and one "Warp Speed" subset card featuring the fastest running backs. Also included in the set are one "Rookie Update" card, two "The Golden Domers Class of '93" subset cards featuring Notre Dame players who made it to the 1993 NFL rookie class, one Monday Night Football card, and two "Monday Night Moment" subset cards. Each card carries its number and the word "Prototype" on the back.
FB941 Troy Aikman 1.25 3.00
FB942 Jeff Hostetler .40 1.00
FB943 Emmitt Smith 2.00 5.00
FB944 Jerry Rice 1.50 4.00
FB945 Barry Foster .40 1.00
RL1 Troy Aikman 1.50 4.00
RM1 Emmitt Smith 2.50 6.00
RU941 Drew Bledsoe .75 2.00
RU942 Derrick Lassic .40 1.00
RU943 Rick Mirer .40 1.00
RU944 Jerome Bettis .75 2.00
MNF941 Steve Young 1.00 2.50
MNF942 Steve Young 1.00 2.50
MNF943 Barry Foster .40 1.00
SL2 Jerry Rice 2.00 5.00

1994 Action Packed

The 1994 Action Packed football set contains 198 standard-size cards. The cards were issued in two series of 120 and 78. The 120th card has a special twist. It is a Troy Aikman Back-To-Back Super Bowl card with Troy on the front holding up a number 1 of his first Super Bowl and on the back holding two fingers up to signify his second win. There are 12 Braille cards in this set. The cards are numbered on the back and checklisted below according to teams. Second series cards include rookies and traded players, Quarterback Club (172-184) and Golden Domers (193-198). Rookie Cards include Derrick Alexander, Mario Bates, Isaac Bruce, Lake Dawson, Trent Dilfer, Bert Emanuel, Marshall Faulk, William Floyd, Gus Frerotte, Greg Hill, Charles Johnson, Byron Bam Morris, Errict Rhett, Darnay Scott and Heath Shuler.
COMPLETE SET (198) 20.00 50.00
COMP.SERIES 1 (120) 10.00 25.00
COMP.SERIES 2 (78) 10.00 25.00
1 Michael Haynes .10 .30
2 Andre Rison .10 .30
3 Mike Pritchard .05 .15
4 Eric Pegram .05 .15
5 Deion Sanders .30 .75
6 Jim Kelly .25 .60
7 Andre Reed .10 .30
8 Thurman Thomas .25 .60
9 Bruce Smith .25 .60
10 Cornelius Bennett .10 .30
11 Nate Odomes .05 .15
12 Richard Dent .10 .30
13 Donnell Woolford .05 .15
14 Harold Green .05 .15
15 David Klingler .05 .15
16 Eric Metcalf .10 .30
17 Michael Dean Perry .10 .30
18 Michael Jackson .10 .30
19 Vinny Testaverde .10 .30
20 Troy Aikman .60 1.50
21 Michael Irvin .25 .60
22 Emmitt Smith 1.00 2.50
23 Jay Novacek .10 .30
24 Alvin Harper .10 .30
25 Charles Haley .10 .30
26 John Elway 1.25 3.00
27 Shannon Sharpe .10 .30
28 Rod Bernstine .05 .15
29 Simon Fletcher .05 .15
30 Barry Sanders 1.00 2.50
31 Herman Moore .25 .60
32 Pat Swilling .05 .15
33 Chris Spielman .10 .30
34 Brett Favre 1.25 3.00
35 Sterling Sharpe UER .25 .60
36 Reggie White .25 .60
37 Jackie Harris .05 .15
38 Tony Bennett .05 .15
39 LeRoy Butler .05 .15
40 Warren Moon .25 .60
41 Ernest Givins .10 .30
42 Haywood Jeffires .10 .30
43 Webster Slaughter .05 .15
44 Ray Childress .05 .15
45 Gary Brown .05 .15
46 Jeff George .25 .60
47 Roosevelt Potts .05 .15
48 Quentin Coryatt .05 .15
49 Joe Montana 1.25 3.00
50 Derrick Thomas .25 .60
51 Neil Smith .10 .30
52 Marcus Allen .25 .60
53 Willie Davis .10 .30
54 Jerome Bettis .40 1.00
55 Sean Gilbert .05 .15
56 Chris Miller .05 .15
57 Jeff Hostetler .10 .30
58 Tim Brown .25 .60
59 Anthony Smith .05 .15
60 Greg Townsend .05 .15
61 Terry McDaniel .05 .15
62 Dan Marino 1.25 3.00
63 Irving Fryar .10 .30
64 Keith Jackson .05 .15
65 Terry Kirby .25 .60
66 Bryan Cox .05 .15
67 Chris Doleman .05 .15
68 Cris Carter .30 .75
69 John Randle .10 .30
70 Drew Bledsoe .60 1.50
71 Ben Coates .10 .30
72 Vincent Brisby .10 .30
73 Rickey Jackson .05 .15
74 Eric Martin .05 .15
75 Renaldo Turnbull .05 .15
76 Rodney Hampton .10 .30
77 Mike Sherrard .05 .15
78 Phil Simms .10 .30
79 Keith Hamilton .05 .15
80 Rob Moore .10 .30
81 Brad Baxter .05 .15
82 Boomer Esiason .10 .30
83 Johnny Johnson .05 .15
84 Ronnie Lott .10 .30
85 Randall Cunningham .25 .60
86 Herschel Walker .10 .30
87 Eric Allen .05 .15
88 Clyde Simmons .05 .15
89 Seth Joyner .05 .15
90 Calvin Williams .10 .30
91 Garrison Hearst .25 .60
92 Steve Beuerlein .10 .30
93 Ricky Proehl .05 .15
94 Ronald Moore .05 .15
95 Barry Foster .05 .15
96 Neil O'Donnell .25 .60
97 Eric Green .05 .15
98 Rod Woodson .10 .30
99 Greg Lloyd .10 .30
100 Kevin Greene .10 .30
101 Stan Humphries .10 .30
102 Anthony Miller .10 .30
103 Junior Seau .25 .60
104 Leslie O'Neal .05 .15
105 Ronnie Harmon .05 .15
106 Jerry Rice .60 1.50
107 Ricky Watters .10 .30
108 Steve Young .50 1.25
109 Brent Jones .10 .30
110 John Taylor .10 .30
111 Rick Mirer .25 .60
112 Chris Warren .10 .30
113 Cortez Kennedy .10 .30
114 Brian Blades .10 .30
115 Eugene Robinson .05 .15
116 Reggie Cobb .05 .15
117 Hardy Nickerson .10 .30
118 Reggie Brooks .10 .30
119 Darrell Green .05 .15
120 Troy Aikman Super Bowl .75 2.00
121 Dan Wilkinson RC .10 .30
122 Marshall Faulk RC 3.00 8.00
123 Heath Shuler RC .25 .60
124 Willie McGinest RC .25 .60
125 Trev Alberts RC .10 .30
126 Trent Dilfer RC .75 2.00
127 Bryant Young RC .40 1.00
128 Sam Adams RC .10 .30
129 Antonio Langham RC .10 .30
130 Jamir Miller RC .10 .30
131 John Thierry RC .05 .15
132 Aaron Glenn RC .25 .60
133 Joe Johnson RC .05 .15
134 Bernard Williams .05 .15
135 Wayne Gandy .05 .15
136 Charles Johnson RC .25 .60
137 Dewayne Washington RC .10 .30
138 Todd Steussie RC .10 .30
139 Tim Bowens RC .10 .30
140 Johnnie Morton RC 1.00 2.50
141 Rob Fredrickson RC .10 .30
142 Shante Carver RC .05 .15
143 Thomas Lewis RC .10 .30
144 Greg Hill RC .25 .60
145 Henry Ford .05 .15
146 Jeff Burris RC .10 .30
147 William Floyd RC .25 .60
148 Derrick Alexander WR RC .25 .60
149 Darnay Scott RC .50 1.25
150 Isaac Bruce RC 3.00 6.00
151 Errict Rhett RC .25 .60
152 Kevin Lee RC .05 .15
153 Chuck Levy RC .05 .15
154 David Palmer RC .25 .60
155 Ryan Yarborough RC .05 .15
156 Charlie Garner RC .75 2.00
157 Mario Bates RC .25 .60
158 Bert Emanuel RC .25 .60
159 Bucky Brooks RC .05 .15
160 Donnell Bennett RC .25 .60
161 Tydus Winans RC .05 .15
162 Andre Coleman RC .05 .15
163 Calvin Jones RC .05 .15
164 LeShon Johnson RC .10 .30
165 Doug Brien RC .05 .15
166 Byron Bam Morris RC .10 .30
167 Lake Dawson RC .10 .30
168 Perry Klein RC .05 .15
169 Doug Nussmeier RC .05 .15
170 Lamont Warren RC .05 .15
171 Gus Frerotte RC UER 1.00 2.50
172 Troy Aikman QC .60 1.50
173 Randall Cunningham QC .25 .60
174 John Elway QC 1.00 2.50
175 Jim Everett QC .05 .15
176 Drew Bledsoe QC .40 1.00
177 Jim Kelly QC .10 .30
178 Dan Marino QC 1.00 2.50
179 Chris Miller QC .05 .15
180 Warren Moon QC .10 .30
181 Rick Mirer QC .25 .60
182 Jeff Hostetler QC .05 .15
183 Brett Favre QC 1.25 2.50
184 Steve Young QC .40 1.00
185 Anthony Miller .10 .30
186 Michael Haynes .10 .30
187 Mike Pritchard .05 .15
188 Jeff George .25 .60
189 Lewis Tillman .05 .15
190 Ken Norton .10 .30
191 Erik Kramer .10 .30
192 Richard Dent .10 .30
193 Rick Mirer GD .25 .60
194 Jerome Bettis GD .25 .60
195 Reggie Brooks GD .05 .15
196 Tom Carter GD .05 .15
197 Irv Smith GD .05 .15
198 Rocket Ismail GD .10 .30

1994 Action Packed Braille

30 Barry Sanders 2.50 5.00
36 Reggie White .60 1.25
38 Tony Bennett .10 .30
40 Warren Moon .60 1.25
59 Anthony Smith .10 .30
70 Drew Bledsoe 1.50 3.00
78 Phil Simms .25 .60
82 Boomer Esiason .25 .60
98 Rod Woodson .25 .60
108 Steve Young 1.25 2.50
113 Cortez Kennedy .25 .60
118 Reggie Brooks .25 .60

1994 Action Packed Gold Signatures

6 Jim Kelly 1.00 2.00
15 David Klingler .20 .50
20 Troy Aikman 2.50 5.00
21 Michael Irvin 1.00 2.00
22 Emmitt Smith 4.00 8.00
26 John Elway 5.00 10.00
30 Barry Sanders 4.00 8.00
34 Brett Favre 5.00 10.00
40 Warren Moon 1.00 2.00
56 Chris Miller .20 .50
57 Jeff Hostetler .40 1.00
62 Dan Marino 5.00 10.00
70 Drew Bledsoe 2.50 5.00
78 Phil Simms .40 1.00
82 Boomer Esiason .40 1.00
85 Randall Cunningham 1.00 2.00
96 Neil O'Donnell 1.00 2.00
106 Jerry Rice 2.50 5.00
108 Steve Young 2.00 4.00
111 Rick Mirer 1.00 2.00

1994 Action Packed 24K Gold

Randomly inserted in foil packs, this 42-card standard-size set features 24K versions of the Quarterback Club (1-20), Catching Fire (21-30), and Warp Speed (31-42) inserts. In design, these cards are identical to their regular issue counterparts, except for the gold on the fronts. The cards are numbered on the back with a "G" prefix.
COMPLETE SET (55) 200.00 400.00
STATED ODDS 1:96
G1 Troy Aikman 6.00 15.00
G2 Randall Cunningham 3.00 8.00
G3 John Elway 12.50 30.00
G4 Boomer Esiason 2.50 6.00
G5 Jim Everett 2.50 6.00
G6 Brett Favre 12.50 30.00
G7 Jerry Rice 8.00 20.00
G8 Jeff Hostetler 2.00 5.00
G9 Jim Kelly 4.00 10.00
G10 David Klingler 2.00 5.00
G11 Bernie Kosar 2.50 6.00
G12 Dan Marino 12.50 30.00
G13 Chris Miller 2.00 5.00
G14 Warren Moon 3.00 8.00
G15 Neil O'Donnell 2.50 6.00
G16 Michael Irvin 4.00 10.00
G17 Phil Simms 3.00 8.00
G18 Steve Young 5.00 12.00
G19 Rick Mirer 2.50 6.00
G20 Drew Bledsoe 4.00 10.00
G21 Jerry Rice 8.00 20.00
G22 Sterling Sharpe 3.00 8.00
G23 Michael Irvin 4.00 10.00
G24 Andre Rison 2.50 6.00
G25 Anthony Miller 2.50 6.00
G26 Tim Brown 3.00 8.00
G27 Andre Reed 3.00 8.00
G28 Herman Moore 2.50 6.00
G29 Irving Fryar 2.50 6.00
G30 Shannon Sharpe 3.00 8.00
G31 Emmitt Smith 12.50 30.00
G32 Barry Sanders 10.00 25.00
G33 Thurman Thomas 3.00 8.00
G34 Jerome Bettis 5.00 12.00
G35 Barry Foster 2.00 5.00
G36 Ricky Watters 2.50 6.00
G37 Rodney Hampton 2.00 5.00
G38 Chris Warren 2.00 5.00
G39 Eric Pegram 2.00 5.00
G40 Reggie Brooks 2.00 5.00
G41 Marcus Allen 3.00 8.00
G42 Ronald Moore 2.00 5.00
G43 Troy Aikman QC 8.00 20.00
G44 Randall Cunningham QC 4.00 10.00
G45 John Elway QC 15.00 40.00
G46 Jim Everett QC 2.50 6.00
G47 Drew Bledsoe QC 5.00 12.00
G48 Jim Kelly QC 5.00 12.00
G49 Dan Marino QC 15.00 40.00
G50 Chris Miller QC 2.50 6.00
G51 Warren Moon QC 4.00 10.00
G52 Rick Mirer QC 4.00 10.00
G53 Jeff Hostetler QC 2.50 6.00
G54 Brett Favre QC 15.00 40.00
G55 Steve Young QC 6.00 15.00

1994 Action Packed Catching Fire

This 10-card standard-size set highlights the hottest receivers in the NFL. The fronts feature embossed color action photos of the player catching a pass while surrounded by metallic foil flames. The backs carry another player shot and a player profile. The cards are numbered on the back with an "R" prefix.
COMPLETE SET (10) 4.00 10.00
R1 Jerry Rice 1.50 3.00
R2 Sterling Sharpe .60 1.25
R3 Michael Irvin .60 1.25
R4 Andre Rison .25 .60
R5 Anthony Miller .25 .60
R6 Tim Brown .60 1.25
R7 Andre Reed .25 .60
R8 Herman Moore .60 1.25
R9 Irving Fryar .25 .60
R10 Shannon Sharpe .25 .60

1994 Action Packed Fantasy Forecast

This 42-card set provides a scouting report on 42 of the top football players. The cards measure the standard size (2 1/2" by 3 1/2"). The fronts feature embossed color action player photos, with a football in a corner that is covered with heat sensitive ink. When you touch the football, it reveals what number you should draft the player if you were fielding a fantasy football team.
COMPLETE SET (42) 6.00 15.00
FF1 Rodney Hampton .07 .20
FF2 Steve Young .40 1.00
FF3 Michael Irvin .15 .40
FF4 Emmitt Smith 1.00 2.00
FF5 Troy Aikman .40 1.00
FF6 Jerry Rice .40 1.00
FF7 Brett Favre 1.00 2.00
FF8 Jerome Bettis .30 .75
FF9 Reggie Brooks .07 .20
FF10 John Elway 1.00 2.00
FF11 Jim Kelly .15 .40
FF12 Dan Marino 1.00 2.00
FF13 Randall Cunningham .15 .40
FF14 Sterling Sharpe .15 .40
FF15 Chris Warren .07 .20
FF16 Andre Rison .07 .20
FF17 Mike Pritchard .02 .10
FF18 Barry Sanders 1.00 2.00
FF19 Marcus Allen .15 .40
FF20 Thurman Thomas .15 .40
FF21 Eric Pegram .02 .10
FF22 Barry Foster .02 .10
FF23 Anthony Miller .07 .20
FF24 Shannon Sharpe .07 .20
FF25 Tim Brown .15 .40
FF26 Ricky Watters .07 .20
FF27 Ernest Givins .07 .20
FF28 Cris Carter .20 .50
FF29 Willie Davis .07 .20
FF30 Warren Moon .15 .40
FF31 Joe Montana 1.00 2.00
FF32 Herman Moore .15 .40
FF33 Terry Kirby .15 .40
FF34 Eric Green .02 .10
FF35 Michael Jackson .07 .20
FF36 Johnny Johnson .02 .10
FF37 Calvin Williams .07 .20
FF38 Michael Haynes .07 .20
FF39 Irving Fryar .07 .20
FF40 Gary Brown .02 .10
FF41 Jeff Hostetler .07 .20
FF42 Keith Jackson .02 .10

1994 Action Packed Quarterback Challenge

Inserted one per special retail pack through Foot Action stores, this set of 12 quarterbacks features card fronts that are silver embossed with an outline of the player's face. The backs contain photos from the Quarterback Challenge competition and a brief write-up.
COMPLETE SET (12) 8.00 20.00
ONE PER SPECIAL RETAIL PACK
FA1 Steve Young .60 1.25
FA2 John Elway 1.50 3.00
FA3 Troy Aikman .75 1.50
FA4 Randall Cunningham .25 .60
FA5 Warren Moon .25 .60
FA6 Brett Favre 1.50 3.00
FA7 Rick Mirer .25 .60
FA8 Drew Bledsoe .75 1.50
FA9 Boomer Esiason .10 .30
FA10 Jeff Hostetler .10 .30
FA11 Jim Kelly .25 .60
FA12 Dan Marino 1.50 3.00

1994 Action Packed Quarterback Club

These cards were randomly inserted into packs and measure the standard-size. The fronts feature a silver foil player headshot, while the backs carry another color player action photo.
COMPLETE SET (20) 8.00 20.00
QB1 Troy Aikman .75 1.50
QB2 Randall Cunningham .25 .60
QB3 John Elway 1.50 3.00
QB4 Boomer Esiason .10 .30
QB5 Jim Everett .05 .15
QB6 Brett Favre 1.50 3.00
QB7 Jerry Rice .75 1.50
QB8 Jeff Hostetler .10 .30
QB9 Jim Kelly .25 .60
QB10 David Klingler .05 .15
QB11 Bernie Kosar .05 .15
QB12 Dan Marino 1.50 3.00
QB13 Chris Miller .05 .15
QB14 Warren Moon .25 .60
QB15 Neil O'Donnell .25 .60
QB16 Michael Irvin .25 .60
QB17 Phil Simms .10 .30
QB18 Steve Young .60 1.25
QB19 Rick Mirer .25 .60
QB20 Drew Bledsoe .75 1.50

1994 Action Packed Warp Speed

This 12-card standard-size set showcases the fastest running backs in the NFL. The horizontal fronts feature embossed color player action photos with a colored foil design made to give the feel of a time tunnel vortex. The player's name and words "Warp Speed" in gold lettering surround the player. The horizontal backs carry another player action shot and behind-the-scene stories that capture the essence of the speed game.
COMPLETE SET (12) 4.00 10.00
WS1 Emmitt Smith 1.50 3.00
WS2 Barry Sanders 1.50 3.00
WS3 Thurman Thomas .30 .75
WS4 Jerome Bettis .60 1.25
WS5 Barry Foster .07 .20
WS6 Ricky Watters .15 .40
WS7 Rodney Hampton .15 .40
WS8 Chris Warren .15 .40
WS9 Eric Pegram .07 .20
WS10 Reggie Brooks .15 .40
WS11 Marcus Allen .30 .75
WS12 Ronald Moore .07 .20

1994 Action Packed Badge of Honor Pins

This set of 25 pins measures approximately 1 1/2" by 1". The pins came in packs of four inside a cardboard holder. The back of the holder contained a checklist for the set. Each box contained three packs of 4-pins along with one of five different black pin "albums" to house five of the pins. On a bronze background, the fronts feature color player portraits with a gold border. The player's last name appears in gold lettering at the bottom. The Action Packed logo is above the picture, while the year 1994 inside a football icon is below. The backs carry the copyrights "1994 Action Packed" and "1994 NFL/NFL QB Club." The pins are unnumbered and checklisted below in alphabetical order. A 24K Gold parallel version of each pin was also produced and randomly inserted in packs.
COMPLETE SET (25) 12.00 30.00
*24K GOLD PINS: 7.5X TO 20X
1 Troy Aikman .80 2.00
2 Drew Bledsoe .80 2.00
3 Bubby Brister .10 .30
4 Randall Cunningham .30 .75
5 John Elway 1.60 4.00
6 Boomer Esiason .20 .50
7 Jim Everett .10 .30
8 Brett Favre 1.60 4.00
9 Jim Harbaugh .20 .50
10 Jeff Hostetler .10 .30
11 Michael Irvin .30 .75
12 Jim Kelly .30 .75
13 David Klingler .10 .30
14 Bernie Kosar .10 .30
15 Dan Marino 1.60 4.00
16 Chris Miller .10 .30
17 Rick Mirer .10 .30
18 Warren Moon .30 .75
19 Neil O'Donnell .10 .30
20 Jerry Rice .80 2.00
21 Mark Rypien .10 .30
22 Barry Sanders 1.60 4.00
23 Phil Simms .20 .50
24 Emmitt Smith 1.20 3.00
25 Steve Young .60 1.50

1994 Action Packed Mammoth

Large versions of the basic cards, this 25-card set spotlights some of the NFL's top names. The cards were offered to dealers by Action Packed. Twenty-five thousand of each card were produced and they are individually numbered. Card MM25 was not issued. These cards measure 7 1/2" by 10 1/2". Three prototype cards and three series 2 cards were produced as well and priced below. We've assigned card numbers to the six and none is considered part of the complete set. The two 24K Gold prototypes were randomly inserted in 28-count Mammoth sets sold to hobby dealers.
COMPLETE SET (25) 45.00 100.00
MM1 Troy Aikman 3.00 8.00
MM2 Drew Bledsoe 2.50 6.00
MM3 Barry Sanders 5.00 12.00
MM4 Chris Miller .75 2.00
MM5 Randall Cunningham 1.60 4.00
MM6 John Elway 5.00 12.00
MM7 Boomer Esiason 1.50 3.00
MM8 Jim Everett .75 2.00
MM9 Brett Favre 5.00 12.00
MM10 Jim Harbaugh 1.50 3.00
MM11 Jeff Hostetler .75 2.00
MM12 Michael Irvin 1.60 4.00
MM13 Jim Kelly 1.60 4.00
MM14 David Klingler .75 2.00
MM15 Bernie Kosar .75 2.00
MM16 Dan Marino 5.00 12.00
MM17 Rick Mirer .75 2.00
MM18 Warren Moon 1.60 4.00
MM19 Neil O'Donnell .75 2.00
MM20 Jerry Rice 3.00 8.00
MM21 Mark Rypien .75 2.00
MM22 Phil Simms 1.50 3.00
MM23 Emmitt Smith 4.00 10.00
MM24 Steve Young 2.00 5.00
MM26 Bubby Brister .75 2.00
2MM1 Troy Aikman 3.00 8.00
Series 2 card
2MM2 Michael Irvin 1.60 4.00
2MM6 Emmitt Smith 4.00 10.00
Series 2 card
P1 Troy Aikman Prototype 3.00 8.00
P2 Emmitt Smith Proto.24K Gold 12.00 30.00
P3 Troy Aikman Proto.24K Gold 8.00 20.00

1994 Action Packed CoaStars

Issued in six-card shrink wrapped retail sheets, these "coaster cards" have rounded corners and measure roughly 3 1/4" by 3 1/4". The front of each features a borderless player action shot that is full color within the 2 3/4" diameter central circle. The player's name and position appear in an arc at the upper right. The back features a borderless color player action shot, with the player's name and '93 away statistics appearing near the bottom. The coasters are numbered on the front but have been listed below in 6-card panels since that is the most common form in which they are traded.
COMPLETE SET (5) 10.00 20.00
1 Aik 2.00 4.00
Brister
RCunn
Elway
Moon
Rice
2 Aik 2.00 4.00
Mirer
Cmiller
Simms
Kosar
Bsanders
3 Bledsoe 3.00 6.00
Marin
O'D
Kelly
Everett
Klingler
4 Bled 1.50 3.00
ESmith
Rypien
Esiason
Syoung
Harbaugh
5 Elway 3.00 6.00
Kelly
Aik
Rice
Marin
ES

1995 Action Packed Promos

Wrapped in a cello pack, four cards from this standard-size set were issued to preview the design of the 1995 Action Packed series. An Emmitt Smith Rocket Man Prototype card was later released and added to the checklist below. The original four promo cards feature two regular cards, one "Armed Forces" card, and one ad card. The cards are essentially identical to their regular issue counterparts, except for the word "Promo" or "Prototype" stamped on the cardbacks.
1 Jerry Rice 1.00 2.50
2 Emmitt Smith 1.60 4.00
AF4 Steve Young .80 2.00
RM1 Emmitt Smith 2.00 5.00
NNO Action Packed Ad Card .20 .50

1995 Action Packed

This 126-card standard size set is the first Action Packed set issued by Pinnacle Brands. The fronts display full-bleed, embossed color action photos, with the team's helmet, player's name and the words "Action Packed 1995" on the right side for veterans and on the left side for rookies. The backs feature statistics, a player photo, and brief biographical information. Rookie Cards include Ki-Jana Carter, Kerry Collins, Joey Galloway, Steve McNair, Rashaan Salaam, J.J. Stokes, Michael Westbrook and Tyrone Wheatley.
COMPLETE SET (126) 7.50 20.00
1 Jerry Rice .60 1.50
2 Emmitt Smith 1.00 2.50
3 Drew Bledsoe .40 1.00
4 Ben Coates .08 .25
5 Jim Everett .02 .10
6 Warren Moon .08 .25
7 Herman Moore .20 .50
8 Deion Sanders .40 1.00
9 Rick Mirer .08 .25
10 Natrone Means .08 .25
11 Jeff Blake RC .50 1.25
12 William Floyd .08 .25
13 Steve Young .50 1.25
14 John Elway 1.25 3.00
15 Brett Favre 1.25 3.00
16 Marshall Faulk .75 2.00
17 Heath Shuler .08 .25
18 Ricky Watters .08 .25
19 Michael Haynes .08 .25
20 Troy Aikman .60 1.50
21 Dan Marino 1.25 3.00
22 Byron Bam Morris .02 .10
23 Marcus Allen .20 .50
24 Carl Pickens .08 .25
25 Rodney Hampton .08 .25
26 Dave Brown .08 .25
27 Jerome Bettis .20 .50
28 Jim Kelly .20 .50
29 Andre Reed .08 .25
30 Michael Irvin .20 .50
31 Barry Sanders 1.00 2.50
32 Chris Warren .08 .25
33 Jeff Hostetler .08 .25
34 Alvin Harper .02 .10
35 Rob Moore .08 .25
36 Steve McNair RC 2.00 5.00
37 Rashaan Salaam RC .08 .25
38 Joey Galloway RC 1.00 2.50
39 J.J. Stokes RC .20 .50
40 Michael Westbrook RC .20 .50
41 Kerry Collins RC 1.25 3.00
42 Ki-Jana Carter RC .20 .50
43 Boomer Esiason .08 .25
44 Chris Spielman .08 .25
45 Vinny Testaverde .08 .25
46 Kevin Williams WR .08 .25
47 Ronnie Harmon .02 .10
48 Fred Barnett .08 .25
49 Harvey Williams .02 .10
50 Reggie White .20 .50
51 Brent Jones .02 .10
52 Henry Ellard .08 .25
53 Cris Carter .20 .50
54 Leroy Hoard .02 .10
55 Trent Dilfer .20 .50
56 Raymont Harris .02 .10
57 Garrison Hearst .20 .50
58 Lewis Tillman .02 .10
59 Mark Brunell .40 1.00
60 Bruce Smith .20 .50
61 Lake Dawson .08 .25
62 Bert Emanuel .20 .50
63 Eric Green .02 .10
64 Barry Foster .08 .25
65 Jeff Graham .02 .10
66 Curtis Conway .20 .50
67 Herschel Walker .08 .25
68 Edgar Bennett .08 .25
69 Mario Bates .08 .25
70 Irving Fryar .08 .25
71 Gary Brown .02 .10
72 Cortez Kennedy .08 .25
73 John Taylor .02 .10
74 Jeff George .08 .25
75 Shannon Sharpe .08 .25
76 Andre Rison .08 .25
77 Mike Sherrard .02 .10
78 Errict Rhett .08 .25
79 Junior Seau .20 .50
80 Willie Davis .08 .25
81 Craig Erickson .02 .10
82 Torrance Small .02 .10
83 Randall Cunningham .20 .50
84 Robert Brooks .20 .50
85 Terance Mathis .08 .25
86 Rod Woodson .08 .25
87 Anthony Miller .08 .25
88 Stan Humphries .08 .25
89 Chris Miller .02 .10
90 Steve Beuerlein .08 .25
91 Steve Bono .08 .25
92 Frank Reich .02 .10
93 Cory Fleming .02 .10
94 Isaac Bruce .30 .75
95 Dave Meggett .02 .10
96 Jackie Harris .02 .10
97 J.J. Birden .02 .10
98 Flipper Anderson .02 .10
99 Johnnie Morton .08 .25
100 Michael Timpson .02 .10
101 Derek Brown RBK .02 .10
102 Ricky Ervins .02 .10
103 Derrick Alexander DE RC .02 .10
104 Dave Barr RC .02 .10
105 Tony Boselli RC .20 .50
106 Kyle Brady RC .20 .50
107 Mark Bruener RC .08 .25
108 Kevin Carter RC .20 .50
109 Neil O'Donnell .08 .25
110 Derrick Alexander WR .20 .50
111 Charlie Garner .20 .50
112 Darnay Scott .08 .25
113 Scott Mitchell .08 .25
114 Charles Johnson .08 .25
115 Greg Hill .08 .25
116 Ty Law RC 1.00 2.50
117 Frank Sanders RC .20 .50
118 James O. Stewart RC .75 2.00
119 James A.Stewart RC .02 .10
120 Kordell Stewart RC 1.00 2.50
121 Rob Johnson RC .60 1.50
122 John Walsh RC .02 .10
123 Stoney Case RC .02 .10
124 Tyrone Wheatley RC .75 2.00
125 Sherman Williams RC .02 .10
126 Ray Zellars RC .08 .25

1995 Action Packed Quick Silver

COMPLETE SET (126) 40.00 100.00
*STARS: 2.5X TO 6X BASIC CARDS
*RCs: 1.5X TO 4X BASIC CARDS
STATED ODDS 1:6

1995 Action Packed 24K Gold

This 21-card standard-size set was randomly inserted into packs. The cards are similar in design to the basic issue. The player's name, Action Packed logo and the "24 Kt Gold" logo are imprinted in gold. The cards are numbered with a "G" suffix.
COMPLETE SET (21) 75.00 200.00
STATED ODDS 1:72
1G Jerry Rice 8.00 20.00
2G Emmitt Smith 12.50 30.00
3G Drew Bledsoe 3.00 8.00
4G Warren Moon 2.50 6.00
5G Deion Sanders 4.00 10.00
6G Natrone Means 2.00 5.00
7G Steve Young 5.00 12.00
8G John Elway 10.00 25.00
9G Brett Favre 12.50 30.00
10G Marshall Faulk 8.00 20.00
11G Heath Shuler 2.00 5.00
12G Troy Aikman 6.00 15.00
13G Dan Marino 12.50 30.00
14G Jerome Bettis 3.00 8.00
15G Jim Kelly 4.00 10.00
16G Michael Irvin 4.00 10.00
17G Barry Sanders 10.00 25.00
18G Steve McNair 8.00 20.00
19G Rashaan Salaam 2.00 5.00
20G Kerry Collins 4.00 15.00
21G Ki-Jana Carter 2.00 5.00

1995 Action Packed Armed Forces

This 12-card horizontally designed, standard-size set was randomly inserted into packs at the rate of 1:24. This set featured leading passers. Braille parallel versions of each card were also randomly inserted at the rate of 1:96 packs.
COMPLETE SET (12) 25.00 60.00
*BRAILLES: .5X TO 1.2X BASIC INSERTS
AF1 Drew Bledsoe 2.00 5.00
AF2 Dan Marino 6.00 15.00
AF3 Troy Aikman 3.00 8.00
AF4 Steve Young 2.50 6.00
AF5 Brett Favre 6.00 15.00
AF6 Heath Shuler 1.25 3.00
AF7 Dave Brown 1.00 2.50
AF8 Jeff Blake 1.25 3.00
AF9 John Elway 5.00 12.00
AF10 Rick Mirer 1.25 3.00
AF11 Kerry Collins 2.00 5.00
AF12 Steve McNair 3.00 8.00

1995 Action Packed G-Force

This horizontal 12 card standard-size set was randomly inserted into packs. This set features leading running backs. The full-bleed fronts contain two photos. One photo is a full-color action embossed shot while the other is a ghosted head photo. The words "Ground Force" are located in the upper left corner. Running horizontally up the left side of the back, are the player's name and his 1994 yards per carry average. The rest of the card back contains a player photo and information about his running ability.
COMPLETE SET (12) 10.00 20.00
STATED ODDS 1:36 HOB
GF1 Emmitt Smith 5.00 10.00
GF2 Barry Sanders 5.00 10.00
GF3 Marshall Faulk 4.00 8.00
GF4 Natrone Means .40 1.00
GF5 Chris Warren .40 1.00
GF6 Jerome Bettis 1.00 2.00
GF7 Errict Rhett .40 1.00
GF8 Byron Bam Morris .15 .40
GF9 Ki-Jana Carter .30 .75
GF10 Mario Bates .40 1.00
GF11 Ricky Watters .40 1.00
GF12 Tyrone Wheatley 1.50 3.00

1995 Action Packed Rocket Men

This horizontal 18 card standard-size set was randomly inserted at approximately one in 12 jumbo packs. The full-bleed fronts contain one photo with a "swirl" in the background. The words "Rocket Man" are located on the left side of the card. Running horizontally on the bottom of the card is the player's name. The rest of the card back contains two player photos and information.
COMPLETE SET (18) 50.00 100.00
STATED ODDS 1:12 JUM
RM1 Marshall Faulk 5.00 10.00
RM2 Emmitt Smith 6.00 12.00
RM3 Barry Sanders 6.00 12.00
RM4 Natrone Means .60 1.25
RM5 Errict Rhett .60 1.25
RM6 Ki-Jana Carter .40 1.00

RM7 Tyrone Wheatley 2.00 4.00
RM8 Drew Bledsoe 2.50 5.00
RM9 Dan Marino 8.00 15.00
RM10 Steve Young 3.00 6.00
RM11 Troy Aikman 4.00 8.00
RM12 Brett Favre 8.00 15.00
RM13 Kerry Collins 2.50 6.00
RM14 Steve McNair 5.00 10.00
RM15 Heath Shuler .60 1.25
RM16 Jerry Rice 4.00 8.00
RM17 Michael Irvin 1.25 2.50
RM18 Herman Moore 1.25 2.50
RM1P Emmitt Smith Promo .75 2.00

1995 Action Packed Brian Piccolo

This single card was issued by Action Packed to honor the 25th anniversary of the passing of Brian Piccolo. Ech card was serial numbered to 2500.

1 Brian Piccolo 5.00 12.00

1996 Action Packed Promos

This three-card set was issued to preview the 1996 Action Packed series. The cards are identical to their regular issue counterparts, except for the word "Promo" printed in black on the card back.

COMPLETE SET (4) 8.00 20.00
1 Emmitt Smith 1.60 4.00
3 Jerry Rice Studs 6.00 15.00
16 Steve Young .80 2.00
105 Neil O'Donnell .40 1.00

1996 Action Packed

The 1996 Action Packed set was issued by Pinnacle in one series totalling 126 standard-size cards. The set was issued in three different pack forms. Retail and Hobby packs each contained five cards per pack while the magazine packs contained four cards per pack. For the first time, these cards had square corners instead of the traditional round corners. Cards numbered 115-126 are a subset titled "Eyeing the Storm". There are no Rookie Cards in this set.

COMPLETE SET (126) 12.50 25.00
1 Emmitt Smith 1.50 3.00
2 Dan Marino 1.25 3.00
3 Isaac Bruce .25 .60
4 Eric Zeier .05 .15
5 Ben Coates .10 .30
6 Jim Kelly .25 .60
7 Rodney Hampton .10 .30
8 Greg Lloyd .10 .30
9 Reggie White .25 .60
10 Derrick Thomas .25 .60
11 Jerry Rice .75 2.00
12 Drew Bledsoe .40 1.00
13 Cris Carter .25 .60
14 Troy Aikman .75 2.00
15 Steve McNair .60 1.50
16 Steve Young .60 1.50
17 Ricky Watters .10 .30
18 Brett Favre 2.00 4.00
19 Michael Westbrook .25 .60
20 Charles Haley .10 .30
21 Heath Shuler .10 .30
22 Tim Brown .25 .60
23 Kerry Collins .25 .60
24 Hugh Douglas .10 .30
25 Marcus Allen .25 .60
26 Steve Bono .05 .15
27 Curtis Martin .60 1.50
28 Wayne Chrebet .40 1.00
29 Dave Brown .05 .15
30 James O. Stewart .10 .30
31 Chris Sanders .10 .30
32 Deion Sanders .40 1.00
33 Rodney Thomas .05 .15
34 Rashaan Salaam .10 .30
35 Curtis Conway .25 .60
36 Harvey Williams .05 .15
37 William Floyd .10 .30
38 Carl Pickens .10 .30
39 Herman Moore .10 .30
40 Stan Humphries .10 .30
41 Orlando Thomas .05 .15
42 Bert Emanuel .10 .30
43 Yancey Thigpen .10 .30
44 Darick Holmes .05 .15
45 Mario Bates .10 .30
46 Greg Hill .10 .30
47 Errict Rhett .10 .30
48 Erik Kramer .05 .15
49 Garrison Hearst .10 .30
50 Jim Everett .05 .15
51 Barry Sanders 1.25 3.00
52 Eric Metcalf .05 .15
53 Marshall Faulk .30 .75
54 Junior Seau .25 .60
55 Bruce Smith .10 .30
56 Kordell Stewart .25 .60
57 Edgar Bennett .10 .30
58 Joey Galloway .25 .60
59 Jeff Hostetler .05 .15
60 Frank Sanders .10 .30
61 John Elway 1.25 3.00
62 Tyrone Wheatley .10 .30
63 Jeff George .10 .30
64 Ken Norton, Jr. .05 .15
65 Bryan Cox .05 .15
66 Bryce Paup .05 .15
67 Larry Centers .10 .30
68 Bernie Parmalee .05 .15
69 Jeff Graham .05 .15
70 Rick Mirer .10 .30
71 Chris Warren .10 .30
72 Charlie Garner .10 .30
73 Robert Brooks .25 .60
74 Jim Harbaugh .10 .30
75 Tamarick Vanover .10 .30
76 Napoleon Kaufman .25 .60
77 Warren Moon .10 .30
78 Vincent Brisby .05 .15
79 Ki-Jana Carter .10 .30
80 Michael Irvin .25 .60
81 Trent Dilfer .25 .60
82 Byron Bam Morris .05 .15
83 Mark Brunell .40 1.00
84 Jeff Blake .25 .60
85 Kevin Williams .05 .15
86 Rod Woodson .10 .30
87 Andre Reed .10 .30
88 Erric Pegram .05 .15
89 Anthony Miller .10 .30
90 Gus Frerotte .10 .30
91 Quinn Early .05 .15
92 Daryl Johnston .10 .30
93 Tony Martin .10 .30
94 Terrell Davis .60 1.50
95 Brent Jones .05 .15
96 Mark Chmura .10 .30
97 Kyle Brady .05 .15
98 J.J. Stokes .25 .60
99 Rodney Peete .05 .15
100 Natrone Means .10 .30
101 Sherman Williams .05 .15
102 Brian Blades .05 .15
103 Brett Perriman .05 .15
104 Antonio Freeman .25 .60
105 Neil O'Donnell .10 .30
106 Craig Heyward .05 .15
107 Derek Loville .05 .15
108 Jay Novacek .05 .15
109 Scott Mitchell .10 .30
110 Bill Brooks .05 .15
111 Shannon Sharpe .10 .30
112 Jake Reed .10 .30
113 Derrick Moore .05 .15
114 Steve Atwater .05 .15
115 Darren Woodson ETS .10 .30
116 Junior Seau ETS .25 .60
117 Quentin Coryatt ETS .05 .15
118 Bruce Smith ETS .10 .30
119 Rod Woodson ETS .10 .30
120 Charles Haley ETS .10 .30
121 Derrick Thomas ETS .10 .30
122 Ken Norton, Jr. ETS .05 .15
123 Steve Atwater ETS .05 .15
124 Greg Lloyd ETS .10 .30
125 Reggie White ETS .25 .60
126 Bryan Cox ETS .05 .15

1996 Action Packed Artist's Proofs

COMPLETE SET (126) 200.00 400.00
*AP STARS: 4X TO 10X BASIC CARDS
STATED ODDS 1:24 HOB, 1:30 RET

1996 Action Packed 24K Gold

Randomly inserted in packs at a rate of one in 72 Retail and Hobby packs, this 14-card insert set features leading NFL players. These cards have the words "24 Karat" printed in the lower right corner.

COMPLETE SET (14) 100.00 200.00
STATED ODDS 1:72 HOB/RET
1 Brett Favre 12.50 30.00
2 Michael Irvin 4.00 10.00
3 Drew Bledsoe 3.00 8.00
4 Jerry Rice 8.00 20.00
5 Troy Aikman 6.00 15.00
6 Dan Marino 12.50 30.00
7 Errict Rhett 2.00 5.00
8 Curtis Martin 3.00 8.00
9 Steve Young 5.00 12.00
10 Barry Sanders 10.00 25.00
11 Marshall Faulk 2.50 6.00
12 Isaac Bruce 2.50 6.00
13 John Elway 12.50 30.00
14 Emmitt Smith 12.50 30.00

1996 Action Packed Ball Hog

Randomly inserted in packs at a rate of one in 23 regular packs and one in 29 magazine packs, this 12-card insert set uses embossed leather-like technology on the front of the card. These cards feature the player's portrait against a football-like background.

COMPLETE SET (12) 20.00 50.00
STATED ODDS 1:23HOB/RET, 1:29MAG
1 Carl Pickens .60 1.50
2 Terrell Davis 3.00 8.00
3 Jerry Rice 4.00 10.00
4 Barry Sanders 6.00 15.00
5 Marshall Faulk 1.50 4.00
6 Isaac Bruce 1.25 3.00
7 Michael Irvin 1.25 3.00
8 Cris Carter 1.25 3.00
9 Rashaan Salaam .60 1.50
10 Herman Moore .60 1.50
11 Chris Warren .60 1.50
12 Emmitt Smith 6.00 15.00

1996 Action Packed Jumbos

These oversized cards were parallel to the regular issue cards, other than in size and numbering. They were inserted one per box in special retail packaging as a chiptopper insert.

COMPLETE SET (4) 6.00 15.00
ONE PER RETAIL BOX
1 Emmitt Smith 2.50 6.00
2 Drew Bledsoe .75 2.00
3 Troy Aikman 1.50 4.00
4 Brett Favre 3.00 8.00

1996 Action Packed Longest Yard

Randomly inserted in packs at a rate of one in 24 magazine packs, this 12-card insert set features leading players.

COMPLETE SET (12) 50.00 120.00
STATED ODDS 1:24 MAG
1 Brett Favre 12.50 30.00
Robert Brooks
2 Tamarick Vanover 1.00 2.50
3 Joey Galloway 2.00 5.00
4 Kerry Collins 2.00 5.00
5 Jeff Blake 2.00 5.00
6 Jerry Rice 6.00 15.00
7 Barry Sanders 10.00 25.00
8 Rodney Thomas .50 1.25
9 Herman Moore 1.00 2.50
10 Emmitt Smith 10.00 25.00
11 Terrell Davis 5.00 12.00
12 Cris Carter 2.00 5.00

1996 Action Packed Sculptor's Proof

Randomly inserted in packs at a rate of one in 192 Hobby and Retail packs and one in 288 Magazine packs, these cards were part of a redemption program. Out of the packs, a collector would acquire a redemption card that would be mailed in, with a $2.50 postage fee, for a pewter metal version of the card. The redemption offer expired on November 1, 1996. We've listed prices below for the pewter cards.

COMPLETE SET (14) 100.00 250.00
REDEMPT.ODDS 1:192H/R, 1:288MAG
1 Dan Marino 12.50 30.00
2 Deion Sanders 3.00 8.00
3 Joey Galloway 2.00 5.00
4 Brett Favre 12.50 30.00
5 Barry Sanders 10.00 25.00
6 Michael Irvin 2.00 5.00
7 Drew Bledsoe 3.00 8.00
8 Emmitt Smith 10.00 25.00
9 Curtis Martin 5.00 12.00
10 Steve Young 5.00 12.00
11 John Elway 12.50 30.00
12 Jerry Rice 6.00 15.00
13 Errict Rhett 1.00 2.50
14 Troy Aikman 6.00 15.00

1996 Action Packed Studs

Randomly inserted in packs at a rate of 1:161 Hobby and Retail packs, this six-card insert set features NFL players sporting their diamond stud earrings. These cards are numbered out of 1500 sets produced and each contains a genuine diamond chip. A 24K Gold parallel set was produced and released through a redemption offer. The 24K Gold cards are sequencially numbered of 200-sets produced

COMPLETE SET (6) 50.00 120.00
STATED ODDS 1:161 HOB/RET
STATED PRINT RUN 1500 #'d SETS
*24K STUDS: .6X TO 1.5X BASIC INSERTS
24K PRINT RUN 200 SERIAL #'d SETS
1 Emmitt Smith 20.00 50.00
2 Deion Sanders 12.50 30.00
3 Jerry Rice 15.00 40.00
4 Michael Irvin 7.50 20.00
5 Kordell Stewart 7.50 20.00
6 Ricky Watters 6.00 15.00

1997 Action Packed

The 1997 Action Packed set was issued in one series totaling 125 cards and was distributed in five card packs with a suggested retail price of $2.99. The fronts feature embossed color action player photos on a pebble-grained pigskin background. The backs carry another player photo with a faded background version of it and career statistics. Three promo cards were produced to promote the set.

COMPLETE SET (125) 12.00 30.00
1 Jerry Rice 1.25 2.50
2 Troy Aikman 1.25 2.50
3 Ricky Watters .25 .60
4 Dan Marino 2.00 5.00
5 Emmitt Smith 2.00 4.00
6 Warren Moon .40 1.00
7 Rashaan Salaam .15 .40
8 Drew Bledsoe .60 1.50
9 Eddie George .40 1.00
10 John Elway 2.00 5.00
11 Robert Brooks .25 .60
12 Scott Mitchell .25 .60
13 Isaac Bruce .40 1.00
14 Marshall Faulk .50 1.25
15 Steve Bono .25 .60
16 Barry Sanders 1.50 4.00
17 Brett Favre 2.50 5.00
18 Curtis Martin .50 1.25
19 Keyshawn Johnson .40 1.00
20 Dave Brown .15 .40
21 Frank Sanders .25 .60
22 Gus Frerotte .15 .40
23 Eric Metcalf .25 .60
24 Thurman Thomas .40 1.00
25 Steve Young .60 1.50
26 Alvin Harper .15 .40
27 Mark Brunell .60 1.50
28 Kordell Stewart .40 1.00
29 Terry Glenn .40 1.00
30 Junior Seau .40 1.00
31 Karim Abdul-Jabbar .25 .60
32 Jeff Hostetler .15 .40
33 Rodney Hampton .25 .60
34 Irving Fryar .25 .60
35 Cris Carter .40 1.00
36 James O.Stewart .25 .60
37 Marcus Allen .40 1.00
38 Napoleon Kaufman .40 1.00
39 Shannon Sharpe .25 .60
40 LeShon Johnson .15 .40
41 Tony Banks .25 .60
42 Lawrence Phillips .15 .40
43 Kerry Collins .40 1.00
44 Curtis Conway .25 .60
45 Jim Harbaugh .25 .60
46 Garrison Hearst .25 .60
47 Trent Dilfer .40 1.00
48 Terance Mathis .25 .60
49 Jerome Bettis .40 1.00
50 Chris Sanders .15 .40
51 Deion Sanders .40 1.00
52 Herman Moore .25 .60
53 Elvis Grbac .25 .60
54 O.J. McDuffie .25 .60
55 Ben Coates .25 .60
56 Jim Kelly .40 1.00
57 J.J. Stokes .25 .60
58 Terrell Davis .50 1.25
59 Stan Humphries .25 .60
60 Carl Pickens .25 .60
61 Neil O'Donnell .25 .60
62 Edgar Bennett .25 .60
63 Yancey Thigpen .25 .60
64 Bert Emanuel .25 .60
65 Amani Toomer .25 .60
66 Jeff Blake .25 .60
67 Eddie Kennison .25 .60
68 Jason Dunn .15 .40
69 Rob Moore .25 .60
70 Andre Rison .25 .60
71 Vinny Testaverde .25 .60
72 Henry Ellard .15 .40
73 Dale Carter .15 .40
74 Tony Martin .25 .60
75 Jim Everett .15 .40
76 Joey Galloway .25 .60
77 Mike Alstott .40 1.00
78 Kevin Hardy .15 .40
79 Jake Reed .25 .60
80 Tim Brown .40 1.00
81 Sean Dawkins .15 .40
82 Bobby Engram .25 .60
83 Michael Irvin .40 1.00
84 Rickey Dudley .25 .60
85 Chris Chandler .25 .60
86 Keith Jackson .15 .40
87 Muhsin Muhammad .25 .60
88 Tamarick Vanover .25 .60
89 Chris Warren .25 .60
90 Johnnie Morton .25 .60
91 Terry Allen .40 1.00
92 Stanley Pritchett .15 .40
93 Charles Johnson .25 .60
94 Chris T. Jones .15 .40
95 Winslow Oliver .15 .40
96 Anthony Miller .15 .40
97 Tyrone Wheatley .25 .60
98 Robert Smith .25 .60
99 Eric Moulds .40 1.00
100 Hardy Nickerson .15 .40
101 Derrick Alexander WR .25 .60
102 Michael Haynes .15 .40
103 Jamal Anderson .40 1.00
104 Marvin Harrison .40 1.00
105 Antonio Freeman .40 1.00
106 Dorsey Levens .40 1.00
107 Natrone Means .25 .60
108 Keenan McCardell .25 .60
109 Mark Chmura .25 .60
110 Darren Woodson .15 .40
111 Brett Favre DD 1.25 2.50
112 Emmitt Smith DD .75 2.00
113 Junior Seau DD .40 1.00
114 Jerry Rice DD .50 1.25
115 Barry Sanders DD .75 2.00
116 Bruce Smith DD .15 .40
117 Troy Aikman DD .50 1.25
118 Bryan Cox DD .15 .40
119 Zach Thomas DD .40 1.00
120 Reggie White DD .40 1.00
121 Ben Coates DD .25 .60
122 Jerome Bettis DD .40 1.00
123 Michael Irvin DD .25 .60
124 Quentin Coryatt DD .15 .40
125 Checklist Card .15 .40
P28 Kordell Stewart Promo .75 2.00
P45 Jim Harbaugh Promo .20 .50

1997 Action Packed First Impressions

COMPLETE SET (125) 200.00 400.00
*SINGLES: 2X TO 5X BASIC CARDS
STATED ODDS 1:12 HOB, 1:15 MAG

1997 Action Packed Gold Impressions

COMPLETE SET (125) 400.00 800.00
*SINGLES: 4X TO 10X BASIC CARDS
STATED ODDS 1:35 HOB, 1:44 MAG

1997 Action Packed 24K Gold

Randomly inserted in hobby packs at a rate of one in 71, this 15-card set features color player photos of some of the league's premier players. Card fronts feature Action Packed's Prime Frost printing technology with 24K Gold foil highlights. Magazine packs (4-card packs) also contained the inserts at a rate of 1:89.

COMPLETE SET (15) 100.00 200.00
STATED ODDS 1:71 HOB, 1:89 MAG
1 Brett Favre 12.50 30.00
2 Steve Young 4.00 10.00
3 Terrell Davis 3.00 8.00
4 Barry Sanders 10.00 25.00
5 Isaac Bruce 3.00 8.00
6 Deion Sanders 4.00 10.00
7 Dan Marino 10.00 25.00
8 Jim Harbaugh 2.50 6.00
9 Jerry Rice 8.00 20.00
10 John Elway 12.50 30.00
11 Herman Moore 2.00 5.00
12 Troy Aikman 6.00 15.00
13 Emmitt Smith 10.00 25.00
14 Drew Bledsoe 3.00 8.00
15 Eddie George 2.50 6.00

1997 Action Packed Crash Course

Randomly inserted in hobby packs at a rate of one in 23, this 18-card set features color player photos of some of the league's toughest superstars and is printed on rainbow holographic foil. Magazine packs (4-card packs) also contained the cards at a rate of 1:29.

COMPLETE SET (18) 30.00 80.00
STATED ODDS 1:23 HOB, 1:29 MAG
1 Dan Marino 8.00 20.00
2 Troy Aikman 4.00 10.00
3 Barry Sanders 6.00 15.00
4 Emmitt Smith 6.00 15.00
5 Brett Favre 8.00 20.00
6 John Elway 8.00 20.00
7 Keyshawn Johnson 1.50 4.00
8 Jim Harbaugh 1.00 2.50
9 Kerry Collins 1.50 4.00
10 Karim Abdul-Jabbar 1.00 2.50
11 Eddie Kennison 1.00 2.50
12 Curtis Martin 2.00 5.00
13 Tony Banks 1.00 2.50
14 Dorsey Levens 1.50 4.00
15 Jerome Bettis 1.50 4.00
16 Drew Bledsoe 2.50 6.00
17 Marvin Harrison 1.50 4.00
18 Jerry Rice 4.00 10.00

1997 Action Packed Extra Points 10

Pinnacle Brands released a special retail pack version of the 1997 Action Packed set that included one Extra Point player game piece per pack. The game pieces included only the player's name (no photo) and a set "point" amount or either 10 or 100 points. The collector that submitted the most points for any one player received that player's actual production embossing die used for his card from the 1996 Action Packed set. The offer expired on December 31, 1997.

COMPLETE SET (100) 4.00 10.00
COMMON CARD (1-100) .02 .10
SEMISTARS .05 .15
UNLISTED STARS .08 .25
*100 POINT: .6X TO 1.5X 10 POINT

1997 Action Packed Pinnacle Scoring Core Preview

These 12 cards were randomly inserted into extra point packs. The cards are unnumbered and we have listed them in alphabetical order.

COMPLETE SET (12) 40.00 100.00
RANDOM INSERTS IN AP EXTRA POINTS
1 Karim Abdul-Jabbar 2.00 5.00
2 Troy Aikman 8.00 20.00
3 Tim Biakabutuka 2.00 5.00
4 Drew Bledsoe 5.00 12.00
5 Robert Brooks 2.00 5.00
6 Mark Brunell 5.00 12.00
7 John Elway 15.00 40.00
8 Terry Glenn 3.00 8.00
9 Garrison Hearst 2.00 5.00
10 Michael Irvin 3.00 8.00
11 Shannon Sharpe 2.00 5.00
12 Steve Young 5.00 12.00

1997 Action Packed Studs

Randomly inserted in hobby packs at a rate of one in 167, this nine-card set features NFL superstars who wear diamond stud earrings. Only 1500 sets were produced and each card is individually numbered with each including a genuine diamond chip. Magazine packs (4-card packs) also contained the cards at a rate of 1:209.

COMPLETE SET (9) 75.00 150.00
STATED ODDS 1:167 HOB, 1:209 MAG
STATED PRINT RUN 1500 #'d SETS
1 Deion Sanders 10.00 25.00
2 Barry Sanders 20.00 50.00
3 Eddie George 7.50 20.00
4 Jerry Rice 15.00 40.00
5 Kordell Stewart 6.00 15.00
6 Emmitt Smith 15.00 40.00
7 Terrell Davis 10.00 25.00
8 Keyshawn Johnson 7.50 20.00
9 Robert Smith 6.00 15.00
P4 Jerry Rice Promo 2.00 5.00
Studs Card

1990 Action Packed All-Madden

This 58-card standard-size set honors the members of the annual team selected by CBS analyst John Madden. The set was released both in six-card packs as well as in a factory set. This set features a borderless design on the front and an action shot of the player and a brief description on the back about what qualifies the player to be on the All-Madden Team. The back also features a portrait shot of the player and a portrait shot of John Madden as well. The set also has some of the features standard in Action Packed sets, rounded corners, and the All-Madden Team logo in embossed, raised letters as well as the players' photos being raised. The Neal Anderson prototype (P12) is not included in the complete set as it was passed out to dealers prior to the mass distribution of the set. The Anderson prototype was also available as a special magazine insert in SCD.

COMPLETE SET (58) 4.00 10.00
COMP.FACT SET (58) 5.00 10.00
1 Joe Montana .75 2.00
2 Jerry Rice .50 1.25
3 Charles Haley .08 .25
4 Steve Wisniewski .08 .25
5 Dave Meggett .08 .25
6 Ottis Anderson .08 .25
7 Nate Newton .08 .25
8 Warren Moon .15 .40
9 Emmitt Smith 1.25 3.00
10 Jackie Slater .05 .15
11 Pepper Johnson .05 .15
12 Lawrence Taylor .15 .40
13 Sterling Sharpe .15 .40
14 Sean Landeta .05 .15
15 Richard Dent .08 .25
16 Neal Anderson .08 .25
17 Bruce Matthews .08 .25
18 Matt Millen .08 .25
19 Reggie White .15 .40
20 Greg Townsend .08 .25
21 Troy Aikman .50 1.25
22 Don Mosebar .05 .15
23 Jeff Zimmerman .05 .15
24 Rod Woodson .15 .40
25 Keith Byars .08 .25
26 Randall Cunningham .15 .40
27 Reyna Thompson .05 .15
28 Marcus Allen .15 .40
29 Gary Clark .15 .40
30 Anthony Carter .08 .25
31 Bubba Paris .05 .15
32 Ronnie Lott .08 .25
33 Erik Howard .05 .15
34 Ernest Givins .08 .25
35 Mike Munchak .08 .25
36 Jim Lachey .05 .15
37 Merril Hoge UER .05 .15
38 Darrell Green .08 .25
39 Pierce Holt .05 .15
40 Jerome Brown .08 .25
41 William Perry UER .08 .25
42 Michael Carter .05 .15
43 Keith Jackson .08 .25
44 Kevin Fagan .05 .15
45 Mark Carrier DB .08 .25
46 Fred Barnett .08 .25
47 Barry Sanders .75 2.00
48 Pat Swilling and .08 .25
49 Sam Mills and .05 .15
50 Jacob Green .05 .15
51 Stan Brock .05 .15
52 Dan Hampton .08 .25
53 Brian Noble .05 .15
54 John Elliott .05 .15
55 Matt Bahr .05 .15
56 Bill Parcells CO .08 .25
57 Art Shell CO .08 .25
58 All-Madden Team Trophy .05 .15
P12 Neal Anderson Proto. .40 1.00

1991 Action Packed All-Madden

In its second year, this 52-card standard-size set honors the selections to the All-Madden Team. The cards were issued in foil packs as well as in factory sets. Each of the cards in the set was also available in a randomly inserted 24K Gold parallel version.

COMPLETE SET (52) 4.00 10.00
COMP.FACT SET (52) 5.00 10.00
1 Mark Rypien .08 .25
2 Erik Kramer .08 .25
3 Jim McMahon .08 .25
4 Jesse Sapolu .05 .15
5 Jay Hilgenberg .05 .15
6 Howard Ballard .05 .15
7 Lomas Brown .05 .15
8 John Elliott .05 .15
9 Joe Jacoby .05 .15
10 Jim Lachey .05 .15
11 Anthony Munoz .08 .25
12 Nate Newton .05 .15
13 Will Wolford .05 .15
14 Jerry Ball .05 .15
15 Jerome Brown .08 .25
16 William Perry .08 .25
17 Charles Mann .05 .15
18 Clyde Simmons .05 .15
19 Reggie White .15 .40
20 Eric Allen .05 .15
21 Darrell Green .05 .15
22 Bennie Blades .05 .15
23 Chuck Cecil .05 .15
24 Rickey Dixon .05 .15
25 David Fulcher .05 .15
26 Ronnie Lott .15 .40
27 Emmitt Smith 1.25 3.00
28 Neal Anderson .08 .25
29 Robert Delpino .05 .15
30 Barry Sanders .75 2.00
31 Thurman Thomas .15 .40
32 Cornelius Bennett .08 .25
33 Rickey Jackson .08 .25
34 Seth Joyner .08 .25
35 Wilber Marshall .05 .15
36 Clay Matthews .08 .25
37 Chris Spielman .08 .25
38 Pat Swilling .08 .25
39 Fred Barnett .08 .25
40 Gary Clark .08 .25
41 Michael Irvin .15 .40
42 Art Monk .08 .25
43 Jerry Rice .50 1.25
44 John Taylor .08 .25
45 Tom Waddle .05 .15
46 Kevin Butler .05 .15
47 Bill Bates .08 .25
48 Greg Manusky .05 .15
49 Elvis Patterson .05 .15
50 Steve Tasker .08 .25
51 John Daly .15 .40
52 All-Madden Team Trophy .05 .15

1991 Action Packed All-Madden 24K Gold

COMPLETE SET (52) 150.00 300.00
*24K GOLD CARDS: 10X TO 25X

1992 Action Packed All-Madden

For the third consecutive year, Action Packed has issued a 55-card standard-size set to honor the toughest players in the game as picked by sportscaster John Madden. For hobby dealers only, Action Packed inserted two prototype cards of upcoming products in each display box of All-Madden Team foil packs. Moreover, 24K Gold leaf versions of each card were randomly inserted in foil packs.

COMPLETE SET (55) 4.00 10.00
1 Emmitt Smith .75 2.00
2 Reggie White .15 .40
3 Deion Sanders .40 1.00
4 Wilber Marshall .05 .15
5 Barry Sanders .75 2.00
6 Derrick Thomas .08 .25
7 Troy Aikman .50 1.25
8 Eric Allen .05 .15
9 Cris Carter .15 .40
10 Jerry Rice .50 1.25
11 Rickey Jackson .05 .15
12 Bubba McDowell .05 .15
13 Jack Del Rio .05 .15
14 Nate Newton .05 .15
15 John Elliott .05 .15
16 Fred Barnett .05 .15
17 Mike Singletary .08 .25
18 Lawrence Taylor .08 .25
19 Bruce Matthews .05 .15
20 Pat Swilling .08 .25
21 Charles Haley .08 .25
22 Andre Rison .15 .40
23 Seth Joyner .08 .25
24 Steve Young .40 1.00
25 Gary Clark .08 .25
26 Jerry Ball .05 .15
27 Michael Irvin .15 .40
28 Haywood Jeffires .08 .25
29 Kevin Ross .05 .15
30 Chris Doleman .05 .15
31 Vai Sikahema .05 .15
32 Ricky Watters .08 .25
33 Henry Thomas .05 .15
34 Mike Kenn .05 .15
35 Erik Williams .08 .25
36 Neil Smith .15 .40
37 Mark Schlereth .05 .15
38 Steve Wallace .05 .15
39 Randall McDaniel .05 .15
40 Kurt Gouveia .05 .15
41 Al Noga .05 .15
42 Tom Rathman .05 .15
43 Harris Barton .05 .15
44 Mel Gray .05 .15
45 Keith Byars .05 .15
46 Todd Scott .05 .15
47 Brent Jones .05 .15
48 Audray McMillian .05 .15
49 Ray Childress .05 .15
50 Dennis Smith .05 .15
51 Mark McMillian .05 .15
52 Sean Gilbert .05 .15
53 Pierce Holt .05 .15
54 Daryl Johnston .08 .25
55 Madden Cruiser (Bus) .05 .15

1992 Action Packed All-Madden 24K Gold

COMPLETE SET (55) 200.00 400.00
*24K GOLDS: 10X TO 25X BASIC CARDS

1993 Action Packed All-Madden

This 42-card standard-size set marks the fourth consecutive year Action Packed honored the toughest players in the game as picked by sportscaster John Madden, and commemorated the 10th anniversary of his All-Madden Team by featuring his all-time favorites from the last 10 years. Action Packed produced 1,000 numbered cases and distributed them only through hobby distributors and dealers. Every case contained a certificate for an uncut sheet of the set autographed by John Madden. Also, 24K gold versions of some of the cards were randomly inserted in packs. A Troy Aikman prototype card was produced as well and priced at the end of our checklist. It is not considered part of the set.

COMPLETE SET (42) 4.00 10.00
1 Troy Aikman .50 1.25
2 Bill Bates .08 .25
3 Mark Bavaro .07 .20
4 Jim Burt .07 .20
5 Gary Clark .07 .20
6 Richard Dent .08 .25
7 Gary Fencik .07 .20
8 Darrell Green .07 .20
9 Roy Green .07 .20
10 Russ Grimm .07 .20
11 Charles Haley .07 .20
12 Dan Hampton .07 .20
13 Lester Hayes .07 .20
14 Mike Haynes .07 .20
15 Jay Hilgenberg .07 .20
16 Michael Irvin .15 .40
17 Joe Jacoby .07 .20
18 Steve Largent .15 .40
19 Howie Long .15 .40
20 Ronnie Lott .08 .25
21 Dan Marino .75 2.00
22 Jim McMahon .08 .25
23 Matt Millen .07 .20
24 Art Monk .08 .25
25 Joe Montana .75 2.00
26 Anthony Munoz .08 .25
27 Nate Newton .07 .20
28 Walter Payton .15 .40
29 William Perry .08 .25
30 Jack Reynolds .07 .20
31 Jerry Rice .50 1.25
32 Barry Sanders .75 2.00
33 Sterling Sharpe .08 .25
34 Mike Singletary .08 .25
35 Jackie Slater .07 .20
36 Emmitt Smith .75 2.00
37 Pat Summerall .08 .25
38 Lawrence Taylor .15 .40
39 Jeff Van Note .07 .20
40 Reggie White .15 .40
41 Otis Wilson .07 .20
42 Jack Youngblood .07 .20
P1 Troy Aikman Prototype 1.00 2.50
NNO Uncut Sheet AUTO/1000 40.00 80.00

1993 Action Packed All-Madden 24K Gold

These twelve 24K gold standard-size cards were randomly inserted in packs of 1993 Action Packed 10th Anniversary All-Madden Team. Except for the richer tone of the 24K gold foil and the words "24Kt. Gold" stamped on the front in gold foil, the design is identical to the regular 10th Anniversary All-Madden cards. Each was numbered of 1750-cards produced.

COMPLETE SET (12) 150.00 300.00
1G Troy Aikman 12.50 30.00
2G Michael Irvin 5.00 12.00
3G Ronnie Lott 3.00 8.00
4G Dan Marino 20.00 50.00
5G Joe Montana 20.00 50.00
6G Walter Payton 7.50 20.00
7G Jerry Rice 12.50 30.00
8G Barry Sanders 20.00 50.00
9G Sterling Sharpe 3.00 8.00
10G Emmitt Smith 20.00 50.00
11G Lawrence Taylor 5.00 12.00
12G Reggie White 7.50 20.00

1994 Action Packed All-Madden

In this 41-card standard-size set, Action Packed presented the 10th Annual All Madden team. Each card has a 24K version; these gold cards were seeded approximately one per box. In addition to the top players, each pack included a "Smash Mouth" scratch-and-win game card with various Sony TV models and All-Madden 24K cards as prizes. Also, non-winning cards were redeemable for one 11th Annual All-Madden Team Prototype card. The contest ran through June 30, 1995. The embossed fronts feature a borderless design that incorporates the band-aid logo. The backs feature Madden's comments on the player and a color headshot of Madden. An uncut sheet of the complete set signed by John Madden and numbered of 1000 was also distributed as an inducement to purchase cases of the product.

COMPLETE SET (41) 4.00 10.00
1 Emmitt Smith .75 2.00
2 Jerome Bettis .30 .75
3 Steve Young .30 .75
4 Jerry Rice .50 1.25
5 Richard Dent .08 .25
6 Junior Seau .15 .40
7 Harris Barton .05 .15
8 Steve Wallace .05 .15
9 Keith Byars .05 .15
10 Michael Irvin .15 .40
11 Joe Montana .75 2.00
12 Jesse Sapolu .05 .15
13 Rickey Jackson .05 .15
14 Ronnie Lott .08 .25
15 Donnell Woolford .05 .15
16 Reggie White .15 .40
17 John Taylor .05 .15
18 Bruce Matthews .05 .15
19 Ronald Moore .05 .15
20 Bill Bates .08 .25
21 Steve Hendrickson .05 .15
22 Eric Allen .05 .15
23 Monte Coleman .05 .15
24 Mark Collins .05 .15
25 Barry Sanders .75 2.00
26 Erik Williams .05 .15
27 Phil Simms .08 .25
28 Chris Zorich .05 .15
29 Troy Aikman .50 1.25
30 Charles Haley .05 .15
31 Darrell Green .05 .15
32 Sean Gilbert .05 .15
33 Kevin Gogan .05 .15
34 Rodney Hampton .08 .25
35 Chris Doleman .05 .15
36 Nate Newton .05 .15
37 Jackie Slater .05 .15
38 Ricky Watters .08 .25
39 LeRoy Butler .05 .15
40 Gary Clark .05 .15
41 Sterling Sharpe .08 .25
P1 Emmitt Smith Proto. 1.00 2.50
NNO Uncut Sheet AUTO/1000 40.00 80.00

1994 Action Packed All-Madden 24K Gold

Each card in the 1994 Action Packed 10th Annual All-Madden series had a 24K version; these gold cards were seeded approximately one per box. The embossed fronts feature a borderless design that incorporates the band-aid logo. The words "24 Kt. Gold" are stamped on the front to distinguish these cards from their regular series counterparts. The backs feature Madden's comments on the player and a color headshot.

COMPLETE SET (41) 250.00 500.00
*24K GOLDS: 10X TO 25X BASIC CARDS
1G Emmitt Smith 20.00 50.00
2G Jerome Bettis 8.00 20.00
3G Steve Young 8.00 20.00
4G Jerry Rice 12.50 30.00
5G Richard Dent 2.50 6.00
6G Junior Seau 4.00 10.00
7G Harris Barton 1.50 4.00
8G Steve Wallace 1.50 4.00
9G Keith Byars 1.50 4.00
10G Michael Irvin 4.00 10.00
11G Joe Montana 20.00 50.00
12G Jesse Sapolu 1.50 4.00
13G Rickey Jackson 1.50 4.00
14G Ronnie Lott 2.50 6.00
15G Donnell Woolford 1.50 4.00
16G Reggie White 4.00 10.00
17G John Taylor 1.50 4.00
18G Bruce Matthews 1.50 4.00
19G Ronald Moore 1.50 4.00
20G Bill Bates 2.50 6.00
21G Steve Hendrickson 1.50 4.00
22G Eric Allen 1.50 4.00
23G Monte Coleman 1.50 4.00
24G Mark Collins 1.50 4.00
25G Barry Sanders 20.00 50.00
26G Erik Williams 1.50 4.00
27G Phil Simms 2.50 6.00
28G Chris Zorich 1.50 4.00
29G Troy Aikman 12.50 30.00
30G Charles Haley 1.50 4.00
31G Darrell Green 1.50 4.00
32G Sean Gilbert 1.50 4.00
33G Kevin Gogan 1.50 4.00
34G Rodney Hampton 2.50 6.00
35G Chris Doleman 1.50 4.00
36G Nate Newton 1.50 4.00
37G Jackie Slater 1.50 4.00
38G Ricky Watters 2.50 6.00
39G LeRoy Butler 1.50 4.00
40G Gary Clark 1.50 4.00
41G Sterling Sharpe 2.50 6.00

1993 Action Packed Monday Night Football Prototypes

These six standard-size cards were issued to show the design of the 1993 Action Packed ABC Monday Night Football series. On a gold-foil background with black borders, the horizontal fronts feature cut-out embossed color player photos. The set title "ABC's Monday Night Football" is printed across the top between two helmets representing the teams that played. The cards highlight two of the 1992 season's best games. The date of the game is given in each side border, while the player's name is printed in the bottom black border. On the back, a gold foil border stripe carrying the words "ABC's Monday Night Football" edges the left side of the card. The rest of the back consists of a rose-colored panel that displays a color head shot, the scoring broken down by quarter, a summary of the player's performance, and various logos. The disclaimer "1993 Prototype" is printed diagonally across the back.

COMPLETE SET (6) 10.00 25.00
MN1 Barry Sanders 4.00 10.00
MN2 Steve Young 1.60 4.00
MN3 Emmitt Smith 4.00 10.00
MN4 Thurman Thomas 1.00 2.50
MN5 Barry Foster .60 1.50
MN6 Warren Moon 1.00 2.50

1993 Action Packed Monday Night Football

Previewing the top players and match-ups for the 1993 games, this 81-card standard-size set consists of cards for each game of the 1993 Monday Night Football schedule. In addition to featuring the top players in the games, the set also includes a card for each of the three ABC Monday Night Football announcers and a card with all three announcers together. The card numbering was done chronologically. Moreover, 250 individually numbered gold Mint cards of each card were produced, and winning certificates for these were randomly inserted in the foil packs. Certificates entitling the collector to an all-expense paid trip to the Pro Bowl were also randomly inserted in the packs. A limited number of 24K Gold foil stamped versions of all the cards were randomly inserted throughout the foil packs. Finally, Chiptopper preview cards were packed two per hobby box.

COMPLETE SET (81) 4.00 10.00
1 Michael Irvin .10 .30
2 Charles Haley .02 .10
3 Art Monk .07 .20
4 Earnest Byner .02 .10
5 Tom Rathman .02 .10
6 John Taylor .02 .10
7 Bernie Kosar .02 .10
8 Clay Matthews .02 .10
9 Simon Fletcher .02 .10
10 John Elway .80 2.00
11 Joe Montana .80 2.00
12 Derrick Thomas .07 .20
13 Rod Woodson .10 .30
14 Gary Anderson K .02 .10
15 Chris Miller .07 .20
16 Andre Rison .07 .20
17 Mark Rypien .02 .10
18 Charles Mann .02 .10
19 John Offerdahl .02 .10
20 Pete Stoyanovich .02 .10
21 Warren Moon .10 .30
22 Lorenzo White .02 .10
23 Haywood Jeffires .02 .10
24 Andre Reed .07 .20
25 Darryl Talley .02 .10
26 Tim Brown .10 .30
27 Howie Long .10 .30
28 Steve Atwater .02 .10
29 Karl Mecklenburg .02 .10
30 Chris Doleman .02 .10
31 Terry Allen .10 .30
32 Richard Dent .02 .10
33 Neal Anderson .02 .10
34 Darrell Green .02 .10
35 Chip Lohmiller .02 .10
36 Jim Kelly .10 .30
37 Cornelius Bennett .02 .10
38 Brett Favre .80 2.00
39 Sterling Sharpe .07 .20
40 Reggie White .10 .30
41 Neil Smith .02 .10
42 Nick Lowery .02 .10
43 Thurman Thomas .10 .30
44 Bruce Smith .10 .30
45 Barry Foster .02 .10
46 Neil O'Donnell .07 .20
47 Rickey Jackson .02 .10
48 Morten Andersen .02 .10
49 Brent Jones .02 .10
50 Ricky Watters .07 .20
51 Leslie O'Neal .02 .10
52 Marion Butts .02 .10
53 Anthony Miller .07 .20
54 Jeff George .07 .20
55 Steve Emtman .02 .10
56 Herschel Walker .07 .20
57 Randall Cunningham .10 .30
58 Clyde Simmons .02 .10
59 Emmitt Smith .80 2.00
60 Ken Norton Jr. .07 .20
61 Troy Aikman .40 1.00
62 Eric Green .02 .10
63 Greg Lloyd .07 .20
64 Bryan Cox .02 .10
65 Mark Higgs .02 .10
66 Phil Simms .07 .20
67 Lawrence Taylor .07 .20
68 Rodney Hampton .07 .20
69 Wayne Martin .02 .10
70 Vaughn Dunbar .02 .10
71 Keith Jackson .07 .20
72 Dan Marino .80 2.00
73 Junior Seau .07 .20

74 Stan Humphries .07 .20
75 Fred Barnett .07 .20
76 Seth Joyner .02 .10
77 Steve Young .30 .75
78 Jerry Rice .40 1.00
79 Dan Dierdorf ANN .07 .20
80 Frank Gifford ANN .10 .30
81 Al Michaels ANN .07 .20
HW1 Hank Williams Jr. .30 .75

1993 Action Packed Monday Night Football Mint Parallel

COMPLETE SET (81) 500.00 800.00
*MINT CARDS: 30X TO 80X BASIC CARDS

1993 Action Packed Monday Night Football 24K Gold

COMPLETE SET (8) 75.00 150.00
*24K GOLDS: 12X TO 30X BASIC CARDS

1994 Action Packed Monday Night Football

Issued in a silver cardboard box, these 71 standard-size cards have rounded corners and feature embossed color action player photos on their silver foil-bordered fronts (except the announcer cards 61-71 are borderless). These cards are sequenced in the order of their planned Monday Night matchup. The horizontal back carries at its lower right a color action player cutout silhouetted against the full moon. The player's name and position appear within the silver-foil margin at the top. The back also carries a Monday Night matchup that gives a sneak preview of the game, as well as a Monday Night Fact.

COMPLETE SET (71) 4.00 10.00
1 Jeff Hostetler .07 .20
2 Terry McDaniel .02 .10
3 Steve Young .30 .75
4 Jerry Rice .40 1.00
5 Donnell Woolford .02 .10
6 Eric Allen .02 .10
7 Herschel Walker .07 .20
8 Barry Sanders .80 2.00
9 Herman Moore .10 .30
10 Emmitt Smith .60 1.50
11 Michael Irvin .10 .30
12 John Elway .80 2.00
13 Jim Kelly .10 .30
14 Andre Reed .07 .20
15 Gary Brown .02 .10
16 Ernest Givins .02 .10
17 Barry Foster .07 .20
18 Rod Woodson .07 .20
19 Warren Moon .10 .30
20 Cris Carter .10 .30
21 Rodney Hampton .07 .20
22 Derrick Thomas .07 .20
23 Marcus Allen .10 .30
24 Shannon Sharpe .07 .20
25 Cody Carlson .02 .10
26 Haywood Jeffires .02 .10
27 Randall Cunningham .10 .30
28 Calvin Williams .02 .10
29 Brett Favre .80 2.00
30 Sterling Sharpe .07 .20
31 Chris Zorich .02 .10
32 Dante Jones .02 .10
33 Mike Sherrard .02 .10
34 Keith Hamilton .02 .10
35 Charles Haley .02 .10
36 Thurman Thomas .10 .30
37 Bruce Smith .07 .20
38 Greg Lloyd .02 .10
39 Michael Brooks .02 .10
40 Jumbo Elliott .02 .10
41 Ray Childress .02 .10
42 Bruce Matthews .02 .10
43 Ricky Watters .07 .20
44 Brent Jones .07 .20
45 Morten Andersen .02 .10
46 Tim Brown .10 .30
47 Anthony Smith .02 .10
48 Natrone Means .10 .30
49 Rickey Jackson .02 .10
50 Joe Montana .80 2.00
51 Neil Smith .07 .20
52 Dan Marino .80 2.00
53 Keith Jackson .02 .10
54 Troy Aikman .40 1.00
55 Jay Novacek .07 .20
56 Junior Seau .07 .20
57 John Taylor .07 .20
58 Tim McDonald .02 .10
59 John Randle .07 .20
60 Henry Thomas .02 .10
61 Meredith .10 .30
Cosell
Gifford
62 Meredith .10 .30
Cosell
63 Meredith .10 .30
Cosell
Gifford
64 Howard Cosell ANN .10 .30
65 Meredith .10 .30
Cosell
Gifford
66 Keith Jackson ANN .02 .10
67 Don Meredith ANN .10 .30
68 Howard Cosell ANN .10 .30
69 Chris Hinton .02 .10
70 Brent Musburger ANN .02 .10
71 Lynn Swann ANN .07 .20

1994 Action Packed Monday Night Football Silver

This 12-card standard-size set was randomly inserted in packs at the rate of 1:96. Other than Howard Cosell, all the players featured play offense. In addition to these cards, 25 certificates for a sterling silver card of Dallas Cowboy stars Troy Aikman, Michael Irvin and Emmitt Smith were included in packs at the rate of 1:60,000 packs.

COMPLETE SET (12) 120.00 300.00
1S Steve Young 10.00 25.00
2S Jerry Rice 12.00 30.00
3S Barry Sanders 20.00 50.00
4S Emmitt Smith 16.00 40.00
5S John Elway 20.00 50.00
6S Jim Kelly 6.00 15.00
7S Warren Moon 6.00 15.00
8S Randall Cunningham 6.00 15.00
9S Brett Favre 20.00 50.00
10S Dan Marino 20.00 50.00
11S Troy Aikman 12.00 30.00
12S Howard Cosell 6.00 15.00

1995 Action Packed Monday Night Football Promos

Wrapped in a cello pack, this four-card standard-size set was issued to preview the design of the 1995 Action Packed ABC MNF series. The set features two regular cards, one "Night Flights" insert card, and an ad card. The cards are identical to their regular issue counterparts, except for the word "Promo" stamped in yellow block lettering on their backs.

1 Steve Young .80 2.00
3A Troy Aikman 1.20 3.00
3B Drew Bledsoe 1.20 3.00
NNO NMFB Ad Card .20 .50

1995 Action Packed Monday Night Football

This 126-card standard size set was issued by Pinnacle Brands. A parallel set was also inserted called Highlights. Rookie Cards include Ki-Jana Carter, Kerry Collins, Joey Galloway, Steve McNair, Rashaan Salaam, Kordell Stewert, J.J. Stokes and Michael Westbrook in the subset "The Night is Young".

COMPLETE SET (126) 10.00 15.00
1 Jerry Rice .40 1.00
2 Barry Sanders .75 2.00
3 Troy Aikman .40 1.00
4 Jerome Bettis .08 .25
5 Tim Brown .08 .25
6 Marcus Allen .08 .25
7 Jeff Blake RC .30 .75
8 Rodney Hampton .05 .15
9 Reggie White .08 .25
10 Warren Moon .08 .25
11 William Floyd .02 .10
12 Cris Carter .08 .25
13 Stan Humphries .05 .15
14 Herschel Walker .05 .15
15 Dave Brown .02 .10
16 Jim Everett .02 .10
17 Mario Bates .05 .15
18 Terance Mathis .02 .10
19 Chris Spielman .02 .10
20 Neil O'Donnell .05 .15
21 Anthony Miller .02 .10
22 Steve Bono .05 .15
23 Henry Ellard .02 .10
24 Dave Meggett .02 .10
25 Flipper Anderson .02 .10
26 Rocket Ismail .05 .15
27 Leroy Hoard .02 .10
28 Steve Young .30 .75
29 Marshall Faulk .20 .50
30 Dan Marino .75 2.00
31 Errict Rhett .05 .15
32 Michael Irvin .08 .25
33 Byron Bam Morris .02 .10
34 Heath Shuler .05 .15
35 Jim Kelly .08 .25
36 Deion Sanders .25 .60
37 Jeff Hostetler .05 .15
38 Jeff George .08 .25
39 Alvin Harper .02 .10
40 Barry Foster .02 .10
41 Craig Erickson .02 .10
42 Vinny Testaverde .05 .15
43 Andre Reed .05 .15
44 Eric Green .02 .10
45 Bruce Smith .05 .15
46 Frank Reich .02 .10
47 Shannon Sharpe .05 .15
48 Chris Miller .02 .10
49 Darnay Scott .05 .15
50 Eric Metcalf .05 .15
51 Mike Sherrard .02 .10
52 Lorenzo White .02 .10
53 Scott Mitchell .05 .15
54 Jay Novacek .02 .10
55 Emmitt Smith .60 1.50
56 Drew Bledsoe .40 1.00
57 Natrone Means .05 .15
58 John Elway .75 2.00
59 Herman Moore .20 .50
60 Brett Favre .75 2.00
61 Ricky Watters .05 .15
62 Andre Rison .05 .15
63 Junior Seau .05 .15
64 Randall Cunningham .08 .25
65 Chris Warren .05 .15
66 Garrison Hearst .08 .25
67 Ben Coates .05 .15
68 Rick Mirer .05 .15
69 Johnny Mitchell .02 .10
70 Trent Dilfer .08 .25
71 Carl Pickens .05 .15
72 Craig Heyward .02 .10
73 Greg Lloyd .02 .10
74 Boomer Esiason .05 .15
75 Greg Hill .02 .10
76 Lewis Tillman .02 .10
77 Willie Davis .02 .10
78 Brent Jones .02 .10
79 Michael Haynes .02 .10
80 Daryl Johnston .05 .15
81 Steve Beuerlein .05 .15
82 Ki-Jana Carter NY RC .08 .25
83 Steve McNair NY RC .75 2.00
84 Michael Westbrook NY RC .40 1.00
85 Kerry Collins NY RC 1.00 2.50
86 Joey Galloway NY RC .50 1.25
87 Kyle Brady NY RC .08 .25
88 J.J. Stokes NY RC .30 .75
89 Tyrone Wheatley NY RC .40 1.00
90 Rashaan Salaam NY RC .08 .25
91 Napoleon Kaufman NY RC .40 1.00
92 Frank Sanders NY RC .30 .75
93 Stoney Case NY RC .02 .10
94 Todd Collins NY RC .50 1.25
95 James O. Stewart NY RC .50 1.25
96 Kordell Stewart NY RC .60 1.50
97 Joe Aska NY .05 .15
98 Terrell Fletcher NY RC .02 .10
99 Rob Johnson NY RC .40 1.00
100 Steve Young C .15 .40
101 Jerry Rice C .20 .50
102 Emmitt Smith C .40 1.00
103 Barry Sanders C .40 1.00
104 Marshall Faulk C .15 .40
105 Drew Bledsoe C .20 .50
106 Dan Marino C .40 1.00
107 Troy Aikman C .20 .50
108 John Elway C .40 1.00
109 Brett Favre C .40 1.00
110 Michael Irvin C .08 .25
111 Heath Shuler C .05 .15
112 Warren Moon C .08 .25
113 Chris Warren C .05 .15
114 Natrone Means C .05 .15
115 Errict Rhett C .05 .15
116 Byron Bam Morris C .02 .10
117 Randall Cunningham C .08 .25
118 Jim Kelly C .08 .25
119 Jeff Hostetler C .02 .10
120 Barry Foster C .02 .10
121 Jim Everett C .05 .15
122 Neil O'Donnell C .05 .15
123 Jerome Bettis C .08 .25
124 Ricky Watters C .05 .15
125 Joe Montana C .75 2.00
126 Rodney Hampton C .05 .15

1995 Action Packed Monday Night Football Highlights

COMP.HIGHLIGHTS (126) 60.00 150.00
*HIGHLIGHTS STARS: 3X TO 8X
*HIGHLIGHTS RCs: 1.2X TO 3X

1995 Action Packed Monday Night Football 24K Gold

This horizontal 12 card set was randomly inserted at a rate of one in 72 packs. The fronts feature two shots of the player, one being the basic photo and the other using the same image enlarged in the background. The cards are printed on rainbow holographic foil with a "24KT Team" logo running vertically along the left side of the card, the player's name written horizontally along the lower right hand side and the Action Packed 24KT Gold logo on the lower left side. The backs have a single photo running vertically with statistical information about the player.

COMPLETE SET (12) 125.00 300.00
1 Emmitt Smith 15.00 40.00
2 Barry Sanders 20.00 50.00
3 Marshall Faulk 7.50 20.00
4 Dan Marino 20.00 50.00
5 Steve Young 10.00 25.00
6 Drew Bledsoe 10.00 25.00
7 Troy Aikman 12.50 30.00
8 John Elway 20.00 50.00
9 Brett Favre 25.00 50.00
10 Ki-Jana Carter 4.00 10.00
11 Steve McNair 12.50 30.00
12 Kerry Collins 8.00 20.00

1995 Action Packed Monday Night Football Night Flight

This 12 card set was randomly inserted into packs at a rate of one in 48. It features 12 members of the NFL Quarterback Club with a rainbow holographic background. The card fronts are vertical with the player's name running along the left side of the card and the "Night Flights" logo in the bottom center. The card backs are horizontal with the player's photo on the left side and his name running over the photo. A brief summary of the player is listed on the right side.

COMPLETE SET (12) 45.00 60.00
1 Steve Young 2.00 5.00
2 Dan Marino 5.00 12.00
3 Drew Bledsoe 2.00 5.00
4 Troy Aikman 2.50 6.00
5 John Elway 5.00 12.00
6 Brett Favre 5.00 12.00
7 Heath Shuler .75 2.00
8 Dave Brown .75 2.00
9 Steve McNair 2.50 6.00
10 Kerry Collins 2.00 5.00
11 Warren Moon 1.25 3.00
12 Jeff Hostetler .75 2.00

1995 Action Packed Monday Night Football Reverse Angle

This 18 card set was randomly inserted into hobby packs at a rate of one in 24. The set focuses on top stars making unusual plays. The card fronts show the player on the right side of the card, with the "Reverse Angle" logo located in the top left corner and the player's name running vertically along the same side. The card backs are very similar to the fronts with the name running vertically on the left side, the shot of the player located at the bottom and information on the player above the photo. Reportedly, fewer than 1500 sets were made.

COMPLETE SET (18) 30.00 60.00
1 Emmitt Smith 3.00 8.00
2 Barry Sanders 4.00 10.00
3 Steve Young 1.50 4.00
4 Marshall Faulk 1.25 3.00
5 Randall Cunningham 1.00 2.50
6 Deion Sanders 1.25 3.00
7 John Elway 4.00 10.00
8 Brett Favre 4.00 10.00
9 William Floyd .60 1.50
10 Ricky Watters 1.00 2.50
11 Ben Coates .60 1.50
12 Rod Woodson .60 1.50
13 Marcus Allen 1.00 2.50
14 Eric Metcalf .60 1.50
15 Keith Byars .60 1.50
16 Jerry Rice 2.00 5.00
17 Alvin Harper .60 1.50
18 Eric Green .60 1.50

1995 Action Packed Rookies/Stars Prototypes

This four-card set was produced to promote the release of the 1995 Action Packed Rookies/Stars release. Each of the three player cards is essentially a parallel of the base issue with the word 'prototype' stamped on the back.

12 Barry Sanders 1.00 2.50
18 Dan Marino 1.00 2.50
38 Troy Aikman .60 1.50
NNO Ad Card .20 .50

1995 Action Packed Rookies/Stars

This 105-card standard size set was issued by Pinnacle Brands. The fronts display full-bleed, embossed color action photos, with the player's name and team logo running along the bottom of the card. The Action Packed Rookies and Stars logo is located in the top left hand corner. The horizontal backs feature season and career statistics, a player photo as well as biographical information. A parallel set called Stargazers was also inserted into packs. Rookie Cards include Ki-Jana Carter, Kerry Collins, Joey Galloway, Curtis Martin, Steve McNair, Rashaan Salaam, Kordell Stewert, J.J. Stokes and Michael Westbrook.

COMPLETE SET (105) 7.50 20.00
1 Steve Young .50 1.25
2 Steve Bono .08 .25
3 Natrone Means .08 .25
4 Steve Beuerlein .08 .25
5 Neil O'Donnell .08 .25
6 Marshall Faulk .75 2.00
7 Ricky Watters .08 .25
8 Gary Brown .02 .10
9 Jeff Hostetler .08 .25
10 Robert Brooks .20 .50
11 Johnny Mitchell .02 .10
12 Barry Sanders 1.00 2.50
13 Dave Brown .08 .25
14 John Elway 1.25 3.00
15 Garrison Hearst .20 .50
16 Jim Everett .02 .10
17 Michael Irvin .20 .50
18 Dan Marino 1.25 3.00
19 Jeff George .08 .25
20 Ben Coates .08 .25
21 Charles Johnson .08 .25
22 Carl Pickens .08 .25
23 Deion Sanders .40 1.00
24 Errict Rhett .08 .25
25 Steve Walsh .02 .10
26 Bruce Smith .20 .50
27 Andre Rison .08 .25
28 Warren Moon .08 .25
29 Terry Allen .08 .25
30 Desmond Howard .08 .25
31 Shannon Sharpe .08 .25
32 Dave Krieg .02 .10
33 Byron Bam Morris .02 .10
34 Rodney Hampton .08 .25
35 Scott Mitchell .08 .25
36 Alvin Harper .02 .10
37 Robert Smith .20 .50
38 Troy Aikman .60 1.50
39 William Floyd .08 .25
40 Randall Cunningham .20 .50
41 Mario Bates .08 .25
42 Reggie White .20 .50
43 Chris Chandler .08 .25
44 Erik Kramer .02 .10
45 Emmitt Smith 1.00 2.50
46 Irving Fryar .08 .25
47 Jeff Blake RC .30 .75
48 Drew Bledsoe .40 1.00
49 Anthony Miller .08 .25
50 Marcus Allen .20 .50
51 Leroy Hoard .02 .10
52 Stan Humphries .08 .25
53 Eric Green .02 .10
54 Herschel Walker .08 .25
55 Junior Seau .20 .50
56 Terance Mathis .08 .25
57 Boomer Esiason .08 .25
58 Lorenzo White .02 .10
59 Tim Brown .20 .50
60 Brett Favre 1.25 3.00
61 Craig Erickson .02 .10
62 Rod Woodson .08 .25
63 Frank Reich .02 .10
64 Cris Carter .20 .50
65 Jerry Rice .60 1.50
66 Greg Hill .08 .25
67 Andre Reed .08 .25
68 Trent Dilfer .20 .50
69 Eric Metcalf .08 .25
70 Jim Kelly .20 .50
71 Herman Moore .20 .50
72 Vinny Testaverde .08 .25
73 Jeff Graham .02 .10
74 Edgar Bennett .08 .25
75 Jerome Bettis .20 .50
76 Heath Shuler .08 .25
77 Chris Warren .08 .25
78 Reggie Brooks .08 .25
79 Rick Mirer .08 .25
80 Chris Miller .02 .10
81 Napoleon Kaufman RC .50 1.25
82 Christian Fauria RC .08 .25
83 Todd Collins RC .60 1.50
84 J.J. Stokes RC .20 .50
85 Mark Bruener RC .08 .25
86 Frank Sanders RC .20 .50
87 Chad May RC .02 .10
88 Kordell Stewart RC .60 1.50
89 Ki-Jana Carter RC .20 .50
90 Curtis Martin RC 1.25 3.00
91 Sherman Williams RC .02 .10
92 Terrell Davis RC 1.00 2.50
93 Chris Sanders RC .08 .25
94 Kyle Brady RC .20 .50
95 Tyrone Wheatley RC .50 1.25
96 Rodney Thomas RC .08 .25
97 James O. Stewart RC .50 1.25
98 Kerry Collins RC 1.00 2.50
99 Rashaan Salaam RC .08 .25
100 Stoney Case RC .02 .10
101 Steve McNair RC 1.25 3.00
102 Joey Galloway RC .60 1.50
103 Michael Westbrook RC .20 .50
104 Eric Zeier RC .20 .50
105 Ray Zellars RC .08 .25

1995 Action Packed Rookies/Stars Stargazers

COMPLETE SET (105) 80.00 200.00
*STARS: 5X TO 12X BASIC CARDS
*RCs: 3X TO 8X BASIC CARDS
STATED ODDS 1:6

1995 Action Packed Rookies/Stars 24K Gold

This 14 card set was randomly inserted into packs at a rate of one in 72 packs. The card fronts feature a shot of the player with the player's name and the "24KT Gold Team" phrase listed vertically along the right hand side of the card. The fronts utilize a "prime frost" technology along the right hand side with a black background on the left. The card backs are horizontal with a player shot and brief commentary.

COMPLETE SET (14) 150.00 300.00
STATED ODDS 1:72
1 Steve Young 8.00 20.00
2 Brett Favre 20.00 50.00
3 Rashaan Salaam 1.25 3.00
4 Tyrone Wheatley 6.00 15.00
5 Marshall Faulk 12.50 30.00
6 Rick Mirer 1.50 4.00
7 Troy Aikman 10.00 25.00
8 John Elway 20.00 50.00
9 Dan Marino 20.00 50.00
10 Barry Sanders 15.00 40.00
11 Jerry Rice 10.00 25.00
12 Emmitt Smith 15.00 40.00
13 Michael Irvin 3.00 8.00
14 Drew Bledsoe 6.00 15.00

1995 Action Packed Rookies/Stars Bustout

This 12 card set was randomly inserted into jumbo packs only. The fronts feature a silver foil etched design in the background with a shot of the player over it. The player's name is listed vertically along the right side of the card with the "Bustout '95" logo under it. The card backs feature a player shot, brief commentary and the player's name and team logo on the left side of the card.

COMPLETE SET (12) 25.00 50.00
STATED ODDS 1:12
1 Marshall Faulk 6.00 12.00
2 Barry Sanders 8.00 15.00
3 Emmitt Smith 8.00 15.00
4 Natrone Means .75 1.50
5 Errict Rhett .75 1.50
6 Byron Bam Morris .25 .60
7 Terry Allen .75 1.50
8 Rodney Hampton .75 1.50
9 Ricky Watters .75 1.50
10 Chris Warren .75 1.50
11 Jerome Bettis 1.50 3.00
12 Gary Brown .25 .60

1995 Action Packed Rookies/Stars Closing Seconds

This 12 card set was randomly inserted into hobby packs only at a rate of one in 36. The fronts have two photos of the player, one in the foreground and the other shadowed behind it. The fronts are printed with rainbow holographic foil and have the player's name in the top left corner with the "Closing Seconds" logo running horizontally along the bottom. The vertical backs feature a shot of the player with his name, position and team located directly underneath along with a short commentary running to the left of the player.

COMPLETE SET (12) 60.00 120.00
STATED ODDS 1:36 HOB
1 Dan Marino 12.50 25.00
2 Steve Young 5.00 10.00
3 Jerry Rice 6.00 12.00
4 Emmitt Smith 10.00 20.00
5 Barry Sanders 10.00 20.00
6 Brett Favre 12.50 25.00
7 Drew Bledsoe 4.00 8.00
8 Troy Aikman 6.00 12.00
9 John Elway 12.50 25.00
10 Dave Brown 1.00 2.00
11 Warren Moon 1.00 2.00
12 Jim Kelly 2.00 4.00

1995 Action Packed Rookies/Stars Instant Impressions

This 12 card set was randomly inserted into packs at a rate of one in 24. The cards utilize a silver "micro-etched" technology. The fronts contain a player shot with his name written in script along the bottom of the card and the "Instant Impressions" logo located in the upper left hand corner. The horizontal backs feature a shot of the player along the right side of the card with a brief commentary located to the left. The player's name runs vertically along the left side of the card on a red background.

COMPLETE SET (12) 30.00 60.00
STATED ODDS 1:24
1 Ki-Jana Carter 1.00 2.00
2 Steve McNair 6.00 12.00
3 Kerry Collins 3.00 8.00
4 Michael Westbrook 1.00 2.00
5 Joey Galloway 3.00 6.00
6 J.J. Stokes 1.00 2.00
7 Rashaan Salaam .40 1.00
8 Tyrone Wheatley 2.50 5.00
9 Eric Zeier 1.00 2.00
10 Curtis Martin 6.00 12.00
11 Napoleon Kaufman 2.50 5.00
12 Kyle Brady 1.00 2.00

2010 Adrenalyn XL

1 Adrian Wilson .15 .40
2 Andre Roberts RC .50 1.25
3 Anthony Becht .15 .40
4 Chris Wells .15 .40
5 Clark Haggans .15 .40
6 Darnell Dockett .15 .40
7 Dominique Rodgers-Cromartie .15 .40
8 Joey Porter .15 .40
9 Larry Fitzgerald .20 .50
10 Matt Leinart .15 .40
11 Steve Breaston .15 .40
12 Tim Hightower .15 .40
13 Curtis Lofton .15 .40
14 Erik Coleman .15 .40
15 Jason Snelling .20 .50
16 Jerious Norwood .15 .40
17 John Abraham .15 .40
18 Jonathan Babineaux .15 .40
19 Matt Ryan .20 .50
20 Michael Jenkins .15 .40
21 Michael Turner .15 .40
22 Mike Peterson .15 .40
23 Roddy White .15 .40
24 Tony Gonzalez .20 .50
25 Anquan Boldin .15 .40
26 Dawan Landry .15 .40
27 Derrick Mason .15 .40
28 Ed Reed .20 .50
29 Joe Flacco .20 .50
30 Mark Clayton .15 .40
31 Ray Lewis .25 .60
32 Ray Rice .15 .40
33 Terrell Suggs .15 .40
34 Todd Heap .15 .40
35 Trevor Pryce .15 .40
36 Willis McGahee .15 .40
37 Aaron Schobel .15 .40
38 Bryan Scott .15 .40
39 C.J. Spiller RC .40 1.00
40 Derek Schouman .15 .40
41 Fred Jackson .20 .50
42 George Wilson .15 .40
43 Jairus Byrd .20 .50
44 James Hardy .15 .40
45 Kyle Williams .15 .40
46 Lee Evans .20 .50
47 Marcus Stroud .15 .40
48 Marshawn Lynch .20 .50
49 Paul Posluszny .15 .40
50 Trent Edwards .15 .40
51 Brandon LaFell RC .60 1.50
52 Charles Godfrey .15 .40
53 Chris Gamble .15 .40
54 Dante Rosario .15 .40
55 DeAngelo Williams .15 .40
56 James Anderson .15 .40
57 Jimmy Clausen RC .40 1.00
58 Jon Beason .15 .40
59 Jonathan Stewart .15 .40
60 Matt Moore .15 .40
61 Richard Marshall .15 .40
62 Steve Smith .20 .50
63 Tyler Brayton .15 .40
64 Brian Urlacher .25 .60
65 Charles Tillman .20 .50
66 Chester Taylor .15 .40
67 Danieal Manning .15 .40
68 Devin Hester .20 .50
69 Earl Bennett .20 .50
70 Greg Olsen .20 .50
71 Hunter Hillenmeyer .15 .40
72 Jay Cutler .15 .40
73 Johnny Knox .15 .40
74 Julius Peppers .20 .50
75 Lance Briggs .20 .50
76 Matt Forte .15 .40
77 Zack Bowman .15 .40
78 Antonio Bryant .15 .40
79 Antwan Odom .15 .40
80 Bernard Scott .15 .40
81 Carson Palmer .20 .50
82 Cedric Benson .15 .40
83 Dhani Jones .15 .40
84 Jermaine Gresham RC .40 1.00
85 Chad Ochocinco .15 .40
86 Johnathan Joseph .15 .40
87 Jordan Shipley RC .40 1.00
88 Keith Rivers .15 .40
89 Leon Hall .15 .40
90 Rey Maualuga .15 .40
91 Roy Williams S .15 .40
92 Abram Elam RC .25 .60
93 Ben Watson .15 .40
94 Colt McCoy RC .50 1.25
95 D'Qwell Jackson .15 .40
96 Eric Barton .15 .40
97 Eric Wright .15 .40
98 Jake Delhomme .15 .40
99 Jerome Harrison .15 .40
100 Josh Cribbs .15 .40
101 Mohamed Massaquoi .20 .50
102 Montario Hardesty RC .40 1.00
103 Sheldon Brown .15 .40
104 Anthony Spencer .15 .40
105 Bradie James .15 .40
106 DeMarcus Ware .20 .50
107 Dez Bryant RC 1.00 2.50
108 Felix Jones .15 .40
109 Jason Witten .20 .50
110 Keith Brooking .15 .40
111 Marion Barber .20 .50
112 Mike Jenkins .15 .40
113 Miles Austin .15 .40
114 Roy Williams WR .15 .40
115 Tony Romo .20 .50
116 Andre Goodman .15 .40
117 Brandon Stokley .15 .40
118 Brian Dawkins .15 .40
119 Champ Bailey .20 .50
120 D.J. Williams .15 .40
121 Daniel Graham .15 .40
122 Demaryius Thomas RC 1.00 2.50
123 Eddie Royal .15 .40
124 Elvis Dumervil .15 .40
125 Knowshon Moreno .15 .40
126 Kyle Orton .15 .40
127 Mario Haggan .15 .40
128 Renaldo Hill .15 .40
129 Tim Tebow RC 5.00 12.00
130 Brandon Pettigrew .15 .40
131 Bryant Johnson .15 .40
132 Calvin Johnson .25 .60
133 Cliff Avril .15 .40
134 DeAndre Levy .15 .40
135 Jahvid Best RC .40 1.00
136 Kevin Smith .15 .40
137 Kyle Vanden Bosch .15 .40
138 Louis Delmas .15 .40
139 Marvin White .15 .40
140 Matthew Stafford .20 .50
141 Nate Burleson .15 .40
142 Ndamukong Suh RC .75 2.00
143 A.J. Hawk .15 .40
144 Aaron Rodgers .50 1.25
145 Brandon Jackson .15 .40
146 Charles Woodson .25 .60
147 Clay Matthews .25 .60
148 Donald Driver .20 .50
149 Greg Jennings .15 .40
150 Jermichael Finley .15 .40
151 Jordy Nelson .20 .50
152 Nick Barnett .15 .40
153 Nick Collins .15 .40
154 Ryan Grant .20 .50
155 Andre Davis .15 .40
156 Andre Johnson .20 .50
157 Ben Tate RC .40 1.00
158 Brian Cushing .15 .40
159 DeMeco Ryans .15 .40
160 Glover Quin .15 .40
161 Kareem Jackson RC .40 1.00
162 Kevin Walter .20 .50
163 Mario Williams .20 .50
164 Matt Schaub .15 .40
165 Owen Daniels .15 .40
166 Steve Slaton .15 .40
167 Anthony Gonzalez .15 .40
168 Antoine Bethea .15 .40
169 Austin Collie .15 .40
170 Bob Sanders .20 .50
171 Clint Session .15 .40
172 Dallas Clark .15 .40
173 Donald Brown .15 .40
174 Dwight Freeney .15 .40
175 Joseph Addai .15 .40
176 Peyton Manning .60 1.50
177 Reggie Wayne .20 .50
178 Robert Mathis .15 .40
179 Aaron Kampman .20 .50
180 Daryl Smith .15 .40
181 David Garrard .15 .40
182 Derek Cox .15 .40
183 Derrick Harvey .15 .40
184 Gerald Alexander .15 .40
185 Justin Durant .15 .40
186 Marcedes Lewis .15 .40
187 Maurice Jones-Drew .15 .40
188 Mike Sims-Walker .15 .40
189 Mike Thomas .20 .50
190 Rashad Jennings .15 .40
191 Rashean Mathis .15 .40
192 Troy Williamson .15 .40
193 Brandon Flowers .15 .40
194 Chris Chambers .15 .40
195 Demorrio Williams .15 .40
196 Dexter McCluster RC .50 1.25
197 Dwayne Bowe .20 .50
198 Eric Berry RC .60 1.50
199 Glenn Dorsey .15 .40
200 Jamaal Charles .20 .50
201 Leonard Pope .15 .40
202 Matt Cassel .15 .40
203 Mike Vrabel .15 .40
204 Tamba Hali .15 .40
205 Thomas Jones .15 .40
206 Anthony Fasano .15 .40
207 Brandon Marshall .20 .50
208 Chad Henne .20 .50
209 Channing Crowder .15 .40
210 Davone Bess .15 .40
211 Greg Camarillo .15 .40
212 Karlos Dansby .15 .40
213 Ricky Williams .20 .50
214 Ronnie Brown .15 .40
215 Vontae Davis .15 .40
216 Yeremiah Bell .15 .40
217 Adrian Peterson .25 .60
218 Antoine Winfield .15 .40
219 Bernard Berrian .15 .40
220 Brett Favre 1.50 4.00
221 Cedric Griffin .15 .40
222 E.J. Henderson .15 .40
223 Jared Allen .15 .40
224 Percy Harvin .15 .40
225 Sidney Rice .15 .40
226 Toby Gerhart RC .40 1.00
227 Visanthe Shiancoe .20 .50
228 Devin McCourty RC .50 1.25
229 Jerod Mayo .20 .50
230 Julian Edelman .25 .60
231 Laurence Maroney .15 .40
232 Randy Moss .20 .50
233 Rob Gronkowski RC 1.25 3.00
234 Sammy Morris .15 .40
235 Tom Brady .60 1.50
236 Ty Warren .15 .40
237 Vince Wilfork .15 .40
238 Wes Welker .20 .50
239 Alex Brown .15 .40
240 Devery Henderson .15 .40
241 Drew Brees .25 .60
242 Jeremy Shockey .15 .40
243 Jonathan Vilma .15 .40
244 Lance Moore .15 .40
245 Marques Colston .15 .40
246 Pierre Thomas .15 .40
247 Reggie Bush .15 .40
248 Roman Harper .15 .40
249 Scott Shanle .15 .40
250 Tracy Porter .15 .40
251 Ahmad Bradshaw .15 .40
252 Antrel Rolle .15 .40
253 Brandon Jacobs .15 .40
254 Eli Manning .20 .50
255 Hakeem Nicks .15 .40
256 Justin Tuck .15 .40
257 Kevin Boss .15 .40
258 Mario Manningham .15 .40
259 Mathias Kiwanuka .15 .40
260 Michael Boley .15 .40
261 Usi Umenyiora .15 .40
262 Steve Smith USC .15 .40
263 Terrell Thomas .15 .40
264 Antonio Cromartie .15 .40
265 Bart Scott .15 .40
266 Braylon Edwards .15 .40
267 Darrelle Revis .15 .40
268 Dustin Keller .15 .40
269 Jerricho Cotchery .15 .40
270 Jim Leonhard .15 .40
271 Kris Jenkins .15 .40
272 LaDainian Tomlinson .25 .60
273 Mark Sanchez .15 .40
274 Santonio Holmes .15 .40
275 Shaun Ellis .15 .40
276 Shonn Greene .15 .40
277 Bruce Gradkowski .15 .40
278 Chaz Schilens .15 .40
279 Darren McFadden .15 .40
280 Darrius Heyward-Bey .20 .50
281 Kamerion Wimbley .15 .40
282 Kirk Morrison .15 .40
283 Louis Murphy .15 .40
284 Michael Bush .15 .40
285 Nnamdi Asomugha .15 .40
286 Richard Seymour .15 .40
287 Rolando McClain RC .40 1.00
288 Tyvon Branch .15 .40
289 Zach Miller .15 .40
290 Brent Celek .15 .40
291 DeSean Jackson .20 .50
292 Ellis Hobbs .15 .40
293 Hank Baskett .15 .40
294 Jeremy Maclin .15 .40
295 Kevin Kolb .15 .40
296 LeSean McCoy .25 .60
297 Michael Vick .20 .50
298 Mike Patterson .15 .40
299 Quintin Mikell .15 .40
300 Stewart Bradley .15 .40
301 Antwaan Randle El .15 .40
302 Ben Roethlisberger .25 .60
303 Brett Keisel .20 .50
304 Bryant McFadden .15 .40
305 Heath Miller .15 .40
306 Hines Ward .20 .50
307 James Farrior .15 .40
308 James Harrison .25 .60
309 Mewelde Moore .15 .40
310 Mike Wallace .15 .40
311 Rashard Mendenhall .15 .40
312 Troy Polamalu .25 .60
313 William Gay .15 .40
314 Antonio Gates .20 .50
315 Darren Sproles .20 .50
316 Eric Weddle .15 .40
317 Kevin Ellison .15 .40
318 Legedu Naanee .15 .40
319 Malcom Floyd .15 .40
320 Philip Rivers .25 .60
321 Quentin Jammer .15 .40
322 Ryan Mathews RC .40 1.00
323 Shaun Phillips .15 .40
324 Shawne Merriman .15 .40
325 Stephen Cooper .15 .40
326 Vincent Jackson .15 .40
327 Alex Smith QB .20 .50
328 Dashon Goldson .15 .40
329 Frank Gore .20 .50
330 Glen Coffee .15 .40
331 Josh Morgan .20 .50
332 Manny Lawson .15 .40
333 Michael Crabtree .15 .40
334 Michael Lewis .15 .40
335 Patrick Willis .20 .50
336 Takeo Spikes .15 .40
337 Vernon Davis .15 .40
338 Aaron Curry .20 .50
339 Colin Cole RC .15 .40
340 Deion Branch .15 .40
341 Golden Tate RC .50 1.25
342 John Carlson .15 .40
343 Josh Wilson .15 .40
344 Julius Jones .15 .40
345 Justin Forsett .20 .50
346 Lofa Tatupu .15 .40
347 Marcus Trufant .15 .40
348 Matt Hasselbeck .15 .40
349 T.J. Houshmandzadeh .15 .40
350 Chris Long .15 .40
351 Daniel Fells RC .60 1.50
352 Danny Amendola .25 .60
353 Donnie Avery .15 .40
354 James Butler .15 .40
355 James Laurinaitis .20 .50
356 Kenneth Darby .15 .40
357 Leonard Little .15 .40
358 Mardy Gilyard RC .40 1.00
359 Oshiomogho Atogwe .15 .40
360 Ron Bartell .15 .40
361 Sam Bradford RC .50 1.25
362 Steven Jackson .15 .40
363 Aqib Talib .15 .40
364 Arrelious Benn RC .40 1.00
365 Barrett Ruud .15 .40
366 Cadillac Williams .15 .40
367 Derrick Ward .15 .40
368 Earnest Graham .15 .40
369 Geno Hayes .15 .40
370 Gerald McCoy RC .40 1.00
371 Josh Freeman .20 .50
372 Kellen Winslow Jr. .15 .40
373 Michael Clayton .15 .40
374 Ronde Barber .15 .40
375 Tanard Jackson .15 .40
376 Bo Scaife .15 .40
377 Chris Hope .15 .40
378 Chris Johnson .15 .40
379 Cortland Finnegan .15 .40
380 Javon Ringer .15 .40
381 Justin Gage .15 .40
382 Kenny Britt .15 .40
383 Michael Griffin .15 .40
384 Nate Washington .15 .40
385 Stephen Tulloch .15 .40
386 Vince Young .15 .40
387 William Hayes .15 .40
388 Albert Haynesworth .15 .40
389 Brian Orakpo .15 .40
390 Chris Cooley .15 .40
391 Clinton Portis .15 .40
392 DeAngelo Hall .15 .40
393 Devin Thomas .15 .40
394 Donovan McNabb .20 .50
395 LaRon Landry .15 .40
396 Larry Johnson .15 .40
397 London Fletcher .20 .50
398 Willie Parker .15 .40
399 Reed Doughty .15 .40
400 Santana Moss .20 .50

2010 Adrenalyn XL Extra

STATED ODDS 1:8 BOOSTER
E1 Adrian Wilson 1.00 2.50
E2 Tony Gonzalez 1.25 3.00
E3 Joe Flacco 1.25 3.00
E4 Paul Posluszny 1.00 2.50
E5 Jon Beason 1.00 2.50
E6 Matt Forte 1.00 2.50
E7 Cedric Benson 1.00 2.50
E8 Jerome Harrison 1.00 2.50
E9 Jason Witten 1.25 3.00
E10 Brian Dawkins 1.00 2.50
E11 Kevin Smith 1.00 2.50
E12 Greg Jennings 1.00 2.50
E13 Mario Williams 1.25 3.00
E14 Dallas Clark 1.00 2.50
E15 Mike Sims-Walker 1.00 2.50
E16 Thomas Jones 1.00 2.50
E17 Ricky Williams 1.25 3.00
E18 Jared Allen 1.00 2.50
E19 Wes Welker 1.25 3.00
E20 Marques Colston 1.00 2.50
E21 Justin Tuck 1.00 2.50
E22 Santonio Holmes 1.00 2.50
E23 Richard Seymour 1.00 2.50
E24 Kevin Kolb 1.00 2.50
E25 Ben Roethlisberger 1.50 4.00
E26 Shawne Merriman 1.00 2.50
E27 Vernon Davis 1.00 2.50
E28 Julius Jones 1.00 2.50
E29 Donnie Avery 1.00 2.50
E30 Kellen Winslow Jr. 1.00 2.50
E31 Kenny Britt 1.00 2.50
E32 Clinton Portis 1.00 2.50

2010 Adrenalyn XL Extra Signature

STATED ODDS 1:8 BOOSTER
ES1 Tim Hightower 2.00 5.00
ES2 Michael Turner 2.00 5.00
ES3 Anquan Boldin 2.00 5.00
ES4 Fred Jackson 2.50 6.00
ES5 DeAngelo Williams 2.00 5.00
ES6 Brian Urlacher 3.00 8.00
ES7 Chad Ochocinco 2.00 5.00
ES8 Mohamed Massaquoi 2.50 6.00
ES9 DeMarcus Ware 2.50 6.00
ES10 Knowshon Moreno 2.00 5.00
ES11 Matthew Stafford 2.50 6.00
ES12 Charles Woodson 3.00 8.00
ES13 Matt Schaub 2.00 5.00
ES14 Reggie Wayne 2.50 6.00
ES15 David Garrard 2.00 5.00
ES16 Dwayne Bowe 2.50 6.00
ES17 Ronnie Brown 2.00 5.00
ES18 Brett Favre 6.00 15.00
ES19 Randy Moss 2.50 6.00
ES20 Reggie Bush 2.00 5.00
ES21 Brandon Jacobs 2.00 5.00
ES22 Darrelle Revis 2.00 5.00
ES23 Nnamdi Asomugha 2.00 5.00
ES24 LeSean McCoy 3.00 8.00
ES25 Troy Polamalu 3.00 8.00
ES26 Antonio Gates 2.50 6.00
ES27 Frank Gore 2.50 6.00
ES28 Matt Hasselbeck 2.00 5.00
ES29 James Laurinaitis 2.50 6.00
ES30 Cadillac Williams 2.00 5.00
ES31 Vince Young 2.00 5.00
ES32 Albert Haynesworth 2.00 5.00

2010 Adrenalyn XL Special

STATED ODDS 1:2 BOOSTER
S1 Joey Porter .50 1.25
S2 Matt Leinart .50 1.25
S3 John Abraham .50 1.25
S4 Roddy White .50 1.25
S5 Ed Reed .60 1.50
S6 Ray Rice .50 1.25
S7 Aaron Schobel .50 1.25
S8 Lee Evans .60 1.50
S9 Jonathan Stewart .50 1.25
S10 Matt Moore .50 1.25
S11 Devin Hester .60 1.50
S12 Julius Peppers .60 1.50
S13 Dhani Jones .50 1.25
S14 Rey Maualuga .50 1.25

S15 Jake Delhomme .50 1.25
S16 Sheldon Brown .50 1.25
S17 Marion Barber .60 1.50
S18 Miles Austin .50 1.25
S19 Elvis Dumervil .50 1.25
S20 Kyle Orton .50 1.25
S21 Julian Peterson .50 1.25
S22 Nate Burleson .50 1.25
S23 A.J. Hawk .50 1.25
S24 Ryan Grant .60 1.50
S25 DeMeco Ryans .50 1.25
S26 Steve Slaton .50 1.25
S27 Dwight Freeney .50 1.25
S28 Joseph Addai .50 1.25
S29 Aaron Kampman .60 1.50
S30 Rashean Mathis .50 1.25
S31 Demorrio Williams .50 1.25
S32 Jamaal Charles .60 1.50
S33 Karlos Dansby .50 1.25
S34 Vontae Davis .50 1.25
S35 Percy Harvin .50 1.25
S36 Sidney Rice .50 1.25
S37 Jerod Mayo .60 1.50
S38 Vince Wilfork .50 1.25
S39 Jeremy Shockey .50 1.25
S40 Jonathan Vilma .50 1.25
S41 Kevin Boss .50 1.25
S42 Mathias Kiwanuka .50 1.25
S43 LaDainian Tomlinson .75 2.00
S44 Shonn Greene .50 1.25
S45 Darrius Heyward-Bey .60 1.50
S46 Zach Miller .50 1.25
S47 Brent Celek .50 1.25
S48 Jeremy Maclin .50 1.25
S49 James Harrison .75 2.00
S50 Rashard Mendenhall .50 1.25
S51 Darren Sproles .60 1.50
S52 Vincent Jackson .50 1.25
S53 Alex Smith QB .60 1.50
S54 Michael Crabtree .50 1.25
S55 Jordan Babineaux .50 1.25
S56 Lofa Tatupu .50 1.25
S57 Chris Long .50 1.25
S58 Sam Bradford .50 1.25
S59 Michael Clayton .50 1.25
S60 Ronde Barber .50 1.25
S61 Cortland Finnegan .50 1.25
S62 Justin Gage .50 1.25
S63 London Fletcher .60 1.50
S64 Santana Moss .60 1.50

2010 Adrenalyn XL Ultimate Signature

STATED ODDS 1:23 BOOSTER
U1 Larry Fitzgerald 2.50 6.00
U2 Matt Ryan 2.50 6.00
U3 Ray Lewis 3.00 8.00
U4 Trent Edwards 2.00 5.00
U5 Steve Smith 2.50 6.00
U6 Jay Cutler 2.00 5.00
U7 Carson Palmer 2.50 6.00
U8 Josh Cribbs 2.00 5.00
U9 Tony Romo 2.50 6.00
U10 Champ Bailey 2.50 6.00
U11 Calvin Johnson 3.00 8.00
U12 Aaron Rodgers 6.00 15.00
U13 Andre Johnson 2.50 6.00
U14 Peyton Manning 8.00 20.00
U15 Maurice Jones-Drew 2.00 5.00
U16 Matt Cassel 2.00 5.00
U17 Brandon Marshall 2.50 6.00
U18 Adrian Peterson 3.00 8.00
U19 Tom Brady 8.00 20.00
U20 Drew Brees 3.00 8.00
U21 Eli Manning 2.50 6.00
U22 Mark Sanchez 2.00 5.00
U23 Darren McFadden 2.00 5.00
U24 DeSean Jackson 2.50 6.00
U25 Hines Ward 2.50 6.00
U26 Philip Rivers 3.00 8.00
U27 Patrick Willis 2.50 6.00
U28 T.J. Houshmandzadeh 2.00 5.00
U29 Steven Jackson 2.00 5.00
U30 Josh Freeman 2.50 6.00
U31 Chris Johnson 2.00 5.00
U32 Donovan McNabb 2.50 6.00

2011 Adrenalyn XL Super Bowl XLV Promos

These two cards were released at the 2011 Super Bowl Card Show in Dallas as part of a wrapper redemption program at the Panini booth.
1 Dez Bryant 5.00 12.00
2 Tim Tebow 5.00 12.00

2011 Adrenalyn XL

1 Adrian Wilson .15 .40
2 Beanie Wells .15 .40
3 Darnell Dockett .15 .40
4 Jay Feely .15 .40
5 Kevin Kolb .15 .40
6 Larry Fitzgerald .20 .50
7 Paris Lenon .15 .40
8 Patrick Peterson RC .75 2.00
9 Ryan Williams RC .40 1.00
10 Todd Heap .15 .40
11 Brent Grimes RC .40 1.00
12 Curtis Lofton .15 .40
13 John Abraham .15 .40
14 Julio Jones RC 1.25 3.00
15 Matt Bryant RC .40 1.00
16 Matt Ryan .20 .50
17 Michael Turner .15 .40
18 Ray Edwards .15 .40
19 Roddy White .15 .40
20 Tony Gonzalez .20 .50
21 Anquan Boldin .15 .40
22 Billy Cundiff .15 .40
23 Ed Reed .20 .50
24 Haloti Ngata .15 .40
25 Joe Flacco .20 .50
26 Ray Lewis .25 .60
27 Ray Rice .15 .40
28 Ricky Williams .20 .50
29 Terrell Suggs .15 .40
30 Torrey Smith RC .40 1.00
31 C.J. Spiller .15 .40
32 Donald Jones .15 .40
33 Fred Jackson .15 .40
34 Jairus Byrd .15 .40
35 Marcell Dareus RC .40 1.00
36 Rian Lindell .15 .40
37 Ryan Fitzpatrick .15 .40
38 Shawne Merriman .15 .40
39 Steve Johnson .15 .40
40 Terrence McGee .15 .40
41 Cam Newton RC 2.00 5.00
42 Charles Johnson .15 .40
43 Chris Gamble .15 .40
44 DeAngelo Williams .15 .40
45 Greg Olsen .20 .50
46 James Anderson .15 .40
47 Jon Beason .15 .40
48 Jonathan Stewart .15 .40
49 Olindo Mare .15 .40
50 Steve Smith .20 .50
51 Brian Urlacher .25 .60
52 Charles Tillman .20 .50
53 Devin Hester .20 .50
54 Jay Cutler .15 .40
55 Johnny Knox .15 .40
56 Julius Peppers .20 .50
57 Lance Briggs .20 .50
58 Marion Barber .15 .40
59 Matt Forte .15 .40
60 Robbie Gould .15 .40
61 A.J. Green RC 1.00 2.50
62 Andy Dalton RC .75 2.00
63 Cedric Benson .15 .40
64 Jermaine Gresham .15 .40
65 Jordan Shipley .15 .40
66 Keith Rivers .15 .40
67 Leon Hall .15 .40
68 Mike Nugent .15 .40
69 Reggie Nelson .15 .40
70 Rey Maualuga .15 .40
71 Ben Watson .15 .40
72 Colt McCoy .15 .40
73 D'Qwell Jackson .15 .40
74 Jabaal Sheard RC .40 1.00
75 Joe Haden .15 .40
76 Josh Cribbs .15 .40
77 Mohamed Massaquoi .15 .40
78 Peyton Hillis .15 .40
79 Phil Dawson .15 .40
80 T.J. Ward .15 .40
81 Anthony Spencer .15 .40
82 David Buehler RC .40 1.00
83 DeMarcus Ware .20 .50
84 Dez Bryant .25 .60
85 Felix Jones .15 .40
86 Jason Witten .20 .50
87 Jay Ratliff .20 .50
88 Mike Jenkins .15 .40
89 Miles Austin .15 .40
90 Tony Romo .20 .50
91 Brandon Lloyd .15 .40
92 Brian Dawkins .15 .40
93 Champ Bailey .20 .50
94 Elvis Dumervil .15 .40
95 Knowshon Moreno .15 .40
96 Kyle Orton .15 .40
97 Matt Prater RC 8.00 20.00
98 Tim Tebow .25 .60
99 Von Miller RC .60 1.50
100 Willis McGahee .15 .40
101 Brandon Pettigrew .15 .40
102 Calvin Johnson .25 .60
103 Jahvid Best .15 .40
104 Jason Hanson .15 .40
105 Louis Delmas .15 .40
106 Matthew Stafford .20 .50
107 Ndamukong Suh .20 .50
108 Nick Fairley RC .40 1.00
109 Stephen Tulloch .15 .40
110 Titus Young RC .40 1.00
111 Aaron Rodgers .40 1.00
112 A.J. Hawk .15 .40
113 Charles Woodson .25 .60
114 Clay Matthews .25 .60
115 Donald Driver .20 .50
116 Greg Jennings .15 .40
117 Jermichael Finley .15 .40
118 Mason Crosby .15 .40
119 Nick Collins .15 .40
120 Ryan Grant .15 .40
121 Andre Johnson .20 .50
122 Arian Foster .15 .40
123 Brian Cushing .15 .40
124 DeMeco Ryans .15 .40
125 Johnathan Joseph .15 .40
126 Kevin Walter .15 .40
127 Mario Williams .15 .40
128 Matt Schaub .15 .40
129 Neil Rackers .15 .40
130 Owen Daniels .15 .40
131 Adam Vinatieri .15 .40
132 Antoine Bethea .15 .40
133 Dallas Clark .15 .40
134 Dwight Freeney .15 .40
135 Ernie Sims .15 .40
136 Joseph Addai .15 .40
137 Peyton Manning .50 1.25
138 Pierre Garcon .20 .50
139 Reggie Wayne .20 .50
140 Robert Mathis .15 .40
141 Aaron Kampman .20 .50
142 Blaine Gabbert RC .40 1.00
143 Luke McCown .15 .40
144 Dawan Landry .15 .40
145 Josh Scobee .15 .40
146 Marcedes Lewis .15 .40
147 Maurice Jones-Drew .15 .40
148 Mike Thomas .20 .50
149 Paul Posluszny .15 .40
150 Rashean Mathis .15 .40
151 Brandon Flowers .15 .40
152 Dwayne Bowe .20 .50
153 Eric Berry .20 .50
154 Glenn Dorsey .15 .40
155 Jamaal Charles .20 .50
156 Jonathan Baldwin RC .40 1.00
157 Matt Cassel .15 .40
158 Ryan Succop .15 .40
159 Tamba Hali .15 .40
160 Thomas Jones .15 .40
161 Anthony Fasano .15 .40
162 Brandon Marshall .20 .50
163 Cameron Wake .20 .50
164 Chad Henne .20 .50
165 Dan Carpenter RC .40 1.00
166 Daniel Thomas RC .40 1.00
167 Karlos Dansby .15 .40
168 Reggie Bush .15 .40
169 Vontae Davis .15 .40
170 Yeremiah Bell .15 .40
171 Adrian Peterson .25 .60
172 Antoine Winfield .15 .40
173 Christian Ponder RC .40 1.00
174 Donovan McNabb .20 .50
175 E.J. Henderson .15 .40
176 Jared Allen .15 .40
177 Kevin Williams .15 .40
178 Percy Harvin .15 .40
179 Ryan Longwell .15 .40
180 Visanthe Shiancoe .20 .50
181 Aaron Hernandez .20 .50
182 Albert Haynesworth .15 .40
183 BenJarvus Green-Ellis .15 .40
184 Chad Ochocinco .15 .40
185 Devin McCourty .15 .40
186 Jerod Mayo .15 .40
187 Stephen Gostkowski .25 .60
188 Tom Brady .60 1.50
189 Vince Wilfork .15 .40
190 Wes Welker .20 .50
191 Cameron Jordan RC .50 1.25
192 Darren Sproles .20 .50
193 Drew Brees .25 .60
194 Garrett Hartley .15 .40
195 Jonathan Vilma .15 .40
196 Lance Moore .15 .40
197 Mark Ingram RC .60 1.50
198 Marques Colston .15 .40
199 Roman Harper .15 .40
200 Will Smith .15 .40
201 Ahmad Bradshaw .15 .40
202 Antrel Rolle .15 .40
203 Brandon Jacobs .15 .40
204 Eli Manning .20 .50
205 Hakeem Nicks .15 .40
206 Justin Tuck .15 .40
207 Lawrence Tynes .15 .40
208 Mario Manningham .15 .40
209 Michael Boley .15 .40
210 Terrell Thomas .15 .40
211 Antonio Cromartie .15 .40
212 Darrelle Revis .15 .40
213 David Harris .15 .40
214 Jim Leonhard .15 .40
215 LaDainian Tomlinson .25 .60
216 Mark Sanchez .15 .40
217 Nick Folk .15 .40
218 Plaxico Burress .15 .40
219 Santonio Holmes .15 .40
220 Shonn Greene .15 .40
221 Darren McFadden .15 .40
222 Jacoby Ford .20 .50
223 Jason Campbell .15 .40
224 Kevin Ross .15 .40
225 Louis Murphy .15 .40
226 Michael Huff .15 .40
227 Richard Seymour .15 .40
228 Rolando McClain .15 .40
229 Sebastian Janikowski .20 .50
230 Tyvon Branch .15 .40
231 Alex Henery RC .50 1.25
232 Brent Celek .15 .40
233 DeSean Jackson .20 .50
234 Dominique Rodgers-Cromartie .15 .40
235 Jason Babin .15 .40
236 Jeremy Maclin .15 .40
237 LeSean McCoy .25 .60
238 Michael Vick .20 .50
239 Nnamdi Asomugha .15 .40
240 Trent Cole .15 .40
241 Aaron Smith .15 .40
242 Ben Roethlisberger .25 .60
243 Heath Miller .15 .40
244 Hines Ward .20 .50
245 James Harrison .20 .50
246 LaMarr Woodley .15 .40
247 Mike Wallace .15 .40
248 Rashard Mendenhall .15 .40
249 Shaun Suisham .15 .40
250 Troy Polamalu .25 .60
251 Antonio Gates .15 .40
252 Bob Sanders .15 .40
253 Eric Weddle .15 .40
254 Mike Tolbert .15 .40
255 Nate Kaeding .15 .40
256 Philip Rivers .25 .60
257 Ryan Mathews .20 .50
258 Shaun Phillips .15 .40
259 Takeo Spikes .15 .40
260 Vincent Jackson .15 .40
261 Aldon Smith RC .40 1.00
262 Alex Smith QB .20 .50
263 Braylon Edwards .15 .40
264 Carlos Rogers .15 .40
265 David Akers .15 .40
266 Frank Gore .20 .50
267 Justin Smith .15 .40
268 Michael Crabtree .15 .40
269 Patrick Willis .20 .50
270 Vernon Davis .15 .40
271 Aaron Curry .15 .40
272 Chris Clemons .15 .40
273 David Hawthorne .15 .40
274 Jeff Reed .15 .40
275 Marcus Trufant .15 .40
276 Marshawn Lynch .20 .50
277 Mike Williams USC .15 .40
278 Sidney Rice .15 .40
279 Tarvaris Jackson .15 .40
280 Zach Miller .15 .40
281 Al Harris .15 .40
282 Chris Long .15 .40
283 Danny Amendola .20 .50
284 Donnie Avery .15 .40
285 James Laurinaitis .15 .40
286 Josh Brown .15 .40
287 Mike Sims-Walker .20 .50
288 Quintin Mikell .15 .40
289 Sam Bradford .15 .40
290 Steven Jackson .15 .40
291 Adrian Clayborn RC .40 1.00
292 Aqib Talib .15 .40
293 Arrelious Benn .15 .40
294 Connor Barth RC .40 1.00
295 Gerald McCoy .15 .40
296 Josh Freeman .20 .50
297 Kellen Winslow Jr. .15 .40
298 LeGarrette Blount .20 .50
299 Mike Williams .20 .50
300 Ronde Barber .15 .40
301 Barrett Ruud .15 .40
302 Chris Johnson .15 .40
303 Cortland Finnegan .15 .40
304 Jake Locker RC .40 1.00
305 Javon Ringer .15 .40
306 Kenny Britt .15 .40
307 Matt Hasselbeck .15 .40
308 Michael Griffin .15 .40
309 Rob Bironas .15 .40
310 Will Witherspoon .15 .40
311 Anthony Armstrong .20 .50
312 Brian Orakpo .20 .50
313 Chris Cooley .15 .40
314 DeAngelo Hall .15 .40
315 Graham Gano RC .40 1.00
316 LaRon Landry .15 .40
317 London Fletcher .20 .50
318 Rex Grossman .15 .40
319 Santana Moss .20 .50
320 Tim Hightower .15 .40

2011 Adrenalyn XL Extra

1 Kevin Kolb 1.00 2.50
2 Michael Turner 1.00 2.50
3 Ed Reed 1.25 3.00
4 Marcell Dareus .60 1.50
5 Cam Newton 3.00 8.00
6 Devin Hester 1.25 3.00
7 Keith Rivers 1.00 2.50
8 Josh Cribbs 1.00 2.50
9 Jason Witten 1.25 3.00
10 Knowshon Moreno 1.00 2.50
11 Matthew Stafford 1.25 3.00
12 Charles Woodson 1.50 4.00
13 Matt Schaub 1.00 2.50
14 Reggie Wayne 1.25 3.00
15 Luke McCown 1.00 2.50
16 Tamba Hali 1.00 2.50
17 Cameron Wake 1.25 3.00
18 Percy Harvin 1.00 2.50
19 Jerod Mayo 1.00 2.50
20 Jonathan Vilma 1.00 2.50
21 Justin Tuck 1.00 2.50
22 Santonio Holmes 1.00 2.50
23 Jacoby Ford 1.25 3.00
24 DeSean Jackson 1.25 3.00
25 James Harrison 1.25 3.00
26 Eric Weddle 1.00 2.50
27 Vernon Davis 1.00 2.50
28 Marshawn Lynch 1.25 3.00
29 Chris Long 1.00 2.50
30 Kellen Winslow Jr. 1.00 2.50
31 Barrett Ruud 1.00 2.50
32 Chris Cooley 1.00 2.50

2011 Adrenalyn XL Extra Signature

1 Adrian Wilson 2.00 5.00
2 Roddy White 2.00 5.00
3 Joe Flacco 2.50 6.00
4 Steve Johnson 2.00 5.00
5 Steve Smith 2.50 6.00
6 Julius Peppers 2.50 6.00
7 Cedric Benson 2.00 5.00
8 Colt McCoy 2.00 5.00
9 DeMarcus Ware 2.50 6.00
10 Champ Bailey 2.50 6.00
11 Ndamukong Suh 2.50 6.00
12 Clay Matthews 3.00 8.00
13 Arian Foster 2.00 5.00
14 Dwight Freeney 2.00 5.00
15 Paul Posluszny 2.00 5.00
16 Dwayne Bowe 2.50 6.00
17 Reggie Bush 2.00 5.00
18 Jared Allen 2.00 5.00
19 Wes Welker 2.50 6.00
20 Marques Colston 2.00 5.00
21 Hakeem Nicks 2.00 5.00
22 Mark Sanchez 2.00 5.00
23 Richard Seymour 2.00 5.00
24 Nnamdi Asomugha 2.00 5.00
25 Ben Roethlisberger 3.00 8.00
26 Antonio Gates 2.00 5.00
27 Frank Gore 2.50 6.00
28 Sidney Rice 2.00 5.00
29 Sam Bradford 2.00 5.00
30 Ronde Barber 2.00 5.00
31 Cortland Finnegan 2.00 5.00
32 London Fletcher 2.50 6.00

2011 Adrenalyn XL Special

1 Todd Heap .50 1.25
2 Curtis Lofton .50 1.25
3 Ray Rice .50 1.25
4 Fred Jackson .50 1.25
5 DeAngelo Williams .50 1.25
6 Jay Cutler .50 1.25
7 A.J. Green .75 2.00
8 Joe Haden .50 1.25
9 Dez Bryant .75 2.00
10 Elvis Dumervil .50 1.25
11 Jahvid Best .50 1.25
12 Greg Jennings .50 1.25
13 Mario Williams .50 1.25
14 Adam Vinatieri .50 1.25
15 Marcedes Lewis .50 1.25
16 Matt Cassel .50 1.25
17 Karlos Dansby .50 1.25
18 Visanthe Shiancoe .60 1.50
19 Aaron Hernandez .60 1.50
20 Mark Ingram .50 1.25
21 Ahmad Bradshaw .50 1.25
22 LaDainian Tomlinson .75 2.00
23 Sebastian Janikowski .60 1.50
24 LeSean McCoy .75 2.00
25 Hines Ward .60 1.50
26 Vincent Jackson .50 1.25
27 Michael Crabtree .50 1.25
28 Zach Miller .50 1.25
29 James Laurinaitis .50 1.25
30 LeGarrette Blount .60 1.50
31 Rob Bironas .50 1.25
32 Brian Orakpo .60 1.50

2011 Adrenalyn XL Ultimate Signature

1 Larry Fitzgerald 2.50 6.00
2 Matt Ryan 2.50 6.00
3 Ray Lewis 3.00 8.00
4 Ryan Fitzpatrick 2.00 5.00
5 Jon Beason 2.00 5.00
6 Brian Urlacher 3.00 8.00
7 Rey Maualuga 2.00 5.00
8 Peyton Hillis 2.00 5.00
9 Tony Romo 2.50 6.00
10 Brandon Lloyd 2.00 5.00
11 Calvin Johnson 3.00 8.00
12 Aaron Rodgers 5.00 12.00
13 Andre Johnson 2.50 6.00
14 Peyton Manning 6.00 15.00
15 Maurice Jones-Drew 2.00 5.00
16 Jamaal Charles 2.50 6.00
17 Brandon Marshall 2.50 6.00
18 Adrian Peterson 3.00 8.00
19 Tom Brady 8.00 20.00
20 Drew Brees 3.00 8.00
21 Eli Manning 2.50 6.00
22 Darrelle Revis 2.00 5.00
23 Darren McFadden 2.00 5.00
24 Michael Vick 2.50 6.00
25 Troy Polamalu 3.00 8.00
26 Philip Rivers 3.00 8.00
27 Patrick Willis 2.50 6.00
28 Aaron Curry 2.00 5.00
29 Steven Jackson 2.00 5.00
30 Josh Freeman 2.50 6.00
31 Chris Johnson 2.00 5.00
32 Santana Moss 2.50 6.00

1972 All Pro Graphics

These 8 1/2" by 10 1/2" color photos were produced by All Pro Graphics Inc. of Miami Florida. Each card carries an attractive color photo of the player with a facsimile signature on the front and the player's name above the photo. The cardbacks include biographical player information and carry the company name "Dimensional Sales Corporation, All Pro Graphics" all in lower case letters. Any additions to the checklist below are appreciated.
1 Buck Buchanan 7.50 15.00
2 Nick Buoniconti 7.50 15.00
3 Mike Curtis 6.00 12.00
4 Len Dawson 12.50 25.00
5 Mel Farr 5.00 10.00
6 Ted Hendricks 6.00 12.00
7 Leroy Kelly 7.50 15.00
8 Jim Kiick 6.00 12.00
9 Willie Lanier 6.00 12.00
10 Archie Manning 10.00 20.00
11 Earl Morrall 6.00 12.00
12 Steve Owens 6.00 12.00
13 Altie Taylor 5.00 10.00
14 Otis Taylor 6.00 12.00
15 Garo Yepremian 6.00 12.00

1973 All Pro Graphics

These 8" by 10" color photos were produced by All Pro Graphics Inc. of Miami Florida around 1973. Each blankbacked photo carries an attractive color photo of the player with a facsimile signature. Below the photo are the manufacturer's name on the left and the player's name on the right side. This list is thought to be incomplete as All Pro Graphics issued many photos in varying styles over a number of years. Any additions are appreciated.
1 John Brockington 6.00 12.00
2 Wally Chambers 5.00 10.00
3 Mike Curtis 6.00 12.00
4 Roman Gabriel 7.50 15.00
5 Joe Greene 12.00 20.00
6 John Hadl 7.50 15.00
7 Ron Johnson 5.00 10.00
8 Steve Owens 7.50 15.00
9 Alan Page 7.50 15.00
10 Jim Plunkett 7.50 15.00
11 Jan Stenerud 6.00 12.00

1991 All World Troy Aikman Promos

This set consists of six standard-size cards. The cards feature the same color action photo of Aikman, with ball cocked behind his head ready to pass. On the first three cards, the top of the photo is oval-shaped and framed by yellow stripes. The space above the oval as well as the stripe at the bottom carrying player information are purple. The outer border is green. Inside green borders, the horizontal back has a color close-up photo, biography (there were French, Spanish, and English versions), and statistics. On the second three cards listed below, the player photo is tilted slightly to the right and framed by a thin green border. Yellow stripes above and below the picture carry information, and the outer border is black-and-white speckled. The backs have a similar design and display a close-up color head shot and biographical and statistical information on a pastel green panel. All versions use the same color action photo, but differ in that the photo is cropped differently on the green-border cards compared to the speckled-border cards. All cards are numbered on the back as number 1.
COMPLETE SET (6) 6.00 15.00
COMMON CARD (1A-1F) 1.20 3.00

1992 All World

The 1992 All World NFL football set contains 300 standard-size cards. The production run was reported to be 8000 foil cases, but many collectors feel the actual print run number fell slightly short of 8000. There are 12 cards per foil pack and 26 per rack pack. Ten rookies and ten "Legends in the Making" cards, embossed with gold-foil stars, were randomly inserted in the foil packs. Likewise, autographed cards by Joe Namath (1,000), Jim Brown (1,000), and Desmond Howard (2,500) were inserted in both foil and rack packs. Although the player's name is not printed on the front, his autograph and number do appear. A special double-fold card (TR1) of the three autographed cards was inserted only in the rack packs. It is distinguished from the regular issue triple cards by foil-stamping. The regular card backs have a second color player photo, with player information (biography and player profile) in a horizontally oriented box alongside the picture. Topical subsets featured include Legends in the Making (1-10) and Greats of the Game (266-300). Rookie Cards include Edgar Bennett, Steve Bono, Terrell Buckley, Dale Carter, Marco Coleman, Quentin Coryatt, Vaughn Dunbar, Steve Emtman, Desmond Howard (AW had exclusive rights), Carl Pickens, and Tommy Vardell. A Desmond Howard promo card was released and is priced at the end of our checklist.
COMPLETE SET (300) 6.00 15.00
1 Emmitt Smith LM .25 .60
2 Thurman Thomas LM .02 .10
3 Deion Sanders LM .08 .25
4 Randall Cunningham LM .02 .10
5 Michael Irvin LM .02 .10
6 Bruce Smith LM .02 .10
7 Jeff George LM .02 .10
8 Derrick Thomas LM .02 .10
9 Andre Rison LM .08 .25
10 Troy Aikman LM .15 .40
11 Quentin Coryatt RC .01 .05
12 Carl Pickens RC .08 .25
13 Steve Emtman RC .01 .05
14 Derek Brown TE RC .01 .05
15 Desmond Howard RC .20 .50
16 Troy Vincent RC .01 .05
17 David Klingler RC .01 .05
18 Vaughn Dunbar RC .01 .05
19 Terrell Buckley RC .01 .05
20 Jimmy Smith RC 1.25 3.00
21 Marquez Pope RC .01 .05
22 Kurt Barber RC .01 .05
23 Robert Harris RC .01 .05
24 Tony Sacca RC .01 .05
25 Alonzo Spellman RC .02 .10
26 Shane Collins RC .01 .05
27 Chris Mims RC .01 .05
28 Siran Stacy RC .01 .05
29 Edgar Bennett RC .08 .25
30 Sean Gilbert RC .02 .10
31 Eugene Chung RC .01 .05
32 Levon Kirkland RC .01 .05
33 Chuck Smith RC .01 .05
34 Chester McGlockton RC .02 .10
35 Ashley Ambrose RC .08 .25
36 Phillippi Sparks RC .01 .05
37 Darryl Williams RC .01 .05
38 Tracy Scroggins RC .01 .05
39 Mike Gaddis RC .01 .05
40 Tony Brooks RC .01 .05
41 Steve Israel RC .01 .05
42 Patrick Rowe RC .01 .05
43 Shane Dronett RC .01 .05
44 Mike Pawlawski RC .01 .05
45 Dale Carter RC .02 .10
46 Tyji Armstrong RC .01 .05
47 Kevin Smith RC .01 .05
48 Courtney Hawkins RC .02 .10
49 Marco Coleman RC .01 .05
50 Tommy Vardell RC .01 .05
51 Ray Ethridge RC .01 .05
52 Robert Porcher RC .08 .25
53 Todd Collins RC .01 .05
54 Robert Jones RC .01 .05
55 Tommy Maddox RC .75 2.00
56 Dana Hall RC .01 .05
57 Leon Searcy RC .01 .05
58 Robert Brooks RC .30 .75
59 Darren Woodson RC .08 .25
60 Jeremy Lincoln RC .01 .05
61 Sean Jones .01 .05
62 Howie Long .08 .25
63 Rich Gannon .08 .25
64 Keith Byars .01 .05
65 John Taylor .02 .10
66 Burt Grossman .01 .05
67 Chris Hinton .01 .05
68 Brad Muster .01 .05
69 Cris Dishman .01 .05
70 Russell Maryland .01 .05
71 Harvey Williams .02 .10
72 Broderick Thomas .01 .05
73 Louis Lipps .01 .05
74 Erik Kramer .01 .05
75 David Fulcher .01 .05
76 Andre Tippett .01 .05
77 Timm Rosenbach .01 .05
78 Mark Rypien .01 .05
79 James Lofton .02 .10
80 Dan Saleaumua .01 .05
81 John L. Williams .01 .05
82 Kevin Fagan .01 .05
83 Flipper Anderson .01 .05
84 Michael Dean Perry .02 .10
85 Mark Higgs .01 .05
86 Pat Swilling .01 .05
87 Pierce Holt .01 .05
88 John Elway .50 1.25
89 Bill Brooks .02 .10
90 Rob Moore .02 .10
91 Junior Seau .08 .25
92 Wendell Davis .01 .05
93 Brian Noble .01 .05
94 Ernest Givins .02 .10
95 Phil Simms .02 .10
96 Eric Dickerson .02 .10
97 Bennie Blades .01 .05
98 Gary Anderson RB .01 .05
99 Erric Pegram .01 .05
100 Hart Lee Dykes .01 .05
101 Charles Haley .02 .10
102 Bruce Smith .08 .25
103 Nick Lowery .01 .05
104 Webster Slaughter .01 .05
105 Ray Childress .01 .05
106 Gene Atkins .01 .05
107 Bruce Armstrong .01 .05
108 Anthony Miller .08 .25
109 Eric Thomas .01 .05
110 Greg Townsend .01 .05
111 Anthony Carter .02 .10
112 James Hasty .01 .05
113 Chris Miller .01 .05
114 Sammie Smith .01 .05
115 Bubby Brister .02 .10
116 Mark Clayton .02 .10
117 Richard Johnson CB .01 .05
118 Bernie Kosar .02 .10
119 Lionel Washington .01 .05
120 Gary Clark .02 .10
121 Anthony Munoz .08 .25
122 Brent Jones .02 .10
123 Thurman Thomas .08 .25
124 Lee Williams .01 .05
125 Jessie Hester .01 .05
126 Andre Ware .02 .10
127 Patrick Hunter .01 .05
128 Erik Howard .01 .05
129 Keith Jackson .02 .10
130 Troy Aikman .30 .75
131 Mike Singletary .02 .10
132 Carnell Lake .01 .05
133 Jeff Hostetler .02 .10
134 Alonzo Highsmith .01 .05
135 Vaughan Johnson .01 .05
136 Louis Oliver .01 .05
137 Mel Gray .02 .10
138 Al Toon .02 .10
139 Bubba McDowell .01 .05
140 Ronnie Lott .02 .10
141 Deion Sanders .20 .50
142 Jim Harbaugh .08 .25
143 Gary Zimmerman .02 .10
144 Ernie Jones .01 .05
145 Cortez Kennedy .02 .10
146 Jeff Cross .01 .05
147 Floyd Turner UER .01 .05
148 Mike Tomczak .01 .05
149 Lorenzo White .01 .05
150 Mark Carrier DB .01 .05
151 John Stephens .01 .05
152 Jerry Rice .30 .75
153 Jim Kelly .08 .25
154 Al Smith .01 .05
155 Duane Bickett .01 .05
156 Brett Perriman .08 .25
157 Boomer Esiason .02 .10
158 Neil Smith .08 .25
159 Eddie Anderson .01 .05
160 Browning Nagle .01 .05
161 John Friesz .02 .10
162 Robert Delpino .01 .05
163 Darren Lewis .01 .05
164 Roger Craig .02 .10
165 Keith McCants .01 .05
166 Stephone Paige .01 .05
167 Steve Broussard .01 .05
168 Gaston Green .01 .05
169 Ethan Horton .01 .05
170 Lewis Billups .01 .05
171 Mike Merriweather .01 .05
172 Randall Cunningham .08 .25
173 Leonard Marshall .01 .05
174 Jay Novacek .02 .10
175 Irving Fryar .02 .10
176 Randal Hill .01 .05
177 Keith Henderson .01 .05
178 Brad Baxter .01 .05
179 William Fuller .01 .05
180 Leslie O'Neal .02 .10
181 Steve Smith .01 .05
182 Joe Montana .50 1.25
183 Eric Green .02 .10
184 Rodney Peete .02 .10
185 Lawrence Dawsey .02 .10
186 Brian Mitchell .02 .10
187 Rickey Jackson .01 .05
188 Christian Okoye .02 .10
189 David Wyman .01 .05
190 Jessie Tuggle .01 .05
191 Ronnie Harmon .01 .05
192 Andre Reed .08 .25
193 Chris Doleman .02 .10
194 Leroy Hoard .01 .05
195 Mark Ingram .01 .05
196 Willie Gault .02 .10
197 Eugene Lockhart .01 .05
198 Jim Everett .02 .10
199 Doug Smith .01 .05
200 Clarence Verdin .01 .05
201 Steve Bono RC .08 .25
202 Mark Vlasic .01 .05
203 Fred Barnett .02 .10
204 Henry Thomas .01 .05
205 Shaun Gayle .01 .05
206 Rod Bernstine .01 .05
207 Harold Green .02 .10
208 Dan McGwire .01 .05
209 Marv Cook .01 .05
210 Emmitt Smith .60 1.50
211 Merril Hoge .01 .05
212 Darion Conner .01 .05
213 Mike Sherrard .01 .05
214 Jeff George .08 .25
215 Craig Heyward .01 .05
216 Henry Ellard .02 .10
217 Lawrence Taylor .08 .25
218 Jerry Ball .01 .05
219 Tom Rathman .01 .05
220 Warren Moon .08 .25
221 Ricky Proehl .01 .05
222 Sterling Sharpe .08 .25
223 Earnest Byner .01 .05
224 Jay Schroeder .01 .05
225 Vance Johnson .01 .05
226 Cornelius Bennett .02 .10
227 Ken O'Brien .01 .05
228 Ferrell Edmunds .01 .05
229 Eric Allen .01 .05
230 Derrick Thomas .08 .25
231 Cris Carter .20 .50
232 Jon Vaughn .01 .05
233 Eric Metcalf .02 .10
234 William Perry .02 .10
235 Vinny Testaverde .02 .10
236 Chip Banks .01 .05
237 Brian Blades .02 .10
238 Calvin Williams .01 .05
239 Andre Rison .08 .25
240 Neil O'Donnell .02 .10
241 Michael Irvin .08 .25
242 Gary Plummer .01 .05
243 Nick Bell .01 .05
244 Ray Crockett .01 .05
245 Sam Mills .01 .05
246 Haywood Jeffires .01 .05
247 Steve Young .25 .60
248 Martin Bayless .01 .05
249 Dan Marino .50 1.25
250 Carl Banks .01 .05
251 Keith McKeller .01 .05
252 Aaron Wallace .01 .05
253 Lamar Lathon .01 .05
254 Derrick Fenner .01 .05
255 Vai Sikahema .01 .05
256 Keith Sims .01 .05
257 Rohn Stark .01 .05
258 Reggie Roby .01 .05
259 Tony Zendejas .01 .05
260 Harris Barton .01 .05
261 Checklist 1-100 .01 .05
262 Checklist 101-200 .01 .05
263 Checklist 201-300 .01 .05
264 Rookies Checklist .01 .05
265 Greats Checklist .01 .05
266 Joe Namath GG .08 .25
267 Joe Namath GG .08 .25
268 Joe Namath GG .08 .25
269 Joe Namath GG .08 .25
270 Joe Namath GG .08 .25
271 Jim Brown GG .08 .25
272 Jim Brown GG .08 .25
273 Jim Brown GG .08 .25
274 Jim Brown GG .08 .25
275 Jim Brown GG .08 .25
276 Vince Lombardi GG .08 .25
277 Jim Thorpe GG .01 .05
278 Tom Fears GG .01 .05
279 John Henry Johnson GG .01 .05
280 Gale Sayers GG .02 .10
281 Willie Brown GG .01 .05
282 Doak Walker GG .01 .05
283 Dick Lane GG .01 .05
284 Otto Graham GG .02 .10
285 Hugh McElhenny GG .01 .05
286 Roger Staubach GG .08 .25
287 Steve Largent GG .08 .25
288 Otis Taylor GG .01 .05
289 Sam Huff GG .01 .05
290 Harold Carmichael GG .01 .05
291 Steve Van Buren GG .01 .05
292 Gino Marchetti GG .01 .05
293 Tony Dorsett GG .02 .10
294 Leo Nomellini GG .01 .05
295 Jack Lambert GG .01 .05
296 Joe Theismann GG .02 .10
297 Bobby Layne GG .01 .05
298 John Stallworth GG .01 .05
299 Paul Hornung GG .02 .10
300 Don Maynard GG .01 .05
A1 Desmond Howard AU/1000 10.00 25.00
A2 Jim Brown AU/1000 25.00 50.00
A3 Joe Namath AU/1000 25.00 60.00
P1 Desmond Howard Promo .40 1.00
TRI D.Howard 1.25 3.00
J.Brown
Nam.

1992 All World Greats/Rookies

One of these 20 standard-size cards was inserted into every 1992 All World rack pack. Reportedly, 60,000 of each card were produced. The cards are numbered with an "SG" prefix.
COMPLETE SET (20) 4.00 10.00
ONE PER RACK PACK
SG1 Troy Aikman .75 2.00
SG2 Thurman Thomas .30 .75
SG3 Andre Rison .20 .50
SG4 Emmitt Smith 1.50 4.00
SG5 Derrick Thomas .30 .75
SG6 Joe Namath .30 .75
SG7 Jim Brown .30 .75
SG8 Roger Staubach .30 .75
SG9 Gale Sayers .20 .50
SG10 Jim Thorpe .20 .50
SG11 Quentin Coryatt .20 .50
SG12 Carl Pickens .30 .75
SG13 Steve Emtman .08 .25
SG14 Derek Brown TE .08 .25
SG15 Desmond Howard .30 .75
SG16 Troy Vincent .08 .25
SG17 David Klingler .20 .50
SG18 Vaughn Dunbar .08 .25
SG19 Terrell Buckley .08 .25
SG20 Jimmy Smith 1.25 3.00

1992 All World Legends/Rookies

Randomly inserted in the foil packs, this insert set consists of ten standard-size Legends in the Making cards (1-10) and ten Rookie (11-20) cards. Reportedly, 5000 of each card were produced. The cards were numbered with an "L" prefix.

COMPLETE SET (20) 15.00 35.00
RANDOM INSERTS IN FOIL PACKS
L1 Emmitt Smith 4.00 10.00
L2 Thurman Thomas .75 2.00
L3 Deion Sanders 1.25 3.00
L4 Randall Cunningham .75 2.00
L5 Michael Irvin .75 2.00
L6 Bruce Smith .40 1.00
L7 Jeff George .40 1.00
L8 Derrick Thomas .40 1.00
L9 Andre Rison .40 1.00
L10 Troy Aikman 2.00 5.00
L11 Quentin Coryatt .40 1.00
L12 Carl Pickens .75 2.00
L13 Steve Emtman .40 1.00
L14 Derek Brown TE .40 1.00
L15 Desmond Howard .40 1.00
L16 Troy Vincent .40 1.00
L17 David Klingler .40 1.00
L18 Vaughn Dunbar .40 1.00
L19 Terrell Buckley .40 1.00
L20 Jimmy Smith 2.50 6.00

1966 American Oil All-Pro

The 1966 American Oil All-Pro set featured 20 stamps, each measuring approximately 15/16" by 1 1/8". To participate in the contest, the consumer needed to acquire an 8 1/2" by 11" collection sheet from a participating American Oil dealer. This sheet is horizontally oriented and presents rules governing the contest as well as 20 slots in which to paste the stamps. The 20 slots are arranged in five rows in the shape of an inverted triangle (6, 5, 4, 3, and 2 stamps per row as one moves from top to bottom) with the prizes listed to the left of each row. The consumer also received envelopes from participating dealers that contained small sheets of three perforated player stamps each. Each 3-stamp sheet was numbered with a letter as noted below making some of the stamps known double prints. Each stamp features a color head shot with the player wearing his helmet. After separating the stamps, the consumer was instructed to paste them on the matching squares of the collection sheet. If all the stamps in a particular prize group row were collected, the consumer won that particular prize. Top prize for all six stamps in the top group was a 1967 Ford Mustang. The other prizes were $250, $25, $5, and $1 for five-, four-, three-, and two-stamp prize groups respectively. Prizes were to be redeemed within 15 days after the closing of the promotion, but no later than March 1, 1967 in any event. Complete three stamp panels carry a 50 percent premium. The stamps are blank backed and unnumbered, and have been checklisted below alphabetically. Wayne Walker and Tommy Nobis were required to win $1; Herb Adderley and Dave Parks and Lenny Moore were required to win $5; John Unitas and Dave Jones, Mick Tingelhoff, and Alex Karras were required to win $25; Dick Butkus and Charley Johnson, Gary Ballman, Frank Ryan, and Willie Davis were required to win $250; and Gary Collins and Tucker Frederickson, Pete Retzlaff, Sam Huff, Gale Sayers, and Bob Lilly were required to win the 1967 Mustang. The winner cards indicated below are not priced (and not considered necessary for a complete set) since each is thought to have been largely redeemed and very few sales have been reported on existing copies. A 3-stamp advertising strip (roughly 3 1/4" by 6 3/4") was also produced and listed below.
COMPLETE SET (15) 100.00 200.00
WRAPPER 3.00 8.00
1 Herb Adderley
2 Gary Ballman 5.00 12.00
3 Dick Butkus
4 Gary Collins
5 Willie Davis 6.00 15.00
6 Tucker Frederickson 5.00 12.00
7 Sam Huff 10.00 20.00
8 Charley Johnson C/L 6.00 15.00
9 Deacon Jones 8.00 20.00
10 Alex Karras 8.00 20.00
11 Bob Lilly 12.50 25.00
12 Lenny Moore 12.50 25.00
13 Tommy Nobis 6.00 15.00
14 Dave Parks 5.00 12.00
15 Pete Retzlaff 5.00 12.00
16 Frank Ryan 5.00 12.00
17 Gale Sayers 20.00 35.00
18 Mick Tingelhoff 6.00 15.00
19 Johnny Unitas
20 Wayne Walker 100.00 200.00
NNO Ad Strip 75.00 150.00
NNO Saver Sheet 50.00 100.00

1967 American Oil All-Pro

The 1967 American Oil All-Pro set featured 21-stamps with each measuring approximately 7/8" by 1 1/8". The contestant needed to acquire an 8 1/2" by 11" collection sheet from a participating American Oil dealer on which he would place the stamps. The sheet was arranged in five rows with the prize level listed above each row. Each 3-stamp sheet was numbered with a letter as noted below. The consumer received envelopes from participating dealers that contained sheets of two perforated player stamps and one Mustang car stamp. Note that the Jim Taylor sheet contained a "Service Award" stamp instead of a second player. If all stamps in a particular prize group were collected, the consumer won that particular prize: the grand prize of a 1968 Ford Mustang, $100, $25, $5, or $1 cash. The $1 prize could be won by acquiring the stamps of Johnny Morris, Tommy Nobis, and Jim Taylor. The $5 prize required the stamps of Timmy Brown, Jimmy Orr, Fran Tarkenton, and Brady Keys. The $25 prize required stamps of John Unitas, Bob Hayes, Bill Brown, and Junior Coffey. The $100 prize required Gary Collins, Sonny Jurgensen, Charley Johnson, Gale Sayers, and Merlin Olsen. To win the 1968 Mustang required stamps of Bart Starr, Wayne Walker, Charley Taylor, Larry Wilson, and Ken Willard. The "winning" player for each prize group is fairly scarce, (and not neccessary for a

complete set) since each is thought to have been largely redeemed. Each stamp front features a color action player photo. The stamps are blank-backed and unnumbered and have been checklisted below alphabetically.
COMPLETE SET (19) 350.00 600.00
1 Bill Brown F 15.00 30.00
2 Timmy Brown J 15.00 30.00
3 Junior Coffey H 15.00 30.00
4 Gary Collins E 15.00 30.00
5 Bob Hayes D 25.00 40.00
6 Charley Johnson J 15.00 30.00
7 Sonny Jurgensen B 30.00 50.00
8 Brady Keys B 15.00 30.00
9 Johnny Morris A/M/P 15.00 30.00
10 Tommy Nobis 60.00 100.00
($1 winner)
11 Merlin Olsen M/P 25.00 35.00
12 Jimmy Orr H 15.00 30.00
13 Gale Sayers 60.00 100.00
($100 winner)
14 Bart Starr A 60.00 100.00
15 Fran Tarkenton 30.00 50.00
($5 winner)
16 Charley Taylor E 20.00 35.00
17 Jim Taylor N 40.00 75.00
18 John Unitas
($25 winner)
19 Wayne Walker
(Winner 1968 Mustang)
20 Ken Willard F 15.00 30.00
21 Larry Wilson A/D 18.00 30.00
NNO Saver Sheet 50.00 100.00

1968 American Oil Mr. and Mrs.

This 32-card set was produced by Glendinning Companies and distributed by the American Oil Company. The cards measure approximately 2 1/8" by 3 7/16". The set is made up of 16 player cards and 16 wife/family cards that were originally connected by perforation in pairs. The cards were distributed as pieces of the "Mr. and Mrs. NFL" game. If a matched pair (i.e. a player card and his wife/family card) were obtained, the holder was an instant winner of either a 1969 Ford (choice of Mustang Mach I or Country Squire), $500, $100, $10, $5, $1, or 50-cents. The cards are most frequently found as detached halves. The horizontally oriented fronts feature action color player photos or color family photos featuring the wife. On the player card, the player's name is printed above the picture. On the wife card, the woman's married name (i.e. Mrs. Bobby Mitchell) and a caption defining the activity shown are above the picture. Each card is bordered in a different color and the prize corresponding to that card is printed in the border. The backs of the cards vary. In each pair that were originally connected, the wife card back features contest rules in a blue box on a red background with darker red car silhouettes. The player card back carries the game title (Mr. and Mrs. NFL), the American Oil Company logo, and the words "Win 1969 Fords and Cash" on the same background. In addition, attached to each pair at either end and forming a 12" strip, two more cardlike pieces contained further information and a game piece for predicting the 1969 Super Bowl scores. The smaller of the two (approximately 1 7/8" by 2 1/8") is printed with the NFL players and the corresponding prizes. The larger of the two (2 1/8" by 3 1/4") is the game piece for the second part of the contest with blanks for recording a score prediction for one NFL and one AFL team. This piece was mailed in to Super Bowl Scoreboard in New York. Each correct entry would share equally in the $100,000 Super Bowl Scoreboard cash prize. The cards are checklisted below alphabetically. The prize corresponding to each married couple is listed under the tougher of the pair. Prices listed are for single cards. Complete two-card panels are valued at approximately double the value of the individual cards. There are 16 tougher pieces that were the cards needed to win prizes. These 16 are not considered necessary for a complete set.
COMPLETE SET (16) 100.00 200.00
1 Kermit Alexander 250.00 400.00
2 Mrs. Kermit Alexander 6.00 12.00
3 Jim Bakken 6.00 12.00
4 Mrs. Jim Bakken 50.00 80.00
5 Gary Collins
6A Mrs. Gary Collins 6.00 12.00
6B Mrs. Gary Collins 6.00 12.00
Enjoying the Outdoors, pink frame
7 Jim Grabowski
8 Mrs. Jim Grabowski 6.00 12.00
9 Earl Gros 50.00 80.00
10 Mrs. Earl Gros 6.00 12.00
11 Deacon Jones 12.00 20.00
12 Mrs. Deacon Jones
13 Billy Lothridge
14 Mrs. Billy Lothridge 6.00 12.00
15 Tom Matte 10.00 15.00
16 Mrs. Tom Matte
17 Bobby Mitchell 90.00 150.00
18 Mrs. Bobby Mitchell 6.00 12.00
19 Joe Morrison 6.00 12.00
20 Mrs. Joe Morrison
21A Dave Osborn 6.00 12.00
21B Dave Osborn silver frame
22 Mrs. Dave Osborn
23 Dan Reeves 40.00 80.00
24 Mrs. Dan Reeves 6.00 12.00
25 Gale Sayers 25.00 40.00
26 Mrs. Gale Sayers
27 Norm Snead 60.00 100.00
28 Mrs. Norm Snead 6.00 12.00
29 Steve Stonebreaker 6.00 12.00
30 Mrs. Steve Stonebreaker 6.00 12.00
31 Wayne Walker 50.00 80.00
32 Mrs. Wayne Walker 6.00 12.00

1968 American Oil Winners Circle

This set of 12 perforated game cards measures approximately 2 5/8" by 2 1/8". There are "left side" and "right side" game cards which had to be matched to win a car or a cash prize. The "right side" game cards have a color drawing of a sports personality in a circle on the left, surrounded by laurel leaf twigs, and a short career summary on the right. There is a color bar on the bottom of the game piece carrying a dollar amount and the words "right side". The "left side" game cards carry a rectangular drawing of a sports personality or a photo of a Camaro or a Corvette. A different color bar with a dollar amount and the words "left side" are under the picture. On a dark blue background, the "right side" backs carry the rules of the game, and the "left side" cards show a "Winners Circle". The cards are unnumbered and checklisted below in alphabetical order.
COMPLETE SET (12) 75.00 150.00
11 Gale Sayers 7.50 15.00
Left side
12 Bart Starr 10.00 20.00
Right side

1961 American Tract Society

These cards are quite attractive and feature the "pure card" concept that is always popular with collectors (no card borders simply pure photo on front). The cards are numbered on the back and are skip-numbered below due to the fact that these singles are part of a much larger (sport and non-sport) set. The issue features Christian ballplayers giving first-person testimonies on the cardbacks describing how Jesus has changed their lives. These cards are often referred to as "Tracards." Each measures approximately 2 3/4" X 3 1/2". Many of the baseball subjects contain variations. No known variations exist for the football cards.
21 Donn Moomaw 10.00 20.00
50 Joe Romig 10.00 20.00

1992 Americana

COMPLETE SET (250) 8.00 20.00
UNOPENED BOX (36 PACKS) 15.00 25.00
UNOPENED PACK (12 CARDS) .75 1.00
COMMON CARD (1-250) .12 .30

2012 Americana Heroes and Legends Historical Items

STATED PRINT RUN 12-299
NO PRICING ON CARDS #'d UNDER 25
3 Jim Thorpe/25 100.00 175.00

2012 Americana Heroes and Legends Summer/Winter Games

COMPLETE SET (30) 20.00 50.00
18 Jim Thorpe 1.50 4.00

2012 Americana Heroes and Legends Summer/Winter Games Materials

STATED PRINT RUN 25-499
18 Jim Thorpe/25

1994 AmeriVox Quarterback Legends Phone Cards

This set of 5-phone cards was issued by AmeriVox mounted on a large cardboard backer. The backer contained brief information about each player and was serial numbered of 2000-sets produced. The cards themselves feature artist's renderings of the player along with the QB Legends logo. Each carried an initial phone time value of $10.
COMPLETE SET (5) 15.00 25.00
1 George Blanda 3.00 6.00
2 Len Dawson 3.00 5.00
3 Otto Graham 4.00 8.00
4 Bob Griese 3.00 5.00
5 Sonny Jurgensen 3.00 5.00

1993 Anti-Gambling Postcards

COMPLETE SET (13) 6.00 15.00
9 Jim Kelly FB 1.00 2.50
10 Bernie Kosar FB .60 1.50

1987 A Question of Sport UK

These cards are part of a British board game "A Question of Sport" in which participants attempt to name an athlete by seeing a picture of them. These white bordered, full color cards measure 2 1/4" by 3 1/2" and have a back that contains only the player's name on a green background. The copyright on the box is 1986, but the game was released in early 1987. We've arranged the unnumbered cards alphabetically below.
COMPLETE SET (240) 20.00 40.00
69 Eric Dickerson .40 1.00
84 John Elway 1.50 4.00
155 Dan Marino 1.50 4.00
163 Joe Montana 2.00 5.00
166 Joe Morris .40 1.00

1992 A Question of Sport UK

These cards are part of a British board game "A Question of Sport" in which participants attempt to name an athlete by seeing a picture of them. These white bordered, full color cards measure 2 1/4" by 3 1/2" and have a back that contains only the player's name. We've arranged the unnumbered cards alphabetically below.
COMPLETE SET (80) 20.00 50.00
54 Joe Montana 2.00 5.00

1994 A Question of Sport UK

These cards are part of a British board game "A Question of Sport" in which participants attempt to name an athlete by seeing a picture of them. These white bordered, full color cards measure 2 1/4" by 3 1/2" and have a back that contains only the player's name surrounded by a blue border on white card stock. We've arranged the unnumbered cards alphabetically below.
COMPLETE SET (79) 20.00 50.00
46 Dan Marino 2.00 5.00
48 Joe Montana 2.00 5.00
58 Jerry Rice 1.50 4.00

1991 Arena Holograms

The 1991 Arena Hologram cards were distributed through hobby dealers and feature famous athletes. According to Arena, production quantities were limited to 250,000 of each card. The standard-size hologram cards have on the horozontially oriented backs a color photo of the player in a tuxedo. Ken Griffey Jr. Frank Thomas, David Robinson, Joe Montana and Barry Sanders all signed cards with each being serial numbered by hand. A card-sized certificate of authenticity was also issued with each signed card.
COMPLETE SET (5) 3.20 8.00
1 Joe Montana .80 2.00
4 Barry Sanders .60 1.50
AU4 Barry Sanders AU/2500 40.00 80.00
AU6 Joe Montana AU/2500 40.00 80.00

1991 Arena Holograms 12th National

These standard-size cards have on their fronts a 3-D silver-colored emblem on a white background with orange borders. Though the back of each card salutes a different superstar, the players themselves are not pictured; instead, one finds pictures of a football; hockey stick and puck; basketball; and baseball in glove respectively. The cards are numbered on the front.
COMPLETE SET (4) 4.00 10.00
1 Joe Montana 1.25 3.00

1992 Arena Holograms

The 1992 Arena Hologram Joe Montana card is very much like the 1991 release. The cardbacks are essentially the same except for the card number (1 versus 1A) and the print run; 99,000 for the 1992 card. The photo on the '92 card shows Montana against a background image of the Golden Gate Bridge.
1A Joe Montana 1.25 3.00

1998 Arizona Rattlers AFL

This set was sponsored by Elete Cards, Inc. and features members of the Arizona Rattlers of the Arena Football League. Each card includes the team name and player name running vertically on the left hand side of the front along with a color player photo. The cardbacks are also printed in color and feature another player photo and a player bio.
COMPLETE SET (27) 15.00 30.00
1 Darrin Kenney .50 1.25
2 Tom Gibson .50 1.25
3 Bryan Hooks .50 1.25
4 Barry Voorhees .50 1.25
5 Junior Green .50 1.25
6 Tony Henderson .50 1.25
7 Marvin Bagley .50 1.25
8 Flint Fleming .50 1.25
9 Sherdrick Bonner .60 1.50
10 Hunkie Cooper .50 1.25
11 Randy Gatewood .50 1.25
12 Bob McMillen .50 1.25
13 Shawn Parnell .50 1.25
14 Calvin Schexnayder .50 1.25
15 Bo Kelly .50 1.25
16 Donnie Davis .50 1.25
17 Cedric Walker .50 1.25
18 Cecil Doggette .50 1.25
19 Mark Tucker .50 1.25
20 Herb Duncan .50 1.25
21 Joe Burch .50 1.25
22 Craig Ritter .50 1.25
23 Tim Watson .50 1.25
24 Brian Easter .50 1.25
25 Danny White CO/GM 1.25 3.00
26 Jayme Washel .50 1.25
27 Cedric Tillman .50 1.25

1984 Arizona Wranglers Carl's Jr.

This ten-card USFL set was sponsored by Carl's Jr. Restaurants and distributed by the local police department in Tempe, Arizona. The cards measure approximately 2 1/2" by 3 5/8". On the front, the company logo and name appears in the lower right hand corner, and the USFL logo in the lower left hand corner. These emblems and the team name "Arizona Wranglers" on the top are in red print. The black and white posed photo in the middle has the player's name and position below in black ink. The back includes biographical information and an advertisement for Carl's Jr. Restaurants. The cards are listed below alphabetically, with the jersey number after the player's name.
COMPLETE SET (10) 50.00 80.00
1 George Allen CO 15.00 40.00
2 Luther Bradley 27 2.00 5.00
3 Trumaine Johnson 2 2.00 5.00
4 Greg Landry 11 6.00 15.00
5 Kit Lathrop 70 2.00 5.00
6 John Lee 64 2.00 5.00
7 Keith Long 33 2.00 5.00
8 Alan Risher 7 2.00 5.00
9 Tim Spencer 46 3.00 8.00
10 Lenny Willis 89 2.00 5.00

1984 Arizona Wranglers Team Sheets

These eight (approximately) 8" by 10" glossy, horizontally oriented sheets feature the 1984 Arizona Wranglers of the USFL. Each sheet features two rows of four black-and-white photos each, with player identification printed immediately beneath the picture. The team and USFL logos fill out the bottom corners. The backs are blank. Each sheet is numbered at the bottom in the middle "X of 8."
COMPLETE SET (8) 30.00 60.00
1 Edward Diethrich PRES 5.00 12.00
2 Clay Brown 3.00 8.00
3 Larry Douglas 3.00 8.00
4 Dave Huffman/ 4.00 10.00
5 Kit Lathrop 3.00 8.00
6 Tom Piette 2.00 5.00
7 Robert Smith 5.00 12.00
8 Rob Taylor 5.00 12.00

2007 Artifacts

This 200-card set was released in June, 2007. The set was issued into the hobby in four-card packs, with a $9.99 SRP which came 10 packs to a box. Cards numbered 1-100 feature veterans in their 2006 team alphabetical order while cards numbered 101-200 feature 2007 NFL rookies. Cards numbered 101-150 and 151-200 are both sequenced in first name alphabetical order.
COMP.SET w/o RC's (100) 15.00 40.00
1 Matt Leinart .30 .75
2 Edgerrin James .40 1.00
3 Larry Fitzgerald .40 1.00
4 Anquan Boldin .30 .75
5 Michael Vick .40 1.00
6 Warrick Dunn .30 .75
7 Alge Crumpler .40 1.00
8 Steve McNair .40 1.00
9 Willis McGahee .30 .75
10 Mark Clayton .30 .75
11 J.P. Losman .30 .75
12 Anthony Thomas .30 .75
13 Lee Evans .40 1.00
14 Jake Delhomme .30 .75
15 DeShaun Foster .40 1.00
16 Steve Smith .40 1.00
17 Rex Grossman .30 .75
18 Cedric Benson .30 .75
19 Brian Urlacher .50 1.25
20 Carson Palmer .40 1.00
21 Rudi Johnson .30 .75
22 Chad Johnson .30 .75
23 T.J. Houshmandzadeh .30 .75
24 Charlie Frye .40 1.00
25 Braylon Edwards .30 .75
26 Kellen Winslow .30 .75
27 Tony Romo .60 1.50
28 Julius Jones .30 .75
29 Terrell Owens .40 1.00
30 Terry Glenn .40 1.00
31 Jay Cutler .30 .75
32 Travis Henry .40 1.00
33 Javon Walker .40 1.00
34 Jon Kitna .30 .75
35 Kevin Jones .30 .75
36 Roy Williams WR .30 .75
37 Mike Furrey .40 1.00
38 Brett Favre 1.00 2.50
39 Greg Jennings .30 .75
40 Donald Driver .40 1.00
41 David Carr .30 .75
42 Ron Dayne .40 1.00
43 Andre Johnson .40 1.00
44 Peyton Manning 1.25 3.00
45 Joseph Addai .30 .75
46 Marvin Harrison .40 1.00
47 Reggie Wayne .40 1.00
48 David Garrard .30 .75
49 Fred Taylor .30 .75
50 Maurice Jones-Drew .30 .75
51 Trent Green .30 .75
52 Larry Johnson .30 .75
53 Tony Gonzalez .40 1.00
54 Daunte Culpepper .40 1.00
55 Ronnie Brown .30 .75
56 Chris Chambers .30 .75
57 Tarvaris Jackson .30 .75
58 Chester Taylor .30 .75
59 Travis Taylor .30 .75
60 Tom Brady 1.50 4.00
61 Laurence Maroney .40 1.00
62 Reche Caldwell .30 .75
63 Drew Brees .50 1.25
64 Deuce McAllister .40 1.00
65 Reggie Bush .30 .75
66 Marques Colston .30 .75
67 Eli Manning .40 1.00
68 Brandon Jacobs .30 .75
69 Plaxico Burress .30 .75
70 Chad Pennington .30 .75
71 Leon Washington .30 .75
72 Laveranues Coles .30 .75
73 Ronald Curry .30 .75
74 LaMont Jordan .40 1.00
75 Randy Moss .40 1.00
76 Donovan McNabb .40 1.00
77 Brian Westbrook .30 .75
78 Reggie Brown .30 .75
79 Ben Roethlisberger .50 1.25
80 Willie Parker .40 1.00
81 Hines Ward .40 1.00
82 Santonio Holmes .30 .75
83 Philip Rivers .50 1.25
84 LaDainian Tomlinson .50 1.25
85 Antonio Gates .50 1.25
86 Matt Hasselbeck .30 .75
87 Shaun Alexander .30 .75
88 Deion Branch .30 .75
89 Marc Bulger .30 .75
90 Steven Jackson .30 .75
91 Torry Holt .40 1.00
92 Chris Simms .30 .75
93 Cadillac Williams .40 1.00
94 Joey Galloway .40 1.00
95 Vince Young .30 .75
96 LenDale White .40 1.00
97 Drew Bennett .30 .75
98 Jason Campbell .30 .75
99 Clinton Portis .30 .75
100 Santana Moss .40 1.00
101 Aaron Ross RC 1.50 4.00
102 Aaron Rouse RC 1.50 4.00
103 Alvin Banks RC 2.00 5.00
104 Anthony Spencer RC 2.00 5.00
105 Ben Patrick RC 2.00 5.00
106 Brandon Siler RC 1.50 4.00
107 Buster Davis RC 2.00 5.00
108 Clark Harris RC 2.00 5.00
109 Chris Henry RC 1.50 4.00
110 Chris Houston RC 1.50 4.00
111 Courtney Taylor RC 1.50 4.00
112 Dallas Baker RC 1.50 4.00
113 Danny Ware RC 2.50 6.00
114 Darius Walker RC 1.50 4.00
115 Darrelle Revis RC 2.00 5.00
116 David Ball RC 1.50 4.00
117 D'Juan Woods RC 1.50 4.00
118 Drew Tate RC 2.00 5.00
119 Dwayne Wright RC 1.50 4.00
120 Isaiah Stanback RC 1.50 4.00
121 Garrett Wolfe RC 1.50 4.00
122 Gary Russell RC 2.00 5.00
123 Jared Zabransky RC 1.50 4.00
124 Jarvis Moss RC 1.50 4.00
125 Jason Hill RC 1.50 4.00
126 Justin Harrell RC 1.50 4.00
127 John Beck RC 1.50 4.00
128 Johnnie Lee Higgins RC 1.50 4.00
129 Kolby Smith RC 1.50 4.00
130 LaMarr Woodley RC 3.00 8.00
131 Le'Ron McClain RC 2.50 6.00
132 Levi Brown RC 1.50 4.00
133 Mason Crosby RC 2.00 5.00
134 Matt Moore RC 2.50 6.00
135 Matt Trannon RC 1.50 4.00
136 Ahmad Bradshaw RC 2.50 6.00
137 Michael Griffin RC 1.50 4.00
138 Paul Williams RC 1.50 4.00
139 Rhema McKnight RC 1.50 4.00
140 Martrez Milner RC 1.50 4.00
141 Scott Chandler RC 2.50 6.00
142 Selvin Young RC 1.50 4.00
143 Steve Breaston RC 1.50 4.00
144 Matt Spaeth RC 2.50 6.00
145 DeMarcus Tank Tyler RC 1.50 4.00
146 Thomas Clayton RC 2.00 5.00
147 Tim Crowder RC 2.00 5.00
148 Tony Ugoh RC 1.50 4.00
149 Trent Edwards RC 1.50 4.00
150 Tyler Palko RC 2.50 6.00
151 Adam Carriker SP RC 1.50 4.00
152 Adrian Peterson SP RC 8.00 20.00
153 Alan Branch SP RC 1.50 4.00
154 Amobi Okoye SP RC 2.00 5.00
155 Anthony Gonzalez SP RC 1.50 4.00
156 Antonio Pittman SP RC 1.50 4.00
157 Aundrae Allison SP RC 1.50 4.00
158 Brady Quinn SP RC 1.50 4.00
159 Brandon Jackson SP RC 1.50 4.00
160 Brian Leonard SP RC 1.50 4.00
161 Calvin Johnson SP RC 5.00 12.00
162 Chansi Stuckey SP RC 2.00 5.00
163 Charles Johnson SP RC 1.50 4.00
164 Chris Leak SP RC 1.50 4.00
165 Craig Buster Davis SP RC 1.50 4.00
166 David Clowney SP RC 1.50 4.00
167 Daymeion Hughes SP RC 1.50 4.00
168 DeShawn Wynn SP RC 1.50 4.00
169 Drew Stanton SP RC 1.50 4.00
170 Dwayne Bowe SP RC 1.50 4.00
171 Dwayne Jarrett SP RC 2.00 5.00
172 Gaines Adams SP RC 2.00 5.00
173 Greg Olsen SP RC 2.50 6.00
174 Jamaal Anderson SP RC 2.00 5.00
175 JaMarcus Russell SP RC 1.50 4.00
176 Joe Thomas SP RC 2.50 6.00
177 Joel Filani SP RC 1.50 4.00
178 Jordan Palmer SP RC 2.00 5.00
179 Kenneth Darby SP RC 1.50 4.00
180 Kenny Irons SP RC 1.50 4.00
181 Kevin Kolb SP RC 2.00 5.00
182 LaRon Landry SP RC 2.50 6.00
183 Lawrence Timmons SP RC 2.50 6.00
184 Leon Hall SP RC 1.50 4.00
185 Lorenzo Booker SP RC 2.00 5.00
186 Marcus McCauley SP RC 1.50 4.00
187 Marshawn Lynch SP RC 3.00 8.00
188 Michael Bush SP RC 1.50 4.00
189 Patrick Willis SP RC 2.50 6.00
190 Paul Posluszny SP RC 1.50 4.00
191 Quentin Moses SP RC 1.50 4.00
192 Reggie Nelson SP RC 1.50 4.00
193 Robert Meachem SP RC 2.00 5.00
194 Sidney Rice SP RC 2.00 5.00
195 Steve Smith USC SP RC 1.50 4.00
196 Ted Ginn Jr. SP RC 2.00 5.00
197 Tony Hunt SP RC 1.50 4.00
198 Troy Smith SP RC 1.50 4.00
199 Tyrone Moss SP RC 1.50 4.00
200 Zach Miller SP RC 1.50 4.00

2007 Artifacts Bronze

*ROOKIES 101-200: 2X TO 5X BASIC CARDS
STATED PRINT RUN 25 SER.#'d SETS

2007 Artifacts Gold

*VETS/70-99: 3X TO 8X BASIC CARDS
*VETS/45-69: 4X TO 10X BASIC CARDS
*VETS/30-44: 5X TO 12X BASIC CARDS
*VETS/20-29: 6X TO 15X BASIC CARDS
*VETS/10-19: 8X TO 20X BASIC CARDS
*ROOKIES 101-200: 1X TO 2.5X BASIC CARDS
ROOKIES PRINT RUN 99 SER.#'d SETS

2007 Artifacts Green

*VETS 1-100: 3X TO 8X BASIC CARDS
*ROOKIES 101-200: 1X TO 2.5X BASIC CARDS
STATED PRINT RUN 99 SER.#'d SETS

2007 Artifacts Red

*VETS: 3X TO 8X BASIC CARDS
STATED PRINT RUN 99 SER.#'d SETS

2007 Artifacts AFC/NFC Apparel

STATED PRINT RUN 325 SER.#'d SETS
*RED/250: .4X TO 1X BASIC JSYs
*GOLD/99: .5X TO 1.2X BASIC JSYs
*BRONZE/75: .5X TO 1.2X BASIC JSYs
*GREEN: .4X TO 1X BASIC JSYs
*PATCH/50: .8X TO 2X BASIC JSYs
*PATCH RED/25: 1X TO 2.5X BASIC JSYs
AB Anquan Boldin 2.00 5.00
AG Ahman Green 2.50 6.00
AJ Andre Johnson 2.50 6.00
BD Brian Dawkins 3.00 8.00
BE Braylon Edwards 2.00 5.00
BF Brett Favre 6.00 15.00
BR Ben Roethlisberger 3.00 8.00
BU Brian Urlacher 3.00 8.00
BW Brian Westbrook 2.00 5.00
CJ Chad Johnson 2.00 5.00
CP1 Carson Palmer 2.50 6.00
CP2 Clinton Portis 2.00 5.00
DB Drew Brees 3.00 8.00
DC David Carr 2.00 5.00
EM Eli Manning 2.50 6.00
HW Hines Ward 2.50 6.00
JO LaMont Jordan 2.50 6.00
KJ Kevin Jones 2.00 5.00
LF Larry Fitzgerald 2.50 6.00
LJ Larry Johnson 2.00 5.00
LM Laurence Maroney 2.50 6.00
LT LaDainian Tomlinson 3.00 8.00
MB Marc Bulger 2.00 5.00
MF Marshall Faulk 2.50 6.00
MH Marvin Harrison 2.50 6.00
ML Matt Leinart 2.00 5.00
MV Michael Vick 2.50 6.00
PM Peyton Manning 8.00 20.00
RB1 Ronnie Brown 2.00 5.00
RB2 Reggie Bush 2.00 5.00
RL Ray Lewis 3.00 8.00
RM Randy Moss 2.50 6.00
SA Shaun Alexander 2.00 5.00
SJ Steven Jackson 2.00 5.00
SM Santana Moss 2.50 6.00
TB1 Tatum Bell 2.00 5.00
TB2 Tom Brady 10.00 25.00
TG Tony Gonzalez 2.50 6.00
TO Terrell Owens 2.50 6.00
WM Willis McGahee 2.00 5.00

2007 Artifacts AFC/NFC Apparel Autographs

STATED PRINT RUN 15 SER.#'d SETS
UNPRICED PATCH AUTOS #'d TO 5
UNPRICED RARE AUTOS #'d TO 1

2007 Artifacts Awesome Artifacts

STATED PRINT RUN 50 SER.#'d SETS
*PATCH/10: 1X TO 2.5X BASIC JSYs
PATCH PRINT RUN 10 SER.#'d SETS
AAAB Anquan Boldin 2.50 6.00
AABE Tatum Bell 2.50 6.00
AABF Brett Favre 8.00 20.00
AABR Ben Roethlisberger 4.00 10.00
AABU Reggie Bush 2.50 6.00
AACB Champ Bailey 3.00 8.00
AACP Carson Palmer 3.00 8.00
AADB Drew Brees 4.00 10.00
AADM Donovan McNabb 3.00 8.00
AAEM Eli Manning 3.00 8.00
AAHA Matt Hasselbeck 2.50 6.00
AAHW Hines Ward 3.00 8.00
AAJD Jake Delhomme 2.50 6.00
AAKJ Kevin Jones 2.50 6.00
AALF Larry Fitzgerald 3.00 8.00
AALJ Larry Johnson 2.50 6.00
AALM Laurence Maroney 3.00 8.00
AALT LaDainian Tomlinson 4.00 10.00
AAMB Marc Bulger 2.50 6.00
AAMF Marshall Faulk 3.00 8.00
AAMH Marvin Harrison 3.00 8.00
AAML Matt Leinart 2.50 6.00
AAMV Michael Vick 3.00 8.00
AAPE Chad Pennington 2.50 6.00
AAPM Peyton Manning 10.00 25.00
AAPR Philip Rivers 4.00 10.00
AARB Ronnie Brown 2.50 6.00
AARL Ray Lewis 4.00 10.00
AARW Reggie Wayne 3.00 8.00
AASA Shaun Alexander 2.50 6.00
AASJ Steven Jackson 2.50 6.00
AATB Tom Brady 30.00 60.00
AATG Trent Green 2.50 6.00
AATP Troy Polamalu 4.00 10.00
AAUR Brian Urlacher 4.00 10.00
AAWI Roy Williams WR 2.50 6.00
AAWP Willie Parker 3.00 8.00

2007 Artifacts NFL Artifacts

STATED PRINT RUN 325 SER.#'d SETS
*RED/250: .4X TO 1X BASIC JSYs
RED PRINT RUN 250 SER.#'d SETS
*GOLD/99: .5X TO 1.2X BASIC JSYs
GOLD PRINT RUN 99 SER.#'d SETS
*BRONZE/75: .5X TO 1.2X BASIC JSYs
BRONZE PRINT RUN 75 SER.#'d SETS
*GREEN: X TO X BASIC JSYs
*PATCH/50: .8X TO 2X BASIC JSYs
PATCH PRINT RUN 50 SER.#'d SETS
*PATCH RED/25: 1X TO 2.5X BASIC JSYs
PATCH RED PRINT RUN 25 SER.#'d SETS
NFLAB Anquan Boldin 2.00 5.00
NFLAG Ahman Green 2.50 6.00
NFLAJ Andre Johnson 2.50 6.00
NFLBD Brian Dawkins 3.00 8.00
NFLBE Ben Roethlisberger 3.00 8.00
NFLBF Brett Favre 6.00 15.00
NFLBL Byron Leftwich 2.00 5.00
NFLBR Tom Brady 10.00 25.00
NFLBU Brian Urlacher 3.00 8.00
NFLBW Brian Westbrook 2.00 5.00
NFLCA David Carr 2.00 5.00
NFLCM Curtis Martin 2.50 6.00
NFLCP Carson Palmer 2.50 6.00
NFLCW Cadillac Williams 2.50 6.00
NFLDB Drew Bledsoe 2.50 6.00
NFLDC Daunte Culpepper 2.50 6.00
NFLDM Donovan McNabb 2.50 6.00
NFLDR Drew Brees 3.00 8.00
NFLED Braylon Edwards 2.00 5.00
NFLEM Eli Manning 2.50 6.00
NFLFG Frank Gore 2.50 6.00
NFLGR Trent Green 2.00 5.00
NFLHA Marvin Harrison 2.50 6.00
NFLHW Hines Ward 2.50 6.00
NFLJD Jake Delhomme 2.00 5.00
NFLJO LaMont Jordan 2.50 6.00
NFLJP Jake Plummer 2.00 5.00
NFLJS Jeremy Shockey 2.00 5.00
NFLJU Julius Peppers 2.50 6.00
NFLKC Kevin Curtis 2.00 5.00
NFLKJ Kevin Jones 2.00 5.00
NFLLF Larry Fitzgerald 2.50 6.00
NFLLJ Larry Johnson 2.00 5.00
NFLLM Laurence Maroney 2.50 6.00
NFLLT LaDainian Tomlinson 3.00 8.00
NFLMA Dan Marino 6.00 15.00
NFLMB Marc Bulger 2.00 5.00
NFLMC Deuce McAllister 2.50 6.00
NFLMF Marshall Faulk 2.50 6.00
NFLMH Matt Hasselbeck 2.00 5.00
NFLML Matt Leinart 2.00 5.00
NFLMV Michael Vick 2.50 6.00
NFLMW Mike Williams 2.00 5.00
NFLPH Priest Holmes 2.50 6.00
NFLPM Peyton Manning 8.00 20.00
NFLPR Philip Rivers 3.00 8.00
NFLRB Reggie Bush 2.00 5.00
NFLRJ Rudi Johnson 2.00 5.00
NFLRL Ray Lewis 3.00 8.00
NFLRM Randy Moss 2.50 6.00
NFLRO Ronnie Brown 2.00 5.00
NFLSA Shaun Alexander 2.00 5.00
NFLSJ Steven Jackson 2.00 5.00
NFLSM Santana Moss 2.50 6.00
NFLTA Lofa Tatupu 2.00 5.00
NFLTB Tatum Bell 2.00 5.00
NFLTE Tedy Bruschi 2.50 6.00
NFLTG Tony Gonzalez 2.50 6.00
NFLTO Terrell Owens 2.50 6.00
NFLWM Willis McGahee 2.00 5.00

2007 Artifacts NFL Artifacts Dual

STATED PRINT RUN 99 SER.#'d SETS
*PATCH/25: .8X TO 2X BASIC JSYs
PATCH PRINT RUN 25 SER.#'d SETS
BJ M.Bulger/S.Jackson 6.00 15.00
BL R.Bush/M.Leinart 15.00 40.00
BM T.Brady/L.Maroney 8.00 20.00
BU B.Urlacher/C.Bailey 8.00 20.00
CJ D.Carr/A.Johnson 5.00 12.00
DD D.Brees/D.McAllister 6.00 15.00
EF B.Edwards/C.Frye 5.00 12.00
FG B.Favre/A.Green 15.00 40.00
FR B.Favre/B.Roethlisberger 15.00 40.00
HA M.Hasselbeck/S.Alexander 6.00 15.00
HW M.Harrison/R.Wayne 6.00 15.00
JB L.Johnson/T.Bell 6.00 15.00
JO C.Johnson/T.Owens 6.00 15.00
JU T.Jones/B.Urlacher 8.00 20.00
KT K.Jones/T.Bell 5.00 12.00
LC M.Leinart/J.Cutler 4.00 10.00
LF M.Leinart/L.Fitzgerald 10.00 25.00
MB P.Manning/T.Brady 15.00 40.00
MD C.Martin/C.Dillon 6.00 15.00
MH P.Manning/M.Harrison 12.00 30.00
MM D.Marino/P.Manning 25.00 60.00
MR E.Manning/P.Rivers 6.00 15.00
MS E.Manning/J.Shockey 6.00 15.00
MW D.McNabb/B.Westbrook 8.00 20.00
OJ T.Owens/J.Jones 6.00 15.00
PE P.Manning/E.Manning 12.00 30.00
PL J.Peppers/R.Lewis 6.00 15.00
PP C.Palmer/C.Pennington 6.00 15.00
PR P.Manning/R.Wayne 12.00 30.00
PW C.Pennington/C.Martin 6.00 15.00
RL R.Bush/L.Maroney 12.00 30.00
RT P.Rivers/L.Tomlinson 6.00 15.00
RW B.Roethlisberger/H.Ward 8.00 20.00
SB S.Smith/A.Boldin 5.00 12.00
TJ L.Tomlinson/L.Johnson 6.00 15.00
UB B.Urlacher/T.Bruschi 6.00 15.00
VC M.Vick/A.Crumpler 6.00 15.00
VM M.Vick/D.McNabb 8.00 20.00
WF R.Williams WR/L.Fitzgerald 6.00 15.00
WP H.Ward/W.Parker 8.00 20.00

2007 Artifacts NFL Artifacts Triple

STATED PRINT RUN 75 SER.#'d SETS
*PATCH/15: .8X TO 2X BASIC JSYs
PATCH PRINT RUN 15 SER.#'d SETS
BHL Bulger/Hasselbeck/Leinart 10.00 25.00
BMD Bush/Maroney/J-Drew 20.00 40.00
BPG Brees/Pennington/Green 6.00 15.00
BRD Bailey/Reed/Dawkins 10.00 25.00
FBM Favre/Brady/Manning 25.00 60.00
FBR Favre/Brady/Roethlisberger 25.00 60.00
GCS Gates/Crumpler/Shockey 6.00 15.00
JJB Jackson/Jones/Brown 8.00 20.00
JSF Johnson/Smith/Fitzgerald 8.00 20.00
LBW Leinart/Bush/Williams 20.00 40.00
LFB Leinart/Fitzgerald/Boldin 12.00 30.00
MHW Manning/Harrison/Wayne 20.00 50.00
MRR Eli/Rivers/Roethlisberger 10.00 25.00
MVP McNabb/Vick/Palmer 10.00 25.00
PLU Peppers/Lewis/Urlacher 10.00 25.00
RPW Roethlisberger/Parker/Ward 15.00 40.00
RTG Rivers/Tomlinson/Gates 12.00 30.00
TAJ Tomlinson/Alexander/Johnson 10.00 25.00
WMW Ward/Moulds/Williams WR 6.00 15.00
YLC Young/Leinart/Cutler 5.00 12.00

2007 Artifacts NFL Equipment

UNPRICED EQUIPMENT PRINT RUN 15

2007 Artifacts NFL Facts

NFAB Anquan Boldin .75 2.00
NFAC Antonio Cromartie .75 2.00
NFAG Antonio Gates 1.25 3.00
NFAH Anttaj Hawthorne .75 2.00
NFAJ Adam Jones .75 2.00
NFAL Shaun Alexander .75 2.00
NFAR Aaron Rodgers 3.00 8.00
NFAS Alex Smith QB 1.00 2.50
NFAV Jason Avant .75 2.00
NFAW Andrew Walter .75 2.00
NFAY Ashton Youboty .75 2.00
NFBB Bernard Berrian .75 2.00
NFBC Brian Calhoun .75 2.00
NFBD Brian Dawkins 1.25 3.00
NFBE Braylon Edwards .75 2.00
NFBET Josh Betts .75 2.00
NFBG Bruce Gradkowski .75 2.00
NFBH Ben Hartsock .75 2.00
NFBI Darnell Bing .75 2.00
NFBJ Brad Johnson 1.00 2.50
NFBL Byron Leftwich .75 2.00
NFBM Brandon Marshall 1.00 2.50
NFBN Brandon Jacobs .75 2.00
NFBP Brodney Pool .75 2.00
NFBR Mark Brunell 1.00 2.50
NFBS Brad Smith .75 2.00
NFBT Ben Troupe .75 2.00
NFBU Marc Bulger .75 2.00
NFBW Ben Watson .75 2.00
NFBY Dominique Byrd .75 2.00
NFCB Chris Brown .75 2.00
NFCE Cedric Benson .75 2.00
NFCF Ciatrick Fason .75 2.00
NFCG Chris Gamble .75 2.00
NFCH Chris Henry .75 2.00
NFCJ Chad Jackson .75 2.00
NFCL Brandon Chillar .75 2.00
NFCO Keary Colbert .75 2.00
NFCP Carson Palmer 1.00 2.50
NFCR Carlos Rogers .75 2.00
NFCRU Alge Crumpler 1.00 2.50
NFCU Jay Cutler .75 2.00
NFCW Corey Webster .75 2.00
NFDA Derek Anderson .75 2.00
NFDB Drew Bledsoe 1.00 2.50
NFDC Deuce McAllister 1.00 2.50
NFDE DeAngelo Hall .75 2.00
NFDF D'Brickashaw Ferguson .75 2.00
NFDG David Givens .75 2.00
NFDH Derek Hagan .75 2.00
NFDJ D.J. Shockley .75 2.00
NFDM Derrick Mason .75 2.00
NFDO Dan Orlovsky .75 2.00
NFDR Drew Bennett .75 2.00
NFDS Darren Sproles 1.00 2.50
NFEJ Edgerrin James 1.00 2.50
NFEL John Elway 2.00 5.00
NFEM Eli Manning 1.00 2.50
NFER Erasmus James .75 2.00
NFES Eric Shelton .75 2.00
NFEW Ernest Wilford .75 2.00
NFFG Frank Gore 1.00 2.50
NFFO DeShaun Foster 1.00 2.50
NFFR Charlie Frye 1.00 2.50
NFGA Robert Gallery .75 2.00
NFGJ Greg Jones .75 2.00
NFGL Greg Lee .75 2.00
NFGN Chad Greenway .75 2.00
NFGO Tony Gonzalez 1.00 2.50
NFGR Ahman Green 1.00 2.50
NFHA Dante Hall .75 2.00
NFHAC Darrell Hackney .75 2.00
NFHAR Jerome Harrison .75 2.00
NFHAS Mike Hass .75 2.00
NFHE Devery Henderson .75 2.00
NFHI Tye Hill .75 2.00
NFHK A.J. Hawk .75 2.00
NFHM Heath Miller .75 2.00
NFHO T.J. Houshmandzadeh .75 2.00
NFHOW Thomas Howard .75 2.00
NFIB Isaac Bruce 1.25 3.00
NFJA Joseph Addai .75 2.00
NFJB James Butler .75 2.00
NFJC Jason Campbell .75 2.00
NFJE Jerricho Cotchery .75 2.00
NFJEN Greg Jennings .75 2.00
NFJF Justin Fargas .75 2.00
NFJG Joey Galloway 1.00 2.50
NFJH Joe Horn .75 2.00
NFJJ Julius Jones .75 2.00
NFJL J.P. Losman .75 2.00
NFJM Johnnie Morant .75 2.00
NFJN Jerious Norwood .75 2.00
NFJO Chad Johnson .75 2.00
NFJP Jim Plunkett 1.00 2.50
NFJT Joe Theismann 1.25 3.00
NFJV Jonathan Vilma .75 2.00
NFJW Jimmy Williams .75 2.00
NFKA Kay-Jay Harris .75 2.00
NFKB Kyle Boller .75 2.00
NFKC Kellen Clemens .75 2.00
NFKE Keyshawn Johnson 1.00 2.50
NFKH Kelly Holcomb .75 2.00
NFKJ Kelly Jennings .75 2.00
NFKL Joe Klopfenstein .75 2.00
NFKM Kirk Morrison .75 2.00
NFKN Kevin Burnett .75 2.00
NFKU Kenechi Udeze .75 2.00
NFKV Kevin Jones .75 2.00
NFKW Kellen Winslow .75 2.00
NFLA Larry Johnson .75 2.00
NFLC Luis Castillo .75 2.00
NFLE Marcedes Lewis .75 2.00
NFLF Larry Fitzgerald 1.00 2.50
NFLJ LaMont Jordan 1.00 2.50
NFLL Brandon Lloyd .75 2.00
NFLM Laurence Maroney 1.00 2.50
NFLO Lofa Tatupu .75 2.00
NFLP Leonard Pope .75 2.00
NFLT LaDainian Tomlinson 1.25 3.00
NFLU Luke McCown .75 2.00
NFLW LenDale White 1.00 2.50
NFMA Mark Bradley .75 2.00
NFMAR Mario Williams 1.00 2.50
NFMB Marion Barber 1.00 2.50
NFMC Michael Clayton .75 2.00
NFMD Maurice Jones-Drew .75 2.00
NFME Mewelde Moore .75 2.00
NFMH Michael Huff 1.00 2.50
NFMI Mike Bell 1.00 2.50
NFMJ Marlin Jackson .75 2.00
NFML Matt Leinart .75 2.00
NFMM Marcus McNeill .75 2.00
NFMN Martin Nance .75 2.00
NFMO Ryan Moats .75 2.00
NFMOS Sinorice Moss 1.00 2.50
NFMQ Mike Quick .75 2.00
NFMR Michael Robinson 1.00 2.50
NFMS Maurice Stovall .75 2.00
NFMV Michael Vick 1.00 2.50
NFMW Mike Williams .75 2.00
NFNB Nate Burleson .75 2.00
NFOD Owen Daniels .75 2.00
NFOJ Omar Jacobs .75 2.00
NFOL Drew Olson .75 2.00
NFPE Chris Perry .75 2.00
NFPM Peyton Manning 3.00 8.00
NFPN Chad Pennington .75 2.00
NFPR Philip Rivers 1.25 3.00
NFRB Ronnie Brown .75 2.00
NFRC Reche Caldwell .75 2.00
NFRE Reggie Bush .75 2.00
NFRG Rex Grossman .75 2.00
NFRI Rocket Ismail 1.00 2.50
NFRJ Rudi Johnson .75 2.00
NFRM Reggie McNeal .75 2.00
NFRO Ben Roethlisberger 1.25 3.00
NFROD Cory Rodgers .75 2.00
NFRU Barrett Ruud .75 2.00
NFRW Roy Williams WR .75 2.00
NFRY Courtney Roby .75 2.00
NFSA Santana Moss 1.00 2.50
NFSAM B.J. Sams .75 2.00
NFSC Matt Schaub .75 2.00
NFSH Santonio Holmes .75 2.00
NFSI Ernie Sims .75 2.00
NFSJ Steven Jackson .75 2.00
NFSM Shawne Merriman .75 2.00
NFSP Samie Parker .75 2.00
NFSS Steve Smith 1.00 2.50
NFTA Tarvaris Jackson .75 2.00
NFTB Tatum Bell .75 2.00
NFTD Thomas Davis .75 2.00
NFTE Terrence Whitehead .75 2.00
NFTG Trent Green .75 2.00
NFTH Tommie Harris .75 2.00
NFTJ Taylor Jacobs .75 2.00
NFTO Todd Heap .75 2.00
NFTR Travis Henry 1.00 2.50
NFTS Terrell Suggs .75 2.00
NFTT Tyson Thompson .75 2.00
NFTW Travis Wilson .75 2.00
NFTY Troy Williamson .75 2.00
NFVD Vernon Davis .75 2.00
NFVM Vernand Morency 1.00 2.50
NFVW Vince Wilfork .75 2.00
NFVY Vince Young .75 2.00
NFWA Kelley Washington .75 2.00
NFWAS Leon Washington .75 2.00
NFWAY Reggie Wayne 1.00 2.50
NFWB Will Blackmon .75 2.00
NFWE Brian Westbrook .75 2.00
NFWH Roddy White .75 2.00
NFWHI Charlie Whitehurst .75 2.00
NFWI Roy Williams S .75 2.00
NFWIL Demetrius Williams .75 2.00
NFWL Reggie Williams 1.00 2.50
NFWM Willis McGahee .75 2.00
NFWP Willie Parker 1.00 2.50
NFWS Will Smith .75 2.00

2007 Artifacts NFL Facts Autographs

AC Antonio Cromartie 5.00 12.00
AI Anttaj Hawthorne 5.00 12.00
AJ Adam Jones 5.00 12.00
AR Aaron Rodgers 125.00 200.00
AS Alex Smith QB 6.00 15.00
AV Jason Avant 5.00 12.00
AW Andrew Walter 5.00 12.00
AY Ashton Youboty 5.00 12.00
BB Bernard Berrian 5.00 12.00
BC Brian Calhoun 5.00 12.00
BD Brian Dawkins 20.00 40.00
BE Braylon Edwards 5.00 12.00
BET Josh Betts 5.00 12.00
BG Bruce Gradkowski 5.00 12.00
BH Ben Hartsock 5.00 12.00
BI Darnell Bing 5.00 12.00
BJ Brad Johnson 6.00 15.00
BL Byron Leftwich 5.00 12.00
BN Brandon Jacobs 5.00 12.00
BP Brodney Pool 5.00 12.00
BR Mark Brunell 6.00 15.00
BS Brad Smith 5.00 12.00
BT Ben Troupe 5.00 12.00
BU Marc Bulger 5.00 12.00
BW Ben Watson 5.00 12.00
BY Dominique Byrd 5.00 12.00
CB Chris Brown 5.00 12.00
CF Ciatrick Fason 5.00 12.00
CG Chris Gamble 5.00 12.00
CH Chris Henry 5.00 12.00
CJ Chad Jackson 5.00 12.00
CL Brandon Chillar 5.00 12.00
CO Keary Colbert 5.00 12.00
CP Carson Palmer 8.00 20.00
CR Carlos Rogers 5.00 12.00
CRU Alge Crumpler 6.00 15.00
CU Jay Cutler 5.00 12.00
CW Corey Webster 5.00 12.00
DA Derek Anderson 5.00 12.00
DB Drew Bledsoe 10.00 25.00
DC Deuce McAllister 6.00 15.00
DE DeAngelo Hall 5.00 12.00
DG David Givens 5.00 12.00
DH Derek Hagan 5.00 12.00
DJ D.J. Shockley 5.00 12.00
DM Derrick Mason 5.00 12.00
DO Dan Orlovsky 5.00 12.00
DR Drew Bennett 5.00 12.00
DS Darren Sproles 6.00 15.00
EJ Edgerrin James 6.00 15.00
EM Eli Manning 30.00 60.00
ER Erasmus James 5.00 12.00
ES Eric Shelton 5.00 12.00
EW Ernest Wilford 5.00 12.00
FG Frank Gore 6.00 15.00
FO DeShaun Foster 6.00 15.00
FR Charlie Frye 6.00 15.00
GA Robert Gallery 5.00 12.00
GJ Greg Jones 5.00 12.00
GL Greg Lee 5.00 12.00
GR Ahman Green 6.00 15.00
HA Dante Hall 5.00 12.00
HAC Darrell Hackney 5.00 12.00
HAR Jerome Harrison 5.00 12.00
HAS Mike Hass 5.00 12.00
HE Devery Henderson 5.00 12.00
HI Tye Hill 5.00 12.00
HK A.J. Hawk 5.00 12.00
HM Heath Miller 5.00 12.00

HO T.J. Houshmandzadeh 5.00 12.00
HOW Thomas Howard 5.00 12.00
IB Isaac Bruce 8.00 20.00
JA Joseph Addai 5.00 12.00
JB James Butler 5.00 12.00
JC Jason Campbell 5.00 12.00
JE Jerricho Cotchery 5.00 12.00
JEN Greg Jennings 5.00 12.00
JF Justin Fargas 5.00 12.00
JG Joey Galloway 6.00 15.00
JH Joe Horn 5.00 12.00
JJ Julius Jones 5.00 12.00
JL J.P. Losman 5.00 12.00
JM Johnnie Morant 5.00 12.00
JN Jerious Norwood 5.00 12.00
JO Chad Johnson 5.00 12.00
JP Jim Plunkett 10.00 25.00
JT Joe Theismann 12.00 30.00
JV Jonathan Vilma 5.00 12.00
JW Jimmy Williams 5.00 12.00
KA Kay-Jay Harris 5.00 12.00
KB Kyle Boller 5.00 12.00
KC Kellen Clemens 5.00 12.00
KE Keyshawn Johnson 6.00 15.00
KH Kelly Holcomb 5.00 12.00
KJ Kelly Jennings 5.00 12.00
KL Joe Klopfenstein 5.00 12.00
KM Kirk Morrison 5.00 12.00
KN Kevin Burnett 5.00 12.00
KU Kenechi Udeze 5.00 12.00
KV Kevin Jones 5.00 12.00
KW Kellen Winslow 5.00 12.00
LA Larry Johnson 5.00 12.00
LC Luis Castillo 5.00 12.00
LE Marcedes Lewis 5.00 12.00
LJ LaMont Jordan 6.00 15.00
LL Brandon Lloyd 5.00 12.00
LM Laurence Maroney 6.00 15.00
LP Leonard Pope 5.00 12.00
LT LaDainian Tomlinson 25.00 60.00
LU Luke McCown 5.00 12.00
LW LenDale White 6.00 15.00
MA Mark Bradley 5.00 12.00
MAR Mario Williams 6.00 15.00
MB Marion Barber 6.00 15.00
MC Michael Clayton 5.00 12.00
MD Maurice Jones-Drew 5.00 12.00
ME Mewelde Moore 5.00 12.00
MH Michael Huff 6.00 15.00
MI Mike Bell 6.00 15.00
MJ Marlin Jackson 5.00 12.00
ML Matt Leinart 5.00 12.00
MM Marcus McNeill 5.00 12.00
MN Martin Nance 5.00 12.00
MO Ryan Moats 5.00 12.00
MOS Sinorice Moss 6.00 15.00
MQ Mike Quick 5.00 12.00
MR Michael Robinson 6.00 15.00
MS Maurice Stovall 5.00 12.00
MV Michael Vick 20.00 50.00
NB Nate Burleson 5.00 12.00
OD Owen Daniels 5.00 12.00
OJ Omar Jacobs 5.00 12.00
OL Drew Olson 5.00 12.00
PE Chris Perry 5.00 12.00
PN Chad Pennington 5.00 12.00
RB Ronnie Brown 5.00 12.00
RC Reche Caldwell 5.00 12.00
RE Reggie Bush 8.00 20.00
RG Rex Grossman 5.00 12.00
RI Rocket Ismail 6.00 15.00
RJ Rudi Johnson 5.00 12.00
RM Reggie McNeal 5.00 12.00
ROD Cory Rodgers 5.00 12.00
RU Barrett Ruud 5.00 12.00
RW Roy Williams WR 5.00 12.00
RY Courtney Roby 5.00 12.00
SA Santana Moss 6.00 15.00
SAM B.J. Sams 5.00 12.00
SC Matt Schaub 5.00 12.00
SH Santonio Holmes 5.00 12.00
SI Ernie Sims 5.00 12.00
SM Shawne Merriman 5.00 12.00
SP Samie Parker 5.00 12.00
TA Tarvaris Jackson 5.00 12.00
TB Tatum Bell 5.00 12.00
TD Thomas Davis 5.00 12.00
TE Terrence Whitehead 5.00 12.00
TG Trent Green 5.00 12.00
TH Tommie Harris 5.00 12.00
TJ Taylor Jacobs 5.00 12.00
TO Todd Heap 5.00 12.00
TR Travis Henry 6.00 15.00
TS Terrell Suggs 8.00 20.00
TT Tyson Thompson 5.00 12.00
TW Travis Wilson 5.00 12.00
TY Troy Williamson 5.00 12.00
VD Vernon Davis 5.00 12.00
VM Vernand Morency 6.00 15.00
VW Vince Wilfork 5.00 12.00
VY Vince Young 5.00 12.00
WA Kelley Washington 5.00 12.00
WAS Leon Washington 5.00 12.00
WAY Reggie Wayne 6.00 15.00
WB Will Blackmon 5.00 12.00
WE Brian Westbrook 5.00 12.00
WH Roddy White 5.00 12.00
WHI Charlie Whitehurst 5.00 12.00
WI Roy Williams S 5.00 12.00
WIL Demetrius Williams 5.00 12.00
WL Reggie Williams 6.00 15.00
WM Willis McGahee 5.00 12.00
WP Willie Parker 6.00 15.00
WS Will Smith 5.00 12.00

2007 Artifacts Photo Shoot Flashback Fabrics

STATED PRINT RUN 350 SER.#'d SETS
*GREEN: .3X TO .8X BASIC INSERTS
AH A.J. Hawk 2.00 5.00
AJ Adam Jones 2.00 5.00
AS Alex Smith QB 2.50 6.00
AW Andrew Walter 2.00 5.00
BB Bernard Berrian 2.00 5.00
BE Braylon Edwards 2.00 5.00
BL Byron Leftwich 2.00 5.00
BR Ben Roethlisberger 3.00 8.00
BW Ben Watson 2.00 5.00
CF Charlie Frye 2.50 6.00
CJ Chad Jackson 2.00 5.00
CL Michael Clayton 2.00 5.00
CP Carson Palmer 2.50 6.00
CR Carlos Rogers 2.00 5.00
CW Cadillac Williams 2.50 6.00
DC Dallas Clark 2.50 6.00
DH DeAngelo Hall 2.00 5.00
DW DeAngelo Williams 2.00 5.00
EM Eli Manning 2.50 6.00
JC Jason Campbell 2.00 5.00
JJ Julius Jones 2.00 5.00
JL J.P. Losman 2.00 5.00
JN Jerious Norwood 2.00 5.00
JO Andre Johnson 2.50 6.00
KC Kellen Clemens 2.00 5.00
KJ Kevin Jones 2.00 5.00
KW Kellen Winslow 2.00 5.00
LE Lee Evans 2.50 6.00
LF Larry Fitzgerald 2.50 6.00
LM Laurence Maroney 2.50 6.00
LW LenDale White 2.50 6.00
MC Mark Clayton 2.00 5.00
MD Maurice Jones-Drew 2.00 5.00
MJ Michael Jenkins 2.00 5.00
ML Matt Leinart 2.00 5.00
MS Matt Schaub 2.00 5.00
PE Chris Perry 2.00 5.00
PR Philip Rivers 3.00 8.00
RB Reggie Bush 2.00 5.00
RO Ronnie Brown 2.00 5.00
RW Reggie Williams 2.50 6.00
SH Santonio Holmes 2.00 5.00
SJ Steven Jackson 2.00 5.00
TB Tatum Bell 2.00 5.00
TW Troy Williamson 2.00 5.00
VD Vernon Davis 2.00 5.00
VY Vince Young 2.00 5.00
WA Leon Washington 2.00 5.00
WH Roddy White 2.00 5.00
WI Roy Williams WR 2.00 5.00

2007 Artifacts Photo Shoot Flashback Fabrics Autographs

UNPRICED AUTO PRINT RUN 10

2007 Artifacts Rookie Autographs

STATED PRINT RUN 10-30
SERIAL #'d TO 10 NOT PRICED
109 Chris Henry/25 10.00 25.00
111 Courtney Taylor/30 10.00 25.00
112 Dallas Baker/25 10.00 25.00
114 Darius Walker/25 10.00 25.00
115 Darrelle Revis/30 12.00 30.00
118 Drew Tate/30 12.00 30.00
119 Dwayne Wright/25 10.00 25.00
121 Garrett Wolfe/25 10.00 25.00
122 Gary Russell/25 12.00 30.00
123 Jared Zabransky/25
125 Jason Hill/25 10.00 25.00
127 John Beck/25 10.00 25.00
128 Johnnie Lee Higgins/25 10.00 25.00
134 Matt Moore/30 15.00 40.00
137 Michael Griffin/30 10.00 25.00
139 Rhema McKnight/25 10.00 25.00
141 Scott Chandler/30 15.00 40.00
142 Selvin Young/25 10.00 25.00
149 Trent Edwards/25 10.00 25.00
150 Tyler Palko/30 15.00 40.00
151 Adam Carriker/30 10.00 25.00
153 Alan Branch/30 10.00 25.00
154 Amobi Okoye/25 12.00 30.00
155 Anthony Gonzalez/25 40.00 80.00
156 Antonio Pittman/25 10.00 25.00
157 Aundrae Allison/30 10.00 25.00
159 Brandon Jackson/25 10.00 25.00
160 Brian Leonard/25 10.00 25.00
164 Chris Leak/30 10.00 25.00
165 Craig Buster Davis/25 10.00 25.00
166 David Clowney/25 10.00 25.00
167 Daymeion Hughes/30 10.00 25.00
169 Drew Stanton/25 10.00 25.00
170 Dwayne Bowe/25 25.00 50.00
171 Dwayne Jarrett/25 12.00 30.00
172 Gaines Adams/25 12.00 30.00
173 Greg Olsen/25 15.00 40.00
174 Jamaal Anderson/30 12.00 30.00
176 Joe Thomas/25 15.00 40.00
177 Joel Filani/30 10.00 25.00
180 Kenny Irons/25 10.00 25.00
182 LaRon Landry/25 15.00 40.00
183 Lawrence Timmons/30 15.00 40.00
184 Leon Hall/25 10.00 25.00
186 Marcus McCauley/30 10.00 25.00
188 Michael Bush/25 30.00 60.00
189 Patrick Willis/25 40.00 80.00
190 Paul Posluszny/25 10.00 25.00
191 Quentin Moses/25 10.00 25.00
193 Robert Meachem/25 12.00 30.00
194 Sidney Rice/25 12.00 30.00
195 Steve Smith USC/25 15.00 40.00
199 Tyrone Moss/30 10.00 25.00

1978 Atlanta Convention

This 24-card standard-size set features circular black-and-white player photos framed in light green and bordered in white. The player's name is printed in black across the top with his position, team name, and logo at the bottom. The white backs carry the player's name and career information. The cards are unnumbered and checklisted below in alphabetical order. Almost all of the players in this set played for the Braves at one time.
COMPLETE SET (24) 7.50 15.00
19 Tommy Nobis .75 1.50

1988 Athletes in Action

The set features six Texas Rangers (1-6) and six Dallas Cowboys (7-12). The cards are standard size, 2 1/2" by 3 1/2". The fronts display color action player photos bordered in white. The words "Athletes in Action" are printed in black across the lower edge of the picture. The backs carry a player quote, a salvation message, and the player's favorite Scripture.
COMPLETE SET (12) 5.00 12.00
7 Tom Landry CO 1.25 3.00
8 Steve Pelluer .50 1.25
9 Gordon Banks .50 1.25
10 Bill Bates .60 1.50
11 Doug Cosbie .50 1.25
12 Herschel Walker .75 2.00

1996 Athletes In Action

This set was sponsored and distributed by Athletes in Action. Each card includes a color photo on the front with an inspirational message from the player on the back.
COMPLETE SET (10) 5.00 10.00
1 Cris Carter 1.50 4.00
2 Howard Cross .40 1.00
3 Trent Dilfer .50 1.25
4 Irving Fryar .60 1.50
5 Brent Jones .40 1.00
6 John Kidd .40 1.00
7 Doug Pelfrey .40 1.00
8 Frank Reich .40 1.00
9 Ken Ruettgers .40 1.00
10 Steve Wallace .40 1.00

2002 Atomic

Released in June 2002, this 150-card base set includes 100 vetarans and 50 rookies prodcued in a die cut design. The rookies are shortprinted (serial numbered of 465) and inserted in hobby packs at a rate of 4:21 and retail packs at a rate of 1:25. Hobby product contains 5 cards per pack/20 packs per box/16 boxes per case. The S.R.P. is $5.99. Retail product contains 3 cards per pack/24 packs ber box/16 boxes per case. The S.R.P. is $2.99. Cards numbered from 1-100 feature veterans while cards numbered 101 through 150 feature rookies. Please note that cards 151-170, that feature rookies which made their name during the 2002 season, were only available in packs of 2002 Pacific Heads Update.
COMP.SET w/o SP's (100) 20.00 50.00
1 David Boston .40 1.00
2 Thomas Jones .40 1.00
3 Jake Plummer .40 1.00
4 Jamal Anderson .50 1.25
5 Warrick Dunn .40 1.00
6 Michael Vick .50 1.25
7 Jamal Lewis .50 1.25
8 Chris Redman .40 1.00
9 Travis Taylor .40 1.00
10 Travis Henry .40 1.00
11 Eric Moulds .40 1.00
12 Peerless Price .40 1.00
13 Muhsin Muhammad .40 1.00
14 Lamar Smith .40 1.00
15 Chris Weinke .40 1.00
16 Marty Booker .40 1.00
17 Jim Miller .40 1.00
18 Anthony Thomas .50 1.25
19 Corey Dillon .40 1.00
20 Jon Kitna .40 1.00
21 Peter Warrick .40 1.00
22 Tim Couch .40 1.00
23 Kevin Johnson .40 1.00
24 Quincy Morgan .40 1.00
25 Quincy Carter .40 1.00
26 Joey Galloway .50 1.25
27 Emmitt Smith 1.00 2.50
28 Terrell Davis .50 1.25
29 Brian Griese .40 1.00
30 Ed McCaffrey .50 1.25
31 Rod Smith .50 1.25
32 Scotty Anderson .40 1.00
33 Az-Zahir Hakim .40 1.00
34 Mike McMahon .40 1.00
35 Brett Favre 1.25 3.00
36 Terry Glenn .50 1.25
37 Ahman Green .50 1.25
38 James Allen .40 1.00
39 Corey Bradford .40 1.00
40 Jermaine Lewis .40 1.00
41 Marvin Harrison .50 1.25
42 Edgerrin James .50 1.25
43 Peyton Manning 1.50 4.00
44 Mark Brunell .50 1.25
45 Jimmy Smith .50 1.25
46 Fred Taylor .40 1.00
47 Tony Gonzalez .50 1.25
48 Trent Green .40 1.00
49 Priest Holmes .40 1.00
50 Chris Chambers .40 1.00
51 Jay Fiedler .50 1.25
52 Ricky Williams .50 1.25
53 Michael Bennett .40 1.00
54 Daunte Culpepper .50 1.25
55 Randy Moss .50 1.25
56 Tom Brady 3.00 8.00
57 Troy Brown .40 1.00
58 Antowain Smith .50 1.25
59 Aaron Brooks .40 1.00
60 Joe Horn .40 1.00
61 Deuce McAllister .50 1.25
62 Tiki Barber .50 1.25
63 Kerry Collins .40 1.00
64 Ron Dayne .50 1.25
65 Wayne Chrebet .40 1.00
66 Curtis Martin .50 1.25
67 Vinny Testaverde .40 1.00
68 Tim Brown .60 1.50
69 Rich Gannon .50 1.25
70 Charlie Garner .50 1.25
71 Jerry Rice 1.25 3.00
72 Correll Buckhalter .40 1.00
73 Donovan McNabb .50 1.25
74 Duce Staley .40 1.00
75 Jerome Bettis .60 1.50
76 Kordell Stewart .40 1.00
77 Hines Ward .50 1.25
78 Isaac Bruce .60 1.50
79 Marshall Faulk .50 1.25
80 Torry Holt .50 1.25
81 Kurt Warner .50 1.25
82 Drew Brees 1.25 3.00
83 Tim Dwight .40 1.00
84 Doug Flutie .50 1.25
85 LaDainian Tomlinson .60 1.50
86 Jeff Garcia .40 1.00
87 Garrison Hearst .40 1.00
88 Terrell Owens .50 1.25
89 Shaun Alexander .40 1.00
90 Trent Dilfer .40 1.00
91 Darrell Jackson .50 1.25
92 Mike Alstott .40 1.00
93 Brad Johnson .50 1.25
94 Keyshawn Johnson .50 1.25
95 Eddie George .50 1.25
96 Derrick Mason .40 1.00
97 Steve McNair .50 1.25
98 Stephen Davis .40 1.00
99 Rod Gardner .40 1.00
100 Jacquez Green .40 1.00
101 Damien Anderson RC 1.50 4.00
102 Ladell Betts RC 2.50 6.00
103 Antonio Bryant RC 2.50 6.00
104 Reche Caldwell RC 2.00 5.00
105 Kelly Campbell RC 2.00 5.00
106 David Carr RC 1.50 4.00
107 Rohan Davey RC 2.50 6.00
108 Andre Davis RC 1.50 4.00
109 T.J. Duckett RC 1.50 4.00
110 DeShaun Foster RC 2.50 6.00
111 David Garrard RC 2.00 5.00
112 Lamar Gordon RC 2.00 5.00
113 William Green RC 2.00 5.00
114 Joey Harrington RC 1.50 4.00
115 Kurt Kittner RC 1.50 4.00
116 Ashley Lelie RC 1.50 4.00
117 Josh McCown RC 2.50 6.00
118 Clinton Portis RC 2.50 6.00
119 Patrick Ramsey RC 2.00 5.00
120 Antwaan Randle El RC 2.00 5.00
121 Josh Reed RC 2.00 5.00
122 Luke Staley RC 1.50 4.00
123 Donte Stallworth RC 2.50 6.00
124 Marquise Walker RC 1.50 4.00
125 Brian Westbrook RC 3.00 8.00
126 Jason McAddley RC 2.00 5.00
127 Josh Scobey RC 2.00 5.00
128 Kahlil Hill RC 1.50 4.00
129 Ron Johnson RC 2.00 5.00
130 Julius Peppers RC 4.00 10.00
131 Adrian Peterson RC 2.00 5.00
132 Woody Dantzler RC 2.00 5.00
133 Roy Williams RC 1.50 4.00
134 Najeh Davenport RC 1.50 4.00
135 Javon Walker RC 2.50 6.00
136 Jabar Gaffney RC 1.50 4.00
137 John Henderson RC 2.00 5.00
138 Leonard Henry RC 1.50 4.00
139 Daniel Graham RC 2.00 5.00
140 Jeremy Shockey RC 2.50 6.00
141 Ronald Curry RC 1.50 4.00
142 Napoleon Harris RC 2.00 5.00
143 Freddie Milons RC 1.50 4.00
144 Lito Sheppard RC 2.50 6.00
145 Eric Crouch RC 2.50 6.00
146 Robert Thomas RC 1.50 4.00
147 Quentin Jammer RC 2.50 6.00
148 Maurice Morris RC 2.00 5.00
149 Travis Stephens RC 1.50 4.00
150 Cliff Russell RC 1.50 4.00
151 Dameon Hunter RC 1.50 4.00
152 Javin Hunter RC 1.50 4.00
153 Tellis Redmon RC 1.50 4.00
154 Chester Taylor RC 2.50 6.00
155 Randy Fasani RC 1.50 4.00
156 Jamin Elliott RC 1.50 4.00
157 Chad Hutchinson RC 1.50 4.00
158 Eddie Drummond RC 1.50 4.00
159 Craig Nall RC 2.00 5.00
160 Jarrod Baxter RC 1.50 4.00
161 Jonathan Wells RC 2.00 5.00
162 Shaun Hill RC 2.50 6.00
163 Deion Branch RC 2.50 6.00
164 J.T. O'Sullivan RC 2.00 5.00
165 Tim Carter RC 2.00 5.00
166 Daryl Jones RC 1.50 4.00
167 Lee Mays RC 1.50 4.00
168 Seth Burford RC 1.50 4.00
169 Brandon Doman RC 1.50 4.00
170 Jerramy Stevens RC 2.50 6.00

2002 Atomic Gold

*VETS/80-98: 2.5X TO 6X BASIC CARDS
*ROOKIES/80-98: .8X TO 2X
*VETS/30-49: 4X TO 10X BASIC CARDS
*ROOKIES/30-49: 1.2X TO 3X
*VETS/20-29: 5X TO 12X BASIC CARDS
*ROOKIES/20-29: 1.5X TO 4X
GOLD PRINT RUN 1-98
SERIAL #'d UNDER 20 NOT PRICED

2002 Atomic Non Die Cut

*VETS 1-100: 1X TO 2.5X BASIC CARDS
*ROOKIES 101-150: .25X TO .6X
NON DIE-CUT/600 ODDS 13:21
STATED PRINT RUN 600 SER.#'d SETS

2002 Atomic Red

*VETS 1-100: 1.5X TO 4X BASIC CARDS
*ROOKIES 101-150: .4X TO 1X
STATED ODDS 4:21

2002 Atomic Retail Rookies

*ROOKIES: .08X TO .2X BASE CARD HI
RETAIL VERSION NOT SERIAL #'d

2002 Atomic Arms Race

This 18-card set is randomly inserted in hobby packs at a rate of 1:21 and retail packs at a rate of 1:49.
COMPLETE SET (18) 20.00 50.00
STATED ODDS 1:21
1 Michael Vick 1.00 2.50
2 Tim Couch .75 2.00
3 Brian Griese .75 2.00
4 Joey Harrington .75 2.00
5 Brett Favre 2.50 6.00
6 David Carr .75 2.00
7 Peyton Manning 3.00 8.00
8 Mark Brunell 1.00 2.50
9 Daunte Culpepper 1.00 2.50
10 Tom Brady 6.00 15.00
11 Aaron Brooks .75 2.00
12 Donovan McNabb 1.00 2.50
13 Kurt Warner 1.00 2.50
14 Drew Brees 2.50 6.00
15 Doug Flutie 1.00 2.50
16 Jeff Garcia .75 2.00
17 Steve McNair 1.00 2.50
18 Patrick Ramsey 1.00 2.50

2002 Atomic Countdown To Stardom

This 18-card set is inserted in packs at a rate of 2:21. Cards feature some of the NFL's top rookies for 2002.
COMPLETE SET (18) 12.00 30.00
STATED ODDS 2:21
1 Josh McCown .75 2.00
2 T.J. Duckett .50 1.25
3 Josh Reed .60 1.50
4 DeShaun Foster .75 2.00
5 William Green .60 1.50
6 Antonio Bryant .75 2.00
7 Ashley Lelie .50 1.25
8 Clinton Portis .75 2.00
9 Joey Harrington .50 1.25
10 Javon Walker .75 2.00
11 David Carr .50 1.25
12 Jabar Gaffney .50 1.25
13 Donte Stallworth .75 2.00
14 Brian Westbrook 1.00 2.50
15 Lamar Gordon .60 1.50
16 Reche Caldwell .60 1.50
17 Maurice Morris .60 1.50
18 Patrick Ramsey .60 1.50

2002 Atomic Fusion Force

This 18-card set is inserted in hobby packs at a rate of 1:41 and retail packs at a rate of 1:97. Set features top rookies and veterans for the 2002 season.
COMPLETE SET (18) 30.00 80.00
STATED ODDS 1:41
1 T.J. Duckett 1.00 2.50
2 Michael Vick 1.25 3.00
3 DeShaun Foster 1.50 4.00
4 Anthony Thomas 1.25 3.00
5 William Green 1.25 3.00
6 Emmitt Smith 2.50 6.00
7 Terrell Davis 1.25 3.00
8 Ashley Lelie 1.00 2.50
9 Joey Harrington 1.00 2.50
10 Brett Favre 3.00 8.00
11 David Carr 1.00 2.50
12 Randy Moss 1.25 3.00
13 Donte Stallworth 1.50 4.00
14 Jerry Rice 3.00 8.00
15 Marshall Faulk 1.25 3.00
16 Kurt Warner 1.25 3.00
17 LaDainian Tomlinson 1.50 4.00
18 Patrick Ramsey 1.25 3.00

2002 Atomic Game Worn Jerseys

This 98-card set is inserted into hobby packs at a rate of 3:21 and retail packs at a rate of 1:49. The cards feature silver foil and a swatch of game-worn jersey. Card #38 was not released.
STATED ODDS 3:21 HOBBY
*GOLD/25: 1X TO 2.5X BASIC JERSEYS
GOLD PRINT RUN 25 SER.#'d SETS
1 David Boston/350 2.00 5.00
2 Freddie Jones/277 2.00 5.00
3 Joel Makovicka/238 2.00 5.00
4 Jake Plummer/132 2.00 5.00
5 Jamal Anderson/333 2.50 6.00
6 Warrick Dunn/106 2.00 5.00
7 Shawn Jefferson/261 2.00 5.00
8 Maurice Smith/259 2.00 5.00
9 Dave Moore/277 2.00 5.00
10 Peerless Price/249 2.00 5.00
11 Jay Riemersma/251 2.00 5.00
12 Lamar Smith/259 2.00 5.00
13 Rabih Abdullah/270 2.00 5.00
14 Chris Chandler/352 2.50 6.00
15 Brian Urlacher/141 3.00 8.00
16 Dez White/246 2.00 5.00
17 Corey Dillon/210 2.00 5.00
18 Scott Mitchell/268 2.50 6.00
19 Akili Smith/264 2.50 6.00
20 Takeo Spikes/283 2.00 5.00
21 Tim Couch/261 2.00 5.00
22 Jammi German/276 2.00 5.00
23 Jamel White/270 2.00 5.00
24 La'Roi Glover/279 2.00 5.00
25 Emmitt Smith/257 5.00 12.00
26 Darren Woodson/281 2.50 6.00
27 Mike Anderson/333 2.00 5.00
28 Terrell Davis/270 2.50 6.00
29 Gus Frerotte/272 2.00 5.00
30 Brian Griese/125 2.00 5.00
31 Howard Griffith/264 2.00 5.00
32 Deltha O'Neal/231 2.00 5.00
33 Shannon Sharpe/278 2.50 6.00
34 Charlie Batch/257 2.00 5.00
35 Az-Zahir Hakim/59 2.00 5.00
36 Brett Favre/247 6.00 15.00
37 Antonio Freeman/358 3.00 8.00
39 Ahman Green/242 2.50 6.00
40 Dorsey Levens/219 2.50 6.00
41 James Allen/241 2.00 5.00
42 Avion Black/262 2.00 5.00
43 Jermaine Lewis/283 2.00 5.00
44 Charlie Rogers/296 2.00 5.00
45 Qadry Ismail/275 2.00 5.00
46 Trent Green/346 2.00 5.00
47 Tony Richardson/282 2.00 5.00
48 Ricky Williams/348 2.50 6.00
49 Cris Carter/199 3.00 8.00
50 Corey Chavous/262 2.00 5.00
51 Daunte Culpepper/346 2.50 6.00
52 Jim Kleinsasser/273 3.00 8.00
53 Randy Moss/179 2.50 6.00
54 Tom Brady/95 15.00 40.00
55 Donald Hayes/264 2.00 5.00
56 Curtis Jackson/206 2.00 5.00
57 Patrick Pass/254 2.00 5.00
58 Aaron Brooks/267 2.00 5.00
59 Bryan Cox/276 2.50 6.00
60 Jerome Pathon/80 2.00 5.00
61 Robert Wilson/287 2.00 5.00
62 Tiki Barber/153 2.50 6.00
63 Kerry Collins/111 2.00 5.00
64 Ron Dayne/354 2.50 6.00
65 Laveranues Coles/243 2.50 6.00
66 James Jett/287 2.50 6.00
67 Randy Jordan/238 2.00 5.00
68 Jerry Rice/323 6.00 15.00
69 Cecil Martin/267 2.00 5.00
70 Donovan McNabb/357 2.50 6.00
71 Brian Mitchell/266 2.50 6.00
72 Jerome Bettis/337 3.00 8.00
73 Mark Bruener/289 2.50 6.00
74 Troy Edwards/262 2.00 5.00
75 Kordell Stewart/340 2.00 5.00
76 Isaac Bruce/351 3.00 8.00
77 Trung Canidate/300 2.00 5.00
78 Ernie Conwell/266 2.00 5.00
79 Marshall Faulk/355 2.50 6.00
80 Torry Holt/77 2.50 6.00
81 Kurt Warner/191 2.50 6.00
82 Aeneas Williams /268 2.00 5.00
83 Stephen Alexander/261 2.00 5.00
84 Drew Brees/248 6.00 15.00
85 Tim Dwight/112 2.00 5.00
86 Terrell Fletcher/262 2.00 5.00
87 Doug Flutie/328 2.50 6.00
88 Ronney Jenkins/292 2.00 5.00
89 Fred Beasley/244 2.00 5.00
90 Shaun Alexander/356 2.00 5.00
91 Itula Mili/262 2.00 5.00
92 Ken Dilger/253 2.00 5.00
93 Michael Pittman/229 2.50 6.00
94 Eddie George/183 2.50 6.00
95 Jevon Kearse/253 2.00 5.00
96 Erron Kinney/247 2.00 5.00
97 Steve McNair/371 2.50 6.00
98 Dameyune Craig/265 2.00 5.00
99 Stephen Davis/304 2.00 5.00

2002 Atomic Game Worn Jersey Patches

Cards from this 97-card set were inserted into hobby packs only at a rate of 1:21. The cards feature a patch swatch from a game-worn jersey and were individually serial numbered. Cards #38 and #84 were not released.
PATCH/2-150 ODDS 1:21 HOBBY
1 David Boston/100 3.00 8.00
3 Joel Makovicka/100 3.00 8.00
5 Jamal Anderson/100 4.00 10.00
6 Warrick Dunn/32 4.00 10.00
7 Shawn Jefferson/100 3.00 8.00
8 Maurice Smith/100 3.00 8.00
9 Dave Moore/100 3.00 8.00
11 Jay Riemersma/29 4.00 10.00
12 Lamar Smith/100 3.00 8.00
13 Rabih Abdullah/100 3.00 8.00
14 Chris Chandler/30 5.00 12.00
16 Dez White/76 3.00 8.00
17 Corey Dillon/80 3.00 8.00
18 Scott Mitchell/100 4.00 10.00
19 Akili Smith/100 4.00 10.00
20 Takeo Spikes/100 3.00 8.00
21 Tim Couch/75 3.00 8.00
22 Jammi German/150 3.00 8.00
23 Jamel White/100 3.00 8.00
24 La'Roi Glover/100 3.00 8.00
25 Emmitt Smith/38 20.00 50.00
26 Darren Woodson/100 4.00 10.00
27 Mike Anderson/75 3.00 8.00
28 Terrell Davis/75 4.00 10.00
29 Gus Frerotte/100 3.00 8.00
31 Howard Griffith/100 3.00 8.00
33 Shannon Sharpe/100 4.00 10.00
35 Az-Zahir Hakim/60 3.00 8.00
36 Brett Favre/100 20.00 50.00
37 Antonio Freeman/100 5.00 12.00
39 Ahman Green/100 4.00 10.00
40 Dorsey Levens/100 4.00 10.00
43 Jermaine Lewis/150 3.00 8.00
44 Charlie Rogers/100 3.00 8.00
45 Qadry Ismail/100 3.00 8.00
46 Trent Green/100 3.00 8.00
47 Tony Richardson/100 3.00 8.00
48 Ricky Williams/95 4.00 10.00
49 Cris Carter/80 5.00 12.00
50 Corey Chavous/100 3.00 8.00
51 Daunte Culpepper/75 4.00 10.00
52 Jim Kleinsasser/100 5.00 12.00
53 Randy Moss/28 5.00 12.00
54 Tom Brady/50 25.00 60.00
55 Donald Hayes/150 3.00 8.00
56 Curtis Jackson/150 3.00 8.00
57 Patrick Pass/100 3.00 8.00
58 Aaron Brooks/100 3.00 8.00
59 Bryan Cox/100 4.00 10.00
61 Robert Wilson/100 3.00 8.00
62 Tiki Barber/25 6.00 15.00
64 Ron Dayne/75 4.00 10.00
65 Laveranues Coles/90 4.00 10.00
66 James Jett/100 4.00 10.00
67 Randy Jordan/100 3.00 8.00
68 Jerry Rice/75 10.00 25.00
69 Cecil Martin/100 3.00 8.00
70 Donovan McNabb/95 4.00 10.00
71 Brian Mitchell/100 4.00 10.00
72 Jerome Bettis/75 10.00 25.00
73 Mark Bruener/100 4.00 10.00
74 Troy Edwards/100 3.00 8.00
75 Kordell Stewart/75 3.00 8.00
76 Isaac Bruce/99 5.00 12.00
77 Trung Canidate/100 3.00 8.00
78 Ernie Conwell/100 3.00 8.00
79 Marshall Faulk/95 4.00 10.00
80 Torry Holt/100 4.00 10.00
81 Kurt Warner/20 20.00 40.00
82 Aeneas Williams/38 4.00 10.00
85 Tim Dwight/25 5.00 12.00
86 Terrell Fletcher/22 5.00 12.00
87 Doug Flutie/20 6.00 15.00
88 Ronney Jenkins/21 5.00 12.00
89 Fred Beasley/100 3.00 8.00
90 Shaun Alexander/95 3.00 8.00
91 Itula Mili/100 3.00 8.00
92 Ken Dilger/100 3.00 8.00
93 Michael Pittman/110 4.00 10.00
94 Eddie George/75 4.00 10.00
96 Erron Kinney/100 3.00 8.00
97 Steve McNair/80 4.00 10.00

2002 Atomic Super Colliders

This 9-card set is randomly inserted into hobby packs at a rate of 1:21 and retail packs at a rate of 1:49. Cards feature top runningbacks from both the AFC and NFC.
COMPLETE SET (9) 7.50 15.00
STATED ODDS 1:21
1 Anthony Thomas .75 2.00
2 Corey Dillon .60 1.50
3 Emmitt Smith 1.50 4.00
4 Edgerrin James .75 2.00
5 Ricky Williams .75 2.00
6 Jerome Bettis 1.00 2.50
7 Marshall Faulk .75 2.00
8 LaDainian Tomlinson 1.00 2.50
9 Shaun Alexander .60 1.50

1995 AT&T Steve Young Snoopy Bowl Phone Cards

1 Steve Young/15,000 2.50 6.00
2 Steve Young/15,000 2.50 6.00
3 Steve Young/15,000 2.50 6.00
4 Steve Young Jumbo/10,000 3.00 8.00

1998 Aurora

The 1998 Pacific Aurora set was issued in one series totalling 200 cards. The 6-card packs retail for $2.99 each. Each card is printed on super-thick 24-point card. Each gold-foiled card features color action photography with a head shot of the featured player in the upper right corner. The backs offer the latest player information and statistics along with a challenging trivia question.
COMPLETE SET (200) 30.00 60.00
1 Rob Moore .25 .60
2 Jake Plummer .40 1.00
3 Frank Sanders .25 .60
4 Eric Swann .15 .40
5 Jamal Anderson .40 1.00
6 Chris Chandler .25 .60
7 Byron Hanspard .15 .40
8 Terance Mathis .25 .60
9 O.J. Santiago .15 .40
10 Chuck Smith .15 .40
11 Jessie Tuggle .15 .40
12 Jay Graham .15 .40
13 Jim Harbaugh .25 .60
14 Michael Jackson .15 .40
15 Pat Johnson RC .60 1.50
16 Jermaine Lewis .25 .60
17 Errict Rhett .25 .60
18 Rod Woodson .25 .60
19 Quinn Early .15 .40
20 Andre Reed .25 .60
21 Antowain Smith .40 1.00
22 Bruce Smith .25 .60
23 Thurman Thomas .40 1.00
24 Ted Washington .15 .40
25 Michael Bates .15 .40
26 Rae Carruth .15 .40
27 Kerry Collins .25 .60
28 Fred Lane .15 .40
29 Wesley Walls .25 .60
30 Edgar Bennett .15 .40
31 Curtis Conway .25 .60
32 Curtis Enis RC .40 1.00
33 Walt Harris .15 .40
34 Erik Kramer .15 .40
35 Barry Minter .15 .40
36 Jeff Blake .25 .60
37 Corey Dillon .40 1.00
38 Carl Pickens .25 .60
39 Darnay Scott .25 .60
40 Troy Aikman .75 2.00
41 Michael Irvin .40 1.00
42 Deion Sanders .40 1.00
43 Emmitt Smith 1.50 3.00
44 Chris Warren .25 .60
45 Terrell Davis .40 1.00
46 John Elway 1.50 4.00
47 Brian Griese RC 1.50 4.00
48 Ed McCaffrey .25 .60
49 John Mobley .15 .40
50 Shannon Sharpe .25 .60
51 Neil Smith .25 .60
52 Rod Smith WR .25 .60
53 Stephen Boyd .15 .40
54 Scott Mitchell .25 .60
55 Herman Moore .25 .60
56 Johnnie Morton .25 .60
57 Robert Porcher .15 .40
58 Barry Sanders 1.25 3.00
59 Robert Brooks .25 .60
60 Mark Chmura .25 .60
61 Brett Favre 2.00 4.00
62 Antonio Freeman .40 1.00
63 Vonnie Holliday RC .60 1.50
64 Dorsey Levens .40 1.00
65 Ross Verba .15 .40
66 Reggie White .40 1.00
67 Elijah Alexander .15 .40
68 Ken Dilger .15 .40
69 Marshall Faulk .50 1.25
70 Marvin Harrison .40 1.00
71 Peyton Manning RC 8.00 20.00
72 Bryan Barker .15 .40
73 Mark Brunell .40 1.00
74 Keenan McCardell .25 .60
75 Jimmy Smith .25 .60
76 James Stewart .25 .60
77 Derrick Alexander WR .25 .60
78 Kimble Anders .25 .60
79 Donnell Bennett .15 .40
80 Elvis Grbac .25 .60
81 Andre Rison .25 .60
82 Rashaan Shehee RC .60 1.50
83 Derrick Thomas .40 1.00
84 Karim Abdul-Jabbar .40 1.00
85 Trace Armstrong .15 .40
86 Charles Jordan .15 .40
87 Dan Marino 1.50 4.00
88 O.J. McDuffie .25 .60
89 Zach Thomas .40 1.00
90 Cris Carter .40 1.00
91 Charles Evans .15 .40
92 Andrew Glover .15 .40
93 Brad Johnson .40 1.00
94 Randy Moss RC 5.00 12.00
95 John Randle .25 .60
96 Jake Reed .25 .60
97 Robert Smith .40 1.00
98 Bruce Armstrong .15 .40
99 Drew Bledsoe .60 1.50
100 Ben Coates .25 .60
101 Robert Edwards RC .60 1.50
102 Terry Glenn .40 1.00
103 Willie McGinest .15 .40
104 Sedrick Shaw .15 .40
105 Tony Simmons RC .60 1.50
106 Chris Slade .15 .40
107 Billy Joe Hobert .15 .40
108 Qadry Ismail .25 .60
109 Heath Shuler .15 .40
110 Lamar Smith .25 .60
111 Ray Zellars .15 .40
112 Tiki Barber .40 1.00
113 Chris Calloway .15 .40
114 Ike Hilliard .25 .60
115 Joe Jurevicius RC .75 2.00
116 Danny Kanell .25 .60
117 Amani Toomer .25 .60
118 Charles Way .15 .40
119 Tyrone Wheatley .25 .60
120 Wayne Chrebet .40 1.00
121 John Elliott .15 .40
122 Glenn Foley .25 .60
123 Scott Frost RC .15 .40
124 Aaron Glenn .15 .40
125 Keyshawn Johnson .40 1.00
126 Curtis Martin .40 1.00
127 Vinny Testaverde .25 .60
128 Tim Brown .40 1.00
129 Rickey Dudley .15 .40
130 Jeff George .25 .60
131 James Jett .25 .60
132 Napoleon Kaufman .40 1.00
133 Darrell Russell .15 .40
134 Charles Woodson RC 1.50 4.00
135 James Darling RC .15 .40
136 Koy Detmer .40 1.00
137 Irving Fryar .25 .60
138 Charlie Garner .25 .60
139 Bobby Hoying .25 .60
140 Chad Lewis .25 .60
141 Duce Staley .50 1.25
142 Kevin Turner .15 .40
143 Jerome Bettis .40 1.00
144 Will Blackwell .15 .40
145 Mark Bruener .15 .40
146 Dermontti Dawson .30 .75
147 Charles Johnson .15 .40
148 Levon Kirkland .15 .40
149 Tim Lester .15 .40
150 Kordell Stewart .40 1.00
151 Tony Banks .25 .60
152 Isaac Bruce .40 1.00
153 Robert Holcombe RC .60 1.50
154 Eddie Kennison .25 .60
155 Amp Lee .15 .40
156 Jerald Moore .15 .40
157 Charlie Jones .15 .40
158 Freddie Jones .15 .40
159 Ryan Leaf RC .75 2.00
160 Natrone Means .25 .60
161 Junior Seau .40 1.00
162 Bryan Still .15 .40
163 Marc Edwards .15 .40
164 Merton Hanks .15 .40
165 Garrison Hearst .40 1.00
166 Terrell Owens .40 1.00
167 Jerry Rice .75 2.00
168 J.J. Stokes .25 .60
169 Bryant Young .15 .40
170 Steve Young .50 1.25
171 Chad Brown .15 .40
172 Joey Galloway .25 .60
173 Walter Jones .15 .40
174 Cortez Kennedy .15 .40
175 Jon Kitna .40 1.00
176 James McKnight .40 1.00
177 Warren Moon .40 1.00
178 Michael Sinclair .15 .40
179 Mike Alstott .40 1.00
180 Reidel Anthony .25 .60
181 Derrick Brooks .40 1.00
182 Trent Dilfer .40 1.00
183 Warrick Dunn .40 1.00
184 Hardy Nickerson .15 .40
185 Warren Sapp .25 .60
186 Willie Davis .15 .40
187 Eddie George .40 1.00
188 Steve McNair .40 1.00
189 Jon Runyan .15 .40
190 Chris Sanders .15 .40
191 Frank Wycheck .15 .40
192 Stephen Alexander RC .60 1.50
193 Terry Allen .40 1.00
194 Stephen Davis .15 .40
195 Cris Dishman .15 .40
196 Gus Frerotte .15 .40
197 Darrell Green .25 .60
198 Skip Hicks RC .60 1.50
199 Dana Stubblefield .15 .40
200 Michael Westbrook .25 .60
S1 Warrick Dunn Sample .40 1.00

1998 Aurora Championship Fever

Randomly inserted in packs at an overall rate of one per pack, this 50-card set is an insert to the Aurora base set release. The fronts feature color action photos with gold foil borders running vertically on both sides of the card. The featured player's name and team name sits in the lower right corner. Four different parallel sets with varying foil colored borders were also made. As an added bonus, Pro Bowl running back Warrick Dunn autographed 100 total cards in this set.
COMP.GOLD SET (50) 20.00 50.00
OVERALL ODDS ONE PER PACK
*COPPER/20: 15X TO 40X BASIC INSERTS
COPPER/20 INSERTED IN HOBBY PACKS
*PLAT.BLUE/100: 4X TO 10X BASIC INSERTS
PLAT.BLUE/100 INSERTED IN HOB/RET
*RED: 1.2X TO 3X BASIC INSERTS
RED ODDS 4:25 SPECIAL RETAIL
*SILVER/250: 2X TO 5X BASIC INSERTS
SILVER/250 INSERTED IN RETAIL PACKS
1 Jake Plummer .40 1.00
2 Antowain Smith .40 1.00
3 Bruce Smith .50 1.25
4 Kerry Collins .40 1.00
5 Kevin Greene .40 1.00
6 Jeff Blake .40 1.00
7 Corey Dillon .40 1.00
8 Carl Pickens .30 .75
9 Troy Aikman 1.00 2.50
10 Michael Irvin .50 1.25
11 Deion Sanders .50 1.25
12 Emmitt Smith 1.50 4.00
13 Terrell Davis .50 1.25
14 John Elway 2.00 5.00
15 Shannon Sharpe .50 1.25
16 Herman Moore .30 .75
17 Barry Sanders 1.50 4.00
18 Brett Favre 2.00 5.00
19 Antonio Freeman .40 1.00
20 Dorsey Levens .40 1.00
21 Marshall Faulk .50 1.25
22 Peyton Manning 4.00 10.00
23 Mark Brunell .40 1.00
24 Elvis Grbac .30 .75
25 Andre Rison .40 1.00
26 Rashaan Shehee .30 .75
27 Derrick Thomas .50 1.25
28 Dan Marino 2.00 5.00
29 Cris Carter .50 1.25
30 Robert Smith .40 1.00
31 Drew Bledsoe .50 1.25
32 Robert Edwards .30 .75
33 Terry Glenn .40 1.00
34 Danny Kanell .30 .75
35 Keyshawn Johnson .40 1.00
36 Tim Brown .50 1.25
37 Napoleon Kaufman .30 .75
38 Bobby Hoying .30 .75
39 Jerome Bettis .50 1.25
40 Kordell Stewart .40 1.00
41 Ryan Leaf .30 .75
42 Jerry Rice 1.00 2.50
43 Steve Young .60 1.50
44 Joey Galloway .40 1.00
45 Mike Alstott .50 1.25
46 Trent Dilfer .40 1.00
47 Warrick Dunn .40 1.00
47AU Warrick Dunn AU/100 20.00 50.00
48 Eddie George .50 1.25
49 Steve McNair .50 1.25
50 Gus Frerotte .30 .75

1998 Aurora Cubes

Inserted one per hobby box, this 20-card hobby set features color action player photos printed on cubes. Each side of a cube displays a different action photo of the same player with head shot of that player printed on the cube's top.
COMPLETE SET (20) 75.00 150.00
ONE PER HOBBY BOX
1 Corey Dillon 2.00 5.00
2 Troy Aikman 4.00 10.00
3 Emmitt Smith 6.00 15.00
4 Terrell Davis 2.00 5.00
5 John Elway 8.00 20.00
6 Barry Sanders 6.00 15.00
7 Brett Favre 8.00 20.00
8 Dorsey Levens 2.00 5.00
9 Peyton Manning 12.00 30.00
10 Mark Brunell 2.00 5.00
11 Dan Marino 8.00 20.00
12 Drew Bledsoe 3.00 8.00
13 Napoleon Kaufman 2.00 5.00
14 Jerome Bettis 2.00 5.00
15 Kordell Stewart 2.00 5.00
16 Ryan Leaf 1.25 3.00
17 Jerry Rice 4.00 10.00
18 Steve Young 2.50 6.00
19 Warrick Dunn 2.00 5.00
20 Eddie George 2.00 5.00

1998 Aurora Face Mask Cel Fusions

Randomly inserted in packs at a rate of one in 73, this 20-card set is an insert to the Pacific Aurora base set. Each card features a foiled and etched player profiled against a die-cut helmet that is fused to a face mask. The set boasts the trading card technology of today.
COMPLETE SET (20) 150.00 250.00
STATED ODDS 1:73
1 Corey Dillon 3.00 8.00
2 Troy Aikman 6.00 15.00
3 Emmitt Smith 10.00 25.00
4 Terrell Davis 3.00 8.00
5 John Elway 12.50 30.00
6 Barry Sanders 10.00 25.00
7 Brett Favre 12.50 30.00
8 Antonio Freeman 3.00 8.00
9 Peyton Manning 15.00 40.00
10 Mark Brunell 3.00 8.00
11 Dan Marino 12.50 30.00
12 Drew Bledsoe 5.00 12.00
13 Napoleon Kaufman 3.00 8.00
14 Jerome Bettis 3.00 8.00
15 Kordell Stewart 3.00 8.00
16 Ryan Leaf 1.50 4.00
17 Jerry Rice 6.00 15.00
18 Steve Young 4.00 10.00
19 Warrick Dunn 3.00 8.00
20 Eddie George 3.00 8.00

1998 Aurora Gridiron Laser Cuts

Randomly inserted in hobby packs only at the rate of four per 37, this 20-card hobby insert set features color portraits of

top players printed on laser-cut cards.
COMPLETE SET (20) 30.00 80.00
STATED ODDS 4:37 HOBBY
1 Jake Plummer 1.50 4.00
2 Corey Dillon 1.50 4.00
3 Troy Aikman 3.00 8.00
4 Emmitt Smith 5.00 12.00
5 Terrell Davis 1.50 4.00
6 John Elway 6.00 15.00
7 Barry Sanders 5.00 12.00
8 Brett Favre 6.00 15.00
9 Peyton Manning 12.00 30.00
10 Mark Brunell 1.50 4.00
11 Dan Marino 6.00 15.00
12 Drew Bledsoe 2.50 6.00
13 Jerome Bettis 1.50 4.00
14 Kordell Stewart 1.50 4.00
15 Ryan Leaf 1.25 3.00
16 Jerry Rice 3.00 8.00
17 Steve Young 2.00 5.00
18 Warrick Dunn 1.50 4.00
19 Eddie George 1.50 4.00
20 Steve McNair 1.50 4.00

1998 Aurora NFL Command

Randomly inserted in packs at a rate of one in 361, this 10-card set is an insert to the Pacific Aurora base set. The fronts feature color action photos in the forefront with an image of a leather football in the background.
STATED ODDS 1:361
1 Terrell Davis 4.00 10.00
2 John Elway 15.00 40.00
3 Barry Sanders 12.50 30.00
4 Brett Favre 15.00 40.00
5 Peyton Manning 30.00 80.00
6 Mark Brunell 4.00 10.00
7 Dan Marino 15.00 40.00
8 Drew Bledsoe 6.00 15.00
9 Ryan Leaf 4.00 10.00
10 Warrick Dunn 4.00 10.00

1999 Aurora

This 200 card set, issued in August 1999, was released in six card packs. These cards are sequenced in alphabetical order by teams which are also in alphabetical order. Rookie Cards in this set include Tim Couch, Edgerrin James and Ricky Williams. Terrell Owens signed 197 cards which were radomly inserted into packs.
COMPLETE SET (150) 15.00 40.00
1 David Boston RC .25 .60
2 Larry Centers .15 .40
3 Rob Moore .15 .40
4 Adrian Murrell .15 .40
5 Jake Plummer .15 .40
6 Jamal Anderson .20 .50
7 Chris Chandler .20 .50
8 Tim Dwight .20 .50
9 Terance Mathis .15 .40
10 O.J. Santiago .15 .40
11 Priest Holmes .15 .40
12 Michael Jackson .15 .40
13 Jermaine Lewis .15 .40
14 Ray Lewis .25 .60
15 Michael McCrary .15 .40
16 Doug Flutie .25 .60
17 Eric Moulds .15 .40
18 Peerless Price RC .25 .60
19 Antowain Smith .15 .40
20 Bruce Smith .20 .50
21 Steve Beuerlein .20 .50
22 Tim Biakabutuka .20 .50
23 Kevin Greene .25 .60
24 Muhsin Muhammad .15 .40
25 Wesley Walls .20 .50
26 Curtis Conway .20 .50
27 Bobby Engram .15 .40
28 Curtis Enis .15 .40
29 Erik Kramer .20 .50
30 Cade McNown RC .25 .60
31 Jeff Blake .20 .50
32 Corey Dillon .15 .40
33 Carl Pickens .20 .50
34 Darnay Scott .15 .40
35 Akili Smith RC .25 .60
36 Tim Couch RC .30 .75
37 Ty Detmer .15 .40
38 Kevin Johnson RC .30 .75
39 Terry Kirby .15 .40
40 Troy Aikman .30 .75
41 Michael Irvin .25 .60
42 Rocket Ismail .20 .50
43 Deion Sanders .20 .50
44 Emmitt Smith .40 1.00
45 Bubby Brister .15 .40
46 Terrell Davis .20 .50
47 Brian Griese .15 .40
48 Ed McCaffrey .20 .50
49 Shannon Sharpe .20 .50
50 Rod Smith .20 .50
51 Charlie Batch .15 .40
52 Sedrick Irvin RC .25 .60
53 Herman Moore .20 .50
54 Johnnie Morton .20 .50
55 Barry Sanders .40 1.00
56 Robert Brooks .20 .50
57 Brett Favre .50 1.25
58 Antonio Freeman UER .20 .50
59 Dorsey Levens .20 .50
60 Derrick Mayes .15 .40
61 Marvin Harrison .20 .50
62 Edgerrin James RC .40 1.00
63 Peyton Manning .75 2.00
64 Jerome Pathon .15 .40
65 Tavian Banks .15 .40
66 Mark Brunell .20 .50
67 Keenan McCardell .20 .50
68 Jimmy Smith .20 .50
69 Fred Taylor .15 .40
70 Derrick Alexander .15 .40
71 Kimble Anders .15 .40
72 Mike Cloud RC .25 .60
73 Elvis Grbac .15 .40
74 Andre Rison .20 .50
75 Karim Abdul-Jabbar .15 .40
76 James Johnson RC .25 .60
77 Dan Marino .50 1.25
78 O.J. McDuffie .20 .50
79 Lamar Thomas .15 .40
80 Cris Carter .25 .60
81 Daunte Culpepper RC .40 1.00
82 Randall Cunningham .20 .50
83 Randy Moss .20 .50
84 John Randle .25 .60
85 Robert Smith .15 .40
86 Drew Bledsoe .20 .50
87 Ben Coates .20 .50
88 Kevin Faulk RC .25 .60
89 Terry Glenn .20 .50
90 Ty Law .25 .60
91 Cam Cleeland .15 .40
92 Andre Hastings .15 .40
93 Billy Joe Hobert .15 .40
94 Ricky Williams RC .40 1.00
95 Tiki Barber .20 .50
96 Kent Graham .15 .40
97 Ike Hilliard .15 .40
98 Charles Way .15 .40
99 Wayne Chrebet .15 .40
100 Keyshawn Johnson .20 .50
101 Curtis Martin .20 .50
102 Vinny Testaverde .15 .40
103 Dedric Ward .15 .40
104 Tim Brown .25 .60
105 Rickey Dudley .15 .40
106 James Jett .15 .40
107 Napoleon Kaufman .15 .40
108 Charles Woodson .25 .60
109 Jeff Graham .15 .40
110 Charles Johnson .15 .40
111 Donovan McNabb RC 2.00 5.00
112 Duce Staley .15 .40
113 Jerome Bettis .25 .60
114 Troy Edwards RC .25 .60
115 Courtney Hawkins .15 .40
116 Kordell Stewart .15 .40
117 Amos Zereoue RC .25 .60
118 Isaac Bruce .25 .60
119 Marshall Faulk .20 .50
120 Joe Germaine RC .30 .75
121 Torry Holt RC .50 1.25
122 Amp Lee .15 .40
123 Charlie Jones .15 .40
124 Ryan Leaf .20 .50
125 Natrone Means .20 .50
126 Junior Seau .20 .50
127 Garrison Hearst .15 .40
128 Terrell Owens .20 .50
129 Jerry Rice .60 1.50
130 J.J. Stokes .15 .40
131 Steve Young .30 .75
132 Chad Brown .15 .40
133 Joey Galloway .20 .50
134 Brock Huard RC .25 .60
135 Jon Kitna .15 .40
136 Ricky Watters .20 .50
137 Mike Alstott .15 .40
138 Reidel Anthony .15 .40
139 Trent Dilfer .15 .40
140 Warrick Dunn .15 .40
141 Jacquez Green .15 .40
142 Shaun King RC .25 .60
143 Eddie George .20 .50
144 Steve McNair .20 .50
145 Yancey Thigpen .15 .40
146 Frank Wycheck .20 .50
147 Champ Bailey RC .50 1.25
148 Skip Hicks .15 .40
149 Brad Johnson .20 .50
150 Michael Westbrook .15 .40
AU1 T.Owens AUTO/197 20.00 40.00

1999 Aurora Pinstripes

*PINSTRIPES: .4X TO 1X BASIC CARDS

1999 Aurora Premiere Date

*VETS: 10X TO 25X BASIC CARDS
*ROOKIES: 6X TO 15X BASIC CARDS
*PINSTRIPE PD: .4X TO 1X PREM.DATE
PREMIERE DATE/77 ODDS 1:25 HOB
PREMIERE DATE PRINT RUN 77

1999 Aurora Canvas Creations

These cards, inserted at a rate of one in 193, feature 10 leading players image against a real canvas background.
COMPLETE SET (10) 40.00 100.00
STATED ODDS 1:193
1 Troy Aikman 4.00 10.00
2 Terrell Davis 2.50 6.00
3 Barry Sanders 5.00 12.00
4 Brett Favre 6.00 15.00
5 Peyton Manning 10.00 25.00
6 Dan Marino 6.00 15.00
7 Randy Moss 2.50 6.00
8 Drew Bledsoe 2.50 6.00
9 Steve Young 4.00 10.00
10 Jon Kitna 2.00 5.00

1999 Aurora Championship Fever

Inserted at a rate of four in 25, these 20 cards feature some of the leading players in football. Three different parallel sets were also produced with each featuring a different foil color.
COMPLETE SET (20) 20.00 40.00
STATED ODDS 4:25
*COPPER/20: 10X TO 25X BASIC INSERTS
*PLAT.BLUE/100: 5X TO 12X BASIC INSERTS
*SILVER/250: 3X TO 8X BASIC INSERTS
1 Jake Plummer .30 .75
2 Jamal Anderson .40 1.00
3 Tim Couch .40 1.00
4 Troy Aikman .60 1.50
5 Emmitt Smith .75 2.00
6 Terrell Davis .40 1.00
7 Barry Sanders .75 2.00
8 Brett Favre 1.00 2.50
9 Peyton Manning 1.50 4.00
10 Fred Taylor .30 .75
11 Dan Marino 1.00 2.50
12 Randy Moss
13 Drew Bledsoe .40 1.00
14 Ricky Williams .50 1.25
15 Keyshawn Johnson .40 1.00
16 Terrell Owens .40 1.00
17 Jerry Rice 1.25 3.00
18 Steve Young .60 1.50
19 Jon Kitna .30 .75
20 Eddie George .40 1.00

1999 Aurora Complete Players

Randomly inserted in both hobby and retail packs, these 10 cards are considered to be among the NFL's premier players. Each of these players have a photo on each side and were made on 10-point double laminated stock with full foil.
STATED PRINT RUN 299 SER.#'d SETS
*HOLOGOLD/25: 1.5X TO 4X BASIC INSERT
HOLOGOLD/25 INSERTS IN HOB/RET
1 Troy Aikman 4.00 10.00
2 Terrell Davis 2.50 6.00
3 Barry Sanders 5.00 12.00
4 Brett Favre 6.00 15.00
5 Peyton Manning 10.00 25.00
6 Dan Marino 6.00 15.00
7 Randy Moss 2.50 6.00
8 Drew Bledsoe 2.50 6.00
9 Jerry Rice 8.00 20.00
10 Steve Young 4.00 10.00

1999 Aurora Leather Bound

Inserted at a rate of two in 25 hobby packs, these 20 cards feature 20 leading players set off by a laminated leather football on card with white foil embossed laces.
COMPLETE SET (20) 50.00 100.00
STATED ODDS 2:25 HOBBY
1 Jake Plummer .75 2.00
2 Jamal Anderson 1.00 2.50
3 Tim Couch .75 2.00
4 Troy Aikman 1.50 4.00
5 Emmitt Smith 2.00 5.00
6 Terrell Davis 1.00 2.50
7 Barry Sanders 2.00 5.00
8 Brett Favre 2.50 6.00
9 Peyton Manning 4.00 10.00
10 Fred Taylor .75 2.00
11 Dan Marino 2.50 6.00
12 Randy Moss 1.00 2.50
13 Drew Bledsoe 1.00 2.50
14 Ricky Williams 1.00 2.50
15 Curtis Martin 1.00 2.50
16 Jerome Bettis 1.25 3.00
17 Jerry Rice 3.00 8.00
18 Steve Young 1.50 4.00
19 Jon Kitna .75 2.00
20 Eddie George 1.00 2.50

1999 Aurora Styrotechs

Issued at a rate of one in 25 packs, these 20 cards of leading players are featured in close-ups photos with their helmets on. The cards are printed on styrene with Pacific's full foil process.
COMPLETE SET (20) 60.00 120.00
STATED ODDS 1:25
1 Jake Plummer 1.00 2.50
2 Jamal Anderson 1.25 3.00
3 Tim Couch 1.00 2.50
4 Troy Aikman 2.00 5.00
5 Emmitt Smith 2.50 6.00
6 Terrell Davis 1.25 3.00
7 Barry Sanders 2.50 6.00
8 Brett Favre 3.00 8.00
9 Peyton Manning 5.00 12.00
10 Fred Taylor 1.00 2.50
11 Dan Marino 3.00 8.00
12 Randy Moss 1.25 3.00
13 Drew Bledsoe 1.25 3.00
14 Ricky Williams 1.25 3.00
15 Curtis Martin 1.25 3.00
16 Jerry Rice 4.00 10.00
17 Steve Young 2.00 5.00
18 Joey Galloway 1.25 3.00
19 Jon Kitna 1.00 2.50
20 Eddie George 1.25 3.00

2000 Aurora

Released as a 150-card set, Aurora features a card design that utilizes both portrait photography and acton photography. A color player portrait photo is placed on the left side of the card, while a black and white player action photo is set against a circle in the upper right hand corner of the card. Background colors are set to match the featured player's team colors, and cards are accented with gold foil highlights. Aurora was packaged in 36-pack boxes with packs containing six cards each.
COMPLETE SET (150) 12.50 30.00
1 David Boston .15 .40
2 Thomas Jones RC .30 .75
3 Rob Moore .15 .40
4 Jake Plummer .15 .40
5 Frank Sanders .15 .40
6 Jamal Anderson .20 .50
7 Chris Chandler .20 .50
8 Tim Dwight .20 .50
9 Doug Johnson RC .25 .60
10 Tony Banks .15 .40
11 Qadry Ismail .15 .40
12 Jamal Lewis RC .40 1.00
13 Chris Redman RC .25 .60
14 Travis Taylor RC .25 .60
15 Doug Flutie .20 .50
16 Rob Johnson .20 .50
17 Eric Moulds .15 .40
18 Peerless Price .20 .50
19 Antowain Smith .20 .50
20 Steve Beuerlein .20 .50
21 Tim Biakabutuka .20 .50
22 Patrick Jeffers .15 .40
23 Muhsin Muhammad .15 .40
24 Curtis Enis .15 .40
25 Cade McNown .15 .40
26 Marcus Robinson .20 .50
27 Dez White RC .25 .60
28 Corey Dillon .15 .40
29 Ron Dugans RC .25 .60
30 Darnay Scott .20 .50
31 Akili Smith .15 .40
32 Peter Warrick RC .25 .60
33 Tim Couch .20 .50
34 JaJuan Dawson RC .25 .60
35 Kevin Johnson .15 .40
36 Dennis Northcutt RC .25 .60
37 Travis Prentice RC .25 .60
38 Troy Aikman .30 .75
39 Rocket Ismail .20 .50
40 Emmitt Smith .40 1.00
41 Jason Tucker .15 .40
42 Terrell Davis .20 .50
43 Olandis Gary .20 .50
44 Brian Griese .15 .40
45 Ed McCaffrey .20 .50
46 Rod Smith .20 .50
47 Charlie Batch .15 .40
48 Germane Crowell .15 .40
49 Reuben Droughns RC .25 .60
50 Herman Moore .15 .40
51 Barry Sanders .40 1.00
52 Brett Favre .50 1.25
53 Bubba Franks RC .25 .60
54 Antonio Freeman .20 .50
55 Dorsey Levens .20 .50
56 Bill Schroeder .20 .50
57 Marvin Harrison .20 .50
58 Edgerrin James .20 .50
59 Peyton Manning .60 1.50
60 Terrence Wilkins .15 .40
61 Mark Brunell .20 .50
62 Keenan McCardell .20 .50
63 Jimmy Smith .20 .50
64 R.Jay Soward RC .25 .60
65 Shyrone Stith RC .25 .60
66 Fred Taylor .15 .40
67 Derrick Alexander .15 .40
68 Donnell Bennett .15 .40
69 Tony Gonzalez .20 .50
70 Elvis Grbac .15 .40
71 Sylvester Morris RC .25 .60
72 Damon Huard .15 .40
73 James Johnson .15 .40
74 Dan Marino .50 1.25
75 Tony Martin .20 .50
76 O.J. McDuffie .20 .50
77 Quinton Spotwood RC .25 .60
78 Cris Carter .25 .60
79 Daunte Culpepper .20 .50
80 Randy Moss .20 .50
81 Robert Smith .15 .40
82 Troy Walters RC .25 .60
83 Drew Bledsoe .20 .50
84 Tom Brady RC 20.00 50.00
85 Kevin Faulk .15 .40
86 Terry Glenn .20 .50
87 J.R. Redmond RC .25 .60
88 Marc Bulger RC .30 .75
89 Sherrod Gideon RC .25 .60
90 Keith Poole .15 .40
91 Ricky Williams .20 .50
92 Kerry Collins .15 .40
93 Ron Dayne RC .40 1.00
94 Ike Hilliard .15 .40
95 Amani Toomer .15 .40
96 Wayne Chrebet .15 .40
97 Laveranues Coles RC .30 .75
98 Curtis Martin .20 .50
99 Chad Pennington RC .30 .75
100 Vinny Testaverde .15 .40
101 Tim Brown .25 .60
102 Rich Gannon .20 .50
103 Napoleon Kaufman .20 .50
104 Jerry Porter RC .40 1.00
105 Tyrone Wheatley .15 .40
106 Charles Johnson .15 .40
107 Donovan McNabb .20 .50
108 Todd Pinkston RC .25 .60
109 Duce Staley .15 .40
110 Jerome Bettis .25 .60
111 Plaxico Burress RC .30 .75
112 Troy Edwards .15 .40
113 Richard Huntley .15 .40
114 Tee Martin RC .25 .60
115 Kordell Stewart .15 .40
116 Isaac Bruce .25 .60
117 Trung Canidate RC .25 .60
118 Marshall Faulk .20 .50
119 Torry Holt .20 .50
120 Kurt Warner .40 1.00
121 Jermaine Fazande .15 .40
122 Trevor Gaylor RC .25 .60
123 Jim Harbaugh .20 .50
124 Junior Seau .20 .50
125 Giovanni Carmazzi RC .25 .60
126 Charlie Garner .20 .50
127 Terrell Owens .20 .50
128 Jerry Rice .60 1.50
129 J.J. Stokes .20 .50
130 Steve Young .30 .75
131 Shaun Alexander RC .40 1.00
132 Christian Fauria .15 .40
133 Jon Kitna .15 .40
134 Derrick Mayes .15 .40
135 Ricky Watters .20 .50
136 Mike Alstott .15 .40
137 Warrick Dunn .15 .40
138 Jacquez Green .15 .40
139 Joe Hamilton RC .25 .60
140 Shaun King .15 .40
141 Eddie George .20 .50
142 Jevon Kearse .15 .40
143 Steve McNair .20 .50
144 Yancey Thigpen .15 .40
145 Frank Wycheck .20 .50
146 Albert Connell .15 .40
147 Stephen Davis .15 .40
148 Todd Husak RC .25 .60
149 Brad Johnson .20 .50
150 Michael Westbrook .15 .40
S1 Jon Kitna Sample .40 1.00

2000 Aurora Pinstripes

COMPLETE SET (50) 30.00 50.00
*VETERANS: 1.2X TO 3X BASIC CARDS
*ROOKIES: .8X TO 2X BASIC CARDS

2000 Aurora Premiere Date

*VETERANS: 8X TO 20X BASIC CARDS
*ROOKIES: 5X TO 12X BASIC CARDS
*PD PINSTRIPE: .4X TO 1X PREM.DATE
STATED PRINT RUN 85 SER.#'d SETS
84 Tom Brady 150.00 300.00

2000 Aurora Autographs

Randomly inserted in packs, this set features the base card design enhanced with an authentic player autograph. Most of the autographs were signed in gold ink. Each card includes Pacific's seal of authenticity. We've included the print run numbers below that were released by Pacific. Coles, Dugans, Lewis, Pennington, Travis Taylor, Hamilton, Droughns, and Stephen Davis were inserted in 2001 Crown Royale packs. Jimmy Smith was inserted in both 2000 Aurora and 2001 Crown Royale packs. Some cards were issued as redemptions with an expiration date of 3/31/2001.

ANNOUNCED PRINT RUNS BELOW
2 Thomas Jones/350* 6.00 15.00
12 Jamal Lewis/325* 8.00 20.00
14 Travis Taylor/150* 6.00 15.00
26 Marcus Robinson/350* 8.00 20.00
27 Dez White/350* 6.00 15.00
29 Ron Dugans/250* 6.00 15.00
32 Peter Warrick 6.00 15.00
34 JaJuan Dawson/350* 6.00 15.00
43 Olandis Gary/350* 8.00 20.00
49 Reuben Droughns/350* 6.00 15.00
61 Mark Brunell/100* 10.00 25.00
63 Jimmy Smith/350* 8.00 20.00
66 Fred Taylor 6.00 15.00
71 Sylvester Morris/350* 6.00 15.00
77 Quinton Spotwood/350* 6.00 15.00
88 Marc Bulger/350* 8.00 20.00
93 Ron Dayne/150* 10.00 25.00
97 Laveranues Coles/250* 8.00 20.00
99 Chad Pennington/150* 6.00 15.00
131 Shaun Alexander/350* 8.00 20.00
139 Joe Hamilton/350* 6.00 15.00
147 Stephen Davis/335* 6.00 15.00

2000 Aurora Championship Fever

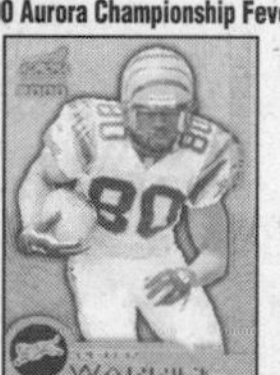

Randomly inserted in packs at the rate of two in 37, this 20-card set features player photos on an all foil card with gold foil accents. Backgrounds are concentric circles on a blue-tone true-life background.
COMPLETE SET (20) 12.50 30.00
STATED ODDS 4:37
*COPPER/160: 2X TO 5X BASIC INSERTS
*PLAT.BLUE/145: 2X TO 5X BASIC INSERTS
PLAT.BLUE PRINT RUN 145 SER.#'d SETS
*SILVER/310: .8X TO 2X BASIC INSERTS
SILVER PRINT RUN 310 SER.#'d SETS
1 Thomas Jones .25 .60
2 Jamal Lewis .30 .75
3 Peter Warrick .20 .50
4 Tim Couch .25 .60
5 Emmitt Smith .50 1.25
6 Olandis Gary .25 .60
7 Marvin Harrison .25 .60
8 Edgerrin James .25 .60
9 Mark Brunell .25 .60
10 Fred Taylor .20 .50
11 Randy Moss .25 .60
12 Chad Pennington .25 .60
13 Plaxico Burress .25 .60
14 Marshall Faulk .25 .60
15 Kurt Warner .50 1.25
16 Shaun Alexander .30 .75
17 Jon Kitna .20 .50
17AU Jon Kitna AUTO 6.00 15.00
18 Eddie George .25 .60
19 Shaun King .20 .50
20 Stephen Davis .20 .50

2000 Aurora Game Worn Jerseys

Randomly inserted in packs, this 10-card set features full color player action photography coupled with a swatch of a game worn jersey. The jersey swatch is circular and placed in the lower left hand corner of the card, and a border along the bottom of the card contains Pacific's Authentic Game Worn Jersey stamp.
UNPRICED PATCH PRINT RUN 10
1 Olandis Gary 3.00 8.00
2 Brett Favre 8.00 20.00
3 Mark Brunell 3.00 8.00
4 Cris Carter 4.00 10.00
5 Randy Moss 3.00 8.00
6 Ricky Williams 3.00 8.00
7 Donovan McNabb 3.00 8.00
8 Duce Staley 2.50 6.00
9 Junior Seau 3.00 8.00
10 Steve McNair 3.00 8.00

2000 Aurora Helmet Styrotechs

Randomly inserted in packs at the rate of one in 37, this 20-card set features 30pt card stock. Each card features a player photograph and is die cut around the player helmet background.
COMPLETE SET (20) 40.00 80.00
STATED ODDS 1:37
1 Jake Plummer .50 1.25
2 Cade McNown .50 1.25
3 Tim Couch .60 1.50
4 Troy Aikman 1.00 2.50
5 Emmitt Smith 1.25 3.00
6 Barry Sanders 1.25 3.00
7 Terrell Davis .60 1.50
8 Brett Favre 1.50 4.00
9 Edgerrin James .60 1.50
10 Peyton Manning 2.00 5.00
11 Mark Brunell .60 1.50
12 Fred Taylor .50 1.25
13 Drew Bledsoe .60 1.50
14 Ricky Williams .60 1.50
15 Randy Moss .60 1.50
16 Kurt Warner 1.25 3.00
17 Jerry Rice 2.00 5.00
18 Jon Kitna .50 1.25
19 Shaun King .50 1.25
20 Eddie George .60 1.50

2000 Aurora Rookie Draft Board

Randomly seeded in Hobby packs at the rate of two in 37, this 20-card set features action photography with foil accents on the front, and a chalkboard surface on the back.
COMPLETE SET (20) 20.00 50.00
STATED ODDS 2:37 HOB
1 Thomas Jones .50 1.25
2 Jamal Lewis .60 1.50
3 Chris Redman .40 1.00
4 Travis Taylor .40 1.00
5 Peter Warrick .40 1.00
6 Dez White .40 1.00
7 Dennis Northcutt .40 1.00
8 Travis Prentice .40 1.00
9 Reuben Droughns .40 1.00
10 R.Jay Soward .40 1.00
11 Sylvester Morris .40 1.00
12 J.R. Redmond .40 1.00
13 Ron Dayne .60 1.50
14 Laveranues Coles .50 1.25
15 Chad Pennington .50 1.25
16 Plaxico Burress .50 1.25
17 Tee Martin .40 1.00
18 Trung Canidate .40 1.00
19 Giovanni Carmazzi .40 1.00
20 Shaun Alexander .60 1.50

2000 Aurora Team Players

Randomly inserted in packs at the rate of one in 37, this 20-card set features card numbers 1-10 in A and B versions. When combined, the A and B versions make a larger card featuring two players from the same team. A versions are found in Hobby packs only and B versions are found in Retail packs only at the same insertion ratio.
COMP.HOBBY SET (10) 7.50 20.00
COMP.RETAIL SET (10) 7.50 20.00
1A-10A STATED ODDS 1:37 HOBBY
1B-10B STATED ODDS 1:37 RETAIL
1A Troy Aikman 1.00 2.50
1B Emmitt Smith 1.25 3.00
2A Terrell Davis .60 1.50
2B Brian Griese .50 1.25
3A Antonio Freeman .60 1.50
3B Brett Favre 1.50 4.00
4A Peyton Manning 2.00 5.00
4B Edgerrin James .60 1.50
5A Fred Taylor .50 1.25
5B Mark Brunell .60 1.50
6A Randy Moss .60 1.50
6B Cris Carter .75 2.00
7A Marshall Faulk .60 1.50
7B Kurt Warner 1.25 3.00
8A Jerry Rice 2.00 5.00
8B Terrell Owens .60 1.50
9A Steve McNair .60 1.50
9B Eddie George .60 1.50
10A Stephen Davis .50 1.25
10B Brad Johnson .60 1.50

1945 Autographs Playing Cards

Cards from this set are part of a playing card game released in 1945 by Leister Game Co. of Toledo Ohio. The cards feature a photo of a famous person, such as an actor or writer, or athlete on the top half of the card with his signature across the middle. A photo appears in the upper left hand corner along with some biographical information about him printed in orange in the center. The bottom half of the cardfront features a drawing along with information about a second personality in the same field or vocation. Those two characters are featured on another card with the positions reversed top and bottom. Note that a card number was also used in the upper left corner with each pair being featured on two of the same card number. We've listed the player who's photo appears on the card first, followed by the personality featured at the bottom of the card.
COMPLETE SET (55) 200.00 400.00
7A Knute Rockne CO 10.00 20.00
Bernie Bierman
7A Bernie Bierman CO 10.00 20.00
Knute Rockne CO
10 Tom Harmon 12.50 25.00
Red Grange
10 Red Grange 12.50 25.00
Tom Harmon

1959 Bazooka

The 1959 Bazooka football cards made up the back of the Bazooka Bubble Gum boxes of that year. The cards are blank backed and measure approximately 2 13/16" by 4 15/16". Comparable to the Bazooka baseball cards of that year, they are relatively difficult to obtain and fairly attractive considering they form part of the box. The full boxes contained 20 pieces of chewing gum. The cards are unnumbered but have been numbered alphabetically in the checklist below for your convenience. The cards marked with SP in the checklist below were apparently printed in shorter supply and are more difficult to find. The catalog number for this set is R414-15A. The value of complete intact boxes would be 50 percent greater than the prices listed below.
COMPLETE SET (18) 6000.00 9500.00
1 Alan Ameche 175.00 300.00
2 Jon Arnett 150.00 250.00
3 Jim Brown 400.00 700.00
4 Rick Casares 200.00 350.00
5A Charley Conerly SP 350.00 500.00
5B Charley Conerly SP 350.00 500.00
6 Howard Ferguson 175.00 300.00
7 Frank Gifford 200.00 350.00
8 Lou Groza SP 1250.00 1800.00
9 Bobby Layne 200.00 350.00
10 Eddie LeBaron 175.00 300.00
11 Woodley Lewis 150.00 250.00
12 Ollie Matson 175.00 300.00
13 Joe Perry 175.00 300.00
14 Pete Retzlaff 150.00 250.00
15 Tobin Rote 150.00 250.00
16 Y.A. Tittle 250.00 400.00
17 Tom Tracy SP 1500.00 2500.00
18 Johnny Unitas 350.00 650.00

1971 Bazooka

The 1971 Bazooka football cards were issued as twelve panels of three on the backs of Bazooka Bubble Gum boxes. Consequently, cards are seen in panels of three or as individual cards which have been cut from panels of three. The individual cards measure approxiamtely 1 15/16" by 2 5/8" and the panels of three measure 2 5/8" by 5 7/8". The 36 individual blank-backed cards are numbered on the card front. The checklist below presents prices for the individual cards. Complete panels are worth 25 percent more than the sum of the individual players making up the panel; complete boxes are worth approximately 50 percent more (i.e., an additional 25 percent premium) than the sum of the three players on the box. With regard to cut single cards, the mid-panel cards (2, 5, 8, ...) seem to be somewhat easier to find in nice shape.
COMPLETE SET (36) 300.00 450.00
1 Joe Namath 25.00 50.00
2 Larry Brown 6.00 12.00
3 Bobby Bell 6.00 12.00
4 Dick Butkus 18.00 30.00
5 Charlie Sanders 6.00 12.00
6 Chuck Howley 6.00 12.00
7 Gale Gillingham 5.00 10.00
8 Leroy Kelly 6.00 12.00
9 Floyd Little 6.00 12.00
10 Dan Abramowicz 5.00 10.00
11 Sonny Jurgensen 10.00 20.00
12 Andy Russell 5.00 10.00
13 Tommy Nobis 6.00 12.00
14 O.J. Simpson 10.00 20.00
15 Tom Woodeshick 5.00 10.00
16 Roman Gabriel 6.00 12.00
17 Claude Humphrey 5.00 10.00
18 Merlin Olsen 7.50 15.00
19 Daryle Lamonica 6.00 12.00
20 Fred Cox 5.00 10.00
21 Bart Starr 30.00 50.00
22 John Brodie 7.50 15.00
23 Jim Nance 5.00 10.00
24 Gary Garrison 5.00 10.00
25 Fran Tarkenton 12.50 25.00
26 Johnny Robinson 5.00 10.00
27 Gale Sayers 18.00 30.00
28 Johnny Unitas 30.00 50.00
29 Jerry LeVias 5.00 10.00
30 Virgil Carter 5.00 10.00
31 Bill Nelsen 5.00 10.00
32 Dave Osborn 5.00 10.00
33 Matt Snell 5.00 10.00
34 Larry Wilson 6.00 12.00
35 Bob Griese 15.00 25.00
36 Lance Alworth 10.00 20.00

1972 Bazooka Official Signals

This 12-card set was issued on the bottom of Bazooka Bubble Gum boxes. The box bottom measures approximately 6 1/4" by 2 7/8". The bottoms are numbered in the upper left corner and the text appears between cartoon characters on the sides of the bottom. The material is entitled "A children's guide to TV football," having been extracted from the book Football Lingo. Cards 1-8 provide definitions of numerous terms associated with football. Card number 9 lists the six different officials and describes their responsibilities. Cards 10-12 picture the officials' signals and explain their meanings. The value of complete intact boxes would be 50 percent greater than the prices listed below.
COMPLETE SET (12) 62.50 125.00
1 Football Lingo 6.00 12.00
2 Football Lingo 6.00 12.00
3 Football Lingo 6.00 12.00
4 Football Lingo 6.00 12.00
5 Football Lingo 6.00 12.00
6 Football Lingo 6.00 12.00
7 Football Lingo 6.00 12.00
8 Football Lingo 6.00 12.00
9 Officials' Duties 6.00 12.00
10 Officials' Duties 6.00 12.00
11 Officials' Signals 6.00 12.00
12 Officials' Signals 6.00 12.00

2004 Bazooka

Bazooka initially released in early September 2004. The base set consists of 220-cards including 55 rookies at the end of the set. Hobby boxes contained 24-packs of 8-cards and carried an S.R.P. of $2 per pack. Two parallel sets and a variety of inserts can be found seeded in hobby and retail packs highlighted by an assortment of jersey memorabilia inserts.
COMPLETE SET (220) 20.00 50.00
1 Peyton Manning .75 2.00
2 Rod Gardner .20 .50
3 Marc Bulger .20 .50
4 Champ Bailey .25 .60
5 Moe Williams .20 .50
6 Andre' Davis .20 .50
7 Corey Dillon .20 .50
8 Trent Green .20 .50
9 Daunte Culpepper .25 .60
10 Chad Pennington .20 .50
11 Hines Ward .25 .60
12 Tim Brown .30 .75
13 Jerome Pathon .20 .50
14 Drew Brees .30 .75
15 Eddie George .25 .60
16 Duce Staley .20 .50
17 Marques Tuiasosopo .20 .50
18 Willis McGahee .20 .50
19 T.J. Duckett .20 .50
20 Brian Urlacher .30 .75
21 Ashley Lelie .20 .50
22 Robert Ferguson .20 .50
23 Tai Streets .20 .50
24 Junior Seau .30 .75
25 Priest Holmes .20 .50
26 Ty Law .30 .75
27 Correll Buckhalter .20 .50
28 Plaxico Burress .20 .50
29 Brad Johnson .25 .60
30 Shaun Alexander .20 .50
31 Mark Brunell .25 .60
32 Julian Peterson .25 .60
33 Marcel Shipp .20 .50
34 Kyle Boller .20 .50
35 Rudi Johnson .20 .50
36 Quincy Carter .20 .50
37 Jabar Gaffney .20 .50
38 Reggie Wayne .25 .60
39 Deion Branch .20 .50
40 Terrell Owens .25 .60
41 Chris Brown .20 .50
42 Bobby Engram .20 .50
43 Josh Reed .20 .50
44 Thomas Jones .20 .50
45 Stephen Davis .20 .50
46 Mike Anderson .20 .50
47 Javon Walker .20 .50
48 Edgerrin James .25 .60
49 Randy McMichael .20 .50
50 Deuce McAllister .25 .60
51 Nate Burleson .25 .60
52 Jevon Kearse .20 .50
53 Jay Fiedler .20 .50
54 Patrick Ramsey .25 .60
55 Brian Westbrook .20 .50
56 Tyrone Calico .25 .60
57 Alge Crumpler .25 .60
58 Josh McCown .25 .60
59 Quincy Morgan .20 .50
60 Jeff Garcia .20 .50
61 Garrison Hearst .20 .50
62 Chad Johnson .20 .50
63 Byron Leftwich .20 .50
64 Donald Driver .25 .60
65 Ricky Williams .25 .60
66 Todd Pinkston .20 .50
67 Amani Toomer .20 .50
68 David Givens .20 .50
69 Jerome Bettis .30 .75
70 Derrick Mason .20 .50
71 Darrell Jackson .25 .60
72 Kassim Osgood .20 .50
73 Todd Heap .20 .50
74 Warrick Dunn .20 .50
75 Brett Favre .60 1.50
76 Chris Chambers .20 .50
77 Fred Taylor .20 .50
78 Charles Rogers .20 .50
79 Onterrio Smith .20 .50
80 Joe Horn .20 .50
81 Justin McCareins .20 .50
82 Ike Hilliard .20 .60
83 Kevan Barlow .20 .50
84 Charlie Garner .25 .60
85 Anquan Boldin .20 .50
86 Anthony Thomas .25 .60
87 Julius Peppers .25 .60
88 Dat Nguyen .20 .50
89 Peerless Price .20 .50
90 Randy Moss .25 .60
91 Jamie Sharper .20 .50
92 Travis Henry .20 .50
93 Terrell Suggs .20 .50
94 Joey Galloway .25 .60
95 Torry Holt .25 .60
96 Freddie Mitchell .20 .50
97 Jerry Porter .20 .50
98 Dwight Freeney .20 .50
99 Joey Harrington .20 .50
100 Michael Vick .25 .60
101 Kelley Washington .20 .50
102 Marty Booker .20 .50
103 Tim Rattay .20 .50
104 Derrick Brooks .20 .50
105 Laveranues Coles .20 .50
106 Ray Lewis .30 .75
107 Jon Kitna .20 .50
108 Terry Glenn .25 .60
109 Steve Smith .30 .75
110 Ahman Green .25 .60
111 Andre Johnson .25 .60
112 Dallas Clark .20 .50
113 Kevin Faulk .20 .50
114 Michael Bennett .20 .50
115 Tony Gonzalez .25 .60
116 Michael Strahan .25 .60
117 Tommy Maddox .20 .50
118 Isaac Bruce .30 .75
119 Brandon Lloyd .25 .60
120 Steve McNair .25 .60
121 Keith Brooking .20 .50
122 Drew Bledsoe .25 .60
123 Peter Warrick .20 .50
124 Antonio Bryant .25 .60
125 Clinton Portis .20 .50
126 Kelly Holcomb .20 .50
127 Jake Delhomme .20 .50
128 Rod Smith .25 .60
129 Lee Suggs .25 .60
130 Domanick Davis .20 .50
131 Carson Palmer .25 .60
132 Kerry Collins .20 .50
133 Teyo Johnson .20 .50
134 Curtis Martin .25 .60
135 Matt Hasselbeck .20 .50
136 Cedrick Wilson .20 .50
137 Eric Moulds .20 .50
138 Keyshawn Johnson .25 .60
139 Dante Hall .20 .50
140 Jamal Lewis .25 .60
141 Kelly Campbell .20 .50
142 Jeremy Shockey .20 .50
143 Jerry Rice .60 1.50
144 Kurt Warner .25 .60
145 Jake Plummer .20 .50
146 Keenan McCardell .20 .50
147 Jimmy Smith .25 .60
148 Zach Thomas .25 .60
149 Eddie Kennison .25 .60
150 Tom Brady 1.25 3.00
151 Donte' Stallworth .20 .50
152 John Abraham .20 .50
153 Koren Robinson .20 .50
154 Rex Grossman .20 .50
155 Donovan McNabb .25 .60
156 David Carr .20 .50
157 David Boston .20 .50
158 Tiki Barber .25 .60
159 Santana Moss .25 .60
160 LaDainian Tomlinson .30 .75
161 Justin Fargas .25 .60
162 Troy Brown .20 .50
163 Marshall Faulk .25 .60
164 Aaron Brooks .20 .50
165 Marvin Harrison .25 .60
166 Kevin Jones RC .50 1.25
167 Michael Clayton RC .50 1.25
168 Bernard Berrian RC .40 1.00
169 Ben Watson RC .50 1.25
170 Philip Rivers RC 1.25 3.00
171 Vince Wilfork RC .60 1.50
172 Jason Babin RC .60 1.50
173 Marcus Tubbs RC .40 1.00
174 Sean Taylor RC 2.50 6.00
175 Larry Fitzgerald RC 1.50 4.00
176 Craig Krenzel RC .40 1.00
177 Cedric Cobbs RC .40 1.00
178 Lee Evans RC .60 1.50
179 Johnnie Morant RC .40 1.00
180 Kellen Winslow RC .40 1.00
181 Mewelde Moore RC .50 1.25
182 Carlos Francis RC .40 1.00
183 Josh Harris RC .40 1.00
184 Julius Jones RC .40 1.00
185 Reggie Williams RC .40 1.00
186 DeAngelo Hall RC .60 1.50
187 D.J. Williams RC .60 1.50
188 Cody Pickett RC .40 1.00
189 Dunta Robinson RC .40 1.00
190 J.P. Losman RC .40 1.00
191 Jonathan Vilma RC .50 1.25
192 Jerricho Cotchery RC .50 1.25
193 Keary Colbert RC .40 1.00
194 Ben Troupe RC .40 1.00
195 Drew Henson RC .40 1.00
196 Chris Gamble RC .40 1.00
197 Samie Parker RC .40 1.00
198 Tatum Bell RC .40 1.00
199 Robert Gallery RC .50 1.25
200 Eli Manning RC 3.00 8.00
201 Ahmad Carroll RC .40 1.00
202 Devery Henderson RC .40 1.00
203 Matt Schaub RC .40 1.00
204 Greg Jones RC .40 1.00
205 Roy Williams RC .40 1.00
206 Tommie Harris RC .50 1.25
207 Jeff Smoker RC .50 1.25
208 Kenechi Udeze RC .50 1.25
209 Derrick Hamilton RC .40 1.00
210 Ben Roethlisberger RC 3.00 8.00
211 Darius Watts RC .40 1.00
212 John Navarre RC .40 1.00
213 Ernest Wilford RC .50 1.25
214 Rashaun Woods RC .40 1.00
215 Steven Jackson RC .60 1.50
216 Michael Jenkins RC .40 1.00
217 Will Smith RC .50 1.25
218 Devard Darling RC .40 1.00
219 Chris Perry RC .40 1.00
220 Luke McCown RC .40 1.00

2004 Bazooka Gold

COMPLETE SET (220) 40.00 80.00
*GOLD STARS: 1.2X TO 3X BASE CARD HI
*GOLD ROOKIES: .8X TO 2X BASE CARD HI
ONE GOLD PER PACK

2004 Bazooka Minis

COMPLETE SET (220) 40.00 80.00
*MINI STARS: 1.2X TO 3X BASE CARD HI
*MINI ROOKIES: .8X TO 2X BASE CARD HI
MINI STATED ODDS 1:1

2004 Bazooka All-Stars Jerseys

STATED ODDS 1:17
BASAB Alex Bannister 3.00 8.00
BASAC Alge Crumpler 3.00 8.00
BASAW Aeneas Williams 3.00 8.00
BASBM Brock Marion 3.00 8.00
BASCC Corey Chavous 3.00 8.00
BASCH Casey Hampton 3.00 8.00
BASCM Chris McAlister 3.00 8.00

BASDB Dre Bly 3.00 8.00
BASDM Derrick Mason 3.00 8.00
BASER Ed Reed 4.00 10.00
BASFA Flozell Adams 3.00 8.00
BASFB Fred Beasley 3.00 8.00
BASJA Jerry Azumah 3.00 8.00
BASJO Jonathan Ogden 3.00 8.00
BASJP Julian Peterson 3.00 8.00
BASJW Jeff Wilkins 3.00 8.00
BASJWO Jerome Woods 3.00 8.00
BASKJ Kris Jenkins 3.00 8.00
BASKM Kevin Mawae 3.00 8.00
BASKBU Keith Bulluck 3.00 8.00
BASLG La'Roi Glover 3.00 8.00
BASLL Leonard Little 3.00 8.00
BASMR Marco Rivera 3.00 8.00
BASMV Mike Vanderjagt 3.00 8.00
BASOP Orlando Pace 3.00 8.00
BASPS Patrick Surtain 3.00 8.00
BASRB Ruben Brown 3.00 8.00
BASRS Richard Seymour 4.00 10.00
BASRW Roy Williams S 4.00 10.00
BASSE Shaun Ellis 3.00 8.00
BASTR Tony Richardson 3.00 8.00
BASTS Takeo Spikes 3.00 8.00
BASTV Troy Vincent 3.00 8.00
BASWJ Walter Jones 3.00 8.00
BASWS Will Shields 3.00 8.00

2004 Bazooka College Collection Jerseys

STATED ODDS 1:115
BCCAB Anquan Boldin 4.00 10.00
BCCCP Carson Palmer 5.00 12.00
BCCCPI Cody Pickett 4.00 10.00
BCCDA Derek Abney 3.00 8.00
BCCDD Devard Darling 3.00 8.00
BCCJRT J.R. Tolver 3.00 8.00
BCCLD Lane Danielsen 3.00 8.00
BCCMS Matt Schaub 8.00 20.00
BCCWW Wes Welker 6.00 15.00

2004 Bazooka Comics

COMPLETE SET (24) 10.00 25.00
STATED ODDS 1:4
1 Anquan Boldin .50 1.25
2 Brett Favre 1.50 4.00
3 Bruce Smith .60 1.50
4 Clinton Portis .50 1.25
5 Dante Hall .50 1.25
6 Domanick Davis .50 1.25
7 Jamal Lewis .60 1.50
8 Jerry Rice 1.50 4.00
9 LaDainian Tomlinson .75 2.00
10 Marvin Harrison .60 1.50
11 Mike Vanderjagt .50 1.25
12 New England Patriots .50 1.25
13 Peyton Manning 2.00 5.00
14 Priest Holmes .50 1.25
15 Randy Moss .60 1.50
16 Shannon Sharpe .60 1.50
17 Steve McNair .60 1.50
18 Terrell Suggs .50 1.25
19 Tom Brady 3.00 8.00
20 Tony Gonzalez .60 1.50
21 Torry Holt .60 1.50
22 Michael Vick .60 1.50
23 Ricky Williams .60 1.50
24 Jake Delhomme .50 1.25

2004 Bazooka Originals Jerseys

STATED ODDS 1:21
BOBB Bernard Berrian 2.50 6.00
BOBR Ben Roethlisberger 8.00 20.00
BOBT Ben Troupe 2.00 5.00
BOBW Ben Watson 2.00 5.00
BOCC Cedric Cobbs 2.00 5.00
BOCP Chris Perry 2.50 6.00
BODD Devard Darling 2.00 5.00
BODH DeAngelo Hall 2.50 6.00
BODHA Derrick Hamilton 2.00 5.00
BODHE Devery Henderson 2.00 5.00
BODR Dunta Robinson 2.00 5.00
BODW Darius Watts 2.00 5.00
BOEM Eli Manning 8.00 20.00
BOGJ Greg Jones 2.50 6.00
BOJJ Julius Jones 3.00 8.00
BOJPL J.P. Losman 2.50 6.00
BOKC Keary Colbert 2.00 5.00
BOKJ Kevin Jones 3.00 8.00
BOKW Kellen Winslow Jr. 2.50 6.00
BOLE Lee Evans 2.50 6.00
BOLF Larry Fitzgerald 5.00 12.00
BOLM Luke McCown 2.50 6.00
BOMC Michael Clayton 2.50 6.00
BOMJ Michael Jenkins 2.00 5.00
BOMM Mewelde Moore 2.00 5.00
BOMS Matt Schaub 5.00 12.00
BOPR Philip Rivers 5.00 12.00
BORG Robert Gallery 2.00 5.00
BORW Roy Williams WR 2.50 6.00
BORWI Reggie Williams 2.00 5.00
BORWO Rashaun Woods 2.50 6.00
BOSJ Steven Jackson 5.00 12.00
BOTB Tatum Bell 2.50 6.00

2004 Bazooka Rookie Roundup Jerseys

STATED ODDS 1:115
RRBT Ben Troupe 3.00 8.00
RRDR Dunta Robinson 2.50 6.00
RRJT Joey Thomas 2.50 6.00
RRKR Keiwan Ratliff 2.50 6.00
RRKS Keith Smith 2.50 6.00
RRPR Philip Rivers 10.00 20.00
RRRC Ricardo Colclough 3.00 8.00
RRRG Robert Gallery 3.00 8.00
RRTA Tim Anderson 4.00 10.00

2004 Bazooka Stickers

STATED ODDS 1:4
1 Bailey/Law/Hall/Robinson .60 1.50
2 Kearse/Peppers/Freeney/Strahan 1.00 2.50
3 Abra/Urlach/Seau/Vilma 1.25 3.00
4 Peterson/Nguyen/Sharper/Suggs .60 1.50
5 Brooks/Lewis/Brook/Thom 1.00 2.50
6 P.Mann/Favre/McNbb/Vick 2.50 6.00
7 Pennin/Culpep/Brady/McNair 2.50 6.00
8 Brunell/Garcia/Warner/Collins 1.00 2.50
9 Boller/Palmer/Gross/Leftw 1.25 3.00
10 Green/Bulger/Hassel/Delh 1.00 2.50
11 Kitna/Brees/Fiedler/Holcomb 1.00 2.50
12 Rattay/McCown/Tuiasosopo/Carter .50 1.25
13 Johnson/Madd/Bled/Plum 1.00 2.50
14 Carr/Brooks/Harring/Rams 1.00 2.50
15 Dillon/Staley/Garner/Hearst .60 1.50
16 George/Davis/Bettis/Martin 1.00 2.50
17 McAllis/Portis/Tomlin/A.Grn 1.00 2.50
18 Holmes/Lewis/Ri.Will/Faulk 1.25 3.00
19 Johnson/Suggs/Davis/West. 1.00 2.50
20 Fargas/Brown/McGahee/Smith 1.00 2.50
21 Taylor/Alexander/James/Henry 1.00 2.50
22 Anderson/Buckhalter/Faulk/Williams .60 1.50
23 Dunn/Barber/Bennett/Jones .60 1.50
24 Shipp/Barlow/Duckett/Thomas .60 1.50
25 McMichael/Crumpler/Clark/Johnson .60 1.50
26 Gonzalez/Shockey/Heap/Hall 1.00 2.50
27 Toomer/Horn/Smith/Moulds .60 1.50
28 Bruce/McCardell/Driver/Brown .60 1.50
29 Boldin/Johnson/Rogers/Calico 1.00 2.50
30 J.Rice/R.Smith/T.Brwn/Glnn 2.00 5.00
31 Mason/Ward/Coles/Jackson 1.00 2.50
32 Moss/Smith/Porter/Chambers 1.00 2.50
33 Campbell/Osgood/Lloyd/Ferguson .50 1.25
34 Booton/Owens/Calloway/Johnson 1.00 2.50
35 R.Moss/C.Jhn/Harris/Holt 1.25 3.00
36 Gardner/Wayne/McCareins/Morgan .60 1.50
37 Burress/Lelie/Robinson/Stallworth .60 1.50
38 Price/Booker/Kennison/Pinkston .60 1.50
39 Hilliard/Pathon/Streets/Engram .50 1.25
40 Davis/Reed/Gaffney/Bryant .50 1.25
41 Burleson/Branch/Washington/Walker .60 1.50
42 Wilson/Givens/Warrick/Mitchell .60 1.50
43 Wltrk/Hrrs/Lhmn/Wllms 1.00 2.50
44 Smith/Udeze/Babin/Gallery 1.00 2.50
45 Eli/Rivers/Roeth/Losman 4.00 10.00
46 Jacksn/Perry/K.Jones/Bell 2.00 5.00
47 Watts/Colbert/Hamilton/Berrian 1.25 3.00
48 Winsl/Watson/Troupe/Darl 1.00 2.50
49 Harris/Smoker/Navarre/Pickett .75 2.00
50 Fitz/Ro.Will/Re.Willi/Evans 2.50 6.00
51 Schaub/L.McCow/Kren/Hens 2.00 5.00
52 Francis/Parker/Cotchery/Wilford .75 2.00
53 Taylor/Carroll/Gamb/Morant 1.00 2.50
54 J.Jones/G.Jones/Mre/Cobbs 1.25 3.00
55 Clayton/Jenkins/Wds/Hend. 1.50 4.00

2004 Bazooka Tattoos

COMPLETE SET (33) 6.00 15.00
STATED ODDS 1:6
1 Arizona Cardinals .30 .75
2 Atlanta Falcons .30 .75
3 Baltimore Ravens .30 .75
4 Buffalo Bills .40 1.00
5 Carolina Panthers .30 .75
6 Chicago Bears .40 1.00
7 Cincinnati Bengals .30 .75
8 Cleveland Browns .30 .75
9 Dallas Cowboys .50 1.25
10 Denver Broncos .40 1.00
11 Detroit Lions .30 .75
12 Green Bay Packers .50 1.25
13 Houston Texans .30 .75
14 Indianapolis Colts .30 .75
15 Jacksonville Jaguars .30 .75
16 Kansas City Chiefs .40 1.00
17 Miami Dolphins .40 1.00
18 Minnesota Vikings .30 .75
19 New England Patriots .40 1.00
20 New Orleans Saints .30 .75
21 New York Giants .40 1.00
22 New York Jets .40 1.00
23 Oakland Raiders .50 1.25
24 Philadelphia Eagles .30 .75
25 Pittsburgh Steelers .40 1.00
26 St. Louis Rams .30 .75
27 San Diego Chargers .30 .75
28 San Francisco 49ers .50 1.25
29 Seattle Seahawks .30 .75
30 Tampa Bay Buccaneers .30 .75
31 Tennessee Titans .30 .75
32 Washington Redskins .50 1.25
33 Bazooka Logo .30 .75

2005 Bazooka

This 220-card set was released in August, 2005. The set was issued into the hobby in six-card packs with an $1.99 SRP which came 24 packs to a box. Cards numbered 1-165 feature veterans while cards 166-220 feature 2005 rookies.
COMPLETE SET (220) 20.00 50.00
COMP.SET w/o RC's (165) 10.00 25.00
1 Willis McGahee .20 .50
2 Aaron Brooks .20 .50
3 Allen Rossum .20 .50
4 Brett Favre .60 1.50
5 Donovan McNabb .25 .60
6 Torry Holt .25 .60
7 Michael Vick .25 .60
8 David Carr .20 .50
9 Eric Moulds .20 .50
10 Chad Pennington .20 .50
11 Larry Fitzgerald .30 .75
12 Tom Brady 1.25 3.00
13 Derrick Brooks .20 .50
14 Brandon Stokley .20 .50
15 Justin McCareins .20 .50
16 Champ Bailey .25 .60
17 Jake Delhomme .20 .50
18 Peyton Manning .75 2.00
19 Keyshawn Johnson .25 .60
20 Daunte Culpepper .25 .60
21 Chester Taylor .25 .60
22 Kurt Warner .25 .60
23 Cedrick Wilson .20 .50
24 Brian Westbrook .20 .50
25 Rodney Harrison .20 .50
26 Clinton Portis .20 .50
27 A.J. Feeley .20 .50
28 Curtis Martin .25 .60
29 Chris Perry .20 .50
30 Randy Moss .25 .60
31 Darrell Jackson .20 .50
32 Edgerrin James .25 .60
33 Ben Roethlisberger .50 1.25
34 Kevin Jones .20 .50
35 LaMont Jordan .25 .60
36 Jerome Bettis .30 .75
37 Ahman Green .25 .60
38 Tyrone Calico .20 .50
39 Anquan Boldin .20 .50
40 Dante Hall .20 .50
41 Todd Heap .20 .50
42 Corey Dillon .20 .50
43 Julius Peppers .25 .60
44 Antonio Bryant .20 .50
45 Dunta Robinson .20 .50
46 Michael Pittman .20 .50
47 Billy Volek .20 .50
48 Jimmy Smith .25 .60
49 Carson Palmer .25 .60
50 Derrick Blaylock .20 .50
51 Deuce McAllister .25 .60
52 Ray Lewis .30 .75
53 Chad Johnson .20 .50
54 Zach Thomas .25 .60
55 Julius Jones .20 .50
56 D.J. Williams .20 .50
57 Stephen Davis .20 .50
58 Greg Jones .20 .50
59 J.P. Losman .20 .50
60 Trent Green .20 .50
61 Drew Bennett .25 .60
62 Joe Horn .20 .50
63 Mewelde Moore .20 .50
64 Alge Crumpler .25 .60
65 Javon Walker .20 .50
66 Jake Plummer .20 .50
67 Aaron Stecker .20 .50
68 Keary Colbert .20 .50
69 Joey Harrington .20 .50
70 Brian Urlacher .30 .75
71 Jeremy Shockey .20 .50
72 Duce Staley .20 .50
73 Tim Rattay .20 .50
74 Jerry Porter .20 .50
75 Steven Jackson .20 .50
76 David Givens .20 .50
77 Byron Leftwich .20 .50
78 T.J. Duckett .20 .50
79 Jason Witten .25 .60
80 Andre Johnson .25 .60
81 Amani Toomer .20 .50
82 Kellen Winslow .20 .50
83 Kyle Boller .20 .50
84 Santana Moss .25 .60
85 Antonio Gates .30 .75
86 Lee Evans .25 .60
87 Larry Johnson .20 .50
88 Plaxico Burress .20 .50
89 Reuben Droughns .20 .50
90 Eli Manning .50 1.25
91 Lito Sheppard .25 .60
92 DeAngelo Hall .20 .50
93 Josh McCown .25 .60
94 Eric Parker .20 .60
95 Drew Brees .30 .75
96 Fred Taylor .20 .50
97 Jonathan Vilma .20 .50
98 Michael Strahan .25 .60
99 Dwight Freeney .20 .50
100 Kerry Collins .20 .50
101 Hines Ward .25 .60
102 Lee Suggs .20 .50
103 Luke McCown .20 .50
104 Laveranues Coles .20 .50
105 LaDainian Tomlinson .30 .75
106 Jeff Garcia .20 .50
107 Michael Clayton .20 .50
108 DeShaun Foster .25 .60
109 Rex Grossman .20 .50
110 Priest Holmes .20 .50
111 Roy Williams WR .20 .50
112 Drew Henson .20 .50
113 Derrick Mason .20 .50
114 Michael Bennett .20 .50
115 Chris Simms .20 .50
116 Isaac Bruce .30 .75
117 Deion Branch .20 .50
118 Rudi Johnson .20 .50
119 Nate Burleson .20 .50
120 Warrick Dunn .20 .50
121 Brian Griese .20 .50
122 T.J. Houshmandzadeh .20 .50
123 Jamaar Taylor .20 .50
124 Drew Bledsoe .25 .60
125 Najeh Davenport .20 .50
126 Charles Rogers .20 .50
127 Ronald Curry .20 .50
128 Chris Brown .20 .50
129 Doug Gabriel .20 .50
130 Todd Pinkston .20 .50
131 Marc Bulger .20 .50
132 Marshall Faulk .25 .60
133 Marvin Harrison .25 .60
134 Matt Hasselbeck .20 .50
135 Tiki Barber .25 .60
136 Muhsin Muhammad .20 .50
137 Kevan Barlow .20 .50
138 Chris Chambers .20 .50
139 Donald Driver .25 .60
140 Jamal Lewis .25 .60
141 Rashaun Woods .20 .50
142 Steve McNair .25 .60
143 Reggie Wayne .25 .60
144 Jevon Kearse .20 .50
145 Domanick Davis .20 .50
146 Donte Stallworth .20 .50
147 Chris Gamble .20 .50
148 Philip Rivers .30 .75
149 Sean Taylor .30 .75
150 Antwaan Randle El .20 .50
151 Koren Robinson .20 .50
152 Tatum Bell .20 .50
153 Tony Gonzalez .25 .60
154 Reggie Williams .20 .50
155 Onterrio Smith .20 .50
156 Patrick Ramsey .25 .60
157 Thomas Jones .20 .50
158 Michael Jenkins .20 .50
159 Rod Smith .25 .60
160 Trent Dilfer .20 .50
161 Randy McMichael .20 .50
162 Terrell Owens .25 .60
163 Travis Henry .20 .50
164 Travis Taylor .20 .50
165 Shaun Alexander .20 .50
166 J.J. Arrington RC .50 1.25
167 Cedric Benson RC .40 1.00
168 Carlos Rogers RC .60 1.50
169 Troy Williamson RC .40 1.00
170 Ronnie Brown RC .50 1.25
171 Jason Campbell RC .40 1.00
172 Alvin Pearman RC .40 1.00
173 Reggie Brown RC .40 1.00
174 Lionel Gates RC .40 1.00
175 Derek Anderson RC .50 1.25
176 Craphonso Thorpe RC .40 1.00
177 Frank Gore RC .75 2.00
178 David Greene RC .40 1.00
179 Vincent Jackson RC .60 1.50
180 Adam Jones RC .50 1.25
181 Derrick Johnson RC .50 1.25
182 Stefan LeFors RC .40 1.00
183 Heath Miller RC .75 2.00
184 Ryan Moats RC .50 1.25
185 Vernand Morency RC .40 1.00
186 Brandon Jacobs RC .50 1.25
187 Kyle Orton RC .40 1.00
188 Roscoe Parrish RC .40 1.00
189 Courtney Roby RC .40 1.00
190 Aaron Rodgers RC 6.00 12.00
191 Marion Barber RC .40 1.00
192 Antrel Rolle RC .60 1.50
193 Airese Currie RC .40 1.00
194 Alex Smith QB RC 1.50 4.00
195 Andrew Walter RC .40 1.00
196 Roddy White RC .60 1.50
197 Cadillac Williams RC .40 1.00
198 Mike Williams .50 1.25
199 Rasheed Marshall RC .50 1.25
200 Charlie Frye RC .40 1.00
201 Justin Miller RC .40 1.00
202 Fabian Washington RC .40 1.00
203 Mark Bradley RC .40 1.00
204 Adrian McPherson RC .40 1.00
205 Marcus Spears RC .40 1.00
206 Matt Jones RC .40 1.00
207 Darren Sproles RC .60 1.50
208 Eric Shelton RC .40 1.00
209 Fred Gibson RC .40 1.00
210 Anthony Davis RC .40 1.00
211 Mark Clayton RC .40 1.00
212 Braylon Edwards RC .40 1.00
213 Ciatrick Fason RC .40 1.00
214 DeMarcus Ware RC 1.25 3.00
215 Dan Orlovsky RC .40 1.00
216 Maurice Clarett .50 1.25
217 Erasmus James RC .40 1.00
218 Chris Henry RC .50 1.25
219 Jerome Mathis RC .60 1.50
220 Terrence Murphy RC .40 1.00

2005 Bazooka Blue

COMPLETE SET (220) 40.00 80.00
*VETS: 1X TO 2.5X BASIC CARDS
*ROOKIES: .6X TO 1.5X BASIC CARDS
ONE BLUE CARD PER PACK

2005 Bazooka Gold

*VETS: 1X TO 2.5X BASIC CARDS
*ROOKIES: .6X TO 1.5X BASIC CARDS
ONE GOLD CARD PER PACK

2005 Bazooka All-Stars Jerseys

GROUP A ODDS 1:259
GROUP B ODDS 1:75
GROUP C ODDS 1:69
GROUP D ODDS 1:84
BAAF Alan Faneca B 8.00 20.00
BAAJ Andre Johnson C 3.00 8.00
BABD Brian Dawkins A 4.00 10.00
BABW Brian Waters D 2.50 6.00
BADB Dre Bly A 2.50 6.00
BAIR Ike Reese B 2.50 6.00
BAJH Jeff Hartings B 5.00 12.00
BAJHO Joe Horn B 2.50 6.00
BAJL John Lynch B 3.00 8.00
BAJT Jeremiah Trotter A 2.50 6.00
BAKW Kevin Williams C 2.50 6.00
BALG La'Roi Glover D 2.50 6.00
BALI Larry Izzo C 2.50 6.00
BALS Lito Sheppard A 3.00 8.00
BAMB Matt Birk D 2.50 6.00
BAMR Marco Rivera C 2.50 6.00
BAMS Marcus Stroud C 2.50 6.00
BAMW Marcus Washington B 2.50 6.00
BAOK Olin Kreutz C 3.00 8.00
BAOP Orlando Pace C 2.50 6.00
BARJ Rudi Johnson B 2.50 6.00
BASA Sam Adams C 2.50 6.00
BASH Steve Hutchinson D 3.00 8.00
BASL Shane Lechler B 2.50 6.00
BATJ Tory James C 2.50 6.00
BATM Terrence McGee B 3.00 8.00
BATP Troy Polamalu D 4.00 10.00
BATS Takeo Spikes B 2.50 6.00
BATS Terrell Suggs D 2.50 6.00
BAWH William Henderson B 2.50 6.00
BAWJ Walter Jones D 2.50 6.00
BAWS Will Shields C 2.50 6.00

2005 Bazooka Comics

STATED ODDS 1:4
1 Peyton Manning 1.50 4.00
2 Ben Roethlisberger 1.00 2.50
3 Jonathan Vilma .40 1.00
4 Torry Holt .50 1.25
5 Peyton Manning 1.50 4.00
6 Curtis Martin .50 1.25
7 Ed Reed .50 1.25
8 Jerome Bettis .60 1.50
9 Reggie Wayne .50 1.25
10 Drew Brees .60 1.50
11 Randy Moss .50 1.25
12 Michael Vick .50 1.25
13 Brett Favre 1.25 3.00
14 Daunte Culpepper .50 1.25
15 Terrell Owens .50 1.25
16 Tom Brady 2.50 6.00
17 LaDainian Tomlinson .60 1.50
18 Donovan McNabb .50 1.25
19 Alex Smith QB 1.50 4.00
20 Aaron Rodgers 5.00 12.00
21 Cadillac Williams .40 1.00
22 Cedric Benson .40 1.00
23 Mike Williams .50 1.25
24 Braylon Edwards .40 1.00

2005 Bazooka Originals Jerseys

STATED ODDS 1:15
BOAJ Adam Jones 1.50 4.00
BOARO Antrel Rolle 2.50 6.00
BOAS Alex Smith QB 6.00 15.00
BOAW Andrew Walter 1.50 4.00
BOBE Braylon Edwards 1.50 4.00
BOCF Ciatrick Fason 1.50 4.00
BOCFR Charlie Frye 1.50 4.00
BOCR Courtney Roby 1.50 4.00
BOCRO Carlos Rogers 2.50 6.00
BOCW Cadillac Williams 1.50 4.00
BOES Eric Shelton 1.50 4.00
BOFG Frank Gore 3.00 8.00
BOJC Jason Campbell 1.50 4.00
BOJJA J.J. Arrington 2.00 5.00
BOKO Kyle Orton 1.50 4.00
BOMB Mark Bradley 1.50 4.00
BOMC Maurice Clarett 1.50 4.00
BOMCL Mark Clayton 1.50 4.00
BOMJ Matt Jones 1.50 4.00
BORB Ronnie Brown 2.00 5.00
BORBR Reggie Brown 1.50 4.00
BORM Ryan Moats 1.50 4.00
BORP Roscoe Parrish 1.50 4.00
BORW Roddy White 2.50 6.00
BOSL Stefan LeFors 1.50 4.00
BOTM Terrence Murphy 1.50 4.00
BOTW Troy Williamson 1.50 4.00
BOVJ Vincent Jackson 2.50 6.00
BOVM Vernand Morency 1.50 4.00

2005 Bazooka Rookie Threads

STATED ODDS 1:69
BZRAJ Adam Jones 2.00 5.00
BZRAR Antrel Rolle 3.00 8.00
BZRAW Andrew Walter 2.00 5.00
BZRCF Charlie Frye 2.00 5.00
BZRCF Ciatrick Fason 2.00 5.00
BZRCR Courtney Roby 2.00 5.00
BZRFG Frank Gore 4.00 10.00
BZRJC Jason Campbell 2.00 5.00
BZRKO Kyle Orton 2.00 5.00
BZRMB Mark Bradley 2.00 5.00
BZRMC Mark Clayton 2.00 5.00
BZRRW Roddy White 3.00 8.00
BZRTM Terrence Murphy Grn 2.00 5.00
BZRTM2 Terrence Murphy Wht 2.00 5.00
BZRVJ Vincent Jackson 3.00 8.00
BZRVM Vernand Morency 2.00 5.00

2005 Bazooka Stickers

STATED ODDS 1:4
1 Bailey/Gamble/Hall/Robinsn .60 1.50
2 Wlliams/Vlma/Shpprd/Taylr .75 2.00
3 Urlchr/Brooks/Lewis/Thms .75 2.00
4 Freeney/Kearse/Pppers/Strhn .60 1.50
5 Crmplr/Gates/Shcky/Wnslw .75 2.00
6 Wttn/McMchl/Heap/Gnzlz .60 1.50
7 Wstbrk/McNbb/TO/Pnkstn .60 1.50
8 Pnnngtn/Boller/Blgr/Rttay .50 1.25
9 Simms/Culppr/Vick/Rvrs .75 2.00
10 Volek/Delhmme/Clins/Dilfr .50 1.25
11 Feeley/Carr/Brees/McCown .75 2.00
12 Roeth/Hnsn/Hrngtn/Rmsy 1.25 3.00
13 Griese/Lftwch/Lsmn/Grssmn .50 1.25
14 Favre/Plmmr/Wrnr/McCwn 1.50 4.00
15 Brks/Grcia/Hsslbck/Peytn 2.00 5.00
16 Plmr/Bldsoe/McNair/Green .60 1.50
17 Stckr/Port/Taylr/J.Jns .50 1.25
18 J.Lewis/Pitt/O.Smth/T.Jns .60 1.50
19 Bettis/Alxndr/Dcktt/Bell .75 2.00
20 Mrtn/Deuce/Dvnprt/McGhe .60 1.50
21 C.Brwn/Hall/L.Jhn/S.Jck .50 1.25
22 A.Grn/C.Tylr/Bnntt/Brbr .60 1.50
23 E.Jmes/Brlow/Hlms/Dvis .60 1.50
24 Blaylck/LT/Droughns/Rudi .75 2.00
25 C.Prry/D.Dvs/L.Sggs/M.Mre .50 1.25
26 Foster/G.Jns/Jordan/Dunn .60 1.50
27 Staly/K.Jns/M.Flk/Henry .60 1.50
28 Dillon/Brnch/Hrrsn/Brady 3.00 8.00
29 Brynt/Jcksn/Gvns/Roy WR .50 1.25
30 Bldn/Rndle El/Stkley/TJ .50 1.25
31 Brce/J.Tylr/J.Smth/Brlsn .75 2.00
32 C.Jhn/Port/Clbrt/Wyne .60 1.50
33 Gbrl/Ward/Mi.Cly/R.Smth .60 1.50
34 J.Wlkr/Fitz/Coles/L.Evns .75 2.00
35 Toom/Keysh/Mhsn/Curry .60 1.50
36 C.Rgrs/Jnkns/S.Mss/T.Tylr .60 1.50
37 Mason/Prkr/Horn/Woods .50 1.25
38 Donte/D.Benn/Mlds/R.Mss .60 1.50
39 Wlsn/Chmbrs/Burrs/Holt .60 1.50
40 Drvr/McCrns/Rbnsn/Harrsn .60 1.50
41 Rssm/A.Jhn/Re.Wll/Cali .60 1.50
42 Rdgrs/Smth QB/Waltr/Eli 5.00 12.00
43 McPher/Frye/Orlov/Orton .40 1.00
44 D.Grn/D.Andr/Cmpbll/Lefrs .50 1.25
45 Pear/Bensn/J.Arrin/Ro.Brwn .50 1.25
46 Gore/L.Gates/Moats/Mrncy .75 2.00
47 Jcbs/Carnell/Sprls/M.Brbr .60 1.50
48 A.Davis/Fasn/Shltn/Clarett .50 1.25
49 Ward/D.Jhn/Jamos/Spears 1.25 3.00
50 Roll/Rogers/Fabian/J.Mllr .75 2.00
51 A.Jns/Roby/H.Mllr/Mathis .75 2.00
52 Thrpe/Re.Brwn/TWill/V.Jck .60 1.50
53 Crrie/M.Will/R.White/Parrsh .60 1.50
54 Gbsn/Brdley/M.Jnes/Mrshll .60 1.50
55 B.Edw/C.Hnry/Clytn/Mrphy .50 1.25

2005 Bazooka Window Clings

COMPLETE SET (34) 6.00 15.00
STATED ODDS 1:6
1 Arizona Cardinals .30 .75
2 Atlanta Falcons .30 .75
3 Baltimore Ravens .30 .75
4 Buffalo Bills .40 1.00
5 Carolina Panthers .30 .75
6 Chicago Bears .40 1.00
7 Cincinnati Bengals .30 .75
8 Cleveland Browns .30 .75
9 Dallas Cowboys .50 1.25
10 Denver Broncos .40 1.00
11 Detroit Lions .30 .75
12 Green Bay Packers .50 1.25
13 Houston Texans .30 .75
14 Indianapolis Colts .30 .75
15 Jacksonville Jaguars .30 .75
16 Kansas City Chiefs .40 1.00
17 Miami Dolphins .40 1.00
18 Minnesota Vikings .30 .75
19 New England Patriots .40 1.00
20 New Orleans Saints .30 .75
21 New York Giants .40 1.00
22 New York Jets .40 1.00
23 Oakland Raiders .50 1.25
24 Philadelphia Eagles .30 .75
25 Pittsburgh Steelers .40 1.00
26 St. Louis Rams .30 .75
27 San Diego Chargers .30 .75
28 San Francisco 49ers .50 1.25
29 Seattle Seahawks .30 .75
30 Tampa Bay Buccaneers .30 .75
31 Tennessee Titans .30 .75
32 Washington Redskins .50 1.25
33 NFL Shield .30 .75
34 Bazooka Joe .30 .75

1964 Bears McCarthy Postcards

This 11-card set of the Chicago Bears features posed and action player photos taken by J.D. McCarthy and printed on postcard-size cards. Each is unnumbered and checklisted below in alphabetical order.
COMPLETE SET (11) 45.00 90.00
1 Charlie Bivins 2.50 5.00
2 Ronnie Bull 4.00 8.00
3 Mike Ditka 15.00 25.00
4 John Farrington 2.50 5.00
5 Sid Luckman CO 7.50 15.00
6 Joe Marconi 4.00 8.00
7 Billy Martin HB 2.50 5.00
8 Billy Martin E 2.50 5.00
9 Johnny Morris 4.00 8.00
10 Mike Rabold 2.50 5.00
11 Gene Schroeder CO 2.50 5.00

1967 Bears Pro's Pizza

These cards are actually discs that measure roughly 4 3/4" in diameter. They were printed on Pro's Pizza packages sold in the Chicago area and at stadiums. The player's image, with the athlete dressed in street clothes, appears on the front and the backs are blank.
COMPLETE SET (12) 3000.00 4500.00
1 Doug Atkins 175.00 300.00
2 Ronnie Bull 150.00 250.00
3 Dick Butkus 500.00 800.00
4 Mike Ditka 500.00 800.00
5 Dick Evey 150.00 250.00
6 Johnny Morris 150.00 250.00
7 Richie Petitbon 150.00 250.00
8 Jim Purnell 150.00 250.00
9 Mike Pyle 150.00 250.00
10 Gale Sayers 500.00 800.00
11 Roosevelt Taylor 150.00 250.00
12 Bob Wetoska 150.00 250.00

1967 Bears Team Issue

These black and white player photos were released by the Chicago Bears around 1967. Each measures approximately 5" by 7" and includes the player's name, his position (spelled out in full) and team name below the photo. They are blankbacked and unnumbered. Any additions to this list are appreciated.
COMPLETE SET (10) 75.00 125.00
1 Ronnie Bull 6.00 12.00
2 Rudy Bukich 5.00 10.00
3 Jack Concannon 5.00 10.00
4 Joe Fortunato 5.00 10.00
5 Richie Petitbon 6.00 12.00
6 Jim Purnell 5.00 10.00
7 Mike Pyle 5.00 10.00
8 Mike Rabold 5.00 10.00
9 Gale Sayers 15.00 30.00
10 Roosevelt Taylor 6.00 12.00

1968-69 Bears Team Issue

The Chicago Bears issued these black and white glossy photos for fans primarily for autograph purposes and mail requests. Each measures roughly 8" by 10" and includes the player's name and team name below the photo. Many also include the player's position or abbreviated position initials below the photo. As is common with many team issued photos, they were issued during more than one season and many contain different printed type styles and sizes. Any additions to this checklist are appreciated.
COMPLETE SET (43) 200.00 400.00
1 Doug Buffone 5.00 10.00
2 Ronnie Bull 6.00 12.00
3 Dick Butkus 15.00 30.00
4 Jim Cadile 5.00 10.00
5 Virgil Carter 5.00 10.00
6 Jack Concannon 5.00 10.00
7 Frank Cornish 5.00 10.00
8 Frank Cornish 5.00 10.00
9 Austin Denney 5.00 10.00
10 Dick Evey 5.00 10.00
11 Dick Evey 5.00 10.00
12 Bobby Joe Green 5.00 10.00
13 Willie Holman 5.00 10.00
14 Mike Hull 5.00 10.00
15 Randy Jackson 5.00 10.00
16 John Johnson DT 5.00 10.00
17 Jimmy Jones TE 5.00 10.00
18 Doug Kriewald 5.00 10.00
19 Rudy Kuechenberg 5.00 10.00
20 Ralph Kurek 5.00 10.00
21 Andy Livingston 5.00 10.00
22 Garry Lyle 5.00 10.00
23 Wayne Mass 5.00 10.00
24 Bennie McRae 5.00 10.00
25 Ed O'Bradovich 5.00 10.00
26 Richie Petitbon 6.00 12.00
27 Loyd Phillips 5.00 10.00
28 Loyd Phillips 5.00 10.00
29 Brian Piccolo 15.00 30.00
30 Brian Piccolo 15.00 30.00
31 Bob Pickens 5.00 10.00
32 Jim Purnell 5.00 10.00
33 Mike Pyle 5.00 10.00
34 Larry Rakestraw 5.00 10.00
35 Mike Reilly 5.00 10.00
36 Gale Sayers 18.00 30.00
37 Gale Sayers 18.00 30.00
38 Gale Sayers 18.00 30.00
39 Joe Taylor 5.00 10.00
40 Roosevelt Taylor 6.00 12.00
41 Cecil Turner 5.00 10.00
42 Bob Wallace 5.00 10.00
43 Bob Wetoska 5.00 10.00

1968 Bears Tasco Prints

1 Dick Butkus 20.00 40.00
2 Gale Sayers 20.00 40.00

1969 Bears Kroger

Similar to the Chiefs set issued the same year, this eight-card release was sponsored by Kroger Stores and measures approximately 8" by 9 3/4." The fronts feature a color painting of the player by artist John Wheeldon with the player's name inscribed across the bottom of the picture. he back has player biographical and statistical information and a brief note about the artist.
COMPLETE SET (8) 150.00 300.00
1 Dick Butkus 40.00 80.00
2 Virgil Carter 8.00 12.00
3 Jack Concannon 10.00 15.00
4 Dick Gordon 8.00 12.00
5 Bennie McRae 8.00 12.00
6 Brian Piccolo 60.00 100.00
7 Gale Sayers 35.00 60.00
8 Roosevelt Taylor 10.00 15.00

1971 Bears Team Issue

These twelve black and white photos were released as a set by the Chicago Bears in 1971. Each measures approximately 4 1/2" by 7" and includes the player's name and team name below the photo. They are blankbacked and unnumbered.
COMPLETE SET (12) 75.00 125.00
1 Doug Buffone 5.00 10.00
2 Dick Butkus 12.50 25.00
3 Rich Coady 5.00 10.00
4 Jack Concannon 5.00 10.00
5 Bobby Douglass 6.00 12.00
6 Dick Gordon 5.00 10.00
7 Jim Grabowski 5.00 10.00
8 Willie Holman 5.00 10.00
9 Randy Jackson 5.00 10.00
10 Gale Sayers 12.50 25.00
11 George Seals 5.00 10.00
12 Aaron Thomas 5.00 10.00

1973 Bears Team Issue Color

The NFLPA worked with many teams in 1973 to issued photo packs to be sold at stadium concession stands. Each measures approximately 7" by 8-5/8" and features a color player photo with a blank back. A small sheet with a player checklist was included in each 12-photo pack. These twelve color photos are thought to have also been released by Jewel Foods in Chicago.
COMPLETE SET (12) 40.00 80.00
1 Doug Buffone 5.00 8.00
2 Dick Butkus 10.00 20.00
3 Bobby Douglass 5.00 10.00
4 George Farmer 5.00 8.00
5 Carl Garrett 5.00 8.00
6 Jimmy Gunn 5.00 8.00
7 Jim Harrison 5.00 8.00
8 Willie Holman 5.00 8.00
9 Mac Percival 5.00 8.00
10 Jim Seymour 5.00 8.00
11 Don Shy 5.00 8.00
12 Cecil Turner 5.00 8.00

1973 Bears Team Sheets

This set of photos of the Chicago Bears was distributed on glossy paper stock each measuring approximately 8" by 10". The fronts feature black-and-white player and/or coach portraits with eight pictures to a sheet along with the Bears helmet and team name. The backs are blank and the sheets are not numbered.
COMPLETE SET (7) 35.00 60.00
1 Lionel Antoine 5.00 8.00
Bob Asher
Rich Coady
Craig Cotto
2 Buffone 6.00 12.00
Butkus
Chambers
Gunn
Holman
McGee
Os
3 Clark 5.00 8.00
Ellis
Graham
Lawson
Rives
Sanderson
Pe
4 Clemons 5.00 8.00
Hale
Horton
Hrivnak
Janet
Jeter
Lyle
5 Douglass 6.00 10.00
Farmer
Huff
Garrett
Harrison
Kozins#
6 Abe Gibron 5.00 8.00
Zeke Bratkowski
Chuck Cherundolo
Whi
7 Coaches 10.00 20.00
Players

1974 Bears Team Sheets

This set of photos of the Chicago Bears was distributed on six glossy sheets with each measuring approximately 8" by 10". The fronts feature black-and-white player or coach portraits with eight pictures to a sheet along with the year of issue. The backs are blank and the sheets are numbered on the fronts 1-5.
COMPLETE SET (5) 25.00 40.00
1 Sheet 1 6.00 10.00
2 Sheet 2 10.00 15.00
3 Sheet 3 5.00 8.00
4 Sheet 4 5.00 8.00
5 Sheet 5 5.00 8.00

1976 Bears Coke Discs

The cards in this 22-player disc set are unnumbered so they are listed below alphabetically. All players in the set are members of the Chicago Bears suggesting that these cards were issued as part of a local Chicago Coca-Cola promotion. The discs measure approximately 3 3/8" in diameter but with the hang tab intact the whole card is 5 1/4" long. There are two versions of the Doug Plank disc (green and yellow) and two versions of Clemons (yellow and orange); both of these variations were printed in the same quantities as all the other cards in the set and hence are not that difficult to find. The discs were produced by Mike Schechter Associates (MSA). These cards are frequently found with their hang tabs intact and hence they are priced that way in the list below. The back of each disc contains the phrase, "Coke adds life to ... halftime fun." The set price below includes all the variation cards. The set is also noteworthy in that it contains another card (albeit round) of Walter Payton in 1976, the same year as his Topps Rookie Card.
COMPLETE SET (24) 50.00 100.00
1 Lionel Antoine 1.00 2.50
2 Bob Avellini 1.25 3.00
3 Waymond Bryant 1.00 2.50
4 Doug Buffone 1.25 3.00
5 Wally Chambers 1.25 3.00
6A Craig Clemons 1.00 2.50
6B Craig Clemons 1.00 2.50
7 Allan Ellis 1.00 2.50
8 Roland Harper 1.00 2.50
9 Mike Hartenstine 1.00 2.50
10 Noah Jackson 1.00 2.50
11 Virgil Livers 1.00 2.50
12 Jim Osborne 1.00 2.50
13 Bob Parsons 1.25 3.00
14 Walter Payton 40.00 75.00
15 Dan Peiffer 1.00 2.50
16A Doug Plank 1.25 3.00
16B Doug Plank 1.25 3.00
17 Bo Rather 1.00 2.50
18 Don Rives 1.00 2.50
19 Jell Sevy 1.00 2.50
20 Ron Shanklin 1.00 2.50
21 Revie Sorey 1.00 2.50
22 Roger Stillwell 1.00 2.50

1980 Bears Team Sheets

This set of photos was released by the Bears. Each measures roughly 8" by 10" and features 8-players or coaches on each sheet. The sheets are blankbacked and numbered on the fronts of 7.
COMPLETE SET (7) 20.00 40.00
1 Neill Armstrong 2.00 5.00
Jerry Frei
Dale Haupt
Hank Kuhl
2 Ted Albrecht 3.00 8.00
Bob Avellini
Brian Baschnagel
Gary
3 Gary Fencik 3.00 8.00
Robert Fisher
Wentford Gaines
Kris
4 Bruce Herron 2.00 5.00
Tom Hicks
Noah Jackson
Dan Jiggett
5 Willie McClendon 6.00 15.00
Rocco Moore
Jerry Muckensturm
6 Mike Phipps 3.00 8.00
Doug Plank
Ron Rydalch
Terry Schmid
7 Matt Suhey 2.00 5.00
Paul Tabor
Bob Thomas
Mike Ulmer
Le

1981 Bears Police

The 1981 Chicago Bears police set contains 24 unnumbered cards. The cards measure approximately 2 5/8" by 4 1/8". Although uniform numbers appear on the fronts of the cards, they have been listed alphabetically in the checklist below. The set is sponsored by the Kiwanis Club, the local law enforcement agency and the Chicago Bears. Appearing on the backs along with a Chicago Bears helmet are "Chicago Bears Tips". The card backs have blue print with orange accent. The Kiwanis logo and Chicago Bears helmet appear on the fronts of the cards.
COMPLETE SET (24) 12.50 25.00
1 Ted Albrecht .30 .75
2 Neill Armstrong CO .40 1.00
3 Brian Baschnagel .40 1.00
4 Gary Campbell .30 .75
5 Robin Earl .30 .75
6 Allan Ellis .30 .75
7 Vince Evans .60 1.50
8 Gary Fencik .50 1.25
9 Dan Hampton 1.00 2.50
10 Roland Harper .40 1.00
11 Mike Hartenstine .30 .75
12 Tom Hicks .30 .75
13 Noah Jackson .40 1.00
14 Dennis Lick .30 .75
15 Jerry Muckensturm .30 .75
16 Dan Neal .30 .75
17 Jim Osborne .30 .75
18 Alan Page 1.00 2.50
19 Walter Payton 5.00 12.00
20 Doug Plank .40 1.00
21 Terry Schmidt .30 .75
22 James Scott .30 .75
23 Revie Sorey .40 1.00
24 Rickey Watts .30 .75

1987 Bears Ace Fact Pack

This 33-card set was made in West Germany (by Ace Fact Pack) for distribution in England. The cards measure approximately 2 1/4" by 3 5/8" and feature rounded corners and a playing card type design on the back. The 22 player cards in the set have been checklisted below in alphabetical order.
COMPLETE SET (33) 125.00 250.00
1 Todd Bell 1.50 4.00
2 Mark Bortz 1.50 4.00
3 Kevin Butler 2.00 5.00
4 Jim Covert 2.00 5.00
5 Richard Dent 4.00 10.00
6 Dave Duerson 1.50 4.00
7 Gary Fencik 2.00 5.00
8 Willie Gault 2.00 5.00
9 Dan Hampton 4.00 10.00
10 Jay Hilgenberg 2.00 5.00
11 Wilber Marshall 2.00 5.00
12 Jim McMahon 10.00 25.00
13 Steve McMichael 2.50 6.00
14 Emery Moorehead 1.50 4.00
15 Keith Ortega 1.50 4.00
16 Walter Payton 50.00 100.00
17 William Perry 3.00 8.00
18 Mike Richardson 1.50 4.00
19 Mike Singletary 10.00 25.00
20 Matt Suhey 2.00 5.00
21 Keith Van Horne 1.50 4.00
22 Otis Wilson 1.50 4.00
23 Bears Helmet 1.50 4.00
24 Bears Information 1.50 4.00
25 Bears Uniform 1.50 4.00
26 Game Record Holders 1.50 4.00
27 Season Record Holders 1.50 4.00
28 Career Record Holders 1.50 4.00
29 Record 1967-86 1.50 4.00
30 1986 Team Statistics 1.50 4.00
31 All-Time Greats 1.50 4.00
32 Roll of Honour 1.50 4.00
33 Soldier Field 1.50 4.00

1994 Bears 75th Anniversary Sheets

Throughout the 1994 season, these ten 10 3/4" by 7 5/8" Hall of Fame Collector Series sheets were inserted in Game Day programs sold at Soldier's Field. Commemorating the 75th anniversary of the NFL and the Chicago Bears, the sheets were inserted one per program and could be removed by tearing the perforation. On a light blue card face, the fronts feature a montage of sepia-tone action player photos of Chicago Bear Hall of Famers. The backs feature a WGN AM radio 720 advertisement on the left half and player information on the right half. The sheets are numbered on the front "(X of 10)" and listed in chronological order.
COMPLETE SET (10) 20.00 50.00
1 George Halas OWN CO 2.00 5.00
2 Doug Atkins 1.20 3.00
3 Walter Payton 10.00 15.00
4 Dan Fortmann 2.00 5.00
5 Dick Butkus 3.20 8.00
6 Bill George 2.00 5.00
7 Gale Sayers 3.20 8.00
8 Bill Hewitt 1.60 4.00
9 Roy(Link) Lyman 1.20 3.00
10 Bronko Nagurski 1.60 4.00

1994 Bears Toyota

Sponsored by Toyota, this two-card standard-size set commemorates October 31, 1994, the day the jerseys were retired for Dick Butkus and Gale Sayers, two Chicago Bear Hall of Famers. The fronts display color action player photos inside white and orange borders. The team's 75th anniversary logo, player information, and the sponsor logo are overprinted on the picture. The backs carry a color closeup photo, career summary, and career highlights. The cards are unnumbered and checklisted below in alphabetical order.
1 Dick Butkus 15.00 30.00
2 Gale Sayers 15.00 30.00

1995 Bears Program Sheets

These eight sheets measure approximately 8" by 10" and appeared in regular season issues of the Bears' GameDay program. The set features large action photos of various individuals involved in the Chicago Bears Super Bowl XX championship. The sheets are listed below in chronological order.
COMPLETE SET (8) 20.00 50.00
1 Mike Ditka 2.40 6.00

2 Walter Payton 4.80 12.00
3 Jim McMahon 2.40 6.00
4 Mike Singletary 3.20 8.00
Gary Fencik
5 Richard Dent 2.40 6.00
6 William Perry 2.40 6.00
7 Otis Wilson 2.00 5.00
8 Wilber Marshall 2.00 5.00

1995 Bears Super Bowl XX 10th Anniversary Kemper

The Chicago Bears, in conjunction with Kemper Mutual Funds, produced this 20-card set commemorating the 10th anniversary of the Chicago Bears winning Super Bowl XX. The fronts feature color action player photos from that championship team with the player's name, position, and jersey number in a vertical blue strip on the left. The backs display a small player portrait with the player's name, biographical information, and 1985 season and postseason highlights. The cards are unnumbered and checklisted below in alphabetical order.

COMPLETE SET (20) 10.00 25.00
1 Mark Bortz .40 1.00
2 Kevin Butler .40 1.00
3 Jim Covert .40 1.00
4 Richard Dent .60 1.50
5 Dave Duerson .40 1.00
6 Gary Fencik .40 1.00
7 Willie Gault .60 1.50
8 Dan Hampton .60 1.50
9 Jay Hilgenberg .40 1.00
10 Wilber Marshall .60 1.50
11 Dennis McKinnon .40 1.00
12 Jim McMahon 1.20 3.00
13 Steve McMichael .40 1.00
14 Walter Payton 3.20 8.00
15 William Perry .60 1.50
16 Mike Singletary 1.00 2.50
17 Matt Suhey .40 1.00
18 Tom Thayer .40 1.00
19 Keith Van Horne .40 1.00
20 Otis Wilson .40 1.00

1995 Bears Super Bowl XX Montgomery Ward Cards/Coins

The Chicago Bears, in conjunction with Montgomery Ward Stores, produced this 8-card and 8-coin set commemorating the 10th anniversary of the Chicago Bears winning Super Bowl XX. The card fronts feature color action player photos from that championship team with the player's name and position in a diagonal blue and orange strip. The backs display the complete 8-card checklist and individual card numbers. We've listed the cards below using a "CA" prefix. The coin fronts feature a player from the championship team with the player's name and jersey number. The backs display the Bears Super Bowl XX logo. The coins are unnumbered but have been listed below alphabetically using a "CO" prefix. A cardboard holder was produced to house the set that featured all the players included in the set.

COMP.CARD/COIN SET (16) 9.60 24.00
COMPLETE CARD SET (8) 4.80 12.00
COMPLETE COIN SET (8) 4.80 12.00
CA1 Mike Ditka .80 2.00
CA2 Kevin Butler .50 1.25
CA3 Dan Hampton .50 1.25
CA4 Richard Dent .60 1.50
CA5 Gary Fencik .50 1.25
CA6 Walter Payton .50 1.25
CA7 Jim McMahon .75 2.00
CA8 Mike Ditka .80 2.00
CO1 Kevin Butler .50 1.25
CO2 Richard Dent .60 1.50
CO3 Mike Ditka CO .80 2.00
CO4 Gary Fencik .50 1.25
CO5 Dan Hampton .50 1.25
CO6 Jim McMahon .75 2.00
CO7 Walter Payton 2.40 6.00
CO8 Super Bowl Trophy .50 1.25
NNO Set Display Holder .40 1.00

1996 Bears Illinois State Lottery

These "cards" were actually issued as Illinois State Lottery tickets. It is common to find them stratched since the potential lottery prize far outweighed the value of the ticket unscratched. Each includes a small color photo of the player along with the rules for the contest.

COMPLETE SET (5) 1.20 3.00
1 Richard Dent .20 .50
2 Mike Ditka .40 1.00
3 Dan Hampton .20 .50
4 William Perry .08 .25
5 Gale Sayers .40 1.00

1997 Bears Collector's Choice

Upper Deck released several team sets in 1997 in a blister pack wrapper. Each of the 14-cards in this set are very similar to the base Collector's Choice cards except for the card numbering on the back. A cover/checklist card was added featuring the team helmet.

COMPLETE SET (14) 1.25 3.00
CH1 Raymont Harris .08 .25
CH2 Jeff Jaeger .07 .20
CH3 Curtis Conway .08 .25
CH4 Walt Harris .07 .20
CH5 Bobby Engram .08 .25
CH6 Rick Mirer .08 .25
CH7 Rashaan Salaam .08 .25
CH8 Darnell Autry .08 .25
CH9 Alonzo Spellman .07 .20
CH10 Bryan Cox .07 .20
CH11 Tom Carter .07 .20
CH12 Tyrone Hughes .07 .20
CH13 Anthony Marshall .07 .20
CH14 Chicago Bears CL .07 .20

1997 Bears Score

This 15-card set of the Chicago Bears was distributed in five-card packs with a suggested retail price of $1.99. The fronts feature color action player photos with white borders and the player's name and team logo printed in team color foil at the bottom. The backs carry player information and career statistics. Platinum Team parallel cards were randomly seeded in packs featuring all foil cardfronts.

COMPLETE SET (15) 2.40 6.00
*PLATINUM TEAMS: 1X TO 2X
1 Rashaan Salaam .15 .40
2 Curtis Conway .15 .40
3 Erik Kramer .15 .40
4 Bobby Engram .30 .75
5 Bryan Cox .08 .25
6 Walt Harris .08 .25
7 Raymont Harris .30 .75
8 Michael Timpson .08 .25
9 Tony Carter .08 .25
10 Alonzo Spellman .08 .25
11 Donnell Woolford .08 .25
12 Barry Minter .08 .25
13 Mark Carrier DB .08 .25
14 Marty Carter .08 .25
15 Rick Mirer .30 .75

1998 Bears Fan Convention

This set of cards was printed on white stock and distributed at the 1998 Chicago Bears Fan Convention. Each card features a blue border with the Fan Convention logo and a player photo on the front and player information on the back. The cards were not numbered.

COMPLETE SET (56) 10.00 25.00
1 Doug Atkins .30 .75
2 Bob Avellini .08 .25
3 Brian Baschnagel .08 .25
4 Mark Bortz .08 .25
5 Doug Buffone .08 .25
6 Ronnie Bull .08 .25
7 Dick Butkus 2.00 4.00
8 Marty Carter .08 .25
9 George Connor .15 .40
10 Curtis Conway .30 .75
11 Jim Covert .08 .25
12 Wendell Davis WR .08 .25
13 Richard Dent .30 .75
14 Bobby Douglass .08 .25
15 Dave Duerson .08 .25
16 Bobby Engram .15 .40
17 Willie Gault .15 .40
18 George Halas 1.00 2.50
19 Dan Hampton .15 .40
20 Roland Harper .08 .25
21 Mike Hartenstine .08 .25
22 Andy Heck .08 .25
23 Jay Hilgenberg .08 .25
24 Jeff Jaeger .08 .25
25 Dan Jiggetts .15 .40
26 Glen Kozlowski .08 .25
27 Sid Luckman .60 1.50
28 Dennis McKinnon .08 .25
29 Jim McMahon .40 1.00
30 Barry Minter .08 .25
31 Emery Moorehead .08 .25
32 Jim Morrissey .08 .25
33 Brad Muster .08 .25
34 Jim Osborne .08 .25
35 Walter Payton 4.00 8.00
36 Todd Perry .08 .25
37 Doug Plank .08 .25
38 Mike Pyle .08 .25
39 Ron Rivera .08 .25
40 Thomas Sanders .08 .25
41 Gale Sayers 2.00 4.00
42 Terry Schmidt .08 .25
43 Carl Simpson .08 .25
44 Mike Singletary .30 .75
45 Ed Sprinkle .08 .25
46 Matt Suhey .08 .25
47 John Thierry .08 .25
48 Bob Thomas .08 .25
49 James Thornton .08 .25
50 Chris Villarrial .08 .25
51 Tom Waddle .08 .25
52 Bill Wade .15 .40
53 Ryan Wetnight .08 .25
54 James Williams T .08 .25
55 Otis Wilson .08 .25
56 Announcers .08 .25

1999 Bears Fan Convention

This set was distributed at the 1999 Chicago Bears Fan Convention in complete set form. Each card features a white border with the Fan Convention logo and a player photo on the front and player information on the back. The cards were not numbered.

COMPLETE SET (45) 10.00 25.00
1 Brian Baschnagel .08 .25
2 Mark Bortz .08 .25
3 Doug Buffone .08 .25
4 Ronnie Bull .08 .25
5 Rick Casares .15 .40
6 George Connor .15 .40
7 Jim Covert .08 .25
8 Richard Dent .30 .75
9 Allan Ellis .08 .25
10 Curtis Enis .75 2.00
11 Gary Fencik .08 .25
12 Jim Flanigan .08 .25
13 George Halas .80 2.00
14 Dan Hampton .15 .40
15 Roland Harper .08 .25
16 Walt Harris .08 .25
17 Mike Hartenstine .08 .25
18 Jay Hilgenberg .08 .25
19 Dick Jauron CO .15 .40
20 Stan Jones .30 .75
21 Glen Kozlowski .08 .25
22 Ricardo McDonald .08 .25
23 Dennis McKinnon .08 .25
24 Glyn Milburn .08 .25
25 Barry Minter .08 .25
26 Emery Moorehead .08 .25
27 Jim Morrissey .08 .25
28 Jim Osborne .08 .25
29 Tony Parrish .08 .25
30 Walter Payton 3.00 6.00
31 Doug Plank .08 .25
32 Mike Pyle .08 .25
33 Marcus Robinson 2.40 6.00
34 Todd Sauerbrun .08 .25
35 Gale Sayers 1.20 3.00
36 Mike Singletary .30 .75
37 Tom Thayer .08 .25
38 James Thornton .08 .25
39 Tom Waddle .08 .25
40 Bill Wade .15 .40
41 Mike Wells .08 .25
42 Ryan Wetnight .08 .25
43 Otis Wilson .08 .25
44 Bears Fan Club Logo .08 .25
45 Checklist Card .08 .25

2003 Bears Upper Deck Van Kampen

This set was sponsored by Van Kampen Investments, produced by Upper Deck, and features 5-young members of the Chicago Bears. The cards are printed in a horizontal format and are numbered on the backs.

COMPLETE SET (5) 10.00 20.00
1 Michael Haynes 1.25 3.00
2 Rex Grossman 5.00 12.00
3 Charles Tillman 1.25 3.00
4 Lance Briggs 1.25 3.00
5 Justin Gage 1.50 4.00

2004 Bears Legends Activa Medallions

COMPLETE SET (21) 40.00 80.00
1 Doug Atkins 1.50 4.00
2 Brian Baschnagel 1.25 3.00
3 George Blanda 1.50 4.00
4 Doug Buffone 1.25 3.00
5 Ronnie Bull 1.25 3.00
6 Dick Butkus 2.00 5.00
7 Mike Ditka 1.50 4.00
8 Bobby Douglass 1.25 3.00
9 Gary Fencik 1.25 3.00
10 Bill George 1.25 3.00
11 Red Grange 2.00 5.00
12 George Halas 2.00 5.00
13 Dan Hampton 1.25 3.00
14 Sid Luckman 1.50 4.00
15 Jim McMahon 1.50 4.00
16 Bronko Nagurski 2.00 5.00
17 Walter Payton 2.50 6.00
18 Richie Petitbon 1.25 3.00
19 Brian Piccolo 2.50 6.00
20 Gale Sayers 2.00 5.00
21 Mike Singletary 1.50 4.00

2005 Bears Playoff Prestige National Convention

This set was issued for the 2005 National Sport Collectors Convention held in Chicago. Collectors who purchased the early bird VIP card show package received this 6-card set featuring members of the Chicago Bears. The cards were produced in the design of a Playoff Prestige product but included a special "2005 Chicago National" logo printed on the cardfronts

COMPLETE SET (6) 8.00 15.00
1 Brian Urlacher 1.25 3.00
2 Rex Grossman .75 2.00
3 Thomas Jones .75 2.00
4 Kyle Orton 1.00 2.50
5 Cedric Benson 1.25 3.00
6 Mark Bradley .75 2.00

2005 Bears Super Bowl XX Activa Medallions

COMPLETE SET (25) 30.00 60.00
1 Mark Bortz 1.25 3.00
2 Maury Buford 1.25 3.00
3 Kevin Butler 1.25 3.00
4 Jim Covert 1.25 3.00
5 Richard Dent 1.50 4.00
6 Mike Ditka 1.50 4.00
7 Dave Duerson 1.25 3.00
8 Gary Fencik 1.25 3.00
9 Leslie Frazier 1.25 3.00
10 Willie Gault 1.25 3.00
11 Dan Hampton 1.50 4.00
12 Wilber Marshall 1.25 3.00
13 Dennis McKinnon 1.25 3.00
14 Jim McMahon 1.50 4.00
15 Steve McMichael 1.25 3.00
16 Emery Moorehead 1.25 3.00
17 Walter Payton 2.50 6.00
18 William Perry 1.25 3.00
19 Ron Rivera 1.25 3.00
20 Mike Singletary 1.50 4.00
21 Matt Suhey 1.25 3.00
22 Tom Thayer 1.25 3.00
23 Keith Van Horne 1.25 3.00
24 Otis Wilson 1.25 3.00
25 Bears Logo 1.00 2.50

2005 Bears Topps National Convention

This set was issued at the Topps booth at the 2005 National Sports Collectors Convention in Chicago. Collectors who presented 5-Topps football wrappers from packs opened at the show received a complete set. While no mention of the card show is given on the cards, they were produced with the Topps 50th Anniversary logo printed in yellow on the cardfronts and a special card numbering scheme XX of 6.

COMPLETE SET (6) 4.00 8.00
1 Rex Grossman .40 1.00
2 Brian Urlacher .60 1.50
3 Cedric Benson .60 1.50
4 Mark Bradley .40 1.00
5 Kyle Orton .50 1.25
6 Gale Sayers .60 1.50

2006 Bears Chicago Tribune

COMPLETE SET (41) 12.50 25.00
1 Mark Anderson 2 .75 2.00
2 Brendon Ayanbadejo 2 .40 1.00
3 Cedric Benson 1 .40 1.00
4 Bernard Berrian 2 .40 1.00
5 Lance Briggs 1 .50 1.25
6 Alex Brown 2 .40 1.00
7 Ruben Brown 3 .40 1.00
8 Desmond Clark 1 .40 1.00
9 Rashied Davis 2 .40 1.00
10 Roberto Garza 1 .40 1.00
11 John Gilmore 3 .40 1.00
12 Robbie Gould 1 .60 1.50
13 Brian Griese 3 .40 1.00
14 Rex Grossman 1 .40 1.00
15 Tommie Harris 1 .40 1.00
16 Devin Hester 3 .75 2.00
17 Hunter Hillenmeyer 3 .40 1.00
18 Todd Johnson 1 .40 1.00
19 Thomas Jones 2 .40 1.00
20 Olin Kreutz 1 .40 1.00
21 Danieal Manning 1 .60 1.50
22 Ricky Manning Jr. 3 .40 1.00
23 Brad Maynard 2 .40 1.00
24 Jason McKie 3 .40 1.00
25 Fred Miller 2 .40 1.00
26 Muhsin Muhammad 2 .40 1.00
27 Adewale Ogunleye 3 .40 1.00
28 Adrian Peterson 3 .50 1.25
29 Gabe Reid 1 .40 1.00
30 Ron Rivera 2 .40 1.00
31 Ian Scott 1 .40 1.00
32 Lovie Smith CO 3 .50 1.25
33 John Tait 2 .40 1.00
34 Charles Tillman 3 .50 1.25
35 Ron Turner 1 .40 1.00
36 Brian Urlacher 3 .60 1.50
37 Nathan Vasher 2 .40 1.00
38 Cameron Worrell 2 .40 1.00
TC1 Title Card #1 .20 .50
TC2 Title Card #2 .20 .50
TC3 Title Card #3 .20 .50

2006 Bears Topps

COMPLETE SET (12) 3.00 6.00
CHI1 Nathan Vasher .25 .60
CHI2 Thomas Jones .25 .60
CHI3 Kyle Orton .25 .60
CHI4 Alex Brown .25 .60
CHI5 Lance Briggs .30 .75
CHI6 Mark Bradley .25 .60
CHI7 Rex Grossman .25 .60
CHI8 Cedric Benson .25 .60
CHI9 Brian Urlacher .40 1.00
CHI10 Brian Griese .25 .60
CHI11 Muhsin Muhammad .25 .60
CHI12 Devin Hester .50 1.25

2007 Bears Topps

COMPLETE SET (12) 2.50 5.00
1 Brian Urlacher .60 1.50
2 Rex Grossman .40 1.00
3 Cedric Benson .40 1.00
4 Bernard Berrian .40 1.00
5 Desmond Clark .40 1.00
6 Devin Hester .50 1.25
7 Tommie Harris .40 1.00
8 Alex Brown .40 1.00
9 Robbie Gould .40 1.00
10 Mike Brown .50 1.25
11 Muhsin Muhammad .40 1.00
12 Greg Olsen .60 1.50

2007 Bears Upper Deck

This set was issued in two perforated 9-card panels; one panel featuring offensive players and the other defensive players. A Jewel-Osco ad card was also included on each panel.

COMPLETE SET (18) 6.00 12.00
1 Devin Hester .40 1.00
2 Robbie Gould .30 .75
3 Desmond Clark .30 .75
4 Bernard Berrian .30 .75
5 NFC Champs Sheet 1 .20 .50
6 Muhsin Muhammad .30 .75
7 Greg Olsen .50 1.25
8 Olin Kreutz .30 .75
9 Cedric Benson .30 .75
10 Tommie Harris .30 .75
11 Ricky Manning .30 .75
12 Hunter Hillenmeyer .30 .75
13 Brian Urlacher .50 1.25
14 NFC Champs Sheet 2 .20 .50
15 Lance Briggs .40 1.00
16 Nathan Vasher .30 .75
17 Charles Tillman .40 1.00
18 Brendon Ayanbadejo .30 .75

2008 Bears Topps

COMPLETE SET (12) 2.50 5.00
1 Brian Urlacher .60 1.50
2 Devin Hester .50 1.25
3 Desmond Clark .40 1.00
4 Tommie Harris .40 1.00
5 Cedric Benson .40 1.00
6 Lance Briggs .50 1.25
7 Rex Grossman .40 1.00
8 Adrian Peterson .40 1.00
9 Greg Olsen .50 1.25
10 Adewale Ogunleye .40 1.00
11 Matt Forte .60 1.50
12 Earl Bennett .60 1.50

2010 Bears Chicago Tribune Fathead Tradeables

These six Bears Fathead Tradeables were issued inside copies of the Chicago Tribune sold through Jewel-Osco stores in the Chicago area. Each unnumbered Fathead features a sticker back that includes an advertisement for the paper which differenitates it from base set.

COMPLETE SET (6) 5.00 12.00
1 Lance Briggs .75 2.00
2 Jay Cutler .60 1.50
3 Matt Forte .60 1.50
4 Devin Hester .75 2.00
5 Julius Peppers .75 2.00
6 Brian Urlacher 1.00 2.50

2012 Bears Chicago Tribune Fathead Tradeables

COMPLETE SET (6) 2.50 6.00
1 Lance Briggs .50 1.25
2 Jay Cutler .40 1.00
3 Matt Forte .40 1.00
4 Devin Hester .50 1.25
5 Brandon Marshall .50 1.25
6 Julius Peppers .50 1.25

2013 Bears Chicago Tribune Fathead Tradeables

COMPLETE SET (6) 2.50 6.00
1 Lance Briggs .50 1.25
2 Jay Cutler .40 1.00
3 Robbie Gould .40 1.00
4 Brandon Marshall .50 1.25
5 Julius Peppers .50 1.25
6 Charles Tillman .50 1.25

1968 Bengals Royal Crown Photos

These black and white blankbacked photos measure roughly 4" by 5 5/8" and feature members of the Bengals. Printed below the player photo are "Compliments of Royal Crown Cola" along with the player's name. A facsimile autograph is also included across each photo.

1 Frank Buncom 10.00 20.00
2 Sherrill Headrick 10.00 20.00
3 Dewey Warren 10.00 20.00
4 Ernie Wright 10.00 20.00

1968 Bengals Team Issue

The Cincinnati Bengals issued and distributed these player photos. Each measures approximately 8 1/2" by 11" and features a black and white photo. The player's name and position appear in the bottom border below the photo..

COMPLETE SET (15) 100.00 200.00
1 Al Beauchamp 7.50 15.00
2 Paul Brown CO 15.00 25.00
3 Frank Buncom 7.50 15.00
4 Greg Cook 7.50 15.00
5 Sherrill Headrick 7.50 15.00
6 Bob Johnson 7.50 15.00
7 Warren McVea 7.50 15.00
8 Jess Phillips 7.50 15.00
10 Fletcher Smith 7.50 15.00
11 Bill Staley 7.50 15.00
12 John Stofa 7.50 15.00
13 Bob Trumpy 7.50 15.00
14 Dewey Warren 7.50 15.00
15 Ernie Wright 7.50 15.00
16 Sam Wyche 10.00 20.00

1969 Bengals Team Issue

COMPLETE SET (6) 40.00 80.00
1 Paul Brown 10.00 20.00
2 Greg Cook 6.00 12.00
3 Bill Bergey 7.50 15.00
4 Bob Johnson 6.00 12.00
5 Horst Muhlmann 6.00 12.00
6 Paul Robinson 6.00 12.00

1969 Bengals Tresler Comet

The 1969 Tresler Comet set contains 20 cards featuring Cincinnati Bengals only. The cards measure 2 1/2" by 3 1/2". The set is quite attractive in its sepia and orange color front with a facsimile autograph of the player portrayed. The cards are unnumbered but have been listed below in alphabetical order for convenience. The card of Bob Johnson is much scarcer than the other cards, although some collectors and dealers consider Howard Fest, Harry Gunner, and Warren McVea to be somewhat more difficult to find as well. The backs contain biographical and statistical data of the player and the Tresler Comet logo. An offer to obtain a free set of these cards at a Tresler Comet (gasoline) dealer is stated at the bottom on the back.

COMPLETE SET (20) 300.00 450.00
1 Al Beauchamp 5.00 10.00
2 Bill Bergey 6.00 12.00
3 Royce Berry 5.00 10.00
4 Paul Brown CO 25.00 40.00
5 Frank Buncom 5.00 10.00
6 Greg Cook 5.00 10.00
7 Howard Fest SP 30.00 50.00
8 Harry Gunner SP 30.00 50.00
9 Bobby Hunt 5.00 10.00
10 Bob Johnson SP 75.00 125.00
11 Charley King 5.00 10.00
12 Dale Livingston 5.00 10.00
13 Warren McVea SP 30.00 50.00
14 Bill Peterson 5.00 10.00
15 Jess Phillips 5.00 10.00
16 Andy Rice 5.00 10.00
17 Bill Staley 5.00 10.00
18 Bob Trumpy 6.00 12.00
19 Ernie Wright 5.00 10.00
20 Sam Wyche 7.50 15.00

1971 Bengals Team Issue

The Bengals issued this photo pack set in 1971. Each borderless photo measures roughly 4 3/4" by 6 3/4" and features a facsimile autograph of the player over the photo. The cardbacks are blank and unnumbered. The set was typically released in an envelope labeled "Travel With the Champs" with the checklist on the outside of the envelope.

COMPLETE SET (6) 30.00 60.00
1 Virgil Carter 6.00 12.00
2 Greg Cook 6.00 12.00
3 Bob Johnson 6.00 12.00
4 Horst Muhlman 6.00 12.00
5 Lamar Parrish 6.00 12.00
6 Mike Reid 7.50 15.00

1972-74 Bengals Team Issue

The Bengals issued this set of player photos in the mid-1970s. Each measures roughly 8" by 10" and was printed on glossy black and white stock. The photos are blankbacked and unnumbered and checklisted below in alphabetical order. Each photo typically includes the player's name, position (spelled out) and team name below the photo seperated by dashes. The type sizes and styles vary with many of the photos in this list suggesting that they were issued in different years. Any additions to the list below are appreciated.

1 Doug Adams 5.00 10.00
2 Ken Anderson 7.50 15.00
3 Ken Avery 5.00 10.00
4 Al Beauchamp 5.00 10.00
5A Royce Berry wht jsy 5.00 10.00
5B Royce Berry brwn jsy 5.00 10.00
6 Lyle Blackwood 5.00 10.00
7 Paul Brown CO 7.50 15.00
8 Ron Carpenter 5.00 10.00
9 Virgil Carter wht jsy 5.00 10.00
10 Tommy Casanova 5.00 10.00
11 Al Chandler 5.00 10.00
12 Steve Chomyszak 5.00 10.00
13 Boobie Clark 6.00 12.00
14 Charles Clark 5.00 10.00
15 Wayne Clark 5.00 10.00
16 Bruce Coslet 5.00 10.00
17 Neal Craig 5.00 10.00
18 Isaac Curtis 5.00 10.00
19 Charles Davis 5.00 10.00
20 Doug Dressler 5.00 10.00
21 Lenvil Elliott 5.00 10.00
22 Mike Ernst 5.00 10.00
23 Howard Fest 5.00 10.00
24 Dave Green 5.00 10.00
25 Vern Holland 5.00 10.00
26 Bernard Jackson 5.00 10.00
27 Bob Johnson wht jsy 6.00 12.00
28 Ken Johnson DT 5.00 10.00
29 Charlie Joiner 7.50 15.00
30 Evan Jolitz wht jsy 5.00 10.00
31 Bob Jones S 5.00 10.00
32 Tim Kearney 5.00 10.00
33 Bill Kollar 5.00 10.00
34 Dave Lapham 5.00 10.00
35 Steve Lawson 5.00 10.00
36 Jim LeClair 5.00 10.00
37 Dave Lewis wht jsy 5.00 10.00
38 Pat Matson 5.00 10.00
39 Rufus Mayes 5.00 10.00
40 John McDaniel 5.00 10.00
41 Horst Muhlmann 5.00 10.00
42 Chip Myers 5.00 10.00
43 Lemar Parrish 6.00 12.00
44 Ron Pritchard 5.00 10.00
45 Mike Reid 6.00 12.00
46 Ken Riley 6.00 12.00
47 Paul Robinson wht jsy 5.00 10.00
48 Ken Sawyer wht jsy 5.00 10.00
49 John Shinners 5.00 10.00
50 Fletcher Smith 5.00 10.00
51 Bob Trumpy 6.00 12.00
52 Stan Walters 5.00 10.00
53 Sherman White 5.00 10.00
54 Fred Willis wht jsy 5.00 10.00

1976 Bengals MSA Cups

This set of plastic cups was issued for the Cincinnati Bengals in 1976 and licensed through MSA. Each features an artist's rendering of a Bengals' player. Some players also appeared in the nationally issued 1976 MSA Cups set with only slight differences in each. The unnumbered cups are listed below alphabetically. Confirmed additions to this checklist are appreciated.

1 Ken Anderson 5.00 10.00
2 Archie Griffin 4.00 8.00
3 Essex Johnson 3.00 6.00

1975-77 Bengals Team Issue

The Bengals issued this set of player photos between 1975 and 1977. Each measures roughly 5" by 8" with a black and white photo. The photos are blankbacked and unnumbered and checklisted below in alphabetical order. Each card includes the player's name, position initials and team name below the photo in large all capital letters. They look very similar to the 1978-79 photos but feature a larger type size. The white border below the player image is generally smaller as well but some players were also issued with a larger border and larger type size which would indicate a multiple year issue.

1 Al Beauchamp 4.00 8.00
2 Lyle Blackwood 4.00 8.00
3 Billy Brooks 4.00 8.00
4A Bob Brown 4.00 8.00
4B Bob Brown 4.00 8.00
5 Glenn Bujnoch 4.00 8.00
6 Gary Burley 4.00 8.00
7 Glenn Cameron 4.00 8.00
8 Ron Carpenter 4.00 8.00
9 Tommy Casanova 4.00 8.00
10 Boobie Clark 4.00 8.00
11 Marvin Cobb 4.00 8.00
12 Bruce Coslet 4.00 8.00
13 Brad Cousino 4.00 8.00
14 Isaac Curtis 5.00 10.00
15 Tony Davis 4.00 8.00
16 Lenvil Elliott 4.00 8.00
17 Greg Fairchild 4.00 8.00
18 Howard Fest 4.00 8.00
19 Stan Fritts 4.00 8.00
20A Vern Holland 4.00 8.00
20B Vern Holland 4.00 8.00
21 Ron Hunt 4.00 8.00
22 Bob Johnson 4.00 8.00
23 Essex Johnson 4.00 8.00
24 Ken Johnson 4.00 8.00
25 Charlie Joiner 6.00 12.00
26 Bill Kollar 4.00 8.00
27 Al Krevis 4.00 8.00
28A Dave Lapham 4.00 8.00
28B Dave Lapham 4.00 8.00
29 Jim LeClair 4.00 8.00
30 Rufus Mayes 4.00 8.00
31A John McDaniel 4.00 8.00
31B John McDaniel 4.00 8.00
32 Pat McInally 4.00 8.00
33 Maulty Moore 4.00 8.00
34 Melvin Morgan 4.00 8.00
35 Jack Novak 4.00 8.00
36 Lemar Parrish 5.00 10.00
37 Scott Perry 4.00 8.00
38A Ron Pritchard 4.00 8.00
38B Ron Pritchard 4.00 8.00
39 John Reaves 4.00 8.00
40 Ken Riley 5.00 10.00
41 Willie Shelby 4.00 8.00
42A John Shinners 4.00 8.00
42B John Shinners 4.00 8.00
43 Rick Walker 4.00 8.00
44 Sherman White 4.00 8.00
45 Ed Williams 4.00 8.00
46A Reggie Williams 5.00 10.00
46B Reggie Williams 5.00 10.00

1978-79 Bengals Team Issue

The Bengals issued this set of player photos in 1978. The 5 x 8 black and white photos are blankbacked and unnumbered and checklisted below in alphabetical order. Each card includes the player's name, position (spelled out) and team name below the photo. They look very similar to the 1975-77 photos but feature a smaller type size and a larger white border below the player image.

COMPLETE SET (30) 100.00 200.00
1 Ken Anderson 6.00 12.00
2 Chris Bahr 4.00 8.00
3 Don Bass 4.00 8.00
4 Louis Breeden 4.00 8.00
5 Ross Browner 4.00 8.00
6 Glenn Bujnoch 4.00 8.00
7 Gary Burley 4.00 8.00
8 Blair Bush 4.00 8.00
9 Glenn Cameron 4.00 8.00
10 Marvin Cobb 4.00 8.00
11 Jim Corbett 4.00 8.00
12 Tom DePaso 4.00 8.00
13 Tom Dinkel 4.00 8.00
14 Mark Donahue 4.00 8.00
15 Eddie Edwards 4.00 8.00
16 Lenvil Elliott 4.00 8.00
17 Archie Griffin 6.00 12.00
18 Ray Griffin 4.00 8.00
19 Bo Harris 4.00 8.00
20 Ron Hunt 4.00 8.00
21 Pete Johnson 5.00 10.00
22 Dave Lapham 4.00 8.00
23 Dennis Law 4.00 8.00
24 Jim LeClair 4.00 8.00
25 Pat McInally 4.00 8.00
26 Ken Riley 5.00 10.00
27 Ron Shumon 4.00 8.00
28 Dave Turner 4.00 8.00
29 Ted Vincent 4.00 8.00
30 Wilson Whitley 4.00 8.00

1982 Bengals Nu-Maid Butter Tubs

This set of butter cups or tubs was released by Nu-Maid and Miami Margarine in 1982 in the Cincinnati area. Each includes color illustrations of the featured player and measures roughly 3 3/4" tall and 3" in diameter.

COMPLETE SET (7) 25.00 40.00
1 Ken Anderson 4.00 10.00
2 Cris Collinsworth 3.00 8.00
3 Archie Griffin 3.00 8.00
4 Pete Johnson 2.50 6.00
5 Jim LeClair 2.50 6.00
6 Anthony Munoz 4.00 10.00
7 Reggie Williams 2.50 6.00

1997 Bengals Team Sheets

COMPLETE SET (9) 15.00 30.00
1 Mike Brown PRES/Bruce Coslet CO/Dick LeBeau CO/Ken Anderson CO/Paul Ale 1.50 4.00
2 John Garrett CO/Ray Horton CO/Tim Krumrie CO/Al Roberts CO/Kim Wood CO# 1.50 4.00
3 Marco Battaglia/Eric Bieniemy/Ken Blackman/Jeff Blake/Rich Braham/Darr 2.00 5.00
4 Brentson Buckner/Steve Bush/Ki-Jana Carter/Andre Collins/John Copeland# 2.00 5.00
5 Ty Douthard/David Dunn/Boomer Esiason/James Francis/Scottie Graham/Bil 3.00 8.00
6 Mike Jenkins/Lee Johnson/Rod Jones/Roger Jones/Jevon Langford/Anthone 1.50 4.00
7 Tony McGee/Brian Milne/Greg Myers/Bo Orlando/Rod Payne/Doug Pelfrey/C 2.00 5.00
8 Kevin Sargent/Corey Sawyer/Darnay Scott/Sam Shade/Jimmy Spencer/Ramond 2.00 5.00
9 Tom Tumulty/Gunnard Twyner/Kimo Von Oelhoffen/Joe Walter/Erik Wilhelm/ 1.50 4.00

1998 Bengals Team Sheets

COMPLETE SET (6) 10.00 25.00
1 Bruce Coslet CO 1.50 4.00
Dick LeBeau Asst. CO
Ken Anderson CO
Paul Alexander CO

2 Bob Wylie 2.00 5.00
Ashley Ambrose
Willie Anderson
Michael Bankston
Marco Battagl
3 Anthony Brown 2.00 5.00
Steve Bush
Ki-Jana Carter
John Copeland
Harry Deligianis#
4 Artrell Hawkins 1.50 4.00
James Hundon
Willie Jackson
Lee Johnson
Rod Jones
Paul
5 Greg Myers 2.00 5.00
Neil Oâ€™Donnell
Rod Payne
Doug Pelfrey
Carl Pickens
Andre Pu
6 Scott Shaw 1.50 4.00
Brian Simmons
Clyde Simmons
Takeo Spikes
Glen Steele
Mike T

2003 Bengals Upper Deck Gold Star Chili

This set was sponsored by Gold Star Chili, produced by Upper Deck, and features members of the Cincinnati Bengals. The cards are printed in a horizontal format and are numbered on the backs.

COMPLETE SET (17) 10.00 20.00
1 Jon Kitna .75 2.00
2 Carson Palmer 2.50 6.00
3 Tory James .30 .75
4 Corey Dillon .75 2.00
5 Kevin Hardy .30 .75
6 Brian Simmons .30 .75
7 Willie Anderson .30 .75
8 Matt O'Dwyer .30 .75
9 Levi Jones .30 .75
10 Peter Warrick .75 2.00
11 Reggie Kelly .30 .75
12 Chad Johnson .40 1.00
13 Justin Smith .40 1.00
14 Tony Williams .30 .75
15 John Thornton .30 .75
16 Marvin Lewis CO .75 2.00
NNO Coupon Card .40 1.00

2006 Bengals Topps

COMPLETE SET (12) 3.00 5.00
CIN1 Deltha O'Neal .25 .60
CIN2 Chad Johnson .25 .60
CIN3 Carson Palmer .30 .75
CIN4 Shayne Graham .25 .60
CIN5 Chris Perry .30 .75
CIN6 Rudi Johnson .25 .60
CIN7 Odell Thurman .25 .60
CIN8 T.J. Houshmandzadeh .25 .60
CIN9 David Pollack .25 .60
CIN10 Tory James .25 .60
CIN11 Reggie McNeal .25 .60
CIN12 Johnathan Joseph .30 .75

2007 Bengals Activa Medallions

COMPLETE SET (22) 30.00 60.00
1 Paul Brown 1.50 4.00
2 Ken Anderson 1.50 4.00
3 James Brooks 1.25 3.00
4 Cris Collinsworth 1.50 4.00
5 Isaac Curtis 1.25 3.00
6 Boomer Esiason 1.50 4.00
7 David Fulcher 1.25 3.00
8 Anthony Munoz 1.50 4.00
9 Ken Riley 1.25 3.00
10 Ickey Woods 1.25 3.00
11 Willie Anderson 1.25 3.00
12 Robert Geathers 1.25 3.00
13 Shayne Graham 1.25 3.00
14 T.J. Houshmandzadeh 1.50 4.00
15 Chad Johnson 1.50 4.00
16 Rudi Johnson 1.25 3.00
17 Levi Jones 1.25 3.00
18 Johnathan Joseph 1.25 3.00
19 Marvin Lewis 1.25 3.00
20 Carson Palmer 2.00 5.00
21 Justin Smith 1.25 3.00
22 40th Anniversary Logo 1.25 3.00

2007 Bengals Topps

COMPLETE SET (12) 2.50 5.00
1 Carson Palmer .50 1.25
2 Rudi Johnson .40 1.00
3 Chad Johnson .40 1.00
4 Madieu Williams .40 1.00
5 T.J. Houshmandzadeh .40 1.00
6 Robert Geathers .40 1.00
7 Landon Johnson .40 1.00
8 Kenny Irons .40 1.00
9 Justin Smith .50 1.25
10 Shayne Graham .40 1.00
11 Leon Hall .40 1.00
12 Johnathan Joseph .40 1.00

2008 Bengals Topps

COMPLETE SET (12) 2.50 5.00
1 Carson Palmer .50 1.25
2 Chad Johnson .40 1.00
3 Kenny Watson .40 1.00
4 T.J. Houshmandzadeh .40 1.00
5 Rudi Johnson .40 1.00
6 Leon Hall .40 1.00
7 Keith Rivers .40 1.00
8 Reggie Kelly .40 1.00
9 Johnathan Joseph .40 1.00
10 Dexter Jackson .60 1.50
11 Jerome Simpson .50 1.25
12 Andre Caldwell .40 1.00

1951 Berk Ross

The 1951 Berk Ross set consists of 72 cards (each measuring approximately 2 1/16" by 2 1/2") with tinted photographs, divided evenly into four series (designated in the checklist as 1, 2, 3 and 4). The cards were marketed in boxes containing two card panels, without gum, and the set includes stars of other sports as well as baseball players. The set is sometimes still found in the original packaging. Intact panels command a premium over the listed prices. The catalog designation for this set is W532-1. In every series the first ten cards are baseball players; the set has a heavy emphasis on Yankees and Phillies players as they were in the World Series the year before. The set includes the first card of Bob Cousy as well as a card of Whitey Ford in his Rookie Card year.

COMPLETE SET (72) 900.00 1500.00
1-14 Leon Hart 7.50 15.00
Football
1-15 James Martin 6.00 12.00
Football
2-14 Doak Walker 10.00 20.00
Football
2-15 Emil Sitko 6.00 12.00
Football
3-14 Wade Walker 7.50 15.00
Football
3-15 Rodney Franz 6.00 12.00
Football
4-14 Arnold Galiffa 6.00 12.00
Football
4-15 Charlie Justice 7.50 15.00
Football

1960 Bills Team Issue

Issued by the team, this set of 40 black-and-white photos each measures roughly 4 7/8" by 6 3/4" and was given to 1960 Bills season ticketholders in complete set form. The photos are unnumbered and checklisted below in alphabetical order. The photos are frequently found personally autographed.

COMPLETE SET (40) 250.00 400.00
1 Bill Atkins 7.50 15.00
2 Bob Barrett 7.50 15.00
3 Phil Blazer 7.50 15.00
4 Bob Brodhead 7.50 15.00
5 Dick Brubaker 7.50 15.00
6 Bernie Buzyniski 7.50 15.00
7 Wray Carlton 7.50 15.00
8 Don Chelf 7.50 15.00
9 Monte Crockett 7.50 15.00
10 Bob Dove CO 7.50 15.00
11 Elbert Dubenion 10.00 20.00
12 Fred Ford 7.50 15.00
13 Dick Gallagher GM 7.50 15.00
14 Darrell Harper 7.50 15.00
15 Harvey Johnson CO 7.50 15.00
16 Jack Johnson 7.50 15.00
17 Billy Kinard DB 7.50 15.00
18 Joe Kulbacki 7.50 15.00
19 John Laraway 7.50 15.00
20 Richie Lucas 7.50 15.00
21 Archie Matsos 7.50 15.00
22 Rich McCabe 7.50 15.00
23 Dan McGrew 7.50 15.00
24 Chuck McMurtry 7.50 15.00
25 Ed Meyer 7.50 15.00
26 Ed Muelhaupt 7.50 15.00
27 Tom O'Connell 7.50 15.00
28 Harold Olson 7.50 15.00
29 Buster Ramsey CO 7.50 15.00
30 Floyd Reid CO 7.50 15.00
31 Tom Rychlec 7.50 15.00
32 Joe Schaffer 7.50 15.00
33 John Scott 7.50 15.00
34 Bob Sedlock 7.50 15.00
35 Carl Smith 7.50 15.00
36 Jim Sorey 7.50 15.00
37 Laverne Torczon 7.50 15.00
38 Jim Wagstaff 7.50 15.00
39 Ralph Wilson OWN 15.00 30.00
40 Mack Yoho 7.50 15.00

1963 Bills Jones-Rich Dairy

This set of 40-crude drawings features members of the Buffalo Bills and were produced in a variety of versions and variations, but not all players have been verified for all versions. These "cards" are actually either blankbacked cardboard cut-outs from the sides of milk cartons or actual cap liners originally inserted into milk bottles. The bottle cap liners were produced with or without a small pull-out tab on the fronts and include the Jones-Rich logo on the backs. The flat (non-tab) version of the bottle caps liners were also produced in two versions with one being printed with a slightly larger player name printed on the front and larger company logo printed on the back. It is not yet known which players appeared in the large versus small print or the flat versus tab cap version. The milk carton version was produced in both a red and black ink variety with a further slight difference being found in the red ink variety (some can be found with a red ink circle around the player image along with the yellow ink dotted line). Most, if not all, of the players appear to be available in both varieties as well as both milk cap versions. The black ink carton variety seems to be very difficult to find. These circular cards measure approximately 1" in diameter and are frequently found miscut, i.e., off-centered. A display sheet that featured Bill's owner, Ralph Wilson, and Head Coach, Lou Saban, was also produced to house some of the caps and liners. Collectors at the time were challenged to complete a line-up of the 1963 Bills team, attach the caps and liners to the sheet and mail it in for a chance to win tickets to a Bill's game. The ACC catalog designation for this set is F118-1.

*CAP LINERS: .5X TO 1.2X CARTON CUT-OUTS
1 Ray Abruzzese 150.00 300.00
2 Art Baker 150.00 300.00
3 Stew Barber 200.00 350.00
4 Glenn Bass 150.00 300.00
5 Dave Behrman 150.00 300.00
6 Al Bemiller 150.00 300.00
7 Wray Carlton 150.00 300.00
8 Carl Charon 150.00 300.00
9 Monte Crockett 150.00 300.00
10 Wayne Crow 150.00 300.00
11 Tom Day 150.00 300.00
12 Elbert Dubenion 200.00 350.00
13 Jim Dunaway 200.00 350.00
14 Booker Edgerson 150.00 300.00
15 Cookie Gilchrist 250.00 400.00

16 Dick Hudson	150.00	300.00
17 Frank Jackunas	150.00	300.00
18 Harry Jacobs	150.00	300.00
19 Jack Kemp	500.00	800.00
20 Roger Kochman	150.00	300.00
21 Daryle Lamonica	250.00	400.00
22 Charley Leo	150.00	300.00
23 Marv Matuszak	150.00	300.00
24 Bill Miller	150.00	300.00
25 Leroy Moore	150.00	300.00
26 Harold Olson	150.00	300.00
27 Herb Paterra	150.00	300.00
28 Ken Rice	150.00	300.00
29 Henry Rivera	150.00	300.00
30 Ed Rutkowski	150.00	300.00
31 George Saimes	150.00	300.00
32 Tom Sestak	150.00	300.00
33 Billy Shaw	250.00	400.00
34 Mike Stratton	150.00	300.00
35 Gene Sykes	150.00	300.00
36 John Tracey	150.00	300.00
37 Ernie Warlick	150.00	300.00
38 Willie West	150.00	300.00
39 Mack Yoho	150.00	300.00
40 Sid Youngelman	150.00	300.00
NNO Display Sheet	500.00	750.00

1965 Bills Matchbooks

This 1965 Buffalo Bills release contains at least 3-different matchbooks. Each features a Bills player printed in blue on white paper stock along with the team's 1965 season schedule. Any additions to the checklist below would be greatly appreciated.

COMPLETE SET (3)	40.00	75.00
1 Elbert Dubenion	18.00	30.00
2 Billy Shaw	20.00	35.00
3 Tom Sestak	15.00	25.00

1965 Bills Super Duper Markets

Super Duper Food Markets offered these black-and-white (approximately 8 1/2" by 11") Buffalo Bills photos to shoppers during the fall of 1965. The photos were a weekly giveaway during the football season by Super Duper markets in western New York. The photos are unnumbered and checklisted below in alphabetical order.

COMPLETE SET (10)	150.00	250.00
1 Glenn Bass	7.50	15.00
2 Elbert Dubenion	10.00	20.00
3 Billy Joe	7.50	15.00
4 Jack Kemp	40.00	80.00
5 Daryle Lamonica	25.00	40.00
6 Tom Sestak	7.50	15.00
7 Billy Shaw	10.00	20.00
8 Mike Stratton	7.50	15.00
9 Ernie Warlick	7.50	15.00
10 Team Photo	15.00	30.00

1965 Bills Team Issue

Issued by the team, this set of black-and-white photos each measures roughly 8" by 10" and was issued to fulfill fan requests and for player appearances in the mid 1960s. Unless noted below, the text within the bottom border includes the player's name in all caps, his position in lower case letters, and the team name in all caps. The photos are unnumbered, blankbacked, and checklisted below in alphabetical order.

1 Cookie Gilchrist	7.50	15.00
2 Daryle Lamonica	10.00	20.00
3 Tom Janik	6.00	12.00

1965 Bills Volpe Tumblers

These Bills artist's renderings were part of a plastic cup tumbler produced in 1965 and distributed through Sunoco gasoline stations. The noted sports artist Volpe created the artwork which includes an action scene and a player portrait. These paper inserts are unnumbered, each measures approximately 5" by 8 1/2" and is curved in the shape required to fit inside a plastic cup.

COMPLETE SET (12)	300.00	500.00
1 Glenn Bass	25.00	40.00
2 Butch Byrd	30.00	50.00
3 Wray Carlton	25.00	40.00
4 Tom Day	25.00	40.00
5 Billy Joe	30.00	50.00
6 Jack Kemp	60.00	100.00
7 Daryle Lamonica	40.00	75.00
8 Lou Saban CO	30.00	50.00
9 George Saimes	25.00	40.00
10 Tom Sestak	25.00	40.00
11 Billy Shaw	35.00	60.00
12 Mike Stratton	30.00	50.00

1966 Bills Matchbooks

The 1966 Bills Matchbook set features the team's 1966 season schedule along with a blue player photo and sponsor logos. Any additions to the checklist below would be greatly appreciated.

COMPLETE SET (4)	100.00	175.00
1 Butch Byrd	7.50	15.00
2 Elbert Dubenion	18.00	30.00
3 Jack Kemp	75.00	125.00
4 Mike Stratton	15.00	25.00

1967 Bills Jones-Rich Dairy

Through a special mail-in offer, Jones-Rich Milk Co. offered this set of six Buffalo Bills' highlight action photos from the 1965 and 1966 seasons. These black-and-white photos measure approximately 8 1/2" by 11".

COMPLETE SET (6)	75.00	125.00
1 George Butch Byrd	12.50	25.00
2 Wray Carlton	12.50	25.00
3 Hagood Clarke	10.00	20.00
4 Paul Costa	10.00	20.00
5 Jim Dunaway	10.00	20.00
6 Jack Spikes	12.50	25.00

1967 Bills Matchbooks

The 1967 Buffalo Bills matchbook set contains 4-different matchbooks. Each includes the team's 1967 season schedule along with a player photo printed in blue ink. Any additions to the checklist below would be greatly appreciated.

COMPLETE SET (4)	50.00	80.00
1 Bobby Burnett	15.00	25.00
2 Butch Byrd	18.00	30.00
3 Roland McDole	15.00	25.00
4 Ed Rutkowski	15.00	25.00

1967 Bills Team Issue

Issued by the team, this set of black-and-white photos each measures roughly 8" by 10" and was issued to fulfill fan requests and for player appearances in the mid 1960s. Unless noted below, the text within the bottom border includes on the far left the photographer's ID, then (in all caps) the player's position, his name, and the team name, followed by the team logo on the far right. The photos are unnumbered, blankbacked, and checklisted below in alphabetical order.

1 Joe Collier CO	6.00	12.00
2 Jack Kemp	20.00	35.00

1968 Bills Matchbooks

This Buffalo Bills matchbook set contains only one known matchbook. It includes the team's 1968 season schedule along with a player photo printed in black ink. Any additions to the checklist below would be appreciated.

1 Keith Lincoln	25.00	40.00
2 Billy Shaw	25.00	40.00

1972 Bills Buffalo News Posters

These posters were created by the Buffalo News and issued as "pages" in the daily newspapers during the 1972 season. Each large poster includes a color artist's rendition of a Bills player on the front with a typical newspaper page back. We've included the date when the photo appeared when known.

COMPLETE SET (10)	50.00	100.00
1 Paul Costa	4.00	10.00
2 Al Cowlings	4.00	10.00
3 Paul Guidry	4.00	10.00
4 J.D. Hill	4.00	10.00
5 Spike Jones	4.00	10.00
6 Reggie McKenzie	6.00	15.00
7 Wayne Patrick	4.00	10.00
8 Walt Patulski	4.00	10.00
9 Dennis Shaw	5.00	12.00
10 O.J. Simpson	12.50	25.00

1973 Bills Buffalo News Posters

These posters were created by the Buffalo News and issued as "pages" in the daily newspapers during the 1973 season. Each large poster includes a color artist's rendition of a Bills player on the front with a typical newspaper page back. We've included the date when the photo appeared when known. Any additions to this list are appreciated.

COMPLETE SET (16)	75.00	150.00
1 Jim Braxton	4.00	10.00
2 Bob Chandler	5.00	12.00
3 Jim Cheyunski	4.00	10.00
4 Earl Edwards	4.00	10.00
5 Joe Ferguson	6.00	15.00
6 Tony Greene	4.00	10.00
7 Bob James	4.00	10.00
8 Bruce Jarvis	4.00	10.00
9 Reggie McKenzie	6.00	15.00
10 Ahmad Rashad	6.00	15.00
11 Lou Saban CO	4.00	10.00
12 Paul Seymour	4.00	10.00
13 Dennis Shaw	5.00	12.00
14 O.J. Simpson	15.00	30.00
15 John Skorupan	4.00	10.00
16 Larry Watkins	4.00	10.00

1973 Bills Team Issue Color

The NFLPA worked with many teams in 1973 to issued photo packs to be sold at stadium concession stands. Each measures approximately 7" by 8-5/8" and features a color player photo with a blank back. A small sheet with a player checklist was included in each 6-photo pack.

COMPLETE SET (12)	40.00	80.00
1 Jim Braxton	4.00	8.00
2 Bob Chandler	4.00	8.00
3 Jim Cheyunski	4.00	8.00
4 Earl Edwards	4.00	8.00
5 Joe Ferguson	5.00	10.00
6 Dave Foley	4.00	8.00
7 Robert James	4.00	8.00
8 Reggie McKenzie	4.00	8.00
9 Jerry Patton	4.00	8.00
10 Walt Patulski	4.00	8.00
11 John Skorupan	4.00	8.00
12 O.J. Simpson	10.00	20.00

1974 Bills Buffalo News Posters

These posters were created by the Buffalo News and issued as "pages" in the daily newspapers during the 1974 season. Each large poster includes a color artist's rendition of a Bills player on the front with a typical newspaper page back. We've included the date when the photo appeared when known. Any additions to this list are appreciated.

COMPLETE SET (12)	60.00	120.00
1 Doug Allen	4.00	10.00
2 Jim Braxton	4.00	10.00
3 Joe DeLamielleure	6.00	15.00
4 Reuben Gant	4.00	10.00
5 Dwight Harrison	4.00	10.00
6 Mike Kadish	4.00	10.00
7 John Leypoldt	4.00	10.00
8 Reggie McKenzie	6.00	15.00
9 Mike Montler	4.00	10.00
10 Walt Patulski	4.00	10.00
11 Ahmad Rashad	6.00	15.00
12 O.J. Simpson	12.50	25.00

1975 Bills Buffalo News Posters

These posters were created by the Buffalo News and issued as "pages" in the daily newspapers during the 1975 season. Each large poster includes a color artist's rendition of a Bills player on the front with a typical newspaper page back. We've included the date when the photo appeared when known. Any additions to this list are appreciated.

COMPLETE SET (13)	50.00	100.00
1 Marv Bateman	3.00	8.00
2 Bo Cornell	3.00	8.00
3 Don Croft	3.00	8.00
4 Dave Foley	3.00	8.00
5 Gary Hayman	3.00	8.00
6 John Holland	3.00	8.00
7 Merv Krakau	3.00	8.00
8 Gary Marangi	3.00	8.00
9 Willie Parker	3.00	8.00
10 Tom Ruud	3.00	8.00
11 Pat Toomay	3.00	8.00
12 Vic Washington	3.00	8.00
13 Jeff Winans	3.00	8.00

1976 Bills Buffalo News Posters

These posters were created by the Buffalo News and issued as "pages" in the daily newspapers during the 1976 season. Each large poster includes a color artist's rendition of a Bills player on the front with a typical newspaper page back. We've included the date when the photo appeared when known. Any additions to this list are appreciated.

COMPLETE SET (11)	40.00	80.00
1 Bill Adams	3.00	8.00
2 Mario Clark	3.00	8.00
3 Joe Ferguson	5.00	12.00
4 Steve Freeman	3.00	8.00
5 Dan Jilek	3.00	8.00
6 Doug Jones	3.00	8.00
7 Ken Jones	3.00	8.00
8 Merv Krakau	3.00	8.00
9 Gary Marangi	3.00	8.00
10 Eddie Ray	3.00	8.00
11 Sherman White	3.00	8.00

1976 Bills McDonald's

This set of three photos was sponsored by McDonald's in conjunction with WBEN-TV. These "Player of the Week" photos were given away free with the purchase of a Quarter Pounder at participating McDonald's restaurants of Western New York. The offer was valid while supplies lasted but ended Nov. 28, 1976. Each photo measures approximately 8" by 10" and features a posed color close-up photo bordered in white. The player's name and team name are printed in black in the bottom white border, and his facsimile autograph is inscribed across the photo toward the lower right corner. The top portion of the back has biographical information, career summary, and career statistics (except the McKenzie back omits statistics). Inside a rectangle, the bottom portion describes the promotion and presents the 1976-77 football schedule on WBEN-TV. The photos are unnumbered and are checklisted below alphabetically.

COMPLETE SET (3)	12.50	25.00
1 Bob Chandler	4.00	8.00
2 Joe Ferguson	6.00	12.00
3 Reggie McKenzie	4.00	8.00

1977 Bills Buffalo News Posters

These posters were created by the Buffalo News and issued as "pages" in the daily newspapers during the 1977 season. Each large poster includes a color artist's rendition of a Bills player on the front with a typical newspaper page back. We've included the date when the photo appeared when known. Any additions to this list are appreciated.

COMPLETE SET (8)	30.00	60.00
1 Joe Devlin	3.00	8.00
2 Phil Dokes	3.00	8.00
3 Bill Dunstan	3.00	8.00
4 Roland Hooks	3.00	8.00
5 Ken Johnson	3.00	8.00
6 Keith Moody	3.00	8.00
7 Shane Nelson	3.00	8.00
8 Ben Williams	3.00	8.00

1978 Bills Buffalo News Posters

These posters were created by the Buffalo News and issued as "pages" in the daily newspapers during the 1978 season. Each large poster includes a color artist's rendition of a Bills player on the front with a typical newspaper page back. We've included the date when the photo appeared when known. Any additions to this list are appreciated.

1 Dee Hardison	6.00	8.00
2 Scott Hutchinson	6.00	8.00
3 Frank Lewis	4.00	10.00
4 Terry Miller	6.00	8.00
5 Charles Romes	6.00	8.00
6 Lucius Sanford	6.00	8.00

1978 Bills Postcards

These Bills Team Issue photos were sent out to fans requesting autographs. The cardbacks include a message from the player to fans along with an area for the fan's name and address similar to a postcard. We've included prices below for unsigned copies of the cards. Two different Simpson photos were released that contain the same cardback.

COMPLETE SET (5)	20.00	40.00
1 Jim Braxton	2.00	4.00
2 Bob Chandler	3.00	6.00
3 Joe Ferguson	3.00	6.00
4 O.J. Simpson	7.50	15.00
5 O.J. Simpson	7.50	15.00

1978 Bills Team Issue

This set of 8" by 10" black and white photos was issued by the Bills around 1978. Each photo was produced in one of two styles: with player name, position, and team name below the photo, or with jersey number, player name, position, and team name below. All photos also include the photographer's notation (Photo by Robert L. Smith) below the photo. Each is blankbacked and listed alphabetically below.

COMPLETE SET (22)	35.00	60.00
1 Mario Celotto	2.00	4.00
2 Mike Collier	2.00	4.00
3 Elbert Drungo	2.00	4.00
4 Mike Franckowiak	2.00	4.00
5 Tom Graham	2.00	4.00
6 Will Grant	2.00	4.00
7 Tony Greene	2.00	4.00
8 Dee Hardison	2.00	4.00
9 Scott Hutchinson	2.00	4.00
10 Dennis Johnson	2.00	4.00
11 Ken Johnson	2.00	4.00
12 Mike Kadish	2.00	4.00
13 Frank Lewis	2.50	5.00
14 John Little	2.00	4.00
15 Carson Long	2.00	4.00
16 David Mays	2.00	4.00
17 Terry Miller	2.00	4.00
18 Keith Moody	2.00	4.00
19 Bill Munson	2.50	5.00
20 Shane Nelson	2.00	4.00
21 Lucius Sanford	2.00	4.00
22 Connie Zelencik	2.00	4.00

1979 Bills Bell's Market

The 1979 Bell's Market Buffalo Bills set contains 11 photos which were issued one per week, with purchase, at Bell's Markets during the football season. The cards measure approximately 7 5/8" by 10" and were printed on thin stock. The Bills' logo as well as the Bell's Markets logo appears on the back along with information and statistics about the players. The cards show the player portrayed in action in full color. The photos are unnumbered and are listed below in alphabetical order by name.

COMPLETE SET (11)	20.00	40.00
1 Curtis Brown	1.50	3.00
2 Bob Chandler	3.00	6.00
3 Joe DeLamielleure	2.00	4.00
4 Joe Ferguson	4.00	8.00
5 Reuben Gant	2.00	4.00
6 Dee Hardison	1.50	3.00
7 Frank Lewis	2.00	4.00
8 Reggie McKenzie	2.00	4.00
9 Terry Miller	2.00	4.00
10 Shane Nelson	1.50	3.00
11 Lucius Sanford	1.50	3.00

1979 Bills Buffalo News Posters

These posters were created by the Buffalo News and issued as "pages" in the daily newspapers during the 1979 season. Each large poster includes a color artist's rendition of a Bills player on the front with a typical newspaper page back. We've included the date when the photo appeared when known. Any additions to this list are appreciated.

1 Curtis Brown	3.00	8.00
2 Jerry Butler	4.00	10.00
3 Jim Haslett	3.00	8.00
4 Isiah Robertson	4.00	10.00
5 Fred Smerlas	3.00	8.00

1980 Bills Bell's Market

The 1980 Bell's Market Buffalo Bills cards were available in ten strips of two (connected together by a perforation) or singly as 20 individual cards. The individual cards measure approximately 2 1/2" by 3 1/2". The cards are in full color and contain a red frame line on the front. The back features blue printing listing player biographies, statistics and the Bell's Markets logo. The prices below are for the individual cards. The value of a connected pair is approximately the sum of the two individual cards listed below. The pairings were as follows: 1-2, 3-4, 5-6, 7-8, 9-10, 11-12, 13-14, 15-16, 17-18, and 19-20.

COMPLETE SET (20)	5.00	10.00
1 Curtis Brown	.20	.50
2 Shane Nelson	.20	.50
3 Jerry Butler	.30	.75
4 Joe Ferguson	.60	1.50
5 Joe Cribbs	.40	1.00
6 Reggie McKenzie	.30	.75
7 Joe Devlin	.30	.75
8 Ken Jones	.20	.50
9 Steve Freeman	.20	.50
10 Mike Kadish	.20	.50
11 Jim Haslett	.75	2.00
12 Isiah Robertson	.30	.75
13 Frank Lewis	.30	.75
14 Jeff Nixon	.20	.50
15 Nick Mike-Mayer	.20	.50
16 Jim Ritcher	.30	.75
17 Charles Romes	.20	.50
18 Fred Smerlas	.40	1.00
19 Ben Williams	.20	.50
20 Roland Hooks	.20	.50

1980 Bills Buffalo News Posters

These posters were created by the Buffalo News and issued as "pages" in the daily newspapers during the 1979 season. Each large poster includes a color artist's rendition of a Bills player on the front with a typical newspaper page back. We've included the date when the photo appeared when known. Any additions to this list are appreciated.

COMPLETE SET (9)	30.00	60.00
1 Joe Cribbs	4.00	10.00
2 Conrad Dobler	4.00	10.00
3 Joe Ferguson	4.00	10.00
4 Roosevelt Leaks	3.00	8.00
5 Reggie McKenzie	5.00	12.00
6 Nick Mike-Mayer	3.00	8.00
7 Jeff Nixon	3.00	8.00
8 Lou Piccone	3.00	8.00
9 Team Picture	4.00	10.00

1981 Bills Buffalo News Posters

These posters were created by the Buffalo News and issued as "pages" in the daily newspapers during the 1981 season. Each poster is smaller than what was issued in prior years and an actual player photo is included instead of a color artist's rendition. The backs are a typical newspaper page. We've included the date when the photo appeared when known.

COMPLETE SET (16)	40.00	80.00
1 Mark Brammer 11/1/1981	2.50	6.00
2 Curtis Brown 9/20/1981	2.50	6.00
3 Jerry Butler 11/15/1981	3.00	8.00
4 Greg Cater 11/29/1981	2.50	6.00
5 Joe Cribbs 12/13/1981	3.00	8.00
6 Conrad Dobler 10/11/1981	3.00	8.00
7 Joe Ferguson 9/6/1981	3.00	8.00
8 Will Grant 9/13/1981	2.50	6.00
9 Shane Nelson 12/6/1981	2.50	6.00
10 Lou Piccone 11/22/1981	2.50	6.00
11 Charles Romes 10/18/1981	2.50	6.00
12 Lucius Sanford 10/4/1981	2.50	6.00
13 Fred Smerlas 10/25/1981	2.50	6.00
14 Sherman White 11/8/1981	2.50	6.00
15 Ben Williams 9/27/1981	2.50	6.00
16 Team Picture 12/20/1981	3.00	8.00

1982 Bills Buffalo News Posters

These posters were created by the Buffalo News and issued as "pages" in the daily newspapers during the 1981 season. Each poster is smaller than what was issued in prior years and an actual player photo is included instead of a color artist's rendition. The backs are a typical newspaper page. We've included the date when the photo appeared when known.

COMPLETE SET (8)	25.00	50.00
1 Mario Clark 10/31/1982	2.50	6.00
2 Joe Devlin 10/17/1982	2.50	6.00
3 Ken Jones 10/3/1982	2.50	6.00
4 Frank Lewis 9/26/1982	3.00	8.00
5 Reggie McKenzie 10/24/1982	4.00	10.00
6 Booker Moore 9/12/1982	2.50	6.00
7 Jeff Nixon 9/19/1982	2.50	6.00
8 Perry Tuttle 10/10/1982	2.50	6.00

1983 Bills Buffalo News Posters

These posters were created by the Buffalo News and issued as "pages" in the daily newspapers during the 1981 season. Each poster is smaller than what was issued in prior years and an actual player photo is included instead of a color artist's rendition. The backs are a typical newspaper page. We've included the date when the photo appeared when known.

COMPLETE SET (16)	40.00	80.00
1 Buster Barnett 10/30/1983	2.50	6.00
2 Jon Borchardt 10/9/1983	2.50	6.00
3 Greg Cater 11/6/1983	2.50	6.00
4 Byron Franklin 11/27/1983	2.50	6.00
5 Steve Freeman 10/16/1983	2.50	6.00
6 Tony Hunter 9/4/1983	2.50	6.00
7 Trey Junkin 11/20/1983	2.50	6.00
8 Chris Keating 12/4/1983	2.50	6.00
9 Matt Kofler 9/18/1983	2.50	6.00
10 Rod Kush 9/25/1983	2.50	6.00
11 Roosevelt Leaks 12/11/1983	3.00	8.00
12 Eugene Marve 10/2/1983	2.50	6.00
13 Jim Ritcher 11/13/1983	2.50	6.00
14 Fred Smerlas 10/23/1983	2.50	6.00
15 Darryl Talley 9/11/1983	3.00	8.00
16 Team Picture 12/18/1983	3.00	8.00

1986 Bills Sealtest

These panels were issued on the sides of half-gallon Sealtest milk cartons. The Freeman and Marve panels were issued on the sides of vitamin D cartons, and the Kelly and Romes panels appeared on two percent lowfat cartons. The panels measure approximately 3 5/8" by 7 5/8" and feature a black and white head shot of the player, biographical information, statistics, and career highlights, all in black lettering. The panels are unnumbered and listed below in alphabetical order.

COMPLETE SET (6)	20.00	40.00
1 Greg Bell SP	4.00	10.00
2 Jerry Butler SP	4.00	10.00
3 Steve Freeman	2.00	5.00
4 Jim Kelly	8.00	20.00
5 Eugene Marve	2.00	5.00
6 Charles Romes	2.00	5.00

1987 Bills Police

This eight-card set of Buffalo Bills is numbered on the back. The card backs are printed in gray and black ink on white card stock. Cards measure approximately 2 5/8" by 4 1/8". The set was sponsored by the Buffalo Bills, Erie and Niagara County Sheriff's Departments, Louis Rich Turkey Products, Claussen Pickles, and WBEN Radio. Uniform numbers are printed on the card front along with the player's name and position. The photos in the set were taken by Robert L. Smith, the Bills' official team photographer.

COMPLETE SET (8)	7.50	15.00
1 Marv Levy CO	.75	2.00
2 Bruce Smith	2.00	5.00
3 Joe Devlin	.60	1.50
4 Jim Kelly	2.50	6.00
5 Eugene Marve	.60	1.50
6 Andre Reed	1.50	4.00
7 Pete Metzelaars	.75	2.00
8 John Kidd	.60	1.50

1988 Bills Police

This eight-card set of Buffalo Bills is numbered in the upper right corner of each reverse. Cards measure approximately 2 5/8" by 4 1/8". The set was sponsored by the Buffalo Bills, Erie and Niagara County Sheriff's Departments, Louis Rich Turkey Products, and WBEN Radio. Uniform numbers are printed on the card front along with the player's name and position. The photos in the set were taken by several photographers, each of whom is credited on the lower right front beside the respective photo.

COMPLETE SET (8)	5.00	10.00
1 Steve Tasker	.75	2.00
2 Cornelius Bennett	1.00	2.50
3 Shane Conlan	.60	1.50
4 Mark Kelso	.60	1.50
5 Will Wolford	.60	1.50
6 Chris Burkett	.60	1.50
7 Kent Hull	.60	1.50
8 Art Still	.60	1.50

1989 Bills Police

This eight-card set of Buffalo Bills is numbered in the upper right corner of each reverse. Cards measure approximately 2 1/2" by 3 1/2". The set was sponsored by the Buffalo Bills, Erie County Sheriff's Department, Louis Rich Turkey Products, and WBEN Radio. Uniform numbers are printed on the card front along with the player's name and position. The photos in the set were taken by several photographers, each of whom is credited on the lower right front beside the respective photo.

COMPLETE SET (8)	6.00	12.00
1 Leon Seals	.30	1.50
2 Thurman Thomas	2.00	5.00
3 Jim Ritcher	.60	1.50
4 Scott Norwood	.60	1.50
5 Darryl Talley	.75	2.00
6 Nate Odomes	.60	1.50
7 Leonard Smith	.60	1.50
8 Ray Bentley	.60	1.50

1990 Bills Police

This eight-card set was sponsored by Blue Shield of Western New York, and its company logo graces both sides of the card. The oversized cards measure approximately 4" by 6". The color action player photos on the fronts have red borders on a white card face. The Bills' helmet and player identification appear above the picture, while biography is given below the picture. In black print, the back has career summary, statistics, and "Tips from the Sheriff" in the form of anti-drug and alcohol messages. The cards are unnumbered and checklisted below in alphabetical order.

COMPLETE SET (8)	6.00	15.00
1 Carlton Bailey	.40	1.00
2 Kirby Jackson	.40	1.00
3 Jim Kelly	2.50	6.00
4 James Lofton	.75	2.00
5 Keith McKeller	.40	1.00
6 Mark Pike	.40	1.00
7 Andre Reed	1.25	3.00
8 Jeff Wright	.40	1.00

1991 Bills Buffalo News Posters

These posters were created by the Buffalo News and issued as "pages" in the daily newspapers during the 1991 season. Each large poster includes a color image of a Bills player on the front with a typical newspaper page back. We've included the date when the photo appeared when known.

COMPLETE SET (16)	25.00	50.00
1 Howard Ballard 10/17/1991	1.25	3.00
2 Don Beebe 10/9/1991	1.50	4.00
3 Cornelius Bennett 10/2/1991	1.50	4.00
4 Shane Conlan 9/25/1991	1.25	3.00
5 Kent Hull 10/30/1991	1.25	3.00
6 Jim Kelly 9/5/1991	4.00	10.00
7 James Lofton 10/23/1991	2.00	5.00
8 Keith McKeller 12/18/1991	1.25	3.00
9 Scott Norwood 12/11/1991	1.25	3.00
10 Nate Odomes 11/21/1991	1.25	3.00
11 Andre Reed 9/19/1991	2.00	5.00
12 Leon Seals 11/27/1991	1.25	3.00
13 Bruce Smith 9/11/1991	2.00	5.00
14 Darryl Talley 11/6/1991	1.25	3.00
15 Thurman Thomas 11/13/1991	2.50	6.00
16 Jeff Wright 12/4/1991	1.25	3.00

1991 Bills Police

This eight-card Police standard-size set was sponsored by Blue Shield of Western New York. The cards are printed on white card stock. The top portion of the front features the player's name centered above the team name, with the team helmet and Blue Shield logo on either side. The center features an action player photo while biographical information is printed below. The three-sectioned front is separated by red borders. The backs have player profile, career statistics, and safety tips sponsored by the Erie County Sheriff's Department. The cards are unnumbered and checklisted below alphabetically.

COMPLETE SET (8)	2.40	6.00
1 Howard Ballard	.30	.75
2 Don Beebe	.50	1.25
3 John Davis	.30	.75
4 Kenneth Davis	.50	1.25
5 Mark Kelso	.30	.75
6 Frank Reich	.60	1.50
7 Butch Rolle	.30	.75
8 J.D. Williams	.30	.75

1992 Bills Buffalo News Posters

These posters were created by the Buffalo News and issued as "pages" in the daily newspapers during the 1992 season. Each large poster includes a color image of a Bills player on the front with a typical newspaper page back. We've included the date when the photo appeared when known.

COMPLETE SET (15)	20.00	40.00
1 Carlton Bailey 9/9/1992	1.25	3.00
2 Steve Christie 9/24/1992	1.50	4.00
3 Kenneth Davis 11/18/1992	1.50	4.00
4 Phil Hansen 11/11/1992	1.25	3.00
5 Henry Jones 12/9/1992	1.50	4.00
6 Mark Kelso 9/30/1992	1.25	3.00
7 Pete Metzelaars 10/22/1992	1.25	3.00
7 Brad Lamb 11/4/1992	1.25	3.00
9 Chris Mohr 10/30/1992	1.25	3.00
10 Chris Mohr 11/29/1992	1.25	3.00
11 Nate Odomes 9/16/1992	1.25	3.00
12 Frank Reich 10/7/1992	1.50	4.00
13 Jim Ritcher 12/16/1992	1.25	3.00
14 Steve Tasker 11/25/1992	1.50	4.00
15 Will Wolford 10/15/1992	1.25	3.00

1992 Bills Police

This seven-card set was sponsored by Blue Shield of Western New York. The oversized cards measure approximately 4" by 6" and are printed on white card stock. The top portion of the front features the player's name centered above the team name, with the team helmet and Blue Shield logo on either side. The center features an action color player photo while biographical information is printed below. The three-section front is separated by red borders. The backs have player profile, career statistics, and safety tips sponsored by the Erie County Sheriff's Department. The cards are unnumbered and checklisted below alphabetically.

COMPLETE SET (7)	6.00	12.00
1 Carlton Bailey	.75	2.00
2 Steve Christie	.75	2.00
3 Shane Conlan	.75	2.00
4 Phil Hansen	.75	2.00
5 Henry Jones	1.00	2.50
6 Chris Mohr	.75	2.00
7 Thurman Thomas	2.00	5.00

1993 Bills Buffalo News Posters

These posters were created by the Buffalo News and issued as "pages" in the daily newspapers during the 1993 season. Each large poster includes a color image of a Bills player on the front with a typical newspaper page back. We've included the date when the photo appeared when known.

COMPLETE SET (14)	25.00	50.00
1 Howard Ballard 12/23/1993	1.25	3.00
2 Cornelius Bennett 10/14/1993	1.50	4.00
3 Bill Brooks 11/10/1993	1.50	4.00
4 Russell Copeland 10/6/1993	1.25	3.00
5 Kenneth Davis 12/8/1993	1.50	4.00
6 John Fina 11/18/1993	1.25	3.00
7 Keith Goganious 12/30/1993	1.25	3.00
8 Kent Hull 12/15/1993	1.25	3.00
9 Jim Kelly 9/22/1993	4.00	10.00
10 Andre Reed 9/29/1993	2.00	5.00
11 Darryl Talley 11/23/1993	1.25	3.00
12 Steve Tasker 11/3/1993	1.50	4.00
13 Nate Turner 10/28/1993	1.25	3.00
14 James Williams 10/21/1993	1.25	3.00

1994 Bills Buffalo News Posters

These posters were created by the Buffalo News and issued as "pages" in the daily newspapers during the 1994 season. Each large poster includes a color image of a Bills player on the front with a typical newspaper page back. We've included the date when the photo appeared when known.

COMPLETE SET (16)	25.00	50.00
1 Don Beebe 11/2/1994	1.50	4.00
2 Cornelius Bennett 9/14/1994	1.50	4.00
3 Jeff Burris 10/19/1994	1.25	3.00
4 Jerry Crafts 11/23/1994	1.25	3.00
5 Kenneth Davis 10/12/1994	1.50	4.00
6 Carwell Gardner 9/28/1994	1.25	3.00
7 Henry Jones 11/9/1994	1.50	4.00
8 Yonel Jordan 12/21/1994	1.25	3.00
9 Jim Kelly 10/27/1994	4.00	10.00
10 Mark Maddox 12/7/1994	1.25	3.00
11 Pete Metzelaars 12/15/1994	1.25	3.00
12 Andre Reed 10/6/1994	2.00	5.00
13 Frank Reich 11/30/1994	1.50	4.00
14 Bruce Smith 9/8/1994	2.00	5.00
15 Darryl Talley 11/16/1994	1.25	3.00
16 Thurman Thomas 9/21/1994	3.00	8.00

1994 Bills Police

Sponsored by Coca-Cola and the Sheriff's office in Erie County, this six-card set measures approximately 3" by 5". The fronts feature color action shots framed by a white inner border and an outer border that shades from red to purple as one moves down the card. This outer border is accented by horizontal black lines that become thicker toward the bottom of the card. Alongside a gray stripe carrying the player's name, position, and team helmet, the backs show a black-and-white head shot, biography, and "Tips from the Sheriff." The cards are unnumbered and checklisted below in alphabetical order.

COMPLETE SET (6)	5.00	10.00
1 Bill Brooks	1.00	2.50
2 Kenneth Davis	1.00	2.50
3 John Fina	.75	2.00
4 Phil Hansen	.75	2.00
5 Pete Metzelaars	1.00	2.50
6 Marvcus Patton	.75	2.00

1995 Bills Buffalo News Posters

These posters were created by the Buffalo News and issued as "pages" in the daily newspapers during the 1995 season. Each large poster includes a color image of a Bills player on the front with a typical newspaper page back. We've included the date when the photo appeared when known.

COMPLETE SET (16)	20.00	40.00
1 Justin Armour 10/12/1995	1.00	2.50
2 Bill Brooks 10/25/1995	1.25	3.00
3 Ruben Brown 10/18/2005	1.00	2.50
4 Jeff Burris 9/20/1995	1.00	2.50
5 Russell Copeland 9/27/1995	1.00	2.50
6 John Fina 11/2/1995	1.00	2.50
7 Darick Holmes 11/9/1995	1.00	2.50
8 Kent Hull 11/29/1995	1.00	2.50
9 Jerry Ostroski 12/6/1995	1.00	2.50
10 Bryce Paup 11/15/1995	1.25	3.00
11 Andre Reed 9/13/1995	1.50	4.00
12 Kurt Schulz 10/5/1995	1.25	3.00
13 Bruce Smith 9/6/1995	1.50	4.00
14 Thomas Smith 12/13/1995	1.00	2.50
15 Steve Tasker 12/20/1995	1.25	3.00
16 Ted Washington 11/21/1995	1.00	2.50

1995 Bills Police

This six-card set of the Buffalo Bills was sponsored by Coca-Cola and the Erie County Office of Sheriff. The cards measure approximately 4" by 6" and feature a color action player photo set on a colorful stone-look background. The backs carry player information and a safety tip. The cards are unnumbered and checklisted below in alphabetical order.

COMPLETE SET (6)	5.00	10.00
1 Jeff Burris	.75	2.00
2 Joe Ferguson AIG	1.00	2.50
3 Kent Hull	.75	2.00
4 Adam Lingner	.75	2.00
5 Glenn Parker	.75	2.00
6 Andre Reed	1.50	4.00

1996 Bills Buffalo News Posters

These posters were created by the Buffalo News and issued as "pages" in the daily newspapers during the 1996 season. Each large poster includes a color image of a Bills player on the front with a typical newspaper page back. We've included the date when the photo appeared when known.

COMPLETE SET (15)	20.00	40.00
1 Jeff Burris 11/21/1996	1.00	2.50
2 Todd Collins 10/3/1996	1.00	2.50
3 Quinn Early 9/25/1996	1.25	3.00
4 Jim Jeffcoat 9/11/1996	1.00	2.50
5 Lonnie Johnson 10/9/1996	1.00	2.50
6 Tony Kline 9/19/1996	1.00	2.50
7 Mark Maddox 10/31/1996	1.00	2.50
8 Gabe Northern 10/23/1996	1.00	2.50
9 Bryce Paup 11/6/1996	1.25	3.00
10 Andre Reed 11/26/1996	1.50	4.00
11 Sam Rogers 11/13/1996	1.00	2.50
12 Chris Spielman 9/5/1996	1.25	3.00
13 Steve Tasker 12/11/1996	1.25	3.00
14 Thurman Thomas 12/18/1996	1.50	4.00
15 David White 12/6/1996	1.00	2.50

1996 Bills Police

This five-card set of the Buffalo Bills was sponsored by Coca-Cola and the Erie County Sheriff's Office. The cards measure approximately 4" by 6" and feature a color action player photo with the sponsor logos on the cardfront. The cards are unnumbered but have been checklisted below in alphabetical order.

COMPLETE SET (5)	3.00	8.00
1 Ruben Brown	.75	2.00
2 Mark Maddox	.75	2.00
3 Bryce Paup	1.00	2.50
4 Mark Pike	.75	2.00
5 Kurt Schulz	.75	2.00

1997 Bills Buffalo News Posters

These posters were created by the Buffalo News and issued as "pages" in the daily newspapers during the 1997 season. Each large poster includes a color image of a Bills player on the front with a typical newspaper page back. We've included the date when the photo appeared when known.

COMPLETE SET (16)	20.00	40.00
1 Ruben Brown 10/15/1997	1.00	2.50
2 Todd Collins 9/3/1997	1.00	2.50
3 John Fina 9/24/1997	1.00	2.50
4 Phil Hansen 11/26/1997	1.00	2.50
5 Ken Irvin 10/30/1997	1.00	2.50
6 Lonnie Johnson 10/8/1997	1.00	2.50
7 Henry Jones 11/5/1997	1.25	3.00
8 Eric Moulds 10/22/1997	1.50	4.00
9 Gabe Northern 11/12/1997	1.00	2.50
10 Andre Reed 12/10/1997	1.50	4.00
11 Antowain Smith 12/3/1997	2.00	5.00
12 Thomas Smith 9/10/1997	1.00	2.50
13 Chris Spielman 9/17/1997	1.25	3.00
14 Thurman Thomas 10/1/1997	1.50	4.00
15 Ted Washington 12/17/1997	1.25	3.00
16 Dusty Zeigler 11/19/1997	1.00	2.50

1998 Bills Buffalo News Posters

These posters were created by the Buffalo News and issued as "pages" in the daily newspapers during the 1998 season. Each large poster includes a color image of a Bills player on the front with a typical newspaper page back. We've included the date when the photo appeared when known.

COMPLETE SET (16)	15.00	30.00
1 Ruben Brown 12/1/1998	.75	2.00
2 Sam Cowart 10/21/1998	.75	2.00
3 Quinn Early 10/7/1998	1.00	2.50
4 Doug Flutie 10/14/1998	2.00	5.00
5 Sam Gash 9/23/1998	.75	2.00
6 John Holecek 12/15/1998	.75	2.00
7 Ken Irvin 12/8/1998	.75	2.00
8 Chris Mohr 11/4/1998	.75	2.00
9 Gabe Northern 11/10/1998	.75	2.00
10 Jerry Ostroski 12/23/1998	.75	2.00
11 Jay Riemersma 11/25/1998	.75	2.00
12 Sam Rogers 9/16/1998	.75	2.00
13 Antowain Smith 11/18/1998	1.25	3.00
14 Ted Washington 10/27/1998	1.00	2.50
15 Marcellus Wiley 9/30/1998	.75	2.00
16 Kevin Williams 9/9/1998	.75	2.00

1998 Bills Police

This set was sponsored by Pepsi and the Erie County Sheriff's Office. The cards measure approximately 4" by 6" and feature a color action player photo with the sponsor logos on the cardfront. The cards are unnumbered but have been checklisted below in alphabetical order.

COMPLETE SET (5)	5.00	10.00
1 Steve Christie	1.00	2.50
2 Phil Hansen	1.00	2.50
3 Henry Jones	1.00	2.50
4 Andre Reed	1.50	4.00
5 Ted Washington	1.00	2.50

1999 Bills Bookmarks

This set of bookmarks was distributed by Buffalo area libraries. Each features one Bills player along with the title "Rush for Reading" on the front. The backs include a smaller photo of the player along with his vital statistics. Sponsors included Blue Cross and Blue Shield, Buffalo Bills Youth Foundation and Just Buffalo Literary Center. Each bookmark measures roughly 2 1/2" by 7 1/2" and was printed on thin glossy stock.

COMPLETE SET (5)	6.00	12.00
1 John Fina	1.25	3.00
2 Sam Gash	1.25	3.00
3 John Holecek	1.25	3.00
4 Gabe Northern	1.25	3.00
5 Marcellus Wiley	1.25	3.00

1999 Bills Buffalo News Posters

These posters were created by the Buffalo News and issued as "pages" in the daily newspapers during the 1999 season. Each large poster includes a color image of a Bills player on the front with a typical newspaper page back. We've included the date when the photo appeared when known.

COMPLETE SET (16)	15.00	30.00
1 Ruben Brown 11/17/1999	.75	2.00
2 Sam Cowart 11/10/1999	.75	2.00
3 Doug Flutie 9/15/1999	2.00	5.00
4 Phil Hansen 10/20/1999	.75	2.00
5 John Holecek 10/6/1999	.75	2.00
6 Henry Jones 12/22/1999	1.00	2.50
7 Eric Moulds 10/13/1999	1.25	3.00
8 Peerless Price 12/1/1999	1.50	4.00
9 Andre Reed 10/27/1999	1.25	3.00
10 Kurt Schulz 11/24/1999	1.00	2.50
11 Antowain Smith 9/29/1999	1.25	3.00
12 Thurman Thomas 12/15/1999	1.25	3.00
13 Ted Washington 9/22/1999	1.00	2.50
14 Marcellus Wiley 12/8/1999	.75	2.00
15 Kevin Williams 11/3/1999	.75	2.00
16 Antoine Winfield 12/29/1999	.75	2.00

2000 Bills Bookmarks

This set of bookmarks was sponsored by Blue Cross and Blue Shield and distributed in the Buffalo area. Each features one Bills player along with the title "Rush for Reading" on the front. The backs include a smaller photo of the player along with his vital statistics. Each measures roughly 2 1/2" by 7 1/2" and was printed on thin glossy stock. An additional bookmark was released for the Summer reading program, but is not considered part of the complete set.

COMPLETE SET (4)	5.00	10.00
1 Sam Cowart	.75	2.00
2 Doug Flutie	2.00	5.00
3 Peerless Price	1.25	3.00
4 Jay Riemersma	.75	2.00
5 Marcellus Wiley	1.25	3.00

2000 Bills Buffalo News Posters

These posters were created by the Buffalo News and issued as "pages" in the daily newspapers during the 2000 season. Each large poster includes a color image of a Bills player on the front with a typical newspaper page back. We've included the date when the photo appeared when known.

COMPLETE SET (8)	7.50	15.00
1 Sam Cowart 10/25/2000	.75	2.00
2 John Fina 10/4/2000	.75	2.00
3 John Holecek 10/18/2000	.75	2.00
4 Rob Johnson 11/22/2000	1.00	2.50
5 Henry Jones 12/6/2000	1.00	2.50
6 Sammy Morris 12/13/2000	1.25	3.00
7 Peerless Price 11/15/2000	1.25	3.00
8 Sam Rogers 11/8/2000	.75	2.00

2000 Bills Xerox

These oversized cards (measuring roughly 4 1/4" by 6 1/2") were sponsored by Xerox and feature members of the Buffalo Bills. Each was printed on thin white coated paper stock with a color photo of the featured player on the front and vital stats on the back. The cards were issued to promote Xerox's DocuColor 2060 Digital Press which was used to print the cards. The unnumbered cards are listed below alphabetically.

COMPLETE SET (32)	30.00	50.00
1 Avion Black	.50	1.25
2 Ruben Brown	.50	1.25
3 Bobby Collins	.50	1.25
4 Sam Cowart	.50	1.25
5 John Fina	.50	1.25
6 Erik Flowers	.50	1.25
7 Doug Flutie	2.00	5.00
8 Drew Haddad	.50	1.25
9 Phil Hansen	.50	1.25
10 Robert Hicks	.50	1.25
11 John Holecek	.50	1.25
12 Ken Irvin	.50	1.25
13 Sheldon Jackson	.50	1.25
14 Rob Johnson	1.25	3.00
15 Henry Jones	.75	2.00
16 Jonathan Linton	.75	2.00
17 Corey Moore	.50	1.25
18 Sammy Morris	1.00	2.50
19 Eric Moulds	1.25	3.00
20 Keith Newman	.50	1.25
21 Jerry Ostroski	.50	1.25
22 Joe Panos	.50	1.25
23 DaShon Polk	.50	1.25
24 Peerless Price	2.50	6.00
25 Jay Riemersma	.50	1.25
26 Sam Rogers	.50	1.25
27 Antowain Smith	1.25	3.00
28 Travares Tillman	.50	1.25
29 Ted Washington	.75	2.00
30 Marcellus Wiley	.75	2.00
31 Pat Williams	.75	2.00
32 Antoine Winfield	.50	1.25

2001 Bills Bookmarks

Blue Cross Blue Shield of Western New York sponsored this set of player bookmarks that was distributed in the Buffalo area. Each features one Bills player along with the title "Rush for Reading" on the front at the top. The backs include a smaller photo of the player along with his vital statistics. Each measures roughly 2 1/2" by 7 1/2" and was printed on thin glossy stock. An additional bookmark was released for the Summer reading program, but is not considered part of the complete set.

COMPLETE SET (4)	3.00	8.00
1 Rob Johnson	1.25	3.00
2 Keion Carpenter	.75	2.00
3 Kenyatta Wright	.75	2.00
4 Jonas Jennings	.75	2.00
5 Sammy Morris	1.25	3.00

2002 Bills Bookmarks

For the fourth year, Blue Cross and Blue Shield sponsored a set of player bookmarks that was distributed in the Buffalo area. Each features one Bills player along with the title "Rush for Reading" on the front. The backs include a smaller photo of the player along with his vital statistics. Each measures roughly 2 1/2" by 7 1/2" and was printed on thin glossy stock. An additional bookmark was released for the Summer reading program, but is not considered part of the complete set.

COMPLETE SET (5)	5.00	10.00
1 Drew Bledsoe	2.00	5.00
2 Larry Centers	1.25	3.00
3 Tony Driver	.75	2.00
4 Brian Moorman	.75	2.00
5 Gregg Williams CO	.75	2.00
6 Sammy Morris (Summer Program; Jersey #33)	1.25	3.00

2002 Bills Buffalo News Posters

These posters were created by the Buffalo News and issued as "pages" in the daily newspapers during the 2002 season. Each large poster includes a color image of a Bills player on the front with a typical newspaper page back. We've included the date when the photo appeared when known.

COMPLETE SET (6)	6.00	12.00
1 Travis Henry 10/12/2002	1.25	3.00
2 Eric Moulds 11/23/2002	1.25	3.00
3 Keith Newman 11/16/2002	.75	2.00
4 Eddie Robinson 9/26/2002	.75	2.00
5 Trey Teague 9/20/2002	.75	2.00
6 Pat Williams 10/17/2002	.75	2.00

2003 Bills Bookmarks

For the third straight year, Blue Cross Blue Shield of Western New York sponsored a set of bookmarks that was distributed in the Buffalo area. Each features one Bills player along with the title "Rush for Reading" on the front at the top. The backs include an additional photo of the player along with his vital statistics. Each measures roughly 2 1/2" by 7 1/2" and was printed on very thin high gloss stock. An additional bookmark was released for the Summer reading program and sponsored by UPS. It is priced below, but is not considered part of the complete set.

COMPLETE SET (6)	4.00	10.00
1 Drew Bledsoe	2.00	5.00
2 Sam Gash	.75	2.00
3 Brian Moorman	.75	2.00

4 Gregg Williams CO .75 2.00
5 Mike Williams .75 2.00
6 Coy Wire .75 2.00
7 Sammy Morris 1.25 3.00
(Summer Program; Jersey #31)

2004 Bills Tops Grocery

These large cards (measuring roughly 3 7/8" by 5 1/8") were issued by Tops Grocery Stores in the Buffalo area and could be exchanged at Bills home games for a chance to win a variety of prizes.
COMPLETE SET (5) 4.00 10.00
1 Drew Bledsoe 1.00 2.50
2 London Fletcher 1.00 2.50
3 Travis Henry .75 2.00
4 Pat Williams 1.00 2.50
5 Coy Wire .75 2.00

2004 Bills Xerox

These slightly oversized cards (measuring roughly 2 1/2" by 3 3/4") were sponsored by Xerox and feature members of the Buffalo Bills. Each was printed on thin white coated paper stock with a color photo of the featured player on the front with a thin blue border. A slightly smaller "mini" version of card was also issued measuring roughly 2 1/4" by 3 1/4". The unnumbered cards are listed below aphabetically.
COMPLETE SET (11) 6.00 15.00
*MINI: .4X TO 1X BASIC CARDS
1 Sam Adams .60 1.50
2 Drew Bledsoe .75 2.00
3 Lee Evans 1.00 2.50
4 London Fletcher .75 2.00
5 Travis Henry .60 1.50
6 J.P. Losman .60 1.50
7 Willis McGahee .60 1.50
8 Lawyer Milloy .60 1.50
9 Eric Moulds .60 1.50
10 Takeo Spikes .60 1.50
11 Pat Williams .75 2.00

2005 Bills Merrick Mint Quarters

COMPLETE SET (11) 40.00 80.00
1 Nate Clements 3.00 8.00
2 Lee Evans 5.00 10.00
3 London Fletcher 5.00 10.00
4 J.P. Losman 5.00 10.00
5 Willis McGahee 5.00 10.00
6 Lawyer Milloy 3.00 8.00
7 Eric Moulds 5.00 10.00
8 Aaron Schobel 3.00 8.00
9 Takeo Spikes 3.00 8.00
10 Bills red helmet 3.00 8.00
11 Bills white helmet 3.00 8.00

2005 Bills Xerox

These slightly oversized cards (measuring roughly 2 1/2" by 3 3/4") were sponsored by Xerox and feature members of the Buffalo Bills. Each was printed on white paper stock with a color photo of the featured player on the front with a thick light blue border. The unnumbered cards are listed below aphabetically.
COMPLETE SET (6) 4.00 10.00
1 London Fletcher .75 2.00
2 J.P. Losman .60 1.50
3 Willis McGahee .60 1.50
4 Eric Moulds .60 1.50
5 Mike Mularkey .60 1.50
6 Takeo Spikes .60 1.50

2006 Bills Topps

COMPLETE SET (12) 3.00 6.00
BUF1 Willis McGahee .25 .60
BUF2 Roscoe Parrish .25 .60
BUF3 London Fletcher .30 .75
BUF4 Lee Evans .30 .75
BUF5 J.P. Losman .30 .75
BUF6 Aaron Schobel .25 .60
BUF7 Takeo Spikes .25 .60
BUF8 Troy Vincent .25 .60
BUF9 Kelly Holcomb .25 .60
BUF10 Josh Reed .25 .60
BUF11 Ashton Youboty .25 .60
BUF12 Nate Clements .25 .60

2006 Bills Xerox

These slightly oversized cards (measuring roughly 2 1/2" by 3 3/4") were sponsored by Xerox and feature members of the Buffalo Bills. Each was printed on white paper stock with a color photo of the featured player on the front with a white border at the top but full-bleed sides. The unnumbered cards are listed below aphabetically.
COMPLETE SET (6) 4.00 10.00
1 Nate Clements .60 1.50
2 Lee Evans .75 2.00
3 London Fletcher .75 2.00
4 Willis McGahee .60 1.50
5 Terrence McGee .60 1.50
6 Takeo Spikes .60 1.50

2007 Bills Blue Cross Blue Shield

These oversized cards (measuring roughly 3" by 4-1/2") were sponsored by Blue Cross Blue Shield and feature members of the Buffalo Bills. Each was printed on white paper stock with a color photo of the featured player on the front and the back as well as a "What Moves U" message. The unnumbered cards are listed below aphabetically.
COMPLETE SET (4) 5.00 12.00
1 Lee Evans 1.25 3.00
2 Chris Kelsay 1.00 2.50
3 Rian Lindell 1.00 2.50
4 Marshawn Lynch 2.00 5.00

2007 Bills Topps

COMPLETE SET (12) 3.00 6.00
1 J.P. Losman .40 1.00
2 Lee Evans .50 1.25
3 Peerless Price .40 1.00
4 Aaron Schobel .40 1.00
5 Anthony Thomas .40 1.00
6 Rian Lindell .40 1.00
7 Josh Reed .40 1.00
8 Terrence McGee .40 1.00
9 Donte Whitner .40 1.00
10 Marshawn Lynch .75 2.00
11 Paul Posluszny .40 1.00
12 Trent Edwards .40 1.00

2008 Bills Topps

COMPLETE SET (12) 2.50 5.00
1 Trent Edwards .40 1.00
2 Marshawn Lynch .50 1.25
3 J.P. Losman .40 1.00
4 Aaron Schobel .40 1.00
5 Angelo Crowell .40 1.00
6 Lee Evans .50 1.25
7 Josh Reed .40 1.00
8 Donte Whitner .40 1.00
9 Terrance McGee .40 1.00
10 Roscoe Parrish .40 1.00
11 James Hardy .40 1.00
12 Leodis McKelvin .50 1.25

2009 Bills Breast Cancer Awareness

This three card set was issued at a Bills game in 2009. Each unnumbered card was created by one of the three NFL licensed manufacturers and features the pink ribbon breast cancer awareness logo on the fronts.
COMPLETE SET (3) 2.50 5.00
1 Jerricho Cotchery Topps .60 1.50
2 Thomas Jones Upper Deck .75 2.00
3 Mark Sanchez Panini .60 1.50

2009 Bills Buffalo News Posters

These posters were created by the Buffalo News and issued as "pages" in the daily newspapers during the 2009 season. Each large poster includes a color image of a Bills player(s) on the front with a typical newspaper page back. We've included the date released for each poster.
COMPLETE SET (15) 10.00 25.00
1 Trent Edwards 1.00 2.50
Lee Evans
Josh Reed
Terrell Owens
(9/23/2009)
2 Fred Jackson .75 2.00
(9/30/2009)
3 Aaron Schobel .75 2.00
(10/7/2009)
4 Terrell Owens 1.00 2.50
(10/14/2009)
5 Terrence McGee .75 2.00
(10/21/2009)
6 Jairus Byrd .75 2.00
(10/28/2009)
7 Bills All-Time Team .75 2.00
(11/14/2009)
8 Jim Kelly 50 yrs. 1.25 3.00
(11/11/2009)
9 Thurman Thomas 50 yrs. 1.00 2.50
(11/18/2009)
10 James Lofton 50 yrs. .75 2.00
Pete Metzelaars
Eric Moulds
Andre Reed
(11/25/2009
11 Reuben Brown 50 yrs. .75 2.00
Joe DeLamielleure
Kent Hull
Jim Ritcher
Billy Shaw
12 Tom Sestak 50 yrs. 1.00 2.50
Fred Smerlas
Bruce Smith
(12/9/2009)
13 Cornelius Bennett 50 yrs. .75 2.00
Shane Conlan
Mike Stratton
Darryl Talley
14 Butch Byrd 50 yrs. .75 2.00
Henry Jones
Nate Odomes
George Saimes
(12/23/2009)
15 Steve Christie 50 yrs. .75 2.00
Brian Moorman
Steve Tasker
Marv Levy CO
(12/30/2009

2009 Bills NOCO Medallions

This set of coins or medallions was issued by NOCO Express stores in the Buffalo area over a series of weeks during the 2009 NFL season. Each features a past Buffalo Bill great and an album was issued as well to house the collection. NOCO offered each coin at an SRP of $2.99 and the complete set at $49.99.
COMPLETE SET (14) 30.00 50.00
1 Ruben Brown 1.25 3.00
2 Joe DeLamielleure 1.25 3.00
3 Kent Hull 1.25 3.00
4 Jim Kelly 2.00 5.00
5 Marv Levy CO 1.25 3.00
6 James Lofton 1.50 4.00
7 Pete Metzelaars 1.25 3.00
8 Eric Moulds 1.25 3.00
9 Andre Reed 1.50 4.00
10 Jim Ritcher 1.25 3.00
11 Billy Shaw 1.25 3.00
12 Steve Tasker 1.25 3.00
13 Thurman Thomas 1.50 4.00
NNO Album 1.25 3.00

2010 Bills Dick's Sporting Goods

This set was released by Dick's Sporting Goods Stores in the Buffalo area in 2010. Each features a large color image of a Bills player along with a $10 store coupon attached below the image. With the coupon attached, the cards measure roughly 5" by 9".
COMPLETE SET (3) 3.00 7.50
1 David Nelson 1.00 2.50
2 Garrison Sanborn 1.00 2.50
3 Jonathan Stupar 1.00 2.50

2014 Bills Prestige

COMPLETE SET (8)
1 Mario Williams
2 Kyle Williams
3 C.J. Spiller
4 Fred Jackson
5 Sammy Watkins
6 Aaron Williams
NNO Aaron Williams
NNO Cover Card

1974 Birmingham Americans WFL Cups

These plastic drinking cups were sponsored by Jack's Hamburgers and WBRC-TV Channel 6 in Birmingham and feature members of the WFL Birmingham Americans. Each week of the WFL season a different player was featured on a cup. Any additions to the list below are appreciated.
1 John Andrews 7.50 15.00
2 George Mira 7.50 15.00
3 Paul Robinson 7.50 15.00

1975 Birmingham Vulcans WFL Team Issue 8X10

These photos measure roughly 8" x 10" and include a large black and white player image on the front with only the player's name below photo. The backs are blank.
1 Matthew Reed 7.50 15.00

1975 Birmingham Vulcans WFL Team Issue Dual Photo 8X10

These photos measure roughly 8" x 10" and include black and white images with a smaller head-and-shoulders photo to the left with the player's name and team logo beneath it and a larger action shot to the right. The backs are blank.
1 William Bryant 7.50 15.00
2 Denny Duron 7.50 15.00
3 Larry Estes 7.50 15.00
4 Mike Hayes 7.50 15.00
5 Dennis Homan 7.50 15.00
6 Pat Kelley 7.50 15.00
7 Steve Manstedt 7.50 15.00
8 Johnny Musso 7.50 15.00
9 Ted Powell 7.50 15.00
10 Joe Profit 7.50 15.00
11 Matthew Reed 7.50 15.00
12 Ron Slovensky 7.50 15.00
13 Bob Tatarek 7.50 15.00
14 Larry Willingham 7.50 15.00
15 Wimpy Winther 7.50 15.00
16 Jesse Wolf 7.50 15.00

2000 Birmingham Steeldogs AFL2

This set was given out as a promotional item at a Steeldogs Arena 2 League football game. Each card features a color photo of the player along with his jersey number. The unnumbered cardbacks feature a short player bio. The cards measure slightly larger than standard size at 2 9/16" by 3 9/16'.
COMPLETE SET (20) 5.00 10.00
1 Fred Bishop .25 .60
2 Donald Blackmon .25 .60
3 Cedrick Buchannon .25 .60
4 Chris Edwards .25 .60
5 Tommy Harrison .25 .60
6 Bobby Humphrey CO .40 1.00
7 James Lewis .25 .60
8 Anthony Jordan .25 .60
9 Wes Mitchem .25 .60
10 Sterrick Morgan .25 .60
11 Alphonso Pogue .25 .60
12 Robert Poole .25 .60
13 Jackie Rowan .25 .60
14 Steve Stanley .25 .60
15 Brandon Stewart .25 .60
16 Wayne Thomas .25 .60
17 Mo Thompson .25 .60
18 Adlai Trone .25 .60
19 Troy Williams .25 .60
20 Chris Windsor .25 .60

2002 Birmingham Steeldogs AFL2

This set was issued to promote the Steeldogs Arena League football team. Each standard-sized card features a color photo of the player printed on thin card stock. The unnumbered cardbacks feature a short player bio and a small photo.
COMPLETE SET (21) 5.00 10.00
1 Johnny Anderson .25 .60
2 Cedrick Buchannon .25 .60
3 Michael Feagin .25 .60
4 Jeff Hannah .25 .60
5 Terrance Harris .25 .60
6 Jimmi Henson .25 .60
7 Bobby Humphrey CO .40 1.00
8 Larry Huntington .25 .60
9 Terrance Ingram .25 .60
10 Anthony Jordan .25 .60
11 Montressa Kirby .25 .60
12 James Lewis .25 .60
13 William Mayes .25 .60
14 Jimmy Moore .25 .60
15 Paul Morgan .25 .60
16 Ozell Powell .25 .60
17 Ernest Ross .25 .60
18 Jackie Rowan .25 .60
19 Wayne Thomas .25 .60
20 Jerry Turner .25 .60
21 DeJuan Washington .25 .60

1997 Black Diamond

The 1997 Upper Deck Black Diamond set totals 180-cards and was distributed in six card packs with a suggested retail of $3.49. The set was produced essentially in three series together: Black Diamond (1-90), Double Black Diamond (91-150) inserted one in every four packs, and Triple Black Diamond (151-180) inserted one in every 30 packs. The fronts feature color action player photos reproduced on Light F/X card stock with one, two, or three Black Diamonds on the front designating its rarity. The backs carry player information and statistics.
COMPLETE SET (180) 150.00 300.00
COMP.SERIES 1 (90) 12.50 25.00
1 Alfred Williams .15 .40
2 Alvin Harper .15 .40
3 Andre Hastings .15 .40
4 Andre Reed .25 .60
5 Anthony Johnson .15 .40
6 Anthony Miller .15 .40
7 Byron Bam Morris .15 .40
8 Bobby Hebert .15 .40
9 Bobby Taylor .15 .40
10 Boomer Esiason .25 .60
11 Brett Perriman .15 .40
12 Brian Blades .15 .40
13 Bryan Cox .15 .40
14 Bryant Young .15 .40
15 Bryce Paup .15 .40
16 Carnell Lake .15 .40
17 Cedric Jones .15 .40
18 Chad Brown .15 .40
19 Charlie Garner .25 .60
20 Chris Chandler .25 .60
21 Cornelius Bennett .15 .40
22 Cortez Kennedy .15 .40
23 Cris Carter .40 1.00
24 Dale Carter .15 .40
25 Daryl Gardener .15 .40
26 Derrick Alexander WR .25 .60
27 Derrick Mayes .25 .60
28 Don Beebe .15 .40
29 Eric Allen .15 .40
30 Eric Moulds .40 1.00
31 Errict Rhett .15 .40
32 Frank Sanders .25 .60
33 Glyn Milburn .15 .40
34 Henry Ellard .15 .40
35 Jamal Anderson .40 1.00
36 James O. Stewart .25 .60
37 Jason Dunn .15 .40
38 Jerry Rice 1.25 3.00
39 Jim Everett .15 .40
40 Jim Kelly .40 1.00
41 Joey Galloway .25 .60
42 John Carney .15 .40
43 John Elway 2.00 5.00
44 John Randle .25 .60
45 Karim Abdul-Jabbar .25 .60
46 Keenan McCardell .25 .60
47 Ken Dilger .15 .40
48 Ken Norton .15 .40
49 Ki-Jana Carter .15 .40
50 Kordell Stewart .40 1.00
51 Lawrence Phillips .15 .40
52 Leslie O'Neal .15 .40
53 Mark Chmura .25 .60
54 Marshall Faulk .50 1.25
55 Michael Haynes .15 .40
56 Michael Irvin .40 1.00
57 Michael Jackson .25 .60
58 Michael Westbrook .25 .60
59 Mike Tomczak .15 .40
60 Napoleon Kaufman .40 1.00
61 Neil O'Donnell .25 .60
62 Neil Smith .25 .60
63 O.J. McDuffie .25 .60
64 Orlando Thomas .15 .40
65 Rashaan Salaam .15 .40
66 Regan Upshaw .15 .40
67 Rick Mirer .15 .40
68 Rob Moore .25 .60
69 Ronnie Harmon .15 .40
70 Sam Mills .15 .40
71 Sean Dawkins .15 .40
72 Shawn Jefferson .15 .40
73 Stan Humphries .25 .60
74 Stepfret Williams .15 .40
75 Stephen Davis .40 1.00
76 Steve Atwater .15 .40
77 Terance Mathis .25 .60
78 Terrell Fletcher .15 .40
79 Terry Glenn .40 1.00
80 Terry McDaniel .15 .40
81 Tony McGee .15 .40
82 Trent Dilfer .40 1.00
83 Troy Drayton .15 .40
84 Ty Detmer .25 .60
85 Tyrone Hughes .15 .40
86 Walt Harris .15 .40
87 Wayne Chrebet .40 1.00
88 Wesley Walls .25 .60
89 Willie Davis .15 .40
90 Willie McGinest .15 .40
91 Adrian Murrell .75 2.00
92 Alex Molden .50 1.25
93 Alex Van Dyke .75 2.00
94 Andre Coleman .50 1.25
95 Ben Coates 1.25 3.00
96 Bobby Engram .75 2.00
97 Bruce Smith 1.25 3.00
98 Charles Johnson 1.25 3.00
99 Chris Sanders 1.25 3.00
100 Chris T. Jones 1.25 3.00
101 Chris Warren .75 2.00
102 Darnay Scott 1.25 3.00
103 Dave Brown .75 2.00
104 Derrick Thomas 1.25 3.00
105 Drew Bledsoe 2.50 6.00
106 Edgar Bennett 1.25 3.00
107 Emmitt Smith 7.50 15.00
108 Eric Bjornson .50 1.25
109 Eric Metcalf 1.25 3.00
110 Garrison Hearst .75 2.00
111 Gus Frerotte .75 2.00
112 Hardy Nickerson .50 1.25
113 Herman Moore .75 2.00
114 Hugh Douglas .50 1.25
115 Irving Fryar .75 2.00
116 J.J. Stokes .75 2.00
117 Jake Reed .75 2.00
118 Jeff Hostetler .75 2.00
119 Jeff Lewis .75 2.00
120 Jim Harbaugh .75 2.00
121 Johnnie Morton .75 2.00
122 Jonathan Ogden .50 1.25
123 Kevin Carter .75 2.00
124 Kevin Greene .75 2.00
125 Kevin Hardy .75 2.00
126 Leeland McElroy .50 1.25
127 Mike Alstott 1.25 3.00
128 Muhsin Muhammad 1.25 3.00
129 Natrone Means .75 2.00
130 Quentin Coryatt .50 1.25
131 Ray Lewis 1.50 4.00
132 Ray Zellars .50 1.25
133 Rickey Dudley .75 2.00
134 Ricky Watters .75 2.00
135 Robert Smith 1.25 3.00
136 Scott Mitchell .75 2.00
137 Sean Gilbert .50 1.25
138 Shannon Sharpe .75 2.00
139 Simeon Rice .75 2.00
140 Stanley Pritchett .50 1.25
141 Steve McNair 2.00 5.00
142 Steve Young 4.00 8.00
143 Tamarick Vanover .75 2.00
144 Terry Allen .75 2.00
145 Thurman Thomas 1.25 3.00
146 Tony Banks 1.25 3.00
147 Tony Martin .75 2.00
148 Tyrone Wheatley 1.25 3.00
149 Vinny Testaverde .75 2.00
150 Zach Thomas 1.25 3.00
151 Amani Toomer 3.00 8.00
152 Barry Sanders 10.00 25.00
153 Bobby Hoying 3.00 8.00
154 Brett Favre 12.50 30.00
155 Carl Pickens 3.00 8.00
156 Curtis Conway 3.00 8.00
157 Curtis Martin 5.00 12.00
158 Dan Marino 12.50 30.00
159 Deion Sanders 3.00 8.00
160 Eddie George .40 1.00
161 Eddie Kennison 2.00 5.00
162 Elvis Grbac 3.00 8.00
163 Isaac Bruce 3.00 8.00
164 Jeff Blake 2.00 5.00
165 Jerome Bettis 3.00 8.00
166 Junior Seau 3.00 8.00
167 Kerry Collins 2.00 5.00
168 Keyshawn Johnson 3.00 8.00
169 Larry Centers 2.00 5.00
170 Marcus Allen 3.00 8.00
171 Mark Brunell 4.00 10.00
172 Marvin Harrison 3.00 8.00
173 Reggie White 3.00 8.00
174 Rodney Hampton 2.00 5.00
175 Terrell Davis 5.00 12.00
176 Tim Brown 3.00 8.00
177 Todd Collins 2.00 5.00
178 Troy Aikman 6.00 15.00
179 Tim Biakabutuka 2.00 5.00
180 Warren Moon 3.00 8.00
BD1 Troy Aikman Promo .75 2.00

1997 Black Diamond Gold

*SINGLES: 2.5X TO 6X BASE CARD HI
SINGLE GOLD STATED ODDS 1:15
*DOUBLES: 1.5X TO 4X BASE CARD HI
DOUBLE GOLD ODDS 1:46
*TRIPLES: 2X TO 5X BASE CARD HI
TRIPLE GOLD STATED PRINT RUN 50 SETS

1997 Black Diamond Title Quest

This 20 card insert set features color action player photos of NFL superstars reproduced on a die-cut card utilizing cell technology and gold etching. Only 100 of each card were produced, and they are sequentially numbered.
COMPLETE SET (20) 400.00 800.00
STATED PRINT RUN 100 SERIAL #'d SETS
1 Dan Marino 50.00 120.00
2 Jerry Rice 25.00 60.00
3 Drew Bledsoe 20.00 40.00
4 Emmitt Smith 40.00 100.00
5 Troy Aikman 25.00 60.00
6 Steve Young 20.00 50.00
7 Brett Favre 50.00 120.00
8 John Elway 50.00 120.00
9 Barry Sanders 40.00 100.00
10 Jerome Bettis 12.50 30.00
11 Deion Sanders 12.50 30.00
12 Karim Abdul-Jabbar 5.00 12.00
13 Terrell Davis 15.00 40.00
14 Marshall Faulk 15.00 40.00
15 Curtis Martin 15.00 40.00
16 Eddie George 12.50 30.00
17 Steve McNair 15.00 40.00
18 Terry Glenn 7.50 20.00
19 Joey Galloway 7.50 20.00
20 Keyshawn Johnson 12.50 30.00

1998 Black Diamond

The 1998 Black Diamond set was issued in one series totalling 150 cards. The fronts feature color action player photos reproduced on Light F/X card stock with one, two, three, or four Black Diamonds on the front designating its rarity. The backs carry player information and statistics.
COMPLETE SET (150) 20.00 40.00
1 Kent Graham .15 .40
2 Darrell Russell .15 .40
3 Jim Harbaugh .25 .60
4 Cornelius Bennett .15 .40
5 Troy Vincent .15 .40
6 Natrone Means .25 .60
7 Michael Jackson .15 .40
8 Will Blackwell .15 .40
9 Greg Hill .15 .40
10 Andre Reed .25 .60
11 Darren Bennett .15 .40
12 Dan Marino 1.50 4.00
13 Tim Biakabutuka .25 .60
14 Terrell Owens .40 1.00
15 Cris Carter .40 1.00
16 Darnell Autry .15 .40
17 Joey Galloway .25 .60
18 Terry Glenn .40 1.00
19 Ki-Jana Carter .15 .40
20 Isaac Bruce .40 1.00
21 Shawn Jefferson .15 .40
22 Michael Irvin .40 1.00
23 Warren Sapp .25 .60
24 Dave Brown .15 .40
25 Terrell Davis .40 1.00
26 Frank Wycheck .15 .40
27 Neil O'Donnell .25 .60
28 Scott Mitchell .25 .60
29 Michael Westbrook .25 .60
30 Tim Brown .40 1.00
31 Antonio Freeman .40 1.00
32 Jake Plummer .40 1.00
33 Irving Fryar .25 .60
34 Quentin Coryatt .15 .40
35 Jamal Anderson .40 1.00
36 Jerome Bettis .40 1.00
37 Keenan McCardell .25 .60
38 Derrick Alexander WR .25 .60
39 Stan Humphries .15 .40
40 Andre Rison .25 .60
41 Bruce Smith .25 .60
42 Garrison Hearst .40 1.00
43 Zach Thomas .40 1.00
44 Rae Carruth .15 .40
45 Kevin Greene .25 .60
46 Robert Smith .40 1.00
47 Curtis Conway .25 .60
48 Christian Fauria .15 .40
49 Curtis Martin .40 1.00
50 Dan Wilkinson .15 .40
51 Eddie Kennison .25 .60
52 Mark Fields .15 .40
53 Anthony Miller .15 .40
54 Mike Alstott .40 1.00
55 Tiki Barber .40 1.00
56 Neil Smith .25 .60
57 Gus Frerotte .15 .40
58 Adrian Murrell .25 .60
59 Johnnie Morton .25 .60
60 O.J. McDuffie .25 .60
61 Napoleon Kaufman .40 1.00
62 Robert Brooks .25 .60
63 Byron Hanspard .15 .40
64 Ty Detmer .25 .60
65 Mark Brunell .40 1.00
66 Byron Bam Morris .15 .40
67 Kordell Stewart .40 1.00
68 Elvis Grbac .25 .60
69 Antowain Smith .40 1.00
70 Junior Seau .40 1.00
71 Tony Gonzalez .40 1.00
72 Anthony Johnson .15 .40
73 Steve Young .50 1.25
74 Brian Manning .15 .40
75 Erik Kramer .15 .40
76 Warren Moon .40 1.00
77 Torrian Gray .15 .40
78 Carl Pickens .25 .60
79 Tony Banks .25 .60
80 Willie McGinest .15 .40
81 Deion Sanders .40 1.00
82 Warrick Dunn .40 1.00
83 Danny Wuerffel .25 .60
84 Rod Smith WR .25 .60
85 Steve McNair .40 1.00
86 Danny Kanell .25 .60
87 Herman Moore .25 .60
88 Brian Mitchell .15 .40
89 James Farrior .15 .40
90 Reggie White .40 1.00
91 Simeon Rice .25 .60
92 James Jett .25 .60
93 Marshall Faulk .50 1.25
94 Chris Chandler .25 .60
95 Mike Mamula .15 .40
96 Jimmy Smith .25 .60
97 Jamie Sharper .15 .40
98 Carnell Lake .15 .40
99 Marcus Allen .40 1.00
100 Thurman Thomas .40 1.00
101 Freddie Jones .15 .40
102 Karim Abdul-Jabbar .40 1.00
103 Kerry Collins .25 .60
104 Jerry Rice .75 2.00
105 Brad Johnson .40 1.00
106 Raymont Harris .15 .40
107 Lamar Smith .25 .60
108 Drew Bledsoe .60 1.50
109 Corey Dillon .40 1.00
110 Lawrence Phillips .15 .40
111 Heath Shuler .15 .40
112 Emmitt Smith 1.25 3.00
113 Reidel Anthony .25 .60
114 Ike Hilliard .25 .60
115 Shannon Sharpe .25 .60
116 Chris Sanders .15 .40
117 Keyshawn Johnson .40 1.00
118 Barry Sanders 1.25 3.00
119 Cris Dishman .15 .40
120 Jeff George .25 .60
121 Dorsey Levens .40 1.00
122 Rob Moore .25 .60
123 Ricky Watters .25 .60
124 Marvin Harrison .40 1.00
125 Vinny Testaverde .25 .60
126 Charles Johnson .15 .40
127 Renaldo Wynn .15 .40
128 Todd Collins QB .15 .40
129 Tony Martin .25 .60
130 Derrick Thomas .40 1.00
131 Wesley Walls .25 .60
132 Rod Woodson .25 .60
133 Troy Drayton .15 .40
134 Bryan Cox .15 .40
135 Shawn Springs .15 .40
136 Jake Reed .25 .60
137 Jeff Blake .25 .60
138 Craig Heyward .15 .40
139 Ben Coates .25 .60
140 Troy Aikman .75 2.00
141 Trent Dilfer .40 1.00
142 Troy Davis .15 .40
143 John Elway 1.50 4.00
144 Eddie George .40 1.00
145 Rodney Hampton .25 .60
146 Ed McCaffrey .25 .60
147 Terry Allen .40 1.00
148 Wayne Chrebet .40 1.00
149 Brett Favre 1.50 4.00
150 Daryl Johnston .25 .60

1998 Black Diamond Double

COMPLETE SET (150) 50.00 100.00
*DOUBLE STARS: 1X TO 2X BASIC CARDS
STATED ODDS ONE PER PACK

1998 Black Diamond Quadruple

*QUAD.STARS: 10X TO 25X BASIC CARDS
QUADRUPLE STATED PRINT RUN 50 SETS

1998 Black Diamond Triple

COMPLETE SET (150) 150.00 300.00
*TRIPLE STARS: 2.5X TO 6X
STATED ODDS 1:5

1998 Black Diamond Premium Cut

Randomly inserted in packs at the rate of one in seven, this 30-card set features color action photos of top stars printed in a Light F/X card design with a single black diamond.
COMPLETE SET (30) 100.00 200.00
SINGLE DIAMOND STATED ODDS 1:7
*DOUBLE DIAM: .6X TO 1.5X BASIC INSERTS
DOUBLE DIAMOND STATED ODDS 1:15
*TRIPLE DIAMONDS: .8X TO 2X BASIC INSERTS
TRIPLE DIAMOND STATED ODDS 1:30
*QUAD VERTICALS: 1.5X TO 4X
QUAD VERTICAL STATED ODDS 1:180
PC1 Karim Abdul-Jabbar 2.50 6.00
PC2 Troy Aikman 5.00 12.00
PC3 Kerry Collins 1.50 4.00
PC4 Drew Bledsoe 4.00 10.00
PC5 Barry Sanders 8.00 20.00
PC6 Marcus Allen 2.50 6.00
PC7 John Elway 10.00 25.00
PC8 Adrian Murrell 1.50 4.00
PC9 Junior Seau 2.50 6.00
PC10 Eddie George 2.50 6.00
PC11 Antowain Smith 2.50 6.00
PC12 Reggie White 2.50 6.00
PC13 Dan Marino 10.00 25.00
PC14 Joey Galloway 1.50 4.00
PC15 Kordell Stewart 2.50 6.00
PC16 Terry Allen 2.50 6.00
PC17 Napoleon Kaufman 2.50 6.00
PC18 Curtis Martin 2.50 6.00
PC19 Steve Young 3.00 8.00
PC20 Rod Smith WR 1.50 4.00
PC21 Mark Brunell 2.50 6.00
PC22 Emmitt Smith 8.00 20.00
PC23 Rae Carruth 1.00 2.50
PC24 Brett Favre 10.00 25.00
PC25 Jeff George 1.50 4.00
PC26 Terry Glenn 2.50 6.00
PC27 Warrick Dunn 2.50 6.00
PC28 Herman Moore 1.50 4.00
PC29 Cris Carter 2.50 6.00
PC30 Terrell Davis 2.50 6.00

1998 Black Diamond Premium Cut Quadruple Horizontal

PC1 Karim Abdul-Jabbar 7.50 20.00
PC2 Troy Aikman 100.00 200.00
PC3 Kerry Collins 7.50 20.00
PC4 Drew Bledsoe 40.00 100.00
PC5 Barry Sanders 125.00 250.00
PC6 Marcus Allen 12.50 30.00
PC7 John Elway 200.00 400.00
PC8 Adrian Murrell 6.00 15.00
PC9 Junior Seau 7.50 20.00
PC10 Eddie George 12.50 30.00
PC11 Antowain Smith 7.50 20.00
PC12 Reggie White 7.50 20.00
PC13 Dan Marino 175.00 300.00
PC14 Joey Galloway 6.00 15.00
PC15 Kordell Stewart 15.00 40.00
PC16 Terry Allen 7.50 20.00
PC17 Napoleon Kaufman 7.50 20.00
PC18 Curtis Martin 12.50 30.00
PC19 Steve Young 40.00 100.00
PC20 Rod Smith WR 6.00 15.00
PC21 Mark Brunell 12.50 30.00
PC22 Emmitt Smith 125.00 250.00
PC23 Rae Carruth 6.00 15.00
PC24 Brett Favre 150.00 300.00
PC25 Jeff George 6.00 15.00
PC26 Terry Glenn 7.50 20.00
PC27 Warrick Dunn 100.00 250.00
PC28 Herman Moore 7.50 20.00
PC29 Cris Carter 12.50 30.00
PC30 Terrell Davis 15.00 40.00

1998 Black Diamond Rookies

The 1998 Black Diamond Rookies set was issued in one series totalling 120 cards and distributed in six-card packs with a suggested retail price of $3.99. The fronts feature color action photos of 90 top veterans and 30 rookie players reproduced on Light F/X foil cards with one, two, three, or four Black Diamonds on the front designating its rarity. The backs carry player information and statistics. The 30 Rookie cards were seeded in packs at the rate of 1:4.
COMPLETE SET (120) 50.00 100.00
1 Jake Plummer .30 .75
2 Adrian Murrell .20 .50
3 Frank Sanders .20 .50
4 Jamal Anderson .30 .75
5 Chris Chandler .20 .50
6 Tony Martin .20 .50
7 Jim Harbaugh .20 .50
8 Errict Rhett .20 .50
9 Michael Jackson .10 .30
10 Rob Johnson .20 .50
11 Antowain Smith .30 .75
12 Thurman Thomas .30 .75
13 Fred Lane .10 .30
14 Kerry Collins .10 .30
15 Rae Carruth .10 .30
16 Erik Kramer .10 .30
17 Edgar Bennett .10 .30
18 Curtis Conway .20 .50
19 Corey Dillon .30 .75
20 Neil O'Donnell .20 .50
21 Carl Pickens .20 .50
22 Troy Aikman .60 1.50
23 Emmitt Smith 1.00 2.50
24 Deion Sanders .30 .75
25 John Elway 1.25 3.00
26 Terrell Davis .30 .75
27 Rod Smith .20 .50
28 Barry Sanders 1.00 2.50
29 Johnnie Morton .20 .50
30 Herman Moore .20 .50
31 Brett Favre 1.25 3.00
32 Antonio Freeman .30 .75
33 Dorsey Levens .30 .75
34 Marshall Faulk .40 1.00
35 Marvin Harrison .30 .75
36 Zack Crockett .10 .30
37 Mark Brunell .30 .75
38 Jimmy Smith .20 .50
39 Keenan McCardell .20 .50
40 Elvis Grbac .20 .50
41 Andre Rison .20 .50
42 Derrick Alexander .20 .50
43 Dan Marino 1.25 3.00
44 Karim Abdul-Jabbar .30 .75
45 Zach Thomas .30 .75
46 Brad Johnson .30 .75
47 Cris Carter .30 .75
48 Robert Smith .30 .75
49 Drew Bledsoe .50 1.25
50 Terry Glenn .30 .75
51 Ben Coates .20 .50
52 Danny Wuerffel .20 .50
53 Lamar Smith .20 .50
54 Sean Dawkins .10 .30
55 Danny Kanell .20 .50
56 Tiki Barber .30 .75
57 Ike Hilliard .20 .50
58 Curtis Martin .30 .75
59 Vinny Testaverde .20 .50
60 Keyshawn Johnson .30 .75
61 Napoleon Kaufman .30 .75
62 Jeff George .20 .50
63 Tim Brown .30 .75
64 Bobby Hoying .20 .50
65 Charlie Garner .20 .50
66 Duce Staley .40 1.00
67 Kordell Stewart .30 .75
68 Jerome Bettis .30 .75
69 Charles Johnson .10 .30
70 Tony Banks .20 .50
71 Isaac Bruce .30 .75
72 Eddie Kennison .20 .50
73 Natrone Means .20 .50
74 Bryan Still .10 .30
75 Junior Seau .30 .75
76 Steve Young .40 1.00
77 Jerry Rice .60 1.50
78 Garrison Hearst .30 .75
79 Ricky Watters .20 .50
80 Joey Galloway .20 .50
81 Warren Moon .10 .30
82 Warrick Dunn .30 .75
83 Trent Dilfer .30 .75
84 Bert Emanuel .20 .50
85 Steve McNair .30 .75
86 Eddie George .30 .75
87 Yancey Thigpen .10 .30
88 Leslie Shepherd .10 .30
89 Terry Allen .30 .75
90 Michael Westbrook .20 .50
91 Peyton Manning RC 12.00 30.00
92 Jacquez Green RC .75 2.00
93 Fred Taylor RC 1.50 4.00
94 Terry Fair RC .75 2.00
95 Pat Johnson RC .75 2.00
96 Corey Chavous RC 1.00 2.50
97 Randy Moss RC 8.00 20.00
98 Curtis Enis RC .50 1.25
99 Rashaan Shehee RC .75 2.00
100 Kevin Dyson RC 1.00 2.50
101 Shaun Williams RC .75 2.00
102 Grant Wistrom RC .75 2.00
103 John Avery RC .75 2.00
104 Brian Griese RC 2.00 5.00
105 Ryan Leaf RC 1.00 2.50
106 Jerome Pathon RC 1.00 2.50
107 Sam Cowart RC .75 2.00
108 Germane Crowell RC .75 2.00
109 Ahman Green RC 4.00 10.00
110 Greg Ellis RC .50 1.25
111 Robert Holcombe RC .75 2.00
112 Marcus Nash RC .50 1.25
113 Duane Starks RC .50 1.25
114 Andre Wadsworth RC .75 2.00
115 Takeo Spikes RC 1.00 2.50
116 Eric Brown RC .50 1.25
117 Robert Edwards RC .75 2.00
118 Charlie Batch RC 1.00 2.50
119 Mikhael Ricks RC .75 2.00
120 Charles Woodson RC 4.00 10.00
S13 Dan Marino SAMPLE .75 2.00

1998 Black Diamond Rookies Double

*VETS/3000: 1.2X TO 3X BASIC CARDS
*ROOKIES/2500: .6X TO 1.5X BASIC CARDS

1998 Black Diamond Rookies Quadruple

*QUAD VETS: 8X TO 20X BASIC CARDS
*QUAD ROOKIES: 2X TO 5X
91 Peyton Manning 100.00 200.00

1998 Black Diamond Rookies Triple

*VETS/1500: 2.5X TO 6X BASIC CARDS
*ROOKIES/1000: 1X TO 2.5X

1998 Black Diamond Rookies Jumbos

Cards from this set were released at the 1999 Super Bowl Card Show. Each is essentially a jumbo (roughly 5" by 7") parallel version of the player's 1998 Upper Deck Black Diamond Rookies card without the foil printing.
COMPLETE SET (8) 16.00 40.00
91 Peyton Manning 5.00 12.00
97 Randy Moss 3.00 8.00
98 Curtis Enis .80 2.00
100 Kevin Dyson .80 2.00
104 Brian Griese 3.00 6.00
105 Ryan Leaf 2.00 4.00
118 Charlie Batch 2.00 5.00
120 Charles Woodson 2.00 5.00

1998 Black Diamond Rookies Sheer Brilliance

Randomly inserted in hobby packs only, this 30-card hobby insert set features color photos of top players with a Quadruple Black Diamond designation. Each card is crash-numbered to the player's uniform number multiplied by 25. This number follows the player's name in the checklist below.
COMPLETE SET (30) 100.00 200.00
EXTREMES SER.#'d TO PLAYER'S JERSEY NO.
B1 Dan Marino/1300 6.00 15.00
B2 Troy Aikman/800 5.00 12.00
B3 Brett Favre/400 12.50 30.00
B4 Ryan Leaf/1600 1.25 3.00
B5 Peyton Manning/1800 12.00 30.00
B6 Barry Sanders/2000 5.00 12.00
B7 Emmitt Smith/2200 4.00 10.00
B8 John Elway/700 10.00 25.00
B9 Steve Young/800 3.00 8.00
B10 Steve McNair/900 2.50 6.00
B11 Antowain Smith/2300 1.25 3.00
B12 Corey Dillon/2800 1.00 2.50
B13 Terrell Davis/3000 1.25 3.00
B14 Mark Brunell/800 4.00 10.00
B15 Charles Woodson/2400 4.00 10.00
B16 Brian Griese/1400 3.00 8.00
B17 Curtis Martin/2800 1.25 3.00
B18 Keyshawn Johnson/1900 1.25 3.00
B19 Kordell Stewart/1000 1.25 3.00
B20 Eddie George/2700 1.25 3.00
B21 Drew Bledsoe/1100 4.00 10.00
B22 Jake Plummer/1600 1.25 3.00
B23 Warren Moon/100 7.50 20.00
B24 Curtis Enis/3900 1.00 2.50
B25 John Avery/2000 1.00 2.50
B26 Randy Moss/1800 8.00 20.00
B27 Rob Johnson/1100 1.50 4.00
B28 Warrick Dunn/2800 1.25 3.00
B29 Terry Allen/2100 1.25 3.00
B30 Robert Smith/2600 1.25 3.00

1998 Black Diamond Rookies Extreme Brilliance

Randomly inserted in hobby packs only, this 30-card hobby insert set features color photos of top players with a Quadruple Black Diamond designation. Each card is crash-numbered to the player's actual uniform number. This number follows the player's name in the checklist below.
STATED PRINT RUN 1-39
B6 Barry Sanders/20 125.00 250.00
B7 Emmitt Smith/22 100.00 200.00
B11 Antowain Smith/23 20.00 50.00
B12 Corey Dillon/28 20.00 50.00
B13 Terrell Davis/30 30.00 80.00
B15 Charles Woodson/24 25.00 60.00
B17 Curtis Martin/28 20.00 50.00
B20 Eddie George/27 20.00 50.00
B24 Curtis Enis/39 15.00 40.00
B25 John Avery/20 12.00 30.00
B28 Warrick Dunn/28 20.00 50.00
B29 Terry Allen/21 20.00 50.00
B30 Robert Smith/26 15.00 40.00

1998 Black Diamond Rookies White Onyx

Randomly inserted in packs, this 30-card set features color action player photos printed on cards with Pearl Light F/X treatment and with a Quadruple Black Diamond designation. Each card is crash-numbered to 2250. A Black Onyx parallel version of this insert set was also produced with a foil shift to Black Light F/X and each card numbered 1 of 1.
COMPLETE SET (30) 100.00 200.00
STATED PRINT RUN 2250 SERIAL #'d SETS
UNPRICED BLACK ONYZ #'d TO 1
ON1 Peyton Manning 20.00 50.00
ON2 Corey Dillon 2.00 5.00
ON3 Jerome Bettis 2.00 5.00
ON4 Brett Favre 8.00 20.00
ON5 Napoleon Kaufman 2.00 5.00
ON6 Joey Galloway 1.25 3.00
ON7 John Elway 8.00 20.00
ON8 Troy Aikman 4.00 10.00
ON9 Robert Smith 2.00 5.00
ON10 Kordell Stewart 2.00 5.00
ON11 Garrison Hearst 2.00 5.00
ON12 Curtis Enis 1.00 2.50
ON13 Dan Marino 8.00 20.00
ON14 Jimmy Smith 1.25 3.00
ON15 Steve Young 2.50 6.00
ON16 Ryan Leaf 2.00 5.00
ON17 Steve McNair 2.00 5.00
ON18 Randy Moss 12.00 30.00
ON19 Curtis Martin 2.00 5.00
ON20 Barry Sanders 6.00 15.00
ON21 Rob Johnson 1.25 3.00
ON22 Emmitt Smith 6.00 15.00
ON23 Jake Plummer 2.00 5.00
ON24 Antonio Freeman 2.00 5.00
ON25 Mark Brunell 2.00 5.00
ON26 Warrick Dunn 2.00 5.00
ON27 Eddie George 2.00 5.00
ON28 Jerry Rice 4.00 10.00
ON29 Drew Bledsoe 3.00 8.00
ON30 Terrell Davis 2.00 5.00

1999 Black Diamond

Released as a 150-card base set, the 1999 Upper Deck Black diamond features 110 regular issue veteran cards and 40 rookie subset cards inserted at one in four packs. Cards fronts are all foil and are enhanced with laser etching. Black Diamond was released both as Hobby and Retail, and was packaged in 30-pack boxes containg 6-cards per pack and carried a suggested retail of $3.99.
COMPLETE SET (150) 60.00 120.00
COMP.SET w/o SPs (110) 10.00 20.00
1 Adrian Murrell .25 .00

2 Jake Plummer .25 .60
3 Rob Moore .25 .60
4 Frank Sanders .25 .60
5 Jamal Anderson .30 .75
6 Terance Mathis .25 .60
7 Chris Chandler .30 .75
8 Tim Dwight .30 .75
9 Jermaine Lewis .25 .60
10 Priest Holmes .25 .60
11 Peter Boulware .25 .60
12 Doug Flutie .40 1.00
13 Antowain Smith .25 .60
14 Eric Moulds .25 .60
15 Bruce Smith .30 .75
16 Rae Carruth .25 .60
17 Muhsin Muhammad .25 .60
18 Wesley Walls .30 .75
19 Tim Biakabutuka .30 .75
20 Curtis Enis .25 .60
21 Curtis Conway .30 .75
22 Bobby Engram .25 .60
23 Darnay Scott .25 .60
24 Corey Dillon .25 .60
25 Jeff Blake .30 .75
26 Ty Detmer .25 .60
27 Terry Kirby .25 .60
28 Leslie Shepherd .25 .60
29 Emmitt Smith .60 1.50
30 Troy Aikman .50 1.25
31 Michael Irvin .40 1.00
32 Rocket Ismail .30 .75
33 Brian Griese .25 .60
34 Terrell Davis .30 .75
35 Shannon Sharpe .30 .75
36 Rod Smith .30 .75
37 Barry Sanders .60 1.50
38 Herman Moore .30 .75
39 Charlie Batch .25 .60
40 Johnnie Morton .30 .75
41 Brett Favre .75 2.00
42 Dorsey Levens .30 .75
43 Antonio Freeman .30 .75
44 Mark Chmura .25 .60
45 Peyton Manning 1.25 3.00
46 Jerome Pathon .25 .60
47 Marvin Harrison .30 .75
48 Fred Taylor .25 .60
49 Mark Brunell .30 .75
50 Jimmy Smith .30 .75
51 Keenan McCardell .30 .75
52 Andre Rison .30 .75
53 Elvis Grbac .25 .60
54 Derrick Alexander WR .25 .60
55 Tony Gonzalez .30 .75
56 Dan Marino .75 2.00
57 Oronde Gadsden .25 .60
58 O.J. McDuffie .30 .75
59 Randy Moss .30 .75
60 Randall Cunningham .30 .75
61 Cris Carter .40 1.00
62 Robert Smith .25 .60
63 Drew Bledsoe .30 .75
64 Terry Glenn .30 .75
65 Ben Coates .30 .75
66 Billy Joe Hobert .25 .60
67 Eddie Kennison .30 .75
68 Cam Cleeland .25 .60
69 Gary Brown .25 .60
70 Ike Hilliard .25 .60
71 Amani Toomer .25 .60
72 Vinny Testaverde .25 .60
73 Keyshawn Johnson .30 .75
74 Curtis Martin .30 .75
75 Wayne Chrebet .25 .60
76 Tim Brown .40 1.00
77 Rickey Dudley .25 .60
78 Napoleon Kaufman .25 .60
79 Charles Woodson .40 1.00
80 Duce Staley .25 .60
81 Doug Pederson .25 .60
82 Charles Johnson .25 .60
83 Kordell Stewart .25 .60
84 Jerome Bettis .40 1.00
85 Courtney Hawkins .25 .60
86 Isaac Bruce .40 1.00
87 Marshall Faulk .30 .75
88 Trent Green .25 .60
89 Jim Harbaugh .30 .75
90 Junior Seau .30 .75
91 Natrone Means .30 .75
92 Lawrence Phillips .30 .75
93 Steve Young .50 1.25
94 Terrell Owens .30 .75
95 Jerry Rice 1.00 2.50
96 Jon Kitna .25 .60
97 Ricky Watters .30 .75
98 Joey Galloway .30 .75
99 Shawn Springs .25 .60
100 Warrick Dunn .25 .60
101 Trent Dilfer .25 .60
102 Reidel Anthony .25 .60
103 Mike Alstott .25 .60
104 Steve McNair .30 .75
105 Eddie George .30 .75
106 Kevin Dyson .25 .60
107 Yancey Thigpen .25 .60
108 Michael Westbrook .25 .60
109 Brad Johnson .30 .75
110 Skip Hicks .25 .60
111 Tim Couch RC 1.00 2.50
112 Akili Smith RC .75 2.00
113 Ricky Williams RC 1.25 3.00
114 Donovan McNabb RC 6.00 15.00
115 Edgerrin James RC 1.25 3.00
116 Cade McNown RC .75 2.00
117 Daunte Culpepper RC 1.25 3.00
118 Shaun King RC .75 2.00
119 Brock Huard RC .75 2.00
120 Joe Germaine RC 1.00 2.50
121 Troy Edwards RC .75 2.00
122 Champ Bailey RC 1.50 4.00
123 Kevin Faulk RC .75 2.00
124 David Boston RC .75 2.00
125 Kevin Johnson RC 1.00 2.50
126 Torry Holt RC 1.50 4.00
127 James Johnson RC .75 2.00
128 Peerless Price RC .75 2.00
129 D'Wayne Bates RC .75 2.00
130 Cecil Collins RC .75 2.00
131 Na Brown RC .75 2.00
132 Rob Konrad RC .75 2.00
133 Joel Makovicka RC .75 2.00
134 Dameane Douglas RC .75 2.00
135 Scott Covington RC .75 2.00
136 Daylon McCutcheon RC .75 2.00
137 Chris Claiborne RC .75 2.00
138 Karsten Bailey RC .75 2.00
139 Mike Cloud RC .75 2.00
140 Sean Bennett RC .75 2.00
141 Jermaine Fazande RC .75 2.00
142 Chris McAlister RC .75 2.00
143 Ebenezer Ekuban RC .75 2.00
144 Jeff Paulk RC .75 2.00
145 Jim Kleinsasser RC 1.25 3.00
146 Bobby Collins RC .75 2.00
147 Andy Katzenmoyer RC 1.00 2.50
148 Jevon Kearse RC 1.00 2.50
149 Amos Zereoue RC .75 2.00
150 Sedrick Irvin RC .75 2.00
WPBD W.Payton Jsy AU/34 1000.00 1500.00

1999 Black Diamond Diamond Cut

COMPLETE SET (150) 100.00 200.00
*DIAMOND CUT STARS: 1.5X TO 4X HI COL.
1-110 STATED ODDS 1:7
*DIAMOND CUT RCs: .5X TO 1.2X
111-150 STATED ODDS 1:12

1999 Black Diamond Final Cut

*FINAL CUT STARS: 10X TO 25X
1-110 FINAL CUT PRINT RUN 100 SER.#'d SETS
*FINAL CUT RCs: 2.5X TO 6X
111-150 FINAL CUT PRINT RUN 50 #'d SETS

1999 Black Diamond A Piece of History

Randomly inserted in Hobby packs at the rate of one in 179 and Retail packs at the rate of one in 359, this 26-card set features a single diamond swatch of a game-used football. Double and Triple diamond swatch versions were released also.

COMPLETE SET (26) 300.00 600.00
H STATED ODDS 1:179 HOBBY
HR STATED ODDS 1:359 HOB/RET
*DOUBLE DIAMONDS: .6X TO 1.5X HI COL.
DOUBLE H STATED ODDS 1:1079 HOBBY
DOUBLE HR ODDS 1:1079 HOB/RET
AS Akili Smith H 6.00 15.00
BF Brett Favre H/R 20.00 50.00
BG Brian Griese H 8.00 20.00
BH Brock Huard H 6.00 15.00
CB Charlie Batch H/R 8.00 20.00
CM Cade McNown H/R 5.00 12.00
DBL Drew Bledsoe H 10.00 25.00
DBO David Boston H 6.00 15.00
DC Daunte Culpepper H/R 15.00 40.00
DF Doug Flutie H/R 8.00 20.00
DM Dan Marino H/R 25.00 60.00
DMC Donovan McNabb H/R 20.00 50.00
EJ Edgerrin James H 15.00 40.00
ES Emmitt Smith H 15.00 40.00
HM Herman Moore H 5.00 12.00
JP Jake Plummer H 6.00 15.00
JR Jerry Rice H/R 10.00 25.00
RM Randy Moss H 10.00 25.00
RW Ricky Williams H/R 10.00 25.00
SY Steve Young H/R 12.50 30.00
TA Troy Aikman H/R 15.00 40.00
TB Tim Brown H/R 8.00 20.00
TC Tim Couch H 8.00 20.00
TD Terrell Davis H 8.00 20.00
TH Torry Holt H/R 8.00 20.00
WD Warrick Dunn H 8.00 20.00

1999 Black Diamond Diamonation

Randomly inserted in packs at the rate of one in six, this 20-card set features 20 of the NFL's elite in a full holo-foil sparkle card stock. Card backs carry a "D" prefix.

COMPLETE SET (20) 20.00 50.00
STATED ODDS 1:6
D1 Brett Favre 3.00 8.00
D2 Eddie George 1.00 2.50
D3 Terrell Davis 1.00 2.50
D4 Jerome Bettis 1.00 2.50
D5 Randall Cunningham 1.00 2.50
D6 Jon Kitna 1.00 2.50
D7 Troy Aikman 2.00 5.00
D8 Marshall Faulk 1.25 3.00
D9 Steve Young 1.25 3.00
D10 Warrick Dunn 1.00 2.50
D11 Jake Plummer .60 1.50
D12 Fred Taylor 1.00 2.50
D13 Antonio Freeman 1.00 2.50
D14 Peyton Manning 3.00 8.00
D15 Randy Moss 2.50 6.00
D16 Steve McNair 1.00 2.50
D17 Emmitt Smith 2.00 5.00
D18 Terrell Owens 1.00 2.50
D19 Kordell Stewart .60 1.50
D20 Ricky Williams 1.50 4.00

1999 Black Diamond Gallery

Randomly seeded in packs at the rate of one in 14, this 10-card set features portrait-style photography of some of the NFL's most collected players. Card backs carry a "G" prefix.

COMPLETE SET (10) 20.00 50.00
STATED ODDS 1:14
G1 Akili Smith 1.25 3.00
G2 Barry Sanders 5.00 12.00
G3 Curtis Martin 1.50 4.00
G4 Drew Bledsoe 2.00 5.00
G5 Emmitt Smith 3.00 8.00
G6 Keyshawn Johnson 1.50 4.00
G7 Jerry Rice 3.00 8.00
G8 Tim Couch 1.50 4.00
G9 Terrell Owens 1.50 4.00
G10 Troy Aikman 3.00 8.00

1999 Black Diamond Might

Randomly inserted in packs at the rate on one in 12, this 10-card set focuses on some of the NFL's powerhouse players. Card fronts are all foil with a sparkle effect. Card backs carry a "DM" prefix.

COMPLETE SET (10) 10.00 25.00
STATED ODDS 1:12
DM1 Antowain Smith 1.00 2.50
DM2 Steve McNair 1.00 2.50
DM3 Corey Dillon 1.00 2.50
DM4 Dan Marino 3.00 8.00
DM5 Eddie George 1.00 2.50
DM6 Jerome Bettis 1.00 2.50
DM7 Jerry Rice 2.00 5.00
DM8 Randall Cunningham 1.00 2.50
DM9 Brian Griese 1.00 2.50
DM10 Joey Galloway .60 1.50

1999 Black Diamond Myriad

Randomly inserted in packs at the rate of one in 29, this 10-card set features full color action photos of top players. Card backs carry an "M" prefix.

COMPLETE SET (10) 25.00 60.00
STATED ODDS 1:29
M1 Barry Sanders 5.00 12.00
M2 Randy Moss 4.00 10.00
M3 Terrell Davis 1.50 4.00
M4 Brett Favre 5.00 12.00
M5 Jamal Anderson 1.50 4.00
M6 Mark Brunell 1.50 4.00
M7 Donovan McNabb 10.00 25.00
M8 Steve Young 2.00 5.00
M9 Ricky Williams 5.00 12.00
M10 Warrick Dunn 1.50 4.00

1999 Black Diamond Skills

Randomly inserted in packs at the rate of one in 29, this 10-card set highlights the most versatile and skilled players in professional football today. Card backs carry an "S" prefix.

COMPLETE SET (10) 40.00 80.00
STATED ODDS 1:29
S1 Drew Bledsoe 2.00 5.00
S2 Fred Taylor 1.50 4.00
S3 Dan Marino 5.00 12.00
S4 Jake Plummer 1.00 2.50
S5 Kurt Warner 7.50 20.00
S6 Marshall Faulk 2.00 5.00
S7 Randy Moss 4.00 10.00
S8 Peyton Manning 5.00 12.00
S9 Keyshawn Johnson 1.50 4.00
S10 Tim Couch 1.50 4.00

2000 Black Diamond

Released in October of 2000, Black Diamond Features a 180 card base set comprised of 120 veteran cards, 30 Rookie Gems sequentially numbered to 2400, and 30 Rookie Jersey Gems showcasing a swatch of a jersey in the shape of an "R" and inserted at one in 23 Hobby and one in 72 Retail packs. Black Diamond was packaged in 24-pack boxes with packs containing six cards and carried a suggested retial price of $3.99

COMP.SET w/o SP's (120) 6.00 15.00
151-180 ROOKIE JSY ODDS 1:23H, 1:72R
1 Jake Plummer .20 .50
2 David Boston .20 .50
3 Frank Sanders .20 .50
4 Tim Dwight .25 .60
5 Chris Chandler .25 .60
6 Jamal Anderson .25 .60
7 Shawn Jefferson .20 .50
8 Terance Mathis .20 .50
9 Qadry Ismail .20 .50
10 Tony Banks .20 .50
11 Shannon Sharpe .25 .60
12 Peerless Price .25 .60
13 Rob Johnson .25 .60
14 Eric Moulds .20 .50
15 Antowain Smith .25 .60
16 Muhsin Muhammad .20 .50
17 Patrick Jeffers .20 .50
18 Steve Beuerlein .25 .60
19 Tim Biakabutuka .25 .60
20 Cade McNown .20 .50
21 Marcus Robinson .25 .60
22 Eddie Kennison .20 .50
23 Bobby Engram .20 .50
24 Akili Smith .20 .50
25 Corey Dillon .20 .50
26 Darnay Scott .25 .60
27 Tim Couch .25 .60
28 Kevin Johnson .20 .50
29 Errict Rhett .25 .60
30 Troy Aikman .40 1.00
31 Emmitt Smith .50 1.25
32 Rocket Ismail .25 .60
33 Joey Galloway .25 .60
34 Terrell Davis .25 .60
35 Olandis Gary .25 .60
36 Brian Griese .20 .50
37 Ed McCaffrey .25 .60
38 Rod Smith .25 .60
39 Charlie Batch .20 .50
40 Germane Crowell .20 .50
41 Johnnie Morton .25 .60
42 James Stewart .20 .50
43 Brett Favre .60 1.50
44 Antonio Freeman .25 .60
45 Dorsey Levens .25 .60
46 Peyton Manning .75 2.00
47 Edgerrin James .25 .60
48 Marvin Harrison .25 .60
49 Terrence Wilkins .20 .50
50 Mark Brunell .25 .60
51 Fred Taylor .20 .50
52 Jimmy Smith .25 .60
53 Keenan McCardell .25 .60
54 Elvis Grbac .20 .50
55 Tony Gonzalez .25 .60
56 Derrick Alexander .20 .50
57 James Johnson .20 .50
58 Tony Martin .25 .60
59 Damon Huard .20 .50
60 Oronde Gadsden .25 .60
61 Randy Moss .25 .60
62 Robert Smith .20 .50
63 Cris Carter .30 .75
64 Daunte Culpepper .25 .60
65 Drew Bledsoe .25 .60
66 Terry Glenn .25 .60
67 Sean Morey RC .20 .50
68 Ricky Williams .25 .60
69 Keith Poole .20 .50
70 Jake Reed .25 .60
71 Jeff Blake .25 .60
72 Kerry Collins .20 .50
73 Amani Toomer .20 .50
74 Joe Montgomery .20 .50
75 Ike Hilliard .20 .50
76 Ray Lucas .20 .50
77 Curtis Martin .25 .60
78 Vinny Testaverde .20 .50
79 Wayne Chrebet .20 .50
80 Tim Brown .30 .75
81 Rich Gannon .25 .60
82 Tyrone Wheatley .20 .50
83 Rickey Dudley .20 .50
84 Napoleon Kaufman .25 .60
85 Duce Staley .20 .50
86 Donovan McNabb .25 .60
87 Torrance Small .20 .50
88 Charles Johnson .20 .50
89 Kent Graham .20 .50
90 Troy Edwards .20 .50
91 Jerome Bettis .30 .75
92 Kordell Stewart .20 .50
93 Marshall Faulk .25 .60
94 Kurt Warner .50 1.25
95 Torry Holt .25 .60
96 Isaac Bruce .30 .75
97 Jermaine Fazande .20 .50
98 Ryan Leaf .25 .60
99 Jeff Graham .20 .50
100 Moses Moreno .20 .50
101 Jerry Rice .75 2.00
102 Terrell Owens .25 .60
103 Jeff Garcia .20 .50
104 Ricky Watters .25 .60
105 Jon Kitna .20 .50
106 Derrick Mayes .20 .50
107 Charlie Rogers .20 .50
108 Warrick Dunn .20 .50
109 Shaun King .20 .50
110 Mike Alstott .20 .50
111 Keyshawn Johnson .25 .60
112 Eddie George .25 .60
113 Steve McNair .25 .60
114 Kevin Dyson .25 .60
115 Kevin Daft .20 .50
116 Jevon Kearse .20 .50
117 Brad Johnson .25 .60
118 Stephen Davis .20 .50
119 Michael Westbrook .20 .50
120 Jeff George .25 .60
121 Kwame Cavil RC .50 1.25
122 Corey Moore RC .50 1.25
123 Sebastian Janikowski RC .75 2.00
124 Troy Walters RC .50 1.25
125 Mike Anderson RC .50 1.25
126 Tom Brady RC 200.00 400.00
127 Spergon Wynn RC .50 1.25
128 Tim Rattay RC .60 1.50
129 Giovanni Carmazzi RC .50 1.25
130 Chris Cole RC .60 1.50
131 Demario Brown RC .50 1.25
132 Chris Coleman RC .50 1.25
133 Michael Wiley RC .50 1.25
134 JaJuan Dawson RC .50 1.25
135 Deon Dyer RC .50 1.25
136 Trevor Gaylor RC .50 1.25
137 Todd Husak RC .50 1.25
138 Darrell Jackson RC .50 1.25
139 Erron Kinney RC .50 1.25
140 Anthony Lucas RC .50 1.25
141 Rondell Mealey RC .50 1.25
142 Chad Morton RC .60 1.50
143 Leon Murray RC .50 1.25
144 Mareno Philyaw RC .50 1.25
145 Gari Scott RC .50 1.25
146 Paul Smith RC .50 1.25
147 Terrelle Smith RC .50 1.25
148 Shyrone Stith RC .50 1.25
149 Bashir Yamini RC .50 1.25
150 Windrell Hayes RC .50 1.25
151 Courtney Brown JSY RC 3.00 8.00
152 Corey Simon JSY RC 3.00 8.00
153 R.Jay Soward JSY RC 2.50 6.00
154 Chris Redman JSY RC 2.50 6.00
155 Joe Hamilton JSY RC 2.50 6.00
156 Chad Pennington JSY RC 3.00 8.00
157 Tee Martin JSY RC 2.50 6.00
158 Ron Dayne JSY RC 4.00 10.00
159 Shaun Alexander JSY RC 4.00 10.00
160 Thomas Jones JSY RC 3.00 8.00
161 Reuben Droughns JSY RC 2.50 6.00
162 Jamal Lewis JSY RC 4.00 10.00
163 J.R. Redmond JSY RC 2.50 6.00
164 Travis Prentice JSY RC 2.50 6.00
165 Trung Canidate JSY RC 2.50 6.00
166 Brian Urlacher JSY RC 12.00 30.00
167 Anthony Becht JSY RC 2.50 6.00
168 Bubba Franks JSY RC 2.50 6.00
169 Peter Warrick JSY RC 2.50 6.00
170 Plaxico Burress JSY RC 3.00 8.00
171 Sylvester Morris JSY RC 2.50 6.00
172 Dez White JSY RC 2.50 6.00
173 Travis Taylor JSY RC 2.50 6.00
174 Todd Pinkston JSY RC 2.50 6.00
175 Dennis Northcutt JSY RC 2.50 6.00
176 Jerry Porter JSY RC 4.00 10.00
177 Laveranues Coles JSY RC 3.00 8.00
178 Danny Farmer JSY RC 2.50 6.00
179 Curtis Keaton JSY RC 2.50 6.00
180 Ron Dugans JSY RC 2.50 6.00

2000 Black Diamond Gold

*VETS 1-120: 1.2X TO 3X BASIC CARDS
1-120 VETERAN PRINT RUN 1000
*ROOKIES 121-150: .5X TO 1.2X
121-150 ROOKIE PRINT RUN 500
*ROOKIE JSY 151-180.: .6X TO 1.5X
151-180 ROOKIE JSY PRINT RUN 100
126 Tom Brady 400.00 800.00
166 Brian Urlacher JSY 20.00 50.00

2000 Black Diamond Diamonation

Randomly inserted in packs at the rate of one in eight, this 10-card set features full color action photography on a foil card stock with gold foil stamping highlights.

COMPLETE SET (10) 3.00 8.00
STATED ODDS 1:8
D1 Marshall Faulk .40 1.00
D2 Marcus Robinson .40 1.00
D3 Eddie George .40 1.00
D4 Kurt Warner .75 2.00
D5 Amani Toomer .30 .75
D6 Muhsin Muhammad .30 .75
D7 Jevon Kearse .30 .75
D8 Jon Kitna .30 .75
D9 Terrell Davis .40 1.00
D10 Tony Gonzalez .40 1.00

2000 Black Diamond Might

Randomly inserted in packs at the rate of one in 11, this 15-card set features full color action photography on a purple foil card stock with gold foil highlights.

COMPLETE SET (15) 7.50 20.00
STATED ODDS 1:11
DM1 Fred Taylor .40 1.00
DM2 Edgerrin James .50 1.25
DM3 Cade McNown .40 1.00
DM4 Randy Moss
DM5 Shaun King .40 1.00
DM6 Keyshawn Johnson .50 1.25
DM7 Jamal Anderson .50 1.25
DM8 Ricky Williams .50 1.25
DM9 Jerry Rice 1.50 4.00
DM10 Isaac Bruce .60 1.50
DM11 Peyton Manning 1.50 4.00
DM12 Mark Brunell .50 1.25
DM13 Tim Couch .50 1.25
DM14 Akili Smith .40 1.00
DM15 Emmitt Smith 1.00 2.50

2000 Black Diamond Skills

Randomly inserted in packs at the rate of one in 11, this 15-card set features top NFL players on a red/orange foil card stock with gold foil highlights.

COMPLETE SET (15) 7.50 20.00
STATED ODDS 1:11
DS1 Eddie George .50 1.25
DS2 Brett Favre 1.25 3.00
DS3 Marshall Faulk .50 1.25
DS4 Rob Johnson .50 1.25
DS5 Kevin Johnson .40 1.00
DS6 Randy Moss
DS7 Peyton Manning 1.50 4.00
DS8 Kurt Warner 1.00 2.50
DS9 Jake Plummer .40 1.00
DS10 Troy Aikman .75 2.00
DS11 Daunte Culpepper .50 1.25
DS12 Drew Bledsoe .50 1.25
DS13 Vinny Testaverde .40 1.00
DS14 Marvin Harrison .50 1.25
DS15 Charlie Batch .40 1.00

1993 Bleachers Troy Aikman Promos

Issued to herald the release of the three-card 23K Gold Border Troy Aikman set, these unnumbered standard-size promo cards feature a borderless color photo of Aikman in his UCLA uniform. The Bleachers logo at the upper right is highlighted by gold-foil bars above and below. The words "1 of 10,000 Promos" appears vertically in gold foil near the right edge. The back carries Aikman's career highlights over a ghosted black-and-white version of the front photo. The cards are unnumbered. Several versions of this promo card were produced by Bleachers for various events, such as the 1993 Comicfest and Tri-Star's 1994 Houston card show with the event's title printed in gold foil lettering on the cardfront.

COMPLETE SET (4) 1.20 3.00
COMMON CARD (1-4) .40 1.00

1993 Bleachers 23K Troy Aikman

These three standard-size cards feature on their fronts color photos of Aikman with wide gold outer borders, and colored and gold-foil inner borders. Aikman's name, team, and position are stamped in gold foil near the bottom. The back carries at the top the set's production number out of a total of 10,000 produced. Below are Aikman's name, biography, and stats and highlights for the team Aikman is pictured playing for on the front. A facsimile Aikman autograph appears in gold foil at the bottom. The cards are numbered on the back as "X of 3". A promo card was also distributed that features Aikman in a Cowboys uniform.

COMPLETE SET (3) 6.00 15.00
COMMON CARD (1-3) 2.00 5.00
P1 Troy Aikman Promo 2.00 5.00
(Cowboys)

1994 Bleachers 23K Troy Aikman

Bleachers again produced a 23K Gold card of Troy Aikman in 1994. The gold card was issued in a blue box along with a more traditional appearing card. The 2-card set was limited to 10,000 produced.

COMMON CARD (1-2) 2.00 5.00

1995 Bleachers 23K Emmitt Smith

Issued in a cello-wrapped cardboard sleeve, these four standard-size cards capture Emmitt Smith during his high school, collegiate, and pro career. The fronts of the regular-issue cards feature color player photos inside a 23K gold outer border and a black-and-white inner border. The back carries at the top the set's production number (of 10,000). Below are biography, statistics, a color head shot, and gold-foil on black autographs and images at the bottom. The promo card has a full-bleed color player photo on its front, and an advertisement and career summary on its back. Each set included a certificate of authenticity.

COMPLETE SET (3) 6.00 15.00
COMMON CARD (1-3) 2.50 6.00
NNO Emmitt Smith Promo 1.20 3.00

1994-97 Bleachers

This card group features embossed player images on 23 Karat all-gold sculptured cards. Each card was sold individually and packaged in a clear acrylic holder along with a Certificate of Authenticity inside a collectible foil-stamped box. The cards are unnumbered and checklisted below in alphabetical order. Each card is serially numbered. The continuation line includes: year, brand, and number of cards issued when known.

1 Troy Aikman 5.00 12.00
(3-Time Champs)/1996 Classic 10,000
2 Troy Aikman (Diamond Star) 5.00 12.00
1995 Classic 10,000
3 Troy Aikman/Emmitt Smith 6.00 15.00
4 Troy Aikman/Emmitt Smith 6.00 15.00
5 Troy Aikman 8.00 20.00
Emmitt Smith
(Jumbo, 1995 4,995)
6 Drew Bledsoe 5.00 12.00
1995 Classic 10,000
7 Marshall Faulk 4.00 10.00
1994 Classic 10,000
8 John Elway 2.50 6.00
(1997 Gems of the NFL)
9 Brett Favre 8.00 20.00
1996 Score Board 10,000
10 Brett Favre (Diamond Star) 8.00 20.00
1996 ScoreBoard 10,000
11 Brett Favre 8.00 20.00
1997 Score Board 10,000
12 Eddie George/1997 Classic 1,996 8.00 20.00
13 Keyshawn Johnson 4.00 10.00
1996 10,000
14 Dan Marino 8.00 20.00
1995 Upper Deck 10,000
15 Joe Montana 5.00 12.00
1995 Upper Deck 10,000
16 Joe Montana UDDS 5.00 12.00
17 Joe Namath/1997 10,000 5.00 12.00
18 Emmitt Smith 6.00 15.00
(1995 MVP; 10,000)
19 Emmitt Smith 6.00 15.00
(Season TD Record)
(1996 Classic 20,000)
20 Emmitt Smith 6.00 15.00
(Diamond Star)/1996 Classic 10,000
21 Emmitt Smith 6.00 15.00
3 time rushing champion/1995/20,000
22 Super Bowl XXX 3.00 8.00
(Color Logo)/1996 Score Board 1,996
23 Super Bowl XXX 2.50 6.00
(Gold)/1996 Score Board 7,850
24 Super Bowl XXXI 3.00 8.00
(Color Logo)/1997 Score Board 1,997
25 Super Bowl XXXI 2.50 6.00
(Gold)/1997 Score Board 4,850
26 Super Bowl Champions 2.50 6.00
1997 Score Board 50,000

2007 Bloomington Extreme

COMPLETE SET (30) 6.00 12.00
1 Team Card .20 .50
2 Ted Schmitz CO .20 .50
3 Reggie Gray .20 .50
4 Steve LaFalce .20 .50
5 Peter Christofilakos .20 .50
6 Dusty Burk .20 .50
7 Glenn Johnson .20 .50
8 Tom Kudyba .20 .50
9 Mike Crumpier .20 .50
10 Dion Brown .20 .50
11 Shatone Powers .20 .50
12 Lamar Baker .20 .50
13 Rocky Harvey .20 .50
14 Terrill Mayberry .20 .50
15 Jason Hutton .20 .50
16 Dorian Pitts .20 .50
17 Ramon Barber .20 .50
18 Eric Johnson DL .20 .50
19 Martin Wilson .20 .50
20 Calvin Jones .20 .50
21 Rachman Crable .20 .50
22 Chad Walker .20 .50
23 Quince Holman .20 .50
24 Luke Wickman .20 .50
25 Evan Triggs .20 .50
26 Jamarkus Gorman .20 .50
27 Chris Burgess .20 .50
28 Nick Ruud .20 .50
29 James Walton .20 .50
30 Dance Team .20 .50

1948 Bowman

The 1948 Bowman set is considered the first football set of the modern era. The set consists of 108 cards measuring 2 1/16" by 2 1/2". Cards were issued in one-card penny packs. The entire front is comprised of a black and white photo. The backs contain a write-up and an offer for a football. The cards were printed in three sheets; the third sheet (containing all the card numbers divisible by three, i.e., 3, 6, 9, 12, 15, etc.) being printed in much lesser quantities. Hence, cards with numbers divisible by three are substantially more valuable than the other cards in the set. The second sheet (numbers 2, 5, 8, 11, 14, etc.) is also regarded as slightly tougher to obtain than the first sheet (numbers 1, 4, 7, 10, 13, etc.) which contains the most plentiful cards. An album with which to house the set was produced. Key Rookie Cards in this set are Sammy Baugh, Charley Conerly, Sid Luckman, Johnny Lujack, Pete Pihos, Bulldog Turner, Steve Van Buren, and Bob Waterfield.

COMPLETE SET (108) 4500.00 7000.00
WRAPPER (1-CENT) 150.00 250.00
1 Joe Tereshinski RC 80.00 150.00
2 Larry Olsonoski RC 15.00 25.00
3 Johnny Lujack SP RC 250.00 350.00
4 Ray Poole RC 12.00 20.00
5 Bill DeCorrevont RC 15.00 25.00
6 Paul Briggs SP RC 65.00 100.00
7 Steve Van Buren RC 125.00 200.00
8 Kenny Washington RC 40.00 60.00
9 Nolan Luhn SP RC 65.00 100.00
10 Chris Iversen RC 12.00 20.00
11 Jack Wiley RC 15.00 25.00
12 Charley Conerly SP RC 250.00 350.00
13 Hugh Taylor RC 15.00 25.00
14 Frank Seno RC 15.00 25.00
15 Gil Bouley SP RC 65.00 100.00
16 Tommy Thompson RC 20.00 35.00
17 Charley Trippi RC 60.00 100.00
18 Vince Banonis SP RC 65.00 100.00
19 Art Faircloth RC 12.00 20.00
20 Clyde Goodnight RC 15.00 25.00
21 Bill Chipley SP RC 65.00 100.00
22 Sammy Baugh RC 350.00 500.00
23 Don Kindt RC 15.00 25.00
24 John Koniszewski SP RC 65.00 100.00
25 Pat McHugh RC 12.00 20.00
26 Bob Waterfield RC 125.00 200.00
27 Tony Compagno SP RC 65.00 100.00
28 Paul Governali RC 15.00 25.00
29 Pat Harder RC 40.00 60.00
30 Vic Lindskog SP RC 65.00 100.00
31 Salvatore Rosato RC 12.00 20.00
32 John Mastrangelo RC 15.00 25.00
33 Fred Gehrke SP RC 65.00 100.00
34 Bosh Pritchard RC 12.00 20.00
35 Mike Micka RC 15.00 25.00
36 Bulldog Turner SP RC 150.00 250.00
37 Len Younce RC 12.00 20.00
38 Pat West RC 15.00 25.00
39 Russ Thomas SP RC 65.00 100.00
40 James Peebles RC 12.00 20.00
41 Bob Skoglund RC 15.00 25.00
42 Walt Stickle SP RC 65.00 100.00
43 Whitey Wistert RC 15.00 25.00
44 Paul Christman RC 40.00 60.00
45 Jay Rhodemyre SP RC 65.00 100.00
46 Tony Minisi RC 12.00 20.00
47 Bob Mann RC 15.00 25.00
48 Mal Kutner SP RC 75.00 125.00
49 Dick Poillon RC 12.00 20.00
50 Charles Cherundolo RC 15.00 25.00
51 Gerald Cowhig SP RC 65.00 100.00
52 Neill Armstrong RC UER 15.00 25.00
53 Frank Maznicki RC 15.00 25.00
54 John Sanchez SP RC 65.00 100.00
55 Frank Reagan RC 12.00 20.00
56 Jim Hardy RC 15.00 25.00
57 John Badaczewski SP 65.00 100.00
58 Robert Nussbaumer RC 12.00 20.00
59 Mervin Pregulman RC 15.00 25.00
60 Elbie Nickel SP RC 75.00 125.00
61 Alex Wojciechowicz RC 90.00 150.00
62 Walt Schlinkman RC 15.00 25.00
63 Pete Pihos SP RC 150.00 225.00
64 Joseph Sulaitis RC 12.00 20.00
65 Mike Holovak RC 30.00 50.00
66 Cy Souders SP RC 65.00 100.00
67 Paul McKee RC 12.00 20.00
68 Bill Moore RC 15.00 25.00
69 Frank Minini SP RC 65.00 100.00
70 Jack Ferrante RC 12.00 20.00
71 Les Horvath RC 35.00 50.00
72 Ted Fritsch Sr. SP RC 75.00 125.00
73 Tex Coulter RC 15.00 25.00
74 Boley Dancewicz RC 15.00 25.00
75 Dante Mangani SP RC 65.00 100.00
76 James Hefti RC 12.00 20.00
77 Paul Sarringhaus RC 15.00 25.00
78 Joe Scott SP RC 65.00 100.00
79 Bucko Kilroy RC 15.00 25.00
80 Bill Dudley RC 75.00 125.00
81 Mar.Goldberg SP RC 75.00 125.00
82 John Cannady RC 12.00 20.00
83 Perry Moss RC 15.00 25.00
84 Harold Crisler SP RC 75.00 125.00
85 Bill Gray RC 12.00 20.00
86 John Clement RC 15.00 25.00
87 Dan Sandifer SP RC 65.00 100.00
88 Ben Kish RC 12.00 20.00
89 Herbert Banta RC 15.00 25.00
90 Bill Garnaas SP RC 65.00 100.00
91 Jim White RC 18.00 30.00
92 Frank Barzilauskas RC 15.00 25.00
93 Vic Sears SP RC 65.00 100.00
94 John Adams RC 12.00 20.00
95 George McAfee RC 90.00 150.00
96 Ralph Heywood SP RC 65.00 100.00
97 Joe Muha RC 12.00 20.00
98 Fred Enke RC 15.00 25.00
99 Harry Gilmer SP RC 100.00 175.00
100 Bill Miklich RC 12.00 20.00
101 Joe Gottlieb RC 15.00 25.00
102 Bud Angsman SP RC 75.00 125.00
103 Tom Farmer RC 12.00 20.00
104 Bruce Smith RC 40.00 75.00
105 Bob Cifers SP RC 65.00 100.00
106 Ernie Steele RC 12.00 20.00
107 Sid Luckman RC 175.00 300.00
108 Buford Ray SP RC 250.00 400.00
NNO c 200.00 350.00

1950 Bowman

After a one year hiatus, Bowman issued its first color football set for 1950. The set comprises 144 cards measuring 2 1/16" by 2 1/2". Cards were issued in six-card nickel packs with two pieces of gum. The fronts contain a black and white photo that was colored in. The card backs, which contain a write-up, feature black printing except for the player's name and the logo for the "5-Star Bowman Picture Card Collectors Club" which are both in red. The set features the Rookie Cards of Tony Canadeo, Glenn Davis, Tom Fears, Otto Graham, Lou Groza, Elroy Hirsch, Dante Lavelli, Marion Motley, Joe Perry, and Y.A. Tittle. With a few exceptions the set numbering is arranged so that trios of players from the same team are numbered together in sequence.

COMPLETE SET (144) 3000.00 4500.00
WRAPPER (5-CENT) 100.00 175.00
1 Doak Walker 150.00 250.00
2 John Greene RC 18.00 25.00
3 Bob Nowasky RC 18.00 25.00
4 Jonathan Jenkins RC 18.00 25.00
5 Y.A.Tittle RC 175.00 250.00
6 Lou Groza RC 100.00 175.00
7 Alex Agase RC 20.00 30.00
8 Mac Speedie RC 30.00 50.00
9 Tony Canadeo RC 50.00 90.00
10 Larry Craig RC 20.00 30.00
11 Ted Fritsch Sr. 20.00 30.00
12 Joe Golding RC 18.00 25.00
13 Martin Ruby RC 18.00 25.00
14 George Taliaferro 20.00 30.00
15 Tank Younger RC 30.00 50.00
16 Glenn Davis RC 75.00 125.00
17 Bob Waterfield 75.00 125.00
18 Val Jansante RC 18.00 25.00
19 Joe Geri RC 18.00 25.00
20 Jerry Nuzum RC 18.00 25.00
21 Elmer Bud Angsman 18.00 25.00
22 Billy Dewell 18.00 25.00
23 Steve Van Buren 50.00 90.00
24 Cliff Patton RC 18.00 25.00
25 Bosh Pritchard 18.00 25.00
26 Johnny Lujack 50.00 80.00
27 Sid Luckman 75.00 125.00
28 Bulldog Turner 35.00 60.00
29 Bill Dudley 35.00 60.00
30 Hugh Taylor 20.00 30.00
31 George Thomas RC 18.00 25.00
32 Ray Poole 18.00 25.00
33 Travis Tidwell RC 18.00 25.00
34 Gail Bruce RC 18.00 25.00
35 Joe Perry RC 125.00 200.00
36 Frankie Albert RC 30.00 50.00
37 Bobby Layne 125.00 200.00
38 Leon Hart 25.00 40.00
39 B.Hoernschemeyer RC 20.00 30.00
40 Dick Barwegan RC 18.00 25.00
41 Adrian Burk RC 20.00 30.00
42 Barry French RC 18.00 25.00
43 Marion Motley RC 150.00 250.00
44 Jim Martin 20.00 30.00
45 Otto Graham RC 300.00 450.00
46 Al Baldwin RC 18.00 25.00
47 Larry Coutre RC 20.00 30.00
48 John Rauch 18.00 25.00
49 Sam Tamburo RC 18.00 25.00
50 Mike Swistowicz RC 18.00 25.00
51 Tom Fears RC 90.00 150.00
52 Elroy Hirsch RC 125.00 225.00
53 Dick Huffman RC 18.00 25.00
54 Bob Gage RC 18.00 25.00
55 Buddy Tinsley RC 18.00 25.00
56 Bill Blackburn RC 18.00 25.00
57 John Cochran RC 18.00 25.00
58 Bill Fischer 18.00 25.00
59 Whitey Wistert 20.00 30.00
60 Clyde Scott RC 18.00 25.00
61 Walter Barnes RC 18.00 25.00
62 Bob Perina RC 18.00 25.00
63 Bill Wightkin RC 18.00 25.00
64 Bob Goode RC 18.00 25.00
65 Al Demao RC 18.00 25.00
66 Harry Gilmer 20.00 30.00
67 Bill Austin RC 18.00 25.00
68 Joe Scott 18.00 25.00
69 Tex Coulter 20.00 30.00
70 Paul Salata RC 18.00 25.00
71 Emil Sitko 20.00 30.00
72 Bill Johnson C RC 18.00 25.00
73 Don Doll RC 18.00 25.00
74 Dan Sandifer RC 18.00 25.00
75 John Panelli RC 18.00 25.00
76 Bill Leonard RC 18.00 25.00
77 Bob Kelly RC 18.00 25.00
78 Dante Lavelli RC 100.00 175.00
79 Tony Adamle RC 20.00 30.00
80 Dick Wildung RC 18.00 25.00
81 Tobin Rote RC 30.00 50.00
82 Paul Burris RC 18.00 25.00
83 Lowell Tew RC 18.00 25.00
84 Barney Poole RC 18.00 25.00
85 Fred Naumetz RC 18.00 25.00
86 Dick Hoerner RC 18.00 25.00
87 Bob Reinhard RC 18.00 25.00
88 Howard Hartley RC 18.00 25.00
89 Darrell Hogan RC 18.00 25.00
90 Jerry Shipkey RC 18.00 25.00
91 Frank Tripucka 20.00 30.00
92 Buster Ramsey RC 18.00 25.00
93 Pat Harder 20.00 30.00
94 Vic Sears RC 18.00 25.00
95 Tommy Thompson QB 20.00 30.00
96 Bucko Kilroy 20.00 30.00
97 George Connor 30.00 50.00
98 Fred Morrison RC 18.00 25.00
99 Jim Keane RC 18.00 25.00
100 Sammy Baugh 150.00 250.00
101 Harry Ulinski 18.00 25.00
102 Frank Spaniel RC 18.00 25.00
103 Charley Conerly 50.00 90.00
104 Dick Hensley RC 18.00 25.00
105 Eddie Price RC 18.00 25.00
106 Ed Carr RC 18.00 25.00
107 Leo Nomellini 45.00 75.00
108 Verl Lillywhite RC 18.00 25.00
109 Wallace Triplett RC 18.00 25.00
110 Joe Watson RC 18.00 25.00
111 Cloyce Box RC 20.00 30.00
112 Billy Stone RC 18.00 25.00
113 Earl Murray RC 18.00 25.00
114 Chet Mutryn RC 20.00 30.00
115 Ken Carpenter RC 20.00 30.00
116 Lou Rymkus RC 20.00 30.00
117 Dub Jones RC 25.00 40.00
118 Clayton Tonnemaker 18.00 25.00
119 Walt Schlinkman RC 18.00 25.00
120 Billy Grimes RC 18.00 25.00
121 George Ratterman RC 20.00 30.00
122 Bob Mann 18.00 25.00
123 Buddy Young RC 30.00 50.00
124 Jack Zilly RC 18.00 25.00
125 Tom Kalmanir RC 18.00 25.00
126 Frank Sinkovitz RC 18.00 25.00
127 Elbert Nickel 20.00 30.00
128 Jim Finks RC 40.00 75.00
129 Charley Trippi 35.00 60.00
130 Tom Wham RC 18.00 25.00
131 Ventan Yablonski RC 18.00 25.00
132 Chuck Bednarik 75.00 125.00
133 Joe Muha 18.00 25.00
134 Pete Pihos 45.00 80.00
135 Washington Serini RC 18.00 25.00
136 George Gulyanics RC 18.00 25.00
137 Ken Kavanaugh 20.00 30.00
138 Howie Livingston RC 18.00 25.00
139 Joe Tereshinski 18.00 25.00
140 Jim White 25.00 40.00
141 Gene Roberts RC 18.00 25.00
142 Bill Swiacki 20.00 30.00
143 Norm Standlee RC 18.00 25.00
144 Knox Ramsey RC 50.00 100.00

1951 Bowman

The 1951 Bowman set of 144 numbered cards witnessed an increase in card size from previous Bowman football sets. Cards were issued in six-card nickel packs and one-card penny packs. The cards were enlarged from the previous year to 2 1/16" by 3 1/8". The set is very similar in format to the baseball card set of that year. The fronts feature black and white photos that were colored in. The player's name is in a bar toward the bottom that runs from the right border toward the middle of the photo. A team logo or mascot is on top of the bar. The card backs are printed in maroon and blue on gray card stock and contain a write-up. The set features the Rookie Cards of Tom Landry, Emlen Tunnell, and Norm Van Brocklin. The Bill Walsh in this set went to Notre Dame and is not the Bill Walsh who coached the San Francisco 49ers in the 1980s. The set numbering is arranged so that two, three, or four players from the same team are together. Three blank backed proof cards have recently been uncovered and added to the listings below. The proofs are very similar to the corresponding base card. However, the artwork varies somewhat versus the base card.

COMPLETE SET (144) 2500.00 3500.00
WRAPPER (1-CENT) 150.00 250.00
WRAPPER (5-CENT) 175.00 300.00
1 Weldon Humble RC 50.00 80.00
2 Otto Graham 150.00 250.00
3 Mac Speedie 20.00 35.00
4 Norm Van Brocklin RC 200.00 300.00
5 Woodley Lewis RC 15.00 25.00
6 Tom Fears 30.00 50.00
7 George Musacco RC 12.00 20.00
8 George Taliaferro 15.00 25.00
9 Barney Poole 12.00 20.00
10 Steve Van Buren 35.00 60.00
11 Whitey Wistert 15.00 25.00
12 Chuck Bednarik 50.00 80.00
13 Bulldog Turner 30.00 50.00
14 Bob Williams RC 12.00 20.00
15 Johnny Lujack 35.00 60.00
16 Roy Rebel Steiner 12.00 20.00
17 Jug Girard 15.00 25.00
18 Bill Neal RC 12.00 20.00
19 Travis Tidwell 12.00 20.00
20 Tom Landry RC 350.00 500.00
21 Arnie Weinmeister RC 35.00 60.00
22 Joe Geri 12.00 20.00
23 Bill Walsh C RC 15.00 30.00
24 Fran Rogel 12.00 20.00
25 Doak Walker 35.00 60.00
26 Leon Hart 20.00 35.00
27 Thurman McGraw RC 12.00 20.00
28 Buster Ramsey 12.00 20.00
29 Frank Tripucka 20.00 35.00
30 Don Paul DB RC 12.00 20.00
31 Alex Loyd RC 12.00 20.00
32 Y.A.Tittle 75.00 135.00
33 Verl Lillywhite 12.00 20.00
34 Sammy Baugh 110.00 175.00
35 Chuck Drazenovich RC 12.00 20.00
36 Bob Goode 12.00 20.00
37 Horace Gillom RC 15.00 25.00
38 Lou Rymkus 15.00 25.00
39 Ken Carpenter 12.00 20.00
40 Bob Waterfield 45.00 75.00
41 Vitamin Smith RC 15.00 25.00
42 Glenn Davis 35.00 60.00
43 Dan Edwards RC 12.00 20.00
44 John Rauch 12.00 20.00
45 Zollie Toth RC 12.00 20.00
46 Pete Pihos 35.00 60.00
47 Russ Craft RC 12.00 20.00
48 Walter Barnes 12.00 20.00
49 Fred Morrison 12.00 20.00
50 Ray Bray RC 12.00 20.00
51 Ed Sprinkle RC 15.00 25.00
52 Floyd Reid RC 12.00 20.00
53 Billy Grimes 12.00 20.00
54 Ted Fritsch Sr. 15.00 25.00
55 Al DeRogatis RC 15.00 25.00
56 Charley Conerly 45.00 75.00
57 Jon Baker RC 12.00 20.00
58 Tom McWilliams 12.00 20.00
59 Jerry Shipkey 12.00 20.00
60 Lynn Chandnois RC 15.00 25.00
61 Don Doll 12.00 20.00
62 Lou Creekmur 30.00 50.00
63 Bob Hoernschemeyer 15.00 25.00
64 Tom Wham 12.00 20.00
65 Bill Fischer 12.00 20.00
66 Robert Nussbaumer 12.00 20.00
67 Gordy Soltau RC 12.00 20.00
68 Visco Grgich RC 12.00 20.00
69 John Strzykalski RC 12.00 20.00
70 Pete Stout RC 12.00 20.00
71 Paul Lipscomb RC 12.00 20.00
72 Harry Gilmer 20.00 35.00
73 Dante Lavelli 30.00 50.00
74 Dub Jones 15.00 25.00
75 Lou Groza 45.00 75.00
76 Elroy Hirsch 45.00 75.00
77 Tom Kalmanir 12.00 20.00
78 Jack Zilly 12.00 20.00

79 Bruce Alford RC 12.00 20.00
80 Art Weiner 12.00 20.00
81 Brad Ecklund RC 12.00 20.00
82 Bosh Pritchard 12.00 20.00
83 John Green RC 12.00 20.00
84 Ebert Van Buren RC 12.00 20.00
85 Julie Rykovich RC 12.00 20.00
86 Fred Davis 12.00 20.00
87 John Hoffman RC 12.00 20.00
88 Tobin Rote 15.00 25.00
89 Paul Burris 12.00 20.00
90 Tony Canadeo 30.00 50.00
91 Emlen Tunnell RC 60.00 100.00
92 Otto Schnellbacher RC 12.00 20.00
93 Ray Poole 12.00 20.00
94 Darrell Hogan 12.00 20.00
95 Frank Sinkovitz 12.00 20.00
96 Ernie Stautner 60.00 100.00
97 Elmer Bud Angsman 12.00 20.00
98 Jack Jennings RC 12.00 20.00
99 Jerry Groom RC 12.00 20.00
100 John Prchlik RC 12.00 20.00
101 J. Robert Smith RC 12.00 20.00
102 Bobby Layne 75.00 135.00
103 Frankie Albert 20.00 35.00
104 Gail Bruce 12.00 20.00
105 Joe Perry 45.00 75.00
106 Leon Heath RC 12.00 20.00
107 Ed Quirk RC 12.00 20.00
108 Hugh Taylor 15.00 25.00
109 Marion Motley 60.00 100.00
110 Tony Adamle 12.00 20.00
111 Alex Agase 15.00 25.00
112 Tank Younger 20.00 35.00
113 Bob Boyd RC 12.00 20.00
114 Jerry Williams RC 12.00 20.00
115 Joe Golding 12.00 20.00
116 Sherman Howard RC 12.00 20.00
117 John Wozniak RC 12.00 20.00
118 Frank Reagan 12.00 20.00
119 Vic Sears 12.00 20.00
120 Clyde Scott 12.00 20.00
121 George Gulyanics 12.00 20.00
122 Bill Wightkin 12.00 20.00
123 Chuck Hunsinger RC 12.00 20.00
124 Jack Cloud 12.00 20.00
125 Abner Wimberly RC 12.00 20.00
126 Dick Wildung 12.00 20.00
127 Eddie Price 12.00 20.00
128 Joe Scott 12.00 20.00
129 Jerry Nuzum 12.00 20.00
130 Jim Finks 20.00 35.00
131 Bob Gage 12.00 20.00
132 Bill Swiacki 15.00 25.00
133 Joe Watson 12.00 20.00
134 Ollie Cline RC 12.00 20.00
135 Jack Lininger RC 12.00 20.00
136 Fran Polsfoot RC 12.00 20.00
137 Charley Trippi 30.00 50.00
138 Ventan Yablonski 12.00 20.00
139 Emil Sitko 12.00 20.00
140 Leo Nomellini 30.00 60.00
141 Norm Standlee 12.00 20.00
142 Eddie Saenz RC 12.00 20.00
143 Al Demao 12.00 20.00
144 Bill Dudley 75.00 150.00
NNO Johnny Lujack Proof 175.00 300.00
NNO Bob Gage Proof 75.00 125.00
NNO Darrell Hogan Proof 75.00 125.00

1952 Bowman Large

One of two different sized sets produced by Bowman in 1952, the large version measures 2 1/2" by 3 3/4". Cards were issued in five-card, five-cent packs. The 144-card issue is identical to the smaller version in every respect except size. Either horizontal or vertical fronts contain a player portrait, a white banner with the player's name and a bar containing the team name and logo. Horizontal backs have a small write-up, previous year's stats and biographical information. Certain numbers were systematically printed in lesser quantities due to the fact that Bowman apparently could not fit each 72-card series on their respective sheets. The affected cards are those which are divisible by nine (i.e. 9, 18, 27 etc.) and those which are numbered one more than those divisible by nine (i.e. 10, 19, 28 etc.). These short-print cards are marked in the checklist below by SP. The set features NFL veterans and college players that entered the pro ranks in '52. The set features the Rookie Cards of Paul Brown, Jack Christiansen, Art Donovan, Frank Gifford, George Halas, Yale Lary, Gino Marchetti, Ollie Matson, Hugh McElhenny, and Andy Robustelli. The last card in the set, No. 144 Jim Lansford, is among the toughest football cards to acquire. It is generally accepted among hobbyists that the card was located at the bottom right corner of the production sheet and was subject to much abuse including numerous poor cuts. The problem was such that many copies never made it out of the factory as they were discarded. This card is also indicated below by SP.

COMPLETE SET (144) 9500.00 12500.00
WRAPPER (5-CENT) 30.00 60.00
1 Norm Van Brocklin SP 350.00 500.00
2 Otto Graham 200.00 300.00
3 Doak Walker 60.00 100.00
4 Steve Owen CO RC 50.00 80.00
5 Frankie Albert 30.00 50.00
6 Laurie Niemi RC 20.00 35.00
7 Chuck Hunsinger 20.00 35.00
8 Ed Modzelewski 30.00 50.00
9 Joe Spencer SP RC 40.00 75.00
10 Chuck Bednarik SP 200.00 350.00
11 Barney Poole 20.00 35.00
12 Charley Trippi 40.00 75.00
13 Tom Fears 40.00 75.00
14 Paul Brown CO RC 150.00 250.00
15 Leon Hart 30.00 50.00
16 Frank Gifford RC 350.00 500.00
17 Y.A.Tittle 200.00 300.00
18 Charlie Justice SP 100.00 175.00
19 George Connor SP 100.00 175.00
20 Lynn Chandnois 20.00 35.00
21 Billy Howton RC 30.00 50.00
22 Kenneth Snyder RC 20.00 35.00
23 Gino Marchetti RC 150.00 250.00
24 John Karras 20.00 35.00
25 Tank Younger 30.00 50.00
26 Tommy Thompson LB RC 20.00 35.00
27 Bob Miller SP RC 200.00 300.00
28 Kyle Rote SP RC 100.00 175.00
29 Hugh McElhenny RC 150.00 250.00
30 Sammy Baugh 225.00 350.00
31 Jim Dooley RC 25.00 45.00
32 Ray Mathews 20.00 35.00
33 Fred Cone RC 20.00 35.00
34 Al Pollard RC 20.00 35.00
35 Brad Ecklund 20.00 35.00
36 John Hancock SP RC 250.00 350.00
37 Elroy Hirsch SP 125.00 200.00
38 Keever Jankovich RC 20.00 35.00
39 Emlen Tunnell 75.00 125.00
40 Steve Dowden RC 20.00 35.00
41 Claude Hipps RC 20.00 35.00
42 Norm Standlee 20.00 35.00
43 Dick Todd CO RC 20.00 35.00
44 Babe Parilli 30.00 50.00
45 Steve Van Buren SP 200.00 300.00
46 Art Donovan SP RC 250.00 350.00
47 Bill Fischer 20.00 35.00
48 George Halas CO RC 160.00 275.00
49 Jerrell Price 20.00 35.00
50 John Sandusky RC 25.00 40.00
51 Ray Beck 20.00 35.00
52 Jim Martin 25.00 45.00
53 Joe Bach CO RC 20.00 35.00
54 Glen Christian SP RC 40.00 75.00
55 Andy Davis SP RC 40.00 75.00
56 Tobin Rote 25.00 50.00
57 Wayne Millner CO RC 50.00 90.00
58 Zollie Toth 20.00 35.00
59 Jack Jennings 20.00 35.00
60 Bill McColl RC 20.00 35.00
61 Les Richter RC 35.00 60.00
62 Walt Michaels RC 25.00 45.00
63 Charley Conerly SP 500.00 750.00
64 Howard Hartley SP 40.00 75.00
65 Jerome Smith RC 20.00 35.00
66 James Clark RC 20.00 35.00
67 Dick Logan RC 20.00 35.00
68 Wayne Robinson RC 20.00 35.00
69 James Hammond RC 20.00 35.00
70 Gene Schroeder RC 20.00 35.00
71 Tex Coulter 25.00 45.00
72 John Schweder SP RC 400.00 600.00
73 Vitamin Smith SP 75.00 125.00
74 Joe Campanella RC 25.00 40.00
75 Joe Kuharich CO RC 30.00 50.00
76 Herman Clark RC 25.00 40.00
77 Dan Edwards 25.00 40.00
78 Bobby Layne 175.00 300.00
79 Bob Hoernschemeyer 30.00 50.00
80 John Carr Blount RC 25.00 40.00
81 John Kastan SP RC 90.00 150.00
82 Harry Minarik SP RC 90.00 150.00
83 Joe Perry 75.00 125.00
84 Buddy Parker CO RC 30.00 50.00
85 Andy Robustelli RC 125.00 200.00
86 Dub Jones 30.00 50.00
87 Mal Cook RC 25.00 40.00
88 Billy Stone 25.00 40.00
89 George Taliaferro 30.00 50.00
90 Thomas Johnson SP RC 90.00 150.00
91 Leon Heath SP 60.00 100.00
92 Pete Pihos 60.00 100.00
93 Fred Benners RC 25.00 40.00
94 George Tarasovic RC 25.00 40.00
95 Buck Shaw CO RC 25.00 40.00
96 Bill Wightkin 25.00 40.00
97 John Wozniak 25.00 40.00
98 Bobby Dillon RC 30.00 50.00
99 Joe Stydahar SP RC 450.00 650.00
100 Dick Alban SP RC 90.00 150.00
101 Arnie Weinmeister 35.00 60.00
102 Bobby Cross RC 25.00 40.00
103 Don Paul DB 25.00 40.00
104 Buddy Young 35.00 60.00
105 Lou Groza 75.00 125.00
106 Ray Pelfrey RC 25.00 40.00
107 Maurice Nipp RC 25.00 40.00
108 Hubert Johnston SP RC 450.00 650.00
109 Vol.Quinlan SP RC 60.00 100.00
110 Jack Simmons RC 25.00 40.00
111 George Ratterman 30.00 50.00
112 John Badaczewski RC 25.00 40.00
113 Bill Reichardt 25.00 40.00
114 Art Weiner 25.00 40.00
115 Keith Flowers RC 25.00 40.00
116 Russ Craft 25.00 40.00
117 Jim O'Donahue SP RC 90.00 150.00
118 Darrell Hogan SP 60.00 100.00
119 Frank Ziegler RC 25.00 40.00
120 Dan Towler 35.00 60.00
121 Fred Williams RC 25.00 40.00
122 Jimmy Phelan CO RC 25.00 40.00
123 Eddie Price 25.00 40.00
124 Chet Ostrowski RC 25.00 40.00
125 Leo Nomellini 60.00 100.00
126 Steve Romanik SP RC 200.00 300.00
127 Ollie Matson SP RC 200.00 300.00
128 Dante Lavelli 50.00 90.00
129 Jack Christiansen RC 100.00 175.00
130 Dom Moselle RC 25.00 40.00
131 John Rapacz RC 25.00 40.00
132 Chuck Ortmann UER RC 25.00 40.00
133 Bob Williams 25.00 40.00
134 Chuck Ulrich RC 25.00 40.00
135 Gene Ronzani CO SP RC 450.00 700.00
136 Bert Rechichar SP 60.00 100.00
137 Bob Waterfield 75.00 125.00
138 Bobby Walston RC 30.00 50.00
139 Jerry Shipkey 25.00 40.00
140 Yale Lary RC 125.00 200.00
141 Gordy Soltau 25.00 40.00
142 Tom Landry 450.00 600.00
143 John Papit RC 25.00 40.00
144 Jim Lansford SP RC 1800.00 3000.00

1952 Bowman Small

One of two different sized sets issued by Bowman in 1952, this 144-card set is identical in every respect to the large version except for the smaller size of 2 1/16" by 3 1/8". Cards were issued in one-card penny packs. The fronts are either horizontal or vertical and feature a player protrait, a white banner with the player's name and a bar containing the team name and logo. All backs are horizontal and contain a brief write-up, previous year's stats and a bio. The set features NFL veterans and college players that entered the pro ranks in '52. The set features the Rookie Cards of Paul Brown, Jack Christiansen, Art Donovan, Frank Gifford, George Halas, Yale Lary, Gino Marchetti, Ollie Matson, Hugh McElhenny, and Andy Robustelli.

COMPLETE SET (144) 3500.00 5000.00
WRAPPER (1-CENT) 40.00 60.00
1 Norm Van Brocklin 200.00 350.00
2 Otto Graham 125.00 200.00
3 Doak Walker 35.00 60.00
4 Steve Owen CO RC 35.00 60.00
5 Frankie Albert 20.00 35.00
6 Laurie Niemi RC 15.00 25.00
7 Chuck Hunsinger 15.00 25.00
8 Ed Modzelewski 20.00 35.00
9 Joe Spencer RC 15.00 25.00
10 Chuck Bednarik 45.00 75.00
11 Barney Poole 15.00 25.00
12 Charley Trippi 35.00 60.00
13 Tom Fears 35.00 60.00
14 Paul Brown CO RC 90.00 150.00
15 Leon Hart 20.00 35.00
16 Frank Gifford 200.00 400.00
17 Y.A.Tittle 75.00 125.00
18 Charlie Justice 30.00 50.00
19 George Connor 20.00 35.00
20 Lynn Chandnois 15.00 25.00
21 Billy Howton RC 25.00 40.00
22 Kenneth Snyder RC 15.00 25.00
23 Gino Marchetti RC 75.00 125.00
24 John Karras 15.00 25.00
25 Tank Younger 20.00 35.00
26 Tommy Thompson LB RC 15.00 25.00
27 Bob Miller RC 15.00 25.00
28 Kyle Rote RC 30.00 50.00
29 Hugh McElhenny RC 100.00 175.00
30 Sammy Baugh 150.00 250.00
31 Jim Dooley RC 18.00 30.00
32 Ray Mathews 15.00 25.00
33 Fred Cone RC 15.00 25.00
34 Al Pollard RC 15.00 25.00
35 Brad Ecklund 15.00 25.00
36 John Lee Hancock RC 15.00 25.00
37 Elroy Hirsch 35.00 60.00
38 Keever Jankovich 15.00 25.00
39 Emlen Tunnell 30.00 50.00
40 Steve Dowden RC 15.00 25.00
41 Claude Hipps 15.00 25.00
42 Norm Standlee 15.00 25.00
43 Dick Todd CO RC 15.00 25.00
44 Babe Parilli 20.00 35.00
45 Steve Van Buren 40.00 75.00
46 Art Donovan RC 125.00 200.00
47 Bill Fischer 15.00 25.00
48 George Halas CO RC 150.00 250.00
49 Jerrell Price 15.00 25.00
50 John Sandusky RC 15.00 25.00
51 Ray Beck 15.00 25.00
52 Jim Martin 18.00 30.00
53 Joe Bach CO RC 15.00 25.00
54 Glen Christian RC 15.00 25.00
55 Andy Davis RC 15.00 25.00
56 Tobin Rote 18.00 30.00
57 Wayne Millner RC CO 30.00 50.00
58 Zollie Toth 15.00 25.00
59 Jack Jennings 15.00 25.00
60 Bill McColl RC 15.00 25.00
61 Les Richter RC 35.00 60.00
62 Walt Michaels RC 18.00 30.00
63 Charley Conerly 40.00 75.00
64 Howard Hartley 15.00 25.00
65 Jerome Smith RC 15.00 25.00
66 James Clark 15.00 25.00
67 Dick Logan 15.00 25.00
68 Wayne Robinson RC 15.00 25.00
69 James Hammond 15.00 25.00
70 Gene Schroeder RC 15.00 25.00
71 Tex Coulter 18.00 30.00
72 John Schweder 15.00 25.00
73 Vitamin Smith 20.00 35.00
74 Joe Campanella RC 18.00 30.00
75 Joe Kuharich CO RC 20.00 35.00
76 Herman Clark 18.00 30.00
77 Dan Edwards 18.00 30.00
78 Bobby Layne 90.00 150.00
79 Bob Hoernschemeyer 20.00 35.00
80 John Carr Blount RC 18.00 30.00
81 John Kastan RC 18.00 30.00
82 Harry Minarik 18.00 30.00
83 Joe Perry 40.00 75.00
84 Buddy Parker CO RC 20.00 35.00
85 Andy Robustelli RC 75.00 125.00
86 Dub Jones 20.00 35.00
87 Mal Cook 18.00 30.00
88 Billy Stone 18.00 30.00
89 George Taliaferro 20.00 35.00
90 Thomas Johnson RC 18.00 30.00
91 Leon Heath 18.00 30.00
92 Pete Pihos 35.00 50.00
93 Fred Benners 18.00 30.00
94 George Tarasovic RC 18.00 30.00
95 Buck Shaw CO RC 18.00 30.00
96 Bill Wightkin 18.00 30.00
97 John Wozniak 18.00 30.00
98 Bobby Dillon RC 20.00 35.00
99 Joe Stydahar RC CO 50.00 80.00
100 Dick Alban RC 18.00 30.00
101 Arnie Weinmeister 25.00 40.00
102 Bobby Cross RC 18.00 30.00
103 Don Paul DB 18.00 30.00
104 Buddy Young 25.00 40.00
105 Lou Groza 45.00 75.00
106 Ray Pelfrey 18.00 30.00
107 Maurice Nipp RC 18.00 30.00
108 Hubert Johnston RC 18.00 30.00
109 Volney Quinlan RC 18.00 30.00
110 Jack Simmons RC 18.00 30.00
111 George Ratterman 20.00 35.00
112 John Badaczewski 18.00 30.00
113 Bill Reichardt 18.00 30.00
114 Art Weiner 18.00 30.00
115 Keith Flowers RC 18.00 30.00
116 Russ Craft 18.00 30.00
117 Jim O'Donahue RC 18.00 30.00
118 Darrell Hogan 18.00 30.00
119 Frank Ziegler RC 18.00 30.00
120 Dan Towler 25.00 40.00
121 Fred Williams RC 18.00 30.00
122 Jimmy Phelan CO RC 18.00 30.00
123 Eddie Price 18.00 30.00
124 Chet Ostrowski RC 18.00 30.00
125 Leo Nomellini 40.00 75.00
126 Steve Romanik RC 18.00 30.00
127 Ollie Matson RC 75.00 125.00
128 Dante Lavelli 35.00 60.00
129 Jack Christiansen RC 50.00 80.00
130 Dom Moselle RC 18.00 30.00
131 John Rapacz RC 18.00 30.00
132 Chuck Ortmann UER RC 18.00 30.00
133 Bob Williams 18.00 30.00
134 Chuck Ulrich RC 18.00 30.00
135 Gene Ronzani CO RC 18.00 30.00
136 Bert Rechichar 20.00 35.00
137 Bob Waterfield 45.00 75.00
138 Bobby Walston RC 20.00 35.00
139 Jerry Shipkey 18.00 30.00
140 Yale Lary RC 50.00 80.00
141 Gordy Soltau 18.00 30.00
142 Tom Landry 250.00 400.00
143 John Papit RC 18.00 30.00
144 Jim Lansford RC 100.00 175.00

1953 Bowman

The 1953 Bowman set of 96 cards measures approximately 2 1/2" by 3 3/4". Cards were issued in five-card, five-cent packs. The set is somewhat smaller in number than would be thought since Bowman was the only major producer of football cards during this year. The fronts feature a player portrait with a football that contains player and team names. Horizontal backs contain a brief write-up, previous year's stats, a bio and a quiz. There are 24 cards marked SP in the checklist below which are considered in shorter supply than the other cards in the set. The Bill Walsh in this set went to Notre Dame and is not the Bill Walsh who coached the San Francisco 49ers in the 1980s. The most notable Rookie Card in this set is Eddie LeBaron.

COMPLETE SET (96) 2500.00 3500.00
WRAPPER (5-CENT) 90.00 150.00
1 Eddie LeBaron RC 75.00 125.00
2 John Dottley 18.00 30.00
3 Babe Parilli 20.00 35.00
4 Bucko Kilroy 20.00 35.00
5 Joe Tereshinski 18.00 30.00
6 Doak Walker 45.00 75.00
7 Fran Polsfoot 18.00 30.00
8 Sisto Averno RC 18.00 30.00
9 Marion Motley 45.00 100.00
10 Pat Brady RC 18.00 30.00
11 Norm Van Brocklin 75.00 125.00
12 Bill McColl 18.00 30.00
13 Jerry Groom 18.00 30.00
14 Al Pollard 18.00 30.00
15 Dante Lavelli 30.00 50.00
16 Eddie Price 18.00 30.00
17 Charley Trippi 30.00 50.00
18 Elbert Nickel 20.00 35.00
19 George Taliaferro 20.00 35.00
20 Charley Conerly 50.00 80.00
21 Bobby Layne 75.00 125.00
22 Elroy Hirsch 60.00 100.00
23 Jim Finks 25.00 40.00
24 Chuck Bednarik 45.00 75.00
25 Kyle Rote 25.00 40.00
26 Otto Graham 100.00 200.00
27 Harry Gilmer 20.00 35.00
28 Tobin Rote 20.00 35.00
29 Billy Stone 18.00 30.00
30 Buddy Young 25.00 40.00
31 Leon Hart 25.00 40.00
32 Hugh McElhenny 45.00 75.00
33 Dale Samuels 18.00 30.00
34 Lou Creekmur 30.00 50.00
35 Tom Catlin RC 18.00 30.00
36 Tom Fears 35.00 60.00
37 George Connor 25.00 40.00
38 Bill Walsh C 18.00 30.00
39 Leo Sanford SP RC 30.00 50.00
40 Horace Gillom 20.00 35.00
41 John Schweder SP 30.00 50.00
42 Tom O'Connell RC 18.00 30.00
43 Frank Gifford SP 175.00 300.00
44 Frank Continetti SP RC 30.00 50.00
45 John Olszewski SP RC 30.00 50.00
46 Dub Jones 20.00 35.00
47 Don Paul LB SP RC 30.00 50.00
48 Gerald Weatherly RC 18.00 30.00
49 Fred Bruney SP RC 30.00 50.00
50 Jack Scarbath RC 18.00 30.00
51 John Karras 18.00 30.00
52 Al Conway RC 18.00 30.00
53 Emlen Tunnell SP 75.00 125.00
54 Gern Nagler SP RC 30.00 50.00
55 Kenneth Snyder SP 30.00 50.00
56 Y.A.Tittle 90.00 150.00
57 John Rapacz SP 30.00 50.00
58 Harley Sewell SP RC 30.00 50.00
59 Don Bingham RC 18.00 30.00
60 Darrell Hogan 18.00 30.00
61 Tony Curcillo RC 18.00 30.00
62 Ray Renfro SP RC 35.00 60.00
63 Leon Heath 18.00 30.00
64 Tex Coulter SP 30.00 50.00
65 Dewayne Douglas RC 18.00 30.00
66 J. Robert Smith SP 30.00 50.00
67 Bob McChesney SP RC 30.00 50.00
68 Dick Alban SP 30.00 50.00
69 Andy Kozar RC 18.00 30.00
70 Merwin Hodel SP RC 30.00 50.00
71 Thurman McGraw 18.00 30.00
72 Cliff Anderson RC 18.00 30.00
73 Pete Pihos 35.00 60.00
74 Julie Rykovich 18.00 30.00
75 John Kreamcheck SP RC 30.00 50.00
76 Lynn Chandnois 18.00 30.00
77 Cloyce Box SP 30.00 50.00
78 Ray Mathews 18.00 30.00
79 Bobby Walston 20.00 35.00
80 Jim Dooley 18.00 30.00
81 Pat Harder SP 30.00 50.00
82 Jerry Shipkey 18.00 30.00
83 Bobby Thomason RC 18.00 30.00
84 Hugh Taylor 20.00 35.00
85 George Ratterman 20.00 35.00
86 Don Stonesifer RC 18.00 30.00
87 John Williams SP RC 30.00 50.00
88 Leo Nomellini 30.00 50.00
89 Frank Ziegler 18.00 30.00
90 Don Paul DB UER 18.00 30.00
91 Tom Dublinski 18.00 30.00
92 Ken Carpenter 18.00 30.00
93 Ted Marchibroda RC 30.00 50.00
94 Chuck Drazenovich 18.00 30.00
95 Lou Groza SP 75.00 125.00
96 William Cross SP RC 50.00 100.00

1954 Bowman

Measuring 2 1/2" by 3 3/4", the 1954 set consists of 128 cards. Cards were issued in seven-card five-cent packs and one-card penny packs. Toward the bottom of the photo is a white banner that contains the player's name, team name and mascot. The card backs feature the player's name in black print inside a red outline of a football. The player's statistical information from the previous season and a quiz are also on back. The "Whizzer" White in the set (125) is not Byron White, the Supreme Court Justice, but Wilford White. Wilford is the father of former Dallas Cowboys quarterback Danny White. The Bill Walsh in this set went to Notre Dame and is not the Bill Walsh who coached the San Francisco 49ers in the 1980s. The mid-series, cards 65-96, is very tough to find in relationship to other series. Rookie Cards in this set include Doug Atkins and George Blanda.

COMPLETE SET (128) 1200.00 1800.00
WRAPPER (1-CENT) 10.00 15.00
WRAPPER (5-CENT) 25.00 30.00
1 Ray Mathews 15.00 30.00
2 John Huzvar RC 3.00 5.00
3 Jack Scarbath 3.00 5.00
4 Doug Atkins RC 30.00 50.00
5 Bill Stits RC 3.00 5.00
6 Joe Perry 18.00 30.00
7 Kyle Rote 7.50 15.00
8 Norm Van Brocklin 25.00 50.00
9 Pete Pihos 12.00 20.00
10 Babe Parilli 4.00 8.00
11 Zeke Bratkowski RC 15.00 25.00
12 Ollie Matson 15.00 25.00
13 Pat Brady 3.00 5.00
14 Fred Enke 3.00 5.00
15 Harry Ulinski 3.00 5.00
16 Bob Garrett RC 3.00 5.00
17 Bill Bowman RC 3.00 5.00
18 Leo Rucka RC 3.00 5.00
19 John Cannady 3.00 5.00
20 Tom Fears 15.00 25.00
21 Norm Willey RC 3.00 5.00
22 Floyd Reid 3.00 5.00
23 George Blanda RC 100.00 175.00
24 Don Doheney RC 3.00 5.00
25 John Schweder 3.00 5.00
26 Bert Rechichar 3.00 5.00
27 Harry Dowda RC 3.00 5.00
28 John Sandusky 3.00 5.00
29 Les Bingaman RC 7.50 15.00
30 Joe Arenas RC 3.00 5.00
31 Ray Wietecha RC 3.00 5.00
32 Elroy Hirsch 18.00 30.00
33 Harold Giancanelli RC 3.00 5.00
34 Billy Howton 4.00 8.00
35 Fred Morrison 3.00 5.00
36 Bobby Cavazos RC 3.00 5.00
37 Darrell Hogan 3.00 5.00
38 Buddy Young 4.00 8.00
39 Charlie Justice 12.00 20.00
40 Otto Graham 50.00 80.00
41 Doak Walker 20.00 35.00
42 Y.A.Tittle 35.00 60.00
43 Buford Long RC 3.00 5.00
44 Volney Quinlan 3.00 5.00
45 Bobby Thomason 3.00 5.00
46 Fred Cone 3.00 5.00
47 Gerald Weatherly 3.00 5.00
48 Don Stonesifer 3.00 5.00
49A Lynn Chandnois ERR 3.00 5.00
49B Lynn Chandnois COR 3.00 5.00
50 George Taliaferro 3.00 5.00
51 Dick Alban 3.00 5.00
52 Lou Groza 20.00 35.00
53 Bobby Layne 35.00 60.00
54 Hugh McElhenny 20.00 40.00
55 Frank Gifford 60.00 100.00
56 Leon McLaughlin RC 3.00 5.00
57 Chuck Bednarik 20.00 40.00
58 Art Hunter RC 3.00 5.00
59 Bill McColl 3.00 5.00
60 Charley Trippi 15.00 25.00
61 Jim Finks 7.50 15.00
62 Bill Lange G RC 3.00 5.00
63 Laurie Niemi 3.00 5.00
64 Ray Renfro 4.00 8.00
65 Dick Chapman SP RC 15.00 25.00
66 Bob Hantla SP RC 15.00 25.00
67 Ralph Starkey SP RC 15.00 25.00
68 Don Paul LB SP 15.00 25.00
69 Kenneth Snyder SP 15.00 25.00
70 Tobin Rote SP 18.00 30.00
71 Art DeCarlo SP RC 15.00 25.00
72 Tom Keane SP RC 15.00 25.00
73 Hugh Taylor SP 18.00 30.00
74 Warren Lahr SP RC 15.00 25.00
75 Jim Neal SP RC 15.00 25.00
76 Leo Nomellini SP 35.00 60.00
77 Dick Yelvington SP RC 15.00 25.00
78 Les Richter SP 18.00 30.00
79 Bucko Kilroy SP 18.00 30.00
80 John Martinkovic SP RC 15.00 25.00
81 Dale Dodrill SP RC 15.00 25.00
82 Ken Jackson SP RC 15.00 25.00
83 Paul Lipscomb SP 15.00 25.00
84 John Bauer SP RC 15.00 25.00
85 Lou Creekmur SP 30.00 50.00
86 Eddie Price SP 15.00 25.00
87 Kenneth Farragut SP RC 15.00 25.00
88 Dave Hanner SP RC 18.00 30.00
89 Don Boll SP RC 15.00 25.00
90 Chet Hanulak SP RC 15.00 25.00
91 Thurman McGraw SP 15.00 25.00
92 Don Heinrich SP RC 18.00 30.00
93 Dan McKown SP RC 15.00 25.00
94 Bob Fleck SP RC 15.00 25.00
95 Jerry Hilgenberg SP RC 15.00 25.00
96 Bill Walsh C SP 15.00 25.00
97A Tom Finnin ERR 35.00 60.00
97B Tom Finnan COR RC 4.00 8.00
98 Paul Barry RC 3.00 5.00
99 Chick Jagade 3.00 5.00
100 Jack Christiansen 12.00 25.00
101 Gordy Soltau 3.00 5.00
102A Emlen Tunnel ERR 15.00 25.00
102B Emlen Tunnell COR 12.00 20.00
102C Emlen Tunnell COR 12.00 20.00
103 Stan West RC 3.00 5.00
104 Jerry Williams 3.00 5.00
105 Veryl Switzer RC 3.00 5.00
106 Billy Stone 3.00 5.00
107 Jerry Watford RC 3.00 5.00
108 Elbert Nickel 4.00 8.00
109 Ed Sharkey RC 3.00 5.00
110 Steve Meilinger RC 3.00 5.00
111 Dante Lavelli 12.00 20.00
112 Leon Hart 7.50 15.00
113 Charley Conerly 18.00 30.00
114 Richard Lemmon RC 3.00 5.00
115 Al Carmichael RC 3.00 5.00
116 George Connor 12.00 20.00
117 John Olszewski 3.00 5.00
118 Ernie Stautner 15.00 25.00
119 Ray Smith RC 3.00 5.00
120 Neil Worden RC 3.00 5.00
121 Jim Dooley 3.00 5.00
122 Arnold Galiffa 3.00 5.00
123 Kline Gilbert RC 3.00 5.00
124 Bob Hoernschemeyer 4.00 8.00
125 Wilford White RC 7.50 15.00
126 Art Spinney RC 3.00 5.00
127 Joe Koch RC 3.00 5.00
128 John Lattner RC 40.00 80.00

1955 Bowman

The 1955 Bowman set of 160 cards was Bowman's last sports issue before the company was purchased by Topps in January of 1956. The cards were issued in seven-card, five-cent packs and one-card penny packs and measure approximately 2 1/2" by 3 3/4". The fronts contain player photos with the player name and team logo at the bottom and the team name at the top. The card backs are printed in red and blue on gray card stock and a short player bio is included. On the bottom of most of the card backs is a play diagram. Cards 65-160 are slightly more difficult to obtain. The notable Rookie Cards in this set are Alan Ameche, Len Ford, Frank Gatski, John Henry Johnson, Mike McCormack, Jim Ringo, Bob St. Clair, and Pat Summerall.

COMPLETE SET (160) 1000.00 1600.00
WRAPPER (1-CENT) 150.00 225.00
WRAPPER (5-CENT) 60.00 120.00
1 Doak Walker 40.00 75.00
2 Mike McCormack RC 18.00 30.00
3 John Olszewski 3.00 5.00
4 Dorne Dibble RC 3.00 5.00
5 Lindon Crow RC 3.00 5.00
6 Hugh Taylor UER 4.00 8.00
7 Frank Gifford 35.00 60.00
8 Alan Ameche RC 25.00 40.00
9 Don Stonesifer 3.00 5.00
10 Pete Pihos 7.50 15.00
11 Bill Austin 3.00 5.00
12 Dick Alban 3.00 5.00
13 Bobby Walston 4.00 8.00
14 Len Ford RC 25.00 40.00
15 Jug Girard 3.00 5.00
16 Charley Conerly 15.00 25.00
17 Volney Peters RC 3.00 5.00
18 Max Boydston RC 3.00 5.00
19 Leon Hart 6.00 12.00
20 Bert Rechichar 3.00 5.00
21 Lee Riley RC 3.00 5.00
22 Johnny Carson RC 3.00 5.00
23 Harry Thompson 3.00 5.00
24 Ray Wietecha 3.00 5.00
25 Ollie Matson 15.00 25.00
26 Eddie LeBaron 7.50 15.00
27 Jack Simmons 3.00 5.00
28 Jack Christiansen 7.50 15.00
29 Bucko Kilroy 4.00 8.00
30 Tom Keane 3.00 5.00
31 Dave Leggett RC 3.00 5.00
32 Norm Van Brocklin 25.00 40.00
33 Harlon Hill RC 6.00 12.00
34 Robert Haner RC 3.00 5.00
35 Veryl Switzer 3.00 5.00
36 Dick Stanfel RC 6.00 12.00
37 Lou Groza 15.00 25.00
38 Tank Younger 6.00 12.00
39 Dick Flanagan RC 3.00 5.00
40 Jim Dooley 3.00 5.00
41 Ray Collins RC 3.00 5.00
42 John Henry Johnson RC 25.00 50.00
43 Tom Fears 7.50 15.00
44 Joe Perry 18.00 30.00
45 Gene Brito RC 3.00 5.00
46 Bill Johnson C 3.00 5.00
47 Dan Towler 6.00 12.00
48 Dick Moegle RC 4.00 8.00
49 Kline Gilbert 3.00 5.00
50 Les Gobel RC 3.00 5.00
51 Ray Krouse RC 3.00 5.00
52 Pat Summerall RC 35.00 70.00
53 Ed Brown RC 7.50 15.00
54 Lynn Chandnois 3.00 5.00
55 Joe Heap RC 3.00 5.00
56 John Hoffman 3.00 5.00
57 Howard Ferguson RC 3.00 5.00
58 Bobby Watkins RC 3.00 5.00
59 Charlie Ane RC 3.00 5.00
60 Ken MacAfee E RC 4.00 8.00
61 Ralph Guglielmi RC 4.00 8.00
62 George Blanda 35.00 60.00
63 Kenneth Snyder 3.00 5.00
64 Chet Ostrowski 3.00 5.00
65 Buddy Young 7.50 15.00
66 Gordy Soltau 5.00 8.00
67 Eddie Bell RC 5.00 8.00
68 Ben Agajanian RC 6.00 12.00
69 Tom Dahms RC 5.00 8.00
70 Jim Ringo RC 30.00 50.00
71 Bobby Layne 45.00 75.00
72 Y.A.Tittle 45.00 75.00
73 Bob Gaona RC 5.00 8.00
74 Tobin Rote 6.00 12.00
75 Hugh McElhenny 18.00 30.00
76 John Kreamcheck 5.00 8.00
77 Al Dorow RC 6.00 12.00
78 Bill Wade 7.50 15.00
79 Dale Dodrill 5.00 8.00
80 Chuck Drazenovich 5.00 8.00
81 Billy Wilson RC 6.00 12.00
82 Les Richter 6.00 12.00
83 Pat Brady 5.00 8.00
84 Bob Hoernschemeyer 6.00 12.00
85 Joe Arenas 5.00 8.00
86 Len Szafaryn UER RC 5.00 8.00
87 Rick Casares RC 12.00 20.00
88 Leon McLaughlin 5.00 8.00
89 Charley Toogood RC 5.00 8.00
90 Tom Bettis RC 5.00 8.00
91 John Sandusky 5.00 8.00
92 Bill Wightkin 5.00 8.00
93 Darrel Brewster RC 5.00 8.00
94 Marion Campbell 7.50 15.00
95 Floyd Reid 5.00 8.00
96 Chick Jagade 5.00 8.00
97 George Taliaferro 5.00 8.00
98 Carlton Massey RC 5.00 8.00
99 Fran Rogel 5.00 8.00
100 Alex Sandusky RC 5.00 8.00
101 Bob St.Clair RC 30.00 60.00
102 Al Carmichael 5.00 8.00
103 Carl Taseff RC 5.00 8.00
104 Leo Nomellini 15.00 25.00
105 Tom Scott 5.00 8.00
106 Ted Marchibroda 7.50 15.00
107 Art Spinney 5.00 8.00
108 Wayne Robinson 5.00 8.00
109 Jim Ricca RC 5.00 8.00
110 Lou Ferry RC 5.00 8.00
111 Roger Zatkoff RC 5.00 8.00
112 Lou Creekmur 7.50 15.00
113 Kenny Konz RC 5.00 8.00
114 Doug Eggers RC 5.00 8.00
115 Bobby Thomason 5.00 8.00
116 Bill McPeak RC 5.00 8.00
117 William Brown RC 5.00 8.00
118 Royce Womble RC 5.00 8.00
119 Frank Gatski RC 20.00 40.00
120 Jim Finks 7.50 15.00
121 Andy Robustelli 15.00 25.00
122 Bobby Dillon 5.00 8.00
123 Leo Sanford 5.00 8.00
124 Elbert Nickel 6.00 12.00
125 Wayne Hansen RC 5.00 8.00
126 Buck Lansford RC 5.00 8.00
127 Gern Nagler 5.00 8.00
128 Jim Salsbury RC 5.00 8.00
129 Dale Atkeson RC 5.00 8.00
130 John Schweder 5.00 8.00
131 Dave Hanner 6.00 12.00
132 Eddie Price 5.00 8.00
133 Vic Janowicz 15.00 30.00
134 Ernie Stautner 15.00 25.00
135 James Parmer RC 5.00 8.00
136 Emlen Tunnell UER 12.00 20.00
137 Kyle Rote 7.50 15.00
138 Norm Willey 5.00 8.00
139 Charley Trippi 12.00 20.00
140 Billy Howton 6.00 12.00
141 Bobby Clatterbuck RC 5.00 8.00
142 Bob Boyd 5.00 8.00
143 Bob Toneff RC 6.00 12.00
144 Jerry Helluin RC 5.00 8.00
145 Adrian Burk 5.00 8.00
146 Walt Michaels 6.00 12.00
147 Zollie Toth 5.00 8.00
148 Frank Varrichione RC 5.00 8.00
149 Dick Bielski RC 5.00 8.00
150 George Ratterman 6.00 12.00
151 Mike Jarmoluk RC 5.00 8.00
152 Tom Landry 125.00 200.00
153 Ray Renfro 6.00 12.00
154 Zeke Bratkowski 6.00 12.00
155 Jerry Norton RC 5.00 8.00
156 Maurice Bassett RC 5.00 8.00
157 Volney Quinlan 5.00 8.00
158 Chuck Bednarik 18.00 30.00
159 Don Colo RC 5.00 8.00
160 L.G. Dupre RC 20.00 40.00

1991 Bowman

Resurrected by Topps after a 36 year hiatus, Bowman returned to the football card playing field with a 561-card standard-size set. The cards retain some of the qualities from early Bowman products. As far as layout, the backs resemble those of the 1950s. They are printed in black and green on gray and have a write-up, bio and stats from the previous season. The cards are checklisted below alphabetically according to teams. Subsets include Rookie Superstars (1-11), League Leaders (273-283) and Road to Super Bowl XXV (547-557). Rookie Cards include Alvin Harper, Randal Hill, Derek Loville, Herman Moore, Mike Pritchard, Ricky Watters, and Harvey Williams.

COMP.FACT.SET (561) 12.00 30.00
COMPLETE SET (561) 8.00 20.00
1 Jeff George RS .08 .25
2 Richmond Webb RS .01 .05
3 Emmitt Smith RS .50 1.25
4 Mark Carrier DB RS UER .01 .05
5 Steve Christie RS .01 .05
6 Keith Sims RS .01 .05
7 Rob Moore RS UER .08 .25
8 Johnny Johnson RS .01 .05
9 Eric Green RS .01 .05
10 Ben Smith RS .01 .05
11 Tory Epps RS .01 .05
12 Andre Rison .02 .10
13 Shawn Collins .01 .05
14 Chris Hinton .01 .05
15 Deion Sanders .15 .40
16 Darion Conner .01 .05
17 Michael Haynes .08 .25
18 Chris Miller .02 .10
19 Jessie Tuggle .01 .05
20 Scott Fulhage .01 .05
21 Bill Fralic .01 .05
22 Floyd Dixon .01 .05
23 Oliver Barnett .01 .05
24 Mike Rozier .01 .05
25 Tory Epps .01 .05
26 Tim Green .01 .05
27 Steve Broussard .01 .05
28 Bruce Pickens RC .01 .05
29 Mike Pritchard RC .08 .25
30 Andre Reed .02 .10
31 Darryl Talley .01 .05
32 Nate Odomes .01 .05
33 Jamie Mueller .01 .05
34 Leon Seals .01 .05
35 Keith McKeller .01 .05
36 Al Edwards .01 .05
37 Butch Rolle .01 .05
38 Jeff Wright RC .01 .05
39 Will Wolford .01 .05
40 James Williams .01 .05
41 Kent Hull .01 .05
42 James Lofton .02 .10
43 Frank Reich .02 .10
44 Bruce Smith .08 .25
45 Thurman Thomas .08 .25
46 Leonard Smith .01 .05
47 Shane Conlan .01 .05
48 Steve Tasker .02 .10
49 Ray Bentley .01 .05
50 Cornelius Bennett .02 .10
51 Stan Thomas .01 .05
52 Shaun Gayle .01 .05
53 Wendell Davis .01 .05
54 James Thornton .01 .05
55 Mark Carrier DB .02 .10
56 Richard Dent .02 .10
57 Ron Morris .01 .05
58 Mike Singletary .02 .10
59 Jay Hilgenberg .01 .05
60 Donnell Woolford .01 .05
61 Jim Covert .01 .05
62 Jim Harbaugh .08 .25
63 Neal Anderson .02 .10
64 Brad Muster .01 .05
65 Kevin Butler .01 .05
66 Trace Armstrong UER .01 .05
67 Ron Cox .01 .05
68 Peter Tom Willis .01 .05
69 Johnny Bailey .01 .05
70 Mark Bortz UER .01 .05
71 Chris Zorich RC .08 .25
72 Lamar Rogers RC .01 .05
73 David Grant UER .01 .05
74 Lewis Billups .01 .05
75 Harold Green .02 .10
76 Ickey Woods .01 .05
77 Eddie Brown .01 .05
78 David Fulcher .01 .05
79 Anthony Munoz .02 .10
80 Carl Zander .01 .05
81 Rodney Holman .01 .05
82 James Brooks .02 .10
83 Tim McGee .01 .05
84 Boomer Esiason .02 .10
85 Leon White .01 .05
86 James Francis UER .01 .05
87 Mitchell Price RC .01 .05
88 Ed King RC .01 .05
89 Eric Turner RC .02 .10
90 Rob Burnett RC .02 .10
91 Leroy Hoard .02 .10
92 Kevin Mack UER .01 .05
93 Thane Gash UER .01 .05
94 Gregg Rakoczy .01 .05
95 Clay Matthews .02 .10
96 Eric Metcalf .02 .10
97 Stephen Braggs .01 .05
98 Frank Minnifield .01 .05
99 Reggie Langhorne .01 .05
100 Mike Johnson .01 .05
101 Brian Brennan .01 .05
102 Anthony Pleasant .01 .05
103 Godfrey Myles UER RC .01 .05
104 Russell Maryland RC .08 .25
105 James Washington RC .01 .05
106 Nate Newton .02 .10
107 Jimmie Jones .01 .05
108 Jay Novacek .08 .25
109 Alexander Wright .01 .05
110 Jack Del Rio .02 .10
111 Jim Jeffcoat .01 .05
112 Mike Saxon .01 .05
113 Troy Aikman .30 .75
114 Issiac Holt .01 .05
115 Ken Norton .02 .10
116 Kelvin Martin .01 .05
117 Emmitt Smith 1.00 2.50
118 Ken Willis .01 .05
119 Daniel Stubbs .01 .05
120 Michael Irvin .08 .25
121 Danny Noonan .01 .05
122 Alvin Harper RC .08 .25
123 Reggie Johnson RC .01 .05
124 Vance Johnson .01 .05
125 Steve Atwater .01 .05
126 Greg Kragen .01 .05
127 John Elway .50 1.25
128 Simon Fletcher .01 .05
129 Wymon Henderson .01 .05
130 Ricky Nattiel .01 .05
131 Shannon Sharpe .20 .50
132 Ron Holmes .01 .05
133 Karl Mecklenburg .01 .05
134 Bobby Humphrey .01 .05
135 Clarence Kay .01 .05
136 Dennis Smith .01 .05
137 Jim Juriga .01 .05
138 Melvin Bratton .01 .05
139 Mark Jackson UER .01 .05
140 Michael Brooks .01 .05
141 Alton Montgomery .01 .05
142 Mike Croel RC .01 .05
143 Mel Gray .02 .10
144 Michael Cofer .01 .05
145 Jeff Campbell .01 .05
146 Dan Owens .01 .05
147 Robert Clark UER .01 .05
148 Jim Arnold .01 .05
149 William White .01 .05
150 Rodney Peete .02 .10
151 Jerry Ball .01 .05
152 Bennie Blades .01 .05
153 Barry Sanders UER .50 1.25
154 Andre Ware .02 .10
155 Lomas Brown .01 .05
156 Chris Spielman .02 .10
157 Kelvin Pritchett RC .02 .10
158 Herman Moore RC .08 .25
159 Chris Jacke .01 .05
160 Tony Mandarich .01 .05
161 Perry Kemp .01 .05
162 Johnny Holland .01 .05
163 Mark Lee .01 .05
164 Anthony Dilweg .01 .05
165 Scott Stephen RC .01 .05
166 Ed West .01 .05
167 Mark Murphy .01 .05
168 Darrell Thompson .01 .05
169 James Campen RC .01 .05
170 Jeff Query .01 .05
171 Brian Noble .01 .05
172 Sterling Sharpe UER .08 .25
173 Robert Brown .01 .05
174 Tim Harris .01 .05
175 LeRoy Butler .02 .10
176 Don Majkowski .01 .05
177 Vinnie Clark RC .01 .05
178 Esera Tuaolo RC .01 .05
179 Lorenzo White UER .01 .05
180 Warren Moon .08 .25
181 Sean Jones .02 .10
182 Curtis Duncan .01 .05
183 Al Smith .01 .05
184 Richard Johnson CB RC .01 .05
185 Tony Jones WR .01 .05
186 Bubba McDowell .01 .05
187 Bruce Matthews .02 .10
188 Ray Childress .01 .05
189 Haywood Jeffires .02 .10
190 Ernest Givins .02 .10
191 Mike Munchak .02 .10
192 Greg Montgomery .01 .05
193 Cody Carlson RC .01 .05
194 Johnny Meads .01 .05
195 Drew Hill UER .01 .05
196 Mike Dumas RC .01 .05
197 Darryll Lewis RC .02 .10
198 Rohn Stark .01 .05
199 Clarence Verdin UER .01 .05
200 Mike Prior .01 .05
201 Eugene Daniel .01 .05
202 Dean Biasucci .01 .05
203 Jeff Herrod .01 .05
204 Keith Taylor .01 .05
205 Jon Hand .01 .05
206 Pat Beach .01 .05
207 Duane Bickett .01 .05
208 Jessie Hester UER .01 .05
209 Chip Banks .01 .05
210 Ray Donaldson .01 .05
211 Bill Brooks .01 .05
212 Jeff George .08 .25
213 Tony Siragusa RC .20 .50
214 Albert Bentley .01 .05
215 Joe Valerio RC .01 .05
216 Chris Martin .01 .05
217 Christian Okoye .01 .05
218 Stephone Paige .01 .05
219 Percy Snow .01 .05
220 David Szott RC .01 .05
221 Derrick Thomas .08 .25
222 Todd McNair .01 .05
223 Albert Lewis .01 .05
224 Neil Smith .08 .25
225 Barry Word .01 .05
226 Robb Thomas .01 .05
227 John Alt .01 .05
228 Jonathan Hayes .01 .05
229 Kevin Ross .01 .05
230 Nick Lowery .01 .05
231 Tim Grunhard .01 .05
232 Dan Saleaumua .01 .05
233 Steve DeBerg .01 .05
234 Harvey Williams RC .08 .25
235 Nick Bell RC UER .01 .05
236 Mervyn Fernandez UER .01 .05
237 Howie Long .08 .25
238 Marcus Allen .08 .25
239 Eddie Anderson .01 .05

Card	Low	High
240 Ethan Horton	.01	.05
241 Lionel Washington	.01	.05
242 Steve Wisniewski UER	.01	.05
243 Bo Jackson UER	.10	.30
244 Greg Townsend	.01	.05
245 Jeff Jaeger	.01	.05
246 Aaron Wallace	.01	.05
247 Garry Lewis	.01	.05
248 Steve Smith	.01	.05
249 Willie Gault UER	.01	.05
250 Scott Davis	.01	.05
251 Jay Schroeder	.01	.05
252 Don Mosebar	.01	.05
253 Todd Marinovich RC	.01	.05
254 Irv Pankey	.01	.05
255 Flipper Anderson	.01	.05
256 Tom Newberry	.01	.05
257 Kevin Greene	.02	.10
258 Mike Wilcher	.01	.05
259 Bern Brostek	.01	.05
260 Buford McGee	.01	.05
261 Cleveland Gary	.01	.05
262 Jackie Slater	.01	.05
263 Henry Ellard	.02	.10
264 Alvin Wright	.01	.05
265 Darryl Henley RC	.01	.05
266 Damone Johnson RC	.01	.05
267 Frank Stams	.01	.05
268 Jerry Gray	.01	.05
269 Jim Everett	.02	.10
270 Pat Terrell	.01	.05
271 Todd Lyght RC	.01	.05
272 Aaron Cox	.01	.05
273 Barry Sanders LL	.20	.50
274 Jerry Rice LL	.15	.40
275 Derrick Thomas LL	.08	.25
276 Mark Carrier DB LL	.02	.10
277 Warren Moon LL	.08	.25
278 Randall Cunningham LL	.02	.10
279 Nick Lowery LL	.01	.05
280 Clarence Verdin LL	.01	.05
281 Thurman Thomas LL	.08	.25
282 Mike Horan LL	.01	.05
283 Flipper Anderson LL	.01	.05
284 John Offerdahl	.01	.05
285 Dan Marino UER	.50	1.25
286 Mark Clayton	.02	.10
287 Tony Paige	.01	.05
288 Keith Sims	.01	.05
289 Jeff Cross	.01	.05
290 Pete Stoyanovich	.01	.05
291 Ferrell Edmunds	.01	.05
292 Reggie Roby	.01	.05
293 Louis Oliver	.01	.05
294 Jarvis Williams	.01	.05
295 Sammie Smith	.01	.05
296 Richmond Webb	.01	.05
297 J.B. Brown	.01	.05
298 Jim C.Jensen	.01	.05
299 Mark Duper	.02	.10
300 David Griggs	.01	.05
301 Randal Hill RC	.02	.10
302 Aaron Craver RC	.01	.05
303 Keith Millard	.01	.05
304 Steve Jordan	.01	.05
305 Anthony Carter	.02	.10
306 Mike Merriweather	.01	.05
307 Audray McMillian RC UER	.01	.05
308 Randall McDaniel	.02	.10
309 Gary Zimmerman	.02	.10
310 Carl Lee	.01	.05
311 Reggie Rutland	.01	.05
312 Hassan Jones	.01	.05
313 Kirk Lowdermilk UER	.01	.05
314 Herschel Walker	.02	.10
315 Chris Doleman	.01	.05
316 Joey Browner	.01	.05
317 Wade Wilson	.02	.10
318 Henry Thomas	.01	.05
319 Rich Gannon	.08	.25
320 Al Noga UER	.01	.05
321 Pat Harlow RC	.01	.05
322 Bruce Armstrong	.01	.05
323 Maurice Hurst	.01	.05
324 Brent Williams	.01	.05
325 Chris Singleton	.01	.05
326 Jason Staurovsky	.01	.05
327 Marvin Allen	.01	.05
328 Hart Lee Dykes	.01	.05
329 Johnny Rembert	.01	.05
330 Andre Tippett	.01	.05
331 Greg McMurtry	.01	.05
332 John Stephens	.01	.05
333 Ray Agnew	.01	.05
334 Tommy Hodson	.01	.05
335 Ronnie Lippett	.01	.05
336 Marv Cook	.01	.05
337 Tommy Barnhardt RC	.01	.05
338 Dalton Hilliard	.01	.05
339 Sam Mills	.01	.05
340 Morten Andersen	.01	.05
341 Stan Brock	.01	.05
342 Brett Maxie	.01	.05
343 Steve Walsh	.01	.05
344 Vaughan Johnson	.01	.05
345 Rickey Jackson	.01	.05
346 Renaldo Turnbull	.01	.05
347 Joel Hilgenberg	.01	.05
348 Toi Cook RC	.01	.05
349 Robert Massey	.01	.05
350 Pat Swilling	.02	.10
351 Eric Martin	.01	.05
352 Rueben Mayes UER	.01	.05
353 Vince Buck	.01	.05
354 Brett Perriman	.08	.25
355 Wesley Carroll RC	.01	.05
356 Jarrod Bunch RC	.01	.05
357 Pepper Johnson	.01	.05
358 Dave Meggett	.02	.10
359 Mark Collins	.01	.05
360 Sean Landeta	.01	.05
361 Maurice Carthon	.01	.05
362 Mike Fox UER	.01	.05
363 Jeff Hostetler	.02	.10
364 Phil Simms	.02	.10
365 Leonard Marshall	.01	.05
366 Gary Reasons	.01	.05
367 Rodney Hampton	.08	.25
368 Greg Jackson RC	.01	.05
369 Jumbo Elliott	.01	.05
370 Bob Kratch RC	.01	.05
371 Lawrence Taylor	.08	.25
372 Erik Howard	.01	.05
373 Carl Banks	.01	.05
374 Stephen Baker	.01	.05
375 Mark Ingram	.02	.10
376 Browning Nagle RC	.01	.05
377 Jeff Lageman	.01	.05
378 Ken O'Brien	.01	.05
379 Al Toon	.02	.10
380 Joe Prokop	.01	.05
381 Tony Stargell	.01	.05
382 Blair Thomas	.01	.05
383 Erik McMillan	.01	.05
384 Dennis Byrd	.01	.05
385 Freeman McNeil	.01	.05
386 Brad Baxter	.01	.05
387 Mark Boyer	.01	.05
388 Terance Mathis	.02	.10
389 Jim Sweeney	.01	.05
390 Kyle Clifton	.01	.05
391 Pat Leahy	.01	.05
392 Rob Moore	.08	.25
393 James Hasty	.01	.05
394 Blaise Bryant RC	.01	.05
395A Jesse Campbell ERR RC	.40	1.00
395B Jesse Campbell COR RC	.01	.05
396 Keith Jackson	.02	.10
397 Jerome Brown	.01	.05
398 Keith Byars	.01	.05
399 Seth Joyner	.02	.10
400 Mike Bellamy	.01	.05
401 Fred Barnett	.08	.25
402 Reggie Singletary RC	.01	.05
403 Reggie White	.08	.25
404 Randall Cunningham	.08	.25
405 Byron Evans	.01	.05
406 Wes Hopkins	.01	.05
407 Ben Smith	.01	.05
408 Roger Ruzek	.01	.05
409 Eric Allen UER	.01	.05
410 Anthony Toney UER	.01	.05
411 Clyde Simmons	.01	.05
412 Andre Waters	.01	.05
413 Calvin Williams	.02	.10
414 Eric Swann RC	.08	.25
415 Eric Hill	.01	.05
416 Tim McDonald	.01	.05
417 Luis Sharpe	.01	.05
418 Ernie Jones UER	.01	.05
419 Ken Harvey	.02	.10
420 Ricky Proehl	.01	.05
421 Johnny Johnson	.01	.05
422 Anthony Bell	.01	.05
423 Timm Rosenbach	.01	.05
424 Rich Camarillo	.01	.05
425 Walter Reeves	.01	.05
426 Freddie Joe Nunn	.01	.05
427 Anthony Thompson UER	.01	.05
428 Bill Lewis	.01	.05
429 Jim Wahler RC	.01	.05
430 Cedric Mack	.01	.05
431 Mike Jones DE RC	.01	.05
432 Ernie Mills RC	.02	.10
433 Tim Worley	.01	.05
434 Greg Lloyd	.08	.25
435 Dermontti Dawson	.02	.10
436 Louis Lipps	.01	.05
437 Eric Green	.01	.05
438 Donald Evans	.01	.05
439 D.J. Johnson	.01	.05
440 Tunch Ilkin	.01	.05
441 Bubby Brister	.01	.05
442 Chris Calloway	.01	.05
443 David Little	.01	.05
444 Thomas Everett	.01	.05
445 Carnell Lake	.01	.05
446 Rod Woodson	.08	.25
447 Gary Anderson K	.01	.05
448 Merril Hoge	.01	.05
449 Gerald Williams	.01	.05
450 Eric Moten RC	.01	.05
451 Marion Butts	.02	.10
452 Leslie O'Neal	.02	.10
453 Ronnie Harmon	.01	.05
454 Gill Byrd	.01	.05
455 Junior Seau	.08	.25
456 Nate Lewis RC	.01	.05
457 Leo Goeas	.01	.05
458 Burt Grossman	.01	.05
459 Courtney Hall	.01	.05
460 Anthony Miller	.02	.10
461 Gary Plummer	.01	.05
462 Billy Joe Tolliver	.01	.05
463 Lee Williams	.01	.05
464 Arthur Cox	.01	.05
465 John Kidd UER	.01	.05
466 Frank Cornish	.01	.05
467 John Carney	.01	.05
468 Eric Bieniemy RC	.01	.05
469 Don Griffin	.01	.05
470 Jerry Rice	.30	.75
471 Keith DeLong	.01	.05
472 John Taylor	.02	.10
473 Brent Jones	.08	.25
474 Pierce Holt	.01	.05
475 Kevin Fagan	.01	.05
476 Bill Romanowski	.01	.05
477 Dexter Carter	.01	.05
478 Guy McIntyre	.01	.05
479 Joe Montana	.50	1.25
480 Charles Haley	.02	.10
481 Mike Cofer	.01	.05
482 Jesse Sapolu	.01	.05
483 Eric Davis	.01	.05
484 Mike Sherrard	.01	.05
485 Steve Young	.30	.75
486 Darryl Pollard	.01	.05
487 Tom Rathman	.01	.05
488 Michael Carter	.01	.05
489 Ricky Watters RC	.60	1.50
490 John Johnson RC	.01	.05
491 Eugene Robinson	.01	.05
492 Andy Heck	.01	.05
493 John L. Williams	.01	.05
494 Norm Johnson	.01	.05
495 David Wyman	.01	.05
496 Derrick Fenner UER	.01	.05
497 Rick Donnelly	.01	.05
498 Tony Woods	.01	.05
499 Derrick Loville RC	.01	.05
500 Dave Krieg	.02	.10
501 Joe Nash	.01	.05
502 Brian Blades	.02	.10
503 Cortez Kennedy	.08	.25
504 Jeff Bryant	.01	.05
505 Tommy Kane	.01	.05
506 Travis McNeal	.01	.05
507 Terry Wooden	.01	.05
508 Chris Warren	.08	.25
509A Dan McGwire ERR RC	.01	.05
509B Dan McGwire COR RC	.01	.05
510 Mark Robinson	.01	.05
511 Ron Hall	.01	.05
512 Paul Gruber	.01	.05
513 Harry Hamilton	.01	.05
514 Keith McCants	.01	.05
515 Reggie Cobb	.01	.05
516 Steve Christie UER	.01	.05
517 Broderick Thomas	.01	.05
518 Mark Carrier WR	.08	.25
519 Vinny Testaverde	.02	.10
520 Ricky Reynolds	.01	.05
521 Jesse Anderson	.01	.05
522 Reuben Davis	.01	.05
523 Wayne Haddix	.01	.05
524 Gary Anderson RB UER	.01	.05
525 Bruce Hill	.01	.05
526 Kevin Murphy	.01	.05
527 Lawrence Dawsey RC	.02	.10
528 Ricky Ervins RC	.02	.10
529 Charles Mann	.01	.05
530 Jim Lachey	.01	.05
531 Mark Rypien UER	.02	.10
532 Darrell Green	.01	.05
533 Stan Humphries	.08	.25
534 Jeff Bostic UER	.01	.05
535 Earnest Byner	.01	.05
536 Art Monk UER	.02	.10
537 Don Warren	.01	.05
538 Darryl Grant	.01	.05
539 Wilber Marshall	.01	.05
540 Kurt Gouveia RC	.01	.05
541 Markus Koch	.01	.05
542 Andre Collins	.01	.05
543 Chip Lohmiller	.01	.05
544 Alvin Walton	.01	.05
545 Gary Clark	.08	.25
546 Ricky Sanders	.01	.05
547 Redskins vs. Eagles	.01	.05
548 Bengals vs. Oilers	.01	.05
549 Dolphins vs. Chiefs	.01	.05
550 Bears vs. Saints UER	.01	.05
551 Playoffs Thurman Thomas	.02	.10
552 49ers vs. Redskins	.01	.05
553 Giants vs. Bears	.01	.05
554 Playoffs Bo Jackson	.02	.10
555 AFC Championship	.01	.05
556 NFC Championship	.01	.05
557 Super Bowl XXV	.01	.05
558 Checklist 1-140	.01	.05
559 Checklist 141-280	.01	.05
560 Checklist 281-420 UER	.01	.05
561 Checklist 421-561 UER	.01	.05

1992 Bowman

The 1992 Bowman football set consists of 573 standard-size glossy cards that were issued 14 per foil pack. The set includes 45 foil cards that are broken into three subsets: 28 Team Leader (TL) cards, 12 Playoff Star (PS) cards and five cards highlighting the longest plays (LP) of the 1991 season (field goal, run, reception, kick return, and punt). The foil cards were issued one per pack and include a number of short-prints which are designated by SP in the checklist below. Rookie Cards include Steve Bono and Jackie Harris.

Card	Low	High
COMPLETE SET (573)	25.00	50.00
1 Reggie White	.40	1.00
2 Johnny Meads	.08	.25
3 Chip Lohmiller	.08	.25
4 James Lofton	.20	.50
5 Ray Horton	.08	.25
6 Rich Moran	.08	.25
7 Howard Cross	.08	.25
8 Mike Horan	.08	.25
9 Erik Kramer	.20	.50
10 Steve Wisniewski	.08	.25
11 Michael Haynes	.20	.50
12 Donald Evans	.08	.25
13 Michael Irvin FOIL	.40	1.00
14 Gary Zimmerman	.08	.25
15 John Friesz	.20	.50
16 Mark Carrier WR	.40	1.00
17 Mark Duper	.08	.25
18 James Thornton	.08	.25
19 Jon Hand	.08	.25
20 Sterling Sharpe	.40	1.00
21 Jacob Green	.08	.25
22 Wesley Carroll	.08	.25
23 Clay Matthews	.20	.50
24 Kevin Greene	.20	.50
25 Brad Baxter	.08	.25
26 Don Griffin	.08	.25
27 Robert Delpino	.60	1.50
28 Lee Johnson	.08	.25
29 Jim Wahler	.08	.25
30 Leonard Russell	.20	.50
31 Eric Moore	.08	.25
32 Dino Hackett	.08	.25
33 Simon Fletcher	.08	.25
34 Al Edwards	.08	.25
35 Brad Edwards	.08	.25
36 James Joseph	.08	.25
37 Rodney Peete	.20	.50
38 Ricky Reynolds	.08	.25
39 Eddie Anderson	.08	.25
40 Ken Clarke	.08	.25
41 Tony Bennett	.20	.50
42 Larry Brown DB	.08	.25
43 Ray Childress	.08	.25
44 Mike Kenn	.08	.25
45 Vestee Jackson	.08	.25
46 Neil O'Donnell	.20	.50
47 Bill Brooks	.08	.25
48 Kevin Butler	.08	.25
49 Joe Phillips	.08	.25
50 Cortez Kennedy	.20	.50
51 Rickey Jackson	.08	.25
52 Vinnie Clark	.08	.25
53 Michael Jackson	.20	.50
54 Ernie Jones	.08	.25
55 Tom Newberry	.08	.25
56 Pat Harlow	.08	.25
57 Craig Taylor	.08	.25
58 Joe Prokop	.08	.25
59 Warren Moon FOIL SP	.75	2.00
60 Jeff Lageman	.08	.25
61 Neil Smith	.40	1.00
62 Jim Jeffcoat	.08	.25
63 Bill Fralic	.08	.25
64 Mark Schlereth RC	.08	.25
65 Keith Byars	.08	.25
66 Jeff Hostetler	.20	.50
67 Joey Browner	.08	.25
68 Bobby Hebert FOIL SP	.60	1.50
69 Keith Sims	.08	.25
70 Warren Moon	.40	1.00
71 Pio Sagapolutele RC	.08	.25
72 Cornelius Bennett	.20	.50
73 Greg Davis	.08	.25
74 Ronnie Harmon	.08	.25
75 Ron Hall	.08	.25
76 Howie Long	.40	1.00
77 Greg Lewis	.08	.25
78 Carnell Lake	.08	.25
79 Ray Crockett	.08	.25
80 Tom Waddle	.08	.25
81 Vincent Brown	.08	.25
82 Bill Brooks	.20	.50
83 John L. Williams	.08	.25
84 Floyd Turner	.08	.25
85 Scott Radecic	.08	.25
86 Anthony Munoz	.20	.50
87 Lonnie Young	.08	.25
88 Dexter Carter	.08	.25
89 Tony Zendejas	.08	.25
90 Tim Jorden	.08	.25
91 LeRoy Butler	.08	.25
92 Richard Brown RC	.08	.25
93 Erric Pegram	.20	.50
94 Sean Landeta	.08	.25
95 Clyde Simmons	.08	.25
96 Martin Mayhew	.08	.25
97 Jarvis Williams	.08	.25
98 Barry Word	.08	.25
99 John Taylor FOIL	.20	.50
100 Emmitt Smith	3.00	8.00
101 Leon Seals	.08	.25
102 Marion Butts	.08	.25
103 Mike Merriweather	.08	.25
104 Ernest Givins	.20	.50
105 Wymon Henderson	.08	.25
106 Robert Wilson	.08	.25
107 Bobby Hebert	.08	.25
108 Terry McDaniel	.08	.25
109 Jerry Ball	.08	.25
110 John Taylor	.20	.50
111 Rob Moore	.20	.50
112 Thurman Thomas FOIL	.40	1.00
113 Checklist 1-115	.08	.25
114 Brian Blades	.20	.50
115 Larry Kelm	.08	.25
116 James Francis	.08	.25
117 Rod Woodson	.40	1.00
118 Trace Armstrong	.08	.25
119 Eugene Daniel	.08	.25
120 Andre Tippett	.08	.25
121 Chris Jacke	.08	.25
122 Jessie Tuggle	.08	.25
123 Chris Chandler	.40	1.00
124 Tim Johnson	.08	.25
125 Mark Collins	.08	.25
126 Aeneas Williams SP	.60	1.50
127 James Jones DT	.08	.25
128 George Jamison	.08	.25
129 Deron Cherry	.08	.25
130 Mark Clayton	.20	.50
131 Keith DeLong	.08	.25
132 Marcus Allen	.40	1.00
133 Joe Walter RC	.08	.25
134 Reggie Rutland	.08	.25
135 Kent Hull	.08	.25
136 Jeff Feagles	.08	.25
137 Ronnie Lott FOIL SP	.75	2.00
138 Henry Rolling	.08	.25
139 Gary Anderson RB	.08	.25
140 Morten Andersen	.08	.25
141 Cris Dishman	.08	.25
142 David Treadwell	.08	.25
143 Kevin Gogan	.08	.25
144 James Hasty	.08	.25
145 Robert Delpino	.08	.25
146 Patrick Hunter	.08	.25
147 Gary Anderson K	.08	.25
148 Chip Banks	.08	.25
149 Dan Fike	.08	.25
150 Chris Miller	.20	.50
151 Hugh Millen	.08	.25
152 Courtney Hall	.08	.25
153 Gary Clark	.20	.50
154 Michael Brooks	.08	.25
155 Jay Hilgenberg	.08	.25
156 Tim McDonald	.08	.25
157 Andre Tippett	.20	.50
158 Doug Riesenberg	.08	.25
159 Bill Maas	.08	.25
160 Fred Barnett	.20	.50
161 Pierce Holt	.08	.25
162 Brian Noble	.08	.25
163 Harold Green	.08	.25
164 Joel Hilgenberg	.08	.25
165 Mervyn Fernandez	.08	.25
166 John Offerdahl	.08	.25
167 Shane Conlan	.08	.25
168 Mark Higgs FOIL SP	.60	1.50
169 Bubba McDowell	.08	.25
170 Barry Sanders	2.50	6.00
171 Larry Roberts	.08	.25
172 Herschel Walker	.20	.50
173 Steve McMichael	.20	.50
174 Kelly Stouffer	.08	.25
175 Louis Lipps	.08	.25
176 Jim Everett	.20	.50
177 Tony Tolbert	.08	.25
178 Mike Baab	.08	.25
179 Eric Swann	.20	.50
180 Emmitt Smith FOIL SP	5.00	12.00
181 Tim Brown	.40	1.00
182 Dennis Smith	.08	.25
183 Moe Gardner	.08	.25
184 Derrick Walker	.08	.25
185 Reyna Thompson	.08	.25
186 Esera Tuaolo	.08	.25
187 Jeff Wright	.08	.25
188 Mark Rypien	.08	.25
189 Quinn Early	.20	.50
190 Christian Okoye	.08	.25
191 Keith Jackson	.20	.50
192 Doug Smith	.08	.25
193 John Elway FOIL	4.00	10.00
194 Reggie Cobb	.08	.25
195 Reggie Roby	.08	.25
196 Clarence Verdin	.08	.25
197 Jim Breech	.08	.25
198 Jim Sweeney	.08	.25
199 Marv Cook	.08	.25
200 Ronnie Lott	.20	.50
201 Mel Gray	.20	.50
202 Maury Buford	.08	.25
203 Lorenzo Lynch	.08	.25
204 Jesse Sapolu	.08	.25
205 Steve Jordan	.08	.25
206 Don Majkowski	.08	.25
207 Flipper Anderson	.08	.25
208 Ed King	.08	.25
209 Tony Woods	.08	.25
210 Ron Heller	.08	.25
211 Greg Kragen	.08	.25
212 Scott Case	.08	.25
213 Tommy Barnhardt	.08	.25
214 Charles Mann	.08	.25
215 David Griggs	.08	.25
216 Kenneth Davis FOIL SP	.60	1.50
217 Lamar Lathon	.08	.25
218 Nate Odomes	.08	.25
219 Vinny Testaverde	.20	.50
220 Rod Bernstine	.08	.25
221 Barry Sanders FOIL	4.00	10.00
222 Carlton Haselrig RC	.08	.25
223 Steve Beuerlein	.20	.50
224 John Alt	.08	.25
225 Pepper Johnson	.08	.25
226 Checklist 116-230	.08	.25
227 Irv Eatman	.08	.25
228 Greg Townsend	.08	.25
229 Mark Jackson	.08	.25
230 Robert Blackmon	.08	.25
231 Terry Allen	.40	1.00
232 Bennie Blades	.08	.25
233 Sam Mills	.40	1.00
234 Richmond Webb	.08	.25
235 Richard Dent	.20	.50
236 Alonzo Mitz RC	.08	.25
237 Steve Young	2.00	5.00
238 Pat Swilling	.08	.25
239 James Campen	.08	.25
240 Earnest Byner	.08	.25
241 Pat Terrell	.08	.25
242 Carwell Gardner	.08	.25
243 Charles McRae	.08	.25
244 Vince Newsome	.08	.25
245 Eric Hill	.08	.25
246 Steve Young FOIL	2.00	5.00
247 Nate Lewis	.08	.25
248 William Fuller	.08	.25
249 Andre Waters	.08	.25
250 Dean Biasucci	.08	.25
251 Andre Rison	.20	.50
252 Brent Williams	.08	.25
253 Todd McNair	.08	.25
254 Jeff Davidson RC	.08	.25
255 Art Monk	.20	.50
256 Kirk Lowdermilk	.08	.25
257 Bob Golic	.08	.25
258 Michael Irvin	.40	1.00
259 Eric Green	.08	.25
260 David Fulcher	.20	.50
261 Damone Johnson	.08	.25
262 Marc Spindler	.08	.25
263 Alfred Williams	.08	.25
264 Donnie Elder	.08	.25
265 Keith McKeller	.08	.25
266 Steve Bono RC	.40	1.00
267 Jumbo Elliott	.08	.25
268 Randy Hilliard RC	.08	.25
269 Rufus Porter	.08	.25
270 Neal Anderson	.08	.25
271 Dalton Hilliard	.08	.25
272 Michael Zordich RC	.08	.25
273 Cornelius Bennett FOIL	.20	.50
274 Louie Aguiar RC	.08	.25
275 Aaron Craver	.08	.25
276 Tony Bennett	.08	.25
277 Terry Wooden	.08	.25
278 Mike Munchak	.20	.50
279 Chris Hinton	.08	.25
280 John Elway	2.50	6.00
281 Randall McDaniel	.08	.25
282 Brad Baxter	.20	.50
283 Wes Hopkins	.08	.25
284 Scott Davis	.08	.25
285 Mark Tuinei	.08	.25
286 Broderick Thompson	.08	.25
287 Henry Ellard	.20	.50
288 Adrian Cooper	.08	.25
289 Don Warren	.08	.25
290 Rodney Hampton	.20	.50
291 Kevin Ross	.08	.25
292 Mark Carrier DB	.08	.25
293 Ian Beckles	.08	.25
294 Gene Atkins	.08	.25
295 Mark Rypien FOIL	.20	.50
296 Eric Metcalf	.20	.50
297 Howard Ballard	.08	.25
298 Nate Newton	.08	.25
299 Dan Owens	.08	.25
300 Tim McGee	.08	.25
301 Greg McMurtry	.08	.25
302 Walter Reeves	.08	.25
303 Jeff Herrod	.08	.25
304 Darren Comeaux	.08	.25
305 Pete Stoyanovich	.08	.25
306 Johnny Holland	.08	.25
307 Jay Novacek	.20	.50
308 Steve Broussard	.08	.25
309 Darrell Green	.08	.25
310 Sam Mills	.08	.25
311 Tim Barnett	.08	.25
312 Steve Atwater	.08	.25
313 Tom Waddle FOIL	.20	.50
314 Felix Wright	.08	.25
315 Sean Jones	.08	.25
316 Jim Harbaugh	.40	1.00
317 Eric Allen	.08	.25
318 Don Mosebar	.08	.25
319 Rob Taylor	.08	.25
320 Terance Mathis	.20	.50
321 Leroy Hoard	.20	.50
322 Kenneth Davis	.08	.25
323 Guy McIntyre	.08	.25
324 Deron Cherry	.20	.50
325 Tunch Ilkin	.08	.25
326 Willie Green	.08	.25
327 Darryl Henley	.08	.25
328 Shawn Jefferson	.08	.25
329 Greg Jackson	.08	.25
330 John Roper	.08	.25
331 Bill Lewis	.08	.25
332 Rodney Holman	.08	.25
333 Bruce Armstrong	.08	.25
334 Robb Thomas	.08	.25
335 Alvin Harper	.20	.50
336 Brian Jordan	.20	.50
337 Morten Andersen	.20	.50
338 Dermontti Dawson	.20	.50
339 Checklist 231-345	.08	.25
340 Louis Oliver	.08	.25
341 Paul McJulien RC	.08	.25
342 Karl Mecklenburg	.08	.25
343 Lawrence Dawsey	.20	.50
344 Kyle Clifton	.08	.25
345 Jeff Bostic	.08	.25
346 Cris Carter	.60	1.50
347 Al Smith	.08	.25
348 Mark Kelso	.08	.25
349 Art Monk FOIL	.40	1.00
350 Michael Carter	.08	.25
351 Ethan Horton	.08	.25
352 Andy Heck	.08	.25
353 Gill Fenerty	.08	.25
354 David Brandon RC	.08	.25
355 Anthony Johnson	.40	1.00
356 Mike Golic	.08	.25
357 Ferrell Edmunds	.08	.25
358 Dennis Gibson	.08	.25
359 Gill Byrd	.08	.25
360 Todd Lyght	.08	.25
361 Jayice Pearson RC	.08	.25
362 John Rade	.08	.25
363 Keith Van Horne	.08	.25
364 John Kasay	.08	.25
365 Broderick Thomas	.60	1.50
366 Ken Harvey	.08	.25
367 Rich Gannon	.40	1.00
368 Darrell Thompson	.08	.25
369 Jon Vaughn	.08	.25
370 Jesse Solomon	.08	.25
371 Erik McMillan	.08	.25
372 Bruce Matthews	.08	.25
373 Wilber Marshall	.08	.25
374 Brian Blades	.60	1.50
375 Vance Johnson	.08	.25
376 Eddie Brown	.08	.25
377 Don Beebe	.08	.25
378 Brent Jones	.20	.50
379 Matt Bahr	.08	.25
380 Dwight Stone	.08	.25
381 Tony Casillas	.08	.25
382 Jay Schroeder	.08	.25
383 Byron Evans	.08	.25
384 Dan Saleaumua	.08	.25
385 Wendell Davis	.08	.25
386 Ron Holmes	.08	.25
387 George Thomas RC	.08	.25
388 Ray Berry	.08	.25
389 Eric Martin	.08	.25
390 Kevin Mack	.08	.25
391 Natu Tuatagaloa RC	.08	.25
392 Bill Romanowski	.08	.25
393 Nick Bell FOIL SP	.60	1.50
394 Grant Feasel	.08	.25
395 Eugene Lockhart	.08	.25
396 Lorenzo White	.08	.25
397 Mike Farr	.08	.25
398 Eric Bieniemy	.08	.25
399 Kevin Murphy	.08	.25
400 Luis Sharpe	.08	.25
401 Jessie Tuggle	.60	1.50
402 Cleveland Gary	.08	.25
403 Tony Mandarich	.08	.25
404 Bryan Cox	.20	.50
405 Marvin Washington	.08	.25
406 Fred Stokes	.08	.25
407 Duane Bickett	.08	.25
408 Leonard Marshall	.08	.25
409 Barry Foster	.20	.50
410 Thurman Thomas	.40	1.00
411 Willie Gault	.20	.50
412 Vinson Smith RC	.08	.25
413 Mark Bortz	.08	.25
414 Johnny Johnson	.08	.25
415 Rodney Hampton FOIL	.40	1.00
416 Steve Wallace	.08	.25
417 Fuad Reveiz	.08	.25
418 Derrick Thomas	.20	.50
419 Jackie Harris RC	.40	1.00
420 Derek Russell	.08	.25
421 David Grant	.08	.25
422 Tommy Kane	.08	.25
423 Stan Brock	.08	.25
424 Haywood Jeffires	.20	.50
425 Broderick Thomas	.08	.25
426 John Kidd	.08	.25
427 Shawn McCarthy RC	.20	.50
428 Jim Arnold	.08	.25
429 Scott Fulhage	.08	.25
430 Jackie Slater	.08	.25
431 Scott Galbraith RC	.08	.25
432 Roger Ruzek	.08	.25
433 Irving Fryar	.20	.50
434A D.Thomas FOIL ERR 494	.40	1.00
434B D.Thomas FOIL COR	.40	1.00
435 D.J. Johnson	.08	.25
436 Jim C.Jensen	.08	.25
437 James Washington	.08	.25
438 Phil Hansen	.08	.25
439 Rohn Stark	.08	.25
440 Jarrod Bunch	.08	.25
441 Todd Marinovich	.08	.25
442 Brett Perriman	.40	1.00
443 Eugene Robinson	.08	.25
444 Robert Massey	.08	.25
445 Nick Lowery	.08	.25
446 Rickey Dixon	.08	.25
447 Jim Lachey	.08	.25
448 Johnny Hector	.20	.50
449 Gary Plummer	.08	.25
450 Robert Brown	.08	.25
451 Gaston Green	.08	.25
452 Checklist 346-459	.08	.25
453 Darion Conner	.08	.25
454 Mike Cofer	.08	.25
455 Craig Heyward	.20	.50
456 Anthony Carter	.20	.50
457 Pat Coleman RC	.08	.25
458 Jeff Bryant	.08	.25
459 Mark Gunn RC	.08	.25
460 Stan Thomas	.08	.25
461 Simon Fletcher	.60	1.50
462 Ray Agnew	.08	.25
463 Jessie Hester	.08	.25
464 Rob Burnett	.08	.25
465 Mike Croel	.08	.25
466 Mike Pitts	.08	.25
467 Darryl Talley	.08	.25
468 Rich Camarillo	.08	.25
469 Reggie White FOIL	.40	1.00
470 Nick Bell	.08	.25
471 Tracy Hayworth RC	.08	.25
472 Eric Thomas	.08	.25
473 Paul Gruber	.08	.25
474 David Richards	.08	.25
475 T.J. Turner	.08	.25
476 Mark Ingram	.08	.25
477 Tim Grunhard	.08	.25
478 Marion Butts FOIL	.20	.50
479 Tom Rathman	.08	.25
480 Brian Mitchell	.20	.50
481 Bryce Paup	.40	1.00
482 Mike Pritchard	.20	.50
483 Ken Norton Jr.	.20	.50
484 Roman Phifer	.08	.25
485 Greg Lloyd	.20	.50
486 Brett Maxie	.08	.25
487 Richard Dent FOIL SP	.60	1.50
488 Curtis Duncan	.08	.25
489 Chris Burkett	.08	.25
490 Travis McNeal	.08	.25
491 Carl Lee	.08	.25
492 Clarence Kay	.08	.25
493 Tom Thayer	.08	.25
494 Erik Kramer FOIL SP	.75	2.00
495 Perry Kemp	.08	.25
496 Jeff Jaeger	.08	.25
497 Eric Sanders	.08	.25
498 Burt Grossman	.08	.25
499 Ben Smith	.08	.25
500 Keith McCants	.08	.25
501 John Stephens	.08	.25
502 John Rienstra	.08	.25
503 Jim Ritcher	.08	.25
504 Harris Barton	.08	.25
505 Andre Rison FOIL SP	.75	2.00
506 Chris Martin	.08	.25
507 Freddie Joe Nunn	.08	.25
508 Mark Higgs	.08	.25
509 Norm Johnson	.08	.25
510 Stephen Baker	.08	.25
511 Ricky Sanders	.08	.25
512 Ray Donaldson	.08	.25
513 David Fulcher	.08	.25
514 Gerald Williams	.08	.25
515 Toi Cook	.08	.25
516 Chris Warren	.40	1.00
517 Jeff Gossett	.08	.25
518 Ken Lanier	.08	.25
519 Haywood Jeffires FOIL SP	.75	2.00
520 Kevin Glover	.08	.25
521 Mo Lewis	.08	.25
522 Bern Brostek	.08	.25
523 Bo Orlando RC	.08	.25
524 Mike Saxon	.08	.25
525 Seth Joyner	.08	.25
526 John Carney	.08	.25
527 Jeff Cross	.08	.25
528 Gary Anderson K FOIL SP	.60	1.50
529 Chuck Cecil	.08	.25
530 Tim Green	.08	.25
531 Kevin Porter	.08	.25
532 Chris Spielman	.20	.50
533 Willie Drewrey	.08	.25
534 Chris Singleton UER	.08	.25
535 Matt Stover	.08	.25
536 Andre Collins	.08	.25
537 Erik Howard	.08	.25
538 Steve Tasker	.20	.50
539 Anthony Thompson	.08	.25
540 Charles Haley	.20	.50
541 Mike Merriweather	.20	.50
542 Henry Thomas	.08	.25
543 Scott Stephen	.08	.25
544 Bruce Kozerski	.08	.25
545 Tim McKyer	.08	.25
546 Chris Doleman	.08	.25
547 Riki Ellison	.08	.25
548 Mike Prior	.08	.25
549 Dwayne Harper	.08	.25
550 Bubby Brister	.08	.25
551 Dave Meggett	.20	.50
552 Greg Montgomery	.08	.25
553 Kevin Mack	.20	.50
554 Mark Stepnoski	.20	.50
555 Kenny Walker	.08	.25
556 Eric Moten	.08	.25
557 Michael Stewart	.08	.25
558 Calvin Williams	.20	.50
559 Johnny Hector	.08	.25
560 Tony Paige	.08	.25
561 Tim Newton	.08	.25
562 Brad Muster	.08	.25
563 Aeneas Williams	.20	.50
564 Herman Moore	.40	1.00
565 Checklist 460-573	.08	.25
566 Jerome Henderson	.08	.25
567 Danny Copeland	.08	.25
568 Alexander Wright	.20	.50
569 Tim Harris	.08	.25
570 Jonathan Hayes	.08	.25
571 Tony Jones T	.08	.25
572 Carlton Bailey RC	.08	.25
573 Vaughan Johnson	.08	.25

1993 Bowman

The 423 standard-size cards comprising the 1993 Bowman set feature full-bleed photos. Each foil pack contained one foil card and each jumbo pack contained two foil cards. A solid Rookie Card crop includes Jerome Bettis, Drew Bledsoe, Vincent Brisby, Reggie Brooks, Mark Brunell, Curtis Conway, Troy Drayton, Garrison Hearst, Qadry Ismail, O.J. McDuffie, Natrone Means, Rick Mirer, Robert Smith, Dana Stubblefield and Kevin Williams.

Card	Low	High
COMPLETE SET (423)	12.00	30.00
1 Troy Aikman FOIL	1.50	3.00
2 John Parrella RC	.07	.20
3 Dana Stubblefield RC	.30	.75
4 Mark Higgs	.07	.20
5 Tom Carter RC	.15	.40
6 Nate Lewis	.07	.20
7 Vaughn Hebron RC	.07	.20
8 Ernest Givins	.15	.40
9 Vince Buck	.07	.20
10 Lovon Kirkland	.07	.20
11 J.J. Birden	.07	.20
12 Steve Jordan	.07	.20
13 Simon Fletcher	.07	.20
14 Willie Green	.07	.20
15 Pepper Johnson	.07	.20
16 Roger Harper RC	.07	.20
17 Rob Moore	.15	.40
18 David Lang	.07	.20
19 David Klingler	.07	.20
20 Garrison Hearst RC	.75	2.00
21 Anthony Johnson	.15	.40
22 Eric Curry RC	.15	.40
23 Nolan Harrison	.07	.20
24 Earl Dotson RC	.07	.20
25 Leonard Russell	.15	.40
26 Doug Riesenberg	.07	.20
27 Dwayne Harper	.07	.20
28 Richard Dent	.15	.40
29 Victor Bailey RC	.07	.20
30 Junior Seau	.30	.75
31 Steve Tasker	.15	.40
32 Kurt Gouveia	.07	.20
33 Renaldo Turnbull UER	.07	.20
34 Dale Carter	.07	.20
35 Russell Maryland	.07	.20
36 Dana Hall	.07	.20
37 Marco Coleman	.07	.20
38 Greg Montgomery	.07	.20
39 Deon Figures RC	.07	.20
40 Troy Drayton RC	.15	.40
41 Eric Metcalf	.15	.40
42 Michael Husted RC	.07	.20
43 Harry Newsome	.07	.20
44 Kelvin Pritchett	.07	.20
45 Andre Rison FOIL	.30	.75
46 John Copeland RC	.15	.40
47 Greg Biekert RC	.07	.20
48 Johnny Johnson	.07	.20
49 Chuck Cecil	.07	.20
50 Rick Mirer RC	.60	1.50
51 Rod Bernstine	.07	.20
52 Steve McMichael	.15	.40
53 Roosevelt Potts RC	.07	.20
54 Mike Sherrard	.07	.20
55 Terrell Buckley	.07	.20
56 Eugene Chung	.07	.20
57 Kimble Anders RC	.30	.75
58 Daryl Johnston	.30	.75
59 Harris Barton	.07	.20
60 Thurman Thomas FOIL	.60	1.50
61 Eric Martin	.07	.20
62 Reggie Brooks RC	.15	.40
63 Eric Bieniemy	.07	.20
64 John Offerdahl	.07	.20
65 Wilber Marshall	.07	.20
66 Mark Carrier WR	.15	.40
67 Merril Hoge	.07	.20
68 Cris Carter	.30	.75
69 Marty Thompson RC	.07	.20
70 Randall Cunningham FOIL	.60	1.50
71 Winston Moss	.07	.20
72 Doug Pelfrey RC	.07	.20
73 Jackie Slater	.07	.20
74 Pierce Holt	.07	.20
75 Hardy Nickerson	.15	.40
76 Chris Burkett	.07	.20
77 Michael Brandon	.07	.20
78 Tom Waddle	.07	.20
79 Walter Reeves	.07	.20
80 Lawrence Taylor FOIL	.30	.75
81 Wayne Simmons RC	.07	.20
82 Brent Williams	.07	.20
83 Shannon Sharpe	.30	.75
84 Robert Blackmon	.07	.20
85 Keith Jackson	.15	.40
86 A.J. Johnson	.07	.20
87 Ryan McNeil RC	.30	.75
88 Michael Dean Perry	.15	.40
89 Russell Copeland RC	.15	.40
90 Sam Mills	.07	.20
91 Courtney Hall	.07	.20
92 Gino Torretta RC	.15	.40
93 Artie Smith RC	.07	.20
94 David Whitmore	.07	.20
95 Charles Haley	.15	.40
96 Rod Woodson	.30	.75
97 Lorenzo White	.07	.20
98 Tom Scott RC	.07	.20
99 Tyji Armstrong	.07	.20
100 Boomer Esiason	.15	.40
101 Rocket Ismail FOIL	.30	.75
102 Mark Carrier DB	.07	.20
103 Broderick Thompson	.07	.20
104 Bob Whitfield	.07	.20
105 Ben Coleman RC	.07	.20
106 Jon Vaughn	.07	.20
107 Marcus Buckley RC	.07	.20
108 Cleveland Gary	.07	.20
109 Ashley Ambrose	.07	.20
110 Reggie White FOIL	.60	1.50
111 Arthur Marshall RC	.07	.20
112 Greg McMurtry	.07	.20
113 Mike Johnson	.07	.20
114 Tim McGee	.07	.20
115 John Carney	.07	.20
116 Neil Smith	.30	.75
117 Mark Stepnoski	.07	.20
118 Don Beebe	.07	.20
119 Scott Mitchell	.30	.75
120 Randall McDaniel	.07	.20
121 Chidi Ahanotu RC	.07	.20
122 Ray Childress	.07	.20
123 Tony McGee RC	.15	.40
124 Marc Boutte	.07	.20
125 Ronnie Lott	.15	.40
126 Jason Elam RC	.30	.75
127 Martin Harrison RC	.07	.20
128 Leonard Renfro RC	.07	.20
129 Jessie Armstead RC	.15	.40
130 Quentin Coryatt	.15	.40
131 Luis Sharpe	.07	.20
132 Bill Maas	.07	.20
133 Jesse Solomon	.07	.20
134 Kevin Greene	.15	.40
135 Derek Brown RBK RC	.15	.40
136 Greg Townsend	.07	.20
137 Neal Anderson	.07	.20
138 John L. Williams	.07	.20
139 Vincent Brisby RC	.30	.75
140 Barry Sanders FOIL	2.00	5.00
141 Charles Mann	.07	.20
142 Ken Norton	.15	.40
143 Eric Moten	.07	.20
144 John Alt	.07	.20
145 Dan Footman RC	.07	.20
146 Bill Brooks	.07	.20
147 James Thornton	.07	.20
148 Martin Mayhew	.07	.20
149 Andy Harmon	.15	.40
150 Dan Marino FOIL	2.50	6.00
151 Micheal Barrow RC	.30	.75
152 Flipper Anderson	.07	.20
153 Jackie Harris	.07	.20
154 Todd Kelly RC	.07	.20
155 Dan Williams RC	.07	.20
156 Harold Green	.07	.20
157 David Treadwell	.07	.20
158 Chris Doleman	.07	.20
159 Eric Hill	.07	.20
160 Lincoln Kennedy RC	.07	.20
161 Devon McDonald RC	.07	.20
162 Natrone Means RC	.30	.75
163 Rick Hamilton RC	.07	.20
164 Kelvin Martin	.07	.20
165 Jeff Hostetler	.15	.40
166 Mark Brunell RC	1.50	4.00
167 Tim Barnett	.07	.20
168 Ray Crockett	.07	.20
169 William Perry	.15	.40
170 Michael Irvin	.30	.75
171 Marvin Washington	.07	.20
172 Irving Fryar	.15	.40
173 Scott Sisson RC	.07	.20
174 Gary Anderson K	.07	.20
175 Bruce Smith	.30	.75
176 Clyde Simmons	.07	.20

177 Russell White RC .15 .40
178 Irv Smith RC .07 .20
179 Mark Wheeler .07 .20
180 Warren Moon .30 .75
181 Del Speer RC .07 .20
182 Henry Thomas .07 .20
183 Keith Kartz .07 .20
184 Ricky Ervins .07 .20
185 Phil Simms .15 .40
186 Tim Brown .30 .75
187 Willis Peguese .07 .20
188 Rich Moran .07 .20
189 Robert Jones .07 .20
190 Craig Heyward .15 .40
191 Ricky Watters .30 .75
192 Stan Humphries .15 .40
193 Larry Webster .07 .20
194 Brad Baxter .07 .20
195 Randal Hill .07 .20
196 Robert Porcher .07 .20
197 Patrick Robinson RC .07 .20
198 Ferrell Edmunds .07 .20
199 Melvin Jenkins .07 .20
200 Joe Montana FOIL 2.50 6.00
201 Marv Cook .07 .20
202 Henry Ellard .15 .40
203 Calvin Williams .15 .40
204 Craig Erickson .15 .40
205 Steve Atwater .07 .20
206 Najee Mustafaa .07 .20
207 Darryl Talley .07 .20
208 Jarrod Bunch .07 .20
209 Tim McDonald .07 .20
210 Patrick Bates RC .07 .20
211 Sean Jones .07 .20
212 Leslie O'Neal .15 .40
213 Mike Golic .07 .20
214 Mark Clayton .07 .20
215 Leonard Marshall .07 .20
216 Curtis Conway RC .60 1.50
217 Andre Hastings RC .15 .40
218 Barry Word .07 .20
219 Will Wolford .07 .20
220 Desmond Howard .15 .40
221 Rickey Jackson .07 .20
222 Alvin Harper .15 .40
223 William White .07 .20
224 Steve Broussard .07 .20
225 Aeneas Williams .07 .20
226 Michael Brooks .07 .20
227 Reggie Cobb .07 .20
228 Derrick Walker .07 .20
229 Marcus Allen .30 .75
230 Jerry Ball .07 .20
231 J.B. Brown .07 .20
232 Terry McDaniel .07 .20
233 LeRoy Butler .07 .20
234 Kyle Clifton .07 .20
235 Henry Jones .07 .20
236 Shane Conlan .07 .20
237 Michael Bates RC .07 .20
238 Vincent Brown .07 .20
239 William Fuller .07 .20
240 Ricardo McDonald .07 .20
241 Gary Zimmerman .07 .20
242 Fred Barnett .15 .40
243 Elvis Grbac RC 1.50 4.00
244 Myron Baker RC .07 .20
245 Steve Emtman .07 .20
246 Mike Compton RC .30 .75
247 Mark Jackson .07 .20
248 Santo Stephens RC .07 .20
249 Tommie Agee .07 .20
250 Broderick Thomas .07 .20
251 Fred Baxter RC .07 .20
252 Andre Collins .07 .20
253 Ernest Dye RC .07 .20
254 Raylee Johnson RC .15 .40
255 Rickey Dixon .07 .20
256 Ron Heller .07 .20
257 Joel Steed .07 .20
258 Everett Lindsay RC .07 .20
259 Tony Smith RB .07 .20
260 Sterling Sharpe UER .30 .75
261 Tommy Vardell .07 .20
262 Morten Andersen .07 .20
263 Eddie Robinson .07 .20
264 Jerome Bettis RC 4.00 8.00
265 Alonzo Spellman .07 .20
266 Harvey Williams .15 .40
267 Jason Belser RC .07 .20
268 Derek Russell .07 .20
269 Derrick Lassic RC .07 .20
270 Steve Young FOIL 1.50 3.00
271 Adrian Murrell RC .30 .75
272 Lewis Tillman .07 .20
273 O.J.McDuffie RC .30 .75
274 Marty Carter .07 .20
275 Ray Seals .07 .20
276 Earnest Byner .07 .20
277 Marion Butts .07 .20
278 Chris Spielman .15 .40
279 Carl Pickens .15 .40
280 Drew Bledsoe RC 2.50 6.00
281 Mark Kelso .07 .20
282 Eugene Robinson .07 .20
283 Eric Allen .07 .20
284 Ethan Horton .07 .20
285 Greg Lloyd .15 .40
286 Anthony Carter .15 .40
287 Edgar Bennett .30 .75
288 Bobby Hebert .07 .20
289 Haywood Jeffires .15 .40
290 Glyn Milburn RC .30 .75
291 Bernie Kosar .15 .40
292 Jumbo Elliott .07 .20
293 Jessie Hester .07 .20
294 Brent Jones .15 .40
295 Carl Banks .07 .20
296 Brian Washington .07 .20
297 Steve Beuerlein .15 .40
298 John Lynch RC .75 2.00
299 Troy Vincent .07 .20
300 Emmitt Smith FOIL 2.50 5.00
301 Chris Zorich .07 .20
302 Wade Wilson .07 .20
303 Darrien Gordon RC .07 .20
304 Fred Stokes .07 .20
305 Nick Lowery .07 .20
306 Rodney Peete .07 .20
307 Chris Warren .15 .40
308 Herschel Walker .15 .40
309 Aundray Bruce .07 .20
310 Barry Foster FOIL .15 .40
311 George Teague RC .15 .40
312 Darryl Williams .07 .20
313 Thomas Smith RC .15 .40
314 Dennis Brown .07 .20
315 Marvin Jones RC .15 .40
316 Andre Tippett .07 .20
317 Demetrius DuBose RC .07 .20
318 Kirk Lowdermilk .07 .20
319 Shane Dronett .07 .20
320 Terry Kirby RC .30 .75
321 Qadry Ismail RC .30 .75
322 Lorenzo Lynch .07 .20
323 Willie Drewrey .07 .20
324 Jessie Tuggle .07 .20
325 Leroy Hoard .15 .40
326 Mark Collins .07 .20
327 Darrell Green .07 .20
328 Anthony Miller .15 .40
329 Brad Muster .07 .20
330 Jim Kelly FOIL .60 1.50
331 Sean Gilbert .15 .40
332 Tim McKyer .07 .20
333 Scott Mersereau .07 .20
334 Willie Davis .30 .75
335 Brett Favre FOIL 3.00 6.00
336 Kevin Gogan .07 .20
337 Jim Harbaugh .30 .75
338 James Trapp RC .07 .20
339 Pete Stoyanovich .07 .20
340 Jerry Rice FOIL 1.50 3.00
341 Gary Anderson RB .07 .20
342 Carlton Gray RC .07 .20
343 Dermontti Dawson .15 .40
344 Ray Buchanan RC .30 .75
345 Derrick Fenner .07 .20
346 Dennis Smith .07 .20
347 Todd Rucci RC .07 .20
348 Seth Joyner .07 .20
349 Jim McMahon .15 .40
350 Rodney Hampton .15 .40
351 Al Smith .07 .20
352 Steve Everitt RC .07 .20
353 Vinnie Clark .07 .20
354 Eric Swann .15 .40
355 Brian Mitchell .15 .40
356 Will Shields RC .30 .75
357 Cornelius Bennett .15 .40
358 Darrin Smith RC .15 .40
359 Chris Mims .07 .20
360 Blair Thomas .07 .20
361 Dennis Gibson .07 .20
362 Santana Dotson .15 .40
363 Mark Ingram .07 .20
364 Don Mosebar .07 .20
365 Ty Detmer .30 .75
366 Bob Christian RC .07 .20
367 Adrian Hardy .07 .20
368 Vaughan Johnson .07 .20
369 Jim Everett .15 .40
370 Ricky Sanders .07 .20
371 Jonathan Hayes .07 .20
372 Bruce Matthews .07 .20
373 Darren Drozdov RC .30 .75
374 Scott Brumfield RC .07 .20
375 Cortez Kennedy .15 .40
376 Tim Harris .07 .20
377 Neil O'Donnell .30 .75
378 Robert Smith RC 1.25 3.00
379 Mike Caldwell RC .07 .20
380 Burt Grossman .07 .20
381 Corey Miller .07 .20
382 Kevin Williams RC .15 .40
383 Ken Harvey .07 .20
384 Greg Robinson RC .07 .20
385 Harold Alexander RC .07 .20
386 Andre Reed .15 .40
387 Reggie Langhorne .07 .20
388 Courtney Hawkins .07 .20
389 James Hasty .07 .20
390 Pat Swilling .07 .20
391 Chris Slade RC .15 .40
392 Keith Byars .07 .20
393 Dalton Hilliard .07 .20
394 David Williams .07 .20
395 Terry Obee RC .07 .20
396 Heath Sherman .07 .20
397 John Taylor .15 .40
398 Irv Eatman .07 .20
399 Johnny Holland .07 .20
400 John Elway FOIL 2.50 6.00
401 Clay Matthews .15 .40
402 Dave Meggett .07 .20
403 Eric Green .07 .20
404 Bryan Cox .07 .20
405 Jay Novacek .15 .40
406 Kenneth Davis .07 .20
407 Lamar Thomas RC .07 .20
408 Lance Gunn RC .07 .20
409 Audray McMillian .07 .20
410 Derrick Thomas FOIL .60 1.50
411 Rufus Porter .07 .20
412 Coleman Rudolph RC .07 .20
413 Mark Rypien .07 .20
414 Duane Bickett .07 .20
415 Chris Singleton .07 .20
416 Mitch Lyons RC .07 .20
417 Bill Fralic .07 .20
418 Gary Plummer .07 .20
419 Ricky Proehl .07 .20
420 Howie Long .30 .75
421 Willie Roaf RC .60 1.50
422 Checklist 1-212 .07 .20
423 Checklist 213-423 .07 .20

1994 Bowman

The 1994 Bowman set consists of 390 standard-size cards. The set includes a 30-card foil subset (215-244, one per pack) of rookies. Rookie Cards include Mario Bates, Isaac Bruce, Lake Dawson, Trent Dilfer, Bert Emanuel, William Floyd, Marshall Faulk, Gus Frerotte, Charles Johnson, Errict Rhett, Darnay Scott and Heath Shuler.

COMPLETE SET (390) 15.00 40.00
1 Dan Wilkinson RC .15 .40
2 Marshall Faulk RC 6.00 15.00
3 Heath Shuler RC .30 .75
4 Willie McGinest RC .30 .75
5 Trent Dilfer RC 1.25 3.00
6 Brent Jones .15 .40
7 Sam Adams RC .15 .40
8 Randy Baldwin .07 .20
9 Jamir Miller RC .15 .40
10 John Thierry RC .07 .20
11 Aaron Glenn RC .30 .75
12 Joe Johnson RC .07 .20
13 Bernard Williams RC .07 .20
14 Wayne Gandy RC .07 .20
15 Aaron Taylor RC .07 .20
16 Charles Johnson RC .30 .75
17 Dewayne Washington RC .15 .40
18 Bernie Kosar .15 .40
19 Johnnie Morton RC 1.00 2.50
20 Rob Fredrickson RC .15 .40
21 Shante Carver RC .07 .20
22 Thomas Lewis RC .15 .40
23 Greg Hill RC .30 .75
24 Cris Dishman .07 .20
25 Jeff Burris RC .15 .40
26 Isaac Davis RC .07 .20
27 Bert Emanuel RC .30 .75
28 Allen Aldridge RC .07 .20
29 Kevin Lee RC .07 .20
30 Chris Brantley RC .07 .20
31 Rich Braham RC .07 .20
32 Ricky Watters .15 .40
33 Quentin Coryatt .07 .20
34 Hardy Nickerson .15 .40
35 Johnny Johnson .07 .20
36 Ken Harvey .07 .20
37 Chris Zorich .07 .20
38 Chris Warren .15 .40
39 David Palmer RC .30 .75
40 Chris Miller .07 .20
41 Ken Ruettgers .07 .20
42 Joe Panos RC .07 .20
43 Mario Bates RC .30 .75
44 Harry Colon .07 .20
45 Barry Foster .07 .20
46 Steve Tasker .15 .40
47 Richmond Webb .07 .20
48 James Folston RC .07 .20
49 Erik Williams .07 .20
50 Rodney Hampton .15 .40
51 Derek Russell .07 .20
52 Greg Montgomery .07 .20
53 Anthony Phillips .07 .20
54 Andre Coleman RC .07 .20
55 Gary Brown .07 .20
56 Neil Smith .15 .40
57 Myron Baker .07 .20
58 Sean Dawkins RC .30 .75
59 Marvin Washington .07 .20
60 Steve Beuerlein .15 .40
61 Brentson Buckner RC .07 .20
62 William Gaines RC .07 .20
63 LeShon Johnson RC .15 .40
64 Errict Rhett RC .30 .75
65 Jim Everett .15 .40
66 Desmond Howard .15 .40
67 Jack Del Rio .07 .20
68 Isaac Bruce RC 6.00 12.00
69 Van Malone RC .07 .20
70 Jim Kelly .30 .75
71 Leon Lett .07 .20
72 Greg Robinson .07 .20
73 Ryan Yarborough RC .07 .20
74 Terry Wooden .07 .20
75 Eric Allen .07 .20
76 Ernest Givins .15 .40
77 Marcus Spears RC .07 .20
78 Thomas Randolph RC .07 .20
79 Willie Clark RC .07 .20
80 John Elway 1.50 4.00
81 Aubrey Beavers RC .07 .20
82 Jeff Cothran RC .07 .20
83 Norm Johnson .07 .20
84 Donnell Bennett RC .30 .75
85 Phillippi Sparks .07 .20
86 Scott Mitchell .15 .40
87 Bucky Brooks RC .07 .20
88 Courtney Hawkins .07 .20
89 Kevin Greene .15 .40
90 Doug Nussmeier RC .07 .20
91 Floyd Turner .07 .20
92 Anthony Newman .07 .20
93 Vinny Testaverde .15 .40
94 Ronnie Lott .15 .40
95 Troy Aikman .75 2.00
96 John Taylor .15 .40
97 Henry Ellard .15 .40
98 Carl Lee .07 .20
99 Terry McDaniel .07 .20
100 Joe Montana 1.50 4.00
101 David Klingler .07 .20
102 Bruce Walker RC .07 .20
103 Rick Cunningham RC .07 .20
104 Robert Delpino .07 .20
105 Mark Ingram .07 .20
106 Leslie O'Neal .07 .20
107 Darrell Thompson .07 .20
108 Dave Meggett .07 .20
109 Chris Gardocki .07 .20
110 Andre Rison .15 .40
111 Kelvin Martin .07 .20
112 Marcus Robertson .07 .20
113 Jason Gildon RC 1.25 3.00
114 Mel Gray .07 .20
115 Tommy Vardell .07 .20
116 Dexter Carter .07 .20
117 Scottie Graham RC .15 .40
118 Horace Copeland .07 .20
119 Cornelius Bennett .15 .40
120 Chris Maumalanga RC .07 .20
121 Mo Lewis .07 .20
122 Toby Wright RC .07 .20
123 George Hegamin RC .07 .20
124 Chip Lohmiller .07 .20
125 Calvin Jones RC .07 .20
126 Steve Shine .07 .20
127 Chuck Levy RC .07 .20
128 Sam Mills .07 .20
129 Terance Mathis .15 .40
130 Randall Cunningham .30 .75
131 John Fina .07 .20
132 Reggie White .30 .75
133 Tom Waddle .07 .20
134 Chris Calloway .07 .20
135 Kevin Mawae RC .30 .75
136 Lake Dawson RC .15 .40
137 Alai Kalaniuvalu .07 .20
138 Tom Nalen RC .30 .75
139 Cody Carlson .07 .20
140 Dan Marino 1.50 4.00
141 Harris Barton .07 .20
142 Don Mosebar .07 .20
143 Romeo Bandison .07 .20
144 Bruce Smith .30 .75
145 Warren Moon .30 .75
146 David Lutz .07 .20
147 Dermontti Dawson .15 .40
148 Ricky Proehl .07 .20
149 Lou Benfatti RC .07 .20
150 Craig Erickson .07 .20
151 Sean Gilbert .07 .20
152 Zefross Moss .07 .20
153 Darnay Scott RC .50 1.25
154 Courtney Hall .07 .20
155A Brian Mitchell .07 .20
155B Mike Fox UER .07 .20
(intended to be card 366)
156 Joe Burch UER RC .07 .20
157 Terry Mickens .07 .20
158 Jay Novacek .15 .40
159 Chris Gedney .07 .20
160 Bruce Matthews .07 .20
161 Marlo Perry RC .07 .20
162 Vince Buck .07 .20
163 Michael Bates .07 .20
164 Willie Davis .15 .40
165 Mike Pritchard .07 .20
166 Doug Riesenberg .07 .20
167 Herschel Walker .15 .40
168 Tim Ruddy RC .07 .20
169 William Floyd RC .30 .75
170 John Randle .15 .40
171 Winston Moss .07 .20
172 Thurman Thomas .30 .75
173 Eric England RC .07 .20
174 Vincent Brisby .15 .40
175 Greg Lloyd .15 .40
176 Paul Gruber .07 .20
177 Brad Ottis RC .07 .20
178 George Teague .07 .20
179 Willie Jackson RC .30 .75
180 Barry Sanders 1.25 3.00
181 Brian Washington .07 .20
182 Michael Jackson .15 .40
183 Jason Mathews RC .07 .20
184 Chester McGlockton .07 .20
185 Tydus Winans RC .07 .20
186 Michael Haynes .15 .40
187 Erik Kramer .15 .40
188 Chris Doleman .07 .20
189 Haywood Jeffires .15 .40
190 Larry Whigham RC .07 .20
191 Shawn Jefferson .07 .20
192 Pete Stoyanovich .07 .20
193 Rod Bernstine .07 .20
194 William Thomas .07 .20
195 Marcus Allen .30 .75
196 Dave Brown .15 .40
197 Harold Bishop RC .07 .20
198 Lorenzo Lynch .07 .20
199 Dwight Stone .07 .20
200 Jerry Rice .75 2.00
201 Rocket Ismail .15 .40
202 LeRoy Butler .07 .20
203 Glenn Parker .07 .20
204 Bruce Armstrong .07 .20
205 Shane Conlan .07 .20
206 Russell Maryland .07 .20
207 Herman Moore .30 .75
208 Eric Martin .07 .20
209 John Friesz .15 .40
210 Boomer Esiason .15 .40
211 Jim Harbaugh .30 .75
212 Harold Green .07 .20
213 Perry Klein RC .07 .20
214 Eric Metcalf .15 .40
215 Steve Everitt .07 .20
216 Victor Bailey .07 .20
217 Lincoln Kennedy .07 .20
218 Glyn Milburn .15 .40
219 John Copeland .07 .20
220 Drew Bledsoe .75 2.00
221 Kevin Williams WR .15 .40
222 Roosevelt Potts .07 .20
223 Troy Drayton .07 .20
224 Terry Kirby .30 .75
225 Ronald Moore .07 .20
226 Tyrone Hughes .15 .40
227 Wayne Simmons .07 .20
228 Tony McGee .07 .20
229 Derek Brown RBK .07 .20
230 Jason Elam .15 .40
231 Qadry Ismail .30 .75
232 O.J. McDuffie .30 .75
233 Mike Caldwell .07 .20
234 Reggie Brooks .15 .40
235 Rick Mirer .30 .75
236 Steve Tovar .07 .20
237 Patrick Robinson .07 .20
238 Tom Carter .07 .20
239 Ben Coates .15 .40
240 Jerome Bettis .50 1.25
241 Garrison Hearst .30 .75
242 Natrone Means .30 .75
243 Dana Stubblefield .15 .40
244 Willie Roaf .07 .20
245 Cortez Kennedy .15 .40
246 Todd Steussie RC .15 .40
247 Pat Coleman .07 .20
248 David Wyman .07 .20
249 Jeremy Lincoln .07 .20
250 Carlester Crumpler .07 .20
251 Dale Carter .07 .20
252 Corey Raymond RC .07 .20
253 Bryan Cox .07 .20
254 Charlie Garner RC 1.25 3.00
255 Jeff Hostetler .15 .40
256 Shane Bonham RC .07 .20
257 Thomas Everett .07 .20
258 John Jackson T .07 .20
259 Terry Irving RC .07 .20
260 Corey Sawyer .15 .40
261 Rob Waldrop RC .07 .20
262 Curtis Conway .30 .75
263 Winfred Tubbs RC .15 .40
264 Sean Jones .07 .20
265 James Washington .07 .20
266 Lonnie Johnson RC .07 .20
267 Rob Moore .15 .40
268 Flipper Anderson .07 .20
269 Jon Hand .07 .20
270 Joe Patton RC .07 .20
271 Howard Ballard .07 .20
272 Fernando Smith RC .07 .20
273 Jessie Tuggle .07 .20
274 John Alt .07 .20
275 Corey Miller .07 .20
276 Gus Frerotte RC 1.25 3.00
277 Jeff Cross .07 .20
278 Kevin Smith .07 .20
279 Corey Louchiey RC .07 .20
280 Micheal Barrow .07 .20
281 Jim Flanigan RC .15 .40
282 Calvin Williams .15 .40
283 Jeff Jaeger .07 .20
284 John Reece RC .07 .20
285 Jason Hanson .07 .20
286 Kurt Haws RC .07 .20
287 Eric Davis .07 .20
288 Maurice Hurst .07 .20
289 Kirk Lowdermilk .07 .20
290 Rod Woodson .15 .40
291 Andre Reed .15 .40
292 Vince Workman .07 .20
293 Wayne Martin .07 .20
294 Keith Lyle RC .07 .20
295 Brett Favre 1.50 4.00
296 Doug Brien RC .07 .20
297 Junior Seau .30 .75
298 Randall McDaniel .07 .20
299 Johnny Mitchell .07 .20
300 Emmitt Smith 1.25 3.00
301 Michael Brooks .07 .20
302 Steve Jackson .07 .20
303 Jeff George .30 .75
304 Irving Fryar .15 .40
305 Derrick Thomas .30 .75
306 Dante Jones .07 .20
307 Darrell Green .07 .20
308 Mark Bavaro .07 .20
309 Eugene Robinson .07 .20
310 Shannon Sharpe .15 .40
311 Michael Timpson .07 .20
312 Kevin Mitchell RC .07 .20
313 Stevon Moore .07 .20
314 Eric Swann .15 .40
315 James Buslic RC .30 .75
316 Robert Brooks .30 .75
317 Pete Pierson RC .07 .20
318 Jim Sweeney .07 .20
319 Anthony Smith .07 .20
320 Rohn Stark .07 .20
321 Gary Anderson K .07 .20
322 Robert Porcher .07 .20
323 Darryl Talley .07 .20
324 Stan Humphries .15 .40
325 Shelly Hammonds RC .07 .20
326 Jim McMahon .15 .40
327 Lamont Warren RC .07 .20
328 Chris Penn RC .07 .20
329 Tony Woods .07 .20
330 Raymont Harris RC .30 .75
331 Mitch Davis RC .07 .20
332 Michael Irvin .30 .75
333 Kent Graham .15 .40
334 Brian Blades .15 .40
335 Lomas Brown .07 .20
336 Willie Drewrey .07 .20
337 Russell Freeman .07 .20
338 Eric Zomalt RC .07 .20
339 Santana Dotson .15 .40
340 Sterling Sharpe .15 .40
341 Ray Crittenden RC .07 .20
342 Perry Carter RC .07 .20
343 Austin Robbins .07 .20
344 Mike Wells RC .07 .20
345 Toddrick McIntosh RC .07 .20
346 Mark Carrier WR .15 .40
347 Eugene Daniel .07 .20
348 Tre Johnson RC .07 .20
349 D.J. Johnson .07 .20
350 Steve Young .60 1.50
351 Jim Pyne RC .07 .20
352 Jocelyn Borgella RC .07 .20
353 Pat Carter .07 .20
354 Sam Rogers RC .07 .20
355 Jason Sehorn RC .50 1.25
356 Darren Carrington .07 .20
357 Lamar Smith RC 1.50 4.00
358 James Burton RC .07 .20
359 Darrin Smith .07 .20
360 Marco Coleman .07 .20
361 Webster Slaughter .07 .20
362 Lewis Tillman .07 .20
363 David Alexander .07 .20
364 Bradford Banta RC .07 .20
365 Erric Pegram .07 .20
367 Jeff Lageman .07 .20
368 Kurt Gouveia .07 .20
369 Tim Brown .30 .75
370 Seth Joyner .07 .20
371 Irv Eatman .07 .20
372 Dorsey Levens RC 1.50 4.00
373 Anthony Pleasant .07 .20
374 Henry Jones .07 .20
375 Cris Carter .40 1.00
376 Morten Andersen .07 .20
377 Neil O'Donnell .30 .75
378 Tyronne Drakeford RC .07 .20
379 John Carney .07 .20
380 Vincent Brown .07 .20
381 J.J. Birden .07 .20
382 Chris Spielman .15 .40
383 Mark Bortz .07 .20
384 Ray Childress .07 .20
385 Carlton Bailey .07 .20
386 Charles Haley .15 .40
387 Shane Dronett .07 .20
388 Jon Vaughn .07 .20
389 Checklist 1-195 .07 .20
390 Checklist 196-390 .07 .20

1995 Bowman

This 357-card standard size set was issued by Topps. Parallel sets of the expansion team cards and rookie draft picks were included. The expansion team parallel had extra gold foil while the draft pick parallel had a "First Round" stamp on the front. Rookie Cards in this set include Jeff Blake, Ki-Jana Carter, Kerry Collins, Joey Galloway, Napoleon Kaufman, Steve McNair, Curtis Martin, Rashan Salaam, Chris Sanders, Kordell Stewart, J.J. Stokes, Rodney Thomas, Tamarick Vanover and Michael Westbrook.

COMPLETE SET (357) 25.00 60.00
1 Ki-Jana Carter RC .30 .75
2 Tony Boselli RC .30 .75
3 Steve McNair RC 3.00 8.00
4 Michael Westbrook RC .25 .60
5 Kerry Collins RC 2.00 5.00
6 Kevin Carter RC .30 .75
7 Mike Mamula RC .07 .20
8 Joey Galloway RC 1.50 4.00
9 Kyle Brady RC .30 .75
10 J.J. Stokes RC .30 .75
11 Derrick Alexander DE RC .07 .20
12 Warren Sapp RC 1.50 4.00
13 Mark Fields RC .30 .75
14 Ruben Brown RC .30 .75
15 Ellis Johnson RC .07 .20
16 Hugh Douglas RC .30 .75
17 Mike Pelton RC .07 .20
18 Napoleon Kaufman RC 1.25 3.00
19 James O. Stewart RC 1.00 2.50
20 Luther Elliss RC .07 .20
21 Rashaan Salaam RC .15 .40
22 Tyrone Poole RC .30 .75
23 Ty Law RC 1.25 3.00
24 Korey Stringer RC .25 .60
25 Billy Milner RC .07 .20
26 Devin Bush RC .07 .20
27 Mark Bruener RC .15 .40
28 Derrick Brooks RC 1.50 4.00
29 Blake Brockermeyer RC .07 .20
30 Alundis Brice RC .07 .20
31 Trezelle Jenkins RC .07 .20
32 Craig Newsome RC .07 .20
33 Fred Barnett .10 .30
34 Ray Childress .05 .15
35 Chris Miller .05 .15
36 Charles Haley .10 .30
37 Ray Crittenden .05 .15
38 Gus Frerotte .10 .30
39 Jeff George .10 .30
40 Dan Marino 1.25 3.00
41 Shawn Lee .05 .15
42 Herman Moore .25 .60
43 Chris Calloway .05 .15
44 Jeff Graham .05 .15
45 Ray Buchanan .05 .15
46 Doug Pelfrey .05 .15
47 Lake Dawson .10 .30
48 Glenn Parker .05 .15
49 Terry McDaniel .05 .15
50 Rod Woodson .10 .30
51 Santana Dotson .05 .15
52 Anthony Miller .10 .30
53 Bo Orlando .05 .15
54 David Palmer .10 .30
55 William Floyd .10 .30
56 Edgar Bennett .10 .30
57 Jeff Blake RC 1.00 2.50
58 Anthony Pleasant .05 .15
59 Quinn Early .10 .30
60 Bobby Houston .05 .15
61 Terrell Fletcher RC .07 .20
62 Gary Brown .05 .15
63 Dwayne Sabb .05 .15
64 Roman Phifer .05 .15
65 Sherman Williams RC .07 .20
66 Roosevelt Potts .05 .15
67 Darnay Scott .10 .30
68 Charlie Garner .25 .60
69 Bert Emanuel .25 .60
70 Herschel Walker .10 .30
71 Lorenzo Styles RC .07 .20
72 Andre Coleman .05 .15
73 Tyronne Drakeford .05 .15
74 Jay Novacek .10 .30
75 Raymont Harris .05 .15
76 Tamarick Vanover RC .30 .75
77 Tom Carter .05 .15
78 Eric Green .05 .15
79 Patrick Hunter .05 .15
80 Jeff Hostetler .10 .30
81 Robert Blackmon .05 .15
82 Anthony Cook RC .07 .20
83 Craig Erickson .05 .15
84 Glyn Milburn .05 .15
85 Greg Lloyd .10 .30
86 Brent Jones .05 .15
87 Barrett Brooks RC .07 .20
88 Alvin Harper .05 .15
89 Sean Jones .05 .15
90 Cris Carter .25 .60
91 Russell Copeland .05 .15
92 Frank Sanders RC .30 .75
93 Mo Lewis .05 .15
94 Michael Haynes .10 .30
95 Andre Rison .10 .30
96 Jesse James RC .07 .20
97 Stan Humphries .10 .30
98 James Hasty .05 .15
99 Ricardo McDonald .05 .15
100 Jerry Rice .60 1.50
101 Chris Hudson RC .07 .20
102 Dave Meggett .05 .15
103 Brian Mitchell .05 .15
104 Mike Johnson .05 .15
105 Kordell Stewart RC 1.50 4.00
106 Michael Brooks .05 .15
107 Steve Walsh .05 .15
108 Eric Metcalf .10 .30
109 Ricky Watters .10 .30
110 Brett Favre 1.25 3.00
111 Aubrey Beavers .05 .15
112 Brian Williams LB RC .07 .20
113 Eugene Robinson .05 .15
114 Matt O'Dwyer RC .07 .20
115 Micheal Barrow .05 .15
116 Rocket Ismail .10 .30
117 Scott Gragg RC .07 .20
118 Leon Lett .05 .15
119 Reggie Roby .05 .15
120 Marshall Faulk .75 2.00
121 Jack Jackson RC .07 .20
122 Keith Byars .05 .15
123 Eric Hill .05 .15
124 Todd Sauerbrun RC .07 .20
125 Dexter Carter .05 .15
126 Vinny Testaverde .10 .30
127 Shane Conlan .05 .15
128 Terrance Shaw RC .07 .20
129 Willie Roaf .05 .15
130 Jim Kelly .25 .60
131 Neil O'Donnell .10 .30
132 Ray McElroy RC .07 .20
133 Ed McDaniel .05 .15
134 Brian Gelzheiser RC .07 .20
135 Marcus Allen .25 .60
136 Carl Pickens .10 .30
137 Mike Verstegan RC .07 .20
138 Chris Mims .05 .15
139 Darryl Pounds RC .07 .20
140 Emmitt Smith 1.25 2.50
141 Mike Frederick RC .07 .20
142 Henry Ellard .10 .30
143 Willie McGinest .10 .30
144 Michael Roan RC .07 .20
145 Chris Spielman .10 .30
146 Darryl Talley .05 .15
147 Randall Cunningham .25 .60
148 Andrew Greene RC .07 .20
149 George Teague .05 .15
150 Tyrone Hughes .10 .30
151 Ron Davis RC .07 .20
152 Stevon Moore .05 .15
153 Merton Hanks .05 .15
154 Darren Perry .05 .15
155 Dave Brown .10 .30
156 Mike Morton RC .07 .20
157 Seth Joyner .05 .15
158 Bryan Cox .05 .15
159 Corey Fuller RC .07 .20
160 John Elway 1.25 3.00
161 Dewayne Washington .10 .30
162 Chris Warren .10 .30
163 Jeff Kopp RC .07 .20
164 Sean Dawkins .10 .30
165 Mark Carrier DB .05 .15
166 Andre Hastings .10 .30
167 Derek West RC .07 .20
168 Glenn Montgomery .05 .15
169 Trent Dilfer .25 .60
170 Rob Johnson RC 1.00 2.50
171 Todd Scott .05 .15
172 Charles Johnson .10 .30
173 Kez McCorvey RC .07 .20
174 Rob Fredrickson .05 .15
175 Corey Sawyer .05 .15
176 Brett Perriman .10 .30
177 Ken Dilger RC .30 .75
178 Dana Stubblefield .10 .30
179 Eric Allen .05 .15
180 Drew Bledsoe .40 1.00
181 Tyrone Davis RC .07 .20
182 Reggie Brooks .10 .30
183 Dale Carter .10 .30
184 William Henderson RC 1.25 3.00
185 Reggie White .25 .60
186 Lorenzo White .05 .15
187 Leslie O'Neal .10 .30
188 Stoney Case RC .07 .20
189 Jeff Burris .05 .15
190 Leroy Hoard .05 .15
191 Thomas Randolph .05 .15
192 Rodney Thomas RC .15 .40
193 Quentin Coryatt .10 .30
194 Terry Wooden .05 .15
195 David Sloan RC .07 .20
196 Bernie Parmalee .10 .30
197 Zack Crockett RC .15 .40
198 Troy Aikman .60 1.50
199 Bruce Smith .25 .60
200 Eric Zeier RC .30 .75
201 Anthony Smith .05 .15
202 Jake Reed .10 .30
203 Hardy Nickerson .05 .15
204 Patrick Riley RC .07 .20
205 Bruce Matthews .05 .15
206 Larry Centers .10 .30
207 Troy Drayton .05 .15
208 John Burrough RC .07 .20
209 Jason Elam .10 .30
210 Donnell Woolford .05 .15
211 Sam Shade RC .07 .20
212 Kevin Greene .10 .30
213 Ronald Moore .05 .15
214 Shane Hannah RC .07 .20
215 Jim Everett .05 .15
216 Scott Mitchell .10 .30
217 Antonio Freeman RC 1.25 3.00
218 Tony McGee .05 .15
219 Clay Matthews .10 .30
220 Neil Smith .10 .30
221 Mark Williams FOIL .15 .40
222 Derrick Graham FOIL RC .15 .40
223 Mike Hollis FOIL .15 .40
224 Darion Conner FOIL .15 .40
225 Steve Beuerlein FOIL .15 .40
226 Rod Smith DB FOIL .15 .40
227 James Williams LB FOIL .15 .40
228 Bob Christian FOIL .15 .40
229 Jeff Lageman FOIL .15 .40
230 Frank Reich FOIL .15 .40
231 Harry Colon FOIL .15 .40
232 Carlton Bailey FOIL .15 .40
233 Mickey Washington FOIL .15 .40
234 Shawn Bouwens FOIL .15 .40
235 Don Beebe FOIL .15 .40
236 Kelvin Pritchett FOIL .15 .40
237 Tommy Barnhardt FOIL .15 .40
238 Mike Dumas FOIL .15 .40
239 Brett Maxie FOIL .15 .40
240 Desmond Howard FOIL .15 .40
241 Sam Mills FOIL .15 .40
242 Keith Goganious FOIL .15 .40
243 Bubba McDowell FOIL .15 .40
244 Vinnie Clark FOIL .15 .40
245 Lamar Lathon FOIL .15 .40
246 Bryan Barker FOIL .15 .40
247 Darren Carrington FOIL .15 .40
248 Jay Barker RC .07 .20
249 Eric Davis .05 .15
250 Heath Shuler .10 .30
251 Donta Jones RC .07 .20
252 LeRoy Butler .05 .15
253 Michael Zordich .05 .15
254 Cortez Kennedy .10 .30
255 Brian DeMarco RC .07 .20
256 Randal Hill .05 .15
257 Michael Irvin .25 .60
258 Natrone Means .10 .30
259 Linc Harden RC .07 .20
260 Jerome Bettis .25 .60
261 Tony Bennett .05 .15
262 Dameian Jeffries RC .07 .20
263 Cornelius Bennett .10 .30
264 Chris Zorich .05 .15
265 Bobby Taylor RC .30 .75
266 Terrell Buckley .05 .15
267 Troy Dumas RC .07 .20
268 Rodney Hampton .10 .30
269 Steve Everitt .05 .15
270 Mel Gray .05 .15
271 Antonio Armstrong RC .07 .20
272 Jim Harbaugh .10 .30
273 Gary Clark .05 .15
274 Tau Pupua RC .07 .20
275 Warren Moon .10 .30
276 Corey Croom .05 .15
277 Tony Berti RC .07 .20
278 Shannon Sharpe .10 .30
279 Boomer Esiason .10 .30
280 Aeneas Williams .05 .15
281 Lethon Flowers RC .07 .20
282 Derek Brown TE .05 .15
283 Charlie Williams RC .07 .20
284 Dan Wilkinson .10 .30
285 Mike Sherrard .05 .15
286 Evan Pilgrim RC .07 .20
287 Kimble Anders .10 .30
288 Greg Jefferson RC .07 .20
289 Ken Norton .10 .30
290 Terance Mathis .10 .30
291 Torey Hunter RC .07 .20
292 Ken Harvey .05 .15
293 Irving Fryar .10 .30
294 Michael Reed RC .07 .20
295 Andre Reed .10 .30
296 Vencie Glenn .05 .15
297 Corey Swinson .05 .15
298 Harvey Williams .05 .15
299 Willie Davis .10 .30
300 Barry Sanders 1.00 2.50
301 Curtis Martin RC 3.00 8.00
302 Johnny Mitchell .05 .15
303 Daryl Johnston .10 .30
304 Lorenzo Lynch .05 .15
305 Christian Fauria RC .15 .40
306 Sean Gilbert .10 .30
307 Ray Zellars RC .15 .40
308 William Strong RC .07 .20
309 Jack Del Rio .05 .15
310 Junior Seau .25 .60
311 Justin Armour RC .07 .20
312 Eric Bjornson RC .07 .20
313 Vincent Brown .05 .15
314 Darius Holland RC .07 .20
315 Chad May RC .07 .20
316 Simon Fletcher .05 .15
317 Roell Preston RC .10 .30
318 John Thierry .05 .15
319 Orlando Thomas RC .07 .20
320 Zach Wiegert RC .07 .20
321 Derrick Alexander WR .25 .60
322 Chris Cowart RC .07 .20
323 Chris Sanders RC .15 .40
324 Robert Brooks .25 .60
325 Todd Collins RC 1.00 2.50
326 Ken Irvin RC .07 .20
327 Erric Pegram .10 .30
328 Damien Covington RC .07 .20
329 Brendan Stai RC .07 .20
330 James A.Stewart RC .07 .20
331 Jessie Tuggle .05 .15
332 Marco Coleman .05 .15
333 Steve Young .50 1.25
334 Greg Hill .10 .30
335 Darryl Williams .05 .15
336 Calvin Williams .10 .30
337 Cris Dishman .05 .15
338 Anthony Morgan .05 .15
339 Renaldo Turnbull .05 .15
340 Rick Mirer .10 .30
341 Tim Brown .25 .60
342 Dennis Gibson .05 .15
343 Brad Baxter .05 .15
344 Henry Jones .05 .15
345 Johnny Bailey .05 .15
346 Rocket Ismail .10 .30
347 Richmond Webb .05 .15
348 Robert Jones .05 .15
349 Garrison Hearst .25 .60
350 Errict Rhett .10 .30
351 Steve Atwater .05 .15
352 Joe Cain .05 .15
353 Ben Coates .10 .30
354 Aaron Glenn .05 .15
355 Antonio Langham .05 .15
356 Eugene Daniel .05 .15
357 Tim Bowens .05 .15

1995 Bowman Expansion Team Gold

EXPANSION GOLDS: 1.5X TO 3X BASIC CARDS
STATED ODDS 1:12

1995 Bowman First Round Picks

COMPLETE SET (27) 30.00 60.00
STATED ODDS 1:12
1 Ki-Jana Carter .60 1.50
2 Tony Boselli .60 1.50
3 Steve McNair 6.00 15.00
4 Michael Westbrook .50 1.25
5 Kerry Collins 4.00 10.00
6 Kevin Carter .60 1.50
7 Mike Mamula .15 .40
8 Joey Galloway 3.00 8.00
9 Kyle Brady .60 1.50
10 J.J.Stokes .60 1.50
11 Derrick Alexander DE .15 .40
12 Warren Sapp 3.00 8.00
13 Mark Fields .60 1.50
14 Ruben Brown .60 1.50
15 Ellis Johnson .15 .40
16 Hugh Douglas .60 1.50
18 Napoleon Kaufman 2.50 6.00
19 James O. Stewart 2.00 5.00
20 Luther Elliss .15 .40
21 Rashaan Salaam .30 .75
22 Tyrone Poole .60 1.50
23 Ty Law 2.50 6.00
28 Derrick Brooks 3.00 8.00
32 Craig Newsome .15 .40
76 Tamarick Vanover .60 1.50
92 Frank Sanders .60 1.50
200 Eric Zeier .60 1.50

1998 Bowman

The 1998 Bowman set was issued in one series totalling 220 standard size cards. The 10-card packs retail for $2.50 each. The cards feature 150 veteran players and 70 prospects. The gold-foil fronts feature a silver and blue logo design for the prospect cards, while the veteran cards show a silver and red design. A 220-card Bowman Inter-State parallel set was also produced which indicated what state the pictured player was from. The card backs display a custom-tailored vanity plate. One card from this parallel set was inserted in every pack.

COMPLETE SET (220) 20.00 50.00
1 Peyton Manning RC 10.00 25.00
2 Keith Brooking RC .60 1.50
3 Duane Starks RC .30 .75
4 Takeo Spikes RC .60 1.50
5 Andre Wadsworth RC .50 1.25
6 Greg Ellis RC .30 .75
7 Brian Griese RC 1.25 3.00
8 Germane Crowell RC .50 1.25
9 Jerome Pathon RC .60 1.50
10 Ryan Leaf RC .60 1.50
11 Fred Taylor RC 1.00 2.50
12 Robert Edwards RC .50 1.25
13 Grant Wistrom RC .50 1.25
14 Robert Holcombe RC .50 1.25
15 Tim Dwight RC .60 1.50
16 Jacquez Green RC .50 1.25
17 Marcus Nash RC .30 .75
18 Jason Peter RC .30 .75
19 Anthony Simmons RC .50 1.25
20 Curtis Enis RC .30 .75
21 John Avery RC .50 1.25
22 Pat Johnson RC .50 1.25
23 Joe Jurevicius RC .60 1.50
24 Brian Simmons RC .50 1.25
25 Kevin Dyson RC .60 1.50
26 Skip Hicks RC .50 1.25
27 Hines Ward RC 3.00 8.00
28 Tavian Banks RC .50 1.25
29 Ahman Green RC 1.50 4.00
30 Tony Simmons RC .50 1.25
31 Charles Johnson .10 .30
32 Freddie Jones .10 .30
33 Joey Galloway .20 .50
34 Tony Banks .20 .50
35 Jake Plummer .30 .75
36 Reidel Anthony .20 .50
37 Steve McNair .30 .75
38 Michael Westbrook .20 .50
39 Chris Sanders .10 .30
40 Isaac Bruce .30 .75
41 Charlie Garner .20 .50
42 Wayne Chrebet .30 .75
43 Michael Strahan .20 .50
44 Brad Johnson .30 .75
45 Mike Alstott .30 .75
46 Tony Gonzalez .30 .75
47 Johnnie Morton .20 .50
48 Darnay Scott .20 .50
49 Rae Carruth .10 .30
50 Terrell Davis .30 .75
51 Jermaine Lewis .20 .50
52 Frank Sanders .20 .50
53 Byron Hanspard .10 .30

54 Gus Frerotte .10 .30
55 Terry Glenn .30 .75
56 J.J. Stokes .20 .50
57 Will Blackwell .10 .30
58 Keyshawn Johnson .30 .75
59 Tiki Barber .30 .75
60 Dorsey Levens .30 .75
61 Zach Thomas .30 .75
62 Corey Dillon .30 .75
63 Antowain Smith .30 .75
64 Michael Sinclair .10 .30
65 Rod Smith .20 .50
66 Trent Dilfer .30 .75
67 Warren Sapp .20 .50
68 Charles Way .10 .30
69 Tamarick Vanover .10 .30
70 Drew Bledsoe .50 1.25
71 John Mobley .10 .30
72 Kerry Collins .20 .50
73 Peter Boulware .10 .30
74 Simeon Rice .20 .50
75 Eddie George .30 .75
76 Fred Lane .10 .30
77 Jamal Anderson .30 .75
78 Antonio Freeman .30 .75
79 Jason Sehorn .20 .50
80 Curtis Martin .30 .75
81 Bobby Hoying .20 .50
82 Garrison Hearst .30 .75
83 Glenn Foley .20 .50
84 Danny Kanell .20 .50
85 Kordell Stewart .30 .75
86 O.J. McDuffie .20 .50
87 Marvin Harrison .30 .75
88 Bobby Engram .20 .50
89 Chris Slade .10 .30
90 Warrick Dunn .30 .75
91 Ricky Watters .20 .50
92 Rickey Dudley .10 .30
93 Terrell Owens .30 .75
94 Karim Abdul-Jabbar .30 .75
95 Napoleon Kaufman .30 .75
96 Darrell Green .20 .50
97 Levon Kirkland .10 .30
98 Jeff George .20 .50
99 Andre Hastings .10 .30
100 John Elway 1.25 3.00
101 John Randle .20 .50
102 Andre Rison .20 .50
103 Keenan McCardell .20 .50
104 Marshall Faulk .40 1.00
105 Emmitt Smith 1.00 2.50
106 Robert Brooks .20 .50
107 Scott Mitchell .20 .50
108 Shannon Sharpe .20 .50
109 Deion Sanders .30 .75
110 Jerry Rice .60 1.50
111 Erik Kramer .10 .30
112 Michael Jackson .10 .30
113 Aeneas Williams .10 .30
114 Terry Allen .30 .75
115 Steve Young .40 1.00
116 Warren Moon .30 .75
117 Junior Seau .30 .75
118 Jerome Bettis .30 .75
119 Irving Fryar .20 .50
120 Barry Sanders 1.00 2.50
121 Tim Brown .30 .75
122 Chad Brown .10 .30
123 Ben Coates .20 .50
124 Robert Smith .30 .75
125 Brett Favre 1.25 3.00
126 Derrick Thomas .30 .75
127 Reggie White .30 .75
128 Troy Aikman .60 1.50
129 Jeff Blake .20 .50
130 Mark Brunell .30 .75
131 Curtis Conway .20 .50
132 Wesley Walls .20 .50
133 Thurman Thomas .30 .75
134 Chris Chandler .20 .50
135 Dan Marino 1.25 3.00
136 Larry Centers .10 .30
137 Shawn Jefferson .10 .30
138 Andre Reed .20 .50
139 Jake Reed .20 .50
140 Cris Carter .30 .75
141 Elvis Grbac .20 .50
142 Mark Chmura .20 .50
143 Michael Irvin .30 .75
144 Carl Pickens .20 .50
145 Herman Moore .20 .50
146 Marvin Jones .10 .30
147 Terance Mathis .20 .50
148 Rob Moore .20 .50
149 Bruce Smith .20 .50
150 Rob Johnson CL .10 .30
151 Leslie Shepherd .10 .30
152 Chris Spielman .10 .30
153 Tony McGee .10 .30
154 Kevin Smith .10 .30
155 Bill Romanowski .10 .30
156 Stephen Boyd .10 .30
157 James Stewart .20 .50
158 Jason Taylor .20 .50
159 Troy Drayton .10 .30
160 Mark Fields .10 .30
161 Jessie Armstead .10 .30
162 James Jett .20 .50
163 Bobby Taylor .10 .30
164 Kimble Anders .20 .50
165 Jimmy Smith .20 .50
166 Quentin Coryatt .10 .30
167 Bryant Westbrook .10 .30
168 Neil Smith .20 .50
169 Darren Woodson .10 .30
170 Ray Buchanan .10 .30
171 Earl Holmes .10 .30
172 Ray Lewis .30 .75
173 Steve Broussard .10 .30
174 Derrick Brooks .30 .75
175 Ken Harvey .10 .30
176 Darryll Lewis .10 .30
177 Derrick Rodgers .10 .30
178 James McKnight .30 .75
179 Cris Dishman .10 .30
180 Hardy Nickerson .10 .30
181 Charles Woodson RC 1.50 4.00
182 Randy Moss RC 5.00 12.00
183 Stephen Alexander RC .50 1.25
184 Samari Rolle RC .30 .75
185 Jamie Duncan RC .30 .75
186 Lance Schulters RC .30 .75
187 Tony Parrish RC .60 1.50
188 Corey Chavous RC .60 1.50
189 Jammi German RC .30 .75
190 Sam Cowart RC .50 1.25
191 Donald Hayes RC .50 1.25
192 R.W. McQuarters RC .50 1.25
193 Az-Zahir Hakim RC .60 1.50
194 Chris Fuamatu-Ma'afala RC .50 1.25
195 Allen Rossum RC .50 1.25
196 Jon Ritchie RC .50 1.25
197 Blake Spence RC .30 .75
198 Brian Alford RC .30 .75
199 Fred Weary RC .30 .75
200 Rod Rutledge RC .30 .75
201 Michael Myers RC .30 .75
202 Rashaan Shehee RC .50 1.25
203 Donovin Darius RC .50 1.25
204 E.G. Green RC .50 1.25
205 Vonnie Holliday RC .50 1.25
206 Charlie Batch RC .60 1.50
207 Michael Pittman RC .75 2.00
208 Artrell Hawkins RC .30 .75
209 Jonathan Quinn RC .60 1.50
210 Kailee Wong RC .30 .75
211 DeShea Townsend RC .30 .75
212 Patrick Surtain RC .60 1.50
213 Brian Kelly RC .50 1.25
214 Tebucky Jones RC .30 .75
215 Pete Gonzalez RC .30 .75
216 Shaun Williams RC .50 1.25
217 Scott Frost RC .30 .75
218 Leonard Little RC .60 1.50
219 Alonzo Mayes RC .30 .75
220 Cordell Taylor RC .30 .75

1998 Bowman Golden Anniversary

*STARS: 25X TO 60X HI COL.
*RCs: 6X TO 15X
STATED ODDS 1:180
STATED PRINT RUN 50 SERIAL #'d SETS
1 Peyton Manning 175.00 300.00

1998 Bowman Interstate

COMPLETE SET (220) 75.00 200.00
*STARS: 1.5X TO 3X BASIC CARDS
*RC'S: .6X TO 1.5X BASIC CARDS
STATED ODDS 1:1

1998 Bowman Rookie Autographs

Randomly inserted in packs at the rate of one in 360, this 11-card set features color action player photos with authentic signatures of the pictured player and a blue foil Topps Certified Autograph Issue Stamp. A silver foil parallel version was also produced with an insertion rate of one in 2,401 packs. A rare gold foil parallel version was produced with an insertion rate of one in 7,202 packs.
BLUE STATED ODDS 1:360
A1 Peyton Manning 350.00 500.00
A2 Andre Wadsworth 10.00 25.00
A3 Brian Griese 15.00 40.00
A4 Ryan Leaf 10.00 25.00
A5 Fred Taylor 6.00 15.00
A6 Robert Edwards 10.00 25.00
A7 Randy Moss 75.00 150.00
A8 Curtis Enis 10.00 25.00
A9 Kevin Dyson 10.00 25.00
A10 Charles Woodson 150.00 300.00
A11 Tim Dwight 12.50 30.00

1998 Bowman Rookie Autographs Gold

*GOLD FOILS: 1.2X TO 3X BLUE
1 Peyton Manning 800.00 1200.00
10 Charles Woodson 250.00 600.00

1998 Bowman Rookie Autographs Silver

*SILVER FOIL: .6X TO 1.5X BLUE
1 Peyton Manning 500.00 800.00
10 Charles Woodson 175.00 400.00

1998 Bowman Chrome Preview

Randomly inserted in Bowman packs at the rate of one in 12, this 10-card set features color action player photos of five rookies and five veterans printed using the technology created for the 1998 Bowman Chrome set which was released later in the year. A Refractor parallel version of this set was also produced with an insertion rate of 1:48.
COMPLETE SET (10) 20.00 50.00
STATED ODDS 1:12
*REFRACTORS: .75X TO 2X BASIC INSERTS
REFRACTOR STATED ODDS 1:48
BCP1 Peyton Manning 12.00 30.00
BCP2 Curtis Enis .60 1.50
BCP3 Kevin Dyson 1.25 3.00
BCP4 Robert Edwards .60 1.50
BCP5 Ryan Leaf 1.25 3.00
BCP6 Brett Favre 6.00 15.00
BCP7 John Elway 6.00 15.00
BCP8 Barry Sanders 5.00 12.00
BCP9 Kordell Stewart 1.50 4.00
BCP10 Terrell Davis 1.50 4.00

1998 Bowman Scout's Choice

Randomly inserted in packs at the rate of one in 12, this 14-card set features borderless color action photos of new players with serious potential printed on double-etched foil cards.
COMPLETE SET (14) 20.00 50.00
STATED ODDS 1:12
SC1 Peyton Manning 12.00 30.00
SC2 John Avery 1.00 2.50
SC3 Grant Wistrom 1.00 2.50
SC4 Kevin Dyson 1.25 3.00
SC5 Andre Wadsworth 1.00 2.50
SC6 Joe Jurevicius 1.25 3.00
SC7 Charles Woodson 3.00 8.00
SC8 Takeo Spikes 1.25 3.00
SC9 Fred Taylor 2.00 5.00
SC10 Ryan Leaf 1.25 3.00
SC11 Robert Edwards 1.00 2.50
SC12 Randy Moss 8.00 20.00
SC13 Pat Johnson 1.00 2.50
SC14 Curtis Enis .60 1.50

1999 Bowman

The 1999 Bowman set was released in mid October of 1999 as a 220-card single series set featuring 150 veteran players along with 70 rookie cards. The veteran cards are done in a silver and red design action shot and the rookies are done in a silver and blue logo design. Key rookies found within this set include Ricky Williams, Edgerrin James, and Tim Couch. A 220-card Bowman Interstate Parallel was also produced at a rate of 1 per pack which shows which state each player originated from. Also exists is a 220 card Bowman Gold Parallel which is identical to the regular base set card exept for the Team name being done in a gold foil. Authentic Signed Rookie autographed cards are also randomly inserted in packs. Also included is the 10 card Late Bloomers/Early Risers insert set featuring top second year players as well as veteran stars such as Dan Marino and Mark Brunell.
COMPLETE SET (220) 15.00 40.00
1 Dan Marino .50 1.25
2 Michael Westbrook .15 .40
3 Yancey Thigpen .15 .40
4 Tony Martin .20 .50
5 Michael Strahan .20 .50
6 Dedric Ward .15 .40
7 Joey Galloway .20 .50
8 Bobby Engram .15 .40
9 Frank Sanders .15 .40
10 Jake Plummer .15 .40
11 Eddie Kennison .20 .50
12 Curtis Martin .20 .50
13 Chris Spielman .20 .50
14 Trent Dilfer .15 .40
15 Tim Biakabutuka .20 .50
16 Elvis Grbac .15 .40
17 Charlie Batch .15 .40
18 Takeo Spikes .15 .40
19 Tony Banks .20 .50
20 Doug Flutie .25 .60
21 Ty Law .25 .60
22 Isaac Bruce .25 .60
23 James Jett .15 .40
24 Kent Graham .15 .40
25 Derrick Mayes .15 .40
26 Amani Toomer .15 .40
27 Ray Lewis .25 .60
28 Shawn Springs .15 .40
29 Warren Sapp .20 .50
30 Jamal Anderson .20 .50
31 Byron Bam Morris .15 .40
32 Johnnie Morton .20 .50
33 Terance Mathis .15 .40
34 Terrell Davis .20 .50
35 John Randle .25 .60
36 Vinny Testaverde .15 .40
37 Junior Seau .20 .50
38 Reidel Anthony .15 .40
39 Brad Johnson .20 .50
40 Emmitt Smith .40 1.00
41 Mo Lewis .15 .40
42 Terry Glenn .20 .50
43 Dorsey Levens .20 .50
44 Thurman Thomas .20 .50
45 Rob Moore .15 .40
46 Corey Dillon .15 .40
47 Jessie Armstead .20 .50
48 Marshall Faulk .20 .50
49 Charles Woodson .25 .60
50 John Elway .40 1.00
51 Kevin Dyson .15 .40
52 Tony Simmons .15 .40
53 Keenan McCardell .20 .50
54 O.J. Santiago .15 .40
55 Jermaine Lewis .15 .40
56 Herman Moore .20 .50
57 Gary Brown .15 .40
58 Jim Harbaugh .20 .50
59 Mike Alstott .15 .40
60 Brett Favre .50 1.25
61 Tim Brown .25 .60
62 Steve McNair .20 .50
63 Ben Coates .20 .50
64 Jerome Pathon .15 .40
65 Ray Buchanan .15 .40
66 Troy Aikman .30 .75
67 Andre Reed .25 .60
68 Bubby Brister .15 .40
69 Karim Abdul-Jabbar .15 .40
70 Peyton Manning .75 2.00
71 Charles Johnson .15 .40
72 Natrone Means .20 .50
73 Michael Sinclair .15 .40
74 Skip Hicks .15 .40
75 Derrick Alexander .15 .40
76 Wayne Chrebet .15 .40
77 Rod Smith .20 .50
78 Carl Pickens .20 .50
79 Adrian Murrell .15 .40
80 Fred Taylor .15 .40
81 Eric Moulds .15 .40
82 Lawrence Phillips .20 .50
83 Marvin Harrison .20 .50
84 Cris Carter .25 .60
85 Ike Hilliard .15 .40
86 Hines Ward .20 .50
87 Terrell Owens .20 .50
88 Ricky Proehl .15 .40
89 Bert Emanuel .20 .50
90 Randy Moss .20 .50
91 Aaron Glenn .15 .40
92 Robert Smith .15 .40
93 Andre Hastings .15 .40
94 Jake Reed .20 .50
95 Curtis Enis .15 .40
96 Andre Wadsworth .15 .40
97 Ed McCaffrey .20 .50
98 Zach Thomas .20 .50
99 Kerry Collins .15 .40
100 Drew Bledsoe .20 .50
101 Germane Crowell .15 .40
102 Bryan Still .15 .40
103 Chad Brown .15 .40
104 Jacquez Green .15 .40
105 Garrison Hearst .15 .40
106 Napoleon Kaufman .15 .40
107 Ricky Watters .20 .50
108 O.J. McDuffie .20 .50
109 Keyshawn Johnson .20 .50
110 Jerome Bettis .25 .60
111 Duce Staley .15 .40
112 Curtis Conway .20 .50
113 Chris Chandler .20 .50
114 Marcus Nash .15 .40
115 Stephen Alexander .15 .40
116 Darnay Scott .15 .40
117 Bruce Smith .20 .50
118 Priest Holmes .15 .40
119 Mark Brunell .20 .50
120 Jerry Rice .60 1.50
121 Randall Cunningham .20 .50
122 Scott Mitchell .15 .40
123 Antonio Freeman .20 .50
124 Kordell Stewart .15 .40
125 Jon Kitna .15 .40
126 Ahman Green .20 .50
127 Warrick Dunn .15 .40
128 Robert Brooks .20 .50
129 Derrick Thomas .25 .60
130 Steve Young .30 .75
131 Peter Boulware .15 .40
132 Michael Irvin .25 .60
133 Shannon Sharpe .20 .50
134 Jimmy Smith .20 .50
135 John Avery .15 .40
136 Fred Lane .15 .40
137 Trent Green .15 .40
138 Andre Rison .20 .50
139 Antowain Smith .15 .40
140 Eddie George .20 .50
141 Jeff Blake .20 .50
142 Rocket Ismail .20 .50
143 Rickey Dudley .15 .40
144 Courtney Hawkins .15 .40
145 Mikhael Ricks .15 .40
146 J.J. Stokes .15 .40
147 Levon Kirkland .15 .40
148 Deion Sanders .20 .50
149 Barry Sanders .40 1.00
150 Tiki Barber .20 .50
151 David Boston RC .25 .60
152 Chris McAlister RC .25 .60
153 Peerless Price RC .25 .60
154 D'Wayne Bates RC .25 .60
155 Cade McNown RC .25 .60
156 Akili Smith RC .25 .60
157 Kevin Johnson RC .30 .75
158 Tim Couch RC .30 .75
159 Sedrick Irvin RC .25 .60
160 Chris Claiborne RC .25 .60
161 Edgerrin James RC .40 1.00
162 Mike Cloud RC .25 .60
163 Cecil Collins RC .25 .60
164 James Johnson RC .25 .60
165 Rob Konrad RC .25 .60
166 Daunte Culpepper RC .40 1.00
167 Kevin Faulk RC .25 .60
168 Donovan McNabb RC 3.00 8.00
169 Troy Edwards RC .25 .60
170 Amos Zereoue RC .25 .60
171 Karsten Bailey RC .25 .60
172 Brock Huard RC .25 .60
173 Joe Germaine RC .30 .75
174 Torry Holt RC .50 1.25
175 Shaun King RC .25 .60
176 Jevon Kearse RC .30 .75
177 Champ Bailey RC .50 1.25
178 Ebenezer Ekuban RC .25 .60
179 Andy Katzenmoyer .30 .75
180 Antoine Winfield RC .25 .60
181 Jermaine Fazande RC .25 .60
182 Ricky Williams RC .40 1.00
183 Joel Makovicka RC .25 .60
184 Reginald Kelly RC .25 .60
185 Brandon Stokley RC .30 .75
186 L.C. Stevens RC .25 .60
187 Marty Booker RC .25 .60
188 Jerry Azumah .25 .60
189 Ted White RC .25 .60
190 Scott Covington RC .25 .60
191 Tim Alexander RC .25 .60
192 Darrin Chiaverini RC .25 .60
193 Dat Nguyen RC .40 1.00
194 Wane McGarity RC .25 .60
195 Al Wilson RC .40 1.00
196 Travis McGriff RC .25 .60
197 Stacey Mack RC .25 .60
198 Antuan Edwards RC .25 .60
199 Aaron Brooks RC .30 .75
200 De'Mond Parker RC .25 .60
201 Jed Weaver RC .25 .60
202 Madre Hill RC .25 .60
203 Jim Kleinsasser RC .40 1.00
204 Michael Bishop RC .30 .75
205 Michael Basnight RC .25 .60
206 Sean Bennett RC .25 .60
207 Dameane Douglas RC .25 .60
208 Na Brown RC .25 .60
209 Patrick Kerney RC .25 .60
210 Malcolm Johnson RC .25 .60
211 Dre Bly RC .40 1.00
212 Terry Jackson RC .25 .60
213 Eugene Baker RC .25 .60
214 Autry Denson RC .25 .60
215 Darnell McDonald RC .25 .60
216 Charlie Rogers RC .25 .60
217 Joe Montgomery RC .25 .60
218 Cecil Martin RC .25 .60
219 Larry Parker RC .30 .75
220 Mike Peterson RC .25 .60

1999 Bowman Gold

*1-150 VETS: 6X TO 15X BASIC CARDS
*151-220 ROOKIES: 4X TO 10X
STATED PRINT RUN 99 SER.#'d SETS

1999 Bowman Interstate

COMPLETE SET (220) 60.00 150.00
*1-150 VETS: 1.2X TO 3X BASIC CARDS
*151-220 ROOKIES: .8X TO 2X
ONE INTERSTATE PER PACK

1999 Bowman Autographs

Randomly inserted in packs, these hand signed rookie autograph cards were done in 3 color variation levels. Each player respectively signed only one color variation each. The inserted ratios for each color are blue found 1 in 180, silver 1 in 212 and the rare gold version found I in 850 packs. All versions were signed in blue ink. The color of the Topps certified Autograph logo located on the card front is how to determine which of the 3 color levels the card is. Some of the cards were issued via mail redemption cards with an expiration date of 4/30/2000. Donovan McNabb (#A7) and Andy Katzenmoyer (#A25) were never inserted into packs. However, ten years later a number of both cards bearing what appears to be autographs appeared on the secondary market.
GOLD STATED ODDS 1:850
SILVER STATED ODDS 1:212
BLUE STATED ODDS 1:180
A1 Randy Moss G 40.00 100.00
A2 Akili Smith G 8.00 20.00
A3 Edgerrin James G 10.00 25.00
A4 Ricky Williams G 15.00 40.00
A5 Torry Holt G 12.00 30.00
A6 Daunte Culpepper G 10.00 25.00
A7 Donovan McNabb G 8.00 20.00
A8 Tim Couch S 10.00 25.00
A9 Champ Bailey S 12.00 30.00
A10 David Boston S 7.50 20.00
A11 Chris Claiborne S 7.50 20.00
A12 Chris McAlister S 7.50 20.00
A13 Rob Konrad S 6.00 15.00
A14 Mike Cloud S 6.00 15.00
A15 Jermaine Fazande S 6.00 15.00
A16 Brock Huard S 10.00 25.00
A17 Joe Germaine S 6.00 15.00
A18 Sedrick Irvin S 6.00 15.00
A19 Cecil Collins S 6.00 15.00
A20 Karsten Bailey S 6.00 15.00
A21 Antoine Winfield S 7.50 20.00
A22 Cade McNown B 5.00 12.00
A23 Troy Edwards B 6.00 15.00
A24 Jevon Kearse B 10.00 25.00
A25 Andy Katzenmoyer B 6.00 15.00
A26 Kevin Johnson B 5.00 12.00
A27 James Johnson B 6.00 15.00
A28 Kevin Faulk B 7.50 20.00
A29 Shaun King B 6.00 15.00
A30 Peerless Price B 7.50 20.00
A31 D'Wayne Bates B 5.00 12.00
A32 Amos Zereoue B 6.00 15.00

1999 Bowman Late Bloomers/Early Risers

Randomly inserted at a rate of 1 in 12 packs, this 10 card insert set features color action shots of 5 rookies from the 98 class who performed well above scouts expectations and 5 veteran players who have matured into star players over the years.
COMPLETE SET (10) 10.00 25.00
STATED ODDS 1:12
U1 Fred Taylor .75 2.00
U2 Peyton Manning 2.50 6.00
U3 Dan Marino 2.50 6.00
U4 Barry Sanders 2.50 6.00
U5 Randy Moss 2.00 5.00
U6 Mark Brunell .75 2.00
U7 Jamal Anderson .75 2.00
U8 Curtis Martin .75 2.00
U9 Wayne Chrebet .50 1.25
U10 Terrell Davis .75 2.00

1999 Bowman Scout's Choice

Randomly inserted in at a rate of 1 in 12 packs, this 21 card insert set features key rookies which were highly sought after by NFL scouts.
COMPLETE SET (21) 25.00 50.00
STATED ODDS 1:12
SC1 David Boston .60 1.50
SC2 Champ Bailey .75 2.00
SC3 Edgerrin James 2.50 6.00
SC4 Mike Cloud .50 1.25
SC5 Kevin Faulk .60 1.50
SC6 Troy Edwards .50 1.25
SC7 Cecil Collins .25 .60
SC8 Peerless Price .60 1.50
SC9 Torry Holt 1.50 4.00
SC10 Rob Konrad .60 1.50
SC11 Akili Smith .50 1.25
SC12 Daunte Culpepper 2.50 6.00
SC13 D'Wayne Bates .50 1.25
SC14 Donovan McNabb 3.00 8.00
SC15 James Johnson .50 1.25
SC16 Cade McNown .50 1.25
SC17 Kevin Johnson .60 1.50
SC18 Ricky Williams 1.25 3.00
SC19 Karsten Bailey .50 1.25
SC20 Tim Couch .60 1.50
SC21 Shaun King .50 1.25

2000 Bowman Promos

This 6-card set was released at various Topps sponsored events and through its dealer network to promote the 2000 Bowman football release. The cards look very similar to the base set except for the card numbering on the backs.
COMPLETE SET (6) 2.00 5.00
PP1 Stephen Davis .50 1.25
PP2 Charlie Batch .30 .75
PP3 Patrick Jeffers .20 .50
PP4 Torry Holt .50 1.25
PP5 Akili Smith .20 .50
PP6 Fred Taylor .50 1.25

2000 Bowman

Released in early October, Bowman features a 240-card base set. Card numbers 1-140 picture veterans, card numbers 141-165 focus on NFL Europe Prospects, and card numbers 166-240 picture 2000 NFL Draft Picks. Base cards are full color action shots with a brown and black border and gold foil highlights. Bowman was packaged in 24-pack boxes with each pack containing 10 cards and carried a suggested retail price of $3.00. Hobby Collector Packs were released as well, and were packaged in 12-pack boxes with packs containing 21 cards and carried a suggested retail price of $6.00.
COMPLETE SET (240) 250.00 400.00
1 Eddie George .20 .50
2 Ike Hilliard .15 .40
3 Terrell Owens .20 .50
4 James Stewart .15 .40
5 Joey Galloway .20 .50
6 Jake Reed .20 .50
7 Derrick Alexander .15 .40
8 Jeff George .20 .50
9 Kerry Collins .15 .40
10 Tony Gonzalez .20 .50
11 Marcus Robinson .20 .50
12 Charles Woodson .25 .60
13 Germane Crowell .15 .40
14 Yancey Thigpen .15 .40
15 Tony Martin .20 .50
16 Frank Sanders .15 .40
17 Napoleon Kaufman .20 .50
18 Jay Fiedler .20 .50
19 Patrick Jeffers .15 .40
20 Steve McNair .20 .50
21 Herman Moore .15 .40
22 Tim Brown .25 .60
23 Olandis Gary .20 .50
24 Corey Dillon .15 .40
25 Warren Sapp .20 .50
26 Curtis Enis .15 .40
27 Vinny Testaverde .15 .40
28 Tim Biakabutuka .20 .50
29 Kevin Johnson .15 .40
30 Charlie Batch .15 .40
31 Jermaine Fazande .15 .40
32 Shaun King .15 .40
33 Errict Rhett .20 .50
34 O.J. McDuffie .20 .50
35 Bruce Smith .20 .50
36 Antonio Freeman .20 .50
37 Tim Couch .20 .50
38 Duce Staley .15 .40
39 Jeff Blake .20 .50
40 Jim Harbaugh .20 .50
41 Jeff Graham .15 .40
42 Drew Bledsoe .20 .50
43 Mike Alstott .15 .40
44 Terance Mathis .15 .40
45 Antowain Smith .20 .50
46 Johnnie Morton .20 .50
47 Chris Chandler .20 .50
48 Keith Poole .15 .40
49 Ricky Watters .20 .50
50 Darnay Scott .20 .50
51 Damon Huard .15 .40
52 Peerless Price .20 .50
53 Brian Griese .15 .40
54 Frank Wycheck .20 .50
55 Kevin Dyson .20 .50
56 Junior Seau .20 .50
57 Curtis Conway .20 .50
58 Jamal Anderson .20 .50
59 Jim Miller .15 .40
60 Rob Johnson .20 .50
61 Mark Brunell .20 .50
62 Wayne Chrebet .15 .40
63 James Johnson .15 .40
64 Sean Dawkins .15 .40
65 Stephen Davis .15 .40
66 Daunte Culpepper .20 .50
67 Doug Flutie .20 .50
68 Pete Mitchell .15 .40
69 Bill Schroeder .20 .50
70 Terrence Wilkins .15 .40
71 Cade McNown .15 .40
72 Muhsin Muhammad .15 .40
73 E.G. Green .15 .40
74 Edgerrin James .20 .50
75 Troy Edwards .15 .40
76 Terry Glenn .20 .50
77 Tony Banks .15 .40
78 Derrick Mayes .15 .40
79 Curtis Martin .20 .50
80 Kordell Stewart .15 .40
81 Amani Toomer .15 .40
82 Dorsey Levens .20 .50
83 Brad Johnson .20 .50
84 Ed McCaffrey .20 .50
85 Charlie Garner .20 .50
86 Brett Favre .50 1.25
87 J.J. Stokes .20 .50
88 Steve Young .30 .75
89 Jonathan Linton .15 .40
90 Isaac Bruce .25 .60
91 Shawn Jefferson .15 .40
92 Rod Smith .20 .50
93 Champ Bailey .20 .50
94 Ricky Williams .20 .50
95 Priest Holmes .15 .40
96 Corey Bradford .15 .40
97 Eric Moulds .15 .40
98 Warrick Dunn .15 .40
99 Jevon Kearse .15 .40
100 Albert Connell .15 .40
101 Az-Zahir Hakim .15 .40
102 Marvin Harrison .20 .50
103 Qadry Ismail .15 .40
104 Oronde Gadsden .20 .50
105 Rob Moore .15 .40
106 Marshall Faulk .20 .50
107 Steve Beuerlein .20 .50
108 Torry Holt .20 .50
109 Donovan McNabb .20 .50
110 Rich Gannon .20 .50
111 Jerome Bettis .25 .60
112 Peyton Manning .60 1.50
113 Cris Carter .25 .60
114 Jake Plummer .15 .40
115 Kent Graham .15 .40
116 Keenan McCardell .20 .50
117 Tim Dwight .20 .50
118 Fred Taylor .15 .40
119 Jerry Rice .60 1.50
120 Michael Westbrook .15 .40
121 Kurt Warner .40 1.00
122 Jimmy Smith .20 .50
123 Emmitt Smith .40 1.00
124 Terrell Davis .20 .50
125 Randy Moss .20 .50
126 Akili Smith .15 .40
127 Rocket Ismail .20 .50
128 Jon Kitna .15 .40
129 Elvis Grbac .15 .40
130 Wesley Walls .15 .40
131 Torrance Small .15 .40
132 Tyrone Wheatley .16 .40
133 Carl Pickens .20 .50
134 Zach Thomas .20 .50
135 Jacquez Green .15 .40
136 Robert Smith .15 .40
137 Keyshawn Johnson .20 .50
138 Matthew Hatchette .15 .40
139 Troy Aikman .30 .75
140 Charles Johnson .15 .40
141 Terry Battle EP .15 .40
142 Pepe Pearson EP RC .15 .40
143 Cory Sauter EP .15 .40
144 Brian Shay EP .15 .40
145 Marcus Crandell EP RC .15 .40
146 Danny Wuerffel EP .25 .60
147 L.C. Stevens EP .15 .40
148 Ted White EP .15 .40
149 Matt Lytle EP RC .15 .40
150 Vershan Jackson EP RC .15 .40
151 Mario Bailey EP .15 .40
152 Darryl Daniel EP RC .15 .40
153 Sean Morey EP RC .15 .40
154 Jim Kubiak EP RC .15 .40
155 Aaron Stecker EP RC .15 .40
156 Damon Dunn EP RC .15 .40
157 Kevin Daft EP .15 .40
158 Corey Thomas EP .15 .40
159 Deon Mitchell EP RC .15 .40
160 Todd Floyd EP RC .15 .40
161 Norman Miller EP RC .15 .40
162 Jeremaine Copeland EP .15 .40
163 Michael Blair EP .15 .40
164 Ron Powlus EP RC .25 .60
165 Pat Barnes EP .15 .40
166 Dez White RC .25 .60
167 Trung Canidate RC .25 .60
168 Thomas Jones RC .30 .75
169 Courtney Brown RC .30 .75
170 Jamal Lewis RC .40 1.00
171 Chris Redman RC .25 .60
172 Ron Dayne RC .40 1.00
173 Chad Pennington RC .30 .75
174 Plaxico Burress RC .30 .75
175 R.Jay Soward RC .25 .60
176 Travis Taylor RC .25 .60
177 Shaun Alexander RC .40 1.00
178 Brian Urlacher RC 2.50 6.00
179 Danny Farmer RC .25 .60
180 Tee Martin RC .25 .60
181 Sylvester Morris RC .25 .60
182 Curtis Keaton RC .25 .60
183 Peter Warrick RC .25 .60
184 Anthony Becht RC .25 .60
185 Travis Prentice RC .25 .60
186 J.R. Redmond RC .25 .60
187 Bubba Franks RC .25 .60
188 Ron Dugans RC .25 .60
189 Reuben Droughns RC .25 .60
190 Corey Simon RC .30 .75
191 Joe Hamilton RC .25 .60
192 Laveranues Coles RC .30 .75
193 Todd Pinkston RC .25 .60
194 Jerry Porter RC .40 1.00
195 Dennis Northcutt RC .25 .60
196 Tim Rattay RC .30 .75
197 Giovanni Carmazzi RC .25 .60
198 Mareno Philyaw RC .25 .60
199 Avion Black RC .25 .60
200 Chafie Fields RC .25 .60
201 Rondell Mealey RC .25 .60
202 Troy Walters RC .25 .60
203 Frank Moreau RC .25 .60
204 Vaughn Sanders RC .25 .60
205 Sherrod Gideon RC .25 .60
206 Doug Chapman RC .25 .60
207 Marcus Knight RC .25 .60
208 Jamel White RC .25 .60
209 Windrell Hayes RC .25 .60
210 Reggie Jones RC .25 .60
211 Jarious Jackson RC .30 .75
212 Ronney Jenkins RC .25 .60
213 Quinton Spotwood RC .25 .60
214 Rob Morris RC .30 .75
215 Gari Scott RC .25 .60
216 Kevin Thompson RC .25 .60
217 Trevor Insley RC .25 .60
218 Frank Murphy RC .25 .60
219 Patrick Pass RC .25 .60
220 Mike Anderson RC .25 .60
221 Derrius Thompson RC .25 .60
222 John Abraham RC .40 1.00
223 Dante Hall RC .25 .60
224 Chad Morton RC .30 .75
225 Ahmed Plummer RC .25 .60
226 Julian Peterson RC .40 1.00
227 Mike Green RC .30 .75
228 Michael Wiley RC .25 .60
229 Spergon Wynn RC .25 .60
230 Trevor Gaylor RC .25 .60
231 Doug Johnson RC .25 .60
232 Marc Bulger RC .30 .75
233 Ron Dixon RC .25 .60
234 Aaron Shea RC .30 .75
235 Thomas Hamner RC .25 .60
236 Tom Brady RC 150.00 300.00
237 Deltha O'Neal RC .25 .60
238 Todd Husak RC .25 .60
239 Erron Kinney RC .25 .60
240 JaJuan Dawson RC .25 .60

2000 Bowman Gold

*VETS 1-165: 6X TO 15X BASIC CARDS
*ROOKIE 166-240: 5X TO 12X BASIC CARDS
GOLD/99 STATED ODDS 1:60
GOLD PRINT RUN 99 SER.#'d SETS
236 Tom Brady 500.00 1000.00

2000 Bowman ROY Promotion

*ROOKIES: 2.5X TO 6X BASIC CARDS
STATED ODDS 1:76
178 Brian Urlacher WIN 40.00 80.00
220 Mike Anderson WIN 20.00 50.00
236 Tom Brady 300.00 600.00

2000 Bowman Autographs

Randomly inserted in hobby packs at an overall rate of one in 46, and Hobby Collector Packs at the rate of one in 27, this set features authentic player autographs. The actual odds for each card are listed below according to group. Some cards were issued via mail redemption cards which carried an expiration date of September 25, 2001.
GROUP A STATED ODDS 1:7680
GROUP B STATED ODDS 1:480
GROUP C STATED ODDS 1:320
GROUP D STATED ODDS 1:111
GROUP E STATED ODDS 1:138
GROUP F STATED ODDS 1:14346
OVERALL ODDS 1:46 HOBBY
AB Anthony Becht S 4.00 10.00
BU Brian Urlacher B 20.00 50.00
CB Courtney Brown G 6.00 15.00
CK Curtis Keaton B 4.00 10.00
CP Chad Pennington G 6.00 15.00
CR Chris Redman G 5.00 12.00
CS Corey Simon B 5.00 12.00
DF Danny Farmer S 4.00 10.00
DN Dennis Northcutt B 4.00 10.00
DW Dez White B 4.00 10.00
GC Giovanni Carmazzi S 4.00 10.00
JH Joe Hamilton B 4.00 10.00
JL Jamal Lewis S 6.00 15.00
JP Jerry Porter G 8.00 20.00
LC Laveranues Coles B 5.00 12.00
MB Marc Bulger S 5.00 12.00
PB Plaxico Burress G 6.00 15.00
PW Peter Warrick G 5.00 12.00
RD Ron Dayne G 8.00 20.00
SA Shaun Alexander G 8.00 20.00
SM Sylvester Morris B 4.00 10.00
TC Trung Canidate S 4.00 10.00
TG Trevor Gaylor S 4.00 10.00
TJ Thomas Jones G 6.00 15.00
TM Tee Martin B 4.00 10.00
TP Travis Prentice B 4.00 10.00
TR Tim Rattay B 5.00 12.00
TT Travis Taylor S 4.00 10.00
DFR Bubba Franks S 4.00 10.00
RDR Reuben Droughns S 4.00 10.00
RDU Ron Dugans B 4.00 10.00
TPI Todd Pinkston G 5.00 12.00

2000 Bowman Bowman's Best Previews

Randomly inserted in packs at the rate of one in 24, and Hobby Collector Packs at the rate of one in 11, this 10-card set debuits the card stock for 2000 Bowman's Best.
COMPLETE SET (10) 8.00 20.00
STATED ODDS 1:24, 1:11 HCP
BBP1 Peyton Manning 2.00 5.00
BBP2 Stephen Davis .50 1.25
BBP3 Marshall Faulk .60 1.50
BBP4 Marvin Harrison .60 1.50
BBP5 Brett Favre 1.50 4.00
BBP6 Terrell Davis .60 1.50
BBP7 Eddie George .60 1.50
BBP8 Kurt Warner 1.25 3.00
BBP9 Edgerrin James .60 1.50
BBP10 Randy Moss .60 1.50

2000 Bowman Breakthrough Discoveries

Randomly inserted in packs at the rate of one in 12, and Hobby Collector Packs at the rate of one in five, this 10-card set features players that moved from small schools into the NFL and have since left their mark.
COMPLETE SET (10) 3.00 8.00
STATED ODDS 1:12, 1:5 HCP
BD1 Jerry Rice 1.25 3.00
BD2 Kurt Warner .75 2.00
BD3 Wayne Chrebet .30 .75
BD4 Isaac Bruce .50 1.25
BD5 Steve McNair .40 1.00
BD6 Shannon Sharpe .40 1.00
BD7 Andre Reed .50 1.25
BD8 Jimmy Smith .40 1.00
BD9 Darrell Green .40 1.00
BD10 Randy Moss .40 1.00

2000 Bowman Draft Day Relics

Randomly inserted in packs at the rate of one in 386, and Hobby Collector Packs at the rate of one in 193, this four card set features swatches of the jerseys these four players wore on the stage at Draft Day 2000.
STATED ODDS 1:386, 1:196 HCP
CB Courtney Brown 6.00 15.00
CS Chris Samuels 8.00 20.00
PW Peter Warrick 5.00 12.00
TJ Thomas Jones 6.00 15.00

2000 Bowman Road to Success

Randomly inserted in packs at the rate of one in 18, and Hobby Collector Packs at the rate of one in eight, this 10-card set pairs two NFL players who attended the same college.
COMPLETE SET (10) 8.00 20.00
STATED ODDS 1:18, 1:8 HCP
R1 C.Pennington R.Moss .50 1.25
R2 J.Lewis P.Manning 1.50 4.00
R3 R.Soward Key.Johnson .50 1.25
R4 T.Jones G.Crowell .50 1.25
R5 G.Carmazzi W.Chrebet .40 1.00
R6 T.Taylor I.Hilliard .40 1.00
R7 P.Burress M.Muhammad .50 1.25
R8 T.Pinkston B.Favre 1.25 3.00
R9 Syl.Morris J.Smith .50 1.25
R10 P.Warrick D.Sanders .50 1.25

2000 Bowman Rookie Rising

Randomly inserted in packs at the rate of one in 12, and Hobby Collector Packs at one in five, this 10-card set pays tribute to second year stars who have proven their worth in the NFL.
COMPLETE SET (10) 2.50 6.00
STATED ODDS 1:12, 1:5 HCP
RR1 Jevon Kearse .40 1.00
RR2 Edgerrin James .50 1.25
RR3 Champ Bailey .50 1.25
RR4 Zach Thomas .50 1.25
RR5 Marvin Harrison .50 1.25
RR6 Kevin Johnson .40 1.00
RR7 Curtis Martin .50 1.25
RR8 Jerome Bettis .60 1.50
RR9 Fred Taylor .40 1.00
RR10 Terry Glenn .50 1.25

2000 Bowman Scout's Choice

Randomly inserted in packs at the rate of one in 18, and Hobby Collector Packs at one in eight, this 20-card set features 20 top prospects as chosen by professional college scouts.
COMPLETE SET (20) 7.50 20.00
STATED ODDS 1:18, 1:8 HCP
SC1 Shaun Alexander .40 1.00
SC2 Bubba Franks .25 .60
SC3 Travis Prentice .25 .60
SC4 Peter Warrick .25 .60
SC5 Plaxico Burress .30 .75
SC6 Corey Simon .30 .75
SC7 Courtney Brown .30 .75
SC8 Tee Martin .25 .60
SC9 Brian Urlacher 1.25 3.00
SC10 J.R. Redmond .25 .60
SC11 Anthony Becht .25 .60
SC12 Thomas Jones .30 .75
SC13 Giovanni Carmazzi .25 .60
SC14 Jamal Lewis .40 1.00
SC15 Ron Dayne .40 1.00
SC16 R.Jay Soward .25 .60
SC17 Travis Taylor .25 .60
SC18 Chad Pennington .30 .75
SC19 Sylvester Morris .25 .60
SC20 Chris Redman .25 .60

2001 Bowman

Issued in October 2001, this 275 card set continued the Topps tradition of using this brand to feature many young players. The cards were issued in ten-card packs with a SRP of $3 or 21-card HTA packs with a SRP of $6. The regular packs came 24 packs to a box while the HTA packs came 12 packs to a box. Cards from 1-130 are veterans while cards 131 through 275 are rookies.
COMPLETE SET (275) 25.00 60.00
1 Emmitt Smith .40 1.00
2 James Stewart .15 .40
3 Jeff Graham .15 .40
4 Keyshawn Johnson .20 .50
5 Stephen Davis .15 .40
6 Chad Lewis .15 .40
7 Drew Bledsoe .20 .50
8 Fred Taylor .15 .40
9 Mike Anderson .15 .40
10 Tony Gonzalez .20 .50
11 Aaron Brooks .15 .40
12 Vinny Testaverde .15 .40
13 Jerome Bettis .25 .60
14 Marshall Faulk .20 .50
15 Jeff Garcia .15 .40
16 Terry Glenn .20 .50
17 Jay Fiedler .20 .50
18 Ahman Green .20 .50
19 Cade McNown .20 .50
20 Rob Johnson .20 .50
21 Jamal Anderson .20 .50
22 Corey Dillon .15 .40
23 Jake Plummer .15 .40
24 Rod Smith .20 .50
25 Trent Green .15 .40

26 Ricky Williams .20 .50
27 Charlie Garner .20 .50
28 Shaun Alexander .15 .40
29 Jeff George .20 .50
30 Torry Holt .20 .50
31 James Thrash .20 .50
32 Rich Gannon .20 .50
33 Ron Dayne .20 .50
34 Dedric Ward .15 .40
35 Edgerrin James .20 .50
36 Cris Carter .25 .60
37 Derrick Mason .15 .40
38 Brad Johnson .20 .50
39 Charlie Batch .15 .40
40 Joey Galloway .20 .50
41 James Allen .15 .40
42 Tim Biakabutuka .15 .40
43 Ray Lewis .25 .60
44 David Boston .15 .40
45 Kevin Johnson .15 .40
46 Jimmy Smith .20 .50
47 Joe Horn .15 .40
48 Terrell Owens .20 .50
49 Eddie George .25 .60
50 Brett Favre .50 1.25
51 Wayne Chrebet .15 .40
52 Hines Ward .20 .50
53 Warrick Dunn .15 .40
54 Matt Hasselbeck .15 .40
55 Tiki Barber .20 .50
56 Lamar Smith .20 .50
57 Tim Couch .15 .40
58 Eric Moulds .15 .40
59 Shawn Jefferson .15 .40
60 Donald Hayes .15 .40
61 Brian Urlacher .30 .75
62 Steve McNair .20 .50
63 Kurt Warner .40 1.00
64 Tim Brown .25 .60
65 Troy Brown .15 .40
66 Albert Connell .15 .40
67 Peyton Manning .60 1.50
68 Peter Warrick .15 .40
69 Elvis Grbac .20 .50
70 Chris Chandler .20 .50
71 Akili Smith .15 .40
72 Keenan McCardell .20 .50
73 Kerry Collins .15 .40
74 Junior Seau .20 .50
75 Donovan McNabb .20 .50
76 Tony Banks .15 .40
77 Steve Beuerlein .20 .50
78 Daunte Culpepper .20 .50
79 Darrell Jackson .20 .50
80 Isaac Bruce .25 .60
81 Tyrone Wheatley .20 .50
82 Derrick Alexander .15 .40
83 Germane Crowell .15 .40
84 Jon Kitna .15 .40
85 Jamal Lewis .25 .60
86 Ed McCaffrey .20 .50
87 Mark Brunell .20 .50
88 Jeff Blake .20 .50
89 Duce Staley .15 .40
90 Doug Flutie .20 .50
91 Kordell Stewart .15 .40
92 Randy Moss .20 .50
93 Marvin Harrison .20 .50
94 Muhsin Muhammad .15 .40
95 Brian Griese .15 .40
96 Antonio Freeman .25 .60
97 Amani Toomer .15 .40
98 Oronde Gadsden .15 .40
99 Curtis Martin .20 .50
100 Jerry Rice .50 1.25
101 Michael Pittman .20 .50
102 Shannon Sharpe .20 .50
103 Peerless Price .15 .40
104 Bill Schroeder .20 .50
105 Ike Hilliard .15 .40
106 Freddie Jones .15 .40
107 Tai Streets .15 .40
108 Ricky Watters .20 .50
109 Az-Zahir Hakim .15 .40
110 Jacquez Green .15 .40
111 Bobby Shaw .15 .40
112 Johnnie Morton .20 .50
113 Laveranues Coles .20 .50
114 Chad Pennington .15 .40
115 Champ Bailey .20 .50
116 Charles Woodson .25 .60
117 Curtis Conway .20 .50
118 Marcus Robinson .20 .50
119 Michael Westbrook .15 .40
120 Mike Alstott .15 .40
121 Priest Holmes .15 .40
122 Qadry Ismail .15 .40
123 Rocket Ismail .20 .50
124 Shawn Bryson .15 .40
125 Jeff Lewis .15 .40
126 Jeremy Mcdaniel .15 .40
127 Terance Mathis .15 .40
128 Travis Prentice .15 .40
129 Warren Sapp .20 .50
130 Jevon Kearse .15 .40
131 George Layne RC .30 .75
132 Correll Buckhalter RC .30 .75
133 Tony Stewart RC .40 1.00
134 Chris Barnes RC .30 .75
135 A.J. Feeley RC .40 1.00
136 Margin Hooks RC .30 .75
137 Anthony Henry RC .50 1.25
138 Dwight Smith RC .30 .75
139 Torrance Marshall RC .30 .75
140 Gary Baxter RC .30 .75
141 Derek Combs RC .30 .75
142 Marcus Bell DT RC .30 .75
143 Delawrence Grant RC .30 .75
144 Jameel Cook RC .40 1.00
145 Eric Downing RC .30 .75
146 Marlon McCree RC .30 .75
147 Tay Cody RC .30 .75
148 Mario Monds RC .30 .75
149 Kenny Smith RC .30 .75
150 Sedrick Hodge RC .30 .75
151 Marcus Stroud RC .40 1.00
152 Steve Smith RC 1.00 2.50
153 Tyrone Robertson RC .30 .75
154 James Reed RC .30 .75
155 Kris Kocurek RC .30 .75
156 Dan O'Leary RC .30 .75
157 Harold Blackmon RC .30 .75
158 Fred Smoot RC .40 1.00
159 Billy Baber RC .30 .75
160 Jarrod Cooper RC .40 1.00
161 Travis Henry RC .40 1.00
162 David Terrell RC .40 1.00
163 Josh Heupel RC .50 1.25
164 Drew Brees RC 15.00 40.00
165 T.J. Houshmandzadeh RC .40 1.00
166 Rod Gardner RC .40 1.00
167 Richard Seymour RC .50 1.25
168 Koren Robinson RC .40 1.00
169 Scotty Anderson RC .30 .75
170 Marques Tuiasosopo RC .40 1.00
171 John Capel RC .30 .75
172 LaMont Jordan RC .50 1.25
173 James Jackson RC .30 .75
174 Bobby Newcombe RC .40 1.00
175 Anthony Thomas RC .50 1.25
176 Dan Alexander RC .40 1.00
177 Quincy Carter RC .40 1.00
178 Morlon Greenwood RC .30 .75
179 Robert Ferguson RC .50 1.25
180 Sage Rosenfels RC .40 1.00
181 Michael Stone RC .30 .75
182 Chris Weinke RC .40 1.00
183 Travis Minor RC .40 1.00
184 Gerard Warren RC .40 1.00
185 Jamar Fletcher RC .30 .75
186 Andre Carter RC .40 1.00
187 Deuce McAllister RC .50 1.25
188 Dan Morgan RC .40 1.00
189 Todd Heap RC .40 1.00
190 Snoop Minnis RC .30 .75
191 Will Allen RC .50 1.25
192 Freddie Mitchell RC .30 .75
193 Rudi Johnson RC .50 1.25
194 Kevan Barlow RC .40 1.00
195 Jamie Winborn RC .40 1.00
196 Onomo Ojo RC .30 .75
197 Leonard Davis RC .50 1.25
198 Santana Moss RC .50 1.25
199 Chris Chambers RC .30 .75
200 Michael Vick RC 5.00 12.00
201 Michael Bennett RC .40 1.00
202 Mike McMahon RC .40 1.00
203 Jonathan Carter RC .30 .75
204 Jamal Reynolds RC .30 .75
205 Justin Smith RC .60 1.50
206 Quincy Morgan RC .40 1.00
207 Chad Johnson RC .50 1.25
208 Jesse Palmer RC .40 1.00
209 Reggie Wayne RC .60 1.50
210 LaDainian Tomlinson RC 5.00 12.00
211 Andre King RC .30 .75
212 Richmond Flowers RC .30 .75
213 Derrick Blaylock RC .40 1.00
214 Cedrick Wilson RC .40 1.00
215 Zeke Moreno RC .40 1.00
216 Tommy Polley RC .30 .75
217 Damione Lewis RC .40 1.00
218 Aaron Schobel RC .50 1.25
219 Alge Crumpler RC .50 1.25
220 Nate Clements RC .40 1.00
221 Quentin McCord RC .40 1.00
222 Ken-Yon Rambo RC .30 .75
223 Milton Wynn RC .30 .75
224 Derrick Gibson RC .30 .75
225 Chris Taylor RC .30 .75
226 Corey Hall RC .30 .75
227 Vinny Sutherland RC .30 .75
228 Kendrell Bell RC .50 1.25
229 Casey Hampton RC .50 1.25
230 Demetric Evans RC .30 .75
231 Brian Allen RC .30 .75
232 Rodney Bailey RC .30 .75
233 Otis Leverette RC .30 .75
234 Ron Edwards RC .30 .75
235 Michael Jameson RC .30 .75
236 Markus Steele RC .30 .75
237 Jimmy Williams RC .30 .75
238 Roger Knight RC .30 .75
239 Randy Garner RC .30 .75
240 Raymond Perryman RC .30 .75
241 Karon Riley RC .30 .75
242 Adam Archuleta RC .40 1.00
243 Arnold Jackson RC .30 .75
244 Ryan Pickett RC .30 .75
245 Shad Meier RC .30 .75
246 Reggie Germany RC .30 .75
247 Justin McCareins RC .40 1.00
248 Idrees Bashir RC .30 .75
249 Josh Booty RC .40 1.00
250 Eddie Berlin RC .30 .75
251 Heath Evans RC .40 1.00
252 Alex Bannister RC .30 .75
253 Corey Alston RC .30 .75
254 Reggie White RC .30 .75
255 Orlando Huff RC .30 .75
256 Ken Lucas RC .40 1.00
257 Matt Stewart RC .30 .75
258 Cedric Scott RC .30 .75
259 Ronney Daniels RC .30 .75
260 Kevin Kasper RC .30 .75
261 Tony Driver RC .40 1.00
262 Kyle Vanden Bosch RC .50 1.25
263 T.J. Turner RC .30 .75
264 Eric Westmoreland RC .30 .75
265 Ronald Flemons RC .30 .75
266 Eric Kelly RC .30 .75
267 Moran Norris RC .30 .75
268 Damerien McCants RC .40 1.00
269 James Boyd RC .30 .75
270 Keith Adams RC .30 .75
271 B.Manumaleuna RC .40 1.00
272 Dee Brown RC .30 .75
273 Ross Kolodziej RC .30 .75
274 Boo Williams RC .30 .75
275 Patrick Chukwurah RC .30 .75

2001 Bowman Gold

*VETS 1-100: 1.2X TO 3X BASIC CARDS
*ROOKIES 101-275: .6X TO 1.5X
STATED ODDS ONE PER PACK

2001 Bowman 1996 Rookies

Inserted at a rate of one in four packs, Topps issued these 15 cards of players who would have had 1996 Bowman Rookie Cards if Topps had made the Bowman product that year.

COMPLETE SET (15) 10.00 25.00
STATED ODDS 1:4
BRC1 Eric Moulds .60 1.50
BRC2 Ray Lewis 1.00 2.50
BRC3 Tim Biakabutuka .60 1.50
BRC4 Eddie George 1.00 2.50
BRC5 Marvin Harrison .75 2.00
BRC6 Joe Horn .60 1.50
BRC7 Muhsin Muhammad .60 1.50
BRC8 Mike Alstott .60 1.50
BRC9 Amani Toomer .60 1.50
BRC10 Terrell Owens .75 2.00
BRC11 Keyshawn Johnson .75 2.00
BRC12 Terry Glenn .75 2.00
BRC13 Zach Thomas .75 2.00
BRC14 Stephen Davis .60 1.50
BRC15 La'Roi Glover .60 1.50

2001 Bowman Rookie Autographs

Issued at an overall rate of one in 61, these cards feature signatures of some of the leading 2001 NFL rookies. The odds of pulling a specific card ranged from one in 119 to one every 5339 packs. A few players did not return their cards in time for pack-out, those exchange cards were redeemable until November 30, 2003. The Reggie Wayne card appeared on the market much later.

GROUP A STATED ODDS 1:5339
GROUP B STATED ODDS 1:2373
GROUP C STATED ODDS 1:2669
GROUP D STATED ODDS 1:1068
GROUP E STATED ODDS 1:3051
GROUP F STATED ODDS 1:1335
GROUP G STATED ODDS 1:428
GROUP H STATED ODDS 1:1186
GROUP I STATED ODDS 1:119
GROUP J STATED ODDS 1:548
OVERALL STATED ODDS 1:61
BABN Bobby Newcombe H 5.00 12.00
BACC Chris Chambers D 4.00 10.00
BACJ Chad Johnson G 6.00 15.00
BACW Chris Weinke D 5.00 12.00
BADA Dan Alexander I 5.00 12.00
BADB Drew Brees B 150.00 300.00
BADM Dan Morgan I 5.00 12.00
BADR David Rivers J 4.00 10.00
BADT David Terrell D 5.00 12.00
BAJB Josh Booty I 5.00 12.00
BAJH Josh Heupel I 6.00 15.00
BAJJ James Jackson I 4.00 10.00
BAJP Jesse Palmer F 5.00 12.00
BAKB Kevan Barlow G 5.00 12.00
BAKR Koren Robinson C 5.00 12.00
BAKW Kenyatta Walker I 4.00 10.00
BAKYR Ken-Yon Rambo D 4.00 10.00
BAMB Michael Bennett A 5.00 12.00
BAMV Michael Vick B 50.00 100.00
BAQM Quincy Morgan E 5.00 12.00
BARG Rod Gardner G 5.00 12.00
DACM Cantana Moss C 6.00 15.00
BATH Travis Henry G 5.00 12.00
BATM Travis Minor I 5.00 12.00
BARW Reggie Wayne 25.00 50.00

2001 Bowman Rookie Relics

Issued at an overall rate of one in 25, these cards feature swatches from uniforms used at either the Hula or the Senior Bowl. The odds for pulling a specific card ranged from one in 36 to one in 2373. All the players in this set were 2001 NFL Rookies.

GROUP A STATED ODDS 1:2373
GROUP B STATED ODDS 1:1941
GROUP C STATED ODDS 1:1780
GROUP D STATED ODDS 1:419
GROUP E STATED ODDS 1:1127
GROUP F STATED ODDS 1:356
GROUP G STATED ODDS 1:856
GROUP H STATED ODDS 1:382
GROUP I STATED ODDS 1:36
OVERALL STATED ODDS 1:25
BJAA Adam Archuleta E 4.00 10.00
BJAC Alge Crumpler A 6.00 15.00
BJBA Brian Allen I 3.00 8.00
BJBJ Bhawoh Jue I 4.00 10.00
BJBN Bobby Newcombe C 4.00 10.00
BJCT Chris Taylor I 3.00 8.00
BJDB Drew Brees H 12.00 30.00
BJDBU Derrick Burgess I 5.00 12.00
BJDG Derrick Gibson F 3.00 8.00
BJEW Eric Westmoreland I 3.00 8.00
BJFS Fred Smoot F 4.00 10.00
BJJB Jeff Backus I 3.00 8.00
BJJC Jarrod Cooper I 4.00 10.00
BJJH Jabari Holloway I 3.00 8.00
BJJHE Jamie Henderson I 4.00 10.00
BJJJ Jonas Jennings I 3.00 8.00
BJJP Jesse Palmer D 4.00 10.00
BJKK Kevin Kasper I 3.00 8.00
BJLJ LaMont Jordan H 5.00 12.00
BJLM Leonard Myers I 3.00 8.00
BJLT LaDainian Tomlinson G 10.00 25.00
BJMF Mario Fatafehi I 3.00 8.00
BJMMC Mike McMahon F 4.00 10.00
BJMS Michael Stone I 3.00 8.00
BJRG Reggie Germany I 3.00 8.00
BJRW Reggie Wayne D 8.00 20.00
BJSH Steve Hutchinson I 8.00 20.00
BJSR Sage Rosenfels B 5.00 12.00
BJSS Steve Smith I 8.00 20.00
BJTD Tony Dixon I 3.00 8.00
BJTM Travis Minor D 4.00 10.00
BJTS Tony Stewart I 4.00 10.00
BJZM Zeke Moreno I 4.00 10.00

2001 Bowman Rookie Relics Autographs

Randomly inserted at a rate of one in 1780, these cards feature the player's signature on a Rookie Relic card. A few of the players did not return their cards by the time the product went live so they were issued as exchange cards. These cards were redeemable until November 30, 2003.

STATED ODDS 1:1780
BJABN Bobby Newcombe 10.00 25.00
BJADB Drew Brees 100.00 200.00
BJALJ LaMont Jordan 12.00 30.00
BJALT LaDainian Tomlinson 60.00 120.00
BJARW Reggie Wayne 15.00 40.00

2001 Bowman Rookie Reprints

Issued at a rate of one in six, these 15-cards feature reprints of 1950s era Bowman cards.

COMPLETE SET (15) 10.00 25.00
STATED ODDS 1:6
RAA Alan Ameche .75 2.00
RAD Art Donovan 1.00 2.50
RBH Bill Howton .75 2.00
RBT Bulldog Turner 1.00 2.50
RCC Charlie Conerly 1.00 2.50
REH Elroy Hirsch 1.25 3.00
RET Emlen Tunnell .75 2.00
RFG Frank Gifford 1.50 4.00
RGM Gino Marchetti .75 2.00
RLG Lou Groza 1.00 2.50
RNV Norm Van Brocklin 1.25 3.00
ROG Otto Graham 1.25 3.00
RSB Sammy Baugh 1.50 4.00
RSL Sid Luckman 1.00 2.50
RTF Tom Fears .75 2.00
RYT Y.A Tittle 1.50 4.00

2001 Bowman Rookie Reprints Seat Relics

Issued at a rate of one in 713, these three cards feature not only reprints of the players' Bowman card but also include a swatch from a seat used in a stadium where these players first became stars.

STATED ODDS 1:713
RREGB George Blanda 6.00 15.00
RREGM Gino Marchetti 4.00 10.00
RRESB Sammy Baugh 7.50 20.00

2002 Bowman

Released in October, 2002. This set contains 145 rookies and 130 veterans. The Hobby S.R.P. is $3.00/pack. Each hobby pack contains 10 cards. HTA Jumbo S.R.P. is $10.00/pack. Each HTA pack contains 35 cards. Cards numbered 1 through 110 feature veterans while cards numbered 111 through 275 feature rookies.

COMPLETE SET (275) 20.00 50.00
1 Emmitt Smith .40 1.00
2 Drew Brees .50 1.25
3 Duce Staley .15 .40
4 Curtis Martin .20 .50
5 Isaac Bruce .25 .60
6 Stephen Davis .15 .40
7 Darrell Jackson .20 .50
8 James Stewart .15 .40
9 Tim Couch .15 .40
10 Travis Henry .15 .40
11 Thomas Jones .15 .40
12 Jamal Lewis .20 .50
13 Chris Chambers .15 .40
14 Jeff Blake .20 .50
15 Plaxico Burress .15 .40
16 Michael Pittman .20 .50
17 Jeff Garcia .15 .40
18 Tim Brown .25 .60
19 Kent Graham .15 .40
20 Shannon Sharpe .20 .50
21 Corey Dillon .15 .40
22 Muhsin Muhammad .15 .40
23 Tony Gonzalez .20 .50
24 Qadry Ismail .15 .40
25 Mike McMahon .15 .40
26 Edgerrin James .20 .50
27 Daunte Culpepper .20 .50
28 Deuce McAllister .20 .50
29 Kerry Collins .15 .40
30 Eddie George .20 .50
31 Torry Holt .20 .50
32 Todd Pinkston .15 .40
33 Quincy Carter .15 .40
34 Rod Smith .20 .50
35 Michael Vick .20 .50
36 Jim Miller .15 .40
37 Troy Brown .15 .40
38 Wayne Chrebet .15 .40
39 Curtis Conway .20 .50
40 Reidel Anthony .15 .40
41 Mark Brunell .20 .50
42 Chris Weinke .15 .40
43 Eric Moulds .15 .40
44 Ike Hilliard .15 .40
45 Jay Fiedler .20 .50
46 Keyshawn Johnson .20 .50
47 Rod Gardner .15 .40
48 Chris Redman .15 .40
49 James Allen .15 .40
50 Kordell Stewart .15 .40
51 Priest Holmes .15 .40
52 Anthony Thomas .20 .50
53 Peter Warrick .15 .40
54 Jake Plummer .15 .40
55 Jerry Rice .50 1.25
56 Joe Horn .15 .40
57 Derrick Mason .15 .40
58 Kurt Warner .20 .50
59 Antowain Smith .20 .50
60 Randy Moss .20 .50
61 Warrick Dunn .15 .40
62 Laveranues Coles .20 .50
63 LaDainian Tomlinson .25 .60
64 Michael Westbrook .15 .40
65 Travis Taylor .15 .40
66 Brian Griese .15 .40
67 Bill Schroeder .15 .40
68 Ahman Green .20 .50
69 Jimmy Smith .20 .50
70 Charlie Garner .20 .50
71 Terrell Owens .20 .50
72 Brad Johnson .20 .50
73 James Thrash .20 .50
74 Marvin Harrison .20 .50
75 Brett Favre .50 1.25
76 Rocket Ismail .20 .50
77 David Boston .15 .40
78 Jermaine Lewis .15 .40
79 Aaron Brooks .15 .40
80 Shaun Alexander .15 .40
81 Steve McNair .20 .50
82 Marshall Faulk .20 .50
83 Terrell Davis .20 .50
84 Corey Bradford .15 .40
85 David Terrell .15 .40
86 Kevin Johnson .15 .40
87 Jon Kitna .15 .40
88 Az-Zahir Hakim .15 .40
89 Drew Bledsoe .20 .50
90 Garrison Hearst .15 .40
91 Doug Flutie .20 .50
92 Jerome Bettis .25 .60
93 Vinny Testaverde .15 .40
94 Tiki Barber .20 .50
95 Johnnie Morton .20 .50
96 Lamar Smith .15 .40
97 Marcus Robinson .20 .50
98 Fred Taylor .15 .40
99 Tom Brady 1.25 3.00
100 Peyton Manning .60 1.50
101 Donovan McNabb .20 .50
102 Rich Gannon .20 .50
103 Hines Ward .20 .50
104 Michael Bennett .15 .40
105 Ricky Williams .20 .50
106 Germane Crowell .15 .40
107 Joey Galloway .20 .50
108 Amani Toomer .15 .40
109 Trent Green .15 .40
110 Terry Glenn .20 .50
111 Donte Stallworth RC .50 1.25
112 Mike Williams RC .30 .75
113 Kurt Kittner RC .30 .75
114 Josh Reed RC .40 1.00
115 Raonall Smith RC .30 .75
116 David Garrard RC .40 1.00
117 Eric Crouch RC .50 1.25
118 Bryan Thomas RC .30 .75
119 Levi Jones RC .30 .75
120 Andre Davis RC .30 .75
121 Herb Haygood RC .30 .75
122 Josh McCown RC .50 1.25
123 Quentin Jammer RC .50 1.25
124 Cliff Russell RC .30 .75
125 Jeremy Shockey RC .50 1.25
126 Jamin Elliott RC .30 .75
127 Roy Williams RC .30 .75
128 Marquise Walker RC .30 .75
129 Kalimba Edwards RC .40 1.00
130 Daniel Graham RC .40 1.00
131 Freddie Milons RC .30 .75
132 Anthony Weaver RC .30 .75
133 Jake Schifino RC .30 .75
134 Antonio Bryant RC .50 1.25
135 DeShaun Foster RC .50 1.25
136 Antwaan Randle El RC .40 1.00
137 William Green RC .40 1.00
138 Ed Reed RC 2.00 5.00
139 Maurice Morris RC .40 1.00
140 Joey Harrington RC .30 .75
141 T.J. Duckett RC .30 .75
142 Javon Walker RC .50 1.25
143 Albert Haynesworth RC .50 1.25
144 Julius Peppers RC .75 2.00
145 Clinton Portis RC .50 1.25
146 Craig Nall RC .40 1.00
147 Ashley Lelie RC .30 .75
148 Reche Caldwell RC .40 1.00
149 Rohan Davey RC .50 1.25
150 Patrick Ramsey RC .40 1.00
151 Jabar Gaffney RC .30 .75
152 Tank Williams RC .40 1.00
153 Ron Johnson RC .40 1.00
154 Ladell Betts RC .50 1.25
155 Brian Westbrook RC .60 1.50
156 Jamar Martin RC .40 1.00
157 Travis Stephens RC .30 .75
158 Tim Carter RC .40 1.00
159 Darrell Hill RC .30 .75
160 Luke Staley RC .30 .75
161 Randy Fasani RC .30 .75
162 Matt Schobel RC .40 1.00
163 Jon McGraw RC .30 .75
164 Dwight Freeney RC .60 1.50
165 Chad Hutchinson RC .30 .75
166 Adrian Peterson RC .40 1.00
167 Josh Scobey RC .40 1.00
168 Jonathan Wells RC .40 1.00
169 Sam Simmons RC .30 .75
170 Jerramy Stevens RC .50 1.25
171 Jason McAddley RC .40 1.00
172 Ken Simonton RC .30 .75
173 Chester Taylor RC .50 1.25
174 Brandon Doman RC .30 .75
175 Javin Hunter RC .30 .75
176 Eddie Drummond RC .30 .75
177 Andre Lott RC .30 .75
178 Travis Fisher RC .40 1.00
179 Jarvis Green RC .30 .75
180 Ross Tucker RC .30 .75
181 Lamont Brightful RC .30 .75
182 Rocky Calmus RC .40 1.00
183 Wes Pate RC .30 .75
184 Lamar Gordon RC .40 1.00
185 Terry Jones RC .30 .75
186 Kyle Johnson RC .30 .75
187 Daryl Jones RC .30 .75
188 Tellis Redmon RC .30 .75
189 Howard Green RC .30 .75
190 Jarrod Baxter RC .30 .75
191 Delvon Flowers RC .30 .75
192 Kevin Curtis RC .30 .75
193 Kelly Campbell RC .40 1.00
194 Eddie Freeman RC .30 .75
195 Atrews Bell RC .30 .75
196 Omar Easy RC .40 1.00
197 Jeremy Allen RC .30 .75
198 Andra Davis RC .30 .75
199 Jack Brewer RC .30 .75
200 Mike Rumph RC .30 .75
201 Seth Burford RC .30 .75
202 Marquand Manuel RC .30 .75
203 Marques Anderson RC .40 1.00
204 Ben Leber RC .30 .75
205 Ryan Denney RC .30 .75
206 Justin Peelle RC .30 .75
207 Lito Sheppard RC .50 1.25
208 Damien Anderson RC .30 .75
209 Lamont Thompson RC .40 1.00
210 David Priestley RC .30 .75
211 Michael Lewis RC .40 1.00
212 Lee Mays RC .30 .75
213 Alan Harper RC .30 .75
214 Verron Haynes RC .30 .75
215 Chris Hope RC .50 1.25
216 David Thornton RC .30 .75
217 Derek Ross RC .40 1.00
218 Brett Keisel RC 4.00 10.00
219 Joseph Jefferson RC .30 .75
220 Andre Goodman RC .30 .75
221 Robert Royal RC .50 1.25
222 Sheldon Brown RC .50 1.25
223 DeVeren Johnson RC .30 .75
224 Rock Cartwright RC .50 1.25
225 Quincy Monk RC .30 .75
226 Nick Rogers RC .30 .75
227 Kendall Simmons RC .30 .75
228 Joe Burns RC .30 .75
229 Wesly Mallard RC .30 .75
230 Chris Cash RC .30 .75
231 David Givens RC .50 1.25
232 John Owens RC .30 .75
233 Jarrett Ferguson RC .30 .75
234 Randy McMichael RC .50 1.25
235 Chris Baker RC .30 .75
236 Rashad Bauman RC .30 .75
237 Matt Murphy RC .30 .75
238 LaVar Glover RC .40 1.00
239 Steve Bellisari RC .30 .75
240 Chad Williams RC .30 .75
241 Kevin Thomas RC .30 .75
242 Carlos Hall RC .30 .75
243 Nick Greisen RC .30 .75
244 Justin Bannan RC .30 .75
245 Charles Hill RC .30 .75
246 Mark Anelli RC .30 .75
247 Coy Wire RC .40 1.00
248 Darnell Sanders RC .30 .75
249 Larry Foote RC .60 1.50
250 David Carr RC .30 .75
251 Ricky Williams RC .40 1.00
252 Napoleon Harris RC .40 1.00
253 Ennis Haywood RC .30 .75
254 Keyuo Craver RC .30 .75
255 Kahlil Hill RC .30 .75
256 J.T. O'Sullivan RC .40 1.00
257 Woody Dantzler RC .40 1.00
258 Phillip Buchanon RC .50 1.25
259 Charles Grant RC .50 1.25
260 Dusty Bonner RC .30 .75
261 James Allen RC .30 .75
262 Ronald Curry RC .30 .75
263 Deion Branch RC .50 1.25
264 Larry Ned RC .30 .75
265 Mel Mitchell RC .30 .75
266 Kendall Newson RC .30 .75
267 Shaun Hill RC .50 1.25
268 David Pugh RC .30 .75
269 Dante Wesley RC .30 .75
270 Josh Mallard RC .30 .75
271 Akin Ayodele RC .40 1.00
272 Pete Hunter RC .30 .75
273 Kevin McCadam RC .30 .75
274 Jeff Kelly RC .30 .75
275 John Henderson RC .40 1.00

2002 Bowman Gold

*VETS 1-100: 10X TO 25X BASIC CARDS
*ROOKIES 111-275: 6X TO 15X
GOLD/50 ODDS 1:67 HOB, 1:19 HTA
STATED PRINT RUN 50 SER.#'d SETS

2002 Bowman Silver

*VETS 1-110: 3X TO 8X BASIC CARDS
*ROOKIES 111-275: 2.5X TO 6X
SILVER/250 ODDS 1:13 HOB, 1:4 HTA
STATED PRINT RUN 250 SER.#'d SETS

2002 Bowman Uncirculated

*SEALED ROOKIES: 1.2X TO 3X
ANNC'd UNCIRCULATED PRINT RUN 290

2002 Bowman Draft Day Relics

Inserted at an overall rate of 1:103, this set features swatches of jerseys and hats. The jerseys were inserted at a rate of 1:109, and the hats were inserted at a rate of 1:1850.

JSY STATED ODDS 1:109H, 1:31HTA
HAT STATED ODDS 1:1850H, 530HTA
OVERALL ODDS 1:103 HOB, 1:30 HTA
DDHBM Bryant McKinnie Hat 8.00 20.00
DDHDC David Carr Hat 8.00 20.00
DDHJP Julius Peppers Hat 15.00 40.00
DDHMW Mike Williams Hat 8.00 20.00
DDHQJ Quentin Jammer Hat 12.00 30.00
DDJBM Bryant McKinnie JSY 4.00 10.00
DDJDC David Carr JSY 4.00 10.00
DDJJP Julius Peppers JSY 8.00 20.00
DDJMW Mike Williams JSY 4.00 10.00
DDJQJ Quentin Jammer JSY 6.00 15.00

2002 Bowman Fabric of the Future

This set contains jersey cards of some of the NFL's top 2002 rookies. The stated odds were as follows: Group A 1:2308, Group B 1:168, Group C, 1:185, and overall odds 1:85.

GROUP A ODDS 1:2308H, 1:662HTA
GROUP B ODDS 1:168H, 1:48HTA
GROUP C ODDS 1:185H, 1:53HTA
OVERALL ODDS 1:85H, 1:25HTA
FFAB Alex Brown B 5.00 12.00
FFDB Deion Branch C 5.00 12.00
FFDC David Carr B 3.00 8.00
FFDF DeShaun Foster A 5.00 12.00
FFEF Eddie Freeman B 3.00 8.00
FFHG Herb Haygood B 3.00 8.00
FFJM Josh McCown C 5.00 12.00
FFJW Javon Walker B 5.00 12.00
FFJWE Jonathan Wells C 4.00 10.00
FFKC Kelly Campbell B 4.00 10.00
FFKK Kurt Kittner B 3.00 8.00
FFLG Lamar Gordon B 4.00 10.00
FFTC Tim Carter C 4.00 10.00
FFTJ Terry Jones Jr. B 3.00 8.00
FFTS Travis Stephens C 3.00 8.00
FFTW Tank Williams B 4.00 10.00
FFWD Woody Dantzler B 4.00 10.00

2002 Bowman Flashback Autographs

This set contains authentic autographs from many of the NFL's top players. The stated odds for this set were as follows: Group A 1:3070, Group B 1:2308, Group C 1:1711, Group D 1:922, and the overall odds were 1:412.

GROUP A ODDS 1:3070H, 1:883HTA
GROUP B ODDS 1:2308H, 1:662HTA
GROUP C ODDS 1:1711H, 1:488HTA
GROUP D ODDS 1:922H, 1:263HTA
OVERALL ODDS 1:412H, 1:118HTA
RFABF Brett Favre A 100.00 200.00
RFABS Bill Schroeder C 6.00 15.00
RFACC Chris Chambers A 10.00 25.00
RFAJG Jeff Garcia C 6.00 15.00
RFALJ LaMont Jordan D 8.00 20.00
RFALS Lamar Smith B 6.00 15.00
RFALT LaDainian Tomlinson D 15.00 40.00
RFAMR Marcus Robinson B 8.00 20.00

2002 Bowman Flashback Jerseys

This set features cards with jersey swatches from many of the NFL's top up and coming players. Group A stated odds were 1:308, Group B were 1:185, and the overall odds were 1:116.

GROUP A ODDS 1:308H, 1:88HTA
GROUP B ODDS 1:185, 1:53HTA
OVERALL ODDS 1:116, 1:34HTA
RFRCJ Chad Johnson A 2.00 5.00
RFRCW Chris Weinke A 2.00 5.00
RFRDM Deuce McAllister B 2.50 6.00
RFRDT David Terrell B 2.00 5.00
RFRKB Kevan Barlow B 2.00 5.00
RFRMM Snoop Minnis A 2.00 5.00
RFRMV Michael Vick B 2.50 6.00
RFRMMC Mike McMahon A 2.00 5.00
RFRQM Quincy Morgan A 2.00 5.00
RFRRG Rod Gardner B 2.00 5.00
RFRSM Santana Moss A 2.50 6.00

2002 Bowman Signs of the Future

This set contains authentic autographs from some of the top 2002 rookies. Stated odds were as follows: Group A 1:8612, Group B 1:9306, Group C 1:659, and Group D 1:171. The overall odds were 1:133. Please note that some cards were only available via redemption, with the exchange expiration date being 10/31/2004. There was also a Red Ink parallel version of this, with each card being signed in red ink and serial numbered to 50.

GROUP A ODDS 1:18612H, 1:5297HTA
GROUP B ODDS 1:9306H, 1:2649HTA
GROUP C ODDS 1:659H, 1:188HTA
GROUP D ODDS 1:171H, 1:49HTA
OVERALL ODDS 1:133H, 1:39HTA
SFAB Antonio Bryant C 8.00 20.00
SFDC David Carr B 5.00 12.00
SFDG David Garrard D 6.00 15.00
SFDRC Reche Caldwell D 6.00 15.00
SFJG Jabar Gaffney C 5.00 12.00
SFJH Joey Harrington A 10.00 25.00
SFJM Josh McCown D 8.00 20.00
SFJS Jeremy Shockey D 8.00 20.00
SFJW Javon Walker C 8.00 20.00
SFLB Ladell Betts D 8.00 20.00
SFMM Maurice Morris D 6.00 15.00
SFNH Napoleon Harris C 6.00 15.00
SFPR Patrick Ramsey D 6.00 15.00
SFQJ Quentin Jammer D 8.00 20.00
SFRD Rohan Davey D 8.00 20.00
SFTC Tim Carter D 6.00 15.00
SFTJD T.J. Duckett C 5.00 12.00
SFTS Travis Stephens D 5.00 12.00
SFWG William Green C 6.00 15.00

2002 Bowman Signs of the Future Red Ink

This set is a parallel to the Signs of the Future set, with each card being signed in red ink, and serial #'d to 50.

STATED ODDS 1:251 HTA
STATED PRINT RUN 50 SER.#'d SETS
SFAB Antonio Bryant 12.00 30.00
SFDC David Carr 8.00 20.00
SFDG Daniel Graham 10.00 25.00
SFDG David Garrard 10.00 25.00
SFDRC Reche Caldwell 10.00 25.00
SFJG Jabar Gaffney 8.00 20.00
SFJH Joey Harrington 8.00 20.00
SFJM Josh McCown 12.00 30.00
SFJS Jeremy Shockey 12.00 30.00
SFJW Javon Walker 12.00 30.00
SFLB Ladell Betts 12.00 30.00
SFMM Maurice Morris 10.00 25.00
SFNH Napoleon Harris 10.00 25.00
SFPR Patrick Ramsey 10.00 25.00
SFQJ Quentin Jammer 12.00 30.00
SFRD Rohan Davey 12.00 30.00
SFTC Tim Carter 10.00 25.00
SFTJD T.J. Duckett 8.00 20.00
SFTS Travis Stephens 8.00 20.00
SFWG William Green 10.00 25.00

2003 Bowman

Released in October of 2003, this set consists of 275 cards including 110 veterans and 165 rookies. Hobby boxes contained 24 packs of 10 cards. SRP was $3.00. HTA jumbo boxes contained 10 packs of 35 cards and had an SRP of $10.00.

COMPLETE SET (273) 40.00 80.00
1 Brett Favre .60 1.50
2 Jeremy Shockey .20 .50
3 Fred Taylor .20 .50
4 Rich Gannon .25 .60
5 Joey Galloway .25 .60
6 Ray Lewis .30 .75
7 Jeff Blake .25 .60
8 Stacey Mack .20 .50
9 Matt Hasselbeck .20 .50
10 Laveranues Coles .20 .50
11 Brad Johnson .25 .60
12 Tommy Maddox .20 .50
13 Curtis Martin .25 .60
14 Tom Brady 1.25 3.00
15 Ricky Williams .25 .60
16 Stephen Davis .20 .50
17 Chad Johnson .20 .50
18 Joey Harrington .20 .50
19 Tony Gonzalez .25 .60
20 Peerless Price .20 .50
21 LaDainian Tomlinson .30 .75
22 James Thrash .20 .50
23 Charlie Garner .25 .60
24 Eddie George .25 .60
25 Terrell Owens .25 .60
26 Brian Urlacher .30 .75
27 Eric Moulds .20 .50
28 Emmitt Smith .50 1.25
29 Tim Couch .20 .50
30 Jake Plummer .20 .50
31 Marvin Harrison .25 .60
32 Chris Chambers .20 .50
33 Tiki Barber .25 .60
34 Kurt Warner .25 .60
35 Michael Pittman .20 .50
36 Kevin Dyson .20 .50
37 Clinton Portis .20 .50
38 Peyton Manning .75 2.00
39 Travis Taylor .20 .50
40 Jeff Garcia .20 .50
41 Patrick Ramsey .25 .60
42 Shaun Alexander .20 .50
43 Joe Horn .20 .50
44 Daunte Culpepper .25 .60
45 Travis Henry .20 .50
46 Brian Finneran .20 .50
47 William Green .20 .50
48 Kordell Stewart .20 .50
49 Reggie Wayne .25 .60
50 Priest Holmes .20 .50
51 Jay Fiedler .20 .50
52 Corey Dillon .20 .50
53 Jamal Lewis .25 .60
54 Mark Brunell .25 .60
55 Santana Moss .25 .60
56 Duce Staley .20 .50
57 Torry Holt .25 .60
58 Rod Gardner .20 .50
59 Kerry Collins .20 .50
60 Randy Moss .25 .60
61 Jerry Porter .20 .50
62 Plaxico Burress .20 .50
63 Steve McNair .25 .60
64 Muhsin Muhammad .20 .50
65 Drew Bledsoe .25 .60
66 T.J. Duckett .20 .50
67 Ahman Green .25 .60
68 Rod Smith .25 .60
69 Jimmy Smith .25 .60
70 Trent Green .20 .50
71 Tim Brown .30 .75
72 Jerome Bettis .30 .75
73 Isaac Bruce .30 .75
74 Derrick Mason .20 .50
75 Donovan McNabb .25 .60
76 Deuce McAllister .25 .60
77 Zach Thomas .25 .60
78 Garrison Hearst .20 .50
79 Koren Robinson .25 .60
80 Marshall Faulk .25 .60
81 Keyshawn Johnson .30 .75
82 Jake Delhomme .20 .50
83 Marty Booker .20 .50
84 James Stewart .20 .50
85 Corey Bradford .20 .50
86 Derrius Thompson .20 .50
87 Edgerrin James .25 .60
88 Darrell Jackson .25 .60
89 Hines Ward .25 .60
90 David Boston .20 .50
91 Curtis Conway .20 .50
92 David Patten .20 .50
93 Michael Bennett .20 .50
94 Todd Pinkston .20 .50
95 Jerry Rice .60 1.50
96 Jon Kitna .20 .50
97 Ed McCaffrey .25 .60
98 Donald Driver .25 .60
99 Anthony Thomas .25 .60
100 Michael Vick .25 .60
101 Terry Glenn .25 .60
102 Quincy Morgan .20 .50
103 David Carr .20 .50
104 Troy Brown .20 .50
105 Aaron Brooks .20 .50
106 Amani Toomer .20 .50
107 Drew Brees .30 .75
108 Chad Hutchinson .20 .50
109 Warrick Dunn .20 .50
110 Chad Pennington .20 .50
111 Carson Palmer RC .75 2.00
112 Brian St.Pierre RC .40 1.00
113 Keenan Howry RC .40 1.00
114 Sultan McCullough RC .40 1.00
115 Terence Newman RC .60 1.50
116 Kelley Washington RC .40 1.00
117 Musa Smith RC .40 1.00
118 Kevin Williams RC .60 1.50
119 Jordan Gross RC .40 1.00
120 Lance Briggs RC 3.00 8.00
121 Victor Hobson RC .40 1.00
122 Bryant Johnson RC .60 1.50
123 Travis Anglin RC .40 1.00
124 Artose Pinner RC .40 1.00
125 Willis McGahee RC .50 1.25
126 Rashean Mathis RC .40 1.00
127 B.J. Askew RC .50 1.25
128 DeWayne White RC .40 1.00
129 Kevin Curtis RC .40 1.00
130 Tyrone Calico RC .40 1.00
131 Julian Battle RC .50 1.25
132 Ricky Manning RC .50 1.25
133 Cory Redding RC .50 1.25
134 Michael Haynes RC .40 1.00
135 Dallas Clark RC .60 1.50
136 Shaun McDonald RC .50 1.25
137 Marcus Trufant RC .50 1.25
138 Kareem Kelly RC .40 1.00
139 Sam Aiken RC .50 1.25
140 Terrell Suggs RC .50 1.25
141 Gibran Hamdan RC .40 1.00
142 Bobby Wade RC .50 1.25
143 Aaron Walker RC .50 1.25
144 Calvin Pace RC .40 1.00
145 Quentin Griffin RC .50 1.25
146 Ken Dorsey RC .50 1.25
147 Jerome McDougle RC .40 1.00
148 Earnest Graham RC .60 1.50
149 Rashad Moore RC .40 1.00
150 Charles Rogers RC .50 1.25
151 Cecil Sapp RC .40 1.00
152 Cato June RC .75 2.00
153 Ahmaad Galloway RC .50 1.25
154 William Joseph RC .40 1.00
155 Anquan Boldin RC .60 1.50
156 L.J. Smith RC .60 1.50
157 Antwoine Sanders RC .40 1.00
158 Justin Griffith RC .50 1.25
159 Kevin Garrett RC .40 1.00
160 Teyo Johnson RC .50 1.25
161 Chris Crocker RC .50 1.25
162 Brad Banks RC .50 1.25
163 Justin Gage RC .50 1.25
164 Doug Gabriel RC .50 1.25
165 Terry Pierce RC .40 1.00
166 Bradie James RC .60 1.50
167 Bennie Joppru RC .40 1.00
168 Malaefou Mackenzie RC .40 1.00
169 Terrence Edwards RC .40 1.00
170 E.J. Henderson RC .50 1.25
171 Tony Romo RC 6.00 15.00
172 DeWayne Robertson RC .50 1.25
173 Dwone Hicks RC .40 1.00
174 Carl Ford RC .40 1.00
175 Byron Leftwich RC .50 1.25
176 Ken Hamlin RC .60 1.50
177 Domanick Davis RC .50 1.25
178 Adrian Madise RC .40 1.00
179 Siddeeq Shabazz RC .40 1.00
180 Dave Ragone RC .40 1.00
181 Mike Seidman RC .40 1.00
182 Brooks Bollinger RC .50 1.25
183 DeAndrew Rubin RC .40 1.00
184 Mike Pinkard RC .40 1.00
185 Nate Burleson RC .50 1.25
186 LaBrandon Toefield RC .40 1.00
187 Angelo Crowell RC .50 1.25
188 J.R. Tolver RC .50 1.25
189 Osi Umenyiora RC .75 2.00
190 Larry Johnson RC .50 1.25
191 Nick Barnett RC .60 1.50
192 Brandon Drumm RC .40 1.00
193 Rien Long RC .40 1.00
194 Zuriel Smith RC .40 1.00
195 Onterrio Smith RC .40 1.00
196 Ronald Bellamy RC .50 1.25
197 Kenny Peterson RC .50 1.25
198 Charles Tillman RC 2.00 5.00
199 Chaun Thompson RC .40 1.00
200 Andre Johnson RC 1.00 2.50
201 Gerald Hayes RC .50 1.25
202 Terrence Holt RC .50 1.25
203 Ovie Mughelli RC .50 1.25
204 Talman Gardner RC .40 1.00
205 Bethel Johnson RC .40 1.00
206 Avon Cobourne RC .40 1.00
207 Brandon Lloyd RC .60 1.50
208 Andre Woolfolk RC .40 1.00
209 George Wrighster RC .40 1.00
210 Justin Fargas RC .60 1.50
211 Jimmy Kennedy RC .50 1.25
212 Arnaz Battle RC .60 1.50
213 Marquel Blackwell RC .40 1.00
214 Walter Young RC .40 1.00
215 Kliff Kingsbury RC .60 1.50
216 Kawika Mitchell RC .60 1.50
217 Drayton Florence RC .60 1.50
218 Jeremi Johnson RC .40 1.00
219 Billy McMullen RC .40 1.00
220 Lee Suggs RC .40 1.00
221 David Kircus RC .50 1.25
222 Rod Babers RC .40 1.00
223 Jon Olinger RC .40 1.00
224 Ty Warren RC .50 1.25
225 Kyle Boller RC .40 1.00
226 Danny Curley RC .40 1.00
227 Andrew Pinnock RC .50 1.25
228 Kirk Farmer RC .50 1.25
229 Tully Banta-Cain RC .60 1.50
230 Alonzo Jackson RC .40 1.00
231 Anthony Adams RC .50 1.25
232 Trent Smith RC .50 1.25
233 Seneca Wallace RC .50 1.25

234 Shane Walton RC .40 1.00
235 Chris Brown RC .40 1.00
236 Dahrran Diedrick RC .40 1.00
237 Juston Wood RC .40 1.00
238 Mike Doss RC .60 1.50
239 Visanthe Shiancoe RC .60 1.50
240 Rex Grossman RC .50 1.25
241 David Young RC .40 1.00
242 Jimmy Wilkerson RC .50 1.25
243 Jason Witten RC 1.50 4.00
244 Dennis Weathersby RC .40 1.00
245 Taylor Jacobs RC .40 1.00
246 Chris Davis RC .50 1.25
247 LaTarence Dunbar RC .40 1.00
248 Eugene Wilson RC .60 1.50
249 Ryan Hoag RC .40 1.00
250 Chris Simms RC .40 1.00
251 Ike Taylor RC .60 1.50
252 Brock Forsey RC .50 1.25
253 Curt Anes RC .40 1.00
254 Taco Wallace RC .40 1.00
255 Johnathan Sullivan RC .40 1.00
256 David Tyree RC .50 1.25
257 Troy Polamalu RC 6.00 15.00
258 Nate Hybl RC .50 1.25
259 Spencer Nead RC .40 1.00
260 Boss Bailey RC .50 1.25
261 LaMarcus McDonald RC .40 1.00
262 Casey Moore RC .40 1.00
263 Pisa Tinoisamoa RC .60 1.50
264 Willie Ponder RC .40 1.00
265 Donald Lee RC .50 1.25
266 Nnamdi Asomugha RC .60 1.50
267 Sammy Davis RC .50 1.25
268 Joffrey Reynolds RC .40 1.00
269 Eddie Moore RC .40 1.00
270 Tony Hollings RC .50 1.25
271 Nick Maddox RC .40 1.00
272 Kevin Walter RC 1.00 2.50
273 Dan Klecko RC .50 1.25
274 Antwan Peek RC .40 1.00
275 Tyler Brayton RC .50 1.25

2003 Bowman Uncirculated Gold

*GOLD: 2.5X TO 6X BASIC CARDS
STATED ODDS ONE PER HTA BOX
171 Tony Romo 25.00 50.00
257 Troy Polamalu 40.00 100.00

2003 Bowman Uncirculated Silver

*ROOKIES: 2X TO 5X BASIC CARDS
ONE EXCH CARD PER HTA BOX
STATED PRINT RUN 111 SETS
171 Tony Romo 60.00 120.00
257 Troy Polamalu 30.00 80.00

2003 Bowman Draft Day Selection Relics

This set features jersey and hat swatches from the 2003 NFL Draft. Stated hat odds were 1:1352 hobby packs and 1:415 HTA packs. Stated jersey odds were 1:79 hobby packs and 1:37 HTA packs.
JSY STATED ODDS 1:79H, 1:37HTA
CAP STATED ODDS 1:1352H, 1:415HTA
DHBL Byron Leftwich Cap 2.50 6.00
DHCP Carson Palmer Cap 4.00 10.00
DHCR Charles Rogers Cap 2.50 6.00
DHDR DeWayne Robertson Cap 2.50 6.00
DHJK Jimmy Kennedy Cap 2.50 6.00
DHTN Terence Newman Cap 3.00 8.00
DJBL Byron Leftwich JSY 2.00 5.00
DJCP Carson Palmer JSY 3.00 8.00
DJCR Charles Rogers JSY 2.00 5.00
DJDR0 DeWayne Robertson JSY 2.00 5.00
DJJK Jimmy Kennedy JSY 2.00 5.00
DJTN Terence Newman JSY 2.50 6.00
DJTS Terrell Suggs JSY 2.00 5.00

2003 Bowman Fabric of the Future

This set features player worn jersey swatches. Stated odds are listed below.
GROUP A STATED ODDS 1:621H, 1:178HTA
GROUP B STATED ODDS 1:724H, 1:218HTA
GROUP C STATED ODDS 1:55H, 1:26HTA
FAAB Anquan Boldin A 2.50 6.00
FAAJ Andre Johnson A 4.00 10.00
FAAP Artose Pinner A 1.50 4.00
FABJ Bryant Johnson C 2.50 6.00
FABL Byron Leftwich A 2.00 5.00
FABSP Brian St.Pierre A 1.50 4.00
FACB Chris Brown C 1.50 4.00
FACP Carson Palmer A 3.00 8.00
FACR Charles Rogers C 2.00 5.00
FADR Dave Ragone C 1.50 4.00
FAJF Justin Fargas B 2.50 6.00
FAKB Kyle Boller A 1.50 4.00
FAKK Kliff Kingsbury C 2.50 6.00
FALJ Larry Johnson C 2.00 5.00
FAOS Onterrio Smith C 1.50 4.00
FARG Rex Grossman B 2.00 5.00
FATJ Taylor Jacobs A 1.50 4.00
FATJO Teyo Johnson C 2.00 5.00
FAWM Willis McGahee C 2.00 5.00

2003 Bowman Fabric of the Future Doubles

Inserted at a rate of 1:3475 hobby packs and 1:999 HTA packs, this set features two player worn jersey swatches. Each card is serial numbered to 50.
DUAL JSY/50 ODDS 1:3475H, 1:999HTA
STATED PRINT RUN 50 SER.#'d SETS
FADBG K.Boller/R.Grossman 2.50 6.00
FADMJ W.McGahee/L.Johnson 2.50 6.00
FADPL C.Palmer/B.Leftwich 4.00 10.00
FADRJ C.Rogers/A.Johnson 5.00 12.00
FADSR C.Simms/D.Ragone 2.00 5.00

2003 Bowman Franchise Future Jerseys

Inserted at a rate of 1:1738 hobby packs and 1:495 HTA packs, this set features two jersey swatches. Each card is numbered to 50.
DUAL JSY/50 ODDS 1:1738H,1:495HTA
STATED PRINT RUN 50 SER.#'d SETS
FFBM D.Bledsoe/W.McGahee 2.50 6.00
FFCJ D.Carr/A.Johnson 5.00 12.00
FFDP C.Dillon/C.Palmer 4.00 10.00
FFDW C.Dillon/K.Washington 2.00 5.00
FFLB R.Lewis/K.Boller 3.00 8.00
FFLS R.Lewis/T.Suggs 3.00 8.00
FFMC S.McNair/T.Calico 2.50 6.00
FFPR C.Pennington/D.Robertson 2.50 6.00
FFSL J.Smith/B.Leftwich 2.50 6.00
FFUG B.Urlacher/R.Grossman 3.00 8.00

2003 Bowman Franchise Jerseys

Serial numbered to 199, this set features jersey swatches. The stated odds for cards in Group A were 1:8838 hobby packs and 1:2448 HTA packs. The stated odds for cards in Group B were 1:473 hobby packs and 1:139 HTA packs.
GROUP A/99 ODDS 1:8838H, 1:2448HTA
GROUP B/199 ODDS 1:473H, 1:139HTA
STATED PRINT RUN 99-199
FRBU Brian Urlacher/199 3.00 8.00
FRCD Corey Dillon/199 2.00 5.00
FRCP Chad Pennington/199 2.00 5.00
FRDB Drew Bledsoe/199 2.50 6.00
FRDC David Carr/199 2.00 5.00
FRDM Deuce McAllister/199 2.50 6.00
FRJS Jimmy Smith/199 2.50 6.00
FRRL Ray Lewis/199 3.00 8.00
FRSM Steve McNair/99 2.50 6.00
FRTB Tim Brown/199 3.00 8.00

2003 Bowman Future Jerseys

Serial numbered to 199, this set features game jersey swatches of some of the NFL's top 2003 rookies. The stated odds were 1:425 hobby packs and 1:128 HTA packs.
JSY/199 ODDS 1:425H, 1:128HTA
STATED PRINT RUN 199 SER.#'d SETS
FUAJ Andre Johnson 5.00 12.00
FUBL Byron Leftwich 2.50 6.00
FUCP Carson Palmer 4.00 10.00
FUDR DeWayne Robertson 2.50 6.00
FUKB Kyle Boller 2.00 5.00
FUKW Kelley Washington 2.00 5.00
FURG Rex Grossman 2.50 6.00
FUTC Tyrone Calico 2.00 5.00
FUTS Terrell Suggs 2.50 6.00
FUWM Willis McGahee 2.50 6.00

2003 Bowman Paydirt Previews

Inserted at a rate of 1:869 hobby packs and 1:251 HTA packs, this set features game used pylon swatches from the 2003 Senior Bowl. There is also a gold parallel version sequentially numbered to 25 that was inserted at a rate of 1:3475 hobby packs and 1:999 HTA packs.
STATED ODDS 1:869H, 1:251HTA
*GOLD/25: .8X TO 2X BASIC PYLON
GOLD/25 ODDS 1:3475H, 1:999HTA
PYPBJ Bryant Johnson 4.00 10.00
PYPCP Carson Palmer 8.00 20.00
PYPCS Chris Simms 2.50 6.00
PYPDR Dave Ragone 2.50 6.00
PYPJF Justin Fargas 4.00 10.00
PYPKB Kyle Boller 2.50 6.00
PYPLJ Larry Johnson 3.00 8.00
PYPTC Tyrone Calico 2.50 6.00
PYPTG Talman Gardner 2.50 6.00
PYPTJ Taylor Jacobs 2.50 6.00

2003 Bowman Pigskin Previews

Inserted at a rate of 1:869 hobby packs and 1:251 HTA packs, this set features game used football swatches from the 2003 Senior Bowl. There is also a gold parallel version sequentially numbered to 25 that was inserted at a rate of 1:3475 hobby packs and 1:999 HTA packs.
STATED ODDS 1:869H, 1:251HTA
*GOLD/25: .8X TO 2X BASIC FB
GOLD/25 ODDS 1:3475H, 1:999HTA
PGPCP Carson Palmer 10.00 25.00
PGPCS Chris Simms 2.50 6.00
PGPDR Dave Ragone 2.50 6.00
PGPJF Justin Fargas 4.00 10.00
PGPKB Kyle Boller 2.50 6.00
PGPLJ Larry Johnson 3.00 8.00
PGPTG Talman Gardner 2.50 6.00
PGPTJ Taylor Jacobs 2.50 6.00
PGPTC Tyrone Calico 2.50 6.00

2003 Bowman Signs of the Future Autographs

This set contains authentic player autographs. Stated odds are listed below. Please note that Charles Rogers, Lee Suggs, Musa Smith, and Quentin Griffin, were only available in packs via redemption, with the exchange expiration date being 9/30/2005.
GROUP A/B ODDS 1:8837H, 1:2548HTA
GROUP C STATED ODDS 1:2918H, 1:941HTA
GROUP D STATED ODDS 1:1242H, 1:455HTA
GROUP E, F STATED ODDS 1:1748H, 1:785HTA
GROUP G STATED ODDS 1:2494H, 1:941HTA
GROUP H STATED ODDS 1:1830H, 698HTA
GROUP I STATED ODDS 1:869H, 309HTA
GROUP J STATED ODDS 1:351H, 1:111HTA
GROUP K STATED ODDS 1:519H, 158HTA
GROUP L STATED ODDS 1:157H, 1:64HTA
GROUP M STATED ODDS 1:39H, 1:18HTA
SFAC Avon Cobourne I 3.00 8.00
SFAJ Andre Johnson C 25.00 50.00
SFBB Brad Banks F 4.00 10.00
SFBJ Bryant Johnson D 5.00 12.00
SFBM Billy McMullen M 3.00 8.00
SFCB Chris Brown D 3.00 8.00
SFCS Chris Simms A 5.00 12.00
SFEG Earnest Graham M 5.00 12.00
SFJF Justin Fargas K 5.00 12.00
SFJT Jason Thomas F 3.00 8.00
SFKB Kyle Boller D 3.00 8.00
SFKD Ken Dorsey A 6.00 15.00
SFKK Kareem Kelly M 3.00 8.00
SFKW Kelley Washington G 3.00 8.00
SFLJ Larry Johnson B 12.00 30.00
SFLT LaBrandon Toefield M 3.00 8.00
SFMB Marquel Blackwell M 3.00 8.00
SFMS Musa Smith L 3.00 8.00
SFNB Nate Burleson M 4.00 10.00
SFOS Onterrio Smith H 3.00 8.00
SFQG Quentin Griffin M 4.00 10.00
SFRG Rex Grossman E 4.00 10.00
SFRL ReShard Lee J 5.00 12.00
SFSA Sam Aiken M 4.00 10.00
SFTC Tyrone Calico L 3.00 8.00
SFTG Talman Gardner M 3.00 8.00
SFTJ Teyo Johnson L 4.00 10.00
SFTJA Taylor Jacobs E 3.00 8.00
SFTS Terrell Suggs J 4.00 10.00

2003 Bowman Signs of the Future Autographs Doubles

Inserted at a rate of 1:3475 hobby packs and 1:999 HTA packs, this set features two authentic player autographs. Please note that the Charles Rogers/Andre Johnson card was only available in packs via redemption, with the exchange expiration date being 9/30/2005. Each card is serial numbered to 50.
STATED ODDS 1:3475H, 1:999 HTA
STATED PRINT RUN 50 SER.#'d SETS
SFDBG K.Boller/R.Grossman 4.00 10.00
SFDJF L.Johnson/J.Fargas 12.00 30.00
SFDJW T.Jacobs/K.Washington 10.00 25.00
SFDPL C.Palmer/B.Leftwich 25.00 60.00
SFDRJ C.Rogers/A.Johnson 40.00 80.00

2003 Bowman Signs of the Future Autographs Triples

Inserted at a rate of 1:11456 hobby packs and 1:3264 HTA packs, this set features three authentic player autographs. Please note that cards PLB and RJJ were only available in packs via redemption, with the exchange expiration being 9/30/2005. Each card is serial numbered to 25.
STATED ODDS 1:11456H, 1:3264HTA
STATED PRINT RUN 25 SER.#'d SETS
JSF Johnson/Smith/Fargas 20.00 50.00
RJJ Rogers/Johnson/Johnson 50.00 100.00

2004 Bowman

Bowman initially released in late October 2004. The base set consists of 275-cards including 165-rookies. Hobby boxes contained 24-packs of 10-cards and carried an S.R.P. of $3 per pack. Three parallel sets were issued including the hobby only First Edition release and the one-per box Uncirculated Gold sealed card. A variety of inserts can be found seeded in hobby and retail packs highlighted by the Coaches Autographs and Rookie Autographs signed Inserts.
COMPLETE SET (275) 30.00 60.00
1 Brett Favre .60 1.50
2 Jay Fiedler .10 .30
3 Andre Davis .10 .30
4 Travis Henry .20 .50
5 Jimmy Smith .20 .50
6 Santana Moss .25 .60
7 Correll Buckhalter .20 .50
8 Randy Moss .25 .60
9 Edgerrin James .25 .60
10 Marc Bulger .20 .50
11 Derrick Mason .20 .50
12 Mark Brunell .25 .60
13 Donte' Stallworth .20 .50
14 Deion Branch .20 .50
15 Jake Plummer .20 .50
16 Steve Smith .30 .75
17 Jon Kitna .20 .50
18 Andre Johnson .25 .60
19 A.J. Feeley .20 .50
20 Drew Bledsoe .25 .60
21 Antonio Bryant .25 .60
22 Reggie Wayne .25 .60
23 Thomas Jones .20 .50
24 Alge Crumpler .25 .60
25 Anquan Boldin .20 .50
26 Tim Rattay .10 .30
27 Charlie Garner .20 .50
28 James Thrash .10 .30
29 Koren Robinson .20 .50
30 Terrell Owens .25 .60
31 Amani Toomer .20 .50
32 Kelly Campbell .10 .30
33 Patrick Ramsey .25 .60
34 Plaxico Burress .20 .50
35 Chad Pennington .20 .50
36 Fred Taylor .20 .50
37 Domanick Davis .20 .50
38 DeShaun Foster .20 .50
39 T.J. Duckett .20 .50
40 Ahman Green .25 .60
41 Lee Suggs .25 .60
42 Tony Gonzalez .25 .60
43 Rich Gannon .20 .50
44 Kevan Barlow .20 .50
45 Torry Holt .25 .60
46 Aaron Brooks .20 .50
47 Tyrone Calico .20 .50
48 Keenan McCardell .10 .30
49 Hines Ward .25 .60
50 LaDainian Tomlinson .30 .75
51 Dante Hall .20 .50
52 Marcus Pollard .10 .30
53 Corey Dillon .20 .50
54 Justin McCareins .20 .50
55 Stephen Davis .20 .50
56 Jeff Garcia .20 .50
57 Ashley Lelie .20 .50
58 Javon Walker .20 .50
59 Kyle Boller .20 .50
60 Chad Johnson .20 .50
61 Anthony Thomas .20 .50
62 Byron Leftwich .20 .50
63 David Boston .20 .50
64 Onterrio Smith .20 .50
65 Deuce McAllister .25 .60
66 Antwaan Randle El .20 .50
67 Justin Fargas .20 .50
68 Laveranues Coles .20 .50
69 Quincy Morgan .20 .50
70 Priest Holmes .20 .50
71 Robert Ferguson .20 .50
72 Charles Rogers .20 .50
73 Drew Brees .30 .75
74 Matt Hasselbeck .20 .50
75 Peyton Manning .75 2.00
76 Rudi Johnson .20 .50
77 Jake Delhomme .20 .50
78 Tiki Barber .25 .60
79 Brad Johnson .20 .50
80 Steve McNair .25 .60
81 Willis McGahee .20 .50
82 Josh McCown .25 .60
83 Garrison Hearst .20 .50
84 Quincy Carter .20 .50
85 Ricky Williams .25 .60
86 Trent Green .20 .50
87 Curtis Martin .25 .60
88 Jerry Porter .20 .50
89 Brian Westbrook .20 .50
90 Clinton Portis .20 .50
91 Eric Moulds .20 .50
92 Marcel Shipp .20 .50
93 Joey Harrington .20 .50
94 David Carr .20 .50
95 Marvin Harrison .25 .60
96 Joe Horn .20 .50
97 Chris Chambers .20 .50
98 Darrell Jackson .25 .60
99 Eddie George .20 .50
100 Donovan McNabb .25 .60
101 Marshall Faulk .25 .60
102 Rex Grossman .20 .50
103 Tai Streets .10 .30
104 Jeremy Shockey .20 .50
105 Jamal Lewis .25 .60
106 Tom Brady 1.25 3.00
107 Shaun Alexander .20 .50
108 Carson Palmer .25 .60
109 Daunte Culpepper .25 .60
110 Michael Vick .25 .60
111 Eli Manning RC 5.00 12.00
112 Kevin Jones RC .50 1.25
113 Philip Rivers RC 1.25 3.00
114 Ben Roethlisberger RC 6.00 15.00
115 Roy Williams RC .40 1.00
116 Tommie Harris RC .50 1.25
117 Vontez Duff RC .40 1.00
118 Karlos Dansby RC .50 1.25
119 Thomas Tapeh RC .50 1.25
120 Matt Schaub RC .40 1.00
121 Dexter Reid RC .40 1.00
122 Jonathan Smith RC .40 1.00
123 Ricardo Colclough RC .40 1.00
124 Jeff Dugan RC .40 1.00
125 Larry Fitzgerald RC 2.50 6.00
126 Gibril Wilson RC .60 1.50
127 Sean Taylor RC 2.50 6.00
128 Marquise Hill RC .40 1.00
129 Ernest Wilford RC .50 1.25
130 Cedric Cobbs RC .40 1.00
131 Rich Gardner RC .50 1.25
132 Chris Cooley RC .50 1.25
133 Kenechi Udeze RC .50 1.25
134 John Navarre RC .40 1.00
135 Ben Troupe RC .40 1.00
136 Dave Ball RC .50 1.25
137 Antwan Odom RC .40 1.00
138 Stuart Schweigert RC .50 1.25
139 Derek Abney RC .40 1.00
140 Keary Colbert RC .40 1.00
141 Jeris McIntyre RC .40 1.00
142 Matt Kranchick RC .50 1.25
143 Rodney Leisle RC .40 1.00
144 Vince Wilfork RC .60 1.50
145 Lee Evans RC .60 1.50
146 Darnell Dockett RC .60 1.50
147 Jeremy LeSueur RC .40 1.00
148 Gilbert Gardner RC .40 1.00
149 Amon Gordon RC .40 1.00
150 Darius Watts RC .40 1.00
151 Junior Siavii RC .60 1.50
152 Igor Olshansky RC .50 1.25
153 Courtney Watson RC .40 1.00
154 D.J. Williams RC .60 1.50
155 Mewelde Moore RC .50 1.25
156 Teddy Lehman RC .40 1.00
157 Nathan Vasher RC .60 1.50
158 Randy Starks RC .40 1.00
159 Isaac Sopoaga RC .40 1.00
160 Drew Henson RC .40 1.00
161 Erik Coleman RC .50 1.25
162 Robert Kent RC .40 1.00
163 Jammal Lord RC .40 1.00
164 Richard Seigler RC .40 1.00
165 Jeff Smoker RC .50 1.25
166 Niko Koutouvides RC .40 1.00
167 Adimchinobe Echemandu RC .50 1.25
168 Matt Mauck RC .40 1.00
169 Brandon Miree RC .40 1.00
170 Dunta Robinson RC .40 1.00
171 B.J. Symons RC .60 1.50
172 Courtney Anderson RC .40 1.00
173 Bruce Perry RC .40 1.00
174 Shaun Phillips RC .50 1.25
175 Greg Jones RC .40 1.00
176 Ryan Krause RC .40 1.00
177 Charlie Anderson RC .40 1.00
178 Tank Johnson RC .40 1.00
179 Dwan Edwards RC .40 1.00
180 Julius Jones RC .40 1.00
181 Chad Lavalais RC .40 1.00
182 Tim Anderson RC .60 1.50
183 Jarrett Payton RC .60 1.50
184 Matt Ware RC .60 1.50
185 DeAngelo Hall RC .60 1.50
186 Ben Hartsock RC .40 1.00
187 Bradlee Van Pelt RC .60 1.50
188 Michael Boulware RC .60 1.50
189 Keith Smith RC .40 1.00
190 Michael Jenkins RC .40 1.00
191 Quincy Wilson RC .40 1.00
192 Dontarrious Thomas RC .50 1.25
193 Sloan Thomas RC .50 1.25
194 Tony Hargrove RC .40 1.00
195 Ben Watson RC .50 1.25
196 Craig Krenzel RC .40 1.00
197 Jason Babin RC .60 1.50
198 Jim Sorgi RC .50 1.25
199 Triandos Luke RC .40 1.00
200 Kellen Winslow RC .40 1.00
201 Patrick Crayton RC .60 1.50
202 Michael Waddell RC .40 1.00
203 Chris Gamble RC .40 1.00
204 Josh Harris RC .40 1.00
205 Devard Darling RC .40 1.00
206 Shawntae Spencer RC .40 1.00
207 Will Smith RC .50 1.25
208 Samie Parker RC .40 1.00
209 Darrion Scott RC .60 1.50
210 Chris Perry RC .40 1.00
211 P.K. Sam RC .40 1.00
212 Wes Welker RC 2.00 5.00
213 Ryan Dinwiddie RC .40 1.00
214 Rod Davis RC .40 1.00
215 Casey Clausen RC .50 1.25
216 Clarence Moore RC .40 1.00
217 D.J. Hackett RC .40 1.00
218 Casey Bramlet RC .40 1.00
219 Jared Lorenzen RC .50 1.25
220 Devery Henderson RC .40 1.00
221 Sean Jones RC .40 1.00
222 Maurice Mann RC .40 1.00
223 Jared Allen RC 2.00 5.00
224 Bruce Thornton RC .40 1.00
225 Tatum Bell RC .40 1.00
226 Leon Joe RC .40 1.00
227 Tim Euhus RC .40 1.00
228 John Standeford RC .40 1.00
229 Reggie Torbor RC .40 1.00
230 Rashaun Woods RC .40 1.00
231 Jason Shivers RC .40 1.00
232 Jason Peters RC .50 1.25
233 Ahmad Carroll RC .40 1.00
234 Jason David RC .60 1.50
235 Keyaron Fox RC .50 1.25
236 Corey Williams RC .50 1.25
237 Raheem Orr RC .40 1.00
238 Carlos Francis RC .40 1.00
239 Von Hutchins RC .40 1.00
240 Marcus Tubbs RC .60 1.50
241 Daryl Smith RC .40 1.00
242 Robert Gallery RC .50 1.25
243 Sean Tufts RC .40 1.00
244 Marquis Cooper RC .40 1.00
245 Bernard Berrian RC .40 1.00
246 Derrick Strait RC .40 1.00
247 Travis LaBoy RC .60 1.50
248 Johnnie Morant RC .40 1.00
249 Caleb Miller RC .40 1.00
250 Michael Clayton RC .50 1.25
251 Will Poole RC .60 1.50
252 Andy Hall RC .40 1.00
253 Demorrio Williams RC .60 1.50
254 Chris Thompson RC .40 1.00
255 Derrick Hamilton RC .40 1.00
256 Glenn Earl RC .40 1.00
257 Jonathan Vilma RC .50 1.25
258 Donnell Washington RC .50 1.25
259 Drew Carter RC .50 1.25
260 Steven Jackson RC .60 1.50
261 Jamaar Taylor RC .40 1.00
262 Nate Lawrie RC .40 1.00
263 Cody Pickett RC .40 1.00
264 Keiwan Ratliff RC .40 1.00
265 Luke McCown RC .40 1.00
266 Jerricho Cotchery RC .50 1.25
267 Joey Thomas RC .40 1.00
268 Shawn Andrews RC .60 1.50
269 Derrick Ward RC .60 1.50
270 Reggie Williams RC .40 1.00
271 Rod Rutherford RC .40 1.00
272 Michael Turner RC .40 1.00
273 Michael Gaines RC .40 1.00
274 Will Allen RC .50 1.25
275 J.P. Losman RC .40 1.00

2004 Bowman First Edition

COMPLETE SET (275) 60.00 120.00
*FIRST EDIT.VETS: .8X TO 2X BASE CARD
*FIRST ED.ROOKIES: .6X TO 1.5X

2004 Bowman Gold

COMPLETE SET (110) 12.50 30.00
*GOLD STARS: 1X TO 2.5X BASE CARD HI
ONE GOLD PER PACK

2004 Bowman Uncirculated Gold

*GOLD BORDER: 2.5X TO 6X BASIC CARDS
ANNOUNCED PRINT RUN 110 SETS

2004 Bowman Uncirculated White

*UNCIR.WHITE VETS: 3X TO 8X BASIC CARD
*UNCIR.WHITE ROOKIES: 2X TO 5X
ONE WHITE BORDER PER HOB/HTA BOX
STATED PRINT RUN 165 SER.#'d SETS

2004 Bowman Coaches Autographs

BRC STATED ODDS 1:2160 HOB
BRP STATED ODDS 1:1440 HOB
BRCJM Jim Mora Jr. 10.00 25.00
BRCMM Mike Mularkey 8.00 20.00
BRPGK Gary Kubiak 12.00 30.00
BRPSP Sean Payton 75.00 125.00

2004 Bowman Draft Day Selections Relics

CAP & JSY-CAP/25 ODDS 1:8640 HOB
JSY GROUP A ODDS 1:1728 H
JSY GROUP B ODDS 1:1481 H
JSY GROUP C ODDS 1:788 H
JSY GROUP D ODDS 1:540 H
JSY GROUP E ODDS 1:465 H
DHBR Ben Roethlisberger Cap 60.00 120.00
DHDH DeAngelo Hall Cap
DHKW Kellen Winslow Cap
DHRG Robert Gallery Cap
DHRW Roy Williams WR Cap
DJBR Ben Roethlisberger Jsy B 15.00 40.00
DJDEM E.Mann Jsy-Jsy/500 20.00 50.00
DJDH DeAngelo Hall Jsy B 5.00 12.00
DJEM Eli Manning Jsy A 20.00 50.00
DJHBR Roethlisberger Jsy-Cap 100.00 200.00
DJHDH DeAngelo Hall Jsy-Cap 12.50 30.00
DJHRG Robert Gallery Jsy-Cap 12.50 30.00
DJHRW Williams WR Jsy-Cap 20.00 50.00
DJKW Kellen Winslow Jsy D 3.00 8.00
DJRG Robert Gallery Jsy C 4.00 10.00
DJRW Roy Williams WR Jsy E 3.00 8.00

2004 Bowman Fabric of the Future

GROUP A ODDS 1:2908 H
GROUP B ODDS 1:1728 H
GROUP C ODDS 1:717 H
GROUP D ODDS 1:575 H
GROUP E ODDS 1:949 H
GROUP F ODDS 1:182 H
GROUP G ODDS 1:480 H
GROUP H ODDS 1:92 H
GROUP I ODDS 1:126 H
FFBR Ben Roethlisberger D 15.00 40.00
FFBT Ben Troupe C 2.50 6.00
FFDH DeAngelo Hall D 4.00 10.00
FFDR Dunta Robinson A 3.00 8.00
FFEM Eli Manning B 15.00 40.00
FFKJ Kevin Jones F 3.00 8.00
FFKW Kellen Winslow Jr. G 2.50 6.00
FFLE Lee Evans H 4.00 10.00
FFLM Luke McCown F 2.50 6.00
FFMJ Michael Jenkins E 2.50 6.00
FFPR Philip Rivers C 10.00 25.00
FFRW Roy Williams WR I 2.50 6.00
FFRWI Reggie Williams H 2.50 6.00
FFSJ Steven Jackson I 4.00 10.00
FFTB Tatum Bell H 2.50 6.00

2004 Bowman Fabric of the Future Doubles

STATED ODDS 1:2936 HOB
STATED PRINT RUN 50 SER.#'d SETS
FFDEJ Lee Evans 6.00 15.00
Michael Jenkins
FFDHR De.Hall/D.Robinson 6.00 15.00
FFDJB K.Jones/T.Bell 5.00 12.00
FFDMW E.Manning/Re.Williams 20.00 50.00
FFDWT K.Winslow Jr./B.Troupe 4.00 10.00

2004 Bowman Fast Forward Dual Jersey

STATED PRINT RUN 199 SER.#'d SETS
FFWBR T.Brady/P.Rivers 15.00 40.00
FFWCR Culpepper/Roethlisberger 12.00 30.00
FFWFJ M.Faulk/S.Jackson 4.00 10.00
FFWHW T.Holt/Ro.Williams WR 3.00 8.00
FFWMM J.McCown/L.McCown 3.00 8.00

2004 Bowman Rookie Autographs Blue

BLUE STATED ODDS 1:766 HOB
111 Eli Manning 60.00 120.00
112 Kevin Jones 15.00 40.00
113 Philip Rivers 40.00 80.00
114 Ben Roethlisberger 90.00 150.00
115 Roy Williams WR 12.00 30.00

2004 Bowman Rookie Autographs Red

*RED AUTO/25: .8X TO 2X BLUE AUTO
RED/25 STATED ODDS 1:7033 HOB
111 Eli Manning 250.00 400.00
114 Ben Roethlisberger 150.00 300.00

2004 Bowman Signs of the Future Autographs

GROUP A ODDS 1:2160 H
GROUP B ODDS 1:3398 H
GROUP C ODDS 1:1938 H
GROUP D ODDS 1:1239 H
GROUP E ODDS 1:866 H
GROUP F ODDS 1:192 H
GROUP G ODDS 1:443 H
GROUP H ODDS 1:91 H
GROUP I ODDS 1:345 H
GROUP J ODDS 1:69 H
SFCC Cedric Cobbs 3.00 8.00
SFCCL Casey Clausen H 4.00 10.00
SFCP Cody Pickett H 3.00 8.00
SFCPE Chris Perry H 3.00 8.00
SFEW Ernest Wilford J 4.00 10.00
SFGJ Greg Jones F 3.00 8.00
SFJC Jerricho Cotchery J 4.00 10.00
SFJH Josh Harris H 3.00 8.00
SFJN John Navarre J 3.00 8.00
SFJPL J.P. Losman C 3.00 8.00
SFJS Jeff Smoker I 4.00 10.00
SFKC Keary Colbert E 3.00 8.00
SFKJ Kevin Jones A 6.00 15.00
SFLE Lee Evans G 5.00 12.00
SFMC Michael Clayton D 4.00 10.00
SFMJ Michael Jenkins J 3.00 8.00
SFMM Mewelde Moore H 4.00 10.00
SFMS Matt Schaub F 10.00 25.00
SFPR Philip Rivers A 20.00 50.00
SFRWO Rashaun Woods B 4.00 10.00
SFTB Tatum Bell F 3.00 8.00

2004 Bowman Signs of the Future Autographs Dual

STATED ODDS 1:4383 HOB
STATED PRINT RUN 50 SER.#'d SETS
SFDFE L.Fitzgerald/L.Evans 20.00 50.00
SFDJJ S.Jackson/K.Jones 8.00 20.00
SFDLC J.P.Losman/Mi.Clayton 6.00 15.00
SFDMR E.Manning/P.Rivers 75.00 150.00

2005 Bowman

This 275-card set was released in October, 2005. The set was issued in the hobby in 10-card packs with an $3 SRP which came 24 packs to a box. Cards numbered 1-109 feature veterans while cards numbered 110-275 feature NFL rookies.
COMP.SET w/o AU's (270) 25.00 60.00
UNPRICED GOLD PRINT RUN 1
UNPRICED PRINT PLATES SER.#'d TO 1
1 Peyton Manning .75 2.00
2 Antonio Gates .30 .75
3 Priest Holmes .20 .50
4 Anquan Boldin .20 .50
5 Donovan McNabb .25 .60
6 Drew Bennett .25 .60
7 Michael Vick .25 .60
8 David Carr .20 .50
9 Drew Brees .30 .75
10 Trent Green .20 .50
11 Drew Bledsoe .25 .60
12 Randy Moss .25 .60
13 Terrell Owens .25 .60
14 Donte Stallworth .20 .50
15 Alge Crumpler .25 .60
16 Jake Plummer .20 .50
17 Curtis Martin .25 .60
18 Jason Witten .25 .60
19 Tom Brady 1.25 3.00
20 Thomas Jones .20 .50
21 Tiki Barber .25 .60
22 Maurice Carthon CO .20 .50
23 Rex Grossman .20 .50
24 Brett Favre .60 1.50
25 Marshall Faulk .25 .60
26 LaMont Jordan .25 .60
27 Kurt Warner .25 .60
28 Corey Dillon .20 .50
29 Julius Jones .20 .50
30 Ahman Green .25 .60
31 Jamal Lewis .25 .60
32 Ben Roethlisberger .50 1.25
33 Keary Colbert .20 .50
34 Mike Nolan CO RC .25 .60
35 Joey Harrington .20 .50
36 Brian Westbrook .20 .50
37 Domanick Davis .20 .50
38 Carson Palmer .25 .60
39 Stephen Davis .20 .50
40 Eli Manning .50 1.25
41 Edgerrin James .25 .60
42 Jonathan Vilma .20 .50
43 Brad Childress CO RC .25 .60
44 Willis McGahee .20 .50
45 Steve McNair .25 .60
46 Plaxico Burress .20 .50
47 Rudi Johnson .20 .50
48 Jerry Porter .20 .50
49 Chad Pennington .20 .50
50 Charles Rogers .20 .50
51 Patrick Ramsey .25 .60
52 Dwight Freeney .20 .50
53 Brian Griese .20 .50
54 Jerome Bettis .30 .75
55 Tim Lewis CO .20 .50
56 Aaron Brooks .20 .50
57 Matt Hasselbeck .20 .50
58 Chris Chambers .20 .50
59 Kyle Boller .20 .50
60 Brandon Lloyd .20 .50
61 Marc Bulger .20 .50
62 Isaac Bruce .30 .75
63 Jake Delhomme .20 .50
64 Chad Johnson .20 .50
65 Shaun Alexander .20 .50
66 Kevin Jones .20 .50
67 Eric Moulds .20 .50
68 Laveranues Coles .20 .50
69 A.J. Feeley .20 .50
70 Sean Taylor .30 .75
71 Romeo Crennel CO RC .30 .75
72 Ashley Lelie .20 .50
73 Nick Saban CO RC .30 .75
74 Deuce McAllister .25 .60
75 Kerry Collins .20 .50
76 Chris Brown .20 .50
77 Steven Jackson .20 .50
78 Nate Burleson .20 .50
79 LaDainian Tomlinson .30 .75
80 Darrell Jackson .20 .50
81 Torry Holt .25 .60
82 Lee Suggs .20 .50
83 Lee Evans .25 .60
84 Santana Moss .25 .60
85 Jeremy Shockey .20 .50
86 Hines Ward .25 .60
87 Muhsin Muhammad .20 .50
88 Daunte Culpepper .25 .60
89 Deion Branch .20 .50
90 DeShaun Foster .25 .60
91 Travis Henry .20 .50
92 Jerry Rice .60 1.50
93 Reggie Wayne .25 .60
94 Roy Williams WR .20 .50
95 Michael Jenkins .20 .50
96 Tatum Bell .20 .50
97 Andre Johnson .25 .60
98 Dante Hall .20 .50
99 Javon Walker .20 .50
100 Larry Fitzgerald .30 .75
101 Joe Horn .20 .50
102 Marvin Harrison .25 .60
103 Fred Taylor .20 .50
104 Byron Leftwich .20 .50
105 Tony Gonzalez .25 .60
106 T.J. Houshmandzadeh .20 .50
107 J.P. Losman .20 .50
108 Michael Clayton .20 .50
109 Clinton Portis .20 .50
110 Ted Cottrell CO RC .20 .50
111 Braylon Edwards RC .40 1.00
112 Aaron Rodgers RC 10.00 20.00
113 Ronnie Brown RC .50 1.25
114 Alex Smith QB RC 1.50 4.00
115 Cadillac Williams RC .40 1.00
116 Ciatrick Fason RC .40 1.00
117 Derrick Johnson RC .50 1.25
118 Carlos Rogers RC .60 1.50
119 Ryan Moats RC .40 1.00
120 Alvin Pearman RC .40 1.00
121 Stefan LeFors RC .40 1.00
122 Brandon Jacobs RC .50 1.25
123 Kyle Orton RC .40 1.00
124 Marion Barber RC .40 1.00
125 Mark Bradley RC .40 1.00
126 Travis Johnson RC .40 1.00
127 Antrel Rolle RC .60 1.50
128 Jason Campbell RC .40 1.00
129 DeMarcus Ware RC 1.25 3.00
130 Frank Gore RC .75 2.00
131 Justin Miller RC .40 1.00
132 J.J. Arrington RC .50 1.25
133 Marcus Spears RC .40 1.00
134 Roddy White RC .60 1.50
135 Fabian Washington RC .40 1.00
136 Vincent Jackson RC .60 1.50
137 Erasmus James RC .40 1.00
138 Roscoe Parrish RC .40 1.00
139 Airese Currie RC .40 1.00
140 Heath Miller RC .75 2.00
141 Mike Patterson RC .40 1.00
142 Troy Williamson RC .40 1.00
143 Terrence Murphy RC .40 1.00
144 Dan Orlovsky RC .40 1.00
145 Eric Shelton RC .40 1.00
146 Thomas Davis RC .40 1.00
147 Cedric Benson RC .40 1.00
148 Noah Herron RC .40 1.00
149 Vernand Morency RC .40 1.00
150 Darren Sproles RC .60 1.50
151 Alex Smith TE RC .40 1.00
152 Mark Clayton RC .40 1.00
153 Craphonso Thorpe RC .40 1.00
154 Mike Williams .50 1.25
155 Anthony Davis RC .40 1.00
156 Charlie Frye RC .40 1.00
157 Fred Gibson RC .40 1.00
158 Reggie Brown RC .40 1.00
159 Andrew Walter RC .40 1.00
160 Adam Jones RC .40 1.00
161 David Greene RC .40 1.00
162 Maurice Clarett .40 1.00
163 Courtney Roby RC .40 1.00
164 Derek Anderson RC .50 1.25
165 Matt Jones RC .40 1.00
166 Chris Henry RC .50 1.25
167 Shaun Cody RC .50 1.25
168 Khalif Barnes RC .40 1.00
169 Matt Roth RC .40 1.00
170 Lionel Gates RC .40 1.00
171 Kevin Burnett RC .50 1.25
172 Taylor Stubblefield RC .40 1.00
173 Zach Tuiasosopo RC .40 1.00
174 Alex Barron RC .40 1.00
175 Mike Nugent RC .50 1.25
176 Barrett Ruud RC .50 1.25
177 Brock Berlin RC .40 1.00
178 Kirk Morrison RC .60 1.50
179 David Pollack RC .40 1.00
180 Ryan Fitzpatrick RC .60 1.50
181 Kay-Jay Harris RC .40 1.00
182 Dan Cody RC .40 1.00
183 Chad Owens RC .40 1.00
184 Stanley Wilson RC .50 1.25
185 Rasheed Marshall RC .50 1.25
186 Bryant McFadden RC .50 1.25
187 Joel Dreessen RC .50 1.25
188 Donte Nicholson RC .40 1.00
189 Scott Starks RC .50 1.25
190 Walter Reyes RC .40 1.00
191 Stanford Routt RC .50 1.25
192 Lance Mitchell RC .50 1.25
193 Rian Wallace RC .50 1.25
194 Timmy Chang RC .40 1.00
195 Oshiomogho Atogwe RC .50 1.25
196 Larry Brackins RC .40 1.00
197 Jovan Witherspoon RC .40 1.00
198 Boomer Grigsby RC .60 1.50
199 Darryl Blackstock RC .40 1.00
200 Jerome Mathis RC .60 1.50
201 Ellis Hobbs RC .60 1.50
202 Dante Ridgeway RC .40 1.00
203 James Kilian RC .40 1.00
204 Patrick Estes RC .40 1.00
205 Justin Tuck RC .50 1.25
206 Channing Crowder RC .50 1.25
207 Dustin Fox RC .50 1.25
208 Marlin Jackson RC .40 1.00
209 Luis Castillo RC .50 1.25
210 Paris Warren RC .50 1.25
211 J.R. Russell RC .40 1.00
212 Cedric Houston RC .60 1.50
213 Corey Webster RC .50 1.25
214 Craig Bragg RC .40 1.00
215 Tab Perry RC .40 1.00
216 Ryan Riddle RC .40 1.00
217 Gino Guidugli RC .40 1.00
218 Deandra Cobb RC .40 1.00
219 Travis Daniels RC .50 1.25
220 Marcus Maxwell RC .40 1.00
221 Eric King RC .40 1.00
222 Matt Cassel RC .40 1.00
223 Justin Green RC .60 1.50
224 Steve Savoy RC .40 1.00
225 Shawne Merriman RC .60 1.50
226 Damien Nash RC .50 1.25
227 T.A. McLendon RC .40 1.00
228 Vincent Fuller RC .50 1.25
229 Jordan Beck RC .50 1.25
230 Lofa Tatupu RC .50 1.25
231 Will Peoples RC .50 1.25
232 Chad Friehauf RC .50 1.25
233 Brady Poppinga RC .60 1.50
234 Anttaj Hawthorne RC .40 1.00
235 Adrian McPherson RC .40 1.00
236 Nick Collins RC .60 1.50
237 Roydell Williams RC .50 1.25
238 Craig Ochs RC .50 1.25
239 Billy Bajema RC .40 1.00
240 Jon Goldsberry RC .60 1.50
241 Jared Newberry RC .50 1.25
242 Odell Thurman RC .60 1.50
243 Kelvin Hayden RC .50 1.25
244 Jamaal Brimmer RC .40 1.00
245 Jonathan Babineaux RC .40 1.00
246 Bo Scaife RC .50 1.25
247 Chris Spencer RC .60 1.50
248 Manuel White RC .50 1.25
249 Josh Davis RC .40 1.00
250 Bryan Randall RC .50 1.25
251 James Butler RC .50 1.25
252 Harry Williams RC .50 1.25
253 Leroy Hill RC .60 1.50
254 Josh Bullocks RC .50 1.25
255 Alfred Fincher RC .50 1.25
256 Antonio Perkins RC .50 1.25
257 Bobby Purify RC .50 1.25
258 Rick Razzano RC .40 1.00
259 Darrent Williams RC .60 1.50
260 Darian Durant RC .40 1.00
261 Fred Amey RC .40 1.00
262 Ronald Bartell RC .50 1.25
263 Kerry Rhodes RC .50 1.25
264 Jerome Carter RC .40 1.00
265 Marcus Randall RC .50 1.25
266 Nehemiah Broughton RC .50 1.25
267 Keron Henry RC .40 1.00
268 Jerome Collins RC .50 1.25
269 Trent Cole RC .60 1.50
270 Alphonso Hodge RC .40 1.00
271 Brandon Jones RC .50 1.25
272 Chase Lyman RC .40 1.00
273 Marviel Underwood RC .50 1.25
274 Maurice Washington RC .40 1.00
275 Madison Hedgecock RC .60 1.50

2005 Bowman Bronze

COMPLETE SET (275) 75.00 150.00
*VETS: 1X TO 2.5X BASIC CARDS
*ROOKIES: .8X TO 2X BASIC CARDS
ONE BRONZE PER PACK

2005 Bowman First Edition

COMPLETE SET (275) 60.00 120.00
*VETS: .8X TO 2X BASIC CARDS
*ROOKIES: .6X TO 1.5X BASIC CARDS

2005 Bowman Silver

*VETS:/200 2X TO 5X BASIC CARDS
*ROOKIES/200: 1.2X TO 3X BASIC CARDS
SILVER/200 ODDS 1:12 H/R, 1:6 JUM

2005 Bowman Coaches Autographs

PROSPECT ODDS 1:2058H, 1:398J, 1:2139R
COACH ROOK.ODDS 1:4171H, 1:792J, 1:4598R
BCPBC Brad Childress 12.00 30.00
BCPMC Maurice Carthon 10.00 25.00
BCPTC Ted Cottrell 10.00 25.00
BCPTL Tim Lewis 10.00 25.00
BRCMN Mike Nolan 12.00 30.00
BRCRC Romeo Crennel 12.00 30.00

2005 Bowman Draft Day Selections Relics

GROUP A JERSEY 1:1208H, 1:365J, 1:1282R
GROUP B JERSEY 1:305H, 1:92J, 1:321R
CAP & JSY-CAP/25 ODDS 1:15,244H, 1:4557J
UNPRICED 1/1 STATED ODDS 1:147,360
DHAR Antrel Rolle Cap 15.00 30.00
DHARO Aaron Rodgers Cap 50.00 100.00
DHCB Cedric Benson Cap 15.00 40.00
DHRB Ronnie Brown Cap 25.00 50.00
DJAR Antrel Rolle Jsy A 6.00 15.00
DJARO Aaron Rodgers Jsy B 20.00 50.00
DJCB Cedric Benson Jsy B 6.00 15.00
DJHAR Antrel Rolle Jsy-Cap 12.50 30.00
DJHARO Aaron Rodgers Jsy-Cap 50.00 100.00
DJHCB Cedric Benson Jsy-Cap 15.00 40.00
DJHRB Ronnie Brown Jsy-Cap 25.00 50.00
DJRB Ronnie Brown Jsy B 10.00 20.00

2005 Bowman Fabric of the Future

GROUP A ODDS 1:1364H, 1:400J, 1:1472R
GROUP B ODDS 1:43 H, 1:18 J, 1:132 R
*GOLD/100: .6X TO 1.5X BASIC JSY
GOLD/100 ODDS 1:1002H, 1:330J, 1:1074R
UNPRICED LETTER PRINT RUN 1
FFARO Antrel Rolle B 4.00 10.00
FFAS Alex Smith QB B 10.00 25.00
FFAW Andrew Walter B 2.50 6.00
FFCR Carlos Rogers A 4.00 10.00
FFES Eric Shelton B 2.50 6.00
FFFG Frank Gore B 5.00 12.00
FFJJA J.J. Arrington B 3.00 8.00
FFMC Maurice Clarett B 2.50 6.00
FFRB Reggie Brown B 2.50 6.00
FFRM Ryan Moats B 2.50 6.00
FFRP Roscoe Parrish B 2.50 6.00
FFRW Roddy White B 4.00 10.00
FFSL Stefan LeFors B 2.50 6.00
FFVJ Vincent Jackson B 4.00 10.00
FFVM Vernand Morency B 2.50 6.00

2005 Bowman Fabric of the Future Doubles

DOUBLE/50 ODDS 1:6056H, 1:2170J, 1:6624R
FFDCJ M.Clayton/M.Jones 8.00 20.00
FFDEW B.Edwards/T.Williamson
FFDRJ A.Rolle/A.Jones
FFDSC A.Smith QB/J.Campbell 15.00 40.00
FFDWB C.Williams/Ro.Brown 15.00 40.00

2005 Bowman Rookie Autographs

STATED ODDS 1:1249 H, 1:249 J, 1:1485 R
111 Braylon Edwards 8.00 20.00
112 Aaron Rodgers 250.00 400.00
113 Ronnie Brown 10.00 25.00
114 Alex Smith QB 15.00 40.00
115 Cadillac Williams 8.00 20.00

2005 Bowman Signs of the Future Autographs

GROUP A ODDS 1:7247H, 1:2940J, 1:7997R
GROUP B ODDS 1:1373H, 1:1072J, 1:1764R
GROUP C ODDS 1:408H, 1:229J, 1:476R
GROUP D ODDS 1:1107H, 1:779J, 1:1230R
GROUP E ODDS 1:385H, 1:171J, 1:634R
GROUP F ODDS 1:557H, 1:432J, 1:758R

GROUP G ODDS 1:200H, 1:80J, 1:756R
GROUP H ODDS 1:292H, 1:126J, 1:1171R
GROUP I ODDS 1:193H, 1:84J, 1:1688R
GROUP J ODDS 1:156H, 1:58J, 1:649R
GROUP K ODDS 1:86H, 1:36J, 1:130R
SFAM Adrian McPherson J
SFAP Alvin Pearman G 3.00 8.00
SFAR Antrel Rolle C 5.00 12.00
SFAS Alex Smith QB E 12.00 30.00
SFBE Braylon Edwards A 3.00 8.00
SFBJ Brandon Jacobs H 8.00 20.00
SFCBR Craig Bragg K 3.00 8.00
SFCF Ciatrick Fason C 3.00 8.00
SFCFR Charlie Frye B 3.00 8.00
SFCFRE Charles Frederick F 3.00 8.00
SFCH Cedric Houston E 5.00 12.00
SFCO Chad Owens K 3.00 8.00
SFCR Courtney Roby K 3.00 8.00
SFCT Craphonso Thorpe C 3.00 8.00
SFDJ Derrick Johnson I 4.00 10.00
SFDO Dan Orlovsky D 3.00 8.00
SFDP David Pollack B 3.00 8.00
SFES Eric Shelton C 3.00 8.00
SFFG Frank Gore J 6.00 15.00
SFHM Heath Miller C 6.00 15.00
SFJC Jason Campbell C 3.00 8.00
SFLM Lance Mitchell G 4.00 10.00
SFMB Mark Bradley K 3.00 8.00
SFMBA Marion Barber C 3.00 8.00
SFMC Mark Clayton C 3.00 8.00
SFMCL Maurice Clarett E 3.00 8.00
SFMW Mike Williams D 4.00 10.00
SFRB Reggie Brown B 3.00 8.00
SFRM Ryan Moats H 3.00 8.00
SFRP Roscoe Parrish J 3.00 8.00
SFRW Roddy White I 5.00 12.00
SFSL Stefan LeFors K 3.00 8.00
SFTM Terrence Murphy I 3.00 8.00
SFTS Taylor Stubblefield F 3.00 8.00
SFTW Troy Williamson G 3.00 8.00
SFVJ Vincent Jackson E 5.00 12.00
SFVM Vernand Morency G 3.00 8.00

2005 Bowman Signs of the Future Autographs Dual

DUAL AU/50 ODDS 1:7247H, 1:1248J, 1:7997R
SFDBB Ro.Brown/C.Benson 25.00 60.00
SFDBW Ro.Brown/C.Williams 25.00 60.00
SFDSR A.Smith QB/A.Rodgers 200.00 350.00
SFDWC T.Williamson/M.Clayton 20.00 50.00
SFDWE M.Williams/B.Edwards 50.00 120.00

2005 Bowman Throwback Threads Jerseys

STATED ODDS 1:76 H, 1:32 J, 1:137 R
*GOLD/50: .6X TO 1.5X BASIC JSY
GOLD/50 ODDS 1:2695 H, 1:701J, 1:2484R
BRTAW Andrew Walter 2.50 6.00
BRTCF Ciatrick Fason 2.50 6.00
BRTCR Courtney Roby 2.50 6.00
BRTCFR Charlie Frye 2.50 6.00
BRTES Eric Shelton 2.50 6.00
BRTFG Frank Gore 5.00 12.00
BRTKO Kyle Orton 2.50 6.00
BRTMB Mark Bradley 2.50 6.00
BRTRM Ryan Moats 2.50 6.00
BRTRP Roscoe Parrish 2.50 6.00
BRTSL Stefan LeFors 2.50 6.00
BRTVJ Vincent Jackson 4.00 10.00
BRTVM Vernand Morency 2.50 6.00

2006 Bowman

This 275-card set was released in October, 2006. The set was issued into the hobby in 10-card packs, with a $3 SRP, which came 24 packs to a box. Cards numbered 1 100 feature veterans (and a couple of newly-hired head coaches) while cards numbered 101-275 feature 2006 rookies.
COMPLETE SET (275) 25.00 60.00
UNPRICED PRINT PLATES SER.#'d TO 1
UNPRICED RED SER.#'d TO 1
1 Plaxico Burress .20 .50
2 Lee Evans .25 .60
3 Shaun Alexander .20 .50
4 Muhsin Muhammad .20 .50
5 Jamal Lewis .25 .60
6 Brett Favre .60 1.50
7 Jake Plummer .20 .50
8 Clinton Portis .20 .50
9 Deuce McAllister .25 .60
10 Rod Marinelli CO RC .20 .50
11 Tom Brady 1.00 2.50
12 Torry Holt .25 .60
13 T.J. Houshmandzadeh .20 .50
14 Rudi Johnson .20 .50
15 Priest Holmes .20 .50
16 Tatum Bell .20 .50
17 Carson Palmer .25 .60
18 Jeremy Shockey .20 .50
19 Willis McGahee .20 .50
20 Shawne Merriman .25 .60
21 Alge Crumpler .25 .60
22 Terrell Owens .25 .60
23 Marion Barber .30 .75
24 Fred Taylor .20 .50
25 Dante Hall .20 .50
26 Steve Smith .30 .75
27 Mike McCarthy CO RC .20 .50
28 Brad Johnson .25 .60
29 Reggie Wayne .25 .60
30 David Carr .20 .50
31 DeShaun Foster .25 .60
32 Julius Jones .20 .50
33 Tony Gonzalez .25 .60
34 Chad Johnson .20 .50
35 Javon Walker .25 .60
36 Curtis Martin .25 .60
37 Marc Bulger .20 .50
38 Peyton Manning .75 2.00
39 LaMont Jordan .25 .60
40 LaDainian Tomlinson .30 .75
41 Tiki Barber .25 .60
42 Darrell Jackson .25 .60
43 Byron Leftwich .20 .50
44 J.P. Losman .25 .60
45 Dwight Freeney .20 .50
46 Kevin Jones .20 .50
47 Drew Brees .30 .75
48 Isaac Bruce .30 .75
49 Hines Ward .25 .60
50 Drew Bledsoe .25 .60
51 Randy Moss .25 .60
52 Roy Williams WR .20 .50
53 Edgerrin James .25 .60
54 Donte Stallworth .20 .50
55 Odell Thurman .20 .50
56 Chester Taylor .25 .60
57 Ahman Green .25 .60
58 Steven Jackson .20 .50
59 Randy McMichael .20 .50
60 Larry Fitzgerald .25 .60
61 Ben Roethlisberger .40 1.00
62 Charlie Frye .25 .60
63 Daunte Culpepper .25 .60
64 Keary Colbert .20 .50
65 Santana Moss .25 .60
66 Patrick Ramsey .25 .60
67 Mark Clayton .20 .50
68 Jonathan Vilma .20 .50
69 Gary Kubiak CO .20 .50
70 Michael Jenkins .20 .50
71 Jake Delhomme .20 .50
72 Marvin Harrison .25 .60
73 Aaron Rodgers .75 2.00
74 Trent Green .20 .50
75 Andre Johnson .25 .60
76 Chris Chambers .20 .50
77 Matt Hasselbeck .20 .50
78 Chris Brown .20 .50
79 Reggie Brown .20 .50
80 Eli Manning .25 .60
81 Warrick Dunn .20 .50
82 Kurt Warner .25 .60
83 Corey Dillon .20 .50
84 Antonio Gates .30 .75
85 Anquan Boldin .20 .50
86 Terry Glenn .25 .60
87 Donovan McNabb .25 .60
88 Steve McNair .25 .60
89 Drew Bennett .25 .60
90 Jason Witten .25 .60
91 Alex Smith QB .25 .60
92 Joe Horn .20 .50
93 Eric Moulds .20 .50
94 Domanick Davis .20 .50
95 Billy Volek .20 .50
96 Deion Branch .20 .50
97 Chris Cooley .20 .50
98 Todd Heap UER .20 .50
99 Larry Johnson .20 .50
100 Chad Pennington .20 .50
101 Willie Parker .25 .60
102 Brandon Lloyd .20 .50
103 Cadillac Williams .25 .60
104 Rod Smith .25 .60
105 Philip Rivers .30 .75
106 Ronnie Brown .25 .60
107 Reuben Droughns .25 .60
108 Braylon Edwards .20 .50
109 Joey Galloway .25 .60
110 Michael Vick .25 .60
111 Reggie Bush RC .60 1.50
112 Matt Leinart RC .40 1.00
113 Vince Young RC .40 1.00
114 Jay Cutler RC .50 1.25
115 Santonio Holmes RC .50 1.25
116 LenDale White RC .40 1.00
117 DeAngelo Williams RC .50 1.25
118 Mario Williams RC .60 1.50
119 A.J. Hawk RC .50 1.25
120 Joseph Addai RC .40 1.00
121 Leonard Pope RC .60 1.50
122 Tamba Hali RC .60 1.50
123 Bruce Gradkowski RC .50 1.25
124 Jerome Harrison RC .40 1.00
125 Jason Allen RC .50 1.25
126 Laurence Maroney RC .40 1.00
127 Mathias Kiwanuka RC .60 1.50
128 Brodrick Bunkley RC .50 1.25
129 Brian Calhoun RC .40 1.00
130 Bobby Carpenter RC .40 1.00
131 Johnathan Joseph RC .50 1.25
132 Maurice Stovall RC .40 1.00
133 Anthony Fasano RC .40 1.00
134 Travis Wilson RC .40 1.00
135 Chad Jackson RC .40 1.00
136 D'Brickashaw Ferguson RC .40 1.00
137 Tarvaris Jackson RC .40 1.00
138 Omar Jacobs RC .40 1.00
139 Reggie McNeal RC .40 1.00
140 Jerious Norwood RC .40 1.00
141 Haloti Ngata RC .50 1.25
142 Jason Avant RC .40 1.00
143 Brandon Marshall RC .75 2.00
144 Tye Hill RC .40 1.00
145 Manny Lawson RC .50 1.25
146 Brandon Williams RC .40 1.00
147 Demetrius Williams RC .40 1.00
148 Michael Huff RC .50 1.25
149 Mike Hass RC .40 1.00
150 Vernon Davis RC .50 1.25
151 Donte Whitner RC .50 1.25
152 Marcedes Lewis RC .40 1.00
153 Michael Robinson RC .40 1.00
154 Maurice Drew RC .60 1.50
155 Sinorice Moss RC .40 1.00
156 Brodie Croyle RC .40 1.00
157 Derek Hagan RC .50 1.25
158 Chad Greenway RC .60 1.50
159 Kellen Clemens RC .40 1.00
160 Skyler Green RC .40 1.00
161 Devin Hester RC .75 2.00
162 Jeremy Bloom RC .40 1.00
163 Ashton Youboty RC .40 1.00
164 Kamerion Wimbley RC .50 1.25
165 Charlie Whitehurst RC .40 1.00
166 Devin Aromashodu RC .40 1.00
167 Darnell Bing RC .50 1.25
168 Adam Jennings RC .50 1.25
169 Joe Klopfenstein RC .40 1.00
170 Jeff Webb RC .50 1.25
171 D.J. Shockley RC .50 1.25
172 Daniel Bullocks RC .40 1.00
173 Marcus Vick RC .40 1.00
174 Greg Jennings RC .60 1.50
175 David Thomas RC .40 1.00
176 Thomas Howard RC .40 1.00
177 Todd Watkins RC .40 1.00
178 Leon Washington RC .40 1.00
179 Winston Justice RC .50 1.25
180 Lawrence Vickers RC .50 1.25
181 Bernard Pollard RC .50 1.25
182 Davin Joseph RC .50 1.25
183 Abdul Hodge RC .40 1.00
184 Pat Watkins RC .50 1.25
185 Jon Alston RC .50 1.25
186 Ernie Sims RC .40 1.00
187 Jovon Bouknight RC .50 1.25
188 D'Qwell Jackson RC .40 1.00
189 Wali Lundy RC .40 1.00
190 Corey Bramlet RC .50 1.25
191 Jonathan Orr RC .50 1.25
192 Gerald Riggs RC .50 1.25
193 Antonio Cromartie RC .50 1.25
194 Will Blackmon RC .40 1.00
195 Chris Gocong RC .50 1.25
196 David Pittman RC .60 1.50
197 Quinn Sypniewski RC .50 1.25
198 A.J. Nicholson RC .40 1.00
199 Richard Marshall RC .50 1.25
200 Kevin McMahan RC .50 1.25
201 Cedric Humes RC .40 1.00
202 J.D. Runnels RC .50 1.25
203 Darryl Tapp RC .50 1.25
204 Charles Davis RC .50 1.25
205 Brad Smith RC .50 1.25
206 Tim Massaquoi RC .50 1.25
207 Nate Salley RC .50 1.25
208 Matt Shelton RC .60 1.50
209 Brett Basanez RC .60 1.50
210 Demario Minter RC .50 1.25
211 Marques Hagans RC .40 1.00
212 Rocky McIntosh RC .40 1.00
213 Anthony Mix RC .50 1.25
214 Hank Baskett RC .40 1.00
215 Jimmy Williams RC .40 1.00
216 Andre Hall RC .50 1.25
217 Cody Hodges RC .50 1.25
218 Greg Lee RC .40 1.00
219 Danieal Manning RC .60 1.50
220 Jason Hatcher RC .60 1.50
221 Ben Obomanu RC .50 1.25
222 Dusty Dvoracek RC .60 1.50
223 Ingle Martin RC .50 1.25
224 Marcus McNeill RC .40 1.00
225 DeMeco Ryans RC .50 1.25
226 Dwayne Slay RC .40 1.00
227 Domenik Hixon RC .60 1.50
228 John David Washington RC .40 1.00
229 P.J. Daniels RC .40 1.00
230 Kelly Jennings RC .50 1.25
231 Josh Betts RC .50 1.25
232 Marques Colston RC .60 1.50
233 John McCargo RC .40 1.00
234 P.J. Pope RC .60 1.50
235 Gabe Watson RC .40 1.00
236 Paul Pinegar RC .40 1.00
237 Ray Edwards RC .60 1.50
238 Elvis Dumervil RC .60 1.50
239 Travis Lulay RC .50 1.25
240 Alan Zemaitis RC .40 1.00
241 Bennie Brazell RC .50 1.25
242 Jeff King RC .50 1.25
243 Damien Rhodes RC .50 1.25
244 Orien Harris RC .50 1.25
245 David Anderson RC .50 1.25
246 Roman Harper RC .50 1.25
247 Garrett Mills RC .50 1.25
248 Anthony Schlegel RC .50 1.25
249 David Kirtman RC .50 1.25
250 Omar Gaither RC .60 1.50
251 Freddie Keiaho RC .50 1.25
252 J.J. Outlaw RC .50 1.25
253 Willie Reid RC .50 1.25
254 Tony Scheffler RC .60 1.50
255 Dee Webb RC .50 1.25
256 Drew Olson RC .40 1.00
257 Tim Day RC .50 1.25
258 Martin Nance RC .40 1.00
259 Spencer Havner RC .50 1.25
260 Ko Simpson RC .50 1.25
261 Jesse Mahelona RC .50 1.25
262 Owen Daniels RC .60 1.50
263 Mike Bell RC .40 1.00
264 Anwar Phillips RC .50 1.25
265 Erik Meyer RC .40 1.00
266 Delanie Walker RC .75 2.00
267 Dominique Byrd RC .40 1.00
268 Eric Smith RC .50 1.25
269 Darrell Hackney RC .50 1.25
270 Freddie Roach RC .50 1.25
271 James Anderson RC .40 1.00
272 Anthony Smith RC .60 1.50
273 Quinton Ganther RC .40 1.00
274 Nick Mangold RC .50 1.25
275 Gerris Wilkinson RC .40 1.00

2006 Bowman Blue

*VETERANS: 1.5X TO 4X BASIC CARDS
*ROOKIES: .8X TO 2X BASIC CARDS
STATED PRINT RUN 500 SER.#'d SETS

2006 Bowman Gold

*VETERANS: .8X TO 2X BASIC CARDS
*ROOKIES: .6X TO 1.5X BASIC CARDS
ONE GOLD PER PACK

2006 Bowman White

*VETERANS: 2.5X TO 6X BASIC CARDS
*ROOKIES: 1.5X TO 4X BASIC CARDS
STATED PRINT RUN 125 SER.#'d SETS

2006 Bowman Rookie Autographs

AUTO/199 ODDS 1:2500 RETAIL
UNPRICED PRINT PLATES #'d TO 1
111 Reggie Bush 10.00 25.00
112 Matt Leinart 6.00 15.00
113 Vince Young 6.00 15.00
114 Jay Cutler 8.00 20.00
115 Santonio Holmes 8.00 20.00
116 LenDale White 6.00 15.00
117 DeAngelo Williams 8.00 20.00
118 Mario Williams 10.00 25.00
119 A.J. Hawk 8.00 20.00
120 Joseph Addai 6.00 15.00

2006 Bowman Draft Day Selections Relics

CAP ODDS 1:14,500 RET
JERSEY ODDS 1:275 RET
JERSEY/CAP/25 ODDS 1:28,000 RET
NFL LOGO 1/1 CARDS NOT PRICED
DHDF D.Ferguson Cap
DHML Matt Leinart Cap
DHMW Mario Williams Cap
DHRB Reggie Bush Cap
DHVD Vernon Davis Cap
DHVY Vince Young Cap
DJDF D.Ferguson Jsy 3.00 8.00
DJML Matt Leinart Jsy 5.00 12.00
DJMW Mario Williams Jsy 4.00 10.00
DJRB Reggie Bush Jsy 5.00 12.00
DJHDF Ferguson Jsy-Cap/25 10.00 25.00
DJHML M.Leinart Jsy-Cap/25 20.00 50.00
DJHMW M.Williams Jsy-Cap/25 20.00 40.00
DJHRB R.Bush Jsy-Cap/25 1.00 25.00

2006 Bowman Fabric of the Future

GROUP A ODDS 1:5275 H, 1:5300 R
GROUP B ODDS 1:112 H, 1:160 R
GROUP C ODDS 1:200 H, 1:210 R
*GOLD/100: .6X TO 1.5X BASIC INSERTS
GOLD/100 ODDS 1:1000 RET
UNPRICED LOGO PATCHES #'d TO 1
FFAH A.J. Hawk B 2.00 5.00
FFBC Brian Calhoun C 1.50 4.00
FFCJ Chad Jackson B 1.50 4.00
FFCW Charlie Whitehurst C 1.50 4.00
FFDH Derek Hagan B 2.00 5.00
FFDW DeAngelo Williams A 2.00 5.00
FFKC Kellen Clemens C 1.50 4.00
FFLM Laurence Maroney B 1.50 4.00
FFLW LenDale White C 1.50 4.00
FFMD Maurice Drew B 2.50 6.00
FFMH Michael Huff B 2.00 5.00
FFML Matt Leinart B 1.50 4.00
FFMR Michael Robinson C 1.50 4.00
FFMW Mario Williams B 2.50 6.00
FFRB Reggie Bush B 2.50 6.00
FFSH Santonio Holmes B 2.00 5.00
FFSM Sinorice Moss B 1.50 4.00
FFTJ Tarvaris Jackson C 1.50 4.00
FFVD Vernon Davis B 2.00 5.00
FFVY Vince Young B 1.50 4.00

2006 Bowman Fabric of the Future Dual

DUAL/50 ODDS 1:900 RET
HD S.Holmes/V.Davis 8.00 20.00
LB M.Leinart/R.Bush 3.00 8.00
WB L.White/R.Bush 3.00 8.00
WW D.Williams/M.Williams 10.00 25.00
YL V.Young/M.Leinart 5.00 12.00

2006 Bowman Rookie Coaches Autographs

STATED ODDS 1:5250 RET
BRCMM Mike McCarthy 30.00 80.00
BRCRM Rod Marinelli 4.00 10.00

2006 Bowman Rookie Rewind Jerseys

GROUP A ODDS 1:1450 HOB/RET
GROUP B ODDS 1:45 HOB, 1:260 RET
*GOLD/50: 1X TO 2.5X BASIC INSERTS
GOLD/50 ODDS 1:3200 RET
BRRAH A.J. Hawk B 4.00 10.00
BRRCJ Chad Jackson B 2.50 6.00
BRRDW DeAngelo Williams B 4.00 10.00
BRRKC Kellen Clemens B 2.50 6.00
BRRLM Laurence Maroney B 3.00 8.00
BRRLW LenDale White B 3.00 8.00
BRRMH Michael Huff B 2.50 6.00
BRRML Matt Leinart B 4.00 10.00
BRRMW Mario Williams B 2.50 6.00
BRRRB Reggie Bush B 3.00 8.00
BRRSH Santonio Holmes A 3.00 8.00
BRRSM Sinorice Moss B 2.50 6.00
BRRTJ Tarvaris Jackson B 2.50 6.00
BRRVD Vernon Davis B 3.00 8.00
BRRVY Vince Young B 2.00 5.00

2006 Bowman Signs of the Future

GROUP A ODDS 1:850 H, 1:1500 R
GROUP B ODDS 1:745 H, 1:750 R
GROUP C ODDS 1:1700 H/R
GROUP D ODDS 1:420 H, 1:440 R
GROUP E ODDS 1:300 H, 1:310 R
GROUP F ODDS 1:33 H, 1:89 R
*GOLD/50: .6X TO 1.5X BASIC INSERTS
GOLD/50 ODDS 1:1200 R
SFAF Anthony Fasano F 5.00 12.00
SFBC Brodie Croyle A 20.00 40.00
SFBM Brandon Marshall A 10.00 20.00
SFBS Brad Smith E 4.00 10.00
SFBW Brandon Williams F 5.00 12.00
SFCG Chad Greenway F 4.00 10.00
SFCJ Chad Jackson A 6.00 15.00
SFDA Devin Aromashodu A 5.00 12.00
SFDF D'Brickashaw Ferguson F 4.00 10.00
SFDH Derek Hagan B 4.00 10.00
SFDM DonTrell Moore F 4.00 10.00
SFDO Drew Olson D 5.00 12.00
SFDT David Thomas F 5.00 12.00
SFGJ Greg Jennings F 10.00 25.00
SFIM Ingle Martin E 5.00 12.00
SFJA Joseph Addai B 15.00 40.00
SFJK Joe Klopfenstein F 3.00 8.00
SFJN Jerious Norwood F 7.50 15.00
SFJW Jeff Webb F 4.00 10.00
SFKC Kellen Clemens F 7.50 15.00
SFLP Leonard Pope F 3.00 8.00
SFLW Leon Washington F 12.00 30.00
SFMD Maurice Drew F 15.00 30.00
SFMH Mike Hass F 4.00 10.00
SFML Marcedes Lewis D 4.00 10.00
SFMN Martin Nance F 4.00 10.00
SFMR Michael Robinson F 5.00 12.00
SFMS Maurice Stovall F 5.00 12.00
SFOJ Omar Jacobs D 4.00 10.00
SFSG Skyler Green E 4.00 10.00
SFTJ Tarvaris Jackson F 6.00 15.00
SFTWI Travis Wilson F 3.00 8.00
SFTW Todd Watkins C 5.00 12.00
SFBCA Brian Calhoun E 4.00 10.00
SFMHU Michael Huff B 6.00 15.00

2006 Bowman Signs of the Future Dual

DUAL/50 ODDS 1:9200 RET
UNPRICED GOLD PRINT RUN 10 SETS
BY R.Bush/V.Young 8.00 20.00
JH C.Jackson/S.Holmes 20.00 50.00
LC M.Leinart/J.Cutler 30.00 60.00
MA L.Maroney/J.Addai 25.00 60.00
WW L.White/D.Williams 20.00 50.00

2007 Bowman

This 275-card set was released in October, 2007. The set was issued into the hobby in 10-card packs, with a $3 SRP, which came 24 packs to a box. Cards numbered 1-110 feature veterans while cards 111-275 feature 2007 NFL rookies.
COMPLETE SET (275) 20.00 50.00
UNPRICED PRINT PLATE PRINT RUN 1
UNPRICED RED PRINT RUN 1
1 Matt Leinart .20 .50
2 Matt Schaub .20 .50
3 Jason Campbell .20 .50
4 Steve McNair .25 .60
5 J.P. Losman .20 .50
6 Jake Delhomme .20 .50
7 Rex Grossman .20 .50
8 Carson Palmer .25 .60
9 Tony Romo .40 1.00
10 Jay Cutler .20 .50
11 Brett Favre .60 1.50
12 Peyton Manning .75 2.00
13 Trent Green .20 .50
14 Tom Brady 1.00 2.50
15 Drew Brees .30 .75
16 Eli Manning .25 .60
17 Chad Pennington .20 .50
18 Donovan McNabb .25 .60
19 Ben Roethlisberger .30 .75
20 Philip Rivers .30 .75
21 Alex Smith QB .25 .60
22 Matt Hasselbeck .20 .50
23 Marc Bulger .20 .50
24 Vince Young .20 .50
25 Edgerrin James .25 .60
26 Warrick Dunn .20 .50
27 Jamal Lewis .25 .60
28 Willis McGahee .20 .50
29 DeShaun Foster .25 .60
30 DeAngelo Williams .20 .50
31 Cedric Benson .20 .50
32 Thomas Jones .20 .50
33 Rudi Johnson .20 .50
34 Julius Jones .20 .50
35 Dominic Rhodes .20 .50
36 Joseph Addai .20 .50
37 Fred Taylor .20 .50
38 Maurice Jones-Drew .20 .50
39 Larry Johnson .20 .50
40 Ronnie Brown .20 .50
41 Chester Taylor .20 .50
42 Laurence Maroney .25 .60
43 Deuce McAllister .25 .60
44 Reggie Bush .20 .50
45 Brandon Jacobs .20 .50
46 Brian Westbrook .20 .50
47 Willie Parker .25 .60
48 LaDainian Tomlinson .30 .75
49 Frank Gore .25 .60
50 Shaun Alexander .20 .50
51 Steven Jackson .20 .50
52 Cadillac Williams .25 .60
53 Clinton Portis .20 .50
54 Michael Turner .20 .50
55 Anquan Boldin .20 .50
56 Larry Fitzgerald .25 .60
57 Derrick Mason .20 .50
58 Lee Evans .25 .60
60 Steve Smith .25 .60
60 Muhsin Muhammad .20 .50
61 Chad Johnson .20 .50
62 T.J. Houshmandzadeh .20 .50
63 Braylon Edwards .20 .50
64 Terrell Owens .25 .60
65 Terry Glenn .25 .60
66 Javon Walker .25 .60
67 Mike Furrey .25 .60
68 Roy Williams WR .20 .50
69 Donald Driver .25 .60
70 Greg Jennings .20 .50
71 Andre Johnson .25 .60
72 Reggie Wayne .25 .60
73 Marvin Harrison .25 .60
74 Matt Jones .25 .60
75 Chris Chambers .20 .50
76 Troy Williamson .20 .50
77 Devery Henderson .20 .50
78 Joe Horn .20 .50
79 Marques Colston .20 .50
80 Plaxico Burress .20 .50
81 Amani Toomer .20 .50
82 Jerricho Cotchery .20 .50
83 Laveranues Coles .20 .50
84 Randy Moss .25 .60
85 Donte Stallworth .25 .60
86 Reggie Brown .20 .50
87 Hines Ward .25 .60
88 Santonio Holmes .20 .50
89 Keenan McCardell .20 .50
90 Eric Parker .20 .50
91 Arnaz Battle .20 .50
92 Antonio Bryant .20 .50
93 Deion Branch .20 .50
94 Darrell Jackson .20 .50
95 Kevin Curtis .20 .50
96 Torry Holt .25 .60
97 Isaac Bruce .30 .75
98 Antwaan Randle El .20 .50
99 Santana Moss .25 .60
100 Alge Crumpler .25 .60
101 Kellen Winslow .20 .50
102 Tony Gonzalez .25 .60
103 Jeremy Shockey .20 .50
104 Antonio Gates .30 .75
105 Vernon Davis .20 .50
106 Tarvaris Jackson .20 .50
107 Travis Henry .25 .60
108 Drew Bennett .20 .50
109 Todd Heap .20 .50
110 Byron Leftwich .20 .50
111 JaMarcus Russell RC .40 1.00
112 Brady Quinn RC .40 1.00
113 Drew Stanton RC .40 1.00
114 Troy Smith RC .40 1.00
115 Kevin Kolb RC .50 1.25
116 Trent Edwards RC .40 1.00
117 John Beck RC .40 1.00
118 Jordan Palmer RC .50 1.25
119 Chris Leak RC .40 1.00
120 Isaiah Stanback RC .40 1.00
121 Tyler Palko RC .60 1.50
122 Jared Zabransky RC .40 1.00
123 Jeff Rowe RC .40 1.00
124 Zac Taylor RC .50 1.25
125 Lester Ricard RC .50 1.25
126 Adrian Peterson RC 5.00 12.00
127 Marshawn Lynch RC .75 2.00
128 Brandon Jackson RC .40 1.00
129 Michael Bush RC .40 1.00
130 Kenny Irons RC .40 1.00
131 Antonio Pittman RC .40 1.00
132 Tony Hunt RC .40 1.00
133 Darius Walker RC .40 1.00
134 Dwayne Wright RC .40 1.00
135 Lorenzo Booker RC .50 1.25
136 Kenneth Darby RC .40 1.00
137 Chris Henry RB RC .40 1.00
138 Selvin Young RC .40 1.00
139 Brian Leonard RC .40 1.00
140 Ahmad Bradshaw RC .60 1.50
141 Gary Russell RC .50 1.25
142 Kolby Smith RC .40 1.00
143 Thomas Clayton RC .50 1.25
144 Garrett Wolfe RC .40 1.00
145 Calvin Johnson RC 3.00 8.00
146 Ted Ginn Jr. RC .50 1.25
147 Dwayne Jarrett RC .50 1.25
148 Dwayne Bowe RC .40 1.00
149 Sidney Rice RC .50 1.25
150 Robert Meachem RC .50 1.25
151 Anthony Gonzalez RC .40 1.00
152 Craig Buster Davis RC .40 1.00
153 Aundrae Allison RC .40 1.00
154 Chansi Stuckey RC .50 1.25
155 David Clowney RC .40 1.00
156 Steve Smith USC RC .40 1.00
157 Courtney Taylor RC .40 1.00
158 Paul Williams RC .40 1.00
159 Johnnie Lee Higgins RC .40 1.00
160 Rhema McKnight RC .40 1.00
161 Jason Hill RC .40 1.00
162 Dallas Baker RC .40 1.00
163 Greg Olsen RC .60 1.50
164 Yamon Figurs RC .40 1.00
165 Scott Chandler RC .60 1.50
166 Matt Spaeth RC .60 1.50
167 Ben Patrick RC .50 1.25
168 Clark Harris RC .50 1.25
169 Martrez Milner RC .40 1.00
170 Joe Newton RC .40 1.00
171 Alan Branch RC .40 1.00
172 Amobi Okoye RC .50 1.25
173 DeMarcus Tank Tyler RC .40 1.00
174 Justin Harrell RC .40 1.00
175 Brandon Mebane RC .50 1.25
176 Gaines Adams RC .50 1.25
177 Jamaal Anderson RC .50 1.25
178 Adam Carriker RC .40 1.00
179 Jarvis Moss RC .40 1.00
180 Charles Johnson RC .40 1.00
181 Anthony Spencer RC .50 1.25
182 Quentin Moses RC .40 1.00
183 LaMarr Woodley RC .75 2.00
184 Victor Abiamiri RC .40 1.00
185 Ray McDonald RC .50 1.25
186 Tim Crowder RC .50 1.25
187 Patrick Willis RC .60 1.50
188 Brandon Siler RC .40 1.00
189 David Harris RC .40 1.00
190 Buster Davis RC .50 1.25
191 Lawrence Timmons RC .60 1.50
192 Paul Posluszny RC .40 1.00
193 Jon Beason RC .40 1.00
194 Rufus Alexander RC .40 1.00
195 Earl Everett RC .40 1.00
196 Stewart Bradley RC .40 1.00
197 Prescott Burgess RC .40 1.00
198 Leon Hall RC .40 1.00
199 Darrelle Revis RC .50 1.25
200 Aaron Ross RC .40 1.00
201 Daymeion Hughes RC .40 1.00
202 Marcus McCauley RC .40 1.00
203 Chris Houston RC .40 1.00
204 Tanard Jackson RC .40 1.00
205 Jonathan Wade RC .40 1.00
206 Josh Wilson RC .50 1.25
207 Eric Wright RC .40 1.00
208 A.J. Davis RC .40 1.00
209 David Irons RC .40 1.00
210 LaRon Landry RC .60 1.50
211 Reggie Nelson RC .40 1.00
212 Michael Griffin RC .40 1.00
213 Brandon Meriweather RC .50 1.25
214 Eric Weddle RC .50 1.25
215 Aaron Rouse RC .40 1.00
216 Josh Gattis RC .40 1.00
217 Joe Thomas RC .60 1.50
218 Levi Brown RC .40 1.00
219 Tony Ugoh RC .40 1.00
220 Ryan Kalil RC .40 1.00
221 Joe Staley RC .50 1.25
222 Steve Breaston RC .40 1.00
223 Jacoby Jones RC .40 1.00
224 Ryne Robinson RC .50 1.25
225 Chris Davis RC .40 1.00
226 Le'Ron McClain RC .60 1.50
227 Joel Filani RC .40 1.00
228 Gerald Alexander RC .40 1.00
229 Justise Hairston RC .50 1.25
230 Nate Ilaoa RC .50 1.25
231 Brett Ratliff RC .60 1.50
232 Kyle Steffes RC .40 1.00
233 Jesse Pellot-Rosa RC .40 1.00
234 Roy Hall RC .60 1.50
235 Brannon Condren RC .40 1.00
236 Clint Session RC .50 1.25
237 Dan Bazuin RC .50 1.25
238 Michael Okwo RC .50 1.25
239 Kevin Payne RC .40 1.00
240 Legedu Naanee RC .50 1.25
241 Jarrett Hicks RC .50 1.25
242 Sonny Shackelford RC .40 1.00
243 Arron Sears RC .50 1.25
244 Justin Durant RC .60 1.50
245 Ikaika Alama-Francis RC .60 1.50
246 Sabby Piscitelli RC .40 1.00
247 Quincy Black RC .60 1.50
248 Jay Alford RC .40 1.00
249 Anthony Waters RC .50 1.25
250 Laurent Robinson RC .60 1.50
251 Brian Robison RC .60 1.50
252 Jay Moore RC .50 1.25
253 Stephen Nicholas RC .50 1.25
254 John Bowie RC .40 1.00
255 Brian Smith RC .40 1.00
256 Marvin White RC .40 1.00
257 Fred Bennett RC .40 1.00
258 Kevin Boss RC .60 1.50
259 Dante Rosario RC .60 1.50
260 Brent Celek RC .40 1.00
261 Orenthal O'Neal RC .40 1.00
262 Reagan Mauia RC .40 1.00
263 Deon Anderson RC .50 1.25
264 Tyler Ecker RC .50 1.25
265 Michael Allan RC .40 1.00
266 Jordan Kent RC .50 1.25
267 John Broussard RC .50 1.25
268 Chandler Williams RC .50 1.25
269 Jason Snelling RC .40 1.00
270 Derek Stanley RC .50 1.25
271 Zach Miller RC .40 1.00
272 Ramzee Robinson RC .40 1.00
273 Michael Johnson RC .50 1.25
274 Syndric Steptoe RC .50 1.25
275 Tarell Brown RC .60 1.50

2007 Bowman Blue

*VETS 1-110: 2X TO 5X BASIC CARDS
*ROOKIES 111-275: 1X TO 2.5X BASIC CARDS
BLUE/500 ODDS 1:13 HOB

2007 Bowman Gold

*VETS 1-110: 1.2X TO 3X BASIC CARDS
*ROOKIES 111-275: .6X TO 1.5X BASIC CARDS
ONE GOLD PER PACK

2007 Bowman Orange

*VETS 1-110: 2.5X TO 6X BASIC CARDS
*ROOKIES 111-275: 1.2X TO 3X BASIC CARDS
ORANGE/250 ODDS 1:26 HOB

2007 Bowman Draft Day Selections Relics

CAP ODDS 1:3650 HOB
JERSEY GROUP A ODDS 1:345 HOB
JERSEY GROUP B ODDS 1:291 HOB
JERSEY-CAP ODDS 1:16,416 HOB
DCAP Adrian Peterson Cap 6.00 15.00
DCBQ Brady Quinn Cap 6.00 15.00
DCGA Gaines Adams Cap 6.00 15.00
DCJR JaMarcus Russell Cap 6.00 15.00
DJAP Adrian Peterson Jsy A 6.00 15.00
DJBQ Brady Quinn Jsy B 8.00 20.00
DJCJ Calvin Johnson Jsy B 8.00 20.00
DJGA Gaines Adams Jsy B 4.00 10.00
DJJR JaMarcus Russell Jsy A 6.00 15.00
DJCAP Adrian Peterson Jsy-Cap 10.00 25.00
DJCBQ Brady Quinn Jsy-Cap 8.00 20.00
DJCGA Gaines Adams Jsy-Cap 4.00 10.00
DJCJR JaMarcus Russell Jsy-Cap 6.00 15.00

2007 Bowman Fabric of the Future

STATED ODDS 1:30 HOB
*GOLD/100: .5X TO 1.2X BASIC INSERTS
GOLD/100 ODDS 1:458 HOB
FFAG Anthony Gonzalez 1.50 4.00
FFAP Adrian Peterson 5.00 12.00
FFAPI Antonio Pittman 1.50 4.00
FFBJ Brandon Jackson 1.50 4.00
FFBL Brian Leonard 1.50 4.00
FFBQ Brady Quinn 1.50 4.00
FFCH Chris Henry RB 1.50 4.00
FFCJ Calvin Johnson 5.00 12.00
FFDB Dwayne Bowe 1.50 4.00
FFDJ Dwayne Jarrett 2.00 5.00
FFDS Drew Stanton 1.50 4.00
FFGA Gaines Adams 2.00 5.00
FFGO Greg Olsen 2.50 6.00
FFGW Garrett Wolfe 1.50 4.00
FFJB John Beck 1.50 4.00
FFJH Jason Hill 1.50 4.00
FFJLH Johnnie Lee Higgins 1.50 4.00
FFJR JaMarcus Russell 1.50 4.00
FFJT Joe Thomas 2.50 6.00
FFKI Kenny Irons 1.50 4.00
FFKK Kevin Kolb 2.00 5.00
FFLB Lorenzo Booker 2.00 5.00
FFMB Michael Bush 1.50 4.00
FFML Marshawn Lynch 3.00 8.00
FFPW Patrick Willis 2.50 6.00
FFPWI Paul Williams 1.50 4.00
FFRM Robert Meachem 2.00 5.00
FFSR Sidney Rice 2.00 5.00
FFSS Steve Smith USC 1.50 4.00
FFTE Trent Edwards 1.50 4.00
FFTG Ted Ginn Jr. 2.00 5.00
FFTH Tony Hunt 3.00 8.00
FFTS Troy Smith 1.50 4.00
FFYF Yamon Figurs 3.00 8.00

2007 Bowman Fabric of the Future Dual

DUAL/50 ODDS 1:7359
*GOLD/25: .6X TO 1.5X BASIC DUALS
DUAL GOLD/25 ODDS 1:14,850 HOB
GB T.Ginn/D.Bowe 6.00 15.00
PJ A.Peterson/C.Johnson 20.00 50.00
PQ A.Peterson/B.Quinn 15.00 40.00
RJ J.Russell/C.Johnson 12.00 30.00
RQ J.Russell/B.Quinn 8.00 20.00

2007 Bowman Rookie Autographs

GROUP A/25 ODDS 1:14,000 HOB
GROUP B/199 ODDS 1:303 HOB
BAVAG Anthony Gonzalez/199 6.00 15.00
BAVAP Adrian Peterson/25 175.00 300.00
BAVBJ Brandon Jackson/199 6.00 15.00
BAVBL Brian Leonard/199 6.00 15.00
BAVBQ Brady Quinn/199 6.00 15.00
BAVCD Craig Buster Davis/199 6.00 15.00
BAVCH Chris Henry RB/199 6.00 15.00
BAVCJ Calvin Johnson/25 100.00 175.00
BAVDB Dwayne Bowe/199 6.00 15.00
BAVDS Drew Stanton/199 6.00 15.00
BAVGA Gaines Adams/199 8.00 20.00
BAVJB John Beck/199 6.00 15.00
BAVJH Jason Hill/199 6.00 15.00
BAVJR JaMarcus Russell/25 12.00 30.00
BAVKK Kevin Kolb/199 8.00 20.00
BAVMB Michael Bush/199 6.00 15.00
BAVML Marshawn Lynch/199 25.00 50.00
BAVRM Robert Meachem/199 8.00 20.00
BAVSS Steve Smith USC/199 6.00 15.00
BAVTG Ted Ginn Jr/199 8.00 20.00

2007 Bowman Rookie Coaches Autographs

STATED ODDS 1:1030 HOB
BP Bobby Petrino 6.00 15.00
CC Cam Cameron 8.00 20.00
KW Ken Whisenhunt 6.00 15.00
LK Lane Kiffin 6.00 15.00

2007 Bowman Signs of the Future

GROUP A ODDS 1:2753 HOB
GROUP B ODDS 1:3300 HOB
GROUP C ODDS 1:327 HOB
GROUP D ODDS 1:97 HOB
GROUP E ODDS 1:916 HOB
GROUP F ODDS 1:273 HOB
GROUP G ODDS 1:60 HOB
*GOLD/50: .5X TO 1.2X BASIC GRP A
*GOLD/50: .6X TO 1.5X BASIC GRP B-G
GOLD/50 ODDS 1:650 HOB
SFAA Aundrae Allison D 3.00 8.00
SFAG Anthony Gonzalez B 3.00 8.00
SFBQ Brady Quinn A 10.00 25.00
SFCD Chris Davis C 3.00 8.00
SFCL Chris Leak G 3.00 8.00
SFCT Courtney Taylor C 3.00 8.00
SFDT Drew Tate G 4.00 10.00
SFDW Dwayne Wright D 3.00 8.00
SFDWA Darius Walker D 3.00 8.00
SFGW Garrett Wolfe D 3.00 8.00
SFJF Joel Filani G 3.00 8.00
SFJHA Justise Hairston D 4.00 10.00
SFJH Jason Hill G 3.00 8.00
SFJP Jordan Palmer D 4.00 10.00
SFJR Jeff Rowe D 3.00 8.00
SFKD Kenneth Darby G 3.00 8.00
SFKS Kolby Smith G 3.00 8.00
SFLB Lorenzo Booker C 4.00 10.00
SFLG Luke Getsy D 5.00 12.00
SFLR Laurent Robinson C 5.00 12.00
SFLT Lawrence Timmons F 5.00 12.00
SFML Marshawn Lynch A 20.00 40.00
SFMM Matt Moore G 5.00 12.00
SFPW Paul Williams D 3.00 8.00
SFRH Roy Hall F 5.00 12.00
SFRM Rhema McKnight E 3.00 8.00
SFRR Ryne Robinson G 4.00 10.00
SFSB Steve Breaston G 3.00 8.00
SFTE Trent Edwards C 3.00 8.00
SFTP Tyler Palko D 5.00 12.00
SFZM Zach Miller F 3.00 8.00
SFZT Zac Taylor G 4.00 10.00

2007 Bowman Signs of the Future Dual

DUAL/50 ODDS 1:4200 HOB
UNPRICED DUAL GOLD/10 ODDS 1:22,464
EL T.Edwards/M.Lynch 20.00 50.00
JM D.Jarrett/R.Meachem 10.00 25.00
QG B.Quinn/T.Ginn Jr. 15.00 40.00
SB D.Stanton/J.Beck 15.00 40.00
WD P.Williams/C.Davis 10.00 25.00

2008 Bowman

This set was released on October 29, 2008. The base set consists of 275 cards. Cards 1-110 feature veterans, and cards 111-275 are rookies.
COMPLETE SET (275) 30.00 60.00
1 Drew Brees .25 .60
2 Tom Brady .75 2.00
3 Peyton Manning .60 1.50
4 Carson Palmer .20 .50
5 Ben Roethlisberger .25 .60
6 Eli Manning .20 .50
7 Tony Romo .20 .50
8 Vince Young .15 .40
9 Matt Hasselbeck .15 .40
10 David Garrard .15 .40
11 Jay Cutler .15 .40
12 Derek Anderson .15 .40
13 Philip Rivers .25 .60
14 Donovan McNabb .20 .50
15 Matt Leinart .15 .40
16 Jason Campbell .15 .40
17 JaMarcus Russell .15 .40
18 Jeff Garcia .15 .40
19 Brodie Croyle .20 .50
20 Marc Bulger .15 .40
21 Trent Edwards .15 .40
22 Kyle Boller .15 .40
23 Tarvaris Jackson .15 .40
24 Matt Schaub .15 .40
25 Aaron Rodgers .50 1.25
26 Steven Jackson .15 .40
27 Willie Parker .20 .50
28 Clinton Portis .15 .40
29 Adrian Peterson .25 .60
30 LaDainian Tomlinson .25 .60
31 Marion Barber .15 .40
32 Brian Westbrook .15 .40
33 Fred Taylor .15 .40
34 Marshawn Lynch .20 .50
35 Joseph Addai .15 .40
36 Willis McGahee .15 .40
37 Frank Gore .20 .50
38 Julius Jones .15 .40
39 Thomas Jones .15 .40
40 Cedric Benson .15 .40
41 LenDale White .15 .40
42 Ryan Grant .20 .50
43 Laurence Maroney .20 .50
44 Brandon Jacobs .15 .40
45 Jamal Lewis .20 .50
46 Larry Johnson .15 .40
47 Rudi Johnson .15 .40
48 Ahmad Bradshaw .15 .40
49 Justin Fargas .15 .40
50 Reggie Bush .15 .40
51 Maurice Jones-Drew .15 .40
52 Michael Turner .15 .40
53 Ronnie Brown .15 .40
54 DeAngelo Williams .15 .40
55 Edgerrin James .20 .50
56 Chad Johnson .15 .40
57 Reggie Wayne .20 .50
58 Anquan Boldin .15 .40
59 Randy Moss .20 .50
60 Plaxico Burress .15 .40
61 Terrell Owens .20 .50
62 Andre Johnson .20 .50
63 Larry Fitzgerald .20 .50
64 Braylon Edwards .15 .40
65 Steve Smith .20 .50
66 Greg Jennings .15 .40
67 Torry Holt .20 .50
68 T.J. Houshmandzadeh .15 .40
69 Jerricho Cotchery .15 .40
70 Joey Galloway .20 .50
71 Santonio Holmes .15 .40

72 Lee Evans .20 .50
73 Dwayne Bowe .20 .50
74 Laurent Robinson .15 .40
75 Wes Welker .20 .50
76 Roy Williams WR .15 .40
77 Brandon Marshall .20 .50
78 Hines Ward .20 .50
79 Donald Driver .20 .50
80 Calvin Johnson .25 .60
81 Marques Colston .15 .40
82 Chris Chambers .15 .40
83 Amani Toomer .15 .40
84 Bernard Berrian .15 .40
85 Sidney Rice .15 .40
86 Anthony Gonzalez .15 .40
87 Steve Smith USC .20 .50
88 Ted Ginn Jr. .15 .40
89 Isaac Bruce .25 .60
90 Derrick Mason .15 .40
91 Roddy White .15 .40
92 Bobby Engram .15 .40
93 Reggie Williams .20 .50
94 Donte Stallworth .15 .40
95 Santana Moss .15 .40
96 Laveranues Coles .15 .40
97 Jerry Porter .15 .40
98 Shaun McDonald .15 .40
99 Dallas Clark .15 .40
100 Tony Gonzalez .20 .50
101 Kellen Winslow .15 .40
102 Antonio Gates .20 .50
103 Jason Witten .20 .50
104 Chris Cooley .15 .40
105 Brett Favre .50 1.25
106 Bob Sanders .20 .50
107 John Harbaugh CO .15 .40
108 Jon Kitna .15 .40
109 Tony Sparano CO .15 .40
110 Mike Smith CO .15 .40
111 Ryan Clady RC .50 1.25
112 Branden Albert RC .50 1.25
113 Gosder Cherilus RC .50 1.25
114 Duane Brown RC .40 1.00
115 Brandon Flowers RC .50 1.25
116 Quentin Groves RC .50 1.25
117 Jason Jones RC .50 1.25
118 Kendall Langford RC .50 1.25
119 Brad Cottam RC .40 1.00
120 Antwaun Molden RC .40 1.00
121 Bryan Smith RC .40 1.00
122 DaJuan Morgan RC .50 1.25
123 Craig Stevens RC .40 1.00
124 Tom Zbikowski RC .50 1.25
125 Andre Fluellen RC .40 1.00
126 Cliff Avril RC .60 1.50
127 Tyvon Branch RC .50 1.25
128 Justin King RC .50 1.25
129 Jeremy Thompson RC .40 1.00
130 William Hayes RC .40 1.00
131 Will Franklin RC .50 1.25
132 Marcus Smith RC .50 1.25
133 Dwight Lowery RC .50 1.25
134 Reggie Corner RC .40 1.00
135 Kenny Iwebema RC .40 1.00
136 Quintin Demps RC .50 1.25
137 Jack Williams RC .40 1.00
138 Craig Steltz RC .40 1.00
139 Bryan Kehl RC .40 1.00
140 Justin Tryon RC .40 1.00
141 Arman Shields RC .50 1.25
142 Paul Hubbard RC .40 1.00
143 Jonathan Wilhite RC .40 1.00
144 Thomas DeCoud RC .40 1.00
145 Derek Fine RC .40 1.00
146 Stanford Keglar RC .40 1.00
147 Kenneth Moore RC .40 1.00
148 Robert James RC .40 1.00
149 Jalen Parmele RC .50 1.25
150 Brandon Carr RC .50 1.25
151 Gary Barnidge RC .60 1.50
152 Zack Bowman RC .50 1.25
153 Lex Hilliard RC .50 1.25
154 Mario Urrutia RC .40 1.00
155 Adrian Arrington RC .40 1.00
156 Jerome Felton RC .40 1.00
157 Chaz Schilens RC .50 1.25
158 Steve Johnson RC .75 2.00
159 Tim Hightower RC .50 1.25
160 Alex Brink RC .50 1.25
161 Brett Swain RC .40 1.00
162 Matt Slater RC .60 1.50
163 Justin Harper RC .40 1.00
164 Kevin Robinson RC .40 1.00
165 Pierre Garcon RC .75 2.00
166 Matt Ryan RC 1.25 3.00
167 Brian Brohm RC .40 1.00
168 Andre Woodson RC .40 1.00
169 Chad Henne RC .50 1.25
170 Joe Flacco RC .75 2.00
171 John David Booty RC .40 1.00
172 Colt Brennan RC .50 1.25
173 Dennis Dixon RC .40 1.00
174 Erik Ainge RC .40 1.00
175 Josh Johnson RC .40 1.00
176 Kevin O'Connell RC .40 1.00
177 Matt Flynn RC .40 1.00
178 Jaymar Johnson RC .40 1.00
179 Marcus Thomas RC .50 1.25
180 Darren McFadden RC .40 1.00
181 Rashard Mendenhall RC .40 1.00
182 Jonathan Stewart RC .60 1.50
183 Felix Jones RC .40 1.00
184 Jamaal Charles RC .60 1.50
185 Chris Johnson RC .50 1.25
186 Ray Rice RC .40 1.00
187 Mike Hart RC .40 1.00
188 Kevin Smith RC .40 1.00
189 Steve Slaton RC .40 1.00
190 Matt Forte RC .60 1.50
191 Tashard Choice RC .40 1.00
192 Cory Boyd RC .40 1.00
193 Allen Patrick RC .40 1.00
194 Thomas Brown RC .40 1.00
195 Justin Forsett RC .50 1.25
196 Harry Douglas RC .50 1.25
197 DeSean Jackson RC .75 2.00
198 Malcolm Kelly RC .40 1.00
199 Limas Sweed RC .40 1.00
200 Mario Manningham RC .40 1.00
201 James Hardy RC .40 1.00
202 Early Doucet RC .40 1.00
203 Donnie Avery RC .50 1.25
204 Dexter Jackson RC .60 1.50
205 Devin Thomas RC .40 1.00
206 Jordy Nelson RC 1.25 3.00
207 Keenan Burton RC .40 1.00
208 Earl Bennett RC .60 1.50
209 Jerome Simpson RC .50 1.25
210 Andre Caldwell RC .40 1.00
211 Josh Morgan RC .40 1.00
212 Eddie Royal RC .40 1.00
213 Fred Davis RC .40 1.00
214 John Carlson RC .40 1.00
215 Martellus Bennett RC .50 1.25
216 Martin Rucker RC .40 1.00
217 Jermichael Finley RC .40 1.00
218 Dustin Keller RC .50 1.25
219 Jacob Tamme RC .50 1.25
220 Kellen Davis RC .40 1.00
221 Owen Schmitt RC .40 1.00
222 Jacob Hester RC .40 1.00
223 Chris Williams RC .40 1.00
224 Jake Long RC .60 1.50
225 Sam Baker RC .40 1.00
226 Jeff Otah RC .40 1.00
227 Glenn Dorsey RC .40 1.00
228 Sedrick Ellis RC .40 1.00
229 Kentwan Balmer RC .40 1.00
230 Pat Sims RC .50 1.25
231 Marcus Harrison RC .40 1.00
232 Dre Moore RC .40 1.00
233 Paul Smith RC .40 1.00
234 Trevor Laws RC .40 1.00
235 Chris Long RC .50 1.25
236 Vernon Gholston RC .40 1.00
237 Derrick Harvey RC .40 1.00
238 Calais Campbell RC .50 1.25
239 Phillip Merling RC .40 1.00
240 Chris Ellis RC .40 1.00
241 Lawrence Jackson RC .40 1.00
242 Dan Connor RC .40 1.00
243 Curtis Lofton RC .50 1.25
244 Jerod Mayo RC .60 1.50
245 Tavares Gooden RC .40 1.00
246 Kyle Wright RC .40 1.00
247 Philip Wheeler RC .50 1.25
248 Marcus Monk RC .50 1.25
249 Jonathan Goff RC .40 1.00
250 Keith Rivers RC .40 1.00
251 Lavelle Hawkins RC .50 1.25
252 Xavier Adibi RC .40 1.00
253 Chauncey Washington RC .50 1.25
254 Bruce Davis RC .50 1.25
255 Jordon Dizon RC .40 1.00
256 Shawn Crable RC .40 1.00
257 Geno Hayes RC .40 1.00
258 D.Rodgers-Cromartie RC .50 1.25
259 Chevis Jackson RC .40 1.00
260 Terrence Wheatley RC .40 1.00
261 Mike Jenkins RC .40 1.00
262 Aqib Talib RC .60 1.50
263 Leodis McKelvin RC .50 1.25
264 Terrell Thomas RC .40 1.00
265 Reggie Smith RC .40 1.00
266 Antoine Cason RC .50 1.25
267 Patrick Lee RC .40 1.00
268 Tracy Porter RC .50 1.25
269 Charles Godfrey RC .40 1.00
270 Kenny Phillips RC .40 1.00
271 Marcus Henry RC .40 1.00
272 DJ Hall RC .40 1.00
273 Xavier Omon RC .40 1.00
274 Tyrell Johnson RC .40 1.00
275 Ryan Torain RC .50 1.25

2008 Bowman Blue

*VETS 1-110: 2.5X TO 6X BASIC CARDS
*ROOKIES 111-275: 1X TO 2.5X BASIC CARDS
BLUE/500 ODDS 1:11 HOB

2008 Bowman Gold

*VETS 1-110: 1.2X TO 3X BASIC CARDS
*ROOKIES 111-275: .6X TO 1.5X BASIC CARDS
ONE GOLD PER PACK

2008 Bowman Orange

*VETS 1-110: 3X TO 8X BASIC CARDS
*ROOKIES 111-275: 1.2X TO 3X BASIC CARDS
ORANGE/250 ODDS 1:21 HOB

2008 Bowman Red

UNPRICED RED 1/1 ODDS 1:2540

2008 Bowman Draft Day Selections Relics

GROUP A JSY ODDS 1:578 HOB
GROUP B JSY ODDS 1:685 HOB
CAP STATED ODDS 1:5300 HOB
JSY-CAP/25 ODDS 1:18,124 HOB
DCCL Chris Long Cap 10.00 25.00
DCDM Darren McFadden Cap 3.00 8.00
DCJL Jake Long Cap 10.00 25.00
DCMR Matt Ryan Cap 20.00 50.00
DCVG Vernon Gholston Cap 10.00 25.00
DJCL Chris Long Jsy 5.00 12.00
DJDM Darren McFadden Jsy 2.50 6.00
DJJL Jake Long Jsy 5.00 12.00
DJMR Matt Ryan Jsy 8.00 20.00
DJVG Vernon Gholston Jsy 5.00 12.00
DJCCL Chris Long Jsy-Cap/25
DJCDM D.McFadden Jsy-Cap/25 6.00 15.00
DJCJL Jake Long Jsy-Cap/25
DJCMR Matt Ryan Jsy-Cap/25
DJCVG V.Gholston Jsy-Cap/25

2008 Bowman Fabric of the Future

GROUP A ODDS 1:115 HOB
GROUP B ODDS 1:59 HOB
*GOLD/100: .6X TO 1.5X BASIC JSY
GOLD/100 ODDS 1:1312 HOB
FFAC Andre Caldwell B 2.00 5.00
FFDJ Dexter Jackson B 3.00 8.00
FFDJ DeSean Jackson A 4.00 10.00
FFDK Dustin Keller B 2.50 6.00
FFDT Devin Thomas B 2.00 5.00
FFEB Earl Bennett B 3.00 8.00
FFED Early Doucet A 2.00 5.00
FFER Eddie Royal B 2.00 5.00
FFGD Glenn Dorsey B 2.00 5.00
FFJB John David Booty A 2.00 5.00
FFJC Jamaal Charles B 3.00 8.00
FFHD Harry Douglas B 2.50 6.00
FFJL Jake Long A 3.00 8.00
FFJN Jordy Nelson A 6.00 15.00
FFJS Jerome Simpson B 2.50 6.00
FFKO Kevin O'Connell B 2.00 5.00
FFKS Kevin Smith A 2.00 5.00
FFMF Matt Forte A 3.00 8.00
FFMM Mario Manningham A 2.00 5.00
FFSS Steve Slaton A 2.00 5.00

2008 Bowman Fabric of the Future Dual

DUAL/50 ODDS 1:10,611 HOB
DUAL GOLD/25 ODDS 1:21,781 HOB
FFDAT D.Avery/D.Thomas
FFDMJ D.McFadden/F.Jones
FFDRF M.Ryan/J.Flacco
FFDRM M.Ryan/D.McFadden 5.00 12.00
FFDSM J.Stewart/R.Mendenhall

2008 Bowman Signs of the Future

GROUP A ODDS 1:4414 HOB
GROUP B ODDS 1:795 HOB
GROUP C ODDS 1:154 HOB
GROUP D ODDS 1:49 HOB
*GOLD/50: .6X TO 1.5X BASIC AUTO
GOLD/50 ODDS 1:706 HOB
SFAA Adrian Arrington C 3.00 8.00
SFAA Anthony Alridge D 3.00 8.00
SFAC Andre Caldwell C 3.00 8.00
SFAP Allen Patrick C 3.00 8.00
SFBB Brian Brohm A 6.00 15.00
SFCW Chauncey Washington C 4.00 10.00
SFDH DJ Hall C 3.00 8.00
SFDM Darren McFadden A 3.00 8.00
SFDR Darius Reynaud C 3.00 8.00
SFDS Dantrell Savage D 4.00 10.00
SFEB Earl Bennett B 5.00 12.00
SFHD Harry Douglas B 4.00 10.00
SFJF Justin Forsett D 4.00 10.00
SFJF Joe Flacco A 6.00 15.00
SFJJ Josh Johnson B 3.00 8.00
SFJJ Jaymar Johnson D 3.00 8.00
SFJS Jonathan Stewart A 10.00 25.00
SFKB Keenan Burton D 3.00 8.00
SFMF Matt Flynn C 3.00 8.00
SFMF Matt Forte B 15.00 40.00
SFMH Marcus Henry C 3.00 8.00
SFMR Matt Ryan A 50.00 100.00
SFMS Marcus Smith D 4.00 10.00
SFPS Paul Smith C 3.00 8.00
SFRT Ryan Torain C 4.00 10.00
SFSK Sam Keller D 3.00 8.00
SFTC Tashard Choice B 3.00 8.00
SFXO Xavier Omon D 3.00 8.00

2008 Bowman Signs of the Future Dual

DUAL AUTO/50 ODDS 1:3923
UNPRICED GOLD/10 ODDS 1:32,100
SFDDL Dorsey/J.Long EXCH 12.00 30.00
SFDHM C.Henne/M.Manningham 15.00 40.00
SFDJS C.Jhnsn/K.Smith 15.00 40.00
SFDNH J.Nelson/J.Hardy 20.00 40.00
SFDRM M.Ryan/D.McFadden 40.00 100.00

2010 Bowman Target Exclusive

ONE PER SPECIAL TARGET BOX OVERALL
*GOLD: .6X TO 1.5X BASIC INSERTS
TC1 Tim Tebow 1.50 4.00
TC2 C.J. Spiller .50 1.25
TC3 Dez Bryant 1.25 3.00
TC4 Golden Tate .60 1.50
TC5 Sam Bradford .60 1.50
TC6 Ryan Mathews .50 1.25
TC7 Jahvid Best .50 1.25
TC8 Colt McCoy .60 1.50
TC9 Demaryius Thomas 1.25 3.00
TC10 Jimmy Clausen .50 1.25
TC11 Ndamukong Suh 1.00 2.50
TC12 Arrelious Benn .50 1.25
TC13 Ben Tate .50 1.25
TC14 Jonathan Dwyer .50 1.25
TC15 Eric Berry .75 2.00

2010 Bowman Wal-Mart Exclusive

ONE PER SPECIAL WAL-MART BOX OVERALL
*GOLD: .6X TO 1.5X BASIC INSERTS
WC1 Tim Tebow 1.50 4.00
WC2 C.J. Spiller .50 1.25
WC3 Dez Bryant 1.25 3.00
WC4 Golden Tate .60 1.50
WC5 Sam Bradford .60 1.50
WC6 Ryan Mathews .50 1.25
WC7 Jahvid Best .50 1.25
WC8 Colt McCoy .60 1.50
WC9 Demaryius Thomas 1.25 3.00
WC10 Jimmy Clausen .50 1.25
WC11 Ndamukong Suh 1.00 2.50
WC12 Arrelious Benn .50 1.25
WC13 Ben Tate .50 1.25
WC14 Jonathan Dwyer .50 1.25
WC15 Eric Berry .75 2.00

2011 Bowman Target Exclusive

ODDS 1:6 TARGET, 1:1 TRGT BLASTER
*GRAY: .5X TO 1.2X BASIC INSERTS
TC1 Blaine Gabbert .60 1.50
TC2 Jake Locker .60 1.50
TC3 Cam Newton 3.00 8.00
TC4 Ryan Mallett .60 1.50
TC5 Mark Ingram 1.00 2.50
TC6 Ryan Williams .60 1.50
TC7 Mikel Leshoure .60 1.50
TC8 A.J. Green 1.50 4.00
TC9 Julio Jones 2.00 5.00
TC10 Jonathan Baldwin .60 1.50
TC11 Marcell Dareus .60 1.50
TC12 Von Miller 1.00 2.50
TC13 Andy Dalton 1.25 3.00
TC14 Kyle Rudolph .60 1.50
TC15 Christian Ponder .60 1.50

2011 Bowman Wal-Mart Exclusive

ODDS 1:6 WAL-MART, 1:1 WLMRT BLASTER
*GRAY: .5X TO 1.2X BASIC INSERTS
WC1 Blaine Gabbert .60 1.50
WC2 Jake Locker .60 1.50
WC3 Cam Newton 3.00 8.00
WC4 Ryan Mallett .60 1.50
WC5 Mark Ingram 1.00 2.50
WC6 Ryan Williams .60 1.50
WC7 Mikel Leshoure .60 1.50
WC8 A.J. Green 1.50 4.00
WC9 Julio Jones 2.00 5.00
WC10 Jonathan Baldwin .60 1.50
WC11 Marcell Dareus .60 1.50
WC12 Von Miller 1.00 2.50
WC13 Andy Dalton 1.25 3.00
WC14 Kyle Rudolph .60 1.50
WC15 Christian Ponder .60 1.50

2012 Bowman

COMP.SET w/o SP's (200) 20.00 50.00
THREE ROOKIES PER PACK OVERALL
ROOKIE SP ODDS 1:39 HOB/RET
MANN/TEBOW SP ODDS 1:488 HOB/RET
1 Cam Newton .30 .75
2 Miles Austin .20 .50
3 Hakeem Nicks .20 .50
4 Michael Vick .25 .60
5 Brandon Marshall .25 .60
6 Brandon Lloyd .20 .50
7 Eric Decker .20 .50
8 Eli Manning .25 .60
9 Carson Palmer .25 .60
10 LeSean McCoy .30 .75
11 Andy Dalton .25 .60
12 Steve Breaston .20 .50
13 Fred Jackson .25 .60
14 Beanie Wells .20 .50
15 Greg Jennings .20 .50
16 DeSean Jackson .25 .60
17 Frank Gore .25 .60
18 Anquan Boldin .20 .50
19 Vincent Jackson .20 .50
20 Calvin Johnson .30 .75
21 Ryan Mathews .25 .60
22 Josh Freeman .25 .60
23 Rashard Mendenhall .20 .50
24 Aaron Hernandez .25 .60
25 Chris Johnson .20 .50
26 Jason Witten .25 .60
27 Mike Williams .25 .60
28 Tony Romo .25 .60
29 Mark Sanchez .20 .50
30 Arian Foster .25 .60
31 Dwayne Bowe .25 .60
32 Cedric Benson .20 .50
33 Von Miller .25 .60
34 Denarius Moore .20 .50
35 Matt Ryan .25 .60
36 Mike Wallace .20 .50
37 Steve Johnson .25 .60
38 Matt Flynn .20 .50
39 Patrick Willis .25 .60
40 Adrian Peterson .30 .75
41 Santonio Holmes .20 .50
42 Victor Cruz .25 .60
43 Roddy White .20 .50
44 Jason Pierre-Paul .20 .50
45 Matthew Stafford .25 .60
46 Ahmad Bradshaw .20 .50
47 Fred Davis .20 .50
48 Matt Hasselbeck .20 .50
49 Jermichael Finley .20 .50
50 Tom Brady .75 2.00
51 Steven Jackson .20 .50
52 Jay Cutler .20 .50
53 Sam Bradford .20 .50
54 Ryan Fitzpatrick .20 .50
55 Michael Bush .20 .50
56 Mario Williams .20 .50
57 Jeremy Maclin .20 .50
58 Michael Turner .20 .50
59 Wes Welker .25 .60
60 Ray Rice .20 .50
61 Marshawn Lynch .25 .60
62 Torrey Smith .20 .50
63 A.J. Green .30 .75
64 Darren Sproles .25 .60
65 Julio Jones .30 .75
66 Philip Rivers .30 .75
67 Alex Smith QB .25 .60
68 DeMarco Murray .25 .60
69 Rob Gronkowski .30 .75
70 Drew Brees .30 .75
71 DeMarcus Ware .30 .75
72 Larry Fitzgerald .25 .60
73 Matt Schaub .20 .50
74 Vernon Davis .20 .50
75 Maurice Jones-Drew .20 .50
76 Joe Flacco .25 .60
77 Dez Bryant .30 .75
78 Colt McCoy .25 .60
79 Reggie Bush .20 .50
80 Andre Johnson .25 .60
81 Willis McGahee .20 .50
82 Percy Harvin .20 .50
83 Tony Gonzalez .25 .60
84 Steve Smith .25 .60
85 LeGarrette Blount .25 .60
86 Jordy Nelson .25 .60
87 Shonn Greene .20 .50
88 Jared Allen .20 .50
89 Plaxico Burress .20 .50
90 Matt Forte .20 .50
91 Antonio Brown .30 .75
92 Jimmy Graham .30 .75
93 Marques Colston .20 .50
94 Doug Baldwin .30 .75
95 David Nelson .20 .50
96 Darren McFadden .20 .50
97 Ben Tate .20 .50
98 Ben Roethlisberger .30 .75
99 James Starks .20 .50
100 Aaron Rodgers .50 1.25
101 Fletcher Cox RC .50 1.25
102 Dont'a Hightower RC .50 1.25
103A Chris Polk RC right .30 .75
103B Chris Polk SP left 2.50 6.00
104A Ryan Lindley RC throw .30 .75
104B R.Lindley SP two hands 2.50 6.00
105 Jerel Worthy RC .30 .75
106 Alfonzo Dennard RC .30 .75
107A Kellen Moore RC wht .40 1.00
107B Kellen Moore SP blu 3.00 8.00
108 Tank Carder RC .50 1.25
109A Jarius Wright RC right .30 .75
109B Jarius Wright SP left 5.00 12.00
110A Ryan Tannehill RC drop .50 1.25
110B Ryan Tannehill SP pass 4.00 10.00
111A Isaiah Pead RC at chin .30 .75
111B Isaiah Pead SP at waist 2.50 6.00
112 Ronnie Hillman RC .30 .75
113A C.Fleener RC at chest .30 .75
113B C.Fleener SP at waist 2.50 6.00
114A T.Streeter RC closed .30 .75
114B T.Streeter SP open 2.50 6.00
115 Cam Johnson RC .50 1.25
116A R.Wilson RC pass 3.00 8.00
116B R.Wilson SP drop 25.00 50.00
117A Nick Toon RC .30 .75
117B Nick Toon SP 2.50 6.00
118 Tauren Poole RC .30 .75
119A Robert Turbin RC .30 .75
119B Robert Turbin SP 2.50 6.00
120A T.Richardson RC at waist .30 .75
120B T.Richardson SP at chin 2.50 6.00
121 Brock Osweiler RC .30 .75
122 Zach Brown RC .30 .75
123A Jeff Fuller RC .30 .75
white jersey
123B Jeff Fuller SP 2.50 6.00
green jersey
124A Jordan White RC running .40 1.00
124B Jordan White SP catch 3.00 8.00
125 Gerell Robinson RC .30 .75
126 Chandler Jones RC .30 .75
127 Vick Ballard RC .40 1.00
128 Matt Kalil RC .30 .75
129A K.Wright RC rght hnd .30 .75
129B K.Wright SP both hnds 2.50 6.00
130A J.Blackmon RC green .30 .75
130B J.Blackmon SP white 5.00 12.00
131 Davin Meggett RC .30 .75
132A L.James RC white .30 .75
132B L.James SP red 2.50 6.00
133 Cordy Glenn RC .40 1.00
134 Courtney Upshaw RC .40 1.00
135 Patrick Witt RC .40 1.00
136 Greg Childs RC .30 .75
137A Alshon Jeffery RC run .60 1.50
137B A.Jeffery SP catch 5.00 12.00
138 Rishard Matthews RC .30 .75
139A Jacory Harris RC pass .40 1.00
139B Jacory Harris SP run 3.00 8.00
140A M.Floyd RC ball at waist .30 .75
140B M.Floyd SP ball at chin 2.50 6.00
141 Eric Page RC .40 1.00
142A C.Harnish RC blue .30 .75
142B C.Harnish SP white 2.50 6.00
143 Mark Barron RC .30 .75
144 Jared Crick RC .30 .75
145A K.Cousins RC forward 1.25 3.00
145B K.Cousins SP back 10.00 25.00
146 Chase Minnifield RC .40 1.00
147 Lavonte David RC .50 1.25
148 Whitney Mercilus RC .30 .75
149A Bernard Pierce RC run .30 .75
149B Bernard Pierce SP catch 2.50 6.00
150A Andrew Luck RC w/ball 3.00 8.00
150B And.Luck SP w/o ball 15.00 40.00
151A A.J. Jenkins RC wht .30 .75
151B A.J. Jenkins SP org 2.50 6.00
152A M.Sanu RC w/ball .50 1.25
152B M.Sanu SP w/o ball 4.00 10.00
153A David Wilson RC blu .30 .75
153B David Wilson SP wht 2.50 6.00
154 Riley Reiff RC .30 .75
155A Doug Martin RC .50 1.25
155B Doug Martin SP 4.00 10.00
156 Nick Perry RC .40 1.00
157 Michael Brockers RC .30 .75
158 Vinny Curry RC .40 1.00
159 Orson Charles RC .30 .75
160A Morris Claiborne RC blu .30 .75
160B Morris Claiborne SP slvr 2.50 6.00
161A B.Weeden RC brown .30 .75
161B B.Weeden SP white 2.50 6.00
162 Marc Tyler RC .30 .75
163A Bobby Rainey RC wht .30 .75
163B Bobby Rainey SP purp 2.50 6.00
164 Dan Herron RC .30 .75
165A Cyrus Gray RC wht .30 .75
165B Cyrus Gray SP red 2.50 6.00
166 Chris Rainey RC .30 .75
167 Markelle Martin RC .40 1.00
168A B.Quick RC w/ball .30 .75
168B B.Quick SP w/o ball 2.50 6.00
169 Devon Still RC .40 1.00
170A Quinton Coples RC wht .30 .75
170B Quinton Coples SP grn 2.50 6.00
171A Nick Foles RC .75 2.00
171B Nick Foles SP 6.00 15.00
172A T.Hilton RC forward .60 1.50
172B T.Y. Hilton SP left 5.00 12.00
173 David DeCastro RC .30 .75
174A Lamar Miller RC left .50 1.25
174B Lamar Miller SP right 4.00 10.00
175 Billy Winn RC .50 1.25
176A D.Allen RC w/o ball .30 .75
176B D.Allen SP w/ball 2.50 6.00
177 Peter Konz RC .30 .75
178 Janoris Jenkins RC .40 1.00
179 Chris Givens RC .30 .75
180A M.Ingram RC left .30 .75
180B M.Ingram SP right 2.50 6.00
181A D.Posey RC w/o ball .30 .75
181B D.Posey SP w/ball 2.50 6.00
182A R.Randle RC waist .30 .75
182B R.Randle SP shldr 2.50 6.00
183 Juron Criner RC .30 .75
184 Brandon Bolden RC .30 .75
185A D.Kirkpatrick RC wht .30 .75
185B D.Kirkpatrick SP orng 2.50 6.00
186A Austin Davis RC 1.00 2.50
186B Austin Davis SP 20.00 50.00
187A Jermaine Kearse RC .50 1.25
187B Jermaine Kearse SP 4.00 10.00
188 Brandon Thompson RC .40 1.00
189A M.McNutt RC rght hnd .30 .75
189B M.McNutt SP bth hnds 2.50 6.00
190 Luke Kuechly RC .75 2.00
191A Dwight Jones RC .30 .75
191B Dwight Jones SP 2.50 6.00
192 Dontari Poe RC .30 .75
193 B.J. Cunningham RC .30 .75
194 Marvin Jones RC .30 .75
195 Andre Branch RC .30 .75
196A Case Keenum RC wht .60 1.50
196B Case Keenum SP blu 5.00 12.00
197A Ryan Broyles RC blu .30 .75
197B Ryan Broyles SP wht 2.50 6.00
198A Joe Adams RC waist .30 .75
198B Joe Adams SP chest 2.50 6.00
199 Stephen Hill RC .30 .75
200A Robert Griffin RC pass .40 1.00
200B Robert Griffin SP run 3.00 8.00
PMSP Peyton Manning SP 15.00 40.00
TTSP Tim Tebow SP 10.00 25.00

2012 Bowman Gold

*GOLD: .8X TO 2X BASIC CARDS
RANDOM INSERTS IN RETAIL PACKS

2012 Bowman Green

*GREEN/25: 6X TO 15X BASIC CARDS
GREEN/25 ODDS 1:390 HOB/RET

2012 Bowman Purple

*PURPLE: .6X TO 1.5X BASIC CARDS
THREE PER SPECIAL RETAIL PACK

2012 Bowman Silver

*SILVER/99: 3X TO 8X BASIC CARDS
SILVER/99 ODDS 1:98 HOB/RET

2012 Bowman Accolades

STATED ODDS 1:12 RETAIL
BACAL Andrew Luck 4.00 10.00
BACDA Dwayne Allen .40 1.00
BACJB Justin Blackmon .40 1.00
BACLK Luke Kuechly 1.00 2.50
BACMC Morris Claiborne .40 1.00
BACRG Robert Griffin III .50 1.25
BACTR Trent Richardson .40 1.00
BACAL2 Andrew Luck 4.00 10.00
BACAL3 Andrew Luck 4.00 10.00
BACRG2 Robert Griffin III .50 1.25

2012 Bowman Accolades Autographs

STATED ODDS 1:699 RETAIL
BACAAL Andrew Luck 125.00 250.00
BACADA Dwayne Allen 10.00 25.00
BACAJB Justin Blackmon 5.00 12.00
BACALK Luke Kuechly 12.00 30.00
BACARG Robert Griffin III 15.00 40.00
BACATR Trent Richardson 20.00 50.00
BACAAL2 Andrew Luck 125.00 250.00
BACAAL3 Andrew Luck 125.00 250.00
BACARG2 Robert Griffin III 15.00 40.00

2012 Bowman All-American Autographs

STATED ODDS 1:3100 RET
BAAAAL Andrew Luck 150.00 250.00
BAAACF Coby Fleener 6.00 15.00
BAAADA Dwayne Allen 6.00 15.00
BAAADS Devon Still 8.00 20.00
BAAAJB Justin Blackmon 6.00 15.00
BAAAJW Jerel Worthy 6.00 15.00
BAAAKW Kendall Wright 6.00 15.00
BAAALK Luke Kuechly 15.00 40.00
BAAAMK Matt Kalil 6.00 15.00
BAAARB Ryan Broyles 40.00 80.00
BAAARG Robert Griffin III 8.00 20.00
BAAATR Trent Richardson 6.00 15.00

2012 Bowman All-Americans

STATED ODDS 1:6 RETAIL
BAAAL Andrew Luck 3.00 8.00
BAACF Coby Fleener .30 .75
BAADA Dwayne Allen .30 .75
BAADK Dre Kirkpatrick .30 .75
BAADS Devon Still .40 1.00
BAAJB Justin Blackmon .30 .75
BAAJW Jerel Worthy .30 .75
BAAKW Kendall Wright .30 .75
BAALJ LaMichael James .30 .75
BAALK Luke Kuechly .75 2.00
BAAMC Morris Claiborne .30 .75
BAAMI Melvin Ingram .30 .75
BAAMK Matt Kalil .30 .75
BAARB Ryan Broyles .30 .75
BAARG Robert Griffin III .40 1.00
BAATR Trent Richardson .30 .75

2012 Bowman Autographs Dual

DUAL AU/25 ODDS 1:386 HOB,1:11,515 RET
BDAHM J.Harris/L.Miller
BDALG A.Luck/R.Griffin III 100.00 200.00
BDAMM K.Moore/D.Martin 20.00 50.00
BDAPK C.Polk/J.Kearse 15.00 40.00
BDARK Richardson/Kirkpatrick 30.00 80.00
BDATM V.Miller/R.Tannehill 25.00 50.00
BDAVW M.Vick/D.Wilson 15.00 40.00
BDAWA J.Wright/J.Adams 25.00 50.00

2012 Bowman Autographs Triple

TRIPLE AU/25 ODDS 1:740 HOB,1:24,700 RET
BTAFWJ Floyd/Wright/Jeffery 30.00 60.00
BTAHMS Harris/Miller/Streeter
BTAMTG Miller/Tannehill/Gray 30.00 60.00
BTATGF Tannehill/Gray/Fuller 30.00 60.00

2012 Bowman Combine Competition

STATED ODDS 1:4 HOB/RET
CCCI Q.Coples/M.Ingram .30 .75
CCCK Claiborne/Kirkpatrick .30 .75
CCCP Claiborne/P.Peterson .30 .75
CCFC N.Foles/K.Cousins 1.25 3.00
CCFW M.Floyd/K.Wright .30 .75
CCGN R.Griffin III/C.Newton .50 1.25
CCHJ S.Hill/C.Johnson .50 1.25
CCJP L.James/C.Polk .30 .75
CCLG A.Luck/R.Griffin III 3.00 8.00
CCLH R.Lindley/C.Harnish .30 .75
CCLN A.Luck/C.Newton 3.00 8.00
CCMR L.Miller/C.Rainey .50 1.25
CCMW D.Martin/D.Wilson .50 1.25
CCPS D.Poe/N.Suh .40 1.00
CCSR M.Sanu/R.Randle .50 1.25

2012 Bowman Inside the Numbers

STATED ODDS 1:8 HOB/RET
ITNAB Ahmad Bradshaw .50 1.25
ITNAF Arian Foster .60 1.50
ITNAJ Andre Johnson .60 1.50
ITNAS Alex Smith QB .60 1.50
ITNBG Blaine Gabbert .50 1.25
ITNBT Ben Tate .50 1.25
ITNBW Beanie Wells .50 1.25
ITNCN Cam Newton .75 2.00
ITNDB Drew Brees .75 2.00
ITNDK Dustin Keller .50 1.25
ITNGO Greg Olsen .60 1.50
ITNJF Jacoby Ford .50 1.25
ITNJM Jeremy Maclin .50 1.25
ITNLB LeGarrette Blount .60 1.50
ITNMC Marques Colston .50 1.25
ITNMF Matt Forte .50 1.25
ITNML Marshawn Lynch .60 1.50
ITNMR Matt Ryan .60 1.50
ITNMS Mark Sanchez .50 1.25
ITNMV Michael Vick .60 1.50
ITNMW Mike Wallace .50 1.25
ITNPH Percy Harvin .50 1.25
ITNPT Pierre Thomas .50 1.25
ITNPW Patrick Willis .60 1.50
ITNRG Rob Gronkowski .75 2.00
ITNRH Roy Helu .50 1.25
ITNRL Ray Lewis .75 2.00
ITNRM Rashard Mendenhall .50 1.25
ITNRW Roddy White .50 1.25
ITNSB Sam Bradford .50 1.25
ITNSG Shonn Greene .50 1.25
ITNSH Santonio Holmes .50 1.25
ITNSJ Steve Johnson .60 1.50
ITNVM Von Miller .60 1.50
ITNABR Antonio Brown .75 2.00
ITNMFL Malcom Floyd .50 1.25
ITNMSC Matt Schaub .50 1.25
ITNMWI Mike Williams .60 1.50
ITNPHI Peyton Hillis .50 1.25
ITNRMA Ryan Mathews .60 1.50

2012 Bowman Inside the Numbers Autographs

STATED ODDS 1:117 HOB, 1:1606 RET
ITNAAB Ahmad Bradshaw 6.00 15.00
ITNAABR Antonio Brown 10.00 25.00
ITNABG Blaine Gabbert 6.00 15.00
ITNACN Cam Newton 40.00 80.00
ITNAJM Jeremy Maclin 6.00 15.00
ITNAMS Mark Sanchez 6.00 15.00
ITNAMSC Matt Schaub 6.00 15.00
ITNAMV Michael Vick SP 10.00 25.00
ITNAPH Percy Harvin 6.00 15.00
ITNAPW Patrick Willis 15.00 40.00
ITNARH Roy Helu 6.00 15.00
ITNASB Sam Bradford 15.00 40.00
ITNAVM Von Miller 8.00 20.00

2012 Bowman Inside the Numbers Relics

STATED ODDS 1:35 RETAIL
ITNRAB Ahmad Bradshaw 2.50 6.00
ITNRAD Andy Dalton 3.00 8.00
ITNRAF Arian Foster 3.00 8.00
ITNRAG A.J. Green 4.00 10.00
ITNRBG Blaine Gabbert 2.50 6.00
ITNRBT Ben Tate 2.50 6.00
ITNRCN Cam Newton 6.00 15.00
ITNRCP Christian Ponder 2.50 6.00
ITNRDB Drew Brees 4.00 10.00
ITNRDK Dustin Keller 2.50 6.00
ITNRDM DeMarco Murray 3.00 8.00
ITNRDT Daniel Thomas 2.50 6.00
ITNRGL Greg Little 2.50 6.00
ITNRGO Greg Olsen 3.00 8.00
ITNRJF Jacoby Ford 2.50 6.00
ITNRJJ Julio Jones 4.00 10.00
ITNRJL Jake Locker 4.00 10.00
ITNRJM Jeremy Maclin 2.50 6.00
ITNRMA Miles Austin 2.50 6.00
ITNRMF Matt Forte 2.50 6.00
ITNRMI Mark Ingram 3.00 8.00
ITNRMR Matt Ryan 3.00 8.00
ITNRMS Mark Sanchez 2.50 6.00
ITNRMSC Matt Schaub 2.50 6.00
ITNRMV Michael Vick 3.00 8.00
ITNRMWI Mike Williams 3.00 8.00
ITNRPH Percy Harvin 2.50 6.00
ITNRPT Pierre Thomas 2.50 6.00
ITNRRG Rob Gronkowski 4.00 10.00
ITNRRH Roy Helu 2.50 6.00
ITNRRL Ray Lewis 4.00 10.00
ITNRRMA Ryan Mathews 3.00 8.00
ITNRRW Roddy White 2.50 6.00
ITNRSB Sam Bradford 2.50 6.00
ITNRSG Shonn Greene 2.50 6.00
ITNRSJ Steve Johnson 3.00 8.00
ITNRTS Torrey Smith 2.50 6.00
ITNRVM Von Miller 3.00 8.00

2012 Bowman Inside the Numbers Relic Autographs

STATED ODDS 1:207 HOB, 1:8680 RET
ITNARAB Ahmad Bradshaw 10.00 25.00
ITNARBG Blaine Gabbert 10.00 25.00
ITNARJM Jeremy Maclin 10.00 25.00
ITNARMS Mark Sanchez
ITNARMSC Matt Schaub 10.00 25.00
ITNARMV Michael Vick
ITNARPH Percy Harvin 10.00 25.00
ITNARRH Roy Helu 10.00 25.00
ITNARSB Sam Bradford
ITNARVM Von Miller 12.00 30.00

2012 Bowman Rookie Autographs

ONE AU PER HOBBY PACK OVERALL
EXCH EXPIRATION: 5/31/2015
103 Chris Polk SP 6.00 15.00
104 Ryan Lindley 2.50 6.00
105 Jerel Worthy 2.50 6.00
107 Kellen Moore 3.00 8.00
109 Jarius Wright SP 3.00 8.00
110 Ryan Tannehill SP 15.00 40.00
111 Isaiah Pead SP 3.00 8.00
112 Ronnie Hillman 2.50 6.00
113 Coby Fleener 2.50 6.00
114 Tommy Streeter SP 3.00 8.00
116 Russell Wilson
117 Nick Toon SP 5.00 12.00
119 Robert Turbin SP 3.00 8.00
120 Trent Richardson SP 15.00 40.00
121 Brock Osweiler SP 3.00 8.00
123 Jeff Fuller 2.50 6.00
129 Kendall Wright SP 8.00 20.00
130 Justin Blackmon SP 3.00 8.00
132 LaMichael James 2.50 6.00
135 Patrick Witt 3.00 8.00
136 Greg Childs 2.50 6.00
137 Alshon Jeffery SP 15.00 30.00
139 Jacory Harris 4.00 10.00
140 Michael Floyd 2.50 6.00
142 Chandler Harnish 2.50 6.00
143 Mark Barron 6.00 15.00
145 Kirk Cousins SP 12.00 30.00
149 Bernard Pierce SP 3.00 8.00
150 Andrew Luck SP 125.00 250.00
152 Mohamed Sanu SP 6.00 15.00
153 David Wilson SP 15.00 30.00
155 Doug Martin SP 5.00 12.00
161 Brandon Weeden SP 10.00 25.00
165 Cyrus Gray SP 3.00 8.00
166 Chris Rainey 6.00 15.00
168 Brian Quick SP 6.00 15.00
169 Devon Still SP 4.00 10.00
171 Nick Foles 12.00 30.00
172 T.Y. Hilton SP 6.00 15.00
173 David DeCastro 8.00 20.00
174 Lamar Miller 4.00 10.00
176 Dwayne Allen 4.00 10.00
178 Janoris Jenkins 3.00 8.00
179 Chris Givens 4.00 10.00
180 Melvin Ingram 2.50 6.00
181 DeVier Posey SP 3.00 8.00
182 Rueben Randle SP 3.00 8.00
183 Juron Criner 4.00 10.00
185 Dre Kirkpatrick EXCH 2.50 6.00
187 Jermaine Kearse 6.00 15.00
189 Marvin McNutt 2.50 6.00
191 Dwight Jones 2.50 6.00
192 Dontari Poe 2.50 6.00
196 Case Keenum 5.00 12.00
197 Ryan Broyles 2.50 6.00
198 Joe Adams 2.50 6.00
200 Robert Griffin III SP 4.00 10.00

2012 Bowman Rookie Autographs Red Ink

RED INK/15: X TO X BASIC AU
RED INK/15* ODDS 1:55 HOBBY
150 Andrew Luck 400.00 600.00
200 Robert Griffin III 12.00 30.00

2012 Bowman Rookie Team Helmet Autographs

STATED ODDS 1:1 HOB OVERALL, 1:88 RET
BCRAAJ Alshon Jeffery 6.00 15.00
BCRAAL Andrew Luck 125.00 250.00
BCRABO Brock Osweiler 3.00 8.00
BCRABP Bernard Pierce 3.00 8.00
BCRABQ Brian Quick 3.00 8.00
BCRABW Brandon Weeden 3.00 8.00
BCRACF Coby Fleener 3.00 8.00
BCRACG Cyrus Gray 3.00 8.00
BCRACGR Chris Givens 3.00 8.00
BCRACP Chris Polk 3.00 8.00
BCRADA Dwayne Allen 3.00 8.00
BCRADJ Dwight Jones 5.00 12.00
BCRADK Dre Kirkpatrick 3.00 8.00
BCRADM Doug Martin 5.00 12.00
BCRADP DeVier Posey 3.00 8.00
BCRADS Devon Still 4.00 10.00
BCRADW David Wilson 3.00 8.00
BCRAIP Isaiah Pead 3.00 8.00
BCRAJA Joe Adams 3.00 8.00
BCRAJB Justin Blackmon 3.00 8.00
BCRAJF Jeff Fuller 3.00 8.00
BCRAJK Jermaine Kearse 8.00 20.00
BCRAJWR Jarius Wright 6.00 15.00
BCRAKC Kirk Cousins 12.00 30.00
BCRAKM Kellen Moore 4.00 10.00
BCRAKW Kendall Wright 3.00 8.00
BCRALJ LaMichael James 3.00 8.00
BCRALK Luke Kuechly 8.00 20.00
BCRALM Lamar Miller 5.00 12.00
BCRAMF Michael Floyd 3.00 8.00
BCRAMK Matt Kalil 3.00 8.00
BCRAMM Marvin McNutt 3.00 8.00
BCRAMS Mohamed Sanu 8.00 20.00
BCRANF Nick Foles 12.00 30.00
BCRANT Nick Toon 3.00 8.00
BCRARG Robert Griffin III 4.00 10.00
BCRARR Rueben Randle 3.00 8.00
BCRART Ryan Tannehill 5.00 12.00
BCRARTU Robert Turbin 3.00 8.00
BCRATH T.Y. Hilton 6.00 15.00
BCRATR Trent Richardson 3.00 8.00
BCRATS Tommy Streeter 3.00 8.00

2012 Bowman Rookie Team Helmet Autographs Red Ink

RED INK/15: 1X TO 2.5X BASIC INSERTS
RED INK/15* ODDS 1:75 HOBBY
BCRAAL Andrew Luck 300.00 600.00
BCRARG Robert Griffin III 10.00 25.00

2013 Bowman

COMPLETE SET (220) 12.00 30.00
1 Adrian Peterson .30 .75
2 Matthew Stafford .25 .60
3 Torrey Smith .20 .50
4 Maurice Jones-Drew .20 .50
5 Darrelle Revis .20 .50
6 Denarius Moore .20 .50
7 Antonio Brown .30 .75
8 Reggie Wayne .25 .60
9 Patrick Peterson .20 .50
10 Eli Manning .25 .60
11 Cameron Wake .20 .50
12 Luke Kuechly .25 .60
13 Ndamukong Suh .25 .60
14 Jamaal Charles .25 .60
15 Andre Johnson .20 .50
16 Victor Cruz .25 .60
17 NaVorro Bowman .25 .60
18 Demaryius Thomas .25 .60
19 Marshawn Lynch .25 .60
20 Andrew Luck .50 1.25
21 Tony Romo .25 .60
22 Chris Long .20 .50
23 Jason Witten .25 .60
24 James Laurinaitis .25 .60
25 Russell Wilson .60 1.50
26 Matt Schaub .20 .50
27 Ben Roethlisberger .30 .75
28 Jermichael Finley .20 .50
29 Brandon Marshall .25 .60
30 Ray Rice .20 .50
31 Bobby Wagner .20 .50
32 Cam Newton .30 .75
33 Stevan Ridley .20 .50
34 Philip Rivers .30 .75
35 LeSean McCoy .30 .75
36 Jeremy Kerley .20 .50
37 Trent Richardson .20 .50
38 Richard Sherman .30 .75
39 Pierre Garcon .25 .60
40 Aaron Rodgers .50 1.25
41 Rob Gronkowski .30 .75
42 Justin Blackmon .20 .50
43 Kyle Rudolph .20 .50
44 Julio Jones .30 .75
45 Frank Gore .25 .60
46 Robert Quinn .25 .60
47 Matt Forte .20 .50
48 Jermaine Gresham .25 .60
49 Aaron Hernandez .25 .60
50 Tom Brady .75 2.00
51 Matt Ryan .25 .60
52 DeMarco Murray .25 .60
53 Roddy White .20 .50
54 Nick Fairley .20 .50
55 Mike Williams .25 .60
56 Hakeem Nicks .20 .50
57 Jeremy Maclin .20 .50
58 Jordy Nelson .25 .60
59 Mikel Leshoure .20 .50
60 Drew Brees .30 .75
61 T.Y. Hilton .25 .60
62 Ryan Mathews .25 .60
63 Steve Johnson .25 .60
64 Jared Allen .20 .50
65 Jimmy Graham .30 .75
66 Christian Ponder .20 .50
67 Michael Crabtree .20 .50
68 Joe Flacco .25 .60
69 Kendall Wright .20 .50
70 Arian Foster .25 .60
71 Darren McFadden .25 .60
72 Andy Dalton .25 .60
73 Jake Locker .25 .60
74 Cecil Shorts .20 .50
75 Larry Fitzgerald .25 .60
76 Josh Freeman .25 .60
77 Ryan Tannehill .25 .60
78 Joe Haden .20 .50
79 C.J. Spiller .20 .50
80 A.J. Green .30 .75
81 Tony Gonzalez .25 .60
82 Vincent Jackson .20 .50
83 Clay Matthews .30 .75
84 Earl Thomas .25 .60
85 Doug Martin .25 .60
86 Josh Gordon .20 .50
87 Jacquizz Rodgers .25 .60
88 Dez Bryant .30 .75
89 Eric Decker .20 .50
90 Calvin Johnson .30 .75
91 Chris Johnson .20 .50
92 Brandon Weeden .20 .50
93 Sam Bradford .20 .50
94 Von Miller .25 .60
95 David Wilson .20 .50
96 Daryl Washington .20 .50
97 Vick Ballard .20 .50
98 Aldon Smith .20 .50
99 Alfred Morris .20 .50
100 Peyton Manning .60 1.50
101 Colin Kaepernick .25 .60
102 J.J. Watt .25 .60
103 Jason Pierre-Paul .20 .50
104 Nick Foles .25 .60
105 Troy Polamalu .30 .75
106 Randall Cobb .25 .60
107 Brian Orakpo .25 .60
108 BenJarvus Green-Ellis .25 .60
109 Brian Hartline .20 .50
110 Robert Griffin III .20 .50

111 Dion Sims RC .25 .60
112 Desmond Trufant RC .25 .60
113 Chase Thomas RC .25 .60
114 Tyler Bray RC .25 .60
115 Datone Jones RC .25 .60
116 Ezekiel Ansah RC .25 .60
117 Knile Davis RC .25 .60
118 Khaseem Greene RC .25 .60
119 Zach Ertz RC .50 1.25
120 Jarvis Jones RC .25 .60
121 Stedman Bailey RC .25 .60
122 Johnathan Hankins RC .25 .60
123 Le'Veon Bell RC .75 2.00
124 Sharrif Floyd RC .25 .60
125 Luke Joeckel RC .25 .60
126 Joseph Randle RC .25 .60
127 EJ Manuel RC .25 .60
128 Mike Glennon RC .25 .60
129 Zach Line RC .25 .60
130 Tavon Austin RC .30 .75
131 Quinton Patton RC .25 .60
132 Dion Jordan RC .25 .60
133 Sheldon Richardson RC .25 .60
134 Tavarres King RC .25 .60
135 Montee Ball RC .25 .60
136 Arthur Brown RC .25 .60
137 Johnthan Banks RC .25 .60
138 Christine Michael RC .25 .60
139 Andre Ellington RC .25 .60
140 Eddie Lacy RC .25 .60
141 Philip Lutzenkirchen RC .40 1.00
142 Dee Milliner RC .25 .60
143 Matt Scott RC .25 .60
144 Rex Burkhead RC .30 .75
145 Matt Elam RC .25 .60
146 Brandon Jenkins RC .30 .75
147 Jesse Williams RC .40 1.00
148 Lonnie Pryor RC .25 .60
149 Shawn Williams RC .25 .60
150 Geno Smith RC .25 .60
151 Mike Gillislee RC .25 .60
152 Markus Wheaton RC .25 .60
153 Corey Fuller RC .25 .60
154 Collin Klein RC .30 .75
155 Stepfan Taylor RC .25 .60
156 Miguel Maysonet RC .25 .60
157 Kenjon Barner RC .25 .60
158 Xavier Rhodes RC .25 .60
159 Eric Reid RC .30 .75
160 Alex Okafor RC .25 .60
161 Dennis Johnson RC .25 .60
162 Jordan Reed RC .40 1.00
163 Johnathan Franklin RC .25 .60
164 T.J. McDonald RC .25 .60
165 Ryan Nassib RC .25 .60
166 Terrance Williams RC .25 .60
167 D.J. Harper RC .30 .75
168 Star Lotulelei RC .30 .75
169 Chance Warmack RC .25 .60
170 Tyler Eifert RC .25 .60
171 Cordarrelle Patterson RC .25 .60
172 Kenny Vaccaro RC .25 .60
173 Chris Gragg RC .25 .60
174 Damontre Moore RC .25 .60
175 Keenan Allen RC .50 1.25
176 Eric Fisher RC .25 .60
177 Kenny Stills RC .25 .60
178 John Simon RC .40 1.00
179 Denard Robinson RC .25 .60
180 DeAndre Hopkins RC .60 1.50
181 Barkevious Mingo RC .25 .60
182 Tyler Wilson RC .25 .60
183 Marquise Goodwin RC .25 .60
184 Joseph Fauria RC .25 .60
185 Logan Ryan RC .30 .75
186 Sam Montgomery RC .25 .60
187 Alec Ogletree RC .25 .60
188 Nico Johnson RC .30 .75
189 Kevin Minter RC .25 .60
190 Bjoern Werner RC .25 .60
191 Kerwynn Williams RC .25 .60
192 Brad Sorensen RC .25 .60
193 Spencer Ware RC .25 .60
194 Ryan Swope RC .25 .60
195 Aaron Mellette RC .25 .60
196 Justin Hunter RC .25 .60
197 Cobi Hamilton RC .25 .60
198 Chris Harper RC .25 .60
199 Ryan Otten RC .25 .60
200 Manti Te'o RC .30 .75
201 Nickell Robey RC .30 .75
202 Ray Graham RC .25 .60
203 Bacarri Rambo RC .30 .75
204 Robert Woods RC .40 1.00
205 Tyrann Mathieu RC .40 1.00
206 Conner Vernon RC .25 .60
207 Aaron Dobson RC .25 .60
208 Marcus Lattimore RC .25 .60
209 Robert Lester RC .25 .60
210 Giovani Bernard RC .25 .60
211 Gavin Escobar RC .25 .60
212 Da'Rick Rogers RC .25 .60
213 Jordan Poyer RC .25 .60
214 Zac Dysert RC .25 .60
215 John Jenkins RC .25 .60
216 Jawan Jamison RC .25 .60
217 David Amerson RC .25 .60
218 Sean Renfree RC .30 .75
219 Landry Jones RC .25 .60
220 Matt Barkley RC .25 .60
221 Leon Sandcastle (Deion) SP 10.00 25.00

2013 Bowman Black

*1-110 VETS: .8X TO 2X BASIC CARDS
TWO VETERANS PER HOBBY PACK
*111-220 ROOKIES: .5X TO 1.2X BASIC RC
FOUR ROOKIES PER HOBBY PACK

2013 Bowman Blue

*1-110 VETS/99: 2.5X TO 6X BASIC CARDS
*111-220 ROOKIES/499: 1X TO 2.5X BASIC RC

2013 Bowman Gold

*1-110 VETS/75: 2.5X TO 6X BASIC CARDS
*111-220 ROOKIES/399: 1X TO 2.5X BASIC RC

2013 Bowman Green

*111-220 ROOKIES/99: 1.5X TO 4X BASIC RC

2013 Bowman Orange

*1-110 VETS/50: 4X TO 10X BASIC CARDS
*111-220 ROOKIES/299: 1.2X TO 3X BASIC RC

2013 Bowman Purple

*1-110 VETS: 1.2X TO 3X BASIC CARDS
*111-220 ROOKIES: .8X TO 2X BASIC RC

2013 Bowman Rainbow Black

*1-110 VETS: 1.2X TO 3X BASIC CARDS
*111-220 ROOKIES: .8X TO 2X BASIC RC

2013 Bowman Rainbow Blue

*1-110 VETS/99: 2.5X TO 6X BASIC CARDS
*111-220 ROOKIES/499: 1X TO 2.5X BASIC RC

2013 Bowman Rainbow Gold

*1-110 VETS/75: 2.5X TO 6X BASIC CARDS
*111-220 ROOKIES/399: 1X TO 2.5X BASIC RC

2013 Bowman Rainbow Orange

*1-110 VETS/50: 4X TO 10X BASIC CARDS
*111-220 ROOKIES/299: 1.2X TO 3X BASIC RC

2013 Bowman Rainbow Prism

*111-220 ROOKIES/99: 1.5X TO 4X BASIC RC

2013 Bowman Rainbow Purple

*1-110 VETS: 2X TO 5X BASIC CARDS
*111-220 ROOKIES: 1.2X TO 3X BASIC RC
RANDOM INSERTS IN RETAIL

2013 Bowman Rainbow Red

*1-110 VETS/25: 6X TO 15X BASIC CARDS
*111-220 ROOKIES/199: 1.2X TO 3X BASIC RC

2013 Bowman Red

*1-110 VETS/25: 6X TO 15X BASIC CARDS
*111-220 ROOKIES/199: 1.2X TO 3X BASIC RC

2013 Bowman Silver Ice

*1-110 VETS: 2X TO 5X BASIC CARDS
*111-220 ROOKIES: 1.2X TO 3X BASIC RC
STATED ODDS 1:7 HOB

2013 Bowman Silver Ice Green

*1-110 VETS/50: 4X TO 10X BASIC CARDS
*111-220 ROOKIES/50: 2X TO 5X BASIC RC

2013 Bowman Silver Ice Red

*1-110 VETS/25: 6X TO 15X BASIC CARDS
*111-220 ROOKIES/25: 4X TO 10X BASIC RC

2013 Bowman Chrome Rookie Autograph Redemption

PLAYERS PICTURED IN NFL UNIFORMS
EXCH EXPIRATION: 6/30/2016
BAAD Aaron Dobson EXCH
BAAE Andre Ellington 8.00 20.00
BACP Cordarrelle Patterson EXCH 8.00 20.00
BADH DeAndre Hopkins 20.00 50.00
BAEL Eddie Lacy 8.00 20.00
BAEM EJ Manuel 8.00 20.00
BAGB Giovanni Bernard 8.00 20.00
BAGE Gavin Escobar 8.00 20.00
BAGS Geno Smith 8.00 20.00
BAJF Johnathan Franklin 8.00 20.00
BAJH Justin Hunter 20.00 40.00
BAJR Jordan Reed EXCH 12.00 30.00
BAJRA Joseph Randle 8.00 20.00
BAKA Keenan Allen 15.00 40.00
BAKD Knile Davis 8.00 20.00
BAKS Kenny Stills EXCH 8.00 20.00
BALB Le'Veon Bell 40.00 80.00
BALJ Landry Jones EXCH
BAMBA Montee Ball EXCH 8.00 20.00
BAMB Matt Barkley 8.00 20.00
BAMG Mike Gillislee 8.00 20.00
BAMGL Mike Glennon EXCH
BAMGO Marquise Goodwin EXCH
BAML Marcus Lattimore 8.00 20.00
BAMT Manti Te'o EXCH 10.00 25.00
BAMW Markus Wheaton 8.00 20.00
BAQP Quinton Patton EXCH
BARN Ryan Nassib EXCH
BARW Robert Woods EXCH 12.00 30.00
BASB Stedman Bailey EXCH
BAST Stepfan Taylor 8.00 20.00
BATA Tavon Austin 10.00 25.00
BATE Tyler Eifert EXCH 8.00 20.00
BATW Terrance Williams 20.00 40.00
BATWI Tyler Wilson EXCH
BAZE Zach Ertz EXCH 15.00 40.00

2013 Bowman Die Cut

STATED ODDS 1:4 HOB
*BLUE/25: 1.2X TO 3X BASIC INSERTS
*PRISM/50: .8X TO 2X BASIC INSERTS
BDCAD Andy Dalton 1.25 3.00
BDCAF Arian Foster 1.25 3.00
BDCAJ Andre Johnson 1.00 2.50
BDCAJG A.J. Green 1.50 4.00
BDCAL Andrew Luck 2.50 6.00
BDCAM Alfred Morris 1.00 2.50
BDCAP Adrian Peterson 1.50 4.00
BDCAR Aaron Rodgers 2.50 6.00
BDCBM Brandon Marshall 1.25 3.00
BDCBR Ben Roethlisberger 1.50 4.00
BDCCJ Chris Johnson 1.00 2.50
BDCCJO Calvin Johnson 1.50 4.00
BDCCJS C.J. Spiller 1.00 2.50
BDCCM Clay Matthews 1.50 4.00
BDCCN Cam Newton 1.50 4.00
BDCDB Dez Bryant 1.50 4.00
BDCDBR Drew Brees 1.50 4.00
BDCDM Doug Martin 1.25 3.00
BDCDT Demaryius Thomas 1.25 3.00
BDCDW David Wilson 1.00 2.50
BDCED Eric Decker 1.00 2.50
BDCEM Eli Manning 1.25 3.00
BDCFG Frank Gore 1.25 3.00
BDCJB Justin Blackmon 1.00 2.50
BDCJC Jamaal Charles 1.25 3.00
BDCJG Jimmy Graham 1.50 4.00
BDCJJ Julio Jones 1.50 4.00
BDCJJW J.J. Watt 1.25 3.00
BDCJW Jason Witten 1.25 3.00
BDCLF Larry Fitzgerald 1.25 3.00
BDCLM LeSean McCoy 1.50 4.00
BDCMJD Maurice Jones-Drew 1.00 2.50
BDCML Marshawn Lynch 1.25 3.00
BDCMR Matt Ryan 1.25 3.00
BDCPM Peyton Manning 3.00 8.00
BDCRC Randall Cobb 1.25 3.00
BDCRG Rob Gronkowski 1.50 4.00
BDCRG3 Robert Griffin III 1.00 2.50
BDCRR Ray Rice 1.00 2.50
BDCRT Ryan Tannehill 1.25 3.00
BDCRW Reggie Wayne 1.25 3.00
BDCRWH Roddy White 1.00 2.50
BDCRWI Russell Wilson 3.00 8.00
BDCTB Tom Brady 4.00 10.00
BDCTG Tony Gonzalez 1.25 3.00
BDCTP Troy Polamalu 1.50 4.00
BDCTR Trent Richardson 1.00 2.50
BDCVC Victor Cruz 1.25 3.00
BDCVJ Vincent Jackson 1.00 2.50
BDCVM Von Miller 1.25 3.00

2013 Bowman Mini

ONE PER HOBBY PACK
52BAB Arthur Brown .30 .75
52BAD Aaron Dobson .30 .75
52BAE Andre Ellington .30 .75
52BAM Aaron Mellette .30 .75
52BAO Alex Okafor .30 .75
52BAOG Alec Ogletree .30 .75
52BBJ Brandon Jenkins .40 1.00
52BBM Barkevious Mingo .30 .75
52BBR Bacarri Rambo .40 1.00
52BBS Brad Sorensen .30 .75
52BBW Bjoern Werner .30 .75
52BCF Corey Fuller .30 .75
52BCG Chris Gragg .30 .75
52BCH Cobi Hamilton .30 .75
52BCHA Chris Harper .30 .75
52BCK Collin Klein .40 1.00
52BCM Christine Michael .30 .75
52BCP Cordarrelle Patterson .30 .75
52BCT Chase Thomas .30 .75
52BCV Conner Vernon .30 .75
52BCW Chance Warmack .30 .75
52BDA David Amerson .30 .75
52BDEJ Dennis Johnson .30 .75
52BDH DeAndre Hopkins .75 2.00
52BDJ Datone Jones .30 .75
52BDJH D.J. Harper .40 1.00
52BDJO Dion Jordan .30 .75
52BDM Damontre Moore .30 .75
52BDMI Dee Milliner .30 .75
52BDR Denard Robinson .30 .75
52BDRO Da'Rick Rogers .30 .75
52BDS Dion Sims .30 .75
52BDT Desmond Trufant .30 .75
52BEA Ezekiel Ansah .30 .75
52BEF Eric Fisher .30 .75
52BEL Eddie Lacy .30 .75
52BEM EJ Manuel .30 .75
52BER Eric Reid .40 1.00
52BERE Sean Renfree .40 1.00
52BGB Giovani Bernard .30 .75
52BGE Gavin Escobar .30 .75
52BGS Geno Smith .30 .75
52BJB Johnthan Banks .30 .75
52BJF Joseph Fauria .30 .75
52BJFR Johnathan Franklin .30 .75
52BJH Justin Hunter .30 .75
52BJHA Johnathan Hankins .30 .75
52BJJ Jarvis Jones .30 .75
52BJJA Jawan Jamison .30 .75
52BJE John Jenkins .30 .75
52BJP Jordan Poyer .30 .75
52BJR Jordan Reed .50 1.25
52BJRA Joseph Randle .30 .75
52BJS John Simon .50 1.25
52BJW Jesse Williams .50 1.25
52BKA Keenan Allen .60 1.50
52BKB Kenjon Barner .30 .75
52BKD Knile Davis .30 .75
52BKG Khaseem Greene .30 .75
52BKM Kevin Minter .30 .75
52BKS Kenny Stills .30 .75
52BKV Kenny Vaccaro .30 .75
52BKW Kerwynn Williams .30 .75
52BLB Le'Veon Bell 1.00 2.50
52BLJ Luke Joeckel .30 .75
52BLJO Landry Jones .30 .75
52BLP Lonnie Pryor .30 .75
52BLR Logan Ryan .40 1.00
52BLS Leon Sandcastle (Deion) 4.00 10.00
52BMB Matt Barkley .30 .75
52BMBA Montee Ball .30 .75
52BME Matt Elam .30 .75
52BMG Mike Glennon .30 .75
52BMGI Mike Gillislee .30 .75
52BMGO Marquise Goodwin .30 .75
52BML Marcus Lattimore .30 .75
52BMM Miguel Maysonet .30 .75
52BMS Matt Scott .30 .75
52BMT Manti Te'o .40 1.00
52BMW Markus Wheaton .30 .75
52BNJ Nico Johnson .40 1.00
52BNR Nickell Robey .40 1.00
52BPL Philip Lutzenkirchen .50 1.25
52BQP Quinton Patton .30 .75
52BRB Rex Burkhead .40 1.00
52BRG Ray Graham .30 .75
52BRL Robert Lester .30 .75
52BRN Ryan Nassib .30 .75
52BRS Ryan Swope .30 .75
52BRW Robert Woods .50 1.25
52BSB Stedman Bailey .30 .75
52BSF Sharrif Floyd .30 .75
52BSL Star Lotulelei .40 1.00
52BSM Sam Montgomery .30 .75
52BSRI Sheldon Richardson .30 .75
52BST Stepfan Taylor .30 .75
52BSW Spencer Ware .30 .75
52BSWI Shawn Williams .30 .75
52BTA Tavon Austin .40 1.00
52BTB Tyler Bray .30 .75
52BTE Tyler Eifert .30 .75
52BTK Tavarres King .30 .75
52BTM T.J. McDonald .30 .75
52BTMA Tyrann Mathieu .50 1.25
52BTR Theo Riddick .30 .75
52BTW Terrance Williams .30 .75
52BTWI Tyler Wilson .30 .75
52BXR Xavier Rhodes .30 .75
52BZD Zac Dysert .30 .75
52BZE Zach Ertz .60 1.50

2013 Bowman Mini Autographs

EXCH EXPIRATION: 6/30/2016
52BAD Aaron Dobson 6.00 15.00
52BAE Andre Ellington 2.50 6.00
52BAO Alex Okafor 2.50 6.00
52BAOG Alec Ogletree 2.50 6.00
52BBJ Brandon Jenkins 3.00 8.00
52BBM Barkevious Mingo 2.50 6.00
52BBR Bacarri Rambo 3.00 8.00
52BBW Bjoern Werner SP 4.00 10.00
52BCHA Chris Harper 5.00 12.00
52BCM Christine Michael 2.50 6.00
52BCP Cordarrelle Patterson SP 2.50 6.00
52BCT Chase Thomas 3.00 8.00
52BCV Conner Vernon 4.00 10.00
52BCW Chance Warmack SP 4.00 10.00
52BDH DeAndre Hopkins SP 8.00 20.00
52BDJ Datone Jones 2.50 6.00
52BDJO Dion Jordan 2.50 6.00
52BDM Damontre Moore 2.50 6.00
52BDMI Dee Millliner SP EXCH 2.50 6.00
52BDR Denard Robinson 2.50 6.00
52BDRO Da'Rick Rogers SP 6.00 15.00
52BDT Desmond Trufant 5.00 12.00
52BEA Ezekiel Ansah 2.50 6.00
52BEF Eric Fisher 2.50 6.00
52BEL Eddie Lacy SP 12.00 30.00
52BEM EJ Manuel SP 15.00 40.00
52BER Eric Reid 5.00 12.00
52BGS Geno Smith SP 2.50 6.00
52BJF Joseph Fauria 3.00 8.00
52BJH Justin Hunter SP EXCH 10.00 25.00
52BJHA Johnathan Hankins 4.00 10.00
52BJJ Jarvis Jones SP 15.00 30.00
52BJE John Jenkins 4.00 10.00
52BJP Jordan Poyer 2.50 6.00
52BJR Jordan Reed SP 4.00 10.00
52BJS John Simon SP 4.00 10.00
52BJW Jesse Williams 5.00 12.00
52BKA Keenan Allen SP 6.00 15.00
52BKB Kenjon Barner 2.50 6.00
52BKD Knile Davis 6.00 15.00
52BKG Khaseem Greene 5.00 12.00
52BKS Kenny Stills 2.50 6.00
52BKV Kenny Vaccaro 2.50 6.00
52BKW Kerwynn Williams 2.50 6.00
52BLB Le'Veon Bell 15.00 40.00
52BLJ Luke Joeckel SP 2.50 6.00
52BLJO Landry Jones SP 2.50 6.00
52BMB Matt Barkley SP 15.00 40.00
52BMBA Montee Ball SP 10.00 25.00
52BME Matt Elam 5.00 12.00
52BMG Mike Glennon SP 2.50 6.00
52BMGI Mike Gillislee SP 2.50 6.00
52BMGO Marquise Goodwin 2.50 6.00
52BML Marcus Lattimore 2.50 6.00
52BMS Matt Scott 2.50 6.00
52BMT Manti Te'o SP 10.00 25.00
52BMW Markus Wheaton SP 2.50 6.00
52BNJ Nico Johnson 6.00 15.00
52BPL Philip Lutzenkirchen 4.00 10.00
52BQP Quinton Patton 10.00 25.00
52BRB Rex Burkhead 3.00 8.00
52BRG Ray Graham 3.00 8.00
52BRL Robert Lester 3.00 8.00
52BRN Ryan Nassib SP 25.00 50.00
52BRW Robert Woods SP 15.00 30.00
52BSB Stedman Bailey 8.00 20.00
52BSM Sam Montgomery 2.50 6.00
52BST Stepfan Taylor 2.50 6.00
52BSWI Shawn Williams 2.50 6.00
52BTA Tavon Austin SP 3.00 8.00
52BTB Tyler Bray SP 15.00 30.00
52BTE Tyler Eifert SP 2.50 6.00
52BTK Tavarres King 2.50 6.00
52BTM T.J. McDonald 2.50 6.00
52BTMA Tyrann Mathieu EXCH 4.00 10.00
52BTR Theo Riddick 2.50 6.00
52BTWI Tyler Wilson SP 30.00 60.00
52BXR Xavier Rhodes SP 2.50 6.00
52BZD Zac Dysert 2.50 6.00
52BZE Zach Ertz 6.00 15.00

2013 Bowman Relics

STATED ODDS 1:20 HOB, 1:38 RET
*BLUE/99: .5X TO 1.2X BASIC JSY
*GOLD/50: .6X TO 1.5X BASIC JSY
*ORANGE/25: .8X TO 2X BASIC JSY
BRAD Andy Dalton 2.50 6.00
BRAH Aaron Hernandez 2.50 6.00
BRAJH A.J. Hawk 2.00 5.00
BRAL Andrew Luck 5.00 12.00
BRAM Alfred Morris 2.00 5.00
BRAR Andre Roberts 2.00 5.00
BRBL Brandon LaFell 2.00 5.00
BRBW Brandon Weeden 2.00 5.00
BRCJS C.J. Spiller 2.00 5.00
BRCN Cam Newton 3.00 8.00
BRCS Cecil Shorts 2.00 5.00
BRDBR Dez Bryant 3.00 8.00
BRDM Doug Martin 2.50 6.00
BRDMU DeMarco Murray 2.50 6.00
BRDR Darrelle Revis 2.00 5.00
BRDT Demaryius Thomas 2.50 6.00
BRED Eric Decker 2.00 5.00
BRET Earl Thomas 2.50 6.00
BRGT Golden Tate 2.00 5.00
BRJD Jonathan Dwyer 2.00 5.00
BRJG Jermaine Gresham 2.50 6.00
BRJJ Julio Jones 3.00 8.00
BRJM Jeremy Maclin 2.00 5.00
BRJR Jacquizz Rodgers 2.50 6.00
BRKM Knowshon Moreno 2.00 5.00
BRKW Kendall Wright 2.00 5.00
BRMI Mark Ingram 2.50 6.00
BRML Mikel Leshoure 2.00 5.00
BRMWI Mike Williams 2.50 6.00
BRNF Nick Foles 2.50 6.00
BRNS Ndamukong Suh 2.50 6.00
BRPA Prince Amukamara 2.00 5.00
BRPP Patrick Peterson 2.00 5.00
BRRG Rob Gronkowski 3.00 8.00
BRRG3 Robert Griffin III 2.00 5.00
BRRL Ray Lewis 3.00 8.00
BRRM Ryan Mathews 2.50 6.00
BRRT Ryan Tannehill 2.50 6.00
BRRW Russell Wilson 6.00 15.00
BRSB Sam Bradford 2.00 5.00
BRSR Stevan Ridley 2.00 5.00
BRTR Trent Richardson 2.00 5.00
BRTRO Tony Romo 2.50 6.00
BRTS Torrey Smith 2.00 5.00
BRVM Von Miller 2.50 6.00

2014 Bowman

COMPLETE SET (220) 12.00 30.00
R1 Marqise Lee RC .20 .50
R2 Kyle Van Noy RC .20 .50
R3 Scott Crichton RC .15 .40
R4 Jason Verrett RC .15 .40
R5 Dominique Easley RC .15 .40
R6 Austin Seferian-Jenkins RC .15 .40
R7 Josh Huff RC .20 .50
R8 Odell Beckham Jr. RC 2.00 5.00
R9 Johnny Manziel RC .25 .60
R10 Jerome Smith RC .15 .40
R11 Jeff Mathews RC .20 .50
R12 Isaiah Crowell RC .20 .50
R13 Blake Bortles RC .20 .50
R14 Carlos Hyde RC .20 .50
R15 Ed Stinson RC .25 .60
R16 Jalen Saunders RC .15 .40
R17 Gabe Jackson RC .15 .40
R18 Antonio Andrews RC .15 .40
R19 Mike Davis RC .15 .40
R20 David Fales RC .15 .40
R21 Zach Mettenberger RC .15 .40
R22 A.J. McCarron RC .15 .40
R23 Ha Ha Clinton-Dix RC .20 .50
R24 Michael Sam RC .15 .40
R25 Cody Hoffman RC .15 .40
R26 Greg Robinson RC .15 .40
R27 Jarvis Landry RC .30 .75
R28 Jeremy Hill RC .20 .50
R29 Ryan Grant RC .15 .40
R30 James Wilder Jr. RC .20 .50
R31 Bradley Roby RC .15 .40
R32 Ahmad Dixon RC .15 .40
R33 Antone Exum RC .15 .40
R34 C.J. Mosley RC .20 .50
R35 Robert Herron RC .15 .40
R36 Kony Ealy RC .20 .50
R37 Teddy Bridgewater RC .25 .60
R38 De'Anthony Thomas RC .15 .40
R39 Anthony Johnson RC .15 .40
R40 Xavier Grimble RC .20 .50
R41 Dion Bailey RC .15 .40
R42 Taylor Hart RC .20 .50
R43 Deone Bucannon RC .15 .40
R44 Lache Seastrunk RC .15 .40
R45 Arthur Lynch RC .15 .40
R46 Paul Richardson RC .20 .50
R47 Lamarcus Joyner RC .20 .50
R48 Craig Loston RC .15 .40
R49 Kareem Martin RC .15 .40
R50 Stephen Morris RC .15 .40
R51 Marion Grice RC .15 .40
R52 George Atkinson RC .15 .40
R53 Eric Ebron RC .20 .50
R54 Khalil Mack RC .60 1.50
R55 Derek Carr RC 1.00 2.50
R56 Jake Matthews RC .15 .40
R57 Tre Mason RC .15 .40
R58 Anthony Barr RC .15 .40
R59 Rajion Neal RC .15 .40
R60 Cyrus Kouandjio RC .20 .50
R61 Adrian Hubbard RC .20 .50
R62 Stephon Tuitt RC .25 .60
R63 Brandon Coleman RC .15 .40
R64 Logan Thomas RC .15 .40
R65 Morgan Breslin RC .25 .60
R66 Mike Evans RC .40 1.00
R67 Christian Jones RC .20 .50
R68 Damien Williams RC .15 .40
R69 Devin Street RC .15 .40
R70 Sammy Watkins RC .25 .60
R71 Silas Redd RC .20 .50
R72 C.J. Fiedorowicz RC .15 .40
R73 Antonio Richardson RC .25 .60
R74 Connor Shaw RC .15 .40
R75 Dri Archer RC .15 .40
R76 Jared Abbrederis RC .15 .40
R77 Jace Amaro RC .15 .40
R78 Aaron Donald RC .40 1.00
R79 Louis Nix III RC .15 .40
R80 Ra'Shede Hageman RC .15 .40
R81 Loucheiz Purifoy RC .15 .40
R82 Tommy Rees RC .20 .50
R83 Bishop Sankey RC .15 .40
R84 Will Sutton RC .20 .50
R85 Charles Sims RC .15 .40
R86 Brandin Cooks RC .25 .60
R87 Jackson Jeffcoat RC .20 .50
R88 Allen Robinson RC .25 .60
R89 Cyril Richardson RC .15 .40
R90 Aaron Murray RC .15 .40
R91 Trey Millard RC .20 .50
R92 Jadeveon Clowney RC .20 .50
R93 Bryn Renner RC .15 .40
R94 Yawin Smallwood RC .15 .40
R95 LaDarius Perkins RC .15 .40
R96 Aaron Colvin RC .15 .40
R97 Donte Moncrief RC .15 .40
R98 Alfred Blue RC .15 .40
R99 Tajh Boyd RC .15 .40
R100 James White RC .30 .75
R101 Andre Williams RC .15 .40
R102 Trent Murphy RC .15 .40
R103 Chris Smith RC .15 .40
R104 Ka'Deem Carey RC .15 .40
R105 Jimmy Garoppolo RC 1.25 3.00
R106 Taylor Lewan RC .15 .40
R107 Ryan Shazier RC .25 .60
R108 Darqueze Dennard RC .20 .50
R109 Allen Hurns RC .20 .50
R110 Jordan Matthews RC .25 .60
V1 Adrian Peterson .30 .75
V2 Eddie Lacy .20 .50
V3 Tyrann Mathieu .25 .60
V4 Alshon Jeffery .25 .60
V5 Michael Floyd .20 .50
V6 Calvin Johnson .30 .75
V7 Stevan Ridley .20 .50
V8 Zac Stacy .20 .50
V9 Russell Wilson .50 1.25
V10 T.Y. Hilton .25 .60
V11 Aaron Rodgers .60 1.50
V12 Kiko Alonso .20 .50
V13 Clay Matthews .30 .75
V14 Terrelle Pryor .20 .50
V15 Aaron Dobson .20 .50
V16 LeSean McCoy .30 .75
V17 J.J. Watt .30 .75
V18 Denard Robinson .20 .50
V19 Luke Kuechly .25 .60
V20 Marshawn Lynch .25 .60
V21 Alfred Morris .20 .50
V22 Le'Veon Bell .25 .60
V23 Mike Wallace .20 .50
V24 Ryan Tannehill .25 .60
V25 Terrell Suggs .20 .50
V26 Demaryius Thomas .25 .60
V27 Charles Clay .20 .50
V28 Rob Gronkowski .30 .75
V29 Larry Fitzgerald .25 .60
V30 DeSean Jackson .25 .60
V31 Dez Bryant .30 .75
V32 Ryan Mathews .25 .60
V33 Sheldon Richardson .20 .50
V34 Andre Johnson .25 .60
V35 Drew Brees .30 .75
V36 Reggie Wayne .25 .60
V37 Andrew Luck .40 1.00
V38 Montee Ball .20 .50
V39 Wes Welker .25 .60
V40 Cecil Shorts .20 .50
V41 Tamba Hali .20 .50
V42 Tyler Eifert .25 .60
V43 Jordy Nelson .25 .60
V44 Randall Cobb .25 .60
V45 Antonio Brown .30 .75
V46 Ray Rice .20 .50
V47 Denarius Moore .20 .50
V48 DeMarcus Ware .25 .60
V49 Frank Gore .25 .60
V50 Patrick Peterson .20 .50
V51 DeAndre Hopkins .25 .60
V52 Earl Thomas .25 .60
V53 Percy Harvin .20 .50
V54 Matt Ryan .25 .60
V55 Von Miller .25 .60
V56 Tom Brady .75 2.00
V57 DeMarco Murray .25 .60
V58 Lamar Miller .20 .50
V59 Maurice Jones-Drew .20 .50
V60 Jake Locker .25 .60
V61 Julius Thomas .20 .50
V62 Keenan Allen .25 .60
V63 Pierre Garcon .25 .60
V64 Cam Newton .30 .75
V65 Michael Crabtree .20 .50
V66 Robert Griffin III .20 .50
V67 Tavon Austin .20 .50
V68 Vernon Davis .20 .50
V69 Tony Romo .25 .60
V70 Kendall Wright .20 .50
V71 Chris Johnson .20 .50
V72 Jordan Cameron .20 .50
V73 Golden Tate .25 .60
V74 Richard Sherman .30 .75
V75 Knowshon Moreno .20 .50
V76 Dion Jordan .20 .50
V77 Matt Forte .20 .50
V78 Brandon Marshall .20 .50
V79 Colin Kaepernick .25 .60
V80 Peyton Manning .60 1.50
V81 Doug Martin .25 .60
V82 EJ Manuel .20 .50
V83 Reggie Bush .20 .50
V84 Julio Jones .30 .75
V85 Terrance Williams .20 .50
V86 Geno Smith .20 .50
V87 Coby Fleener .20 .50
V88 Darrelle Revis .20 .50
V89 Trent Richardson .20 .50
V90 Vincent Jackson .20 .50
V91 Eric Decker .20 .50
V92 Giovani Bernard .20 .50
V93 C.J. Spiller .20 .50
V94 Jamaal Charles .25 .60
V95 Cordarrelle Patterson .20 .50
V96 Jason Pierre-Paul .20 .50
V97 Geno Atkins .20 .50
V98 Robert Quinn .25 .60
V99 A.J. Green .30 .75
V100 Torrey Smith .20 .50
V101 Matthew Stafford .25 .60
V102 Victor Cruz .25 .60
V103 Patrick Willis .25 .60
V104 Andre Ellington .20 .50
V105 Marlon Brown .20 .50
V106 Steve Johnson .25 .60
V107 Jordan Reed .20 .50
V108 Arian Foster .25 .60
V109 Kenny Stills .20 .50
V110 Jimmy Graham .30 .75

2014 Bowman Black

COMPLETE SET (220) 15.00 40.00
*VETS: .5X TO 1.2X BASIC CARDS
*ROOKIES: .5X TO 1.2X BASIC RC

2014 Bowman Blue

*VETS/99: 2X TO 5X BASIC CARDS
*ROOKIES/499: 1.2X TO 3X BASIC RC

2014 Bowman Gold

*V1-V110 VETS/75: 2.5X TO 6X BASIC CARDS
*R1-R110 ROOKIES/399: 1.2X TO 3X BASIC RC

2014 Bowman Green

*ROOKIES/99: 2X TO 5X BASIC RC

2014 Bowman Orange

*VETS/50: 3X TO 8X BASIC CARDS
*ROOKIES/299: 1.2X TO 3X BASIC RC

2014 Bowman Purple

*VETS: 1.5X TO 4X BASIC CARDS
*ROOKIES: 1X TO 2.5X BASIC RC

2014 Bowman Rainbow Black

*VETS: .8X TO 2X BASIC CARDS
*ROOKIES: .8X TO 2X BASIC RC

2014 Bowman Rainbow Blue

*VETS/99: 2X TO 5X BASIC CARDS
*ROOKIES/499: 1.2X TO 3X BASIC RC

2014 Bowman Rainbow Gold

*VETS/75: 2.5X TO 6X BASIC CARDS
*ROOKIES/399: 1.2X TO 3X BASIC RC

2014 Bowman Rainbow Orange

*VETS/50: 3X TO 8X BASIC CARDS
*ROOKIES/299: 1.2X TO 3X BASIC RC

2014 Bowman Rainbow Orange Ice

*VETS/50: 4X TO 10X BASIC CARDS
*ROOKIES/50: 4X TO 10X BASIC RC
V80 Peyton Manning 10.00 25.00

2014 Bowman Rainbow Purple

*VETS: 2X TO 5X BASIC CARDS
*ROOKIES: 1.2X TO 3X BASIC RC

2014 Bowman Rainbow Red

*VETS/25: 6X TO 15X BASIC CARDS
*ROOKIES/199: 1.5X TO 4X BASIC RC

2014 Bowman Rainbow Silver Ice

*VETS: 2X TO 5X BASIC CARDS
*ROOKIES: 2X TO 5X BASIC RC

2014 Bowman Red

*VETS/25: 6X TO 15X BASIC CARDS
*ROOKIES/199: 1.5X TO 4X BASIC RC

2014 Bowman '50 Bowman Mini

ONE PER PACK
50B1 Lamarcus Joyner .30 .75
50B2 Allen Hurns .30 .75
50B3 Bishop Sankey .25 .60
50B4 Deone Bucannon .25 .60
50B5 Silas Redd .30 .75
50B6 Ha Ha Clinton-Dix .30 .75
50B7 Cyrus Kouandjio .30 .75
50B8 Adrian Hubbard .30 .75
50B9 Brandon Coleman .25 .60
50B10 Logan Thomas .25 .60
50B11 Devin Street .25 .60
50B12 Kony Ealy .30 .75
50B13 Chris Smith .25 .60
50B14 Brandin Cooks .40 1.00
50B15 Mike Evans .60 1.50
50B16 Jarvis Landry .50 1.25
50B17 Cyril Richardson .25 .60
50B18 Jimmy Garoppolo 2.00 5.00
50B19 Loucheiz Purifoy .25 .60
50B20 Stephon Tuitt .40 1.00
50B21 Paul Richardson .30 .75
50B22 Connor Shaw .25 .60
50B23 Trey Millard .30 .75
50B24 Dri Archer .25 .60
50B25 Jeff Mathews .30 .75
50B26 Odell Beckham Jr. .60 1.50
50B27 Ahmad Dixon .25 .60
50B28 Cody Hoffman .25 .60
50B29 Johnny Manziel .40 1.00
50B30 Josh Huff .30 .75
50B31 Derek Carr 1.50 4.00
50B32 Anthony Barr .25 .60
50B33 Bradley Roby .25 .60
50B34 Bryn Renner .25 .60
50B35 Khalil Mack 1.00 2.50
50B36 Christian Jones .30 .75
50B37 Marion Grice .25 .60
50B38 Gabe Jackson .25 .60
50B39 Mike Davis .25 .60
50B40 Robert Herron .25 .60
50B41 Craig Loston .25 .60
50B42 Arthur Lynch .25 .60
50B43 C.J. Mosley .30 .75
50B44 Jason Verrett .25 .60
50B45 Kyle Van Noy .30 .75
50B46 C.J. Fiedorowicz .25 .60
50B47 Xavier Grimble .30 .75
50B48 Stephen Morris .25 .60
50B49 Taylor Lewan .25 .60
50B50 Scott Crichton .25 .60
50B51 Allen Robinson .40 1.00
50B52 Carlos Hyde .30 .75
50B53 James White .50 1.25
50B54 Dominique Easley .25 .60
50B55 LaDarius Perkins .25 .60
50B56 Jalen Saunders .25 .60
50B57 Antonio Richardson .40 1.00
50B58 Trent Murphy .25 .60
50B59 Jordan Matthews .40 1.00
50B60 Ryan Grant .25 .60
50B61 Jeremy Hill .30 .75
50B62 Antone Exum .25 .60
50B63 Rajion Neal .25 .60
50B64 Morgan Breslin .40 1.00
50B65 Jared Abbrederis .25 .60
50B66 Taylor Hart .30 .75
50B67 Jackson Jeffcoat .30 .75
50B68 Teddy Bridgewater .40 1.00
50B69 Zach Mettenberger .25 .60
50B70 George Atkinson .25 .60
50B71 Damien Williams .25 .60
50B72 Darqueze Dennard .30 .75
50B73 David Fales .25 .60
50B74 Tajh Boyd .25 .60
50B75 Charles Sims .25 .60
50B76 Aaron Donald .60 1.50
50B77 Ed Stinson .40 1.00
50B78 Donte Moncrief .25 .60
50B79 Louis Nix III .25 .60
50B80 Greg Robinson .25 .60
50B81 Blake Bortles .30 .75
50B82 Anthony Johnson .25 .60
50B83 Ra'Shede Hageman .25 .60
50B84 Ka'Deem Carey .25 .60
50B85 De'Anthony Thomas .25 .60
50B86 Kareem Martin .25 .60
50B87 Will Sutton .30 .75
50B88 Tre Mason .25 .60
50B89 Austin Seferian-Jenkins .25 .60
50B90 Eric Ebron .30 .75
50B91 Antonio Andrews .25 .60
50B92 Yawin Smallwood .25 .60
50B93 James Wilder Jr. .30 .75
50B94 Isaiah Crowell .30 .75
50B95 Alfred Blue .25 .00
50B96 Aaron Colvin .25 .60
50B97 Michael Sam .25 .60
50B98 Aaron Murray .25 .60
50B99 Jerome Smith .25 .60
50B100 Tommy Rees .30 .75
50B101 Marqise Lee .30 .75
50B102 Jace Amaro .25 .60
50B103 Andre Williams .25 .60
50B104 A.J. McCarron .25 .60
50B105 Ryan Shazier .40 1.00
50B106 Lache Seastrunk .25 .60
50B107 Jadeveon Clowney .30 .75
50B108 Dion Bailey .25 .60
50B109 Jake Matthews .25 .60
50B110 Sammy Watkins .40 1.00

2014 Bowman '50 Bowman Mini Autographs

MINI AU/99 STATED ODDS 1:41
EXCH EXPIRATION: 5/31/2017
1 Stephen Morris 3.00 8.00
2 LaDarius Perkins 3.00 8.00
3 Trent Murphy 3.00 8.00
4 Jace Amaro 3.00 8.00
5 Jason Verrett 3.00 8.00
7 Brandin Cooks 5.00 12.00
8 Devin Street 3.00 8.00
11 Zach Mettenberger 3.00 8.00
12 Mike Evans 12.00 30.00
13 Teddy Bridgewater 5.00 12.00
14 Tommy Rees 4.00 10.00
15 Jared Abbrederis 8.00 20.00
16 Aaron Colvin 3.00 8.00
17 George Atkinson 3.00 8.00
18 Dominique Easley 3.00 8.00
19 Marqise Lee 12.00 30.00
20 Ha Ha Clinton-Dix 4.00 10.00
21 Arthur Lynch 3.00 8.00
22 Khalil Mack 12.00 30.00
23 Kyle Van Noy 4.00 10.00
24 Ka'Deem Carey 6.00 15.00
25 Brandon Coleman 3.00 8.00
26 Donte Moncrief 3.00 8.00
27 Ra'Shede Hageman EXCH 3.00 8.00
28 Mike Davis 3.00 8.00
29 Jarvis Landry 6.00 15.00
30 Cyril Richardson 3.00 8.00
31 Bradley Roby 3.00 8.00
32 Paul Richardson 8.00 20.00
35 Craig Loston 3.00 8.00
36 James White 6.00 15.00
37 Trey Millard 4.00 10.00
38 Christian Jones 4.00 10.00
39 Austin Seferian-Jenkins 3.00 8.00
40 De'Anthony Thomas 3.00 8.00
41 Jordan Matthews 5.00 12.00
42 Lamarcus Joyner 4.00 10.00
43 A.J. McCarron 15.00 40.00
45 Marion Grice 3.00 8.00
46 Isaiah Crowell 4.00 10.00
47 Derek Carr 15.00 40.00
48 Aaron Murray 3.00 8.00
49 Ryan Shazier 5.00 12.00
50 Eric Ebron 4.00 10.00
51 Tajh Boyd 3.00 8.00
52 Bishop Sankey 8.00 20.00
53 Stephon Tuitt 5.00 12.00
54 C.J. Mosley 4.00 10.00
55 Will Sutton 4.00 10.00
57 Jadeveon Clowney 4.00 10.00
58 Allen Robinson 5.00 12.00
59 C.J. Fiedorowicz 3.00 8.00
61 Loucheiz Purifoy 3.00 8.00
62 Damien Williams 3.00 8.00
63 Sammy Watkins 5.00 12.00
64 Chris Smith 3.00 8.00
65 Silas Redd 4.00 10.00
67 Blake Bortles 4.00 10.00
68 Jerome Smith 3.00 8.00
69 James Wilder Jr. 4.00 10.00
70 Taylor Lewan 3.00 8.00
71 Jake Matthews 3.00 8.00
72 Charles Sims 3.00 8.00
73 Xavier Grimble 4.00 10.00
74 Odell Beckham Jr. 30.00 60.00
75 Robert Herron 3.00 8.00
77 Josh Huff 4.00 10.00
81 Tre Mason 3.00 8.00
83 Johnny Manziel 5.00 12.00
85 Jimmy Garoppolo 20.00 40.00
86 Deone Bucannon 3.00 8.00
88 Gabe Jackson 4.00 10.00
91 Cody Hoffman 3.00 8.00
104 Carlos Hyde 4.00 10.00
105 Louis Nix III 3.00 8.00

2014 Bowman Chrome Rookie Autographs College Blue Refractors

*BLUE/99: .6X TO 1.5X BASIC INSERTS
79 Odell Beckham Jr. 60.00 125.00

2014 Bowman Chrome Rookie Autographs College Gold Refractors

*GOLD/75: .8X TO 2X BASIC INSERTS
79 Odell Beckham Jr. 75.00 150.00

2014 Bowman Chrome Rookie Autographs College Orange Refractors

*ORANGE/50: 1X TO 2.5X BASIC INSERTS
79 Odell Beckham Jr. 75.00 150.00

2014 Bowman Chrome Rookie Autographs College Red Refractors

*RED/25: 1.5X TO 4X BASIC AU
79 Odell Beckham Jr. 100.00 200.00
107 Jimmy Garoppolo 250.00 400.00

2014 Bowman Chrome Rookie Autographs College Refractors

FOUR AUs PER BOWMAN HOBBY BOX OVERALL
1 Stephen Morris 2.50 6.00
2 LaDarius Perkins 2.50 6.00
3 Trent Murphy 2.50 6.00
4 Jace Amaro 2.50 6.00
5 Jason Verrett 2.50 6.00
6 Antone Exum 2.50 6.00
8 Jarvis Landry 5.00 12.00
9 Jeremy Hill 3.00 8.00
10 Jared Abbrederis 2.50 6.00
12 Johnny Manziel 6.00 15.00
13 Mike Evans 6.00 15.00
14 Teddy Bridgewater 4.00 10.00
16 Devin Street 2.50 6.00
17 Aaron Colvin 2.50 6.00
18 Ha Ha Clinton-Dix 3.00 8.00
19 Dominique Easley 2.50 6.00
20 Allen Robinson 4.00 10.00
21 Lamarcus Joyner 3.00 8.00
22 Arthur Lynch 2.50 6.00
23 Khalil Mack 10.00 25.00
24 Kyle Van Noy 3.00 8.00
25 Tajh Boyd 2.50 6.00
26 Ka'Deem Carey 2.50 6.00
27 Donte Moncrief 2.50 6.00
29 Ra'Shede Hageman 2.50 6.00
30 Damien Williams 2.50 6.00
31 Robert Herron 2.50 6.00
32 Brandon Coleman 2.50 6.00
33 Gabe Jackson 2.50 6.00
34 Bradley Roby 2.50 6.00
35 Brandin Cooks 4.00 10.00
36 Carlos Hyde 3.00 8.00
37 Tre Mason 8.00 20.00
38 Craig Loston 2.50 6.00
39 Jerome Smith 2.50 6.00
40 Trey Millard 3.00 8.00
41 Christian Jones 3.00 8.00
42 Austin Seferian-Jenkins 2.50 6.00
43 De'Anthony Thomas 2.50 6.00
44 Paul Richardson 3.00 8.00
45 Deone Bucannon 2.50 6.00
46 A.J. McCarron 2.50 6.00
48 Marion Grice 2.50 6.00
49 Isaiah Crowell 3.00 8.00
50 Derek Carr 40.00 80.00
51 Aaron Murray 2.50 6.00
52 Eric Ebron 3.00 8.00
53 Ryan Shazier 4.00 10.00
54 Cyril Richardson 2.50 6.00
55 Zach Mettenberger 2.50 6.00
56 Bishop Sankey 10.00 25.00
57 Stephon Tuitt 4.00 10.00
58 C.J. Mosley 3.00 8.00
59 Will Sutton 3.00 8.00
60 Mike Davis 2.50 6.00
61 Jadeveon Clowney 3.00 8.00
62 Jordan Matthews 4.00 10.00
63 C.J. Fiedorowicz 2.50 6.00
65 Loucheiz Purifoy 2.50 6.00
66 James White 5.00 12.00
67 Sammy Watkins 4.00 10.00
68 Chris Smith 2.50 6.00
69 Silas Redd 3.00 8.00
72 George Atkinson 2.50 6.00
73 James Wilder Jr. 3.00 8.00
75 Jake Matthews 2.50 6.00
76 Charles Sims 2.50 6.00
77 Xavier Grimble 3.00 8.00
78 Marqise Lee 3.00 8.00
79 Odell Beckham Jr. 25.00 60.00
82 Darqueze Dennard 3.00 8.00
87 Tommy Rees 3.00 8.00
91 Connor Shaw 2.50 6.00
93 Josh Huff 3.00 8.00
99 Scott Crichton 2.50 6.00
101 Cody Hoffman 2.50 6.00
105 Ahmad Dixon 2.50 6.00
106 Andre Williams 2.50 6.00
107 Jimmy Garoppolo 60.00 125.00
109 Blake Bortles 3.00 8.00

2014 Bowman Die Cut

COMPLETE SET (50) 25.00 50.00
*BLUE/99: 1X TO 2.5X BASIC INSERTS
1 Terrance Williams .60 1.50
2 Reggie Wayne .75 2.00
3 Kenny Stills .60 1.50
4 Dez Bryant 1.00 2.50
5 Giovani Bernard .60 1.50
6 Drew Brees 1.00 2.50
7 DeAndre Hopkins .75 2.00
8 Victor Cruz .75 2.00
9 Demaryius Thomas .75 2.00
10 Peyton Manning 2.00 5.00
11 EJ Manuel .60 1.50
12 Andrew Luck 1.25 3.00
13 Jordy Nelson .75 2.00
14 Frank Gore .75 2.00
15 Andre Ellington .60 1.50
16 Keenan Allen .75 2.00
17 Arian Foster .75 2.00
18 Tom Brady 2.50 6.00
19 A.J. Green 1.00 2.50
20 Jamaal Charles .75 2.00
21 Marshawn Lynch .75 2.00

22 Jimmy Graham 1.00 2.50
23 DeSean Jackson .75 2.00
24 Reggie Bush .60 1.50
25 Rob Gronkowski 1.00 2.50
26 Ray Rice .60 1.50
27 LeSean McCoy 1.00 2.50
28 Matthew Stafford .75 2.00
29 Wes Welker .75 2.00
30 Andre Johnson .75 2.00
31 Coby Fleener .60 1.50
32 Matt Forte .60 1.50
33 Geno Smith .60 1.50
34 Russell Wilson 1.50 4.00
35 Knowshon Moreno .60 1.50
36 Robert Griffin III .60 1.50
37 Zac Stacy .60 1.50
38 Alshon Jeffery .75 2.00
39 Eddie Lacy .60 1.50
40 Adrian Peterson 1.00 2.50
41 Cam Newton 1.00 2.50
42 Calvin Johnson 1.00 2.50
43 T.Y. Hilton .75 2.00
44 Brandon Marshall .60 1.50
45 Colin Kaepernick .75 2.00
46 Larry Fitzgerald .75 2.00
47 Aaron Rodgers 2.00 5.00
48 Julius Thomas .60 1.50
49 Alfred Morris .60 1.50
50 Vernon Davis .60 1.50

2014 Bowman Relics

*BLUE/99: .5X TO 1.2X BASIC INSERTS
*GOLD/50: .6X TO 1.5X BASIC INSERTS
*ORANGE/25: 1X TO 2.5X BASIC JSY
1 Andy Dalton 2.00 5.00
2 LeSean McCoy 2.50 6.00
3 Alshon Jeffery 2.00 5.00
4 Earl Thomas 2.00 5.00
5 Champ Bailey 2.00 5.00
6 Manti Te'o 2.00 5.00
7 Le'Veon Bell 2.00 5.00
8 Robert Woods 2.00 5.00
9 Randall Cobb 2.00 5.00
10 Arian Foster 2.00 5.00
11 Robert Griffin III 1.50 4.00
12 Nick Foles 2.00 5.00
13 T.Y. Hilton 2.00 5.00
14 Andre Ellington 1.50 4.00
15 EJ Manuel 1.50 4.00
16 Jake Locker 2.00 5.00
17 Geno Smith 1.50 4.00
18 Jordan Reed 1.50 4.00
19 DeMarco Murray 2.00 5.00
20 Andrew Luck 4.00 10.00
21 DeAndre Hopkins 2.00 5.00
22 Dwayne Bowe 2.00 5.00
23 Sam Bradford 1.50 4.00
24 Terrance Williams 1.50 4.00
25 Ezekiel Ansah 1.50 4.00
26 Julio Jones 2.50 6.00
27 Rob Gronkowski 2.50 6.00
28 Cordarrelle Patterson 1.50 4.00
29 Giovani Bernard 1.50 4.00
30 Lamar Miller 1.50 4.00
31 Doug Martin 2.00 5.00
32 Stevan Ridley 1.50 4.00
33 Joe Flacco 2.00 5.00
34 Eric Decker 1.50 4.00
35 Eddie Lacy 1.50 4.00
36 Mike Glennon 2.00 5.00
37 A.J. Green 2.50 6.00
38 Matt Forte 1.50 4.00
39 Ryan Tannehill 2.00 5.00
40 Keenan Allen 2.00 5.00
41 Aaron Dobson 1.50 4.00
42 Cam Newton 2.50 6.00
43 Prince Amukamara 1.50 4.00
44 Torrey Smith 1.50 4.00
45 Von Miller 2.00 5.00

2014 Bowman Rookie Autographs

EXCH EXPIRATION: 5/31/2017
19 Mike Evans 15.00 40.00
27 Jarvis Landry 12.00 30.00
AM Aaron Murray EXCH 30.00 60.00
AR Allen Robinson EXCH
BB Blake Bortles EXCH
BC Brandin Cooks EXCH
BS Bishop Sankey EXCH 6.00 15.00
CH Carlos Hyde EXCH 8.00 20.00
CL Cody Latimer EXCH 8.00 20.00
CM C.J. Mosley EXCH
CS Charles Sims EXCH 8.00 20.00
DA Davante Adams EXCH 10.00 25.00
DF David Fales EXCH 6.00 15.00
DM Donte Moncrief EXCH 6.00 15.00
DT De'Anthony Thomas EXCH 6.00 15.00
EE Eric Ebron EXCH 8.00 20.00
JC Jadeveon Clowney EXCH 8.00 20.00
JG Jimmy Garoppolo EXCH
JH Jeremy Hill EXCH 8.00 20.00
JM Johnny Manziel EXCH 40.00 80.00
KB Kelvin Benjamin EXCH 10.00 25.00
KC Ka'Deem Carey EXCH 6.00 15.00
KM Khalil Mack EXCH 25.00 50.00
LT Logan Thomas EXCH
ML Marqise Lee EXCH 8.00 20.00
OB Odell Beckham Jr. EXCH
PR Paul Richardson EXCH 12.00 30.00
SW Sammy Watkins EXCH 10.00 25.00
TB Tajh Boyd EXCH 6.00 15.00
TM Tre Mason EXCH 6.00 15.00
TS Tom Savage EXCH 6.00 15.00
TW Terrance West EXCH 6.00 15.00
AJM A.J. McCarron EXCH 25.00 50.00
ASJ Austin Seferian-Jenkins EXCH 6.00 15.00
BCO Brandon Coleman EXCH 6.00 15.00
CSH Connor Shaw EXCH 6.00 15.00
DAR Dri Archer EXCH 6.00 15.00
DFR Devonta Freeman EXCH 20.00 40.00
JMA Jordan Matthews EXCH 12.00 30.00
TBR Teddy Bridgewater EXCH 10.00 25.00

2015 Bowman

R1 Marcus Peters RC .25 .60
R2 Trae Waynes RC .15 .40
R3 Ifo Ekpre-Olomu RC .15 .40
R4 P.J. Williams RC .20 .50
R5 Kevin Johnson RC .15 .40
R6 Randy Gregory RC .15 .40
R7 Dante Fowler RC .25 .60
R8 Arik Armstead RC .15 .40
R9 Hau'oli Kikaha RC .20 .50
R10 Leonard Williams RC .15 .40
R11 Michael Bennett RC .15 .40
R12 Danny Shelton RC .15 .40
R13 Vic Beasley RC .20 .50
R14 Shaq Thompson RC .20 .50
R15 Benardrick McKinney RC .15 .40
R16 Eric Kendricks RC .15 .40
R17 Andrus Peat RC .15 .40
R18 Brandon Scherff RC .25 .60
R19 Cedric Ogbuehi RC .15 .40
R20 Dezmin Lewis RC .15 .40
R21 Ereck Flowers RC .20 .50
R22 Marcus Mariota RC .60 1.50
R23 Jameis Winston RC 2.00 5.00
R24 Brett Hundley RC .15 .40
R25 Bryce Petty RC .15 .40
R26 Sean Mannion RC .15 .40
R27 T.J. Yeldon RC .15 .40
R28 Todd Gurley RC .60 1.50
R29 Melvin Gordon RC 1.50 4.00
R30 Michael Dyer RC .25 .60
R31 Mike Davis RC .15 .40
R32 Duke Johnson RC .25 .60
R33 Ameer Abdullah RC .25 .60
R34 Karlos Williams RC .15 .40
R35 Jeremy Langford RC .15 .40
R36 Malcolm Brown RC .20 .50
R37 Carl Davis RC .20 .50
R38 Landon Collins RC .20 .50
R39 Cody Prewitt RC .20 .50
R40 Devin Funchess RC .25 .60
R41 Nick O'Leary RC .15 .40
R42 Jeff Heuerman RC .20 .50
R43 Ben Koyack RC .25 .60
R44 Amari Cooper RC .50 1.25
R45 Dorial Green-Beckham RC .15 .40
R46 Jaelen Strong RC .20 .50
R47 DeVante Parker RC .25 .60
R48 Nelson Agholor RC .20 .50
R49 Rashad Greene RC .15 .40
R50 Stefon Diggs RC .40 1.00
R51 Ty Montgomery RC .15 .40
R52 Sammie Coates RC .20 .50
R53 Antwan Goodley RC .15 .40
R54 Justin Hardy RC .15 .40
R55 Tyler Lockett RC .25 .60
R56 Deontay Greenberry RC .15 .40
R57 Garrett Grayson RC .15 .40
R58 Bo Wallace RC .15 .40
R59 Jay Ajayi RC .25 .60
R60 Javorius Allen RC .20 .50
R61 Tevin Coleman RC .20 .50
R62 Matt Jones RC .15 .40
R63 David Cobb RC .15 .40
R64 Austin Hill RC .15 .40
R65 Levi Norwood RC .15 .40
R66 Clive Walford RC .15 .40
R67 Tyler Kroft RC .20 .50
R68 Alvin Dupree RC .20 .50
R69 Eli Harold RC .15 .40
R70 Shane Ray RC .15 .40
R71 Malcom Brown RC .15 .40
R72 Eddie Goldman RC .15 .40
R73 Alex Carter RC .15 .40
R74 Jalen Collins RC .15 .40
R75 Kevin White RC .20 .50
R76 Josh Harper RC .15 .40
R77 T.J. Clemmings RC .15 .40
R78 Nate Orchard RC .15 .40
R79 Maxx Williams RC .15 .40
R80 Tony Lippett RC .15 .40
R81 Cameron Artis-Payne RC .15 .40
R82 Vince Mayle RC .20 .50
R83 Dres Anderson RC .15 .40
R84 Phillip Dorsett RC .15 .40
R85 Shane Carden RC .15 .40
R86 Jamison Crowder RC .20 .50
R87 Danielle Hunter RC .20 .50
R88 Lorenzo Mauldin RC .15 .40
R89 Paul Dawson RC .20 .50
R90 Owamagbe Odighizuwa RC .20 .50
R91 David Johnson RC .40 1.00
R92 Senquez Golson RC .15 .40
R93 D'Joun Smith RC .25 .60
R94 Jesse James RC .20 .50
R95 Devin Smith RC .15 .40
R96 Brandon Bridge RC .15 .40
R97 Tre McBride RC .15 .40
R98 Titus Davis RC .20 .50
R99 Josh Robinson RC .15 .40
R100 Cody Fajardo RC .20 .50
R101 Dominique Brown RC .15 .40
R102 Devante Davis RC .20 .50
R103 Denzel Perryman RC .15 .40
R104 Kenny Bell RC .25 .60
R105 Marcus Murphy RC .15 .40
R106 Breshad Perriman RC .15 .40
R107 Blake Sims RC .15 .40
R108 Terrence Magee RC .25 .60
R109 Nick Marshall RC .25 .60
R110 Nick Montana RC .25 .60
V1 Julio Jones .30 .75
V2 Larry Fitzgerald .25 .60
V3 Michael Floyd .20 .50
V4 John Brown .25 .60
V5 Sammy Watkins .25 .60
V6 Roddy White .20 .50
V7 Carson Palmer .25 .60
V8 Steve Smith .25 .60
V9 Joe Flacco .25 .60
V10 Matt Forte .20 .50
V11 Torrey Smith .20 .50
V12 EJ Manuel .20 .50
V13 C.J. Spiller .20 .50
V14 Matt Ryan .25 .60
V15 Kelvin Benjamin .25 .60
V16 Greg Olsen .25 .60
V17 Cam Newton .30 .75
V18 Robert Woods .25 .60
V19 Dennis Pitta .20 .50
V20 Jay Cutler .20 .50
V21 Martellus Bennett .20 .50
V22 Brandon Marshall .20 .50
V23 Alshon Jeffery .25 .60
V24 A.J. Green .30 .75
V25 Johnny Manziel .25 .60
V26 Giovani Bernard .20 .50
V27 Andy Dalton .25 .60
V28 Isaiah Crowell .20 .50
V29 Terrance West .20 .50
V30 DeMarco Murray .25 .60
V31 Terrance Williams .20 .50
V32 Tony Romo .25 .60
V33 Dez Bryant .30 .75
V34 Julius Thomas .20 .50
V35 Peyton Manning .60 1.50
V36 Montee Ball .20 .50
V37 Emmanuel Sanders .25 .60
V38 Demaryius Thomas .25 .60
V39 Calvin Johnson .30 .75
V40 Matthew Stafford .25 .60
V41 Golden Tate .20 .50
V42 Joique Bell .20 .50
V43 Reggie Bush .20 .50
V44 Randall Cobb .25 .60
V45 Jordy Nelson .25 .60
V46 Aaron Rodgers .60 1.50
V47 Eddie Lacy .20 .50
V48 DeAndre Hopkins .25 .60
V49 J.J. Watt .30 .75
V50 Jadeveon Clowney .20 .50
V51 Andre Johnson .25 .60
V52 Arian Foster .25 .60
V53 T.Y. Hilton .25 .60
V54 Reggie Wayne .25 .60
V55 Andrew Luck .40 1.00
V56 Allen Hurns .20 .50
V57 Blake Bortles .20 .50
V58 Marqise Lee .20 .50
V59 Alex Smith .25 .60
V60 Jamaal Charles .25 .60
V61 Knowshon Moreno .20 .50
V62 Mike Wallace .20 .50
V63 Ryan Tannehill .25 .60
V64 Odell Beckham Jr. .30 .75
V65 Teddy Bridgewater .25 .60
V66 Kyle Rudolph .20 .50
V67 Shane Vereen .25 .60
V68 Julian Edelman .30 .75
V69 Rob Gronkowski .30 .75
V70 Tom Brady .75 2.00
V71 Brandin Cooks .25 .60
V72 Mark Ingram .25 .60
V73 Drew Brees .30 .75
V74 Pierre Thomas .20 .50
V75 Jimmy Graham .30 .75
V76 Victor Cruz .25 .60
V77 Eli Manning .25 .60
V78 Jeremy Hill .20 .50
V79 Chris Ivory .25 .60
V80 LeSean McCoy .30 .75
V81 Eric Decker .20 .50
V82 Derek Carr .30 .75
V83 Rod Streater .20 .50
V84 Jeremy Maclin .20 .50
V85 Darren Sproles .25 .60
V86 Zach Ertz .25 .60
V87 Nick Foles .25 .60
V88 Jarvis Landry .25 .60
V89 Le'Veon Bell .25 .60
V90 Antonio Brown .30 .75
V91 Ben Roethlisberger .30 .75
V92 Philip Rivers .30 .75
V93 Vernon Davis .20 .50
V94 Colin Kaepernick .25 .60
V95 Marshawn Lynch .25 .60
V96 Carlos Hyde .20 .50
V97 Frank Gore .25 .60
V98 Anquan Boldin .20 .50
V99 Percy Harvin .20 .50
V100 Russell Wilson .40 1.00
V101 Tre Mason .25 .60
V102 Doug Martin .25 .60
V103 Mike Evans .25 .60
V104 Jake Locker .25 .60
V105 Robert Griffin III .20 .50
V106 Bishop Sankey .20 .50
V107 Pierre Garcon .25 .60
V108 Alfred Morris .20 .50
V109 Kendall Wright .20 .50
V110 DeSean Jackson .25 .60

2015 Bowman Black

*VETS: .5X TO 1.2X BASIC CARDS
*ROOKIES: .5X TO 1.2X BASIC RC

2015 Bowman Blue

*VETS/99: 2X TO 5X BASIC CARDS
*ROOKIES/499: 1.2X TO 3X BASIC RC

2015 Bowman Gold

*V1-V110 VETS/75: 2.5X TO 6X BASIC CARDS
*R1-R110 ROOKIES/399: 1.2X TO 3X BASIC RC

2015 Bowman Green

*ROOKIES/99: 2X TO 5X BASIC RC

2015 Bowman Orange

*VETS/50: 3X TO 8X BASIC CARDS
*ROOKIES/299: 1.2X TO 3X BASIC RC

2015 Bowman Purple

*VETS: 1.5X TO 4X BASIC CARDS
*ROOKIES: 1X TO 2.5X BASIC RC

2015 Bowman Rainbow Black

*VETS: .8X TO 2X BASIC CARDS
*ROOKIES: .8X TO 2X BASIC RC

2015 Bowman Rainbow Blue

*VETS/99: 2X TO 5X BASIC CARDS
*ROOKIES/499: 1.2X TO 3X BASIC RC

2015 Bowman Rainbow Electric Yellow

*ROOKIES/99: 2X TO 5X BASIC RC

2015 Bowman Rainbow Gold

*VETS/75: 2.5X TO 6X BASIC CARDS
*ROOKIES/299: 1.2X TO 3X BASIC RC

2015 Bowman Rainbow Orange

*VETS/50: 3X TO 8X BASIC CARDS
*ROOKIES/299: 1.2X TO 3X BASIC RC

2015 Bowman Rainbow Orange Ice

*VETS/50: 4X TO 10X BASIC CARDS
*ROOKIES/50: 4X TO 10X BASIC RC

2015 Bowman Rainbow Red

*VETS/25: 6X TO 15X BASIC CARDS
*ROOKIES/199: 1.5X TO 4X BASIC RC

2015 Bowman Rainbow Silver Ice

*VETS: 2X TO 5X BASIC CARDS
*ROOKIES: 2X TO 5X BASIC RC

2015 Bowman Red

*VETS/25: 6X TO 15X BASIC CARDS
*ROOKIES/199: 1.5X TO 4X BASIC RC

2015 Bowman '48 Bowman Mini

BMAA Ameer Abdullah .40 1.00
BMAC Amari Cooper .75 2.00
BMAD Alvin Dupree .30 .75
BMAG Antwan Goodley .25 .60
BMAP Andrus Peat .25 .60
BMBB Brandon Bridge .25 .60
BMBH Brett Hundley .25 .60
BMBK Ben Koyack .40 1.00
BMBP Bryce Petty .25 .60
BMBS Brandon Scherff .40 1.00
BMBW Bo Wallace .25 .60
BMCA Cameron Artis-Payne .25 .60
BMCD Carl Davis .30 .75
BMCF Cody Fajardo .30 .75
BMCO Cedric Ogbuehi .25 .60
BMCP Cody Prewitt .30 .75
BMCW Clive Walford .25 .60
BMDA Dres Anderson .25 .60
BMDB Dominique Brown .25 .60
BMDC David Cobb .25 .60
BMDD Devante Davis .30 .75
BMDF Devin Funchess .40 1.00
BMDH Danielle Hunter .30 .75
BMDJ Duke Johnson .40 1.00
BMDL Dezmin Lewis .25 .60
BMDP DeVante Parker .40 1.00
BMDS D'Joun Smith .40 1.00
BMEF Ereck Flowers .30 .75
BMEG Eddie Goldman .25 .60
BMEH Eli Harold .25 .60
BMEK Eric Kendricks .25 .60
BMGG Garrett Grayson .25 .60
BMHK Hauoli Kikaha .30 .75
BMIE Ifo Ekpre-Olomu .25 .60
BMJA Jay Ajayi .40 1.00
BMJC Jalen Collins .25 .60
BMJH Jeff Heuerman .30 .75
BMJJ Jesse James .30 .75
BMJL Jeremy Langford .25 .60
BMJR Josh Robinson .25 .60
BMJS Jaelen Strong .30 .75
BMJW Jameis Winston .60 1.50
BMKB Kenny Bell .40 1.00
BMKJ Kevin Johnson .25 .60
BMKW Karlos Williams .25 .60
BMLC Landon Collins .30 .75
BMLM Lorenzo Mauldin .25 .60
BMLN Levi Norwood .25 .60
BMLW Leonard Williams .25 .60
BMMB Malcolm Brown .30 .75
BMMD Michael Dyer .40 1.00
BMMG Melvin Gordon .60 1.50
BMMJ Matt Jones .25 .60
BMMM Marcus Mariota 1.00 2.50
BMMM Marcus Murphy .25 .60
BMMW Maxx Williams .25 .60
BMNA Nelson Agholor .30 .75
BMNM Nick Marshall .40 1.00
BMNO Nick O'Leary .25 .60
BMOO Owamagbe Odighizuwa .30 .75
BMPD Paul Dawson .30 .75
BMPW P.J. Williams .30 .75
BMRG Rashad Greene .25 .60
BMSC Sammie Coates .30 .75
BMSD Stefon Diggs .60 1.50
BMSG Senquez Golson .25 .60
BMSM Sean Mannion .25 .60
BMSR Shane Ray .25 .60
BMST Shaq Thompson .30 .75
BMTC Tevin Coleman .30 .75
BMTD Titus Davis .30 .75
BMTG Todd Gurley 1.00 2.50
BMTL Tyler Lockett .40 1.00
BMTM Ty Montgomery .25 .60
BMTW Trae Waynes .25 .60
BMTY T.J. Yeldon .25 .60
BMVB Vic Beasley .30 .75
BMVM Vince Mayle .30 .75
BMAAR Arik Armstead .25 .60
BMACA Alex Carter .25 .60
BMAHI Austin Hill .25 .60
BMBMC Benardrick McKinney .25 .60
BMBPE Breshad Perriman .25 .60
BMBSI Blake Sims .25 .60
BMDFO Dante Fowler .40 1.00
BMDGB Dorial Green-Beckham .25 .60
BMDGR Deontay Greenberry .25 .60
BMDJO David Johnson .60 1.50
BMDPE Denzel Perryman .25 .60
BMDSH Danny Shelton .25 .60
BMDSM Devin Smith .25 .60
BMJAL Javorius Allen .30 .75
BMJCR Jamison Crowder .30 .75
BMJHA Justin Hardy .25 .60
BMKWH Kevin White .30 .75
BMMBE Michael Bennett .25 .60
BMMBR Malcom Brown .25 .60
BMMDA Mike Davis .25 .60
BMMPE Marcus Peters .40 1.00
BMNMO Nick Montana .40 1.00
BMNOR Nate Orchard .25 .60
BMPDO Phillip Dorsett .25 .60
BMRGR Randy Gregory .25 .60
BMSCA Shane Carden .25 .60
BMTCL T.J. Clemmings .25 .60
BMTKR Tyler Kroft .30 .75
BMTLI Tony Lippett .25 .60
BMTMA Terrence Magee .40 1.00
BMTMC Tre McBride .25 .60
BMJHAR Josh Harper .25 .60

2015 Bowman '48 Bowman Mini Autographs

STATED ODDS 1:35 HOBBY
BMAAA Ameer Abdullah 5.00 12.00
BMAAC Amari Cooper 40.00 80.00
BMAAD Alvin Dupree 4.00 10.00
BMAAP Andrus Peat 3.00 8.00
BMABH Brett Hundley 3.00 8.00
BMABK Ben Koyack 5.00 12.00
BMABP Bryce Petty 3.00 8.00
BMABS Brandon Scherff 5.00 12.00
BMACA Cameron Artis-Payne 3.00 8.00
BMACO Cedric Ogbuehi 3.00 8.00
BMACW Clive Walford 3.00 8.00
BMADA Dres Anderson 3.00 8.00
BMADB Dominique Brown 3.00 8.00
BMADC David Cobb 3.00 8.00
BMADF Devin Funchess 5.00 12.00
BMADJ Duke Johnson 5.00 12.00
BMADP DeVante Parker 8.00 20.00
BMADS Devin Smith 3.00 8.00
BMAEF Ereck Flowers 4.00 10.00
BMAEG Eddie Goldman 3.00 8.00
BMAEH Eli Harold 3.00 8.00
BMAEK Eric Kendricks 3.00 8.00
BMAIE Ifo Ekpre-Olomu 3.00 8.00
BMAJA Jay Ajayi 5.00 12.00
BMAJJ Jesse James 4.00 10.00
BMAJL Jeremy Langford 3.00 8.00
BMAJR Josh Robinson 3.00 8.00
BMAJS Jaelen Strong 8.00 20.00
BMAJW Jameis Winston 8.00 20.00
BMAKW Karlos Williams 3.00 8.00
BMALC Landon Collins 4.00 10.00
BMALM Lorenzo Mauldin 3.00 8.00
BMALW Leonard Williams 3.00 8.00
BMAMB Malcolm Brown 4.00 10.00
BMAMJ Matt Jones 3.00 8.00
BMAMM Marcus Mariota 50.00 100.00
BMAMW Maxx Williams 3.00 8.00
BMANA Nelson Agholor 4.00 10.00
BMAOO Owamagbe Odighizuwa 4.00 10.00
BMAPD Phillip Dorsett 3.00 8.00
BMAPW P.J. Williams 4.00 10.00
BMARG Rashad Greene 3.00 8.00
BMASC Sammie Coates 4.00 10.00
BMASD Stefon Diggs 8.00 20.00
BMASR Shane Ray 3.00 8.00
BMAST Shaq Thompson 4.00 10.00
BMATC Tevin Coleman 4.00 10.00
BMATG Todd Gurley 30.00 60.00
BMATL Tyler Lockett 5.00 12.00
BMATW Trae Waynes 3.00 8.00
BMATY T.J. Yeldon 3.00 8.00
BMAVB Vic Beasley 4.00 10.00
BMAAAR Arik Armstead 3.00 8.00
BMAACA Alex Carter 3.00 8.00
BMAAHI Austin Hill 3.00 8.00
BMABPE Breshad Perriman 3.00 8.00
BMABSI Blake Sims 3.00 8.00
BMADFO Dante Fowler Jr. 5.00 12.00
BMADGB Dorial Green-Beckham 3.00 8.00
BMADGR Deontay Greenberry 3.00 8.00
BMADJO David Johnson 10.00 25.00
BMADSH Danny Shelton 3.00 8.00
BMAJCR Jamison Crowder 4.00 10.00
BMAJHA Justin Hardy 3.00 8.00
BMAKWH Kevin White 4.00 10.00
BMALCO La'el Collins 4.00 10.00
BMAMBE Michael Bennett 3.00 8.00
BMAMBR Malcom Brown 3.00 8.00
BMAMDA Mike Davis 3.00 8.00
BMAMPE Marcus Peters 5.00 12.00
BMANOR Nate Orchard 3.00 8.00
BMAPDA Paul Dawson 4.00 10.00
BMARGR Randy Gregory 3.00 8.00
BMATJC T.J. Clemmings 3.00 8.00
BMATKR Tyler Kroft 4.00 10.00
BMATLI Tony Lippett 3.00 8.00
BMATMC Tre McBride 3.00 8.00
BMAJHAR Josh Harper 3.00 8.00

2015 Bowman Chrome Rookie Autographs Refractors

RCRAAA Arik Armstead 2.50 6.00
RCRAAAB Ameer Abdullah 4.00 10.00
RCRAAC Amari Cooper 15.00 40.00
RCRAAD Alvin Dupree 3.00 8.00
RCRAAHI Austin Hill 2.50 6.00
RCRAAP Andrus Peat 2.50 6.00
RCRABB Brandon Bridge 2.50 6.00
RCRABH Brett Hundley 2.50 6.00
RCRABK Ben Koyack 4.00 10.00
RCRABP Bryce Petty 2.50 6.00
RCRABPR Breshad Perriman 2.50 6.00
RCRABS Brandon Scherff 4.00 10.00
RCRABSI Blake Sims 2.50 6.00
RCRABW Bo Wallace 2.50 6.00
RCRACA Cameron Artis-Payne 2.50 6.00
RCRACD Carl Davis 3.00 8.00
RCRACF Cody Fajardo 3.00 8.00
RCRACW Clive Walford 2.50 6.00
RCRADA Dres Anderson 2.50 6.00
RCRADB Dominique Brown 2.50 6.00
RCRADC David Cobb 2.50 6.00
RCRADD Devante Davis 3.00 8.00
RCRADF Dante Fowler Jr. 4.00 10.00
RCRADFU Devin Funchess 4.00 10.00
RCRADGB Dorial Green-Beckham 2.50 6.00
RCRADGR Deontay Greenberry 2.50 6.00
RCRADJ Duke Johnson 4.00 10.00
RCRADJO David Johnson 15.00 30.00
RCRADJS D'Joun Smith 4.00 10.00
RCRADPA DeVante Parker 4.00 10.00
RCRADS Danny Shelton 2.50 6.00
RCRADSM Devin Smith 2.50 6.00
RCRAEF Ereck Flowers 3.00 8.00
RCRAEGO Eddie Goldman 2.50 6.00
RCRAEK Eric Kendricks 2.50 6.00
RCRAHK Hauoli Kikaha 3.00 8.00
RCRAIE Ifo Ekpre-Olomu 2.50 6.00
RCRAJA Jay Ajayi 4.00 10.00
RCRAJAL Javorius Allen 3.00 8.00
RCRAJC Jamison Crowder 3.00 8.00
RCRAJHA Justin Hardy 2.50 6.00
RCRAJHAR Josh Harper 2.50 6.00
RCRAJHE Jeff Heuerman 3.00 8.00
RCRAJJ Jesse James 3.00 8.00
RCRAJL Jeremy Langford 2.50 6.00
RCRAJR Josh Robinson 2.50 6.00
RCRAJST Jaelen Strong 3.00 8.00
RCRAJW Jameis Winston 25.00 50.00
RCRAKJ Kevin Johnson 2.50 6.00
RCRAKWH Kevin White 3.00 8.00
RCRALC La'el Collins 3.00 8.00
RCRALCO Landon Collins 3.00 8.00
RCRALN Levi Norwood 2.50 6.00
RCRALW Leonard Williams 2.50 6.00
RCRAMBR Malcolm Brown 3.00 8.00
RCRAMBRO Malcom Brown 2.50 6.00
RCRAMDA Mike Davis 2.50 6.00
RCRAMJ Matt Jones 2.50 6.00
RCRAMM Marcus Mariota 50.00 100.00
RCRAMW Maxx Williams 2.50 6.00
RCRANA Nelson Agholor 3.00 8.00
RCRANM Nick Marshall 4.00 10.00
RCRAOO Owamagbe Odighizuwa 3.00 8.00
RCRAPD Phillip Dorsett 2.50 6.00
RCRAPDA Paul Dawson 3.00 8.00
RCRAPW P.J. Williams 3.00 8.00
RCRARG Randy Gregory 2.50 6.00
RCRARGR Rashad Greene 2.50 6.00
RCRASC Shane Carden 2.50 6.00
RCRASCO Sammie Coates 3.00 8.00
RCRASD Stefon Diggs 6.00 15.00
RCRASG Senquez Golson 2.50 6.00
RCRASM Sean Mannion 2.50 6.00
RCRASRA Shane Ray 2.50 6.00
RCRAST Shaq Thompson 3.00 8.00
RCRATC Tevin Coleman 3.00 8.00
RCRATG Todd Gurley 25.00 50.00
RCRATJC T.J. Clemmings 2.50 6.00
RCRATKR Tyler Kroft 3.00 8.00
RCRATL Tyler Lockett 4.00 10.00
RCRATLI Tony Lippett 2.50 6.00
RCRATMA Terrence Magee 4.00 10.00
RCRATMC Tre McBride 2.50 6.00
RCRATW Trae Waynes 2.50 6.00
RCRATY T.J. Yeldon 2.50 6.00
RCRAVB Vic Beasley 3.00 8.00

2015 Bowman Chrome Rookie Autographs Refractors Blue

RCRAAC Amari Cooper 25.00 60.00
RCRAMM Marcus Mariota 75.00 150.00

2015 Bowman Chrome Rookie Autographs Refractors Gold

*GOLD/75: .8X TO 2X BASIC INSERTS
RCRAAC Amari Cooper 30.00 80.00
RCRAMM Marcus Mariota 75.00 150.00
RCRATG Todd Gurley 30.00 80.00

2015 Bowman Chrome Rookie Autographs Refractors Orange

*ORANGE/50: 1X TO 2.5X BASIC INSERTS
RCRAAC Amari Cooper 40.00 100.00
RCRAMM Marcus Mariota 100.00 200.00
RCRATG Todd Gurley 75.00 150.00

2015 Bowman Chrome Rookie Autographs Refractors Red Wave

*RED/25: 1.5X TO 4X BASIC AU
RCRAMM Marcus Mariota 300.00 500.00
RCRATG Todd Gurley 100.00 200.00

2015 Bowman Die Cut

*BLUE/99: 1X TO 2.5X BASIC INSERTS
BCDCAB Antonio Brown 1.00 2.50
BCDCAF Arian Foster .75 2.00
BCDCAL Andrew Luck 1.25 3.00
BCDCAM Alfred Morris .60 1.50
BCDCAR Aaron Rodgers 2.00 5.00
BCDCBC Brandin Cooks .75 2.00
BCDCBM Brandon Marshall .60 1.50
BCDCBR Ben Roethlisberger 1.00 2.50
BCDCBS Bishop Sankey .60 1.50
BCDCCH Carlos Hyde .60 1.50
BCDCCJ Calvin Johnson 1.00 2.50
BCDCCK Colin Kaepernick .75 2.00
BCDCDB Dez Bryant 1.00 2.50
BCDCDC Derek Carr 1.00 2.50
BCDCDM DeMarco Murray .75 2.00
BCDCDT Demaryius Thomas .75 2.00
BCDCEL Eddie Lacy .60 1.50
BCDCGB Giovani Bernard .60 1.50
BCDCJC Jadeveon Clowney .60 1.50
BCDCJE Julian Edelman 1.00 2.50
BCDCJG Jimmy Graham 1.00 2.50
BCDCJH Jeremy Hill .60 1.50
BCDCJJ Julio Jones 1.00 2.50
BCDCJL Jarvis Landry .75 2.00
BCDCJM Johnny Manziel .75 2.00
BCDCKB Kelvin Benjamin .75 2.00
BCDCLB Le'Veon Bell .75 2.00
BCDCLM LeSean McCoy 1.00 2.50
BCDCME Mike Evans .75 2.00
BCDCMF Michael Floyd .60 1.50
BCDCMS Matthew Stafford .75 2.00
BCDCMW Mike Wallace .60 1.50
BCDCOB Odell Beckham Jr. 1.00 2.50
BCDCPM Peyton Manning 2.00 5.00
BCDCPR Philip Rivers 1.00 2.50
BCDCRC Randall Cobb .75 2.00
BCDCRW Reggie Wayne .75 2.00
BCDCSW Sammy Watkins .75 2.00
BCDCTB Teddy Bridgewater .75 2.00
BCDCTM Tre Mason .75 2.00
BCDCTS Torrey Smith .60 1.50
BCDCVC Victor Cruz .75 2.00
BCDCAJG A.J. Green 1.00 2.50
BCDCDBR Drew Brees 1.00 2.50
BCDCJCH Jamaal Charles .75 2.00
BCDCJJW J.J. Watt 1.00 2.50
BCDCMFO Matt Forte .60 1.50
BCDCMLY Marshawn Lynch .75 2.00
BCDCRWI Russell Wilson 1.25 3.00
BCDCTBR Tom Brady 2.50 6.00

2015 Bowman Die Cut Autographs

BCDCAB Antonio Brown 25.00 50.00
BCDCAM Alfred Morris 6.00 15.00
BCDCBC Brandin Cooks 8.00 20.00
BCDCDC Derek Carr 40.00 80.00
BCDCEL Eddie Lacy 6.00 15.00
BCDCGB Giovani Bernard 6.00 15.00
BCDCJC Jamaal Charles 12.00 30.00
BCDCJH Jeremy Hill 6.00 15.00
BCDCKB Kelvin Benjamin 8.00 20.00
BCDCME Mike Evans 8.00 20.00
BCDCMF Matt Forte 6.00 15.00
BCDCOB Odell Beckham Jr. 30.00 60.00
BCDCSW Sammy Watkins 8.00 20.00
BCDCAJG A.J. Green 12.00 30.00
BCDCJCL Jadeveon Clowney 6.00 15.00

2015 Bowman Relics

*BLUE/99: .5X TO 1.2X BASIC INSERTS
*GOLD/50: .6X TO 1.5X BASIC INSERTS
*ORANGE/25: 1X TO 2.5X BASIC JSY
BRAE Andre Ellington 1.50 4.00
BRAL Andrew Luck 3.00 8.00
BRAW Andre Williams 1.50 4.00
BRBB Blake Bortles 1.50 4.00
BRBC Brandin Cooks 2.00 5.00
BRBS Bishop Sankey 1.50 4.00
BRCH Carlos Hyde 1.50 4.00
BRCL Cody Latimer 1.50 4.00
BRCN Cam Newton 2.50 6.00
BRCP Cordarrelle Patterson 1.50 4.00
BRDA Davante Adams 2.00 5.00
BRDC Derek Carr 2.50 6.00
BRDF Devonta Freeman 2.00 5.00
BRDH DeAndre Hopkins 2.00 5.00
BRDM Doug Martin 2.00 5.00
BRDT Demaryius Thomas 2.00 5.00
BREE Eric Ebron 1.50 4.00
BRET Earl Thomas 2.00 5.00
BRGB Giovani Bernard 1.50 4.00
BRJC Jadeveon Clowney 1.50 4.00
BRJG Jimmy Garoppolo 3.00 8.00
BRJH Jeremy Hill 1.50 4.00
BRJJ Julio Jones 2.50 6.00
BRJM Johnny Manziel 2.00 5.00
BRKA Keenan Allen 2.00 5.00
BRKB Kelvin Benjamin 2.00 5.00
BRKW Kendall Wright 1.50 4.00
BRLB Le'Veon Bell 2.00 5.00
BRMB Montee Ball 1.50 4.00
BRME Mike Evans 2.00 5.00
BRMF Michael Floyd 1.50 4.00
BRMW Markus Wheaton 1.50 4.00
BRNF Nick Foles 2.00 5.00
BROB Odell Beckham Jr. 2.50 6.00
BRRG Robert Griffin III 1.50 4.00
BRRT Ryan Tannehill 2.00 5.00
BRRW Russell Wilson 3.00 8.00
BRSW Sammy Watkins 2.00 5.00
BRTB Teddy Bridgewater 2.00 5.00
BRTM Tre Mason 2.00 5.00
BRTW Terrance West 1.50 4.00
BRVM Von Miller 2.00 5.00
BRAJG A.J. Green 2.50 6.00
BRAJO Andre Johnson 2.00 5.00
BRJHU Justin Hunter 1.50 4.00

2015 Bowman 5x7 NFL Draft

COMPLETE SET (25) 30.00 50.00
*GOLD/49: 1X TO 2.5X BASIC CARDS/199
26 Jameis Winston 1.00 2.50
27 Marcus Mariota 1.50 4.00
28 Dante Fowler Jr. .60 1.50
29 Amari Cooper 1.25 3.00
30 Brandon Scherff .60 1.50
31 Leonard Williams .40 1.00
32 Kevin White .50 1.25
33 Vic Beasley .50 1.25
34 Ereck Flowers .50 1.25
35 Todd Gurley 1.50 4.00
36 Trae Waynes .40 1.00
37 Danny Shelton .40 1.00
38 Andrus Peat .40 1.00
39 DeVante Parker .60 1.50
40 Melvin Gordon 1.00 2.50
41 Kevin Johnson .40 1.00
42 Arik Armstead .40 1.00
43 Shaq Thompson .50 1.25
44 Cedric Ogbuehi .40 1.00
45 Bud Dupree .50 1.25
46 Shane Ray .40 1.00
47 D.J. Humphries .40 1.00
48 Shaq Thompson .50 1.25
49 Breshad Perriman .40 1.00
50 Byron Jones .60 1.50

1998 Bowman Chrome

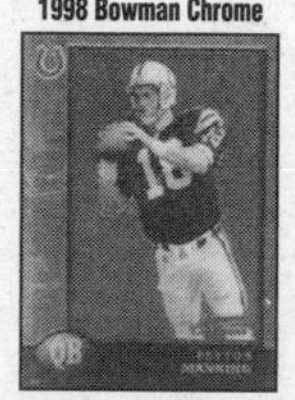

The 1998 Bowman Chrome set was issued in one series totalling 220 cards and was distributed in four-card packs with a suggested retail price of $3. The set features color action photos of 150 veteran players and 70 top prospects printed on chromium metalized cards. The veteran cards display a silver and red design, while the prospect cards carry a silver and blue logo design.

COMPLETE SET (220) 50.00 100.00
1 Peyton Manning RC 25.00 60.00
2 Keith Brooking RC 1.25 3.00
3 Duane Starks RC .75 2.00
4 Takeo Spikes RC 1.00 2.50
5 Andre Wadsworth RC 1.25 3.00
6 Greg Ellis RC 1.00 2.50
7 Brian Griese RC 1.50 4.00
8 Germane Crowell RC .75 2.00
9 Jerome Pathon RC 1.00 2.50
10 Ryan Leaf RC 1.00 2.50
11 Fred Taylor RC 1.50 4.00
12 Robert Edwards RC 1.00 2.50
13 Grant Wistrom RC .75 2.00
14 Robert Holcombe RC .75 2.00
15 Tim Dwight RC 1.25 3.00
16 Jacquez Green RC 1.00 2.50
17 Marcus Nash RC .75 2.00
18 Jason Peter RC .75 2.00
19 Anthony Simmons RC .75 2.00
20 Curtis Enis RC 1.00 2.50
21 John Avery RC 1.00 2.50
22 Pat Johnson RC 1.00 2.50
23 Joe Jurevicius RC 1.25 3.00
24 Brian Simmons RC .75 2.00
25 Kevin Dyson RC 1.00 2.50
26 Skip Hicks RC 1.00 2.50
27 Hines Ward RC 7.50 15.00
28 Tavian Banks RC 1.00 2.50
29 Ahman Green RC 1.50 4.00
30 Tony Simmons RC 1.00 2.50
31 Charles Johnson .25 .60
32 Freddie Jones .25 .60
33 Joey Galloway .30 .75
34 Tony Banks .30 .75
35 Jake Plummer .25 .60
36 Reidel Anthony .25 .60
37 Steve McNair .30 .75
38 Michael Westbrook .30 .75
39 Chris Sanders .25 .60
40 Isaac Bruce .40 1.00
41 Charlie Garner .30 .75
42 Wayne Chrebet .25 .60
43 Michael Strahan .30 .75
44 Brad Johnson .30 .75
45 Mike Alstott .25 .60
46 Tony Gonzalez .30 .75
47 Johnnie Morton .30 .75
48 Darnay Scott .30 .75
49 Rae Carruth .25 .60
50 Terrell Davis .30 .75
51 Jermaine Lewis .25 .60
52 Frank Sanders .25 .60
53 Byron Hanspard .25 .60
54 Gus Frerotte .25 .60
55 Terry Glenn .30 .75
56 J.J. Stokes .30 .75
57 Will Blackwell .25 .60
58 Keyshawn Johnson .30 .75
59 Tiki Barber .30 .75
60 Dorsey Levens .30 .75
61 Zach Thomas .30 .75
62 Corey Dillon .25 .60
63 Antowain Smith .30 .75
64 Michael Sinclair .25 .60
65 Rod Smith .30 .75
66 Trent Dilfer .30 .75
67 Warren Sapp .30 .75
68 Charles Way .25 .60
69 Tamarick Vanover .25 .60
70 Drew Bledsoe .30 .75
71 John Mobley .25 .60
72 Kerry Collins .25 .60
73 Peter Boulware .25 .60
74 Simeon Rice .30 .75
75 Eddie George .30 .75
76 Fred Lane .25 .60
77 Jamal Anderson .30 .75
78 Antonio Freeman .40 1.00
79 Jason Sehorn .30 .75
80 Curtis Martin .30 .75
81 Bobby Hoying .30 .75
82 Garrison Hearst .25 .60
83 Glenn Foley .25 .60
84 Danny Kanell .25 .60
85 Kordell Stewart .25 .60
86 O.J. McDuffie .30 .75
87 Marvin Harrison .30 .75
88 Bobby Engram .25 .60
89 Chris Slade .25 .60
90 Warrick Dunn .25 .60
91 Ricky Watters .30 .75
92 Rickey Dudley .25 .60
93 Terrell Owens .30 .75
94 Karim Abdul-Jabbar .25 .60
95 Napoleon Kaufman .25 .60
96 Darrell Green .40 1.00
97 Levon Kirkland .25 .60
98 Jeff George .30 .75
99 Andre Hastings .25 .60
100 John Elway .60 1.50
101 John Randle .40 1.00
102 Andre Rison .30 .75
103 Keenan McCardell .30 .75
104 Marshall Faulk .30 .75
105 Emmitt Smith .60 1.50
106 Robert Brooks .30 .75
107 Scott Mitchell .30 .75
108 Shannon Sharpe .30 .75
109 Deion Sanders .30 .75
110 Jerry Rice 1.00 2.50
111 Erik Kramer .25 .60
112 Michael Jackson .25 .60
113 Aeneas Williams .25 .60
114 Terry Allen .30 .75
115 Steve Young .50 1.25
116 Warren Moon .40 1.00
117 Junior Seau .30 .75
118 Jerome Bettis .40 1.00
119 Irving Fryar .30 .75
120 Barry Sanders .60 1.50
121 Tim Brown .40 1.00
122 Chad Brown .25 .60
123 Ben Coates .30 .75
124 Robert Smith .25 .60
125 Brett Favre .75 2.00
126 Derrick Thomas .40 1.00
127 Reggie White .40 1.00
128 Troy Aikman .50 1.25
129 Jeff Blake .30 .75
130 Mark Brunell .30 .75
131 Curtis Conway .30 .75
132 Wesley Walls .30 .75
133 Thurman Thomas .30 .75
134 Chris Chandler .30 .75
135 Dan Marino .75 2.00
136 Larry Centers .25 .60
137 Shawn Jefferson .25 .60
138 Andre Reed .40 1.00
139 Jake Reed .30 .75
140 Cris Carter .40 1.00
141 Elvis Grbac .30 .75
142 Mark Chmura .25 .60
143 Michael Irvin .40 1.00
144 Carl Pickens .30 .75
145 Herman Moore .30 .75
146 Marvin Jones .25 .60
147 Terance Mathis .25 .60
148 Rob Moore .25 .60
149 Bruce Smith .30 .75
150 Rob Johnson CL .30 .75
151 Leslie Shepherd .25 .60
152 Chris Spielman .30 .75
153 Tony McGee .25 .60
154 Kevin Smith .25 .60
155 Bill Romanowski .30 .75
156 Stephen Boyd .25 .60
157 James Stewart .25 .60
158 Jason Taylor .30 .75
159 Troy Drayton .25 .60
160 Mark Fields .25 .60
161 Jessie Armstead .25 .60
162 James Jett .25 .60
163 Bobby Taylor .30 .75
164 Kimble Anders .25 .60
165 Jimmy Smith .30 .75
166 Quentin Coryatt .25 .60
167 Bryant Westbrook .25 .60
168 Neil Smith .30 .75
169 Darren Woodson .30 .75
170 Ray Buchanan .30 .75
171 Earl Holmes .25 .60
172 Ray Lewis .40 1.00
173 Steve Broussard .25 .60
174 Derrick Brooks .40 1.00
175 Ken Harvey .25 .60
176 Darryll Lewis .25 .60
177 Derrick Rodgers .25 .60
178 James McKnight .25 .60
179 Cris Dishman .25 .60
180 Hardy Nickerson .25 .60
181 Charles Woodson RC 3.00 8.00
182 Randy Moss RC 6.00 15.00
183 Stephen Alexander RC 1.00 2.50
184 Samari Rolle RC .75 2.00
185 Jamie Duncan RC .75 2.00
186 Lance Schulters RC .75 2.00
187 Tony Parrish RC 1.00 2.50
188 Corey Chavous RC 1.00 2.50
189 Jammi German RC .75 2.00
190 Sam Cowart RC 1.00 2.50
191 Donald Hayes RC .75 2.00
192 R.W. McQuarters RC 1.25 3.00
193 Az-Zahir Hakim RC 1.00 2.50
194 Chris Fuamatu-Ma'afala RC 1.00 2.50
195 Allen Rossum RC 1.00 2.50
196 Jon Ritchie RC 1.00 2.50
197 Blake Spence RC .75 2.00
198 Brian Alford RC .75 2.00
199 Fred Weary RC .75 2.00
200 Rod Rutledge RC .75 2.00
201 Michael Myers RC .75 2.00
202 Rashaan Shehee RC .75 2.00
203 Donovin Darius RC .75 2.00
204 E.G. Green RC 1.00 2.50
205 Vonnie Holliday RC 1.00 2.50
206 Charlie Batch RC 1.25 3.00
207 Michael Pittman RC 1.25 3.00
208 Artrell Hawkins RC .75 2.00
209 Jonathan Quinn RC 1.00 2.50
210 Kailee Wong RC .75 2.00
211 Deshea Townsend RC .75 2.00
212 Patrick Surtain RC 1.00 2.50
213 Brian Kelly RC .75 2.00
214 Tebucky Jones RC .75 2.00
215 Pete Gonzalez RC .75 2.00
216 Shaun Williams RC 1.00 2.50
217 Scott Frost RC .75 2.00
218 Leonard Little RC 1.00 2.50
219 Alonzo Mayes RC .75 2.00
220 Cordell Taylor RC .75 2.00

1998 Bowman Chrome Golden Anniversary

*31-180 VETS/50: 10X TO 25X BASIC CARDS
*1-30/181-220 ROOK/50: 2X TO 5X BASIC RC
STATED ODDS 1:138
STATED PRINT RUN 50 SER.#'d SETS
1 Peyton Manning 200.00 350.00
27 Hines Ward 60.00 120.00

1998 Bowman Chrome Interstate

COMPLETE SET (220) 400.00 800.00
*31-180 VETS: 1.2X TO 3X BASIC CARDS
*1-30/181-220 ROOK: .6X TO 1.2X BASIC RC
STATED ODDS 1:4

1998 Bowman Chrome Interstate Refractors

*31-180 VETS: 4X TO 10X BASIC CARDS
*1-30/181-220 ROOK: 1.5X TO 4X BASIC RC
STATED ODDS 1:24
1 Peyton Manning 125.00 250.00

1998 Bowman Chrome Refractors

*31-180 VETS: 2.5X TO 6X BASIC CARDS
*1-30/181-220 ROOK: 1X TO 2.5X BASIC RC
STATED ODDS 1:12
1 Peyton Manning 40.00 100.00

1999 Bowman Chrome

The 1999 Bowman Chrome set was releases as a 220-card set parallels the base 1999 Bowman release. The set contains 150 veteran cards and 70 top rookies on an enhanced all-foil card stock. Each rookie card features the "Bowman Chrome Rookie" logo, and highlights and trim appear in blue, while on veteran cards they appear in red. 1999 Bowman chrome was packaged in 24-pack boxes containing four cards per pack. Packs carried a suggested retail price of $3.00.

COMPLETE SET (220) 40.00 80.00
1 Dan Marino .75 2.00
2 Michael Westbrook .25 .60
3 Yancey Thigpen .25 .60
4 Tony Martin .30 .75
5 Michael Strahan .30 .75
6 Dedric Ward .25 .60
7 Joey Galloway .30 .75
8 Bobby Engram .25 .60
9 Frank Sanders .25 .60
10 Jake Plummer .25 .60
11 Eddie Kennison .30 .75
12 Curtis Martin .30 .75
13 Chris Spielman .30 .75
14 Trent Dilfer .25 .60
15 Tim Biakabutuka .30 .75
16 Elvis Grbac .25 .60
17 Charlie Batch .25 .60
18 Takeo Spikes .25 .60
19 Tony Banks .30 .75
20 Doug Flutie .40 1.00
21 Ty Law .40 1.00
22 Isaac Bruce .40 1.00
23 James Jett .25 .60
24 Kent Graham .25 .60
25 Derrick Mayes .25 .60
26 Amani Toomer .25 .60
27 Ray Lewis .40 1.00
28 Shawn Springs .25 .60
29 Warren Sapp .30 .75
30 Jamal Anderson .30 .75
31 Byron Bam Morris .25 .60
32 Johnnie Morton .30 .75
33 Terance Mathis .25 .60
34 Terrell Davis .30 .75
35 John Randle .40 1.00
36 Vinny Testaverde .25 .60
37 Junior Seau .30 .75
38 Reidel Anthony .25 .60
39 Brad Johnson .30 .75
40 Emmitt Smith .60 1.50
41 Mo Lewis .25 .60
42 Terry Glenn .30 .75
43 Dorsey Levens .30 .75
44 Thurman Thomas .30 .75
45 Rob Moore .25 .60
46 Corey Dillon .25 .60
47 Jessie Armstead .30 .75
48 Marshall Faulk .30 .75
49 Charles Woodson .40 1.00
50 John Elway .60 1.50
51 Kevin Dyson .25 .60
52 Tony Simmons .25 .60
53 Keenan McCardell .30 .75
54 O.J. Santiago .25 .60
55 Jermaine Lewis .25 .60
56 Herman Moore .30 .75
57 Gary Brown .25 .60
58 Jim Harbaugh .30 .75
59 Mike Alstott .25 .60
60 Brett Favre .75 2.00
61 Tim Brown .40 1.00
62 Steve McNair .30 .75
63 Ben Coates .30 .75
64 Jerome Pathon .25 .60
65 Ray Buchanan .25 .60
66 Troy Aikman .50 1.25
67 Andre Reed .40 1.00
68 Bubby Brister .25 .60
69 Karim Abdul-Jabbar .25 .60
70 Peyton Manning 1.25 3.00
71 Charles Johnson .25 .60
72 Natrone Means .30 .75
73 Michael Sinclair .25 .60
74 Skip Hicks .25 .60
75 Derrick Alexander .25 .60
76 Wayne Chrebet .25 .60
77 Rod Smith .30 .75
78 Carl Pickens .30 .75
79 Adrian Murrell .25 .60
80 Fred Taylor .25 .60
81 Eric Moulds .25 .60
82 Lawrence Phillips .30 .75
83 Marvin Harrison .30 .75
84 Cris Carter .40 1.00
85 Ike Hilliard .25 .60
86 Hines Ward .30 .75
87 Terrell Owens .30 .75
88 Ricky Proehl .25 .60
89 Bert Emanuel .30 .75
90 Randy Moss .30 .75
91 Aaron Glenn .25 .60
92 Robert Smith .25 .60
93 Andre Hastings .25 .60
94 Jake Reed .30 .75
95 Curtis Enis .25 .60
96 Andre Wadsworth .25 .60
97 Ed McCaffrey .30 .75
98 Zach Thomas .30 .75
99 Kerry Collins .25 .60
100 Drew Bledsoe .30 .75
101 Germane Crowell .25 .60
102 Bryan Still .25 .60
103 Chad Brown .25 .60
104 Jacquez Green .25 .60
105 Garrison Hearst .25 .60
106 Napoleon Kaufman .25 .60
107 Ricky Watters .30 .75
108 O.J. McDuffie .30 .75
109 Keyshawn Johnson .30 .75
110 Jerome Bettis .40 1.00
111 Duce Staley .25 .60
112 Curtis Conway .30 .75
113 Chris Chandler .30 .75
114 Marcus Nash .25 .60
115 Stephen Alexander .25 .60
116 Darnay Scott .25 .60
117 Bruce Smith .30 .75
118 Priest Holmes .25 .60
119 Mark Brunell .30 .75
120 Jerry Rice 1.00 2.50
121 Randall Cunningham .30 .75
122 Scott Mitchell .25 .60
123 Antonio Freeman .30 .75
124 Kordell Stewart .25 .60
125 Jon Kitna .25 .60
126 Ahman Green .30 .75
127 Warrick Dunn .25 .60
128 Robert Brooks .30 .75
129 Derrick Thomas .40 1.00
130 Steve Young .50 1.25
131 Peter Boulware .25 .60
132 Michael Irvin .40 1.00
133 Shannon Sharpe .30 .75
134 Jimmy Smith .30 .75
135 John Avery .25 .60
136 Fred Lane .25 .60
137 Trent Green .25 .60
138 Andre Rison .30 .75
139 Antowain Smith .25 .60
140 Eddie George .30 .75
141 Jeff Blake .30 .75
142 Rocket Ismail .30 .75
143 Rickey Dudley .25 .60
144 Courtney Hawkins .25 .60
145 Mikhael Ricks .25 .60
146 J.J. Stokes .25 .60
147 Levon Kirkland .25 .60
148 Deion Sanders .30 .75
149 Barry Sanders .60 1.50
150 Tiki Barber .30 .75
151 David Boston RC .40 1.00
152 Chris McAlister RC .40 1.00
153 Peerless Price RC .40 1.00
154 D'Wayne Bates RC .40 1.00
155 Cade McNown RC .40 1.00
156 Akili Smith RC .40 1.00
157 Kevin Johnson RC .50 1.25
158 Tim Couch RC .50 1.25
159 Sedrick Irvin RC .40 1.00
160 Chris Claiborne RC .40 1.00
161 Edgerrin James RC .60 1.50
162 Mike Cloud RC .40 1.00
163 Cecil Collins RC .40 1.00
164 James Johnson RC .40 1.00
165 Rob Konrad RC .40 1.00
166 Daunte Culpepper RC .60 1.50
167 Kevin Faulk RC .40 1.00
168 Donovan McNabb RC 1.25 3.00
169 Troy Edwards RC .40 1.00
170 Amos Zereoue RC .40 1.00
171 Karsten Bailey RC .40 1.00
172 Brock Huard RC .40 1.00
173 Joe Germaine RC .50 1.25
174 Torry Holt RC .75 2.00
175 Shaun King RC .40 1.00
176 Jevon Kearse RC .50 1.25
177 Champ Bailey RC .75 2.00
178 Ebenezer Ekuban RC .40 1.00
179 Andy Katzenmoyer RC .50 1.25
180 Antoine Winfield RC .40 1.00
181 Jermaine Fazande RC .40 1.00
182 Ricky Williams RC .60 1.50
183 Joel Makovicka RC .40 1.00
184 Reginald Kelly RC .40 1.00
185 Brandon Stokley RC .50 1.25
186 L.C. Stevens RC .40 1.00
187 Marty Booker RC .40 1.00
188 Jerry Azumah RC .40 1.00
189 Ted White RC .40 1.00
190 Scott Covington RC .40 1.00
191 Tim Alexander RC .40 1.00
192 Darrin Chiaverini RC .40 1.00
193 Dat Nguyen RC .60 1.50
194 Wane McGarity RC .40 1.00
195 Al Wilson RC .60 1.50
196 Travis McGriff RC .40 1.00
197 Stacey Mack RC .40 1.00
198 Antuan Edwards RC .40 1.00
199 Aaron Brooks RC .50 1.25
200 De'Mond Parker RC .40 1.00
201 Jed Weaver RC .40 1.00
202 Madre Hill RC .40 1.00
203 Jim Kleinsasser RC .60 1.50
204 Michael Bishop RC .50 1.25
205 Michael Basnight RC .40 1.00
206 Sean Bennett RC .40 1.00
207 Dameane Douglas RC .40 1.00
208 Na Brown RC .40 1.00
209 Patrick Kerney RC .40 1.00
210 Malcolm Johnson RC .40 1.00
211 Dre Bly RC .60 1.50
212 Terry Jackson RC .40 1.00
213 Eugene Baker RC .40 1.00
214 Autry Denson RC .40 1.00
215 Darnell McDonald RC .40 1.00
216 Charlie Rogers RC .40 1.00
217 Joe Montgomery RC .40 1.00
218 Cecil Martin RC .40 1.00
219 Larry Parker RC .50 1.25
220 Mike Peterson RC .40 1.00

1999 Bowman Chrome Gold

*VETS 1-150: 2.5X TO 6X BASIC CARDS
*ROOKIES 151-220: 1.5X TO 4X
STATED ODDS 1:24

1999 Bowman Chrome Gold Refractors

*VETS 1-150: 10X TO 25X BASIC CARDS
*ROOKIES 151-220: 6X TO 15X
GOLD REF/25 STATED ODDS 1:253
STATED PRINT RUN 25 SER.#'d SETS

1999 Bowman Chrome Interstate

COMPLETE SET (220) 200.00 400.00
*VETS 1-150: 1X TO 2.5X BASIC CARDS
*ROOKIES 151-220: .6X TO 1.5X
STATED ODDS 1:4

1999 Bowman Chrome Interstate Refractors

*VETS 1-150: 5X TO 12X BASIC CARDS
*ROOKIES 151-220: 3X TO 8X
STATED PRINT RUN 100 SER.#'d SETS

1999 Bowman Chrome Refractors

COMPLETE SET (220) 400.00 800.00
*VETS 1-150: 2X TO 5X BASIC CARDS
*ROOKIES 151-220: 1.2X TO 3X
STATED ODDS 1:12

1999 Bowman Chrome Scout's Choice

Randomly inserted in packs at the rate on one in 12, this 21-card set features top rookies that are expected to have an impact on the NFL in the years to come. Each card is borderless and features Topps double-etched foil technology. Card backs carry an "SC" prefix.

COMPLETE SET (21) 25.00 50.00
STATED ODDS 1:12
*REFRACTORS: 1X TO 2.5X BASIC INSERTSL.
REFRACTOR STATED ODDS 1:60
SC1 David Boston .40 1.00
SC2 Champ Bailey .60 1.50
SC3 Edgerrin James 2.00 5.00
SC4 Mike Cloud .25 .60
SC5 Kevin Faulk .40 1.00
SC6 Troy Edwards .25 .60
SC7 Cecil Collins .20 .50
SC8 Peerless Price .40 1.00
SC9 Torry Holt 1.25 3.00
SC10 Rob Konrad .40 1.00
SC11 Akili Smith .25 .60
SC12 Daunte Culpepper 2.00 5.00
SC13 D'Wayne Bates .25 .60
SC14 Donovan McNabb 2.50 6.00
SC15 James Johnson .25 .60
SC16 Cade McNown .25 .60
SC17 Kevin Johnson .40 1.00
SC18 Ricky Williams 1.00 2.50
SC19 Karsten Bailey .25 .60
SC20 Tim Couch .40 1.00
SC21 Shaun King .25 .60

1999 Bowman Chrome Stock in the Game

Randomly inserted in packs at the rate of one in 21, this 18-card set features players divided up into three categories. IPO consists of six rookies, Growth features six players with less than five years in the NFL, and Blue Chips features six of the NFL's proven performers. Card backs carry an "S" prefix.

COMPLETE SET (18) 20.00 40.00
STATED ODDS 1:21
*REFRACTOR: 1X TO 2.5X BASIC INSERTS
REFRACTOR STATED ODDS 1:105
S1 Joe Germaine .30 .75
S2 Jevon Kearse .60 1.50
S3 Sedrick Irvin .30 .75
S4 Brock Huard .30 .75
S5 Amos Zereoue .30 .75
S6 Andy Katzenmoyer .30 .75
S7 Randy Moss 2.50 6.00
S8 Jake Plummer 1.00 2.50
S9 Keyshawn Johnson .60 1.50
S10 Fred Taylor 1.00 2.50
S11 Eddie George 1.00 2.50
S12 Peyton Manning 3.00 8.00
S13 Dan Marino 3.00 8.00
S14 Terrell Davis 1.00 2.50
S15 Brett Favre 3.00 8.00
S16 Jamal Anderson .60 1.50
S17 Steve Young 1.25 3.00
S18 Jerry Rice 2.00 5.00

2000 Bowman Chrome

Released in Late December 2000, Bowman Chrome features a 270-card base set divided up into 140 Veteran Cards, 105 Rookie Cards, and 25 NFL Europe Prospects. Cards utilize the same base design as 2000 Bowman consisting of a full color player action shot and black and brown borders, but are enhanced with an all foil card stock. Several rookie cards were limited to just 499 copies which were inserted in packs at the rate of one in 134. Bowman Chrome was packaged in 24-pack boxes with packs containing four cards and carried a suggested retial price of $3.00.

SP ROOKIE/499 ODDS 1:134
1 Eddie George .30 .75
2 Ike Hilliard .25 .60
3 Terrell Owens .30 .75
4 James Stewart .25 .60
5 Joey Galloway .30 .75
6 Jake Reed .30 .75
7 Derrick Alexander .25 .60
8 Jeff George .30 .75
9 Kerry Collins .25 .60
10 Tony Gonzalez .30 .75
11 Marcus Robinson .30 .75
12 Charles Woodson .40 1.00
13 Germane Crowell .25 .60
14 Yancey Thigpen .25 .60
15 Tony Martin .30 .75
16 Frank Sanders .25 .60
17 Napoleon Kaufman .30 .75
18 Jay Fiedler .30 .75
19 Patrick Jeffers .25 .60
20 Steve McNair .30 .75
21 Herman Moore .25 .60
22 Tim Brown .40 1.00
23 Olandis Gary .30 .75
24 Corey Dillon .25 .60
25 Warren Sapp .30 .75
26 Curtis Enis .25 .60
27 Vinny Testaverde .25 .60
28 Tim Biakabutuka .30 .75
29 Kevin Johnson .25 .60
30 Charlie Batch .25 .60
31 Jermaine Fazande .25 .60
32 Shaun King .25 .60
33 Errict Rhett .30 .75
34 O.J. McDuffie .30 .75
35 Bruce Smith .30 .75
36 Antonio Freeman .30 .75
37 Tim Couch .30 .75
38 Duce Staley .25 .60
39 Jeff Blake .30 .75
40 Jim Harbaugh .30 .75
41 Jeff Graham .25 .60
42 Drew Bledsoe .30 .75
43 Mike Alstott .25 .60
44 Terance Mathis .25 .60
45 Antowain Smith .30 .75
46 Johnnie Morton .30 .75
47 Chris Chandler .30 .75
48 Keith Poole .25 .60
49 Ricky Watters .30 .75
50 Darnay Scott .30 .75
51 Damon Huard .25 .60
52 Peerless Price .30 .75
53 Brian Griese .25 .60
54 Frank Wycheck .30 .75
55 Kevin Dyson .30 .75
56 Junior Seau .30 .75
57 Curtis Conway .30 .75
58 Jamal Anderson .30 .75
59 Jim Miller .25 .60
60 Rob Johnson .30 .75
61 Mark Brunell .30 .75
62 Wayne Chrebet .25 .60
63 James Johnson .25 .60
64 Sean Dawkins .25 .60
65 Stephen Davis .25 .60
66 Daunte Culpepper .30 .75
67 Doug Flutie .30 .75
68 Pete Mitchell .25 .60
69 Bill Schroeder .30 .75
70 Terrence Wilkins .25 .60
71 Cade McNown .25 .60
72 Muhsin Muhammad .25 .60
73 E.G. Green .25 .60
74 Edgerrin James .30 .75
75 Troy Edwards .25 .60
76 Terry Glenn .30 .75
77 Tony Banks .25 .60
78 Derrick Mayes .25 .60
79 Curtis Martin .30 .75
80 Kordell Stewart .25 .60
81 Amani Toomer .25 .60
82 Dorsey Levens .30 .75
83 Brad Johnson .30 .75
84 Ed McCaffrey .30 .75
85 Charlie Garner .30 .75
86 Brett Favre .75 2.00
87 J.J. Stokes .30 .75
88 Steve Young .50 1.25
89 Jonathan Linton .25 .60
90 Isaac Bruce .40 1.00
91 Shawn Jefferson .25 .60
92 Rod Smith .30 .75
93 Champ Bailey .30 .75
94 Ricky Williams .30 .75
95 Priest Holmes .25 .60
96 Corey Bradford .25 .60
97 Eric Moulds .25 .60
98 Warrick Dunn .25 .60
99 Jevon Kearse .25 .60
100 Albert Connell .25 .60
101 Az-Zahir Hakim .25 .60
102 Marvin Harrison .30 .75
103 Qadry Ismail .25 .60
104 Oronde Gadsden .30 .75
105 Rob Moore .25 .60
106 Marshall Faulk .30 .75
107 Steve Beuerlein .30 .75
108 Torry Holt .30 .75
109 Donovan McNabb .30 .75
110 Rich Gannon .30 .75
111 Jerome Bettis .40 1.00
112 Peyton Manning 1.00 2.50
113 Cris Carter .40 1.00
114 Jake Plummer .25 .60
115 Kent Graham .25 .60
116 Keenan McCardell .30 .75
117 Tim Dwight .30 .75
118 Fred Taylor .25 .60
119 Jerry Rice 1.00 2.50
120 Michael Westbrook .25 .60
121 Kurt Warner .60 1.50
122 Jimmy Smith .30 .75
123 Emmitt Smith .60 1.50
124 Terrell Davis .30 .75
125 Randy Moss .30 .75
126 Akili Smith .25 .60
127 Rocket Ismail .30 .75
128 Jon Kitna .25 .60
129 Elvis Grbac .25 .60
130 Wesley Walls .25 .60
131 Torrance Small .25 .60
132 Tyrone Wheatley .25 .60
133 Carl Pickens .30 .75
134 Zach Thomas .30 .75
135 Jacquez Green .25 .60
136 Robert Smith .25 .60
137 Keyshawn Johnson .30 .75
138 Matthew Hatchette .25 .60
139 Troy Aikman .50 1.25
140 Charles Johnson .25 .60
141 Terry Battle EP .25 .60
142 Pepe Pearson EP RC .25 .60
143 Cory Sauter EP .25 .60
144 Brian Shay EP .25 .60
145 Marcus Crandell EP RC .25 .60
146 Danny Wuerffel EP .40 1.00
147 L.C. Stevens EP .25 .60
148 Ted White EP .25 .60
149 Matt Lytle EP RC .25 .60
150 Vershan Jackson EP RC .25 .60
151 Mario Bailey EP .25 .60
152 Darryl Daniel EP RC .25 .60
153 Sean Morey EP RC .25 .60
154 Jim Kubiak EP RC .25 .60
155 Aaron Stecker EP RC .25 .60
156 Damon Dunn EP RC .25 .60
157 Kevin Daft EP .25 .60
158 Corey Thomas EP .25 .60
159 Deon Mitchell EP RC .25 .60
160 Todd Floyd EP RC .25 .60
161 Norman Miller EP RC .25 .60
162 Jeremaine Copeland EP .25 .60
163 Michael Blair EP .25 .60
164 Ron Powlus EP RC .40 1.00
165 Pat Barnes EP .25 .60
166 Dez White RC 1.00 2.50
167 Trung Canidate SP RC 6.00 15.00
168 Thomas Jones SP RC 8.00 20.00
169 Courtney Brown SP RC 8.00 20.00
170 Jamal Lewis SP RC 10.00 25.00
171 Chris Redman SP RC 6.00 15.00
172 Ron Dayne SP RC 10.00 25.00
173 Chad Pennington SP RC 8.00 20.00
174 Plaxico Burress SP RC 8.00 20.00
175 R.Jay Soward SP RC 6.00 15.00
176 Travis Taylor SP RC 6.00 15.00
177 Shaun Alexander SP RC 10.00 25.00
178 Brian Urlacher RC 5.00 12.00
179 Danny Farmer RC 1.00 2.50
180 Tee Martin SP RC 6.00 15.00
181 Sylvester Morris SP RC 6.00 15.00
182 Curtis Keaton RC 1.00 2.50
183 Peter Warrick SP RC 6.00 15.00
184 Anthony Becht RC 1.00 2.50
185 Travis Prentice SP RC 6.00 15.00
186 J.R. Redmond SP RC 6.00 15.00
187 Bubba Franks SP RC 6.00 15.00
188 Ron Dugans SP RC 6.00 15.00
189 Reuben Droughns RC 1.00 2.50
190 Corey Simon RC 1.25 3.00
191 Joe Hamilton RC 1.00 2.50
192 Laveranues Coles RC 1.25 3.00
193 Todd Pinkston SP RC 6.00 15.00
194 Jerry Porter SP RC 10.00 25.00
195 Dennis Northcutt RC 1.00 2.50
196 Tim Rattay RC 1.25 3.00
197 Giovanni Carmazzi RC 1.00 2.50
198 Mareno Philyaw RC 1.00 2.50
199 Avion Black RC 1.00 2.50
200 Chafie Fields RC 1.00 2.50
201 Rondell Mealey RC 1.00 2.50
202 Troy Walters RC 1.00 2.50
203 Frank Moreau RC 1.00 2.50
204 Vaughn Sanders RC 1.00 2.50
205 Sherrod Gideon RC 1.00 2.50
206 Doug Chapman RC 1.00 2.50
207 Marcus Knight RC 1.00 2.50
208 Jamel White RC 1.00 2.50
209 Windrell Hayes RC 1.00 2.50
210 Reggie Jones RC 1.00 2.50
211 Jarious Jackson RC 1.25 3.00
212 Ronney Jenkins RC 1.00 2.50
213 Quinton Spotwood RC 1.00 2.50
214 Rob Morris RC 1.25 3.00
215 Gari Scott RC 1.00 2.50
216 Kevin Thompson RC 1.00 2.50
217 Trevor Insley RC 1.00 2.50
218 Frank Murphy RC 1.00 2.50
219 Patrick Pass RC 1.00 2.50
220 Mike Anderson RC 1.00 2.50
221 Derrius Thompson RC 1.00 2.50
222 John Abraham RC 1.50 4.00
223 Dante Hall RC 1.00 2.50
224 Chad Morton RC 1.25 3.00
225 Ahmed Plummer RC 1.00 2.50
226 Julian Peterson RC 1.50 4.00
227 Mike Green RC 1.25 3.00
228 Michael Wiley RC 1.00 2.50
229 Spergon Wynn RC 1.00 2.50
230 Trevor Gaylor RC 1.00 2.50
231 Doug Johnson RC 1.00 2.50
232 Marc Bulger RC 1.25 3.00
233 Ron Dixon RC 1.00 2.50
234 Aaron Shea RC 1.25 3.00
235 Thomas Hamner RC 1.00 2.50
236 Tom Brady RC 300.00 600.00
237 Deltha O'Neal RC 1.00 2.50
238 Todd Husak RC 1.00 2.50
239 Erron Kinney RC 1.00 2.50
240 JaJuan Dawson RC 1.00 2.50
241 Nick Williams .25 .60
242 Deon Grant RC 1.00 2.50
243 Brad Hoover RC 1.25 3.00
244 Kamil Loud .25 .60
245 Rashard Anderson RC 1.00 2.50
246 Clint Stoerner RC 1.50 4.00
247 Antwan Harris RC 1.00 2.50
248 Jason Webster RC 1.00 2.50
249 Kevin McDougal RC 1.00 2.50
250 Tony Scott RC 1.00 2.50
251 Thabiti Davis RC 1.00 2.50
252 Ian Gold RC 1.00 2.50
253 Sammy Morris RC 1.00 2.50
254 Raynoch Thompson RC 1.00 2.50
255 Jeremy McDaniel .25 .60
256 Terrelle Smith RC 1.00 2.50
257 Deon Dyer RC 1.00 2.50
258 Na'il Diggs RC 1.00 2.50
259 Brandon Short RC 1.00 2.50
260 Mike Brown RC 1.00 2.50
261 John Engelberger RC 1.00 2.50
262 Rogers Beckett RC 1.00 2.50
263 JaJuan Seider RC 1.00 2.50
264 Desmond Kitchings RC 1.00 2.50
265 Reggie Davis RC 1.00 2.50
266 Corey Moore RC 1.00 2.50
267 Cornelius Griffin RC 1.00 2.50
268 Stockar McDougle RC 1.00 2.50
269 James Williams RC 1.00 2.50
270 Darrell Jackson RC 1.00 2.50

2000 Bowman Chrome Refractors

*VETS 1-165: 1.5X TO 4X BASIC CARDS
1-165 VETERAN STATED ODDS 1:12
*ROOKIE 166-270: 1.5X TO 4X BASIC CARD
166-270 ROOKIE ODDS 1:281
*ROOKIE/99: .6X TO 1.5X BASIC RC/499
ROOKIE SP/99 ODDS 1:659
ROOKIE SP PRINT RUN 99
236 Tom Brady 1200.00 3000.00

2000 Bowman Chrome By Selection

Randomly inserted in packs at the rate of one in 24, this 10-card set pairs two top NFL players of the same position and draft selection. Card stock is silver foil and features both players on the front.

COMPLETE SET (10) 10.00 25.00
STATED ODDS 1:24 H/R
*REFRACTOR: 1.2X TO 3X BASIC INSERTS
REFRACTOR STATED ODDS 1:240 H/R
B1 T.Aikman / D.Bledsoe 1.00 2.50
B2 M.Faulk / D.McNabb .60 1.50
B3 R.Williams / J.Lewis .75 2.00
B4 R.Moss / Syl.Morris .60 1.50
B5 S.Alexander / M.Harrison .75 2.00
B6 T.Couch / P.Manning 2.00 5.00
B7 E.James / P.Warrick .60 1.50
B8 J.Smith / T.Pinkston .60 1.50
B9 S.McNair / A.Smith .60 1.50
B10 P.Burress / J.Galloway .60 1.50

2000 Bowman Chrome Ground Breakers

Randomly inserted in packs at the rate of one in 12, this 10-card set features player action photography on an all maroon and silver foil card stock with the words ground breakers in yellow along the left side of the card front.

COMPLETE SET (10) 4.00 10.00
STATED ODDS 1:12 H/R
*REFRACTOR: 1.2X TO 3X BASIC INSERTS
REFRACTOR STATED ODDS 1:120 H/R
GB1 Edgerrin James .50 1.25
GB2 Eddie George .50 1.25
GB3 Jerome Bettis .60 1.50
GB4 Fred Taylor .40 1.00
GB5 Curtis Martin .50 1.25
GB6 Errict Rhett .50 1.25
GB7 Marshall Faulk .50 1.25
GB8 Karim Abdul-Jabbar .40 1.00
GB9 Olandis Gary .50 1.25
GB10 Terrell Davis .50 1.25

2000 Bowman Chrome Rookie Autographs

Randomly inserted in packs at the rate of one in 5247 hobby and 1:5292 retail, this set consists of the first 25 serial numbered copies of ten top rookies with each carrying an authentic player autograph.

FIRST 25 ROOKIE CARDS WERE SIGNED
AUTO/25* ODDS 1:5247 HOB, 1:5292 RET
168 Thomas Jones 25.00 60.00
170 Jamal Lewis 50.00 120.00
172 Ron Dayne 30.00 80.00
173 Chad Pennington 25.00 60.00
174 Plaxico Burress 25.00 60.00
175 R.Jay Soward 20.00 50.00
177 Shaun Alexander 100.00 200.00
181 Sylvester Morris 20.00 50.00
183 Peter Warrick 20.00 50.00
185 Travis Prentice 20.00 50.00

2000 Bowman Chrome Rookie of the Year

Randomly inserted at the rate of one per box as a box topper, this 10-card set features players that have taken Rookie of the Year honors in the past two decades. Cards are all silver foil with a yellow frame around the player and the words rookie of the year appear along the top in yellow.

COMPLETE SET (10) 4.00 10.00
STATED ODDS ONE PER BOX
R1 Santana Dotson .50 1.25
R2 Jerome Bettis .75 2.00
R3 Marshall Faulk .60 1.50
R4 Curtis Martin .60 1.50
R5 Eddie George .60 1.50
R6 Warrick Dunn .50 1.25
R7 Charles Woodson .75 2.00
R8 Randy Moss .60 1.50
R9 Jevon Kearse .50 1.25
R10 Edgerrin James .60 1.50

2000 Bowman Chrome Scout's Choice Update

Randomly inserted in packs at the rate of one in 24, this ten card set features top rookies from the 2000 draft on an all foil card with a green border along the top and the right side of the card. A player action photo is featured with a small circular closeup of the players face in the upper right hand corner.

COMPLETE SET (10) 7.50 20.00
STATED ODDS 1:24 H/R
*REFRACTOR: 1.2X TO 3X BASIC INSERTS
REFRACTOR STATED ODDS 1:240 H/R
SCU1 Shaun Alexander .60 1.50
SCU2 Brian Urlacher 2.00 5.00
SCU3 Courtney Brown .50 1.25
SCU4 Jamal Lewis .60 1.50
SCU5 Sylvester Morris .40 1.00
SCU6 Plaxico Burress .50 1.25
SCU7 Ron Dayne .60 1.50
SCU8 Thomas Jones .50 1.25
SCU9 Corey Simon .50 1.25
SCU10 Travis Taylor .40 1.00

2000 Bowman Chrome Shattering Performers

Randomly inserted in packs at the rate of one in 16, this 20-card set features top break out players on an all foil card stock with a colorful background resembling shattered glass.

COMPLETE SET (20) 15.00 40.00
STATED ODDS 1:16 H/R
*REFRACTOR: 1.2X TO 3X BASIC INSERTS
REFRACTOR STATED ODDS 1:160 H/R
SP1 Kurt Warner 1.25 3.00
SP2 Peyton Manning 2.00 5.00
SP3 Brian Griese .50 1.25
SP4 Daunte Culpepper .60 1.50
SP5 Elvis Grbac .50 1.25
SP6 Stephen Davis .50 1.25
SP7 Charlie Garner .60 1.50
SP8 Mike Anderson .50 1.25
SP9 Marshall Faulk .60 1.50
SP10 Robert Smith .50 1.25
SP11 Tiki Barber .60 1.50
SP12 Edgerrin James .60 1.50
SP13 Isaac Bruce .75 2.00
SP14 Rod Smith .60 1.50
SP15 Jimmy Smith .60 1.50
SP16 Torry Holt .60 1.50
SP17 Keenan McCardell .60 1.50
SP18 Marcus Robinson .60 1.50
SP19 Marvin Harrison .60 1.50
SP20 Randy Moss .60 1.50

2001 Bowman Chrome

This 255 card set was released in four card packs which came packaged 24 to a box. Cards numbered 1-110 featured vets while cards numbered 111-255 featured rookies and were inserted at a rate of one every three packs. These rookie cards are serial numbered to 1999 and were printed with Refractor printing technology.

COMPLETE SET (255) 150.00 300.00
COMP.SET w/o SP's (110) 10.00 25.00
ROOKIE/1999 ODDS 1:3 HOBBY
1 Emmitt Smith .60 1.50
2 James Stewart .25 .60
3 Jeff Graham .25 .60
4 Keyshawn Johnson .30 .75
5 Stephen Davis .25 .60
6 Chad Lewis .25 .60
7 Drew Bledsoe .30 .75
8 Fred Taylor .25 .60
9 Mike Anderson .25 .60
10 Tony Gonzalez .30 .75
11 Aaron Brooks .25 .60
12 Vinny Testaverde .25 .60
13 Jerome Bettis .40 1.00
14 Marshall Faulk .30 .75
15 Jeff Garcia .25 .60
16 Terry Glenn .30 .75
17 Jay Fiedler .30 .75
18 Ahman Green .30 .75
19 Cade McNown .30 .75
20 Rob Johnson .30 .75
21 Jamal Anderson .30 .75
22 Corey Dillon .25 .60
23 Jake Plummer .25 .60
24 Rod Smith .30 .75
25 Trent Green .25 .60
26 Ricky Williams .30 .75
27 Charlie Garner .30 .75
28 Shaun Alexander .25 .60
29 Jeff George .30 .75
30 Torry Holt .30 .75
31 James Thrash .30 .75
32 Rich Gannon .30 .75
33 Ron Dayne .30 .75
34 Dedric Ward .25 .60
35 Edgerrin James .30 .75
36 Cris Carter .40 1.00
37 Derrick Mason .25 .60
38 Brad Johnson .30 .75
39 Charlie Batch .25 .60
40 Joey Galloway .30 .75
41 James Allen .25 .60
42 Tim Biakabutuka .25 .60
43 Ray Lewis .40 1.00
44 David Boston .25 .60
45 Kevin Johnson .25 .60
46 Jimmy Smith .30 .75
47 Joe Horn .25 .60
48 Terrell Owens .30 .75
49 Eddie George .40 1.00
50 Brett Favre .75 2.00
51 Wayne Chrebet .25 .60
52 Hines Ward .30 .75
53 Warrick Dunn .25 .60
54 Matt Hasselbeck .25 .60
55 Tiki Barber .30 .75
56 Lamar Smith .30 .75
57 Tim Couch .25 .60
58 Eric Moulds .25 .60
59 Shawn Jefferson .25 .60
60 Donald Hayes .25 .60
61 Brian Urlacher .50 1.25
62 Steve McNair .30 .75
63 Kurt Warner .60 1.50
64 Tim Brown .40 1.00
65 Troy Brown .25 .60
66 Albert Connell .25 .60
67 Peyton Manning 1.00 2.50
68 Peter Warrick .25 .60
69 Elvis Grbac .30 .75
70 Chris Chandler .30 .75
71 Akili Smith .25 .60
72 Keenan McCardell .30 .75
73 Kerry Collins .25 .60
74 Junior Seau .30 .75
75 Donovan McNabb .30 .75
76 Tony Banks .25 .60
77 Steve Beuerlein .30 .75
78 Daunte Culpepper .30 .75
79 Darrell Jackson .30 .75
80 Isaac Bruce .40 1.00
81 Tyrone Wheatley .30 .75
82 Derrick Alexander .25 .60
83 Germane Crowell .25 .60
84 Jon Kitna .25 .60
85 Jamal Lewis .40 1.00
86 Ed McCaffrey .30 .75
87 Mark Brunell .30 .75
88 Jeff Blake .30 .75
89 Duce Staley .25 .60
90 Doug Flutie .30 .75
91 Kordell Stewart .25 .60
92 Randy Moss .30 .75
93 Marvin Harrison .30 .75
94 Muhsin Muhammad .25 .60
95 Brian Griese .25 .60
96 Antonio Freeman .40 1.00
97 Amani Toomer .25 .60
98 Oronde Gadsden .25 .60
99 Curtis Martin .30 .75
100 Jerry Rice .75 2.00
101 Michael Pittman .30 .75
102 Shannon Sharpe .30 .75
103 Peerless Price .25 .60
104 Bill Schroeder .30 .75
105 Ike Hilliard .25 .60
106 Freddie Jones .25 .60
107 Tai Streets .25 .60
108 Ricky Watters .30 .75
109 Az-Zahir Hakim .25 .60
110 Jacquez Green .25 .60
111 George Layne RC 2.00 5.00
112 Correll Buckhalter RC 2.00 5.00
113 Tony Stewart RC 2.50 6.00
114 Chris Barnes RC 2.00 5.00
115 A.J. Feeley RC 2.50 6.00
116 Margin Hooks RC 2.00 5.00
117 Anthony Henry RC 3.00 8.00
118 Dwight Smith RC 2.00 5.00
119 Torrance Marshall RC 2.00 5.00
120 Gary Baxter RC 2.00 5.00
121 Derek Combs RC 2.00 5.00
122 Marcus Bell RC 2.00 5.00
123 DeLawrence Grant RC 2.00 5.00
124 Jameel Cook RC 2.50 6.00
125 Eric Downing RC 2.00 5.00
126 Marlon McCree RC 2.00 5.00
127 Tay Cody RC 2.00 5.00
128 Mario Monds RC 2.00 5.00
129 Kenny Smith RC 2.00 5.00
130 Sedrick Hodge RC 2.00 5.00
131 Marcus Stroud RC 2.50 6.00
132 Steve Smith RC 10.00 25.00
133 Tyrone Robertson RC 2.00 5.00
134 James Reed RC 2.00 5.00
135 Kris Kocurek RC 2.00 5.00
136 Dan O'Leary RC 2.00 5.00
137 Harold Blackmon RC 2.00 5.00
138 Fred Smoot RC 2.50 6.00
139 Billy Baber RC 2.00 5.00
140 Jarrod Cooper RC 2.50 6.00
141 Travis Henry RC 2.50 6.00
142 David Terrell RC 2.50 6.00
143 Josh Heupel RC 3.00 8.00
144 Drew Brees RC 250.00 400.00
145 T.J. Houshmandzadeh RC 2.50 6.00
146 Rod Gardner RC 2.50 6.00
147 Richard Seymour RC 3.00 8.00
148 Koren Robinson RC 2.50 6.00
149 Scotty Anderson RC 2.00 5.00
150 Marques Tuiasosopo RC 2.50 6.00
151 John Capel RC 2.00 5.00
152 LaMont Jordan RC 3.00 8.00
153 James Jackson RC 2.00 5.00
154 Bobby Newcombe RC 2.50 6.00
155 Anthony Thomas RC 3.00 8.00
156 Dan Alexander RC 2.50 6.00
157 Quincy Carter RC 2.50 6.00
158 Morlon Greenwood RC 2.00 5.00
159 Robert Ferguson RC 3.00 8.00
160 Sage Rosenfels RC 2.50 6.00
161 Michael Stone RC 2.00 5.00
162 Chris Weinke RC 2.50 6.00
163 Travis Minor RC 2.50 6.00
164 Gerard Warren RC 2.50 6.00
165 Jamar Fletcher RC 2.00 5.00
166 Andre Carter RC 2.50 6.00
167 Deuce McAllister RC 3.00 8.00
168 Dan Morgan RC 2.50 6.00
169 Todd Heap RC 2.50 6.00
170 Snoop Minnis RC 2.00 5.00
171 Will Allen RC 3.00 8.00
172 Freddie Mitchell RC 2.00 5.00
173 Rudi Johnson RC 3.00 8.00
174 Kevan Barlow RC 2.50 6.00
175 Jamie Winborn RC 2.50 6.00
176 Onome Ojo RC 2.00 5.00
177 Leonard Davis RC 3.00 8.00
178 Santana Moss RC 3.00 8.00
179 Chris Chambers RC 2.00 5.00
180 Michael Vick RC 12.00 30.00
181 Michael Bennett RC 2.50 6.00
182 Mike McMahon RC 2.50 6.00
183 Jonathan Carter RC 2.00 5.00
184 Jamal Reynolds RC 2.00 5.00
185 Justin Smith RC 4.00 10.00
186 Quincy Morgan RC 2.50 6.00
187 Chad Johnson RC 8.00 20.00
188 Jesse Palmer RC 2.50 6.00
189 Reggie Wayne RC 15.00 20.00
190 LaDainian Tomlinson RC 15.00 40.00
191 Andre King RC 2.00 5.00
192 Richmond Flowers RC 2.00 5.00
193 Derrick Blaylock RC 2.50 6.00
194 Cedrick Wilson RC 2.50 6.00
195 Zeke Moreno RC 2.50 6.00
196 Tommy Polley RC 2.00 5.00
197 Damione Lewis RC 2.50 6.00
198 Aaron Schobel RC 3.00 8.00
199 Alge Crumpler RC 3.00 8.00
200 Nate Clements RC 2.50 6.00
201 Quentin McCord RC 2.50 6.00
202 Ken-Yon Rambo RC 2.00 5.00
203 Milton Wynn RC 2.00 5.00
204 Derrick Gibson RC 2.00 5.00
205 Chris Taylor RC 2.00 5.00
206 Corey Hall RC 2.00 5.00
207 Vinny Sutherland RC 2.00 5.00
208 Kendrell Bell RC 3.00 8.00
209 Casey Hampton RC 3.00 8.00
210 Demetric Evans RC 2.00 5.00
211 Brian Allen RC 2.00 5.00
212 Rodney Bailey RC 2.00 5.00
213 Otis Leverette RC 2.00 5.00
214 Ron Edwards RC 2.00 5.00
215 Michael Jameson RC 2.00 5.00
216 Markus Steele RC 2.00 5.00
217 Jimmy Williams RC 2.00 5.00
218 Roger Knight RC 2.00 5.00
219 Randy Garner RC 2.00 5.00
220 Raymond Perryman RC 2.00 5.00
221 Karon Riley RC 2.00 5.00
222 Adam Archuleta RC 2.50 6.00
223 Arnold Jackson RC 2.00 5.00
224 Ryan Pickett RC 2.00 5.00
225 Shad Meier RC 2.00 5.00
226 Reggie Germany RC 2.00 5.00
227 Justin McCareins RC 2.50 6.00
228 Idrees Bashir RC 2.00 5.00
229 Josh Booty RC 2.50 6.00
230 Eddie Berlin RC 2.00 5.00
231 Heath Evans RC 2.50 6.00
232 Alex Bannister RC 2.00 5.00
233 Corey Alston RC 2.00 5.00
234 Reggie White RC 2.00 5.00
235 Orlando Huff RC 2.00 5.00
236 Ken Lucas RC 2.50 6.00
237 Matt Stewart RC 2.00 5.00
238 Cedric Scott RC 2.00 5.00
239 Ronney Daniels RC 2.00 5.00
240 Kevin Kasper RC 2.00 5.00
241 Tony Driver RC 2.50 6.00
242 Kyle Vanden Bosch RC 3.00 8.00
243 T.J. Turner RC 2.00 5.00
244 Eric Westmoreland RC 2.00 5.00
245 Ronald Flemons RC 2.00 5.00
246 Eric Kelly RC 2.00 5.00
247 Moran Norris RC 2.00 5.00
248 Damerien McCants RC 2.50 6.00
249 James Boyd RC 2.00 5.00
250 Keith Adams RC 2.00 5.00
251 B.Manumaleuna RC 2.50 6.00
252 Dee Brown RC 2.00 5.00
253 Ross Kolodziej RC 2.00 5.00
254 Boo Williams RC 2.00 5.00
255 Patrick Chukwurah RC 2.00 5.00

2001 Bowman Chrome Gold Refractors

*STARS: 5X TO 12X HI COL.
*ROOKIES: 1.2X TO 3X HI COL.
STATED PRINT RUN 99 SER.#'d SETS
STATED ODDS 1:38 HOBBY
144 Drew Brees 1700.00 2500.00
180 Michael Vick 60.00 80.00
190 LaDainian Tomlinson 75.00 200.00

2001 Bowman Chrome Xfractors

*VETS 1-110: 2.5X TO 6X BASIC CARDS
*ROOKIES 111-255: .8X TO 2X
STATED ODDS 1:23 HOBBY
144 Drew Brees 800.00 1200.00
180 Michael Vick 30.00 80.00
190 LaDainian Tomlinson 40.00 100.00

2001 Bowman Chrome 1996 Rookies

Issued at a stated odds of one in 16, these cards featured 15 leading rookies of 1996 who never had 1996 Bowman cards because that set was never issued.

COMPLETE SET (15) 15.00 40.00
STATED ODDS 1:16 HOBBY
BRC1 Eric Moulds 1.50 4.00
BRC2 Ray Lewis 2.50 6.00
BRC3 Tim Biakabutuka 1.50 4.00
BRC4 Eddie George 2.50 6.00
BRC5 Marvin Harrison 2.50 6.00
BRC6 Joe Horn 1.50 4.00
BRC7 Muhsin Muhammad 1.50 4.00
BRC8 Mike Alstott 2.50 6.00
BRC9 Amani Toomer 1.50 4.00
BRC10 Terrell Owens 2.50 6.00
BRC11 Keyshawn Johnson 2.50 6.00
BRC12 Terry Glenn 1.50 4.00
BRC13 Zach Thomas 2.50 6.00
BRC14 Stephen Davis 2.50 6.00
BRC15 La'Roi Glover 1.00 2.50

2001 Bowman Chrome Autographs

Inserted at overall odds of one in 315 hobby packs for the veterans and 1:772 hobby for the rookies, 28 players signed cards for this product. Deuce McAllister did not sign cards in time for inclusion in packs and therefore his redemption cards could be exchanged until December 31, 2003.

GROUP A STATED ODDS 1:947
GROUP B STATED ODDS 1:473
OVERALL STATED ODDS 1:315 HOBBY
ROOKIE STATED ODDS 1:772 HOBBY
BCAT Anthony Thomas 12.00 30.00
BCBN Bobby Newcombe 10.00 25.00
BCCC Chris Chambers 8.00 20.00
BCCJ Chad Johnson 40.00 100.00
BCCW Chris Weinke 10.00 25.00

BCDA Dan Alexander 10.00 25.00
BCDB Drew Brees 400.00 700.00
BCDBO David Boston 8.00 20.00
BCDM1 Derrick Mason 8.00 20.00
BCDM3 Dan Morgan 10.00 25.00
BCDT David Terrell 10.00 25.00
BCJH Josh Heupel 12.00 30.00
BCJHO Joe Horn 8.00 20.00
BCJJ James Jackson 8.00 20.00
BCJP Jesse Palmer 10.00 25.00
BCKB Kevan Barlow 10.00 25.00
BCLJ LaMont Jordan 12.00 30.00
BCLT LaDainian Tomlinson 200.00 400.00
BCMB Michael Bennett 10.00 25.00
BCMV Michael Vick 300.00 600.00
BCQC Quincy Carter 10.00 25.00
BCQM Quincy Morgan 10.00 25.00
BCRG Rod Gardner 10.00 25.00
BCRGE Reggie Germany 8.00 20.00
BCRW Reggie Wayne 125.00 250.00
BCSM Santana Moss 15.00 40.00
BCTH Travis Henry 10.00 25.00
BCTM Travis Minor 10.00 25.00

2001 Bowman Chrome Draft Day Relics

Inserted at odds of one in 131 for jersey cards and one in 2,129 for hat cards, these 11-cards feature leading rookies of 2001 along with pieces of equipment worn by the featured player on draft day.

JSY STATED ODDS 1:131 HOBBY
CAP STATED ODDS 1:2129 HOBBY
DHDT David Terrell Cap 7.50 20.00
DHJS Justin Smith Cap 7.50 20.00
DHLD Leonard Davis Cap 7.50 20.00
DHLT LaDainian Tomlinson Cap 15.00 40.00
DHMV Michael Vick Cap 15.00 40.00
DJDT David Terrell JSY 4.00 10.00
DJJS Justin Smith JSY 5.00 12.00
DJKW Kenyatta Walker JSY 4.00 10.00
DJLD Leonard Davis JSY 4.00 10.00
DJLT LaDainian Tomlinson JSY 12.00 30.00
DJMV Michael Vick JSY 15.00 40.00

2001 Bowman Chrome Rookie Relics

Inserted at overall odds of one in 78, these 23 cards feature game-worn swatches taken from game-used uniforms at either the Hula or the Senior bowls.

GROUP A STATED ODDS 1:9648
GROUP B STATED ODDS 1:1730
GROUP C STATED ODDS 1:902
GROUP D STATED ODDS 1:2376
GROUP E STATED ODDS 1:664
GROUP F STATED ODDS 1:379
GROUP G STATED ODDS 1:505
GROUP H STATED ODDS 1:676
GROUP I STATED ODDS 1:574
GROUP J STATED ODDS 1:789
OVERALL ODDS 1:78 HOBBY
BCRBA Brian Allen 3.00 8.00
BCRBJ Bhawoh Jue 4.00 10.00
BCRDB Drew Brees 30.00 60.00
BCRDBU Derrick Burgess 5.00 12.00
BCREW Eric Westmoreland 3.00 8.00
BCRJB Jeff Backus 3.00 8.00
BCRJC Jarrod Cooper 4.00 10.00
BCRJH Jabari Holloway 3.00 8.00
BCRJJ Jonas Jennings 3.00 8.00
BCRJP Jesse Palmer 4.00 10.00
BCRJHE Jamie Henderson 4.00 10.00
BCRKK Kevin Kasper 3.00 8.00
BCRLJ LaMont Jordan 5.00 12.00
BCRLM Leonard Myers 3.00 8.00
BCRMF Mario Fatafehi 3.00 8.00
BCRMS Michael Stone 3.00 8.00
BCRRG Reggie Germany 3.00 8.00
BCRRW Reggie Wayne 10.00 25.00
BCRSH Steve Hutchinson 8.00 20.00
BCRSS Steve Smith 10.00 25.00
BCRTD Tony Dixon 3.00 8.00
BCRTS Tony Stewart 4.00 10.00
BCRZM Zeke Moreno 4.00 10.00

2001 Bowman Chrome Rookie Reprints

Issued at stated odds of one in 24, these 16 cards feature reprints of some all-time greats Bowman Rookie Cards.

COMPLETE SET (16) 20.00 40.00
STATED ODDS 1:24 HOBBY
RAA Alan Ameche 1.25 3.00
RAD Art Donovan 1.50 4.00
RBH Bill Howton 1.25 3.00
RBT Bulldog Turner 1.50 4.00
RCC Charlie Conerly 1.50 4.00
REH Elroy Hirsch 2.00 5.00
RET Emlen Tunnell 1.25 3.00
RFG Frank Gifford 2.50 6.00
RGM Gino Marchetti 1.25 3.00
RLG Lou Groza 1.50 4.00
RNV Norm Van Brocklin 2.00 5.00
ROG Otto Graham 2.00 5.00
RSB Sammy Baugh 2.50 6.00
RSL Sid Luckman 1.50 4.00
RTF Tom Fears 1.25 3.00
RYT Y.A Tittle 2.50 6.00

2002 Bowman Chrome

Released in December 2002, this set features 110 veterans and 140 rookies. Cards 111-220 were inserted at a rate of 1:2. Cards 221-250 were signed and inserted at the following rates: Group A 1:134, Group B 1:162, Group C 1:140, Group D 1:91, Group E 1:68, and Group F 1:150. Boxes contained 18 packs of 4 cards.

COMP.SET w/o SP's (110) 10.00 25.00
1 Emmitt Smith .60 1.50
2 Drew Brees .75 2.00
3 Duce Staley .25 .60
4 Curtis Martin .30 .75
5 Isaac Bruce .40 1.00
6 Stephen Davis .25 .60
7 Darrell Jackson .30 .75
8 James Stewart .25 .60
9 Tim Couch .25 .60
10 Travis Henry .25 .60
11 Thomas Jones .25 .60
12 Jamal Lewis .30 .75
13 Chris Chambers .25 .60
14 Jeff Blake .30 .75
15 Plaxico Burress .25 .60
16 Michael Pittman .30 .75
17 Jeff Garcia .25 .60
18 Tim Brown .40 1.00
19 Kent Graham .25 .60
20 Shannon Sharpe .30 .75
21 Corey Dillon .25 .60
22 Muhsin Muhammad .25 .60
23 Tony Gonzalez .30 .75
24 Qadry Ismail .25 .60
25 Mike McMahon .25 .60
26 Edgerrin James .30 .75
27 Daunte Culpepper .30 .75
28 Deuce McAllister .30 .75
29 Kerry Collins .25 .60
30 Eddie George .30 .75
31 Torry Holt .30 .75
32 Todd Pinkston .25 .60
33 Quincy Carter .25 .60
34 Rod Smith .30 .75
35 Michael Vick .30 .75
36 Jim Miller .25 .60
37 Troy Brown .25 .60
38 Wayne Chrebet .25 .60
39 Curtis Conway .30 .75
40 Reidel Anthony .25 .60
41 Mark Brunell .30 .75
42 Chris Weinke .25 .60
43 Eric Moulds .25 .60
44 Ike Hilliard .25 .60
45 Jay Fiedler .30 .75
46 Keyshawn Johnson .30 .75
47 Rod Gardner .25 .60
48 Chris Redman .25 .60
49 James Allen .25 .60
50 Kordell Stewart .25 .60
51 Priest Holmes .25 .60
52 Anthony Thomas .30 .75
53 Peter Warrick .25 .60
54 Jake Plummer .25 .60
55 Jerry Rice .75 2.00
56 Joe Horn .25 .60
57 Derrick Mason .25 .60
58 Kurt Warner .30 .75
59 Antowain Smith .30 .75
60 Randy Moss .30 .75
61 Warrick Dunn .25 .60
62 Laveranues Coles .30 .75
63 LaDainian Tomlinson .40 1.00
64 Michael Westbrook .25 .60
65 Travis Taylor .25 .60
66 Brian Griese .25 .60
67 Bill Schroeder .25 .60
68 Ahman Green .30 .75
69 Jimmy Smith .30 .75
70 Charlie Garner .30 .75
71 Terrell Owens .30 .75
72 Brad Johnson .30 .75
73 James Thrash .30 .75
74 Marvin Harrison .30 .75
75 Brett Favre .75 2.00
76 Rocket Ismail .30 .75
77 David Boston .25 .60
78 Jermaine Lewis .25 .60
79 Aaron Brooks .25 .60
80 Shaun Alexander .25 .60
81 Steve McNair .30 .75
82 Marshall Faulk .30 .75
83 Terrell Davis .30 .75
84 Corey Bradford .25 .60
85 David Terrell .25 .60
86 Kevin Johnson .25 .60
87 Jon Kitna .25 .60
88 Az-Zahir Hakim .25 .60
89 Drew Bledsoe .30 .75
90 Garrison Hearst .25 .60
91 Doug Flutie .30 .75
92 Jerome Bettis .40 1.00
93 Vinny Testaverde .25 .60
94 Tiki Barber .30 .75
95 Johnnie Morton .30 .75
96 Lamar Smith .25 .60
97 Marcus Robinson .30 .75
98 Fred Taylor .25 .60
99 Tom Brady 6.00 15.00
100 Peyton Manning 1.00 2.50
101 Donovan McNabb .30 .75
102 Rich Gannon .30 .75
103 Hines Ward .30 .75
104 Michael Bennett .25 .60
105 Ricky Williams .30 .75
106 Germane Crowell .25 .60
107 Joey Galloway .30 .75
108 Amani Toomer .25 .60
109 Trent Green .25 .60
110 Terry Glenn .30 .75
111 Donte Stallworth RC 1.50 4.00
112 Mike Williams RC 1.00 2.50
113 Kurt Kittner RC 1.00 2.50
114 Josh Reed RC 1.25 3.00
115 Raonall Smith RC 1.00 2.50
116 David Garrard RC 1.25 3.00
117 Eric Crouch RC 1.50 4.00
118 Levi Jones RC 1.00 2.50
119 Quentin Jammer RC 1.50 4.00
120 Cliff Russell RC 1.00 2.50
121 Jamin Elliott RC 1.00 2.50
122 Roy Williams RC 1.00 2.50
123 Marquise Walker RC 1.00 2.50
124 Kalimba Edwards RC 1.25 3.00
125 Daniel Graham RC 1.25 3.00
126 Anthony Weaver RC 1.00 2.50
127 Antonio Bryant RC 1.50 4.00
128 DeShaun Foster RC 1.50 4.00
129 Antwaan Randle El RC 1.25 3.00
130 William Green RC 1.25 3.00
131 Joey Harrington RC 1.00 2.50
132 T.J. Duckett RC 1.00 2.50
133 Javon Walker RC 1.50 4.00
134 Albert Haynesworth RC 1.50 4.00
135 Julius Peppers RC 2.50 6.00
136 Clinton Portis RC 1.50 4.00
137 Ashley Lelie RC 1.00 2.50
138 Reche Caldwell RC 1.25 3.00
139 Rohan Davey RC 1.50 4.00
140 Patrick Ramsey RC 1.25 3.00
141 Ron Johnson RC 1.25 3.00
142 Jamar Martin RC 1.25 3.00
143 Travis Stephens RC 1.00 2.50
143AU Travis Stephens AU 4.00 10.00
144 Darrell Hill RC 1.00 2.50
145 Jon McGraw RC 1.00 2.50
146 Javin Hunter RC 1.00 2.50
146AU Javin Hunter AU 4.00 10.00
147 Eddie Drummond RC 1.00 2.50
148 Andre Lott RC 1.00 2.50
149 Travis Fisher RC 1.25 3.00
150 Lamont Brightful RC 1.00 2.50
151 Rocky Calmus RC 1.25 3.00
152 Wes Pate RC 1.00 2.50
152AU Wes Pate AU 4.00 10.00
153 Lamar Gordon RC 1.25 3.00
154 Terry Jones RC 1.00 2.50
155 Kyle Johnson RC 1.00 2.50
155AU Kyle Johnson AU 4.00 10.00
156 Daryl Jones RC 1.00 2.50
157 Tellis Redmon RC 1.00 2.50
158 Jarrod Baxter RC 1.00 2.50
159 Delvon Flowers RC 1.00 2.50
160 Kelly Campbell RC 1.25 3.00
161 Eddie Freeman RC 1.00 2.50
162 Atrews Bell RC 1.00 2.50
163 Omar Easy RC 1.25 3.00
164 Jeremy Allen RC 1.00 2.50
165 Andra Davis RC 1.00 2.50
166 Mike Rumph RC 1.00 2.50
167 Seth Burford RC 1.00 2.50
168 Marquand Manuel RC 1.00 2.50
169 Marques Anderson RC 1.25 3.00
170 Ben Leber RC 1.00 2.50
171 Ryan Denney RC 1.00 2.50
172 Justin Peelle RC 1.00 2.50
173 Lito Sheppard RC 1.50 4.00
174 Damien Anderson RC 1.00 2.50
175 Lamont Thompson RC 1.25 3.00
176 David Priestley RC 1.00 2.50
177 Michael Lewis RC 1.25 3.00
178 Lee Mays RC 1.00 2.50
179 Alan Harper RC 1.00 2.50
180 Verron Haynes RC 1.00 2.50
181 Chris Hope RC 1.50 4.00
182 Derek Ross RC 1.25 3.00
183 Joseph Jefferson RC 1.00 2.50
184 Carlos Hall RC 1.00 2.50
185 Robert Royal RC 1.50 4.00
186 Sheldon Brown RC 1.50 4.00
187 DeVeren Johnson RC 1.00 2.50
188 Rock Cartwright RC 1.50 4.00
189 Kendall Simmons RC 1.00 2.50
190 Joe Burns RC 1.00 2.50
191 David Givens RC 1.50 4.00
192 John Owens RC 1.00 2.50
193 Jarrett Ferguson RC 1.00 2.50
194 Randy McMichael RC 1.50 4.00
195 Chris Baker RC 1.00 2.50
196 Rashad Bauman RC 1.00 2.50
197 Matt Murphy RC 1.00 2.50
198 Steve Bellisari RC 1.00 2.50
199 Jeff Kelly RC 1.00 2.50
200 Mark Anelli RC 1.00 2.50
201 Darnell Sanders RC 1.00 2.50
202 Coy Wire RC 1.25 3.00
203 Ricky Williams RC 1.25 3.00
204 Napoleon Harris RC 1.25 3.00
205 Ennis Haywood RC 1.00 2.50
206 Keyuo Craver RC 1.00 2.50
207 Kahlil Hill RC 1.00 2.50
208 J.T. O'Sullivan RC 1.25 3.00
209 Woody Dantzler RC 1.25 3.00
210 Phillip Buchanon RC 1.50 4.00
211 Charles Grant RC 1.50 4.00
212 Dusty Bonner RC 1.00 2.50
213 James Allen RC 1.00 2.50
214 Ronald Curry RC 1.00 2.50
215 Deion Branch RC 1.50 4.00
216 Larry Ned RC 1.00 2.50
217 Kendall Newson RC 1.00 2.50
218 Shaun Hill RC 1.50 4.00
219 Akin Ayodele RC 1.25 3.00
220 John Henderson RC 1.25 3.00
221 Andre Davis AU A RC 4.00 10.00
222 Bryan Thomas AU A RC 4.00 10.00
223 Brian Westbrook AU C RC 8.00 20.00
224 Chad Hutchinson AU C RC 4.00 10.00
225 Craig Nall AU D RC 5.00 12.00
226 David Carr AU A RC 10.00 25.00
227 Dwight Freeney AU D RC 20.00 40.00
228 Adrian Peterson AU A RC 8.00 20.00
229 Randy Fasani AU E RC 4.00 10.00
230 Ed Reed AU A RC 40.00 80.00
231 Freddie Milons AU B RC 4.00 10.00
232 Herb Haygood AU E RC 4.00 10.00
233 Jabar Gaffney AU A RC 4.00 10.00
234 Josh McCown AU A RC 6.00 15.00
235 Jeremy Shockey AU A RC 12.00 30.00
236 Jake Schifino AU F RC 4.00 10.00
237 Josh Scobey AU E RC 5.00 12.00
238 Jonathan Wells AU D RC 5.00 12.00
239 Ladell Betts AU A RC 8.00 20.00
240 Luke Staley AU E RC 4.00 10.00
241 Maurice Morris AU B RC 5.00 12.00
242 Matt Schobel AU D RC 5.00 12.00
243 Sam Simmons AU C RC 4.00 10.00
244 Tim Carter AU A RC 5.00 12.00
245 Tank Williams AU E RC 5.00 12.00
246 Jerramy Stevens AU A RC 6.00 15.00
247 Jason McAddley AU C RC 5.00 12.00
248 Ken Simonton AU D RC 4.00 10.00
249 Chester Taylor AU F RC 6.00 15.00
250 Brandon Doman AU C RC 4.00 10.00

2002 Bowman Chrome Refractors

*VETS 1-110: 1.5X TO 4X BASIC CARDS
*ROOKIES 111-220: 1X TO 2.5X
REFRACTOR/500 ODDS 1:6
STATED PRINT RUN 500 SER.#'d SETS

2002 Bowman Chrome Refractors Gold

*VETS 1-110: 5X TO 12X BASIC CARDS
*ROOKIES 111-220: 2.5X TO 6X
REFRACTOR GOLD/50 ODDS 1:60
STATED PRINT RUN 50 SER.#'d SETS

2002 Bowman Chrome Xfractors

*VETS 1-110: 2.5X TO 6X BASIC CARDS
*ROOKIES 111-220: 1.5X TO 4X
1-220 XFRACTOR/250 ODDS 1:12
1-220 PRINT RUN 250 SER.#'d SETS
*ROOKIE AU 221-250: .8X TO 2X
221-250 ROOKIE AU/250 ODDS 1:391
230 Ed Reed AU 75.00 150.00

2002 Bowman Chrome Uncirculated

*ROOKIES: .5X TO 1.2X BASIC CARDS
ANNC'd UNSIGNED PRINT RUN 172
UNPRICED ANNC'd AUTO PRINT RUN 10

2003 Bowman Chrome

Released in November of 2003, this set consists of 246 cards, including 110 veterans and 136 rookies. Rookies 221-246 feature authentic player autographs and are seeded as follows: Group A: 1:3897, Group B: 1:333, Group C: 1:195, Group D: 1:28, and Group E: 1:99. In addition, Gold Refractor Rookie Autographs are seeded 1:542. Please note that card #180 (Rex Grossman) can be found signed and unsigned. Taylor Jacobs, Bryant Johnson, Talman Gardner, and LaBrandon Toefield were issued as exchange cards in packs with an expiration date of 11/30/2005. Boxes contained 18 packs of 4 cards. SRP was $4.00.

COMP.SET w/o SP's (110) 10.00 25.00
COMP.SET w/o AU's (220) 50.00 100.00
ROOKIE AU GROUP A ODDS 1:3897
ROOKIE AU GROUP B ODDS 1:333
ROOKIE AU GROUP C ODDS 1:195
ROOKIE AU GROUP D ODDS 1:28
ROOKIE AU GROUP E ODDS 1:99
1 Brett Favre .75 2.00
2 Jeremy Shockey .25 .60
3 Fred Taylor .25 .60
4 Rich Gannon .30 .75
5 Joey Galloway .30 .75
6 Ray Lewis .40 1.00
7 Jeff Blake .30 .75
8 Stacey Mack .25 .60
9 Matt Hasselbeck .25 .60
10 Laveranues Coles .25 .60
11 Brad Johnson .30 .75
12 Tommy Maddox .25 .60
13 Curtis Martin .30 .75
14 Tom Brady 1.50 4.00
15 Ricky Williams .30 .75
16 Stephen Davis .25 .60
17 Chad Johnson .25 .60
18 Joey Harrington .25 .60
19 Tony Gonzalez .30 .75
20 Peerless Price .25 .60
21 LaDainian Tomlinson .40 1.00
22 James Thrash .25 .60
23 Charlie Garner .30 .75
24 Eddie George .30 .75
25 Terrell Owens .30 .75
26 Brian Urlacher .40 1.00
27 Eric Moulds .25 .60
28 Emmitt Smith .60 1.50
29 Tim Couch .25 .60
30 Jake Plummer .25 .60
31 Marvin Harrison .30 .75
32 Chris Chambers .25 .60
33 Tiki Barber .30 .75
34 Kurt Warner .30 .75
35 Michael Pittman .25 .60
36 Kevin Dyson .25 .60
37 Clinton Portis .25 .60
38 Peyton Manning 1.00 2.50
39 Travis Taylor .25 .60
40 Jeff Garcia .25 .60
41 Patrick Ramsey .30 .75
42 Shaun Alexander .25 .60
43 Joe Horn .25 .60
44 Daunte Culpepper .30 .75
45 Travis Henry .25 .60
46 Brian Finneran .25 .60
47 William Green .25 .60
48 Kordell Stewart .25 .60
49 Reggie Wayne .30 .75
50 Priest Holmes .25 .60
51 Jay Fiedler .25 .60
52 Corey Dillon .25 .60
53 Jamal Lewis .30 .75
54 Mark Brunell .30 .75
55 Santana Moss .30 .75
56 Duce Staley .25 .60
57 Torry Holt .30 .75
58 Rod Gardner .25 .60
59 Kerry Collins .25 .60
60 Randy Moss .30 .75
61 Jerry Porter .25 .60
62 Plaxico Burress .25 .60
63 Steve McNair .30 .75
64 Muhsin Muhammad .25 .60
65 Drew Bledsoe .30 .75
66 T.J. Duckett .25 .60
67 Ahman Green .30 .75
68 Rod Smith .30 .75
69 Jimmy Smith .30 .75
70 Trent Green .25 .60
71 Tim Brown .40 1.00
72 Jerome Bettis .40 1.00
73 Isaac Bruce .40 1.00
74 Derrick Mason .25 .60
75 Donovan McNabb .30 .75
76 Deuce McAllister .30 .75
77 Zach Thomas .30 .75
78 Garrison Hearst .25 .60
79 Koren Robinson .30 .75
80 Marshall Faulk .30 .75
81 Keyshawn Johnson .40 1.00
82 Jake Delhomme .25 .60
83 Marty Booker .25 .60
84 James Stewart .25 .60
85 Corey Bradford .25 .60
86 Derrius Thompson .25 .60
87 Edgerrin James .30 .75
88 Darrell Jackson .30 .75
89 Hines Ward .30 .75
90 David Boston .25 .60
91 Curtis Conway .25 .60
92 David Patten .25 .60
93 Michael Bennett .25 .60
94 Todd Pinkston .25 .60
95 Jerry Rice .75 2.00
96 Jon Kitna .25 .60
97 Ed McCaffrey .30 .75
98 Donald Driver .30 .75
99 Anthony Thomas .30 .75
100 Michael Vick .30 .75
101 Terry Glenn .30 .75
102 Quincy Morgan .25 .60
103 David Carr .25 .60
104 Troy Brown .25 .60
105 Aaron Brooks .25 .60
106 Amani Toomer .25 .60
107 Drew Brees .40 1.00
108 Chad Hutchinson .25 .60
109 Warrick Dunn .25 .60
110 Chad Pennington .25 .60
111 Brian St.Pierre RC 1.25 3.00
112 Keenan Howry RC 1.25 3.00
113 Sultan McCullough RC 1.25 3.00
114 Terence Newman RC 2.00 5.00
115 Kelley Washington RC 1.25 3.00
116 Musa Smith RC 1.25 3.00
117 Victor Hobson RC 1.25 3.00
118 Travis Anglin RC 1.25 3.00
119 Artose Pinner RC 1.25 3.00
120 Rashean Mathis RC 1.25 3.00
121 DeWayne White RC 1.25 3.00
122 Kevin Curtis RC 1.25 3.00
123 Tyrone Calico RC 1.25 3.00
124 Ricky Manning RC 1.50 4.00
125 Cory Redding RC 1.50 4.00
126 Dallas Clark RC 2.00 5.00
127 Marcus Trufant RC 1.50 4.00
128 Terrell Suggs RC 1.50 4.00
129 Aaron Walker RC 1.50 4.00
130 Calvin Pace RC 1.25 3.00
131 Ken Dorsey RC 1.50 4.00
132 Earnest Graham RC 2.00 5.00
133 Cecil Sapp RC 1.25 3.00
134 William Joseph RC 1.25 3.00
135 Anquan Boldin RC 2.00 5.00
136 Justin Griffith RC 1.50 4.00
137 Teyo Johnson RC 1.50 4.00
138 Chris Crocker RC 1.50 4.00
139 Doug Gabriel RC 1.50 4.00
140 Terry Pierce RC 1.25 3.00
141 Bradie James RC 2.00 5.00
142 Terrence Edwards RC 1.25 3.00
143 E.J. Henderson RC 1.50 4.00
144 Tony Romo RC 25.00 50.00
145 DeWayne Robertson RC 1.50 4.00
146 Dwone Hicks RC 1.25 3.00
147 Carl Ford RC 1.25 3.00
148 Ken Hamlin RC 2.00 5.00
149 Adrian Madise RC 1.25 3.00
150 Siddeeq Shabazz RC 1.25 3.00
151 Dave Ragone RC 1.25 3.00
152 Mike Seidman RC 1.25 3.00
153 DeAndrew Rubin RC 1.25 3.00
154 Mike Pinkard RC 1.25 3.00
155 Nate Burleson RC 1.50 4.00
156 Angelo Crowell RC 1.50 4.00
157 J.R. Tolver RC 1.50 4.00
158 Osi Umenyiora RC 2.50 6.00
159 Nick Barnett RC 2.00 5.00
160 Brandon Drumm RC 1.25 3.00
161 Rien Long RC 1.25 3.00
162 Zuriel Smith RC 1.25 3.00
163 Onterrio Smith RC 1.25 3.00
164 Kenny Peterson RC 1.50 4.00
165 Chaun Thompson RC 1.25 3.00
166 Terrence Holt RC 1.50 4.00
167 Ovie Mughelli RC 1.50 4.00
168 Bethel Johnson RC 1.25 3.00
169 Avon Cobourne RC 1.25 3.00
170 Andre Woolfolk RC 1.25 3.00
171 George Wrighster RC 1.25 3.00
172 Justin Fargas RC 2.00 5.00
173 Marquel Blackwell RC 1.25 3.00
174 Walter Young RC 1.25 3.00
175 Kawika Mitchell RC 2.00 5.00
176 Drayton Florence RC 2.00 5.00
177 Jeremi Johnson RC 1.25 3.00
178 Lee Suggs RC 1.25 3.00
179 David Kircus RC 1.50 4.00
180 Rex Grossman RC 1.50 4.00
180AU Rex Grossman AU B 12.00 30.00
181 Jon Olinger RC 1.25 3.00
182 Dan Curley RC 1.25 3.00
183 Andrew Pinnock RC 1.50 4.00
184 Kirk Farmer RC 1.50 4.00
185 Charles Rogers RC 1.50 4.00
186 Alonzo Jackson RC 1.25 3.00
187 Trent Smith RC 1.50 4.00
188 Seneca Wallace RC 1.50 4.00
189 Shane Walton RC 1.25 3.00
190 Chris Brown RC 1.25 3.00
191 Dahrran Diedrick RC 1.25 3.00
192 Juston Wood RC 1.25 3.00
193 Mike Doss RC 2.00 5.00
194 Visanthe Shiancoe RC 2.00 5.00
195 Andre Johnson RC 3.00 8.00
196 Dennis Weathersby RC 1.25 3.00
197 Chris Davis RC 1.50 4.00
198 LaTarence Dunbar RC 1.25 3.00
199 Eugene Wilson RC 2.00 5.00
200 Ryan Hoag RC 1.25 3.00
201 Chris Simms RC 1.25 3.00
202 Curt Anes RC 1.25 3.00
203 Taco Wallace RC 1.25 3.00
204 David Tyree RC 1.50 4.00
205 Nate Hybl RC 1.50 4.00
206 Willis McGahee RC 1.50 4.00
207 Casey Moore RC 1.25 3.00
208 Pisa Tinoisamoa RC 2.00 5.00
209 Willie Ponder RC 1.25 3.00
210 Donald Lee RC 1.50 4.00
211 Nnamdi Asomugha RC 2.00 5.00
212 Sammy Davis RC 1.50 4.00
213 Joffrey Reynolds RC 1.25 3.00
214 Eddie Moore RC 1.25 3.00
215 Tony Hollings RC 1.50 4.00
216 Nick Maddox RC 1.25 3.00
217 Kevin Walter RC 3.00 8.00
218 Dan Klecko RC 1.50 4.00
219 Antwan Peek RC 1.25 3.00
220 Tyler Brayton RC 1.50 4.00
221 Byron Leftwich AU B RC 6.00 15.00
222 Bobby Wade AU D RC 5.00 12.00
223 Jerome McDougle AU C RC 5.00 12.00
224 Michael Haynes AU D RC 4.00 10.00
225 Taylor Jacobs AU C RC 5.00 12.00
226 Shaun McDonald AU D RC 5.00 12.00
228 Talman Gardner AU D RC 4.00 10.00
229 Domanick Davis AU D RC 5.00 12.00
230 Jason Witten AU D RC 30.00 60.00
231 Kyle Boller AU B RC 5.00 12.00
232 L.J. Smith AU C RC 8.00 20.00
233 Boss Bailey AU C RC 6.00 15.00
234 Billy McMullen AU D RC 4.00 10.00
235 Larry Johnson AU B RC 12.00 30.00
236 Kareem Kelly AU E RC 4.00 10.00
237 Carson Palmer AU A RC 25.00 60.00
238 Quentin Griffin AU D RC 5.00 12.00
239 Kevin Garrett AU E RC 4.00 10.00
240 Charles Tillman AU E RC 25.00 50.00
241 Arnaz Battle AU D RC 5.00 12.00
242 Brooks Bollinger AU E RC 5.00 12.00
243 LaBrandon Toefield AU D RC 4.00 10.00
244 Sam Aiken AU D RC 5.00 12.00
245 Justin Gage AU D RC 5.00 12.00
246 Gibran Hamdan AU D RC 4.00 10.00

2003 Bowman Chrome Refractors

*VETS 1-110: 2X TO 5X BASIC CARDS
*ROOKIES 111-220: .8X TO 2X
REFRACTOR/500 ODDS 1:7
STATED PRINT RUN 500 SER.#'d SETS
144 Tony Romo 60.00 100.00

2003 Bowman Chrome Uncirculated Blue Refractors

ONE EXCH CARD PER BOX
STATED PRINT RUN 235 SETS
144 Tony Romo 60.00 100.00

2003 Bowman Chrome Gold Refractors

*VETS 1-110: 6X TO 15X BASIC CARDS
*ROOKIES 111-220: 2.5X TO 6X
1-220 STATED ODDS 1:67
*ROOKIE AUs 221-246: 1.5X TO 4X
221-246 STATED ODDS 1:542
STATED PRINT RUN 50 SER.#'d SETS
144 Tony Romo 125.00 200.00
230 Jason Witten AU 100.00 200.00
235 Larry Johnson AU 15.00 40.00
237 Carson Palmer AU 60.00 120.00

2003 Bowman Chrome Red Refractors

*ROOKIES 111-220: 1.2X TO 3X
OVERALL ODDS ONE PER BOX
111-220 PRINT RUN 235 SER.#'d SETS
221-246 UNPRICED AU PRINT RUN 10
#'d/10 NOT PRICED DUE TO SCARCITY
144 Tony Romo 60.00 100.00

2003 Bowman Chrome Xfractors

*VETS 1-110: 2.5X TO 6X BASIC CARDS
*ROOKIES 111-220: 1X TO 2.5X
XFRACTOR/250 STATED ODDS 1:13
STATED PRINT RUN 250 SER.#'d SETS
144 Tony Romo 60.00 100.00

2004 Bowman Chrome

Bowman Chrome initially released in early December 2004. The base set consists of 245-cards including 110-rookies (issued one per pack) and 25-autographed rookie cards. Six of the signed rookies were serial numbered to just 199-copies. Hobby boxes contained 18-packs of 4-cards and carried an S.R.P. of $4 per pack. Six parallel sets can be found seeded in hobby and retail packs.

COMP.SET w/o SP's (220) 75.00 150.00
COMP.SET w/o RC's (110) 12.50 30.00
ROOKIE AU/199 GROUP A ODDS 1:603
ROOKIE AU GROUP B ODDS 1:1293
ROOKIE AU GROUP C ODDS 1:359
ROOKIE AU GROUP D ODDS 1:21
1 Brett Favre .75 2.00
2 Jay Fiedler .25 .60
3 Andre Davis .25 .60
4 Travis Henry .25 .60
5 Jimmy Smith .30 .75
6 Santana Moss .30 .75
7 Correll Buckhalter .25 .60
8 Randy Moss .30 .75
9 Edgerrin James .30 .75
10 Marc Bulger .25 .60
11 Derrick Mason .25 .60
12 Mark Brunell .30 .75
13 Donte Stallworth .25 .60
14 Deion Branch .25 .60
15 Jake Plummer .25 .60
16 Steve Smith .40 1.00
17 Jon Kitna .25 .60
18 Andre Johnson .30 .75
19 A.J. Feeley .25 .60
20 Drew Bledsoe .30 .75
21 Antonio Bryant .30 .75
22 Reggie Wayne .30 .75
23 Thomas Jones .25 .60
24 Alge Crumpler .30 .75
25 Anquan Boldin .25 .60
26 Tim Rattay .25 .60
27 Charlie Garner .30 .75
28 James Thrash .25 .60
29 Koren Robinson .25 .60
30 Terrell Owens .30 .75
31 Amani Toomer .25 .60
32 Kelly Campbell .25 .60
33 Patrick Ramsey .30 .75
34 Plaxico Burress .25 .60
35 Chad Pennington .25 .60
36 Fred Taylor .25 .60
37 Domanick Davis .25 .60
38 DeShaun Foster .30 .75
39 T.J. Duckett .25 .60
40 Ahman Green .30 .75
41 Lee Suggs .30 .75
42 Tony Gonzalez .30 .75
43 Rich Gannon .30 .75
44 Kevan Barlow .25 .60
45 Torry Holt .30 .75
46 Aaron Brooks .25 .60
47 Tyrone Calico .30 .75
48 Keenan McCardell .25 .60
49 Hines Ward .30 .75
50 LaDainian Tomlinson .40 1.00
51 Dante Hall .25 .60
52 Marcus Pollard .25 .60
53 Corey Dillon .25 .60
54 Justin McCareins .25 .60
55 Stephen Davis .25 .60
56 Jeff Garcia .25 .60
57 Ashley Lelie .25 .60
58 Javon Walker .25 .60
59 Kyle Boller .25 .60
60 Chad Johnson .25 .60
61 Anthony Thomas .30 .75
62 Byron Leftwich .25 .60
63 David Boston .25 .60
64 Onterrio Smith .25 .60
65 Deuce McAllister .30 .75
66 Antwaan Randle El .25 .60
67 Justin Fargas .30 .75
68 Laveranues Coles .25 .60
69 Quincy Morgan .25 .60
70 Priest Holmes .25 .60
71 Robert Ferguson .25 .60
72 Charles Rogers .25 .60
73 Drew Brees .40 1.00
74 Matt Hasselbeck .25 .60
75 Peyton Manning 1.00 2.50
76 Rudi Johnson .25 .60
77 Jake Delhomme .25 .60
78 Tiki Barber .30 .75
79 Brad Johnson .30 .75
80 Steve McNair .30 .75
81 Willis McGahee .25 .60
82 Josh McCown .30 .75
83 Garrison Hearst .25 .60
84 Quincy Carter .25 .60
85 Ricky Williams .30 .75
86 Trent Green .25 .60
87 Curtis Martin .30 .75
88 Jerry Porter .25 .60
89 Brian Westbrook .25 .60
90 Clinton Portis .25 .60
91 Eric Moulds .25 .60
92 Marcel Shipp .25 .60
93 Joey Harrington .25 .60
94 David Carr .25 .60
95 Marvin Harrison .30 .75
96 Joe Horn .25 .60
97 Chris Chambers .25 .60
98 Darrell Jackson .30 .75
99 Eddie George .30 .75
100 Donovan McNabb .30 .75
101 Marshall Faulk .30 .75
102 Rex Grossman .25 .60
103 Tai Streets .25 .60
104 Jeremy Shockey .25 .60
105 Jamal Lewis .30 .75
106 Tom Brady 1.50 4.00
107 Shaun Alexander .25 .60
108 Carson Palmer .30 .75
109 Daunte Culpepper .30 .75
110 Michael Vick .30 .75
111 Roethlis AU/199 RC 150.00 250.00
112 Tommie Harris RC 1.25 3.00
113 Thomas Tapeh RC 1.25 3.00
114 Matt Schaub RC 1.00 2.50
115 Jonathan Smith RC 1.00 2.50
116 Ricardo Colclough RC 1.00 2.50
117 Jeff Dugan RC 1.00 2.50
118 Larry Fitzgerald RC 4.00 10.00
119 Gibril Wilson RC 1.50 4.00
120 Sean Taylor RC 6.00 15.00
121 Marquise Hill RC 1.00 2.50
122 Cedric Cobbs RC 1.00 2.50
123 Rich Gardner RC 1.25 3.00
124 Chris Cooley RC 1.25 3.00
125 Ben Troupe RC 1.00 2.50
126 Antwan Odom RC 1.00 2.50
127 Stuart Schweigert RC 1.25 3.00
128 Derek Abney RC 1.00 2.50
129 Keary Colbert RC 1.00 2.50
130 Jeris McIntyre RC 1.00 2.50
131 Matt Kranchick RC 1.25 3.00
132 Rodney Leisle RC 1.00 2.50
133 Vince Wilfork RC 1.50 4.00
134 Darnell Dockett RC 1.50 4.00
135 Jeremy LeSueur RC 1.00 2.50
136 Gilbert Gardner RC 1.00 2.50
137 Amon Gordon RC 1.00 2.50
138 Darius Watts RC 1.00 2.50
139 Junior Siavii RC 1.00 2.50
140 Igor Olshansky RC 1.25 3.00
141 Mewelde Moore RC 1.25 3.00
142 Nathan Vasher RC 1.50 4.00
143 Randy Starks RC 1.00 2.50
144 Isaac Sopoaga RC 1.00 2.50
145 Drew Henson RC 1.00 2.50
146 Erik Coleman RC 1.25 3.00
147 Robert Kent RC 1.00 2.50
148 Jammal Lord RC 1.00 2.50
149 Richard Seigler RC 1.00 2.50
150 Niko Koutouvides RC 1.00 2.50
151 Brandon Miree RC 1.00 2.50
152 Dunta Robinson RC 1.00 2.50
153 Courtney Anderson RC 1.00 2.50
154 Bruce Perry RC 1.00 2.50
155 Shaun Phillips RC 1.25 3.00
156 Greg Jones RC 1.00 2.50
157 Tank Johnson RC 1.00 2.50
158 Dwan Edwards RC 1.00 2.50
159 Julius Jones RC 1.00 2.50
160 Chad Lavalais RC 1.00 2.50
161 Tim Anderson RC 1.25 3.00
162 Jarrett Payton RC 1.25 3.00
163 Matt Ware RC 1.50 4.00
164 DeAngelo Hall RC 1.50 4.00
165 Ben Hartsock RC 1.00 2.50
166 Keith Smith RC 1.00 2.50
167 Michael Jenkins RC 1.00 2.50
168 Quincy Wilson RC 1.00 2.50
169 Dontarrious Thomas RC 1.25 3.00
170 Tony Hargrove RC 1.00 2.50
171 Ben Watson RC 1.25 3.00
172 Triandos Luke RC 1.00 2.50
173 Kellen Winslow RC 1.00 2.50
174 Patrick Crayton RC 1.50 4.00
175 Devard Darling RC 1.00 2.50
176 Shawntae Spencer RC 1.00 2.50
177 Will Smith RC 1.25 3.00
178 Darrion Scott RC 1.25 3.00
179 Wes Welker RC 4.00 10.00
180 Ryan Dinwiddie RC 1.00 2.50
181 Rod Davis RC 1.00 2.50
182 Casey Clausen RC 1.25 3.00
183 Clarence Moore RC 1.00 2.50
184 D.J. Hackett RC 1.00 2.50
185 Devery Henderson RC 1.00 2.50
186 Sean Jones RC 1.00 2.50
187 Bruce Thornton RC 1.00 2.50
188 Tatum Bell RC 1.00 2.50
189 Tim Euhus RC 1.00 2.50
190 John Standeford RC 1.00 2.50
191 Reggie Torbor RC 1.00 2.50
192 Rashaun Woods RC 1.00 2.50
193 Jason Shivers RC 1.00 2.50
194 Ahmad Carroll RC 1.00 2.50
195 Keyaron Fox RC 1.25 3.00
196 Von Hutchins RC 1.00 2.50
197 Marcus Tubbs RC 1.00 2.50
198 Daryl Smith RC 1.00 2.50
199 Robert Gallery RC 1.25 3.00
200 Marquis Cooper RC 1.00 2.50
201 Bernard Berrian RC 1.00 2.50
202 Derrick Strait RC 1.00 2.50
203 Travis LaBoy RC 1.25 3.00
204 Caleb Miller RC 1.00 2.50
205 Michael Clayton RC 1.25 3.00
206 Will Poole RC 1.50 4.00
207 Derrick Hamilton RC 1.00 2.50
208 Glenn Earl RC 1.00 2.50
209 Donnell Washington RC 1.25 3.00
210 Nate Lawrie RC 1.00 2.50
211 Keiwan Ratliff RC 1.00 2.50
212 Luke McCown RC 1.00 2.50
213 Joey Thomas RC 1.00 2.50
214 Shawn Andrews RC 1.25 3.00
215 Derrick Ward RC 1.50 4.00
216 Reggie Williams RC 1.00 2.50
217 Rod Rutherford RC 1.00 2.50
218 Michael Gaines RC 1.00 2.50
219 Will Allen RC 1.25 3.00
220 J.P. Losman RC 1.00 2.50
221 Roy Williams AU/199 RC 4.00 10.00
222 Kevin Jones AU/199 RC 10.00 25.00
223 Philip Rivers AU/199 RC 100.00 200.00
224 Steven Jackson AU/199 RC 4.00 10.00
225 Eli Manning AU/199 RC 125.00 250.00
226 Cody Pickett AU D RC 4.00 10.00
227 P.K. Sam AU D RC 4.00 10.00
228 Maurice Mann AU D RC 4.00 10.00
229 Andy Hall AU D RC 4.00 10.00
230 Chris Perry AU D RC 4.00 10.00
231 Ernest Wilford AU C RC 5.00 12.00
232 Kenechi Udeze AU D RC 5.00 12.00
233 Michael Boulware AU D RC 6.00 15.00
234 B.J. Symons AU D RC 4.00 10.00
235 Jared Lorenzen AU D RC 5.00 12.00
236 Matt Mauck AU D RC 4.00 10.00
237 Carlos Francis AU D RC 4.00 10.00
238 Michael Turner AU D RC 4.00 10.00
239 Lee Evans AU B RC 10.00 25.00
240 Jerricho Cotchery AU D RC 5.00 12.00
241 John Navarre AU D RC 4.00 10.00
242 Jonathan Vilma AU D RC 4.00 10.00
243 Josh Harris AU D RC 4.00 10.00
244 Jeff Smoker AU C RC 5.00 12.00
245 Jamaar Taylor AU D RC 4.00 10.00

2004 Bowman Chrome Blue Refractors

UNPRICED BLUE REF.PRINT RUN 1 SET

2004 Bowman Chrome Gold Refractors

*STARS: 8X TO 20X BASE CARD HI
*ROOKIES: 3X TO 8X BASE CARD HI
1-220 STATED ODDS 1:59
*ROOKIE AUTOS: 1.2X TO 3X BASE CARD HI
ROOKIE AUTO STATED ODDS 1:646
STATED PRINT RUN 50 SER.#'d SETS
111 Ben Roethlisberger AU 300.00 500.00
223 Philip Rivers AU 200.00 350.00
224 Steven Jackson AU 15.00 40.00
225 Eli Manning AU 350.00 500.00

2004 Bowman Chrome Red Refractors

*ROOKIES 112-220: 2X TO 5X
112-220 PRINT RUN 210 SER.#'d SETS
UNPRICED 111/221-245 AU PRINT RUN 10
ONE RED REFRACTOR PER HOBBY BOX

2004 Bowman Chrome Refractors

*STARS: 2X TO 5X BASE CARD HI
*ROOKIES: .8X TO 2X BASE CARD HI
STATED ODDS 1:6
STATED PRINT RUN 500 SER.#'d SETS

2004 Bowman Chrome Uncirculated White Refractors

*ROOKIES 112-220: 1.5X TO 4X
STATED PRINT RUN 210 SETS

2004 Bowman Chrome Xfractors

*STARS: 2.5X TO 6X BASE CARD HI
*ROOKIES: 1.2X TO 3X BASE CARD HI
STATED ODDS 1:12
STATED PRINT RUN 250 SER.#'d SETS

2004 Bowman Chrome Super Bowl XXXIX Unsigned Draft Picks

This set was released in factory set form by Topps in a clear plastic box at the Super Bowl XXXIX Card Show in Jacksonville. The cards are nearly identical to the basic issue Bowman Chrome signed Rookie Cards except for the obvious lack of autographs and lack of the Topps Authenticity hologram on the backs. Note also that the in-pack signed cards also have a ghosted out box on the fronts in which the players affixed their signatures.

COMPLETE SET (26) 75.00 150.00
111 Ben Roethlisberger 25.00 50.00
221 Roy Williams WR 2.00 5.00
222 Kevin Jones 2.50 6.00
223 Philip Rivers 6.00 15.00
224 Steven Jackson 3.00 8.00
225 Eli Manning 25.00 50.00
226 Cody Pickett 2.00 5.00
227 P.K. Sam 2.00 5.00
228 Maurice Mann 2.00 5.00
229 Andy Hall 2.00 5.00
230 Chris Perry 2.00 5.00
231 Ernest Wilford 2.50 6.00
232 Kenechi Udeze 2.50 6.00
233 Michael Boulware 3.00 8.00
234 B.J. Symons 2.00 5.00
235 Jared Lorenzen 2.50 6.00
236 Matt Mauck 2.00 5.00
237 Carlos Francis 2.00 5.00
238 Michael Turner 2.00 5.00
239 Lee Evans 3.00 8.00
240 Jerricho Cotchery 2.50 6.00
241 John Navarre 2.00 5.00
242 Jonathan Vilma 2.50 6.00
243 Josh Harris 2.00 5.00
244 Jeff Smoker 2.50 6.00
245 Jamaar Taylor 2.00 5.00

2005 Bowman Chrome

This 259-card set was released in January, 2006. The set was issued in the hobby in four-card packs wirth an $4 SRP which came 18 packs to a box. Cards numbered 1-109 feature veterans while cards 110-259 feature rookies. Cards numbered 221-259 were signed by the player and a few players (221-227) signed fewer cards (199 serial numbered sets). Those rookies with 199 serial numbered signatures were inserted at a stated rate of one in 685 hobby and one in 1348 retail packs. The other signed rookies were inserted at different rates depending on what autograph group they belonged to.

COMP.SET w/o AU's (220) 40.00 100.00
COMP.SET w/o RC's (110) 12.50 30.00
ROOK.AU GROUP A ODDS 1:381 H, 1:1011 R
ROOK.AU GROUP B ODDS 1:156 H, 1:449 R
ROOK.AU GROUP C ODDS 1:318 H, 1:899 R
ROOK.AU GROUP D ODDS 1:296 H, 1:899 R
ROOK.AU GROUP E ODDS 1:281 H, 1:809 R
ROOK.AU GROUP F ODDS 1:132 H, 404 R
ROOK.AU GROUP G ODDS 1:39 H, 1:108 R
ROOKIE AU/199 ODDS 1:685 H, 1:1348 R
UNPRICED PRINT.PLATE 1/1 ODDS 1:975 H
1 Peyton Manning 1.00 2.50
2 Priest Holmes .25 .60
3 Anquan Boldin .25 .60
4 Michael Vick .30 .75
5 Drew Brees .40 1.00
6 Terrell Owens .30 .75
7 Curtis Martin .30 .75
8 Tom Brady 1.50 4.00
9 Maurice Carthon CO .25 .60
10 Brett Favre .75 2.00
11 Marshall Faulk .30 .75
12 Corey Dillon .25 .60
13 Julius Jones .25 .60
14 Jamal Lewis .30 .75
15 Keary Colbert .25 .60
16 Joey Harrington .25 .60
17 Domanick Davis .25 .60
18 Eli Manning .60 1.50
19 Brad Childress CO .30 .75
20 Steve McNair .30 .75
21 Plaxico Burress .25 .60
22 Chad Pennington .25 .60
23 Patrick Ramsey .30 .75
24 Brian Griese .25 .60
25 Matt Hasselbeck .25 .60
26 Chris Chambers .25 .60
27 Marc Bulger .25 .60
28 Jake Delhomme .25 .60
29 Shaun Alexander .25 .60
30 Laveranues Coles .25 .60
31 A.J. Feeley .25 .60
32 Ashley Lelie .25 .60
33 Deuce McAllister .30 .75
34 Chris Brown .25 .60
35 Nate Burleson .25 .60
36 Darrell Jackson .25 .60
37 Lee Evans .30 .75
38 Jeremy Shockey .25 .60
39 Muhsin Muhammad .25 .60
40 Deion Branch .25 .60
41 DeShaun Foster .30 .75
42 Reggie Wayne .30 .75
43 Michael Jenkins .25 .60
44 Andre Johnson .30 .75
45 Javon Walker .25 .60

46 Joe Horn .25 .60
47 Fred Taylor .25 .60
48 Tony Gonzalez .30 .75
49 J.P. Losman .25 .60
50 Clinton Portis .25 .60
51 Randy Moss .30 .75
52 Jake Plummer .25 .60
53 Tiki Barber .30 .75
54 Edgerrin James .30 .75
55 Jerome Bettis .40 1.00
56 Brandon Lloyd .25 .60
57 Romeo Crennel CO .40 1.00
58 Antonio Gates .40 1.00
59 Donovan McNabb .30 .75
60 Drew Bennett .30 .75
61 David Carr .25 .60
62 Trent Green .25 .60
63 Drew Bledsoe .30 .75
64 Donte Stallworth .25 .60
65 Alge Crumpler .30 .75
66 Jason Witten .30 .75
67 Thomas Jones .25 .60
68 Rex Grossman .25 .60
69 LaMont Jordan .30 .75
70 Kurt Warner .30 .75
71 Ahman Green .30 .75
72 Ben Roethlisberger .60 1.50
73 Mike Nolan CO .30 .75
74 Brian Westbrook .25 .60
75 Carson Palmer .30 .75
76 Stephen Davis .25 .60
77 Jonathan Vilma .25 .60
78 Willis McGahee .25 .60
79 Rudi Johnson .25 .60
80 Jerry Porter .25 .60
81 Charles Rogers .25 .60
82 Dwight Freeney .25 .60
83 Tim Lewis CO .25 .60
84 Aaron Brooks .25 .60
85 Kyle Boller .25 .60
86 Isaac Bruce .40 1.00
87 Chad Johnson .25 .60
88 Kevin Jones .25 .60
89 Eric Moulds .25 .60
90 Sean Taylor .40 1.00
91 Chris Perry .25 .60
92 Kerry Collins .25 .60
93 Steven Jackson .25 .60
94 LaDainian Tomlinson .40 1.00
95 Torry Holt .30 .75
96 Lee Suggs .25 .60
97 Santana Moss .30 .75
98 Hines Ward .30 .75
99 Daunte Culpepper .30 .75
100 Travis Henry .25 .60
101 Ricky Williams .30 .75
102 Roy Williams WR .25 .60
103 Tatum Bell .25 .60
104 Dante Hall .25 .60
105 Larry Fitzgerald .40 1.00
106 Marvin Harrison .30 .75
107 Byron Leftwich .25 .60
108 T.J. Houshmandzadeh .25 .60
109 Michael Clayton .25 .60
110 Ted Cottrell CO .25 .60
111 Carlos Rogers RC 1.25 3.00
112 Kyle Orton RC .75 2.00
113 Marion Barber RC .75 2.00
114 Mark Bradley RC .75 2.00
115 Travis Johnson RC .75 2.00
116 Antrel Rolle RC 1.25 3.00
117 Jason Campbell RC .75 2.00
118 Justin Miller RC .75 2.00
119 J.J. Arrington RC 1.00 2.50
120 Marcus Spears RC .75 2.00
121 Vincent Jackson RC 1.25 3.00
122 Erasmus James RC .75 2.00
123 Heath Miller RC 1.50 4.00
124 Eric Shelton RC .75 2.00
125 Cedric Benson RC .75 2.00
126 Mark Clayton RC .75 2.00
127 Anthony Davis RC .75 2.00
128 Charlie Frye RC .75 2.00
129 Fred Gibson RC .75 2.00
130 Reggie Brown RC .75 2.00
131 Andrew Walter RC .75 2.00
132 Adam Jones RC .75 2.00
133 David Greene RC .75 2.00
134 Maurice Clarett .75 2.00
135 Roscoe Parrish RC .75 2.00
136 Chris Henry RC 1.00 2.50
137 Mike Nugent RC 1.00 2.50
138 Kevin Burnett RC 1.00 2.50
139 Matt Roth RC .75 2.00
140 Barrett Ruud RC 1.00 2.50
141 Kirk Morrison RC 1.25 3.00
142 Brock Berlin RC .75 2.00
143 Bryant McFadden RC 1.00 2.50
144 Scott Starks RC 1.00 2.50
145 Stanford Routt RC 1.00 2.50
146 Oshiomogho Atogwe RC 1.00 2.50
147 Jovan Witherspoon RC .75 2.00
148 Boomer Grigsby RC 1.25 3.00
149 Lance Mitchell RC 1.00 2.50
150 Darryl Blackstock RC .75 2.00
151 Ellis Hobbs RC 1.25 3.00
152 James Kilian RC .75 2.00
153 Willie Parker .30 .75
154 Justin Tuck RC 1.00 2.50
155 Luis Castillo RC 1.00 2.50
156 Paris Warren RC 1.00 2.50
157 Corey Webster RC 1.00 2.50
158 Tab Perry RC .75 2.00
159 Rian Wallace RC 1.00 2.50
160 Joel Dreessen RC 1.00 2.50
161 Khalif Barnes RC .75 2.00
162 David Pollack RC .75 2.00
163 Zach Tuiasosopo RC .75 2.00
164 Ryan Riddle RC .75 2.00
165 Travis Daniels RC 1.00 2.50
166 Eric King RC .75 2.00
167 Justin Green RC 1.25 3.00
168 Manuel White RC 1.00 2.50
169 Jordan Beck RC 1.00 2.50
170 Lofa Tatupu RC 1.00 2.50
171 Will Peoples RC 1.00 2.50
172 Chad Friehauf RC 1.00 2.50
173 Brady Poppinga RC 1.25 3.00
174 Anttaj Hawthorne RC .75 2.00
175 Nick Collins RC 1.25 3.00
176 Craig Ochs RC 1.00 2.50
177 Billy Bajema RC .75 2.00
178 Jon Goldsberry RC 1.25 3.00
179 Jared Newberry RC 1.00 2.50
180 Odell Thurman RC 1.25 3.00
181 Kelvin Hayden RC 1.00 2.50
182 Jamaal Brimmer RC .75 2.00
183 Jonathan Babineaux RC .75 2.00
184 Bo Scaife RC 1.00 2.50
185 Bryan Randall RC 1.00 2.50
186 James Butler RC 1.00 2.50
187 Harry Williams RC 1.00 2.50
188 Leroy Hill RC 1.25 3.00
189 Josh Bullocks RC 1.00 2.50
190 Alfred Fincher RC 1.00 2.50
191 Antonio Perkins RC 1.00 2.50
192 Bobby Purify RC 1.00 2.50
193 Darrent Williams RC 1.25 3.00
194 Darian Durant RC .75 2.00
195 Fred Amey RC .75 2.00
196 Ronald Bartell RC 1.00 2.50
197 Kerry Rhodes RC 1.00 2.50
198 Jerome Carter RC .75 2.00
199 Roddy White RC 1.25 3.00
200 Nehemiah Broughton RC 1.00 2.50
201 Keron Henry RC .75 2.00
202 Jerome Collins RC 1.00 2.50
203 Trent Cole RC 1.25 3.00
204 Alphonso Hodge RC .75 2.00
205 Marviel Underwood RC 1.00 2.50
206 Marlin Jackson RC .75 2.00
207 Madison Hedgecock RC 1.25 3.00
208 Chris Spencer RC 1.25 3.00
209 Vincent Fuller RC 1.00 2.50
210 Marcus Maxwell RC .75 2.00
211 Dustin Fox RC 1.00 2.50
212 Timmy Chang RC .75 2.00
213 Walter Reyes RC .75 2.00
214 Donte Nicholson RC .75 2.00
215 Stanley Wilson RC 1.00 2.50
216 Dan Cody RC .75 2.00
217 Alex Barron RC .75 2.00
218 Taylor Stubblefield RC .75 2.00
219 Shaun Cody RC 1.00 2.50
220 Steve Savoy RC .75 2.00
221 Aaron Rodgers AU/199 RC 450.00 750.00
222 Alex Smith QB AU/199 RC 40.00 80.00
223 Bray.Edwards AU/199 RC 8.00 20.00
224 Cadill.Williams AU/199 RC 8.00 20.00
225 Mike Williams AU/199 10.00 25.00
226 Ronnie Brown AU/199 RC 10.00 25.00
227 T.Williamson AU/199 RC 8.00 20.00
228 Dante Ridgeway AU B RC 4.00 10.00
229 Channing Crowder AU G RC 5.00 12.00
230 Chase Lyman AU E RC 4.00 10.00
231 Courtney Roby AU F RC 4.00 10.00
232 Damien Nash AU G RC 5.00 12.00
233 Dan Orlovsky AU C RC 4.00 10.00
234 Fabian Washington AU B RC 4.00 10.00
235 Shawne Merriman AU B RC 6.00 15.00
236 Cedric Houston AU G RC 6.00 15.00
237 Alex Smith TE AU D RC 4.00 10.00
238 Brandon Jones AU B RC 5.00 12.00
239 Alvin Pearman AU G RC 4.00 10.00
240 Derek Anderson AU C RC 5.00 12.00
241 J.R. Russell AU G RC 4.00 10.00
242 Jerome Mathis AU F RC 6.00 15.00
243 Josh Davis AU A RC 4.00 10.00
244 Kay-Jay Harris AU G RC 4.00 10.00
245 Rasheed Marshall AU F RC 5.00 12.00
246 Matt Jones AU/199 RC 8.00 20.00
247 Chad Owens AU G RC 4.00 10.00
248 Larry Brackins AU A RC 4.00 10.00
249 Matt Cassel AU G RC 4.00 10.00
250 Noah Herron AU G RC 4.00 10.00
251 Roydell Williams AU G RC 5.00 12.00
252 Ryan Fitzpatrick AU F RC 6.00 15.00
253 Derrick Johnson AU E RC 5.00 12.00
254 DeMarcus Ware AU D RC 12.00 30.00
255 Brandon Jacobs AU A RC 8.00 20.00
256 Craig Bragg AU G RC 4.00 10.00
257 Ryan Moats AU G RC 4.00 10.00
258 Stefan LeFors AU G RC 4.00 10.00
259 Frank Gore AU B RC 15.00 30.00

2005 Bowman Chrome Blue Refractors

*VETS: 2.5X TO 6X BASIC CARDS
*ROOKIES: .8X TO 2X BASIC CARDS
BLUE REF/250 ODDS 1:24 H, 1:23 R

2005 Bowman Chrome Bronze Refractors

*VETS: 3X TO 8X BASIC CARDS
*ROOKIES 111-220: 1X TO 2.5X BASIC CARDS
1-220 BRONZE REF/150 ODDS 1:39H, 1:40R
*BRONZE AU/50: .8X TO 2X BASE AU
*BRONZE AU/50: .4X TO 1X BASE AU/199
AU BRONZE REF/50 ODDS 1:630 H, 1:815 R
221 Aaron Rodgers AU 700.00 1000.00
222 Alex Smith QB AU 60.00 120.00

2005 Bowman Chrome Gold Refractors

UNPRICED GOLD REF.1/1 ODDS 1:5904 H/R

2005 Bowman Chrome Red Refractors

*VETS: 2X TO 5X BASIC CARDS
*ROOKIES: .6X TO 1.5X BASIC CARDS
STATED ODDS 1:5

2005 Bowman Chrome Silver Refractors

*VETS: 5X TO 12X BASIC CARDS
*ROOKIE 111-220: 1.5X TO 4X BASIC CARD
1-220 SILVER REF/50 ODDS 1:118H, 1:119R
UNPRICED AU SILVER REF. PRINT RUN 10

2005 Bowman Chrome Uncirculated Green Refractors

*ROOKIES/399: .8X TO 2X BASIC CARDS

2005 Bowman Chrome Uncirculated Green Xfractors

*ROOKIES: 2X TO 5X BASIC CARDS
STATED PRINT RUN 50 SER.#'d SETS

2005 Bowman Chrome Felt Back Flashback

FELT BACK/199 ODDS 1:399 H, 1:533 R
1 Randy Moss 6.00 15.00
2 Michael Vick 6.00 15.00
3 Brett Favre 15.00 40.00
4 LaDainian Tomlinson 8.00 20.00
5 Marvin Harrison 6.00 15.00
6 Curtis Martin 6.00 15.00
7 Peyton Manning 12.00 30.00
8 Tom Brady 30.00 80.00
9 Daunte Culpepper 6.00 15.00
10 Shaun Alexander 5.00 12.00
11 Ronnie Brown 6.00 15.00
12 Alex Smith QB 20.00 50.00
13 Cadillac Williams 5.00 12.00
14 Troy Williamson 5.00 12.00
15 Braylon Edwards 5.00 12.00

2006 Bowman Chrome

This 275-card set was released in January, 2007. The set was issued in four-card packs, with a $4 SRP, which came 18 packs to a box. Cards numbered 1-110 and 221-275 are 2006 rookies. Interestingly, cards numbered 1-55 were inserted in 2006 Bowman packs.

COMPLETE SET (275) 100.00 200.00
COMP.SHORT SET (55) 15.00 40.00
COMP.VET SET (110) 8.00 20.00
1-55 INSERTED IN BOWMAN PACKS
UNPRICED RED REF. SER.#'d TO 5
UNPRICED SUPERFRACT.1/1 ODDS 1:4687
UNPRICED PRINT PLATE/1 ODDS 1:1177
1 Devin Aromashodu RC .50 1.25
2 Daniel Bullocks RC .50 1.25
3 Winston Justice RC .60 1.50
4 Lawrence Vickers RC .60 1.50
5 Bernard Pollard RC .60 1.50
6 Abdul Hodge RC .50 1.25
7 Jovon Bouknight RC .60 1.50
8 Wali Lundy RC .50 1.25
9 Jonathan Orr RC .60 1.50
10 Gerald Riggs RC .60 1.50
11 Chris Gocong RC .60 1.50
12 David Pittman RC .60 1.50
13 Quinn Sypniewski RC .60 1.50
14 Richard Marshall RC .50 1.25
15 Darryl Tapp RC .60 1.50
16 Charles Davis RC .60 1.50
17 Tim Massaquoi RC .60 1.50
18 DeMario Minter RC .60 1.50
19 Hank Baskett RC .50 1.25
20 Andre Hall RC .60 1.50
21 Cody Hodges RC .60 1.50
22 Greg Lee RC .50 1.25
23 Danieal Manning RC .75 2.00
24 Jason Hatcher RC .75 2.00
25 Ben Obomanu RC .60 1.50
26 Dusty Dvoracek RC .75 2.00
27 Domenik Hixon RC .60 1.50
28 Josh Betts RC .60 1.50
29 Marques Colston RC .75 2.00
30 P.J. Pope RC .50 1.25
31 Gabe Watson RC .50 1.25
32 Alan Zemaitis RC .50 1.25
33 Jeff King RC .60 1.50
34 Damien Rhodes RC .60 1.50
35 Orien Harris RC .60 1.50
36 David Anderson RC .60 1.50
37 Garrett Mills RC .60 1.50
38 Anthony Schlegel RC .60 1.50
39 Omar Gaither RC .60 1.50
40 Freddie Keiaho RC .60 1.50
41 J.J. Outlaw RC .60 1.50
42 Tony Scheffler RC .75 2.00
43 Dee Webb RC .60 1.50
44 Drew Olson RC .50 1.25
45 Martin Nance RC .50 1.25
46 Ko Simpson RC .60 1.50
47 Jesse Mahelona RC .60 1.50
48 Owen Daniels RC .75 2.00
49 Delanie Walker RC 1.00 2.50
50 Eric Smith RC .60 1.50
51 Darrell Hackney RC .60 1.50
52 Freddie Roach RC .60 1.50
53 James Anderson RC .50 1.25
54 Anthony Smith RC .75 2.00
55 Gerris Wilkinson RC .50 1.25
56 Tamba Hali RC 1.50 4.00
57 Jerome Harrison RC 1.00 2.50
58 Jason Allen RC 1.25 3.00
59 Brodrick Bunkley RC 1.25 3.00
60 Bobby Carpenter RC 1.00 2.50
61 Johnathan Joseph RC 1.25 3.00
62 Travis Wilson RC 1.00 2.50
63 Reggie McNeal RC 1.00 2.50
64 Haloti Ngata RC 1.25 3.00
65 Manny Lawson RC 1.25 3.00
66 Donte Whitner RC 1.25 3.00
67 Derek Hagan RC 1.25 3.00
68 Devin Hester RC 2.00 5.00
69 Jeremy Bloom RC 1.00 2.50
70 Ashton Youboty RC 1.00 2.50
71 Kamerion Wimbley RC 1.25 3.00
72 Charlie Whitehurst RC 1.00 2.50
73 Darnell Bing RC 1.25 3.00
74 Adam Jennings RC 1.25 3.00
75 Tim Day RC 1.25 3.00
76 Jeff Webb RC 1.25 3.00
77 D.J. Shockley RC 1.25 3.00
78 Marcus Vick RC 1.00 2.50
79 Thomas Howard RC 1.00 2.50
80 Todd Watkins RC 1.00 2.50
81 Davin Joseph RC 1.25 3.00
82 Pat Watkins RC 1.25 3.00
83 Jon Alston RC 1.00 2.50
84 Ernie Sims RC 1.00 2.50
85 D'Qwell Jackson RC 1.00 2.50
86 Corey Bramlet RC 1.25 3.00
87 Antonio Cromartie RC 1.25 3.00
88 A.J. Nicholson RC 1.00 2.50
89 Kevin McMahan RC 1.25 3.00
90 J.D. Runnels RC 1.25 3.00
91 Nate Salley RC 1.25 3.00
92 Matt Shelton RC 1.50 4.00
93 Brett Basanez RC 1.50 4.00
94 Rocky McIntosh RC 1.00 2.50
95 Anthony Mix RC 1.25 3.00
96 Jimmy Williams RC 1.00 2.50
97 Marcus McNeill RC 1.00 2.50
98 DeMeco Ryans RC 1.25 3.00
99 Dwayne Slay RC 1.00 2.50
100 John David Washington RC 1.00 2.50
101 P.J. Daniels RC 1.00 2.50
102 Kelly Jennings RC 1.25 3.00
103 John McCargo RC 1.00 2.50
104 Paul Pinegar RC 1.00 2.50
105 Ray Edwards RC 1.50 4.00
106 Elvis Dumervil RC 1.50 4.00
107 Travis Lulay RC 1.25 3.00
108 Bennie Brazell RC 1.25 3.00
109 Dominique Byrd RC 1.00 2.50
110 Nick Mangold RC 1.25 3.00
111 Plaxico Burress .25 .60
112 Shaun Alexander .25 .60
113 Muhsin Muhammad .25 .60
114 Jake Plummer .25 .60
115 Deuce McAllister .30 .75
116 T.J. Houshmandzadeh .25 .60
117 Carson Palmer .30 .75
118 Willis McGahee .25 .60
119 Terrell Owens .30 .75
120 Fred Taylor .25 .60
121 Dante Hall .25 .60
122 Brad Johnson .30 .75
123 Reggie Wayne .30 .75
124 DeShaun Foster .30 .75
125 Tony Gonzalez .30 .75
126 Javon Walker .30 .75
127 Marc Bulger .25 .60
128 LaDainian Tomlinson .40 1.00
129 Byron Leftwich .25 .60
130 Dwight Freeney .25 .60
131 Kevin Jones .25 .60
132 Hines Ward .30 .75
133 Randy Moss .30 .75
134 Edgerrin James .30 .75
135 Ahman Green .30 .75
136 Steven Jackson .25 .60
137 Ben Roethlisberger .50 1.25
138 Daunte Culpepper .30 .75
139 Santana Moss .30 .75
140 Jonathan Vilma .25 .60
141 Gary Kubiak CO .25 .60
142 Marvin Harrison .30 .75
143 Trent Green .25 .60
144 Chris Chambers .25 .60
145 Chris Brown .25 .60
146 Eli Manning .30 .75
147 Corey Dillon .25 .60
148 Anquan Boldin .25 .60
149 Donovan McNabb .30 .75
150 Drew Bennett .30 .75
151 Jason Witten .30 .75
152 Eric Moulds .25 .60
153 Billy Volek .25 .60
154 Chris Cooley .25 .60
155 Larry Johnson .25 .60
156 Willie Parker .30 .75
157 Cadillac Williams .30 .75
158 Philip Rivers .40 1.00
159 Reuben Droughns .30 .75
160 Joey Galloway .30 .75
161 Lee Evans .30 .75
162 Jamal Lewis .30 .75
163 Brett Favre .75 2.00
164 Clinton Portis .25 .60
165 Rod Marinelli CO .25 .60
166 Tom Brady 1.25 3.00
167 Torry Holt .30 .75
168 Rudi Johnson .25 .60
169 Priest Holmes .25 .60
170 Tatum Bell .25 .60
171 Jeremy Shockey .25 .60
172 Shawne Merriman .30 .75
173 Alge Crumpler .30 .75
174 Marion Barber .30 .75
175 Steve Smith .40 1.00
176 Mike McCarthy CO .25 .60
177 David Carr .25 .60
178 Julius Jones .25 .60
179 Chad Johnson .25 .60
180 Curtis Martin .30 .75
181 Peyton Manning 1.00 2.50
182 LaMont Jordan .30 .75
183 Tiki Barber .30 .75
184 Darrell Jackson .25 .60
185 J.P. Losman .25 .60
186 Drew Brees .30 .75
187 Isaac Bruce .40 1.00
188 Drew Bledsoe .30 .75
189 Roy Williams WR .25 .60
190 Donte Stallworth .25 .60
191 Odell Thurman .25 .60
192 Chester Taylor .30 .75
193 Randy McMichael .25 .60
194 Larry Fitzgerald .30 .75
195 Charlie Frye .30 .75
196 Keary Colbert .25 .60
197 Patrick Ramsey .30 .75
198 Mark Clayton .25 .60
199 Michael Jenkins .25 .60
200 Jake Delhomme .25 .60
201 Aaron Rodgers 1.00 2.50
202 Andre Johnson .30 .75
203 Matt Hasselbeck .25 .60
204 Reggie Brown .25 .60
205 Warrick Dunn .25 .60
206 Kurt Warner .30 .75
207 Antonio Gates .40 1.00
208 Terry Glenn .30 .75
209 Steve McNair .30 .75
210 Alex Smith QB .30 .75
211 Joe Horn .25 .60
212 Domanick Davis .25 .60
213 Deion Branch .25 .60
214 Todd Heap .25 .60
215 Chad Pennington .25 .60
216 Brandon Lloyd .25 .60
217 Rod Smith .30 .75
218 Ronnie Brown .30 .75
219 Braylon Edwards .25 .60
220 Michael Vick .30 .75
221 Vince Young RC 1.00 2.50
222 Jay Cutler RC 1.25 3.00
223 Reggie Bush RC 1.50 4.00
224 Matt Leinart RC 1.00 2.50
225 Vernon Davis RC 1.25 3.00
226 A.J. Hawk RC 1.25 3.00
227 Santonio Holmes RC 1.25 3.00
228 DeAngelo Williams RC 1.25 3.00
229 LenDale White RC 1.00 2.50
230 Sinorice Moss RC 1.00 2.50
231 Joseph Addai RC 1.00 2.50
232 Mike Bell RC 1.00 2.50
233 Will Blackmon RC 1.00 2.50
234 Brian Calhoun RC 1.00 2.50
235 Kellen Clemens RC 1.00 2.50
236 Brodie Croyle RC 1.00 2.50
237 Maurice Drew RC 1.50 4.00
238 Anthony Fasano RC 1.00 2.50
239 D'Brickashaw Ferguson RC 1.00 2.50
240 Quinton Ganther RC 1.00 2.50
241 Bruce Gradkowski RC 1.25 3.00
242 Skyler Green RC 1.00 2.50
243 Chad Greenway RC 1.50 4.00
244 Marques Hagans RC 1.00 2.50
245 Michael Huff RC 1.25 3.00
246 Cedric Humes RC 1.00 2.50
247 Tarvaris Jackson RC 1.00 2.50
248 Omar Jacobs RC 1.00 2.50
249 Greg Jennings RC 1.50 4.00
250 Mathias Kiwanuka RC 1.50 4.00
251 Joe Klopfenstein RC 1.00 2.50
252 Marcedes Lewis RC 1.00 2.50
253 Brandon Marshall RC 2.00 5.00
254 Ingle Martin RC 1.25 3.00
255 Dontrell Moore RC 1.25 3.00
256 Jerious Norwood RC 1.00 2.50
257 Leonard Pope RC 1.50 4.00
258 Willie Reid RC 1.25 3.00
259 Michael Robinson RC 1.00 2.50
260 Brad Smith RC 1.25 3.00
261 Maurice Stovall RC 1.00 2.50
262 David Thomas RC 1.00 2.50
263 Leon Washington RC 1.00 2.50
264 Brandon Williams RC 1.00 2.50
265 Demetrius Williams RC 1.00 2.50
266 Tye Hill RC 1.00 2.50
267 Mike Hass RC 1.00 2.50
268 Jason Avant RC 1.00 2.50
269 Chad Jackson RC 1.00 2.50
270 Laurence Maroney RC 1.00 2.50
271 Anwar Phillips RC 1.25 3.00
272 David Kirtman RC 1.25 3.00
273 Roman Harper RC 1.25 3.00
274 Spencer Havner RC 1.25 3.00
275 Erik Meyer RC 1.00 2.50

2006 Bowman Chrome Blue Refractors

*BLUE REF 1-55: 3X TO 8X BASIC CARDS
1-55 BLUE REF/150 ODDS 1:262 BOWMAN
*BLUE REF 111-220: 4X TO 10X BASIC CARDS
*BLUE REF 56-110/221-275: 1.5X TO 4X
56-275 BLUE REF/150 ODDS 1:44

2006 Bowman Chrome Gold Refractors

*GOLD REF 1-55: 4X TO 10X BASIC CARDS
1-55 GOLD REF/50 ODDS 1:770 BOWMAN
*GOLD REF 111-220: 5X TO 12X BASIC CARDS
*GOLD REF 56-110/221-275: 2X TO 5X
56-275 GOLD REF/50 ODDS 1:133

2006 Bowman Chrome Orange Refractors

*ORANGE 1-55: 5X TO 12X BASIC CARDS
1-55 ORANGE/25 ODDS 1:1525 BOWMAN
*ORANGE 111-220: 8X TO 20X BASIC CARDS
*ORANGE 56-110/221-275: 2.5X TO 6X
56-275 ORANGE/25 ODDS 1:267
221 Vince Young 6.00 15.00
222 Jay Cutler 8.00 20.00

2006 Bowman Chrome Red Refractors

1-55 RED REF. ODDS 1:7600 BOWMAN
56-275 RED REF ODDS 1:1335 CHROME
UNPRICED RED REF PRINT RUN 5

2006 Bowman Chrome Refractors

*REF 1-55: 2X TO 5X BASIC CARDS
1-55 REF/500 ODDS 1:80 BOWMAN
*REF 111-220: 2X TO 5X BASIC CARDS
*REF 56-110-221-275: 1X TO 2.5X
56-275 REFRACTOR ODDS 1:4

2006 Bowman Chrome Superfractors

UNPRICED SUPERFRACTOR 1/1 ODDS 1:4687

2006 Bowman Chrome Uncirculated Rookies

*UNCIRC/519: 1X TO 2.5X BASIC CARDS
UNCIRCULATED/519 ODDS 1:BOX

2006 Bowman Chrome Xfractors

*XFRACTOR 1-55: 2.5X TO 6X BASIC CARDS
XFRACTOR/250 ODDS 1:155 BOWMAN
*XFRACTOR 111-220: 2.5X TO 6X
*XFRACTOR 56-110/221-275: 1.2X TO 3X
56-220 XFRACTOR/250 ODDS 1:27

2006 Bowman Chrome Felt Back Flashback

STATED PRINT RUN 199 SER.#'d SETS
*REF/25: 1X TO 2.5X BASIC INSERTS
1 Santonio Holmes
2 Vince Young 4.00 10.00
3 Matt Leinart 4.00 10.00
4 Reggie Bush 6.00 15.00
5 Vernon Davis 5.00 12.00
6 Joseph Addai 4.00 10.00
7 Omar Jacobs 4.00 10.00
8 Jay Cutler 5.00 12.00
9 D'Brickashaw Ferguson 4.00 10.00
10 Laurence Maroney 4.00 10.00
11 DeAngelo Williams 5.00 12.00
12 Tarvaris Jackson 4.00 10.00
13 LenDale White 4.00 10.00
14 Sinorice Moss 4.00 10.00
15 Chad Jackson 4.00 10.00

2006 Bowman Chrome Rookie Autographs

AUTO/199 STATED ODDS 1:615
AUTO GROUP A ODDS 1:320
AUTO GROUP B ODDS 1:220
AUTO GROUP C ODDS 1:208
AUTO GROUP D ODDS 1:29
UNPRICED PRINT PLATE/1 ODDS 1:5503
UNPRICED RED REF/5 ODDS 1:6550
UNPRICED SUPERFRACT/1 ODDS 1:21,768
UNPRICED UNCIRCULATED PRINT RUN 10
221 Vince Young/199 6.00 15.00
222 Jay Cutler/199 8.00 20.00
223 Reggie Bush/199 10.00 25.00
224 Matt Leinart/199 6.00 15.00
225 Vernon Davis/199 8.00 20.00
226 A.J. Hawk/199 8.00 20.00
227 Santonio Holmes/199 8.00 20.00
228 DeAngelo Williams/199 8.00 20.00
229 LenDale White/199 6.00 15.00
230 Sinorice Moss/199 6.00 15.00
231 Joseph Addai A 4.00 10.00
232 Mike Bell D 3.00 8.00
233 Will Blackmon C 3.00 8.00
234 Brian Calhoun A 4.00 10.00
236 Brodie Croyle A 4.00 10.00
237 Maurice Drew A 10.00 25.00
238 Anthony Fasano D 3.00 8.00
239 D'Brickashaw Ferguson B 3.00 8.00
240 Quinton Ganther D 3.00 8.00
241 Bruce Gradkowski A 5.00 12.00
242 Skyler Green A 4.00 10.00
243 Chad Greenway D 5.00 12.00
244 Marques Hagans D 3.00 8.00
245 Michael Huff A 5.00 12.00
246 Cedric Humes D 3.00 8.00
247 Tarvaris Jackson D 3.00 8.00
248 Omar Jacobs A 4.00 10.00
249 Greg Jennings A 6.00 15.00
250 Mathias Kiwanuka D 5.00 12.00
251 Joe Klopfenstein C 3.00 8.00
252 Marcedes Lewis A 4.00 10.00
253 Brandon Marshall D 10.00 25.00
254 Ingle Martin D 4.00 10.00
256 Jerious Norwood C 3.00 8.00
257 Leonard Pope D 5.00 12.00
258 Willie Reid D 4.00 10.00
259 Michael Robinson B 3.00 8.00
260 Brad Smith A 5.00 12.00
261 Maurice Stovall B 3.00 8.00
262 David Thomas D 3.00 8.00
263 Leon Washington A 4.00 10.00
264 Brandon Williams D 3.00 8.00
265 Demetrius Williams A 4.00 10.00
266 Tye Hill D 3.00 8.00
268 Jason Avant B 3.00 8.00
269 Chad Jackson A 4.00 10.00
270 Laurence Maroney A 4.00 10.00

2006 Bowman Chrome Rookie Autographs Blue Refractors

*BLUE REF/75: .8X TO 2X BASIC AUTO
*BLUE REF/75: .6X TO 1.5X GROUP A AU
*BLUE REF/75: .4X TO 1X BASIC AU/199
BLUE REFRACTOR/75 ODDS 1:349

2006 Bowman Chrome Rookie Autographs Gold Refractors

*GOLD REF/50: 1.2X TO 3X BASIC AUTO
*GOLD REF/50: 1X TO 2.5X GROUP A AU
*GOLD REF/50: .6X TO 1.5X AUTO/199
GOLD REFRACT/50 ODDS 1:527

2006 Bowman Chrome Rookie Autographs Orange Refractors

*ORANGE REF/25: 2X TO 5X BASIC AUTO
*ORANGE REF/25: 1.5X TO 4X GROUP A AU
*ORANGE REF/25: 1X TO 2.5X AUTO/199
ORANGE REF/25 ODDS 1:1075

2007 Bowman Chrome

This 220-card set was released in November, 2007. Cards numbered 1-110 all are 2007 NFL rookies while cards 111-220 feature veterans. Cards numbered 1-55 were inserted earlier in the year in the 2007 Bowman product.

COMPLETE SET (220) 30.00 80.00
COMP.SHORT SET (55) 8.00 20.00
COMP.VET SET (110) 6.00 15.00
1-55 INSERTED IN BOWMAN PACKS
UNPRICED 1-55 RED REF/5 ODDS 1:6884 BOW
UNPR.56-220 RED REF/5 ODDS 1:1628 CHR
UNPR.1-55 SUPERFR/1 ODDS 1:14,227 BOW
UNPR.56-220 SUPERFR/1 ODDS 1:6528 CHR
UNPRICED PRINT.PLATE/1 ODDS 1:1632 CHR
BC1 Kenny Irons RC .40 1.00
BC2 David Clowney RC .40 1.00
BC3 Courtney Taylor RC .40 1.00
BC4 Amobi Okoye RC .50 1.25
BC5 Jamaal Anderson RC .50 1.25
BC6 Adam Carriker RC .40 1.00
BC7 Jarvis Moss RC .40 1.00
BC8 Anthony Spencer RC .50 1.25
BC9 Jon Beason RC .40 1.00
BC10 Darrelle Revis RC .50 1.25
BC11 Aaron Ross RC .40 1.00
BC12 Reggie Nelson RC .40 1.00
BC13 Michael Griffin RC .40 1.00
BC14 Brandon Meriweather RC .50 1.25
BC15 Tyler Palko RC .60 1.50
BC16 Jared Zabransky RC .40 1.00
BC17 Lester Ricard RC .50 1.25
BC18 Darius Walker RC .40 1.00
BC19 Ahmad Bradshaw RC .60 1.50
BC20 Thomas Clayton RC .50 1.25
BC21 Rhema McKnight RC .40 1.00
BC22 Scott Chandler RC .60 1.50
BC23 Matt Spaeth RC .60 1.50
BC24 Ben Patrick RC .50 1.25
BC25 Clark Harris RC .50 1.25
BC26 Martrez Milner RC .40 1.00
BC27 Joe Newton RC .40 1.00
BC28 DeMarcus Tank Tyler RC .40 1.00
BC29 Justin Harrell RC .40 1.00
BC30 LaMarr Woodley RC .75 2.00
BC31 David Harris RC .40 1.00
BC32 Buster Davis RC .50 1.25
BC33 Rufus Alexander RC .40 1.00
BC34 Earl Everett RC .40 1.00
BC35 Stewart Bradley RC .40 1.00
BC36 Prescott Burgess RC .40 1.00
BC37 Daymeion Hughes RC .40 1.00
BC38 Marcus McCauley RC .40 1.00
BC39 Chris Houston RC .40 1.00
BC40 David Irons RC .40 1.00
BC41 Levi Brown RC .40 1.00
BC42 Joe Staley RC .50 1.25
BC43 Steve Breaston RC .40 1.00
BC44 Le'Ron McClain RC .60 1.50
BC45 Joel Filani RC .40 1.00
BC46 Justise Hairston RC .50 1.25
BC47 Nate Ilaoa RC .50 1.25
BC48 Brett Ratliff RC .50 1.25
BC49 Roy Hall RC .50 1.25
BC50 Legedu Naanee RC .50 1.25
BC51 Jarrett Hicks RC .50 1.25
BC52 Sonny Shackelford RC .40 1.00
BC53 Jordan Kent RC .40 1.00
BC54 John Broussard RC .40 1.00
BC55 Chandler Williams RC .40 1.00
BC56 JaMarcus Russell RC 1.00 2.50
BC57 Brady Quinn RC 1.00 2.50
BC58 Drew Stanton RC 1.00 2.50
BC59 Troy Smith RC 1.00 2.50
BC60 Kevin Kolb RC 1.25 3.00
BC61 Trent Edwards RC 1.00 2.50
BC62 John Beck RC 1.00 2.50
BC63 Jordan Palmer RC 1.25 3.00
BC64 Chris Leak RC 1.00 2.50
BC65 Adrian Peterson RC 10.00 25.00
BC66 Marshawn Lynch RC 2.00 5.00
BC67 Brandon Jackson RC 1.00 2.50
BC68 Michael Bush RC 1.00 2.50
BC69 Antonio Pittman RC 1.00 2.50
BC70 Tony Hunt RC 1.00 2.50
BC71 Lorenzo Booker RC 1.25 3.00
BC72 Chris Henry RC 1.00 2.50
BC73 Brian Leonard RC 1.00 2.50
BC74 Garrett Wolfe RC 1.00 2.50
BC75 Calvin Johnson RC 8.00 20.00
BC76 Ted Ginn RC 1.25 3.00
BC77 Dwayne Jarrett RC 1.25 3.00
BC78 Dwayne Bowe RC 1.00 2.50
BC79 Sidney Rice RC 1.25 3.00
BC80 Robert Meachem RC 1.25 3.00
BC81 Anthony Gonzalez RC 1.00 2.50
BC82 Craig Buster Davis RC 1.00 2.50
BC83 Aundrae Allison RC 1.00 2.50
BC84 Chansi Stuckey RC 1.25 3.00
BC85 Alan Branch RC 1.00 2.50
BC86 Steve Smith USC RC 1.00 2.50
BC87 Paul Williams RC 1.00 2.50
BC88 Johnnie Lee Higgins RC 1.00 2.50
BC89 Jason Hill RC 1.00 2.50
BC90 Greg Olsen RC 1.50 4.00
BC91 Yamon Figurs RC 1.00 2.50
BC92 Gaines Adams RC 1.25 3.00
BC93 Patrick Willis RC 1.50 4.00
BC94 Joe Thomas RC 1.50 4.00
BC95 Isaiah Stanback RC 1.00 2.50
BC96 Paul Posluszny RC 1.00 2.50
BC97 Jeff Rowe RC 1.00 2.50
BC98 Zac Taylor RC 1.25 3.00
BC99 Dwayne Wright RC 1.00 2.50
BC100 Kenneth Darby RC 1.00 2.50
BC101 Selvin Young RC 1.00 2.50
BC102 Gary Russell RC 1.25 3.00
BC103 Kolby Smith RC 1.00 2.50
BC104 Dallas Baker RC 1.00 2.50
BC105 Jacoby Jones RC 1.00 2.50
BC106 Ryne Robinson RC 1.25 3.00
BC107 Chris Davis RC 1.00 2.50
BC108 Laron Landry RC 1.50 4.00
BC109 Leon Hall RC 1.00 2.50
BC110 Lawrence Timmons RC 1.50 4.00
BC111 Matt Leinart .25 .60
BC112 Jason Campbell .25 .60
BC113 J.P. Losman .25 .60
BC114 Rex Grossman .25 .60
BC115 Tony Romo .50 1.25
BC116 Brett Favre .75 2.00
BC117 Trent Green .25 .60
BC118 Drew Brees .40 1.00
BC119 Chad Pennington .25 .60
BC120 Ben Roethlisberger .40 1.00
BC121 Alex Smith QB .30 .75
BC122 Marc Bulger .25 .60
BC123 Edgerrin James .30 .75
BC124 Jamal Lewis .30 .75
BC125 DeShaun Foster .30 .75
BC126 Cedric Benson .25 .60
BC127 Rudi Johnson .25 .60
BC128 Dominic Rhodes .25 .60
BC129 Fred Taylor .25 .60
BC130 Larry Johnson .25 .60
BC131 Chester Taylor .25 .60
BC132 Deuce McAllister .30 .75
BC133 Brandon Jacobs .25 .60
BC134 Willie Parker .30 .75
BC135 Frank Gore .30 .75
BC136 Steven Jackson .25 .60
BC137 Clinton Portis .25 .60
BC138 Anquan Boldin .25 .60
BC139 Derrick Mason .25 .60
BC140 Steve Smith .30 .75
BC141 Chad Johnson .25 .60
BC142 Braylon Edwards .25 .60
BC143 Terry Glenn .30 .75
BC144 Mike Furrey .30 .75
BC145 Donald Driver .30 .75
BC146 Andre Johnson .30 .75
BC147 Marvin Harrison .30 .75
BC148 Chris Chambers .25 .60
BC149 Devery Henderson .25 .60
BC150 Marques Colston .25 .60
BC151 Amani Toomer .25 .60
BC152 Laveranues Coles .25 .60
BC153 Donte Stallworth .30 .75
BC154 Hines Ward .30 .75
BC155 Keenan McCardell .25 .60
BC156 Arnaz Battle .25 .60
BC157 Deion Branch .25 .60
BC158 Kevin Curtis .25 .60
BC159 Isaac Bruce .40 1.00
BC160 Santana Moss .30 .75
BC161 Kellen Winslow .25 .60
BC162 Jeremy Shockey .25 .60
BC163 Vernon Davis .25 .60
BC164 Travis Henry .30 .75
BC165 Todd Heap .25 .60
BC166 Matt Schaub .25 .60
BC167 Steve McNair .30 .75
BC168 Jake Delhomme .25 .60
BC169 Carson Palmer .30 .75
BC170 Jay Cutler .25 .60
BC171 Peyton Manning 1.00 2.50
BC172 Tom Brady 1.25 3.00
BC173 Eli Manning .30 .75
BC174 Donovan McNabb .30 .75
BC175 Philip Rivers .40 1.00
BC176 Matt Hasselbeck .25 .60
BC177 Vince Young .25 .60
BC178 Warrick Dunn .25 .60
BC179 Willis McGahee .25 .60
BC180 DeAngelo Williams .25 .60
BC181 Thomas Jones .25 .60
BC182 Julius Jones .25 .60
BC183 Joseph Addai .25 .60
BC184 Maurice Jones-Drew .25 .60
BC185 Ronnie Brown .25 .60
BC186 Laurence Maroney .30 .75
BC187 Reggie Bush .25 .60
BC188 Brian Westbrook .25 .60
BC189 LaDainian Tomlinson .40 1.00
BC190 Shaun Alexander .25 .60
BC191 Cadillac Williams .30 .75
BC192 Michael Turner .25 .60
BC193 Larry Fitzgerald .30 .75
BC194 Lee Evans .30 .75
BC195 Muhsin Muhammad .25 .60
BC196 T.J. Houshmandzadeh .25 .60
BC197 Terrell Owens .30 .75
BC198 Javon Walker .30 .75
BC199 Roy Williams WR .25 .60
BC200 Greg Jennings .25 .60
BC201 Reggie Wayne .30 .75
BC202 Matt Jones .30 .75
BC203 Troy Williamson .25 .60
BC204 Joe Horn .25 .60
BC205 Plaxico Burress .25 .60
BC206 Jerricho Cotchery .25 .60
BC207 Randy Moss .30 .75
BC208 Reggie Brown .25 .60
BC209 Santonio Holmes .25 .60
BC210 Eric Parker .25 .60
BC211 Antonio Bryant .25 .60
BC212 Darrell Jackson .25 .60
BC213 Torry Holt .30 .75
BC214 Antwaan Randle El .25 .60
BC215 Alge Crumpler .30 .75
BC216 Tony Gonzalez .30 .75
BC217 Antonio Gates .40 1.00
BC218 Tarvaris Jackson .25 .60
BC219 Drew Bennett .25 .60
BC220 Byron Leftwich .25 .60

2007 Bowman Chrome Blue Refractors

*1-55 BLUE REF/150: 2.5X TO 6X
*56-110 BLUE REF/150: 1X TO 2.5X
*111-220 BLUE REF/150: 3X TO 8X
1-55 BLUE REF/150 ODDS 1:228 BOW
56-220 BLUE REF/150 ODDS 1:55 CHR
BC65 Adrian Peterson 100.00 200.00
BC75 Calvin Johnson 30.00 80.00

2007 Bowman Chrome Gold Refractors

*1-55 GOLD REF/50: 4X TO 10X BASIC CARDS
*56-110 GOLD REF/50: 1.5X TO 4X
*111-220 GOLD REF/50: 5X TO 12X
1-55 GOLD REF/50 ODDS 1:685 BOW
56-220 GOLD REF/50 ODDS 1:164 CHR
BC65 Adrian Peterson 150.00 300.00
BC75 Calvin Johnson 50.00 120.00

2007 Bowman Chrome Orange Refractors

*1-55 ORNGE REF/25: 5X TO 12X BASIC CARDS
*56-110 ORNGE REF/25: 2X TO 5X
*111-220 ORNGE REF/25: 6X TO 15X
1-55 ORANGE REF/25 ODDS 1:1377 BOW HOB
56-220 ORNGE REF/25 ODDS 1:327 CHR
BC65 Adrian Peterson 250.00 500.00
BC75 Calvin Johnson 100.00 200.00

2007 Bowman Chrome Refractors

*1-55 REFRACT/500: 1.5X TO 4X BASIC CARDS
*56-110 REF: .6X TO 1.5X BASIC CARDS
*111-220 REF: 2X TO 5X BASIC CARDS
1-55 REF/500 ODDS 1:68 BOW
56-220 REFRACTOR ODDS 1:4 CHR
BC65 Adrian Peterson 20.00 50.00

2007 Bowman Chrome Uncirculated Rookies

*ROOKIES/1079: .8X TO 2X BASIC CARDS
UNCIRCULATED/1079 ONE PER CHROME BOX
BC65 Adrian Peterson 15.00 40.00

2007 Bowman Chrome Xfractors

*1-55 XFRACT/275: 2X TO 5X BASIC CARDS
*56-110 XFRACT/250: .8X TO 2X BASIC CARDS
*111-220 XFRACT/250: 2.5X TO 6X
1-55 XFRACTOR/275 ODDS 1:124 BOW
56-220 XFRACTOR/250 ODDS 1:33 CHR
BC65 Adrian Peterson 25.00 60.00
BC75 Calvin Johnson 20.00 50.00

2007 Bowman Chrome Rookie Autographs

UNPRICED PRINT PLATE ODDS 1:6700
UNPRICED RED REF/5 ODDS 1:5655
UNPRICED SUPERFR/1 ODDS 1:20,368
UNPRICED UNCIRC AUTO PRINT RUN 10
BC56 JaMarcus Russell B 5.00 12.00
BC57 Brady Quinn B 5.00 12.00
BC58 Drew Stanton C 5.00 12.00
BC59 Troy Smith C 5.00 12.00
BC60 Kevin Kolb D 5.00 12.00
BC61 Trent Edwards E 3.00 8.00
BC62 John Beck D 3.00 8.00
BC63 Jordan Palmer E 4.00 10.00
BC64 Chris Leak K 3.00 8.00
BC65 Adrian Peterson B 75.00 150.00
BC66 Marshawn Lynch C 30.00 60.00
BC67 Brandon Jackson I 3.00 8.00
BC68 Michael Bush I 3.00 8.00
BC69 Antonio Pittman D 3.00 8.00
BC70 Tony Hunt J 3.00 8.00
BC71 Lorenzo Booker G 4.00 10.00
BC72 Chris Henry K 3.00 8.00
BC73 Brian Leonard C 5.00 12.00
BC74 Garrett Wolfe J 3.00 8.00
BC75 Calvin Johnson A 75.00 150.00
BC76 Ted Ginn C 6.00 15.00
BC77 Dwayne Jarrett C 6.00 15.00
BC78 Dwayne Bowe C 5.00 12.00
BC79 Sidney Rice C 20.00 50.00
BC80 Robert Meachem C 6.00 15.00
BC81 Anthony Gonzalez E 3.00 8.00
BC82 Craig Buster Davis L 3.00 8.00
BC83 Aundrae Allison G 3.00 8.00
BC84 Chansi Stuckey J 4.00 10.00
BC85 Alan Branch H 3.00 8.00
BC86 Steve Smith USC E 3.00 8.00
BC87 Paul Williams I 3.00 8.00
BC88 Johnnie Lee Higgins L 3.00 8.00
BC89 Jason Hill K 3.00 8.00
BC90 Greg Olsen E 5.00 12.00
BC91 Yamon Figurs L 3.00 8.00
BC92 Gaines Adams C 6.00 15.00
BC93 Patrick Willis D 5.00 12.00
BC94 Joe Thomas E 5.00 12.00
BC95 Isaiah Stanback K 3.00 8.00
BC96 Paul Posluszny K 3.00 8.00
BC97 Jeff Rowe I 3.00 8.00
BC99 Dwayne Wright I 3.00 8.00
BC100 Kenneth Darby L 3.00 8.00
BC101 Selvin Young L 3.00 8.00
BC102 Gary Russell I 4.00 10.00
BC103 Kolby Smith K 3.00 8.00
BC104 Dallas Baker J 3.00 8.00
BC105 Jacoby Jones L 3.00 8.00
BC106 Ryne Robinson J 4.00 10.00
BC107 Chris Davis L 3.00 8.00
BC108 LaRon Landry I 5.00 12.00
BC109 Leon Hall F 3.00 8.00
BC110 Lawrence Timmons F 5.00 12.00

2007 Bowman Chrome Rookie Autographs Blue Refractors

*BLUE REF/75: .5X TO 1.2X GROUP B/C AU
*BLUE REF/75: .6X TO 1.5X GROUP D AU
*BLUE REF/75: .8X TO 2X BASIC AUTO
BLUE REF/25 GROUP A ODDS 1:50,900
BLUE REF/75 GROUP B ODDS 1:309
BC57 Brady Quinn 6.00 15.00
BC65 Adrian Peterson 100.00 200.00
BC75 Calvin Johnson/25 100.00 200.00

2007 Bowman Chrome Rookie Autographs Gold Refractors

*GOLD REF/50: .6X TO 1.5X GROUP B/C AU
*GOLD REF/50: 1X TO 2.5X GROUP D AU
*GOLD REF/50: 1.2X TO 3X BASIC AUTO
GOLD REF/15 GROUP A ODDS 1:92,545
GOLD REF/50 GROUP B ODDS 1:467
BC57 Brady Quinn 10.00 25.00
BC65 Adrian Peterson 125.00 250.00
BC75 Calvin Johnson/15 125.00 250.00

2007 Bowman Chrome Rookie Autographs Orange Refractors

*ORANGE REF/25: 1X TO 2.5X GROUP C AU
*ORANGE REF/25: 1.2X TO 3X GROUP D AU
*ORANGE REF/25: 1.5X TO 4X BASIC AUTO
UNPRICED ORG/10 GRP A ODDS 1:169,666
ORANGE REF/25 GROUP B ODDS 1:955
BC57 Brady Quinn 12.00 30.00
BC65 Adrian Peterson 150.00 300.00
BC66 Marshawn Lynch 75.00 125.00
BC75 Calvin Johnson/10 200.00 400.00

2008 Bowman Chrome

This set was released on November 19, 2008. The base set consists of 220 cards. Cards 1-110 feature rookies, and cards 111-220 are veterans. Cards 1-55 can be found in regular Bowman packs.

COMPLETE SET (220) 40.00 80.00
COMP.SER.1 SET (55) 10.00 25.00
COMP.SER.2 SET (165) 30.00 60.00
1-55 INSERTED TWO PER BOWMAN PACK
UNPRICED 56-220 PRINT PLATE/1 ODDS 1:797 BOW CHR

BC1 Ryan Clady RC .40 1.00
BC2 Branden Albert RC .40 1.00
BC3 Gosder Cherilus RC .40 1.00
BC4 Duane Brown RC .30 .75
BC5 Brandon Flowers RC .40 1.00
BC6 Quentin Groves RC .40 1.00
BC7 Jason Jones RC .40 1.00
BC8 Kendall Langford RC .40 1.00
BC9 Brad Cottam RC .30 .75
BC10 Antwaun Molden RC .30 .75
BC11 Bryan Smith RC .30 .75
BC12 DaJuan Morgan RC .40 1.00
BC13 Craig Stevens RC .30 .75
BC14 Tom Zbikowski RC .40 1.00
BC15 Andre Fluellen RC .30 .75
BC16 Cliff Avril RC .50 1.25
BC17 Tyvon Branch RC .40 1.00
BC18 Justin King RC .40 1.00
BC19 Jeremy Thompson RC .30 .75
BC20 William Hayes RC .30 .75
BC21 Will Franklin RC .40 1.00
BC22 Marcus Smith RC .40 1.00
BC23 Dwight Lowery RC .40 1.00
BC24 Reggie Corner RC .30 .75
BC25 Kenny Iwebema RC .30 .75
BC26 Quintin Demps RC .40 1.00
BC27 Jack Williams RC .30 .75
BC28 Craig Steltz RC .30 .75
BC29 Bryan Kehl RC .30 .75
BC30 Justin Tryon RC .30 .75
BC31 Arman Shields RC .40 1.00
BC32 Paul Hubbard RC .30 .75
BC33 Jonathan Wilhite RC .30 .75
BC34 Thomas DeCoud RC .30 .75
BC35 Derek Fine RC .30 .75
BC36 Stanford Keglar RC .30 .75
BC37 Kenneth Moore RC .30 .75
BC38 Robert James RC .30 .75
BC39 Jalen Parmele RC .40 1.00
BC40 Brandon Carr RC .40 1.00
BC41 Gary Barnidge RC .50 1.25
BC42 Zack Bowman RC .40 1.00
BC43 Lex Hilliard RC .40 1.00
BC44 Mario Urrutia RC .30 .75
BC45 Adrian Arrington RC .30 .75
BC46 Jerome Felton RC .30 .75
BC47 Chaz Schilens RC .40 1.00
BC48 Steve Johnson RC .60 1.50
BC49 Tim Hightower RC .40 1.00
BC50 Alex Brink RC .40 1.00
BC51 Brett Swain RC .30 .75
BC52 Matt Slater RC .50 1.25
BC53 Justin Harper RC .30 .75
BC54 Kevin Robinson RC .30 .75
BC55 Pierre Garcon RC .60 1.50
BC56 John David Booty RC .60 1.50
BC57 Brian Brohm RC .60 1.50
BC58 Kevin O'Connell RC .60 1.50
BC59 Matt Ryan RC 2.00 5.00
BC60 Chad Henne RC .75 2.00
BC61 Joe Flacco RC 1.25 3.00
BC62 Colt Brennan RC .75 2.00
BC63 Paul Smith RC .60 1.50
BC64 Eric Ainge RC .60 1.50
BC65 Kyle Wright RC .60 1.50
BC66 Josh Johnson RC .60 1.50
BC67 Dennis Dixon RC .60 1.50
BC68 Andre Woodson RC .60 1.50
BC69 Matt Forte RC 1.00 2.50
BC70 Felix Jones RC .60 1.50
BC71 Darren McFadden RC .60 1.50
BC72 Rashard Mendenhall RC .60 1.50
BC73 Ray Rice RC .60 1.50
BC74 Steve Slaton RC .60 1.50
BC75 Jonathan Stewart RC 1.00 2.50
BC76 Chris Johnson RC .75 2.00
BC77 Kevin Smith RC .60 1.50
BC78 Jamaal Charles RC 2.50 6.00
BC79 Ryan Torain RC .75 2.00
BC80 Mike Hart RC .60 1.50
BC81 Chauncey Washington RC .75 2.00
BC82 Dustin Keller RC .75 2.00
BC83 John Carlson RC .60 1.50
BC84 Andre Caldwell RC .60 1.50
BC85 Dexter Jackson RC 1.00 2.50
BC86 Malcolm Kelly RC .60 1.50
BC87 Donnie Avery RC .75 2.00
BC88 Devin Thomas RC .60 1.50
BC89 Jordy Nelson RC 2.00 5.00
BC90 James Hardy RC .60 1.50
BC91 Eddie Royal RC .60 1.50
BC92 Jerome Simpson RC .75 2.00
BC93 DeSean Jackson RC 1.25 3.00
BC94 Limas Sweed RC .60 1.50
BC95 Earl Bennett RC 1.00 2.50
BC96 Early Doucet RC .60 1.50
BC97 Harry Douglas RC .75 2.00
BC98 Mario Manningham RC .60 1.50
BC99 Lavelle Hawkins RC .75 2.00
BC100 Marcus Monk RC .75 2.00
BC101 Marcus Henry RC .60 1.50
BC102 Tashard Choice RC .60 1.50
BC103 DJ Hall RC .60 1.50
BC104 Jake Long RC 1.00 2.50
BC105 Jacob Hester RC .60 1.50
BC106 Owen Schmitt RC .60 1.50
BC107 Jerod Mayo RC 1.00 2.50
BC108 Chris Long RC .75 2.00
BC109 Vernon Gholston RC .60 1.50
BC110 Glenn Dorsey RC .60 1.50
BC111 Drew Brees .40 1.00
BC112 Tom Brady 1.25 3.00
BC113 Peyton Manning 1.00 2.50
BC114 Carson Palmer .30 .75
BC115 Ben Roethlisberger .40 1.00
BC116 Eli Manning .30 .75
BC117 Tony Romo .30 .75
BC118 Vince Young .25 .60
BC119 Matt Hasselbeck .25 .60
BC120 David Garrard .25 .60
BC121 Jay Cutler .25 .60
BC122 Derek Anderson .25 .60
BC123 Philip Rivers .40 1.00
BC124 Donovan McNabb .30 .75
BC125 Matt Leinart .25 .60
BC126 Jason Campbell .25 .60
BC127 JaMarcus Russell .25 .60
BC128 Jeff Garcia .25 .60
BC129 Brodie Croyle .30 .75
BC130 Marc Bulger .25 .60
BC131 Trent Edwards .25 .60
BC132 Kyle Boller .25 .60
BC133 Tarvaris Jackson .25 .60
BC134 Matt Schaub .25 .60
BC135 Aaron Rodgers .75 2.00
BC136 Steven Jackson .25 .60
BC137 Willie Parker .30 .75
BC138 Clinton Portis .25 .60
BC139 Adrian Peterson .40 1.00
BC140 LaDainian Tomlinson .40 1.00
BC141 Marion Barber .25 .60
BC142 Brian Westbrook .25 .60
BC143 Fred Taylor .25 .60
BC144 Marshawn Lynch .30 .75
BC145 Joseph Addai .25 .60
BC146 Willis McGahee .25 .60
BC147 Frank Gore .30 .75
BC148 Julius Jones .25 .60
BC149 Thomas Jones .25 .60
BC150 Cedric Benson .25 .60
BC151 LenDale White .25 .60
BC152 Ryan Grant .30 .75
BC153 Laurence Maroney .30 .75
BC154 Brandon Jacobs .25 .60
BC155 Jamal Lewis .30 .75
BC156 Larry Johnson .25 .60
BC157 Rudi Johnson .25 .60
BC158 Ahmad Bradshaw .25 .60
BC159 Justin Fargas .25 .60
BC160 Reggie Bush .25 .60
BC161 Maurice Jones-Drew .25 .60
BC162 Michael Turner .25 .60
BC163 Ronnie Brown .25 .60
BC164 DeAngelo Williams .25 .60
BC165 Edgerrin James .30 .75
BC166 Chad Johnson .25 .60
BC167 Reggie Wayne .30 .75
BC168 Anquan Boldin .25 .60
BC169 Randy Moss .30 .75
BC170 Plaxico Burress .25 .60
BC171 Terrell Owens .30 .75
BC172 Andre Johnson .30 .75
BC173 Larry Fitzgerald .30 .75
BC174 Braylon Edwards .25 .60
BC175 Steve Smith .30 .75
BC176 Greg Jennings .25 .60
BC177 Torry Holt .30 .75
BC178 T.J. Houshmandzadeh .25 .60
BC179 Jerricho Cotchery .25 .60
BC180 Joey Galloway .30 .75
BC181 Santonio Holmes .25 .60
BC182 Lee Evans .30 .75
BC183 Dwayne Bowe .30 .75
BC184 Laurent Robinson .25 .60
BC185 Wes Welker .30 .75
BC186 Roy Williams WR .25 .60
BC187 Brandon Marshall .30 .75
BC188 Hines Ward .30 .75
BC189 Donald Driver .30 .75
BC190 Calvin Johnson .40 1.00
BC191 Marques Colston .25 .60
BC192 Chris Chambers .25 .60
BC193 Amani Toomer .25 .60
BC194 Bernard Berrian .25 .60
BC195 Sidney Rice .25 .60
BC196 Anthony Gonzalez .25 .60
BC197 Steve Smith USC .30 .75
BC198 Ted Ginn Jr. .25 .60
BC199 Isaac Bruce .40 1.00
BC200 Derrick Mason .25 .60
BC201 Roddy White .25 .60
BC202 Bobby Engram .25 .60
BC203 Reggie Williams .30 .75
BC204 Donte Stallworth .25 .60
BC205 Santana Moss .25 .60
BC206 Laveranues Coles .25 .60
BC207 Jerry Porter .25 .60
BC208 Shaun McDonald .25 .60
BC209 Dallas Clark .25 .60
BC210 Tony Gonzalez .30 .75
BC211 Kellen Winslow .25 .60
BC212 Antonio Gates .30 .75
BC213 Jason Witten .30 .75
BC214 Chris Cooley .25 .60
BC215 Brett Favre .75 2.00
BC216 Bob Sanders .30 .75
BC217 John Harbaugh CO RC .25 .60
BC218 Jon Kitna .25 .60
BC219 Tony Sparano CO RC .25 .60
BC220 Mike Smith CO RC .25 .60

2008 Bowman Chrome Blue Refractors

*1-55 ROOKIES: 2.5X TO 6X BASIC CARDS
1-55 BLUE REF/150 ODDS 1:192 BOW
*56-110 ROOKIES: 1.2X TO 3X BASIC CARDS
*111-220 VETS: 2.5X TO 6X BASIC CARDS
56-110 BLUE REF/150 ODDS 1:31 BOW CHR
BC59 Matt Ryan 30.00 60.00

2008 Bowman Chrome Gold Refractors

*1-55 ROOKIES: 4X TO 10X BASIC CARDS
1-55 GOLD REF/50 ODDS 1:575 BOW
*56-110 ROOKIES: 2.5X TO 6X BASIC CARDS
*111-220 VETS: 5X TO 12X BASIC CARDS
56-220 GOLD REF/50 ODDS 1:93 BOW CHR
BC59 Matt Ryan 40.00 100.00

2008 Bowman Chrome Orange Refractors

*1-55 ROOKIES: 6X TO 15X BASIC CARDS
1-55 ORANGE REF/25 ODDS 1:1139 BOW
*56-110 ROOKIES: 4X TO 10X BASIC CARDS
*111-220 VETS: 8X TO 20X BASIC CARDS
56-220 ORANGE REF/25 ODDS 1:185 BOW CHR
BC59 Matt Ryan 60.00 120.00

2008 Bowman Chrome Red Refractors

UNPRICED 1-55 RED REF/5 ODDS 1:4800 BOW
UNPRICED 56-220 RED REF/5 ODDS 1:940 BOW CHR

2008 Bowman Chrome Refractors

*1-55 ROOKIES: 1.5X TO 4X BASIC CARDS
1-55 REFRACTOR/500 ODDS 1:57 BOW
*56-110 ROOKIES: .6X TO 1.5X BASIC CARDS
*111-220 VETS: 1.2X TO 3X BASIC CARDS
56-220 REF INSERTED IN BOW CHR

2008 Bowman Chrome Rookies Bronze

*BRONZE/329: .8X TO 2X BASIC CARDS
BRONZE/329 ODDS 1:36 BOW CHR

2008 Bowman Chrome Rookies Silver

*SILVER: 1X TO 2.5X BASIC INSERTS
SILVER/199 ODDS 1:54 BOW CHR

2008 Bowman Chrome Superfractors

UNPRICED 1-55 SUPER/1 ODDS 1:11,770 BOW
UNPRICED 56-220 SUPER/1 ODDS 1:3200 BOW CHR

2008 Bowman Chrome Xfractors

*1-55 ROOKIES: 2X TO 5X BASIC CARDS
1-55 XFRACTOR/275 ODDS 1:103 BOW
*56-110 ROOKIES: 1X TO 2.5X BASIC CARDS
*111-220 VETS: 2X TO 5X BASIC CARDS
56-220 XFRCT/250 ODDS 1:19 BOW CHR

2008 Bowman Chrome Rookie Autographs

GROUP A ODDS 1:1380 HOB
GROUP B ODDS 1:865 HOB
GROUP C ODDS 1:878 HOB
GROUP D ODDS 1:172 HOB
GROUP E ODDS 1:662 HOB
GROUP F ODDS 1:134 HOB
GROUP G ODDS 1:33 HOB
UNPRICED RED REF/5 ODDS 1:2225 BOW CHR
UNPRICED SUPER/1 ODDS 1:10,481 BOW CHR
UNPRICED PRNT PLTE/1 ODDS 1:3518 BW CHR
UNPRICED SILVER/10 ODDS 1:1170 BOW CHR
BC59 Matt Ryan A 50.00 100.00
BC60 Chad Henne B 6.00 15.00
BC61 Joe Flacco A 30.00 60.00
BC70 Felix Jones A 6.00 15.00
BC72 Rashard Mendenhall A 6.00 15.00
BC73 Ray Rice B 5.00 12.00
BC76 Chris Johnson C 25.00 60.00

2008 Bowman Chrome Rookie Autographs Blue Refractors

*BLUE REFRACT/35: .6X TO 1.5X GREEN AU
BLUE REFRACT/35 ODDS 1:371 BOW CHR
BC59 Matt Ryan 100.00 200.00
BC76 Chris Johnson 10.00 25.00

2008 Bowman Chrome Rookie Autographs Gold Refractors

*GOLD REFRACT/25: .8X TO 2X GREEN AU
GOLD REFRACT/25 ODDS 1:532 BOW CHR
UNPRICED GOLD REF JSY AU PRINT RUN 10
BC59 Matt Ryan 100.00 200.00
BC76 Chris Johnson 12.00 30.00

2008 Bowman Chrome Rookie Autographs Green

GREEN AU/150 ODDS 1:93 BOWMAN
BC56 John David Booty 5.00 12.00
BC57 Brian Brohm 5.00 12.00
BC58 Kevin O'Connell 5.00 12.00
BC59 Matt Ryan 60.00 125.00
BC60 Chad Henne 6.00 15.00
BC62 Colt Brennan 6.00 15.00
BC63 Paul Smith 5.00 12.00
BC64 Erik Ainge 5.00 12.00
BC66 Josh Johnson 5.00 12.00
BC67 Dennis Dixon 5.00 12.00
BC68 Andre Woodson 5.00 12.00
BC69 Matt Forte 10.00 25.00
BC70 Felix Jones 5.00 12.00
BC71 Darren McFadden 5.00 12.00
BC72 Rashard Mendenhall 5.00 12.00
BC73 Ray Rice 5.00 12.00
BC74 Steve Slaton 5.00 12.00
BC75 Jonathan Stewart 8.00 20.00
BC76 Chris Johnson 6.00 15.00
BC77 Kevin Smith 5.00 12.00
BC78 Jamaal Charles 8.00 20.00
BC79 Ryan Torain 6.00 15.00
BC80 Mike Hart 5.00 12.00
BC81 Chauncey Washington 6.00 15.00
BC82 Dustin Keller 6.00 15.00
BC83 John Carlson 5.00 12.00
BC84 Andre Caldwell 5.00 12.00
BC85 Dexter Jackson 8.00 20.00
BC86 Malcolm Kelly 5.00 12.00
BC87 Donnie Avery 6.00 15.00
BC88 Devin Thomas 5.00 12.00
BC89 Jordy Nelson 20.00 40.00
BC90 James Hardy 5.00 12.00
BC91 Eddie Royal 5.00 12.00
BC92 Jerome Simpson 6.00 15.00
BC93 DeSean Jackson 12.00 30.00
BC94 Limas Sweed 5.00 12.00
BC95 Earl Bennett 8.00 20.00
BC96 Early Doucet 5.00 12.00
BC97 Harry Douglas 6.00 15.00
BC98 Mario Manningham 10.00 25.00
BC99 Lavelle Hawkins 6.00 15.00
BC100 Marcus Monk 6.00 15.00
BC101 Marcus Henry 5.00 12.00
BC102 Tashard Choice 5.00 12.00
BC103 DJ Hall 5.00 12.00
BC104 Jake Long 8.00 20.00
BC105 Jacob Hester 5.00 12.00
BC106 Owen Schmitt 5.00 12.00
BC107 Jerod Mayo 8.00 20.00
BC108 Chris Long 6.00 15.00
BC109 Vernon Gholston 5.00 12.00
BC110 Glenn Dorsey EXCH 5.00 12.00

2008 Bowman Chrome Rookie Autographs Orange Refractors

*ORANGE REFRACT/15: 1X TO 2.5X GREEN AU
ORANGE REFRACT/15 ODDS 1:760 BOW CHR
BC59 Matt Ryan 250.00 400.00
BC76 Chris Johnson 15.00 40.00

2008 Bowman Chrome Rookie Coaches Autographs

STATED ODDS 1:1550 BOW HOB
BRCJH John Harbaugh 12.00 30.00
BRCMS Mike Smith 8.00 20.00
BRCTS Tony Sparano 10.00 25.00

2009 Bowman Chrome

COMPLETE SET (165) 40.00 100.00
1 Drew Brees .30 .75
2 Ben Roethlisberger .30 .75
3 Eli Manning .25 .60
4 Tony Romo .25 .60
5 Philip Rivers .30 .75
6 Aaron Rodgers .60 1.50
7 Marc Bulger .20 .50
8 Jay Cutler .20 .50
9 Matt Ryan .25 .60
10 Tom Brady 1.00 2.50
11 Carson Palmer .25 .60
12 Peyton Manning .75 2.00
13 Kerry Collins .20 .50
14 Kurt Warner .25 .60
15 Jason Campbell .20 .50
16 Chad Pennington .20 .50
17 Trent Edwards .20 .50
18 Matt Schaub .20 .50
19 Donovan McNabb .25 .60
20 Jared Allen .20 .50
21 Kyle Orton .20 .50
22 JaMarcus Russell .20 .50
23 Joe Flacco .25 .60
24 Jake Delhomme .20 .50
25 David Garrard .20 .50
26 Matt Cassel .20 .50
27 Derek Anderson .20 .50
28 Steven Jackson .20 .50
29 Clinton Portis .20 .50
30 Adrian Peterson .30 .75
31 LaDainian Tomlinson .30 .75
32 Marion Barber .25 .60
33 Brian Westbrook .20 .50
34 Frank Gore .25 .60
35 Chris Johnson .20 .50
36 Michael Turner .20 .50
37 Brandon Jacobs .20 .50
38 Steve Slaton .20 .50
39 Matt Forte .20 .50
40 Leon Washington .20 .50
41 Fred Taylor .20 .50
42 Joseph Addai .20 .50
43 Willis McGahee .20 .50
44 Marshawn Lynch .25 .60
45 Thomas Jones .20 .50
46 DeAngelo Williams .20 .50
47 Earnest Graham .20 .50
48 Jamal Lewis .25 .60
49 John Carlson .25 .60
50 Ryan Grant .25 .60
51 Ronnie Brown .20 .50
52 Jonathan Stewart .20 .50
53 Kevin Boss .20 .50
54 Darren McFadden .30 .75
55 Maurice Jones-Drew .20 .50
56 LenDale White .20 .50
57 Pierre Thomas .20 .50
58 LaMarr Woodley .20 .50
59 Warrick Dunn .20 .50
60 Sammy Morris .20 .50
61 Reggie Bush .20 .50
62 Kevin Smith .20 .50
63 Ricky Williams .25 .60
64 Felix Jones .20 .50
65 Anquan Boldin .20 .50
66 Andre Johnson .25 .60
67 Larry Fitzgerald .25 .60
68 Steve Smith .25 .60
69 Greg Jennings .20 .50
70 Santana Moss .25 .60
71 Brandon Marshall .25 .60
72 T.J. Houshmandzadeh .20 .50
73 Eddie Royal .20 .50
74 Chad Ochocinco .20 .50
75 Troy Polamalu .30 .75
76 Terrell Owens .25 .60
77 Braylon Edwards .20 .50
78 Randy Moss .25 .60
79 Reggie Wayne .25 .60
80 Wes Welker .25 .60
81 Roddy White .20 .50
82 Dwayne Bowe .25 .60
83 Lance Moore .20 .50
84 Tim Hightower .20 .50
85 Antonio Bryant .20 .50
86 Jerricho Cotchery .20 .50
87 Laveranues Coles .20 .50
88 Derrick Mason .20 .50
89 Peyton Hillis .25 .60
90 Greg Camarillo .25 .60
91 DeSean Jackson .25 .60
92 Ed Reed .25 .60
93 Lee Evans .25 .60
94 Hines Ward .25 .60
95 Calvin Johnson .30 .75
96 Steve Smith USC .25 .60
97 Bernard Berrian .20 .50
98 Chris Cooley .20 .50
99 Tony Gonzalez .25 .60
100 Kevin Walter .25 .60
101 Antonio Gates .25 .60
102 Jason Witten .25 .60
103 Dallas Clark .20 .50
104 Joey Porter .25 .60
105 Patrick Willis .25 .60
106 DeMarcus Ware .25 .60
107 James Harrison .30 .75
108 Charles Woodson .30 .75
109 Oshiomogho Atogwe .20 .50
110 Justin Tuck .20 .50
111 Matthew Stafford RC 6.00 15.00
112 Josh Freeman RC .60 1.50
113 Nate Davis RC .60 1.50
114 Rhett Bomar RC .60 1.50
115 Mark Sanchez RC .60 1.50
116 Chris Wells RC .60 1.50
117 Javon Ringer RC .60 1.50
118 Deon Butler RC .60 1.50
119 Brandon Pettigrew RC .60 1.50
120 LeSean McCoy RC 1.50 4.00
121 Darrius Heyward-Bey RC 1.00 2.50
122 Ramses Barden RC .60 1.50
123 Derrick Williams RC .60 1.50
124 Hakeem Nicks RC .75 2.00
125 Aaron Curry RC 1.00 2.50
126 Patrick Turner RC .60 1.50
127 Knowshon Moreno RC .60 1.50
128 Brian Robiskie RC .60 1.50
129 Stephen McGee RC .60 1.50
130 Kenny Britt RC 1.00 2.50
131 Mohamed Massaquoi RC .60 1.50
132 Donald Brown RC .60 1.50
133 Juaquin Iglesias RC .60 1.50
134 Andre Brown RC .75 2.00
135 Michael Crabtree RC 1.00 2.50
136 Glen Coffee RC .60 1.50
137 Shonn Greene RC .60 1.50
138 Percy Harvin RC .60 1.50
139 Pat White RC .75 2.00
140 Jeremy Maclin RC .75 2.00
141 Jason Smith RC .60 1.50
142 Tyson Jackson RC .60 1.50
143 Mike Wallace RC 1.00 2.50
144 Mike Thomas RC .60 1.50
145 B.J. Raji RC .75 2.00
146 Aaron Maybin RC .75 2.00
147 Brian Orakpo RC .75 2.00
148 Malcolm Jenkins RC .60 1.50
149 Brian Cushing RC .60 1.50
150 Brian Hartline RC 1.00 2.50
151 Mike Goodson RC .75 2.00
152 Louis Murphy RC .60 1.50
153 Austin Collie RC .60 1.50
154 Gartrell Johnson RC .60 1.50
155 Johnny Knox RC .75 2.00
156 Kenny McKinley RC .60 1.50
157 Jarett Dillard RC .60 1.50
158 Brooks Foster RC .60 1.50
159 Tom Brandstater RC .75 2.00
160 Mike Teel RC .60 1.50
161 Cedric Peerman RC .60 1.50
162 Brandon Gibson RC .75 2.00
163 James Davis RC .60 1.50
164 Curtis Painter RC .60 1.50
165 Brandon Tate RC .75 2.00

2009 Bowman Chrome Blue Refractors

*VETS 1-110: 4X TO 10X BASIC CARDS
*ROOKIES 111-165: 1X TO 2.5X BASIC CARDS
BLUE REF/150 ODDS 1:20 HOB
111 Matthew Stafford 30.00 80.00

2009 Bowman Chrome Gold Refractors

*VETS 1-110: 6X TO 15X BASIC CARDS
*ROOKIES 111-165: 2X TO 5X BASIC CARDS
GOLD REF/50 ODDS 1:59 HOB
111 Matthew Stafford 60.00 150.00

2009 Bowman Chrome Green Refractors

*VETS 1-110: 5X TO 12X BASIC CARDS
*ROOKIES 111-165: 1.2X TO 3X BASIC CARDS
GREEN REF/99 ODDS 1:30
111 Matthew Stafford 30.00 80.00

2009 Bowman Chrome Orange Refractors

*VETS 1-110: 8X TO 20X BASIC CARDS
*ROOKIES 111-165: 2.5X TO 6X BASIC CARDS
ORANGE REF/25 ODDS 1:118 HOB
111 Matthew Stafford 100.00 200.00

2009 Bowman Chrome Refractors

*VETS 1-110: 2X TO 5X BASIC CARDS
*ROOKIES 111-165: .5X TO 1.2X BASIC CARDS
REFRACTOR STATED ODDS 1:4

2009 Bowman Chrome Rookies Bronze

*ROOKIES 111-165: .6X TO 1.5X BASIC CARDS
BRONZE ROOKIE PRINT RUN 225 SER.#'d SETS

2009 Bowman Chrome Rookies Silver

*ROOKIES 111-165: 1X TO 2.5X BASIC CARDS
SILVER ROOKIE PRINT RUN 99 SER.#'d SETS

2009 Bowman Chrome Xfractors

*VETS 1-110: 2.5X TO 6X BASIC CARDS
*ROOKIES 111-165: .6X TO 1.5X BASIC CARDS
XFRACTOR/250 ODDS 1:12 HOB

2009 Bowman Chrome NFL Letter Autographs

JL James Laurinaitis/22* 12.00 30.00
TB Tom Brandstater/22* 12.00 30.00

2009 Bowman Chrome Rookie Autographs

GROUP A ODDS 1:655 HOB
GROUP B ODDS 1:165 HOB
GROUP C ODDS 1:174 HOB
GROUP D ODDS 1:186 HOB
GROUP E ODDS 1:39 HOB
111 Matthew Stafford A 40.00 100.00
112 Josh Freeman A 3.00 8.00
113 Nate Davis E 3.00 8.00
114 Rhett Bomar E 3.00 8.00
115 Mark Sanchez A 3.00 8.00
116 Chris Wells B 10.00 25.00
117 Javon Ringer D 3.00 8.00
118 Deon Butler E 3.00 8.00
119 Brandon Pettigrew B 3.00 8.00
120 LeSean McCoy B 15.00 40.00
121 Darrius Heyward-Bey A 5.00 12.00
122 Ramses Barden E 6.00 15.00
123 Derrick Williams D 3.00 8.00
124 Hakeem Nicks B 4.00 10.00
125 Aaron Curry B 5.00 12.00
126 Patrick Turner E 3.00 8.00
127 Knowshon Moreno A 3.00 8.00
128 Brian Robiskie B 6.00 15.00
129 Stephen McGee C 3.00 8.00
130 Kenny Britt B 5.00 12.00
131 Mohamed Massaquoi C 3.00 8.00
132 Donald Brown B 8.00 20.00
133 Juaquin Iglesias C 3.00 8.00
134 Andre Brown E 4.00 10.00
135 Michael Crabtree A 5.00 12.00
136 Glen Coffee C 3.00 8.00
137 Shonn Greene C 4.00 10.00
138 Percy Harvin C 3.00 8.00
139 Pat White B 4.00 10.00
140 Jeremy Maclin B 8.00 20.00
141 Jason Smith B 3.00 8.00
142 Tyson Jackson C 3.00 8.00
143 Mike Wallace D 5.00 12.00
144 Mike Thomas E 3.00 8.00
147 Brian Orakpo D 4.00 10.00
149 Brian Cushing D 8.00 20.00
150 Brian Hartline E 8.00 20.00
151 Mike Goodson E 4.00 10.00
153 Austin Collie E 3.00 8.00
154 Gartrell Johnson E 3.00 8.00
155 Johnny Knox E 4.00 10.00
157 Jarett Dillard E 3.00 8.00
158 Brooks Foster E 3.00 8.00
159 Tom Brandstater E 4.00 10.00
160 Mike Teel E 3.00 8.00
161 Cedric Peerman E 3.00 8.00
162 Brandon Gibson E 4.00 10.00
163 James Davis E 3.00 8.00
164 Curtis Painter E 3.00 8.00
165 Brandon Tate E 4.00 10.00

2009 Bowman Chrome Rookie Autographs Blue Refractors

*BLUE REF/35: .6X TO 1.5X BASIC AUTO
BLUE REF/35 ODDS 1:222 HOB
111 Matthew Stafford 150.00 300.00
112 Josh Freeman 5.00 12.00

2009 Bowman Chrome Rookie Autographs Gold Refractors

*GOLD REF/25: 1X TO 2.5X BASIC AUTO
GOLD REF/25 ODDS 1:308 HOB
111 Matthew Stafford 250.00 400.00

2009 Bowman Chrome Rookie Autographs Orange Refractors

*ORANGE REF/15: 1.2X TO 3X BASIC AUTO
ORANGE REF/15 ODDS 1:498 HOB
111 Matthew Stafford 300.00 500.00
112 Josh Freeman 10.00 25.00

2010 Bowman Chrome Rookie Preview Inserts

STATED ODDS 1:12 TOPPS CHROME HOB
*REFRACT/99: 2.5X TO 6X BASIC INSERTS
BCR1 Tim Tebow 2.00 5.00
BCR2 C.J. Spiller .60 1.50
BCR3 Dez Bryant 1.50 4.00
BCR4 Golden Tate .75 2.00
BCR5 Sam Bradford .75 2.00
BCR6 Ryan Mathews .60 1.50
BCR7 Jahvid Best .60 1.50
BCR8 Colt McCoy .75 2.00
BCR9 Demaryius Thomas 1.50 4.00
BCR10 Jimmy Clausen .60 1.50
BCR11 Ndamukong Suh 1.25 3.00
BCR12 Arrelious Benn .60 1.50
BCR13 Ben Tate .60 1.50
BCR14 Jonathan Dwyer .60 1.50
BCR15 Eric Berry 1.00 2.50
BCR16 Damian Williams .60 1.50
BCR17 Armanti Edwards .75 2.00
BCR18 Emmanuel Sanders 1.00 2.50
BCR19 Rolando McClain .60 1.50
BCR20 Andre Roberts .75 2.00
BCR21 Eric Decker .75 2.00
BCR22 Joe McKnight .60 1.50
BCR23 Brandon LaFell 1.00 2.50
BCR24 Jordan Shipley .60 1.50
BCR25 Rob Gronkowski 2.00 5.00
BCR26 Dexter McCluster .75 2.00
BCR27 Jermaine Gresham .60 1.50
BCR28 Montario Hardesty .60 1.50
BCR29 Toby Gerhart .60 1.50
BCR30 Gerald McCoy .60 1.50

2010 Bowman Chrome Rookie Preview Inserts Autographs

AU/25 ODDS 1:2058 TOPPS CHROME
BCRA1 Tim Tebow 75.00 200.00
BCRA2 C.J. Spiller 12.00 30.00
BCRA3 Dez Bryant 100.00 200.00
BCRA4 Golden Tate 15.00 40.00
BCRA5 Sam Bradford 15.00 40.00
BCRA6 Ryan Mathews 12.00 30.00
BCRA7 Jahvid Best 12.00 30.00
BCRA8 Colt McCoy 15.00 40.00
BCRA9 Demaryius Thomas 40.00 80.00
BCRA10 Jimmy Clausen 12.00 30.00
BCRA11 Ndamukong Suh 75.00 150.00
BCRA12 Arrelious Benn 12.00 30.00
BCRA13 Ben Tate 12.00 30.00
BCRA14 Jonathan Dwyer 15.00 40.00
BCRA15 Eric Berry 20.00 50.00
BCRA16 Damian Williams 12.00 30.00
BCRA17 Armanti Edwards 15.00 40.00
BCRA18 Emmanuel Sanders 20.00 50.00
BCRA19 Rolando McClain 12.00 30.00
BCRA20 Andre Roberts 30.00 60.00
BCRA21 Eric Decker 15.00 40.00
BCRA22 Joe McKnight 12.00 30.00
BCRA23 Brandon LaFell 15.00 40.00
BCRA24 Jordan Shipley 12.00 30.00
BCRA25 Rob Gronkowski 100.00 175.00
BCRA26 Dexter McCluster 15.00 40.00
BCRA27 Jermaine Gresham 12.00 30.00
BCRA28 Montario Hardesty 12.00 30.00
BCRA29 Toby Gerhart 12.00 30.00
BCRA30 Gerald McCoy 12.00 30.00

2011 Bowman Chrome Rookie Preview Inserts

COMPLETE SET (30) 25.00 50.00
STATED ODDS 1:12 TOPPS CHROME HOB
*REFRACTOR/99: 3X TO 8X BASIC INSERTS
BCR1 Blaine Gabbert .60 1.50
BCR2 Jake Locker .60 1.50
BCR3 Cam Newton 3.00 8.00
BCR4 Ryan Mallett .60 1.50
BCR5 Mark Ingram 1.00 2.50
BCR6 Ryan Williams .60 1.50
BCR7 Mikel Leshoure .60 1.50
BCR8 A.J. Green 1.50 4.00
BCR9 Julio Jones 2.00 5.00
BCR10 Jon Baldwin .60 1.50
BCR11 Marcell Dareus .60 1.50
BCR12 Von Miller 1.00 2.50
BCR13 Andy Dalton 1.25 3.00
BCR14 Kyle Rudolph .60 1.50
BCR15 Christian Ponder .60 1.50
BCR16 Blaine Gabbert .60 1.50
BCR17 Jake Locker .60 1.50
BCR18 Cam Newton 3.00 8.00
BCR19 Ryan Mallett .60 1.50
BCR20 Mark Ingram 1.00 2.50
BCR21 Ryan Williams .60 1.50
BCR22 Mikel Leshoure .60 1.50
BCR23 A.J. Green 1.50 4.00
BCR24 Julio Jones 2.00 5.00
BCR25 Jon Baldwin .60 1.50
BCR26 Marcell Dareus .60 1.50
BCR27 Von Miller 1.00 2.50
BCR28 Andy Dalton 1.25 3.00
BCR29 Kyle Rudolph .60 1.50
BCR30 Christian Ponder .60 1.50

2011 Bowman Chrome Rookie Preview Inserts Autographs

STATED ODDS 1:477 TOP.CHROME HOB
BCAR1 Blaine Gabbert 12.00 30.00
BCAR2 Jake Locker 12.00 30.00
BCAR3 Cam Newton 200.00 400.00
BCAR4 Ryan Mallett 12.00 30.00
BCAR5 Mark Ingram 20.00 50.00
BCAR6 Ryan Williams 20.00 50.00
BCAR7 Mikel Leshoure 15.00 40.00
BCAR8 A.J. Green 30.00 80.00
BCAR9 Julio Jones
BCAR10 Jon Baldwin 12.00 30.00
BCAR11 Marcell Dareus 12.00 30.00
BCAR12 Von Miller 30.00 80.00
BCAR13 Andy Dalton 25.00 60.00
BCAR14 Kyle Rudolph 15.00 40.00
BCAR15 Christian Ponder 12.00 30.00
BCAR16 Blaine Gabbert 12.00 30.00
BCAR17 Jake Locker 12.00 30.00
BCAR18 Cam Newton 200.00 400.00
BCAR19 Ryan Mallett 12.00 30.00
BCAR20 Mark Ingram 20.00 50.00
BCAR21 Ryan Williams 20.00 50.00
BCAR22 Mikel Leshoure 15.00 40.00
BCAR23 A.J. Green 30.00 80.00
BCAR24 Julio Jones
BCAR25 Jon Baldwin 12.00 30.00
BCAR26 Marcell Dareus 12.00 30.00
BCAR27 Von Miller 30.00 80.00
BCAR28 Andy Dalton 25.00 60.00
BCAR29 Kyle Rudolph 15.00 40.00
BCAR30 Christian Ponder 12.00 30.00

2013 Bowman Chrome Rookie Autographs Gold Refractors

GOLD STATED PRINT RUN 75
*BLUE/99: .3X TO .8X GOLD AU/75
RCRAAB Arthur Brown 5.00 12.00
RCRAAD Aaron Dobson 5.00 12.00
RCRAAE Andre Ellington 5.00 12.00
RCRAAM Aaron Mellette 5.00 12.00
RCRAAO Alex Okafor 5.00 12.00
RCRAAOG Alec Ogletree 5.00 12.00
RCRABJ Brandon Jenkins 6.00 15.00
RCRABM Barkevious Mingo 5.00 12.00
RCRABW Bjoern Werner 5.00 12.00
RCRACF Corey Fuller 5.00 12.00
RCRACHA Chris Harper 5.00 12.00
RCRACM Christine Michael 5.00 12.00
RCRACP Cordarrelle Patterson 5.00 12.00
RCRACV Conner Vernon 5.00 12.00
RCRACW Chance Warmack 5.00 12.00
RCRADEJ Dennis Johnson 5.00 12.00
RCRADH DeAndre Hopkins 15.00 40.00
RCRADJ Datone Jones 5.00 12.00
RCRADJO Dion Jordan 5.00 12.00
RCRADM Damontre Moore 5.00 12.00
RCRADMI Dee Milliner 5.00 12.00
RCRADR Denard Robinson 5.00 12.00
RCRADRO Da'Rick Rogers 5.00 12.00
RCRADT Desmond Trufant 5.00 12.00
RCRAEA Ezekiel Ansah 4.00 10.00
RCRAEL Eddie Lacy 5.00 12.00
RCRAEM EJ Manuel 5.00 12.00
RCRAER Eric Fisher 5.00 12.00
RCRAERE Eric Reid 15.00 40.00
RCRAJFA Joseph Fauria 5.00 12.00
RCRAJH Johnathan Hankins 5.00 12.00
RCRAJHU Justin Hunter 12.00 30.00
RCRAJJ Jarvis Jones 5.00 12.00
RCRAJJA Jawan Jamison 8.00 20.00
RCRAJJE John Jenkins 5.00 12.00
RCRAJP Jordan Poyer 5.00 12.00
RCRAJR Jordan Reed 8.00 20.00
RCRAKA Keenan Allen 10.00 25.00
RCRAKB Kenjon Barner 5.00 12.00
RCRAKD Knile Davis 10.00 25.00
RCRAKG Khaseem Greene 5.00 12.00
RCRAKS Kenny Stills 5.00 12.00
RCRAKV Kenny Vaccaro 5.00 12.00
RCRAKW Kerwynn Williams 5.00 12.00
RCRALB Le'Veon Bell 25.00 60.00
RCRALJ Luke Joeckel 5.00 12.00
RCRALJO Landry Jones 5.00 12.00
RCRALP Lonnie Pryor 5.00 12.00
RCRAMBA Montee Ball 12.00 30.00
RCRAME Matt Elam 5.00 12.00
RCRAMG Mike Glennon 5.00 12.00
RCRAMGI Mike Gillislee 5.00 12.00
RCRAMGO Marquise Goodwin 5.00 12.00
RCRAML Marcus Lattimore 5.00 12.00
RCRAMS Matt Scott 5.00 12.00
RCRAMT Manti Te'o 12.00 30.00
RCRAMW Markus Wheaton 5.00 12.00
RCRAPL Philip Lutzenkirchen 8.00 20.00
RCRAQP Quinton Patton 15.00 40.00
RCRARG Ray Graham 5.00 12.00
RCRARN Ryan Nassib 15.00 40.00
RCRARS Ryan Swope 5.00 12.00
RCRARW Robert Woods 8.00 20.00
RCRASB Stedman Bailey 5.00 12.00
RCRASM Sam Montgomery 5.00 12.00
RCRASR Sheldon Richardson 10.00 25.00
RCRAST Stepfan Taylor 5.00 12.00
RCRASWI Shawn Williams 5.00 12.00
RCRATA Tavon Austin 6.00 15.00
RCRATB Tyler Bray 5.00 12.00
RCRATE Tyler Eifert 5.00 12.00
RCRATJM T.J. McDonald 5.00 12.00
RCRATK Tavarres King 5.00 12.00
RCRATWI Tyler Wilson 5.00 12.00
RCRAXR Xavier Rhodes 5.00 12.00
RCRAZD Zac Dysert 5.00 12.00
RCRAZE Zach Ertz 10.00 25.00

2013 Bowman Chrome Rookie Autographs Orange Refractors

*ORANGE/50: .4X TO 1X BLUE AU/75
RCRAEL Eddie Lacy 5.00 12.00

2013 Bowman Chrome Rookie Autographs Red Refractors

*RED/25: .6X TO 1.5X GOLD AU/75
RED STATED PRINT RUN 25
RCRAEL Eddie Lacy 8.00 20.00
RCRALB Le'Veon Bell 50.00 100.00
RCRAMBA Montee Ball 25.00 60.00

2013 Bowman Chrome Rookie Autographs Refractors

*REFRACTOR: .2X TO .5X GOLD AU/75
*REFRACTOR SP: .3X TO .8X GOLD AU/75
RCRAEL Eddie Lacy 2.50 6.00
RCRAEM EJ Manuel SP 4.00 10.00
RCRAGS Geno Smith 2.50 6.00
RCRAMB Matt Barkley 6.00 15.00
RCRAMBA Montee Ball SP 10.00 25.00

2013 Bowman Chrome Rookie Dual Autograph Refractors

STATED PRINT RUN 25 SER.#'d SETS
EXCH EXPIRATION: 6/30/2016
BDAAA T.Austin/K.Allen EXCH 20.00 50.00
BDABL G.Bernard/E.Lacy 10.00 25.00
BDABT M.Ball/S.Taylor 20.00 50.00
BDAPH Patterson/D.Hopkins 20.00 50.00
BDASB M.Barkley/G.Smith 10.00 25.00

2014 Bowman Chrome

COMP.SET w/o SP's (220) 25.00 50.00
SP STATED ODDS 1:430
1 Eddie Lacy .20 .50
2 Tyrann Mathieu .25 .60
3 Patrick Peterson .20 .50
4 Darrelle Revis .20 .50
5 J.J. Watt .30 .75
6 Cameron Wake .20 .50
7 Dion Jordan .20 .50
8 Robert Quinn .25 .60
9 DeMarcus Ware .25 .60
10 Jason Pierre-Paul .20 .50
11 Geno Atkins .20 .50
12 Bobby Wagner .20 .50
13 Luke Kuechly .25 .60
14 Von Miller .25 .60
15 Patrick Willis .25 .60
16 Clay Matthews .30 .75
17 Terrell Suggs .20 .50
18 Tamba Hali .20 .50
19 EJ Manuel .20 .50
20 Matthew Stafford .25 .60
21 Aaron Rodgers .60 1.50
22 Andrew Luck .40 1.00
23 Robert Griffin III .20 .50
24 Peyton Manning .60 1.50
25 Cam Newton .30 .75
26 Geno Smith .20 .50
27 Drew Brees .30 .75
28 Tom Brady .75 2.00
29 Colin Kaepernick .25 .60
30 Russell Wilson .50 1.25
31 Eric Berry .25 .60
32 Ryan Tannehill .25 .60
33 Matt Ryan .25 .60
34 Jake Locker .25 .60
35 Richard Sherman .30 .75
36 Tony Romo .25 .60
37 Giovani Bernard .20 .50
38 Jamaal Charles .25 .60
39 Marshawn Lynch .25 .60
40 Frank Gore .25 .60
41 Matt Forte .20 .50
42 Doug Martin .25 .60
43 Andre Ellington .20 .50
44 Alfred Morris .20 .50
45 Mike Glennon .25 .60
46 Arian Foster .25 .60
47 Zac Stacy .20 .50
48 Bernard Pierce .20 .50
49 Reggie Bush .20 .50
50 LeSean McCoy .30 .75
51 Le'Veon Bell .25 .60
52 Nick Foles .25 .60
53 Chris Johnson .20 .50
54 Knowshon Moreno .20 .50
55 Jimmy Graham .30 .75
56 DeMarco Murray .25 .60
57 Maurice Jones-Drew .20 .50
58 Trent Richardson .20 .50
59 Jay Cutler .20 .50
60 Montee Ball .20 .50
61 Stevan Ridley .20 .50
62 Ryan Mathews .25 .60
63 Earl Thomas .25 .60
64 Jordan Cameron .20 .50
65 Dez Bryant .30 .75
66 Ben Roethlisberger .30 .75
67 C.J. Spiller .20 .50
68 Rob Gronkowski .30 .75
69 Julius Thomas .20 .50
70 Vernon Davis .20 .50
71 Jason Witten .25 .60
72 Kyle Rudolph .20 .50
73 Tavon Austin .20 .50
74 Eric Decker .20 .50
75 Calvin Johnson .30 .75
76 Julio Jones .30 .75
77 T.Y. Hilton .25 .60
78 DeSean Jackson .25 .60
79 Jordan Reed .20 .50
80 A.J. Green .30 .75
81 Jordy Nelson .25 .60
82 Brandon Marshall .20 .50
83 DeAndre Hopkins .25 .60
84 Victor Cruz .25 .60
85 Keenan Allen .25 .60
86 Terrance Williams .20 .50
87 Rueben Randle .20 .50
88 Larry Fitzgerald .25 .60
89 Cecil Shorts .20 .50
90 Demaryius Thomas .25 .60
91 Kenny Stills .20 .50
92 Kendall Wright .20 .50
93 Reggie Wayne .25 .60
94 Wes Welker .25 .60
95 Eli Manning .25 .60
96 Torrey Smith .20 .50
97 Marques Colston .20 .50
98 Michael Floyd .20 .50
99 Pierre Garcon .25 .60
100 Antonio Gates .20 .50
101 Alshon Jeffery .25 .60
102 Antonio Brown .30 .75
103 Philip Rivers .30 .75
104 Andre Johnson .25 .60
105 Percy Harvin .20 .50
106 Vincent Jackson .20 .50
107 Mike Wallace .20 .50
108 Randall Cobb .25 .60
109 Michael Crabtree .20 .50
110 Cordarrelle Patterson .20 .50
111 Jason Verrett RC .30 .75
112 Bradley Roby RC .30 .75
113 Trent Murphy RC .30 .75
114 Stephon Tuitt RC .50 1.25
115A Jadeveon Clowney RC .40 1.00
115B Jadeveon Clowney SP 2.50 6.00
116 Arthur Lynch RC .30 .75
117 Cody Hoffman RC .30 .75
118 Ra'Shede Hageman RC .30 .75
119 Dominique Easley RC .30 .75
120 Will Sutton RC .40 1.00
121 Trey Millard RC .40 1.00
122 Anthony Barr RC .30 .75
123A Khalil Mack RC 1.25 3.00
123B Khalil Mack SP 8.00 20.00
124 C.J. Mosley RC .40 1.00
125A Teddy Bridgewater RC .50 1.25
125B Teddy Bridgewater SP 3.00 8.00
126 Kyle Van Noy RC .40 1.00
127 Jake Matthews RC .30 .75
128 Taylor Lewan RC .30 .75
129 Ryan Shazier RC .50 1.25
130A Johnny Manziel RC .50 1.25
130B Johnny Manziel SP 3.00 8.00
131A Zach Mettenberger RC .30 .75
131B Zach Mettenberger SP 2.00 5.00
132A Tajh Boyd RC .30 .75
132B Tajh Boyd SP 2.00 5.00
133 Stephen Morris RC .30 .75
134A Aaron Murray RC .30 .75
134B Aaron Murray SP 2.00 5.00
135A Derek Carr RC 2.00 5.00
135B Derek Carr SP 12.00 30.00
136 Dion Bailey RC .30 .75
137A Charles Sims RC .30 .75
137B Charles Sims SP 2.00 5.00
138 Lache Seastrunk RC .30 .75
139A Ka'Deem Carey RC .30 .75
139B Ka'Deem Carey SP 2.00 5.00
140A Bishop Sankey RC .30 .75
140B Bishop Sankey SP 2.00 5.00
141A De'Anthony Thomas RC .30 .75
141B De'Anthony Thomas SP 2.00 5.00
142 Marion Grice RC .30 .75
143A Aaron Colvin RC .30 .75
143B James White SP 4.00 10.00

144 Silas Redd RC .40 1.00
145A A.J. McCarron RC .30 .75
145B A.J. McCarron SP 2.00 5.00
146 Isaiah Crowell RC .40 1.00
147 Damien Williams RC .30 .75
148 James White RC .60 1.50
149 Ahmad Dixon RC .30 .75
150 Ha Ha Clinton-Dix RC .40 1.00
152 Deone Bucannon RC .30 .75
153A Eric Ebron RC .40 1.00
153B Eric Ebron SP 2.50 6.00
154A Jace Amaro RC .30 .75
154B Jace Amaro SP 2.00 5.00
155A Sammy Watkins RC .50 1.25
155B Sammy Watkins SP 3.00 8.00
156 C.J. Fiedorowicz RC .30 .75
157A Xavier Grimble RC .40 1.00
157B Xavier Grimble SP 2.50 6.00
158A Austin Seferian-Jenkins RC .30 .75
158B Austin Seferian-Jenkins SP 2.00 5.00
159 Jalen Saunders RC .30 .75
160A Marqise Lee RC .40 1.00
160B Marqise Lee SP 2.50 6.00
161A Allen Robinson RC .50 1.25
161B Allen Robinson SP 3.00 8.00
162A Jordan Matthews RC .50 1.25
162B Jordan Matthews SP 3.00 8.00
163A Paul Richardson RC .40 1.00
163B Paul Richardson SP 2.50 6.00
164A Jarvis Landry RC .60 1.50
164B Jarvis Landry SP 4.00 10.00
165A Brandin Cooks RC .50 1.25
165B Brandin Cooks SP 3.00 8.00
166 Brandon Coleman RC .30 .75
167A Donte Moncrief RC .30 .75
167B Donte Moncrief SP 2.00 5.00
168A Jared Abbrederis RC .30 .75
168B Jared Abbrederis SP 2.00 5.00
169 Devin Street RC .30 .75
170A Mike Evans RC .75 2.00
170B Mike Evans SP 5.00 12.00
171 Mike Davis RC .30 .75
172A Robert Herron RC .30 .75
172B Robert Herron SP 2.00 5.00
173 Kareem Martin RC .30 .75
174 Michael Campanaro RC .30 .75
175A Jimmy Garoppolo RC 2.50 6.00
175B Jimmy Garoppolo SP 15.00 40.00
176 Cyrus Kouandjio RC .40 1.00
177A David Fales RC .30 .75
177B David Fales SP 2.00 5.00
178 Scott Crichton RC .30 .75
179A Logan Thomas RC .30 .75
179B Logan Thomas SP 2.00 5.00
180A Kelvin Benjamin RC .50 1.25
180B Kelvin Benjamin SP 3.00 8.00
181 Antonio Andrews RC .30 .75
182 Cassius Marsh RC .40 1.00
183 Rajion Neal RC .30 .75
184A Josh Huff RC .40 1.00
184B Josh Huff SP 2.50 6.00
185A Andre Williams RC .30 .75
185B Andre Williams SP 2.00 5.00
186 Connor Shaw RC .30 .75
187A Dri Archer RC .30 .75
187B Dri Archer SP 2.00 5.00
188 Ryan Grant RC .30 .75
189 Darqueze Dennard RC .40 1.00
190A Odell Beckham Jr. RC .75 2.00
190B Odell Beckham Jr. SP
191 Troy Niklas RC .30 .75
192A Jeremy Hill RC .40 1.00
192B Jeremy Hill SP 2.50 6.00
193A Martavis Bryant RC .40 1.00
193B Martavis Bryant SP 2.50 6.00
194A Tom Savage RC .30 .75
194B Tom Savage SP 2.00 5.00
195A Blake Bortles RC .40 1.00
195B Blake Bortles SP 2.50 6.00
196 Kony Ealy RC .40 1.00
197A Davante Adams RC .50 1.25
197B Davante Adams SP 3.00 8.00
198 Greg Robinson RC .30 .75
199 Aaron Donald RC .75 2.00
200A Michael Sam RC .30 .75
200B Michael Sam SP 2.00 5.00
201A Cody Latimer RC .40 1.00
201B Cody Latimer SP 2.50 6.00
202A Terrance West RC .30 .75
202B Terrance West SP 2.00 5.00
203A Devonta Freeman RC .50 1.25
203B Devonta Freeman SP 3.00 8.00
204 Shaquelle Evans RC .30 .75
205A Tre Mason RC .30 .75
205B Tre Mason SP 2.00 5.00
206A Kevin Norwood RC .30 .75
206B Kevin Norwood SP 2.00 5.00
207A Bruce Ellington RC .30 .75
207B Bruce Ellington SP 2.00 5.00
208 Calvin Pryor RC .30 .75
209 Lorenzo Taliaferro RC .30 .75
210A Carlos Hyde RC .40 1.00
210B Carlos Hyde SP 2.50 6.00
211 Garrett Gilbert RC .30 .75
212 Henry Josey RC .30 .75
213 Richard Rodgers RC .50 1.25
214 Jeff Janis RC .30 .75
215 Jerick McKinnon RC .40 1.00
216 Justin Gilbert RC .30 .75
217 Colt Lyerla RC .50 1.25
218 Jordan Lynch RC .40 1.00
219 John Brown RC .50 1.25
220 Timmy Jernigan RC .30 .75
222 Pierre Desir RC .30 .75

2014 Bowman Chrome Black Refractors

*VETS/299: 2X TO 5X BASIC CARDS
*ROOKIES/299: 1.2X TO 3X BASIC CARDS
STATED ODDS 1:17
175 Jimmy Garoppolo 20.00 40.00
190 Odell Beckham Jr. 12.00 30.00

2014 Bowman Chrome Blue Refractors

*VETS/199: 2X TO 5X BASIC CARDS
*ROOKIES/199: 1.2X TO 3X BASIC CARDS
STATED ODDS 1:25
175 Jimmy Garoppolo 25.00 60.00
190 Odell Beckham Jr. 12.00 30.00

2014 Bowman Chrome Bubbles Refractors

*VETS/99: 2.5X TO 6X BASIC CARDS
*ROOKIES/99: 1.5X TO 4X BASIC CARDS
STATED ODDS 1:50
190 Odell Beckham Jr. 15.00 40.00

2014 Bowman Chrome Gold Refractors

*VETS/50: 8X TO 20X BASIC CARDS
*ROOKIES/50: 5X TO 12X BASIC CARDS
STATED ODDS 1:98
175 Jimmy Garoppolo 60.00 125.00
190 Odell Beckham Jr. 50.00 80.00

2014 Bowman Chrome Pulsar Refractors

*VETS/271: 2X TO 5X BASIC CARDS
*ROOKIES/271: 1.2X TO 3X BASIC CARDS
STATED ODDS 1:18
175 Jimmy Garoppolo 25.00 50.00
190 Odell Beckham Jr. 12.00 30.00

2014 Bowman Chrome Red Refractors

*VETS/25: 12X TO 30X BASIC CARDS
*ROOKIES/25: 8X TO 20X BASIC CARDS
STATED ODDS 1:195
175 Jimmy Garoppolo 40.00 80.00
190 Odell Beckham Jr. 75.00 150.00

2014 Bowman Chrome Refractors

*VETS: 1.2X TO 3X BASIC CARDS
*ROOKIES: .8X TO 2X BASIC CARDS
STATED ODDS 1:4 HOBBY
190 Odell Beckham Jr. 6.00 15.00

2014 Bowman Chrome Bowman's Best Die Cut

STATED ODDS 1:9
*GOLD/50: 1X TO 2.5X BASIC INSERTS
BBAM A.J. McCarron .60 1.50
BBAMU Aaron Murray .60 1.50
BBAW Andre Williams .60 1.50
BBBB Blake Bortles .75 2.00
BBBC Brandin Cooks 1.00 2.50
BBBS Bishop Sankey .60 1.50
BBCH Carlos Hyde .75 2.00
BBCL Cody Latimer .75 2.00
BBCS Charles Sims .60 1.50
BBDA Davante Adams 1.00 2.50
BBDC Derek Carr 4.00 10.00
BBDF Devonta Freeman 1.00 2.50
BBEE Eric Ebron .75 2.00
BBJC Jadeveon Clowney .75 2.00
BBJG Jimmy Garoppolo 5.00 12.00
BBJH Jeremy Hill .75 2.00
BBJL Jarvis Landry 1.25 3.00
BBJM Johnny Manziel 1.00 2.50
BBJMA Jordan Matthews 1.00 2.50
BBKB Kelvin Benjamin 1.00 2.50
BBKC Ka'Deem Carey .60 1.50
BBME Mike Evans 1.50 4.00
BBML Marqise Lee .75 2.00
BBOB Odell Beckham Jr. 8.00 20.00
BBSW Sammy Watkins 1.00 2.50
BBTB Teddy Bridgewater 1.00 2.50
BBTBO Tajh Boyd .60 1.50
BBTM Tre Mason .60 1.50
BBTS Tom Savage .60 1.50
BBTW Terrance West .60 1.50

2014 Bowman Chrome Future of the Franchise Minis Die Cut

STATED ODDS 1:18
*GOLD/332: .6X TO 1.5X BASIC INSERTS
FFBB Blake Bortles .75 2.00
FFBC Brandin Cooks 1.00 2.50
FFBS Bishop Sankey .60 1.50
FFDC Derek Carr 4.00 10.00
FFEE Eric Ebron .75 2.00
FFJC Jadeveon Clowney .75 2.00
FFJG Jimmy Garoppolo 5.00 12.00
FFJM Johnny Manziel 1.00 2.50
FFJMA Jordan Matthews 1.00 2.50
FFKB Kelvin Benjamin 1.00 2.50
FFME Mike Evans 1.50 4.00
FFOB Odell Beckham Jr. 1.50 4.00
FFSW Sammy Watkins 1.00 2.50
FFTB Teddy Bridgewater 1.00 2.50
FFTM Tre Mason .60 1.50

2014 Bowman Chrome Rookie Autographs Refractors

*BASE REF.AU: .2X TO .5X GOLD AU/50
STATED ODDS 1:24
EXCH EXPIRATION: 12/31/2017
RCRADC Derek Carr 125.00 250.00
RCRAJG Jimmy Garoppolo 60.00 125.00
RCRAOB Odell Beckham Jr. 50.00 100.00

2014 Bowman Chrome Rookie Autographs Blue Refractors

*BLUE AU/199: .25X TO .6X GOLD AU/50
RCRAOB Odell Beckham Jr. 50.00 100.00

2014 Bowman Chrome Rookie Autographs Bubbles Refractors

*BUBBLES AU/99: .3X TO .8X GOLD AU/50
RCRAOB Odell Beckham Jr. 60.00 125.00

2014 Bowman Chrome Rookie Autographs Gold Refractors

EXCH EXPIRATION: 12/31/2017
RCRAAA Antonio Andrews 5.00 12.00
RCRAAB Anthony Barr 5.00 12.00
RCRAAD Aaron Donald 40.00 100.00
RCRAAHU Allen Hurns 6.00 15.00
RCRAAL Arthur Lynch 5.00 12.00
RCRAAM A.J. McCarron 25.00 50.00
RCRAAMU Aaron Murray 5.00 12.00
RCRAAR Allen Robinson 8.00 20.00
RCRAASJ Austin Seferian-Jenkins 5.00 12.00
RCRAAW Andre Williams 5.00 12.00
RCRABB Blake Bortles 6.00 15.00
RCRABC Brandin Cooks 8.00 20.00
RCRABCO Brandon Coleman 5.00 12.00
RCRABE Bruce Ellington 5.00 12.00
RCRABS Bishop Sankey 8.00 20.00
RCRACHO Cody Hoffman 5.00 12.00
RCRACJF C.J. Fiedorowicz 5.00 12.00
RCRACJM C.J. Mosley 6.00 15.00
RCRACL Cody Latimer 10.00 25.00
RCRACLY Colt Lyerla 8.00 20.00
RCRACP Calvin Pryor 5.00 12.00
RCRACS Charles Sims 5.00 12.00
RCRACSH Connor Shaw 5.00 12.00
RCRACW Corey Washington 8.00 20.00
RCRADA Davante Adams 15.00 40.00
RCRADAR Dri Archer 5.00 12.00
RCRADB Deone Bucannon 5.00 12.00
RCRADBA Dion Bailey 5.00 12.00
RCRADC Derek Carr 200.00 400.00
RCRADD Darqueze Dennard 6.00 15.00
RCRADE Dominique Easley 5.00 12.00
RCRADF Devonta Freeman 20.00 50.00
RCRADFA David Fales 5.00 12.00
RCRADM Donte Moncrief 12.00 30.00
RCRADS Devin Street 5.00 12.00
RCRADW Damien Williams 5.00 12.00
RCRAEE Eric Ebron 6.00 15.00
RCRAHCD Ha Ha Clinton-Dix 6.00 15.00
RCRAIC Isaiah Crowell 6.00 15.00
RCRAJA Jace Amaro 5.00 12.00
RCRAJAB Jared Abbrederis 5.00 12.00
RCRAJB John Brown 8.00 20.00
RCRAJC Jadeveon Clowney 6.00 15.00
RCRAJG Jimmy Garoppolo 125.00 250.00
RCRAJH Jeremy Hill 6.00 15.00
RCRAJHU Josh Huff 6.00 15.00
RCRAJJ Jeff Janis 5.00 12.00
RCRAJL Jarvis Landry 10.00 25.00
RCRAJM Johnny Manziel 12.00 30.00
RCRAJMA Jake Matthews 5.00 12.00
RCRAJMAT Jordan Matthews 8.00 20.00
RCRAJV Jason Verrett 5.00 12.00
RCRAJW James White 10.00 25.00
RCRAKB Kelvin Benjamin 8.00 20.00
RCRAKE Kony Ealy 6.00 15.00
RCRAKN Kevin Norwood 5.00 12.00
RCRAKVN Kyle Van Noy 6.00 15.00
RCRALS Lache Seastrunk 5.00 12.00
RCRALT Logan Thomas 5.00 12.00
RCRALTA Lorenzo Taliaferro 5.00 12.00
RCRAMB Martavis Bryant 6.00 15.00
RCRAMD Mike Davis 5.00 12.00
RCRAME Mike Evans 12.00 30.00
RCRAMG Marion Grice 5.00 12.00
RCRAML Marqise Lee 6.00 15.00
RCRAMS Michael Sam 5.00 12.00
RCRAOB Odell Beckham Jr. 100.00 200.00
RCRAPR Paul Richardson 6.00 15.00
RCRARH Robert Herron 5.00 12.00
RCRARR Richard Rodgers 8.00 20.00
RCRARS Ryan Shazier 8.00 20.00
RCRARSH Ra'Shede Hageman 5.00 12.00
RCRASE Shaquelle Evans
RCRASM Stephen Morris 5.00 12.00
RCRASR Silas Redd 6.00 15.00
RCRAST Stephon Tuitt 8.00 20.00
RCRASW Sammy Watkins 8.00 20.00
RCRATB Teddy Bridgewater 8.00 20.00
RCRATBO Tajh Boyd 5.00 12.00
RCRATMI Trey Millard 6.00 15.00
RCRATN Troy Niklas 5.00 12.00
RCRATS Tom Savage 5.00 12.00
RCRATW Terrance West 5.00 12.00
RCRAWS Will Sutton
RCRAXG Xavier Grimble 6.00 15.00
RCRAZM Zach Mettenberger 5.00 12.00
RSRAGG Garrett Gilbert 5.00 12.00

2014 Bowman Chrome Topps Shelf Rookies

STATED ODDS 1:18
*GOLD/50: 1X TO 2.5X BASIC INSERTS
*XFRACTORS/10: 2.5X TO 6X BASIC INSERTS
TSRAM A.J. McCarron .60 1.50
TSRAMU Aaron Murray .60 1.50
TSRAW Andre Williams .60 1.50
TSRBB Blake Bortles .75 2.00
TSRBC Brandin Cooks 1.00 2.50
TSRBS Bishop Sankey .60 1.50
TSRCH Carlos Hyde .75 2.00
TSRCL Cody Latimer .75 2.00
TSRCS Charles Sims .60 1.50
TSRDA Davante Adams 1.00 2.50
TSRDC Derek Carr 4.00 10.00
TSRDF Devonta Freeman 1.00 2.50
TSREE Eric Ebron .75 2.00
TSRJC Jadeveon Clowney .75 2.00
TSRJG Jimmy Garoppolo 8.00 20.00
TSRJH Jeremy Hill .75 2.00
TSRJL Jarvis Landry 1.25 3.00
TSRJM Johnny Manziel 1.00 2.50
TSRJMA Jordan Matthews 1.00 2.50
TSRKB Kelvin Benjamin 1.00 2.50
TSRKC Ka'Deem Carey .60 1.50
TSRME Mike Evans 1.50 4.00
TSRML Marqise Lee .75 2.00
TSROB Odell Beckham Jr. 1.50 4.00
TSRSW Sammy Watkins 1.00 2.50
TSRTB Teddy Bridgewater 1.00 2.50
TSRTBO Tajh Boyd .60 1.50
TSRTM Tre Mason .60 1.50
TSRTS Tom Savage .60 1.50
TSRTW Terrance West .60 1.50

2009 Bowman Draft

COMPLETE SET (220) 20.00 40.00
1 Drew Brees .25 .60
2 Ben Roethlisberger .25 .60
3 Eli Manning .20 .50
4 Tony Romo .20 .50
5 Philip Rivers .25 .60
6 Aaron Rodgers .50 1.25
7 Brett Favre .50 1.25
8 Jay Cutler .15 .40
9 Matt Ryan .20 .50
10 Tom Brady .75 2.00
11 Carson Palmer .20 .50
12 Peyton Manning .60 1.50
13 Kerry Collins .15 .40
14 Kurt Warner .20 .50
15 Jason Campbell .15 .40
16 Chad Pennington .15 .40
17 Trent Edwards .15 .40
18 Matt Schaub .15 .40
19 Donovan McNabb .20 .50
20 Jared Allen .15 .40
21 Kyle Orton .15 .40
22 JaMarcus Russell .15 .40
23 Joe Flacco .20 .50
24 Jake Delhomme .15 .40
25 David Garrard .15 .40
26 Matt Cassel .15 .40
27 Derek Anderson .15 .40
28 Steven Jackson .15 .40
29 Clinton Portis .15 .40
30 Adrian Peterson .25 .60
31 LaDainian Tomlinson .25 .60
32 Marion Barber .20 .50
33 Brian Westbrook .15 .40
34 Frank Gore .20 .50
35 Chris Johnson .15 .40
36 Michael Turner .15 .40
37 Brandon Jacobs .15 .40
38 Steve Slaton .15 .40
39 Matt Forte .15 .40
40 Leon Washington .15 .40
41 Fred Taylor .15 .40
42 Joseph Addai .15 .40
43 Willis McGahee .15 .40
44 Marshawn Lynch .20 .50
45 Thomas Jones .15 .40
46 DeAngelo Williams .15 .40
47 Earnest Graham .15 .40
48 Jamal Lewis .20 .50
49 John Carlson .20 .50
50 Ryan Grant .20 .50
51 Ronnie Brown .15 .40
52 Jonathan Stewart .15 .40
53 Kevin Boss .15 .40
54 Darren McFadden .25 .60
55 Maurice Jones-Drew .15 .40
56 LenDale White .15 .40
57 Pierre Thomas .15 .40
58 LaMarr Woodley .15 .40
59 Warrick Dunn .15 .40
60 Sammy Morris .15 .40
61 Reggie Bush .15 .40
62 Kevin Smith .15 .40
63 Ricky Williams .20 .50
64 Felix Jones .15 .40
65 Anquan Boldin .15 .40
66 Andre Johnson .20 .50
67 Larry Fitzgerald .20 .50
68 Steve Smith .20 .50
69 Greg Jennings .15 .40
70 Santana Moss .20 .50
71 Brandon Marshall .20 .50
72 T.J. Houshmandzadeh .15 .40
73 Eddie Royal .15 .40
74 Chad Johnson .15 .40
75 Troy Polamalu .25 .60
76 Terrell Owens .20 .50
77 Braylon Edwards .15 .40
78 Randy Moss .20 .50
79 Reggie Wayne .20 .50
80 Wes Welker .20 .50
81 Roddy White .15 .40
82 Dwayne Bowe .20 .50
83 Lance Moore .15 .40
84 Tim Hightower .15 .40
85 Antonio Bryant .15 .40
86 Jerricho Cotchery .15 .40
87 Laveranues Coles .15 .40
88 Derrick Mason .15 .40
89 Peyton Hillis .20 .50
90 Greg Camarillo .20 .50
91 DeSean Jackson .20 .50
92 Ed Reed .20 .50
93 Lee Evans .20 .50
94 Hines Ward .20 .50
95 Calvin Johnson .25 .60
96 Steve Smith USC .20 .50
97 Bernard Berrian .15 .40
98 Chris Cooley .15 .40
99 Tony Gonzalez .20 .50
100 Kevin Walter .20 .50
101 Antonio Gates .20 .50
102 Jason Witten .20 .50
103 Dallas Clark .15 .40
104 Joey Porter .20 .50
105 Patrick Willis .20 .50
106 DeMarcus Ware .20 .50
107 James Harrison .25 .60
108 Charles Woodson .25 .60
109 Oshiomogho Atogwe .15 .40
110 Justin Tuck .15 .40
111 Matthew Stafford RC 2.00 5.00
112 Brian Orakpo RC .50 1.25
113 Michael Oher RC .60 1.50
114 Michael Crabtree RC .60 1.50
115 Andre Smith RC .40 1.00
116 Knowshon Moreno RC .40 1.00
117 Aaron Curry RC .60 1.50
118 Gartrell Johnson RC .40 1.00
119 Jason Smith RC .40 1.00
120 James Laurinaitis RC .40 1.00
121 Chris Wells RC .40 1.00
122 Glen Coffee RC .40 1.00
123 Eugene Monroe RC .40 1.00
124 Rey Maualuga RC .60 1.50
125 Malcolm Jenkins RC .40 1.00
126 Michael Johnson RC .40 1.00
127 Javon Ringer RC .40 1.00
128 B.J. Raji RC .50 1.25
129 Donald Brown RC .40 1.00
130 Clint Sintim RC .40 1.00
131 Brian Cushing RC .40 1.00
132 Brandon Pettigrew RC .40 1.00
133 Alphonso Smith RC .40 1.00
134 Vontae Davis RC .40 1.00
135 Jeremy Maclin RC .50 1.25
136 John Parker Wilson RC .40 1.00
137 Peria Jerry RC .40 1.00
138 Chase Coffman RC .40 1.00
139 Darius Butler RC .50 1.25
140 Jamon Meredith RC .40 1.00
141 Alex Mack RC .40 1.00
142 Jarett Dillard RC .40 1.00
143 Mike Mickens RC .40 1.00
144 William Moore RC .40 1.00
145 Austin Collie RC .40 1.00
146 Fili Moala RC .40 1.00
147 Percy Harvin RC .40 1.00
148 Jared Cook Jr. RC .50 1.25
149 Rashad Jennings RC .50 1.25
150 Rhett Bomar RC .40 1.00
151 Sen'Derrick Marks RC .40 1.00
152 Duke Robinson RC .40 1.00
153 Everette Brown RC .40 1.00
154 Darrius Heyward-Bey RC .60 1.50
155 Jeremy Childs RC .40 1.00
156 Darius Passmore RC .40 1.00
157 Brooks Foster RC .40 1.00
158 Tyson Jackson RC .40 1.00
159 James Casey RC .50 1.25
160 Marcus Freeman RC .40 1.00
161 Max Unger RC .60 1.50
162 Josh Freeman RC .40 1.00
163 Victor Harris RC .50 1.25
164 Derrick Williams RC .40 1.00
165 Jonathan Luigs RC .40 1.00
166 Graham Harrell RC .40 1.00
167 Pat White RC .50 1.25
168 Chase Daniel RC .50 1.25
169 Mike Goodson RC .50 1.25
170 LeSean McCoy RC 1.00 2.50
171 James Davis RC .40 1.00
172 Ramses Barden RC .40 1.00
173 Juaquin Iglesias RC .40 1.00
174 Cedric Peerman RC .40 1.00
175 Kenny Britt RC .60 1.50
176 Marlon Lucky RC .40 1.00
177 Mohamed Massaquoi RC .40 1.00
178 Louis Murphy RC .40 1.00
179 Tyrell Sutton RC .40 1.00
180 Andre Brown RC .50 1.25
181 Brandon Tate RC .50 1.25
182 Kory Sheets RC .50 1.25
183 Arian Foster RC 1.00 2.50
184 Demetrius Byrd RC .50 1.25
185 Hunter Cantwell RC .40 1.00
186 Brandon Gibson RC .50 1.25
187 Brian Robiskie RC .40 1.00
188 Dannell Ellerbe RC .50 1.25
189 Cornelius Ingram RC .40 1.00
190 Mark Sanchez RC .40 1.00
191 Kenny McKinley RC .40 1.00
192 Travis Beckum RC .40 1.00
193 Jeremiah Johnson RC .40 1.00
194 P.J. Hill RC .40 1.00
195 Deon Butler RC .40 1.00
196 Clay Matthews RC 1.50 4.00
197 Patrick Chung RC .40 1.00
198 Patrick Turner RC .40 1.00
199 Darry Beckwith RC .40 1.00
200 Nate Davis RC .40 1.00
201 Stephen McGee RC .40 1.00
202 Aaron Kelly RC .40 1.00
203 Ian Johnson RC .40 1.00
204 Brian Hoyer RC .60 1.50
205 Shonn Greene RC .40 1.00
206 Sammie Stroughter RC .40 1.00
207 Cullen Harper RC .40 1.00
208 Devin Moore RC .40 1.00
209 Quan Cosby RC .40 1.00
210 Hakeem Nicks RC .50 1.25
211 Kevin Ellison RC .40 1.00
212 Phil Loadholt RC .50 1.25
213 Scott McKillop RC .40 1.00
214 Brad Lester RC .40 1.00
215 Michael Hamlin RC .40 1.00
216 Fenuki Tupou RC .40 1.00
217 Terrance Taylor RC .50 1.25
218 Zack Follett RC .40 1.00
219 Aaron Maybin RC .50 1.25
220 Worrell Williams RC .40 1.00

2009 Bowman Draft Blue

*VETS: 3X TO 8X BASIC CARDS
*ROOKIES: 1X TO 2.5X BASIC CARDS
BLUE/199 ODDS 1:32 HOB

2009 Bowman Draft Bronze

*VETS: 4X TO 10X BASIC CARDS
*ROOKIES: 1.2X TO 3X BASIC CARDS
BRONZE/99 ODDS 1:67 HOB

2009 Bowman Draft Gold

*VETS: 12X TO 30X BASIC CARDS
*ROOKIES: 3X TO 8X BASIC CARDS
GOLD/10 ODDS 1:668 HOB

2009 Bowman Draft Orange

COMPLETE SET (220) 75.00 150.00
*VETS: 1.2X TO 3X BASIC CARDS
*ROOKIES: .5X TO 1.2X BASIC CARDS
ONE BASE PARALLEL PER PACK

2009 Bowman Draft Silver

*VETS: 5X TO 12X BASIC CARDS
*ROOKIES: 1.5X TO 4X BASIC CARDS
SILVER/50 ODDS 1:131 HOB

2009 Bowman Draft White

COMPLETE SET (220) 100.00 200.00
*VETS: 1.5X TO 4X BASIC CARDS
*ROOKIES: .6X TO 1.5X BASIC CARDS
WHITE/299 ODDS 1:22 HOB

2009 Bowman Draft All-Star Alumni

COMPLETE SET (10) 6.00 15.00
STATED ODDS 1:6
*BRONZE/99: 1X TO 2.5X BASIC INSERTS
BRONZE PRINT RUN 99 SER.#'d SETS
*GOLD/10: 4X TO 10X BASIC INSERTS
GOLD PRINT RUN 10 SER.#'d SETS
*SILVER/50: 1.2X TO 3X BASIC INSERTS
SILVER PRINT RUN 50 SER.#'d SETS
AA1 Matt Ryan .60 1.50
AA2 Eli Manning .60 1.50
AA3 Peyton Manning 2.00 5.00
AA4 Adrian Peterson .75 2.00
AA5 Andre Johnson .60 1.50
AA6 Steve Slaton .50 1.25
AA7 Matt Forte .50 1.25
AA8 Larry Fitzgerald .60 1.50
AA9 Eddie Royal .50 1.25
AA10 DeAngelo Williams .50 1.25

2009 Bowman Draft All-Star Alumni Combos

COMPLETE SET (10) 8.00 20.00
STATED ODDS 1:12
*BRONZE/99: .8X TO 2X BASIC INSERTS
BRONZE PRINT RUN 99 SER.#'d SETS
*GOLD/10: 3X TO 8X BASIC INSERTS
GOLD PRINT RUN 10 SER.#'d SETS
*SILVER/50: 1X TO 2.5X BASIC INSERTS
SILVER PRINT RUN 50 SER.#'d SETS
AAC1 M.Ryan/Kiwanuka .75 2.00
AAC2 E.Manning/P.Willis .75 2.00
AAC3 P.Manning/J.Mayo 2.50 6.00
AAC4 A.Johnson/Winslow .75 2.00
AAC5 J.Addai/D.Bowe .60 1.50
AAC6 M.Lynch/D.Jackson .75 2.00
AAC7 B.Marshall/K.Smith .75 2.00
AAC8 R.Bush/T.Polamalu 1.00 2.50
AAC9 T.Brady/B.Edwards 3.00 8.00
AAC10 L.Fitzgerald/D.Revis .75 2.00

2009 Bowman Draft College Letter Patch Autographs

GROUP A ODDS 1:915
GROUP B ODDS 1:1250
GROUP C ODDS 1:375
GROUP D ODDS 1:336
GROUP E ODDS 1:160
GROUP F ODDS 1:125
GROUP G ODDS 1:104
TOTAL PRINT RUNS GIVEN BELOW
EXCH EXPIRATION: 5/31/2012
AB Andre Brown F/920* 6.00 15.00
AC Austin Collie E/690* 5.00 12.00
ACU Aaron Curry A/100* 20.00 50.00
AF Arian Foster D/468* 12.00 30.00
AK Aaron Kelly F/920* 5.00 12.00
BC Brian Cushing A/63* 8.00 20.00
BF Brooks Foster G/1038* 5.00 12.00
BG Brandon Gibson G/1038 6.00 15.00
BO Brian Orakpo C/270* 12.00 30.00
BP Brandon Pettigrew D/360* 5.00 12.00
CC Chase Coffman B/105* 6.00 15.00
CD Chase Daniel A/72* 10.00 25.00
CH Cullen Harper D/480* 5.00 12.00
CP Cedric Peerman E/700* 5.00 12.00
CW Chris Wells A/60* 25.00 50.00
DB Donald Brown C/275* 6.00 15.00
DBY Demetrius Byrd F/920* 6.00 15.00
DHB Darrius Heyward-Bey B/130* 10.00 25.00
DM Devin Moore D/460* 5.00 12.00
DP Darius Passmore G/1040* 5.00 12.00
DW Derrick Williams C/232* 6.00 15.00
GC Glen Coffee E/690* 5.00 12.00
GH Graham Harrell A/84* 20.00 50.00
GJ Gartrell Johnson F/945* 5.00 12.00
HN Hakeem Nicks A/85* 10.00 25.00
IJ Ian Johnson G/1050* 5.00 12.00
JC Jeremy Childs F/930* 5.00 12.00
JCO Jared Cook D/360* 6.00 15.00
JD Jarett Dillard G/1050* 5.00 12.00
JDA James Davis C 6.00 15.00
JF Josh Freeman B/112* 6.00 15.00
JI Juaquin Iglesias B 6.00 15.00
JJ Jeremiah Johnson E/700 5.00 12.00
JL James Laurinaitis B/132* 15.00 40.00
JM Jeremy Maclin A/54* 15.00 40.00
JMS Matthew Stafford A/64* 60.00 150.00
JPW John Parker Wilson B/120* 6.00 15.00
JR Javon Ringer C/240* 6.00 15.00
JW Jaison Williams G/1040* 6.00 15.00
KB Kenny Britt C/230* 10.00 25.00
KM Knowshon Moreno A/78* 8.00 20.00
KS Kory Sheets G/1050* 6.00 15.00
LM Louis Murphy F/930* 5.00 12.00
LMC LeSean McCoy C/260* 20.00 50.00
MC Michael Crabtree A/56* 12.00 30.00
MJ Malcolm Jenkins A/56* 8.00 20.00
MJO Michael Johnson D/455* 5.00 12.00
ML Marlon Lucky G/1035* 5.00 12.00
MM Mohamed Massaquoi E/702* 5.00 12.00
MS Mark Sanchez A/56* 30.00 80.00
ND Nate Davis A/100* 8.00 20.00
PH Percy Harvin A/90* 8.00 20.00
PJH P.J. Hill E/692* 5.00 12.00
PW Pat White A/85* 10.00 25.00
QC Quan Cosby F/920* 5.00 12.00
RB Ramses Barden C/240* 6.00 15.00
RBO Rhett Bomar B115* 6.00 15.00
RJ Rashad Jennings C232* 8.00 20.00
RM Rey Maualuga A/64* 12.00 30.00
SG Shonn Greene C/216* 6.00 15.00
SS Sammie Stroughter F/920* 5.00 12.00
TS Tyrell Sutton E/690* 5.00 12.00

2009 Bowman Draft College Logo Patch Autographs

VARIATIONS: .4X TO 1X BASIC INSERTS
GROUP A/25 ODDS 1:5800
GROUP B/40 ODDS 1:1700
GROUP C/75 ODDS 1:399
GROUP D/250 ODDS 1:224
GROUP E/300 ODDS 1:301
EXCH EXPIRATION: 5/31/2012
AB Andre Brown/300 NCS 6.00 15.00
AC Austin Collie/250 BYU 5.00 12.00
AF Arian Foster/75 T 15.00 40.00
BG B.Gibson/300 Cougars 6.00 15.00
CD Chase Daniel/40 Missouri 10.00 25.00
CP Cedric Peerman/250 V 5.00 12.00
CW Chris Wells/40 Ohio State 30.00 80.00
DB Donald Brown/40 UConn 8.00 20.00
DM Devin Moore/75 UW 6.00 15.00
DW D.Williams/75 paw print 10.00 25.00
GC Glen Coffee/250 A 12.00 30.00
GH Graham Harrell/40 TT 12.00 30.00
HN Hakeem Nicks/75 NC 8.00 20.00
IJ Ian Johnson 5.00 12.00
JC Jared Cook/75 C 8.00 20.00
JD Jarett Dillard/300 R 5.00 12.00
JF J.Freeman/75 wildcat head 6.00 15.00
JI Juaquin Iglesias/75 OU 6.00 15.00
JJ Jeremiah Johnson/250 O 5.00 12.00
JL J.Laurinaitis/75 Ohio State 15.00 40.00
JM Jeremy Maclin/40 Missouri 10.00 25.00
KB Kenny Britt/75 R 10.00 25.00
KM Knowshon Moreno/25 G 10.00 25.00
KS Kory Sheets P 6.00 15.00
LM Louis Murphy/300 Gators 5.00 12.00
MC Michael Crabtree/25 TT 15.00 40.00
MM Mohamed Massaquoi/250 G 5.00 12.00
MS Matthew Stafford/25 G 60.00 150.00
ND Nate Davis/40 Hemet 8.00 20.00
PH Percy Harvin/40 Gators 8.00 20.00
QC Quan Cosby/300 UT 5.00 12.00
RB Ramses Barden/75 CP 15.00 30.00
RJ Rashad Jennings/75 LU 8.00 20.00
TS Tyrell Sutton/250 NU 5.00 12.00
WM William Moore/75 Missouri 6.00 15.00
JDA James Davis/75 EXCH 6.00 15.00
JPW John Parker Wilson/75 A 15.00 30.00
LMC LeSean McCoy/40 20.00 50.00
MSA Mark Sanchez/25 USC 40.00 100.00
PJH P.J. Hill/250 W 5.00 12.00
RBO Rhett Bomar/75 SH Paw 6.00 15.00

2009 Bowman Draft Rivals

COMPLETE SET (10) 10.00 25.00
STATED ODDS 1:12
*BRONZE/99: .8X TO 2X BASIC INSERTS
BRONZE PRINT RUN 99 SER.#'d SETS
*GOLD/10: 3X TO 8X BASIC INSERTS
GOLD PRINT RUN 10 SER.#'d SETS
*SILVER/50: 1X TO 2.5X BASIC INSERTS
SILVER PRINT RUN 50 SER.#'d SETS
R1 J.Maclin/V.Davis .50 1.25
R2 P.White/L.McCoy 1.00 2.50
R3 J.Ringer/D.Williams .40 1.00
R4 T.Taylor/C.Wells .40 1.00
R5 K.Moreno/P.Harvin .40 1.00
R6 J.Johnson/Stroughter .40 1.00
R7 J.Laurinaitis/D.Butler .40 1.00
R8 A.Smith/S.Marks .40 1.00
R9 M.Lucky/J.Iglesias .40 1.00
R10 W.Williams/Maualuga .60 1.50

2009 Bowman Draft Rookie All-Stars

COMPLETE SET (20) 20.00 40.00
STATED ODDS 1:6
*BRONZE/99: .8X TO 2X BASIC INSERTS
BRONZE PRINT RUN 99 SER.#'d SETS
*GOLD/10: 3X TO 8X BASIC INSERTS
GOLD PRINT RUN 10 SER.#'d SETS
*SILVER/50: 1X TO 2.5X BASIC INSERTS
SILVER PRINT RUN 50 SER.#'d SETS
AS1 Knowshon Moreno .40 1.00
AS2 Brian Orakpo .50 1.25
AS3 Rey Maualuga .60 1.50
AS4 Chris Wells .40 1.00
AS5 Michael Crabtree .60 1.50
AS6 Aaron Curry .60 1.50
AS7 Jeremy Maclin .50 1.25
AS8 Chase Coffman .40 1.00
AS9 Darrius Heyward-Bey .60 1.50
AS10 Matthew Stafford 2.00 5.00
AS11 Vontae Davis .40 1.00
AS12 James Davis .40 1.00
AS13 Percy Harvin .40 1.00
AS14 Brandon Pettigrew .40 1.00
AS15 Malcolm Jenkins .40 1.00
AS16 Shonn Greene .40 1.00
AS17 Javon Ringer .40 1.00
AS18 LeSean McCoy 1.00 2.50
AS19 Hakeem Nicks .50 1.25
AS20 Mark Sanchez .40 1.00

2009 Bowman Draft Rookie All-Stars Combos

COMPLETE SET (10) 8.00 20.00
STATED ODDS 1:12
*BRONZE/99: .8X TO 2X BASIC INSERTS
BRONZE PRINT RUN 99 SER.#'d SETS
*GOLD/10: 3X TO 8X BASIC INSERTS
GOLD PRINT RUN 10 SER.#'d SETS
*SILVER/50: 1X TO 2.5X BASIC INSERTS
SILVER PRINT RUN 50 SER.#'d SETS
ASC1 L.Murphy/P.Harvin .40 1.00
ASC2 M.Stafford/K.Moreno 2.00 5.00
ASC3 C.Daniel/C.Coffman .50 1.25
ASC4 M.Jenkins/J.Laurinaitis .40 1.00
ASC5 M.Sanchez/C.Matthews 1.50 4.00
ASC6 G.Harrell/M.Crabtree .60 1.50
ASC7 B.Cushing/R.Maualuga .40 1.00
ASC8 A.Curry/A.Smith .40 1.00
ASC9 C.Harper/J.Davis .40 1.00
ASC10 J.Iglesias/D.Robinson .40 1.00

2009 Bowman Draft Rookie Autographs

GROUP A ODDS 1:229
GROUP B ODDS 1:66
GROUP C ODDS 1:1050
GROUP D ODDS 1:200
GROUP E ODDS 1:725
GROUP F ODDS 1:575
111 Matthew Stafford A 30.00 80.00
112 Brian Orakpo A 6.00 15.00
114 Michael Crabtree A 8.00 20.00
116 Knowshon Moreno A 5.00 12.00
117 Aaron Curry A 8.00 20.00
118 Gartrell Johnson B 4.00 10.00
120 James Laurinaitis A 5.00 12.00
121 Chris Wells A 10.00 25.00
122 Glen Coffee B 4.00 10.00
124 Rey Maualuga A 8.00 20.00
125 Malcolm Jenkins A 5.00 12.00
126 Michael Johnson A 5.00 12.00
127 Javon Ringer A 5.00 12.00
129 Donald Brown A 5.00 12.00
131 Brian Cushing A 5.00 12.00
132 Brandon Pettigrew A 5.00 12.00
135 Jeremy Maclin A 6.00 15.00
136 John Parker Wilson B 4.00 10.00
138 Chase Coffman A 5.00 12.00
142 Jarett Dillard B 4.00 10.00
145 Austin Collie E 4.00 10.00
147 Percy Harvin A 5.00 12.00
148 Jared Cook A 6.00 15.00
149 Rashad Jennings A 6.00 15.00
150 Rhett Bomar A 5.00 12.00
154 Darrius Heyward-Bey A 8.00 20.00
155 Jeremy Childs B 4.00 10.00
156 Darius Passmore B 4.00 10.00
157 Brooks Foster D 4.00 10.00
159 James Casey 5.00 12.00
162 Josh Freeman A 5.00 12.00
164 Derrick Williams A 5.00 12.00
166 Graham Harrell A 10.00 25.00
167 Pat White A 5.00 12.00
168 Chase Daniel A 6.00 15.00
170 LeSean McCoy A 15.00 40.00
171 James Davis A 5.00 12.00
172 Ramses Barden A 5.00 12.00
173 Juaquin Iglesias A 5.00 12.00
174 Cedric Peerman D 4.00 10.00
175 Kenny Britt A 8.00 20.00
176 Marlon Lucky B 4.00 10.00
177 Mohamed Massaquoi B 4.00 10.00
179 Tyrell Sutton B 4.00 10.00
180 Andre Brown B 5.00 12.00
182 Kory Sheets D 5.00 12.00
183 Arian Foster B 10.00 25.00
184 Demetrius Byrd B 5.00 12.00
186 Brandon Gibson B 5.00 12.00
190 Mark Sanchez A 5.00 12.00
193 Jeremiah Johnson B 4.00 10.00
194 P.J. Hill B 4.00 10.00
200 Nate Davis A 5.00 12.00
201 Stephen McGee 4.00 10.00
202 Aaron Kelly B 4.00 10.00
203 Ian Johnson D 4.00 10.00
205 Shonn Greene A 5.00 12.00
206 Sammie Stroughter F 4.00 10.00
207 Cullen Harper A 5.00 12.00
208 Devin Moore B 4.00 10.00
209 Quan Cosby C 4.00 10.00
210 Hakeem Nicks A 6.00 15.00

2009 Bowman Draft Rookie Autographs Bronze

BRONZE/99 STATED ODDS 1:115
*SILVER/50: .5X TO 1.2X BRONZE/99 AU
SILVER/50 ODDS 1:220
EXCH EXPIRATION: 5/31/2012
111 Matthew Stafford 40.00 100.00
112 Brian Orakpo 6.00 15.00
114 Michael Crabtree 8.00 20.00
116 Knowshon Moreno 5.00 12.00
117 Aaron Curry 8.00 20.00
118 Gartrell Johnson 5.00 12.00
120 James Laurinaitis 5.00 12.00
121 Chris Wells 5.00 12.00
122 Glen Coffee 5.00 12.00
124 Rey Maualuga 8.00 20.00
125 Malcolm Jenkins 5.00 12.00
126 Michael Johnson 5.00 12.00
127 Javon Ringer 5.00 12.00
129 Donald Brown 5.00 12.00
131 Brian Cushing 5.00 12.00
132 Brandon Pettigrew 5.00 12.00
135 Jeremy Maclin 6.00 15.00
136 John Parker Wilson 5.00 12.00
138 Chase Coffman 5.00 12.00
142 Jarett Dillard 5.00 12.00
145 Austin Collie 5.00 12.00
147 Percy Harvin 5.00 12.00
148 Jared Cook 6.00 15.00
149 Rashad Jennings 6.00 15.00
150 Rhett Bomar 5.00 12.00
154 Darrius Heyward-Bey 8.00 20.00
155 Jeremy Childs 5.00 12.00
156 Darius Passmore 5.00 12.00
157 Brooks Foster 5.00 12.00
159 James Casey 6.00 15.00
162 Josh Freeman 5.00 12.00
164 Derrick Williams 5.00 12.00
166 Graham Harrell 12.00 30.00
167 Pat White 6.00 15.00
168 Chase Daniel 6.00 15.00
170 LeSean McCoy 12.00 30.00
171 James Davis 5.00 12.00
172 Ramses Barden 5.00 12.00
173 Juaquin Iglesias 5.00 12.00
174 Cedric Peerman 5.00 12.00
175 Kenny Britt 8.00 20.00
176 Marlon Lucky 5.00 12.00
177 Mohamed Massaquoi 5.00 12.00
179 Tyrell Sutton 5.00 12.00
180 Andre Brown 6.00 15.00
182 Kory Sheets 6.00 15.00
183 Arian Foster 12.00 30.00
184 Demetrius Byrd 6.00 15.00
186 Brandon Gibson 6.00 15.00
190 Mark Sanchez 5.00 12.00
193 Jeremiah Johnson 5.00 12.00
194 P.J. Hill 5.00 12.00
200 Nate Davis 5.00 12.00
201 Stephen McGee 5.00 12.00
202 Aaron Kelly 5.00 12.00
203 Ian Johnson 5.00 12.00
205 Shonn Greene 5.00 12.00
206 Sammie Stroughter 5.00 12.00
207 Cullen Harper 5.00 12.00
208 Devin Moore 5.00 12.00
209 Quan Cosby 5.00 12.00
210 Hakeem Nicks 6.00 15.00

2009 Bowman Draft Superlatives

COMPLETE SET (10) 6.00 15.00
STATED ODDS 1:6
*BRONZE/99: 1X TO 2.5X BASIC INSERTS
BRONZE PRINT RUN 99 SER.#'d SETS
*GOLD/10: 4X TO 10X BASIC INSERTS
GOLD PRINT RUN 10 SER.#'d SETS
*SILVER/50: 1.2X TO 3X BASIC INSERTS
SILVER PRINT RUN 50 SER.#'d SETS
S1 Chase Coffman .30 .75
S2 Brian Orakpo .40 1.00
S3 Aaron Curry .50 1.25
S4 Andre Smith .30 .75
S5 Rey Maualuga .50 1.25
S6 Graham Harrell .30 .75
S7 Shonn Greene .30 .75
S8 Brian Orakpo .40 1.00
S9 Michael Crabtree .50 1.25
S10 Malcolm Jenkins .30 .75

2000 Bowman Reserve

Released in late November 2000, Bowman Reserve features a 125-card base set consisting of 100 Veterans and 25 Rookies sequentially numbered to 999. Base cards are printed on an all foil chromium refractor stock and carry an embossed Bowman Reserve logo behind action photography. Bowman Reserve was released in boxes containing 10 packs and one Rookie Autographed Mini Helmet. Boxes carried a suggested retail price of $129.99.

COMP.SET w/o RCs (100) 15.00 40.00
1 Chad Pennington RC 3.00 8.00
2 Shaun Alexander RC 4.00 10.00
3 Thomas Jones RC 3.00 8.00
4 Courtney Brown RC 3.00 8.00
5 Curtis Keaton RC 2.50 6.00
6 Jerry Porter RC 4.00 10.00
7 Jamal Lewis RC 4.00 10.00
8 Ron Dayne RC 4.00 10.00
9 R.Jay Soward RC 2.50 6.00
10 Tee Martin RC 2.50 6.00
11 Travis Taylor RC 2.50 6.00
12 Plaxico Burress RC 3.00 8.00
13 Giovanni Carmazzi RC 2.50 6.00
14 Sylvester Morris RC 2.50 6.00
15 Chris Redman RC 2.50 6.00
16 Trung Canidate RC 2.50 6.00
17 J.R. Redmond RC 2.50 6.00
18 Bubba Franks RC 2.50 6.00
19 Travis Prentice RC 2.50 6.00
20 Peter Warrick RC 2.50 6.00
21 Frank Sanders .25 .60
22 Edgerrin James .30 .75
23 Marcus Robinson .30 .75
24 Mike Alstott .25 .60
25 Jerry Rice 1.00 2.50
26 Marshall Faulk .30 .75
27 Brad Johnson .30 .75
28 Elvis Grbac .25 .60
29 Wayne Chrebet .25 .60
30 Akili Smith .25 .60
31 Rob Johnson .30 .75
32 Brett Favre .75 2.00
33 Ricky Williams .30 .75
34 Donovan McNabb .30 .75
35 Cris Carter .40 1.00
36 Ricky Watters .30 .75
37 Steve McNair .30 .75
38 Stephen Davis .25 .60
39 Fred Taylor .25 .60
40 Rocket Ismail .30 .75
41 Terry Glenn .30 .75
42 Ed McCaffrey .30 .75
43 Patrick Jeffers .25 .60
44 Jake Plummer .25 .60
45 Doug Flutie .30 .75
46 Terrell Davis .30 .75
47 Marvin Harrison .30 .75
48 Amani Toomer .25 .60
49 Tyrone Wheatley .25 .60
50 Charlie Garner .30 .75
51 Jevon Kearse .25 .60
52 Michael Westbrook .25 .60
53 Eddie George .30 .75
54 Robert Smith .25 .60
55 Keyshawn Johnson .30 .75
56 Torry Holt .30 .75
57 Jon Kitna .25 .60
58 Curtis Conway .30 .75
59 Jeff Garcia .25 .60
60 Randy Moss .30 .75
61 Jimmy Smith .30 .75
62 James Stewart .25 .60
63 Troy Aikman .50 1.25
64 Cade McNown .25 .60
65 Natrone Means .30 .75
66 Jamal Anderson .30 .75
67 Warrick Dunn .25 .60
68 Kordell Stewart .25 .60
69 Duce Staley .25 .60
70 Rich Gannon .30 .75
71 Curtis Martin .30 .75
72 Kerry Collins .25 .60
73 Jeff Blake .30 .75
74 Drew Bledsoe .30 .75
75 Kevin Dyson .30 .75
76 Tony Gonzalez .30 .75

77 Mark Brunell .30 .75
78 Peyton Manning 1.00 2.50
79 Dorsey Levens .30 .75
80 Germane Crowell .25 .60
81 Brian Griese .25 .60
82 Steve Beuerlein .30 .75
83 Eric Moulds .25 .60
84 Tony Banks .25 .60
85 Chris Chandler .30 .75
86 Isaac Bruce .40 1.00
87 Terrell Owens .30 .75
88 Jerome Bettis .40 1.00
89 Daunte Culpepper .30 .75
90 Emmitt Smith .60 1.50
91 Curtis Enis .25 .60
92 Shaun King .25 .60
93 Tim Brown .40 1.00
94 Antonio Freeman .30 .75
95 Charlie Batch .25 .60
96 Tim Couch .30 .75
97 Corey Dillon .25 .60
98 Muhsin Muhammad .25 .60
99 Joey Galloway .30 .75
100 Kurt Warner .60 1.50
101 David Boston .25 .60
102 Rod Smith .30 .75
103 Derrick Mayes .25 .60
104 Tony Martin .30 .75
105 Darnay Scott .30 .75
106 Joe Horn .30 .75
107 Troy Edwards .25 .60
108 James Johnson .25 .60
109 Vinny Testaverde .25 .60
110 Qadry Ismail .25 .60
111 Andre Reed .40 1.00
112 Zach Thomas .30 .75
113 Ike Hilliard .25 .60
114 Herman Moore .25 .60
115 Kevin Johnson .25 .60
116 Shawn Jefferson .25 .60
117 Terance Mathis .25 .60
118 Peerless Price .30 .75
119 Bert Emanuel .25 .60
120 Terrence Wilkins .25 .60
121 Mike Anderson RC 2.50 6.00
122 Dez White RC 2.50 6.00
123 Todd Pinkston RC 2.50 6.00
124 Reuben Droughns RC 2.50 6.00
125 Danny Farmer RC 2.50 6.00

2000 Bowman Reserve Autographs

Randomly inserted in Hobby packs at the rate of one in 10, this 8-card set features a player action shot set against a gold background with the bottom fourth of the card, below the name box, whited out. Player autographs appear in the white out portion of the card.

STATED ODDS 1:10 HOBBY
DC Daunte Culpepper 6.00 15.00
EJ Edgerrin James 6.00 15.00
GC Germane Crowell 5.00 12.00
KJ Kevin Johnson 5.00 12.00
MF Marshall Faulk 20.00 50.00
MR Marcus Robinson 6.00 15.00
TG Tony Gonzalez 15.00 40.00
TH Torry Holt 6.00 15.00

2000 Bowman Reserve Mini Helmet Autographs

Randomly inserted at the rate of one per Hobby Gift box, this set features autographed mini helmets by some of the top rookies from the 2000 draft. The helmets feature the Topps authenticity hologram and are checklisted in alphabetical order.

ONE PER HOBBY GIFT BOX
1 Shaun Alexander 20.00 50.00
2 Courtney Brown 12.50 25.00
3 Plaxico Burress 20.00 50.00
4 Trung Canidate 12.50 25.00
5 Giovanni Carmazzi 12.50 25.00
6 Laveranues Coles 12.50 25.00
7 Ron Dayne 15.00 40.00
8 Danny Farmer 12.50 25.00
9 Darrell Jackson 15.00 40.00
10 Thomas Jones 15.00 40.00
11 Jamal Lewis 15.00 40.00
12 Sylvester Morris 12.50 25.00
13 Chad Pennington 30.00 60.00
14 Todd Pinkston 12.50 25.00
15 Travis Prentice 12.50 25.00
16 Chris Redman 12.50 25.00
17 J.R. Redmond 12.50 25.00
18 R.Jay Soward 12.50 25.00
19 Brian Urlacher 50.00 100.00
20 Peter Warrick 15.00 40.00
21 Dez White 12.50 25.00
22 Mike Anderson 15.00 40.00

2000 Bowman Reserve Pro Bowl Jerseys

Randomly seeded in Hobby packs at the rate of one in 20, this 47-card set features player portrait shots set against a gold background coupled with a swatch of a game worn jersey from the 2000 Pro Bowl in the shape of the NFL Shield logo.

STATED ODDS 1:10 HOBBY
PBBJ Brad Johnson 8.00 20.00
PBBM Bruce Matthews 6.00 15.00
PBCB Chad Brown 6.00 15.00
PBCC Cris Carter 10.00 25.00
PBCD Corey Dillon 6.00 15.00
PBCK Cortez Kennedy 8.00 20.00
PBCL Carnell Lake 6.00 15.00
PBCW Charles Woodson 10.00 25.00
PBDB Derrick Brooks 6.00 15.00
PBDR Darrell Russell 6.00 15.00
PBEG Eddie George 8.00 20.00
PBEJ Edgerrin James 8.00 20.00
PBEM Emmitt Smith 12.00 30.00
PBFW Frank Wycheck 8.00 20.00
PBGM Glyn Milburn 6.00 15.00
PBHN Hardy Nickerson 6.00 15.00
PBIB Isaac Bruce 10.00 25.00
PBJA Jessie Armstead 6.00 15.00
PBJK Jevon Kearse 6.00 15.00
PBJS Jimmy Smith 8.00 20.00
PBKH Kevin Hardy 6.00 15.00
PBKJ Keyshawn Johnson 8.00 20.00
PBKM Kevin Mawae 6.00 15.00
PBKW Kurt Warner 15.00 40.00
PBLM Lawyer Milloy 6.00 15.00
PBMA Mike Alstott 6.00 15.00
PBMB Mark Brunell 8.00 20.00
PBMF Marshall Faulk 8.00 20.00
PBMH Marvin Harrison 8.00 20.00
PBMM Michael McCrary 6.00 15.00
PBMS Michael Strahan 8.00 20.00
PBPB Peter Boulware 6.00 15.00
PBRG Rich Gannon 8.00 20.00
PBRM Randy Moss 8.00 20.00
PBRM Randall McDaniel 8.00 20.00
PBRP Robert Porcher 6.00 15.00
PBRW Rod Woodson 10.00 25.00
PBSB Steve Beuerlein 8.00 20.00
PBSD Stephen Davis 6.00 15.00
PBSG Sam Gash 6.00 15.00
PBSM Sam Madison 6.00 15.00
PBTG Tony Gonzalez 8.00 20.00
PBTL Todd Lyght 6.00 15.00
PBTT Tom Tupa 6.00 15.00
PBWR Willie Roaf 6.00 15.00
PBWS Warren Sapp 8.00 20.00
PBWW Wesley Walls 6.00 15.00

2000 Bowman Reserve Rookie Autographs

Randomly inserted in Retail packs, this 15-card set features top 2000 rookies in action coupled with an authentic player autograph.

OVERALL STAT.ODDS 1:41 RETAIL
CB Courtney Brown 6.00 15.00
CP Chad Pennington 6.00 15.00
CR Chris Redman 5.00 12.00
DW Dez White 5.00 12.00
JL Jamal Lewis 8.00 20.00
JR J.R. Redmond 5.00 12.00
PB Plaxico Burress 6.00 15.00
PW Peter Warrick 5.00 12.00
RD Ron Dayne 8.00 20.00
RS R.Jay Soward 5.00 12.00
SA Shaun Alexander 5.00 12.00
SM Sylvester Morris 5.00 12.00
TC Trung Canidate 5.00 12.00
TJ Thomas Jones 6.00 15.00
TP Travis Prentice 5.00 12.00

2000 Bowman Reserve Rookie Premier Jerseys

Randomly inserted in Hobby packs, this 2-card set features jersey swatches from these two players in their "first worn" NFL Jerseys. Action photography is set against a blue background and the jersey swatch is in the shape of the NFL logo shield.

RPW Peter Warrick 5.00 12.00
RRDU Ron Dugans 5.00 12.00

2006 Bowman Sterling

This 195-card set was released in November, 2006. The set was issued in five-card packs, with a $50 SRP, which came six packs to a box. The set is a mix of rookies, some of whom signed their cards, and veterans with game-worn jersey swatches. A few of the veterans also signed their cards.

COMP.RC SET (50) 20.00 50.00
1 Jon Alston RC .75 2.00
2 Daniel Bullocks RC .75 2.00
3 Damien Rhodes RC 1.00 2.50
4 Josh Betts RC 1.00 2.50
5 Garrett Mills RC 1.00 2.50
6 Anthony Schlegel RC 1.00 2.50
7 Lawrence Vickers RC 1.00 2.50
8 Abdul Hodge RC .75 2.00
9 Kevin McMahan RC 1.00 2.50
10 Orien Harris RC 1.00 2.50
11 Charles Davis RC 1.00 2.50
12 Haloti Ngata RC 1.00 2.50
13 Kelly Jennings RC 1.00 2.50
14 Corey Bramlet RC 1.00 2.50
15 Manny Lawson RC 1.00 2.50
16 David Kirtman RC 1.00 2.50
17 Jeremy Bloom RC .75 2.00
18 Jason Allen RC 1.00 2.50
19 Owen Daniels RC 1.25 3.00
20 Ray Edwards RC 1.25 3.00
21 DeMario Minter RC 1.00 2.50
22 Ernie Sims RC .75 2.00
23 Jovon Bouknight RC 1.00 2.50
24 Sinorice Moss RC .75 2.00
25 Travis Lulay RC 1.00 2.50
26 Quinn Sypniewski RC 1.00 2.50
27 T.J. Rushing RC .75 2.00
28 J.J. Outlaw RC 1.00 2.50
29 Donte Whitner RC 1.00 2.50
30 Freddie Keiaho RC 1.00 2.50
31 Rocky McIntosh RC .75 2.00
32 Tamba Hali RC 1.25 3.00
33 Johnathan Joseph RC 1.00 2.50
34 Omar Gaither RC 1.00 2.50
35 Elvis Dumervil RC 1.25 3.00
36 Thomas Howard RC .75 2.00
37 Gabe Watson RC .75 2.00
38 Tony Scheffler RC 1.25 3.00
39 Tim Massaquoi RC 1.00 2.50
40 Chris Gocong RC 1.00 2.50
41 Ko Simpson RC 1.00 2.50
42 D'Qwell Jackson RC .75 2.00
43 James Anderson RC .75 2.00
44 P.J. Pope RC 1.25 3.00
45 Bennie Brazell RC 1.00 2.50
46 Jeff King RC 1.00 2.50
47 Dusty Dvoracek RC 1.25 3.00
48 Dee Webb RC 1.00 2.50
49 Jimmy Williams RC .75 2.00
50 Danieal Manning RC 1.25 3.00
AC1 Antonio Cromartie AU RC 4.00 10.00
AC2 Alge Crumpler JSY 4.00 10.00
AF Anthony Fasano AU RC 3.00 8.00
AH1 A.J. Hawk JSY RC 2.50 6.00
AH2 A.J. Hawk JSY AU 8.00 20.00
AHA Andre Hall AU RC 4.00 10.00
AJ Adam Jennings AU RC 4.00 10.00
AW Al Wilson JSY 3.00 8.00
AY Ashton Youboty AU RC 3.00 8.00
AZ Alan Zemaitis AU RC 3.00 8.00
BB Brett Basanez AU RC 5.00 12.00
BC1 Brian Calhoun JSY RC 2.00 5.00
BC2 Brian Calhoun JSY AU 5.00 12.00
BCR Brodie Croyle AU RC SP 12.00 30.00
BF Brett Favre JSY 10.00 25.00
BG Bruce Gradkowski AU RC 4.00 10.00
BM Brandon Marshall JSY RC 4.00 10.00
BO Ben Obomanu AU RC 4.00 10.00
BS1 Bob Sanders JSY 4.00 10.00
BS2 Brad Smith AU RC SP 4.00 10.00
BW1 Brandon Williams JSY RC 2.00 5.00
BW2 Brandon Williams JSY AU 5.00 12.00
CB1 Chris Brown JSY 3.00 8.00
CB2 Chris Brown JSY AU 5.00 12.00
CG Chad Greenway AU RC 5.00 12.00
CH Cedric Humes AU RC 3.00 8.00
CHO Cody Hodges AU RC 4.00 10.00
CJ Chad Jackson JSY RC 2.00 5.00
CM Curtis Martin JSY 4.00 10.00
CP Carson Palmer JSY 4.00 10.00
CW Charlie Whitehurst JSY RC 2.00 5.00
DAN David Anderson AU RC 4.00 10.00
DB1 Derrick Burgess JSY 3.00 8.00
DB2 Dominique Byrd AU RC 3.00 8.00
DEH Derek Hagan JSY RC 2.50 6.00
DEW Demetrius Williams JSY RC 2.00 5.00
DF Dwight Freeney JSY 3.00 8.00
DFE D.Ferguson AU RC SP 3.00 8.00
DHA Darrell Hackney AU RC SP 4.00 10.00
DHE Devin Hester AU RC 8.00 20.00
DHI Domenik Hixon AU RC 5.00 12.00
DM Donovan McNabb JSY 4.00 10.00
DOL Drew Olson AU RC 3.00 8.00
DON Deltha O'Neal JSY SP
DRY DeMeco Ryans AU RC 4.00 10.00
DS1 Darren Sharper JSY 3.00 8.00
DS2 D.J. Shockley AU RC 4.00 10.00
DT David Thomas AU RC 3.00 8.00
DW DeAngelo Williams JSY RC 2.50 6.00
DWA Delanie Walker AU RC 6.00 15.00
GJ Greg Jennings AU RC 5.00 12.00
HB Hank Baskett AU RC 3.00 8.00
IM Ingle Martin AU RC 4.00 10.00
JA1 Joseph Addai AU RC 12.00 30.00
JA2 Jason Avant JSY RC 2.00 5.00
JD Jake Delhomme JSY 3.00 8.00
JH Jerome Harrison AU RC 3.00 8.00
JJ Julius Jones JSY 3.00 8.00
JK1 Joe Klopfenstein JSY RC 2.00 5.00
JK2 Joe Klopfenstein JSY AU 5.00 12.00
JL Jamal Lewis JSY 4.00 10.00
JM Jerome Mathis JSY 3.00 8.00
JN1 Jerious Norwood JSY RC 2.00 5.00
JN2 Jerious Norwood AU 3.00 8.00
JN3 Jerious Norwood JSY AU 5.00 12.00
JO Jonathan Orr AU RC 4.00 10.00
JP Julius Peppers JSY 4.00 10.00
JS Jeremy Shockey JSY 3.00 8.00
JSM Jimmy Smith JSY 4.00 10.00
JT Jeremiah Trotter JSY 3.00 8.00
JW Javon Walker JSY 4.00 10.00
JWE Jeff Webb AU RC 4.00 10.00
KC1 Kellen Clemens JSY RC 2.00 5.00
KC2 Kellen Clemens JSY AU 5.00 12.00
KR Koren Robinson JSY 3.00 8.00
KW Kamerion Wimbley AU RC 4.00 10.00
LB Lance Briggs JSY 4.00 10.00
LE Lee Evans JSY 4.00 10.00
LF Larry Fitzgerald JSY 4.00 10.00
LJ Larry Johnson JSY 3.00 8.00
LM Laurence Maroney JSY RC 2.00 5.00
LN Lorenzo Neal JSY 3.00 8.00
LP Leonard Pope AU RC SP 5.00 12.00
LW LenDale White JSY RC 2.00 5.00
LWA1 Leon Washington JSY RC 2.00 5.00
LWA2 Leon Washington JSY AU 5.00 12.00
MB Marion Barber JSY 4.00 10.00
MBE Mike Bell AU RC 3.00 8.00
MD Maurice Drew JSY RC 3.00 8.00
MH Marvin Harrison JSY 4.00 10.00
MHA Marques Hagans AU RC 3.00 8.00
MHU Michael Huff JSY RC 2.50 6.00
MIH Mike Hass AU RC SP 3.00 8.00
MK Mathias Kiwanuka AU RC 5.00 12.00
ML Matt Leinart JSY RC 2.00 5.00
MLE Marcedes Lewis JSY RC 2.00 5.00
MN Martin Nance AU RC 3.00 8.00
MR1 Michael Robinson JSY RC 2.00 5.00
MR2 Michael Robinson JSY AU 5.00 12.00
MS Michael Strahan JSY 4.00 10.00
MST Marcus Stroud JSY 3.00 8.00
MST1 Maurice Stovall JSY RC 2.00 5.00
MST2 Maurice Stovall AU 3.00 8.00
MV Michael Vick JSY 4.00 10.00
MW1 Mario Williams JSY RC 3.00 8.00
MW2 Mario Williams JSY AU 8.00 20.00
OJ Omar Jacobs JSY RC 2.00 5.00
OU Osi Umenyiora JSY 3.00 8.00
PB Plaxico Burress JSY 3.00 8.00
PM Peyton Manning JSY 12.00 30.00
PP Paul Pinegar AU RC SP 3.00 8.00
QG Quinton Ganther AU RC 3.00 8.00
RB1 Reggie Bush JSY RC 3.00 8.00
RB2 Reggie Bush JSY AU SP 8.00 20.00
RB3 Ronnie Brown JSY 4.00 10.00
RBA Ronde Barber JSY 3.00 8.00
RJ Rudi Johnson JSY AU 5.00 12.00
RM Reggie McNeal AU RC 3.00 8.00
RS Rod Smith JSY 4.00 10.00
RW Reggie Wayne JSY 4.00 10.00
RWI Roy Williams S JSY 3.00 8.00
SG Skyler Green AU RC SP 3.00 8.00
SH1 Santonio Holmes JSY RC 2.50 6.00
SH2 S.Holmes JSY AU SP 15.00 40.00
SMO Santana Moss JSY 4.00 10.00
SR Shaun Rogers JSY 3.00 8.00
SS Steve Smith JSY AU SP 20.00 40.00
TB Tatum Bell JSY AU 5.00 12.00
TBA Tiki Barber JSY 4.00 10.00
TG Tony Gonzalez JSY 4.00 10.00
TH Tommie Harris JSY 3.00 8.00
THO Torry Holt JSY 4.00 10.00
TJ1 Tarvaris Jackson JSY RC 2.00 5.00
TJ2 Tarvaris Jackson JSY AU 10.00 25.00
TW Travis Wilson JSY RC 2.00 5.00
TYH Tye Hill AU RC 3.00 8.00
VD1 Vernon Davis JSY RC 2.50 6.00
VD2 Vernon Davis JSY AU SP 6.00 15.00
VY1 Vince Young JSY RC 2.00 5.00
VY2 Vince Young JSY AU SP 5.00 12.00
WB Will Blackmon AU RC 3.00 8.00
WD Warrick Dunn JSY 3.00 8.00
WJ Winston Justice AU RC 4.00 10.00
WR Willie Reid AU RC 4.00 10.00
ZT Zach Thomas JSY 4.00 10.00

2006 Bowman Sterling Black Refractors

*ROOKIES 1-50: 3X TO 8X BASIC CARDS
*VET JSYs: .8X TO 2X BASIC CARDS
*ROOKIE JSYs: .8X TO 2X BASIC CARDS
*ROOKIE AUs: .8X TO 2X BASIC CARDS
*VET JSY AU: .8X TO 2X BASIC CARDS
*ROOKIE JSY AU: .8X TO 2X BASIC CARDS
STATED PRINT RUN 25 SER.#'d SETS
DHE Devin Hester AU 15.00 40.00
RB2 Reggie Bush AU JSY 15.00 40.00

2006 Bowman Sterling Red Refractors

UNPRICED RED REF PRINT RUN 1

2006 Bowman Sterling Refractors

*ROOKIES 1-50: 1.5X TO 4X BASIC CARDS
*VET JSYs: .5X TO 1.2X BASIC CARDS
*ROOK JSYs: .5X TO 1.2X BASIC CARDS
*ROOK AUs: .5X TO 1.2X BASIC CARDS
*VET JSY AU: .4X TO 1X BASIC CARDS
*ROOK JSY AU: .4X TO 1X BASIC CARDS
STATED PRINT RUN 199 SER.#'d SETS
DHE Devin Hester AU 10.00 25.00

2006 Bowman Sterling Gold Relic Autographs

BF Brett Favre/50 100.00 200.00
CB Chris Brown/250 5.00 12.00
EM Eli Manning/100 50.00 80.00
JJ Julius Jones/75 20.00 50.00
LJ Larry Johnson/250 10.00 25.00
MH Marvin Harrison/50 25.00 60.00
MV Michael Vick/50 40.00 80.00
PM Peyton Manning/100 100.00 175.00
SMO Santana Moss/50 20.00 50.00

2006 Bowman Sterling Gold Rookie Autographs

PRINT RUN 450-900 SER.#'d SETS
AF Anthony Fasano/900 4.00 10.00
BCR Brodie Croyle/900 4.00 10.00
BG Bruce Gradkowski/900 5.00 12.00
BO Ben Obomanu/900 5.00 12.00
BS Brad Smith/500 5.00 12.00
CG Chad Greenway/900 6.00 15.00
CHO Cody Hodges/900 5.00 12.00
DAN David Anderson/900 5.00 12.00
DHA Darrell Hackney/500 5.00 12.00
DHI Domenik Hixon/450 6.00 15.00
DS D.J. Shockley/900 5.00 12.00
DT David Thomas/900 4.00 10.00
GJ Greg Jennings/900 6.00 15.00
HB Hank Baskett/500 4.00 10.00
IM Ingle Martin/900 5.00 12.00
JA Joseph Addai/900 8.00 20.00
JH Jerome Harrison/900 4.00 10.00
JN Jerious Norwood/900 4.00 10.00
LP Leonard Pope/900 6.00 15.00
MBE Mike Bell/900 4.00 10.00
MHA Marques Hagans/450 4.00 10.00
MIH Mike Hass/900 4.00 10.00
MST Maurice Stovall/900 4.00 10.00
RM Reggie McNeal/900 4.00 10.00
SG Skyler Green/700 4.00 10.00
WB Will Blackmon/900 4.00 10.00
WR Willie Reid/900 5.00 12.00

2006 Bowman Sterling Dual Autographs

STATED PRINT RUN 20-600
CAB J.Addai/M.Bell/600 6.00 15.00
CBS R.Bush/E.Smith/20 20.00 50.00
CCC Cutler/K.Clemens/50 30.00 60.00
CCF K.Clemens/B.Favre/20 125.00 250.00
CDL V.Davis/M.Lewis/600 8.00 20.00
CHJ Holmes/C.Jackson/200 15.00 40.00
CJS C.Johnson/S.Smith/20 25.00 60.00
CJT B.Jackson/L.Tomlinson/20 75.00 150.00
CLM M.Leinart/J.Montana/20 125.00 250.00
CMB Maroney/M.Bell/600 6.00 15.00
CMH Si.Moss/S.Holmes/400 12.00 30.00
CMM P.Manning/E.Manning/20 175.00 350.00
CNE J.Namath/J.Elway/20 125.00 250.00
CVF M.Vick/B.Favre/20 150.00 300.00
CWH Ma.Williams/Hawk/300 15.00 40.00
CWW L.White/DeA.Will/50 30.00 80.00
CYC V.Young/E.Campbell/20 60.00 120.00

2007 Bowman Sterling

This 208-card set was released in September, 2007. The set was issued into the hobby in five-card packs, with a $50 SRP, which came six packs to a box. The set contains a mix of Rookie Cards (1-50); veteran cards with game-worn jersey swatches and Rookie Cards with either player-worn jersey swatches or Rookie Cards with both player-worn swatches and a signature.

UNPRICED PRINT.PLATES #'d TO 1
1 Levi Brown RC 1.50 4.00
2 Darrelle Revis RC 2.00 5.00
3 Lawrence Timmons RC 2.50 6.00
4 Justin Harrell RC 1.50 4.00
5 Jarvis Moss RC 1.50 4.00
6 Michael Griffin RC 1.50 4.00
7 Aaron Ross RC 1.50 4.00
8 Reggie Nelson RC 1.50 4.00
9 Brandon Meriweather RC 2.00 5.00
10 Jon Beason RC 1.50 4.00
11 Anthony Spencer RC 2.00 5.00
12 David Irons RC 1.50 4.00
13 Matt Spaeth RC 2.50 6.00
14 Zak DeOssie RC 2.00 5.00
15 Matt Moore RC 2.50 6.00
16 Brett Ratliff RC 2.50 6.00
17 John Broussard RC 2.00 5.00
18 Chandler Williams RC 2.00 5.00
19 Chansi Stuckey RC 2.00 5.00
20 Derek Stanley RC 2.00 5.00
21 Ahmad Bradshaw RC 2.50 6.00
22 Jason Snelling RC 1.50 4.00
23 Tyler Palko RC 2.50 6.00
24 Tyrone Moss RC 1.50 4.00
25 Drew Tate RC 2.00 5.00
26 Joe Staley RC 2.00 5.00
27 Ben Grubbs RC 2.00 5.00
28 Eric Weddle RC 2.00 5.00
29 Chris Houston RC 1.50 4.00
30 Justin Durant RC 2.50 6.00
31 Eric Wright RC 1.50 4.00
32 Josh Wilson RC 2.00 5.00
33 Tim Crowder RC 2.00 5.00
34 Victor Abiamiri RC 1.50 4.00
35 Ramzee Robinson RC 1.50 4.00
36 Jonathan Wade RC 1.50 4.00
37 Aaron Rouse RC 1.50 4.00
38 Daymeion Hughes RC 1.50 4.00
39 Ray McDonald RC 2.00 5.00
40 Tanard Jackson RC 1.50 4.00
41 Martrez Milner RC 1.50 4.00
42 Le'Ron McClain RC 2.50 6.00
43 Kevin Boss RC 2.50 6.00
44 C.J. Gaddis RC 1.50 4.00
45 Rufus Alexander RC 1.50 4.00
46 Courtney Taylor RC 1.50 4.00
47 Prescott Burgess RC 1.50 4.00
48 Jordan Kent RC 2.00 5.00
49 Ben Patrick RC 2.00 5.00
50 Tyler Thigpen RC 2.50 6.00
AA Aundrae Allison AU RC 2.50 6.00
AB Anquan Boldin JSY 3.00 8.00
ABR Alan Branch AU RC 2.50 6.00
AC Adam Carriker AU RC 2.50 6.00
ACR Alge Crumpler JSY 4.00 10.00
AG1 Anthony Gonzalez JSY RC 2.00 5.00
AG2 Anthony Gonzalez JSY AU 4.00 10.00
AGA Antonio Gates JSY 5.00 12.00
AJ Andre Johnson JSY 4.00 10.00
AO Amobi Okoye AU RC 3.00 8.00
AP1 Antonio Pittman JSY RC 2.00 5.00
AP2 Antonio Pittman JSY AU 4.00 10.00
APE1 Adrian Peterson JSY RC 6.00 15.00
APE2 Adrian Peterson JSY AU 125.00 250.00
AS Aaron Schobel JSY 3.00 8.00
AT Adalius Thomas JSY 3.00 8.00
AW Adrian Wilson JSY 3.00 8.00
BE Braylon Edwards JSY 3.00 8.00
BF Brett Favre JSY 10.00 25.00
BJ1 Brandon Jackson JSY RC 2.00 5.00
BJ2 Brandon Jackson JSY AU 4.00 10.00
BL1 Brian Leonard JSY RC 2.00 5.00
BL2 Brian Leonard JSY AU 4.00 10.00
BQ1 Brady Quinn JSY RC 2.00 5.00
BQ2 Brady Quinn JSY AU 12.00 30.00
BW Brian Westbrook JSY 3.00 8.00
CD Craig Buster Davis AU RC 2.50 6.00
CDA Chris Davis AU RC 2.50 6.00
CH1 Chris Henry JSY RC 2.00 5.00
CH2 Chris Henry JSY AU 4.00 10.00
CJ Chad Johnson JSY 3.00 8.00
CJO1 Calvin Johnson JSY RC 6.00 15.00
CJO2 Calvin Johnson JSY AU 75.00 150.00
CL Chris Leak AU RC 2.50 6.00
CM Chris McAlister JSY 3.00 8.00
CP Chad Pennington JSY 3.00 8.00
CPO Clinton Portis JSY 3.00 8.00
DB1 Dwayne Bowe JSY RC 2.00 5.00
DB2 Dwayne Bowe JSY AU 4.00 10.00
DBA Dallas Baker AU RC 2.50 6.00
DC David Clowney AU RC 2.50 6.00
DD Donald Driver JSY 4.00 10.00
DH DeAngelo Hall JSY 3.00 8.00
DHA David Harris AU RC 2.50 6.00
DJ1 Dwayne Jarrett JSY RC 2.50 6.00
DJ2 Dwayne Jarrett JSY AU 5.00 12.00
DM Deuce McAllister JSY 4.00 10.00
DS1 Drew Stanton JSY RC 2.00 5.00
DS2 Drew Stanton JSY AU 4.00 10.00
DW Darius Walker AU RC 2.50 6.00
DWA DeMarcus Ware JSY 4.00 10.00
DWR Dwayne Wright AU RC 2.50 6.00
EJ Edgerrin James JSY 4.00 10.00
ER Ed Reed JSY 4.00 10.00
FG Frank Gore JSY 4.00 10.00
GA1 Gaines Adams JSY RC 2.50 6.00
GA2 Gaines Adams JSY AU 5.00 12.00
GO1 Greg Olsen JSY RC 3.00 8.00
GO2 Greg Olsen JSY AU 6.00 15.00
GR Gary Russell AU RC 3.00 8.00
GW1 Garrett Wolfe JSY RC 2.00 5.00
GW2 Garrett Wolfe JSY AU 4.00 10.00
IS Isaiah Stanback AU RC 2.50 6.00
JA Jamaal Anderson AU RC 3.00 8.00
JAD Joseph Addai JSY 3.00 8.00
JB1 John Beck JSY RC 2.00 5.00
JB2 John Beck JSY AU 4.00 10.00
JC Jerricho Cotchery JSY 3.00 8.00
JF Joel Filani AU RC 2.50 6.00
JH1 Jason Hill JSY RC 2.00 5.00
JH2 Jason Hill JSY AU 4.00 10.00
JHA Justise Hairston AU RC 3.00 8.00
JJ Jacoby Jones AU RC 6.00 15.00
JJO James Jones AU RC 2.50 6.00
JL J.P. Losman JSY 3.00 8.00
JLH1 Johnnie Lee Higgins JSY RC 2.00 5.00
JLH2 Johnnie Lee Higgins JSY AU 4.00 10.00
JLY John Lynch JSY 4.00 10.00
JM Justin Miller JSY 3.00 8.00
JP Jordan Palmer AU RC 3.00 8.00
JPE Julian Peterson JSY 3.00 8.00
JR1 JaMarcus Russell JSY RC 2.00 5.00
JR2 JaMarcus Russell JSY AU 12.00 30.00
JRO Jeff Rowe AU RC 2.50 6.00
JT Jason Taylor JSY 4.00 10.00
JTH1 Joe Thomas JSY RC 3.00 8.00
JTH2 Joe Thomas JSY AU 6.00 15.00
JW Javon Walker JSY 4.00 10.00
JZ Jared Zabransky AU RC 2.50 6.00
KD Ken Darby AU RC 2.50 6.00
KI1 Kenny Irons JSY RC 2.00 5.00
KI2 Kenny Irons JSY AU 4.00 10.00
KK1 Kevin Kolb JSY RC 2.50 6.00
KK2 Kevin Kolb JSY AU 5.00 12.00
KS Kolby Smith AU RC 2.50 6.00
LB1 Lorenzo Booker JSY RC 2.50 6.00
LB2 Lorenzo Booker JSY AU 5.00 12.00
LC Laveranues Coles JSY 3.00 8.00
LG Luke Getsy AU RC 4.00 10.00
LH Leon Hall AU RC 2.50 6.00
LN Legedu Naanee AU RC 3.00 8.00
LR Laurent Robinson AU RC 4.00 10.00
LW LaMarr Woodley AU RC 6.00 15.00
MB Marc Bulger JSY 3.00 8.00
MBU1 Michael Bush JSY RC 2.00 5.00
MBU2 Michael Bush JSY AU 4.00 10.00
MH Matt Hasselbeck JSY 3.00 8.00
ML1 Marshawn Lynch JSY RC 4.00 10.00
ML2 Marshawn Lynch JSY AU 20.00 40.00
MS Michael Strahan JSY 4.00 10.00
MST Mack Strong JSY 3.00 8.00
MW Mike Walker AU RC 4.00 10.00
PB Plaxico Burress JSY 3.00 8.00
PP Paul Posluszny AU RC 2.50 6.00
PW1 Patrick Willis JSY RC 3.00 8.00
PW2 Patrick Willis JSY AU 6.00 15.00
PWI1 Paul Williams JSY RC 2.00 5.00
PWI2 Paul Williams JSY AU 4.00 10.00
RB Reggie Brown JSY 3.00 8.00
RBR Ronnie Brown JSY 3.00 8.00
RH Roy Hall AU RC 4.00 10.00
RM Rhema McKnight AU RC 2.50 6.00
RMA Rashean Mathis JSY 3.00 8.00
RME1 Robert Meachem JSY RC 2.50 6.00
RME2 Robert Meachem JSY AU 5.00 12.00
RR Ryne Robinson AU RC 3.00 8.00
RW Reggie Wayne JSY 4.00 10.00
RWI Roy Williams S JSY 3.00 8.00
RWL Roy Williams WR JSY 3.00 8.00
SD Steve Dreaston AU RC 2.50 6.00
SC Scott Chandler AU RC 4.00 10.00
SH Steve Hutchinson JSY 4.00 10.00
SJ Steven Jackson JSY 3.00 8.00
SR1 Sidney Rice JSY RC 2.50 6.00
SR2 Sidney Rice JSY AU 5.00 12.00
SS1 Steve Smith USC JSY RC 2.00 5.00
SS2 Steve Smith USC JSY AU 10.00 25.00
SSM Steve Smith JSY 4.00 10.00
SY Selvin Young AU RC 2.50 6.00
TC Thomas Clayton AU RC 3.00 8.00
TE1 Trent Edwards JSY RC 2.00 5.00
TE2 Trent Edwards JSY AU 4.00 10.00
TG1 Ted Ginn JSY RC 2.50 6.00
TG2 Ted Ginn JSY AU 5.00 12.00
TH1 Tony Hunt JSY RC 2.00 5.00
TH2 Tony Hunt JSY AU 4.00 10.00
THO T.J. Houshmandzadeh JSY 3.00 8.00
TS1 Troy Smith JSY RC 2.00 5.00
TS2 Troy Smith JSY AU 10.00 25.00
WD Warrick Dunn JSY 3.00 8.00
WP Willie Parker JSY 4.00 10.00
WPI Willie Parker PB JSY 4.00 10.00
WS Will Smith JSY 3.00 8.00
YF1 Yamon Figurs JSY RC 2.00 5.00
YF2 Yamon Figurs JSY AU 4.00 10.00
ZM Zach Miller AU RC 2.50 6.00
ZT Zac Taylor AU RC 3.00 8.00
ZTH Zach Thomas JSY 4.00 10.00

2007 Bowman Sterling Black Refractors

*ROOKIES 1-50: 1.5X TO 4X BASIC CARDS
*VET JSYs: .8X TO 2X BASIC CARDS
*ROOKIE AUs: .8X TO 2X BASIC CARDS
*ROOKIE JSY: 1X TO 2.5X BASIC CARDS
*ROOK JSY AU/25: 1X TO 2.5X
JSY AU/10 CARDS NOT PRICED
STATED PRINT RUN 10-25

2007 Bowman Sterling Refractors

*ROOKIES 1-50: .6X TO 2X BASIC CARDS
*VET JSYs: .5X TO 1.2X BASIC CARDS
*ROOK AUs: .5X TO 1.2X BASIC CARDS
*ROOKIE JSY: .6X TO 1.5X BASIC CARDS
*ROOK JSY AU/199: .5X TO 1.2X
STATED PRINT RUN 25-199
APE2 A.Peterson JSY AU/25 250.00 500.00
BQ2 B.Quinn JSY AU/25 8.00 20.00
CJO2 Cal.Johnson JSY AU/25 150.00 300.00
JR2 J.Russell JSY AU/25 20.00 50.00
ML2 M.Lynch JSY AU/25 40.00 80.00

2007 Bowman Sterling Red Refractors

UNPRICED RED REF. PRINT RUN 1

2007 Bowman Sterling Dual Autograph Gold Refractors

STATED PRINT RUN 20-400
AA J.Ander/G.Adams/250 8.00 20.00
BL R.Bush/M.Leinart/20 40.00 100.00
BO A.Branch/A.Okoye/400 8.00 20.00
BS R.Bush/B.Sanders/20 125.00 250.00
BST J.Beck/D.Stanton/150 6.00 15.00
EK T.Edwards/Kolb/150 15.00 40.00
EM J.Elway/D.Marino/20 250.00 400.00
FJ M.Faulk/S.Jackson/20 50.00 120.00
II K.Irons/D.Irons/250 8.00 20.00
JB D.Jarrett/D.Bowe/150 12.00 30.00
JT L.Johnson/Tomlinson/20 40.00 100.00
LB Leonard/M.Bush/250 8.00 20.00
LP M.Lynch/A.Peterson/25 200.00 400.00
MB J.Montana/T.Brady/20 300.00 400.00
MW S.Merriman/P.Willis/250 12.00 30.00
NS Namath/Starr/20 175.00 300.00
OM G.Olsen/Z.Miller/250 10.00 25.00
PG Pittman/A.Gonzalez/250 12.00 30.00
QM B.Quinn/J.Montana/20 150.00 300.00
RJ J.Russell/C.Johnson/20 40.00 100.00
RJO J.Rice/C.Johnson/20 200.00 350.00
RQ J.Russell/B.Quinn/20 30.00 80.00
SA Staubach/Aikman/20 125.00 200.00
SG T.Smith/T.Ginn Jr./250 12.00 30.00
SJ S.Smith USC/D.Jarrett/150 12.00 30.00
SM P.Simms/E.Manning/20 100.00 175.00
WJ R.Will.WR/C.Johnson/20 50.00 120.00
YC V.Young/E.Campbell/20 60.00 120.00

2007 Bowman Sterling Gold Relic Autographs

STATED PRINT RUN 25-250
AG Anthony Gonzalez/250 8.00 20.00
AP Adrian Peterson/25 150.00 300.00
BJ Brandon Jackson/250 8.00 20.00
BL Brian Leonard/150 8.00 20.00
BQ Brady Quinn/25 40.00 100.00
CH Chris Henry/150 8.00 20.00
CJ Calvin Johnson/25 125.00 250.00
DB Dwayne Bowe/150 8.00 20.00
DJ Dwayne Jarrett/150 10.00 25.00
DS Drew Stanton/150 8.00 20.00
FG Frank Gore/25 20.00 40.00
GA Gaines Adams/250 10.00 25.00
GO Greg Olsen/250 12.00 30.00
JB John Beck/250 8.00 20.00
JH Johnnie Lee Higgins/250 8.00 20.00
JR JaMarcus Russell/25 20.00 50.00
KI Kenny Irons/150 8.00 20.00
KK Kevin Kolb/150 10.00 25.00
LJ Larry Johnson/25 20.00 50.00
MB Michael Bush/150 8.00 20.00
ML Matt Leinart/25 25.00 60.00
MLY Marshawn Lynch/100 40.00 80.00
RB Reggie Bush/25 30.00 80.00
RM Robert Meachem/150 10.00 25.00
SR Sidney Rice/150 10.00 25.00
SS Steve Smith USC/150 12.00 30.00
TG Ted Ginn/100 12.00 30.00
TS Troy Smith/150 12.00 30.00
VY Vince Young/25 25.00 60.00
YF Yamon Figurs/250 8.00 20.00

2007 Bowman Sterling Gold Rookie Autographs

STATED PRINT RUN 25-1800
AG Anthony Gonzalez/250 4.00 10.00
AP Adrian Peterson/25 150.00 300.00
AR Aaron Ross/1800 3.00 8.00
BL Brian Leonard/400 4.00 10.00
BQ Brady Quinn/25 30.00 80.00
CD Craig Buster Davis/250 4.00 10.00
CH Chris Henry/400 4.00 10.00
CJ Calvin Johnson/25 125.00 200.00
CS Chansi Stuckey/1800 4.00 10.00
CT Courtney Taylor/1800 3.00 8.00
DB Dwayne Bowe/100 5.00 12.00
DJ Dwayne Jarrett/100 6.00 15.00
DS Drew Stanton/100 5.00 12.00
DT Drew Tate/1800 4.00 10.00
GO Greg Olsen/250 6.00 15.00
JB John Beck/250 4.00 10.00
JF Joel Filani/1000 3.00 8.00
JR JaMarcus Russell/25 15.00 40.00
KI Kenny Irons/50 6.00 15.00
KK Kevin Kolb/100 6.00 15.00
LT Lawrence Timmons/1800 5.00 12.00
ML Marshawn Lynch/50 20.00 50.00
MM Matt Moore/1800 5.00 12.00
RM Robert Meachem/100 10.00 25.00
SR Sidney Rice/100 6.00 15.00
SS Steve Smith USC/100 10.00 25.00
TG Ted Ginn Jr./50 8.00 20.00
TM Tyrone Moss/1800 3.00 8.00
TP Tyler Palko/1800 5.00 12.00
ZD Zak DeOssie/1800 4.00 10.00

2008 Bowman Sterling

This set was released on August 27, 2008. The base set consists of 195 cards. Cards 1-50 feature rookies, cards 51-100 are jersey cards of vererans serial numbered of 389, and cards 101-175 are different types of rookie cards. Some are autographed, some contain jerseys and are serial numbered of 569, and others are autographed jerseys.

JSY VET/389 ODDS 1:4
JSY ROOKIE/569 ODDS 1:4
UNPRICED PRINT.PLATES #'d TO 1
UNPRICED RED REFRACTOR #'d TO 1
1 Leodis McKelvin RC 1.50 4.00
2 Antoine Cason RC 1.50 4.00
3 Brandon Flowers RC 1.50 4.00
4 Tracy Porter RC 1.50 4.00
5 Patrick Lee RC 1.25 3.00
6 Terrence Wheatley RC 1.25 3.00
7 Terrell Thomas RC 1.25 3.00
8 Charles Godfrey RC 1.25 3.00
9 Chevis Jackson RC 1.25 3.00
10 Reggie Smith RC 1.25 3.00
11 Antwaun Molden RC 1.25 3.00
12 Lawrence Jackson RC 1.25 3.00
13 Josh Morgan RC 1.25 3.00
14 Calais Campbell RC 1.50 4.00
15 Quentin Groves RC 1.50 4.00
16 Tim Hightower RC 1.50 4.00
17 Kendall Langford RC 1.50 4.00
18 Chris Ellis RC 1.25 3.00
19 Bryan Smith RC 1.25 3.00
20 Cliff Avril RC 2.00 5.00
21 Sedrick Ellis RC 1.25 3.00
22 Kentwan Balmer RC 1.25 3.00
23 Trevor Laws RC 1.25 3.00
24 Pat Sims RC 1.50 4.00
25 Andre Fluellen RC 1.25 3.00
26 Marcus Harrison RC 1.25 3.00
27 Branden Albert RC 1.50 4.00
28 Matt Slater RC 2.00 5.00
29 Curtis Lofton RC 1.50 4.00
30 Jordon Dizon RC 1.25 3.00
31 Tavares Gooden RC 1.25 3.00
32 Shawn Crable RC 1.25 3.00
33 Bruce Davis RC 1.50 4.00
34 Philip Wheeler RC 1.50 4.00
35 Ryan Clady RC 1.50 4.00
36 Xavier Omon RC 1.25 3.00
37 Gosder Cherilus RC 1.50 4.00
38 Jalen Parmele RC 1.50 4.00
39 Duane Brown RC 1.25 3.00
40 Tyrell Johnson RC 1.25 3.00
41 Tom Zbikowski RC 1.50 4.00
42 Thomas DeCoud RC 1.25 3.00
43 Martellus Bennett RC 1.50 4.00
44 Brad Cottam RC 1.25 3.00
45 Marcus Thomas RC 1.50 4.00
46 Jermichael Finley RC 1.25 3.00
47 Kenneth Moore RC 1.25 3.00
48 Arman Shields RC 1.50 4.00
49 Thomas Brown RC 1.25 3.00
50 Will Franklin RC 1.50 4.00
51 Drew Brees JSY 4.00 10.00
52 Tom Brady JSY 12.00 30.00
53 Peyton Manning JSY 10.00 25.00
54 Carson Palmer JSY 3.00 8.00
55 Ben Roethlisberger JSY 4.00 10.00
56 Eli Manning JSY 3.00 8.00
57 Tony Romo JSY 3.00 8.00
58 Vince Young JSY 2.50 6.00
59 Steven Jackson JSY 2.50 6.00
60 Willie Parker JSY 3.00 8.00
61 Clinton Portis JSY 2.50 6.00
62 Adrian Peterson JSY 8.00 20.00
63 LaDainian Tomlinson JSY 4.00 10.00
64 Marion Barber JSY 2.50 6.00
65 Brian Westbrook JSY 2.50 6.00
66 Fred Taylor JSY 2.50 6.00
67 Marshawn Lynch JSY 3.00 8.00
68 Joseph Addai JSY 2.50 6.00
69 Willis McGahee JSY 2.50 6.00
70 Frank Gore JSY 3.00 8.00
71 Chad Johnson JSY 2.50 6.00
72 Reggie Wayne JSY 3.00 8.00
73 Anquan Boldin JSY 2.50 6.00
74 Randy Moss JSY 3.00 8.00
75 Plaxico Burress JSY 2.50 6.00
76 Terrell Owens JSY 3.00 8.00
77 Andre Johnson JSY 3.00 8.00
78 Larry Fitzgerald JSY 3.00 8.00
79 Braylon Edwards JSY 2.50 6.00
80 Steve Smith JSY 3.00 8.00
81 Derek Anderson JSY 2.50 6.00
82 Edgerrin James JSY 3.00 8.00
83 Brendon Ayanbadejo JSY 2.50 6.00
84 Rob Bironas JSY 2.50 6.00
85 Shane Lechler JSY 2.50 6.00
86 Darren Sharper JSY 2.50 6.00
87 Brian Westbrook JSY 2.50 6.00
88 Nick Folk JSY 3.00 8.00
89 Tony Richardson JSY 2.50 6.00
90 Torry Holt JSY 3.00 8.00
91 Aaron Kampman JSY 4.00 10.00
92 Dan Koppen JSY 2.50 6.00
93 Mike Vrabel JSY 3.00 8.00
94 Terence Newman JSY 3.00 8.00
95 T.J. Houshmandzadeh JSY 2.50 6.00
96 Jared Allen JSY 2.50 6.00
97 James Harrison JSY RC 10.00 25.00
98 Chris Cooley JSY 3.00 8.00
99 Vince Wilfork JSY 2.50 6.00
100 Ken Hamlin JSY 3.00 8.00
101 D.Rodgers-Cromartie AU RC 4.00 10.00
102 Mike Jenkins AU RC 3.00 8.00
103 Aqib Talib AU RC 5.00 12.00
104 Vernon Gholston AU RC 3.00 8.00
105 Derrick Harvey AU RC 3.00 8.00
106 Owen Schmitt AU RC 3.00 8.00
107 Keith Rivers AU RC 3.00 8.00
108 Dan Connor AU RC 3.00 8.00
109 Sam Baker AU RC 3.00 8.00
110 Dennis Dixon AU RC 3.00 8.00
111 Josh Johnson AU RC 3.00 8.00
112 Erik Ainge AU RC 3.00 8.00
113 Colt Brennan AU RC 3.00 8.00
114 Andre Woodson AU RC 3.00 8.00
115 Matt Flynn AU RC 3.00 8.00
116 Anthony Morelli AU RC 3.00 8.00
117 Kyle Wright AU RC 3.00 8.00
118 Tashard Choice AU RC 3.00 8.00
119 Jacob Hester AU RC 3.00 8.00
120 Mike Hart AU RC 3.00 8.00
121 Anthony Alridge AU RC 3.00 8.00
122 Justin Forsett AU RC 4.00 10.00
123 Jerod Mayo AU RC 8.00 20.00
124 Allen Patrick AU RC 3.00 8.00
125 Ryan Torain AU RC 4.00 10.00
126 Chauncey Washington AU RC 4.00 10.00
127 DaJuan Morgan AU RC 4.00 10.00
128 Chris Long AU RC 4.00 10.00
129 Kenny Phillips AU RC 3.00 8.00
130 John Carlson AU RC 3.00 8.00
131 Fred Davis AU RC 3.00 8.00
132 Martin Rucker AU RC 3.00 8.00
133 Paul Smith AU RC 3.00 8.00
134 Keenan Burton AU RC 3.00 8.00
135 Adrian Arrington AU RC 3.00 8.00
136 Marcus Smith AU RC 4.00 10.00
137 DJ Hall AU RC 3.00 8.00
138 Marcus Monk AU RC 4.00 10.00
139 Darius Reynaud AU RC 3.00 8.00
140 Marcus Henry AU RC 3.00 8.00
141 Glenn Dorsey JSY RC 1.50 4.00
142A Jake Long JSY RC 2.50 6.00
142B Jake Long JSY AU 8.00 20.00
143A John David Booty JSY RC 1.50 4.00
143B John David Booty JSY AU 5.00 12.00
144A Brian Brohm JSY RC 1.50 4.00
144B Brian Brohm JSY AU 5.00 12.00
145 Kevin O'Connell JSY RC 1.50 4.00
146A Matt Ryan JSY RC 5.00 12.00
146B Matt Ryan JSY AU 25.00 60.00
147A Chad Henne JSY RC 2.00 5.00
147B Chad Henne JSY AU 6.00 15.00
148A Joe Flacco JSY RC 3.00 8.00
148B Joe Flacco JSY AU 10.00 25.00
149 Matt Forte JSY RC 2.50 6.00
150A Felix Jones JSY RC 1.50 4.00
150B Felix Jones JSY AU 5.00 12.00
151A Darren McFadden JSY RC 1.50 4.00
151B Darren McFadden JSY AU 5.00 12.00
152A R.Mendenhall JSY RC 1.50 4.00
152B R.Mendenhall JSY AU 5.00 12.00
153A Ray Rice JSY RC 1.50 4.00
153B Ray Rice JSY AU 5.00 12.00
154A Steve Slaton JSY RC 1.50 4.00
154B Steve Slaton JSY AU 5.00 12.00
155A Jonathan Stewart JSY RC 2.50 6.00
155B Jonathan Stewart JSY AU 8.00 20.00
156A Chris Johnson JSY RC 2.00 5.00
156B Chris Johnson JSY AU 6.00 15.00
157A Kevin Smith JSY RC 1.50 4.00
157B Kevin Smith JSY AU 5.00 12.00
158A Jamaal Charles JSY RC 2.50 6.00
158B Jamaal Charles JSY AU 8.00 20.00
159 Dustin Keller JSY RC 2.00 5.00
160 Andre Caldwell JSY RC 1.50 4.00
161 Dexter Jackson JSY RC 2.50 6.00
162A Malcolm Kelly JSY RC 1.50 4.00
162B Malcolm Kelly JSY AU 5.00 12.00
163A Donnie Avery JSY RC 2.00 5.00
163B Donnie Avery JSY AU 6.00 15.00
164 Devin Thomas JSY RC 1.50 4.00
165 Jordy Nelson JSY RC 5.00 12.00
166A James Hardy JSY RC 1.50 4.00
166B James Hardy JSY AU 5.00 12.00
167 Eddie Royal JSY RC 1.50 4.00
168 Jerome Simpson JSY RC 2.00 5.00
169A DeSean Jackson JSY RC 3.00 8.00
169B DeSean Jackson JSY AU 10.00 25.00
170A Limas Sweed JSY RC 1.50 4.00
170B Limas Sweed JSY AU 5.00 12.00
171 Earl Bennett JSY RC 2.50 6.00
172 Early Doucet JSY RC 1.50 4.00
173 Harry Douglas JSY RC 2.00 5.00
174 Mario Manningham JSY RC 1.50 4.00

2008 Bowman Sterling Black Refractors

*ROOKIES 1-50: 1X TO 2.5X BASIC CARDS
1-50 ROOKIE/50 ODDS 1:25
*VET JSYs 51-100: .6X TO 1.5X BASIC JSY
51-100 VET JSY/50 ODDS 1:26
*ROOKIE AU 101-140: .6X TO 1.5X BASIC AU
101-140 ROOKIE AU/50 ODDS 1:33
*ROOK.JSY/50: .8X TO 2X BASIC JSY
141-174 ROOKIE JSY/50 ODDS 1:38
*ROOK.JSY AU/50: .6X TO 1.5X BASIC JSY AU
141-174 ROOK.JSY AU/50 ODDS 1:65
113 Colt Brennan AU 6.00 15.00
146B Matt Ryan JSY AU 75.00 150.00
148B Joe Flacco JSY AU 15.00 40.00
151B Darren McFadden JSY AU 8.00 20.00
153B Ray Rice JSY AU 8.00 20.00
156B Chris Johnson JSY AU 10.00 25.00

2008 Bowman Sterling Gold Refractors

*ROOKIES 1-50: 1.2X TO 3X BASIC CARDS
1-50 ROOKIE/25 ODDS 1:50
*VET JSYs 51-100: .8X TO 2X BASIC JSY
51-100 VET JSY/25 ODDS 1:53
*ROOKIE AU 101-140: .8X TO 2X BASIC AU
101-140 ROOKIE AU/25 ODDS 1:66
*ROOK.JSY/50: 1X TO 2.5X BASIC JSY
141-174 ROOKIE JSY/50 ODDS 1:77
*ROOK.JSY AU/25: .8X TO 2X BASIC JSY AU
141-174 ROOK.JSY AU/25 ODDS 1:131
115 Matt Flynn AU 6.00 15.00
146B Matt Ryan JSY AU 125.00 200.00
148B Joe Flacco JSY AU 25.00 60.00
150B Felix Jones JSY AU 12.00 30.00
151B Darren McFadden JSY AU 30.00 60.00
152B Rashard Mendenhall JSY AU 12.00 30.00
153B Ray Rice JSY AU 12.00 30.00
155B Jonathan Stewart JSY AU 30.00 80.00
156B Chris Johnson JSY AU 15.00 40.00

2008 Bowman Sterling Refractors

*ROOKIES 1-50: .8X TO 2X BASIC CARDS
1-50 ROOKIE/199 ODDS 1:7
*VET JSYs 51-100: .5X TO 1.2X BASIC JSY
51-100 VET JSY/199 ODDS 1:7
*ROOKIE AU 101-140: .5X TO 1.2X BASIC AU
101-140 ROOKIE AU/199 ODDS 1:8
*ROOK.JSY/199: .6X TO 1.5X BASIC JSY
141-174 ROOKIE JSY/199 ODDS 1:10
*ROOK.JSY AU/199: .5X TO 1.2X BASIC JSY AU
141-174 ROOK.JSY AU/199 ODDS 1:27
141-174 ROOK.JSY AU/99 ODDS 1:80
115 Matt Flynn AU 4.00 10.00
146B Matt Ryan JSY AU/99 50.00 100.00
148B Joe Flacco JSY AU/99 20.00 50.00
150B Felix Jones JSY AU/99 6.00 15.00
151B Darren McFadden JSY AU/99 12.00 30.00
152B R.Mendenhall JSY AU/99 6.00 15.00
153B Ray Rice JSY AU 6.00 15.00
156B Chris Johnson JSY AU 8.00 20.00

2008 Bowman Sterling Blue Refractor Rookie Autographs

ISSUED VIA MAIL AS BONUS CARDS
BA1 Matt Ryan 30.00 80.00
BA2 Ryan Torain 4.00 10.00
BA3 Darren McFadden 3.00 8.00
BA4 Tashard Choice 3.00 8.00
BA5 Keenan Burton 3.00 8.00
BA6 Andre Caldwell 3.00 8.00
BA7 Kenny Phillips 3.00 8.00
BA8 Dan Connor 3.00 8.00
BA9 Mike Jenkins 3.00 8.00
BA10 Derrick Harvey 3.00 8.00

2008 Bowman Sterling Dual Autograph Gold Refractors

GROUP A ODDS 1:327
GROUP B ODDS 1:26
A1 M.Ryan/McFadden A 50.00 100.00
A2 M.Ryan/T.Brady A 300.00 600.00
A3 Peterson/McFadden A 50.00 100.00
A4 Eli/Manningham A 60.00 120.00
A5 M.Barber/F.Jones B 12.00 30.00
A6 Westbrook/D.Jackson B 30.00 80.00
A7 J.Flacco/P.Manning A 125.00 200.00
A8 Edwards/D.Anderson A 15.00 40.00
A9 R.Moss/T.Brady A 250.00 400.00
A10 E.Ainge/D.Keller B 8.00 20.00
A11 M.Monk/K.Burton B 8.00 20.00
A12 R-Cromartie/Jenkins B 8.00 20.00
A13 M.Hart/C.Henne B 20.00 50.00
A14 V.Gholston/C.Long B 8.00 20.00
A15 J.Hester/L.Tomlinson A 30.00 60.00
A16 Booty/Washington B 6.00 15.00
A17 M.Flynn/K.Wright B 6.00 15.00
A18 A.Patrick/R.Torain B 8.00 20.00
A19 Arrington/Manningham B 6.00 15.00
A20 J.Johnson/A.Morelli B 6.00 15.00

2008 Bowman Sterling Dual Autograph Relic Gold

GROUP A/25 ODDS 1:374
GROUP B/75 ODDS 1:37
AR1 McFadden/F.Jones/25 10.00 25.00
AR2 Ryan/McFadden/25 60.00 150.00
AR3 M.Ryan/B.Brohm/25 40.00 100.00
AR4 Stewart/Mendnhll/25 15.00 40.00
AR5 J.Flacco/R.Rice/75 60.00 120.00
AR6 Henne/Manningham/75 10.00 25.00
AR7 Doucet/Dorsey/75 EXCH 8.00 20.00
AR8 J.Long/Henne/75 20.00 50.00
AR9 B.Brohm/C.Henne/75 10.00 25.00
AR10 D.Keller/J.Long/75 12.00 30.00
AR11 O'Connell/J.Booty/75 8.00 20.00
AR12 C.Johnson/M.Forte/75 15.00 40.00
AR13 M.Ryan/Douglas/25 75.00 150.00
AR14 S.Slaton/J.Charles/75 12.00 30.00
AR15 Dorsey/J.Long/75 EXCH 12.00 30.00
AR16 K.Smith/R.Rice/75 8.00 20.00
AR17 D.Avery/D.Thomas/75 10.00 25.00
AR18 D.Thomas/M.Kelly/75 8.00 20.00
AR19 J.Nelson/J.Hardy/75 25.00 60.00
AR20 D.Jcksn/Smpsn/75 15.00 40.00
AR21 Simpson/Caldwell/75 10.00 25.00
AR22 Manninghm/Jacksn/75 12.00 30.00
AR23 McFadden/Stewart/25 30.00 80.00
AR24 F.Jones/C.Johnson/75 10.00 25.00
AR25 E.Royal/E.Bennett/75 8.00 20.00
AR26 Flacco/Avery/75 30.00 80.00
AR27 J.Flacco/M.Ryan/25 100.00 200.00
AR28 Caldwell/H.Douglas/75 10.00 25.00
AR29 E.Bennett/M.Forte/75 12.00 30.00
AR30 C.Jhnsn/K.Smith/75 15.00 40.00

2008 Bowman Sterling Gold Relic Autographs

GROUP C/235 ODDS 1:34
GROUP B/100 ODDS 1:70
GROUP A/20 ODDS 1:254
52 Tom Brady/20 200.00 350.00
53 Peyton Manning/20 100.00 200.00
56 Eli Manning/20 75.00 150.00
62 Adrian Peterson/20 100.00 200.00
68 Joseph Addai/20 12.00 30.00
81 Derek Anderson/20 12.00 30.00
143 John David Booty/235 4.00 10.00
144 Brian Brohm/20 15.00 40.00
145 Kevin O'Connell/100 6.00 15.00
146 Matt Ryan/20 60.00 120.00
147 Chad Henne/100 8.00 20.00
148 Joe Flacco/20 12.00 30.00
149 Matt Forte/235 20.00 50.00
150 Felix Jones/20 10.00 25.00
151 Darren McFadden/20 20.00 50.00
152 Rashard Mendenhall/20 10.00 25.00
153 Ray Rice/100 6.00 15.00
154 Steve Slaton/100 6.00 15.00
155 Jonathan Stewart/20 20.00 50.00
156 Chris Johnson/235 8.00 20.00
157 Kevin Smith/235 4.00 10.00
158 Jamaal Charles/100 10.00 25.00
159 Dustin Keller/235 5.00 12.00
162 Malcolm Kelly/235 4.00 10.00
163 Donnie Avery/235 8.00 20.00
164 Devin Thomas/100 6.00 15.00
165 Jordy Nelson/100 25.00 50.00
166 James Hardy/100 6.00 15.00
169 DeSean Jackson/235 15.00 40.00
170 Limas Sweed/100 6.00 15.00

2008 Bowman Sterling Gold Rookie Autographs

GROUP D/1050 ODDS 1:6
GROUP C/400 ODDS 1:18
GROUP B/250 ODDS 1:42
GROUP A/25 ODDS 1:523
115 Matt Flynn/400 3.00 8.00
116 Anthony Morelli/1050 2.50 6.00
117 Kyle Wright/400 3.00 8.00
118 Tashard Choice/400 3.00 8.00
121 Anthony Alridge/1050 2.50 6.00
122 Justin Forsett/400 4.00 10.00
124 Allen Patrick/1050 2.50 6.00
125 Ryan Torain/1050 3.00 8.00
127 DaJuan Morgan/1050 3.00 8.00
131 Fred Davis/400 3.00 8.00
134 Keenan Burton/1050 2.50 6.00
135 Adrian Arrington/1050 2.50 6.00
137 DJ Hall/400 3.00 8.00
138 Marcus Monk/1050 3.00 8.00
142 Jake Long/250 8.00 20.00
146 Matt Ryan/25 125.00 200.00
148 Joe Flacco/25 25.00 60.00
149 Matt Forte/1050 12.00 30.00
151 Darren McFadden/25 20.00 50.00
152 Rashard Mendenhall/25 8.00 20.00
155 Jonathan Stewart/25 25.00 60.00
156 Chris Johnson/400 4.00 10.00
160 Andre Caldwell/1050 2.50 6.00
167 Eddie Royal/250 3.00 8.00
168 Jerome Simpson/250 5.00 12.00
171 Earl Bennett/400 5.00 12.00
172 Early Doucet/250 4.00 10.00
173 Harry Douglas/400 4.00 10.00
174 Mario Manningham/250 4.00 10.00

2008 Bowman Sterling Jerseys Blue

*BLUE VETS: .4X TO 1X BASIC JSY
BLUE VETS/349 ODDS 1:4
*BLUE ROOKIES: .4X TO 1X BASIC JSY
BLUE ROOKIE/399 ODDS 1:5

2008 Bowman Sterling Jerseys Green

*GREEN VETS: .4X TO 1X BASIC JSY
GREEN VET/249 ODDS 1:6
*GREEN ROOKIE: .5X TO 1.2X BASIC JSY
GREEN ROOKIE/299 ODDS 1:7

2008 Bowman Sterling Jerseys Large Swatch

*LARGE SWATCH: .5X TO 1.2X BASIC JSY
LARGE SWATCH/309 ODDS 1:6

2008 Bowman Sterling Rookie Blue Refractors

COMPLETE SET (10) 20.00 50.00
BS1 Matt Ryan 3.00 8.00
BS2 Joe Flacco 2.00 5.00
BS3 Darren McFadden 1.00 2.50
BS4 Jonathan Stewart 1.50 4.00
BS5 Matt Forte 1.50 4.00
BS6 Ray Rice 1.00 2.50
BS7 Chris Johnson 1.25 3.00
BS8 DeSean Jackson 2.00 5.00
BS9 Eddie Royal 1.00 2.50
BS10 Jerod Mayo 1.50 4.00

2008 Bowman Sterling Rookie Blue Refractors Autographs

BSA1 Matt Ryan 30.00 60.00

2009 Bowman Sterling

1-50 ROOKIE PRINT RUN 799
VET JERSEY PRINT RUN 719-999
1 Eugene Monroe RC 1.25 3.00
2 Sean Smith RC 1.25 3.00
3 Andre Smith RC 1.25 3.00
4 B.J. Raji RC 1.50 4.00
5 Peria Jerry RC 1.25 3.00
6 Tony Fiammetta RC 1.25 3.00
7 Jairus Byrd RC 2.00 5.00
8 Louis Murphy RC 1.25 3.00
9 David Veikune RC 1.50 4.00
10 Alphonso Smith RC 1.25 3.00
11 Alex Mack RC 1.25 3.00
12 Jeremiah Johnson RC 1.25 3.00
13 Vontae Davis RC 1.25 3.00
14 Javarris Williams RC 1.50 4.00
15 Darius Butler RC 1.50 4.00
16 Everette Brown RC 1.25 3.00
17 Quinn Johnson RC 1.25 3.00
18 Robert Ayers RC 1.25 3.00
19 Patrick Chung RC 1.25 3.00
20 Richard Quinn RC 1.50 4.00
21 Fili Moala RC 1.25 3.00
22 Louis Delmas RC 1.50 4.00
23 Paul Kruger RC 2.00 5.00
24 Connor Barwin RC 1.50 4.00
25 Victor Harris RC 1.50 4.00
26 Bear Pascoe RC 1.50 4.00
27 Michael Mitchell RC 1.25 3.00
28 Larry English RC 1.50 4.00
29 Bernard Scott RC 2.00 5.00
30 Rashad Johnson RC 1.25 3.00
31 Ron Brace RC 1.50 4.00
32 Jake O'Connell RC 1.25 3.00
33 Gerald McRath RC 1.50 4.00
34 Eric Wood RC 1.25 3.00
35 Asher Allen RC 1.25 3.00
36 Darcel McBath RC 1.25 3.00
37 Mike Mickens RC 1.25 3.00
38 Eben Britton RC 1.50 4.00
39 Frank Summers RC 2.00 5.00
40 Kevin Barnes RC 1.25 3.00
41 Max Unger RC 2.00 5.00
42 Tyrone McKenzie RC 1.50 4.00
43 Michael Oher RC 2.00 5.00
44 Andy Levitre RC 1.50 4.00
45 Marcus Freeman RC 1.25 3.00
46 Scott McKillop RC 1.25 3.00
47 Evander Hood RC 2.00 5.00
48 Quinten Lawrence RC 1.25 3.00
49 Phil Loadholt RC 1.50 4.00
50 Clint Sintim RC 1.25 3.00
51 B.Roethlisberger JSY/249 4.00 10.00
52 Clinton Portis JSY/39 4.00 10.00
53A Steven Jackson JSY/719 2.00 5.00
54 Jamaal Charles JSY/999 2.50 6.00
55 Wes Welker JSY/189 3.00 8.00
56A Jonathan Stewart JSY/189 2.50 6.00
57 Aaron Rodgers JSY/249 15.00 40.00
58 Thomas Jones JSY/249 2.50 6.00
59 Calvin Johnson JSY/719 3.00 8.00
60 Andre Johnson JSY/189 3.00 8.00
61 Matt Forte JSY/999 2.00 5.00
62 Hines Ward JSY/39 5.00 12.00
63 JaMarcus Russell JSY/189 2.50 6.00
64 Jerricho Cotchery JSY/249 2.50 6.00
65A Ray Rice JSY/999 2.00 5.00
66 Eddie Royal JSY/999 2.00 5.00
67 Brian Westbrook JSY/249 2.50 6.00
68A Dwayne Bowe JSY/249 3.00 8.00
69A Marshawn Lynch JSY/249 3.00 8.00
70 Larry Fitzgerald JSY/249 3.00 8.00
71A Philip Rivers JSY/249 4.00 10.00
72 Jake Long JSY/999 2.00 5.00
73 Steve Smith USC JSY/999 2.50 6.00
74 Brady Quinn JSY/189 2.50 6.00
75 Steve Smith JSY/249 3.00 8.00
76 D.McNabb JSY/249 3.00 8.00
77 Jordy Nelson JSY/999 2.50 6.00
78 Dustin Keller JSY/999 2.00 5.00
79 Chester Taylor JSY/249 2.50 6.00
80A D.Williams JSY/999 2.00 5.00
81 Ronnie Brown JSY/719 2.00 5.00
82 Santana Moss JSY/249 3.00 8.00
83 Lee Evans JSY/719 2.50 6.00
84 Donnie Avery JSY/999 2.00 5.00
85 M.Jones-Drew JSY/249 2.50 6.00
86 Anthony Gonzalez JSY/39 4.00 10.00
87 Joseph Addai JSY/189 2.50 6.00
88 Marques Colston JSY/249 2.50 6.00
89 Willie Parker JSY/189 2.50 6.00
90 Ted Ginn JSY/249 2.50 6.00
91 Greg Olsen JSY/719 2.50 6.00
92 Brian Urlacher JSY/719 3.00 8.00
93 Donald Driver JSY/249 3.00 8.00
94 Trent Edwards JSY/189 2.50 6.00
95 Antonio Gates JSY/999 2.50 6.00
96 Ryan Grant JSY/249 3.00 8.00
97 Santonio Holmes JSY/189 2.50 6.00
98A Chad Ochocinco JSY/249 2.50 6.00
99A Brandon Marshall JSY/999 2.50 6.00
100 Anquan Boldin JSY/719 2.00 5.00
101 Brandon Gibson AU/399 RC 3.00 8.00
102 M.Jenkins AU/499 RC 2.50 6.00
103 Ian Johnson AU/999 RC 2.00 5.00
104 William Moore AU/999 RC 2.00 5.00
105 Brian Cushing AU/499 RC 2.50 6.00
106 Gartrell Johnson AU/499 RC 2.50 6.00
107 R.Jennings AU/999 RC 2.50 6.00
108 Devin Moore AU/699 RC 2.00 5.00
109 Rey Maualuga AU/299 RC 5.00 12.00
110 Cedric Peerman AU/999 RC 2.00 5.00
111 Kory Sheets AU/999 RC 2.50 6.00
112 Jaison Williams AU/999 RC 2.50 6.00
113 Jeremy Childs AU/999 RC 2.00 5.00
114 Demetrius Byrd AU/999 RC 2.50 6.00
115 Arian Foster AU/599 RC 5.00 12.00
116 Manuel Johnson AU/299 RC 3.00 8.00
117 Jarett Dillard AU/399 RC 2.50 6.00
118 J.Laurinaitis AU/299 RC 6.00 15.00
119 James Davis AU/999 RC 2.00 5.00
120 Marlon Lucky AU/999 RC 2.00 5.00
121 P.J. Hill AU/699 RC 2.00 5.00
122 S.Stroughter AU/299 RC 3.00 8.00
123 Quan Cosby AU/299 RC 3.00 8.00
124 Tyrell Sutton AU/399 RC 2.50 6.00
125 Mike Goodson AU RC 2.50 6.00
126 Chase Coffman AU/399 RC 2.50 6.00
127 Kenny McKinley AU/299 RC 3.00 8.00
128 C.Ingram AU/499 RC 2.50 6.00
129 Marko Mitchell AU/499 RC 2.50 6.00
130 Chase Daniel AU/299 RC 4.00 10.00
131 Brooks Foster AU/999 RC 2.00 5.00
132 Mike Teel AU/299 RC 3.00 8.00
133 Aaron Kelly AU/999 RC 2.00 5.00
134 Brian Hoyer AU/299 RC 5.00 12.00
135 Johnny Knox AU/499 RC 3.00 8.00
136 Brandon Tate AU/499 RC 3.00 8.00
137 T.Underwood AU/499 RC 2.50 6.00
138 Travis Beckum AU/499 RC 2.50 6.00
139 Brian Hartline AU/499 RC 6.00 15.00
140 Shawn Nelson AU/699 RC 2.00 5.00
141 Chris Ogbonnaya AU/699 RC 2.50 6.00
142 Tom Brandstater AU/299 RC 4.00 10.00
143 Curtis Painter AU/499 RC 2.50 6.00
144 Jared Cook AU/499 RC 3.00 8.00
145 James Casey AU/999 RC 2.50 6.00
146A M.Stafford JSY/749 RC 8.00 20.00
146B M.Stafford JSY AU/40 75.00 150.00
147A Josh Freeman JSY/749 RC 1.50 4.00
147B Josh Freeman JSY AU/40
148A Nate Davis JSY/749 RC 1.50 4.00
148B Nate Davis JSY AU/250 5.00 12.00
149A Rhett Bomar JSY/749 RC 1.50 4.00
150A M.Sanchez JSY/749 RC 1.50 4.00
150B M.Sanchez JSY AU/40 12.00 30.00
151A Chris Wells JSY/749 RC 1.50 4.00
151B Chris Wells JSY AU/100 20.00 50.00
152A Javon Ringer JSY/749 RC 1.50 4.00
152B Javon Ringer JSY AU/599 4.00 10.00
153A Deon Butler JSY/749 RC 1.50 4.00
154A B.Pettigrew JSY/749 RC 1.50 4.00
154B B.Pettigrew JSY AU/600 4.00 10.00
155A L.McCoy JSY/749 RC 4.00 10.00
155B L.McCoy JSY AU/150 25.00 50.00
156A D.Heyward-Bey JSY/749 RC 2.50 6.00
156B D.Heyward-Bey JSY AU/40 15.00 40.00
157A Ramses Barden JSY/749 RC 1.50 4.00
157B Ramses Barden JSY AU/600 4.00 10.00
158A Derrick Williams JSY/749 RC 1.50 4.00
158B Derrick Williams JSY AU/600 4.00 10.00
159 Tyson Jackson JSY/749 RC 1.50 4.00
160A Hakeem Nicks JSY/749 RC 2.00 5.00
161 Mike Wallace JSY/749 RC 2.50 6.00
162 Jason Smith JSY/749 RC 1.50 4.00
163A Aaron Curry JSY/749 RC 3.00 8.00
163B Aaron Curry JSY AU/400 6.00 15.00
164A Patrick Turner JSY/749 RC 1.50 4.00
165A K.Moreno JSY/749 RC 1.50 4.00
165B K.Moreno JSY AU/40 10.00 26.00
166A Brian Robiskie JSY/749 RC 1.50 4.00
166B Brian Robiskie JSY AU/400 4.00 10.00
167A S.McGee JSY/749 RC 1.50 4.00
167B S.McGee JSY AU/500 4.00 10.00
168A Kenny Britt JSY/749 RC 2.50 6.00
168B Kenny Britt JSY AU/500 6.00 15.00
169A M.Massaquoi JSY/749 RC 1.50 4.00
169B M.Massaquoi JSY AU/200 5.00 12.00
170A Donald Brown JSY/749 RC 1.50 4.00
170B Donald Brown JSY AU/40 15.00 40.00
171 Mike Thomas JSY/749 RC 1.50 4.00
172A Juaquin Iglesias JSY/749 RC 1.50 4.00
173A Andre Brown JSY/749 RC 2.00 5.00
173B Andre Brown JSY AU/500 5.00 12.00
174A Glen Coffee JSY/749 RC 1.50 4.00
174B Glen Coffee JSY AU/500 4.00 10.00
175A M.Crabtree JSY/749 RC 2.50 6.00
175B M.Crabtree JSY AU/40 10.00 25.00
176A Shonn Greene JSY/749 RC 1.50 4.00
176B Shonn Greene JSY AU/500 4.00 10.00
177A Percy Harvin JSY/749 RC 1.50 4.00
177B Percy Harvin JSY AU/200 5.00 12.00
178A Pat White JSY/749 RC 2.00 5.00
178B Pat White JSY AU/50 12.00 30.00
179A Jeremy Maclin JSY/749 RC 2.00 5.00
179B Jeremy Maclin JSY AU/50 15.00 40.00
180A P.Manning JSY AU/30 60.00 120.00
181A Greg Jennings JSY AU/300 4.00 10.00
182 Jamaal Charles JSY AU/425 5.00 12.00
183A A.Peterson JSY AU/30 75.00 150.00
184 Donnie Avery JSY AU/425 4.00 10.00
185 Harry Douglas JSY AU/500 4.00 10.00
186 Devin Thomas JSY AU/300 4.00 10.00
187A D.McFadden JSY AU/30 20.00 50.00
188A Tony Romo JSY AU/30 40.00 80.00
189A Frank Gore JSY AU/30 15.00 40.00
190A Tom Brady JSY AU/30 125.00 250.00
191A Joe Flacco JSY AU/50 25.00 60.00
192 Drew Brees JSY AU/30 40.00 80.00
193A L.Tomlinson JSY AU/30 25.00 50.00
194A Reggie Bush JSY AU/30 20.00 50.00
195 R.Mendenhall JSY AU/30 10.00 25.00

2009 Bowman Sterling Black Refractors

*1-50 ROOKIES: 1.2X TO 3X BASIC RCs
1-50 ROOKIES PRINT RUN 50
*VET JSY/50: .5X TO 1.2X REFRCT.JSY/199
*VET JSY/15: .5X TO 1.2X REFRCT.JSY/25
51-100 VET JERSEY PRINT RUN 15-50
*ROOK AU/25: .5X TO 1.2X REFRACT.AU/75
101-145 ROOKIE AUTO PRINT RUN 25
*ROOK JSY/50: .5X TO 1.2X REFRACT.JSY/199
146-179 ROOKIE JERSEY PRINT RUN 50
*VET JSY AU/15: .5X TO 1.2X REF.JSY AU/25
*RK JSY AU/15: .5X TO 1.2X REF.JSY AU/25
115 Arian Foster AU 12.00 30.00
146B Matthew Stafford JSY AU 150.00 300.00
147B Josh Freeman JSY AU 8.00 20.00
150B Mark Sanchez JSY AU 30.00 80.00
177B Percy Harvin JSY AU 8.00 20.00

2009 Bowman Sterling Gold Refractors

*1-50 ROOKIES: 1.5X TO 4X BASIC RCs
1-50 ROOKIES PRINT RUN 25
*VET JSY/25: .6X TO 1.5X REFRCT.JSY/199
*VET JSY/10: .6X TO 1.5X REFRCT.JSY/25
51-100 VET JERSEY PRINT RUN 10-25
*ROOK JSY/25: .6X TO 1.5X REFRACT.JSY/199
146-179 ROOKIE JERSEY PRINT RUN 25

2009 Bowman Sterling Refractors

*1-50 ROOKIES: .6X TO 1.5X BASIC RCs
1-50 ROOKIE PRINT RUN 299
COMMON VET JSY/199 2.50 6.00
VET JSY/199 SEMIS 3.00 8.00
VET JSY/199 UNL.STARS 4.00 10.00
COMMON VET JSY/25 6.00 15.00
VET JSY/25 UNL.STARS 8.00 20.00
51-100 VET JERSEY PRINT RUN 25-199
COMMON ROOKIE AU/75 5.00 12.00
ROOKIE AU/75 UNL.STR 6.00 15.00
101-145 ROOKIE AUTO PRINT RUN 75
COMMON ROOKIE JSY/199 2.50 6.00
ROOKIE JSY/199 UNL.STR 3.00 8.00
ROOKIE JERSEY PRINT RUN 199
COMMON ROOKIE JSY AU/25 10.00 25.00
*VET JSY AU: .6X TO 1.5X JSY AU/300-500
*VET JSY AU: .4X TO 1X BSE JSY AU/30-50
146-195 JERSEY AUTO PRINT RUN 25
104 William Moore AU 4.00 10.00
105 Brian Cushing AU 4.00 10.00
108 Devin Moore AU 4.00 10.00
109 Rey Maualuga AU 6.00 15.00
110 Cedric Peerman AU 4.00 10.00
117 Jarett Dillard AU 4.00 10.00
118 James Laurinaitis AU 4.00 10.00
119 James Davis AU 4.00 10.00
129 Marko Mitchell AU 4.00 10.00
130 Chase Daniel AU 5.00 12.00
134 Brian Hoyer AU 6.00 15.00
135 Johnny Knox AU 5.00 12.00
139 Brian Hartline AU 8.00 20.00
146A Matthew Stafford JSY 12.00 30.00
146B Matthew Stafford JSY AU 199.00 200.00
147A Josh Freeman JSY 2.00 5.00
147B Josh Freeman JSY AU 6.00 15.00
148A Nate Davis JSY 2.00 5.00
148B Nate Davis JSY AU 6.00 15.00
150A Mark Sanchez JSY 2.00 5.00
150B Mark Sanchez JSY AU 25.00 60.00
151A Chris Wells JSY 2.00 5.00
151B Chris Wells JSY AU 6.00 15.00
154A Brandon Pettigrew JSY 2.00 5.00
154B Brandon Pettigrew JSY AU 6.00 15.00
155A LeSean McCoy JSY 5.00 12.00
155B LeSean McCoy JSY AU 15.00 40.00
156A Darrius Heyward-Bey JSY 3.00 8.00
156B Darrius Heyward-Bey JSY AU 10.00 25.00
160A Hakeem Nicks JSY 2.50 6.00
161 Mike Wallace JSY 3.00 8.00
163A Aaron Curry JSY 3.00 8.00
163B Aaron Curry JSY AU 10.00 25.00
165A Knowshon Moreno JSY 2.00 5.00
165B Knowshon Moreno JSY AU 15.00 40.00
168A Kenny Britt JSY 3.00 8.00
168B Kenny Britt JSY AU 10.00 25.00
170A Donald Brown JSY 2.00 5.00
170B Donald Brown JSY AU 20.00 50.00
174A Glen Coffee JSY 2.00 5.00
174B Glen Coffee JSY AU 6.00 15.00
175A Michael Crabtree JSY 3.00 8.00
175B Michael Crabtree JSY AU 15.00 40.00
176A Shonn Greene JSY 2.00 5.00
176B Shonn Greene JSY AU 6.00 15.00
177A Percy Harvin JSY 2.00 5.00
177B Percy Harvin JSY AU 6.00 15.00
178A Pat White JSY 2.50 6.00
178B Pat White JSY AU 25.00 60.00
179A Jeremy Maclin JSY 2.50 6.00
179B Jeremy Maclin JSY AU 8.00 20.00

2009 Bowman Sterling Xfractors

*1-50 ROOKIES: .8X TO 2X BASIC RCs
1-50 ROOKIE PRINT RUN 100
51-195 UNPRICED PRINT RUN 5

2009 Bowman Sterling Dual Autograph Gold Refractors

STATED PRINT RUN 10-125
SERIAL #'d UNDER 15 NOT PRICED
EXCH EXPIRATION: 8/31/2012
BM D.Brown/Moreno/15 20.00 50.00
BR K.Britt/J.Ringer/125 10.00 25.00
BW D.Butler/D.Williams/125 10.00 25.00
CI J.Cutler/J.Iglesias/25 30.00 60.00
FM Freeman/S.McGee/25 30.00 60.00
HM P.Harvin/J.Maclin/125 15.00 40.00
HW S.Holms/M.Wallce/125 25.00 50.00
JB B.Jacobs/A.Brown/75 10.00 25.00
JG T.Jones/S.Greene/75 20.00 50.00
JM D.Jackson/Maclin/15 25.00 60.00
MH McFadd/Hywrd-Bey/15 30.00 60.00
MM L.McCoy/J.Maclin/75 25.00 50.00
MW L.McCoy/C.Wells/15 50.00 100.00
PH Peterson/P.Harvin/15 125.00 250.00
PW Pettigrew/D.Will/125 10.00 25.00
TW M.Thms/M.Wllce/125 12.00 30.00
WF Winslow/Freeman/15 30.00 60.00
WR L.White/Ringer/125 10.00 25.00
WT P.White/P.Turner/125 25.00 60.00

2010 Bowman Sterling

EXCH EXPIRATION: 12/31/2013
1 Javier Arenas RC 1.00 2.50
2 Deji Karim RC 1.25 3.00
3 Chris Cook RC 1.00 2.50
4 Derrick Morgan RC 1.00 2.50
5 Carlos Dunlap RC 1.00 2.50
6 Bryan Bulaga RC 1.00 2.50
7 Akwasi Owusu-Ansah RC 1.00 2.50
8 Nate Allen RC 1.50 4.00
9 Brian Price RC 1.00 2.50
10 Dan Williams RC 1.00 2.50
11 Terrence Cody RC 1.00 2.50
12 Mike Iupati RC 1.50 4.00
13 Joe Haden RC 1.50 4.00
14 Russell Okung RC 1.00 2.50
15 Devin McCourty RC 1.25 3.00
16 Dezmon Briscoe RC 1.00 2.50
17 Daryl Washington RC 1.00 2.50
18 Trent Williams RC 1.25 3.00
19 Brandon Spikes RC 1.00 2.50
20 Jared Odrick RC 1.25 3.00
21 Victor Cruz RC 2.00 5.00
22 Charles Brown RC 1.00 2.50
23 Everson Griffen RC 1.00 2.50
24 Dorin Dickerson RC 1.00 2.50
25 Jerry Hughes RC 1.00 2.50
26 Linval Joseph RC 1.00 2.50
27 Tony Moeaki RC 1.25 3.00
28 Ed Dickson RC 1.00 2.50
29 Patrick Robinson RC 1.25 3.00
30 Corey Wootton RC 1.00 2.50
31 Morgan Burnett RC 1.25 3.00
32 Taylor Mays RC 1.00 2.50
33 Maurkice Pouncey RC 1.25 3.00
34 Brandon Graham RC 1.25 3.00
35 Rodger Saffold RC 1.00 2.50
36 Koa Misi RC 1.25 3.00
37 Jerome Murphy RC 1.25 3.00
38 Kyle Wilson RC 1.00 2.50
39 Lamarr Houston RC 1.25 3.00
40 LeGarrette Blount RC 2.00 5.00
41 Vladimir Ducasse RC 1.50 4.00
42 Cam Thomas RC 1.25 3.00
43 Jermaine Cunningham RC 1.00 2.50
44 Antonio Brown RC 8.00 20.00
45 David Gettis RC 1.00 2.50
46 Dominique Franks RC 1.00 2.50
47 Garrett Graham RC 1.00 2.50
48 Jason Worilds RC 1.00 2.50
49 Keiland Williams RC 1.25 3.00
50 Sam Shields RC 3.00 8.00
BSAAB Arrelious Benn AU B 3.00 8.00
BSAAD Anthony Dixon AU D 2.50 6.00
BSAAH Aaron Hernandez AU D 12.00 30.00
BSAAM Anthony McCoy AU D 2.50 6.00
BSAAR Andre Roberts AU B 4.00 10.00
BSABL Brandon LaFell AU C 4.00 10.00
BSACJS C.J. Spiller AU A 3.00 8.00
BSACMI Carlton Mitchell AU D 2.50 6.00
BSACS Charles Scott AU D 2.50 6.00
BSADD Dennis Dixon AU D 5.00 12.00
BSADM Dexter McCluster AU B 4.00 10.00
BSADR David Reed AU D 2.50 6.00
BSADS Darryl Sharpton AU D RC 2.50 6.00
BSADT Demaryius Thomas AU A 8.00 20.00
BSADW Damian Williams AU C 2.50 6.00
BSAEB Eric Berry AU C 4.00 10.00
BSAED Eric Decker AU C 3.00 8.00
BSAES Emmanuel Sanders AU D 4.00 10.00
BSAGJ Greg Jennings AU A 3.00 8.00
BSAGM Gerald McCoy AU A 3.00 8.00
BSAGT Golden Tate AU B 4.00 10.00
BSAHN Hakeem Nicks AU B 8.00 20.00
BSAJB Jahvid Best AU A 3.00 8.00
BSAJC Jonathan Crompton AU D RC 2.50 6.00
BSAJD Jonathan Dwyer AU C 2.50 6.00
BSAJF Jacoby Ford AU D 2.50 6.00
BSAJG Jimmy Graham AU C 1.00 25.00
BSAJJ James Jones AU D 3.00 8.00
BSAJP J.Pierre-Paul AU D RC 4.00 10.00
BSAJS Jordan Shipley AU D 2.50 6.00
BSAJSK John Skelton AU D 4.00 10.00
BSAKJ Kareem Jackson AU D RC 2.50 6.00
BSAME Marcus Easley AU D 2.50 6.00
BSAMG Mardy Gilyard AU D 2.50 6.00
BSAMH Montario Hardesty AU B 3.00 8.00
BSAMW Mike Williams AU D 10.00 25.00
BSANS Ndamukong Suh AU A 6.00 15.00
BSAPH Percy Harvin AU A 10.00 25.00
BSARAB Arrelious Benn JSY AU B 4.00 10.00
BSARAD Anthony Dixon JSY AU D 4.00 10.00
BSARAE A.Edwards JSY AU C 5.00 12.00
BSARAP A.Peterson JSY AU A 50.00 100.00
BSARAR Andre Roberts JSY AU C 5.00 12.00
BSARBE Braylon Edwards JSY AU D 5.00 12.00
BSARBL Brandon LaFell JSY AU C 6.00 15.00
BSARBT Ben Tate JSY AU A 4.00 10.00
BSARC Riley Cooper AU D 2.50 6.00
BSARCJS C.J. Spiller JSY AU A 4.00 10.00
BSARCM Colt McCoy JSY AU A 5.00 12.00
BSARDBR Drew Brees JSY AU A 50.00 100.00
BSARDM D.McCluster JSY AU B 5.00 12.00
BSARDT D.Thomas JSY AU A 15.00 30.00
BSARDW D.Williams JSY AU C 4.00 10.00
BSAREB Eric Berry JSY AU B 5.00 12.00
BSARED Eric Decker JSY AU C 5.00 12.00
BSARES E.Sanders JSY AU D 6.00 15.00
BSARFJ Felix Jones JSY AU A 6.00 15.00
BSARG Rob Gronkowski AU C 25.00 50.00
BSARGM Gerald McCoy JSY AU A 4.00 10.00
BSARGT Golden Tate JSY AU B 5.00 12.00
BSARJB Jahvid Best JSY AU A 4.00 10.00
BSARJC Jimmy Clausen JSY AU A 4.00 10.00
BSARJD Jonathan Dwyer JSY AU C 4.00 10.00
BSARJG J.Graham JSY AU D 40.00 60.00
BSARJS Jordan Shipley JSY AU D 4.00 10.00
BSARLT L.Tomlinson JSY AU A 20.00 40.00
BSARM Ryan Mathews AU A 3.00 8.00
BSARMC Matt Cassel JSY AU B 8.00 20.00
BSARME Marcus Easley JSY AU B 4.00 10.00
BSARMG Mardy Gilyard JSY AU C 4.00 10.00
BSARMH M.Hardesty JSY AU A 4.00 10.00
BSARMJD M.Jones-Drew JSY AU A 10.00 25.00
BSARMK Mike Kafka JSY AU A 5.00 12.00
BSARMW Mike Williams JSY AU D 4.00 10.00
BSARNS N.Suh JSY AU A 8.00 20.00
BSARR Ray Rice AU A 8.00 20.00
BSARRC Riley Cooper JSY AU B 4.00 10.00
BSARRG R.Gronkowski JSY AU C 15.00 40.00
BSARRM R.Mathews JSY AU A 4.00 10.00
BSARRME R.Meachem JSY AU A 5.00 12.00
BSARSB S.Bradford JSY AU A 5.00 12.00
BSARSC Sean Canfield JSY AU C 4.00 10.00
BSARTG Toby Gerhart JSY AU B 4.00 10.00
BSARTP Taylor Price JSY AU C 4.00 10.00
BSARTT Tim Tebow JSY AU A 25.00 60.00
BSASB Sam Bradford AU A 4.00 10.00
BSASC Sean Canfield AU D 2.50 6.00
BSASG Shonn Greene AU A 6.00 15.00
BSASL Sean Lee AU C RC 8.00 20.00
BSASR Sidney Rice AU A 10.00 25.00
BSASW Sean Weatherspoon AU D RC 2.50 6.00
BSATA Tyson Alualu AU D RC 2.50 6.00
BSATG Toby Gerhart AU B 3.00 8.00
BSATPR Taylor Price AU D 2.50 6.00
BSATT Tim Tebow AU A 25.00 60.00
BSATW T.J. Ward AU D RC 4.00 10.00
BSAVJ Vincent Jackson AU A 6.00 15.00
BSAZR Zac Robinson AU D 3.00 8.00
BSRAB Arrelious Benn JSY B RC 2.00 5.00
BSRAD Anthony Dixon JSY A RC 2.50 6.00
BSRAE A.Edwards JSY B RC 2.50 6.00
BSRAH A.Hernandez JSY A RC 4.00 10.00
BSRAM Anthony McCoy JSY B RC 2.00 5.00
BSRAP Adrian Peterson JSY B 4.00 10.00
BSRAR Andre Roberts JSY B RC 2.50 6.00
BSRAS Alex Smith QB JSY A 4.00 10.00
BSRBL Brandon LaFell JSY B RC 3.00 8.00
BSRBS Bob Sanders JSY A 4.00 10.00
BSRBT Ben Tate JSY B RC 2.00 5.00
BSRBU Brian Urlacher JSY A 5.00 12.00
BSRCB Cedric Benson JSY A 3.00 8.00
BSRCBA Champ Bailey JSY A 5.00 12.00
BSRCC Chris Cooley JSY A 5.00 12.00
BSRCJS C.J. Spiller JSY B RC 2.00 5.00
BSRCM Colt McCoy JSY B RC 2.50 6.00
BSRCMI Carlton Mitchell JSY A RC 2.50 6.00
BSRCS Charles Scott JSY A RC 2.50 6.00
BSRDB Dez Bryant JSY B RC 8.00 20.00
BSRDJW D.J. Williams JSY A 3.00 8.00
BSRDL Dan LeFevour JSY A RC 2.50 6.00
BSRDM D.McCluster JSY B RC 2.50 6.00
BSRDMC Donovan McNabb JSY A 4.00 10.00
BSRDR David Reed JSY A RC 2.50 6.00
BSRDT D.Thomas JSY B RC 5.00 12.00
BSRDW D.Williams JSY B RC 2.00 5.00
BSREB Eric Berry JSY B RC 3.00 8.00
BSRED Eric Decker JSY B RC 2.50 6.00
BSRES E.Sanders JSY B RC 3.00 8.00
BSRET Earl Thomas JSY A RC 6.00 15.00
BSRGM Gerald McCoy JSY A RC 2.50 6.00
BSRGT Golden Tate JSY B RC 2.50 6.00
BSRJB Jahvid Best JSY B RC 2.00 5.00
BSRJC Jimmy Clausen JSY B RC 2.00 5.00
BSRJD Jonathan Dwyer JSY B RC 2.00 5.00
BSRJF Jacoby Ford JSY A RC 2.50 6.00
BSRJG Jimmy Graham JSY A RC 6.00 15.00
BSRJGR J.Gresham JSY B RC 2.00 5.00
BSRJM Joe McKnight JSY B RC 2.00 5.00
BSRJN Jordy Nelson JSY A 4.00 10.00
BSRJS Jordan Shipley JSY B RC 3.00 8.00
BSRJSK John Skelton JSY A RC 4.00 10.00
BSRJST James Starks JSY B RC 3.00 8.00
BSRJWI Jason Witten JSY A 5.00 12.00
BSRKO Kyle Orton JSY A 3.00 8.00
BSRKS Kevin Smith JSY A 3.00 8.00
BSRMB Marion Barber JSY A 4.00 10.00
BSRMBU Michael Bush JSY A 3.00 8.00
BSRME Marcus Easley JSY B RC 2.00 5.00
BSRMG Mardy Gilyard JSY B RC 2.00 5.00
BSRMH M.Hardesty JSY B RC 2.00 5.00
BSRMK Mike Kafka JSY B RC 2.50 6.00
BSRML Matt Leinart JSY A 3.00 8.00
BSRMW Mike Williams JSY B RC 2.00 5.00
BSRMWI Mario Williams JSY A 4.00 10.00
BSRNS N.Suh JSY B RC 4.00 10.00
BSRRC Riley Cooper JSY A RC 2.50 6.00
BSRRG R.Gronkowski JSY B RC 6.00 15.00
BSRRM Ryan Mathews JSY B RC 2.00 5.00
BSRRMC R.McClain JSY B RC 2.00 5.00
BSRRS Richard Seymour JSY A 3.00 8.00
BSRSB S.Bradford JSY B RC 2.50 6.00
BSRSC Sean Canfield JSY A RC 2.50 6.00
BSRSM Santana Moss JSY A 4.00 10.00
BSRSS Steve Slaton JSY A 3.00 8.00
BSRTG Toby Gerhart JSY B RC 2.00 5.00
BSRTH Tommie Harris JSY A 3.00 8.00
BSRTHE Todd Heap JSY A 3.00 8.00
BSRTP Tony Pike JSY A RC 2.50 6.00
BSRTPR Taylor Price JSY B RC 2.00 5.00
BSRTT Tim Tebow JSY B RC 6.00 15.00
BSRVJ Vincent Jackson JSY A 3.00 8.00
BSRZR Zac Robinson JSY A RC 3.00 8.00

2010 Bowman Sterling Black Refractors

*1-50 ROOKIES: 1X TO 2.5X BASIC CARDS
*ROOKIE AU: .6X TO 1.5X BASIC AU A-B
*ROOKIE AU: .8X TO 2X BASIC AU C-D
*ROOKIE JSY: .5X TO 1.2X BASIC JSY A-B
*ROOKIE JSY: .6X TO 1.5X BASIC JSY C-D
*VET AU: .6X TO 1.5X BASIC CARDS
*VET JSY: .5X TO 1.2X BASIC CARDS
STATED PRINT RUN 50 SER.#'d SETS
EXCH EXPIRATION: 12/31/2013
BSABW Chris Wells AU EXCH 6.00 15.00
BSACM Colt McCoy AU 6.00 15.00
BSADBR Drew Brees AU 40.00 80.00
BSAJCL Jimmy Clausen AU 5.00 12.00
BSATT Tim Tebow AU 30.00 80.00

2010 Bowman Sterling Blue Refractors

*1-50 ROOKIES: .8X TO 2X BASIC CARDS
*ROOKIE AU: .5X TO 1.2X BASIC AU A-B
*ROOKIE AU: .6X TO 1.5X BASIC AU C-D
*ROOKIE JSY: .4X TO 1X BASIC JSY A-B
*ROOKIE JSY: .5X TO 1.2X BASIC JSY C-D
*ROOKIE JSY AU: .5X TO 1.2X BASIC CARDS
*VET AU: .6X TO 1.5X BASIC CARDS
*VET JSY: .4X TO 1X BASIC CARDS
*VET JSY AU: .5X TO 1.2X BASIC CARDS
STATED PRINT RUN 99 SER.#'d SETS
EXCH EXPIRATION: 12/31/2013

2010 Bowman Sterling Gold Refractors

*1-50 ROOKIES: 2X TO 5X BASIC CARDS
*ROOKIE AU: 1X TO 2.5X BASIC AU A-B
*ROOKIE AU: 1.2X TO 3X BASIC AU C-D
*ROOKIE JSY: .6X TO 1.5X BASIC JSY A-B
*ROOKIE JSY: .8X TO 2X BASIC JSY C-D
*ROOKIE JSY AU: 1.2X TO 3X BASIC CARDS
*VET AU: .8X TO 2X BASIC CARDS
*VET JSY: .6X TO 1.5X BASIC CARDS
*VET JSY AU: .8X TO 2X BASIC CARDS
STATED PRINT RUN 25 SER.#'d SETS
EXCH EXPIRATION: 12/31/2013
BSADB Dez Bryant AU 75.00 150.00
BSADBR Drew Brees AU 50.00 100.00
BSARAP Adrian Peterson JSY AU 60.00 120.00
BSARNS Ndamukong Suh JSY AU 40.00 100.00
BSARTT Tim Tebow JSY AU 75.00 200.00
BSATT Tim Tebow AU 40.00 100.00
BSRTT Tim Tebow JSY 12.00 30.00

2010 Bowman Sterling Refractors

*1-50 ROOKIES: .6X TO 1.5X BASIC CARDS
*ROOKIE JSY: .4X TO 1X BASIC JSY A
*ROOKIE JSY: .5X TO 1.2X BASIC JSY B
*VETERAN JSY: .4X TO 1X BASIC CARDS
STATED PRINT RUN 299 SER.#'d SETS

2010 Bowman Sterling Dual Autographs

STATED PRINT RUN 25 SER.#'d SETS
BC S.Bradford/J.Clausen 20.00 40.00
BM S.Bradford/C.McCoy 20.00 40.00
BT E.Berry/E.Thomas 30.00 60.00
MB R.Mathews/J.Best 12.00 30.00
MBE D.McCluster/J.Best 25.00 60.00
MH C.McCoy/M.Hardesty 25.00 60.00
MM Mathews/McCluster 12.00 30.00
MS G.McCoy/N.Suh 25.00 60.00
SB C.Spiller/J.Best 12.00 30.00
SM C.Spiller/R.Mathews 12.00 30.00
ST C.Spiller/D.Thomas 25.00 50.00

2010 Bowman Sterling Dual Autographed Relic Black Refractors

STATED PRINT RUN 25 SER.#'d SETS
*BASIC DUAL: .4X TO 1X BLACK REF/25
EXCH EXPIRATION: 12/31/2013
BC S.Bradford/J.Clausen 30.00 60.00
BD A.Benn/E.Decker 20.00 50.00
BG Bradford/Gilyard 30.00 60.00
BM S.Bradford/C.McCoy 30.00 60.00
BTH E.Berry/E.Thomas 30.00 60.00
BW D.Bryant/M.Williams 40.00 80.00
CL J.Clausen/B.LaFell 20.00 50.00
CT J.Clausen/G.Tate 15.00 40.00
DR F.Decker/A.Roberts 20.00 50.00
DT J.Dwyer/D.Thomas 20.00 50.00
GD T.Gerhart/E.Decker 20.00 50.00
GDW T.Gerhart/J.Dwyer 15.00 40.00
CH Cronkowski/Hernandez 60.00 100.00
HD M.Hardesty/J.Dwyer
LE B.LaFell/A.Edwards 12.00 30.00
LW B.LaFell/M.Williams 15.00 40.00
MB R.Mathews/J.Best 12.00 30.00
MBE D.McCluster/J.Best 20.00 50.00
MH C.McCoy/M.Hardesty 25.00 60.00
MM R.Mathews/McCluster 12.00 30.00
MS G.McCoy/N.Suh 20.00 50.00
MSH C.McCoy/J.Shipley 25.00 60.00
MT D.McCluster/D.Thomas 20.00 50.00
PG T.Price/R.Gronkowski 25.00 50.00
RG Roberts/Gilyard EXCH 12.00 30.00
SB C.Spiller/J.Best 12.00 30.00
SD E.Sanders/J.Dwyer 15.00 40.00
SE C.Spiller/M.Easley 12.00 30.00
SS J.Shipley/E.Sanders 15.00 40.00
ST C.Spiller/D.Thomas 20.00 50.00
TD D.Thomas/E.Decker 20.00 50.00
TDI B.Tate/A.Dixon 15.00 40.00
TT G.Tate/B.Tate 15.00 40.00
TTH G.Tate/D.Thomas 20.00 50.00
WB M.Williams/A.Benn 20.00 40.00

2010 Bowman Sterling Dual Jersey Box Topper

ONE PER HOBBY BOX
*BLACK REF/25: .6X TO 1.5X BASIC INSERTS
*BLUE REF/50: .5X TO 1.2X BASIC INSERTS
*REF/69: .5X TO 1.2X BASIC INSERTS
BB D.Bryant/J.Best 6.00 15.00
BC S.Bradford/J.Clausen 2.00 5.00
BG S.Bradford/M.Gilyard 2.00 5.00
BM E.Berry/D.McCluster 2.00 5.00
BMC S.Bradford/C.McCoy 2.00 5.00
BS J.Best/C.Spiller 5.00 12.00
BT E.Berry/E.Thomas 4.00 10.00
BTE D.Bryant/D.Thomas 6.00 15.00
BW D.Bryant/M.Williams 6.00 15.00
CL J.Clausen/B.LaFell 2.50 6.00
CT J.Clausen/G.Tate 2.00 5.00
DS J.Dwyer/E.Sanders 2.50 6.00
DT J.Dwyer/D.Thomas 4.00 10.00
GM A.Gates/R.Mathews 6.00 15.00
MH C.McCoy/M.Hardesty 2.00 5.00
MS C.McCoy/J.Shipley 5.00 12.00
PG A.Peterson/T.Gerhart 6.00 15.00
RB T.Romo/D.Bryant 6.00 15.00
SE C.Spiller/M.Easley 4.00 10.00
ST S.Slaton/B.Tate 3.00 8.00
TD T.Tebow/E.Decker 8.00 20.00
TDE D.Thomas/E.Decker 5.00 12.00
TT T.Tebow/D.Thomas 8.00 20.00
WB M.Williams/A.Benn 4.00 10.00
WM P.Willis/R.McClain 3.00 8.00

2011 Bowman Sterling

EXCH EXPIRATION: 12/31/2014
1 Patrick Peterson RC 1.50 4.00
2 Aldon Smith RC .75 2.00
3 J.J. Watt RC 4.00 10.00
4 Nick Fairley RC .75 2.00
5 Robert Quinn RC .75 2.00
6 Ryan Kerrigan RC 1.00 2.50
7 James Carpenter RC 1.00 2.50
8 Jacquizz Rodgers RC .75 2.00
9 Niles Paul RC .75 2.00
10 Derek Sherrod RC .75 2.00
11 Aaron Williams RC .75 2.00
12 Akeem Ayers RC .75 2.00
13 Tandon Doss RC .75 2.00
14 Cecil Shorts RC .75 2.00
15 Lance Kendricks RC .75 2.00
16 Marvin Austin RC .75 2.00
17 Rob Housler RC .75 2.00
18 Roy Helu RC .75 2.00
19 Tyrod Taylor RC 1.50 4.00
20 Casey Matthews RC .75 2.00
21 Julius Thomas RC 1.00 2.50
22 Johnny White RC .75 2.00
23 Jeremy Kerley RC 1.25 3.00
24 Denarius Moore RC .75 2.00
25 T.J. Yates RC .75 2.00
26 Da'Rel Scott RC .75 2.00
27 Nathan Enderle RC .75 2.00
28 Ryan Whalen RC .75 2.00
29 Muhammad Wilkerson RC .75 2.00
30 Greg Jones RC 1.00 2.50
31 Virgil Green RC .75 2.00
32 Ryan Taylor RC 1.00 2.50
33 Justin Houston RC 1.00 2.50
34 Brooks Reed RC 1.00 2.50
35 Mike Pouncey RC 1.25 3.00
36 Prince Amukamara RC .75 2.00
37 Jimmy Smith RC .75 2.00
38 Da'Quan Bowers RC .75 2.00
39 Greg Salas RC .75 2.00
40 Dion Lewis RC 1.00 2.50
41 Mark Herzlich RC .75 2.00
42 Jabaal Sheard RC .75 2.00
43 Adrian Clayborn RC .75 2.00
44 Cameron Heyward RC 1.00 2.50
45 Tyron Smith RC 1.00 2.50
46 Rahim Moore RC .75 2.00
48 Ricky Stanzi RC .75 2.00
49 Anthony Allen RC .75 2.00
50 Kris Durham RC .75 2.00
BSAAA Akeem Ayers AU 2.50 6.00
BSAAB Ahmad Bradshaw AU 5.00 12.00
BSAABR Antonio Brown AU 10.00 25.00
BSAAC Adrian Clayborn AU 5.00 12.00
BSAAG Alex Green AU 2.50 6.00
BSAAP Austin Pettis AU 2.50 6.00
BSAAS Aldon Smith AU 8.00 20.00
BSAAW Adrian Wilson AU 5.00 12.00
BSABL Brandon Lloyd AU 5.00 12.00
BSABP Bilal Powell AU 3.00 8.00
BSADA Darvin Adams AU 2.50 6.00
BSADB Davone Bess AU 5.00 12.00
BSADBO Da'Quan Bowers AU 2.50 6.00
BSADC Delone Carter AU 2.50 6.00
BSADH Dwayne Harris AU 2.50 6.00
BSADL Dion Lewis AU 3.00 8.00
BSADM DeMarco Murray AU 5.00 12.00
BSADT Daniel Thomas AU 2.50 6.00
BSAEG Edmond Gates AU 2.50 6.00
BSAGL Greg Little AU 3.00 8.00
BSAGM Greg McElroy AU 4.00 10.00
BSAGS Greg Salas AU 2.50 6.00
BSAJB Jon Baldwin AU 5.00 12.00
BSAJG Jabar Gaffney AU 5.00 12.00
BSAJH Jamie Harper AU 2.50 6.00
BSAJHO Justin Houston AU 3.00 8.00
BSAJJE Jerrel Jernigan AU 2.50 6.00
BSAJR Jacquizz Rodgers AU 2.50 6.00
BSAJT Jordan Todman AU 2.50 6.00
BSAKH Kendall Hunter AU 2.50 6.00
BSALH Leonard Hankerson AU 2.50 6.00
BSALS Luke Stocker AU RC 2.50 6.00
BSAMF Malcom Floyd AU 5.00 12.00
BSAML Mikel Leshoure AU 2.50 6.00
BSAMLE Marcedes Lewis AU 5.00 12.00
BSAMM Mike McNeill AU 4.00 10.00
BSAMP Mike Pouncey AU RC 4.00 10.00
BSAMT Mike Thomas AU 5.00 12.00
BSAMW Mike Wallace AU 5.00 12.00
BSARC Randall Cobb AU 4.00 10.00
BSARMA Robert Mathis AU 8.00 20.00
BSART Ryan Torain AU 5.00 12.00
BSARW Ryan Williams AU 2.50 6.00
BSASR Stevan Ridley AU 2.50 6.00
BSASV Shane Vereen AU 3.00 8.00
BSATJ Taiwan Jones AU 2.50 6.00
BSATS Torrey Smith AU 2.50 6.00
BSATT Tyrod Taylor AU 5.00 12.00
BSATTO Terrence Toliver AU 3.00 8.00
BSATY Titus Young AU 2.50 6.00
BSAVB Vincent Brown AU 2.50 6.00
BSRAD Andy Dalton JSY RC 3.00 8.00
BSRAG Alex Green JSY RC 1.50 4.00
BSRAH Albert Haynesworth JSY 2.50 8.00
BSRAJG A.J. Green JSY RC 4.00 10.00
BSRAJH A.J. Hawk JSY 2.50 6.00
BSRAP Austin Pettis JSY RC 1.50 4.00
BSRAS Alex Smith QB JSY 3.00 8.00
BSRBG Blaine Gabbert JSY RC 1.50 4.00
BSRBP Bilal Powell JSY RC 2.00 5.00
BSRBU Brian Urlacher JSY 4.00 10.00
BSRCC Chris Cooley JSY 4.00 10.00
BSRCK C.Kaepernick JSY RC 2.50 6.00
BSRCN Cam Newton JSY RC 8.00 20.00
BSRCP Christian Ponder JSY RC 1.50 4.00
BSRCS Cecil Shorts JSY 1.50 4.00
BSRDC Delone Carter JSY RC 1.50 4.00
BSRDHE Devin Hester JSY 3.00 8.00
BSRDL Dion Lewis JSY 2.00 5.00
BSRDM DeMarco Murray JSY RC 3.00 8.00
BSRDT Daniel Thomas JSY RC 1.50 4.00
BSRDW DeAngelo Williams JSY 2.50 6.00
BSREG Edmond Gates JSY RC 1.50 4.00
BSREM Eli Manning JSY 3.00 8.00
BSRER Eddie Royal JSY 2.50 6.00
BSRGL Greg Little JSY RC 2.00 5.00
BSRGS Greg Salas JSY 1.50 4.00
BSRJB Jon Baldwin JSY RC 1.50 4.00
BSRJH Jamie Harper JSY RC 1.50 4.00
BSRJJ Julio Jones JSY RC 5.00 12.00
BSRJJE Jerrel Jernigan JSY RC 1.50 4.00
BSRJL Jake Locker JSY RC 1.50 4.00
BSRJP Julius Peppers JSY 3.00 8.00
BSRJT Jordan Todman JSY RC 1.50 4.00
BSRKH Kendall Hunter JSY RC 1.50 4.00
BSRKO Kyle Orton JSY 2.50 6.00
BSRKR Kyle Rudolph JSY RC 1.50 4.00
BSRLH L.Hankerson JSY RC 1.50 4.00
BSRMD Marcell Dareus JSY RC 1.50 4.00
BSRMF Matt Forte JSY 2.50 6.00
BSRMI Mark Ingram JSY RC 2.50 6.00
BSRML Mikel Leshoure JSY RC 1.50 4.00
BSRPA Prince Amukamara JSY 1.50 4.00
BSRRC Randall Cobb JSY RC 2.50 6.00
BSRRM Ryan Mallett JSY RC 1.50 4.00
BSRRR Ray Rice JSY 2.50 6.00
BSRRW Ryan Williams JSY RC 1.50 4.00
BSRSB Sam Bradford JSY 2.50 6.00
BSRSR Stevan Ridley JSY RC 1.50 4.00
BSRSV Shane Vereen JSY RC 2.00 5.00
BSRTJ Taiwan Jones JSY RC 1.50 4.00
BSRTR Tony Romo JSY 3.00 8.00
BSRTS Torrey Smith JSY RC 1.50 4.00
BSRTY Titus Young JSY RC 1.50 4.00
BSRVB Vincent Brown JSY RC 1.50 4.00
BSRVM Von Miller JSY RC 2.50 6.00
BSARAG Alex Green JSY AU 4.00 10.00
BSARAJG A.J. Green JSY AU 15.00 40.00
BSARAP Austin Pettis JSY AU 4.00 10.00
BSARBP Bilal Powell JSY AU 5.00 12.00
BSARCB Champ Bailey JSY AU 15.00 30.00
BSARCK C.Kaepernick JSY AU 6.00 15.00
BSARCP Christian Ponder JSY AU 4.00 10.00
BSARDC Delone Carter JSY AU 4.00 10.00
BSARDH DeAngelo Hall JSY AU 6.00 15.00
BSARDK Dustin Keller JSY AU 6.00 15.00
BSARDM D.Murray JSY AU 8.00 20.00
BSARDMA Derrick Mason JSY AU 6.00 15.00
BSARDT Daniel Thomas JSY AU 4.00 10.00
BSARGL Greg Little JSY AU 5.00 12.00
BSARGO Greg Olsen JSY AU 8.00 20.00
BSARJB Jon Baldwin JSY AU 4.00 10.00
BSARJH Jamie Harper JSY AU 5.00 12.00
BSARJE Jerrel Jernigan JSY AU 4.00 10.00
BSARJR Jacquizz Rodgers JSY AU 4.00 10.00
BSARJT Jordan Todman JSY AU 4.00 10.00
BSARKH Kendall Hunter JSY AU 4.00 10.00
BSARKR Kyle Rudolph JSY AU 4.00 10.00
BSARLH L.Hankerson JSY AU 4.00 10.00
BSARMD Marcell Dareus JSY AU 4.00 10.00
BSARML Mikel Leshoure JSY AU 4.00 10.00
BSARNF Nick Fairley JSY AU 4.00 10.00
BSARRC Randall Cobb JSY AU 6.00 15.00
BSARRM Ryan Mallett JSY AU 4.00 10.00
BSARRW Ryan Williams JSY AU 4.00 10.00
BSARSJ Steve Johnson JSY AU 12.00 30.00

BSARSR Stevan Ridley JSY AU 4.00 10.00
BSARSRI Sidney Rice JSY AU 6.00 15.00
BSARSV Shane Vereen JSY AU 5.00 12.00
BSARTJ Taiwan Jones JSY AU 4.00 10.00
BSARTS Torrey Smith JSY AU 4.00 10.00
BSARTY Titus Young JSY AU 4.00 10.00
BSARVB Vincent Brown JSY AU 4.00 10.00
BSARVM Von Miller JSY AU 10.00 25.00
BSARZM Zach Miller JSY AU 6.00 15.00

2011 Bowman Sterling Black Refractors

*1-50 ROOKIES/50: 1.2X TO 3X BASIC CARDS
*VETERAN AU/50: .6X TO 1.5X BASIC AU
*ROOKIE AU/50: .8X TO 2X BASIC AU
STATED PRINT RUN 50 SER.#'d SETS
BSAAF Arian Foster AU 15.00 40.00
BSARH Roy Helu AU 5.00 12.00
BSATP Terrelle Pryor AU 8.00 20.00

2011 Bowman Sterling Blue Refractors

*1-50 ROOKIES/99: 1X TO 2.5X BASIC CARDS
*VETERAN AU/99: .5X TO 1.2X BASIC AU
*ROOKIE AU/99: .6X TO 1.5X BASIC AU
*VETERAN JSY/99: .5X TO 1.2X BASIC JSY
*ROOKIE JSY/99: .6X TO 1.5X BASIC JSY
*VET JSY AU/50: .5X TO 1.2X BASIC JSY AU
*ROOK.JSY AU/99: .5X TO 1.2X BASE JSY AU
STATED PRINT RUN 99 SER.#'d SETS
EXCH EXPIRATION: 12/31/2014
BSAAF Arian Foster AU 12.00 30.00
BSARM Ryan Mallett AU 4.00 10.00
BSARAD Andy Dalton JSY AU 10.00 25.00
BSARCP Christian Ponder JSY AU 5.00 12.00
BSARJJ Julio Jones JSY AU 30.00 60.00

2011 Bowman Sterling Gold Refractors

*1-50 ROOKIES/25: 1.5X TO 4X BASIC CARDS
*VETERAN JSY/25: .8X TO 2X BASIC JSY
*ROOKIE JSY/25: 1X TO 2.5X BASIC JSY
*VETERAN AU/25: .8X TO 2X BASIC AU
*ROOKIE AU/25: 1X TO 2.5X BASIC AU
*VET JSY AU/25: .6X TO 1.5X BASIC JSY AU
*ROOK.JSY AU/25: 1X TO 2.5X BASE JSY AU
STATED PRINT RUN 25 SER.#'d SETS
BSAAD Andy Dalton AU 40.00 80.00
BSAAF Arian Foster AU 20.00 50.00
BSAAJG A.J. Green AU 50.00 100.00
BSACN Cam Newton AU 75.00 150.00
BSACP Christian Ponder AU 6.00 15.00
BSAJL Jake Locker AU 6.00 15.00
BSAMI Mark Ingram AU 10.00 25.00
BSAPM Peyton Manning AU 75.00 150.00
BSARH Roy Helu AU 6.00 15.00
BSARM Ryan Mallett AU
BSATP Terrelle Pryor AU 10.00 25.00
BSARAD Andy Dalton JSY AU 50.00 125.00
BSARCN Cam Newton JSY AU 125.00 250.00
BSARJJ Julio Jones JSY AU
BSARJL Jake Locker JSY AU 10.00 25.00
BSARMI Mark Ingram JSY AU 15.00 40.00

2011 Bowman Sterling Pulsar Refractors

*1-50 ROOK/15: 2.5X TO 6X BASIC CARDS
*VETERAN JSY/15: 1.2X TO 3X BASIC JSY
*ROOKIE JSY/15: 1.5X TO 4X BASIC JSY
*VET AU/15: .5X TO 1.2X GOLD REF/25
*ROOK.AU/15: .5X TO 1.2X GOLD REF/25
*VET JSY AU/15: .5X TO 1.2X GOLD REF/25
*ROOK.JSY AU/15: .5X TO 1.2X GLD REF/25
STATED PRINT RUN 15 SER.#'d SETS
BSAAD Andy Dalton AU 40.00 100.00
BSAAJG A.J. Green AU 90.00 150.00
BSAAS Aldon Smith AU 40.00 100.00
BSACN Cam Newton AU 150.00 300.00
BSAJL Jake Locker AU 8.00 20.00
BSAMI Mark Ingram AU 12.00 30.00
BSARM Ryan Mallett AU
BSARAD Andy Dalton JSY AU 60.00 150.00
BSARAJG A.J. Green JSY AU 100.00 175.00
BSARCN Cam Newton JSY AU 200.00 400.00
BSARDM D.Murray JSY AU 25.00 60.00
BSARJJ Julio Jones JSY AU
BSARJL Jake Locker JSY AU 12.00 30.00

2011 Bowman Sterling Refractors

*1-50 ROOKIES/299: .6X TO 1.5X BASIC CARDS
*VETERAN JSY/299: .4X TO 1X BASIC JSY
*ROOKIE JSY/299: .4X TO 1X BASIC JSY
STATED PRINT RUN 299 SER.#'d SETS

2011 Bowman Sterling Dual Autographs

STATED PRINT RUN 25 SER.#'d SETS
BSDABS J.Baldwin/T.Smith 6.00 15.00
BSDACG R.Cobb/A.Green 10.00 25.00
BSDADG A.Dalton/A.Green 30.00 60.00
BSDAKH C.Kaepernick/K.Hunter 30.00 80.00
BSDALG J.Locker/B.Gabbert 8.00 20.00
BSDALY M.Leshoure/T.Young 12.00 30.00
BSDAMD V.Miller/M.Dareus
BSDANI C.Newton/M.Ingram 40.00 80.00
BSDAPR C.Ponder/K.Rudolph 20.00 50.00
BSDAVR S.Vereen/S.Ridley 10.00 25.00

2011 Bowman Sterling Dual Autographed Relics Pulsar Refractors

STATED PRINT RUN 5-60
BSPDARBR B.Powell/S.Ridley/60 12.00 30.00
BSPDARCG R.Cobb/A.Green/35 8.00 20.00
BSPDARCY R.Cobb/T.Young/35 8.00 20.00
BSPDARHC J.Harper/D.Carter/60 10.00 25.00
BSPDARHJ Hankrsn/Jernigan/35 12.00 30.00
BSPDARHP Hankerson/Paul/60 12.00 30.00
BSPDARLH Little/Hankerson/35 12.00 30.00
BSPDARMH D.Murray/K.Hunter 12.00 30.00
BSPDARSD T.Smith/T.Doss/60 6.00 15.00
BSPDARTB Todman/V.Brown/60 10.00 25.00
BSPDARTG D.Thomas/Gates/60 12.00 30.00
BSPDARTJ J.Todman/T.Jones/60 10.00 25.00
BSPDARTP D.Thomas/Powell/60 12.00 30.00
BSPDARVP S.Vereen/B.Powell/60 8.00 20.00
BSPDARVR S.Vereen/S.Ridley/60 12.00 30.00
BSPDARWH R.Williams/Hunter/35 12.00 30.00
BSPDARYP T.Young/A.Pettis/35 10.00 25.00

2011 Bowman Sterling Dual Jersey Box Topper

ONE DUAL JSY PER HOBBY BOX
*BLACK REF/25: .8X TO 2X BASIC DUAL
*BLUE REF/50: .6X TO 1.5X BASIC DUAL
*PULSAR REF/15: 1X TO 2.5X BASIC DUAL
*REFRACT/75: .5X TO 1.2X BASIC DUAL
BSDRBM T.Brady/R.Mallett 8.00 20.00
BSDRBS J.Baldwin/T.Smith 2.00 5.00
BSDRCB R.Cobb/A.Green 3.00 8.00
BSDRDM A.Dalton/R.Mallett 4.00 10.00
BSDRFB Fitzgerald/J.Baldwin 2.50 6.00
BSDRGD A.Green/A.Dalton 10.00 25.00
BSDRGJ A.Green/J.Jones 8.00 20.00
BSDRGP Gabbert/C.Ponder 2.00 5.00
BSDRIJ M.Ingram/J.Jones 6.00 15.00
BSDRIW M.Ingram/R.Williams 3.00 8.00
BSDRJD J.Jones/M.Dareus 6.00 15.00
BSDRKH Kaepernick/Hunter 3.00 8.00
BSDRLH J.Locker/J.Harper 6.00 15.00
BSDRLY Leshoure/T.Young 5.00 12.00
BSDRMH S.Moss/Hankerson 2.50 6.00
BSDRMJ McFadden/T.Jones 4.00 10.00
BSDRMR R.Mallett/S.Ridley 2.00 5.00
BSDRNC J.Nelson/R.Cobb 3.00 8.00
BSDRNL C.Newton/J.Locker 10.00 25.00
BSDRPM Peterson/D.Murray 4.00 10.00
BSDRRP Rudolph/C.Ponder 2.00 5.00
BSDRTB J.Todman/V.Brown 2.00 5.00
BSDRTR M.Turner/J.Rodgers 2.00 5.00
BSDRVR S.Vereen/S.Ridley 2.50 6.00
BSDRYP T.Young/A.Pettis 2.00 5.00

2011 Bowman Sterling Relics Jumbo Black Refractors

STATED PRINT RUN 50 SER.#'d SETS
BSRJRAD Andy Dalton 6.00 15.00
BSRJRAG Alex Green 3.00 8.00
BSRJRAJG A.J. Green 8.00 20.00
BSRJRAP Austin Pettis 3.00 8.00
BSRJRBG Blaine Gabbert 3.00 8.00
BSRJRBP Bilal Powell 4.00 10.00
BSRJRCK Colin Kaepernick 5.00 12.00
BSRJRCN Cam Newton 15.00 40.00
BSRJRCP Christian Ponder 3.00 8.00
BSRJRCS Cecil Shorts 3.00 8.00
BSRJRDC Delone Carter 3.00 8.00
BSRJRDL Dion Lewis 4.00 10.00
BSRJRDM DeMarco Murray 6.00 15.00
BSRJRDT Daniel Thomas 3.00 8.00
BSRJREG Edmond Gates 3.00 8.00
BSRJRGL Greg Little 4.00 10.00
BSRJRGS Greg Salas 3.00 8.00
BSRJRJB Jon Baldwin 3.00 8.00
BSRJRJH Jamie Harper 3.00 8.00
BSRJRJJ Julio Jones 10.00 25.00
BSRJRJJE Jerrel Jernigan 3.00 8.00
BSRJRJL Jake Locker 3.00 8.00
BSRJRJT Jordan Todman 3.00 8.00
BSRJRKH Kendall Hunter 3.00 8.00
BSRJRKR Kyle Rudolph 3.00 8.00
BSRJRLH Leonard Hankerson 3.00 8.00
BSRJRMD Marcell Dareus 3.00 8.00
BSRJRMI Mark Ingram 5.00 12.00
BSRJRML Mikel Leshoure 3.00 8.00
BSRJRPA Prince Amukamara 3.00 8.00
BSRJRRC Randall Cobb 5.00 12.00
BSRJRRM Ryan Mallett 3.00 8.00
BSRJRRW Ryan Williams 3.00 8.00
BSRJRSR Stevan Ridley 3.00 8.00
BSRJRSV Shane Vereen 4.00 10.00
BSRJRTJ Taiwan Jones 3.00 8.00
BSRJRTS Torrey Smith 3.00 8.00
BSRJRTY Titus Young 3.00 8.00
BSRJRVB Vincent Brown 3.00 8.00
BSRJRVM Von Miller 5.00 12.00

2012 Bowman Sterling

COMP.ROOKIE SET (100) 75.00 150.00
EXCH EXPIRATION: 12/31/2015
1 Robert Griffin III RC .75 2.00
2 Chandler Jones RC .60 1.50
3 Riley Reiff RC .60 1.50
4 Stephen Hill RC .60 1.50
5 Russell Wilson RC 6.00 15.00
6 Michael Brockers RC .60 1.50
7 Greg Childs RC .60 1.50
8 Ryan Broyles RC .60 1.50
9 Orson Charles RC .60 1.50
10 Ryan Tannehill RC 1.00 2.50
11 Ronnie Hillman RC .60 1.50
12 Bobby Rainey RC .60 1.50
13 Vick Ballard RC .75 2.00
14 Matt Kalil RC .60 1.50
15 Mohamed Sanu RC 1.00 2.50
16 Dont'a Hightower RC 1.00 2.50
17 David DeCastro RC .60 1.50
18 Kevin Zeitler RC .60 1.50
19 Kirk Cousins RC 2.50 6.00
20 Michael Floyd RC .60 1.50
21 Chris Givens RC .60 1.50
22 Peter Konz RC .60 1.50
23 Tavon Wilson RC .75 2.00
24 Alshon Jeffery RC 1.25 3.00
25 Rueben Randle RC .60 1.50
26 Shea McClellin RC .75 2.00
27 Coby Fleener RC .60 1.50
28 Derek Wolfe RC .75 2.00
29 Chandler Harnish RC .60 1.50
30 Brandon Weeden RC .60 1.50
31 Bobby Wagner RC 1.00 2.50
32 Kendall Reyes RC .60 1.50
33 Brandon Boykin RC .75 2.00
34 Dontari Poe RC .60 1.50
35 Nick Toon RC .60 1.50
36 Isaiah Pead RC .60 1.50
37 Jeff Fuller RC .60 1.50
38 Travis Benjamin RC .60 1.50
39 Jerel Worthy RC .60 1.50
40 Morris Claiborne RC .60 1.50
41 Juron Criner RC .60 1.50
42 Janoris Jenkins RC .75 2.00
43 T.J. Graham RC .60 1.50
44 Brandon Thompson RC .75 2.00
45 Bernard Pierce RC .60 1.50
46 Dre Kirkpatrick RC .60 1.50
47 Nick Perry RC .75 2.00
48 Chris Rainey RC .60 1.50
49 Kellen Moore RC .75 2.00
50 Trent Richardson RC .60 1.50
51 Terrance Ganaway RC .75 2.00
52 Quinton Coples RC .60 1.50
53 Dan Herron RC .60 1.50
54 Lamar Miller RC 1.00 2.50
55 Rishard Matthews RC .60 1.50
56 Michael Egnew RC .60 1.50
57 Nick Foles RC 1.50 4.00
58 Jonathan Martin RC .60 1.50
59 Tommy Streeter RC .60 1.50
60 Kendall Wright RC .60 1.50
61 Mark Barron RC .60 1.50
62 Vinny Curry RC .75 2.00
63 Cordy Glenn RC .75 2.00
64 Dwight Bentley RC .75 2.00
65 Ryan Lindley RC .60 1.50
66 Jeff Demps RC .75 2.00
67 Cyrus Gray RC .60 1.50
68 Jarius Wright RC .60 1.50
69 Zach Brown RC .60 1.50
70 David Wilson RC .60 1.50
71 A.J. Jenkins RC .60 1.50
72 Mychal Kendricks RC 1.00 2.50
73 Brian Quick RC .60 1.50
74 Luke Kuechly RC 1.50 4.00
75 Courtney Upshaw RC .75 2.00
76 LaMichael James RC .60 1.50
77 Harrison Smith RC .60 1.50
78 Brock Osweiler RC .60 1.50
79 Whitney Mercilus RC .60 1.50
80 Justin Blackmon RC .60 1.50
81 DeVier Posey RC .60 1.50
82 Melvin Ingram RC .60 1.50
83 T.Y. Hilton RC 1.25 3.00
84 Marvin McNutt RC .60 1.50
85 Robert Turbin RC .60 1.50
86 Joe Adams RC .60 1.50
87 Fletcher Cox RC 1.00 2.50
88 Lavonte David RC 1.00 2.50
89 Bruce Irvin RC .75 2.00
90 Doug Martin RC 1.00 2.50
91 Keshawn Martin RC .75 2.00
92 Andre Branch RC .60 1.50
93 Dwayne Allen RC .60 1.50
94 Josh Gordon RC 1.50 4.00
95 Devon Still RC .75 2.00
96 Stephon Gilmore RC .75 2.00
97 Case Keenum RC 1.25 3.00
98 Chris Polk RC .60 1.50
99 Marvin Jones RC .60 1.50
100 Andrew Luck RC 25.00 50.00
AU1 Robert Griffin III AU 3.00 8.00
AU5 Russell Wilson AU 60.00 125.00
AU8 Ryan Broyles AU 2.50 6.00
AU10 Ryan Tannehill AU 4.00 10.00
AU11 Ronnie Hillman AU 2.50 6.00
AU13 Vick Ballard AU 6.00 15.00
AU14 Matt Kalil AU 2.50 6.00
AU15 Mohamed Sanu AU 4.00 10.00
AU17 David DeCastro AU 2.50 6.00
AU19 Kirk Cousins AU 12.00 30.00
AU20 Michael Floyd AU 2.50 6.00
AU24 Alshon Jeffery AU 8.00 20.00
AU25 Rueben Randle AU 2.50 6.00
AU27 Coby Fleener AU 2.50 6.00
AU29 Chandler Harnish AU 2.50 6.00
AU30 Brandon Weeden AU 2.50 6.00
AU34 Dontari Poe AU 2.50 6.00
AU35 Nick Toon AU 2.50 6.00
AU36 Isaiah Pead AU 2.50 6.00
AU38 Travis Benjamin AU 2.50 6.00
AU41 Juron Criner AU 2.50 6.00
AU43 T.J. Graham AU 2.50 6.00
AU49 Kellen Moore AU 3.00 8.00
AU50 Trent Richardson AU 2.50 6.00
AU54 Lamar Miller AU 4.00 10.00
AU56 Michael Egnew AU 2.50 6.00
AU57 Nick Foles AU 15.00 40.00
AU60 Kendall Wright AU 2.50 6.00
AU67 Cyrus Gray AU 2.50 6.00
AU68 Jarius Wright AU 2.50 6.00
AU70 David Wilson AU 2.50 6.00
AU71 A.J. Jenkins AU 2.50 6.00
AU73 Brian Quick AU 2.50 6.00
AU74 Luke Kuechly AU 15.00 40.00
AU76 LaMichael James AU 2.50 6.00
AU78 Brock Osweiler AU 2.50 6.00
AU80 Justin Blackmon AU 2.50 6.00
AU82 Melvin Ingram AU 2.50 6.00
AU84 Marvin McNutt AU 2.50 6.00
AU90 Doug Martin AU 4.00 10.00
AU94 Josh Gordon AU 6.00 15.00
AU95 Devon Still AU 3.00 8.00
AU97 Case Keenum AU 5.00 12.00
AU100 Andrew Luck AU 125.00 200.00
AU103 Jorvorskie Lane AU 3.00 8.00
AU104 Harrison Smith AU 5.00 12.00
AU105 Bobby Wagner AU 6.00 15.00
AU106 Dan Herron AU 2.50 6.00
AU107 Orson Charles AU 2.50 6.00
AU108 Stephon Gilmore AU 3.00 8.00
AU111 Rod Streater AU 4.00 10.00
AU113 Fletcher Cox AU 4.00 10.00
AU115 Taylor Thompson AU 3.00 8.00
AU117 Alfred Morris AU 2.50 6.00
AU120 Akeem Ayers AU 4.00 10.00
AU121 Brandon Pettigrew AU 4.00 10.00
AU122 C.J. Spiller AU 6.00 15.00
AU123 Jerod Mayo AU 4.00 10.00
AU124 Antrel Rolle AU 4.00 10.00
AU125 Kenny Britt AU 4.00 10.00
AU126 Jimmy Graham AU 6.00 15.00
AU127 Eddie Royal AU 4.00 10.00
AU128 Mikel Leshoure AU 4.00 10.00
BSARBQ Brian Quick JSY AU 3.00 8.00
BSARCF Coby Fleener JSY AU 3.00 8.00
BSARCGR Cyrus Gray JSY AU 3.00 8.00
BSARCR Chris Rainey JSY AU EXCH 3.00 8.00
BSARDA Dwayne Allen JSY AU 3.00 8.00
BSARDH D.Hightower JSY AU EXCH 5.00 12.00
BSARDP DeVier Posey JSY AU 3.00 8.00
BSARGC Greg Childs JSY AU 3.00 8.00
BSARJA Joe Adams JSY AU 3.00 8.00
BSARJR Juron Criner JSY AU 3.00 8.00
BSARJW Jarius Wright JSY AU 3.00 8.00
BSARLK Luke Kuechly JSY AU 15.00 30.00
BSARME Michael Egnew JSY AU 3.00 8.00
BSARNT Nick Toon JSY AU 3.00 8.00
BSARRB Ryan Broyles JSY AU 6.00 15.00
BSARRH Ronnie Hillman JSY AU 3.00 8.00
BSARRTU R.Turbin JSY AU EXCH 6.00 15.00
BSARTJG T.J. Graham JSY AU 3.00 8.00
BSARTYH T.Y. Hilton JSY AU 6.00 15.00
BSJRRAJ Alshon Jeffery JSY 3.00 8.00
BSJRRAJJ A.J. Jenkins JSY 1.50 4.00
BSJRRAL Andrew Luck JSY 12.00 30.00
BSJRRBO Brock Osweiler JSY 1.50 4.00
BSJRRBP Bernard Pierce JSY 1.50 4.00
BSJRRBQ Brian Quick JSY 1.50 4.00
BSJRRBW Brandon Weeden JSY 1.50 4.00
BSJRRCF Coby Fleener JSY 1.50 4.00
BSJRRCG Chris Givens JSY 1.50 4.00
BSJRRCGR Cyrus Gray JSY 1.50 4.00
BSJRRCR Chris Rainey JSY 1.50 4.00
BSJRRDA Dwayne Allen JSY 1.50 4.00
BSJRRDH Dont'a Hightower JSY 2.50 6.00
BSJRRDK Dre Kirkpatrick JSY 1.50 4.00
BSJRRDM Doug Martin JSY 2.50 6.00
BSJRRDP DeVier Posey JSY 1.50 4.00
BSJRRDW David Wilson JSY 1.50 4.00
BSJRRGC Greg Childs JSY 1.50 4.00
BSJRRIP Isaiah Pead JSY 1.50 4.00
BSJRRJA Joe Adams JSY 1.50 4.00
BSJRRJB Justin Blackmon JSY 1.50 4.00
BSJRRJR Juron Criner JSY 1.50 4.00
BSJRRJW Jarius Wright JSY 1.50 4.00
BSJRRKW Kendall Wright JSY 1.50 4.00
BSJRRLJ LaMichael James JSY 1.50 4.00
BSJRRLM Lamar Miller JSY 2.50 6.00
BSJRRME Michael Egnew JSY 1.50 4.00
BSJRRMF Michael Floyd JSY 1.50 4.00
BSJRRMS Mohamed Sanu JSY 2.50 6.00
BSJRRNF Nick Foles JSY 4.00 10.00
BSJRRNT Nick Toon JSY 1.50 4.00
BSJRRRB Ryan Broyles JSY 1.50 4.00
BSJRRRG Robert Griffin III JSY 2.00 5.00
BSJRRRH Ronnie Hillman JSY 1.50 4.00
BSJRRRR Rueben Randle JSY 1.50 4.00
BSJRRRT Ryan Tannehill JSY 2.50 6.00
BSJRRRTU Robert Turbin JSY 1.50 4.00
BSJRRRW Russell Wilson JSY 8.00 20.00
BSJRRSH Stephen Hill JSY 1.50 4.00
BSJRRTJG T.J. Graham JSY 1.50 4.00
BSJRRTR Trent Richardson JSY 1.50 4.00
BSJRRTYH T.Y. Hilton JSY 3.00 8.00
BSJVRAD Andy Dalton JSY/99 4.00 10.00
BSJVRAG A.J. Green JSY/99 5.00 12.00
BSJVRAH Aaron Hernandez JSY/99 4.00 10.00
BSJVRCB Champ Bailey JSY/99 4.00 10.00
BSJVRCJ Chris Johnson JSY/99 3.00 8.00
BSJVRCN Cam Newton JSY/99 5.00 12.00
BSJVRDM DeMarco Murray JSY/99 4.00 10.00
BSJVRLM LeSean McCoy JSY/99 5.00 12.00
BSJVRMC Marques Colston JSY/99 3.00 8.00
BSJVRMI Mark Ingram JSY/99 4.00 10.00
BSJVRMV Michael Vick JSY/99 4.00 10.00
BSJVRMW Mike Wallace JSY/99 3.00 8.00
BSJVRPW Patrick Willis JSY/99 4.00 10.00
BSJVRSG Shonn Greene JSY/99 3.00 8.00
BSJVRSH Santonio Holmes JSY/99 3.00 8.00

2012 Bowman Sterling Black Refractors

*1-100 ROOKIES/75: 1.2X TO 3X BASIC RC
*ROOKIE JSY/75: .6X TO 1.5X BASIC JSY
*VET JSY/50: .5X TO 1.2X BASIC JSY/99
100 Andrew Luck 50.00 120.00
AU5 Russell Wilson AU 100.00 200.00
AU8 Ryan Broyles AU 8.00 20.00
AU10 Ryan Tannehill AU 6.00 15.00
AU11 Ronnie Hillman AU 4.00 10.00
AU13 Vick Ballard AU 10.00 25.00
AU14 Matt Kalil AU 4.00 10.00
AU15 Mohamed Sanu AU 6.00 15.00
AU17 David DeCastro AU 4.00 10.00
AU19 Kirk Cousins AU 20.00 50.00
AU20 Michael Floyd AU 4.00 10.00
AU24 Alshon Jeffery AU 15.00 40.00
AU25 Rueben Randle AU 4.00 10.00
AU27 Coby Fleener AU 4.00 10.00
AU29 Chandler Harnish AU 4.00 10.00
AU30 Brandon Weeden AU 4.00 10.00
AU34 Dontari Poe AU 4.00 10.00
AU35 Nick Toon AU 4.00 10.00
AU36 Isaiah Pead AU 4.00 10.00
AU38 Travis Benjamin AU 4.00 10.00
AU41 Juron Criner AU 4.00 10.00
AU43 T.J. Graham AU 4.00 10.00
AU49 Kellen Moore AU 5.00 12.00
AU54 Lamar Miller AU 6.00 15.00
AU56 Michael Egnew AU 4.00 10.00
AU57 Nick Foles AU 40.00 100.00
AU60 Kendall Wright AU 4.00 10.00
AU67 Cyrus Gray AU 4.00 10.00
AU68 Jarius Wright AU 4.00 10.00
AU70 David Wilson AU 4.00 10.00
AU71 A.J. Jenkins AU 4.00 10.00
AU73 Brian Quick AU 4.00 10.00
AU74 Luke Kuechly AU 20.00 50.00
AU76 LaMichael James AU 4.00 10.00
AU78 Brock Osweiler AU 4.00 10.00
AU80 Justin Blackmon AU 4.00 10.00
AU82 Melvin Ingram AU 4.00 10.00
AU84 Marvin McNutt AU 4.00 10.00
AU90 Doug Martin AU 6.00 15.00
AU94 Josh Gordon AU 10.00 25.00
AU95 Devon Still AU 5.00 12.00
AU97 Case Keenum AU 8.00 20.00
AU100 Andrew Luck AU 150.00 300.00

2012 Bowman Sterling Blue Refractors

*1-100 ROOKIES/99: 1X TO 2.5X BASIC RC
*AU1-AU128 ROOK.AU/99: .5X TO 1.2X BASIC AU
*ROOKIE JSY/99: .6X TO 1.5X BASIC JSY
*VET JSY/75: .5X TO 1.2X BASIC JSY/99
100 Andrew Luck 40.00 100.00
BSARAJ Alshon Jeffery JSY AU 15.00 30.00
BSARAJJ A.J. Jenkins JSY AU 4.00 10.00
BSARAL Andrew Luck JSY AU 100.00 200.00
BSARBO Brock Osweiler JSY AU 4.00 10.00
BSARBQ Brian Quick JSY AU 4.00 10.00
BSARBW B.Weeden JSY AU 4.00 10.00
BSARCF Coby Fleener JSY AU 4.00 10.00
BSARCGR Cyrus Gray JSY AU 4.00 10.00
BSARDA Dwayne Allen JSY AU EXCH 4.00 10.00
BSARDH D.Hightower JSY AU 6.00 15.00
BSARDM Doug Martin JSY AU 6.00 15.00
BSARDP DeVier Posey JSY AU 4.00 10.00
BSARDW David Wilson JSY AU 4.00 10.00
BSARGC Greg Childs JSY AU 4.00 10.00
BSARIP Isaiah Pead JSY AU 4.00 10.00
BSARJA Joe Adams JSY AU EXCH 4.00 10.00
BSARJB J.Blackmon JSY AU 4.00 10.00
BSARJG Josh Gordon JSY AU 10.00 25.00
BSARJR Juron Criner JSY AU 4.00 10.00
BSARJW Jarius Wright JSY AU 4.00 10.00
BSARKW Kendall Wright JSY AU 4.00 10.00
BSARLJ L.James JSY AU 4.00 10.00
BSARLK Luke Kuechly JSY AU 25.00 50.00
BSARLM Lamar Miller JSY AU 6.00 15.00
BSARME Michael Egnew JSY AU 4.00 10.00
BSARMF Michael Floyd JSY AU 4.00 10.00
BSARMS Mohamed Sanu JSY AU 6.00 15.00
BSARNF Nick Foles JSY AU 20.00 50.00
BSARNT Nick Toon JSY AU 4.00 10.00
BSARRB Ryan Broyles JSY AU 8.00 20.00
BSARRH Ronnie Hillman JSY AU 4.00 10.00
BSARRR Rueben Randle JSY AU 4.00 10.00
BSARRT Ryan Tannehill JSY AU 6.00 15.00
BSARRTU Robert Turbin JSY AU EXCH 4.00 10.00
BSARRW R.Wilson JSY AU 60.00 125.00
BSARSH Stephen Hill JSY AU 4.00 10.00
BSARTJG T.J. Graham JSY AU 4.00 10.00
BSARTYH T.Y. Hilton JSY AU 8.00 20.00

2012 Bowman Sterling Gold Refractors

*1-100 ROOKIES/50: 1.5X TO 4X BASIC RC
*ROOK.AU/25: .6X TO 1.5X BLACK REF AU/50
*ROOK.JSY AU/66: .5X TO 1.2X BLU REF/99
*ROOK.PATCH/65: 1X TO 2.5X BASIC JSY
*VET PATCH/25: .6X TO 1.5X BASIC JSY/99
5 Russell Wilson 30.00 80.00
100 Andrew Luck 100.00 200.00
AU5 Russell Wilson AU 150.00 250.00
AU10 Ryan Tannehill AU 10.00 25.00
AU100 Andrew Luck AU 250.00 500.00
BSARAL Andrew Luck JSY AU 200.00 350.00
BSARRW R.Wilson JSY AU 125.00 200.00

2012 Bowman Sterling Prism Refractors

*1-100 ROOKIES/25: 2.5X TO 6X BASIC RC
*ROOK.AU/15: .8X TO 2X BLACK REF AU/50
*ROOK.JSY AU/36: .6X TO 1.5X BLU REF/99
*ROOK.PATCH/47: 1X TO 2.5X BASIC JSY
*VET PATCH/15: .8X TO X2 BASIC JSY/99
5 Russell Wilson 50.00 100.00
100 Andrew Luck 125.00 250.00
AU5 Russell Wilson AU 175.00 300.00
AU10 Ryan Tannehill AU 12.00 30.00
AU19 Kirk Cousins AU 25.00 60.00
AU97 Case Keenum AU 15.00 40.00
AU100 Andrew Luck AU 350.00 600.00
BSARAL Andrew Luck JSY AU 300.00 450.00
BSARBO Brock Osweiler JSY AU 6.00 15.00
BSARRW Russell Wilson JSY AU 150.00 250.00

2012 Bowman Sterling Dual Autographed Relics Prism Refractors

EXCH EXPIRATION: 12/31/2015
AT N.Toon/J.Adams/110 8.00 20.00
BF Blackmon/M.Floyd/15 8.00 20.00
BP Ballard/D.Posey EXCH 12.00 30.00
BS Benjamin/M.Sanu/110 8.00 20.00
CH J.Criner/T.Hilton
FA D.Allen/Fleener/110 5.00 12.00
FW N.Foles/R.Wilson/20 75.00 150.00
GR C.Gray/C.Rainey EXCH 12.00 30.00
GW Graham/J.Wright/110 5.00 12.00
HK D.Hightower/L.Kuechly 15.00 40.00
HO Hillman/Osweiler/110 5.00 12.00
HR S.Hill/R.Randle/20 8.00 20.00
HS M.Sanu/T.Hilton/110 10.00 25.00
HT Turbin/R.Hillman EXCH 15.00 30.00
JB Broyles/Jeffery/110 12.00 30.00
JJ L.James/A.Jenkins/20 8.00 20.00
JR Randle/A.Jeffery/20 15.00 40.00
KP Kuechly/D.Poe EXCH 25.00 50.00
LF A.Luck/M.Floyd/15 150.00 300.00
MW D.Martin/D.Wilson/20 12.00 30.00
PG D.Poe/C.Gray/110 5.00 12.00
QJ A.Jeffery/B.Quick/20 15.00 40.00
QP B.Quick/I.Pead/20 8.00 20.00
RB Blckmn/Rchrdsn/15 8.00 20.00
RW Rchrdsn/Wden/15 8.00 20.00
SK Sanu/Kirkpatrick EXCH 12.00 30.00
TE Tannehill/M.Egnew/15 12.00 30.00
TH S.Hill/R.Tannehill/15 12.00 30.00
WF K.Wright/M.Floyd/15 8.00 20.00
WG J.Gordon/K.Wright/120 20.00 50.00
WO Weeden/Osweiler/15 8.00 20.00
WR R.Randle/D.Wilson 8.00 20.00
WT Turbin/R.Wilson EXCH 75.00 135.00

2012 Bowman Sterling Dual Autographs

STATED PRINT RUN 25 SER.#'d SETS
BSDACT M.Colston/N.Toon 12.00 30.00
BSDACW V.Cruz/D.Wilson 12.00 30.00
BSDAGC P.Garcon/R.Griffin III 12.00 30.00
BSDAJJ A.Jenkins/L.James 10.00 25.00
BSDAJM D.Martin/V.Jackson 15.00 40.00
BSDAJW K.Wright/C.Johnson 15.00 40.00
BSDALW K.Wright/A.Luck 100.00 200.00
BSDAMC J.Criner/D.Moore 10.00 25.00
BSDAPT R.Turbin/I.Pead 10.00 25.00
BSDARB L.Robinson/Blackmon 10.00 25.00

2012 Bowman Sterling Relics Jumbo

*BLACK REF/45: .6X TO 1.5X BASIC JSY/99
*BLUE REF/60: .5X TO 1.2X BASIC JSY/99
*GOLD REF/25: .8X TO 2X BASIC JSY/99
BSJRPAJ Alshon Jeffery 5.00 12.00
BSJRPAL Andrew Luck 15.00 40.00
BSJRPBO Brock Osweiler 2.50 6.00
BSJRPBP Bernard Pierce 2.50 6.00
BSJRPBQ Brian Quick 2.50 6.00
BSJRPBW Brandon Weeden 2.50 6.00
BSJRPCF Coby Fleener 2.50 6.00
BSJRPDA Dwayne Allen 2.50 6.00
BSJRPDM Doug Martin 4.00 10.00
BSJRPDP DeVier Posey 2.50 6.00
BSJRPDW David Wilson 2.50 6.00
BSJRPIP Isaiah Pead 2.50 6.00
BSJRPJA Joe Adams 4.00 10.00
BSJRPJB Justin Blackmon 2.50 6.00
BSJRPJC Juron Criner 2.50 6.00
BSJRPJW Jarius Wright 2.50 6.00
BSJRPKW Kendall Wright 2.50 6.00
BSJRPLJ LaMichael James 2.50 6.00
BSJRPLM Lamar Miller 4.00 10.00
BSJRPME Michael Egnew 2.50 6.00
BSJRPMF Michael Floyd 2.50 6.00
BSJRPMS Mohamed Sanu 4.00 10.00
BSJRPNF Nick Foles 6.00 15.00
BSJRPNT Nick Toon 2.50 6.00
BSJRPRB Ryan Broyles 2.50 6.00
BSJRPRG Robert Griffin III 3.00 8.00
BSJRPRH Ronnie Hillman 2.50 6.00
BSJRPRR Rueben Randle 2.50 6.00
BSJRPRT Ryan Tannehill 4.00 10.00
BSJRPRW Russell Wilson 12.00 30.00
BSJRPSH Stephen Hill 2.50 6.00
BSJRPTR Trent Richardson 2.50 6.00
BSJRPAJJ A.J. Jenkins 2.50 6.00
BSJRPRTU Robert Turbin 2.50 6.00
BSJRPTJG T.J. Graham 2.50 6.00

2013 Bowman Sterling

1 Peyton Manning 1.50 4.00
2 Cordarrelle Patterson RC .50 1.25
3 Denard Robinson RC .50 1.25
4 LeSean McCoy .40 1.00
5 DeAndre Hopkins RC 1.25 3.00
6 Lonnie Pryor RC .50 1.25
7 Eric Fisher RC .50 1.25
8 Tyler Wilson RC .50 1.25
9 Dez Bryant .40 1.00
10 Tom Brady 1.00 2.50
11 Josh Boyce RC .50 1.25
12 Eli Manning .30 .75
13 Luke Joeckel RC .50 1.25
14 Tyler Eifert RC .50 1.25
15 Andre Ellington RC .50 1.25
16 Le'Veon Bell RC 1.50 4.00
17 Stepfan Taylor RC .50 1.25
18 Chris Harper RC .50 1.25
19 Ezekiel Ansah RC .50 1.25
20 Aaron Rodgers .60 1.50
21 Kenny Vaccaro RC .50 1.25
22 Desmond Trufant RC .50 1.25
24 Knile Davis RC .50 1.25
25 Geno Smith RC .50 1.25
26 Jamar Taylor RC .50 1.25
27 Jordan Reed RC .75 2.00
28 Theo Riddick RC .50 1.25
29 Tyler Bray RC .50 1.25
30 Drew Brees .40 1.00
31 Ryan Swope RC .50 1.25
32 J.J. Watt .30 .75
33 Ray Graham RC .50 1.25
34 Zach Ertz RC 1.00 2.50
35 D.J. Hayden RC .50 1.25
36 Stedman Bailey RC .50 1.25
37 Kenjon Barner RC .50 1.25
38 Damontre Moore RC .50 1.25
39 Keenan Allen RC 1.00 2.50
40 Joe Flacco .30 .75
41 Corey Fuller RC .50 1.25
42 Kenny Stills RC .50 1.25
43 John Jenkins RC .50 1.25
44 Zac Dysert RC .50 1.25
45 Dion Jordan RC .50 1.25
46 Robert Woods RC .75 2.00
47 Christine Michael RC .50 1.25
48 Tavarres King RC .50 1.25
49 Justin Hunter RC .50 1.25
50 Andrew Luck .60 1.50
51 Vance McDonald RC .60 1.50
52 Montee Ball RC .50 1.25
53 A.J. Green .40 1.00
54 Matt Barkley RC .50 1.25
55 Manti Te'o RC .60 1.50
56 Kerwynn Williams RC .50 1.25
57 Gavin Escobar RC .50 1.25
58 Aaron Mellette RC .50 1.25
59 Cam Newton .40 1.00
60 Adrian Peterson .40 1.00
61 Markus Wheaton RC .50 1.25
62 Alex Okafor RC .50 1.25
63 Xavier Rhodes RC .50 1.25
64 Eddie Lacy RC .50 1.25
65 Aaron Dobson RC .50 1.25
66 Chris Gragg RC .50 1.25
67 Ryan Nassib RC .50 1.25
68 Rodney Smith RC .50 1.25
69 Ace Sanders RC .60 1.50
70 Calvin Johnson .40 1.00
71 Cobi Hamilton RC .50 1.25
72 Jamaal Charles .30 .75
73 Marcus Lattimore RC .50 1.25
74 Chris Thompson RC .50 1.25
75 EJ Manuel RC .50 1.25
76 Jarvis Jones RC .50 1.25
77 Da'Rick Rogers RC .50 1.25
78 Marquise Goodwin RC .50 1.25
79 Blidi Wreh-Wilson RC .60 1.50
80 Russell Wilson .75 2.00
81 Brandon Marshall .30 .75
82 Miguel Maysonet RC .50 1.25
83 Jordan Poyer RC .50 1.25
84 Matt Ryan .30 .75
85 Mike Glennon RC .50 1.25
86 Giovani Bernard RC .50 1.25
87 Sheldon Richardson RC .50 1.25
88 Dan Buckner RC .50 1.25
89 Eric Reid RC .60 1.50
90 Colin Kaepernick .30 .75
91 Mike Gillislee RC .50 1.25
92 Tavon Austin RC .60 1.50
93 Quinton Patton RC .50 1.25
94 Dee Milliner RC .50 1.25
95 Johnathan Franklin RC .50 1.25
96 Terrance Williams RC .50 1.25
97 Landry Jones RC .50 1.25
98 Joseph Randle RC .50 1.25
99 Dion Sims RC .50 1.25
100 Robert Griffin III .25 .60

2013 Bowman Sterling Black Refractors

*VETS/75: 2.5X TO 6X BASIC CARDS
*ROOKIES/75: 1X TO 2.5X BASIC RC

2013 Bowman Sterling Blue Wave Refractors

*VETS/99: 2X TO 5X BASIC CARDS
*ROOKIES/99: .8X TO 2X BASIC RC

2013 Bowman Sterling Gold Refractors

*VETS/50: 3X TO 8X BASIC CARDS
*ROOKIES/50: 1.2X TO 3X BASIC RC

2013 Bowman Sterling Prism Refractors

*VETS/25: 4X TO 10X BASIC CARDS
*ROOKIES/25: 1.5X TO 4X BASIC RC

2013 Bowman Sterling Autographs

BSAAD Aaron Dobson 2.00 5.00
BSAAE Andre Ellington 2.00 5.00
BSAAO Alex Okafor 2.00 5.00
BSAAS Ace Sanders 2.00 5.00
BSABM Barkevious Mingo 2.00 5.00
BSACG Chris Gragg 2.00 5.00
BSACH Cobi Hamilton 2.00 5.00
BSACHA Chris Harper 2.00 5.00
BSACM Christine Michael 2.00 5.00
BSACP Cordarrelle Patterson 2.00 5.00
BSADH DeAndre Hopkins 5.00 12.00
BSADJ Dion Jordan 2.00 5.00
BSADM Dee Milliner 2.00 5.00
BSADR Denard Robinson 2.00 5.00
BSADRO Da'Rick Rogers 2.00 5.00
BSAEA Ezekiel Ansah 2.00 5.00
BSAEF Eric Fisher 2.00 5.00
BSAEJM EJ Manuel 5.00 12.00
BSAEL Eddie Lacy 2.00 5.00
BSAER Eric Reid 4.00 10.00
BSAGB Giovani Bernard 2.00 5.00
BSAGE Gavin Escobar 2.00 5.00
BSAGS Geno Smith 2.00 5.00
BSAJB Joique Bell 5.00 12.00
BSAJBO Josh Boyce 2.00 5.00
BSAJF Johnathan Franklin 2.00 5.00
BSAJH Justin Hunter 2.00 5.00
BSAJJ Jarvis Jones 2.00 5.00
BSAJJE John Jenkins 2.00 5.00
BSAJR Joseph Randle 2.00 5.00
BSAJRE Jordan Reed 3.00 8.00
BSAKA Keenan Allen 6.00 15.00
BSAKB Kenjon Barner 2.00 5.00
BSAKD Knile Davis 2.00 5.00
BSAKS Kenny Stills 2.00 5.00
BSALB Le'Veon Bell 12.00 30.00
BSALJ Landry Jones 2.00 5.00
BSALJO Luke Joeckel 2.00 5.00
BSAMB Matt Barkley 2.00 5.00
BSAMBA Montee Ball 2.00 5.00
BSAMG Mike Glennon 2.00 5.00
BSAMGI Mike Gillislee 2.00 5.00
BSAMGO Marquise Goodwin 2.00 5.00
BSAML Marcus Lattimore 2.00 5.00
BSAMT Manti Te'o 2.50 6.00
BSAMW Markus Wheaton 2.00 5.00
BSAQP Quinton Patton 2.00 5.00
BSARG Ray Graham 2.00 5.00
BSARN Ryan Nassib SP EXCH 6.00 15.00
BSARS Ryan Swope 2.00 5.00
BSARW Robert Woods 3.00 8.00
BSASB Stedman Bailey 2.00 5.00
BSAST Stepfan Taylor 2.00 5.00
BSATA Tavon Austin 2.50 6.00
BSATB Tyler Bray 2.00 5.00
BSATE Tyler Eifert 2.00 5.00
BSATK Tavarres King 2.00 5.00
BSAVM Vance McDonald 2.50 6.00
BSAXR Xavier Rhodes 2.00 5.00
BSAZD Zac Dysert 2.00 5.00
BSAZE Zach Ertz 4.00 10.00

2013 Bowman Sterling Autographs Black Refractors

*BLACK ROOK/50: .6X TO 1.5X BASE AU
EXCH EXPIRATION: 11/30/2016
BSAAL Andrew Luck 50.00 100.00
BSABGE BenJarvus Green-Ellis 6.00 15.00
BSABO Brian Orakpo 6.00 15.00
BSACJS C.J. Spiller 5.00 12.00
BSACS Cecil Shorts 5.00 12.00
BSAEL Eddie Lacy 3.00 8.00
BSAFG Frank Gore 8.00 20.00
BSAGO Greg Olsen 6.00 15.00
BSAGT Golden Tate 5.00 12.00
BSAHN Haloti Ngata 5.00 12.00
BSAJAJ Janoris Jenkins 5.00 12.00
BSAJG Jermaine Gresham 6.00 15.00
BSAJK Jeremy Kerley 5.00 12.00
BSAPM Peyton Manning 100.00 200.00
BSARC Randall Cobb
BSARG3 Robert Griffin III 5.00 12.00
BSASJ Steve Johnson 6.00 15.00
BSASR Stevan Ridley 5.00 12.00

2013 Bowman Sterling Autographs Blue Wave Refractors

*BLUE ROOK/99: .5X TO 1.2X BASE AU
BSABGE BenJarvus Green-Ellis 5.00 12.00
BSABO Brian Orakpo 5.00 12.00
BSACJS C.J. Spiller 4.00 10.00
BSACM Christine Michael 2.50 6.00
BSACS Cecil Shorts 4.00 10.00
BSAFG Frank Gore
BSAGO Greg Olsen 5.00 12.00
BSAGT Golden Tate 4.00 10.00
BSAHN Haloti Ngata 4.00 10.00
BSAJB Joique Bell EXCH 6.00 15.00
BSAJG Jermaine Gresham 5.00 12.00
BSAJK Jeremy Kerley 4.00 10.00
BSAJW Jarius Wright 4.00 10.00
BSAMC Michael Crabtree

2013 Bowman Sterling Autographs Gold Refractors

*GOLD/25: .6X TO 1.5X BLACK REF/50
BSAEL Eddie Lacy 5.00 12.00
BSAPM Peyton Manning 100.00 200.00
BSARG3 Robert Griffin III 8.00 20.00

2013 Bowman Sterling Autographs Prism Refractors

*PRISM/25: .8X TO 2X BLACK REF/50
BSAAL Andrew Luck 100.00 200.00
BSAPM Peyton Manning 200.00 350.00

2013 Bowman Sterling Dual Autographs

BSDAAB T.Austin/S.Bailey 8.00 20.00
BSDABD K.Davis/M.Ball 6.00 15.00
BSDABW M.Barkley/R.Woods
BSDAEE Z.Ertz/T.Eifert
BSDAJA D.Jordan/E.Ansah 6.00 15.00
BSDALF J.Franklin/E.Lacy 6.00 15.00
BSDAMH D.Hayden/D.Milliner 6.00 15.00
BSDAMS G.Smith/E.Manuel 6.00 15.00
BSDATE M.Te'o/T.Eifert 8.00 20.00
BSDATEL S.Taylor/A.Ellington 6.00 15.00

2013 Bowman Sterling Jumbo Rookie Patches Blue Wave Refractors

*BLACK REF/50: .5X TO 1.2X BLUE WAVE/171
*GOLD REF/25: .6X TO 1.5X BLUE WAVE/171
*PRISM REF/10: 1X TO 2.5X BLUE WAVE/171
BSJRPAD Aaron Dobson 2.00 5.00
BSJRPAE Andre Ellington 4.00 10.00
BSJRPCM Christine Michael 2.00 5.00
BSJRPCP Cordarrelle Patterson 2.00 5.00
BSJRPDH DeAndre Hopkins 5.00 12.00
BSJRPDJ Dion Jordan 2.00 5.00
BSJRPDR Denard Robinson 2.00 5.00
BSJRPEJM EJ Manuel 5.00 12.00
BSJRPEL Eddie Lacy 2.00 5.00
BSJRPGB Giovani Bernard 2.00 5.00
BSJRPGE Gavin Escobar 2.00 5.00
BSJRPGS Geno Smith 2.00 5.00
BSJRPJF Johnathan Franklin 2.00 5.00
BSJRPJH Justin Hunter 2.00 5.00
BSJRPJR Joseph Randle 2.00 5.00
BSJRPJRE Jordan Reed 3.00 8.00
BSJRPKA Keenan Allen 8.00 20.00
BSJRPKD Knile Davis 2.00 5.00
BSJRPKS Kenny Stills 2.00 5.00
BSJRPLB Le'Veon Bell 12.00 30.00
BSJRPLJ Landry Jones 2.00 5.00
BSJRPMB Matt Barkley 2.00 5.00
BSJRPMBA Montee Ball 2.00 5.00
BSJRPMG Mike Glennon 2.00 5.00
BSJRPMGI Mike Gillislee 2.00 5.00
BSJRPMGO Marquise Goodwin 2.00 5.00
BSJRPML Marcus Lattimore 2.00 5.00
BSJRPMT Manti Te'o 2.50 6.00
BSJRPMW Markus Wheaton 2.00 5.00
BSJRPQP Quinton Patton 2.00 5.00
BSJRPRN Ryan Nassib 2.00 5.00
BSJRPRW Robert Woods 3.00 8.00
BSJRPSB Stedman Bailey 2.00 5.00
BSJRPST Stepfan Taylor 2.00 5.00
BSJRPTA Tavon Austin 2.50 6.00
BSJRPTE Tyler Eifert 2.00 5.00
BSJRPTW Tyler Wilson 2.00 5.00
BSJRPTWI Terrance Williams 2.00 5.00
BSJRPVM Vance McDonald 2.50 6.00
BSJRPZE Zach Ertz 4.00 10.00

2013 Bowman Sterling Prism Refractor Dual Autographed Dual Relics

BSPDARAG Goodwin/Austin/35 6.00 15.00
BSPDARAT M.Te'o/K.Allen/35 10.00 25.00
BSPDARBE Bernard/Eifert/35 5.00 12.00
BSPDARBER Barkley/Ertz/15
BSPDARBW Woods/Barkley/15 30.00 60.00
BSPDARBWH Wheaton/Bell/35 15.00 40.00
BSPDARDB K.Davis/T.Bray/35 4.00 10.00
BSPDARER J.Reed/T.Eifert/75 6.00 15.00
BSPDAREW Escobar/Williams/75 4.00 10.00
BSPDARFR Randle/Franklin/75 4.00 10.00
BSPDARGR M.Gillislee/J.Reed/75 6.00 15.00
BSPDARJA E.Ansah/D.Jordan/35 5.00 12.00
BSPDARLB E.Lacy/M.Ball/35 4.00 10.00
BSPDARLF J.Franklin/E.Lacy/75 4.00 10.00
BSPDARLP Lattimore/Patton/35 5.00 12.00
BSPDARLR Robnsn/Lattmre/75 4.00 10.00
BSPDARMH Michael/Harper/75 4.00 10.00
BSPDARMS Manuel/Smith/15 12.00 30.00
BSPDARMW Manuel/Woods/15 15.00 40.00
BSPDARPH Hunter/Patterson/15 10.00 25.00
BSPDARPM McDonald/Patton/35 12.00 30.00
BSPDARRP Robinson/Patton/35 5.00 12.00
BSPDARSB K.Stills/K.Barner/75 4.00 10.00
BSPDARSBA Smith/Barkley/15 12.00 30.00
BSPDARSN G.Smith/R.Nassib/15 12.00 30.00
BSPDARTE S.Taylor/A.Ellington/75 4.00 10.00
BSPDARTEI M.Te'o/T.Eifert/35 6.00 15.00
BSPDARWA R.Woods/K.Allen/35 12.00 30.00
BSPDARWG Glennon/Wilson/15

2013 Bowman Sterling Relics

*VET BLACK/50: .4X TO 1X JSY/99
*ROOK.BLK/75: .6X TO 1.5X JSY/1206-1214
*VET BLU/75: .4X TO 1X JSY/99
*ROOK.BLU/99: .6X TO 1.5X JSY/1206-1214
*VET GOLD/30: .5X TO 1.2X JSY/99
*ROOK.GOLD/50: .8X TO 2X JSY/1206-1214
*VET PRISM/15: .8X TO 2X JSY/99
*ROOK.PRISM/30: 1X TO 2.5X JSY/1206-1214
BSJRRAD Aaron Dobson/1214 1.25 3.00
BSJRRAE Andre Ellington/1214 1.25 3.00
BSJRRCM Christine Michael/1214 1.25 3.00
BSJRRCP Cordarrelle Patterson/1206 1.25 3.00
BSJRRDH DeAndre Hopkins/1206 3.00 8.00
BSJRRDJ Dion Jordan/1214 1.25 3.00
BSJRRDR Denard Robinson/1206 1.25 3.00
BSJRREJM EJ Manuel/1206 3.00 8.00
BSJRREL Eddie Lacy/1206 1.25 3.00
BSJRRGB Giovani Bernard/1206 1.25 3.00
BSJRRGE Gavin Escobar/1214 1.25 3.00
BSJRRGS Geno Smith/1206 1.25 3.00
BSJRRJF Johnathan Franklin/1214 1.25 3.00
BSJRRJH Justin Hunter/1214 1.25 3.00
BSJRRJR Joseph Randle/1214 1.25 3.00
BSJRRJRE Jordan Reed/1214 3.00 8.00
BSJRRKA Keenan Allen/1214 2.50 6.00
BSJRRKD Knile Davis/1214 1.25 3.00
BSJRRKS Kenny Stills/1214 1.25 3.00
BSJRRLB Le'Veon Bell/1206 4.00 10.00
BSJRRLJ Landry Jones/1214 1.25 3.00
BSJRRMB Matt Barkley/1206 1.25 3.00
BSJRRMBA Montee Ball/1206 1.25 3.00
BSJRRMG Mike Glennon/1214 1.25 3.00
BSJRRMGI Mike Gillislee/1214 1.25 3.00
BSJRRMGO Marquise Goodwin/1214 1.25 3.00
BSJRRML Marcus Lattimore/1214 1.25 3.00
BSJRRMT Manti Te'o/1206 1.50 4.00
BSJRRMW Markus Wheaton/1214 1.25 3.00
BSJRRQP Quinton Patton/1214 1.25 3.00
BSJRRRN Ryan Nassib/1214 1.25 3.00
BSJRRRW Robert Woods/1214 2.00 5.00
BSJRRSB Stedman Bailey/1214 1.25 3.00
BSJRRST Stepfan Taylor/1214 1.25 3.00
BSJRRTA Tavon Austin/1206 1.50 4.00
BSJRRTE Tyler Eifert/1214 1.25 3.00
BSJRRTW Tyler Wilson/1214 1.25 3.00
BSJRRTWI T.Williams/1214 1.25 3.00
BSJRRVM Vance McDonald/1214 1.50 4.00
BSJRRZE Zach Ertz/1214 2.50 6.00
BSJVRAD Andy Dalton/99 4.00 10.00
BSJVRAJG A.J. Green/99 5.00 12.00
BSJVRAL Andrew Luck/99 8.00 20.00
BSJVRCK Colin Kaepernick/99 4.00 10.00
BSJVRDB Dez Bryant/99 6.00 15.00
BSJVRDJ DeSean Jackson/99 4.00 10.00
BSJVRDM Doug Martin/99 4.00 10.00
BSJVRED Eric Decker/99 5.00 12.00
BSJVRJC Jamaal Charles/99 4.00 10.00
BSJVRJJ Julio Jones/99 5.00 12.00
BSJVRJL Jake Locker/99 4.00 10.00
BSJVRMJD Maurice Jones-Drew/99 3.00 8.00
BSJVRRC Randall Cobb/99 4.00 10.00
BSJVRRG3 Robert Griffin III/99 3.00 8.00
BSJVRVM Von Miller/99 4.00 10.00

2013 Bowman Sterling Rookie Autograph Relics

*BLUE/125: .6X TO 1.5X JSY AU/361
*BLUE/125: .5X TO 1.2X JSY AU/130-200
*GOLD/75: .8X TO 2X JSY AU/361
*GOLD/75: .6X TO 1.5X JSY AU/130-200
*PRISM/55: .8X TO 2X JSY AU/361
*PRISM/55: .6X TO 1.5X JSY AU/130-200
EXCH EXPIRATION: 11/30/2016
BSARAD Aaron Dobson/166 3.00 8.00
BSARAE Andre Ellington/361 2.50 6.00
BSARCM Christine Michael/166 3.00 8.00
BSARCP C.Patterson/130 3.00 8.00
BSARDH DeAndre Hopkins/130 8.00 20.00
BSARDJ Dion Jordan/166 3.00 8.00
BSARDR Denard Robinson/361 2.50 6.00
BSAREJM EJ Manuel/130 3.00 8.00
BSAREL Eddie Lacy/166 3.00 8.00
BSARGB Giovani Bernard/166 3.00 8.00
BSARGE Gavin Escobar/361 5.00 12.00
BSARGS Geno Smith/130 3.00 8.00
BSARJF Johnathan Franklin/200 3.00 8.00
BSARJH Justin Hunter/166 3.00 8.00
BSARJR Joseph Randle/200 3.00 8.00
BSARJRE Jordan Reed/361 4.00 10.00
BSARKA Keenan Allen/361 6.00 15.00
BSARKD Knile Davis/361 2.50 6.00
BSARKS Kenny Stills/361 2.50 6.00
BSARLB Le'Veon Bell/166 10.00 25.00
BSARLJ Landry Jones/200 3.00 8.00
BSARMB Matt Barkley/130 3.00 8.00
BSARMBA Montee Ball/166 3.00 8.00
BSARMG Mike Glennon/130 3.00 8.00
BSARMGI Mike Gillislee/361 2.50 6.00
BSARMGO Marquise Goodwin/361 2.50 6.00
BSARML Marcus Lattimore EXCH 3.00 8.00
BSARMT Manti Te'o/130 4.00 10.00
BSARMW Markus Wheaton/200 3.00 8.00
BSARQP Quinton Patton/361 2.50 6.00
BSARRN Ryan Nassib/166 3.00 8.00
BSARRW Robert Woods/166 5.00 12.00
BSARSB Stedman Bailey/361 2.50 6.00
BSARST Stepfan Taylor/200 3.00 8.00
BSARTA Tavon Austin/130 4.00 10.00
BSARTE Tyler Eifert/166 3.00 8.00
BSARTW Tyler Wilson/166 3.00 8.00
BSARTWI Terrance Williams/200 3.00 8.00
BSARVM Vance McDonald/361 3.00 8.00
BSARZE Zach Ertz/200 6.00 15.00

2014 Bowman Sterling

COMPLETE SET (100) 50.00 100.00
1 Blake Bortles RC .60 1.50
2 Sammy Watkins RC .75 2.00
3 Teddy Bridgewater RC .75 2.00
4 Johnny Manziel RC .75 2.00

5 Jadeveon Clowney RC .60 1.50
6 Greg Robinson RC .50 1.25
7 Jake Matthews RC .50 1.25
8 Derek Carr RC 3.00 8.00
9 Khalil Mack RC 2.00 5.00
10 Mike Evans RC 1.25 3.00
11 Anthony Barr RC .50 1.25
12 Kony Ealy RC .60 1.50
13 Taylor Lewan RC .50 1.25
14 Justin Gilbert RC .50 1.25
15 Kelvin Benjamin RC .75 2.00
16 Aaron Donald RC 1.25 3.00
17 Eric Ebron RC .60 1.50
18 Odell Beckham Jr. RC 6.00 15.00
19 Louis Nix RC .50 1.25
20 Ha Ha Clinton-Dix RC .60 1.50
21 Calvin Pryor RC .50 1.25
22 Ra'Shede Hageman RC .50 1.25
23 Darqueze Dennard RC .60 1.50
24 Jason Verrett RC .50 1.25
25 Marqise Lee RC .60 1.50
26 C.J. Mosley RC .60 1.50
27 Zack Martin RC .60 1.50
28 Jace Amaro RC .50 1.25
29 Brandin Cooks RC .75 2.00
30 Timmy Jernigan RC .50 1.25
31 Cyrus Kouandjio RC .60 1.50
32 Zach Mettenberger RC .50 1.25
33 Allen Robinson RC .75 2.00
34 Carlos Hyde RC .60 1.50
35 Austin Seferian-Jenkins RC .50 1.25
36 Jarvis Landry RC 1.00 2.50
37 Kyle Van Noy RC .60 1.50
38 Jimmy Garoppolo RC 4.00 10.00
39 Davante Adams RC .75 2.00
40 Martavis Bryant RC .60 1.50
41 Jordan Matthews RC .75 2.00
42 Troy Niklas RC .50 1.25
43 Tre Mason RC .50 1.25
44 Bishop Sankey RC .50 1.25
45 Lache Seastrunk RC .50 1.25
46 Charles Sims RC .50 1.25
47 Loucheiz Purifoy RC .50 1.25
48 C.J. Fiedorowicz RC .50 1.25
49 Josh Huff RC .60 1.50
50 Cody Latimer RC .60 1.50
51 Aaron Murray RC .50 1.25
52 Paul Richardson RC .60 1.50
53 Arthur Lynch RC .50 1.25
54 A.J. McCarron RC .50 1.25
55 Jeremy Hill RC .60 1.50
56 Logan Thomas RC .50 1.25
57 Ka'Deem Carey RC .50 1.25
58 Andre Williams RC .50 1.25
59 Devonta Freeman RC .75 2.00
60 Robert Herron RC .50 1.25
61 Craig Loston RC .50 1.25
62 Brandon Coleman RC .50 1.25
63 Michael Sam RC .50 1.25
64 Ryan Grant RC .50 1.25
65 Jared Abbrederis RC .50 1.25
66 Tajh Boyd RC .50 1.25
67 De'Anthony Thomas RC .50 1.25
68 Terrance West RC .50 1.25
69 Yawin Smallwood RC .50 1.25
70 Xavier Grimble RC .60 1.50
71 Trent Murphy RC .50 1.25
72 Tom Savage RC .50 1.25
73 Storm Johnson RC .50 1.25
74 Stephon Tuitt RC .75 2.00
75 Shaquelle Evans RC .50 1.25
76 Ryan Shazier RC .75 2.00
77 Pierre Desir RC .50 1.25
78 Mike Davis RC .50 1.25
79 Marion Grice RC .50 1.25
80 Marcus Roberson RC .60 1.50
81 Kevin Norwood RC .50 1.25
82 Kareem Martin RC .50 1.25
83 Jordan Lynch RC .60 1.50
84 Jeff Janis RC .50 1.25
85 Jeff Mathews RC .60 1.50
86 Jalen Saunders RC .50 1.25
87 Henry Josey RC .50 1.25
88 Dri Archer RC .50 1.25
89 Donte Moncrief RC .50 1.25
90 Dion Bailey RC .50 1.25
91 Devin Street RC .50 1.25
92 Deone Bucannon RC .50 1.25
93 Damien Williams RC .50 1.25
94 Cody Hoffman RC .50 1.25
95 Caraun Reid RC .60 1.50
96 Bruce Ellington RC .50 1.25
97 Antone Exum RC .50 1.25
98 Ahmad Dixon RC .50 1.25
99 Aaron Colvin RC .50 1.25
100 Garrett Gilbert RC .50 1.25

2014 Bowman Sterling Black Refractors

*BLACK/75: .75X TO 2X BASIC CARDS
18 Odell Beckham Jr. 20.00 40.00

2014 Bowman Sterling Blue Wave Refractors

*BLUE WAVE/25: 1.2X TO 3X BASIC CARDS
18 Odell Beckham Jr. 25.00 50.00

2014 Bowman Sterling Gold Refractors

*ORANGE/99: .75X TO 2X BASIC CARDS

2014 Bowman Sterling Pulsar Refractors

*PULSAR/50: 1X TO 2.5X BASIC CARDS

2014 Bowman Sterling Autographs

*BASE AU: .3X TO .8X GOLD AU/99
BSAJG Jimmy Garoppolo 30.00 60.00

2014 Bowman Sterling Autographs Black Refractors

*BLACK/50: .5X TO 1.2X GOLD/99

2014 Bowman Sterling Autographs Blue Wave Refractors

*BLUE WAVE/15: .75X TO 2X GOLD/99

2014 Bowman Sterling Autographs Gold Refractors

BSAAB Anthony Barr 2.50 6.00
BSAAD Aaron Donald 6.00 15.00
BSAAM A.J. McCarron 2.50 6.00
BSAAMU Aaron Murray 2.50 6.00
BSAAR Allen Robinson 4.00 10.00
BSAARI Antonio Richardson 4.00 10.00
BSAASJ Austin Seferian-Jenkins 2.50 6.00
BSABB Blake Bortles 3.00 8.00
BSABC Brandin Cooks 4.00 10.00
BSABCO Brandon Coleman 2.50 6.00
BSABS Bishop Sankey 2.50 6.00
BSACJF C.J. Fiedorowicz 2.50 6.00
BSACL Colt Lyerla 4.00 10.00
BSACLA Cody Latimer 3.00 8.00
BSACSH Connor Shaw 2.50 6.00
BSADA Davante Adams 4.00 10.00
BSADAR Dri Archer 2.50 6.00
BSADC Derek Carr 25.00 60.00
BSADD Darqueze Dennard 3.00 8.00
BSADF David Fales 2.50 6.00
BSADFR Devonta Freeman 4.00 10.00
BSADS Devin Street 2.50 6.00
BSAEE Eric Ebron 3.00 8.00
BSAGR Greg Robinson 2.50 6.00
BSAHCD Ha Ha Clinton-Dix 3.00 8.00
BSAJA Jace Amaro 2.50 6.00
BSAJAB Jared Abbrederis 2.50 6.00
BSAJB John Brown 4.00 10.00
BSAJC Jadeveon Clowney 3.00 8.00
BSAJH Jeremy Hill 3.00 8.00
BSAJHU Josh Huff 3.00 8.00
BSAJL Jarvis Landry 8.00 20.00
BSAJLY Jordan Lynch 3.00 8.00
BSAJM Johnny Manziel 4.00 10.00
BSAJMA Jordan Matthews 4.00 10.00
BSAJMC Jerick McKinnon 3.00 8.00
BSAJV Jason Verrett 2.50 6.00
BSAJW James White 5.00 12.00
BSAKB Kelvin Benjamin 4.00 10.00
BSAKC Ka'Deem Carey 2.50 6.00
BSAKN Kevin Norwood 2.50 6.00
BSALN Louis Nix 2.50 6.00
BSALS Lache Seastrunk 2.50 6.00
BSALT Logan Thomas 2.50 6.00
BSAMB Martavis Bryant 3.00 8.00
BSAMD Mike Davis 2.50 6.00
BSAME Mike Evans 12.00 30.00
BSAMG Marion Grice 2.50 6.00
BSAML Marqise Lee 3.00 8.00
BSAOB Odell Beckham Jr. 40.00 80.00
BSAPR Paul Richardson 3.00 8.00
BSARH Robert Herron 2.50 6.00
BSARN Rajion Neal 2.50 6.00
BSASE Shaquelle Evans 2.50 6.00
BSASJ Storm Johnson 2.50 6.00
BSASW Sammy Watkins 4.00 10.00
BSATB Teddy Bridgewater 4.00 10.00
BSATBO Tajh Boyd 2.50 6.00
BSATN Troy Niklas 2.50 6.00
BSATS Tom Savage 2.50 6.00
BSATW Terrance West 2.50 6.00
BSAXG Xavier Grimble 3.00 8.00
BSAZM Zach Mettenberger 2.50 6.00
BSAZMA Zack Martin 3.00 8.00

2014 Bowman Sterling Autographs Pulsar Refractors

*PULSAR/25: .6X TO 1.5X GOLD/99

2014 Bowman Sterling Bronze Autographs

BSAAJG A.J. Green
BSABB Blake Bortles 4.00 10.00
BSABC Brandin Cooks 6.00 15.00
BSACP Cordarrelle Patterson 5.00 12.00
BSADB Drew Brees 25.00 50.00
BSADC Derek Carr 25.00 50.00
BSAEE Eric Ebron 4.00 10.00
BSAEL Eddie Lacy 5.00 12.00
BSAGB Giovani Bernard 5.00 12.00
BSAJC1 Jadeveon Clowney 4.00 10.00
BSAJC2 Jordan Cameron 5.00 12.00
BSAJM Johnny Manziel 5.00 12.00
BSAMB Montee Ball 5.00 12.00
BSAME Mike Evans 8.00 20.00
BSANF Nick Foles 6.00 15.00
BSAOB Odell Beckham Jr. 40.00 80.00
BSARW Russell Wilson
BSASW Sammy Watkins 5.00 12.00
BSATB Teddy Bridgewater 5.00 12.00

2014 Bowman Sterling Bronze Autographs Black Refractors

*BLACK/50: .5X TO 1.2X BRONZE AU/99
BSAOB Odell Beckham Jr. 40.00 100.00

2014 Bowman Sterling Bronze Autographs Pulsar Refractors

*PULSAR/25: .6X TO 1.5X BRONZE AU/99

2014 Bowman Sterling Dual Autographed Relic Patches Pulsar Refractors

BSPDARAB T.Boyd/J.Amaro 5.00 12.00
BSPDARAL D.Adams/C.Latimer 8.00 20.00
BSPDARAT D.Thomas/D.Archer 5.00 12.00
BSPDARBC T.Brdgwtr/D.Carr 60.00 120.00
BSPDARBE K.Benjamin/M.Evans 50.00 80.00
BSPDARBECO B.Cooks/O.Bckhm 60.00 125.00
BSPDARBH O.Beckham/J.Hill 60.00 125.00
BSPDARBL M.Lee/B.Bortles 6.00 15.00
BSPDARBM J.Mnzl/T.Brdgwtr 25.00 50.00
BSPDARBR B.Bortles/A.Robinson 8.00 20.00
BSPDARBW O.Bckhm/A.Wllms 60.00 125.00
BSPDARCM K.Mack/D.Carr 200.00 300.00
BSPDARCS J.Clowney/T.Savage 6.00 15.00
BSPDARCW B.Cooks/S.Watkins 8.00 20.00
BSPDARDS T.Savage/A.Donald 12.00 30.00
BSPDAREBSJ A.Jenkins/E.Ebron 6.00 15.00
BSPDARES M.Evans/C.Sims 12.00 30.00
BSPDARESJ A.Jenkins/M.Evans 20.00 50.00
BSPDARGS J.Grpplo/T.Svge 12.00 30.00
BSPDARHL J.Hill/J.Landry 25.00 50.00
BSPDARHM A.McCarron/J.Hill 12.00 30.00
BSPDARLB J.Landry/O.Beckham 60.00 125.00
BSPDARLR A.Robinson/M.Lee 8.00 20.00
BSPDARMB J.Manziel/B.Bortles 30.00 60.00
BSPDARME J.Manziel/M.Evans 30.00 80.00
BSPDARMH T.Mason/C.Hyde 6.00 15.00
BSPDARMM A.Mrry/A.McCrrn 30.00 60.00
BSPDARMS B.Sankey/T.Mason 5.00 12.00
BSPDARSH C.Hyde/B.Sankey 6.00 15.00
BSPDARSJS A.Jenkins/C.Sims 5.00 12.00
BSPDARTM D.Thomas/A.Murray 5.00 12.00
BSPDARWABO S.Watkins/T.Boyd 8.00 20.00
BSPDARWB S.Watkins/M.Bryant 8.00 20.00
BSPDARWE M.Evans/S.Watkins 12.00 30.00
BSPDARWT D.Freeman/T.West 20.00 50.00

2014 Bowman Sterling Dual Autographs

BSDABH G.Bernard/J.Hill 5.00 12.00
BSDABL M.Lee/B.Bortles 5.00 12.00
BSDABW O.Beckham/A.Williams 60.00 120.00
BSDACS J.Clowney/T.Savage 5.00 12.00
BSDAHT D.Thomas/C.Hyde 5.00 12.00
BSDAMB B.Bortles/J.Manziel 30.00 80.00
BSDAMS B.Sankey/T.Mason
BSDASE M.Stafford/E.Ebron 20.00 40.00
BSDASH C.Hyde/B.Sankey 5.00 12.00
BSDAWE S.Watkins/M.Evans 30.00 60.00

2014 Bowman Sterling Jumbo Rookie Patches Blue Wave Refractors

RANDOM INSERTS IN BOX TOPPER PACKS
*GOLD/75: .5X TO 1.2X BASIC PATCH
*BLACK/50: .6X TO 1.5X BASIC PATCH
*PULSAR/25: .75X TO 2X BASIC PATCH
BSJRPAM A.J. McCarron 2.00 5.00
BSJRPAR Allen Robinson 3.00 8.00
BSJRPAW Andre Williams 2.00 5.00
BSJRPBB Blake Bortles 2.50 6.00
BSJRPBC Brandin Cooks 3.00 8.00
BSJRPBS Bishop Sankey 2.00 5.00
BSJRPCH Carlos Hyde 2.50 6.00
BSJRPCL Cody Latimer 2.50 6.00
BSJRPCS Charles Sims 2.00 5.00
BSJRPDA Davante Adams 3.00 8.00
BSJRPDC Derek Carr 10.00 25.00
BSJRPDF Devonta Freeman 3.00 8.00
BSJRPDM Donte Moncrief 2.00 5.00
BSJRPDT De'Anthony Thomas 2.00 5.00
BSJRPEE Eric Ebron 2.50 6.00
BSJRPJA Jace Amaro 2.00 5.00
BSJRPJC Jadeveon Clowney 2.50 6.00
BSJRPJG Jimmy Garoppolo 15.00 40.00
BSJRPJH Jeremy Hill 2.50 6.00
BSJRPJL Jarvis Landry 4.00 10.00
BSJRPJM Jordan Matthews 3.00 8.00
BSJRPKB Kelvin Benjamin 3.00 8.00
BSJRPKC Ka'Deem Carey 2.00 5.00
BSJRPKM Khalil Mack 8.00 20.00
BSJRPLT Logan Thomas 2.00 5.00
BSJRPME Mike Evans 5.00 12.00
BSJRPML Marqise Lee 2.50 6.00
BSJRPOB Odell Beckham Jr. 5.00 12.00
BSJRPPR Paul Richardson 2.50 6.00
BSJRPSW Sammy Watkins 3.00 8.00
BSJRPTB Teddy Bridgewater 3.00 8.00
BSJRPTM Tre Mason 2.00 5.00
BSJRPTS Tom Savage 2.00 5.00
BSJRPTW Terrance West 2.00 5.00
BSJRPAMU Aaron Murray 2.00 5.00
BSJRPASJ Austin Seferian-Jenkins 2.00 5.00
BSJRPCJF C.J. Fiedorowicz 2.00 5.00
BSJRPDAR Dri Archer 2.00 5.00
BSJRPJMA Johnny Manziel 3.00 8.00
BSJRPTBO Tajh Boyd 2.00 5.00

2014 Bowman Sterling Purple Wave Autographs Refractors

APWAM Aaron Murray 6.00 15.00
APWAR Allen Robinson 10.00 25.00
APWASJ Austin Seferian-Jenkins 6.00 15.00
APWAW Andre Williams 6.00 15.00
APWBC Brandin Cooks 10.00 25.00
APWBS Bishop Sankey 6.00 15.00
APWCH Carlos Hyde EXCH 8.00 20.00
APWCS Charles Sims 6.00 15.00
APWDA Dri Archer 6.00 15.00
APWDAD Davante Adams 10.00 25.00
APWEE Eric Ebron 8.00 20.00
APWJA Jace Amaro 6.00 15.00
APWJG Jimmy Garoppolo 25.00 50.00
APWJH Jeremy Hill 8.00 20.00
APWJMA Jordan Matthews 10.00 25.00
APWKB Kelvin Benjamin 10.00 25.00
APWKC Ka'Deem Carey 6.00 15.00
APWLT Logan Thomas 6.00 15.00
APWME Mike Evans 30.00 60.00
APWML Marqise Lee 8.00 20.00
APWOB Odell Beckham Jr. 50.00 100.00
APWPR Paul Richardson 8.00 20.00
APWSW Sammy Watkins 10.00 25.00
APWTM Tre Mason 6.00 15.00
APWTS Tom Savage 6.00 15.00

2014 Bowman Sterling Relics

*GOLD/99: .5X TO 1.2X BASIC JSY
*BLACK/75: .5X TO 1.2X BASIC JSY
*PULSAR/50: .6X TO 1.5X BASIC JSY
BSRDRAM A.J. McCarron 1.25 3.00
BSRDRAR Allen Robinson 2.00 5.00
BSRDRAW Andre Williams 1.25 3.00
BSRDRBB Blake Bortles 1.50 4.00
BSRDRBC Brandin Cooks 2.00 5.00
BSRDRBS Bishop Sankey 1.25 3.00
BSRDRCH Carlos Hyde 1.50 4.00
BSRDRCL Cody Latimer 1.50 4.00
BSRDRCS Charles Sims 1.25 3.00
BSRDRDA Davante Adams 2.00 5.00
BSRDRDC Derek Carr 8.00 20.00
BSRDRDF Devonta Freeman 2.00 5.00
BSRDRDM Donte Moncrief 1.25 3.00
BSRDRDT De'Anthony Thomas 1.25 3.00
BSRDREE Eric Ebron 1.50 4.00
BSRDRJA Jace Amaro 1.25 3.00
BSRDRJC Jadeveon Clowney 1.50 4.00
BSRDRJG Jimmy Garoppolo 10.00 25.00
BSRDRJH Jeremy Hill 1.50 4.00
BSRDRJL Jarvis Landry 2.50 6.00
BSRDRJM Jordan Matthews 2.00 5.00
BSRDRJW James White 2.50 6.00
BSRDRKB Kelvin Benjamin 2.00 5.00
BSRDRKC Ka'Deem Carey 1.25 3.00
BSRDRKM Khalil Mack 5.00 12.00
BSRDRLT Logan Thomas 1.25 3.00
BSRDRME Mike Evans 3.00 8.00
BSRDRML Marqise Lee 1.50 4.00
BSRDROB Odell Beckham Jr. 3.00 8.00
BSRDRPR Paul Richardson 1.50 4.00
BSRDRSW Sammy Watkins 2.00 5.00
BSRDRTB Teddy Bridgewater 2.00 5.00
BSRDRTM Tre Mason 1.25 3.00
BSRDRTS Tom Savage 1.25 3.00
BSRDRTW Terrance West 1.25 3.00
BSRDRAMU Aaron Murray 1.25 3.00
BSRDRASJ Austin Seferian-Jenkins 1.25 3.00
BSRDRDAR Dri Archer 1.25 3.00
BSRDRJMA Johnny Manziel 2.00 5.00
BSRDRTBO Tajh Boyd 1.25 3.00

2014 Bowman Sterling Rookie Autograph Relics

*BASIC AU: .3X TO .8X GOLD/99
BSARJG Jimmy Garoppolo 40.00 80.00

2014 Bowman Sterling Rookie Autograph Relics Black Refractors

*BLACK/50: .5X TO 1.2X GOLD/99
BSARJG Jimmy Garoppolo 60.00 125.00
BSAROB Odell Beckham Jr. 40.00 100.00

2014 Bowman Sterling Rookie Autograph Relics Gold Refractors

BSARAD Aaron Donald 10.00 25.00
BSARAM Aaron Murray 3.00 8.00
BSARAMC A.J. McCarron 3.00 8.00
BSARAR Allen Robinson 5.00 12.00
BSARAS Austin Seferian-Jenkins 3.00 8.00
BSARAW Andre Williams 3.00 8.00
BSARBB Blake Bortles
BSARBC Brandin Cooks 5.00 12.00
BSARBS Bishop Sankey 3.00 8.00
BSARCH Carlos Hyde 4.00 10.00
BSARCL Cody Latimer 4.00 10.00
BSARCSI Charles Sims 3.00 8.00
BSARDA Davante Adams 5.00 12.00
BSARDAR Dri Archer 3.00 8.00
BSARDC Derek Carr 30.00 80.00
BSARDF Devonta Freeman 5.00 12.00
BSARDM Donte Moncrief 3.00 8.00
BSARDT De'Anthony Thomas 3.00 8.00
BSAREE Eric Ebron 4.00 10.00
BSARJA Jace Amaro 3.00 8.00
BSARJC Jadeveon Clowney
BSARJG Jimmy Garoppolo 50.00 100.00
BSARJH Josh Huff 4.00 10.00
BSARJHI Jeremy Hill 4.00 10.00
BSARJL Jarvis Landry 6.00 15.00
BSARJM Johnny Manziel
BSARJMA Jordan Matthews 5.00 12.00
BSARJMC Jerick McKinnon 4.00 10.00
BSARJW James White 6.00 15.00
BSARKB Kelvin Benjamin 5.00 12.00
BSARKC Ka'Deem Carey 3.00 8.00
BSARKM Khalil Mack
BSARLT Logan Thomas 3.00 8.00
BSARMB Martavis Bryant 4.00 10.00
BSARME Mike Evans
BSARML Marqise Lee 4.00 10.00
BSAROB Odell Beckham Jr. 30.00 80.00
BSARPR Paul Richardson 4.00 10.00
BSARSW Sammy Watkins
BSARTB Teddy Bridgewater
BSARTBO Tajh Boyd 3.00 8.00
BSARTM Tre Mason 3.00 8.00
BSARTS Tom Savage 3.00 8.00
BSARTW Terrance West 3.00 8.00
BSARZM Zach Mettenberger 3.00 8.00

2014 Bowman Sterling Rookie Autograph Relics Green Refractors

*GREEN/75: .4X TO 1X GOLD/99
BSARJG Jimmy Garoppolo 60.00 125.00
BSAROB Odell Beckham Jr. 30.00 80.00

2014 Bowman Sterling Rookie Autograph Relics Pulsar Refractors

*PULSAR/25: .6X TO 1.5X GOLD/99
BSARJG Jimmy Garoppolo 75.00 150.00
BSARJM Johnny Manziel 8.00 20.00
BSAROB Odell Beckham Jr. 50.00 125.00
BSARSW Sammy Watkins 8.00 20.00
BSARTB Teddy Bridgewater 8.00 20.00

1995 Bowman's Best

This 180 card set was issued by Topps and broken down into two subsets: Bowman's Best Black for veterans (V1-V90) and Bowman's Best Blue for rookies (R1-R90). Rookie Cards in this set include Mark Bruener, Ki-Jana Carter, Kerry Collins, Joey Galloway, Darrick Holmes, Napoleon Kaufman, Steve McNair, Curtis Martin, Chris Sanders, Frank Sanders, Rashaan Salaam, Kordell Stewart, Tamarick Vanover and Michael Westbrook

COMPLETE SET (180) 40.00 100.00
R1 Ki-Jana Carter RC .60 1.50
R2 Tony Boselli RC .60 1.50
R3 Steve McNair RC 5.00 12.00
R4 Michael Westbrook RC .60 1.50
R5 Kerry Collins RC 2.50 6.00
R6 Kevin Carter RC .60 1.50
R7 Mike Mamula RC .15 .40
R8 Joey Galloway RC 2.50 6.00
R9 Kyle Brady RC .60 1.50
R10 Ray McElroy RC .15 .40
R11 Derrick Alexander DE RC .15 .40
R12 Warren Sapp RC 2.50 6.00
R13 Mark Fields RC .60 1.50
R14 Ruben Brown RC .60 1.50
R15 Ellis Johnson RC .15 .40
R16 Hugh Douglas RC .60 1.50
R17 Alundis Brice RC .15 .40
R18 Napoleon Kaufman RC 2.00 5.00
R19 James O. Stewart RC 1.25 3.00
R20 Luther Elliss RC .15 .40
R21 Rashaan Salaam RC .30 .75
R22 Tyrone Poole RC .60 1.50
R23 Ty Law RC 1.50 4.00
R24 Korey Stringer RC .50 1.25
R25 Billy Milner RC .15 .40
R26 Roell Preston RC .30 .75
R27 Mark Bruener RC .30 .75
R28 Derrick Brooks RC 2.50 6.00
R29 Blake Brockermeyer RC .15 .40
R30 Mike Frederick RC .15 .40
R31 Trezelle Jenkins RC .15 .40
R32 Craig Newsome RC .15 .40
R33 Matt O'Dwyer RC .15 .40
R34 Terrance Shaw RC .15 .40
R35 Anthony Cook RC .15 .40
R36 Darick Holmes RC .30 .75
R37 Cory Raymer RC .15 .40
R38 Zach Wiegert RC .15 .40
R39 Sam Shade RC .15 .40
R40 Brian DeMarco RC .15 .40
R41 Ron Davis RC .15 .40
R42 Orlando Thomas RC .15 .40
R43 Derek West RC .15 .40
R44 Ray Zellars RC .30 .75
R45 Todd Collins RC 2.00 5.00
R46 Linc Harden RC .15 .40
R47 Frank Sanders RC .60 1.50
R48 Ken Dilger RC .60 1.50
R49 Barrett Robbins RC .15 .40
R50 Bobby Taylor RC 1.00 2.50
R51 Terrell Fletcher RC .15 .40
R52 Jack Jackson RC .15 .40
R53 Jeff Kopp RC .15 .40
R54 Brendan Stai RC .15 .40
R55 Corey Fuller RC .15 .40
R56 Todd Sauerbrun RC .15 .40
R57 Dameian Jeffries RC .15 .40
R58 Troy Dumas RC .15 .40
R59 Charlie Williams RC .15 .40
R60 Kordell Stewart RC 2.50 6.00
R61 Jay Barker RC .15 .40
R62 Jesse James RC .15 .40
R63 Shane Hannah RC .15 .40
R64 Rob Johnson RC 1.50 4.00
R65 Darius Holland RC .15 .40
R66 William Henderson RC 2.00 5.00
R67 Chris Sanders RC .30 .75
R68 Darryl Pounds RC .15 .40
R69 Melvin Tuten RC .15 .40
R70 David Sloan RC .15 .40
R71 Chris Hudson RC .15 .40
R72 William Strong RC .15 .40
R73 Brian Williams LB RC .15 .40
R74 Curtis Martin RC 6.00 15.00
R75 Mike Verstegen RC .15 .40
R76 Justin Armour RC .15 .40
R77 Lorenzo Styles RC .15 .40
R78 Oliver Gibson RC .15 .40
R79 Zack Crockett RC .30 .75
R80 Tau Pupua RC .15 .40
R81 Tamarick Vanover RC .60 1.50
R82 Steve McLaughlin RC .15 .40
R83 Sean Harris RC .15 .40
R84 Eric Zeier RC .60 1.50
R85 Rodney Young RC .15 .40
R86 Chad May RC .15 .40
R87 Evan Pilgrim RC .15 .40
R88 James A.Stewart RC .15 .40
R89 Torey Hunter RC .15 .40
R90 Antonio Freeman RC 1.50 4.00
V1 Rob Moore .25 .60
V2 Craig Heyward .25 .60
V3 Jim Kelly .50 1.25
V4 John Kasay .10 .30
V5 Jeff Graham .10 .30
V6 Jeff Blake RC 1.00 2.50
V7 Antonio Langham .10 .30
V8 Troy Aikman 1.25 3.00
V9 Simon Fletcher .10 .30
V10 Barry Sanders 2.00 5.00
V11 Edgar Bennett .25 .60
V12 Ray Childress .10 .30
V13 Ray Buchanan .10 .30
V14 Desmond Howard .25 .60
V15 Dale Carter .25 .60
V16 Troy Vincent .10 .30
V17 David Palmer .25 .60
V18 Ben Coates .25 .60
V19 Derek Brown .10 .30
V20 Dave Brown .25 .60
V21 Mo Lewis .10 .30
V22 Harvey Williams .10 .30
V23 Randall Cunningham .50 1.25
V24 Kevin Greene .25 .60
V25 Junior Seau .50 1.25
V26 Merton Hanks .10 .30
V27 Cortez Kennedy .25 .60
V28 Troy Drayton .10 .30
V29 Hardy Nickerson .10 .30
V30 Brian Mitchell .10 .30
V31 Raymont Harris .10 .30
V32 Keith Goganious .10 .30
V33 Andre Reed .25 .60
V34 Terance Mathis .25 .60
V35 Garrison Hearst .50 1.25
V36 Glyn Milburn .10 .30
V37 Emmitt Smith 2.00 5.00
V38 Vinny Testaverde .25 .60
V39 Darnay Scott .25 .60
V40 Mickey Washington .10 .30
V41 Craig Erickson .10 .30
V42 Chris Chandler .50 1.25
V43 Brett Favre 2.50 6.00
V44 Scott Mitchell .25 .60
V45 Chris Slade .10 .30
V46 Warren Moon .25 .60
V47 Dan Marino 2.50 6.00
V48 Greg Hill .25 .60
V49 Rocket Ismail .25 .60
V50 Bobby Houston .10 .30
V51 Rodney Hampton .25 .60
V52 Jim Everett .10 .30
V53 Rick Mirer .25 .60
V54 Steve Young 1.00 2.50
V55 Dennis Gibson .10 .30
V56 Rod Woodson .25 .60
V57 Calvin Williams .25 .60
V58 Tom Carter .10 .30
V59 Trent Dilfer .50 1.25
V60 Shane Conlan .10 .30
V61 Cornelius Bennett .25 .60
V62 Eric Metcalf .25 .60
V63 Frank Reich .10 .30
V64 Eric Hill .10 .30
V65 Erik Kramer .10 .30
V66 Michael Irvin .50 1.25
V67 Tony McGee .10 .30
V68 Andre Rison .25 .60
V69 Shannon Sharpe .25 .60
V70 Quentin Coryatt .25 .60
V71 Robert Brooks .50 1.25
V72 Steve Beuerlein .25 .60
V73 Herman Moore .50 1.25
V74 Jack Del Rio .10 .30
V75 Dave Meggett .10 .30
V76 Pete Stoyanovich .10 .30
V77 Neil Smith .25 .60
V78 Corey Miller .10 .30
V79 Tim Brown .50 1.25
V80 Tyrone Hughes .25 .60
V81 Boomer Esiason .25 .60
V82 Natrone Means .25 .60
V83 Chris Warren .25 .60
V84 Byron Bam Morris .10 .30
V85 Jerry Rice 1.25 3.00
V86 Michael Zordich .10 .30
V87 Errict Rhett .25 .60
V88 Henry Ellard .25 .60
V89 Chris Miller .10 .30
V90 John Elway 2.50 6.00

1995 Bowman's Best Refractors

COMPLETE SET (180) 200.00 500.00
*STARS: 1.2X TO 3X BASIC CARDS
*ROOKIES: 1.2X TO 3X BASIC CARDS
STATED ODDS 1:6

1995 Bowman's Best Mirror Images Draft Picks

This 15-card set was randomly inserted into packs at a ratio of 1:2. The cards feature the top 15 draft picks from 1994 and 1995 "back-to-back." Each card is numbered according to the player's draft position. Cards were also available as Refractor parallels inserted at a rate of one in 18 packs.

COMPLETE SET (15) 10.00 25.00
STATED ODDS 1:4
*REFRACTORS: 2.5X TO 5X BASIC INSERTS
REFRACTOR STATED ODDS 1:36
1 Ki.Carter D.Wilkinson .75 2.00
2 M.Faulk T.Boselli 2.00 5.00
3 S.McNair H.Shuler 3.00 8.00
4 Westbrook McGinest .75 2.00
5 K.Collins T.Alberts 1.50 4.00
6 T.Dilfer Kev.Carter .75 2.00
7 B.Young M.Mamula .75 2.00
8 J.Galloway S.Adams 1.50 4.00
9 A.Langham K.Brady .50 1.25
10 J.J.Stokes J.Miller .75 2.00
11 Thierry Alexander DE .75 2.00
12 A.Glenn W.Sapp .50 1.25
13 Joe Johnson Fields .75 2.00
14 B.Williams R.Brown .75 2.00
15 W.Gandy E.Johnson .50 1.25

1996 Bowman's Best

The 1996 Bowman's Best set was issued in one series totalling 180 cards. The six-card packs retail for $5.00 each. The fronts of the 135 veterans' cards feature color action player photos in a gold design. The cards for the 45 draft picks display color action player photos in a silver design. The backs carry player information and statistics.

COMPLETE SET (180) 40.00 80.00
1 Emmitt Smith 1.25 3.00
2 Kordell Stewart .30 .75
3 Mark Chmura .20 .50
4 Sean Dawkins .10 .30
5 Steve Young .60 1.50
6 Tamarick Vanover .20 .50
7 Scott Mitchell .20 .50
8 Aaron Hayden .10 .30
9 William Thomas .10 .30
10 Dan Marino 1.50 4.00
11 Curtis Conway .30 .75
12 Steve Atwater .10 .30
13 Derrick Brooks .30 .75
14 Rick Mirer .20 .50
15 Mark Brunell .40 1.00
16 Garrison Hearst .20 .50
17 Eric Turner .10 .30
18 Mark Carrier WR .10 .30
19 Darnay Scott .20 .50
20 Steve McNair .60 1.50
21 Jim Everett .10 .30
22 Wayne Chrebet .40 1.00
23 Ben Coates .20 .50
24 Harvey Williams .10 .30
25 Michael Westbrook .30 .75
26 Kevin Carter .10 .30
27 Dave Brown .10 .30
28 Jake Reed .20 .50
29 Thurman Thomas .30 .75
30 Jeff George .20 .50
31 Carnell Lake .10 .30
32 J.J. Stokes .30 .75
33 Jay Novacek .10 .30
34 Brett Perriman .10 .30
35 Robert Brooks .30 .75
36 Neil Smith .20 .50
37 Chris Zorich .10 .30
38 Micheal Barrow .10 .30
39 Quentin Coryatt .10 .30
40 Kerry Collins .30 .75
41 Aeneas Williams .10 .30
42 James O.Stewart .20 .50
43 Warren Moon .20 .50
44 Willie McGinest .10 .30
45 Rodney Hampton .20 .50
46 Jeff Hostetler .10 .30
47 Darrell Green .10 .30
48 Warren Sapp .10 .30
49 Troy Drayton .10 .30
50 Junior Seau .30 .75
51 Mike Mamula .10 .30
52 Antonio Langham .10 .30
53 Eric Metcalf .10 .30
54 Adrian Murrell .20 .50
55 Joey Galloway .30 .75
56 Anthony Miller .20 .50
57 Carl Pickens .20 .50
58 Bruce Smith .20 .50
59 Merton Hanks .10 .30
60 Troy Aikman .75 2.00
61 Erik Kramer .10 .30
62 Tyrone Poole .10 .30
63 Michael Jackson .20 .50
64 Rob Moore .20 .50
65 Marcus Allen .30 .75
66 Orlando Thomas .10 .30
67 Dave Meggett .10 .30
68 Trent Dilfer .30 .75
69 Herman Moore .20 .50
70 Brett Favre 1.50 4.00
71 Blaine Bishop .10 .30
72 Eric Allen .10 .30
73 Bernie Parmalee .10 .30
74 Kyle Brady .10 .30
75 Terry McDaniel .10 .30
76 Rodney Peete .10 .30
77 Yancey Thigpen .20 .50
78 Stan Humphries .20 .50
79 Craig Heyward .10 .30
80 Rashaan Salaam .20 .50
81 Shannon Sharpe .20 .50
82 Jim Harbaugh .20 .50
83 Vinnie Clark .10 .30
84 Steve Bono .10 .30
85 Drew Bledsoe .40 1.00
86 Ken Norton .10 .30
87 Brian Mitchell .10 .30
88 Hardy Nickerson .10 .30
89 Todd Lyght .10 .30
90 Barry Sanders 1.25 3.00
91 Robert Blackmon .10 .30
92 Larry Centers .20 .50
93 Jim Kelly .30 .75
94 Lamar Lathon .10 .30
95 Cris Carter .30 .75
96 Hugh Douglas .20 .50
97 Michael Strahan .20 .50
98 Lee Woodall .10 .30
99 Michael Irvin .30 .75
100 Marshall Faulk .40 1.00
101 Terance Mathis .10 .30
102 Eric Zeier .10 .30
103 Marty Carter .10 .30
104 Steve Tovar .10 .30
105 Isaac Bruce .30 .75
106 Tony Martin .20 .50
107 Dale Carter .10 .30
108 Terry Kirby .20 .50
109 Tyrone Hughes .10 .30
110 Bryce Paup .10 .30
111 Errict Rhett .20 .50
112 Ricky Watters .20 .50
113 Chris Chandler .20 .50
114 Edgar Bennett .20 .50
115 John Elway 1.50 4.00
116 Sam Mills .10 .30
117 Seth Joyner .10 .30
118 Jeff Lageman .10 .30
119 Chris Calloway .10 .30
120 Curtis Martin .60 1.50
121 Ken Harvey .10 .30
122 Eugene Daniel .10 .30
123 Tim Brown .30 .75
124 Mo Lewis .10 .30
125 Jeff Blake .30 .75
126 Jessie Tuggle .10 .30
127 Vinny Testaverde .20 .50
128 Chris Warren .20 .50
129 Terrell Davis .60 1.50
130 Greg Lloyd .20 .50
131 Deion Sanders .40 1.00
132 Derrick Thomas .30 .75
133 Darryll Lewis .10 .30
134 Reggie White .30 .75
135 Jerry Rice .75 2.00
136 Tony Banks RC .30 .75
137 Derrick Mayes RC .30 .75
138 Leeland McElroy RC .20 .50
139 Bryan Still RC .20 .50
140 Tim Biakabutuka RC .30 .75
141 Rickey Dudley RC .30 .75
142 Tory James RC .20 .50
143 Lawyer Milloy RC .30 .75
144 Mike Ulufale RC .10 .30
145 Bobby Engram RC .30 .75
146 Willie Anderson RC .10 .30
147 Terrell Owens RC 6.00 12.00
148 Jonathan Ogden RC 3.00 8.00
149 Darrius Johnson RC .10 .30
150 Kevin Hardy RC .30 .75
151 Simeon Rice RC .40 1.00
152 Alex Molden RC .10 .30
153 Cedric Jones RC .10 .30
154 Duane Clemons RC .10 .30
155 Karim Abdul-Jabbar RC .30 .75
156 Dedric Mathis RC .10 .30
157 John Michels RC .10 .30
158 Winslow Oliver RC .10 .30
159 Stepfret Williams RC .10 .30
160 Eddie Kennison RC .30 .75
161 Marcus Coleman RC .10 .30
162 Tedy Bruschi RC 6.00 15.00
163 Detron Smith RC .10 .30
164 Ray Lewis RC 15.00 40.00
165 Marvin Harrison RC 4.00 10.00
166 Je'rod Cherry RC .10 .30
167 Jerris McPhail RC .10 .30
168 Eric Moulds RC 1.00 2.50
169 Walt Harris RC .10 .30
170 Eddie George RC 3.00 8.00
171 Jermaine Lewis RC .30 .75
172 Jeff Lewis RC .20 .50
173 Ray Mickens RC .10 .30
174 Amani Toomer RC 2.00 5.00
175 Zach Thomas RC 1.25 3.00
176 Lawrence Phillips RC .20 .50
177 John Mobley RC .10 .30
178 Anthony Dorsett RC .10 .30
179 DeRon Jenkins RC .10 .30
180 Keyshawn Johnson RC 2.50 6.00

1996 Bowman's Best Atomic Refractors

*ATOMIC REF.VETS: 5X TO 12X
*ATOMIC REF.ROOKIES: 2X TO 5X
STATED ODDS 1:48 HOBBY, 1:80 RETAIL
162 Tedy Bruschi 50.00 100.00
164 Ray Lewis 300.00 600.00

1996 Bowman's Best Refractors

COMP.REF.SET (180) 125.00 250.00
*REFRACT.VETS: 1.5X TO 4X BASE CARD
*REFRACTOR ROOKIES: .8X TO 2X
STATED ODDS 1:12 HOBBY, 1:20 RETAIL
162 Tedy Bruschi 25.00 60.00
164 Ray Lewis 125.00 200.00

1996 Bowman's Best Bets

Randomly inserted in hobby packs at a rate of 1:12, and retail at 1:20 packs, this nine-card set features borderless color action player photos of nine 1996 NFL rookies and was printed using Topps' chromium technology. Parallel Refractor (1:48 odds hobby, 1:80 packs retail) and Atomic Refractor (1:96 odds hobby, 1:160 retail) cards were also produced.

COMPLETE SET (9) 15.00 30.00
STATED ODDS 1:12 HOBBY, 1:20 RETAIL
*ATOMIC REF: 1.2X TO 3X BASIC INSERTS
ATOMIC ODDS 1:96 HOB, 1:160 RET
*REFRACTORS: .8X TO 2X BASIC INSERTS
REFRACTOR ODDS 1:48 HOB, 1:80 RET
1 Keyshawn Johnson 1.50 4.00
2 Lawrence Phillips .10 .30
3 Tim Biakabutuka .25 .60
4 Eddie George 2.00 5.00
5 John Mobley .05 .15
6 Eddie Kennison .25 .60
7 Marvin Harrison 4.00 10.00
8 Amani Toomer 1.25 3.00
9 Bobby Engram .25 .60

1996 Bowman's Best Cuts

Randomly inserted in hobby packs at a rate of 1:24, and 1:40 retail, this 15-card set features color action player photos of NFL stars and was printed on a die cut chromium foil card stock. Parallel Refractor (1:48 odds hobby, 1:96 retail) and Atomic Refractor (1:96 odds hobby, 1:160 retail) cards were also produced.

COMPLETE SET (15) 30.00 80.00
STATED ODDS 1:24 HOBBY, 1:40 RETAIL
*ATOMIC REF: 1X TO 2.5X BASIC INSERTS
ATOMIC ODDS 1:96 HOB, 1:160 RET
*REFRACTORS: .6X TO 1.5X BASIC INSERTS
REFRACTOR ODDS 1:48 HOB. 1:96 RET
1 Dan Marino 5.00 12.00
2 Emmitt Smith 4.00 10.00
3 Rashaan Salaam .50 1.25
4 Herman Moore .50 1.25
5 Brett Favre 5.00 12.00
6 Marshall Faulk 1.25 3.00
7 John Elway 5.00 12.00
8 Curtis Martin 2.00 5.00
9 Deion Sanders 1.25 3.00
10 Jerry Rice 2.50 6.00
11 Terrell Davis 2.00 5.00
12 Kerry Collins 1.00 2.50
13 Steve Young 2.00 5.00
14 Troy Aikman 2.50 6.00
15 Barry Sanders 4.00 10.00

1996 Bowman's Best Mirror Images

Randomly inserted in hobby packs at a rate of 1:48, and 1:80 retail, this nine-card set features double-sided cards with color photos of four top players from the same position. One side displays an AFC veteran alongside an AFC young star. The opposite side shows an NFC veteran next to an NFC young star. Parallel Refractor (1:96 odds hobby, 1:160 retail) and Atomic Refractor (1:192 odds hobby, 1:320 retail) cards were also produced.

COMPLETE SET (9) 40.00 100.00
STATED ODDS 1:48 HOBBY, 1:80 RETAIL
*ATOMIC REF: .8X TO 2X BASIC INSERTS
ATOMIC ODDS 1:192 HOB, 1:320 RET
*REFRACTORS: .6X TO 1.5X BASIC INSERTS
REFRACTOR ODDS 1:96 HOB, 1:160 RET
1 Marino/Young/Coll/Brnll 10.00 25.00
2 Favre/Grb/Elway/Bleds 10.00 25.00
3 Aikmn/Frer/Harb/Blake 5.00 12.00
4 E.Smth/Rhett/Warr/Mrtin 7.50 20.00
5 B.Sand/Sala/T.Thm/T.Dvis 7.50 20.00
6 Hamp/Phill/Allen/Faulk 4.00 10.00
7 J.Rice/Brce/T.Brwn/Gallo 5.00 12.00
8 C.Carter Cnwy Pckns K.John. 3.00 8.00
9 Brooks Westb. Miller McDuf. 2.00 5.00

1996 Bowman's Best Super Bowl XXXI

*SUPER BOWL XXXI: 1.5X TO 4X BASIC CARDS

1997 Bowman's Best

The 1997 Bowman's Best set was issued in one series totalling 125 cards and was distributed in six-card packs with a suggested retail price of $5. The fronts feature color action photos of 95 veteran players with a gold design and 30 top rookies on silver-designed cards. The backs carry player information and statistics.

COMPLETE SET (125) 15.00 30.00
1 Brett Favre 1.50 4.00
2 Larry Centers .25 .60
3 Trent Dilfer .40 1.00
4 Rodney Hampton .25 .60
5 Wesley Walls .25 .60
6 Jerome Bettis .40 1.00
7 Keyshawn Johnson .40 1.00
8 Keenan McCardell .25 .60
9 Terry Allen .40 1.00
10 Troy Aikman .75 2.00
11 Tony Banks .25 .60
12 Ty Detmer .25 .60
13 Chris Chandler .25 .60
14 Marshall Faulk .50 1.25
15 Heath Shuler .15 .40
16 Stan Humphries .25 .60
17 Bryan Cox .15 .40
18 Chris Spielman .15 .40
19 Derrick Thomas .40 1.00
20 Steve Young .50 1.25
21 Desmond Howard .25 .60
22 Jeff Blake .25 .60
23 Michael Jackson .25 .60
24 Cris Carter .40 1.00
25 Joey Galloway .25 .60
26 Simeon Rice .25 .60
27 Reggie White .40 1.00
28 Dave Brown .15 .40
29 Mike Alstott .40 1.00
30 Emmitt Smith 1.25 3.00
31 Anthony Johnson .15 .40
32 Mark Brunell .50 1.25
33 Ricky Watters .25 .60
34 Terrell Davis .50 1.25
35 Ben Coates .25 .60
36 Gus Frerotte .15 .40
37 Andre Reed .25 .60
38 Isaac Bruce .40 1.00
39 Junior Seau .40 1.00
40 Eddie George .40 1.00
41 Adrian Murrell .25 .60
42 Jake Reed .25 .60
43 Karim Abdul-Jabbar .25 .60
44 Scott Mitchell .25 .60
45 Ki-Jana Carter .15 .40
46 Curtis Conway .25 .60
47 Jim Harbaugh .25 .60
48 Tim Brown .40 1.00
49 Mario Bates .15 .40
50 Jerry Rice .75 2.00
51 Byron Bam Morris .15 .40
52 Marcus Allen .40 1.00
53 Errict Rhett .15 .40
54 Steve McNair .50 1.25
55 Kerry Collins .40 1.00
56 Bert Emanuel .25 .60
57 Curtis Martin .50 1.25
58 Bryce Paup .15 .40
59 Brad Johnson .40 1.00
60 John Elway 1.50 4.00
61 Natrone Means .25 .60
62 Deion Sanders .40 1.00
63 Tony Martin .25 .60
64 Michael Westbrook .25 .60
65 Chris Calloway .15 .40
66 Antonio Freeman .40 1.00
67 Rob Johnson .40 1.00
68 Kent Graham .15 .40
69 O.J. McDuffie .25 .60

70 Barry Sanders 1.25 3.00
71 Chris Warren .25 .60
72 Kordell Stewart .40 1.00
73 Thurman Thomas .40 1.00
74 Marvin Harrison .40 1.00
75 Carl Pickens .25 .60
76 Brent Jones .15 .40
77 Irving Fryar .25 .60
78 Neil O'Donnell .25 .60
79 Elvis Grbac .25 .60
80 Drew Bledsoe .50 1.25
81 Shannon Sharpe .25 .60
82 Vinny Testaverde .25 .60
83 Chris Sanders .15 .40
84 Herman Moore .25 .60
85 Jeff George .25 .60
86 Bruce Smith .25 .60
87 Robert Smith .25 .60
88 Kevin Hardy .15 .40
89 Kevin Greene .25 .60
90 Dan Marino 1.50 4.00
91 Michael Irvin .40 1.00
92 Garrison Hearst .25 .60
93 Lake Dawson .15 .40
94 Lawrence Phillips .15 .40
95 Terry Glenn .40 1.00
96 Jake Plummer RC 2.00 5.00
97 Byron Hanspard RC .25 .60
98 Bryant Westbrook RC .15 .40
99 Troy Davis RC .25 .60
100 Danny Wuerffel RC .40 1.00
101 Tony Gonzalez RC 2.50 6.00
102 Jim Druckenmiller RC .25 .60
103 Kevin Lockett RC .25 .60
104 Renaldo Wynn RC .15 .40
105 James Farrior RC .40 1.00
106 Rae Carruth RC .15 .40
107 Tom Knight RC .15 .40
108 Corey Dillon RC 2.00 5.00
109 Kenny Holmes RC .40 1.00
110 Orlando Pace RC .40 1.00
111 Reidel Anthony RC .40 1.00
112 Chad Scott RC .25 .60
113 Antowain Smith RC 1.25 3.00
114 David LaFleur RC .15 .40
115 Yatil Green RC .25 .60
116 Darrell Russell RC .15 .40
117 Joey Kent RC .40 1.00
118 Darnell Autry RC .25 .60
119 Peter Boulware RC .40 1.00
120 Shawn Springs RC .25 .60
121 Ike Hilliard RC .60 1.50
122 Dwayne Rudd RC .40 1.00
123 Reinard Wilson RC .25 .60
124 Michael Booker RC .15 .40
125 Warrick Dunn RC 1.50 4.00

1997 Bowman's Best Atomic Refractors

COMPLETE SET (125) 300.00 600.00
*VETERANS: 3X TO 8X BASIC CARDS
*ROOKIE STARS: 1.5X TO 4X BASIC RC
ATOMIC REF.STATED ODDS 1:24
101 Tony Gonzalez 30.00 60.00

1997 Bowman's Best Refractors

COMPLETE SET (125) 200.00 400.00
*VETERANS: 2X TO 5X BASIC CARDS
*ROOKIES: 1.2X TO 3X BASIC RC
REFRACTOR STATED ODDS 1:12

1997 Bowman's Best Autographs

Randomly inserted in packs at the rate of one in 131, this 10-card set features autographed photos of seven rookies on silver design cards and three veterans on gold design ones. A Topps "Certified Autograph Issue" logo is stamped on each card. The cards are numbered and checklisted below according to their numbers in the base set.

COMPLETE SET (10) 75.00 150.00
BASE AUTOGRAPH STATED ODDS 1:131
*ATOMIC REFRACTORS: 1.5X TO 4X
ATOMIC REFRACTOR ODDS 1:4733
*REFRACTORS: .8X TO 2X
REFRACTOR STATED ODDS 1:1578
22 Jeff Blake 6.00 15.00
44 Scott Mitchell 6.00 15.00
47 Jim Harbaugh 12.00 30.00
99 Troy Davis 6.00 15.00
102 Jim Druckenmiller 6.00 15.00
113 Antowain Smith 12.50 30.00
114 David LaFleur 6.00 15.00
120 Shawn Springs 6.00 15.00
121 Ike Hilliard 7.50 20.00
125 Warrick Dunn 20.00 40.00

1997 Bowman's Best Cuts

Randomly inserted in packs at the rate of one in 24, this 20-card set features color action photos of NFL superstars printed on die-cut cards. The backs carry information about the player.

COMPLETE SET (20) 40.00 100.00
STATED ODDS 1:24
*ATOMIC REF: 1X TO 2.5X BASIC INSERTS
ATOMIC REF.STATED ODDS 1:96
*REFRACTORS: .6X TO 1.5X BASIC INSERTS
REFRACTOR STATED ODDS 1:48
BC1 Orlando Pace .60 1.50
BC2 Eddie George 1.25 3.00
BC3 John Elway 5.00 12.00
BC4 Tony Gonzalez 3.00 8.00
BC5 Brett Favre 5.00 12.00
BC6 Shawn Springs .40 1.00
BC7 Warrick Dunn 2.50 6.00
BC8 Troy Aikman 2.50 6.00
BC9 Terry Glenn 1.25 3.00
BC10 Dan Marino 5.00 12.00
BC11 Jake Plummer 2.50 6.00
BC12 Ike Hilliard 1.00 2.50
BC13 Emmitt Smith 4.00 10.00
BC14 Steve Young 1.50 4.00
BC15 Barry Sanders 4.00 10.00
BC16 Jim Druckenmiller .40 1.00
BC17 Drew Bledsoe 1.50 4.00
BC18 Antowain Smith 2.00 5.00
BC19 Mark Brunell 1.50 4.00
BC20 Jerry Rice 2.50 6.00

1997 Bowman's Best Mirror Images

Randomly inserted in packs at the rate of one in 48, this 10-card set features double-sided cards with color photos of an AFC veteran alongside an AFC up-and-coming star on one side and an NFC veteran beside an NFC young star on the other side.

COMPLETE SET (10) 50.00 120.00
STATED ODDS 1:48
*ATOMIC REFRACT: 1X TO 2.5X BASIC INSERTS
ATOMIC REF.STATED ODDS 1:192
*REFRACTORS: .6X TO 1.5X BASIC INSERTS
REFRACTOR STATED ODDS 1:96
MI1 Favre/Frerotte/Elway/Brunell 10.00 25.00
MI2 Young/Banks/Marino/Bledsoe 10.00 25.00
MI3 Aikman/Collins/Testa/Stewart 6.00 15.00
MI4 Smith/Levens/M.All/E.Geor 7.50 20.00
MI5 B.Sand/Rhett/Thom/C.Martin 7.50 20.00
MI6 T.Davis/Watt/J.And/Warren 5.00 12.00
MI7 Rice/Bruce/Martin/Harrison 6.00 15.00
MI8 Moore/Conway/Brown/Glenn 2.00 5.00
MI9 Irvin/Kennis/Pick/K.Johnson 1.50 4.00
MI10 Walls/J.Dunn/Sharpe/Dudley 1.50 4.00

1997-98 Bowman's Best Jumbos

This set of 16-cards was sold in complete set form (for $59.95) directly to collectors through Topps' TSC Zone magazine/catalog. Each set included 16-cards, of which three were Refractors and one an Atomic Refractor. A certificate of authenticity accompanied each set with each numbered of 500-sets produced. Thus these "factory sets" would essentially need to be broken to put together a complete 16-card set of any one version. Each card is a parallel to its base 1997 Bowman's Best card except for the card numbering. Super Bowl and Pro Bowl logo versions were produced as well and distributed at those corresponding events.

COMPLETE SET (16) 24.00 60.00
*ATOMIC REFRACT: 2X TO 5X BASE CARD
*REFRACTORS: 1.2X TO 3X BASE CARD
1 Brett Favre 4.00 10.00
2 Barry Sanders 4.00 10.00
3 Emmitt Smith 3.20 8.00
4 John Elway 4.00 10.00
5 Tim Brown 1.25 3.00
6 Eddie George .75 2.00
7 Troy Aikman 2.00 5.00
8 Drew Bledsoe 1.50 4.00
9 Dan Marino 4.00 10.00
10 Jerry Rice 2.00 5.00
11 Junior Seau .75 2.00
12 Antowain Smith .75 2.00
13 Warrick Dunn 1.25 3.00
14 Jim Druckenmiller .50 1.25
15 Terrell Davis 3.20 8.00
16 Curtis Martin 1.20 3.00

1997-98 Bowman's Best Pro Bowl Jumbos

This oversized card (4" by 6") set was distributed by Topps to card dealers at the 1998 Pro Bowl show in Hawaii. Each card is essentially an enlarged parallel of a base 1997 Bowman's Best football card. A Pro Bowl logo has been added to each card as well as an additional card number (of 16-cards in the set). Both Refractor and Atomic Refractor parallels were produced for all 16-cards in the set. Reportedly, just 100-Refractor sets and 25-Atomic Refractor sets were produced.

COMPLETE SET (16) 24.00 60.00
*ATOMIC REFRACT: 15X TO 30X BASE CARD
*REFRACTORS: 6X TO 15X BASE CARD
1 Brett Favre 4.00 10.00
2 Barry Sanders 4.00 10.00
3 Emmitt Smith 3.20 8.00
4 John Elway 4.00 10.00
5 Tim Brown .80 2.00
6 Eddie George 1.60 4.00
7 Troy Aikman 2.00 5.00
8 Drew Bledsoe 2.00 5.00
9 Dan Marino 4.00 10.00
10 Jerry Rice 2.00 5.00
11 Junior Seau .50 1.25
12 Antowain Smith 1.20 3.00
13 Warrick Dunn 1.50 4.00
14 Jim Druckenmiller .50 1.25
15 Terrell Davis 3.20 8.00
16 Curtis Martin 1.20 3.00

1997-98 Bowman's Best Pro Bowl Promos 5X7

This six card set was issued to promote the Bowman brand and feature players in the 1998 Pro Bowl. These cards were issued at the Pro Bowl show in Hawaii and at their measurement of 5"x7" are slightly bigger than the 4' by 6' versions usually seen.

COMPLETE SET (6) 16.00 40.00
*ATOMIC REFRACT: 15X TO 30X BASE CARD
*REFRACTORS: 7.5X TO 15X BASE CARD
1 Brett Favre 4.00 10.00
2 Barry Sanders 4.00 10.00
3 Emmitt Smith 3.20 8.00
4 John Elway 4.00 10.00
5 Tim Brown 1.20 3.00
6 Eddie George 1.60 4.00

1997-98 Bowman's Best Super Bowl Jumbos

This oversized card (4" by 6") set was distributed by Topps to card dealers at the 1998 Super Bowl Show. Each card is essentially an enlarged parallel of a base 1997 Bowman's Best football card. The Super Bowl logo was added to each card.

COMPLETE SET (16) 24.00 60.00
*REFRACTORS: 6X TO 15X BASE CARD
1 Brett Favre 4.00 10.00
2 Barry Sanders 4.00 10.00
3 Emmitt Smith 3.20 8.00
4 John Elway 4.00 10.00
5 Tim Brown .80 2.00
6 Eddie George 1.60 4.00
7 Troy Aikman 2.00 5.00
8 Drew Bledsoe 2.00 5.00
9 Dan Marino 4.00 10.00
10 Jerry Rice 2.00 5.00
11 Junior Seau .50 1.25
12 Antowain Smith 1.20 3.00
13 Warrick Dunn 1.50 4.00
14 Jim Druckenmiller .50 1.25
15 Terrell Davis 3.20 8.00
16 Curtis Martin 1.20 3.00

1998 Bowman's Best

The 1998 Bowman's Best set was issued in one series totalling 125 cards and was distributed in six-card packs with a suggested retail price of $5. The fronts feature color action photos of 100 key veterans with a radiant gold design and 25 top rookies printed on silver-designed cards all printed on 26 pt. stock. The backs carry player information.

COMPLETE SET (125) 30.00 80.00
1 Emmitt Smith 1.25 3.00
2 Reggie White .40 1.00
3 Jake Plummer .40 1.00
4 Ike Hilliard .15 .40
5 Isaac Bruce .15 .40
6 Trent Dilfer .40 1.00
7 Ricky Watters .25 .60
8 Jeff George .25 .60
9 Wayne Chrebet .40 1.00
10 Brett Favre 1.50 4.00
11 Terry Allen .40 1.00
12 Bert Emanuel .15 .40
13 Andre Reed .25 .60
14 Andre Rison .25 .60
15 Jeff Blake .25 .60
16 Steve McNair .40 1.00
17 Joey Galloway .25 .60
18 Irving Fryar .25 .60
19 Dorsey Levens .40 1.00
20 Jerry Rice .75 2.00
21 Kerry Collins .25 .60
22 Michael Jackson .15 .40
23 Kordell Stewart .40 1.00
24 Junior Seau .40 1.00
25 Jimmy Smith .25 .60
26 Michael Westbrook .25 .60
27 Eddie George .40 1.00
28 Cris Carter .40 1.00
29 Jason Sehorn .25 .60
30 Warrick Dunn .40 1.00
31 Garrison Hearst .40 1.00
32 Erik Kramer .15 .40
33 Chris Chandler .25 .60
34 Michael Irvin .40 1.00
35 Marshall Faulk .50 1.25
36 Warren Moon .40 1.00
37 Rickey Dudley .15 .40
38 Drew Bledsoe .60 1.50
39 Antowain Smith .40 1.00
40 Terrell Davis .40 1.00
41 Gus Frerotte .15 .40
42 Robert Brooks .25 .60
43 Tony Banks .25 .60
44 Terrell Owens .40 1.00
45 Edgar Bennett .15 .40
46 Rob Moore .25 .60
47 J.J. Stokes .25 .60
48 Yancey Thigpen .15 .40
49 Elvis Grbac .25 .60
50 John Elway 1.50 4.00
51 Charles Johnson .15 .40
52 Karim Abdul-Jabbar .40 1.00
53 Carl Pickens .25 .60
54 Peter Boulware .15 .40
55 Chris Warren .15 .40
56 Terance Mathis .25 .60
57 Andre Hastings .15 .40
58 Jake Reed .25 .60
59 Mike Alstott .15 .40
60 Mark Brunell .40 1.00
61 Herman Moore .25 .60
62 Troy Aikman .75 2.00
63 Fred Lane .15 .40
64 Rod Smith .25 .60
65 Terry Glenn .40 1.00
66 Jerome Bettis .40 1.00
67 Derrick Thomas .40 1.00
68 Marvin Harrison .40 1.00
69 Adrian Murrell .15 .40
70 Curtis Martin .40 1.00
71 Bobby Hoying .25 .60
72 Darrell Green .25 .60
73 Sean Dawkins .15 .40
74 Robert Smith .40 1.00
75 Antonio Freeman .40 1.00
76 Scott Mitchell .25 .60
77 Curtis Conway .25 .60
78 Rae Carruth .15 .40
79 Jamal Anderson .40 1.00
80 Dan Marino 1.50 4.00
81 Brad Johnson .40 1.00
82 Danny Kanell .25 .60
83 Charlie Garner .25 .60
84 Rob Johnson .25 .60
85 Natrone Means .25 .60
86 Tim Brown .40 1.00
87 Keyshawn Johnson .40 1.00
88 Ben Coates .25 .60
89 Derrick Alexander .25 .60
90 Steve Young .50 1.25
91 Shannon Sharpe .25 .60
92 Corey Dillon .40 1.00
93 Bruce Smith .25 .60
94 Errict Rhett .25 .60
95 Jim Harbaugh .15 .40
96 Napoleon Kaufman .40 1.00
97 Glenn Foley .25 .60
98 Tony Gonzalez .40 1.00
99 Keenan McCardell .25 .60
100 Barry Sanders 1.25 3.00
101 Charles Woodson RC 2.00 5.00
102 Tim Dwight RC 1.00 2.50
103 Marcus Nash RC .50 1.25
104 Joe Jurevicius RC 1.00 2.50
105 Jacquez Green RC .75 2.00
106 Kevin Dyson RC 1.00 2.50
107 Keith Brooking RC 1.00 2.50
108 Andre Wadsworth RC .75 2.00
109 Randy Moss RC 5.00 12.00
110 Robert Edwards RC .75 2.00
111 Pat Johnson RC .75 2.00
112 Peyton Manning RC 15.00 40.00
113 Duane Starks RC .50 1.25
114 Grant Wistrom RC .75 2.00
115 Anthony Simmons RC .75 2.00
116 Takeo Spikes RC 1.00 2.50
117 Tony Simmons RC .75 2.00
118 Jerome Pathon RC 1.00 2.50
119 Ryan Leaf RC 1.00 2.50
120 Skip Hicks RC .75 2.00
121 Curtis Enis RC .50 1.25
122 Germane Crowell RC .75 2.00
123 John Avery RC .75 2.00
124 Hines Ward RC 5.00 10.00
125 Fred Taylor RC 1.50 4.00

1998 Bowman's Best Atomic Refractors

*VETS/100: 10X TO 25X BASIC CARDS
*ROOKIES: 4X TO 10X BASIC CARDS
STATED ODDS 1:103
112 Peyton Manning 200.00 350.00

1998 Bowman's Best Refractors

COMPLETE SET (125) 250.00 500.00
*STARS: 3X TO 8X BASIC CARDS
*ROOKIES: 1.2X TO 3X BASIC CARDS
STATED ODDS 1:25

1998 Bowman's Best Autographs

Randomly inserted in packs at the rate of one in 158, this 20-card set features cards signed by 10 different players. Each player has two card versions with different poses on each. The seven veteran cards display a gold design with the three rookie cards have silver backgrounds. Each card is stamped with the Topps "Certified Autograph Issue" logo. A refractive parallel version of this set was also produced and seeded in packs at the rate of 1:840. An Atomic Refractor parallel version was produced and seeded at the rate of 1:2,521 packs.

STATED ODDS 1:158
1A Jake Plummer 10.00 25.00
1B Jake Plummer 10.00 25.00
2A Jason Sehorn 6.00 15.00
2B Jason Sehorn 6.00 15.00
3A Corey Dillon 10.00 25.00
3B Corey Dillon 10.00 25.00
4A Tim Brown 15.00 40.00
4B Tim Brown 15.00 40.00
5A Keenan McCardell 6.00 15.00
5B Keenan McCardell 6.00 15.00
6A Kordell Stewart 7.50 20.00
6B Kordell Stewart 7.50 20.00
7A Peyton Manning 300.00 500.00
7B Peyton Manning 300.00 500.00
8A Danny Kanell 6.00 15.00
8B Danny Kanell 6.00 15.00
9A Fred Taylor 10.00 25.00
9B Fred Taylor 10.00 25.00
10A Curtis Enis 6.00 15.00
10B Curtis Enis 6.00 15.00

1998 Bowman's Best Autographs Atomic Refractors

*ATOMIC REF: 1.2X TO 3X BASIC AU
7A Peyton Manning 1000.00 1800.00
7B Peyton Manning 1000.00 1800.00

1998 Bowman's Best Autographs Refractors

*REFRACTOR: .8X TO 2X BASIC AU
7A Peyton Manning 350.00 600.00
7B Peyton Manning 350.00 600.00

1998 Bowman's Best Mirror Image Fusion

Randomly inserted in packs at the rate of one in 48, this 20-card set features color action photos of two top players in the same position printed on double-sided die-cut cards. A refractor parallel version of this set was produced, seeded in packs at the rate of 1:630, and sequentially numbered to 100. An Atomic Refractor parallel version was also produced, seeded in packs at the rate of 1:2,521, and sequentially numbered to 25.

COMPLETE SET (20) 75.00 150.00
STATED ODDS 1:48
*ATOMIC REF/25: 4X TO 10X BASIC INSERTS
*REFRACTOR/100: 1.5X TO 4X BASIC INSERTS
MI1 T.Davis J.Avery 2.50 6.00
MI2 E.Smith C.Enis 6.00 15.00
MI3 B.Sanders S.Hicks 6.00 15.00
MI4 E.George R.Edwards 2.50 6.00
MI5 J.Bettis F.Taylor 2.50 6.00
MI6 M.Brunell R.Loaf 2.50 6.00
MI7 J.Elway B.Griese 7.50 20.00
MI8 D.Marino P.Manning 12.00 30.00
MI9 B.Favre C.Batch 6.00 15.00
MI10 D.Bledsoe J.Quinn 3.00 8.00
MI11 T.Brown K.Dyson 2.50 6.00
MI12 H.Moore G.Crowell 1.50 4.00
MI13 J.Galloway J.Pathon 1.50 4.00
MI14 C.Carter J.Green 2.50 6.00
MI15 J.Rice R.Moss 12.50 25.00
MI16 J.Seau T.Spikes 2.50 6.00
MI17 J.Randle J.Peter 1.50 4.00
MI18 R.White A.Wadsworth 1.50 4.00
MI19 P.Boulware A.Simmons 1.50 4.00
MI20 D.Thomas B.Simmons 1.50 4.00

1998 Bowman's Best Performers

Randomly inserted in packs at the rate of one in 12, this 10-card set features color action photos of 1997 top college players. The backs carry player information. A refractor parallel version of this set was produced, seeded in packs at the rate of 1:630, and sequentially numbered to 200. An Atomic Refractor parallel version was also produced, seeded in packs at the rate of 1:2,521, and sequentially numbered to 50.

COMPLETE SET (10) 20.00 40.00
STATED ODDS 1:12
*ATOMIC REFRACTOR/50: 4X TO 10X
ATOMIC REFRACTOR/50 ODDS 1:2521
*REFRACTOR/200: 1.5X TO 4X
REFRACTOR/200 ODDS 1:630
BP1 Peyton Manning 10.00 25.00
BP2 Charles Woodson 2.50 6.00
BP3 Skip Hicks .75 2.00
BP4 Andre Wadsworth .75 2.00
BP5 Randy Moss 6.00 15.00
BP6 Marcus Nash .50 1.25
BP7 Ahman Green 2.50 6.00
BP8 Anthony Simmons .75 2.00
BP9 Tavian Banks 1.25 3.00
BP10 Ryan Leaf 1.00 2.50

1998-99 Bowman's Best Super Bowl Promos

These cards were distributed as a wrapper redemption at the 1999 Super Bowl Card Show. Each is essentially a parallel version to the base 1998 Bowman's Best card including the Super Bowl XXXIII logo on the cardfronts.

COMPLETE SET (6) 16.00 40.00
101 Charles Woodson 1.50 4.00
110 Robert Edwards 1.00 2.50
112 Peyton Manning 15.00 25.00
119 Ryan Leaf 2.00 5.00
121 Curtis Enis 1.00 2.50
125 Fred Taylor 4.00 8.00

1999 Bowman's Best Previews

COMPLETE SET (6) 6.00 15.00
PP1 Brett Favre 2.00 5.00
PP2 Warrick Dunn .75 2.00
PP3 Herman Moore .60 1.50
PP4 Tim Couch .75 2.00
PP5 Curtis Martin 1.00 2.50
PP6 Mark Brunell .75 2.00

1999 Bowman's Best

Released as a 133-card set, the 1999 Bowman's Best is comprised of 90 Star Veteran cards, 10 Best Performers cards and 33 Rookie cards inserted at one per pack. Base cards are all foil and feature laser etched highlights in the background. Bowman's Best was packaged in 24-pack boxes with six cards per pack.

COMPLETE SET (133) 30.00 80.00
1 Randy Moss .25 .60
2 Skip Hicks .20 .50
3 Robert Smith .20 .50
4 Drew Bledsoe .25 .60
5 Tim Brown .30 .75
6 Marshall Faulk .25 .60
7 Terance Mathis .20 .50
8 Sean Dawkins .20 .50
9 Ed McCaffrey .25 .60
10 Jamal Anderson .25 .60
11 Antonio Freeman .25 .60
12 Terry Kirby .20 .50
13 Vinny Testaverde .20 .50
14 Eddie George .25 .60
15 Ricky Watters .25 .60
16 Johnnie Morton .25 .60
17 Natrone Means .25 .60
18 Terry Glenn .25 .60
19 Michael Westbrook .20 .50
20 Doug Flutie .30 .75
21 Jake Plummer .20 .50
22 Darnay Scott .20 .50
23 Andre Rison .25 .60
24 Jon Kitna .20 .50
25 Dan Marino .60 1.50
26 Ike Hilliard .20 .50
27 Warrick Dunn .20 .50
28 Jerome Bettis .30 .75
29 Curtis Conway .25 .60
30 Emmitt Smith .50 1.25
31 Jimmy Smith .25 .60
32 Isaac Bruce .30 .75
33 Jerry Rice .75 2.00
34 Curtis Martin .25 .60
35 Steve McNair .25 .60
36 Jeff Blake .25 .60
37 Rob Moore .20 .50
38 Dorsey Levens .25 .60
39 Terrell Davis .25 .60
40 John Elway .50 1.25
41 Trent Dilfer .20 .50
42 Joey Galloway .25 .60
43 Keyshawn Johnson .25 .60
44 O.J. McDuffie .25 .60
45 Fred Taylor .20 .50
46 Andre Reed .30 .75
47 Frank Sanders .20 .50
48 Keenan McCardell .25 .60
49 Elvis Grbac .20 .50
50 Barry Sanders .50 1.25
51 Terrell Owens .25 .60
52 Trent Green .20 .50
53 Brad Johnson .25 .60
54 Rich Gannon .25 .60
55 Randall Cunningham .25 .60
56 Tony Martin .25 .60
57 Rod Smith .25 .60
58 Eric Moulds .20 .50
59 Yancey Thigpen .20 .50
60 Brett Favre .60 1.50
61 Cris Carter .30 .75
62 Marvin Harrison .25 .60
63 Chris Chandler .25 .60
64 Antowain Smith .20 .50
65 Carl Pickens .25 .60
66 Shannon Sharpe .25 .60
67 Mike Alstott .20 .50
68 J.J. Stokes .20 .50
69 Ben Coates .25 .60
70 Peyton Manning 1.00 2.50
71 Duce Staley .20 .50
72 Michael Irvin .30 .75
73 Tim Biakabutuka .25 .60
74 Priest Holmes .20 .50
75 Steve Young .40 1.00
76 Jerome Pathon .20 .60
77 Wayne Chrebet .20 .50
78 Bert Emanuel .25 .60
79 Curtis Enis .20 .50
80 Mark Brunell .25 .60
81 Herman Moore .25 .60
82 Corey Dillon .20 .50
83 Jim Harbaugh .25 .60
84 Gary Brown .20 .50
85 Kordell Stewart .20 .50
86 Garrison Hearst .20 .50
87 Rocket Ismail .25 .60
88 Charlie Batch .20 .50
89 Napoleon Kaufman .20 .50
90 Troy Aikman .40 1.00
91 Brett Favre BP .50 1.25
92 Randy Moss BP .20 .50
93 Terrell Davis BP .20 .50
94 Barry Sanders BP .40 1.00
95 Peyton Manning BP .75 2.00
96 Troy Edwards BP .15 .40
97 Cade McNown BP .15 .40
98 Edgerrin James BP .25 .60
99 Torry Holt BP .30 .75
100 Tim Couch BP .20 .50
101 Chris Claiborne RC .40 1.00
102 Brock Huard RC .40 1.00
103 Amos Zereoue RC .40 1.00
104 Sedrick Irvin RC .40 1.00
105 Kevin Faulk RC .40 1.00
106 Ebenezer Ekuban RC .40 1.00
107 Daunte Culpepper RC .60 1.50
108 Rob Konrad RC .40 1.00
109 James Johnson RC .40 1.00
110 Kurt Warner RC 4.00 10.00
111 Mike Cloud RC .40 1.00
112 Andy Katzenmoyer RC .50 1.25
113 Jevon Kearse RC .50 1.25
114 Akili Smith RC .40 1.00
115 Edgerrin James RC .60 1.50
116 Cecil Collins RC .40 1.00
117 Chris McAlister RC .40 1.00
118 Donovan McNabb RC 2.50 6.00
119 Kevin Johnson RC .50 1.25
120 Torry Holt RC .75 2.00
121 Antoine Winfield RC .40 1.00
122 Michael Bishop RC .50 1.25
123 Joe Germaine RC .50 1.25
124 David Boston RC .40 1.00
125 D'Wayne Bates RC .40 1.00
126 Champ Bailey RC .75 2.00
127 Cade McNown RC .40 1.00
128 Shaun King RC .40 1.00
129 Peerless Price RC .40 1.00
130 Troy Edwards RC .40 1.00
131 Karsten Bailey RC .40 1.00
132 Tim Couch RC .50 1.25
133 Ricky Williams RC .60 1.50
C1 Rookie Class Photo 2.00 5.00

1999 Bowman's Best Atomic Refractors

*VETS 1-100: 6X TO 15X BASIC CARDS
*ROOKIES 101-133: 4X TO 10X
1-133 ATOMIC REF/100 ODDS 1:69
C1 ROOKIE CLASS/35 ODDS 1:26,880

1999 Bowman's Best Refractors

*VETS 1-100: 3X TO 8X BASIC CARDS
*ROOKIES 101-133: 2X TO 5X
1-133 REFRACTOR/400 ODDS 1:17
C1 ROOKIE CLASS REF/125 ODDS 1:7429

1999 Bowman's Best Autographs

Randomly inserted, this 3-card set features authentic autographs of Fred Taylor and Jake Plummer with odds of one in every 915 packs, and Randy Moss who is found one in every 9129 packs. Some cards were issued via exchange cards that carried an expiration date of 9/30/2000. Each autographed card carries the "Topps Certified Autograph Stamp."

A1-A2 STATED ODDS 1:915
ROY1 STATED ODDS 1:9129
A1 Fred Taylor 12.50 30.00
A2 Jake Plummer 10.00 25.00
ROY1 Randy Moss ROY 50.00 100.00

1999 Bowman's Best Franchise Best

Randomly inserted in packs at the rate of one in 20, this 9-card set features a franchise player who carries his team. Card backs carry an "FB" prefix.

COMPLETE SET (9) 25.00 50.00
STATED ODDS 1:20
FB1 Dan Marino 5.00 12.00
FB2 Fred Taylor 1.50 4.00
FB3 Emmitt Smith 3.00 8.00
FB4 Terrell Davis 1.50 4.00
FB5 Brett Favre 5.00 12.00
FB6 Tim Couch 1.50 4.00
FB7 Peyton Manning 5.00 12.00
FB8 Eddie George 1.50 4.00
FB9 Randy Moss 4.00 10.00

1999 Bowman's Best Franchise Favorites

Randomly inserted in packs at the rate of one in 153, this 2-card set features franchise favorites of yesterday and today. Card backs carry an "F" prefix.

STATED ODDS 1:153
F1 T.Dorsett R.Staubach 4.00 10.00
F2 R.Moss F.Tarkenton 6.00 15.00

1999 Bowman's Best Franchise Favorites Autographs

Randomly inserted, this 6-card set features authentic autographs of past and present NFL stars. Card FA1 can be found inserted at one in 4599 packs, Cards FA2 and FA5 can be found inserted at one in 1017 packs, Cards FA3 and FA6 combined are inserted at one in 9129, and Card FA4 is inserted at one in 9129 packs for an overall ration of one in 703.

FA1 STATED ODDS 1:4599
FA2/FA5 COMBINED STATED ODDS 1:1017
FA3/FA6 COMBINED STATED ODDS 1:9129
FA4 STATED ODDS 1:9129
OVERALL STATED ODDS 1:703
FA1 Tony Dorsett 35.00 60.00
FA2 Roger Staubach 50.00 80.00
FA3 T.Dorsett/R.Staubach 90.00 150.00
FA4 Randy Moss 50.00 100.00
FA5 Fran Tarkenton 30.00 50.00
FA6 R.Moss/F.Tarkenton 100.00 200.00

1999 Bowman's Best Future Foundations

Randomly inserted in packs at the rate of one in 20, this 18-card set features top rookies who are expected to lead their teams in the years to come. Card backs carry an "FF" prefix.

COMPLETE SET (18) 25.00 50.00
STATED ODDS 1:20
FF1 Tim Couch .60 1.50
FF2 David Boston .60 1.50
FF3 Donovan McNabb 3.00 8.00
FF4 Troy Edwards .60 1.25
FF5 Ricky Williams 1.25 3.00
FF6 Daunte Culpepper 2.50 6.00
FF7 Torry Holt 1.50 4.00
FF8 Cade McNown .50 1.25
FF9 Akili Smith .50 1.25
FF10 Edgerrin James 2.50 6.00
FF11 Cecil Collins .30 .75
FF12 Peerless Price .60 1.50
FF13 Kevin Johnson .60 1.50
FF14 Champ Bailey .75 2.00
FF15 Mike Cloud .50 1.25
FF16 D'Wayne Bates .50 1.25
FF17 Shaun King .50 1.25
FF18 James Johnson .50 1.25

1999 Bowman's Best Honor Roll

Randomly inserted in packs at the rate of one in 40, this 8-card set features past Heisman Trophy winners and #1 draft picks who have proven their worth in the NFL. Card backs carry an "H" prefix.

COMPLETE SET (8) 20.00 40.00
STATED ODDS 1:40
H1 Peyton Manning 6.00 15.00
H2 Drew Bledsoe 2.50 6.00
H3 Doug Flutie 2.00 5.00
H4 Tim Couch 2.00 5.00
H5 Charles Woodson 1.25 3.00
H6 Ricky Williams 2.50 6.00
H7 Tim Brown 2.00 5.00
H8 Eddie George 2.00 5.00

1999 Bowman's Best Legacy

Randomly inserted in packs at the rate of one in 102, this 3-card set features Texas Legends and Heisman Trophy Winners Ricky Williams and Earl Campbell. Each player is featured on his own card which is printed on 26-point stock, and on a combination card featuring both players. Card backs carry an "L" prefix.

COMPLETE SET (3) 10.00 25.00
STATED ODDS 1:102
L1 Ricky Williams 3.00 8.00
L2 Earl Campbell 3.00 8.00
L3 R.Williams E.Campbell 6.00 15.00

1999 Bowman's Best Legacy Autographs

Randomly inserted, this 3-card set parallels the base Legacy insert set with cards that feature authentic autographs. LA1 odds are one in 4599 packs, LA2 odds are one in 2040, and the combination card, LA3 is liseted at one in 18108 packs giving this insert set total odds of one in 1311. Card backs carry an "LA" prefix.

LA1 STATED ODDS 1:4599
LA2 STATED ODDS 1:2040
LA3 STATED ODDS 1:18,108
OVERALL STATED ODDS 1:1311
LA1 Ricky Williams 20.00 50.00
LA2 Earl Campbell 20.00 50.00
LA3 R.Williams/E.Campbell 100.00 200.00

1999 Bowman's Best Rookie Locker Room Autographs

Randomly inserted, this set features authentic autographs from some of this year's top rookies. R1, R4, and R5 were inserted one in every 305 packs, and R2 and R3 were inserted 1:915 packs on average. Some cards were issued via mail redemptions that carried an expiration date of 9/30/2000. Donovan McNabb (#RA2) never signed cards for the set.

RA1/RA4/RA5 STATED ODDS 1:305
RA2/RA3 STATED ODDS 1:915
RA1 Tim Couch 7.50 20.00
RA3 Edgerrin James 20.00 50.00
RA4 David Boston 7.50 20.00
RA5 Torry Holt 10.00 25.00

1999 Bowman's Best Rookie Locker Room Jerseys

Randomly inserted in packs at the rate one in 229 packs, this 4-card set features swatches of game-used jerseys from some of the hottest 1999 rookies. The cards were skip numbered and the backs carry an "RU" prefix. Some cards were issued via mail redemptions that carried an expiration date of 9/30/2000.

STATED ODDS 1:229
RU2 Donovan McNabb 25.00 60.00
RU3 Kevin Faulk 7.50 20.00
RU5 Torry Holt 12.50 30.00
RU6 Ricky Williams 12.50 30.00

2000 Bowman's Best

Released in mid-November 2000, Bowman's Best features a 150-card base set consisting of 90 veteran cards, 10 dual player Best Performer cards, and 50 rookies inserted at the rate of one in 11 and sequentially numbered to 1499. Base cards are all refractive foil with a border along the top and full beed photography along the sides and bottom. Bowman's Best was packaged in 24-pack boxes with packs containing five cards and carried a suggested retail price of $5.00.

COMP.SET w/o SP's (100) 7.50 20.00
1 Troy Edwards .20 .50
2 Kurt Warner .50 1.25
3 Steve McNair .25 .60
4 Terry Glenn .25 .60
5 Charlie Batch .20 .50
6 Patrick Jeffers .20 .50
7 Jake Plummer .20 .50
8 Derrick Alexander .20 .50
9 Joey Galloway .25 .60
10 Tony Banks .20 .50
11 Robert Smith .20 .50
12 Jerry Rice .75 2.00
13 Jeff Garcia .20 .50
14 Michael Westbrook .20 .50
15 Curtis Conway .25 .60
16 Brian Griese .20 .50
17 Peyton Manning .75 2.00
18 Daunte Culpepper .25 .60
19 Frank Sanders .20 .50
20 Muhsin Muhammad .20 .50
21 Corey Dillon .20 .50
22 Brett Favre .60 1.50
23 Warrick Dunn .20 .50
24 Tim Brown .30 .75
25 Kerry Collins .20 .50
26 Brad Johnson .25 .60
27 Rocket Ismail .25 .60
28 Jamal Anderson .25 .60
29 Jimmy Smith .25 .60
30 Torry Holt .25 .60
31 Duce Staley .20 .50
32 Drew Bledsoe .25 .60
33 Jerome Bettis .30 .75
34 Keyshawn Johnson .25 .60
35 Fred Taylor .20 .50
36 Akili Smith .20 .50
37 Rob Johnson .25 .60
38 Elvis Grbac .20 .50
39 Antonio Freeman .25 .60
40 Curtis Enis .20 .50
41 Terance Mathis .20 .50
42 Terrell Davis .25 .60
43 Randy Moss .25 .60
44 Jon Kitna .20 .50
45 Curtis Martin .25 .60
46 Terrell Owens .25 .60
47 Robert Smith .20 .50
48 Albert Connell .20 .50
49 Edgerrin James .25 .60
50 Tony Gonzalez .25 .60
51 Eric Moulds .25 .60
52 Natrone Means .20 .50
53 Carl Pickens .25 .60
54 Mark Brunell .25 .60
55 Rob Moore .20 .50
56 Marshall Faulk .25 .60
57 Stephen Davis .20 .50
58 Rich Gannon .25 .60
59 Ricky Williams .25 .60
60 Emmitt Smith .50 1.25
61 Germane Crowell .20 .50
62 Doug Flutie .25 .60
63 O.J. McDuffie .25 .60
64 Chris Chandler .25 .60
65 Qadry Ismail .20 .50
66 Tim Couch .25 .60
67 James Stewart .20 .50
68 Marvin Harrison .25 .60
69 Cris Carter .30 .75
70 Cade McNown .20 .50
71 Marcus Robinson .25 .60
72 Steve Beuerlein .25 .60
73 Jevon Kearse .20 .50
74 Eddie George .25 .60
75 Donovan McNabb .25 .60
76 Jeff Blake .25 .60
77 Wayne Chrebet .20 .50
78 Kordell Stewart .20 .50
79 Steve Young .40 1.00
80 Mike Alstott .20 .50
81 Ricky Watters .25 .60
82 Charlie Garner .25 .60
83 Troy Aikman .40 1.00
84 Dorsey Levens .25 .60
85 Ike Hilliard .20 .50
86 Shaun King .20 .50
87 Isaac Bruce .30 .75
88 Tyrone Wheatley .20 .50
89 Amani Toomer .20 .50
90 Ed McCaffrey .25 .60
91 E.James M.Faulk BP .15 .40
92 D.Bledsoe B.Johnson BP .15 .40
93 J.Smith R.Moss BP .15 .40
94 E.George S.Davis BP .20 .50
95 M.Brunell T.Aikman BP .25 .60
96 M.Harrison C.Carter BP .20 .50
97 C.Martin E.Smith BP .30 .75
98 T.Brown I.Bruce BP .20 .50
99 F.Taylor R.Williams BP .15 .40
100 K.Warner P.Manning BP .50 1.25
101 Shaun Alexander RC 2.50 6.00
102 Thomas Jones RC 2.00 5.00
103 Courtney Brown RC 2.00 5.00
104 Curtis Keaton RC 1.50 4.00
105 Jerry Porter RC 2.50 6.00
106 Corey Simon RC 2.00 5.00
107 Dez White RC 1.50 4.00
108 Jamal Lewis RC 2.50 6.00
109 Ron Dayne RC 2.50 6.00
110 R.Jay Soward RC 1.50 4.00
111 Tee Martin RC 1.50 4.00
112 Brian Urlacher RC 8.00 20.00
113 Reuben Droughns RC 1.50 4.00
114 Travis Taylor RC 1.50 4.00
115 Plaxico Burress RC 2.00 5.00
116 Chad Pennington RC 2.00 5.00
117 Sylvester Morris RC 1.50 4.00
118 Ron Dugans RC 1.50 4.00
119 Joe Hamilton RC 1.50 4.00
120 Chris Redman RC 1.50 4.00
121 Trung Canidate RC 1.50 4.00
122 J.R. Redmond RC 1.50 4.00
123 Danny Farmer RC 1.50 4.00
124 Todd Pinkston RC 1.50 4.00
125 Dennis Northcutt RC 1.50 4.00
126 Laveranues Coles RC 2.00 5.00
127 Bubba Franks RC 1.50 4.00
128 Travis Prentice RC 1.50 4.00
129 Peter Warrick RC 1.50 4.00
130 Anthony Becht RC 1.50 4.00
131 Ike Charlton RC 1.50 4.00
132 Shaun Ellis RC 2.00 5.00
133 Sean Morey RC 1.50 4.00
134 Sebastian Janikowski RC 2.50 6.00
135 Aaron Stecker RC 1.50 4.00
136 Ronney Jenkins RC 1.50 4.00
137 Jamel White RC 1.50 4.00
138 Nick Williams 1.50 4.00
139 Andy McCullough 1.50 4.00
140 Kevin Daft 1.50 4.00
141 Thomas Hamner RC 1.50 4.00
142 Tim Rattay RC 2.00 5.00
143 Spergon Wynn RC 1.50 4.00
144 Brandon Short RC 1.50 4.00
145 Chad Morton RC 2.00 5.00
146 Gari Scott RC 1.50 4.00
147 Frank Murphy RC 1.50 4.00
148 James Williams RC 1.50 4.00
149 Windrell Hayes RC 1.50 4.00
150 Doug Johnson RC 1.50 4.00

2000 Bowman's Best Acetate Parallel

*VETS 1-100: 3X TO 8X BASIC CARDS
*ROOKIES 101-150: .5X TO 1.2X
ACETATE/250 STATED ODDS 1:22
ACETATE PRINT RUN 250 SER.#'d SETS

2000 Bowman's Best Autographs

Randomly inserted in packs at the overall rate of 1:2395 for veteran players and 1:83 for rookies, this 21-card set features both veteran players and rookies. Full color action photography is combined with a white-out card bottom with player autographs and a Genuine Issue Autograph stamp in gold foil. Many cards were issued through redemption cards that carried an expiration date of 10/31/2001.

GROUP 1 VETS STATED ODDS 1:8369
GROUP 2 VETS STATED ODDS 1:3348
OVERALL STATED ODDS 1:2395
GROUP A ROOKIES STATED ODDS 1:98
GROUP B ROOKIES STATED ODDS 1:1860
GROUP C ROOKIES STATED ODDS 1:8369
GROUP D ROOKIES STATED ODDS 1:837
OVERALL ROOKIE STATED ODDS 1:83
BBBU Brian Urlacher 25.00 60.00
BBCB Courtney Brown SP 6.00 15.00
BBCP Chad Pennington 6.00 15.00
BBDF Danny Farmer 5.00 12.00
BBJH Joe Hamilton 5.00 12.00
BBJL Jamal Lewis 8.00 20.00
BBJM Joe Montana 60.00 120.00
BBJR J.R. Redmond 5.00 12.00
BBLC Laveranues Coles 6.00 15.00
BBPB Plaxico Burress 15.00 30.00
BBPW Peter Warrick 5.00 12.00
BBRD Ron Dayne 8.00 20.00
BBRDR Reuben Droughns 5.00 12.00
BBRDU Ron Dugans 5.00 12.00
BBRM Randy Moss 40.00 80.00
BBRS R.Jay Soward 5.00 12.00
BBSA Shaun Alexander 8.00 20.00
BBSM Sylvester Morris 5.00 12.00
BBTJ Thomas Jones 6.00 15.00
BBTM Tee Martin 5.00 12.00
BBTPR Travis Prentice 5.00 12.00

2000 Bowman's Best Best of the Game Autographs

Randomly inserted in packs at the rate of one in 837, this 2-card set features 1999 Rookie of the Year Edgerrin James and 1999 Player of the Year Kurt Warner. Cards contain full color action photography and a fade to white along the bottom third of the card where the player's autograph and a Certified Autograph stamp are prominently displayed.

STATED ODDS 1:837
BG1 Edgerrin James 10.00 25.00
BG2 Kurt Warner 20.00 50.00

2000 Bowman's Best Bets

Randomly inserted in packs at the rate of one in 19, this 13-card set spotlights top 2000 rookies in action on an all foil card showing the rookie's current team logo in the background. Cards are die cut along the top edge in a spiked semi-circle.

COMPLETE SET (13) 6.00 15.00
STATED ODDS 1:19

B1 Jamal Lewis	.40	1.00
B2 Plaxico Burress	.30	.75
B3 Chad Pennington	.30	.75
B4 Sylvester Morris	.25	.60
B5 Shaun Alexander	.40	1.00
B6 Peter Warrick	.25	.60
B7 Travis Taylor	.25	.60
B8 Courtney Brown	.30	.75
B9 R.Jay Soward	.25	.60
B10 Ron Dayne	.40	1.00
B11 Jerry Porter	.40	1.00
B12 Curtis Keaton	.25	.60
B13 Thomas Jones	.30	.75

2000 Bowman's Best Franchise 2000

Randomly inserted in packs at the rate of one in 12, this 20-card set features 20 team leaders who have taken the lead role on their teams. Cards feature full color action photography and an all foil card stock.

COMPLETE SET (20)	12.50	30.00
STATED ODDS 1:12		
F1 Curtis Martin	.50	1.25
F2 Eddie George	.50	1.25
F3 Emmitt Smith	1.00	2.50
F4 Stephen Davis	.40	1.00
F5 Cade McNown	.40	1.00
F6 Drew Bledsoe	.50	1.25
F7 Zach Thomas	.50	1.25
F8 Mark Brunell	.50	1.25
F9 Tim Brown	.60	1.50
F10 Akili Smith	.40	1.00
F11 Peyton Manning	1.50	4.00
F12 Terrell Davis	.50	1.25
F13 Brett Favre	1.25	3.00
F14 Randy Moss	.50	1.25
F15 Kurt Warner	1.00	2.50
F16 Ricky Williams	.50	1.25
F17 Jerry Rice	1.50	4.00
F18 Jake Plummer	.40	1.00
F19 Tim Couch	.50	1.25
F20 Warren Sapp	.50	1.25

2000 Bowman's Best Pro Bowl Jerseys

Randomly seeded in packs at the rate of one in 112, this 14-card set features a color portrait shot of each player and a swatch of a player worn Pro Bowl jersey in the shape of the 2000 Hawaii Pro Bowl logo.

STATED ODDS 1:112		
BJQB Brad Johnson	6.00	15.00
CWCB Charles Woodson	8.00	20.00
DBOLB Derrick Brooks	5.00	12.00
EJRB Edgerrin James	6.00	15.00
IBWR Isaac Bruce	8.00	20.00
JKDE Jevon Kearse	5.00	12.00
JSWR Jimmy Smith	6.00	15.00
KJWR Keyshawn Johnson	6.00	15.00
KWQB Kurt Warner	12.00	30.00
MBQB Mark Brunell	6.00	15.00
MFRB Marshall Faulk	6.00	15.00
MHWR Marvin Harrison	6.00	15.00
RMWR Randy Moss	6.00	15.00
SDRB Stephen Davis	5.00	12.00

2000 Bowman's Best Year by Year

Randomly inserted in packs at the rate of one in 20, this 12-card set features dual NFL stars paired because they both made their debuts during the same season. Cards are all gold foil with red foil highlights.

COMPLETE SET (12)	6.00	15.00
STATED ODDS 1:20		
Y1 P.Manning R.Moss	1.50	4.00
Y2 Key.Johnson E.George	.50	1.25
Y3 T.Brown T.Thomas	.60	1.50
Y4 D.Bledsoe J.Bettis	.60	1.50
Y5 E.James R.Williams	.50	1.25
Y6 T.Aikman D.Sanders	.75	2.00
Y7 I.Bruce M.Faulk	.60	1.50
Y8 J.Seau E.Smith	1.00	2.50
Y9 C.Martin T.Davis	.50	1.25
Y10 B.Johnson J.Smith	.50	1.25
Y11 B.Favre R.Watters	1.25	3.00
Y12 P.Warrick P.Burress	.50	1.25

2000 Bowman's Best Promos

COMPLETE SET (6)	1.50	4.00
PP1 Kurt Warner	.30	.75
PP2 Marvin Harrison	.30	.75
PP3 Terrell Davis	.30	.75
PP4 Marshall Faulk	.30	.75
PP5 Stephen Davis	.20	.50
PP6 Eddie George	.20	.50

2001 Bowman's Best

This 170 card set was issued in November, 2001. The set was issued in five card packs with a SRP of $5. The packs come 24 to a box and either six or 12 boxes to a case. The first 90 cards were all veteran cards, cards 91-100 are two player best performer cards, cards 101-120 are rookie relics and cards 121-170 are all rookies. The rookie relic cards are serial numbered to 999 while the other rookies are serial numbered to 1499.

COMP.SET w/o SP's (100)	7.50	20.00
1 Jerry Rice	.60	1.50
2 Doug Flutie	.25	.60
3 Drew Bledsoe	.25	.60
4 Edgerrin James	.25	.60
5 Muhsin Muhammad	.20	.50
6 Charlie Batch	.20	.50
7 Marshall Faulk	.25	.60
8 Trent Green	.20	.50
9 Rich Gannon	.25	.60
10 Emmitt Smith	.50	1.25
11 Steve McNair	.25	.60
12 Darrell Jackson	.25	.60
13 Amani Toomer	.20	.50
14 Jimmy Smith	.25	.60
15 Kevin Johnson	.20	.50
16 Ray Lewis	.30	.75
17 Peter Warrick	.20	.50
18 Cris Carter	.30	.75
19 Jerome Bettis	.30	.75
20 Keyshawn Johnson	.25	.60
21 Joey Galloway	.25	.60
22 Chris Chandler	.25	.60
23 Brett Favre	.60	1.50
24 Aaron Brooks	.20	.50
25 Kurt Warner	.50	1.25
26 Jeff Graham	.20	.50
27 Curtis Martin	.25	.60
28 Mike Anderson	.20	.50
29 Eric Moulds	.20	.50
30 David Boston	.20	.50
31 Elvis Grbac	.25	.60
32 James Stewart	.20	.50
33 Randy Moss	.25	.60
34 Donovan McNabb	.25	.60
35 Matt Hasselbeck	.20	.50
36 Stephen Davis	.20	.50
37 Brad Johnson	.25	.60
38 Jamal Anderson	.25	.60
39 Tim Biakabutuka	.20	.50
40 Antonio Freeman	.30	.75
41 Mark Brunell	.25	.60
42 Tiki Barber	.25	.60
43 Charlie Garner	.25	.60
44 Eddie George	.30	.75
45 Ricky Williams	.25	.60
46 Rob Johnson	.25	.60
47 Jake Plummer	.20	.50
48 Peyton Manning	.75	2.00
49 Lamar Smith	.25	.60
50 Corey Dillon	.20	.50
51 Derrick Alexander	.20	.50
52 Troy Brown	.20	.50
53 Wayne Chrebet	.20	.50
54 Shaun Alexander	.20	.50
55 Jeff George	.25	.60
56 Tim Brown	.30	.75
57 Brian Griese	.20	.50
58 Cade McNown	.25	.60
59 Jamal Lewis	.30	.75
60 Germane Crowell	.20	.50
61 Junior Seau	.25	.60
62 Warrick Dunn	.20	.50
63 Isaac Bruce	.30	.75
64 Terry Glenn	.25	.60
65 Fred Taylor	.20	.50
66 Tim Couch	.20	.50
67 Akili Smith	.20	.50
68 Tony Gonzalez	.25	.60
69 Kerry Collins	.20	.50
70 James Thrash	.25	.60
71 Terrell Owens	.25	.60
72 Derrick Mason	.20	.50
73 Tyrone Wheatley	.25	.60
74 Oronde Gadsden	.20	.50
75 Ahman Green	.25	.60
76 Jon Kitna	.20	.50
77 Tony Banks	.20	.50
78 Marvin Harrison	.25	.60
79 Daunte Culpepper	.25	.60
80 Vinny Testaverde	.20	.50
81 Chad Lewis	.20	.50
82 Torry Holt	.25	.60
83 Jeff Garcia	.20	.50
84 Rod Smith	.25	.60
85 Marcus Robinson	.25	.60
86 Keenan McCardell	.25	.60
87 Joe Horn	.20	.50
88 Kordell Stewart	.20	.50
89 Jay Fiedler	.25	.60
90 Ed McCaffrey	.25	.60
91 E.George/S.Davis	.30	.75
92 P.Manning/J.Garcia	.75	2.00
93 R.Smith/T.Holt	.25	.60
94 E.James/M.Faulk	.25	.60
95 E.Grbac/D.Culpepper	.25	.60
96 M.Harrison/R.Moss	.25	.60
97 M.Anderson/E.Smith	.50	1.25
98 B.Griese/K.Warner	.50	1.25
99 M.Muhammad/E.McCaffrey	.25	.60
100 E.Moulds/T.Owens	.25	.60
101 David Terrell JSY RC	2.50	6.00
102 Kevan Barlow JSY RC	2.50	6.00
103 Quincy Morgan JSY RC	2.50	6.00
104 Chris Weinke JSY RC	2.50	6.00
105 Josh Heupel JSY RC	3.00	8.00
106 Chris Chambers JSY RC	2.00	5.00
107 Reggie Wayne JSY RC	4.00	10.00
108 Gerard Warren JSY RC	2.50	6.00
109 Freddie Mitchell JSY RC	2.00	5.00
110 Anthony Thomas JSY RC	3.00	8.00
111 Robert Ferguson JSY RC	3.00	8.00
112 Deuce McAllister JSY RC	3.00	8.00
113 Travis Henry JSY RC	2.50	6.00
114 Rod Gardner JSY RC	2.50	6.00
115 Michael Bennett JSY RC	2.50	6.00
116 Santana Moss JSY RC	3.00	8.00
117 Chad Johnson JSY RC	3.00	8.00
118 Jesse Palmer JSY RC	2.50	6.00
119 James Jackson JSY RC	2.00	5.00
120 Dan Morgan JSY RC	2.50	6.00
121 Drew Brees RC	75.00	150.00
122 Travis Minor RC	1.50	4.00
123 Quincy Carter RC	1.50	4.00
124 LaDainian Tomlinson RC	10.00	25.00
125 Michael Vick RC	15.00	30.00
126 Ryan Pickett RC	1.25	3.00
127 Mike McMahon RC	1.50	4.00
128 Alex Bannister RC	1.25	3.00
129 A.J. Feeley RC	1.50	4.00
130 Shad Meier RC	1.25	3.00
131 Jamie Winborn RC	1.50	4.00
132 Fred Smoot RC	1.50	4.00
133 Milton Wynn RC	1.25	3.00
134 Onome Ojo RC	1.25	3.00
135 Jonathan Carter RC	1.25	3.00
136 Todd Heap RC	1.50	4.00
137 Bobby Newcombe RC	1.50	4.00
138 Tony Stewart RC	1.50	4.00
139 Torrance Marshall RC	1.25	3.00
140 Jamal Reynolds RC	1.25	3.00
141 Jamar Fletcher RC	1.25	3.00
142 Richard Seymour RC	2.00	5.00
143 Tay Cody RC	1.25	3.00
144 Koren Robinson RC	1.50	4.00
145 Eddie Berlin RC	1.25	3.00
146 Damione Lewis RC	1.50	4.00
147 Marques Tuiasosopo RC	1.50	4.00
148 Snoop Minnis RC	1.25	3.00
149 Chris Barnes RC	1.25	3.00
150 Leonard Davis RC	2.00	5.00
151 Vinny Sutherland RC	1.25	3.00
152 Rudi Johnson RC	2.00	5.00
153 Derrick Gibson RC	1.25	3.00
154 Dan Alexander RC	1.50	4.00
155 Damerien McCants RC	1.50	4.00
156 Adam Archuleta RC	1.50	4.00
157 Correll Buckhalter RC	1.25	3.00
158 LaMont Jordan RC	2.00	5.00
159 Quentin McCord RC	1.50	4.00
160 Justin Smith RC	2.50	6.00
161 Nate Clements RC	1.50	4.00
162 Alge Crumpler RC	2.00	5.00
163 Dan O'Leary RC	1.25	3.00
164 Sage Rosenfels RC	1.50	4.00
165 Andre Carter RC	1.50	4.00
166 Marcus Stroud RC	1.50	4.00
167 Will Allen RC	2.00	5.00
168 Tommy Polley RC	1.25	3.00
169 Justin McCareins RC	1.50	4.00
170 Josh Booty RC	1.50	4.00

2001 Bowman's Best Autographs

Randomly inserted at different odds ranging anywhere from one in 53 to one in 3158, with overall odds at one in 23, this is a 33-card set featuring some of the key rookies of 2001. A few players did not sign their cards in time to be included in the packs and those cards were available as redemptions with an expiration date of November 1, 2003.

GROUP A STATED ODDS 1:3158 H,1:5376 R		
GROUP B STATED ODDS 1:2398 H,1:3974 R		
GROUP C STATED ODDS 1:1593 H,1:2688 R		
GROUP D STATED ODDS 1:530 H,1:880 R		
GROUP E STATED ODDS 1:53 H,1:88 R		
GROUP F STATED ODDS 1:868 H,1:1451 R		
GROUP G STATED ODDS 1:340 H,1:568 R		
GROUP H STATED ODDS 1:502 H,1:838 R		
GROUP I STATED ODDS 1:68 H,1:113 R		
OVERALL STATED ODDS 1:23 H,1:39 R		
BBAT Anthony Thomas I	6.00	15.00
BBBU Brian Urlacher	40.00	80.00
BBCC Chris Chambers E	4.00	10.00
BBCJ Chad Johnson H	12.00	30.00
BBCW Chris Weinke E	5.00	12.00
BBDA Dan Alexander E	5.00	12.00
BBDBR Drew Brees E	300.00	500.00
BBDMO Dan Morgan I	5.00	12.00
BBDR David Rivers I	4.00	10.00
BBDT David Terrell G	5.00	12.00
BBEM Eric Moulds E	4.00	10.00
BBJH Joe Horn E	4.00	10.00
BBJHE Josh Heupel I	6.00	15.00
BBJJ James Jackson E	4.00	10.00
BBJL Jamal Lewis C	6.00	15.00
BBJP Jesse Palmer D	5.00	12.00
BBKB Kevan Barlow E	5.00	12.00
BBLS Lamar Smith E	5.00	12.00
BBLT LaDainian Tomlinson I	75.00	125.00
BBMB Michael Bennett E	5.00	12.00
BBMV Michael Vick A	60.00	120.00
BBQM Quincy Morgan E	5.00	12.00
BBRF Robert Ferguson E	6.00	15.00
BBRG Rod Gardner D	5.00	12.00
BBRM Randy Moss C	30.00	60.00
BBRW Reggie Wayne E	25.00	50.00
BBSD Stephen Davis F	4.00	10.00
BBSM Santana Moss E	6.00	15.00
BBSMO Sammy Morris E	4.00	10.00
BBTD Tim Dwight I	5.00	12.00
BBTH Travis Henry E	5.00	12.00
BBTO Terrell Owens E	15.00	40.00
BBTW Terrence Wilkins G	4.00	10.00

2001 Bowman's Best Bets

This set, issued at a rate of one in 12, featured 13 of the leading rookies of 2001 in a "playing card" style format.

COMPLETE SET (10)	10.00	25.00
STATED ODDS 1:12 HOB/RET		
BB1 Drew Brees	10.00	25.00
BB2 Michael Vick	.75	2.00
BB3 David Terrell	.40	1.00
BB4 Michael Bennett	.40	1.00
BB5 LaDainian Tomlinson	1.50	4.00
BB6 Koren Robinson	.40	1.00
BB7 Chris Weinke	.40	1.00
BB8 Rod Gardner	.40	1.00
BB9 Reggie Wayne	.60	1.50
BB10 Deuce McAllister	.50	1.25
BB11 Freddie Mitchell	.30	.75
BB12 Chad Johnson	.50	1.25
BB13 Santana Moss	.50	1.25

2001 Bowman's Best Franchise Favorites Relics

This four card set, inserted at overall odds of one in 414 featured relics from each of the two players featured on the card. They were originally issued in packs as redemption cards with an expiration date of 11/1/2003. The photographs and swatches used on the cards came from the 2001 Pro Bowl.

GROUP A STATED ODDS 1:9648H,1:16,619R		
GROUP B STATED ODDS 1:1593 H,1:2688 R		
GROUP C STATED ODDS 1:1360 H,1:2285 R		
GROUP D STATED ODDS 1:1059 H,1:1760 R		
OVERALL STATED ODDS 1:414 H, 1:692 R		
FFCC Culpepper/C.Carter A	20.00	50.00
FFGJ E.George/E.James D	12.00	30.00
FFSG J.Smith/T.Gonzalez B	7.50	20.00
FFWW C.Woodson/R.Woodson C	10.00	25.00

2001 Bowman's Best Impact Players

This set, inserted at a rate of one in four, features 20 of the leading offensive threats in the NFL. The card design implies that these players are breaking down the walls to play.

COMPLETE SET (20)	6.00	15.00
STATED ODDS 1:4 HOB/RET		
IP1 Randy Moss	.40	1.00
IP2 Peyton Manning	1.25	3.00
IP3 Eddie George	.50	1.25
IP4 Elvis Grbac	.40	1.00
IP5 Marshall Faulk	.40	1.00
IP6 Marvin Harrison	.40	1.00
IP7 Tony Gonzalez	.40	1.00
IP8 Corey Dillon	.30	.75
IP9 Rod Smith	.40	1.00
IP10 Daunte Culpepper	.40	1.00
IP11 Edgerrin James	.40	1.00
IP12 Terrell Owens	.40	1.00
IP13 Eric Moulds	.30	.75
IP14 Kurt Warner	.75	2.00
IP15 Donovan Mcnabb	.40	1.00
IP16 Isaac Bruce	.50	1.25
IP17 Jeff Garcia	.30	.75
IP18 Cris Carter	.50	1.25
IP19 Stephen Davis	.30	.75
IP20 Torry Holt	.40	1.00

2001 Bowman's Best Vintage Best

This set, inserted at a rate of one in four, honors some of the all time NFL greats.

COMPLETE SET (10)	5.00	12.00
STATED ODDS 1:4 HOB/RET		
VBDB Dick Butkus	.60	1.50
VBDJ Deacon Jones	.40	1.00
VBED Eric Dickerson	.40	1.00
VBFG Frank Gifford	.50	1.25
VBGS Gale Sayers	.50	1.25
VBJB Jim Brown	.60	1.50
VBJM Joe Montana	2.00	5.00
VBJN Joe Namath	.75	2.00
VBLT Lawrence Taylor	.50	1.25
VBPH Paul Hornung	.50	1.25

2002 Bowman's Best

Released in mid-November 2002, this set consists of 90 veterans, 27 rookie jerseys, and 50 rookie autographs. The rookie autographs were inserted at an overall rate of 1:3 packs. Boxes contained 10-packs of 5-cards each. The pack SRP was $15.

COMP.SET w/o SP's (90)	15.00	40.00
ROOKIE AU STATED ODDS 1:3		
1 Peyton Manning	1.25	3.00
2 Chris Weinke	.30	.75
3 Daunte Culpepper	.40	1.00
4 Deuce McAllister	.40	1.00
5 Duce Staley	.30	.75
6 Koren Robinson	.30	.75
7 Emmitt Smith	.75	2.00
8 Jamal Lewis	.40	1.00
9 Jake Plummer	.30	.75
10 Tim Brown	.50	1.25
11 LaDainian Tomlinson	.50	1.25
12 Derrick Mason	.30	.75
13 Keyshawn Johnson	.40	1.00
14 Priest Holmes	.30	.75
15 Marcus Robinson	.40	1.00
16 Drew Bledsoe	.40	1.00
17 Troy Brown	.30	.75
18 Ahman Green	.40	1.00
19 Edgerrin James	.40	1.00
20 Hines Ward	.40	1.00
21 Marshall Faulk	.40	1.00
22 Rod Gardner	.30	.75
23 Amani Toomer	.30	.75
24 Ricky Williams	.40	1.00
25 Peter Warrick	.30	.75
26 Ray Lewis	.50	1.25
27 Warrick Dunn	.30	.75
28 Jermaine Lewis	.30	.75
29 Mark Brunell	.40	1.00
30 Randy Moss	.40	1.00
31 Laveranues Coles	.40	1.00
32 Kordell Stewart	.30	.75
33 Darrell Jackson	.40	1.00
34 Jeff Garcia	.30	.75
35 Eddie George	.40	1.00
36 Tim Dwight	.30	.75
37 Trent Green	.30	.75
38 Quincy Carter	.30	.75
39 Mike McMahon	.30	.75
40 Corey Dillon	.30	.75
41 Corey Bradford	.30	.75
42 Aaron Brooks	.30	.75
43 Todd Pinkston	.30	.75
44 Isaac Bruce	.50	1.25
45 Shane Matthews	.30	.75
46 Eric Moulds	.30	.75
47 Anthony Thomas	.40	1.00
48 David Boston	.30	.75
49 Kevin Johnson	.30	.75
50 Brett Favre	1.00	2.50
51 Ron Dayne	.40	1.00
52 Donovan McNabb	.40	1.00
53 Brad Johnson	.40	1.00
54 Garrison Hearst	.30	.75
55 Jimmy Smith	.40	1.00
56 Muhsin Muhammad	.30	.75
57 Michael Vick	.40	1.00
58 Kerry Collins	.30	.75
59 Jerome Bettis	.50	1.25
60 Trent Dilfer	.30	.75
61 Torry Holt	.40	1.00
62 Stephen Davis	.30	.75
63 Steve McNair	.40	1.00
64 Marvin Harrison	.40	1.00
65 Zach Thomas	.40	1.00
66 Antowain Smith	.40	1.00
67 Joe Horn	.30	.75
68 Jim Miller	.30	.75
69 Travis Taylor	.30	.75
70 James Allen	.30	.75
71 Tom Brady	2.50	6.00
72 Tiki Barber	.40	1.00
73 Doug Flutie	.40	1.00
74 Rich Gannon	.40	1.00
75 Kurt Warner	.40	1.00
76 Michael Pittman	.40	1.00
77 Curtis Martin	.40	1.00
78 Plaxico Burress	.30	.75
79 Terrell Owens	.40	1.00
80 Tony Gonzalez	.40	1.00
81 Michael Bennett	.30	.75
82 Brian Griese	.30	.75
83 Tim Couch	.30	.75
84 Shaun Alexander	.30	.75
85 Drew Brees	1.00	2.50
86 Vinny Testaverde	.30	.75
87 Chris Chambers	.30	.75
88 David Terrell	.30	.75
89 Rod Smith	.40	1.00
90 Jerry Rice	1.00	2.50
91 David Carr JSY RC	2.00	5.00
92 Joey Harrington JSY RC	2.00	5.00
93 Marquise Walker JSY RC	2.00	5.00
94 Ladell Betts JSY RC	3.00	8.00
95 David Garrard JSY RC	2.50	6.00
96 Antwaan Randle El JSY RC	2.50	6.00
97 Antonio Bryant JSY RC	3.00	8.00
98 Eric Crouch JSY RC	3.00	8.00
99 Tim Carter JSY RC	2.50	6.00
100 William Green JSY RC	2.50	6.00
101 Rohan Davey JSY RC	3.00	8.00
102 Julius Peppers JSY RC	5.00	12.00
103 Donte Stallworth JSY RC	3.00	8.00
104 Ashley Lelie JSY RC	2.00	5.00
105 Jeremy Shockey JSY RC	3.00	8.00
106 Javon Walker JSY RC	3.00	8.00
107 Patrick Ramsey JSY RC	2.50	6.00
108 Roy Williams JSY RC	2.00	5.00
109 T.J. Duckett JSY RC	2.00	5.00
110 Jabar Gaffney JSY RC	2.00	5.00
111 Andre Davis JSY RC	2.00	5.00
112 Reche Caldwell JSY RC	2.50	6.00
113 Josh McCown JSY RC	3.00	8.00
114 Maurice Morris JSY RC	2.50	6.00
115 Ron Johnson JSY RC	2.50	6.00
116 DeShaun Foster JSY RC	3.00	8.00
117 Clinton Portis JSY RC	3.00	8.00
118 Aaron Lockett AU RC	3.00	8.00
119 Robert Thomas AU RC	3.00	8.00
121 Atrews Bell AU RC	3.00	8.00
122 Brandon Doman AU RC	3.00	8.00
124 Bryan Thomas AU RC	3.00	8.00
125 Bryant McKinnie AU RC	3.00	8.00
126 Chad Hutchinson AU RC	3.00	8.00
127 Charles Grant AU RC	5.00	12.00
128 Chester Taylor AU RC	5.00	12.00
129 Craig Nall AU RC	4.00	10.00
130 Deion Branch AU RC	6.00	15.00
131 Doug Jolley AU RC	3.00	8.00
132 Dwight Freeney AU RC	6.00	15.00
133 Ed Reed AU RC	20.00	50.00
134 Freddie Milons AU RC	3.00	8.00
135 Herb Haygood AU RC	3.00	8.00
136 J.T. O'Sullivan AU RC	4.00	10.00
137 Jake Schifino AU RC	3.00	8.00
138 Jason McAddley AU RC	4.00	10.00
139 Jeff Kelly AU RC	3.00	8.00
140 Jerramy Stevens AU RC	5.00	12.00
141 John Henderson AU RC	4.00	10.00
142 Jonathan Wells AU RC	4.00	10.00
143 Josh Scobey AU RC	4.00	10.00
144 Kelly Campbell AU RC	4.00	10.00
145 Kahlil Hill AU RC	3.00	8.00
146 Kalimba Edwards AU RC	4.00	10.00
147 Ken Simonton AU RC	3.00	8.00
148 Kurt Kittner AU RC	3.00	8.00
149 Lamar Gordon AU RC	4.00	10.00
150 Leonard Henry AU RC	3.00	8.00
151 Lito Sheppard AU RC	5.00	12.00
152 Luke Staley AU RC	3.00	8.00
153 Matt Schobel AU RC	4.00	10.00
154 Mike Rumph AU RC	3.00	8.00
155 Najeh Davenport AU RC	3.00	8.00
156 Napoleon Harris AU RC	4.00	10.00
158 Quentin Jammer AU RC	5.00	12.00
159 Randy Fasani AU RC	3.00	8.00
160 Ronald Curry AU RC	3.00	8.00
161 Ryan Sims AU RC	5.00	12.00
162 Sam Simmons AU RC	3.00	8.00
163 Seth Burford AU RC	3.00	8.00
164 Tellis Redmon AU RC	3.00	8.00
165 Terry Charles AU RC	3.00	8.00
166 Tracey Wistrom AU RC	4.00	10.00
167 Verron Haynes AU RC	3.00	8.00
168 Wes Pate AU RC	3.00	8.00
169 Wendell Bryant AU RC	3.00	8.00
170 Damien Anderson AU RC	3.00	8.00

2002 Bowman's Best Blue

*VETS 1-90: 2X TO 5X BASIC CARDS
1-90 VET/300 ODDS 1:5
1-90 VET PRINT RUN 300
*ROOKIE JSY 91-117: .5X TO 1.2X
ROOKIE JSY/399 ODDS 1:13
ROOKIE JSY PRINT RUN 399 SER.#'d SETS
*ROOKIE AU 118-170: .5X TO 1.2X
ROOKIE AU/399 ODDS 1:6
ROOKIE AU PRINT RUN 399 SER.#'d SETS

2002 Bowman's Best Gold

*VETS 1-90: 10X TO 25X BASIC CARDS
1-90 VETERAN/25 ODDS 1:62
1-90 VETERAN PRINT RUN 25
*ROOKIE JSY 91-117: 1.5X TO 3X
91-117 ROOKIE JSY/99 ODDS 1:51
91-117 ROOKIE JSY PRINT RUN 99
*ROOKIE AU 118-170: 1X TO 2.5X
118-170 ROOKIE AU/99 ODDS 1:26
118-170 ROOKIE AU PRINT RUN 99

2002 Bowman's Best Red

*VETS: 3X TO 8X BASIC CARDS
1-90 VETERAN/200 ODDS 1:9
1-90 VETERAN PRINT RUN 200
*ROOKIE JSY 91-117: 1X TO 2X
91-117 ROOKIE JSY/199 ODDS 1:25
ROOKIE JSY PRINT RUN 199 SER.#'d SETS
*ROOKIE AU 118-170: .8X TO 1.5X
118-170 ROOKIE AU/199 ODDS 1:13
ROOKIE AU PRINT RUN 199 SER.#'d SETS

2002 Bowman's Best Uncirculated

*SEALED JSY: 1.5X TO 4X BASIC JSY
*SEALED AU: 1X TO 3X BASIC AU
EXCH CARD STATED ODDS 1:89
ANNOUNCED PRINT RUN 20

2003 Bowman's Best

Released in October of 2003, this set consists of 173 cards including 80 veterans and 95 rookies. Rookies 81-90 are not short printed. Rookies 91-115 feature jersey swatches, and were inserted at a rate of 1:5. Rookies 116-175 feature authentic player autographs and were inserted at a rate of 1:136. Boxes contained 10 packs of 5 cards. Please note that cards 270 and 275 were never released.

COMP.SET w/o SP's (80)	12.50	30.00
ROOKIE JSY STATED ODDS 1:5		
ROOKIE AU STATED ODDS 1:136		
1 Terrell Owens	.50	1.25
2 Peerless Price	.40	1.00
3 Joey Harrington	.40	1.00
4 Ricky Williams	.50	1.25
5 David Boston	.40	1.00
6 Troy Brown	.40	1.00
7 Deuce McAllister	.50	1.25
8 Marvin Harrison	.50	1.25
9 Ahman Green	.50	1.25
10 Emmitt Smith	1.00	2.50
11 Brian Urlacher	.60	1.50
12 Jamal Lewis	.50	1.25
13 Keyshawn Johnson	.60	1.50
14 Kurt Warner	.50	1.25
15 Rod Gardner	.40	1.00
16 Plaxico Burress	.40	1.00
17 Chad Pennington	.40	1.00
18 Jeremy Shockey	.40	1.00
19 Donovan McNabb	.50	1.25
20 T.J. Duckett	.40	1.00
21 Fred Taylor	.40	1.00
22 Daunte Culpepper	.50	1.25
23 Tiki Barber	.50	1.25
24 Brian Griese	.40	1.00
25 Chad Johnson	.40	1.00
26 Julius Peppers	.60	1.50
27 Chad Hutchinson	.40	1.00
28 Eddie George	.50	1.25
29 Torry Holt	.50	1.25
30 Drew Brees	.60	1.50
31 Rich Gannon	.50	1.25
32 Trent Green	.40	1.00
33 Clinton Portis	.40	1.00
34 Tom Brady	2.50	6.00
35 Aaron Brooks	.40	1.00
36 Ray Lewis	.60	1.50
37 David Carr	.40	1.00
38 Chris Chambers	.40	1.00
39 Brad Johnson	.50	1.25
40 Tommy Maddox	.40	1.00
41 Curtis Martin	.50	1.25
42 Travis Henry	.40	1.00
43 Brett Favre	1.25	3.00
44 Randy Moss	.50	1.25
45 Jimmy Smith	.50	1.25
46 Joey Galloway	.50	1.25
47 Derrick Mason	.40	1.00
48 Darrell Jackson	.50	1.25
49 Curtis Conway	.40	1.00
50 Michael Vick	.50	1.25
51 Rod Smith	.50	1.25
52 Muhsin Muhammad	.40	1.00
53 Drew Bledsoe	.50	1.25
54 Michael Bennett	.40	1.00
55 Joe Horn	.40	1.00
56 Stephen Davis	.40	1.00
57 Isaac Bruce	.60	1.50
58 Shaun Alexander	.40	1.00
59 Jerry Rice	1.25	3.00
60 Peyton Manning	1.50	4.00
61 Tony Gonzalez	.50	1.25
62 Jake Plummer	.40	1.00
63 Tim Couch	.40	1.00
64 Marty Booker	.40	1.00
65 Corey Dillon	.40	1.00
66 Steve McNair	.50	1.25
67 Jeff Garcia	.40	1.00
68 Hines Ward	.50	1.25
69 Laveranues Coles	.40	1.00
70 Amani Toomer	.40	1.00
71 Eric Moulds	.40	1.00
72 Donald Driver	.50	1.25
73 Jay Fiedler	.40	1.00
74 Charlie Garner	.50	1.25
75 Priest Holmes	.40	1.00
76 Edgerrin James	.50	1.25
77 Kerry Collins	.40	1.00
78 LaDainian Tomlinson	.60	1.50
79 Mark Brunell	.50	1.25
80 Marshall Faulk	.50	1.25
81 Lee Suggs RC	1.00	2.50
82 William Joseph RC	1.00	2.50
83 Brandon Lloyd RC	1.50	4.00
84 Nick Barnett RC	1.50	4.00
85 Andre Woolfolk RC	1.00	2.50
86 Jimmy Kennedy RC	1.25	3.00
87 Kliff Kingsbury RC	1.50	4.00
88 Andrew Williams RC	1.00	2.50
89 Mike Doss RC	1.50	4.00
90 Troy Polamalu RC	12.00	30.00
91 Bryant Johnson JSY RC	3.00	8.00
92 Justin Fargas JSY RC	3.00	8.00
93 Terence Newman JSY RC	3.00	8.00
94 Brian St.Pierre JSY RC	2.00	5.00
95 DeWayne Robertson JSY RC	2.50	6.00
96 Dave Ragone JSY RC	2.00	5.00
97 Teyo Johnson JSY RC	2.50	6.00
98 Bethel Johnson JSY RC	2.00	5.00
99 Tyrone Calico JSY RC	2.00	5.00
100 Carson Palmer JSY RC	4.00	10.00
101 Marcus Trufant JSY RC	2.50	6.00
102 Nate Burleson JSY RC	2.50	6.00
103 Musa Smith JSY RC	2.00	5.00
104 Anquan Boldin JSY RC	3.00	8.00
105 Chris Simms JSY RC	2.00	5.00
106 Taylor Jacobs JSY RC	2.00	5.00
107 Dallas Clark JSY RC	3.00	8.00
108 Seneca Wallace JSY RC	2.50	6.00
109 Ken Dorsey JSY RC	2.50	6.00
110 Willis McGahee JSY RC	2.50	6.00
111 Chris Brown JSY RC	2.00	5.00
112 Terrell Suggs JSY RC	2.50	6.00
113 Kelley Washington JSY RC	2.00	5.00
114 Onterrio Smith JSY RC	2.00	5.00
115 Rex Grossman JSY RC	2.50	6.00
116 LaBrandon Toefield AU RC	3.00	8.00
117 Sam Aiken AU RC	4.00	10.00
118 Malaefou Mackenzie AU RC	3.00	8.00
119 David Tyree AU RC	4.00	10.00
120 Jerome McDougle AU RC	3.00	8.00
121 DeWayne White AU RC	3.00	8.00
122 Zuriel Smith AU RC	3.00	8.00
123 Shaun McDonald AU RC	4.00	10.00
124 Andre Johnson AU/199 RC	40.00	80.00
125 Ahmaad Galloway AU RC	4.00	10.00
126 Keenan Howry AU RC	3.00	8.00
127 Kareem Kelly AU RC	3.00	8.00
128 Brooks Bollinger AU RC	4.00	10.00
129 Arnaz Battle AU RC	5.00	12.00
130 Adrian Madise AU RC	3.00	8.00
131 LaTarence Dunbar AU RC	3.00	8.00
132 L.J. Smith AU RC	5.00	12.00
133 B.J. Askew AU RC	4.00	10.00
134 Michael Haynes AU RC	3.00	8.00
135 David Kircus AU RC	4.00	10.00
136 Kyle Boller AU/199 RC	5.00	12.00
137 Domanick Davis AU RC	4.00	10.00
138 Osi Umenyiora AU RC	12.00	30.00
139 Bobby Wade AU RC	4.00	10.00
140 Boss Bailey AU RC	4.00	10.00
141 Billy McMullen AU RC	3.00	8.00
142 Doug Gabriel AU RC	4.00	10.00
143 J.R. Tolver AU RC	4.00	10.00
144 Gibran Hamdan AU RC	3.00	8.00
145 Walter Young AU RC	3.00	8.00
146 Carl Ford AU RC	3.00	8.00
147 Andrew Pinnock AU RC	4.00	10.00
148 Byron Leftwich AU/199 RC	12.00	30.00
149 Ty Warren AU RC	4.00	10.00
150 Visanthe Shiancoe AU RC	5.00	12.00
151 Justin Gage AU RC	4.00	10.00
152 Brock Forsey AU RC	4.00	10.00
153 Casey Moore AU RC	3.00	8.00
154 Juston Wood AU RC	3.00	8.00
155 Aaron Walker AU RC	4.00	10.00
156 Trent Smith AU RC	4.00	10.00
157 Travis Anglin AU RC	3.00	8.00
158 Jeremi Johnson AU RC	3.00	8.00
159 Justin Griffith AU RC	4.00	10.00
160 Chris Davis AU RC	4.00	10.00
161 J.T. Wall AU RC	3.00	8.00
162 Larry Johnson AU/199 RC	6.00	15.00
163 Jon Olinger AU RC	3.00	8.00
164 Donald Lee AU RC	4.00	10.00
165 Taco Wallace AU RC	3.00	8.00
166 DeAndrew Rubin AU RC	3.00	8.00
167 Ryan Hoag AU RC	3.00	8.00
168 Kevin Williams AU RC	6.00	15.00
169 Ovie Mughelli AU RC	4.00	10.00
171 Brandon Drumm AU RC	3.00	8.00
172 Brad Banks AU RC	4.00	10.00
173 Talman Gardner AU RC	3.00	8.00
174 Jason Witten AU RC	30.00	60.00

2003 Bowman's Best Blue

*VETS 1-80: 1X TO 2.5X BASE CARD		
*ROOKIES 81-90: .8X TO 2X BASE CARD		
OVERALL BLUE STATED ODDS 1:3		
*ROOK.JSY 91-115: .5X TO 1.2X		
ROOKIE JSY BLUE STATED ODDS 1:12		
*ROOK.AU/116-174: .5X TO 1.2X BASE CARD		
*ROOK.AU/50: .6X TO 1.5X BASE AU/199		
ROOKIE AU BLUE STATED ODDS 1:5		
BLUE PRINT RUN 499 SER.#'d SETS		
90 Troy Polamalu	30.00	80.00

2003 Bowman's Best Red

*VETS 1-80: 3X TO 8X BASE CARDS		
*ROOKIES 81-90: 2.5X TO 6X BASE CARD		
*ROOK.JSY: 1X TO 2.5X BASE CARD		
ROOKIE JSY RED STATED ODDS 1:110		
*ROOK.AU/50: 1X TO 2.5X BASE AU RC		
*ROOK.AU/25: 1X TO 2.5X BASE AU/199		
ROOKIE AU RED STATED ODDS 1:50		
OVERALL RED/25-50 ODDS 1:30		
RED PRINT RUN 25-50		
90 Troy Polamalu	100.00	175.00

2003 Bowman's Best Best Coverage Jersey Duals

Inserted at a rate of 1:464, this set features two game jersey swatches. Each card is serial numbered to 25.

DUAL JSY/25 ODDS 1:464		
STATED PRINT RUN 25 SER.#'d SETS		
BCFB B.Favre/K.Boller	15.00	40.00
BCGJ E.George/L.Johnson	6.00	15.00
BCJJ K.Johnson/B.Johnson	8.00	20.00
BCKS J.Kearse/T.Suggs	6.00	15.00
BCOR T.Owens/C.Rogers	6.00	15.00
BCRJ J.Rice/A.Johnson	15.00	40.00
BCSJ J.Smith/T.Jacobs	6.00	15.00
BCTF F.Taylor/J.Fargas	8.00	20.00
BCTM L.Tomlinson/W.McGahee	8.00	20.00
BCWP K.Warner/C.Palmer	10.00	25.00

2003 Bowman's Best Double Coverage Autographs

Inserted at a rate of 1:454, this set features two authentic player autographs. Each card is serial numbered to 50.

DUAL AUTO/50 ODDS 1:454		
STATED PRINT RUN 50 SER.#'d SETS		
DCABG K.Boller/R.Grossman	5.00	12.00
DCAMJ W.McGahee/L.Johnson	25.00	60.00
DCAPL C.Palmer/B.Leftwich	25.00	60.00

2003 Bowman's Best Double Coverage Jerseys

Inserted at a rate of 1:151, this set features two jersey swatches. Each card is serial numbered to 50.

DUAL JSY/50 ODDS 1:151		
STATED PRINT RUN 50 SER.#'d SETS		
DCRBC N.Burleson/K.Curtis	2.50	6.00
DCRBG K.Boller/R.Grossman	2.50	6.00
DCRBJ A.Boldin/B.Johnson	3.00	8.00
DCRCJ D.Clark/T.Johnson	3.00	8.00
DCRCW T.Calico/K.Washington	2.00	5.00
DCRFB J.Fargas/C.Brown	3.00	8.00
DCRJJ B.Johnson/T.Jacobs	2.00	5.00
DCRMJ W.McGahee/L.Johnson	2.50	6.00
DCRNT T.Newman/M.Trufant	3.00	8.00
DCRPL C.Palmer/B.Leftwich	4.00	10.00
DCRRJ C.Rogers/A.Johnson	5.00	12.00
DCRRW D.Ragone/S.Wallace	2.50	6.00
DCRSR T.Suggs/D.Robertson	2.50	6.00
DCRSS M.Smith/O.Smith	2.00	5.00
DCRSPK B.St.Pierre/K.Kingsbury	3.00	8.00

2003 Bowman's Best Single Coverage Autographs

Inserted at a rate of 1:151, this set features authentic player autographs. Each card is serial numbered to 100.

AUTO/100 STATED ODDS 1:151		
STATED PRINT RUN 100 SER.#'d SETS		
SCADD Donald Driver	15.00	40.00
SCAHW Hines Ward	20.00	50.00
SCAJT Jason Taylor	12.00	30.00
SCALC Laveranues Coles	8.00	20.00
SCAMH Marvin Harrison	10.00	25.00
SCAMS Michael Strahan	12.00	30.00
SCATH Travis Henry	8.00	20.00
SCATM Tommy Maddox	8.00	20.00

2003 Bowman's Best Single Coverage Jerseys

Inserted at a rate of 1:151, this set features game worn jersey swatches. Each card is serial numbered to 100.

JSY/100 STATED ODDS 1:151		
STATED PRINT RUN 100 SER.#'d SETS		
SCREG Eddie George	2.50	6.00
SCRFT Fred Taylor	2.00	5.00
SCRJK Jevon Kearse	2.00	5.00
SCRJR Jerry Rice	6.00	15.00
SCRJS Jimmy Smith	2.50	6.00
SCRKJ Keyshawn Johnson	3.00	8.00
SCRKW Kurt Warner	2.50	6.00
SCRLT LaDainian Tomlinson	3.00	8.00
SCRTO Terrell Owens	2.50	6.00

2003 Bowman's Best Ultimate Coverage Jersey Autographs

Inserted at a rate of 1:921, this set features two jersey swatches and two authentic autographs. Each card is serial numbered to 25.

DUAL JSY AUTO/25 ODDS 1:921		
UCBG K.Boller/R.Grossman	15.00	40.00
UCMJ W.McGahee/L.Johnson	30.00	80.00
UCPL C.Palmer/B.Leftwich	50.00	100.00

2004 Bowman's Best

Bowmanâ€™s Best initially released in late November 2004. The base set consists of 188-cards including 10-rookie cards, 25-rookie jersey cards, and 58-rookie autographed cards. Five of the signed rookies were serial numbered to just 199-copies. Hobby boxes contained 10-packs of 5-cards and carried an S.R.P. of $15 per pack. Two parallel sets and a variety of inserts can be found seeded in hobby and retail packs highlighted by the Double Coverage Autographs and Ultimate Coverage Jersey Autograph inserts.

COMP.SET w/o SP's (100)	25.00	50.00
RC JSY GROUP A ODDS 1:130		
RC JSY GROUP B ODDS 1:236		
RC JSY GROUP C ODDS 1:86		
RC JSY GROUP D ODDS 1:88		
RC JSY GROUP E ODDS 1:31		
RC JSY GROUP F ODDS 1:27		
RC JSY GROUP G ODDS 1:50		
RC JSY GROUP H ODDS 1:89		
RC JSY GROUP I ODDS 1:29		
RC AU/199 STATED ODDS 1:311		
RC AU STATED ODDS 1:3		
1 Brett Favre	1.00	2.50
2 Chris Chambers	.30	.75
3 Kyle Boller	.30	.75
4 Brian Urlacher	.50	1.25
5 Marvin Harrison	.40	1.00
6 Matt Hasselbeck	.30	.75
7 Aaron Brooks	.30	.75
8 Curtis Martin	.40	1.00
9 Keenan McCardell	.30	.75
10 Terrell Owens	.40	1.00
11 Jimmy Smith	.40	1.00
12 Garrison Hearst	.30	.75
13 Joe Horn	.30	.75
14 David Carr	.30	.75
15 Tom Brady	2.00	5.00
16 Shaun Alexander	.30	.75
17 Tommy Maddox	.30	.75
18 Tiki Barber	.40	1.00
19 Trent Green	.30	.75
20 Anquan Boldin	.30	.75
21 Peerless Price	.30	.75
22 Jake Delhomme	.30	.75
23 Eric Moulds	.30	.75
24 Quincy Carter	.30	.75
25 Steve McNair	.40	1.00
26 Tim Rattay	.30	.75
27 Laveranues Coles	.30	.75
28 Corey Dillon	.30	.75
29 Byron Leftwich	.30	.75
30 Chad Pennington	.30	.75
31 Koren Robinson	.30	.75
32 Plaxico Burress	.30	.75
33 Steve Smith	.50	1.25
34 Warrick Dunn	.30	.75
35 Jamal Lewis	.40	1.00
36 Charles Rogers	.30	.75
37 Tony Gonzalez	.40	1.00
38 Jake Plummer	.30	.75
39 Chad Johnson	.30	.75
40 Peyton Manning	1.25	3.00
41 Daunte Culpepper	.40	1.00
42 Fred Taylor	.30	.75
43 Amani Toomer	.30	.75
44 Santana Moss	.40	1.00
45 Deuce McAllister	.40	1.00
46 Rex Grossman	.30	.75
47 Ray Lewis	.50	1.25
48 Hines Ward	.40	1.00
49 Darrell Jackson	.40	1.00
50 Randy Moss	.40	1.00
51 Carson Palmer	.40	1.00
52 Rod Smith	.40	1.00
53 Drew Bledsoe	.40	1.00
54 Brad Johnson	.40	1.00
55 Travis Henry	.30	.75
56 Joey Harrington	.30	.75
57 Edgerrin James	.40	1.00
58 Kurt Warner	.40	1.00
59 Josh McCown	.40	1.00
60 Clinton Portis	.30	.75
61 Brian Westbrook	.30	.75
62 Marc Bulger	.30	.75
63 Charlie Garner	.40	1.00
64 Torry Holt	.40	1.00
65 LaDainian Tomlinson	.50	1.25
66 Mark Brunell	.40	1.00
67 Derrick Mason	.30	.75
68 Andre Johnson	.40	1.00
69 Keyshawn Johnson	.40	1.00
70 Ahman Green	.40	1.00
71 Rudi Johnson	.30	.75
72 Stephen Davis	.30	.75
73 Jeff Garcia	.30	.75
74 Michael Strahan	.40	1.00
75 Michael Vick	.40	1.00
76 Ricky Williams	.40	1.00
77 Domanick Davis	.30	.75
78 Priest Holmes	.30	.75
79 Marshall Faulk	.40	1.00
80 Donovan McNabb	.40	1.00
81 Dunta Robinson RC	1.00	2.50
82 Robert Gallery RC	1.25	3.00
83 Ben Troupe RC	1.00	2.50
84 Antwan Odom RC	1.00	2.50
85 Brandon Miree RC	1.00	2.50
86 Darnell Dockett RC	1.50	4.00
87 Vince Wilfork RC	1.50	4.00
88 Randy Starks RC	1.00	2.50
89 Chris Cooley RC	1.25	3.00
90 Dwan Edwards RC	1.00	2.50
91 Patrick Crayton RC	1.50	4.00
92 Sean Jones RC	1.00	2.50
93 Sean Ryan RC	1.00	2.50
94 Chris Gamble RC	1.00	2.50
95 Will Smith RC	1.25	3.00
96 Sloan Thomas RC	1.25	3.00
97 Tim Euhus RC	1.00	2.50
98 Tommie Harris RC	1.25	3.00
99 Will Poole RC	1.50	4.00
100 Karlos Dansby RC	1.25	3.00
101 Bernard Berrian JSY RC D	1.50	4.00
102 DeAngelo Hall JSY RC A	2.50	6.00
103 Mewelde Moore JSY RC G	2.00	5.00
104 Rashaun Woods JSY RC G	1.50	4.00
105 Reggie Williams JSY RC	1.50	4.00
106 Derrick Hamilton JSY RC F	1.50	4.00
107 Kellen Winslow JSY RC C	1.50	4.00
108 Devard Darling JSY RC D	1.50	4.00
109 Michael Clayton JSY RC B	2.00	5.00
110 Larry Fitzgerald JSY RC E	6.00	15.00
111 Greg Jones JSY RC E	1.50	4.00
112 Chris Perry JSY RC H	1.50	4.00
113 Lee Evans JSY RC F	2.50	6.00
114 Tatum Bell JSY RC E	1.50	4.00
115 Steven Jackson JSY RC I	2.50	6.00
116 Matt Schaub JSY RC A	6.00	15.00
117 Ben Troupe JSY	1.50	4.00
118 Devery Henderson JSY RC F	1.50	4.00
119 Ben Watson JSY RC E	2.00	5.00
120 J.P. Losman JSY RC I	1.50	4.00
121 Keary Colbert JSY RC F	1.50	4.00
122 Darius Watts JSY RC C	1.50	4.00
123 Cedric Cobbs JSY RC D	1.50	4.00
124 Luke McCown JSY RC A	1.50	4.00
125 Michael Jenkins JSY RC A	1.50	4.00
126 Eli Manning AU/199 RC	50.00	100.00
127 Roy Williams AU/199 RC	8.00	20.00
128 Kevin Jones AU/199 RC	10.00	25.00
129 Philip Rivers AU/199 RC	40.00	80.00
130 Roethlisbergr AU/199 RC	100.00	175.00
131 Carlos Francis AU RC	3.00	8.00
132 Bradlee Van Pelt AU RC	4.00	10.00
133 Michael Turner AU RC	6.00	15.00
134 Kenechi Udeze AU RC	4.00	10.00
135 Jeff Smoker AU RC	4.00	10.00
136 Josh Harris AU RC	3.00	8.00
137 Derrick Strait AU RC	3.00	8.00
138 Jonathan Vilma AU RC	4.00	10.00
139 Triandos Luke AU RC	3.00	8.00
140 Jim Sorgi AU RC	4.00	10.00
141 Ryan Krause AU RC	3.00	8.00
142 Julius Jones AU RC	3.00	8.00
143 Mark Jones AU RC	3.00	8.00
144 P.K. Sam AU RC	3.00	8.00
145 B.J. Symons AU RC	3.00	8.00
146 Adimchinobe Echemandu AU RC	4.00	10.00
147 Casey Bramlet AU RC	3.00	8.00
148 Clarence Moore AU RC	3.00	8.00
149 D.J. Williams AU RC	5.00	12.00
150 Jeris McIntyre AU RC	3.00	8.00
151 Jerricho Cotchery AU RC	4.00	10.00
152 Andy Hall AU RC	3.00	8.00
153 Samie Parker AU RC	3.00	8.00

154 Maurice Mann AU RC 3.00 8.00
155 Jonathan Smith AU RC 3.00 8.00
156 Derrick Ward AU RC 5.00 12.00
157 D.J. Hackett AU RC 3.00 8.00
158 Craig Krenzel AU RC 3.00 8.00
159 Jared Lorenzen AU RC 4.00 10.00
160 Cody Pickett AU RC 3.00 8.00
161 Jamaar Taylor AU RC 3.00 8.00
162 Michael Boulware AU RC 5.00 12.00
163 Matt Mauck AU RC 3.00 8.00
164 John Navarre AU RC 3.00 8.00
165 Ahmad Carroll AU RC 3.00 8.00
166 Bruce Perry AU RC 3.00 8.00
167 Erik Jensen AU RC 3.00 8.00
168 Matt Kranchick AU RC 4.00 10.00
169 Courtney Anderson AU RC 3.00 8.00
170 Nate Lawrie AU RC 3.00 8.00
171 Thomas Tapeh AU RC 4.00 10.00
172 Courtney Watson AU RC 3.00 8.00
173 Drew Carter AU RC 4.00 10.00
174 Ricardo Colclough AU RC 4.00 10.00
175 Dontarrious Thomas AU RC 4.00 10.00
176 Ernest Wilford AU RC 4.00 10.00
177 Quincy Wilson AU RC 3.00 8.00
178 Derek Abney AU RC 3.00 8.00
179 Jeff Dugan AU RC 3.00 8.00
180 Ben Hartsock AU RC 3.00 8.00
181 Matt Kegel AU RC 5.00 12.00
182 Derrick Knight AU RC 3.00 8.00
183 Teddy Lehman AU RC 3.00 8.00
184 Johnnie Morant AU RC 3.00 8.00
185A B.Sanders AU RC Long AU 40.00 100.00
185B B.Sanders AU RC Short AU 10.00 25.00
186 Michael Gaines AU RC 3.00 8.00
187 Daryl Smith AU RC 3.00 8.00
188 Jason Babin AU RC 5.00 12.00

2004 Bowman's Best Green

*VETS: .8X TO 2X BASIC CARDS
*ROOKIES 81-100: .6X TO 1.5X BASIC CARDS
1-100 GREEN STATED ODDS 1:3
*ROOKIE JSYs 101-125: .5X TO 1.2X
*ROOKIE AUs 126-188: .5X TO 1.2X
GREEN AU STATED ODDS 1:5
GREEN PRINT RUN 499 SER.#'d SETS
185 Bob Sanders AU 15.00 40.00

2004 Bowman's Best Red

*VETS: 2.5X TO 6X BASIC CARDS
*ROOKIES 81-100: 2X TO 5X BASIC CARDS
*ROOKIE JSYs 101-125: 1X TO 2.5X
*ROOKIE AUs 126-188: 1X TO 2.5X
RED STATED ODDS 1:26
RED AU STATED ODDS 1:46
RED PRINT RUN 50 SER.#'d SETS

2004 Bowman's Best Best Coverage Jersey Duals

STATED ODDS 1:1088
STATED PRINT RUN 25 SER.#'d SETS
BCBF A.Boldin/L.Fitzgerald 10.00 25.00
BCBR T.Brady/P.Rivers 20.00 50.00
BCMM P.Manning/E.Manning 12.00 30.00
BCMR E.Manning/B.Roethlisberger 12.00 30.00
BCWJ R.Williams/K.Jones 6.00 15.00

2004 Bowman's Best Double Coverage Autographs

STATED ODDS 1:532
STATED PRINT RUN 50 SER.#'d SETS
DCAJE S.Jackson/L.Evans 6.00 15.00
DCAMF E.Manning/Fitzgerald 75.00 150.00
DCAPJ C.Perry/K.Jones 20.00 50.00
DCARW Rivers/Ro.Williams WR 30.00 80.00

2004 Bowman's Best Double Coverage Jerseys

GROUP A STATED ODDS 1:5747
GROUP B STATED ODDS 1:295
STATED PRINT RUN 50 SER.#'d SETS
DCEJ L.Evans/M.Jenkins B 4.00 10.00
DCFW Fitzgerald/Re.Williams B 10.00 25.00
DCJB J.Jones/T.Bell B 2.50 6.00
DCJJ S.Jackson/K.Jones B 4.00 10.00
DCMR E.Manning/Roeth./25 A 12.00 30.00
DCPJ C.Perry/G.Jones B 2.50 6.00
DCRL P.Rivers/J.Losman B 12.00 30.00
DCSM M.Schaub/L.McCown B 4.00 10.00
DCWC Ro.Will WR/Clayton B 3.00 8.00
DCWW Winslow/Watson B 3.00 8.00

2004 Bowman's Best Single Coverage Autographs

STATED ODDS 1:532
STATED PRINT RUN 50 SER.#'d SETS
SCACP Chad Pennington 10.00 25.00
SCADD Domanick Davis 10.00 25.00
SCADH Dante Hall 10.00 25.00
SCAPM Peyton Manning 40.00 80.00

2004 Bowman's Best Single Coverage Jerseys

STATED ODDS 1:265
STATED PRINT RUN 50 SER.#'d SETS
SCAB Anquan Boldin 2.50 6.00
SCCB Champ Bailey 3.00 8.00
SCCC Chris Chambers 2.50 6.00
SCDB Drew Bledsoe 3.00 8.00
SCES Emmitt Smith 6.00 15.00
SCPM Peyton Manning 10.00 25.00
SCRW Ricky Williams 3.00 8.00
SCTB Tom Brady 15.00 40.00

2004 Bowman's Best Ultimate Coverage Jersey Autographs

STATED ODDS 1:1087
STATED PRINT RUN 25 SER.#'d SETS
UCFW Fitzgerald/Ro.Will.WR 50.00 100.00
UCJP S.Jackson/C.Perry 10.00 25.00
UCJR K.Jones/Roethlisberger 100.00 200.00
UCMR E.Manning/P.Rivers 125.00 250.00

2005 Bowman's Best

This 172-card set was released in November, 2005. The set was issued in the hobby through five-card packs with a $10 SRP which came 10 packs to a box. Cards numbered 1-50 feature veterans while cards numbered 51-167 feature rookies. Five different players were issued in both signed an unsigned versions. Cards numbered 51-100 (with the exception of the few variations specifically notated) had neither signatures nor player-worn jersey swatches. Cards numbered 101-127 had player-worn jersey swatches and cards numbered 128-167 were all signed by the player. The rookie jersey cards were issued to a stated print run of 799 serial numbered sets and were inserted at a stated rate of one in 14. The signed rookie cards were issued either to a stated print run of 199 or 999 serial numbered sets. The cards numbered to 199 were inserted at a stated rate of one in 296 and the cards numbered to 999 were inserted at a stated rate of one in eight. A few players did not return their signatures in time for pack out and those cards could be redeemed until October 31, 2007.

COMP.SET w/o SPs (100) 15.00 40.00
ROOKIE JSY STATED ODDS 1:14
ROOKIE JSY PRINT RUN 799 SER.#'d SETS
ROOKIE AU/999 STATED ODDS 1:8
ROOKIE AU/199 STATED ODDS 1:296
ROOKIE AU PRINT RUN 999 SER.#'d SETS
UNPRICED GOLD PRINT RUN 1 SET
UNPRICED PRINT.PLATE PRINT RUN 1 SET
1 Tiki Barber .30 .75
2 Peyton Manning 1.00 2.50
3 Tony Gonzalez .30 .75
4 Terrell Owens .30 .75
5 Brett Favre .75 2.00
6 Rudi Johnson .25 .60
7 Hines Ward .30 .75
8 Andre Johnson .30 .75
9 Tom Brady 1.50 4.00
10 LaDainian Tomlinson .40 1.00
11 Daunte Culpepper .30 .75
12 Muhsin Muhammad .25 .60
13 Dwight Freeney .25 .60
14 Curtis Martin .30 .75
15 Eli Manning .60 1.50
16 Willis McGahee .25 .60
17 Steve McNair .30 .75
18 Jamal Lewis .30 .75
19 Reggie Wayne .30 .75
20 Trent Green .25 .60
21 Isaac Bruce .40 1.00
22 Edgerrin James .30 .75
23 Marc Bulger .25 .60
24 Torry Holt .30 .75
25 Deuce McAllister .30 .75
26 Jake Plummer .25 .60
27 Randy Moss .30 .75
28 Drew Brees .40 1.00
29 Ahman Green .30 .75
30 Marvin Harrison .30 .75
31 Michael Vick .30 .75
32 Julius Jones .25 .60
33 Matt Hasselbeck .25 .60
34 Priest Holmes .30 .75
35 Drew Bennett .30 .75
36 Donovan McNabb .30 .75
37 Chad Johnson .30 .75
38 Fred Taylor .25 .60
39 Chris Brown .25 .60
40 Jake Delhomme .25 .60
41 Joe Horn .25 .60
42 Chad Pennington .25 .60
43 Corey Dillon .25 .60
44 Byron Leftwich .25 .60
45 Javon Walker .25 .60
46 Ben Roethlisberger .60 1.50
47 Eric Moulds .25 .60
48 Domanick Davis .25 .60
49 Steven Jackson .25 .60
50 Shaun Alexander .25 .60
51 Stanford Routt RC 1.25 3.00
52 Marion Barber RC 1.25 3.00
53 Matt Roth RC 1.00 2.50
54 James Kilian RC 1.00 2.50
55 Alex Barron RC 1.00 2.50
56 Madison Hedgecock RC 1.50 4.00
57 Patrick Estes RC 1.00 2.50
58 Bryant McFadden RC 1.25 3.00
59 Dan Cody RC 1.00 2.50
60 Justin Miller RC 1.00 2.50
61 Paris Warren RC 1.25 3.00
62 Marcus Spears RC 1.25 3.00
63 Odell Thurman RC 1.50 4.00
64 Craphonso Thorpe RC 1.00 2.50
65 Dustin Fox RC 1.25 3.00
66 David Pollack RC 1.00 2.50
67 Anthony Davis RC 1.00 2.50
68 Mike Nugent RC 1.00 2.50
69 David Greene RC 1.00 2.50
70 Rick Razzano RC 1.00 2.50
70AU Rick Razzano AU 3.00 8.00
71 Mike Patterson RC 1.00 2.50
72 Derek Anderson RC 1.25 3.00
72AU Derek Anderson AU 4.00 10.00
73 Marlin Jackson RC 1.00 2.50
73AU Marlin Jackson AU 3.00 8.00
74 Boomer Grigsby RC 1.50 4.00
75 Kevin Burnett RC 1.25 3.00
76 Ryan Riddle RC 1.00 2.50
77 Brock Berlin RC 1.00 2.50
78 Khalif Barnes RC 1.25 3.00
79 Marcus Maxwell RC 1.00 2.50
80 Fred Gibson RC 1.00 2.50
81 T.A. McLendon RC 1.00 2.50
82 Kirk Morrison RC 1.50 4.00
83 Sean Considine RC 1.25 3.00
84 Luis Castillo RC 1.00 2.50
85 Darryl Blackstock RC 1.00 2.50
86 Airese Currie RC 1.00 2.50
87 Corey Webster RC 1.25 3.00
88 Kurt Campbell RC 1.00 2.50
89 Ellis Hobbs RC 1.50 4.00
90 Timmy Chang RC 1.00 2.50
91 Travis Johnson RC 1.00 2.50
92 Eric Moore RC 1.00 2.50
93 Barrett Ruud RC 1.25 3.00
94 Erasmus James RC 1.00 2.50
95 Anttaj Hawthorne RC 1.00 2.50
96 Manuel White RC 1.25 3.00
97 Rian Wallace RC 1.25 3.00
98 Justin Tuck RC 1.25 3.00
99 Travis Daniels RC 1.25 3.00
100 Donte Nicholson RC 1.00 2.50
101 Matt Jones JSY RC 1.50 4.00
102 J.J. Arrington JSY RC 2.00 5.00
103 Mark Bradley JSY RC 1.50 4.00
104 Reggie Brown JSY RC 1.50 4.00
105 Jason Campbell JSY RC 1.50 4.00
106 Maurice Clarett JSY 1.50 4.00
107 Mark Clayton JSY RC 1.50 4.00
108 Braylon Edwards JSY RC 1.50 4.00
109 Ciatrick Fason JSY RC 1.50 4.00
110 Charlie Frye JSY RC 1.50 4.00
111 Frank Gore JSY RC 3.00 8.00
112 Vincent Jackson JSY RC 2.50 6.00
113 Adam Jones JSY RC 1.50 4.00
114 Stefan LeFors JSY 1.50 4.00
114AU Stefan LeFors AU RC 3.00 8.00
115 Ryan Moats JSY 1.50 4.00
115AU Ryan Moats AU RC 3.00 8.00
116 Vernand Morency JSY RC 1.50 4.00
117 Terrence Murphy JSY RC 1.50 4.00
118 Kyle Orton JSY RC 1.50 4.00
119 Roscoe Parrish JSY RC 1.50 4.00
120 Courtney Roby JSY RC 1.50 4.00
121 Carlos Rogers JSY RC 2.50 6.00
122 Antrel Rolle JSY RC 2.50 6.00
123 Eric Shelton JSY RC 1.50 4.00
124 Andrew Walter JSY RC 1.50 4.00
125 Roddy White JSY RC 2.50 6.00
126 Cadillac Williams JSY RC 1.50 4.00
127 Troy Williamson JSY RC 1.50 4.00
128 Cedric Benson AU/199 RC 15.00 40.00
129 Aaron Rodgers AU/199 RC 350.00 500.00
130 Alex Smith QB AU/199 RC 25.00 60.00
131 Mike Williams AU/199 8.00 20.00
132 Ronnie Brown AU/199 RC 15.00 40.00
133 Adrian McPherson AU RC 3.00 8.00
134 Brandon Jacobs AU RC 8.00 20.00
135 Chad Owens AU RC 3.00 8.00
136 Chase Lyman AU RC 3.00 8.00
137 Chris Henry AU RC 4.00 10.00
138 Craig Bragg AU RC 3.00 8.00
139 Damien Nash AU RC 4.00 10.00
140 Dante Ridgeway AU RC 3.00 8.00
141 Darren Sproles AU RC 8.00 20.00
142 Deandra Cobb AU RC 3.00 8.00
143 Gino Guidugli AU RC 3.00 8.00
144 J.R. Russell AU RC 3.00 8.00
145 Jerome Mathis AU RC 5.00 12.00
146 Josh Davis AU RC 3.00 8.00
147 Kay-Jay Harris AU RC 3.00 8.00
148 Larry Brackins AU RC 3.00 8.00
149 Matt Cassel AU RC 6.00 15.00
150 Noah Herron AU RC 3.00 8.00
151 Rasheed Marshall AU RC 4.00 10.00
152 Roydell Williams AU RC 4.00 10.00
153 Ryan Fitzpatrick AU RC 5.00 12.00
154 Steve Savoy AU RC 3.00 8.00
155 Tab Perry AU RC 3.00 8.00
156 Shawne Merriman AU RC 5.00 12.00
157 Charles Frederick AU RC 3.00 8.00
158 Alvin Pearman AU RC 3.00 8.00
159 Channing Crowder AU RC 4.00 10.00
160 Fabian Washington AU RC 4.00 10.00
161 Dan Orlovsky AU RC 3.00 8.00
162 Derrick Johnson AU RC 4.00 10.00
163 Alex Smith TE AU RC 3.00 8.00
164 Cedric Houston AU RC 5.00 12.00
165 Brandon Jones AU RC 4.00 10.00
166 DeMarcus Ware AU RC 10.00 25.00
167 Lionel Gates AU RC 3.00 8.00

2005 Bowman's Best Blue

*VETS 1-50: 1.2X TO 3X BASIC CARDS
*ROOK.51-100: .5X TO 1.2X BASIC CARDS
BLUE 1-100 STATED ODDS 1:3
1-100 PRINT RUN 1399 SER.#'d SETS
*ROOKIE JSYs 101-127: .5X TO 1.2X
BLUE JSY STATED ODDS 1:37
*ROOKIE AUs: .5X TO 1.2X BASE CARDS
BLUE AU STATED ODDS 1:25
101-167 PRINT RUN 299 SER.#'d SETS

2005 Bowman's Best Bronze

*VETS 1-50: 2.5X TO 6X BASIC CARDS
*ROOK.51-100: 1X TO 2.5X BASIC CARDS
BRONZE 1-100 STATED ODDS 1:15
1-100 PRINT RUN 199 SER.#'d SETS
*ROOKIE JSYs 101-127: .6X TO 1.5X
BRONZE JSY STATED ODDS 1:111
*ROOKIE AUs: .6X TO 1.5X BASE CARDS
BRONZE AU STATED ODDS 1:75
101-167 PRINT RUN 99 SER.#'d SETS

2005 Bowman's Best Gold

GOLD 1:100 STATED ODDS 1:2340
GOLD JSY STATED ODDS 1:8796
GOLD AU STATED ODDS 1:5943
UNPRICED GOLD PRINT RUN 1 SET

2005 Bowman's Best Green

*VETS 1-50: 1.5X TO 4X BASIC CARDS
*ROOK.51-100: .6X TO 1.5X BASIC CARDS
GREEN 1-100 STATED ODDS 1:4
1-100 PRINT RUN 799 SER.#'d SETS
*ROOKIE JSYs 101-127: .4X TO 1X
GREEN JSY STATED ODDS 1:19
*ROOKIE AUs: .4X TO 1X BASE CARDS
GREEN AU STATED ODDS 1:13
101-167 PRINT RUN 599 SER.#'d SETS

2005 Bowman's Best Red

*VETS 1-50: 2X TO 5X BASIC CARDS
*ROOK.51-100: .8X TO 2X BASIC CARDS
RED 1-100 STATED ODDS 1:6
1-100 PRINT RUN 499 SER.#'d SETS
*ROOKIE JSYs 101-127: .5X TO 1.2X
RED JSY STATED ODDS 1:55
*ROOKIE AUs: .5X TO 1.2X BASE CARDS
RED AU STATED ODDS 1:37
101-167 PRINT RUN 199 SER.#'d SETS

2005 Bowman's Best Silver

*VETS 1-50: 5X TO 12X BASIC CARDS
*ROOK.51-100: 1.5X TO 4X BASIC CARDS
SILVER 1-100 STATED ODDS 1:117
*ROOKIE JSYs 101-127: .8X TO 2X
SILVER JSY STATED ODDS 1:471
*ROOKIE AUs: .8X TO 2X BASE CARDS
SILVER AU STATED ODDS 1:318
1-167 PRINT RUN 25 SER.#'d SETS
153 Ryan Fitzpatrick AU 50.00 100.00

2005 Bowman's Best Best Coverage Jersey Duals

DUAL/25 STATED ODDS 1:1278
BCRAT J.Arrington/L.Tomlinson 12.50 30.00
BCRBV M.Vick/Ro.Brown
BCRCF B.Favre/J.Campbell
BCRCH Ma.Clayton/T.Holt 10.00 25.00
BCREH B.Edwards/M.Harrison 20.00 50.00
BCRJM M.Jones/R.Moss 20.00 50.00
BCRJR A.Jones/E.Reed 10.00 25.00
BCRSB A.Smith QB/T.Brady 30.00 80.00
BCRWC Culpep/Williamson 10.00 25.00
BCRWG A.Green/C.Williams 30.00 60.00

2005 Bowman's Best Double Coverage Autographs

DUAL AU/50 STATED ODDS 1:1525
DCABW M.Williams/Ro.Brown 40.00 100.00
DCACW C.Williams/Campbell 40.00 100.00
DCAEW Edwards/Williamson 30.00 80.00
DCARS Rodgers/A.Smith QB 200.00 400.00

2005 Bowman's Best Double Coverage Jerseys

DUAL/50 STATED ODDS 1:609
DCRBM Re.Brown/R.Moats 5.00 12.00
DCRCE B.Edwards/M.Clayton 10.00 25.00
DCRCG F.Gore/M.Clarett 6.00 15.00
DCRFA C.Fason/J.Arrington 5.00 12.00
DCRFC C.Frye/J.Campbell 6.00 15.00
DCRJR A.Jones/A.Rolle 5.00 12.00
DCRSW A.Smith QB/A.Walter 10.00 25.00
DCRWB C.Williams/Ro.Brown 15.00 40.00
DCRWJ M.Jones/T.Williamson 5.00 12.00
DCRWJA R.White/V.Jackson

2005 Bowman's Best Single Coverage Autographs

AUTO/50 STATED ODDS 1:1221
SCABR Ben Roethlisberger 60.00 120.00
SCADB Deion Branch 15.00 30.00
SCAJB Jim Brown 60.00 120.00
SCAJN Joe Namath 50.00 100.00
SCAPM Peyton Manning 60.00 120.00

2005 Bowman's Best Single Coverage Jerseys

JERSEY/50 STATED ODDS 1:604
SCRAJ Adam Jones 5.00 12.00
SCRAS Alex Smith QB 15.00 40.00
SCRBE Braylon Edwards 4.00 10.00
SCRCW Cadillac Williams 4.00 10.00
SCRJA J.J. Arrington 5.00 12.00
SCRJC Jason Campbell 4.00 10.00
SCRMC Mark Clayton 4.00 10.00
SCRMJ Matt Jones 4.00 10.00
SCRRB Ronnie Brown 5.00 12.00
SCRTW Troy Williamson 4.00 10.00

2005 Bowman's Best Ultimate Coverage Jersey Autographs

DUAL AU/25 STATED ODDS 1:2533
UCBJ M.Jones/Ro.Brown 30.00 80.00
UCEC B.Edwards/M.Clayton 30.00 80.00
UCSC A.Smith QB/Campbell 40.00 100.00
UCSM A.Smith QB/P.Mann 100.00 200.00
UCWW C.Willms/Williamson 30.00 80.00

1977 Bowmar Reading Kit

The 50-card series consisting of the Bowmar NFL Reading Kit was originally issued to promote reading within school classrooms. The cards would be used to reward school children who correctly answered the questions relating to the biography on the cards. It was distributed in complete set form along with study materials, card dividers, and a colorful storage box. Each card measures roughly 8 3/8" by 13" and includes a color photo on front with a text intensive cardback.

COMPLETE SET (50) 100.00 200.00
1 Terry Metcalf 2.00 4.00
2 O.J. Simpson 2.00 4.00
3 Paul Brown 4.00 8.00
4 George Izo 2.00 4.00
5 Ernie Davis 4.00 8.00
6 Fred Gehrke 2.00 4.00
Bob Waterfield
7 Bronko Nagurski 2.00 4.00
8 Don Hutson 2.00 4.00
9 Growth of Pro Football .75 2.00
Helmets
10 The Men in the Striped Shirts .75 2.00
Referees
11 Bert Jones 2.00 4.00
12 Jack Lambert 4.00 8.00
13 Charley Taylor 2.00 4.00
14 Frank Gifford 4.00 8.00
15 Roger Staubach 7.50 15.00
16 Joe Namath 10.00 20.00
17 Teddy Roosevelt 2.00 4.00
18 Sammy Baugh 4.00 8.00
19 George Halas 4.00 8.00
20 Y. A. Tittle 4.00 8.00
21 Dan Abramowicz 2.00 4.00
22 Fran Tarkenton 4.00 8.00
23 Johnny Unitas 10.00 20.00
24 Vince Lombardi 6.00 12.00
25 Csonka 2.00 4.00
Clarence Davis
26 Ken Houston 2.00 4.00
27 Don Shula 5.00 10.00
28 LeBaron 2.00 4.00
T.McDonald
Cl.Davis
G.Pruitt
29 Jim Brown 7.50 15.00
30 Franco Harris 2.00 4.00
31 Lydell Mitchell 2.00 4.00
Franco Harris
32 Players No One Watches 2.00 4.00
33 Gale Sayers 4.00 8.00
34 Tom Dempsey 2.00 4.00
35 Sonny Jurgensen 2.00 4.00
36 George Blanda 2.00 4.00
37 Bart Starr 10.00 20.00
38 Chuck Noll 6.00 12.00
Terry Bradshaw
39 Longest Football Game 2.00 4.00
40 Rocky Bleier 2.00 4.00
41 Walter Payton 15.00 25.00
42 Ken Anderson 2.00 4.00
43 Stadiums: From the Coliseum to the Superdome .75 2.00
44 Coldest Championship Game 5.00 10.00
Bart Starr
45 Jim Bakken 2.00 4.00
46 PP and K: A Super Bowl for Young Players .75 2.00
47 Game that Made Pro Football 2.00 4.00
48 Purple People Eaters 2.00 4.00
49 Super Game 4.00 8.00
R.Staubach
J.Lambert
P.Pearson
50 Pro Bowl: A Dream that Came True 2.00 4.00

1987 Bowmar Reading Kit

This set is essentially a re-issue of the 50-card 1977 release, but has been paired down to only 40-cards. The Bowmar NFL Reading Kit was originally issued to promote reading within school classrooms. The large cards would be used to reward school children who correctly answered the questions relating to the biography on the cards. It was distributed in complete set form along with study materials, card dividers, and a colorful storage box. Each card measures roughly 8 3/8" by 13" and includes a color photo on front with a text intensive cardback.

COMPLETE SET (40) 125.00 200.00
1 Dan Marino 10.00 25.00
2 O.J. Simpson 1.50 4.00
3 Walter Payton 10.00 25.00
4 George Izo 1.50 4.00
5 Ernie Davis 3.00 8.00
6 Fred Gehrke 1.50 4.00
Bob Waterfield
7 Bronko Nagurski 1.50 4.00
8 Joe Morris 1.50 4.00
Lionel James
9 Growth of Pro Football Helmets 1.50 4.00
10 The Men in the Striped Shirts 1.50 4.00
Referees
11 Frank Gifford 3.00 8.00
12 Roger Staubach 3.00 8.00
13 Joe Namath 8.00 20.00
14 Teddy Roosevelt .75 2.00
15 William Perry 1.50 4.00
16 George Halas 3.00 8.00
17 Eat to Win .75 2.00
18 Fran Tarkenton 3.00 8.00
19 Johnny Unitas 6.00 15.00
20 Vince Lombardi 6.00 15.00
21 Marcus Allen 4.00 10.00
22 Don Shula 3.00 8.00
23 Monday Night Football 3.00 8.00
24 Jim Brown 4.00 10.00
25 Franco Harris 1.50 4.00
26 Players no one Watches 1.50 4.00
27 Gale Sayers 3.00 8.00
28 Tom Dempsey 1.50 4.00
29 Stadiums: From the Coliseum to the Superdome .75
30 Eric Dickerson 1.50 4.00
Craig James
31 Dan Fouts 3.00 8.00
32 Chuck Noll 5.00 12.00
Terry Bradshaw
33 Longest Football Game 1.50 4.00
34 Ken Anderson 1.50 4.00
35 Coldest Championship Game 3.00 8.00
36 Jim Bakken 1.50 4.00
37 Game That Made Pro Football 1.50 4.00
38 Purple People Eaters 1.50 4.00
39 Super Game 3.00 8.00
40 Pro Bowl Dream 1.50 4.00

1950 Bread for Health

The 1950 Bread for Health football card (actually bread end labels) set contains 32 bread-end labels of players in the National Football League. The cards (actually paper thin labels) measure approximately 2 3/4" by 2 3/4". These labels are not usually found in top condition due to the difficulty in removing them from the bread package. While all the bakeries who issued this set are not presently known, Fisher's Bread in the New Jersey, New York and Pennsylvania area and NBC Bread in the Michigan area are two of the bakeries that have been confirmed to date. As with many of the bread label sets of the early 1950's, an album to house the set was probably issued. Each label contains the B.E.B. copyright found on so many of the labels of this period. Labels which contain "Bread for Energy" at the bottom are not a part of the set but part of a series of movie, western and sport stars issued during the same approximate time period. The catalog designation for this set is D290-15. The cards are unnumbered but are arranged alphabetically below for convenience.

COMPLETE SET (32) 8000.00 12000.00
1 Frankie Albert 150.00 300.00
2 Elmer Bud Angsman 125.00 250.00
3 Dick Barwegan 125.00 250.00
4 Sammy Baugh 500.00 800.00
5 Charley Conerly 200.00 400.00
6 Glenn Davis 150.00 300.00
7 Don Doll 150.00 300.00
8 Tom Fears 200.00 350.00
9 Harry Gilmer 150.00 300.00
10 Otto Graham 500.00 800.00
11 Pat Harder 150.00 300.00
12 Bobby Layne 400.00 700.00
13 Sid Luckman 400.00 700.00
14 Johnny Lujack 250.00 500.00
15 John Panelli 150.00 300.00
16 Barney Poole 150.00 300.00
17 George Ratterman 150.00 300.00
18 Tobin Rote 150.00 300.00
19 Jack Russell 200.00 400.00
20 Lou Rymkus 150.00 300.00
21 Joe Signaigo 150.00 300.00
22 Mac Speedie 200.00 400.00
23 Bill Swiacki 150.00 300.00
24 Tommy Thompson QB 150.00 300.00
25 Y.A. Tittle 300.00 600.00
26 Clayton Tonnemaker 150.00 300.00
27 Charley Trippi 150.00 300.00
28 Bulldog Turner 200.00 400.00
29 Steve Van Buren 200.00 400.00
30 Bill Walsh C 150.00 300.00
31 Bob Waterfield 250.00 500.00
32 Jim White 150.00 300.00

1951 Bread For Energy

The 1951 Bread for Energy bread end labels set contains 11 known labels of players in the National Football League, professional basketball, pro boxing, and famous actors. Each measures approximately 2 3/4" by 2 3/4" with the corners cut out in typical bread label style. These labels are not usually found in top condition due to the difficulty in removing them from the bread package. While all the bakeries who issued this set are not presently known, Junge's Brand Bread in the New England area is one bakery that has been confirmed. As with many of the bread label sets of the early 1950's, an album to house the set was probably issued. Each label was printed with a red, yellow, and blue background. The cards are unnumbered but are arranged alphabetically within subject below.

37 Otto Graham FB 800.00 1200.00
38 Johnny Lujack FB 200.00 400.00
39 Johnny Rauch FB 150.00 300.00
40 Buddy Young FB 150.00 300.00

1985 Breakers Team Issue

These 5" by 7" black and white photos were issued by the 1985 Portland Breakers of the USFL. Unless noted below, each includes a studio portrait of the featured player with a dress shirt on - not a jersey. The player's name, jersey number and position are typed on the back of each. The Tim Mazzetti includes his name printed below the photo with the team name "New Orleans Breakers" as well.

COMPLETE SET (10) 25.00 50.00
1 Jearld Baylis 2.00 5.00
2 Allen Hughes 2.00 5.00
3 Dan Hurley 2.00 5.00
4 Louis Jackson 2.00 5.00
5 Tim Mazzetti 2.00 5.00
6 Ben Needham 2.00 5.00
7 Joe Restic 2.00 5.00
8 Matt Robinson 2.50 6.00
9 Dan Ross 2.50 6.00
10 Vince Williams 2.00 5.00

2011 Breast Cancer Awareness

Cards from this set were issued four at a time at home games for each team in 2011. Each card was created by one of the two NFL licensed manufacturers for one of their brands (Topps or Panini Gridiron Gear) and features the pink ribbon breast cancer awareness logo on the front. Gridiron Gear cards were also inserted into 2011 Gridiron Gear packs.

1 Beanie Wells PGG/250 .60 1.50
2 Kevin Kolb PGG/250 .60 1.50
3 Larry Fitzgerald T .75 2.00
4 Adrian Wilson T .60 1.50
5 Tony Gonzalez T .75 2.00
8 John Abraham T .60 1.50
9 Joe Flacco T .75 2.00
11 Ray Rice PGG/250 .60 1.50
12 Ed Reed T .75 2.00
13 Steve Johnson PGG/250 .60 1.50
14 Ryan Fitzpatrick T .60 1.50
15 Marcell Dareus PGG/250 .50 1.25
16 C.J. Spiller T .60 1.50
17 Cam Newton T 2.50 6.00
18 Steve Smith T .75 2.00
19 Jonathan Stewart PGG/250 .60 1.50
20 DeAngelo Williams PGG/250 .60 1.50
21 Lance Briggs T .75 2.00
22 Jay Cutler PGG/250 .60 1.50
23 Matt Forte T .60 1.50
24 Brian Urlacher PGG/250 1.00 2.50
25 A.J. Green PGG/250 1.25 3.00
26 Andy Dalton PGG/250 1.00 2.50
27 Jermaine Gresham T .60 1.50
28 Jordan Shipley T .60 1.50
29 Josh Cribbs T .60 1.50
30 Greg Little PGG/250 .60 1.50
31 Peyton Hillis PGG/250 .60 1.50
32 Colt McCoy T .60 1.50
34 Felix Jones T .60 1.50
35 Tony Romo T .75 2.00
37 Von Miller PGG/250 .75 2.00
38 Champ Bailey T .75 2.00
39 Kyle Orton T .60 1.50
40 Tim Tebow PGG/250 1.00 2.50
41 Jahvid Best T .60 1.50
42 Calvin Johnson PGG/250 1.00 2.50
43 Matthew Stafford T .75 2.00
44 Ndamukong Suh PGG/250 .75 2.00
45 A.J. Hawk T .60 1.50
46 Aaron Rodgers T 1.50 4.00
47 Charles Woodson PGG/250 1.00 2.50
48 Clay Matthews PGG/250 1.00 2.50
49 Andre Johnson PGG/250 .75 2.00
50 Matt Schaub T .60 1.50
51 Mario Williams T .60 1.50
52 Arian Foster PGG/250 .60 1.50
54 Dwight Freeney T .60 1.50
55 Peyton Manning T 2.00 5.00
57 David Garrard T .60 1.50
58 Maurice Jones-Drew T .60 1.50
60 Blaine Gabbert PGG/250 .50 1.25
61 Dwayne Bowe PGG/250 .75 2.00
62 Matt Cassel T .60 1.50
63 Derrick Johnson T .60 1.50
64 Jamaal Charles PGG/250 .75 2.00
65 Davone Bess T .60 1.50
66 Daniel Thomas PGG/250 .50 1.25
67 Chad Henne T .75 2.00
70 Christian Ponder PGG/250 .50 1.25
71 Percy Harvin T .60 1.50
72 Adrian Peterson T 1.00 2.50
73 Chad Ochocinco PGG/250 .60 1.50
74 Wes Welker T .75 2.00
75 Jerod Mayo T .60 1.50
77 Drew Brees T 1.00 2.50
79 Jonathan Vilma T .60 1.50
80 Mark Ingram PGG/250 .75 2.00
81 Ahmad Bradshaw PGG/250 .60 1.50
82 Eli Manning T .75 2.00
83 Hakeem Nicks PGG/250 .60 1.50
84 Justin Tuck T .60 1.50
86 Mark Sanchez T .60 1.50
87 Nick Mangold T .60 1.50
88 Darrelle Revis PGG/250 .60 1.50
89 Michael Bush T .60 1.50
92 Richard Seymour T .60 1.50
93 DeSean Jackson PGG/250 .75 2.00
94 LeSean McCoy PGG/250 1.00 2.50
95 Asante Samuel T .60 1.50
96 Michael Vick T .75 2.00
97 Mike Wallace PGG/250 .60 1.50
98 Ben Roethlisberger T 1.00 2.50
99 Hines Ward PGG/250 .75 2.00
100 Troy Polamalu T 1.00 2.50
102 Vincent Jackson PGG/250 .60 1.50
103 Philip Rivers T 1.00 2.50
104 Ryan Mathews T .75 2.00
105 Michael Crabtree T .60 1.50
106 Josh Morgan PGG/250 .60 1.50
107 Frank Gore T .75 2.00
109 Earl Thomas T .75 2.00
111 Sidney Rice PGG/250 .60 1.50
112 Mike Williams USC T .60 1.50
114 Steven Jackson T .60 1.50
116 Chris Long T .60 1.50
117 LeGarrette Blount T .75 2.00
118 Josh Freeman T .75 2.00
119 Mike Williams PGG/250 .75 2.00
120 Kellen Winslow PGG/250 .60 1.50
121 Matt Hasselbeck T .60 1.50
122 Akeem Ayers PGG/250 .50 1.25
124 Nate Washington T .60 1.50
125 Chris Cooley T .60 1.50
126 LaRon Landry T .60 1.50

1992 Breyers Bookmarks

This 66-card set (of bookmarks) was produced by Breyers to promote reading in the home cities of eleven NFL teams. The bookmarks measure approximately 2" by 8". The fronts feature a cut-out player photo superimposed on a yellow - background decorated with open books. A lighter yellow panel above the player contains a player profile and a biography. The player's name appears in a black stripe that borders the panel. The Breyers logo and the words "Reading Team" appear on an electronic billboard design. The backs list book selections found at the library, the American Library Association logo, and the sponsor logo. The cards are numbered on the front and are arranged in team order.

COMPLETE SET (66) 100.00 250.00
1 Greg Townsend 1.00 2.50
2 Steve Wisniewski 1.00 2.50
3 Art Shell CO 1.60 4.00
4 Jeff Jaeger 1.00 2.50
5 Lisa O'Day 1.00 2.50
6 Los Angeles Raiders 1.00 2.50
7 Jerry Rice 6.00 15.00
8 Don Griffin 1.00 2.50
9 John Taylor 1.00 2.50
10 Joe Montana 25.00 40.00
11 Michael Walter 1.00 2.50
12 San Francisco 49ers 1.00 2.50
13 Junior Seau 1.60 4.00
14 John Friesz 1.00 2.50
15 Ronnie Harmon 1.00 2.50
16 Marion Butts 1.00 2.50
17 Gill Byrd 1.00 2.50
18 San Diego Chargers 1.00 2.50
19 Kelly Stouffer 1.00 2.50
20 John Kasay 1.00 2.50
21 Andy Heck 1.00 2.50
22 Jacob Green 1.00 2.50
23 Eugene Robinson 1.00 2.50
24 Seattle Seahawks 1.00 2.50
25 Pat Swilling 1.60 4.00
26 Vaughan Johnson 1.00 2.50
27 Bobby Hebert 1.00 2.50
28 Floyd Turner 1.00 2.50
29 Rickey Jackson 1.00 2.50
30 New Orleans Saints 1.00 2.50
31 Harvey Williams 1.60 4.00
32 Derrick Thomas 2.00 5.00
33 Bill Maas 1.00 2.50
34 Tim Grunhard 1.00 2.50
35 Jonathan Hayes 1.00 2.50
36 Kansas City Chiefs 1.00 2.50
37 Rich Gannon
38 Tim Irwin 1.00 2.50
39 Audray McMillian 1.00 2.50
40 Gary Zimmerman 1.00 2.50
41 Hassan Jones 1.00 2.50
42 Minnesota Vikings 1.00 2.50
43 Eric Green 1.00 2.50
44 Louis Lipps 1.00 2.50
45 Rod Woodson 1.60 4.00
46 Merril Hoge 1.00 2.50
47 Gary Anderson RB 1.00 2.50
48 Pittsburgh Steelers 1.00 2.50
49 Anthony Johnson 1.00 2.50
50 Bill Brooks 1.00 2.50
51 Jeff Herrod 1.00 2.50
52 Mike Prior 1.00 2.50
53 Jeff George 1.60 4.00
54 Indianapolis Colts 1.00 2.50
55 Troy Aikman 6.00 15.00
56 Jay Novacek 1.60 4.00
57 Emmitt Smith 18.00 30.00
58 Michael Irvin 2.40 6.00
59 Dorie Braddy 1.00 2.50
60 Dallas Cowboys 1.00 2.50
61 Clay Matthews 1.60 4.00
62 Tommy Vardell 1.00 2.50
63 Eric Turner 1.00 2.50
64 Mike Johnson 1.00 2.50
65 James Jones DT 1.00 2.50
66 Cleveland Browns 1.00 2.50

1990 British Petroleum

This 36-card standard-size set was issued two cards at a time by British Petroleum gas stations throughout California in association with Talent Network Inc. of Skokie, Illinois. There were five winning player cards issued in the following quantities. Andre Tippett: $5 - 990 cards, Freeman McNeil: $10 - 325 cards, Clay Matthews: $100 - 18 cards, Tim Harris: $1,000 - three cards, and Deion Sanders $10,000 - one card. Most of these winning cards are not valued as collectibles in the checklist below as they were more valuable as prize winners. The set has multiple players numbered 1, 3, 6, 8, and 10, and we have arranged each group of same-numbered cards into alphabetical order. Each game piece was two NFL football cards inside a cardboard frame, with full-color head shots in uniform of the player. Cards are frequently found in less than Mint condition due to the fact that glue was applied to the obverses of the cards in the manufacturing process. There were 36 cards in the set, and the object of the game was to collect two adjacent numbers, 1-2, 3-4, 5-6, 7-8, or 9-10. One number was easy to get, but the other was difficult. The game redemptions expired in October 1991. Each card was produced in two different card back variations: black with contest rules and advertising design featuring full color football scene.

COMPLETE SET (36) 40.00 80.00
*CONTEST BACK: .4X TO 1X
1A John Elway 5.00 12.00
1B Boomer Esiason .40 1.00
1C Jim Everett .40 1.00
1D Bernie Kosar .40 1.00
1E Karl Mecklenburg .30 .75
1F Bruce Smith .75 2.00
2 Deion Sanders/1* WIN
3A Roger Craig .40 1.00
3B Randall Cunningham .75 2.00
3C Keith Jackson .40 1.00
3D Dan Marino 6.00 15.00
3E Freddie Joe Nunn .30 .75
3F Jerry Rice 3.00 8.00
3G Vinny Testaverde .40 1.00
3H John L. Williams .30 .75
4 Tim Harris/3* WIN
5 Clay Matthews/18* WIN
6A Neal Anderson .30 .75
6B Duane Bickett .30 .75
6C Ronnie Lott .75 2.00
6D Anthony Munoz .40 1.00
6E Christian Okoye .30 .75
6F Barry Sanders 5.00 12.00
7 Freeman McNeil/325* WIN
8A Cornelius Bennett .40 1.00
8B Anthony Carter .40 1.00
8C Jim Kelly 1.50 4.00
8D Louis Lipps .30 .75
8E Phil Simms .75 2.00
8F Billy Ray Smith .30 .75
8G Lawrence Taylor .75 2.00
9 Andre Tippett/990* WIN
10A Bo Jackson .75 2.00
10B Howie Long .75 2.00
10C Don Majkowski .30 .75
10D Art Monk .40 1.00
10E Warren Moon .40 1.00
10F Mike Singletary .75 2.00
10G Al Toon .40 1.00
10H Herschel Walker .75 2.00
10I Reggie White 1.25 3.00

1962 Broncos Team Issue

The Broncos issued several series of player photos in the early 1960s with some invariably being released in multiple years. Each of the photos in this group are black-and-white and measure approximately 8" by 10" and are blankbacked. The line of text below the image contains the following from left to right: player name and team name in all caps.

1 George Herring/(dropping back to pass) 7.50 15.00
2 George Herring/(running pose) 7.50 15.00
3 George Herring/(punting pose) 7.50 15.00
4 Tom Higginbotham 7.50 15.00

1963 Broncos Team Issue

The Broncos issued several series of player photos in the early 1960s with some invariably being released in multiple years. Each of the photos in this group are black-and-white and measure approximately 8" by 10" and are blankbacked. The line of text below the image contains the following from left to right: player name, position spelled out, height, weight and team name in all caps.

1 George Herring/(portrait) 7.50 15.00
2 George Herring/(handing off the ball) 7.50 15.00
3 Jack Hill 7.50 15.00
4 Jerry Hopkins 7.50 15.00

1967-68 Broncos Team Issue

The Broncos issued several series of player photos in the late 1960s through early 1970s with many invariably being released in multiple years. The format is the same for most of the sets with only subtle differences in the type (size and style) and information contained below the photo. Each of the photos in this group are black-and-white measuring approximately 5" by 7" and are blankbacked and unnumbered. The line of text contains the following from left to right: player name, position (completely spelled out), height, weight, and team name. We've included what is thought to be the year of issue. The 1967 photos were printed with both upper and lower case lettering, while the 1968 issue was done in all caps. We've listed the only known photos in the set.

COMPLETE SET (4) 25.00 50.00
1 Carl Cunningham 67 7.50 15.00
2 Al Denson 67 7.50 15.00
3 Wallace Dickey 68 7.50 15.00
4 Charlie Greer 68 7.50 15.00

1969 Broncos Team Issue

The Broncos issued several series of player photos in the 1960s and 1970s with many invariably being released in multiple years. The format is the same for most of the sets with only subtle differences in the type (size and style) and information contained below the photo. Each of these black-and-white photos measures approximately 5" by 7" and is blankbacked and unnumbered. The line of text for the 1969 issue contains the following from left to right: player name (in all caps), position (spelled out in all caps), height, weight, and team name (in all caps). We've listed the only known photos in the set.

COMPLETE SET (16) 100.00 200.00
1 Tom Beer 7.50 15.00
2 Phil Brady 7.50 15.00
3 Sam Brunelli 7.50 15.00
4 George Burrell 7.50 15.00
5 Grady Cavness 7.50 15.00
6 Ken Criter 7.50 15.00
7 Al Denson 7.50 15.00
8 John Embree 7.50 15.00
9 Walter Highsmith 7.50 15.00
10 Gus Hollomon 7.50 15.00
11 Pete Liske 7.50 15.00
12 Rex Mirich 7.50 15.00
13 Tom Oberg 7.50 15.00
14 Frank Richter 7.50 15.00
15 Paul Smith 7.50 15.00
16 Bob Young 7.50 15.00

1970 Broncos Carlson-Frink Dairy Coaches

These large (roughly 6" by 11 7/8") cards were issued by Carlson-Frink Dairy in the Denver area about 1970. Each is blankbacked and features a black and white photo of a then current Denver Broncos coach. A written "Football Tip" is also included below the coach's photo. The set includes just one unique photo for each coach but it is included on five different card numbers that begin with the first initial of the coach's last name. The "Football Tip" is unique to each of the five cards per coach. Lou Saban has also been found only in an unnumbered card version. Any confirmed additions to this list are appreciated.

COMPLETE SET (36) 2500.00 4000.00
COMP.SHORT SET (8) 500.00 800.00
C1 Joe Collier 60.00 100.00
C2 Joe Collier 60.00 100.00
C3 Joe Collier 60.00 100.00
C4 Joe Collier 60.00 100.00
C5 Joe Collier 60.00 100.00
D1 Whitey Dovell 60.00 100.00
D2 Whitey Dovell 60.00 100.00
D3 Whitey Dovell 60.00 100.00
D4 Whitey Dovell 60.00 100.00
D5 Whitey Dovell 60.00 100.00
E1 Hunter Enis 60.00 100.00
E2 Hunter Enis 60.00 100.00
E3 Hunter Enis 60.00 100.00
E4 Hunter Enis 60.00 100.00
E5 Hunter Enis 60.00 100.00
G1 Fred Gehrke 60.00 100.00
G2 Fred Gehrke 60.00 100.00
G3 Fred Gehrke 60.00 100.00
G4 Fred Gehrke 60.00 100.00
G5 Fred Gehrke 60.00 100.00
J1 Stan Jones 75.00 125.00
J2 Stan Jones 75.00 125.00
J3 Stan Jones 75.00 125.00
J4 Stan Jones 75.00 125.00
J5 Stan Jones 75.00 125.00
M1 Dick MacPherson 60.00 100.00
M2 Dick MacPherson 60.00 100.00
M3 Dick MacPherson 60.00 100.00
M4 Dick MacPherson 60.00 100.00
M5 Dick MacPherson 60.00 100.00
R1 Sam Rutigliano 75.00 125.00
R2 Sam Rutigliano 75.00 125.00
R3 Sam Rutigliano 75.00 125.00
R4 Sam Rutigliano 75.00 125.00
R5 Sam Rutigliano 75.00 125.00
S1 Lou Saban 75.00 125.00
S2 Lou Saban 75.00 125.00
S3 Lou Saban 75.00 125.00
S4 Lou Saban 75.00 125.00
S5 Lou Saban 75.00 125.00
NNO Lou Saban 75.00 125.00

1970 Broncos Team Issue

The Broncos issued several series of player photos in the 1960s and 1970s with many invariably being released in multiple years. The format is the same for most of the sets with only subtle differences in the type (size and style) and information contained below the photo. Each of these black-and-white photos measures approximately 5" by 7" and is blankbacked and unnumbered. The line of text for the 1970 issue contains the following from left to right: player name (in upper and lower case), position (initials), and team name (in upper and lower case). We've listed the only known photos in the set.

COMPLETE SET (11) 50.00 100.00
1 Bob Anderson 6.00 12.00
2 Dave Costa 6.00 12.00
3 Ken Criter 6.00 12.00
4 Mike Current 6.00 12.00
5 Fred Forsberg 6.00 12.00
6 Charles Greer 6.00 12.00
7 Larry Kaminski 6.00 12.00
8 Fran Lynch 6.00 12.00
9 Mike Schnitker 6.00 12.00
10 Paul Smith 6.00 12.00
11 Dave Washington 6.00 12.00

1970 Broncos Texaco

The Broncos and Texaco released this set in 1970. Each card is actually an artist's rendering in an 8" by 10" format. The backs are unnumbered and contain extensive player information as well information about the artist, Von Schroeder.

COMPLETE SET (10) 100.00 175.00
1 Bob Anderson RB 7.50 15.00
2 Dave Costa 7.50 15.00
3 Pete Duranko 7.50 15.00
4 George Goeddeke SP 15.00 30.00
5 Mike Haffner 7.50 15.00
6 Rich Jackson 7.50 15.00
7 Larry Kaminski 7.50 15.00
8 Floyd Little 10.00 20.00
9 Pete Liske SP 15.00 30.00
10 Bill Van Heusen 7.50 15.00

1971 Broncos Team Issue 5x7

The Broncos issued several series of player photos in the 1960s and 1970s with many invariably being released in multiple years. The format is the same for most of the sets with only subtle differences in the type (size and style) and information contained below the photo. Each of these black-and-white photos measures approximately 5" by 7" and is blankbacked and unnumbered. The line of text for the 1971 issue contains the following from left to right: player name (in upper and lower case), height, weight, position (initials), and team name (in upper and lower case). We've listed the only known photos in the set.

COMPLETE SET (6) 25.00 40.00
1 Jack Gehrke 4.00 8.00
2 Dwight Harrison 4.00 8.00
3 Randy Montgomery 4.00 8.00
4 Steve Ramsey 4.00 8.00
5 Roger Shoals 4.00 8.00
6 Olen Underwood 4.00 8.00

1971-72 Broncos Team Issue 8x10

The Broncos issued several series of player photos in the 1960s and 1970s with many invariably being released in multiple years. The format is roughly the same for most of the sets with only subtle differences in the type (size and style) and information contained below the photo. Each of these black-and-white photos measures approximately 8" by 10" and is blankbacked and unnumbered.

COMPLETE SET (10) 50.00 100.00
1 Lyle Alzado 7.50 15.00
2 Mike Current 5.00 10.00
3 Fred Forsberg 5.00 10.00
4 Charles Greer 5.00 10.00
5 Don Horn 5.00 10.00
6 Bill McKoy 5.00 10.00
7 George Saimes 5.00 10.00
8 Paul Smith 5.00 10.00
9 Bill Thompson 5.00 10.00
10 Jim Turner 5.00 10.00
Don Horn

1972 Broncos Team Issue

The Broncos issued several series of player photos in the 1960s and 1970s with many invariably being released in multiple years. The format is the same for most of the sets with only subtle differences in the type (size and style) and information contained below the photo. Each of these black-and-white photos measures approximately 5" by 7" and is blankbacked and unnumbered. The line of text for the 1972 issue contains the following from left to right: player name (in all caps), position (initials in all caps), and team city and team name (in all caps). We've listed only the known photos in the set, additions to this list are welcomed.

COMPLETE SET (6) 25.00 50.00
1 Carter Campbell 5.00 10.00
2 Cornell Gordon 5.00 10.00
3 Larron Jackson 5.00 10.00
4 Tommy Lyons 5.00 10.00
5 Bobby Maples 5.00 10.00
6 Jerry Simmons 5.00 10.00

1973 Broncos Team Issue

The Broncos issued several series of player photos in the 1960s and 1970s with many invariably being released in multiple years. The format is the same for most of the sets with only subtle differences in the type (size and style) and information contained below the photo. Each of these black-and-white photos measures approximately 5" by 7" and is blankbacked and unnumbered. The line of text for the 1973 issue contains the following from left to right: player name (in all caps), position (initials in all caps) followed by a comma, and team city and team name (in all caps). We've listed only the known photos in the set, additions to this list are welcomed.

COMPLETE SET (16) 75.00 150.00
1 Lyle Alzado 6.00 12.00
2 Otis Armstrong 6.00 12.00
3 Barney Chavous 5.00 10.00
4 Mike Current 5.00 10.00
5 Joe Dawkins 5.00 10.00
6 John Grant 5.00 10.00
7 Larron Jackson 73 5.00 10.00
8 Calvin Jones 5.00 10.00
9 Larry Kaminski 5.00 10.00
10 Bill Laskey 5.00 10.00
11 Tom Lyons 5.00 10.00
12 Randy Montgomery 5.00 10.00
13 Riley Odoms 5.00 10.00
14 Oliver Ross 5.00 10.00
15 Ed Smith 5.00 10.00
16 Bill Van Heusen 5.00 10.00

1975 Broncos Team Issue

The Broncos issued several series of player photos in the 1960s and 1970s with many invariably being released in multiple years. The format is very similar for most of the sets with only subtle differences in the type (size and style) and information contained below the photo. Each of these black-and-white photos measures approximately 5" by 7" and is blankbacked and unnumbered. The line of text for the 1975 issue contains the following from left to right: player name (in all caps), position (initials in all caps), and team city (in all caps). We've listed only the known photos in the set, additions to this list are welcomed.

COMPLETE SET (15) 60.00 120.00
1 Stan Rogers 5.00 10.00
2 John Rowser 5.00 10.00
3 Bob Swenson 5.00 10.00
4 Paul Smith 5.00 10.00
5 Jeff Severson 5.00 10.00
6 Boyd Brown 5.00 10.00
7 Rubin Carter 5.00 10.00
8 Jack Dolbin 5.00 10.00
9 Mike Franckowiak 5.00 10.00
10 Randy Gradishar 6.00 12.00
11 Paul Howard 5.00 10.00
12 Claudie Minor 5.00 10.00
13 Phil Olsen 5.00 10.00
14 Steve Ramsey 5.00 10.00
15 Joe Rizzo 5.00 10.00

1976 Broncos Team Issue

The Broncos issued several series of player photos in the 1960s and 1970s with many invariably being released in multiple years. The format is very similar for most of the sets with only subtle differences in the type (size and style) and information contained below the photo. Each of these black-and-white photos measures approximately 5" by 7" and is blankbacked and unnumbered. The line of text for the 1975 issue contains the following from left to right: player name (in upper and lower case letters), position (initials or spelled out fully in upper and lower case), and team city (in upper and lower case). We've listed only the known photos in the set, additions to this list are welcomed.

1 Randy Poltl 5.00 10.00
2 Earlie Thomas 5.00 10.00

1977 Broncos Burger King Glasses

Burger King restaurants released this set of 6-drinking glasses during the 1977 NFL season in Denver area stores. Each features a black and white photo of a Broncos player with his name and team name below the picture.

COMPLETE SET (6) 45.00 90.00
1 Lyle Alzado 12.50 25.00
2 Randy Gradishar 10.00 20.00
3 Tom Jackson 10.00 20.00
4 Craig Morton 12.50 25.00
5 Haven Moses 7.50 15.00
6 Riley Odoms 7.50 15.00

1977 Broncos Orange Crush Cans

This can set features player images of the Denver Broncos printed on Orange Crush Soda cans. The set is unnumbered and checklisted below in alphabetical order. Reportedly, there were 64-different cans made. Any additions to the below list are appreciated.

COMPLETE SET (64) 200.00 350.00
1 Henry Allison 2.50 5.00
2 Lyle Alzado 5.00 10.00
3 Steve Antonopulos TR 2.50 5.00
4 Otis Armstrong 4.00 8.00
5 Rick Baska 2.50 5.00
6 Ronnie Bill EQ MGR 2.50 5.00
7 Marv Braden CO 2.50 5.00
8 Rubin Carter 2.50 5.00
9 Barney Chavous 3.00 6.00
10 Joe Collier CO 2.50 5.00
11 Bucky Dilts 2.50 5.00
12 Jack Dolbin 3.00 6.00
13 Larry Elliot EQ MGR 2.50 5.00
14 Larry Evans 2.50 5.00
15 Dave Frei DIR 2.50 5.00
16 Steve Foley 3.00 6.00
17 Ron Egloff 2.50 5.00
18 Bob Gambold CO 2.50 5.00
19 Fred Gehrke GM 2.50 5.00
20 Tom Glassic 2.50 5.00
21 Randy Gradishar 5.00 10.00
22 John Grant 2.50 5.00
23 Ken Gray CO 2.50 5.00
24 Paul Howard 2.50 5.00
25 Allen Hurst TR 2.50 5.00
26 Glenn Hyde 2.50 5.00
27 Bernard Jackson 2.50 5.00
28 Tom Jackson 5.00 10.00
29 Jim Jensen 2.50 5.00
30 Stan Jones CO 4.00 8.00
31 Rob Lytle 3.00 6.00
32 Jon Keyworth 3.00 6.00
33 Brison Manor 2.50 5.00
34 Bobby Maples 2.50 5.00
35 Andy Maurer 2.50 5.00
36 Red Miller CO 4.00 8.00
37 Claudie Minor 2.50 5.00
38 Mike Montler 2.50 5.00
39 Myrel Moore CO 2.50 5.00
40 Craig Morton 5.00 10.00
41 Haven Moses 4.00 8.00
42 Rob Nairne 2.50 5.00
43 Riley Odoms 3.00 6.00
44 Babe Parilli CO 3.00 6.00
45 Bob Peck 2.50 5.00
46 Craig Penrose 2.50 5.00
47 Lonnie Perrin 2.50 5.00
48 Fran Polstoot CO 2.50 5.00
49 Randy Poltl 2.50 5.00
50 Randy Rich 2.50 5.00
51 Larry Riley 2.50 5.00
52 Joe Rizzo 2.50 5.00
53 Paul Roach CO 2.50 5.00
54 Steve Schindler 2.50 5.00
55 John Schultz 2.50 5.00
56 Paul Smith 3.00 6.00
57 Gail Stuckey 2.50 5.00
58 Bob Swenson 2.50 5.00
59 Bill Thompson 3.00 6.00
60 Godwin Turk 2.50 5.00
61 Jim Turner 3.00 6.00
62 Rick Upchurch 4.00 8.00
63 Norris Weese 2.50 5.00
64 Louis Wright 3.00 6.00

1980 Broncos Stamps Police

The 1980 Denver Broncos set are not cards but stamps each measuring approximately 3" by 3". Each stamp actually contains three smaller stamps, two player stamps and the Denver Broncos logo stamp. The set is co-sponsored by Albertson's, the Kiwanis Club, and the local law enforcement agency. A different stamp pair was given away each week for nine weeks by Albertson's food stores in the Denver Metro area. The set is unnumbered, although player uniform numbers appear on each small stamp. The set has been listed below in alphabetical order based on the player stamp on the left side. The back of each pair states "Support your local Law Enforcement Agency" and gives instructions on how to reach the police by phone. The backs of the stamps contain 1980 NFL and NFL Player's Association copyright dates. There was also a poster (to hold the stamps) issued which originally was priced at 99 cents. It was a color action picture of four Broncos tackling a Chargers running back measuring approximately 21" by 29"; the poster is much more difficult to find now than the set of stamps.

COMPLETE SET (9) 7.50 15.00
1 Barney Chavous .60 1.50
2 Bernard Jackson .60 1.50
3 Tom Jackson 1.25 3.00
4 Brison Manor .60 1.50
5 Claudie Minor .60 1.50
6 Craig Morton 1.25 3.00
7 Jim Turner .75 2.00
8 Rick Upchurch 1.00 2.50
9 Louis Wright .75 2.00

1982 Broncos Police

The 1982 Denver Broncos set contains 15 unnumbered cards. The cards measure approximately 2 5/8" by 4 1/8". The uniform numbers, which appear on the fronts of the cards, are used in the checklist below. The set was sponsored by the Colorado Springs Police Department and features "Broncos Tips" and the Broncos helmet logo on the back. Card backs feature black print on white card stock. The fronts contain both the Denver helmet logo and the logo of the Colorado Springs Police Department. The cards of Barney Chavous and Randy Gradishar are supposedly harder to find than the other cards in the set, with Chavous considered the more difficult of the two. In addition Riley Odoms and Dave Preston seem to be harder to find.

COMPLETE SET (15) 75.00 150.00
7 Craig Morton 4.00 10.00
11 Luke Prestridge 1.50 4.00
20 Louis Wright 1.50 4.00
24 Rick Parros 1.50 4.00
36 Bill Thompson 1.50 4.00
41 Rob Lytle 1.50 4.00
46 Dave Preston SP 4.00 10.00
51 Bob Swenson 1.50 4.00
53 Randy Gradishar SP 20.00 50.00
57 Tom Jackson 4.00 10.00
60 Paul Howard 1.50 4.00
68 Rubin Carter 1.50 4.00
79 Barney Chavous SP 20.00 50.00
80 Rick Upchurch 2.50 6.00
88 Riley Odoms SP 4.00 10.00

1984 Broncos KOA

These cards were issued as part of a KOA "Match 'N Win" and KOA/Denver Broncos Silver Anniversary Sweepstakes. They were distributed at any participating Dairy Queen or Safeway in the Metro Denver area between September 17 and November 11, 1984. The cards measure approximately 2" by 4", with a tab at the bottom (measuring 1 1/8" in length). The front has a black and white photo of the player from the waist up. Above the photo the card reads "KOA Official Denver Broncos Memory Series" in blue print with white outlining. The lower portion of the photo is covered over by three items: 1) player number, name, and position; 2) a logo of the original American Football League and the sponsor's name or logo (Rocky Mountain News, Kodak, Dairy Queen, Wood Bros. Homes, KMGH-TV-7 Denver, Safeway, and Armour). The picture and these items are enframed by a color border on a color background. There were three each of eight different color schemes used. The tab portion of the card has three silver footballs that were to be scratched off with a coin. The back lists the rules governing the sweepstakes. There are four players marked as SP in the checklist below who are supposedly tougher to find than the others; they are Bobby Anderson, Randy Gradishar, Floyd Little, and Claudie Minor. The cards are unnumbered but are listed below in uniform number order. The prices listed refer to unscratched cards.

COMPLETE SET (24) 100.00 200.00
7 Craig Morton 5.00 12.00
11 Bob Anderson SP 5.00 12.00
12 Charley Johnson 4.00 10.00
15 Jim Turner 3.00 8.00
21 Gene Mingo 3.00 8.00
22 Fran Lynch 3.00 8.00
23 Goose Gonsoulin 3.00 8.00
24 Otis Armstrong 4.00 10.00
24 Willie Brown 5.00 12.00
25 Haven Moses 4.00 10.00
36 Bill Thompson 3.00 8.00
42 Bill Van Heusen 3.00 8.00
44 Floyd Little SP 8.00 20.00
53 Randy Gradishar SP 8.00 20.00
71 Claudie Minor SP 5.00 12.00
72 Sam Brunelli 3.00 8.00
74 Mike Current 3.00 8.00
75 Eldon Danenhauer 3.00 8.00
78 Marv Montgomery 3.00 8.00
81 Billy Masters 3.00 8.00
82 Bob Scarpitto 3.00 8.00
87 Lionel Taylor 4.00 10.00
87 Rich Jackson 3.00 8.00
88 Riley Odoms 3.00 8.00

1984 Broncos Pizza Hut Glasses

This set of small glasses was distributed and sponsored by Pizza Hut to commemorate the Denver Broncos 25th anniversary. Each glass includes color artist's renderings of 6-different Broncos all-time greats.

COMPLETE SET (4) 15.00 25.00
1 Alzado 5.00 12.00
Glassic
Gons
T.Jack
Trip
Watson
2 Bryan 3.00 8.00
Murl
Moses
Thomp
Upch
Van Heu
3 Chav 3.00 8.00
Grad
Odoms
Smith
Turner
Wright
4 R.Jack 2.00 5.00
C.John
Little
Minor
Swen
Tayl

1987 Broncos Ace Fact Pack

This 33-card set measures approximately 2 1/4" by 3 5/8". This set consists of 22 player cards and 11 organizational cards. These cards, which were issued in Great Britain and made in West Germany (by Ace Fact Pack), have a playing card design on the back. The cards are checklisted below in alphabetical order.

COMPLETE SET (33) 150.00 300.00
1 Keith Bishop 1.25 3.00
2 Bill Bryan 1.25 3.00
3 Mark Cooper 1.25 3.00
4 John Elway 125.00 250.00
5 Steve Foley 1.25 3.00
6 Mike Harden 1.25 3.00
7 Ricky Hunley 1.25 3.00
8 Vance Johnson 2.00 5.00
9 Rulon Jones 1.25 3.00
10 Rich Karlis 1.25 3.00
11 Clarence Kay 1.25 3.00
12 Ken Lanier 1.25 3.00
13 Karl Mecklenburg 3.00 8.00
14 Chris Norman 1.25 3.00
15 Jim Ryan 1.25 3.00
16 Dennis Smith 2.00 5.00
17 Dave Studdard 1.25 3.00
18 Andre Townsend 1.25 3.00
19 Steve Watson 2.00 5.00
20 Gerald Willhite 1.25 3.00
21 Sammy Winder 2.00 5.00
22 Louis Wright 2.00 5.00
23 Broncos Helmet 1.25 3.00
24 Broncos Information 1.25 3.00
25 Broncos Uniform 1.25 3.00
26 Game Record Holders 1.25 3.00
27 Season Record Holders 1.25 3.00
28 Career Record Holders 1.25 3.00
29 Record 1967-86 1.25 3.00
30 1986 Team Statistics 1.25 3.00
31 All-Time Greats 1.25 3.00
32 Roll of Honour 1.25 3.00
33 Denver Mile High 1.25 3.00

1987 Broncos Orange Crush

This nine-card set of Denver Broncos' ex-players was sponsored by Orange Crush and KOA Radio. The cards are standard size, 2 1/2" by 3 1/2", and feature black and white photos inside a blue and orange frame. The set is a salute to the "Ring of Famers," Denver's best players in its history as a franchise. Card backs (written in black, orange, and blue on white card stock) feature a capsule biography and indicate the year of induction into the Ring of Fame. Reportedly 1.35 million cards were distributed over a three-week period at participating 7-Eleven and Albertsons stores in Denver and surrounding areas.

COMPLETE SET (9) 4.00 8.00
1 Bill Thompson .40 1.00
2 Lionel Taylor .50 1.25
3 Goose Gonsoulin .30 .75
4 Paul Smith .30 .75
5 Rich Jackson .30 .75
6 Charley Johnson .40 1.00
7 Floyd Little .75 2.00
8 Frank Tripucka .40 1.00
9 Gerald Phipps .30 .75

1997 Broncos Collector's Choice

Upper Deck released several team sets in 1997 in a blister pack wrapper. Each of the 14-cards in this set are very similar to the base Collector's Choice cards except for the card numbering on the cardback. A cover/checklist card was added featuring the team helmet.

COMPLETE SET (14) 1.60 4.00
DN1 Tory James .02 .10
DN2 Terrell Davis .50 1.25
DN3 Tyrone Braxton .02 .10
DN4 John Mobley .05 .15
DN5 Bill Romanowski .02 .10
DN6 Vaughn Hebron .02 .10
DN7 Trevor Pryce .05 .15
DN8 Alfred Williams .02 .10
DN9 John Elway .60 1.50
DN10 Shannon Sharpe .08 .25
DN11 Steve Atwater .05 .15
DN12 Neil Smith .08 .25
DN13 Darrien Gordon .05 .15
DN14 Broncos Logo .20 .50
Checklist

1997 Broncos Score

This 15-card set of the Denver Broncos was distributed in five-card packs with a suggested retail price of $1.99. The fronts feature color action player photos with white borders and the player's name and team logo printed in team color foil at the bottom. The backs carry player information and career statistics. Platinum Team parallel cards were randomly seeded in packs featuring all foil cardfronts.

COMPLETE SET (15) 4.00 10.00
*PLATINUM TEAMS: 1X TO 2X
1 John Elway 1.20 3.00
2 Shannon Sharpe .30 .75
3 Anthony Miller .15 .40
4 Terrell Davis 1.00 2.50
5 Bill Romanowski .08 .25
6 Ed McCaffrey .15 .40
7 John Mobley .15 .40
8 Alfred Williams .08 .25
9 Steve Atwater .15 .40
10 Jeff Lewis .15 .40
11 Aaron Craver .08 .25
12 Rod Smith WR .50 1.25
13 Tyrone Braxton .08 .25
14 Ray Crockett .08 .25
15 Allen Aldridge .08 .25

2006 Broncos Topps

COMPLETE SET (12) 3.00 6.00
DEN1 Domonique Foxworth .25 .60
DEN2 Rod Smith .30 .75
DEN3 John Lynch .25 .60
DEN4 Tatum Bell .25 .60
DEN5 Brandon Marshall .50 1.25
DEN6 D.J. Williams .25 .60
DEN7 Jake Plummer .25 .60
DEN8 Ashley Lelie .25 .60
DEN9 Ron Dayne .30 .75
DEN10 Champ Bailey .30 .75
DEN11 Javon Walker .30 .75
DEN12 Jay Cutler .30 .75

2007 Broncos Topps

COMPLETE SET (12) 2.50 5.00
1 Jay Cutler .40 1.00
2 Rod Smith .50 1.25
3 Champ Bailey .50 1.25
4 Mike Bell .50 1.25
5 Travis Henry .50 1.25
6 Brandon Marshall .50 1.25
7 Elvis Dumervil .40 1.00
8 Javon Walker .50 1.25
9 Dre Bly .40 1.00
10 Jason Elam .40 1.00
11 John Lynch .50 1.25
12 D J Williams .40 1.00

2008 Broncos Topps

COMPLETE SET (12) 2.50 5.00
1 Jay Cutler .40 1.00
2 Selvin Young .40 1.00
3 Brandon Marshall .50 1.25
4 Champ Bailey .50 1.25
5 Tony Scheffler .40 1.00
6 Travis Henry .40 1.00
7 Brandon Stokley .40 1.00
8 Dre Bly .40 1.00
9 Elvis Dumervil .40 1.00
10 D.J. Williams .40 1.00
11 John Lynch .50 1.25
12 Eddie Royal .40 1.00

2014 Broncos Panini Super Bowl XLVIII

COMPLETE SET (10) 3.00 8.00
1 Peyton Manning 1.25 3.00
2 Knowshon Moreno .40 1.00
3 Montee Ball .40 1.00
4 Eric Decker .40 1.00
5 Demaryius Thomas .50 1.25
6 Wes Welker .50 1.25
7 Julius Thomas .40 1.00
8 Danny Trevathan .40 1.00
9 Shaun Phillips .40 1.00
10 Matt Prater .60 1.50

2014 Broncos Score

COMPLETE SET (10) 2.50 6.00
1 Peyton Manning 1.25 3.00
2 Von Miller .50 1.25
3 Julius Thomas .40 1.00
4 Demaryius Thomas .50 1.25
5 Terrance Knighton .40 1.00
6 DeMarcus Ware .50 1.25
7 Aqib Talib .40 1.00
SS1 Sam Schmidt IRL .60 1.50
SS2 Sam Schmidt Project IRL .60 1.50
NNO Coupon Card .20 .50

1986 Brownell Heisman

This large-sized black and white set features drawings of past Heisman Trophy winners by Art Brownell. The set (first 50-cards) was originally available as part of a promotion. They are unnumbered and blank backed so they have been assigned numbers below in chronological order according to when each player won the Heisman Trophy. Since Archie Griffin of Ohio State won the Heisman in both 1974 and 1975 there is only one card for him. The Vinny Testaverde and Tim Brown cards were produced at a later date. The cards measure approximately 7 15/16" by 10".

COMPLETE SET (52) 350.00 600.00
1 Jay Berwanger 4.00 10.00
2 Larry Kelley 4.00 10.00
3 Clint Frank 4.00 10.00
4 Davey O'Brien 4.00 10.00
5 Nile Kinnick 8.00 20.00
6 Tom Harmon 4.00 10.00
7 Bruce Smith 4.00 10.00
8 Frank Sinkwich 4.00 10.00
9 Angelo Bertelli 4.00 10.00
10 Les Horvath 4.00 10.00
11 Doc Blanchard 5.00 12.00
12 Glenn Davis 5.00 12.00
13 Johnny Lujack 8.00 20.00
14 Doak Walker 6.00 15.00
15 Leon Hart 4.00 10.00
16 Vic Janowicz 5.00 12.00
17 Dick Kazmaier 4.00 10.00
18 Bill Vessels 4.00 10.00
19 John Lattner 5.00 12.00
20 Alan Ameche 5.00 12.00
21 Howard Cassady 4.00 10.00
22 Paul Hornung 8.00 20.00
23 John David Crow 4.00 10.00
24 Pete Dawkins 4.00 10.00
25 Billy Cannon 5.00 12.00
26 Joe Bellino 4.00 10.00
27 Ernie Davis 12.00 30.00
28 Terry Baker RB 4.00 10.00
29 Roger Staubach 15.00 40.00
30 John Huarte 4.00 10.00
31 Mike Garrett 4.00 10.00
32 Steve Spurrier 6.00 15.00
33 Gary Beban 4.00 10.00
34 O.J. Simpson 8.00 20.00
35 Steve Owens 4.00 10.00
36 Jim Plunkett 5.00 12.00
37 Pat Sullivan 4.00 10.00
38 Johnny Rodgers 4.00 10.00
39 John Cappelletti 4.00 10.00
40 Archie Griffin 5.00 12.00
41 Tony Dorsett 10.00 25.00
42 Earl Campbell 8.00 20.00
43 Billy Sims 4.00 10.00
44 Charles White 4.00 10.00
45 George Rogers 4.00 10.00
46 Marcus Allen 10.00 25.00
47 Herschel Walker 5.00 12.00
48 Mike Rozier 4.00 10.00
49 Doug Flutie 8.00 20.00
50 Bo Jackson 5.00 12.00
51 Vinny Testaverde 6.00 15.00
52 Tim Brown 10.00 25.00

1946 Browns Sears

These eight cards measure approximately 2 1/2" by 4". They were issued by Sears and Roebuck and feature players from the debut season of the Cleveland Browns. The cards were printed on heavy white paper stock and include a black and white photo of the featured player on the front with a team schedule on back. Cardfronts also included a message to follow the Browns and shop at Sears Stores. Several very early cards of Hall of Famers are included in this set. We have checklisted this set in alphabetical order.

COMPLETE SET (8) 1000.00 1800.00
1 Ernie Blandin 90.00 150.00
2 Jim Daniell 90.00 150.00
3 Fred Evans 90.00 150.00
4 Frank Gatski 150.00 250.00
5 Otto Graham 350.00 600.00
6 Dante Lavelli 175.00 300.00
7 Mel Maceau 90.00 150.00
8 George Young 125.00 200.00

1948 Browns Sohio

These large (measure either 8" by 9 7/8" or 7 3/4" by 9 7/8") black and white photos are issued by Cleveland area Sohio stores in 1948. They are very simiar to the 1949 release and were printed on heavy card stock and each includes a black and white photo along with brief biographical information on the cardfronts and "Compliments of Sohio" printed within the bottom border. Since the photos are unnumbered, we have sequenced them in alphabetical order.

COMPLETE SET (3) 150.00 300.00
1 Horace Gillom 25.00 50.00
2 Marion Motley 100.00 175.00
3 Bill Willis 40.00 80.00

1949 Browns Sohio

These large black and white photos were issued by Cleveland area Sohio stores in 1949 as a complete set in an envelope. The exact size of each photo varies slightly by as much as 1/16" but roughly each measures 8" by 9 3/4". They were printed on heavy card stock and each includes a black and white photo along with brief biographical information on the cardfronts. Since the photos are unnumbered, we have sequenced them in alphabetical order. Note that most of the photos in this release have been reproduced with slight differences in paper stock and size.

COMPLETE SET (11) 500.00 800.00
1 Bob Gaudio 25.00 40.00
2 Otto Graham 175.00 300.00
3 Lou Groza 90.00 150.00
4 Lin Houston 25.00 40.00
5 Weldon Humble 25.00 40.00
6 Tommy James 25.00 40.00
7 Edgar Jones 30.00 50.00
8 Dante Lavelli 60.00 100.00
9 Marion Motley 100.00 175.00
10 Lou Saban 30.00 50.00
11 Mac Speedie 50.00 80.00

1950 Browns Team Issue 6x9

This set of team-issued photos measures approximately 6 1/4" by 9" and was printed on thin paper stock and issued as a set. The fronts feature black-and-white posed action shots framed by white borders with a facsimile autogrpah near the bottoom of the photo. The cardbacks are blank and unnumbered and the photos are checklisted below in alphabetical order.

COMPLETE SET (25) 600.00 1000.00
1 Tony Adamle 18.00 30.00
2 Paul Brown 50.00 80.00
3 Rex Bumgardner 18.00 30.00
4 Frank Gatski 30.00 50.00
5 Abe Gibron 18.00 30.00
6 Otto Graham 125.00 200.00
7 Forrest Grigg 18.00 30.00
8 Lou Groza 60.00 100.00
9 Hal Herring 18.00 30.00
10 Lin Houston 18.00 30.00
11 Tommy James 18.00 30.00
12 Dub Jones 20.00 35.00
13 Warren Lahr 18.00 30.00
14 Dante Lavelli 40.00 75.00
15 Cliff Lewis 18.00 30.00
16 Dom Moselle 18.00 30.00
17 Marion Motley 60.00 100.00
18 Derrell F. Palmer 18.00 30.00
19 Don Phelps 18.00 30.00
20 John Russell 18.00 30.00
21 Lou Rymkus 20.00 35.00
22 Mac Speedie 30.00 50.00
23 Thomas Thompson 18.00 30.00
24 Bill Willis 35.00 60.00
25 George Young 25.00 40.00

1950 Browns Team Issue 8x10

This set of Cleveland Browns photos measures approximately 8" by 10" and features black and white posed action shots framed by white borders. The year is an estimate based upon when the players appeared on the same Browns' team. The player's name appears in a small white box close to the bottom of the photo and the cardbacks are blank. Each is unnumbered and checklisted below in alphabetical order. It is thought that the set could have been released by Sohio. These photos are identical to the 1954 set and some players may have been issued both years. Any additions to either checklist is appreciated.

COMPLETE SET (11) 400.00 750.00
1 Tony Adamle 25.00 40.00
2 Otto Graham 125.00 200.00
3 Horace Gillom 25.00 40.00
4 Chubby Grigg 25.00 40.00
5 Lou Groza 75.00 125.00
6 Lin Houston 25.00 40.00
7 Dub Jones 30.00 50.00
8 Dante Lavelli 40.00 75.00
9 Marion Motley 75.00 125.00
10 Mac Speedie 35.00 60.00
11 Bill Willis 35.00 60.00

1951 Browns Team Issue 6x9

This set of team-issued photos measures approximately 6 1/2" by 9" and features black and white posed action shots framed by white borders. The set was distributed in an attractive off-white envelope with orange and brown trim titled "Cleveland Browns Photographs". The set is similar to the 1950 issue, but the player's name appears in script close to the photo. The backs are blank. The cards are unnumbered and checklisted below in alphabetical order.

COMPLETE SET (25) 600.00 1000.00
1 Tony Adamle 18.00 30.00
2 Alex Agase 18.00 30.00
3 Rex Bumgardner 18.00 30.00
4 Emerson Cole 18.00 30.00
5 Len Ford 35.00 60.00
6 Frank Gatski 30.00 50.00
7 Horace Gillom 18.00 30.00
8 Ken Gorgal 18.00 30.00
9 Otto Graham 125.00 200.00
10 Forrest Grigg 18.00 30.00
11 Lou Groza 60.00 100.00
12 Hal Herring 18.00 30.00
13 Lin Houston 18.00 30.00
14 Weldon Humble 18.00 30.00
15 Tommy James 18.00 30.00
16 Dub Jones 20.00 35.00
17 Warren Lahr 18.00 30.00
18 Dante Lavelli 40.00 75.00
19 Cliff Lewis 18.00 30.00
20 Marion Motley 60.00 100.00
21 Lou Rymkus 20.00 35.00
22 Mac Speedie 30.00 50.00
23 Tommy Thompson LB 18.00 30.00
24 Bill Willis 35.00 60.00
25 George Young 25.00 40.00

1952 Browns Team Issue

This set of team-issued photos measures approximately 8" by 10" and features black and white posed action shots framed by white borders. Each photo was issued with the player's name, position, and team name stamped on the back making it quite different than other Browns photos of the era. The photos are unnumbered and checklisted below in alphabetical order.

1 Doug Atkins 25.00 40.00
2 Darrel Brewster 15.00 30.00
3 Ken Carpenter 15.00 30.00
4 Tom Catlin 15.00 30.00
5 Don Colo 15.00 30.00
6 Gene Donaldson 15.00 30.00
7 Abe Gibron 15.00 30.00
8 Horace Gillom 15.00 30.00
9 Jerry Helluin 15.00 30.00
10 Sherm Howard 15.00 30.00
11 Dub Jones 20.00 35.00
12 Warren Lahr 15.00 30.00
13 Chuck Noll 30.00 50.00
14 Derrell Palmer 15.00 30.00
15 George Ratterman 15.00 30.00
16 Ray Renfro 20.00 35.00
17 John Sandusky 15.00 30.00
18 Tommy Thompson 15.00 30.00

1953 Browns Carling Beer

This set of ten black and white posed action shots was sponsored by Carling Black Label Beer and features members of the Cleveland Browns. The pictures measure approximately 8" by 12 1/4" and have white borders. The sponsor's name and the team name appear below the picture in black lettering. The photos are very similar to the 1954 issue but with several different players and four players with different images. Each is unnumbered and the backs are blank. The serial number in the lower right corner on the fronts reads "DBL 54" plus a unique letter for each player. The photos were shot against a background of an open field with trees.

COMPLETE SET (10) 250.00 400.00
54F Dante Lavelli 25.00 40.00
54G Otto Graham 75.00 125.00
54H Lou Groza 40.00 75.00
54J Dub Jones 20.00 35.00
54K Gorgal 18.00 30.00
54L Len Ford 25.00 40.00
54M Bill Willis 25.00 40.00
54N Thompson 18.00 30.00
54O Frank Gatski 20.00 35.00
54P Jagade 18.00 30.00

1953 Browns Team Issue

The Cleveland Browns issued and distributed this 12-photo set. Each measures approximately 0 1/2" by 10 1/4" and features a black and white photo. The player's name and position appear in a small white box near the photo.

COMPLETE SET (12) 300.00 450.00
1 Len Ford 20.00 35.00
2 Frank Gatski 20.00 35.00
3 Abe Gibron 15.00 25.00
4 Ken Gorgal 12.00 20.00
5 Otto Graham 75.00 135.00
6 Lou Groza 35.00 60.00
7 Harry Jagade 12.00 20.00
8 Dub Jones 15.00 25.00
9 Dante Lavelli 30.00 50.00
10 Ray Renfro 15.00 25.00
11 Tommy Thompson 15.00 25.00
12 Bill Willis 20.00 35.00

1954 Browns Fisher Foods

This 10-card set features 8 1/2" by 10 1/2" black-and-white photos of the 1954 Cleveland Browns sponsored by Fisher Foods. The photos are very similar to many of the Browns Team Issue sets of the era but can be differentiated by the "Fisher Foods" type within the bottom border. Some or all of the photos an also be found missing the Fisher Foods name. The backs are blank. The cards are unnumbered and checklisted below in alphabetical order.

COMPLETE SET (10) 250.00 400.00
1 Darrel Brewster 12.00 20.00
2 Tom Catlin 12.00 20.00
3 Len Ford 20.00 35.00
4 Otto Graham 60.00 100.00
5 Lou Groza 30.00 50.00
6 Kenny Konz 15.00 25.00
7 Dante Lavelli 25.00 40.00
8 Mike McCormack 20.00 35.00
9 Fred Morrison 12.00 20.00
10 Chuck Noll 60.00 100.00

1954 Browns Team Issue

This photo set features 8 1/2" by 10 1/2" black-and-white photos of the 1954 Cleveland Browns. The photos are very similar to many of the Browns Team Issue sets of the era and are identical to the Fisher Foods set except for the omission of the company name in the bottom border. The player's name and position appear inside a box found near the player's image. The backs are blank. The cards are unnumbered and checklisted below in alphabetical order.

COMPLETE SET (10) 250.00 400.00
1 Tom Catlin 12.00 20.00
2 Len Ford 20.00 35.00
3 Abe Gibron 12.00 20.00
4 Otto Graham 60.00 100.00
5 Lou Groza 30.00 50.00
6 Dante Lavelli 25.00 40.00
7 Mike McCormack 20.00 35.00
8 Fred Morrison 12.00 20.00
9 Chuck Noll 60.00 100.00
10 Tommy Thompson 12.00 20.00

1954 Browns Team Issue 8x10

The Cleveland Browns released this set of photos with each measuring approximately 8" by 10" - slightly smaller than the Fisher Foods photos. The photos feature black and white posed action shots framed by white borders with just the player's name on the front. The year is an estimate based upon when the players appeared on the same Browns' team. Each is blankbacked and unnumbered and checklisted below in alphabetical order. It is thought that the set could have been released by Sohio. These photos are identical in style to the 1947 set and some players may have been issued both years. Any additions to either checklist is appreciated.

COMPLETE SET (8) 90.00 150.00
1 Darrell Brewster 12.00 20.00
2 Len Ford 15.00 25.00
3 Kenny Konz 12.00 20.00
4 Warren Lahr 12.00 20.00
5 Mike McCormack 15.00 25.00
6 Fred Morrison 12.00 20.00
7 Don Phelps 12.00 20.00
8 Tommy Thompson 12.00 20.00

1955-56 Browns Team Issue

This set consists of 8 1/2" by 10" posed player photos, with white borders and blank backs. Most of the photos are poses shot from the waist up; a few (Colo, Ford, and Lahr) picture the player in an action pose. The player's name and position are printed in the bottom white border in large letters. The photos are unnumbered and checklisted below in alphabetical order.

COMPLETE SET (23) 250.00 400.00
1 Maurice Bassett 7.50 15.00
2 Harold Bradley 7.50 15.00
3 Darrell(Pete) Brewster 7.50 15.00
4 Don Colo 7.50 15.00
5 Len Ford 15.00 25.00
6 Bobby Freeman 7.50 15.00
7 Bob Gain 7.50 15.00
8 Frank Gatski 15.00 25.00
9 Abe Gibron 7.50 15.00
10 Lou Groza 25.00 40.00
11 Tommy James 7.50 15.00
12 Dub Jones 10.00 20.00
13 Kenny Konz 7.50 15.00
14 Warren Lahr 7.50 15.00
15 Dante Lavelli 18.00 30.00
16 Carlton Massey 7.50 15.00
17 Mike McCormack 15.00 25.00
18 Walt Michaels 10.00 20.00
19 Chuck Noll 40.00 75.00
20 Babe Parilli 10.00 20.00
21 Don Paul DB 7.50 15.00
22 Ray Renfro 10.00 20.00
23 George Ratterman 10.00 20.00

1954 Browns Carling Beer

This set of black and white posed action shots was sponsored by Carling Black Label Beer and features members of the Cleveland Browns. The pictures measure approximately 8" by 12 1/4" and have white borders. The sponsor's name and the team name appear below the picture in black lettering. The photos are very similar to the 1953 issue with several new players and updated pictures on four players. Each of the backs are blank and the photo numbering in the lower right corner reads "DBL 54" followed by a unique letter for each player. We've included those numbers/letters below when known. The photos were shot against a background of an open field with trees.

COMPLETE SET (10) 300.00 500.00
1 Darrel Brewster 18.00 30.00
2 Tom Catlin 18.00 30.00
3 Len Ford 25.00 40.00
4 Otto Graham 75.00 125.00
5 Lou Groza 40.00 75.00
6 Kenny Konz 18.00 30.00
7 Dante Lavelli 25.00 40.00
8 Mike McCormack 20.00 35.00
9 Fred Morrison 18.00 30.00
10 Chuck Noll 50.00 100.00

1955 Browns Color Postcards

Measuring approximately 6" by 9", these color postcards feature Cleveland Browns players. The cards have rounded corners are are thought to have been distributed directly by the Browns.

COMPLETE SET (6) 125.00 225.00
1 Maurice Bassett 12.50 25.00
2 Don Colo 12.50 25.00
3 Frank Gatski 25.00 40.00
4 Lou Groza 40.00 75.00
5 Dante Lavelli 35.00 60.00
6 George Ratterman 12.50 25.00

1956 Browns Team Issue

This set was issued by the Cleveland Browns. Each photo is very similar to the 1954-55 set except for the size which is 6 3/4" by 8 1/2." All are black and white player photos with white borders and blankbacks. The player's name and position are printed in the bottom white border. The photos are unnumbered and checklisted below in alphabetical order.

COMPLETE SET (7) 125.00 200.00
1 Otto Graham 35.00 60.00
2 Dante Lavelli 15.00 25.00
3 Carlton Massey 7.50 15.00
4 Chuck Noll 25.00 50.00
5 Babe Parilli 10.00 20.00
6 George Ratterman 10.00 20.00
7 Ray Renfro 10.00 20.00

1958 Browns Carling Beer

This set of black-and-white posed action shots was sponsored by Carling Black Label Beer and features members of the Cleveland Browns. The pictures measure approximately 8 1/2" by 11 1/2" and have white borders. The sponsor's name and the team name appear below the picture in black lettering. The backs are blank and the pictures are numbered on the fronts with a "DBL" prefix on the card numbers.

COMPLETE SET (10) 350.00 600.00
227A Ray Renfro 20.00 40.00
227B Jim Brown 150.00 250.00
227C Art Hunter 20.00 40.00
227D Lowe Wren 20.00 40.00
227E Vince Costello 20.00 40.00
227F Chuck Noll 60.00 120.00
227G Paul Wiggin 20.00 40.00
227H Lou Groza 30.00 60.00
227I Bob Gain 20.00 40.00
227J Milt Plum 25.00 50.00

1958-59 Browns Team Issue

These cards are an unnumbered, blank-backed, team issue set of black and white photographs of the Cleveland Browns measuring approximately 8 1/2" by 10 1/2". The set features posed action shots of players whose name and position appear in a white reverse-out block burned into the bottom of each picture. The photos are very similar to the 1961 Browns Team Issue therefore differences are included below for player in both sets. The unnumbered cards are listed below alphabetically.

COMPLETE SET (28) 175.00 300.00
1 Leroy Bolden 6.00 12.00
2 Lew Carpenter 6.00 12.00
3 Tom Catlin 6.00 12.00
4 Don Colo 6.00 12.00
5 Vince Costello 6.00 12.00
6 Galen Fiss 6.00 12.00
7 Bob Gain 6.00 12.00
8 Gene Hickerson 10.00 20.00
9 Art Hunter 6.00 12.00
10 Hank Jordan 10.00 20.00
11 Ken Konz 6.00 12.00
12 Warren Lahr 6.00 12.00
13 Willie McClung 6.00 12.00
14 Mike McCormack 7.50 15.00
15 Walt Michaels 7.50 15.00
16 Bobby Mitchell 10.00 20.00
17 Ed Modzelewski 6.00 12.00
18 Jim Ninowski 6.00 12.00
19 Chuck Noll 12.50 25.00
20 Fran O'Brien 6.00 12.00
21 Bernie Parrish 6.00 12.00
22 Don Paul 6.00 12.00
23 Milt Plum 7.50 15.00
24 Bill Quinlan 6.00 12.00
25 Ray Renfro 7.50 15.00
26 Jim Shofner 7.50 15.00
27 Paul Wiggin 6.00 12.00
28 Lowe Wren 6.00 12.00

1959 Browns Carling Beer

This set of black and white posed action shots was sponsored by Carling Black Label Beer and features members of the Cleveland Browns. The pictures measure approximately 8 1/2" by 11 1/2" and have white borders. The sponsor's name and the team name appear below the picture in black lettering. The backs are typically blank and were printed on glossy paper stock. The pictures are numbered in the lower right corner on the fronts. The photos were shot against a background of an open field with trees. The set is dated by the fact that Billy Howton's last year with Cleveland was 1959. This set was reprinted in the late 1980's; the reprints are on slightly thicker cardboard stock and typically show the Henry M. Barr stamp on the back.

COMPLETE SET (10) 350.00 600.00
302A Leroy Bolden 25.00 40.00
302B Vince Costello 25.00 40.00
302C Galen Fiss 25.00 40.00
302D Jim Brown 100.00 200.00
302E Lou Groza 40.00 75.00

302F Walt Michaels	30.00	50.00
302G Bobby Mitchell	35.00	60.00
302J Bob Gain	25.00	40.00
302K Bill Howton	30.00	50.00
302H Milt Plum	30.00	50.00

1959 Browns Shell Posters

This set of posters was distributed by Shell Oil in 1959. The pictures are black and white drawings with a light sepia color and measure approximately 11 3/4" by 13 3/4". The unnumbered posters are arranged alphabetically by the player's last name and feature members of the Cleveland Browns. Any additions to this list are appreciated.

COMPLETE SET (4)	75.00	125.00
1 Preston Carpenter	15.00	25.00
2 Lou Groza	30.00	50.00
3 Milt Plum	18.00	30.00
4 Jim Ray Smith	15.00	25.00

1960 Browns Team Issue

These large photos are an unnumbered, blank-backed, team issue set of black and white photographs of the Cleveland Browns. Each measures approximately 6" by 9 1/8" and was printed on thin glossy paper stock. The set features posed action shots of players with a facsimile autograph across the image. The cardbacks are blank and they are listed below alphabetically.

COMPLETE SET (32)	300.00	500.00
1 Sam Baker	6.00	12.00
2 Jim Brown	50.00	80.00
3 Paul Brown CO	15.00	30.00
4 Vince Costello	6.00	12.00
5 Len Dawson	30.00	50.00
6 Bob Denton	6.00	12.00
7 Ross Fichtner	6.00	12.00
8 Galen Fiss	6.00	12.00
9 Don Fleming	6.00	12.00
10 Bobby Franklin	6.00	12.00
11 Bob Gain	6.00	12.00
12 Prentice Gautt	6.00	12.00
13 Gene Hickerson	10.00	20.00
14 Jim Houston	6.00	12.00
15 Rich Kreitling	6.00	12.00
16 Dave Lloyd	6.00	12.00
17 Mike McCormack	10.00	20.00
18 Walt Michaels	7.50	15.00
19 Bobby Mitchell	12.50	25.00
20 John Morrow	6.00	12.00
21 Rich Mostardo	6.00	12.00
22 Fred Murphy	6.00	12.00
23 Gern Nagler	6.00	12.00
24 Bernie Parrish	6.00	12.00
25 Floyd Peters	6.00	12.00
26 Milt Plum	7.50	15.00
27 Jim Prestel	6.00	12.00
28 Dick Schafrath	7.50	15.00
29 Jim Shofner	7.50	15.00
30 Jim Ray Smith	6.00	12.00
31 Paul Wiggin	6.00	12.00
32 John Wooten	6.00	12.00

1961 Browns Carling Beer

This set of ten black and white posed action shots was sponsored by Carling Black Label Beer and features members of the Cleveland Browns. The pictures measure approximately 8 1/2" by 11 1/2" and have white borders. The sponsor's name and the team name appear below the picture in black lettering. The banks are blank. The pictures are numbered in the lower right corner on the fronts. The set is dated by the fact that Jim Houston's first year was 1960 and Bobby Mitchell and Milt Plum's last year with the Browns was 1961.

COMPLETE SET (10)	350.00	600.00
439A Milt Plum	30.00	50.00
439B Mike McCormack	30.00	50.00
439C Bob Gain	25.00	40.00
439D John Morrow	25.00	40.00
439E Jim Brown	100.00	200.00
439F Bobby Mitchell	35.00	60.00
439G Bobby Franklin	25.00	40.00
439H Jim Ray Smith	25.00	40.00
439K Jim Houston	25.00	40.00
439L Ray Renfro	30.00	50.00

1961 Browns National City Bank

The 1961 National City Bank Cleveland Browns football card set contains 36 brown and white cards each measuring approximately 2 1/2" by 3 9/16". The cards were issued in sheets of six cards, with each sheet of six given a set number and each individual card within the sheet given a player number. In the checklist below the cards have been numbered consecutively from one to 36. On the actual card, set/sheet number one will appear on cards 1 through 6, set number two on cards 7 through 12, etc. The front of the card states that the card is a "Quarterback Club Brownie Card". The backs of the cards contain the card number, a short biography and an ad for the National City Bank. Cards still in uncut (sheet of six) form are valued at one to two times the sum of the single card prices listed below. Len Dawson's card predates his 1963 Fleer Rookie Card by two years. It has been reported that cards #25-30 are in shorter supply than the rest.

COMPLETE SET (36)	1200.00	2000.00
1 Mike McCormack	30.00	60.00
2 Jim Brown	300.00	500.00
3 Leon Clarke	20.00	35.00
4 Walt Michaels	25.00	40.00
5 Jim Ray Smith	20.00	35.00
6 Quarterback Club	40.00	80.00
7 Len Dawson	250.00	400.00
8 John Morrow	20.00	35.00
9 Bernie Parrish	25.00	40.00
10 Floyd Peters	25.00	40.00
11 Paul Wiggin	25.00	40.00
12 John Wooten	25.00	40.00
13 Ray Renfro	25.00	40.00
14 Galen Fiss	20.00	35.00
15 Dave Lloyd	20.00	35.00
16 Dick Schafrath	30.00	50.00
17 Ross Fichtner	20.00	35.00
18 Gern Nagler	20.00	35.00
19 Rich Kreitling	20.00	35.00
20 Duane Putnam	20.00	35.00
21 Vince Costello	20.00	35.00
22 Jim Shofner	25.00	40.00
23 Sam Baker	25.00	40.00
24 Bob Gain	25.00	40.00
25 Lou Groza	100.00	175.00
26 Don Fleming	35.00	60.00
27 Tom Watkins	30.00	50.00
28 Jim Houston	35.00	60.00
29 Larry Stephens	30.00	50.00
30 Bobby Mitchell	90.00	150.00
31 Bobby Franklin	20.00	35.00
32 Charley Ferguson	20.00	35.00
33 Johnny Brewer	20.00	35.00
34 Bob Crespino	20.00	35.00
35 Milt Plum	35.00	60.00
36 Preston Powell	20.00	35.00

1961 Browns Team Issue Large

These large photo cards are an unnumbered, blank-backed, team issue set of black and white photographs of the Cleveland Browns measuring approximately 8 1/2" by 10 1/2". The set features posed action shots of players whose name and position appear in a white reverse-out block burned into the bottom of each picture. The cards are listed below alphabetically.

COMPLETE SET (20)	175.00	300.00
1 Jim Brown	50.00	75.00
2 Galen Fiss	6.00	12.00
3 Don Fleming	6.00	12.00
4 Bobby Franklin	6.00	12.00
5 Bob Gain	6.00	12.00
6 Jim Houston	6.00	12.00
7 Rich Kreitling	6.00	12.00
8 Dave Lloyd	6.00	12.00
9 Mike McCormack	12.00	20.00
10 Bobby Mitchell	15.00	25.00
11 John Morrow	6.00	12.00
12 Bernie Parrish	6.00	12.00
13 Milt Plum	7.50	15.00
14 Ray Renfro	7.50	15.00
15 Dick Schafrath	7.50	15.00
16 Jim Shofner	7.50	15.00
17 Jim Ray Smith	6.00	12.00
18 Tom Watkins	6.00	12.00
19 Paul Wiggin	6.00	12.00
20 John Wooten	6.00	12.00

1961 Browns Team Issue Small

These photos are an unnumbered, blank-backed, team issue set of black and white images of the Cleveland Browns. The photos are virtually identical to the 1960 Team Issue set except for the slightly different size. Each measures approximately 6 1/8" by 9" and was printed on thin glossy paper stock. The set features posed action shots of players with a facsimile autograph across the image. Many of the same photos were used for the 1961 Browns National City card set. The cardbacks are blank and the photos are listed below alphabetically.

COMPLETE SET (30)	200.00	350.00
1 Sam Baker	5.00	10.00
2 Jim Brown	50.00	75.00
3 Paul Brown CO	15.00	25.00
4 Vince Costello	5.00	10.00
5 Len Dawson	25.00	40.00
6 Charley Ferguson	5.00	10.00
7 Ross Fichtner	5.00	10.00
8 Galen Fiss	5.00	10.00
9 Don Fleming	5.00	10.00
10 Bobby Franklin	5.00	10.00
11 Bob Gain	5.00	10.00
12 Prentice Gautt	5.00	10.00
13 Lou Groza	15.00	25.00
14 Jim Houston	5.00	10.00
15 Dave Lloyd	5.00	10.00
16 Mike McCormack	7.50	15.00
17 Walt Michaels	6.00	12.00
18 Bobby Mitchell	10.00	20.00
19 John Morrow	5.00	10.00
20 Bernie Parrish	5.00	10.00
21 Floyd Peters	5.00	10.00
22 Milt Plum	6.00	12.00
23 Preston Powell	5.00	10.00
24 Duane Putnam	5.00	10.00
25 Ray Renfro	6.00	12.00
26 Jim Shofner	6.00	12.00
27 Jim Ray Smith	5.00	10.00
28 Tom Watkins	5.00	10.00
29 Paul Wiggin	5.00	10.00
30 John Wooten	5.00	10.00

1963 Browns Team Issue

These large photos measure approximately 7 1/2" by 9 1/2" and feature a black-and-white player photo on blankbacked glossy paper stock. Each includes the player's name, position (initials) and team name in the bottom border. They are very similar in design to the 1964-66 set, but can be differentiated by the 1/4" space between the player's name, position, and team name. The photos are unnumbered and checklisted below in alphabetical order.

COMPLETE SET (28)	150.00	250.00
1 Johnny Brewer	5.00	10.00
2 Monte Clark	5.00	10.00
3 Blanton Collier CO	5.00	10.00
4 Gary Collins	6.00	12.00
5 Vince Costello	5.00	10.00
6 Bob Crespino	5.00	10.00
7 Ross Fichtner	5.00	10.00
8 Galen Fiss	5.00	10.00
9 Bob Gain	5.00	10.00
10 Bill Glass	5.00	10.00
11 Ernie Green	6.00	12.00
12 Lou Groza	10.00	20.00
13 Gene Hickerson	7.50	15.00
14 Jim Houston	5.00	10.00
15A Tom Hutchinson	5.00	10.00
15B Tom Hutchinson	5.00	10.00
16 Rich Kreitling	5.00	10.00
17 Mike Lucci	6.00	12.00
18 John Morrow	5.00	10.00
19 Jim Ninowski	6.00	12.00
20 Frank Parker	5.00	10.00
21 Bernie Parrish	5.00	10.00
22 Ray Renfro	6.00	12.00
23 Dick Schafrath	5.00	10.00
24 Jim Shofner	6.00	12.00
25 Ken Webb	5.00	10.00
26 Paul Wiggin	5.00	10.00
27 John Wooten	5.00	10.00

1964-66 Browns Team Issue Large

These large photos measure approximately 7 3/8" by 9 3/8" and feature a black-and-white player photo on blankbacked glossy paper stock. Each includes the player's name, position (initials) and team name in the bottom border. They are very similar in design to the 1963 set, but can be differentiated by the 1" space between the player's name, position, and team name. The Blanton Collier and John Wooten photos are the only exception to this design. Some players were issued over several years with no differences in the photos or only very slight differences in the photo cropping or text as noted below. Each photo is unnumbered and checklisted below in alphabetical order.

COMPLETE SET (42)	250.00	400.00
1 Walter Beach	5.00	10.00
2 Larry Benz	5.00	10.00
3 John Brewer	5.00	10.00
4 John Brown T	5.00	10.00
5 Jim Brown	35.00	60.00
6 Monte Clark	5.00	10.00
7 Blanton Collier CO	5.00	10.00
8 Gary Collins	6.00	12.00
9 Gary Collins	6.00	12.00
10 Vince Costello	5.00	10.00
11 Vince Costello	5.00	10.00
12 Galen Fiss	5.00	10.00
13 Galen Fiss	5.00	10.00
14 Bill Glass DE	5.00	10.00
15 Bill Glass DE	5.00	10.00
16 Ernie Green	5.00	10.00
17 Lou Groza	12.00	20.00
18 Gene Hickerson	7.50	15.00
19 Gene Hickerson	7.50	15.00
20 Jim Houston LB	5.00	10.00
21 Jim Houston LB	5.00	10.00
22 Jim Kanicki	5.00	10.00
23 Jim Kanicki	5.00	10.00
24 Leroy Kelly	12.00	20.00
25 Dick Modzelewski	5.00	10.00
26 Milt Morin	5.00	10.00
27 John Morrow	5.00	10.00
28 John Morrow	5.00	10.00
29 Jim Ninowski	6.00	12.00
30 Frank Parker	5.00	10.00
31 Bernie Parrish	5.00	10.00
32 Walter Roberts	5.00	10.00
33 Frank Ryan	6.00	12.00
34 Frank Ryan	6.00	12.00
35 Dick Schafrath	5.00	10.00
36 Dick Schafrath	5.00	10.00
37 Paul Warfield	15.00	25.00
38 Paul Warfield	15.00	25.00
39 Paul Wiggin	5.00	10.00
40 Paul Wiggin	5.00	10.00
41 John Wooten	5.00	10.00
42 John Wooten	5.00	10.00

1964-66 Browns Team Issue Small

1 Vince Costello	5.00	10.00
2 Ross Fichtner	5.00	10.00
3 Ernie Green	5.00	10.00
4 Gene Hickerson	7.50	15.00
5 Jim Kanicki	5.00	10.00
6 Rich Kreitling	5.00	10.00
7 Dick Scharath	5.00	10.00

1965 Browns Volpe Tumblers

These Browns artist's renderings were part of a plastic cup tumbler product produced in 1965, which celebrated the 1964 Browns World Championship. These cups were promoted by Fisher's, Fazio's and Costa's Supermarkets in Cleveland The noted sports artist Volpe created the artwork which includes an action scene and a player portrait. The "cards" are unnumbered, each measures approximately 5" by 8 1/2" and is curved in the shape required to fit inside a plastic cup.

COMPLETE SET (12)	350.00	600.00
1 Jim Brown	75.00	125.00
2 Blanton Collier CO	20.00	35.00
3 Gary Collins	25.00	40.00
4 Vince Costello	20.00	35.00
5 Bill Glass	20.00	35.00
6 Lou Groza	40.00	75.00
7 Jim Houston	25.00	40.00
8 Jim Kanicki	20.00	35.00
9 Dick Modzelewski	25.00	40.00
10 Frank Ryan	25.00	40.00
11 Dick Schafrath	25.00	40.00
12 Paul Warfield	40.00	75.00

1966 Browns Team Sheets

Each of these team issued sheets features four black and white player photos and measures roughly 8" x10". The player's name, position and team name appear below each photo and the cardbacks are blank. Any additions to list below are appreciated.

COMPLETE SET (8)	25.00	50.00
1 E.Barnes	2.50	5.00
B.Matheson		
J.Gregory		
L.Conjar		
2 J.Brewer	2.50	5.00
J.Houston		
J.Kanicki		
P.Wiggin		
3 G.Collins	3.00	6.00
F.Ryan		
F.Hoaglin		
J.Wooten		
4 B.Davis	2.50	5.00
R.Smith		
D.Schafrath		
M.Morin		
5 R.Fichtner	6.00	12.00
M.Howell		
M.Clark		
P.Warfield		
6 G.Hickerson	5.00	10.00
B.Collier		
E.Green		
L.Kelly		
7 W.Johnson	6.00	12.00
B.Glass		
E.Kellerman		
L.Groza		
8 G.Lane	2.50	5.00
D.Lindsey		
V.Costello		
F.Parker		

1968 Browns Team Issue 7x8

The Cleveland Browns issued and distributed this set of player photos around 1968. Each measures approximately 6 7/8" by 8 1/2" and features a black and white photo on the front and a blank back. The player's name, position (spelled out), and team name appear in the bottom border below the photo. There is also a facsimile autograph of the featured player printed on each photo. Any additions to this list are appreciated.

COMPLETE SET (7)	50.00	100.00
1 Gary Collins	6.00	12.00
2 Ernie Green	5.00	10.00
3 Leroy Kelly	10.00	20.00
4 Bill Nelsen	6.00	12.00
5 Frank Ryan	6.00	12.00
6 Dick Schafrath	6.00	12.00
7 Paul Warfield	12.50	25.00

1968 Browns Team Issue 8x10

The Cleveland Browns issued and distributed this set of player photos. Each measures approximately 8" by 10" and features a black and white photo. The player's name and position appear in the bottom border below the photo. Any additions to this list are appreciated.

COMPLETE SET (12)	75.00	135.00
1 Don Cockroft	5.00	10.00
2 Gary Collins	6.00	12.00
3 Ernie Green	5.00	10.00
4 Jack Gregory	5.00	10.00
5 Gene Hickerson	7.50	15.00
6 Ernie Kellerman	5.00	10.00
7 Leroy Kelly	10.00	20.00
8 Milt Morin	5.00	10.00
9 Frank Ryan	6.00	12.00
10 Marvin Upshaw	5.00	10.00
11 Paul Warfield	12.50	25.00
12 Coaching Staff	6.00	12.00

1968 Browns Team Sheets

These 8" by 10" sheets were issued primarily to the media for use as player images for print. Each features 7 or 8-players and coaches with the player's name beneath his picture. The sheets are blankbacked and unnumbered. Any additions to this list are appreciated.

1 Collier	6.00	15.00
Houston		
Keller.		
Hick.		
Kelly		
Warfield		
Schaf		
2 Howell	5.00	12.00
Kanicki		
Greg.		
Collins		
Lindsey		
Math.		
Mitch		
N		

1969 Browns Team Issue

The Cleveland Browns issued and distributed this set of player photos in the late 1960s. They closely resemble other photos issued by the team throughout the decade. Each measures approximately 7 1/2" by 9 1/2" and features a black and white photo. The player's name, position (spelled out completely), and team name appear in the bottom border below the photo with roughly a 1/2" to 1" white space between the words.

COMPLETE SET (27)	150.00	225.00
1 Bill Andrews	5.00	10.00
2 Erich Barnes	5.00	10.00
3 Monte Clark	5.00	10.00
4 Don Cockroft	5.00	10.00
5 Gary Collins	6.00	12.00
6 Ben Davis	5.00	10.00
7 John DeMarie	5.00	10.00
8 Jack Gregory	5.00	10.00
9 Gene Hickerson	7.50	15.00
10 Fred Hoaglin	5.00	10.00
11 Jim Houston	5.00	10.00
12 Mike Howell	5.00	10.00
13 Ron Johnson	6.00	12.00
14 Jim Kanicki	5.00	10.00
15 Walter Johnson	5.00	10.00
16 Ernie Kellerman	5.00	10.00
17 Leroy Kelly	12.00	20.00
18 Dale Lindsey	5.00	10.00
19 Bob Matheson	5.00	10.00
20 Reece Morrison	5.00	10.00
21 Milt Morin	5.00	10.00
22 Bill Nelsen	6.00	12.00
23 Dick Schafrath	5.00	10.00
24 Ron Snidow	5.00	10.00
25 Walt Sumner	5.00	10.00
26 Marvin Upshaw	5.00	10.00
27 Paul Warfield	12.50	25.00

1971 Browns Boy Scouts

These standard sized cards were issued for the Boy Scouts as rewards for the 1971 "Roundup" membership drive in the Cleveland area. Each was printed on thin stock and features a black and white photo of a Browns player on the front and Boy Scouts membership information on the backs. The cards are often found with the player's autograph on the back as well as the member's hand written name.

1 Jim Houston	20.00	50.00
2 Leroy Kelly	40.00	75.00
3 Bill Nelsen	35.00	60.00
4 Bo Scott	20.00	50.00

1978 Browns Wendy's

This set of oversized (roughly 5" by 7") black and white photos was sponsored by Wendy's. Each includes a Browns player photo with the player's name below the photo and to the left and the Wendy's logo to the right. The backs are blank and unnumbered. Any additions to the list below are appreciated.

COMPLETE SET (19)	100.00	200.00
1 Dick Ambrose	6.00	12.00
2 Ron Bolton	6.00	12.00
3 Larry Colliins	6.00	12.00
4 Oliver Davis	6.00	12.00
5 Johnny Evans	6.00	12.00
6 Ricky Feacher	6.00	12.00
7 Dave Graf	6.00	12.00
8 Charlie Hall	6.00	12.00
9 Calvin Hill	7.50	15.00
10 Gerald Irons	6.00	12.00
11 Robert L. Jackson	6.00	12.00
12 Ricky Jones	6.00	12.00
13 Clay Mathews	10.00	20.00
14 Cleo Miller	6.00	12.00
15 Mark Miller	6.00	12.00
16 Sam Rutigliano CO	6.00	12.00
17 Henry Sheppard	6.00	12.00
18 Mickey Sims	6.00	12.00
19 Gerry Sullivan	6.00	12.00

1979 Browns Team Sheets

The 1979 Browns Team Issue Sheets were issued to fans and total six known sheets. Each measures roughly 8" by 10" and includes seven or eight small black and white player photos.

COMPLETE SET (6)	12.50	25.00
1 Clinton Burrell	1.50	3.00
Clarence Scott		
Willis Adams		
Law		
2 Oliver Davis	2.50	5.00
Ricky Feacher		
Charlie Hall		
Don Coc		
3 Jack Gregory	1.50	3.00
Dave Graf		
Cleo Miller		
Ricky Jones#		
4 Art Modell	2.50	5.00
Sam Rutigliano		
Jerry Sherk		
Greg Prui		
5 Henry Sheppard	3.00	6.00
Mike Pruitt		
Gerry Sullivan		
Curti		
6 Mickey Sims	2.50	5.00
Mark Miller		
Clay Matthews		
Robert E.		

1981 Browns Team Issue

This set of 8" by 10" glossy photos was released by the team for fan mail requests and player appearances. Each is blankbacked with many being found with the photogapher, Henry Barr Studios, notation on the backs along with a stamped player name. Otherwise, there is no player name or team name for identification on the fronts. Any additions to this list are appreciated.

COMPLETE SET (13)	30.00	60.00
1 Lyle Alzado	4.00	10.00
2 Dick Ambrose	2.50	6.00
3 Ron Bolton	2.50	6.00
4 Steve Cox	2.50	6.00
5 Thom Darden	2.50	6.00
6 Joe DeLamielleure	3.00	8.00
7 Ricky Feacher	2.50	6.00
8 Dino Hall	2.50	6.00
9 Bob Jackson	2.50	6.00
10 R.L. Jackson	2.50	6.00
11 Dave Logan	3.00	8.00
12 Paul McDonald	2.50	6.00
13 Mike Pruitt	3.00	8.00

1981 Browns Wendy's Glasses

Each of these drinking glasses includes a front and back picture of a Cleveland Browns player. The front picture is a brown and white drawing of a player within a star, with the players name below the picture. The back contained an action drawing of that particular player. Wendy's stores sponsored the promotion and distributed the glasses in 1981. The set is catalogued in alphabetical order below.

COMPLETE SET (4)	15.00	30.00
1 Lyle Alzado	4.00	10.00
2 Doug Dieken	2.50	6.00
3 Mike Pruitt	3.00	8.00
4 Brian Sipe	3.00	8.00

1982 Browns Nu-Maid Butter Tubs

This set of butter cups or tubs was released by Nu-Maid and Miami Margarine in 1982. Each includes color illustrations of the featured player and measures roughly 3 3/4" tall and 3" in diameter.

COMPLETE SET (7)	15.00	30.00
1 Tom Cousineau	2.00	5.00
2 Doug Dieken	2.00	5.00
3 Dave Logan	2.00	5.00
4 Ozzie Newsome	3.00	8.00
5 Mike Pruitt	2.50	6.00
6 Dan Ross	2.00	5.00
7 Clarence Scott	2.00	5.00

1984 Browns Team Sheets

These 8" by 10" sheets were issued primarily to the media for use as player images for print. Each features 8-players or coaches with the player's jersey number, name, and position beneath his picture. The sheets are blankbacked and unnumbered.

COMPLETE SET (8)	16.00	40.00
1 willis Adams	2.00	5.00
Dick Ambrose		
Mike Baab		
Matt Bah		
2 Clinton Burrell	2.50	6.00
Earnest Byner		
Reggie Camp		
B		
3 Joe DeLamielleure	2.50	6.00
Tom Deleone		
Doud Dieken		
Han		
4 Elvis Franks	2.00	5.00
Bob Golic		
Boyce Green		
Al Gross#		
5 Eddie Johnson	4.00	10.00
Lawrence Johnson		
David Marshall		
6 Art Modell	6.00	15.00
Bill Davis		
Paul Warfield		
Calvin Hil		
7 Terry Nugent	4.00	10.00
Rod Perry		
Mike Pruitt		
Dave Puzzuo		
8 Sam Rutigliano CO	2.00	5.00

1985 Browns Coke/Mr. Hero

This 48-card set was issued as six sheets of eight cards each featuring players on the Cleveland Browns. Each card measures approximately 2 3/4" by 3 1/4". Each sheet was numbered; the sheet number is given after each player in the checklist below. The cards are otherwise unnumbered except for uniform number as they are listed below. The bottom of each sheet had coupons for discounts on food and drink from the sponsors.

COMPLETE SET (48)	10.00	25.00
7 Jeff Gossett 4	.30	.75
9 Matt Bahr 1	.30	.75
16 Paul McDonald 4	.30	.75
18 Gary Danielson 5	.30	.75
19 Bernie Kosar 6	1.00	2.50
20 Don Rogers DB	.30	.75
22 Felix Wright 2	.30	.75
26 Greg Allen 3	.20	.50
27 Al Gross 2	.20	.50
29 Hanford Dixon 5	.30	.75
30 Boyce Green 1	.20	.50
31 Frank Minnifield 1	.30	.75
34 Kevin Mack 3	.50	1.25
37 Chris Rockins 1	.20	.50
38 Johnny Davis 5	.20	.50
44 Earnest Byner 2	.60	1.50
47 Larry Braziel 4	.20	.50
50 Tom Cousineau 6	.30	.75
51 Eddie Johnson 2	.20	.50
55 Curtis Weathers 1	.20	.50
56 Chip Banks 6	.30	.75
57 Clay Matthews 5	.60	1.50
58 Scott Nicolas 1	.20	.50
61 Mike Baab 4	.30	.75
62 George Lilja 5	.20	.50
63 Cody Risien 6	.30	.75
65 Mark Krerowicz 3	.20	.50
68 Robert Jackson G 4	.20	.50
69 Dan Fike 2	.20	.50
72 Dave Puzzuoli 1	.20	.50
74 Paul Farren 2	.20	.50
77 Rickey Bolden 3	.20	.50
78 Carl Hairston 2	.30	.75
79 Bob Golic 6	.30	.75
80 Willis Adams 2	.20	.50
81 Harry Holt 3	.20	.50
82 Ozzie Newsome 3	1.00	2.50
83 Fred Banks 3	.20	.50
84 Glen Young 1	.20	.50
85 Clarence Weathers 6	.20	.50
86 Brian Brennan 5	.30	.75
87 Travis Tucker 6	.20	.50
88 Reggie Langhorne 5	.30	.75
89 John Jefferson 4	.40	1.00
91 Sam Clancy 4	.30	.75
96 Reggie Camp 5	.20	.50
99 Keith Baldwin 6	.20	.50
NNO Action Photo 3	.60	1.50

1987 Browns Louis Rich

This five-card set was originally produced as a food product insert for Louis Rich products. Apparently, the promotion was canceled, and collectors were known to have acquired these cards directly from the Cleveland office of Oscar Mayer, which produces the Louis Rich brand. On card number 4 below, the player was unidentified as a question mark, and it is rumored that this was intended to be part of a contest in the promotion. Both Dante Lavelli and Dub Jones wore number 86. Jones wore uniform number 86 in his earlier years with the Browns, in 1952 he began to wear number 40. Also that same year Lavelli changed from wearing number 56 to number 86, Jones' former uniform number. The plastic helmet dates the photo as after 1952 since the Browns changed to this type of helmet in 1952. Therefore, Dante Lavelli appears to be the correct identification. The oversized cards measure approximately 5" by 7 1/8" and are printed on heavy white card stock. The fronts feature full-bleed sepia-toned player photos. An orange diagonal cuts across the lower left corner and carries the set title ("Memorable Moments by Louis Rich"), uniform number, and player's name. The backs are blank. The cards are unnumbered and checklisted below in alphabetical order.

COMPLETE SET (5)	35.00	60.00
1 Jim Brown	10.00	25.00
B.Mitchell		
2 Otto Graham	6.00	15.00
3 Lou Groza	4.00	10.00
4 Dante Lavelli	4.00	10.00
5 Marion Motley	4.00	10.00

1987 Browns Oh Henry Cups

This set of 20-ounce cups was sponsored by Oh Henry! and distributed in the Cleveland area. Each includes a picture of three-Browns players and sponsor logos. Any additions to the list below are appreciated.

1 Brennan	3.00	8.00
Byner		
Golic		
2 Curtis Dickey	4.00	10.00
Kevin Mack		
Ozzie Newsome		

1987 Browns Team Issue

The Cleveland Browns issued this set of black and white player photos. Each card measures roughly 5" by 7" and includes the player's jersey number, name, position initials, and team name below the photo. The cards are blankbacked and unnumbered.

COMPLETE SET (9)	16.00	40.00
1 Mike Baab	2.00	5.00
2 Earnest Byner	3.00	8.00
3 Reggie Camp	2.00	5.00
4 Bob Golic	2.00	5.00
5 Al Gross	2.00	5.00
6 Mike Junkin	2.00	5.00
7 Reggie Langhorne	2.50	6.00
8 Gerald McNeil	2.00	5.00
9 Frank Minnifield	2.50	6.00

1989 Browns Wendy's Cups

This set of 32-ounce cups was sponsored and distributed by Wendy's Restaurant in the Cleveland area. Each includes a picture of two-Browns players and sponsor logos. Any additions to the list below are appreciated.

COMPLETE SET (3)	8.00	20.00
1 Ozzie Newsome	3.00	8.00
Cody Risien		
2 Hanford Dixon	2.50	6.00
Frank Minnifield		
3 Brian Brennan	2.50	6.00
Webster Slaughter		

1992 Browns Sunoco

Featuring Cleveland Browns' Hall of Famers, this 24-card set was produced by NFL Properties for an Ohio-area promotion sponsored by Sunoco. Two AM radio stations, WMMS 100.7 and WHK 14.20, cosponsored the set. The cards were available in cello packs that contained a cover card, a player card, and an official sweepstakes entry blank. Some packs contained autograph cards of featured players who were still living. The grand prize offered to the winner was a trip for two to the Super Bowl in Pasadena, California. One player card shown at the Pro Football Hall of Fame would entitle the holder to receive up to three complimentary admissions when up to three admissions were purchased. The offer expired August 31, 1993. The fronts of the cover cards have the words "The Cleveland Browns' Collection" printed in black near the top. A Browns helmet is near the center with the player's name printed below it. The words "Hall of Famer Limited Edition" are printed at the bottom with the Sunoco logo. The backs are simple showing only the Pro Football Hall of Fame logo and sponsors' logos. The player cards exhibit a mix of color and black-and-white full-bleed photos with the player's last name printed in oversized orange letters at the bottom. The Sunoco logo is superimposed on the player's name. The backs are sandstone-textured in varying pastel shades and display a ghosted picture of the player. A career summary and the year the player was inducted into the Hall of Fame are overprinted in black. The player cards are numbered on the back. The cover cards are unnumbered but are checklisted below as they appear in the set and assigned corresponding card numbers with a "C" suffix. There was also an album produced for this set.

COMPLETE SET (24)	6.00	15.00
COMMON CARD (1-12)	.30	.75
COMMON COVER CARD (1-12C)	.10	.25
1 Otto Graham	.80	2.00
1C Otto Graham	.08	.25
2 Paul Brown CO	.60	1.50
2C Paul Brown CO	.08	.25
3 Marion Motley	.60	1.50
3C Marion Motley	.08	.25
4 Jim Brown	1.60	4.00
4C Jim Brown	.20	.50
5 Lou Groza	.60	1.50
5C Lou Groza	.08	.25
6 Dante Lavelli	.50	1.25
6C Dante Lavelli	.08	.25
7 Len Ford	.30	.75
7C Len Ford	.08	.25
8 Bill Willis	.30	.75
8C Bill Willis	.08	.25
9 Bobby Mitchell	.50	1.25
9C Bobby Mitchell	.08	.25
10 Paul Warfield	.60	1.50
10C Paul Warfield	.08	.25
11 Mike McCormack	.30	.75
11C Mike McCormack	.08	.25
12 Frank Gatski	.30	.75
12C Frank Gatski	.08	.25

1999 Browns Giant Eagle Cards

This set was distributed in 4-card packs over the course of 6-weeks during the 1999 NFL season by participating Giant Eagle stores in the Northeast Ohio area. Each card includes a full color player photo on the front along with the player's last name and year.

COMPLETE SET (24)	8.00	20.00
1 Ty Detmer	.30	.75
2 Marc Edwards	.20	.50
3 Jim Pyne	.20	.50
4 Kevin Johnson	1.60	4.00
5 Jerry Ball	.20	.50
6 John Jurkovic	.20	.50
7 Marlon Forbes	.20	.50
8 Marquez Pope	.20	.50
9 Orlando Brown	.20	.50
10 Daylon McCutcheon	.20	.50
11 Irv Smith	.20	.50
12 Dave Wohlabaugh	.20	.50
13 Terry Kirby	.20	.50
14 Lomas Brown	.20	.50
15 Jamir Miller	.20	.50
16 John Thierry	.20	.50
17 Corey Fuller	.20	.50
18 Chris Spielman	.30	.75
19 Roy Barker	.20	.50
20 Antonio Langham	.20	.50
21 Tim Couch	4.00	10.00
22 Derrick Alexander DE	.20	.50
23 Chris Gardocki	.20	.50
24 Leslie Shepherd	.20	.50
NNO Card Album	1.60	4.00

1999 Browns Giant Eagle Coins

This set was distributed over the course of 6-weeks during the 1999 NFL season by participating Giant Eagle stores in the Northeast Ohio area along with the card set. Each coin includes a player image on the front along with the player's name. A backer board was also included with each coin that featured a player photo and brief bio very similar to a card. We've priced the coin/backer board combos below.

COMPLETE SET (8)	8.00	20.00
1 Jerry Ball	.40	1.00
2 Orlando Brown	.40	1.00
3 Tim Couch	6.00	15.00
4 Ty Detmer	.60	1.50
5 Corey Fuller	.40	1.00
6 John Jurkovic	.40	1.00
7 Terry Kirby	.40	1.00
8 Chris Spielman	.60	1.50

2004 Browns Donruss Playoff National

This 6-card set was issued vto persons who purchased the VIP package at the 2004 National convention in Cleveland. Each card features bronze foil highlights on the front and is number "x/6" on the back. A silver foil version of the Kellen Winslow Jr. card was also produced and given away. It features Pepsi and Pizza Hut sponsorship logos on the front and no card number on the back.

COMPLETE SET (6)	6.00	15.00
1 Kellen Winslow Jr.	3.00	8.00
2 Quincy Morgan	.75	2.00
3 Andre Davis	.50	1.25
4 William Green	.75	2.00
5 Lee Suggs	1.00	2.50
6 Jeff Garcia	1.00	2.50
NNO Kellen Winslow Jr. Silver	2.00	5.00

2004 Browns Fleer Tradition National

This set was issued as a 9-card perforated sheet inserted into 525,000 issues of the July 18, 2004 Cleveland Plain Dealer newspaper. A 10th card of Kellen Winslow Jr. was distributed only at the Fleer booth at The Natonal. Each card was produced in the design of the 2004 Fleer Tradition set with an orange border instead of white. The cards are also re-numbered 1-10. Finally a cut version of the 10-card set, along with a Kellen Winslow Jr. Throwback Threads card, was also issued to persons purchasing the VIP package for the show.

COMPLETE SET (10)	5.00	12.00
1 Jeff Garcia	.60	1.50
2 Lee Suggs	.60	1.50
3 Quincy Morgan	.50	1.25
4 William Green	.50	1.25
5 Andre Davis	.30	.75
6 Courtney Brown	.50	1.25
7 Dennis Northcutt	.30	.75
8 Luke McCown	.60	1.50
9 Andra Davis	.30	.75
10 Kellen Winslow Jr.	2.00	5.00
NNO Kellen Winslow Jr. Threads	5.00	12.00

2006 Browns Topps

COMPLETE SET (12)	3.00	6.00
CLE1 Lee Suggs	.25	.60
CLE2 Charlie Frye	.30	.75
CLE3 Braylon Edwards	.25	.60
CLE4 Kamerion Wimbley	.30	.75
CLE5 Dennis Northcutt	.25	.60
CLE6 Reuben Droughns	.30	.75
CLE7 Ken Dorsey	.20	.50
CLE8 Kellen Winslow	.25	.60
CLE9 Willie McGinest	.25	.60
CLE10 Joe Jurevicius	.25	.60
CLE11 D'Qwell Jackson	.25	.60
CLE12 Travis Wilson	.25	.60

2007 Browns Topps

COMPLETE SET (12)	4.00	8.00
1 Braylon Edwards	.40	1.00
2 Kellen Winslow	.40	1.00
3 Charlie Frye	.50	1.25
4 Joe Jurevicius	.40	1.00
5 Kamerion Wimbley	.40	1.00
6 Jerome Harrison	.40	1.00
7 Jamal Lewis	.50	1.25
8 Sean Jones	.40	1.00
9 Phil Dawson	.40	1.00
10 Andra Davis	.40	1.00
11 Brady Quinn	.40	1.00
12 Joe Thomas	.60	1.50

2008 Browns Topps

COMPLETE SET (12)	2.00	4.00
1 Kellen Winslow	.40	1.00
2 Derek Anderson	.40	1.00
3 Jamal Lewis	.50	1.25
4 Braylon Edwards	.40	1.00
5 Donte Stallworth	.40	1.00
6 Joe Jurevicius	.40	1.00
7 Sean Jones	.40	1.00
8 Joe Thomas	.50	1.25
9 Brady Quinn	.40	1.00
10 Joshua Cribbs	.40	1.00
11 Martin Rucker	.40	1.00
12 Beau Bell	.50	1.25

1978 Buccaneers Team Issue

These 8" by 10" black and white Photos were issued by the Buccaneers for player signing sessions and to fill fan requests. Each includes the player's name, his position initials and the team name below the player photo in all capital letters. It is believed that there were more photos issued in the series, thus any additional submissions would be welcomed.

1 Ricky Bell	3.00	6.00
2 Dave Pear	2.50	5.00
3 Lee Roy Selmon	6.00	12.00

1978 Buccaneers Team Sheets

This set consists of 8" by 10" glossy photo sheets that display eight black-and-white player/coach photos. Each individual photo on the sheet measures approximately 2 1/8" by 3 1/4". Two Buccaneers logos appear in the upper left and right corners of the sheet. The backs are blank. The sheets are unnumbered and checklisted below alphabetically according to the player featured in the upper left corner.

COMPLETE SET (4)	20.00	40.00
1 Sheet 1	7.50	15.00
2 Sheet 2	4.00	8.00
3 Sheet 3	4.00	8.00
4 Sheet 4	6.00	12.00

1979 Buccaneers Team Issue

These 8 1/2" by 11" black and white blank backed photos were given out for publicity purposes by the Buccaneers. Each includes the player's name, his position (spelled out) and the team name below the player photo. It is believed that there were more photos issued in the series, thus any additional submissions would be welcomed.

1 Jimmy DuBose	2.50	5.00
2 Doug Williams	4.00	8.00

1980 Buccaneers Police

This set is complete at 56 cards measuring approximately 2 5/8" by 4 1/8". Since there are no numbers on the cards, the set has been listed in alphabetical order by player. In addition to player cards, an assortment of coaches, mascots, and Swash-Buc-Lers (cheerleaders) are included. The set was sponsored by the Greater Tampa Chamber of Commerce Law Enforcement Council, the local law enforcement agencies, and Coca-Cola. Tips from the Buccaneers are written on the backs. The fronts contain the Tampa Bay helmet logo. Cards are also available with a tougher Paradyne (Corporation) cardback sponsorship.

COMPLETE SET (56)	75.00	150.00
*PARADYNE BACKS: 1.5X TO 2.5X		
1 Ricky Bell	3.00	8.00
2 Rick Berns	1.50	4.00
3 Tom Blanchard	1.25	3.00
4 Scot Brantley	1.25	3.00
5 Aaron Brown LB	1.25	3.00
6 Cedric Brown	1.25	3.00
7 Mark Cotney	1.25	3.00
8 Randy Crowder	1.25	3.00
9 Gary Davis	1.25	3.00
10 Johnny Davis	1.50	4.00
11 Tony Davis	1.25	3.00
12 Jerry Eckwood	2.00	5.00
13 Chuck Fusina	1.50	4.00
14 Jimmie Giles	2.00	5.00
15 Isaac Hagins	1.25	3.00
16 Charley Hannah	1.25	3.00
17 Andy Hawkins	1.25	3.00
18 Kevin House	2.00	5.00
19 Cecil Johnson	1.25	3.00
20 Gordon Jones	1.50	4.00
21 Curtis Jordan	1.25	3.00
22 Bill Kollar	1.25	3.00
23 Jim Leonard	1.25	3.00
24 David Lewis	1.50	4.00
25 Reggie Lewis	1.25	3.00
26 David Logan	1.50	4.00
27 Larry Mucker	1.25	3.00
28 Jim O'Bradovich	1.50	4.00
29 Mike Rae	1.25	3.00
30 Dave Reavis	1.25	3.00
31 Danny Reece	1.25	3.00
32 Greg Roberts	1.25	3.00
33 Gene Sanders	1.25	3.00
34 Dewey Selmon	2.00	5.00
35 Lee Roy Selmon	8.00	20.00
36 Ray Snell	1.25	3.00
37 Dave Stalls	1.25	3.00
38 Norris Thomas	1.25	3.00
39 Mike Washington	1.25	3.00
40 Doug Williams	4.00	10.00
41 Steve Wilson	1.25	3.00
42 Richard Wood	1.50	4.00
43 George Yarno	1.25	3.00
44 Garo Yepremian	2.00	5.00
45 Logo Card	1.25	3.00
46 Team Photo	2.00	5.00
47 Hugh Culverhouse OWN	1.50	4.00
48 John McKay CO	1.50	4.00
49 Mascot Capt. Crush	1.25	3.00
50 Cheerleaders:	1.50	4.00
51 Swash-Buc-Lers	1.50	4.00
52 Swash-Buc-Lers	1.50	4.00
53 Swash-Buc-Lers	1.50	4.00
54 Swash-Buc-Lers	1.50	4.00
55 Swash-Buc-Lers (Pass	1.50	4.00
56 Swash-Buc-Lers	1.50	4.00

1980 Buccaneers Team Issue

These paper thin 5" by 7" black and white blank backed photos were given out for publicity purposes. Each includes the player's name (all caps), a facsimile signature, and the team name (all caps) below the player photo. It is believed that there were more photos issued in the series, thus any additional submissions would be welcomed.

COMPLETE SET (5)	12.50	25.00
1 Jerry Eckwood	2.00	5.00

2 Lee Roy Selmon 3.00 8.00
3 1980 Team Photo 2.00 5.00
4 Doug Williams 3.00 8.00
5 Garo Yepremian 2.00 5.00

1982 Buccaneers Shell

Sponsored by Shell Oil Co., these 32 paper-thin blank-backed cards measure approximately 1 1/2" by 2 1/2" and feature color action player photos. The photos are borderless, except at the bottom, where the player's name, his team's helmet, and the Shell logo appear in a white margin. The cards are unnumbered and checklisted below in alphabetical order.

COMPLETE SET (32) 25.00 50.00
1 Theo Bell .50 1.25
2 Scot Brantley .50 1.25
3 Cedric Brown .50 1.25
4 Bill Capece .50 1.25
5 Neal Colzie .50 1.25
6 Mark Cotney .50 1.25
7 Hugh Culverhouse OWN .50 1.25
8 Jeff Davis .50 1.25
9 Jerry Eckwood .50 1.25
10 Sean Farrell .50 1.25
11 Jimmie Giles .60 1.50
12 Hugh Green .60 1.50
13 Charley Hannah .50 1.25
14 Andy Hawkins .50 1.25
15 John Holt .50 1.25
16 Kevin House .60 1.50
17 Cecil Johnson .50 1.25
18 Gordon Jones .50 1.25
19 David Logan .50 1.25
20 John McKay CO .60 1.50
21 James Owens .50 1.25
22 Greg Roberts .50 1.25
23 Gene Sanders .50 1.25
24 Lee Roy Selmon 4.00 10.00
25 Ray Snell .50 1.25
26 Larry Swider .50 1.25
27 Norris Thomas .50 1.25
28 Mike Washington .50 1.25
29 James Wilder .60 1.50
30 Doug Williams 2.50 6.00
31 Steve Wilson .50 1.25
32 Richard Wood .50 1.25

1984 Buccaneers Police

This unnumbered 56-card set features the Tampa Bay Buccaneers players, cheerleaders, and other personnel. Cards measure approximately 2 5/8" by 4 1/8". Backs are printed in red ink on thin white card stock and feature "Kids and Kops Tips from the Buccaneers". Cards were sponsored by the Greater Tampa Chamber of Commerce Community Security Council and the local law enforcement agencies. In action (IA) cards were issued as an additional card for three players. The cards are essentially ordered below alphabetically according to the player's name with the exception of the non-player cards who are listed first.

COMPLETE SET (56) 30.00 75.00
1 Swash-Buc-Lers .75 2.00
2 Hugh Culverhouse OWN .40 1.00
3 John McKay (25 Years .60 1.50
4 John McKay CO .60 1.50
5 Defensive Action .60 1.50
6 Fred Acorn .40 1.00
7 Obed Ariri .40 1.00
8 Adger Armstrong .40 1.00
9 Jerry Bell .40 1.00
10 Theo Bell .60 1.50
11 Byron Braggs .40 1.00
12 Scot Brantley .40 1.00
13 Cedric Brown .40 1.00
14 Keith Browner .40 1.00
15 John Cannon .40 1.00
16 Jay Carroll .40 1.00
17 Gerald Carter .40 1.00
18 Melvin Carver .40 1.00
19 Jeremiah Castille .40 1.00
20 Mark Cotney .40 1.00
21 Steve Courson .40 1.00
22 Jeff Davis .40 1.00
23 Steve DeBerg 2.00 5.00
24 Sean Farrell .40 1.00
25 Frank Garcia .40 1.00
26 Jimmie Giles .75 2.00
27 Hugh Green 1.25 3.00
28 Hugh Green IA .60 1.50
29 Randy Grimes .40 1.00
30 Ron Heller .60 1.50
31 John Holt .40 1.00
32 Kevin House .75 2.00
33 Noah Jackson .40 1.00
34 Cecil Johnson .40 1.00
35 Ken Kaplan .40 1.00
36 Blair Kiel .60 1.50
37 David Logan .60 1.50
38 Brison Manor .40 1.00
39 Michael Morton .40 1.00
40 James Owens .40 1.00
41 Beasley Reece .60 1.50
42 Gene Sanders .40 1.00
43 Lee Roy Selmon 5.00 12.00
44 Lee Roy Selmon IA 3.00 8.00
45 Danny Spradlin .40 1.00
46 Kelly Thomas .40 1.00
47 Norris Thomas .40 1.00
48 Jack Thompson .75 2.00
49 Perry Tuttle .40 1.00
50 Chris Washington .40 1.00
51 Mike Washington .40 1.00
52 James Wilder .75 2.00
53 James Wilder IA .60 1.50
54 Steve Wilson .40 1.00
55 Mark White .40 1.00
56 Richard Wood .60 1.50

1989 Buccaneers Police

This ten-card set measures 2 5/8" by 4 1/8" and features members of the Tampa Bay Buccaneers. The fronts of the cards feature an action color shot along with the identification of the player and his position and uniform number. The back of the card features biographical information, some text, one line of career statistics, and the card number. This set was sponsored by IMC Fertilizer, Inc. and the Polk County Law Enforcement Office.

COMPLETE SET (10) 20.00 50.00
1 Vinny Testaverde 15.00 25.00
2 Mark Carrier WR 3.00 8.00
3 Randy Grimes 1.25 3.00
4 Paul Gruber 2.00 5.00
5 Ron Hall 2.00 5.00
6 William Howard 1.25 3.00
7 Curt Jarvis 1.25 3.00
8 Ervin Randle 1.25 3.00
9 Ricky Reynolds 2.00 5.00
10 Rob Taylor T 1.25 3.00

2006 Buccaneers Topps

COMPLETE SET (12) 3.00 6.00
TB1 Chris Simms .25 .60
TB2 Simeon Rice .25 .60
TB3 Michael Clayton .25 .60
TB4 Derrick Brooks .25 .60
TB5 Cadillac Williams .30 .75
TB6 Joey Galloway .30 .75
TB7 Edell Shepherd .25 .60
TB8 Mike Alstott .25 .60
TB9 Ronde Barber .25 .60
TB10 Alex Smith TE .25 .60
TB11 Maurice Stovall .25 .60
TB12 Bruce Gradkowski .30 .75

2007 Buccaneers Topps

COMPLETE SET (12) 2.00 5.00
1 Alex Smith TE .40 1.00
2 Cadillac Williams .60 1.25
3 Michael Clayton .40 1.00
4 Bruce Gradkowski .40 1.00
5 Cato June .40 1.00
6 Chris Simms .40 1.00
7 Joey Galloway .50 1.25
8 Derrick Brooks .40 1.00
9 Ronde Barber .40 1.00
10 Jeff Garcia .40 1.00
11 Mike Alstott .40 1.00
12 Gaines Adams .50 1.25

2008 Buccaneers Topps

COMPLETE SET (12) 2.00 4.00
1 Joey Galloway .50 1.25
2 Jeff Garcia .40 1.00
3 Brian Griese .40 1.00
4 Warrick Dunn .40 1.00
5 Ernest Graham .40 1.00
6 Gaines Adams .40 1.00
7 Cadillac Williams .50 1.25
8 Ike Hilliard .40 1.00
9 Ronde Barber .40 1.00
10 Derrick Brooks .40 1.00
11 Aqib Talib .60 1.50
12 Dexter Jackson .60 1.50

2009 Buccaneers Donruss Super Bowl XLIII Promos

This set was issued at the Donruss/Playoff booth during the 2009 Super Bowl Card Show in Tampa, Florida. A complete set was given to any collector that opened a specified number of football card packs at the booth during the show.

COMPLETE SET (4) 3.00 6.00
1 Derrick Brooks .60 1.50
2 Earnest Graham .60 1.50
3 Ronde Barber .60 1.50
4 Jeff Garcia .60 1.50

2009 Buccaneers Upper Deck Super Bowl XLIII Promos

This set was issued at the Upper Deck booth during the 2009 Super Bowl Card Show in Tampa, Florida. A complete set was given to any collector that opened a specified number of football card packs at the booth during the show.

COMPLETE SET (4) 3.00 6.00
5 Derrick Brooks .60 1.50
6 Antonio Bryant .60 1.50
7 Jeff Garcia .60 1.50
8 Aqib Talib .60 1.50

1976 Buckmans Discs

The 1976 Buckmans football disc set of 20 is unnumbered and features star players from the National Football League. The circular cards measure approximately 3 3/8" in diameter. The players' pictures are in black and white with a colored arc serving as the disc border. Four stars complete the border at the top. The backs of the most common version contain the address of the Buckmans Ice Cream outlet in Rochester, New York. A much scarcer blankbacked version of the set was also prodcued and though to have been issued in packages of Safelon lunch bags. Another version that reads "Customized Sports Discs" on the back exists and is thought to have been issued as promotional pieces or samples. The MSA marking, signifying Michael Schechter Associates, is featured on the backs as well. Since the set is unnumbered, the cards are listed below alphabetically by player's name.

COMPLETE SET (20) 40.00 80.00
*BLANKBACK: 4X TO 10X
*CUSTOMIZED: 8X TO 20X
1 Otis Armstrong 1.00 2.50
2 Steve Bartkowski 1.00 2.50
3 Terry Bradshaw 15.00 25.00
4 Doug Buffone .75 2.00
5 Wally Chambers .75 2.00
6 Chuck Foreman 1.00 2.50
7 Roman Gabriel 1.25 3.00
8 Mel Gray 1.00 2.50
9 Franco Harris 5.00 10.00
10 James Harris 1.00 2.50
11 Jim Hart 1.00 2.50
12 Gary Huff .75 2.00
13 Billy Kilmer 1.00 2.50
14 Terry Metcalf 1.00 2.50
15 Jim Otis .75 2.00
16 Jim Plunkett 1.25 3.00
17 Greg Pruitt 1.00 2.50
18 Roger Staubach 15.00 25.00
19 Jan Stenerud 1.00 2.50
20 Roger Wehrli 1.00 2.50

2002 Buffalo Destroyers AFL

This set was sponsored by Dave and Adams Card World and features members of the 2002 Buffalo Destroyers Arena Football League team. Each includes a color player photo on the front and a brief player bio on back.

COMPLETE SET (17) 6.00 15.00
1 Thomas Bailey .40 1.00
2 Ray Bentley CO .30 .75
3 Eddie Brown .40 1.00
4 David Caldwell .30 .75
5 Derrick Chachere .30 .75
6 Bret Cooper .30 .75
7 Lamart Cooper UER .40 1.00
8 Jerry Crafts .30 .75
9 Kerwin Hairston .30 .75
10 Carlos James .30 .75
11 Corey Johnson .30 .75
12 Juan Long .30 .75
13 Kevin Mason .30 .75
14 Steve McLaughlin .30 .75
15 Fred McNair .50 1.25
16 Hardy Mitchell .30 .75
17 Cover Card .30 .75

1972 Burger King Ice Milk Cups

These white cups with brown detail were issued in 1972 by Burger King to promote their Ice Milk dessert. These cups are approximately 4" high and feature a detailed portrait on the front of the cup with a biography on the back and a Burger King logo at the bottom. The cups are listed below in alphabetical order. These thin cups are condition sensitive since they are highly susceptible to cracking.

1 Dan Abramowicz 6.00 12.00
2 Julius Adams 6.00 12.00
3 Bob Anderson 6.00 12.00
4 Dick Anderson 6.00 12.00
5 George Andrie 6.00 12.00
6 Jim Bakken 6.00 12.00
7 Pete Banaszak 6.00 12.00
8 Pete Beathard 6.00 12.00
9 Bill Bergey 7.50 15.00
10 Forrest Blue 6.00 12.00
11 Terry Bradshaw 20.00 40.00
12 John Brockington 6.00 12.00
13 Buck Buchanan 7.50 15.00
14 Norm Bulaich 6.00 12.00
15 Nick Buoniconti 7.50 15.00
16 Virgil Carter 6.00 12.00
17 Richard Caster 6.00 12.00
18 Jack Concannon 6.00 12.00
19 Dave Costa 6.00 12.00
20 Larry Csonka 10.00 20.00
21 Mike Curtis 6.00 12.00
22 Len Dawson 12.50 25.00
23 Bobby Douglass 6.00 12.00
24 Bobby Duhon 6.00 12.00
25 Carl Eller 7.50 15.00
26 Mel Farr 6.00 12.00
27 Manny Fernandez 6.00 12.00
28 John Fuqua 7.50 15.00
29 Walt Garrison 6.00 12.00
30 John Gilliam 6.00 12.00
31 Dick Gordon 6.00 12.00
32 Joe Greene 10.00 20.00
33 Bob Griese
34 John Hadl 7.50 15.00
35 Don Hansen 6.00 12.00
36 Cliff Harris 7.50 15.00
37 Dave Herman 6.00 12.00
38 J.D. Hill 6.00 12.00
39 Jim Houston 6.00 12.00
40 Delles Howell 6.00 12.00
41 Rich Jackson 6.00 12.00
42 Ron Johnson 6.00 12.00
43 Walter Johnson 6.00 12.00
44 Clint Jones 6.00 12.00
45 Deacon Jones 10.00 20.00
46 Lee Roy Jordan 10.00 20.00
47 Leroy Kelly 10.00 20.00
48 Leroy Keyes 6.00 12.00
49 Jim Kiick 7.50 15.00
50 George Kunz 6.00 12.00
51 Jake Kupp 6.00 12.00
52 Greg Landry 7.50 15.00
53 Willie Lanier 7.50 15.00
54 Pete Liske 6.00 12.00
55 Floyd Little 7.50 15.00
56 Mike Lucci 6.00 12.00
57 Jim Lynch 6.00 12.00
58 Milt Morin 6.00 12.00
59 Earl Morrall 7.50 15.00
60 Mercury Morris 7.50 15.00
61 Haven Moses 6.00 12.00
62 John Niland 6.00 12.00
63 Frank Nunley 6.00 12.00
64 Merlin Olsen 10.00 20.00
65 Steve Owens 7.50 15.00
66 Lemar Parrish 6.00 12.00
67 Dan Pastorini 6.00 12.00
68 Jim Plunkett 10.00 20.00
69 Ed Podolak 6.00 12.00
70 Ron Pritchard 6.00 12.00
71 Isiah Robertson 6.00 12.00
72 Dave Robinson 6.00 12.00
73 Tim Rossovich 6.00 12.00
74 Andy Russell 7.50 15.00
75 Charlie Sanders 7.50 15.00
76 Jake Scott 7.50 15.00
77 George Seals 6.00 12.00
78 Dennis Shaw 6.00 12.00
79 Jackie Smith 7.50 15.00
80 Jerry Smith 6.00 12.00
81 Royce Smith 6.00 12.00
82 Jack Snow 6.00 12.00
83 Walt Sweeney 6.00 12.00
84 Steve Tannen 6.00 12.00
85 Fran Tarkenton 12.50 25.00
86 Altie Taylor 6.00 12.00
87 Otis Taylor 7.50 15.00
88 Billy Truax 6.00 12.00
89 Bob Tucker 6.00 12.00
90 Randy Vataha 6.00 12.00
91 Paul Warfield 10.00 20.00
92 Gene Washington 7.50 15.00
93 George Webster 6.00 12.00
94 Dave Wilcox 7.50 15.00
95 Ken Willard 6.00 12.00
96 Larry Wilson 10.00 20.00
97 Garo Yepremian 6.00 12.00

1995 Burger King/Sports Illustrated College Legends Cups

In 1995, Burger King in conjunction with Sports Illustrated produced a series of 32 oz. Stadium style drinking cups which featured an array of notable college players by position on each cup. These colorful cups were produced by both Alpha Products and Packer Plastics.

COMPLETE SET 16.00 40.00
1 Coaches 4.80 12.00
Bobby Bowden
Woody Hayes
Lou Holtz
Tom
2 Defense 2.40 6.00
Cornelius Bennett
Hugh Green
Joe Greene
3 Quarterbacks 4.80 12.00
Kerry Collins
Ty Detmer
Doug Fluti
4 Receivers# 3.20 8.00
5 Running Backs 4.80 12.00
Marcus Allen
Ki-Jana Carter
Tony

1932 Briggs Chocolate

This set was issued by C.A. Briggs Chocolate company in 1932. The cards feature 31-different sports with each card including an artist's rendering of a sporting event. Although players are not named, it is thought that most were modeled after famous athletes of the time. The cardbacks include a written portion about the sport and an offer from Briggs for free baseball equipment for building a compete set of cards.

11 Football 800.00 1200.00

1976 Canada Dry Cans

Canada Dry released soda cans in 1976 featuring the logos of NFL teams along with a brief history of the featured team. The pricing below is for opened cans.

COMPLETE SET (28) 100.00 200.00
1 Atlanta Falcons 4.00 8.00
2 Baltimore Colts 4.00 8.00
3 Buffalo Bills 5.00 10.00
4 Chicago Bears 4.00 8.00
5 Cincinnati Bengals 4.00 8.00
6 Cleveland Browns 5.00 10.00
7 Dallas Cowboys 7.50 15.00
8 Denver Broncos 4.00 8.00
9 Detroit Lions 4.00 8.00
10 Green Bay Packers 7.50 15.00
11 Houston Oilers 4.00 8.00
12 Kansas City Chiefs 4.00 8.00
13 Los Angeles Rams 4.00 8.00
14 Miami Dolphins 7.50 15.00
15 Minnesota Vikings 5.00 10.00
16 New England Patriots 4.00 8.00
17 New Orleans Saints 4.00 8.00
18 New York Giants 5.00 10.00
19 New York Jets 5.00 10.00
20 Oakland Raiders 7.50 15.00
21 Philadelphia Eagles 4.00 8.00
22 Pittsburgh Steelers 5.00 10.00
23 St. Louis Cardinals 4.00 8.00
24 San Diego Chargers 4.00 8.00
25 San Francisco 49ers 5.00 10.00
26 Seattle Seahawks 4.00 8.00
27 Tampa Bay Buccaneers 4.00 8.00
28 Washington Redskins 7.50 15.00

1964 Caprolan Nylon All-Star Buttons

These buttons were issued in the mid-1960s and feature a black and white image of an AFL or NFL player. The fronts also feature the words " A Caprolan Nylon All-Star Performer" along with the player's name printed in blue ink above the photo. Any additions to this list are appreciated.

COMPLETE SET (5) 100.00 200.00
1 Maxie Baughan 25.00 40.00
2 Gino Cappelletti 25.00 40.00
3 Matt Hazeltine UER 25.00 40.00
4 Merlin Olsen 30.00 50.00
5 Andy Robustelli 30.00 50.00

1967 Caprolan Nylon Photos

These 8" x 10" glossy black-and-white photos were issued to promote the Caprolan company. Each includes the player's name, team name, and "A Caprolan All-Star" below the image.

1 Gary Ballman 12.50 25.00
2 Gino Cappelletti 12.50 25.00
3 Mike Ditka 20.00 40.00
4 Matt Hazeltine 12.50 25.00
5 Pete Retzlaff 12.50 25.00
6 Andy Robustelli 15.00 30.00
7 Frank Ryan 12.50 25.00

1953 Cardinals Team Issue

Photos in this set of the Chicago Cardinals measure approximately 8" by 10" and feature a black-and-white player image on the front printed on high gloss stock. The player's name and position can sometimes be found written on the backs but no player identification is otherwise given. The photos are unnumbered and checklisted below in alphabetical order.

COMPLETE SET (31) 350.00 600.00
1 Cliff Anderson 10.00 20.00
2 Roy Barni 10.00 20.00
3 Tom Bienemann 10.00 20.00
4 Al Campana 10.00 20.00
5 Nick Chickillo 10.00 20.00
6 Billy Cross 10.00 20.00
7 Tony Curcillo 10.00 20.00
8 Jerry Groom 10.00 20.00
9 Ed Husmann 10.00 20.00
10 Don Joyce 10.00 20.00
11 Ed Listopad 10.00 20.00
12 Ollie Matson 15.00 30.00
13 Gern Nagler 10.00 20.00
14 Johnny Olszewski 10.00 20.00
15 John Panelli 10.00 20.00
16 Volney Peters 10.00 20.00
17 Gordon Polofsky 10.00 20.00
18 Jim Psaltis 10.00 20.00
19 Ray Ramsey 10.00 20.00
20 Jack Simmons 10.00 20.00
21 Emil Sitko 10.00 20.00
22 Don Stonesifer 10.00 20.00
23 Joe Stydahar CO 12.50 25.00
24 Leo Sugar 10.00 20.00
25 Dave Suminski 10.00 20.00
26 Pat Summerall 15.00 30.00
27 Bill Svoboda 10.00 20.00
28 Charley Trippi 12.50 25.00
29 Fred Wallner 10.00 20.00
30 Jerry Watford 10.00 20.00
31 Team Photo 12.50 25.00

1960 Cardinals Mayrose Franks

The Mayrose Franks set of 11 cards features players on the St. Louis (Football) Cardinals and first hit store shelves in Septmber 1960. The cards are plastic coated (they were intended as inserts in hot dog and bacon packages) with slightly rounded corners and are numbered. The cards measure approximately 2 1/2" by 3 1/2". The fronts, with a black and white photograph of the player and a red background, contain the card number, player statistics and the Cardinal's logo. The backs contain a description of the Big Mayrose Football Contest.

COMPLETE SET (11) 80.00 125.00
1 Don Gillis 6.00 12.00
2 Frank Fuller 6.00 12.00
3 George Izo 6.00 12.00
4 Woodley Lewis 6.00 12.00
5 King Hill 6.00 12.00
6 John David Crow 7.50 15.00
7 Bill Stacy 6.00 12.00
8 Ted Bates 6.00 12.00
9 Mike McGee 6.00 12.00
10 Bobby Joe Conrad 6.00 12.00
11 Ken Panfil 6.00 12.00

1961 Cardinals Jay Publishing

This 12-card set features (approximately) 5" by 7" black-and-white player photos. The pictures show players in traditional poses with the quarterback preparing to throw, the runner heading downfield, and the defensive player ready for the tackle. These cards were packaged 12 to a packet and originally sold for 25 cents. The backs are blank. The cards are unnumbered and checklisted below in alphabetical order.

COMPLETE SET (12) 40.00 80.00
1 Joe Childress 4.00 8.00
2 Sam Etcheverry 4.00 8.00
3 Ed Henke 4.00 8.00
4 Jimmy Hill 4.00 8.00
5 Bill Koman 4.00 8.00
6 Roland McDole 4.00 8.00
7 Mike McGee 4.00 8.00
8 Dale Meinert 4.00 8.00
9 Jerry Norton 4.00 8.00
10 Sonny Randle 4.00 8.00
11 Joe Robb 4.00 8.00
12 Billy Stacy 4.00 8.00

1963-64 Cardinals Team Issue

The Cardinals likely issued these photos over a period of years during the mid-1960s. Each measures approximately 5" by 7" and features a black and white player photo along with player information below the photo. Some photos contain only the player's name, positon and team name in all caps, while others also include the player's height and weight with the team name in upper and lower case letters. They are unnumbered and blankbacked and listed below alphabetically.

COMPLETE SET (15) 100.00 175.00
1 Taz Anderson 6.00 12.00
2 Garland Boyette 6.00 12.00
3 Don Brumm 6.00 12.00
4A Jim Burson 6.00 12.00
4B Jim Burson 6.00 12.00
5 Irv Goode 6.00 12.00
6 John Houser 6.00 12.00
7 Bill Koman 6.00 12.00
8 Ernie McMillan 6.00 12.00
9A Luke Owens 6.00 12.00
9B Luke Owens 6.00 12.00
10 Bob Paremore 6.00 12.00
11A Bob Reynolds 6.00 12.00
11B Bob Reynolds 6.00 12.00
12 Joe Robb 6.00 12.00
13 Sam Silas 6.00 12.00
14 Jerry Stovall 6.00 12.00
15A Bill Triplett 6.00 12.00
15B Bill Triplett 6.00 12.00

1965 Cardinals Big Red Biographies

This set was featured during the 1965 football season as the side panels of half-gallon milk cartons from Adams Dairy in St. Louis. When cut, the cards measure approximately 3 1/16" by 5 9/16". The printing on the cards is in purple and orange. All cards feature members of the St. Louis Cardinals. The catalog designation for this set is F112. Two different Cardinals logos in the upper right hand corner we used on the cards, but no variations of the same card are known. We've identified known logo versions below with: 1) cards featuring the white jersey Cardinal beneath the Arch, and 2) cards featuring the red jersey Cardinal and no Arch. Complete milk cartons would be valued at double the prices listed below.

COMPLETE SET (27) 3000.00 5000.00
1 Monk Bailey 150.00 250.00
2 Jim Bakken 1 175.00 300.00
3 Don Brumm 2 150.00 250.00
4 Jim Burson 150.00 250.00
5 Joe Childress 2 150.00 250.00
6 Willis Crenshaw 1 150.00 250.00
7 Bob DeMarco 1 150.00 250.00
8 Pat Fischer 1 150.00 250.00
9 Billy Gambrell 150.00 250.00
10 Irv Goode 1 150.00 250.00
11 Ken Gray 1 150.00 250.00
12 Charley Johnson 2 175.00 300.00
13 Bill Koman 1 150.00 250.00
14 Dave Meggysey 1 150.00 250.00
15 Dale Meinert 2 150.00 250.00
16 Mike Melinkovich 1 150.00 250.00
17 Sonny Randle 150.00 250.00
18 Bob Reynolds 1 150.00 250.00
19 Joe Robb 150.00 250.00
20 Marion Rushing 150.00 250.00
21 Sam Silas 150.00 250.00
22 Carl Silvestri 1 150.00 250.00
23 Dave Simmons 1 150.00 250.00
24 Jackie Smith 1 200.00 350.00
25 Bill(Thunder) Thornton 1 150.00 250.00
26 Bill Triplett 2 150.00 250.00
27 Herschel Turner 1 150.00 250.00

1965 Cardinals McCarthy Postcards

This two-card set features posed player photos of the Cardinals team printed on postcard-size cards. The cards are unnumbered and checklisted below in alphabetical order.

1 Dick Lane 2.50 5.00
2 Ollie Matson 2.50 5.00

1965 Cardinals Team Issue

This 10-card set of the St. Louis Cardinals measures approximately 7 3/8" by 9 3/8" and features black-and-white player photos in a white border. The player's name, position and team are printed in the wide bottom margin. The backs are blank. The cards are unnumbered and checklisted below in alphabetical order.

COMPLETE SET (10) 60.00 120.00
1 Don Brumm 6.00 12.00
2 Bobby Joe Conrad 6.00 12.00
3 Bob DeMarco 6.00 12.00
4 Charley Johnson 7.50 15.00
5 Ernie McMillan 6.00 12.00
6 Dale Meinert 6.00 12.00
7 Luke Owens 6.00 12.00
8 Sonny Randle 6.00 12.00
9 Joe Robb 6.00 12.00
10 Jerry Stovall 6.00 12.00

1967 Cardinals Team Issue

These photos are very similar in design to several other Cardinals Team Issue releases. Like the other sets, this set was likely released over a period of years. Each photo measures approximately 5" by 7" and features a black and white player photo along with player information below the photo. The player's name and positon are in all caps with the team name in upper and lower case letters. They are unnumbered and blankbacked and listed below alphabetically.

COMPLETE SET (16) 90.00 150.00
1 Don Brumm 6.00 12.00
2 Charlie Bryant 6.00 12.00
3 Jim Burson 6.00 12.00
4 Irv Goode 6.00 12.00
5 Mal Hammack 6.00 12.00
6 Bill Koman 6.00 12.00
7 Chuck Logan 6.00 12.00
8 Dave Long 6.00 12.00
9 John McDowell 6.00 12.00
10 Ernie McMillan 6.00 12.00
11 Dave O'Brien OL 6.00 12.00
12 Bob Reynolds 6.00 12.00
13 Joe Robb 6.00 12.00
14 Roy Shivers 6.00 12.00
15 Chuck Walker 6.00 12.00
16 Bobby Williams DB 6.00 12.00

1969 Cardinals Team Issue

These photos are very similar in design to several other Cardinals Team Issue releases. Like the other sets, this set was likely released over a period of years. Each photo measures approximately 5" by 7" and features a black and white player photo along with player information below the photo. The player's name and positon are in all caps with the team name in upper and lower case letters. The type size and style differs slightly from one photo to the next, but all include a slightly wider or round letter "C" in the word Cardinals than the 1971 set. They are unnumbered and blankbacked and listed below alphabetically.

COMPLETE SET (31) 150.00 250.00
1 Robert Atkins 5.00 10.00
2 Jim Bakken 6.00 12.00
3 Bob Brown 5.00 10.00
4 Terry Brown 5.00 10.00
5 Willis Crenshaw 5.00 10.00
6 Jerry Daanen 5.00 10.00
7 Irv Goode 5.00 10.00
8 Chip Healy 5.00 10.00
9 Fred Heron 5.00 10.00
10 King Hill 5.00 10.00
11 Fred Hyatt 5.00 10.00
12 Rolf Krueger 5.00 10.00
13 MacArthur Lane 6.00 12.00
14 Ernie McMillan 5.00 10.00
15 Wayne Mulligan 5.00 10.00
16 Dave Olerich 5.00 10.00
17 Bob Reynolds 5.00 10.00
18 Jamie Rivers 5.00 10.00
19 Johnny Roland 5.00 10.00
20 Rocky Rosema 5.00 10.00
21 Bob Rowe 5.00 10.00
22 Lonnie Sanders 5.00 10.00
23 Joe Schmiesing 5.00 10.00
24 Roy Shivers 5.00 10.00
25 Cal Snowden 5.00 10.00
26 Rick Sortun 5.00 10.00
27 Chuck Walker 5.00 10.00
28 Clyde Williams 5.00 10.00
29 Dave Williams 5.00 10.00
30 Charley Winner CO 5.00 10.00
31 Nate Wright 5.00 10.00

1971 Cardinals Team Issue

These photos are very similar in design to many other Cardinals Team Issue set listings. Like the others, these photos were likely released over a period of years. Each photo measures approximately 5" by 7" and features a black and white player photo along with player information below the photo. The player's name and positon are in all caps with the team name in upper and lower case letters. The type size and style differs slightly from one photo to the next, but all include a slightly more narrow letter "C" in the word Cardinals than the 1969 set. They are unnumbered and blankbacked and listed below alphabetically.

COMPLETE SET (22) 100.00 175.00
1 Tom Banks 5.00 10.00
2 Dale Hackbart 5.00 10.00
3 Jim Hargrove 5.00 10.00
4 Fred Heron 5.00 10.00
5 Bob Hollway CO 5.00 10.00
6 Mike McGill 5.00 10.00
7 Dave Meggysey 5.00 10.00
8 Terry Miller LB 5.00 10.00
9 Don Parish 5.00 10.00
10 Charlie Pittman 5.00 10.00
11 Rocky Rosema 5.00 10.00
12 Lonnie Sanders 5.00 10.00
13 Joe Schmiesing 5.00 10.00
14 Mike Siwek 5.00 10.00
15 Larry Stegent 5.00 10.00
16 Norm Thompson 5.00 10.00
17 Tim Van Galder 5.00 10.00
18 Chuck Walker 5.00 10.00
19 Dave Williams 5.00 10.00
20 Larry Willingham 5.00 10.00
21 Nate Wright 5.00 10.00
22 Ron Yankowski 5.00 10.00

1972 Cardinals Team Issue

The Cardinals issued these photos likely over a period of years. Each measures approximately 5" by 7" and features a black and white player photo along with the player's name, positon, height, weight, and team name below the photo. The type size and style used is virtually the same for all of the photos and the team name reads "St. Louis Cardinals." The player's name is printed in upper and lower case letters. They are unnumbered and blankbacked and listed below alphabetically.

COMPLETE SET (37) 125.00 225.00
1 Jeff Allen 4.00 8.00
2 Tom Banks 4.00 8.00
3 Craig Baynham 4.00 8.00
4 Pete Beathard 4.00 8.00
5 Tom Beckman 4.00 8.00
6 Terry Brown 4.00 8.00
7 Gary Cuozzo 5.00 10.00
8 Paul Dickson 4.00 8.00
9 Miller Farr 4.00 8.00
10 Walker Gillette 4.00 8.00
11 John Gilliam 5.00 10.00
12 Dale Hackbart 4.00 8.00
13 Jim Hargrove 4.00 8.00
14 Jim Hart 6.00 12.00
15 Fred Heron 4.00 8.00
16 George Hoey 4.00 8.00
17 Bob Hollway CO 4.00 8.00
18 Chuck Hutchison 4.00 8.00
19 Fred Hyatt 4.00 8.00
20 Martin Imhof 4.00 8.00
21 Jeff Lyman 4.00 8.00
22 Mike McGill 4.00 8.00
23 Ernie McMillan 4.00 8.00
24 Terry Miller LB 4.00 8.00
25 Bobby Moore 10.00 20.00
(Ahmad Rashad)
26 Wayne Mulligan 4.00 8.00
27 Bob Reynolds 4.00 8.00
28 Jamie Rivers 4.00 8.00
29 Johnny Roland 5.00 10.00
30 Bob Rowe 4.00 8.00
31 Roy Shivers 4.00 8.00
32 Tim Van Galder 4.00 8.00
33 Chuck Walker 4.00 8.00
34 Eric Washington 4.00 8.00
35 Clyde Williams 4.00 8.00
36 Larry Willingham 4.00 8.00
37 Ron Yankowski 4.00 8.00

1973 Cardinals Team Issue

The Cardinals issued these photos likely over a period of years as this set looks very similar to the 1972 issue. Each measures approximately 5" by 7" and features a black and white player photo along with the player's name, positon, height, weight, and team name below the photo. The type size and style used is different than the 1972 set and varies slightly from photo to photo. The team name reads "St. Louis Football Cardinals" on all these photos unless noted below. They are unnumbered and blankbacked and listed below alphabetically.

COMPLETE SET (43) 150.00 250.00
1 Donny Anderson 5.00 10.00
2 Tom Banks 4.00 8.00
3 Chuck Beatty 4.00 8.00
4 Tom Beckman 4.00 8.00
5 Willie Belton 4.00 8.00
6 Leon Burns 4.00 8.00
7 Dave Butz 4.00 8.00
8 Steve Conley 4.00 8.00
9 Dwayne Crump 4.00 8.00
10 Ron Davis 4.00 8.00
11 Rod Dowhower CO 4.00 8.00
12 Miller Farr 4.00 8.00
13 Ken Garrett 4.00 8.00
14 Joe Gibbs CO 15.00 30.00
15 Walker Gillette 4.00 8.00
16 Jim Hanifan CO 4.00 8.00
17 Sid Hall CO 4.00 8.00
18 Chuck Hutchison 4.00 8.00
19 Fred Hyatt 4.00 8.00
20 Martin Imhoff 4.00 8.00
21 Gary Keithley 4.00 8.00
22 Don Maynard 6.00 12.00
23 Ernie McMillan 4.00 8.00
25 Terry Miller LB 4.00 8.00
26 Wayne Mulligan 4.00 8.00
27 Jim Otis 5.00 10.00
28 Marv Owens 4.00 8.00
29 Ara Person 4.00 8.00
30 Ahmad Rashad 7.50 15.00
31 John Richardson 4.00 8.00
32 Jamie Rivers 4.00 8.00
33 Johnny Roland 4.00 8.00
34 Don Shy 4.00 8.00
35 Jackie Simpson CO 4.00 8.00
36 Maurice Spencer 4.00 8.00
37 Jeff Staggs 4.00 8.00
38 Norm Thompson 4.00 8.00
39 Jim Tolbert 4.00 8.00
40 Eric Washington 4.00 8.00
41 Bob Wicks 4.00 8.00
42 Ray Willsey CO 4.00 8.00
43 Bob Young 4.00 8.00
24A Terry Metcalf 5.00 10.00
24B Terry Metcalf 5.00 10.00

1974 Cardinals Team Issue

The Cardinals issued these photos likely over a period of years as this set looks very similar to the 1972 and 1973 issues. Each measures approximately 5" by 7" and features a black and white player photo along with the player's name, positon, height, weight, and team name below the photo. The type size and style used is different than the 1972 and 1973 sets with the 1974 printing being slightly larger. The team name reads "St. Louis Football Cardinals" on all these photos with most, but not all, being in all capitals letters. They are unnumbered and blankbacked and listed below alphabetically.

COMPLETE SET (17) 50.00 100.00
1 Tom Banks 4.00 8.00
2 Jim Champion CO 4.00 8.00
3 Gene Hamlin 4.00 8.00
4 Reggie Harrison 4.00 8.00
5 Eddie Moss 4.00 8.00
6 Steve Neils 4.00 8.00
7 Jim Otis 5.00 10.00
8 Ken Reaves 4.00 8.00
9 Hal Roberts 4.00 8.00
10 Hurles Scales 4.00 8.00
11 Wayne Sevier CO 4.00 8.00
12 Dennis Shaw 4.00 8.00
13 Maurice Spencer 4.00 8.00
14 Larry Stallings 4.00 8.00
15 Scott Stringer 4.00 8.00
16 Earl Thomas 4.00 8.00
17 Cal Withrow 4.00 8.00

1976 Cardinals Team Issue

The St. Louis Cardinals issued this series of player photos quite possibly over a number of years. Each photo is very similar in design and is only differentiated by the size and type style of the print. The unnumbered black and white photos measure approximately 5 1/8" by 7" and all, except John Zook, include the player's name, position, height and weight below the photo along with "St. Louis Football Cardinals." The team name printed on the cards varies in size and print type from photo to photo. Although they likely were issued over a period of years, we've included them all as a 1976 release since all players performed for that year's team.

COMPLETE SET (51) 150.00 300.00
1 Mark Arneson 4.00 8.00
2 Jim Bakken 5.00 10.00
3 Rodrigo Barnes 4.00 8.00
4 Al Beauchamp 4.00 8.00
5 Bob Bell 4.00 8.00
6 Tom Brahaney 4.00 8.00
7 Leo Brooks 4.00 8.00
8 J.V. Cain 4.00 8.00
9 Don Coryell CO 5.00 10.00
10 Dwayne Crump 4.00 8.00
11 Charlie Davis 4.00 8.00
12 Mike Dawson 4.00 8.00
13 Dan Dierdorf 6.00 12.00
14 Conrad Dobler 5.00 10.00
15 Bill Donckers 4.00 8.00
16 Clarence Duren 4.00 8.00
17 Roger Finnie 4.00 8.00
18 Carl Gersbach 4.00 8.00
19 Harry Gilmer CO 5.00 10.00
20 Mel Gray 5.00 10.00
21 Tim Gray 4.00 8.00
22 Gary Hammond 4.00 8.00
23 Ike Harris 4.00 8.00
24 Jim Hart 5.00 10.00
25 Steve Jones 4.00 8.00
26 Terry Joyce 4.00 8.00
27 Tim Kearney 4.00 8.00
28 Jerry Latin 4.00 8.00
29 Mike McGraw 4.00 8.00
30 Terry Metcalf 5.00 10.00
31 Wayne Morris 4.00 8.00
32 Steve Neils 4.00 8.00
33 Brad Oates 4.00 8.00
34 Steve Okoniewski 4.00 8.00
35 Walt Patulski 4.00 8.00
36 Ken Reaves 4.00 8.00
37 Mike Sensibaugh 4.00 8.00
38 Jeff Severson 4.00 8.00
39 Jackie Smith 6.00 12.00
40 Larry Stallings 4.00 8.00
41 Norm Thompson 4.00 8.00
42 Pat Tilley 5.00 10.00
43 Jim Tolbert 4.00 8.00
44 Marvin Upshaw 4.00 8.00
45 Roger Wehrli 5.00 10.00
46 Jeff West 4.00 8.00
47 Ray White 4.00 8.00
48 Sam Wyche 5.00 10.00
49 Ron Yankowski 4.00 8.00
50 Bob Young 4.00 8.00
51 John Zook 4.00 8.00

1977-78 Cardinals Team Issue

The St. Louis Cardinals issued this series of player photos quite possibly over a number of years. Each photo is nearly identical in design. The unnumbered black and white photos measure approximately 5 1/8" by 7" and all include the player's name, position, height and weight below the photo along with "ST. LOUIS FOOTBALL CARDINALS" in all capital letters. We've cataloged them all as a 1977-78 release since all of the players performed during those years and the type style matches on each photo.

COMPLETE SET (28) 100.00 200.00
1 Kurt Allerman 4.00 8.00
2 Dan Audick 4.00 8.00
3 John Barefield 4.00 8.00
4 Tim Black 4.00 8.00
5 Dan Brooks CO 4.00 8.00
6 Duane Carrell 4.00 8.00
7 Al Chandler 4.00 8.00
8 Jim Childs 4.00 8.00
9 George Collins 4.00 8.00
10 Dan Dierdorf 5.00 10.00
11 Bob Giblin 4.00 8.00
12 Randy Gill 4.00 8.00
13 Doug Greene 4.00 8.00
14 Ken Greene 4.00 8.00
15 Willard Harrell 4.00 8.00
16 Jim Hart 5.00 10.00
17 Steve Little 4.00 8.00
18 Steve Pisarkiewicz 4.00 8.00
19 Bob Pollard 4.00 8.00
20 Eason Ramson 4.00 8.00
21 Keith Simons 4.00 8.00
22 Perry Smith 4.00 8.00
23 Dave Stief 4.00 8.00
24 Terry Stieve 4.00 8.00
25 Ken Stone 4.00 8.00
26 Pat Tilley 5.00 10.00
27 Eric Williams 4.00 8.00
28 Keith Wortman 4.00 8.00

1980 Cardinals Police

The 15-card 1980 St. Louis Cardinals set was sponsored by the local law enforcement agency, the St. Louis Cardinals, KMOX Radio (which broadcasts the Cardinals' games), and Community Federal Savings and Loan: the last three of which have their logos on the backs of the cards. The cards measure approximately 2 5/8" by 4 1/8". The set is unnumbered but has been listed by player uniform number in the checklist below. The backs present "Cardinal Tips" and information on how to contact a police officer by telephone. Card backs feature black print with red trim on white card stock. Ottis Anderson appears in his Rookie Card year.

COMPLETE SET (15) 7.50 15.00
17 Jim Hart .75 2.00
22 Roger Wehrli .60 1.50
24 Wayne Morris .30 .75
32 Ottis Anderson 1.00 2.50
33 Theotis Brown .30 .75
37 Ken Greene .30 .75
55 Eric Williams LB .30 .75
56 Tim Kearney .30 .75
59 Calvin Favron .30 .75
68 Terry Stieve .30 .75
72 Dan Dierdorf 1.25 3.00
73 Mike Dawson .30 .75
82 Bob Pollard .30 .75
83 Pat Tilley .50 1.25
85 Mel Gray .60 1.50

1980 Cardinals Team Issue

The St. Louis Cardinals issued this series of player photos around 1980. Each photo is very similar in design to the 1976 issue and is only differentiated by slight differences in type size and style. The unnumbered black and white photos measure approximately 5 1/8" by 7" and all include the player's name, position, height and weight below the photo along with "St. Louis Football Cardinals."

COMPLETE SET (12) 30.00 60.00
1 Mark Arneson 2.50 6.00
2 Tom Banks 2.50 6.00
3 Joe Bostic 3.00 8.00

4 Dan Dierdorf 4.00 10.00
4 Barney Cotton 2.50 6.00
5 Calvin Favron 2.50 6.00
6 Harry Gilmer CO 3.00 8.00
7 Tim Kearney 2.50 6.00
7 Jim Hart 3.00 8.00
8 Dave Stief 2.50 6.00
9 Ken Stone 2.50 6.00
10 Ron Yankowski 2.50 6.00

1982 Cardinals Nu-Maid Butter Tubs

This set of butter cups or tubs was released by Nu-Maid and Miami Margarine in 1982. Each includes color illustrations of the featured player and measures roughly 3 3/4" tall and 3" in diameter.

COMPLETE SET (6) 12.50 25.00
1 Ottis Anderson 2.50 6.00
2 Dan Dierdorf 3.00 8.00
3 Roy Green 2.00 5.00
4 Curtis Greer 2.00 5.00
5 Neil Lomax 2.00 5.00
6 Pat Tilley 2.00 5.00

1988 Cardinals Holsum

This 12-card standard-size full-color set features players of the Phoenix Cardinals; cards were available only in Holsum Bread packages. The set was co-produced by Mike Schechter Associates on behalf of the NFL Players Association. Card fronts have a color photo within a green border and the backs are printed in black ink on white card stock.

COMPLETE SET (12) 20.00 50.00
1 Roy Green 2.50 6.00
2 Stump Mitchell 2.00 5.00
3 J.T. Smith 2.00 5.00
4 E.J. Junior 2.00 5.00
5 Cedric Mack 1.50 4.00
6 Curtis Greer 1.50 4.00
7 Lonnie Young 1.50 4.00
8 David Galloway 1.50 4.00
9 Luis Sharpe 1.50 4.00
10 Leonard Smith 1.50 4.00
11 Ron Wolfley 1.50 4.00
12 Earl Ferrell 1.50 4.00

1988 Cardinals Smokey

This set of Phoenix Cardinals was issued through local Fire Prevention agencies and sponsored by Blue Cross/Blue Shield. Each unnumbered card is oversized (roughly 5" by 7") and includes a message from Smokey the Bear on the cardback.

COMPLETE SET (16) 25.00 60.00
1 Carl Carter 1.50 4.00
2 David Galloway 1.50 4.00
3 Roy Green 2.00 5.00
4 Don Holmes 1.50 4.00
5 Shawn Knight 1.50 4.00
6 Cedric Mack 1.50 4.00
7 Jay Novacek 2.50 6.00
8 Walter Reeves 1.50 4.00
9 J.T. Smith 2.00 5.00
10 Lance Smith 1.50 4.00
11 Tom Tupa 1.50 4.00
12 Jim Wahler 1.50 4.00
13 Karl Wilson 1.50 4.00
14 Ron Wolfley 1.50 4.00
15 Lonnie Young 1.50 4.00
16 Michael Zordich 1.50 4.00

1989 Cardinals Holsum

The 1989 Holsum Phoenix Cardinals set features 16 standard-size cards. The set was co-produced by Mike Schechter Associates on behalf of the NFL Players Association. The fronts have helmetless color mug shots; the vertically oriented backs have bios, stats, and card numbers.

COMPLETE SET (16) 12.50 25.00
1 Roy Green 1.00 2.50
2 J.T. Smith .75 2.00
3 Neil Lomax .75 2.00
4 Stump Mitchell .75 2.00
5 Vai Sikahema .75 2.00
6 Lonnie Young .60 1.50
7 Robert Awalt .60 1.50
8 Cedric Mack .60 1.50
9 Earl Ferrell .60 1.50
10 Ron Wolfley .60 1.50
11 Bob Clasby .60 1.50
12 Luis Sharpe .60 1.50
13 Steve Alvord .60 1.50
14 David Galloway .60 1.50
15 Freddie Joe Nunn .60 1.50
16 Niko Noga .60 1.50

1989 Cardinals Police

The 1989 Police Phoenix Cardinals set contains 15 cards measuring approximately 2 5/8" by 4 3/16". The fronts have white borders and color action photos; the vertically oriented backs have brief bios, career highlights, and safety messages. The set features members of the Phoenix Cardinals. The set was also sponsored by Louis Rich Meats and KTSP-TV. The cards are unnumbered except for uniform number which is prominently displayed on both sides of the card. Two cards were given out every two weeks during the season. It has been reported that 1.6 million cards were produced; 100,000 of each player. Derek Kennard's card was supposedly withdrawn at some time during the promotion after he was arrested. Reportedly, Freddie Joe Nunn was also planned for inclusion in this set but was withdrawn as well.

COMPLETE SET (15) 10.00 25.00
5 Gary Hogeboom .50 1.25
24 Ron Wolfley .40 1.00
30 Stump Mitchell .50 1.25
31 Earl Ferrell .40 1.00
36 Vai Sikahema .50 1.25
43 Lonnie Young .40 1.00
46 Tim McDonald .75 2.00
65 David Galloway .40 1.00
67 Luis Sharpe .50 1.25
70 Derek Kennard SP 3.00 8.00
79 Bob Clasby .40 1.00
80 Robert Awalt .40 1.00
81 Roy Green .60 1.50
84 J.T. Smith .50 1.25
85 Jay Novacek 1.50 4.00

1990 Cardinals Police

This 16-card police set was sponsored by Louis Rich Meats and KTSP-TV. The cards measure approximately 2 5/8" by 4 1/4". The color action player photos on the fronts have maroon borders, with player information below the pictures in the bottom border. The team and NFL logos overlay the upper corners of the pictures. The backs have biography, a "Cardinal Rule" in the form of a safety tip, and sponsor logos. The cards are unnumbered (except for the prominent display of the player's uniform number) and checklisted below in alphabetical order.

COMPLETE SET (16) 3.20 8.00
1 Anthony Bell .20 .50
2 Joe Bugel CO .20 .50
3 Rich Camarillo .10 .30
4 Roy Green .40 1.00
5 Ken Harvey .40 1.00
6 Eric Hill .50 1.25
7 Tim McDonald .30 .75
8 Tootie Robbins .10 .30
9 Timm Rosenbach .30 .75
10 Luis Sharpe .20 .50
11 Vai Sikahema .20 .50
12 J.T. Smith .30 .75
13 Lance Smith .10 .30
14 Jim Wahler .10 .30
15 Ron Wolfley .10 .30
16 Lonnie Young .10 .30

1992 Cardinals Police

Sponsored by KTVK-TV (Channel 3) and the Arizona Public Service Co., this 16-card set measures the standard-size. The fronts display color player photos bordered above and partially on the left by stripes that fade from red to yellow. In the lower left corner, an electronic scoreboard gives the player's jersey number and position. Beneath the team name and logo, the player's name and jersey number are printed between two red stripes toward the bottom of the card. The horizontal backs present biographical information and, on a red panel, recycling and conservation tips. The cards are unnumbered and checklisted below in alphabetical order.

COMPLETE SET (16) 4.80 12.00
1 Joe Bugel CO .20 .50
2 Rich Camarillo .20 .50
3 Ed Cunningham .20 .50
4 Greg Davis .20 .50
5 Ken Harvey .40 1.00
6 Randal Hill .30 .75
7 Ernie Jones .30 .75
8 Mike Jones .20 .50
9 Tim McDonald .40 1.00
10 Freddie Joe Nunn .20 .50
11 Ricky Proehl .30 .75
12 Timm Rosenbach .20 .50
13 Tony Sacca .30 .75
14 Lance Smith .20 .50
15 Eric Swann .60 1.50
16 Aeneas Williams .50 1.25

1994 Cardinals Police

The cards are unnumbered, but listed below alphabetically. They feature a color player photo surrounded by a maroon and orange border. The set is thought to be complete at four cards.

COMPLETE SET (4) 4.00 10.00
1 Greg Davis 1.00 2.50
2 Anthony Edwards 1.00 2.50
3 Terry Hoage 1.00 2.50
4 Aeneas Williams 1.40 3.50

2006 Cardinals Topps

COMPLETE SET (12) 5.00 8.00
ARI1 J.J. Arrington .20 .50
ARI2 Antrel Rolle .20 .50
ARI3 Karlos Dansby .20 .50
ARI4 Kurt Warner .30 .75
ARI5 Neil Rackers .20 .50
ARI6 Anquan Boldin .25 .60
ARI7 Larry Fitzgerald .30 .75
ARI8 Edgerrin James .30 .75
ARI9 Adrian Wilson .20 .50
ARI10 Bryant Johnson .20 .50
ARI11 Matt Leinart .75 2.00
ARI12 Leonard Pope .30 .75

2007 Cardinals Topps

COMPLETE SET (12) 2.50 5.00
1 Matt Leinart .40 1.00
2 Edgerrin James .50 1.25
3 Larry Fitzgerald .50 1.25
4 Anquan Boldin .40 1.00
5 Kurt Warner .50 1.25
6 Bryant Johnson .40 1.00
7 Leonard Pope .40 1.00
8 Marcel Shipp .40 1.00
9 Adrian Wilson .40 1.00
10 Karlos Dansby .40 1.00
11 Neil Rackers .40 1.00
12 Levi Brown .40 1.00

2008 Cardinals Donruss Playoff Super Bowl XLII Card Show

These cards were issued at the 2008 Super Bowl Card Show. Collectors could obtain one card in exchange for wrappers from 2007 Donruss Playoff football card packs opened at the show.

COMPLETE SET (4) 1.50 4.00
9 Karlos Dansby .30 .75
10 Matt Leinart .60 1.50
11 Anquan Boldin .40 1.00
12 Larry Fitzgerald .40 1.00

2008 Cardinals Topps

COMPLETE SET (12) 2.50 5.00
1 Matt Leinart .40 1.00
2 Kurt Warner .50 1.25
3 Edgerrin James .50 1.25
4 Larry Fitzgerald .50 1.25
5 Anquan Boldin .40 1.00
6 Antrel Rolle .40 1.00
7 Darnell Dockett .40 1.00
8 Roderick Hood .40 1.00
9 Karlos Dansby .40 1.00
10 Leonard Pope .40 1.00
11 Early Doucet .40 1.00
12 Calais Campbell .50 1.25

2008 Cardinals Topps Super Bowl XLII Card Show

These cards were issued at the 2008 Super Bowl Card Show. Collectors could obtain one card in exchange for wrappers from 2007 Topps football card packs opened at the show.

COMPLETE SET (4) 1.50 4.00
1 Larry Fitzgerald .40 1.00
2 Matt Leinart .60 1.50
3 Anquan Boldin .40 1.00
4 Kurt Warner .50 1.25

2008 Cardinals Upper Deck Super Bowl XLII Card Show

These cards were issued at the 2008 Super Bowl Card Show. Collectors could obtain one card in exchange for wrappers from 2007 Upper Deck football card packs opened at the show.

5 Matt Leinart .60 1.50
7 Edgerrin James .50 1.25
8 Adrian Wilson .30 .75

2009 Cardinals Donruss Super Bowl XLIII

This set was issued at the Donruss/Playoff booth during the 2009 Super Bowl Card Show in Tampa, Florida. A complete set of Steelers and Cardinals was given to any collector that purchased a Score Super Bowl XLIII factory set at the booth during the show.

COMPLETE SET (9) 4.00 8.00
1 Kurt Warner .50 1.25
2 Larry Fitzgerald .50 1.25
3 Anquan Boldin .40 1.00
4 Edgerrin James .50 1.25
5 Tim Hightower .40 1.00
6 Steve Breaston .50 1.25
7 Dominique Rodgers-Cromartie .40 1.00
8 Karlos Dansby .40 1.00
9 Adrian Wilson .40 1.00

2014 Cardinals Topps 5x7 Super Bowl XLIX

COMPLETE SET (9) 12.00 20.00
40 Calais Campbell 1.00 2.50
41 Tyrann Mathieu 1.25 3.00
175 Carson Palmer 1.25 3.00
194 Ted Ginn 1.00 2.50
210 Andre Roberts 1.00 2.50
222 Andre Ellington 1.00 2.50
302 Larry Fitzgerald 1.25 3.00
319 Michael Floyd 1.00 2.50
325 Antonio Cromartie 1.00 2.50

2015 Cardinals Panini Super Bowl XLIV

COMPLETE SET (9) 3.00 8.00
1 Carson Palmer .50 1.25
2 Ryan Lindley .40 1.00
3 Andre Ellington .40 1.00
4 Larry Fitzgerald .50 1.25
5 Michael Floyd .40 1.00
6 John Brown .50 1.25
7 Patrick Peterson .40 1.00
8 Tyrann Mathieu .50 1.25
9 Chandler Catanzaro .40 1.00

1993 Cardz Flintstones NFL Promos

This six-card promo standard-size set features color cartoons of Flintstones characters in NFL uniforms. The characters are set against a sky blue background with white borders. The team name appears in large print in team colors. The backs display statistics and team records for 1992 against team-colored backgrounds with white borders. The cards are numbered on the back, and the word prototype appears next to the card number.

COMPLETE SET (6) 1.60 4.00
1 Fred Flintstone .30 .75
2 Fred Flintstone .30 .75
3 Fred and Barney .30 .75
4 Fred and Barney .30 .75
5 Fred Flintstone .30 .75
6 Fred, Barney and Dino .30 .75

1993 Cardz Flintstones NFL

This 110-card standard-size set was produced by CARDZ under license granted by Turner Home Entertainment and the NFL. Randomly packed in eight-card foil packs were three holograms and one Tekchrome card. The fronts feature color action shots of Fred Flintstone, Barney, and other Flintstones characters in NFL colors and uniforms against a light blue background with white borders. The team name and logo also appear on the front. The backs carry either statistics, trivia questions, team records, or team schedules on team-colored backgrounds. Four bonus cards are randomly inserted in the eight-card foil packs: three holograms and one Tekchrome card. The cards are numbered on the back and are divided into the categories of Team Draft Picks (1-28), Team Schedules (29-56), Team Stats (57-84), Stone Age Signals (85-100), Activity Cards (101-110), and Bonus Cards (H1-H3, T1).

COMPLETE SET (114) 3.20 8.00
COMMON CARD (1-110) .04 .10

1998 Cris Carter Energizer/Target

These oversized cards (roughly 5" x 7") were released at Target stores and feature different photos and stats on the career of Cris Carter. Each cardback contains player information, a serial number of 5400-sets produced, and and a card number.

COMPLETE SET (4) 6.00 15.00
COMMON CARD (1-4) 1.60 4.00

1989 CBS Television Announcers

This ten-card set (with cards measuring approximately 2 3/4" by 3 7/8") features those members of the 1989 CBS Football Announcing team who had been involved in professional football. The front of the card features a color action shot from the person's professional career bordered in orange and superimposed over a green football field with a white yard stripe. The words "Going the extra yard" appear in red block lettering at the card top, while the words "NFL on CBS" appear in the lower right corner. The backs are horizontally oriented and have a black and white studio portrait head shot of the announcer. Biography and career highlights are bordered in red. It has been reported that 500 sets were distributed to various CBS outlets and publication sources. The set was split into two series of five announcers each and are unnumbered.

COMPLETE SET (10) 200.00 350.00
WRAPPER 7.50 15.00
1 Terry Bradshaw 40.00 80.00
2 Dick Butkus 25.00 50.00
3 Irv Cross 4.00 10.00
4 Dan Fouts 10.00 25.00
5 Pat Summerall 8.00 20.00
6 Gary Fencik 4.00 10.00
7 Dan Jiggetts 4.00 10.00
8 John Madden 30.00 60.00
9 Ken Stabler 40.00 80.00
10 Hank Stram 6.00 15.00

2008 Americana Celebrity Cuts

COMPLETE SET (100) 125.00 200.00
STATED PRINT RUN 499 SERIAL #'d SETS
*CENTURY SILVER/50: .6X TO 1.5X BASE
*CENTURY GOLD/25: .75X TO 2X BASE
UNPRICED CENTURY PLATINUM #'d TO 1
46 Knute Rockne 2.00 5.00

2008 Americana Celebrity Cuts Century Material

RANDOM INSERTS IN PACKS
PRINT RUNS B/WN 5-100 COPIES
NO PRICING ON QTY OF 5
46 Knute Rockne Jkt/100 30.00 60.00

2008 Americana Celebrity Cuts Century Material Prime

RANDOM INSERTS IN PACKS
PRINT RUNS B/WN 1-50 COPIES PER
NO PRICING ON QTY OF 12 OR LESS
46 Knute Rockne Jkt/50 40.00 80.00

2008 Americana Celebrity Cuts Century Material Combo

RANDOM INSERTS IN PACKS
PRINT RUNS B/WN 5-50 COPIES PER
NO PRICING ON QTY OF 10 OR LESS
46 Knute Rockne Jkt/50 40.00 80.00

2008 CenTex Barracudas IFL

COMPLETE SET (8) 4.00 8.00
1 James Brown .75 2.00
2 Olan Coleman .40 1.00
3 Tim Cook .40 1.00
4 Lance Garner .40 1.00
5 Rolandus Johnson .40 1.00
6 Roderick Knight .40 1.00
7 Taurean Robinson .40 1.00
8 J.R. Turner .40 1.00

2009 Certified

COMP.SET w/o RC's (125) 20.00 40.00
ROOKIE AUTO PRINT RUN 99-499
ROOKIE JSY AU PRINT RUN 229-399
1 Anquan Boldin .25 .60
2 Edgerrin James .30 .75
3 Kurt Warner .30 .75
4 Larry Fitzgerald .30 .75
5 Tim Hightower .25 .60
6 Jerious Norwood .25 .60
7 Matt Ryan .30 .75
8 Michael Turner .25 .60
9 Roddy White .25 .60
10 Derrick Mason .25 .60
11 Joe Flacco .30 .75
12 Ray Rice .25 .60
13 Willis McGahee .25 .60
14 James Hardy .30 .75
15 Lee Evans .30 .75
16 Terrell Owens .30 .75
17 Marshawn Lynch .30 .75
18 DeAngelo Williams .25 .60
19 Jake Delhomme .25 .60
20 Jonathan Stewart .25 .60
21 Steve Smith .30 .75
22 Brian Urlacher .40 1.00
23 Greg Olsen .30 .75
24 Jay Cutler .25 .60
25 Matt Forte .25 .60
26 Carson Palmer .30 .75
27 Cedric Benson .25 .60
28 Chad Ochocinco .25 .60
29 Laveranues Coles .25 .60
30 Brady Quinn .25 .60
31 Braylon Edwards .25 .60
32 Jamal Lewis .30 .75
33 Jason Witten .30 .75
34 Marion Barber .30 .75
35 Roy Williams WR .25 .60
36 Tony Romo .30 .75
37 Brandon Marshall .30 .75
38 Correll Buckhalter .25 .60
39 Eddie Royal .25 .60
40 Kyle Orton .25 .60
41 Calvin Johnson .40 1.00
42 Daunte Culpepper .30 .75
43 Kevin Smith .25 .60
44 Aaron Rodgers .75 2.00
45 A.J. Hawk .25 .60
46 Donald Driver .30 .75
47 Greg Jennings .25 .60
48 Ryan Grant .30 .75
49 Andre Johnson .30 .75
50 Matt Schaub .25 .60
51 Owen Daniels .25 .60
52 Steve Slaton .25 .60
53 Anthony Gonzalez .25 .60
54 Dallas Clark .25 .60
55 Joseph Addai .25 .60
56 Peyton Manning 1.00 2.50
57 Reggie Wayne .30 .75
58 David Garrard .25 .60
59 Torry Holt .30 .75
60 Maurice Jones-Drew .25 .60
61 Dwayne Bowe .30 .75
62 Larry Johnson .25 .60
63 Matt Cassel .25 .60
64 Tony Gonzalez .30 .75
65 Chad Pennington .25 .60
66 Ricky Williams .30 .75
67 Ronnie Brown .25 .60
68 Ted Ginn .25 .60
69 Adrian Peterson .40 1.00
70 Bernard Berrian .25 .60
71 Brett Favre 5.00 12.00
72 Laurence Maroney .30 .75
73 Randy Moss .30 .75
74 Tom Brady 1.25 3.00
75 Wes Welker .30 .75
76 Drew Brees .40 1.00
77 Jeremy Shockey .25 .60
78 Lance Moore .25 .60
79 Marques Colston .25 .60
80 Reggie Bush .25 .60
81 Brandon Jacobs .25 .60
82 Eli Manning .30 .75
83 Kevin Boss .25 .60
84 Jerricho Cotchery .25 .60
85 Leon Washington .25 .60
86 Thomas Jones .25 .60
87 Darren McFadden .40 1.00
88 JaMarcus Russell .25 .60
89 Justin Fargas .25 .60
90 Zach Miller .25 .60
91 Brian Westbrook .25 .60
92 DeSean Jackson .30 .75
93 Donovan McNabb .30 .75
94 Kevin Curtis .25 .60
95 Ben Roethlisberger .40 1.00
96 Willie Parker .25 .60
97 Santonio Holmes .25 .60
98 Hines Ward .30 .75
99 Antonio Gates .30 .75
100 LaDainian Tomlinson .40 1.00
101 Philip Rivers .40 1.00
102 Vincent Jackson .25 .60
103 Frank Gore .30 .75
104 Patrick Willis .30 .75
105 Isaac Bruce .40 1.00
106 Vernon Davis .25 .60
107 Julius Jones .25 .60
108 Matt Hasselbeck .25 .60
109 Deion Branch .25 .60
110 T.J. Houshmandzadeh .25 .60
111 Donnie Avery .25 .60
112 Marc Bulger .25 .60
113 Steven Jackson .25 .60
114 Antonio Bryant .25 .60
115 Cadillac Williams .30 .75
116 Derrick Ward .25 .60
117 Kellen Winslow Jr. .25 .60
118 Chris Johnson .25 .60
119 Justin Gage .25 .60
120 Kerry Collins .25 .60
121 LenDale White .25 .60
122 Chris Cooley .25 .60
123 Clinton Portis .25 .60
124 Jason Campbell .25 .60
125 Santana Moss .30 .75
126 Aaron Brown RC 1.25 3.00
127 Aaron Kelly AU/499 RC 2.50 6.00
128 Aaron Maybin RC 1.25 3.00
129 Anthony Hill RC 1.00 2.50
130 Austin Collie AU/399 RC 2.50 6.00
131 B.J. Raji AU/199 RC 3.00 8.00
132 Bear Pascoe RC 1.25 3.00
133 Bernard Scott RC 1.50 4.00
134 Brandon Gibson AU/399 RC 3.00 8.00
135 Brandon Tate AU/299 RC 3.00 8.00
136 Brian Cushing AU/199 RC 2.50 6.00
137 Brian Hartline RC 1.50 4.00
138 Brian Orakpo AU/199 RC 3.00 8.00
139 Brooks Foster AU/399 RC 2.50 6.00
140 Cameron Morrah AU/399 RC 2.50 6.00
141 Cedric Peerman AU/149 RC 2.50 6.00
142 Chase Coffman AU/399 RC 2.50 6.00
143 Chris Ogbonnaya RC 1.25 3.00
144 Clay Matthews AU/199 RC 20.00 50.00
145 Clint Sintim AU/199 RC 2.50 6.00
146 Cornelius Ingram AU/399 RC 2.50 6.00
147 Curtis Painter RC 1.00 2.50
148 Dan Gronkowski RC 1.00 2.50
149 Darius Passmore RC 1.00 2.50
150 David Johnson RC 1.25 3.00
151 Davon Drew RC 1.00 2.50
152 Demetrius Byrd AU/249 RC 3.00 8.00
153 Devin Moore AU/199 RC 2.50 6.00
154 D.Edison AU/399 RC 2.50 6.00
155 Eddie Williams RC 1.25 3.00
156 Everette Brown AU/299 RC 2.50 6.00
157 Frank Summers RC 1.50 4.00
158 Fui Vakapuna RC 1.25 3.00
159 Gartrell Johnson RC 1.00 2.50
160 Hunter Cantwell AU/399 RC 2.50 6.00
161 James Casey AU/199 RC 3.00 8.00
162 J.Laurinaitis AU/299 RC 6.00 15.00
163 James Davis RC 1.00 2.50
164 Jared Cook AU/299 RC 3.00 8.00
165 Jarett Dillard AU/399 RC 2.50 6.00
166 Javarris Williams RC 1.25 3.00
167 John Phillips RC 1.50 4.00
168 Johnny Knox AU/499 RC 8.00 20.00
169 Keith Null RC 1.25 3.00
170 Kenny McKinley AU/399 RC 2.50 6.00
171 Kevin Ogletree AU/499 RC 3.00 8.00
172 Kory Sheets AU/249 RC 3.00 8.00
173 Larry English AU/99 RC 3.00 8.00
174 Louis Murphy AU/299 RC 2.50 6.00
175 Louis Delmas RC 1.25 3.00
176 Malcolm Jenkins AU/299 RC 2.50 6.00
177 Manuel Johnson RC 1.00 2.50
178 Marko Mitchell RC 1.00 2.50
179 Michael Mitchell RC 1.00 2.50
180 M.Goodson AU/399 RC EXCH 1.50 4.00
181 Mike Teel RC 1.00 2.50
182 Nathan Brown RC 1.25 3.00
183 P.J. Hill AU/499 RC 2.50 6.00
184 Patrick Chung RC 1.00 2.50
185 Quan Cosby AU/349 RC 2.50 6.00
186 Quinn Johnson AU/399 RC 2.50 6.00
187 Quinten Lawrence RC 1.00 2.50
188 R.Jennings AU/499 RC 3.00 8.00
189 Rey Maualuga AU/199 RC 4.00 10.00
190 Richard Quinn RC 1.25 3.00
191 Robert Ayers RC 1.00 2.50
192 Sammie Stroughter RC 1.00 2.50
193 S.Nelson EXCH AU RC 1.00 2.50
194 Sherrod Martin RC 1.00 2.50
195 Tiquan Underwood RC 1.00 2.50
196 T.Brandstater AU/99 RC 3.00 8.00
197 T.Fiammetta AU/399 RC 2.50 6.00
198 Travis Beckum AU/399 RC 2.50 6.00
199 Tyrell Sutton AU/499 RC 2.50 6.00
200 Vontae Davis AU/299 RC 2.50 6.00
201 Barry Sanders JSY/250 8.00 20.00
202 Brett Favre JSY/250 10.00 25.00
203 Charlie Joiner JSY/250 3.00 8.00
204 Dan Marino JSY/250 10.00 25.00
205 Emmitt Smith JSY/250 8.00 20.00
206 Eric Dickerson JSY/250 4.00 10.00
207 Franco Harris JSY/250 5.00 12.00
208 Gene Upshaw JSY/250 3.00 8.00
209 Jerry Rice JSY/250 10.00 25.00
210 Jim Brown JSY/150 6.00 15.00
211 Joe Montana JSY/250 15.00 40.00
212 Joe Namath JSY/100 6.00 15.00
213 John Elway JSY/250 8.00 20.00
214 Lawrence Taylor JSY/250 5.00 12.00
215 Merlin Olsen JSY/250 3.00 8.00
216 Roger Staubach JSY/250 6.00 15.00
217 Ronnie Lott JSY/250 4.00 10.00
218 Steve Largent JSY/250 5.00 12.00
219 Thurman Thomas JSY/250 4.00 10.00
220 Troy Aikman JSY/250 6.00 15.00
221 M.Stafford JSY AU/249 RC 40.00 100.00
222 J.Smith JSY AU/249 RC 4.00 10.00
223 T.Jackson JSY AU/229 RC 4.00 10.00
224 A.Curry JSY AU/249 RC 6.00 15.00
225 M.Sanchez JSY AU/249 RC 4.00 10.00
226 D.Hywrd-By JSY AU/249 RC 6.00 15.00
227 M.Crabtree JSY AU/249 RC 6.00 15.00
228 K.Moreno JSY AU/249 RC 4.00 10.00
229 J.Freeman JSY AU/249 RC 4.00 10.00
230 J.Maclin JSY AU/249 RC 5.00 12.00
231 B.Pettigrew JSY AU/399 RC 4.00 10.00
232 P.Harvin JSY AU/249 RC 4.00 10.00
233 D.Brown JSY AU/249 RC 8.00 20.00
234 H.Nicks JSY AU RC/249 5.00 12.00
235 K.Britt JSY AU/399 RC 6.00 15.00
236 C.Wells JSY AU/249 RC 4.00 10.00
237 B.Robiskie JSY AU/399 RC 4.00 10.00
238 P.White JSY AU/249 RC 5.00 12.00
239 Massaquoi JSY AU/249 RC 8.00 20.00
240 L.McCoy JSY AU/249 RC 10.00 25.00
241 S.Greene JSY AU/399 RC 4.00 10.00
242 G.Coffee JSY AU/399 RC 4.00 10.00
243 D.Williams JSY AU/249 RC 4.00 10.00
244 J.Ringer JSY AU/399 RC 4.00 10.00
245 M.Wallace JSY AU/399 RC 6.00 15.00
246 R.Barden JSY AU/249 RC 4.00 10.00
247 P.Turner JSY AU/349 RC 4.00 10.00
248 D.Butler JSY AU/399 RC 4.00 10.00
249 J.Iglesias JSY AU/249 RC 4.00 10.00
250 S.McGee JSY AU/249 RC 4.00 10.00
251 M.Thomas JSY AU/249 RC 4.00 10.00
252 A.Brown JSY AU/249 RC 5.00 12.00
253 R.Bomar JSY AU/249 RC 4.00 10.00
254 N.Davis JSY AU/249 RC 4.00 10.00

2009 Certified Mirror Blue

*1-125 VETS: 4X TO 10X BASIC CARDS
*126-200 ROOKIES: .5X TO 1.2X MIRROR RED
1-200 MIRROR BLUE PRINT RUN 100
*ROOK.JSY AU/50: .6X TO 1.5X BASIC CARD
*ROOK.JSY AU/25: .8X TO 2X BASIC CARDS
201-234 JSY AU MIRR.BLUE PRINT RUN 25-50
71 Brett Favre 15.00 40.00
221 Matthew Stafford JSY AU/25 60.00 120.00
225 Mark Sanchez JSY AU/25 8.00 20.00
227 Michael Crabtree JSY AU/25 12.00 30.00

2009 Certified Mirror Gold

*1-125 VETS: 6X TO 15X BASIC CARDS
*126-200 ROOKIES: .8X TO 2X MIRROR RED
1-200 MIRROR GOLD PRINT RUN 25
*201-234 JSY AU/25: .8X TO 2X BASIC CARDS
201-234 JSY AU MIR.GOLD PRINT RUN 10-25
71 Brett Favre 40.00 80.00

2009 Certified Mirror Red

*MIRROR RED: 3X TO 8X BASIC CARDS
COMMON ROOKIE 2.00 5.00
ROOKIE SEMISTARS 2.50 6.00
ROOKIE UNL.STARS 3.00 8.00
MIRROR RED PRINT RUN 250
71 Brett Favre 12.00 30.00
130 Austin Collie 2.00 5.00
131 B.J. Raji 2.50 6.00
136 Brian Cushing 2.00 5.00
138 Brian Orakpo 2.50 6.00
144 Clay Matthews 8.00 20.00
162 James Laurinaitis 2.00 5.00
168 Johnny Knox 2.50 6.00
189 Rey Maualuga 3.00 8.00
191 Robert Ayers 2.00 5.00

2009 Certified Certified Potential

STATED PRINT RUN 1000 SER.#'d SETS
*BLUE/50: .6X TO 1.5X BASIC INSERTS
*GOLD/25: .8X TO 2X BASIC INSERTS
*RED/100: .5X TO 1.2X BASIC INSERTS
1 Glen Coffee .50 1.25
2 LeSean McCoy 1.25 3.00
3 Rhett Bomar .50 1.25
4 Ramses Barden .50 1.25
5 Deon Butler .50 1.25
6 Stephen McGee .50 1.25
7 Andre Brown .60 1.50
8 Nate Davis .50 1.25
9 Javon Ringer .50 1.25
10 Matthew Stafford 2.50 6.00
11 Tyson Jackson .50 1.25
12 Mark Sanchez .50 1.25
13 Michael Crabtree .75 2.00
14 Josh Freeman .50 1.25
15 Brandon Pettigrew .50 1.25
16 Donald Brown .50 1.25
17 Kenny Britt .75 2.00
18 Brian Robiskie .50 1.25
19 Pat White .60 1.50
20 Mohamed Massaquoi .50 1.25
21 Shonn Greene .50 1.25
22 Chris Wells .50 1.25
23 Hakeem Nicks .60 1.50
24 Percy Harvin .50 1.25
25 Jeremy Maclin .60 1.50
26 Knowshon Moreno .50 1.25
27 Darrius Heyward-Bey .75 2.00
28 Aaron Curry .75 2.00
29 Jason Smith .50 1.25
30 Derrick Williams .50 1.25
31 Mike Wallace .75 2.00
32 Patrick Turner .50 1.25
33 Juaquin Iglesias .50 1.25
34 Mike Thomas .50 1.25

2009 Certified Certified Potential Autographs

STATED PRINT RUN 10-25
1 Glen Coffee/25 5.00 12.00
5 Deon Butler/25 5.00 12.00
9 Javon Ringer/25 5.00 12.00
15 Brandon Pettigrew/25 5.00 12.00
17 Kenny Britt/25 8.00 20.00
21 Shonn Greene/25 5.00 12.00
31 Mike Wallace/25 8.00 20.00

2009 Certified Certified Potential Materials

STATED PRINT RUN 100 SER.#'d SETS
*PRIME/25: .8X TO 2X BASIC JSY
PRIME PRINT RUN 25 SER.#'d SETS
1 Glen Coffee 1.50 4.00
2 LeSean McCoy 4.00 10.00
3 Rhett Bomar 1.50 4.00
4 Ramses Barden 1.50 4.00
5 Deon Butler 1.50 4.00
6 Stephen McGee 1.50 4.00
7 Andre Brown 2.00 5.00
8 Nate Davis 1.50 4.00
9 Javon Ringer 1.50 4.00
10 Matthew Stafford 6.00 15.00
11 Tyson Jackson 1.50 4.00
12 Mark Sanchez 1.50 4.00
13 Michael Crabtree 2.50 6.00
14 Josh Freeman 1.50 4.00
15 Brandon Pettigrew 1.50 4.00
16 Donald Brown 1.50 4.00
17 Kenny Britt 2.50 6.00
18 Brian Robiskie 1.50 4.00
19 Pat White 2.00 5.00
20 Mohamed Massaquoi 1.50 4.00
21 Shonn Greene 1.50 4.00
22 Chris Wells 1.50 4.00
23 Hakeem Nicks 2.00 5.00
24 Percy Harvin 1.50 4.00
25 Jeremy Maclin 2.00 5.00
26 Knowshon Moreno 1.50 4.00
27 Darrius Heyward-Bey 2.50 6.00
28 Aaron Curry 2.50 6.00
29 Jason Smith 1.50 4.00
30 Derrick Williams 1.50 4.00
31 Mike Wallace 2.50 6.00
32 Patrick Turner 1.50 4.00
33 Juaquin Iglesias 1.50 4.00
34 Mike Thomas 1.50 4.00

2009 Certified Fabric of the Game

STATED PRINT RUN 10-99
SERIAL #'d UNDER 19 NOT PRICED
2 Aaron Ross/99 2.50 6.00
4 A.J. Hawk/99 2.50 6.00
5 Alan Page/99 3.00 8.00
6 Alex Karras/99 4.00 10.00
7 Andre Johnson/60 3.00 8.00
11 Antonio Gates/99 3.00 8.00
12 Bart Starr/99 8.00 20.00
14 Ben Watson/99 2.50 6.00
16 Bertrand Berry/99 2.50 6.00
17 Bob Griese/99 5.00 12.00
18 Bob Sanders/99 3.00 8.00
20 Terence Newman/99 2.50 6.00
22 Brandon Stokley/99 2.50 6.00
27 Cadillac Williams/50 4.00 10.00
28 Carson Palmer/99 3.00 8.00
30 Chris Cooley/99 2.50 6.00
34 Dan Fouts/99 4.00 10.00
35 Darrelle Revis/99 2.50 6.00
37 Dave Casper/99 3.00 8.00
38 D'Brickashaw Ferguson/99 2.50 6.00
41 DeMeco Ryans/90 3.00 8.00
42 Derek Anderson/99 2.50 6.00
43 Derrick Mason/35 3.00 8.00
45 Devery Henderson/99 2.50 6.00
46 Devin Hester/99 3.00 8.00
48 Donovan McNabb/99 3.00 8.00
49 Drew Brees/99 4.00 10.00
51 Dwight Freeney/99 2.50 6.00
52 Earl Campbell/99 5.00 12.00
54 Edgerrin James/19 5.00 12.00
55 Eli Manning/99 3.00 8.00
59 Hank Baskett/99 2.50 6.00
61 Jamal Lewis/99 3.00 8.00
62 JaMarcus Russell/99 2.50 6.00
68 Jevon Kearse/88 2.50 6.00
69 Jim Kelly/99 5.00 12.00
71 John Mackey/99 4.00 10.00
73 Joseph Addai/99 2.50 6.00
74 Josh Reed/99 2.50 6.00
78 Justin McCareins/99 2.50 6.00
79 Keith Bulluck/99 2.50 6.00
84 Lance Alworth/99 4.00 10.00
85 LaRon Landry/99 2.50 6.00
89 Len Dawson/99 5.00 12.00
91 Lenny Moore /99 3.00 8.00
93 Mario Williams/99 3.00 8.00
95 Mark Clayton/99 2.50 6.00
97 Mathias Kiwanuka/99 2.50 6.00
99 Matt Hasselbeck/99 2.50 6.00
100 Matt Ryan/99 3.00 8.00
102 Maurice Jones-Drew/99 2.50 6.00
104 Mike Brown/99 2.50 6.00
105 Nate Burleson/99 2.50 6.00
106 Nick Barnett/99 2.50 6.00
108 Ozzie Newsome/99 4.00 10.00
109 Patrick Crayton/99 2.50 6.00
111 Paul Hornung/99 5.00 12.00
112 Peyton Manning/99 10.00 25.00
113 Philip Rivers/99 4.00 10.00
115 Ray Lewis/99 4.00 10.00
116 Reggie Brown/99 2.50 6.00
119 Richard Seymour/99 2.50 6.00
120 Ricky Williams/99 3.00 8.00
122 Roger Craig/99 4.00 10.00
124 Ryan Grant/60 3.00 8.00
127 Sebastian Janikowski/99 2.50 6.00
128 Shaun Ellis/99 2.50 6.00
129 Sidney Rice/99 2.50 6.00
130 Sinorice Moss/99 3.00 8.00
131 Sonny Jurgensen/99 4.00 10.00
132 Steve Slaton/99 2.50 6.00
133 Steve Smith/99 3.00 8.00
134 Steve Smith USC/99 3.00 8.00
135 Steve Young/99 6.00 15.00
136 Steven Jackson/99 2.50 6.00
138 Terrell Suggs/99 2.50 6.00
139 Thomas Jones/99 2.50 6.00
140 Todd Heap/55 3.00 8.00
141 Tom Brady/99 12.00 30.00
143 Tony Romo/99 3.00 8.00
144 Trent Edwards/99 2.50 6.00
146 Vincent Jackson/99 2.50 6.00
147 Warren Moon/99 5.00 12.00
149 Willis McGahee/99 2.50 6.00
150 Zach Miller/99 2.50 6.00

2009 Certified Fabric of the Game NFL Die Cut Prime

COMMON CARD/15-25 6.00 15.00
SEMISTARS/15-25 8.00 20.00
UNL.STARS/15-25 10.00 25.00
NFL DC PRIME PRINT RUN 1-25
34 Dan Fouts/25 10.00 25.00
52 Earl Campbell/25 12.00 30.00
69 Jim Kelly/25 12.00 30.00
100 Matt Ryan/25 8.00 20.00
135 Steve Young/25 15.00 40.00
141 Tom Brady/25 30.00 80.00
143 Tony Romo/25 8.00 20.00

2009 Certified Fabric of the Game Prime

PRIME STATED PRINT RUN 1-50
13 Ben Roethlisberger/50 5.00 12.00
34 Dan Fouts/25 6.00 15.00
100 Matt Ryan/50 4.00 10.00
135 Steve Young/50 8.00 20.00
141 Tom Brady/50 15.00 40.00
143 Tony Romo/35 4.00 10.00

2009 Certified Fabric of the Game Team Die Cut

STATED PRINT RUN 2-25
12 Bart Starr/25 20.00 50.00
34 Dan Fouts/25 10.00 25.00
69 Jim Kelly/25 12.00 30.00
89 Len Dawson/20 12.00 30.00
100 Matt Ryan/25 8.00 20.00
111 Paul Hornung/25 12.00 30.00
112 Peyton Manning/25 25.00 60.00
135 Steve Young/25 15.00 40.00
141 Tom Brady/24 30.00 80.00
143 Tony Romo/25 8.00 20.00

2009 Certified Fabric of the Game Jersey Number Autographs

STATED PRINT RUN 2-25
4 A.J. Hawk/25 12.00 30.00
5 Alan Page/25 15.00 40.00
6 Alex Karras/25 20.00 50.00
7 Andre Johnson/15 15.00 40.00
12 Bart Starr/25 75.00 125.00
17 Bob Griese/25 25.00 60.00
34 Dan Fouts/25 20.00 50.00
37 Dave Casper/25 15.00 40.00
41 DeMeco Ryans/25 15.00 40.00
45 Devery Henderson/25 12.00 30.00
49 Drew Brees/15 40.00 80.00
52 Earl Campbell/25 25.00 60.00
59 Hank Baskett/25 12.00 30.00
63 James Jones/25 12.00 30.00
69 Jim Kelly/25 25.00 60.00
71 John Mackey/25 20.00 50.00
84 Lance Alworth/25 30.00 80.00
85 LaRon Landry/25 12.00 30.00
89 Len Dawson/25 25.00 60.00
91 Lenny Moore/25 15.00 40.00
96 Marques Colston/25 12.00 30.00
108 Ozzie Newsome/25 20.00 50.00
109 Patrick Crayton/25 12.00 30.00
111 Paul Hornung/25 25.00 60.00
122 Roger Craig/25 20.00 50.00
129 Sidney Rice/25 12.00 30.00
131 Sonny Jurgensen/25 20.00 50.00
135 Steve Young/25 30.00 80.00
146 Vincent Jackson/25 12.00 30.00
147 Warren Moon/25 25.00 60.00

2009 Certified Fabric of the Game College

STATED PRINT RUN 20-100
*PRIME/20-25: .8X TO 2X BASIC JSY/100
*PRIME/25: .5X TO 1.2X BASIC JSY/20
1 Matthew Stafford/100 8.00 20.00
2 Tyson Jackson/100 2.00 5.00
3 Mark Sanchez/20 3.00 8.00
4 Brian Orakpo/100 2.50 6.00
6 Brian Cushing/100 2.00 5.00
7 Josh Freeman/100 2.00 5.00
8 Jeremy Maclin/100 2.50 6.00
9 Donald Brown/100 2.00 5.00
10 Chris Wells/100 2.00 5.00
11 James Laurinaitis/100 2.00 5.00
12 Rey Maualuga/100 3.00 8.00
13 Mohamed Massaquoi/100 2.00 5.00
14 LeSean McCoy/100 5.00 12.00
15 Derrick Williams/100 2.00 5.00
16 Brandon Tate/100 2.50 6.00
17 Ramses Barden/100 2.00 5.00
18 Chase Coffman/100 2.00 5.00
19 Juaquin Iglesias/100 2.00 5.00
20 Kenny McKinley/100 2.00 5.00
21 Rhett Bomar/100 2.00 5.00
23 Brandon Gibson/100 2.50 6.00
24 Graham Harrell/100 2.00 5.00
25 Quan Cosby/100 2.00 5.00

2009 Certified Fabric of the Game College Combos

STATED PRINT RUN 50 SER.#'d SETS
1 M.Kelly/Iglesias 3.00 8.00
2 Sweed/Orakpo 4.00 10.00
3 Dorsey/T.Jackson 3.00 8.00
4 J.Charles/Cosby 4.00 10.00
5 Connor/D.Williams 3.00 8.00
6 Rivers/Cushing 3.00 8.00
7 Coffman/Maclin 4.00 10.00
9 Fitzgerald/L.McCoy 8.00 20.00
10 Stafford/Sanchez 8.00 20.00

2009 Certified Freshman Fabric Jumbo

STATED PRINT RUN 100 SER.#'d SETS
*MIRROR BLUE/50: .5X TO 1.2X BASIC JSY/99
*MIRROR GOLD/25: .8X TO 2X BASIC JSY/99
221 Matthew Stafford 10.00 25.00
222 Jason Smith 2.00 5.00
223 Tyson Jackson 2.00 5.00
224 Aaron Curry 3.00 8.00
225 Mark Sanchez 2.00 5.00
226 Darrius Heyward-Bey 3.00 8.00
227 Michael Crabtree 3.00 8.00
228 Knowshon Moreno 2.00 5.00
229 Josh Freeman 2.00 5.00
230 Jeremy Maclin 2.50 6.00
231 Brandon Pettigrew 2.00 5.00
232 Percy Harvin 2.00 5.00
233 Donald Brown 2.00 5.00
234 Hakeem Nicks 2.50 6.00
235 Kenny Britt 3.00 8.00
236 Chris Wells 2.00 5.00
237 Brian Robiskie 2.00 5.00
238 Pat White 2.50 6.00
239 Mohamed Massaquoi 2.00 5.00
240 LeSean McCoy 5.00 12.00
241 Shonn Greene 2.00 5.00
242 Glen Coffee 2.00 5.00
243 Derrick Williams 2.00 5.00
244 Javon Ringer 2.00 5.00
245 Mike Wallace 3.00 8.00
246 Ramses Barden 2.00 5.00
247 Patrick Turner 2.00 5.00
248 Deon Butler 2.00 5.00
249 Juaquin Iglesias 2.00 5.00
250 Stephen McGee 2.00 5.00
251 Mike Thomas 2.00 5.00
252 Andre Brown 2.50 6.00
253 Rhett Bomar 2.00 5.00
254 Nate Davis 2.00 5.00

2009 Certified Gold Team

STATED PRINT RUN 1000 SER.#'d SETS
*MIRROR/100: .8X TO 2X BASIC INSERTS
1 Tom Brady 2.50 6.00
2 Adrian Peterson .75 2.00
3 Tony Romo .60 1.50
4 Ben Roethlisberger .75 2.00
5 Brian Westbrook .50 1.25
6 Clinton Portis .50 1.25
7 Andre Johnson .60 1.50
8 Larry Fitzgerald .60 1.50
9 Calvin Johnson .75 2.00
10 Reggie Bush .50 1.25

2009 Certified Gold Team Materials Prime

STATED PRINT RUN 25 SER.#'d SETS
*BASE MATER/250: .25X TO .6X PRIME/25
1 Tom Brady 20.00 50.00
3 Tony Romo 5.00 12.00
5 Brian Westbrook 4.00 10.00
7 Andre Johnson 5.00 12.00
10 Reggie Bush 4.00 10.00

2009 Certified Mirror Blue Materials

1-122 MIRROR BLUE VET PRINT RUN 15-100
*LEGEND JSY/35-50: .6X TO 1.5X BASE JSY
201-220 MIRR.BLUE LEGEND PRINT RUN 35-50
*MIRR.RED LEGEND/50-100: .3X TO .8X
1 Anquan Boldin/100 2.50 6.00
2 Edgerrin James/100 3.00 8.00
4 Larry Fitzgerald/65 3.00 8.00
7 Matt Ryan/100 3.00 8.00
8 Michael Turner/100 2.50 6.00
10 Derrick Mason/100 2.50 6.00
13 Willis McGahee/100 2.50 6.00
16 Terrell Owens/100 3.00 8.00
17 Marshawn Lynch/100 3.00 8.00
19 Jake Delhomme/100 2.50 6.00
21 Steve Smith/100 3.00 8.00
24 Jay Cutler/15 4.00 10.00
26 Carson Palmer/100 3.00 8.00
27 Cedric Benson/35 3.00 8.00
29 Laveranues Coles/70 2.50 6.00
30 Brady Quinn/100 2.50 6.00
32 Jamal Lewis/100 3.00 8.00
34 Marion Barber/35 4.00 10.00
36 Tony Romo/100 5.00 12.00
38 Correll Buckhalter/100 2.50 6.00
45 A.J. Hawk/100 2.50 6.00
52 Steve Slaton/100 2.50 6.00
54 Dallas Clark/100 2.50 6.00
55 Joseph Addai/100 2.50 6.00
56 Peyton Manning/100 10.00 25.00
57 Reggie Wayne/100 3.00 8.00
59 Torry Holt/100 3.00 8.00
60 Maurice Jones-Drew/100 2.50 6.00
66 Ricky Williams/100 3.00 8.00
74 Tom Brady/100 12.00 30.00
76 Drew Brees/100 4.00 10.00
77 Jeremy Shockey/100 2.50 6.00
79 Marques Colston/60 2.50 6.00

80 Reggie Bush/70 2.50 6.00
82 Eli Manning/100 3.00 8.00
84 Jerricho Cotchery/100 2.50 6.00
86 Thomas Jones/100 2.50 6.00
87 Darren McFadden/100 4.00 10.00
88 JaMarcus Russell/100 2.50 6.00
89 Justin Fargas/100 2.50 6.00
90 Zach Miller/100 2.50 6.00
93 Donovan McNabb/100 3.00 8.00
96 Willie Parker/100 2.50 6.00
97 Santonio Holmes/100 2.50 6.00
99 Antonio Gates/100 3.00 8.00
101 Philip Rivers/100 4.00 10.00
102 Vincent Jackson/100 2.50 6.00
108 Matt Hasselbeck/100 2.50 6.00
109 Deion Branch/100 2.50 6.00
112 Marc Bulger/100 2.50 6.00
113 Steven Jackson/100 2.50 6.00
115 Cadillac Williams/100 3.00 8.00
122 Chris Cooley/95 2.50 6.00
201 Barry Sanders/50 12.00 30.00
202 Brett Favre/50 15.00 40.00
203 Charlie Joiner/50 5.00 12.00
204 Dan Marino/50 15.00 40.00
205 Emmitt Smith/50 12.00 30.00
206 Eric Dickerson/50 6.00 15.00
207 Franco Harris/50 8.00 20.00
208 Gene Upshaw/50 5.00 12.00
209 Jerry Rice/50 10.00 25.00
210 Jim Brown/50 10.00 25.00
211 Joe Montana/50 25.00 60.00
212 Joe Namath/35 10.00 25.00
213 John Elway/50 12.00 30.00
214 Lawrence Taylor/50 8.00 20.00
215 Merlin Olsen/50 5.00 12.00
216 Roger Staubach/50 10.00 25.00
217 Ronnie Lott/50 6.00 15.00
218 Steve Largent/50 8.00 20.00
219 Thurman Thomas/50 6.00 15.00
220 Troy Aikman/50 10.00 25.00

2009 Certified Mirror Gold Materials

1-125 VETERAN PRINT RUN 5-50
*201-220 LEGEND/16-25: .8X TO 2X BASE JSY
201-220 LEGEND PRINT RUN 8-25
7 Matt Ryan/50 4.00 10.00
36 Tony Romo/50 6.00 15.00
74 Tom Brady/50 15.00 40.00

2009 Certified Mirror Red Materials

*MIRR.RED LEGEND/50-100: .3X TO .8X
201-220 LEGEND PRINT RUN 50-100

2009 Certified Mirror Gold Signatures

5-116 VET MIRROR GOLD PRINT RUN 10-25
*127-200 ROOK.AU/25: .8X TO 2X BASE AU RC
127-200 ROOKIE MIRR.GOLD PRINT RUN 25
201-220 LEGEND JSY AU MIRR.GOLD PRINT RUN 13-25
SERIAL #'d UNDER 20 NOT PRICED
5 Tim Hightower/25 5.00 12.00
6 Jerious Norwood/25 5.00 12.00
12 Ray Rice/25 5.00 12.00
14 James Hardy/25 6.00 15.00
25 Matt Forte/25 10.00 25.00
43 Kevin Smith/25 5.00 12.00
45 A.J. Hawk/25 5.00 12.00
52 Steve Slaton/25 5.00 12.00
76 Drew Brees/25 50.00 100.00
79 Marques Colston/25 5.00 12.00
94 Kevin Curtis/25 5.00 12.00
102 Vincent Jackson/25 5.00 12.00
104 Patrick Willis/25 6.00 15.00
111 Donnie Avery/24 5.00 12.00
116 Derrick Ward/25 5.00 12.00
201 Barry Sanders JSY/25 75.00 150.00
202 Brett Favre JSY/25 100.00 200.00
204 Dan Marino JSY/25 125.00 200.00
205 Emmitt Smith JSY/20 90.00 150.00
206 Eric Dickerson JSY/25 25.00 60.00
207 Franco Harris JSY/25 25.00 60.00
208 Gene Upshaw JSY/25 25.00 50.00
209 Jerry Rice JSY/25 75.00 150.00
210 Jim Brown JSY/25 40.00 80.00
211 Joe Montana JSY/25 75.00 150.00
212 Joe Namath JSY/25 50.00 100.00
213 John Elway JSY/25 75.00 150.00
214 Lawrence Taylor JSY/25 25.00 60.00
215 Merlin Olsen JSY/25 15.00 40.00
216 Roger Staubach JSY/25 40.00 80.00
217 Ronnie Lott JSY/25 20.00 50.00
218 Steve Largent JSY/25 25.00 60.00
219 Thurman Thomas JSY/25 20.00 50.00
220 Troy Aikman JSY/25 30.00 80.00

2009 Certified Rookie Fabric of the Game

STATED PRINT RUN 100 SER.#'d SETS
*TEAM DC/25: .8X TO 2X BASIC JSY/100
1 Tyson Jackson 1.50 4.00
2 Mark Sanchez 1.50 4.00
3 Michael Crabtree 2.50 6.00
4 Josh Freeman 1.50 4.00
5 Brandon Pettigrew 1.50 4.00
6 Donald Brown 1.50 4.00
7 Kenny Britt 2.50 6.00
8 Brian Robiskie 1.50 4.00
9 Mohamed Massaquoi 1.50 4.00
10 Shonn Greene 1.50 4.00
11 Derrick Williams 1.50 4.00
12 Mike Wallace 2.50 6.00
13 Patrick Turner 1.50 4.00
14 Juaquin Iglesias 1.50 4.00
15 Mike Thomas 1.50 4.00
16 Rhett Bomar 1.50 4.00
17 Andre Brown 2.00 5.00
18 Nate Davis 1.50 4.00
19 Javon Ringer 1.50 4.00
20 Stephen McGee 1.50 4.00
21 Deon Butler 1.50 4.00
22 Ramses Barden 1.50 4.00
23 Chris Wells 5.00 12.00
24 Glen Coffee 1.50 4.00
25 LeSean McCoy 4.00 10.00
26 Pat White 2.00 5.00
27 Matthew Stafford 6.00 15.00
28 Jason Smith 1.50 4.00
29 Aaron Curry 2.50 6.00
30 Darrius Heyward-Bey 2.50 6.00
31 Knowshon Moreno 1.50 4.00
32 Jeremy Maclin 2.00 5.00
33 Percy Harvin 1.50 4.00
34 Hakeem Nicks 2.00 5.00

2009 Certified Rookie Fabric of the Game Jersey Number Autographs

STATED PRINT RUN 10-25
5 Brandon Pettigrew/25 6.00 15.00
7 Kenny Britt/25 10.00 25.00
8 Brian Robiskie/25 6.00 15.00
10 Shonn Greene/25 6.00 15.00
12 Mike Wallace/25 10.00 25.00
19 Javon Ringer/25 6.00 15.00
21 Deon Butler/25 6.00 15.00
24 Glen Coffee/25 6.00 15.00

2009 Certified Rookie Fabric of the Game Combos

STATED PRINT RUN 100 SER.#'d SETS
*PRIME/25: .6X TO 1.5X BASIC COMBO/100
1 Stafford/Pettigrew 8.00 20.00
2 P.White/P.Turner 2.50 6.00
3 J.Smith/T.Jackson 2.00 5.00
4 Sanchez/Greene 2.00 5.00
5 Ringer/Britt 3.00 8.00
6 Maclin/L.McCoy 5.00 12.00
7 Heyward-Bey/Crabtree 3.00 8.00
8 Moreno/C.Wells 2.00 5.00
9 Robiskie/Massaquoi 2.00 5.00
10 Coffee/N.Davis 2.00 5.00
11 McGee/J.Freeman 2.00 5.00
12 Nicks/Barden 2.50 6.00
13 Bomar/Harvin 2.00 5.00
14 Stafford/Sanchez 8.00 20.00
15 D.Williams/Butler 2.00 5.00

2009 Certified Souvenir Stamps College Materials

STATED PRINT RUN 99 SER.#'d SETS
*PRIME/25: .6X TO 1.5X BASIC JSY/99
1 Chris Wells 2.00 5.00
2 Donald Brown 2.00 5.00
3 Jeremy Maclin 2.50 6.00
4 Josh Freeman 2.00 5.00
5 Brandon Tate 2.50 6.00
6 Derrick Williams 2.00 5.00
7 LeSean McCoy 5.00 12.00
8 Mohamed Massaquoi 2.00 5.00
9 Mark Sanchez 2.00 5.00
10 Tyson Jackson 2.00 5.00
11 Matthew Stafford 10.00 25.00
12 Juaquin Iglesias 2.00 5.00
13 Brian Orakpo 2.50 6.00
14 Brian Cushing 2.00 5.00
15 James Laurinaitis 5.00 12.00
16 Rey Maualuga 3.00 8.00
17 Chase Coffman 2.00 5.00
18 Brandon Gibson 2.50 6.00
19 Graham Harrell 2.00 5.00
20 Quan Cosby 2.00 5.00
21 Jeremiah Johnson 2.00 5.00
22 Kenny McKinley 2.00 5.00

2009 Certified Souvenir Stamps Material Pro Team Logos

STATED PRINT RUN 99 SER.#'d SETS
*PRIME/25: .6X TO 1.5X BASIC JSY/99
*1969 STAMP/50: .5X TO 1.2X BASIC JSY/99
1 Shonn Greene 2.00 5.00
2 Hakeem Nicks 2.50 6.00
3 Jeremy Maclin 2.50 6.00
4 Darrius Heyward-Bey 3.00 8.00
5 Jason Smith 2.00 5.00
6 Mike Wallace 3.00 8.00
7 Juaquin Iglesias 2.00 5.00
8 Rhett Bomar 2.00 5.00
9 Glen Coffee 2.00 5.00
10 LeSean McCoy 5.00 12.00
11 Deon Butler 2.00 5.00
12 Andre Brown 2.50 6.00
13 Javon Ringer 2.00 5.00
14 Tyson Jackson 2.00 5.00
15 Michael Crabtree 3.00 8.00
16 Brandon Pettigrew 2.00 5.00
17 Kenny Britt 3.00 8.00
18 Pat White 2.50 6.00
19 Mike Thomas 2.00 5.00
20 Patrick Turner 2.00 5.00
21 Derrick Williams 2.00 5.00
22 Aaron Curry 3.00 8.00
23 Knowshon Moreno 2.00 5.00
24 Percy Harvin 2.00 5.00
25 Chris Wells 2.00 5.00
26 Mohamed Massaquoi 2.00 5.00
27 Brian Robiskie 2.00 5.00
28 Donald Brown 2.00 5.00
29 Josh Freeman 2.00 5.00
30 Mark Sanchez 2.00 5.00
31 Matthew Stafford 8.00 20.00
32 Nate Davis 2.00 5.00
33 Stephen McGee 2.00 5.00
34 Ramses Barden 2.00 5.00

2009 Certified Souvenir Stamps Material Autographs Pro Team Logos

PRO TEAM LOGO AU PRINT RUN 15-20
*1960 STAMP MAT.AU/20: .4X TO 1X
*PRO TEAM LOGO PRIME AU/15: .4X TO 1X
1 Shonn Greene/20 6.00 15.00
2 Hakeem Nicks/20 8.00 20.00
3 Jeremy Maclin/15 8.00 20.00
4 Darrius Heyward-Bey/20 10.00 25.00
5 Jason Smith/20 6.00 15.00
6 Mike Wallace/20 10.00 25.00
7 Juaquin Iglesias/15 6.00 15.00
8 Rhett Bomar/20 6.00 15.00
9 Glen Coffee/20 6.00 15.00
10 LeSean McCoy/15 15.00 40.00
11 Deon Butler/20 6.00 15.00
12 Andre Brown/20 8.00 20.00
13 Javon Ringer/20 6.00 15.00
14 Tyson Jackson/15 6.00 15.00
15 Michael Crabtree/20 10.00 25.00
16 Brandon Pettigrew/20 6.00 15.00
17 Kenny Britt/20 10.00 25.00
18 Pat White/20 8.00 20.00
19 Mike Thomas/20 6.00 15.00
20 Patrick Turner/20 6.00 15.00
21 Derrick Williams/15 6.00 15.00
22 Aaron Curry/20 10.00 25.00
23 Knowshon Moreno/20 6.00 15.00
24 Percy Harvin/20 6.00 15.00
25 Chris Wells/15 6.00 15.00
26 Mohamed Massaquoi/15 6.00 15.00
27 Brian Robiskie/20 6.00 15.00
28 Donald Brown/15 6.00 15.00
29 Josh Freeman/15 6.00 15.00
30 Mark Sanchez/15 6.00 15.00
31 Matthew Stafford/15 75.00 150.00
32 Nate Davis/20 6.00 15.00
33 Stephen McGee/20 6.00 15.00
34 Ramses Barden/20 6.00 15.00

2010 Certified

COMP.SET w/o SP's (150) 15.00 40.00
151-170 LEGEND JSY PRINT RUN 150-250
171-270 ROOKIE PRINT RUN 999
271-304 ROOK.JSY AU PRINT RUN 199-699
EXCH EXPIRATION: 5/3/2012
1 Chris Wells .25 .60
2 Larry Fitzgerald .30 .75
3 Tim Hightower .25 .60
4 Steve Breaston .25 .60
5 Matt Ryan .30 .75
6 Michael Turner .25 .60
7 Roddy White .25 .60
8 Tony Gonzalez .30 .75
9 Michael Jenkins .25 .60
10 Anquan Boldin .25 .60
11 Derrick Mason .25 .60
12 Joe Flacco .30 .75
13 Ray Lewis .40 1.00
14 Ray Rice .25 .60
15 Fred Jackson .30 .75
16 Lee Evans .30 .75
17 Marshawn Lynch .30 .75
18 Ryan Fitzpatrick .25 .60
19 DeAngelo Williams .25 .60
20 Jonathan Stewart .25 .60
21 Matt Moore .25 .60
22 Steve Smith .30 .75
23 Brian Urlacher .40 1.00
24 Devin Hester .30 .75
25 Greg Olsen .30 .75
26 Jay Cutler .25 .60
27 Matt Forte .25 .60
28 Leon Hall .25 .60
29 Carson Palmer .30 .75
30 Cedric Benson .25 .60
31 Chad Ochocinco .25 .60
32 Terrell Owens .30 .75
33 Ben Watson .25 .60
34 Jake Delhomme .25 .60
35 Jerome Harrison .25 .60
36 Josh Cribbs .25 .60
37 Mohamed Massaquoi .30 .75
38 Felix Jones .25 .60
39 Jason Witten .30 .75
40 Marion Barber .30 .75
41 Miles Austin .25 .60
42 Tony Romo .30 .75
43 Eddie Royal .25 .60
44 Brandon Lloyd .25 .60
45 Knowshon Moreno .25 .60
46 Kyle Orton .25 .60
47 Brandon Pettigrew .25 .60
48 Calvin Johnson .40 1.00
49 Matthew Stafford .30 .75
50 Nate Burleson .25 .60
51 Aaron Rodgers .75 2.00
52 Donald Driver .30 .75
53 Greg Jennings .25 .60
54 Jermichael Finley .25 .60
55 Ryan Grant .30 .75
56 Andre Johnson .30 .75
57 Kevin Walter .30 .75
58 Matt Schaub .25 .60
59 Owen Daniels .25 .60
60 Arian Foster .30 .75
61 Austin Collie .25 .60
62 Dallas Clark .25 .60
63 Joseph Addai .25 .60
64 Peyton Manning 1.00 2.50
65 Pierre Garcon .30 .75
66 Reggie Wayne .30 .75
67 David Garrard .25 .60
68 Maurice Jones-Drew .25 .60
69 Mike Sims-Walker .25 .60
70 Mike Thomas .30 .75
71 Chris Chambers .25 .60
72 Dwayne Bowe .30 .75
73 Jamaal Charles .30 .75
74 Matt Cassel .25 .60
75 Thomas Jones .25 .60
76 Brandon Marshall .30 .75
77 Brian Hartline .30 .75
78 Chad Henne .30 .75
79 Davone Bess .25 .60
80 Anthony Fasano .25 .60
81 Ronnie Brown .25 .60
82 Adrian Peterson .40 1.00
83 Bernard Berrian .25 .60
84 Brett Favre .75 2.00
85 Percy Harvin .25 .60
86 Sidney Rice .25 .60
87 Visanthe Shiancoe .30 .75
88 Laurence Maroney .25 .60
89 Randy Moss .30 .75
90 Tom Brady 1.00 2.50
91 Wes Welker .30 .75
92 Devery Henderson .25 .60
93 Drew Brees .40 1.00
94 Jeremy Shockey .25 .60
95 Marques Colston .25 .60
96 Pierre Thomas .25 .60
97 Brandon Jacobs .25 .60
98 Ahmad Bradshaw .25 .60
99 Eli Manning .30 .75
100 Hakeem Nicks .25 .60
101 Steve Smith USC .25 .60
102 Braylon Edwards .25 .60
103 Jerricho Cotchery .25 .60
104 LaDainian Tomlinson .40 1.00
105 Mark Sanchez .25 .60
106 Santonio Holmes .25 .60
107 Shonn Greene .25 .60
108 Darren McFadden .25 .60
109 Jason Campbell .25 .60
110 Darrius Heyward-Bey .30 .75
111 Zach Miller .25 .60
112 Brent Celek .25 .60
113 DeSean Jackson .30 .75
114 Jeremy Maclin .25 .60
115 Michael Vick .30 .75
116 LeSean McCoy .40 1.00
117 Antwaan Randle El .25 .60
118 Ben Roethlisberger .40 1.00
119 Heath Miller .25 .60
120 Hines Ward .30 .75
121 Rashard Mendenhall .25 .60
122 Troy Polamalu .40 1.00
123 Antonio Gates .30 .75
124 Darren Sproles .30 .75
125 Philip Rivers .40 1.00
126 Vincent Jackson .25 .60
127 Brian Westbrook .25 .60
128 Frank Gore .30 .75
129 Josh Morgan .30 .75
130 Michael Crabtree .25 .60
131 Vernon Davis .25 .60
132 Deion Branch .25 .60
133 John Carlson .25 .60
134 Julius Jones .25 .60
135 Matt Hasselbeck .25 .60
136 T.J. Houshmandzadeh .25 .60
137 Donnie Avery .25 .60
138 James Laurinaitis .30 .75
139 Steven Jackson .25 .60
140 Cadillac Williams .25 .60
141 Josh Freeman .30 .75
142 Kellen Winslow Jr. .25 .60
143 Bo Scaife .25 .60
144 Chris Johnson .25 .60
145 Kenny Britt .25 .60
146 Vince Young .25 .60
147 Chris Cooley .25 .60
148 Clinton Portis .25 .60
149 Donovan McNabb .30 .75
150 Santana Moss .30 .75
151 Jerry Rice JSY/250 6.00 15.00
153 Irving Fryar JSY/250 4.00 10.00
154 John Taylor JSY/150 4.00 10.00
155 Paul Warfield JSY/250 4.00 10.00
156 Emmitt Smith JSY/250 8.00 20.00
157 Bruce Smith JSY/150 4.00 10.00
158 Cris Carter JSY/250 5.00 12.00
159 Rickey Jackson JSY/250 4.00 10.00
160 Len Dawson JSY/150 6.00 15.00
161 Lenny Moore JSY/250 3.00 8.00
162 Jack Youngblood JSY/250 4.00 10.00
163 Terry Bradshaw JSY/250 6.00 15.00
164 Todd Christensen JSY/250 4.00 10.00
165 Earl Campbell JSY/195 5.00 12.00
166 Raymond Berry JSY/250 4.00 10.00
167 Bo Jackson JSY/250 6.00 15.00
168 Curtis Martin JSY/150 4.00 10.00
169 Ernie Davis JSY/150 12.00 30.00
170 Ronnie Lott JSY/250 4.00 10.00
171 Aaron Hernandez RC 1.25 3.00
172 Andrew Quarless RC 1.25 3.00
173 Lamarr Houston RC 1.50 4.00
174 Anthony Armstrong RC 2.50 6.00
175 Anthony Dixon RC 1.25 3.00
176 Anthony McCoy RC 1.25 3.00
177 Antonio Brown RC 10.00 25.00
178 Cody Grimm RC 2.50 6.00
179 Blair White RC 1.25 3.00
180 Brandon Banks RC 2.50 6.00
181 Brandon Graham RC 1.50 4.00
182 Brandon Spikes RC 1.25 3.00
183 Brody Eldridge RC 2.00 5.00
184 Bryan Bulaga RC 1.25 3.00
185 Carlos Dunlap RC 1.25 3.00
186 Carlton Mitchell RC 1.25 3.00
187 Chad Jones RC 1.25 3.00
188 Chris Cook RC 1.25 3.00
189 Chris Gronkowski RC 2.00 5.00
190 Chris Ivory RC 3.00 8.00
191 Clay Harbor RC 1.25 3.00
192 Corey Wootton RC 1.25 3.00
193 Dan LeFevour RC 1.25 3.00
194 Danario Alexander RC 1.25 3.00
195 Daryl Washington RC 1.25 3.00
196 David Gettis RC 1.25 3.00
197 David Nelson RC 2.00 5.00
198 David Reed RC 1.25 3.00
199 Deji Karim RC 1.50 4.00
200 Dennis Pitta RC 1.25 3.00
201 Derrick Morgan RC 1.25 3.00
202 Devin McCourty RC 1.50 4.00
203 Dezmon Briscoe RC 1.25 3.00
204 Dominique Curry RC 1.50 4.00
205 Dominique Franks RC 1.25 3.00
206 Donald Jones RC 2.00 5.00
207 Isaac Redman RC 15.00 30.00
208 Duke Calhoun RC 1.50 4.00
209 Earl Thomas RC 3.00 8.00
210 Ed Dickson RC 1.25 3.00
211 Everson Griffen RC 1.25 3.00
212 Fendi Onobun RC 1.50 4.00
213 Garrett Graham RC 1.25 3.00
214 Jacoby Ford RC 1.25 3.00
215 James Starks RC 1.50 4.00
216 Jarrett Brown RC 1.25 3.00
217 Javier Arenas RC 1.25 3.00
218 Jason Pierre-Paul RC 2.00 5.00
219 Jason Worilds RC 1.25 3.00
220 Jeremy Horne RC 1.50 4.00
221 Jerry Hughes RC 1.25 3.00
222 Jimmy Graham RC 3.00 8.00
223 Joe Haden RC 2.00 5.00
224 Joe Webb RC 1.25 3.00
225 John Conner RC 1.25 3.00
226 John Skelton RC 1.50 4.00
227 T.J. Ward RC 2.00 5.00
228 Joique Bell RC 1.25 3.00
229 Tyson Alualu RC 1.25 3.00
230 Jonathan Stupar RC 2.00 5.00
231 Mickey Shuler RC 2.00 5.00
232 Kareem Jackson RC 1.25 3.00
233 Keiland Williams RC 1.50 4.00
234 Keith Toston RC 2.00 5.00
235 Kerry Meier RC 1.50 4.00
236 Kyle Williams RC 2.00 5.00
237 Kyle Wilson RC 1.25 3.00
238 Lonyae Miller RC 1.50 4.00
239 Marc Mariani RC 2.00 5.00
240 Marlon Moore RC 2.00 5.00
241 Matt Willis RC 2.00 5.00
242 Max Hall RC 2.00 5.00
243 Max Komar RC 2.00 5.00
244 Michael Hoomanawanui RC 2.00 5.00
245 Morgan Burnett RC 1.50 4.00
246 Nate Allen RC 2.00 5.00
247 Nate Byham RC 1.25 3.00
248 NaVorro Bowman RC 2.50 6.00
249 Koa Misi RC 1.50 4.00
250 Patrick Robinson RC 1.50 4.00
251 Perrish Cox RC 1.50 4.00
252 Preston Parker RC 1.50 4.00
253 Ricky Sapp RC 1.25 3.00
254 Riley Cooper RC 1.25 3.00
255 Roberto Wallace RC 1.50 4.00
256 Russell Okung RC 1.25 3.00
257 Rusty Smith RC 2.00 5.00
258 Sean Canfield RC 1.25 3.00
259 Sean Lee RC 2.50 6.00
260 Sean Weatherspoon RC 1.25 3.00
261 Sergio Kindle RC 1.25 3.00
262 Seyi Ajirotutu RC 1.25 3.00
263 Stephen Williams RC 2.00 5.00
264 Taylor Mays RC 1.25 3.00
265 Jared Odrick RC 1.50 4.00
266 Thaddeus Lewis RC 1.50 4.00
267 Tony Moeaki RC 1.50 4.00
268 Tony Pike RC 1.25 3.00
269 Trent Williams RC 1.50 4.00
270 Victor Cruz RC 2.50 6.00
271 A.Roberts JSY AU/699 RC 4.00 10.00
272 A.Edwards JSY AU/699 RC 4.00 10.00
273 A.Benn JSY AU/499 RC 3.00 8.00
274 Ben Tate JSY AU/699 RC 3.00 8.00
275 B.LaFell JSY AU/599 RC 5.00 12.00
276 C.J. Spiller JSY AU/349 RC 4.00 10.00
277 Colt McCoy JSY AU/349 RC 5.00 12.00
278 D.Williams JSY AU/599 RC 3.00 8.00
279 D.Thomas JSY AU/599 RC 8.00 20.00
280 McClstr JSY/599 RC No AU 4.00 10.00
281 D.Bryant JSY AU/349 RC 30.00 60.00
282 E.Sanders JSY AU/699 RC 6.00 15.00
283 Eric Berry JSY AU/699 RC 6.00 15.00
284 Eric Decker JSY AU/699 RC 4.00 10.00
285 Gerald McCoy JSY AU/199 RC 4.00 10.00
286 G.Tate JSY AU/349 RC 5.00 12.00
287 Jahvid Best JSY AU/499 RC 3.00 8.00
288 J.Gresham JSY AU/699 RC 3.00 8.00
289 J.Clausen JSY AU/299 RC 4.00 10.00
290 J.McKnight JSY AU/699 RC 6.00 15.00
291 J.Dwyer JSY AU/699 RC 3.00 8.00
292 J.Shipley JSY AU/599 RC 3.00 8.00
293 M.Easley JSY AU/699 RC 3.00 8.00
294 M.Gilyard JSY AU/699 RC 3.00 8.00
295 Mike Kafka JSY AU/699 RC 4.00 10.00
296 M.Williams JSY AU/699 RC 3.00 8.00
297 M.Hardesty JSY AU/699 RC 3.00 8.00
298 N.Suh JSY AU/599 RC 6.00 15.00
299 R.Grnkwski JSY AU/699 RC 25.00 50.00
300 R.McClain JSY AU/699 RC 3.00 8.00
301 R.Mathews JSY AU/349 RC 4.00 10.00
302 S.Bradford JSY AU/299 RC 5.00 12.00
303 Taylor Price JSY AU/699 RC 3.00 8.00
304 Tim Tebow JSY AU/299 RC 15.00 40.00
305 T.Gerhart JSY AU/599 RC 3.00 8.00

2010 Certified Mirror Blue

*VETS: 3X TO 8X BASIC CARDS
*RK.JSY AU: .6X TO 1.5X JSY AU RC/499-699
*RK.JSY AU: .5X TO 1.2X JSY AU RC/199-349
STATED PRINT RUN 50 SER.#'d SETS
EXCH EXPIRATION: 5/3/2012
281 Dez Bryant JSY AU 50.00 100.00
302 Sam Bradford JSY AU 6.00 15.00
304 Tim Tebow JSY AU 25.00 60.00

2010 Certified Mirror Gold

*VETS: 5X TO 12X BASIC CARDS
*RK.JSY AU: 1.5X TO 4X JSY AU RC/499-699
*RK.JSY AU: 1.2X TO 3X JSY AU RC/199-349
STATED PRINT RUN 25 SER.#'d SETS
EXCH EXPIRATION: 5/3/2012
276 C.J. Spiller JSY AU 12.00 30.00
281 Dez Bryant JSY AU 90.00 150.00
302 Sam Bradford JSY AU 15.00 40.00
304 Tim Tebow JSY AU 50.00 120.00

2010 Certified Mirror Red

*VETS 1-150: 2.5X TO 6X BASIC CARDS
1-150 VETERAN PRINT RUN 250
*LEGEND JSY: .5X TO 1.2X BASIC CARDS
151-170 LEGEND JSY PRINT RUN 60-100
152 Jack Lambert JSY/60 8.00 20.00

2010 Certified Platinum Blue

*VETS: 3X TO 8X BASIC CARDS
STATED PRINT RUN 100 SER.#'d SETS

2010 Certified Platinum Red

*VETS/999: 1.5X TO 4X BASIC CARDS
STATED PRINT RUN 999 SER.#'d SETS

2010 Certified Certified Potential

STATED PRINT RUN 999 SER.#'d SETS
*BLUE/50: .6X TO 1.5X BASIC INSERT/999
*GOLD/25: .8X TO 2X BASIC INSERT/999
*RED/100: .5X TO 1.2X BASIC INSERT/999
1 Dez Bryant 1.25 3.00
2 Eric Decker .60 1.50
3 Jahvid Best .50 1.25
4 Joe McKnight .50 1.25
5 Marcus Easley .50 1.25
6 Mike Williams .50 1.25
7 Sam Bradford .60 1.50
8 Toby Gerhart .50 1.25
9 Brandon LaFell .75 2.00
10 Colt McCoy .60 1.50
11 Jordan Shipley .50 1.25
12 Dexter McCluster .60 1.50
13 Eric Berry .75 2.00
14 Andre Roberts .60 1.50
15 Gerald McCoy .50 1.25
16 Ryan Mathews .50 1.25
17 Taylor Price .50 1.25
18 Ndamukong Suh 1.00 2.50
19 Damian Williams .50 1.25
20 Golden Tate .60 1.50
21 Rob Gronkowski 1.50 4.00
22 C.J. Spiller .50 1.25
23 Armanti Edwards .60 1.50
24 Tim Tebow 1.50 4.00
25 Jermaine Gresham .50 1.25
26 Emmanuel Sanders .75 2.00
27 Mardy Gilyard .50 1.25
28 Rolando McClain .50 1.25
29 Demaryius Thomas 1.25 3.00
30 Arrelious Benn .50 1.25
31 Jonathan Dwyer .50 1.25
32 Mike Kafka .60 1.50
33 Jimmy Clausen .50 1.25
34 Montario Hardesty .50 1.25
35 Ben Tate .50 1.25

2010 Certified Certified Potential Autographs

STATED PRINT RUN 25-50
EXCH EXPIRATION: 5/3/2012
1 Dez Bryant/50 30.00 60.00
2 Eric Decker/50 5.00 12.00
3 Jahvid Best/50 4.00 10.00
4 Joe McKnight/50 4.00 10.00
5 Marcus Easley/50 4.00 10.00
6 Mike Williams/50 4.00 10.00
7 Sam Bradford/25 6.00 15.00
8 Toby Gerhart/50 4.00 10.00
9 Brandon LaFell/50 6.00 15.00
10 Colt McCoy/25 6.00 15.00
11 Jordan Shipley/50 4.00 10.00
13 Eric Berry/50 6.00 15.00
14 Andre Roberts/50 5.00 12.00
16 Ryan Mathews/50 4.00 10.00
17 Taylor Price/50 4.00 10.00
18 Ndamukong Suh/50 8.00 20.00
19 Damian Williams/50 4.00 10.00
20 Golden Tate/50 5.00 12.00
21 Rob Gronkowski/50 25.00 50.00
22 C.J. Spiller/25 5.00 12.00
23 Armanti Edwards/50 5.00 12.00
24 Tim Tebow/25 25.00 60.00
25 Jermaine Gresham/50 4.00 10.00
26 Emmanuel Sanders/50 6.00 15.00
27 Mardy Gilyard/50 4.00 10.00
28 Rolando McClain/50 4.00 10.00
29 Demaryius Thomas/50 10.00 25.00
30 Arrelious Benn/50 4.00 10.00
31 Jonathan Dwyer/50 4.00 10.00
32 Mike Kafka/50 5.00 12.00
33 Jimmy Clausen/25 5.00 12.00
34 Montario Hardesty/50 4.00 10.00
35 Ben Tate/50 4.00 10.00

2010 Certified Certified Potential Materials

STATED PRINT RUN 75-250
*PRIME/50: .6X TO 1.5X BASIC JSY/250
*PRIME/50: .5X TO 1.2X BASIC JSY/75
1 Dez Bryant/250 6.00 15.00
2 Eric Decker/250 2.00 5.00
3 Jahvid Best/250 1.50 4.00
4 Joe McKnight/250 1.50 4.00
5 Marcus Easley/250 1.50 4.00
6 Mike Williams/250 1.50 4.00
7 Sam Bradford/250 2.00 5.00
8 Toby Gerhart/250 1.50 4.00
9 Brandon LaFell/250 2.50 6.00
10 Colt McCoy/250 2.00 5.00
11 Jordan Shipley/250 1.50 4.00
12 Dexter McCluster/250 2.00 5.00
13 Eric Berry/250 2.50 6.00
14 Andre Roberts/250 2.00 5.00
15 Gerald McCoy/250 1.50 4.00
16 Ryan Mathews/75 1.50 4.00
17 Taylor Price/250 1.50 4.00
18 Ndamukong Suh/250 3.00 8.00
19 Damian Williams/250 1.50 4.00
20 Golden Tate/250 2.00 5.00
21 Rob Gronkowski/250 5.00 12.00
22 C.J. Spiller/250 1.50 4.00
23 Armanti Edwards/250 2.00 5.00
24 Tim Tebow/250 5.00 12.00
25 Jermaine Gresham/250 1.50 4.00
26 Emmanuel Sanders/250 2.50 6.00
27 Mardy Gilyard/250 1.50 4.00
28 Rolando McClain/250 1.50 4.00
29 Demaryius Thomas/250 4.00 10.00
30 Arrelious Benn/250 1.50 4.00
31 Jonathan Dwyer/250 1.50 4.00
32 Mike Kafka/250 2.00 5.00
33 Jimmy Clausen/250 1.50 4.00
34 Montario Hardesty/250 1.50 4.00
35 Ben Tate/250 1.50 4.00

2010 Certified Fabric of the Game

STATED PRINT RUN 35-250
1 Adrian Peterson/250 4.00 10.00
3 Alan Page/250 4.00 10.00
4 Alex Karras/250 4.00 10.00
11 Bart Starr/250 8.00 20.00
13 Bernie Kosar/250 4.00 10.00
14 Bill Bates/250 5.00 12.00
15 Bo Jackson/250 6.00 15.00
16 Bob Griese/250 5.00 12.00
17 Bob Hayes/100 5.00 12.00
18 Bob Lilly/250 4.00 10.00
19 Boomer Esiason/250 4.00 10.00
20 Brent Jones/50 4.00 10.00
21 Brett Favre/125 8.00 20.00
22 Buck Buchanan/250 5.00 12.00
25 Carson Palmer/250 3.00 8.00
26 Cedric Benson/125 2.50 6.00
27 Charles Woodson/250 5.00 12.00
28 Charley Taylor/250 3.00 8.00
29 Charlie Joiner/250 3.00 8.00
30 Chuck Howley/250 4.00 10.00
31 Cliff Harris/120 4.00 10.00
32 Clinton Portis/125 2.50 6.00
33 Craig James/250 3.00 8.00
34 Dan Fouts/250 4.00 10.00
35 Dan Marino/250 8.00 20.00
36 Darren Woodson/35 8.00 20.00
37 D.D. Lewis/250 4.00 10.00
38 Deacon Jones/250 4.00 10.00
40 Deion Sanders/250 4.00 10.00
42 Derrick Thomas/250 8.00 20.00
44 Dick Butkus/250 6.00 15.00
45 Don Maynard/250 4.00 10.00
46 Don Meredith/100 12.00 30.00
48 Doug Flutie/250 4.00 10.00
51 Ed Too Tall Jones/250 3.00 8.00
52 Ed McCaffrey/250 3.00 8.00
53 Eddie George/250 4.00 10.00
54 Eddie Royal/200 2.50 6.00
55 Emmitt Smith/250 8.00 20.00
56 Forrest Gregg/250 5.00 12.00
57 Fran Tarkenton/250 5.00 12.00
58 Franco Harris/250 5.00 12.00
60 Fred Biletnikoff/250 5.00 12.00
61 Gale Sayers/250 5.00 12.00
62 Greg Olsen/250 3.00 8.00
63 Harvey Martin/100 4.00 10.00
64 Henry Ellard/250 3.00 8.00
65 Hank Jordan/250 5.00 12.00
67 Howie Long/250 5.00 12.00
68 Jackie Slater/250 3.00 8.00
69 Jared Allen/250 2.50 6.00
70 Jason Witten/250 3.00 8.00
71 Jay Cutler/250 2.50 6.00
72 Jerricho Cotchery/250 2.50 6.00
73 Jerry Rice/250 6.00 15.00
74 Jim Brown/250 8.00 20.00
75 Jim Kelly/250 5.00 12.00
76 Jim McMahon/250 5.00 12.00
77 Jim Otto/250 3.00 8.00
78 Jim Plunkett/200 4.00 10.00
79 Joe Flacco/250 3.00 8.00
80 Joe Greene/160 6.00 15.00
81 Joe Klecko/140 3.00 8.00
82 Joe Montana/250 8.00 20.00
83 Joe Namath/250 8.00 20.00
85 John Elway/250 8.00 20.00
86 John Taylor/35 6.00 15.00
87 Joseph Addai/250 2.50 6.00
89 Josh Freeman/115 3.00 8.00
90 Junior Seau/250 4.00 10.00
91 Justin Gage/140 2.50 6.00
92 Ken Stabler/250 6.00 15.00
94 Keyshawn Johnson/170 3.00 8.00
95 Joe Perry/100 6.00 15.00
96 Laurence Maroney/250 2.50 6.00
97 L.C. Greenwood/250 6.00 15.00
98 Len Dawson/100 5.00 12.00
100 Mark Sanchez/250 2.50 6.00
102 Knowshon Moreno/250 2.50 6.00
104 Merlin Olsen/250 3.00 8.00
106 Michael Irvin/250 6.00 15.00
107 Mohamed Massaquoi/165 3.00 8.00
109 Ozzie Newsome/250 4.00 10.00
110 Paul Warfield/100 4.00 10.00
111 Peyton Manning/250 10.00 25.00
112 Phil Simms/250 5.00 12.00
113 Philip Rivers/250 4.00 10.00
115 Randy Moss/100 3.00 8.00
116 Randy White/140 5.00 12.00
117 Ray Lewis/250 5.00 12.00
119 Raymond Berry/250 4.00 10.00
122 Rickey Jackson/250 3.00 8.00
123 Robert Meachem/250 2.50 6.00
124 Rod Smith/250 3.00 8.00
125 Rod Woodson/250 6.00 15.00
126 Roger Craig/250 4.00 10.00
127 Roger Staubach/250 6.00 15.00
128 Santana Moss/100 3.00 8.00
129 Sidney Rice/250 2.50 6.00
130 Sonny Jurgensen/250 5.00 12.00
131 Steve Largent/250 5.00 12.00
133 Steve Smith USC/125 2.50 6.00
134 Steven Jackson/125 2.50 6.00
135 Terrell Davis/150 4.00 10.00
136 Terry Bradshaw/250 6.00 15.00
137 Thurman Thomas/145 4.00 10.00
138 Brian Orakpo/250 3.00 8.00
139 Tom Rathman/250 3.00 8.00
140 Tony Dorsett/250 5.00 12.00
141 Tony Romo/125 3.00 8.00
142 Troy Aikman/250 6.00 15.00
143 Troy Polamalu/215 4.00 10.00
144 Vince Young/250 2.50 6.00
145 Walter Payton/250 15.00 30.00
146 Warren Moon/130 6.00 15.00
147 Wayne Chrebet/100 3.00 8.00
148 William Perry/250 3.00 8.00
149 Willie Brown/250 3.00 8.00
150 Bo Scaife/250 2.50 6.00

2010 Certified Fabric of the Game NFL Die Cut Prime

STATED PRINT RUN 1-25
1 Adrian Peterson/25 12.00 30.00
5 Andre Johnson/25 10.00 25.00
7 Antwaan Randle El/25 8.00 20.00
10 Barry Sanders/25 25.00 60.00
15 Bo Jackson/15 20.00 50.00
16 Bob Griese/25 15.00 40.00
24 Calvin Johnson/25 12.00 30.00
25 Carson Palmer/25 10.00 25.00
26 Cedric Benson/25 8.00 20.00
27 Charles Woodson/25 12.00 30.00
30 Chuck Howley/15 12.00 30.00
32 Clinton Portis/25 8.00 20.00
34 Dan Fouts/25 12.00 30.00
36 Darren Woodson/25 20.00 50.00
37 D.D. Lewis/25 12.00 30.00
39 DeAngelo Williams/25 8.00 20.00
41 DeMarcus Ware/25 12.00 30.00
42 Derrick Thomas/25 40.00 100.00
47 Donald Driver/25 10.00 25.00
48 Doug Flutie/25 12.00 30.00
50 Dustin Keller/25 8.00 20.00
51 Ed Too Tall Jones/25 10.00 25.00
52 Ed McCaffrey/25 10.00 25.00
54 Eddie Royal/25 8.00 20.00
55 Emmitt Smith/25 25.00 60.00
57 Fran Tarkenton/25 15.00 40.00
62 Greg Olsen/25 10.00 25.00
64 Henry Ellard/25 10.00 25.00
66 Hines Ward/20 10.00 25.00
67 Howie Long/25 15.00 40.00
69 Jared Allen/25 8.00 20.00
70 Jason Witten/25 10.00 25.00
72 Jerricho Cotchery/25 8.00 20.00
73 Jerry Rice/25 20.00 50.00
78 Jim Plunkett/25 12.00 30.00
82 Joe Montana/25 25.00 60.00
84 Tom Brady/25 30.00 80.00
87 Joseph Addai/25 8.00 20.00
90 Junior Seau/25 12.00 30.00
94 Keyshawn Johnson/25 10.00 25.00
96 Laurence Maroney/25 8.00 20.00
101 Marshawn Lynch/25 10.00 25.00
102 Knowshon Moreno/25 8.00 20.00
106 Michael Irvin/25 15.00 40.00
107 Mohamed Massaquoi/25 10.00 25.00
111 Peyton Manning/25 30.00 80.00
113 Philip Rivers/25 12.00 30.00
115 Randy Moss/25 10.00 25.00
117 Ray Lewis/25 15.00 40.00
120 Reggie Bush/25 8.00 20.00
123 Robert Meachem/25 8.00 20.00
124 Rod Smith/25 10.00 25.00
126 Roger Craig/25 12.00 30.00
128 Santana Moss/25 10.00 25.00
129 Sidney Rice/25 8.00 20.00
131 Steve Largent/25 15.00 40.00
132 Steve Smith/25 10.00 25.00
134 Steven Jackson/25 8.00 20.00
135 Terrell Davis/25 12.00 30.00
138 Brian Orakpo/25 10.00 25.00
143 Troy Polamalu/25 12.00 30.00
144 Vince Young/25 8.00 20.00
147 Wayne Chrebet/25 10.00 25.00
150 Bo Scaife/25 8.00 20.00

2010 Certified Fabric of the Game Prime

PRIME STATED PRINT RUN 2-50
1 Adrian Peterson/50 6.00 15.00
3 Alan Page/25 8.00 20.00
4 Alex Karras/21 8.00 20.00
5 Andre Johnson/50 5.00 12.00
7 Antwaan Randle El/50 4.00 10.00
10 Barry Sanders/50 12.00 30.00
13 Bernie Kosar/50 6.00 15.00
14 Bill Bates/45 6.00 15.00
16 Bob Griese/50 8.00 20.00
17 Bob Hayes/20 10.00 25.00
23 Buck Buchanan/25 8.00 20.00
24 Calvin Johnson/50 6.00 15.00
25 Carson Palmer/15 6.00 15.00
26 Cedric Benson/50 4.00 10.00
27 Charles Woodson/50 10.00 25.00
30 Chuck Howley/25 8.00 20.00
32 Clinton Portis/50 4.00 10.00
33 Craig James/50 5.00 12.00
34 Dan Fouts/25 8.00 20.00
36 Darren Woodson/50 10.00 25.00
37 D.D. Lewis/25 8.00 20.00
39 DeAngelo Williams/50 4.00 10.00
41 DeMarcus Ware/30 6.00 15.00
42 Derrick Thomas/50 20.00 50.00
44 Dick Butkus/25 12.00 30.00
45 Don Maynard/15 8.00 20.00
46 Don Meredith/25 20.00 50.00
47 Donald Driver/50 5.00 12.00
48 Doug Flutie/50 6.00 15.00
50 Dustin Keller/30 4.00 10.00
51 Ed Too Tall Jones/50 5.00 12.00
52 Ed McCaffrey/50 5.00 12.00
53 Eddie George/50 6.00 15.00
54 Eddie Royal/50 4.00 10.00
55 Emmitt Smith/50 12.00 30.00
57 Fran Tarkenton/50 8.00 20.00
58 Franco Harris/25 10.00 25.00
60 Fred Biletnikoff/25 10.00 25.00
61 Gale Sayers/50 8.00 20.00
62 Greg Olsen/50 5.00 12.00
63 Harvey Martin/25 6.00 15.00
64 Henry Ellard/50 5.00 12.00
65 Hank Jordan/15 10.00 25.00
66 Hines Ward/50 5.00 12.00
68 Jackie Slater/25 6.00 15.00
69 Jared Allen/50 4.00 10.00
70 Jason Witten/50 5.00 12.00
72 Jerricho Cotchery/50 4.00 10.00
73 Jerry Rice/25 12.00 30.00
74 Jim Brown/15 15.00 40.00
75 Jim Kelly/20 10.00 25.00
76 Jim McMahon/25 10.00 25.00
77 Jim Otto/25 6.00 15.00
78 Jim Plunkett/50 6.00 15.00
79 Joe Flacco/30 5.00 12.00
82 Joe Montana/50 12.00 30.00
83 Joe Namath/15 15.00 40.00
84 Tom Brady/50 15.00 40.00
90 Junior Seau/50 6.00 15.00
91 Justin Gage/20 5.00 12.00
92 Ken Stabler/25 12.00 30.00
93 Kevin Boss/40 4.00 10.00
94 Keyshawn Johnson/50 5.00 12.00
95 Joe Perry/15 12.00 30.00
96 Laurence Maroney/50 4.00 10.00
98 Len Dawson/15 10.00 25.00
101 Marshawn Lynch/50 5.00 12.00
102 Knowshon Moreno/50 4.00 10.00
106 Michael Irvin/50 8.00 20.00
107 Mohamed Massaquoi/50 5.00 12.00
108 Owen Daniels/35 4.00 10.00
110 Paul Warfield/15 8.00 20.00
111 Peyton Manning/50 15.00 40.00
112 Phil Simms/25 8.00 20.00
113 Philip Rivers/48 6.00 15.00
114 Priest Holmes/35 5.00 12.00
115 Randy Moss/50 5.00 12.00
117 Ray Lewis/50 8.00 20.00
118 Ray Rice/35 4.00 10.00
120 Reggie Bush/50 4.00 10.00
122 Rickey Jackson/15 6.00 15.00
123 Robert Meachem/50 4.00 10.00
124 Rod Smith/50 5.00 12.00
126 Roger Craig/50 6.00 15.00
128 Santana Moss/50 5.00 12.00
129 Sidney Rice/50 4.00 10.00
131 Steve Largent/50 8.00 20.00
132 Steve Smith/50 5.00 12.00
133 Steve Smith USC/50 4.00 10.00
134 Steven Jackson/50 4.00 10.00
135 Terrell Davis/50 6.00 15.00
137 Thurman Thomas/50 6.00 15.00
138 Brian Orakpo/50 5.00 12.00
139 Tom Rathman/50 5.00 12.00
143 Troy Polamalu/50 6.00 15.00
144 Vince Young/50 4.00 10.00
145 Walter Payton/25 25.00 60.00
147 Wayne Chrebet/50 5.00 12.00
148 William Perry/25 6.00 15.00
149 Willie Brown/25 6.00 15.00
150 Bo Scaife/50 4.00 10.00

2010 Certified Fabric of the Game Team Die Cut

STATED PRINT RUN 5-25
1 Adrian Peterson/15 10.00 25.00
3 Alan Page/25 10.00 25.00
11 Bart Starr/25 20.00 50.00
14 Bill Bates/15 10.00 25.00
15 Bo Jackson/25 15.00 40.00
16 Bob Griese/20 12.00 30.00
18 Bob Lilly/25 10.00 25.00
19 Boomer Esiason/25 10.00 25.00
23 Buck Buchanan/25 12.00 30.00
25 Carson Palmer/25 8.00 20.00
27 Charles Woodson/25 15.00 40.00
28 Charley Taylor/25 8.00 20.00
29 Charlie Joiner/25 8.00 20.00
30 Chuck Howley/25 10.00 25.00
32 Clinton Portis/15 6.00 15.00
34 Dan Fouts/25 10.00 25.00
35 Dan Marino/25 20.00 50.00
37 D.D. Lewis/25 10.00 25.00
38 Deacon Jones/25 10.00 25.00
40 Deion Sanders/25 10.00 25.00
42 Derrick Thomas/15 40.00 100.00
44 Dick Butkus/25 15.00 40.00
45 Don Maynard/25 10.00 25.00
48 Doug Flutie/25 10.00 25.00
51 Ed Too Tall Jones/25 8.00 20.00
52 Ed McCaffrey/25 8.00 20.00
53 Eddie George/25 10.00 25.00
54 Eddie Royal/25 6.00 15.00
55 Emmitt Smith/25 20.00 50.00
56 Forrest Gregg/25 12.00 30.00
57 Fran Tarkenton/25 12.00 30.00
58 Franco Harris/25 12.00 30.00
60 Fred Biletnikoff/25 12.00 30.00
61 Gale Sayers/25 12.00 30.00
62 Greg Olsen/25 8.00 20.00

64 Henry Ellard/25 8.00 20.00
65 Hank Jordan/25 12.00 30.00
68 Jackie Slater/25 8.00 20.00
69 Jared Allen/25 6.00 15.00
71 Jay Cutler/25 6.00 15.00
72 Jerricho Cotchery/15 6.00 15.00
74 Jim Brown/25 20.00 50.00
75 Jim Kelly/25 12.00 30.00
76 Jim McMahon/25 12.00 30.00
77 Jim Otto/25 8.00 20.00
78 Jim Plunkett/25 10.00 25.00
79 Joe Flacco/25 8.00 20.00
80 Joe Greene/25 15.00 40.00
82 Joe Montana/25 20.00 50.00
83 Joe Namath/25 20.00 50.00
85 John Elway/25 20.00 50.00
87 Joseph Addai/25 6.00 15.00
89 Josh Freeman/25 8.00 20.00
90 Junior Seau/25 10.00 25.00
92 Ken Stabler/25 15.00 40.00
94 Keyshawn Johnson/25 8.00 20.00
100 Mark Sanchez/25 6.00 15.00
102 Knowshon Moreno/25 6.00 15.00
104 Merlin Olsen/25 8.00 20.00
106 Michael Irvin/25 12.00 30.00
10/ Mohamed Massaquoi/25 8.00 20.00
109 Ozzie Newsome/25 10.00 25.00
111 Peyton Manning/25 25.00 60.00
112 Phil Simms/25 10.00 25.00
116 Randy White/25 12.00 30.00
117 Ray Lewis/25 12.00 30.00
118 Ray Rice/15 6.00 15.00
119 Raymond Berry/25 10.00 25.00
122 Rickey Jackson/25 8.00 20.00
123 Robert Meachem/25 6.00 15.00
124 Rod Smith/25 8.00 20.00
126 Roger Craig/25 10.00 25.00
127 Roger Staubach/25 12.00 30.00
129 Sidney Rice/25 6.00 15.00
130 Sonny Jurgensen/25 12.00 30.00
131 Steve Largent/25 12.00 30.00
136 Terry Bradshaw/25 15.00 40.00
138 Brian Orakpo/25 8.00 20.00
139 Tom Rathman/25 8.00 20.00
140 Tony Dorsett/25 12.00 30.00
142 Troy Aikman/25 15.00 40.00
144 Vince Young/25 6.00 15.00
145 Walter Payton/25 30.00 80.00
146 Warren Moon/25 15.00 40.00
147 Wayne Chrebet/15 8.00 20.00
149 Willie Brown/25 8.00 20.00
150 Bo Scaife/25 6.00 15.00

2010 Certified Fabric of the Game Combos Prime

PRIME PRINT RUN 25 SER.#'d SETS
*BASE CMBO/70-100: .25X TO .6X PRIME/25
1 T.Brady/P.Manning 20.00 50.00
2 L.Fitzgerald/C.Wells 6.00 15.00
3 S.Rice/C.Woodson 12.00 30.00
4 F.Gore/P.Willis 6.00 15.00
5 B.Urlacher/D.Hester 8.00 20.00
6 A.Peterson/C. Johnson 10.00 25.00
7 R.Moss/D.Revis 6.00 15.00
8 R.Bush/D.Henderson 5.00 12.00
9 R.Williams/J.Charles 6.00 15.00
10 D.Jackson/T.Newman 6.00 15.00
11 A.Johnson/C.Johnson 8.00 20.00
12 T.Romo/E.Manning 6.00 15.00
14 M.Barber/F.Jones 6.00 15.00
15 D.Ware/W.Smith 6.00 15.00

2010 Certified Fabric of the Game Jersey Number Autographs

STATED PRINT RUN 5-25
EXCH EXPIRATION: 5/3/2012
1 Adrian Peterson/15 90.00 150.00
3 Alan Page/25 15.00 40.00
4 Alex Karras/25 15.00 40.00
11 Bart Starr/25 75.00 135.00
13 Bernie Kosar/25 15.00 40.00
14 Bill Bates/25 20.00 50.00
15 Bo Jackson/25 40.00 80.00
16 Bob Griese/25 20.00 50.00
18 Bob Lilly/25 20.00 50.00
19 Boomer Esiason/25 15.00 40.00
20 Brent Jones/25 12.00 30.00
21 Brett Favre/10
24 Calvin Johnson/15 20.00 50.00
25 Carson Palmer/9
26 Cedric Benson/15 12.00 30.00
28 Charley Taylor/25 12.00 30.00
29 Charlie Joiner/25 12.00 30.00
30 Chuck Howley/25 15.00 40.00
33 Craig James/25 12.00 30.00
34 Dan Fouts/25 25.00 60.00
35 Dan Marino/25 100.00 175.00
36 Darren Woodson/25 25.00 50.00
37 D.D. Lewis/25 15.00 40.00
38 Deacon Jones/25 15.00 40.00
40 Deion Sanders/25 40.00 80.00
44 Dick Butkus/25 40.00 80.00
45 Don Maynard/25 15.00 40.00
48 Doug Flutie/25 15.00 40.00
51 Ed Too Tall Jones/25 20.00 50.00
52 Ed McCaffrey/25 12.00 30.00
53 Eddie George/25 20.00 50.00
55 Emmitt Smith/10
56 Forrest Gregg/25 12.00 30.00
57 Fran Tarkenton/25 25.00 60.00
58 Franco Harris/25 25.00 50.00
60 Fred Biletnikoff/25 20.00 50.00
61 Gale Sayers/25 30.00 60.00
64 Henry Ellard/25 15.00 40.00
67 Howie Long/25 30.00 60.00
68 Jackie Slater/25
70 Jason Witten/10
71 Jay Cutler/15 12.00 30.00
73 Jerry Rice/5
74 Jim Brown/25 50.00 100.00
75 Jim Kelly/25 25.00 60.00
76 Jim McMahon/25 15.00 40.00
77 Jim Otto/25 15.00 40.00
78 Jim Plunkett/25 15.00 40.00
79 Joe Flacco/10
80 Joe Greene/25 30.00 60.00
81 Joe Klecko/25 12.00 30.00
82 Joe Montana/13
83 Joe Namath/21 50.00 100.00
84 Tom Brady/12
85 John Elway/25 75.00 150.00
86 John Taylor/25 15.00 40.00
90 Junior Seau/25 40.00 80.00
92 Ken Stabler/25 40.00 80.00
94 Keyshawn Johnson/25 12.00 30.00
95 Joe Perry/25 30.00 60.00
97 L.C. Greenwood/25 12.00 30.00
98 Len Dawson/25 20.00 50.00
100 Mark Sanchez/25 15.00 40.00
102 Knowshon Moreno/5
104 Merlin Olsen/12
106 Michael Irvin/25 40.00 80.00
109 Ozzie Newsome/25 15.00 40.00
110 Paul Warfield/25 15.00 40.00
111 Peyton Manning/25 75.00 150.00
112 Phil Simms/25 25.00 50.00
113 Philip Rivers/10
114 Priest Holmes/19 12.00 30.00
116 Randy White/26 30.00 80.00
118 Ray Rice/25 12.00 30.00
119 Raymond Berry/25 15.00 40.00
122 Rickey Jackson/10
124 Rod Smith/25 15.00 40.00
125 Rod Woodson/25 50.00 100.00
126 Roger Craig/25 15.00 40.00
127 Roger Staubach/25 60.00 120.00
129 Sidney Rice/25 10.00 25.00
130 Sonny Jurgensen/25 20.00 50.00
131 Steve Largent/25 20.00 50.00
135 Terrell Davis/25 15.00 40.00
137 Thurman Thomas/25 30.00 60.00
139 Tom Rathman/25 12.00 30.00
140 Tony Dorsett/25 40.00 80.00
141 Tony Romo/10
142 Troy Aikman/25 40.00 80.00
143 Troy Polamalu/25 75.00 150.00
144 Vince Young/10
146 Warren Moon/25 30.00 60.00
147 Wayne Chrebet/25 12.00 30.00
148 William Perry/25 15.00 40.00
149 Willie Brown/25 15.00 40.00

2010 Certified Gold Team

STATED PRINT RUN 999 SER.#'d SETS
*MIRROR/100: .8X TO 2X BASIC INSERTS
1 Chris Johnson .75 2.00
2 Steven Jackson .75 2.00
3 Peyton Manning 3.00 8.00
4 Wes Welker 1.00 2.50
5 Brett Favre 2.50 6.00
6 Adrian Peterson 1.25 3.00
7 Larry Fitzgerald 1.00 2.50
8 Andre Johnson 1.00 2.50
9 Drew Brees 1.25 3.00
10 Aaron Rodgers 2.50 6.00

2010 Certified Gold Team Materials

STATED PRINT RUN 100-250
2 Steven Jackson/100 2.50 6.00
3 Peyton Manning/125 10.00 25.00
5 Brett Favre/125 8.00 20.00
6 Adrian Peterson/250 4.00 10.00

2010 Certified Gold Team Materials Prime

STATED PRINT RUN 10-50
1 Chris Johnson/50 4.00 10.00
2 Steven Jackson/50 4.00 10.00
3 Peyton Manning/50 15.00 40.00
4 Wes Welker/50 5.00 12.00
5 Brett Favre/10
6 Adrian Peterson/50 6.00 15.00
8 Andre Johnson/50 5.00 12.00

2010 Certified Mirror Blue Materials

*LEGEND JSY: .6X TO 1.5X BASIC JSY
BLUE STATED PRINT RUN 15-100
12 Joe Flacco/100 3.00 8.00
13 Ray Lewis/100 5.00 12.00
19 DeAngelo Williams/40 3.00 8.00
20 Jonathan Stewart/20 4.00 10.00
24 Devin Hester/100 3.00 8.00
25 Greg Olsen/100 3.00 8.00
26 Jay Cutler/100 2.50 6.00
27 Matt Forte/100 2.50 6.00
29 Carson Palmer/100 3.00 8.00
30 Cedric Benson/100 2.50 6.00
31 Chad Ochocinco/40 3.00 8.00
32 Terrell Owens/100 3.00 8.00
37 Mohamed Massaquoi/100 3.00 8.00
38 Felix Jones/100 2.50 6.00
39 Jason Witten/100 3.00 8.00
40 Marion Barber/100 3.00 8.00
42 Tony Romo/100 3.00 8.00
43 Eddie Royal/100 2.50 6.00
45 Knowshon Moreno/100 2.50 6.00
46 Kyle Orton/100 2.50 6.00
48 Calvin Johnson/60 5.00 12.00
53 Greg Jennings/15 4.00 10.00
55 Ryan Grant/100 3.00 8.00
58 Matt Schaub/100 2.50 6.00
62 Dallas Clark/100 2.50 6.00
63 Joseph Addai/100 2.50 6.00
64 Peyton Manning/100 10.00 25.00
67 David Garrard/100 2.50 6.00
68 Maurice Jones-Drew/100 2.50 6.00
69 Mike Sims-Walker/100 2.50 6.00
72 Dwayne Bowe/100 3.00 8.00
73 Jamaal Charles/100 3.00 8.00
74 Matt Cassel/100 2.50 6.00
76 Brandon Marshall/40 4.00 10.00
82 Adrian Peterson/100 4.00 10.00
84 Brett Favre/100 8.00 20.00
85 Percy Harvin/100 2.50 6.00
86 Sidney Rice/100 2.50 6.00
88 Laurence Maroney/100 2.50 6.00
89 Randy Moss/100 3.00 8.00
90 Tom Brady/100 10.00 25.00
92 Devery Henderson/100 2.50 6.00
94 Jeremy Shockey/100 2.50 6.00
102 Braylon Edwards/100 2.50 6.00
103 Jerricho Cotchery/100 2.50 6.00
105 Mark Sanchez/100 2.50 6.00
108 Darren McFadden/100 2.50 6.00
109 Jason Campbell/100 2.50 6.00
112 Brent Celek/100 2.50 6.00
119 Heath Miller/25 4.00 10.00
121 Rashard Mendenhall/100 2.50 6.00
122 Troy Polamalu/100 4.00 10.00
123 Antonio Gates/100 3.00 8.00
125 Philip Rivers/100 4.00 10.00
126 Vincent Jackson/100 2.50 6.00
128 Frank Gore/100 3.00 8.00
131 Vernon Davis/100 2.50 6.00
139 Steven Jackson/100 2.50 6.00
141 Josh Freeman/100 3.00 8.00
143 Bo Scaife/100 2.50 6.00
144 Chris Johnson/100 2.50 6.00
145 Kenny Britt/100 2.50 6.00
146 Vince Young/100 2.50 6.00
148 Clinton Portis/100 2.50 6.00
150 Santana Moss/100 3.00 8.00
151 Jerry Rice/50 12.00 30.00
152 Jack Lambert/50 10.00 25.00
153 Irving Fryar/50 5.00 12.00
154 John Taylor/50 5.00 12.00
155 Paul Warfield/50 6.00 15.00
156 Emmitt Smith/50 12.00 30.00
157 Bruce Smith/50 6.00 15.00
158 Cris Carter/50 8.00 20.00
159 Rickey Jackson/50 5.00 12.00
160 Len Dawson/50 8.00 20.00
161 Lenny Moore/50 5.00 12.00
162 Jack Youngblood/50 5.00 12.00
163 Terry Bradshaw/50 10.00 25.00
164 Todd Christensen/50 5.00 12.00
165 Earl Campbell/50 8.00 20.00
166 Raymond Berry/50 6.00 15.00
167 Bo Jackson/50 10.00 25.00
168 Curtis Martin/50 6.00 15.00
169 Ernie Davis/50 30.00 80.00
170 Ronnie Lott/50 6.00 15.00
271 Andre Roberts/50 3.00 8.00
272 Armanti Edwards/50 3.00 8.00
273 Arrelious Benn/50 2.50 6.00
274 Ben Tate/50 2.50 6.00
275 Brandon LaFell/50 4.00 10.00
276 C.J. Spiller/50 2.50 6.00
277 Colt McCoy/50 3.00 8.00
278 Damian Williams/50 2.50 6.00
279 Demaryius Thomas/50 6.00 15.00
280 Dexter McCluster/50 3.00 8.00
281 Dez Bryant/50 10.00 25.00
282 Emmanuel Sanders/50 4.00 10.00
283 Eric Berry/50 4.00 10.00
284 Eric Decker/50 3.00 8.00
285 Gerald McCoy/50 2.50 6.00
286 Golden Tate/50 3.00 8.00
287 Jahvid Best/50 2.50 6.00
288 Jermaine Gresham/50 2.50 6.00
289 Jimmy Clausen/50 2.50 6.00
290 Joe McKnight/50 2.50 6.00
291 Jonathan Dwyer/50 2.50 6.00
292 Jordan Shipley/50 2.50 6.00
293 Marcus Easley/50 2.50 6.00
294 Mardy Gilyard/50 2.50 6.00
295 Mike Kafka/50 3.00 8.00
296 Mike Williams/50 2.50 6.00
297 Montario Hardesty/50 2.50 6.00
298 Ndamukong Suh/50 5.00 12.00
299 Rob Gronkowski/50 8.00 20.00
300 Rolando McClain/50 2.50 6.00
301 Ryan Mathews/50 2.50 6.00
302 Sam Bradford/50 3.00 8.00
303 Taylor Price/50 2.50 6.00
304 Tim Tebow/50 8.00 20.00
305 Toby Gerhart/50 2.50 6.00

2010 Certified Mirror Gold Materials

*GLD LEG/25: .8X TO 2X BASE JSY
*GLD ROOKIE/25: .6X TO 1.5X BLUE/50
GOLD STATED PRINT RUN 15-50
1 Chris Wells/5
5 Matt Ryan/15 5.00 12.00
7 Roddy White/50 3.00 8.00
12 Joe Flacco/50 4.00 10.00
13 Ray Lewis/50 6.00 15.00
14 Ray Rice/50 3.00 8.00
16 Lee Evans/50 4.00 10.00
17 Marshawn Lynch/50 4.00 10.00
19 DeAngelo Williams/50 3.00 8.00
20 Jonathan Stewart/50 3.00 8.00
22 Steve Smith/50 4.00 10.00
24 Devin Hester/50 4.00 10.00
25 Greg Olsen/50 4.00 10.00
26 Jay Cutler/50 3.00 8.00
27 Matt Forte/50 3.00 8.00
29 Carson Palmer/50 4.00 10.00
30 Cedric Benson/50 3.00 8.00
31 Chad Ochocinco/50 3.00 8.00
37 Mohamed Massaquoi/50 4.00 10.00
38 Felix Jones/50 3.00 8.00
39 Jason Witten/50 4.00 10.00
40 Marion Barber/50 4.00 10.00
42 Tony Romo/50 4.00 10.00
43 Eddie Royal/50 3.00 8.00
45 Knowshon Moreno/50 3.00 8.00
46 Kyle Orton/50 3.00 8.00
48 Calvin Johnson/50 5.00 12.00
49 Matthew Stafford/20 5.00 12.00
52 Donald Driver/50 4.00 10.00
55 Ryan Grant/50 4.00 10.00
56 Andre Johnson/50 4.00 10.00
62 Dallas Clark/50 3.00 8.00
63 Joseph Addai/50 3.00 8.00
64 Peyton Manning/50 12.00 30.00
67 David Garrard/50 3.00 8.00
68 Maurice Jones-Drew/50 3.00 8.00
69 Mike Sims-Walker/50 3.00 8.00
72 Dwayne Bowe/50 4.00 10.00
73 Jamaal Charles/50 4.00 10.00
74 Matt Cassel/50 3.00 8.00
81 Ronnie Brown/50 3.00 8.00
82 Adrian Peterson/50 5.00 12.00
83 Bernard Berrian/50 3.00 8.00
84 Brett Favre/25 12.00 30.00
85 Percy Harvin/50 3.00 8.00
86 Sidney Rice/50 3.00 8.00
87 Visanthe Shiancoe/50 4.00 10.00
88 Laurence Maroney/50 3.00 8.00
89 Randy Moss/50 4.00 10.00
90 Tom Brady/50 12.00 30.00
91 Wes Welker/50 4.00 10.00
92 Devery Henderson/50 3.00 8.00
94 Jeremy Shockey/50 3.00 8.00
97 Brandon Jacobs/50 3.00 8.00
98 Ahmad Bradshaw/50 3.00 8.00
102 Braylon Edwards/50 3.00 8.00
103 Jerricho Cotchery/50 3.00 8.00
108 Darren McFadden/50 3.00 8.00
112 Brent Celek/50 3.00 8.00
117 Antwaan Randle El/50 3.00 8.00
120 Hines Ward/50 4.00 10.00
121 Rashard Mendenhall/50 3.00 8.00
122 Troy Polamalu/50 5.00 12.00
123 Antonio Gates/50 4.00 10.00
124 Darren Sproles/50 4.00 10.00
125 Philip Rivers/50 5.00 12.00
126 Vincent Jackson/50 3.00 8.00
128 Frank Gore/50 4.00 10.00
131 Vernon Davis/50 3.00 8.00
132 Deion Branch/50 3.00 8.00
139 Steven Jackson/50 3.00 8.00
140 Cadillac Williams/50 3.00 8.00
143 Bo Scaife/50 3.00 8.00
144 Chris Johnson/50 3.00 8.00
145 Kenny Britt/50 3.00 8.00
146 Vince Young/50 3.00 8.00
147 Chris Cooley/50 3.00 8.00
148 Clinton Portis/50 3.00 8.00
150 Santana Moss/50 4.00 10.00
151 Jerry Rice/25 12.00 30.00
153 Irving Fryar/25 6.00 15.00
154 John Taylor/25 6.00 15.00
155 Paul Warfield/25 8.00 20.00
156 Emmitt Smith/25 15.00 40.00
157 Bruce Smith/25 8.00 20.00
158 Cris Carter/25 10.00 25.00
159 Rickey Jackson/25 6.00 15.00
160 Len Dawson/25 10.00 25.00
161 Lenny Moore/25 6.00 15.00
163 Terry Bradshaw/25 12.00 30.00
164 Todd Christensen/25 6.00 15.00
167 Bo Jackson/25 12.00 30.00
168 Curtis Martin/25 8.00 20.00
169 Ernie Davis/25 40.00 100.00

2010 Certified Mirror Blue Signatures

BLUE PRINT RUN 50 SER.#'d SETS
*RED/200-250: .3X TO .8X BLUE AU/50
EXCH EXPIRATION: 5/3/2012
171 Aaron Hernandez 4.00 10.00
175 Anthony Dixon 4.00 10.00
176 Anthony McCoy 4.00 10.00
177 Antonio Brown 15.00 40.00
179 Blair White 4.00 10.00
181 Brandon Graham 5.00 12.00
182 Brandon Spikes 4.00 10.00
184 Bryan Bulaga 4.00 10.00
185 Carlos Dunlap 4.00 10.00
186 Carlton Mitchell 4.00 10.00
187 Chad Jones 4.00 10.00
189 Chris Gronkowski 6.00 15.00
192 Corey Wootton 4.00 10.00
193 Dan LeFevour 4.00 10.00
194 Danario Alexander 4.00 10.00
196 David Gettis 4.00 10.00
199 Deji Karim 5.00 12.00
201 Derrick Morgan 4.00 10.00
202 Devin McCourty 5.00 12.00
203 Dezmon Briscoe 4.00 10.00
204 Dominique Curry 5.00 12.00
205 Dominique Franks 4.00 10.00
206 Donald Jones 6.00 15.00
209 Earl Thomas 12.00 30.00
210 Ed Dickson 4.00 10.00
211 Everson Griffen 4.00 10.00
212 Fendi Onobun 5.00 12.00
213 Garrett Graham 4.00 10.00
214 Jacoby Ford 4.00 10.00
215 James Starks 5.00 12.00
216 Jarrett Brown 4.00 10.00
217 Javier Arenas 8.00 20.00
218 Jason Pierre-Paul 6.00 15.00
219 Jason Worilds 4.00 10.00
221 Jerry Hughes 4.00 10.00
222 Jimmy Graham 12.00 30.00
223 Joe Haden 6.00 15.00
225 John Conner 4.00 10.00
226 John Skelton 5.00 12.00
228 Joique Bell 4.00 10.00
229 Tyson Alualu 4.00 10.00
231 Mickey Shuler 6.00 15.00
235 Kerry Meier 5.00 12.00
238 Lonyae Miller 5.00 12.00
244 Michael Hoomanawanui 6.00 15.00
245 Morgan Burnett 5.00 12.00
249 Koa Misi 5.00 12.00
250 Patrick Robinson 5.00 12.00
251 Perrish Cox 5.00 12.00
252 Preston Parker 5.00 12.00
253 Ricky Sapp 4.00 10.00
254 Riley Cooper 4.00 10.00
257 Rusty Smith 15.00 30.00
258 Sean Canfield 4.00 10.00
259 Sean Lee 8.00 20.00
260 Sean Weatherspoon 4.00 10.00
261 Sergio Kindle 4.00 10.00
262 Seyi Ajirotutu 4.00 10.00
264 Taylor Mays 4.00 10.00
266 Thaddeus Lewis 5.00 12.00
268 Tony Pike 4.00 10.00

2010 Certified Mirror Gold Signatures

*GOLD ROOK.171-268: .5X TO 1.2X BLUE AU
GOLD STATED PRINT RUN 5-25
EXCH EXPIRATION: 5/3/2012
1 Chris Wells/25 8.00 20.00
7 Roddy White/25 8.00 20.00
8 Tony Gonzalez/15 10.00 25.00
14 Ray Rice/25 12.00 30.00
20 Jonathan Stewart/15 8.00 20.00
36 Josh Cribbs/25 8.00 20.00
38 Felix Jones/25 12.00 30.00
45 Knowshon Moreno/25 8.00 20.00
46 Kyle Orton/25 8.00 20.00
55 Ryan Grant/25 12.00 30.00
58 Matt Schaub/25 8.00 20.00
61 Austin Collie/25 12.00 30.00
62 Dallas Clark/15 15.00 40.00
64 Peyton Manning/18 60.00 120.00
72 Dwayne Bowe/15 10.00 25.00
73 Jamaal Charles/25 10.00 25.00
83 Bernard Berrian/25 8.00 20.00
86 Sidney Rice/25 8.00 20.00
87 Visanthe Shiancoe/15
97 Brandon Jacobs/15 8.00 20.00
102 Braylon Edwards/25 8.00 20.00
106 Santonio Holmes/25 8.00 20.00
107 Shonn Greene/25 8.00 20.00
112 Brent Celek/25 12.00 30.00
114 Jeremy Maclin/25 8.00 20.00
119 Heath Miller/25 8.00 20.00
121 Rashard Mendenhall/25 8.00 20.00
122 Troy Polamalu/25 100.00 175.00
126 Vincent Jackson/25 8.00 20.00
140 Cadillac Williams/15 8.00 20.00
145 Kenny Britt/25 8.00 20.00
147 Chris Cooley/15
149 Donovan McNabb/25 25.00 50.00
151 Jerry Rice JSY/25 75.00 150.00
153 Irving Fryar JSY/25 15.00 40.00
154 John Taylor JSY/25 15.00 40.00
155 Paul Warfield JSY/24 15.00 40.00
157 Bruce Smith JSY/25 30.00 60.00
159 Rickey Jackson JSY/25 30.00 60.00
160 Len Dawson JSY/25 25.00 60.00
161 Lenny Moore JSY/25 EXCH 15.00 40.00
164 Todd Christensen JSY/25 20.00 50.00
168 Curtis Martin JSY/25 30.00 60.00

2010 Certified Rookie Fabric of the Game

STATED PRINT RUN 35-250
*TEAM DC/25: .8X TO 2X BASIC JSY/250
*TEAM DC/25: .5X TO 1.2X BASIC JSY/35
1 Colt McCoy/250 2.00 5.00
2 Sam Bradford/250 2.00 5.00
3 Jordan Shipley/250 1.50 4.00
4 Gerald McCoy/250 1.50 4.00
5 Rob Gronkowski/250 5.00 12.00
6 Emmanuel Sanders/250 2.50 6.00
7 Arrelious Benn/250 1.50 4.00
8 Ben Tate/250 1.50 4.00
9 Dez Bryant/250 4.00 10.00
10 Dexter McCluster/250 2.00 5.00
11 Mike Kafka/250 2.00 5.00
12 Tim Tebow/250 5.00 12.00
13 Mike Williams/250 1.50 4.00
14 Eric Berry/250 2.50 6.00
15 Eric Decker/250 2.00 5.00
16 C.J. Spiller/250 1.50 4.00
17 Ndamukong Suh/250 3.00 8.00
18 Marcus Easley/250 1.50 4.00
19 Taylor Price/250 1.50 4.00
20 Montario Hardesty/250 1.50 4.00
21 Rolando McClain/250 1.50 4.00
22 Jahvid Best/250 1.50 4.00
23 Brandon LaFell/250 2.50 6.00
24 Mardy Gilyard/250 1.50 4.00
25 Jonathan Dwyer/250 1.50 4.00
26 Andre Roberts/250 2.00 5.00
27 Jermaine Gresham/250 1.50 4.00
28 Toby Gerhart/250 1.50 4.00
29 Ryan Mathews/35 2.50 6.00
30 Joe McKnight/250 1.50 4.00
31 Jimmy Clausen/250 1.50 4.00
32 Damian Williams/250 1.50 4.00
33 Armanti Edwards/250 2.00 5.00
34 Demaryius Thomas/250 4.00 10.00
35 Golden Tate/250 2.00 5.00

2010 Certified Rookie Fabric of the Game Jersey Number Autographs

STATED PRINT RUN 25 SER.#'d SETS
EXCH EXPIRATION: 5/3/2012
1 Colt McCoy 8.00 20.00
2 Sam Bradford 8.00 20.00
3 Jordan Shipley 6.00 15.00
4 Gerald McCoy 6.00 15.00
5 Rob Gronkowski 30.00 60.00
6 Emmanuel Sanders 10.00 25.00
7 Arrelious Benn 6.00 15.00
8 Ben Tate 6.00 15.00
9 Dez Bryant 50.00 100.00
11 Mike Kafka 8.00 20.00
12 Tim Tebow 40.00 100.00
13 Mike Williams 6.00 15.00
14 Eric Berry 10.00 25.00
15 Eric Decker 8.00 20.00
16 C.J. Spiller 6.00 15.00
17 Ndamukong Suh 12.00 30.00
18 Marcus Easley 6.00 15.00
19 Taylor Price 6.00 15.00
20 Montario Hardesty 6.00 15.00
21 Rolando McClain 6.00 15.00
22 Jahvid Best 6.00 15.00
23 Brandon LaFell 10.00 25.00
24 Mardy Gilyard 6.00 15.00
25 Jonathan Dwyer 6.00 15.00
26 Andre Roberts 8.00 20.00
27 Jermaine Gresham 6.00 15.00
28 Toby Gerhart 6.00 15.00
29 Ryan Mathews 6.00 15.00
30 Joe McKnight 6.00 15.00
31 Jimmy Clausen 6.00 15.00
32 Damian Williams 6.00 15.00
33 Armanti Edwards 8.00 20.00
34 Demaryius Thomas 15.00 40.00
35 Golden Tate 8.00 20.00

2010 Certified Shirt Off My Back Combos Prime

PRIME PRINT RUN 25 SER.#'d SETS
*BASE COMBO/100: .25X TO .6X PRIME/25
1 B.Berrian/V.Shiancoe 6.00 15.00
2 C.Williams/R.Brown 5.00 12.00
3 C.Palmer/M.Sanchez 6.00 15.00
4 D.Driver/G.Jennings 6.00 15.00
6 B.Jacobs/A.Bradshaw 8.00 20.00
7 L.Murphy/D.McFadden 5.00 12.00
9 J.Flacco/R.Rice 6.00 15.00
10 D.Williams/J.Stewart 5.00 12.00
12 P.Rivers/E.Manning 8.00 20.00
13 S.Moss/C.Cooley 6.00 15.00
14 V.Young/B.Scaife 5.00 12.00
15 J.Addai/M.Lynch 6.00 15.00

2010 Certified Shirt Off My Back Materials

STATED PRINT RUN 55-250
1 Antonio Gates/250 3.00 8.00
4 Steven Jackson/125 2.50 6.00
6 Maurice Jones-Drew/250 2.50 6.00
7 Tony Romo/125 3.00 8.00
8 Frank Gore/250 3.00 8.00
9 Vernon Davis/250 2.50 6.00
10 Kenny Britt/55 3.00 8.00
13 Steve Slaton/250 2.50 6.00
14 Vincent Jackson/250 2.50 6.00
15 Darren McFadden/250 2.50 6.00
17 Reggie Bush/110 2.50 6.00
18 Laurence Maroney/70 3.00 8.00
20 Mark Sanchez/250 2.50 6.00
21 Kevin Kolb/250 2.50 6.00
22 Brett Favre/100 8.00 20.00
24 Philip Rivers/150 4.00 10.00
25 Percy Harvin/250 2.50 6.00
27 Carson Palmer/125 3.00 8.00
28 Jason Witten/250 3.00 8.00
30 Vince Young/250 2.50 6.00
31 Matt Forte/250 2.50 6.00
32 Jeremy Shockey/250 2.50 6.00
33 Charles Woodson/125 4.00 10.00

2010 Certified Shirt Off My Back Materials Prime

COMMON CARD/35-50 4.00 10.00
SEMISTARS/35-50 5.00 12.00
UNL.STARS/35-50 6.00 15.00
COMMON CARD/15-20 6.00 15.00
UNL.STARS/15-20 8.00 20.00
STATED PRINT RUN 10-50
1 Antonio Gates/50 5.00 12.00
2 Lee Evans/50 5.00 12.00
3 Chad Ochocinco/50 4.00 10.00
4 Steven Jackson/50 4.00 10.00
6 Maurice Jones-Drew/50 4.00 10.00
7 Tony Romo/50 5.00 12.00
8 Frank Gore/50 5.00 12.00
9 Vernon Davis/50 4.00 10.00
10 Kenny Britt/35 4.00 10.00
11 Matt Ryan/20 6.00 15.00
12 Chris Cooley/50 6.00 15.00
13 Steve Slaton/50 4.00 10.00
14 Vincent Jackson/50 4.00 10.00
15 Darren McFadden/50 4.00 10.00
16 DeMarcus Ware/20 6.00 15.00
17 Reggie Bush/50 4.00 10.00
18 Laurence Maroney/50 4.00 10.00
20 Mark Sanchez/15 5.00 12.00
21 Kevin Kolb/50 4.00 10.00
22 Brett Favre/10
23 Ronnie Brown/50 4.00 10.00
24 Philip Rivers/50 6.00 15.00
25 Percy Harvin/45 4.00 10.00
26 Darren Sproles/50 5.00 12.00
27 Carson Palmer/50 5.00 12.00
28 Jason Witten/50 5.00 12.00
30 Vince Young/50 4.00 10.00
31 Matt Forte/50 4.00 10.00
32 Jeremy Shockey/50 4.00 10.00
33 Charles Woodson/50 6.00 15.00
35 Clinton Portis/50 4.00 10.00

2010 Certified National Convention

COMPLETE SET (6) 12.00 30.00
*BLUE/25: 1.2X TO 3X BASIC CARDS
*GREEN/50: 1X TO 2.5X BASIC CARDS
CM Colt McCoy .75 2.00
DM Donovan McNabb 1.00 2.50
PM Peyton Manning 3.00 8.00
RL Ray Lewis 1.25 3.00
SB Sam Bradford .75 2.00
TT Tim Tebow 2.00 5.00

2011 Certified

COMP.SET w/o SP's (150) 15.00 40.00
151-250 ROOKIE PRINT RUN 999
251-286 JSY AU RC PRINT RUN 299-499
287-306 LEGEND JSY PRINT RUN 49-99
1 Beanie Wells .25 .60
2 Larry Fitzgerald .30 .75
3 Steve Breaston .25 .60
4 Tim Hightower .25 .60
5 Jason Snelling .25 .60
6 Matt Ryan .30 .75
7 Michael Turner .25 .60
8 Roddy White .25 .60
9 Tony Gonzalez .30 .75
10 Anquan Boldin .25 .60
11 Joe Flacco .30 .75
12 Ray Lewis .40 1.00
13 Ray Rice .25 .60
14 Todd Heap .25 .60
15 C.J. Spiller .25 .60
16 Fred Jackson .25 .60
17 Lee Evans .30 .75
18 Ryan Fitzpatrick .25 .60
19 Steve Johnson .25 .60
20 DeAngelo Williams .25 .60
21 Mike Goodson .25 .60
22 Brandon LaFell .25 .60
23 Steve Smith .30 .75
24 Brian Urlacher .40 1.00
25 Devin Hester .30 .75
26 Jay Cutler .25 .60
27 Julius Peppers .30 .75
28 Matt Forte .25 .60
29 Carson Palmer .30 .75
30 Dhani Jones .25 .60
31 Chad Ochocinco .25 .60
32 Jordan Shipley .25 .60
33 Jermaine Gresham .25 .60
34 Ben Watson .25 .60
35 Colt McCoy .25 .60
36 Josh Cribbs .25 .60
37 Peyton Hillis .25 .60
38 Dez Bryant .40 1.00
39 Felix Jones .25 .60
40 Jason Witten .30 .75
41 Miles Austin .25 .60
42 Tony Romo .30 .75
43 Brandon Lloyd .25 .60
44 Eddie Royal .25 .60
45 Jabar Gaffney .25 .60
46 Knowshon Moreno .25 .60
47 Tim Tebow .40 1.00
48 Brandon Pettigrew .25 .60
49 Calvin Johnson .40 1.00
50 Jahvid Best .25 .60
51 Matthew Stafford .30 .75
52 Ndamukong Suh .30 .75
53 Aaron Rodgers .60 1.50
54 Clay Matthews .40 1.00
55 Donald Driver .30 .75
56 Greg Jennings .25 .60
57 Charles Woodson .40 1.00
58 Andre Johnson .30 .75
59 Arian Foster .25 .60
60 Brian Cushing .25 .60
61 Kevin Walter .25 .60
62 Matt Schaub .25 .60
63 Austin Collie .25 .60
64 Dallas Clark .25 .60
65 Dwight Freeney .25 .60
66 Peyton Manning .75 2.00
67 Reggie Wayne .30 .75
68 Paul Posluszny .25 .60
69 Marcedes Lewis .25 .60
70 Maurice Jones-Drew .25 .60
71 Mike Sims-Walker .30 .75
72 Mike Thomas .30 .75
73 Dwayne Bowe .30 .75
74 Jamaal Charles .30 .75
75 Matt Cassel .25 .60
76 Tony Moeaki .25 .60
77 Brandon Marshall .30 .75
78 Brian Hartline .30 .75
79 Chad Henne .30 .75
80 Davone Bess .25 .60
81 Ronnie Brown .30 .75
82 Adrian Peterson .40 1.00
83 Percy Harvin .25 .60
84 Sidney Rice .25 .60
85 Jared Allen .25 .60
86 Visanthe Shiancoe .30 .75
87 Jerod Mayo .25 .60
88 Danny Woodhead .30 .75
89 Deion Branch .25 .60
90 Tom Brady 1.00 2.50
91 Wes Welker .30 .75
92 Drew Brees .40 1.00
93 Lance Moore .25 .60
94 Marques Colston .25 .60
95 Pierre Thomas .25 .60
96 Reggie Bush .25 .60
97 Brandon Jacobs .25 .60
98 Eli Manning .30 .75
99 Hakeem Nicks .25 .60
100 Mario Manningham .25 .60
101 Steve Smith USC .25 .60
102 Braylon Edwards .25 .60
103 LaDainian Tomlinson .40 1.00
104 Mark Sanchez .25 .60
105 Santonio Holmes .25 .60
106 Shonn Greene .25 .60
107 Darren McFadden .25 .60
108 Nnamdi Asomugha .25 .60
109 Louis Murphy .25 .60
110 Jacoby Ford .30 .75
111 DeSean Jackson .30 .75
112 Jeremy Maclin .25 .60
113 LeSean McCoy .40 1.00
114 Michael Vick .30 .75
115 Ben Roethlisberger .40 1.00
116 Hines Ward .30 .75
117 Mike Wallace .25 .60
118 Rashard Mendenhall .25 .60
119 Troy Polamalu .40 1.00
120 Antonio Gates .25 .60
121 Malcom Floyd .25 .60
122 Mike Tolbert .25 .60
123 Philip Rivers .40 1.00
124 Ryan Mathews .30 .75
125 Frank Gore .30 .75
126 Michael Crabtree .25 .60
127 Patrick Willis .30 .75
128 Vernon Davis .25 .60
129 John Carlson .25 .60
130 Marshawn Lynch .30 .75
131 Matt Hasselbeck .25 .60
132 Mike Williams USC .25 .60
133 Danny Amendola .30 .75
134 James Laurinaitis .25 .60
135 Sam Bradford .25 .60
136 Steven Jackson .25 .60
137 Cadillac Williams .25 .60
138 Josh Freeman .30 .75
139 Kellen Winslow Jr. .25 .60
140 LeGarrette Blount .30 .75
141 Mike Williams .30 .75
142 Bo Scaife .25 .60
143 Chris Johnson .25 .60
144 Kenny Britt .25 .60
145 Nate Washington .25 .60
146 Stephen Tulloch .25 .60
147 Chris Cooley .25 .60
148 Donovan McNabb .30 .75
149 London Fletcher .30 .75
150 Santana Moss .30 .75
151 Aaron Williams RC 1.25 3.00
152 Adrian Clayborn RC 1.25 3.00
153 Ahmad Black RC 1.50 4.00
154 Akeem Ayers RC 1.25 3.00
155 Aldon Smith RC 1.25 3.00
156 Aldrick Robinson RC 1.50 4.00
157 Allen Bradford RC 1.25 3.00
158 Anthony Allen RC 1.25 3.00
159 Anthony Castonzo RC 1.25 3.00
160 Baron Batch RC 1.50 4.00
161 Brandon Harris RC 1.25 3.00
162 Brooks Reed RC 1.50 4.00
163 Bruce Carter RC 1.25 3.00
164 Cameron Heyward RC 1.50 4.00
165 Cameron Jordan RC 1.50 4.00
166 Cecil Shorts RC 1.25 3.00
167 Chris Culliver RC 1.25 3.00
168 Corey Liuget RC 1.25 3.00
169 D.J. Williams RC 1.25 3.00
170 Danny Watkins RC 1.25 3.00
171 Da'Quan Bowers RC 1.25 3.00
172 Da'Rel Scott RC 1.25 3.00
173 David Ausberry RC 1.25 3.00
174 DeMarco Sampson RC 1.25 3.00
175 DeMarcus Van Dyke RC 1.50 4.00
176 Denarius Moore RC 1.25 3.00
177 Derek Sherrod RC 1.25 3.00
178 Dion Lewis RC 1.50 4.00
179 Dontay Moch RC 1.25 3.00
180 Dwayne Harris RC 1.25 3.00
181 Evan Royster RC 1.25 3.00
182 Gabe Carimi RC 1.50 4.00
183 Greg Jones RC 1.50 4.00
184 Greg McElroy RC 2.00 5.00
185 Greg Salas RC 1.25 3.00
186 J.J. Watt RC 6.00 15.00
187 Jabaal Sheard RC 1.25 3.00
188 Jacquizz Rodgers RC 1.25 3.00
189 Jaiquawn Jarrett RC 1.25 3.00
190 James Carpenter RC 1.50 4.00
191 Jarvis Jenkins RC 1.25 3.00
192 Jay Finley RC 1.50 4.00
193 Jeremy Kerley RC 2.00 5.00
194 Jimmy Smith RC 1.25 3.00
195 Johnny White RC 1.25 3.00
196 Jonas Mouton RC 1.50 4.00
197 Jordan Cameron RC 1.50 4.00
198 Julius Thomas RC 1.50 4.00
199 Jurrell Casey RC 1.25 3.00
200 Justin Houston RC 1.50 4.00
201 Kealoha Pilares RC 1.25 3.00
202 Kelvin Sheppard RC 1.25 3.00
203 Kris Durham RC 1.25 3.00
204 Lance Kendricks RC 1.25 3.00
205 Lee Smith RC 1.50 4.00
206 Luke Stocker RC 1.25 3.00
207 Marcus Cannon RC 1.25 3.00
208 Marcus Gilbert RC 2.00 5.00
209 Marcus Gilchrist RC 1.25 3.00
210 Martez Wilson RC 1.25 3.00
211 Marvin Austin RC 1.25 3.00
212 Mason Foster RC 1.25 3.00
213 Mike Pouncey RC 2.00 5.00
214 Muhammad Wilkerson RC 1.25 3.00
215 Nate Irving RC 1.50 4.00
216 Nate Solder RC 1.25 3.00
217 Nathan Enderle RC 1.25 3.00
218 Nick Fairley RC 1.25 3.00
219 Niles Paul RC 1.25 3.00
220 Orlando Franklin RC 1.50 4.00
221 Owen Marecic RC 1.25 3.00
222 Patrick Peterson RC 2.50 6.00
223 Phil Taylor RC 1.25 3.00
224 Prince Amukamara RC 1.25 3.00
225 Quinton Carter RC 1.25 3.00
226 Rahim Moore RC 1.25 3.00
227 Ras-I Dowling RC 1.25 3.00
228 Richard Gordon RC 1.25 3.00
229 Ricky Stanzi RC 1.25 3.00
230 Robert Housler RC 1.25 3.00
231 Robert Quinn RC 1.25 3.00
232 Rodney Hudson RC 1.25 3.00
233 Ronald Johnson RC 1.25 3.00
234 Roy Helu RC 1.25 3.00
235 Ryan Kerrigan RC 1.50 4.00
236 Ryan Whalen RC 1.25 3.00
237 Scotty McKnight RC 1.25 3.00
238 Shane Bannon RC 1.25 3.00
239 Stanley Havili RC 1.25 3.00
240 Stefen Wisniewski RC 2.00 5.00
241 Stephen Burton RC 1.25 3.00
242 Stephen Paea RC 1.25 3.00
243 T.J. Yates RC 1.25 3.00
244 Tandon Doss RC 1.25 3.00
245 Terrell McClain RC 1.50 4.00
246 Terrelle Pryor RC 2.00 5.00
247 Tyler Sash RC 1.25 3.00
248 Tyrod Taylor RC 2.50 6.00
249 Tyron Smith RC 1.50 4.00
250 Virgil Green RC 1.25 3.00
251 Andy Dalton JSY AU/499 RC 8.00 20.00
252 Cam Newton JSY AU/299 RC 50.00 100.00
253 A.J. Green JSY AU/299 RC 25.00 50.00
254 T.Jones JSY AU/499 RC 4.00 10.00
255 D.Murray JSY AU/499 RC 8.00 20.00
256 Torrey Smith JSY AU/499 RC 4.00 10.00
257 Ryan Mallett JSY AU/299 RC 5.00 12.00
258 S.Ridley JSY AU/499 RC 4.00 10.00
259 Austin Pettis JSY AU/499 RC 4.00 10.00
260 Shane Vereen JSY AU/499 RC 5.00 12.00
261 T.Young JSY AU/499 RC 4.00 10.00
262 M.Leshoure JSY AU/499 RC 4.00 10.00
263 C.Ponder JSY AU/299 RC 5.00 12.00
264 J.Todman JSY AU/499 RC 4.00 10.00
265 V. Brown JSY AU/499 RC 4.00 10.00
266 V.Miller JSY AU/499 RC 15.00 40.00
267 K.Rudolph JSY AU/499 RC 4.00 10.00
268 J.Baldwin JSY AU/499 RC 4.00 10.00
269 Jake Locker JSY AU/299 RC 5.00 12.00
270 J.Harper JSY AU/499 RC 4.00 10.00
271 Mark Ingram JSY AU/299 RC 8.00 20.00
272 L.Hankerson JSY AU/499 RC 4.00 10.00
273 J.Jernigan JSY AU/499 RC 4.00 10.00
274 D.Carter JSY AU/499 RC 4.00 10.00
275 B.Gabbert JSY AU/299 RC 5.00 12.00
276 Julio Jones JSY AU/499 RC 30.00 60.00
277 M.Dareus JSY AU/499 RC 4.00 10.00
278 R.Williams JSY AU/499 RC 4.00 10.00
279 Clyde Gates JSY AU/499 RC 4.00 10.00
280 D.Thomas JSY AU/499 RC 4.00 10.00
281 Greg Little JSY AU/499 RC 5.00 12.00
282 C.Kaepernick JSY AU/499 RC 6.00 15.00
283 Alex Green JSY AU/499 RC 4.00 10.00
284 R.Cobb JSY AU/499 RC 6.00 15.00
285 B.Powell JSY AU/499 RC 5.00 12.00
286 K. Hunter JSY AU/499 RC 4.00 10.00
287 Dan Marino JSY/99 12.00 30.00
288 Barry Sanders JSY/99 10.00 25.00
289 Brett Favre JSY/99 12.00 30.00
290 Bart Starr JSY/49 12.00 30.00
291 Deion Sanders JSY/99 8.00 20.00
292 Emmitt Smith JSY/99 10.00 25.00
293 Gale Sayers JSY/49 8.00 20.00
294 Jerry Rice JSY/99 10.00 25.00
295 Jim Brown JSY/49 10.00 25.00
296 Joe Montana JSY/99 10.00 25.00
297 Joe Namath JSY/99 10.00 25.00
298 John Elway JSY/99 10.00 25.00
299 Marshall Faulk JSY/99 5.00 12.00
300 Jim Kelly JSY/99 6.00 15.00
301 Terry Bradshaw JSY/49 10.00 25.00
302 Derrick Thomas JSY/49 25.00 50.00
303 Bob Griese JSY/99 6.00 15.00
304 Phil Simms JSY/99 5.00 12.00
305 Troy Aikman JSY/99 8.00 20.00
306 Dick Lane JSY/99 5.00 12.00

2011 Certified Mirror Blue

*VETS/100: 3X TO 8X BASIC CARDS
*RK.JSY AU/50: .6X TO 1.5X JSY AU/499
*RK.JSY AU/50: .5X TO 1.2X JSY AU/299
*LEGEND JSY/50: .5X TO 1.2X JSY/99
*LEGEND JSY/25: .5X TO 1.2X JSY/49

2011 Certified Mirror Gold

*1-150 VETS/25: 5X TO 12X BASIC CARDS
*ROOK.JSY AU/25: 1.2X TO 3X AU RC/499
*ROOK.JSY AU/25: 1X TO 2.5X AU RC/299
*LEG.JSY/25: .6X TO 1.5X JSY/49-99
STATED PRINT RUN 25 SER.#'d SETS
263 Christian Ponder JSY AU 12.00 30.00
269 Jake Locker JSY AU 12.00 30.00
271 Mark Ingram JSY AU 20.00 50.00
276 Julio Jones JSY AU 75.00 150.00

2011 Certified Mirror Red

*1-150 VETS/250: 2.5X TO 6X BASIC CARDS
1-150 VETERAN PRINT RUN 250
*LEG JSY/75-100: .4X TO 1X JSY/99
*LEG JSY/75-100: .3X TO .8X JSY/49
*LEG JSY/50: .4X TO 1X JSY/49
287-306 LEGEND JSY PRINT RUN 75-100

2011 Certified Platinum Blue

*VETS/100: 3X TO 8X BASIC CARDS
STATED PRINT RUN 100 SER.#'d SETS

2011 Certified Platinum Gold

*VETS/25: 5X TO 12X BASIC CARDS
STATED PRINT RUN 25 SER.#'d SETS

2011 Certified Platinum Red

*VETS 1-150: 1.5X TO 4X BASIC CARDS
RANDOM INSERTS IN PACKS

2011 Certified Certified Potential

STATED PRINT RUN 999 SER.#'d SETS
1 A.J. Green 1.50 4.00
2 Alex Green .60 1.50
3 Andy Dalton 1.25 3.00
4 Austin Pettis .60 1.50
5 Bilal Powell .75 2.00
6 Blaine Gabbert .60 1.50
7 Cam Newton 3.00 8.00
8 Christian Ponder .60 1.50
9 Clyde Gates .60 1.50
10 Colin Kaepernick 1.00 2.50
11 Daniel Thomas .60 1.50
12 Delone Carter .60 1.50
13 DeMarco Murray 1.25 3.00
14 Greg Little .75 2.00
15 Jake Locker .60 1.50
16 Jamie Harper .60 1.50
17 Jerrel Jernigan .60 1.50
18 Jonathan Baldwin .60 1.50
19 Jordan Todman .60 1.50

20 Julio Jones 2.00 5.00
21 Kendall Hunter .60 1.50
22 Kyle Rudolph .60 1.50
23 Leonard Hankerson .60 1.50
24 Marcell Dareus .60 1.50
25 Mark Ingram 1.00 2.50
26 Mikel Leshoure .60 1.50
27 Randall Cobb 1.00 2.50
28 Ryan Mallett .60 1.50
29 Ryan Williams .60 1.50
30 Shane Vereen .75 2.00
31 Stevan Ridley .60 1.50
32 Taiwan Jones .60 1.50
33 Titus Young .60 1.50
34 Torrey Smith .60 1.50
35 Vincent Brown .60 1.50
36 Von Miller 1.00 2.50

2011 Certified Certified Potential Autographs

STATED PRINT RUN 25-50
1 A.J. Green/35 20.00 50.00
2 Alex Green/50 4.00 10.00
3 Andy Dalton/50 8.00 20.00
4 Austin Pettis/50 4.00 10.00
5 Bilal Powell/50 5.00 12.00
6 Blaine Gabbert/35 4.00 10.00
7 Cam Newton/35 50.00 100.00
8 Christian Ponder/35 4.00 10.00
9 Clyde Gates/50 4.00 10.00
10 Colin Kaepernick/50 6.00 15.00
11 Daniel Thomas/50 4.00 10.00
12 Delone Carter/50 4.00 10.00
13 DeMarco Murray/50 8.00 20.00
14 Greg Little/50 5.00 12.00
15 Jake Locker/35 4.00 10.00
16 Jamie Harper/50 4.00 10.00
17 Jerrel Jernigan/50 4.00 10.00
18 Jonathan Baldwin/50 8.00 20.00
19 Jordan Todman/50 4.00 10.00
20 Julio Jones/50 20.00 40.00
21 Kendall Hunter/50 4.00 10.00
22 Kyle Rudolph/50 4.00 10.00
23 Leonard Hankerson/50 4.00 10.00
24 Marcell Dareus/50 EXCH 4.00 10.00
25 Mark Ingram/35 6.00 15.00
26 Mikel Leshoure/50 4.00 10.00
27 Randall Cobb/50 6.00 15.00
28 Ryan Mallett/35 4.00 10.00
29 Ryan Williams/50 4.00 10.00
30 Shane Vereen/50 5.00 12.00
31 Stevan Ridley/50 4.00 10.00
32 Taiwan Jones/50 4.00 10.00
33 Titus Young/50 4.00 10.00
34 Torrey Smith/50 4.00 10.00
35 Vincent Brown/50 4.00 10.00
36 Von Miller/25 10.00 25.00

2011 Certified Certified Potential Materials

STATED PRINT RUN 250 SER.#'d SETS
*PRIME/50: .6X TO 1.5X BASIC JSY/250
1 A.J. Green 4.00 10.00
2 Alex Green 1.50 4.00
3 Andy Dalton 3.00 8.00
4 Austin Pettis 1.50 4.00
5 Bilal Powell 2.00 5.00
6 Blaine Gabbert 1.50 4.00
7 Cam Newton 8.00 20.00
8 Christian Ponder 1.50 4.00
9 Clyde Gates 1.50 4.00
10 Colin Kaepernick 2.50 6.00
11 Daniel Thomas 1.50 4.00
12 Delone Carter 1.50 4.00
13 DeMarco Murray 3.00 8.00
14 Greg Little 2.00 5.00
15 Jake Locker 1.50 4.00
16 Jamie Harper 1.50 4.00
17 Jerrel Jernigan 1.50 4.00
18 Jonathan Baldwin 1.50 4.00
19 Jordan Todman 1.50 4.00
20 Julio Jones 5.00 12.00
21 Kendall Hunter 1.50 4.00
22 Kyle Rudolph 1.50 4.00
23 Leonard Hankerson 1.50 4.00
24 Marcell Dareus 1.50 4.00
25 Mark Ingram 2.50 6.00
26 Mikel Leshoure 1.50 4.00
27 Randall Cobb 2.50 6.00
28 Ryan Mallett 1.50 4.00
29 Ryan Williams 1.50 4.00
30 Shane Vereen 2.00 5.00
31 Stevan Ridley 1.50 4.00
32 Taiwan Jones 1.50 4.00
33 Titus Young 1.50 4.00
34 Torrey Smith 1.50 4.00
35 Vincent Brown 1.50 4.00
36 Von Miller 2.50 6.00

2011 Certified Fabric of the Game

STATED PRINT RUN 20-250
1 Adrian Peterson/150 4.00 10.00
2 Anquan Boldin/25 4.00 10.00
3 Arian Foster/25 4.00 10.00
4 Santana Moss/150 3.00 8.00
5 Dallas Clark/25 4.00 10.00
6 Carson Palmer/25 5.00 12.00
7 Beanie Wells/25 4.00 10.00
8 Ben Roethlisberger/25 6.00 15.00
9 Bo Scaife/49 3.00 8.00
10 Ray Rice/25 4.00 10.00
11 Devin Hester/25 5.00 12.00
12 Darrelle Revis/25 4.00 10.00
13 Clay Matthews/25 8.00 20.00
14 Tim Tebow/25 8.00 20.00
16 LeSean McCoy/25 6.00 15.00
17 Jonathan Stewart/25 4.00 10.00
18 Knowshon Moreno/25 4.00 10.00
19 Tony Romo/25 5.00 12.00
21 Louis Murphy/25 4.00 10.00
22 Peyton Hillis/25 4.00 10.00
23 Ryan Fitzpatrick/25 4.00 10.00
25 Dwight Freeney/25 4.00 10.00
27 James Harrison/25 8.00 20.00
28 Ray Lewis/25 6.00 15.00
29 Peyton Manning/99 8.00 20.00
30 Ryan Mathews/25 5.00 12.00
32 Patrick Willis/250 3.00 8.00
33 Matt Schaub/25 4.00 10.00
35 Lee Evans/49 4.00 10.00
36 Marques Colston/250 2.50 6.00
37 Jason Witten/250 4.00 10.00
38 Eddie George/49 5.00 12.00
39 Ed Too Tall Jones/49 4.00 10.00
40 Eric Dickerson/49 5.00 12.00
41 Forrest Gregg/25 5.00 12.00
42 Fran Tarkenton/25 8.00 20.00
43 Franco Harris/25 8.00 20.00
44 Fred Biletnikoff/25 8.00 20.00
45 Fred Dryer/250 3.00 8.00
46 Garo Yepremian/49 4.00 10.00
47 Gene Upshaw/150 3.00 8.00
48 George Blanda/25 6.00 15.00
49 Henry Jordan/250 4.00 10.00
50 Howie Long/25 8.00 20.00
51 Priest Holmes/25 5.00 12.00
52 Randall Cunningham/250 4.00 10.00
53 Randy White/49 6.00 15.00
54 Raymond Berry/25 6.00 15.00
55 Richard Dent/25 5.00 12.00
56 Rod Woodson/25 10.00 25.00
57 Jan Stenerud/25 5.00 12.00
58 Dan Hampton/250 3.00 8.00
59 Steve Bartkowski/49 5.00 12.00
60 Steve Young/250 6.00 15.00
62 Thurman Thomas/25 6.00 15.00
63 Jay Novacek/25 6.00 15.00
64 Warren Sapp/250 4.00 10.00
66 Willie Brown/25 5.00 12.00
67 Bernie Kosar/25 6.00 15.00
68 Bert Jones/20 5.00 12.00
69 Billy Sims/55 5.00 12.00
70 Daryle Lamonica/25 5.00 12.00
71 Bob Hayes/25 8.00 20.00
72 Bob Lilly/25 6.00 15.00
73 Don Maynard/25 6.00 15.00
74 Doug Flutie/250 4.00 10.00
75 Carl Eller/25 5.00 12.00
76 Alan Page/25 5.00 12.00
77 Alex Karras/25 6.00 15.00
78 Dick Butkus/25 10.00 25.00
79 Bo Jackson/49 8.00 20.00
80 Chuck Foreman/49 4.00 10.00
81 John Fuqua/49 5.00 12.00
82 John Hadl/49 4.00 10.00
84 John Matuszak/250 5.00 12.00
85 Junior Seau/49 5.00 12.00
86 Keith Jackson/100 5.00 12.00
87 Ken Anderson/100 4.00 10.00
88 Keyshawn Johnson/20 6.00 15.00
89 Larry Little/49 4.00 10.00
90 Lee Roy Selmon/49 6.00 15.00
91 Len Dawson/49 6.00 15.00
92 Marcus Allen/250 5.00 12.00
94 Mark Carrier DB/250 3.00 8.00
95 Mark Duper/49 4.00 10.00
97 Michael Irvin/250 5.00 12.00
98 Mike Alstott/49 4.00 10.00
99 Irving Fryar/49 4.00 10.00
100 Dan Fouts/49 5.00 12.00

2011 Certified Fabric of the Game NFL Die Cut Prime

STATED PRINT RUN 5-25
1 Adrian Peterson/25 8.00 20.00
2 Anquan Boldin/25 5.00 12.00
4 Santana Moss/25 6.00 15.00
5 Dallas Clark/15 5.00 12.00
10 Ray Rice/25 5.00 12.00
13 Clay Matthews/25 10.00 25.00
14 Tim Tebow/25 15.00 40.00
17 Jonathan Stewart/25 5.00 12.00
18 Knowshon Moreno/25 5.00 12.00
19 Tony Romo/25 6.00 15.00
20 DeAngelo Hall/25 5.00 12.00
21 Louis Murphy/15 5.00 12.00
24 Danny Woodhead/20 6.00 15.00
25 Dwight Freeney/25 5.00 12.00
26 David Harris/25 5.00 12.00
27 James Harrison/25 10.00 25.00
28 Ray Lewis/24 15.00 40.00
30 Ryan Mathews/25 6.00 15.00
31 Roddy White/25 5.00 12.00
32 Patrick Willis/15 6.00 15.00
36 Marques Colston/25 5.00 12.00
37 Jason Witten/25 8.00 20.00
38 Eddie George/25 8.00 20.00
40 Eric Dickerson/25 8.00 20.00
41 Forrest Gregg/25 6.00 15.00
42 Fran Tarkenton/15 10.00 25.00
43 Franco Harris/25 10.00 25.00
44 Fred Biletnikoff/25 10.00 25.00
51 Priest Holmes/25 6.00 15.00
52 Randall Cunningham/25 8.00 20.00
53 Randy White/25 10.00 25.00
54 Raymond Berry/25 8.00 20.00
55 Richard Dent/25 6.00 15.00
56 Rod Woodson/25 12.00 30.00
59 Steve Bartkowski/25 8.00 20.00
60 Steve Young/15 12.00 30.00
62 Thurman Thomas/15 8.00 20.00
63 Jay Novacek/25 8.00 20.00
64 Warren Sapp/25 8.00 20.00
65 Wayne Chrebet/25 6.00 15.00
66 Willie Brown/15 6.00 15.00
67 Bernie Kosar/25 8.00 20.00
69 Billy Sims/15 8.00 20.00
71 Bob Hayes/25 10.00 25.00
72 Bob Lilly/25 8.00 20.00
74 Doug Flutie/25 8.00 20.00
76 Alan Page/25 6.00 15.00
78 Dick Butkus/25 12.00 30.00
79 Bo Jackson/15 12.00 30.00
80 Chuck Foreman/15 6.00 15.00
82 John Hadl/25 6.00 15.00
86 Keith Jackson/25 10.00 25.00
87 Ken Anderson/25 8.00 20.00
88 Keyshawn Johnson/15 8.00 20.00
89 Larry Little/20 6.00 15.00
90 Lee Roy Selmon/25 10.00 25.00
92 Marcus Allen/25 10.00 25.00
93 Curtis Martin/25 8.00 20.00
94 Mark Carrier DB/25 6.00 15.00
95 Mark Duper/25 6.00 15.00
98 Mike Alstott/15 6.00 15.00
100 Dan Fouts/25 8.00 20.00

2011 Certified Fabric of the Game Prime

STATED PRINT RUN 5-50
1 Adrian Peterson/50 6.00 15.00
2 Anquan Boldin/50 4.00 10.00
4 Santana Moss/50 5.00 12.00
8 Ben Roethlisberger/15 8.00 20.00
10 Ray Rice/50 4.00 10.00
12 Darrelle Revis/25 5.00 12.00
13 Clay Matthews/50 8.00 20.00
14 Tim Tebow/50 8.00 20.00
17 Jonathan Stewart/50 4.00 10.00
18 Knowshon Moreno/50 4.00 10.00
19 Tony Romo/50 5.00 12.00
20 DeAngelo Hall/50 4.00 10.00
21 Louis Murphy/25 5.00 12.00
24 Danny Woodhead/25 6.00 15.00
25 Dwight Freeney/50 4.00 10.00
26 David Harris/25 5.00 12.00
27 James Harrison/50 8.00 20.00
30 Ryan Mathews/50 5.00 12.00
31 Roddy White/50 4.00 10.00
32 Patrick Willis/50 5.00 12.00
35 Lee Evans/50 5.00 12.00
36 Marques Colston/50 4.00 10.00
37 Jason Witten/50 6.00 15.00
38 Eddie George/50 6.00 15.00
40 Eric Dickerson/50 6.00 15.00
41 Forrest Gregg/50 5.00 12.00
42 Fran Tarkenton/25 10.00 25.00
43 Franco Harris/50 8.00 20.00
44 Fred Biletnikoff/25 10.00 25.00
48 George Blanda/50 6.00 15.00
51 Priest Holmes/50 5.00 12.00
52 Randall Cunningham/50 6.00 15.00
53 Randy White/50 8.00 20.00
54 Raymond Berry/50 6.00 15.00
55 Richard Dent/50 5.00 12.00
56 Rod Woodson/50 10.00 25.00
59 Steve Bartkowski/50 6.00 15.00
60 Steve Young/25 15.00 40.00
62 Thurman Thomas/25 8.00 20.00
63 Jay Novacek/50 6.00 15.00
64 Warren Sapp/50 6.00 15.00
65 Wayne Chrebet/50 5.00 12.00
66 Willie Brown/50 5.00 12.00
67 Bernie Kosar/50 6.00 15.00
71 Bob Hayes/50 8.00 20.00
72 Bob Lilly/50 6.00 15.00
74 Doug Flutie/50 6.00 15.00
76 Alan Page/45 5.00 12.00
78 Dick Butkus/50 10.00 25.00
80 Chuck Foreman/25 6.00 15.00
81 John Fuqua/25 8.00 20.00
82 John Hadl/50 5.00 12.00
84 John Matuszak/25 10.00 25.00
85 Junior Seau/15 8.00 20.00
86 Keith Jackson/50 8.00 20.00
87 Ken Anderson/50 6.00 15.00
88 Keyshawn Johnson/30 6.00 15.00
89 Larry Little/50 5.00 12.00
90 Lee Roy Selmon/50 8.00 20.00
92 Marcus Allen/50 8.00 20.00
93 Curtis Martin/50 6.00 15.00
94 Mark Carrier DB/50 5.00 12.00
95 Mark Duper/50 5.00 12.00
98 Mike Alstott/50 5.00 12.00
100 Dan Fouts/25 8.00 20.00

2011 Certified Fabric of the Game Team Die Cut

STATED PRINT RUN 5-25
1 Adrian Peterson/25 6.00 15.00
2 Anquan Boldin/25 4.00 10.00
4 Santana Moss/25 5.00 12.00
5 Dallas Clark/25 4.00 10.00
7 Beanie Wells/25 4.00 10.00
8 Ben Roethlisberger/25 6.00 15.00
9 Bo Scaife/25 4.00 10.00
12 Darrelle Revis/25 4.00 10.00
13 Clay Matthews/25 8.00 20.00
16 LeSean McCoy/25 6.00 15.00
18 Knowshon Moreno/25 4.00 10.00
19 Tony Romo/25 5.00 12.00
21 Louis Murphy/25 4.00 10.00
24 Danny Woodhead/15 5.00 12.00
25 Dwight Freeney/25 4.00 10.00
27 James Harrison/25 6.00 15.00
29 Peyton Manning/15 12.00 30.00
32 Patrick Willis/25 5.00 12.00
33 Matt Schaub/25 4.00 10.00
35 Lee Evans/25 5.00 12.00
36 Marques Colston/25 4.00 10.00
37 Jason Witten/25 8.00 20.00
38 Eddie George/25 6.00 15.00
39 Ed Too Tall Jones/25 5.00 12.00
40 Eric Dickerson/25 6.00 15.00
45 Fred Dryer/25 5.00 12.00
46 Garo Yepremian/25 5.00 12.00
47 Gene Upshaw/25 5.00 12.00
49 Henry Jordan/25 6.00 15.00
52 Randall Cunningham/25 6.00 15.00
55 Richard Dent/25 5.00 12.00
57 Jan Stenerud/25 5.00 12.00
58 Dan Hampton/25 5.00 12.00
59 Steve Bartkowski/25 6.00 15.00
60 Steve Young/25 10.00 25.00
61 Ted Hendricks/25 5.00 12.00
63 Jay Novacek/25 6.00 15.00
64 Warren Sapp/25 6.00 15.00
67 Bernie Kosar/25 6.00 15.00
69 Billy Sims/25 6.00 15.00
74 Doug Flutie/25 6.00 15.00
77 Alex Karras/25 6.00 15.00
80 Chuck Foreman/25 5.00 12.00
82 John Hadl/25 5.00 12.00
84 John Matuszak/25 8.00 20.00
85 Junior Seau/25 6.00 15.00
86 Keith Jackson/25 8.00 20.00
87 Ken Anderson/25 6.00 15.00
90 Lee Roy Selmon/25 8.00 20.00
92 Marcus Allen/25 8.00 20.00
94 Mark Carrier DB/25 5.00 12.00
95 Mark Duper/25 5.00 12.00
97 Michael Irvin/25 8.00 20.00
98 Mike Alstott/25 5.00 12.00

2011 Certified Fabric of the Game Combos

STATED PRINT RUN 50-150
*PRIME/14-25: .6X TO 1.5X BASIC COMBO
2 Aikman/S.Bradford/150 8.00 20.00
3 B.Kosar/C.McCoy/150 5.00 12.00
4 Polamalu/E.Reed/100 6.00 15.00
5 R.Woodson/Revis/75 6.00 15.00
6 J.Namath/Bradford/100 8.00 20.00
7 Cunningham/Vick/150 5.00 12.00
8 E.Jones/D.Ware/100 5.00 12.00
9 Dickerson/McFadden/150 5.00 12.00
10 E.George/C.Johnson/150 5.00 12.00
11 C.Eller/J.Allen/150 8.00 20.00
12 G.Sayers/M.Forte/150 8.00 20.00
13 F.Harris/J.Fuqua/50 8.00 20.00

2011 Certified Fabric of the Game Jersey Number Autographs

STATED PRINT RUN 4-25
12 Darrelle Revis/25 12.00 30.00
16 LeSean McCoy/15 20.00 50.00
18 Knowshon Moreno/15 12.00 30.00
29 Peyton Manning/15 60.00 120.00
32 Patrick Willis/25 20.00 50.00
33 Matt Schaub/15 12.00 30.00
35 Lee Evans/15 15.00 40.00
37 Jason Witten/15
39 Ed Too Tall Jones/25 15.00 40.00
40 Eric Dickerson/25 20.00 50.00
41 Forrest Gregg/25 15.00 40.00
43 Franco Harris/25 40.00 80.00
44 Fred Biletnikoff/25 25.00 60.00
47 Gene Upshaw/15 15.00 40.00
50 Howie Long/25 25.00 60.00
51 Priest Holmes/25 15.00 40.00
52 Randall Cunningham/25 20.00 50.00
53 Randy White/25 20.00 50.00
54 Raymond Berry/25 20.00 50.00
57 Jan Stenerud/25 15.00 40.00
59 Steve Bartkowski/25 12.00 30.00
66 Willie Brown/25 15.00 40.00
70 Daryle Lamonica/25 12.00 30.00
72 Bob Lilly/25 20.00 50.00
73 Don Maynard/25 20.00 50.00
76 Alan Page/25 15.00 40.00
77 Alex Karras/25 20.00 50.00
79 Bo Jackson/25 40.00 80.00
85 Junior Seau/25 50.00 100.00
88 Keyshawn Johnson/15 15.00 40.00
89 Larry Little/20 15.00 40.00
90 Lee Roy Selmon/25 20.00 50.00
91 Len Dawson/25 30.00 80.00
92 Marcus Allen/25 20.00 50.00
95 Mark Duper/25 15.00 40.00
97 Michael Irvin/25 25.00 60.00
98 Mike Alstott/25 15.00 40.00

2011 Certified Gold Team

STATED PRINT RUN 999 SER.#'d SETS
1 Andre Johnson 1.00 2.50
2 Michael Vick 1.00 2.50
3 Aaron Rodgers 2.00 5.00
4 Peyton Manning 2.50 6.00
5 Larry Fitzgerald 1.00 2.50
6 Ray Lewis 1.25 3.00
7 Darrelle Revis .75 2.00
8 Tom Brady 3.00 8.00
9 Adrian Peterson 1.25 3.00
10 Troy Polamalu 1.25 3.00

2011 Certified Gold Team Materials

STATED PRINT RUN 10-250
*PRIME/50: .6X TO 1.5X BASIC JSY/100-125
1 Andre Johnson/28 6.00 15.00
2 Michael Vick/250 3.00 8.00
3 Aaron Rodgers/125 12.00 30.00
4 Peyton Manning/10
5 Larry Fitzgerald/100 4.00 10.00
6 Ray Lewis/250 4.00 10.00
7 Darrelle Revis/100 3.00 8.00
8 Tom Brady/200 10.00 25.00
9 Adrian Peterson/100 5.00 12.00

2011 Certified Hometown Heroes Autographs

STATED PRINT RUN 1-30
4 Asante Samuel/30 EXCH
5 Brandon Meriweather/25 6.00 15.00
18 Jared Allen/20 25.00 50.00

2011 Certified Hometown Heroes Materials

STATED PRINT RUN 25-250
1 Aaron Rodgers/125 12.00 30.00
2 Adrian Peterson/150 4.00 10.00
3 Antonio Gates/250 2.50 6.00
6 Brian Urlacher/250 4.00 10.00
7 Calvin Johnson/150 4.00 10.00
8 Ben Roethlisberger/200 4.00 10.00
10 Chris Johnson/200 2.50 6.00
11 DeMarcus Ware/250 4.00 10.00
12 DeSean Jackson/250 3.00 8.00
14 Dwayne Bowe/25 6.00 15.00
15 Eli Manning/250 3.00 8.00
16 Frank Gore/250 3.00 8.00
17 Hines Ward/250 4.00 10.00
18 Jared Allen/250 4.00 10.00
19 Joe Flacco/250 3.00 8.00
20 Larry Fitzgerald/100 4.00 10.00
21 Mark Sanchez/250 2.50 6.00
22 Matt Ryan/250 3.00 8.00
23 Maurice Jones-Drew/100 3.00 8.00
24 Michael Turner/250 2.50 6.00
25 Miles Austin/250 2.50 6.00
26 Percy Harvin/250 2.50 6.00
27 Reggie Wayne/250 3.00 8.00
28 Santana Moss/50 5.00 12.00
29 Steve Smith/100 4.00 10.00
30 Steven Jackson/250 2.50 6.00
31 Tom Brady/100 10.00 25.00
33 Vernon Davis/150 2.50 6.00
34 Wes Welker/50 5.00 12.00

2011 Certified Hometown Heroes Materials Prime

STATED PRINT RUN 1-50
2 Adrian Peterson/50 10.00 25.00
3 Antonio Gates/50 6.00 15.00
6 Brian Urlacher/25 12.00 30.00
7 Calvin Johnson/50 10.00 25.00
10 Chris Johnson/50 6.00 15.00
11 DeMarcus Ware/50 10.00 25.00
12 DeSean Jackson/50 8.00 20.00
14 Dwayne Bowe/50 8.00 20.00
15 Eli Manning/15 10.00 25.00
18 Jared Allen/50 10.00 25.00
23 Maurice Jones-Drew/50 6.00 15.00
24 Michael Turner/50 6.00 15.00
25 Miles Austin/50 6.00 15.00
27 Reggie Wayne/25 10.00 25.00
28 Santana Moss/50 8.00 20.00
29 Steve Smith/25 10.00 25.00
30 Steven Jackson/50 6.00 15.00
33 Vernon Davis/50 6.00 15.00
34 Wes Welker/50 8.00 20.00

2011 Certified Hometown Heroes Materials Autographs Prime

STATED PRINT RUN 1-25
4 Asante Samuel/25 EXCH
18 Jared Allen/20 40.00 80.00
28 Santana Moss/20 15.00 40.00

2011 Certified Mirror Gold Materials

MIRROR GOLD PRINT RUN 5-25
*BLUE/50: .3X TO .8X GOLD JSY/25
7 Michael Turner/25 4.00 10.00
8 Roddy White/25 4.00 10.00
9 Tony Gonzalez/25 5.00 12.00
10 Anquan Boldin/25 4.00 10.00
12 Ray Lewis/25 6.00 15.00
13 Ray Rice/25 4.00 10.00
15 C.J. Spiller/25 4.00 10.00
16 Fred Jackson/25 8.00 20.00
17 Lee Evans/25 5.00 12.00
20 DeAngelo Williams/25 4.00 10.00
23 Steve Smith/25 5.00 12.00
24 Brian Urlacher/25 6.00 15.00
26 Jay Cutler/25 4.00 10.00
27 Julius Peppers/25 5.00 12.00
28 Matt Forte/25 4.00 10.00
32 Jordan Shipley/25 4.00 10.00
35 Colt McCoy/25 4.00 10.00
37 Peyton Hillis/25 4.00 10.00
39 Felix Jones/25 4.00 10.00
40 Jason Witten/25 6.00 15.00
41 Miles Austin/25 4.00 10.00
42 Tony Romo/25 5.00 12.00
43 Brandon Lloyd/25 4.00 10.00
46 Knowshon Moreno/25 4.00 10.00
47 Tim Tebow/25 6.00 15.00
49 Calvin Johnson/25 6.00 15.00
50 Jahvid Best/25 4.00 10.00
52 Ndamukong Suh/25 5.00 12.00
53 Aaron Rodgers/25 15.00 40.00
54 Clay Matthews/25 6.00 15.00
65 Dwight Freeney/25 4.00 10.00
67 Reggie Wayne/25 5.00 12.00
70 Maurice Jones-Drew/25 4.00 10.00
72 Mike Thomas/25 5.00 12.00
73 Dwayne Bowe/25 5.00 12.00
74 Jamaal Charles/25 5.00 12.00
75 Matt Cassel/25 4.00 10.00
77 Brandon Marshall/25 5.00 12.00
78 Brian Hartline/25 5.00 12.00
79 Chad Henne/25 5.00 12.00
82 Adrian Peterson/25 6.00 15.00
85 Jared Allen/25 6.00 15.00
86 Visanthe Shiancoe/25 5.00 12.00
91 Wes Welker/25 5.00 12.00
94 Marques Colston/25 4.00 10.00
98 Eli Manning/25 5.00 12.00
99 Hakeem Nicks/25 4.00 10.00
103 LaDainian Tomlinson/25 6.00 15.00
105 Santonio Holmes/25 4.00 10.00
107 Darren McFadden/25 4.00 10.00
109 Louis Murphy/25 4.00 10.00
110 Jacoby Ford/25 5.00 12.00
111 DeSean Jackson/25 5.00 12.00
112 Jeremy Maclin/25 4.00 10.00
117 Mike Wallace/25 4.00 10.00
118 Rashard Mendenhall/25 4.00 10.00
119 Troy Polamalu/25 6.00 15.00
120 Antonio Gates/25 4.00 10.00
121 Malcom Floyd/25 4.00 10.00
123 Philip Rivers/25 6.00 15.00
124 Ryan Mathews/25 5.00 12.00
127 Patrick Willis/25 5.00 12.00
128 Vernon Davis/25 4.00 10.00
134 James Laurinaitis/25 4.00 10.00
135 Sam Bradford/25 4.00 10.00
136 Steven Jackson/25 4.00 10.00
139 Kellen Winslow Jr./25 4.00 10.00
143 Chris Johnson/25 4.00 10.00
144 Kenny Britt/25 4.00 10.00
145 Nate Washington/25 4.00 10.00
147 Chris Cooley/25 4.00 10.00
149 London Fletcher/15 6.00 15.00
150 Santana Moss/25 5.00 12.00
251 Andy Dalton/25 8.00 20.00
252 Cam Newton/25 20.00 50.00
253 A.J. Green/25 10.00 25.00
254 Taiwan Jones/25 4.00 10.00
255 DeMarco Murray/25 8.00 20.00
256 Torrey Smith/25 4.00 10.00
257 Ryan Mallett/25 4.00 10.00
258 Stevan Ridley/25 4.00 10.00
259 Austin Pettis/25 4.00 10.00
260 Shane Vereen/25 5.00 12.00
261 Titus Young/25 4.00 10.00
262 Mikel Leshoure/25 4.00 10.00
263 Christian Ponder/25 4.00 10.00
264 Jordan Todman/25 4.00 10.00
265 Vincent Brown/25 4.00 10.00
266 Von Miller/25 6.00 15.00
267 Kyle Rudolph/25 4.00 10.00
268 Jonathan Baldwin/25 4.00 10.00
269 Jake Locker/25 4.00 10.00
270 Jamie Harper/25 4.00 10.00
271 Mark Ingram/25 6.00 15.00
272 Leonard Hankerson/25 4.00 10.00
273 Jerrel Jernigan/25 4.00 10.00
274 Delone Carter/25 4.00 10.00
275 Blaine Gabbert/25 4.00 10.00
276 Julio Jones/25 12.00 20.00
277 Marcell Dareus/25 4.00 10.00
278 Ryan Williams/25 4.00 10.00
279 Clyde Gates/25 4.00 10.00
280 Daniel Thomas/25 4.00 10.00
281 Greg Little/25 5.00 12.00
282 Colin Kaepernick/25 6.00 15.00
283 Alex Green/25 4.00 10.00
284 Randall Cobb/25 6.00 15.00
285 Bilal Powell/25 5.00 12.00
286 Kendall Hunter/25 4.00 10.00

2011 Certified Mirror Gold Signatures

*GOLD ROOKIE/25: .8X TO 2X RED/100-250
STATED PRINT RUN 25 SER.#'d SETS
246 Terrelle Pryor 10.00 25.00
287 Dan Marino JSY/25 100.00 200.00
288 Barry Sanders JSY/25 60.00 120.00
289 Brett Favre JSY/25 100.00 200.00
291 Deion Sanders JSY/25 40.00 80.00
292 Emmitt Smith JSY/25 100.00 175.00
294 Jerry Rice JSY/25 100.00 175.00
295 Jim Brown JSY/25 EXCH 40.00 80.00
296 Joe Montana JSY/25 100.00 200.00
297 Joe Namath JSY/25 100.00 200.00
298 John Elway JSY/25 75.00 150.00
299 Marshall Faulk JSY/25 30.00 60.00
300 Jim Kelly JSY/25 30.00 60.00
303 Bob Griese JSY/25 30.00 60.00
304 Phil Simms JSY/25 20.00 50.00
305 Troy Aikman JSY/25 EXCH 40.00 80.00

2011 Certified Mirror Red Signatures

MIRROR RED AU PRINT RUN 100-250
*MIRR.BLUE/50-100: .5X TO 1.2X RED/100-250
152 Adrian Clayborn/250 3.00 8.00
153 Ahmad Black/250 4.00 10.00
154 Akeem Ayers/250 3.00 8.00
155 Aldon Smith/250 3.00 8.00
156 Aldrick Robinson/250 4.00 10.00
157 Allen Bradford/250 3.00 8.00
158 Anthony Allen/250 3.00 8.00
159 Anthony Castonzo/250 3.00 8.00
161 Brandon Harris/250 3.00 8.00
164 Cameron Heyward/250 4.00 10.00
165 Cameron Jordan/250 4.00 10.00
166 Cecil Shorts/250 3.00 8.00
168 Corey Liuget/250 3.00 8.00
169 D.J. Williams/250 3.00 8.00
171 Da'Quan Bowers/250 3.00 8.00
172 Da'Rel Scott/250 3.00 8.00
176 Denarius Moore/250 8.00 20.00
178 Dion Lewis/250 4.00 10.00
180 Dwayne Harris/250 3.00 8.00
181 Evan Royster/250 3.00 8.00
183 Greg Jones/250 4.00 10.00
184 Greg McElroy/250 5.00 12.00
185 Greg Salas/250 3.00 8.00
186 J.J. Watt/250 50.00 100.00
188 Jacquizz Rodgers/250 3.00 8.00
193 Jeremy Kerley/250 5.00 12.00
194 Jimmy Smith/250 3.00 8.00
195 Johnny White/250 3.00 8.00
197 Jordan Cameron/250 4.00 10.00
198 Julius Thomas/250 4.00 10.00
200 Justin Houston/250 4.00 10.00
201 Kealoha Pilares/250 3.00 8.00
203 Kris Durham/250 3.00 8.00
204 Lance Kendricks/250 3.00 8.00
206 Luke Stocker/250 3.00 8.00
207 Marcus Cannon/100 3.00 8.00
210 Martez Wilson/250 3.00 8.00
217 Nathan Enderle/250 3.00 8.00
219 Niles Paul/250 3.00 8.00
221 Owen Marecic/250 3.00 8.00
223 Phil Taylor/250 3.00 8.00
224 Prince Amukamara/250 6.00 15.00
225 Quinton Carter/250 3.00 8.00
226 Rahim Moore/250 3.00 8.00
229 Ricky Stanzi/250 3.00 8.00
230 Robert Housler/250 3.00 8.00
233 Ronald Johnson/250 3.00 8.00
234 Roy Helu/250 3.00 8.00
235 Ryan Kerrigan/250 6.00 15.00
236 Ryan Whalen/250 3.00 8.00
237 Scotty McKnight/250 3.00 8.00
238 Shane Bannon/250 3.00 8.00
239 Stanley Havili/250 3.00 8.00
241 Stephen Burton/250 3.00 8.00
242 Stephen Paea/150 3.00 8.00
243 T.J. Yates/250 3.00 8.00
244 Tandon Doss/250 3.00 8.00
247 Tyler Sash/250 3.00 8.00
248 Tyrod Taylor/250 6.00 15.00
249 Tyron Smith/250 4.00 10.00

2011 Certified Rookie Fabric of the Game

STATED PRINT RUN 150-250
*TEAM DC/25: .8X TO 2X JSY/150-250
*TEAM DC/10: 1.2X TO 3X JSY/150-250
1 Clyde Gates/250 1.50 4.00
2 Jonathan Baldwin/250 1.50 4.00
3 A.J. Green/250 4.00 10.00
4 Mark Ingram/250 2.50 6.00
5 Von Miller/250 2.50 6.00
6 Torrey Smith/250 1.50 4.00
7 Blaine Gabbert/250 1.50 4.00
8 Greg Little/250 2.00 5.00
9 Ryan Mallett/250 1.50 4.00
10 Kendall Hunter/250 1.50 4.00
11 Andy Dalton/250 3.00 8.00
12 Colin Kaepernick/250 2.50 6.00
13 Stevan Ridley/250 1.50 4.00
14 Mikel Leshoure/250 1.50 4.00
15 Jamie Harper/250 1.50 4.00
16 Austin Pettis/250 1.50 4.00
17 Alex Green/250 1.50 4.00
18 Jake Locker/250 1.50 4.00
19 Kyle Rudolph/250 1.50 4.00
20 Ryan Williams/250 1.50 4.00
21 Titus Young/250 1.50 4.00
22 Randall Cobb/250 2.50 6.00
23 Delone Carter/250 1.50 4.00
24 Cam Newton/250 8.00 20.00
25 Bilal Powell/250 2.00 5.00
26 Jerrel Jernigan/250 1.50 4.00
27 Vincent Brown/150 1.50 4.00
28 DeMarco Murray/250 3.00 8.00
29 Christian Ponder/250 1.50 4.00
30 Julio Jones/250 5.00 12.00
31 Shane Vereen/250 2.00 5.00
32 Taiwan Jones/250 1.50 4.00
33 Daniel Thomas/250 1.50 4.00
34 Jordan Todman/250 1.50 4.00
35 Leonard Hankerson/250 1.50 4.00
36 Marcell Dareus/250 1.50 4.00

2011 Certified Rookie Fabric of the Game Jersey Number Autographs

STATED PRINT RUN 25-50
*PRIME/15-25: .5X TO 1.2X AU/25-50
1 Clyde Gates/50 6.00 15.00
2 Jonathan Baldwin/50 12.00 30.00
3 A.J. Green/30 40.00 80.00
4 Mark Ingram/30 10.00 25.00
5 Von Miller/25 15.00 40.00
6 Torrey Smith/50 6.00 15.00
7 Blaine Gabbert/30 6.00 15.00
8 Greg Little/50 8.00 20.00
9 Ryan Mallett/30 6.00 15.00
10 Kendall Hunter/50 6.00 15.00
11 Andy Dalton/50 12.00 30.00
12 Colin Kaepernick/50 10.00 25.00
13 Stevan Ridley/50 6.00 15.00
14 Mikel Leshoure/50 6.00 15.00
15 Jamie Harper/50 6.00 15.00
16 Austin Pettis/50 6.00 15.00
17 Alex Green/50 6.00 15.00
18 Jake Locker/30 6.00 15.00
19 Kyle Rudolph/50 6.00 15.00
20 Ryan Williams/50 6.00 15.00
21 Titus Young/50 6.00 15.00
22 Randall Cobb/50 10.00 25.00
23 Delone Carter/50 6.00 15.00
24 Cam Newton/30 60.00 125.00
25 Bilal Powell/50 8.00 20.00
26 Jerrel Jernigan/50 6.00 15.00
27 Vincent Brown/50 6.00 15.00
28 DeMarco Murray/50 12.00 30.00
29 Christian Ponder/30 6.00 15.00
30 Julio Jones/50 30.00 60.00
31 Shane Vereen/50 8.00 20.00
32 Taiwan Jones/50 6.00 15.00
33 Daniel Thomas/50 6.00 15.00
34 Jordan Todman/50 6.00 15.00
35 Leonard Hankerson/50 6.00 15.00
36 Marcell Dareus/50 EXCH 6.00 15.00

2011 Certified Shirt Off My Back Materials

*JSY/150-250: .4X TO 1X FOTG/150-250
*PRIME/50: .6X TO 1.5X JSY/150-250
STATED PRINT RUN 150-250

2011 Certified Shirt Off My Back Materials Combos

STATED PRINT RUN 25-100
*PRM/18-25: .8X TO 2X CMBO/50-100
*PRIME/25: .5X TO 1.2X COMBO/25
1 A.Green/A.Dalton/100 5.00 12.00
2 S.Smith/C.Newton/100 10.00 25.00
3 M.Ryan/J.Jones/100 6.00 15.00
4 M.Colston/M.Ingram/100 3.00 8.00
5 A.Peterson/C.Ponder/100 8.00 20.00
6 C.Johnson/M.Leshoure/75 6.00 15.00
7 Jones-Drew/B.Gabbert/50 2.00 5.00
8 D.Bowe/J.Baldwin/25 8.00 20.00
9 T.Romo/D.Murray/100 4.00 10.00
10 D.Clark/D.Carter/100 3.00 8.00
11 A.Gates/V.Brown/100 3.00 8.00
12 K.Britt/J.Locker/100 2.00 5.00
13 C.Cooley/L.Hankerson/100 3.00 8.00
14 V.Davis/C.Kaepernick/100 5.00 12.00
15 J.Flacco/T.Smith/100 4.00 10.00

2012 Certified

COMP.SET w/o SP's (150) 12.00 30.00
151-200 IMMORTAL PRINT RUN 999
251-315 ROOKIE PRINT RUN 999
316-350 JSY AU PRINT RUN 299-499
EXCH EXPIRATION: 4/17/2014
1 Brandon Lloyd .25 .60
2 Rob Gronkowski .40 1.00
3 Stevan Ridley .25 .60
4 Tom Brady 1.00 2.50
5 Wes Welker .30 .75
6 Darrelle Revis .25 .60
7 Mark Sanchez .25 .60
8 Santonio Holmes .25 .60
9 Shonn Greene .25 .60
10 Tim Tebow .40 1.00
11 Brian Hartline .30 .75
12 Cameron Wake .30 .75
13 Davone Bess .25 .60
14 Karlos Dansby .25 .60
15 Reggie Bush .25 .60
16 Fred Jackson .30 .75
17 Mario Williams .25 .60
18 Ryan Fitzpatrick .25 .60
19 Steve Johnson .30 .75
20 Anquan Boldin .25 .60
21 Ed Reed .30 .75
22 Joe Flacco .30 .75
23 Ray Lewis .40 1.00
24 Ray Rice .25 .60
25 Antonio Brown .40 1.00
26 Ben Roethlisberger .40 1.00
27 Mike Wallace .25 .60
28 Rashard Mendenhall .25 .60
29 A.J. Green .40 1.00
30 Andy Dalton .30 .75
31 BenJarvus Green-Ellis .30 .75
32 Jermaine Gresham .25 .60
33 Colt McCoy .30 .75
34 D'Qwell Jackson .25 .60
35 Greg Little .25 .60
36 Montario Hardesty .25 .60
37 Andre Johnson .30 .75
38 Arian Foster .30 .75
39 Matt Schaub .25 .60
40 Owen Daniels .25 .60
41 Chris Johnson .25 .60
42 Jared Cook .25 .60
43 Kenny Britt .25 .60
44 Nate Washington .25 .60
45 Blaine Gabbert .25 .60
46 Laurent Robinson .25 .60
47 Maurice Jones-Drew .25 .60
48 Mike Thomas .30 .75
49 Austin Collie .25 .60
50 Donald Brown .25 .60
51 Dwight Freeney .25 .60
52 Reggie Wayne .30 .75
53 Demaryius Thomas .40 1.00
54 Eric Decker .25 .60
55 Peyton Manning 1.25 3.00
56 Von Miller .30 .75
57 Willis McGahee .25 .60
58 Antonio Gates .30 .75
59 Malcom Floyd .25 .60
60 Philip Rivers .40 1.00
61 Ryan Mathews .30 .75
62 Carson Palmer .30 .75
63 Darren McFadden .25 .60
64 Darrius Heyward-Bey .25 .60
65 Jacoby Ford .25 .60
66 Dwayne Bowe .30 .75
67 Jamaal Charles .30 .75
68 Matt Cassel .25 .60
69 Steve Breaston .25 .60
70 Tamba Hali .25 .60
71 Ahmad Bradshaw .25 .60
72 Eli Manning .30 .75
73 Hakeem Nicks .25 .60
74 Jason Pierre-Paul .25 .60
75 Victor Cruz .30 .75
76 DeMeco Ryans .25 .60
77 DeSean Jackson .30 .75
78 Jeremy Maclin .25 .60
79 LeSean McCoy .40 1.00
80 Michael Vick .30 .75
81 DeMarco Murray .30 .75
82 Dez Bryant .40 1.00
83 Jason Witten .30 .75
84 Miles Austin .25 .60
85 Tony Romo .30 .75
86 DeAngelo Hall .25 .60
87 Fred Davis .25 .60
88 Jabar Gaffney .25 .60
89 Pierre Garcon .30 .75
90 Santana Moss .30 .75
91 Aaron Rodgers .60 1.50
92 Charles Woodson .40 1.00
93 Greg Jennings .25 .60
94 Jermichael Finley .25 .60
95 Jordy Nelson .30 .75
96 Brandon Pettigrew .25 .60
97 Calvin Johnson .40 1.00
98 Matthew Stafford .30 .75
99 Ndamukong Suh .30 .75
100 Stephen Tulloch .25 .60
101 Brandon Marshall .30 .75
102 Brian Urlacher .40 1.00
103 Devin Hester .30 .75
104 Jay Cutler .25 .60
105 Matt Forte .25 .60
106 Adrian Peterson .40 1.00
107 Chad Greenway .30 .75
108 Christian Ponder .25 .60
109 Jared Allen .25 .60
110 Percy Harvin .25 .60
111 Darren Sproles .30 .75
112 Drew Brees .40 1.00
113 Jimmy Graham .40 1.00
114 Mark Ingram .30 .75
115 Marques Colston .25 .60
116 Julio Jones .40 1.00
117 Matt Ryan .30 .75
118 Michael Turner .25 .60
119 Roddy White .25 .60
120 Tony Gonzalez .30 .75
121 Cam Newton .40 1.00
122 DeAngelo Williams .25 .60
123 James Anderson .25 .60
124 Jonathan Stewart .25 .60
125 Steve Smith .30 .75
126 Josh Freeman .30 .75
127 Kellen Winslow Jr. .25 .60
128 LeGarrette Blount .30 .75
129 Mike Williams .30 .75
130 Vincent Jackson .25 .60
131 Alex Smith .30 .75
132 Frank Gore .30 .75
133 Michael Crabtree .25 .60
134 Randy Moss .30 .75
135 Vernon Davis .25 .60
136 Beanie Wells .25 .60
137 Daryl Washington .25 .60
138 Kevin Kolb .25 .60
139 Larry Fitzgerald .30 .75
140 Patrick Peterson .25 .60
141 Doug Baldwin .40 1.00
142 Golden Tate .25 .60
143 Marshawn Lynch .30 .75
144 Matt Flynn .25 .60
145 Sidney Rice .25 .60
146 Cortland Finnegan .25 .60
147 James Laurinaitis .25 .60
148 Lance Kendricks .25 .60
149 Sam Bradford .25 .60
150 Steven Jackson .25 .60
151 Alan Page IMM 1.00 2.50
152 Andre Rison IMM 1.25 3.00
153 Art Monk IMM 1.50 4.00
154 Barry Sanders IMM 2.50 6.00
155 Bernie Kosar IMM 1.25 3.00
156 Bill Romanowski IMM 1.00 2.50
157 Bo Jackson IMM 2.00 5.00
158 Bobby Engram IMM 1.00 2.50
159 Boomer Esiason IMM 1.25 3.00
160 Bruce Matthews IMM 1.00 2.50
161 Bryant Young IMM 1.00 2.50
162 Christian Okoye IMM 1.25 3.00
163 Craig James IMM 1.00 2.50
164 Cris Carter IMM 1.50 4.00
165 Curtis Martin IMM 1.25 3.00
166 Dan Fouts IMM 1.25 3.00
167 Darren Woodson IMM 1.25 3.00
168 Daryle Lamonica IMM 1.00 2.50
169 Doug Flutie IMM 1.25 3.00
170 Drew Bledsoe IMM 1.25 3.00
171 Dwight Clark IMM 1.25 3.00
172 Ed McCaffrey IMM 1.00 2.50
173 Emmitt Smith IMM 2.50 6.00
174 Eric Dickerson IMM 1.25 3.00
175 Erik Williams IMM 1.00 2.50
176 Fred Taylor IMM 1.00 2.50
177 Fred Williamson IMM 1.00 2.50
178 Haywood Jeffires IMM 1.00 2.50
179 Henry Ellard IMM 1.00 2.50
180 Herman Moore IMM 1.00 2.50
181 Irving Fryar IMM 1.00 2.50
182 Jack Lambert IMM 1.50 4.00
183 Jamal Lewis IMM 1.00 2.50
184 James Lofton IMM 1.00 2.50
185 Jim Kelly IMM 1.50 4.00
186 Jim McMahon IMM 1.25 3.00
187 Jimmy Orr IMM 1.00 2.50
188 Joey Galloway IMM 1.00 2.50
189 John Riggins IMM 1.25 3.00
190 John Taylor IMM 1.25 3.00
191 Keith Jackson IMM 1.00 2.50
192 Lee Roy Jordan IMM 1.00 2.50
193 Mark Duper IMM 1.00 2.50
194 Mike Curtis IMM 1.00 2.50
195 Priest Holmes IMM 1.00 2.50
196 Rod Smith IMM 1.00 2.50
197 Sam Huff IMM 1.25 3.00
198 Shaun Alexander IMM 1.00 2.50
199 Steve Largent IMM 1.50 4.00
200 Willie Brown IMM 1.00 2.50
251 Alfred Morris RC .75 2.00
252 Andre Branch RC .75 2.00
253 B.J. Coleman RC .75 2.00
254 B.J. Cunningham RC .75 2.00
255 Bobby Wagner RC 1.25 3.00
256 Bruce Irvin RC 1.00 2.50
257 Case Keenum RC 1.50 4.00
258 Chandler Harnish RC .75 2.00
259 Chandler Jones RC .75 2.00
260 Chris Rainey RC .75 2.00
261 Courtney Upshaw RC 1.00 2.50
262 Cyrus Gray RC .75 2.00
263 Dan Herron RC .75 2.00
264 Danny Coale RC .75 2.00
265 David DeCastro RC .75 2.00
266 Devon Still RC 1.00 2.50
267 Devon Wylie RC .75 2.00
268 Dont'a Hightower RC 1.25 3.00
269 Dontari Poe RC .75 2.00
270 Dre Kirkpatrick RC .75 2.00
271 Fletcher Cox RC 1.25 3.00
272 George Iloka RC .75 2.00
273 Greg Childs RC .75 2.00
274 Harrison Smith RC .75 2.00
275 Janoris Jenkins RC 1.00 2.50
276 Jared Crick RC .75 2.00
277 Jonathan Martin RC .75 2.00
278 Juron Criner RC .75 2.00
279 Kellen Moore RC 1.00 2.50
280 Keshawn Martin RC 1.00 2.50
281 Kevin Zeitler RC .75 2.00
282 Kirk Cousins RC 3.00 8.00
283 Ladarius Green RC .75 2.00
284 LaVon Brazill RC 1.25 3.00
285 Lavonte David RC 1.25 3.00
286 Luke Kuechly RC 2.00 5.00
287 Mark Barron RC .75 2.00
288 Marquis Maze RC .75 2.00
289 Marvin Jones RC .75 2.00
290 Marvin McNutt RC .75 2.00
291 Matt Kalil RC .75 2.00
292 Melvin Ingram RC .75 2.00
293 Michael Brockers RC .75 2.00
294 Michael Smith RC 1.00 2.50
295 Morris Claiborne RC .75 2.00
296 Mychal Kendricks RC 1.25 3.00
297 Nick Perry RC 1.00 2.50
298 Orson Charles RC .75 2.00
299 Quinton Coples RC .75 2.00
300 Riley Reiff RC .75 2.00
301 Ronnell Lewis RC .75 2.00
302 Ryan Lindley RC .75 2.00
303 Shea McClellin RC 1.00 2.50
304 Stephon Gilmore RC 1.00 2.50
305 T.Y. Hilton RC 1.50 4.00
306 Terrance Ganaway RC 1.00 2.50
307 Tim Benford RC .75 2.00
308 Tommy Streeter RC .75 2.00
309 Travis Benjamin RC .75 2.00
310 Vick Ballard RC 1.00 2.50
311 Vinny Curry RC 1.00 2.50
312 Whitney Mercilus RC .75 2.00
313 Zach Brown RC .75 2.00
314 Eric Page RC 1.00 2.50
315 Vontaze Burfict RC 1.00 2.50
316 A.Luck JSY AU/299 RC 60.00 125.00
317 R.Griffin III JSY AU/299 RC 5.00 12.00
318 T.Richardson JSY AU/299 RC 4.00 10.00

319 J.Blackmon JSY AU/299 RC 4.00 10.00
320 R.Tannehill JSY AU/299 RC 6.00 15.00
321 M.Floyd JSY AU/399 RC 3.00 8.00
322 K. Wright JSY AU/399 RC 3.00 8.00
323 B.Weeden JSY AU/299 RC 4.00 10.00
324 A.Jenkins JSY AU/499 RC EXCH 3.00 8.00
325 Doug Martin JSY AU/399 RC 5.00 12.00
326 David Wilson JSY AU/499 RC 3.00 8.00
327 A.Jeffery JSY AU/499 RC 12.00 30.00
328 B.Pierce JSY AU/499 RC 3.00 8.00
329 Brian Quick JSY AU/499 RC 3.00 8.00
330 B.Osweiler JSY AU/399 RC 3.00 8.00
331 Coby Fleener JSY AU/499 RC 3.00 8.00
332 D.Posey JSY AU/499 RC 3.00 8.00
333 Dwayne Allen JSY AU/499 RC 3.00 8.00
334 Isaiah Pead JSY AU/499 RC 3.00 8.00
335 C.Givens JSY AU/499 RC 3.00 8.00
336 J.Adams JSY AU/499 RC 3.00 8.00
337 Lamar Miller JSY AU/399 RC 5.00 12.00
338 L.James JSY AU/499 RC 3.00 8.00
339 M.Egnew JSY AU/499 RC EXCH 3.00 8.00
340 M.Sanu JSY AU/499 RC EXCH 5.00 12.00
341 N.Foles JSY AU/499 RC 15.00 40.00
342 Nick Toon JSY AU/499 RC 3.00 8.00
343 Robert Turbin JSY AU/499 RC 3.00 8.00
344 R.Hillman JSY AU/499 RC 3.00 8.00
345 R.Randle JSY AU/499 RC 3.00 8.00
346 R. Wilson JSY AU/499 RC 40.00 80.00
347 Ryan Broyles JSY AU/499 RC 3.00 8.00
348 Stephen Hill JSY AU/499 RC 3.00 8.00
349 T.J. Graham JSY AU/499 RC 3.00 8.00
350 Jarius Wright JSY AU/499 RC 3.00 8.00

2012 Certified Mirror Blue

*VETS/100: 3X TO 8X BASIC CARDS
*LEGENDS/100: .8X TO 2X LEGEND/999
*ROOKIES/100: 1X TO 2.5X BASIC RC/999
*RK.JSY AU/49: .8X TO 2X JSY AU RC/399-499
*RK.JSY AU/49: .6X TO 1.5X JSY AU RC/299
STATED PRINT RUN 100 SER.#'d SETS
EXCH EXPIRATION: 4/17/2014
316 Andrew Luck JSY AU 100.00 200.00
346 Russell Wilson JSY AU 75.00 150.00

2012 Certified Mirror Gold

*VETS/25: 5X TO 12X BASIC CARDS
*LEGENDS/25: 1.2X TO 3X LEGEND/999
*ROOKIES/25: 1.5X TO 4X BASIC RC/999
*RK.JSY AU/25: 1.2X TO 3X JSY AU RC/399-499
*RK.JSY AU/25: 1X TO 2.5X JSY AU RC/299
STATED PRINT RUN 25 SER.#'d SETS
316 Andrew Luck JSY AU 150.00 300.00
346 Russell Wilson JSY AU 100.00 200.00

2012 Certified Mirror Red

*VETS/250: 2.5X TO 6X BASIC CARDS
*LEGENDS/250: .6X TO 1.5X LEGEND/999
*ROOKIES/250: .8X TO 2X BASIC RC/999
STATED PRINT RUN 250 SER.#'d SETS

2012 Certified Certified Rookie Materials

STATED PRINT RUN 299 SER.#'d SETS
*PRIME/49: .6X TO 1.5X BASIC JSY/299
1 Rueben Randle 1.50 4.00
2 Russell Wilson 10.00 25.00
3 Ryan Broyles 1.50 4.00
4 Stephen Hill 1.50 4.00
5 T.J. Graham 1.50 4.00
6 Ryan Tannehill 2.50 6.00
7 Jarius Wright 1.50 4.00
8 Dwayne Allen 1.50 4.00
9 DeVier Posey 1.50 4.00
10 Coby Fleener 1.50 4.00
11 Brock Osweiler 1.50 4.00
12 Brian Quick 1.50 4.00
13 Bernard Pierce 1.50 4.00
14 Alshon Jeffery 3.00 8.00
15 David Wilson 1.50 4.00
16 Doug Martin 2.50 6.00
17 A.J. Jenkins 1.50 4.00
18 Brandon Weeden 1.50 4.00
19 Kendall Wright 1.50 4.00
20 Michael Floyd 1.50 4.00
21 Ronnie Hillman 1.50 4.00
22 Robert Turbin 1.50 4.00
23 Nick Toon 1.50 4.00
24 Nick Foles 4.00 10.00
25 Mohamed Sanu 2.50 6.00
26 Michael Egnew 1.50 4.00
27 LaMichael James 1.50 4.00
28 Lamar Miller 2.50 6.00
29 Joe Adams 1.50 4.00
30 Chris Givens 1.50 4.00
31 Isaiah Pead 1.50 4.00
32 Andrew Luck 12.00 30.00
33 Robert Griffin III 2.00 5.00
34 Trent Richardson 1.50 4.00
35 Justin Blackmon 1.50 4.00

2012 Certified Certified Skills Materials

*SKILLS JSY/299: .4X TO 1X ROOKIE JSY/299
*PRIME/49: .6X TO 1.5X BASIC JSY/299

2012 Certified Elway Collection Materials

COMMON ELWAY/99 15.00 40.00

2012 Certified Essential Autographs

3 Deion Sanders/15 30.00 60.00
4 Franco Harris/15
6 Jerome Bettis/20 30.00 60.00
9 Marcus Allen/15
12 Ronnie Lott/20 20.00 40.00

2012 Certified Fabric of the Game

*PRIME/40-49: .6X TO 1.5X FOTG/99-199
*PRIME/25: .8X TO 2X FOTG/99-199
*PRIME/25: .6X TO 1.5X FOTG/49
*TEAM DC/15-25: .8X TO 2X FOTG/99-199
*TEAM DC/25: .6X TO 1.5X FOTG/48-49
*TEAM DC/25: .5X TO 1.2X FOTG/25
*PRIME TEAM DC/15: 1X TO 2.5X FOTG
1 Bart Starr/99 8.00 20.00
2 Brett Favre/99 8.00 20.00
3 Bob Griese/99 5.00 12.00
4 Brian Urlacher/99 5.00 12.00
5 Cris Collinsworth/199 4.00 10.00
6 Danny White/99 5.00 12.00
7 David Harris/25
8 Devery Henderson/99 2.50 6.00
9 Doug Flutie/199 4.00 10.00
10 Earl Campbell/13
11 Ed Too Tall Jones/199 4.00 10.00
12 Eli Manning/99 3.00 8.00
13 Felix Jones/199 2.50 6.00
14 Forrest Gregg/49 4.00 10.00
15 Fran Tarkenton/49 6.00 15.00
16 Fred Dryer/199 5.00 12.00
17 Haloti Ngata/199 3.00 8.00
18 Jay Cutler/199 2.50 6.00
19 Jerry Rice/99 8.00 20.00
20 Jim Otto/99 3.00 8.00
21 Jim Plunkett/399 4.00 10.00
22 Joe Flacco/99 3.00 8.00
23 Joe Montana/199 12.00 30.00
24 John Brodie/99 5.00 12.00
25 John Elway/199 8.00 20.00
26 John Hadl/99 4.00 10.00
27 John Randle/49 4.00 10.00
28 Junior Seau/199 4.00 10.00
29 Mark Sanchez/10
30 Matt Cassel/199 2.50 6.00
31 Matt Schaub/49 3.00 8.00
33 Miles Austin/199 2.50 6.00
34 Pierre Thomas/199 2.50 6.00
35 Randall Cunningham/199 4.00 10.00
36 Ronnie Lott/199 4.00 10.00
37 Sterling Sharpe/99 4.00 10.00
38 Tamba Hali/48 5.00 12.00
39 Tony Dorsett/199 5.00 12.00
40 Will Smith/199 2.50 6.00
41 Doug Williams/99 4.00 10.00
42 Mark Duper/199 3.00 8.00
43 Bernie Kosar/99 4.00 10.00
44 Amani Toomer/199 2.50 6.00
45 Tiki Barber/25 5.00 12.00
46 Priest Holmes/199 2.50 6.00
47 Jamal Lewis/49 3.00 8.00
48 Kurt Warner/199 3.00 8.00
49 Dan Fouts/199 4.00 10.00
50 Jim Kelly/199 5.00 12.00

2012 Certified Fabric of the Game Jersey Number Autographs Prime

11 Ed Too Tall Jones/25 15.00 40.00
13 Felix Jones/25 15.00 40.00
19 Jerry Rice/15 100.00 200.00
21 Jim Plunkett/25 20.00 50.00
34 Pierre Thomas/25 15.00 40.00
35 Randall Cunningham/25 20.00 50.00
37 Sterling Sharpe/25 20.00 50.00
42 Mark Duper/25 20.00 50.00
46 Priest Holmes/25 15.00 40.00

2012 Certified Gold Team Materials

*PRIME/49: .6X TO 1.5X BASIC JSY/99
*PRIME/20-25: .8X TO 2X BASIC JSY/99
1 Tom Brady/99 10.00 25.00
2 Maurice Jones-Drew/99 2.50 6.00
3 Ray Rice/99 2.50 6.00
4 Michael Turner/99 2.50 6.00
5 LeSean McCoy/49 5.00 12.00
6 Arian Foster/49 4.00 10.00
7 Frank Gore/99 3.00 8.00
8 Adrian Peterson/25 6.00 15.00
9 Steven Jackson/99 2.50 6.00
10 Drew Brees/99 4.00 10.00
11 Matthew Stafford/99 3.00 8.00
12 Eli Manning/99 3.00 8.00
14 Philip Rivers/49 5.00 12.00
15 Tony Romo/99 3.00 8.00
16 Matt Ryan/99 3.00 8.00
17 Joe Flacco/99 3.00 8.00
18 Michael Vick/25 5.00 12.00
20 Jay Cutler/99 2.50 6.00
21 Jonathan Stewart/25 4.00 10.00
23 Wes Welker/99 3.00 8.00
24 Larry Fitzgerald/49 4.00 10.00
25 Steve Smith/99 3.00 8.00
26 Roddy White/99 2.50 6.00
27 Hakeem Nicks/99 2.50 6.00
28 Dwayne Bowe/99 3.00 8.00

2012 Certified Mirror Blue Materials

*316-350 ROOKIES/49: .5X TO 1.2X RED/149
STATED PRINT RUN 1-99
1 Dez Bryant/15 6.00 15.00
4 Jermaine Gresham/15 4.00 10.00
5 Steve Johnson/15 5.00 12.00
8 Drew Brees/49 5.00 12.00
9 Zach Miller/99 2.50 6.00
10 Reggie Wayne/99 3.00 8.00
11 Michael Vick/99 3.00 8.00
12 Brian Urlacher/49 5.00 12.00
13 Ray Lewis/99 4.00 10.00
14 Devery Henderson/99 2.50 6.00
17 Charles Woodson/25 8.00 20.00
18 Tom Brady/99 10.00 25.00
19 Steve Smith/99 3.00 8.00
22 Brent Celek/25 4.00 10.00
23 Andre Johnson/25 5.00 12.00
24 Troy Polamalu/40 5.00 12.00
25 DeMarcus Ware/24 6.00 15.00
26 Anquan Boldin/49 3.00 8.00
27 Jason Witten/99 3.00 8.00
28 Tony Romo/99 3.00 8.00
30 Eli Manning/49 4.00 10.00
32 Philip Rivers/49 5.00 12.00
33 Steven Jackson/99 2.50 6.00
34 Michael Turner/49 3.00 8.00
35 Larry Fitzgerald/25 5.00 12.00
36 Matt Schaub/49 3.00 8.00
38 Wes Welker/75 4.00 10.00
39 Jared Allen/25 4.00 10.00
43 Frank Gore/49 4.00 10.00
44 Roddy White/99 2.50 6.00
45 Ryan Fitzpatrick/20 4.00 10.00
46 Matt Cassel/99 2.50 6.00
47 Maurice Jones-Drew/99 2.50 6.00
48 Jay Cutler/99 2.50 6.00
50 Mario Williams/99 2.50 6.00
52 London Fletcher/99 3.00 8.00
54 Tamba Hali/25 4.00 10.00
56 Devin Hester/49 4.00 10.00
57 Miles Austin/99 2.50 6.00
58 Owen Daniels/25 4.00 10.00
59 Marques Colston/99 2.50 6.00
61 Heath Miller/49 3.00 8.00
63 Dwayne Bowe/99 3.00 8.00
64 Darrelle Revis/25 4.00 10.00
67 Matt Ryan/99 3.00 8.00
72 Jamaal Charles/49 4.00 10.00
73 Ray Rice/99 2.50 6.00
74 Joe Flacco/49 4.00 10.00
76 Matthew Stafford/99 3.00 8.00
80 LeSean McCoy/25 6.00 15.00
81 Shonn Greene/99 2.50 6.00
82 Arian Foster/49 4.00 10.00
83 Michael Crabtree/25 4.00 10.00
84 Jeremy Maclin/49 3.00 8.00
85 Percy Harvin/99 2.50 6.00
86 Hakeem Nicks/49 3.00 8.00
93 Jerod Mayo/99 2.50 6.00
94 Lance Briggs/99 3.00 8.00
95 Patrick Willis/99 4.00 10.00
96 Pierre Thomas/99 2.50 6.00
97 Nnamdi Asomugha/49 3.00 8.00
98 Brandon Stokley/99 2.50 6.00
99 Cortland Finnegan/49 3.00 8.00
100 Chris Cooley/99 2.50 6.00
202 Yale Lary/19 5.00 12.00
203 Ken Stabler/99 5.00 12.00
204 Kurt Warner/99 4.00 10.00
206 Doug Williams/99 4.00 10.00
207 Warren Moon/99 5.00 12.00
208 Walter Payton/99 10.00 25.00
209 Marcus Allen/99 5.00 12.00
210 Troy Aikman/99 6.00 15.00
212 Rocket Ismail/75 5.00 12.00
214 Tommy McDonald/25 6.00 15.00
215 Paul Warfield/75 5.00 12.00
216 Merlin Olsen/99 4.00 10.00
217 Tiki Barber/99 4.00 10.00
219 Terry Bradshaw/99 6.00 15.00
220 Jimmy Smith/25 5.00 12.00
221 Ted Hendricks/99 4.00 10.00
222 Steve Young/99 6.00 15.00
223 Steve McNair/99 4.00 10.00
224 Keyshawn Johnson/49 5.00 12.00
225 Steve Bartkowski/20 6.00 15.00
226 Marshall Faulk/99 4.00 10.00
227 Sonny Jurgensen/25 8.00 20.00
230 Lance Alworth/49 6.00 15.00
231 Ronnie Lott/99 4.00 10.00
232 Mark Gastineau/25 5.00 12.00
233 Roger Staubach/99 6.00 15.00
235 Len Dawson/49 6.00 15.00
236 Raymond Berry/99 4.00 10.00
237 Ray Nitschke/40 6.00 15.00
238 Randy White/99 4.00 10.00
239 Randall Cunningham/99 4.00 10.00
241 Phil Simms/99 4.00 10.00
243 Paul Hornung/99 6.00 15.00
245 Warrick Dunn/20 5.00 12.00
247 Mike Singletary/15 8.00 20.00
248 Mike Ditka/99 5.00 12.00
249 Mike Alstott/99 3.00 8.00

2012 Certified Mirror Gold Materials

*316-350 ROOKIES/49: .6X TO 1.5X RED/149
STATED PRINT RUN 1-49
9 Zach Miller/25 6.00 15.00
13 Ray Lewis/35 8.00 20.00
14 Devery Henderson/49 4.00 10.00
16 Tony Gonzalez/49 5.00 12.00
27 Jason Witten/49 5.00 12.00
28 Tony Romo/49 5.00 12.00
30 Eli Manning/25 8.00 20.00
38 Wes Welker/49 5.00 12.00
44 Roddy White/15 6.00 15.00
47 Maurice Jones-Drew/25 6.00 15.00
52 London Fletcher/49 5.00 12.00
54 Tamba Hali/30 5.00 12.00
56 Devin Hester/25 8.00 20.00
57 Miles Austin/49 4.00 10.00
59 Marques Colston/49 4.00 10.00
63 Dwayne Bowe/25 8.00 20.00
71 Chris Johnson/49 4.00 10.00
72 Jamaal Charles/25 8.00 20.00
73 Ray Rice/30 5.00 12.00
75 Matt Forte/45 4.00 10.00
84 Jeremy Maclin/25 6.00 15.00
86 Hakeem Nicks/25 6.00 15.00
92 Ryan Mathews/49 5.00 12.00
96 Pierre Thomas /49 4.00 10.00
97 Nnamdi Asomugha/49 4.00 10.00
99 Cortland Finnegan/25 6.00 15.00
201 Mark Carrier/49 5.00 12.00
205 Wayne Chrebet/49 5.00 12.00
206 Doug Williams/49 6.00 15.00
208 Walter Payton/35 25.00 50.00
210 Troy Aikman/49 10.00 25.00
211 Amani Toomer/49 5.00 12.00
212 Rocket Ismail/49 6.00 15.00
213 Tony Dorsett/49 8.00 20.00
218 Thurman Thomas/49 6.00 15.00
220 Jimmy Smith/29 6.00 15.00
221 Ted Hendricks/49 6.00 15.00
223 Steve McNair/49 6.00 15.00
224 Keyshawn Johnson/49 6.00 15.00
225 Steve Bartkowski/49 6.00 15.00
226 Marshall Faulk/49 6.00 15.00
229 Shannon Sharpe/49 6.00 15.00
231 Ronnie Lott/49 6.00 15.00
233 Roger Staubach/19 20.00 50.00
234 Rickey Jackson/25 8.00 20.00
236 Raymond Berry/20 10.00 25.00
238 Randy White/49 6.00 15.00
239 Randall Cunningham/49 6.00 15.00
240 Larry Little/25 8.00 20.00
244 Ozzie Newsome/49 6.00 15.00
245 Warrick Dunn/49 5.00 12.00
246 Marvin Harrison/49 6.00 15.00
248 Mike Ditka/49 8.00 20.00
249 Mike Alstott/49 5.00 12.00

2012 Certified Mirror Red Materials

STATED PRINT RUN 2-199
3 Jacoby Ford/25 4.00 10.00
4 Jermaine Gresham/49 3.00 8.00
5 Steve Johnson/199 3.00 8.00
6 Andy Dalton/25 5.00 12.00
7 DeMarco Murray/25 5.00 12.00
8 Drew Brees/99 4.00 10.00
9 Zach Miller/199 2.50 6.00
10 Reggie Wayne/199 3.00 8.00
11 Michael Vick/199 3.00 8.00
12 Brian Urlacher/99 4.00 10.00
13 Ray Lewis/199 4.00 10.00
14 Devery Henderson/199 2.50 6.00
17 Charles Woodson/49 6.00 15.00
18 Tom Brady/199 10.00 25.00
19 Steve Smith/65 4.00 10.00
20 Dwight Freeney/49 3.00 8.00
22 Brent Celek/49 3.00 8.00
23 Andre Johnson/49 4.00 10.00
25 DeMarcus Ware/99 4.00 10.00
26 Anquan Boldin/99 2.50 6.00
27 Jason Witten/199 3.00 8.00
28 Tony Romo/199 3.00 8.00
30 Eli Manning/99 3.00 8.00
32 Philip Rivers/99 4.00 10.00
33 Steven Jackson/199 2.50 6.00
34 Michael Turner/149 2.50 6.00
35 Larry Fitzgerald/49 4.00 10.00
36 Matt Schaub/80 2.50 6.00
38 Wes Welker/115 3.00 8.00
39 Jared Allen/49 3.00 8.00
43 Frank Gore/99 3.00 8.00
45 Ryan Fitzpatrick/45 3.00 8.00
46 Matt Cassel/199 2.50 6.00
47 Maurice Jones-Drew/199 2.50 6.00
48 Jay Cutler/199 2.50 6.00
49 DeAngelo Williams/25 4.00 10.00
50 Mario Williams/199 2.50 6.00
52 London Fletcher/199 3.00 8.00
54 Tamba Hali/75 3.00 8.00
56 Devin Hester/99 3.00 8.00
57 Miles Austin/199 2.50 6.00
58 Owen Daniels/49 3.00 8.00
59 Marques Colston/199 2.50 6.00
60 Adrian Peterson/25 6.00 15.00
61 Heath Miller/99 2.50 6.00
63 Dwayne Bowe/199 3.00 8.00
64 Darrelle Revis/99 2.50 6.00
65 Ahmad Bradshaw/199 2.50 6.00
67 Matt Ryan/199 3.00 8.00
69 Jonathan Stewart/25 4.00 10.00
72 Jamaal Charles/99 3.00 8.00
73 Ray Rice/199 2.50 6.00
74 Joe Flacco/99 3.00 8.00
76 Matthew Stafford/199 3.00 8.00
78 Josh Freeman/25 5.00 12.00
80 LeSean McCoy/49 5.00 12.00
81 Shonn Greene/199 2.50 6.00
82 Arian Foster/99 3.00 8.00
83 Michael Crabtree/49 3.00 8.00
84 Jeremy Maclin/99 2.50 6.00
85 Percy Harvin/199 2.50 6.00
86 Hakeem Nicks/99 2.50 6.00
88 Mike Wallace/25 4.00 10.00
93 Jerod Mayo/199 2.50 6.00
94 Lance Briggs/199 3.00 8.00
95 Patrick Willis/99 4.00 10.00
96 Pierre Thomas/95 2.50 6.00
97 Nnamdi Asomugha/99 2.50 6.00
98 Brandon Stokley/199 2.50 6.00
99 Cortland Finnegan/99 2.50 6.00
100 Chris Cooley/199 2.50 6.00
203 Ken Stabler/199 5.00 12.00
204 Kurt Warner/199 4.00 10.00
206 Doug Williams/199 4.00 10.00
207 Warren Moon/199 5.00 12.00
208 Walter Payton/199 10.00 25.00
209 Marcus Allen/199 5.00 12.00
210 Troy Aikman/199 6.00 15.00
211 Amani Toomer/25 5.00 12.00
212 Rocket Ismail/199 4.00 10.00
213 Tony Dorsett/75 6.00 15.00
214 Tommy McDonald/80 4.00 10.00
216 Merlin Olsen/199 4.00 10.00
217 Tiki Barber/199 4.00 10.00
219 Terry Bradshaw/199 6.00 15.00
220 Jimmy Smith/75 4.00 10.00
221 Ted Hendricks/199 4.00 10.00
222 Steve Young/199 6.00 15.00
223 Steve McNair/199 4.00 10.00
224 Keyshawn Johnson/145 4.00 10.00
225 Steve Bartkowski/199 4.00 10.00
226 Marshall Faulk/199 4.00 10.00
227 Sonny Jurgensen/75 6.00 15.00
228 Sid Luckman/50 12.00 30.00
230 Lance Alworth/99 6.00 15.00
231 Ronnie Lott/199 4.00 10.00
232 Mark Gastineau/65 4.00 10.00
233 Roger Staubach/199 6.00 15.00
235 Len Dawson/149 5.00 12.00
236 Raymond Berry/199 4.00 10.00
237 Ray Nitschke/149 5.00 12.00
238 Randy White/199 4.00 10.00
239 Randall Cunningham/199 4.00 10.00
240 Larry Little/19 5.00 12.00
241 Phil Simms/199 4.00 10.00
242 Y.A. Tittle/20 8.00 20.00
243 Paul Hornung/199 6.00 15.00
244 Ozzie Newsome/50 5.00 12.00
248 Mike Ditka/199 5.00 12.00
249 Mike Alstott/199 3.00 8.00
250 Lenny Moore/15 5.00 12.00
316 Andrew Luck/149 15.00 40.00
317 Robert Griffin III/149 2.50 6.00
318 Trent Richardson/149 2.00 5.00
319 Justin Blackmon/149 2.00 5.00
320 Ryan Tannehill/149 3.00 8.00
321 Michael Floyd/149 2.00 5.00
322 Kendall Wright/149 2.00 5.00
323 Brandon Weeden/149 2.00 5.00
324 A.J. Jenkins/149 2.00 5.00
325 Doug Martin/149 3.00 8.00
326 David Wilson/140 2.00 5.00
327 Alshon Jeffery/149 4.00 10.00
328 Bernard Pierce/149 2.00 5.00
329 Brian Quick/149 2.00 5.00
330 Brock Osweiler/149 2.00 5.00
331 Coby Fleener/149 2.00 5.00
332 DeVier Posey/149 2.00 5.00
333 Dwayne Allen/149 2.00 5.00
334 Isaiah Pead/149 2.00 5.00
335 Chris Givens/149 2.00 5.00
336 Joe Adams/149 2.00 5.00
337 Lamar Miller/149 3.00 8.00
338 LaMichael James/149 2.00 5.00
339 Michael Egnew/149 2.00 5.00
340 Mohamed Sanu/149 3.00 8.00
341 Nick Foles/149 5.00 12.00
342 Nick Toon/149 2.00 5.00
343 Robert Turbin/149 2.00 5.00
344 Ronnie Hillman/149 2.00 5.00
345 Rueben Randle/149 2.00 5.00
346 Russell Wilson/149 12.00 30.00
347 Ryan Broyles/149 2.00 5.00
348 Stephen Hill/149 2.00 5.00
349 T.J. Graham/149 2.00 5.00
350 Jarius Wright/149 2.00 5.00

2012 Certified Mirror Blue Signatures

*250-315 ROOKIES/49: .6X TO 1.5X RED/250-350
STATED PRINT RUN
1 Brandon Lloyd/49 5.00 12.00
2 Rob Gronkowski/49 15.00 40.00
8 Santonio Holmes/49 5.00 12.00
11 Brian Hartline/49 6.00 15.00
15 Reggie Bush/49 8.00 20.00
16 Fred Jackson/49 15.00 30.00
17 Mario Williams/49 5.00 12.00
18 Ryan Fitzpatrick/49 5.00 12.00
19 Steve Johnson/49 6.00 15.00
20 Anquan Boldin/49 5.00 12.00
28 Rashard Mendenhall/49 5.00 12.00
29 A.J. Green/49 12.00 30.00
30 Andy Dalton/49 12.00 30.00
31 BenJarvus Green-Ellis/49 6.00 15.00
32 Jermaine Gresham/49 5.00 12.00
35 Greg Little/49 5.00 12.00
40 Owen Daniels/49 5.00 12.00
45 Blaine Gabbert/49 8.00 20.00
53 Demaryius Thomas/15 10.00 25.00
55 Peyton Manning/25 150.00 225.00
56 Von Miller/49 8.00 20.00
58 Antonio Gates/49 6.00 15.00
64 Darrius Heyward-Bey/49 5.00 12.00
65 Jacoby Ford/49 5.00 12.00
71 Ahmad Bradshaw/49 5.00 12.00
74 Jason Pierre-Paul/49 12.00 30.00
75 Victor Cruz/49 6.00 15.00
79 LeSean McCoy/49 8.00 20.00
83 Jason Witten/49 12.00 30.00
85 Tony Romo/49 20.00 50.00
87 Fred Davis/49 8.00 20.00
88 Jabar Gaffney/49 5.00 12.00
89 Pierre Garcon/49 6.00 15.00
95 Jordy Nelson/49 8.00 20.00
96 Brandon Pettigrew/49 5.00 12.00
98 Matthew Stafford/25 15.00 40.00
103 Devin Hester/49 6.00 15.00
108 Christian Ponder/49 5.00 12.00
109 Jared Allen/49 12.00 30.00
110 Percy Harvin/49 8.00 20.00
111 Darren Sproles/49 8.00 20.00
114 Mark Ingram/25 8.00 20.00
115 Marques Colston/25 6.00 15.00
117 Matt Ryan/49 25.00 50.00
118 Michael Turner/49 5.00 12.00
119 Roddy White/49 8.00 15.00
128 LeGarrette Blount/49 6.00 15.00
129 Mike Williams/49 6.00 15.00
130 Vincent Jackson/49 5.00 12.00
136 Beanie Wells/49 5.00 12.00
143 Marshawn Lynch/49 6.00 15.00
144 Matt Flynn/49 5.00 12.00
147 James Laurinaitis/49 8.00 20.00
148 Lance Kendricks/49 5.00 12.00
149 Sam Bradford/49 5.00 12.00
159 Boomer Esiason/49 12.00 30.00
168 Daryle Lamonica/49 6.00 15.00
169 Doug Flutie/49 12.00 30.00
175 Erik Williams/49 6.00 15.00
177 Fred Williamson/49 6.00 15.00
186 Jim McMahon/49 12.00 30.00
187 Jimmy Orr/49 6.00 15.00
192 Lee Roy Jordan/49 8.00 20.00
193 Mark Duper/49 8.00 20.00
194 Mike Curtis/49 6.00 15.00
197 Sam Huff/49 8.00 20.00
199 Steve Largent/37 15.00 40.00
200 Willie Brown/49 8.00 20.00

2012 Certified Mirror Gold Signatures

*250-315 ROOKIES/25: .8X TO 2X RED/250-350
STATED PRINT RUN 4-25
EXCH EXPIRATION: 4/17/2014
1 Brandon Lloyd/25 6.00 15.00
2 Rob Gronkowski/25 25.00 50.00
4 Tom Brady/25
8 Santonio Holmes/25 6.00 15.00
10 Tim Tebow/25 EXCH 25.00 60.00
11 Brian Hartline/25 8.00 20.00
15 Reggie Bush/25 10.00 25.00
16 Fred Jackson/25 20.00 40.00
17 Mario Williams/25 6.00 15.00
18 Ryan Fitzpatrick/25 6.00 15.00
19 Steve Johnson/25 8.00 20.00
20 Anquan Boldin/25 6.00 15.00
24 Ray Rice/21 6.00 15.00
28 Rashard Mendenhall/25 6.00 15.00
29 A.J. Green/25 12.00 30.00
30 Andy Dalton/25 15.00 40.00
31 BenJarvus Green-Ellis/25 8.00 20.00
32 Jermaine Gresham/25 6.00 15.00
35 Greg Little/25 6.00 15.00
40 Owen Daniels/25 6.00 15.00
45 Blaine Gabbert/25 10.00 25.00
56 Von Miller/25 10.00 25.00
58 Antonio Gates/25 8.00 20.00
64 Darrius Heyward-Bey/25 6.00 15.00
65 Jacoby Ford/25 6.00 15.00
71 Ahmad Bradshaw/25 6.00 15.00
74 Jason Pierre-Paul/25 15.00 40.00
75 Victor Cruz/25 8.00 20.00
79 LeSean McCoy/25 10.00 25.00
83 Jason Witten/25 25.00 50.00
85 Tony Romo/25 25.00 50.00
87 Fred Davis/25 10.00 25.00
88 Jabar Gaffney/25 6.00 15.00
89 Pierre Garcon/25 8.00 20.00
95 Jordy Nelson/25 10.00 25.00
96 Brandon Pettigrew/25 6.00 15.00
98 Matthew Stafford/25 15.00 40.00
103 Devin Hester/25 8.00 20.00
108 Christian Ponder/25 6.00 15.00
109 Jared Allen/25 15.00 40.00
110 Percy Harvin/25 10.00 25.00
111 Darren Sproles/25 10.00 25.00
115 Marques Colston/25 6.00 15.00
117 Matt Ryan/25 30.00 60.00
118 Michael Turner/25 6.00 15.00
119 Roddy White/25 10.00 25.00
121 Cam Newton/25 30.00 60.00
122 DeAngelo Williams/25 6.00 15.00
125 Steve Smith/25 8.00 20.00
128 LeGarrette Blount/25 8.00 20.00
129 Mike Williams/25 8.00 20.00
130 Vincent Jackson/25 6.00 15.00
131 Alex Smith/25 15.00 40.00
132 Frank Gore/25 8.00 20.00
136 Beanie Wells/25 6.00 15.00
143 Marshawn Lynch/25 8.00 20.00
144 Matt Flynn/25 6.00 15.00
147 James Laurinaitis/25 10.00 25.00
148 Lance Kendricks/25 6.00 15.00
149 Sam Bradford/25 15.00 40.00
151 Alan Page/25 8.00 20.00
157 Bo Jackson/25 40.00 80.00
159 Boomer Esiason/25 15.00 40.00
164 Cris Carter/25 12.00 30.00
165 Curtis Martin/25 15.00 40.00
168 Daryle Lamonica/25 8.00 20.00
169 Doug Flutie/25 15.00 40.00
174 Eric Dickerson/25 20.00 50.00
175 Erik Williams/25 8.00 20.00
177 Fred Williamson/25 8.00 20.00
182 Jack Lambert/25 25.00 50.00
184 James Lofton/25 8.00 20.00
186 Jim McMahon/25 15.00 40.00
187 Jimmy Orr/25 8.00 20.00
192 Lee Roy Jordan/25 10.00 25.00
193 Mark Duper/25 10.00 25.00
194 Mike Curtis/25 8.00 20.00
195 Priest Holmes/25 12.00 30.00
197 Sam Huff/25 10.00 25.00
199 Steve Largent/25 20.00 50.00
200 Willie Brown/25 10.00 25.00
251 Alfred Morris/25 5.00 12.00

2012 Certified Mirror Red Signatures

STATED PRINT RUN 250-350
251 Alfred Morris/350 2.50 6.00
252 Andre Branch/250 2.50 6.00
253 B.J. Coleman/250 2.50 6.00
254 B.J. Cunningham/350 2.50 6.00
255 Bobby Wagner/350 4.00 10.00
256 Bruce Irvin/350 3.00 8.00
257 Case Keenum/250 5.00 12.00
258 Chandler Harnish/350 2.50 6.00
259 Chandler Jones/250 EXCH 2.50 6.00
260 Chris Rainey/250 2.50 6.00
261 Courtney Upshaw/350 3.00 8.00
262 Cyrus Gray/350 2.50 6.00
263 Dan Herron/250 EXCH 2.50 6.00
264 Danny Coale/350 2.50 6.00
265 David DeCastro/350 2.50 6.00
266 Devon Still/350 3.00 8.00
267 Devon Wylie/350 2.50 6.00
268 Dont'a Hightower/250 4.00 10.00
269 Dontari Poe/250 2.50 6.00
270 Dre Kirkpatrick/250 2.50 6.00
271 Fletcher Cox/350 4.00 10.00
272 George Iloka/250 2.50 6.00
273 Greg Childs/350 2.50 6.00
274 Harrison Smith/350 5.00 12.00
275 Janoris Jenkins/250 3.00 8.00
276 Jared Crick/250 EXCH 2.50 6.00
277 Jonathan Martin/250 2.50 6.00
278 Juron Criner/350 2.50 6.00
279 Kellen Moore/350 3.00 8.00
280 Keshawn Martin/350 3.00 8.00
281 Kevin Zeitler/350 2.50 6.00
282 Kirk Cousins/350 10.00 25.00
283 Ladarius Green/350 2.50 6.00
284 LaVon Brazill/350 4.00 10.00
285 Lavonte David/250 4.00 10.00
286 Luke Kuechly/250 6.00 15.00
287 Mark Barron/350 2.50 6.00
288 Marquis Maze/350 2.50 6.00
289 Marvin Jones/350 2.50 6.00
290 Marvin McNutt/250 2.50 6.00
291 Matt Kalil/250 EXCH 2.50 6.00
292 Melvin Ingram/250 EXCH 2.50 6.00
293 Michael Brockers/250 EXCH 2.50 6.00
294 Michael Smith/250 EXCH 3.00 8.00
295 Morris Claiborne/250 2.50 6.00
296 Mychal Kendricks/250 4.00 10.00
297 Nick Perry/250 3.00 8.00
298 Orson Charles/350 2.50 6.00
299 Quinton Coples/250 2.50 6.00
300 Riley Reiff/250 2.50 6.00
301 Ronnell Lewis/350 2.50 6.00
302 Ryan Lindley/350 2.50 6.00
303 Shea McClellin/350 3.00 8.00
304 Stephon Gilmore/350 3.00 8.00
305 T.Y. Hilton/250 5.00 12.00
306 Terrance Ganaway/250 3.00 8.00
307 Tim Benford/350 2.50 6.00
308 Tommy Streeter/250 2.50 6.00
309 Travis Benjamin/350 2.50 6.00
310 Vick Ballard/250 3.00 8.00
311 Vinny Curry/350 3.00 8.00
312 Whitney Mercilus/250 2.50 6.00
313 Zach Brown/350 2.50 6.00
314 Eric Page/350 3.00 8.00
315 Vontaze Burfict/250 3.00 8.00

2012 Certified Rookie Fabric of the Game

*FOTG/199: .4X TO 1X ROOKIE JSY/299
STATED PRINT RUN 199 SER.#'d SETS
*PRIME FOTG/49: .6X TO 1.5X ROOKIE JSY/299
*TEAM DC FOTG/49: .5X TO 1.2X ROOK.JSY/299
*TEAM DC PRIME/25: .8X TO 2X ROOK.JSY/299

2012 Certified Rookie Fabric of the Game Team Die Cut Autographs

STATED PRINT RUN 25 SER.#'d SETS
*PRIME/15: .5X TO 1.2X JSY AU/25
1 Andrew Luck 150.00 250.00
2 Robert Griffin III 10.00 25.00
3 Trent Richardson 8.00 20.00
4 Justin Blackmon 8.00 20.00
5 Ryan Tannehill 12.00 30.00
6 Michael Floyd 8.00 20.00
7 Kendall Wright 8.00 20.00
8 Brandon Weeden 8.00 20.00
9 A.J. Jenkins 8.00 20.00
10 Doug Martin 12.00 30.00
11 David Wilson 8.00 20.00
12 Alshon Jeffery 25.00 60.00
13 Bernard Pierce 8.00 20.00
14 Brian Quick 8.00 20.00
15 Brock Osweiler 8.00 20.00
16 Coby Fleener 8.00 20.00
17 DeVier Posey 8.00 20.00
18 Dwayne Allen 8.00 20.00
19 Isaiah Pead 8.00 20.00
20 Chris Givens 8.00 20.00
21 Joe Adams 8.00 20.00
22 Lamar Miller 12.00 30.00
23 LaMichael James 8.00 20.00
24 Michael Egnew 8.00 20.00
25 Mohamed Sanu 12.00 30.00
26 Nick Foles 20.00 50.00
27 Nick Toon 8.00 20.00
28 Robert Turbin 8.00 20.00
29 Ronnie Hillman EXCH 8.00 20.00
30 Rueben Randle 8.00 20.00
31 Russell Wilson 100.00 200.00
32 Ryan Broyles 8.00 20.00
33 Stephen Hill 8.00 20.00
34 T.J. Graham 8.00 20.00
35 Jarius Wright 8.00 20.00

2012 Certified Rookie Fabric of the Game Combos

STATED PRINT RUN 149 SER.#'d SETS
*PRIME/49: .6X TO 1.5X BASIC COMBO/149
1 A.Luck/B.Weeden 10.00 25.00
2 R.Tannehill/R.Wilson 8.00 20.00
3 B.Osweiler/R.Griffin III 2.00 5.00
4 T.Richardson/I.Pead 1.50 4.00
5 D.Wilson/D.Martin 2.50 6.00
6 L.James/R.Hillman 1.50 4.00
7 J.Blackmon/A.Jenkins 1.50 4.00
8 K.Wright/M.Floyd 1.50 4.00
9 B.Quick/R.Broyles 3.00 8.00
10 A.Jeffery/S.Hill 3.00 8.00

2013 Certified

201 300 ROOKIE PRINT RUN 999
301-340 ROOK.JSY AU PRINT RUN 399-499
1 Joe Flacco .30 .75
2 Torrey Smith .25 .60
3 Jacoby Jones .25 .60
4 Ray Rice .25 .60
5 Terrell Suggs .25 .60
6 Andy Dalton .30 .75
7 A.J. Green .40 1.00
8 BenJarvus Green-Ellis .30 .75
9 Jermaine Gresham .30 .75
10 Brandon Weeden .25 .60
11 Josh Gordon .25 .60
12 Greg Little .25 .60
13 Trent Richardson .25 .60
14 Ben Roethlisberger .40 1.00
15 Antonio Brown .40 1.00
16 Plaxico Burress .25 .60
17 Jonathan Dwyer .25 .60
18 Troy Polamalu .40 1.00
19 Matt Schaub .25 .60
20 Andre Johnson .25 .60
21 Arian Foster .30 .75
22 Owen Daniels .25 .60
23 J.J. Watt .30 .75
24 Andrew Luck .60 1.50
25 Reggie Wayne .30 .75
26 T.Y. Hilton .30 .75
27 Vick Ballard .25 .60
28 Dwayne Allen .25 .60
29 Blaine Gabbert .25 .60
30 Cecil Shorts .25 .60
31 Justin Blackmon .25 .60
32 Maurice Jones-Drew .25 .60
33 Marcedes Lewis .25 .60
34 Jake Locker .30 .75
35 Kenny Britt .25 .60
36 Kendall Wright .25 .60
37 Chris Johnson .25 .60
38 Steve Johnson .30 .75
39 C.J. Spiller .25 .60
40 Fred Jackson .30 .75
41 Scott Chandler .25 .60
42 Ryan Tannehill .30 .75
43 Mike Wallace .25 .60
44 Brian Hartline .25 .60
45 Daniel Thomas .25 .60
46 Dustin Keller .25 .60
47 Tom Brady 1.00 2.50
48 Danny Amendola .30 .75
49 Stevan Ridley .25 .60
50 Rob Gronkowski .40 1.00
51 Tim Tebow .30 .75
52 Mark Sanchez .25 .60
53 Santonio Holmes .25 .60
54 Jeremy Kerley .25 .60
55 Bilal Powell .25 .60
56 Peyton Manning .75 2.00
57 Demaryius Thomas .30 .75
58 Wes Welker .30 .75
59 Eric Decker .25 .60
60 Von Miller .30 .75
61 Alex Smith .30 .75
62 Dwayne Bowe .30 .75
63 Jonathan Baldwin .25 .60
64 Jamaal Charles .30 .75
65 Eric Berry .30 .75
66 Matt Flynn .25 .60
67 Denarius Moore .25 .60
68 Jacoby Ford .25 .60
69 Darren McFadden .30 .75
70 Philip Rivers .40 1.00
71 Robert Meachem .25 .60
72 Malcom Floyd .25 .60
73 Ryan Mathews .30 .75
74 Antonio Gates .30 .75
75 Jay Cutler .25 .60
76 Brandon Marshall .30 .75
77 Matt Forte .25 .60
78 Lance Briggs .30 .75
79 Matthew Stafford .30 .75
80 Calvin Johnson .40 1.00
81 Reggie Bush .25 .60
82 Mikel Leshoure .25 .60
83 Brandon Pettigrew .25 .60
84 Aaron Rodgers .60 1.50
85 Jordy Nelson .30 .75
86 Randall Cobb .30 .75
87 Clay Matthews .40 1.00
88 Christian Ponder .25 .60
89 Greg Jennings .25 .60
90 Adrian Peterson .40 1.00
91 Kyle Rudolph .25 .60
92 Matt Ryan .30 .75
93 Julio Jones .40 1.00
94 Roddy White .25 .60
95 Steven Jackson .25 .60
96 Tony Gonzalez .30 .75
97 Cam Newton .40 1.00
98 Steve Smith .30 .75
99 Brandon LaFell .25 .60
100 Jonathan Stewart .25 .60
101 Luke Kuechly .30 .75
102 Drew Brees .40 1.00
103 Marques Colston .25 .60
104 Darren Sproles .30 .75
105 Mark Ingram .30 .75
106 Jimmy Graham .40 1.00
107 Josh Freeman .30 .75
108 Vincent Jackson .25 .60
109 Mike Williams .30 .75
110 Doug Martin .30 .75
111 Tony Romo .30 .75
112 Dez Bryant .40 1.00
113 Miles Austin .25 .60
114 DeMarco Murray .30 .75
115 Jason Witten .30 .75
116 Eli Manning .30 .75
117 Hakeem Nicks .25 .60
118 Victor Cruz .30 .75
119 Andre Brown .30 .75
120 David Wilson .25 .60
121 Michael Vick .30 .75
122 DeSean Jackson .30 .75
123 Jeremy Maclin .25 .60
124 LeSean McCoy .40 1.00
125 Brent Celek .25 .60
126 Robert Griffin III .25 .60
127 Pierre Garcon .30 .75
128 Santana Moss .30 .75
129 Alfred Morris .25 .60
130 Brian Orakpo .30 .75
131 Carson Palmer .30 .75
132 Larry Fitzgerald .30 .75
133 Michael Floyd .25 .60
134 Rashard Mendenhall .25 .60
135 Patrick Peterson .25 .60
136 Colin Kaepernick .30 .75
137 Michael Crabtree .25 .60
138 Anquan Boldin .25 .60
139 Frank Gore .30 .75
140 Vernon Davis .25 .60
141 Russell Wilson .75 2.00
142 Percy Harvin .25 .60
143 Sidney Rice .25 .60
144 Marshawn Lynch .30 .75
145 Richard Sherman .40 1.00
146 Sam Bradford .25 .60
147 Chris Givens .25 .60
148 Isaiah Pead .25 .60
149 Daryl Richardson .25 .60
150 Jared Cook .25 .60
151 Andre Rison IMM 1.00 2.50
152 Art Monk IMM 1.25 3.00
153 Barry Sanders IMM 3.00 8.00
154 Bart Starr IMM 2.00 5.00
155 Bernie Kosar IMM 1.00 2.50
156 Bo Jackson IMM 1.50 4.00
157 Boomer Esiason IMM 1.00 2.50
158 Brett Favre IMM 2.50 6.00
159 Bruce Smith IMM 1.00 2.50
160 Cris Carter IMM 1.25 3.00
161 Dan Fouts IMM 1.00 2.50
162 Dan Marino IMM 2.50 6.00
163 Deion Sanders IMM 1.00 2.50
164 Dick Butkus IMM 1.50 4.00
165 Doug Flutie IMM 1.00 2.50
166 Doug Williams IMM 1.00 2.50
167 Drew Bledsoe IMM 1.00 2.50
168 Earl Campbell IMM 1.25 3.00
169 Eddie George IMM 1.00 2.50
170 Emmitt Smith IMM 2.00 5.00
171 Eric Dickerson IMM 1.00 2.50
172 Fred Taylor IMM .75 2.00
173 Gale Sayers IMM 1.25 3.00
174 Jay Novacek IMM 1.00 2.50
175 Jerome Bettis IMM 1.25 3.00
176 Jerry Rice IMM 2.00 5.00
177 Jamal Lewis IMM .75 2.00
178 Jim Brown IMM 1.50 4.00
179 Jim McMahon IMM 1.00 2.50
180 Joe Montana IMM 6.00 15.00
181 Joe Namath IMM 1.50 4.00
182 John Elway IMM 2.00 5.00
183 Ken Stabler IMM 1.25 3.00
184 Kurt Warner IMM 1.00 2.50
185 LaDainian Tomlinson IMM 1.00 2.50
186 Lance Alworth IMM 1.00 2.50
187 Larry Csonka IMM 1.25 3.00
188 Marcus Allen IMM 1.25 3.00
189 Marshall Faulk IMM 1.00 2.50
190 Michael Irvin IMM 1.25 3.00
191 Phil Simms IMM 1.00 2.50
192 Shannon Sharpe IMM 1.00 2.50
193 Steve Young IMM 1.50 4.00
194 Terry Bradshaw IMM 2.00 5.00
195 Tim Brown IMM 1.25 3.00
196 Tony Dorsett IMM 1.25 3.00
197 Terrell Davis IMM 1.00 2.50
198 Troy Aikman IMM 1.50 4.00
199 Walter Payton IMM 2.50 6.00
200 Warren Moon IMM 1.25 3.00
201 Aaron Dobson RC .60 1.50
202 Aaron Mellette RC .60 1.50
203 Ace Sanders RC .60 1.50
204 Alec Ogletree RC .60 1.50
205 Alex Okafor RC .60 1.50
206 Andre Ellington RC .60 1.50
207 Arthur Brown RC .60 1.50
208 Barkevious Mingo RC .60 1.50
209 Bjoern Werner RC .60 1.50
210 Chance Warmack RC .60 1.50
211 Chris Gragg RC .60 1.50
212 Chris Harper RC .60 1.50
213 Christine Michael RC .60 1.50
214 Blidi Wreh-Wilson RC .75 2.00
215 Conner Vernon RC .60 1.50
216 Cordarrelle Patterson RC .60 1.50
217 Corey Fuller RC .60 1.50
218 D.J. Hayden RC .60 1.50
219 Damontre Moore RC .60 1.50
220 Da'Rick Rogers RC .60 1.50
221 Robert Alford RC .60 1.50
222 Datone Jones RC .60 1.50
223 DeAndre Hopkins RC 1.50 4.00
224 Dee Milliner RC .60 1.50
225 Denard Robinson RC .60 1.50
226 Desmond Trufant RC .60 1.50
227 Dion Jordan RC .60 1.50
228 Dion Sims RC .60 1.50
229 Eddie Lacy RC .60 1.50
230 EJ Manuel RC .60 1.50
231 Eric Fisher RC .60 1.50
232 Eric Reid RC .75 2.00
233 Ezekiel Ansah RC .60 1.50
234 Gavin Escobar RC .60 1.50
235 Geno Smith RC .60 1.50
236 Giovani Bernard RC .60 1.50
237 Jamar Taylor RC .60 1.50
238 Jarvis Jones RC .60 1.50
239 Cornellius Carradine RC .60 1.50
240 Johnathan Cyprien RC .60 1.50
241 Johnathan Franklin RC .60 1.50
242 Jasper Collins RC .60 1.50
243 Johnthan Banks RC .60 1.50
244 Jordan Poyer RC .60 1.50
245 Jordan Reed RC 1.00 2.50
246 Joseph Randle RC .60 1.50
247 Josh Boyce RC .60 1.50
248 Justin Hunter RC .60 1.50
249 Keenan Allen RC 1.25 3.00
250 Kenjon Barner RC .60 1.50
251 Kenny Stills RC .60 1.50
252 Kenny Vaccaro RC .60 1.50
253 Kevin Minter RC .60 1.50
254 Knile Davis RC .60 1.50
255 Landry Jones RC .60 1.50
256 Le'Veon Bell RC 2.00 5.00
257 Dennis Johnson RC .60 1.50
258 D.J. Fluker RC .60 1.50
259 Manti Te'o RC .75 2.00
260 Marcus Davis RC .60 1.50
261 Marcus Lattimore RC .60 1.50
262 Margus Hunt RC .60 1.50
263 Markus Wheaton RC .60 1.50
264 Marquess Wilson RC 1.00 2.50
265 Marquise Goodwin RC .60 1.50
266 Matt Barkley RC .60 1.50
267 Matt Elam RC .60 1.50
268 Brad Sorensen RC .60 1.50
269 Mike Gillislee RC .60 1.50
270 Mike Glennon RC .60 1.50
271 Montee Ball RC .60 1.50
272 Nick Kasa RC .60 1.50
273 Phillip Thomas RC .60 1.50
274 Quinton Patton RC .60 1.50
275 Rex Burkhead RC .75 2.00
276 Robert Woods RC 1.00 2.50
277 Rodney Smith RC .60 1.50
278 Ryan Nassib RC .60 1.50
279 Ryan Otten RC .60 1.50
280 Ryan Swope RC .60 1.50
281 Sam Montgomery RC .60 1.50
282 Dustin Hopkins RC .60 1.50
283 Mychal Rivera RC .60 1.50
284 Kerwynn Williams RC .60 1.50
285 Chris Thompson RC .60 1.50
286 Stedman Bailey RC .60 1.50
287 Stepfan Taylor RC .60 1.50
288 Tavarres King RC .60 1.50
289 Tavon Austin RC .75 2.00
290 Terrance Williams RC .60 1.50
291 Theo Riddick RC .60 1.50
292 Travis Kelce RC 1.50 4.00

293 Tyler Bray RC .60 1.50
294 Tyler Eifert RC .60 1.50
295 Tyler Wilson RC .60 1.50
296 Tyrann Mathieu RC 1.00 2.50
297 Vance McDonald RC .75 2.00
298 Xavier Rhodes RC .60 1.50
299 Zac Dysert RC .60 1.50
300 Zach Ertz RC 1.25 3.00
301 Aaron Dobson JSY AU/399 2.50 6.00
302 Andre Ellington JSY AU/499 2.50 6.00
303 Christine Michael JSY AU/499 2.50 6.00
304 C.Patterson JSY AU/399 2.50 6.00
305 DeAndre Hopkins JSY AU/499 8.00 20.00
306 Denard Robinson JSY AU/399 2.50 6.00
307 Dion Jordan JSY AU/399 2.50 6.00
308 Eddie Lacy JSY AU/399 2.50 6.00
309 EJ Manuel JSY AU/399 2.50 6.00
310 Gavin Escobar JSY AU/399 2.50 6.00
311 Geno Smith JSY AU/399 2.50 6.00
312 Giovani Bernard JSY AU/499 2.50 6.00
313 J.Franklin JSY AU/499 2.50 6.00
314 Jordan Reed JSY AU/399 4.00 10.00
315 Joseph Randle JSY AU/499 2.50 6.00
316 Justin Hunter JSY AU/399 2.50 6.00
317 Keenan Allen JSY AU/499 5.00 12.00
318 Kenny Stills JSY AU/399 2.50 6.00
319 Knile Davis JSY AU/399 2.50 6.00
320 Landry Jones JSY AU/499 2.50 6.00
321 Le'Veon Bell JSY AU/499 12.00 30.00
322 Manti Te'o JSY AU/399 3.00 8.00
323 Marcus Lattimore JSY AU/499 2.50 6.00
324 M.Wheaton JSY AU/499 2.50 6.00
325 M.Goodwin JSY AU/399 2.50 6.00
326 Matt Barkley JSY AU/399 2.50 6.00
327 Mike Gillislee JSY AU/399 2.50 6.00
328 Mike Glennon JSY AU/499 2.50 6.00
329 Montee Ball JSY AU/499 2.50 6.00
330 Quinton Patton JSY AU/499 2.50 6.00
331 Robert Woods JSY AU/399 4.00 10.00
332 Ryan Nassib JSY AU/399 2.50 6.00
333 Stedman Bailey JSY AU/399 2.50 6.00
334 Stepfan Taylor JSY AU/499 2.50 6.00
335 Tavon Austin JSY AU/399 3.00 8.00
336 T.Williams JSY AU/499 2.50 6.00
337 Tyler Eifert JSY AU/399 2.50 6.00
338 Tyler Wilson JSY AU/499 2.50 6.00
339 V.McDonald JSY AU/399 3.00 8.00
340 Zach Ertz JSY AU/499 5.00 12.00

2013 Certified Mirror Blue

*1-150 VETS/100: 2.5X TO 6X BASIC CARDS
*151-200 IMM/100: .8X TO 2X BASIC IMM/999
*201-300 ROOK/100: 1X TO 2.5X BASIC RC/999
*301-340 RK JSY AU/100: .6X TO 1.5X

2013 Certified Mirror Blue Signatures

*GOLD ROOK/25: .6X TO 1.5X BLUE AU/100
*GOLD ROOK/25: .5X TO 1.2X BLUE AU/49
10 Brandon Weeden/25 6.00 15.00
26 T.Y. Hilton/25 8.00 20.00
28 Dwayne Allen/25 6.00 15.00
30 Cecil Shorts/25 6.00 15.00
31 Justin Blackmon/25 6.00 15.00
35 Kenny Britt/25 6.00 15.00
46 Dustin Keller/25 6.00 15.00
54 Jeremy Kerley/25 6.00 15.00
69 Darren McFadden/25 8.00 20.00
83 Brandon Pettigrew/25 6.00 15.00
86 Randall Cobb/25 8.00 20.00
91 Kyle Rudolph/25 6.00 15.00
101 Luke Kuechly/25 8.00 20.00
107 Josh Freeman/25 8.00 20.00
110 Doug Martin/25 8.00 20.00
120 David Wilson/25 6.00 15.00
123 Jeremy Maclin/25 6.00 15.00
133 Michael Floyd/25 6.00 15.00
135 Patrick Peterson/25 10.00 25.00
137 Michael Crabtree/25 6.00 15.00
139 Frank Gore/25 8.00 20.00
143 Sidney Rice/25 6.00 15.00
147 Chris Givens/25 6.00 15.00
149 Daryl Richardson/25 6.00 15.00
150 Jared Cook/25 6.00 15.00
151 Andre Rison/25 8.00 20.00
201 Aaron Dobson/25 5.00 12.00
203 Ace Sanders/100 3.00 8.00
206 Andre Ellington/25 5.00 12.00
207 Arthur Brown/100 3.00 8.00
208 Barkevious Mingo/100 3.00 8.00
209 Bjoern Werner/100 3.00 8.00
210 Chance Warmack/100 3.00 8.00
211 Chris Gragg/100 3.00 8.00
212 Chris Harper/100 3.00 8.00
213 Christine Michael/25 5.00 12.00
214 Blidi Wreh-Wilson/100 4.00 10.00
215 Conner Vernon/100 3.00 8.00
216 Cordarrelle Patterson/25 5.00 12.00
217 Corey Fuller/100 3.00 8.00
218 D.J. Hayden/100 6.00 15.00
219 Damontre Moore/100 3.00 8.00
220 Da'Rick Rogers/100 3.00 8.00
221 Robert Alford/100 3.00 8.00
222 Datone Jones/100 3.00 8.00
223 DeAndre Hopkins/25 12.00 30.00
226 Desmond Trufant/100 3.00 8.00
227 Dion Jordan/25 5.00 12.00
229 Eddie Lacy/25 5.00 12.00
231 Eric Fisher/100 3.00 8.00
234 Gavin Escobar/25 5.00 12.00
235 Geno Smith/25 5.00 12.00
236 Giovani Bernard/25 5.00 12.00
237 Jamar Taylor/100 3.00 8.00
238 Jarvis Jones/100 3.00 8.00
239 Cornellius Carradine/100 3.00 8.00
240 Johnathan Cyprien/100 3.00 8.00
241 Johnathan Franklin/25 5.00 12.00
242 Jasper Collins/100 3.00 8.00
243 Johnthan Banks/100 3.00 8.00
244 Jordan Poyer/100 3.00 8.00
245 Jordan Reed/25 8.00 20.00
246 Joseph Randle/25 5.00 12.00
247 Josh Boyce/100 3.00 8.00
249 Keenan Allen/25 10.00 25.00
250 Kenjon Barner/100 3.00 8.00
251 Kenny Stills/25 5.00 12.00
254 Knile Davis/25 5.00 12.00
255 Landry Jones/25 5.00 12.00
256 Le'Veon Bell/25 15.00 40.00
257 Dennis Johnson/100 3.00 8.00
258 D.J. Fluker/100 3.00 8.00
259 Manti Te'o/25 6.00 15.00
260 Marcus Davis/100 3.00 8.00
261 Marcus Lattimore/25 5.00 12.00
262 Margus Hunt/100 3.00 8.00
263 Markus Wheaton/25 5.00 12.00
264 Marquess Wilson/100 5.00 12.00
265 Marquise Goodwin/25 5.00 12.00
266 Matt Barkley/25 5.00 12.00
267 Matt Elam/100 3.00 8.00
268 Brad Sorensen/100 3.00 8.00
270 Mike Glennon/25 5.00 12.00
271 Montee Ball/25 5.00 12.00
273 Phillip Thomas/100 3.00 8.00
274 Quinton Patton/25 5.00 12.00
275 Rex Burkhead/100 4.00 10.00
277 Rodney Smith/100 3.00 8.00
279 Ryan Otten/100 3.00 8.00
280 Ryan Swope/100 3.00 8.00
281 Sam Montgomery/100 3.00 8.00
282 Dustin Hopkins/100 3.00 8.00
283 Mychal Rivera/100 3.00 8.00
284 Kerwynn Williams/100 3.00 8.00
285 Chris Thompson/100 3.00 8.00
287 Steptan Taylor/25 5.00 12.00
288 Tavarres King/100 3.00 8.00
289 Tavon Austin/25 6.00 15.00
290 Terrance Williams/25 5.00 12.00
291 Theo Riddick/100 3.00 8.00
293 Tyler Bray/100 3.00 8.00
294 Tyler Eifert/25 5.00 12.00
295 Tyler Wilson/25 5.00 12.00
296 Tyrann Mathieu/49 6.00 15.00
297 Vance McDonald/25 6.00 15.00
298 Xavier Rhodes/100 3.00 8.00
299 Zac Dysert/100 3.00 8.00
300 Zach Ertz/25 10.00 25.00

2013 Certified Mirror Gold

*1-150 VETS/25: 3X TO 8X BASIC CARDS
*151-200 IMM/25: 1X TO 2.5X BASIC IMM/999
*201-300 ROOK/25: 1.2X TO 3X BASIC RC/999
*301-340 RK JSY AU/25: 1X TO 2.5X

2013 Certified Mirror Red

*1-150 VETS/250: 1.5X TO 4X BASIC CARDS
*151-200 IMM/250: .5X TO 1.2X BASIC IMM/999
*201-300 ROOK/250: .6X TO 1.5X BASIC RC/999
*301-340 RK JSY AU/199-250: .5X TO 1.2X

2013 Certified Mirror Red Materials

*BLUE/99: .4X TO 1X RED/99-299
*BLUE/49: .5X TO 1.2X RED/99-199
*BLUE/25: .6X TO 1.5X RED/99
*BLUE/25: .5X TO 1.2X RED/49
*BLUE ROOKIE/49: .5X TO 1.2X RED/149
*GOLD/49: .5X TO 1.2X RED/99-299
*GOLD/20-25: .6X TO 1.5X RED/99-199
*GOLD/20: .5X TO 1.2X RED/49
*GOLD ROOKIE/25: .6X TO 1.5X RED/149
1 Adrian Peterson/99 4.00 10.00
2 A.J. Green/99 4.00 10.00
3 Alfred Morris/199 2.50 6.00
4 Andy Dalton/99 3.00 8.00
5 Antonio Gates/99 3.00 8.00
6 Arian Foster/99 3.00 8.00
7 BenJarvus Green-Ellis/199 3.00 8.00
8 Brandon Marshall/49 4.00 10.00
9 Brandon Weeden/299 2.50 6.00
10 Brent Celek/199 2.50 6.00
11 Brian Hartline/299 2.50 6.00
12 Christian Ponder/199 2.50 6.00
13 C.J. Spiller/299 2.50 6.00
14 Darren McFadden/299 3.00 8.00
15 Darren Sproles/199 3.00 8.00
16 DeMarco Murray/199 3.00 8.00
17 DeMarcus Ware/299 4.00 10.00
18 Demaryius Thomas/199 3.00 8.00
20 Derrick Johnson/299 2.50 6.00
21 DeSean Jackson/299 3.00 8.00
22 Dexter McCluster/199 3.00 8.00
23 Dez Bryant/99 4.00 10.00
24 D'Qwell Jackson/299 2.50 6.00
25 Drew Brees/99 4.00 10.00
26 Dwayne Bowe/299 3.00 8.00
27 Eli Manning/99 3.00 8.00
28 Eric Berry/299 3.00 8.00
29 Eric Decker/199 2.50 6.00
30 Fred Davis/199 2.50 6.00
31 Fred Jackson/299 3.00 8.00
32 Golden Tate/199 2.50 6.00
33 Greg Little/299 2.50 6.00
34 Greg Olsen/99 3.00 8.00
35 Hakeem Nicks/99 2.50 6.00
36 Haloti Ngata/299 2.50 6.00
37 Jacob Tamme/299 2.50 6.00
38 Jamaal Charles/199 3.00 8.00
39 Jason Witten/199 3.00 8.00
40 Jay Cutler/99 2.50 6.00
41 Jeremy Kerley/199 2.50 6.00
42 Jeremy Maclin/199 2.50 6.00
43 Jermaine Gresham/299 3.00 8.00
44 Jimmy Graham/99 4.00 10.00
45 Joe Flacco/199 3.00 8.00
46 Joe Haden/299 2.50 6.00
47 Jonathan Baldwin/299 2.50 6.00
48 Jonathan Stewart/199 2.50 6.00
49 Josh Freeman/99 3.00 8.00
50 Josh Gordon/199 2.50 6.00
51 Julio Jones/99 4.00 10.00
52 Julius Peppers/199 3.00 8.00
53 Justin Blackmon/199 2.50 6.00
54 Kenny Britt/299 2.50 6.00
55 Knowshon Moreno/299 2.50 6.00
56 Kyle Rudolph/99 2.50 6.00
57 Lance Briggs/299 3.00 8.00
58 Larry Fitzgerald/99 3.00 8.00
59 Leonard Hankerson/299 2.50 6.00
60 LeSean McCoy/199 4.00 10.00
61 Malcom Floyd/199 2.50 6.00
62 Marcedes Lewis/199 2.50 6.00
63 Marques Colston/199 2.50 6.00
64 Matt Forte/199 2.50 6.00
65 Matt Ryan/199 3.00 8.00
66 Matt Schaub/99 2.50 6.00
67 Matthew Stafford/99 3.00 8.00
68 Maurice Jones-Drew/99 2.50 6.00
70 Michael Vick/99 3.00 8.00
71 Miles Austin/199 2.50 6.00
72 Peyton Manning/199 15.00 40.00
73 Philip Rivers/199 4.00 10.00
74 Ray Rice/199 2.50 6.00
75 Reggie Wayne/99 4.00 10.00
76 Robert Griffin III/99 2.50 6.00
77 Robert Meachem/199 2.50 6.00
78 Roddy White/199 2.50 6.00
79 Ronnie Hillman/199 2.50 6.00
80 Ryan Kerrigan/299 2.50 6.00
81 Ryan Mathews/199 3.00 8.00
82 Ryan Tannehill/199 3.00 8.00
83 Sam Bradford/299 2.50 6.00
84 Santana Moss/199 3.00 8.00
85 Santonio Holmes/199 2.50 6.00
86 Sean Lee/99 3.00 8.00
87 Sidney Rice/199 2.50 6.00
88 Steve Johnson/199 3.00 8.00
89 Steve Smith/99 3.00 8.00
90 Tamba Hali/199 2.50 6.00
91 Terrell Suggs/199 2.50 6.00
92 Tom Brady/199 10.00 25.00
93 Tony Gonzalez/49 4.00 10.00
94 Tony Romo/199 3.00 8.00
95 Torrey Smith/99 2.50 6.00
96 Trent Richardson/99 2.50 6.00
97 Vernon Davis/99 2.50 6.00
98 Vincent Jackson/99 2.50 6.00
99 Von Miller/199 3.00 8.00
100 Chris Johnson/99 2.50 6.00
301 Aaron Dobson 1.50 4.00
302 Andre Ellington 1.50 4.00
303 Christine Michael 1.50 4.00
304 Cordarrelle Patterson 1.50 4.00
305 DeAndre Hopkins 4.00 10.00
306 Denard Robinson 1.50 4.00
307 Dion Jordan 1.50 4.00
308 Eddie Lacy 1.50 4.00
309 EJ Manuel 1.50 4.00
310 Gavin Escobar 1.50 4.00
311 Geno Smith 1.50 4.00
312 Giovani Bernard 1.50 4.00
313 Johnathan Franklin 1.50 4.00
314 Jordan Reed 2.50 6.00
315 Joseph Randle 1.50 4.00
316 Justin Hunter 1.50 4.00
317 Keenan Allen 3.00 8.00
318 Kenny Stills 1.50 4.00
319 Knile Davis 1.50 4.00
320 Landry Jones 1.50 4.00
321 Le'Veon Bell 5.00 12.00
322 Manti Te'o 2.00 5.00
323 Marcus Lattimore 1.50 4.00
324 Markus Wheaton 1.50 4.00
325 Marquise Goodwin 1.50 4.00
326 Matt Barkley 1.50 4.00
327 Mike Gillislee 1.50 4.00
328 Mike Glennon 1.50 4.00
329 Montee Ball 1.50 4.00
330 Quinton Patton 1.50 4.00
331 Robert Woods 2.50 6.00
332 Ryan Nassib 1.50 4.00
333 Stedman Bailey 1.50 4.00
334 Stepfan Taylor 1.50 4.00
335 Tavon Austin 2.00 5.00
336 Terrance Williams 1.50 4.00
337 Tyler Eifert 1.50 4.00
338 Tyler Wilson 1.50 4.00
339 Vance McDonald 2.00 5.00
340 Zach Ertz 3.00 8.00

2013 Certified Mirror Red Signatures

*RED/799-999: .2X TO .5X BLUE AU/49
*RED/299-499: .25X TO .6X BLUE AU/49
*RED/99: .3X TO .8X BLUE AU/49
*RED/49: .3X TO .8X BLUE AU/25
230 EJ Manuel/49 4.00 10.00
235 Geno Smith/49 4.00 10.00
252 Kenny Vaccaro/299 2.50 6.00
276 Robert Woods/49 6.00 15.00

2013 Certified Emmitt Smith Collection Materials

COMMON EMMITT/25 20.00 50.00

2013 Certified Fabric of the Game Team Die Cut

*PRIME/49: .8X TO 2X BASIC JSY/99
*PRIME/41-49: .6X TO 1.5X BASIC JSY/49
1 Amani Toomer/99 3.00 8.00
3 Bill Romanowski/99 6.00 15.00
4 Ted Hendricks/49 6.00 15.00
5 Dan Marino/49 15.00 40.00
6 Marvin Harrison/99 4.00 10.00
7 Marshall Faulk/49 6.00 15.00
8 Shaun Alexander/99 3.00 8.00
9 Cris Collinsworth/99 5.00 12.00
11 Jim Kelly/99 5.00 12.00
12 LaDainian Tomlinson/49 5.00 12.00
13 Jerry Rice/49 15.00 40.00
14 Jim McMahon/49 5.00 12.00
15 Joe Namath/49 12.00 30.00
16 John Elway/49 10.00 25.00
17 Kurt Warner/49 12.00 30.00
18 Mike Singletary/49 6.00 15.00
19 Ronnie Lott/49 10.00 25.00
20 Steve Largent/49 6.00 15.00

2013 Certified Platinum Blue

*1-150 VETS/100: 2.5X TO 6X BASIC CARDS
*151-200 IMM/100: .8X TO 2X BASIC IMM/999
*201-300 ROOK/100: 1X TO 2.5X BASIC RC/999

2013 Certified Platinum Gold

*1-150 VETS/25: 3X TO 8X BASIC CARDS
*151-200 IMM/25: 1X TO 2.5X BASIC IMM/999
*201-300 ROOK/25: 1.2X TO 3X BASIC RC/999

2013 Certified Platinum Red

*1-150 VETS: 1.2X TO 3X BASIC CARDS
*151-200 IMM: .4X TO 1X BASIC IMM/999
*201-300 ROOK: .5X TO 1.2X BASIC RC/999

2013 Certified Potential Materials

1 Aaron Dobson 1.25 3.00
2 Andre Ellington 1.25 3.00
3 Christine Michael 1.25 3.00
4 Cordarrelle Patterson 1.25 3.00
5 DeAndre Hopkins 3.00 8.00
6 Denard Robinson 1.25 3.00
7 Eddie Lacy 1.25 3.00
8 EJ Manuel 3.00 8.00
9 Gavin Escobar 1.25 3.00
10 Geno Smith 1.25 3.00
11 Giovani Bernard 1.25 3.00
12 Johnathan Franklin 1.25 3.00
13 Jordan Reed 2.00 5.00
14 Joseph Randle 1.25 3.00
15 Justin Hunter 1.25 3.00
16 Keenan Allen 2.50 6.00
17 Kenny Stills 1.25 3.00
18 Knile Davis 1.25 3.00
19 Landry Jones 1.25 3.00
20 Le'Veon Bell 4.00 10.00
21 Manti Te'o 1.50 4.00
22 Marcus Lattimore 1.25 3.00
23 Markus Wheaton 1.25 3.00
24 Marquise Goodwin 1.25 3.00
25 Matt Barkley 1.25 3.00
26 Mike Gillislee 2.00 5.00
27 Mike Glennon 1.25 3.00
28 Montee Ball 1.25 3.00
29 Quinton Patton 1.25 3.00
30 Robert Woods 2.00 5.00
31 Ryan Nassib 1.25 3.00
32 Stedman Bailey 1.25 3.00
33 Steptan Taylor 2.00 5.00
34 Tavon Austin 1.50 4.00
35 Terrance Williams 1.25 3.00
36 Dion Jordan 1.25 3.00
37 Tyler Eifert 1.25 3.00
38 Tyler Wilson 1.50 4.00
39 Vance McDonald 1.50 4.00
40 Zach Ertz 2.50 6.00

2013 Certified Rookie Fabric of the Game Team Die Cut

*PRIME/49: .6X TO 1.5X BASIC JSY/99
1 Aaron Dobson 2.00 5.00
2 Andre Ellington 2.00 5.00
3 Christine Michael 2.00 5.00
4 Cordarrelle Patterson 2.00 5.00
5 DeAndre Hopkins 5.00 12.00
6 Denard Robinson 2.00 5.00
7 Eddie Lacy 2.00 5.00
8 EJ Manuel 5.00 12.00
9 Gavin Escobar 2.00 5.00
10 Geno Smith 2.00 5.00
11 Giovani Bernard 2.00 5.00
12 Johnathan Franklin 2.00 5.00
13 Jordan Reed 3.00 8.00
14 Joseph Randle 2.00 5.00
15 Justin Hunter 2.00 5.00
16 Keenan Allen 4.00 10.00
17 Kenny Stills 2.00 5.00
18 Knile Davis 2.00 5.00
19 Landry Jones 1.50 4.00
20 Le'Veon Bell 6.00 15.00
21 Manti Te'o 2.50 6.00
22 Marcus Lattimore 2.00 5.00
23 Markus Wheaton 2.00 5.00
24 Marquise Goodwin 2.00 5.00
25 Matt Barkley 2.00 5.00
26 Mike Gillislee 3.00 8.00
27 Mike Glennon 2.00 5.00
28 Montee Ball 2.00 5.00
29 Quinton Patton 2.00 5.00
30 Robert Woods 3.00 8.00
31 Ryan Nassib 2.00 5.00
32 Stedman Bailey 2.00 5.00
33 Steptan Taylor 3.00 8.00
34 Tavon Austin 2.50 6.00
35 Terrance Williams 2.00 5.00
36 Dion Jordan 2.00 5.00
37 Tyler Eifert 2.00 5.00
38 Tyler Wilson 2.00 5.00
39 Vance McDonald 2.50 6.00
40 Zach Ertz 4.00 10.00

2013 Certified Rookie Fabric of the Game Team Die Cut Autographs

*PRIME/15: .5X TO 1.2X BASIC AU/25
1 Aaron Dobson 8.00 20.00
2 Andre Ellington 8.00 20.00
3 Christine Michael 8.00 20.00
4 Cordarrelle Patterson 8.00 20.00
5 DeAndre Hopkins 30.00 60.00
7 Eddie Lacy 8.00 20.00
8 EJ Manuel 30.00 80.00
9 Gavin Escobar 8.00 20.00
10 Geno Smith 8.00 20.00
11 Giovani Bernard 8.00 20.00
12 Johnathan Franklin 8.00 20.00
13 Jordan Reed 12.00 30.00
14 Joseph Randle 8.00 20.00
16 Keenan Allen 15.00 40.00
17 Kenny Stills 8.00 20.00
18 Knile Davis 8.00 20.00
19 Landry Jones 8.00 20.00
20 Le'Veon Bell 25.00 60.00
21 Manti Te'o 10.00 25.00
22 Marcus Lattimore 8.00 20.00
23 Markus Wheaton 8.00 20.00
24 Marquise Goodwin 8.00 20.00
25 Matt Barkley 8.00 20.00
27 Mike Glennon 8.00 20.00
28 Montee Ball 8.00 20.00
29 Quinton Patton 8.00 20.00
30 Robert Woods 12.00 30.00
33 Steptan Taylor 8.00 20.00
34 Tavon Austin 10.00 25.00
35 Terrance Williams 8.00 20.00
36 Dion Jordan 8.00 20.00
37 Tyler Eifert 8.00 20.00
38 Tyler Wilson 8.00 20.00
39 Vance McDonald 10.00 25.00
40 Zach Ertz 15.00 40.00

2013 Certified Skills Materials

*PRIME/49: .8X TO 2X BASIC JSY/99-299
*PRIME/49: .6X TO 1.5X BASIC JSY/49
*PRIME/25: 1X TO 2.5X BASIC JSY/99-299
*PRIME/25: .8X TO 2X BASIC JSY/49
1 A.J. Green/199 4.00 10.00
2 Alfred Morris/299 2.50 6.00
3 Andrew Luck/299 6.00 15.00
4 Antonio Gates/99 3.00 8.00
5 Arian Foster/49 4.00 10.00
6 Brandon Marshall/25
7 Christian Ponder/299 2.50 6.00
8 C.J. Spiller/299 2.50 6.00
9 Darren McFadden/299 3.00 8.00
10 Darren Sproles/99 3.00 8.00
11 DeMarco Murray/99 3.00 8.00
12 Demaryius Thomas/299 3.00 8.00
13 Colin Kaepernick/299 3.00 8.00
14 DeSean Jackson/299 3.00 8.00
15 Dez Bryant/49 5.00 12.00
16 Drew Brees/99 4.00 10.00
17 Dwayne Bowe/299 3.00 8.00
18 Eli Manning/299 3.00 8.00
19 Eric Decker/99 2.50 6.00
20 Hakeem Nicks/99 2.50 6.00
21 Jamaal Charles/299 3.00 8.00
22 Jeremy Maclin/299 2.50 6.00
23 Jimmy Graham/49 5.00 12.00
24 Joe Flacco/299 3.00 8.00
25 Julio Jones/99 4.00 10.00
26 Larry Fitzgerald/99 3.00 8.00
27 LeSean McCoy/299 4.00 10.00
28 Marques Colston/299 2.50 6.00
29 Matt Forte/299 2.50 6.00
30 Matt Ryan/299 3.00 8.00
31 Matthew Stafford/49 4.00 10.00
33 Michael Vick/299 3.00 8.00
34 Peyton Manning/299 20.00 50.00
35 Ray Rice/299 2.50 6.00
36 Robert Griffin III/299 2.50 6.00
37 Sidney Rice/99 2.50 6.00
38 Tony Romo/299 3.00 8.00
39 Torrey Smith/99 2.50 6.00
40 Trent Richardson/299 2.50 6.00

2014 Certified

101-175 ROOKIE PRINT RUN 999
176-200 IMMORTAL PRINT RUN 999
301-340 ROOK.JSY AU PRINT RUN 199-699
1 Carson Palmer .30 .75
2 Larry Fitzgerald .30 .75
3 Andre Ellington .25 .60
4 Patrick Peterson .25 .60
5 Matt Ryan .30 .75
6 Julio Jones .40 1.00
7 Steven Jackson .25 .60
8 Joe Flacco .30 .75
9 Steve Smith .30 .75
10 Bernard Pierce .25 .60
11 EJ Manuel .25 .60
12 Steve Johnson .30 .75
13 C.J. Spiller .25 .60
14 Cam Newton .40 1.00
15 DeAngelo Williams .25 .60
16 Luke Kuechly .30 .75
17 Jay Cutler .25 .60
18 Brandon Marshall .30 .75
19 Alshon Jeffery .30 .75
20 Andy Dalton .30 .75
21 A.J. Green .40 1.00
22 Giovani Bernard .25 .60
23 Brian Hoyer .25 .60
24 Josh Gordon .25 .60
25 Ben Tate .25 .60
26 Tony Romo .30 .75
27 Dez Bryant .40 1.00
28 DeMarco Murray .30 .75
29 Peyton Manning .75 2.00
30 Demaryius Thomas .30 .75
31 Montee Ball .25 .60
32 DeMarcus Ware .30 .75
33 Matthew Stafford .30 .75
34 Calvin Johnson .40 1.00
35 Reggie Bush .25 .60
36 Aaron Rodgers .75 2.00
37 Jordy Nelson .30 .75
38 Eddie Lacy .25 .60
39 Arian Foster .30 .75
40 Andre Johnson .30 .75
41 J.J. Watt .40 1.00
42 Andrew Luck .50 1.25
43 Hakeem Nicks .25 .60
44 Trent Richardson .25 .60
45 Justin Blackmon .25 .60
46 Ace Sanders .25 .60
47 Toby Gerhart .25 .60
48 Alex Smith .30 .75
49 Dwayne Bowe .30 .75
50 Jamaal Charles .30 .75
51 Ryan Tannehill .30 .75
52 Mike Wallace .25 .60
53 Knowshon Moreno .25 .60
54 Cordarrelle Patterson .25 .60
55 Greg Jennings .25 .60
56 Adrian Peterson .40 1.00
57 Tom Brady 1.00 2.50
58 Rob Gronkowski .40 1.00
59 Darrelle Revis .25 .60
60 Drew Brees .40 1.00
61 Jimmy Graham .40 1.00
62 Jairus Byrd .25 .60
63 Eli Manning .30 .75
64 Victor Cruz .30 .75
65 Rashad Jennings .25 .60
66 Geno Smith .25 .60
67 Michael Vick .30 .75
68 Eric Decker .25 .60
69 Matt Schaub .25 .60
70 Darren McFadden .25 .60
71 Maurice Jones-Drew .25 .60
72 Nick Foles .30 .75
73 Jeremy Maclin .25 .60
74 LeSean McCoy .40 1.00
75 Ben Roethlisberger .40 1.00
76 Antonio Brown .40 1.00
77 Le'Veon Bell .30 .75
78 Philip Rivers .40 1.00
79 Keenan Allen .30 .75
80 Ryan Mathews .30 .75
81 Colin Kaepernick .30 .75
82 Michael Crabtree .25 .60
83 Anquan Boldin .25 .60
84 Aldon Smith .25 .60
85 Russell Wilson .60 1.50
86 Percy Harvin .25 .60
87 Marshawn Lynch .30 .75
88 Richard Sherman .40 1.00
89 Sam Bradford .25 .60
90 Tavon Austin .25 .60
91 Zac Stacy .25 .60
92 Josh McCown .25 .60
93 Vincent Jackson .25 .60
94 Doug Martin .30 .75
95 Jake Locker .30 .75
96 Dexter McCluster .30 .75
97 Kendall Wright .25 .60
98 Robert Griffin III .25 .60
99 DeSean Jackson .30 .75
100 Alfred Morris .25 .60
101 Aaron Donald RC 1.50 4.00
102 Aaron Murray RC .60 1.50
103 Anthony Barr RC .60 1.50
104 Bradley Roby RC .60 1.50
105 Brandon Coleman RC .60 1.50
106 Brett Smith RC .60 1.50
107 Bruce Ellington RC .60 1.50
108 C.J. Fiedorowicz RC .60 1.50
109 C.J. Mosley RC .75 2.00
110 Calvin Pryor RC .60 1.50
111 Chris Borland RC .60 1.50
112 Chris Smith RC .60 1.50
113 Crockett Gillmore RC .75 2.00
114 Cyril Richardson RC .60 1.50
115 Cyrus Kouandjio RC .75 2.00
116 Darqueze Dennard RC .75 2.00
117 David Fales RC .60 1.50
118 Dee Ford RC .60 1.50
119 DeMarcus Lawrence RC .75 2.00
120 Devin Street RC .60 1.50
121 Deone Bucannon RC .60 1.50
122 Dominique Easley RC .60 1.50
123 Ego Ferguson RC .60 1.50
124 Greg Robinson RC .60 1.50
125 Ha Ha Clinton-Dix RC .75 2.00
126 Jace Amaro RC .60 1.50
127 Jackson Jeffcoat RC .75 2.00
128 Jake Matthews RC .60 1.50
129 Jalen Saunders RC .60 1.50
130 James White RC 1.25 3.00
131 James Wilder Jr. RC .75 2.00
132 Jared Abbrederis RC .60 1.50
133 Jason Verrett RC .60 1.50
134 Jerick McKinnon RC .75 2.00
135 Jimmie Ward RC .75 2.00
136 John Brown RC 1.00 2.50
137 Josh Huff RC .75 2.00
138 Justin Gilbert RC .60 1.50
139 Kony Ealy RC .75 2.00
140 Kyle Fuller RC .60 1.50
141 Kyle Van Noy RC .75 2.00
142 L'Damian Washington RC .75 2.00
143 Lache Seastrunk RC .60 1.50
144 Lamarcus Joyner I RC .75 2.00
145 Lorenzo Taliaferro RC .60 1.50
146 Louis Nix III RC .60 1.50
147 Marcus Roberson RC .75 2.00
148 Marcus Smith RC .60 1.50
149 Marion Grice RC .60 1.50
150 Martavis Bryant RC .75 2.00
151 Michael Campanaro RC .60 1.50
152 Michael Sam RC .60 1.50
153 Mike Davis RC .60 1.50
154 Pierre Desir RC .60 1.50
155 Ra'Shede Hageman RC .60 1.50
156 Richard Rodgers RC 1.00 2.50
157 Ryan Shazier RC 1.00 2.50
158 Scott Crichton RC .60 1.50
159 Shaq Evans RC .60 1.50
160 Shayne Skov RC .60 1.50
161 Stephon Tuitt RC 1.00 2.50
162 Storm Johnson RC .60 1.50
163 Taylor Lewan RC .60 1.50
164 Telvin Smith RC .60 1.50
165 Tevin Reese RC .60 1.50
166 Timmy Jernigan RC .60 1.50
167 Travis Swanson RC .60 1.50
168 Trent Murphy RC .60 1.50
169 Trevor Reilly RC .60 1.50
170 Troy Niklas RC .60 1.50
171 Tyler Gaffney RC .60 1.50
172 Xavier Su'A-Filo RC .75 2.00
173 Yawin Smallwood RC .60 1.50
174 Zach Mettenberger RC .60 1.50
175 Zack Martin RC .75 2.00
176 Barry Sanders IMM 2.00 5.00
177 Bo Jackson IMM 1.50 4.00
178 Bob Griese IMM 1.25 3.00
179 Brett Favre IMM 2.50 6.00
180 Dave Casper IMM .75 2.00
181 Deion Sanders IMM 1.00 2.50
182 Earl Campbell IMM 1.25 3.00
183 Emmitt Smith IMM 2.00 5.00
184 Eric Dickerson IMM 1.00 2.50
185 Fran Tarkenton IMM 1.25 3.00
186 Franco Harris IMM 1.25 3.00
187 Gale Sayers IMM 1.25 3.00
188 Jerome Bettis IMM 1.25 3.00
189 Jerry Rice IMM 2.00 5.00
190 John Elway IMM 2.00 5.00
191 Kurt Warner IMM 1.00 2.50
192 Lance Alworth IMM 1.00 2.50
193 Marcus Allen IMM 1.25 3.00
194 Marshall Faulk IMM 1.00 2.50
195 Michael Irvin IMM 1.25 3.00
196 Paul Warfield IMM 1.00 2.50
197 Roger Staubach IMM 1.50 4.00
198 Steve Young IMM 1.50 4.00
199 Terry Bradshaw IMM 1.50 4.00
200 Tim Brown IMM 1.25 3.00
201 Aaron Murray JSY AU/699 RC 3.00 8.00
202 A.J. McCarron JSY AU/199 RC 5.00 12.00
203 Allen Robinson JSY AU/699 RC 5.00 12.00
204 Andre Williams JSY AU/699 RC 3.00 8.00
205 Asa Watson JSY AU/699 RC 3.00 8.00
206 A.Seferian-Jenkins JSY AU/699 RC 3.00 8.00
207 Bishop Sankey JSY AU/699 RC 3.00 8.00
208 Blake Bortles JSY AU/199 RC 6.00 15.00
211 Charles Sims JSY AU/699 RC 3.00 8.00
212 Cody Latimer JSY AU/699 RC 6.00 15.00
213 Connor Shaw JSY AU/699 RC 3.00 8.00
215 D.Thomas JSY AU/699 RC 3.00 8.00
216 Derek Carr JSY AU/199 RC 50.00 100.00
218 Donte Moncrief JSY AU/699 RC 3.00 8.00
220 Eric Ebron JSY AU/699 RC 4.00 10.00
221 Jadeveon Clowney JSY AU/199 RC 6.00 15.00
222 Jarvis Landry JSY AU/699 RC 8.00 20.00
224 Jimmy Garoppolo JSY AU/199 RC 50.00 100.00
225 Johnny Manziel JSY AU/199 RC 15.00 40.00
226 Jordan Matthews JSY AU/699 RC 5.00 12.00
227 Ka'Deem Carey JSY AU/699 RC 6.00 15.00
228 Kelvin Benjamin JSY AU/699 RC 5.00 12.00
229 Khalil Mack JSY AU/699 RC 25.00 50.00
230 Logan Thomas JSY AU/699 RC 3.00 8.00
231 Marqise Lee JSY AU/699 RC 4.00 10.00
232 Mike Evans JSY AU/199 RC 12.00 30.00
235 Sammy Watkins JSY AU/199 RC 8.00 20.00
237 Teddy Bridgewater JSY AU/199 RC 8.00 20.00
238 Terrance West JSY AU/699 RC 3.00 8.00
239 Tom Savage JSY AU/699 RC 3.00 8.00

2014 Certified Blue

*1-100 VETS/99 2.5X TO 6X BASIC CARDS
*101-175 ROOK/99: 1X TO 2.5X BASIC RC/999
*176-200 IMM/99: .8X TO 2X BASIC IMM/999
1-200 STATED PRINT RUN 99 SER.#'d SETS
*201-239 RK JSY AU/25-99: .6X TO 1.5X JSY AU/199-699
*201-239 RK JSY AU/25: 1X TO 2.5X JSY AU/699
201-239 STATED PRINT RUN 25-99
223 Jeremy Hill JSY AU/99 6.00 15.00
224 Jimmy Garoppolo JSY AU/25 75.00 150.00

2014 Certified Camo Blue

*1-100 VETS/100 2.5X TO 6X BASIC CARDS
*101-175 ROOK/100: 1X TO 2.5X BASIC RC/999
*176-200 IMM/100: .8X TO 2X BASIC IMM/999
STATED PRINT RUN 100 SER.#'d SETS

2014 Certified Camo Gold

*1-100 VETS/25: 3X TO 8X BASIC CARDS
*101-175 ROOK/25: 1.2X TO 3X BASIC RC/999
*176-200 IMM/25: 1X TO 2.5X BASIC IMM/999
STATED PRINT RUN 25 SER.#'d SETS

2014 Certified Camo Red

*1-100 VETS: 1.2X TO 3X BASIC CARDS
*101-175 ROOK/149: 1X TO 2.5X BASIC RC/999
*176-200 IMM/149: .8X TO 2X BASIC IMM/999
101-200 STATED PRINT RUN 149

2014 Certified Gold

*1-100 VETS/25: 3X TO 8X BASIC CARDS
*101-175 ROOK/25: 1.2X TO 3X BASIC RC/999
*176-200 IMM/25: 1X TO 2.5X BASIC IMM/999
STATED PRINT RUN 25 SER.#'d SETS

2014 Certified Mirror Gold

*1-100 VETS/25: 3X TO 8X BASIC CARDS
*101-175 ROOK/25: 1.2X TO 3X BASIC RC/999
*176-200 IMM/25: 1X TO 2.5X BASIC IMM/999
*201-239 RK JSY AU/25: 1X TO 2.5X JSY AU/699
STATED PRINT RUN 25 SER.#'d SETS
UNPRICED PRINT RUN 10

2014 Certified Mirror Red Signatures

*BLUE/25: .5X TO 1.2X RED/45-49
SAB Arrelious Benn/49 5.00 12.00
SAD Aaron Dobson/49 5.00 12.00
SBJ Bo Jackson/15
SBM Bruce Matthews/49 8.00 20.00
SBR Bill Romanowski/25 20.00 50.00
SCG Clyde Gates/49 5.00 12.00
SCH Cobi Hamilton/49 5.00 12.00
SCM Clay Matthews/15
SCP Cordarrelle Patterson/49 10.00 25.00
SCT Chris Thompson/49 6.00 15.00
SDA Dwayne Allen/49 8.00 20.00
SDC Dave Casper/49 5.00 12.00
SDH1 Dwayne Harris/49 12.00 30.00
SDH2 DeAndre Hopkins/45 8.00 20.00
SDJ Dennis Johnson/49 5.00 12.00
SDL D.D. Lewis/49 20.00 40.00
SDP Dennis Pitta/49 5.00 12.00
SEM EJ Manuel/25 6.00 15.00
SER Eric Reid/49 6.00 15.00
SGB Giovani Bernard/49 5.00 12.00
SGE Gavin Escobar/49 10.00 25.00
SGS1 Gale Sayers/25 10.00 25.00
SGS2 Geno Smith/25 6.00 15.00
SHM Herman Moore/49 6.00 15.00
SJH Justin Hunter/49 5.00 12.00
SJJ Janoris Jenkins/49 5.00 12.00
SJK1 Jeremy Kerley/49 5.00 12.00
SJK2 Jim Kiick/49 5.00 12.00
SJL Jamal Lewis/49 6.00 15.00
SJT1 John Taylor/49 5.00 12.00
SJT2 Jordan Todman/49 5.00 12.00
SKA Kiko Alonso/49 5.00 12.00
SKB Kenjon Barner/49 5.00 12.00
SKJ Keith Jackson/49 8.00 20.00
SKM Kevin Minter/49 5.00 12.00
SKS Kenny Stills/49 5.00 12.00
SLB Le'Veon Bell/49 10.00 25.00
SLW Luke Willson/49 6.00 15.00
SMB Marlon Brown/49 5.00 12.00
SMG Marquise Goodwin/49 5.00 12.00
SML Marcus Lattimore/49 6.00 15.00
SMS Mark Stepnoski/25 20.00 50.00
SNF Nick Foles/49 15.00 30.00
SRW Robert Woods/49 6.00 15.00
STD Trent Dilfer/49 5.00 12.00
STG Ted Ginn Jr./49 8.00 20.00
STH1 T.Y. Hilton/49 6.00 15.00
STH2 Trindon Holliday/49 5.00 12.00
STM Tyrann Mathieu/49 6.00 15.00
SVS Vai Sikahema/49 5.00 12.00

2014 Certified Red

*1-100 VETS/249: 1.5X TO 4X BASIC CARDS
*101-175 ROOK/249: .6X TO 1.5X BASIC RC/999
*176-200 IMM/249: .5X TO 1.2X BASIC IMM/999
1-200 STATED PRINT RUN 49
*201-239 RK JSY AU/49-249: .5X TO 1.2X
*301-340 RK JSY AU/49: .8X TO 2X BASIC JSY AU/699
201-239 JSY AU PRINT RUN 49-249
209 Brandin Cooks JSY AU/249 6.00 15.00
210 Carlos Hyde JSY AU/249 5.00 12.00
211 Charles Sims JSY AU/249 4.00 10.00
219 Dri Archer JSY AU/249 4.00 10.00
224 Jimmy Garoppolo JSY AU/49 75.00 150.00
234 Paul Richardson JSY AU/249 5.00 12.00
236 Tajh Boyd JSY AU/249 4.00 10.00

2014 Certified Fabric of the Game Autographs

UNPRICED PRINT RUN 10
3 EJ Manuel/15 8.00 20.00
6 Michael Floyd/25 8.00 20.00
8 Shaun Alexander/25 8.00 20.00
9 Richard Sherman/25 90.00 150.00
10 Rahim Moore/25 8.00 20.00
12 Montee Ball/25 8.00 20.00
15 Le'Veon Bell/25 10.00 25.00
16 Eddie Lacy/25 8.00 20.00
17 C.J. Spiller/25 8.00 20.00
18 Pierre Thomas/25 8.00 20.00
19 Jeremy Kerley/25 8.00 20.00
21 Ronnie Brown/25 8.00 20.00
22 Doug Martin/25 12.00 30.00
23 Kellen Winslow Jr./25 8.00 20.00
25 Matt Schaub/25 8.00 20.00

2014 Certified Gold Team Autographs

1 C.J. Spiller/25 6.00 15.00
5 Doug Martin/15
7 Russell Wilson/15
8 Andy Dalton/15 10.00 25.00
12 Eddie Lacy/25 6.00 15.00
13 Jamaal Charles/15
14 Jordy Nelson/25 40.00 100.00
20 Richard Sherman/25 40.00 100.00

2014 Certified Mirror Materials

*RED/149-299: .4X TO 1X BASIC JSY/199-499
*RED/99: .5X TO 1.2X BASIC JSY/199
*RED/49: .5X TO 1.2X BASIC JSY/99
*BLUE/49-99: .5X TO 1.2X BASIC JSY/199-499
*BLUE/25: .6X TO 1.5X BASIC JSY/99
*GOLD/25: .8X TO 2X BASIC JSY/499
MAB Antonio Brown/299 4.00 10.00
MAF Arian Foster/499 3.00 8.00
MAL Andrew Luck/199 6.00 15.00
MCK Colin Kaepernick/99 4.00 10.00
MCN Cam Newton/499 4.00 10.00
MDB Dez Bryant/199 4.00 10.00
MDM Doug Martin/299 3.00 8.00
MJC Jay Cutler/499 2.50 6.00
MJG Jimmy Graham/199 4.00 10.00
MJM Joe Montana/499 8.00 20.00
MKA Keenan Allen/199 3.00 8.00
MLM LeSean McCoy/199 4.00 10.00
MMF Matt Forte/499 2.50 6.00
MMS Michael Strahan/299 3.00 8.00
MON Ozzie Newsome/499 3.00 8.00
MPM Peyton Manning/499 8.00 20.00
MRB Reggie Bush/199 2.50 6.00
MRG Robert Griffin III/199 2.50 6.00
MRW Russell Wilson/99 8.00 20.00
MWM Warren Moon/499 4.00 10.00

2014 Certified New Generation Autographs Mirror Red

*BLUE/99: .5X TO 1.2X RED/199
*BLUE/49: .5X TO 1.2X RED/99
*BLUE/25: .5X TO 1.2X RED/49
*GOLD/25: .8X TO 2X RED/199
1 Johnny Manziel/25 8.00 20.00
2 Blake Bortles/25 6.00 15.00
3 Teddy Bridgewater/25 8.00 20.00
4 Sammy Watkins/25
5 A.J. McCarron/25 5.00 12.00
6 Jimmy Garoppolo/25 75.00 150.00
7 Derek Carr/25 40.00 80.00
8 Jadeveon Clowney/25 6.00 15.00
9 Marqise Lee/25
10 Mike Evans/25 12.00 30.00
11 Kelvin Benjamin/25 8.00 20.00
13 Bishop Sankey/49 3.00 8.00
14 Andre Williams/49 3.00 8.00
15 Anthony Barr/99 2.50 6.00
16 Bradley Roby/199 2.00 5.00
17 Ha Ha Clinton-Dix/199 2.50 6.00
18 Khalil Mack/199 20.00 40.00
19 Allen Robinson/49 5.00 12.00
20 Austin Seferian-Jenkins/49 3.00 8.00
22 Carlos Hyde/49 4.00 10.00
23 Cody Latimer/199 6.00 15.00
24 Jeremy Hill/49 4.00 10.00
25 Logan Thomas/25 5.00 12.00
26 Charles Sims/49 3.00 8.00
27 Terrance West/199 2.00 5.00
28 De'Anthony Thomas/199 2.00 5.00
29 Jarvis Landry/99 6.00 15.00
30 Donte Moncrief/199 2.00 5.00
31 Dri Archer/199 2.00 5.00
32 Eric Ebron/25 6.00 15.00
33 Jace Amaro/49 3.00 8.00
34 Aaron Donald/49 10.00 25.00
35 Calvin Pryor/199 2.00 5.00
36 Michael Sam/199 2.00 5.00
37 Lamarcus Joyner I/199 2.50 6.00
38 Brandin Cooks/49 5.00 12.00
39 Darqueze Dennard/199 2.50 6.00

2014 Certified New Generation Materials

*RED/299: .5X TO 1.2X BASIC JSY/599
*BLUE/99: .6X TO 1.5X BASIC JSY/599
*GOLD/49: .8X TO 2X BASIC JSY/599
NGAM1 A.J. McCarron 1.25 3.00
NGAM2 Aaron Murray 1.25 3.00
NGAR Allen Robinson 2.00 5.00
NGAS Austin Seferian-Jenkins 1.25 3.00
NGAW1 Asa Watson 1.25 3.00
NGAW2 Andre Williams 1.25 3.00
NGBB Blake Bortles 1.50 4.00
NGBC Brandin Cooks 2.00 5.00
NGBS Bishop Sankey 1.25 3.00
NGCH Carlos Hyde 1.50 4.00
NGCL Cody Latimer 1.50 4.00
NGCS1 Connor Shaw 1.25 3.00
NGCS2 Charles Sims 1.25 3.00
NGDA1 Davante Adams 2.00 5.00
NGDA2 Dri Archer 1.25 3.00
NGDC Derek Carr 8.00 20.00
NGDF Devonta Freeman 2.00 5.00
NGDM Donte Moncrief 1.25 3.00
NGDT De'Anthony Thomas 1.25 3.00
NGEE Eric Ebron 1.50 4.00
NGJC Jadeveon Clowney 1.50 4.00
NGJG Jimmy Garoppolo 10.00 25.00
NGJH Jeremy Hill 1.50 4.00
NGJL Jarvis Landry 2.50 6.00
NGJM1 Johnny Manziel 2.00 5.00
NGJM2 Jordan Matthews 2.00 5.00
NGKB Kelvin Benjamin 2.00 5.00
NGKC Ka'Deem Carey 1.25 3.00
NGKM Khalil Mack 5.00 12.00
NGLT Logan Thomas 1.25 3.00
NGME Mike Evans 3.00 8.00
NGML Marqise Lee 1.50 4.00
NGOB Odell Beckham Jr. 3.00 8.00
NGPR Paul Richardson 1.50 4.00
NGSW Sammy Watkins 2.00 5.00
NGTB1 Tajh Boyd 1.25 3.00
NGTB2 Teddy Bridgewater 2.00 5.00
NGTM Tre Mason 1.25 3.00
NGTS Tom Savage 1.25 3.00
NGTW Terrance West 1.25 3.00

2014 Certified Potential Autographs

*BLUE/99: .6X TO 1.5X BASIC AU/399
*BLUE/25: .8X TO 2X BASIC AU/399
*BLUE/25: .6X TO 1.5X BASIC AU/99-149
*GOLD/15-25: .8X TO 2X BASIC AU/399
PAB Anthony Barr/99 2.50 6.00
PAD Aaron Donald/99 8.00 20.00
PAJ A.J. McCarron/25 4.00 10.00
PAM Aaron Murray/99 2.50 6.00
PAR Allen Robinson/99 4.00 10.00
PAS Austin Seferian-Jenkins/99 2.50 6.00
PAW Andre Williams/99 2.50 6.00
PBB Blake Bortles/25 5.00 12.00
PBC Brandin Cooks/99 4.00 10.00
PBO Tajh Boyd/25 4.00 10.00
PBR Bradley Roby/399 2.00 5.00
PBS Bishop Sankey/25 4.00 10.00
PCF C.J. Fiedorowicz/399 2.00 5.00
PCH Cody Hoffman/399 2.00 5.00
PCL Cody Latimer/399 4.00 10.00
PCM C.J. Mosley/399 2.50 6.00
PCN Connor Shaw/99 2.50 6.00
PCP Calvin Pryor/399 2.00 5.00
PCS Charles Sims/25 4.00 10.00
PDA Dri Archer/399 2.00 5.00
PDC Derek Carr/25 20.00 50.00
PDD Darqueze Dennard/399 2.50 6.00
PDE Dee Ford/399 2.00 5.00
PDF David Fales/25 4.00 10.00
PDM Donte Moncrief/399 2.00 5.00
PDT De'Anthony Thomas/399 2.00 5.00
PDV Devonta Freeman/25 6.00 15.00
PEE Eric Ebron/25 5.00 12.00
PGR Greg Robinson/399 2.00 5.00
PHC Ha Ha Clinton-Dix/399 2.50 6.00
PHU Josh Huff/399 2.50 6.00
PJA Jace Amaro/25 4.00 10.00
PJC Jadeveon Clowney/25 5.00 12.00
PJE Jerick McKinnon/399 5.00 12.00
PJG Jimmy Garoppolo/25 75.00 150.00
PJH Jeremy Hill/25 5.00 12.00
PJI Jimmie Ward/399 2.50 6.00
PJJ Jeff Janis/399 6.00 15.00
PJK Jake Matthews/399 2.00 5.00
PJL Jarvis Landry/99 10.00 25.00
PJM Johnny Manziel/25 6.00 15.00
PJO Jordan Matthews/399 3.00 8.00
PJR Jared Abbrederis/399 5.00 12.00
PJV Jason Verrett/399 2.00 5.00
PJW James Wilder Jr./399 2.50 6.00
PKB Kelvin Benjamin/25 6.00 15.00
PKC Ka'Deem Carey/149 2.50 6.00
PKE Kony Ealy/399 2.50 6.00
PKF Kyle Fuller/399 2.00 5.00
PKM Khalil Mack/399 15.00 40.00
PKN Kevin Norwood/399 2.00 5.00
PKV Kyle Van Noy/399 2.50 6.00
PLJ Lamarcus Joyner I/399 2.50 6.00
PLS Lache Seastrunk/25
PLT Logan Thomas/25 4.00 10.00
PMB Martavis Bryant/399 2.50 6.00
PMD Mike Davis/399 2.00 5.00
PME Mike Evans/25 10.00 25.00
PML Marqise Lee/25
PMS Michael Sam/399 2.00 5.00
PPR Paul Richardson/25 5.00 12.00
PRS Ryan Shazier/399 3.00 8.00
PSE Shaq Evans/399 2.00 5.00
PSS Shayne Skov/399 2.00 5.00
PSW Sammy Watkins/25 6.00 15.00
PTB Teddy Bridgewater/25 6.00 15.00
PTG Tyler Gaffney/99 2.50 6.00
PTJ Timmy Jernigan/399 2.00 5.00
PTM Trent Murphy/399 2.00 5.00
PTN Troy Niklas/99 2.50 6.00
PTO Tom Savage/99 2.50 6.00
PTR Trevor Reilly/399 2.00 5.00
PTS Telvin Smith/399 2.00 5.00
PTW Terrance West/399 2.00 5.00
PZM Zack Martin/399 4.00 10.00

2014 Certified Potential Autographs Mirror Red

*RED/149: .5X TO 1.2X BASIC AU/399
*RED/49: .5X TO 1.2X BASIC AU/99-149
*RED/20: .4X TO 1X BASIC AU/25
PJC Jadeveon Clowney/20 5.00 12.00
PJG Jimmy Garoppolo/20 100.00 200.00
PTB Teddy Bridgewater/20 6.00 15.00

2014 Certified Pro Bowl Bound

*RED/249: .5X TO 1.2X BASIC INSERTS
*BLUE/99: .6X TO 1.5X BASIC INSERTS
1 Tom Brady 2.50 6.00
2 Peyton Manning 2.00 5.00
3 Drew Brees 1.00 2.50
4 Russell Wilson 1.50 4.00
5 Jamaal Charles .75 2.00
6 Marshawn Lynch .75 2.00
7 Adrian Peterson 1.00 2.50
8 LeSean McCoy 1.00 2.50
9 Dez Bryant 1.00 2.50
10 A.J. Green 1.00 2.50
11 Brandon Marshall .60 1.50
12 Julius Thomas .60 1.50
13 Jimmy Graham 1.00 2.50
14 J.J. Watt 1.00 2.50
15 Robert Quinn .75 2.00
16 Ndamukong Suh .75 2.00
17 Luke Kuechly .75 2.00
18 Patrick Peterson .60 1.50
19 Richard Sherman 1.00 2.50

2014 Certified Pro Bowl Bound Gold

*GOLD/25: 1.2X TO 3X BASIC INSERTS
1 Tom Brady 10.00 25.00
2 Peyton Manning 12.00 30.00
4 Russell Wilson 8.00 20.00

2014 Certified Rookie Retro

*RED/249: .5X TO 1.2X BASIC INSERTS
*BLUE/99: .6X TO 1.5X BASIC INSERTS
*GOLD/25: 1X TO 2.5X BASIC INSERTS
RR1 Johnny Manziel .75 2.00
RR2 Blake Bortles .60 1.50
RR3 Teddy Bridgewater .75 2.00
RR4 Sammy Watkins .75 2.00
RR5 A.J. McCarron .50 1.25
RR6 Jimmy Garoppolo 4.00 10.00
RR7 Derek Carr 3.00 8.00
RR8 Jadeveon Clowney .60 1.50
RR9 Marqise Lee .60 1.50
RR10 Mike Evans 1.25 3.00
RR11 Kelvin Benjamin .75 2.00
RR12 Tom Savage .50 1.25
RR13 Eric Ebron .60 1.50
RR14 Tre Mason .50 1.25
RR15 David Fales .50 1.25
RR16 Logan Thomas .50 1.25
RR17 Andre Williams .50 1.25
RR18 Bishop Sankey .50 1.25
RR19 Zack Martin .60 1.50
RR20 Charles Sims .50 1.25
RR21 Jeremy Hill .60 1.50
RR22 Lache Seastrunk .50 1.25
RR23 Aaron Murray .50 1.25
RR24 Brandin Cooks .75 2.00
RR25 Ka'Deem Carey .50 1.25
RR26 Allen Robinson .75 2.00
RR27 Carlos Hyde .60 1.50
RR28 Jace Amaro .50 1.25
RR29 Jarvis Landry 1.00 2.50
RR30 Odell Beckham Jr. 1.25 3.00
RR31 Paul Richardson .60 1.50
RR32 Devonta Freeman .75 2.00
RR33 Austin Seferian-Jenkins .50 1.25
RR34 Greg Robinson .50 1.25
RR35 Tajh Boyd .50 1.25
RR36 Aaron Donald 1.25 3.00
RR37 Anthony Barr .50 1.25
RR38 Troy Niklas .50 1.25
RR39 Tyler Gaffney .50 1.25
RR40 C.J. Mosley .60 1.50
RR41 Marcus Smith .50 1.25
RR42 Taylor Lewan .50 1.25
RR43 Darqueze Dennard .60 1.50
RR44 Dee Ford .50 1.25
RR45 Ha Ha Clinton-Dix .60 1.50
RR46 Jake Matthews .50 1.25
RR47 Khalil Mack 2.00 5.00
RR48 Justin Gilbert .50 1.25
RR49 Cody Latimer .60 1.50
RR50 Michael Sam .50 1.25

2014 Certified Sky's the Limit

*RED/249: .5X TO 1.2X BASIC INSERTS
*BLUE/99: .6X TO 1.5X BASIC INSERTS
*GOLD/25: 1X TO 2.5X BASIC INSERTS
SKY1 Jadeveon Clowney .60 1.50
SKY2 Khalil Mack 2.00 5.00
SKY3 Johnny Manziel .75 2.00
SKY4 Blake Bortles .60 1.50
SKY5 Teddy Bridgewater .75 2.00
SKY6 A.J. McCarron .50 1.25
SKY7 Jimmy Garoppolo 4.00 10.00
SKY8 Derek Carr 3.00 8.00
SKY9 Tom Savage .50 1.25
SKY10 Logan Thomas .50 1.25
SKY11 Aaron Murray .50 1.25
SKY12 Tre Mason .50 1.25
SKY13 Andre Williams .50 1.25
SKY14 Bishop Sankey .50 1.25
SKY15 Charles Sims .50 1.25
SKY16 Jeremy Hill .60 1.50
SKY17 Lache Seastrunk .50 1.25
SKY18 Carlos Hyde .60 1.50
SKY19 Eric Ebron .60 1.50
SKY20 Jace Amaro .50 1.25
SKY21 Sammy Watkins .75 2.00
SKY22 Mike Evans 1.25 3.00
SKY23 Kelvin Benjamin .75 2.00
SKY24 Brandin Cooks .75 2.00
SKY25 Cody Latimer .60 1.50
SKY26 Allen Robinson .75 2.00
SKY27 Jarvis Landry 1.00 2.50
SKY28 Odell Beckham Jr. 1.25 3.00
SKY29 Justin Gilbert .50 1.25
SKY30 Marqise Lee .60 1.50

2015 Certified

1 Russell Wilson .50 1.25
2 Robert Griffin III .25 .60
3 Jeremy Maclin .25 .60
4 Tom Brady 1.00 2.50
5 Terrance West .25 .60
6 Antonio Gates .25 .60
7 Richard Sherman .40 1.00
8 Eric Decker .25 .60
9 Zach Mettenberger .25 .60
10 Andrew Luck .50 1.25
11 Eddie Lacy .25 .60
12 Brandon Marshall .25 .60
13 Victor Cruz .30 .75
14 LeSean McCoy .40 1.00
15 Kenny Stills .25 .60
16 Cordarrelle Patterson .25 .60
17 Philip Rivers .40 1.00
18 A.J. Green .40 1.00
19 Odell Beckham Jr. .40 1.00
20 Sammy Watkins .30 .75
21 Aaron Rodgers .75 2.00
22 Andy Dalton .30 .75
23 Devin Hester .30 .75
24 Joe Flacco .30 .75
25 Ryan Tannehill .30 .75
26 Bishop Sankey .25 .60
27 Jordy Nelson .30 .75
28 Doug Martin .30 .75
29 Brian Hartline .30 .75
30 Jonathan Stewart .25 .60
31 Vincent Jackson .25 .60
32 Jason Witten .30 .75
33 Teddy Bridgewater .30 .75
34 Rob Gronkowski .40 1.00
35 Randall Cobb .30 .75
36 Elvis Dumervil .25 .60
37 Denard Robinson .25 .60
38 Tre Mason .30 .75
39 Julian Edelman .40 1.00
40 Demaryius Thomas .30 .75
41 Tony Romo .30 .75
42 Johnny Manziel .30 .75
43 Matthew Stafford .30 .75
44 Frank Gore .30 .75
45 Carson Palmer .30 .75
46 Eli Manning .30 .75
47 Keenan Allen .30 .75
48 Geno Smith .25 .60
49 Peyton Manning .75 2.00
50 Allen Hurns .25 .60
51 Mark Ingram .30 .75
52 Andre Johnson .30 .75
53 Darren McFadden .25 .60
54 Matt Ryan .30 .75
55 Steve Smith Sr. .30 .75
56 Lamar Miller .25 .60
57 Alshon Jeffery .30 .75
58 Marshawn Lynch .30 .75
59 Joique Bell .25 .60
60 DeMarco Murray .30 .75
61 Tavon Austin .25 .60
62 Jay Cutler .25 .60
63 Julio Jones .40 1.00
64 Emmanuel Sanders .30 .75
65 Torrey Smith .25 .60
66 Dwayne Bowe .30 .75
67 Ben Roethlisberger .40 1.00
68 Arian Foster .30 .75
69 Mike Evans .30 .75
70 Calvin Johnson .40 1.00
71 Dez Bryant .40 1.00
72 Andre Ellington .25 .60
73 Jamaal Charles .30 .75
74 Jordan Matthews .30 .75
75 Derek Carr .40 1.00
76 Reggie Bush .25 .60
77 Alex Smith .30 .75
78 Larry Fitzgerald .30 .75
79 J.J. Watt .40 1.00
80 Le'Veon Bell .30 .75
81 Cam Newton .40 1.00
82 Nick Foles .30 .75
83 Kelvin Benjamin .30 .75
84 Adrian Peterson .40 1.00
85 Antonio Brown .40 1.00
86 Pierre Garcon .30 .75
87 EJ Manuel .25 .60
88 Colin Kaepernick .30 .75
89 Giovani Bernard .25 .60
90 Matt Forte .25 .60
91 Justin Hunter .25 .60
92 Ryan Mallett .30 .75
93 Michael Crabtree .25 .60
94 Sam Bradford .25 .60
95 Trent Richardson .25 .60
96 Brandin Cooks .30 .75
97 T.Y. Hilton .30 .75
98 Drew Brees .40 1.00
99 Alfred Morris .25 .60
100 Blake Bortles .25 .60
101 Joe Montana IMM 3.00 8.00
102 John Elway IMM 2.00 5.00
103 Terry Bradshaw IMM 1.50 4.00
104 Barry Sanders IMM 2.00 5.00
105 Warren Moon IMM 1.25 3.00
106 Joe Greene IMM 1.25 3.00
107 Brian Urlacher IMM 1.25 3.00
108 Troy Aikman IMM 1.50 4.00
109 Dan Marino IMM 2.50 6.00
110 Gale Sayers IMM 1.25 3.00
111 Lawrence Taylor IMM 1.25 3.00
112 Emmitt Smith IMM 2.00 5.00
113 LaDainian Tomlinson IMM 1.00 2.50
114 Marcus Allen IMM 1.25 3.00
115 Rod Woodson IMM 1.00 2.50
116 Mike Ditka IMM 1.25 3.00
117 Jerry Rice IMM 2.00 5.00
118 Franco Harris IMM 1.25 3.00
119 Kurt Warner IMM 1.00 2.50
120 Brett Favre IMM 2.50 6.00
121 Bo Jackson IMM 1.50 4.00
122 Steve Young IMM 1.50 4.00
123 Deion Sanders IMM 1.00 2.50
124 Jerome Bettis IMM 1.25 3.00
125 Eric Dickerson IMM 1.00 2.50
126 Bud Dupree RC .75 2.00
127 Arik Armstead RC .60 1.50
128 Ben Koyack RC 1.00 2.50
129 Benardrick McKinney RC .60 1.50
130 Blake Bell RC 1.00 2.50
131 Cameron Artis-Payne RC .60 1.50
132 Clive Walford RC .60 1.50
133 Danielle Hunter RC .75 2.00
134 Dante Fowler Jr. RC 1.00 2.50
135 Da'Ron Brown RC .60 1.50
136 Darren Waller RC .75 2.00
137 Davis Tull RC .60 1.50
138 Denzel Perryman RC .60 1.50
139 Derron Smith RC .60 1.50
140 Dezmin Lewis RC .60 1.50
141 Doran Grant RC 1.00 2.50
142 Eli Harold RC .60 1.50
143 Eric Kendricks RC .60 1.50
144 Eric Rowe RC .60 1.50
145 Geneo Grissom RC .60 1.50
146 Gerald Christian RC .75 2.00
147 Hau'oli Kikaha RC .75 2.00
148 Ifo Ekpre-Olomu RC .60 1.50
149 Jalen Collins RC .60 1.50
150 Jaquiski Tartt RC .60 1.50
151 Jeff Heuerman RC .75 2.00
152 Jesse James RC .75 2.00
153 J.J. Nelson RC .60 1.50
154 Josh Robinson RC .60 1.50
155 Josh Shaw RC 1.00 2.50
156 Kaelin Clay RC .60 1.50
157 Ronald Darby RC .60 1.50
158 Kenny Bell RC 1.00 2.50
159 Kenny Hilliard RC .60 1.50
160 Charles Gaines RC 1.00 2.50
161 Gerod Holliman RC 1.00 2.50
162 Kevin Johnson RC .60 1.50
163 Kwon Alexander RC .75 2.00
164 Landon Collins RC .75 2.00
165 Lorenzo Doss RC .60 1.50
166 Lorenzo Mauldin RC .60 1.50
167 Marcus Murphy RC .60 1.50
168 Marcus Peters RC 1.00 2.50
169 Mario Alford RC .60 1.50
170 Mario Edwards Jr. RC .60 1.50
171 Markus Golden RC .60 1.50
172 MyCole Pruitt RC .60 1.50
173 Nate Orchard RC .60 1.50
174 Nick Boyle RC .60 1.50
175 Nick O'Leary RC .60 1.50
176 Owamagbe Odighizuwa RC .75 2.00
177 P.J. Williams RC .75 2.00
178 Paul Dawson RC .75 2.00
179 Preston Smith RC .75 2.00
180 Quinten Rollins RC 1.25 3.00
181 Randy Gregory RC .60 1.50
182 Senquez Golson RC .60 1.50
183 Shane Ray RC .60 1.50
184 Shaq Thompson RC .75 2.00
185 Stephone Anthony RC .60 1.50
186 Steven Nelson RC .60 1.50
187 Tony Lippett RC .60 1.50
188 Trae Waynes RC .60 1.50
189 Tre McBride RC .60 1.50
190 Trey Flowers RC 1.00 2.50
191 Tyler Kroft RC .75 2.00
192 Vic Beasley Jr. RC .75 2.00
193 Danny Shelton RC .60 1.50
194 Eddie Goldman RC .60 1.50
195 Jordan Phillips RC .60 1.50
196 Malcom Brown RC .60 1.50
197 Andrus Peat RC .60 1.50
198 Brandon Scherff RC 1.00 2.50
199 Cedric Ogbuehi RC .60 1.50
200 Ereck Flowers RC .75 2.00
201 Buck Allen JSY AU RC/799 4.00 10.00
202 David Johnson JSY AU RC/799 15.00 30.00
203 Devin Smith JSY AU RC/799 3.00 8.00
204 Dorial Green-Beckham JSY AU RC/799 3.00 8.00
205 Jamison Crowder JSY AU RC/799 4.00 10.00
206 Jeremy Langford JSY AU RC/799 10.00 25.00
207 Justin Hardy JSY AU RC/799 3.00 8.00
208 Matt Jones JSY AU RC/799 3.00 8.00
209 Mike Davis JSY AU RC/799 3.00 8.00
210 Phillip Dorsett JSY AU RC/799 3.00 8.00
211 Rashad Greene JSY AU RC/799 3.00 8.00
212 Sammie Coates JSY AU RC/799 4.00 10.00
213 Sean Mannion JSY AU RC/799 3.00 8.00
214 Stefon Diggs JSY AU RC/799 8.00 20.00
215 Ty Montgomery JSY AU RC/799 3.00 8.00
216 Tyler Lockett JSY AU RC/799 5.00 12.00
217 Vince Mayle JSY AU RC/799 4.00 10.00
218 Devin Funchess JSY AU RC/599 5.00 12.00
219 Chris Conley JSY AU RC/399 4.00 10.00
220 Leonard Williams JSY AU RC/399 4.00 10.00
221 David Cobb JSY AU RC/299 4.00 10.00
222 Duke Johnson JSY AU RC/299 6.00 15.00
223 Jay Ajayi JSY AU RC/299 6.00 15.00
224 Maxx Williams JSY AU RC/299 4.00 10.00
225 Tevin Coleman JSY AU RC/249 5.00 12.00
226 Amari Cooper JSY AU RC/199 15.00 40.00
227 Ameer Abdullah JSY AU RC/199 8.00 20.00
228 Breshad Perriman JSY AU RC/199 5.00 12.00
229 Brett Hundley JSY AU RC/199 5.00 12.00
230 Bryce Petty JSY AU RC/199 5.00 12.00
231 DeVante Parker JSY AU RC/199 8.00 20.00
232 Jaelen Strong JSY AU RC/199 6.00 15.00
233 Jameis Winston JSY AU RC/199 12.00 30.00
234 Kevin White JSY AU RC/199 6.00 15.00
235 Marcus Mariota JSY AU RC/199 20.00 50.00
236 Melvin Gordon JSY AU RC/199 12.00 30.00
237 Nelson Agholor JSY AU RC/199 6.00 15.00
238 T.J. Yeldon JSY AU RC/199 5.00 12.00
239 Todd Gurley JSY AU RC/199 20.00 50.00
240 Garrett Grayson JSY AU RC/199 5.00 12.00
241 K.Williams JSY AU RC/199 EXCH 5.00 12.00

2015 Certified Mirror Blue

*VETS/50: 3X TO 8X BASIC CARDS
*IMM/50: 1X TO 2.5X BASIC CARDS/999
*ROOKIES/50: 1.2X TO 3X BASIC CARDS/999
*201-241 RK JSY AU/99: .8X TO 2X JSY AU/599-799
*201-241 RK JSY AU/25: 1X TO 2.5X JSY AU/249-399
*201-241 RK JSY AU/25: 1.2X TO 3X JSY AU/199

2015 Certified Mirror Gold

*VETS/25: 4X TO 10X BASIC CARDS
*IMM/25: 1.5X TO 4X BASIC CARDS/999
*ROOKIES/25: 1.2X TO 3X BASIC CARDS/999
*201-241 RK JSY AU/25: 1.2X TO 3X JSY AU/599-799
*201-241 RK JSY AU/15-25: 1X TO 2.5X JSY AU/249-399
*201-241 RK JSY AU/15-25: .8X TO 2X JSY AU/199

2015 Certified Mirror Red

*VETS/99: 2.5X TO 6X BASIC CARDS
*IMM/99: .8X TO 2X BASIC CARDS/999
*ROOKIES/99: 1X TO 2.5X BASIC CARDS/999
*201-241 RK JSY AU/299: .5X TO 1.2X JSY AU/599-799
*201-241 RK JSY AU/149: .5X TO 1.2X JSY AU/249-399
*201-241 RK JSY AU/75: .6X TO 1.5X JSY AU/249-399
*201-241 RK JSY AU/75: .5X TO 1.2X JSY AU/199
*201-241 RK JSY AU/49: .6X TO 1.5X JSY AU/199

2015 Certified Mirror Silver

*VETS/499: 1.5X TO 4X BASIC CARDS
*IMM/499: .5X TO 1.2X BASIC CARDS/999
*ROOKIES/499: .6X TO 1.5X BASIC CARDS/999

2015 Certified Fabric of the Game

*PRIME/49: .5X TO 1.2X BASIC JSY/99
*PRIME/25-35: .6X TO 1.5X BASIC JSY/99
*PRIME/15: .8X TO 2X BASIC JSY/99
*PRIME/25-30: .5X TO 1.2X BASIC JSY/49-50
*PRIME/15: .5X TO 1.2X BASIC JSY/25
*PRIME/21: .4X TO 1X BASIC JSY/25
FOTGAB Antonio Brown/35 5.00 12.00
FOTGAD Andy Dalton/99 3.00 8.00
FOTGAE Andre Ellington/49 3.00 8.00
FOTGAG A.J. Green/49 5.00 12.00
FOTGAP Adrian Peterson/99 4.00 10.00
FOTGAS Ace Sanders/99 2.50 6.00
FOTGAW Andre Williams/99 2.50 6.00
FOTGBB Blake Bortles/25 4.00 10.00
FOTGBC Brandin Cooks/99 3.00 8.00
FOTGBF Brett Favre/50 12.00 30.00
FOTGBJ Bo Jackson/50 6.00 15.00
FOTGBR Tim Brown/25 6.00 15.00
FOTGBS Bishop Sankey/99 2.50 6.00
FOTGBU Brian Urlacher/54 5.00 12.00
FOTGCC Cris Collinsworth/99 3.00 8.00
FOTGCH Carlos Hyde/99 2.50 6.00
FOTGCK Colin Kaepernick/99 3.00 8.00
FOTGCN Cam Newton/99 4.00 10.00
FOTGCP Cordarrelle Patterson/99 2.50 6.00
FOTGDA Davante Adams/99 3.00 8.00
FOTGDC Derek Carr/99 4.00 10.00
FOTGDH Dan Hampton/99 2.50 6.00
FOTGDM Dan Marino/49 10.00 25.00
FOTGDMC Darren McFadden/99 2.50 6.00
FOTGDMU DeMarco Murray/25 5.00 12.00
FOTGDT Demaryius Thomas/50 4.00 10.00
FOTGEC Earl Campbell/49 5.00 12.00
FOTGED Eric Dickerson/49 4.00 10.00
FOTGES Emmanuel Sanders/99 3.00 8.00
FOTGJB Jerome Bettis/94 4.00 10.00
FOTGJC1 Jay Cutler/99 2.50 6.00
FOTGJC2 Jamaal Charles/25 5.00 12.00
FOTGJD Jadeveon Clowney/99 2.50 6.00
FOTGJE John Elway/99 6.00 15.00
FOTGJF Johnny Manziel/99 3.00 8.00
FOTGJG Jimmy Garoppolo/99 5.00 12.00
FOTGJH Jeremy Hill/99 2.50 6.00
FOTGJL Jarvis Landry/25 5.00 12.00
FOTGJM Jordan Matthews/99 3.00 8.00
FOTGJN Joe Namath/24 8.00 20.00
FOTGJO Joe Montana/81 15.00 40.00
FOTGJT Joe Theismann/49 5.00 12.00
FOTGKB Kelvin Benjamin/99 3.00 8.00
FOTGLB Le'Veon Bell/73 3.00 8.00
FOTGLF Larry Fitzgerald/11
FOTGLM Lamar Miller/99 2.50 6.00
FOTGLT Lawrence Taylor/56 5.00 12.00
FOTGLTO LaDainian Tomlinson/25 5.00 12.00
FOTGMA Marcus Allen/49 5.00 12.00
FOTGMB Martellus Bennett/25 4.00 10.00
FOTGME Mike Evans/99 3.00 8.00
FOTGML Marqise Lee/99 2.50 6.00
FOTGMO Montee Ball/49 3.00 8.00
FOTGMR Matt Ryan/25 5.00 12.00
FOTGMS Mohamed Sanu/35 3.00 8.00
FOTGMT Manti Te'o/25 5.00 12.00
FOTGNS Ndamukong Suh/10
FOTGOB Odell Beckham Jr./99 4.00 10.00
FOTGPM Peyton Manning/49 12.00 30.00
FOTGPR Philip Rivers/15
FOTGRS Roger Staubach/25
FOTGRT Ryan Tannehill/35 4.00 10.00
FOTGRW Russell Wilson/12
FOTGRY Ricky Williams/99 3.00 8.00
FOTGSW Sammy Watkins/99 3.00 8.00
FOTGSY Steve Young/49 6.00 15.00
FOTGTA Troy Aikman/99 5.00 12.00
FOTGTB Teddy Bridgewater/99 3.00 8.00
FOTGTD Tony Dorsett/99 4.00 10.00
FOTGTDA Terrell Davis/99 3.00 8.00
FOTGTK Travis Kelce/99 4.00 10.00
FOTGTM Tre Mason/99 3.00 8.00
FOTGTR Tony Romo/99 3.00 8.00
FOTGWM Warren Moon/35 5.00 12.00
FOTGWP Walter Payton/99 15.00 40.00

2015 Certified Fabric of the Game Signatures

FOTGAB Antonio Brown/25 30.00 60.00
FOTGAL Andrew Luck/49 90.00 150.00
FOTGBJ Bo Jackson/99 30.00 80.00
FOTGBS Barry Sanders/25 90.00 150.00
FOTGBU Brian Urlacher/25
FOTGCK Colin Kaepernick/25 15.00 40.00
FOTGDB Drew Brees/25 30.00 60.00
FOTGDF Doug Flutie/25 15.00 40.00
FOTGDH Devin Hester/49 12.00 30.00
FOTGDM Dan Marino/25 100.00 200.00
FOTGDT Demaryius Thomas/99 10.00 25.00
FOTGDW Danny Woodhead/25 15.00 40.00
FOTGDZ Dez Bryant/99 30.00 60.00
FOTGJC Jay Cutler/15
FOTGJG Jimmy Garoppolo/49 20.00 50.00
FOTGJN Jordy Nelson/99 10.00 25.00
FOTGMR Matt Ryan/25 15.00 40.00
FOTGMS Matthew Stafford/25 15.00 40.00
FOTGRG Rob Gronkowski/99 20.00 50.00
FOTGRS Richard Sherman/49 40.00 80.00
FOTGTR Tony Romo/25 30.00 60.00
FOTGWA DeMarcus Ware/25 15.00 40.00

2015 Certified Gold Team

*RED/199: .5X TO 1.2X BASIC INSERTS
*BLUE/99: .6X TO 1.5X BASIC INSERTS
*GOLD/50: .8X TO 2X BASIC INSERTS
*PURPLE/25: 1X TO 2.5X BASIC INSERTS
GT1 Tom Brady 2.50 6.00
GT2 Peyton Manning 2.00 5.00
GT3 Aaron Rodgers 2.00 5.00
GT4 Calvin Johnson 1.00 2.50
GT5 Dez Bryant 1.00 2.50
GT6 Demaryius Thomas .75 2.00
GT7 Jamaal Charles .75 2.00
GT8 Marshawn Lynch .75 2.00
GT9 Matt Forte .60 1.50
GT10 J.J. Watt 1.00 2.50

2015 Certified Gold Team Signatures

GSAL Andrew Luck/25
GSCN Cam Newton/25
GSJW J.J. Watt/25
GSML Marshawn Lynch/25 30.00 60.00
GSMR Matt Ryan/25 12.00 30.00
GSRG Rob Gronkowski/25

2015 Certified Legends

*RED/199: .5X TO 1.2X BASIC INSERTS
*BLUE/99: .6X TO 1.5X BASIC INSERTS
*GOLD/50: .8X TO 2X BASIC INSERTS
*PURPLE/25: 1X TO 2.5X BASIC INSERTS
CL1 Deion Sanders 1.25 3.00
CL2 Dan Marino 3.00 8.00
CL3 John Elway 2.50 6.00
CL4 Joe Namath 2.00 5.00
CL5 Brian Urlacher 1.50 4.00
CL6 Emmitt Smith 2.50 6.00
CL7 Steve Young 2.00 5.00
CL8 Eric Dickerson 1.25 3.00
CL9 Barry Sanders 2.50 6.00
CL10 Gale Sayers 1.50 4.00
CL11 Terry Bradshaw 2.00 5.00
CL12 Walter Payton 3.00 8.00
CL13 Franco Harris 1.50 4.00
CL14 Jerome Bettis 1.50 4.00
CL15 Bo Jackson 2.00 5.00
CL16 Joe Montana 4.00 10.00
CL17 Troy Aikman 2.00 5.00
CL18 Brett Favre 3.00 8.00
CL19 Earl Campbell 1.50 4.00
CL20 Marcus Allen 1.50 4.00

2015 Certified New Generation Dual Jerseys

*RED/249: .5X TO 1.2X BASIC JSY/799
*BLUE/99: .6X TO 1.5X BASIC JSY/99
*GOLD/25: 1X TO 2.5X BASIC JSY/799
NGALA A.Cooper/T.Yeldon 5.00 12.00
NGATL J.Hardy/T.Coleman 2.00 5.00
NGCHI J.Langford/K.White 2.00 5.00
NGCLE D.Johnson/V.Mayle 2.50 6.00
NGFSU J.Winston/R.Greene 6.00 15.00
NGMIA D.Parker/J.Ajayi 2.50 6.00
NGMIN M.Williams/S.Diggs 4.00 10.00
NGNYJ B.Petty/L.Williams 1.50 4.00
NGQB1 B.Hundley/G.Grayson 1.50 4.00
NGRB1 M.Gordon/M.Davis 4.00 10.00
NGSTL S.Mannion/T.Gurley 6.00 15.00
NGTEN D.G.Beckham/M.Mariota 5.00 12.00
NGUSC B.Allen/N.Agholor 2.00 5.00
NGWR1 S.Coates/T.Montgomery 2.00 5.00
NGWR2 D.Smith/P.Dorsett 1.50 4.00

2015 Certified New Generation Jerseys

*RED/249: .5X TO 1.2X BASIC JSY/799
*BLUE/99: .6X TO 1.5X BASIC JSY/799
*GOLD/25: .8X TO 2X BASIC JSY/799
NGAA Ameer Abdullah 2.00 5.00
NGAC Amari Cooper 4.00 10.00
NGBH Brett Hundley 1.25 3.00
NGBP Bryce Petty 1.25 3.00
NGCC Chris Conley 1.25 3.00
NGDF Devin Funchess 2.00 5.00
NGDG Dorial Green-Beckham 1.25 3.00
NGDJ David Johnson 3.00 8.00
NGDP DeVante Parker 2.00 5.00
NGDS Devin Smith 1.25 3.00
NGDU Duke Johnson 2.00 5.00
NGGG Garrett Grayson 1.25 3.00
NGJC Jamison Crowder 1.50 4.00
NGJS Jaelen Strong 1.50 4.00
NGJW Jameis Winston 6.00 15.00
NGKW Kevin White 1.50 4.00
NGMG Melvin Gordon 3.00 8.00
NGMJ Matt Jones 1.25 3.00
NGMM Marcus Mariota 5.00 12.00
NGMW Maxx Williams 1.25 3.00
NGNA Nelson Agholor 1.50 4.00
NGPD Phillip Dorsett 1.25 3.00
NGPE Breshad Perriman 1.25 3.00
NGSC Sammie Coates 1.50 4.00
NGSM Sean Mannion 1.25 3.00
NGTC Tevin Coleman 1.50 4.00
NGTG Todd Gurley 5.00 12.00
NGTL Tyler Lockett 2.00 5.00
NGTM Ty Montgomery 1.25 3.00
NGTY T.J. Yeldon 1.25 3.00

2015 Certified Potential Autographs

*BASE AU/249-299: .5X TO 1.2X SILVER AU/150
*BASE AU/299: .6X TO 1.5X SILVER AU/99
*BASE AU/199: .4X TO 1X SILVER AU/150
*BASE AU/125-150: .5X TO 1.2X SILVER AU/99
*BASE AU/99: .5X TO 1.2X SILVER AU/40

2015 Certified Potential Autographs Mirror Blue

*BLUE/50: .6X TO 1.5X SILVER AU/150
*BLUE/50: .5X TO 1.2X SILVER AU/150
*BLUE/15: .6X TO 1.5X SILVER AU/49-50
*BLUE/15: .5X TO 1.2X SILVER AU/25
CPDV DeVante Parker/15
CPJW Jameis Winston/15
CPMG Melvin Gordon/15
CPMM Marcus Mariota/15

2015 Certified Potential Autographs Mirror Purple

*PURPLE/25: .8X TO 2X SILVER AU/150
*PURPLE/25: .6X TO 1.5X SILVER AU/99

2015 Certified Potential Autographs Mirror Silver

CPAA Ameer Abdullah/49 6.00 15.00
CPAG Antwan Goodley/150 2.50 6.00
CPBB Blake Bell/99 5.00 12.00
CPBD Bud Dupree/99 4.00 10.00
CPBK Ben Koyack/150 4.00 10.00
CPBM Benardrick McKinney/99 3.00 8.00
CPBP Bryce Petty/49 4.00 10.00
CPCD Carl Davis/150 3.00 8.00
CPCW Clive Walford/99 3.00 8.00
CPDA DeAndrew White/99 5.00 12.00
CPDF Devin Funchess/49 6.00 15.00
CPDFJ Dante Fowler Jr./99 5.00 12.00
CPDG Deontay Greenberry/150 2.50 6.00
CPDH Danielle Hunter/99 4.00 10.00
CPDL Dezmin Lewis/150 2.50 6.00
CPDP Denzel Perryman/150 2.50 6.00
CPDS Danny Shelton/99 3.00 8.00
CPDW Darren Waller/99 4.00 10.00
CPEG Eddie Goldman/99 3.00 8.00
CPEH Eli Harold/150 2.50 6.00
CPEK Eric Kendricks/150 2.50 6.00
CPER Eric Rowe/150 2.50 6.00
CPGG Garrett Grayson/25 5.00 12.00
CPJH Josh Harper/150 2.50 6.00
CPJJ Jesse James/150 3.00 8.00
CPJN J.J. Nelson/150 2.50 6.00
CPJR Josh Robinson/150 2.50 6.00
CPKA Kwon Alexander/150 3.00 8.00
CPKB Kenny Bell/150 4.00 10.00
CPKJ Kevin Johnson/150 2.50 6.00
CPKV Kevin White/20 8.00 20.00
CPLC Landon Collins/99 4.00 10.00
CPMA Mario Alford/150 2.50 6.00
CPMD Michael Dyer/150 4.00 10.00
CPMM Marcus Mariota/25 40.00 80.00
CPMP Marcus Peters/99 5.00 12.00
CPMY MyCole Pruitt/150 2.50 6.00
CPNA Nelson Agholor/49 5.00 12.00
CPNO Nick O'Leary/150 2.50 6.00
CPRG Randy Gregory/99 3.00 8.00
CPTG Todd Gurley/25 20.00 50.00
CPTM Tre McBride/150 2.50 6.00
CPTY T.J. Yeldon/49 4.00 10.00

2015 Certified Rookie Gold Team

*RED/199: .5X TO 1.2X BASIC INSERTS
*BLUE/99: .6X TO 1.5X BASIC INSERTS
*GOLD/50: .8X TO 2X BASIC INSERTS
*PURPLE/25: 1X TO 2.5X BASIC INSERTS
RGT1 Marcus Mariota 2.00 5.00
RGT2 Jameis Winston 1.25 3.00
RGT3 Kevin White .60 1.50
RGT4 Todd Gurley 2.00 5.00
RGT5 Melvin Gordon 1.25 3.00
RGT6 Amari Cooper 1.50 4.00
RGT7 DeVante Parker .75 2.00
RGT8 Breshad Perriman .50 1.25
RGT9 Bryce Petty .50 1.25
RGT10 Garrett Grayson .50 1.25

2015 Certified Scorching Swatches

*RED/249: .5X TO 1.2X BASIC JSY/
*BLUE/99: .6X TO 1.5X BASIC JSY/399
*GOLD/25: 1X TO 2.5X BASIC JSY/399
SSAA Ameer Abdullah 2.00 5.00
SSAC Amari Cooper 4.00 10.00
SSBA Buck Allen 1.50 4.00
SSBH Brett Hundley 1.25 3.00
SSBP Bryce Petty 1.25 3.00
SSDC David Cobb 1.25 3.00
SSDP DeVante Parker 2.00 5.00
SSGG Garrett Grayson 1.25 3.00
SSJA Jay Ajayi 2.00 5.00
SSJW Jameis Winston 6.00 15.00
SSKW Kevin White 1.50 4.00
SSMG Melvin Gordon 3.00 8.00
SSMM Marcus Mariota 5.00 12.00
SSTG Todd Gurley 5.00 12.00

2015 Certified Signatures

CSAC Amari Cooper/25 15.00 40.00
CSAH Allen Hurns/199 2.00 5.00
CSBO Branden Oliver/299 2.50 6.00
CSLT Lorenzo Taliaferro/299 2.00 5.00
CSMB Martavis Bryant/199 2.00 5.00
CSOO Owamagbe Odighizuwa/299 2.50 6.00
CSPW P.J. Williams/299 2.50 6.00
CSRD Ronald Darby/299 2.00 5.00
CSSA Stephone Anthony/299 2.00 5.00
CSSC Shane Carden/150 2.50 6.00
CSSR Shane Ray/150 8.00 20.00
CSST Shaq Thompson/150 3.00 8.00
CSTD Titus Davis/299 2.50 6.00
CSTF Trey Flowers/299 3.00 8.00
CSTH Taylor Heinicke/299 3.00 8.00
CSTL Tony Lippett/199 2.00 5.00
CSTM Terrence Magee/199 3.00 8.00
CSTMC Tre McBride/299 2.00 5.00
CSTR Trey Williams/199 2.50 6.00
CSTW Trae Waynes/150 2.50 6.00
CSVB Vic Beasley Jr./150 3.00 8.00

2015 Certified Signatures Mirror Blue

CSAD Aaron Donald/25 8.00 20.00
CSAH Allen Hurns/50 4.00 10.00
CSBL Brandon LaFell/25 5.00 12.00
CSBO Branden Oliver/50 5.00 12.00
CSDP DeVante Parker/15
CSEL Eddie Lacy/25 5.00 12.00
CSFB Fred Biletnikoff/50 10.00 25.00
CSGG Garrett Grayson/15 6.00 15.00
CSIC Isaiah Crowell/50 4.00 10.00
CSJB John Brown/50 5.00 12.00
CSJF Justin Forsett/25 6.00 15.00
CSJS Jaelen Strong/15
CSLM Latavius Murray/50 15.00 40.00
CSLT Lorenzo Taliaferro/50 4.00 10.00
CSMB Martavis Bryant/50 4.00 10.00
CSOO Owamagbe Odighizuwa/50 5.00 12.00
CSPW P.J. Williams/50 5.00 12.00
CSRD Ronald Darby/50 4.00 10.00
CSSA Stephone Anthony/50 4.00 10.00
CSSC Shane Carden/50 4.00 10.00
CSSR Shane Ray/50 4.00 10.00
CSST Shaq Thompson/50 5.00 12.00
CSTD Titus Davis/50 5.00 12.00
CSTF Trey Flowers/50 6.00 15.00
CSTH Taylor Heinicke/50 6.00 15.00
CSTI Timothy Wright/50 4.00 10.00
CSTL Tony Lippett/50 4.00 10.00
CSTM Terrence Magee/50 6.00 15.00
CSTMC Tre McBride/50 4.00 10.00
CSTR Trey Williams/50 5.00 12.00
CSTW Trae Waynes/50 4.00 10.00
CSVB Vic Beasley Jr./50 5.00 12.00
CSZM Zach Mettenberger/25

2015 Certified Signatures Mirror Purple

CSAH Allen Hurns/25 5.00 12.00
CSBO Branden Oliver/25 6.00 15.00
CSFB Fred Biletnikoff/25
CSIC Isaiah Crowell/25 5.00 12.00
CSJB John Brown/25 6.00 15.00
CSLM Latavius Murray/25
CSLT Lorenzo Taliaferro/25 5.00 12.00
CSMB Martavis Bryant/25 5.00 12.00
CSOO Owamagbe Odighizuwa/25 6.00 15.00
CSPW P.J. Williams/25 6.00 15.00
CSRD Ronald Darby/25 5.00 12.00
CSSA Stephone Anthony/25 5.00 12.00
CSSC Shane Carden/25 5.00 12.00
CSSR Shane Ray/25 5.00 12.00
CSST Shaq Thompson/25
CSTD Titus Davis/25 6.00 15.00
CSTF Trey Flowers/25 8.00 20.00
CSTH Taylor Heinicke/25 8.00 20.00
CSTI Timothy Wright/25
CSTL Tony Lippett/25 5.00 12.00
CSTM Terrence Magee/25 8.00 20.00
CSTMC Tre McBride/25 5.00 12.00
CSTR Trey Williams/25 6.00 15.00
CSTW Trae Waynes/25 5.00 12.00
CSVB Vic Beasley Jr./25

2015 Certified Signatures Mirror Red

CSAC Amari Cooper/15 30.00 60.00
CSAD Allen Hurns/99 3.00 8.00
CSBO Branden Oliver/99 4.00 10.00
CSDP DeVante Parker/20 8.00 20.00
CSEL Eddie Lacy/49 4.00 10.00
CSFB Fred Biletnikoff/99 8.00 20.00
CSGG Garrett Grayson/25 5.00 12.00
CSJB John Brown/75 4.00 10.00
CSJW Jameis Winston/20 60.00 120.00
CSKW Kevin White/15 6.00 15.00
CSLM Latavius Murray/75 12.00 30.00
CSLT Lorenzo Taliaferro/99 3.00 8.00
CSMB Martavis Bryant/99 3.00 8.00
CSMG Melvin Gordon/15 12.00 30.00
CSMM Marcus Mariota/15 30.00 60.00
CSOO Owamagbe Odighizuwa/99 4.00 10.00
CSPW P.J. Williams/99 4.00 10.00
CSRD Ronald Darby/99 3.00 8.00
CSSA Stephone Anthony/99 3.00 8.00
CSSC Shane Carden/75 3.00 8.00
CSSR Shane Ray/75 3.00 8.00
CSST Shaq Thompson/75 4.00 10.00
CSTD Titus Davis/99 4.00 10.00
CSTF Trey Flowers/99 5.00 12.00
CSTG Todd Gurley/15 20.00 50.00
CSTH Taylor Heinicke/99 5.00 12.00
CSTI Timothy Wright/99 3.00 8.00
CSTL Tony Lippett/75 3.00 8.00
CSTM Terrence Magee/75 5.00 12.00
CSTMC Tre McBride/99 3.00 8.00
CSTR Trey Williams/99 4.00 10.00
CSTW Trae Waynes/75 3.00 8.00
CSVB Vic Beasley Jr./75 4.00 10.00

2015 Certified Signatures Mirror Silver

CSAC Amari Cooper/20
CSAD Allen Hurns/150 2.50 6.00
CSBO Branden Oliver/150 3.00 8.00
CSDP DeVante Parker/25 8.00 20.00
CSEL Eddie Lacy/99 3.00 8.00
CSJB John Brown/150 3.00 8.00
CSJW Jameis Winston/35 75.00 150.00
CSKW Kevin White/20
CSLM Latavius Murray/150 10.00 25.00
CSLT Lorenzo Taliaferro/150 2.50 6.00
CSMB Martavis Bryant/150 2.50 6.00
CSMM Marcus Mariota/20 30.00 60.00
CSOO Owamagbe Odighizuwa/150 3.00 8.00
CSPW P.J. Williams/150 3.00 8.00
CSRD Ronald Darby/150 2.50 6.00
CSSA Stephone Anthony/150 2.50 6.00
CSSC Shane Carden/99 3.00 8.00
CSSR Shane Ray/99 3.00 8.00
CSST Shaq Thompson/99 4.00 10.00
CSTD Titus Davis/150 3.00 8.00
CSTF Trey Flowers/150 4.00 10.00
CSTG Todd Gurley/25 20.00 50.00
CSTH Taylor Heinicke/150 4.00 10.00
CSTL Tony Lippett/150 2.50 6.00
CSTM Terrence Magee/150 4.00 10.00
CSTMC Tre McBride/150 2.50 6.00
CSTR Trey Williams/150 3.00 8.00
CSTW Trae Waynes/99 3.00 8.00
CSVB Vic Beasley Jr./99 4.00 10.00

2015 Certified Skills

*RED/199: .5X TO 1.2X BASIC INSERTS
*BLUE/99: .6X TO 1.5X BASIC INSERTS
*GOLD/50: .8X TO 2X BASIC INSERTS
*PURPLE/25: 1X TO 2.5X BASIC INSERTS
SK1 Tom Brady 2.50 6.00
SK2 Russell Wilson 1.25 3.00
SK3 Colin Kaepernick .75 2.00
SK4 Larry Fitzgerald .75 2.00
SK5 Mike Evans .75 2.00
SK6 Drew Brees 1.00 2.50
SK7 Kelvin Benjamin .75 2.00
SK8 Julio Jones 1.00 2.50
SK9 Aaron Rodgers 2.00 5.00
SK10 Calvin Johnson 1.00 2.50
SK11 DeSean Jackson .75 2.00
SK12 Dez Bryant 1.00 2.50
SK13 Odell Beckham Jr. 1.00 2.50
SK14 DeMarco Murray .75 2.00
SK15 Keenan Allen .75 2.00
SK16 Peyton Manning 2.00 5.00
SK17 Andrew Luck 1.25 3.00
SK18 Antonio Brown 1.00 2.50
SK19 Johnny Manziel .75 2.00
SK20 Brandon Marshall .60 1.50

2015 Certified Stars

*RED/199: .5X TO 1.2X BASIC INSERTS
*BLUE/99: .6X TO 1.5X BASIC INSERTS
*GOLD/50: .8X TO 2X BASIC INSERTS
*PURPLE/25: 1X TO 2.5X BASIC INSERTS
S1 Dez Bryant 1.00 2.50
S2 Kelvin Benjamin .75 2.00
S3 Calvin Johnson 1.00 2.50
S4 Derek Carr 1.00 2.50
S5 Sammy Watkins .75 2.00
S6 Ryan Tannehill .75 2.00
S7 Brandon Marshall .60 1.50
S8 Johnny Manziel .75 2.00
S9 DeMarco Murray .75 2.00
S10 Jay Cutler .60 1.50
S11 Ben Roethlisberger 1.00 2.50
S12 Matt Ryan .75 2.00
S13 Le'Veon Bell .75 2.00
S14 Peyton Manning 2.00 5.00
S15 Nick Foles .75 2.00
S16 Eli Manning .75 2.00
S17 Aaron Rodgers 2.00 5.00
S18 Alfred Morris .60 1.50
S19 Tony Romo .75 2.00
S20 Russell Wilson 1.25 3.00
S21 Jordy Nelson .75 2.00
S22 Mike Evans .75 2.00
S23 Cam Newton 1.00 2.50
S24 Matthew Stafford .75 2.00
S25 Andy Dalton .75 2.00
S26 Colin Kaepernick .75 2.00
S27 Jamaal Charles .75 2.00
S28 Teddy Bridgewater .75 2.00
S29 Larry Fitzgerald .75 2.00
S30 Richard Sherman 1.00 2.50
S31 J.J. Watt 1.00 2.50
S32 Tom Brady 2.50 6.00
S33 Demaryius Thomas .75 2.00
S34 Bishop Sankey .60 1.50
S35 Andrew Luck 1.25 3.00
S36 Drew Brees 1.00 2.50
S37 Philip Rivers 1.00 2.50
S38 Joe Flacco .75 2.00
S39 Odell Beckham Jr. 1.00 2.50
S40 Blake Bortles .60 1.50

2016 Certified

1 Antonio Gates .25 .60
2 Tony Romo .30 .75
3 Kenny Britt .25 .60
4 Aaron Rodgers .75 2.00
5 Blake Bortles .25 .60
6 Tom Brady 1.00 2.50
7 Adrian Peterson .40 1.00
8 Julio Jones .40 1.00
9 Amari Cooper .40 1.00
10 Greg Olsen .30 .75
11 Colin Kaepernick .30 .75
12 Darren McFadden .25 .60
13 Jameis Winston .40 1.00
14 Jordy Nelson .30 .75
15 Allen Hurns .25 .60
16 Julian Edelman .40 1.00
17 Stefon Diggs .30 .75
18 Devonta Freeman .30 .75
19 Sam Bradford .25 .60
20 Jay Cutler .25 .60
21 Carlos Hyde .25 .60
22 Dez Bryant .40 1.00
23 Doug Martin .30 .75
24 Randall Cobb .30 .75
25 Allen Robinson .30 .75
26 Rob Gronkowski .40 1.00
27 Drew Brees .40 1.00
28 Joe Flacco .30 .75
29 DeMarco Murray .30 .75
30 Matt Forte .25 .60
31 Torrey Smith .25 .60
32 Jason Witten .30 .75
33 Vincent Jackson .25 .60
34 Eddie Lacy .25 .60
35 Alex Smith .30 .75
36 Ryan Fitzpatrick .25 .60
37 Mark Ingram .30 .75
38 Justin Forsett .30 .75
39 Jordan Matthews .30 .75
40 Alshon Jeffery .30 .75
41 Russell Wilson .50 1.25
42 Peyton Manning .75 2.00
43 Mike Evans .30 .75
44 J.J. Watt .40 1.00
45 Jamaal Charles .30 .75
46 Brandon Marshall .25 .60
47 Brandin Cooks .30 .75
48 Steve Smith Sr. .30 .75
49 Ben Roethlisberger .40 1.00
50 Andy Dalton .30 .75
51 Marshawn Lynch .30 .75
52 Demaryius Thomas .30 .75
53 Marcus Mariota .40 1.00
54 Jeremy Langford .30 .75
55 Jeremy Maclin .25 .60
56 Darrelle Revis .25 .60
57 Eli Manning .30 .75
58 Tyrod Taylor .30 .75
59 Le'Veon Bell .30 .75
60 Jeremy Hill .25 .60
61 Jimmy Graham .40 1.00
62 Emmanuel Sanders .40 1.00
63 Delanie Walker .25 .60
64 DeAndre Hopkins .30 .75
65 Ryan Tannehill .30 .75
66 Carson Palmer .30 .75
67 Odell Beckham Jr. .40 1.00
68 LeSean McCoy .40 1.00
69 Antonio Brown .40 1.00
70 A.J. Green .40 1.00
71 Richard Sherman .40 1.00
72 Matthew Stafford .30 .75
73 Kirk Cousins .40 1.00
74 Andrew Luck .50 1.25
75 Lamar Miller .25 .60
76 Larry Fitzgerald .30 .75
77 Rashad Jennings .25 .60
78 Sammy Watkins .40 1.00
79 Philip Rivers .40 1.00
80 Robert Griffin III .25 .60
81 Todd Gurley .40 1.00
82 Calvin Johnson .40 1.00
83 Jordan Reed .25 .60
84 Frank Gore .30 .75
85 Jarvis Landry .30 .75
86 Chris Johnson .25 .60
87 Derek Carr .40 1.00
88 Cam Newton .40 1.00
89 Ryan Mathews .30 .75
90 Isaiah Crowell .25 .60
91 Tavon Austin .25 .60
92 Ameer Abdullah .25 .60
93 Pierre Garcon .30 .75
94 T.Y. Hilton .30 .75
95 Teddy Bridgewater .30 .75
96 Matt Ryan .30 .75
97 Latavius Murray .25 .60
98 Jonathan Stewart .25 .60
99 Keenan Allen .30 .75
100 Gary Barnidge .25 .60
101 Joe Namath IMM 1.50 4.00
102 Kurt Warner IMM 1.00 2.50
103 Barry Sanders IMM 2.00 5.00
104 Shannon Sharpe IMM 1.25 3.00
105 Rod Woodson IMM 1.00 2.50
106 Terrell Davis IMM 1.00 2.50
107 Steve Young IMM 1.50 4.00
108 Mike Ditka IMM 1.25 3.00
109 Terry Bradshaw IMM 1.50 4.00
110 Michael Strahan IMM 1.00 2.50
111 Dan Marino IMM 2.50 6.00
112 Earl Campbell IMM 1.25 3.00
113 Troy Aikman IMM 1.50 4.00
114 Bo Jackson IMM 1.50 4.00
115 Gale Sayers IMM 1.25 3.00
116 Marcus Allen IMM 1.00 2.50
117 Brian Urlacher IMM 1.25 3.00
118 Cris Carter IMM 1.25 3.00
119 Brett Favre IMM 2.50 6.00
120 Jim Kelly IMM 1.25 3.00
121 Michael Irvin IMM 1.25 3.00
122 Curtis Martin IMM 1.00 2.50
123 Roger Staubach IMM 1.50 4.00
124 Bruce Smith IMM 1.00 2.50
125 Marshall Faulk IMM 1.00 2.50
126 Jerome Bettis IMM 1.25 3.00
127 John Riggins IMM 1.00 2.50
128 Larry Csonka IMM 1.00 2.50
129 Jerry Rice IMM 2.00 5.00
130 Tony Dorsett IMM 1.25 3.00
131 Edgerrin James IMM 1.00 2.50
132 Emmitt Smith IMM 2.00 5.00
133 Joe Montana IMM 3.00 8.00
134 Franco Harris IMM 1.25 3.00
135 John Elway IMM 2.00 5.00
136 Jalen Ramsey RC 1.00 2.50
137 Demarcus Ayers RC .60 1.50
138 Keanu Neal RC .60 1.50
139 Tyler Higbee RC .60 1.50
140 Vernon Butler RC .60 1.50
141 Emmanuel Ogbah RC .75 2.00
142 Jacoby Brissett RC .75 2.00
143 Noah Spence RC .60 1.50
144 Zac Brooks RC .75 2.00
145 A'Shawn Robinson RC .60 1.50
146 DeForest Buckner RC .60 1.50
147 Daniel Braverman RC .60 1.50
148 Shaq Lawson RC .60 1.50
149 Temarrick Hemingway RC .60 1.50
150 Roberto Aguayo RC .60 1.50
151 Kevin Dodd RC .60 1.50
152 Kelvin Taylor RC .60 1.50

153 Reggie Ragland RC .60 1.50
154 Seth DeValve RC .75 2.00
155 Jakeem Grant RC .60 1.50
156 Leonard Floyd RC .75 2.00
157 Devin Fuller RC .75 2.00
158 Darron Lee RC .60 1.50
159 Jerell Adams RC .60 1.50
160 Nate Sudfeld RC .60 1.50
161 Jaylon Smith RC .60 1.50
162 Darius Jackson RC .75 2.00
163 Kamalei Correa RC .60 1.50
164 Tajae Sharpe RC .75 2.00
165 Kolby Listenbee RC .60 1.50
166 Eli Apple RC .75 2.00
167 Charone Peake RC .60 1.50
168 William Jackson III RC .75 2.00
169 David Morgan RC 1.00 2.50
170 Jake Rudock RC .60 1.50
171 Myles Jack RC .75 2.00
172 Dwayne Washington RC .75 2.00
173 Austin Johnson RC .60 1.50
174 Jordan Payton RC .60 1.50
175 Mike Thomas RC 1.00 2.50
176 Vernon Hargreaves III RC 1.00 2.50
177 Kenny Lawler RC 1.00 2.50
178 Artie Burns RC .75 2.00
179 Rico Gathers RC .60 1.50
180 Brandon Allen RC .60 1.50
181 Chris Jones RC .60 1.50
182 Daniel Lasco RC .60 1.50
183 Malcolm Mitchell RC .60 1.50
184 Tyreek Hill RC 2.50 6.00
185 Aaron Burbridge RC .60 1.50
186 Sheldon Rankins RC .75 2.00
187 Austin Hooper RC .60 1.50
188 Kenny Clark RC .60 1.50
189 Thomas Duarte RC .60 1.50
190 Jeff Driskel RC .60 1.50
191 Xavien Howard RC .75 2.00
192 Keith Marshall RC .60 1.50
193 Cody Core RC .60 1.50
194 Rashard Higgins RC .60 1.50
195 Devin Lucien RC .75 2.00
196 Karl Joseph RC .60 1.50
197 Nick Vannett RC .60 1.50
198 Robert Nkemdiche RC .75 2.00
199 Beau Sandland RC 1.00 2.50
200 Brandon Doughty RC .60 1.50
201 Jared Goff/149 JSY AU RC 50.00 100.00
202 Carson Wentz/149 JSY AU RC 100.00 200.00
203 Joey Bosa/299 JSY AU RC 8.00 20.00
204 Ezekiel Elliott/149 JSY AU RC EXCH 75.00 150.00
205 Corey Coleman/149 JSY AU RC 8.00 20.00
206 Will Fuller/149 JSY AU RC 8.00 20.00
207 Josh Doctson/299 JSY AU RC 5.00 12.00
208 Laquon Treadwell/149 JSY AU RC 25.00 50.00
209 Paxton Lynch/149 JSY AU RC 5.00 12.00
210 Hunter Henry/299 JSY AU RC 5.00 12.00
211 Sterling Shepard/299 JSY AU RC 5.00 12.00
212 Derrick Henry/149 JSY AU RC 12.00 30.00
213 Michael Thomas/149 JSY AU RC 10.00 25.00
214 Christian Hackenberg/299 JSY AU RC 4.00 10.00
215 Kenyan Drake/499 JSY AU RC 8.00 20.00
216 Braxton Miller/299 JSY AU RC 4.00 10.00
217 Leonte Carroo/299 JSY AU RC 4.00 10.00
218 C.J. Prosise/299 JSY AU RC 4.00 10.00
219 DeAndre Washington/499 JSY AU RC 3.00 8.00
220 Cody Kessler/299 JSY AU RC 4.00 10.00
221 Tyler Boyd/299 JSY AU RC 5.00 12.00
222 Connor Cook/149 JSY AU RC 6.00 15.00
223 Chris Moore/499 JSY AU RC 4.00 10.00
224 Ricardo Louis/499 JSY AU RC 3.00 8.00
225 Pharoh Cooper/299 JSY AU RC 4.00 10.00
226 Tyler Ervin/499 JSY AU RC 3.00 8.00
227 Demarcus Robinson/499 JSY AU RC 3.00 8.00
228 Kenneth Dixon/299 JSY AU RC 4.00 10.00
229 Dak Prescott/299 JSY AU RC 30.00 60.00
230 Devontae Booker/299 JSY AU RC 5.00 12.00
231 Cardale Jones/149 JSY AU RC 5.00 12.00
232 Paul Perkins/299 JSY AU RC 4.00 10.00
233 Jordan Howard/299 JSY AU RC 10.00 25.00
234 Wendell Smallwood/499 JSY AU RC 3.00 8.00
235 Jonathan Williams/499 JSY AU RC 4.00 10.00
236 Kevin Hogan/499 JSY AU RC 4.00 10.00
237 Trevor Davis/499 JSY AU RC 3.00 8.00
238 Alex Collins/299 JSY AU RC 5.00 12.00
239 Keenan Reynolds/499 JSY AU RC 4.00 10.00
240 Moritz Bohringer/499 JSY AU RC 8.00 20.00

2016 Certified Mirror Blue

*VETS/50: 3X TO 8X BASIC CARDS
*IMM/50: 1X TO 2.5X BASIC CARDS/999
*ROOKIES/50: 1.2X TO 3X BASIC CARDS/999
*201-240 RK JSY AU/50: 1X TO 2.5X JSY AU/499
*201-240 RK JSY AU/50: .8X TO 2X JSY AU/299
*201-240 RK JSY AU/50: .6X TO 1.5X JSY AU/149
202 Carson Wentz JSY AU 125.00 250.00
204 Ezekiel Elliott JSY AU 125.00 250.00

2016 Certified Mirror Gold

*VETS/25: 4X TO 10X BASIC CARDS
*IMM/25: 1.5X TO 4X BASIC CARDS/999
*ROOKIES/25: 1.2X TO 3X BASIC CARDS/999
*201-240 RK JSY AU/25: 1.2X TO 3X JSY AU/499
*201-240 RK JSY AU/25: 1X TO 2.5X JSY AU/299
*201-240 RK JSY AU/25: .8X TO 2X JSY AU/149
202 Carson Wentz JSY AU 150.00 300.00
204 Ezekiel Elliott JSY AU 150.00 300.00

2016 Certified Mirror Orange

*VETS/225: 1.5X TO 4X BASIC CARDS
*IMM/225: .5X TO 1.2X BASIC CARDS/999
*ROOKIES/225: .6X TO 1.5X BASIC CARDS/999
*201-240 RK JSY AU/349: .5X TO 1.2X JSY AU/499
*201-240 RK JSY AU/199: .5X TO 1.2X JSY AU/229
*201-240 RK JSY AU/99: .5X TO 1.2X JSY AU/149
202 Carson Wentz/99 JSY AU 100.00 200.00
204 Ezekiel Elliott/99 JSY AU 100.00 200.00

2016 Certified Mirror Red

*VETS/99: 2.5X TO 6X BASIC CARDS
*IMM/99: .8X TO 2X BASIC CARDS/999
*ROOKIES/99: 1X TO 2.5X BASIC CARDS/999
*201-240 RK JSY AU/249: .5X TO 1.2X JSY AU/499
*201-240 RK JSY AU/99: .6X TO 1.5X JSY AU/299
*201-240 RK JSY AU/75: .5X TO 1.2X JSY AU/149
202 Carson Wentz/75 JSY AU 100.00 200.00
204 Ezekiel Elliott/75 JSY AU 100.00 200.00
229 Dak Prescott/99 JSY AU 40.00 100.00

2016 Certified Mirror Silver

*VETS/499: 1.5X TO 4X BASIC CARDS
*IMM/499: .5X TO 1.2X BASIC CARDS/999
*ROOKIES/499: .6X TO 1.5X BASIC CARDS/999

2016 Certified Champions

*RED/99: .6X TO 1.5X BASIC INSERTS
*BLUE/50: .8X TO 2X BASIC INSERTS
*GOLD/25: 1X TO 2.5X BASIC INSERTS
1 Russell Wilson 1.25 3.00
2 Terry Bradshaw 1.25 3.00
3 Kurt Warner .75 2.00
4 Roger Staubach 1.25 3.00
5 Brett Favre 2.00 5.00
6 Marcus Allen .75 2.00
7 Emmitt Smith 1.50 4.00
8 Joe Montana 2.50 6.00
9 Peyton Manning 2.00 5.00
10 Jim McMahon .75 2.00
11 Aaron Rodgers 2.00 5.00
12 Larry Csonka .75 2.00
13 John Elway 1.50 4.00
14 Joe Namath 1.25 3.00
15 Troy Aikman 1.25 3.00
16 Bob Griese 1.00 2.50
17 Michael Irvin 1.00 2.50
18 Jerry Rice 1.50 4.00
19 Tom Brady 2.50 6.00
20 John Riggins .75 2.00

2016 Certified EPIX Jerseys Play

*GAME/50: .6X TO 1.5X PLAY JSY
*GAME/25: .8X TO 2X PLAY JSY
*SEASON/25: .8X TO 2X PLAY JSY
1 Jeremy Hill 2.00 5.00
2 Marcus Mariota 3.00 8.00
3 Amari Cooper 3.00 8.00
4 Ryan Tannehill 2.50 6.00
5 Blake Bortles 2.00 5.00
6 Larry Fitzgerald 2.50 6.00
7 Eli Manning 2.50 6.00
8 Philip Rivers 3.00 8.00
9 Jameis Winston 3.00 8.00
10 Von Miller 2.50 6.00
11 Jordan Reed 2.00 5.00
12 Odell Beckham Jr. 3.00 8.00
13 Andy Dalton 2.50 6.00
14 Todd Gurley 3.00 8.00
15 Champ Bailey 2.50 6.00

2016 Certified Fabric of the Game

*PRIME/49: .5X TO 1.2X BASIC JSY/99
*PRIME/25: .5X TO 1.2X BASIC JSY/29
1 Stefon Diggs/99 3.00 8.00
2 Eric Ebron/99 2.50 6.00
3 Jeremy Hill/99 2.50 6.00
4 A.J. Green/25 6.00 15.00
5 Joe Haden/99 2.50 6.00
6 Andy Dalton/49 4.00 10.00
7 Mark Ingram/25 5.00 12.00
8 Carlos Hyde/99 2.50 6.00
9 Odell Beckham Jr./99 4.00 10.00
10 Devin Funchess/99 2.50 6.00
11 T.J. Yeldon/99 2.50 6.00
13 Jeremy Langford/99 3.00 8.00
14 Dre Kirkpatrick/99 2.50 6.00
15 Julius Thomas/99 2.50 6.00
16 Antonio Gates/49 3.00 8.00
17 Marshall Faulk/25 5.00 12.00
18 Champ Bailey/99 3.00 8.00
19 Ozzie Newsome/49 4.00 10.00
20 Devonta Freeman/99 3.00 8.00
21 Tim Tebow/49 10.00 25.00
22 Jadeveon Clowney/99 2.50 6.00
23 Jerry Rice/25
24 Allen Hurns/99 2.50 6.00
25 Kendall Wright/99 2.50 6.00
26 Barry Sanders/25
27 Matt Ryan/49 4.00 10.00
28 Cole Beasley/99 4.00 10.00
29 Philip Rivers/49 5.00 12.00
30 Donte Moncrief/99 3.00 8.00
31 Todd Gurley/99 4.00 10.00
32 Jameis Winston/99 4.00 10.00
33 Jimmy Garoppolo/99 5.00 12.00
34 Allen Robinson/99 3.00 8.00
35 Khalil Mack/99 4.00 10.00
36 Blake Bortles/99 2.50 6.00
37 Matthew Stafford/25 5.00 12.00
38 Cris Carter/25 12.00 30.00
39 Phillip Dorsett/99 2.50 6.00
40 Dorial Green-Beckham/99 2.50 6.00
42 Jamison Crowder/99 2.50 6.00
43 John Riggins/25 5.00 12.00
44 Amari Cooper/99 4.00 10.00
45 Larry Fitzgerald/49 4.00 10.00
46 Brandin Cooks/99 3.00 8.00
47 Melvin Gordon/99 3.00 8.00
48 DeAngelo Hall/99 3.00 8.00
50 Duke Johnson/99 2.50 6.00
51 Von Miller/49 4.00 10.00
52 Jarvis Landry/99 3.00 8.00
53 Jordan Matthews/99 3.00 8.00
54 Ameer Abdullah/99 2.50 6.00
55 LeSean McCoy/49 5.00 12.00
56 Buck Allen/99 2.50 6.00
57 Mike Evans/99 3.00 8.00
58 Delanie Walker/99 2.50 6.00
59 Ryan Tannehill/49 4.00 10.00
60 Earl Thomas/25 5.00 12.00
61 Warren Moon/25 12.00 30.00
62 Jay Ajayi/99 3.00 8.00
63 Jordan Reed/49 3.00 8.00
64 Andrew Luck/25 8.00 20.00
65 Marcus Mariota/99 4.00 10.00
66 Cameron Wake/99 2.50 6.00
67 Nelson Agholor/99 2.50 6.00
68 Derek Carr/99 4.00 10.00
69 Sammy Watkins/49 5.00 12.00
70 Eli Manning/49 4.00 10.00

2016 Certified Fabric of the Game Signatures

*PRIME/49: .5X TO 1.2X BASIC JSY AU/99
FGSCO Chris Cooley/25 5.00 12.00
FGSDGB Dorial Green-Beckham/99 3.00 8.00
FGSEE Eric Ebron/25 5.00 12.00
FGSJC Jamison Crowder/99 3.00 8.00
FGSJH Justin Hunter/25 5.00 12.00
FGSJL Jeremy Langford/99 4.00 10.00
FGSJS Jaelen Strong/25 5.00 12.00
FGSKB Kelvin Benjamin/25 6.00 15.00
FGSKS Kenny Stills/25 5.00 12.00
FGSKW Karlos Williams/99 3.00 8.00
FGSMJ Matt Jones/99 4.00 10.00
FGSMT Manti Te'o/25 5.00 12.00
FGSNA Nelson Agholor/25 5.00 12.00
FGSTB Teddy Bridgewater/25
FGSTR Tom Rathman/25 5.00 12.00
FGSTY T.J. Yeldon/99 3.00 8.00

2016 Certified Gamers

*ORANGE/149: .5X TO 1.2X BASIC INSERTS
*ORANGE/99: .6X TO 1.5X BASIC INSERTS
*RED/75-99: .6X TO 1.5X BASIC INSERTS
*BLUE/50: .8X TO 2X BASIC INSERTS
*GOLD/25: 1X TO 2.5X BASIC INSERTS
1 Andy Dalton 1.50 4.00
2 Blake Bortles 1.25 3.00
3 Jarvis Landry 1.50 4.00
4 Jeremy Hill 1.25 3.00
5 Karlos Williams 1.25 3.00
6 T.J. Yeldon 1.25 3.00
7 Tyler Eifert 1.50 4.00
8 Aqib Talib 1.25 3.00
9 DeMarcus Ware 1.50 4.00
10 Keenan Allen 1.50 4.00
11 Philip Rivers 2.00 5.00
12 Allen Robinson 1.50 4.00
13 Geno Atkins 1.25 3.00
14 Marcell Dareus 1.25 3.00
15 Aaron Rodgers 8.00 20.00

2016 Certified Gold Team

*RED/99: .6X TO 1.5X BASIC INSERTS
*BLUE/50: .8X TO 2X BASIC INSERTS
*GOLD/25: 1X TO 2.5X BASIC INSERTS
1 Peyton Manning 1.25 3.00
2 Tom Brady 1.50 4.00
3 Todd Gurley .60 1.50
4 Aaron Rodgers 1.25 3.00
5 Odell Beckham Jr. .60 1.50
6 Russell Wilson .75 2.00
7 Jameis Winston .60 1.50
8 Cam Newton .60 1.50
9 Marcus Mariota .60 1.50
10 Andrew Luck .75 2.00
11 Joey Bosa .75 2.00
12 Derrick Henry 1.00 2.50
13 Paxton Lynch .40 1.00
14 Ezekiel Elliott 2.00 5.00
15 Connor Cook .50 1.25
16 Laquon Treadwell .50 1.25
17 Carson Wentz 4.00 10.00
18 Josh Doctson .50 1.25
19 Jared Goff 2.50 6.00
20 Michael Thomas .75 2.00

2016 Certified Gridiron Signatures

*RED/75: .4X TO 1X BASIC AU/99
*BLUE/50: .5X TO 1.2X BASIC AU/99
*GOLD/25: .6X TO 1.5X BASIC AU/99
*GOLD/15: .5X TO 1.2X BASIC AU/25
GSBM Byron Marshall/99 4.00 10.00
GSCC Connor Cook/25 8.00 20.00
GSCW Carson Wentz/25 75.00 150.00
GSDH Derrick Henry/25 15.00 40.00
GSDR Demarcus Robinson/99 4.00 10.00
GSJB Jacoby Brissett/99 5.00 12.00
GSJC Jeremy Cash/99 5.00 12.00
GSJG Jared Goff/25 40.00 100.00
GSJS Jaylon Smith/99 4.00 10.00
GSKF Kendall Fuller/99 5.00 12.00
GSKH Kevin Hogan/99 5.00 12.00
GSKR KeiVarae Russell/99 4.00 10.00
GSMJ Myles Jack/99 5.00 12.00
GSNP Nelson Spruce/99 4.00 10.00
GSNS Nate Sudfeld/99 4.00 10.00
GSPL Paxton Lynch/25 6.00 15.00
GSRN Robert Nkemdiche/99 5.00 12.00
GSSC Su'a Cravens/99 4.00 10.00
GSTB Trevone Boykin/99 4.00 10.00
GSVB Vonn Bell/99 5.00 12.00

2016 Certified New Generation Jerseys

*ORANGE/399: .5X TO 1.2X BASIC JSY
*RED/299: .5X TO 1.2X BASIC JSY
*BLUE/50: .8X TO 2X BASIC JSY
*GOLD/25: 1X TO 2.5X BASIC JSY
1 Jared Goff 8.00 20.00
2 Carson Wentz 12.00 30.00
3 Joey Bosa 2.50 6.00
4 Ezekiel Elliott 8.00 20.00
5 Corey Coleman 2.00 5.00
6 Will Fuller 2.00 5.00
7 Josh Doctson 1.50 4.00
8 Laquon Treadwell 1.50 4.00
9 Paxton Lynch 1.25 3.00
10 Hunter Henry 1.50 4.00
11 Sterling Shepard 1.50 4.00
12 Derrick Henry 3.00 8.00
13 Michael Thomas 2.50 6.00
14 Christian Hackenberg 1.25 3.00
15 Kenyan Drake 2.00 5.00
16 Braxton Miller 1.25 3.00
17 Leonte Carroo 1.25 3.00
18 C.J. Prosise 1.25 3.00
19 Moritz Bohringer 1.25 3.00
20 Cody Kessler 1.25 3.00
21 Tyler Boyd 1.50 4.00
22 Connor Cook 1.50 4.00
23 Chris Moore 1.50 4.00
24 Paul Perkins 1.25 3.00
25 Ricardo Louis 1.25 3.00
26 Pharoh Cooper 1.25 3.00
27 Demarcus Robinson 1.25 3.00
28 Kenneth Dixon 1.25 3.00
29 Dak Prescott 6.00 15.00
30 Cardale Jones 1.25 3.00

2016 Certified Potential Autographs

*RED/75: .4X TO 1X BASIC AU/99
*BLUE/50: .5X TO 1.2X BASIC AU/99
CPSAB Aaron Burbridge/99 3.00 8.00
CPSAC Alex Collins/99 4.00 10.00
CPSAG Aaron Green/99 3.00 8.00
CPSAH Austin Hooper/99 3.00 8.00
CPSAR A'Shawn Robinson/99 3.00 8.00
CPSBA Bralon Addison/99 3.00 8.00
CPSBD Brandon Doughty/99 3.00 8.00
CPSBM Braxton Miller/99 3.00 8.00
CPSCC Connor Cook/25 25.00 60.00
CPSCH Christian Hackenberg/49 4.00 10.00
CPSCJ Cardale Jones/49 4.00 10.00
CPSCK Cody Kessler/99 3.00 8.00
CPSCO Corey Coleman/99 5.00 12.00
CPSCW Carson Wentz/25 40.00 80.00
CPSDB Devontae Booker/99 4.00 10.00
CPSDH Derrick Henry/25 12.00 30.00
CPSDL Darron Lee/99 3.00 8.00
CPSDP Dak Prescott/99 40.00 80.00
CPSDW De'Runnya Wilson/99 3.00 8.00
CPSEE Ezekiel Elliott/49 60.00 125.00
CPSHH Hunter Henry/99 4.00 10.00
CPSJA Jarran Reed/99 3.00 8.00
CPSJB Joey Bosa/99 6.00 15.00
CPSJD Josh Doctson/49
CPSJG Jared Goff/25 50.00 100.00
CPSJH Jordan Howard/99 8.00 20.00
CPSJR Jalen Ramsey/99 5.00 12.00
CPSJW Jonathan Williams/99 4.00 10.00
CPSKD Kenyan Drake/99 5.00 12.00
CPSKE Kenneth Dixon/99 EXCH 3.00 8.00
CPSKL Kenny Lawler/99 5.00 12.00
CPSKT Kelvin Taylor/99 3.00 8.00
CPSLC Leonte Carroo/99 3.00 8.00
CPSLT Laquon Treadwell/49 30.00 60.00
CPSMA Mackensie Alexander/99 3.00 8.00
CPSMT Michael Thomas/49 8.00 20.00
CPSPC Pharoh Cooper/99 3.00 8.00
CPSPL Paxton Lynch/25 5.00 12.00
CPSPP Paul Perkins/99 3.00 8.00
CPSRH Rashard Higgins/99 3.00 8.00
CPSRR Reggie Ragland/99 3.00 8.00
CPSSL Shaq Lawson/99 3.00 8.00
CPSSP C.J. Prosise/99 3.00 8.00
CPSSS Sterling Shepard/99 4.00 10.00
CPSTB Tyler Boyd/99 4.00 10.00
CSPTM Tre Madden/99 3.00 8.00
CPSVH Vernon Hargreaves III/99 5.00 12.00
CPSWF Will Fuller/49 6.00 15.00

2016 Certified Potential Autographs Mirror Gold

*GOLD/25: .5X TO 1.2X BASIC AU/49
*GOLD/25: .6X TO 1.5X BASIC AU/99
*GOLD/15: .5X TO 1.2X BASIC AU/25

2016 Certified Signatures

*RED/60: .5X TO 1.2X BASIC AU/99
*BLUE/40: .5X TO 1.2X BASIC AU/99
*GOLD/25: .6X TO 1.5X BASIC AU/99
2 Warrick Dunn/25 15.00 30.00
3 Antonio Freeman/25 15.00 30.00
4 Blake Bortles/25 15.00 30.00
5 Brandon Jacobs/35 4.00 10.00
6 Brett Hundley/25 10.00 25.00
7 Brian Mitchell/99 10.00 25.00
8 Bryce Brown/99 3.00 8.00
9 Bryce Petty/99 3.00 8.00
10 Bubba Franks/35 4.00 10.00
11 C.J. Fiedorowicz/99 4.00 10.00
12 Cameron Artis-Payne/99 3.00 8.00
13 Case Keenum/99 4.00 10.00
14 Champ Bailey/35 15.00 30.00
15 Charles Mann/99 8.00 20.00
16 Charles Sims/99 3.00 8.00
18 Clinton Portis/20
19 Crockett Gillmore/99 3.00 8.00
20 Dallas Clark/24 5.00 12.00
21 David Carr/35 4.00 10.00
23 Fred Williamson/33 4.00 10.00
24 Dexter Manley/99 15.00 40.00
25 Dhani Jones/35 4.00 10.00
26 Donald Driver/25 15.00 30.00
27 Dorial Green-Beckham/99 3.00 8.00
28 EJ Manuel/25 5.00 12.00
30 Eric Ebron/35 4.00 10.00
31 Forrest Gregg/25 20.00 40.00
32 Fred Biletnikoff/25 12.00 30.00
33 Fred Taylor/25 10.00 25.00
34 Greg Jennings/25 5.00 12.00
35 Hakeem Nicks/25 5.00 12.00
36 Jackie Smith/35 4.00 10.00
37 Jamal Lewis/35 5.00 12.00
38 Jamison Crowder/99 3.00 8.00
39 Jason Verrett/99 3.00 8.00
40 Jeff Janis/99 3.00 8.00
41 Jeremy Langford/99 4.00 10.00
43 Jesse James/99 3.00 8.00
44 Jimmy Garoppolo/35 8.00 20.00
45 Joe Theismann/25 25.00 50.00
48 Bob Lilly/35 5.00 12.00
49 Karlos Williams/99 3.00 8.00
50 Kelvin Benjamin/35 5.00 12.00
51 Bill Romanowski/23 5.00 12.00
52 Kenny Stills/35 4.00 10.00
53 Kevin White/35 4.00 10.00
54 Kony Ealy/99 3.00 8.00
55 La'el Collins/99 3.00 8.00
56 Lance Briggs/35 5.00 12.00
57 Landon Collins/99 3.00 8.00
58 Larry Csonka/25 25.00 50.00
59 Latavius Murray/99 3.00 8.00
60 Lawrence Taylor/25 15.00 40.00
61 Malcolm Smith/35 6.00 15.00
62 Manti Te'o/35 4.00 10.00
63 Mark Chmura/35 10.00 25.00
64 Marqise Lee/35 4.00 10.00
65 Matt Jones/99 4.00 10.00
66 Matt Schaub/25 5.00 12.00
67 Melvin Gordon/25
68 Michael Floyd/35 4.00 10.00
69 Michael Strahan/15 15.00 40.00
70 Mike Curtis/35 4.00 10.00
71 Mike Quick/35 4.00 10.00
72 Nelson Agholor/35 4.00 10.00
74 Plaxico Burress/35 4.00 10.00
75 Reggie Wayne/25 6.00 15.00
76 Ricky Sanders/99 6.00 15.00
77 Ricky Williams/35 5.00 12.00
78 Robert Brooks/35 10.00 25.00
79 Robert Mathis/35 4.00 10.00
81 Ron Mix/99 3.00 8.00
82 Ronnie Brown/25 5.00 12.00
83 Steve Johnson/35 5.00 12.00
84 T.J. Yeldon/99 3.00 8.00
85 Teddy Bridgewater/25 12.00 30.00
86 Tim Brown/25 30.00 60.00
87 Trent Dilfer/35 4.00 10.00
88 Vincent Jackson/35 4.00 10.00
89 Wes Welker/15 25.00 50.00
90 Zach Mettenberger/99 3.00 8.00

2016 Certified Signed and Certified

*RED/75: .4X TO 1X BASIC AU/99
*BLUE/50: .5X TO 1.2X BASIC AU/99
SCAJ Austin Johnson/99 3.00 8.00
SCAW Adolphus Washington/99 3.00 8.00
SCCC Corey Coleman/35 6.00 15.00
SCCH Christian Hackenberg/35 4.00 10.00
SCCJ Cardale Jones/25 5.00 12.00
SCCP C.J. Prosise/35 4.00 10.00
SCDB DeForest Buckner/99 3.00 8.00
SCDB2 Daniel Braverman/99 6.00 15.00
SCDV Dan Vitale/99 3.00 8.00
SCEA Eli Apple/99 4.00 10.00
SCEE Ezekiel Elliott/25 60.00 125.00
SCEO Emmanuel Ogbah/99 4.00 10.00
SCGG Glenn Gronkowski/99 3.00 8.00
SCJD Josh Doctson/25 6.00 15.00
SCJWL Jordan Williams-Lambert/99 3.00 8.00
SCKC Konny Clark/99 3.00 8.00
SCLT Laquon Treadwell/25 30.00 60.00
SCMC Maliek Collins/99 3.00 8.00
SCMT Michael Thomas/25 10.00 25.00
SCNV Nick Vannett/99 3.00 8.00
SCPP Paul Perkins/35 4.00 10.00
SCRL Ricardo Louis/99 3.00 8.00
SCSC Shilique Calhoun/99 8.00 20.00
SCSR Sheldon Rankins/99 4.00 10.00
SCSW Scooby Wright III/99 3.00 8.00
SCTS Tajae Sharpe/99 4.00 10.00
SCVB Vernon Butler/99 3.00 8.00
SCWF Will Fuller/35 6.00 15.00
SCWJ William Jackson III/99 4.00 10.00
SCXH Xavien Howard/99 4.00 10.00

2016 Certified Signed and Certified Mirror Gold

*GOLD/25: .6X TO 1.5X BASIC AU/99
*GOLD/25: .5X TO 1.2X BASIC AU/35
*GOLD/15: .5X TO 1.2X BASIC AU/25
SCEE Ezekiel Elliott/15 125.00 250.00

2016 Certified Skills

*RED/99: .6X TO 1.5X BASIC INSERTS
*BLUE/50: .8X TO 2X BASIC INSERTS
*GOLD/25: 1X TO 2.5X BASIC INSERTS
1 Odell Beckham Jr. 1.00 2.50
2 A.J. Green 1.00 2.50
3 Eli Manning .75 2.00
4 Julian Edelman 1.00 2.50
5 Adrian Peterson 1.00 2.50
6 Darrelle Revis .60 1.50
7 Peyton Manning 2.00 5.00
8 J.J. Watt 1.00 2.50
9 Antonio Brown 1.00 2.50
10 Aaron Rodgers 2.00 5.00
11 Allen Robinson .75 2.00
12 Drew Brees 1.00 2.50
13 Larry Fitzgerald .75 2.00
14 Marcus Peters .60 1.50
15 Doug Martin .75 2.00
16 Richard Sherman 1.00 2.50
17 Devonta Freeman .75 2.00
18 Khalil Mack 1.00 2.50
19 DeAndre Hopkins .75 2.00
20 Russell Wilson 1.25 3.00
21 Demaryius Thomas .75 2.00
22 Dez Bryant 1.00 2.50
23 Rob Gronkowski 1.00 2.50
24 Tyrann Mathieu .75 2.00
25 Todd Gurley 1.00 2.50
26 Josh Norman .60 1.50
27 Julio Jones 1.00 2.50
28 Tom Brady 2.50 6.00
29 Brandon Marshall .60 1.50
30 Cam Newton 1.00 2.50

2016 Certified Sunday Certified

*RED/99: .6X TO 1.5X BASIC INSERTS
*BLUE/50: .8X TO 2X BASIC INSERTS
*GOLD/25: 1X TO 2.5X BASIC INSERTS
1 Aaron Rodgers 2.00 5.00
2 Julian Edelman 1.00 2.50
3 J.J. Watt 1.00 2.50
4 Jameis Winston 1.00 2.50
5 Odell Beckham Jr. 1.00 2.50
6 Le'Veon Bell .75 2.00
7 Clay Matthews 1.00 2.50
8 Cam Newton 1.00 2.50
9 Russell Wilson 1.25 3.00
10 Teddy Bridgewater .75 2.00
11 Dez Bryant 1.00 2.50
12 Amari Cooper 1.00 2.50
13 Marshawn Lynch .75 2.00
14 Eli Manning .75 2.00
15 Tony Romo .75 2.00
16 A.J. Green 1.00 2.50
17 Drew Brees 1.00 2.50
18 Jordy Nelson .75 2.00
19 Peyton Manning 2.00 5.00
20 Ryan Tannehill .75 2.00
21 Richard Sherman 1.00 2.50
22 Marcus Mariota 1.00 2.50
23 Rob Gronkowski 1.00 2.50
24 Eddie Lacy .60 1.50
25 Luke Kuechly .75 2.00
26 Ben Roethlisberger 1.00 2.50
27 Antonio Brown 1.00 2.50
28 Calvin Johnson 1.00 2.50
29 Tom Brady 2.50 6.00
30 Andrew Luck 1.25 3.00

2017 Certified

1 Cam Newton .40 1.00
2 Matt Ryan .30 .75
3 Russell Wilson .50 1.25
4 Dak Prescott .40 1.00
5 Joe Flacco .30 .75
6 Cameron Meredith .25 .60
7 Ben Roethlisberger .40 1.00
8 Marcus Mariota .40 1.00
9 Drew Brees .40 1.00
10 Eli Manning .30 .75
11 Julio Jones .40 1.00
12 Aaron Rodgers .75 2.00
13 Odell Beckham Jr. .40 1.00
14 Andy Dalton .30 .75
15 Tom Brady 1.00 2.50
16 Jameis Winston .30 .75
17 Philip Rivers .40 1.00
18 Matthew Stafford .30 .75
19 A.J. Green .40 1.00
20 Sammy Watkins .40 1.00
21 LeSean McCoy .40 1.00
22 Matt Forte .25 .60
23 Eric Decker .25 .60
24 Jay Ajayi .30 .75
25 Jarvis Landry .30 .75
26 Ryan Tannehill .30 .75
27 Rob Gronkowski .40 1.00
28 Julian Edelman .40 1.00
29 Demaryius Thomas .30 .75
30 Von Miller .30 .75
31 Alex Smith .30 .75
32 Tyreek Hill .40 1.00
33 Eric Berry .30 .75
34 Melvin Gordon .30 .75
35 Joey Bosa .40 1.00
36 Derek Carr .40 1.00
37 Amari Cooper .40 1.00
38 Khalil Mack .40 1.00
39 Isaiah Crowell .25 .60
40 Jamie Collins .25 .60
41 Antonio Brown .40 1.00
42 Le'Veon Bell .30 .75
43 J.J. Watt .40 1.00
44 DeAndre Hopkins .30 .75
45 Jadeveon Clowney .25 .60
46 Andrew Luck .50 1.25
47 T.Y. Hilton .30 .75
48 Blake Bortles .25 .60
49 Allen Robinson .30 .75
50 Derrick Henry .30 .75
51 Delanie Walker .25 .60
52 Ezekiel Elliott .50 1.25
53 Dez Bryant .40 1.00
54 Jason Witten .30 .75
55 Landon Collins .25 .60
56 Carson Wentz .50 1.25
57 Jordan Matthews .25 .60
58 Kirk Cousins .40 1.00
59 Robert Kelley .25 .60
60 Jordan Reed .25 .60
61 Larry Fitzgerald .30 .75
62 Carson Palmer .30 .75
63 David Johnson .40 1.00
64 Patrick Peterson .25 .60
65 Jared Goff .40 1.00
66 Todd Gurley II .40 1.00
67 Aaron Donald .40 1.00
68 Carlos Hyde .25 .60
69 Jeremy Kerley .25 .60
70 Doug Baldwin .30 .75
71 Jimmy Graham .40 1.00
72 Richard Sherman .40 1.00
73 Alshon Jeffery .30 .75
74 Leonard Floyd .25 .60
75 Marvin Jones Jr. .25 .60
76 Golden Tate III .25 .60
77 Jordy Nelson .30 .75
78 Randall Cobb .30 .75
79 Clay Matthews .30 .75
80 Stefon Diggs .30 .75
81 Adrian Peterson .40 1.00
82 Harrison Smith .25 .60
83 Sam Bradford .25 .60
84 Devonta Freeman .30 .75
85 Vic Beasley Jr. .25 .60
86 Greg Olsen .30 .75
87 Kelvin Benjamin .30 .75
88 Luke Kuechly .30 .75
89 Brandin Cooks .30 .75
90 Mark Ingram .30 .75
91 Mike Evans .30 .75
92 Mike Glennon .30 .75
93 Jordan Howard .40 1.00
94 DeMarco Murray .30 .75
95 Lamar Miller .25 .60
96 Michael Thomas .40 1.00
97 Terrelle Pryor Sr. .25 .60
98 Josh Norman .25 .60
99 Kyle Rudolph .25 .60
100 Travis Kelce .40 1.00
101 Calvin Johnson IMM 1.25 3.00
102 Randy Moss IMM 1.00 2.50
103 John Riggins IMM 1.00 2.50
104 Franco Harris IMM 1.25 3.00
105 Troy Aikman IMM 1.50 4.00
106 LaDainian Tomlinson IMM 1.00 2.50
107 Kurt Warner IMM 1.00 2.50
108 Morten Andersen IMM .75 2.00
109 Terrell Davis IMM 1.00 2.50
110 Steve Young IMM 1.50 4.00
111 Howie Long IMM 1.25 3.00
112 Terry Bradshaw IMM 2.00 5.00
113 Peyton Manning IMM 2.50 6.00
114 Jerome Bettis IMM 1.25 3.00
115 Marcus Allen IMM 1.00 2.50
116 Michael Strahan IMM 1.00 2.50
117 Steve Largent IMM 1.25 3.00
118 Dan Marino IMM 2.50 6.00
119 Jerry Rice IMM 2.00 5.00
120 Deion Sanders IMM 1.00 2.50
121 Brian Urlacher IMM 1.25 3.00
122 Emmitt Smith IMM 2.00 5.00
123 Michael Irvin IMM 1.25 3.00
124 Ickey Woods IMM .75 2.00
125 Brett Favre IMM 2.50 6.00
126 Dick Butkus IMM 1.50 4.00
127 Heath Miller IMM .75 2.00
128 Warren Moon IMM 1.25 3.00
129 Earl Campbell IMM 1.25 3.00
130 Ray Lewis IMM 1.25 3.00
131 Jeff Garcia IMM .75 2.00
132 Bruce Smith IMM 1.00 2.50
133 Tim Brown IMM 1.25 3.00
134 Doug Flutie IMM 1.00 2.50
135 Jim McMahon IMM 1.00 2.50
136 Myles Garrett RC 2.00 5.00
137 Josh Malone RC .60 1.50
138 Chad Hansen RC .60 1.50
139 Donnel Pumphrey RC .75 2.00
140 Ryan Switzer RC .75 2.00
141 Brian Hill RC .60 1.50
142 Shelton Gibson RC .60 1.50
143 Chad Williams RC .60 1.50
144 Jehu Chesson RC .75 2.00
145 Tarik Cohen RC 1.25 3.00
146 Rodney Adams RC .60 1.50
147 Isaiah McKenzie RC .60 1.50
148 DeAngelo Yancey RC .60 1.50
149 Trent Taylor RC .75 2.00
150 T.J. Logan RC 1.00 2.50
151 Solomon Thomas RC .60 1.50
152 Jamal Adams RC .60 1.50
153 Marshon Lattimore RC .75 2.00
154 Haason Reddick RC .60 1.50
155 Derek Barnett RC .75 2.00
156 Malik Hooker RC .60 1.50
157 Marlon Humphrey RC .60 1.50
158 Jonathan Allen RC .75 2.00
159 Adoree' Jackson RC .75 2.00
160 Garett Bolles RC .60 1.50
161 Jarrad Davis RC .75 2.00
162 Charles Harris RC .60 1.50
163 Gareon Conley RC .60 1.50
164 Jabrill Peppers RC 1.00 2.50
165 Takkarist McKinley RC .60 1.50
166 Tre'Davious White RC .60 1.50
167 Taco Charlton RC .60 1.50
168 David Njoku RC .75 2.00
169 T.J. Watt RC 2.00 5.00
170 Reuben Foster RC .60 1.50
171 Ryan Ramczyk RC .60 1.50
172 Kevin King RC .75 2.00
173 Cam Robinson RC .60 1.50
174 Budda Baker RC .60 1.50
175 Marcus Maye RC .60 1.50
176 Marcus Williams RC .60 1.50
177 Sidney Jones RC .60 1.50
178 Gerald Everett RC .60 1.50
179 Adam Shaheen RC .60 1.50
180 Quincy Wilson RC .60 1.50
181 Tyus Bowser RC .60 1.50
182 Ryan Anderson RC .60 1.50
183 Justin Evans RC .60 1.50
184 DeMarcus Walker RC .60 1.50
185 Teez Tabor RC .75 2.00
186 Raekwon McMillan RC .60 1.50
187 Dalvin Tomlinson RC .60 1.50
188 Obi Melifonwu RC .60 1.50
189 Zach Cunningham RC .75 2.00
190 Tanoh Kpassagnon RC .75 2.00
191 Chidobe Awuzie RC .75 2.00
192 Josh Jones RC .60 1.50
193 Chris Wormley RC .60 1.50
194 Jordan Willis RC .60 1.50
195 Duke Riley RC .60 1.50
196 Derek Rivers RC .75 2.00
197 Fabian Moreau RC .60 1.50
198 Eddie Vanderdoes RC .60 1.50
199 Shaquill Griffin RC .75 2.00
200 Jourdan Lewis RC .60 1.50
201 Mitchell Trubisky JSY AU/149 RC 50.00 100.00
202 Leonard Fournette JSY AU/149 RC 15.00 40.00
203 Corey Davis JSY AU/149 RC 8.00 20.00
204 Mike Williams JSY AU/149 RC 8.00 20.00
205 Christian McCaffrey JSY AU/149 RC 25.00 50.00
206 John Ross III JSY AU/149 RC 6.00 15.00
207 Patrick Mahomes II JSY AU/149 RC 250.00 500.00
208 Deshaun Watson JSY AU/149 RC 60.00 125.00
209 O.J. Howard JSY AU/199 RC 6.00 15.00
210 Evan Engram JSY AU/299 RC 5.00 12.00
211 Zay Jones JSY AU/299 RC 5.00 12.00
212 Curtis Samuel JSY AU/199 RC 6.00 15.00
213 Dalvin Cook JSY AU/149 RC 30.00 60.00
214 Joe Mixon JSY AU/499 RC 6.00 15.00
215 DeShone Kizer JSY AU/149 RC 5.00 12.00
216 JuJu Smith-Schuster JSY AU/149 RC 12.00 30.00
217 Alvin Kamara JSY AU/299 RC 15.00 40.00
218 Cooper Kupp JSY AU/499 RC 5.00 12.00
219 Taywan Taylor JSY AU/499 RC EXCH 3.00 8.00
220 ArDarius Stewart JSY AU/499 RC 3.00 8.00
221 Carlos Henderson JSY AU/299 RC 4.00 10.00
222 Chris Godwin JSY AU/499 RC 4.00 10.00
223 Kareem Hunt JSY AU/499 RC 10.00 25.00
224 Davis Webb JSY AU/299 RC 4.00 10.00
225 D'Onta Foreman JSY AU/299 RC 5.00 12.00
226 C.J. Beathard JSY AU/299 RC 4.00 10.00
227 James Conner JSY AU/499 RC 25.00 50.00
228 Amara Darboh JSY AU/299 RC 4.00 10.00
229 Kenny Golladay JSY AU/499 RC 5.00 12.00
230 Dede Westbrook JSY AU/199 RC 5.00 12.00
231 Samaje Perine JSY AU/299 RC 4.00 10.00
232 Josh Reynolds JSY AU/499 RC 3.00 8.00
233 Mack Hollins JSY AU/499 RC 3.00 8.00
234 Joe Williams JSY AU/499 RC 3.00 8.00
235 Jamaal Williams JSY AU/499 RC 8.00 20.00
236 R. Joshua Dobbs JSY AU/499 RC 4.00 10.00
237 Wayne Gallman JSY AU/299 RC 5.00 12.00
238 Marlon Mack JSY AU/499 RC 5.00 12.00
239 Jeremy McNichols JSY AU/499 RC 3.00 8.00
240 Nathan Peterman JSY AU/199 RC 6.00 15.00

2017 Certified Mirror Blue

*VETS/50: 3X TO 8X BASIC CARDS
*IMM/50: 1X TO 2.5X BASIC CARDS/999
*ROOKIES/50: 1.2X TO 3X BASIC CARDS/999
*201-240 RK JSY AU/50: 1X TO 2.5X JSY AU/499
*201-240 RK JSY AU/50: .8X TO 2X JSY AU/299
*201-240 RK JSY AU/50: .6X TO 1.5X JSY AU/149-199
201 Mitchell Trubisky JSY AU 75.00 150.00
207 Patrick Mahomes II JSY AU 400.00 800.00
208 Deshaun Watson JSY AU 100.00 200.00

2017 Certified Mirror Gold

*VETS/25: 4X TO 10X BASIC CARDS
*IMM/25: 1.5X TO 4X BASIC CARDS/999
*ROOKIES/25: 1.2X TO 3X BASIC CARDS/999
*201-240 RK JSY AU/25: 1.2X TO 3X JSY AU/499
*201-240 RK JSY AU/25: 1X TO 2.5X JSY AU/299
*201-240 RK JSY AU/25: .8X TO 2X JSY AU/149-199
201 Mitchell Trubisky JSY AU 100.00 200.00
207 Patrick Mahomes II JSY AU 500.00 1000.00
208 Deshaun Watson JSY AU 150.00 250.00

2017 Certified Mirror Orange

*VETS/299: 1.5X TO 4X BASIC CARDS
*IMM/299: .5X TO 1.2X BASIC CARDS/999
*ROOKIES/199: .6X TO 1.5X BASIC CARDS/999
*201-240 RK JSY AU/349: .5X TO 1.2X JSY AU/499
*201-240 RK JSY AU/199: .6X TO 1.5X JSY AU/499
*201-240 RK JSY AU/199: .5X TO 1.2X JSY AU/299
*201-240 RK JSY AU/99: .5X TO 1.2X JSY AU/149-199
201 Mitchell Trubisky JSY AU/99 60.00 125.00
207 Patrick Mahomes II JSY AU/99 300.00 600.00
208 Deshaun Watson JSY AU/99 75.00 150.00

2017 Certified Mirror Red

*VETS/99: 2.5X TO 6X BASIC CARDS
*IMM/99: .8X TO 2X BASIC CARDS/999
*ROOKIES/99: 1X TO 2.5X BASIC CARDS/999
*201-240 RK JSY AU/249: .5X TO 1.2X JSY AU/499
*201-240 RK JSY AU/99: .8X TO 2X JSY AU/499
*201-240 RK JSY AU/99: .6X TO 1.5X JSY AU/299
*201-240 RK JSY AU/75: .5X TO 1.2X JSY AU/149-199
201 Mitchell Trubisky JSY AU/75 60.00 125.00
207 Patrick Mahomes II JSY AU/75 300.00 600.00
208 Deshaun Watson JSY AU/75 75.00 150.00

2017 Certified Mirror Silver

*VETS/499: 1.5X TO 4X BASIC CARDS
*IMM/499: .5X TO 1.2X BASIC CARDS/999
*ROOKIES/499: .6X TO 1.5X BASIC CARDS/999

2017 Certified Accomplishments

*RED/99: .6X TO 1.5X BASIC INSERTS
*BLUE/50: .8X TO 2X BASIC INSERTS
*GOLD/25: 1X TO 2.5X BASIC INSERTS
1 Matt Ryan .75 2.00
2 Khalil Mack 1.00 2.50
3 Dak Prescott 1.00 2.50
4 Joey Bosa 1.00 2.50
5 Jordy Nelson .75 2.00
6 Tom Brady 2.50 6.00
7 Pat McAfee .75 2.00
8 Kyle Juszczyk .60 1.50
9 Antonio Brown 1.00 2.50
10 Eli Manning .75 2.00
11 Cam Newton 1.00 2.50
12 Eric Berry .75 2.00
13 LaDainian Tomlinson .75 2.00
14 Aaron Rodgers 2.00 5.00
15 Adrian Peterson 1.00 2.50
16 J.J. Watt 1.00 2.50
17 Luke Kuechly .75 2.00
18 Brian Urlacher 1.00 2.50
19 Brett Favre 2.00 5.00
20 Jerome Bettis 1.00 2.50
21 Tim Brown 1.00 2.50
22 Kurt Warner .75 2.00
23 Deion Sanders .75 2.00
24 Terrell Davis .75 2.00
25 Steve Young 1.25 3.00
26 Terry Bradshaw 1.50 4.00
27 Ben Roethlisberger 1.00 2.50
28 Von Miller .75 2.00
29 Randy Moss .75 2.00
30 Odell Beckham Jr. 1.00 2.50

2017 Certified Clutch Performers Jerseys

*ORANGE/199: .4X TO 1X BASIC JSY/199-399
*ORANGE/75-99: .4X TO 1X BASIC JSY/75
*RED/75-99: .5X TO 1.2X BASIC JSY/199-399
*RED/50: .5X TO 1.2X BASIC JSY/75-99
*BLUE/50: .6X TO 1.5X BASIC JSY/199-399
*BLUE/25: .6X TO 1.5X BASIC JSY/25
*GOLD/25: .8X TO 2X BASIC JSY/199-399
*GOLD/25: .5X TO 1.2X BASIC JSY/50
1 Dak Prescott 2.50 6.00
2 Antonio Brown 4.00 10.00
3 Tom Brady 10.00 25.00
4 Drew Brees 4.00 10.00
5 Tony Dorsett 3.00 8.00
6 Rob Gronkowski 3.00 8.00
7 Russell Wilson 3.00 8.00
8 Steve Young 4.00 10.00
9 Peyton Manning 8.00 20.00
10 Dan Bailey 1.50 4.00
11 David Johnson 2.50 6.00
12 Eric Dickerson 3.00 8.00
13 Ezekiel Elliott 3.00 8.00
14 Derek Carr 2.50 6.00
15 Jameis Winston 2.00 5.00

2017 Certified Fabric of the Game

*PRIME/49: .5X TO 1.2X BASIC JSY/99
*PRIME/25: .6X TO 1.5X BASIC JSY/99
*PRIME/25: .5X TO 1.2X BASIC JSY/49-50
*PRIME/20: .6X TO 1.5X BASIC JSY/40
1 Dak Prescott 3.00 8.00
2 Allen Robinson 2.50 6.00
3 Amari Cooper 3.00 8.00
4 Andrew Luck 4.00 10.00
5 Andy Dalton 2.50 6.00
6 Barry Sanders 5.00 12.00
7 Russell Wilson 4.00 10.00
8 Blake Bortles 2.00 5.00
9 Bo Jackson 4.00 10.00
10 Tom Brady 12.00 30.00
11 Boomer Esiason 3.00 8.00
12 Brian Urlacher 5.00 12.00
13 Carlos Hyde 2.00 5.00
14 Cam Newton 3.00 8.00
15 Carson Wentz 4.00 10.00
16 Curtis Martin 4.00 10.00
17 Dan Bailey 2.00 5.00
18 Davante Adams 2.50 6.00
19 David Johnson 3.00 8.00
20 DeAndre Hopkins 2.50 6.00
21 DeAndre Washington 2.00 5.00
22 Derek Carr 3.00 8.00
23 Derrick Henry 2.50 6.00
24 Devonta Freeman 2.50 6.00
25 Devontae Booker 2.00 5.00
26 Drew Brees 5.00 12.00
27 Earl Thomas III 2.50 6.00
28 Eric Berry 3.00 8.00
29 Eric Ebron 2.00 5.00
30 Ezekiel Elliott 4.00 10.00
31 Geno Atkins 2.00 5.00
32 Giovani Bernard 2.00 5.00
33 Hunter Henry 2.00 5.00
34 Jameis Winston 2.50 6.00
35 James White 2.50 6.00
36 Jamison Crowder 2.00 5.00
37 Jared Goff 3.00 8.00
38 Jarvis Landry 2.50 6.00
39 Jay Ajayi 2.50 6.00
40 Jeremy Hill 2.00 5.00
41 Joey Bosa 3.00 8.00
42 Jordan Howard 3.00 8.00
43 Jordan Reed 2.00 5.00
44 Kelvin Benjamin 2.50 6.00
45 Kenyan Drake 2.00 5.00
46 Khalil Mack 3.00 8.00
47 Kurt Warner 4.00 10.00
48 Luke Kuechly 2.50 6.00
49 Malcolm Mitchell 2.50 6.00
50 Marcus Mariota 3.00 8.00
51 Melvin Gordon 2.50 6.00
52 Michael Thomas 3.00 8.00
53 Paul Perkins 2.00 5.00
54 Paxton Lynch 2.00 5.00
55 Philip Rivers 4.00 10.00
57 Steve Young 5.00 12.00
58 Terrell Davis 3.00 8.00
59 Terry Bradshaw 6.00 15.00
60 Todd Gurley II 3.00 8.00
61 Travis Kelce 3.00 8.00
62 Ty Montgomery 2.00 5.00
63 Tyreek Hill 3.00 8.00
64 Von Miller 2.50 6.00
65 Wendell Smallwood 2.00 5.00
66 Will Fuller V 2.00 5.00
67 Zach Ertz 2.50 6.00
68 Corey Coleman 2.00 5.00
69 Eddie George 3.00 8.00
70 Mike Ditka 5.00 12.00
71 Jadeveon Clowney 2.00 5.00
72 Franco Harris 3.00 8.00
73 Jim Kelly 3.00 8.00
74 Jimmy Garoppolo 4.00 10.00
75 Odell Beckham Jr. 3.00 8.00

2017 Certified Fabric of the Game Signatures

*PRIME: .5X TO 1.2X BASIC JSY AU
2 Carson Wentz 75.00 150.00
3 Drew Brees 40.00 80.00
4 Shaun Alexander 10.00 25.00
5 Ezekiel Elliott 40.00 80.00
6 Jared Goff 20.00 50.00
7 Jordan Howard 6.00 15.00
9 Michael Thomas 5.00 12.00
10 Tyler Eifert 5.00 12.00
11 Tyreek Hill 5.00 12.00
15 Eric Berry 8.00 20.00
16 Jameis Winston 15.00 40.00
17 Melvin Gordon 6.00 15.00
18 Wes Welker 6.00 15.00
19 David Johnson 15.00 40.00
20 Derek Carr 25.00 50.00
21 Allen Robinson 5.00 12.00
23 Emmanuel Sanders 5.00 12.00
24 Curtis Martin 10.00 25.00
25 Hines Ward 20.00 50.00

2017 Certified Gamers Jerseys

*ORANGE/75: .4X TO 1X BASIC JSY/99
*RED/50: .5X TO 1.2X BASIC JSY/99
*RED/25: .5X TO 1.2X BASIC JSY/50
*BLUE/25: .6X TO 1.5X BASIC JSY/99

1 Demaryius Thomas 2.50 6.00
2 Devonta Freeman 2.50 6.00
3 Dez Bryant 3.00 8.00
4 Eli Manning 2.50 6.00
5 Alex Smith 2.50 6.00
7 Ndamukong Suh 2.50 6.00
8 Jarvis Landry 2.50 6.00
9 Jay Ajayi 2.50 6.00
10 Tyrod Taylor 2.50 6.00
11 Philip Rivers 3.00 8.00
12 Ryan Tannehill 2.50 6.00
13 Blake Bortles 2.00 5.00
14 Matthew Stafford 3.00 8.00
15 DeMarcus Ware 2.50 6.00

2017 Certified Gold Team

*RED/99: .6X TO 1.5X BASIC INSERTS
*BLUE/50: .8X TO 2X BASIC INSERTS
*GOLD/25: 1X TO 2.5X BASIC INSERTS
1 Tom Brady 1.50 4.00
2 Ezekiel Elliott .75 2.00
3 Antonio Brown .60 1.50
4 Derek Carr .60 1.50
5 Julio Jones .60 1.50
6 Aaron Rodgers 1.25 3.00
7 Von Miller .50 1.25
8 J.J. Watt .60 1.50
9 Luke Kuechly .50 1.25
10 Khalil Mack .60 1.50
11 Deshaun Watson 2.50 6.00
12 Mitchell Trubisky 2.00 5.00
13 DeShone Kizer .40 1.00
14 Patrick Mahomes II 12.00 30.00
15 Leonard Fournette 1.25 3.00
16 Dalvin Cook 1.00 2.50
17 Christian McCaffrey 1.00 2.50
18 Mike Williams .60 1.50
19 Corey Davis .60 1.50
20 John Ross III .50 1.25

2017 Certified Gridiron Signatures

*RED/75: .4X TO 1X BASIC AU/99
*RED/35: .4X TO 1X BASIC AU/50
*BLUE/50: .5X TO 1.2X BASIC AU/99
*BLUE/25: .5X TO 1.2X BASIC AU/50
*GOLD/25: .6X TO 1.5X BASIC AU/99
1 Marshon Lattimore 4.00 10.00
2 Donnel Pumphrey 4.00 10.00
3 Jonathan Allen 5.00 12.00
4 Jerod Evans 4.00 10.00
5 Artavis Scott 3.00 8.00
6 Quincy Wilson 3.00 8.00
7 Sidney Jones 3.00 8.00
8 Jabrill Peppers 6.00 15.00
9 Jake Butt 4.00 10.00
10 Adoree' Jackson 4.00 10.00
12 Marlon Humphrey 3.00 8.00
13 Matthew Dayes 3.00 8.00
15 Josh Malone 3.00 8.00
16 Jamal Adams 3.00 8.00
17 Chad Hansen 3.00 8.00
18 Malik Hooker 3.00 8.00
19 Chad Kelly 3.00 8.00
20 Raekwon McMillan 3.00 8.00

2017 Certified New Generation Jerseys

*ORANGE/399: .5X TO 1.2X BASIC JSY
*RED/299: .5X TO 1.2X BASIC JSY
*BLUE/50: .8X TO 2X BASIC JSY
*GOLD/25: 1X TO 2.5X BASIC JSY
1 Mitchell Trubisky 5.00 12.00
2 Leonard Fournette 5.00 12.00
3 Corey Davis 2.00 5.00
4 Mike Williams 2.00 5.00
5 Christian McCaffrey 5.00 12.00
6 John Ross III 1.50 4.00
7 Patrick Mahomes II 15.00 40.00
8 Deshaun Watson 6.00 15.00
9 O.J. Howard 1.50 4.00
10 Evan Engram 1.50 4.00
11 R. Joshua Dobbs 1.50 4.00
12 Samaje Perine 1.25 3.00
13 Dalvin Cook 5.00 12.00
14 Joe Mixon 2.50 6.00
15 DeShone Kizer 1.25 3.00
16 JuJu Smith-Schuster 3.00 8.00
17 Alvin Kamara 5.00 12.00
18 Cooper Kupp 2.00 5.00
19 Taywan Taylor 1.25 3.00
20 ArDarius Stewart 1.25 3.00
21 Carlos Henderson 1.25 3.00
22 Chris Godwin 1.50 4.00
23 Kareem Hunt 2.50 6.00
24 Davis Webb 1.25 3.00
25 D'Onta Foreman 1.50 4.00
26 C.J. Beathard 1.25 3.00
27 James Conner 2.50 6.00
28 Amara Darboh 1.25 3.00
29 Kenny Golladay 2.00 5.00
30 Dede Westbrook 1.25 3.00

2017 Certified Potential Signatures

*RED/75: .4X TO 1X BASIC AU/99
*RED/35: .4X TO 1X BASIC AU/50
*BLUE/50: .5X TO 1.2X BASIC AU/99
*BLUE/25: .5X TO 1.2X BASIC AU/50
*GOLD/25: .6X TO 1.5X BASIC AU/99
1 Jerod Evans 4.00 10.00
2 Jonathan Allen 5.00 12.00
3 Jabrill Peppers 6.00 15.00
4 Marlon Humphrey 3.00 8.00
5 Jamal Adams 3.00 8.00
6 Chad Kelly 3.00 8.00
7 Marshon Lattimore 4.00 10.00
8 Quincy Wilson 3.00 8.00
9 Adoree' Jackson 4.00 10.00
11 Malik Hooker 3.00 8.00
12 Isaiah Ford 3.00 8.00
13 Sidney Jones 3.00 8.00
14 Desmond King 4.00 10.00
15 Derek Barnett 10.00 25.00
16 Carl Lawson 3.00 8.00
17 Charles Harris 3.00 8.00
18 Tim Williams 4.00 10.00
19 Matthew Dayes 3.00 8.00
20 Shelton Gibson 3.00 8.00
21 Stacy Coley 3.00 8.00
22 Josh Malone 3.00 8.00
23 Cordrea Tankersley 4.00 10.00
24 Tre'Davious White 3.00 8.00
25 Taco Charlton 3.00 8.00
26 Solomon Thomas 3.00 8.00
27 Raekwon McMillan 3.00 8.00
28 Zach Cunningham 4.00 10.00
29 Jarrad Davis 4.00 10.00
31 Chad Hansen 3.00 8.00
32 Donnel Pumphrey 4.00 10.00
33 Ryan Switzer 4.00 10.00
34 Brian Hill 3.00 8.00
35 Jake Butt 4.00 10.00
36 Travis Rudolph 3.00 8.00
37 Artavis Scott 3.00 8.00
38 Haason Reddick 3.00 8.00
39 Brad Kaaya 4.00 10.00
40 Cameron Sutton 3.00 8.00
42 Gareon Conley 10.00 25.00
43 DeMarcus Walker 3.00 8.00
44 Jordan Leggett 3.00 8.00
45 T.J. Watt 15.00 40.00
46 Jordan Willis 3.00 8.00
47 Elijah Hood 3.00 8.00
48 Elijah Qualls 3.00 8.00
49 Caleb Brantley 3.00 8.00

2017 Certified Rookie Roll Call Signatures

1 Dalvin Cook/50 10.00 25.00
2 Taywan Taylor/75 3.00 8.00
3 Mike Williams/50 6.00 15.00
4 Zay Jones/75 4.00 10.00
5 Deshaun Watson/50 50.00 100.00
6 ArDarius Stewart/75 3.00 8.00
7 Christian McCaffrey/50 50.00 100.00
8 John Ross III/50 5.00 12.00
9 Davis Webb/75 3.00 8.00
10 Mitchell Trubisky/50 40.00 80.00
11 Corey Davis/50 6.00 15.00
12 Carlos Henderson/75 3.00 8.00
13 D'Onta Foreman/75 4.00 10.00
14 Cooper Kupp/75 5.00 12.00
15 DeShone Kizer/50 4.00 10.00
16 JuJu Smith-Schuster/50 10.00 25.00
17 Samaje Perine/99 3.00 8.00
18 Evan Engram/75 8.00 20.00
19 Dede Westbrook/75
20 Patrick Mahomes II/50 150.00 300.00
21 Chris Godwin/99 4.00 10.00
22 Alvin Kamara/75 12.00 30.00
23 Joe Mixon/99 6.00 15.00
24 Curtis Samuel/75 4.00 10.00
25 Leonard Fournette/50
26 Kareem Hunt/99 6.00 15.00
28 O.J. Howard/50 5.00 12.00
29 Wayne Gallman/99 4.00 10.00
30 Amara Darboh/75 3.00 8.00

2017 Certified Rookie Roll Call Signatures Mirror Blue

*BLUE/50: .5X TO 1.2X BASIC AU/75-99
*BLUE/25: .6X TO 1.5X BASIC AU/75-99

2017 Certified Rookie Roll Call Signatures Mirror Gold

*GOLD/25: .6X TO 1.5X BASIC AU/75-99

2017 Certified Rookie Roll Call Signatures Mirror Red

*RED/75: .4X TO 1X BASIC AU/75-99
*RED/50: .5X TO 1.2X BASIC AU/75-99
*RED/75: .4X TO 1X BASIC AU/75-99
5 Deshaun Watson/25 60.00 125.00
20 Patrick Mahomes II/25 200.00 400.00
25 Leonard Fournette/25 40.00 80.00

2017 Certified Shutdown

*RED/99: .6X TO 1.5X BASIC INSERTS
*BLUE/50: .8X TO 2X BASIC INSERTS
*GOLD/25: 1X TO 2.5X BASIC INSERTS
1 Luke Kuechly .75 2.00
2 Richard Sherman 1.00 2.50
3 Earl Thomas III .75 2.00
4 Leonard Floyd .60 1.50
5 J.J. Watt 1.00 2.50
6 Jadeveon Clowney .60 1.50
7 Joey Bosa 1.00 2.50
8 Vic Beasley Jr. .60 1.50
9 Eric Berry .75 2.00
10 Patrick Peterson .60 1.50
11 Von Miller .75 2.00
12 Khalil Mack 1.00 2.50
13 Clay Matthews .75 2.00
14 Jalen Ramsey .60 1.50
15 Josh Norman .60 1.50
16 Brent Grimes .60 1.50
17 Derrick Johnson .60 1.50
18 Cameron Heyward .60 1.50
19 Aaron Donald 1.00 2.50
20 Ndamukong Suh .75 2.00
21 Geno Atkins .60 1.50
22 Vontaze Burfict .60 1.50
23 Kam Chancellor 1.00 2.50
24 Tyrann Mathieu .75 2.00
25 Landon Collins .60 1.50
26 James Harrison .75 2.00
27 Harrison Smith .60 1.50
28 Sean Lee .75 2.00
29 Ryan Kerrigan .60 1.50
30 Lorenzo Alexander .60 1.50

2018 Certified

1 Richard Sherman .40 1.00
2 Jimmy Garoppolo .50 1.25
3 Jerick McKinnon .25 .60
4 Mitchell Trubisky .40 1.00
5 Allen Robinson .30 .75
6 Jordan Howard .40 1.00
7 A.J. Green .40 1.00
8 Andy Dalton .30 .75
9 Joe Mixon .30 .75
10 LeSean McCoy .40 1.00
11 A.J. McCarron .25 .60
12 Kelvin Benjamin .30 .75
13 Case Keenum .30 .75
14 Emmanuel Sanders .40 1.00
15 Von Miller .30 .75
16 Tyrod Taylor .30 .75
17 Jarvis Landry .30 .75
18 Josh Gordon .25 .60
19 Carlos Hyde .25 .60
20 Jameis Winston .30 .75
21 Mike Evans .30 .75
22 Cameron Brate .25 .60
23 Sam Bradford .25 .60
24 Chandler Jones .25 .60
25 David Johnson .40 1.00
26 Larry Fitzgerald .30 .75
27 Philip Rivers .40 1.00
28 Melvin Gordon .30 .75
29 Keenan Allen .30 .75
30 Patrick Mahomes II 1.00 2.50
31 Kareem Hunt .30 .75
32 Tyreek Hill .40 1.00
33 Andrew Luck .50 1.25
34 T.Y. Hilton .30 .75
35 Ezekiel Elliott .50 1.25
36 Dak Prescott .40 1.00
37 DeMarcus Lawrence .25 .60
38 Sean Lee .30 .75
39 Ryan Tannehill .30 .75
40 Kenyan Drake .25 .60
41 DeVante Parker .30 .75
42 Carson Wentz .50 1.25
43 Malcolm Jenkins .25 .60
44 Jay Ajayi .30 .75
45 Matt Ryan .30 .75
46 Devonta Freeman .30 .75
47 Julio Jones .40 1.00
48 Eli Manning .30 .75
49 Odell Beckham Jr. .40 1.00
50 Landon Collins .25 .60
51 Blake Bortles .25 .60
52 Leonard Fournette .40 1.00
53 Jalen Ramsey .30 .75
54 Matthew Stafford .30 .75
55 LeGarrette Blount .30 .75
56 Golden Tate III .25 .60
57 Aaron Rodgers .75 2.00
58 Jimmy Graham .40 1.00
59 Clay Matthews .30 .75
60 Randall Cobb .30 .75
61 Cam Newton .40 1.00
62 Devin Funchess .25 .60
63 Julius Peppers .30 .75
64 Greg Olsen .30 .75
65 Tom Brady 1.00 2.50
66 Julian Edelman .40 1.00
67 Chris Hogan .25 .60
68 Derek Carr .40 1.00
69 Jordy Nelson .30 .75
70 Khalil Mack .40 1.00
71 Jared Goff .40 1.00
72 Todd Gurley II .40 1.00
73 Robert Woods .30 .75
74 Joe Flacco .30 .75
75 Terrell Suggs .25 .60
76 Alex Collins .25 .60
77 Alex Smith .30 .75
78 Josh Norman .25 .60
79 Jordan Reed .25 .60
80 Drew Brees .40 1.00
81 Alvin Kamara .30 .75
82 Michael Thomas .40 1.00
83 Russell Wilson .50 1.25
84 Earl Thomas III .30 .75
85 Doug Baldwin .30 .75
86 Antonio Brown .40 1.00
87 Le'Veon Bell .30 .75
88 Ben Roethlisberger .40 1.00
89 J.J. Watt .40 1.00
90 DeAndre Hopkins .30 .75
91 Deshaun Watson .50 1.25
92 Marcus Mariota .40 1.00
93 Derrick Henry .40 1.00
94 Delanie Walker .25 .60
95 Kirk Cousins .40 1.00
96 Dalvin Cook .30 .75
97 Stefon Diggs .30 .75
98 Josh McCown .25 .60
99 Isaiah Crowell .25 .60
100 Jamal Adams .30 .75
101 Bruce Matthews IMM .75 2.00
102 Cris Carter IMM 1.25 3.00
103 Darren Woodson IMM 1.00 2.50
104 Jeremy Shockey IMM .75 2.00
105 John Lynch IMM 1.00 2.50
106 Rod Woodson IMM 1.25 3.00
107 Shaun Alexander IMM .75 2.00
108 Ty Law IMM 1.25 3.00
109 Vinny Testaverde IMM .75 2.00
110 Warren Sapp IMM 1.00 2.50
111 Warrick Dunn IMM .75 2.00
112 Curley Culp IMM 1.00 2.50
113 Charlie Joiner IMM .75 2.00
114 Dan Dierdorf IMM .75 2.00
115 Dermontti Dawson IMM 1.00 2.50
116 Donnie Shell IMM .75 2.00
117 Jack Ham IMM 1.00 2.50
118 Jim Taylor IMM 1.00 2.50
119 Joe Theismann IMM 1.25 3.00
120 Jonathan Ogden IMM 1.00 2.50
121 Marshall Faulk IMM 1.00 2.50
122 Paul Hornung IMM 1.25 3.00
123 Randall McDaniel IMM 1.00 2.50
124 Randy Moss IMM 1.00 2.50
125 Rocky Bleier IMM 1.00 2.50
126 Tony Gonzalez IMM 1.00 2.50
127 Walter Jones IMM .75 2.00
128 Jack Youngblood IMM .75 2.00
129 Mike Ditka IMM 1.25 3.00
130 Terry Bradshaw IMM 2.00 5.00
131 Roger Staubach IMM 1.50 4.00
132 Barry Sanders IMM 2.00 5.00
133 Bruce Smith IMM 1.00 2.50
134 Randy White IMM 1.00 2.50
135 Marcus Allen IMM 1.25 3.00
136 Luke Falk RC .75 2.00
137 Denzel Ward RC 1.50 4.00
138 Shaquem Griffin RC 1.00 2.50
139 Minkah Fitzpatrick RC 1.25 3.00
140 Terrell Edmunds RC 2.00 5.00
141 Roquan Smith RC 2.00 5.00
142 Dallas Goedert RC .75 2.00
143 Deon Cain RC .75 2.00
144 Derwin James RC 1.25 3.00
145 Arden Key RC .60 1.50
146 Auden Tate RC .60 1.50
147 Carlton Davis RC .75 2.00
148 Cedrick Wilson Jr. RC .60 1.50
149 John Kelly RC .75 2.00
150 Harold Landry RC .60 1.50
151 Isaiah Oliver RC .60 1.50
152 Jaire Alexander RC 1.00 2.50
153 Jordan Lasley RC .60 1.50
154 Joshua Jackson RC 1.25 3.00
155 Leighton Vander Esch RC 2.00 5.00
156 Malik Jefferson RC .75 2.00
157 Marcus Davenport RC 1.25 3.00
158 Mark Andrews RC 1.00 2.50
159 Mike Hughes RC 1.00 2.50
160 Rashaan Evans RC 1.00 2.50
161 Ronnie Harrison RC .75 2.00
162 Sam Hubbard RC .75 2.00
163 Tremaine Edmunds RC 1.25 3.00
164 Daron Payne RC 1.00 2.50
165 Justin Reid RC .60 1.50
166 Maurice Hurst RC .75 2.00
167 Tanner Lee RC .75 2.00
168 Justin Jackson RC .75 2.00
169 Trey Quinn RC .60 1.50
170 Josh Adams RC 1.25 3.00
171 Antonio Callaway RC .75 2.00
172 Derrick Nnadi RC .60 1.50
173 Donte Jackson RC 1.00 2.50
174 Duke Dawson RC .60 1.50
175 Dorance Armstrong Jr. RC .60 1.50
176 Austin Proehl RC .60 1.50
177 Dalton Schultz RC .75 2.00
178 Simmie Cobbs Jr. RC 1.00 2.50
179 Dylan Cantrell RC .60 1.50
180 Braxton Berrios RC .60 1.50
181 Chase Edmonds RC .60 1.50
182 Ray-Ray McCloud RC .60 1.50
183 Rasheem Green RC .60 1.50
184 Ian Thomas RC .60 1.50
185 Fred Warner RC .60 1.50
186 Jerome Baker RC .75 2.00
187 Jalyn Holmes RC 1.00 2.50
188 Lorenzo Carter RC .60 1.50
189 M.J. Stewart RC .60 1.50
190 Taven Bryan RC .60 1.50
191 Tyquan Lewis RC .75 2.00
192 Harrison Phillips RC .60 1.50
193 Chad Thomas RC .60 1.50
194 Richie James RC .60 1.50
195 Quenton Nelson RC 1.00 2.50
196 Mike McGlinchey RC 1.25 3.00
197 Kolton Miller RC 1.00 2.50
198 Isaiah Wynn RC .60 1.50
199 Roc Thomas RC .75 2.00
200 Vita Vea RC 1.00 2.50
201 Saquon Barkley JSY AU/175 RC 100.00 200.00
202 Mason Rudolph JSY AU/199 RC 12.00 30.00
203 Lamar Jackson JSY AU/99 RC 100.00 200.00
204 Josh Allen JSY AU/175 RC 30.00 60.00
205 Sam Darnold JSY AU/175 RC 30.00 80.00
206 Baker Mayfield JSY AU/175 RC 100.00 200.00
207 Derrius Guice JSY AU/175 RC 10.00 25.00
208 Jaleel Scott JSY AU/499 RC 3.00 8.00
209 Josh Rosen JSY AU/175 RC 15.00 40.00
210 Kyle Lauletta JSY AU/349 RC 5.00 12.00
211 Calvin Ridley JSY AU/175 RC 12.00 30.00
212 J'Mon Moore JSY AU/499 RC 3.00 8.00
213 Marquez Valdes-Scantling JSY AU/499 RC 4.00 10.00
214 Anthony Miller JSY AU/299 RC 6.00 15.00
215 D.J. Chark JSY AU/499 RC 4.00 10.00
216 Dante Pettis JSY AU/399 RC 5.00 12.00
217 Nick Chubb JSY AU/199 RC 15.00 40.00
218 Mike Gesicki JSY AU/349 RC 4.00 10.00
219 Ronald Jones II JSY AU/299 RC 4.00 10.00
220 Hayden Hurst JSY AU/399 RC 4.00 10.00
221 Mark Walton JSY AU/499 RC 4.00 10.00
222 Royce Freeman JSY AU/399 RC 4.00 10.00
223 Kerryon Johnson JSY AU/399 RC 5.00 12.00
224 Rashaad Penny JSY AU/349 RC 5.00 12.00
225 Kalen Ballage JSY AU/499 RC 4.00 10.00
226 Nyheim Hines JSY AU/499 RC 4.00 10.00
227 Ito Smith JSY AU/499 RC 4.00 10.00
228 James Washington JSY AU/249 RC 8.00 20.00
229 Keke Coutee JSY AU/399 RC 4.00 10.00
230 Courtland Sutton JSY AU/199 RC 8.00 20.00
231 Bradley Chubb JSY AU/399 RC 5.00 12.00
232 D.J. Moore JSY AU/249 RC 8.00 20.00
233 Jaylen Samuels JSY AU/499 RC 4.00 10.00
234 DaeSean Hamilton JSY AU/499 RC 4.00 10.00
235 Tre'Quan Smith JSY AU/499 RC 5.00 12.00
236 Sony Michel JSY AU/199 RC 15.00 40.00
237 Christian Kirk JSY AU/199 RC 8.00 20.00
238 Daurice Fountain JSY AU/499 RC 4.00 10.00
239 Mike White JSY AU/499 RC 4.00 10.00
240 Michael Gallup JSY AU/499 RC 6.00 15.00

2018 Certified Mirror Blue

*VETS/50: 3X TO 8X BASIC CARDS
*IMM: 1X TO 2.5X BASIC CARDS
*ROOKIES: 1.2X TO 3X BASIC CARDS
*ROOK JSY AU/50: .8X TO 2X BASIC JSY AU/299
*ROOK JSY AU/50: 1X TO 2.5X BASIC JSY AU/349-499
*ROOK JSY AU/50: .6X TO 1.5X BASIC JSY AU/175-199
*ROOK JSY AU/35: .5X TO 1.2X BASIC JSY AU/99
201 Saquon Barkley JSY AU/50 150.00 300.00
206 Baker Mayfield JSY AU/50 150.00 300.00

2018 Certified Mirror Gold

*VETS: 4X TO 10X BASIC CARDS
*IMM: 1.2X TO 3X BASIC CARDS
*ROOKIES: 1.5X TO 4X BASIC CARDS
*ROOK JSY AU/25: 1.2X TO 3X BASIC JSY AU/349-499
*ROOK JSY AU/25: 1X TO 2.5X BASIC JSY AU/299
*ROOK JSY AU/25: .8X TO 2X BASIC JSY AU/175-199
*ROOK JSY AU/15: .8X TO 2X BASIC JSY AU/99
201 Saquon Barkley JSY AU/25 250.00 400.00
206 Baker Mayfield JSY AU/25 175.00 350.00

2018 Certified Mirror Orange

*VETS: 2X TO 5X BASIC CARDS
*IMM: .8X TO 2X BASIC CARDS
*ROOKIES: 1X TO 2.5X BASIC CARDS
*ROOK JSY AU/349: .4X TO 1X BASIC JSY AU/349-499
*ROOK JSY AU/249-299: .5X TO 1.2X BASIC JSY AU/349-499
*ROOK JSY AU/249: .4X TO 1X BASIC JSY AU/299
*ROOK JSY AU/99: .5X TO 1.2X BASIC JSY AU/175-199
201 Saquon Barkley JSY AU/99 150.00 250.00
206 Baker Mayfield JSY AU/99 125.00 250.00

2018 Certified Mirror Red

*VETS: 2.5X TO 6X BASIC CARDS
*IMM: .8X TO 2X BASIC CARDS
*ROOKIES: 1X TO 2.5X BASIC CARDS
*ROOK JSY AU/249: .5X TO 1.2X BASIC JSY AU/349-499
*ROOK JSY AU/149: .6X TO 1.5X BASIC JSY AU/349-499
*ROOK JSY AU/99: .8X TO 2X BASIC JSY AU/349-499
*ROOK JSY AU/99: .6X TO 1.5X BASIC JSY AU/299
*ROOK JSY AU/75: .5X TO 1.2X BASIC JSY AU/175-199
201 Saquon Barkley JSY AU/75 150.00 250.00
206 Baker Mayfield JSY AU/75 125.00 250.00

2018 Certified Mirror Silver

*VETS: 1.5X TO 4X BASIC CARDS
*IMM: .5X TO 1.2X BASIC CARDS
*ROOKIES: .6X TO 1.5X BASIC CARDS

2018 Certified Champions

*RED/99: .6X TO 1.5X BASIC INSERTS
*BLUE/50: .8X TO 2X BASIC INSERTS
*GOLD/25: 1X TO 2.5X BASIC INSERTS
1 Tony Dorsett 1.00 2.50
2 Tom Brady 2.50 6.00
3 Jeremy Shockey .60 1.50
4 Terrence Cody .60 1.50
5 Derrick Brooks .60 1.50
6 Charles Woodson 1.00 2.50
7 Marcus Allen 1.00 2.50
8 Ed Reed .75 2.00
9 Joe Namath 1.25 3.00
10 Michael Irvin 1.00 2.50
11 Jimmy Johnson .75 2.00
12 Brandon LaFell .60 1.50
13 Dont'a Hightower .60 1.50
14 Ronald Darby .60 1.50
15 Barry Switzer .75 2.00

2018 Certified Clutch Performers Jerseys

*ORANGE/199: .4X TO 1X BASIC JSY/399
*RED/99: .5X TO 1.2X BASIC JSY/399
*BLUE/50: .6X TO 1.5X BASIC JSY/399
*GOLD/25: .8X TO 2X BASIC JSY/399
1 Carson Wentz 3.00 8.00
2 Russell Wilson 3.00 8.00
3 Antonio Brown 2.50 6.00
4 Davante Adams 2.00 5.00
5 Marcus Mariota 2.50 6.00
6 Stefon Diggs 2.00 5.00
7 Blake Bortles 1.50 4.00
8 Matthew Stafford 2.00 5.00
10 Deshaun Watson 3.00 8.00
12 Alvin Kamara 2.00 5.00
13 JuJu Smith-Schuster 2.50 6.00
14 Christian McCaffrey 2.50 6.00
15 Kareem Hunt 2.00 5.00

2018 Certified Diamonds

*RED/99: .6X TO 1.5X BASIC INSERTS
*BLUE/50: .8X TO 2X BASIC INSERTS
*GOLD/25: 1X TO 2.5X BASIC INSERTS
1 Adam Vinatieri .60 1.50
2 Alvin Kamara .75 2.00
3 Andre Reed .75 2.00
4 Antonio Brown 1.00 2.50
5 Antonio Gates .60 1.50
6 Charles Haley 1.00 2.50
7 Curtis Martin .75 2.00
8 Dak Prescott 1.00 2.50
9 David Johnson 1.00 2.50
10 Devonta Freeman .75 2.00
11 Drew Pearson .75 2.00
12 James Harrison .75 2.00
13 Jay Ajayi .75 2.00
14 Jordan Howard 1.00 2.50
15 Josh Norman .60 1.50
16 JuJu Smith-Schuster 1.00 2.50
17 Kareem Hunt .75 2.00
18 Kurt Warner .75 2.00
19 Kwon Alexander .60 1.50
20 Malcolm Butler 1.00 2.50
21 Michael Strahan .75 2.00
22 Priest Holmes .60 1.50
23 Rodney Harrison .75 2.00
24 Telvin Smith .60 1.50
25 Terrell Davis .75 2.00
26 Tom Brady 2.50 6.00
27 Tony Romo .75 2.00
28 Tyreek Hill 1.00 2.50
29 Warren Moon 1.00 2.50
30 Zach Thomas .75 2.00

2018 Certified Fabric of the Game

*PRIME/49: .5X TO 1.2X BASIC JSY/99
*PRIME/25: .6X TO 1.5X BASIC JSY/99
*PRIME/15-20: .8X TO 2X BASIC JSY/99
1 Matt Ryan/99 2.50 6.00
2 Takkarist McKinley/99 2.00 5.00
3 Joe Flacco/99 2.50 6.00
4 Terrell Suggs/99 2.00 5.00
5 Jim Kelly/99 3.00 8.00
6 Thurman Thomas/99 2.50 6.00
7 Greg Olsen/99 2.50 6.00
8 Luke Kuechly/99 2.50 6.00
9 Kyle Fuller/99 2.00 5.00
10 Jabrill Peppers/99 2.00 5.00
11 Tony Romo/99 2.50 6.00
12 Golden Tate III/99 2.00 5.00
13 Matthew Stafford/99 2.50 6.00
15 Clay Matthews/99 2.50 6.00
16 Lamar Miller/99 2.00 5.00
17 Jack Doyle/99 2.00 5.00
18 Blake Bortles/99 2.00 5.00
19 Spencer Ware/99 2.00 5.00
20 Latavius Murray/99 2.00 5.00
21 Quincy Enunwa/99 2.00 5.00
22 Derek Carr/49 4.00 10.00
23 Marshawn Lynch/99 2.50 6.00
24 T.J. Watt/99 2.50 6.00
25 Matt Breida/99 2.50 6.00
26 Doug Baldwin/99 2.50 6.00
27 Tyler Lockett/99 2.50 6.00
28 Mike Evans/99 2.50 6.00
29 DeSean Jackson/99 2.50 6.00
30 Taylor Lewan/99 2.00 5.00
31 Marcus Mariota/99 3.00 8.00
32 Brandon Scherff/99 2.00 5.00
33 David Johnson/99 3.00 8.00
34 Devonta Freeman/99 2.50 6.00
35 Christian McCaffrey/99 3.00 8.00
36 Devin Funchess/99 2.00 5.00
37 Jordan Howard/99 3.00 8.00
38 Earl Thomas III/99 2.50 6.00
39 Mitchell Trubisky/99 3.00 8.00
40 Joe Mixon/99 2.50 6.00
41 Corey Coleman/99 2.00 5.00
42 Duke Johnson/99 2.00 5.00
44 Dak Prescott/99 3.00 8.00
45 Devontae Booker/99 2.00 5.00
46 Davante Adams/99 2.50 6.00
47 Ty Montgomery/99 2.00 5.00
48 DeAndre Hopkins/99 2.50 6.00
49 Deshaun Watson/99 4.00 10.00
50 D'Onta Foreman/99 2.00 5.00
51 Dede Westbrook/99 2.00 5.00
52 Leonard Fournette/99 3.00 8.00
53 Kareem Hunt/99 2.50 6.00
54 Patrick Mahomes II/99 8.00 20.00
55 Jared Goff/99 3.00 8.00
56 Cooper Kupp/99 2.50 6.00
57 Kenyan Drake/99 2.00 5.00
58 Dalvin Cook/99 2.50 6.00
59 James White/99 2.50 6.00
60 Alvin Kamara/99 2.50 6.00
61 Evan Engram/99 2.00 5.00
62 Sterling Shepard/99 2.50 6.00
63 Amari Cooper/99 3.00 8.00
64 Carson Wentz/99 4.00 10.00
65 Nelson Agholor/99 2.00 5.00
66 JuJu Smith-Schuster/49 4.00 10.00
67 Melvin Gordon/99 2.50 6.00
68 Todd Gurley II/99 3.00 8.00
69 O.J. Howard/99 2.00 5.00
70 Corey Davis/99 2.50 6.00
71 Derrick Henry/99 3.00 8.00
72 Jamison Crowder/99 2.00 5.00
73 Josh Doctson/99 2.00 5.00
74 Samaje Perine/99 2.00 5.00
75 Joey Bosa/99 3.00 8.00

2018 Certified Fabric of the Game Signatures

*PRIME/25: .5X TO 1.2X BASIC JSY AU/49
*PRIME/15: .5X TO 1.2X BASIC JSY AU/25
8 Patrick Mahomes II/25 25.00 60.00
12 Brian Dawkins/15
13 Travis Kelce/25 10.00 25.00
14 Dalvin Cook/25
15 Devin Funchess/25
16 Jordan Howard/25 10.00 25.00
17 Stefon Diggs/25
18 Harrison Smith/49 25.00 50.00
19 Brett Keisel/49 5.00 12.00
20 JuJu Smith-Schuster/49 10.00 25.00
21 Duke Johnson/49 5.00 12.00
22 Justin Houston/49 5.00 12.00
23 Alvin Kamara/49 10.00 25.00
24 Kareem Hunt/25 8.00 20.00
25 T.J. Watt/49 6.00 15.00

2018 Certified Gamers Jerseys

*ORANGE/149: .4X TO 1X BASIC JSY/199-299
*ORANGE/99: .5X TO 1.2X BASIC JSY/199-299
*RED/75-99: .5X TO 1.2X BASIC JSY/199-299
*BLUE/50: .6X TO 1.5X BASIC JSY/199-299
*GOLD/25: .8X TO 2X BASIC JSY/199-299
*GOLD/15: 1X TO 2.5X BASIC JSY/199-299
1 Calais Campbell/299 1.50 4.00
2 Sebastian Janikowski/299 1.50 4.00
4 A.J. Green/299 2.50 6.00
5 Andy Dalton/299 2.00 5.00
7 Ezekiel Elliott/199 3.00 8.00
8 Dez Bryant/199 2.50 6.00
9 C.J. Anderson/299 2.00 5.00
11 DeVante Parker/299 2.00 5.00
12 Ryan Tannehill/299 2.00 5.00
13 Alshon Jeffery/299 2.00 5.00
14 Dak Prescott/299 2.50 6.00
15 Jordan Reed/299 1.50 4.00

2018 Certified Gold Team

*RED/99: .6X TO 1.5X BASIC INSERTS
*BLUE/50: .8X TO 2X BASIC INSERTS
*GOLD/25: 1X TO 2.5X BASIC INSERTS
*GOLD ETCH/25: 1X TO 2.5X BASIC INSERTS
1 Aaron Rodgers 1.25 3.00
2 Carson Wentz .75 2.00
3 Jimmy Garoppolo .75 2.00
4 Tom Brady 1.50 4.00
5 Ezekiel Elliott .75 2.00
6 Jared Goff .60 1.50
7 Antonio Brown .60 1.50
8 Brian Urlacher .60 1.50
9 Michael Strahan .50 1.25
10 Alvin Kamara .50 1.25
11 Baker Mayfield 4.00 10.00
12 Saquon Barkley 3.00 8.00
13 Sam Darnold 2.50 6.00
14 D.J. Moore .75 2.00
15 Calvin Ridley 1.00 2.50
16 Sony Michel 1.25 3.00
17 Josh Allen 1.50 4.00
18 Josh Rosen 1.25 3.00
19 Lamar Jackson 2.50 6.00
20 Bradley Chubb .60 1.50

2018 Certified Gridiron Signatures

*RED/75: .4X TO 1X BASIC AU/99
*BLUE/50: .5X TO 1.2X BASIC AU/99
*GOLD/25: .6X TO 1.5X BASIC AU/99
1 Dallas Goedert 4.00 10.00
2 Minkah Fitzpatrick 6.00 15.00
3 Roquan Smith 10.00 25.00
4 Maurice Hurst 4.00 10.00
5 Mark Andrews 5.00 12.00
6 Derwin James 6.00 15.00
7 Denzel Ward 8.00 20.00
8 Joshua Jackson 6.00 15.00
9 Arden Key 3.00 8.00
10 Jaire Alexander 5.00 12.00
11 Tremaine Edmunds 10.00 25.00
12 Rashaan Evans 5.00 12.00
13 Mike Hughes 5.00 12.00
14 Leighton Vander Esch 10.00 25.00
15 Antonio Callaway 4.00 10.00
16 Daron Payne 5.00 12.00
17 Vita Vea 5.00 12.00
18 Dylan Cantrell 3.00 8.00
19 Marcus Davenport 6.00 15.00
20 Roc Thomas 4.00 10.00

2018 Certified New Generation Jerseys

*ORANGE/399: .5X TO 1.2X BASIC JSY
*RED/299: .5X TO 1.2X BASIC JSY
*BLUE/50: .8X TO 2X BASIC JSY
*GOLD/25: 1X TO 2.5X BASIC JSY
1 Saquon Barkley 10.00 25.00
2 Mason Rudolph 3.00 8.00
3 Lamar Jackson 5.00 12.00
4 Josh Allen 4.00 10.00
5 Sam Darnold 6.00 15.00
6 Baker Mayfield 8.00 20.00
7 Derrius Guice 2.50 6.00
8 Josh Rosen 6.00 15.00
9 Kyle Lauletta 2.00 5.00
10 Calvin Ridley 3.00 8.00
11 Anthony Miller 2.00 5.00
12 D.J. Chark 1.50 4.00
13 Dante Pettis 2.00 5.00
14 Nick Chubb 4.00 10.00
15 Mike Gesicki 1.50 4.00
16 Ronald Jones II 1.25 3.00
17 Hayden Hurst 1.50 4.00
18 Mark Walton 1.50 4.00
19 Royce Freeman 1.50 4.00
20 Kerryon Johnson 2.00 5.00
21 Rashaad Penny 2.00 5.00
22 Nyheim Hines 1.50 4.00
23 James Washington 2.50 6.00
24 Keke Coutee 1.50 4.00
25 Courtland Sutton 2.00 5.00
26 Bradley Chubb 2.00 5.00
27 D.J. Moore 2.50 6.00
28 Sony Michel 4.00 10.00
29 Christian Kirk 2.00 5.00
30 Michael Gallup 2.50 6.00

2018 Certified Potential Signatures

*RED/75: .5X TO 1.2X BASIC AU/99
*BLUE/50: .5X TO 1.2X BASIC AU/99
*GOLD/25: .6X TO 1.5X BASIC AU/99
1 Auden Tate 3.00 8.00
2 Austin Proehl 3.00 8.00
3 Braxton Berrios 3.00 8.00
4 Carlton Davis 4.00 10.00
5 Cedrick Wilson Jr. 3.00 8.00
6 Chase Edmonds 3.00 8.00
7 Dalton Schultz 4.00 10.00
8 Riley Ferguson 5.00 12.00
9 Derrick Nnadi 3.00 8.00
11 Dorance Armstrong Jr. 3.00 8.00
12 Duke Dawson 3.00 8.00
13 Fred Warner 3.00 8.00
14 Harold Landry 3.00 8.00
15 Ian Thomas 3.00 8.00
16 Isaiah Oliver 3.00 8.00
17 Simmie Cobbs Jr. 5.00 12.00
18 John Kelly 4.00 10.00
19 Jordan Lasley 3.00 8.00
20 Josh Adams 6.00 15.00
21 Justin Jackson 4.00 10.00
22 Justin Reid 3.00 8.00
23 Luke Falk 4.00 10.00
24 Malik Jefferson 4.00 10.00
25 Rasheem Green 3.00 8.00
26 Ray-Ray McCloud 3.00 8.00
27 Ronnie Harrison 4.00 10.00
28 Sam Hubbard 4.00 10.00
29 Shaquem Griffin 10.00 25.00
30 Tanner Lee
31 Terrell Edmunds 10.00 25.00
32 Trey Quinn 3.00 8.00
33 Ogbonnia Okoronkwo 5.00 12.00
34 Orlando Brown 5.00 12.00
35 DeAndre Goolsby 3.00 8.00
36 Lavon Coleman 4.00 10.00
37 Mike McGlinchey 6.00 15.00
38 Quenton Nelson 12.00 30.00
39 Chad Thomas 3.00 8.00
40 Harrison Phillips 3.00 8.00
41 Tyquan Lewis
42 Lorenzo Carter 3.00 8.00
43 M.J. Stewart 3.00 8.00
44 Jalyn Holmes 5.00 12.00
45 Jerome Baker 4.00 10.00
46 Kyzir White
47 Troy Fumagalli 4.00 10.00
48 Ryan Izzo 3.00 8.00
49 Austin Allen 4.00 10.00
50 Logan Woodside

2018 Certified Rookie Roll Call Signatures

*RED/75: .4X TO 1X BASIC AU/99
*RED/60: .5X TO 1.2X BASIC AU/75
*RED/35: .4X TO 1X BASIC AU/35-50
*RED/25: .5X TO 1.2X BASIC AU/35-50
*BLUE/50: .5X TO 1.2X BASIC AU/75-99
*BLUE/25: .5X TO 1.2X BASIC AU/35-50
1 Baker Mayfield/20
2 Saquon Barkley/25 100.00 200.00
3 Sam Darnold/25 40.00 80.00
4 Bradley Chubb/25 8.00 20.00
5 Josh Allen/25 20.00 50.00
6 Josh Rosen/25 15.00 40.00
7 D.J. Moore/35 8.00 20.00
8 Hayden Hurst/35 EXCH 5.00 12.00
9 Calvin Ridley/35 10.00 25.00
10 Rashaad Penny/35 EXCH
11 Sony Michel/35 12.00 30.00
12 Keke Coutee/99 4.00 10.00
13 Nick Chubb/50 12.00 30.00
14 Ronald Jones II/50 4.00 10.00
15 Courtland Sutton/75 5.00 12.00
16 Mike Gesicki/75 4.00 10.00
17 Kerryon Johnson/75 5.00 12.00
18 Dante Pettis/99 5.00 12.00
19 Christian Kirk/99 5.00 12.00
20 Anthony Miller/99 5.00 12.00
21 Derrius Guice/99 8.00 20.00
22 James Washington/99 6.00 15.00
23 D.J. Chark/99
24 Royce Freeman/99 4.00 10.00
25 Mason Rudolph/99 8.00 20.00
26 Michael Gallup/99 6.00 15.00
27 Kyle Lauletta/99 5.00 12.00
28 J'Mon Moore/99 3.00 8.00
29 Jaylen Samuels/99 4.00 10.00
30 Mike White/99 4.00 10.00

2018 Certified Rookie Roll Call Signatures Mirror Gold

*GOLD/25: .6X TO 1.5X BASIC AU/75-99
*GOLD/15: .6X TO 1.5X BASIC AU/35-50
*GOLD/15: .5X TO 1.2X BASIC AU/25
*GOLD/15: .4X TO 1X BASIC AU/20
2 Saquon Barkley/15 250.00 400.00

2018 Certified Seal of Approval

*RED/99: .6X TO 1.5X BASIC INSERTS
*BLUE/50: .8X TO 2X BASIC INSERTS
*GOLD/25: 1X TO 2.5X BASIC INSERTS
1 Carson Wentz 1.25 3.00
2 Tom Brady 2.50 6.00
3 Dak Prescott 1.00 2.50
4 Antonio Brown 1.00 2.50
5 Ezekiel Elliott 1.25 3.00
6 Aaron Rodgers 2.00 5.00
7 Rob Gronkowski 1.00 2.50
8 Adam Thielen 1.00 2.50
9 Russell Wilson 1.25 3.00
10 Odell Beckham Jr. 1.00 2.50
11 Derek Carr 1.00 2.50
12 Julio Jones 1.00 2.50
13 Todd Gurley II 1.00 2.50
14 Deshaun Watson 1.25 3.00
15 Matthew Stafford .75 2.00
16 Cam Newton 1.00 2.50
17 Ben Roethlisberger 1.00 2.50
18 Jimmy Garoppolo 1.25 3.00
19 Le'Veon Bell .75 2.00
20 Kirk Cousins 1.00 2.50
21 Jarvis Landry .75 2.00
22 Alex Smith .75 2.00
23 Drew Brees 1.00 2.50
24 T.Y. Hilton .75 2.00
25 Matt Ryan .75 2.00
26 David Johnson 1.00 2.50
27 Leonard Fournette 1.00 2.50
28 Melvin Gordon .75 2.00
29 A.J. Green 1.00 2.50
30 Mike Evans .75 2.00
31 Kareem Hunt .75 2.00
32 Case Keenum .75 2.00
33 J.J. Watt 1.00 2.50
34 Dalvin Cook .75 2.00
35 Larry Fitzgerald .75 2.00

2018 Certified Signatures

*RED/60: .5X TO 1.2X BASIC AU/99
*RED/35-40: .4X TO 1X BASIC AU/50
*RED/25: .4X TO 1X BASIC AU/30
*RED/15: .4X TO 1X BASIC AU/20
*BLUE/50: .5X TO 1.2X BASIC AU/99
*BLUE/25-30: .5X TO 1.2X BASIC AU/50
*GOLD/25: .6X TO 1.5X BASIC AU/99
*GOLD/25: .5X TO 1.2X BASIC AU/40-50
*GOLD/15: .6X TO 1.5X BASIC AU/50
27 Charles Harris/50 4.00 10.00
31 Michael Bennett/20 6.00 15.00
32 Marvin Jones Jr./20 6.00 15.00
33 Carlos Hyde/20 6.00 15.00
34 Nelson Agholor/20 6.00 15.00
35 Manti Te'o/20 6.00 15.00
36 Vinny Testaverde/20 12.00 30.00
37 Zach Ertz/30
38 Gerald McCoy/30 5.00 12.00
39 Chris Thompson/30 5.00 12.00
40 Bruce Matthews/30 5.00 12.00
41 Brett Keisel/30 5.00 12.00
42 Steve Atwater/30 6.00 15.00
43 Mark Schlereth/30 5.00 12.00
44 Justin Tucker/30 12.00 30.00
45 Alex Collins/30 5.00 12.00
47 Chandler Jones/30 5.00 12.00
48 Brian Orakpo/30 5.00 12.00
49 Fletcher Cox/30 5.00 12.00
50 Jermaine Kearse/30
51 C.J. Mosley/30 6.00 15.00
52 Tavon Austin/30 5.00 12.00
53 Eric Weddle/30 5.00 12.00
54 Pierre Garcon/30 6.00 15.00
55 Dan Bailey/30
58 Willis McGahee/50 4.00 10.00
59 Eric Berry/50 8.00 20.00
60 Jerick McKinnon/50 4.00 10.00
61 Ron Dayne/50 4.00 10.00
62 Delanie Walker/50 4.00 10.00
63 Xavier Rhodes/50 4.00 10.00
64 Melvin Ingram/50 4.00 10.00
65 Dhani Jones/20 6.00 15.00
66 John Kuhn/50 4.00 10.00
67 D'Onta Foreman/50 4.00 10.00
69 Dede Westbrook/50 4.00 10.00
71 Sterling Shepard/50 5.00 12.00
72 Alvin Kamara/50 15.00 40.00
73 Gilbert Brown/50 4.00 10.00
74 Morten Andersen/50 4.00 10.00
75 Steve Grogan/50 4.00 10.00
76 Ted Johnson/50 4.00 10.00
77 Randall McDaniel/50 10.00 25.00
78 Marquette King/50 4.00 10.00
79 Samaje Perine/50 4.00 10.00
80 Geno Atkins/50
82 Jamison Crowder/40 4.00 10.00
83 Walter Jones/60 6.00 15.00
84 Aaron Jones/50 5.00 12.00
85 LeGarrette Blount/30 6.00 15.00
86 James Conner/50 6.00 15.00
87 Ryan Switzer/99 3.00 8.00
88 Artie Burns/99 5.00 12.00
90 Quincy Wilson/99 3.00 8.00
91 Tarik Cohen/50 5.00 12.00
92 T.J. Watt/50 5.00 12.00
94 Vonn Bell/99 3.00 8.00
95 Joe Mixon/30 6.00 15.00
96 Blake Martinez/99 3.00 8.00
97 Preston Smith/99 3.00 8.00
98 Preston Brown/99 3.00 8.00
99 Jack Doyle/50 4.00 10.00
100 Tyler Matakevich/99 3.00 8.00

2019 Certified

1 Tom Brady 1.00 2.50
2 Sony Michel .40 1.00
3 Julian Edelman .40 1.00
4 Josh Allen .40 1.00
5 LeSean McCoy .40 1.00
6 Kenyan Drake .25 .60
7 DeVante Parker .30 .75
8 Sam Darnold .40 1.00
9 Le'Veon Bell .30 .75
10 Jamison Crowder .25 .60
11 Lamar Jackson .40 1.00
12 Mark Ingram II .30 .75
13 Earl Thomas III .30 .75
14 Andy Dalton .30 .75
15 Joe Mixon .30 .75
16 A.J. Green .40 1.00
17 Baker Mayfield .60 1.50
18 Nick Chubb .40 1.00
19 Odell Beckham Jr. .40 1.00
20 Jarvis Landry .30 .75
21 Ben Roethlisberger .30 .75
22 James Conner .40 1.00
23 JuJu Smith-Schuster .40 1.00
24 T.J. Watt .30 .75
25 Deshaun Watson .50 1.25
26 DeAndre Hopkins .30 .75
27 J.J. Watt .40 1.00
28 Andrew Luck .50 1.25
29 Marlon Mack .25 .60
30 T.Y. Hilton .30 .75
31 Nick Foles .30 .75
32 Leonard Fournette .40 1.00
33 Jalen Ramsey .30 .75
34 Marcus Mariota .40 1.00
35 Derrick Henry .40 1.00
36 Corey Davis .30 .75
37 Joe Flacco .30 .75
38 Phillip Lindsay .40 1.00
39 Courtland Sutton .30 .75
40 Patrick Mahomes II 1.00 2.50
41 Damien Williams .25 .60
42 Travis Kelce .40 1.00
43 Philip Rivers .40 1.00
44 Melvin Gordon III .30 .75
45 Keenan Allen .30 .75
46 Joey Bosa .30 .75
47 Derek Carr .40 1.00
48 Antonio Brown .40 1.00
49 Tyrell Williams .25 .60
50 Dak Prescott .40 1.00
51 Ezekiel Elliott .50 1.25
52 Amari Cooper .40 1.00
53 Leighton Vander Esch .30 .75
54 Eli Manning .30 .75
55 Saquon Barkley .50 1.25
56 Sterling Shepard .30 .75
57 Carson Wentz .50 1.25
58 DeSean Jackson .30 .75
59 Alshon Jeffery .30 .75
60 Case Keenum .30 .75
61 Adrian Peterson .40 1.00
62 Derrius Guice .30 .75
63 Mitchell Trubisky .40 1.00
64 Tarik Cohen .30 .75
65 Anthony Miller .30 .75
66 Khalil Mack .40 1.00

67 Matthew Stafford .30 .75
68 Kenny Golladay .25 .60
69 Kerryon Johnson .30 .75
70 Aaron Rodgers .75 2.00
71 Aaron Jones .30 .75
72 Davante Adams .30 .75
73 Kirk Cousins .40 1.00
74 Dalvin Cook .30 .75
75 Stefon Diggs .30 .75
76 Adam Thielen .40 1.00
77 Matt Ryan .40 1.00
78 Julio Jones .40 1.00
79 Calvin Ridley .30 .75
80 Cam Newton .40 1.00
81 Christian McCaffrey .40 1.00
82 D.J. Moore .30 .75
83 Drew Brees .40 1.00
84 Alvin Kamara .30 .75
85 Michael Thomas .40 1.00
86 Jameis Winston .30 .75
87 Mike Evans .30 .75
88 Chris Godwin .25 .60
89 Josh Rosen .40 1.00
90 David Johnson .40 1.00
91 Larry Fitzgerald .30 .75
92 Jared Goff .40 1.00
93 Todd Gurley II .40 1.00
94 Cooper Kupp .30 .75
95 Jimmy Garoppolo .40 1.00
96 Dante Pettis .30 .75
97 George Kittle .25 .60
98 Russell Wilson .50 1.25
99 Doug Baldwin .30 .75
100 Tyler Lockett .30 .75
101 Barry Sanders IMM 2.50 6.00
102 Brian Dawkins IMM 1.50 4.00
103 Calvin Johnson IMM 1.25 3.00
104 Chris Spielman IMM 1.00 2.50
105 Dan Fouts IMM 1.25 3.00
106 Dan Marino IMM 3.00 8.00
107 Devin Hester IMM 1.25 3.00
108 Ed Reed IMM 1.25 3.00
109 Emmitt Smith IMM 2.50 6.00
110 James Harrison IMM 1.25 3.00
111 Jason Taylor IMM 1.25 3.00
112 Jerome Bettis IMM 1.50 4.00
113 Jerry Rice IMM 2.50 6.00
114 Jim Kelly IMM 1.50 4.00
115 John Elway IMM 2.50 6.00
116 Johnny Unitas IMM 2.50 6.00
117 Kellen Winslow IMM 1.25 3.00
118 Lawrence Taylor IMM 1.50 4.00
119 Mike Alstott IMM 1.00 2.50
120 Neal Anderson IMM 1.00 2.50
121 Pat Tillman IMM 1.50 4.00
122 Peyton Manning IMM 3.00 8.00
123 Randy Moss IMM 1.25 3.00
124 Reggie White IMM 1.50 4.00
125 Russ Grimm IMM 1.00 2.50
126 Terrell Davis IMM 1.25 3.00
127 Tim Brown IMM 1.25 3.00
128 Troy Aikman IMM 2.00 5.00
129 Warren Moon IMM 1.50 4.00
130 Zach Thomas IMM 1.00 2.50
131 Darnell Savage Jr. RC 1.25 3.00
132 Emanuel Hall RC .75 2.00
133 Greedy Williams RC 2.50 6.00
134 Stanley Morgan Jr. RC 1.25 3.00
135 Dexter Lawrence RC 1.25 3.00
136 Clayton Thorson RC 1.25 3.00
137 Jaylon Ferguson RC .75 2.00
138 Karan Higdon RC 1.00 2.50
139 Brian Burns RC 1.00 2.50
140 Rodney Anderson RC 1.00 2.50
141 Rashan Gary RC 1.50 4.00
142 Trayvon Mullen Jr. RC 1.25 3.00
143 Deandre Baker RC 2.00 5.00
144 Julian Love RC 1.00 2.50
145 Devin White RC 2.50 6.00
146 Dillon Mitchell RC 1.00 2.50
147 Ed Oliver RC 1.25 3.00
148 Alex Barnes RC 1.00 2.50
149 Jalen Hurd RC 1.00 2.50
150 Johnathan Abram RC .75 2.00
151 Dexter Williams RC 1.00 2.50
152 David Sills V RC 2.50 6.00
153 Lil'Jordan Humphrey RC 1.00 2.50
154 Rock Ya-Sin RC 1.00 2.50
155 Antoine Wesley RC .75 2.00
156 Deionte Thompson RC 1.00 2.50
157 Emmanuel Butler RC 1.25 3.00
158 Penny Hart RC 1.00 2.50
159 Preston Williams RC .75 2.00
160 Byron Murphy RC .75 2.00
161 Kelvin Harmon RC 1.25 3.00
162 Travis Homer RC .75 2.00
163 Trace McSorley RC 2.00 5.00
164 Tyree Jackson RC 2.00 5.00
165 Anthony Johnson RC 1.00 2.50
166 Christian Wilkins RC 3.00 8.00
167 Zach Allen RC 1.25 3.00
168 Gardner Minshew II RC 1.25 3.00
169 Mack Wilson RC 1.00 2.50
170 Trayveon Williams RC 1.00 2.50
171 Taylor Rapp RC .75 2.00
172 Jonah Williams RC 2.00 5.00
173 KeeSean Johnson RC .75 2.00
174 Jordan Scarlett RC .75 2.00
175 Josh Oliver RC .75 2.00
176 Kaden Smith RC .75 2.00
177 Jeffery Simmons RC .75 2.00
178 Clelin Ferrell RC 1.25 3.00
179 Ben Banogu RC 1.50 4.00
180 Chase Winovich RC 2.50 6.00
181 Christian Miller RC 1.50 4.00
182 Devin Bush II RC 3.00 8.00
183 Dre'Mont Jones RC 1.00 2.50
184 Drew Sample RC .75 2.00
185 Jace Sternberger RC 1.00 2.50
186 Jachai Polite RC 1.00 2.50
187 Jalen Jelks RC 1.00 2.50
188 Jamel Dean RC 1.50 4.00
189 Juan Thornhill RC .75 2.00
190 Justin Layne RC 1.50 4.00
191 L.J. Collier RC .75 2.00
192 Mike Weber RC 1.25 3.00
193 Montez Sweat RC 2.50 6.00
194 Nasir Adderley RC 1.00 2.50
195 Quinnen Williams RC .75 2.00
196 Ryquell Armstead RC .75 2.00
197 Terry Godwin II RC 1.00 2.50
198 Travis Fulgham RC .75 2.00
199 Josh Allen RC 3.00 8.00
200 Terry Beckner Jr. RC .75 2.00
201 Dwayne Haskins JSY AU/199 RC 50.00 100.00
202 Kyler Murray JSY AU/199 RC 100.00 200.00
203 Daniel Jones JSY AU/199 RC 30.00 60.00
204 Josh Jacobs JSY AU/299 RC 20.00 50.00
205 Damien Harris JSY AU/399 RC 8.00 20.00
206 Darrell Henderson JSY AU/499 RC 8.00 20.00
207 Marquise Brown JSY AU/299 RC EXCH 12.00 30.00
208 D.K. Metcalf JSY AU/399 RC 15.00 40.00
209 A.J. Brown JSY AU/399 RC 8.00 20.00
210 Nick Bosa JSY AU/299 RC 15.00 40.00
211 Noah Fant JSY AU/499 RC 6.00 15.00
212 T.J. Hockenson JSY AU/499 RC 12.00 30.00
213 Irv Smith Jr. JSY AU/499 RC 10.00 25.00
214 Drew Lock JSY AU/199 RC 30.00 60.00
215 Will Grier JSY AU/299 RC 12.00 30.00
216 Ryan Finley JSY AU/499 RC 6.00 15.00
217 David Montgomery JSY AU/499 RC 15.00 40.00
218 Justice Hill JSY AU/499 RC 5.00 12.00
219 Tony Pollard JSY AU/499 RC 8.00 20.00
220 N'Keal Harry JSY AU/299 RC 12.00 30.00
221 Parris Campbell JSY AU/499 RC EXCH 8.00 20.00
222 Hakeem Butler JSY AU/499 RC 6.00 15.00
223 Deebo Samuel JSY AU/399 RC 8.00 20.00
224 J.J. Arcega-Whiteside JSY AU/499 RC 5.00 12.00
225 Mecole Hardman Jr. JSY AU/399 RC 15.00 40.00
226 Jarrett Stidham JSY AU/499 RC 12.00 30.00
227 Easton Stick JSY AU/499 RC 10.00 25.00
228 Miles Sanders JSY AU/499 RC 12.00 30.00
229 Devin Singletary JSY AU/499 RC 8.00 20.00
230 Alexander Mattison JSY AU/499 RC 6.00 15.00
231 Andy Isabella JSY AU/499 RC 5.00 12.00
232 Terry McLaurin JSY AU/499 RC 4.00 10.00
233 Diontae Johnson JSY AU/499 RC 10.00 25.00
234 Miles Boykin JSY AU/499 RC 4.00 10.00
235 Gary Jennings Jr. JSY AU/499 RC 5.00 12.00
236 Bryce Love JSY AU/399 RC 5.00 12.00
237 Benny Snell Jr. JSY AU/499 RC EXCH 10.00 25.00
238 Riley Ridley JSY AU/499 RC 5.00 12.00
239 Darius Slayton JSY AU/499 RC 5.00 12.00
240 Hunter Renfrow JSY AU/499 RC 6.00 15.00

2019 Certified Mirror Silver

*VETS/450: 1.5X TO 4X BASIC CARDS
*IMM/299: .4X TO 1X BASIC CARDS/399
*ROOK/299: .5X TO 1.2X BASIC CARDS/399

2019 Certified Mirror Blue

*VETS/50: 3X TO 8X BASIC CARDS
*IMM/50: .8X TO 2X BASIC CARDS/399
*ROOK/50: 1X TO 2.5X BASIC CARDS/399
*ROOK JSY AU/99: .8X TO 2X BASIC JSY AU/399-499
*ROOK JSY AU/49: .8X TO 2X BASIC JSY AU/199-299
202 Kyler Murray JSY AU/49 200.00 400.00

2019 Certified Mirror Blue Etch

*ROOK JSY AU/20: 1.5X TO 4X BASIC JSY AU/399-499
*ROOK JSY AU/20: 1.2X TO 3X BASIC JSY AU/199-299
202 Kyler Murray JSY AU 300.00 600.00

2019 Certified Mirror Gold

*VETS/25: 4X TO 10X BASIC CARDS
*IMM/25: .8X TO 2X BASIC CARDS
*ROOK/25: 1X TO 2.5X BASIC CARDS
*ROOK JSY AU/25: 1.2X TO 3X BASIC JSY AU/399-499
*ROOK JSY AU/25: 1X TO 2.5X BASIC JSY AU
202 Kyler Murray JSY AU 250.00 500.00

2019 Certified Mirror Gold Etch

*VETS/25: 4X TO 10X BASIC CARDS

2019 Certified Mirror Orange

*VETS/199: 2X TO 5X BASIC CARDS
*IMM/199: .5X TO 1.2X BASIC CARDS
*ROOK/199: .6X TO 1.5X BASIC CARDS
*ROOK JSY AU/299: .5X TO 1.2X BASIC JSY AU/399-499
*ROOK JSY AU/299: .4X TO 1X BASIC JSY AU/199-299
*ROOK JSY AU/149: .5X TO 1.2X BASIC JSY AU/199-299
202 Kyler Murray JSY AU/149 125.00 250.00

2019 Certified Mirror Red

*VETS/99: 2.5X TO 6X BASIC CARDS
*IMM/99: .6X TO 1.5X BASIC CARDS/399
*ROOK/99: .8X TO 2X BASIC CARDS/399
*ROOK JSY AU/199: .6X TO 1.5X BASIC JSY AU/399-499
*ROOK JSY AU/99: .6X TO 1.5X BASIC JSY AU/199-299
202 Kyler Murray JSY AU/99 150.00 300.00

2019 Certified Mirror Red Etch

*ROOK JSY AU/25: 1.2X TO 3X BASIC JSY AU/399-499
*ROOK JSY AU/25: 1X TO 2.5X BASIC JSY AU/199-299
202 Kyler Murray JSY AU 250.00 500.00

2019 Certified Mirror Teal

*VETS/35: 3X TO 8X BASIC CARDS
*IMM/399: ..8X TO 2X BASIC CARDS/399
*ROOK/399: 1X TO 2.5X BASIC CARDS/399
*ROOK JSY AU/35-50: 1X TO 2.5X BASIC JSY AU/399-499
*ROOK JSY AU/35-50: .8X TO 2X BASIC JSY AU/199-299
202 Kyler Murray JSY AU/35 200.00 400.00

2019 Certified Mirror Teal Etch

*ROOK JSY AU/15: 1.5X TO 4X BASIC JSY AU/399-499
*ROOK JSY AU/15: 1.2X TO 3X BASIC JSY AU/199-299
202 Kyler Murray JSY AU 300.00 600.00

2019 Certified Diamonds

*TEAL/35: .8X TO 2X BASIC INSERTS
*GOLD/25: 1X TO 2.5X BASIC INSERTS
1 Von Miller .75 2.00
2 Patrick Mahomes II 2.50 6.00
3 Lamar Jackson 1.00 2.50
4 Jalen Ramsey .75 2.00
5 Tom Brady 2.50 6.00
6 Kirk Cousins 1.00 2.50
7 Ezekiel Elliott 1.25 3.00
8 Saquon Barkley 1.25 3.00
9 Davante Adams .75 2.00
10 Josh Allen 1.00 2.50
11 JuJu Smith-Schuster 1.00 2.50
12 Travis Kelce 1.00 2.50
13 Myles Garrett .60 1.50
14 Kerryon Johnson .75 2.00
15 T.Y. Hilton .75 2.00
16 Marcus Mariota 1.00 2.50
17 J.J. Watt 1.00 2.50
18 Christian McCaffrey 1.00 2.50
19 Alvin Kamara .75 2.00
20 Julio Jones 1.00 2.50
21 Mike Evans .75 2.00
22 Todd Gurley II 1.00 2.50
23 Zach Ertz .75 2.00
24 George Kittle .60 1.50
25 Patrick Peterson .60 1.50

2019 Certified Fabric of the Game

*PRIME/35-50: .6X TO 1.5X BASIC JSY/299
*PRIME/35-50: .5X TO 1.2X BASIC JSY/85
*PRIME/25: .8X TO 2X BASIC JSY/299
*PRIME/15: 1X TO 2.5X BASIC JSY/299
1 Johnny Unitas/50 6.00 15.00
2 Josh Allen/299 2.50 6.00
3 LeSean McCoy/85 3.00 8.00
4 Kenyan Drake/299 1.50 4.00
5 Sam Darnold/299 2.50 6.00
6 Baker Mayfield/299 4.00 10.00
7 Nick Chubb/299 2.50 6.00
8 Saquon Barkley/299 3.00 8.00
9 Aaron Rodgers/299 5.00 12.00
10 Ezekiel Elliott/299 3.00 8.00
11 Drew Brees/299 2.50 6.00
12 Sony Michel/299 2.50 6.00
13 Philip Rivers/299 2.50 6.00
14 Melvin Gordon III/299 2.00 5.00
15 Patrick Mahomes II/299 6.00 15.00
16 Leonard Fournette/299 2.50 6.00
17 Derrick Henry/299 2.50 6.00
18 Marcus Mariota/299 2.50 6.00
19 Marquez Valdes-Scantling/299 2.00 5.00
20 Corey Davis/299 2.00 5.00
21 Sterling Shepard/299 2.00 5.00
22 Matt Ryan/299 2.50 6.00
23 Calvin Ridley/299 2.00 5.00
24 Lamar Jackson/299 2.50 6.00
25 Christian McCaffrey/299 2.50 6.00
26 Mitchell Trubisky/299 2.50 6.00
27 Greg Olsen/299 2.00 5.00
28 A.J. Green/50 4.00 10.00
29 Von Miller/299 2.00 5.00
30 Kerryon Johnson/299 2.00 5.00
31 Matthew Stafford/299 2.00 5.00
32 DeAndre Hopkins/299 2.00 5.00
35 Jared Goff/299 2.50 6.00
36 Dalvin Cook/299 2.00 5.00
37 Derek Carr/299 2.50 6.00
38 JuJu Smith-Schuster/299 2.50 6.00
39 Matt Breida/299 1.50 4.00
40 Jameis Winston/299 2.00 5.00

2019 Certified Gamers Jerseys

*ORANGE/199: .4X TO 1X BASIC JSY/199-299
*ORANGE/125-149: .5X TO 1.2X BASIC JSY/199-299
*RED/75-99: .5X TO 1.2X BASIC JSY/199-299
*BLUE/75: .5X TO 1.2X BASIC JSY/199-299
*BLUE/50: .6X TO 1.5X BASIC JSY/199-299
*TEAL/35: .6X TO 1.5X BASIC JSY/199-299
*TEAL/35: .5X TO 1.2X BASIC JSY/100
*GOLD/25: .8X TO 2X BASIC JSY/199-299
*GOLD/25: .6X TO 1.5X BASIC JSY/100
1 Kenyan Drake/199 1.50 4.00
2 DeVante Parker/199 2.00 5.00
3 Josh Allen/299 2.50 6.00
4 LeSean McCoy/100 3.00 8.00
5 Dede Westbrook/299 1.50 4.00
6 Andy Dalton/199 2.00 5.00
7 A.J. Green/199 2.50 6.00
8 A.J. Bouye/200 1.50 4.00
9 JuJu Smith-Schuster/100 3.00 8.00
10 Minkah Fitzpatrick/200 1.50 4.00
11 Dak Prescott/50 4.00 10.00
12 Ezekiel Elliott/50 5.00 12.00
13 Byron Jones/299 1.50 4.00
14 Tyler Boyd/299 1.50 4.00
15 Royce Freeman/299 1.50 4.00
16 Cam Newton/50 4.00 10.00
17 Emmanuel Sanders/299 2.50 6.00
18 Albert Wilson/299 1.50 4.00
19 Tyron Smith/299 1.50 4.00
20 Joe Mixon/299 2.00 5.00

2019 Certified Gold Team

*TEAL/35: .8X TO 2X BASIC INSERTS
*GOLD/25: 1X TO 2.5X BASIC INSERTS
1 Matt Ryan .60 1.50
2 Patrick Mahomes II 1.50 4.00
3 Tom Brady 1.50 4.00
4 Baker Mayfield 1.00 2.50
5 John Elway 1.00 2.50
6 Brett Favre 1.25 3.00
7 Ezekiel Elliott .75 2.00
8 Roger Staubach .75 2.00
9 Antonio Brown .60 1.50
10 Charles Woodson .50 1.25
11 Ben Roethlisberger .50 1.25
12 Deshaun Watson .75 2.00
13 Carson Wentz .75 2.00
14 Melvin Gordon III .50 1.25
15 Jared Goff .60 1.50
16 Deion Sanders .50 1.25
17 Ray Lewis .60 1.50
18 Tiki Barber .40 1.00
19 Peyton Manning 1.25 3.00
20 Mitchell Trubisky .60 1.50

2019 Certified Record Breakers

*TEAL/35: .8X TO 2X BASIC INSERTS
*GOLD/25: 1X TO 2.5X BASIC INSERTS
1 Adam Vinatieri .60 1.50
2 Saquon Barkley 1.25 3.00
3 Zach Ertz .75 2.00
4 Aaron Rodgers 2.00 5.00
5 Baker Mayfield 1.50 4.00
6 Drew Brees 1.00 2.50
7 Jerry Rice 1.50 4.00
8 Emmitt Smith 1.50 4.00
9 Devin Hester .75 2.00
10 Peyton Manning 2.00 5.00
11 Eric Dickerson 1.00 2.50
12 LaDainian Tomlinson .75 2.00
13 Calvin Johnson .75 2.00
14 Randy Moss .75 2.00
15 Derrick Henry 1.00 2.50

2019 Certified Rookie Roll Call Signatures

101 Daniel Jones/99 20.00 50.00
102 Dwayne Haskins/99 40.00 80.00
103 Nick Bosa/99 10.00 25.00
104 T.J. Hockenson/99 8.00 20.00
105 Marquise Brown/50 EXCH 12.00 30.00
106 Kyler Murray/50 100.00 200.00
107 Darrell Henderson/99 8.00 20.00
108 Josh Jacobs/99 25.00 50.00
109 Drew Lock/50 20.00 50.00
110 D.K. Metcalf/99 10.00 25.00
111 A.J. Brown/99 8.00 20.00
112 David Montgomery/99 12.00 30.00
113 Parris Campbell/99 EXCH 8.00 20.00
114 Mecole Hardman Jr./99 8.00 20.00
115 N'Keal Harry/99 15.00 40.00

2019 Certified Rookie Roll Call Signatures Mirror Gold

*GOLD/25: .6X TO 1.5X BASIC AU/99
*GOLD/25: .5X TO 1.2X BASIC AU/50

2019 Certified Rookie Roll Call Signatures Mirror Teal

*TEAL/35: .5X TO 1.2X BASIC AU/99
*TEAL/35: .4X TO 1X BASIC AU/50

2019 Certified Rookie Signatures

131 Darnell Savage Jr. 6.00 15.00
132 Emanuel Hall 3.00 8.00
133 Greedy Williams 10.00 25.00
134 Stanley Morgan Jr. 5.00 12.00
135 Dexter Lawrence 5.00 12.00
136 Clayton Thorson 5.00 12.00
137 Jaylon Ferguson 3.00 8.00
138 Karan Higdon 4.00 10.00
139 Brian Burns 4.00 10.00
140 Rodney Anderson 4.00 10.00
141 Rashan Gary 6.00 15.00
142 Trayvon Mullen Jr. 5.00 12.00
143 Deandre Baker 8.00 20.00
144 Julian Love 4.00 10.00
145 Devin White 10.00 25.00
146 Dillon Mitchell 4.00 10.00
147 Ed Oliver 6.00 15.00
148 Alex Barnes 4.00 10.00
149 Jalen Hurd 4.00 10.00
150 Johnathan Abram 3.00 8.00
151 Dexter Williams 4.00 10.00
152 David Sills V 10.00 25.00
153 Lil'Jordan Humphrey 4.00 10.00
154 Rock Ya-Sin 4.00 10.00
155 Antoine Wesley 3.00 8.00
156 Deionte Thompson 4.00 10.00
157 Emmanuel Butler 5.00 12.00
158 Penny Hart 4.00 10.00
159 Preston Williams 3.00 8.00
161 Kelvin Harmon 5.00 12.00
162 Travis Homer 3.00 8.00
163 Trace McSorley 8.00 20.00
164 Tyree Jackson 8.00 20.00
165 Anthony Johnson 4.00 10.00
166 Christian Wilkins 12.00 30.00
167 Zach Allen 5.00 12.00
168 Gardner Minshew II 5.00 12.00
169 Mack Wilson 4.00 10.00
170 Trayveon Williams 4.00 10.00

2019 Certified Rookie Signatures Mirror Etch

*ETCH/25: .6X TO 1.5X BASIC AU/149

2019 Certified Rookie Signatures Mirror Gold

*GOLD/25: .6X TO 1.5X BASIC AU/149

2019 Certified Superb Swatches

*PRIME/50: .6X TO 1.5X BASIC JSY/299
*PRIME/25: .8X TO 2X BASIC JSY/299
*PRIME/15: 1X TO 2.5X BASIC JSY/299
*PRIME/15: .6X TO 1.5X BASIC JSY/50
1 Patrick Mahomes II/299 6.00 15.00
2 Todd Gurley II/299 2.50 6.00
3 Cooper Kupp/299 2.00 5.00
4 T.Y. Hilton/299 2.00 5.00
5 Marcus Mariota/299 2.50 6.00
6 Matthew Stafford/299 2.00 5.00
7 Josh Allen/299 2.50 6.00
9 DeAndre Hopkins/299 2.00 5.00
10 Lamar Jackson/299 2.50 6.00
11 Christian McCaffrey/299 2.50 6.00
12 Mike Williams/299 1.50 4.00
13 Calvin Ridley/299 2.00 5.00
14 Hunter Henry/299 1.50 4.00
15 Kyle Rudolph/299 1.50 4.00
16 Joe Mixon/299 2.00 5.00
17 Davante Adams/299 2.00 5.00
18 Tyler Boyd/299 1.50 4.00
19 Alvin Kamara/299 2.00 5.00
20 Kenny Golladay/299 1.50 4.00
21 Michael Gallup/299 2.50 6.00
22 James Conner/299 2.50 6.00
23 Jared Goff/299 2.50 6.00
24 DeVante Parker/299 2.00 5.00
25 Baker Mayfield/299 4.00 10.00
26 Ronald Jones II/299 1.50 4.00
27 Derrius Guice/299 2.00 5.00
28 Matt Ryan/299 2.50 6.00
29 Ben Roethlisberger/299 2.00 5.00
30 J.J. Watt/299 2.50 6.00
31 Derek Carr/299 2.50 6.00
32 DeSean Jackson/50 3.00 8.00
33 Nyheim Hines/299 2.00 5.00
35 Russell Wilson/299 3.00 8.00
36 Doug Baldwin/299 2.00 5.00
37 Christian Kirk/299 1.50 4.00
38 Dede Westbrook/299 1.50 4.00
39 Saquon Barkley/299 3.00 8.00
40 Adam Thielen/299 2.50 6.00

2017 Certified Cuts

1 Ezekiel Elliott .50 1.25
2 Dak Prescott .40 1.00
3 Jason Witten .30 .75
4 Dez Bryant .40 1.00
5 Eli Manning .30 .75
6 Odell Beckham Jr. .40 1.00
7 Brandon Marshall .25 .60
8 Carson Wentz .50 1.25
9 Alshon Jeffery .30 .75
10 Jordan Matthews .25 .60
11 Kirk Cousins .40 1.00
12 Robert Kelley .25 .60
13 Jamison Crowder .25 .60
14 Jordan Reed .25 .60
15 Carson Palmer .30 .75
16 David Johnson .40 1.00
17 Larry Fitzgerald .30 .75
18 Jared Goff .40 1.00
19 Todd Gurley II .40 1.00
20 Brian Hoyer .25 .60
21 Carlos Hyde .25 .60
22 Russell Wilson .50 1.25
23 Thomas Rawls .25 .60
24 Eddie Lacy .25 .60
25 Jimmy Graham .40 1.00
26 Mike Glennon .30 .75
27 Jordan Howard .40 1.00
28 Kevin White .25 .60
29 Matthew Stafford .30 .75
30 Ameer Abdullah .25 .60
31 Marvin Jones Jr. .25 .60
32 Aaron Rodgers .75 2.00
33 Davante Adams .30 .75
34 Jordy Nelson .30 .75
35 Clay Matthews .30 .75
36 Sam Bradford .25 .60
37 Latavius Murray .25 .60
38 Stefon Diggs .30 .75
39 Matt Ryan .30 .75
40 Devonta Freeman .30 .75
41 Julio Jones .40 1.00
42 Tevin Coleman .30 .75
43 Cam Newton .40 1.00
44 Kelvin Benjamin .30 .75
45 Julius Peppers .30 .75
46 Drew Brees .40 1.00
47 Adrian Peterson .40 1.00
48 Michael Thomas .40 1.00
49 Jameis Winston .30 .75
50 Mike Evans .30 .75
51 DeSean Jackson .30 .75
52 Tyrod Taylor .30 .75
53 LeSean McCoy .40 1.00
54 Sammy Watkins .40 1.00
55 Ryan Tannehill .30 .75
56 Jay Ajayi .30 .75
67 Jarvis Landry .30 .75
58 Tom Brady 1.00 2.50
59 Rob Gronkowski .40 1.00
60 Julian Edelman .40 1.00
61 Brandin Cooks .30 .75
62 Matt Forte .25 .60
63 Darron Lee .25 .60
64 Paxton Lynch .25 .60
65 Trevor Siemian .25 .60
66 Von Miller .30 .75
67 Alex Smith .30 .75
68 Tyreek Hill .40 1.00
69 Travis Kelce .40 1.00
70 Philip Rivers .40 1.00
71 Melvin Gordon .30 .75
72 Joey Bosa .40 1.00
73 Marshawn Lynch .30 .75
74 Derek Carr .40 1.00
75 Amari Cooper .40 1.00
76 Khalil Mack .40 1.00
77 Joe Flacco .30 .75
78 Kenneth Dixon .25 .60
79 Andy Dalton .30 .75
80 A.J. Green .40 1.00
81 Tyler Eifert .30 .75
82 Cody Kessler .25 .60
83 Isaiah Crowell .25 .60
84 Corey Coleman .25 .60
85 Ben Roethlisberger .40 1.00
86 Le'Veon Bell .30 .75
87 Antonio Brown .40 1.00
88 James Harrison .30 .75
89 Lamar Miller .25 .60
90 DeAndre Hopkins .30 .75
91 J.J. Watt .40 1.00
92 Andrew Luck .50 1.25
93 Frank Gore .30 .75
94 T.Y. Hilton .30 .75
95 Blake Bortles .25 .60
96 Allen Robinson .30 .75
97 Jalen Ramsey .25 .60
98 Marcus Mariota .40 1.00
99 DeMarco Murray .30 .75
100 Derrick Henry .30 .75
101 Jerry Rice 2.50 6.00
102 Jim Brown 2.00 5.00
103 Lawrence Taylor 1.50 4.00
104 Joe Montana 4.00 10.00
105 Walter Payton 3.00 8.00
106 Johnny Unitas 2.50 6.00
107 Peyton Manning 3.00 8.00
108 Charles Haley 1.50 4.00
109 Ronnie Lott 1.25 3.00
110 Warren Moon 1.50 4.00
111 Joe Greene 1.50 4.00
112 Barry Sanders 2.50 6.00
113 Ray Lewis 1.50 4.00
114 Brett Favre 3.00 8.00
115 Gale Sayers 1.50 4.00
116 John Elway 2.50 6.00
117 John Hannah 1.00 2.50
118 Dan Marino 3.00 8.00
119 Bob Lilly 1.25 3.00
120 Emmitt Smith 2.50 6.00
121 Bruce Smith 1.25 3.00
122 Deion Sanders 1.25 3.00
123 Raymond Berry 1.25 3.00
124 Lance Alworth 1.25 3.00
125 Rod Woodson 1.25 3.00
126 John Riggins 1.25 3.00
127 Roger Staubach 2.00 5.00
128 Red Grange 2.00 5.00
129 Terry Bradshaw 2.50 6.00
130 Eric Dickerson 1.50 4.00
131 Earl Campbell 1.50 4.00
132 Mike Singletary 1.50 4.00
133 Jack Ham 1.25 3.00
134 LaDainian Tomlinson 1.25 3.00
135 Randy White 1.25 3.00
136 Randy Moss 1.25 3.00
137 Kellen Winslow 1.25 3.00
138 Marshall Faulk 1.25 3.00
139 Ozzie Newsome 1.25 3.00
140 Tony Dorsett 1.50 4.00
141 Troy Aikman 2.00 5.00
142 Steve Young 2.00 5.00
143 Ted Hendricks 1.00 2.50
144 Marcus Allen 1.25 3.00
145 Ed Reed 1.25 3.00
146 Kurt Warner 1.25 3.00
147 Fran Tarkenton 1.50 4.00
148 Michael Irvin 1.50 4.00
149 Michael Strahan 1.25 3.00
150 Joe Namath 2.00 5.00
151 Brad Kaaya RC .75 2.00
152 Jerod Evans RC 1.00 2.50
153 Chad Kelly RC .75 2.00
154 Brian Hill RC .75 2.00
155 Donnel Pumphrey RC 1.00 2.50
156 Matthew Dayes RC .75 2.00
157 Elijah McGuire RC .75 2.00
158 Aaron Jones RC 2.00 5.00
159 Elijah Hood RC .75 2.00
160 De'Angelo Henderson RC .75 2.00
161 Tarik Cohen RC 1.50 4.00
162 T.J. Logan RC 1.25 3.00
163 Marlon Humphrey RC .75 2.00
164 Marshon Lattimore RC 1.00 2.50
165 Adoree' Jackson RC 1.00 2.50
166 Quincy Wilson RC .75 2.00
167 Sidney Jones RC .75 2.00
168 Tre'Davious White RC .75 2.00
169 Cameron Sutton RC .75 2.00
170 Gareon Conley RC .75 2.00
171 Chidobe Awuzie RC 1.00 2.50
172 Kevin King RC 1.00 2.50
173 Dalvin Tomlinson RC .75 2.00
174 Jonathan Allen RC 1.00 2.50
175 Derek Barnett RC 1.00 2.50
176 Charles Harris RC .75 2.00
177 Taco Charlton RC .75 2.00
178 DeMarcus Walker RC .75 2.00
179 Solomon Thomas RC .75 2.00
180 Jabrill Peppers RC 1.25 3.00
181 Marcus Maye RC .75 2.00
182 T.J. Watt RC 2.50 6.00
183 Malik McDowell RC .75 2.00
184 Haason Reddick RC .75 2.00
185 Jamal Adams RC .75 2.00
186 Montravius Adams RC 1.00 2.50
187 Raekwon McMillan RC .75 2.00
188 Zach Cunningham RC 1.00 2.50
189 Jarrad Davis RC 1.00 2.50
190 Malik Hooker RC .75 2.00
191 Jake Butt RC 1.00 2.50
192 Adam Shaheen RC .75 2.00
193 Gerald Everett RC .75 2.00
194 Noah Brown RC 1.00 2.50
195 Shelton Gibson RC .75 2.00
196 Josh Malone RC .75 2.00
197 Chad Hansen RC .75 2.00
198 Chad Williams RC .75 2.00
199 Trent Taylor RC 1.00 2.50
200 Ryan Switzer RC 1.00 2.50
201 Deshaun Watson JSY AU/49 RC 60.00 125.00
202 Mitchell Trubisky JSY AU/49 RC 50.00 100.00
203 DeShone Kizer JSY AU/49 RC 6.00 15.00
204 Patrick Mahomes II JSY AU/49 RC 250.00 500.00
205 C.J. Beathard JSY AU/299 RC 4.00 10.00
206 Davis Webb JSY AU/99 RC 5.00 12.00
207 Nathan Peterman JSY AU/99 RC 6.00 15.00
208 R. Joshua Dobbs JSY AU/299 RC 5.00 12.00
209 Leonard Fournette JSY AU/49 RC 20.00 50.00
210 Dalvin Cook JSY AU/40 RC 15.00 40.00
211 Christian McCaffrey JSY AU/49 RC 40.00 80.00
212 D'Onta Foreman JSY AU/199 RC 5.00 12.00
213 Alvin Kamara JSY AU/200 RC 25.00 60.00
214 Samaje Perine JSY AU/299 RC 4.00 10.00
215 Wayne Gallman JSY AU/299 RC 5.00 12.00
216 Kareem Hunt JSY AU/299 RC 12.00 30.00
217 Jeremy McNichols JSY AU/299 RC 4.00 10.00
218 James Conner JSY AU/299 RC 8.00 20.00
219 Joe Mixon JSY AU/299 RC 8.00 20.00
220 Marlon Mack JSY AU/299 RC 6.00 15.00
221 O.J. Howard JSY AU/99 RC 6.00 15.00
222 Mike Williams JSY AU/49 RC 10.00 25.00
223 Corey Davis JSY AU/49 RC 10.00 25.00
224 John Ross III JSY AU/49 RC 8.00 20.00
225 JuJu Smith-Schuster JSY AU/49 RC 15.00 40.00
226 Zay Jones JSY AU/99 RC 6.00 15.00
227 Curtis Samuel JSY AU/199 RC 5.00 12.00
228 Dede Westbrook JSY AU/299 RC 4.00 10.00
229 Carlos Henderson JSY AU/299 RC 4.00 10.00
230 Chris Godwin JSY AU/299 RC 5.00 12.00
231 Joe Williams JSY AU/299 RC 4.00 10.00
232 Cooper Kupp JSY AU/299 RC 6.00 15.00
233 Amara Darboh JSY AU/299 RC 4.00 10.00
234 Jamaal Williams JSY AU/299 RC 4.00 10.00
235 ArDarius Stewart JSY AU/299 RC 4.00 10.00
236 Kenny Golladay JSY AU/299 RC 6.00 15.00
237 Josh Reynolds JSY AU/299 RC 4.00 10.00
238 Taywan Taylor JSY AU/299 RC 4.00 10.00
239 Mack Hollins JSY AU/299 RC 4.00 10.00
240 Evan Engram JSY AU/299 RC 5.00 12.00

2017 Certified Cuts Rookie Cuts Blue

*BLUE/25: .8X TO 2X BASIC JSY AU/199-299

2017 Certified Cuts Rookie Cuts Red

*RED/99: .5X TO 1.2X BASIC JSY AU/199-299
*RED/49: .6X TO 1.5X BASIC JSY AU/199-299
*RED/25: .8X TO 2X BASIC JSY AU/199-299
*RED/25: .6X TO 1.5X BASIC JSY AU/99
*RED/25: .5X TO 1.2X BASIC JSY AU/49
*RED/15: .6X TO 1.5X BASIC JSY AU/49
201 Deshaun Watson JSY AU/15 125.00 250.00
202 Mitchell Trubisky JSY AU/15 75.00 150.00
204 Patrick Mahomes II JSY AU/15 200.00 400.00

2017 Certified Cuts Silver

*VETS: 2.5X TO 6X BASIC CARDS
*RET: 1X TO 2.5X BASIC CARDS
*ROOKIES: .8X TO 2X BASIC CARDS

2017 Certified Cuts Canton Bound

*SILVER/99: .6X TO 1.5X BASIC INSERTS
1 Tom Brady 2.50 6.00
2 Drew Brees 1.00 2.50
3 Aaron Rodgers 2.00 5.00
4 Ben Roethlisberger 1.00 2.50
5 Eli Manning .75 2.00
6 Randy Moss .75 2.00
7 Le'Veon Bell .75 2.00
8 Ezekiel Elliott 1.25 3.00
9 LeSean McCoy 1.00 2.50
10 David Johnson 1.00 2.50
11 Julio Jones 1.00 2.50
12 Larry Fitzgerald .75 2.00
13 Antonio Brown 1.00 2.50
14 Odell Beckham Jr. 1.00 2.50
15 Jason Witten .75 2.00
16 Steve Smith .75 2.00
17 Von Miller .75 2.00
18 Richard Sherman 1.00 2.50
19 James Harrison .75 2.00
20 Julius Peppers .75 2.00

2017 Certified Cuts Contemporaries Dual Memorabilia

1 E.Smith/T.Aikman/25 10.00 25.00
2 D.Johnson/L.Bell/99 4.00 10.00
3 M.Stafford/C.Johnson/25 6.00 15.00
4 G.Olsen/J.Graham/45 5.00 12.00
5 H.Miller/H.Ward/49 4.00 10.00
6 D.Carr/D.Brees/99 4.00 10.00
7 D.Baldwin/R.Wilson/25 8.00 20.00
8 M.Ditka/J.Witten/25 6.00 15.00
9 M.Ryan/D.Freeman/99 3.00 8.00
10 T.Gurley II/E.Elliott/99 5.00 12.00
11 K.Warner/M.Faulk/99 3.00 8.00
12 C.Wentz/P.Lynch/99 5.00 12.00
13 J.Kelly/T.Thomas/99 4.00 10.00
14 C.Matthews/L.Kuechly/99 3.00 8.00
15 J.Montana/P.Holmes/49 12.00 30.00
16 E.Sanders/A.Brown/99 4.00 10.00
17 A.Talib/C.Harris/99 2.50 6.00
18 T.Kelce/R.Gronkowski/99 4.00 10.00
19 E.Thomas III/R.Sherman/99 4.00 10.00
20 D.Johnson/R.Lewis/99 4.00 10.00
21 E.Elliott/D.Prescott/99 5.00 12.00
22 J.Peppers/V.Miller/25 5.00 12.00
23 C.Newton/K.Benjamin/49 5.00 12.00
24 A.Vinatieri/D.Bailey/99 2.50 6.00
25 C.Wentz/J.Matthews/99 5.00 12.00
26 E.Berry/H.Clinton-Dix/49 4.00 10.00
27 D.Walker/M.Mariota/99 4.00 10.00
28 R.Moss/H.Ward/25 5.00 12.00
29 D.Henry/D.Murray/99 3.00 8.00
30 P.Manning/T.Brady/25 15.00 40.00
31 M.Evans/J.Winston/99 3.00 8.00
32 E.Smith/T.Davis/25 10.00 25.00
33 T.Lockett/R.Wilson/99 5.00 12.00
34 W.Payton/E.Campbell/25 12.00 30.00
35 K.White/J.Howard/99 4.00 10.00
36 R.Staubach/T.Bradshaw/25 10.00 25.00
37 P.Perkins/S.Shepard/99 3.00 8.00
38 D.Bryant/O.Beckham Jr./25 6.00 15.00
39 K.Allen/M.Gordon/99 3.00 8.00
40 J.Elway/J.Kelly/25 10.00 25.00

2017 Certified Cuts Future Legends Memorabilia

*SILVER/49: .8X TO 2X BASIC JSY
1 Nathan Peterman 2.00 5.00
2 Zay Jones 2.00 5.00
3 Christian McCaffrey 5.00 12.00
4 Curtis Samuel 2.00 5.00
5 Mitchell Trubisky 5.00 12.00
6 Joe Mixon 3.00 8.00
7 John Ross III 2.00 5.00
8 DeShone Kizer 1.50 4.00
9 Carlos Henderson 1.50 4.00
10 Kenny Golladay 2.50 6.00
11 Jamaal Williams 1.50 4.00
12 Deshaun Watson 8.00 20.00
13 D'Onta Foreman 2.00 5.00
14 Marlon Mack 2.50 6.00
15 Leonard Fournette 5.00 12.00
16 Dede Westbrook 1.50 4.00
17 Patrick Mahomes II 12.00 30.00
18 Kareem Hunt 4.00 10.00
19 Mike Williams 2.50 6.00
20 Cooper Kupp 2.50 6.00
21 Josh Reynolds 1.50 4.00
22 Dalvin Cook 4.00 10.00
23 Alvin Kamara 3.00 8.00
24 Davis Webb 1.50 4.00
25 Wayne Gallman 2.00 5.00
26 Evan Engram 2.00 5.00
27 ArDarius Stewart 1.50 4.00
28 Mack Hollins 1.50 4.00
29 R. Joshua Dobbs 2.00 5.00
30 James Conner 3.00 8.00
31 JuJu Smith-Schuster 3.00 8.00
32 C.J. Beathard 1.50 4.00
33 Joe Williams 1.50 4.00
34 Amara Darboh 1.50 4.00
35 Jeremy McNichols 1.50 4.00
36 O.J. Howard 2.00 5.00
37 Chris Godwin 2.00 5.00
38 Corey Davis 2.50 6.00
39 Taywan Taylor 1.50 4.00
40 Samaje Perine 1.50 4.00

2017 Certified Cuts Heritage Collection

*SILVER/99: .6X TO 1.5X BASIC INSERTS
1 Emmitt Smith 1.50 4.00
2 John Riggins .75 2.00
3 Derrick Thomas .75 2.00
4 Dan Marino 2.00 5.00
5 Randy Moss .75 2.00
6 Reggie White 1.00 2.50
7 Joe Montana 2.50 6.00
8 John Elway 1.50 4.00
9 Peyton Manning 2.00 5.00
10 Walter Payton 2.00 5.00
11 Barry Sanders 1.50 4.00
12 Brett Favre 2.00 5.00
13 Tom Landry 1.25 3.00
14 Jim Brown 1.25 3.00
15 Terry Bradshaw 1.50 4.00
16 Earl Campbell 1.00 2.50
17 Jim Taylor .75 2.00
18 Jerry Rice 1.50 4.00
19 Steve Largent 1.00 2.50
20 Jim Thorpe 1.25 3.00

2017 Certified Cuts Highlight Reels

*SILVER/99: .6X TO 1.5X BASIC INSERTS
1 Antonio Brown 1.00 2.50
2 Jordy Nelson .75 2.00
3 Mike Evans .75 2.00
4 Davante Adams .75 2.00
5 Odell Beckham Jr. 1.00 2.50
6 Michael Thomas 1.00 2.50
7 Dez Bryant 1.00 2.50
8 Kelvin Benjamin .75 2.00
9 Julio Jones 1.00 2.50
10 Tyreek Hill 1.00 2.50
11 David Johnson 1.00 2.50
12 Ezekiel Elliott 1.25 3.00
13 DeMarco Murray .75 2.00
14 Jay Ajayi .75 2.00
15 Le'Veon Bell .75 2.00
16 Jordan Howard 1.00 2.50
17 Cam Newton 1.00 2.50
18 Dak Prescott 1.00 2.50
19 Drew Brees 1.00 2.50
20 Matt Ryan .75 2.00
21 Aaron Rodgers 2.00 5.00
22 Russell Wilson 1.25 3.00
23 Carson Wentz 1.25 3.00
24 Derek Carr 1.00 2.50
25 Marcus Mariota 1.00 2.50

2017 Certified Cuts Historical Pieces

1 Joe Theismann/99 4.00 10.00
2 Barry Sanders/99 6.00 15.00
3 Bo Jackson/99 5.00 12.00
4 Champ Bailey/99 3.00 8.00
5 Clinton Portis/99 2.50 6.00
6 Dan Marino/99 8.00 20.00
8 Dwight Clark/99 3.00 8.00
9 Earl Campbell/99 4.00 10.00
11 Fran Tarkenton/99 4.00 10.00
12 Franco Harris/99 4.00 10.00
14 Jerome Bettis/99 4.00 10.00
15 Jim Kelly/99 4.00 10.00
18 Joe Montana/99 10.00 25.00
19 John Riggins/99 3.00 8.00
21 Kurt Warner/99 3.00 8.00
22 LaDainian Tomlinson/99 3.00 8.00
23 Lance Alworth/99 3.00 8.00
30 Priest Holmes/99 2.50 6.00
31 Ray Lewis/99 4.00 10.00
32 Ricky Williams/99 3.00 8.00
34 Steve Young/99 5.00 12.00
36 Terrell Davis/99 3.00 8.00
37 Terry Bradshaw/99 6.00 15.00
39 Troy Aikman/99 5.00 12.00

2017 Certified Cuts Memorable Moments

*SILVER/99: .6X TO 1.5X BASIC INSERTS
1 Dwight Clark 1.00 2.50
2 Franco Harris 1.25 3.00
3 Herman Edwards 1.00 2.50
4 Roger Staubach 1.50 4.00
5 Tom Brady 3.00 8.00
6 James Harrison 1.00 2.50
7 Bo Jackson 1.50 4.00
8 John Elway 2.00 5.00
9 Dan Marino 2.50 6.00
10 DeSean Jackson 1.00 2.50
11 Chuck Bednarik 1.00 2.50
12 Tony Dorsett 1.25 3.00
13 Earl Campbell
14 Marcus Allen 1.00 2.50
15 Emmitt Smith 2.00 5.00

2017 Certified Cuts Modern Cuts

2 Isaiah Crowell/149 3.00 8.00
3 Robert Kelley/149 3.00 8.00
4 LeGarrette Blount/99 5.00 12.00
7 Joey Bosa/99 6.00 15.00
8 Thomas Rawls/99 4.00 10.00
9 Malcolm Mitchell/149 4.00 10.00
10 DeMarco Murray/99 5.00 12.00
11 Quincy Enunwa/149 3.00 8.00
12 Carson Wentz/49 10.00 25.00
13 Derek Carr/49 8.00 20.00
14 Ameer Abdullah/149 3.00 8.00
15 Drew Brees/15
17 John Brown/149 4.00 10.00
18 Jamison Crowder/149 3.00 8.00
19 Mike Evans/49 6.00 15.00
20 LeSean McCoy/149 5.00 12.00
21 Jordan Howard/149 5.00 12.00
22 Sterling Shepard/149 4.00 10.00
23 Tyreek Hill/149 10.00 25.00
24 David Johnson/99 12.00 30.00
25 John Kuhn/149 3.00 8.00
26 Brandin Cooks/99 5.00 12.00
27 Latavius Murray/149 3.00 8.00
28 Cole Beasley/149 5.00 12.00
30 Marcus Mariota/15

2017 Certified Cuts Modern Cuts Blue

*BLUE/25: .8X TO 2X BASIC AU/149
*BLUE/15: 1X TO 2.5X BASIC AU/149

2017 Certified Cuts Modern Cuts Red

*RED/99: .5X TO 1.2X BASIC AU/149
*RED/49: .6X TO 1.5X BASIC AU/149
*RED/49: .5X TO 1.2X BASIC AU/99
*RED/25: .6X TO 1.5X BASIC AU/99
*RED/25: .5X TO 1.2X BASIC AU/49

2017 Certified Cuts Retired Cuts

*RED/15: .5X TO 1.2X BASIC AU/25
3 Dan Hampton/15 8.00 20.00
6 Jeff Saturday/15 15.00 40.00
9 Louis Lipps/25 6.00 15.00
10 Jim Zorn/25 6.00 15.00
11 Neil Smith/25 6.00 15.00
15 Bill Bates/25 6.00 15.00
23 Troy Brown/25 6.00 15.00
25 Roger Craig/15 10.00 25.00
26 Sterling Sharpe/15 15.00 40.00
27 Charles Haley/15 12.00 30.00

1968 Champion Corn Flakes

These cards were thought to have been issued on Champion Corn Flakes boxes around 1968, but the year has yet to have been confirmed. Each card measures approximately 2 1/16" by 3 3/16, is blankbacked, and features perforations on the edges. The cardfronts feature a color action player photo surrounded by a thin black border on three sides with the player's name and number at the bottom within a thick black border. The cards are apparently reprints of Sports Illustrated posters that were made available in the late 1960s. The card number consists of a numerical team code and AFL or NFL league letter assigned to each team (Examples. 7N for Packers and NFL, 6A for Chiefs and AFL) followed by the player's jersey number. Any additional confirmed information or additions to this list are appreciated. The recently discovered Floyd Little and Lance Rentzel cards were apparently issued without a player image on the cardfronts and have not yet been priced due to perceived scarcity.

1A35 Jim Nance 35.00 60.00
1N34 Junior Coffey 35.00 60.00
1N60 Tommy Nobis 50.00 80.00
2A15 Jack Kemp 125.00 200.00
2N41 Tom Matte 50.00 80.00
2N88 John Mackey 50.00 80.00
3A42 Warren McVea UER 35.00 60.00
3N40 Gale Sayers 175.00 300.00
3N51 Dick Butkus 175.00 300.00
4A44 Floyd Little ERR No Photo
4N13 Frank Ryan 50.00 80.00
4N44 Leroy Kelly 60.00 100.00
5A90 George Webster 50.00 80.00
5N19 Lance Rentzel ERR No Photo
5N30 Dan Reeves 60.00 100.00
5N74 Bob Lilly 125.00 200.00
6A16 Len Dawson 125.00 200.00
6A21 Mike Garrett 35.00 60.00
6N20 Lem Barney 50.00 80.00
6N24 Mel Farr 35.00 60.00
7A12 Bob Griese 150.00 250.00
7A39 Larry Csonka 150.00 250.00
7N15 Bart Starr 300.00 500.00
7N33 Jim Grabowski 50.00 80.00
7N66 Ray Nitschke 125.00 200.00
8A12 Joe Namath 300.00 500.00
8A13 Don Maynard 90.00 150.00
8A83 George Sauer 50.00 80.00
8N18 Roman Gabriel 60.00 100.00
8N75 Deacon Jones 60.00 100.00
9A13 Daryle Lamonica 60.00 100.00
9A40 Pete Banaszak 35.00 60.00
9N30 Bill Brown RB 35.00 60.00
9N84 Gene Washington Vik 35.00 60.00
10A19 Lance Alworth 125.00 200.00
10A21 John Hadl 60.00 100.00
10N17 Billy Kilmer 50.00 80.00
10N31 Jim Taylor 125.00 200.00
11N45 Homer Jones 35.00 60.00
12N16 Norm Snead 50.00 80.00
12N18 Ben Hawkins 35.00 60.00
13N10 Kent Nix 35.00 60.00
13N24 Andy Russell 50.00 80.00
13N47 Marv Woodson 35.00 60.00
14N12 Charley Johnson 50.00 80.00
14N25 Jim Bakken 35.00 60.00
15N12 John Brodie 75.00 125.00
16N9 Sonny Jurgensen 90.00 150.00
16N42 Charley Taylor 50.00 80.00

1960 Chargers Team Issue 5x7

The Chargers released these photos in 1960 - their only year in Los Angeles. Each measures approximately 5" by 7" and includes a black and white photo on the cardfront with a blankback. The player's name appears below the photo to the left with the team name oriented to the right.

1 Charlie Flowers 7.50 15.00
2 Jim Sears 7.50 15.00

1960 Chargers Team Issue 8x10

The Chargers released these photos in 1960 - their only year in Los Angeles. Each measures approximately 5" by 7" and includes a black and white photo on the cardfront with a blankback. The player's name appears below the photo to the left with the team name oriented to the right.

1 Howie Ferguson 10.00 20.00
2 Jack Kemp 20.00 40.00

1961 Chargers Golden Tulip

The 1961 Golden Tulip Chips football card set contains 22 black and white cards featuring San Diego (Los Angeles in 1960) Chargers AFL players. The cards measure approximately 2" by 3" and are commonly found with roughly cut or irregularly shaped edges. The fronts contain the player's name, a short biography, and vital statistics. The backs, which are the same for all cards, contain an ad for XETV television, a premium offer for (approximately) 8" by 10" photos and an ad for a free ticket contest. The cards are unnumbered but have been numbered in alphabetical order in the checklist below for your convenience. The catalog designation for this set is F395.

COMPLETE SET (22) 1200.00 1800.00
1 Ron Botchan 40.00 75.00
2 Howard Clark 40.00 75.00
3 Fred Cole 40.00 75.00
4 Sam DeLuca 40.00 75.00
5 Orlando Ferrante 40.00 75.00
6 Charlie Flowers 40.00 75.00
7 Dick Harris 40.00 75.00
8 Emil Karas 40.00 75.00
9 Jack Kemp 300.00 500.00
10 Dave Kocourek 40.00 75.00
11 Bob Laraba 40.00 75.00
12 Paul Lowe 50.00 100.00
13 Paul Maguire 50.00 100.00
14 Charlie McNeil 40.00 75.00
15 Ron Mix 75.00 150.00
16 Ron Nery 40.00 75.00
17 Don Norton 40.00 75.00
18 Volney Peters 40.00 75.00
19 Don Rogers 40.00 75.00
20 Maury Schleicher 50.00 100.00
21 Ernie Wright 50.00 100.00
22 Bob Zeman 40.00 75.00

1961 Chargers Golden Tulip Premiums

These oversized (roughly 8" by 10") photos were issued as premiums for collectors in 1961. Each was mailed in exchange for 5-Golden Tulip cards of the featured player. The photos are black and white and include a facsimile player autograph on the front along with a small Golden Tulip Potato Chips logo.

1 Charlie Flowers 125.00 200.00
2 Dick Harris 125.00 200.00
3 Jack Kemp 350.00 600.00
4 Dave Kocourek 125.00 200.00
5 Paul Maguire 150.00 250.00
6 Charlie McNeil 125.00 200.00
7 Ron Mix 175.00 300.00
8 Don Norton 125.00 200.00
9 Volney Peters 125.00 200.00
10 Don Rogers 125.00 200.00
11 Ernie Wright 150.00 250.00
12 Bob Zeman 125.00 200.00

1961-64 Chargers Team Issue 8x10

The Chargers released these photos over a number of seasons. Each measures approximately 8" by 10" and includes a black and white photo on the cardfront with a blankback. The player's name appears below the photo and to the left with the team name oriented to the right. As is common with many team issued photos, the text style and size varies slightly from photo to photo. We've noted known photo variations below and added a number in parenthesis for other players with reported variations.

1 Chuck Allen 7.50 15.00
2 Lance Alworth (2) 15.00 30.00
3 Alworth 12.50 25.00
Kocourek
Carolan
4 Alworth 12.50 25.00
D.Norton
Kocourek
Carolan
5 Ernie Barnes 7.50 15.00
6 George Blair 7.50 15.00
7 Frank Buncom 7.50 15.00
8 Reg Carolan 7.50 15.00
9 Ron Carpenter 7.50 15.00
10 Bert Coan 7.50 15.00
11 Sam DeLuca (2) 7.50 15.00
12 Hunter Enis 7.50 15.00
13 Earl Faison 7.50 15.00
14 Claude Gibson 7.50 15.00
15 Sid Gillman 10.00 20.00
16 Ken Graham 7.50 15.00
17 George Gross 7.50 15.00
18 Sam Gruneisen 7.50 15.00
19 John Hadl 12.50 25.00
20 John Hadl 12.50 25.00
Willie Frazier
21 Dick Harris 7.50 15.00
22 Bill Hudson 7.50 15.00
Richard Hudson
23 Richard Hudson 7.50 15.00
24 Bob Jackson 7.50 15.00
25 Emil Karas 7.50 15.00
26A Jack Kemp 15.00 30.00
26B Jack Kemp 15.00 30.00
26C Jack Kemp 15.00 30.00
27 Keith Kinderman 7.50 15.00
28 Gary Kirner 7.50 15.00
29 Dave Kocourek (2) 7.50 15.00
30 Ernie Ladd (3) 10.00 20.00
31 Bob Lane (2) 7.50 15.00
32 Keith Lincoln (3) 10.00 20.00
33 Paul Lowe (2) 10.00 20.00
34A Jacque MacKinnon 7.50 15.00
34B Jacque MacKinnon 7.50 15.00
34C Jacque MacKinnon 7.50 15.00
34D Jacque MacKinnon 7.50 15.00
35 Joe Madro 7.50 15.00
36A Paul Maguire 10.00 20.00
36B Paul Maguire 10.00 20.00
37 Charlie McNeil (2) 7.50 15.00
38 Tommy Minter 7.50 15.00
39 Bob Mitinger 7.50 15.00
40 Ron Mix 12.50 25.00
41 Ron Nery 7.50 15.00
42 Don Norton 7.50 15.00
43 Ernie Park 7.50 15.00
44 Bob Petrich (2) 7.50 15.00
45 Bo Roberson 7.50 15.00
46 Jerry Robinson 7.50 15.00
47 Don Rogers 7.50 15.00
48 Tobin Rote (2) 10.00 20.00
49 Tobin Rote 10.00 20.00
Keith Linclon
50 Alvin Roy 10.00 20.00
Keith Linclon
51 Henry Schmidt 7.50 15.00
52 Pat Shea 7.50 15.00
53 Walt Sweeney (2) 7.50 15.00
54 Jim Warren 7.50 15.00
55 Dick Westmoreland (2) 7.50 15.00
56 Bud Whitehead 7.50 15.00
57 Ernie Wright (2) 7.50 15.00
58 1964 Coaching Staff 7.50 15.00
59 1961 Team Photo 10.00 20.00
60 1962 Team Photo 10.00 20.00
61 1963 Team Photo 10.00 20.00
62 1964 Team Photo 10.00 20.00

1962 Chargers Golden Arrow Dairy Bottle Caps

This set of milk caps was issued in 1962, and possibly 1963, by the Golden Arrow Dairy in the San Diego area. Each blankbacked paper milk bottle cap features a black and white drawing of a player or other AFL or team subject along with the team name printed above and his position printed bleow the image. These milk caps are exceedingly scarce and were cataloged for the first time in 2008. The saver sheet is a white paper poster with a football field printed on it along with spaces to align the milk caps into a football play formation. The saver sheet reports that 35 different player caps were produced, therefore it is thought that our list below is not fully complete.

1 Chuck Allen 75.00 150.00
2 Lance Alworth 175.00 300.00
3 Ernie Barnes 75.00 150.00
4 Jim Bates 75.00 150.00
5 Frank Buncom 75.00 150.00
6 Bert Coan 75.00 150.00
7 Earl Faison 75.00 150.00
8 Joe Foss Comm. 75.00 150.00
9 Claude Gibson 75.00 150.00
10 Sid Gillman CO 100.00 200.00
11 George Gross 75.00 150.00
12 John Hadl 150.00 250.00
13 Dick Harris 75.00 150.00
14 Barron Hilton Pres. 75.00 150.00
15 Bill Hudson 75.00 150.00
16 Dick Hudson 75.00 150.00
17 Bob Jackson 75.00 150.00
18 Emil Karas 75.00 150.00
19 Jack Kemp 200.00 400.00
20 Ernie Ladd 100.00 200.00
21 Keith Lincoln 100.00 200.00
22 Paul Lowe 100.00 200.00
23 Jacque MacKinnon 75.00 150.00
24 Paul Maguire 100.00 200.00
25 Bob Mitinger 75.00 150.00
26 Ron Mix 150.00 250.00
27 Ron Nery 75.00 150.00
28 Don Norton 75.00 150.00
29 Sherman Plunkett 75.00 150.00
30 Don Rogers 75.00 150.00
31 Tobin Rote 100.00 200.00
32 Maury Schleicher 75.00 150.00
33 Mark Schmidt 75.00 150.00
34 Bud Whitehead 75.00 150.00
35 Ernie Wright 75.00 150.00
36 Saver Sheet 75.00 150.00

1962 Chargers Union Oil

The set was sponsored by Union 76. All players featured in the set are members of the San Diego Chargers. They are derived from sketches by the artist, Patrick. The cards are black and white, approximately 6" by 8" with player biography and Union Oil logo on backs. The catalog designation for the set is UO35-2. The cards were reportedly issued with an album with 24 spaces for the photos. The key cards in this set are quarterback Jack Kemp, who would later gain fame as a politician, as well as cards issued during the rookie season of future Hall of Famer Lance Alworth and star quarterback John Hadl.

COMPLETE SET (16) 350.00 600.00
1 Chuck Allen 10.00 20.00
2 Lance Alworth 75.00 125.00
3 Earl Faison 10.00 20.00
4 John Hadl 25.00 40.00
5 Dick Harris 10.00 20.00
6 Bill Hudson 10.00 20.00
7 Jack Kemp 125.00 250.00
8 Dave Kocourek 10.00 20.00
9 Ernie Ladd 20.00 35.00
10 Keith Lincoln 12.50 25.00
11 Paul Lowe 12.50 25.00
12 Charlie McNeil 10.00 20.00
13 Ron Mix 20.00 35.00
14 Ron Nery 10.00 20.00
15 Don Norton 10.00 20.00
16 Team Photo 15.00 30.00

1962-63 Chargers Team Issue 5x7

The Chargers released these photos over a number of seasons. Each measures approximately 5" by 7" and includes a black and white photo on the cardfront with a blankback. The player's name appears below the photo to the left, while the team name appears on the right. The type styles and sizes vary slightly from photo to photo and many players were issued with photo variations as noted below.

1964 Chargers Team Issue

Photos from this set, measuring approximately 5 1/2" by 8 1/2", were issued over a number of years. Each features black and white close-up player photos on off-white linen weave paper (same as 1965-67 Chargers Team Issue). The player's facsimile autograph is centered beneath each picture above the team name. The 1964 issue has biographical and statistical information on the backs that helps to identify the year of issue. Because the set is unnumbered, players and coaches are listed alphabetically.

COMPLETE SET (36) 150.00 300.00
1 Chuck Allen 6.00 12.00
2 Lance Alworth 12.50 25.00
3 George Blair 6.00 12.00
4 Frank Buncom 6.00 12.00
5 Earl Faison 6.00 12.00
6 Sid Gillman CO 7.50 15.00
7 George Gross 6.00 12.00
8 Sam Gruneisen 6.00 12.00
9 Walt Hackett CO 6.00 12.00
10 John Hadl 10.00 20.00
11 Dick Harris 6.00 12.00
12 Bob Jackson 6.00 12.00
13 Emil Karas 6.00 12.00
14 Dave Kocourek 6.00 12.00
15 Ernie Ladd 7.50 15.00
16 Keith Lincoln 7.50 15.00
17 Paul Lowe 7.50 15.00
18 Jacque MacKinnon 6.00 12.00
19 Joe Madro CO 6.00 12.00
20 Gerry McDougall 6.00 12.00
21 Charlie McNeil 6.00 12.00
22 Bob Mitinger 6.00 12.00
23 Ron Mix 10.00 20.00
24 Chuck Noll CO 10.00 20.00
25 Don Norton 6.00 12.00
26 Bob Petrich 6.00 12.00
27 Jerry Robinson 6.00 12.00
28 Don Rogers 6.00 12.00
29 Tobin Rote 7.50 15.00
30 Hank Schmidt 6.00 12.00
31 Pat Shea 6.00 12.00
32 Walt Sweeney 7.50 15.00
33 Dick Westmoreland 6.00 12.00
34 Bud Whitehead 6.00 12.00
35 Ernie Wright 6.00 12.00
36 1963 Team Photo 7.50 15.00

1965-67 Chargers Team Issue

This team issue set, with photos measuring approximately 5 1/2" by 8 1/2", was issued over at least a couple of years, with a few personnel changes reflected each year. This series features black and white close-up player photos on off-white linen weave paper. The player's facsimile autograph is centered beneath each picture above the team name. Some photos were issued with biographical information on the back (primarily in 1964 and 1966), while others have blank backs (issued primarily in 1967). We've included known variations below, but the checklist is thought to be incomplete. Because the set is unnumbered, players and coaches are listed alphabetically. This set is interesting in that it features an early issue of Bum Phillips.

1A Chuck Allen 6.00 12.00
blank backed
1B Chuck Allen 6.00 12.00
1966 bio on back
2A Jim Allison 6.00 12.00
blank backed
2B Jim Allison 6.00 12.00
1966 bio on back
3A Lance Alworth 25.00 40.00
blank backed
3B Lance Alworth 25.00 40.00
1966 bio on back
4A Tom Bass CO 6.00 12.00
blank backed
4B Tom Bass CO 6.00 12.00
1966 bio on back
5A Joe Beauchamp 6.00 12.00
blank backed
6A Frank Buncom 6.00 12.00
blank backed
6B Frank Buncom 6.00 12.00
1966 bio on back
7A Ron Carpenter 6.00 12.00
blank backed
7B Ron Carpenter 6.00 12.00
1966 bio on back
8A Richard Degen 6.00 12.00
blank backed
9A Steve DeLong 6.00 12.00
blank backed
9B Steve DeLong 6.00 12.00
1966 bio on back
10A Speedy Duncan 6.00 12.00
blank backed
10B Speedy Duncan 6.00 12.00
1966 bio on back
11A Earl Faison 6.00 12.00
(1966 bio on back
12A John Farris 6.00 12.00
(blank backed
12B John Farris 6.00 12.00
(1966 bio on back
13A Gene Foster 6.00 12.00
blank backed
13B Gene Foster 6.00 12.00
1966 bio on back
14A Willie Frazier 6.00 12.00
blank backed
15A Gary Garrison 6.00 12.00
blank backed
15B Gary Garrison 6.00 12.00
1966 bio on back
16A Sid Gillman CO 7.50 15.00
blank backed
16B Sid Gillman CO 7.50 15.00
coaching record on back
through 1965)
17A Kenny Graham 6.00 12.00
blank backed)
17B Kenny Graham 6.00 12.00
1966 bio on back)
18A Jim Griffin 6.00 12.00
(blank backed)
18B Jim Griffin 6.00 12.00
(1966 bio on back)
19A George Gross 6.00 12.00
blank backed)
19B George Gross 6.00 12.00
1967 bio on back)
20A Sam Gruneisen 6.00 12.00
blank backed)
20B Sam Gruneisen 6.00 12.00
1966 bio on back)
21A Walt Hackett CO 6.00 12.00
(blank backed)
22A John Hadl 15.00 25.00
(blank backed)
22B John Hadl 15.00 25.00
(1966 bio on back)
23A Dick Harris 6.00 12.00
blank backed)
23B Dick Harris 6.00 12.00
1966 bio on back)
24A Dan Henning 6.00 12.00
blank backed)
25A Bob Horton 6.00 12.00
26A Harry Johnston CO 6.00 12.00
blank backed)
27A Howard Kindig 6.00 12.00
blank backed)
28A Gary Kirner 6.00 12.00
(blank backed)
28B Gary Kirner 6.00 12.00
(1966 bio on back)
29A Dave Kocourek 6.00 12.00
(1966 bio on back)
30A Ernie Ladd 7.50 15.00
(1966 bio on back)
31A Mike London 6.00 12.00
(1966 bio on back)
32A Jacque MacKinnon 6.00 12.00
blank backed)
32B Jacque MacKinnon 6.00 12.00
1966 bio on back)
33A Joe Madro CO 6.00 12.00
blank backed)
33B Joe Madro CO 6.00 12.00
1966 bio on back)
34A Lloyd McCoy 6.00 12.00
(blank backed)
35A Ed Mitchell 6.00 12.00
blank backed)
35B Ron Mix 10.00 20.00
(blank backed)
36A Fred Moore 6.00 12.00
blank backed)
36B Fred Moore 6.00 12.00
1966 bio on back)
37A Chuck Noll CO 10.00 20.00
(blank backed)
38A Don Norton 6.00 12.00
blank backed)
38B Don Norton 6.00 12.00
1966 bio on back)
39A Terry Owens 6.00 12.00
(blank backed)
39B Terry Owens 6.00 12.00
(1966 bio on back)
40A Bob Petrich 6.00 12.00
(blank backed)
40B Bob Petrich 6.00 12.00
(1966 bio on back)
41A Bum Phillips CO 7.50 15.00
blank backed)
42A Dave Plump 6.00 12.00
blank backed)
43A Rick Redman 6.00 12.00
blank backed)
43B Rick Redman 6.00 12.00
1966 bio on back)
44A Houston Ridge 6.00 12.00
blank backed)
45A Hank Schmidt 6.00 12.00
(blank backed)
46A Pat Shea 6.00 12.00
blank backed)
46B Pat Shea 6.00 12.00
(1966 bio on back)
47A Jackie Simpson CO 6.00 12.00
blank backed)
48A Walt Sweeney 7.50 15.00
blank backed)
48B Walt Sweeney 7.50 15.00
1966 bio on back)
49A Sammy Taylor 6.00 12.00
49B Steve Tensi 6.00 12.00
blank backed)
50A Herb Travenio 6.00 12.00
51A John Travis 6.00 12.00
blank backed)
52A Dick Van Raaphorst 6.00 12.00
blank backed)
53A Charlie Waller CO 6.00 12.00
blank backed)
53B Charlie Waller CO 6.00 12.00
1966 bio on back)
54A Bud Whitehead 6.00 12.00
blank backed)
54B Bud Whitehead 6.00 12.00
1966 bio on back)
55A Nat Whitmyer 6.00 12.00
blank backed)
55B Nat Whitmyer 6.00 12.00
1966 bio on back)
56A Ernie Wright 7.50 15.00
blank backed)
56B Ernie Wright 7.50 15.00
1966 bio on back)
57A Bob Zeman 6.00 12.00
(1966 bio on back)
58A 1965 Team Photo 10.00 20.00
58B 1966 Team Photo 10.00 20.00

1965-69 Chargers Team Issue 8x10

The Chargers released these photos over a number of seasons. Each measures approximately 8" by 10" and includes a black and white photo on the cardfront with a blankback. The player's name appears below the photo to the left, with the player's position spelled out in the middle and the team name to the right. Each also includes the newer Chargers' team logo with the goalpost style H. The text style and size varies slightly from photo to photo and the checklist is thought to be incomplete. Any additions to this list are appreciated.

1966-68 Chargers Team Issue 5X7

The Chargers released these photos over a number of seasons. Each measures approximately 5" by 7" and includes a black and white photo on the cardfront with a blankback. The player's name appears below the photo to the left with his position centered. The Chargers' team name appears on the right and is in the style with the goalpost shaped H. The type styles and sizes can vary slightly from photo to photo.

COMPLETE SET (15) 60.00 120.00
1 Harold Akin 5.00 10.00
2 Scott Appleton 5.00 10.00
3 Tom Denman CO 5.00 10.00
4 Ken Dyer 5.00 10.00
5 Willie Frazier 5.00 10.00
6 Barron Hilton OWN 5.00 10.00
7 Brad Hubbert 5.00 10.00
8 Harry Johnston CO 5.00 10.00
9 Irv Kaze OFF 5.00 10.00
10 Paul Lowe 6.00 12.00
11 Don Norton 5.00 10.00
12 Dick Van Raaphorst 5.00 10.00
13 Charlie Waller CO 5.00 10.00
14 Bob Wells 5.00 10.00
15 Bob Zeman 5.00 10.00

1968 Chargers Team Issue 7x9

The Chargers released these photos over a number of seasons. Each measures approximately 7" by 9" and includes a black and white photo on the cardfront with a blankback. The player's name appears below the photo to the left with his position centered. The Chargers' team name appears on the right and is in the style with the goalpost shaped H. The type styles and sizes can vary slightly from photo to photo.

COMPLETE SET (23) 100.00 200.00
1 Chuck Allen 5.00 10.00
2A Lance Alworth 12.50 25.00
2B Lance Alworth 12.50 25.00
3 Scott Appleton 5.00 10.00
4 Jon Brittenum 5.00 10.00
5 Steve DeLong 5.00 10.00
6 Les Duncan 6.00 12.00
7 Dick Farley 5.00 10.00
8 Gene Foster 5.00 10.00
9 Willie Frazier 5.00 10.00
10 Gary Garrison 5.00 10.00
11 Ken Graham 5.00 10.00
12 Sam Gruneisen 5.00 10.00
13 John Hadl 7.50 15.00
14 Bob Howard 5.00 10.00
15 Gary Kirner 5.00 10.00
16 Larry Little 10.00 20.00
17 Ron Mix 10.00 20.00
18 Terry Owens 5.00 10.00
19 Dick Post 5.00 10.00
20 Rick Redman 5.00 10.00
21 Houston Ridge 5.00 10.00
22 Jeff Staggs 5.00 10.00
23 Walt Sweeney 5.00 10.00

1968 Chargers Team Issue 8x11

This set featuring members of the 1968 San Diego Chargers features sepia toned player photos measuring approximately 8 1/2" by 11". The backs are blank. The cards are unnumbered and checklisted below in alphabetical order. The 1968 photos are nearly identical to the 1969 issue but can be differentiated by the slightly larger type size. Also, most of the photos were produced with the facsimile autograph appearing over the image of the player.

COMPLETE SET (8) 50.00 100.00
1 Lance Alworth 12.50 25.00
2 John Hadl 7.50 15.00
3 Bob Howard 6.00 12.00
4 Brad Hubbert 6.00 12.00
5 Ron Mix 7.50 15.00
6 Dick Post 6.00 12.00
7 Jeff Staggs 6.00 12.00
8 Walt Sweeney 6.00 12.00

1968 Chargers Volpe Tumblers

These Chargers artist's renderings were part of a plastic cup tumbler product produced in 1968 and distributed by White Front Stores. The noted sports artist Volpe created the artwork which includes an action scene and a player portrait. Each is unnumbered, measures approximately 5" by 8 1/2" when flat, and is curved in the shape required to fit inside a plastic cup. The manufacturer notation PGC (Programs General Corp) is printed on each piece as well. There are thought to be 6-cups included in this set. Any additions to this list are appreciated.

1 Chuck Allen 20.00 40.00
2 Kenny Graham 20.00 40.00
3 John Hadl 25.00 50.00
4 Dick Post 20.00 40.00

1969 Chargers Team Issue 8x11

This set of the 1969 San Diego Chargers was issued by the team. Each features a black-and-white player photo measuring approximately 8 1/2" by 11". The backs are blank. The cards are unnumbered and checklisted below in alphabetical order. The 1969 photos are nearly identical to the 1968 issue but can be differentiated by the smaller type size. Also all of the photos were produced with the facsimile autograph appearing away from the player image.

COMPLETE SET (11) 60.00 120.00
1 Lance Alworth 10.00 20.00
2 Les Duncan 5.00 10.00
3 Gary Garrison 5.00 10.00
4 Kenny Graham 5.00 10.00
5 John Hadl 7.50 15.00
6 Ron Mix 7.50 15.00
7 Dick Post 5.00 10.00
8 Jeff Staggs 5.00 10.00
9 Walt Sweeney 6.00 12.00
10 Russ Washington 5.00 10.00
11 Team Photo 6.00 12.00

1970 Chargers Team Issue 8X10

This set of photos featuring the 1970 San Diego Chargers was issued by the team. Each features a black-and-white player photo measuring approximately 8" by 10" with blank backs. The player's name is included below the image oriented to the left with his position in the center and the Chargers' team name to the right. Each player is pictured in a posed kneeling photo with his hand on his helmet which includes the player's jersey number. The photos are unnumbered and checklisted below in alphabetical order.

COMPLETE SET (20) 75.00 150.00
1 Lance Alworth 10.00 20.00
2 Bob Babich 5.00 10.00
3 Pete Barnes 5.00 10.00
4 Joe Beauchamp 5.00 10.00
5 Ron Billingsley 5.00 10.00
6 Gene Ferguson 5.00 10.00
7 Gene Foster 5.00 10.00
8 Mike Garrett 6.00 12.00
9 Gary Garrison 5.00 10.00
10 Ira Gordon 5.00 10.00
11 Sam Gruneisen 5.00 10.00
12 Jim Hill 5.00 10.00
13 Bob Howard 5.00 10.00
14 Joe Owens 5.00 10.00
15 Dennis Partee 5.00 10.00
16 Dick Post 5.00 10.00
17 Jeff Staggs 5.00 10.00
18 Walt Sweeney 6.00 12.00
19 Jim Tolbert 5.00 10.00
20 Russ Washington 5.00 10.00

1974 Chargers Team Issue

Photos in this set were issued by the team to fulfill fan requests. Each features a black-and-white player photo measuring approximately 8 1/2" by 11" with blank backs. The team name "Chargers" is printed to the far left below the image and the player's name and position (spelled out) are oriented to the far right side. The photos are unnumbered and checklisted below in alphabetical order.

1 Harrison Davis 5.00 10.00
2 Jesse Freitas 5.00 10.00
3 John Teerlink 5.00 10.00

1976 Chargers Dean's Photo

This 10-card set was sponsored by Dean's Photo Service and features nine San Diego Chargers' players. The cards were released on an uncut perforated sheet with each card measuring approximately 5" by 8." The player photos are black and white, but the team helmet is printed in color. The cards are blank backed and unnumbered.

COMPLETE SET (10) 30.00 60.00
1 Pat Curran 2.50 5.00
2 Chris Fletcher 2.50 5.00
3 Dan Fouts 10.00 20.00
4 Gary Garrison 3.00 6.00
5 Louie Kelcher 3.00 6.00
6 Joe Washington 3.00 6.00
7 Russ Washington 2.50 5.00
8 Doug Wilkerson 2.50 5.00
9 Don Woods 2.50 5.00
10 Schedule Card 2.50 5.00

1976 Chargers Team Sheets

The San Diego Chargers issued these sheets of black-and-white player photos around 1976. Each measures roughly 8" by 10 1/4" and was printed on glossy stock with white borders. Each sheet includes photos of 3-players and/or coaches. Below each player's image is his jersey number, his name, position and the team name. The photos are blankbacked.

COMPLETE SET (16) 75.00 125.00
1 Charles Anthony 5.00 10.00
Doug Wilkerson
Louie Kelcher
2 Ken Bernich 4.00 8.00
Mark Markovich
Floyd Rice
3 Bob Brown 4.00 8.00
Coy Bacon
Dwight McDonald
4 Booker Brown 4.00 8.00
Billy Shields
Ira Gordon
5 Earnel Durden CO 4.00 8.00
Bobb McKittrick CO
Howard Mudd CO
6 Rudy Feldman CO 4.00 8.00
Dick Coury CO
George Dickson CO
7 Jesse Freitas 4.00 8.00
Mike Williams
Glen Bonner
8 Mike Fuller 4.00 8.00
Chris Fletcher
Sam Williams
9 Gary Garrison 5.00 10.00
Dennis Partee
Don Woods
10 Don Goode 4.00 8.00
Ed Flanagan
Carl Gersbach
11 Neal Jeffrey 10.00 20.00
Dan Fouts
Ray Wersching
12 Dave Lowe/Terry Owens/John Teerlinck 4.00 8.00
13 Tommy Prothro CO 5.00 10.00
John David Crow CO
Jackie Simpson CO
14 Bob Thomas 4.00 8.00
Joe Beauchamp
Bo Matthews
15 Charles Wadnelk 4.00 8.00
Harrison Davis
Wayne Stewart
16 Russ Washington 5.00 10.00
Fred Dean
Gary Johnson

1981 Chargers Jack in the Box Prints

These large prints were issued by Jack in the Box stores in 1981. Each features an artist's rendering of a group of Chargers players on the front and a write-up of the featured players on the back.

COMPLETE SET (4) 30.00 75.00
1 Charger Power 8.00 20.00
2 Air Coryell 12.00 30.00
3 Powerline 6.00 15.00
4 Very Special Teams 6.00 15.00

1981 Chargers Police

The 1981 San Diego Chargers set contains 24 unnumbered cards of 22 subjects. The cards measure approximately 2 5/8" by 4 1/8". The cards are listed in the checklist below by the uniform number which appears on the fronts of the cards. The set is sponsored by the Kiwanis Club, the local law enforcement agency, and Pepsi-Cola. A Chargers helmet logo and "Chargers Tips" appear on the card backs. The card backs have black print with blue trim on white card stock. The Kiwanis and Chargers helmet logos appear on the fronts. Fouts and Winslow each exist with two different safety tips on the backs; the variations are distinguished below by the first few words of the safety tip. The complete set price below includes the variation cards.

COMPLETE SET (24) 40.00 75.00
6 Rolf Benirschke 1.00 2.50
14A Dan Fouts 6.00 15.00
14B Dan Fouts 3.00 8.00
18 Charlie Joiner 2.00 5.00
25 John Cappelletti 1.00 2.50
28 Willie Buchanon .75 2.00
29 Mike Williams .75 2.00
43 Bob Gregor .75 2.00
44 Pete Shaw .75 2.00
46 Chuck Muncie 1.00 2.50
51 Woodrow Lowe .75 2.00
57 Linden King .75 2.00
59 Cliff Thrift .75 2.00
62 Don Macek .75 2.00
63 Doug Wilkerson .75 2.00
66 Billy Shields .75 2.00
67 Ed White .75 2.00
68 Leroy Jones .75 2.00
70 Russ Washington .75 2.00
74 Louie Kelcher 1.00 2.50
79 Gary Johnson .75 2.00
80A Kellen Winslow 5.00 12.00
80B Kellen Winslow 3.00 8.00
NNO Don Coryell CO 1.00 2.50

1982 Chargers Police

The 1982 San Diego Chargers Police set contains 16 unnumbered cards. The cards measure approximately 2 5/8" by 4 1/8". Although uniform numbers appear on the fronts of the cards, the set has been listed below in alphabetical order. The set is sponsored by the Kiwanis Club, the local law enforcement agency, and Pepsi-Cola. Chargers Tips, in addition to the helmet logo of the Chargers, the Pepsi-Cola logo and a police logo appear on the backs. Card backs have black printing with blue accent on white backs. The Kiwanis logo and Chargers helmet appear on the fronts of the cards.

COMPLETE SET (16) 20.00 40.00
1 Rolf Benirschke 1.00 2.50
2 James Brooks 1.50 4.00
3 Wes Chandler 1.50 4.00
4 Dan Fouts 3.00 8.00
5 Tim Fox 1.00 2.50
6 Gary Johnson 1.00 2.50
7 Charlie Joiner 2.50 6.00
8 Louie Kelcher 1.00 2.50
9 Linden King .75 2.00
10 Bruce Laird .75 2.00
11 David Lewis .75 2.00
12 Don Macek .75 2.00
13 Billy Shields .75 2.00
14 Eric Sievers .75 2.00
15 Russ Washington .75 2.00
16 Kellen Winslow 3.00 8.00

1985 Chargers Kodak

This set was sponsored by Kodak and measures approximately 5 1/2" by 8 1/2". The fronts have white borders and action color photos. The player's name, position, and a Chargers helmet icon appear below the picture. The backs have biographical information. The set is listed below in alphabetical order by player's name. It is thought that the checklist could be incomplete. Any additions to this list are appreciated.

COMPLETE SET (43) 50.00 100.00
1 Jesse Bendross .75 2.00
2 Rolf Benirschke 1.25 3.00
3 Carlos Bradley .75 2.00
4 Maury Buford .75 2.00
5 Gill Byrd 1.25 3.00
6 Wes Chandler 2.00 5.00
7 Sam Claphan .75 2.00
8 Don Coryell CO 1.25 3.00
9 Bobby Duckworth .75 2.00
10 Chuck Ehin .75 2.00
11 Bill Elko .75 2.00
12 Keith Ferguson .75 2.00
13 Dan Fouts 6.00 15.00
14 Andrew Gissinger .75 2.00
15 Derrel Gofourth .75 2.00
16 Mike Green .75 2.00
17 Keith Guthrie .75 2.00
18 Pete Holohan .75 2.00
19 Earnest Jackson 1.25 3.00
20 Lionel James 1.25 3.00
21 Charlie Joiner 4.00 10.00
22 Bill Kay .75 2.00
23 Linden King .75 2.00
24 Chuck Loewen .75 2.00
25 Woodrow Lowe .75 2.00
26 Don Macek .75 2.00
27 Bruce Mathison .75 2.00
28 Buford McGee .75 2.00
29 Dennis McKnight .75 2.00
30 Miles McPherson .75 2.00
31 Derrie Nelson .75 2.00
32 Vince Osby .75 2.00
33 Fred Robinson .75 2.00
34 Eric Sievers .75 2.00
35 Billy Ray Smith 1.25 3.00
36 Lucious Smith .75 2.00
37 Cliff Thrift .75 2.00
38 John Turner .75 2.00
39 Danny Walters .75 2.00
40 Ed White .75 2.00
41 Doug Wilkerson .75 2.00
42 Lee Williams 1.25 3.00
43 Kellen Winslow 4.00 10.00

1986 Chargers Kodak

This set of 48-photos featuring the San Diego Chargers was sponsored by Kodak and measures approximately 5 1/2" by 8 1/2". The fronts feature color action photos with white borders. Biographical information is given below the photo between the Chargers' helmet on the left and the Kodak logo on the right. The backs are blank. The photos are unnumbered and checklisted below in alphabetical order.

COMPLETE SET (48) 50.00 100.00
1 Curtis Adams .75 2.00
2 Gary Anderson RB 1.50 4.00
3 Jesse Bendross .75 2.00
4 Rolf Benirschke 1.25 3.00
5 Carlos Bradley .75 2.00
6 Gill Byrd 1.25 3.00
7 Wes Chandler 1.25 3.00
8 Sam Claphan .75 2.00
9 Don Coryell CO 1.25 3.00
10 Jeffery Dale .75 2.00
11 Wayne Davis .75 2.00
12 Jerry Doerger .75 2.00
13 Chuck Ehin .75 2.00
14 Chris Faulkner .75 2.00
15 Mark Fellows .75 2.00
16 Dan Fouts 5.00 12.00
17 Mike Green LB .75 2.00
18 Mike Guendling .75 2.00
19 John Hendy .75 2.00
20 Mark Herrmann .75 2.00
21 Pete Holohan 1.25 3.00
22 Lionel James 1.25 3.00
23 Trumaine Johnson .75 2.00
24 Charlie Joiner 3.00 8.00
25 David King .75 2.00
26 Linden King .75 2.00
27 Gary Kowalski .75 2.00
28 Jim Lachey 1.25 3.00
29 Woodrow Lowe .75 2.00
30 Don Macek .75 2.00
31 Buford McGee .75 2.00
32 Dennis McKnight .75 2.00
33 Ralf Mojsiejenko .75 2.00
34 Derrie Nelson .75 2.00
35 Ron O'Bard .75 2.00
36 Fred Robinson .75 2.00
37 Eric Sievers .75 2.00
38 Tony Simmons DE .75 2.00
39 Billy Ray Smith 1.25 3.00
40 Lucious Smith .75 2.00
41 Alex G. Spanos PRES .75 2.00
42 Tim Spencer 1.25 3.00
43 Bob Thomas K .75 2.00
44 Rich Umphrey .75 2.00
45 Danny Walters .75 2.00
46 Ed White .75 2.00
47 Lee Williams 1.25 3.00
48 Earl Wilson .75 2.00

1987 Chargers Junior Chargers Tickets

This 11" by 8 1/2" perforated sheet features two rows of six coupons each. The coupons resemble tickets, with each coupon measuring approximately 1 7/8" by 4 1/4". They were given to members of the Coca-Cola Junior Chargers club. Edged below by a mustard stripe, a powder blue strip at the top carries the coupon's subtitle. The large middle panel of the ticket carries a color action player photo with white borders and the player's name immediately below. Another powder blue stripe at the bottom of the coupon reads "Sec. Row Seat" in imitation of an actual ticket. The horizontal backs vary in their content, consisting of either a membership card, season schedule, Coca-Cola Junior Chargers club, preseason pass, or various coupons to attractions in the San Diego area. The coupons are unnumbered and are listed below in alphabetical order by subject.

COMPLETE SET (12) 20.00 35.00
1 Gary Anderson RB 1.50 4.00
2 Rolf Benirschke 1.25 3.00
3 Wes Chandler 1.50 4.00
4 Jeffery Dale 1.25 3.00
5 Dan Fouts 2.50 6.00
6 Pete Holohan 1.25 3.00
7 Lionel James 1.25 3.00
8 Don Macek 1.25 3.00
9 Dennis McKnight 1.25 3.00
10 Al Saunders CO 1.25 3.00
11 Billy Ray Smith 1.25 3.00
12 Kellen Winslow 2.00 5.00

1987 Chargers Police

The 1987 San Diego Chargers Police set contains 21 numbered cards. The cards measure approximately 2 5/8" by 4 1/8". Uniform numbers appear on the fronts of the cards. The set is sponsored by the San Diego Chargers, Oscar Mayer, and local law enforcement agencies. The Chargers helmet logo, "Chargers Tips," and the Oscar Mayer logo appear on the backs. Card backs have black printing on white backs. The Chargers helmet along with height, weight, age, and experience statistics appear on the fronts of the cards. Card 13 was never issued apparently for superstitious reasons. Cards 3 (Benirschke released) and 17 (Walters arrested) were distributed in lesser quantities and hence are a little tougher to find, especially Benirschke. Chip Banks (22) was the player substituted in the set for Rolf Benirschke.

COMPLETE SET (21) 10.00 25.00
1 Alex Spanos OWN .30 .75
2 Gary Anderson RB .60 1.50
3 Rolf Benirschke SP 2.50 6.00
4 Gill Byrd .30 .75
5 Wes Chandler .60 1.50
6 Sam Claphan .30 .75
7 Jeffery Dale .30 .75
8 Pete Holohan .30 .75
9 Lionel James .30 .75
10 Jim Lachey .30 .75
11 Woodrow Lowe .30 .75
12 Don Macek .30 .75
14 Dan Fouts 1.50 4.00
15 Eric Sievers .30 .75
16 Billy Ray Smith .30 .75
17 Danny Walters SP 2.00 5.00
18 Lee Williams .30 .75
19 Kellen Winslow 1.25 3.00
20 Al Saunders CO .30 .75
21 Dennis McKnight .30 .75
22 Chip Banks .30 .75

1987 Chargers Smokey

This 48-card set features players of the San Diego Chargers in a set sponsored by the California Forestry Department. The cards measure approximately 5 1/2" by 8 1/2"; card fronts show a full-color action photo of the player. Card backs have a forestry safety tip cartoon with Smokey the Bear. Cards are unnumbered but are ordered below in alphabetical order according to the subject's last name. Cards of Donald Brown, Mike Douglas, and Fred Robinson were withdrawn after they were cut from the team and the card of Don Coryell was withdrawn after he was replaced as head coach.

COMPLETE SET (48) 50.00 100.00
1 Curtis Adams .75 2.00
2 Ty Allert .75 2.00
3 Gary Anderson RB 1.25 3.00
4 Rolf Benirschke 1.00 2.50
5 Thomas Benson 1.00 2.50
6 Donald Brown SP 3.00 8.00
7 Gill Byrd 1.00 2.50
8 Wes Chandler 1.25 3.00
9 Sam Claphan .75 2.00
10 Don Coryell CO SP 3.00 8.00
11 Jeffery Dale .75 2.00
12 Wayne Davis .75 2.00
13 Mike Douglass SP 3.00 8.00
14 Chuck Ehin .75 2.00
15 James Fitzpatrick .75 2.00
16 Tom Flick .75 2.00
17 Dan Fouts 4.00 10.00
18 Dee Hardison .75 2.00
19 Andy Hawkins .75 2.00
20 John Hendy .75 2.00
21 Mark Herrmann 1.00 2.50
22 Pete Holohan 1.00 2.50
23 Lionel James 1.00 2.50
24 Trumaine Johnson .75 2.00
25 Charlie Joiner 2.50 6.00
26 Gary Kowalski .75 2.00
27 Jim Lachey 1.00 2.50
28 Jim Leonard .75 2.00
29 Woodrow Lowe .75 2.00
30 Don Macek .75 2.00
31 Buford McGee .75 2.00
32 Dennis McKnight .75 2.00
33 Ralf Mojsiejenko .75 2.00
34 Derrie Nelson .75 2.00
35 Leslie O'Neal 1.50 4.00
36 Gary Plummer 1.00 2.50
37 Fred Robinson SP 3.00 8.00
38 Eric Sievers .75 2.00
39 Billy Ray Smith 1.00 2.50
40 Tim Spencer 1.00 2.50
41 Kenny Taylor .75 2.00
42 Terry Unrein .75 2.00
43 Jeff Walker .75 2.00
44 Danny Walters .75 2.00
45 Lee Williams 1.00 2.50
46 Earl Wilson .75 2.00
47 Kellen Winslow 3.00 8.00
48 Kevin Wyatt .75 2.00

1988 Chargers Police

The 1988 Police San Diego Chargers set contains 12 cards each measuring approximately 2 5/8" by 4". The fronts are white and navy blue with color photos, and the backs feature career highlights and safety tips.

COMPLETE SET (12) 3.00 8.00
1 Gary Anderson RB .40 1.00
2 Rod Bernstine .40 1.00
3 Gill Byrd .30 .75
4 Vencie Glenn .30 .75
5 Lionel James .30 .75
6 Babe Laufenberg .30 .75
7 Don Macek .20 .50
8 Mark Malone .30 .75
9 Dennis McKnight .20 .50
10 Anthony Miller .75 2.00
11 Billy Ray Smith .30 .75
12 Lee Williams .30 .75

1988 Chargers Smokey

This 52-card set features players of the San Diego Chargers in a set sponsored by the California Forestry Department.

The cards measure approximately 5" by 8"; card fronts show a full-color action photo of the player. Card backs have a forestry safety tip cartoon with Smokey Bear. Cards are unnumbered but are ordered below in numerical order according to the subject's uniform number as listed on the card's front and back. There is a variation on the Spanos card, which was originally issued indicating he bought the Chargers in 1987 and was quickly corrected to 1984. There are 35 cards which are easier to obtain as they were available all year and 18 cards (marked below by SP) who are more difficult to find as their cards were withdrawn after they were cut from the team, retired, traded, or put on injured reserve. The set is considered complete with only one Spanos card.

COMPLETE SET (52) 30.00 60.00
2 Ralf Mojsiejenko .60 1.50
9 Mark Herrmann SP .75 2.00
10 Vince Abbott .60 1.50
13 Mark Vlasic .60 1.50
14 Dan Fouts 1.50 4.00
20 Barry Redden .60 1.50
22 Gill Byrd .75 2.00
23 Danny Walters SP .75 2.00
25 Vencie Glenn .60 1.50
26 Lionel James .75 2.00
27 Daniel Hunter SP .75 2.00
34 Elvis Patterson .60 1.50
36 Mike Davis SP .75 2.00
40 Gary Anderson RB 1.00 2.50
42 Curtis Adams .60 1.50
43 Tim Spencer .75 2.00
44 Martin Bayless .60 1.50
50 Gary Plummer .75 2.00
52 Jeff Jackson .60 1.50
54 Billy Ray Smith .75 2.00
55 Steve Busick SP .75 2.00
56 Chip Banks SP .75 2.00
57 Thomas Benson SP .75 2.00
58 David Brandon .60 1.50
60 Dennis McKnight .60 1.50
61 Ken Dallafior .60 1.50
62 Don Macek .60 1.50
68 Gary Kowalski .60 1.50
69 Les Miller .60 1.50
70 James Fitzpatrick .60 1.50
71 Mike Charles .60 1.50
72 Karl Wilson .60 1.50
74 Jim Lachey SP 1.25 3.00
75 Joe Phillips .60 1.50
76 Broderick Thompson .60 1.50
77 Sam Claphan SP .75 2.00
78 Chuck Ehin SP .75 2.00
79 Curtis Rouse SP .75 2.00
80 Kellen Winslow 1.50 4.00
81 Timmie Ware SP .75 2.00
82 Rod Bernstine .75 2.00
85 Eric Sievers .60 1.50
86 Jamie Holland .60 1.50
88 Pete Holohan SP .75 2.00
89 Wes Chandler SP 1.50 4.00
92 Dee Hardison SP .75 2.00
94 Randy Kirk .60 1.50
96 Keith Baldwin SP .75 2.00
98 Terry Unrein SP .75 2.00
99 Lee Williams .60 1.50
NNO Al Saunders CO .60 1.50
NNO Alex G. Spanos ERR SP 2.00 5.00
NNO Alex G. Spanos COR .60 1.50

1989 Chargers Junior Chargers Tickets

This perforated sheet features two rows of six cards each. If the cards were separated, they would measure 1 7/8" by 3 5/8". The color action player photos are bordered in white and the cards are designed like game tickets. A bonus gift is listed at the top of each card and the player's name printed below the photo. The set was sponsored by Ralph's and XTRA. The backs contain information about the bonus gift or discount available to the ticket holder. The coupons are unnumbered and are listed below in alphabetical order by subject.

COMPLETE SET (12) 12.50 25.00
1 Gary Anderson RB 1.50 3.00
2 Gill Byrd 1.25 2.50
3 Quinn Early 1.50 3.00
4 Vencie Glenn 1.25 2.50
5 Jamie Holland .75 2.00
6 Don Macek .75 2.00
7 Dennis McKnight .75 2.00
8 Anthony Miller 1.50 3.00
9 Ralf Mojsiejenko .75 2.00
10 Leslie O'Neal 1.25 2.50
11 Billy Ray Smith 1.25 2.50
12 Lee Williams 1.25 2.50

1989 Chargers Knudsen Dairy Milk Cartons

This set of six half-gallon milk cartons features an image of a Chargers player and a safety tip to youngsters on one of its panels. Each was printed in blue on white stock and issued by Knudsen's Dairy.

COMPLETE SET (5) 20.00 40.00
1 Gill Byrd 3.00 8.00
2 Don Macek 3.00 8.00
3 Anthony Miller 4.00 10.00
4 Leslie O'Neal 4.00 10.00
5 Gary Plummer 3.00 8.00

1989 Chargers Police

The 1989 Police San Diego Chargers set contains 12 cards measuring approximately 2 5/8" by 4 3/16". The fronts have white borders and color action photos; the vertically oriented backs have brief bios, career highlights, and safety messages. The set was sponsored by Louis Rich Co. The set was given away in two six-card panels; the first group at the Chargers' October 22nd home game and the other at the November 5th game.

COMPLETE SET (12) 4.00 10.00
1 Tim Spencer .30 .75
2 Vencie Glenn .30 .75
3 Gill Byrd .30 .75
4 Jim McMahon .60 1.50
5 David Richards .20 .50
6 Don Macek .20 .50
7 Billy Ray Smith .30 .75
8 Gary Plummer .30 .75
9 Lee Williams .30 .75
10 Leslie O'Neal .40 1.00
11 Anthony Miller .60 1.50
12 Broderick Thompson .20 .50

1989 Chargers Smokey

This 48-card set is very similar in style to the Smokey Chargers set of the previous year. This set gives the 1989 date on the bottom of every reverse. Cards are unnumbered except for uniform number which appears on the card front and back. The cards are ordered below by uniform number. The cards measure approximately 5" by 8". Each card back shows a different fire safety cartoon.

COMPLETE SET (48) 25.00 60.00
2 Ralf Mojsiejenko .60 1.50
6 Steve DeLine .60 1.50
10 Vince Abbott .60 1.50
13 Mark Vlasic .60 1.50
16 Mark Malone .75 2.00
20 Barry Redden .60 1.50
22 Gill Byrd .75 2.00
23 Roy Bennett .60 1.50
25 Vencie Glenn .75 2.00
26 Lionel James .75 2.00
30 Sam Seale .60 1.50
31 Leonard Coleman .60 1.50
34 Elvis Patterson .60 1.50
40 Gary Anderson RB .75 2.00
42 Curtis Adams .60 1.50
43 Tim Spencer .75 2.00
44 Martin Bayless .60 1.50
48 Pat Miller .60 1.50
50 Gary Plummer .75 2.00
51 Cedric Figaro .60 1.50
52 Jeff Jackson .60 1.50
53 Chuck Faucette .60 1.50
54 Billy Ray Smith .75 2.00
57 Keith Browner .60 1.50
58 David Brandon .60 1.50
59 Ken Woodard .60 1.50
60 Dennis McKnight .60 1.50
61 Ken Dallafior .60 1.50
65 David Richards .60 1.50
66 Dan Rosado .60 1.50
69 Les Miller .60 1.50
70 James Fitzpatrick .60 1.50
71 Mike Charles .60 1.50
72 Karl Wilson .60 1.50
73 Darrick Brilz .60 1.50
75 Joe Phillips .75 2.00
76 Broderick Thompson .60 1.50
82 Rod Bernstine .75 2.00
83 Anthony Miller 1.25 3.00
86 Jamie Holland .60 1.50
87 Quinn Early .75 2.00
88 Arthur Cox .60 1.50
89 Darren Flutie 1.25 3.00
91 Leslie O'Neal .75 2.00
93 Tyrone Keys .60 1.50
95 Joe Campbell LB .60 1.50
97 George Hinkle .60 1.50
99 Lee Williams .75 2.00

1990 Chargers Junior Chargers Tickets

Cards from this set resemble game tickets with each being a coupon good for discounts from local businesses. Each measures approximately 1 7/8" by 4 1/4" with the small lower portion of the coupon intact. They were given to members of the Junior Chargers club. Each coupon carries its own subtitle near the top. The large middle panel of the ticket carries a color action player photo with white borders and the player's name immediately below. A yellow stripe at the bottom of the coupon reads "Sec. Row Seat" similar to an actual ticket. The horizontal backs vary in their content, consisting of either a membership card, season schedule, Coca-Cola Junior Chargers club, preseason pass, or various coupons to attractions in the San Diego area. The coupons are unnumbered and are listed below in alphabetical order by subject.

COMPLETE SET (12) 12.50 25.00
1 Joe Phillips .75 2.00
2 Quinn Early 1.50 3.00
3 Arthur Cox .75 2.00
4 Joe Caravello .75 2.00
5 Courtney Hall .75 2.00
6 Tim Spencer 1.25 2.50
7 Darrin Nelson .75 2.00
8 Billy Joe Tolliver 1.25 2.50
9 Anthony Miller 1.50 3.00
10 Sam Seale .75 2.00
11 Burt Grossman .75 2.00
12 Gary Plummer 1.25 2.50

1990 Chargers Knudsen

This six-card set (of bookmarks) which measures approximately 2" by 8" was produced by Knudsen's to help promote readership by people under 15 years old in the San Diego area. They were given out in San Diego libraries on a weekly basis. The set was sponsored by Knudsen, American Library Association, and the San Diego Public Library. Between the Knudsen company name, the front features a color action photo of the player superimposed on a football stadium. The field is green, the bleachers are yellow with gray print, and the scoreboard above the player reads "The Reading Team". The box below the player gives brief biographical information and player highlights. The back has logos of the sponsors and describes two books that are available at the public library. We have checklisted this set in alphabetical order because they are otherwise unnumbered except for the player's uniform number displayed on the card front.

COMPLETE SET (6) 6.00 15.00
1 Marion Butts 1.20 3.00
2 Anthony Miller 1.60 4.00
3 Leslie O'Neal 1.20 3.00
4 Gary Plummer 1.20 3.00
5 Billy Ray Smith 1.00 2.50
6 Billy Joe Tolliver 1.00 2.50

1990 Chargers Police

This 12-card set measures approximately 2 5/8" by 4 1/8" and features members of the 1990 San Diego Chargers. The set was sponsored by Louis Rich Meats. The card fronts have full-color photos framed by solid blue borders while the backs have brief biographies of the players and limited personal information. There is also a safety tip on the back of the card. The set was issued in two six-card panels or sheets (but is also found as individual cards). The cards are numbered on the back.

COMPLETE SET (12) 3.20 8.00
1 Martin Bayless .20 .50
2 Marion Butts .30 .75
3 Gill Byrd .20 .50
4 Burt Grossman .20 .50
5 Ronnie Harmon .30 .75
6 Anthony Miller .50 1.25
7 Leslie O'Neal .40 1.00
8 Joe Phillips .20 .50
9 Gary Plummer .30 .75
10 Billy Ray Smith .20 .50
11 Billy Joe Tolliver .30 .75
12 Lee Williams .30 .75

1990 Chargers Smokey

This attractive 36-card set was distributed in the San Diego area and features members of the Chargers. The cards measure approximately 5" by 8" and are very similar in style to previous Chargers Smokey issues. Since the cards are unnumbered except for uniform number, they are ordered below in that manner. The cardbacks contain a fire safety cartoon and very brief biographical information.

COMPLETE SET (36) 16.00 40.00
11 Billy Joe Tolliver .50 1.25
13 Mark Vlasic .50 1.25
15 David Archer 1.00 2.50
20 Darrin Nelson .40 1.00
22 Gill Byrd .50 1.25
24 Lester Lyles .40 1.00
25 Vencie Glenn .50 1.25
30 Sam Seale .40 1.00
31 Craig McEwen .40 1.00
35 Marion Butts .50 1.25
43 Tim Spencer .50 1.25
44 Martin Bayless .40 1.00
46 Joe Caravello .40 1.00
50 Gary Plummer .50 1.25
51 Cedric Figaro .40 1.00
53 Courtney Hall .40 1.00
54 Billy Ray Smith .50 1.25
58 David Brandon .40 1.00
59 Ken Woodard .40 1.00
60 Dennis McKnight .40 1.00
65 David Richards .40 1.00
69 Les Miller .40 1.00
75 Joe Phillips .50 1.25
76 Broderick Thompson .40 1.00
78 Joel Patten .40 1.00
79 Joey Howard .40 1.00
80 Wayne Walker WR .40 1.00
82 Rod Bernstine .50 1.25
83 Anthony Miller 1.00 2.50
85 Andy Parker .40 1.00
87 Quinn Early .60 1.50
88 Arthur Cox .40 1.00
91 Leslie O'Neal .60 1.50
92 Burt Grossman .50 1.25
97 George Hinkle .40 1.00
99 Lee Williams .50 1.25

1991 Chargers Vons

The 12-card Vons Chargers set was issued on panels measuring approximately 6 5/8" by 3 1/2". Two perforated lines divide the panels into three sections: a standard size (2 1/2" by 3 1/2") player card, a 1991 Junior Charger Official Membership Card, and a Sea World of California discount coupon. The player cards have color action player photos on the fronts, with yellow borders on a white card face. A Charger helmet and the words "Junior Chargers" appear at the top of the card. In a horizontal format with dark blue print, the back has biography, career highlights, and sponsors' logos. The cards are unnumbered and checklisted below in alphabetical order.

COMPLETE SET (12) 4.00 10.00
1 Rod Bernstine .30 .75
2 Gill Byrd .30 .75
3 Burt Grossman .30 .75
4 Ronnie Harmon .30 .75
5 Anthony Miller .60 1.50
6 Leslie O'Neal .40 1.00
7 Gary Plummer .30 .75
8 Junior Seau .80 2.00
9 Billy Ray Smith .30 .75
10 Broderick Thompson .20 .50
11 Billy Joe Tolliver .30 .75
12 Lee Williams .30 .75

1992 Chargers Louis Rich

Sponsored by Louis Rich, this 52-card oversized set measures approximately 5" by 8". The fronts feature full-bleed glossy color action photos that are framed by a thin white line. The player's jersey number, name, and position appear at the lower left corner, while the sponsor logo and a replica of the team helmet are printed in the lower right corner. In addition to biographical information, the backs are dominated by a large advertisement for Louis Rich products. The cards are unnumbered and checklisted below in alphabetical order.

COMPLETE SET (52) 20.00 40.00
1 Sam Anno .40 1.00
2 Johnnie Barnes .40 1.00
3 Rod Bernstine .50 1.25
4 Eric Bieniemy .50 1.25
5 Anthony Blaylock .40 1.00
6 Brian Brennan .40 1.00
7 Marion Butts .60 1.50
8 Gill Byrd .50 1.25
9 John Carney .50 1.25
10 Darren Carrington .40 1.00
11 Robert Claborne .40 1.00
12 Floyd Fields .40 1.00
13 Donald Frank .40 1.00
14 Bob Gagliano .40 1.00
15 Leo Goeas .40 1.00
16 Burt Grossman .40 1.00
17 Courtney Hall .40 1.00
18 Delton Hall .40 1.00
19 Ronnie Harmon .50 1.25
20 Steve Hendrickson .40 1.00
21 Stan Humphries .60 1.50
22 Shawn Jefferson .50 1.25
23 John Kidd .40 1.00
24 Shawn Lee .40 1.00
25 Nale Lewis .50 1.25
26 Eugene Marve .40 1.00
27 Deems May .40 1.00
28 Anthony Miller .60 1.50
29 Chris Mims .50 1.25
30 Eric Moten .40 1.00
31 Kevin Murphy .40 1.00
32 Pat O'Hara .40 1.00
33 Leslie O'Neal .50 1.25
34 Gary Plummer .50 1.25
35 Marquez Pope .40 1.00
36 Alfred Pupunu .40 1.00
37 Stanley Richard .40 1.00
38 David Richards .40 1.00
39 Henry Rolling .40 1.00
40 Bobby Ross CO .50 1.25
41 Junior Seau 1.00 2.50
42 Harry Swayne .40 1.00
43 Broderick Thompson .40 1.00
44 George Thornton .40 1.00
45 Peter Tuipulotu .40 1.00
46 Sean Vanhorse .40 1.00
47 Derrick Walker .40 1.00
48 Reggie E. White .40 1.00
49 Curtis Whitley .40 1.00
50 Blaise Winter .40 1.00
51 Duane Young .40 1.00
52 Mike Zandofsky .40 1.00

1993 Chargers D.A.R.E.

The San Diego Chargers issued this 30-card set sponsored by the local Police and the D.A.R.E. program. Each cardfront includes a color photo surrounded by a yellow border. Cardbacks include a short player bio and a public service message. The unnumbered cards are arranged below alphabetically.

COMPLETE SET (30) 3.20 8.00
1 Sam Anno .07 .20
2 Stan Brock .07 .20
3 Marion Butts .10 .30
4 Gill Byrd .07 .20
5 John Carney .10 .30
6 Darren Carrington .07 .20
7 Brian Davis .07 .20
8 Donald Frank .07 .20
9 John Friesz .10 .30
10 Burt Grossman .07 .20
11 Courtney Hall .07 .20
12 Ronnie Harmon .10 .30
13 Steve Hendrickson .07 .20
14 Stan Humphries .20 .50
15 John Kidd .07 .20
16 Shawn Lee .07 .20
17 Nate Lewis .07 .20
18 Joe Milinichik .07 .20
19 Anthony Miller .20 .50
20 Leslie O'Neal .20 .50
21 Gary Plummer .10 .30
22 Bobby Ross CO .10 .30
23 Junior Seau .40 1.00
24 Alex Spanos OWN .07 .20
25 Harry Swayne .07 .20
26 Sean Vanhorse .07 .20
27 Derrick Walker .07 .20
28 Jerrol Williams .07 .20
29 Blaise Winter .07 .20
30 Mike Zandofsky .07 .20

1993 Chargers Police

These 32 standard-size cards of the San Diego Chargers feature color player action shots on their blue- and yellow-bordered fronts. The player's name appears in vertical blue lettering within the inner yellow border on the left. The California Highway Patrol (CHP) shield logo appears at the lower left. The white back is framed by a thin blue line and carries the player's name at the top, followed below by position and biography. A safety message at the bottom from the CHP's "Designated Driver" campaign cautions against driving while intoxicated. Natrone Means is featured during his Rookie season.

COMPLETE SET (32) 6.00 15.00
1 Darrien Gordon .15 .40
2 Natrone Means 1.00 2.50
3 John Friesz .15 .40
4 Stan Humphries .40 1.00
5 Anthony Miller .40 1.00
6 Marion Butts .30 .75
7 Ronnie Harmon .30 .75
8 Stanley Richard .15 .40
9 Leslie O'Neal .30 .75
10 Harry Swayne .08 .25
11 Junior Seau .60 1.50
12 Courtney Hall .15 .40
13 Gary Plummer .15 .40
14 Eric Moten .08 .25
15 Chris Mims .30 .75
16 Burt Grossman .15 .40
17 Blaise Winter .08 .25
18 Donald Frank .08 .25
19 Sean Vanhorse .08 .25
20 John Carney .08 .25
21 Floyd Fields .08 .25
22 Gill Byrd .15 .40
23 Shawn Jefferson .15 .40
24 Shawn Lee .08 .25
25 Alfred Pupunu .15 .40
26 Marquez Pope .08 .25
27 Darren Carrington .08 .25
28 Duane Young .08 .25
29 Derrick Walker .08 .25
30 Deems May .08 .25
31 Nate Lewis .15 .40
32 Bobby Ross CO .30 .75

1994 Chargers Castrol

This 52-card set was co-sponsored by Castrol and Pepboys. The cards measure approximately 5" by 8" and are printed on white cardboard stock. The fronts feature full-bleed color action photos, except at the bottom where a white stripe carries the player's name, uniform number, and sponsor logos. In blue print over a ghosted NFL emblem, the backs show biography and sponsor advertisements. The cards are unnumbered and checklisted below in alphabetical order.

COMPLETE SET (52) 20.00 40.00
1 Johnnie Barnes .40 1.00
2 Eric Bieniemy .50 1.25
3 David Binn .40 1.00
4 Stan Brock .40 1.00
5 Jeff Brohm .40 1.00
6 Lewis Bush .40 1.00
7 John Carney .50 1.25
8 Darren Carrington .40 1.00
9 Eric Castle .40 1.00
10 Willie Clark .40 1.00
11 Joe Cocozzo .40 1.00
12 Andre Coleman .40 1.00
13 Rodney Culver .40 1.00
14 Isaac Davis .40 1.00
15 Reuben Davis .40 1.00
16 Greg Engel .40 1.00
17 Dennis Gilbert .40 1.00
18 Gale Gilbert .40 1.00
19 Darrien Gordon .50 1.25
20 David Griggs .40 1.00
21 Courtney Hall .40 1.00
22 Ronnie Harmon .50 1.25
23 Dwayne Harper .40 1.00
24 Rodney Harrison 1.50 4.00
25 Steve Hendrickson .40 1.00
26 Stan Humphries .60 1.50
27 Shawn Jefferson .50 1.25
28 Raylee Johnson .40 1.00
29 Eric Jonassen .40 1.00
30 Aaron Laing .40 1.00
31 Shawn Lee .40 1.00
32 Deems May .40 1.00
33 Natrone Means 1.00 2.50
34 Joe Milinichik .40 1.00
35 Doug Miller .40 1.00
36 Chris Mims .40 1.00
37 Shannon Mitchell .40 1.00
38 Leslie O'Neal .60 1.50
39 Vaughn Parker .40 1.00
40 John Parrella .40 1.00
41 Alfred Pupunu .40 1.00
42 Stanley Richard .40 1.00
43 Junior Seau 1.20 3.00
44 Mark Seay .40 1.00
45 Harry Swayne .40 1.00
46 Cornell Thomas .40 1.00
47 Sean Van Horse .40 1.00
48 Bryan Wagner .40 1.00
49 Reggie E. White .40 1.00
50 Curtis Whitley .40 1.00
51 Duane Young .40 1.00
52 Lonnie Young .40 1.00

1994 Chargers Pro Mags/Pro Tags

Issued in a black cardboard box and featuring the San Diego Chargers, this set consists of six Pro Mags and six Pro Tags, both with rounded corners and measuring 2 1/8" by 3 3/8". Each box is individually numbered out of 750. The magnets and tags are unnumbered and checklisted below in alphabetical order, first the magnets (1-6) and then the tags (7-12).

COMPLETE SET (12) 10.00 25.00
1 Stan Humphries .80 2.00
2 Tony Martin .80 2.00
3 Natrone Means 1.00 2.50
4 Leslie O'Neal .60 1.50
5 Junior Seau 1.20 3.00
6 Mark Seay .60 1.50
7 Stan Humphries .80 2.00
8 Tony Martin .80 2.00
9 Natrone Means 1.00 2.50
10 Leslie O'Neal .60 1.50
11 Junior Seau 1.20 3.00
12 Mark Seay .60 1.50

1995 Chargers Police

This 16-card set of the San Diego Chargers sponsored by the California Highway patrol features color player photos with a white inner and blue outer border. The backs carry player information and a safety message.

COMPLETE SET (16) 3.20 8.00
1 John Carney .25 .60
2 Stan Humphries .30 .75
3 Natrone Means .40 1.00
4 Darrien Gordon .20 .50
5 Courtney Hall .20 .50
6 Junior Seau .50 1.25
7 Harry Swayne .20 .50
8 Tony Martin .30 .75
9 Mark Seay .20 .50
10 Chris Mims .25 .60
11 Shawn Lee .20 .50
12 Leslie O'Neal .25 .60
13 Reuben Davis .20 .50
14 Darren Bennett .25 .60
15 Gale Gilbert .20 .50
16 Bobby Ross CO .25 .60
Chief Don Watkins

2006 Chargers Topps

COMPLETE SET (12) 3.00 6.00
SD1 Vincent Jackson .25 .60
SD2 LaDainian Tomlinson .40 1.00
SD3 Eric Parker .25 .60
SD4 Antonio Gates .40 1.00
SD5 Shawne Merriman .30 .75
SD6 Darren Sproles .40 1.00
CD7 Donnie Edwards .25 .60
SD8 Philip Rivers .40 1.00
SD9 Keenan McCardell .30 .75
SD10 Quentin Jammer .25 .60
SD11 Antonio Cromartie .30 .75
SD12 Charlie Whitehurst .25 .60

2007 Chargers Topps

COMPLETE SET (12) 2.50
1 Philip Rivers .60 1.50
2 LaDainian Tomlinson .60 1.50
3 Antonio Gates .60 1.50
4 Eric Parker .40 1.00
5 Shaun Phillips .40 1.00
6 Vincent Jackson .40 1.00
7 Shawne Merriman .40 1.00
8 Michael Turner .40 1.00
9 Luis Castillo .40 1.00
10 Nate Kaeding .40 1.00
11 Craig Davis .40 1.00
12 Eric Weddle .50 1.25

2008 Chargers Topps

COMPLETE SET (12) 2.50 5.00
1 Antonio Gates .50 1.25
2 LaDainian Tomlinson .60 1.50
3 Philip Rivers .60 1.50
4 Shawne Merriman .40 1.00
5 Antonio Cromartie .40 1.00
6 Chris Chambers .40 1.00
7 Jamal Williams .40 1.00
8 Shaun Phillips .40 1.00
9 Vincent Jackson .40 1.00
10 Luis Castillo .40 1.00
11 Clinton Hart .40 1.00
12 Jacob Hester .40 1.00

1993 Charlotte Rage AFL

This set was issued by the Charlotte Rage and sponsored by Matthews Equipment. Each card includes a color photo of the featured player or personality on the front with a blue and red striped framed on a white border. The cardbacks include a sponsorship logo with a player bio and stats.

1 Davis Smith .75 2.00
2 Mike Black .75 2.00
3 Andre Johnson .75 2.00
4 Peda Samuel .75 2.00
5 Tony Kimbrough .75 2.00
6 Andy Kelly 1.50 4.00
7 Chris Poston .75 2.00
8 John Burch .75 2.00
9 Tiger Greene 1.00 2.50
10 Steve Wilks .75 2.00
11 Sean Doctor .75 2.00
12 Terry Langston .75 2.00
13 Junior Jackson .75 2.00
14 Tony Bowick .75 2.00
15 Scott Miller .75 2.00
16 Pete Antoniou .75 2.00
17 Danny Smith .75 2.00
18 Mike Renna .75 2.00
19 Ryan Bethea .75 2.00
20 Kubanai Kalombo .75 2.00
21 Marlin Brown .75 2.00
22 Billy Marsh .75 2.00
23 Matthews Equip. Employees .75 2.00
24 Mascot .75 2.00
25 Cheerleaders .75 2.00
26 Assistant Coaches .75 2.00
27 Cliff Stoudt CO 1.00 2.50
28 Cover Card .75 2.00

1970 Chase and Sanborn Stickers

This 26-card set features colored stickers of team logos on silver backgrounds. The backs carry a Chase and Sanborn Coffee send-in ad for a complete set of the 26 NFL team emblems. The cards are unnumbered and checklisted below in alphabetical order according to team nickname.

COMPLETE SET (26) 150.00 300.00
1 Chicago Bears 7.50 15.00
2 Cincinnati Bengals 7.50 15.00
3 Buffalo Bills 7.50 15.00
4 Denver Broncos 7.50 15.00
5 Cleveland Browns 7.50 15.00
6 St.Louis Cardinals 7.50 15.00
7 San Diego Chargers 7.50 15.00
8 Kansas City Chiefs 7.50 15.00
9 Baltimore Colts 7.50 15.00
10 Dallas Cowboys 10.00 20.00
11 Miami Dolphins 7.50 15.00
12 Philadelphia Eagles 7.50 15.00
13 Atlanta Falcons 7.50 15.00
14 San Francisco 49ers 7.50 15.00
15 New York Giants 7.50 15.00
16 New York Jets 7.50 15.00
17 Detroit Lions 7.50 15.00
18 Houston Oilers 7.50 15.00
19 Green Bay Packers 10.00 20.00
20 New England Patriots 7.50 15.00
21 Oakland Raiders 10.00 20.00
22 Los Angeles Rams 7.50 15.00
23 Washington Redskins 10.00 20.00
24 New Orleans Saints 7.50 15.00
25 Pittsburgh Steelers 7.50 15.00
26 Minnesota Vikings 7.50 15.00

1969 Chemtoy AFL Superballs

These little high bouncing 1" balls were produced by Chemtoy and featured AFL players. The player's picture is on the front with their name and team affiliation on the back of the paper piece inside the ball. Since these are not numbered, we have sequenced them in alphabetical order.

COMPLETE SET (26) 600.00 1000.00
1 Lance Alworth 60.00 100.00
2 Pete Beathard 18.00 30.00
3 Bobby Bell 30.00 50.00
4 Emerson Boozer 18.00 30.00
5 Nick Buoniconti 35.00 60.00
6 Billy Cannon 25.00 40.00
7 Gino Cappelletti 25.00 40.00
8 Jack Clancy 18.00 30.00
9 Larry Csonka 60.00 100.00
10 Ben Davidson 25.00 40.00
11 Len Dawson 60.00 100.00
12 Mike Garrett 18.00 30.00
13 Bob Griese 80.00 120.00
14 John Hadl 30.00 50.00
15 Jack Kemp 90.00 150.00
16 Don Maynard 50.00 80.00
17 Ron McDole 18.00 30.00
18 Ron Mix 30.00 50.00
20 Dick Post 18.00 30.00
20 Jim Otto 30.00 50.00
21 George Saimes 18.00 30.00
22 George Sauer 18.00 30.00
23 Jan Stenerud 30.00 50.00
24 Matt Snell 25.00 40.00
25 Jim Turner 18.00 30.00
26 George Webster 18.00 30.00

1983 Chicago Blitz Team Sheets

Each of these sheets measures approximately 10" by 8" and features two rows with four players per row. The first sheet presents the coaching staff, while the other seven sheets feature players. The individual photos measure 2 1/4" by 2 1/2" and have white borders. The photos are head-and-shoulders shots, with player information immediately below. A title between two team logos running across the bottom of the sheets completes them. The sheets are unnumbered.

COMPLETE SET (7) 16.00 40.00
1 Coaching Staff 6.00 15.00
2 Luther Bradley 4.00 10.00
Ed.Brown S
3 Mack Boatner 2.00 5.00
4 Robert Barnes 2.00 5.00
5 Junior Ah You 2.00 5.00
6 Jim Fahnhorst 2.00 5.00
7 Marcus Anderson 2.00 5.00

2003 Chicago Rush AFL

This set was produced by Multi-Ad, sponsored by Cort Furniture, and distributed by the Rush. Each card was produced with a dark blue border on one side with the year of issue and the team name. The cardbacks are numbered in small print at the bottom and feature brief player bios.

COMPLETE SET (30) 6.00 12.00
1 Team Photo .20 .50
2 Dameon Porter .30 .75
3 Anthony Ladd .20 .50
4 Chad Salisbury .30 .75
5 Cedric Walker .20 .50
6 Billy Dicken .40 1.00
7 Cornelius Bonner .30 .75
8 Lindsay Fleshman .30 .75
9 Brian Ah Yat .20 .50
10 Marvin Taylor .20 .50
11 Keith Gispert .20 .50
12 Antonio Chatman .20 .50
13 Levelle Brown .20 .50
14 DeJuan Alfonzo .20 .50
15 Jamie McGourty .20 .50
16 Bob McMillen .20 .50
17 Frank Moore .20 .50
18 Tony Bowick .20 .50
19 Marcus McKenzie .20 .50
20 Furnell Hankton .20 .50
21 James Baron .20 .50
22 Riley Kleinhesselink .20 .50
23 Jerry Montgomery .20 .50
24 John Moyer .20 .50
25 Mike Hohensee CO .20 1.00
26 Assistant Coaches .20 .50
Walt Housman
Stan Davis
Dave Witthun
27 Rush Dancers .20 .50
28 Rush Logo .20 .50
29 AFL NBC Logo .20 .50
30 Cort Furniture Logo .20 .50

2004 Chicago Rush AFL

This set was produced by Multi-Ad and distributed by the Rush. Each card is horizontal in format and produced with a dark blue border on the right side with the year of issue in the center and the player image to the left. The cardbacks are numbered and feature brief player bios.

COMPLETE SET (30) 6.00 12.00
1 Cover Card .20 .50
2 Raymond Philyaw .30 .75
3 Sam Clemons .30 .75
4 Chad Salisbury .30 .75
5 Greg Williams S .20 .50
6 Corey Sawyer .30 .75
7 Lindsay Fleshman .30 .75
8 Kareem Larrimore .30 .75
9 Jeremy McDaniel .20 .50
10 Keith Gispert .20 .50
11 Etu Molden .20 .50
12 Levelle Brown .20 .50
13 Donnie Caldwell .20 .50
14 DeJuan Alfonzo .20 .50
15 Jamie McGourty .20 .50
16 Bob McMillen .20 .50
17 Colin Greczek .20 .50
18 Frank Moore .20 .50
19 Salem Simon .20 .50
20 James Baron .20 .50
21 Riley Kleinhesselink .20 .50
22 John Thomas .20 .50
23 John Sikora .20 .50
24 John Moyer .20 .50
25 Mike Hohensee CO .20 1.00
26 Assistant Coaches .20 .50
Dave Witthun
Walt Housman
Brian Schwartze
27 Rush Dancers .20 .50
28 Lindsay Fleshman .20 .50
Season Ticket Ad
29 AFL on NBC Ad .20 .50
30 Cort Furniture Coupon .20 .50

2006 Chicago Rush AFL

COMPLETE SET (36) 10.00 20.00
1 CORT Sponsor Card .30 .75
2 Carlos Wright .30 .75
3 C.J. Johnson .30 .75
4 Russell Shaw .30 .75
5 Dan Frantz .30 .75
6 Nick Myers .30 .75
7 Marvin Taylor .30 .75
8 Michael Bishop .50 1.25
9 Asad Abdul-Khaliq .30 .75
10 Bobby Sippio .40 1.00
11 Matt D'Orazio .30 .75
12 Woody Dantzler .40 1.00
13 Todd Howard .30 .75
14 Buchie Ibeh .30 .75
15 Etu Molden .30 .75
16 Levelle Brown .30 .75
17 Dennison Robinson .30 .75
18 Marcus Moore .30 .75
19 DeJuan Alfonzo .30 .75
20 Jeremy Unertl .30 .75
21 Bob McMillen .30 .75
22 Curtis Eason .30 .75
23 Khreem Smith .30 .75
24 Tango McCauley .30 .75
25 Frank Moore .30 .75
26 Brian Sump .30 .75
27 D.J. Bleisath .30 .75
28 Charlie Cook .30 .75
29 Joe Peters .30 .75
30 Darain Tate .30 .75
31 John Sikora .30 .75
32 John Moyer .30 .75
33 Mike Hohensee CO .30 1.00
34 Asst Coaches .30 .75
35 Rush Dancers .30 .75
36 Grabowski (Mascot) .30 .75

2007 Chicago Rush AFL

COMPLETE SET (36) 6.00 12.00
1 Sponsor Card .20 .50
2 Woody Dantzler .40 1.00
3 Russell Shaw .20 .50
4 Bobby Sippio .30 .75
5 Dan Frantz .20 .50
6 Nick Myers .20 .50
7 James Sadler .20 .50
8 Russ Michna .20 .50
9 Matt D'Orazio .30 .75
10 Rob Mager .20 .50
11 Kevin Beard .20 .50
12 Etu Molden .30 .75
13 Rui Nakanishi .20 .50
14 Jonathan Ordway .20 .50
15 Dennison Robinson .20 .50
16 DeJuan Alfonzo .20 .50
17 Jeremy Unertl .20 .50
18 Bob McMillen .20 .50
19 Curtis Eason .20 .50
20 Frank Moore .20 .50
21 D.J. Bleisath .20 .50
22 Jason Thomas .20 .50
23 Joe Peters .20 .50
24 Robert Boss .20 .50
25 E.J. Burt .20 .50
26 Demetrios Walker .20 .50
27 John Sikora .20 .50
28 John Moyer .20 .50
29 Mike Hohensee (HC) .20 1.00
30 Asst Coaches .20 .50
31 Rush Dancers .20 .50
32 Grabowski (Mascot) .20 .50
33 Team Records .20 .50
34 Team Records .20 .50
35 Arena Bowl XX .20 .50
36 Team Schedule .20 .50

2008 Chicago Rush AFL

COMPLETE SET (36) 6.00 12.00
1 Cort Ad Card .20 .50
2 Damian Harrell .40 1.00
3 Donovan Morgan .20 .50
4 Talib Wise .20 .50
5 Dan Frantz .20 .50
6 Carlos Hendricks .20 .50
7 Reggie Gray .20 .50
8 James Sadler .20 .50
9 Russ Michna .20 .50
10 Ryan Dennard .20 .50
11 Clinton Solomon .20 .50
12 Rob Mager .20 .50
13 Sherdrick Bonner .30 .75
14 Liam Ezekiel .20 .50
15 Jonathan Ordway .20 .50
16 Dennison Robinson .20 .50
17 DeJuan Alfonzo .20 .50
18 Matt Kinsinger .20 .50
19 Jeremy Unertl .20 .50
20 Dan Alexander .30 .75
21 Beau Elliott .20 .50
22 Khreem Smith .20 .50
23 Nick Zeck .20 .50
24 Travis Latendresse .20 .50
25 Joe Peters .20 .50
26 Robert Boss .20 .50
27 James Baron .20 .50
28 Demetrios Walker .20 .50
29 John Sikora .20 .50
30 John Moyer .20 .50
31 Mike Hohensee CO .20 1.00
32 Assistant Coaches .20 .50
Scott Bailey
Walt Hoisman
Ryan Leonard
Bob McMillen
33 Adrenaline Dancers .20 .50
34 Grabowski - Mascot .20 .50
35 Rush Team Records .20 .50
36 Rush Team Records .20 .50

1963-65 Chiefs Fairmont Dairy

These cards were featured as the side panels of half-gallon milk cartons in the Kansas City area by Fairmont Dairy. Similar cards were apparently issued during more than one season as there are several styles with different sizes and colors. Any one individual card can be identified using either the age of the player or "years pro" that is printed on the card. The cards below were likely issued between 1963 and 1965 based upon this information or have not been confirmed as to year of issue. When cut, each card measures approximately 2 1/4" by 3 1/4" to the outside dotted line. The printing on the cards is in red and may also have been printed in black as well. The fronts feature close-up player photos with the player's biographical information appearing to the right. The cards have blank backs as is the case with most milk carton issues. Complete milk cartons would be valued at double the prices listed below. Additions to the list below are welcomed.

1 Bobby Bell 300.00 500.00
2 Mel Branch 200.00 350.00
(Age: 27; 1964 issue
3 Len Dawson 350.00 600.00
4 Dave Grayson 200.00 350.00
5 Abner Haynes 250.00 400.00
6 Sherrill Headrick 200.00 350.00
7 Dave Hill 200.00 350.00
8 Bobby Hunt 200.00 350.00
9 Frank Jackson 200.00 350.00
10 Curtis McClinton 250.00 400.00
11 Bobby Ply 200.00 350.00
12 Al Reynolds 200.00 350.00
13 Smokey Stover 200.00 350.00

1965 Chiefs Team Issue 8 x 10

This set of photos was released around 1965. Each features a Chiefs player on glossy photographic stock measuring roughly 8" by 10." The player's position (initials), name and team name is spelled out below the player's photo. The photo backs are blank and can often be found with a photographer's imprint and year of issue. These photos look very similar to the 1967 set, but the team name is roughly 1 3/4" to 1 7/8" long. Any additions to this list are appreciated.

COMPLETE SET (17) 100.00 200.00
1 Pete Beathard 7.50 15.00
2 Buck Buchanan 12.50 25.00
3 Ed Budde 7.50 15.00
4 Chris Burford 7.50 15.00
5 Len Dawson 20.00 35.00
6 Sherrill Headrick 7.50 15.00
7 Mack Lee Hill 7.50 15.00
8 E.J. Holub 7.50 15.00
9 Bobby Hunt 7.50 15.00
10 Frank Jackson 7.50 15.00
11 Ed Lothamer 7.50 15.00
12 Jerry Mays 7.50 15.00
13 Curtis McClinton 10.00 20.00
14 Johnny Robinson 10.00 20.00
15 Jim Tyrer 10.00 20.00
16 Fred Williamson 10.00 20.00
17 Jerrel Wilson 7.50 15.00

1966 Chiefs Team Issue

The Kansas City Chiefs issued these player photos around 1966. Some likely were released over a period years. The type style and size varies slightly from photo to photo. Each measures roughly 7 1/4" by 9 1/2" and features a black and white photo. They are unnumbered and checklisted below in alphabetical order. Any additions to the list are appreciated.

COMPLETE SET (15) 125.00 250.00
1 Pete Beathard 7.50 15.00
2 Bobby Bell 10.00 20.00
3 Tommy Brooker 7.50 15.00
4 Ed Budde 7.50 15.00
5 Bert Coan 7.50 15.00
6 Len Dawson 15.00 30.00
7 Mike Garrett 7.50 15.00
8 Sherrill Headrick 7.50 15.00
9 Jerry Mays 7.50 15.00
10 Curtis McClinton 7.50 15.00
11 Bobby Ply 7.50 15.00
12 Johnny Robinson 7.50 15.00
13 Hank Stram CO 12.50 25.00
14 Otis Taylor 10.00 20.00
15 Fred Williamson 10.00 20.00

1967 Chiefs Fairmont Dairy

These cards were featured as the side panels of half-gallon milk cartons in the Kansas City area by Fairmont Dairy. Similar cards were apparently issued during more than one season as there are several styles with different sizes and colors. Any one individual card can be identified using the age of the player that is printed on the card. The cards below were issued in 1967 based upon this information and we've noted that below when known. When cut, each card measures approximately 2 3/8" by 3 3/8" to the outside dotted line. The printing on all confirmed cards is in red but may also have been printed in black as well. The fronts feature a close-up player photo with the player's team, his name, position, height, weight, age, and college information appearing to the right. The cards have blank backs as is the case with most milk carton issues. Complete milk cartons would be valued at double the prices listed below. Additions to the list below are welcomed.

COMPLETE SET (23) 1500.00 2500.00
1 Fred Arbanas 175.00 300.00
2 Pete Beathard 175.00 300.00
3 Bobby Bell 250.00 400.00
4 Aaron Brown 150.00 250.00
5 Buck Buchanan 250.00 400.00

6 Ed Budde	150.00	250.00
7 Chris Burford	175.00	300.00
8 Bert Coan	150.00	250.00
9 Len Dawson	350.00	600.00
10 Mike Garrett	175.00	300.00
11 Jon Gilliam	150.00	250.00
12 E.J. Holub	175.00	300.00
13 Bobby Hunt	150.00	250.00
14 Chuck Hurston	150.00	250.00
15 Ed Lothamer	150.00	250.00
16 Curtis McClinton	175.00	300.00
17 Curt Merz	150.00	250.00
18 Willie Mitchell	150.00	250.00
19 Johnny Robinson	175.00	300.00
20 Otis Taylor	200.00	350.00
21 Jim Tyrer	175.00	300.00
22 Fred Williamson	200.00	350.00
23 Jerrel Wilson	150.00	250.00

1967 Chiefs Team Issue

This set of photos was released around 1967. Each features a Chiefs player on glossy stock measuring roughly 8" by 10." The player's name and team name is spelled out below the player's photo with some photos also including the player's position listed before his name. These photos look very similar to the 1965 set, but the team name is roughly 1 1/2" long. Any additions to this list are appreciated.

COMPLETE SET (11)	100.00	175.00
1 Bobby Bell	10.00	20.00
2 Aaron Brown	7.50	15.00
3 Ed Budde	7.50	15.00
4 Chris Burford	7.50	15.00
5 Bert Coan	7.50	15.00
6 Len Dawson	15.00	30.00
7 Willie Lanier	10.00	20.00
8 Curt Merz	7.50	15.00
9 Jan Stenerud	10.00	20.00
10 Otis Taylor	10.00	20.00
11 Jim Tyrer	10.00	20.00

1968 Chiefs Fairmont Dairy

These cards were featured as the side panels of half-gallon milk cartons in the Kansas City area by Fairmont Dairy. Similar cards were apparently issued during more than one season as there are several styles with different sizes and colors. Any one individual card can be identified using the "years pro" of the player that is printed on the card. The cards below were issued in 1968 based upon this information and we've noted that below when known. When cut, each card measures approximately 2 3/8" by 3 3/8" to the outside dotted lines. The printing on the confirmed cards is in red but may also have been printed in black as well. The fronts feature close-up player photos with the player's team, his name, position, biographical information, and years pro appearing to the right. Most were printed with a very thin (roughly 1/16") white border, while a few featured a thicker (roughly 1/4") white border. The cards have blank backs as is the case with most milk carton issues. Complete milk cartons would be valued at double the prices listed below. Additions to the list below are welcomed.

COMPLETE SET (23)	1500.00	2500.00
1 Bud Abell	150.00	250.00
2 Fred Arbanas	175.00	300.00
3 Aaron Brown	150.00	250.00
4 Buck Buchanan	250.00	400.00
5 Ed Budde	150.00	250.00
6 Wendell Hayes	175.00	300.00
7 Dave Hill	150.00	250.00
8 E.J. Holub	175.00	300.00
9 Jim Kearney	150.00	250.00
10 Ernie Ladd	200.00	350.00
11 Willie Lanier	250.00	400.00
12 Jacky Lee	175.00	300.00
13 Ed Lothamer	150.00	250.00
14 Jim Lynch	150.00	250.00
15 Jerry Mays	150.00	250.00
16 Curtis McClinton	175.00	300.00
17 Willie Mitchell	150.00	250.00
18 Johnny Robinson	175.00	300.00
19 Noland Smith	150.00	250.00
20 Jan Stenerud	200.00	350.00
21 Otis Taylor	200.00	350.00
22 Jim Tyrer	175.00	300.00
23 Jerrel Wilson	150.00	250.00

1968 Chiefs Team Issue

The Chiefs issued these player photos in the late 1960s. Each photo measures roughly 8 1/2" by 10 5/16" and features a black and white photo along with a white facsimile autograph. The Len Dawson can be found with either a white or black signature. The player's position initials, name, and team name appear below the photo. They are unnumbered and checklisted below in alphabetical order.

COMPLETE SET (22)	150.00	300.00
1 Bobby Bell	10.00	20.00
2 Buck Buchanan	10.00	20.00
3 Reg Carolan	7.50	15.00
4 Len Dawson WHT	15.00	30.00
5 Len Dawson BLK	15.00	30.00
6 Mike Garrett	7.50	15.00
7 E.J. Holub	7.50	15.00
8 Jim Kearney	7.50	15.00
9 Ernie Ladd	7.50	15.00
10 Willie Lanier	10.00	20.00
11 Jacky Lee	7.50	15.00
12 Ed Lothamer	7.50	15.00
13 Curtis McClinton	7.50	15.00
14 Willie Mitchell	7.50	15.00
15 Frank Pitts	7.50	15.00
16 Johnny Robinson	7.50	15.00
17 Goldie Sellers	7.50	15.00
18 Noland Smith	7.50	15.00
19 Hank Stram CO	12.50	25.00
20 Otis Taylor	10.00	20.00
21 Fred Williamson	10.00	20.00
22 Jerrel Wilson	7.50	15.00

1969 Chiefs Fairmont Dairy

These cards were featured as the side panels of half-gallon milk cartons in the Kansas City area by Fairmont Dairy. Similar cards were apparently issued during more than one season as there are several styles with different sizes and colors. Any one individual card can be identified using either the age of the player or "years pro" that is printed on the card. The cards below were issued in 1969 based upon this information and we've noted that below. When cut, each card measures approximately 1 5/8" by 3 1/2" to the outside dotted line. The printing on the confirmed cards is in black ink but some may also have been printed in red ink as well. The fronts feature close-up player photos with the player's team, his jersey number, his name, position, biographical information, and years pro appearing to the right. The cards have blank backs as is the case with most milk carton issues. Complete milk cartons would be valued at double the prices listed below. Additions to the list below are welcomed.

COMPLETE SET (25)	1800.00	3000.00
1 Fred Arbanas	60.00	100.00
2 Bobby Bell (Years Pro 7)	125.00	200.00
3 Aaron Brown	60.00	100.00
4 Buck Buchanan	100.00	200.00
5 Ed Budde	60.00	100.00
6 Curley Culp (Years Pro 2)	100.00	175.00
7 George Daney	60.00	100.00
8 Len Dawson	200.00	350.00
9 Wendell Hayes	75.00	125.00
10 E.J. Holub	75.00	125.00
11 Ernie Ladd	90.00	150.00
12 Mike Livingston	75.00	125.00
13 Ed Lothamer	60.00	100.00
14 Jim Marsalis (First Year Pro)	60.00	100.00
15 Jerry Mays	60.00	100.00
16 Curtis McClinton	75.00	125.00
17 Willie Mitchell	60.00	100.00
18 Mo Moorman	60.00	100.00
19 Frank Pitts (Years Pro 5)	60.00	100.00
20 Gloster Richardson	60.00	100.00
21 Johnny Robinson	75.00	125.00
22 Otis Taylor	90.00	150.00
23 Emmitt Thomas	75.00	125.00
24 Jim Tyrer	60.00	100.00
25 Jerrel Wilson	60.00	100.00

1969 Chiefs Kroger

This eight-card, unnumbered set was sponsored by Kroger and measures approximately 8" by 9 3/4". The front features a color painting of the player by artist John Wheeldon, with the player's name inscribed across the bottom of the picture. The back has biographical and statistical information about the player and a brief note about the artist.

COMPLETE SET (8)	75.00	150.00
1 Buck Buchanan	10.00	20.00
2 Len Dawson	25.00	40.00
3 Mike Garrett	7.50	15.00
4 Willie Lanier	10.00	20.00
5 Jerry Mays	7.50	15.00
6 Johnny Robinson	7.50	15.00
7 Jan Stenerud	10.00	20.00
8 Jim Tyrer	7.50	15.00

1969 Chiefs Team Issue

These photos of the Kansas City Chiefs measures approximately 8 1/2" by 10 3/8" and feature black-and-white player images with a white border. The player's name and team name are included below each photo. The backs are blank and unnumbered so the photos are checklisted below in alpabetical order.

COMPLETE SET (5)	25.00	50.00
1 Caesar Belser	6.00	12.00
2 Curley Culp	6.00	12.00
3 George Daney	6.00	12.00
4 Mo Moorman	6.00	12.00
5 Frank Pitts	6.00	12.00

1970 Chiefs Team Issue

This 17-card set of the Kansas City Chiefs measures approximately 8" by 10 3/8" and features black-and-white player photos with a white border. The player's facsimile autograph appears across the photo with his name and team name below each photo. The backs are blank and unnumbered so the photos are checklisted below in alpabetical order.

COMPLETE SET (17)	75.00	150.00
1 Fred Arbanas	5.00	10.00
2 Bobby Bell	7.50	15.00
3 Aaron Brown	5.00	10.00
4 Billy Cannon	6.00	12.00
5 Robert Holmes	5.00	10.00
6 Mike Livingston	5.00	10.00
7 Jim Lynch	5.00	10.00
8 Jim Marsalis	5.00	10.00
9 Warren McVea	5.00	10.00
10 Willie Mitchell	5.00	10.00
11 Mo Moorman	5.00	10.00
12 Ed Podolak	5.00	10.00
13 Bob Stein	5.00	10.00
14 Jan Stenerud	7.50	15.00
15 Morris Stroud	5.00	10.00
16 Otis Taylor	6.00	12.00
17 Jerrel Wilson	5.00	10.00

1971 Chiefs Team Issue

This set of photos is a team-issued set. Each photo measures approximately 7 1/4" by 10" and features a black-and-white head shot bordered in white. The player's name and team name are printed in the lower white border, while the player's facsimile autograph is inscribed across the picture. The backs carry biography and career summary; some of the backs also have statistics. The photos are unnumbered and checklisted below in alphabetical order.

COMPLETE SET (13)	60.00	120.00
1 Bobby Bell	7.50	15.00
2 Wendell Hayes	5.00	10.00
3 Ed Lothamer	5.00	10.00
4 Jim Lynch	5.00	10.00
5 Mike Oriard	5.00	10.00
6 Jack Rudnay	5.00	10.00
7 Sid Smith	5.00	10.00
8 Bob Stein	5.00	10.00
9 Jan Stenerud	7.50	15.00
10 Hank Stram CO	7.50	15.00
11 Otis Taylor	6.00	12.00
12 Jim Tyrer	6.00	12.00
13 Marvin Upshaw	5.00	10.00

1972 Chiefs Team Issue

This set of photos was released by the Chiefs. Each photo measures approximately 7 1/4" by 10" and features a black-and-white head shot bordered in white. The player's name and team name are printed in the lower white border, while the player's facsimile autograph is inscribed across the picture. The backs on most carry biography and career summaries and other statistics while some were issued blankbacked as well. The photos are unnumbered and checklisted below in alphabetical order. Any additions to this list are appreciated.

COMPLETE SET (34)	150.00	300.00
1 Mike Adamle	5.00	10.00
2 Nate Allen	5.00	10.00
3 Buck Buchanan	7.50	15.00
4 Ed Budde	5.00	10.00
5 Curley Culp	5.00	10.00
6 George Daney	5.00	10.00
7 Willie Frazier	5.00	10.00
8 Wendell Hayes	5.00	10.00
9 Dave Hill	5.00	10.00
10 Dennis Homan	5.00	10.00
11 Bruce Jankowski	5.00	10.00
12 Jim Kearney	5.00	10.00
13 Jeff Kinney	5.00	10.00
14A Willie Lanier	7.50	15.00
14B Willie Lanier	7.50	15.00
15 Mike Livingston	5.00	10.00
16 Ed Lothamer	5.00	10.00
17 Jim Lynch	5.00	10.00
18 Jim Marsalis	5.00	10.00
19 Larry Marshall	5.00	10.00
20 Mo Moorman	5.00	10.00
21 Mike Oriard	5.00	10.00
22 Jim Otis	5.00	10.00
23 Ed Podolak	5.00	10.00
24 Kerry Reardon	5.00	10.00
25 Jack Rudnay	5.00	10.00
26A Mike Sensibaugh	5.00	10.00
26B Mike Sensibaugh	5.00	10.00
27 Sid Smith	5.00	10.00
28 Jan Stenerud	7.50	15.00
29 Otis Taylor	6.00	12.00
30 Jim Tyrer	5.00	10.00
31 Clyde Werner	5.00	10.00
32 Jerrel Wilson	5.00	10.00
33 Elmo Wright	5.00	10.00
34 Wilbur Young	5.00	10.00

1973 Chiefs Team Issue Color

The NFLPA worked with many teams in 1973 to issued photo packs to be sold at stadium concession stands. Each measures approximately 7" by 8-5/8" and features a color player photo with a blank back. A small sheet with a player checklist was included in each 6-photo pack.

COMPLETE SET (6)	30.00	60.00
1 Len Dawson	7.50	15.00
2 Bobby Bell	5.00	10.00
3 Willie Lanier	5.00	10.00
4 Jan Stenerud	5.00	10.00
5 Otis Taylor	4.00	8.00
6 Aaron Brown	4.00	8.00

1973-74 Chiefs Team Issue 5x7

This 18-card set of the Kansas City Chiefs measures approximately 5" by 7" and features black-and-white player photos with a white border. The backs are blank. The cards are unnumbered and checklisted below in alphabetical order.

COMPLETE SET (18)	60.00	120.00
1 Bob Briggs	4.00	8.00
2 Larry Brunson	4.00	8.00
3 Gary Butler	4.00	8.00
4 Dean Carlson	4.00	8.00
5 Tom Condon	4.00	8.00
6 George Daney	4.00	8.00
7 Andy Hamilton	4.00	8.00
8 Dave Hill	4.00	8.00
9 Jim Kearney	4.00	8.00
10 Mike Livingston	4.00	8.00
11 Jim Marsalis	4.00	8.00
12 Barry Pearson	4.00	8.00
13 Francis Peay	4.00	8.00
14 Kerry Reardon	4.00	8.00
15 Mike Sensibaugh	4.00	8.00
16 Bill Thomas	4.00	8.00
17 Marvin Upshaw	4.00	8.00
18 Clyde Werner	4.00	8.00

1973 Chiefs Team Issue 7x10

This set of the Kansas City Chiefs measures approximately 7 1/4" by 10 1/2" and features black-and-white player photos with a white border. The player's facsimile autograph appears across the photo with his name, position (initials), and team name below each photo. The backs are blank. The cards are unnumbered and checklisted below in alpabetical order.

COMPLETE SET (12)	50.00	100.00
1 Pete Beathard	5.00	10.00
2 Gary Butler	5.00	10.00
3 Dean Carlson	5.00	10.00
4 Willie Ellison	5.00	10.00
5 Andy Hamilton	5.00	10.00
6 Pat Holmes	5.00	10.00
7 Leroy Keyes	5.00	10.00
8 John Lohmeyer	5.00	10.00
9 Al Palewicz	5.00	10.00
10 Francis Peay	5.00	10.00
11 George Seals	5.00	10.00
12 Wayne Walton	5.00	10.00

1974 Chiefs Team Issue 7x10

Photos in this set of the Kansas City Chiefs measure approximately 7 1/4" by 10 1/4" and feature a black-and-white player image with a white border. The player's facsimile autograph appears across the photo with his name, position initials (unless noted below) and team name below each photo in small (1/8") letters. The backs are blank. The cards are unnumbered and checklisted below in alpabetical order.

COMPLETE SET (14)	50.00	100.00
1 Bobby Bell	5.00	10.00
2 Larry Brunson	4.00	8.00
3 Tom Condon	4.00	8.00
4 Len Dawson	7.50	15.00
5 Charlie Getty	4.00	8.00
6 Woody Green	4.00	8.00
7 Dave Jaynes	4.00	8.00
8 Doug Jones	4.00	8.00
9 Tom Keating	4.00	8.00
10 Cleo Miller	4.00	8.00
11 Jim Nicholson	4.00	8.00
12 Bill Thomas	4.00	8.00
13 Bob Thornbladh	4.00	8.00
14 Marvin Upshaw	4.00	8.00

1975 Chiefs Team Issue

Each of these photos measures approximately 7 1/4" by 10" and features a black-and-white head shot bordered in white. The player's name, his position (initials), and team name are printed in the lower white border, while the player's facsimile autograph is inscribed across the picture. The player name and position is printed in a different font (resembles typewriter print) than the 1976 issue. The backs carry a player biography and career summary; some of the backs also have statistics. The photos are unnumbered and checklisted below in alphabetical order. Any additions to this list are appreciated.

COMPLETE SET (19)	75.00	150.00
1 Tony Adams	4.00	8.00
2 Charlie Ane III	4.00	8.00
3 Ken Avery	4.00	8.00
4 Charlie Getty	4.00	8.00
5 Woody Green	4.00	8.00
6 Tim Kearney	4.00	8.00
7 Morris LaGrand	4.00	8.00
8 MacArthur Lane	4.00	10.00
9 Willie Lanier	5.00	10.00
10 Jim Lynch	4.00	8.00
11 Bob Maddox	4.00	8.00
12 Don Martin	4.00	8.00
13 Billy Masters	4.00	8.00
14 John Matuszak	5.00	10.00
15 Bill Peterson	4.00	8.00
16 Jan Stenerud	6.00	12.00
17 Charlie Thomas	4.00	8.00
18 Walter White	4.00	8.00
19 Paul Wiggin CO	4.00	8.00

1976 Chiefs Team Issue

This set of photos was released by the Chiefs with each measuring approximately 7 1/4" by 10." The photos include a black-and-white head shot bordered in white. The player's name appears at the left with his position (initials) in the middle and team name printed in script to the right all within the lower white border. The player's facsimile autograph is inscribed across the picture. The backs carry biography and career summary; some of the backs also have statistics. The photos are unnumbered and checklisted below in alphabetical order. Any additions to this list are appreciated.

COMPLETE SET (31)	100.00	200.00
1 Tony Adams	4.00	8.00
2 Billy Andrews	4.00	8.00
3 Charlie Ane III	4.00	8.00
4 Gary Barbaro	4.00	8.00
5 Larry Brunson	4.00	8.00
6 Tim Collier	4.00	8.00
7 Tom Condon	4.00	8.00
8 Jimbo Elrod	4.00	8.00
9 Lawrence Estes	4.00	8.00
10 Tim Gray	4.00	8.00
11 Matt Herkenhoff	4.00	8.00
12 MacArthur Lane	5.00	10.00
13 Willie Lee	4.00	8.00
14 John Lohmeyer	4.00	8.00
15 Henry Marshall	5.00	10.00
16 Billy Masters	4.00	8.00
17 Pat McNeil	4.00	8.00
18 Mike Nott	4.00	8.00
19 Orrin Olsen	4.00	8.00
20 Whitney Paul	4.00	8.00
21 Jack Rudnay	4.00	8.00
22 Keith Simons	4.00	8.00
23 Jan Stenerud	5.00	10.00
24 Steve Taylor	4.00	8.00
25 Emmitt Thomas	5.00	10.00
26 Rod Walters	4.00	8.00
27 Walter White	4.00	8.00
28 Larry Williams	4.00	8.00
29 Jerrel Wilson	4.00	8.00
30 Jim Wolf	4.00	8.00
31 Wilbur Young	4.00	8.00

1977 Chiefs Team Issue

This set of photos was released by the Chiefs with each measuring approximately 7 1/4" by 10." The photos include a black-and-white head shot bordered in white. The player's name appears at the left with his position in the middle and team name printed in script to the right all below the photo. The player's facsimile autograph is inscribed across the picture. The backs carry biographical information and/or a career summary and statistics. The photos are unnumbered and checklisted below in alphabetical order. Any additions to this list are appreciated.

COMPLETE SET (10)	40.00	80.00
1 Mark Bailey	4.00	8.00
2 Tom Bettis CO	4.00	8.00
3 John Brockington	5.00	10.00
4 Ricky Davis	4.00	8.00
5 Cliff Frazier	4.00	8.00
6 Darius Helton	4.00	8.00
7 Thomas Howard	4.00	8.00
8 Dave Rozumek	4.00	8.00
9 Bob Simmons	4.00	8.00
10 Ricky Wesson	4.00	8.00

1979 Chiefs Frito Lay

These black and white photos include the player's name, position (initials) and team name below the picture on the front. The cardbacks contain an extensive player bio and career statistics.

COMPLETE SET (8)	30.00	60.00
1 Brad Budde	4.00	8.00
2 Steve Gaunty	4.00	8.00
3 Dave Lindstrom	4.00	8.00
4 Arnold Morgado	4.00	8.00
5 Tony Samuels	4.00	8.00
6 Bob Simmons	4.00	8.00
7 Jan Stenerud	5.00	10.00
8 Art Still	4.00	8.00

1979 Chiefs Police

The 1979 Kansas City Chiefs Police set consists of ten cards co-sponsored by Hardee's Restaurants and the Kansas City (Missouri) Police Department, in addition to the Chiefs' football club. The cards measure approximately 2 5/8" by 4 1/8". The card backs discuss a football term and related legal/safety issue in a section entitled "Chief's Tips". The set is unnumbered but the player's uniform number appears on the front of the cards; the cards are numbered and ordered below by uniform number. The Chiefs' helmet logo is found on both the fronts and backs of the cards.

COMPLETE SET (10)	7.50	15.00
1 Bob Grupp	.75	1.50
4 Steve Fuller	1.00	2.00
22 Ted McKnight	.75	1.50
24 Gary Green	.75	1.50
26 Gary Barbaro	.75	1.50
32 Tony Reed	1.00	2.00
58 Jack Rudnay	.75	1.50
67 Art Still	1.00	2.00
73 Bob Simmons	.75	1.50
NNO Marv Levy CO	2.00	4.00

1979 Chiefs Team Issue

This set of Kansas City Chiefs players measures approximately 5" by 7" and features black-and-white player photos with a white border. The fronts include the player's name, position initials, and team name below the photo. The backs contain a player profile and stats but no sponsor logos. The cards are unnumbered and checklisted below in alpabetical order.

COMPLETE SET (20)	75.00	150.00
1 Mike Bell	4.00	8.00
2 Jerry Blanton	4.00	8.00
3 M.L. Carter	4.00	8.00
4 Earl Gant	4.00	8.00
5 Steve Gaunty	4.00	8.00
6 Bob Grupp	4.00	8.00
7 Charles Jackson	4.00	8.00
8 Gerald Jackson	4.00	8.00
9 Ken Kremer	4.00	8.00
10 Dave Lindstrom	4.00	8.00
11 Frank Manumaleuga	4.00	8.00
12 Arnold Morgado	4.00	8.00
13 Horace Perkins	4.00	8.00
14 Cal Peterson	4.00	8.00
15 Jerry Reese	4.00	8.00
16 Tony Samuels	4.00	8.00
17 Bob Simmons	4.00	8.00
18 J.T. Smith	5.00	10.00
19 Art Still	4.00	8.00
20 Mike Williams	4.00	8.00

1980 Chiefs Frito Lay

These black and white photos include the player's name, position initials and team name below the picture on the front. The cardbacks contain an extensive player bio and career statistics along with the Frito Lay logo.

COMPLETE SET (35)	125.00	250.00
1 Gary Barbaro	3.00	8.00
2 Ed Beckman	3.00	8.00
3 Mike Bell	3.00	8.00
4 Horace Belton	3.00	8.00
5 Jerry Blanton	3.00	8.00
6 Brad Budde	3.00	8.00
7 Carlos Carson	3.00	8.00
8 M.L. Carter	3.00	8.00
9 Herb Christopher	3.00	8.00
10 Tom Clements	4.00	10.00
11 Paul Dombrowski	3.00	8.00
12 Steve Fuller	3.00	8.00
13 Charlie Getty	3.00	8.00
14 Gary Green	3.00	8.00
15 Bob Grupp	3.00	8.00
16 James Hadnot	3.00	8.00
17 Eric Harris	3.00	8.00
18 Matt Herkenhoff	3.00	8.00
19 Thomas Howard	3.00	8.00
20 Charles Jackson	3.00	8.00
21 Dave Lindstrom	3.00	8.00
22 Mike Livingston	3.00	8.00
23 Nick Lowery	3.00	8.00
24 Dino Mangiero	3.00	8.00
25 Frank Manumaleuga	3.00	8.00
26 Henry Marshall	3.00	8.00
27 Ted McKnight	3.00	8.00
28 Don Parrish	3.00	8.00
29 Whitney Paul	3.00	8.00
30 Cal Peterson	3.00	8.00
31 Jim Rourke	3.00	8.00
32 J.T. Smith	4.00	10.00
33 Gary Spani	3.00	8.00
34 Art Still	3.00	8.00
35 Mike Williams	3.00	8.00

1980 Chiefs Police

The unnumbered, ten-card, 1980 Kansas City Chiefs Police set has been listed by the player's uniform number in the checklist below. The cards measure approximately 2 5/8" by 4 1/8". The Stenerud card was supposedly distributed on a limited basis and is thus more difficult to obtain. In addition to the Chiefs and the local law enforcement agencies, the set is sponsored by the Kiwanis Club and Frito-Lay, whose logos appear on the backs of the cards. The 1980 date can be found on the back of the cards as can "Chiefs Tips".

COMPLETE SET (10)	5.00	10.00
1 Bob Grupp	.40	1.00
3 Jan Stenerud SP	1.00	1.00
32 Tony Reed	.50	1.25
53 Whitney Paul	.40	1.00
59 Gary Spani	.40	1.00
67 Art Still	.60	1.50
86 J.T. Smith	.60	1.50
99 Mike Bell	.40	1.00
NNO Defensive Team	.50	1.25
NNO Offensive Team	.50	1.25

1980 Chiefs Team Issue

The Kansas City Chiefs issued this set of unnumbered photos that measure approximately 5" by 7" and contain black and white player photos. Each is similar to the Frito Lay photos except that there are no sponsor logos and the backs are blank. Any additions to this checklist would be appreciated.

COMPLETE SET (34)	125.00	250.00
1 Earl Gant	3.00	8.00
2 Bob Grupp	3.00	8.00
3 James Hadnot	3.00	8.00
4 Larry Heater	3.00	8.00
5 Matt Herkenhoff	3.00	8.00
6 Sylvester Hicks	3.00	8.00
7 Thomas Howard	3.00	8.00
8 Charles Jackson	3.00	8.00
9 Gerald Jackson	3.00	8.00
10 Bill Kellar	3.00	8.00
11 Bill Kenney	3.00	8.00
12 Bruce Kirchner	3.00	8.00
13 Ken Kremer	3.00	8.00
14 Frank Manumaleuga	3.00	8.00
15 Dale Markham	3.00	8.00
16 Henry Marshall	3.00	8.00
17 Ted McKnight	3.00	8.00
18 Arnold Morgado	3.00	8.00
19 Don Parrish	3.00	8.00
20 Cal Peterson	3.00	8.00
21 Tony Reed	3.00	8.00
22 Jerry Reese	3.00	8.00
23 Stan Rome	3.00	8.00
24 Donovan Rose	3.00	8.00
25 Jim Rourke	3.00	8.00
26 Jack Rudnay	3.00	8.00
27 Tony Samuels	3.00	8.00
28 Bob Simmons	3.00	8.00
29 Franky Smith	3.00	8.00
30 Kelvin Smith	3.00	8.00
31 Sam Stepney	3.00	8.00
32 Rod Walters	3.00	8.00
33 Mike Williams	3.00	8.00
34 Cecil Youngblood	3.00	8.00

1981 Chiefs Frito Lay

These black and white photos include the player's name, position (initials) and team name below the picture on the front. The cardbacks contain an extensive player bio and career statistics.

1 Mike Bell	3.00	8.00
2 Jerry Blanton	3.00	8.00
3 Curtis Bledsoe	3.00	8.00
4 Lloyd Burruss	3.00	8.00
5 Phil Cancik	3.00	8.00
6 Frank Case	3.00	8.00
7 Deron Cherry	3.00	8.00
8 Tom Condon	3.00	8.00
9 Joe Delaney	4.00	10.00
10 Bob Gagliano	3.00	8.00
11 Eric Harris	3.00	8.00
12 Marvin Harvey	3.00	8.00
13 Billy Jackson	3.00	8.00
14 Dave Klug	3.00	8.00
15 Dave Lindstrom	3.00	8.00
16 Henry Marshall	3.00	8.00
17 Stan Rome	3.00	8.00
18 Jack Rudnay	3.00	8.00
19 Willie Scott	3.00	8.00
20 Bob Simmons	3.00	8.00
21 J.T. Smith	4.00	10.00
22 Art Still	3.00	8.00
23 Roger Taylor	3.00	8.00
24 Todd Thomas	3.00	8.00

1981 Chiefs Police

The 1981 Kansas City Chiefs Police set consists of ten cards, some of which have more than one player pictured. The cards are numbered on the back as well as prominently displaying the player's uniform number on the fronts of the cards. The cards measure approximately 2 5/8" by 4 1/8". The set is sponsored by the area law enforcement agency, the Kiwanis Club, Frito-Lay, and the Kansas City Chiefs. The Kiwanis Club and Frito-Lay logos, in addition to the Chiefs helmet logo, appear on the backs of the cards. Also "Chiefs Tips" are featured on the card backs. The card backs have black print with red accent on white card stock.

COMPLETE SET (10)	1.50	4.00
1 Warpaint and Carla	.15	.40
2 Art Still	.30	.75
3 Steve Fuller and	.20	.50
4 Gary Green	.20	.50
5 Tom Condon Marv Levy	.30	.75
6 J.T. Smith	.30	.75
7 Gary Spani and	.15	.40
8 Nick Lowery and	.30	.75
9 Gary Barbaro	.20	.50
10 Henry Marshall	.15	.40

1982 Chiefs Nu-Maid Butter Tubs

This set of butter cups or tubs was released by Nu-Maid and Miami Margarine in 1982. Each includes color illustrations of the featured player and measures roughly 3 3/4" tall and 3" in diameter.

1 Gary Barbaro	2.00	5.00
2 Joe Delaney	2.00	5.00
3 Jack Rudnay	2.00	5.00
4 Gary Spani	2.00	5.00
5 Art Still	2.00	5.00

1982 Chiefs Police

The 1982 Kansas City Chiefs Police set features ten numbered (on back) cards, some of which portray more than one player. The cards measure approximately 2 5/8" by 4 1/8". The backs deviate somewhat from a standard police set in that a cartoon is utilized to drive home the sage "Chiefs Tips". This set is sponsored by the local law enforcement agency, Frito-Lay, and the Kiwanis Club. The backs contain a 1982 date and logos of the Kiwanis, Frito-Lay, and the Chiefs. Card backs have black print with red accent on white card stock. Each player's uniform number is given on the front of the card.

COMPLETE SET (10)	2.00	5.00
1 Bill Kenney and	.25	.60
2 Steve Fuller and	.40	1.00
3 Matt Herkenhoff	.20	.50
4 Art Still	.30	.75
5 Gary Spani	.20	.50
6 James Hadnot	.25	.60
7 Mike Bell	.25	.60
8 Carol Canfield	.20	.50
9 Gary Green	.25	.60
10 Joe Delaney	.40	1.00

1982 Chiefs Team Issue

This set of Kansas City Chiefs players measures approximately 5" by 7" and features black-and-white player photos with a white border. The fronts include the player's name, position initials, and team name below the photo. The backs contain a player profile and stats but no sponsor logos. The cards are unnumbered and checklisted below in alpabetical order.

1 Mike Bell	3.00	8.00
2 Dean Prater	3.00	8.00

1983 Chiefs Frito Lay

The Kansas City Chiefs issued this set sponsored by Frito Lay. The cards are unnumbered, measure approximately 5" by 7", and contain black and white player photos. The cards can be distinguished from other Chiefs Frito Lay issues by the biographical information contained on the cardback. We've noted the NFL experince years that are included on the cardbacks for easier identification. Seven lines of large text type are presented. Any additions to this checklist would be appreciated.

COMPLETE SET (14)	50.00	100.00
1 Tom Condon	3.00	8.00
2 Ellis Gardner	3.00	8.00
3 Anthony Hancock	3.00	8.00
4 Louis Haynes	3.00	8.00
5 Matt Herkenhoff	3.00	8.00
6 Thomas Howard	3.00	8.00
7 Billy Jackson	3.00	8.00
8 Charles Jackson	3.00	8.00
9 Van Jakes	3.00	8.00
10 Dave Klug	3.00	8.00
11 Dave Lindstrom	3.00	8.00
12 Adam Lingner	3.00	8.00
13 Nick Lowery	3.00	8.00
14 John Zamberlin	3.00	8.00

1983 Chiefs Police

The 1983 Kansas City Chiefs set contains ten numbered cards. The cards measure approximately 2 5/8" by 4 1/8". Sponsored by Frito-Lay, the local law enforcement agency, the Kiwanis Club, and KCTV-5, the set features cartoon "Chiefs Tips" and Crime Tips on the backs. A 1983 date plus logos of the Chiefs, Frito-Lay, the Kiwanis, and KCTV-5 also appear on the backs. Uniform numbers are given on the front of the player's card.

COMPLETE SET (10)	2.00	5.00
1 John Mackovic CO	.40	1.00
2 Tom Condon	.20	.50
3 Gary Spani	.20	.50
4 Carlos Carson	.30	.75
5 Brad Budde	.25	.60
6 Lloyd Burruss	.20	.50
7 Gary Green	.25	.60
8 Mike Bell	.25	.60
9 Nick Lowery	.40	1.00
10 Sandi Byrd	.20	.50

1983 Chiefs Team Issue

This set of Kansas City Chiefs players measures approximately 5" by 7" and features black-and-white player photos with a white border. The fronts include the player's name, position initials, and team name below the photo. The backs contain a player profile and stats but no sponsor logos. The cards are unnumbered and checklisted below in alphabetical order.

COMPLETE SET (20)	60.00	120.00
1 Jim Arnold	3.00	8.00
2 Ed Beckman	3.00	8.00
3 Todd Blackledge	3.00	8.00
4 Jerry Blanton	3.00	8.00
5 Carlos Carson	3.00	8.00
6 Calvin Daniels	3.00	8.00
7 Albert Lewis	4.00	10.00
8 Dave Lindstrom	3.00	8.00
9 David Lutz	3.00	8.00
10 Kyle McNorton	3.00	8.00
11 Stephone Paige	3.00	8.00
12 Steve Potter	3.00	8.00
13 Lawrence Ricks	3.00	8.00
14 Durwood Roquemore	3.00	8.00
15 Bob Rush	3.00	8.00
16 Willie Scott	3.00	8.00
17 Lucious Smith	3.00	8.00
18 Ken Thomas	3.00	8.00
19 James Walker	3.00	8.00
20 Ron Wetzel	3.00	8.00

1984 Chiefs Police

This numbered (on back) ten-card set features the Kansas City Chiefs. Backs contain a "Chiefs Tip" and a "Crime Tip," each with an accompanying cartoon. Cards measure approximately 2 5/8" by 4 1/8". Cards were also sponsored by Frito-Lay and KCTV.

COMPLETE SET (10)	2.00	5.00
1 John Mackovic CO	.30	.75
2 Deron Cherry	.40	1.00
3 Bill Kenney	.25	.60
4 Henry Marshall	.20	.50
5 Nick Lowery	.30	.75
6 Theotis Brown	.25	.60
7 Stephone Paige	.50	1.25
8 Gary Spani and	.30	.75
9 Albert Lewis	.40	1.00
10 Carlos Carson	.30	.75

1984 Chiefs QuikTrip

This 16-card set was sponsored by QuikTrip and measures approximately 5" by 7". The front features a black and white posed photo of the player and the back is blank.

COMPLETE SET (16)	60.00	120.00
1 Mike Bell	3.00	8.00
2 Todd Blackledge	3.00	8.00
3 Brad Budde	3.00	8.00
4 Lloyd Burruss	3.00	8.00
5 Carlos Carson	3.00	8.00
6 Gary Green	3.00	8.00
7 Anthony Hancock	3.00	8.00
8 Eric Harris	3.00	8.00
9 Lamar Hunt OWN	4.00	10.00
10 Bill Kenney	3.00	8.00
11 Ken Kremer	3.00	8.00
12 Nick Lowery	3.00	8.00
13 John Mackovic CO	3.00	8.00
14 J.T. Smith	3.00	8.00
15 Gary Spani	3.00	8.00
16 Art Still	3.00	8.00

1984 Chiefs Team Issue

This set of Kansas City Chiefs players measures approximately 5" by 7" and features black-and-white player photos with a white border. The fronts include the player's name, position initials, and team name below the photo. The backs contain a player profile and stats but no sponsor logos. The cards are unnumbered and checklisted below in alphabetical order. Any additions to this list are appreciated.

1 Brad Budde	3.00	8.00
2 Bill Kenney	3.00	8.00
3 Scott Radecic	3.00	8.00

1985 Chiefs Frito Lay

The Kansas City Chiefs issued this set sponsored by Frito Lay. The cards are unnumbered, measure approximately 5" by 7", and contain black and white player photos. The cards can be distinguished from other Chiefs Frito Lay issues by the biographical information contained on the cardback. Many lines of text are presented with almost a full cardback of information. Any additions to this checklist would be appreciated.

COMPLETE SET (4)	15.00	30.00
1 Pete Koch	3.00	8.00
2 Adam Lingner	3.00	8.00
3 Jeff Paine	3.00	8.00
4 Mark Robinson	3.00	8.00

1985 Chiefs Police

This ten-card set features the Kansas City Chiefs. Cards in the set measure approximately 2 5/8" by 4 1/8". The card back gives the card number and the year of issue; printing is in black and red on white card stock. The set was sponsored by Frito-Lay, KCTV-5, and area law enforcement agencies. Two cartoons are featured on the back of each card picturing a Chiefs Tip and a Crime Tip.

COMPLETE SET (10)	2.00	5.00
1 John Mackovic CO	.30	.75
2 Herman Heard	.20	.50
3 Bill Kenney	.30	.75
4 Der.Cherry L.Burruss	.30	.75
5 Jim Arnold	.20	.50
6 Kevin Ross	.25	.60
7 David Lutz	.20	.50
8 Chiefettes Cheerleaders	.20	.50
9 Bill Maas	.30	.75
10 Art Still	.30	.75

1985 Chiefs Team Issue

This set of Kansas City Chiefs players measures approximately 5" by 7" and features black-and-white player photos with a white border. The fronts include the player's name, position initials, and team name below the photo. The backs contain a player profile and stats but no sponsor logos. The cards are unnumbered and checklisted below in alphabetical order.

COMPLETE SET (7)	25.00	50.00
1 Deron Cherry	3.00	8.00
2 Jeff Paine	3.00	8.00
3 Jerry Blanton	3.00	8.00
4 Anthony Hancock	3.00	8.00
5 Carlos Carson	3.00	8.00
6 Mark Robinson	3.00	8.00
7 Todd Blackledge	3.00	8.00

1986 Chiefs Frito Lay

The Kansas City Chiefs issued this set sponsored by Frito Lay. The cards are unnumbered, measure approximately 5" by 7", and contain black and white player photos. The cards can be distinguished from other Chiefs Frito Lay issues by the biographical information contained on the cardback. We've noted the NFL experince years that are included on the cardbacks for easier identification. Seven lines of large text type are presented. Any additions to this checklist would be appreciated.

COMPLETE SET (7)	25.00	50.00
1 Mark Adickes	3.00	8.00
2 Tom Baugh	3.00	8.00
3 Lewis Colbert	3.00	8.00
4 Rick Donnalley	3.00	8.00
5 Dino Hackett	3.00	8.00
6 Bill Kenney	3.00	8.00
7 Pete Koch	3.00	8.00

1986 Chiefs Louis Rich

The Kansas City Chiefs issued this set sponsored by Louis Rich and The Kansas City Star. The cards are blankbacked, unnumbered, measure approximately 5" by 7", and contain black and white player photos. The cards can be distinguished from other Chiefs Louis Rich issues by the team name appearing in all upper case letters below the player photo. Any additions to this list are appreciated.

COMPLETE SET (5)	20.00	40.00
1 Carlos Carson	3.00	8.00
2 Calvin Daniels	3.00	8.00
3 Herman Heard	3.00	8.00
4 Albert Lewis	4.00	10.00
5 John Mackovic CO	3.00	8.00

1986 Chiefs Police

This ten-card set features the Kansas City Chiefs. Cards in the set measure approximately 2 5/8" by 4 1/8" and the card back gives the card number and the year of issue. Printing is in black and red on white card stock. The set was sponsored by Frito-Lay, KCTV-5, and area law enforcement agencies. Two cartoons are featured on the back of each card picturing a "Chiefs Tip" and a "Crime Tip".

COMPLETE SET (10)	2.50	6.00
1 John Mackovic CO	.30	.75
2 Willie Lanier	.60	1.50
3 Stephone Paige	.30	.75
4 Brad Budde	.20	.50
5 Nick Lowery	.25	.60
6 Scott Radecic	.20	.50
7 Mike Pruitt	.25	.60
8 Albert Lewis	.30	.75
9 Todd Blackledge	.25	.60
10 Deron Cherry	.25	.60

1986 Chiefs Team Issue

The Kansas City Chiefs issued this set of unnumbered photos that measure approximately 5" by 7" and contain black and white player photos. Each is similar to the 1986 Frito Lay photos except that there are no sponsor logos and the backs are blank. Note also that the design is nearly identical to the 1980 Cheifs Team Issue photos except that the player's name is slightly (1/32") larger on the 1986 issue. Any additions to this checklist would be appreciated.

COMPLETE SET (16)	50.00	100.00
1 Boyce Green	3.00	8.00
2 Anthony Hancock	3.00	8.00
3 Emile Harry	3.00	8.00
4 Greg Hill	3.00	8.00
5 Eric Holle	3.00	8.00
6 Brian Jozwiak	3.00	8.00
7 Bill Kenney	3.00	8.00
8 Pete Koch	3.00	8.00
9 Kit Lathrop	3.00	8.00
10 Adam Lingner	3.00	8.00
11 Aaron Pearson	3.00	8.00
12 Mike Pruitt	4.00	10.00
13 Frank Seurer	3.00	8.00
14 Jeff Smith	3.00	8.00
15 Gary Spani	3.00	8.00
16 Art Still	3.00	8.00

1987 Chiefs Louis Rich

The Kansas City Chiefs issued this set sponsored by Louis Rich and The Kansas City Star. The cards are blankbacked, unnumbered, measure approximately 5" by 7", and contain black and white player photos. The cards can be distinguished from other Chiefs Louis Rich issues by the team name appearing in all lower case letters below the player photo. There are 16-known cards in the set. Any additions to this checklist would be appreciated.

COMPLETE SET (16)	40.00	80.00
1 John Alt	2.50	6.00
2 Carlos Carson	2.50	6.00
3 Deron Cherry	2.50	6.00
4 Sherman Cocroft	2.50	6.00
5 Irv Eatman	2.50	6.00
6 Frank Gansz	2.50	6.00
7 Dino Hackett	2.50	6.00
8 Jonathan Hayes	2.50	6.00
9 Bill Kenney	2.50	6.00
10 Albert Lewis	3.00	8.00
11 Nick Lowery	2.50	6.00
12 Bill Maas	2.50	6.00
13 Christian Okoye	3.00	8.00
14 Stephone Paige	2.50	6.00
15 Paul Palmer	2.50	6.00
16 Kevin Ross	2.50	6.00

1987 Chiefs Police

This ten-card set features the Kansas City Chiefs. Cards in the set measure approximately 2 5/8" by 4 1/8". The card back gives the card number and the year of issue; printing is in black and red on white card stock. The set was sponsored by Frito-Lay, US Sprint, KCTV-5, and area law enforcement agencies. Two cartoons are featured on the back of each card picturing a "Chiefs Tip" and a "Crime Tip". Reportedly more than 4.5 million cards were given out by over 275 different

police departments.
COMPLETE SET (10) 1.50 4.00
1 Frank Gansz CO .15 .40
2 Tim Cofield .15 .40
3 Deron Cherry .25 .60
4 Chiefs Cheerleaders .15 .40
5 Jeff Smith RB .15 .40
6 Rick Donnalley .15 .40
7 Lloyd Burruss .20 .50
8 Dino Hackett .15 .40
9 Bill Maas .15 .40
10 Carlos Carson .25 .60

1987 Chiefs Price Chopper

The Kansas City Chiefs issued this set sponsored by Price Chopper. Each card measures approximately 5" by 7" with a black and white player photo on the front. The cardbacks feature a brief player bio and vital statistics along with a "Compliments of Price Chopper" notation at the bottom. The team name appears on the cardfront in all upper case letters below the player photo and to the left. The player's name and position (initial) appear below the photo and to the right of the team name. Any additions to this checklist would be appreciated.
1 Tom Baugh 2.50 6.00
2 Lloyd Burruss 2.50 6.00

1988 Chiefs Gatorade

The Kansas City Chiefs issued this set sponsored by Gatorade. The cardbacks contain the player's name, biographical information and a Gatorade sponsorship logo. Each measures approximately 5" by 7", and features a typical black and white player photo. The team name appears on the cardfront in all lower case letters below the player photo. Any additions to this checklist would be appreciated.
COMPLETE SET (10) 25.00 50.00
1 Kelly Goodburn 2.50 6.00
2 Emile Harry 2.50 6.00
3 Bill Kenney 2.50 6.00
4 Albert Lewis 2.50 6.00
5 Nick Lowery 2.50 6.00
6 Bill Maas 2.50 6.00
7 Stephone Paige 2.50 6.00
8 Kevin Ross 2.50 6.00
9 Angelo Snipes 2.50 6.00
10 Kitrick Taylor 2.50 6.00

1988 Chiefs Police

The 1988 Police Kansas City Chiefs set contains ten numbered cards each measuring approximately 2 5/8" by 4 1/8". There are nine player cards and one coach card. The backs have one "Chiefs Tip" and one "Crime Tip."
COMPLETE SET (10) 2.00 5.00
1 Frank Gansz CO .20 .50
2 Bill Kenney .25 .60
3 Carlos Carson .25 .60
4 Paul Palmer .25 .60
5 Christian Okoye .30 .75
6 Mark Adickes .20 .50
7 Bill Maas .20 .50
8 Albert Lewis .30 .75
9 Deron Cherry .25 .60
10 Stephone Paige .30 .75

1989 Chiefs Price Chopper/Farmland

The Kansas City Chiefs issued this set with each photo sponsored by either Price Chopper or Farmland, but not both. Each card measures approximately 5" by 7" with a black and white player photo on the front. The cardbacks feature a brief player bio and vital statistics along with a "Compliments of Price Chopper" or "Compliments of Farmland" notation at the bottom. The team name appears on the cardfront in all lower case letters below the player photo and to the left. The player's name and position (initial) appear below the team name with the sponsorship logo printed on the far right. Any additions to this checklist would be appreciated.
COMPLETE SET (4) 12.50 25.00
1 Deron Cherry 2.00 5.00
2 Stephone Paige 2.00 5.00
3 Neil Smith 3.00 8.00
4 Derrick Thomas 5.00 12.00

1989 Chiefs Police

The 1989 Police Kansas City Chiefs set contains ten cards measuring approximately 2 5/8" by 4 1/8". The fronts have white borders and color action photos; the horizontally-oriented backs have safety tips. The set was sponsored by Western Auto and KCTV Channel 5. These cards were printed on very thin stock.
COMPLETE SET (10) 2.00 5.00
1 Marty Schottenheimer CO .30 .75
2 Irv Eatman .20 .50
3 Kevin Ross .25 .60
4 Bill Maas .20 .50
5 Chiefs Cheerleaders .20 .50
6 Carlos Carson .25 .60
7 Steve DeBerg .30 .75
8 Jonathan Hayes .25 .60
9 Deron Cherry .25 .60
10 Dino Hackett .20 .50

1991 Chiefs Star Price Chopper

The Kansas City Chiefs issued this set sponsored by The Kansas City Star and Price Chopper stores. The cardbacks are blank and each measures approximately 5" by 7" with a black and white player photo on the front. The team name appears on the cardfront in all lower case letters below the player photo. The player's name and position (initials) appear below the photo in all caps as well. The two sponsor logos appear on either side of the player name. Note that the basic Price Chopper logo is the one used. Any additions to this checklist would be appreciated.
COMPLETE SET (4) 8.00 20.00
1 Derrick Thomas 3.00 6.00
2 Steve DeBerg 1.50 4.00
3 Neil Smith 2.00 5.00
4 Nick Lowery 2.00 5.00

1991 Chiefs Team Issue

The Chiefs issued these 5" by 7" black and white photos in 1991. Each includes a portrait shot of the featured player with his name, position initials, and team name below the photo in all capital letters. They are nearly identical to the 1993 photos, but the team name in 1991 is slightly larger in size (roughly 1 3/4" long). The photo backs are blank.
COMPLETE SET (4) 6.00 15.00
1 Tim Barnett 1.50 4.00
2 Todd McNair 1.50 4.00
3 Tom Sims 1.50 4.00
4 Neil Smith 2.00 5.00

1992 Chiefs Intimidator Bio Sheets

Produced by Intimidator, each of these bio sheets measures approximately 8 1/2" by 10 1/2" and was printed on thick card stock. The fronts display a large glossy color player photo framed by gold foil. The backs carry two black-and-white player photos, pro career summary, college career summary, and personal as well as biographical information. The bio sheets are unnumbered and checklisted below in alphabetical order.
COMPLETE SET (12) 15.00 30.00
1 Dave Krieg 1.50 4.00
2 Albert Lewis 1.25 3.00
3 Nick Lowery 1.25 3.00
4 Bill Maas 1.00 2.50
5 Christian Okoye 1.50 4.00
6 Kevin Ross 1.25 3.00
7 Dan Saleaumua 1.00 2.50
8 Neil Smith 1.50 4.00
9 Percy Snow 1.00 2.50
10 Derrick Thomas 3.00 8.00
11 Harvey Williams 1.25 3.00
12 Barry Word 1.25 3.00

1993 Chiefs Team Issue

The Chiefs issued these 5" by 7" black and white photos in 1993. Each includes a portrait shot of the featured player with his name, position initials, and team name below the photo in all capital letters. They are nearly identical to the 1991 photos, but the team name in 1993 is slightly smaller in size (roughly 1 3/8" to 1 1/2" long). The photo backs are blank.
COMPLETE SET (24) 40.00 80.00
1 Kimble Anders 1.50 4.00
2 Erick Anderson 1.50 4.00
3 Bryan Barker 1.50 4.00
4 J.J. Birden 1.50 4.00
5 Matt Blundin 1.50 4.00
6 Dale Carter 2.00 5.00
7 Keith Cash 1.50 4.00
8 Derrick Graham 1.50 4.00
9 Tim Grunhard 1.50 4.00
10 Tony Hargain 1.50 4.00
11 Jonathan Hayes 1.50 4.00
12 Fred Jones 1.50 4.00
13 Darren Mickell 1.50 4.00
14 Charles Mincy 1.50 4.00
15 Tracy Rogers 1.50 4.00
16 Will Shields 1.50 4.00
17 Ricky Siglar 1.50 4.00
18 Tracy Simien 1.50 4.00
19 Tony Smith 1.50 4.00
20 Jay Taylor 1.50 4.00
21 Doug Terry 1.50 4.00
22 Bennie Thompson 1.50 4.00
23 Joe Valerio 1.50 4.00
24 Todd Young 1.50 4.00

1996 Chiefs Star Price Chopper

The Kansas City Chiefs issued this set sponsored by The Kansas City Star and Price Chopper. The cardbacks are blank and each measures approximately 5" by 7" with a black and white player photo on the front. The team name appears on the cardfront in all upper case letters below the player photo and to the left. The player's name and position (initial) appear below the photo in all caps as well. The two sponsor logos appear on either side of the player name. Note that the Price Chopper "Best Price" logo is the one used. Any additions to this checklist would be appreciated.
COMPLETE SET (15) 25.00 50.00
1 Marcus Allen 3.00 6.00
2 Kimble Anders 1.50 4.00
3 Donnell Bennett 1.50 4.00
4 Steve Bono 1.50 4.00
5 Vaughn Booker 1.50 4.00
6 Mark Collins 1.50 4.00
7 Jeff Criswell 1.50 4.00
8 Anthony Davis 1.50 4.00
9 Len Dawson 3.00 6.00
10 Pellom McDaniels 1.50 4.00
11 Dan Saleaumua 1.50 4.00
12 Derrick Thomas 3.00 6.00
13 Reggie Tongue 1.50 4.00
14 Tamarick Vanover 1.50 4.00
15 Jerome Woods 1.50 4.00

1997 Chiefs Score

This 15-card set of the Kansas City Chiefs was distributed in five-card packs with a suggested retail price of $1.99. The fronts feature color action player photos with white borders and the player's name and team logo printed in team color foil at the bottom. The backs carry player information and career statistics. Platinum Team parallel cards were randomly seeded in packs featuring all foil cardfronts.
COMPLETE SET (15) 2.00 5.00
*PLATINUM TEAMS: 1X TO 2X
1 Lake Dawson .15 .40
2 Tamarick Vanover .15 .40
3 Marcus Allen .30 .75
4 Neil Smith .15 .40
5 Derrick Thomas .30 .75
6 Kimble Anders .15 .40
7 Chris Penn .08 .25
8 Elvis Grbac .15 .40
9 Mark Collins .08 .25
10 Greg Hill .15 .40
11 Reggie Tongue .08 .25
12 James Hasty .08 .25
13 Dale Carter .08 .25
14 Jerome Woods .08 .25
15 Sean LaChapelle .08 .25

2006 Chiefs Donruss Thanksgiving Classic

COMPLETE SET (7) 4.00 8.00
KC1 Trent Green .50 1.25
KC2 Larry Johnson .50 1.25
KC3 Eddie Kennison .50 1.25
KC4 Tony Gonzalez .60 1.50
KC5 Tamba Hali .75 2.00
KC6 Marcus Allen 1.00 2.50
NNO Cover Card CL .20 .50

2006 Chiefs Topps

COMPLETE SET (12) 3.00 6.00
KC1 Derrick Johnson .25 .60
KC2 Larry Johnson .25 .60
KC3 Trent Green .25 .60
KC4 Samie Parker .25 .60
KC5 Tony Gonzalez .30 .75
KC6 Dante Hall .25 .60
KC7 Eddie Kennison .25 .60
KC8 Priest Holmes .25 .60
KC9 Patrick Surtain .25 .60
KC10 Sammy Knight .20 .50
KC11 Tamba Hali .40 1.00
KC12 Brodie Croyle .25 .60

2007 Chiefs Topps

COMPLETE SET (12) 2.50 5.00
1 Tony Gonzalez .50 1.25
2 Trent Green .40 1.00
3 Larry Johnson .40 1.00
4 Derrick Johnson .40 1.00
5 Eddie Kennison .40 1.00
6 Samie Parker .40 1.00
7 Tamba Hali .40 1.00
8 Damon Huard .50 1.25
9 Dwayne Bowe .40 1.00
10 Jared Allen .40 1.00
11 Ty Law .60 1.50
12 Donnie Edwards .40 1.00

2008 Chiefs Topps

COMPLETE SET (12) 2.50 5.00
1 Napoleon Harris .40 1.00
2 Dwayne Bowe .50 1.25
3 Tony Gonzalez .50 1.25
4 Damon Huard .40 1.00
5 Larry Johnson .40 1.00
6 Tamba Hali .40 1.00
7 Brodie Croyle .50 1.25
8 Kolby Smith .40 1.00
9 Donnie Edwards .40 1.00
10 Derrick Johnson .40 1.00
11 Glenn Dorsey .40 1.00
12 Jamaal Charles .60 1.50

1970 Chiquita Team Logo Stickers

In 1970, Chiquita produced team logo stickers for the 26 pro football teams. We have sequenced these unnumbered stickers alphabetically below. Both Boston and New England Patriots versions of that team's sticker were issued allowing that these stickers may have first appeared in the late 1960s.

COMPLETE SET (26) 175.00 350.00
1 Atlanta Falcons 6.00 12.00
2 Baltimore Colts 7.50 15.00
3 Boston Patriots 20.00 40.00
4 Buffalo Bills 7.50 15.00
5 Chicago Bears 7.50 15.00
6 Cincinnati Bengals 6.00 12.00
7 Cleveland Browns 7.50 15.00
8 Dallas Cowboys 10.00 20.00
9 Denver Broncos 7.50 15.00
10 Detroit Lions 6.00 12.00
11 Green Bay Packers 10.00 20.00
12 Houston Oilers 6.00 12.00
13 Kansas City Chiefs 6.00 12.00
14 Los Angeles Rams 6.00 12.00
15 Miami Dolphins 7.50 15.00
16 Minnesota Vikings 7.50 15.00
17 New England Patriots 6.00 12.00
18 New Orleans Saints 6.00 12.00
19 New York Giants 7.50 15.00
20 New York Jets 7.50 15.00
21 Oakland Raiders 10.00 20.00
22 Philadelphia Eagles 6.00 12.00
23 Pittsburgh Steelers 10.00 20.00
24 San Diego Chargers 6.00 12.00
25 San Francisco 49ers 7.50 15.00
26 St. Louis Cardinals 6.00 12.00
27 Washington Redskins 7.50 15.00

1972 Chiquita NFL Slides

This set consists of 13-slides and a plastic viewer for viewing the slides. Each slide measures approximately 3 9/16" by 1 3/4" and features two players (one on each side); each of the 26 NFL teams is represented by one player. Each side has a player summary on its middle portion, with two small color action slides at each end stacked one above the other. When the slide is placed in the viewer, the two bottom slides, which are identical, reveal the first player. Flipping the slide over reveals the other player biography and enables one to view the other two slides, which show the second player. The text on each slide can be found printed in either black or blue ink. Each side of the slides is numbered as listed below. The set is considered complete without the viewer. In 1972, collectors could receive a viewer and a complete set of 13-slides by sending in 35-cents, 5-NFL Logo Stickers from Chiquita bananas, and a cash register receipt showing $15 worth of produce purchases made at the store.
COMPLETE SET (13) 40.00 100.00
*BLUE: .5X TO 1.2X BLACK
1 Joe Greene 12.50 30.00
B.Lilly
3 Bill Bergey 5.00 12.00
G.Collins
5 Walt Sweeney 4.00 10.00
Bub.Smith
7 Larry Wilson 5.00 12.00
Fred Carr
9 Mac Percival 5.00 12.00
John Brodie
11 Lem Barney 5.00 12.00
Ron Yary
13 Curt Knight 4.00 10.00
A.Haymond
15 Floyd Little 5.00 12.00
G.Philbin
17 Jim Mitchell 4.00 10.00
Paul Costa
19 Jake Kupp 4.00 10.00
Ben Hawkins
21 Johnny Robinson 4.00 10.00
G.Webster
23 Mercury Morris 6.00 15.00
Willie Brown
25 Ron Johnson 4.00 10.00
Jon Morris
NNO Yellow Viewer 6.00 15.00
NNO Red Viewer 6.00 15.00
NNO Blue Viewer 6.00 15.00

1970 Clark Volpe

This 66-card set is actually a collection of team sets. Each team subset contains between six and nine cards. These unnumbered cards are listed below alphabetically by player within team as follows: Chicago Bears (1-8), Cincinnati Bengals (9-14), Cleveland Browns (15-21), Detroit Lions (22-30), Green Bay Packers (31-39), Kansas City Chiefs (40-48), Minnesota Vikings (49-57), St. Louis Cardinals (58-66). The cards measure approximately 7 1/2" by 9 15/16" (or 7 1/2" by 14" with mail-in tab intact). The back of the (top) drawing portion describes the mail-in offers for tumblers, posters, etc. The bottom tab is a business-reply mail-in card addressed to Clark Oil and Refining Corporation to the attention of Alex Karras. The artist for these drawings was Nicholas Volpe. The cards are typically found with tabs intact and hence they are priced that way below.
COMPLETE SET (66) 200.00 400.00
1 Ronnie Bull 4.00 8.00
2 Dick Butkus 15.00 30.00
3 Lee Roy Caffey 4.00 8.00
4 Bobby Douglass 4.00 8.00
5 Dick Gordon 4.00 8.00
6 Bennie McRae 4.00 8.00
7 Ed O'Bradovich 4.00 8.00
8 George Seals 4.00 8.00
9 Bill Bergey 5.00 10.00
10 Jess Phillips 4.00 8.00
11 Mike Reid 5.00 10.00
12 Paul Robinson 4.00 8.00
13 Bob Trumpy 5.00 10.00
14 Sam Wyche 5.00 10.00
15 Erich Barnes 4.00 8.00
16 Gary Collins 4.00 8.00
17 Gene Hickerson 5.00 10.00
18 Jim Houston 4.00 8.00
19 Leroy Kelly 6.00 12.00
20 Ernie Kellerman 4.00 8.00
21 Bill Nelsen 4.00 8.00
22 Lem Barney 6.00 12.00
23 Mel Farr 4.00 8.00
24 Larry Hand 4.00 8.00
25 Alex Karras 7.50 15.00
26 Mike Lucci 4.00 8.00
27 Bill Munson 4.00 8.00
28 Charlie Sanders 5.00 10.00
29 Tom Vaughn 4.00 8.00
30 Wayne Walker 4.00 8.00
31 Lionel Aldridge 4.00 8.00
32 Donny Anderson 5.00 10.00
33 Ken Bowman 4.00 8.00
34 Carroll Dale 4.00 8.00
35 Jim Grabowski 4.00 8.00
36 Ray Nitschke 7.50 15.00
37 Dave Robinson 5.00 10.00
38 Travis Williams 4.00 8.00
39 Willie Wood 6.00 12.00
40 Fred Arbanas 4.00 8.00
41 Bobby Bell 6.00 12.00
42 Aaron Brown 4.00 8.00
43 Buck Buchanan 6.00 12.00
44 Len Dawson 12.50 25.00
45 Jim Marsalis 4.00 8.00
46 Jerry Mays 4.00 8.00
47 Johnny Robinson 4.00 8.00
48 Jim Tyrer 4.00 8.00
49 Bill Brown 5.00 10.00
50 Fred Cox 4.00 8.00
51 Gary Cuozzo 4.00 8.00
52 Carl Eller 6.00 12.00
53 Jim Marshall 6.00 12.00
54 Dave Osborn 4.00 8.00
55 Alan Page 7.50 15.00
56 Mick Tingelhoff 5.00 10.00
57 Gene Washington Vik 4.00 8.00
58 Pete Beathard 4.00 8.00
59 John Gilliam 4.00 8.00
60 Jim Hart 5.00 10.00
61 Johnny Roland 4.00 8.00
62 Jackie Smith 6.00 12.00
63 Larry Stallings 4.00 8.00
64 Roger Wehrli 5.00 10.00
65 Dave Williams 4.00 8.00
66 Larry Wilson 6.00 12.00

1992 Classic NFL Game

The 1992 Classic NFL Game football set consists of 60 standard-size cards, a travel game board, player piece and die, rules, and scoreboard. Apparently cards number 13 and 51 were never issued. The game board included with each 60-card blister pack featured a football field and a list of plays at each end with the outcome of each play determining by a roll of the die. The board is folded in half and measures approximately 15 1/2" by 6" after unfolding. The rules for the game are printed on the backs of the Andre Ware and Cris Dishman cards. The cards measure the standard size. The fronts feature color player photos with a dusty rose inner border and a dark blue outer border. The player's name and position appear in a black bar at the lower right corner. The horizontal backs are white and carry a second color player photo, a "personal bio" feature, and five trivia questions with answers.
COMPLETE SET (60) 2.40 6.00
1 Steve Atwater .01 .05
2 Louis Oliver .01 .05
3 Ronnie Lott .02 .10
4 Reggie White .07 .20
5 Cortez Kennedy .02 .10
6 Derrick Thomas .07 .20
7 Pat Swilling .02 .10
8 Cornelius Bennett .02 .10
9 Mark Rypien .02 .10
10 Todd Marinovich .01 .05
11 Steve Young .30 .75
12 Warren Moon .07 .20
14 Hugh Millen .01 .05
15 John Friesz .02 .10
16 John Elway .60 1.50
17 Chris Miller .02 .10
18 Jim Everett .02 .10
19 Emmitt Smith .60 1.50
20 Johnny Johnson .01 .05
21 Thurman Thomas .07 .20
22 Leonard Russell .02 .10
23 Rodney Hampton .02 .10
24 Marion Butts .02 .10
25 Neal Anderson .02 .10
26 Barry Sanders .60 1.50
27 Dexter Carter .01 .05
28 Gaston Green .01 .05
29 Barry Word .01 .05
30 Eric Bieniemy .01 .05
31 Nick Bell .01 .05
32 Reggie Cobb .01 .05
33 Jay Novacek .07 .20
34 Keith Jackson .02 .10
35 Eric Green .02 .10
36 Lawrence Dawsey .02 .10
37 Mike Pritchard .01 .05
38 Michael Haynes .02 .10
39 James Lofton .02 .10
40 Art Monk .02 .10
41 Herman Moore .10 .30
42 Andre Rison .07 .20
43 Wendell Davis .01 .05
44 Sterling Sharpe .02 .10
45 Fred Barnett .02 .10
46 Rob Moore .02 .10
47 Gary Clark .02 .10
48 Wesley Carroll .01 .05
49 Michael Irvin .07 .20
50 John Taylor .02 .10
52 Ray Bentley .01 .05
53 Eric Swann .02 .10
54 Amp Lee .01 .05
55 Darryl Williams .01 .05
56 Wilber Marshall .01 .05
57 Siran Stacy .01 .05
58 Chip Lohmiller .01 .05
59 Rodney Culver .02 .10
60 Tommy Vardell .02 .10
NNO Cris Dishman .01 .05
NNO Andre Ware .02 .10

1992 Classic Show Promos 20

This 20-card standard-size set was issued one card at a time at the various shows throughout the year where Classic maintained a presence or booth. Typically the cards were given out free to attendees while supplies lasted. The cards all read "Promo Card x of 20" prominently on the card back. The cards are done in several different styles depending on the Classic issue that was being promoted by that particular card.
COMPLETE SET (20) 15.00 30.00
4 David Klingler .20 .50
(1992 Sports Spectacular)
6 Quentin Coryatt .20 .50
(July 1992 Arlington Marcus show)
18 David Klingler .20 .50
(1992 Tri-Star Houston)

1992 Classic World Class Athletes

Packaged in a high impact clam shell, this 60-card standard-size set features current and past world class athletes. The production run was 295,000 sets, and an enclosed certificate of limited edition carries the set serial number. A few athletes had autographs randomly inserted into the factory sets. We have noted those cards at the end of our checklist.
COMP.FACT SET (60) 1.60 4.00
55 Desmond Howard FB .05 .15
56 Rocket Ismail FB .05 .15
57 Deion Sanders BB .08 .25
FB

1993 Classic TONX

These 150 TONX (or player caps) were sold in a clear plastic bag; the attached paper display tag advertises that 123 players and 27 quarterbacks from all NFL teams are featured in the set. Each tonx measures approximately 1 5/8" in diameter and features a full-bleed color action player photo.
COMPLETE SET (150) 125.00 200.00
1 Troy Aikman 2.50 6.00
2 Eric Allen .30 .75
3 Terry Allen .60 1.50
4 Morten Andersen .30 .75
5 Neal Anderson .30 .75
6 Flipper Anderson .30 .75
7 Steve Atwater .30 .75
8 Carl Banks .30 .75
9 Patrick Bates .30 .75
10 Cornelius Bennett .40 1.00
11 Rod Bernstine .30 .75
12 Jerome Bettis 3.00 8.00
13 Steve Beuerlein .40 1.00
14 Bennie Blades .30 .75
15 Brian Blades .40 1.00
16 Drew Bledsoe 2.00 5.00
17 Tim Brown .75 2.00
18 Terrell Buckley .30 .75
19 Marion Butts .40 1.00
20 Mark Carrier DB .30 .75
21 Anthony Carter .40 1.00
22 Cris Carter .75 2.00
23 Dale Carter .40 1.00
24 Ray Childress .40 1.00
25 Gary Clark .40 1.00
26 Reggie Cobb .30 .75
27 Marco Coleman .30 .75
28 Curtis Conway .50 1.25
29 John Copeland .40 1.00
30 Quentin Coryatt .30 .75
31 Randall Cunningham .60 1.50
32 Eric Curry .40 1.00
33 Lawrence Dawsey .30 .75
34 Chris Doleman .40 1.00
35 Vaughn Dunbar .30 .75
36 Henry Ellard .40 1.00
37 John Elway 6.00 12.00
38 Steve Emtman .30 .75
39 Ricky Ervins .30 .75
40 Jim Everett .30 .75
41 Brett Favre 6.00 12.00
42 Barry Foster .40 1.00
43 Cleveland Gary .30 .75
44 Jeff George .50 1.25
45 Sean Gilbert .40 1.00
46 Ernest Givins .30 .75
47 Harold Green .30 .75
48 Kevin Greene .40 1.00
49 Paul Gruber .30 .75
50 Charles Haley .40 1.00
51 Rodney Hampton .40 1.00
52 Jim Harbaugh .60 1.50
53 Ronnie Harmon .30 .75
54 Michael Haynes .40 1.00
55 Garrison Hearst .75 2.00
56 Randal Hill .30 .75
57 Merril Hoge .30 .75
58 Pierce Holt .30 .75
59 Jeff Hostetler .40 1.00
60 Stan Humphries .40 1.00
61 Michael Irvin .75 2.00
62 Keith Jackson .40 1.00
63 Rickey Jackson .30 .75
64 Haywood Jeffires .30 .75
65 Pepper Johnson .30 .75
66 Brent Jones .40 1.00
67 Marvin Jones .30 .75
68 Seth Joyner .40 1.00
69 Jim Kelly 1.25 3.00
70 Cortez Kennedy .40 1.00
71 David Klingler .30 .75
72 Bernie Kosar .40 1.00
73 Reggie Langhorne .30 .75
74 Mo Lewis .30 .75
75 Howie Long .75 2.00
76 Ronnie Lott .40 1.00
77 Charles Mann .30 .75
78 Dan Marino 6.00 12.00
79 Todd Marinovich .30 .75
80 Eric Martin .30 .75
81 Clay Matthews .40 1.00
82 Ed McCaffrey .60 1.50
83 O.J. McDuffie .60 1.50
84 Steve McMichael .30 .75
85 Audray McMillian .30 .75
86 Greg McMurtry .30 .75
87 Karl Mecklenburg .30 .75
88 Dave Meggett .30 .75
89 Eric Metcalf .40 1.00
90 Anthony Miller .40 1.00
91 Chris Miller .30 .75
92 Sam Mills .30 .75
93 Rick Mirer .60 1.50
94 Johnny Mitchell .30 .75
95 Art Monk .40 1.00
96 Joe Montana 7.50 15.00
97 Warren Moon .60 1.50
98 Rob Moore .40 1.00
99 Brad Muster .30 .75
100 Browning Nagle .30 .75
101 Ken Norton Jr. .40 1.00
102 Jay Novacek .60 1.50
103 Neil O'Donnell .60 1.50
104 Leslie O'Neal .40 1.00
105 Louis Oliver .30 .75
106 Rodney Peete .40 1.00
107 Michael Dean Perry .40 1.00
108 Carl Pickens .40 1.00
109 Ricky Proehl .30 .75
110 Andre Reed .60 1.50
111 Jerry Rice 3.00 8.00
112 Andre Rison .60 1.50
113 Leonard Russell .40 1.00
114 Mark Rypien .30 .75
115 Barry Sanders 4.00 10.00
116 Deion Sanders 1.50 4.00
117 Junior Seau .60 1.50
118 Shannon Sharpe .60 1.50
119 Sterling Sharpe .40 1.00
120 Clyde Simmons .30 .75
121 Wayne Simmons .30 .75
122 Phil Simms .40 1.00
123 Bruce Smith .60 1.50
124 Emmitt Smith 5.00 12.00
126 Alonzo Spellman .30 .75
127 Pat Swilling .40 1.00
128 John Taylor .40 1.00
129 Lawrence Taylor .60 1.50
130 Broderick Thomas .30 .75
131 Derrick Thomas .60 1.50
132 Thurman Thomas .60 1.50
133 Andre Tippett .30 .75
134 Jessie Tuggle .30 .75
135 Tommy Vardell .30 .75
136 Jon Vaughn .30 .75
137 Clarence Verdin .30 .75
138 Herschel Walker .40 1.00
139 Andre Ware .30 .75
140 Chris Warren .40 1.00
141 Ricky Watters .60 1.50
142 Lorenzo White .30 .75
143 Reggie White .60 1.50
144 Alfred Williams .30 .75
145 Calvin Williams .40 1.00
146 Harvey Williams .40 1.00
147 John L. Williams .30 .75
148 Rod Woodson .60 1.50
149 Barry Word .30 .75
150 Steve Young 2.00 5.00

1993 Classic TONX Previews

NNO Troy Aikman 2.00 5.00
NNO Michael Irvin 1.25 3.00

1993 Classic TONX QB Club

These cards are actually round discs (sometimes called POGs) produced by Classic and named TONX. Each features an image of a quarterback club member and measures roughly 1-1/2" round.
1 Troy Aikman 8.00 20.00
2 Bubby Brister 3.00 8.00
3 Randall Cunningham 4.00 10.00
4 John Elway 12.00 30.00
5 Jim Everett 3.00 8.00
6 Boomer Esiason 4.00 10.00
7 Jim Kelly 5.00 12.00
8 Dan Marino 12.00 30.00
9 Jim Harbaugh 4.00 10.00
10 Jeff Hostetler 3.00 8.00
11 Warren Moon 4.00 10.00
12 Bernie Kosar 4.00 10.00
13 Mark Rypien 3.00 8.00
14 Chris Miller 3.00 8.00
15 David Klingler 3.00 8.00
17 Steve Young 6.00 15.00
18 Brett Favre 12.00 30.00
19 Neil O'Donnell 3.00 8.00

1993-94 Classic C3 Gold Crown Cut Lasercut

Along with the 20-card set checklisted below, the 10,000 members of the 1994 Classic Collectors Gold Crown Club received a 1994 C3 T-shirt, a TONX milk caps collectible sheet, a Classic Games magnet, and a 1994 C3 membership card. In later mailings they also received a 1993 Basketball Draft uncut sheet, a Chris Webber poster, and an autographed card of Jamal Mashburn, along with two promo cards. The sports represented are basketball (1-6), football (7-13), baseball (14-17), and hockey (18-20). The unnumbered checklist carries the set's production number out of the 10,000 produced.
COMPLETE SET (21) 10.00 25.00
7 Drew Bledsoe 1.00 2.50
8 Rick Mirer .40 1.00
9 Garrison Hearst .40 1.00
10 Terry Kirby .40 1.00
11 Glyn Milburn .40 1.00
12 Reggie Brooks .40 1.00
13 Jerome Bettis .75 2.00
NNO Drew Bledsoe/5000 1.25 3.00
Rick Mirer
Presidential Membership

1994 Classic C3 Gold Crown Club

Part of a special issue to Classic Collector's Club members, these standard-size cards feature on their fronts color player action shots that are borderless, except at the bottom, where the player's name appears. His first name is shown at the bottom left within a gray rectangle, which is actually a vertically distorted and ghosted black-and-white player action shot. The last name is shown within a black rectangle edging the bottom right. Another vertically distorted black-and-white player action shot forms a stripe that roughly bisects the back. A color player action shot appears on the left side; the player's name and statistics are shown vertically within white and black panels on the right. As part of the 1994 Classic Collectors Gold Crown Club offer, members also received one of 10,000 individually numbered standard-size white bordered autographed card of Jamal Mashburn. His autograph in blue ink appears across the card face. The back carries the C3 logo and a congratulatory message.
COMPLETE SET (4) 6.00 15.00
CC3 Emmitt Smith 4.00 10.00

1994 Classic International Promos

This four-card standard-size set was given away during the International Sportscard and Memorabilia Expo at the Anaheim Convention Center July 19-24, 1994. The fronts display full-bleed color action shots. The player's name appears in red print on a black bar near the bottom. On a dark screened background, the backs carry the logo for the card show. The cards are unnumbered and checklisted below in alphabetical order.
COMPLETE SET (4) 3.00 8.00
1 Troy Aikman FB 1.25 3.00
3 Marshall Faulk FB 1.25 3.00

1994 Classic National Promos

This five-card standard-size set was issued to promote the 15th National Sports Collectors Convention in Houston August 4-7, 1994. The fronts display full-bleed color action shots. The player's name appears in red print on a black bar near the bottom. On a dark screened background, the backs carry a gold foil National Convention logo. The Hill card was given out on Exhibitor Preview Night, as noted on its back. The cards are unnumbered and checklisted below in alphabetical order.
COMPLETE SET (5) 6.00 15.00
4 Heath Shuler FB .75 2.00
5 Emmitt Smith FB 2.00 5.00

1995 Classic $3 Phone Cards

COMPLETE SET (6) 6.00 15.00
1 Troy Aikman 1.50 4.00
2 Ki-Jana Carter .75 2.00
3 Kerry Collins 1.00 2.50
4 Marshall Faulk 1.00 2.50
5 Steve McNair 1.00 2.50
6 Steve Young 1.25 3.00

1995 Classic Draft Day Jaguars

This 5-card standard-size set was issued on April 22 to salute the Jacksonville Jaguars' inaugural NFL Draft. The cards were given to individuals attending the Jaguars' reception. The fronts display color action player photos, with the team logo, player's name and position, and a 1995 NFL Draft emblem across the bottom. On a background consisting of an enlarged version of the 1995 NFL Draft emblem, the back carries the team logo and a salutation. Reportedly, 5000 sets were made.
COMPLETE SET (5) 8.00 20.00
JJ1 Kerry Collins 1.50 4.00
JJ2 Steve McNair 4.80 12.00
JJ3 Tony Boselli .80 2.00
JJ4 Kevin Carter
JJ5 Ki-Jana Carter 1.20 3.00

1996 Classic NFL Draft Day

This 15-card set was distributed at the 1996 NFL Draft in New York. It was designed to match the top picks with the team that selected them; therefore three players appear with three different team options. NFL veterans and the previous Heisman Award winner are also included. Each set came with a certificate of authenticity numbered of 9,996.
COMPLETE SET (15) 12.00 30.00
1A Keyshawn Johnson 1.20 3.00
1B Keyshawn Johnson 1.50 3.00
1C Keyshawn Johnson .60 1.50
2A Kevin Hardy .80 2.00
2B Kevin Hardy .40 1.00
2C Kevin Hardy .40 1.00
3A Terry Glenn .80 2.00
3B Terry Glenn .80 2.00
3C Terry Glenn .80 2.00
4 Eddie George 2.00 5.00
5 Emmitt Smith 1.60 4.00
6 Troy Aikman 1.00 2.50
7 Drew Bledsoe 1.00 2.50
8 Kerry Collins 1.00 2.50
9 Title Card CL .40 1.00

1996 Classic SP Autographs

This eight-card set was offered as a mail-in order from Score Board Inc. (Classic) and Scott Paper Company. Each card was personally autographed by the player featured on the front and is accompanied by a Score Board certificate of authenticity. The cards were initially offered for $7.95 each with two UPCs or $10.95 without UPC labels. Complete could be had for $54.95 with eight UPCs or $64.95 without. Although the cards contain the 1995 date on the copyright line, they were first offered in early 1996.
COMPLETE SET (8) 40.00 100.00
SP1 Kyle Brady 4.80 12.00
SP2 Kerry Collins 10.00 20.00
SP3 Ron Jaworski 4.80 12.00
SP4 Napoleon Kaufman 6.00 15.00
SP5 Jim Kiick 4.80 12.00
SP6 Steve McNair 14.00 35.00
SP7 Jim Plunkett 6.00 15.00
SP8 Randy White 6.00 15.00

1994 Classic NFL Experience Promos

Classic released this set to preview the design of the 1994 Classic NFL Experience series. The cards feature full-bleed color action shots on the front with the player's name appearing at the bottom. The back clearly states "For Promotional Purposes Only" at the top with the card number (of 6) at the bottom. The Aikman card features a typical Classic NFL Experience card back, while the other five contain an ad for the 1994 Super Bowl Card Show V convention in Atlanta.
COMPLETE SET (6) 6.00 15.00
1 Troy Aikman 1.60 4.00
2 Jerry Rice 1.60 4.00
3 Emmitt Smith 2.40 6.00
4 Derrick Thomas .50 1.25
5 Thurman Thomas .80 2.00
6 Rod Woodson .50 1.25

1994 Classic NFL Experience

These 100 standard-size cards were released by Classic Games in celebration of Super Bowl XXVIII. Classic produced 1,500 sequentially numbered cases that were offered to hobby dealers only. Cards from the 10-card 1994 Classic NFL Experience LPs and 1,994 Troy Aikman Super Bowl XXVII MVP cards were randomly inserted in the eight-card foil packs.
COMPLETE SET (100) 4.00 10.00
1 Checklist 1 .01 .05
2 Checklist 2 .01 .05
3 Bobby Hebert .01 .05
4 Erric Pegram .01 .05
5 Andre Rison .02 .10
6 Deion Sanders .15 .40
7 Cornelius Bennett .02 .10
8 Jim Kelly .07 .20
9 Andre Reed .02 .10
10 Bruce Smith .07 .20
11 Thurman Thomas .07 .20
12 Curtis Conway .07 .20
13 Jim Harbaugh .07 .20
14 John Copeland .01 .05
15 David Klingler .01 .05
16 Carl Pickens .02 .10
17 Eric Metcalf .02 .10
18 Vinny Testaverde .02 .10
19 Eric Turner .01 .05
20 Tommy Vardell .01 .05
21 Troy Aikman .30 .75
22 Michael Irvin .07 .20
23 Emmitt Smith .50 1.25
24 Kevin Williams WR .02 .10
25 John Elway .60 1.50
26 Glyn Milburn .02 .10
27 Shannon Sharpe .02 .10
28 Herman Moore .07 .20
29 Rodney Peete .01 .05
30 Barry Sanders .50 1.25
31 Pat Swilling .01 .05
32 Brett Favre .60 1.50
33 Sterling Sharpe .02 .10
34 Reggie White .07 .20
35 Haywood Jeffires .02 .10
36 Warren Moon .07 .20
37 Webster Slaughter .01 .05
38 Lorenzo White .01 .05
39 Quentin Coryatt .01 .05
40 Jeff George .07 .20
41 Roosevelt Potts .01 .05
42 Marcus Allen .07 .20
43 Joe Montana .60 1.50
44 Neil Smith .02 .10
45 Derrick Thomas .07 .20
46 Tim Brown .07 .20
47 Jeff Hostetler .02 .10
48 Rocket Ismail .02 .10
49 Anthony Smith .01 .05
50 Jerome Bettis .15 .40
51 Jim Everett .02 .10
52 T.J.Rubley RC .01 .05
53 Keith Jackson .01 .05
54 Terry Kirby .07 .20
55 Dan Marino .60 1.50
56 O.J.McDuffie .07 .20
57 Scott Mitchell .02 .10
58 Cris Carter .15 .40
59 Chris Doleman .01 .05
60 Robert Smith .07 .20
61 Drew Bledsoe .25 .60
62 Vincent Brisby .02 .10
63 Derek Brown RBK .01 .05
64 Willie Roaf .01 .05
65 Irv Smith .01 .05
66 Renaldo Turnbull .01 .05
67 Rodney Hampton .02 .10
68 Phil Simms .02 .10
69 Lawrence Taylor .07 .20
70 Boomer Esiason .02 .10
71 Marvin Jones .01 .05
72 Ronnie Lott .02 .10
73 Johnny Mitchell .01 .05
74 Rob Moore .02 .10
75 Victor Bailey .01 .05
76 Randall Cunningham .07 .20
77 Ken O'Brien .01 .05
78 Steve Beuerlein .02 .10
79 Garrison Hearst .07 .20
80 Ronald Moore .01 .05
81 Ricky Proehl .01 .05
82 Deon Figures .01 .05
83 Barry Foster .01 .05
84 Neil O'Donnell .07 .20
85 Rod Woodson .02 .10
86 Natrone Means .07 .20
87 Anthony Miller .02 .10
88 Junior Seau .07 .20
89 Jerry Rice .30 .75
90 Ricky Watters .02 .10
91 Steve Young .30 .75
92 Brian Blades .02 .10
93 Cortez Kennedy .02 .10
94 Rick Mirer .07 .20
95 Stan Humphries .02 .10
96 Eric Curry .01 .05
97 Craig Erickson .01 .05
98 Reggie Brooks .02 .10
99 Desmond Howard .02 .10
100 Mark Rypien .01 .05
QB1 Troy Aikman AU/2500 40.00 80.00
SP1 Troy Aikman SB MVP/1994 15.00 40.00

1994 Classic NFL Experience LPs

Randomly inserted in 1994 Classic NFL Experience packs, these ten standard-size cards feature 1993 first-year players. Reportedly only 2,400 of each card were produced. Each card includes an embossed gold-foil Super Bowl XXVIII logo with "1 of 2,400" printed on it. The cards are numbered on the back with an "LP" prefix. The set is sequenced in alphabetical order.
COMPLETE SET (10) 20.00 50.00
LP1 Jerome Bettis 4.00 10.00
LP2 Drew Bledsoe 6.00 15.00
LP3 Reggie Brooks 1.00 2.50
LP4 Garrison Hearst 2.00 5.00
LP5 Derek Brown RBK .50 1.25
LP6 Terry Kirby 2.00 5.00
LP7 Natrone Means 2.00 5.00
LP8 Glyn Milburn 1.00 2.50
LP9 Rick Mirer 2.00 5.00
LP10 Robert Smith 2.00 5.00

1994 Classic NFL Experience Super Bowl Heroes

COMPLETE SET (5) 5.00 12.00
SBH1 Jerry Rice 1.25 3.00
SBH2 Joe Montana 2.00 5.00
SBH3 Emmitt Smith 1.50 4.00
SBH4 Troy Aikman 1.00 2.50
SBH5 Lawrence Taylor .60 1.50

1995 Classic Draft Day Autographs

Cards from this set were issued in Summer 1995 to honor the NFL Draft. The fronts display a color player photo and a 1995 NFL Draft emblem. On a background consisting of an enlarged version of the 1995 NFL Draft emblem, the back carries the announced print run (of 500) and a brief congratulatory message.
1 Kerry Collins 15.00 30.00
2 Steve McNair 30.00 60.00

1995 Classic National

This 20-card multi-sport set was issued by Classic to commemorate the 16th National Sports Collectors Convention in St. Louis. The set included a certificate of limited edition, with the serial number out of 9,995 sets produced. One thousand Sprint 20-minute phone cards featuring Ki-Jana Carter and Nolan Ryan were also distributed.
COMPLETE SET (20) 8.00 20.00
NC2 Emmitt Smith 1.50 4.00
NC3 Troy Aikman 1.00 2.50
NC6 Steve Young .75 2.00
NC8 Marshall Faulk .75 2.00
NC10 Drew Bledsoe .75 2.00

NC11 Ki-Jana Carter .20 .50
NC12 Kerry Collins .40 1.00
NNO Ki-Jana Carter .75 2.00
Phone Card

1995 Classic NFL Experience

This 110-card standard-size set features color player action shots with team color-coded borders. This set also includes a Miami Dolphins commemorative card featuring legendary head coach Don Shula and quarterback Dan Marino (on average of one per box), and 1,995 sequentially numbered "Emmitt Zone" insert cards. Gold cards were inserted one per hobby pack. The cards are grouped alphabetically within teams and checklisted below according to teams. There was an Emmitt Smith Preview card issued for the set one per box in 1994 Classic Images. It is priced with the Images set. For the 1995 Super Bowl NFL Experience Card Show in Miami, Classic issued a commemorative sheet (roughly 8-3/4" by 11-1/2") honoring the 49ers and Chargers. The blankbacked sheet includes the cardfronts of three players from each of the two teams.

COMPLETE SET (110) 4.00 10.00
1 Seth Joyner .01 .05
2 Clyde Simmons .01 .05
3 Ronald Moore .01 .05
4 Andre Rison .02 .10
5 Bert Emanuel .07 .20
6 Jeff George .02 .10
7 Terance Mathis .02 .10
8 Jim Kelly .07 .20
9 Thurman Thomas .07 .20
10 Andre Reed .02 .10
11 Bruce Smith .07 .20
12 Cornelius Bennett .02 .10
13 Steve Walsh .01 .05
14 Lewis Tillman .01 .05
15 Chris Zorich .01 .05
16 Jeff Blake RC .25 .60
17 Darnay Scott .02 .10
18 Dan Wilkinson .02 .10
19 Eric Metcalf .02 .10
20 Antonio Langham .01 .05
21 Pepper Johnson .01 .05
22 Eric Turner .01 .05
23 Leroy Hoard .01 .05
24 Vinny Testaverde .02 .10
25 Troy Aikman .30 .75
26 Emmitt Smith .50 1.25
27 Michael Irvin .07 .20
28 Alvin Harper .01 .05
29 Charles Haley .02 .10
30 John Elway .60 1.50
31 Leonard Russell .01 .05
32 Shannon Sharpe .02 .10
33 Herman Moore .07 .20
34 Barry Sanders .50 1.25
35 Brett Favre .60 1.50
36 Sterling Sharpe .02 .10
37 Reggie White .07 .20
38 Gary Brown .01 .05
39 Haywood Jeffires .01 .05
40 Quentin Coryatt .02 .10
41 Marshall Faulk .40 1.00
42 Tony Bennett .01 .05
43 Joe Montana .60 1.50
44 Marcus Allen .07 .20
45 Derrick Thomas .07 .20
46 Neil Smith .02 .10
47 Tim Brown .07 .20
48 Jeff Hostetler .02 .10
49 Terry McDaniel .01 .05
50 Jerome Bettis .07 .20
51 Sean Gilbert .02 .10
52 Dan Marino .60 1.50
53 Irving Fryar .02 .10
54 Keith Jackson .01 .05
55 Bernie Parmalee .02 .10
56 Tim Bowens .01 .05
57 Cris Carter .07 .20
58 Terry Allen .02 .10
59 Warren Moon .02 .10
60 John Randle .02 .10
61 Jake Reed .02 .10
62 Drew Bledsoe .20 .50
63 Marion Butts .01 .05
64 Ben Coates .02 .10
65 Derek Brown RBK .01 .05
66 Jim Everett .01 .05
67 Michael Haynes .02 .10
68 Darion Conner .01 .05
69 Rodney Hampton .02 .10
70 Dave Meggett .01 .05
71 Boomer Esiason .02 .10
72 Johnny Johnson .01 .05
73 Ronnie Lott .02 .10
74 Rob Moore .02 .10
75 Mo Lewis .01 .05
76 Randall Cunningham .07 .20
77 Herschel Walker .02 .10
78 Charlie Garner .07 .20
79 Calvin Williams .02 .10
80 Fred Barnett .02 .10
81 William Fuller .01 .05
82 Eric Allen .01 .05
83 Barry Foster .02 .10
84 Neil O'Donnell .02 .10
85 Rod Woodson .02 .10
86 Kevin Greene .02 .10
87 Byron Bam Morris .01 .05
88 Darren Perry .01 .05
89 Greg Lloyd .02 .10
90 Steve Young .25 .60
91 Ricky Watters .02 .10
92 Jerry Rice .30 .75
93 Ken Norton Jr. .02 .10
94 Deion Sanders .15 .40
95 Stan Humphries .02 .10
96 Natrone Means .02 .10
97 Junior Seau .07 .20
98 Leslie O'Neal .02 .10
99 Chris Mims .01 .05
100 Rick Mirer .02 .10
101 Chris Warren .02 .10
102 Brian Blades .02 .10
103 Trent Dilfer .07 .20
104 Errict Rhett .02 .10
105 Heath Shuler .02 .10
106 Henry Ellard .02 .10
107 Ken Harvey .01 .05
108 Gus Frerotte .02 .10
109 Checklist 1 .02 .10
110 Checklist 2 .02 .10
SP1 Marshall Faulk Promo .40 1.00
SP1S M.Faulk Spanish Promo 4.00 10.00
EZ1 E.Smith Zone/1995 10.00 25.00
GC1 Dan Marino .75 2.00
Don Shula
GC2 Dan Marino 1.25 3.00
Don Shula
MD1 Dan Marino 1.25 3.00
Don Shula
PC1 Marshall Faulk Promo .40 1.00
NNO Super Bowl XXIX Sheet .75 2.00

1995 Classic NFL Experience Gold

COMPLETE SET (110) 20.00 40.00
*GOLD CARDS: 1.2X to 3X BASIC CARDS
ONE PER PACK

1995 Classic NFL Experience Rookies

Inserted on average of one in six packs, this insert set honors ten rookies of 1994. The cards are numbered with an "R" prefix. A parallel set printed in Spanish on the cardbacks was also produced and distributed as promos at a card show in Miami.

COMPLETE SET (10) 4.00 8.00
STATED ODDS 1:6 HOB, 1:5 JUM
*SPANISH: .8X TO 2X BASIC INSERTS
R1 Marshall Faulk 4.00 10.00
R2 Bert Emanuel .75 2.00
R3 Charlie Garner .75 2.00
R4 Errict Rhett .40 1.00
R5 Byron Bam Morris .20 .50
R6 Heath Shuler .40 1.00
R7 Trent Dilfer .75 2.00
R8 Darnay Scott .40 1.00
R9 Tim Bowens .20 .50
R10 Antonio Langham .20 .50

1995 Classic NFL Experience Super Bowl Game

This 20-card standard-size set was issued one per special jumbo pack. The set consists of ten stars from each conference. If the card number corresponded to the last digit of the conference representative's score in the 1995 Super Bowl, the collector redeemed the card for a prize. The contest expired on March 6, 1995.

COMPLETE SET (20) 10.00 20.00
ONE PER SPECIAL JUMBO PACK
A0 Marshall Faulk .75 2.00
A1 Natrone Means .07 .20
A2 Thurman Thomas .15 .40
A3 Joe Montana 1.25 3.00
A4 John Elway 1.25 3.00
A5 Rick Mirer .07 .20
A6 Drew Bledsoe WIN .40 1.00
A7 Dan Marino 1.25 3.00
A8 Jim Kelly .15 .40
A9 Marcus Allen .15 .40
N0 Troy Aikman .60 1.50
N1 Steve Young .50 1.25
N2 Jerome Bettis .15 .40
N3 Barry Sanders 1.00 2.50
N4 Randall Cunningham .15 .40
N5 Andre Rison .07 .20
N6 Jerry Rice .60 1.50
N7 Emmitt Smith 1.00 2.50
N8 Michael Irvin .15 .40
N9 Sterling Sharpe WIN .07 .20

1995 Classic NFL Experience Super Bowl Inserts

This five-card set was sold on Home Shopping Network with the regular 1994 NFL Experience set. It was made exclusively for them. The fronts feature color player action shots with the player's name and a Super Bowl XXX highlight at the bottom in a red stripe. The backs carry another color player action shot with the player's name, position, and team name below it along with a brief biography of the player.

COMPLETE SET (5) 4.80 12.00
SBF1 Jerry Rice 1.60 4.00
SBF2 Ricky Watters .80 2.00
SBF3 Natrone Means .80 2.00
SBF4 Steve Young 1.20 3.00
SBF5 Steve Young 1.20 3.00

1995 Classic NFL Experience Throwbacks

Inserted on average of two per box, these standard-size cards are printed on parchment paper to look and feel like an old-time card. The set is arranged in alphabetical order by teams. An autographed version of the Emmitt Smith card was made available via a mail redemption.

COMPLETE SET (28) 50.00 100.00
STATED ODDS 1:12 HOB, 1:10 JUM
T1 Seth Joyner .15 .40
T2 Andre Rison .30 .75
T3 Thurman Thomas .60 1.50
T4 Lewis Tillman .15 .40
T5 Dan Wilkinson .30 .75
T6 Eric Metcalf .30 .75
T7 Emmitt Smith 4.00 10.00
T8 John Elway 5.00 12.00
T9 Barry Sanders 4.00 10.00
T10 Reggie White .60 1.50
T11 Haywood Jeffires .15 .40
T12 Marshall Faulk 3.00 8.00
T13 Joe Montana 5.00 12.00
T14 Jeff Hostetler .30 .75
T15 Jerome Bettis .60 1.50
T16 Dan Marino 5.00 12.00
T17 Warren Moon .30 .75
T18 Drew Bledsoe 1.50 4.00
T19 Jim Everett .15 .40
T20 Dave Meggett .15 .40
T21 Ronnie Lott .30 .75
T22 Randall Cunningham .60 1.50
T23 Rod Woodson .30 .75
T24 Natrone Means .30 .75
T25 Rick Mirer .30 .75
T26 Steve Young 2.00 5.00
T27 Trent Dilfer .60 1.50
T28 Henry Ellard .30 .75
T7AU E.Smith AUTO/1995 75.00 125.00

1996 Classic NFL Experience

This 125 card standard-size set was issued in 10 card packs, with 24 cards in a box and 16 boxes in a case. There were also factory sets issued with Emmitt Smith featured on the front, and was released as part of a retail package that included 12-packs of 1996 NFL Experience as well. There are no key Rookie Cards in this set. Special Super Bowl packs were issued with special parallel versions of these cards. An Emmitt Smith Sculpted Promo card (#XXX) was produced to preview the set. We've included it below in the price listings.

COMPLETE SET (125) 4.00 10.00
COMP.FACT SET (130) 6.00 15.00
1 Emmitt Smith .50 1.25
2 Jerry Rice .30 .75
3 Carl Pickens .02 .10
4 Curtis Conway .07 .20
5 Isaac Bruce .07 .20
6 Marshall Faulk .15 .40
7 Errict Rhett .02 .10
8 Troy Aikman .30 .75
9 Jeff Hostetler .01 .05
10 Dan Marino .60 1.50
11 Barry Sanders .50 1.25
12 Drew Bledsoe .15 .40
13 Ricky Watters .02 .10
14 Natrone Means .02 .10
15 Chris Warren .02 .10
16 Jim Kelly .07 .20
17 Jeff George .02 .10
18 Garrison Hearst .02 .10
19 Brett Favre .60 1.50
20 John Elway .60 1.50
21 Robert Smith .02 .10
22 Steve Bono .01 .05
23 Byron Bam Morris .01 .05
24 Jim Everett .01 .05
25 Steve Young .25 .60
26 Rodney Hampton .02 .10
27 Terry Allen .02 .10
28 Chris Chandler .02 .10
29 Mark Carrier WR .01 .05
30 Desmond Howard .02 .10
31 Erik Kramer .01 .05
32 Irving Fryar .02 .10
33 Jeff Blake .07 .20
34 Vinny Testaverde .02 .10
35 Stan Humphries .02 .10
36 Tim Brown .07 .20
37 Trent Dilfer .07 .20
38 Jim Harbaugh .02 .10
39 Warren Moon .02 .10
40 Ben Coates .02 .10
41 Boomer Esiason .02 .10
42 Rodney Peete .01 .05
43 Gus Frerotte .02 .10
44 Jerome Bettis .07 .20
45 Dave Brown .01 .05
46 William Floyd .02 .10
47 Andre Rison .02 .10
48 Robert Brooks .07 .20
49 Marcus Allen .07 .20
50 Rick Mirer .02 .10
51 Alvin Harper .01 .05
52 Chris Miller .01 .05
53 Eric Metcalf .01 .05
54 Dave Krieg .01 .05
55 Darnay Scott .02 .10
56 Cris Carter .07 .20
57 Lake Dawson .01 .05
58 Haywood Jeffires .01 .05
59 Herman Moore .02 .10
60 Michael Irvin .07 .20
61 Anthony Miller .02 .10
62 Troy Vincent .01 .05
63 Jake Reed .02 .10
64 Michael Haynes .01 .05
65 Scott Mitchell .02 .10
66 Roman Phifer .01 .05
67 Harvey Williams .01 .05
68 Darren Perry .01 .05
69 Brian Mitchell .01 .05
70 Derek Loville .01 .05
71 Junior Seau .07 .20
72 Bruce Smith .02 .10
73 Willie Davis .01 .05
74 Charles Haley .02 .10
75 Mike Sherrard .01 .05
76 Pat Swilling .01 .05
77 Yancey Thigpen .02 .10
78 Bryce Paup .01 .05
79 Eric Green .01 .05
80 Deion Sanders .15 .40
81 Mario Bates .02 .10
82 John Randle .02 .10
83 Charlie Garner .02 .10
84 Chris Doleman .01 .05
85 Robert Porcher .01 .05
86 Rob Moore .02 .10
87 Anthony Pleasant .01 .05
88 Bryan Cox .01 .05
89 Greg Hill .02 .10
90 Reggie White .07 .20
91 Shannon Sharpe .02 .10
92 Leroy Hoard .01 .05
93 John Copeland .01 .05
94 Tony Martin .02 .10
95 Greg Lloyd .02 .10
96 Tony Bennett .01 .05
97 Alonzo Spellman .01 .05
98 Wayne Martin .01 .05
99 Craig Heyward .01 .05
100 Leslie O'Neal .01 .05
101 Andy Harmon .01 .05
102 Edgar Bennett .02 .10
103 Derrick Moore .01 .05
104 Terrell Davis .20 .50
105 Kerry Collins .07 .20
106 Rodney Thomas .01 .05
107 Mark Brunell .15 .40
108 Curtis Martin .20 .50
109 Tyrone Wheatley .02 .10
110 Rashaan Salaam .02 .10
111 Kevin Carter .01 .05
112 Joey Galloway .07 .20
113 Mike Mamula .01 .05
114 Kyle Brady .01 .05
115 James O.Stewart .02 .10
116 Michael Westbrook .07 .20
117 J.J. Stokes .07 .20
118 Wayne Chrebet .15 .40
119 Warren Sapp .01 .05
120 Hugh Douglas .02 .10
121 Jim Flanigan .01 .05
122 Chester McGlockton .01 .05
123 Shawn Lee .01 .05
124 Emmitt Smith CL .10 .30
125 Kerry Collins CL .02 .10
P1 Emmitt Smith Promo .75 2.00

1996 Classic NFL Experience Printer's Proofs

COMPLETE SET (125) 80.00 200.00
*STARS: 5X TO 12X BASIC CARDS
STATED ODDS 1:20
STATED PRINT RUN 499 #'d SETS

1996 Classic NFL Experience Super Bowl Gold

COMPLETE GOLD SET (125) 20.00 50.00
*GOLD CARDS: 1.5X TO 4X BASIC CARDS
STATED PRINT RUN 799 #'d SETS

1996 Classic NFL Experience Super Bowl Red

COMPLETE RED SET (125) 150.00 300.00
*RED CARDS: 15X TO 40X BASIC CARDS
STATED ODDS 1:8 SUPER BOWL PACKS
STATED PRINT RUN 150 #'d SETS

1996 Classic NFL Experience Class of 1995

As a special factory set insert, these five cards were included. These standard-size cards feature various award winners and have the player's portrait against a silver background. The cards are numbered with a "FI" prefix on the back.

COMPLETE SET (5) 2.50 6.00
ONE SET PER NFL EXP.FACTORY SET
FI1 Steve Young .75 2.00
FI2 Emmitt Smith 1.50 4.00
FI3 Deion Sanders .50 1.25
FI4 Rashaan Salaam .10 .30
FI5 Kerry Collins .25 .60

1996 Classic NFL Experience Emmitt Zone

Randomly inserted into packs, this five-card standard-size set features highlights from Emmitt Smith's career. The set breaks down his career into year by year breakdown. The name "Emmitt Smith" is printed down the left side of the front while Emmitt has a picture on the right. The words "Emmitt Zone" are printed in the lower right hand corner. The cards are numbered as "X" of 5 . A special "Emmitt Zone" phone card was issued as well. That card was inserted one every 375 Super Bowl packs and had a calling value of $5.

COMMON CARD (1-5) 20.00 50.00
NNO Emmitt Smith Phone Card 1.25 3.00

1996 Classic NFL Experience Super Bowl Die Cut Promos

This 10-card promo set was given away at the NFL Experience 1996 Super Bowl Card Show in Tempe, Arizona. The cards feature players that are represented on the Classic NFL Experience Super Bowl Die Cut inserts with the fronts displaying what the A and B cards would look like if matched. The backs carry the interactive rules to claim a prize with the Super Bowl Die Cut contest cards. Various prize levels could be attained depending on which group of cards the collector had acquired. Both the show Promos and Die Cut contest cards could be combined to win advanced prizes from Classic.

COMPLETE SET (10) 10.00 20.00
1C Jim Kelly .60 1.50
2C Dan Marino 2.50 6.00
3C Greg Lloyd .30 .75
4C Marcus Allen .60 1.50
5C Tim Brown .60 1.50
6C Emmitt Smith 2.00 5.00
7C Steve Young 1.00 2.50
8C Rashaan Salaam .30 .75
9C Brett Favre 2.50 6.00
10C Isaac Bruce .60 1.50

1996 Classic NFL Experience Super Bowl Die Cut Contest

This 20-card set consists of ten players with each featured on two die-cut cards which fit together to form the Super Bowl XXX logo. The cards are numbered 1A-10A and 1B-10B with the A's having the left side of the Super Bowl logo as a background and the B's the right. The Die Cuts were randomly inserted in the Card Show version of 1996 Classic NFL Experience at the rate of 1:12 packs. Two die-cut cards forming the Super Bowl XXX logo and a show promo card could be redeemed for one of four levels of prizes. The fronts display a color action player photo with the player's name in the gold side border. The backs carry the rules and how to redeem the cards for a prize.

COMPLETE SET (20) 30.00 80.00
STATED ODDS 1:12 SUPER BOWL PACKS
1A Jim Kelly .60 1.50
1B Jim Kelly .60 1.50
2A Dan Marino 5.00 12.00
2B Dan Marino 5.00 12.00
3A Greg Lloyd .30 .75
3B Greg Lloyd .30 .75
4A Marcus Allen .60 1.50
4B Marcus Allen .60 1.50
5A Tim Brown .60 1.50
5B Tim Brown .60 1.50
6A Emmitt Smith 4.00 10.00
6B Emmitt Smith 4.00 10.00
7A Steve Young 2.00 5.00
7B Steve Young 2.00 5.00
8A Rashaan Salaam .30 .75
8B Rashaan Salaam .30 .75
9A Brett Favre 5.00 12.00
9B Brett Favre 5.00 12.00
10A Isaac Bruce .60 1.50
10B Isaac Bruce .60 1.50

1996 Classic NFL Experience Super Bowl Game

These 20 standard-size cards were inserted approximately one every four packs. The cards were winners based on the "box pool" concept in which numbers from each row and column corresponds to the last digit in each team's score. All collectors who sent in winning cards were eligible for the grand prize of a trip for 2 to New Orleans for Super Bowl XXX1. The deadline for mailing in the contest cards were March 8, 1996.

COMPLETE SET (20) 10.00 25.00
STATED ODDS 1:4 HOB, 1:1 SUPER BOWL
A0 Drew Bledsoe .60 1.50
A1 John Elway 2.50 6.00
A2 Harvey Williams .07 .20
A3 Marshall Faulk .60 1.50
A4 Jim Kelly .30 .75
A5 Carl Pickens .15 .40
A6 Stan Humphries .15 .40
A7 Dan Marino WIN 2.50 6.00
A8 Steve Bono .07 .20
A9 Napoleon Kaufman .30 .75
N0 Isaac Bruce .30 .75
N1 Steve Young 1.00 2.50
N2 Michael Westbrook .30 .75
N3 Troy Aikman 1.25 3.00
N4 Barry Sanders 2.00 5.00
N5 Rashaan Salaam .15 .40
N6 Emmitt Smith 2.00 5.00
N7 Jerry Rice WIN 1.25 3.00
N8 Deion Sanders .60 1.50
N9 Kerry Collins .30 .75

1996 Classic NFL Experience Super Bowl Game Redemption

This five-card prize set was a redemption set for Game cards distributed at the 1996 Super Bowl Card Show in Phoenix, Arizona. They have an "SBR" prefix on the card numbers.

COMPLETE SET (5) 3.00 6.00
SBR1 Jay Novacek .20 .50
SBR2 Yancey Thigpen .20 .50
SBR3 Emmitt Smith 1.25 2.50
SBR4 Byron Bam Morris .20 .50
SBR5 Troy Aikman .75 2.00

1996 Classic NFL Experience Sculpted

These cards were inserted approximately one every 15 hobby packs. They feature a die cut pattern with the player's picture against a gold background which features the team's logo. The cards are numbered with an "S" prefix.

COMPLETE SET (20) 40.00 100.00
STATED ODDS 1:15 HOBBY
S1 Kerry Collins .75 2.00
S2 Jeff Blake .75 2.00
S3 Vinny Testaverde .40 1.00
S4 Emmitt Smith 5.00 12.00
S5 Troy Aikman 3.00 8.00
S6 Deion Sanders 1.50 4.00
S7 John Elway 6.00 15.00
S8 Barry Sanders 5.00 12.00
S9 Brett Favre 6.00 15.00
S10 Marshall Faulk 1.50 4.00
S11 Steve Bono .20 .50
S12 Dan Marino 6.00 15.00
S13 Robert Smith .40 1.00
S14 Drew Bledsoe 1.50 4.00
S15 Natrone Means .40 1.00
S16 Steve Young 2.50 6.00
S17 Jerry Rice 3.00 8.00
S18 Isaac Bruce .75 2.00
S19 Errict Rhett .40 1.00
S20 Michael Westbrook .75 2.00

1996 Classic NFL Experience X

These 10 standard-size cards feature leading NFL players. The cards were randomly inserted into hobby packs at a rate of one in 70. The cards are numbered with an "X" prefix.

COMPLETE SET (10) 30.00 80.00
STATED ODDS 1:70 HOBBY
X1 Kerry Collins 1.50 4.00
X2 Rashaan Salaam .75 2.00
X3 Michael Westbrook 1.50 4.00
X4 Terrell Davis 4.00 10.00
X5 Joey Galloway 1.50 4.00
X6 Deion Sanders 3.00 8.00
X7 Steve Young 5.00 12.00
X8 Dan Marino 12.50 30.00
X9 Drew Bledsoe 3.00 8.00
X10 Emmitt Smith 10.00 25.00

1996 Classic Promos

NNO Kerry Collins .60 1.50

1998 Classic Collectibles Commemorative Tickets

1 Mike Alstott 1.00 2.50
2 Peyton Manning 3.00 8.00
3 Kordell Stewart 1.00 2.50

2010 Classics

101-200 ROOKIE PRINT RUN 999
201-250 LEGEND PRINT RUN 999
1 Chris Wells .20 .50
2 Larry Fitzgerald .25 .60
3 Matt Leinart .20 .50
4 Matt Ryan .25 .60
5 Michael Turner .20 .50
6 Roddy White .20 .50
7 Anquan Boldin .20 .50
8 Joe Flacco .25 .60
9 Ray Rice .20 .50
10 Fred Jackson .25 .60
11 Lee Evans .25 .60
12 Marshawn Lynch .25 .60
13 DeAngelo Williams .20 .50
14 Jonathan Stewart .20 .50
15 Steve Smith .25 .60
16 Devin Hester .25 .60
17 Jay Cutler .20 .50
18 Matt Forte .20 .50
19 Carson Palmer .25 .60
20 Cedric Benson .20 .50
21 Chad Ochocinco .20 .50
22 Jake Delhomme .20 .50
23 Josh Cribbs .20 .50
24 Jerome Harrison .20 .50
25 Felix Jones .20 .50
26 Jason Witten .25 .60
27 Miles Austin .20 .50
28 Tony Romo .25 .60
29 Eddie Royal .20 .50
30 Knowshon Moreno .20 .50
31 Kyle Orton .20 .50
32 Calvin Johnson .30 .75
33 Matthew Stafford .25 .60
34 Nate Burleson .20 .50
35 Aaron Rodgers .60 1.50
36 Greg Jennings .20 .50
37 Ryan Grant .25 .60
38 Andre Johnson .25 .60
39 Matt Schaub .20 .50
40 Steve Slaton .20 .50
41 Dallas Clark .20 .50
42 Peyton Manning .75 2.00
43 Pierre Garcon .25 .60
44 Reggie Wayne .25 .60
45 David Garrard .20 .50
46 Maurice Jones-Drew .20 .50
47 Mike Sims-Walker .20 .50
48 Dwayne Bowe .25 .60
49 Jamaal Charles .25 .60
50 Matt Cassel .20 .50
51 Chad Henne .25 .60
52 Ronnie Brown .20 .50
53 Davone Bess .20 .50
54 Adrian Peterson .30 .75
55 Brett Favre .60 1.50
56 Sidney Rice .20 .50
57 Visanthe Shiancoe .25 .60
58 Randy Moss .25 .60
59 Tom Brady .75 2.00
60 Wes Welker .25 .60
61 Devery Henderson .20 .50
62 Drew Brees .30 .75
63 Pierre Thomas .20 .50
64 Brandon Jacobs .20 .50
65 Eli Manning .25 .60
66 Steve Smith USC .20 .50
67 Braylon Edwards .20 .50
68 Mark Sanchez .20 .50
69 Shonn Greene .20 .50
70 Darren McFadden .20 .50
71 Jason Campbell .20 .50
72 Louis Murphy .20 .50
73 Brent Celek .20 .50
74 DeSean Jackson .25 .60
75 Kevin Kolb .20 .50
76 LeSean McCoy .30 .75
77 Ben Roethlisberger .30 .75
78 Rashard Mendenhall .20 .50
79 Hines Ward .25 .60
80 Antonio Gates .25 .60
81 Darren Sproles .25 .60
82 Philip Rivers .30 .75
83 Alex Smith QB .25 .60
84 Frank Gore .25 .60
85 Vernon Davis .20 .50
86 John Carlson .20 .50
87 Matt Hasselbeck .20 .50
88 T.J. Houshmandzadeh .20 .50
89 Danny Amendola .30 .75
90 Donnie Avery .20 .50
91 Steven Jackson .20 .50
92 Cadillac Williams .20 .50
93 Josh Freeman .25 .60
94 Kellen Winslow Jr. .20 .50
95 Chris Johnson .20 .50
96 Kenny Britt .20 .50
97 Vince Young .20 .50
98 Chris Cooley .20 .50
99 Clinton Portis .20 .50
100 Donovan McNabb .25 .60
101 Aaron Hernandez RC 1.25 3.00
102 Andre Anderson RC 1.25 3.00
103 Andre Dixon RC 2.00 5.00
104 Andre Roberts RC 1.50 4.00
105 Anthony Dixon RC 1.25 3.00
106 Anthony McCoy RC 1.25 3.00
107 Antonio Brown RC 10.00 25.00
108 Armanti Edwards RC 1.50 4.00
109 Arrelious Benn RC 1.25 3.00
110 Ben Tate RC 1.25 3.00
111 Blair White RC 1.25 3.00
112 Brandon Graham RC 1.50 4.00
113 Brandon LaFell RC 2.00 5.00
114 Brandon Spikes RC 1.25 3.00
115 Bryan Bulaga RC 1.25 3.00
116 C.J. Spiller RC 1.25 3.00
117 Carlos Dunlap RC 1.25 3.00
118 Carlton Mitchell RC 1.25 3.00
119 Chad Jones RC 1.25 3.00
120 Charles Scott RC 1.25 3.00
121 Chris Cook RC 1.25 3.00
122 Chris McGaha RC 1.25 3.00
123 Colt McCoy RC 1.50 4.00
124 Corey Wootton RC 1.25 3.00
125 Damian Williams RC 1.25 3.00
126 Dan LeFevour RC 1.25 3.00
127 Daryl Washington RC 1.25 3.00
128 David Gettis RC 1.25 3.00
129 Demaryius Thomas RC 3.00 8.00
130 Derrick Morgan RC 1.25 3.00
131 Devin McCourty RC 1.50 4.00
132 Dexter McCluster RC 1.50 4.00
133 Dez Bryant RC 3.00 8.00
134 Dezmon Briscoe RC 1.25 3.00
135 Dominique Franks RC 1.25 3.00
136 Earl Thomas RC 3.00 8.00
137 Ed Dickson RC 1.25 3.00
138 Emmanuel Sanders RC 2.00 5.00
139 Eric Berry RC 2.00 5.00
140 Eric Decker RC 1.50 4.00
141 Everson Griffen RC 1.25 3.00
142 Freddie Barnes RC 1.25 3.00
143 Garrett Graham RC 1.25 3.00
144 Gerald McCoy RC 1.25 3.00
145 Golden Tate RC 1.50 4.00
146 Jacoby Ford RC 1.25 3.00
147 Jahvid Best RC 1.25 3.00
148 James Starks RC 1.50 4.00
149 Jarrett Brown RC 1.25 3.00
150 Jason Pierre-Paul RC 2.00 5.00
151 Jason Worilds RC 1.25 3.00
152 Jeremy Williams RC 1.25 3.00
153 Jermaine Gresham RC 1.25 3.00
154 Jerry Hughes RC 1.25 3.00
155 Jevan Snead RC 1.25 3.00
156 Jimmy Clausen RC 1.25 3.00
157 Jimmy Graham RC 3.00 8.00
158 Joe Haden RC 2.00 5.00
159 Joe McKnight RC 1.25 3.00
160 John Skelton RC 1.50 4.00
161 Jonathan Crompton RC 1.25 3.00
162 Jonathan Dwyer RC 1.25 3.00
163 Jordan Shipley RC 1.25 3.00
164 Kareem Jackson RC 1.25 3.00
165 Kyle Wilson RC 1.25 3.00
166 LeGarrette Blount RC 2.50 6.00
167 Lonyae Miller RC 1.50 4.00
168 Marcus Easley RC 1.25 3.00
169 Mardy Gilyard RC 1.25 3.00
170 Mike Kafka RC 1.50 4.00
171 Mike Williams RC 1.25 3.00
172 Montario Hardesty RC 1.25 3.00
173 Morgan Burnett RC 1.50 4.00
174 Nate Allen RC 2.00 5.00
175 NaVorro Bowman RC 2.50 6.00
176 Ndamukong Suh RC 2.50 6.00
177 Pat Paschall RC 1.25 3.00
178 Patrick Robinson RC 1.50 4.00
179 Perrish Cox RC 1.50 4.00
180 Ricky Sapp RC 1.25 3.00
181 Riley Cooper RC 1.25 3.00
182 Rob Gronkowski RC 4.00 10.00
183 Rolando McClain RC 1.25 3.00
184 Russell Okung RC 1.25 3.00
185 Ryan Mathews RC 1.25 3.00
186 Sam Bradford RC 1.50 4.00
187 Sean Canfield RC 1.25 3.00
188 Sean Lee RC 2.50 6.00
189 Sean Weatherspoon RC 1.25 3.00
190 Sergio Kindle RC 1.25 3.00
191 Seyi Ajirotutu RC 1.25 3.00
192 Shay Hodge RC 1.25 3.00
193 Taylor Mays RC 1.25 3.00
194 Taylor Price RC 1.25 3.00
195 Tim Tebow RC 4.00 10.00
196 Toby Gerhart RC 1.25 3.00
197 Tony Pike RC 1.25 3.00
198 Trent Williams RC 1.50 4.00
199 Tyson Alualu RC 1.25 3.00
200 Zac Robinson RC 1.50 4.00
201 Art Monk 2.00 5.00
202 Barry Sanders 3.00 8.00
203 Bernie Kosar 1.50 4.00
204 Bob Hayes 2.00 5.00
205 Boomer Esiason 1.50 4.00
206 Brent Jones 1.25 3.00
207 Bruce Smith 1.50 4.00
208 Chuck Howley 1.25 3.00
209 Craig James 1.25 3.00
210 Cris Carter 2.00 5.00
211 Curtis Martin 1.50 4.00
212 Dan Marino 4.00 10.00
213 Darren Woodson 1.50 4.00
214 Deion Sanders 1.50 4.00
215 Derrick Thomas 2.00 5.00
216 Doug Flutie 1.50 4.00
217 Ed Too Tall Jones 1.25 3.00
218 Ed McCaffrey 1.25 3.00
219 Eddie George 1.50 4.00
220 Harvey Martin 1.25 3.00
221 Henry Ellard 1.25 3.00
222 Hank Jordan 1.25 3.00
224 Irving Fryar 1.25 3.00
225 Jackie Slater 1.25 3.00
226 Jim Kelly 2.00 5.00
227 Jim Plunkett 1.50 4.00
228 Joe Montana 6.00 15.00
229 John Elway 3.00 8.00
230 John Taylor 1.25 3.00
231 Junior Seau 1.50 4.00
232 Keyshawn Johnson 1.25 3.00
233 L.C. Greenwood 1.25 3.00
234 Mike Singletary 2.00 5.00
235 Gale Sayers 2.00 5.00
236 Mel Blount 1.50 4.00
237 Michael Strahan 1.50 4.00
238 Mike Alstott 1.25 3.00
239 Priest Holmes 1.25 3.00
240 Randall Cunningham 1.50 4.00
241 Rod Smith 1.25 3.00
242 Rod Woodson 1.50 4.00
245 Terrell Davis 1.50 4.00
246 Terry Bradshaw 2.50 6.00
247 Todd Christensen 1.25 3.00
248 Tom Rathman 1.25 3.00
249 Wayne Chrebet 1.25 3.00
250 William Perry 1.25 3.00

2010 Classics Timeless Tributes Gold

*VETS 1-100: 5X TO 12X BASIC CARDS
*ROOKIES 101-200: .8X TO 2X BASIC CARDS
*LEGENDS 201-250: 1X TO 2.5X BASIC CARDS
STATED PRINT RUN 50 SER.#'d SETS

2010 Classics Timeless Tributes Platinum

*VETS 1-100: 8X TO 20X BASIC CARDS
*ROOKIES 101-200: 1X TO 2.5X BASIC CARDS
*LEGENDS 201-250: 1.5X TO 4X BASIC CARDS
STATED PRINT RUN 25 SER.#'d SETS

2010 Classics Timeless Tributes Silver

*VETS 1-100: 4X TO 10X BASIC CARDS
*ROOKIES 101-200: .6X TO 1.5X BASIC CARDS
*LEGENDS 201-250: .8X TO 2X BASIC CARDS
STATED PRINT RUN 100 SER.#'d SETS

2010 Classics Classic Combos

*GOLD/100: .8X TO 2X BASIC INSERTS
*PLATINUM/25: 1.2X TO 3X BASIC INSERTS
1 J.Kelly/B.Smith 2.00 5.00
2 D.Thomas/J.Seau 2.50 6.00
3 B.Hayes/C.Howley 2.00 5.00
4 H.Ellard/J.Slater 1.25 3.00
5 T.Christensen/J.Plunkett 1.50 4.00
6 D.Marino/I.Fryar 3.00 8.00
8 H.Martin/E.Jones 1.50 4.00
9 R.Woodson/D.Woodson 2.00 5.00
10 M.Singletary/M.Strahan 2.00 5.00

2010 Classics Classic Combos Jerseys

STATED PRINT RUN 75 SER.#'d SETS
*PRIME/25: .8X TO 2X BASIC JSY/75
1 J.Kelly/B.Smith 8.00 20.00
2 D.Thomas/J.Seau 20.00 50.00
3 B.Hayes/C.Howley 10.00 25.00
4 H.Ellard/J.Slater 8.00 20.00
5 T.Christensen/J.Plunkett 8.00 20.00
6 D.Marino/I.Fryar 15.00 40.00
8 H.Martin/E.Jones 8.00 20.00
9 R.Woodson/D.Woodson 8.00 20.00
10 M.Singletary/M.Strahan 12.00 30.00

2010 Classics Classic Cuts

STATED PRINT RUN 1-100
SERIAL #'d UNDER 20 NOT PRICED
3 Alex Wojciechowicz/43 30.00 60.00
8 Bert Bell/19 25.00 50.00
9 Bill Dudley/100 15.00 40.00
16 Bulldog Turner/100 30.00 60.00
21 Elroy Hirsch/100 30.00 60.00
23 Dante Lavelli/100 15.00 40.00
25 Don Hutson/50 100.00 175.00
28 Frank Gatski/45 15.00 40.00
30 George Connor/50 25.00 50.00
32 George McAfee/90 20.00 50.00
35 Hank Stram/50 20.00 50.00
36 Jay Berwanger/40 25.00 50.00
39 Jim Ringo/20 40.00 80.00
45 Kyle Rote/45 25.00 50.00
50 Lou Groza/25 40.00 80.00
56 Otto Graham/35 40.00 80.00
58 Paul Brown/50 25.00 60.00
63 Red Badgro/35 30.00 60.00
65 Roosevelt Brown/20 30.00 60.00
72 Tony Canadeo/45 30.00 80.00
73 Walter Payton/25 150.00 300.00
75 Weeb Ewbank/80 25.00 50.00

2010 Classics Classic Quads

*GOLD/100: .8X TO 2X BASIC INSERTS
*PLATINUM/25: 1.2X TO 3X BASIC INSERTS
1 Mntna/Jons/Tylr/Rthmn 5.00 12.00
3 Brdshw/Blnt/Grnwd/Wdsn 2.50 6.00
4 Esiasn/Chrbt/Jhnsn/Mrtin 1.50 4.00
5 Smith/Strhn/Sngltry/Thms 3.00 8.00

2010 Classics Classic Quads Jerseys

STATED PRINT RUN 25 SER.#'d SETS
*PRIME15: .5X TO 1.2X QUAD JSY/25
1 Mntna/Jns/Tylr/Rthmn 30.00 60.00
4 Esiasn/Chrbt/Jhnsn/Mrtn 15.00 30.00
5 Smith/Strhn/Sngltry/Thms 60.00 120.00

2010 Classics Classic Singles

*GOLD/100: .8X TO 2X BASIC INSERTS
*PLATINUM/25: 1.2X TO 3X BASIC INSERTS
1 Bernie Kosar 1.25 3.00
2 Bob Hayes 1.50 4.00
3 Boomer Esiason 1.25 3.00
4 Brent Jones 1.00 2.50
5 Bruce Smith 1.25 3.00
6 Chuck Howley 1.00 2.50
7 Craig James 1.00 2.50
8 Curtis Martin 1.25 3.00
9 Darren Woodson 1.25 3.00
10 Doug Flutie 1.25 3.00
11 Ed McCaffrey 1.00 2.50
12 Harvey Martin 1.00 2.50
13 Henry Ellard 1.00 2.50
14 Hank Jordan 1.00 2.50
15 Jackie Slater 1.00 2.50
16 John Taylor 1.00 2.50
17 L.C. Greenwood 1.00 2.50
18 Gale Sayers 1.50 4.00
19 Mel Blount 1.25 3.00
20 Rod Smith 1.00 2.50
21 Rod Woodson 1.25 3.00
22 Todd Christensen 1.00 2.50
23 Tom Rathman 1.00 2.50
24 Wayne Chrebet 1.00 2.50
25 William Perry 1.00 2.50

2010 Classics Classic Singles Jerseys

STATED PRINT RUN 100-299
*PRIME/50: .6X TO 1.5X JSY/175-299
*PRIME/50: .5X TO 1.2X JSY/100
*PRIME/25: .8X TO 2X JSY/175-299
1 Bernie Kosar/299 5.00 12.00
2 Bob Hayes/199 10.00 25.00
3 Boomer Esiason/299 5.00 12.00
4 Brent Jones/199 4.00 10.00
5 Bruce Smith/200 5.00 12.00
6 Chuck Howley/299 4.00 10.00
7 Craig James/200 4.00 10.00
8 Curtis Martin/200 5.00 12.00
9 Darren Woodson/100 6.00 15.00
10 Doug Flutie/299 5.00 12.00
11 Ed McCaffrey/200 4.00 10.00
12 Harvey Martin/100 5.00 12.00
13 Henry Ellard/299 4.00 10.00
14 Hank Jordan/299 6.00 15.00
15 Jackie Slater/299 4.00 10.00
16 John Taylor/299 4.00 10.00
17 L.C. Greenwood/100 5.00 12.00
18 Gale Sayers/299 8.00 20.00
19 Mel Blount/299 5.00 12.00
20 Rod Smith/299 4.00 10.00
21 Rod Woodson/299 5.00 12.00
22 Todd Christensen/299 4.00 10.00
23 Tom Rathman/299 4.00 10.00
24 Wayne Chrebet/299 4.00 10.00
25 William Perry/175 4.00 10.00

2010 Classics Classic Singles Jerseys Autographs

STATED PRINT RUN 10-25
*PRIME/15: .5X TO 1.2X JSY AU/25
EXCH EXPIRATION: 1/28/2012
1 Bernie Kosar/25 25.00 50.00
3 Boomer Esiason/15 15.00 40.00
4 Brent Jones/10
5 Bruce Smith/15
6 Chuck Howley/20 20.00 50.00
8 Curtis Martin/20 30.00 60.00
11 Ed McCaffrey/15 15.00 40.00
16 John Taylor/15 25.00 50.00
17 L.C. Greenwood/15 15.00 40.00
20 Rod Smith/15
21 Rod Woodson/10
22 Todd Christensen/10
23 Tom Rathman/15
24 Wayne Chrebet/15 20.00 50.00
25 William Perry/10

2010 Classics Classic Triples

*GOLD/100: .8X TO 2X BASIC INSERTS
*PLATINUM/25: 1.2X TO 3X BASIC INSERTS
1 Elway/Kosar/Marino 4.00 10.00
2 Bradshaw/Blount/Grnwd 3.00 8.00
3 Chrebet/Johnson/Martin 1.50 4.00
4 Jones/Taylor/Rathman 1.50 4.00
5 Ellard/Carter/Fryar 2.00 5.00
6 Singletary/Thomas/Seau 2.50 6.00
7 R.Wdsn/Deion/Blount 1.50 4.00
8 Kosar/Cunningham/Kelly 2.00 5.00
9 George/Martin/Holmes 1.50 4.00

2010 Classics Classic Triples Jerseys

STATED PRINT RUN 50 SER.#'d SETS
*PRIME/25: .6X TO 1.5X BASIC JSY/50
1 Elway/Kosar/Marino 25.00 60.00
3 Chrebet/Johnson/Martin 10.00 25.00
4 Jones/Taylor/Rathman 10.00 25.00
5 Ellard/Carter/Fryar 12.00 30.00
6 Singletary/Thomas/Seau 30.00 60.00
7 R.Wdsn/Deion/Blount 15.00 40.00
8 Kosar/Cunningham/Kelly 12.00 30.00
9 George/Martin/Holmes 10.00 25.00

2010 Classics Cowboys 50th Anniversary

1 Roger Staubach 3.00 8.00
2 Troy Aikman 3.00 8.00
3 Emmitt Smith 4.00 10.00
4 Tony Dorsett 2.50 6.00
5 Don Perkins 2.00 5.00
6 Michael Irvin 2.50 6.00
7 Bob Hayes 2.50 6.00
8 Jason Witten 2.00 5.00
9 Erik Williams 1.50 4.00
10 Rayfield Wright 1.50 4.00
11 Larry Allen 2.50 6.00
12 John Niland 1.50 4.00
13 Mark Stepnoski 1.50 4.00
14 Harvey Martin 1.50 4.00
15 Ed Too Tall Jones 1.50 4.00
16 Bob Lilly 2.50 6.00
17 Randy White 2.00 5.00
18 DeMarcus Ware 2.00 5.00
19 Chuck Howley 2.00 5.00
20 Lee Roy Jordan 2.00 5.00
21 Everson Walls 1.50 4.00
22 Mel Renfro 2.00 5.00
23 Darren Woodson 2.00 5.00
24 Cliff Harris 2.00 5.00
25 Mat McBriar 1.50 4.00
26 Rafael Septien 1.50 4.00
27 Deion Sanders 2.00 5.00
28 Bill Bates 2.00 5.00
29 Tom Landry 2.50 6.00
30 Jerry Jones 4.00 10.00

2010 Classics Cowboys 50th Anniversary Autographs

STATED PRINT RUN 5-100
EXCH EXPIRATION: 1/28/2012
SERIAL #'d UNDER 25 NOT PRICED
1 Roger Staubach/10
2 Troy Aikman/10
3 Emmitt Smith/5
4 Tony Dorsett/10
6 Don Perkins/10
6 Michael Irvin/10
8 Jason Witten/10
9 Erik Williams/100 20.00 40.00
10 Rayfield Wright/100 25.00 60.00
11 Larry Allen/100 No AU 6.00 15.00

12 John Niland/100 12.00 30.00
13 Mark Stepnoski/100 12.00 30.00
15 Ed Too Tall Jones/10 EXCH
16 Bob Lilly/10
17 Randy White/10
18 DeMarcus Ware/10
19 Chuck Howley/10
20 Lee Roy Jordan/100 12.00 30.00
21 Everson Walls/100 12.00 30.00
22 Mel Renfro/50 25.00 60.00
24 Cliff Harris/50 20.00 40.00
25 Mat McBriar/100 12.00 30.00
27 Deion Sanders/10
28 Bill Bates/10
30 Jerry Jones/25 EXCH 100.00 200.00

2010 Classics Cowboys 50th Anniversary Autographs Triples

TRIPLE AU PRINT RUN 15
1 Ware/Howley/Jordan 60.00 100.00

2010 Classics Cowboys 50th Anniversary Materials

STATED PRINT RUN 50 SER.#'d SETS
*PRIME/15-25: .6X TO 1.5X BASIC JSY/50
1 Roger Staubach 12.00 30.00
2 Troy Aikman 12.00 30.00
3 Emmitt Smith 15.00 40.00
4 Tony Dorsett 10.00 25.00
6 Michael Irvin 10.00 25.00
7 Bob Hayes 10.00 25.00
8 Jason Witten 8.00 20.00
14 Harvey Martin 8.00 20.00
16 Bob Lilly 8.00 20.00
17 Randy White 8.00 20.00
18 DeMarcus Ware 8.00 20.00
19 Chuck Howley 8.00 20.00
23 Darren Woodson 10.00 25.00
24 Cliff Harris 8.00 20.00
27 Deion Sanders 8.00 20.00
28 Bill Bates 8.00 20.00
29 Tom Landry 25.00 50.00

2010 Classics Cowboys 50th Anniversary Materials Combos

COMBO PRINT RUN 50 SER.#'d SETS
*COMBO PRIME/20: .6X TO 1.5X COMBO JSY
1 R.Staubach/T.Aikman 20.00 50.00
2 B.Lilly/R.White 12.00 30.00
3 D.Woodson/C.Harris 12.00 30.00
4 E.Smith/T.Dorsett 15.00 40.00
5 M.Irvin/B.Hayes 15.00 40.00

2010 Classics Cowboys 50th Anniversary Materials Quads

QUAD PRINT RUN 25 SER.#'d SETS
1 Landry/Stbch/Drstt/Whte 50.00 100.00
2 Smith/Dorstt/Irvin/Hayes 50.00 100.00
3 Stbch/Aikmn/Smith/Drstt 50.00 100.00
4 Martin/Lilly/Whte/Howly 30.00 60.00
5 Hrris/Bts/Wdsn/Sandrs 25.00 50.00

2010 Classics Cowboys 50th Anniversary Materials Triples

STATED PRINT RUN 30 SER.#'d SETS
*PRIME/15: .6X TO 1.5X BASIC TRIPLE/30
1 Landry/White/Martin 40.00 80.00
2 Irvin/Hayes/Witten 25.00 50.00

2010 Classics Dress Code

*GOLD/100: .6X TO 1.5X BASIC INSERTS
*PLATINUM/25: 1X TO 2.5X BASIC INSERTS
1 Matt Schaub 1.00 2.50
2 Eli Manning 1.25 3.00
3 Jonathan Stewart 1.00 2.50
4 Chad Ochocinco 1.00 2.50
5 Andre Johnson 1.25 3.00
6 Roddy White 1.00 2.50
7 Steven Jackson 1.00 2.50
8 Heath Miller 1.00 2.50
9 Calvin Johnson 1.50 4.00
10 Philip Rivers 1.50 4.00
11 Jason Witten 1.25 3.00
12 Matt Ryan 1.25 3.00
13 Wes Welker 1.25 3.00
14 Dallas Clark 1.00 2.50
15 Troy Polamalu 1.50 4.00
16 Santonio Holmes 1.00 2.50
17 Randy Moss 1.25 3.00
18 Antonio Gates 1.25 3.00
19 Steve Smith 1.25 3.00
20 Greg Jennings 1.00 2.50
21 Brandon Jacobs 1.00 2.50
22 Chris Cooley 1.00 2.50
23 Marques Colston 1.00 2.50
24 Donald Driver 1.25 3.00
25 Cadillac Williams 1.00 2.50

2010 Classics Dress Code Jerseys Prime

PRIME PRINT RUN 25-50
*BASIC JSY/175-299: .25X TO .6X PRIME/50
*BASIC JSY/175-299: .2X TO .5X PRIME/25
*BASIC JSY/90: .3X TO .8X PRIME JSY/35
1 Matt Schaub/35 4.00 10.00
2 Eli Manning/50 5.00 12.00
3 Jonathan Stewart/50 4.00 10.00
4 Chad Ochocinco/50 4.00 10.00
5 Andre Johnson/50 5.00 12.00
6 Roddy White/50 4.00 10.00
7 Steven Jackson/50 4.00 10.00
8 Heath Miller/50 4.00 10.00
9 Calvin Johnson/50 6.00 15.00
10 Philip Rivers/50 6.00 15.00
11 Jason Witten/50 5.00 12.00
12 Matt Ryan/25 6.00 15.00
13 Wes Welker/50 5.00 12.00
14 Dallas Clark/50 4.00 10.00
15 Troy Polamalu/50 6.00 15.00
16 Santonio Holmes/50 4.00 10.00
17 Randy Moss/50 5.00 12.00
18 Antonio Gates/50 5.00 12.00
19 Steve Smith/50 5.00 12.00
20 Greg Jennings/50 6.00 15.00
21 Brandon Jacobs/50 4.00 10.00
22 Chris Cooley/50 6.00 15.00
23 Marques Colston/50 4.00 10.00
24 Donald Driver/50 6.00 15.00
25 Cadillac Williams/50 4.00 10.00

2010 Classics Dress Code Jerseys Autographs

JERSEY AUTO PRINT RUN 10-15
EXCH EXPIRATION: 1/28/2012
1 Matt Schaub/10
2 Eli Manning/10
3 Jonathan Stewart/15 15.00 40.00
4 Chad Ochocinco/15 15.00 40.00
5 Andre Johnson/10
6 Roddy White/10
8 Heath Miller/15 15.00 40.00
9 Calvin Johnson/10
10 Philip Rivers/15 25.00 60.00
11 Jason Witten/15 20.00 50.00
12 Matt Ryan/10
18 Antonio Gates/15 20.00 50.00
19 Steve Smith/10
21 Brandon Jacobs/15
22 Chris Cooley/15 15.00 40.00
23 Marques Colston/10
25 Cadillac Williams/10

2010 Classics Flashback Fabrics Jerseys

STATED PRINT RUN 10-500
1 LaDainian Tomlinson/50 5.00 12.00
2 Tony Gonzalez/75 4.00 10.00
3 Ricky Williams/500 2.50 6.00
4 Randy Moss/75 8.00 20.00
6 Kyle Orton/500 2.00 5.00
7 Jay Cutler/500 2.00 5.00
8 Cedric Benson/500 2.00 5.00
9 Terrell Owens/35 5.00 12.00
10 Brian Westbrook/190 2.50 6.00
11 Charles Woodson/160 4.00 10.00
12 Torry Holt/150 3.00 8.00
13 T.J. Houshmandzadeh/15 5.00 12.00
14 Kellen Winslow Jr./10 5.00 12.00
15 Jonathan Vilma/500 2.00 5.00
16 Julius Peppers/260 4.00 10.00
17 Chris Chambers/500 2.00 5.00
18 Nate Burleson/70 3.00 8.00
19 Larry Johnson/80 3.00 8.00
20 Brett Favre/500 8.00 20.00
21 Terrell Owens/190 3.00 8.00
22 Randy Moss/30 5.00 12.00
23 Clinton Portis/130 2.50 6.00
24 Santana Moss/500 2.50 6.00
25 Anquan Boldin/500 2.00 5.00

2010 Classics Flashback Fabrics Jerseys Prime

STATED PRINT RUN 60-200
1 LaDainian Tomlinson/200 5.00 12.00
2 Tony Gonzalez/200 4.00 10.00
3 Ricky Williams/200 4.00 10.00
4 Randy Moss/200 8.00 20.00
5 Jeremy Shockey/200 3.00 8.00
6 Kyle Orton/200 3.00 8.00
8 Cedric Benson/150 3.00 8.00
9 Terrell Owens/200 4.00 10.00
10 Brian Westbrook/200 3.00 8.00
11 Charles Woodson/200 5.00 12.00
12 Torry Holt/200 4.00 10.00
13 T.J. Houshmandzadeh/200 3.00 8.00
14 Kellen Winslow Jr./200 3.00 8.00
15 Jonathan Vilma/175 3.00 8.00
16 Julius Peppers/180 5.00 12.00
17 Chris Chambers/200 3.00 8.00
18 Nate Burleson/100 4.00 10.00
19 Larry Johnson/200 3.00 8.00
21 Terrell Owens/200 4.00 10.00
22 Randy Moss/60 5.00 12.00
23 Clinton Portis/200 3.00 8.00
24 Santana Moss/200 4.00 10.00
25 Anquan Boldin/90 4.00 10.00

2010 Classics Hall of Fame

1 Emmitt Smith 8.00 20.00
2 Jerry Rice 8.00 20.00
3 Russ Grimm 2.00 5.00
4 Rickey Jackson 2.00 5.00
5 Floyd Little 2.00 5.00
6 John Randle 2.50 6.00
7 Dick LeBeau 2.00 5.00

2010 Classics Hall of Fame Autographs

STATED PRINT RUN 50 SER.#'d SETS
EXCH EXPIRATION: 1/28/2012
1 Emmitt Smith 125.00 200.00
2 Jerry Rice 100.00 200.00
3 Russ Grimm 15.00 40.00
4 Rickey Jackson 20.00 50.00
5 Floyd Little 15.00 40.00
6 John Randle 25.00 50.00
7 Dick LeBeau 30.00 60.00

2010 Classics Hall of Fame Materials

STATED PRINT RUN 100 SER.#'d SETS
*PRIME/25: .8X TO 2X BASIC JSY/100
1 Emmitt Smith 12.00 30.00
2 Jerry Rice 10.00 25.00

2010 Classics Membership

*GOLD/100: .6X TO 1.5X BASIC INSERTS
*PLATINUM/25: 1X TO 2.5X BASIC INSERTS
1 Rashard Mendenhall 1.00 2.50
2 Knowshon Moreno 1.00 2.50
3 Mark Sanchez 1.00 2.50
4 Jamaal Charles 1.25 3.00
5 Austin Collie 1.00 2.50
6 Kenny Britt 1.00 2.50
7 LeSean McCoy 1.50 4.00
8 Matt Forte 1.00 2.50
9 Brent Celek 1.00 2.50
10 Darren Sproles 1.25 3.00
11 Felix Jones 1.00 2.50
12 Matthew Stafford 1.25 3.00
13 Visanthe Shiancoe 1.25 3.00
14 Ray Rice 1.00 2.50
15 Miles Austin 1.00 2.50
16 Shonn Greene 1.00 2.50
17 Jeremy Maclin 1.00 2.50
18 Chris Wells 1.00 2.50
19 Pierre Garcon 1.25 3.00
20 Percy Harvin 1.00 2.50
21 Mike Wallace 1.00 2.50
22 Mike Sims-Walker 1.00 2.50
23 Pierre Thomas 1.00 2.50
24 Michael Crabtree 1.00 2.50
25 Kevin Boss 1.00 2.50

2010 Classics Membership VIP Jerseys

STATED PRINT RUN 40-299
*PRIME/50: .6X TO 1.5X BASIC JSY/225-299
*PRIME/50: .4X TO 1X BASIC JSY/40
1 Rashard Mendenhall/299 2.50 6.00
2 Knowshon Moreno/299 2.50 6.00
3 Mark Sanchez/299 2.50 6.00
4 Jamaal Charles/40 5.00 12.00
6 Kenny Britt/299 2.50 6.00
7 LeSean McCoy/299 4.00 10.00
8 Matt Forte/225 2.50 6.00
10 Darren Sproles/299 3.00 8.00
11 Felix Jones/299 2.50 6.00
12 Matthew Stafford/299 3.00 8.00
13 Visanthe Shiancoe/299 3.00 8.00
16 Shonn Greene/299 2.50 6.00
17 Jeremy Maclin/299 2.50 6.00
18 Chris Wells/299 2.50 6.00
20 Percy Harvin/299 2.50 6.00
24 Michael Crabtree/299 2.50 6.00

2010 Classics Monday Night Heroes

*GOLD/100: .6X TO 1.5X BASIC INSERTS
*PLATINUM/25: 1X TO 2.5X BASIC INSERTS
1 Tom Brady 4.00 10.00
2 Dallas Clark 1.00 2.50
3 Ronnie Brown 1.00 2.50
4 Felix Jones 1.00 2.50
5 Aaron Rodgers 3.00 8.00
6 Brett Favre 3.00 8.00
7 Ricky Williams 1.25 3.00
8 Kyle Orton 1.00 2.50
9 DeSean Jackson 1.25 3.00
10 Drew Brees 1.50 4.00
11 Michael Turner 1.00 2.50
12 Ben Roethlisberger 1.50 4.00
13 Rashard Mendenhall 1.00 2.50
14 Ray Rice 1.00 2.50
15 Chris Johnson 1.00 2.50
16 Vince Young 1.00 2.50
17 Drew Brees 1.50 4.00
18 Marques Colston 1.00 2.50
19 Aaron Rodgers 3.00 8.00
20 Jermichael Finley 1.00 2.50
21 Frank Gore 1.25 3.00
22 Eli Manning 1.25 3.00
23 Ahmad Bradshaw 1.00 2.50
24 Jay Cutler 1.00 2.50
25 Adrian Peterson 1.50 4.00

2010 Classics Monday Night Heroes Jerseys

STATED PRINT RUN 100-299
1 Tom Brady/150 8.00 20.00
2 Dallas Clark/299 2.50 6.00
3 Ronnie Brown/150 2.50 6.00
4 Felix Jones/299 2.50 6.00
6 Brett Favre/100 10.00 25.00
7 Ricky Williams/299 3.00 8.00
8 Kyle Orton/299 2.50 6.00
10 Drew Brees/100 5.00 12.00
11 Michael Turner/299 2.50 6.00
12 Ben Roethlisberger/299 4.00 10.00
13 Rashard Mendenhall/100 3.00 8.00
15 Chris Johnson/299 2.50 6.00
16 Vince Young/299 2.50 6.00
17 Drew Brees/250 4.00 10.00
18 Marques Colston/299 2.50 6.00
21 Frank Gore/250 3.00 8.00
22 Eli Manning/299 3.00 8.00
23 Ahmad Bradshaw/299 2.50 6.00
24 Jay Cutler/299 2.50 6.00
25 Adrian Peterson/299 4.00 10.00

2010 Classics Monday Night Heroes Jerseys Prime

STATED PRINT RUN 5-50
SERIAL #'d UNDER 25 NOT PRICED
1 Tom Brady/50 12.00 30.00
2 Dallas Clark/50 4.00 10.00
3 Ronnie Brown/50 4.00 10.00
4 Felix Jones/50 4.00 10.00
5 Aaron Rodgers/25 20.00 50.00
6 Brett Favre/10
7 Ricky Williams/50 5.00 12.00
8 Kyle Orton/50 4.00 10.00
10 Drew Brees/9
11 Michael Turner/50 4.00 10.00
12 Ben Roethlisberger/25 8.00 20.00
13 Rashard Mendenhall/50 4.00 10.00
15 Chris Johnson/50 4.00 10.00
16 Vince Young/50 4.00 10.00
17 Drew Brees/5
18 Marques Colston/50 4.00 10.00
19 Aaron Rodgers/25 10.00 25.00
21 Frank Gore/50 5.00 12.00
22 Eli Manning/50 5.00 12.00
23 Ahmad Bradshaw/50 4.00 10.00
24 Jay Cutler/10

2010 Classics Monday Night Heroes Jerseys Autographs

STATED PRINT RUN 4-15
EXCH EXPIRATION: 1/28/2012
11 Michael Turner/15 12.00 30.00
13 Rashard Mendenhall/15 12.00 30.00
24 Jay Cutler/15 12.00 30.00

2010 Classics Significant Signatures Gold

1-100 VETERAN PRINT RUN 5-50
101-200 ROOKIE PRINT RUN 99-499
201-250 LEGEND PRINT RUN 5-50
EXCH EXPIRATION: 1/28/2012
11 Lee Evans/20
29 Eddie Royal/25 8.00 20.00
30 Knowshon Moreno/20
42 Peyton Manning/18 75.00 150.00
43 Pierre Garcon/25 12.00 30.00
48 Dwayne Bowe/15
57 Visanthe Shiancoe/20 EXCH
63 Pierre Thomas/20 12.00 30.00
67 Braylon Edwards/20
68 Mark Sanchez/15 30.00 60.00
69 Shonn Greene/20 12.00 30.00
72 Louis Murphy/50 8.00 20.00
73 Brent Celek/20 8.00 20.00
96 Kenny Britt/25 8.00 20.00
101 Aaron Hernandez/499 10.00 25.00
102 Andre Anderson/499 3.00 8.00
103 Andre Dixon/499 5.00 12.00
104 Andre Roberts/399 4.00 10.00
105 Anthony Dixon/99 5.00 12.00
106 Anthony McCoy/499 3.00 8.00
107 Antonio Brown/499 25.00 50.00
108 Armanti Edwards/499 6.00 15.00
109 Arrelious Benn/499 3.00 8.00
110 Ben Tate/299 4.00 10.00
111 Blair White/99 5.00 12.00
112 Brandon Graham/499 4.00 10.00
113 Brandon LaFell/399 6.00 15.00
114 Brandon Spikes/99 5.00 12.00
115 Bryan Bulaga/499 3.00 8.00
116 C.J. Spiller/249 4.00 10.00
117 Carlos Dunlap/499 3.00 8.00
118 Carlton Mitchell/499 3.00 8.00
119 Chad Jones/499 3.00 8.00
120 Charles Scott/499 3.00 8.00
121 Chris Cook/499 3.00 8.00
122 Chris McGaha/499 3.00 8.00
123 Colt McCoy/249 5.00 12.00
124 Corey Wootton/499 3.00 8.00
125 Damian Williams/399 3.00 8.00
126 Dan LeFevour/499 6.00 15.00
127 Daryl Washington/99 5.00 12.00
128 David Gettis/499 3.00 8.00
129 Demaryius Thomas/399 8.00 20.00
130 Derrick Morgan/299 4.00 10.00
131 Devin McCourty/499 4.00 10.00
132 Dexter McCluster/399 8.00 20.00
133 Dez Bryant/299 30.00 60.00
134 Dezmon Briscoe/99 5.00 12.00
135 Dominique Franks/399 3.00 8.00
136 Earl Thomas/399 8.00 20.00
137 Ed Dickson/499 3.00 8.00
138 Emmanuel Sanders/499 5.00 12.00
139 Eric Berry/99 8.00 20.00
140 Eric Decker/399 4.00 10.00
141 Everson Griffen/499 3.00 8.00
142 Freddie Barnes/99 5.00 12.00
143 Garrett Graham/399 3.00 8.00
144 Gerald McCoy/399 3.00 8.00
145 Golden Tate/299 5.00 12.00
146 Jacoby Ford/499 10.00 20.00
147 Jahvid Best/399 3.00 8.00
148 James Starks/499 4.00 10.00
149 Jarrett Brown/249 4.00 10.00
150 Jason Pierre-Paul/499 5.00 12.00
151 Jason Worilds/499 3.00 8.00
152 Jeremy Williams/99 5.00 12.00
153 Jermaine Gresham/199 4.00 10.00
154 Jerry Hughes/499 3.00 8.00
155 Jevan Snead/499 3.00 8.00
156 Jimmy Clausen/249 4.00 10.00
157 Jimmy Graham/99 12.00 30.00
158 Joe Haden/399 5.00 12.00
159 Joe McKnight/99 5.00 12.00
160 John Skelton/99 6.00 15.00
161 Jonathan Crompton/499 3.00 8.00
162 Jonathan Dwyer/399 3.00 8.00
163 Jordan Shipley/199 4.00 10.00
164 Kareem Jackson/499 6.00 15.00
165 Kyle Wilson/99 5.00 12.00
166 LeGarrette Blount/499 6.00 15.00
167 Lonyae Miller/499 4.00 10.00
168 Marcus Easley/499 3.00 8.00
169 Mardy Gilyard/499 3.00 8.00
170 Mike Kafka/499 4.00 10.00
171 Mike Williams/99 5.00 12.00
172 Montario Hardesty/399 3.00 8.00
173 Morgan Burnett/499 4.00 10.00
174 Nate Allen/499 5.00 12.00
175 NaVorro Bowman/99 10.00 25.00
176 Ndamukong Suh/299 8.00 20.00
177 Pat Paschall/99 5.00 12.00
178 Patrick Robinson/499 4.00 10.00
179 Perrish Cox/499 4.00 10.00
180 Ricky Sapp/99 5.00 12.00
181 Riley Cooper/499 3.00 8.00
182 Rob Gronkowski/499 25.00 50.00
183 Rolando McClain/299 4.00 10.00
184 Russell Okung/99 5.00 12.00
185 Ryan Mathews/299 4.00 10.00
186 Sam Bradford/249 5.00 12.00
187 Sean Canfield/99 5.00 12.00
188 Sean Lee/499 6.00 15.00
189 Sean Weatherspoon/499 3.00 8.00
190 Sergio Kindle/499 3.00 8.00
191 Seyi Ajirotutu/499 3.00 8.00
192 Shay Hodge/499 3.00 8.00
193 Taylor Mays/499 3.00 8.00
194 Taylor Price/399 3.00 8.00
195 Tim Tebow/249 20.00 50.00
196 Toby Gerhart/299 4.00 10.00
197 Tony Pike/499 6.00 15.00
198 Trent Williams/99 12.00 30.00
200 Zac Robinson/399 4.00 10.00
201 Art Monk/25 40.00 80.00
202 Barry Sanders/25 60.00 120.00
203 Bernie Kosar/50 12.00 30.00
205 Boomer Esiason/15 12.00 30.00
206 Brent Jones/15 10.00 25.00
211 Curtis Martin/50 15.00 40.00
212 Dan Marino/20 75.00 150.00
217 Ed Too Tall Jones/25 20.00 40.00
219 Eddie George/15
224 Irving Fryar/25 10.00 25.00
226 Jim Kelly/20 40.00 80.00
228 Joe Montana/15 90.00 150.00
229 John Elway/15 75.00 150.00
234 Mike Singletary/20 20.00 40.00
238 Mike Alstott/20 20.00 40.00
239 Priest Holmes/20 15.00 30.00
240 Randall Cunningham/20 25.00 50.00
245 Terrell Davis/20 20.00 40.00

2010 Classics Significant Signatures Platinum

*VETERAN/25: .5X TO 1.2X GOLD/50
1-100 VET PRINT RUN 1-25
*ROOKIES/24-25: 1X TO 2.5X GOLD/399-499
*ROOKIES/24-25: .8X TO 2X GOLD/199-299
*ROOKIES/24-25: .6X TO 1.5X GOLD/99
101-200 ROOKIE PRINT RUN 1-25
*LEGEND/25: .5X TO 1.2X GOLD/50
201-250 LEGEND PRINT RUN 1-25
SERIAL #'d UNDER 20 NOT PRICED
123 Colt McCoy/25 10.00 25.00
133 Dez Bryant/25 50.00 120.00
153 Jermaine Gresham/25 8.00 20.00
156 Jimmy Clausen/25 8.00 20.00
185 Ryan Mathews/25 8.00 20.00
195 Tim Tebow/25 40.00 100.00

2010 Classics Sunday's Best

*GOLD/100: .6X TO 1.5X BASIC INSERTS
*PLATINUM/25: 1X TO 2.5X BASIC INSERTS
1 Vernon Davis 1.00 2.50
2 Aaron Rodgers 3.00 8.00
3 Larry Fitzgerald 1.25 3.00
4 Chris Johnson 1.00 2.50
5 DeSean Jackson 1.25 3.00
6 Tony Romo 1.25 3.00
7 Ryan Grant 1.25 3.00
8 Josh Cribbs 1.00 2.50
9 Vince Young 1.00 2.50
10 Sidney Rice 1.00 2.50
11 Vincent Jackson 1.00 2.50
12 DeAngelo Williams 1.00 2.50
13 Carson Palmer 1.25 3.00
14 Maurice Jones-Drew 1.00 2.50
15 Brett Favre 3.00 8.00
16 Drew Brees 1.50 4.00
17 Frank Gore 1.25 3.00
18 Ronnie Brown 1.00 2.50
19 Adrian Peterson 1.50 4.00
20 Peyton Manning 4.00 10.00
21 Reggie Wayne 1.25 3.00
22 Tom Brady 4.00 10.00
23 Devery Henderson 1.00 2.50
24 Ben Roethlisberger 1.50 4.00
25 Marion Barber 1.25 3.00

2010 Classics Sunday's Best Jerseys

STATED PRINT RUN 100-299
1 Vernon Davis/105 2.50 6.00
3 Larry Fitzgerald/299 3.00 8.00
4 Chris Johnson/299 2.50 6.00
6 Tony Romo/299 3.00 8.00
7 Ryan Grant/145 3.00 8.00
8 Josh Cribbs/299 2.50 6.00
9 Vince Young/299 2.50 6.00
10 Sidney Rice/299 2.50 6.00
11 Vincent Jackson/299 2.50 6.00
12 DeAngelo Williams/299 2.50 6.00
13 Carson Palmer/299 3.00 8.00
14 Maurice Jones-Drew/299 2.50 6.00
15 Brett Favre/100 10.00 25.00
16 Drew Brees/100 5.00 12.00
17 Frank Gore/250 3.00 8.00
18 Ronnie Brown/150 2.50 6.00
19 Adrian Peterson/280 4.00 10.00
20 Peyton Manning/299 10.00 25.00
21 Reggie Wayne/299 3.00 8.00
22 Tom Brady/150 10.00 25.00
23 Devery Henderson/299 2.50 6.00
24 Ben Roethlisberger/299 4.00 10.00
25 Marion Barber/299 3.00 8.00

2010 Classics Sunday's Best Jerseys Prime

*PRIME/45-50: .6X TO 1.5X JSY/145-299
*PRIME/25: .8X TO 2X JSY/145-299
PRIME JSY PRINT RUN 9-50
2 Aaron Rodgers/25 15.00 40.00

2010 Classics Sunday's Best Jerseys Autographs

STATED PRINT RUN 5-25
EXCH EXPIRATION: 1/28/2012
1 Vernon Davis/10
4 Chris Johnson/5
6 Tony Romo/10
7 Ryan Grant/25 20.00 50.00
8 Josh Cribbs/15 40.00 80.00
9 Vince Young/10
10 Sidney Rice/10
11 Vincent Jackson/15 15.00 40.00
12 DeAngelo Williams/15 15.00 40.00
13 Carson Palmer/10
14 Maurice Jones-Drew/10
15 Brett Favre/10
16 Drew Brees/5
17 Frank Gore/10
18 Ronnie Brown/10
19 Adrian Peterson/10
20 Peyton Manning/20 60.00 120.00
21 Reggie Wayne/10
22 Tom Brady/5
23 Devery Henderson/25 15.00 40.00
24 Ben Roethlisberger/10

2010 Classics Super Bowl Pigskins

STATED PRINT RUN 4-100
1 Fred Biletnikoff/25 10.00 25.00
2 Bart Starr/24 40.00 80.00
4 Jim Taylor/10
5 Harvey Martin/25 20.00 40.00
6 Jerry Rice/100 15.00 40.00
7 Thurman Thomas/75 12.00 30.00
8 Troy Aikman/4

2010 Classics Super Bowl Pigskins Combos

STATED PRINT RUN 5-25
1 B.Starr/J.Taylor/10
2 R.Staubach/T.Dorsett/10
3 J.Montana/J.Rice/25 30.00 80.00
4 T.Aikman/E.Smith/5

2010 Classics Team Colors

1 Rob Gronkowski 2.50 6.00
2 Rolando McClain .75 2.00
3 Ryan Mathews .75 2.00
4 Sam Bradford 1.00 2.50
5 Taylor Price .75 2.00
6 Tim Tebow 2.50 6.00
7 Toby Gerhart .75 2.00
8 Andre Roberts 1.00 2.50
9 Armanti Edwards 1.00 2.50
10 Arrelious Benn .75 2.00
11 Ben Tate .75 2.00
12 Brandon LaFell 1.25 3.00
13 C.J. Spiller .75 2.00
14 Colt McCoy 1.00 2.50
15 Damian Williams .75 2.00
16 Demaryius Thomas 2.00 5.00
17 Dexter McCluster 1.00 2.50
18 Dez Bryant 2.00 5.00
19 Emmanuel Sanders 1.25 3.00
20 Eric Berry 1.25 3.00
21 Eric Decker 1.00 2.50
22 Gerald McCoy .75 2.00
23 Golden Tate 1.00 2.50
24 Jahvid Best .75 2.00
25 Jermaine Gresham .75 2.00
26 Jimmy Clausen .75 2.00
27 Joe McKnight .75 2.00
28 Jonathan Dwyer .75 2.00
29 Jordan Shipley .75 2.00
30 Marcus Easley .75 2.00
31 Mardy Gilyard .75 2.00
32 Mike Kafka 1.00 2.50
33 Mike Williams .75 2.00
34 Montario Hardesty .75 2.00
35 Ndamukong Suh 1.50 4.00

2010 Classics Team Colors Autographs

STATED PRINT RUN 25 SER.#'d SETS
1 Rob Gronkowski 40.00 80.00
2 Rolando McClain 8.00 20.00
3 Ryan Mathews 8.00 20.00
4 Sam Bradford 10.00 25.00
5 Taylor Price 8.00 20.00
6 Tim Tebow 30.00 80.00
7 Toby Gerhart 8.00 20.00
8 Andre Roberts 10.00 25.00
9 Armanti Edwards 10.00 25.00
10 Arrelious Benn 8.00 20.00
11 Ben Tate 8.00 20.00
12 Brandon LaFell 12.00 30.00
13 C.J. Spiller 8.00 20.00
14 Colt McCoy 10.00 25.00
15 Damian Williams 8.00 20.00
16 Demaryius Thomas 20.00 50.00
17 Dexter McCluster 10.00 25.00
18 Dez Bryant 50.00 100.00
19 Emmanuel Sanders 12.00 30.00
20 Eric Berry 12.00 30.00
21 Eric Decker 10.00 25.00
22 Gerald McCoy 8.00 20.00
23 Golden Tate 10.00 25.00
24 Jahvid Best 8.00 20.00
25 Jermaine Gresham
26 Jimmy Clausen 8.00 20.00
27 Joe McKnight 8.00 20.00
28 Jonathan Dwyer 8.00 20.00
29 Jordan Shipley 8.00 20.00
30 Marcus Easley
31 Mardy Gilyard 8.00 20.00
32 Mike Kafka 10.00 25.00
33 Mike Williams 8.00 20.00
34 Montario Hardesty
35 Ndamukong Suh 15.00 40.00

2010 Classics Team Colors Materials

STATED PRINT RUN 299 SER.#'d SETS
*PRIME/50: .8X TO 2X JSY/299
1 Rob Gronkowski 6.00 15.00
2 Rolando McClain 2.00 5.00
3 Ryan Mathews 2.00 5.00
4 Sam Bradford 2.50 6.00
5 Taylor Price 2.00 5.00
6 Tim Tebow 8.00 20.00
7 Toby Gerhart 2.00 5.00
8 Andre Roberts 2.50 6.00
9 Armanti Edwards 2.50 6.00
10 Arrelious Benn 2.00 5.00
11 Ben Tate 2.00 5.00
12 Brandon LaFell 3.00 8.00
13 C.J. Spiller 2.00 5.00
14 Colt McCoy 2.50 6.00
15 Damian Williams 2.00 5.00
16 Demaryius Thomas 5.00 12.00
17 Dexter McCluster 2.50 6.00
18 Dez Bryant 10.00 25.00
19 Emmanuel Sanders 3.00 8.00
20 Eric Berry 3.00 8.00
21 Eric Decker 2.50 6.00
22 Gerald McCoy 2.00 5.00
23 Golden Tate 2.50 6.00
24 Jahvid Best 2.00 5.00
25 Jermaine Gresham 2.00 5.00
26 Jimmy Clausen 2.00 5.00
27 Joe McKnight 2.00 5.00
28 Jonathan Dwyer 2.00 5.00
29 Jordan Shipley 2.00 5.00
30 Marcus Easley 2.00 5.00
31 Mardy Gilyard 2.00 5.00
32 Mike Kafka 2.50 6.00
33 Mike Williams 2.00 5.00
34 Montario Hardesty 2.00 5.00
35 Ndamukong Suh 4.00 10.00

2016 Classics

1 Amari Cooper .30 .75
2 Joe Flacco .25 .60
3 Nick Foles .25 .60
4 Adrian Peterson .30 .75
5 T.Y. Hilton .25 .60
6A Tom Brady .75 2.00
6B Tom Brady SP 5.00 12.00
7A Cam Newton .30 .75
7B Cam Newton SP 2.00 5.00
8 Lamar Miller .20 .50
9 Mark Ingram .25 .60
10 Jason Witten .25 .60
11 Philip Rivers .30 .75
12 Justin Forsett .25 .60
13A Todd Gurley .30 .75
13B Todd Gurley SP 2.00 5.00
14 Stefon Diggs .25 .60
15 Brian Hoyer .20 .50
16 Rob Gronkowski .30 .75
17 Jonathan Stewart .20 .50
18 Jarvis Landry .25 .60
19 Brandin Cooks .25 .60
20 Sam Bradford .20 .50
21 Melvin Gordon .25 .60
22 Kamar Aiken .20 .50
23 Kenny Britt .20 .50
24 Jay Cutler .20 .50
25 Arian Foster .25 .60
26 Julian Edelman .30 .75
27 Greg Olsen .25 .60
28 Kirk Cousins .30 .75
29A Peyton Manning .60 1.50
29B Peyton Manning SP 4.00 10.00
30 DeMarco Murray .25 .60
31 Keenan Allen .25 .60
32 Isaiah Crowell .20 .50
33 Colin Kaepernick .25 .60
34 Matt Forte .20 .50
35 DeAndre Hopkins .25 .60
36 Ryan Fitzpatrick .20 .50
37A Jameis Winston .30 .75
37B Jameis Winston SP 2.00 5.00
38 Alfred Morris .20 .50
39 Ronnie Hillman .20 .50
40 Jordan Matthews .25 .60
41 Carson Palmer .25 .60
42 Gary Barnidge .20 .50
43 Carlos Hyde .20 .50
44 Alshon Jeffery .25 .60
45 Blake Bortles .20 .50
46 Chris Ivory .25 .60
47 Doug Martin .25 .60
48 DeSean Jackson .25 .60
49 Demaryius Thomas .25 .60
50 Andy Dalton .25 .60
51 Chris Johnson .20 .50
52 Travis Benjamin .20 .50
53 Anquan Boldin .20 .50
54 Matthew Stafford .25 .60
55 Allen Robinson .25 .60
56 Brandon Marshall .20 .50
57 Mike Evans .25 .60
58 Eli Manning .25 .60
59 Alex Smith .25 .60
60 Jeremy Hill .20 .50
61 Larry Fitzgerald .25 .60
62A Aaron Rodgers .60 1.50
62B Aaron Rodgers SP 4.00 10.00
63 Richard Sherman .30 .75
64 Ameer Abdullah .20 .50
65 Allen Hurns .20 .50
66 Tyrod Taylor .25 .60
67 Matt Ryan .25 .60
68 Rashad Jennings .20 .50
69 Jamaal Charles .25 .60
70 A.J. Green .30 .75
71A Russell Wilson .40 1.00
71B Russell Wilson SP 2.50 6.00
72 Eddie Lacy .20 .50
73 Josh Norman .20 .50
74A Calvin Johnson .30 .75
74B Calvin Johnson SP 2.00 5.00
75A Marcus Mariota .30 .75
75B Marcus Mariota SP 2.00 5.00
76 LeSean McCoy .30 .75
77 Devonta Freeman .25 .60
78A Odell Beckham Jr. .30 .75
78B Odell Beckham Jr. SP 6.00 15.00
79 Jeremy Maclin .20 .50
80 Ben Roethlisberger .30 .75
81 Marshawn Lynch .25 .60
82 Jordy Nelson .25 .60
83 J.J. Watt .30 .75
84A Andrew Luck .40 1.00
84B Andrew Luck SP 2.50 6.00
85 Antonio Andrews .20 .50
86 Sammy Watkins .30 .75
87A Julio Jones .30 .75
87B Julio Jones SP 2.00 5.00
88A Tony Romo .25 .60
88B Tony Romo SP 1.50 4.00
89 Derek Carr .30 .75
90 Le'Veon Bell .25 .60
91 Jimmy Graham .30 .75
92 Teddy Bridgewater .25 .60
93 Darrelle Revis .20 .50
94 Frank Gore .25 .60
95 Delanie Walker .20 .50
96 Ryan Tannehill .25 .60
97A Drew Brees .30 .75
97B Drew Brees SP 2.00 5.00
98A Dez Bryant .30 .75
98B Dez Bryant SP 2.00 5.00
99 Latavius Murray .20 .50
100 Antonio Brown .30 .75
101 Michael Strahan .50 1.25
102 Daunte Culpepper .50 1.25
103 Rod Woodson .50 1.25
104 Edgerrin James .50 1.25
105A Terry Bradshaw .75 2.00
105B Terry Bradshaw SP 6.00 15.00
106 Harold Carmichael .40 1.00
107 Jim Plunkett .50 1.25
108 Aeneas Williams .40 1.00
109 Kurt Warner .50 1.25
110 Carl Eller .40 1.00
111 Mike Ditka .60 1.50
112A Deion Sanders .50 1.25
112B Deion Sanders SP 1.50 4.00
113 Roger Craig .50 1.25
114A Emmitt Smith 1.00 2.50
114B Emmitt Smith SP 3.00 8.00
115 Thurman Thomas .50 1.25
116 Herman Edwards .50 1.25
117 Dermontti Dawson .50 1.25
118 Andre Reed .50 1.25
119 LaDainian Tomlinson .50 1.25
120 Champ Bailey .50 1.25
121 Ozzie Newsome .50 1.25
122 Plaxico Burress .40 1.00
123A Roger Staubach .75 2.00
123B Roger Staubach SP 2.50 6.00
124 Eric Dickerson .50 1.25
125 Tim Brown .60 1.50
126 Ickey Woods .40 1.00
127A Joe Montana 1.50 4.00
127B Joe Montana SP 5.00 12.00
128 Antonio Freeman .50 1.25
129 Larry Csonka .50 1.25
130 Charles Haley .60 1.50
131 Paul Hornung .60 1.50
132 Mike Singletary .60 1.50
133 Ron Jaworski .50 1.25
134 Forrest Gregg .40 1.00
135 Tony Dorsett .60 1.50
136 Jackie Slater .40 1.00
137A Joe Namath .75 2.00
137B Joe Namath SP 2.50 6.00
138A Barry Sanders 1.00 2.50
138B Barry Sanders SP 3.00 8.00
139 Lawrence Taylor .60 1.50
140 Charlie Joiner .40 1.00
141 Paul Warfield .50 1.25
142 Don Majkowski .50 1.25
143 Ronnie Lott .50 1.25
144 Fran Tarkenton .60 1.50
145 Torry Holt .50 1.25
146 Jackie Smith .40 1.00
147 Joe Theismann .60 1.50
148 Bo Jackson .75 2.00
149 Len Dawson .60 1.50
150 Cris Carter .60 1.50
151 Randy White .50 1.25
152 Donald Driver .50 1.25
153 Shannon Sharpe .60 1.50
154 Franco Harris .60 1.50
155A Troy Aikman .75 2.00
155B Troy Aikman SP 2.50 6.00
156 James Lofton .50 1.25
157A John Elway 1.00 2.50
157B John Elway SP 3.00 8.00
158 Bob Griese .60 1.50
159 Lenny Moore .40 1.00
160 Cris Collinsworth .50 1.25
161 Raymond Berry .50 1.25
162 Doug Flutie .50 1.25
163 Steve Largent .60 1.50
164 Sonny Jurgensen .50 1.25
165 Warren Moon .60 1.50
166 Jerome Bettis .60 1.50
167 John Randle .50 1.25
168 Bob Lilly .50 1.25
169 Marcus Allen .50 1.25
170 Curtis Martin .50 1.25
171 Ricky Williams .50 1.25
172 Doug Williams .50 1.25
173 Steve Young .75 2.00
174 Fred Biletnikoff .60 1.50
175 Warren Sapp .50 1.25
176A Jerry Rice 1.00 2.50
176B Jerry Rice SP 3.00 8.00
177A John Riggins .50 1.25
177B John Riggins SP 1.50 4.00
178A Brett Favre 1.25 3.00
178B Brett Favre SP 4.00 10.00
179 Mark Chmura .40 1.00
180 Dan Hampton .40 1.00
181 Robert Brooks .50 1.25
182 Dwight Clark .50 1.25
183 Ted Hendricks .40 1.00
184 Fred Taylor .40 1.00
185 Wilbert Montgomery .40 1.00
186A Jim Kelly .60 1.50
186B Jim Kelly SP 2.00 5.00
187 Mike Quick .40 1.00
188 Brian Urlacher .60 1.50
189 Marshall Faulk .50 1.25
190A Dan Marino 1.25 3.00
190B Dan Marino SP 4.00 10.00
191 Rod Smith .50 1.25
192 Earl Campbell .60 1.50
193 Terrell Davis .50 1.25
194 Gale Sayers .60 1.50
195 Willie McGinest .40 1.00
196 Jim McMahon .50 1.25
197 Kellen Winslow .50 1.25
198 Bruce Smith .50 1.25
199A Michael Irvin .60 1.50
199B Michael Irvin SP 2.00 5.00
200 Darrell Green .50 1.25
201 Daniel Lasco RC .25 .60
202 Emmanuel Ogbah RC .30 .75
203 Eli Apple RC .30 .75
204 Jayron Kearse RC .25 .60
205 Jordan Payton RC .25 .60
206 Aaron Burbridge RC .25 .60
207 Kevin Dodd RC .25 .60
208 Brandon Allen RC .25 .60
209 Myles Jack RC .30 .75
210 Corey Coleman RC .40 1.00
211 Scooby Wright III RC .25 .60
212A Ezekiel Elliott RC 1.25 3.00
212B Ezekiel Elliott SP 4.00 10.00
213 Vernon Butler RC .25 .60
214 Jeff Driskel RC .25 .60
215 Jordan Williams RC .25 .60
216 Aaron Green RC .25 .60
217 Kevin Hogan RC .30 .75
218 Brandon Doughty RC .25 .60
219 Nate Sudfeld RC .25 .60
220 Dak Prescott RC 1.25 3.00
221 Shaq Lawson RC .25 .60
222 Sheldon Rankins RC .30 .75
223 Tyler Boyd RC .30 .75
224 Jerell Adams RC .25 .60
225A Josh Doctson RC .30 .75
225B Josh Doctson SP 1.00 2.50
226 Adolphus Washington RC .25 .60
227 Kolby Listenbee RC .25 .60
228 Braxton Miller RC .25 .60
229 Nelson Spruce RC .25 .60
230 Daniel Braverman RC .25 .60
231 Noah Spence RC .25 .60
232 Hunter Henry RC .30 .75
233 Tyler Ervin RC .25 .60
234 Jeremy Cash RC .30 .75
235 Josh Ferguson RC .25 .60
236 Alex Collins RC .30 .75
237A Laquon Treadwell RC .30 .75
237B Laquon Treadwell SP 1.00 2.50
238 Byron Marshall RC .25 .60
239 Nick Vannett RC .25 .60
240 Darron Lee RC .25 .60
241 Shilique Calhoun RC .25 .60
242 Charles Tapper RC .30 .75
243 Vernon Hargreaves III RC .40 1.00
244A Joey Bosa RC .50 1.25
244B Joey Bosa SP 1.50 4.00
245 Kelvin Taylor RC .25 .60
246 Andrew Billings RC .30 .75
247 Laremy Tunsil RC .25 .60
248 C.J. Prosise RC .25 .60
249 Paul Perkins RC .25 .60
250 DeForest Buckner RC .25 .60
251 Sterling Shepard RC .30 .75
252A Jalen Ramsey RC .40 1.00
252B Jalen Ramsey SP 1.25 3.00
253 Vonn Bell RC .30 .75
254 Karl Joseph RC .25 .60
255 Kendall Fuller RC .30 .75
256 Keith Marshall RC .25 .60
257 Leonard Floyd RC .30 .75
258 Cardale Jones RC .25 .60
259A Paxton Lynch RC .25 .60
259B Paxton Lynch SP .75 2.00
260 Glenn Gronkowski RC .25 .60
261 Su'a Cravens RC .25 .60
262A Jared Goff RC 1.50 4.00
262B Jared Goff SP 5.00 12.00
263 Wendell Smallwood RC .25 .60
264 Jonathan Williams RC .30 .75
265 Kenneth Dixon RC .25 .60
266 A'Shawn Robinson RC .25 .60
267 Leonte Carroo RC .25 .60
268A Carson Wentz RC 2.50 6.00
268B Carson Wentz SP 8.00 20.00
269 Pharoh Cooper RC .25 .60
270 Demarcus Robinson RC .25 .60
271 Tajae Sharpe RC .30 .75
272 Jarran Reed RC .25 .60
273 Will Fuller RC .40 1.00
274 Jacoby Brissett RC .30 .75
275 Kenny Clark RC .25 .60
276 Austin Hooper RC .25 .60
277 Mackensie Alexander RC .25 .60
278 Christian Hackenberg RC .25 .60
279 Rashard Higgins RC .25 .60
280A Derrick Henry RC .60 1.50
280B Derrick Henry SP 2.00 5.00
281 Malcolm Mitchell RC .25 .60
282 Kamalei Correa RC .25 .60
283 Tre Madden RC .25 .60
284 Vernon Adams Jr. RC .40 1.00
285 Kenny Lawler RC .40 1.00
286 Austin Johnson RC .25 .60
287 Maliek Collins RC .25 .60
288 Cody Kessler RC .25 .60
289 Reggie Ragland RC .25 .60
290 De'Runnya Wilson RC .25 .60
291 Thomas Duarte RC .25 .60
292 Jaylon Smith RC .25 .60
293 William Jackson III RC .30 .75
294 Jordan Howard RC .60 1.50
295 Kenyan Drake RC .40 1.00
296 Braxton Addison RC .25 .60
297 Michael Thomas RC .50 1.25
298A Connor Cook RC .30 .75
298B Connor Cook SP 1.00 2.50
299 Robert Nkemdiche RC .30 .75
300 Devontae Booker RC .30 .75

2016 Classics Blank Back

*VETS: 4X TO 10X BASIC CARDS
*LEGENDS: 2X TO 5X BASIC CARDS
*ROOKIES: 3X TO 8X BASIC CARDS

2016 Classics Glossy
*VETS: 2X TO 5X BASIC CARDS
*LEGENDS: 1X TO 2.5X BASIC CARDS
*ROOKIES: 1.5X TO 4X BASIC CARDS

2016 Classics Red Back
*VETS: 2.5X TO 6X BASIC CARDS
*LEGENDS: 1X TO 2.5X BASIC CARDS
*ROOKIES: 2X TO 5X BASIC CARDS

2016 Classics Timeless Tributes Bronze
*VETS: 3X TO 8X BASIC CARDS
*LEGENDS: 1.5X TO 4X BASIC CARDS
*ROOKIES: 2.5X TO 6X BASIC CARDS

2016 Classics Timeless Tributes Silver
*VETS: 5X TO 12X BASIC CARDS
*LEGENDS: 2.5X TO 6X BASIC CARDS
*ROOKIES: 4X TO 10X BASIC CARDS

2016 Classics Canton Collections Autographs
CANAW Aeneas Williams/49 8.00 20.00
CANCJ Charlie Joiner/99 10.00 25.00
CANDH Dan Hampton/99 10.00 25.00
CANFT Fran Tarkenton/25 15.00 40.00
CANGS Gale Sayers/25 25.00 60.00
CANJH John Hannah/99 10.00 25.00
CANJS Jackie Smith/49 8.00 20.00
CANJS Jan Stenerud/47 8.00 20.00
CANJS Jackie Slater/49 10.00 25.00
CANLM Lenny Moore/49 8.00 20.00
CANON Ozzie Newsome/49 10.00 25.00
CANPW Paul Warfield/49 10.00 25.00
CANRB Raymond Berry/25 12.00 30.00
CANRL Ronnie Lott/25 25.00 50.00
CANRW Randy White/49 10.00 25.00

2016 Classics Canton Collections Swatches
1 Paul Warfield/99 2.50 6.00
2 Jim Kelly/99 3.00 8.00
3 Steve Young/199 4.00 10.00
4 Troy Aikman/99 4.00 10.00
5 Joe Montana/49 10.00 25.00
6 John Elway/199 5.00 12.00
7 Larry Csonka/99 2.50 6.00
8 Bob Griese/99 3.00 8.00
9 Marcus Allen/199 2.50 6.00
10 Earl Campbell/199 3.00 8.00
11 Roger Staubach/49 5.00 12.00
12 Jim Thorpe/49 5.00 12.00
13 Thurman Thomas/99 2.50 6.00
14 Joe Namath/99 4.00 10.00
15 Tim Brown/99 3.00 8.00
16 Jan Stenerud/199 2.00 5.00
17 Dan Marino/99 6.00 15.00
18 Len Dawson/99 3.00 8.00
19 Mike Ditka/99 3.00 8.00
20 Jerry Rice/99 5.00 12.00

2016 Classics Classic Clashes
*BRONZE: .8X TO 2X BASIC INSERTS
1 E.Manning/T.Romo .60 1.50
2 B.Rthlsbrgr/K.Warner .75 2.00
3 R.Wilson/C.Palmer 1.00 2.50
4 J.Kelly/T.Aikman 1.00 2.50
5 D.Sanders/J.Rice 1.25 3.00
6 P.Manning/T.Brady 2.00 5.00
7 R.Staubach/T.Bradshaw 1.00 2.50
8 R.Wilson/P.Manning 1.50 4.00
9 S.Young/T.Aikman 1.00 2.50
10 J.Norman/O.Beckham .75 2.00
11 A.Rodgers/J.Cutler 1.50 4.00
12 K.Warner/T.Brady 2.00 5.00
13 A.Luck/P.Manning 1.50 4.00
14 D.Revis/R.Sherman .75 2.00
15 J.Elway/J.Montana 2.00 5.00
16 R.Wilson/T.Brady 2.00 5.00
17 B.Favre/J.Elway 1.50 4.00
18 E.Manning/T.Brady 2.00 5.00
19 J.Montana/L.Taylor 2.00 5.00
20 B.Rthlsbrgr/A.Rodgers 1.50 4.00

2016 Classics Classic Combos Memorabilia
1 J.Kelly/T.Thomas/99 4.00 10.00
2 B.Griese/L.Csonka/99 4.00 10.00
3 A.Green/A.Dalton/199 4.00 10.00
4 J.Montana/J.Rice/49 25.00 50.00
5 D.McFadden/T.Romo/199 15.00 30.00
6 J.Landry/R.Tannehill/199 3.00 8.00
7 C.Johnson/M.Stafford/99 4.00 10.00
8 B.Favre/A.Rodgers/25 60.00 100.00
9 J.Jones/M.Ryan/99 4.00 10.00
10 M.Allen/B.Jackson/99 10.00 25.00
11 C.Palmer/L.Fitzgerald/99 3.00 8.00
12 T.Brady/J.Edelman/25 60.00 100.00
13 R.Staubach/T.Aikman/49 25.00 50.00
14 V.Miller/D.Ware/199 3.00 8.00
15 J.Elway/P.Manning/49 30.00 60.00

2016 Classics Classic Material
*PRIME/25: .6X TO 1.5X BASIC JSY/99-199
1 Brian Urlacher/99 3.00 8.00
2 Ozzie Newsome/99 2.50 6.00
3 Carl Eller/99 2.00 5.00
4 Rod Woodson/99 2.50 6.00
5 Antonio Gates/99 2.00 5.00
6 T.Y. Hilton/199 2.50 6.00
7 Doug Flutie/199 2.50 6.00
8 Jan Stenerud/199 2.00 5.00
9 Adrian Peterson/199 3.00 8.00
10 LaDainian Tomlinson/99 2.50 6.00
11 Bruce Smith/199 2.50 6.00
12 Randy White/99 2.50 6.00
13 Charles Haley/199 3.00 8.00
14 Roger Craig/149 2.50 6.00
15 Derek Carr/199 3.00 8.00
16 Tyler Lockett/199 2.50 6.00
17 Drew Brees/49 4.00 10.00
18 Jay Cutler/99 2.00 5.00
19 Ameer Abdullah/199 2.00 5.00
20 Marshawn Lynch/99 2.50 6.00
21 Cam Newton/49 4.00 10.00
22 Ricky Williams/199 2.50 6.00
23 Cordarrelle Patterson/199 2.00 5.00
24 Ronnie Lott/199 2.50 6.00
25 DeSean Jackson/99 2.50 6.00
26 Warren Sapp/30 3.00 8.00
27 Eli Manning/49 3.00 8.00
28 Joe Theismann/199 3.00 8.00
29 Bob Lilly/99 2.50 6.00

2016 Classics Classic Moments
*BRONZE: .8X TO 2X BASIC INSERTS
1 Roger Staubach 1.00 2.50
2 Eli Manning .60 1.50
3 John Riggins .60 1.50
4 Len Dawson .75 2.00
5 Franco Harris .75 2.00
6 Emmitt Smith 1.25 3.00
7 Malcolm Butler .75 2.00
8 Herman Edwards .60 1.50
9 Joe Montana 2.00 5.00
10 Hines Ward .60 1.50
11 Andre Reed .60 1.50
12 Terrell Davis .60 1.50
13 Steve Young 1.00 2.50
14 Dan Marino 1.50 4.00
15 Dwight Clark .60 1.50
16 Michael Strahan .60 1.50
17 Tom Brady 2.00 5.00
18 Tony Dorsett .75 2.00
19 John Elway 1.25 3.00
20 Aaron Donald 1.50 4.00

2016 Classics Future Legends
*BRONZE: .8X TO 2X BASIC INSERTS
1 Jameis Winston .75 2.00
2 Marcus Mariota .75 2.00
3 Todd Gurley .75 2.00
4 David Johnson .75 2.00
5 Thomas Rawls .50 1.25
6 T.J. Yeldon .50 1.25
7 Amari Cooper .75 2.00
8 Stefon Diggs .60 1.50
9 Tyler Lockett .60 1.50
10 Jamison Crowder .50 1.25
11 Joey Bosa .60 1.50
12 Jared Goff 2.00 5.00
13 Paxton Lynch .30 .75
14 Connor Cook .40 1.00
15 Ezekiel Elliott 1.50 4.00
16 Derrick Henry .75 2.00
17 Laquon Treadwell .40 1.00
18 Corey Coleman .50 1.25
19 Carson Wentz 3.00 8.00
20 Josh Doctson .40 1.00

2016 Classics Instant Classics Ink
10 Thurman Thomas/25 12.00 30.00
11 Jack Ham/25 20.00 50.00
12 Darrell Green/25 20.00 50.00
13 Joe Theismann/25 15.00 40.00
14 Hines Ward/25 30.00 60.00
15 Doug Williams/25 12.00 30.00
16 James Lofton/25 12.00 30.00
17 Doug Flutie/49 10.00 25.00
18 Rod Woodson/40 10.00 25.00
19 Ricky Williams/49 10.00 25.00
20 Jim Plunkett/49 10.00 25.00
21 Herman Edwards/49 10.00 25.00
22 Dwight Clark/49 15.00 40.00
23 Roger Craig/49 10.00 25.00
24 Antonio Freeman/49 10.00 25.00
25 Andre Reed/49 10.00 25.00
26 Aeneas Williams/99 6.00 15.00
27 Lenny Moore/25 10.00 25.00
28 Kellen Winslow/99 8.00 20.00
29 Ickey Woods/99
30 Troy Brown/99 12.00 30.00

2016 Classics Monday Night Heroes
*BRONZE: .8X TO 2X BASIC INSERTS
1 Julio Jones .75 2.00
2 Marshall Faulk .60 1.50
3 Le'Veon Bell .60 1.50
4 Cam Newton .75 2.00
5 Drew Brees .75 2.00
6 Eli Manning .60 1.50
7 Bo Jackson 1.00 2.50
8 Alex Smith .60 1.50
9 Tom Brady 2.00 5.00
10 Colin Kaepernick .60 1.50
11 Brandon Marshall .50 1.25
12 Peyton Manning 1.50 4.00
13 DeMarco Murray .60 1.50
14 Jay Cutler .50 1.25
15 Jerry Rice 1.25 3.00
16 Matthew Stafford .60 1.50
17 Earl Campbell .75 2.00
18 Russell Wilson 1.00 2.50
19 Brett Favre 1.50 4.00
20 Andrew Luck 1.00 2.50
21 Aaron Rodgers 1.50 4.00
22 Ricky Williams .60 1.50
23 Carson Palmer .60 1.50
24 Odell Beckham Jr. .75 2.00
25 Steve Young 1.00 2.50

2016 Classics Record Breakers
*BRONZE: .8X TO 2X BASIC INSERTS
1 Thurman Thomas .50 1.25
2 Tom Brady 1.50 4.00
3 Adrian Peterson .60 1.50
4 Peyton Manning 1.25 3.00
5 Dan Marino 1.25 3.00
6 Emmitt Smith 1.00 2.50
7 Brett Favre 1.25 3.00
8 Bruce Smith .50 1.25
9 Tim Brown .60 1.50
10 Tony Dorsett .60 1.50
11 Eli Manning .50 1.25
12 Willie McGinest .40 1.00
13 Gale Sayers .60 1.50
14 Aaron Rodgers 1.25 3.00
15 Tony Romo .50 1.25
16 Jerry Rice 1.00 2.50
17 Barry Sanders 1.00 2.50
18 Eric Dickerson .50 1.25
19 Antonio Gates .40 1.00
20 Calvin Johnson .60 1.50
21 Michael Irvin .60 1.50
22 Ronnie Lott .50 1.25
23 Joe Namath .75 2.00
24 Drew Brees .60 1.50
25 Ben Roethlisberger .60 1.50
26 Rod Woodson .50 1.25
27 John Elway 1.00 2.50
28 LaDainian Tomlinson .50 1.25
29 Larry Fitzgerald .50 1.25
30 Michael Strahan .50 1.25

2016 Classics Sideline Generals Signatures
1 Bill Parcells/25 25.00 60.00
2 Mike Ditka/10
3 Herman Edwards/99 8.00 20.00
4 Mike Singletary/70 10.00 25.00
5 Forrest Gregg/25 12.00 30.00

2016 Classics Significant Signatures
14 Stefon Diggs/99 8.00 20.00
19 Brandin Cooks/25 12.00 30.00
21 Melvin Gordon/25 12.00 30.00
25 Arian Foster/25 12.00 30.00
27 Greg Olsen/25 12.00 30.00
31 Keenan Allen/25 12.00 30.00
32 Isaiah Crowell/49 8.00 20.00
34 Matt Forte/25 10.00 25.00
40 Jordan Matthews/25 12.00 30.00
44 Alshon Jeffery/25 12.00 30.00
45 Blake Bortles/25
57 Mike Evans/25 12.00 30.00
64 Ameer Abdullah/99 6.00 15.00
77 Devonta Freeman/99 8.00 20.00
82 Jordy Nelson/25 12.00 30.00
92 Teddy Bridgewater/25 12.00 30.00
99 Latavius Murray/99 6.00 15.00
102 Daunte Culpepper/35 10.00 25.00
103 Rod Woodson/25 12.00 30.00
106 Harold Carmichael/99 6.00 15.00
107 Jim Plunkett/15 15.00 40.00
108 Aeneas Williams/49 8.00 20.00
110 Carl Eller/75 6.00 15.00
113 Roger Craig/49
115 Thurman Thomas/15
116 Herman Edwards/25 12.00 30.00
117 Dermontti Dawson/99 8.00 20.00
118 Andre Reed/25 12.00 30.00
119 LaDainian Tomlinson/15 15.00 40.00
120 Champ Bailey/49 10.00 25.00
121 Ozzie Newsome/49 10.00 25.00
122 Plaxico Burress/49 8.00 20.00
124 Eric Dickerson/15 15.00 40.00
125 Tim Brown/15 20.00 50.00
126 Ickey Woods/99 6.00 15.00
128 Antonio Freeman/25 12.00 30.00
131 Paul Hornung/25 25.00 60.00
132 Mike Singletary/15 20.00 50.00
133 Ron Jaworski/49 10.00 25.00
136 Jackie Slater/25 10.00 25.00
140 Charlie Joiner/99 6.00 15.00
141 Paul Warfield/25 12.00 30.00
142 Don Majkowski/49 10.00 25.00
143 Ronnie Lott/15 15.00 40.00
144 Fran Tarkenton/15 20.00 50.00
146 Jackie Smith/49 8.00 20.00
147 Joe Theismann/15 20.00 50.00
149 Len Dawson/15 20.00 50.00
151 Randy White/25 12.00 30.00
152 Donald Driver/15 15.00 40.00
154 Franco Harris/15 20.00 50.00
156 James Lofton/15 15.00 40.00
158 Bob Griese/15 20.00 50.00
159 Lenny Moore/49 8.00 20.00
160 Cris Collinsworth/15
161 Raymond Berry/15 15.00 40.00
162 Doug Flutie/25
163 Steve Largent/15 30.00 60.00
165 Warren Moon/15 20.00 50.00
166 Jerome Bettis/15 40.00 80.00
167 John Randle/15 12.00 30.00
168 Bob Lilly/25 12.00 30.00
169 Marcus Allen/15 15.00 40.00
171 Ricky Williams/49 10.00 25.00
172 Doug Williams/15 15.00 40.00
175 Warren Sapp/15 15.00 40.00
179 Mark Chmura/99 6.00 15.00
180 Dan Hampton/25 10.00 25.00
181 Robert Brooks/99 8.00 20.00
182 Dwight Clark/25 12.00 30.00
184 Fred Taylor/15 12.00 30.00
185 Wilbert Montgomery/99 6.00 15.00
187 Mike Quick/49 4.00 10.00
193 Terrell Davis/15 15.00 40.00
194 Gale Sayers/15
195 Willie McGinest/25 10.00 25.00
196 Jim McMahon/15 40.00 80.00
197 Kellen Winslow/49 10.00 25.00
198 Bruce Smith/15 15.00 40.00
200 Darrell Green/15 40.00 80.00
201 Daniel Lasco/299 2.50 6.00
202 Emmanuel Ogbah/299 3.00 8.00
203 Eli Apple/199 3.00 8.00
204 Jayron Kearse/199 2.50 6.00
205 Jordan Payton/299 2.50 6.00
206 Aaron Burbridge/99 3.00 8.00
207 Kevin Dodd/199 2.50 6.00
208 Brandon Allen/199 2.50 6.00
209 Myles Jack/199 3.00 8.00
210 Corey Coleman/49 6.00 15.00
211 Scooby Wright III/299 2.50 6.00
212 Ezekiel Elliott/25 75.00 150.00
213 Vernon Butler/199 2.50 6.00
214 Jeff Driskel/299 2.50 6.00
215 Jordan Williams/299 2.50 6.00
216 Aaron Green/199 2.50 6.00
217 Kevin Hogan/299 3.00 8.00
218 Brandon Doughty/199 2.50 6.00
219 Nate Sudfeld/199 2.50 6.00
220 Dak Prescott/99 40.00 80.00
221 Shaq Lawson/99 3.00 8.00
222 Sheldon Rankins/299 3.00 8.00
224 Jerell Adams/199 2.50 6.00
225 Josh Doctson/25 6.00 15.00
226 Adolphus Washington/299 2.50 6.00
227 Kolby Listenbee/299 2.50 6.00
228 Braxton Miller/49 4.00 10.00
229 Nelson Spruce/99 3.00 8.00
230 Daniel Braverman/299 2.50 6.00
231 Noah Spence/199 2.50 6.00
232 Hunter Henry/99 4.00 10.00
233 Tyler Ervin/199 2.50 6.00
234 Jeremy Cash/199 3.00 8.00
235 Josh Ferguson/199 2.50 6.00
236 Alex Collins/49 5.00 12.00
237 Laquon Treadwell/25 6.00 15.00
238 Byron Marshall/199 2.50 6.00
239 Nick Vannett/199 2.50 6.00
240 Darron Lee/199 2.50 6.00
241 Shilique Calhoun/299 2.50 6.00
242 Charles Tapper/299 3.00 8.00
243 Vernon Hargreaves III/99 5.00 12.00
244 Joey Bosa/99 6.00 15.00
245 Kelvin Taylor/49 4.00 10.00
246 Andrew Billings/299 3.00 8.00
247 Laremy Tunsil/199 2.50 6.00
248 C.J. Prosise/49 4.00 10.00
249 Paul Perkins/49 4.00 10.00
250 DeForest Buckner/99 3.00 8.00
251 Sterling Shepard/99 4.00 10.00
252 Jalen Ramsey/99 5.00 12.00
253 Vonn Bell/199 3.00 8.00
254 Karl Joseph/299 2.50 6.00
255 Kendall Fuller/299 3.00 8.00
256 Keith Marshall/299 2.50 6.00
257 Leonard Floyd/199 3.00 8.00
258 Cardale Jones/49 4.00 10.00
259 Paxton Lynch/25 5.00 12.00
260 Glenn Gronkowski/299 2.50 6.00
261 Su'a Cravens/199 2.50 6.00
262 Jared Goff/25 75.00 150.00
263 Wendell Smallwood/299 2.50 6.00
264 Jonathan Williams/99 4.00 10.00
265 Kenneth Dixon/99 3.00 8.00
266 A'Shawn Robinson/199 2.50 6.00
267 Leonte Carroo/49 4.00 10.00
268 Carson Wentz/25 100.00 200.00
269 Pharoh Cooper/49 4.00 10.00
270 Demarcus Robinson/199 2.50 6.00
271 Tajae Sharpe/299 3.00 8.00
272 Jarran Reed/199 2.50 6.00
273 Will Fuller/49 6.00 15.00
274 Jacoby Brissett/199 3.00 8.00
275 Kenny Clark/299 2.50 6.00
276 Austin Hooper/199 2.50 6.00
277 Mackensie Alexander/199 2.50 6.00
278 Christian Hackenberg/49 4.00 10.00
279 Rashard Higgins/99 12.00 30.00
280 Derrick Henry/25 30.00 60.00
281 Malcolm Mitchell/299 2.50 6.00
282 Kamalei Correa/299 2.50 6.00
283 Tre Madden/299 2.50 6.00
284 Vernon Adams Jr./299 4.00 10.00
285 Kenny Lawler/199 4.00 10.00
286 Austin Johnson/299 2.50 6.00
287 Maliek Collins/299 2.50 6.00
288 Cody Kessler/99 3.00 8.00
289 Reggie Ragland/199 2.50 6.00
290 De'Runnya Wilson/99 3.00 8.00
291 Thomas Duarte/199 2.50 6.00
292 Jaylon Smith/199 2.50 6.00
294 Jordan Howard/49 10.00 25.00
295 Kenyan Drake/99 5.00 12.00
296 Bralon Addison/99 3.00 8.00
297 Michael Thomas/49 8.00 20.00
298 Connor Cook/25 6.00 15.00
299 Robert Nkemdiche/99 20.00 40.00
300 Devontae Booker/99 4.00 10.00

2016 Classics Sunday Stars Swatches
1 Alshon Jeffery/199 3.00 8.00
2 Amari Cooper/199 4.00 10.00
3 Aaron Rodgers/10 25.00 60.00
4 Devonta Freeman/199 3.00 8.00
5 Tom Brady/10 25.00 60.00
6 Stefon Diggs/199 3.00 8.00
7 Larry Fitzgerald/199 3.00 8.00
8 Matt Ryan/99 4.00 10.00
9 A.J. Green/199 4.00 10.00
10 Ryan Tannehill/199 3.00 8.00
11 Andre Ellington/199 2.50 6.00
12 Davante Adams/199 2.50 6.00
13 Tyrod Taylor/149 3.00 8.00
14 Khalil Mack/199 4.00 10.00
15 Jarvis Landry/199 3.00 8.00
16 Teddy Bridgewater/199 3.00 8.00
17 LeSean McCoy/99 5.00 12.00
18 Peyton Manning/99 10.00 25.00
19 Allen Hurns/149 2.50 6.00
20 Sammy Watkins/149 4.00 10.00
21 Andy Dalton/199 3.00 8.00
22 Jameis Winston/199 4.00 10.00
23 Colin Kaepernick/199 3.00 8.00
24 Marcus Mariota/199 4.00 10.00
25 Jeremy Hill/199 2.50 6.00
26 Todd Gurley/199 4.00 10.00
27 Mark Ingram/99 4.00 10.00
28 Philip Rivers/99 5.00 12.00
29 Allen Robinson/199 3.00 8.00
30 Tony Romo/199 3.00 8.00
31 Blake Bortles/199 2.50 6.00
32 Kelvin Benjamin/199 3.00 8.00
33 DeMarcus Ware/199 3.00 8.00
34 Odell Beckham Jr./199 4.00 10.00
35 Joe Flacco/99 4.00 10.00

2016 Classics The Next Level
*BRONZE: .8X TO 2X BASIC INSERTS
1 Michael Irvin .60 1.50
2 Darrelle Revis .40 1.00
3 Thurman Thomas .50 1.25
4 Tom Brady 1.50 4.00
5 Barry Sanders 1.00 2.50
6 Carson Palmer .50 1.25
7 Emmitt Smith 1.00 2.50
8 Todd Gurley .60 1.50
9 LaDainian Tomlinson .50 1.25
10 Odell Beckham Jr. .60 1.50
11 Ricky Williams .50 1.25
12 Richard Sherman .60 1.50
13 Tony Dorsett .60 1.50
14 Philip Rivers .60 1.50
15 Bo Jackson .75 2.00
16 Cam Newton .60 1.50
17 Joe Namath .75 2.00
18 Antonio Brown .60 1.50
19 Lawrence Taylor .60 1.50
20 Larry Fitzgerald .50 1.25
21 Steve Young .75 2.00
22 J.J. Watt .60 1.50
23 Troy Aikman .75 2.00
24 Peyton Manning 1.25 3.00
25 Dan Marino 1.25 3.00
26 Adrian Peterson .60 1.50
27 John Elway 1.00 2.50
28 Julio Jones .60 1.50
29 Marshall Faulk .50 1.25
30 DeAndre Hopkins .50 1.25

2016 Classics Timeless Ink
2 Jim Kiick/99 6.00 15.00
3 Charles Mann/99 6.00 15.00
5 Steve Grogan/99 6.00 15.00
6 Joe Andruzzi/99 6.00 15.00
7 John Hannah/99 6.00 15.00
8 Dan Hampton/99 6.00 15.00
9 Charlie Joiner/99 6.00 15.00
10 Mark Chmura/49 8.00 20.00
11 Sidney Rice/49 8.00 20.00
12 Dallas Clark/49 8.00 20.00
13 Rod Smith/25 12.00 30.00
14 Donald Driver/25 12.00 30.00
15 Bill Parcells/25 15.00 40.00
17 Tim Brown/25 15.00 40.00
28 Robert Brooks/49 10.00 25.00
29 Clinton Portis/49 8.00 20.00
30 Ahman Green/49 10.00 25.00

2017 Classics
SP VARIATION IMAGES ARE SEPIA
1 Tyrod Taylor .25 .60
2 Jarvis Landry .25 .60
3A Tom Brady .75 2.00
3B Tom Brady SP 4.00 10.00
4 Brandon Marshall .20 .50
5 Joe Flacco .25 .60
6A A.J. Green .30 .75
6B A.J. Green SP 1.50 4.00
7 Terrelle Pryor Sr. .20 .50
8A Antonio Brown .30 .75
8B Antonio Brown SP 1.50 4.00
9 DeAndre Hopkins .25 .60
10A Andrew Luck .40 1.00
10B Andrew Luck SP 2.00 5.00
11 Allen Robinson .25 .60
12A Marcus Mariota .30 .75
12B Marcus Mariota SP 1.50 4.00
13 Demaryius Thomas .25 .60
14 Travis Kelce .30 .75
15A Derek Carr .30 .75
15B Derek Carr SP 1.50 4.00
16 Melvin Gordon .25 .60
17A Dak Prescott .30 .75
17B Dak Prescott SP 1.50 4.00
18A Odell Beckham Jr. .30 .75
18B Odell Beckham Jr. SP 1.50 4.00
19A Carson Wentz .40 1.00
19B Carson Wentz SP 2.00 5.00
20 Kirk Cousins .30 .75
21 Jordan Howard .30 .75
22A Matthew Stafford .25 .60
22B Matthew Stafford SP 1.25 3.00
23A Aaron Rodgers .60 1.50
23B Aaron Rodgers SP 3.00 8.00
24 Stefon Diggs .25 .60
25A Matt Ryan .25 .60
25B Matt Ryan SP 1.25 3.00
26A Cam Newton .30 .75
26B Cam Newton SP 1.50 4.00
27 Brandin Cooks .25 .60
28 Jameis Winston .25 .60
29 David Johnson .30 .75
30 Todd Gurley II .30 .75
31A Russell Wilson .40 1.00
31B Russell Wilson SP 2.00 5.00
32 Carlos Hyde .20 .50
33A Von Miller .25 .60
33B Von Miller SP 1.25 3.00
34 Emmanuel Sanders .30 .75
35 LeSean McCoy .30 .75
36 Sammy Watkins .30 .75
37 Ryan Tannehill .25 .60
38 Ndamukong Suh .25 .60
39 Cameron Wake .20 .50
40A Rob Gronkowski .30 .75
40B Rob Gronkowski SP 1.50 4.00
41 Dont'a Hightower .20 .50
42 Matt Forte .20 .50
43 Quincy Enunwa .20 .50
44 Steve Smith Sr. .25 .60
45A Terrell Suggs .20 .50
45B Terrell Suggs SP 1.00 2.50
46A Andy Dalton .25 .60
46B Andy Dalton SP 1.25 3.00
47 Vontaze Burfict .20 .50
48 Isaiah Crowell .20 .50
49A Joe Haden .20 .50
49B Joe Haden SP 1.00 2.50
50 Ben Roethlisberger .30 .75
51A Le'Veon Bell .25 .60
51B Le'Veon Bell SP 1.25 3.00
52A James Harrison .25 .60
52B James Harrison SP 1.25 3.00
53 Vince Wilfork .20 .50
54A J.J. Watt .30 .75
54B J.J. Watt SP 1.50 4.00
55A T.Y. Hilton .25 .60
55B T.Y. Hilton SP 1.25 3.00
56 Frank Gore .25 .60
57 Blake Bortles .20 .50
58 T.J. Yeldon .20 .50
59 Delanie Walker .20 .50
60A DeMarco Murray .25 .60
60B DeMarco Murray SP 1.25 3.00
61A Alex Smith .25 .60
61B Alex Smith SP 1.25 3.00
62 Spencer Ware .20 .50
63A Amari Cooper .30 .75
63B Amari Cooper SP 1.50 4.00
64 Khalil Mack .30 .75
65A Philip Rivers .30 .75
65B Philip Rivers SP 1.50 4.00
66 Keenan Allen .25 .60
67A Ezekiel Elliott .40 1.00
67B Ezekiel Elliott SP 2.00 5.00
68 Dez Bryant .30 .75
69A Jason Witten .25 .60
69B Jason Witten SP 1.25 3.00
70A Eli Manning .25 .60
70B Eli Manning SP 1.25 3.00
71 Landon Collins .20 .50
72 Jordan Matthews .20 .50
73 Ryan Mathews .25 .60
74A Robert Kelley .20 .50
74B Robert Kelley SP 1.00 2.50
75 DeSean Jackson .25 .60
76A Alshon Jeffery .25 .60
76B Alshon Jeffery SP 1.25 3.00
77 Leonard Floyd .20 .50
78 Marvin Jones Jr. .20 .50
79 Ezekiel Ansah .20 .50
80A Jordy Nelson .25 .60
80B Jordy Nelson SP 1.25 3.00
81 Randall Cobb .25 .60
82 Clay Matthews .25 .60
83 Sam Bradford .20 .50
84A Adrian Peterson .30 .75
84B Adrian Peterson SP 1.50 4.00
85A Julio Jones .30 .75
85B Julio Jones SP 1.50 4.00
86 Devonta Freeman .25 .60
87A Greg Olsen .25 .60
87B Greg Olsen SP 1.25 3.00
88A Luke Kuechly .25 .60
88B Luke Kuechly SP 1.25 3.00
89A Drew Brees .30 .75
89B Drew Brees SP 1.50 4.00
90 Mark Ingram .25 .60
91 Mike Evans .25 .60
92 Doug Martin .25 .60
93 Carson Palmer .25 .60
94 Tyrann Mathieu .25 .60
95A Jared Goff .30 .75
95B Jared Goff SP 1.50 4.00
96 Aaron Donald .30 .75
97 Doug Baldwin .25 .60
98A Kam Chancellor .30 .75
98B Kam Chancellor SP 1.50 4.00
99 Colin Kaepernick .25 .60
100 Torrey Smith .20 .50
101 Eric Dickerson .30 .75
102 Champ Bailey .25 .60
103 Andre Reed .25 .60
104 Dexter Manley .25 .60
105 Bo Jackson .40 1.00
106 Ed Reed .25 .60
107 Clinton Portis .20 .50
108 Darren Woodson .25 .60
109 Cris Carter .30 .75
110 Deion Sanders .25 .60
111 Antonio Freeman .25 .60
112 Kurt Warner .25 .60
113 Curtis Martin .25 .60
114 Boomer Esiason .25 .60
115 Dermontti Dawson .25 .60
116 Michael Strahan .25 .60
117 Dave Wilcox .20 .50
118 Brett Favre .60 1.50
119 Ken Stabler .30 .75
120 Rod Woodson .25 .60
121 Doug Flutie .25 .60
122 Archie Manning .25 .60
123 Joe Montana .75 2.00
124 Donald Driver .25 .60
125 Barry Sanders .50 1.25
126 Derrick Brooks .20 .50
127 LaDainian Tomlinson .25 .60
128 Y.A. Tittle .30 .75
129 Joe Namath .40 1.00
130 Dick LeBeau .20 .50
131 Aeneas Williams .20 .50
132 Eddie George .25 .60
133 Jack Ham .25 .60
134 Bob Griese .30 .75
135 Drew Pearson .25 .60
136 Calvin Johnson .30 .75
137 Jim McMahon .25 .60
138 Earl Campbell .30 .75
139 Kellen Winslow .25 .60
140 Bob Lilly .25 .60
141 Fran Tarkenton .30 .75
142 John Randle .20 .50
143 Charley Trippi .20 .50
144 Ickey Woods .20 .50
145 Heath Miller .20 .50
146 Jim Kiick .20 .50
147 Christian Okoye .20 .50
148 Fred Biletnikoff .30 .75
149 Bruce Smith .25 .60
150 Hugh McElhenny .25 .60
151 John Riggins .25 .60
152 Charlie Joiner .20 .50
153 Edgerrin James .25 .60
154 Jerry Rice .50 1.25
155 Dan Fouts .25 .60
156 Harry Carson .20 .50
157 John Elway .50 1.25
158 Carl Eller .20 .50
159 Franco Harris .30 .75
160 Jim Plunkett .25 .60
161 Dan Hampton .20 .50
162 Brian Urlacher .30 .75
163 Dwight Clark .25 .60
164 Charles Haley .30 .75
165 Jerome Bettis .30 .75
166 Don Maynard .25 .60
167 Harold Carmichael .20 .50
168 Jan Stenerud .20 .50
169 Torry Holt .25 .60
170 John Hannah .20 .50
171 Ed "Too Tall" Jones .20 .50
172 Joe Greene .30 .75
173 Dan Marino .60 1.50
174 Emmitt Smith .50 1.25
175 Ray Lewis .30 .75
176 Mike Singletary .30 .75
177 Roger Staubach .40 1.00
178 Roger Craig .25 .60
179 Len Dawson .30 .75
180 Phil McConkey .25 .60
181 Paul Hornung .30 .75
182 Rocky Bleier .25 .60
183 Mark Brunell .25 .60
184 Raymond Berry .25 .60
185 Steve Largent .30 .75
186 Marshall Faulk .25 .60
187 Peyton Manning .60 1.50
188 Ted Hendricks .20 .50
189 Lawrence Taylor .30 .75
190 Rich Gannon .20 .50
191 Terrell Davis .25 .60
192 Michael Irvin .30 .75
193 Ray Guy .20 .50
194 Terry Bradshaw .50 1.25
195 Marcus Allen .25 .60
196 Steve Grogan .20 .50
197 Paul Warfield .25 .60
198 Randy Moss .25 .60
199 Mark Gastineau .20 .50
200 Ricky Williams .25 .60
201 Adoree' Jackson RC .50 1.25
202 Alvin Kamara RC 1.50 4.00
203 Amara Darboh RC .40 1.00
204 ArDarius Stewart RC .40 1.00
205 Artavis Scott RC .40 1.00
206 Brad Kaaya RC .40 1.00
207 Brian Hill RC .40 1.00
208 Bucky Hodges RC .40 1.00
209 Caleb Brantley RC .40 1.00
210 Cam Robinson RC .40 1.00
211 Cameron Sutton RC .40 1.00
212 Carl Lawson RC .40 1.00
213 Carlos Henderson RC .40 1.00
214 Chad Hansen RC .40 1.00
215 Chad Kelly RC .40 1.00
216 Charles Harris RC .40 1.00
217 Christian McCaffrey RC 1.00 2.50
218 Cooper Kupp RC .60 1.50
219 Cordrea Tankersley RC .50 1.25
220 Corey Clement RC .50 1.25
221 Corey Davis RC .60 1.50
222 Curtis Samuel RC .50 1.25
223 Dalvin Cook RC 1.00 2.50
224 Davis Webb RC .40 1.00
225 Dede Westbrook RC .40 1.00
226 DeMarcus Walker RC .40 1.00
227 Derek Barnett RC .50 1.25
228 Deshaun Watson RC 2.50 6.00
229 DeShone Kizer RC .40 1.00
230 Desmond King RC .50 1.25
231 Donnel Pumphrey RC .50 1.25
232 D'Onta Foreman RC .50 1.25
233 Elijah Hood RC .40 1.00
234 Elijah Qualls RC .40 1.00
235 Evan Engram RC .50 1.25
236 Gareon Conley RC .40 1.00
237 Zay Jones RC .50 1.25
238 Isaiah Ford RC .40 1.00
239 Jabrill Peppers RC .60 1.50
240 Jake Butt RC .50 1.25
241 Teez Tabor RC .50 1.25
242 Jamaal Williams RC .40 1.00
243 Jamal Adams RC .40 1.00
244 James Conner RC .75 2.00
245 Jarrad Davis RC .50 1.25
246 Jeremy McNichols RC .40 1.00
247 Jerod Evans RC .50 1.25
248 Joe Mixon RC .75 2.00
249 John Ross RC .50 1.25
250 Jonathan Allen RC .50 1.25
251 Jordan Leggett RC .40 1.00
252 Jordan Willis RC .40 1.00
253 Josh Malone RC .40 1.00
254 Josh Reynolds RC .40 1.00
255 R. Joshua Dobbs RC .50 1.25
256 Jourdan Lewis RC .40 1.00
257 JuJu Smith-Schuster RC 1.00 2.50
258 Kareem Hunt RC .75 2.00
259 KD Cannon RC .40 1.00
260 Leonard Fournette RC 1.25 3.00
261 Malachi Dupre RC .40 1.00
262 Malik Hooker RC .40 1.00
263 Malik McDowell RC .40 1.00
264 Marlon Humphrey RC .40 1.00
265 Marlon Mack RC .60 1.50
266 Marshon Lattimore RC .50 1.25
267 Matthew Dayes RC .40 1.00
268 Mike Williams RC .60 1.50
269 Mitchell Trubisky RC 2.00 5.00
270 Myles Garrett RC 1.25 3.00
271 Nathan Peterman RC .50 1.25
272 Noah Brown RC .50 1.25
273 O.J. Howard RC .50 1.25
274 Patrick Mahomes II RC 5.00 12.00
275 Quincy Wilson RC .40 1.00
276 Raekwon McMillan RC .40 1.00
277 Reuben Foster RC .40 1.00
278 Ryan Switzer RC .50 1.25
279 Samaje Perine RC .40 1.00
280 Shelton Gibson RC .40 1.00
281 Sidney Jones RC .40 1.00
282 Solomon Thomas RC .40 1.00
283 Stacy Coley RC .40 1.00
284 T.J. Watt RC 1.25 3.00
285 Taco Charlton RC .40 1.00
286 Takkarist McKinley RC .40 1.00
287 Tim Williams RC .50 1.25
288 Travis Rudolph RC .40 1.00
289 Tre'Davious White RC .40 1.00
290 Wayne Gallman RC .50 1.25
291 Zach Cunningham RC .50 1.25
292 Gunner Kiel RC .60 1.50
293 Justin Davis RC .60 1.50
294 Haason Reddick RC .40 1.00
295 Obi Melifonwu RC .40 1.00
296 James Quick RC .50 1.25
297 David Njoku RC .50 1.25
298 Shock Linwood RC .50 1.25
299 Chris Godwin RC .50 1.25
300 Taywan Taylor RC .40 1.00

2017 Classics Blank Back
*VETS/50: 2.5X TO 6X BASIC CARDS
*ROOKIES/50: 1.2X TO 3X BASIC CARDS

2017 Classics Blue Back
*VETS/175: 1.5X TO 4X BASIC CARDS
*ROOK/175: .8X TO 2X BASIC CARDS

2017 Classics Glossy
*VETS: 1X TO 2.5X BASIC CARDS
*ROOKIES: .6X TO 1.5X BASIC CARDS

2017 Classics Red Back
*VETS/299: 1.5X TO 4X BASIC CARDS
*ROOK/299: .8X TO 2X BASIC CARDS

2017 Classics Timeless Tributes Gold
*VETS/99: 2X TO 5X BASIC CARDS
*ROOK/99: 1X TO 2.5X BASIC CARDS

2017 Classics Timeless Tributes Orange
*VETS/25: 3X TO 8X BASIC CARDS
*ROOK/25: 1.5X TO 4X BASIC CARDS

2017 Classics Buybacks Autographs
3 Adam Vinatieri/30 15.00 40.00
40 Charles Haley/27 12.00 30.00
43 Clinton Portis/30 8.00 20.00
44 Clinton Portis/30 8.00 20.00
45 Clinton Portis/25 8.00 20.00
46 Clinton Portis/30 8.00 20.00
56 Darren Woodson/30 10.00 25.00
57 Darren Woodson/30 10.00 25.00
59 Deion Branch/15 10.00 25.00
60 Deion Branch/15 10.00 25.00
61 Deion Branch/15 10.00 25.00
72 Don Maynard/20 12.00 30.00
85 Edgerrin James/20 12.00 30.00
86 Edgerrin James/20 12.00 30.00
87 Edgerrin James/19 12.00 30.00
88 Edgerrin James/20 12.00 30.00
89 Edgerrin James/20 12.00 30.00
90 Edgerrin James/20 12.00 30.00
95 Emmanuel Sanders/19 15.00 40.00
116 Heath Miller/25 8.00 20.00
117 Heath Miller/30 8.00 20.00
118 Heath Miller/21 10.00 25.00
125 Ickey Woods/15 10.00 25.00
131 Jason Taylor/20 20.00 50.00
132 Jay Novacek/20 12.00 30.00
153 Jim Plunkett/17 12.00 30.00
168 Kordell Stewart/30 8.00 20.00
169 Kordell Stewart/30 8.00 20.00
170 Kordell Stewart/30 8.00 20.00
171 Kordell Stewart/30 8.00 20.00
195 Mark Brunell/20 12.00 30.00
196 Mark Brunell/20 12.00 30.00
218 Maurice Jones-Drew/30 8.00 20.00
219 Maurice Jones-Drew/30 8.00 20.00
220 Maurice Jones-Drew/30 8.00 20.00
221 Maurice Jones-Drew/30 8.00 20.00
235 Ozzie Newsome/15 12.00 30.00
259 Randall Cunningham/20 12.00 30.00
260 Randall Cunningham/20 12.00 30.00
261 Randall Cunningham/15 12.00 30.00
280 Rich Gannon/30 8.00 20.00
281 Rich Gannon/30 8.00 20.00
282 Rich Gannon/30 8.00 20.00
283 Rich Gannon/30 8.00 20.00
284 Ricky Williams/15 12.00 30.00
285 Ricky Williams/30 10.00 25.00
286 Ricky Williams/30 10.00 25.00
289 Rod Smith/15 30.00 60.00
301 Sterling Sharpe/18 12.00 30.00
305 Steve Atwater/20 12.00 30.00
306 Steve Atwater/20 12.00 30.00
312 Steve Smith Sr./15 12.00 30.00
333 Tim Brown/15 15.00 40.00
334 Tim Brown/15 15.00 40.00
340 Torry Holt/30 10.00 25.00
341 Torry Holt/20 12.00 30.00
342 Torry Holt/20 12.00 30.00
343 Torry Holt/20 12.00 30.00
344 Torry Holt/20 12.00 30.00
353 Troy Brown/30 8.00 20.00
359 Willie McGinest/30 8.00 20.00
360 Willie McGinest/28 8.00 20.00

2017 Classics Canton Collections Swatches
*PRIME/50: .6X TO 1.5X BASIC JSY/299
*PRIME/25: .8X TO 2X BASIC JSY/299
1 Barry Sanders/299 5.00 12.00
2 Brett Favre/99 8.00 20.00
3 Dan Marino/299 6.00 15.00
4 Earl Campbell/299 3.00 8.00
5 Eric Dickerson/299 3.00 8.00
6 Emmitt Smith/299 10.00 25.00
7 Franco Harris/299 3.00 8.00
8 Howie Long/99 4.00 10.00
9 Jim Kelly/299 3.00 8.00
10 John Elway/299 5.00 12.00
11 John Riggins/299 2.50 6.00
12 Marcus Allen/299 2.50 6.00
13 Tony Dorsett/299 3.00 8.00
14 Rod Woodson/299 2.50 6.00
15 Jerome Bettis/299 3.00 8.00
16 Roger Staubach/99 5.00 12.00
17 Steve Young/299 4.00 10.00
18 Terry Bradshaw/299 5.00 12.00
19 Jerry Rice/299 5.00 12.00
20 Paul Hornung/299 3.00 8.00

2017 Classics Career Colors
1 Brett Favre 1.50 4.00
2 Steve Smith Sr. .60 1.50
3 Peyton Manning 1.50 4.00
4 Deion Sanders .60 1.50
5 Steve Young 1.00 2.50
6 Marcus Allen .60 1.50
7 Randy Moss .60 1.50
8 Jerome Bettis .75 2.00
9 Kurt Warner .60 1.50
10 Emmitt Smith 1.25 3.00

2017 Classics Classic Clashes
*GOLD: .75X TO 8X BASIC INSERTS
1 J.Norman/O.Beckham .75 2.00
2 R.Sherman/T.Brady 2.00 5.00
3 L.Kuechly/M.Ryan .60 1.50
4 P.McAfee/M.King .50 1.25
5 M.Butler/R.Wilson 1.00 2.50
6 D.Carr/E.Berry .75 2.00
7 A.Brown/V.Burfict .75 2.00
8 P.Manning/T.Brady 2.00 5.00
9 B.Favre/B.Urlacher 1.50 4.00
10 A.Talib/S.Smith .60 1.50
11 A.Rodgers/N.Suh 1.50 4.00
12 E.Manning/P.Manning 1.50 4.00
13 R.Sherman/P.Peterson .75 2.00
14 J.Montana/S.Young 2.00 5.00
15 A.Rodgers/B.Favre 1.50 4.00
16 T.Bradshaw/R.Staubach 1.25 3.00
17 J.Rice/D.Sanders 1.25 3.00
18 S.Young/T.Aikman 1.00 2.50
19 B.Rthlsbrgr/R.Lewis .75 2.00
20 J.Montana/H.Long 2.00 5.00

2017 Classics Classic Combos Memorabilia
*PRIME/50: .6X TO 1.5X BASIC JSY/199-299
*PRIME/50: .5X TO 1.2X BASIC JSY/99
1 A.Green/A.Dalton/199 4.00 10.00
2 A.Rodgers/J.Nelson/99 12.00 30.00
3 A.Brown/B.Rthlsbrgr/99 5.00 12.00
4 E.Elliott/D.Prescott/299 12.00 30.00
5 T.Hill/D.Hester/299 4.00 10.00
6 E.Manning/O.Beckham/199 4.00 10.00
7 A.Cooper/D.Carr/299 4.00 10.00
8 J.Watt/J.Clowney/299 4.00 10.00
9 J.Jones/M.Ryan/99 5.00 12.00
10 C.Johnson/M.Stafford/99 5.00 12.00
11 J.Winston/M.Evans/299 3.00 8.00
12 S.Young/J.Elway/299 6.00 15.00
13 R.Gronkowski/T.Brady/99 12.00 30.00
14 T.Bradshaw/B.Rthlsbrgr/99 30.00 60.00
15 G.Atkins/V.Burfict/299 2.50 6.00

2017 Classics Combos Autographs
6 R.Williams/R.Brown/25 30.00 60.00
12 J.Klecko/M.Gastineau/25 40.00 80.00
13 R.Dent/D.Hampton/20 30.00 60.00

2017 Classics Flashback Fabrics
*PRIME/50: .6X TO 1.5X BASIC JSY/299-399
*PRIME/25: .8X TO 2X BASIC JSY/299-399
*PRIME/25: .6X TO 1.5X BASIC JSY/99
1 Darren McFadden/399 2.00 5.00
2 Don Maynard/399 2.50 6.00
3 Brett Favre/399 6.00 15.00
4 Brian Urlacher/99 4.00 10.00
5 Alfred Morris/299 2.00 5.00
6 Curtis Martin/399 2.50 6.00
7 Doug Flutie/399 2.50 6.00
8 DeMarcus Ware/399 2.50 6.00
9 DeSean Jackson/399 2.50 6.00
10 Darren Sproles/399 2.50 6.00
11 Anquan Boldin/399 2.00 5.00
12 Peyton Manning/99 8.00 20.00
13 Frank Gore/99 3.00 8.00
14 Jerry Rice/99 6.00 15.00
15 Julius Peppers/299 2.50 6.00
16 Kurt Warner/299 2.50 6.00
17 Boomer Esiason/399 2.50 6.00
18 Bruce Smith/399 2.50 6.00
19 Matt Forte/399 2.00 5.00
20 Michael Crabtree/299 2.00 5.00
21 Mike Wallace/399 2.00 5.00
22 Ndamukong Suh/399 2.50 6.00
23 Rich Gannon/399 2.00 5.00
24 Michael Vick/399 2.50 6.00
25 Robbie Gould/399 2.00 5.00
26 Marvin Jones Jr./399 2.00 5.00
27 Sam Bradford/399 2.00 5.00
28 Brock Osweiler/399 2.00 5.00
29 Carson Palmer/299 2.50 6.00
30 Tim Tebow/399 3.00 8.00
31 Tony Romo/399 2.50 6.00
32 DeMarco Murray/399 2.50 6.00
33 Eric Decker/399 2.00 5.00
34 Ryan Fitzpatrick/399 2.00 5.00
35 Torrey Smith/399 2.00 5.00

2017 Classics Idolized
*GOLD: .8X TO 2X BASIC INSERTS
1 O.Beckham/R.Moss .75 2.00
2 E.Elliott/E.Smith 1.25 3.00
3 J.Montana/D.Prescott 2.00 5.00
4 A.Luck/P.Manning 1.50 4.00
5 T.Bradshaw/B.Rthlsbrgr 1.25 3.00
6 C.Long/H.Long .75 2.00
7 B.Jackson/J.Jones 1.00 2.50
8 B.Urlacher/L.Kuechly .75 2.00
9 F.Tarkenton/M.Stafford .75 2.00
10 A.Brown/H.Ward .75 2.00
11 K.Greene/J.Watt .75 2.00
12 J.Kelly/J.Flacco .75 2.00
13 K.Chancellor/R.Lott .75 2.00
14 D.Green/J.Norman .75 2.00
15 M.Harrison/T.Hilton .60 1.50
16 J.Goff/A.Rodgers 1.50 4.00
17 D.Hester/T.Hill .75 2.00
18 J.Nelson/S.Sharpe .60 1.50
19 R.Wilson/W.Moon 1.00 2.50
20 Brett Favre/Matt Ryan 1.50 4.00

2017 Classics Membership Autographs
1 Ottis Anderson/49 4.00 10.00
3 Neil Smith/49 15.00 40.00
5 Jim Plunkett/15
6 Mark Brunell/25 6.00 15.00
8 Jim McMahon/15 20.00 50.00
9 Morten Andersen/49 10.00 25.00
10 Brett Keisel/49 15.00 40.00
12 Aeneas Williams/25 5.00 12.00
16 Rocky Bleier/15 8.00 20.00
17 Fred Taylor/15 8.00 20.00
18 Kellen Winslow/15 8.00 20.00
21 Torry Holt/15 12.00 30.00
22 Hugh McElhenny/49 10.00 25.00
23 Ricky Williams/15 12.00 30.00
25 Mark Gastineau/25 5.00 12.00
26 Harry Carson/15 6.00 15.00
27 Priest Holmes/15 15.00 40.00
29 Drew Pearson/15 10.00 25.00
30 Champ Bailey/15 15.00 40.00

2017 Classics Record Breakers
*GOLD: .8X TO 2X BASIC INSERTS
1 Cam Newton .60 1.50
2 Dak Prescott .60 1.50
3 Julio Jones .60 1.50
4 Matt Ryan .50 1.25
5 Ezekiel Elliott .75 2.00
6 Drew Brees .60 1.50
7 Jason Witten .50 1.25
8 Antonio Brown .60 1.50
9 Jordy Nelson .50 1.25
10 Tyreek Hill .60 1.50
11 Le'Veon Bell .50 1.25
12 Tom Brady 1.50 4.00
13 Thomas Rawls .40 1.00
14 Jordan Howard .60 1.50
15 Philip Rivers .60 1.50
16 Morten Andersen .40 1.00
17 Franco Harris .60 1.50
18 Brian Urlacher .60 1.50
19 Tim Brown .60 1.50
20 Sebastian Janikowski .40 1.00
21 Peyton Manning 1.25 3.00
22 Jerry Rice 1.00 2.50
23 Warren Moon .60 1.50
24 Brett Favre 1.25 3.00
25 Curtis Martin .50 1.25
26 Emmitt Smith 1.00 2.50
27 Adrian Peterson .60 1.50
28 Larry Fitzgerald .50 1.25
29 John Elway 1.00 2.50
30 Calvin Johnson .60 1.50

2017 Classics Sideline Generals Signatures
2 Jimmy Johnson/25 20.00 40.00
3 Mike Holmgren/15 40.00 80.00
4 Mike Vrabel/25 8.00 20.00
5 Dick LeBeau/49 20.00 40.00

2017 Classics Significant Signatures
1 Tyrod Taylor/25 10.00 25.00
11 Allen Robinson/15 8.00 20.00
14 Travis Kelce/15 10.00 25.00
15 Derek Carr/15 40.00 80.00
16 Melvin Gordon/15 8.00 20.00
19 Carson Wentz/15 75.00 150.00
21 Jordan Howard/49 10.00 25.00
27 Brandin Cooks/15 8.00 20.00
32 Carlos Hyde/25 5.00 12.00
36 Sammy Watkins/15 10.00 25.00
37 Ryan Tannehill/15 8.00 20.00
42 Matt Forte/15 6.00 15.00
43 Quincy Enunwa/49 4.00 10.00
44 Steve Smith Sr./15 8.00 20.00
48 Isaiah Crowell/49 4.00 10.00
49 Joe Haden/25 5.00 12.00
51 Le'Veon Bell/15 EXCH
58 T.J. Yeldon/25 5.00 12.00
59 Delanie Walker/49 4.00 10.00
66 Keenan Allen/25 6.00 15.00
72 Jordan Matthews/20 6.00 15.00
74 Robert Kelley/49 4.00 10.00
75 DeSean Jackson/15 8.00 20.00
80 Jordy Nelson/15 8.00 20.00
81 Randall Cobb/15 8.00 20.00
87 Greg Olsen/15 8.00 20.00
88 Luke Kuechly/15 20.00 50.00
91 Mike Evans/25 6.00 15.00
92 Doug Martin/25 6.00 15.00
96 Aaron Donald/49 6.00 15.00
97 Doug Baldwin/15
100 Torrey Smith/25 5.00 12.00
102 Champ Bailey/15 8.00 20.00
103 Andre Reed/15 8.00 20.00
104 Dexter Manley/99 4.00 10.00
108 Darren Woodson/15 8.00 20.00
111 Antonio Freeman/25 6.00 15.00
114 Boomer Esiason/15 8.00 20.00
115 Dermontti Dawson/25 6.00 15.00
117 Dave Wilcox/49 4.00 10.00
120 Rod Woodson/25 10.00 25.00
124 Donald Driver/15 8.00 20.00
126 Derrick Brooks/25 10.00 25.00
128 Y.A. Tittle/25 8.00 20.00
130 Dick LeBeau/49 15.00 40.00
131 Aeneas Williams/15 6.00 15.00
132 Eddie George/15 8.00 20.00
135 Drew Pearson/25 6.00 15.00
137 Jim McMahon/15 20.00 50.00
139 Kellen Winslow/25 6.00 15.00
140 Bob Lilly/25 6.00 15.00
141 Fran Tarkenton/15 15.00 40.00
143 Charley Trippi/49 4.00 10.00
146 Jim Kiick/25 5.00 12.00
147 Christian Okoye/15 6.00 15.00
150 Hugh McElhenny/49 5.00 12.00
153 Edgerrin James/15 8.00 20.00
156 Harry Carson/49 15.00 40.00
158 Carl Eller/25 5.00 12.00
160 Jim Plunkett/15
161 Dan Hampton/49 4.00 10.00
163 Dwight Clark/25 6.00 15.00
164 Charles Haley/25 8.00 20.00
166 Don Maynard/15 8.00 20.00
168 Jan Stenerud/25 5.00 12.00
169 Torry Holt/15 8.00 20.00
171 Ed "Too Tall" Jones/49
176 Mike Singletary/15 10.00 25.00
178 Roger Craig/25 6.00 15.00
179 Len Dawson/15 15.00 40.00
180 Phil McConkey/49 6.00 12.00
181 Paul Hornung/15 10.00 25.00
182 Rocky Bleier/25 10.00 25.00
183 Mark Brunell/25
184 Raymond Berry/15 8.00 20.00
185 Steve Largent/15 10.00 25.00
188 Ted Hendricks/15 6.00 15.00
191 Terrell Davis/15 8.00 20.00
193 Ray Guy/25 12.00 30.00
195 Marcus Allen/15
197 Paul Warfield/15 8.00 20.00
199 Mark Gastineau/25
200 Ricky Williams/15 8.00 20.00
201 Adoree' Jackson/199 3.00 8.00
202 Alvin Kamara/199 10.00 25.00
203 Amara Darboh/199 2.50 6.00
204 ArDarius Stewart/199 2.50 6.00
205 Artavis Scott/199 2.50 6.00
206 Brad Kaaya/49
207 Brian Hill/199 2.50 6.00
211 Cameron Sutton/199 2.50 6.00
212 Carl Lawson/199 2.50 6.00
213 Carlos Henderson/199 2.50 6.00
214 Chad Hansen/199 2.50 6.00
215 Chad Kelly/199 2.50 6.00
216 Charles Harris/199 2.50 6.00
217 Christian McCaffrey/49 40.00 80.00
218 Cooper Kupp/199 4.00 10.00
220 Corey Clement/199 3.00 8.00
221 Corey Davis/49 6.00 15.00
222 Curtis Samuel/199 3.00 8.00
223 Dalvin Cook/49 10.00 25.00
224 Davis Webb/199 2.50 6.00
225 Dede Westbrook/99 3.00 8.00
226 DeMarcus Walker/199 2.50 6.00
228 Deshaun Watson/25 60.00 125.00
229 DeShone Kizer/25 5.00 12.00
230 Desmond King/199 3.00 8.00
231 Donnel Pumphrey/199 3.00 8.00
232 D'Onta Foreman/99 4.00 10.00
233 Elijah Hood/199 2.50 6.00
234 Elijah Qualls/199 2.50 6.00
235 Evan Engram/199 3.00 8.00
237 Zay Jones/199 3.00 8.00
238 Isaiah Ford/199 2.50 6.00
239 Jabrill Peppers/99 5.00 12.00
240 Jake Butt/199 3.00 8.00
242 Jamaal Williams/199 2.50 6.00
243 Jamal Adams/199 2.50 6.00
244 James Conner/199 5.00 12.00
245 Jarrad Davis/199 3.00 8.00
246 Jeremy McNichols/199 2.50 6.00
247 Jerod Evans/199 3.00 8.00
248 Joe Mixon/199 12.00 30.00
249 John Ross/99 4.00 10.00
250 Jonathan Allen/99 4.00 10.00
251 Jordan Leggett/199 2.50 6.00
252 Jordan Willis/199 2.50 6.00
253 Josh Malone/199 2.50 6.00
254 Josh Reynolds/199 2.50 6.00
255 R. Joshua Dobbs/199 3.00 8.00
257 JuJu Smith-Schuster/49 10.00 25.00
258 Kareem Hunt/199 8.00 20.00
259 KD Cannon/199 2.50 6.00
260 Leonard Fournette/25 15.00 40.00
262 Malik Hooker/199 2.50 6.00
265 Marlon Mack/199 4.00 10.00
266 Marshon Lattimore/199 3.00 8.00
267 Matthew Dayes/199 2.50 6.00
268 Mike Williams/49 6.00 15.00
269 Mitchell Trubisky/25 40.00 80.00
272 Noah Brown/199 3.00 8.00
273 O.J. Howard/99 4.00 10.00
274 Patrick Mahomes II/49 100.00 200.00
275 Quincy Wilson/199 2.50 6.00
276 Raekwon McMillan/199 2.50 6.00
278 Ryan Switzer/199 3.00 8.00
279 Samaje Perine/199 8.00 20.00
280 Shelton Gibson/199 2.50 6.00
281 Sidney Jones/199 2.50 6.00
282 Solomon Thomas/199 2.50 6.00
283 Stacy Coley/199 2.50 6.00
284 T.J. Watt/199 8.00 20.00
285 Taco Charlton/199 2.50 6.00
287 Tim Williams/199 3.00 8.00
288 Travis Rudolph/199 2.50 6.00
289 Tre'Davious White/199 2.50 6.00
290 Wayne Gallman/199 3.00 8.00
291 Zach Cunningham/199 3.00 8.00
292 Gunner Kiel/199 4.00 10.00
293 Justin Davis/199 4.00 10.00
294 Haason Reddick/199 2.50 6.00
295 Obi Melifonwu/199 2.50 6.00
296 James Quick/199 3.00 8.00
299 Chris Godwin/199 3.00 8.00
300 Taywan Taylor/199 2.50 6.00

2017 Classics Significant Signatures Gold
*GOLD/35-49: .6X TO 1.5X BASIC AU/199
*GOLD/35-49: .5X TO 1.2X BASIC AU/99
*GOLD/25: .6X TO 1.5X BASIC AU/99
*GOLD/25: .5X TO 1.2X BASIC AU/49
*GOLD/15: .5X TO 1.2X BASIC AU/25
274 Patrick Mahomes II/25 125.00 250.00

2017 Classics Significant Signatures Orange
*ORANGE/25: .8X TO 2X BASIC AU/199
*ORANGE/25: .6X TO 1.5X BASIC AU/99

2017 Classics Stadium Stars Signatures
1 Thomas Rawls/25 5.00 12.00
6 Aaron Donald/25 8.00 20.00
9 Tedy Bruschi/25 25.00 50.00
10 Luke Kuechly/15 20.00 50.00
11 Demaryius Thomas/15
12 Joe Haden/25 5.00 12.00
14 Landon Collins/25 5.00 12.00
18 Carlos Hyde/49 4.00 10.00
19 Devonta Freeman/15
21 Doug Baldwin/15
24 Victor Cruz/15 8.00 20.00
25 Greg Olsen/15
26 Jadeveon Clowney/25 5.00 12.00
28 Joey Bosa/49

2017 Classics The Next Level
*GOLD: .8X TO 2X BASIC INSERTS
1 Ezekiel Elliott .75 2.00
2 Dak Prescott .60 1.50
3 Tom Brady 1.50 4.00
4 Matt Ryan .50 1.25
5 Greg Olsen .50 1.25
6 Derek Carr .60 1.50
7 Odell Beckham Jr. .60 1.50
8 Heath Miller .40 1.00
9 Matthew Stafford .50 1.25
10 Khalil Mack .60 1.50
11 Brett Favre 1.25 3.00
12 Cam Newton .60 1.50
13 Luke Kuechly .50 1.25
14 Julio Jones .60 1.50
15 Troy Aikman .75 2.00
16 Terry Bradshaw 1.00 2.50
17 Andrew Luck .75 2.00
18 Aaron Rodgers 1.25 3.00
19 Marvin Harrison .50 1.25
20 Jadeveon Clowney .40 1.00
21 Dez Bryant .60 1.50
22 David Johnson .60 1.50
23 Brian Urlacher .60 1.50
24 Eli Manning .50 1.25
25 Drew Brees .60 1.50
26 Joey Bosa .60 1.50
27 Peyton Manning 1.25 3.00
28 Le'Veon Bell .60 1.25
29 Derrick Henry .50 1.25
30 Jameis Winston .50 1.25

2018 Classics
1 Patrick Peterson .20 .50
2 David Johnson .30 .75
3 Larry Fitzgerald .25 .60
4 Matt Ryan .25 .60
5 Julio Jones .30 .75
6 Devonta Freeman .25 .60
7 Tevin Coleman .20 .50
8 Joe Flacco .25 .60
9 Terrell Suggs .20 .50
10 Justin Tucker .20 .50
11 Tyrod Taylor .25 .60
12 LeSean McCoy .30 .75
13 Charles Clay .20 .50
14 Cam Newton .30 .75
15 Christian McCaffrey .30 .75
16 Luke Kuechly .25 .60
17 Mitchell Trubisky .30 .75
18 Jordan Howard .30 .75
19 Tarik Cohen .25 .60
20 Andy Dalton .25 .60
21 A.J. Green .30 .75
22 Joe Mixon .25 .60
23 Josh Gordon .20 .50
24 Isaiah Crowell .20 .50
25 Myles Garrett .30 .75
26 Dak Prescott .30 .75
27 Ezekiel Elliott .40 1.00
28 Dez Bryant .30 .75
29 Jason Witten .25 .60
30 Emmanuel Sanders .30 .75
31 Demaryius Thomas .25 .60
32 Von Miller .25 .60
33 Matthew Stafford .25 .60
34 Golden Tate III .20 .50
35 Theo Riddick .20 .50
36 Aaron Rodgers .60 1.50
37 Jordy Nelson .25 .60
38 Davante Adams .25 .60
39 Randall Cobb .25 .60
40 Deshaun Watson .40 1.00
41 Lamar Miller .20 .50
42 DeAndre Hopkins .25 .60
43 Andrew Luck .40 1.00
44 T.Y. Hilton .25 .60
45 Frank Gore .25 .60
46 Blake Bortles .20 .50
47 Leonard Fournette .30 .75
48 Jalen Ramsey .25 .60
49 Patrick Mahomes II .75 2.00
50 Travis Kelce .30 .75
51 Kareem Hunt .25 .60
52 Tyreek Hill .30 .75
53 Ryan Tannehill .25 .60
54 Jarvis Landry .25 .60
55 Kenyan Drake .20 .50
56 Case Keenum .25 .60
57 Dalvin Cook .25 .60
58 Stefon Diggs .25 .60
59 Tom Brady .75 2.00
60 Brandin Cooks .25 .60
61 Rob Gronkowski .30 .75
62 Drew Brees .30 .75
63 Alvin Kamara .25 .60
64 Michael Thomas .30 .75
65 Eli Manning .25 .60
66 Odell Beckham Jr. .30 .75
67 Evan Engram .20 .50
68 Bilal Powell .20 .50
69 Robby Anderson .20 .50
70 Leonard Williams .20 .50
71 Derek Carr .30 .75
72 Marshawn Lynch .25 .60
73 Amari Cooper .30 .75
74 Carson Wentz .40 1.00
75 Alshon Jeffery .25 .60
76 Jay Ajayi .25 .60
77 Ben Roethlisberger .30 .75
78 Le'Veon Bell .25 .60
79 Antonio Brown .30 .75
80 Philip Rivers .30 .75
81 Melvin Gordon .25 .60
82 Keenan Allen .25 .60
83 Jimmy Garoppolo .40 1.00
84 Carlos Hyde .20 .50
85 Marquise Goodwin .20 .50
86 Russell Wilson .40 1.00
87 Doug Baldwin .25 .60
88 Richard Sherman .30 .75
89 Jared Goff .30 .75
90 Todd Gurley II .30 .75
91 Cooper Kupp .25 .60
92 Jameis Winston .25 .60
93 DeSean Jackson .25 .60
94 Mike Evans .25 .60
95 Marcus Mariota .30 .75
96 Derrick Henry .30 .75
97 Delanie Walker .20 .50
98 Kirk Cousins .30 .75
99 Jordan Reed .20 .50
100 Samaje Perine .20 .50
101 Kurt Warner .25 .60
102 Eric Dickerson .30 .75
103 Jonathan Ogden .25 .60
104 Ed Reed .25 .60
105 Jim Kelly .30 .75
106 Ray Lewis .30 .75
107 Michael Strahan .25 .60
108 Thurman Thomas .25 .60
109 Dick Butkus .40 1.00
110 Mike Ditka .30 .75
111 Brian Urlacher .30 .75
112 Mike Singletary .30 .75
113 Alan Page .20 .50
114 Charlie Joiner .20 .50
115 Ken Anderson .20 .50
116 Mike Wagner .20 .50
117 Ozzie Newsome .25 .60
118 Troy Aikman .40 1.00
119 Larry Allen .30 .75
120 Tony Dorsett .30 .75
121 Randy White .25 .60
122 Rayfield Wright .20 .50
123 Charles Haley .30 .75
124 Terrell Davis .25 .60
125 John Elway .50 1.25
126 Elvin Bethea .20 .50
127 Dick LeBeau .20 .50
128 Barry Sanders .50 1.25
129 Calvin Johnson .30 .75
130 Antonio Freeman .25 .60
131 Brett Favre .60 1.50
132 Gilbert Brown .20 .50
133 Paul Hornung .30 .75
134 Warren Moon .30 .75
135 Raymond Berry .25 .60
136 Edgerrin James .25 .60
137 Maurice Jones-Drew .20 .50
138 Marcus Allen .30 .75
139 Curley Culp .25 .60
140 Jan Stenerud .20 .50
141 Fred Biletnikoff .30 .75
142 Howie Long .30 .75
143 Marshall Faulk .25 .60
144 Larry Little .20 .50
145 Jason Taylor .25 .60
146 Roger Wehrli .20 .50
147 Paul Warfield .25 .60
148 Chris Doleman .20 .50
149 Carl Eller .20 .50
150 Paul Krause .20 .50
151 Ron Yary .20 .50
152 Fran Tarkenton .30 .75
153 Tedy Bruschi .30 .75
154 Ty Law .30 .75
155 Rickey Jackson .20 .50
156 Jim Taylor .25 .60
157 Roger Craig .25 .60
158 Ron Jaworski .25 .60
159 Don Majkowski .25 .60
160 Lenny Moore .20 .50
161 Doug Williams .25 .60
162 John Riggins .25 .60
163 Joe Namath .40 1.00
164 Doug Flutie .25 .60
165 Dan Marino .60 1.50
166 Jim Otto .20 .50
167 Tim Brown .30 .75
168 Bill Bates .20 .50
169 Cliff Branch .20 .50
170 Rich Gannon .25 .60
171 Ken Stabler .30 .75
172 Brian Dawkins .30 .75
173 Jack Lambert .20 .50
174 Hines Ward .25 .60
175 Heath Miller .20 .50
176 Franco Harris .30 .75
177 Jerome Bettis .30 .75
178 Terry Bradshaw .50 1.25
179 LaDainian Tomlinson .25 .60
180 Lance Alworth .25 .60
181 Rodney Harrison .25 .60
182 Steve Young .40 1.00
183 Y.A. Tittle .30 .75
184 Shaun Alexander .20 .50
185 Henry Ellard .20 .50
186 Warren Sapp .25 .60
187 Kellen Winslow .25 .60
188 Joe Theismann .30 .75
189 Charley Taylor .20 .50
190 Clinton Portis .20 .50
191 Emmitt Smith .50 1.25
192 Earl Campbell .30 .75
193 Roger Staubach .40 1.00
194 Tony Gonzalez .25 .60
195 Rod Woodson .30 .75
196 Bruce Smith .25 .60
197 John Hannah .20 .50
198 Peyton Manning .60 1.50
199 Ted Johnson .20 .50
200 Ray Guy .20 .50
201 Minkah Fitzpatrick RC .75 2.00
202 Denzel Ward RC 1.00 2.50
203 Bradley Chubb RC .60 1.50
204 Harold Landry RC .40 1.00
205 Josh Rosen RC 1.25 3.00
206 Sam Darnold RC 2.50 6.00
207 Josh Allen RC 1.50 4.00
208 Baker Mayfield RC 4.00 10.00
209 Lamar Jackson RC 2.50 6.00
210 Mason Rudolph RC 1.00 2.50
211 Kurt Benkert RC .50 1.25
212 Riley Ferguson RC .60 1.50
213 Saquon Barkley RC 3.00 8.00
214 Derrius Guice RC .75 2.00
215 Ronald Jones II RC .40 1.00
216 Nick Chubb RC 1.25 3.00
217 Kerryon Johnson RC .60 1.50
218 Sony Michel RC 1.25 3.00
219 John Kelly RC .50 1.25
220 Rashaad Penny RC .60 1.50
221 Calvin Ridley RC 1.00 2.50
222 Christian Kirk RC .60 1.50
223 Courtland Sutton RC .60 1.50
224 James Washington RC .75 2.00
225 Anthony Miller RC .60 1.50
226 Deontay Burnett RC .50 1.25
227 Michael Gallup RC .75 2.00
228 DJ Chark RC .50 1.25
229 Dallas Goedert RC .50 1.25
230 Deon Cain RC .50 1.25
231 Joshua Jackson RC .75 2.00
232 Isaiah Oliver RC .40 1.00
233 Arden Key RC .40 1.00
234 Quadree Henderson RC .50 1.25
235 Micah Kiser RC .40 1.00
236 Maurice Hurst RC .50 1.25
237 Vita Vea RC .60 1.50
238 Roquan Smith RC 1.25 3.00
239 Malik Jefferson RC .50 1.25
240 Rashaan Evans RC .60 1.50
241 Tremaine Edmunds RC .75 2.00
242 Ogbonnia Okoronkwo RC .60 1.50
243 Luke Falk RC .50 1.25
244 Mike White RC .50 1.25
245 Richie James RC .40 1.00
246 Trey Quinn RC .40 1.00
247 Josh Adams RC .75 2.00
248 Bo Scarbrough RC .50 1.25
249 Royce Freeman RC .50 1.25
250 Akrum Wadley RC .40 1.00
251 Kalen Ballage RC .50 1.25
252 Mark Walton RC .50 1.25
253 Derwin James RC .75 2.00
254 Ronnie Harrison RC .50 1.25
255 Mark Andrews RC .60 1.50
256 Mike Gesicki RC .50 1.25
257 D.J. Moore RC .75 2.00
258 Marcell Ateman RC .50 1.25
259 Simmie Cobbs Jr. RC .60 1.50
260 Allen Lazard RC .40 1.00
261 Dante Pettis RC .60 1.50
262 Jaleel Scott RC .40 1.00
263 Jordan Lasley RC .40 1.00
264 Quin Blanding RC .40 1.00
265 Troy Fumagalli RC .50 1.25
266 Azeem Victor RC .50 1.25
267 Lowell Lotulelei RC .40 1.00
268 Billy Price RC .50 1.25
269 Tarvarus McFadden RC .50 1.25
270 Carlton Davis RC .50 1.25
271 M.J. Stewart RC .40 1.00
272 Jaylen Samuels RC .50 1.25
273 Jaire Alexander RC .60 1.50
274 Brandon Facyson RC .40 1.00
275 Duke Dawson RC .40 1.00
276 Kevin Toliver II RC .50 1.25
277 Tony Brown RC .40 1.00
278 Jordan Thomas RC .50 1.25
279 Sam Hubbard RC .50 1.25
280 Kamryn Pettway RC .60 1.50
281 Javon Wims RC .40 1.00
282 Lorenzo Carter RC .40 1.00
283 Keishawn Bierria RC .40 1.00
284 Dorian O'Daniel RC .40 1.00
285 J.T. Barrett RC .60 1.50
286 Fred Warner RC .40 1.00
287 Davin Bellamy RC .40 1.00
288 Kyle Lauletta RC .60 1.50
289 Justin Jackson RC .50 1.25
290 Dalyn Dawkins RC .40 1.00
291 Ian Thomas RC .40 1.00
292 Christopher Herndon IV RC .40 1.00
293 Dalton Schultz RC .50 1.25
294 Cedrick Wilson Jr. RC .40 1.00
295 Darren Carrington II RC .50 1.25
296 DaeSean Hamilton RC .50 1.25
297 Jester Weah RC .40 1.00
298 Steve Ishmael RC .40 1.00
299 Bryce Bobo RC .40 1.00
300 Robert Foster RC .40 1.00
301 Nick Mullens
302 Baker Mayfield
303 Sam Darnold
304 Lamar Jackson
305 Josh Rosen
306 Josh Allen
307 Saquon Barkley
308 Calvin Ridley
309 Phillip Lindsay
310 D.J. Moore
311 Sony Michel
312 Roquan Smith
313 Denzel Ward
314 Bradley Chubb
315 Courtland Sutton
316 Mason Rudolph
317 Marquez Valdes-Scantling
318 Derwin James
319 Nick Chubb
320 Michael Gallup
321 Rashaad Penny
322 James Washington
323 Kerryon Johnson
324 Kyle Lauletta
325 Ito Smith
326 Tre'Quan Smith
327 Dallas Goedert
328 Christian Kirk
329 Anthony Miller
330 Leighton Vander Esch

2018 Classics Blank Back
*VETS/50: 2.5X TO 6X BASIC CARDS
*ROOKIES/50: 1.2X TO 3X BASIC CARDS

2018 Classics Blue Back
*VETS/175: 1.5X TO 4X BASIC CARDS
*ROOK/175: .8X TO 2X BASIC CARDS

2018 Classics Green Back
*VETS/40: 2.5X TO 6X BASIC CARDS
*ROOKIES/40: 1.2X TO 3X BASIC CARDS
209 Lamar Jackson 10.00 25.00

2018 Classics Premium Edition
*VETS: 1X TO 2.5X BASIC CARDS
*ROOKIES: .6X TO 1.5X BASIC CARDS

2018 Classics Premium Edition Blank Back
*VETS/35: 2.5X TO 6X BASIC CARDS
*ROOKIES/35: 1.2X TO 3X BASIC CARDS

2018 Classics Premium Edition Red Back
*VETS/175: 1.5X TO 4X BASIC CARDS
*ROOK/175: .8X TO 2X BASIC CARDS

2018 Classics Red Back
*VETS/299: 1.5X TO 4X BASIC CARDS
*ROOK/299: .8X TO 2X BASIC CARDS

2018 Classics Timeless Tributes Gold
*VETS/99: 2X TO 5X BASIC CARDS
*ROOKIES/99: 1X TO 2.5X BASIC CARDS
209 Lamar Jackson 10.00 25.00

2018 Classics Timeless Tributes Orange
*VETS/25: 3X TO 8X BASIC CARDS
*ROOKIES/25: 1.5X TO 4X BASIC CARDS
208 Baker Mayfield 15.00 40.00
209 Lamar Jackson 15.00 40.00

2018 Classics Timeless Tributes Premium Edition Gold
*VETS/65: 2.5X TO 6X BASIC CARDS
*ROOKIES/65: 1.2X TO 3X BASIC CARDS
209 Lamar Jackson 10.00 25.00
213 Saquon Barkley 30.00 60.00

2018 Classics Timeless Tributes Premium Edition Orange
*VETS/15: 4X TO 10X BASIC CARDS
*ROOKIES/15: 2X TO 5X BASIC CARDS
209 Lamar Jackson 75.00 150.00
213 Saquon Barkley 50.00 100.00

2018 Classics Award Winners Stickers
1 Tom Brady 2.00 5.00
2 Alvin Kamara .60 1.50
3 Marshon Lattimore .50 1.25
4 Nick Foles .60 1.50

2018 Classics Canton Collection Swatches
*PRIME/25: .8X TO 2X BASIC JSY
1 Terry Bradshaw 5.00 12.00
2 Barry Sanders 5.00 12.00
3 Jerome Bettis 3.00 8.00
4 Jerry Rice 5.00 12.00
5 Howie Long 3.00 8.00
6 John Riggins 2.50 6.00
7 Mike Ditka 3.00 8.00
8 John Elway 5.00 12.00
9 Dan Marino 6.00 15.00
10 Mike Singletary 3.00 8.00
11 Lawrence Taylor 3.00 8.00
12 Joe Montana 8.00 20.00
13 Earl Campbell 3.00 8.00
15 Eric Dickerson 3.00 8.00
16 Thurman Thomas 2.50 6.00
17 Michael Irvin 3.00 8.00
18 Ozzie Newsome 2.50 6.00
19 Brett Favre 6.00 15.00
20 Warren Moon 3.00 8.00

2018 Classics Classic Clashes
*GOLD/99: .6X TO 1.5X BASIC INSERT
1 C.Wentz/D.Prescott 1.00 2.50
2 V.Miller/B.Urlacher .75 2.00
3 A.Green/J.Ramsey .75 2.00
4 B.Sanders/E.Smith 1.25 3.00
5 B.Roethlisberger/T.Brady 2.00 5.00
6 D.Sanders/J.Rice 1.25 3.00
7 A.Brown/O.Beckham Jr. .75 2.00
8 J.Montana/T.Bradshaw 2.00 5.00
9 J.Howard/L.McCoy .75 2.00
10 D.Marino/J.Namath 1.50 4.00
11 A.Rodgers/M.Stafford 1.50 4.00
12 C.Johnson/R.Moss .75 2.00
13 P.Peterson/K.Mack .75 2.00
14 T.Gonzalez/K.Winslow .60 1.50
15 D.Brees/R.Wilson 1.00 2.50

2018 Classics Classic Combos Memorabilia
1 A.Brown/B.Roethlisberger 3.00 8.00
2 M.Irvin/T.Aikman 4.00 10.00
3 D.Baldwin/R.Wilson 4.00 10.00
4 Reggie Wayne 2.50 6.00
5 O.Beckham Jr./E.Manning 3.00 8.00
6 A.Reed/J.Kelly 3.00 8.00
7 T.Hill/K.Hunt 3.00 8.00
8 S.Young/J.Rice 5.00 12.00
9 C.Wentz/Z.Ertz 4.00 10.00
10 B.Bortles/L.Fournette 3.00 8.00
11 T.Brady/R.Gronkowski 8.00 20.00
12 A.Cooper/D.Carr 3.00 8.00
13 J.Jones/M.Ryan 3.00 8.00
14 J.Riggins/J.Theismann 3.00 8.00
15 D.Prescott/E.Elliott 4.00 10.00
16 Ted Hendricks 2.00 5.00
17 A.Rodgers/J.Nelson 6.00 15.00
18 C.Kupp/J.Goff 3.00 8.00
19 M.Stafford/G.Tate III 2.50 6.00
20 J.Elway/T.Davis 5.00 12.00

2018 Classics Classic Materials
*PRIME/50: .6X TO 1.5X BASIC JSY
*PRIME/15: 1X TO 2.5X BASIC JSY
1 Jared Goff 3.00 8.00
2 Troy Aikman 4.00 10.00
3 Cam Newton 3.00 8.00
4 Clay Matthews 2.50 6.00
5 Mitchell Trubisky 3.00 8.00
6 Jim Kelly 3.00 8.00
7 A.J. Green 3.00 8.00
8 Thurman Thomas 2.50 6.00
9 Dak Prescott 3.00 8.00
10 Dan Marino 6.00 15.00
11 Von Miller 2.50 6.00
12 Terrell Suggs 2.00 5.00
13 Aaron Rodgers 6.00 15.00
14 Edgerrin James 2.50 6.00
15 Deshaun Watson 4.00 10.00
17 Leonard Fournette 3.00 8.00
18 Kareem Hunt 2.50 6.00
19 Howie Long 3.00 8.00
20 Fran Tarkenton 3.00 8.00

2018 Classics Composers
*GOLD/99: .6X TO 1.5X BASIC INSERTS
1 Terry Bradshaw 1.25 3.00
2 Peyton Manning 1.50 4.00
3 Jimmy Garoppolo 1.00 2.50
4 Tom Brady 2.00 5.00
5 Matt Ryan .60 1.50
6 Russell Wilson 1.00 2.50
7 Dak Prescott .75 2.00
8 Aaron Rodgers 1.50 4.00
9 Matthew Stafford .60 1.50
10 Cam Newton .75 2.00
11 Mitchell Trubisky .75 2.00
12 Rich Gannon .60 1.50
13 Dan Marino 1.50 4.00
14 John Elway 1.25 3.00
15 Steve Young 1.00 2.50
16 Drew Brees .75 2.00
17 Blake Bortles .50 1.25
18 Carson Wentz 1.00 2.50
19 Derek Carr .75 2.00
20 Eli Manning .60 1.50
21 Ben Roethlisberger .75 2.00
22 Troy Aikman 1.00 2.50
23 Brett Favre 1.50 4.00
24 Jim Kelly .75 2.00
25 Jared Goff .75 2.00
26 Deshaun Watson 1.00 2.50
27 Philip Rivers .75 2.00
28 Andrew Luck 1.00 2.50
29 Warren Moon .75 2.00
30 Joe Flacco .60 1.50

2018 Classics Eras
*GOLD/99: .6X TO 1.5X BASIC INSERTS
1 E.Smith/E.Elliott 1.25 3.00
2 J.Plunkett/D.Carr .75 2.00
3 C.Wentz/R.Jaworski 1.00 2.50
4 L.McCoy/T.Thomas .75 2.00
5 S.Diggs/C.Carter .75 2.00
6 B.Roethlisberger/T.Bradshaw 1.25 3.00
7 R.Wayne/T.Hilton .60 1.50
8 T.Gurley II/E.Dickerson .75 2.00
9 L.Tomlinson/M.Gordon .60 1.50
10 S.Largent/D.Baldwin .75 2.00
11 T.Gonzalez/T.Kelce .75 2.00
12 R.Moss/B.Cooks .60 1.50
13 B.Favre/A.Rodgers 1.50 4.00
14 R.Lewis/T.Suggs .75 2.00
15 D.Freeman/W.Dunn .60 1.50

2018 Classics Full Throttle
*GOLD/99: .6X TO 1.5X BASIC INSERTS
1 Kareem Hunt .60 1.50
2 Devonta Freeman .60 1.50
3 Le'Veon Bell .60 1.50
4 Jerome Bettis .75 2.00
5 Ray Lewis .75 2.00
6 Marshawn Lynch .60 1.50
7 Sean Lee .60 1.50
8 Von Miller .60 1.50
9 Luke Kuechly .60 1.50
10 Richard Sherman .75 2.00
11 Jalen Ramsey .60 1.50
12 Ezekiel Elliott 1.00 2.50
13 Todd Gurley II .75 2.00
14 Champ Bailey .60 1.50
15 Leonard Fournette .75 2.00

2018 Classics High Praise
*GOLD/99: .6X TO 1.5X BASIC INSERTS
1 Peyton Manning 1.50 4.00
2 Jerome Bettis .75 2.00
3 Lawrence Taylor .75 2.00
4 Jerry Rice 1.25 3.00
5 Barry Sanders 1.25 3.00
6 Joe Montana 2.00 5.00
7 Deion Sanders .60 1.50
8 LaDainian Tomlinson .60 1.50
9 Tony Gonzalez .60 1.50
10 Brian Urlacher .75 2.00
11 John Elway 1.25 3.00
12 Marshall Faulk .60 1.50
13 Earl Campbell .75 2.00
14 Charlie Joiner .50 1.25
15 Mike Singletary .75 2.00

2018 Classics Instant Classics
*GOLD/99: .8X TO 2X BASIC INSERTS
1 Tom Brady 1.50 4.00
2 Aaron Rodgers 1.25 3.00
3 Mike Singletary .60 1.50
4 Dan Marino 1.25 3.00
5 Franco Harris .60 1.50
6 Eli Manning .50 1.25
7 Joe Montana 1.50 4.00
8 Adam Vinatieri .40 1.00
9 Joe Namath .75 2.00
10 James Harrison .50 1.25

2018 Classics Saturday Swatches
*PRIME/32-50: .6X TO 1.5X BASIC JSY
*PRIME/17: 1X TO 2.5X BASIC JSY
1 David Johnson 3.00 8.00
2 Corey Davis 2.50 6.00
3 D'Onta Foreman 2.00 5.00
4 Dede Westbrook 2.00 5.00
5 Christian McCaffrey 3.00 8.00
6 Mitchell Trubisky 3.00 8.00
7 Jordan Howard 3.00 8.00
8 DeShone Kizer 2.50 6.00
9 Dak Prescott 3.00 8.00
10 Ezekiel Elliott 4.00 10.00
12 Ameer Abdullah 2.00 5.00
13 Davante Adams 2.50 6.00
14 Deshaun Watson 4.00 10.00
15 Marlon Mack 2.00 5.00
16 Leonard Fournette 3.00 8.00
17 Kareem Hunt 2.50 6.00
18 Jarvis Landry 2.50 6.00
19 Dalvin Cook 2.50 6.00
20 Brandin Cooks 2.50 6.00
21 Alvin Kamara 2.50 6.00
22 Odell Beckham Jr. 3.00 8.00
24 Derek Carr 3.00 8.00
25 Carson Wentz 4.00 10.00
27 Melvin Gordon 2.50 6.00
28 Carlos Hyde 2.00 5.00
30 Jared Goff 3.00 8.00
31 Mike Evans 2.50 6.00
32 Marcus Mariota 3.00 8.00
33 Samaje Perine 2.00 5.00
35 Curtis Samuel 2.00 5.00
36 Will Fuller V 2.00 5.00
37 Jay Ajayi 2.50 6.00
38 Amari Cooper 3.00 8.00
39 Todd Gurley II 3.00 8.00
40 Jameis Winston 2.50 6.00

2018 Classics Significant Signatures
10 Justin Tucker/99 6.00 15.00
15 Christian McCaffrey/15 10.00 25.00
19 Tarik Cohen/25 6.00 15.00
22 Joe Mixon/99 4.00 10.00
31 Demaryius Thomas/25 6.00 15.00
34 Golden Tate III/40 4.00 10.00
39 Randall Cobb/15 12.00 30.00
43 Andrew Luck/15
44 T.Y. Hilton/15
49 Patrick Mahomes II/15 40.00 80.00
50 Travis Kelce/15 10.00 25.00
55 Kenyan Drake/25 5.00 12.00
63 Alvin Kamara/25 20.00 40.00
64 Michael Thomas/25 8.00 20.00
65 Eli Manning/15 8.00 20.00
69 Robby Anderson/20 6.00 15.00
77 Ben Roethlisberger/15 30.00 80.00
82 Keenan Allen/15 8.00 20.00
83 Jimmy Garoppolo/30 90.00 150.00
84 Carlos Hyde/65 4.00 10.00
87 Doug Baldwin/15 8.00 20.00
91 Cooper Kupp/25
97 Delanie Walker/75 3.00 8.00
100 Samaje Perine/25 5.00 12.00
102 Eric Dickerson/25
109 Dick Butkus/20 25.00 50.00
114 Charlie Joiner/99 3.00 8.00
116 Mike Wagner/99 8.00 20.00
119 Larry Allen/15 10.00 25.00
123 Charles Haley/15
124 Terrell Davis/15
126 Elvin Bethea/35 4.00 10.00
127 Dick LeBeau/30
132 Gilbert Brown/99 3.00 8.00
133 Paul Hornung/99 5.00 12.00
139 Curley Culp/99 15.00 40.00
140 Jan Stenerud/99 3.00 8.00
144 Larry Little/35 8.00 20.00
146 Roger Wehrli/99 3.00 8.00
147 Paul Warfield/50 5.00 12.00
148 Chris Doleman/75 3.00 8.00
149 Carl Eller/75 3.00 8.00
150 Paul Krause/20 6.00 15.00
151 Ron Yary/75 6.00 15.00
155 Rickey Jackson/20 6.00 15.00
159 Don Majkowski/99 12.00 30.00
160 Lenny Moore/50 4.00 10.00
161 Doug Williams/35 5.00 12.00
166 Jim Otto/30 10.00 25.00
168 Bill Bates/65 4.00 10.00
181 Rodney Harrison/20 8.00 20.00
183 Y.A. Tittle/65 6.00 15.00
185 Henry Ellard/20 6.00 15.00
187 Kellen Winslow/30 6.00 15.00
189 Charley Taylor/10
195 Rod Woodson/15
197 John Hannah/40 4.00 10.00
199 Ted Johnson/99 8.00 20.00
200 Ray Guy/99 3.00 8.00
205 Josh Rosen/35 40.00 80.00
206 Sam Darnold/35 60.00 125.00
207 Josh Allen/35 50.00 100.00
208 Baker Mayfield/35 100.00 200.00
210 Mason Rudolph/50 15.00 40.00
211 Kurt Benkert/199 3.00 8.00
212 Riley Ferguson/199 4.00 10.00
213 Saquon Barkley/35 75.00 150.00
214 Derrius Guice/49 12.00 30.00
215 Ronald Jones II/99 3.00 8.00
216 Nick Chubb/99 20.00 40.00
217 Kerryon Johnson/99 5.00 12.00
218 Sony Michel/199 8.00 20.00
219 John Kelly/199 3.00 8.00
221 Calvin Ridley/35 20.00 40.00
222 Christian Kirk/99 5.00 12.00
223 Courtland Sutton/199 4.00 10.00
224 James Washington/199 5.00 12.00
225 Anthony Miller/199 4.00 10.00
226 Deontay Burnett/99 4.00 10.00
227 Michael Gallup/199 5.00 12.00
229 Dallas Goedert/99 4.00 10.00
231 Joshua Jackson/99 6.00 15.00
232 Isaiah Oliver/99 3.00 8.00
233 Arden Key/99 3.00 8.00
234 Quadree Henderson/99 4.00 10.00
235 Micah Kiser/99 3.00 8.00
236 Maurice Hurst/199 3.00 8.00
237 Vita Vea/99 5.00 12.00
238 Roquan Smith/199 8.00 20.00
239 Malik Jefferson/99 4.00 10.00
240 Rashaan Evans/99 5.00 12.00
241 Tremaine Edmunds/99 6.00 15.00
243 Luke Falk/99 4.00 10.00
244 Mike White/99 4.00 10.00
245 Richie James/99 3.00 8.00
246 Trey Quinn/99 3.00 8.00
247 Josh Adams/199 5.00 12.00
248 Bo Scarbrough/99 4.00 10.00
249 Royce Freeman/99 4.00 10.00
250 Akrum Wadley/99 3.00 8.00
251 Kalen Ballage/99 4.00 10.00
252 Mark Walton/99 4.00 10.00
253 Derwin James/99 6.00 15.00
254 Ronnie Harrison/99 4.00 10.00
255 Mark Andrews/99 5.00 12.00
256 Mike Gesicki/199 3.00 8.00
257 DJ Moore/199 5.00 12.00
258 Marcell Ateman/99 4.00 10.00
259 Simmie Cobbs Jr./199 4.00 10.00
260 Allen Lazard/99 3.00 8.00
261 Dante Pettis/99 5.00 12.00
262 Jaleel Scott/99 3.00 8.00
263 Jordan Lasley/99 3.00 8.00
264 Quin Blanding/99 3.00 8.00
265 Troy Fumagalli/99 4.00 10.00
266 Azeem Victor/99 4.00 10.00
267 Lowell Lotulelei/99 3.00 8.00
268 Billy Price/99 4.00 10.00
269 Tarvarus McFadden/99 4.00 10.00
270 Carlton Davis/99 4.00 10.00
271 M.J. Stewart/99 3.00 8.00
272 Jaylen Samuels/99 4.00 10.00
273 Jaire Alexander/99 5.00 12.00
274 Brandon Facyson/99 3.00 8.00
275 Duke Dawson/99 3.00 8.00
277 Tony Brown/99 3.00 8.00
279 Sam Hubbard/99 4.00 10.00
280 Kamryn Pettway/75 5.00 12.00
281 Javon Wims/99 3.00 8.00
282 Lorenzo Carter/99 8.00 20.00
283 Keishawn Bierria/99 3.00 8.00
284 Dorian O'Daniel/99 3.00 8.00
285 J.T. Barrett/99 5.00 12.00
286 Fred Warner/99 3.00 8.00
287 Davin Bellamy/99 3.00 8.00
288 Kyle Lauletta/99 5.00 12.00
289 Justin Jackson/99 4.00 10.00
290 Dalyn Dawkins/99 3.00 8.00
291 Ian Thomas/99 3.00 8.00
292 Christopher Herndon IV/99 3.00 8.00
293 Dalton Schultz/99 4.00 10.00
294 Cedrick Wilson Jr./99 3.00 8.00
295 Darren Carrington II/99 4.00 10.00
296 DaeSean Hamilton/99 4.00 10.00
297 Jester Weah/99 3.00 8.00
298 Steve Ishmael/99 3.00 8.00
299 Bryce Bobo/99 3.00 8.00
300 Robert Foster/99 3.00 8.00
301 Nick Mullens/75
302 Baker Mayfield/49
304 Lamar Jackson/49
305 Josh Rosen/49
306 Josh Allen/49
307 Saquon Barkley/49
308 Calvin Ridley/49
309 Phillip Lindsay/75
310 D.J. Moore/75
312 Roquan Smith/75
313 Denzel Ward/75
314 Bradley Chubb/75
315 Courtland Sutton/75
318 Derwin James/75

319 Nick Chubb/49
320 Michael Gallup/75
322 James Washington/75
323 Kerryon Johnson/75
324 Kyle Lauletta/75
327 Dallas Goedert/75
328 Christian Kirk/49
330 Leighton Vander Esch/75

2018 Classics Team Pennants

1 New York Jets 1.00 2.50
2 Pittsburgh Steelers 1.00 2.50
3 Chicago Bears 1.00 2.50
4 Indianapolis Colts 1.00 2.50
5 San Francisco 49ers 1.00 2.50
6 New York Giants FB 1.00 2.50
7 Dallas Cowboys 1.00 2.50
8 Green Bay Packers 1.00 2.50
9 Denver Broncos 1.00 2.50
10 New England Patriots 1.00 2.50
11 New Orleans Saints 1.00 2.50

2018 Classics Vintage Logo Stickers

1 Philadelphia Eagles 1.00 2.50
2 New England Patriots 1.00 2.50
3 Cincinnati Bengals 1.00 2.50
4 Miami Dolphins 1.00 2.50
5 Tampa Bay Buccaneers 1.00 2.50
6 Washington Redskins 1.00 2.50
7 New York Jets 1.00 2.50
8 Pittsburgh Steelers 1.00 2.50
9 Buffalo Bills 1.00 2.50
10 Atlanta Falcons 1.00 2.50
11 Denver Broncos 1.00 2.50
12 Green Bay Packers 1.00 2.50
13 Los Angeles Chargers 1.00 2.50
14 Seattle Seahawks 1.00 2.50
15 Tennessee Titans 1.00 2.50

1995 Cleo Quarterback Club Valentines

These blank-backed red-bordered valentine cards came in 38-card boxes of Cleo Valentines and feature color action photos of eight NFL quarterbacks. The valentines are printed on thin white card stock and measure approximately 2 1/2" by 3 1/2". They came in 4-card perforated sheets, with two rows of two cards each. The back of the box features three bonus cards that are identical to three of the cards inside. We've included those in the complete set price below. Non-mailable envelopes were included in the boxes. The cards are unnumbered and checklisted below in alphabetical order.

COMPLETE SET (11) 1.20 3.00
1A Troy Aikman .15 .40
1B Troy Aikman .20 .50
2 John Elway .25 .60
3A Brett Favre .25 .60
3B Brett Favre .30 .75
4 Jim Kelly .05 .15
5 Dan Marino .25 .60
6A Warren Moon .05 .15
6B Warren Moon .08 .25
7 Phil Simms .05 .15
8 Steve Young .10 .30

1996 Cleo Quarterback Club Valentines

These white-bordered valentine cards came in 40-card boxes with featuring a color action photo of one of eight NFL quarterbacks. The valentines are printed on thin white card stock and each measures approximately 2 1/2" by 5" except Marcus Allen measures 3 3/4" by 5". The back of the box features two bonus cards that are identical to two of the cards inside. We've included those in the complete set price. The cards are unnumbered and checklisted below in alphabetical order.

COMPLETE SET (10) 1.00 2.50
1 Troy Aikman .15 .40
2 Marcus Allen .05 .15
3 Drew Bledsoe .15 .40
4 John Elway .25 .60
5 Jim Kelly .08 .25
6A Junior Seau .05 .15
6B Junior Seau .08 .25
7A Emmitt Smith .25 .60
7B Emmitt Smith .30 .75
8 Steve Young .10 .30

1997 Cleo Quarterback Club Valentines

COMPLETE SET (8) 1.25 3.00
*WINDOW CLINGS: .4X TO 1X
1 T.Aikman/E.Smith .25 .60
2 Drew Bledsoe .10 .25
3 Mark Brunell .10 .25
4 Kerry Collins .10 .25
5 John Elway .20 .50
6 Brett Favre .30 .75
7 Dan Marino .25 .60
8 Jerry Rice .20 .50

1998 Cleo Quarterback Club Valentines

COMPLETE SET (8) 1.25 3.00
1 Drew Bledsoe .14 .40
2 Kerry Collins .08 .25
3 John Elway .25 .60
4 Brett Favre .30 .75
5 Dan Marino .30 .75
6 Steve McNair .08 .25
7 Kordell Stewart .08 .25
8 Steve Young .20 .50

1962 Cleveland Bulldogs UFL Picture Pack

Big League Books produced and distributed this set of 5" by 7" photos for the Cleveland Bulldogs of the United Football League. This semi-pro league was centered in the Midwest and consisted of 7-teams. It's likely that each of the teams had a similar set produced, and any additional information on those would be appreciated.

COMPLETE SET (10) 75.00 150.00
1 Dave Adams 7.50 15.00
Gordon Helms
2 Bob Alford 7.50 15.00
Leo Bland
3 Bob Brodhead 10.00 20.00
4 John Drew 7.50 15.00
Bill Eyesdom
Ed Nemetz
5 Clay Hill 7.50 15.00
Gary Hostetler
6 Clark Kellogg 7.50 15.00
Bill Slacas
7 Dick Louis 7.50 15.00
Frank Mancini
8 Dick Newsome 7.50 15.00
Paul Pirrone
9 Coaching Staff 7.50 15.00
10 Officers 7.50 15.00

1992 Cleveland Thunderbolts Arena

Printed on plain white card stock, these 24 cards are irregularly cut and so vary in size, but are close to standard size. Framed by a purple line, the fronts feature coarsely screened posed black-and-white player photos of the Arena Football League's (AFL) Cleveland Thunderbolts. The player's name and position, along with the logo of the sponsor, Area Temps, appear below the photo. The backs carry the player's name at the top, followed by the team logo, position, jersey number, biography, and career highlights. The cards are unnumbered and checklisted below in alphabetical order.

COMPLETE SET (24) 12.00 30.00
1 Eric Anderson .50 1.25
2 Robert Banks WR .50 1.25
DB
3 Bobby Bounds .50 1.25
4 Marvin Bowman .50 1.25
5 George Cooper .50 1.25
6 Michael Denbrock ACO .50 1.25
7 Chris Drennan .50 1.25
8 Dennis Fitzgerald ACO .50 1.25
9 John Fletcher .50 1.25
10 Andre Giles .50 1.25
11 Chris Harkness .50 1.25
12 Major Harris 2.00 5.00
13 Luther Johnson .50 1.25
14 Marvin Mattox .50 1.25
15 Cedric McKinnon .50 1.25
16 Cleo Miller ACO .80 2.00
17 Tony Missick .50 1.25
18 Anthony Newsom .50 1.25
19 Phil Poirier .50 1.25
20 Alvin Powell .50 1.25
21 Ray Puryear .50 1.25
22 Dave Whinham CO .50 1.25
23 Brian Williams DL .50 1.25
24 Kennedy Wilson .50 1.25

2014 Cleveland Gladiators AFL

COMPLETE SET (17) 7.50 15.00
1 Shane Austin .40 1.00
2 Luke Black .40 1.00
3 Shannon Breen .40 1.00
4 C.J. Cobb .40 1.00
5 Chris Dieker .40 1.00
6 Dominick Goodman .40 1.00
7 Jason Jones .40 1.00
8 Dominic Jones .40 1.00
9 Thyron Lewis .40 1.00
10 Willie McGinnis .40 1.00
11 Marrio Norman .40 1.00
12 Kitt O'Brien .40 1.00
13 Aaron Pettrey .40 1.00
14 Joe Phinisee .40 1.00
15 Chad Schofield .40 1.00
16 Collin Taylor .40 1.00
17 Checklist Card .40 1.00

1963 Coke Caps Chargers

Little is actually known about these recently discovered Coke Caps but they are thought to be a scarce test issue to the more common Coke Cap series released nationally from 1964-1966. Each is similar in format to the 1964 release but coaches were included in this test issue and the player caps include the player's jersey number and position initials below the image. The set includes the earliest known Al Davis football collectible.

1 Lance Alworth 25.00 50.00
2 Frank Buncom 10.00 20.00
3 Reg Carolan 10.00 20.00
4 Al Davis CO 60.00 100.00
5 Wayne Frazier 10.00 20.00
6 Sid Gillman CO 15.00 30.00
7 George Gross 10.00 20.00
8 Sam Gruneisen 10.00 20.00
9 Rufus Guthrie 10.00 20.00
10 John Hadl 15.00 30.00
11 Bob Jackson 10.00 20.00
12 Emil Karas 10.00 20.00
13 Keith Kinderman 10.00 20.00
14 Ernie Ladd 12.50 25.00
15 Keith Lincoln 12.50 25.00
16 Gerry McDougall 10.00 20.00
17 Charlie McNeil 10.00 20.00
18 Ron Mix 15.00 30.00
19 Chuck Noll CO 25.00 50.00
20 Tobin Rote 12.50 25.00
21 Pat Shea 10.00 20.00

1964 Coke Caps All-Stars AFL

These AFL All-Star caps were issued in AFL cities (and a few other cities as well) along with the local team caps as part of the Go with the Pros promotion. The AFL team Cap Saver sheets had separate sections in which to affix the local team's player caps, the AFL team logos, and the All-Stars' caps. The caps measure approximately 1 1/8" in diameter and have the drink logo and a football on the outside, while the inside has the player's face printed in black, with text surrounding the face. The consumer could turn in his completed saver sheet to receive various prizes. The caps are unnumbered, but have been alphabetically listed below. These caps were also produced for 1964 on Sprite and King Size Coke bottles. Sprite caps typically carry a slight premium over the value of the Coke version.

COMPLETE SET (44) 100.00 200.00
1 Tommy Addison 1.75 3.50
2 Dalva Allen 1.75 3.50
3 Lance Alworth 7.50 15.00
4 Houston Antwine 1.75 3.50
5 Fred Arbanas 1.75 3.50
6 Tony Banfield 1.75 3.50
7 Stew Barber 1.75 3.50
8 George Blair 1.75 3.50
9 Mel Branch 1.75 3.50
10 Nick Buoniconti 3.75 7.50
11 Doug Cline 1.75 3.50
12 Eldon Danenhauer 1.75 3.50
13 Clem Daniels 2.00 4.00
14 Larry Eisenhauer 1.75 3.50
15 Earl Faison 1.75 3.50
16 Cookie Gilchrist 2.00 5.00
17 Freddy Glick 1.75 3.50
18 Larry Grantham 2.00 4.00
19 Ron Hall 1.75 3.50
20 Charlie Hennigan 2.00 4.00
21 E.J. Holub 2.00 4.00
22 Ed Husmann 1.75 3.50
23 Jack Kemp 12.50 25.00
24 Dave Kocourek 1.75 3.50
25 Keith Lincoln 2.00 4.00
26 Charles Long 1.75 3.50
27 Paul Lowe 2.00 4.00
28 Archie Matsos 1.75 3.50
29 Jerry Mays 2.00 4.00
30 Ron Mix 3.00 6.00
31 Tom Morrow 1.75 3.50
32 Billy Neighbors 2.00 4.00
33 Jim Otto 3.75 7.50
34 Art Powell 2.00 4.00
35 Johnny Robinson 2.00 4.00
36 Tobin Rote 2.00 4.00
37 Bob Schmidt 1.75 3.50
38 Tom Sestak 1.75 3.50
39 Billy Shaw 2.00 4.00
40 Bob Talamini 1.75 3.50
41 Lionel Taylor 2.00 4.00
42 Jim Tyrer 2.00 4.00
43 Dick Westmoreland 1.75 3.50
44 Fred Williamson 2.00 5.00

1964 Coke Caps All-Stars NFL

These NFL All-Star caps were issued in NFL cities (and a few other cities as well) along with the local team caps as part of the Go with the Pros promotion. The NFL team Cap Saver sheets had separate sections in which to affix the local team's player caps, the NFL team logos, and the All-Stars' caps. The caps measure approximately 1 1/8" in diameter and have the drink logo and a football on the outside, while the inside has the player's face printed in black, with text surrounding the face. The consumer could turn in his completed saver sheet to receive various prizes. The caps are unnumbered, but have been alphabetically listed below. These caps were also produced for 1964 on Sprite and King Size Coke bottles. Sprite caps typically carry a slight premium over the value of the Coke version.

COMPLETE SET (44) 100.00 200.00
1 Doug Atkins 3.00 6.00
2 Terry Barr 1.25 2.50
3 Jim Brown 12.50 25.00
4 Roger Brown 2.00 4.00
5 Roosevelt Brown 2.50 5.00
6 Timmy Brown 2.00 4.00
7 Bobby Joe Conrad 2.00 4.00
8 Willie Davis 3.00 6.00
9 Bob DeMarco 1.25 2.50
10 Darrell Dess 1.25 2.50
11 Mike Ditka 7.50 15.00
12 Bill Forester 1.25 2.50
13 Joe Fortunato 1.25 2.50
14 Bill George 3.00 6.00
15 Ken Gray 1.25 2.50
16 Forrest Gregg 3.00 6.00
17 Roosevelt Grier 2.50 5.00
18 Hank Jordan 3.00 6.00
19 Jim Katcavage 2.00 4.00
20 Jerry Kramer 2.50 5.00
21 Ron Kramer 1.25 2.50
22 Dick Lane 3.00 6.00
23 Dick Lynch 1.25 2.50
24 Gino Marchetti 3.00 6.00
25 Tommy Mason 2.00 4.00
26 Ed Meador 1.25 2.50
27 Bobby Mitchell 3.00 6.00
28 Larry Morris 1.25 2.50
29 Merlin Olsen 4.00 8.00
30 Jim Parker 2.50 5.00
31 Jim Patton 2.00 4.00
32 Myron Pottios 1.25 2.50
33 Jim Ringo 2.50 5.00
34 Dick Schafrath 1.25 2.50
35 Joe Schmidt 3.00 6.00
36 Del Shofner 2.00 4.00
37 Bob St. Clair 2.50 5.00
38 Jim Taylor 4.00 8.00
39 Roosevelt Taylor 2.00 4.00
40 Y.A. Tittle 5.00 10.00
41 Johnny Unitas 7.50 15.00
42 Larry Wilson 3.00 6.00
43 Willie Wood 3.00 6.00
44 Abe Woodson 2.00 4.00

1964 Coke Caps Bears

Coke caps were issued in each NFL city (except for the St.Louis Cardinals) featuring 35-members of that team along with the NFL All-Stars caps as part of the 1964 Go with the Pros promotion. The NFL team Cap Saver sheets had separate sections in which to affix both the local team's caps, the NFL team logos, and the All-Stars' caps. The caps measure approximately 1 1/8" in diameter and have the drink logo and a football on the outside, while the inside has the player's face printed in black with the team name above the photo, the player's name below, his jersey number to the left and his position to the right. Most caps were issued with either a plastic or cork liner on the inside. The consumer could turn in his completed saver sheet (before the expiration date of Nov. 21, 1964) to receive various prizes. The 1964 caps look very similar to those issued in 1965 and 1966 but were numbered only according to the player's jersey number. We've arranged them alphabetically by team for ease in cataloging. Football caps were produced for Coca-Cola, Sprite and King Size Coke bottles. Sprite caps typically carry a slight premium over the value of the Coke version.

COMPLETE SET (35) 75.00 150.00
1 Doug Atkins 4.00 8.00
2 Steve Barnett 1.50 3.00
3 Charlie Bivins 1.50 3.00
4 Rudy Bukich 2.50 4.00
5 Ronnie Bull 2.50 4.00
6 Jim Cadile 1.50 3.00
7 J.C. Caroline 1.50 3.00
8 Rick Casares 2.50 4.00
9 Roger Davis 1.50 3.00
10 Mike Ditka 6.00 12.00
11 John Farrington 1.50 3.00
12 Joe Fortunato 1.50 3.00
13 Willie Galimore 2.50 4.00
14 Bill George 3.50 6.00
15 Larry Glueck 1.50 3.00
16 Bobby Joe Green 1.50 3.00
17 Bob Jencks 1.50 3.00
18 John Johnson 1.50 3.00
19 Stan Jones 3.50 6.00
20 Ted Karras 1.50 3.00
21 Bob Kilcullen 1.50 3.00
22 Roger LeClerc 1.50 3.00
23 Herman Lee 1.50 3.00
24 Earl Leggett 1.50 3.00
25 Joe Marconi 1.50 3.00
26 Bennie McRae 1.50 3.00
27 Johnny Morris 1.50 3.00
28 Larry Morris 1.50 3.00
29 Ed O'Bradovich 1.50 3.00
30 Richie Petitbon 2.50 4.00
31 Mike Pyle 1.50 3.00
32 Roosevelt Taylor 2.50 4.00
33 Bill Wade 2.50 4.00
34 Bob Wetoska 1.50 3.00
35 Dave Whitsell 1.50 3.00
NNO Bears Saver Sheet 15.00 30.00

1964 Coke Caps Browns

Please see the 1964 Coke Caps Bears listing for information on this set.

COMPLETE SET (35) 75.00 150.00
1 Walter Beach 1.50 3.00
2 Larry Benz 1.50 3.00
3 Johnny Brewer 1.50 3.00
4 Jim Brown 15.00 30.00
5 John Brown 1.50 3.00
6 Monte Clark 1.50 3.00
7 Gary Collins 2.50 5.00
8 Vince Costello 1.50 3.00
9 Ross Fichtner 1.50 3.00
10 Galen Fiss 1.50 3.00
11 Bobby Franklin 1.50 3.00
12 Bob Gain 2.00 4.00
13 Bill Glass 2.00 4.00
14 Ernie Green 1.50 3.00
15 Lou Groza 5.00 10.00
16 Gene Hickerson 2.00 4.00
17 Jim Houston 1.50 3.00
18 Tom Hutchinson 1.50 3.00
19 Jim Kanicki 1.50 3.00
20 Mike Lucci 2.00 4.00
21 Dick Modzelewski 2.00 4.00
22 John Morrow 1.50 3.00
23 Jim Ninowski 2.00 4.00
24 Frank Parker 1.50 3.00
25 Bernie Parrish 2.00 4.00
26 Frank Ryan 2.50 5.00
27 Charlie Scales 1.50 3.00
28 Dick Schafrath 2.00 4.00
29 Roger Shoals 1.50 3.00
30 Jim Shorter 1.50 3.00
31 Billy Truax 2.00 4.00
32 Paul Warfield 7.50 15.00
33 Ken Webb 1.50 3.00
34 Paul Wiggin 1.50 3.00
35 John Wooten 2.00 4.00
NNO Browns Saver Sheet 15.00 30.00

1964 Coke Caps Chargers

Coke caps were issued in each AFL city, except Buffalo, featuring 35-members of that team along with the AFL All-Stars caps as part of the 1964 Go with the Pros promotion. The AFL team Cap Saver sheets had separate sections in which to affix both the local team's caps, all of the AFL team logos, and the AFL All-Star caps. The caps measure approximately 1 1/8" in diameter and have the drink logo and a football on the outside, while the inside has the player's face printed in black with the team name above the photo, the player's name below, his jersey number to the left and his position to the right. Most caps were issued with either a plastic or cork liner on the inside. The consumer could turn in his completed saver sheet (before the expiration date of Nov. 21, 1964) to receive various prizes. The 1964 caps look very similar to those issued in 1965 and 1966 but were numbered only according to the player's jersey number. We've arranged them alphabetically by team for ease in cataloging. Football caps were produced for Coca-Cola, Sprite and King Size Coke bottles. Sprite caps typically carry a slight premium over the value of the Coke version.

COMPLETE SET (35) 100.00 175.00
1 Chuck Allen 2.50 5.00
2 Lance Alworth 10.00 20.00
3 George Blair 2.00 4.00
4 Frank Buncom 2.00 4.00
5 Earl Faison 2.50 5.00
6 Kenny Graham 2.00 4.00
7 George Gross 2.00 4.00
8 Sam Gruneisen 2.00 4.00
9 John Hadl 5.00 10.00
10 Dick Harris 2.50 5.00
11 Bob Jackson FB 2.00 4.00
12 Emil Karas 2.00 4.00
13 Dave Kocourek 2.00 4.00
14 Ernie Ladd 5.00 10.00
15 Bob Lane 2.00 4.00
16 Keith Lincoln 3.00 6.00
17 Paul Lowe 3.00 6.00
18 Jacque MacKinnon 2.00 4.00
19 Gerry McDougall 2.00 4.00
20 Charlie McNeil 2.50 5.00
21 Bob Mitinger 2.00 4.00
22 Ron Mix 5.00 10.00
23 Don Norton 2.00 4.00
24 Ernie Park 2.00 4.00
25 Bob Petrich 2.00 4.00
26 Jerry Robinson 2.00 4.00
27 Don Rogers 2.00 4.00
28 Tobin Rote 2.50 5.00
29 Henry Schmidt 2.00 4.00
30 Pat Shea 2.00 4.00
31 Walt Sweeney 2.50 5.00
32 Jim Warren 2.00 4.00
33 Dick Westmoreland 2.50 5.00
34 Bud Whitehead 2.00 4.00
35 Ernie Wright 2.50 5.00
NNO Chargers Saver Sheet 15.00 30.00

1964 Coke Caps Eagles

Please see the 1964 Coke Caps Bears listing for information on this set.

COMPLETE SET (35) 75.00 150.00
1 Mickey Babb 2.00 3.00
2 Sam Baker 2.00 3.00
3 Maxie Baughan 2.00 3.00
4 Ed Blaine 2.00 3.00
5 Bob Brown 2.50 4.00
6 Timmy Brown 2.50 4.00
7 Don Burroughs 2.00 3.00
8 Pete Case 2.00 3.00
9 Jack Concannon 2.50 4.00
10 Claude Crabb 2.00 3.00
11 Glenn Glass 2.00 3.00
12 Ron Goodwin 2.00 3.00
13 Dave Graham 2.00 3.00
14 Earl Gros 2.00 3.00
15 Riley Gunnels 2.00 3.00
16 King Hill 2.50 4.00
17 Lynn Hoyem 2.00 3.00
18 Don Hultz 2.00 3.00
19 Terry Kosens 2.00 3.00
20 Chuck Lamson 2.00 3.00
21 Dave Lloyd 2.00 3.00
22 Red Mack 2.00 3.00
23 Ollie Matson 6.00 10.00
24 John Mellekas 2.00 3.00
25 John Meyers 2.00 3.00
26 Floyd Peters 2.50 4.00
27 Ray Poage 2.00 3.00
28 Nate Ramsey 2.00 3.00
29 Pete Retzlaff 2.50 4.00
30 Jim Ringo 5.00 8.00
31 Jim Skaggs 2.00 3.00
32 Ralph Smith 2.00 3.00
33 Norm Snead 3.00 5.00
34 George Tarasovic 2.00 3.00
35 Tom Woodeshick 2.50 4.00
NNO Eagles Saver Sheet 15.00 30.00

1964 Coke Caps 49ers

Please see the 1964 Coke Caps Bears listing for information on this set.

COMPLETE SET (35) 75.00 150.00
1 Kermit Alexander 2.00 3.00
2 Bruce Bosley 2.00 3.00
3 John Brodie 4.00 8.00
4 Vern Burke 2.00 3.00
5 Bernie Casey 2.50 4.00
6 Dan Colchico 2.00 3.00
7 Clyde Conner 2.00 3.00
8 Bill Cooper 2.00 3.00
9 Tommy Davis 2.50 4.00
10 Leon Donohue 2.00 3.00
11 Mike Dowdle 2.00 3.00
12 Matt Hazeltine 2.00 3.00
13 Jim Johnson 3.00 5.00
14 Billy Kilmer 3.60 6.00
15 Elbert Kimbrough 2.00 3.00
16 Charlie Krueger 2.00 3.00
17 Roland Lakes 2.00 3.00
18 Don Lisbon 2.00 3.00
19 Mike Magac 2.00 3.00
20 Jerry Mertens 2.00 3.00
21 Dave Messer 2.00 3.00
22 Clark Miller 2.00 3.00
23 George Mira 2.50 4.00
24 Dave Parks 2.50 4.00
25 Ed Pine 2.00 3.00
26 Walter Rock 2.00 3.00
27 Len Rohde 2.00 3.00
28 Karl Rubke 2.00 3.00
29 Bob St. Clair 3.00 5.00
30 Charlie Sieminski 2.00 3.00
31 J.D. Smith 2.50 4.00
32 Monty Stickles 2.00 3.00
33 John Thomas 2.00 3.00
34 Jim Vollenweider 2.00 3.00
35 Abe Woodson 2.50 4.00
NNO 49ers Saver Sheet 15.00 30.00

1964 Coke Caps Giants

Please see the 1964 Coke Caps Bears listing for information on this set.

COMPLETE SET (38) 75.00 150.00
1 Roger Anderson 1.50 4.00
2 Erich Barnes 1.50 4.00
3 Bookie Bolin UER 1.50 4.00
4 Ken Byers 1.50 4.00
5 Roosevelt Brown 2.50 6.00
6 Don Chandler 2.00 5.00
7 Bob Crespino 1.50 4.00
8 Darrell Dess 1.50 4.00
9 Ed Dove 1.50 4.00
10 Frank Gifford 5.00 4.00
11 Glynn Griffing 1.50 4.00
12 Jerry Hillebrand 1.50 4.00
13 Lane Howell 1.50 4.00
14 Dick James 1.50 4.00
15 Jim Katcavage 2.00 5.00
16 Charlie Killett 1.50 4.00
17 Phil King 1.50 4.00
18 Lou Kirouac 1.50 4.00
19 Greg Larson 1.50 4.00
20 Joe Don Looney 2.00 5.00
21 John LoVetere 1.50 4.00
22 Dick Lynch 1.50 4.00
23 Jim Moran 1.50 4.00
24 Joe Morrison 2.00 5.00
25 Jimmy Patton 1.50 4.00
26 Dick Pesonen 1.50 4.00
27 Tom Scott 1.50 4.00
28 Del Shofner 2.00 5.00
29 Jack Stroud 1.50 4.00
30 Andy Stynchula 1.50 4.00
31 Aaron Thomas 1.50 4.00
32 Bob Timberlake 1.50 4.00
33 Y.A. Tittle 6.00 12.00
34 Mickey Walker 1.50 4.00
35 Joe Walton 1.50 4.00
36 Allan Webb 1.50 4.00
37 Alex Webster 2.00 5.00
38 Bill Winter 1.50 4.00

1964 Coke Caps Lions

Please see the 1964 Coke Caps Bears listing for information on this set.

COMPLETE SET (35) 75.00 150.00
1 Terry Barr 1.50 3.00
2 Carl Brettschneider 1.50 3.00
3 Roger Brown 2.00 4.00
4 Mike Bundra 1.50 3.00
5 Ernie Clark 1.50 3.00
6 Gail Cogdill 2.00 4.00
7 Larry Ferguson 1.50 3.00
8 Dennis Gaubatz 1.50 3.00
9 Jim Gibbons 2.00 4.00
10 John Gonzaga 1.50 3.00
11 John Gordy 1.50 3.00
12 Tom Hall 1.50 3.00
13 Alex Karras 5.00 10.00
14 Dick Lane 4.00 8.00
15 Dan LaRose 1.50 3.00
16 Yale Lary 4.00 8.00
17 Dick LeBeau 2.00 4.00
18 Dan Lewis 1.50 3.00
19 Gary Lowe 1.50 3.00
20 Bruce Maher 1.50 3.00
21 Darris McCord 1.50 3.00
22 Max Messner 1.50 3.00
23 Earl Morrall 3.00 6.00
24 Nick Pietrosante 2.00 4.00
25 Milt Plum 2.50 5.00
26 Daryl Sanders 1.50 3.00
27 Joe Schmidt 5.00 10.00
28 Bob Scholtz 1.50 3.00
29 J.D. Smith T 2.00 4.00
30 Pat Studstill 2.00 4.00
31 Larry Vargo 1.50 3.00
32 Wayne Walker 2.00 4.00
33 Tom Watkins 1.50 3.00
34 Bob Whitlow 1.50 3.00
35 Sam Williams 1.50 3.00
NNO Lions Saver Sheet 15.00 30.00

1964 Coke Caps National NFL

This set of 68 Coke caps was issued on bottled soft drinks primarily in cities without an NFL team. The caps were issued along with their own Saver Sheet. Each measures approximately 1 1/8" in diameter and has the drink logo and a football on the outside, while the inside has the player's face printed with text surrounding the face. An "NFL ALL STARS" title appears above the player's photo, therefore some players below appear in both this set and the NFL All-Stars set listing. The consumer could turn in his completed saver sheet to receive various prizes. The caps are unnumbered and checklisted below in alphabetical order. Football caps were also produced for Sprite and King Size Coke bottles. Sprite caps typically carry a slight premium over the value of the Coke version.

COMPLETE SET (68) 125.00 250.00
1 Herb Adderley 2.50 5.00
2 Grady Alderman 1.50 3.00
3 Doug Atkins 3.00 6.00
4 Sam Baker 1.50 3.00
5 Erich Barnes 1.50 3.00
6 Terry Barr 1.50 3.00
7 Dick Bass 1.50 3.00
8 Maxie Baughan 1.50 3.00
9 Raymond Berry 3.00 6.00
10 Charley Bradshaw 1.50 3.00
11 Jim Brown 12.50 25.00
12 Roger Brown 1.50 3.00
13 Timmy Brown 1.50 3.00
14 Gail Cogdill 1.50 3.00
15 Tommy Davis 1.50 3.00
16 Willie Davis 1.50 3.00
17 Bob DeMarco 1.50 3.00
18 Darrell Dess 1.50 3.00
19 Buddy Dial 2.00 4.00
20 Mike Ditka 7.50 15.00
21 Galen Fiss 1.50 3.00
22 Lee Folkins 1.50 3.00
23 Joe Fortunato 1.50 3.00
24 Bill Glass 1.50 3.00
25 John Gordy 1.50 3.00
26 Ken Gray 1.50 3.00
27 Forrest Gregg 3.00 6.00
28 Rip Hawkins 1.50 3.00
29 Charley Johnson 2.00 4.00
30 John Henry Johnson 2.50 5.00
31 Hank Jordan 2.50 5.00
32 Jim Katcavage 1.50 3.00
33 Jerry Kramer 2.50 5.00
34 Joe Krupa 1.50 3.00
35 John Lovetere 1.50 3.00
36 Dick Lynch 1.50 3.00
37 John Mackey 3.00 6.00
38 Gino Marchetti 2.50 5.00
39 Joe Marconi 1.50 3.00
40 Tommy Mason 1.50 3.00
41 Dale Meinert 1.50 3.00
42 Lou Michaels 2.00 4.00
43 Bobby Mitchell 3.00 6.00
44 John Morrow 1.50 3.00
45 Merlin Olsen 4.00 8.00
46 Jack Pardee 2.00 4.00
47 Jim Parker 1.50 3.00
48 Bernie Parrish 1.50 3.00
49 Don Perkins 2.00 4.00
50 Richie Petitbon 1.50 3.00
51 Myron Pottios 1.50 3.00
52 Vince Promuto 1.50 3.00
53 Mike Pyle 1.50 3.00
54 Pete Retzlaff 2.00 4.00
55 Jim Ringo 2.50 5.00
56 Joe Rutgens 1.50 3.00
57 Dick Schafrath 1.50 3.00
58 Del Shofner 1.50 3.00
59 Jim Taylor 3.75 7.50
60 Roosevelt Taylor 1.50 3.00
61 Clendon Thomas 1.50 3.00
62 Y.A. Tittle 5.00 10.00
63 John Unitas 7.50 15.00
64 Bill Wade 1.50 3.00
65 Wayne Walker 1.50 3.00
66 Jesse Whittenton 2.00 4.00
67 Larry Wilson 2.50 5.00
68 Abe Woodson 2.00 4.00
NNO NFL All-Star Saver Sheet 15.00 30.00

1964 Coke Caps Oilers

Please see the 1964 Coke Caps Chargers listing for information on this set.

COMPLETE SET (35) 90.00 150.00
1 Scott Appleton 2.00 4.00
2 Johnny Baker 2.00 4.00
3 Tony Banfield 2.00 4.00
4 George Blanda 10.00 20.00
5 Danny Brabham 2.00 4.00
6 Ode Burrell 2.00 4.00
7 Billy Cannon 3.00 6.00
8 Doug Cline 2.00 4.00
9 Bobby Crenshaw 2.00 4.00
10 Gary Cutsinger 2.00 4.00
11 Willard Dewveall 2.00 4.00
12 Mike Dukes 2.00 4.00
13 Staley Faulkner 2.00 4.00
14 Don Floyd 2.00 4.00
15 Freddy Glick 2.00 4.00
16 Tom Goode 2.00 4.00
17 Charlie Hennigan 2.50 5.00
18 Ed Husmann 2.00 4.00
19 Bobby Jancik 2.00 4.00
20 Mark Johnston 2.00 4.00
21 Jacky Lee 2.50 5.00
22 Bob McLeod 2.00 4.00
23 Dudley Meredith 2.00 4.00
24 Rich Michael 2.00 4.00
25 Benny Nelson 2.00 4.00
26 Jim Norton 2.50 5.00
27 Larry Onesti 2.00 4.00
28 Bob Schmidt 2.00 4.00
29 Dave Smith 2.00 4.00
30 Walt Suggs 2.00 4.00
31 Bob Talamini 2.00 4.00
32 Charley Tolar 2.00 4.00
33 Don Trull 2.50 5.00
34 John Varnell 2.00 4.00
35 Hogan Wharton 2.00 4.00

1964 Coke Caps Packers

Please see the 1964 Coke Caps Bears listing for information on this set.

COMPLETE SET (35) 125.00 225.00
1 Herb Adderley 4.00 8.00
2 Lionel Aldridge 3.00 5.00
3 Zeke Bratkowski 3.00 5.00
4 Lee Roy Caffey 2.50 4.00
5 Dennis Claridge 2.50 4.00
6 Dan Currie 2.50 4.00
7 Willie Davis 4.00 8.00
8 Boyd Dowler 3.00 5.00
9 Marv Fleming 3.00 5.00
10 Forrest Gregg 4.00 8.00
11 Hank Gremminger 2.50 4.00
12 Dan Grimm 2.50 4.00
13 Dave Hanner 3.00 5.00
14 Urban Henry 2.50 4.00
15 Paul Hornung 10.00 20.00
16 Bob Jeter 3.00 5.00
17 Hank Jordan 4.00 8.00
18 Ron Kostelnik 2.50 4.00
19 Jerry Kramer 3.00 6.00
20 Ron Kramer 2.50 4.00
21 Norm Masters 2.50 4.00
22 Max McGee 3.00 5.00
23 Frank Mestnik 2.50 4.00
24 Tom Moore 3.00 5.00
25 Ray Nitschke 6.00 12.00
26 Jerry Norton 2.50 4.00
27 Elijah Pitts 3.00 5.00
28 Dave Robinson 3.50 6.00
29 Bob Skoronski 2.50 4.00
30 Bart Starr 12.50 25.00
31 Jim Taylor 6.00 12.00
32 Fuzzy Thurston 4.00 8.00
33 Lloyd Voss 2.50 4.00
34 Jesse Whittenton 2.50 4.00
35 Willie Wood 4.00 8.00
NNO Packers Saver Sheet 20.00 40.00

1964 Coke Caps Patriots

Please see the 1964 Coke Caps Chargers listing for information on this set.

COMPLETE SET (35) 75.00 150.00
1 Tom Addison 2.50 4.00
2 Houston Antwine 2.50 4.00
3 Nick Buoniconti 6.00 10.00
4 Ron Burton 3.00 5.00
5 Gino Cappelletti 3.50 6.00
6 Jim Colclough 2.50 4.00
7 Harry Crump 2.50 4.00
8 Bob Dee 2.50 4.00
9 Bob Dentel 2.50 4.00
10 Larry Eisenhauer 2.50 4.00
11 Dick Felt 2.50 4.00
12 Larry Garron 2.50 4.00
13 Art Graham 3.00 5.00
14 Ron Hall 2.50 4.00
15 Jim Hunt 2.50 4.00
16 Charles Long 2.50 4.00
17 Don McKinnon 2.50 4.00
18 Jon Morris 2.50 4.00
19 Billy Neighbors 2.50 4.00
20 Tom Neumann 2.50 4.00
21 Don Oakes 2.50 4.00
22 Ross O'Hanley 2.50 4.00
23 Babe Parilli 3.00 5.00
24 Jesse Richardson 2.50 4.00
25 Tony Romeo 2.50 4.00
26 Jack Rudolph 2.50 4.00
27 Chuck Shonta 2.50 4.00
28 Al Snyder 2.50 4.00
29 Nick Spinelli 2.50 4.00
30 Bob Suci 2.50 4.00
31 Dave Watson 2.50 4.00
32 Don Webb 2.50 4.00
33 Bob Yates 2.50 4.00
34 Tom Yewcic 2.50 4.00
35 Mack Yoho 2.50 4.00

1964 Coke Caps Raiders

Please see the 1964 Coke Caps Chargers listing for information on this set.

1 Jan Barrett 3.00 6.00
2 Dan Birdwell 3.00 6.00
3 Sonny Bishop 3.00 6.00
4 Bill Budness 3.00 6.00
5 Dave Costa 3.00 6.00
6 Dobie Craig 3.00 6.00
7 Clem Daniels 4.00 8.00
8 Claude Gibson 3.00 6.00
9 Wayne Hawkins 4.00 8.00
10 Ken Herock 3.00 6.00
11 Dick Klein 3.00 6.00
12 Jim McMillin 3.00 6.00
13 Chuck McMurtry 3.00 6.00
14 Mike Mercer 3.00 6.00
15 Al Miller 3.00 6.00
16 Rex Mirich 3.00 6.00
17 Bob Mischak 3.00 6.00
18 Jim Norris 3.00 6.00
19 Jim Otto 7.50 15.00
20 Art Powell 4.00 8.00
21 Warren Powers 3.00 6.00
22 Ken Rice 3.00 6.00
23 Bo Roberson 3.00 6.00
24 Jack Simpson 3.00 6.00
25 Fred Williamson 5.00 10.00
26 Frank Youso 3.00 6.00

1964 Coke Caps Rams

Please see the 1964 Coke Caps Bears listing for information on this set.

COMPLETE SET (35) 75.00 150.00
1 Jon Arnett 2.50 4.00
2 Pervis Atkins 1.50 3.00
3 Terry Baker RB 3.00 5.00
4 Dick Bass 2.50 4.00
5 Charley Britt 1.50 3.00
6 Willie Brown WR 2.50 4.00
7 Joe Carollo 1.50 3.00
8 Don Chuy 1.50 3.00
9 Charlie Cowan 1.50 3.00
10 Lindon Crow 1.50 3.00
11 Carroll Dale 2.50 4.00
12 Roman Gabriel 4.00 8.00
13 Roosevelt Grier 3.00 6.00
14 Mike Henry 1.50 3.00
15 Art Hunter 1.50 3.00
16 Ken Iman 1.50 3.00
17 Deacon Jones 5.00 10.00
18 Cliff Livingston 1.50 3.00
19 Lamar Lundy 2.50 4.00
20 Marlin McKeever 1.50 3.00
21 Ed Meador 1.50 3.00
22 Bill Munson 2.50 4.00
23 Merlin Olsen 6.00 12.00
24 Jack Pardee 2.50 4.00
25 Art Perkins 1.50 3.00
26 Jim Phillips 2.50 4.00
27 Roger Pillath 1.50 3.00
28 Mel Profit 1.50 3.00
29 Joe Scibelli 1.50 3.00
30 Carver Shannon 1.50 3.00
31 Bobby Smith 1.50 3.00
32 Bill Swain 1.50 3.00
33 Frank Varrichione 1.50 3.00
34 Danny Villanueva 1.50 3.00
35 Nat Whitmyer 1.50 3.00
NNO Rams Saver Sheet 15.00 30.00

1964 Coke Caps Redskins

Please see the 1964 Coke Caps Bears listing for information on this set.

COMPLETE SET (35) 90.00 150.00
1 Bill Barnes 2.50 4.00
2 Don Bosseler 2.50 4.00
3 Rod Breedlove 2.50 4.00
4 Frank Budd 2.50 4.00
5 Henry Butsko 2.50 4.00
6 Jimmy Carr 2.50 4.00
7 Bill Clay 2.50 4.00
8 Angelo Coia 2.50 4.00
9 Fred Dugan 2.50 4.00
10 Fred Hageman 2.50 4.00
11 Sam Huff 5.00 10.00
12 George Izo 3.00 5.00
13 Sonny Jurgensen 5.00 10.00
14 Carl Kammerer 2.50 4.00
15 Gordon Kelley 2.50 4.00
16 Bob Khayat 2.50 4.00
17 Paul Krause 3.50 6.00
18 J.W. Lockett 2.50 4.00
19 Riley Mattson 2.50 4.00
20 Bobby Mitchell 4.00 8.00
21 John Nisby 2.50 4.00
22 Fran O'Brien 2.50 4.00
23 John Paluck 2.50 4.00
24 Jack Pardee 3.50 6.00
25 Bob Pellegrini 2.50 4.00
26 Vince Promuto 2.50 4.00
27 Pat Richter 3.00 5.00
28 Johnny Sample 3.00 5.00
29 Lonnie Sanders 2.50 4.00
30 Dick Shiner 2.50 4.00
31 Ron Snidow 2.50 4.00
32 Jim Steffen 2.50 4.00
33 Charley Taylor 5.00 10.00
34 Tom Tracy 3.00 5.00
35 Fred Williams 2.50 4.00
NNO Redskins Saver Sheet 15.00 30.00

1964 Coke Caps Steelers

Please see the 1964 Coke Caps Bears listing for information on this set.

COMPLETE SET (35) 75.00 150.00
1 Art Anderson 2.50 4.00
2 Frank Atkinson 2.50 4.00
3 Gary Ballman 2.50 4.00
4 John Baker 2.50 4.00
5 Charley Bradshaw 2.50 4.00
6 Jim Bradshaw 2.50 4.00
7 Ed Brown 3.00 5.00
8 John Burrell 2.50 4.00
9 Preston Carpenter 3.00 5.00
10 Lou Cordileone 2.50 4.00
11 Willie Daniel 2.50 4.00
12 Dick Haley 2.50 4.00
13 Bob Harrison 2.50 4.00
14 Dick Hoak 3.00 5.00
15 Dan James 2.50 4.00
16 Tom Jenkins 2.50 4.00
17 John Henry Johnson 5.00 10.00
18 Jim Kelly TE 2.50 4.00
19 Brady Keys 2.50 4.00
20 Joe Krupa 2.50 4.00
21 Ray Lemek 2.50 4.00
22 Paul Martha 2.50 4.00
23 Lou Michaels 3.00 5.00
24 Bill Nelsen 3.00 6.00
25 Terry Nofsinger 2.50 4.00
26 Buzz Nutter 2.50 4.00
27 Clarence Peaks 2.50 4.00
28 Myron Pottios 2.50 4.00
29 John Reger 2.50 4.00
30 Mike Sandusky 2.50 4.00
31 Theron Sapp 2.50 4.00
32 Bob Schmitz 2.50 4.00
33 Ron Stehouwer 2.50 4.00
34 Clendon Thomas 2.50 4.00
35 Joe Womack 2.50 4.00

1964 Coke Caps Team Emblems AFL

Each 1964 Coke Caps saver sheet had a section for collecting caps featuring the team emblem for all eight AFL teams. The caps are unnumbered and checklisted below in alphabetical order. These "Coke" caps were also available on Sprite bottles. Sprite caps typically carry a 1.5X-2X premium over the Coke version.

COMPLETE SET (8) 20.00 40.00
1 Boston Patriots 2.50 5.00
2 Buffalo Bills 2.50 5.00
3 Denver Broncos 3.00 6.00
4 Houston Oilers 2.50 5.00
5 Kansas City Chiefs 2.50 5.00
6 New York Jets 2.50 5.00
7 Oakland Raiders 3.00 6.00
8 San Diego Chargers 2.50 5.00

1964 Coke Caps Team Emblems NFL

Each 1964 Coke Caps saver sheet had a section for collecting caps featuring the team emblem for all fourteen NFL teams. The caps are unnumbered and checklisted below in alphabetical order. These "Coke" caps were also available on Sprite bottles. Sprite caps typically carry a 1.5X-2X premium over the Coke version.

COMPLETE SET (14) 30.00 60.00
1 Baltimore Colts 2.50 5.00
2 Chicago Bears 2.50 5.00
3 Cleveland Browns 2.50 5.00
4 Dallas Cowboys 3.00 6.00
5 Detroit Lions 2.50 5.00
6 Green Bay Packers 3.00 6.00
7 Los Angeles Rams 2.50 5.00
8 Minnesota Vikings 2.50 5.00
9 New York Giants 2.50 5.00
10 Philadelphia Eagles 2.50 5.00
11 Pittsburgh Steelers 2.50 5.00
12 San Francisco 49ers 2.50 5.00
13 St. Louis Cardinals 2.50 5.00
14 Washington Redskins 3.00 6.00

1964 Coke Caps Vikings

Please see the 1964 Coke Caps Bears listing for information on this set.

COMPLETE SET (35) 75.00 150.00
1 Grady Alderman 2.50 5.00
2 Hal Bedsole 2.00 4.00
3 Larry Bowie 2.00 4.00
4 Jim Boylan 2.00 4.00
5 Bill Brown 2.50 5.00
6 Bill Butler 2.00 4.00
7 Lee Calland 2.00 4.00
8 John Campbell 2.00 4.00
9 Fred Cox 2.50 5.00
10 Ted Dean 2.00 4.00
11 Bob Denton 2.00 4.00
12 Paul Dickson 2.00 4.00
13 Carl Eller 6.00 10.00
14 Paul Flatley 2.00 4.00
15 Tom Franckhauser 2.00 4.00
16 Rip Hawkins 2.00 4.00
17 Bill Jobko 2.00 4.00
18 Karl Kassulke 2.00 4.00

19 John Kirby 2.00 4.00
20 Bob Lacey 2.00 4.00
21 Errol Linden 2.00 4.00
22 Jim Marshall 6.00 10.00
23 Tommy Mason 2.50 5.00
24 Dave O'Brien 2.00 4.00
25 Palmer Pike 2.00 4.00
26 Jim Prestel 2.00 4.00
27 Jerry Reichow 2.00 4.00
28 George Rose 2.00 4.00
29 Ed Sharockman 2.00 4.00
30 Gordon Smith 2.00 4.00
31 Fran Tarkenton 15.00 25.00
32 Mick Tingelhoff 2.50 5.00
33 Ron Vanderkelen 2.00 4.00
34 Tom Wilson 2.00 4.00
35 Roy Winston 2.50 5.00

1965 Coke Caps All-Stars AFL

These AFL All-Star caps were issued in AFL cities (and a few other cities as well) along with the local team caps as part of the Go with the Pros promotion. The AFL team Cap Saver sheets had separate sections in which to affix both the local team's caps and the All-Stars' caps. The caps measure approximately 1 1/8" in diameter and have the drink logo and a football on the outside, while the inside has the player's face printed in black or red, with text surrounding the face. The consumer could turn in his completed saver sheet to receive various prizes. The caps are numbered with a "C" prefix. The 1965 caps are very similar to the 1966 issue and many of the players are the same in both years. However, the 1965 caps do not have the words "Caramel Colored" on the outside of the cap as do the 1966 caps. These caps were also produced for 1965 on other Coca-Cola products: TAB, Fanta and Sprite. The other drink caps typically carry a slight premium (1.5-2 times) over the value of the Coke version.

COMPLETE SET (34) 87.50 175.00
C37 Jerry Mays 1.50 3.00
C38 Cookie Gilchrist 2.00 4.00
C39 Lionel Taylor 2.00 4.00
C40 Goose Gonsoulin 2.00 4.00
C41 Gino Cappelletti 2.00 4.00
C42 Nick Buoniconti 2.50 5.00
C43 Larry Eisenhauer 1.50 3.00
C44 Babe Parilli 2.00 4.00
C45 Jack Kemp 12.50 25.00
C46 Billy Shaw 2.00 4.00
C47 Scott Appleton 1.50 3.00
C48 Matt Snell 2.00 4.00
C49 Charlie Hennigan 2.00 4.00
C50 Tom Flores 2.50 5.00
C51 Clem Daniels 2.00 4.00
C52 George Blanda 7.50 15.00
C53 Art Powell 2.00 4.00
C54 Jim Otto 5.00 10.00
C55 Larry Grantham 1.50 3.00
C56 Don Maynard 6.00 12.00
C57 Gerry Philbin 1.50 3.00
C58 E.J. Holub 1.50 3.00
C59 Chris Burford 1.50 3.00
C60 Ron Mix 3.75 7.50
C61 Ernie Ladd 3.75 7.50
C62 Fred Arbanas 1.50 3.00
C63 Tom Sestak 1.50 3.00
C64 Elbert Dubenion 2.00 4.00
C65 Mike Stratton 1.50 3.00
C66 Willie Brown 5.00 10.00
C67 Sid Blanks 1.50 3.00
C68 Len Dawson 6.00 12.00
C69 Lance Alworth 6.00 12.00
C70 Keith Lincoln 2.00 4.00

1965 Coke Caps All-Stars NFL

These NFL All-Star caps were issued in NFL cities (and a few other cities as well) along with the local team caps as part of the Go with the Pros promotion. The NFL team Cap Saver sheets had separate sections in which to affix both the local team's caps and the All-Stars' caps. The caps measure approximately 1 1/8" in diameter and have the drink logo and a football on the outside, while the inside has the player's face printed in black or red with text surrounding the face. The 1965 caps are very similar to the 1966 issue and many of the players are the same in both years. However, the 1965 caps do not have the words "Caramel Colored" on the outside of the cap as do the 1966 caps. The consumer could turn in his completed saver sheet to receive various prizes. The caps are numbered with a "C" prefix. These caps were also produced for 1965 on other Coca-Cola products: TAB, Fanta and Sprite. The other drink caps typically carry a slight premium (1.5-2 times) over the value of the Coke version.

COMPLETE SET (34) 50.00 100.00
C37 Sonny Jurgensen 2.50 6.00
C38 Fran Tarkenton 3.00 8.00
C39 Frank Ryan 1.25 3.00
C40 Johnny Unitas 5.00 12.00
C41 Tommy Mason 1.25 3.00
C42 Mel Renfro 1.50 4.00
C43 Ed Meador 1.00 2.50
C44 Paul Krause 1.50 4.00
C45 Irv Cross 1.25 3.00
C46 Bill Brown 1.25 3.00
C47 Joe Fortunato 1.00 2.50
C48 Jim Taylor 2.50 6.00
C49 John Henry Johnson 1.50 4.00
C50 Pat Fischer 1.00 2.50
C51 Bob Boyd DB 1.00 2.50
C52 Terry Barr 1.00 2.50
C53 Charley Taylor 1.50 4.00
C54 Paul Warfield 2.50 6.00
C55 Pete Retzlaff 1.25 3.00
C56 Maxie Baughan 1.00 2.50
C57 Matt Hazeltine 1.00 2.50
C58 Ken Gray 1.00 2.50
C59 Ray Nitschke 2.50 6.00
C60 Myron Pottios 1.00 2.50
C61 Charlie Krueger 1.00 2.50
C62 Deacon Jones 2.00 5.00
C63 Bob Lilly 2.50 6.00
C64 Merlin Olsen 2.00 5.00
C65 Jim Parker 1.50 4.00
C66 Roosevelt Brown 1.50 4.00
C67 Jim Gibbons 1.00 2.50
C68 Mike Ditka 3.00 8.00
C69 Willie Davis 1.50 4.00
C70 Aaron Thomas 1.00 2.50

1965 Coke Caps Bears

Coke caps were again issued for each NFL team in 1965 primarily in that team's local area along with the NFL All-Stars caps as part of the Go with the Pros promotion. The NFL team Cap Saver sheets had separate sections in which to affix both the local team's caps and the All-Stars' caps. The caps measure approximately 1 1/8" in diameter and have the drink logo and a football on the outside, while the inside has the player's face printed in red or black, with the team name above the photo, the player's name below, his position to the right and the cap number to the left. Some teams are also known to exist in a version that features a slightly smaller player photo. Cap numbers included a "C" prefix on all NFL teams except the Giants which had two sets using either a "C" or "G" prefix. The consumer could turn in his completed saver sheet to receive various prizes. The 1965 caps are very similar to the 1966 issue and many of the players are the same in both years. However, the 1965 caps do not have the words "Caramel Colored" on the outside of the cap as do the 1966 caps. Football caps were also produced for 1965 on other Coca-Cola products: Coke lift top, TAB (Low-Calorie Beverage), TAB lift top, Fanta Grape, Fanta Grapefruit, Fanta Orange, King Size Coke and Sprite. The other drink caps typically carry a slight premium over the value of the basic Coke version.

C1 Bennie McRae 1.50 3.00
C2 Johnny Morris 1.50 3.00
C3 Roosevelt Taylor 2.50 4.00
C4 Larry Morris 1.50 3.00
C5 Ed O'Bradovich 1.50 3.00
C6 Richie Petitbon 2.50 4.00
C7 Mike Pyle 1.50 3.00
C8 Dave Whitsell 1.50 3.00
C9 Billy Martin 1.50 3.00
C10 John Johnson 1.50 3.00
C11 Stan Jones 3.50 6.00
C12 Ted Karras 1.50 3.00
C13 Bob Kilcullen 1.50 3.00
C14 Roger LeClerc 1.50 3.00
C15 Herman Lee 1.50 3.00
C16 Earl Leggett 1.50 3.00
C17 Joe Marconi 1.50 3.00
C18 Rudy Bukich 2.50 4.00
C19 Mike Reilly 1.50 3.00
C20 Mike Ditka 6.00 12.00
C21 Dick Evey 1.50 3.00
C22 Joe Fortunato 1.50 3.00
C23 Bill Wade 2.50 4.00
C24 Bill George 3.50 6.00
C25 Larry Glueck 1.50 3.00
C26 Bobby Joe Green 1.50 3.00
C27 Bob Wetoska 1.50 3.00
C28 Doug Atkins 4.00 8.00
C29 Jon Arnett 2.50 4.00
C30 Dick Butkus 18.00 30.00
C31 Charlie Bivins 1.50 3.00
C32 Ronnie Bull 2.50 4.00
C33 Jim Cadile 1.50 3.00
C34 J.C. Caroline 1.50 3.00
C35 Gale Sayers 18.00 30.00
C36 Team Logo 1.50 3.00
NNO Saver Sheet 15.00 30.00

1965 Coke Caps Bills B

Coke caps were again issued for each AFL team in 1965 primarily in that team's local area along with the AFL All-Stars caps as part of the Go with the Pros promotion. The AFL team Cap Saver sheets had separate sections in which to affix both the local team's caps and the All-Stars' caps. The caps measure approximately 1 1/8" in diameter and have the drink logo and a football on the outside, while the inside has the player's face printed in red or black, with the team name above the photo, the player's name below, his position to the right and the cap number to the left. Some teams are also known to exist in a version that features a slightly smaller player photo. Cap numbers included a "C" prefix on all AFL teams except the Jets (J prefix) and Bills (B prefix). The consumer could turn in his completed saver sheet to receive various prizes. The 1965 caps are very similar to the 1966 issue and many of the players are the same in both years. However, the 1965 caps do not have the words "Caramel Colored" on the outside of the cap as do the 1966 caps. Football caps were also produced for 1965 on other Coca-Cola products: TAB, Fanta, King Size Coke and Sprite. The other drink caps typically carry a slight premium over the value of the basic Coke version.

COMPLETE SET (35) 75.00 150.00
*C CAPS: .4X TO 1X B CAPS
B1 Ray Abruzzese 1.50 3.00
B2 Joe Auer 1.50 3.00
B3 Stew Barber 2.00 4.00
B4 Glenn Bass 1.50 3.00
B5 Dave Behrman 1.50 3.00
B6 Al Bemiller 1.50 3.00
B7 George Butch Byrd 2.00 4.00
B8 Wray Carlton 2.00 4.00
B9 Hagood Clarke 1.50 3.00
B10 Jack Kemp 15.00 30.00
B11 Oliver Dobbins 1.50 3.00
B12 Elbert Dubenion 2.00 4.00
B13 Jim Dunaway 2.00 4.00
B14 Booker Edgerson 1.50 3.00
B15 George Flint 1.50 3.00
B16 Pete Gogolak 2.00 4.00
B17 Dick Hudson 2.00 4.00
B18 Harry Jacobs 2.00 4.00
B19 Tom Keating 1.50 3.00
B20 Tom Day 1.50 3.00
B21 Daryle Lamonica 6.00 12.00
B22 Paul Maguire 3.00 6.00
B23 Roland McDole 2.00 4.00
B24 Dudley Meredith 1.50 3.00
B25 Joe O'Donnell 1.50 3.00
B26 Willie Ross 1.50 3.00
B27 Ed Rutkowski 1.50 3.00
B28 George Saimes 2.00 4.00
B29 Tom Sestak 2.00 4.00
B30 Billy Shaw 2.00 4.00
B31 Bob Lee Smith 1.50 3.00
B32 Mike Stratton 2.00 4.00
B33 Gene Sykes 1.50 3.00
B34 John Tracey 1.50 3.00
B35 Ernie Warlick 1.50 3.00
NNO Bills Saver Sheet 15.00 30.00

1965 Coke Caps Bills C

Please see the 1965 Coke Caps Bills B listing for information on this set.

1965 Coke Caps Broncos

Please see the 1965 Coke Caps Bills listing for information on this set.

COMPLETE SET (36) 125.00 225.00
C1 Odell Barry 3.00 6.00
C2 Willie Brown 6.00 12.00
C3 Bob Scarpitto 3.00 6.00
C4 Ed Cooke 3.00 6.00
C5 Al Denson 3.00 6.00
C6 Tom Erlandson 3.00 6.00
C7 Hewritt Dixon 3.00 6.00
C8 Mickey Slaughter 3.00 6.00
C9 Lionel Taylor 4.00 8.00
C10 Jerry Sturm 3.00 6.00
C11 Jerry Hopkins 3.00 6.00
C12 Charlie Mitchell 3.00 6.00
C13 Ray Jacobs 3.00 6.00
C14 Larry Jordan 3.00 6.00
C15 Charlie Janerette 3.00 6.00
C16 Ray Kubala 3.00 6.00
C17 Leroy Moore 3.00 6.00
C18 Bob Breitenstein 3.00 6.00
C19 Eldon Danenhauer 3.00 6.00
C20 Miller Farr 3.00 6.00
C21 Max Leetzow 3.00 6.00
C22 Gene Jeter 3.00 6.00
C23 Tom Janik 3.00 6.00
C24 Gerry Bussell 3.00 6.00
C25 Bob McCullough 3.00 6.00
C26 Jim McMillin 3.00 6.00
C27 Abner Haynes 4.00 8.00
C28 John McGeever 3.00 6.00
C29 Cookie Gilchrist 4.00 8.00
C30 John McCormick 3.00 6.00
C31 Don Shackelford 3.00 6.00
C32 Goose Gonsoulin 3.00 6.00
C33 Jim Perkins 3.00 6.00
C34 Marv Matuszak 3.00 6.00
C35 Jacky Lee 3.00 6.00
C36 Team Logo 3.00 6.00

1965 Coke Caps Browns

Please see the 1965 Coke Caps Bears listing for information on this set.

COMPLETE SET (36) 75.00 125.00
C1 Jim Ninowski 2.50 4.00
C2 Leroy Kelly 5.00 10.00
C3 Lou Groza 4.00 8.00
C4 Gary Collins 2.50 4.00
C5 Bill Glass 2.50 4.00
C6 Bobby Franklin 1.50 3.00
C7 Galen Fiss 1.50 3.00
C8 Ross Fichtner 1.50 3.00
C9 John Wooten 2.50 4.00
C10 Clifton McNeil 1.50 3.00
C11 Paul Wiggin 2.50 4.00
C12 Gene Hickerson 2.50 4.00
C13 Ernie Green 1.50 3.00
C14 Dale Memmelaar 1.50 3.00
C15 Dick Schafrath 1.50 3.00
C16 Sidney Williams 1.50 3.00
C17 Frank Ryan 2.50 4.00
C18 Bernie Parrish 1.50 3.00
C19 Vince Costello 1.50 3.00
C20 John Brown 1.50 3.00
C21 Monte Clark 1.50 3.00
C22 Walter Roberts 1.50 3.00
C23 Johnny Brewer 1.50 3.00
C24 Walter Beach 1.50 3.00
C25 Dick Modzelewski 1.50 3.00
C26 Larry Benz 1.50 3.00
C27 Jim Houston 1.50 3.00
C28 Mike Lucci 1.50 3.00
C29 Mel Anthony 1.50 3.00
C30 Tom Hutchinson 1.50 3.00
C31 John Morrow 1.50 3.00
C32 Jim Kanicki 1.50 3.00
C33 Paul Warfield 5.00 10.00
C34 Jim Garcia 1.50 3.00
C35 Walter Johnson 1.50 3.00
C36 Team Logo 1.50 3.00

1965 Coke Caps Cardinals

Please see the 1965 Coke Caps Bears listing for information on this set.

C1 Pat Fischer 4.00 8.00
C2 Sonny Randle 3.00 6.00
C3 Joe Childress 3.00 6.00
C4 Dave Meggysey 4.00 8.00
C5 Joe Robb 3.00 6.00
C6 Jerry Stovall 3.00 6.00
C7 Ernie McMillan 3.00 6.00
C8 Dale Meinert 3.00 6.00
C9 Irv Goode 3.00 6.00
C10 Bob DeMarco 3.00 6.00
C11 Mal Hammack 3.00 6.00
C12 Jim Bakken 3.00 6.00
C13 Bill Thornton 3.00 6.00
C14 Buddy Humphrey 3.00 6.00
C15 Bill Koman 3.00 6.00
C16 Larry Wilson 5.00 10.00
C17 Ed Cook 3.00 6.00
C18 Prentice Gautt 3.00 6.00
C19 Charlie Johnson 4.00 8.00
C20 Ken Gray 3.00 6.00
C21 Taz Anderson 3.00 6.00
C22 Sam Silas 3.00 6.00
C23 Larry Stallings 3.00 6.00
C24 Don Brumm 3.00 6.00
C25 Bobby Joe Conrad 3.00 6.00
C26 Bill Triplett 3.00 6.00
C27 Luke Owens 3.00 6.00
C28 Jackie Smith 5.00 10.00
C29 Bob Reynolds 3.00 6.00
C30 Abe Woodson 3.00 6.00
C31 Jim Burson 3.00 6.00
C32 Willis Crenshaw 3.00 6.00
C33 Billy Gambrell 3.00 6.00
C34 Tom Redmond 3.00 6.00
C35 Herschel Turner 3.00 6.00
C36 Team Logo 3.00 6.00

1965 Coke Caps Chiefs

Please see the 1965 Coke Caps Bills listing for information on this set.

COMPLETE SET (36)
C1 E.J. Holub 4.00 8.00
C2 Al Reynolds 3.00 6.00
C3 Buck Buchanan 5.00 10.00
C4 Curt Merz 3.00 6.00
C5 Dave Hill 3.00 6.00
C6 Bobby Hunt 3.00 6.00
C7 Jerry Mays 3.00 6.00
C8 Jon Gilliam 3.00 6.00
C9 Walt Corey 3.00 6.00
C10 Curt Farrier 3.00 6.00
C11 Jerry Cornelison 3.00 6.00
C12 Bert Coan 3.00 6.00
C13 Ed Budde 3.00 6.00
C14 Tommy Brooker 3.00 6.00
C15 Bobby Bell 5.00 10.00
C16 Smokey Stover 3.00 6.00
C17 Curtis McClinton 4.00 8.00
C18 Jerrel Wilson 3.00 6.00
C19 Jim Fraser 3.00 6.00
C20 Mack Lee Hill 3.00 6.00
C21 Jim Tyrer 3.00 6.00
C22 Johnny Robinson 4.00 8.00
C23 Bobby Ply 3.00 6.00
C24 Frank Jackson 3.00 6.00
C25 Ed Lothamer 3.00 6.00
C26 Sherrill Headrick 3.00 6.00
C27 Fred Williamson 4.00 8.00
C28 Chris Burford 3.00 6.00
C29 Willie Mitchell 3.00 6.00
C30 Mel Branch 3.00 6.00
C31 Fred Arbanas 3.00 6.00
C32 Hatch Rosdahl 3.00 6.00
C33 Reggie Carolan 3.00 6.00
C34 Len Dawson 6.00 12.00
C35 Pete Beathard 3.00 6.00
C36 Team Logo 2.50 5.00

1965 Coke Caps Colts

Please see the 1965 Coke Caps Bears listing for information on this set.

COMPLETE SET (36) 75.00 150.00
C1 Ted Davis 1.50 3.00
C2 Bob Boyd DB 1.50 3.00
C3 Lenny Moore 6.00 12.00
C4 Lou Kirouac 1.50 3.00
C5 Jimmy Orr 2.00 4.00
C6 Wendell Harris 1.50 3.00
C7 Mike Curtis 4.00 8.00
C8 Jerry Logan 1.50 3.00
C9 Steve Stonebreaker 1.50 3.00
C10 John Mackey 5.00 10.00
C11 Dennis Gaubatz 1.50 3.00
C12 Don Shinnick 1.50 3.00
C13 Dick Szymanski 1.50 3.00
C14 Ordell Braase 1.50 3.00
C15 Lenny Lyles 1.50 3.00
C16 John Campbell 1.50 3.00
C17 Dan Sullivan 1.50 3.00
C18 Lou Michaels 2.00 4.00
C19 Gary Cuozzo 2.00 4.00
C20 Butch Wilson 1.50 3.00
C21 Alex Sandusky 1.50 3.00
C22 Jim Welch 1.50 3.00
C23 Tony Lorick 1.50 3.00
C24 Billy Ray Smith 2.00 4.00
C25 Fred Miller 1.50 3.00
C26 Tom Matte 3.00 6.00
C27 Johnny Unitas 10.00 20.00
C28 Glenn Ressler 1.50 3.00
C29 Alex Hawkins 2.00 4.00
C30 Jim Parker 4.00 8.00
C31 Guy Reese 1.50 3.00
C32 Bob Vogel 1.50 3.00
C33 Jerry Hill 1.50 3.00
C34 Raymond Berry 6.00 12.00
C35 George Preas 1.50 3.00
C36 Team Logo 1.50 3.00
NNO Colts Saver Sheet 15.00 30.00

1965 Coke Caps Cowboys

Please see the 1965 Coke Caps Bears listing for information on this set.

COMPLETE SET (36) 100.00 175.00
C1 Mike Connelly 2.50 5.00
C2 Tony Liscio 2.50 5.00
C3 Maury Youmans 2.50 5.00
C4 Larry Stephens 2.50 5.00
C5 Jim Colvin 2.50 5.00
C6 Malcolm Walker 2.50 5.00
C7 Danny Villanueva 2.50 5.00
C8 Frank Clarke 3.00 6.00
C9 Don Meredith 10.00 20.00
C10 George Andrie 2.50 5.00
C11 Mel Renfro 5.00 10.00
C12 Pettis Norman 2.50 5.00
C13 Buddy Dial 3.00 6.00
C14 Lee Folkins 2.50 5.00
C15 Jerry Rhome 2.50 5.00
C16 Bob Hayes 7.50 15.00
C17 Mike Gaechter 2.50 5.00
C18 Joe Bob Isbell 2.50 5.00
C19 Harold Hays 2.50 5.00
C20 Craig Morton 4.00 8.00
C21 Jake Kupp 2.50 5.00
C22 Cornell Green 2.50 5.00
C23 Perry Lee Dunn 2.50 5.00
C24 Don Talbert 2.50 5.00
C25 Dave Manders 2.50 5.00
C26 Warren Livingston 2.50 5.00
C27 Bob Lilly 7.50 15.00
C28 Chuck Howley 4.00 8.00
C29 Don Bishop 2.50 5.00
C30 Don Perkins 3.00 6.00
C31 Jim Boeke 2.50 5.00
C32 Dave Edwards 2.50 5.00
C33 Lee Roy Jordan 3.00 6.00
C34 Jerry Tubbs 2.50 5.00
C35 Amos Marsh 2.50 5.00
C36 Team Logo 2.00 4.00

1965 Coke Caps Eagles

Please see the 1965 Coke Caps Bears listing for information on this set.

COMPLETE SET (36) 80.00 120.00
C1 Norm Snead 2.50 5.00
C2 Al Nelson 1.50 3.00
C3 Jim Skaggs 1.50 3.00
C4 Glenn Glass 1.50 3.00
C5 Pete Retzlaff 2.00 4.00
C6 Bill Mack 1.50 3.00
C7 Ray Rissmiller 1.50 3.00
C8 Lynn Hoyem 1.50 3.00
C9 King Hill 2.00 4.00
C10 Timmy Brown 2.50 5.00
C11 Ollie Matson 5.00 10.00
C12 Dave Lloyd 2.00 4.00
C13 Jim Ringo 3.50 7.00
C14 Floyd Peters 2.00 4.00
C15 Riley Gunnels 1.50 3.00
C16 Claude Crabb 1.50 3.00
C17 Earl Gros 2.00 4.00
C18 Fred Hill 1.50 3.00
C19 Don Hultz 1.50 3.00
C20 Ray Poage 1.50 3.00
C21 Irv Cross 2.50 5.00
C22 Mike Morgan 1.50 3.00
C23 Maxie Baughan 2.00 4.00
C24 Ed Blaine 1.50 3.00
C25 Jack Concannon 2.00 4.00
C26 Sam Baker 1.50 3.00
C27 Tom Woodeshick 2.00 4.00
C28 Joe Scarpati 1.50 3.00
C29 John Meyers 1.50 3.00
C30 Nate Ramsey 1.50 3.00
C31 George Tarasovic 1.50 3.00
C32 Bob Brown T 2.50 5.00
C33 Ralph Smith 1.50 3.00
C34 Ron Goodwin 1.50 3.00
C35 Dave Graham 1.50 3.00
C36 Team Logo 1.50 3.00
NNO Eagles Saver Sheet 15.00 30.00

1965 Coke Caps Giants C

Please see the 1965 Coke Caps Bears listing for information on this set.

COMPLETE SET (36) 75.00 125.00
C1 Ernie Koy 2.50 4.00
C2 Chuck Mercein 2.50 4.00
C3 Bob Timberlake 1.75 3.00
C4 Jim Katcavage 2.50 4.00
C5 Mickey Walker 1.75 3.00
C6 Roger Anderson 1.75 3.00
C7 Jerry Hillebrand 1.75 3.00
C8 Tucker Frederickson 2.50 4.00
C9 Jim Moran 1.75 3.00
C10 Bill Winter 1.75 3.00
C11 Aaron Thomas 2.50 4.00
C12 Clarence Childs 1.75 3.00
C13 Jim Patton 2.00 4.00
C14 Joe Morrison 2.50 4.00
C15 Homer Jones 2.50 4.00
C16 Dick Lynch 2.50 4.00
C17 John Lovetere 1.75 3.00
C18 Greg Larson 2.50 4.00
C19 Lou Slaby 1.75 3.00
C20 Tom Costello 1.75 3.00
C21 Darrell Dess 1.75 3.00
C22 Frank Lasky 1.75 3.00
C23 Dick Pesonen 1.75 3.00
C24 Tom Scott 1.75 3.00
C25 Erich Barnes 2.50 4.00
C26 Roosevelt Brown 3.50 6.00
C27 Del Shofner 2.50 4.00
C28 Dick James 1.75 3.00
C29 Andy Stynchula 1.75 3.00
C30 Tony Dimidio 1.75 3.00
C31 Steve Thurlow 1.75 3.00
C32 Ernie Wheelwright 1.75 3.00
C33 Bookie Bolin 1.75 3.00
C34 Gary Wood 2.50 4.00
C35 John Contoulis 1.75 3.00
C36 Team Logo 1.75 3.00

1965 Coke Caps Giants G

Please see the 1965 Coke Caps Bears listing for information on this set.

COMPLETE SET (35) 75.00 150.00
G1 Joe Morrison 2.00 4.00
G2 Dick Lynch 2.00 4.00
G3 Andy Stynchula 1.50 3.00
G4 Clarence Childs 1.50 3.00
G5 Aaron Thomas 2.00 4.00
G6 Mickey Walker 1.50 3.00
G7 Bill Winter 1.50 3.00
G8 Bookie Bolin 1.50 3.00
G9 Tom Scott 1.50 3.00
G10 John Lovetere 1.50 3.00
G11 Jim Patton 2.00 4.00
G12 Darrell Dess 1.50 3.00
G13 Dick James 1.50 3.00
G14 Jerry Hillebrand 1.50 3.00
G15 Dick Pesonen 1.50 3.00
G16 Del Shofner 2.00 4.00
G17 Erich Barnes 2.00 4.00
G18 Roosevelt Brown 3.00 6.00
G19 Greg Larson 2.00 4.00
G20 Jim Katcavage 2.00 4.00
G21 Frank Lasky 1.50 3.00
G22 Lou Slaby 1.50 3.00
G23 Jim Moran 1.50 3.00
G24 Roger Anderson 1.50 3.00
G25 Steve Thurlow 1.50 3.00
G26 Ernie Wheelwright 1.50 3.00
G27 Gary Wood 2.00 4.00
G28 Tony Dimidio 1.50 3.00
G29 John Contoulis 1.50 3.00
G30 Tucker Frederickson 2.00 4.00
G31 Bob Timberlake 1.50 3.00
G32 Chuck Mercein 2.00 4.00
G33 Ernie Koy 2.00 4.00
G34 Tom Costello 1.50 3.00
G35 Homer Jones 2.00 4.00
NNO Giants Saver Sheet 15.00 30.00

1965 Coke Caps Jets

Please see the 1965 Coke Caps Bills listing for information on this set.

COMPLETE SET (35) 125.00 200.00
J1 Don Maynard 6.00 12.00
J2 George Sauer Jr. 3.00 6.00
J3 Cosmo Iacavazzi 2.00 4.00
J4 Jim O'Mahoney 2.00 4.00
J5 Matt Snell 3.00 6.00
J6 Clyde Washington 2.00 4.00
J7 Jim Turner 2.50 5.00
J8 Mike Taliaferro 2.00 4.00
J9 Marshall Starks 2.00 4.00
J10 Mark Smolinski 2.00 4.00
J11 Bob Schweickert 2.00 4.00
J12 Paul Rochester 2.00 4.00
J13 Sherman Plunkett 2.50 5.00
J14 Gerry Philbin 2.50 5.00
J15 Pete Perreault 2.00 4.00
J16 Dainard Paulson 2.00 4.00
J17 Joe Namath 30.00 50.00
J18 Winston Hill 2.50 5.00
J19 Dee Mackey 2.00 4.00
J20 Curley Johnson 2.00 4.00
J21 Mike Hudock 2.00 4.00
J22 John Huarte 3.00 6.00
J23 Gordy Holz 2.00 4.00
J24 Gene Heeter 2.50 5.00
J25 Larry Grantham 2.50 5.00
J26 Dan Ficca 2.00 4.00
J27 Sam DeLuca 2.50 5.00
J28 Bill Baird 2.00 4.00
J29 Ralph Baker 2.00 4.00
J30 Wahoo McDaniel 6.00 12.00
J31 Jim Evans 2.00 4.00
J32 Dave Herman 2.50 5.00
J33 John Schmitt 2.00 4.00
J34 Jim Harris 2.00 4.00
J35 Bake Turner 2.50 5.00
NNO Jets Saver Sheet 15.00 30.00

1965 Coke Caps Lions

Please see the 1965 Coke Caps Bears listing for information on this set.

COMPLETE SET (36) 75.00 150.00
C1 Pat Studstill 2.00 4.00
C2 Bob Whitlow 1.50 3.00
C3 Wayne Walker 2.00 4.00
C4 Tom Watkins 1.50 3.00
C5 Jim Simon 1.50 3.00
C6 Sam Williams 1.50 3.00
C7 Terry Barr 1.50 3.00
C8 Jerry Rush 1.50 3.00
C9 Roger Brown 2.00 4.00
C10 Tom Nowatzke 2.00 4.00
C11 Dick Lane 4.00 8.00
C12 Dick Compton 1.50 3.00
C13 Yale Lary 4.00 8.00
C14 Dick Lebeau 2.00 4.00
C15 Dan Lewis 2.00 4.00
C16 Wally Hilgenberg 2.00 4.00
C17 Bruce Maher 1.50 3.00
C18 Darris McCord 1.50 3.00
C19 Hugh McInnis 1.50 3.00
C20 Ernie Clark 1.50 3.00
C21 Gail Cogdill 2.00 4.00
C22 Wayne Rasmussen 1.50 3.00
C23 Joe Don Looney 5.00 10.00
C24 Jim Gibbons 2.00 4.00
C25 John Gonzaga 1.50 3.00
C26 John Gordy 1.50 3.00
C27 Bobby Thompson DB 1.50 3.00
C28 J.D. Smith T 2.00 4.00
C29 Earl Morrall 2.50 5.00
C30 Alex Karras 5.00 10.00
C31 Nick Pietrosante 2.00 4.00
C32 Milt Plum 2.00 4.00
C33 Daryl Sanders 1.50 3.00
C34 Joe Schmidt 5.00 10.00
C35 Bob Scholtz 1.50 3.00
C36 Team Logo 1.50 3.00
NNO Lions Saver Sheet 15.00 30.00

1965 Coke Caps National NFL

This set of 70 Coke caps was issued on bottled soft drinks primarily in cities without an NFL team. The caps were issued along with their own Saver Sheet. Each measures approximately 1 1/8" in diameter and has the drink logo and a football on the outside, while the inside has the player's face printed in black or red, with NFL ALL STARS above the player image. The 1965 caps are very similar to the 1966 issue and many of the players are the same in both years. However, the 1965 caps do not have the words "Caramel Colored" on the outside of the cap as do the 1966 caps. An "NFL ALL STARS" title appears above the player's photo so some caps were issued with this set and the NFL All-Stars set. The consumer could turn in his completed saver sheet to receive various prizes. These caps were also produced for 1965 on other Coca-Cola products: TAB, Fanta and Sprite. The other drink caps typically carry a slight premium (1.5-2 times) over the value of the Coke version.

COMPLETE SET (70) 112.50 225.00
C1 Herb Adderley 2.50 5.00
C2 Yale Lary 2.50 5.00
C3 Dick LeBeau 1.50 3.00
C4 Bill Brown 2.00 4.00
C5 Jim Taylor 3.75 7.50
C6 Joe Fortunato 1.50 3.00
C7 Bob Boyd DB 1.50 3.00
C8 Terry Barr 1.50 3.00
C9 Dick Szymanski 1.50 3.00
C10 Mick Tingelhoff 2.00 4.00
C11 Wayne Walker 1.50 3.00
C12 Matt Hazeltine 1.50 3.00
C13 Ray Nitschke 3.75 7.50
C14 Grady Alderman 1.50 3.00
C15 Charlie Krueger 1.50 3.00
C16 Tommy Mason 1.50 3.00
C17 Willie Wood 2.50 5.00
C18 John Unitas 6.00 12.00
C19 Lenny Moore 3.00 6.00
C20 Fran Tarkenton 5.00 10.00
C21 Deacon Jones 3.00 6.00
C22 Bob Vogel 1.50 3.00
C23 John Gordy 1.50 3.00
C24 Jim Parker 2.50 5.00
C25 Jim Gibbons 1.50 3.00
C26 Merlin Olsen 3.00 6.00
C27 Forrest Gregg 2.50 5.00
C28 Roger Brown 1.50 3.00
C29 Dave Parks 1.50 3.00
C30 Raymond Berry 3.00 6.00
C31 Mike Ditka 6.00 12.00
C32 Gino Marchetti 3.00 6.00
C33 Willie Davis 3.00 6.00
C34 Ed Meador 1.50 3.00
C35 Browns Logo 1.50 3.00
C36 Colts Logo 1.50 3.00
C37 Sam Baker 1.50 3.00
C38 Irv Cross 2.00 4.00
C39 Maxie Baughan 1.50 3.00
C40 Vince Promuto 1.50 3.00
C41 Paul Krause 1.50 3.00
C42 Charley Taylor 3.00 6.00
C43 John Paluck 1.50 3.00
C44 Paul Warfield 5.00 10.00
C45 Dick Modzelewski 1.50 3.00
C46 Myron Pottios 1.50 3.00
C47 Erich Barnes 1.50 3.00
C48 Bill Koman 1.50 3.00
C49 John Thomas 1.50 3.00
C50 Gary Ballman 1.50 3.00
C51 Sam Huff 3.00 6.00
C52 Ken Gray 1.50 3.00
C53 Roosevelt Brown 2.50 5.00
C54 Bobby Joe Conrad 1.50 3.00
C55 Pat Fischer 1.50 3.00
C56 Irv Goode 1.50 3.00
C57 Floyd Peters 1.50 3.00
C58 Charley Johnson 2.00 4.00
C59 John Henry Johnson 3.00 6.00
C60 Charles Bradshaw 1.50 3.00
C61 Jim Ringo 2.50 5.00
C62 Pete Retzlaff 2.00 4.00
C63 Sonny Jurgensen 3.50 7.00
C64 Don Meredith 6.00 12.00
C65 Bob Lilly 5.00 10.00
C66 Bill Glass 1.50 3.00
C67 Dick Schafrath 1.50 3.00
C68 Mel Renfro 3.00 6.00
C69 Jim Houston 1.50 3.00
C70 Frank Ryan 2.00 4.00
NNO NFL Saver Sheet 15.00 30.00

1965 Coke Caps Packers

Please see the 1965 Coke Caps Bears listing for information on this set.

COMPLETE SET (36) 125.00 200.00
C1 Herb Adderley 4.00 8.00
C2 Lionel Aldridge 3.00 5.00
C3 Hank Gremminger 2.50 4.00
C4 Willie Davis 4.00 8.00
C5 Boyd Dowler 3.00 5.00
C6 Marv Fleming 3.00 5.00
C7 Ken Bowman 3.00 5.00
C8 Tom Brown 2.50 4.00
C9 Doug Hart 2.50 4.00
C10 Dan Grimm 2.50 4.00
C11 Dennis Claridge 2.50 4.00
C12 Dave Hanner 3.00 5.00
C13 Tommy Crutcher 2.50 4.00
C14 Fred Thurston 4.00 8.00
C15 Elijah Pitts 3.00 5.00
C16 Lloyd Voss 2.50 4.00
C17 Lee Roy Caffey 2.50 4.00
C18 Dave Robinson 3.50 6.00
C19 Bart Starr 10.00 20.00
C20 Ray Nitschke 6.00 12.00
C21 Max McGee 3.00 5.00
C22 Don Chandler 3.00 5.00
C23 Norman Masters 2.50 4.00
C24 Ron Kostelnik 2.50 4.00
C25 Carroll Dale 3.00 5.00
C26 Hank Jordan 4.00 8.00
C27 Bob Jeter 3.00 5.00
C28 Bob Skoronski 2.50 4.00
C29 Jerry Kramer 3.50 6.00
C30 Willie Wood 4.00 8.00
C31 Paul Hornung 7.50 15.00
C32 Forrest Gregg 4.00 8.00
C33 Zeke Bratkowski 3.00 5.00
C34 Tom Moore 3.00 5.00
C35 Jim Taylor 6.00 12.00
C36 Team Logo 2.50 4.00
NNO Packers Saver Sheet 15.00 30.00

1965 Coke Caps Patriots

Please see the 1965 Coke Caps Bills listing for information on this set.

COMPLETE SET (36) 75.00 135.00
C1 Jon Morris 2.50 4.00
C2 Don Webb 2.50 4.00
C3 Charles Long 2.50 4.00
C4 Tony Romeo 2.50 4.00
C5 Bob Dee 2.50 4.00
C6 Tommy Addison 3.00 5.00
C7 Bob Yates 2.50 4.00
C8 Ron Hall 2.50 4.00
C9 Billy Neighbors 2.50 4.00
C10 Jack Rudolph 2.50 4.00
C11 Don Oakes 2.50 4.00
C12 Tom Yewcic 2.50 4.00
C13 Ron Burton 3.00 5.00
C14 Jim Colclough 2.50 4.00
C15 Larry Garron 2.50 4.00
C16 Dave Watson 2.50 4.00
C17 Art Graham 3.00 5.00
C18 Babe Parilli 3.00 6.00
C19 Jim Hunt 2.50 4.00
C20 Don McKinnon 2.50 4.00
C21 Houston Antwine 2.50 4.00
C22 Nick Buoniconti 5.00 10.00
C23 Ross O'Hanley 2.50 4.00
C24 Gino Cappelletti 3.00 6.00
C25 Chuck Shonta 2.50 4.00
C26 Dick Felt 2.50 4.00
C27 Mike Dukes 2.50 4.00
C28 Larry Eisenhauer 2.50 4.00
C29 Bob Schmidt 2.50 4.00
C30 Len St. Jean 2.50 4.00
C31 J.D. Garrett 2.50 4.00
C32 Jim Whalen 2.50 4.00
C33 Jim Nance 3.00 6.00
C34 Eddie Wilson 2.50 4.00
C35 Lonnie Farmer 2.50 4.00
C36 Boston Patriots Logo 2.50 4.00
NNO Patriots Saver Sheet 15.00 30.00

1965 Coke Caps Raiders

Please see the 1965 Coke Caps Bills listing for information on this set.

COMPLETE SET (36) 100.00 175.00
C1 Fred Biletnikoff 6.00 12.00
C2 Gus Otto 2.50 5.00
C3 Harry Schuh 2.50 5.00
C4 Ken Herock 2.50 5.00
C5 Claude Gibson 2.50 5.00
C6 Cotton Davidson 2.50 5.00
C7 Rich Zecher 2.50 5.00
C8 Ben Davidson 3.00 6.00
C9 Frank Youso 2.50 5.00
C10 Bob Svihus 2.50 5.00
C11 John R. Williamson 2.50 5.00
C12 Dave Grayson 2.50 5.00
C13 Archie Matsos 2.50 5.00
C14 Dave Costa 2.50 5.00
C15 Bo Roberson 2.50 5.00
C16 Alan Miller 2.50 5.00
C17 Billy Cannon 4.00 8.00
C18 Wayne Hawkins 3.00 6.00
C19 Warren Powers 2.50 5.00
C20 Clancy Osborne 2.50 5.00
C21 Dan Conners 2.50 5.00
C22 Jim Otto 5.00 10.00
C23 Clem Daniels 3.00 6.00
C24 Tom Flores 4.00 8.00
C25 Art Powell 3.00 6.00
C26 Rex Mirich 2.50 5.00
C27 Dick Klein 2.50 5.00
C28 Dan Birdwell 2.50 5.00
C29 Dalva Allen 2.50 5.00
C30 Mike Mercer 2.50 5.00
C31 Ken Rice 2.50 5.00
C32 Bill Budness 2.50 5.00
C33 Tommy Morrow 2.50 5.00
C34 Joe Krakoski 2.50 5.00
C35 Bob Mischak 2.50 5.00
C36 Team Logo 2.50 5.00

1965 Coke Caps Rams

Please see the 1965 Coke Caps Bears listing for information on this set.

COMPLETE SET (36) 75.00 125.00
C1 Jerry Richardson 2.50 4.00
C2 Bobby Smith 1.50 3.00
C3 Bill Munson 2.50 4.00
C4 Frank Varrichione 1.50 3.00
C5 Joe Carollo 1.50 3.00
C6 Dick Bass 2.50 4.00
C7 Ken Iman 1.50 3.00
C8 Charlie Cowan 1.50 3.00
C9 Terry Baker 3.00 5.00
C10 Don Chuy 1.50 3.00
C11 Cliff Livingston 1.50 3.00
C12 Lamar Lundy 2.50 4.00
C13 Duane Allen 1.50 3.00
C14 Roman Gabriel 3.00 6.00
C15 Roosevelt Grier 3.00 6.00
C16 Mike Henry 1.50 3.00
C17 Merlin Olsen 5.00 10.00
C18 Deacon Jones 5.00 10.00
C19 Joe Scibelli 1.50 3.00
C20 Marlin McKeever 1.50 3.00
C21 Fred Brown 1.50 3.00
C22 Frank Budka 1.50 3.00
C23 Dan Currie 1.50 3.00
C24 Roger Davis 1.50 3.00
C25 Bruce Gossett 2.50 4.00
C26 Les Josephson 2.50 4.00
C27 Ed Meador 1.50 3.00
C28 Joe Krupa 1.50 3.00
C29 Aaron Martin 1.50 3.00
C30 Tommy McDonald 3.00 5.00
C31 Bucky Pope 1.50 3.00
C32 Jack Snow 2.50 4.00
C33 Joe Wendryhoski 1.50 3.00
C34 Clancy Williams 1.50 3.00
C35 Ben Wilson 1.50 3.00
C36 Team Logo 1.50 3.00

1965 Coke Caps Redskins

Please see the 1965 Coke Caps Bears listing for information on this set.

COMPLETE SET (36) 62.50 125.00
C1 Jimmy Carr 1.50 3.00
C2 Fred Mazurek 1.50 3.00
C3 Lonnie Sanders 1.50 3.00
C4 Jim Steffen 1.50 3.00
C5 John Nisby 1.50 3.00
C6 George Izo 2.50 4.00
C7 Vince Promuto 1.50 3.00
C8 Johnny Sample 2.50 4.00
C9 Pat Richter 2.50 4.00
C10 Preston Carpenter 1.50 3.00
C11 Sam Huff 5.00 10.00
C12 Pervis Atkins 1.50 3.00
C13 Steve Barnett 1.50 3.00
C14 Len Hauss 2.50 4.00
C15 Bill Anderson 1.50 3.00
C16 John Reger 1.50 3.00
C17 George Seals 1.50 3.00
C18 J.W. Lockett 1.50 3.00
C19 Tom Walters 1.50 3.00
C20 Joe Rutgens 1.50 3.00
C21 John Paluck 1.50 3.00
C22 Fran O'Brien 1.50 3.00
C23 Willie Adams 1.50 3.00
C24 Rod Breedlove 1.50 3.00
C25 Bob Pellegrini 1.50 3.00
C26 Bob Jencks 1.50 3.00
C27 Joe Hernandez 1.50 3.00
C28 Sonny Jurgensen 5.00 10.00
C29 Bob Toneff 1.50 3.00
C30 Charley Taylor 5.00 10.00
C31 Dick Shiner 1.50 3.00
C32 Bobby Williams 1.50 3.00
C33 Angelo Coia 1.50 3.00
C34 Ron Snidow 1.50 3.00
C35 Paul Krause 3.00 6.00
C36 Team Logo 1.50 3.00
NNO Redskins Saver Sheet 15.00 30.00

1965 Coke Caps Southern Pros

This set of Coke caps was created for and, apparently, only issued in the south as part of the Go with the Pros promotion. The player selection focused on athletes playing in the south or those who had college careers in the south. Most of the players appear in the various team sets as well but carry a different cap number in this set. The caps measure approximately 1 1/8" in diameter and have the drink logo and a football on the outside, while the inside has the player's face printed in black, with his team name above the photo, the player's name below, his position to the right and the cap number to the left including a "C" prefix. The 1965 caps are very similar to the 1966 issue but the 1965 caps do not have the words "Caramel Colored" on the outside of the cap. Football caps were also produced for 1965 on other Coca-Cola products: TAB (Low-Calorie Beverage), Fanta, King Size Coke and Sprite. The other drink caps typically carry a slight premium over the value of the basic Coke version.

C1 Bart Starr 12.50 25.00
C2 Roman Gabriel 4.00 8.00
C3 Tommy Mason 3.00 6.00
C4 Jim Patton 2.50 5.00
C5 Maxie Baughan 2.50 5.00
C6 Johnny Unitas 12.50 25.00
C7 Richie Petitbon 3.00 6.00
C8 Johnny Brewer 2.50 5.00
C9 Lee Roy Jordan 3.00 6.00
C10 John Gordy 2.50 5.00
C11 Theron Sapp 2.50 5.00
C12 Joe Childress 2.50 5.00
C13 Tommy Davis 2.50 5.00
C14 Sam Huff 4.00 8.00
C15 Clendon Thomas 2.50 5.00
C16 Jerry Stovall 2.50 5.00
C17 George Mira 2.50 5.00
C18 Sonny Jurgensen 6.00 12.00
C19 Jim Taylor 7.50 15.00
C20 Deacon Jones 4.00 8.00
C21 Fran Tarkenton 6.00 12.00
C22 Bookie Bolin 2.50 5.00
C23 Earl Gros 2.50 5.00
C24 Raymond Berry 6.00 12.00
C25 Bill Wade 3.00 6.00
C26 Ernie Green 2.50 5.00
C27 Bob Lilly 6.00 12.00
C28 Yale Lary 4.00 8.00
C29 Jimmy Orr 3.00 6.00
C30 Larry Morris 2.50 5.00
C31 Gene Hickerson 4.00 8.00
C32 Don Meredith 10.00 20.00
C33 Darris McCord 2.50 5.00
C34 Willie Davis 5.00 10.00
C35 Ed Meador 2.50 5.00
C36 Rip Hawkins 2.50 5.00
C37 Clarence Childs 2.50 5.00
C38 Norm Snead 4.00 8.00
C39 Charley Bradshaw 2.50 5.00
C40 Bill Koman 2.50 5.00
C41 J.D. Smith 3.00 6.00
C42 Preston Carpenter 2.50 5.00
C43 Buzz Nutter 2.50 5.00
C44 Sonny Randle 2.50 5.00
C45 John David Crow 3.00 6.00
C46 Tom Tracy 3.00 6.00
C47 Lou Michaels 3.00 6.00
C48 Joe Fortunato 2.50 5.00
C49 Bernie Parrish 2.50 5.00
C50 Harold Hays 2.50 5.00
C51 Pat Studstill 3.00 6.00
C52 Tom Moore 3.00 6.00
C53 Bucky Pope 2.50 5.00
C54 Jim Phillips 2.50 5.00
C55 Darrell Dess 2.50 5.00
C56 Riley Gunnels 2.50 5.00
C57 Don Chandler 2.50 5.00
C58 Tommy McDonald 4.00 8.00
C59 Bobby Walden 2.50 5.00
C60 Frank Lasky 2.50 5.00
C61 Tom Woodeshick 2.50 5.00
C62 Fred Miller 2.50 5.00
C63 Bobby Joe Green 2.50 5.00
C64 Frank Ryan 3.00 6.00
C65 Bob Hayes 7.50 15.00
C66 Hugh McInnis 2.50 5.00
C67 Ben McGee 2.50 5.00
C68 Bobby Joe Conrad 2.50 5.00
C69 Charlie Krueger 2.50 5.00
C70 Rick Casares 3.00 6.00

1965 Coke Caps Steelers

Please see the 1965 Coke Caps Bears listing for information on this set.

COMPLETE SET (36)	75.00	150.00
C1 John Baker	2.00	5.00
C2 Ed Brown	2.00	5.00
C3 Jim Kelly	2.00	5.00
C4 Willie Daniel	2.00	5.00
C5 Bob Harrison	2.00	5.00
C6 Dick Haley	2.00	5.00
C7 Dan James	2.00	5.00
C8 Gary Ballman	2.00	5.00
C9 Brady Keys	2.00	5.00
C10 Charlie Bradshaw	2.00	5.00
C11 Jim Bradshaw	2.00	5.00
C12 Bill Saul	2.00	5.00
C13 Paul Martha	2.00	5.00
C14 Mike Clark	2.00	5.00
C15 Ray Lemek	2.00	5.00
C16 Clarence Peaks	2.00	5.00
C17 Theron Sapp	2.00	5.00
C18 Ray Mansfield	2.00	5.00
C19 Chuck Hinton	2.00	5.00
C20 Bill Nelsen	2.50	6.00
C21 Dan LaRose	2.00	5.00
C22 Buzz Nutter	2.00	5.00
C23 Ben McGee	2.00	5.00
C24 Myron Pottios	2.00	5.00
C25 Max Messner	2.00	5.00
C26 Andy Russell	2.50	6.00
C27 Mike Sandusky	2.00	5.00
C28 Bob Schmitz	2.00	5.00
C29 Ron Stehouwer	2.00	5.00
C30 Clendon Thomas	2.00	5.00
C31 Tommy Wade	2.00	5.00
C32 Dick Hoak	2.00	5.00
C33 Marv Woodson	2.00	5.00
C34 John Burrell	2.00	5.00
C35 John Henry Johnson	4.00	8.00
C36 Team Logo	2.00	5.00

1965 Coke Caps Vikings

Please see the 1965 Coke Caps Bears listing for information on this set.

COMPLETE SET (36)	90.00	150.00
C1 Jerry Reichow	1.25	3.00
C2 Jim Prestel	1.25	3.00
C3 Jim Marshall	3.00	6.00
C4 Errol Linden	1.25	3.00
C5 Bob Lacey	1.25	3.00
C6 Rip Hawkins	1.25	3.00
C7 John Kirby	1.25	3.00
C8 Roy Winston	1.50	4.00
C9 Ron Vanderkelen	1.25	3.00
C10 Gordon Smith	1.25	3.00
C11 Larry Bowie	1.25	3.00
C12 Paul Flatley	1.50	4.00
C13 Grady Alderman	1.50	4.00
C14 Mick Tingelhoff	2.00	5.00
C15 Lee Calland	1.25	3.00
C16 Fred Cox	1.50	4.00
C17 Bill Brown	1.50	4.00
C18 Ed Sharockman	1.25	3.00
C19 George Rose	1.25	3.00
C20 Paul Dickson	1.25	3.00
C21 Tommy Mason	1.50	4.00
C22 Carl Eller	2.00	5.00
C23 Bill Jobko	1.25	3.00
C24 Hal Bedsole	1.25	3.00
C25 Karl Kassulke	1.25	3.00
C26 Fran Tarkenton	7.50	15.00
C27 Tom Hall	1.25	3.00
C28 Archie Sutton	1.25	3.00
C29 Jim Phillips	1.25	3.00
C30 Bill Swain	1.25	3.00
C31 Larry Vargo	1.25	3.00
C32 Bobby Walden	1.25	3.00
C33 Bob Berry	1.50	4.00
C34 Jeff Jordan	1.25	3.00
C35 Lance Rentzel	1.50	4.00
C36 Vikings Logo	1.25	3.00
NNO Vikings Saver Sheet	15.00	30.00

1966 Coke Caps All-Stars AFL

The AFL All-Star caps were issued in AFL cities (and a few other cities as well) along with the local team caps as part of the Score with the Pros promotion. The local team cap saver sheets had separate sections in which to affix both the local team's caps and the All-Stars' caps. The caps measure approximately 1 1/8" in diameter and have the drink logo and a football on the outside, while the inside has the player's face printed in black, with the words "AFL ALL STAR" above the player photo and his name below. The consumer could turn in his completed saver sheet to receive various prizes. The caps are numbered with a "C" prefix. These caps were also produced for 1966 on other Coca-Cola products: Tab, Fanta, Fresca and Sprite. The other drink caps typically carry a slight premium over the value of the basic Coke version.

COMPLETE SET (34)	90.00	150.00
C37 Babe Parilli	1.50	3.00
C38 Mike Stratton	1.00	2.00
C39 Jack Kemp	12.50	25.00
C40 Len Dawson	3.75	7.50
C41 Fred Arbanas	1.00	2.00
C42 Bobby Bell	2.50	5.00
C43 Willie Brown	2.50	5.00
C44 Buck Buchanan	2.50	5.00
C45 Frank Buncom	1.00	2.00
C46 Nick Buoniconti	2.00	4.00
C47 Gino Cappelletti	1.50	3.00
C48 Eldon Danenhauer	1.00	2.00
C49 Clem Daniels	1.50	3.00
C50 Les Speedy Duncan	1.50	3.00
C51 Willie Frazier	1.00	2.00
C52 Cookie Gilchrist	1.50	3.00
C53 Dave Grayson	1.00	2.00
C54 John Hadl	2.00	4.00
C55 Wayne Hawkins	1.00	2.00
C56 Sherrill Headrick	1.00	2.00
C57 Charlie Hennigan	1.50	3.00
C58 E.J. Holub	1.00	2.00
C59 Curley Johnson	1.00	2.00
C60 Keith Lincoln	1.50	3.00
C61 Paul Lowe	1.50	3.00
C62 Don Maynard	3.00	6.00
C63 Jon Morris	1.00	2.00
C64 Joe Namath	15.00	30.00
C65 Jim Otto	2.50	5.00
C66 Dainard Paulson	1.00	2.00
C67 Art Powell	1.50	3.00
C68 Walt Sweeney	1.50	3.00
C69 Bob Talamini	1.00	2.00
C70 Lance Alworth UER	3.75	7.50

1966 Coke Caps All-Stars NFL

These NFL All-Star caps were issued in NFL cities (and a few other cities as well) along with the local team caps as part of the Score with the Pros promotion. The local team cap saver sheets had separate sections in which to affix both the local team's caps and the All-Stars' caps. The caps measure approximately 1 1/8" in diameter and have the drink logo and a football on the outside, while the inside has the player's face printed in black, with the words "NFL ALL STAR" above the player photo and his name below. The consumer could turn in his completed saver sheet to receive various prizes. The caps are numbered with a "C" prefix. These caps were also produced for 1966 on other Coca-Cola products: Tab, Fanta, Fresca and Sprite. The other drink caps typically carry a slight premium over the value of the basic Coke version.

COMPLETE SET (34)	50.00	100.00
C37 Frank Ryan	1.00	2.50
C38 Timmy Brown	1.00	2.50
C39 Tucker Frederickson	.75	2.00
C40 Cornell Green	1.00	2.50
C41 Bob Hayes	1.50	4.00
C42 Charley Taylor	1.25	3.00
C43 Pete Retzlaff	1.00	2.50
C44 Jim Ringo	1.25	3.00
C45 John Wooten	.75	2.00
C46 Dale Meinert	.75	2.00
C47 Bob Lilly	2.00	5.00
C48 Sam Silas	.75	2.00
C49 Roosevelt Brown	1.25	3.00
C50 Gary Ballman	.75	2.00
C51 Gary Collins	.75	2.00
C52 Sonny Randle	.75	2.00
C53 Charlie Johnson UER	1.00	2.50
C54 Herb Adderley	1.25	3.00
C55 Doug Atkins	1.25	3.00
C56 Roger Brown	.75	2.00
C57 Dick Butkus	4.00	10.00
C58 Willie Davis	1.25	3.00
C59 Tommy McDonald	1.00	2.50
C60 Alex Karras	1.50	4.00
C61 John Mackey	1.25	3.00
C62 Ed Meador	.75	2.00
C63 Merlin Olsen	1.50	4.00
C64 Dave Parks	.75	2.00
C65 Gale Sayers	4.00	10.00
C66 Fran Tarkenton	2.50	6.00
C67 Mick Tingelhoff	.75	2.00
C68 Ken Willard	.75	2.00
C69 Willie Wood	1.25	3.00
C70 Bill Brown	1.00	2.50

1966 Coke Caps Bears

Coca-Cola issued its final run of football caps in 1966. Each NFL team had a set released in their area along with the NFL All-Stars caps as part of the "Score with the Pros" promotion. Each team's Saver Sheets had separate sections in which to affix both the local team's caps and the All-Stars' caps. The caps measure approximately 1 1/8" in diameter and have the drink logo and a football on the outside, while the inside has the player's face printed in black with the team name above the photo, the player's name below, his position to the right and the cap number to the left. Some teams are also known to exist in a version that features a slightly smaller player photo. Cap numbers included a "C" prefix on all NFL teams except the Giants which had two versions with either "C" or "G" prefixes. The consumer could turn in his completed saver sheet to receive various prizes. The 1966 caps are very similar to the 1965 issue and many of the players are the same in both years. However, the 1966 caps have the words "Caramel Colored" on the outside of the cap while the 1965 caps do not. Most caps were also produced for 1966 on other Coca-Cola products: Tab (Dietary Beverage), Fanta, Fresca, King Size Coke and Sprite. These other drink caps typically carry a slight premium over the value of the Coke version.

COMPLETE SET (36)	75.00	135.00
C1 Bennie McRae	1.25	2.50
C2 Johnny Morris	1.25	2.50
C3 Roosevelt Taylor	2.00	4.00
C4 Doug Buffone	1.25	2.50
C5 Ed O'Bradovich	1.25	2.50
C6 Richie Petitbon	2.00	4.00
C7 Mike Pyle	1.25	2.50
C8 Dave Whitsell	1.25	2.50
C9 Dick Gordon	1.25	2.50
C10 John Johnson DT	1.25	2.50
C11 Jim Jones	1.25	2.50
C12 Andy Livingston	1.25	2.50
C13 Bob Kilcullen	1.25	2.50
C14 Roger LeClerc	1.25	2.50
C15 Herman Lee	1.25	2.50
C16 Earl Leggett	1.25	2.50
C17 Joe Marconi	1.25	2.50
C18 Rudy Bukich	2.00	4.00
C19 Mike Reilly	1.25	2.50
C20 Mike Ditka	5.00	10.00
C21 Dick Evey	1.25	2.50
C22 Joe Fortunato	1.25	2.50
C23 Bill Wade	3.00	5.00
C24 Jim Purnell	1.25	2.50
C25 Larry Glueck	1.25	2.50
C26 Mike Rabold	1.25	2.50
C27 Bob Wetoska	1.25	2.50
C28 Mike Rabold	1.25	2.50
C29 Jon Arnett	2.00	4.00
C30 Dick Butkus	15.00	25.00
C31 Charlie Bivins	1.25	2.50
C32 Ronnie Bull	2.00	4.00
C33 Jim Cadile	1.25	2.50
C34 George Seals	1.25	2.50
C35 Gale Sayers	15.00	25.00
C36 Bears Logo	1.25	2.50

1966 Coke Caps Bills

Coca-Cola issued its final run of football caps in 1966. Each AFL team had a set released in their area along with the AFL All-Stars caps as part of the "Score with the Pros" promotion. Each team's Saver Sheets had separate sections in which to affix both the local team's caps and the All-Stars' caps. The caps measure approximately 1 1/8" in diameter and have the drink logo and a football on the outside, while the inside has the player's face printed in black with the team name above the photo, the player's name below, his position to the right and the cap number to the left. Some teams are also known to exist in a version that features a slightly smaller player photo. Cap numbers included a "C" prefix on all AFL teams except the Jets (J prefix) and Bills (B prefix). The consumer could turn in his completed saver sheet to receive various prizes. The 1966 caps are very similar to the 1965 issue and many of the players are the same in both years. However, the 1966 caps have the words "Caramel Colored" on the outside of the cap while the 1965 caps do not. Most caps were also produced for 1966 on other Coca-Cola products: Tab, Fanta, Fresca, King Size Coke and Sprite. These other drink caps typically carry a slight premium over the value of the Coke version.

COMPLETE SET (35)	90.00	150.00
B1 Bill Laskey	1.25	2.50
B2 Marty Schottenheimer	6.00	12.00
B3 Stew Barber	2.50	4.00
B4 Glenn Bass	1.25	2.50
B5 Remi Prudhomme	1.25	2.50
B6 Al Bemiller	1.25	2.50
B7 George Butch Byrd	2.50	4.00
B8 Wray Carlton	2.50	4.00
B9 Hagood Clarke	1.25	2.50
B10 Jack Kemp	15.00	30.00
B11 Charley Warner	1.25	2.50
B12 Elbert Dubenion	2.50	4.00
B13 Jim Dunaway	2.50	4.00
B14 Booker Edgerson	2.50	4.00
B15 Paul Costa	1.25	2.50
B16 Henry Schmidt	1.25	2.50
B17 Dick Hudson	1.25	2.50
B18 Harry Jacobs	2.50	4.00
B19 Tom Janik	1.25	2.50
B20 Tom Day	2.50	4.00
B21 Daryle Lamonica	4.00	8.00
B22 Paul Maguire	3.00	6.00
B23 Roland McDole	2.50	4.00
B24 Dudley Meredith	1.25	2.50
B25 Joe O'Donnell	1.25	2.50
B26 Charley Ferguson	1.25	2.50
B27 Ed Rutkowski	1.25	2.50
B28 George Saimes	2.50	4.00
B29 Tom Sestak	2.50	4.00
B30 Billy Shaw	2.50	4.00
B31 Bob Lee Smith	1.25	2.50
B32 Mike Stratton	2.50	4.00
B33 Gene Sykes	1.25	2.50
B34 John Tracey	1.25	2.50
B35 Ernie Warlick	1.25	2.50
NNO Bills Saver Sheet	15.00	30.00

1966 Coke Caps Broncos

Please see the 1966 Coke Caps Bills listing for information on this set.

COMPLETE SET (36)	70.00	120.00
C1 Fred Forsberg	1.50	3.00
C2 Willie Brown DB	5.00	10.00
C3 Bob Scarpitto	2.50	4.00
C4 Butch Davis	1.50	3.00
C5 Al Denson	2.50	4.00
C6 Ron Sbranti	1.50	3.00
C7 John Bramlett	1.50	3.00
C8 Mickey Slaughter	1.50	3.00
C9 Lionel Taylor	3.00	5.00
C10 Jerry Sturm	1.50	3.00
C11 Jerry Hopkins	1.50	3.00
C12 Charlie Mitchell	1.50	3.00
C13 Ray Jacobs	1.50	3.00
C14 Lonnie Wright	1.50	3.00
C15 Goldie Sellers	1.50	3.00
C16 Ray Kubala	1.50	3.00
C17 John Griffin	1.50	3.00
C18 Bob Breitenstein	1.50	3.00
C19 Eldon Danenhauer	1.50	3.00
C20 Wendell Haynes	2.50	4.00
C21 Max Leetzow	1.50	3.00
C22 Nemiah Wilson	2.50	4.00
C23 Jim Thibert	1.50	3.00
C24 Gerry Bussell	1.50	3.00
C25 Bob McCullough	1.50	3.00
C26 Jim McMillin	1.50	3.00
C27 Abner Haynes	3.00	5.00
C28 Darrell Lester	1.50	3.00
C29 Cookie Gilchrist	3.00	5.00
C30 John McCormick	2.50	4.00
C31 Lee Bernet	1.50	3.00
C32 Goose Gonsoulin	2.50	4.00
C33 Scotty Glacken	1.50	3.00
C34 Bob Hadrick	1.50	3.00
C35 Archie Matsos	2.50	4.00
C36 Broncos Logo	1.50	3.00

1966 Coke Caps Browns

Please see the 1966 Coke Caps Bears listing for information on this set.

COMPLETE SET (36)	75.00	125.00
C1 Jim Ninowski	2.00	3.50
C2 Leroy Kelly	4.00	8.00
C3 Lou Groza	4.00	8.00
C4 Gary Collins	2.00	3.50
C5 Bill Glass	2.00	3.50
C6 Dale Lindsey	1.25	2.50
C7 Galen Fiss	1.25	2.50
C8 Ross Fichtner	1.25	2.50
C9 John Wooten	2.00	3.50
C10 Clifton McNeil	1.25	2.50
C11 Paul Wiggin	2.00	3.50
C12 Gene Hickerson	2.00	3.50
C13 Ernie Green	1.25	2.50
C14 Mike Howell	1.25	2.50
C15 Dick Schafrath	1.25	2.50
C16 Sidney Williams	1.25	2.50
C17 Frank Ryan	2.00	3.50
C18 Bernie Parrish	1.25	2.50
C19 Vince Costello	1.25	2.50
C20 John Brown OT	1.25	2.50
C21 Monte Clark	1.25	2.50
C22 Walter Roberts	1.25	2.50
C23 Johnny Brewer	1.25	2.50
C24 Walter Beach	1.25	2.50
C25 Dick Modzelewski	1.25	2.50
C26 Gary Lane	1.25	2.50
C27 Jim Houston	1.25	2.50
C28 Milt Morin	1.25	2.50
C29 Erich Barnes	1.25	2.50
C30 Tom Hutchinson	1.25	2.50
C31 John Morrow	1.25	2.50
C32 Jim Kanicki	1.25	2.50
C33 Paul Warfield	4.00	8.00
C34 Jim Garcia	1.25	2.50
C35 Walter Johnson	1.25	2.50
C36 Browns Logo	1.25	2.50
NNO Browns Saver Sheet	15.00	30.00

1966 Coke Caps Cardinals

Please see the 1966 Coke Caps Bears listing for information on this set.

COMPLETE SET (36)	50.00	100.00
C1 Pat Fischer	1.75	3.50
C2 Sonny Randle	1.75	3.50
C3 Joe Childress	1.25	2.50
C4 Dave Meggysey UER	2.50	5.00
C5 Joe Robb	1.25	2.50
C6 Jerry Stovall	1.25	2.50
C7 Ernie McMillan	1.75	3.50
C8 Dale Meinert	1.25	2.50
C9 Irv Goode	1.25	2.50
C10 Bob DeMarco	1.25	2.50
C11 Mal Hammack	1.25	2.50
C12 Jim Bakken	1.75	3.50
C13 Bill Thornton	1.25	2.50
C14 Buddy Humphrey	1.25	2.50
C15 Bill Koman	1.25	2.50
C16 Larry Wilson	3.00	6.00
C17 Charles Walker	1.25	2.50
C18 Prentice Gautt	1.25	2.50
C19 Charlie Johnson UER	2.00	4.00
C20 Ken Gray	1.25	2.50
C21 Dave Simmons	1.25	2.50
C22 Sam Silas	1.25	2.50
C23 Larry Stallings	1.25	2.50
C24 Don Brumm	1.25	2.50
C25 Bobby Joe Conrad	1.75	3.50
C26 Bill Triplett	1.25	2.50
C27 Luke Owens	1.25	2.50
C28 Jackie Smith	3.00	6.00
C29 Bob Reynolds	1.25	2.50
C30 Abe Woodson	1.75	3.50
C31 Jim Burson	1.25	2.50
C32 Willis Crenshaw	1.25	2.50
C33 Billy Gambrell	1.25	2.50
C34 Ray Ogden	1.25	2.50
C35 Herschel Turner	1.25	2.50
C36 Cardinals Logo	1.25	2.50
NNO Cardinals Saver Sheet	15.00	30.00

1966 Coke Caps Chargers

Please see the 1966 Coke Caps Bills listing for information on this set.

COMPLETE SET (36)	70.00	120.00
C1 John Hadl	4.00	8.00
C2 George Gross	1.50	3.00
C3 Frank Buncom	1.50	3.00
C4 Lance Alworth	4.00	8.00
C5 Paul Lowe	3.00	5.00
C6 Herb Travenio	1.50	3.00
C7 Dick Degen	1.50	3.00
C8 Jacque MacKinnon	1.50	3.00
C9 Les Duncan	2.50	4.00
C10 John Farris	1.50	3.00
C11 Willie Frazier	2.50	4.00
C12 Howard Kindig	1.50	3.00
C13 Pat Shea	1.50	3.00
C14 Fred Moore	1.50	3.00
C15 Bob Petrich	1.50	3.00
C16 Ron Mix	3.00	6.00
C17 Miller Farr	1.50	3.00
C18 Keith Lincoln	3.00	5.00
C19 Sam Gruneisen	1.50	3.00
C20 Jim Allison	1.50	3.00
C21 Chuck Allen	1.50	3.00
C22 Gene Foster	1.50	3.00
C23 Rick Redman	1.50	3.00
C24 Steve DeLong	1.50	3.00
C25 Gary Kirner	1.50	3.00
C26 Steve Tensi	1.50	3.00
C27 Kenny Graham	1.50	3.00
C28 Bud Whitehead	1.50	3.00
C29 Walt Sweeney	1.50	3.00
C30 Bob Zeman	1.50	3.00
C31 Gary Garrison	2.50	4.00
C32 Don Norton	1.50	3.00
C33 Ernie Wright	2.50	4.00
C34 Ron Carpenter	1.50	3.00
C35 Pete Jacques	1.50	3.00
C36 Team Logo	1.50	3.00

1966 Coke Caps Chiefs

Please see the 1966 Coke Caps Bills listing for information on this set.

COMPLETE SET (36)	75.00	150.00
C1 E.J. Holub	2.00	4.00
C2 Al Reynolds	1.50	3.00
C3 Buck Buchanan	4.00	8.00
C4 Curt Merz SP	4.00	8.00
C5 Dave Hill	1.50	3.00
C6 Bobby Hunt	1.50	3.00
C7 Jerry Mays	2.00	4.00
C8 Jon Gilliam	1.50	3.00
C9 Walt Corey	2.00	4.00
C10 Solomon Brannan	1.50	3.00
C11 Aaron Brown	1.50	3.00
C12 Bert Coan	1.50	3.00
C13 Ed Budde	2.00	4.00
C14 Tommy Brooker	1.50	3.00
C15 Bobby Bell	4.00	8.00
C16 Smokey Stover	1.50	3.00
C17 Curtis McClinton	2.00	4.00
C18 Jerrel Wilson	2.00	4.00
C19 Ron Burton	2.00	4.00
C20 Mike Garrett	2.50	5.00
C21 Jim Tyrer	2.00	4.00
C22 Johnny Robinson	2.00	4.00
C23 Bobby Ply	1.50	3.00
C24 Frank Pitts	1.50	3.00
C25 Ed Lothamer	1.50	3.00
C26 Sherrill Headrick	2.00	4.00
C27 Fred Williamson	3.00	6.00
C28 Chris Burford	2.00	4.00
C29 Willie Mitchell	1.50	3.00
C30 Otis Taylor	3.00	6.00
C31 Fred Arbanas	2.00	4.00
C32 Hatch Rosdahl	1.50	3.00
C33 Reg Carolan	1.50	3.00
C34 Len Dawson	6.00	12.00
C35 Pete Beathard	2.00	4.00
C36 Chiefs Logo	1.50	3.00
NNO Chiefs Saver Sheet	15.00	30.00

1966 Coke Caps Colts

Please see the 1966 Coke Caps Bears listing for information on this set.

COMPLETE SET (36)	75.00	135.00
C1 Ted Davis	1.25	2.50
C2 Bob Boyd DB	1.25	2.50
C3 Lenny Moore	5.00	10.00
C4 Jackie Burkett	1.25	2.50
C5 Jimmy Orr	1.50	3.50
C6 Andy Stynchula	1.25	2.50
C7 Mike Curtis	3.00	6.00
C8 Jerry Logan	1.25	2.50
C9 Steve Stonebreaker	1.25	2.50
C10 John Mackey	4.00	8.00
C11 Dennis Gaubatz	1.25	2.50
C12 Don Shinnick	1.25	2.50
C13 Dick Szymanski	1.25	2.50
C14 Ordell Braase	1.25	2.50
C15 Lenny Lyles	1.25	2.50
C16 Rick Kestner	1.25	2.50
C17 Dan Sullivan	1.25	2.50
C18 Lou Michaels	1.50	3.50
C19 Gary Cuozzo	1.50	3.50
C20 Butch Wilson	1.25	2.50
C21 Willie Richardson	1.50	3.50
C22 Jim Welch	1.25	2.50
C23 Tony Lorick	1.25	2.50
C24 Billy Ray Smith	1.50	3.50
C25 Fred Miller	1.25	2.50
C26 Tom Matte	2.50	5.00
C27 Johnny Unitas	7.50	15.00
C28 Glenn Ressler	1.25	2.50
C29 Alvin Haymond	1.50	3.50
C30 Jim Parker	3.00	6.00
C31 Butch Allison	1.25	2.50
C32 Bob Vogel	1.25	2.50
C33 Jerry Hill	1.25	2.50
C34 Raymond Berry	5.00	10.00
C35 Sam Ball	1.25	2.50
C36 Colts Team Logo	1.25	2.50
NNO Colts Saver Sheet	15.00	30.00

1966 Coke Caps Cowboys

Please see the 1966 Coke Caps Bears listing for information on this set.

COMPLETE SET (36)	100.00	175.00
C1 Mike Connelly	2.00	4.00
C2 Tony Liscio	1.50	3.00
C3 Jethro Pugh	2.00	4.00
C4 Larry Stephens	1.50	3.00
C5 Jim Colvin	1.50	3.00
C6 Malcolm Walker	1.50	3.00
C7 Danny Villanueva	1.50	3.00
C8 Frank Clarke	2.00	4.00
C9 Don Meredith	7.50	15.00
C10 George Andrie	2.00	4.00
C11 Mel Renfro	5.00	10.00
C12 Pettis Norman	2.00	4.00
C13 Buddy Dial	2.00	4.00
C14 Pete Gent	2.00	4.00
C15 Jerry Rhome	2.00	4.00
C16 Bob Hayes	7.50	15.00
C17 Mike Gaechter	1.50	3.00
C18 Joe Bob Isbell	1.50	3.00
C19 Harold Hays	1.50	3.00
C20 Craig Morton	4.00	8.00
C21 Jake Kupp	1.50	3.00
C22 Cornell Green	2.00	4.00
C23 Dan Reeves	5.00	10.00
C24 Leon Donohue	1.50	3.00
C25 Dave Manders	1.50	3.00
C26 Warren Livingston	1.50	3.00
C27 Bob Lilly	6.00	12.00
C28 Chuck Howley	3.00	6.00
C29 Don Bishop	2.00	4.00
C30 Don Perkins	2.00	4.00
C31 Jim Boeke	1.50	3.00
C32 Dave Edwards	2.00	4.00
C33 Lee Roy Jordan	3.00	6.00
C34 Obert Logan	1.50	3.00
C35 Ralph Neely	2.00	4.00
C36 Cowboys Logo	1.50	3.00
NNO Cowboys Saver Sheet	15.00	30.00

1966 Coke Caps Eagles

Please see the 1966 Coke Caps Bears listing for information on this set.

COMPLETE SET (36)	75.00	135.00
C1 Norm Snead	2.00	4.00
C2 Al Nelson	1.25	2.50
C3 Jim Skaggs	1.25	2.50
C4 Glenn Glass	1.25	2.50
C5 Pete Retzlaff	1.75	3.50
C6 John Osmond	1.25	2.50
C7 Ray Rissmiller	1.25	2.50
C8 Lynn Hoyem	1.25	2.50
C9 King Hill	1.75	3.50
C10 Timmy Brown	1.75	3.50
C11 Ollie Matson	3.75	7.50
C12 Dave Lloyd	1.75	3.50
C13 Jim Ringo	3.00	6.00
C14 Floyd Peters	1.75	3.50
C15 Gary Pettigrew	1.25	2.50
C16 Frank Molden	1.25	2.50
C17 Earl Gros	1.75	3.50
C18 Fred Hill	1.25	2.50
C19 Don Hultz	1.25	2.50
C20 Ray Poage	1.25	2.50
C21 Aaron Martin	1.25	2.50
C22 Mike Morgan	1.25	2.50
C23 Lane Howell	1.25	2.50
C24 Ed Blaine	1.25	2.50
C25 Jack Concannon	1.75	3.50
C26 Sam Baker	1.25	2.50
C27 Tom Woodeshick	1.75	3.50
C28 Joe Scarpati	1.25	2.50
C29 John Meyers	1.25	2.50
C30 Nate Ramsey	1.75	3.50
C31 Ben Hawkins	1.25	2.50
C32 Bob Brown T	1.75	3.50
C33 Willie Brown WR	1.25	2.50
C34 Ron Goodwin	1.25	2.50
C35 Randy Beisler	1.25	2.50
C36 Team Logo	1.25	2.50
NNO Eagles Saver Sheet	15.00	30.00

1966 Coke Caps Falcons

Please see the 1966 Coke Caps Bears listing for information on this set.

COMPLETE SET (36)	50.00	100.00
C1 Tommy Nobis	4.00	8.00
C2 Ernie Wheelwright	1.75	3.50
C3 Lee Calland	1.25	2.50
C4 Chuck Sieminski	1.25	2.50
C5 Dennis Claridge	1.75	3.50
C6 Ralph Heck	1.25	2.50
C7 Alex Hawkins	1.75	3.50
C8 Dan Grimm	1.75	3.50
C9 Marion Rushing	1.25	2.50
C10 Bobbie Johnson	1.25	2.50
C11 Bobby Franklin	1.25	2.50
C12 Bill McWatters	1.25	2.50
C13 Billy Lothridge	1.75	3.50
C14 Billy Martin E	1.75	3.50
C15 Tom Wilson	1.25	2.50
C16 Dennis Murphy	1.25	2.50
C17 Randy Johnson	1.75	3.50
C18 Guy Reese	1.25	2.50
C19 Frank Marchlewski	1.25	2.50
C20 Don Talbert	1.25	2.50
C21 Errol Linden	1.25	2.50
C22 Dan Lewis	1.25	2.50
C23 Ed Cook	1.25	2.50
C24 Hugh McInnis	1.25	2.50
C25 Frank Lasky	1.25	2.50
C26 Bob Jencks	1.25	2.50
C27 Bill Jobko	1.25	2.50
C28 Nick Rassas	1.25	2.50
C29 Bob Riggle	1.25	2.50
C30 Ken Reaves	1.75	3.50
C31 Bob Sanders	1.25	2.50
C32 Steve Sloan	1.75	3.50
C33 Ron Smith	1.75	3.50
C34 Bob Whitlow	1.25	2.50
C35 Roger Anderson	1.25	2.50
C36 Falcons Logo	1.25	2.50
NNO Falcons Saver Sheet	15.00	30.00

1966 Coke Caps 49ers

Please see the 1966 Coke Caps Bears listing for information on this set.

COMPLETE SET (36)	75.00	135.00
C1 Bernie Casey	1.75	3.50
C2 Bruce Bosley	1.75	3.50
C3 Kermit Alexander	1.75	3.50
C4 John Brodie	3.75	7.50
C5 Dave Parks	1.75	3.50
C6 Len Rohde	1.75	3.50
C7 Walter Rock	1.75	3.50
C8 George Mira	2.50	5.00
C9 Karl Rubke	1.25	2.50
C10 Ken Willard	1.75	3.50
C11 John David Crow UER	2.00	4.00
C12 George Donnelly	1.25	2.50
C13 Dave Wilcox	2.00	4.00
C14 Vern Burke	1.25	2.50
C15 Wayne Swinford	1.25	2.50
C16 Elbert Kimbrough	1.25	2.50
C17 Clark Miller	1.25	2.50
C18 Dave Kopay	1.75	3.50
C19 Joe Cerne	1.25	2.50
C20 Roland Lakes	1.25	2.50
C21 Charlie Krueger	1.75	3.50
C22 Billy Kilmer	2.50	5.00
C23 Jim Johnson	3.00	6.00
C24 Matt Hazeltine	1.75	3.50
C25 Mike Dowdle	1.25	2.50
C26 Jim Wilson	1.25	2.50
C27 Tommy Davis	1.75	3.50
C28 Jim Norton	1.25	2.50
C29 Jack Chapple	1.25	2.50
C30 Ed Beard	1.25	2.50
C31 John Thomas	1.25	2.50
C32 Monty Stickles	1.25	2.50
C33 Kay McFarland	1.25	2.50
C34 Gary Lewis	1.25	2.50
C35 Howard Mudd	1.25	2.50
C36 49ers Logo	1.25	2.50
NNO 49ers Saver Sheet	15.00	30.00

1966 Coke Caps Giants C

Please see the 1966 Coke Caps Bears listing for information on this set.

COMPLETE SET (36)	60.00	100.00
C1 Joe Morrison	2.00	3.50
C2 Dick Lynch	2.00	3.50
C3 Pete Case	2.00	3.50
C4 Clarence Childs	1.50	2.50
C5 Aaron Thomas	2.00	3.50
C6 Jim Carroll	1.50	2.50
C7 Henry Carr	2.00	3.50
C8 Bookie Bolin	1.50	2.50
C9 Roosevelt Davis	1.50	2.50
C10 John Lovetere	1.50	2.50
C11 Jim Patton	2.00	3.50
C12 Wendell Harris	1.50	2.50
C13 Roger LaLonde	1.50	2.50
C14 Jerry Hillebrand	1.50	2.50
C15 Spider Lockhart	2.00	3.50
C16 Del Shofner	2.00	3.50
C17 Earl Morrall	3.00	5.00
C18 Roosevelt Brown	3.00	5.00
C19 Greg Larson	2.00	3.50
C20 Jim Katcavage	2.00	3.50
C21 Smith Reed	1.50	2.50
C22 Lou Slaby	1.50	2.50
C23 Jim Moran	1.50	2.50
C24 Bill Swain	1.50	2.50
C25 Steve Thurlow	1.50	2.50
C26 Olen Underwood	1.50	2.50
C27 Gary Wood	2.00	3.50
C28 Larry Vargo	1.50	2.50
C29 Jim Prestel	1.50	2.50
C30 Tucker Frederickson	2.00	3.50
C31 Bob Timberlake	1.50	2.50
C32 Chuck Mercein	2.50	4.00
C33 Ernie Koy	2.00	3.50
C34 Tom Costello	1.50	2.50
C35 Homer Jones	2.00	3.50
C36 Team Logo	1.50	2.50

1966 Coke Caps Giants G

Please see the 1966 Coke Caps Bears listing for information on this set.

COMPLETE SET (35)	60.00	100.00
G1 Joe Morrison	2.00	3.50
G2 Dick Lynch	2.00	3.50
G3 Pete Case	2.00	3.50
G4 Clarence Childs	1.50	2.50
G5 Aaron Thomas	2.00	3.50
G6 Jim Carroll	1.50	2.50
G7 Henry Carr	2.00	3.50
G8 Bookie Bolin	1.50	2.50
G9 Roosevelt Davis	1.50	2.50
G10 John Lovetere	1.50	2.50
G11 Jim Patton	2.00	3.50
G12 Wendell Harris	1.50	2.50
G13 Roger LaLonde	1.50	2.50
G14 Jerry Hillebrand	1.50	2.50
G15 Spider Lockhart	2.00	3.50
G16 Del Shofner	2.00	3.50
G17 Earl Morrall	2.50	5.00
G18 Roosevelt Brown	2.50	5.00
G19 Greg Larson	2.00	3.50
G20 Jim Katcavage	2.00	3.50
G21 Smith Reed	1.50	2.50
G22 Lou Slaby	1.50	2.50
G23 Jim Moran	1.50	2.50
G24 Bill Swain	1.50	2.50
G25 Steve Thurlow	1.50	2.50
G26 Olen Underwood	1.50	2.50
G27 Gary Wood	2.00	3.50
G28 Larry Vargo	1.50	2.50
G29 Jim Prestel	1.50	2.50
G30 Tucker Frederickson	2.00	3.50
G31 Bob Timberlake	1.50	2.50
G32 Chuck Mercein	2.50	4.00
G33 Ernie Koy	2.00	3.50
G34 Tom Costello	1.50	2.50
G35 Homer Jones	2.00	3.50
NNO Giants Saver Sheet	15.00	30.00

1966 Coke Caps Jets

Please see the 1966 Coke Caps Bills listing for information on this set.

COMPLETE SET (35)	75.00	150.00
J1 Don Maynard	5.00	10.00
J2 George Sauer Jr.	2.50	5.00
J3 Paul Crane	1.25	2.50
J4 Jim Colclough	1.25	2.50
J5 Matt Snell	3.00	6.00
J6 Sherman Lewis	3.00	6.00
J7 Jim Turner	1.75	3.50
J8 Mike Taliaferro	1.25	2.50
J9 Cornell Gordon	1.75	3.50
J10 Mark Smolinski	1.25	2.50
J11 Al Atkinson	1.75	3.50
J12 Paul Rochester	1.25	2.50
J13 Sherman Plunkett	1.25	2.50
J14 Gerry Philbin	1.75	3.50
J15 Pete Lammons	1.75	3.50
J16 Dainard Paulson	1.25	2.50
J17 Joe Namath	25.00	50.00
J18 Winston Hill	1.75	3.50
J19 Dee Mackey	1.25	2.50
J20 Curley Johnson	1.25	2.50
J21 Verlon Biggs	1.75	3.50
J22 Bill Mathis	1.75	3.50
J23 Carl McAdams	1.25	2.50
J24 Bert Wilder	1.25	2.50
J25 Larry Grantham	1.75	3.50
J26 Bill Yearby	1.25	2.50
J27 Sam DeLuca	1.25	2.50
J28 Bill Baird	1.25	2.50
J29 Ralph Baker	1.75	3.50
J30 Ray Abruzzese	1.25	2.50
J31 Jim Hudson	1.25	2.50
J32 Dave Herman	1.75	3.50
J33 John Schmitt	1.25	2.50
J34 Jim Harris	1.25	2.50
J35 Bake Turner	1.75	3.50
NNO Jets Saver Sheet	15.00	30.00

1966 Coke Caps Lions

Please see the 1966 Coke Caps Bears listing for information on this set.

COMPLETE SET (36)	50.00	100.00
C1 Pat Studstill	1.75	3.50
C2 Ed Flanagan	1.75	3.50
C3 Wayne Walker	1.75	3.50
C4 Tom Watkins	1.25	2.50
C5 Tommy Vaughn	1.25	2.50
C6 Jim Kearney	1.25	2.50
C7 Larry Hand	1.75	3.50
C8 Jerry Rush	1.25	2.50
C9 Roger Brown	1.75	3.50
C10 Tom Nowatzke	1.75	3.50
C11 John Henderson	1.25	2.50
C12 Tom Myers QB	1.25	2.50
C13 Ron Kramer	1.75	3.50
C14 Dick LeBeau	1.75	3.50
C15 Amos Marsh	1.75	3.50
C16 Wally Hilgenberg	1.75	3.50
C17 Bruce Maher	1.25	2.50
C18 Darris McCord	1.75	3.50
C19 Ted Karras	1.25	2.50
C20 Ernie Clark	1.25	2.50
C21 Gail Cogdill	1.75	3.50
C22 Wayne Rasmussen	1.25	2.50
C23 Joe Don Looney	4.00	8.00
C24 Jim Gibbons	1.75	3.50
C25 John Gonzaga	1.25	2.50
C26 John Gordy	1.25	2.50
C27 Bobby Thompson	1.25	2.50
C28 J.D. Smith	1.25	2.50
C29 Roger Shoals	1.25	2.50
C30 Alex Karras	3.50	7.00
C31 Nick Pietrosante	1.75	3.50
C32 Milt Plum	2.00	4.00
C33 Daryl Sanders	1.25	2.50
C34 Mike Lucci	1.75	3.50
C35 George Izo	1.75	3.50
C36 Lions Logo	1.25	2.50

1966 Coke Caps National NFL

As part of an advertising promotion, Coca-Cola issued 21 sets of bottle caps, covering the 14 NFL cities, the six AFL cities, and a separate National set for cities not reached by the leagues. This National issue was released primarily in non-NFL cities as part of the Score with the Pros promotion. There was a separate Saver Sheet for the National set. The caps measure approximately 1 1/8" in diameter and have the drink logo and a football on the outside, while the inside has the player's face printed in black, with text surrounding the face. The consumer could turn in his completed saver sheet to receive various prizes. The caps are numbered with a "C" prefix. These caps were also produced for 1966 on other Coca-Cola products: Tab, Fanta, Fresca and Sprite. The other drink caps typically carry a slight premium of 1.5X to 2X the value of the Coke version.

COMPLETE SET (70)	112.50	225.00
C1 Larry Wilson	2.50	5.00
C2 Frank Ryan	1.75	3.50
C3 Norm Snead	1.75	3.50
C4 Mel Renfro	2.50	5.00
C5 Timmy Brown	1.75	3.50
C6 Tucker Frederickson	1.25	2.50
C7 Jim Bakken	1.25	2.50
C8 Paul Krause	2.00	4.00
C9 Irv Cross	1.25	2.50
C10 Cornell Green	1.75	3.50
C11 Pat Fischer	1.25	2.50
C12 Bob Hayes	3.00	6.00
C13 Charley Taylor	2.50	5.00
C14 Pete Retzlaff	1.75	3.50
C15 Jim Ringo	2.50	5.00
C16 Maxie Baughan	1.25	2.50
C17 Chuck Howley	1.50	3.00
C18 John Wooten	1.25	2.50
C19 Bob DeMarco	1.25	2.50
C20 Dale Meinert	1.25	2.50
C21 Gene Hickerson	1.25	2.50
C22 George Andrie	1.25	2.50
C23 Joe Rutgens	1.25	2.50
C24 Bob Lilly	5.00	10.00
C25 Sam Silas	1.25	2.50
C26 Bob Brown OT	1.75	3.50
C27 Dick Schafrath	1.25	2.50
C28 Roosevelt Brown	2.50	5.00
C29 Jim Houston	1.25	2.50
C30 Paul Wiggin	1.25	2.50
C31 Gary Ballman	1.25	2.50
C32 Gary Collins	1.75	3.50
C33 Sonny Randle	1.25	2.50
C34 Charley Johnson	1.75	3.50
C35 Browns Logo	1.25	2.50
C36 Packers Logo	1.25	2.50
C37 Herb Adderley	2.50	5.00
C38 Grady Alderman	1.25	2.50
C39 Doug Atkins	2.50	5.00
C40 Bruce Bosley UER	1.25	2.50
C41 John Brodie UER	2.50	5.00
C42 Roger Brown	1.25	2.50
C43 Bill Brown	1.25	2.50
C44 Dick Butkus	7.50	15.00
C45 Lee Roy Caffey	1.25	2.50
C46 John David Crow UER	1.75	3.50
C47 Willie Davis	2.50	5.00
C48 Mike Ditka	6.00	12.00
C49 Joe Fortunato	1.25	2.50
C50 John Gordy	1.25	2.50
C51 Deacon Jones	2.50	5.00
C52 Alex Karras	3.75	7.50
C53 Dick LeBeau	1.25	2.50
C54 Jerry Logan	1.25	2.50
C55 John Mackey	2.50	5.00
C56 Ed Meador	1.25	2.50
C57 Tommy McDonald	1.75	3.50
C58 Merlin Olsen	3.75	7.50
C59 Jimmy Orr	1.75	3.50
C60 Jim Parker	2.50	5.00
C61 Dave Parks	1.25	2.50
C62 Walter Rock	1.25	2.50
C63 Gale Sayers	7.50	15.00
C64 Pat Studstill	1.25	2.50
C65 Fran Tarkenton	6.00	12.00
C66 Mick Tingelhoff	1.75	3.50
C67 Bob Vogel	1.25	2.50
C68 Wayne Walker	1.25	2.50
C69 Ken Willard	1.25	2.50
C70 Willie Wood	2.50	5.00
NNO National Saver Sheet	7.50	15.00

1966 Coke Caps Oilers

Please see the 1966 Coke Caps Bills listing for information on this set.

COMPLETE SET (36)	62.50	125.00
C1 Scott Appleton	1.50	3.00
C2 George Allen	2.50	4.00
C3 Don Floyd	1.50	3.00
C4 Ronnie Caveness	1.50	3.00
C5 Jim Norton	1.50	3.00
C6 Jacky Lee	2.50	4.00
C7 George Blanda	7.50	15.00
C8 Tony Banfield	2.50	4.00
C9 George Rice	1.50	3.00
C10 Charley Tolar	2.50	4.00
C11 Bobby Jancik	1.50	3.00
C12 Freddy Glick	1.50	3.00
C13 Ode Burrell	2.50	4.00
C14 Walt Suggs	2.50	4.00
C15 Bob McLeod	1.50	3.00
C16 Johnny Baker	1.50	3.00
C17 Danny Brabham	1.50	3.00
C18 Gary Cutsinger	2.50	4.00
C19 Doug Cline	1.50	3.00
C20 Hoyle Granger	2.50	4.00
C21 Bob Talamini	2.50	4.00
C22 Don Trull	2.50	4.00
C23 Charlie Hennigan	2.50	4.00
C24 Sid Blanks	2.50	4.00
C25 Pat Holmes	1.50	3.00
C26 John Frongillo	1.50	3.00
C27 John Wittenborn	1.50	3.00
C28 George Kinney	1.50	3.00
C29 Charles Frazier	1.50	3.00
C30 Ernie Ladd	4.00	8.00
C31 W.K. Hicks	1.50	3.00
C32 Sonny Bishop	2.50	4.00
C33 Larry Elkins	2.50	4.00
C34 Glen Ray Hines	2.50	4.00
C35 Bobby Maples	2.50	4.00
C36 Oilers Logo	1.50	3.00
NNO Oilers Saver Sheet	15.00	30.00

1966 Coke Caps Packers

Please see the 1966 Coke Caps Bears listing for information on this set.

COMPLETE SET (31)	100.00	175.00
C1 Herb Adderley	4.00	8.00
C2 Lionel Aldridge	2.50	4.00
C3 Bob Long	1.50	3.00
C4 Willie Davis	4.00	8.00
C5 Boyd Dowler	2.50	4.00
C6 Marv Fleming	2.50	4.00
C7 Ken Bowman	2.50	4.00
C8 Tom Brown	1.50	3.00
C9 Doug Hart	1.50	3.00
C10 Steve Wright	1.50	3.00
C11 Bill Anderson	1.50	3.00
C12 Bill Curry	2.50	4.00
C13 Tommy Crutcher	1.50	3.00
C14 Fred Thurston	4.00	8.00
C15 Elijah Pitts	2.50	4.00
C16 Lloyd Voss	1.50	3.00
C17 Lee Roy Caffey	1.50	3.00
C18 Dave Robinson	3.00	5.00
C19 Bart Starr	7.50	15.00
C20 Ray Nitschke	5.00	10.00
C21 Max McGee	2.50	4.00
C22 Don Chandler	2.50	4.00
C23 Rich Marshall	1.50	3.00
C24 Ron Kostelnik	1.50	3.00
C25 Carroll Dale	2.50	4.00
C26 Hank Jordan	4.00	8.00
C27 Bob Jeter	2.50	4.00
C28 Bob Skoronski	1.50	3.00
C29 Jerry Kramer	3.00	6.00
C30 Willie Wood	4.00	8.00
C31 Paul Hornung	7.50	15.00
C32 Forrest Gregg	4.00	8.00
C33 Zeke Bratkowski	2.50	4.00
C34 Tom Moore	2.50	4.00
C35 Jim Taylor	5.00	10.00
C36 Packers Team Emblem	1.50	3.00
NNO Packers Saver Sheet	15.00	30.00

1966 Coke Caps Patriots

Please see the 1966 Coke Caps Bills listing for information on this set.

COMPLETE SET (36)	75.00	125.00
C1 Jon Morris	2.50	4.00
C2 Don Webb	1.50	3.00
C3 Charles Long	1.50	3.00
C4 Tony Romeo	1.50	3.00
C5 Bob Dee	2.50	4.00
C6 Tommy Addison	2.50	4.00
C7 Tom Neville	2.50	4.00
C8 Ron Hall	1.50	3.00
C9 White Graves	1.50	3.00
C10 Ellis Johnson	1.50	3.00
C11 Don Oakes	1.50	3.00
C12 Tom Yewcic	1.50	3.00
C13 Tom Hennessey	1.50	3.00
C14 Jay Cunningham	1.50	3.00
C15 Larry Garron	2.50	4.00
C16 Justin Canale	1.50	3.00
C17 Art Graham	2.50	4.00
C18 Babe Parilli	2.50	4.00
C19 Jim Hunt	2.50	4.00
C20 Karl Singer	1.50	3.00
C21 Houston Antwine	2.50	4.00
C22 Nick Buoniconti	3.00	6.00
C23 John Huarte	2.50	5.00
C24 Gino Cappelletti	2.50	4.00
C25 Chuck Shonta	1.50	3.00
C26 Dick Felt	1.50	3.00
C27 Mike Dukes	2.50	4.00
C28 Larry Eisenhauer	2.50	4.00
C29 Jim Fraser	1.50	3.00
C30 Len St. Jean	2.50	4.00

C31 J.D. Garrett 1.50 3.00
C32 Jim Whalen 1.50 3.00
C33 Jim Nance 2.50 5.00
C34 Dick Arrington 1.50 3.00
C35 Lonnie Farmer 1.50 3.00
C36 Patriots Logo 1.50 3.00
NNO Patriots Saver Sheet 15.00 30.00

1966 Coke Caps Raiders

Please see the 1966 Coke Caps Bills listing for information on this set.

COMPLETE SET (36) 70.00 120.00
C1 Fred Biletnikoff 4.00 8.00
C2 Gus Otto 1.50 3.00
C3 Harry Schuh 1.50 3.00
C4 Ken Herock 1.50 3.00
C5 Claude Gibson 1.50 3.00
C6 Cotton Davidson 2.50 4.00
C7 Cliff Kenney 1.50 3.00
C8 Ben Davidson 3.00 5.00
C9 Roger Hagberg 1.50 3.00
C10 Bob Svihus 1.50 3.00
C11 John R. Williamson 1.50 3.00
C12 Dave Grayson 1.50 3.00
C13 Hewritt Dixon 2.50 4.00
C14 Dave Costa 1.50 3.00
C15 Tom Keating 1.50 3.00
C16 Alan Miller 1.50 3.00
C17 Billy Cannon 3.00 5.00
C18 Wayne Hawkins 2.50 4.00
C19 Warren Powers 1.50 3.00
C20 Joe Labruzzo 1.50 3.00
C21 Dan Conners 1.50 3.00
C22 Jim Otto 3.00 6.00
C23 Clem Daniels 2.50 4.00
C24 Tom Flores 3.00 5.00
C25 Art Powell 2.50 4.00
C26 Larry Todd 1.50 3.00
C27 James Harvey 1.50 3.00
C28 Dan Birdwell 1.50 3.00
C29 Carleton Oats 1.50 3.00
C30 Mike Mercer 1.50 3.00
C31 Pete Banaszak 1.50 3.00
C32 Bill Budness 1.50 3.00
C33 Kent McCloughan 1.50 3.00
C34 Howie Williams 1.50 3.00
C35 Rodger Bird 1.50 3.00
C36 Team Logo 1.50 3.00

1966 Coke Caps Rams

Please see the 1966 Coke Caps Bears listing for information on this set.

COMPLETE SET (36) 62.50 125.00
C1 Tom Mack 4.00 8.00
C2 Tom Moore 1.25 2.50
C3 Bill Munson 2.00 3.50
C4 Bill George 3.00 6.00
C5 Joe Carollo 1.25 2.50
C6 Dick Bass 2.00 3.50
C7 Ken Iman 1.25 2.50
C8 Charlie Cowan 2.00 3.50
C9 Terry Baker RB 3.00 5.00
C10 Don Chuy 1.25 2.50
C11 Jack Pardee 2.00 3.50
C12 Lamar Lundy 2.00 3.50
C13 Bill Anderson 1.25 2.50
C14 Roman Gabriel 3.00 6.00
C15 Roosevelt Grier 3.00 6.00
C16 Billy Truax 2.00 3.50
C17 Merlin Olsen 4.00 8.00
C18 Deacon Jones 4.00 8.00
C19 Joe Scibelli 1.25 2.50
C20 Marlin McKeever 1.25 2.50
C21 Doug Woodlief 1.25 2.50
C22 Chuck Lamson 1.25 2.50
C23 Dan Currie 1.25 2.50
C24 Maxie Baughan 2.00 3.50
C25 Bruce Gossett 2.00 3.50
C26 Les Josephson 2.00 3.50
C27 Ed Meador 1.25 2.50
C28 Anthony Guillory 1.25 2.50
C29 Irv Cross 2.00 3.50
C30 Tommy McDonald 3.00 5.00
C31 Bucky Pope 1.25 2.50
C32 Jack Snow 2.00 3.50
C33 Joe Wendryhoski 1.25 2.50
C34 Clancy Williams 1.25 2.50
C35 Ben Wilson 1.25 2.50
C36 Rams Logo 1.25 2.50
NNO Rams Saver Sheet 15.00 30.00

1966 Coke Caps Redskins

Please see the 1966 Coke Caps Bears listing for information on this set.

COMPLETE SET (36) 75.00 125.00
C1 Don Croftcheck 1.50 3.00
C2 Fred Mazurek 1.50 3.00
C3 Lonnie Sanders 1.50 3.00
C4 Jim Steffen 1.50 3.00
C5 Jim Shofner 2.00 4.00
C6 Bill Hunter 1.50 3.00
C7 Vince Promuto 1.50 3.00
C8 Jerry Smith 1.50 3.00
C9 Pat Richter 1.50 3.00
C10 Preston Carpenter 1.50 3.00
C11 Sam Huff 4.00 8.00
C12 Darrell Dess 1.50 3.00
C13 Jim Snowden 1.50 3.00
C14 Len Hauss 1.50 3.00
C15 Chris Hanburger 2.00 4.00
C16 John Reger 1.50 3.00
C17 George Hughley 1.50 3.00
C18 Rickie Harris 1.50 3.00
C19 Tom Walters 1.50 3.00
C20 Joe Rutgens 1.50 3.00
C21 Carl Kammerer 1.50 3.00
C22 Fran O'Brien 1.50 3.00
C23 Willie Adams 1.50 3.00
C24 Bill Clay 1.50 3.00
C25 Charlie Gogolak 1.50 3.00
C26 Dick Lemay 1.50 3.00
C27 Walter Barnes 1.50 3.00
C28 Sonny Jurgensen 4.00 8.00
C29 John Strohmeyer 1.50 3.00
C30 Charley Taylor 4.00 8.00
C31 Dick Shiner 1.50 3.00
C32 Fred Williams 1.50 3.00
C33 Angelo Coia 1.50 3.00
C34 Ron Snidow 1.50 3.00
C35 Paul Krause 2.50 5.00
C36 Team Logo 1.50 3.00

1966 Coke Caps Steelers

Please see the 1966 Coke Caps Bears listing for information on this set.

COMPLETE SET (36) 70.00 120.00
C1 John Baker 1.50 3.00
C2 Mike Lind 2.50 4.00
C3 Ken Kortas 1.50 3.00
C4 Willie Daniel 1.50 3.00
C5 Roy Jefferson 2.50 4.00
C6 Bob Hohn 1.50 3.00
C7 Dan James 1.50 3.00
C8 Gary Ballman 2.50 4.00
C9 Brady Keys 1.50 3.00
C10 Charley Bradshaw 2.50 4.00
C11 Jim Bradshaw 1.50 3.00
C12 Jim Butler 2.50 4.00
C13 Paul Martha 2.50 4.00
C14 Mike Clark 1.50 3.00
C15 Ray Lemek 1.50 3.00
C16 Clarence Peaks 2.50 4.00
C17 Theron Sapp 1.50 3.00
C18 Ray Mansfield 2.50 4.00
C19 Chuck Hinton 1.50 3.00
C20 Bill Nelsen 2.50 4.00
C21 Rod Breedlove 1.50 3.00
C22 Frank Lambert 1.50 3.00
C23 Ben McGee 1.50 3.00
C24 Myron Pottios 2.50 4.00
C25 John Campbell 1.50 3.00
C26 Andy Russell 2.50 5.00
C27 Mike Sandusky 1.50 3.00
C28 Bob Schmitz 1.50 3.00
C29 Riley Gunnels 1.50 3.00
C30 Clendon Thomas 2.50 4.00
C31 Tommy Wade 1.50 3.00
C32 Dick Hoak 2.50 4.00
C33 Marv Woodson 1.50 3.00
C34 Bob Nichols 1.50 3.00
C35 John Henry Johnson 3.00 6.00
C36 Steelers Logo 1.50 3.00
NNO Steelers Saver Sheet 15.00 30.00

1966 Coke Caps Vikings

Please see the 1966 Coke Caps Bears listing for information on this set.

COMPLETE SET (36) 50.00 100.00
C1 Milt Sunde 1.75 3.50
C2 Don Hansen 1.25 2.50
C3 Jim Marshall 3.00 6.00
C4 Jerry Shay 1.25 2.50
C5 Ken Byers 1.25 2.50
C6 Rip Hawkins 1.25 2.50
C7 John Kirby 1.25 2.50
C8 Roy Winston 1.75 3.50
C9 Ron VanderKelen 1.75 3.50
C10 Jim Lindsey 1.25 2.50
C11 Paul Flatley 1.75 3.50
C12 Larry Bowie 1.25 2.50
C13 Grady Alderman 1.75 3.50
C14 Mick Tingelhoff 2.50 5.00
C15 Lonnie Warwick 1.75 3.50
C16 Fred Cox 1.75 3.50
C17 Bill Brown 1.75 3.50
C18 Ed Sharockman 1.75 3.50
C19 George Rose 1.25 2.50
C20 Paul Dickson 1.25 2.50
C21 Tommy Mason 1.75 3.50
C22 Carl Eller 3.00 6.00
C23 Jim Young 1.25 2.50
C24 Hal Bedsole 1.25 2.50
C25 Karl Kassulke 1.75 3.50
C26 Fran Tarkenton 6.00 12.00
C27 Tom Hall 1.25 2.50
C28 Archie Sutton 1.25 2.50
C29 Jim Phillips 1.25 2.50
C30 Gary Larsen 1.75 3.50
C31 Phil King 1.25 2.50
C32 Bobby Walden 1.25 2.50
C33 Bob Berry 1.75 3.50
C34 Jeff Jordan 1.25 2.50
C35 Lance Rentzel 1.75 3.50
C36 Team Logo 1.25 2.50
NNO Vikings Saver Sheet 15.00 30.00

1971 Coke Caps Packers

This is a 22-player set of Coca-Cola bottle caps featuring members of the Green Bay Packers. They have the Coke logo and a football on the outside, while the inside has the player's face printed in black, with the player's name below the picture. The caps measure approximately 1 1/8" in diameter. A cap-saver sheet was also issued to aid in collecting the bottle caps, and the consumer could turn in his completed sheet to receive various prizes. The caps are unnumbered and therefore listed below alphabetically. The caps were also produced in a twist-off version with red printing.

COMPLETE SET (22) 25.00 50.00
*TWIST OFF CAPS: .6X TO 1.5X
1 Ken Bowman 1.00 2.00
2 John Brockington 1.50 3.00
3 Bob Brown DT .75 1.50
4 Fred Carr 1.00 2.00
5 Jim Carter .75 1.50
6 Carroll Dale 1.00 2.00
7 Ken Ellis 1.00 2.00
8 Gale Gillingham 1.00 2.00
9 Dave Hampton .75 1.50
10 Doug Hart .75 1.50
11 Jim Hill .75 1.50
12 Dick Himes .75 1.50
13 Scott Hunter 1.00 2.00
14 MacArthur Lane 1.50 3.00
15 Bill Lueck .75 1.50
16 Al Matthews .75 1.50
17 Rich McGeorge 1.00 1.50
18 Ray Nitschke 3.00 8.00
19 Francis Peay .75 1.50
20 Dave Robinson 1.50 3.00
21 Alden Roche .75 1.50
22 Bart Starr 7.50 15.00
NNO Saver Sheet 12.50 25.00

1971 Coke Fun Kit Photos

These color photos were released around 1971 with packages of Coca-Cola drinks in packages of four. Each is blankbacked, measures roughly 7" by 10" and includes a color photo of the featured player with his name and team name below the photo. The photos were printed on thin white paper stock. No Coca-Cola logos appear on the photos only that of the NFL Player's Association. Any additions to this list are appreciated.

COMPLETE SET (106) 500.00 800.00
1 Donny Anderson 4.00 8.00
2 Tony Baker 3.00 6.00
3 Pete Barnes 3.00 6.00
4 Lem Barney 4.00 8.00
5 Bill Bergey 4.00 8.00
6 Fred Biletnikoff 10.00 18.00
7 George Blanda 12.00 20.00
8 Lee Bouggess 3.00 6.00
9 Marlin Briscoe 3.00 6.00
10 John Brodie 6.00 12.00
11 Larry Brown 4.00 8.00
12 Willie Brown 4.00 8.00
13 Nick Buoniconti 6.00 12.00
14 Dick Butkus 18.00 30.00
15 Butch Byrd 3.00 6.00
16 Fred Carr 3.00 6.00
17 Virgil Carter 3.00 6.00
18 Gary Collins 3.00 6.00
19 Jack Concannon 3.00 6.00
20 Greg Cook 3.00 6.00
21 Dave Costa 3.00 6.00
22 Paul Costa 3.00 6.00
23 Larry Csonka 15.00 25.00
24 Carroll Dale 3.00 6.00
25 Len Dawson 12.00 20.00
26 Tom Dempsey 3.00 6.00
27 Al Dodd 3.00 6.00
28 Fred Dryer 4.00 8.00
29 Carl Eller 4.00 8.00
30 Mel Farr 3.00 6.00
31 Jim Files 3.00 6.00
32 John Fuqua 3.00 6.00
33 Roman Gabriel 6.00 12.00
34 Gary Garrison 3.00 6.00
35 Walt Garrison 4.00 8.00
36 Joe Greene 12.00 20.00
37 Bob Griese 15.00 25.00
38 John Hadl 6.00 12.00
39 Terry Hanratty 3.00 6.00
40 Jim Hart 6.00 12.00
41 Ben Hawkins 3.00 6.00
42 Alvin Haymond 3.00 6.00
43 Eddie Hinton 3.00 6.00
44 Claude Humphrey 3.00 6.00
45 Rich Jackson 3.00 6.00
46 Charley Johnson 3.00 6.00
47 Ron Johnson 4.00 8.00
48 Walter Johnson 3.00 6.00
49 Deacon Jones 10.00 16.00
50 Lee Roy Jordan 6.00 12.00
51 Joe Kapp 4.00 8.00
52 Leroy Kelly 6.00 12.00
53 Curt Knight 3.00 6.00
54 Charlie Krueger 3.00 6.00
55 Jake Kupp 3.00 6.00
56 MacArthur Lane 3.00 6.00
57 Willie Lanier 6.00 12.00
58 Jerry Levias 3.00 6.00
59 Bob Lilly 10.00 18.00
60 Floyd Little 4.00 8.00
61 Mike Lucci 4.00 8.00
62 Jim Marshall 6.00 12.00
62 Dave Manders 3.00 6.00
63 Tom Matte 4.00 8.00
64 Don Maynard 10.00 18.00
65 Mike McCoy 3.00 6.00
66 Jim Mitchell 3.00 6.00
67 Jon Morris 3.00 6.00
68 Joe Namath 25.00 40.00
69 Jim Nance 4.00 8.00
70 Bill Nelsen 4.00 8.00
72 Tommy Nobis 4.00 8.00
73 Merlin Olsen 10.00 15.00
74 Dave Osborn 3.00 6.00
76 Alan Page 6.00 12.00
77 Preston Pearson 4.00 8.00
78 Mac Percival 3.00 6.00
79 Gerry Philbin 3.00 6.00
80 Jess Phillips 3.00 6.00
81 Tom Regner 3.00 6.00
82 Mel Renfro 6.00 12.00
83 Johnny Robinson 3.00 6.00
84 Tim Rossovich 3.00 6.00
85 Charlie Sanders 3.00 6.00
86 Gale Sayers 18.00 30.00
87 Ron Sellers 3.00 6.00
88 Dennis Shaw 3.00 6.00
89 Bubba Smith 6.00 12.00
90 Charlie Smith 3.00 6.00
91 Jerry Smith 3.00 6.00
92 Matt Snell 4.00 8.00
93 Larry Stallings 3.00 6.00
94 Walt Sweeney 3.00 6.00
95 Fran Tarkenton 12.00 20.00
96 Bruce Taylor 3.00 6.00
97 Charley Taylor 6.00 12.00
98 Otis Taylor 4.00 8.00
99 Bill Thompson 3.00 6.00
100 Johnny Unitas 18.00 30.00
101 Harmon Wages 3.00 6.00
102 Paul Warfield 10.00 18.00
103 Gene Washington 49er 4.00 8.00
104 George Webster 3.00 6.00
104 Gene Washington Vik 3.00 6.00
105 Larry Wilson 6.00 12.00
106 Tom Woodeshick 3.00 6.00

1973 Coke Cap Team Logos

This set of caps were issued in bottles of Coca-Cola in the Milwaukee area in 1973. Each clear plastic liner inside the cap features a black and white NFL team logo. The inside liners were to be attached to a saver sheet that could be partially or completely filled in order to be exchanged for various prizes from Coke.

COMPLETE SET (26) 30.00 60.00
1 Atlanta Falcons 1.00 2.50
2 Baltimore Colts 1.25 3.00
3 Buffalo Bills 1.00 2.50
4 Chicago Bears 1.25 3.00
5 Cincinnati Bengals 1.00 2.50
6 Cleveland Browns 1.25 3.00
7 Dallas Cowboys 2.00 4.00
8 Denver Broncos 1.25 3.00
9 Detroit Lions 1.00 2.50
10 Green Bay Packers 2.00 4.00
11 Houston Oilers 1.00 2.50
12 Kansas City Chiefs 1.00 2.50
13 Los Angeles Rams 1.00 2.50
14 Miami Dolphins 2.00 4.00
15 Minnesota Vikings 1.25 3.00
16 New England Patriots 1.00 2.50
17 New Orleans Saints 1.00 2.50
18 New York Giants 1.00 2.50
19 New York Jets 1.00 2.50
20 Oakland Raiders 2.00 4.00
21 Philadelphia Eagles 1.00 2.50
22 Pittsburgh Steelers 2.00 4.00
23 San Diego Chargers 1.00 2.50
24 San Francisco 49ers 2.00 4.00
25 St. Louis Cardinals 1.00 2.50
26 Washington Redskins 2.00 4.00

1973 Coke Prints

These prints were released around 1973 through retailers as an inducement to their customers to purchase Coke flavored Icee or Frozen Coca-Cola drinks. Each measures roughly 8 1/2" x 11" and features a black and white artist's rendering of the player along with two characatures of football players and a facsimile autograph in blue ink. The backs feature a brief write-up on the player printed in blue ink along with either a large Frozen Coke or Icee ad. Some players were issued with both back versions as noted below. Any additions to this checklist are appreciated.

COMPLETE SET (49) 500.00 800.00
1 Danny Abramowicz 10.00 20.00
2 Julius Adams 10.00 20.00
3 Bobby Anderson 10.00 20.00
4 Dick Anderson 12.50 25.00
5 Terry Bradshaw 40.00 75.00
6 Larry Brown 12.50 25.00
7A Nick Buoniconti 15.00 30.00
7B Nick Buoniconti 15.00 30.00
8 Ken Burrow 12.50 25.00
9 Richard Caster 12.50 25.00
10 Larry Csonka 30.00 50.00
11A Mike Curtis 12.50 25.00
11B Mike Curtis 12.50 25.00
12 John Elliott 10.00 20.00
13 Manny Fernandez 10.00 20.00
14A John Fuqua 12.50 25.00
14B John Fuqua 12.50 25.00
15 Walt Garrison 10.00 20.00
16 Joe Greene 25.00 40.00
17A Bob Griese 30.00 50.00
17B Bob Griese 30.00 50.00
18 Paul Guidry 10.00 20.00
19 Don Hansen 10.00 20.00
20A Ted Hendricks 15.00 30.00
20B Ted Hendricks 15.00 30.00
21 Dave Herman 10.00 20.00
22 J.D. Hill 10.00 20.00
23 Fred Hoaglin 10.00 20.00
24 Jim Houston 10.00 20.00
25A Rich Jackson 10.00 20.00
25B Rich Jackson 10.00 20.00
26 Walter Johnson 10.00 20.00
27A Leroy Kelly 15.00 30.00
27B Leroy Kelly 15.00 30.00
28A Jim Kiick 12.50 25.00
28B Jim Kiick 12.50 25.00
29 George Kunz 10.00 20.00
30 Floyd Little 12.50 25.00
31 Archie Manning 15.00 30.00
32 Milt Morin 10.00 20.00
33A Earl Morrall 12.50 25.00
33B Earl Morrall 12.50 25.00
34 Mercury Morris 15.00 30.00
35 Haven Moses 12.50 25.00
36A John Niland 10.00 20.00
36B John Niland 10.00 20.00
37A Walt Patulski 10.00 20.00
37B Walt Patulski 10.00 20.00
38A Jim Plunkett 15.00 30.00
38B Jim Plunkett 15.00 30.00
39 Andy Russell 12.50 25.00
40 Jake Scott 12.50 25.00
41 Jerry Smith 12.50 25.00
42A Royce Smith 10.00 20.00
42B Royce Smith 10.00 20.00
43 Steve Tannen 10.00 20.00
44 Charley Taylor 15.00 30.00
45 Billy Truax 10.00 20.00
46 Randy Vataha 10.00 20.00
47A Rick Volk 10.00 20.00
47B Rick Volk 10.00 20.00
48 Paul Warfield 15.00 30.00
49 Garo Yepremian 10.00 20.00

1981 Coke Caps

In 1981 Coca-Cola included player's photos underneath Coke caps as part of a redemption contest. Apparently the contest was released around the country (Atlanta, Miami, Green Bay area and Dallas confirmed) using a variety of players in each area. At least three different cap saver sheets were issued for the game in each area. It required the consumer collect Coke, Sprite and/or TAB bottle caps of certain players and attach them to the saver sheets. Sheets 1-3 measure approximately 6 3/8" by 9 1/8" and were divided into three 2 1/8" columns. The top of each column has a hole so that the offer could hang on a soft drink bottle. The first column included a picture of Joe Greene with the quote "Look for me and my friends under caps from Coke and TAB." If one found all seven caps required to complete the yellow middle column, a cash prize of a thousand dollars was awarded. If one completed the five caps required by the third column on the front, the prize was one "Mean" Joe jersey. Finally, the first column on the back required four caps in order to win a player T-shirt. It appears this group always contained four players from the local NFL team. The back also presented official rules for the game. The more difficult caps to find were Steve Fuller and Gene Upshaw from the top two prize levels and one local player from the t-shirt prize level (for example Ed Jones for Dallas). These SPs have not been priced below since it is thought very few exist. Another saver sheet features a grouping of 28-players that had to be completed to be eligible to purchase an NFL t-shirt or Joe Greene replica jersey. Since there were many different bottlers around the country involved in the program, the caps can be found in a number of varieties. Many of the standard bottle cap style can be found in white and/or silver and most, if not all, were issued as twist-off caps. We have checklisted the caps below according to their skip-number and any confirmed additions are appreciated.

1 Joe Greene 1.50 4.00
3 Steve Grogan .75 2.00
4 Rich Wingo .60 1.50
5 Steve Bartkowski .75 2.00
6 Mike Siani .60 1.50
7 Drew Pearson 1.50 4.00
10 Ottis Anderson .75 2.00
11 Dan Fouts 2.00 5.00
12 Wesley Walker .75 2.00
13 Nat Moore .75 2.00
14 Rick Upchurch .75 2.00
17 Craig Morton .75 2.00
22 John Riggins 2.00 5.00
23 Harold Carmichael .75 2.00
25 Kim Bokamper .60 1.50
26 Tommy Kramer .75 2.00
29 Ken Anderson 1.25 3.00
30 Greg Pruitt .75 2.00
31 Alfred Jenkins .60 1.50
32 Curtis Dickey SP
33 Bob Breunig .60 1.50
35 Jack Youngblood .75 2.00
36 Ralph Ortega .60 1.50
38 Gene Upshaw SP
47 Steve Fuller SP
49 Walter Payton 6.00 15.00
50 Pete Johnson .60 1.50
51 Ozzie Newsome .75 2.00
53 Ed Too Tall Jones SP
56 Vagas Ferguson .60 1.50
57 Herman Edwards .60 1.50
64 Jerry Robinson .60 1.50
65 Jimmy Cefalo .60 1.50
67 Mike Bell .60 1.50
71 John James .60 1.50
74 Ezra Johnson .60 1.50
82 Joe Washington .75 2.00
86 Harold Jackson .75 2.00
87 James Lofton 1.50 4.00
91 William Andrews .75 2.00
92 Roger Carr .75 2.00
94 Terdell Middleton .60 1.50
95 A.J. Duhe .60 1.50
96 Jeff Siemon .60 1.50
102 Clarence Harmon .75 2.00
106 Matt Blair .60 1.50
107 Benny Barnes .60 1.50
108 Billy Sims 1.25 3.00
109 Lyle Alzado .75 2.00
111 Jeff Van Note .60 1.50
112 Bruce Laird .60 1.50
115 Fred Dryer .75 2.00
118 Keith Krepfle .60 1.50
122 Tony Franklin .60 1.50
124 Ahmad Rashad .75 2.00
127 Robert Newhouse .60 1.50
128 Archie Griffin .75 2.00
130 Alfred Jackson .60 1.50
131 Mike Barnes .60 1.50
134 Elvis Peacock .60 1.50
135 Bob Baumhower .75 2.00
143 Max Runager .60 1.50
146 Charlie Waters .75 2.00
154 Jewerl Thomas .60 1.50
155 Tim Mazzetti .60 1.50
164 Andy Johnson .60 1.50
165 Delvin Williams .60 1.50
166 Isaac Curtis .60 1.50
169 Ed Simonini .60 1.50
172 Pat Thomas .60 1.50
178 Brad Dusek .60 1.50
180 Leon Gray .60 1.50
184 Aundra Thompson .60 1.50
188 Joe Lavender .60 1.50
191 Reggie Rucker .75 2.00
192 Lynn Dickey .75 2.00
NNO Saver Sheet 3 6.00 15.00
NNO Saver Sheet 28 8.00 20.00
NNO Saver Sheet 1 6.00 15.00

1981 Coke

The 1981 Coca-Cola/Topps football set of 84 standard-size cards contains 11 player cards and one header card each from seven National Football League teams. The cards are actually numbered on the back in alphabetical order within team from 1-11; however in the checklist below the cards are numbered 1-77 alphabetically by team. The backs of the header cards carried an offer to receive one (of four) uncut sheet(s) of the 1981 Topps regular series. Similar in design to the Topps cards of that year, these cards contain the Coke logo on both the front and the back. The key cards in the set are Art Monk and Kellen Winslow, both appearing in their "Rookie" year for cards.

COMPLETE SET (84) 25.00 60.00
1 Raymond Butler .15 .40
2 Roger Carr .25 .60
3 Curtis Dickey .25 .60
4 Nesby Glasgow .15 .40
5 Bert Jones .30 .75
6 Bruce Laird .15 .40
7 Greg Landry .25 .60
8 Reese McCall .15 .40
9 Don McCauley .15 .40
10 Herb Orvis .15 .40
11 Ed Simonini .15 .40
12 Pat Donovan .15 .40
13 Tony Dorsett 2.00 5.00
14 Billy Joe DuPree .25 .60
15 Tony Hill .25 .60
16 Ed Too Tall Jones .40 1.00
17 Harvey Martin .25 .60
18 Robert Newhouse .15 .40
19 Drew Pearson .30 .75
20 Charlie Waters .25 .60
21 Danny White .30 .75
22 Randy White .60 1.50
23 Mike Barber .15 .40
24 Elvin Bethea .30 .75
25 Gregg Bingham .15 .40
26 Robert Brazile .25 .60
27 Ken Burrough .15 .40
28 Rob Carpenter .15 .40
29 Leon Gray .15 .40
30 Vernon Perry .15 .40
31 Mike Renfro .15 .40
32 Carl Roaches .15 .40
33 Morris Towns .15 .40
34 Harry Carson .25 .60
35 Mike Dennis .15 .40
36 Mike Friede .15 .40
37 Earnest Gray .15 .40
38 Dave Jennings .15 .40
39 Gary Jeter .15 .40
40 George Martin .15 .40
41 Roy Simmons .15 .40
42 Phil Simms 1.25 3.00
43 Billy Taylor .15 .40
44 Brad Van Pelt .15 .40
45 Ottis Anderson .40 1.00
46 Rush Brown .15 .40
47 Theotis Brown .15 .40
48 Dan Dierdorf .30 .75
49 Mel Gray .25 .60
50 Ken Greene .15 .40
51 Jim Hart .25 .60
52 Doug Marsh .15 .40
53 Wayne Morris .15 .40
54 Pat Tilley .15 .40
55 Roger Wehrli .30 .75
56 Rolf Benirschke .25 .60
57 Fred Dean .25 .60
58 Dan Fouts 1.00 2.50
59 John Jefferson .25 .60
60 Gary Johnson .15 .40
61 Charlie Joiner .50 1.25
62 Louie Kelcher .15 .40
63 Chuck Muncie .25 .60
64 Doug Wilkerson .15 .40
65 Clarence Williams RB .15 .40
66 Kellen Winslow 2.00 5.00
67 Coy Bacon .15 .40
68 Wilbur Jackson .15 .40
69 Karl Lorch .15 .40
70 Rich Milot .15 .40
71 Art Monk 3.00 8.00
72 Mark Moseley .15 .40
73 Mike Nelms .15 .40
74 Lemar Parrish .15 .40
75 Joe Theismann .60 1.50
76 Ricky Thompson .15 .40
77 Joe Washington .25 .60
NNO Baltimore Colts .15 .40
NNO Dallas Cowboys .15 .40
NNO Houston Oilers .15 .40
NNO New York Giants .15 .40
NNO St. Louis Cardinals .15 .40
NNO San Diego Chargers .15 .40
NNO Redskins Header Card .15 .40

1993 Coke Monsters of the Gridiron

Sponsored by Coca-Cola, this 30-card standard-size set was released as a complete set at Super Bowl Card Show V, January 27-30, 1994 in Atlanta. The set was available to the first 10,000 fans at the redemption booth in exchange for ten wrappers from any 1993 NFL-licensed trading card packs. The fronts feature borderless color studio shots of NFL players posed in their uniforms. The players are also dressed in horror costumes and made up to look like "monsters." Three of the cards (10, 19, and 20) feature fanciful color paintings of the players instead of photos. The white back carries the player's name and "monstrous" nickname at the top, followed below by career highlights. The cards are numbered on the back. Television ads featuring Randall Cunningham helped promote this set. The actual in-store promotion consisted of two randomly selected cards included in specially marked multi-packs of Coca-Cola Classic, diet Coke, Caffeine-free diet Coke, and Sprite. An "instant win" scratch-off game piece inside the same multi-packs could entitle the collector to win various prizes, including a gold foil edition of the entire set. Also collectors could obtain a random group of five cards by sending in a proof-of-purchase from any specially marked two-liter bottle. Reportedly more than 100 million collector cards were available nationwide. The promotion ran from Sept. 19 until Halloween, or while supplies lasted. Although the cards carry a 1994 copyright line date, they are considered a 1993 issue.

COMPLETE SET (30) 16.00 40.00
1 Title Card .30 .75
2 Cornelius Bennett .50 1.25
3 Terrell Buckley .30 .75
4 Tony Casillas .30 .75
5 Reggie Cobb .30 .75
6 Marco Coleman .30 .75
7 Shane Conlan .30 .75
8 Randall Cunningham .75 2.00
9 Chris Doleman .30 .75
10 Steve Emtman .30 .75
11 Harold Green .30 .75
12 Michael Haynes .50 1.25
13 Garrison Hearst 1.60 4.00
14 Craig Heyward .30 .75
15 Rickey Jackson .30 .75
16 Joe Jacoby .30 .75
17 Sean Jones .30 .75
18 Cortez Kennedy .50 1.25
19 Howie Long .75 2.00
20 Ronnie Lott .75 2.00
21 Karl Mecklenburg .30 .75
22 Neil O'Donnell .50 1.25
23 Tom Rathman .30 .75
24 Junior Seau .75 2.00
25 Emmitt Smith 6.00 15.00
26 Pat Swilling .30 .75
27 Lawrence Taylor .75 2.00
28 Derrick Thomas .75 2.00
29 Andre Tippett .30 .75
30 Eric Turner .30 .75

1994 Coke Monsters of the Gridiron

This 31-card set was sponsored by Coca-Cola and features color player photos dressed in horror costumes and made to look like monsters. The backs carry a head photo of the player with player information. The set was primarily distributed at the 1995 Super Bowl Card Show VI in Miami in exchange for 10 wrappers from any 1994 NFL card set. A Gold parallel version of the cards was also distributed.

COMPLETE SET (31) 20.00 40.00
*GOLD CARDS: 1X TO 2.5X BASIC CARDS
1 Eric Swann .40 1.00
2 Jessie Tuggle .25 .60
3 Cornelius Bennett .40 1.00
4 Carolina Panthers Mascot .60 1.50
5 Chris Zorich .25 .60
6 Dan Wilkinson .25 .60
7 Eric Turner .25 .60
8 Emmitt Smith 6.00 12.00
9 Steve Atwater .25 .60
10 Pat Swilling .25 .60
11 Sean Jones .25 .60
12 Ray Childress .25 .60
13 Marshall Faulk 4.00 10.00
14 Jacksonville Jaguars Mascot .60 1.50
15 Derrick Thomas .60 1.50
16 Chester McGlockton .25 .60
17 Shane Conlan .25 .60
18 Marco Coleman .25 .60
19 John Randle .40 1.00
20 Bruce Armstrong .25 .60
21 Renaldo Turnbull .25 .60
22 Jumbo Elliott .25 .60
23 Ronnie Lott .60 1.50
24 Randall Cunningham .60 1.50
25 Neil O'Donnell .60 1.50
26 Junior Seau .60 1.50
27 Tom Rathman .25 .60
28 Cortez Kennedy .40 1.00
29 Hardy Nickerson .25 .60
30 Ken Harvey UER .25 .60
NNO Title Card CL .25 .60

1994 Collector's Choice

This standard-size 384-card set features color action player photos. Cards were issued in 12, 13 and 20-card packs. One gold or silver parallel card was inserted per pack. Also issued was a 36-card Spanish promo set and a 260-card full Spanish set. Rookie Cards include Derrick Alexander, Marshall Faulk, William Floyd, Greg Hill, Charles Johnson, Errict Rhett, Darnay Scott and Heath Shuler. A Joe Montana Promo card was produced and priced below.

COMPLETE SET (384) 7.50 20.00
1 Antonio Langham RC .02 .10
2 Aaron Glenn RC .08 .25
3 Sam Adams RC .02 .10
4 Dewayne Washington RC .02 .10
5 Dan Wilkinson RC .02 .10
6 Bryant Young RC .15 .40
7 Aaron Taylor RC .01 .05
8 Willie McGinest RC .08 .25
9 Trev Alberts RC .02 .10
10 Jamir Miller RC .02 .10
11 John Thierry RC .01 .05
12 Heath Shuler RC .08 .25
13 Trent Dilfer RC .50 1.25
14 Marshall Faulk RC 2.00 5.00
15 Greg Hill RC .08 .25
16 William Floyd RC .08 .25
17 Chuck Levy RC .01 .05
18 Charlie Garner RC .50 1.25
19 Mario Bates RC .08 .25
20 Donnell Bennett RC .08 .25
21 LeShon Johnson RC .02 .10
22 Calvin Jones RC .01 .05
23 Darnay Scott RC .20 .50
24 Charles Johnson RC .08 .25
25 Johnnie Morton RC .20 .50
26 Shante Carver RC .01 .05
27 Derrick Alexander WR RC .08 .25
28 David Palmer RC .08 .25
29 Ryan Yarborough RC .01 .05
30 Errict Rhett RC .08 .25
31 James Washington I93 .01 .05
32 Sterling Sharpe I93 .01 .05
33 Drew Bledsoe I93 .08 .25
34 Eric Allen I93 .01 .05
35 Jerome Bettis I93 .08 .25
36 Joe Montana I93 .25 .60
37 John Carney I93 .01 .05
38 Emmitt Smith I93 .20 .50
39 Chris Warren I93 .08 .25
40 Reggie Brooks I93 .01 .05
41 Gary Brown I93 .01 .05
42 Tim Brown I93 .02 .10
43 Eric Pegram I93 .01 .05
44 Ronald Moore I93 .01 .05
45 Jerry Rice I93 .15 .40
46 Ricky Watters TE .02 .10
47 Joe Montana TE .25 .60
48 Reggie Brooks TE .01 .05
49 Rick Mirer TE .08 .25
50 Rocket Ismail TE .02 .10
51 Curtis Conway TE .02 .10
52 Junior Seau TE .08 .25
53 Mark Carrier DB TE .01 .05
54 Ronnie Lott TE .02 .10
55 Marcus Allen TE .08 .25
56 Michael Irvin TE .08 .25
57 Bennie Blades .01 .05
58 Randal Hill .01 .05
59 Brian Blades .02 .10
60 Russell Maryland .01 .05
61 Jim Kelly .08 .25
62 Arthur Marshall .01 .05
63 Webster Slaughter .01 .05
64 Dave Krieg .02 .10
65 Steve Jordan .01 .05
66 Neil O'Donnell .08 .25
67 Andre Reed .02 .10
68 Mike Croel .01 .05
69 Al Smith .01 .05
70 Joe Montana .60 1.50
71 Randall McDaniel .02 .10
72 Greg Lloyd .02 .10
73 Thomas Smith .01 .05
74 Glyn Milburn .02 .10
75 Lorenzo White .01 .05
76 Neil Smith .02 .10
77 John Randle .02 .10
78 Rod Woodson .02 .10
79 Russell Maryland .01 .05
80 Rodney Peete .01 .05
81 Jackie Harris .01 .05
82 James Jett .01 .05
83 Rodney Hampton .02 .10
84 Bill Romanowski .01 .05
85 Ken Norton Jr. .02 .10
86 Barry Sanders .50 1.25
87 Johnny Holland .01 .05
88 Terry McDaniel .01 .05
89 Greg Jackson .01 .05
90 Dana Stubblefield .02 .10
91 Jay Novacek .02 .10
92 Chris Spielman .02 .10
93 Ken Ruettgers .01 .05
94 Greg Robinson .01 .05
95 Mark Jackson .01 .05
96 John Taylor .02 .10
97 Roger Harper .01 .05
98 Jerry Ball .01 .05
99 Keith Byars .01 .05
100 Morten Andersen .01 .05
101 Eric Allen .01 .05
102 Marion Butts .01 .05
103 Michael Haynes .02 .10
104 Rob Burnett .01 .05
105 Marco Coleman .01 .05
106 Derek Brown RBK .01 .05
107 Andy Harmon .01 .05
108 Darren Carrington .01 .05
109 Bobby Hebert .01 .05
110 Mark Carrier WR .02 .10
111 Bryan Cox .01 .05
112 Toi Cook .01 .05
113 Tim Harris .01 .05
114 John Friesz .02 .10
115 Neal Anderson .01 .05
116 Jerome Bettis .15 .40
117 Bruce Armstrong .01 .05
118 Brad Baxter .01 .05
119 Johnny Bailey .01 .05
120 Brian Blades .02 .10
121 Mark Carrier DB .01 .05
122 Shane Conlan .01 .05
123 Drew Bledsoe .25 .60
124 Chris Burkett .01 .05
125 Steve Beuerlein .02 .10
126 Ferrell Edmunds .01 .05
127 Curtis Conway .08 .25
128 Troy Drayton .01 .05
129 Vincent Brown .01 .05
130 Boomer Esiason .02 .10
131 Larry Centers .08 .25
132 Carlton Gray .01 .05
133 Chris Miller .01 .05
134 Eric Metcalf .02 .10
135 Mark Higgs .01 .05
136 Tyrone Hughes .02 .10
137 Randall Cunningham .08 .25
138 Ronnie Harmon .01 .05
139 Andre Rison .02 .10
140 Eric Turner .01 .05
141 Terry Kirby .08 .25
142 Eric Martin .01 .05
143 Seth Joyner .01 .05
144 Stan Humphries .02 .10
145 Deion Sanders .15 .40
146 Vinny Testaverde .02 .10
147 Dan Marino .60 1.50
148 Renaldo Turnbull .01 .05
149 Herschel Walker .02 .10
150 Anthony Miller .02 .10
151 Richard Dent .02 .10
152 Jim Everett .02 .10
153 Ben Coates .02 .10
154 Jeff Lageman .01 .05
155 Garrison Hearst .08 .25
156 Kelvin Martin .01 .05
157 Dante Jones .01 .05
158 Sean Gilbert .01 .05
159 Leonard Russell .01 .05
160 Ronnie Lott .02 .10
161 Randal Hill .01 .05
162 Rick Mirer .08 .25
163 Alonzo Spellman .01 .05
164 Todd Lyght .01 .05
165 Chris Slade .01 .05
166 Johnny Mitchell .01 .05
167 Ronald Moore .01 .05
168 Eugene Robinson .01 .05
169 Chris Hinton .01 .05
170 Dan Footman .01 .05
171 Keith Jackson .01 .05
172 Rickey Jackson .01 .05
173 Heath Sherman .01 .05
174 Chris Mims .01 .05
175 Erric Pegram .01 .05
176 Leroy Hoard .01 .05
177 O.J.McDuffie .08 .25
178 Wayne Martin .01 .05
179 Clyde Simmons .01 .05
180 Leslie O'Neal .01 .05
181 Mike Pritchard .01 .05
182 Michael Jackson .02 .10
183 Scott Mitchell .02 .10
184 Lorenzo Neal .01 .05
185 William Thomas .01 .05
186 Junior Seau .08 .25
187 Chris Gedney .01 .05
188 Tim Lester .01 .05
189 Sam Gash .01 .05
190 Johnny Johnson .01 .05
191 Chuck Cecil .01 .05
192 Cortez Kennedy .02 .10
193 Jim Harbaugh .08 .25
194 Roman Phifer .01 .05
195 Pat Harlow .01 .05
196 Rob Moore .02 .10
197 Gary Clark .02 .10
198 Jon Vaughn .01 .05
199 Craig Heyward .02 .10
200 Michael Stewart .01 .05
201 Greg McMurtry .01 .05
202 Brian Washington .01 .05
203 Ken Harvey .01 .05
204 Chris Warren .02 .10
205 Bruce Smith .08 .25
206 Tom Rouen .01 .05
207 Cris Dishman .01 .05
208 Keith Cash .01 .05
209 Carlos Jenkins .01 .05
210 Levon Kirkland .01 .05
211 Pete Metzelaars .01 .05
212 Shannon Sharpe .02 .10
213 Cody Carlson .01 .05
214 Derrick Thomas .08 .25
215 Emmitt Smith .50 1.25
216 Robert Porcher .01 .05
217 Sterling Sharpe .02 .10
218 Anthony Smith .01 .05
219 Mike Sherrard .01 .05
220 Tom Rathman .01 .05
221 Nate Newton .01 .05
222 Pat Swilling .01 .05
223 George Teague .01 .05
224 Greg Townsend .01 .05
225 Eric Guliford RC .02 .10
226 Leroy Thompson .01 .05
227 Thurman Thomas .08 .25
228 Dan Williams .01 .05
229 Bubba McDowell .01 .05
230 Tracy Simien .01 .05
231 Scottie Graham RC .02 .10
232 Eric Green .01 .05
233 Phil Simms .02 .10
234 Ricky Watters .02 .10
235 Kevin Williams WR .02 .10
236 Brett Perriman .02 .10
237 Reggie White .08 .25
238 Steve Wisniewski .01 .05
239 Mark Collins .01 .05
240 Steve Young .30 .75
241 Steve Tovar .01 .05
242 Jason Belser .01 .05
243 Ray Seals .01 .05
244 Earnest Byner .01 .05
245 Ricky Proehl .01 .05
246 Rich Miano .01 .05
247 Alfred Williams .01 .05
248 Ray Buchanan UER .01 .05
249 Hardy Nickerson .02 .10
250 Brad Edwards .01 .05
251 Jerrol Williams .01 .05
252 Marvin Washington .01 .05
253 Tony McGee .01 .05
254 Jeff George .08 .25
255 Ron Hall .01 .05
256 Tim Johnson .01 .05
257 Willie Roaf .01 .05
258 Corwin Brown RC .01 .05
259 Ricardo McDonald .01 .05
260 Jeff Herrod .01 .05
261 Demetrius DuBose .01 .05
262 Ricky Sanders .01 .05
263 John L. Williams .01 .05
264 John Lynch .08 .25
265 Lance Gunn .01 .05
266 Jessie Hester .01 .05
267 Mark Wheeler .01 .05
268 Chip Lohmiller .01 .05
269 Eric Swann .02 .10
270 Byron Evans .01 .05
271 Gary Plummer .01 .05
272 Roger Duffy RC .01 .05
273 Irv Smith .01 .05
274 Todd Collins .01 .05
275 Robert Blackmon .01 .05
276 Reggie Roby .01 .05
277 Russell Copeland .01 .05
278 Simon Fletcher .01 .05
279 Ernest Givins .02 .10
280 Tim Barnett .01 .05
281 Chris Doleman .01 .05
282 Jeff Graham .01 .05
283 Kenneth Davis .01 .05
284 Vance Johnson .01 .05
285 Haywood Jeffires .02 .10
286 Todd McNair .01 .05
287 Daryl Johnston .02 .10
288 Ryan McNeil .01 .05
289 Terrell Buckley .01 .05

290 Ethan Horton .01 .05
291 Corey Miller .01 .05
292 Marc Logan .01 .05
293 Lincoln Coleman RC .01 .05
294 Derrick Moore .01 .05
295 LeRoy Butler .01 .05
296 Jeff Hostetler .02 .10
297 Qadry Ismail .08 .25
298 Andre Hastings .02 .10
299 Henry Jones .01 .05
300 John Elway .60 1.50
301 Warren Moon .08 .25
302 Willie Davis .02 .10
303 Vencie Glenn .01 .05
304 Kevin Greene .02 .10
305 Marcus Buckley .01 .05
306 Tim McDonald .01 .05
307 Michael Irvin .08 .25
308 Herman Moore .08 .25
309 Brett Favre .60 1.50
310 Rocket Ismail .02 .10
311 Jarrod Bunch .01 .05
312 Don Beebe .01 .05
313 Steve Atwater .01 .05
314 Gary Brown .01 .05
315 Marcus Allen .08 .25
316 Terry Allen .02 .10
317 Chad Brown .01 .05
318 Cornelius Bennett .02 .10
319 Rod Bernstine .01 .05
320 Greg Montgomery .01 .05
321 Kimble Anders .02 .10
322 Charles Haley .02 .10
323 Mel Gray .01 .05
324 Edgar Bennett .08 .25
325 Eddie Anderson .01 .05
326 Derek Brown TE .01 .05
327 Steve Bono .02 .10
328 Alvin Harper .02 .10
329 Willie Green .01 .05
330 Robert Brooks .08 .25
331 Patrick Bates .01 .05
332 Anthony Carter .02 .10
333 Barry Foster .01 .05
334 Bill Brooks .01 .05
335 Jason Elam .02 .10
336 Ray Childress .01 .05
337 J.J. Birden .01 .05
338 Cris Carter .15 .40
339 Deon Figures .01 .05
340 Carlton Bailey .01 .05
341 Brent Jones .02 .10
342 Troy Aikman UER .30 .75
343 Rodney Holman .01 .05
344 Tony Bennett .01 .05
345 Tim Brown .08 .25
346 Michael Brooks .01 .05
347 Martin Harrison .01 .05
348 Jerry Rice .30 .75
349 John Copeland .01 .05
350 Kerry Cash .01 .05
351 Reggie Cobb .01 .05
352 Brian Mitchell .01 .05
353 Derrick Fenner .01 .05
354 Roosevelt Potts .01 .05
355 Courtney Hawkins .01 .05
356 Carl Banks .01 .05
357 Harold Green .01 .05
358 Steve Emtman .01 .05
359 Santana Dotson .02 .10
360 Reggie Brooks .02 .10
361 Terry Obee .01 .05
362 David Klingler .01 .05
363 Quentin Coryatt .01 .05
364 Craig Erickson .01 .05
365 Desmond Howard .02 .10
366 Carl Pickens .02 .10
367 Lawrence Dawsey .01 .05
368 Henry Ellard .02 .10
369 Shaun Gayle .01 .05
370 David Lang .01 .05
371 Anthony Johnson .02 .10
372 Darnell Walker RC .01 .05
373 Pepper Johnson .01 .05
374 Kurt Gouveia .01 .05
375 Louis Oliver .01 .05
376 Lincoln Kennedy .01 .05
377 Anthony Pleasant .01 .05
378 Irving Fryar .02 .10
379 Carolina Panthers Logo .08 .25
380 Jacksonville Jaguars Logo .01 .05
381 Sterling Sharpe CL UER .02 .10
382 Dan Marino ART CL .08 .25
383 Jerry Rice ART CL .08 .25
384 Joe Montana ART CL .08 .25
P19 Joe Montana Promo .75 2.00

1994 Collector's Choice Gold

*STARS: 10X TO 25X BASIC CARDS
*RCs: 6X TO 15X BASIC CARDS
ONE GOLD OR SILVER PER PACK

1994 Collector's Choice Silver

COMPLETE SET (384) 35.00 80.00
*STARS: 1.2X TO 3X BASIC CARDS
*RCS: 1X TO 2X BASIC CARDS
ONE GOLD OR SILVER PER F
TWO SILV/GOLD PER SPECIAL RETAIL

1994 Collector's Choice Crash the Game

Upper Deck produced the first release of Crash the Game in 1994. Each player was produced with two different colored foils on the card front (blue in hobby packs, green in retail packs). If the player featured scored or passed for a touchdown on one, two or three of the game dates included on the cardback, the card could be exchanged for a parallel prize card featuring bronze, silver, or gold foil. We've listed the cards below along with the prize level (B, G, or S) category, if any, that could be redeemed. The expiration date for the contest was April 30, 1995.

COMP.BLUE SET (30) 15.00 40.00
COMP.GREEN SET (30) 15.00 40.00
BLUE FOIL INSERTED IN HOBBY PACKS
GREEN FOIL INSERTED IN RETAIL PACKS
COMP.BRONZE SET (30) 5.00 12.00
*BRONZES: .1X to .3X BASIC INSERTS
ONE SET PER BRONZE WINNER CARD
COMP.SILVER SET (30) 6.00 15.00
*SILVERS: .15X to .4X BASIC INSERTS
ONE SET PER SILVER WINNER CARD
COMP.GOLD SET (30) 10.00 25.00
*GOLDS: .25X to .6X BASIC INSERTS
ONE SET PER GOLD WINNER CARD
C1B Steve Young WIN G 1.00 2.50
C1G Steve Young WIN G 1.00 2.50
C2B Troy Aikman WIN S 1.00 2.50
C2G Troy Aikman WIN B 1.00 2.50
C3B Rick Mirer WIN B .30 .75
C3G Rick Mirer WIN B .30 .75
C4B Trent Dilfer WIN B .50 1.25
C4G Trent Dilfer NO WIN .50 1.25
C5B Dan Marino WIN G 2.00 5.00
C5G Dan Marino WIN S 2.00 5.00
C6B John Elway WIN S 2.00 5.00
C6G John Elway WIN S 2.00 5.00
C7B Heath Shuler WIN S .08 .25
C7G Heath Shuler NO WIN .08 .25
C8B Joe Montana WIN G 2.00 5.00
C8G Joe Montana WIN S 2.00 5.00
C9B D.Bledsoe UER WIN G .75 2.00
C9G D.Bledsoe UER WIN G .75 2.00
C10B Warren Moon WIN S .30 .75
C10G Warren Moon WIN S .30 .75
C11B Marshall Faulk WIN B 2.00 5.00
C11G Marshall Faulk WIN S 2.00 5.00
C12B Th.Thomas WIN B .30 .75
C12G Th.Thomas WIN B .30 .75
C13B Barry Foster WIN B .05 .15
C13G Barry Foster WIN B .05 .15
C14B Gary Brown NO WIN .05 .15
C14G Gary Brown NO WIN .05 .15
C15B Emmitt Smith WIN G 1.50 4.00
C15G Emmitt Smith WIN G 1.50 4.00
C16B Barry Sanders WIN B 1.50 4.00
C16G Barry Sanders WIN B 1.50 4.00
C17B R.Hampton WIN B .10 .30
C17G R.Hampton WIN B .10 .30
C18B Jerome Bettis WIN B .50 1.25
C18G Jerome Bettis NO WIN .50 1.25
C19B Ricky Watters WIN B .10 .30
C19G R.Watters NO WIN .10 .30
C20B Ronald Moore WIN B .05 .15
C20G Ronald Moore WIN B .05 .15
C21B Jerry Rice WIN G 1.00 2.50
C21G Jerry Rice NO WIN 1.00 2.50
C22B Andre Rison WIN G .10 .30
C22G Andre Rison WIN B .10 .30
C23B Michael Irvin NO WIN .30 .75
C23G Michael Irvin WIN S .30 .75
C24B Sterling Sharpe WIN S .10 .30
C24G Sterling Sharpe WIN B .10 .30
C25B Sh.Sharpe NO WIN .10 .30
C25G Sh.Sharpe NO WIN .10 .30
C26B D.Scott NO WIN .20 .50
C26G D.Scott WIN B .20 .50
C27B Andre Reed WIN S .10 .30
C27G Andre Reed WIN B .10 .30
C28B Tim Brown NO WIN .30 .75
C28G Tim Brown WIN S .30 .75
C29B Ch.Johnson WIN B .08 .25
C29G Ch.Johnson NO WIN .08 .25
C30B Irving Fryar NO WIN .10 .30
C30G Irving Fryar NO WIN .10 .30

1994 Collector's Choice Then and Now

This eight card set could be obtained by sending in a Then and Now exchange card. The theme of the set is portraying an active player with one from the same team from yesteryear. Horizontally designed, the fronts feature a color player photo superimposed over holographic background that contains the former player. The back contains a write-up about each player along with a small photo of both.

COMPLETE SET (8) 4.00 10.00
ONE SET PER TRADE CARD BY MAIL
1 Jerome Bettis .50 1.25
Dickerson
2 Tim Brown .40 1.00
F.Biletnikoff
3 Joe Montana .75 2.00
Len Dawson
4 Steve Young 1.00 2.50
Joe Montana
5 Dan Marino 1.25 3.00
Bob Griese
6 Rick Mirer .30 .75
Jim Zorn
NNO Joe Montana Header .75 2.00
NNO Eric Dickerson CL .30 .75

1994 Collector's Choice Spanish Promos NNO

This standard-size set was issued to preview the Collector's Choice Spanish series. The cards are nearly identical to their American counterparts, with the exception that the player profile on the backs have been shortened to create space for the Spanish translation. Also these cards are unnumbered with just a solid black oval where the card number should be. They are checklisted below alphabetically.

COMPLETE SET (36) 36.00 90.00
1 Troy Aikman 6.00 15.00
2 Marcus Allen 2.00 5.00
3 Terry Allen 1.20 3.00
4 Kimble Anders .80 2.00
5 Eddie Anderson .50 1.25
6 Steve Atwater .50 1.25
7 Carlton Bailey .50 1.25
8 Patrick Bates .50 1.25
9 Don Beebe .50 1.25
10 Cornelius Bennett .80 2.00
11 Edgar Bennett .80 2.00
12 Tony Bennett .50 1.25
13 Rod Bernstine .50 1.25
14 J.J.Birden .50 1.25
15 Steve Bono .50 1.25
16 Bill Brooks .50 1.25
17 Michael Brooks .50 1.25
18 Robert Brooks .80 2.00
19 Chad Brown .50 1.25
20 Derek Brown TE .50 1.25
21 Gary Brown .50 1.25
22 Tim Brown 2.00 5.00
23 Anthony Carter .50 1.25
24 Cris Carter 3.00 6.00
25 Ray Childress .50 1.25
26 Jason Elam .50 1.25
27 Deon Figures .50 1.25
28 Barry Foster .50 1.25
29 Mel Gray .50 1.25
30 Willie Green .50 1.25
31 Charles Haley .50 1.25
32 Alvin Harper .50 1.25
33 Martin Harrison .50 1.25
34 Rodney Holman .50 1.25
35 Brent Jones .50 1.25
36 Greg Montgomery .50 1.25

1994 Collector's Choice Spanish

Produced by Upper Deck for sale in Mexico, this 260-card set measures the standard size. The set starts with the subsets Rookie Class 1994 (1-30) and Images of 93 (31-45), followed by 215-regular cards. Each cardback is written in both English and Spanish.

COMPLETE SET (260) 32.00 80.00
1 Antonio Langham .10 .30
2 Aaron Glenn .20 .50
3 Sam Adams .10 .30
4 Dewayne Washington .10 .30
5 Dan Wilkinson .10 .30
6 Bryant Young .10 .30
7 Aaron Taylor .07 .20
8 Willie McGinest .20 .50
9 Trev Alberts .10 .30
10 Jamir Miller .07 .20
11 John Thierry .07 .20
12 Heath Shuler .20 .50
13 Trent Dilfer 2.00 5.00
14 Marshall Faulk 10.00 20.00
15 Greg Hill .10 .30
16 William Floyd .10 .30
17 Chuck Levy .07 .20
18 Charlie Garner .20 .50
19 Mario Bates .10 .30
20 Donnell Bennett .07 .20
21 LeShon Johnson .10 .30
22 Calvin Jones .07 .20
23 Darnay Scott .20 .50
24 Charles Johnson .20 .50
25 Johnnie Morton .20 .50
26 Shante Carver .07 .20
27 Derrick Alexander WR .20 .50
28 David Palmer .10 .30
29 Ryan Yarborough .07 .20
30 Errict Rhett .40 1.00
31 James Washington I93 .07 .20
32 Sterling Sharpe I93 .07 .20
33 Drew Bledsoe I93 1.00 2.50
34 Eric Allen I93 .07 .20
35 Jerome Bettis I93 .50 1.25
36 Joe Montana I93 2.50 5.00
37 John Carney I93 .07 .20
38 Emmitt Smith I93 1.60 4.00
39 Chris Warren I93 .20 .50
40 Reggie Brooks I93 .07 .20
41 Gary Brown I93 .07 .20
42 Tim Brown I93 .20 .50
43 Eric Pegram I93 .07 .20
44 Ronald Moore I93 .07 .20
45 Jerry Rice I93 1.25 3.00
46 Don Beebe .07 .20
47 Steve Atwater .07 .20
48 Gary Brown .07 .20
49 Marcus Allen .20 .50
50 Terry Allen .10 .30
51 Chad Brown .07 .20
52 Cornelius Bennett .10 .30
53 Rod Bernstine .07 .20
54 Greg Montgomery .07 .20
55 Kimble Anders .07 .20
56 Charles Haley .10 .30
57 Mel Gray .07 .20
58 Edgar Bennett .10 .30
59 Eddie Anderson .07 .20
60 Derek Brown TE .07 .20
61 Jim Kelly .20 .50
62 Arthur Marshall .07 .20
63 Webster Slaughter .07 .20
64 Dave Krieg .10 .30
65 Steve Jordan .07 .20
66 Neil O'Donnell .10 .30
67 Andre Reed .10 .30
68 Mike Croel .07 .20
69 Al Smith .07 .20
70 Joe Montana 3.20 8.00
71 Randall McDaniel .07 .20
72 Greg Lloyd .10 .30
73 Thomas Smith .07 .20
74 Glyn Milburn .10 .30
75 Lorenzo White .07 .20
76 Neil Smith .10 .30
77 John Randle .10 .30
78 Rod Woodson .10 .30
79 Russell Maryland .07 .20
80 Rodney Peete .07 .20
81 Jackie Harris .07 .20
82 James Jett .07 .20
83 Rodney Hampton .10 .30
84 Bill Romanowski .07 .20
85 Ken Norton .10 .30
86 Barry Sanders 3.20 8.00
87 Johnny Holland .07 .20
88 Terry McDaniel .07 .20
89 Greg Jackson .07 .20
90 Dana Stubblefield .10 .30
91 Jay Novacek .10 .30
92 Chris Spielman .10 .30
93 Ken Ruettgers .07 .20
94 Greg Robinson .07 .20
95 Mark Jackson .07 .20
96 John Taylor .10 .30
97 Roger Harper .07 .20
98 Jerry Ball .07 .20
99 Keith Byars .07 .20
100 Morten Andersen .07 .20
101 Eric Allen .07 .20
102 Marion Butts .07 .20
103 Michael Haynes .10 .30
104 Rob Burnett .07 .20
105 Marco Coleman .07 .20
106 Derek Brown RBK .07 .20
107 Andy Harmon .07 .20
108 Darren Carrington .07 .20
109 Bobby Hebert .07 .20
110 Mark Carrier WR .10 .30
111 Bryan Cox .07 .20
112 Toi Cook .07 .20
113 Tim Harris .07 .20
114 John Friesz .10 .30
115 Neal Anderson .07 .20
116 Jerome Bettis 1.00 2.50
117 Bruce Armstrong .07 .20
118 Brad Baxter .07 .20
119 Johnny Bailey .07 .20
120 Brian Blades .10 .30
121 Mark Carrier DB UER .07 .20
122 Shane Conlan .07 .20
123 Drew Bledsoe 2.00 5.00
124 Chris Burkett .07 .20
125 Steve Beuerlein .10 .30
126 Ferrell Edmunds .07 .20
127 Curtis Conway .20 .50
128 Troy Drayton .07 .20
129 Vincent Brown .07 .20
130 Boomer Esiason .10 .30
131 Larry Centers .10 .30
132 Carlton Gray .07 .20
133 Chris Miller .07 .20
134 Eric Metcalf .10 .30
135 Mark Higgs .07 .20
136 Tyrone Hughes .10 .30
137 Randall Cunningham .20 .50
138 Ronnie Harmon .07 .20
139 Andre Rison .10 .30
140 Eric Turner .07 .20
141 Terry Kirby .10 .30
142 Eric Martin .07 .20
143 Seth Joyner .07 .20
144 Stan Humphries .10 .30
145 Deion Sanders 1.00 2.50
146 Vinny Testaverde .10 .30
147 Dan Marino 3.20 8.00
148 Renaldo Turnbull .07 .20
149 Herschel Walker .10 .30
150 Anthony Miller .10 .30
151 Richard Dent .10 .30
152 Jim Everett .10 .30
153 Ben Coates .10 .30
154 Jeff Lageman .07 .20
155 Garrison Hearst .80 2.00
156 Kelvin Martin .07 .20
157 Dante Jones .07 .20
158 Sean Gilbert .07 .20
159 Leonard Russell .07 .20
160 Ronnie Lott .10 .30
161 Randal Hill .07 .20
162 Rick Mirer .20 .50
163 Alonzo Spellman .07 .20
164 Todd Lyght .07 .20
165 Chris Slade .07 .20
166 Johnny Mitchell .07 .20
167 Ronald Moore .07 .20
168 Eugene Robinson .07 .20
169 John Copeland .07 .20
170 Kerry Cash .07 .20
171 Reggie Cobb .07 .20
172 Brian Mitchell .07 .20
173 Derrick Fenner .07 .20
174 Roosevelt Potts .07 .20
175 Courtney Hawkins .07 .20
176 Carl Banks .07 .20
177 Harold Green .07 .20
178 Steve Emtman .07 .20
179 Santana Dotson .10 .30
180 Reggie Brooks .10 .30
181 Terry Obee .07 .20
182 David Klingler .07 .20
183 Quentin Coryatt .07 .20
184 Craig Erickson .07 .20
185 Desmond Howard .10 .30
186 Carl Pickens .10 .30
187 Lawrence Dawsey .07 .20
188 Henry Ellard .07 .20
189 Shaun Gayle .07 .20
190 David Lang .07 .20
191 Anthony Johnson .10 .30
192 Darnell Walker .07 .20
193 Pepper Johnson .07 .20
194 Kurt Gouveia .07 .20
195 Louis Oliver .07 .20
196 Lincoln Kennedy .07 .20
197 Anthony Pleasant .07 .20
198 Irving Fryar .10 .30
199 Steve Bono .10 .30
200 Alvin Harper .10 .30
201 Willie Green .07 .20
202 Robert Brooks .20 .50
203 Patrick Bates .07 .20
204 Anthony Carter .10 .30
205 Bruce Smith .20 .50
206 Tom Rouen .07 .20
207 Cris Dishman .07 .20
208 Keith Cash .07 .20
209 Carlos Jenkins .07 .20
210 Levon Kirkland .07 .20
211 Pete Metzelaars .07 .20
212 Shannon Sharpe .10 .30
213 Cody Carlson .07 .20
214 Derrick Thomas .20 .50
215 Emmitt Smith 2.40 6.00
216 Robert Porcher .07 .20
217 Sterling Sharpe .10 .30
218 Anthony Smith .07 .20
219 Mike Sherrard .07 .20
220 Tom Rathman .07 .20
221 Nate Newton .07 .20
222 Pat Swilling .07 .20
223 George Teague .07 .20
224 Greg Townsend .07 .20
225 Eric Guliford .07 .20
226 Leroy Thompson .07 .20
227 Thurman Thomas .20 .50
228 Dan Williams .07 .20
229 Bubba McDowell .07 .20
230 Tracy Simien .07 .20
231 Scottie Graham .10 .30
232 Eric Green .07 .20
233 Phil Simms .10 .30
234 Ricky Watters .10 .30
235 Kevin Williams WR .10 .30
236 Brett Perriman .10 .30
237 Reggie White .20 .50
238 Steve Wisniewski .07 .20
239 Mark Collins .07 .20
240 Steve Young 1.60 4.00
241 Barry Foster .07 .20
242 Bill Brooks .07 .20
243 Jason Elam .10 .30
244 Ray Childress .07 .20
245 J.J. Birden .07 .20
246 Cris Carter .20 .50
247 Deon Figures .07 .20
248 Carlton Bailey .07 .20
249 Brent Jones .10 .30
250 Troy Aikman 2.00 5.00
251 Rodney Holman .07 .20
252 Tony Bennett .07 .20
253 Tim Brown .20 .50
254 Michael Brooks .07 .20
255 Martin Harrison .07 .20
256 Carolina Panthers Logo .20 .50
257 Jacksonville Jaguars Logo .07 .20
258 Dan Marino ART CL .50 1.25
259 Jerry Rice ART CL .40 1.00
260 Joe Montana CL UER .50 1.25

1994-95 Collector's Choice Crash the Super Bowl XXI

Upper Deck produced eight standard-size cards specifically for Super Bowl XXIX. These cards were available at the NFL Experience card show in Miami, in various hobby publications and through the nationally-syndicated "Sports Collector's Radio Network." The set features four players from the AFC champion San Diego Chargers (1-4) and four from the NFC San Francisco 49ers (5-8). If the player featured scored a touchdown in the Super Bowl, the card was redeemable for a special nine-card set. The redemption prize set featured the eight players in the set plus a Super Bowl "header" card. The redemption prize cards' text were rewritten to present a summary of that player's Super Bowl performance.

COMPLETE SET (9) 4.00 10.00
*PRIZES: .4X TO 1X BASIC INSERTS
1 Steve Young WIN 1.00 2.50
2 Jerry Rice WIN 1.20 3.00
3 Brent Jones .30 .75
4 Ricky Watters WIN .40 1.00
5 Stan Humphries WIN .30 .75
6 Natrone Means WIN .40 1.00
7 Ronnie Harmon .30 .75
8 Tony Martin WIN .40 1.00
NNO Header Card .30 .75

1995 Collector's Choice

This 348-card standard-size set features color action player photos with white borders on the front. Subsets include 1995 Rookie Class (1-30, sequenced in draft order), Did You Know (31-50), Jacksonville Jaguars expansion selections (331-338) and Carolina Panthers picks (339-346). The 12-card packs had a suggested retail price of .99 cents. Each pack contained a Player's Club parallel insert card. Inserted one per hobby boxes was a Platinum Player's Club card. Hobby dealers ordering cases directly from Upper Deck received 30 silver Crash the Game cards for their first case ordered and 90 silver Crash the Game cards if they ordered two cases. Rookie Cards in this set include Ki-Jana Carter, Kerry Collins, Joey Galloway, Steve McNair, Rashaan Salaam, J.J.Stokes and Michael Westbrook. A Joe Montana Promo card was produced and priced below.

COMPLETE SET (348) 10.00 20.00
1 Ki-Jana Carter RC .08 .25
2 Tony Boselli RC .08 .25
3 Steve McNair RC 1.00 2.50
4 Michael Westbrook RC .08 .25
5 Kerry Collins RC .60 1.50
6 Kevin Carter RC .08 .25
7 Mike Mamula RC .01 .05
8 Joey Galloway RC .50 1.25
9 Kyle Brady RC .08 .25
10 J.J. Stokes RC .08 .25
11 Derrick Alexander DE RC .01 .05
12 Warren Sapp RC .50 1.25
13 Mark Fields RC .08 .25
14 Tyrone Wheatley RC .40 1.00
15 Napoleon Kaufman RC .40 1.00
16 James O. Stewart RC .40 1.00
17 Luther Elliss RC .01 .05
18 Rashaan Salaam RC .02 .10
19 Ty Law RC .50 1.25
20 Mark Bruener RC .02 .10
21 Derrick Brooks RC .50 1.25
22 Christian Fauria RC .02 .10
23 Ray Zellars RC .02 .10
24 Todd Collins RC .30 .75
25 Sherman Williams RC .01 .05
26 Frank Sanders RC .08 .25
27 Rodney Thomas RC .02 .10
28 Rob Johnson RC .30 .75
29 Steve Stenstrom RC .01 .05
30 James A.Stewart RC .01 .05
31 Barry Sanders DYK .25 .60
32 Marshall Faulk DYK .15 .40
33 Darnay Scott DYK .02 .10
34 Joe Montana DYK .25 .60
35 Michael Irvin DYK .02 .10
36 Jerry Rice DYK .15 .40
37 Errict Rhett DYK .02 .10
38 Drew Bledsoe DYK .08 .25
39 Dan Marino DYK .25 .60
40 Terance Mathis DYK .01 .05
41 Natrone Means DYK .02 .10
42 Tim Brown DYK .02 .10
43 Steve Young DYK .10 .30
44 Mel Gray DYK .01 .05
45 Jerome Bettis DYK .08 .25
46 Aeneas Williams DYK .01 .05
47 Charlie Garner DYK .02 .10
48 Deion Sanders DYK .08 .25
49 Ken Harvey DYK .01 .05
50 Emmitt Smith DYK .20 .50
51 Andre Reed .02 .10
52 Sean Dawkins .02 .10
53 Irving Fryar .02 .10
54 Vincent Brisby .01 .05
55 Rob Moore .02 .10
56 Carl Pickens .02 .10
57 Vinny Testaverde .02 .10
58 Webster Slaughter .01 .05
59 Eric Green .01 .05
60 Anthony Miller .02 .10
61 Lake Dawson .02 .10
62 Tim Brown .08 .25
63 Stan Humphries .02 .10
64 Rick Mirer .02 .10
65 Gary Clark .01 .05
66 Troy Aikman .30 .75
67 Mike Sherrard .01 .05
68 Fred Barnett .02 .10
69 Henry Ellard .02 .10
70 Terry Allen .02 .10
71 Jeff Graham .01 .05
72 Herman Moore .08 .25
73 Brett Favre .60 1.50
74 Trent Dilfer .08 .25
75 Derek Brown RBK .01 .05
76 Andre Rison .02 .10
77 Flipper Anderson .01 .05
78 Jerry Rice .30 .75
79 Thurman Thomas .08 .25
80 Marshall Faulk .40 1.00
81 O.J. McDuffie .08 .25
82 Ben Coates .02 .10
83 Johnny Mitchell .01 .05
84 Darnay Scott .02 .10
85 Derrick Alexander WR .08 .25
86 Micheal Barrow .01 .05
87 Charles Johnson .02 .10
88 John Elway .60 1.50
89 Willie Davis .02 .10
90 James Jett .02 .10
91 Mark Seay .02 .10
92 Brian Blades .02 .10
93 Ricky Proehl .01 .05
94 Charles Haley .02 .10
95 Chris Calloway .01 .05
96 Calvin Williams .02 .10
97 Ethan Horton .01 .05
98 Cris Carter .08 .25
99 Curtis Conway .08 .25
100 Lomas Brown .01 .05
101 Edgar Bennett .02 .10
102 Craig Erickson .01 .05
103 Jim Everett .01 .05
104 Terance Mathis .02 .10
105 Wayne Gandy .01 .05
106 Brent Jones .01 .05
107 Bruce Smith .08 .25
108 Roosevelt Potts .01 .05
109 Dan Marino .60 1.50
110 Michael Timpson .01 .05
111 Boomer Esiason .02 .10
112 David Klingler .02 .10
113 Eric Metcalf .02 .10
114 Lorenzo White .01 .05
115 Neil O'Donnell .02 .10
116 Shannon Sharpe .02 .10
117 Joe Montana .60 1.50
118 Jeff Hostetler .02 .10
119 Ronnie Harmon .01 .05
120 Chris Warren .02 .10
121 Randal Hill .01 .05
122 Alvin Harper .01 .05
123 Dave Brown .02 .10
124 Randall Cunningham .08 .25
125 Heath Shuler .02 .10
126 Jake Reed .02 .10
127 Donnell Woolford .01 .05
128 Scott Mitchell .02 .10
129 Reggie White .08 .25
130 Lawrence Dawsey .01 .05
131 Michael Haynes .02 .10
132 Bert Emanuel .08 .25
133 Troy Drayton .01 .05
134 Merton Hanks .01 .05
135 Jim Kelly .08 .25
136 Tony Bennett .01 .05
137 Terry Kirby .02 .10
138 Drew Bledsoe .20 .50
139 Johnny Johnson .01 .05
140 Dan Wilkinson .02 .10
141 Leroy Hoard .01 .05
142 Gary Brown .01 .05
143 Barry Foster .02 .10
144 Shane Dronett .01 .05
145 Marcus Allen .08 .25
146 Harvey Williams .01 .05
147 Tony Martin .02 .10
148 Rod Stephens .01 .05
149 Ronald Moore .01 .05
150 Michael Irvin .08 .25
151 Rodney Hampton .02 .10
152 Herschel Walker .02 .10
153 Reggie Brooks .02 .10
154 Qadry Ismail .02 .10
155 Chris Zorich .01 .05
156 Barry Sanders .50 1.25
157 Sean Jones .01 .05
158 Errict Rhett .02 .10
159 Tyrone Hughes .02 .10
160 Jeff George .02 .10
161 Chris Miller .01 .05
162 Steve Young .25 .60
163 Cornelius Bennett .02 .10
164 Trev Alberts .01 .05
165 J.B. Brown .01 .05
166 Marion Butts .01 .05
167 Aaron Glenn .01 .05
168 James Francis .01 .05
169 Eric Turner .01 .05
170 Darryll Lewis .01 .05
171 John L. Williams .01 .05
172 Simon Fletcher .01 .05
173 Neil Smith .02 .10
174 Chester McGlockton .02 .10
175 Natrone Means .02 .10
176 Michael Sinclair .01 .05
177 Larry Centers .02 .10
178 Daryl Johnston .02 .10
179 Dave Meggett .01 .05
180 Greg Jackson .01 .05
181 Ken Harvey .01 .05
182 Warren Moon .02 .10
183 Steve Walsh .01 .05
184 Chris Spielman .02 .10
185 Bryce Paup .02 .10
186 Courtney Hawkins .01 .05
187 Willie Roaf .01 .05
188 Chris Doleman .01 .05
189 Jerome Bettis .08 .25
190 Ricky Watters .02 .10
191 Henry Jones .01 .05
192 Quentin Coryatt .02 .10
193 Bryan Cox .01 .05
194 Kevin Turner .01 .05
195 Siupeli Malamala .01 .05
196 Louis Oliver .01 .05
197 Rob Burnett .01 .05
198 Cris Dishman .01 .05
199 Byron Bam Morris .01 .05
200 Ray Crockett .01 .05
201 Jon Vaughn .01 .05
202 Nolan Harrison .01 .05
203 Leslie O'Neal .02 .10
204 Sam Adams .01 .05
205 Eric Swann .02 .10
206 Jay Novacek .02 .10
207 Keith Hamilton .01 .05
208 Charlie Garner .08 .25
209 Tom Carter .01 .05
210 Henry Thomas .01 .05
211 Lewis Tillman .01 .05
212 Pat Swilling .01 .05
213 Terrell Buckley .01 .05
214 Hardy Nickerson .01 .05
215 Mario Bates .02 .10
216 D.J. Johnson .01 .05
217 Robert Young .01 .05
218 Dana Stubblefield .02 .10
219 Jeff Burris .01 .05
220 Floyd Turner .01 .05
221 Troy Vincent .01 .05
222 Willie McGinest .02 .10
223 James Hasty .01 .05
224 Jeff Blake RC .25 .60
225 Stevon Moore .01 .05
226 Ernest Givins .01 .05
227 Greg Lloyd .02 .10
228 Steve Atwater .01 .05
229 Dale Carter .02 .10
230 Terry McDaniel .01 .05
231 John Carney .01 .05
232 Cortez Kennedy .02 .10
233 Clyde Simmons .01 .05
234 Emmitt Smith .50 1.25
235 Thomas Lewis .02 .10
236 William Fuller .01 .05
237 Ricky Ervins .01 .05
238 John Randle .02 .10
239 John Thierry .01 .05
240 Mel Gray .01 .05
241 George Teague .01 .05
242 Charles Wilson Bucs .01 .05
243 Joe Johnson .01 .05
244 Chuck Smith .01 .05
245 Sean Gilbert .02 .10
246 Bryant Young .02 .10
247 Bucky Brooks .01 .05
248 Ray Buchanan .01 .05
249 Tim Bowens .01 .05
250 Vincent Brown .01 .05
251 Marcus Turner .01 .05
252 Derrick Fenner .01 .05
253 Antonio Langham .01 .05
254 Cody Carlson .01 .05
255 Kevin Greene .02 .10
256 Leonard Russell .01 .05
257 Donnell Bennett .02 .10
258 Rocket Ismail .02 .10
259 Alfred Pupunu RC .01 .05
260 Eugene Robinson .01 .05
261 Seth Joyner .01 .05
262 Darren Woodson .02 .10
263 Phillippi Sparks .01 .05
264 Andy Harmon .01 .05
265 Brian Mitchell .01 .05
266 Fuad Reveiz .01 .05
267 Mark Carrier DB .01 .05
268 Johnnie Morton .02 .10
269 LeShon Johnson .02 .10
270 Eric Curry .01 .05
271 Quinn Early .02 .10
272 Elbert Shelley .01 .05
273 Roman Phifer .01 .05
274 Ken Norton Jr. .02 .10
275 Steve Tasker .02 .10
276 Jim Harbaugh .02 .10
277 Aubrey Beavers .01 .05
278 Chris Slade .01 .05
279 Mo Lewis .01 .05
280 Alfred Williams .01 .05
281 Michael Dean Perry UER .01 .05
282 Marcus Robertson .01 .05
283 Rod Woodson .02 .10
284 Glyn Milburn .01 .05
285 Greg Hill .02 .10
286 Rob Fredrickson .01 .05
287 Junior Seau .08 .25
288 Rick Tuten .01 .05
289 Aeneas Williams .01 .05
290 Darrin Smith .01 .05
291 John Booty .01 .05
292 Eric Allen .01 .05
293 Reggie Roby .01 .05
294 David Palmer .02 .10
295 Trace Armstrong .01 .05
296 Dave Krieg .01 .05
297 Robert Brooks .08 .25
298 Brad Culpepper RC .01 .05
299 Wayne Martin .01 .05
300 Craig Heyward .02 .10
301 Isaac Bruce .15 .40
302 Deion Sanders .15 .40
303 Matt Darby .01 .05
304 Kirk Lowdermilk .01 .05
305 Bernie Parmalee .02 .10
306 Leroy Thompson .01 .05
307 Ronnie Lott .02 .10
308 Steve Tovar .01 .05
309 Michael Jackson .02 .10
310 Al Smith .01 .05
311 Chad Brown .02 .10
312 Elijah Alexander .01 .05
313 Kimble Anders .02 .10
314 Anthony Smith .01 .05
315 Andre Coleman .01 .05
316 Terry Wooden .01 .05
317 Garrison Hearst .08 .25
318 Russell Maryland .01 .05
319 Michael Brooks .01 .05
320 Bernard Williams .01 .05
321 Andre Collins .01 .05
322 Dewayne Washington .02 .10
323 Raymont Harris .01 .05
324 Brett Perriman .02 .10
325 LeRoy Butler .01 .05
326 Santana Dotson .01 .05
327 Irv Smith .01 .05
328 Ron George .01 .05
329 Marquez Pope .01 .05
330 William Floyd .02 .10
331 Mickey Washington .01 .05
332 Keith Goganious .01 .05
333 Derek Brown TE .01 .05
334 Steve Beuerlein .02 .10
335 Reggie Cobb .01 .05
336 Jeff Lageman .01 .05
337 Kelvin Martin .01 .05
338 Darren Carrington .01 .05
339 Mark Carrier WR .02 .10
340 Willie Green .01 .05
341 Frank Reich .01 .05
342 Don Beebe .01 .05
343 Lamar Lathon .01 .05
344 Tim McKyer .01 .05
345 Pete Metzelaars .01 .05
346 Vernon Turner .01 .05
347 Dan Marino CL .08 .25
348 Joe Montana CL .08 .25
PC1 Joe Montana Promo .40 1.00
P1 Joe Montana Promo .40 1.00

1995 Collector's Choice Player's Club

COMPLETE SET (348) 25.00 50.00
*STARS: 1X TO 2.5X BASIC CARDS
*RCs: .75X TO 2X BASIC CARDS
ONE PER PACK

1995 Collector's Choice Player's Club Platinum

COMPLETE SET (348) 200.00 400.00
*STARS: 8X TO 20X BASIC CARDS
*RCs: 4X TO 10X BASIC CARDS
STATED ODDS 1:35

1995 Collector's Choice Crash The Game

Thirty offensive players are included in this set. Each player has three different cards with different dates in foil layering on the front for a total of 90 cards. If the player scored or passed for a touchdown, the cards could be redeemed (with $3 check or money order) for a special prize set. Each of the 90 cards were issued in packs in Silver and Gold variations. Silver cards were inserted one every five hobby packs, while the gold varieties were included one every 50 packs. The expiration date for the contest was February 29, 1996. The fronts feature posed player shots against a yellow background, surrounded by multi-colored borders. The backs contain contest information. The 30-card prize sets were issued in four ways: silver foil with "silver set" down the left hand side, silver foil with "touchdown" down the left side, gold foil with "gold set" down the left hand side, and gold foil with "touchdown" down the left side.

COMPLETE SILVER SET (90) 20.00 50.00
SILVER ODDS 1:5 HOB/RET, 1:1 JUM
*GOLD INSERTS: 1.2X TO 3X SILVER
GOLD STATED ODDS 1:50 HOB/RET
COMP.SILVER REDEMPT.(30) 4.00 8.00
*SILVER SET REDEMPTION: .2X TO .5X
*SILVER TD REDEMPTION: .8X TO 2X
COMP.GOLD REDEMPT.(30) 15.00 40.00
*GOLD SET REDEMPTION: .6X TO 1.5X
*GOLD TD REDEMPTION: 2.5X TO 6X
C1A Dan Marino 1.00 2.00
C1B Dan Marino 10/8 W 1.00 2.00
C1C Dan Marino 11/20 W 1.00 2.00
C2A John Elway 1.00 2.00
C2B John Elway 11/12 W 1.00 2.00
C2C John Elway 11/19 W 1.00 2.00
C3A Kerry Collins .25 .60
C3B Kerry Collins 10/29 W .25 .60
C3C Kerry Collins 11/12 W .25 .60
C4A Stan Humphries .02 .10
C4B Stan Humphries 10/9 W .02 .10
C4C Stan Humphries 11/5 W .02 .10
C5A Steve Young .30 .75
C5B Steve Young 10/15 W .30 .75
C5C Steve Young 11/5 L .30 .75
C6A Brett Favre 1.00 2.00
C6B Brett Favre 9/24 W 1.00 2.00
C6C Brett Favre 10/29 W 1.00 2.00
C7A Troy Aikman .40 1.00
C7B Troy Aikman 10/1 L .40 1.00
C7C Troy Aikman 11/12 L .40 1.00
C8A Warren Moon .02 .10
C8B Warren Moon 10/8 W .02 .10
C8C Warren Moon 11/23 W .02 .10
C9A Drew Bledsoe .25 .60
C9B Drew Bledsoe 9/17 L .25 .60
C9C Drew Bledsoe 10/23 W .25 .60
C10A Steve McNair .60 1.25
C10B Steve McNair 10/29 L .60 1.25
C10C Steve McNair 11/19 L .60 1.25
C11A Chris Warren .02 .10
C11B Chris Warren 11/12 W .02 .10
C11C Chris Warren 11/26 L .02 .10
C12A Natrone Means .02 .10
C12B Natrone Means 10/9 W .02 .10
C12C Natrone Means 11/27 L .02 .10
C13A Thurman Thomas .10 .30
C13B Thurman Thomas 10/22 L .10 .30
C13C Thurman Thomas 12/3 L .10 .30
C14A Barry Sanders .75 1.50
C14B Barry Sanders 10/22 L .75 1.50
C14C Barry Sanders 11/23 W .75 1.50
C15A Emmitt Smith .75 1.50
C15B Emmitt Smith 10/29 W .75 1.50
C15C Emmitt Smith 11/19 W .75 1.50
C16A Jerome Bettis .10 .30
C16B Jerome Bettis 10/22 L .10 .30
C16C Jerome Bettis 11/19 L .10 .30
C17A Ki-Jana Carter .05 .15
C17B Ki-Jana Carter 10/1 L .05 .15
C17C Ki-Jana Carter 11/12 L .05 .15
C18A Napoleon Kaufman .20 .50
C18B Napoleon Kaufman 11/5 L .20 .50
C18C Napoleon Kaufman 12/3 L .20 .50
C19A Marshall Faulk .60 1.25
C19B Marshall Faulk 10/1 W .60 1.25
C19C Marshall Faulk 11/5 W .60 1.25
C20A Errict Rhett .02 .10
C20B Errict Rhett 10/22 W .02 .10
C20C Errict Rhett 11/19 W .02 .10
C21A Cris Carter .10 .30
C21B Cris Carter 10/30 L .10 .30
C21C Cris Carter 11/19 W .10 .30
C22A Jerry Rice .40 1.00
C22B Jerry Rice 10/1 W .40 1.00
C22C Jerry Rice 11/26 W .40 1.00
C23A Tim Brown .10 .30
C23B Tim Brown 10/16 L .10 .30
C23C Tim Brown 11/27 L .10 .30
C24A Andre Reed .02 .10
C24B Andre Reed 10/29 L .02 .10
C24C Andre Reed 11/26 L .02 .10
C25A Andre Rison .02 .10
C25B Andre Rison 10/2 L .02 .10
C25C Andre Rison 10/22 L .02 .10
C26A Ben Coates .02 .10
C26B Ben Coates 10/29 L .02 .10
C26C Ben Coates 11/19 L .02 .10
C27A Michael Irvin .10 .30
C27B Michael Irvin 10/15 L .10 .30
C27C Michael Irvin 11/6 W .10 .30
C28B Terance Mathis 10/1 L .02 .10
C28C Terance Mathis 10/12 L .02 .10
C29A Michael Westbrook .10 .30
C29B Michael Westbrook 10/22 L .10 .30
C29C Michael Westbrook 11/19 W .10 .30
C30A Herman Moore .10 .30
C30B Herman Moore 10/15 W .10 .30
C30C Herman Moore 11/12 L .10 .30

1995 Collector's Choice Dan Marino Chronicles

This ten card set was inserted at a rate of one per series one specially marked retail pack and chronicles Dan Marino highlights. Card fronts contain an aqua border with the title "Marino" in gold foil at the top of the card. The feat being highlighted on the card is also written in gold foil on the card fronts. Card backs contain a commentary on the highlight.

COMPLETE SET (10) 6.00 15.00
COMMON CARD (DM1-DM10) .60 1.50
ONE PER SPECIAL RETAIL PACK
DM&J Dan Marino 1.50 4.00

1995 Collector's Choice Joe Montana Chronicles

This ten card set was inserted at a rate of one per series two specially marked retail pack and chronicles Joe Montana highlights. Card fronts contain a red border with the title "Montana" in gold foil at the top of the card. The feat being highlighted on the card is also written in gold foil on the card fronts. Card backs contain a commentary on the highlight. Cards are numbered with a "JM" prefix.

COMPLETE SET (10) 6.00 15.00
COMMON CARD (JM1-JM10) .60 1.50
ONE PER SPECIAL RETAIL PACK
JM8J Joe Montana Jumbo 1.50 4.00

1995 Collector's Choice Update

This 225 card update set was produced late in the 1995 season and the format of the cards are identical to the regular Collector's Choice release. Subsets include Rookie Collection cards featuring first-year players, Expansion cards from Carolina and Jacksonville and The Key cards describing what NFL teams do to stop "key" players on each NFL team. Rookie Cards not included in the first issue include Terrell Davis, Curtis Martin, Kordell Stewart and Tamarick Vanover. Each card has a "U" prefix. Also, a parallel of the cards were randomly inserted in packs as Silver and Gold versions.

COMPLETE SET (225) 7.50 15.00
U111 Mark Brunell .40 1.00

1995 Collector's Choice Update Gold

COMPLETE SET (90) 200.00 400.00
*STARS: 8X TO 20X BASIC CARDS
*RCs: 5X TO 12X BASIC CARDS
U1-U60 STATED ODDS 1:35
U61-U90 STATED ODDS 1:52

1995 Collector's Choice Update Silver

COMPLETE SET (90) 30.00 60.00
*STARS: 1.2X TO 3X BASIC CARDS
*RCs: 1X TO 2.5X BASIC CARDS
U1-U60 STATED ODDS 1:3
U61-U90 STATED ODDS 1:5

1995 Collector's Choice Update Crash the Playoffs

This 18 card set was randomly inserted in packs at a rate of one in five for silver and one in 50 for gold. Each card contains five players representing the same position: quarterback, running back or receiver. If any of the players pictured on the card threw or caught a touchdown pass, or rushed or returned a kick for a touchdown during the 1995 NFL Playoffs and Super Bowl XXX, the card could be exchanged as a winner. Winning cards could be redeemed for the Post Season Heroics set in either Gold foil or silver foil depending on which foil the winning Crash card featured. The expiration date was 2/29/1996.

COMPLETE SET (18) 7.50 20.00
SILVER STATED ODDS 1:5
GOLD STATED ODDS 1:50
CP1 AFC East QB 1.50 3.00
Marino
CP2 AFC Cent QB 1.00 2.50
McNair
Blake
CP3 AFC West QB 1.00 2.50
Elway
CP4 NFC East QB .60 1.50
Aikman
CP5 NFC Central QB 1.50 3.00
Favre
CP6 NFC West QB .60 1.50
Young
Coll
CP7 AFC East RB 1.00 2.50
Martin
CP8 AFC Central RB .20 .50
CP9 AFC West RB .75 2.00
T.Davis
CP10 NFC East RB .30 .75
E.Smith
CP11 NFC Central WR .20 .50
CP12 NFC West RB L .20 .50
CP13 AFC East WR W .20 .50
CP14 AFC Central WR L .20 .50
CP15 AFC West WR .40 1.00
Galloway
CP16 NFC East WR .30 .75
Westbrook
CP17 NFC Central RB 1.50 3.00
Sanders
CP18 NFC West WR .60 1.50
Rice

1995 Collector's Choice Update Post Season Heroics

This 20 card set was available only by redeeming a winning Collectors Choice Update Crash the Playoffs silver or gold card. The cards are similar to regular Collector's Choice cards with the phrase "Post Season Heroics" written across the top of the card in either silver or gold foil. Card backs include regular season and playoff statistics.

COMPLETE SET (20) 5.00 12.00
*GOLDS: 1.2X TO 3X BASIC INSERTS
1 Stan Humphries .07 .20
2 Natrone Means .15 .40
3 Tony Martin .40 1.00
4 Neil O'Donnell .15 .40
5 Byron Bam Morris .07 .20
6 Charles Johnson .15 .40
7 Jim Harbaugh .40 1.00
8 Darick Holmes .15 .40
9 Sean Dawkins .07 .20
10 Steve Young .75 1.50
11 Craig Heyward .07 .20
12 Jerry Rice 1.00 2.00
13 Brett Favre 2.00 4.00
14 Edgar Bennett .15 .40
15 Robert Brooks .15 .40
16 Troy Aikman 1.00 2.00
17 Emmitt Smith 1.50 3.00
18 Michael Irvin .40 1.00
19 Byron Bam Morris .07 .20
20 Larry Brown .07 .20

1995 Collector's Choice Update Stick-Ums

Randomly inserted in packs at a rate of one per pack, this 90-card set features a trading-card size sticker picturing the NFL's top stars. The Stick-Ums were available in three versions - one with four players on a card, one with three players and a team helmet and one with a larger photo of a star player. Stick-Ums Collector books were available through an on-pack offer for $2 and two Collector's Choice Update wrappers.

COMPLETE SET (90) 6.00 12.00
ONE PER HOB.PACK/TWO PER RET.PACK
1 Jeff George .08 .25
2 Kerry Collins .08 .25
3 Jerome Bettis .08 .25
4 Mario Bates .05 .15
5 Steve Young .15 .40
6 Rashaan Salaam .08 .25
7 Barry Sanders .30 .75
8 Brett Favre .40 1.00
9 Warren Moon .08 .25
10 Errict Rhett .05 .15
11 Emmitt Smith .30 .75
12 Rodney Hampton .05 .15
13 Ricky Watters .05 .15
14 Garrison Hearst .08 .25
15 Michael Westbrook .08 .25
16 Jim Kelly .08 .25
17 Marshall Faulk .25 .60
18 Dan Marino .40 1.00
19 Drew Bledsoe .10 .30
20 Kyle Brady .05 .15
21 Ki-Jana Carter .05 .15
22 Andre Rison .05 .15
23 Steve McNair .25 .60
24 James O. Stewart .08 .25
25 Byron Bam Morris .02 .10
26 John Elway .40 1.00
27 Marcus Allen .08 .25
28 Tim Brown .08 .25
29 Natrone Means .05 .15
30 Chris Warren .05 .15
31 Mathis .05 .15
Carr WR
C.Mill
Ever
32 Bruce .05 .15
Metz.
Stubb.
Emanuel
33 J.Rice .10 .30
Doleman
Reich
Brown
34 S.Young .10 .30
Tugg.
Phif.
Hughes
35 S.Mills .02 .10
artr
M.Haynes
Jnes
36 Metcalf .08 .25
T.Poole
Pinkney
37 Andersen .02 .10
Kasay
Dray
38 J.J.Stokes .08 .25
Gilbert
Fields
39 Christian .02 .10
Roaf
Norton
40 Heyward .02 .10
Turnbull
Floyd
41 Har .08 .25
H.Moore
Benn
C.Cart
42 Grahm .08 .25
H.Th
R.White
Dilfer
43 Conwy .08 .25
Mtch
Rob.Smth
Harp
44 Walsh .02 .10
Jones
Q.Ism
Nicker
45 Blades .02 .10
Jurko
Randle
Hawk
46 Thierry .02 .10
L.Elliss
Butler
47 Lions .08 .25
Morton
Brooks
Reed
48 L.Johns .02 .10
Washing
J.Harris
49 Woolford .02 .10
J.A.Stewart
Curry
50 M.Carrier DB .02 .10
Spiel
Sapp
51 Aikman .10 .30
Sherr.
Barnett
Krieg
52 Irvin .05 .15
Calloway
C.Will
Ellard
53 Shuler .08 .25
Will.
Brown
Moore
54 Haley .05 .15
Cunn
Swann
Harvey
55 Lewis .02 .10
Garner
Simm
T.Cart
56 T.Wheatley .05 .15
Taylor
Johnston
57 Croel .02 .10
Evans
A.Williams
58 Mamula .02 .10
Centers
Mitchell
59 F.Sanders .08 .25
Allen
Novacek
60 D.Sanders .08 .25
Walker
S.Palmer
61 Jones .02 .10
Erickson
Kirby
Coales
62 Reed .05 .15
F.Ander
Fryar
J.Mitch
63 Coplnd .05 .15
Dwkns
Brisby
Esia
64 B.Smith .08 .25
McDuf
McGin.
Yarb.
65 C.Martin .25 .60
Potts
Byars
Baxter
66 C.Benn .02 .10
Buchan
M.Coleman
67 Colts .02 .10
Coryatt
B.Cox
Slade
68 E.Green .02 .10
T.Law
M.Washing
69 T.Collins .25 .60
V.Brown
Ron.Mre
70 J.Burris .02 .10
F.Turner
Glenn
71 Pickns .08 .25
Testa
Jeffres
Howard
72 Scott .05 .15
Turner
Brown
O'Don.
73 Klnglr .08 .25
Hoard
Boslli
C.John.
74 Tovr .02 .10
Al Smith
D.Brwn
J.Will.
75 R.Thom .05 .15
L.White
Beu
Greene
76 J.Blake .08 .25
Alexander
Child.
77 E.Zeier .02 .10
M.Gray
R.Cobb
78 T.McNair .05 .15
Lageman
Lloyd
79 R.Johnson .08 .25
Wilk
Woodson
80 Bieniemy .02 .10
Langham
Bruener
81 Sh.Shrp .08 .25
W.Dvis
Hst
S.Hmp.
82 Bernstine .05 .15
Lott
H.Will.
Mirer
83 Miller .08 .25
Smith
Seau
Blades
84 Kfman .05 .15
O'Neal
Adam
Prit.
85 Hill .05 .15
Ismail
Pupunu
Kennedy
86 T.Vanover .05 .15
McGlock
Atwater
87 Bono .05 .15
Fredrick.
T.Martin
88 McDaniel .02 .10
Olivor
Fauria
89 J.Galloway .15 .40
Milburn
Carney
90 T.Fletcher .02 .10
K.Cash
E.Robin.

1996 Collector's Choice

The 1996 Collector's Choice first series containted 375 standard-size cards. The 14-card hobby packs had a suggested retail price of $.99 each. A factory set was produced and sold with ten Stick-Ums inserts and ten Gold foil MVPs inserts. The set features the topical subsets: Rookie Class (1-45) and Season To Remember (46-79). This set has a slightly different design than previous Collector's Choice sets in that the player's name and position was printed either on the side or the bottom. Rookie Cards in this set include Karim Abdul-Jabbar, Tim Biakabutuka, Bobby Engram, Terry Glenn, Eddie George, Keyshawn Johnson and Lawrence Phillips. A Jerry Rice base brand and a Dan Marino unnumbered Promo Crash the Game card were produced to promote the set and are priced below.

COMPLETE SET (375) 10.00 25.00
COMP.FACT.SET (395) 20.00 30.00
1 Keyshawn Johnson RC .40 1.00
2 Kevin Hardy RC .15 .40
3 Simeon Rice RC .30 .75
4 Jonathan Ogden RC .40 1.00
5 Cedric Jones RC .02 .10
6 Lawrence Phillips RC .15 .40
7 Tim Biakabutuka RC .15 .40
8 Terry Glenn RC .40 1.00
9 Rickey Dudley RC .15 .40
10 Regan Upshaw RC .02 .10
11 Walt Harris RC .02 .10
12 Eddie George RC .50 1.25
13 John Mobley RC .02 .10
14 Duane Clemons RC .02 .10
15 Marvin Harrison RC 1.00 2.50
16 Daryl Gardener RC .02 .10
17 Pete Kendall RC .02 .10
18 Marcus Jones RC .02 .10
19 Eric Moulds RC .50 1.25
20 Ray Lewis RC 2.00 5.00
21 Alex Van Dyke RC .07 .20
22 Leeland McElroy RC .07 .20
23 Mike Alstott RC .40 1.00
24 Lawyer Milloy RC .15 .40
25 Marco Battaglia RC .02 .10
26 Je'rod Cherry RC .02 .10
27 Israel Ifeanyi RC .02 .10
28 Bobby Engram RC .15 .40
29 Jason Dunn RC .07 .20
30 Derrick Mayes RC .15 .40
31 Stepfret Williams RC .07 .20
32 Bobby Hoying RC .15 .40
33 Karim Abdul-Jabbar RC .15 .40
34 Danny Kanell RC .15 .40
35 Chris Darkins RC .02 .10
36 Charlie Jones RC .15 .40
37 Tedy Bruschi RC 1.50 4.00
38 Stanley Pritchett RC .07 .20
39 Donnie Edwards RC .15 .40
40 Jeff Lewis RC .07 .20
41 Stephen Davis RC .60 1.50
42 Winslow Oliver RC .02 .10
43 Mercury Hayes RC .02 .10
44 Jon Runyan RC .02 .10
45 Steve Taneyhill RC .02 .10
46 Eric Metcalf SR .02 .10
47 Bryce Paup SR .02 .10
48 Kerry Collins SR .07 .20
49 Rashaan Salaam SR .07 .20
50 Carl Pickens SR .07 .20
51 Emmitt Smith SR .20 .50
52 Michael Irvin SR .07 .20
53 Troy Aikman SR .15 .40
54 Terrell Davis SR .07 .20
55 John Elway SR .30 .75
56 Herman Moore SR .07 .20
57 Brett Favre SR .30 .75
58 Rodney Thomas SR .02 .10
59 Jim Harbaugh SR .07 .20
60 Mark Brunell SR .07 .20
61 Marcus Allen SR .07 .20
62 Tamarick Vanover SR .07 .20
63 Steve Bono SR .02 .10
64 Dan Marino SR .30 .75
65 Warren Moon SR .02 .10
66 Curtis Martin SR .07 .20
67 Tyrone Hughes SR .02 .10
68 Rodney Hampton SR .02 .10
69 Hugh Douglas SR .02 .10
70 Tim Brown SR .07 .20
71 Ricky Watters SR .07 .20
72 Kordell Stewart SR .15 .40
73 Andre Coleman SR .02 .10
74 Jerry Rice SR .15 .40
75 Joey Galloway SR .07 .20
76 Isaac Bruce SR .07 .20
77 Errict Rhett SR .07 .20
78 Michael Westbrook SR .02 .10
79 Brian Mitchell SR .02 .10
80 Aeneas Williams .02 .10
81 Andre Reed .07 .20
82 Brett Maxie .02 .10
83 Jim Flanigan .02 .10
84 Jeff Blake .15 .40
85 Mike Frederick .02 .10
86 Michael Irvin .15 .40
87 Aaron Craver .02 .10
88 Barry Sanders .50 1.25
89 Travis Jervey RC .15 .40
90 Chris Sanders .07 .20
91 Marshall Faulk .15 .40
92 Bryan Schwartz .02 .10
93 Tamarick Vanover .07 .20
94 Troy Vincent .02 .10
95 Robert Smith .07 .20
96 Drew Bledsoe .20 .50
97 Quinn Early .02 .10
98 Wayne Chrebet .15 .40
99 Tim Brown .15 .40
100 Charlie Garner .07 .20
101 Yancey Thigpen .07 .20
102 Isaac Bruce .15 .40
103 Natrone Means .07 .20
104 Jerry Rice .30 .75
105 Chris Warren .07 .20
106 Errict Rhett .07 .20
107 Heath Shuler .07 .20
108 Eric Swann .02 .10
109 Jeff George .07 .20
110 Steve Tasker .02 .10
111 Sam Mills .02 .10
112 Jeff Graham .02 .10
113 Carl Pickens .07 .20
114 Vinny Testaverde .07 .20
115 Emmitt Smith .50 1.25
116 John Elway .60 1.50
117 Henry Thomas .02 .10
118 LeRoy Butler .02 .10
119 Blaine Bishop .02 .10
120 Floyd Turner .02 .10
121 Jeff Lageman .02 .10
122 Kimble Anders .07 .20
123 Bryan Cox .02 .10
124 Qadry Ismail .07 .20
125 Ted Johnson RC .15 .40
126 Wesley Walls .07 .20
127 Rodney Hampton .07 .20
128 Adrian Murrell .07 .20
129 Daryl Hobbs RC .02 .10
130 Ricky Watters .07 .20
131 Carnell Lake .02 .10
132 Toby Wright .02 .10
133 Darren Bennett .02 .10
134 J.J. Stokes .15 .40
135 Eugene Robinson .02 .10
136 Eric Curry .02 .10
137 Tom Carter .02 .10
138 Dave Krieg .02 .10
139 Eric Metcalf .02 .10
140 Bill Brooks .02 .10
141 Pete Metzelaars .02 .10
142 Kevin Butler .02 .10
143 John Copeland .02 .10
144 Keenan McCardell .15 .40
145 Larry Brown .02 .10
146 Jason Elam .07 .20
147 Willie Clay .02 .10
148 Robert Brooks .15 .40
149 Chris Chandler .07 .20
150 Quentin Coryatt .02 .10
151 Pete Mitchell .07 .20
152 Martin Bayless .02 .10
153 Pete Stoyanovich .02 .10
154 Cris Carter .15 .40
155 Jimmy Hitchcock RC .02 .10
156 Mario Bates .07 .20
157 Mike Sherrard .02 .10
158 Boomer Esiason .07 .20
159 Chester McGlockton .02 .10
160 Bobby Taylor .02 .10
161 Kordell Stewart .15 .40
162 Kevin Carter .02 .10
163 Junior Seau .15 .40
164 Derek Loville .02 .10
165 Brian Blades .02 .10
166 Jackie Harris .02 .10
167 Michael Westbrook .15 .40
168 Rob Moore .07 .20
169 Jessie Tuggle .02 .10
170 Darick Holmes .02 .10
171 Tim McKyer .02 .10
172 Erik Kramer .02 .10
173 Harold Green .02 .10
174 Stevon Moore .02 .10
175 Deion Sanders .15 .40
176 Anthony Miller .07 .20
177 Herman Moore .07 .20
178 Brett Favre .60 1.50
179 Rodney Thomas .02 .10
180 Ken Dilger .07 .20
181 Mark Brunell .20 .50
182 Marcus Allen .15 .40
183 Dan Marino .60 1.50
184 John Randle .07 .20
185 Ben Coates .07 .20
186 Tyrone Hughes .02 .10
187 Dave Brown .02 .10
188 Johnny Mitchell .02 .10
189 Harvey Williams .02 .10
190 Andy Harmon .02 .10
191 Kevin Greene .07 .20
192 D'Marco Farr .02 .10
193 Andre Coleman .02 .10
194 Bryant Young .07 .20
195 Rick Mirer .07 .20
196 Horace Copeland .02 .10
197 Leslie Shepherd .02 .10
198 Jamir Miller .02 .10
199 Bert Emanuel .07 .20
200 Steve Christie .02 .10
201 Kerry Collins .15 .40
202 Rashaan Salaam .07 .20
203 Steve Tovar .02 .10
204 Michael Jackson .07 .20
205 Kevin Williams .02 .10
206 Glyn Milburn .02 .10
207 Johnnie Morton .07 .20
208 Antonio Freeman .15 .40
209 Cris Dishman .02 .10
210 Ellis Johnson .02 .10
211 Cedric Tillman .02 .10
212 Steve Bono .02 .10
213 Eric Green .02 .10
214 David Palmer .02 .10
215 Vincent Brisby .02 .10
216 Michael Haynes .02 .10
217 Chris Calloway .02 .10
218 Kyle Brady .02 .10
219 Terry McDaniel .02 .10
220 Calvin Williams .02 .10
221 Greg Lloyd .07 .20
222 Jerome Bettis .15 .40
223 Stan Humphries .07 .20
224 Lee Woodall .02 .10
225 Robert Blackmon .02 .10
226 Warren Sapp .02 .10
227 Brian Mitchell .02 .10
228 Garrison Hearst .07 .20
229 Terance Mathis .02 .10
230 Bryce Paup .02 .10
231 Derrick Moore .02 .10
232 Curtis Conway .15 .40
233 Darnay Scott .07 .20
234 Andre Rison .07 .20
235 Jay Novacek .02 .10
236 Terrell Davis .20 .50
237 David Sloan .02 .10
238 Reggie White .15 .40
239 Todd McNair .02 .10
240 Ray Buchanan .02 .10
241 Steve Beuerlein .07 .20
242 Dan Saleaumua .02 .10
243 Bernie Parmalee .02 .10
244 Warren Moon .07 .20
245 Ty Law .15 .40
246 Torrance Small .02 .10
247 Phillippi Sparks .02 .10
248 Mo Lewis .02 .10
249 Jeff Hostetler .02 .10
250 Rodney Peete .02 .10
251 Byron Bam Morris .02 .10
252 Chris Miller .02 .10
253 Tony Martin .07 .20
254 Eric Davis .02 .10
255 Joey Galloway .15 .40
256 Derrick Brooks .15 .40
257 Ken Harvey .02 .10
258 Frank Sanders .07 .20
259 Morten Andersen .02 .10
260 Marlon Kerner .02 .10
261 Mark Carrier WR .02 .10
262 Mark Carrier DB .02 .10
263 Tony McGee .02 .10
264 Eric Zeier .02 .10
265 Darren Woodson .07 .20
266 Shannon Sharpe .07 .20
267 Brett Perriman .02 .10
268 Edgar Bennett .07 .20
269 Darryll Lewis .02 .10
270 Jim Harbaugh .07 .20
271 Desmond Howard .07 .20
272 Derrick Thomas .15 .40
273 Irving Fryar .07 .20
274 Jake Reed .07 .20
275 Curtis Martin .20 .50
276 Eric Allen .02 .10
277 Thomas Lewis .02 .10
278 Hugh Douglas .07 .20
279 Pat Swilling .02 .10
280 William Thomas .02 .10
281 Norm Johnson .02 .10
282 Roman Phifer .02 .10
283 Chris Mims .02 .10
284 Steve Young .25 .60
285 Cortez Kennedy .02 .10
286 Trent Dilfer .15 .40
287 Terry Allen .07 .20
288 Clyde Simmons .02 .10
289 Craig Heyward .02 .10
290 Jim Kelly .15 .40
291 Tyrone Poole .02 .10
292 Chris Zorich .02 .10
293 Dan Wilkinson .02 .10
294 Antonio Langham .02 .10
295 Troy Aikman .30 .75
296 Steve Atwater .02 .10
297 Scott Mitchell .07 .20
298 Mark Chmura .07 .20
299 Steve McNair .20 .50
300 Tony Bennett .02 .10
301 Willie Jackson .07 .20
302 Neil Smith .07 .20
303 Terry Kirby .07 .20
304 Orlando Thomas .02 .10
305 Willie McGinest .02 .10
306 Wayne Martin .02 .10
307 Michael Brooks .02 .10
308 Marvin Washington .02 .10
309 Nolan Harrison .02 .10
310 William Fuller .02 .10
311 Willie Williams .02 .10
312 Troy Drayton .02 .10
313 Shawn Lee .02 .10
314 Ken Norton .02 .10
315 Terry Wooden .02 .10
316 Hardy Nickerson .02 .10
317 Gus Frerotte .07 .20
318 Oscar McBride .02 .10
319 Merton Hanks .02 .10
320 Justin Armour .02 .10
321 Willie Green .02 .10
322 Roger Jones RC .02 .10
323 Leroy Hoard .02 .10
324 Chris Boniol .02 .10
325 Jason Hanson .02 .10
326 Sean Jones .02 .10
327 Roosevelt Potts .02 .10
328 Greg Hill .07 .20
329 O.J. McDuffie .07 .20
330 Amp Lee .02 .10
331 Chris Slade .02 .10
332 Jim Everett .02 .10
333 Tyrone Wheatley .07 .20
334 Charles Wilson .02 .10
335 Napoleon Kaufman .15 .40
336 Fred Barnett .02 .10
337 Neil O'Donnell .07 .20
338 Sean Gilbert .02 .10
339 Aaron Hayden RC .02 .10
340 Brent Jones .02 .10
341 Christian Fauria .02 .10
342 Alvin Harper .02 .10
343 Henry Ellard .02 .10
344 Willie Davis .02 .10
345 Charles Haley .07 .20
346 Chris Jacke .02 .10
347 Allen Aldridge .02 .10
348 Jeff Herrod .02 .10
349 Rocket Ismail .07 .20
350 Leslie O'Neal .02 .10
351 Marquez Pope .02 .10
352 Brock Marion .02 .10
353 Ernie Mills .02 .10
354 Larry Centers .07 .20
355 Chris Doleman .02 .10
356 Bruce Smith .07 .20
357 John Kasay .02 .10
358 Donnell Woolford .02 .10
359 David Dunn .02 .10
360 Eric Turner .02 .10
361 Sherman Williams .02 .10
362 Chris Spielman .02 .10
363 Craig Newsome .02 .10
364 Sean Dawkins .02 .10
365 James O. Stewart .07 .20
366 Dale Carter .02 .10
367 Marco Coleman .02 .10
368 Dave Meggett .02 .10
369 Irv Smith .02 .10
370 Mike Mamula .02 .10
371 Erric Pegram .02 .10
372 Dana Stubblefield .07 .20
373 Terrance Shaw .02 .10
374 Jerry Rice CL .15 .40
375 Dan Marino CL .15 .40
P1 Jerry Rice Promo .40 1.00
P2 Dan Marino Promo .40 1.00

1996 Collector's Choice A Cut Above

This 10-card set features color action player photos of top NFL stars on a die cut card. The backs carry a small circular head photo with player information and why this particular player was selected for the set. These cards were available one per special retail pack. Jumbo versions (3 1/2" by 5") of some of the cards were released later through Upper Deck Authenticated in complete box set form at a suggested retail price of $10.

COMPLETE SET (10) 5.00 12.00
ONE PER SPECIAL RETAIL PACK
*UDA JUMBO'S: .4X TO 1X BASIC INSERTS
1 Troy Aikman .50 1.25
2 Tim Biakabutuka .25 .60
3 Drew Bledsoe .30 .75
4 Emmitt Smith UER .75 2.00
5 Marshall Faulk .25 .60
6 Brett Favre 1.00 2.50
7 Keyshawn Johnson .60 1.50
8 Deion Sanders .25 .60
9 Lawrence Phillips .25 .60
10 Jerry Rice .50 1.25

1996 Collector's Choice Crash The Game

Randomly inserted in packs at a rate of one in five, this 90-card insert standard-size set was redeemable for a super premium quality card of the winning player. The redemption card will include Light F/X technology and feature a new photo of the player. If the card was a winner a collector could mail in the game card along with $1.75 and receive either a silver or a gold (depending on which game card they had) card. The gold cards were inserted one every 50 packs.

COMPLETE SET (90) 35.00 75.00
SILVER STATED ODDS 1:5
*GOLD CARDS: 2X TO 4X SILVERS
GOLD STATED ODDS 1:50
*GOLD REDEMPTIONS: 5X TO 10X SILV.
*SILVER REDEMPTIONS: 1.5X TO 3X SILV.
ONE PRIZE CARD VIA MAIL PER WINNER
CG1A Dan Marino 9/23 L 1.50 3.00
CG1B Dan Marino 10/27 W 1.50 3.00
CG1C Dan Marino 11/25 W 1.50 3.00
CG2A John Elway 10/6 W 1.50 3.00
CG2B John Elway 10/27 W 1.50 3.00
CG2C John Elway 11/24 W 1.50 3.00
CG3A Jeff Blake 9/29 W .30 .75
CG3B Jeff Blake 10/20 W .30 .75
CG3C Jeff Blake 12/1 W .30 .75
CG4A Drew Bledsoe 9/22 W .40 1.00
CG4B Drew Bledsoe 10/13 L .40 1.00
CG4C Drew Bledsoe 12/1 W .40 1.00
CG5A Steve Young 9/29 L .60 1.25
CG5B Steve Young 10/14 L .60 1.25
CG5C Steve Young 12/8 W .60 1.25
CG6A Brett Favre 10/6 W 1.50 3.00
CG6B Brett Favre 11/3 W 1.50 3.00
CG6C Brett Favre 11/24 W 1.50 3.00
CG7A Jim Kelly 9/22 L .30 .75
CG7B Jim Kelly 10/27 W .30 .75
CG7C Jim Kelly 11/10 W .30 .75
CG8A Scott Mitchell 10/6 W .15 .40
CG8B Scott Mitchell 10/27 W .15 .40
CG8C Scott Mitchell 11/11 L .15 .40
CG9A Jeff George 9/22 W .15 .40
CG9B Jeff George 10/20 L .15 .40
CG9C Jeff George 11/17 L .15 .40
CG10A Erik Kramer 9/29 L .07 .20
CG10B Erik Kramer 10/28 L .07 .20
CG10C Erik Kramer 11/24 L .07 .20
CG11A Jerry Rice 9/22 L .75 1.50
CG11B Jerry Rice 10/27 L .75 1.50
CG11C Jerry Rice 11/17 W .75 1.50
CG12A Michael Irvin 9/30 L .30 .75
CG12B Michael Irvin 10/13 L .30 .75
CG12C Michael Irvin 11/10 L .30 .75
CG13A Joey Galloway 9/22 L .30 .75
CG13B Joey Galloway 10/27 L .30 .75
CG13C Joey Galloway 11/24 L .30 .75
CG14A Cris Carter 9/29 L .30 .75
CG14B Cris Carter 11/3 W .30 .75
CG14C Cris Carter 12/1 W .30 .75
CG15A Carl Pickens 10/6 L .15 .40
CG15B Carl Pickens 10/27 W .15 .40
CG15C Carl Pickens 11/17 W .15 .40
CG16A Herman Moore 9/22 L .15 .40
CG16B Herman Moore 10/13 W .15 .40
CG16C Herman Moore 11/28 L .15 .40
CG17A Isaac Bruce 10/13 L .30 .75
CG17B Isaac Bruce 11/10 W .30 .75
CG17C Isaac Bruce 11/24 W .30 .75
CG18A Tim Brown 9/22 W .30 .75
CG18B Tim Brown 10/21L .30 .75
CG18C Tim Brown 11/24 L .30 .75
CG19A Keysh.Johnson 10/6 L .40 1.00
CG19B Keysh.Johnson 11/10 L .40 1.00
CG19C Keysh.Johnson 12/1 W .40 1.00
CG20A Terry Glenn 10/13 L .40 1.00
CG20B Terry Glenn 11/10 W .40 1.00
CG20C Terry Glenn 12/1 W .40 1.00
CG21A Emmitt Smith 9/22 W 1.25 2.50
CG21B Emmitt Smith 11/3 W 1.25 2.50
CG21C Emmitt Smith 11/28 W 1.25 2.50
CG22A Edgar Bennett 10/6 L .15 .40
CG22B Edgar Bennett 11/3 L .15 .40
CG22C Edgar Bennett 11/18 L .15 .40
CG23A Chris Warren 10/6 L .15 .40
CG23B Chris Warren 10/27 W .15 .40
CG23C Chris Warren 11/17 L .15 .40
CG24A Marshall Faulk 9/23 L .30 .75
CG24B Marshall Faulk 11/3 L .30 .75
CG24C Marshall Faulk 11/24 L .30 .75
CG25A Curtis Martin 9/22 W .40 1.00
CG25B Curtis Martin 10/20 W .40 1.00
CG25C Curtis Martin 12/1 L .40 1.00
CG26A Barry Sanders 9/29 L 1.25 2.50
CG26B Barry Sanders 10/17 W 1.25 2.50
CG26C Barry Sanders 11/17 W 1.25 2.50
CG27A Rashaan Salaam 9/22 L .15 .40
CG27B Rashaan Salaam 10/28 W .15 .40
CG27C Rashaan Salaam 11/17 L .15 .40
CG28A Leeland McElroy 9/29 L .07 .20
CG28B Leeland McElroy 10/27 L .07 .20
CG28C Leeland McElroy 11/17 L .07 .20
CG29A Tim Biakabutuka 9/22 L .15 .40
CG29B Tim Biakabutuka 10/13 L .15 .40
CG29C Tim Biakabutuka 11/3 L .15 .40
CG30A Lawrence Phillips 9/29 L .15 .40
CG30B Lawrence Phillips 10/20 L .15 .40
CG30C Lawrence Phillips 10/27 L .15 .40

1996 Collector's Choice Jumbos 3x5

Cards from this nine-card set were inserted one per special retail blister pack that also included a complete Collector's Choice team set and foil pack from 1996 Collector's Choice. The blister packs containing one of the oversized cards originally retailed for $4.97 each. Each card is an enlarged (3 1/2" by 5") version of that player's Season to Remember subset card from the regular 1996 Collector's Choice set. The card numbering is also the same.

COMPLETE SET (9) 12.00 30.00
48 Kerry Collins 1.00 2.50
49 Rashaan Salaam .60 1.50
51 Emmitt Smith 1.50 4.00
57 Brett Favre 2.00 5.00
60 Mark Brunell 1.25 3.00
64 Dan Marino 2.00 5.00
70 Tim Brown 1.00 2.50
72 Kordell Stewart 1.00 2.50
74 Jerry Rice 1.25 3.00

1996 Collector's Choice Dan Marino A Cut Above

Inserted one per special Collector's Choice six-card retail pack, this 10-card set features color photos of various highlights from Dan Marino's career printed on a die cut card. Jumbo versions (3 1/2" by 5") of the cards were released through Upper Deck Authenticated in complete box set form at a suggested retail price of $10.

COMPLETE SET (10) 6.00 15.00
COMMON CARD (CA1-CA10) .60 1.50
ONE PER SPECIAL RETAIL PACK
*UDA JUMBO CARDS: SAME PRICE

1996 Collector's Choice MVPs

Inserted one per pack, this 45-card insert set highlights each NFL Team's MVP and co-MVP. There was also a gold version of these cards issued they were inserted one every 35 packs. The words MVP are in the upper left corner with the player's name in the lower left. The cards are numbered with a "M" prefix.

COMPLETE SET (45) 4.00 10.00
STATED ODDS 1:1 HOBBY, 2:1 SPEC.RET
*GOLD STARS: 3X TO 8X BASIC INSERTS
TEN GOLDS PER FACTORY SET
GOLD STATED ODDS 1:35
M1 Larry Centers .10 .30
M2 Jeff George .10 .30
M3 Jim Kelly .25 .60
M4 Bryce Paup .05 .15
M5 Kerry Collins .25 .60
M6 Erik Kramer .05 .15
M7 Rashaan Salaam .10 .30
M8 Jeff Blake .25 .60
M9 Carl Pickens .10 .30
M10 Vinny Testaverde .10 .30
M11 Michael Irvin .25 .60
M12 Emmitt Smith 1.00 2.00
M13 John Elway 1.25 2.50
M14 Terrell Davis .30 .75
M15 Herman Moore .10 .30
M16 Barry Sanders 1.00 2.00
M17 Brett Favre 1.25 2.50
M18 Edgar Bennett .10 .30
M19 Rodney Thomas .05 .15
M20 Jim Harbaugh .10 .30
M21 Marshall Faulk .25 .60
M22 Mark Brunell .30 .75
M23 Steve Bono .05 .15
M24 Marcus Allen .25 .60
M25 Dan Marino 1.25 2.50
M26 Bryan Cox .05 .15
M27 Cris Carter .25 .60
M28 Curtis Martin .30 .75
M29 Drew Bledsoe .30 .75
M30 Jim Everett .05 .15
M31 Rodney Hampton .10 .30
M32 Adrian Murrell .10 .30
M33 Tim Brown .25 .60
M34 Rodney Peete .05 .15
M35 Ricky Watters .10 .30
M36 Yancey Thigpen .10 .30
M37 Greg Lloyd .10 .30
M38 Isaac Bruce .25 .60
M39 Tony Martin .10 .30
M40 Junior Seau .25 .60
M41 Steve Young .40 1.00
M42 Jerry Rice .60 1.25
M43 Chris Warren .10 .30
M44 Errict Rhett .10 .30
M45 Brian Mitchell .05 .15

1996 Collector's Choice Stick-Ums

Inserted approximately one every three packs, these thin cards feature images which can be peeled off and applied to various surfaces. The player's picture is identified on the front. The back has a checklist of the set and the cards are numbered with an "S" prefix.

COMPLETE SET (30) 5.00 12.00
STATED ODDS 1:3
TEN PER FACTORY SET
S1 Dan Marino 1.00 2.50
S2 Mike Mamula .05 .15
S3 Errict Rhett .10 .30
S4 Drew Bledsoe .30 .75
S5 Anthony Smith .05 .15
S6 Brett Favre UER 1.00 2.50
S7 Morten Andersen .05 .15
S8 Deion Sanders .25 .60
S9 Jeff George .10 .30
S10 Erik Kramer .05 .15
S11 Jerry Rice .50 1.25
S12 Michael Irvin .25 .60
S13 Greg Lloyd .10 .30
S14 Cris Carter .25 .60
S15 Ken Norton .05 .15
S16 Natrone Means .10 .30
S17 Robert Brooks .25 .60
S18 Bomb .05 .15
Blitz
S19 Kordell Stewart .25 .60
S20 Referee .05 .15
S21 Emmitt Smith .75 2.00
S22 Reggie White .25 .60
S23 Eric Metcalf .05 .15
S24 Jesse Sapolu .05 .15
S25 Curtis Martin .30 .75
S26 Neil Smith .10 .30
S27 Junior Seau .25 .60
S28 TD .05 .15
S29 Yardmarkers .05 .15
S30 Terry McDaniel .05 .15

1996 Collector's Choice Update

The 1996 Collector's Choice Update set was issued in one series totalling 200 cards. The 12-card packs retail for $.99 each. The set contains the topical subsets: Rookie Collection (1-60), Franchise Playmaker (61-90) and Regular cards (91-200).

COMPLETE SET (200) 7.50 15.00
U1 Zach Thomas RC .25 .60
U2 Simeon Rice .20 .50
U3 Jonathan Ogden .30 .75
U4 Eric Moulds .10 .30
U5 Tim Biakabutuka .10 .30
U6 Walt Harris .02 .10
U7 Willie Anderson .02 .10
U8 Ricky Whittle .02 .10
U9 John Mobley .02 .10
U10 Reggie Brown RC .02 .10
U11 John Michels RC .02 .10
U12 Eddie George .25 .60
U13 Marvin Harrison .50 1.25
U14 Kevin Hardy .07 .20
U15 Kavika Pittman RC .02 .10
U16 Daryl Gardener .02 .10
U17 Duane Clemons .02 .10
U18 Terry Glenn .10 .30
U19 Alex Molden RC .02 .10
U20 Cedric Jones .02 .10
U21 Keyshawn Johnson .20 .50
U22 Rickey Dudley .10 .30
U23 Jason Dunn .02 .10
U24 Jamain Stephens .02 .10
U25 Lawrence Phillips .10 .30
U26 Bryan Still RC .07 .20
U27 Israel Ifeanyi .02 .10
U28 Pete Kendall .02 .10
U29 Regan Upshaw .02 .10
U30 Andre Johnson RC .02 .10
U31 Leeland McElroy .02 .10
U32 Ray Lewis 1.00 2.50
U33 Sean Moran RC .02 .10
U34 Muhsin Muhammad RC .40 1.00
U35 Bobby Engram .10 .30

Card	Low	High
U36 Marco Battaglia	.02	.10
U37 Stepfret Williams	.02	.10
U38 Jeff Lewis	.07	.20
U39 Derrick Mayes	.07	.20
U40 Reggie Tongue RC	.02	.10
U41 Tory James RC	.07	.20
U42 Tony Banks RC	.10	.30
U43 Tedy Bruschi	.75	2.00
U44 Mike Alstott	.20	.50
U45 Anthony Dorsett	.02	.10
U46 Tony Brackens RC	.10	.30
U47 Bryant Mix	.02	.10
U48 Karim Abdul-Jabbar	.10	.30
U49 Moe Williams RB RC	.30	.75
U50 Lawyer Milloy	.07	.20
U51 Je'rod Cherry	.02	.10
U52 Amani Toomer RC	.40	1.00
U53 Alex Van Dyke	.07	.20
U54 Lance Johnstone RC	.07	.20
U55 Bobby Hoying	.10	.30
U56 Jon Witman RC	.07	.20
U57 Eddie Kennison RC	.10	.30
U58 Brian Roche RC	.02	.10
U59 Terrell Owens RC	1.00	2.50
U60 Stephen Davis	.30	.75
U61 Jeff George FP	.07	.20
U62 Darick Holmes FP	.02	.10
U63 Kerry Collins FP	.10	.30
U64 Rashaan Salaam FP	.07	.20
U65 Jeff Blake FP	.07	.20
U66 Emmitt Smith FP	.30	.75
U67 Troy Aikman FP	.20	.50
U68 John Elway FP	.40	1.00
U69 Terrell Davis FP	.15	.40
U70 Barry Sanders FP	.30	.75
U71 Herman Moore FP	.07	.20
U72 Brett Favre FP	.40	1.00
U73 Robert Brooks FP	.07	.20
U74 Steve McNair FP	.15	.40
U75 Marshall Faulk FP	.10	.30
U76 Marcus Allen FP	.10	.30
U77 Dan Marino FP	.40	1.00
U78 Warren Moon FP	.02	.10
U79 Drew Bledsoe FP	.10	.30
U80 Curtis Martin FP	.15	.40
U81 Mario Bates FP	.07	.20
U82 Tim Brown FP	.10	.30
U83 Charlie Garner FP	.07	.20
U84 Kordell Stewart FP	.10	.30
U85 Isaac Bruce FP	.10	.30
U86 Tony Martin FP	.02	.10
U87 Jerry Rice FP	.20	.50
U88 J.J. Stokes FP	.10	.30
U89 Joey Galloway FP	.10	.30
U90 Errict Rhett FP	.07	.20
U91 Mike Pritchard	.02	.10
U92 Jerome Bettis	.10	.30
U93 Winslow Oliver	.02	.10
U94 David Klingler	.02	.10
U95 Lawrence Dawsey	.02	.10
U96 Charlie Jones	.07	.20
U97 Dave Krieg	.02	.10
U98 Chris Spielman	.02	.10
U99 Stanley Pritchett	.02	.10
U100 Sean Gilbert	.02	.10
U101 Tommy Vardell	.02	.10
U102 DeRon Jenkins	.02	.10
U103 Larry Bowie	.02	.10
U104 Kyle Wachholtz RC	.02	.10
U105 Brady Smith RC	.02	.10
U106 Steve Walsh	.02	.10
U107 Wesley Walls	.07	.20
U108 Kevin Ross	.02	.10
U109 Willie Clay	.02	.10
U110 Olanda Truitt	.02	.10
U111 Calvin Williams	.02	.10
U112 Chris Doleman	.02	.10
U113 Irving Fryar	.07	.20
U114 Jimmy Spencer	.02	.10
U115 Reggie Barlow RC	.02	.10
U116 Reggie Brown RBK RC	.02	.10
U117 Dixon Edwards	.02	.10
U118 Haywood Jeffires	.02	.10
U119 Santana Dotson	.02	.10
U120 Herschel Walker	.07	.20
U121 Darryl Williams	.02	.10
U122 Bryan Cox	.02	.10
U123 Lamar Thomas	.02	.10
U124 Hendrick Lusk	.02	.10
U125 Jahine Arnold RC	.02	.10
U126 Boomer Esiason	.07	.20
U127 Willie Davis	.02	.10
U128 Pete Stoyanovich	.02	.10
U129 Bill Romanowski	.02	.10
U130 Tim McKyer	.02	.10
U131 Patrick Sapp	.02	.10
U132 Natrone Means	.07	.20
U133 Quinn Early	.02	.10
U134 Leslie O'Neal	.02	.10
U135 Mark Seay	.02	.10
U136 Pete Metzelaars	.02	.10
U137 Jay Leeuwenburg UER RC	.02	.10
U138 Buster Owens	.02	.10
U139 Todd McNair	.02	.10
U140 Eugene Robinson	.02	.10
U141 Sean Salisbury	.02	.10
U142 Eddie Robinson	.02	.10
U143 Jerris McPhail	.02	.10
U144 Ray Farmer RC	.02	.10
U145 Garrison Hearst	.07	.20
U146 Leonard Russell	.02	.10
U147 Roy Barker	.02	.10
U148 Larry Brown	.02	.10
U149 Webster Slaughter	.02	.10
U150 Roman Oben RC	.02	.10
U151 LeShon Johnson	.02	.10
U152 Patrick Bates	.02	.10
U153 Iheanyi Uwaezuoke RC	.10	.30
U154 Scott Slutzker	.02	.10
U155 John Jurkovic	.02	.10
U156 Brian Milne	.02	.10
U157 Mike Sherrard	.02	.10
U158 Neil O'Donnell	.07	.20
U159 Roger Harper	.02	.10
U160 Desmond Howard	.07	.20
U161 Alfred Williams	.02	.10
U162 Ronnie Harmon	.02	.10
U163 Sammie Burroughs RC	.02	.10
U164 Keenan McCardell	.10	.30
U165 Shane Dronett	.02	.10
U166 Jeff Graham	.02	.10
U167 Bill Brooks	.02	.10
U168 Shawn Jefferson	.02	.10
U169 Detron Smith	.02	.10
U170 Danny Kanell	.10	.30
U171 Jevon Langford	.02	.10
U172 Russell Maryland	.02	.10
U173 Scott Milanovich RC	.10	.30
U174 Eric Davis	.02	.10
U175 Ernie Conwell	.02	.10
U176 Kurt Gouveia	.02	.10
U177 Andre Rison	.07	.20
U178 Harold Green	.02	.10
U179 Frank Reich	.02	.10
U180 Glyn Milburn	.02	.10
U181 Nilo Silvan	.02	.10
U182 Cornelius Bennett	.02	.10
U183 Freddie Solomon RC	.02	.10
U184 Pat Terrell	.02	.10
U185 Miles Macik	.02	.10
U186 Bo Orlando	.02	.10
U187 Kelvin Martin	.02	.10
U188 Todd Kinchen	.02	.10
U189 Reggie Brooks	.02	.10
U190 Steve Beuerlein	.07	.20
U191 Marco Coleman	.02	.10
U192 Johnny Johnson	.02	.10
U193 Dedric Mathis	.02	.10
U194 Leon Searcy	.02	.10
U195 Kevin Greene	.07	.20
U196 Daniel Stubbs	.02	.10
U197 Ray Mickens	.02	.10
U198 Devin Wyman	.02	.10
U199 Lorenzo Lynch	.02	.10
U200 Rice Marino CL	.10	.30

1996 Collector's Choice Update Record Breaking Trio

Randomly inserted in packs at the rate of one in 100, this four-card set features color player images of three record breaking players on sepia-colored crowd backgrounds and printed on Light F/X cards. The fourth card displays images of all three players.

Card	Low	High
COMPLETE SET (4)	25.00	60.00
STATED ODDS 1:100		
1 Joe Montana	7.50	15.00
2 Dan Marino	12.50	30.00
3 Jerry Rice	7.50	15.00
4 Mont/Marino/Rice	12.50	25.00

1996 Collector's Choice Update Stick-Ums

Randomly inserted in packs at a rate of one in four, this 30-card set features color player images on re-stickable stickers along with their team helmet and name and position printed in a re-stickable bar. The stickers from this set were made to stick on to their corresponding card in the Collector's Choice Update Stick-Ums Mystery Base Card set.

Card	Low	High
COMPLETE SET (30)	7.50	15.00
STICKER STATED ODDS 1:4		
*MYSTERY BASE: .5X TO 1X BASE CARD HI		
MYSTERY STATED ODDS 1:4		
S1 Jeff George	.15	.40
S2 Darren Bennett	.07	.20
S3 Marcus Allen	.25	.60
S4 Brett Favre	1.00	2.00
S5 Carl Pickens	.15	.40
S6 Troy Aikman	.40	1.00
S7 John Elway	1.00	2.00
S8 Steve Young	.25	.60
S9 Norm Johnson	.07	.20
S10 Kordell Stewart	.25	.60
S11 Drew Bledsoe	.25	.60
S12 Jim Kelly	.25	.60
S13 Dan Marino	1.00	2.00
S14 Joey Galloway	.25	.60
S15 Lawrence Phillips	.25	.60
S16 Reggie White	.25	.60
S17 Kevin Hardy	.15	.40
S18 Isaac Bruce	.25	.60
S19 Keyshawn Johnson	.40	1.00
S20 Barry Sanders	.75	1.50
S21 Deion Sanders	.25	.60
S22 Emmitt Smith	.75	1.50
S23 Chris Warren	.15	.40
S24 Tim Biakabutuka	.25	.60
S25 Terry Glenn	.25	.60
S26 Marshall Faulk	.25	.60
S27 Tamarick Vanover	.07	.20
S28 Curtis Martin	.30	.75
S29 Terrell Davis	.30	.75
S30 Jerry Rice	.40	1.00

1996 Collector's Choice Update You Make The Play

Randomly inserted one in every pack, this 90-card set features color player images on cards that are used in playing a game. Touchdowns, extra points and field goals are scored by drawing cards from stacks of Offensive and Kicking cards. Information cards with rules are inserted one in every five Collector's Choice Update packs. A set of 12 game cards could be obtained from a special mail-in offer.

Card	Low	High
COMPLETE SET (90)	10.00	20.00
ONE PER PACK		
Y1 Norm Johnson	.07	.20
Y2 Jerry Rice	.40	1.00
Y3 Dan Marino	1.00	2.00
Y4 Marshall Faulk	.25	.60
Y5 Neil Smith	.07	.20
Y6 Herman Moore	.15	.40
Y7 Brett Favre	1.00	2.00
Y8 Curtis Martin	.30	.75
Y9 Reggie White	.25	.60
Y10 Cris Carter	.25	.60
Y11 Rick Tuten	.07	.20
Y12 Steve Young	.30	.75
Y13 Barry Sanders	.75	1.50
Y14 Deion Sanders	.25	.60
Y15 Isaac Bruce	.25	.60
Y16 Troy Aikman	.40	1.00
Y17 Emmitt Smith	.75	1.50
Y18 Junior Seau	.25	.60
Y19 Joey Galloway	.25	.60
Y20 Drew Bledsoe	.25	.60
Y21 Jason Elam	.07	.20
Y22 Edgar Bennett	.15	.40
Y23 Greg Lloyd	.07	.20
Y24 Tamarick Vanover	.07	.20
Y25 John Elway	1.00	2.00
Y26 Larry Centers	.15	.40
Y27 Derrick Thomas	.25	.60
Y28 Michael Irvin	.25	.60
Y29 Jeff George	.15	.40
Y30 Thurman Thomas	.25	.60
Y31 Darren Bennett	.07	.20
Y32 Ken Norton	.07	.20
Y33 Carl Pickens	.25	.60
Y34 Jeff Blake	.15	.40
Y35 Craig Heyward	.15	.40
Y36 Aeneas Williams	.07	.20
Y37 Terance Mathis	.15	.40
Y38 Jim Kelly	.25	.60
Y39 Marcus Allen	.25	.60
Y40 Tim McDonald	.07	.20
Y41 Jason Hanson	.07	.20
Y42 Scott Mitchell	.15	.40
Y43 Tim Brown	.25	.60
Y44 Kordell Stewart	.25	.60
Y45 Eric Metcalf	.15	.40
Y46 Norm Johnson	.07	.20
Y47 Jerry Rice	.40	1.00
Y48 Dan Marino	1.00	2.00
Y49 Marshall Faulk	.25	.60
Y50 Neil Smith	.07	.20
Y51 Herman Moore	.15	.40
Y52 Brett Favre	1.00	2.00
Y53 Curtis Martin	.30	.75
Y54 Reggie White	.25	.60
Y55 Cris Carter	.25	.60
Y56 Rick Tuten	.07	.20
Y57 Steve Young	.30	.75
Y58 Barry Sanders	.75	1.50
Y59 Deion Sanders	.25	.60
Y60 Isaac Bruce	.25	.60
Y61 Troy Aikman	.40	1.00
Y62 Emmitt Smith	.75	1.50
Y63 Junior Seau	.25	.60
Y64 Joey Galloway	.25	.60
Y65 Drew Bledsoe	.25	.60
Y66 Jason Elam	.07	.20
Y67 Edgar Bennett	.15	.40
Y68 Greg Lloyd	.07	.20
Y69 Tamarick Vanover	.07	.20
Y70 John Elway	1.00	2.00
Y71 Larry Centers	.15	.40
Y72 Derrick Thomas	.25	.60
Y73 Michael Irvin	.25	.60
Y74 Jeff George	.15	.40
Y75 Thurman Thomas	.25	.60
Y76 Darren Bennett	.07	.20
Y77 Ken Norton	.07	.20
Y78 Carl Pickens	.25	.60
Y79 Jeff Blake	.15	.40
Y80 Craig Heyward	.15	.40
Y81 Aeneas Williams	.07	.20
Y82 Terance Mathis	.15	.40
Y83 Jim Kelly	.25	.60
Y84 Marcus Allen	.25	.60
Y85 Tim McDonald	.07	.20
Y86 Jason Hanson	.07	.20
Y87 Scott Mitchell	.15	.40
Y88 Tim Brown	.25	.60
Y89 Kordell Stewart	.25	.60
Y90 Eric Metcalf	.15	.40

1997 Collector's Choice

This 565-card set was distributed in two series. The first 310-cards were released in 14-card packs with a suggested retail price of $1.29 and featured color action player photos in white borders. The backs carried player information and statistics along with dual numbering that helps collectors put together cards of their favorite NFL team. There were 220 regular player cards, 45 Rookie Class subset cards (1-45), 40 Names of the Game subset cards (46-85), and five checklists which featured collecting tips for new collectors. Series two included 255 different cards with Rookie Collection and Building Blocks subsets.

Card	Low	High
COMPLETE SET (565)	12.50	30.00
COMP.SERIES 1 (310)	7.50	20.00
COMP.FACT.SER.1(330)	10.00	25.00
COMP.SERIES 2 (255)	5.00	12.00
1 Orlando Pace RC	.20	.50
2 Darrell Russell RC	.07	.20
3 Shawn Springs RC	.10	.30
4 Peter Boulware RC	.20	.50
5 Bryant Westbrook RC	.07	.20
6 Tom Knight RC	.07	.20
7 Ike Hilliard RC	.30	.75
8 James Farrior RC	.20	.50
9 Chris Naeole RC	.07	.20
10 Michael Booker RC	.07	.20
11 Warrick Dunn RC	.60	1.50
12 Tony Gonzalez RC	.75	2.00
13 Reinard Wilson RC	.10	.30
14 Yatil Green RC	.10	.30
15 Reidel Anthony RC	.20	.50
16 Kenard Lang RC	.10	.30
17 Kenny Holmes RC	.20	.50
18 Tarik Glenn RC	.20	.50
19 Dwayne Rudd RC	.20	.50
20 Renaldo Wynn RC	.07	.20
21 David LaFleur RC	.07	.20
22 Antowain Smith RC	.50	1.25
23 Jim Druckenmiller RC	.10	.30
24 Rae Carruth RC	.07	.20
25 Jared Tomich RC	.07	.20
26 Chris Canty RC	.07	.20
27 Jake Plummer RC	.75	2.00
28 Troy Davis RC	.10	.30
29 Sedrick Shaw RC	.10	.30
30 Jamie Sharper RC	.10	.30
31 Tiki Barber RC	1.25	3.00
32 Byron Hanspard RC	.10	.30
33 Darnell Autry RC	.10	.30
34 Corey Dillon RC	.75	2.00
35 Joey Kent RC	.20	.50
36 Nathan Davis RC	.07	.20
37 Will Blackwell RC	.10	.30
38 Kim Herring RC	.07	.20
39 Pat Barnes RC	.20	.50
40 Kevin Lockett RC	.10	.30
41 Trevor Pryce RC	.20	.50
42 Matt Russell RC	.07	.20
43 Greg Jones RC	.07	.20
44 Antonio Anderson RC	.07	.20
45 George Jones RC	.10	.30
46 Steve Young NG	.20	.50
47 Jerry Rice NG	.20	.50
48 Curtis Conway NG	.07	.20
49 Jeff Blake NG	.10	.30
50 Carl Pickens NG	.10	.30
51 Bruce Smith NG	.07	.20
52 John Elway NG	.40	1.00
53 Terrell Davis NG	.20	.50
54 Shannon Sharpe NG	.07	.20
55 Junior Seau NG	.07	.20
56 Darren Bennett NG	.07	.20
57 Jim Harbaugh NG	.10	.30
58 Marshall Faulk NG	.20	.50
59 Emmitt Smith NG	.30	.75
60 Troy Aikman NG	.20	.50
61 Deion Sanders NG	.20	.50
62 Dan Marino NG	.40	1.00
63 Ricky Watters NG	.07	.20
64 Mark Brunell NG	.20	.50
65 Keenan McCardell NG	.07	.20
66 Keyshawn Johnson NG	.20	.50
67 Barry Sanders NG	.30	.75
68 Herman Moore NG	.10	.30
69 Eddie George NG	.20	.50
70 Steve McNair NG	.20	.50
71 Brett Favre NG	.40	1.00
72 Reggie White NG	.10	.30
73 Edgar Bennett NG	.07	.20
74 Kerry Collins NG	.10	.30
75 Kevin Greene NG	.07	.20
76 Drew Bledsoe NG	.10	.30
77 Terry Glenn NG	.10	.30
78 Curtis Martin NG	.20	.50
79 Jeff Hostetler NG	.07	.20
80 Napoleon Kaufman NG	.20	.50
81 Isaac Bruce NG	.20	.50
82 Terry Allen NG	.10	.30
83 Joey Galloway NG	.10	.30
84 Kordell Stewart NG	.20	.50
85 Jerome Bettis NG	.20	.50
86 Dana Stubblefield	.07	.20
87 Merton Hanks	.07	.20
88 Terrell Owens	.25	.60
89 Brent Jones	.07	.20
90 Ken Norton Jr.	.07	.20
91 Jerry Rice	.40	1.00
92 Terry Kirby	.10	.30
93 Bryant Young	.07	.20
94 Raymont Harris	.07	.20
95 Jeff Jaeger	.07	.20
96 Curtis Conway	.10	.30
97 Walt Harris	.07	.20
98 Bobby Engram	.10	.30
99 Donnell Woolford	.07	.20
100 Rashaan Salaam	.07	.20
101 Jeff Blake	.10	.30
102 Tony McGee	.07	.20
103 Ashley Ambrose	.07	.20
104 Dan Wilkinson	.07	.20
105 Jevon Langford	.07	.20
106 Darnay Scott	.10	.30
107 David Dunn	.07	.20
108 Eric Moulds	.20	.50
109 Darick Holmes	.07	.20
110 Thurman Thomas	.20	.50
111 Quinn Early	.07	.20
112 Jim Kelly	.20	.50
113 Bryce Paup	.07	.20
114 Bruce Smith	.10	.30
115 Todd Collins	.07	.20
116 Tory James	.07	.20
117 Anthony Miller	.07	.20
118 Terrell Davis	.25	.60
119 Tyrone Braxton	.07	.20
120 John Mobley	.07	.20
121 Bill Romanowski	.07	.20
122 Vaughn Hebron	.07	.20
123 Mike Alstott	.20	.50
124 Errict Rhett	.07	.20
125 Trent Dilfer	.20	.50
126 Courtney Hawkins	.07	.20
127 Hardy Nickerson	.07	.20
128 Donnie Abraham RC	.20	.50
129 Regan Upshaw	.07	.20
130 Kent Graham	.07	.20
131 Rob Moore	.10	.30
132 Simeon Rice	.10	.30
133 LeShon Johnson	.07	.20
134 Frank Sanders	.10	.30
135 Leeland McElroy	.07	.20
136 Seth Joyner	.07	.20
137 Andre Coleman	.07	.20
138 Stan Humphries	.10	.30
139 Charlie Jones	.07	.20
140 Junior Seau	.20	.50
141 Rodney Harrison RC	.40	1.00
142 Darrien Gordon	.07	.20
143 Terrell Fletcher	.07	.20
144 Tamarick Vanover	.10	.30
145 Greg Hill	.07	.20
146 Marcus Allen	.20	.50
147 Lake Dawson	.07	.20
148 Dale Carter	.07	.20
149 Kimble Anders	.10	.30
150 Chris Penn	.07	.20
151 Sean Dawkins	.07	.20
152 Ken Dilger	.07	.20
153 Marvin Harrison	.20	.50
154 Jeff Herrod	.07	.20
155 Jim Harbaugh	.10	.30
156 Cary Blanchard	.07	.20
157 Aaron Bailey	.07	.20
158 Deion Sanders	.20	.50
159 Jim Schwantz RC	.07	.20
160 Michael Irvin	.20	.50
161 Herschel Walker	.10	.30
162 Emmitt Smith	.60	1.50
163 Chris Boniol	.07	.20
164 Eric Bjornson	.07	.20
165 Karim Abdul-Jabbar	.10	.30
166 O.J. McDuffie	.10	.30
167 Troy Drayton	.07	.20
168 Zach Thomas	.20	.50
169 Irving Spikes	.07	.20
170 Shane Burton RC	.10	.30
171 Stanley Pritchett	.07	.20
172 Ty Detmer	.10	.30
173 Chris T. Jones	.07	.20
174 Troy Vincent	.07	.20
175 Brian Dawkins	.20	.50
176 Irving Fryar	.10	.30
177 Charlie Garner	.10	.30
178 Bobby Taylor	.07	.20
179 Jamal Anderson	.20	.50
180 Terance Mathis	.10	.30
181 Craig Heyward	.07	.20
182 Cornelius Bennett	.07	.20
183 Jessie Tuggle	.07	.20
184 Devin Bush	.07	.20
185 Dave Brown	.07	.20
186 Danny Kanell	.07	.20
187 Rodney Hampton	.10	.30
188 Tyrone Wheatley	.10	.30
189 Amani Toomer	.10	.30
190 Phillippi Sparks	.07	.20
191 Thomas Lewis	.07	.20
192 Jimmy Smith	.10	.30
193 Pete Mitchell	.07	.20
194 Natrone Means	.10	.30
195 Mark Brunell	.25	.60
196 Kevin Hardy	.07	.20
197 Tony Brackens	.07	.20
198 Aaron Beasley RC	.07	.20
199 Chris Hudson	.07	.20
200 Wayne Chrebet	.20	.50
201 Keyshawn Johnson	.20	.50
202 Adrian Murrell	.10	.30
203 Neil O'Donnell	.10	.30
204 Hugh Douglas	.07	.20
205 Mo Lewis	.07	.20
206 Glenn Foley	.07	.20
207 Aaron Glenn	.07	.20
208 Johnnie Morton	.10	.30
209 Reggie Brown LB	.10	.30
210 Barry Sanders	.60	1.50
211 Glyn Milburn	.07	.20
212 Bennie Blades	.07	.20
213 Steve McNair	.25	.60
214 Frank Wycheck	.07	.20
215 Chris Sanders	.07	.20
216 Blaine Bishop	.07	.20
217 Willie Davis	.07	.20
218 Darryll Lewis	.07	.20
219 Marcus Robertson	.07	.20
220 Robert Brooks	.10	.30
221 Antonio Freeman	.20	.50
222 Keith Jackson	.07	.20
223 Mark Chmura	.10	.30
224 Brett Favre	.75	2.00
225 Sean Jones	.07	.20
226 Reggie White	.20	.50
227 LeRoy Butler	.07	.20
228 Craig Newsome	.07	.20
229 Wesley Walls	.10	.30
230 Mark Carrier WR	.07	.20
231 Muhsin Muhammad	.10	.30
232 John Kasay	.07	.20
233 Anthony Johnson	.07	.20
234 Kerry Collins	.20	.50
235 Kevin Greene	.10	.30
236 Sam Mills	.07	.20
237 Ben Coates	.10	.30
238 Terry Glenn	.20	.50
239 Willie McGinest	.07	.20
240 Ted Johnson	.07	.20
241 Lawyer Milloy	.10	.30
242 Drew Bledsoe	.25	.60
243 Willie Clay	.07	.20
244 Chris Slade	.07	.20
245 Tim Brown	.20	.50
246 Daryl Hobbs	.07	.20
247 Rickey Dudley	.10	.30
248 Joe Aska	.07	.20
249 Chester McGlockton	.07	.20
250 Rob Fredrickson	.07	.20
251 Terry McDaniel	.07	.20
252 Tony Banks	.10	.30
253 Lawrence Phillips	.07	.20
254 Isaac Bruce	.20	.50
255 Eddie Kennison	.10	.30
256 Kevin Carter	.07	.20
257 Roman Phifer	.07	.20
258 Keith Lyle	.07	.20
259 Vinny Testaverde	.10	.30
260 Derrick Alexander WR	.10	.30
261 Ray Lewis	.30	.75
262 Jermaine Lewis	.20	.50
263 Byron Bam Morris	.07	.20
264 Stevon Moore	.07	.20
265 Antonio Langham	.07	.20
266 Brian Mitchell	.07	.20
267 Henry Ellard	.07	.20
268 Leslie Shepherd	.07	.20
269 Michael Westbrook	.10	.30
270 Jamie Asher	.07	.20
271 Ken Harvey	.07	.20
272 Gus Frerotte	.07	.20
273 Michael Haynes	.07	.20
274 Ray Zellars	.07	.20
275 Jim Everett	.07	.20
276 Tyrone Hughes	.07	.20
277 Joe Johnson	.07	.20
278 Eric Allen	.07	.20
279 Brady Smith	.07	.20
280 Mario Bates	.07	.20
281 Torrance Small	.07	.20
282 John Friesz	.07	.20
283 Brian Blades	.07	.20
284 Chris Warren	.10	.30
285 Joey Galloway	.10	.30
286 Michael Sinclair	.07	.20
287 Lamar Smith	.20	.50
288 Mike Pritchard	.07	.20
289 Jerome Bettis	.20	.50
290 Charles Johnson	.10	.30
291 Mike Tomczak	.07	.20
292 Levon Kirkland	.07	.20
293 Carnell Lake	.07	.20
294 Erric Pegram	.07	.20
295 Kordell Stewart	.20	.50
296 Greg Lloyd	.07	.20
297 Dixon Edwards	.07	.20
298 Cris Carter	.20	.50
299 Brad Johnson	.20	.50
300 Qadry Ismail	.10	.30
301 John Randle	.10	.30
302 Orlando Thomas	.07	.20
303 Dewayne Washington	.07	.20
304 Jake Reed	.10	.30
305 Derrick Alexander DE	.07	.20
306 Eddie George CL	.20	.50
307 Dan Marino CL	.15	.40
308 Curtis Martin CL	.10	.30
309 Troy Aikman CL	.20	.50
310 Marcus Allen CL	.20	.50
311 Jim Druckenmiller	.07	.20
312 Greg Clark RC	.07	.20
313 Darnell Autry	.10	.30
314 Reinard Wilson	.07	.20
315 Corey Dillon	.30	.75
316 Antowain Smith	.20	.50
317 Trevor Pryce	.10	.30
318 Warrick Dunn	.25	.60
319 Reidel Anthony	.10	.30
320 Jake Plummer	.30	.75
321 Tom Knight	.07	.20
322 Freddie Jones RC	.10	.30
323 Tony Gonzalez	.30	.75
324 Pat Barnes	.10	.30
325 Kevin Lockett	.10	.30
326 Tarik Glenn	.08	.25
327 David LaFleur	.07	.20
328 Antonio Anderson	.07	.20
329 Yatil Green	.10	.30
330 Jason Taylor RC	.40	1.00
331 Brian Manning RC	.07	.20
332 Michael Booker	.07	.20
333 Byron Hanspard	.10	.30
334 Ike Hilliard	.20	.50
335 Tiki Barber	.50	1.25
336 Renaldo Wynn	.07	.20
337 Damon Jones RC	.07	.20
338 James Farrior	.10	.30
339 Dedric Ward RC	.10	.30
340 Bryant Westbrook	.07	.20
341 Joey Kent	.20	.50
342 Kenny Holmes	.07	.20
343 Darren Sharper RC	1.25	3.00
344 Rae Carruth	.07	.20
345 Chris Canty	.07	.20
346 Darrell Russell	.07	.20
347 Orlando Pace	.20	.50
348 Peter Boulware	.10	.30
349 Kenard Lang	.07	.20
350 Danny Wuerffel RC	.20	.50
351 Troy Davis	.07	.20
352 Shawn Springs	.10	.30
353 Walter Jones RC	.30	.75
354 Will Blackwell	.07	.20
355 Dwayne Rudd	.07	.20
356 49ers BB	.07	.20
357 Bears BB	.07	.20
358 Bengals BB	.07	.20
359 Bills BB	.07	.20
360 Broncos BB	.10	.30
361 Buccaneers BB	.07	.20
362 Cardinals BB	.10	.30
363 Chargers BB	.07	.20
364 Chiefs BB	.10	.30
365 Colts BB	.10	.30
366 Cowboys BB	.07	.20
367 Dolphins BB	.07	.20
368 Eagles BB	.07	.20
369 Falcons BB	.07	.20
370 Giants BB	.07	.20
371 Jaguars BB	.07	.20
372 Jets BB	.07	.20
373 Lions BB	.07	.20
374 Oilers BB	.07	.20
375 Packers BB	.20	.50
376 Panthers BB	.07	.20
377 Patriots BB	.07	.20
378 Raiders BB	.07	.20
379 Rams BB	.07	.20
380 Ravens BB	.07	.20
381 Redskins BB	.07	.20
382 Saints BB	.07	.20
383 Seahawks BB	.07	.20
384 Steelers BB	.10	.30
385 Vikings BB	.10	.30
386 William Floyd	.10	.30
387 Steve Young	.25	.60
388 Lee Woodall	.07	.20
389 J.J. Stokes	.10	.30
390 Marc Edwards	.07	.20
391 Rod Woodson	.10	.30
392 Jim Schwantz	.07	.20
393 Garrison Hearst	.10	.30
394 Rick Mirer	.07	.20
395 Alonzo Spellman	.07	.20
396 Tom Carter	.07	.20
397 Bryan Cox	.07	.20
398 John Allred RC	.07	.20
399 Ricky Proehl	.07	.20
400 Tyrone Hughes	.07	.20
401 Carl Pickens	.10	.30
402 Tremain Mack RC	.07	.20
403 Boomer Esiason	.10	.30
404 Ki-Jana Carter	.07	.20
405 Steve Tovar	.07	.20
406 Billy Joe Hobert	.10	.30
407 Andre Reed	.10	.30
408 Marcellus Wiley RC	.10	.30
409 Steve Tasker	.07	.20
410 Chris Spielman	.07	.20
411 Alfred Williams	.07	.20
412 John Elway	.75	2.00
413 Shannon Sharpe	.10	.30
414 Steve Atwater	.07	.20
415 Neil Smith	.10	.30
416 Darrien Gordon	.07	.20
417 Jeff Lewis	.07	.20
418 Flipper Anderson	.07	.20
419 Willie Green	.07	.20
420 Jackie Harris	.07	.20
421 Steve Walsh	.07	.20
422 Anthony Parker	.07	.20
423 Ronde Barber RC	.60	1.50
424 Warren Sapp	.10	.30
425 Aeneas Williams	.07	.20
426 Larry Centers	.10	.30
427 Eric Swann	.07	.20
428 Kevin Williams	.07	.20
429 Darren Bennett	.07	.20
430 Tony Martin	.10	.30
431 John Carney	.07	.20
432 Jim Everett	.07	.20
433 William Fuller	.07	.20
434 Latario Rachal RC	.07	.20
435 Erric Pegram	.07	.20
436 Eric Metcalf	.10	.30
437 Jerome Woods	.07	.20
438 Derrick Thomas	.20	.50
439 Elvis Grbac	.10	.30
440 Terry Wooden	.07	.20
441 Andre Rison	.10	.30
442 Brett Perriman	.07	.20
443 Paul Justin	.07	.20
444 Robert Blackmon	.07	.20
445 Carlton Gray	.07	.20
446 Chris Gardocki	.07	.20
447 Marshall Faulk	.25	.60
448 Sammie Burroughs	.07	.20
449 Quentin Coryatt	.07	.20
450 Troy Aikman	.40	1.00
451 Daryl Johnston	.10	.30
452 Tony Tolbert	.07	.20
453 Brock Marion	.07	.20
454 Billy Davis RC	.07	.20
455 Stepfret Williams	.07	.20
456 Anthony Miller	.07	.20
457 Dan Marino	.75	2.00
458 Jerris McPhail	.07	.20
459 Terrell Buckley	.07	.20
460 Daryl Gardener	.07	.20
461 George Teague	.07	.20
462 Derrick Rodgers RC	.07	.20
463 Fred Barnett	.07	.20
464 Darrin Smith	.07	.20
465 Michael Timpson	.07	.20
466 Jon Harris	.07	.20
467 Jason Dunn	.07	.20
468 Bobby Hoying	.10	.30
469 Ricky Watters	.10	.30
470 Derrick Witherspoon	.07	.20
471 Chris Chandler	.10	.30
472 Ray Buchanan	.07	.20
473 Michael Haynes	.07	.20
474 O.J. Santiago RC	.10	.30
475 Morten Andersen	.07	.20
476 Bert Emanuel	.10	.30
477 Chris Calloway	.07	.20
478 Jason Sehorn	.10	.30
479 John Jurkovic	.07	.20
480 Keenan McCardell	.10	.30
481 James O. Stewart	.10	.30
482 Rob Johnson	.20	.50
483 Mike Logan RC	.07	.20
484 Deon Figures	.07	.20
485 Kyle Brady	.07	.20
486 Alex Van Dyke	.07	.20
487 Jeff Graham	.07	.20
488 Jason Hanson	.07	.20
489 Herman Moore	.10	.30
490 Scott Mitchell	.10	.30
491 Tommy Vardell	.07	.20
492 Derrick Mason RC	.40	1.00
493 Rodney Thomas	.07	.20
494 Ronnie Harmon	.07	.20
495 Eddie George	.20	.50
496 Edgar Bennett	.10	.30
497 William Henderson	.10	.30
498 Dorsey Levens	.20	.50
499 Gilbert Brown	.10	.30
500 Steve Bono	.10	.30
501 Derrick Mayes	.10	.30
502 Fred Lane RC	.10	.30
503 Ernie Mills	.07	.20
504 Tim Biakabutuka	.10	.30
505 Michael Bates	.07	.20
506 Winslow Oliver	.07	.20
507 Ty Law	.10	.30
508 Shawn Jefferson	.07	.20
509 Vincent Brisby	.07	.20
510 Henry Thomas	.07	.20
511 Tedy Bruschi	.40	1.00
512 Curtis Martin	.25	.60
513 Jeff George	.10	.30
514 Desmond Howard	.10	.30
515 Napoleon Kaufman	.20	.50
516 Kenny Shedd RC	.07	.20
517 Russell Maryland	.07	.20
518 Lance Johnstone	.07	.20
519 Eric Turner	.07	.20
520 Dexter McCleon RC	.07	.20
521 Craig Heyward	.07	.20
522 Ryan McNeil	.07	.20
523 Mark Rypien	.07	.20
524 Mike Jones LB	.07	.20
525 Jamie Sharper	.07	.20
526 Tony Siragusa	.07	.20
527 Michael Jackson	.10	.30
528 Floyd Turner	.07	.20
529 Eric Green	.07	.20
530 Michael McCrary	.07	.20
531 Jay Graham RC	.10	.30
532 Terry Allen	.20	.50
533 Sean Gilbert	.07	.20
534 Scott Turner	.07	.20
535 Cris Dishman	.07	.20
536 Darrell Green	.10	.30
537 Stephen Davis	.20	.50
538 Alvin Harper	.07	.20
539 Daryl Hobbs	.07	.20
540 Wayne Martin	.07	.20
541 Heath Shuler	.07	.20
542 Andre Hastings	.07	.20
543 Jared Tomich	.07	.20
544 Nicky Savoie RC	.07	.20
545 Cortez Kennedy	.07	.20
546 Warren Moon	.20	.50
547 Chad Brown	.07	.20
548 Willie Williams	.07	.20
549 Bennie Blades	.07	.20
550 Darren Perry	.07	.20
551 Mark Bruener	.07	.20
552 Yancey Thigpen	.10	.30
553 Courtney Hawkins	.07	.20
554 Chad Scott RC	.10	.30
555 George Jones	.10	.30
556 Robert Tate RC	.07	.20
557 Torrian Gray RC	.07	.20
558 Robert Griffith RC	.07	.20
559 Leroy Hoard	.07	.20
560 Robert Smith	.10	.30
561 Randall Cunningham	.20	.50
562 Darrell Russell CL	.07	.20
563 Troy Aikman CL	.20	.50
564 Dan Marino CL	.15	.40
565 Jim Druckenmiller CL	.07	.20

1997 Collector's Choice Crash the Game

Randomly inserted in Series one packs at the rate of one in five, this set consists of 30-players featured on three cards each. A different game date was included on each card. If that player threw or scored a touchdown on that game date, the card was considered a game winner. Winning cards could be redeemed (along with $2) for a foil enhanced card of the featured player. The contest ended 2/20/98.

Card	Low	High
COMPLETE SET (90)	30.00	60.00
COMP.SHORT SET (30)	10.00	20.00
STATED ODDS 1:5 SERIES 1		
COMP.PRIZE SET (19)	15.00	30.00
*PRIZE STARS: 1X TO 2.5X BASE CARD HI		
*PRIZE ROOKIES: .4X TO 1X BASE CARD HI		
1A Troy Aikman	.60	1.50
1B Troy Aikman 11/2 W	.60	1.50
1C Troy Aikman 11/27 W	.60	1.50
2A Dan Marino	1.25	3.00
2B Dan Marino 11/17 W	1.25	3.00
2C Dan Marino 11/30 W	1.25	3.00
3A Steve Young	.40	1.00
3B Steve Young 11/2 L	.40	1.00
3C Steve Young 11/23 W	.40	1.00
4A Brett Favre	1.25	3.00
4B Brett Favre 10/27 W	1.25	3.00
4C Brett Favre 12/1 W	1.25	3.00
5A Drew Bledsoe	.40	1.00
5B Drew Bledsoe 11/9 W	.40	1.00
5C Drew Bledsoe 11/23 L	.40	1.00
6A Jeff Blake 9/28 W	.20	.50
6B Jeff Blake 10/19 L	.20	.50
6C Jeff Blake 11/30 L	.20	.50
7A Mark Brunell	.40	1.00
7B Mark Brunell 10/19 W	.40	1.00
7C Mark Brunell 11/16 W	.40	1.00
8A John Elway	1.25	3.00
8B John Elway 11/9 W	1.25	3.00
8C John Elway 11/30 W	1.25	3.00
9A Vinny Testaverde 9/28 W	.20	.50
9B Vinny Testaverde 10/19 W	.20	.50
9C Vinny Testaverde 11/9 L	.20	.50
10A Steve McNair	.40	1.00
10B Steve McNair 10/26 W	.40	1.00
10C Steve McNair 11/27 W	.40	1.00
11A Jerry Rice	.60	1.50
11B Jerry Rice 10/12 L	.60	1.50
11C Jerry Rice 11/10 L	.60	1.50
12A Terry Glenn	.30	.75
12B Terry Glenn 10/27 L	.30	.75
12C Terry Glenn 11/16 L	.30	.75
13A Michael Jackson 10/5 L	.20	.50
13B Michael Jackson 11/9 L	.20	.50
13C Michael Jackson 11/23 L	.20	.50
14A Tony Martin 9/21 L	.20	.50
14B Tony Martin 10/16 L	.20	.50
14C Tony Martin 11/16 L	.20	.50
15A Isaac Bruce 9/28 L	.30	.75
15B Isaac Bruce 10/12 L	.30	.75
15C Isaac Bruce 11/16 L	.30	.75
16A Cris Carter 9/28 W	.30	.75
16B Cris Carter 11/16 L	.30	.75
16C Cris Carter 12/1 L	.30	.75
17A Shannon Sharpe 10/19 L	.20	.50
17B Shannon Sharpe 11/2 L	.20	.50
17C Shannon Sharpe 11/30 L	.20	.50
18A Rae Carruth 9/29 W	.05	.15
18B Rae Carruth 10/26 L	.05	.15
18C Rae Carruth 11/9 L	.05	.15
19A Ike Hilliard 10/5 L	.25	.60
19B Ike Hilliard 10/19 L	.25	.60
19C Ike Hilliard 11/23 L	.25	.60
20A Yatil Green 9/21 L	.08	.25
20B Yatil Green 10/5 L	.08	.25
20C Yatil Green 11/17 L	.08	.25
21A Terry Allen 10/5 W	.30	.75
21B Terry Allen 10/13 L	.30	.75
21C Terry Allen 11/23 L	.30	.75
22A Emmitt Smith	1.00	2.50
22B Emmitt Smith 11/16 L	1.00	2.50
22C Emmitt Smith 11/23 W	1.00	2.50
23A K.Abdul-Jabbar 10/12 W	.20	.50
23B K.Abdul-Jabbar 11/17 W	.20	.50
23C K.Abdul-Jabbar 11/30 W	.20	.50
24A Barry Sanders	1.00	2.50
24B Barry Sanders 11/9 W	1.00	2.50
24C Barry Sanders 11/27 W	1.00	2.50
25A Terrell Davis	.40	1.00
25B Terrell Davis 11/16 L	.40	1.00
25C Terrell Davis 11/24 W	.40	1.00
26A Jerome Bettis 9/22 L	.30	.75
26B Jerome Bettis 11/3 L	.30	.75
26C Jerome Bettis 11/16 L	.30	.75
27A Ricky Watters 9/28 L	.20	.50
27B Ricky Watters 10/26 L	.20	.50
27C Ricky Watters 11/10 L	.20	.50
28A Curtis Martin	.40	1.00
28B Curtis Martin 10/27 L	.40	1.00
28C Curtis Martin 11/16 L	.40	1.00
29A Byron Hanspard 9/28 L	.08	.25
29B Byron Hanspard 10/26 L	.08	.25
29C Byron Hanspard 11/23 L	.08	.25
30A Warrick Dunn	.40	1.00
30B Warrick Dunn 10/5 W	.40	1.00
30C Warrick Dunn 11/16 L	.40	1.00

1997 Collector's Choice Jumbos

Inserted one per special retail blister pack, each of these five cards is essentially an enlarged version of a base series two Collector's Choice card. Each measures roughly 3 1/2" by 5" and is numbered X of 5. Each pack included one Jumbo card and two series two retail packs for a suggested retail price of $2.99

Card	Low	High
COMPLETE SET (5)	4.00	10.00
1 Troy Aikman	.80	2.00
2 Brett Favre	1.60	4.00
3 Terrell Davis	1.00	2.50
4 Reggie White	.40	1.00
5 Eddie George	.80	2.00

1997 Collector's Choice Mini-Standee

Randomly inserted in Series 2 packs at the rate of one in five, this 30-card set features color images of NFL superstars printed on cards that could be stood up for viewing.

Card	Low	High
COMPLETE SET (30)	12.50	25.00
STATED ODDS 1:5 SERIES 2		
ST1 Jerry Rice	.60	1.50
ST2 Rashaan Salaam	.10	.30
ST3 Jeff Blake	.20	.50
ST4 Antowain Smith	.75	2.00
ST5 John Elway	1.25	3.00
ST6 Errict Rhett	.10	.30
ST7 Jake Plummer	1.50	4.00
ST8 Junior Seau	.30	.75
ST9 Marcus Allen	.30	.75
ST10 Marvin Harrison	.30	.75
ST11 Emmitt Smith	1.00	2.50
ST12 Dan Marino	1.25	3.00
ST13 Ricky Watters	.20	.50
ST14 Jamal Anderson	.30	.75
ST15 Rodney Hampton	.20	.50
ST16 Mark Brunell	.40	1.00
ST17 Keyshawn Johnson	.30	.75
ST18 Barry Sanders	1.00	2.50
ST19 Eddie George	.30	.75
ST20 Brett Favre	1.25	3.00
ST21 Kerry Collins	.30	.75
ST22 Drew Bledsoe	.40	1.00
ST23 Napoleon Kaufman	.30	.75
ST24 Tony Banks	.20	.50
ST25 Vinny Testaverde	.20	.50
ST26 Terry Allen	.30	.75
ST27 Mario Bates	.10	.30
ST28 Joey Galloway	.20	.50
ST29 Jerome Bettis	.30	.75
ST30 Robert Smith	.20	.50

1997 Collector's Choice Names of the Game Jumbos

Inserted one per retail blister pack, these cards feature top NFL players printed on jumbo (3 1/2" by 5") cards. Each card was packaged with two 1997 Collector's Choice retail packs. The entire package carried a suggested retail price of $2.99. An even larger (5" by 7") version of the cards was also produced as a special retail pack insert. This version was actually divided into two different 5-card sets.

Card	Low	High
COMPLETE SET (10)	5.00	12.00
*5X7 CARDS: SAME PRICE		
1 Brett Favre	1.00	2.50

2 Emmitt Smith .80 2.00
3 Curtis Martin .40 1.00
4 Jerome Bettis .40 1.00
5 Terrell Davis .80 2.00
6 Troy Aikman .50 1.25
7 Dan Marino 1.00 2.50
8 Drew Bledsoe .50 1.25
9 Reggie White .40 1.00
10 Eddie George .50 1.25

1997 Collector's Choice Star Quest

Randomly inserted in Series 2 packs, this 90-card tiered insert set features color player photos with different numbers of stars on the cards to signify what particular tier that card belongs to. Cards 1-45 have one star with an insertion rate of 1:1; cards 46-65 have two stars and are inserted 1:21; cards 66-80 have three stars and are inserted 1:71; cards 81-90 have four stars and are inserted 1:145.

COMPLETE SET (90) 150.00 300.00
COMP.SERIES 1 (45) 5.00 10.00
SQ1-SQ45 STATED ODDS 1:1 SERIES 2
SQ46-SQ65 STATED ODDS 1:21 SER.2
SQ66-SQ80 STATED ODDS 1:71 SER.2
SQ81-SQ90 STATED ODDS 1:145 SER.2
SQ1 Frank Sanders .25 .60
SQ2 Jamal Anderson .40 1.00
SQ3 Byron Bam Morris .15 .40
SQ4 Thurman Thomas .40 1.00
SQ5 Muhsin Muhammad .25 .60
SQ6 Bobby Engram .25 .60
SQ7 Carl Pickens .25 .60
SQ8 Deion Sanders .40 1.00
SQ9 Shannon Sharpe .25 .60
SQ10 Herman Moore .25 .60
SQ11 Robert Brooks .25 .60
SQ12 Steve McNair .40 1.00
SQ13 Marshall Faulk .40 1.00
SQ14 Keenan McCardell .25 .60
SQ15 Tamarick Vanover .25 .60
SQ16 Fred Barnett .15 .40
SQ17 Orlando Thomas .15 .40
SQ18 Drew Bledsoe .40 1.00
SQ19 Mario Bates .15 .40
SQ20 Keyshawn Johnson .40 1.00
SQ21 Rodney Hampton .25 .60
SQ22 Darrell Russell .15 .40
SQ23 Irving Fryar .25 .60
SQ24 Charles Johnson .25 .60
SQ25 Stan Humphries .25 .60
SQ26 Terrell Owens .40 1.00
SQ27 Chris Warren .25 .60
SQ28 Isaac Bruce .40 1.00
SQ29 Warrick Dunn .60 1.50
SQ30 Gus Frerotte .15 .40
SQ31 Rocket Ismail .25 .60
SQ32 Natrone Means .25 .60
SQ33 Chris Sanders .15 .40
SQ34 Vinny Testaverde .25 .60
SQ35 Ken Norton Jr. .15 .40
SQ36 Tim Biakabutuka .25 .60
SQ37 Marcus Allen .40 1.00
SQ38 Zach Thomas .40 1.00
SQ39 Derrick Thomas .40 1.00
SQ40 Tyrone Wheatley .25 .60
SQ41 Dorsey Levens .40 1.00
SQ42 Darnay Scott .25 .60
SQ43 Scott Mitchell .25 .60
SQ44 Marvin Harrison .40 1.00
SQ45 Eddie Kennison .25 .60
SQ46 Jake Reed 1.50 4.00
SQ47 Andre Reed 1.50 4.00
SQ48 Neil Smith 1.50 4.00
SQ49 Anthony Johnson 1.00 2.50
SQ50 Napoleon Kaufman 1.50 4.00
SQ51 Terance Mathis 1.50 4.00
SQ52 Tony Martin 1.50 4.00
SQ53 Adrian Murrell 1.50 4.00
SQ54 Glyn Milburn 1.00 2.50
SQ55 Errict Rhett 1.00 2.50
SQ56 Kerry Collins 1.50 4.00
SQ57 Curtis Conway 1.50 4.00
SQ58 Eric Swann 1.00 2.50
SQ59 Michael Jackson 1.50 4.00
SQ60 Ty Detmer 1.50 4.00
SQ61 Michael Irvin 1.50 4.00
SQ62 Terrell Fletcher 1.00 2.50
SQ63 Brian Mitchell 1.00 2.50
SQ64 Tony Banks 1.50 4.00
SQ65 Eddie George 1.50 4.00
SQ66 Kordell Stewart 4.00 10.00
SQ67 Greg Hill 2.50 6.00
SQ68 Karim Abdul-Jabbar 2.50 6.00
SQ69 Cris Carter 4.00 10.00
SQ70 Terry Glenn 4.00 10.00
SQ71 Emmitt Smith 10.00 25.00
SQ72 Jim Harbaugh 4.00 10.00
SQ73 Jeff Blake 4.00 10.00
SQ74 Rashaan Salaam 2.50 6.00
SQ75 Ricky Watters 4.00 10.00
SQ76 Joey Galloway 4.00 10.00
SQ77 Junior Seau 4.00 10.00
SQ78 Dave Brown 2.50 6.00
SQ79 Tim Brown 4.00 10.00
SQ80 Troy Aikman 7.50 20.00
SQ81 Dan Marino 12.50 30.00
SQ82 Brett Favre 10.00 25.00
SQ83 John Elway 12.50 30.00
SQ84 Steve Young 6.00 15.00
SQ85 Mark Brunell 5.00 12.00
SQ86 Barry Sanders 12.50 30.00
SQ87 Jerome Bettis 5.00 12.00
SQ88 Terrell Davis 5.00 12.00
SQ89 Curtis Martin 5.00 12.00
SQ90 Jerry Rice 7.50 20.00

1997 Collector's Choice Stick-Ums

Randomly inserted in Series 1 packs at a rate of one in three, this 30-card set features color player images from each NFL team that can be peeled off and re-stuck anywhere.
Cardbacks contain the set checklist and instructions on how to use the stickers.

COMPLETE SET (30) 4.00 10.00
STATED ODDS 1:3 SERIES 1
S1 Kerry Collins .15 .40
S2 Troy Aikman .30 .75
S3 Steve Young .20 .50
S4 Ricky Watters .08 .25
S5 Cris Carter .15 .40
S6 Terry Allen .15 .40
S7 Bobby Engram .08 .25
S8 Larry Centers .08 .25
S9 Mike Alstott .15 .40
S10 Rodney Hampton .08 .25
S11 Eddie Kennison .08 .25
S12 Jamal Anderson .15 .40
S13 Jim Everett .05 .15
S14 Curtis Martin .20 .50
S15 Keenan McCardell .08 .25
S16 Kordell Stewart .15 .40
S17 John Elway .60 1.50
S18 Terrell Davis .20 .50
S19 Thurman Thomas .15 .40
S20 Marshall Faulk .20 .50
S21 Marcus Allen .15 .40
S22 Tony Martin .08 .25
S23 Dan Marino .60 1.50
S24 Karim Abdul-Jabbar .08 .25
S25 Carl Pickens .08 .25
S26 Eddie George .15 .40
S27 Joey Galloway .08 .25
S28 Napoleon Kaufman .15 .40
S29 Vinny Testaverde .08 .25
S30 Keyshawn Johnson .15 .40

1997 Collector's Choice Turf Champions

Randomly inserted in Series 1 packs, this 90-card set features color action player photos of NFL Superstars. The set consists of four "Tiers" which were randomly inserted in packs according to the following insertion rates: Tier 1 (1-30) inserted 1:1, Tier 2 (31-60) inserted 1:21, Tier 3 (61-80) inserted 1:71, and Tier 4 (81-90) inserted 1:145. Some cards from the top two tiers were produced in a die cut format.

COMPLETE SET (90) 175.00 350.00
COMP.SERIES 1 (30) 3.00 6.00
TC1-TC30 STATED ODDS 1:1H, 2:1R SER.1
TC31-TC60 STATED ODDS 1:21 SER.1
TC61-TC80 STATED ODDS 1:71 SER.1
TC81-TC90 STATED ODDS 1:145 SER.1
TC1 Kerry Collins .15 .40
TC2 Scott Mitchell .15 .40
TC3 Jim Schwantz .08 .25
TC4 Orlando Pace .25 .60
TC5 Troy Davis .15 .40
TC6 Vinny Testaverde .15 .40
TC7 Rocket Ismail .15 .40
TC8 Henry Ellard .08 .25
TC9 Kevin Turner .08 .25
TC10 Bobby Engram .15 .40
TC11 Keyshawn Johnson .25 .60
TC12 Trent Dilfer .25 .60
TC13 Elvis Grbac .15 .40
TC14 Trev Alberts .08 .25
TC15 Kevin Hardy .08 .25
TC16 Warren Sapp .15 .40
TC17 Chris Hudson .08 .25
TC18 Antonio Langham .08 .25
TC19 Jonathan Ogden .08 .25
TC20 Bruce Smith .15 .40
TC21 Marcus Allen .25 .60
TC22 Desmond Howard .15 .40
TC23 Eric Metcalf .15 .40
TC24 Terance Mathis .15 .40
TC25 LeShon Johnson .08 .25
TC26 Kevin Greene .15 .40
TC27 Alex Van Dyke .08 .25
TC28 Jeff Jaeger .08 .25
TC29 Jason Elam .08 .25
TC30 Thomas Lewis .08 .25
TC31 Rick Mirer 1.00 3.00
TC32 Warren Moon 3.00 8.00
TC33 Jim Kelly 3.00 8.00
TC34 Junior Seau 3.00 8.00
TC35 Jeff Hostetler 1.00 3.00
TC36 Neil O'Donnell 2.00 5.00
TC37 Jeff Blake 2.00 5.00
TC38 Kordell Stewart 3.00 8.00
TC39 Terry Glenn 3.00 8.00
TC40 Simeon Rice 2.00 5.00
TC41 Jimmy Smith 2.00 5.00
TC42 Natrone Means 2.00 5.00
TC43 Tony Martin 2.00 5.00
TC44 Charles Johnson 2.00 5.00
TC45 Napoleon Kaufman 3.00 8.00
TC46 Dale Carter 1.00 3.00
TC47 Brett Perriman 1.00 3.00
TC48 Cortez Kennedy 1.00 3.00
TC49 Bryce Paup 1.00 3.00
TC50 Greg Lloyd 1.00 3.00
TC51 Bryant Young 1.00 3.00
TC52 Steve McNair 3.00 8.00
TC53 Garrison Hearst 2.00 5.00
TC54 John Copeland 1.00 3.00
TC55 Eric Curry 1.00 3.00
TC56 Reggie White 3.00 8.00
TC57 Rod Woodson 3.00 8.00
TC58 Andre Rison 2.00 5.00
TC59 Herschel Walker 2.00 5.00
TC60 John Kasay 1.00 3.00
TC61 Emmitt Smith 10.00 25.00
TC62 Dan Marino 12.50 30.00
TC63 Michael Irvin 5.00 12.00
TC64 Drew Bledsoe 5.00 12.00
TC65 Mark Brunell 5.00 12.00
TC66 Jim Harbaugh 3.00 8.00
TC67 Herman Moore 3.00 8.00
TC68 Rashaan Salaam 2.00 5.00
TC69 Ty Detmer 3.00 8.00
TC70 Cris Carter 5.00 12.00
TC71 Chris Warren 3.00 8.00
TC72 Thurman Thomas 5.00 12.00
TC73 Ricky Watters 3.00 8.00
TC74 Tim Brown 5.00 12.00
TC75 Marshall Faulk 5.00 12.00
TC76 Jerome Bettis 5.00 12.00
TC77 Karim Abdul-Jabbar 5.00 12.00
TC78 Deion Sanders 5.00 12.00
TC79 Ben Coates 3.00 8.00
TC80 Andre Reed 3.00 8.00
TC81 Brett Favre 12.50 30.00
TC82 Terrell Davis 5.00 12.00
TC83 Troy Aikman 6.00 15.00
TC84 Carl Pickens 3.00 8.00
TC85 Barry Sanders 10.00 25.00
TC86 Jerry Rice 6.00 15.00
TC87 Curtis Martin 5.00 12.00
TC88 Steve Young 5.00 12.00
TC89 Eddie George 5.00 12.00
TC90 John Elway 12.50 30.00

1997 Collector's Choice Turf Champion Jumbos

These oversize cards were inserted into special retail boxes. This is a limited parallel featuring some of the more popular players included in the regular Turf Champion set.

COMPLETE SET (8) 6.00 15.00
TC1 Kerry Collins .40 1.00
TC62 Dan Marino 1.50 4.00
TC65 Mark Brunell .50 1.25
TC76 Jerome Bettis .50 1.25
TC81 Brett Favre 1.50 4.00
TC83 Troy Aikman .75 2.00
TC88 Steve Young .60 1.50
TC90 John Elway 1.50 4.00

1992 Collector's Edge Prototypes

These six prototype cards were issued before the 1992 regular issue was released to show the design of Collector's Edge cards. The cards were issued in two different styles, with slightly sticky backs with a removable paper protective cover backing or with a non-sticky back.The paper-covered back versions are somewhat more difficult to find. The production figures were reportedly 8,000 for each card.

COMPLETE SET (6) 8.00 20.00
*STICKER BACKS: 1X TO 2X
1 Jim Kelly .80 2.00
2 Randall Cunningham .80 2.00
3 Warren Moon .80 2.00
4 John Elway 3.20 8.00
5 Dan Marino 3.20 8.00
6 Bernie Kosar .60 1.60

1992 Collector's Edge

This 250-card standard-size set was issued in two series of 175 and 75 cards, respectively. Cards were issued six per pack. The cards are printed on plastic stock and production quantities were limited to 100,000 of each card; with every card individually numbered on the back. The cards are checklisted alphabetically according to teams. There are a few cards in the set which were apparently late additions as counterparts have been found with a large "X" on the cardfront. We've listed the X-out variation cards below, but they are not considered part of the complete set. It is thought card number 179 was also changed, but has not been confirmed. Two thousand five hundred cards autographed by John Elway and Ken O'Brien were randomly inserted in first series foil packs as well as factory sets. Randomly inserted in second series (Rookies) packs were 2500 signed Ronnie Lott cards. These card do not feature serial number. A second version of the Ronnie Lott signed card was also produced bearing a different photo and card number RL1. These card feature a hand serial numbering of 2542. Two Rookie/Update Prototype cards were produced as well and listed below.

COMPLETE SET (250) 15.00 35.00
COMP.SERIES 1 (175) 8.00 20.00
COMP.FACT.SER.1 (175) 8.00 20.00
COMP.SERIES 2 (75) 6.00 15.00
COMP.FACT.SER.2 (75) 6.00 15.00
1 Chris Miller .07 .20
2 Steve Broussard .02 .10
3 Mike Pritchard .07 .20
4 Tim Green .02 .10
5 Andre Rison .07 .20
6 Deion Sanders .40 1.00
7 Jim Kelly .15 .40
8 James Lofton .07 .20
9 Andre Reed .07 .20
10 Bruce Smith .15 .40
11 Thurman Thomas .15 .40
12 Cornelius Bennett .07 .20
13 Jim Harbaugh .15 .40
14 William Perry .07 .20
15 Mike Singletary .07 .20
16 Mark Carrier DB .02 .10
17 Kevin Butler .02 .10
18 Tom Waddle .02 .10
19 Boomer Esiason .07 .20
20 David Fulcher .02 .10
21 Anthony Munoz .07 .20
22 Tim McGee .02 .10
23 Harold Green .02 .10
24 Rickey Dixon .02 .10
25 Bernie Kosar .07 .20
26 Michael Dean Perry .07 .20
27 Mike Baab .02 .10
28 Brian Brennan .02 .10
29 Michael Jackson .07 .20
30 Eric Metcalf .07 .20
31 Troy Aikman 1.00 2.50
32 Emmitt Smith 2.50 5.00
33 Michael Irvin .15 .40
34 Jay Novacek .07 .20
35 Issiac Holt .02 .10
36 Ken Norton .07 .20
37 John Elway 1.50 4.00
38 Gaston Green .02 .10
39 Charles Dimry .02 .10
40 Vance Johnson .02 .10
41 Dennis Smith .02 .10
42 David Treadwell .02 .10
43 Michael Young .02 .10
44 Bennie Blades .02 .10
45 Mel Gray .07 .20
46 Andre Ware .02 .10
47 Rodney Peete .07 .20
48 Toby Caston RC .02 .10
49 Herman Moore .15 .40
50 Brian Noble .02 .10
51 Sterling Sharpe .15 .40
52 Mike Tomczak .02 .10
53 Vinnie Clark .02 .10
54 Tony Mandarich .02 .10
55 Ed West .02 .10
56 Warren Moon .15 .40
57 Ray Childress .02 .10
58 Haywood Jeffires .07 .20
59 Al Smith .02 .10
60 Cris Dishman .02 .10
61 Ernest Givins .07 .20
62 Richard Johnson CB .02 .10
63 Eric Dickerson .07 .20
64 Jessie Hester .02 .10
65 Rohn Stark .02 .10
66 Clarence Verdin .02 .10
67 Dean Biasucci .02 .10
68 Duane Bickett .02 .10
69 Jeff George .15 .40
70 Christian Okoye .02 .10
71 Derrick Thomas .15 .40
72 Stephone Paige .02 .10
73 Dan Saleaumua .02 .10
74 Deron Cherry .02 .10
75 Kevin Ross .02 .10
76 Barry Word .02 .10
77 Ronnie Lott .07 .20
78 Greg Townsend .02 .10
79 Willie Gault .07 .20
80 Howie Long .15 .40
81 Winston Moss .02 .10
82 Steve Smith .02 .10
83 Jay Schroeder .02 .10
84 Jim Everett .07 .20
85 Flipper Anderson .02 .10
86 Henry Ellard .07 .20
87 Tony Zendejas .02 .10
88 Robert Delpino .02 .10
89 Pat Terrell .02 .10
90 Dan Marino 1.50 4.00
91 Mark Clayton .07 .20
92 Jim C.Jensen .02 .10
93 Reggie Roby .02 .10
94 Sammie Smith .02 .10
95 Tony Martin .07 .20
96 Jeff Cross .02 .10
97 Anthony Carter .07 .20
98 Chris Doleman .02 .10
99 Wade Wilson .02 .10
100 Cris Carter .30 .75
101 Mike Merriweather .02 .10
102 Gary Zimmerman .02 .10
103 Chris Singleton .02 .10
104 Bruce Armstrong .02 .10
105 Marv Cook .02 .10
106 Andre Tippett .02 .10
107 Tommy Hodson .02 .10
108 Greg McMurtry .02 .10
109 Jon Vaughn .02 .10
110 Vaughan Johnson .02 .10
111 Craig Heyward .07 .20
112 Floyd Turner .02 .10
113 Pat Swilling .02 .10
114 Rickey Jackson .02 .10
115 Steve Walsh .02 .10
116 Phil Simms .07 .20
117 Carl Banks .02 .10
118 Mark Ingram .02 .10
119 Bart Oates .02 .10
120 Lawrence Taylor .15 .40
121 Jeff Hostetler .07 .20
122 Rob Moore .07 .20
123 Ken O'Brien .02 .10
124 Bill Pickel .02 .10
125 Irv Eatman .02 .10
126 Browning Nagle .02 .10
127 Al Toon .07 .20
128 Randall Cunningham .15 .40
129 Eric Allen .02 .10
130 Mike Golic .02 .10
131 Fred Barnett .15 .40
132 Keith Byars .02 .10
133 Calvin Williams .07 .20
134 Randal Hill .02 .10
135 Ricky Proehl .02 .10
136 Lance Smith .02 .10
137 Ernie Jones .02 .10
138 Timm Rosenbach .02 .10
139 Anthony Thompson .02 .10
140 Bubby Brister .02 .10
141 Merril Hoge .02 .10
142 Louis Lipps .02 .10
143 Eric Green .02 .10
144 Gary Anderson K .02 .10
145 Neil O'Donnell .07 .20
146 Rod Bernstine .02 .10
147 John Friesz .07 .20
148 Anthony Miller .07 .20
149 Junior Seau .15 .40
150 Leslie O'Neal .07 .20
151 Nate Lewis .02 .10
152 Steve Young .75 2.00
153 Kevin Fagan .02 .10
154 Charles Haley .07 .20
155 Tom Rathman .02 .10
156 Jerry Rice 1.00 2.50
157 John Taylor .07 .20
158 Brian Blades .07 .20
159 Patrick Hunter .02 .10
160 Cortez Kennedy .07 .20
161 Vann McElroy .02 .10
162 Dan McGwire .02 .10
163 John L. Williams .02 .10
164 Gary Anderson RB .02 .10
165 Broderick Thomas .02 .10
166 Vinny Testaverde .07 .20
167 Lawrence Dawsey .07 .20
168 Paul Gruber .02 .10
169 Keith McCants .02 .10
170 Mark Rypien .02 .10
171 Gary Clark .15 .40
172 Earnest Byner .02 .10
173 Brian Mitchell .07 .20
174 Monte Coleman .02 .10
175 Joe Jacoby .02 .10
176 Tommy Vardell RC .02 .10
177 Troy Vincent RC .02 .10
178 Robert Jones RC .02 .10
179 Marc Boutte RC .02 .10
180 Marco Coleman RC .02 .10
181 Chris Mims RC .07 .20
182 Tony Casillas .07 .20
182X Ray Roberts 30.00 50.00
Large X on front
183 Shane Dronett RC .02 .10
184 Sean Gilbert RC .07 .20
185 Siran Stacy RC .02 .10
186 Tommy Maddox RC 1.25 3.00
187 Steve Israel RC .02 .10
188 Brad Muster .02 .10
188X Casey Weldon 30.00 50.00
189 Shane Collins RC .02 .10
190 Terrell Buckley RC .02 .10
191 Eugene Chung RC .02 .10
192 Leon Searcy RC .02 .10
193 Chuck Smith RC .02 .10
194 Patrick Rowe RC .02 .10
195 Bill Johnson RC .02 .10
196 Gerald Dixon RC .02 .10
197 Robert Porcher RC .15 .40
198 Tracy Scroggins RC .02 .10
199 Jason Hanson RC .07 .20
200 Corey Harris RC .02 .10
201 Eddie Robinson RC .02 .10
202 Steve Emtman RC .02 .10
203 Ashley Ambrose RC .15 .40
204 Greg Skrepenak RC .02 .10
205 Todd Collins RC .02 .10
206 Derek Brown TE RC .02 .10
207 Kurt Barber RC .02 .10
208 Tony Sacca RC .02 .10
209 Mark Wheeler RC .02 .10
210 Kevin Smith RC .02 .10
211 John Fina RC .02 .10
212 Johnny Mitchell RC .02 .10
213 Dale Carter RC .07 .20
214 Bob Spitulski RC .02 .10
215 Phillippi Sparks RC .02 .10
216 Levon Kirkland RC .02 .10
217 Mike Sherrard .02 .10
218 Marquez Pope RC .02 .10
219 Courtney Hawkins RC .07 .20
220 Tyji Armstrong RC .02 .10
221 Keith Jackson .07 .20
222 Clayton Holmes RC .02 .10
223 Quentin Coryatt RC .02 .10
224 Troy Auzenne RC .02 .10
225 David Klingler RC .02 .10
226 Darryl Williams RC .02 .10
227 Carl Pickens RC .15 .40
228 Jimmy Smith RC 2.00 5.00
229 Chester McGlockton RC .07 .20
230 Robert Brooks RC .50 1.25
231 Alonzo Spellman RC .07 .20
232 Darren Woodson RC .15 .40
233 Lewis Billups .02 .10
234 Edgar Bennett RC .15 .40
235 Vaughn Dunbar RC .02 .10
236 Steve Bono RC .15 .40
237 Clarence Kay .02 .10
238 Chris Hinton .02 .10
239 Jimmie Jones .02 .10
240 Vai Sikahema .02 .10
241 Russell Maryland .02 .10
242 Neal Anderson .02 .10
242X Mark Bavaro 30.00 50.00
243 Charles Mann .02 .10
244 Hugh Millen .02 .10
244X Bobby Humphrey 30.00 50.00
245 Roger Craig .07 .20
246 Rich Gannon .15 .40
247 Ricky Ervins .02 .10
247X Marion Butts 12.00 30.00
248 Leonard Marshall .02 .10
249 Eric Dickerson .07 .20
250 Joe Montana 1.50 4.00
RL1 Ronnie Lott AU/2542 7.50 15.00
RU1 Terrell Buckley Proto. .75 2.00
RU2 Tommy Maddox Proto. 1.00 2.50
AU37 John Elway AU/2500 25.00 60.00
AU77 Ronnie Lott AU Bonus 7.50 15.00
AU123 Ken O'Brien AU/2500 3.00 8.00

1992 Collector's Edge Promos

This four-card set was issued to promote the Tuff Stuff Buyer's Club. The Elway card was distributed in all copies of the November issue of Tuff Stuff. More than 250,000 cards were printed; only about 40,000 each of the remaining three cards were printed. One of these was given away with each paid membership in the Buyers Club. The Elway card was also printed with the designations "Proto 1," "Elway Foundation," and "John Elway Dealerships." The number of these additional cards is reportedly less than 50,000 and they are not included in the complete set price. The fronts of these standard-size promo cards have a color action player photo inside a gold frame and dark blue borders. The upper left corner of the picture is cut off. The player's name and position appear in the bottom border, and the team helmet is superimposed at the lower right corner of the picture. Within bright blue borders, the backs carry a color head shot, biography, and statistics on a ghosted version of the front photo. The cards are numbered on the back, and each has a serial number in the bottom border.

COMPLETE SET (4) 4.00 10.00
TS1 John Elway 1.20 3.00
TS2 Ronnie Lott 1.60 4.00
TS3 Jim Everett 1.20 3.00
TS4 Bernie Kosar 1.20 3.00
PROT1 John Elway 3.20 8.00
NNO Elway Foundation 10.00 25.00
NNO Elway Dealerships 10.00 25.00

1993 Collector's Edge Prototypes

These six prototype cards were issued before the 1993 regular issue set was released to show the design of the 1993 Collector's Edge regular series. Forty thousand six-card sets were produced, with each card serial-numbered from 00001 to 40,000 on the backs. The standard-size cards feature color action photos with blue marbleized borders on their fronts. The team helmet appears in the lower right corner. Inside a green marbleized border, the backs have a head shot, biography, and statistics placed on a three-dimensional style gray granite panel. The cards are numbered on the back "Proto X." Also, 8 1/2" by 11" versions of these prototypes were packed in dealer cases. The oversized cards are unnumbered, and the production number is handwritten on the back in a gold-colored permanent marker. Otherwise, the cards are identical to their standard-size counterparts but are valued at two to three times the corresponding values listed below.

COMPLETE SET (6) 4.80 12.00
1 John Elway 2.00 5.00
2 Derrick Thomas .50 1.25
3 Randall Cunningham .50 1.25
4 Thurman Thomas .50 1.25
5 Warren Moon .50 1.25
6 Barry Sanders 2.00 5.00

1993 Collector's Edge RU Prototypes

These five prototypes were issued to herald the design of the regular 1993 Collector's Edge Rookie/Update set. Each card carries a production number on its back. The standard-size cards feature on their fronts color player action shots framed by a thin red line and having blue marbleized borders. The backgrounds of the photos are slightly ghosted, making the image of the featured player stand out. The player's name and position, as well as the team helmet, rest at the bottom. The back has a gray lithic design with green marbleized borders. A color player head shot appears at the upper left. His name, team name and logo, position, and uniform number are shown alongside to the right. Biography and statistics appear below. The cards are numbered on the back with an "RU" prefix.

COMPLETE SET (5) 2.00 5.00
RU1 Garrison Hearst 1.00 2.50
RU2 Reggie White .50 1.25
RU3 Boomer Esiason .30 .75
RU4 Rod Bernstine .30 .75
RU5 Dana Stubblefield .30 .75

1993 Collector's Edge

The 1993 Collector's Edge football set consists of 325 standard-size cards. The production run was limited to 100,000 of each player, with each card serially numbered from 000001 to 100,000. In this year's issue, the cards were printed on heavier, 20-mil, thick plastic stock. Also this year's set added new Team Cards that depict whole-team portraits of the 28 NFL teams. The cards are numbered on the back and checklisted below according to teams. Cards 251-325 comprise the Rookie Update series. Randomly inserted in the foil packs was a factory redemption card that entitled the holder to redeem the card for a factory set, in which every card had the same serial number. The offer expired at noon on February 28, 1994. Two cards commemorating the newest expansion teams in the NFL, the Jacksonville Jaguars and the Carolina Panthers, were produced. The Panthers card, originally numbered 326, was issued very late in the pack production run. Only 4,000 of these cards were issued. The company then produced a second version of the Panthers card as well as a Jaguars card. These are numbered with an "M" prefix. The cards were available by mail and cost $3.95 with a production figure of 25,000. The purple marbleized fronts have a grey granite panel with a welcome to the new expansion team. The team logo appears in the lower right corner. Rookie Cards include Drew Bledsoe, Vincent Brisby, Reggie Brooks, Mark Brunell, Curtis Conway, Garrison Hearst, Billy Jo Hobert, Qadry Ismail, Glyn Milburn, Rick Mirer, Roosevelt Potts, Robert Smith and Dana Stubblefield.

COMPLETE SET (325) 10.00 20.00
COMP.SERIES 1 (250) 5.00 10.00
COMP.SERIES 2 (75) 5.00 10.00
1 Falcons Team Photo .01 .05
2 Michael Haynes .02 .10
3 Chris Miller .02 .10
4 Mike Pritchard .02 .10
5 Andre Rison .02 .10
6 Deion Sanders .20 .50
7 Chuck Smith .01 .05
8 Drew Hill .01 .05
9 Bobby Hebert .01 .05
10 Bills Team Photo .01 .05
11 Matt Darby .01 .05
12 John Fina .01 .05
13 Jim Kelly .08 .25
14 Marvcus Patton RC .02 .10
15 Andre Reed .02 .10
16 Thurman Thomas .08 .25
17 James Lofton .02 .10
18 Bruce Smith .08 .25
19 Bears Team Photo .01 .05
20 Neal Anderson .01 .05
21 Troy Auzenne .01 .05
22 Jim Harbaugh .08 .25
23 Alonzo Spellman .01 .05
24 Tom Waddle .01 .05
25 Darren Lewis .01 .05
26 Wendell Davis .01 .05
27 Will Furrer .01 .05
28 Bengals Team Photo .01 .05
29 David Klingler .01 .05
30 Ricardo McDonald .01 .05
31 Carl Pickens .02 .10
32 Harold Green .01 .05
33 Anthony Munoz .02 .10
34 Darryl Williams .01 .05
35 Browns Team Photo .01 .05
36 Michael Jackson .02 .10
37 Pio Sagapolutele .01 .05
38 Tommy Vardell .01 .05
39 Bernie Kosar .02 .10
40 Michael Dean Perry .02 .10
41 Bill Johnson .01 .05
42 Vinny Testaverde .02 .10
43 Cowboys Team Photo .01 .05
44 Troy Aikman .30 .75
45 Alvin Harper .02 .10
46 Michael Irvin .08 .25
47 Russell Maryland .01 .05
48 Emmitt Smith .60 1.50
49 Kenneth Gant .01 .05
50 Jay Novacek .02 .10
51 Robert Jones .01 .05
52 Clayton Holmes .01 .05
53 Broncos Team Photo .01 .05
54 Mike Croel .01 .05
55 Shane Dronett .01 .05
56 Kenny Walker .01 .05
57 Tommy Maddox .08 .25
58 Dennis Smith .01 .05
59 John Elway .60 1.50
60 Karl Mecklenburg .01 .05
61 Steve Atwater .01 .05
62 Vance Johnson .01 .05
63 Lions Team Photo .01 .05
64 Barry Sanders .50 1.25
65 Andre Ware .01 .05
66 Pat Swilling .01 .05
67 Jason Hanson .01 .05
68 Willie Green .01 .05
69 Herman Moore .08 .25
70 Rodney Peete .01 .05
71 Erik Kramer .02 .10
72 Robert Porcher .01 .05
73 Packers Team Photo .01 .05
74 Terrell Buckley .01 .05
75 Reggie White .08 .25
76 Brett Favre .75 2.00
77 Don Majkowski .01 .05
78 Edgar Bennett .08 .25
79 Ty Detmer .08 .25
80 Sanjay Beach .01 .05
81 Sterling Sharpe .08 .25
82 Oilers Team Photo .01 .05
83 Gary Brown .01 .05
84 Ernest Givins .02 .10
85 Haywood Jeffires .02 .10
86 Corey Harris .01 .05
87 Warren Moon .08 .25
88 Eddie Robinson .01 .05
89 Lorenzo White .01 .05
90 Bo Orlando .01 .05
91 Colts Team Photo .01 .05
92 Quentin Coryatt .02 .10
93 Steve Emtman .01 .05
94 Jeff George .08 .25
95 Jessie Hester .01 .05
96 Rohn Stark .01 .05
97 Ashley Ambrose .01 .05
98 John Baylor .01 .05
99 Chiefs Team Photo .01 .05
100 Tim Barnett .01 .05
101 Derrick Thomas .08 .25
102 Barry Word .01 .05
103 Dale Carter .01 .05
104 Jayice Pearson .01 .05
105 Tracy Simien .01 .05
106 Harvey Williams .02 .10
107 Dave Krieg .02 .10
108 Christian Okoye .01 .05
109 Joe Montana .60 1.50
110 Dolphins Team Photo .01 .05
111 J.B. Brown .01 .05
112 Marco Coleman .01 .05
113 Dan Marino .60 1.50
114 Mark Clayton .01 .05
115 Mark Higgs .01 .05
116 Bryan Cox .01 .05
117 Chuck Klingbeil .01 .05
118 Troy Vincent .01 .05
119 Keith Jackson .02 .10
120 Bruce Alexander .01 .05
121 Vikings Team Photo .01 .05
122 Terry Allen .08 .25
123 Rich Gannon .08 .25
124 Todd Scott .01 .05
125 Cris Carter .08 .25
126 Sean Salisbury .01 .05
127 Jack Del Rio .01 .05
128 Chris Doleman .01 .05
129 Anthony Carter .02 .10
130 Patriots Team Photo .01 .05
131 Eugene Chung .01 .05
132 Todd Collins .01 .05
133 Tommy Hodson .01 .05
134 Leonard Russell .02 .10
135 Jon Vaughn .01 .05
136 Andre Tippett .01 .05
137 Saints Team Photo .01 .05
138 Wesley Carroll .01 .05
139 Richard Cooper .01 .05
140 Vaughn Dunbar .01 .05
141 Fred McAfee .01 .05
142 Torrance Small .01 .05
143 Steve Walsh .01 .05
144 Vaughan Johnson .01 .05
145 Giants Team Photo .01 .05
146 Jarrod Bunch .01 .05
147 Phil Simms .02 .10
148 Carl Banks .01 .05
149 Lawrence Taylor .08 .25
150 Rodney Hampton .02 .10
151 Phillippi Sparks .01 .05
152 Derek Brown TE .01 .05
153 Jets Team Photo .01 .05
154 Boomer Esiason .02 .10
155 Johnny Mitchell .01 .05
156 Rob Moore .02 .10
157 Ronnie Lott .02 .10
158 Browning Nagle .01 .05
159 Johnny Johnson .01 .05
160 Dwayne White .01 .05
161 Blair Thomas .01 .05
162 Eagles Team Photo .01 .05
163 Randall Cunningham .08 .25
164 Fred Barnett .02 .10
165 Siran Stacy .01 .05
166 Keith Byars .01 .05
167 Calvin Williams .02 .10
168 Jeff Sydner .01 .05
169 Tommy Jeter .01 .05
170 Andre Waters .01 .05
171 Phoenix Team Photo .01 .05
172 Steve Beuerlein .02 .10
173 Randal Hill .01 .05
174 Timm Rosenbach .01 .05
175 Ed Cunningham .01 .05
176 Walter Reeves .01 .05
177 Michael Zordich .01 .05
178 Gary Clark .02 .10
179 Ken Harvey .01 .05
180 Steelers Team Photo .01 .05
181 Barry Foster .02 .10
182 Neil O'Donnell .08 .25
183 Leon Searcy .01 .05
184 Bubby Brister .01 .05
185 Merril Hoge .01 .05
186 Joel Steed .01 .05
187 Raiders Team Photo .01 .05
188 Nick Bell .01 .05
189 Eric Dickerson .02 .10
190 Nolan Harrison .01 .05
191 Todd Marinovich .01 .05
192 Greg Skrepenak .01 .05
193 Howie Long .08 .25
194 Jay Schroeder .01 .05
195 Chester McGlockton .02 .10
196 Rams Team Photo .01 .05
197 Jim Everett .02 .10
198 Sean Gilbert .02 .10
199 Steve Israel .01 .05
200 Marc Boutte .01 .05
201 Joe Milinichik .01 .05
202 Henry Ellard .02 .10
203 Jackie Slater .01 .05
204 Chargers Team Photo .01 .05
205 Eric Bieniemy .01 .05
206 Marion Butts .01 .05
207 Nate Lewis .01 .05
208 Junior Seau .08 .25
209 Steve Hendrickson .01 .05
210 Chris Mims .01 .05
211 Harry Swayne .01 .05
212 Marquez Pope .01 .05
213 Donald Frank .01 .05
214 Anthony Miller .02 .10
215 Seahawks Team Photo .01 .05
216 Cortez Kennedy .02 .10
217 Dan McGwire .01 .05
218 Kelly Stouffer .01 .05
219 Chris Warren .02 .10
220 Brian Blades .02 .10
221 Rod Stephens RC .01 .05
222 49ers Team Photo .01 .05
223 Jerry Rice .40 1.00
224 Ricky Watters .08 .25
225 Steve Young .30 .75
226 Tom Rathman .01 .05
227 Dana Hall .01 .05
228 Amp Lee .01 .05
229 Brian Bollinger .01 .05
230 Keith DeLong .01 .05
231 John Taylor .02 .10
232 Buccaneers Team Photo .01 .05
233 Tyji Armstrong .01 .05
234 Lawrence Dawsey .01 .05
235 Mark Wheeler .01 .05
236 Vince Workman .01 .05
237 Reggie Cobb .01 .05
238 Tony Mayberry .01 .05
239 Marty Carter .01 .05
240 Courtney Hawkins .01 .05
241 Ray Seals .01 .05
242 Mark Carrier WR .02 .10
243 Redskins Team Photo .01 .05
244 Mark Rypien .01 .05
245 Ricky Ervins .01 .05
246 Gerald Riggs .01 .05
247 Art Monk .02 .10
248 Mark Schlereth .01 .05
249 Monte Coleman .01 .05
250 Wilber Marshall .01 .05
251 Ben Coleman RC .01 .05
252 Curtis Conway RC .15 .40
253 Ernest Dye RC .01 .05
254 Todd Kelly RC .01 .05
255 Patrick Bates RC .01 .05
256 George Teague RC .02 .10
257 Mark Brunell RC .60 1.50
258 Adrian Hardy .01 .05
259 Dana Stubblefield RC .08 .25
260 Willie Roaf RC .10 .30
261 Irv Smith RC .01 .05
262 Drew Bledsoe RC 1.00 2.50
263 Dan Williams RC .01 .05
264 Jerry Ball .01 .05
265 Mark Clayton .01 .05
266 John Stephens .01 .05
267 Reggie White .08 .25
268 Jeff Hostetler .02 .10
269 Boomer Esiason .02 .10
270 Wade Wilson .01 .05
271 Steve Beuerlein .02 .10
272 Tim McDonald .01 .05
273 Craig Heyward .02 .10
274 Everson Walls .01 .05
275 Stan Humphries .02 .10
276 Carl Banks .01 .05
277 Brad Muster .01 .05
278 Tim Harris .01 .05
279 Gary Clark .02 .10
280 Joe Milinichik .01 .05
281 Leonard Marshall .01 .05
282 Joe Montana .60 1.50
283 Rod Bernstine .01 .05
284 Mark Carrier WR .02 .10
285 Michael Brooks .01 .05
286 Marvin Jones RC .01 .05
287 John Copeland RC .02 .10
288 Eric Curry RC .01 .05
289 Steve Everitt RC .01 .05
290 Tom Carter RC .02 .10
291 Deon Figures RC .01 .05
292A Leonard Renfro ERR RC .01 .05
292B Leonard Renfro COR RC .01 .05
293 Thomas Smith RC .02 .10
294 Carlton Gray RC .01 .05
295 Demetrius DuBose RC .01 .05
296 Coleman Rudolph RC .01 .05
297 John Parrella RC .01 .05
298 Glyn Milburn RC .08 .25
299 Reggie Brooks RC .02 .10
300 Garrison Hearst RC .30 .75
301 John Elway .60 1.50
302 Brad Hopkins RC .01 .05
303 Darrien Gordon RC .01 .05
304 Robert Smith RC .50 1.25
305 Chris Slade RC .02 .10
306 Ryan McNeil RC .08 .25
307 Micheal Barrow RC .08 .25
308 Roosevelt Potts RC .01 .05
309 Qadry Ismail RC .08 .25
310 Reggie Freeman RC .01 .05
311 Vincent Brisby RC .08 .25
312 Rick Mirer RC .08 .25
313 Billy Joe Hobert RC .08 .25
314 Natrone Means RC .08 .25
315 Cary Zimmerman .01 .05
316 Bobby Hebert .01 .05
317 Don Beebe .01 .05
318 Wilber Marshall .01 .05
319 Marcus Allen .08 .25
320 Ronnie Lott .02 .10
321 Ricky Sanders .01 .05
322 Charles Mann .01 .05
323 Simon Fletcher .01 .05
324 Johnny Johnson .01 .05
325 Gary Plummer .01 .05
326 Panthers Insert 10.00 25.00
M326 Panthers Send Away 1.00 2.50
M327 Jaguars Send Away 1.00 2.50
PRO1 John Elway AU/3000 30.00 60.00
CL1 Checklist 1 .07 .20
CL2 Checklist 2 .07 .20
CL3 Checklist 3 .07 .20
CL4 Checklist 4 .07 .20
CL5 Checklist 5 .07 .20
CL6 Checklist 6 .07 .20

1993 Collector's Edge Elway Prisms

Randomly inserted in 1993 Collector's Edge packs, these five standard-size cards feature blue-bordered prismatic foil fronts that carry color cut-outs of John Elway in action against a silver prismatic background. The production number appears below and, further below, career highlights. The cards are numbered on the back with an "E" prefix. There are two versions of each card. Tougher to find early packs contained cards with the serial number starting with "S" and cards found in packs released later had the serial number start with "E". A noted difference between the two versions are the prismatic backgrounds. Every collector who purchased All Star Collection Manager software direct from Taurus Technologies received a free Collector's Edge five-card John Elway (S-prefix) prism set. These cards have a blue (rather than silver) prismatic background on front. Just 500 sets were available through this offer. Titled the "Two Minute Warning" set, these standard-size cards highlight some of Elway's greatest two-minute marches.

COMPLETE E SET (5) 2.00 4.00
COMMON ELWAY (E1-E5) .40 1.00
COMMON ELWAY (S1-S5) 1.25 3.00

1993 Collector's Edge Jumbos

These jumbo cards were inserted as case toppers in 1993 Collector's Edge. Each measures 8 1/2" by 11" and is essentially a parallel to the respective regular issue card minus the card number. They are also individually numbered in gold ink on the cardback.

COMPLETE SET (6) 14.00 35.00
1 Randall Cunningham 2.00 5.00
2 John Elway 4.00 10.00
3 Warren Moon 2.00 5.00
4 Barry Sanders 4.00 10.00
5 Derrick Thomas 2.00 5.00
6 Thurman Thomas 1.60 4.00

1993 Collector's Edge Rookies FX

One of these 25 standard-size cards was inserted in each Rookie/Update foil pack. The cards are numbered on the front with an "F/X" prefix. Gold-colored background versions of these cards were also randomly inserted in packs. Two Prototype cards were produced as well and listed below. They are not considered part of the complete set.

COMPLETE SET (25) 6.00 15.00
ONE PER ROOKIE/UPDATE PACK

*GOLD STARS: 6X TO 15X BASE CARD HI
*GOLD ROOKIES: 3X TO 8X BASE CARD HI
1 Garrison Hearst .30 .75
2 Glyn Milburn .08 .25
3 Demetrius DuBose .01 .05
4 Joe Montana 1.50 3.00
5 Thomas Smith .02 .10
6 Mark Clayton .02 .10
7 Curtis Conway .15 .40
8 Drew Bledsoe 1.25 2.50
9 Todd Kelly .01 .05
10 Stan Humphries .07 .20
11 John Elway 1.50 3.00
12 Troy Aikman .75 1.50
13 Marion Butts .02 .10
14 Alvin Harper .07 .20
15 Drew Hill .02 .10
16 Michael Irvin .20 .50
17 Warren Moon .20 .50
18 Andre Reed .07 .20
19 Andre Rison .07 .20
20 Emmitt Smith UER 1.50 3.00
21 Thurman Thomas .20 .50
22 Ricky Watters .20 .50
23 Calvin Williams .07 .20
24 Steve Young .75 1.50
25 Howie Long .20 .50
P1A Drew Bledsoe Prototype 1.25 2.50
P1B Drew Bledsoe Prototype 1.25 2.50
P2 Drew Bledsoe Prototype 1.25 2.50
P3 Drew Bledsoe Prototype 1.25 2.50
P4 Drew Bledsoe Prototype 1.25 2.50
P5 Drew Bledsoe Prototype 1.25 2.50

1994 Collector's Edge Boss Rookies Update Pop Warner Promos

This six-card set was issued to preview the Boss Rookies Update series. Each card is numbered on the back with P prefix and fronts include the "Pop Warner" notation. A parallel version featuring different cropping on the player photos and an "SRH" prefix on the card numbers was also produced.
COMPLETE SET (6) 3.20 8.00
*SRH PREFIX: .4X TO 1X BASIC CARDS
P1 Trent Dilfer .60 1.50
P2 Marshall Faulk 2.00 4.00
P3 Heath Shuler .20 .50
P4 Errict Rhett .40 1.00
P5 Johnnie Morton .20 .50
P6 Charlie Garner .40 1.00

1994 Collector's Edge

Consisting of 200 cards, this standard size set features full-bleed photos on front with the player's name and team logo at the bottom. The cards are checklisted alphabetically according to teams. There are no key Rookie Cards in this set. A Shannon Sharpe prototype card was produced and is listed at the end of our checklist. It is not considered part of the complete set.
COMPLETE SET (200) 7.50 15.00
1 Mike Pritchard .01 .05
2 Eric Pegram .01 .05
3 Michael Haynes .02 .10
4 Bobby Hebert .01 .05
5 Deion Sanders .20 .50
6 Andre Rison .02 .10
7 Don Beebe .01 .05
8 Mark Kelso .01 .05
9 Darryl Talley .01 .05
10 Cornelius Bennett .02 .10
11 Jim Kelly .08 .25
12 Andre Reed .02 .10
13 Bruce Smith .08 .25
14 Thurman Thomas .08 .25
15 Craig Heyward .02 .10
16 Chris Zorich .01 .05
17 Alonzo Spellman .01 .05
18 Tom Waddle .01 .05
19 Neal Anderson .01 .05
20 Kevin Butler .01 .05
21 Curtis Conway .08 .25
22 Richard Dent .02 .10
23 Jim Harbaugh .08 .25
24 Derrick Fenner .01 .05
25 Harold Green .01 .05
26 David Klingler .01 .05
27 Daniel Stubbs .01 .05
28 Alfred Williams .01 .05
29 John Copeland .01 .05
30 Mark Carrier WR .02 .10
31 Michael Jackson .02 .10
32 Eric Metcalf .02 .10
33 Vinny Testaverde .02 .10
34 Tommy Vardell .01 .05
35 Alvin Harper .02 .10
36 Ken Norton Jr. .02 .10
37 Tony Casillas .01 .05
38 Leon Lett .01 .05
39 Jay Novacek .02 .10
40 Kevin Smith .01 .05
41 Troy Aikman .40 1.00
42 Michael Irvin .08 .25
43 Russell Maryland .01 .05
44 Emmitt Smith .60 1.50
45 Robert Delpino .01 .05
46 Simon Fletcher .01 .05
47 Greg Kragen .01 .05
48 Arthur Marshall .01 .05
49 Steve Atwater .01 .05
50 Rod Bernstine .01 .05
51 John Elway .75 2.00
52 Glyn Milburn .02 .10
53 Shannon Sharpe .02 .10
54 Bennie Blades .01 .05
55 Mel Gray .01 .05
56 Herman Moore .08 .25
57 Pat Swilling .01 .05
58 Chris Spielman .02 .10
59 Rodney Peete .01 .05
60 Andre Ware .01 .05
61 Brett Perriman .02 .10
62 Erik Kramer .02 .10
63 Barry Sanders .60 1.50
64 Mark Clayton .01 .05
65 Chris Jacke .01 .05
66 Terrell Buckley .01 .05
67 Ty Detmer .02 .10
68 Sanjay Beach .01 .05
69 Brian Noble .01 .05
70 Edgar Bennett .08 .25
71 Brett Favre .75 2.00
72 Sterling Sharpe .02 .10
73 Reggie White .08 .25
74 Ernest Givins .02 .10
75 Al Del Greco .01 .05
76 Cris Dishman .01 .05
77 Curtis Duncan .01 .05
78 Webster Slaughter .01 .05
79 Spencer Tillman .01 .05
80 Warren Moon .08 .25
81 Wilber Marshall .01 .05
82 Haywood Jeffires .02 .10
83 Lorenzo White .01 .05
84 Gary Brown .01 .05
85 Reggie Langhorne .01 .05
86 Dean Biasucci .01 .05
87 Steve Emtman .01 .05
88 Jessie Hester .01 .05
89 Quentin Coryatt .01 .05
90 Roosevelt Potts .01 .05
91 Jeff George .08 .25
92 Nick Lowery .01 .05
93 Willie Davis .02 .10
94 Joe Montana .75 2.00
95 Neil Smith .02 .10
96 Marcus Allen .08 .25
97 Derrick Thomas .08 .25
98 Greg Townsend .01 .05
99 Willie Gault .01 .05
100 Ethan Horton .01 .05
101 Jeff Hostetler .02 .10
102 Tim Brown .08 .25
103 Rocket Ismail .02 .10
104 Shane Conlan .01 .05
105 Henry Ellard .02 .10
106 T.J. Rubley .01 .05
107 Sean Gilbert .01 .05
108 Troy Drayton .01 .05
109 Jerome Bettis .15 .40
110 Terry Kirby .08 .25
111 Mark Ingram .01 .05
112 John Offerdahl .01 .05
113 Louis Oliver .01 .05
114 Irving Fryar .02 .10
115 Dan Marino .75 2.00
116 Keith Jackson .01 .05
117 O.J.McDuffie .08 .25
118 Jim McMahon .02 .10
119 Sean Salisbury .01 .05
120 Randall McDaniel .02 .10
121 Jack Del Rio .01 .05
122 Cris Carter .20 .50
123 Chris Doleman .01 .05
124 John Randle .01 .05
125 Vincent Brisby .02 .10
126 Greg McMurtry .01 .05
127 Drew Bledsoe .30 .75
128 Leonard Russell .01 .05
129 Michael Brooks .01 .05
130 Mark Jackson .01 .05
131 Pepper Johnson .01 .05
132 Doug Riesenberg .01 .05
133 Phil Simms .02 .10
134 Rodney Hampton .02 .10
135 Leonard Marshall .01 .05
136 Rob Moore .02 .10
137 Chris Burkett .01 .05
138 Boomer Esiason .02 .10
139 Johnny Johnson .01 .05
140 Ronnie Lott .02 .10
141 Brad Muster .01 .05
142 Renaldo Turnbull .01 .05
143 Willie Roaf .01 .05
144 Rickey Jackson .01 .05
145 Morten Andersen .01 .05
146 Vaughn Dunbar .01 .05
147 Wade Wilson .01 .05
148 Eric Martin .01 .05
149 Seth Joyner .01 .05
150 Calvin Williams .02 .10
151 Vai Sikahema .01 .05
152 Herschel Walker .02 .10
153 Eric Allen .01 .05
154 Fred Barnett .02 .10
155 Randall Cunningham .08 .25
156 Steve Beuerlein .02 .10
157 Gary Clark .02 .10
158 Anthony Edwards .01 .05
159 Randal Hill .01 .05
160 Freddie Joe Nunn .01 .05
161 Garrison Hearst .08 .25
162 Ricky Proehl .01 .05
163 Eric Green .01 .05
164 Levon Kirkland .01 .05
165 Joel Steed .01 .05
166 Deon Figures .01 .05
167 Leroy Thompson .01 .05
168 Barry Foster .01 .05
169 Neil O'Donnell .08 .25
170 Junior Seau .08 .25
171 Leslie O'Neal .01 .05
172 Stan Humphries .02 .10
173 Marion Butts .01 .05
174 Anthony Miller .02 .10
175 Natrone Means .08 .25
176 Odessa Turner .01 .05
177 Dana Stubblefield .02 .10
178 John Taylor .02 .10
179 Ricky Watters .02 .10
180 Steve Young .30 .75
181 Jerry Rice .40 1.00
182 Tom Rathman .01 .05
183 Brian Blades .02 .10
184 Patrick Hunter .01 .05
185 Rick Mirer .08 .25
186 Chris Warren .02 .10
187 Cortez Kennedy .02 .10
188 Reggie Cobb .01 .05
189 Craig Erickson .01 .05
190 Hardy Nickerson .02 .10
191 Lawrence Dawsey .01 .05
192 Broderick Thomas .01 .05
193 Ricky Sanders .01 .05
194 Carl Banks .01 .05
195 Ricky Ervins .01 .05
196 Darrell Green .01 .05
197 Mark Rypien .01 .05
198 Desmond Howard .02 .10
199 Art Monk .02 .10
200 Reggie Brooks .02 .10
P1 Shannon Sharpe Prototype .40 1.00

1994 Collector's Edge Gold

COMPLETE SET (200) 10.00 25.00
*GOLD CARDS: .75X TO 1.5X BASIC CARDS

1994 Collector's Edge Pop Warner

COMPLETE SET (200) 6.00 15.00
*POP WARNER: .4X TO 1X BASE CARD HI

1994 Collector's Edge Pop Warner 22K Gold

COMPLETE SET (200) 30.00 80.00
*PW 22K GOLDS: 2.5X TO 5X BASIC CARDS

1994 Collector's Edge Silver

COMPLETE SET (200) 7.50 20.00
*SILVER CARDS: .5X TO 1.2X BASIC CARDS

1994 Collector's Edge Boss Rookies

This 19-card standard-size set depicts NFL rookies in action shots wearing either their NFL or college uniforms. The cards were printed on transparent plastic and have the "Boss Rookies" logo at top right and the player's name at the bottom. Reportedly 25,000 numbered sets were produced, and each set sold originally for $49.95 with ten Edge foil wrappers.
COMPLETE SET (19) 5.00 12.00
STATED ODDS 1:2 ALL EDGE PACK TYPES
1 Isaac Bruce 1.50 4.00
2 Jeff Burris .10 .30
3 Shante Carver .10 .30
4 Lake Dawson .20 .50
5 Bert Emanuel .30 .75
6 William Floyd .20 .50
7 Wayne Gandy .10 .30
8 Aaron Glenn .30 .75
9 Chris Maumalanga .10 .30
10 David Palmer .30 .75
11 Errict Rhett .30 .75
12 Heath Shuler .30 .75
13 Dewayne Washington .10 .30
14 Bryant Young .20 .50
15 Dan Wilkinson .20 .50
16 Rob Fredrickson .10 .30
17 Calvin Jones .10 .30
18 James Folston .10 .30
19 Marshall Faulk 1.50 4.00

1994 Collector's Edge Boss Rookies Update

The base set version of the 1994 Collector's Edge Boss Rookies Update cards was made available via a mail order offer in complete set form. Each card was printed on clear plastic stock and individually numbered. Two parallel versions were also produced; one with a "Diamond Rookies" logo (mail redemption) and one printed on clear Green card stock (randomly inserted in Pop Warner packs).
COMPLETE FACT.SET (25) 15.00 30.00
*DIAMOND CARDS: 1.5X to 2.5X HI COLUMN
ONE SET PER MAIL REDEMPTION CARD
COMPLETE GREEN SET (25) 12.50 25.00
*GREEN CARDS: .4X TO .75X HI COLUMN
STATED ODDS 1:3 POP WARNER
1 Trent Dilfer 1.00 2.50
2 Jeff Burris .30 .75
3 Shante Carver .30 .75
4 Lake Dawson .50 1.25
5 Bert Emanuel .50 1.25
6 Marshall Faulk 3.00 8.00
7 William Floyd .50 1.25
8 Charlie Garner 1.00 2.50
9 Rob Fredrickson .30 .75
10 Wayne Gandy .30 .75
11 Aaron Glenn .75 2.00
12 Greg Hill .50 1.25
13 Isaac Bruce 3.00 8.00
14 Charles Johnson .50 1.25
15 Johnnie Morton 1.25 3.00
16 Calvin Jones .30 .75
17 Tim Bowens .30 .75
18 David Palmer .75 2.00
19 Errict Rhett .50 1.25
20 Darnay Scott .60 1.50
21 Heath Shuler .50 1.25
22 John Thierry .30 .75
23 Bernard Williams .30 .75
24 Dan Wilkinson .30 .75
25 Bryant Young .50 1.25

1994 Collector's Edge Boss Squad

Randomly inserted in all pack types, this 25-card set showcases eight top quarterbacks, running backs and receivers based on 1993 performance. The plastic transparent cards contain an action photo on front.
COMPLETE SET (25) 6.00 15.00
STATED ODDS 1:2 ALL EDGE PACK TYPES
*SILVERS: .4X TO 1X BASIC INSERTS
STATED ODDS 1:2 POP WARNER
*BRONZE EQII: .4X TO 1X BASIC INSERTS
ONE SET PER EDGEQUEST REDEMPTION
*GOLD HELMETS: .4X TO 1X BASIC INSERTS
ONE SET PER POP WARN.EDGEQUEST RED.
1 John Elway W-2 1.50 4.00
2 Joe Montana 1.50 4.00
3 Vinny Testaverde .07 .20
4 Boomer Esiason .07 .20
5 Steve Young W-1 .60 1.50
6 Troy Aikman .75 2.00
7 Phil Simms .07 .20
8 Bobby Hebert .02 .10
9 Thurman Thomas .20 .50
10 Leonard Russell .02 .10
11 Chris Warren W-2 .07 .20
12 Gary Brown .02 .10
13 Emmitt Smith 1.25 3.00
14 Jerome Bettis .30 .75
15 Eric Pegram .02 .10
16 Barry Sanders W-1 1.25 3.00
17 Reggie Langhorne .02 .10
18 Anthony Miller .07 .20
19 Shannon Sharpe .07 .20
20 Tim Brown .20 .50
21 Sterling Sharpe W-2 .07 .20
22 Jerry Rice W-1 .75 2.00
23 Michael Irvin .20 .50
24 Andre Rison .07 .20
25 Checklist .02 .10

1994 Collector's Edge Boss Squad Promos

These six standard-size clear plastic cards feature on their fronts color action player cutouts set on backgrounds of parallel and converging lines. The player's name appears in orange-yellow lettering within a blue bar near the bottom. The back allows the reverse image of the front photo to show through. They were issued on two different types of uncut sheets. The cards are numbered on the front with a "Boss" prefix.
COMPLETE SET (6) 3.20 8.00
1 Marshall Faulk 1.60 4.00
2 Jerome Bettis .60 1.50
3 Eric Pegram .30 .75
4 Sterling Sharpe .50 1.25
5 Shannon Sharpe .50 1.25
6 Leonard Russell .30 .75

1994 Collector's Edge FX

This seven-card standard-size set was randomly inserted into the various Collector's Edge packs. There are many parallel versions of these cards. The cards with gold shields were also found in Collector's Edge gold packs. Cards with white backs or silver shields were inserted in Collector's Edge retail jumbo packs. Cards featuring silver or gold backs are found in Collector's Edge silver packs. Cards with silver or gold lettering are found in Collector's Edge Pop Warner packs. Also, cards with red lettering were sent out as part of the EdgeQuest redemption program. The cards are transparent with the player's image and the words "Edge F/X" located in the upper left corner. The player is identified near the bottom of the card.
COMPLETE SET (7) 7.50 20.00
STATED ODDS 1:7 GOLD PACKS
*GOLD SHIELDS: .8X to 2X BASIC INSERTS
STATED ODDS 1:200 GOLD PACKS
*WHITE BACKS: .4X TO 1X BASIC INSERTS
STATED ODDS 1:7 RETAIL/JUMBO
*SILVER SHIELDS: 2X to 5X BASIC INSERTS
STATED ODDS 1:200 RETAIL/JUMBO
*SILVER BACKS: .2X TO .5X BASIC INSERTS
STATED ODDS 1:7 SILVER
*GOLD BACKS: 1.2X to 3X BASIC INSERTS
STATED ODDS 1:200 SILVER
*SILVER LETTERS: .4X TO 1X BASIC INSERTS
STATED ODDS 1:7 POP WARNER
*GOLD LETTERS: .8X to 2X BASIC INSERTS
STATED ODDS 1:200 POP WARNER
*RED LETTERS: .3X to .8X BASIC INSERTS
ONE SET PER EDGEQUEST REDEMPTION
*EQ RED LETTER: .4X to 1X BASIC INSERTS
1 John Elway 4.00 8.00
2 Joe Montana 4.00 8.00
3 Troy Aikman 2.00 4.00
4 Emmitt Smith 3.00 6.00
5 Jerome Bettis .75 1.50
6 Anthony Miller .30 .75
7 Sterling Sharpe .30 .75

1995 Collector's Edge

This 205-card standard-size set features full-action color photos on front with the player's name across the left-side. The cards are grouped alphabetically within teams and checklisted below alphabetically according to teams. There are no key Rookie Cards in this set. Many parallels of the basic set exist.
COMPLETE SET (205) 10.00 20.00
1 Anthony Edwards .01 .05
2 Garrison Hearst .08 .25
3 Seth Joyner .01 .05
4 Dave Krieg .01 .05
5 Chuck Levy .01 .05
6 Rob Moore .02 .10
7 J.J. Birden .01 .05
8 Jeff George .02 .10
9 Craig Heyward .02 .10
10 Norm Johnson .01 .05
11 Terance Mathis .02 .10
12 Eric Metcalf .02 .10
13 Chuck Smith .01 .05
14 Darryl Talley .01 .05
15 Cornelius Bennett .02 .10
16 Steve Christie .01 .05
17 Kenneth Davis .01 .05
18 Phil Hansen .01 .05
19 Jim Kelly .08 .25
20 Bryce Paup .02 .10
21 Andre Reed .02 .10
22 Bruce Smith .08 .25
23 Eric Ball .01 .05
24 Don Beebe .01 .05
25 Mark Carrier WR .02 .10
26 Tim McKyer .01 .05
27 Pete Metzelaars .01 .05
28 Sam Mills .02 .10
29 Jack Trudeau .01 .05
30 Mark Carrier DB .01 .05
31 Curtis Conway .08 .25
32 Erik Kramer .01 .05
33 Lewis Tillman .01 .05
34 Michael Timpson .01 .05
35 Steve Walsh .01 .05
36 Chris Zorich .01 .05
37 Jeff Blake RC .25 .60
38 Harold Green .01 .05
39 David Klingler .02 .10
40 Carl Pickens .02 .10
41 Tom Waddle .01 .05
42 Dan Wilkinson .02 .10
43 Leroy Hoard .01 .05
44 Michael Jackson .02 .10
45 Antonio Langham .01 .05
46 Andre Rison .02 .10
47 Vinny Testaverde .02 .10
48 Eric Turner .01 .05
49 Tommy Vardell .01 .05
50 Troy Aikman .40 1.00
51 Charles Haley .02 .10
52 Michael Irvin .08 .25
53 Daryl Johnston .02 .10
54 Leon Lett .01 .05
55 Jay Novacek .02 .10
56 Emmitt Smith .60 1.50
57 Kevin Williams WR .02 .10
58 Steve Atwater .01 .05
59 John Elway .75 2.00
60 Simon Fletcher .01 .05
61 Glyn Milburn .01 .05
62 Anthony Miller .02 .10
63 Leonard Russell .01 .05
64 Shannon Sharpe .02 .10
65 Scott Mitchell .02 .10
66 Herman Moore .08 .25
67 Johnnie Morton .02 .10
68 Brett Perriman .02 .10
69 Barry Sanders .60 1.50
70 Edgar Bennett .02 .10
71 Brett Favre .75 2.00
72 Mark Ingram .01 .05
73 Chris Jacke .01 .05
74 Guy McIntyre .01 .05
75 Reggie White .08 .25
76 Gary Brown .01 .05
77 Ernest Givins .01 .05
78 Mel Gray .01 .05
79 Haywood Jeffires .01 .05
80 Webster Slaughter .01 .05
81 Craig Erickson .01 .05
82 Marshall Faulk .50 1.25
83 Jim Harbaugh .02 .10
84 Roosevelt Potts .01 .05
85 Floyd Turner .01 .05
86 Steve Beuerlein .02 .10
87 Reggie Cobb .01 .05
88 Jeff Lageman .01 .05
89 Mazio Royster .01 .05
90 Marcus Allen .08 .25
91 Steve Bono .02 .10
92 Willie Davis .02 .10
93 Lake Dawson .02 .10
94 Ronnie Lott .02 .10
95 Eric Martin .01 .05
96 Chris Penn .01 .05
97 Tim Brown .08 .25
98 Derrick Fenner .01 .05
99 Rob Fredrickson .01 .05
100 Nolan Harrison .01 .05
101 Jeff Hostetler .02 .10
102 Rocket Ismail .02 .10
103 James Jett .02 .10
104 Chester McGlockton .02 .10
105 Anthony Smith .01 .05
106 Harvey Williams .01 .05
107 Jerome Bettis .08 .25
108 Troy Drayton .01 .05
109 Chris Miller .01 .05
110 Robert Young .01 .05
111 Keith Byars .01 .05
112 Gary Clark .01 .05
113 Bryan Cox .01 .05
114 Jeff Cross .01 .05
115 Irving Fryar .02 .10
116 Randal Hill .01 .05
117 Terry Kirby .02 .10
118 Dan Marino .75 2.00
119 O.J. McDuffie .08 .25
120 Bernie Parmalee .02 .10
121 Terry Allen .02 .10
122 Cris Carter .08 .25
123 Qadry Ismail .02 .10
124 Warren Moon .02 .10
125 John Randle .02 .10
126 Jake Reed .02 .10
127 Fuad Reveiz .01 .05
128 Broderick Thomas .01 .05
129 Drew Bledsoe .25 .60
130 Vincent Brisby .01 .05
131 Ben Coates .02 .10
132 Dave Meggett .01 .05
133 Chris Slade .01 .05
134 Leroy Thompson .01 .05
135 Eric Allen .01 .05
136 Mario Bates .02 .10
137 Quinn Early .01 .05
138 Jim Everett .01 .05
139 Michael Haynes .02 .10
140 Torrance Small .01 .05
141 Dave Brown .02 .10
142 Chris Calloway .01 .05
143 Keith Hamilton .01 .05
144 Rodney Hampton .02 .10
145 Mike Sherrard .01 .05
146 David Treadwell .01 .05
147 Herschel Walker .02 .10
148 Boomer Esiason .02 .10
149 Erik Howard .01 .05
150 Johnny Johnson .01 .05
151 Mo Lewis .01 .05
152 Johnny Mitchell .01 .05
153 Fred Barnett .02 .10
154 Randall Cunningham .08 .25
155 William Fuller .01 .05
156 Charlie Garner .08 .25
157 Greg Jackson .01 .05
158 Ricky Watters .02 .10
159 Calvin Williams .02 .10
160 Barry Foster .02 .10
161 Kevin Greene .02 .10
162 Greg Lloyd .02 .10
163 Byron Bam Morris .01 .05
164 Neil O'Donnell .02 .10
165 Eric Pegram .02 .10
166 John L. Williams .01 .05
167 Rod Woodson .02 .10
168 John Carney .01 .05
169 Stan Humphries .02 .10
170 Natrone Means .02 .10
171 Chris Mims .01 .05
172 Leslie O'Neal .02 .10
173 Alfred Pupunu RC .01 .05
174 Junior Seau .08 .25
175 Mark Seay .02 .10
176 William Floyd .02 .10
177 Jerry Rice .40 1.00
178 Deion Sanders .25 .60
179 Dana Stubblefield .02 .10
180 John Taylor .01 .05
181 Steve Young .30 .75
182 Bryant Young .02 .10
183 Brian Blades .02 .10
184 Cortez Kennedy .02 .10
185 Kelvin Martin .01 .05
186 Rick Mirer .02 .10
187 Ricky Proehl .01 .05
188 Michael Sinclair .01 .05
189 Chris Warren .02 .10
190 Trent Dilfer .08 .25
191 Alvin Harper .01 .05
192 Jackie Harris .01 .05
193 Hardy Nickerson .01 .05
194 Errict Rhett .02 .10
195 Reggie Roby .01 .05
196 Henry Ellard .02 .10
197 Ricky Ervins .01 .05
198 Darrell Green .01 .05
199 Brian Mitchell .01 .05
200 Heath Shuler .02 .10
201 Checklist .01 .05
202 Checklist .01 .05
203 Checklist .01 .05
204 Checklist .01 .05
205 Checklist .01 .05
P1 Natrone Means Promo .20 .50
P2 Chris Warren Promo .20 .50

1995 Collector's Edge Black Label

COMPLETE SET (205) 7.50 20.00
*BLACK LABEL: SAME PRICE AS BASIC CARDS

1995 Collector's Edge Black Label Silver Die Cuts

COMPLETE SET (205) 100.00 200.00
*STARS: 4X TO 10X BASIC CARDS
STATED ODDS 1:24 BLACK LABEL

1995 Collector's Edge Black Label 22K Gold

COMPLETE SET (205) 250.00 500.00
*22K GOLD STARS: 10X TO 25X BASIC CARDS
RANDOM INSERTS IN BLACK LABEL

1995 Collector's Edge Die Cuts

COMPLETE SET (205) 40.00 100.00
*STARS: 2X TO 5X BASIC CARDS

1995 Collector's Edge Gold Logo

COMPLETE SET (205) 7.50 20.00
*GOLD LOGOS: SAME PRICE AS BASIC CARDS

1995 Collector's Edge Nitro 22K

COMPLETE SET (205) 75.00 200.00
*NITRO 22K STARS: 5X TO 12X BASIC CARDS

1995 Collector's Edge 22K Gold

COMPLETE SET (205) 250.00 500.00
*22K GOLD: 10X TO 25X BASIC CARDS
RANDOM INSERTS IN RETAIL PACKS

1995 Collector's Edge 22K Gold 500

*22K GOLD/500: 6X TO 15X BASIC CARDS

1995 Collector's Edge 22K Gold Die Cuts

COMPLETE SET (205) 100.00 250.00
*DIE CUT/500: 5X TO 12X BASIC CARDS
STATED PRINT RUN 500 SERIAL #'d SETS

1995 Collector's Edge Black Label Quantum Motion

This 13-card set was made available via a wrapper mail order redemption. The cards feature Collector's Edge's Quantum Motion printing technology and are individually numbered of 5151. Collectors needed to send 51-1995 Black Label wrappers to Collector's Edge for the 13-card set. For 72-wrappers, collector's received the set along with a numbered (of 2500) giant TimeWarp card featuring Dick Butkus, Jeff Blake, and Junior Seau. All three players signed the card as well. Collector's Edge made available single Quantum Motion cards for 5-wrappers. The 12-card set was later released again as a promo (one per special retail box) for the 1996 President's Reserve release. These promo cards are identical to the original release except that they are not serial numbered. The word "Quantum" appears where the serial number would be otherwise.
COMPLETE SET (13) 20.00 40.00
*UNNUMBERED PROMOS: .2X TO .5X
1 Jerome Bettis .20 .50
2 Jeff Blake .20 .50
3 Drew Bledsoe .50 1.25
4 Cris Carter .20 .50
5 John Elway 1.00 2.50
6 Marshall Faulk .20 .50
7 Terance Mathis .10 .30
8 Byron Bam Morris .05 .15
9 Errict Rhett .05 .15
10 Jerry Rice .50 1.25
11 Deion Sanders .30 .75
12 Heath Shuler .05 .15
13 Checklist Card .05 .15
GTW1 Giant TimeWarp AUTO 25.00 50.00

1995 Collector's Edge EdgeTech

This 37-card set was randomly inserted in regular, Black Label, and special retail packs. The base insert version features a target style round design in the background while some later "parallels" included new player photos and a swirl design created out of footballs in the background. There are actually numerous parallels of the set including a 22K gold set randomly inserted in retail packs, a Quantum set (featuring the football swilr design and new player photos) randomly inserted in Black Label packs, a Quantum die-cut set randomly inserted in Black Label packs and a Circular Prism set inserted one per special retail pack. The Quantum parallel differs from the regular card by having a lenticular front instead of the green background.
COMPLETE SET (37) 15.00 40.00
STATED ODDS 1:12 HOB/RET
*22K GOLDS: 1.2X TO 3X BASIC INSERTS
STATED ODDS 1:120 RETAIL
*BLACK LABEL: .2X TO .5X BASIC INSERTS
STATED ODDS 1:12 BLACK LABEL
*BLACK LABEL 22K: .6X TO 1.5X BASIC INS.
BL 22K STATED ODDS 1:120 BLACK LABEL
*QUANTUMS: 2.5X TO 6X BASIC INSERTS
STATED ODDS 1:120 BLACK LABEL
*QUANT.DIE CUTS: 4X TO 10X BASIC INSERTS
RANDOM INSERTS IN BLACK LABEL PACKS
*CIRCULAR PRISMS: .4X TO 1X BASIC INS.
CIRC.PRISMS: ONE PER JUMBO
1 Dan Marino 3.00 6.00
2 Steve Young 1.25 2.50
3 Rick Mirer .10 .30
4 Emmitt Smith 2.50 5.00
5 John Elway 3.00 6.00
6 Neil O'Donnell .10 .30
7 Marshall Faulk 2.00 4.00
8 Deion Sanders 1.00 2.00
9 Terance Mathis .10 .30
10 Kevin Greene .10 .30
11 Ricky Watters .10 .30
12 Tim Brown .30 .75
13 Antonio Langham .05 .15
14 Lake Dawson .10 .30
15 Jay Novacek .10 .30
16 Herman Moore .30 .75
17 Mark Seay .10 .30
18 Bernie Parmalee .10 .30
19 Drew Bledsoe 1.00 2.00
20 Troy Aikman 1.50 3.00
21 Brett Favre 3.00 6.00
22 Jerry Rice 1.50 3.00
23 Barry Sanders 3.00 8.00
24 Heath Shuler .10 .30
25 Errict Rhett .10 .30
26 Cris Carter .30 .75
27 Jerome Bettis .30 .75
28 Reggie White .30 .75
29 Chris Warren .10 .30
30 Ben Coates .10 .30
31 Bryant Young .10 .30
32 Mel Gray .05 .15
33 Darryl Talley .05 .15
34 Mike Sherrard .05 .15
35 William Floyd .10 .30
36 Alvin Harper .05 .15
37 Checklist (1-36) .05 .15

1995 Collector's Edge Nitro Redemption

Collector's Edge released this set to collectors who accumulated points from the 1995 Nitro Game. Game pieces were randomly inserted into 1995 Edge packs. Collectors were encouraged to watch the NFL games featured on the game piece. If the featured players were declared game winners (based on NFL game stats), the collector could send in the game piece, along with the base brand card of the featured players and $4.95 postage, to receive a Nitro 22K gold foil parallel card. The collector also received 150 Nitro Redemption points that could then be accumulated and traded later for this Nitro Redemption set.
COMPLETE SET (25) 20.00 50.00
1 Warren Moon .25 .60
2 Scott Mitchell .25 .60
3 Jeff Blake .75 2.00
4 Emmitt Smith 4.00 10.00
5 Barry Sanders 4.00 10.00
6 Terance Mathis .25 .60
7 Herman Moore .60 1.50
8 Isaac Bruce .60 1.50
9 Cris Carter .60 1.50
10 Ben Coates .25 .60
11 Shannon Sharpe .25 .60
12 Jay Novacek .25 .60
13 Norm Johnson .10 .30
14 Morten Andersen .10 .30
15 Fuad Reveiz .10 .30
16 Bryce Paup .25 .60
17 Jim Flanigan .10 .30
18 Kevin Carter .10 .30
19 Sam Mills .25 .60
20 Willie McGinest .10 .30
21 Orlando Thomas .10 .30
22 Brett Favre 5.00 12.00
23 Dan Marino 5.00 12.00
24 Jerry Rice 2.50 6.00
25 Larry Brown .10 .30

1995 Collector's Edge Junior Seau Promos

This five card standard-size set features the San Diego Chargers' All-Pro linebacker Junior Seau. Each card celebrates a different year in his five year career. There were several versions produced of each card: blue foil "Promo" stamped, gold foil "Promo" stamped, non-foil base brand, Black Label foil stamped, blue foil stamped "95 National St.Louis," and blue foil stamped "Sack-A-Seau." There are no price differences for the various versions.
COMPLETE SET (5) 2.00 5.00
COMMON CARD (1-5) .40 1.00

1995 Collector's Edge Rookies

This 25 card set was randomly inserted in retail and Black Label packs. The card fronts show the top draft picks from 1995 in their college uniforms. The Black Label version differs from the regular by having the gold Black Label seal in the top left hand corner. Card backs contain biographical information and a short summary on the player.
COMPLETE SET (25) 20.00 40.00
STATED ODDS 1:4 RETAIL
*22K GOLDS: 1.2X TO 3X BASIC INSERTS
22K GOLD ODDS 1:40 RETAIL
*BLACK LABELS: .4X TO 1X BASIC INSERTS
*BL 22K GOLDS: 1.2X TO 3X BASIC INSERTS
1 Derrick Alexander DE .25 .60
2 Tony Boselli .60 1.50
3 Ki-Jana Carter .60 1.50
4 Kevin Carter .60 1.50
5 Kerry Collins 1.25 3.00
6 Steve McNair 2.50 6.00
7 Billy Milner .25 .60
8 Rashaan Salaam .60 1.50
9 Warren Sapp .40 1.00
10 James O. Stewart 1.00 2.50
11 J.J.Stokes .60 1.50
12 Bobby Taylor .60 1.50
13 Tyrone Wheatley UER 1.00 2.50
14 Derrick Brooks 1.25 3.00
15 Reuben Brown .60 1.50
16 Mark Bruener .40 1.00
17 Joey Galloway 1.25 3.00
18 Napoleon Kaufman 1.00 2.50
19 Ty Law 1.00 2.50
20 Craig Newsome .40 1.00
21 Kordell Stewart 1.25 3.00
22 Korey Stringer .50 1.25
23 Zach Wiegert .25 .60
24 Michael Westbrook .60 1.50
25 Checklist .25 .60

1995 Collector's Edge TimeWarp

These cards were randomly inserted in both regular and Black Label packs. Parallels of this set include a 22K gold set inserted in all pack types and a Prism set, where both the front and back of the card have prisms in the background.
COMPLETE SET (21) 25.00 60.00
STATED ODDS 1:400 HOB/RET,1:200 JUM
*22K GOLDS: 2X TO 4X BASIC INSERTS
22K GOLD ODDS 1:4000 HOB/RET
*PRISMS: .4X TO 1X BASIC INSERTS
*BLACK LABEL: .4X TO 1X BASIC INSERTS
BL ODDS 1:200 BLACK LABEL PACKS
*BLACK LABEL 22K: 2X TO 4X BASIC INS.
1 Emmitt Smith 5.00 12.00
Butkus
2 Troy Aikman 3.00 8.00
Marchetti
3 Natrone Means 1.00 2.50
Nitschke
4 Chris Zorich 1.00 2.50
Van Buren
5 Barry Sanders 5.00 12.00
D.Jones
6 Kevin Greene 1.50 4.00
Hornung
7 Charles Haley 1.50 4.00
Len Dawson
8 Marshall Faulk 2.50 6.00
W.Lanier
9 Ronnie Lott 1.50 4.00
Gale Sayers
10 Cris Carter 1.00 2.50
Jack Ham
11 Junior Seau 1.50 4.00
Gale Sayers
12 Reggie White 1.50 4.00
Graham
13 Leslie O'Neal 1.00 2.50
Tittle
14 Drew Bledsoe 2.50 6.00
Hendricks
15 Heath Shuler 1.50 4.00
Lilly
16 Ricky Watters 1.50 4.00
Lamonica
17 Marshall Faulk 2.50 6.00
Butkus
18 Deion Sanders 2.00 5.00
R.Berry
19 Steve Young 2.50 6.00
Youngblood
20 Bruce Smith 1.50 4.00
Baugh
NNO Checklist .20 .50
TW1 Sayers 1.25 3.00
Seau
Butkus

1995 Collector's Edge 12th Man Redemption

Collector's Edge produced this redemption card set for insertion in 1995 Black Label and retail version packs. The letter trade cards pulled from packs were to be assembled by collectors to form the words "12TH MAN." Collectors could trade single card letters to Collector's Edge for promo cards or complete letter sets for the 25-card 12th Man prize set listed below. Postage and handling was $19.95 for complete set redemption and the expiration date was March 1, 1996. Although the prize cards feature a 1996 date on the copyright line, the cards are considered part of the 1995 release.
COMPLETE PRIZE SET (25) 6.00 15.00
COMP.LETTERS SET (7) .30 .75
12TH MAN LETTERS: STATED ODDS 1:9
1 Dan Marino 1.25 3.00
2 Jeff Blake .25 .60
3 Steve Bono .05 .15
4 Brett Favre 1.25 3.00
5 Steve Young .50 1.25
6 Scott Mitchell .05 .15
7 Chris Warren .05 .15
8 Marshall Faulk .75 2.00
9 Byron Bam Morris .02 .10
10 Emmitt Smith 1.00 2.50
11 Barry Sanders 1.00 2.50
12 Rashaan Salaam .15 .40
13 Carl Pickens .05 .15
14 Anthony Miller .05 .15
15 Tim Brown .15 .40
16 Jerry Rice .60 1.50
17 Herman Moore .15 .40
18 Isaac Bruce .15 .40
19 Ben Coates .05 .15
20 Shannon Sharpe .05 .15
21 Alfred Pupunu .02 .10
22 Jackie Harris .02 .10
23 Jay Novacek .05 .15
24 Brent Jones .02 .10
25 Checklist Card .02 .10

1995 Collector's Edge Instant Replay

This 51-card set was produced late in the year by Collector's Edge and replaced last year's Pop Warner set. Rookies included in this set are Kerry Collins, Terrell Davis, Joey Galloway, Steve McNair, J.J. Stokes and Michael Westbrook. In addition to the basic set, there is a Prism parallel set. These cards were inserted approximately one in every two packs. There is also a Micro Mini set, which is an eight card set of Black Label base cards. These cards were inserted at a rate of one in 14 packs. Each card contains 50 total "mini" cards with 25 on each side.
COMPLETE SET (51) 6.00 15.00
1 Jeff George .02 .10
2 Eric Metcalf .02 .10
3 Jim Kelly .07 .20
4 Jeff Blake RC .25 .60
5 Andre Rison .02 .10
6 Troy Aikman .30 .75
7 Michael Irvin .07 .20
8 Emmitt Smith .50 1.25
9 John Elway .60 1.50
10 Terrell Davis RC .75 2.00
11 Herman Moore .07 .20
12 Barry Sanders .50 1.25
13 Brett Favre .60 1.50
14 Marshall Faulk .40 1.00
15 Steve Beuerlein .02 .10
16 Steve Bono .02 .10
17 Tim Brown .07 .20
18 Jeff Hostetler .02 .10
19 Jerome Bettis .07 .20
20 Dan Marino .60 1.50
21 Cris Carter .07 .20
22 Drew Bledsoe .20 .50
23 Ben Coates .02 .10
24 Randall Cunningham .07 .20
25 Terry Kirby .02 .10
26 Ricky Watters .02 .10
27 Kyle Brady .07 .20
28 Byron Bam Morris .01 .05
29 Neil O'Donnell .02 .10
30 Natrone Means .02 .10
31 Junior Seau .07 .20
32 William Floyd .02 .10
33 Jerry Rice .30 .75
34 Deion Sanders .20 .50
35 Steve Young .25 .60
36 Rick Mirer .02 .10
37 Chris Warren .02 .10
38 Trent Dilfer .07 .20
39 Errict Rhett .02 .10
40 Heath Shuler .02 .10
41 Ki-Jana Carter RC .07 .20
42 Kerry Collins RC .60 1.50
43 Steve McNair RC 1.00 2.50
44 Rashaan Salaam RC .02 .10
45 James O. Stewart RC .40 1.00
46 J.J. Stokes RC .07 .20
47 Tyrone Wheatley RC .40 1.00
48 Joey Galloway RC .50 1.25
49 Napoleon Kaufman RC .40 1.00
50 Michael Westbrook RC .07 .20
NNO Checklist Card .01 .05

1995 Collector's Edge Instant Replay Prisms

COMP.PRISM SET (50) 12.00 30.00
*PRISM STARS: 1X TO 2.5X
*PRISM RCs: .5X TO 1.2X
STATED ODDS 1:2

1995 Collector's Edge Instant Replay EdgeTech Die Cuts

This 13-card set was randomly inserted at a rate of one in four regular retail packs and one per pack in special retail packs. The card fronts are die cut in the shape of a helmet at the top of the card with the player's name beneath the shot. The background of the fronts also resemble a football field. Card backs contain the "EdgeTech" logo at the top of the card, with a headshot of the player in a circle underneath it. Also listed are the player's name and biological information. In the background is a shot of the team helmet and a football field.
COMPLETE SET (13) 4.00 10.00
STATED ODDS 1:4 RET, 1:1 SPEC.RET
1 Troy Aikman .60 1.50
2 Drew Bledsoe .40 1.00
3 Tim Brown .15 .40

4 Ben Coates .07 .20
5 Marshall Faulk .75 2.00
6 William Floyd .07 .20
7 Dan Marino 1.25 3.00
8 Errict Rhett .07 .20
9 Deion Sanders .40 1.00
10 Emmitt Smith 1.00 2.50
11 Ricky Watters .07 .20
12 Steve Young .50 1.25
NNO Checklist .02 .10

1995 Collector's Edge Instant Replay Quantum Motion

This complete 22-card set was available in packs in several ways. The first 10-cards plus the checklist were inserted in packs at a rate of one in 12 packs. The other 11-cards were available through a mail redemption, where an exchange card was available for each individual card. Cards 1-10 feature actual game footage on the front of the card and the player's name alternating with the words Quantum Motion. For cards 11-21, exchange cards were available. The exchange cards were gray/black on the top and bottom with the word Quantum written in white over a red background in the center of the card. The cards are numbered out of 21 on the front. Card backs contain lines to fill out to exchange the card for a Quantum card. The redeemed cards feature "double face" fronts that alternate between two different action shots rather than actual game footage. Card backs are the same as the first ten cards.

COMPLETE SET (22) 12.50 30.00
COMP.SERIES 1 (11) 7.50 20.00
COMP.SERIES 2 (11) 4.00 10.00
1-10/CL: STATED ODDS 1:12
11-21: AVAIL. VIA MAIL REDEMPTION
1 Troy Aikman 1.25 3.00
2 Drew Bledsoe .75 2.00
3 Marshall Faulk 1.50 4.00
4 Michael Irvin .30 .75
5 Dan Marino 2.50 6.00
6 Jerry Rice 1.25 3.00
7 Rod Smith 2.00 5.00
8 Emmitt Smith 2.00 5.00
9 Michael Westbrook .10 .30
10 Steve Young 1.00 2.50
11 Erik Kramer .07 .20
12 Jeff Blake .40 1.00
13 Eric Metcalf .15 .40
14 Steve Bono .15 .40
15 Carl Pickens .15 .40
16 Isaac Bruce .30 .75
17 Errict Rhett .15 .40
18 Kerry Collins 1.00 2.50
19 Rashaan Salaam .05 .15
20 Gus Frerotte .15 .40
21 Terry Kirby .15 .40
NNO Checklist .07 .20

1995 Collector's Edge TimeWarp Jumbos

This 42-card set features borderless color player photos and measures approximately 8" by 10". The cards are similar to the regular issue 1995 Collector's Edge TimeWarp cards, except in jumbo format. Initially distributed to hobby dealers but offered later direct to collectors (for $11.95 each), 5000 of each card was produced with every card serial numbered. Signed versions of each of the cards were also available autographed by the Hall of Fame player featured for $23.95 each. The cards were also made available through a 1996 Collector's Edge special retail pack redemption offer for $3.95 each with 12-wrappers of product.

COMPLETE SET (42) 150.00 250.00
1 Dick Butkus 5.00 12.00
Emmitt Smith
2 Dick Butkus 5.00 12.00
Emmitt Smith
3 Gino Marchetti 3.00 8.00
Troy Aikman
4 Gino Marchetti 3.00 8.00
Troy Aikman
5 Ray Nitschke 2.00 5.00
Natrone Means
6 Ray Nitschke 2.00 5.00
Natrone Means
7 Steve Van Buren 1.50 4.00
Chris Zorich
8 Steve Van Buren 1.50 4.00
Chris Zorich
9 Deacon Jones 6.00 15.00
Barry Sanders
10 Deacon Jones 6.00 15.00
Barry Sanders
11 Paul Hornung 2.00 5.00
Kevin Greene
12 Paul Hornung 2.00 5.00
Kevin Greene
13 Len Dawson 2.00 5.00
Charles Haley
14 Len Dawson 2.00 5.00
Charles Haley
15 Willie Lanier 2.50 6.00
Marshall Faulk
16 Willie Lanier 2.50 6.00
Marshall Faulk
17 Gale Sayers 2.00 5.00
Ronnie Lott
18 Gale Sayers 2.00 5.00
Ronnie Lott
19 Jack Ham 2.00 5.00
Cris Carter
20 Jack Ham 2.00 5.00
Cris Carter
21 Gale Sayers 2.00 5.00
Junior Seau
22 Gale Sayers 2.00 5.00
Junior Seau
23 Otto Graham 2.00 5.00
Reggie White
24 Otto Graham 2.00 5.00
Reggie White
25 Y.A.Tittle 2.00 5.00
Leslie O'Neal
26 Y.A.Tittle 2.00 5.00
Leslie O'Neal
27 Daryle Lamonica 1.50 4.00
Ricky Watters
28 Daryle Lamonica 1.50 4.00
Ricky Watters
29 Dick Butkus 2.40 6.00
Marshall Faulk
30 Dick Butkus 2.40 6.00
Marshall Faulk
31 Raymond Berry 2.40 6.00
Deion Sanders
32 Raymond Berry 2.40 6.00
Deion Sanders
33 Jack Youngblood 3.20 8.00
Steve Young
34 Jack Youngblood 3.20 8.00
Steve Young
35 Sammy Baugh 2.00 5.00
Bruce Smith
36 Sammy Baugh 2.00 5.00
Bruce Smith
37 Ted Hendricks 6.00 15.00
Dan Marino
38 Bob Lilly 6.00 15.00
Dan Marino
39 Ted Hendricks 3.20 8.00
Drew Bledsoe
40 Bob Lilly 2.00 5.00
Heath Shuler
41 Dick Butkus 2.00 5.00
Jeff Blake
42 Dick Butkus 2.40 6.00
Michael Westbrook

1995 Collector's Edge TimeWarp Jumbos Autographs

These are the autographed parallel version of the 1995 Collector's Edger TimeWarp Jumbos cards (measure roughly 8" x 10"). Each card was issued direct to the hobby as a single card (initially at $23.95 each) or part of a compete set that could have been purchased direct for $1005.90. The cards were signed by the retired player only and were issued with a separate gold foil certificate of authenticity.

COMPLETE SET (42) 600.00 1000.00
1 Dick Butkus AUTO 20.00 40.00
Emmitt Smith
2 Dick Butkus AUTO 20.00 40.00
Emmitt Smith
3 Gino Marchetti AUTO 12.50 25.00
Troy Aikman
4 Gino Marchetti AUTO 12.50 25.00
Troy Aikman
5 Ray Nitschke AUTO 30.00 60.00
Natrone Means
6 Ray Nitschke AUTO 30.00 60.00
Natrone Means
7 Steve Van Buren AUTO 12.50 25.00
Chris Zorich
8 Steve Van Buren AUTO 12.50 25.00
Chris Zorich
9 Deacon Jones AUTO 12.50 25.00
Barry Sanders
10 Deacon Jones AUTO 12.50 25.00
Barry Sanders
11 Paul Hornung AUTO 20.00 40.00
Kevin Greene
12 Paul Hornung AUTO 20.00 40.00
Kevin Greene
13 Len Dawson AUTO 20.00 40.00
Charles Haley
14 Len Dawson AUTO 20.00 40.00
Charles Haley
15 Willie Lanier AUTO 10.00 20.00
Marshall Faulk
16 Willie Lanier AUTO 10.00 20.00
Marshall Faulk
17 Gale Sayers AUTO 25.00 50.00
Ronnie Lott
18 Gale Sayers AUTO 25.00 50.00
Ronnie Lott
19 Jack Ham AUTO 15.00 30.00
Cris Carter
20 Jack Ham AUTO 15.00 30.00
Cris Carter
21 Gale Sayers AUTO 30.00 60.00
Junior Seau
22 Gale Sayers AUTO 30.00 60.00
Junior Seau
23 Otto Graham AUTO 20.00 40.00
Reggie White
24 Otto Graham AUTO 20.00 40.00
Reggie White
25 Y.A.Tittle AUTO 20.00 40.00
Leslie O'Neal
26 Y.A.Tittle AUTO 20.00 40.00
Leslie O'Neal
27 Daryle Lamonica AUTO 12.50 25.00
Ricky Watters
28 Daryle Lamonica AUTO 12.50 25.00
Ricky Watters
29 Dick Butkus AUTO 20.00 40.00
Marshall Faulk
30 Dick Butkus AUTO 20.00 40.00
Marshall Faulk
31 Raymond Berry AUTO 12.50 25.00
Deion Sanders
32 Raymond Berry AUTO 12.50 25.00
Deion Sanders
33 Jack Youngblood AUTO 10.00 20.00
Steve Young
34 Jack Youngblood AUTO 10.00 20.00
Steve Young
35 Sammy Baugh AUTO 40.00 80.00
Bruce Smith
36 Sammy Baugh AUTO 40.00 80.00
Bruce Smith
37 Ted Hendricks AUTO 12.50 25.00
Dan Marino
38 Bob Lilly AUTO 15.00 30.00
Dan Marino
39 Ted Hendricks AUTO 12.50 25.00
Drew Bledsoe
40 Bob Lilly AUTO 15.00 30.00
Heath Shuler
41 Dick Butkus AUTO 20.00 40.00
Jeff Blake
42 Dick Butkus AUTO 20.00 40.00
Michael Westbrook
GTW1 Butkus AU/Blake AU/Seau AU 30.00 60.00

1995 Collector's Edge TimeWarp Sunday Ticket

Collector's Edge originally released this set through a direct mail order offer at $19.95 per set. Each order also included a group of various free promo and preview cards. The five-card Sunday Ticket set features borderless color action player photos of a current player interacting with a previous player in a fictitious game. The backs carry information about both players on a metallic background with the serial number (of 2500 sets produced). Later a set version numbered of 10,000 was released through a special mail order offer.

COMPLETE SET (5) 4.00 10.00
*NUMBERED OF 10,000: .25X TO .5X
1 Paul Hornung .60 1.50
Chris Zorich
2 Gale Sayers .60 1.50
Kevin Greene
3 Ted Hendricks .60 1.50
Ricky Watters
4 Sammy Baugh .60 1.50
Bruce Smith
5 Dick Butkus 1.60 4.00
Marshall Faulk

1996 Collector's Edge Cowboybilia Promos

This 3-card set looks like the 1996 Cowboybilia series that was inserted into 1996 Collector's Edge Cowboybilia packs, with the difference being the fact that these cards are unsigned, and have "PROMO" stamped across the front of them.

DCA20 Daryl Johnston .80 2.00
DCA21 Jay Novacek .60 1.50
DCA22 Charles Haley .60 1.50

1996 Collector's Edge Dolphinbilia Preview

This card was produced as a Preview to a card set that was never released -- Dolphinbilia. The card features Dan Marino printed on a holofoil card with a 24K logo. Each is serial numbered of 250.

DB127 Dan Marino 24K 4.00 10.00

1996 Collector's Edge 49erbilia Preview

These cards were produced as a Preview to a set that was never released -- 49erbilia. The cards feature the player printed on holofoil card stock with a 24K logo. Each was serial numbered of 250.

206 Jerry Rice 3.20 8.00
211 Steve Young 2.40 6.00

1996 Collector's Edge Packerbilia Preview

This card was produced as a Preview to a card set that was never released -- Packerbilia. The card features Brett Favre printed on a holofoil card with a 24K logo. Each is serial numbered of 250.

PB82 Brett Favre 24K 4.00 10.00

1996 Collector's Edge Promos

These four cards were issued to preview the 1996 Collector's Edge set. The three player cards are numbered on the back.

COMPLETE SET (4) 1.20 3.00
P1 Errict Rhett .60 1.50
P2 Junior Seau .40 1.00
P3 Terry Kirby .20 .50
NNO Cover Card .10 .30

1996 Collector's Edge

The 1996 Collector's Edge set was issued in one series totalling 240 cards. The cards were issued in six card packs with 10 packs per box and 24 boxes per case in retail, hobby, and special retail packaging. The cards are grouped alphabetically within teams and checklisted below alphabetically according to teams. Collector's Edge Cowboybilia packs also contained the base brand and insert cards with the same pack configuration. Draft Redemption cards were also randomly inserted into packs. When redeemed, a collector would receive a card of one of that teams' draft picks selected by the company. A special die cut Crucibles Eddie George promo card was produced, apparently for an insert set never released.

COMPLETE SET (250) 8.00 20.00
1 Larry Centers .07 .20
2 Garrison Hearst .07 .20
3 Dave Krieg .02 .10
4 Rob Moore .07 .20
5 Frank Sanders .07 .20
6 Eric Swann .02 .10
7 Morten Andersen .02 .10
8 Chris Doleman .02 .10
9 Bert Emanuel .07 .20
10 Jeff George .07 .20
11 Craig Heyward .02 .10
12 Terance Mathis .02 .10
13 Clay Matthews .02 .10
14 Eric Metcalf .02 .10
15 Bill Brooks .02 .10
16 Todd Collins .07 .20
17 Russell Copeland .02 .10
18 Jim Kelly .15 .40
19 Bryce Paup .02 .10
20 Andre Reed .07 .20
21 Bruce Smith .07 .20
22 Mark Carrier WR .02 .10
23 Kerry Collins .15 .40
24 Willie Green .02 .10
25 Eric Guliford .02 .10
26 Brett Maxie .02 .10
27 Tim McKyer .02 .10
28 Derrick Moore .02 .10
29 Curtis Conway .15 .40
30 Jim Flanigan .02 .10
31 Jeff Graham .02 .10
32 Robert Green .02 .10
33 Erik Kramer .02 .10
34 Rashaan Salaam .07 .20
35 Alonzo Spellman .02 .10
36 Donnell Woolford .02 .10
37 Chris Zorich .02 .10
38 Eric Bieniemy .02 .10
39 Jeff Blake .15 .40
40 Ki-Jana Carter .07 .20
41 John Copeland .02 .10
42 Harold Green .02 .10
43 Tony McGee .02 .10
44 Carl Pickens .07 .20
45 Darnay Scott .07 .20
46 Bracy Walker RC .02 .10
47 Dan Wilkinson .02 .10
48 Rob Burnett .02 .10
49 Leroy Hoard .02 .10
50 Ernest Hunter .02 .10
51 Michael Jackson .07 .20
52 Stevon Moore .02 .10
53 Anthony Pleasant .02 .10
54 Andre Rison .07 .20
55 Vinny Testaverde .07 .20
56 Eric Zeier .02 .10
57 Troy Aikman .40 1.00
58 Bill Bates .07 .20
59 Shante Carver .02 .10
60 Michael Irvin .15 .40
61 Daryl Johnston .07 .20
62 Jay Novacek .02 .10
63 Deion Sanders .25 .60
64 Emmitt Smith .60 1.50
65 Sherman Williams .02 .10
66 Terrell Davis .30 .75
67 John Elway .50 1.25
68 Ed McCaffrey .07 .20
69 Glyn Milburn .02 .10
70 Anthony Miller .07 .20
71 Michael Dean Perry .02 .10
72 Shannon Sharpe .07 .20
73 Willie Clay .02 .10
74 Scott Mitchell .07 .20
75 Herman Moore .07 .20
76 Johnnie Morton .07 .20
77 Brett Perriman .02 .10
78 Barry Sanders .60 1.50
79 Tracy Scroggins .02 .10
80 Edgar Bennett .07 .20
81 Robert Brooks .15 .40
82 Brett Favre .75 2.00
83 Dorsey Levens .15 .40
84 Craig Newsome .02 .10
85 Wayne Simmons .02 .10
86 Reggie White .15 .40
87 Chris Chandler .07 .20
88 Anthony Cook .02 .10
89 Mel Gray .02 .10
90 Haywood Jeffires .02 .10
91 Darryll Lewis .02 .10
92 Steve McNair .30 .75
93 Todd McNair .02 .10
94 Rodney Thomas .02 .10
95 Trev Alberts .02 .10
96 Tony Bennett .02 .10
97 Quentin Coryatt .02 .10
98 Sean Dawkins .02 .10
99 Ken Dilger .07 .20
100 Marshall Faulk .20 .50
101 Jim Harbaugh .07 .20
102 Ronald Humphrey .02 .10
103 Floyd Turner .02 .10
104 Steve Beuerlein .07 .20
105 Tony Boselli .02 .10
106 Mark Brunell .25 .60
107 Willie Jackson .07 .20
108 Jeff Lageman .02 .10
109 James O. Stewart .07 .20
110 Cedric Tillman .02 .10
111 Marcus Allen .15 .40
112 Kimble Anders .07 .20
113 Steve Bono .02 .10
114 Dale Carter .02 .10
115 Willie Davis .02 .10
116 Lake Dawson .02 .10
117 Dan Saleaumua .02 .10
118 Neil Smith .07 .20
119 Derrick Thomas .15 .40
120 Tamarick Vanover .07 .20
121 Marco Coleman .02 .10
122 Bryan Cox .02 .10
123 Steve Emtman .02 .10
124 Irving Fryar .07 .20
125 Eric Green .02 .10
126 Terry Kirby .07 .20
127 Dan Marino .75 2.00
128 O.J. McDuffie .07 .20
129 Bernie Parmalee .02 .10
130 Troy Vincent .02 .10
131 Cris Carter .15 .40
132 Jack Del Rio .02 .10
133 Qadry Ismail .07 .20
134 Amp Lee .02 .10
135 Warren Moon .07 .20
136 John Randle .07 .20
137 Jake Reed .07 .20
138 Robert Smith .07 .20
139 Drew Bledsoe .25 .60
140 Vincent Brisby .02 .10
141 Ben Coates .07 .20
142 Curtis Martin .30 .75
143 Dave Meggett .02 .10
144 Will Moore .02 .10
145 Chris Slade .02 .10
146 Mario Bates .07 .20
147 Quinn Early .02 .10
148 Jim Everett .02 .10
149 Michael Haynes .02 .10
150 Tyrone Hughes .02 .10
151 Wayne Martin .02 .10
152 Renaldo Turnbull .02 .10
153 Dave Brown .02 .10
154 Chris Calloway .02 .10
155 Rodney Hampton .07 .20
156 Mike Sherrard .02 .10
157 Michael Strahan .07 .20
158 Herschel Walker .07 .20
159 Tyrone Wheatley .07 .20
160 Kyle Brady .02 .10
161 Wayne Chrebet .25 .60
162 Hugh Douglas .07 .20
163 Adrian Murrell .07 .20
164 Todd Scott .02 .10
165 Charles Wilson .02 .10
166 Tim Brown .15 .40
167 Aundray Bruce .02 .10
168 Andrew Glover .02 .10
169 Jeff Hostetler .02 .10
170 Napoleon Kaufman .15 .40
171 Terry McDaniel .02 .10
172 Chester McGlockton .02 .10
173 Pat Swilling .02 .10
174 Harvey Williams .02 .10
175 Fred Barnett .02 .10
176 Randall Cunningham .15 .40
177 William Fuller .02 .10
178 Charlie Garner .07 .20
179 Andy Harmon .02 .10
180 Rodney Peete .02 .10
181 Ricky Watters .07 .20
182 Calvin Williams .02 .10
183 Chad Brown .02 .10
184 Kevin Greene .07 .20
185 Greg Lloyd .07 .20
186 Byron Bam Morris .02 .10
187 Neil O'Donnell .07 .20
188 Erric Pegram .02 .10
189 Kordell Stewart .15 .40
190 Yancey Thigpen .07 .20
191 Rod Woodson .07 .20
192 Darren Bennett .02 .10
193 Ronnie Harmon .02 .10
194 Stan Humphries .07 .20
195 Tony Martin .07 .20
196 Natrone Means .07 .20
197 Leslie O'Neal .02 .10
198 Junior Seau .15 .40
199 Mark Seay .02 .10
200 William Floyd .07 .20
201 Merton Hanks .02 .10
202 Brent Jones .02 .10
203 Derek Loville .02 .10
204 Ken Norton, Jr. .02 .10
205 Gary Plummer .02 .10
206 Jerry Rice .40 1.00
207 J.J. Stokes .15 .40
208 Dana Stubblefield .07 .20
209 John Taylor .02 .10
210 Bryant Young .07 .20
211 Steve Young .30 .75
212 Brian Blades .02 .10
213 Joey Galloway .15 .40
214 Carlton Gray .02 .10
215 Cortez Kennedy .02 .10
216 Rick Mirer .07 .20
217 Chris Warren .07 .20
218 Jerome Bettis .15 .40
219 Isaac Bruce .15 .40
220 Troy Drayton .02 .10
221 D'Marco Farr .02 .10
222 Sean Gilbert .02 .10
223 Chris Miller .02 .10
224 Roman Phifer .02 .10
225 Trent Dilfer .15 .40
226 Santana Dotson .02 .10
227 Alvin Harper .02 .10
228 Jackie Harris .02 .10
229 John Lynch .15 .40
230 Hardy Nickerson .02 .10
231 Errict Rhett .07 .20
232 Warren Sapp .02 .10
233 Terry Allen .07 .20
234 Henry Ellard .02 .10
235 Gus Frerotte .07 .20
236 Ken Harvey .02 .10
237 Brian Mitchell .02 .10
238 Heath Shuler .07 .20
239 James Washington .02 .10
240 Michael Westbrook .15 .40
241 Checklist .02 .10
242 Checklist .02 .10
243 Checklist .02 .10
244 Checklist .02 .10
245 Checklist .02 .10
246 Checklist .02 .10
247 Checklist .02 .10
248 Checklist .02 .10
249 Checklist .02 .10
250 Checklist .02 .10
PR1 Eddie George Promo .20 .50

1996 Collector's Edge Die Cuts

*STARS: 1.2X TO 3X BASIC CARDS
ONE PER SPECIAL RETAIL PACK

1996 Collector's Edge Holofoil

*STARS: 12X TO 30X BASIC CARDS
STATED ODDS 1:48

1996 Collector's Edge Big Easy

This set was distributed as a random insert in various 1996 Collector's Edge pack types. The cards feature metallized foil printing on the cardback with the Big Easy title on the cardfront with a mustard colored background. Each card was numbered of 2000 made and an unnumbered checklist card was produced as well. A gold foil parallel set was later released via mail order. Each was numbered of 3100 made.

COMPLETE SET (19) 25.00 60.00
STATED ODDS 1:72
STATED PRINT RUN 2000 SERIAL #'d SETS
*GOLD FOILS: .2X TO .5X BASIC INSERTS
GOLDS PRINT RUN 3100 SERIAL #'d SETS
GOLD FOILS ISSUED VIA DIRECT MAIL OFFER
1 Kerry Collins 1.00 2.50
2 Rashaan Salaam .50 1.25
3 Troy Aikman 2.50 6.00
4 Deion Sanders 1.50 4.00
5 Emmitt Smith 4.00 10.00
6 Terrell Davis 2.00 5.00
7 Barry Sanders 4.00 10.00
8 Brett Favre 5.00 12.00
9 Marshall Faulk 1.25 3.00
10 Tamarick Vanover .50 1.25
11 Dan Marino 5.00 12.00
12 Drew Bledsoe 1.50 4.00
13 Curtis Martin 2.00 5.00
14 J.J.Stokes 1.00 2.50
15 Joey Galloway 1.00 2.50
16 Isaac Bruce 1.00 2.50
17 Errict Rhett .50 1.25
18 Carl Pickens .50 1.25
NNO Checklist Card .25 .60
P1 Errict Rhett Promo .30 .75

1996 Collector's Edge Cowboybilia

This set was not released through the initial 1996 Cowboybilia pack product, but later in 1997 Cowboybilia Plus packs. The cards are essentially an unsigned version of the Cowboybilia Autographs, were inserted two per pack, and are serial numbered of 10,000 sets produced.

COMPLETE SET (25) 10.00 20.00
TWO PER 1997 COWBOYBILIA PLUS
Q1 Chris Boniol .20 .50
Q2 John Jett .20 .50
Q3 Sherman Williams .20 .50
Q4 Chad Hennings .20 .50
Q5 Larry Allen .20 .50
Q6 Jason Garrett .50 1.25
Q7 Tony Tolbert .20 .50
Q8 Kevin Williams .20 .50
Q9 Mark Tuinei .20 .50
Q10 Larry Brown .20 .50
Q11 Kevin Smith .20 .50
Q12 Darrin Smith .20 .50
Q13 Robert Jones .20 .50
Q14 Nate Newton .20 .50
Q15 Darren Woodson .30 .75
Q16 Leon Lett .30 .75
Q17 Russell Maryland .20 .50
Q18 Erik Williams .20 .50
Q19 Bill Bates .30 .75
Q20 Daryl Johnston .30 .75
Q21 Jay Novacek .30 .75
Q22 Charles Haley .30 .75
Q23 Troy Aikman 1.50 3.00
Q24 Michael Irvin .60 1.50
Q25 Emmitt Smith 2.50 5.00

1996 Collector's Edge Cowboybilia Autographs

These 25-cards feature members of the Dallas Cowboys and were randomly inserted into 1996 Collector's Edge Cowboybilia packs. Each card was signed by the player, except for Troy Aikman, and individually numbered on the cardback. The initial release had the signed cards inserted at the rate of 1:2.5 packs. However, the cards were later re-released as a 1:1.5 pack insert in 1997 Cowboybilia Plus packs that also included two unsigned cards and 6-base set cards. Every other pack contained an autographed Cowboys card or certificate for a signed Cowboys item. Other items included: Signed jerseys, helmets, photos, pennants and footballs. Also 24K Prism parallel cards of Emmitt Smith, Troy Aikman, Michael Irvin and Deion Sanders were inserted at a rate of approximately four per case (one per player per case) in the first release and 1:32.5 in the second release. The Staubach/Pearson signed Hail Mary card was randomly inserted at the rate of 1:192 packs in the first release and 1:134 in the second. The REAP program (Roever Educational Assistance Programs) was the charitable beneficiary of this issue. Lastly, some unsigned versions of many of the cards have been seen on the market leading to the possibility of forged autographs.

STATED ODDS 1:2.5 COWBOYBILIA
STATED PRINT RUN 500-4000 10.00 25.00
DCA1 Chris Boniol/4000 6.00 15.00
DCA2 John Jett/4000 6.00 15.00
DCA3 Sherman Williams/4000 6.00 15.00
DCA4 Chad Hennings/4000 6.00 15.00
DCA5 Larry Allen/4000 15.00 30.00
DCA6 Jason Garrett/4000 10.00 25.00
DCA7 Tony Tolbert/4000 6.00 15.00
DCA8 Kevin Williams/4000 6.00 15.00
DCA9 Mark Tuinei/4000 15.00 30.00
DCA10 Larry Brown/4000 8.00 20.00
DCA11 Kevin Smith/4000 6.00 15.00
DCA12 Darrin Smith/4000 6.00 15.00
DCA13 Robert Jones/4000 6.00 15.00
DCA14 Nate Newton/4000 8.00 20.00
DCA15 Darren Woodson/4000 8.00 20.00
DCA16 Leon Lett/4000 10.00 25.00
DCA17 Russell Maryland/4000 6.00 15.00
DCA18 Erik Williams/4000 8.00 20.00
DCA19 Bill Bates/4000 10.00 25.00
DCA20 Daryl Johnston/2300 25.00 40.00
DCA21 Jay Novacek/2300 20.00 50.00
DCA22 Charles Haley/2300 10.00 25.00
DCA23 Aikman/600 Unsigned 40.00 80.00
DCA24 Michael Irvin/500 100.00 200.00
DCA25 Emmitt Smith/500 75.00 150.00
NNO Staubach/Pear./1000 50.00 120.00

1996 Collector's Edge Cowboybilia 24K Holofoil

These four cards are parallels to the player's 1995 Collector's Edge Holofoil card. To differentiate them, they were printed with a 24K logo. They were randomly inserted into 1996 Collector's Edge Cowboybilia packs at the rate of 1:48 and 1997 Cowboybilia Plus at the rate of 1:32.5.

COMPLETE SET (4) 100.00 200.00
STATED ODDS 1:48 1996 COWBOYBILIA
CB57 Troy Aikman 15.00 40.00
CB60 Michael Irvin 6.00 15.00
CB63 Deion Sanders 10.00 25.00
CB64 Emmitt Smith 25.00 60.00

1996 Collector's Edge Draft Day Redemption

Cards from this 30-card standard-size set were randomly inserted into packs at the rate of 1:8. Each card was redeemable for a top rookie signed by the NFL team whose logo appears on the card. The front features the team helmet and the back contains redemption information. The cards were redeemable until March 3, 1997. There have been two different variations discovered on the backs, one with "Retail-R1" printed near the lower right corner and the other with "Retail-T." Since the cards are unnumbered, they are sequenced in alphabetical order by team.

STATED ODDS 1:8
1 Arizona Cardinals .08 .25
2 Atlanta Falcons .08 .25
3 Buffalo Bills .08 .25
4 Carolina Panthers .08 .25
5 Chicago Bears .08 .25
6 Cincinnati Bengals .08 .25
7 Cleveland Browns .08 .25
8 Dallas Cowboys .08 .25
9 Denver Broncos .08 .25
10 Detroit Lions .08 .25
11 Green Bay Packers .08 .25
12 Houston Oilers .08 .25
13 Indianapolis Colts .08 .25
14 Jacksonville Jaguars .08 .25
15 Kansas City Chiefs .08 .25
16 Los Angeles Raiders .08 .25
17 Miami Dolphins .08 .25
18 Minnesota Vikings .08 .25
19 New England Patriots .08 .25
20 New Orleans Saints .08 .25
21 New York Giants .08 .25
22 New York Jets .08 .25
23 Philadelphia Eagles .08 .25
24 Pittsburgh Steelers .08 .25
25 San Diego Chargers .08 .25
26 San Francisco 49ers .08 .25
27 Seattle Seahawks .08 .25
28 St.Louis Rams .08 .25
29 Tampa Bay Buccaneers .08 .25
30 Washington Redskins .08 .25

1996 Collector's Edge Draft Day Redemption Prizes

This 30-card set features color player photos of the Draft picks of the NFL teams. One of these player cards was received when the trade card for the appropriate team was redeemed. The redemption cards were randomly inserted in packs at the rate of one in eight. The trade cards expired March 3,1997.

COMPLETE SET (30) 25.00 60.00
1 Simeon Rice 1.50 4.00
2 Richard Huntley .75 2.00
3 Jonathan Ogden 2.00 5.00
4 Eric Moulds 1.25 3.00
5 Tim Biakabutuka 1.25 3.00
6 Walt Harris .50 1.25
7 Marco Battaglia .50 1.25
8 Stepfret Williams .50 1.25
9 John Mobley .50 1.25
10 Reggie Brown LB .50 1.25
11 Derrick Mayes .75 2.00
12 Eddie George 2.00 5.00
13 Marvin Harrison 4.00 8.00
14 Kevin Hardy .50 1.25
15 Jerome Woods .50 1.25
16 Karim Abdul-Jabbar .75 2.00
17 Duane Clemons .50 1.25
18 Terry Glenn 1.25 3.00
19 Ricky Whittle .50 1.25
20 Amani Toomer 1.50 4.00
21 Keyshawn Johnson 1.25 3.00
22 Rickey Dudley .75 2.00
23 Bobby Hoying .75 2.00
24 Jahine Arnold .50 1.25
25 Tony Banks .75 2.00
26 Bryan Still .50 1.25
27 Terrell Owens 4.00 8.00
28 Reggie Brown RBK .50 1.25
29 Mike Alstott 1.25 3.00
30 Stephen Davis 2.50 6.00

1996 Collector's Edge Proteges

Randomly inserted (1:164 packs) in all Collector's Edge package types for 1996, these cards feature a top NFL veteran matched with a comparable younger player -- one on each side of the card. Each card is individually numbered and an unnumbered checklist card was produced as well.

COMPLETE SET (13) 30.00 80.00
STATED ODDS 1:164
1 E.Metcalf 2.00 5.00
J.Galloway
2 H.Moore 2.00 5.00
M.Westbrook
3 E.Smith 6.00 15.00
E.Rhett
4 K.Stewart 7.50 20.00
J.Elway
5 T.Davis 7.50 20.00
M.Faulk
6 R.Salaam 2.00 5.00
M.Allen
7 D.Marino 7.50 20.00
D.Bledsoe
8 B.Favre 7.50 20.00
K.Collins
9 T.Brown 2.00 5.00
I.Bruce
10 C.Carter 1.50 4.00
C.Sanders
11 C.Martin 3.00 8.00
C.Warren
12 T.Vanover 2.00 5.00
B.Mitchell
PR1 Rashaan Salaam Promo .40 1.00
NNO Checklist Card .75 2.00

1996 Collector's Edge Quantum Motion

Randomly inserted at a rate of 1:36 1996 retail, hobby and Cowboybilia packs, this 24-card set changes images before your eyes using lenticular printing technology. The cards were also included in the re-release of 1997 Cowboybilia and inserted at the rate of 1:50. They feature top NFL stars in both their current NFL uniform and their college uniform. This set is sequenced in alphabetical order.

COMPLETE SET (25) 30.00 80.00
STATED ODDS 1:36 1996 EDGE PACKS
STATED ODDS 1:50 1997 COWBOYBILIA
*FOIL CARDS: .4X TO 1X BASIC INSERTS
1 Troy Aikman 3.00 8.00
2 Marcus Allen 1.25 3.00
3 Drew Bledsoe 2.00 5.00
4 Tim Brown 1.25 3.00
5 Isaac Bruce 1.25 3.00
6 Mark Brunell 2.00 5.00
7 Kerry Collins 1.25 3.00
8 John Elway 6.00 15.00
9 Marshall Faulk 1.50 4.00
10 Brett Favre 6.00 15.00
11 Jeff George .60 1.50
12 Terry Kirby .60 1.50
13 Dan Marino 6.00 15.00
14 Natrone Means .60 1.50
15 Carl Pickens .60 1.50
16 Errict Rhett .60 1.50
17 Rashaan Salaam .60 1.50
18 Deion Sanders 2.00 5.00
19 Barry Sanders 5.00 12.00
20 Emmitt Smith 5.00 12.00
21 Kordell Stewart 1.25 3.00
22 Tamarick Vanover .60 1.50
23 Michael Westbrook 1.25 3.00
24 Steve Young 2.50 6.00
NNO Checklist Card .30 .75
QM1 Rashaan Salaam Promo .30 .75

1996 Collector's Edge Ripped

Randomly inserted in 1996 hobby, retail and Cowboybilia packs at a rate of 1:12, this 19-card insert set (series one) features celebrities offering their commentary on NFL players. Cards numbered 1-18 with an unnumbered checklist (listed below) were available in 1996 Edge packs. The cards were also included in the re-release of 1997 Cowboybilia Plus and inserted at the rate of 1:6. A series two set (cards numbered 19-36) was released later in 1997 Collector's Edge Masters. A Jeff Blake Promo card was also produced and priced below. In addition, the series one set was produced and sold as a complete 18-card die cut set. Although the die cuts were produced in smaller numbers (500 of each card), they were released in full set form and thus are often available in larger group quantities.

COMP.SERIES 1 (19) 15.00 40.00
STATED ODDS 1:12 1996 EDGE PACKS
STATED ODDS 1:6 1997 COWBOYBILIA
*DIE CUTS: .4X TO 1X BASIC INSERTS
DIE CUTS PRINT RUN 500 SERIAL #'d SETS
DIE CUTS: AVAIL.VIA DIRECT MAIL OFFER
1 Jeff Blake 1.00 2.00
2 Steve Bono .20 .50
3 Terrell Davis 2.00 4.00
4 John Elway 5.00 10.00
6 Brett Favre 5.00 10.00
8 Erik Kramer .20 .50
9 Dan Marino 5.00 10.00
10 Natrone Means .40 1.00
11 Eric Metcalf .20 .50
12 Anthony Miller .40 1.00
13 Herman Moore .40 1.00
14 Errict Rhett .40 1.00
15 Andre Rison .40 1.00
16 Joey Galloway 1.00 2.00
17 Yancey Thigpen .40 1.00
18 Michael Westbrook 1.00 2.00
CK1 Checklist Series 1 .20 .50
R1 Jeff Blake Promo .30 .75

1996 Collector's Edge Too Cool Rookies

Randomly inserted in 1996 retail, hobby and Cowboybilia packs at a rate of one in eight, this 25-card set features some of the best rookies from the 1995 NFL season. The cards were also included in the re-release of 1997 Cowboybilia and inserted at the rate of 1:5. The set is sequenced in alphabetical order. A Michael Westbrook Promo (#TC1) was produced and distributed with the base brand promos.

COMPLETE SET (25) 25.00 50.00
STATED ODDS 1:8 1996 EDGE PACKS
STATED ODDS 1:5 1997 COWBOYBILIA
1 Tony Boselli .25 .60
2 Kyle Brady .25 .60
3 Ki-Jana Carter .60 1.25
4 Kerry Collins 1.25 2.50
5 Todd Collins .60 1.25
6 Terrell Davis 2.50 5.00
7 Hugh Douglas .60 1.25
8 Joey Galloway 1.25 2.50
9 Darius Holland .25 .60
10 Napoleon Kaufman 1.25 2.50
11 Mike Mamula 1.25 2.50
12 Curtis Martin 2.50 5.00
13 Steve McNair 2.50 5.00
14 Billy Milner .25 .60
15 Rashaan Salaam .60 1.25
16 Frank Sanders .60 1.25
17 Warren Sapp .25 .60
18 James O. Stewart .60 1.25
19 J.J. Stokes 1.25 2.50
20 Tamarick Vanover .60 1.25
21 Michael Westbrook 1.25 2.50
22 Tyrone Wheatley .60 1.25
23 Kordell Stewart 1.25 2.50
24 Sherman Williams .25 .60
25 Eric Zeier .25 .60
TC1 Michael Westbrook Promo .30 .75

1996 Collector's Edge All-Stars

This set was released in late 1996, although the tag "Edge '95" appears on the cardfronts. Each is printed on the typical Edge plastic stock and features two color photos of the player on the front.

COMPLETE SET (13) 8.00 20.00
1 Junior Seau .40 1.00
2 Drew Bledsoe 1.20 3.00
3 Marshall Faulk .75 2.00
4 John Elway 2.40 6.00
5 Jerry Rice 1.20 3.00
6 Errict Rhett .40 1.00
7 Jerome Bettis .60 1.50
8 Deion Sanders 1.00 2.50
9 Byron Bam Morris .40 1.00
10 Cris Carter .60 1.50
11 Terrell Davis 2.40 6.00
12 Terance Mathis .40 1.00
13 Checklist Card .40 1.00

1998 Collector's Edge Peyton Manning Promos

These unnumbered cards were issued one at a time either as promos to dealers or promos to buyers of card lots from Shop at Home. Several more special cards were issued with one featuring a facsimile silver foil autograph on the front with serial numbering of 6000 cards made. The other also features a facsimile autograph along with a diamond shaped swatch of football. The cards were unnumbered and feature identical cardbacks.

NNO Peyton Manning/6000 2.00 5.00
NNO Peyton Manning holding jersey 2.00 5.00
NNO Peyton Manning diamond
NNO Peyton Manning FB 4.00 10.00

1998 Collector's Edge Spectrum

This 25-card set features color player photos printed on silver foil stock with shimmering gold foil highlights. The backs carry another player photo and career statistics. The set could be obtained at participating Hobby Direct Shops by redeeming 36-wrappers from the 1998 Supreme Season Review. One random card of the set was received by redeeming three wrappers from Supreme Season Review packs. The cards were also randomly distributed as samples at various card shows throughout the year. An unpriced "Proof" version was also produced for each card.

COMPLETE SET (25) 4.00 10.00
1 Jamal Anderson .15 .40
2 Antowain Smith .15 .40
3 Corey Dillon .40 1.00
4 Emmitt Smith .40 1.00
5 Terrell Davis .40 1.00
6 John Elway .50 1.25
7 Barry Sanders .50 1.25
8 Brett Favre .50 1.25
9 Antonio Freeman .15 .40
10 Marcus Allen .15 .40
11 Dan Marino .50 1.25
12 Cris Carter .15 .40
13 Drew Bledsoe .25 .60
14 Curtis Martin .15 .40
15 Ike Hilliard .05 .15
16 Adrian Murrell .05 .15
17 Tim Brown .15 .40
18 Napoleon Kaufman .08 .25
19 Jerome Bettis .15 .40
20 Kordell Stewart .15 .40
21 Jim Druckenmiller .05 .15
22 Jerry Rice .25 .60
23 Mike Alstott .15 .40
24 Warrick Dunn .30 .75
25 Eddie George .20 .50

1998 Collector's Edge Super Bowl Card Show

This 25-card set was first distributed at the 1998 Super Bowl Card Show in San Diego. Each card was available via a wrapper redemption program and serial numbered of 1000. Three wrappers from a variety of 1997 Edge football products could be redeemed for one card from this set. Each includes a player photo with the Super Bowl XXXII logo on the cardfront. A parallel set was released a month later via another wrapper redemption involving 1997 Edge Extreme and 1998 Advantage wrappers. Collectors could send in 3-wrappers for a single card, from the parallel set, or 36-wrappers for either the AFC (13-cards) or NFC (12-cards) sets. This parallel includes a gold foil AFC or NFC logo on the cardfronts. Edge also released the cards at various shows across the country during 1998. Finally, third and fourth Proof versions of the cards were issued with one set distributed at the 1998 Hawaii Trade Conference event. Each was numbered of 29-sets produced and designated as "Proof" on the cardfronts. The second Proof set was serial numbered to 500.

COMPLETE SET (25) 12.00 30.00
*GOLD FOIL: .4X TO 1X BASIC CARDS
*PROOF 29: 2X TO 5X BASIC CARDS
*PROOF 500: .5X TO 1.2X BASIC CARDS
1 Jamal Anderson .50 1.25
2 Antowain Smith .50 1.25
3 Corey Dillon 1.25 3.00
4 Emmitt Smith 1.20 3.00
5 Terrell Davis 1.20 3.00
6 John Elway 1.60 4.00
7 Barry Sanders 1.60 4.00
8 Brett Favre 1.60 4.00
9 Antonio Freeman .50 1.25
10 Marcus Allen .50 1.25
11 Dan Marino 1.60 4.00
12 Cris Carter .50 1.25

13 Drew Bledsoe .80 2.00
14 Troy Davis .20 .50
15 Ike Hilliard .20 .50
16 Adrian Murrell .30 .75
17 Tim Brown .50 1.25
18 Napoleon Kaufman .50 1.25
19 Jerome Bettis .50 1.25
20 Kordell Stewart .50 1.25
21 Jim Druckenmiller .20 .50
22 Jerry Rice .80 2.00
23 Mike Alstott .50 1.25
24 Warrick Dunn .75 2.00
25 Eddie George .80 2.00

1998 Collector's Edge Super Bowl XXXII

This set was issued directly to dealers who attended the Super Bowl XXXII Card Show. It features players of the Broncos and Packers the two teams which competed in the game. Each card is highlighted with gold or silver foil printing on the cardfronts.

COMPLETE SET (26) 6.00 15.00
*SILVERS: SAME PRICE
1 John Elway 1.50 4.00
2 Terrell Davis 1.00 2.50
3 Shannon Sharpe .20 .50
4 Ed McCaffrey .20 .50
5 Rod Smith WR .30 .75
6 Ray Crockett .10 .30
7 Darrien Gordon .10 .30
8 Bill Romanowski .10 .30
9 Neil Smith .20 .50
10 John Mobley .10 .30
11 Steve Atwater .10 .30
12 Alfred Williams .10 .30
13 Vaughn Hebron .10 .30
14 Brett Favre 1.50 4.00
15 Robert Brooks .20 .50
16 Antonio Freeman .30 .75
17 Dorsey Levens .30 .75
18 Mark Chmura .10 .30
19 Ross Verba .10 .30
20 William Henderson .10 .30
21 Ryan Longwell .10 .30
22 Reggie White .30 .75
23 Bernardo Harris .10 .30
24 LeRoy Butler .10 .30
25 Eugene Robinson .10 .30
T1 Score Board Final Score .10 .30

1999 Collector's Edge Peyton Manning Game Gear Promos

These Game Gear cards were issued one at a time either as promos to dealers or promos to buyers of card lots from Shop at Home. Each includes a diamond shaped swatch of football along with the words "Game Gear" at the top or bottom of the cardfront. The cardbacks are identical for each card and are each numbered simply "PM." We've assigned an additional number below for ease in cataloging.

PM1 Peyton Manning 6.00 15.00
PM2 Peyton Manning 6.00 15.00
PM3 Peyton Manning 6.00 15.00
PM4 Peyton Manning 6.00 15.00
PM5 Peyton Manning 6.00 15.00
PM6 Peyton Manning Triumph 6.00 15.00
PM7 Peyton Manning Triumph 6.00 15.00

1999 Collector's Edge Super Bowl XXXIII

COMPLETE SET (25) 10.00 20.00
A1 Jamal Anderson .40 1.00
A1B Scoreboard .30 .75
A2 Keith Brooking .30 .75
A3 Chris Chandler .40 1.00
A4 Tim Dwight .40 1.00
A5 Jammi German .30 .75
A6 Cornelius Bennett .40 1.00
A7 Ken Oxendine .30 .75
A8 Tony Martin .40 1.00
A9 Terance Mathis .40 1.00
A10 O.J. Santiago .30 .75
A11 Jessie Tuggle .30 .75
B1 Bubby Brister .40 1.00
B2 Ray Crockett .30 .75
B3 Terrell Davis .75 2.00
B4 John Elway 1.50 4.00
B5 Brian Griese .50 1.25
B6 Darrien Gordon .30 .75
B7 Ed McCaffrey .40 1.00
B8 Bill Romanowski .40 1.00
B9 Shannon Sharpe .50 1.25
B10 Howard Griffith .30 .75
B11 Rod Smith .40 1.00
R1 Peyton Manning 1.50 4.00
R2 Randy Moss .75 2.00

2000 Collector's Edge Peyton Manning Destiny

This set was produced in 2000 by Collectors Edge and intended to be released in box set form as well as inserts in various packs at the time. It is thought that some cards did make it into some packs in 2000, but the majority of the cards were released much later after CE suspended their football card operations. Each card in the basic unnumbered set features gold foil highlights on the front. Five additional reprinted cards from other Edge products were also printed along with these 45-cards. Complete sets of all 50-cards in the factory sealed box can often be found. Several numbered parallel versions were also produced with each featuring its own foil color on the front and serial numbering on the back. The most interesting card in the set features a boyhood photo of the three Manning brothers including a very young Eli.

COMPLETE SET (50) 10.00 25.00
*BLUE/75: .8X TO 2X GOLD
BLUE PRINT RUN 75 SER.#'d SETS
*BLUE HOLO/50: .8X TO 2X GOLD
BLUE HOLOFOIL PRINT RUN 50
*GREEN/400: .5X TO 1.2X GOLD
GREEN PRINT RUN 400 SER.#'d SETS
*RED/18: 1.2X TO 3X GOLD
RED PRINT RUN 18 SER.#'d SETS
*RED HOLO/25: 1.2X TO 3X GOLD
RED HOLOFOIL PRINT RUN 25
*GOLD HOLO: .6X TO 1.5X BASIC GOLD
*SILVER HOLO: .6X TO 1.5X BASIC GOLD
PM1 Peyton Manning .40 1.00
PM2 Peyton Manning .40 1.00
PM3 Peyton Manning .40 1.00
PM4 Peyton Manning .40 1.00
PM5 Peyton Manning .40 1.00
PM6 Peyton Manning .40 1.00
PM7 Peyton Manning .40 1.00
PM8 Peyton Manning .40 1.00
PM9 Peyton Manning .40 1.00
PM10 Peyton Manning .40 1.00
PM11 Peyton Manning .40 1.00
PM12 Peyton Manning .40 1.00
PM13 Peyton Manning .40 1.00
PM14 Peyton Manning .40 1.00
PM15 Peyton Manning .40 1.00
PM16 Peyton Manning .40 1.00
PM17 Peyton Manning .40 1.00
PM18 Peyton Manning .40 1.00
PM19 Peyton Manning .40 1.00
PM20 Peyton Manning .40 1.00
PM21 Peyton Manning .40 1.00
PM22 Peyton Manning .40 1.00
PM23 Peyton Manning .40 1.00
PM24 Peyton Manning .40 1.00
PM25 Peyton Manning .40 1.00
PM26 Peyton Manning .40 1.00
PM27 Peyton Manning .40 1.00
PM28 Peyton Manning .40 1.00
PM29 Peyton Manning .40 1.00
PM30 Peyton Manning .40 1.00
PM31 Peyton Manning .40 1.00
PM32 Peyton Manning .40 1.00
PM33 Peyton Manning .40 1.00
PM34 Peyton Manning .40 1.00
PM35 Peyton Manning .40 1.00
PM36 Peyton Manning .40 1.00
PM37 Peyton Manning .40 1.00
PM38 Title Card .08 .25
PM39 Certificate Card .08 .25
PM40 Peyton Manning 98 REV .40 1.00
PM41 Peyton Manning 98 REV .40 1.00
PM42 P.Manning .40 1.00
A.Manning
PM43 P.Manning 2.00 5.00
E.Manning
C.Manning
PM44 Peyton Manning .40 1.00
PM45 Peyton Manning .40 1.00
PM46 Peyton Manning .40 1.00
53 Peyton Manning 99SUP .40 1.00
59 Peyton Manning 00SUP .40 1.00
66 Peyton Manning 99 ODY .40 1.00
67 Peyton Manning 99ADV .40 1.00

2000 Collector's Edge Pro Signature Authentic Unsigned Promos

These unsigned Pro Signature Authentic cards surfaced long after Edge ceased card operations. They follow the style of the 2000 T3 Rookie Ink cards with a different set name at the top of the card and each was printed with gold foil on the fronts. They apparently were samples or promos for veteran signed inserts that were never issued.

AS Akili Smith unsigned 1.50 4.00
DC Daunte Culpepper unsigned 2.00 5.00
GC Germane Crowell unsigned 1.50 4.00
PM Peyton Manning unsigned 3.00 8.00
TC Tim Couch unsigned 1.50 4.00
TH Torry Holt unsigned 2.00 5.00

2000 Collector's Edge Super Bowl XXXIV

COMPLETE SET (25) 8.00 20.00
R1 Isaac Bruce .60 1.50
R2 Kevin Carter .40 1.00
R3 Marshall Faulk .50 1.25
R4 Az-Zahir Hakim .40 1.00
R5 Robert Holcombe .40 1.00
R6 Torry Holt .50 1.25
R7 Tony Horne .40 1.00
R8 Todd Lyght .40 1.00
R9 Kurt Warner 1.00 2.50
R10 Jeff Wilkins .40 1.00
R11 Roland Williams .40 1.00
T1 Al Del Greco .40 1.00
T2 Kevin Dyson .50 1.25
T3 Eddie George .50 1.25
T4 Jackie Harris .40 1.00
T5 Jevon Kearse .40 1.00
T6 Derrick Mason .40 1.00
T7 Steve McNair .50 1.25
T8 Eddie Robinson .40 1.00
T9 Samari Rolle .40 1.00
T10 Yancey Thigpen .40 1.00
T11 Frank Wycheck .50 1.25
AW1 Kurt Warner MVP 1.00 2.50
AW2 Edgerrin James ROY .50 1.25
SB Scoreboard .30 .75

1996 Collector's Edge Advantage Promos

This four-card set was issued to preview the 1996 Collector's Edge Advantage series. The Promo set contains one card from each of three Advantage insert sets and one base set Promo. The fronts feature designs very similar to the regular release while the backs carry the word "Promo." The cards are all numbered 1 with a prefix and, therefore, checklisted below in alphabetical order.

1 Jeff Blake .60 1.50
2 Steve Bono .80 2.00
3 Rashaan Salaam .60 1.50
4 Michael Westbrook .60 1.50

1996 Collector's Edge Advantage

The 1996 Collector's Edge Advantage set was issued in one series totalling 150 cards and features color player photos on front and back embossed gold foil stamped cards. The six-card packs retail for $2.69 each.

COMPLETE SET (150) 10.00 25.00
1 Drew Bledsoe .30 .75
2 Chris Warren .08 .25
3 Eddie George RC .60 1.50
4 Barry Sanders .75 2.00
5 Scott Mitchell .08 .25
6 Carl Pickens .08 .25
7 Tim Brown .20 .50
8 John Elway 1.00 2.50
9 Michael Westbrook .20 .50
10 Cris Carter .20 .50
11 Troy Aikman .50 1.25
12 Ben Coates .08 .25
13 Brett Favre 1.25 2.50
14 Marshall Faulk .25 .60
15 Steve Young .40 1.00
16 Terrell Davis .40 1.00
17 Keyshawn Johnson RC .50 1.25
18 Mario Bates .08 .25
19 Steve McNair .40 1.00
20 Kerry Collins .20 .50
21 Natrone Means .08 .25
22 Kordell Stewart .20 .50
23 Jeff George .08 .25
24 Rick Mirer .08 .25
25 Herman Moore .08 .25
26 Rodney Peete .05 .15
27 Isaac Bruce .20 .50
28 Errict Rhett .08 .25
29 Jerry Rice .50 1.25
30 Rashaan Salaam .08 .25
31 Eric Metcalf .05 .15
32 Jim Kelly .20 .50
33 Jerome Bettis .20 .50
34 Deion Sanders .30 .75
35 J.J. Stokes .20 .50
36 Neil O'Donnell .08 .25
37 Marcus Allen .20 .50
38 Thurman Thomas .20 .50
39 Dan Marino 1.00 2.50
40 Rickey Dudley RC .20 .50
41 Napoleon Kaufman .20 .50
42 Kyle Brady .05 .15
43 Emmitt Smith .75 2.00
44 Tyrone Wheatley .08 .25
45 Jeff Blake .20 .50
46 Reggie White .20 .50
47 Joey Galloway .20 .50
48 Antonio Langham .05 .15
49 Craig Heyward .05 .15
50 Curtis Martin .40 1.00
51 Karim Abdul-Jabbar RC .20 .50
52 Antonio Freeman .20 .50
53 Ki-Jana Carter .08 .25
54 Willie Davis .05 .15
55 Jim Everett .05 .15
56 Gus Frerotte .08 .25
57 Daryl Gardener RC .05 .15
58 Charles Haley .08 .25
59 Michael Irvin .20 .50
60 Keith Jackson .05 .15
61 Cortez Kennedy .05 .15
62 Greg Lloyd .08 .25
63 Tony Martin .08 .25
64 Ken Norton Jr. .05 .15
65 Bobby Hoying RC .20 .50
66 Bryce Paup .05 .15
67 Jake Reed .08 .25
68 Frank Sanders .08 .25
69 Vinny Testaverde .08 .25
70 Regan Upshaw RC .05 .15
71 Tamarick Vanover .08 .25
72 Walt Harris RC .05 .15
73 John Randle .08 .25
74 Ricky Watters .08 .25
75 Terry Allen .08 .25
76 Edgar Bennett .08 .25
77 Larry Centers .08 .25
78 Chris Penn .05 .15
79 Bobby Engram RC .20 .50
80 Irving Fryar .08 .25
81 Charlie Garner .08 .25
82 Rodney Hampton .08 .25
83 Michael Jackson .08 .25
84 O.J. McDuffie .08 .25
85 Shannon Sharpe .08 .25
86 Aaron Hayden .05 .15
87 Muhsin Muhammad RC .40 1.00
88 Rod Woodson .08 .25
89 Levon Kirkland .05 .15
90 Chad Brown .05 .15
91 Junior Seau .20 .50
92 Terry Kirby .08 .25
93 Zach Thomas RC .30 .75
94 Harvey Williams .05 .15
95 Robert Brooks .20 .50
96 Darrell Green .05 .15
97 Chester McGlockton .05 .15
98 Neil Smith .08 .25
99 Eric Swann .05 .15
100 Mike Alstott RC .50 1.25
101 Tim Biakabutuka RC .20 .50
102 Mark Brunell .30 .75
103 Chris Doleman .05 .15
104 Sean Gilbert .05 .15
105 Jim Harbaugh .08 .25
106 Chris T. Jones .08 .25
107 Tyrone Hughes .05 .15
108 Amani Toomer RC .50 1.25
109 Larry Brown .05 .15
110 Kevin Greene .08 .25
111 John Mobley .05 .15
112 Danny Kanell RC .20 .50
113 Kevin Hardy RC .20 .50
114 Brett Perriman .05 .15
115 Simeon Rice RC .50 1.25
116 Chris Sanders .08 .25
117 Dave Brown .05 .15
118 Bryan Cox .05 .15
119 Yancey Thigpen .08 .25
120 Terance Mathis .05 .15
121 Warren Moon .08 .25
122 Derrick Thomas .20 .50
123 Trent Dilfer .20 .50
124 Terry Glenn RC .50 1.25
125 Jeff Hostetler .05 .15
126 Leeland McElroy RC .08 .25
127 Hardy Nickerson .05 .15
128 Steve Bono .05 .15
129 Stanley Pritchett RC .08 .25
130 Dana Stubblefield .08 .25
131 Andre Coleman .05 .15
132 Anthony Miller .08 .25
133 Stan Humphries .08 .25
134 Robert Smith .08 .25
135 Curtis Conway .20 .50
136 Darick Holmes .05 .15
137 Pat Swilling .05 .15
138 Andre Rison .08 .25
139 Erik Kramer .05 .15
140 Jason Dunn RC .08 .25
141 Torrance Small .05 .15
142 Cedric Jones RC .05 .15
143 Derek Loville .05 .15
144 Brian Mitchell .05 .15
145 Eric Moulds RC .60 1.50
146 James O.Stewart .08 .25
147 Bruce Smith .08 .25
148 Keenan McCardell .20 .50
149 Warren Sapp .05 .15
150 Marvin Harrison RC 1.25 3.00

1996 Collector's Edge Advantage Perfect Play Foils

COMPLETE SET (150) 40.00 100.00
*STARS: 3X TO 6X BASIC CARDS
*RCs: 1.5X TO 3X BASIC CARDS
STATED ODDS 1:2

1996 Collector's Edge Advantage Crystal Cuts

Randomly inserted in packs at a rate of one in eight, this 25-card set features a player photo against a background resembling a section of movie film. Each of the pack inserted cards are numbered of 5000 sets made. A silver foil parallel set was produced as well and distributed via mail order. Each silver card is numbered of 3100 made.

COMPLETE SET (25) 50.00 100.00
STATED ODDS 1:8
STATED PRINT RUN 5000 SERIAL #'d SETS
*SILVER FOILS: SAME PRICE
SILVERS PRINT RUN 3100 SERIAL #'d SETS
CC1 Barry Sanders 4.00 10.00
CC2 Eddie George 1.50 4.00
CC3 Curtis Martin 2.00 5.00
CC4 J.J. Stokes 1.00 2.50
CC5 Kyle Brady .30 .75
CC6 Chris Warren .50 1.25
CC7 Jerry Rice 2.50 6.00
CC8 Ben Coates .50 1.25
CC9 Terrell Davis 2.00 5.00
CC10 Marcus Allen 1.00 2.50
CC11 John Elway 5.00 12.00
CC12 Joey Galloway 1.00 2.50
CC13 Dan Marino 5.00 12.00
CC14 Napoleon Kaufman 1.00 2.50
CC15 Emmitt Smith 4.00 10.00
CC16 Eric Metcalf .30 .75
CC17 Kerry Collins 1.00 2.50
CC18 Troy Aikman 2.50 6.00
CC19 Rickey Dudley .50 1.25
CC20 Steve McNair 2.00 5.00
CC21 Steve Young 2.00 5.00
CC22 Isaac Bruce 1.00 2.50
CC23 Kordell Stewart 1.00 2.50
CC24 LeShon Johnson .50 1.25
CC25 Scott Mitchell .50 1.25

1996 Collector's Edge Advantage Video

Randomly inserted in packs at a rate of one in 36, this 25-card set features a player photo . Each is numbered on the back of 2000 sets produced. A die cut parallel set was produced and released primarily through the Shop at Home television program and other mail order outlets. Reported only 300 of each die cut card was produced. Also several cards were released later featuring a gold foil "E" variation cardfront through Shop at Home.

COMPLETE SET (25) 60.00 150.00
STATED ODDS 1:36
STATED PRINT RUN 2000 SERIAL #'d SETS
*DIE CUT/300: 1.2X TO 3X BASIC INSERT/2000
*GOLD E/2000: .4X TO 1X BASIC INSERT/2000
V1 Brett Favre 8.00 20.00
V2 Keyshawn Johnson 2.50 6.00
V3 Deion Sanders 3.00 8.00
V4 Marcus Allen 2.50 6.00
V5 Rashaan Salaam 1.25 3.00
V6 Thurman Thomas 2.50 6.00
V7 Emmitt Smith 6.00 15.00
V8 Isaac Bruce 2.50 6.00
V9 Michael Westbrook 2.50 6.00
V10 Cris Carter 2.50 6.00
V11 Marshall Faulk 3.00 8.00
V12 Jerry Rice 6.00 15.00
V13 Tim Brown 2.50 6.00
V14 Steve Young 4.00 10.00
V15 Eric Metcalf .75 2.00
V16 Chris Warren 1.25 3.00
V17 Drew Bledsoe 2.50 6.00
V18 Barry Sanders 6.00 15.00
V19 Herman Moore 1.25 3.00
V20 Rodney Peete .75 2.00
V21 Troy Aikman 5.00 12.00
V22 Jerome Bettis 2.50 6.00
V23 Errict Rhett 1.25 3.00
V24 Dan Marino 8.00 20.00
V25 Natrone Means 1.25 3.00

1996 Collector's Edge Advantage Game Ball

Randomly inserted in packs at a rate of one in 72, this 37-card set features a medallion cut from an authentic NFL game-used football, with highlights of the game in which the ball was used. A different game ball is paired with each color player photo. The Jerry Rice card was released later in a signed version numbered of 50 in 1998 Edge Masters packs.

STATED ODDS 1:72
RICE AUTO ODDS 1:12,000 98 CE MASTERS
G1 Kordell Stewart 4.00 10.00
G2 Emmitt Smith 25.00 60.00
G3 Brett Favre 25.00 60.00
G4 Steve Young 10.00 25.00
G5 Barry Sanders 20.00 50.00
G6 John Elway 25.00 60.00
G7 Drew Bledsoe 6.00 15.00
G8 Dan Marino 25.00 60.00
G9 Keyshawn Johnson 5.00 12.00
G10 Eddie George 5.00 12.00
G11 Kevin Hardy 4.00 10.00
G12 Terry Glenn 5.00 12.00
G13 Michael Westbrook 4.00 10.00
G14 Joey Galloway 5.00 12.00
G15 John Mobley 4.00 10.00
G16 Curtis Martin 7.50 20.00
G17 Rashaan Salaam 4.00 10.00
G18 J.J. Stokes 4.00 10.00
G19 Kerry Collins 5.00 12.00
G20 Deion Sanders 6.00 15.00
G21 Shannon Sharpe 5.00 12.00
G22 Terry Allen 4.00 10.00
G23 Ricky Watters 4.00 10.00
G24 Marshall Faulk 6.00 15.00
G25 Tim Biakabutuka 4.00 10.00
G26 Troy Aikman 12.00 30.00
G27 Jerry Rice 20.00 50.00
G28 Chris Warren 4.00 10.00
G29 Jeff Blake 5.00 12.00
G30 Carl Pickens 4.00 10.00
G31 Isaac Bruce 5.00 12.00
G32 Terrell Davis 6.00 15.00
G33 Mark Brunell 5.00 12.00
G34 Karim Abdul-Jabbar 4.00 10.00
G35 Herman Moore 4.00 10.00
G36 Cris Carter 6.00 15.00
NNO Checklist Card .40 1.00
G27AU Jerry Rice AU/50 150.00 300.00

1996 Collector's Edge Advantage Role Models

Randomly inserted in packs at a rate of one in 12, this 13-card set featues color player action photos on specially die cut, embossed, metalized cards.

COMPLETE SET (13) 25.00 50.00
STATED ODDS 1:12
RM1 John Elway 6.00 12.00
RM2 Dan Marino 6.00 12.00
RM3 Jerry Rice 3.00 6.00
RM4 Emmitt Smith 5.00 10.00
RM5 Chris Warren .60 1.25
RM6 Tim Brown 1.25 2.50
RM7 Jeff George .60 1.25
RM8 Tyrone Wheatley .60 1.25
RM9 Steve Bono .30 .75
RM10 Kerry Collins 1.25 2.50
RM11 Jerome Bettis 1.25 2.50
RM12 Steve Beuerlein 1.25 2.50
NNO Checklist Card .30 .75

1996 Collector's Edge Advantage Super Bowl Game Ball

Randomly inserted in packs at a rate of one in 164, this 36-card set features a medallion cut from an authentic NFL Super Bowl game-used football with highlights of the Super Bowl game in which the ball was used. Different game balls are paired with each of the 36 color player photos.

STATED ODDS 1:164
SB1 Emmitt Smith 20.00 50.00
SB2 Troy Aikman 25.00 50.00
SB3 Michael Irvin 10.00 25.00
SB4 Deion Sanders 12.00 30.00
SB5 John Elway 30.00 80.00
SB6 Dan Marino 30.00 80.00
SB7 Marcus Allen 10.00 25.00
SB8 Kordell Stewart 10.00 25.00
SB9 Steve Young 20.00 40.00
SB10 Ricky Watters 8.00 20.00
SB11 Jerry Rice 25.00 60.00
SB12 Jim Kelly 12.00 30.00
SB13 Thurman Thomas 10.00 25.00
SB14 Bruce Smith 6.00 15.00
SB15 Stan Humphries 6.00 15.00
SB16 Junior Seau 10.00 25.00
SB17 Natrone Means 8.00 20.00
SB18 Neil O'Donnell 8.00 20.00
SB19 Rod Woodson 10.00 25.00
SB20 Andre Reed 10.00 25.00
SB21 Jeff Hostetler 6.00 15.00
SB22 Dave Meggett 6.00 15.00
SB23 Greg Lloyd 6.00 15.00
SB24 Kevin Greene 10.00 25.00
SB25 Yancey Thigpen 6.00 15.00
SB26 Charles Haley 8.00 20.00
SB27 Byron Bam Morris 6.00 15.00
SB28 Alvin Harper 6.00 15.00
SB29 Ken Norton Jr. 6.00 15.00
SB30 William Floyd 6.00 15.00
SB31 Leslie O'Neal 6.00 15.00
SB32 Jay Novacek 10.00 25.00
SB33 Irving Fryar 8.00 20.00
SB34 Leon Lett 6.00 15.00
SB35 Tony Martin 6.00 15.00
SB36 Mark Collins 6.00 15.00

1998 Collector's Edge Advantage

The 1998 Collector's Edge Advantage set was originally issued in one series totaling 180-cards and was distributed in six-card packs with a suggested retail price of $5.99. The fronts feature large player head shots over an action photo with a shadow version of the head photo in the background. The backs carry player information. Twenty "update" and Rookie Cards were inserted in late issue retail boxes as a box topper.

COMPLETE SET (200) 25.00 60.00
COMP.SHORT SET (180) 20.00 50.00
1 Larry Centers .20 .50
2 Kent Graham .20 .50
3 LeShon Johnson .20 .50
4 Leeland McElroy .20 .50
5 Jake Plummer .50 1.25
6 Jamal Anderson .50 1.25
7 Chris Chandler .30 .75
8 Bert Emanuel .30 .75
9 Byron Hanspard .20 .50
10 O.J. Santiago .20 .50
11 Derrick Alexander WR .30 .75
12 Peter Boulware .20 .50
13 Eric Green .20 .50
14 Michael Jackson .20 .50
15 Byron Bam Morris .20 .50
16 Vinny Testaverde .30 .75
17 Todd Collins .20 .50
18 Quinn Early .20 .50
19 Jim Kelly .50 1.25
20 Andre Reed .30 .75
21 Antowain Smith .50 1.25
22 Steve Tasker .20 .50
23 Thurman Thomas .50 1.25
24 Steve Beuerlein .30 .75
25 Rae Carruth .20 .50
26 Kerry Collins .30 .75
27 Anthony Johnson .20 .50
28 Ernie Mills .20 .50
29 Wesley Walls .30 .75
30 Curtis Conway .30 .75
31 Bobby Engram .30 .75
32 Raymont Harris .20 .50
33 Erik Kramer .20 .50
34 Rick Mirer .20 .50
35 Darnay Scott .30 .75
36 Tony McGee .20 .50
37 Jeff Blake .30 .75
38 Corey Dillon .50 1.25
39 Carl Pickens .30 .75
40 Troy Aikman 1.25 2.50
41 Billy Davis .20 .50
42 David LaFleur .20 .50
43 Anthony Miller .20 .50
44 Emmitt Smith 2.00 4.00
45 Herschel Walker .30 .75
46 Sherman Williams .20 .50
47 Flipper Anderson .20 .50
48 Terrell Davis .50 1.25
49 Jason Elam .20 .50
50 John Elway 2.50 5.00
51 Darrien Gordon .20 .50
52 Ed McCaffrey .30 .75
53 Shannon Sharpe .30 .75
54 Neil Smith .30 .75
55 Rod Smith WR .30 .75
56 Maa Tanuvasa .20 .50
57 Glyn Milburn .20 .50
58 Scott Mitchell .30 .75
59 Herman Moore .30 .75
60 Johnnie Morton .30 .75
61 Barry Sanders 1.50 4.00
62 Tommy Vardell .20 .50
63 Bryant Westbrook .20 .50
64 Robert Brooks .30 .75
65 Mark Chmura .30 .75
66 Brett Favre 2.50 5.00
67 Antonio Freeman .50 1.25
68 Dorsey Levens .50 1.25
69 Bill Schroeder RC .75 2.00
70 Marshall Faulk .60 1.50
71 Jim Harbaugh .30 .75
72 Marvin Harrison .50 1.25
73 Derek Brown TE .20 .50
74 Mark Brunell .50 1.25
75 Rob Johnson .30 .75
76 Keenan McCardell .30 .75
77 Natrone Means .30 .75
78 Jimmy Smith .30 .75
79 James O.Stewart .30 .75
80 Marcus Allen .50 1.25
81 Pat Barnes .20 .50
82 Tony Gonzalez .50 1.25
83 Elvis Grbac .30 .75
84 Greg Hill .20 .50
85 Kevin Lockett .20 .50
86 Andre Rison .30 .75
87 Karim Abdul-Jabbar .50 1.25
88 Fred Barnett .20 .50
89 Troy Drayton .20 .50
90 Dan Marino 2.50 5.00
91 Irving Spikes .20 .50
92 Cris Carter .50 1.25
93 Matthew Hatchette .20 .50
94 Brad Johnson .50 1.25
95 Jake Reed .30 .75
96 Robert Smith .50 1.25
97 Drew Bledsoe .75 2.00
98 Keith Byars .20 .50
99 Ben Coates .30 .75
100 Terry Glenn .50 1.25
101 Shawn Jefferson .20 .50
102 Curtis Martin .50 1.25
103 Dave Meggett .20 .50
104 Troy Davis .20 .50
105 Danny Wuerffel .30 .75
106 Ray Zellars .20 .50
107 Tiki Barber .50 1.25
108 Rodney Hampton .30 .75
109 Ike Hilliard .30 .75
110 Danny Kanell .30 .75
111 Tyrone Wheatley .30 .75
112 Kyle Brady .20 .50
113 Wayne Chrebet .50 1.25
114 Aaron Glenn .20 .50
115 Jeff Graham .20 .50
116 Keyshawn Johnson .50 1.25
117 Adrian Murrell .30 .75
118 Neil O'Donnell .30 .75
119 Heath Shuler .20 .50
120 Tim Brown .50 1.25
121 Rickey Dudley .20 .50
122 Jeff George .30 .75
123 Desmond Howard .30 .75
124 James Jett .30 .75
125 Napoleon Kaufman .50 1.25
126 Chad Levitt RC .20 .50
127 Darrell Russell .20 .50
128 Ty Detmer .30 .75
129 Irving Fryar .30 .75
130 Charlie Garner .30 .75
131 Kevin Turner .20 .50
132 Ricky Watters .30 .75
133 Jerome Bettis .50 1.25
134 Will Blackwell .20 .50
135 Mark Bruener .20 .50
136 Charles Johnson .20 .50
137 George Jones .20 .50
138 Kordell Stewart .50 1.25
139 Yancey Thigpen .20 .50
140 Gary Brown .20 .50
141 Jim Everett .20 .50
142 Terrell Fletcher .20 .50
143 Stan Humphries .20 .50
144 Freddie Jones .30 .75
145 Tony Martin .30 .75
146 Jim Druckenmiller .20 .50
147 Garrison Hearst .50 1.25
148 Brent Jones .20 .50
149 Terrell Owens .50 1.25
150 Jerry Rice 1.25 2.50
151 J.J. Stokes .30 .75
152 Steve Young .60 1.50
153 Steve Broussard .20 .50
154 Joey Galloway .30 .75
155 Jon Kitna .50 1.25
156 Warren Moon .50 1.25
157 Shawn Springs .20 .50
158 Chris Warren .30 .75
159 Tony Banks .30 .75
160 Isaac Bruce .50 1.25
161 Eddie Kennison .30 .75
162 Orlando Pace .20 .50
163 Lawrence Phillips .20 .50
164 Mike Alstott .50 1.25
165 Reidel Anthony .30 .75
166 Horace Copeland .20 .50
167 Trent Dilfer .50 1.25
168 Warrick Dunn .50 1.25
169 Hardy Nickerson .20 .50
170 Karl Williams .20 .50
171 Eddie George .50 1.25
172 Ronnie Harmon .20 .50
173 Joey Kent .30 .75
174 Steve McNair .50 1.25
175 Chris Sanders .20 .50
176 Terry Allen .50 1.25
177 Jamie Asher .20 .50
178 Stephen Davis .20 .50
179 Gus Frerotte .20 .50
180 Leslie Shepherd .20 .50
181 Victor Riley RC .20 .50
182 Curtis Enis RC .20 .50
183 Brian Griese RC .75 2.00
184 Eric Brown RC .20 .50
185 Jacquez Green RC .30 .75
186 Andre Wadsworth RC .30 .75
187 Ryan Leaf RC .40 1.00
188 Rashaan Shehee RC .30 .75
189 Peyton Manning RC 6.00 15.00
190 Flozell Adams RC .20 .50
191 Fred Taylor RC .60 1.50
192 Charlie Batch RC .40 1.00
193 Kevin Dyson RC .40 1.00
194 Charles Woodson RC 1.00 2.50
195 Ahman Green RC 1.00 2.50
196 Randy Moss RC 2.50 6.00
197 Robert Edwards RC .30 .75
198 Reidel Anthony .30 .75
199 Jerome Pathon RC .40 1.00
200 Samari Rolle RC .20 .50

1998 Collector's Edge Advantage Gold

COMPLETE SET (180) 150.00 300.00
*GOLDS: 2X TO 5X BASIC CARDS
STATED ODDS 1:6

1998 Collector's Edge Advantage 50-point

COMPLETE SET (180) 75.00 150.00
*50-POINT: 1X TO 2.5X BASIC CARDS
STATED ODDS 1:1

1998 Collector's Edge Advantage Silver

COMPLETE SET (180) 125.00 250.00
*SILVER VETS: 1.5X TO 4X BASIC CARDS
*SILVER ROOKIES: .8X TO 2X BASIC CARDS
STATED ODDS 1:2

1998 Collector's Edge Advantage Livin' Large

Randomly inserted in packs at the rate of one in 12, this 22-card set features a large color player head photo on a die-cut card.

COMPLETE SET (22) 75.00 150.00
STATED ODDS 1:12
*HOLOFOILS: 2X TO 5X BASIC INSERTS
HOLOFOIL STATED PRINT RUN 100 SETS
1 Leeland McElroy 1.00 2.50
2 Jamal Anderson 2.50 6.00
3 Antowain Smith 2.50 6.00
4 Emmitt Smith 8.00 20.00
5 John Elway 10.00 25.00
6 Barry Sanders 8.00 20.00
7 Elvis Grbac 1.50 4.00
8 Dan Marino 10.00 25.00
9 Cris Carter 2.50 6.00
10 Drew Bledsoe 4.00 10.00
11 Curtis Martin 2.50 6.00
12 Troy Davis 1.00 2.50
13 Ike Hilliard 1.50 4.00
14 Adrian Murrell 1.50 4.00
15 Tim Brown 2.50 6.00
16 Kordell Stewart 2.50 6.00
17 Jerry Rice 5.00 12.00
18 Tony Banks 1.50 4.00
19 Mike Alstott 2.50 6.00
20 Trent Dilfer 2.50 6.00
21 Eddie George 2.50 6.00
22 Steve McNair 2.50 6.00

1998 Collector's Edge Advantage Memorable Moments

Randomly inserted in packs at the rate of one in 360, this 12-card set features actual pieces of game-used footballs embedded into each card. The cards display color player photos printed with gold foil on a metallic background. The cardbacks feature highlights of the game in which the ball was used. Each card is serial numbered of 200 and contains the player's initials before the card number. Some cards were also produced in a promo version in which the words "Media Sample" were printed in gold foil on the cardbacks instead of a serial number. This version appears to be difficult to find so no pricing has yet been established.

COMPLETE SET (12) 125.00 300.00
STATED PRINT 200 SERIAL #'d SETS
STATED ODDS 1:360
1 Carl Pickens 7.50 20.00
2 Terrell Davis 15.00 40.00
3 Herman Moore 12.50 30.00
4 Antonio Freeman 15.00 40.00
5 Jimmy Smith 7.50 20.00
6 Marcus Allen 15.00 40.00
7 Cris Carter 15.00 40.00
8 Curtis Martin 15.00 40.00
9 Napoleon Kaufman 12.50 30.00
10 Joey Galloway 12.50 30.00
11 Warrick Dunn 12.50 30.00
12 Eddie George 15.00 40.00

1998 Collector's Edge Advantage Personal Victory

Randomly inserted in packs at the rate of one in 675, this 6-card set features actual pieces of game-used footballs embedded into each card. The cards display color player photos printed with gold foil on a metallic background. Cardbacks contain highlights of the game in which the ball was used. Each is numbered of 200-sets produced.

STATED PRINT 200 SETS
STATED ODDS 1:675
1 John Elway 40.00 100.00
2 Barry Sanders 30.00 80.00
3 Brett Favre 60.00 150.00
4 Mark Brunell 15.00 40.00
5 Drew Bledsoe 20.00 50.00
6 Jerry Rice 30.00 80.00

1998 Collector's Edge Advantage Prime Connection

Randomly inserted in packs at the rate of one in 36, this 25-card set features color photos of the hottest players from the same team paired together on a metallic double sided card.

COMPLETE SET (25) 250.00 500.00
STATED ODDS 1:36
1 L.Johnson 2.50 6.00
L.McElroy
2 P.Boulware 4.00 10.00
M.Jackson
3 A.Reed 6.00 15.00
A.Smith
4 R.Carruth 2.50 6.00
A.Johnson
5 H.Walker 15.00 40.00
E.Smith
6 T.Davis 15.00 40.00
J.Elway
7 E.McCaffrey 4.00 10.00
S.Sharpe
8 H.Moore 25.00 60.00
B.Sanders
9 B.Favre 25.00 60.00
A.Freeman
10 M.Brunell 6.00 15.00
J.Stewart
11 M.Allen 6.00 15.00
E.Grbac
12 D.Marino 25.00 60.00
Abdul-Jabbar
13 D.Bledsoe 10.00 25.00
B.Coates
14 T.Glenn 7.50 20.00
C.Martin
15 Tr.Davis 4.00 10.00
D.Wuerffel
16 I.Hilliard 4.00 10.00
D.Kanell
17 A.Glenn 4.00 10.00
A.Murrell
18 T.Brown 6.00 15.00
N.Kaufman
19 M.Bruener 6.00 15.00
J.Bettis
20 J.Druckenmiller 6.00 15.00
Owens
21 G.Hearst 10.00 25.00
S.Young
22 T.Banks 6.00 15.00
E.Kennison
23 M.Alstott 6.00 15.00
R.Anthony
24 H.Nickerson 6.00 15.00
W.Dunn
25 E.George 6.00 15.00
S.McNair

1998 Collector's Edge Advantage Showtime

Randomly inserted in packs at the rate of one in 18, this 23-card set features color photos of the hottest stars of the present. The backs carry player information.

COMPLETE SET (23) 100.00 200.00
STATED ODDS 1:18
*HOLOFOILS: 2X TO 4X BASIC INSERTS
HOLOFOIL STATED PRINT RUN 100 SETS
1 LeShon Johnson 1.50 4.00
2 Peter Boulware 1.50 4.00
3 Jim Kelly 4.00 10.00
4 Rae Carruth 1.50 4.00
5 Kerry Collins 2.50 6.00
6 Troy Aikman 8.00 20.00
7 Terrell Davis 4.00 10.00
8 Shannon Sharpe 2.50 6.00
9 Brett Favre 15.00 40.00
10 Mark Brunell 4.00 10.00
11 Keenan McCardell 2.50 6.00
12 Marcus Allen 4.00 10.00
13 Terry Glenn 4.00 10.00
14 Danny Wuerffel 2.50 6.00
15 Danny Kanell 2.50 6.00
16 Aaron Glenn 1.50 4.00
17 Napoleon Kaufman 4.00 10.00
18 Mark Bruener 1.50 4.00
19 Jim Druckenmiller 1.50 4.00
20 Terrell Owens 4.00 10.00
21 Steve Young 5.00 12.00
22 Reidel Anthony 2.50 6.00
23 Warrick Dunn 4.00 10.00

1999 Collector's Edge Advantage Previews

This set was released as a Preview to the 1999 Collector's Edge Advantage base set. Each card is essentially a parallel version of the base set card with the player's initials as the card number along with the word "preview" on the cardbacks.

COMPLETE SET (10) 5.00 12.00
CM Curtis Martin .50 1.25
DF Doug Flutie .60 1.50
DM Dan Marino 1.25 3.00
GH Garrison Hearst .30 .75
JA Jamal Anderson .50 1.25
MB Mark Brunell .60 1.50
PM Peyton Manning 1.00 2.50
RE Robert Edwards .30 .75
RM Randy Moss 1.00 2.50
TD Terrell Davis .75 2.00

1999 Collector's Edge Advantage

The 1999 Collector's Edge Advantage set was issued in one series for a total of 190 cards. The rookie subset cards were short printed. The set features color action photos of NFL stars and draft picks printed on 20-point card stock with silver foil stamping. The backs carry season and career statistics, biographical, and other player information.

COMPLETE SET (190) 25.00 50.00
1 Larry Centers .20 .50
2 Rob Moore .20 .50
3 Adrian Murrell .20 .50
4 Jake Plummer .20 .50
5 Frank Sanders .20 .50
6 Jamal Anderson .25 .60
7 Chris Chandler .25 .60
8 Tim Dwight .25 .60
9 Tony Martin .25 .60
10 Terance Mathis .20 .50
11 O.J. Santiago .20 .50
12 Jim Harbaugh .25 .60
13 Priest Holmes .20 .50
14 Jermaine Lewis .20 .50
15 Rod Woodson .30 .75
16 Eric Zeier .20 .50
17 Doug Flutie .30 .75
18 Sam Gash .20 .50
19 Rob Johnson .25 .60
20 Eric Moulds .20 .50
21 Andre Reed .30 .75
22 Antowain Smith .20 .50
23 Bruce Smith .25 .60
24 Thurman Thomas .25 .60
25 Steve Beuerlein .25 .60
26 Kevin Greene .30 .75
27 Rocket Ismail .25 .60
28 Fred Lane .20 .50
29 Muhsin Muhammad .20 .50
30 Edgar Bennett .25 .60
31 Curtis Conway .25 .60
32 Bobby Engram .20 .50
33 Curtis Enis .20 .50
34 Erik Kramer .25 .60
35 Jeff Blake .25 .60
36 Corey Dillon .20 .50
37 Neil O'Donnell .25 .60
38 Carl Pickens .25 .60
39 Takeo Spikes .20 .50
40 Troy Aikman .40 1.00
41 Billy Davis .20 .50
42 Michael Irvin .30 .75
43 Deion Sanders .25 .60
44 Emmitt Smith .50 1.25
45 Darren Woodson .25 .60
46 Bubby Brister .20 .50
47 Terrell Davis .25 .60
48 John Elway .50 1.25
49 Ed McCaffrey .25 .60
50 Bill Romanowski .25 .60
51 Shannon Sharpe .25 .60
52 Rod Smith .25 .60
53 Charlie Batch .20 .50
54 Germane Crowell .20 .50
55 Herman Moore .25 .60
56 Johnnie Morton .25 .60

57 Barry Sanders	.50	1.25
58 Robert Brooks	.25	.60
59 Brett Favre	.60	1.50
60 Antonio Freeman	.25	.60
61 Darick Holmes	.20	.50
62 Dorsey Levens	.25	.60
63 Roell Preston	.20	.50
64 Marshall Faulk	.25	.60
65 E.G.Green	.20	.50
66 Marvin Harrison	.25	.60
67 Peyton Manning	1.00	2.50
68 Jerome Pathon	.20	.50
69 Mark Brunell	.25	.60
70 Kevin Hardy	.20	.50
71 Keenan McCardell	.25	.60
72 Jimmy Smith	.25	.60
73 Fred Taylor	.20	.50
74 Alvis Whitted	.20	.50
75 Kimble Anders	.20	.50
76 Donnell Bennett	.20	.50
77 Rich Gannon	.25	.60
78 Elvis Grbac	.20	.50
79 Byron Bam Morris	.20	.50
80 Andre Rison	.25	.60
81 Karim Abdul-Jabbar	.20	.50
82 John Avery	.20	.50
83 Oronde Gadsden	.20	.50
84 Sam Madison	.20	.50
85 Dan Marino	.60	1.50
86 O.J. McDuffie	.25	.60
87 Zach Thomas	.25	.60
88 Cris Carter	.30	.75
89 Randall Cunningham	.25	.60
90 Brad Johnson	.25	.60
91 Randy Moss	.25	.60
92 John Randle	.30	.75
93 Jake Reed	.25	.60
94 Robert Smith	.20	.50
95 Drew Bledsoe	.25	.60
96 Ben Coates	.25	.60
97 Robert Edwards	.20	.50
98 Terry Glenn	.25	.60
99 Ty Law	.30	.75
100 Cam Cleeland	.20	.50
101 Kerry Collins	.20	.50
102 Gary Brown	.20	.50
103 Kent Graham	.20	.50
104 Ike Hilliard	.20	.50
105 Joe Jurevicius	.20	.50
106 Danny Kanell	.20	.50
107 Wayne Chrebet	.20	.50
108 Aaron Glenn	.20	.50
109 Keyshawn Johnson	.25	.60
110 Curtis Martin	.25	.60
111 Vinny Testaverde	.20	.50
112 Tim Brown	.30	.75
113 Jeff George	.20	.50
114 James Jett	.20	.50
115 Napoleon Kaufman	.20	.50
116 Charles Woodson	.30	.75
117 Koy Detmer	.20	.50
118 Duce Staley	.20	.50
119 Jerome Bettis	.30	.75
120 Charles Johnson	.20	.50
121 Kordell Stewart	.20	.50
122 Tony Banks	.25	.60
123 Isaac Bruce	.30	.75
124 June Henley RC	.20	.50
125 Ryan Leaf	.25	.60
126 Natrone Means	.25	.60
127 Mikhael Ricks	.20	.50
128 Craig Whelihan	.20	.50
129 Garrison Hearst	.20	.50
130 Terrell Owens	.25	.60
131 Jerry Rice	.75	2.00
132 J.J.Stokes	.20	.50
133 Steve Young	.40	1.00
134 Joey Galloway	.25	.60
135 Ahman Green	.25	.60
136 Jon Kitna	.20	.50
137 Ricky Watters	.25	.60
138 Mike Alstott	.20	.50
139 Reidel Anthony	.20	.50
140 Trent Dilfer	.20	.50
141 Warrick Dunn	.20	.50
142 Jacquez Green	.20	.50
143 Kevin Dyson	.20	.50
144 Eddie George	.25	.60
145 Steve McNair	.25	.60
146 Yancey Thigpen	.20	.50
147 Terry Allen	.25	.60
148 Trent Green	.20	.50
149 Skip Hicks	.20	.50
150 Michael Westbrook	.20	.50
151 Rahim Abdullah RC	.30	.75
152 Champ Bailey RC	.60	1.50
153 Marlon Barnes RC	.30	.75
154 D'Wayne Bates RC	.30	.75
155 Michael Bishop RC	.40	1.00
156 Dre Bly RC	.50	1.25
157 David Boston RC	.30	.75
158 Chris Claiborne RC	.30	.75
159 Tim Couch RC	.40	1.00
160 Daunte Culpepper RC	.50	1.25
161 Autry Denson RC	.30	.75
162 Jared DeVries RC	.30	.75
163 Troy Edwards RC	.30	.75
164 Kris Farris RC	.30	.75
165 Kevin Faulk RC	.30	.75
166 Martin Gramatica RC	.30	.75
167 Torry Holt RC UER	.60	1.50
168 Brock Huard RC	.30	.75
169 Sedrick Irvin RC	.30	.75
170 Edgerrin James RC	.50	1.25
171 James Johnson RC	.30	.75
172 Kevin Johnson RC	.40	1.00
173 Andy Katzenmoyer RC	.40	1.00
174 Jevon Kearse RC	.40	1.00
175 Shaun King RC	.30	.75
176 Rob Konrad RC	.30	.75
177 Chris McAlister RC	.30	.75
178 Darnell McDonald RC	.30	.75
179 Donovan McNabb RC	2.50	6.00
180 Cade McNown RC	.30	.75
181 Dat Nguyen RC	.50	1.25
182 Peerless Price RC	.30	.75
183 Akili Smith RC	.30	.75
184 Tai Streets RC	.40	1.00
185 Cuncho Brown UER RC	.30	.75
186 Ricky Williams RC	.50	1.25
187 Craig Yeast RC	.30	.75
188 Amos Zereoue RC	.30	.75
189 Checklist	.10	.30
190 Checklist	.10	.30

1999 Collector's Edge Advantage Galvanized

COMPLETE SET (190)	150.00	300.00

*1-190 VETS/500: 2X TO 5X BASIC CARDS
1-190 VETERAN PRINT RUN 500
*151-188 ROOKIES/200: 1.5X TO 4X
151-188 ROOKIE PRINT RUN 200

1999 Collector's Edge Advantage Gold Ingot

COMPLETE SET (190)	40.00	80.00

*1-190 VETS: .8X TO 2X BASIC CARDS
*151-188 ROOKIES: .6X TO 1.5X
ONE PER PACK

1999 Collector's Edge Advantage HoloGold

*1-190 VETS/50: 10X TO 25X BASIC CARDS
1-190 VETERANS PRINT RUN 50
*151-188 ROOKIES/20: 10X TO 25X
151-188 ROOKIES PRINT RUN 20

1999 Collector's Edge Advantage Rookie Autographs

This set features all but three of the rookie players contained in the base 1999 Advantage set. Each card includes a cardback that looks and is numbered similar to the base set, but the cardfronts have been re-designed and autographed by the featured player. Cuncho Brown, Torry Holt, Andy Katzenmoyer and Autry Denson did not sign for the set. Blue ink and Red ink versions were signed and hand numbered between 40-80 and 10-13 respectively. Note that Tim Couch, Ricky Williams, and Edgerrin James signed only in blue ink on the base card and did not serial number any blue ink autographs. Couch and Williams do have a red ink serial numbered version, but James does not.

STATED ODDS 1:24
*BLUE INK #'d: 1X TO 2.5X BASIC AU
BLUE INK NUMBERED PRINT RUN 40-80
UNPRICED RED INK PRINT RUN 10-13

151 Rahim Abdullah	4.00	10.00
152 Champ Bailey	6.00	15.00
153 Marlon Barnes	3.00	8.00
154 D'Wayne Bates	4.00	10.00
155 Michael Bishop	5.00	12.00
156 Dre Bly	5.00	12.00
157 David Boston	4.00	10.00
158 Chris Claiborne	3.00	8.00
159 Tim Couch Blue	5.00	12.00
160 Daunte Culpepper	12.00	30.00
162 Jared DeVries	4.00	10.00
163 Troy Edwards	4.00	10.00
164 Kris Farris	3.00	8.00
165 Kevin Faulk	5.00	12.00
166 Martin Gramatica	3.00	8.00
168 Brock Huard	5.00	12.00
169 Sedrick Irvin	3.00	8.00
170 Edgerrin James Blue	10.00	25.00
171 James Johnson	4.00	10.00
172 Kevin Johnson	5.00	12.00
174 Jevon Kearse	6.00	15.00
175 Shaun King	4.00	10.00
176 Rob Konrad	4.00	10.00
177 Chris McAlister	4.00	10.00
178 Darnell McDonald	4.00	10.00
179 Donovan McNabb	15.00	40.00
180 Cade McNown	4.00	10.00
181 Dat Nguyen	5.00	12.00
182 Peerless Price	5.00	12.00
183 Akili Smith	4.00	10.00
184 Tai Streets	5.00	12.00
186 Ricky Williams Blue	10.00	25.00
187 Craig Yeast	4.00	10.00
188 Amos Zereoue	5.00	12.00

1999 Collector's Edge Advantage Jumpstarters

Randomly inserted into packs, this 10-card set features color action photos of ten top 1999 draft picks printed on clear acetate and foil cards. The backs carry commentary by Edge spokesman, Peyton Manning, last year's first overall draft pick. Each card is sequentially numbered to 500.

COMPLETE SET (10)	15.00	40.00
STATED PRINT RUN 500 SERIAL #'d SETS		
JS1 Champ Bailey	1.50	4.00
JS2 David Boston	1.50	4.00
JS3 Tim Couch	1.50	4.00
JS4 Daunte Culpepper	4.00	10.00
JS5 Torry Holt	2.50	6.00
JS6 Donovan McNabb	4.00	10.00
JS7 Cade McNown	1.50	4.00
JS8 Peerless Price	1.50	4.00
JS9 Brock Huard	1.50	4.00
JS10 Ricky Williams	2.00	5.00

1999 Collector's Edge Advantage Memorable Moments

Randomly inserted into packs at the rate of one in 24, this 10-card set features color action player photos of some of the most unforgettable moments of the 1998 NFL season printed on foil board with foil stamping and micro-etching.

COMPLETE SET (10)	40.00	80.00
STATED ODDS 1:24		
MM1 Terrell Davis	2.00	5.00
MM2 Randy Moss	5.00	12.00
MM3 Peyton Manning	6.00	15.00
MM4 Emmitt Smith	4.00	10.00
MM5 Keyshawn Johnson	2.00	5.00
MM6 Dan Marino	6.00	15.00
MM7 John Elway	6.00	15.00
MM8 Doug Flutie	2.00	5.00
MM9 Jerry Rice	4.00	10.00
MM10 Steve Young	2.50	6.00

1999 Collector's Edge Advantage Overture

Randomly inserted into packs at the rate of one in 24, this 10-card set features color action photos of some of football's biggest superstars printed on micro-etched gold foil cards with gold foil stamping.

COMPLETE SET (10)	50.00	100.00
STATED ODDS 1:24		
1 Jamal Anderson	2.00	5.00
2 Terrell Davis	2.00	5.00
3 John Elway	6.00	15.00
4 Brett Favre	6.00	15.00
5 Peyton Manning	6.00	15.00
6 Dan Marino	6.00	15.00
7 Randy Moss	5.00	12.00
8 Jerry Rice	4.00	10.00
9 Barry Sanders	6.00	15.00
10 Emmitt Smith	4.00	10.00

1999 Collector's Edge Advantage Prime Connection

Randomly inserted into packs at the rate of one in four, this 20-card set features color action photos of current and future NFL stars.

COMPLETE SET (20)	30.00	60.00
STATED ODDS 1:4		
PC1 Ricky Williams	1.25	3.00
PC2 Fred Taylor	.60	1.50
PC3 Tim Couch	.60	1.50
PC4 Peyton Manning	1.50	4.00
PC5 Daunte Culpepper	2.50	6.00
PC6 Drew Bledsoe	1.00	2.50
PC7 Torry Holt	1.50	4.00
PC8 Keyshawn Johnson	.60	1.50
PC9 Champ Bailey	.60	1.50
PC10 Charles Woodson	.60	1.50
PC11 Brock Huard	.60	1.50
PC12 Jake Plummer	.60	1.50
PC13 Donovan McNabb	3.00	8.00
PC14 Steve Young	1.00	2.50
PC15 Edgerrin James	2.50	6.00
PC16 Jamal Anderson	.60	1.50
PC17 Cade McNown	.60	1.50
PC18 Mark Brunell	.60	1.50
PC19 Peerless Price	.60	1.50
PC20 Randy Moss	1.25	3.00

1999 Collector's Edge Advantage Shockwaves

Randomly inserted into packs at the rate of one in 12, this 20-card set features color action photos of some of the most exciting NFL players in the game printed on foil board with foil stamping and micro-etching.

COMPLETE SET (20)	50.00	100.00
STATED ODDS 1:12		
SW1 Jamal Anderson	2.00	5.00
SW2 Jake Plummer	1.25	3.00
SW3 Eric Moulds	2.00	5.00
SW4 Troy Aikman	4.00	10.00
SW5 Emmitt Smith	4.00	10.00
SW6 Marshall Faulk	2.50	6.00
SW7 John Elway	6.00	15.00
SW8 Barry Sanders	6.00	15.00
SW9 Brett Favre	6.00	15.00
SW10 Peyton Manning	6.00	15.00
SW11 Mark Brunell	2.00	5.00
SW12 Fred Taylor	2.00	5.00
SW13 Randall Cunningham	2.00	5.00
SW14 Randy Moss	5.00	12.00
SW15 Drew Bledsoe	2.50	6.00
SW16 Keyshawn Johnson	2.00	5.00
SW17 Curtis Martin	2.00	5.00
SW18 Steve Young	2.50	6.00
SW19 Warrick Dunn	2.00	5.00
SW20 Eddie George	2.00	5.00

1999 Collector's Edge Advantage Showtime

Randomly inserted into packs, this 15-card set features color action photos of some of the most collectible stars in the NFL printed on clear acetate with foil stamping. Each card is numbered to 500.

COMPLETE SET (15)	50.00	100.00
STATED PRINT RUN 500 SERIAL #'d SETS		
ST1 Troy Aikman	4.00	10.00
ST2 Jamal Anderson	2.00	5.00
ST3 Mark Brunell	2.00	5.00
ST4 Terrell Davis	2.00	5.00
ST5 Warrick Dunn	2.00	5.00
ST6 Brett Favre	6.00	15.00
ST7 Doug Flutie	2.00	5.00
ST8 Eddie George	2.00	5.00
ST9 Keyshawn Johnson	2.00	5.00
ST10 Peyton Manning	6.00	15.00
ST11 Dan Marino	6.00	15.00
ST12 Randy Moss	5.00	12.00
ST13 Jake Plummer	1.25	3.00
ST14 Jerry Rice	4.00	10.00
ST15 Barry Sanders	6.00	15.00

2000 Collector's Edge EG Previews

These cards were issued to preview the 2000 Edge Graded product. Each is essentially a parallel to the base set card with a new card number. Cards from this set were also graded by PSA and released as Hawaii XV card show promos in February 2000.

COMPLETE SET (7)	3.00	8.00
EG Eddie George	.50	1.25
EJ Edgerrin James	.50	1.25
KW Kurt Warner	.60	1.50
MB Mark Brunell	.40	1.00
MF Marshall Faulk	.50	1.25
PM Peyton Manning	1.25	3.00
TC Tim Couch	.40	1.00

2000 Collector's Edge EG

Released as a 148-card base set, Collector's Edge EG features cards numbered from 1-150 due to the fact that card #93 and #110 were short printed and intended to not be released. Bill Burke (#93) was included on a very limited basis in packs printed with a red embossed stamp over the front of the card. This stamp was meant to enable the card to be pulled from collation during the packaging process. All other base cards were printed on a gold holofoil card stock with the letters "EG" in gold foil. Collector's Edge EG was packaged in 12-pack boxes with each pack containing ten cards and one PSA Graded card and carried a suggested retail price of $21.99.

COMPLETE SET (148)	60.00	120.00
1 Marcus Robinson	.30	.75
2 Adrian Murrell	.25	.60
3 Qadry Ismail	.25	.60
4 Tim Biakabutuka	.30	.75
5 Jamal Anderson	.30	.75
6 Dorsey Levens	.30	.75
7 Robert Smith	.25	.60
8 Tony Banks	.25	.60
9 Yancey Thigpen	.25	.60
10 Elvis Grbac	.25	.60
11 Sedrick Irvin	.25	.60
12 Rob Johnson	.30	.75
13 Frank Sanders	.25	.60
14 Rich Gannon	.30	.75
15 Steve Beuerlein	.30	.75
16 James Stewart	.25	.60
17 Ricky Watters	.30	.75
18 Curtis Enis	.25	.60
19 Eddie Kennison	.25	.60
20 Kerry Collins	.25	.60
21 Ray Lucas	.25	.60
22 Carl Pickens	.30	.75
23 Natrone Means	.30	.75
24 Daunte Culpepper	.30	.75
25 Karim Abdul-Jabbar	.25	.60
26 David Boston	.25	.60
27 Rocket Ismail	.30	.75
28 Jacquez Green	.25	.60
29 Kevin Dyson	.30	.75
30 Chris Chandler	.30	.75
31 Brian Griese	.25	.60
32 Charlie Garner	.30	.75
33 Wayne Chrebet	.25	.60
34 Mike Alstott	.25	.60
35 Germane Crowell	.25	.60
36 Mike Cloud	.25	.60
37 Antowain Smith	.30	.75
38 Jeff George	.30	.75
39 Antonio Freeman	.30	.75
40 Champ Bailey	.30	.75
41 Terrence Wilkins	.25	.60
42 Junior Seau	.30	.75
43 Jimmy Smith	.30	.75
44 Greg Hill	.25	.60
45 Tyrone Wheatley	.25	.60
46 Tony Gonzalez	.30	.75
47 Rod Smith	.30	.75
48 Damon Huard	.25	.60
49 Jerome Bettis	.40	1.00
50 Cris Carter	.40	1.00
51 Darnay Scott	.30	.75
52 Ike Hilliard	.25	.60
53 Errict Rhett	.30	.75
54 Tim Brown	.40	1.00
55 Terry Glenn	.30	.75
56 Jeff Blake	.30	.75
57 Terance Mathis	.25	.60
58 Duce Staley	.25	.60
59 Amani Toomer	.25	.60
60 Terry Allen	.30	.75
61 Corey Dillon	.25	.60
62 Kordell Stewart	.25	.60
63 Az-Zahir Hakim	.25	.60
64 Jim Harbaugh	.30	.75
65 Bill Schroeder	.30	.75
66 O.J. McDuffie	.30	.75
67 Keenan McCardell	.30	.75
68 Terrell Owens	.30	.75
69 Joey Galloway	.30	.75
70 Derrick Alexander	.25	.60
71 Ed McCaffrey	.30	.75
72 Reidel Anthony	.25	.60
73 Michael Irvin	.40	1.00
74 Herman Moore	.25	.60
75 Joe Montgomery	.25	.60
76 Muhsin Muhammad	.25	.60
77 Charles Johnson	.25	.60
78 Michael Westbrook	.25	.60
79 Jevon Kearse	.25	.60
80 Courtney Brown RC	.60	1.50
81 Shaun Alexander RC	.75	2.00
82 R.Jay Soward RC	.50	1.25
83 Sylvester Morris RC	.50	1.25
84 Giovanni Carmazzi RC	.50	1.25
85 J.R. Redmond RC	.50	1.25
86 Sherrod Gideon RC	.50	1.25
87 Tee Martin RC	.50	1.25
88 Dennis Northcutt RC	.50	1.25
89 Troy Walters RC	.50	1.25
90 Joe Hamilton RC	.50	1.25
91 Reuben Droughns RC	.50	1.25
92 Trung Canidate RC	.50	1.25
93A Bill Burke SP	20.00	40.00
93B Bill Burke Red		
94 Tim Rattay RC	.60	1.50
95 Jerry Porter RC	.75	2.00
96 Michael Wiley RC	.50	1.25
97 Anthony Lucas RC	.50	1.25
98 Danny Farmer RC	.50	1.25
99 Travis Prentice RC	.50	1.25
100 Dez White RC	.50	1.25
101 Chad Pennington RC	.60	1.50
102 Chris Redman RC	.50	1.25
103 Thomas Jones RC	.60	1.50
104 Ron Dayne RC	.75	2.00
105 Jamal Lewis RC	.75	2.00
106 Shyrone Stith RC	.50	1.25
107 Peter Warrick RC	.50	1.25
108 Plaxico Burress RC	.60	1.50
109 Travis Taylor RC	.50	1.25
110A LaVar Arrington RC	15.00	40.00
110B LaVar Arrington RC Red	10.00	25.00
111 Terrell Davis	.30	.75
112 Dan Marino	.75	2.00
113 Brad Johnson	.30	.75
114 Isaac Bruce	.40	1.00
115 Eric Moulds	.25	.60
116 Olandis Gary	.30	.75
117 Drew Bledsoe	.30	.75
118 Steve Young	.50	1.25
119 Keyshawn Johnson	.30	.75
120 Emmitt Smith	.60	1.50
121 Warrick Dunn	.25	.60
122 Doug Flutie	.30	.75
123 Troy Edwards	.25	.60
124 Brett Favre	.75	2.00
125 Charlie Batch	.25	.60
126 Curtis Martin	.30	.75
127 Stephen Davis	.25	.60
128 Troy Aikman	.50	1.25
129 Fred Taylor	.25	.60
130 Jerry Rice	1.00	2.50
131 Jon Kitna	.25	.60
132 Steve McNair	.30	.75
133 Jake Plummer	.25	.60
134 Donovan McNabb	.30	.75
135 Ricky Williams	.30	.75
136 Torry Holt	.30	.75
137 James Johnson	.25	.60
138 Kevin Johnson	.25	.60
139 Akili Smith	.25	.60
140 Cade McNown	.25	.60
141 Eddie George	.30	.75
142 Shaun King	.25	.60
143 Marshall Faulk	.30	.75
144 Kurt Warner	.60	1.50
145 Randy Moss	.30	.75
146 Mark Brunell	.30	.75
147 Marvin Harrison	.30	.75
148 Edgerrin James	.30	.75
149 Tim Couch	.30	.75
150 Peyton Manning	1.00	2.50
151 Thomas Jones HN	.60	1.50
152 Jamal Lewis HN	.75	2.00
153 Chris Redman HN	.50	1.25
154 Travis Taylor HN	.50	1.25
155 Brian Urlacher HN RC	2.50	6.00
156 Dez White HN	.50	1.25
157 Ron Dugans HN RC	.50	1.25
158 Peter Warrick HN	.50	1.25
159 Dennis Northcutt HN	.50	1.25
160 Travis Prentice HN	.50	1.25
161 Bubba Franks HN RC	.50	1.25
162 R.Jay Soward HN	.50	1.25
163 Sylvester Morris HN	.50	1.25
164 J.R. Redmond HN	.50	1.25
165 Ron Dayne HN	.75	2.00
166 Anthony Becht HN RC	.50	1.25
167 Laveranues Coles HN RC	.60	1.50
168 Chad Pennington HN	.60	1.50
169 Jerry Porter HN	.75	2.00
170 Todd Pinkston HN RC	.50	1.25
171 Plaxico Burress HN	.60	1.50
172 Tee Martin HN	.50	1.25
173 Trung Canidate HN	.50	1.25
174 Shaun Alexander HN	.75	2.00
175 Joe Hamilton HN	.50	1.25

2000 Collector's Edge EG Brilliant

*VETS 111-150: 2.5X TO 6X BASIC CARDS
*ROOKIES 101-110: 1.2X TO 3X BASIC CARDS
STATED PRINT RUN 500 SERIAL #'d SETS

110 LaVar Arrington	3.00	8.00

2000 Collector's Edge EG Gems Previews

*UNLISTED PREVIEWS: .2X TO .5X BASIC INSERTS

E49 LaVar Arrington	.60	1.50

2000 Collector's Edge EG Gems

Randomly inserted in packs, this 49-card set features full color player action photography set against a split colored foil background. Card #E49, LaVar Arrington, was never included in packs. The right side of the background is a purple foil with the player's name and Edge logo in gold foil, while the right side of the background is a multi-color foil design. Each card is sequentially numbered to 500. Preview cards were produced for some players including an otherwise unreleased LaVar Arrington #49 card.

COMPLETE SET (49)	125.00	250.00
STATED PRINT RUN 500 SER.#'d SETS		
E1 Doug Flutie	.75	2.00
E2 Cade McNown	.60	1.50
E3 Akili Smith	.60	1.50
E4 Tim Couch	.75	2.00
E5 Kevin Johnson	.60	1.50
E6 Troy Aikman	1.25	3.00
E7 Emmitt Smith	1.50	4.00
E8 Terrell Davis	.75	2.00
E9 Brett Favre	2.00	5.00
E10 Marvin Harrison	.75	2.00
E11 Edgerrin James	.75	2.00
E12 Peyton Manning	2.50	6.00
E13 Mark Brunell	.75	2.00
E14 Dan Marino	2.00	5.00
E15 Randy Moss	.75	2.00
E16 Drew Bledsoe	.75	2.00
E17 Ricky Williams	.75	2.00
E18 Keyshawn Johnson	.75	2.00
E19 Curtis Martin	.75	2.00
E20 Donovan McNabb	.75	2.00
E21 Marshall Faulk	.75	2.00
E22 Torry Holt	.75	2.00
E23 Kurt Warner	1.50	4.00
E24 Jerry Rice	2.50	6.00
E25 Steve Young	1.25	3.00
E26 Jon Kitna	.60	1.50
E27 Shaun King	.60	1.50
E28 Eddie George	.75	2.00
E29 Stephen Davis	.60	1.50
E30 Brad Johnson	.75	2.00
E31 Chad Pennington	.75	2.00
E32 Chris Redman	.60	1.50
E33 Tim Rattay	.75	2.00
E34 Tee Martin	.60	1.50
E35 Thomas Jones	.75	2.00
E36 Ron Dayne	1.00	2.50
E37 Jamal Lewis	1.00	2.50
E38 J.R. Redmond	.60	1.50
E39 Travis Prentice	.60	1.50
E40 Shaun Alexander	1.00	2.50
E41 Michael Wiley	.60	1.50
E42 Quinton Spotwood	.60	1.50
E43 Peter Warrick	.60	1.50
E44 Plaxico Burress	.75	2.00
E45 Travis Taylor	.60	1.50
E46 Troy Walters	.60	1.50
E47 R.Jay Soward	.60	1.50
E48 Dez White	.60	1.50
E50 Courtney Brown	.75	2.00

2000 Collector's Edge EG Golden Edge

Randomly inserted in packs, this 50-card set features full color player action photography set against a gold foil backdrop. Player's names and positions are centered below the photograph in gold foil. Each card is sequentially numbered to 2000.

COMPLETE SET (50)	100.00	200.00
STATED PRINT RUN 2000 SER.#'d SETS		
GE1 Jake Plummer	.40	1.00
GE2 Qadry Ismail	.40	1.00
GE3 Doug Flutie	.50	1.25
GE4 Muhsin Muhammad	.40	1.00
GE5 Cade McNown	.40	1.00
GE6 Marcus Robinson	.50	1.25
GE7 Akili Smith	.40	1.00
GE8 Tim Couch	.50	1.25
GE9 Kevin Johnson	.40	1.00
GE10 Troy Aikman	.75	2.00
GE11 Emmitt Smith	1.00	2.50
GE12 Terrell Davis	.50	1.25
GE13 Charlie Batch	.40	1.00
GE14 Brett Favre	1.25	3.00
GE15 Marvin Harrison	.50	1.25
GE16 Edgerrin James	.50	1.25
GE17 Peyton Manning	1.50	4.00
GE18 Mark Brunell	.50	1.25
GE19 Fred Taylor	.40	1.00
GE20 Dan Marino	1.25	3.00
GE21 Randy Moss	.50	1.25
GE22 Drew Bledsoe	.50	1.25
GE23 Ricky Williams	.50	1.25
GE24 Curtis Martin	.50	1.25
GE25 Donovan McNabb	.50	1.25
GE26 Isaac Bruce	.60	1.50
GE27 Marshall Faulk	.50	1.25
GE28 Torry Holt	.50	1.25
GF29 Kurt Warner	1.00	2.50
GE30 Jerry Rice	1.50	4.00
GE31 Jon Kitna	.40	1.00
GE32 Eddie George	.50	1.25
GE33 Steve McNair	.50	1.25
GE34 Stephen Davis	.40	1.00
GE35 Brad Johnson	.50	1.25
GE36 Travis Prentice	.40	1.00
GE37 Dez White	.40	1.00
GE38 Chad Pennington	.50	1.25
GE39 Chris Redman	.40	1.00
GE40 Thomas Jones	.50	1.25
GE41 Ron Dayne	.60	1.50
GE42 Jamal Lewis	.60	1.50
GE43 Shyrone Stith	.40	1.00
GE44 Peter Warrick	.40	1.00
GE45 Plaxico Burress	.50	1.25
GE46 Travis Taylor	.40	1.00
GE48 Shaun Alexander	.60	1.50
GE49 R.Jay Soward	.40	1.00
GE50 Sylvester Morris	.40	1.00

2000 Collector's Edge EG Impeccable

Randomly seeded in packs, this 20-card set features full color player action photography set against an all foil backdrop. The right and left side feature a red foil design that is bisected by a broad blue foil design down the middle of the card. Cards are accented with gold foil highlights and are sequentially numbered to 2000.

COMPLETE SET (20)	40.00	80.00
STATED PRINT RUN 2000 SER.#'d SETS		
I1 Cade McNown	.40	1.00
I2 Tim Couch	.50	1.25
I3 Troy Aikman	.75	2.00
I4 Emmitt Smith	1.00	2.50
I5 Terrell Davis	.50	1.25
I6 Brett Favre	1.25	3.00
I7 Edgerrin James	.50	1.25
I8 Peyton Manning	1.50	4.00
I9 Mark Brunell	.50	1.25
I10 Fred Taylor	.40	1.00
I11 Dan Marino	1.25	3.00
I12 Randy Moss	.50	1.25
I13 Drew Bledsoe	.50	1.25
I14 Ricky Williams	.50	1.25
I15 Curtis Martin	.50	1.25
I16 Marshall Faulk	.50	1.25
I17 Kurt Warner	1.00	2.50
I18 Eddie George	.50	1.25
I19 Steve McNair	.50	1.25
I20 Stephen Davis	.40	1.00

2000 Collector's Edge EG Making the Grade

Randomly seeded in packs, this 29-card set features full color player action photography set against the same picture blown up in the background. The card is borderless, but the background color fades to almost white along the edges. Cards contain gold foil highlights and are sequentially numbered to 2000.

COMPLETE SET (29)	50.00	100.00
STATED PRINT RUN 2000 SER.#'d SETS		
M1 Shaun Alexander	.60	1.50
M2 R.Jay Soward	.40	1.00
M3 Sylvester Morris	.40	1.00
M4 Corey Simon	.50	1.25
M5 J.R. Redmond	.40	1.00
M6 Bubba Franks	.40	1.00
M7 Tee Martin	.40	1.00
M8 Dennis Northcutt	.40	1.00
M9 Courtney Brown	.50	1.25
M10 Joe Hamilton	.40	1.00
M11 Reuben Droughns	.40	1.00
M12 Trung Canidate	.40	1.00
M13 Laveranues Coles	.50	1.25
M14 Brian Urlacher	2.00	5.00
M15 Jerry Porter	.60	1.50
M16 Ron Dugans	.40	1.00
M17 Anthony Becht	.40	1.00
M18 Danny Farmer	.40	1.00
M19 Travis Prentice	.40	1.00
M20 Dez White	.40	1.00
M21 Chad Pennington	.50	1.25
M22 Chris Redman	.40	1.00
M23 Thomas Jones	.50	1.25
M24 Ron Dayne	.60	1.50
M25 Jamal Lewis	.60	1.50
M26 Todd Pinkston	.40	1.00
M27 Peter Warrick	.40	1.00
M28 Plaxico Burress	.50	1.25
M29 Travis Taylor	.40	1.00

2000 Collector's Edge EG Rookie Leatherback Autographs

Randomly inserted in packs, this 29-card set features a full color player action shot set against a black background with designs and the PSA/DNA logo in the lower left hand corner. The card backs are made entirely of game used football leather. The cards are autographed and sequentially numbered to 12.

STATED PRINT RUN 12 SER.#'d SETS		
AB Anthony Becht	30.00	80.00
BF Bubba Franks	30.00	80.00
BU Brian Urlacher	250.00	400.00
CK Curtis Keaton	30.00	80.00
CP Chad Pennington	40.00	100.00
CR Chris Redman	30.00	80.00
CS Corey Simon	40.00	100.00
DF Danny Farmer	30.00	80.00
DN Dennis Northcutt	30.00	80.00
DW Dez White	30.00	80.00
JH Joe Hamilton	30.00	80.00
JL Jamal Lewis	75.00	200.00
JP Jerry Porter	50.00	125.00
JR J.R. Redmond	30.00	80.00
LC Laveranues Coles	40.00	100.00
PB Plaxico Burress	40.00	100.00
PW Peter Warrick	30.00	80.00
RD Ron Dayne	50.00	125.00
RD Reuben Droughns	30.00	80.00
RD Ron Dugans	30.00	80.00
RS R.Jay Soward	30.00	80.00
SA Shaun Alexander	175.00	300.00
SM Sylvester Morris	30.00	80.00
TC Trung Canidate	30.00	80.00
TJ Thomas Jones	40.00	100.00
TM Tee Martin	30.00	80.00
TP Travis Prentice	30.00	80.00
TP Todd Pinkston	30.00	80.00
TT Travis Taylor	30.00	80.00

2000 Collector's Edge EG Uncirculated

*VETS 111-150: 1.2X TO 3X BASIC CARDS
*ROOKIES 101-109: .6X TO 1.5X BASIC CARDS
ANNOUCED PRINT RUN 5000

1997 Collector's Edge Extreme

This 180-card set was distributed in six-card packs with a suggested retail price of $2.29. The fronts feature color action photos of players from all 30 teams printed on thin glossy card stock. The backs carry complete player historical statistics. A much thicker non-glossy "50-Point" parallel set was also issued which is sometimes confused with the base issue set.

COMPLETE SET (180)	7.50	20.00
1 Larry Centers	.10	.30
2 Leeland McElroy	.07	.20
3 Jake Plummer RC	.75	2.00
4 Simeon Rice	.10	.30
5 Eric Swann	.07	.20
6 Jamal Anderson	.20	.50
7 Bert Emanuel	.10	.30
8 Byron Hanspard RC	.10	.30
9 Derrick Alexander WR	.10	.30
10 Peter Boulware RC	.20	.50
11 Michael Jackson	.10	.30
12 Ray Lewis	.30	.75
13 Vinny Testaverde	.10	.30
14 Todd Collins	.07	.20
15 Eric Moulds	.20	.50
17 Andre Reed	.10	.30
18 Bruce Smith	.10	.30
19 Antowain Smith RC	.50	1.25
21 Thurman Thomas	.20	.50
22 Tim Biakabutuka	.10	.30
23 Rae Carruth RC	.07	.20
24 Kerry Collins	.20	.50
25 Anthony Johnson	.07	.20
26 Lamar Lathon	.07	.20
27 Muhsin Muhammad	.10	.30
28 Darnell Autry RC	.10	.30
29 Curtis Conway	.10	.30
30 Bryan Cox	.07	.20
31 Bobby Engram	.10	.30
32 Walt Harris	.07	.20
33 Erik Kramer	.07	.20
34 Rashaan Salaam	.07	.20
35 Jeff Blake	.10	.30
36 Ki-Jana Carter	.07	.20
37 Corey Dillon RC	.75	2.00
38 Carl Pickens	.10	.30
39 Troy Aikman	.40	1.00
40 Dexter Coakley RC	.20	.50
41 Michael Irvin	.20	.50
42 Daryl Johnston	.10	.30
43 David LaFleur RC	.07	.20
44 Anthony Miller	.07	.20
45 Deion Sanders	.20	.50
46 Emmitt Smith	.60	1.50
47 Broderick Thomas	.07	.20
48 Terrell Davis	.25	.60
49 John Elway	.75	2.00
50 John Mobley	.07	.20
51 Shannon Sharpe	.10	.30
52 Neil Smith	.10	.30
53 Checklist	.07	.20
54 Scott Mitchell	.10	.30
55 Herman Moore	.10	.30
56 Barry Sanders	.60	1.50
57 Edgar Bennett	.10	.30
58 Robert Brooks	.10	.30
59 Mark Chmura	.10	.30
60 Brett Favre	.75	2.00
61 Antonio Freeman	.20	.50
62 Dorsey Levens	.20	.50
63 Reggie White	.20	.50
64 Eddie George	.20	.50
65 Darryll Lewis	.07	.20
66 Steve McNair	.25	.60
67 Chris Sanders	.07	.20
68 Marshall Faulk	.25	.60
69 Jim Harbaugh	.10	.30
70 Marvin Harrison	.20	.50
71 Tony Brackens	.07	.20
72 Mark Brunell	.25	.60
73 Kevin Hardy	.07	.20
74 Rob Johnson	.20	.50
75 Keenan McCardell	.10	.30
76 Natrone Means	.10	.30
77 Jimmy Smith	.10	.30
78 Marcus Allen	.20	.50
79 Pat Barnes RC	.20	.50
80 Tony Gonzalez RC	.75	2.00
81 Elvis Grbac	.10	.30
82 Brett Perriman	.07	.20
83 Andre Rison	.10	.30
84 Derrick Thomas	.20	.50
85 Tamarick Vanover	.10	.30
86 Karim Abdul-Jabbar	.10	.30
87 Fred Barnett	.07	.20
88 Terrell Buckley	.07	.20
89 Yatil Green RC	.10	.30
90 Dan Marino	.75	2.00
91 O.J. McDuffie	.10	.30
92 Jason Taylor RC	.40	1.00
93 Zach Thomas	.20	.50
94 Cris Carter	.20	.50
95 Brad Johnson	.20	.50
96 John Randle	.10	.30
97 Jake Reed	.10	.30
98 Robert Smith	.10	.30
99 Drew Bledsoe	.25	.60
100 Chris Canty RC	.07	.20
101 Ben Coates	.10	.30
102 Terry Glenn	.20	.50
103 Ty Law	.10	.30
104 Curtis Martin	.25	.60
105 Willie McGinest	.07	.20
106 Troy Davis RC	.10	.30
108 Wayne Martin	.07	.20
109 Heath Shuler	.07	.20
110 Danny Wuerffel RC	.20	.50
111 Ray Zellars	.07	.20
112 Tiki Barber RC	1.25	3.00
113A Dave Brown	.07	.20
113B Checklist	.07	.20
114 Ike Hilliard RC	.30	.75
115 Jason Sehorn	.10	.30
116 Amani Toomer	.10	.30
117 Tyrone Wheatley	.10	.30
118 Hugh Douglas	.07	.20
119 Aaron Glenn	.07	.20
120 Jeff Graham	.07	.20
121 Keyshawn Johnson	.20	.50
122A Adrian Murrell	.10	.30
122B Bryce Paup UER	.07	.20
123A Neil O'Donnell	.10	.30
123B Chris Spielman UER	.07	.20
124 Tim Brown	.20	.50
125 Jeff George	.10	.30
126 Desmond Howard	.10	.30
127 Napoleon Kaufman	.20	.50
128 Chester McGlockton	.07	.20
129 Darrell Russell RC	.07	.20
130 Ty Detmer	.10	.30
131 Irving Fryar	.10	.30
132 Chris T. Jones	.07	.20
133 Ricky Watters	.10	.30
134 Jerome Bettis	.20	.50
135 Charles Johnson	.10	.30
136 George Jones RC	.10	.30
137 Greg Lloyd	.07	.20
138 Kordell Stewart	.20	.50
139 Yancey Thigpen	.10	.30
140 Jim Everett	.07	.20
141 Stan Humphries	.10	.30
142 Tony Martin	.10	.30
143 Eric Metcalf	.10	.30
144 Junior Seau	.20	.50
145 Jim Druckenmiller RC	.10	.30
146 Kevin Greene	.10	.30
147 Garrison Hearst	.10	.30
148 Terry Kirby	.10	.30
149 Terrell Owens	.25	.60
150 Jerry Rice	.40	1.00
151 Dana Stubblefield	.07	.20
152 Rod Woodson	.10	.30
153 Bryant Young	.07	.20
154 Steve Young	.25	.60
155 Chad Brown	.07	.20
156 John Friesz	.07	.20
157 Joey Galloway	.10	.30
158 Cortez Kennedy	.07	.20
159 Warren Moon	.20	.50
160 Shawn Springs RC	.10	.30
161 Chris Warren	.10	.30
162 Tony Banks	.10	.30
163 Isaac Bruce	.20	.50
164 Eddie Kennison	.10	.30
165 Keith Lyle	.07	.20
166 Orlando Pace RC	.20	.50
167 Lawrence Phillips	.07	.20
168 Checklist	.07	.20
169 Mike Alstott	.20	.50
170 Reidel Anthony RC	.20	.50
171 Warrick Dunn RC	.60	1.50
172 Hardy Nickerson	.07	.20
173 Errict Rhett	.07	.20
174 Warren Sapp	.10	.30
175 Terry Allen	.20	.50
176 Gus Frerotte	.07	.20
177 Sean Gilbert	.07	.20
178 Ken Harvey	.07	.20
179 Jeff Hostetler	.07	.20
180 Michael Westbrook	.10	.30

1997 Collector's Edge Extreme 50-Point

COMPLETE SET (180)	15.00	30.00

*50-POINT: .5X TO 1.2X BASIC CARDS

1997 Collector's Edge Extreme Foil

*FOIL STARS: 1.25X TO 2.5X BASIC CARDS
*FOIL RCs: .5X TO 1X BASIC CARDS
SILVER STATED ODDS 1:2
*GOLD STARS: 2.5X TO 5X BASIC CARDS
*GOLD RCs: 1X TO 2X BASIC CARDS
GOLD STATED ODDS 1:12
*DIE CUT STARS: 7.5X TO 15X BASIC CARDS
*DIE CUT RCs: 3X TO 6X BASIC CARDS
DIE CUT STATED ODDS 1:36

1997 Collector's Edge Extreme Finesse

Randomly inserted in packs at the rate of one in 60, this 25-card set features color action images of star players printed on a frosted clear card with gold foil stamping.

COMPLETE SET (25)	30.00	80.00
STATED ODDS 1:60		
*HOLOFOIL: .5X TO 1.2X BASIC INSERTS		
1 Troy Aikman	2.50	6.00
2 Marcus Allen	1.50	4.00
3 Ben Coates	1.25	3.00
4 Tony Banks	1.25	3.00
5 Jeff Blake	1.25	3.00
6 Tim Brown	1.50	4.00
7 Mark Brunell	1.25	3.00
8 Todd Collins	1.00	2.50
9 Terrell Davis	2.00	5.00
10 Jim Druckenmiller	1.00	2.50
11 John Elway	5.00	12.00
12 Marshall Faulk	2.00	5.00
13 Brett Favre	5.00	12.00
14 Antonio Freeman	1.50	4.00
15 Joey Galloway	1.25	3.00
16 Eddie George	1.50	4.00
17 Terry Glenn	1.25	3.00
18 Marvin Harrison	1.50	4.00
19 Garrison Hearst	1.25	3.00
20 Warrick Dunn	1.50	4.00
21 Muhsin Muhammad	1.25	3.00
22 Jerry Rice	3.00	8.00
23 Barry Sanders	4.00	10.00
24 Emmitt Smith	4.00	10.00
25 Shawn Springs	1.00	2.50

1997 Collector's Edge Extreme Force

Randomly inserted in packs at the rate of one in eight, this 25-card set features color action player photos printed on silver with flow etched designs.

COMPLETE SET (25)	25.00	60.00
STATED ODDS 1:8		
1 Marcus Allen	1.25	3.00
2 Chris Canty	.25	.60
3 Jerome Bettis	1.25	3.00
4 Carl Pickens	.75	2.00
5 Drew Bledsoe	1.50	4.00
6 Robert Brooks	.75	2.00
7 Shannon Sharpe	.75	2.00
8 Tim Brown	1.25	3.00
9 Mark Brunell	1.50	4.00
10 Ben Coates	.75	2.00
11 Todd Collins	.50	1.25
12 Terrell Davis	1.50	4.00
13 John Elway	5.00	12.00
14 Brett Favre	5.00	12.00
15 Antonio Freeman	1.25	3.00
16 Joey Galloway	.75	2.00
17 Warrick Dunn	2.00	5.00

18 Terry Glenn 1.25 3.00
19 Marvin Harrison 1.25 3.00
20 Dan Marino 5.00 12.00
21 Jerry Rice 2.50 6.00
22 Junior Seau 1.25 3.00
23 Tony Banks .75 2.00
24 Emmitt Smith 4.00 10.00
25 Napoleon Kaufman 1.25 3.00

1997 Collector's Edge Extreme Forerunners

This 25-card set features color action player photos printed on clear two-way view cards with a large head shot on the back viewable from the card front and gold foil throughout. Each was serial numbered of 1500 sets produced.

COMPLETE SET (25) 40.00 100.00
STATED PRINT RUN 1500 SERIAL #'d SETS
1 Karim Abdul-Jabbar 1.50 4.00
2 Marcus Allen 2.50 6.00
3 Jerome Bettis 2.50 6.00
4 Drew Bledsoe 3.00 8.00
5 Robert Brooks 1.50 4.00
6 Mark Brunell 3.00 8.00
7 Todd Collins 1.00 2.50
8 Terrell Davis 3.00 8.00
9 John Elway 10.00 25.00
10 Brett Favre 10.00 25.00
11 Joey Galloway 1.50 4.00
12 Eddie George 2.50 6.00
13 Terry Glenn 2.50 6.00
14 Marvin Harrison 2.50 6.00
15 Keyshawn Johnson 2.50 6.00
16 Rob Johnson 2.50 6.00
17 Eddie Kennison 1.50 4.00
18 Dorsey Levens 2.50 6.00
19 Dan Marino 10.00 25.00
20 Steve McNair 3.00 8.00
21 Terrell Owens 3.00 8.00
22 Carl Pickens 1.50 4.00
23 Jerry Rice 5.00 12.00
24 Emmitt Smith 8.00 20.00
25 Kordell Stewart 2.50 6.00

1997 Collector's Edge Extreme Fury

Randomly inserted in packs at the rate of one in 48, this 18-card set features color action player images printed on a Deep Metal card with chromium finish.

COMPLETE SET (18) 50.00 120.00
STATED ODDS 1:48
1 Jerome Bettis 2.50 6.00
2 Terry Glenn 2.50 6.00
3 Drew Bledsoe 3.00 8.00
4 Mark Brunell 2.50 6.00
5 Terrell Davis 3.00 8.00
6 Troy Davis 1.50 4.00
7 Marshall Faulk 3.00 8.00
8 Brett Favre 10.00 25.00
9 Antonio Freeman 2.50 6.00
10 Joey Galloway 1.50 4.00
11 Eddie George 2.50 6.00
12 Eddie Kennison 1.50 4.00
13 Errict Rhett 1.00 2.50
14 Rashaan Salaam 1.00 2.50
15 Emmitt Smith 8.00 20.00
16 Kordell Stewart 2.50 6.00
17 Danny Wuerffel 2.50 6.00
18 Steve Young 3.00 8.00

1997 Collector's Edge Extreme Game Gear Quads

Randomly inserted in packs at the rate of one in 360, this set features color player photos printed on foil card stock with a piece of the player's game used gear mounted on the cardfront. Players can be found with one or more of the following items embedded in the cardfront: ball (B), jersey (J), pants (P), shoes (S).

STATED ODDS 1:360
1F Marcus Allen FB 15.00 40.00
1J Marcus Allen JSY 15.00 40.00
2F Mike Alstott FB 15.00 40.00
2J Mike Alstott JSY 15.00 40.00
2P Mike Alstott Pants 15.00 40.00
2S Mike Alstott Shoes 15.00 40.00
3F Drew Bledsoe FB 20.00 50.00
3J Drew Bledsoe JSY 20.00 50.00
4F Tim Brown FB 12.50 30.00
4J Tim Brown JSY 15.00 30.00
5F Mark Brunell FB 20.00 50.00
5J Mark Brunell JSY 20.00 50.00
5P Mark Brunell Pants 20.00 50.00
5S Mark Brunell Shoes 20.00 50.00
6F Kerry Collins FB 10.00 25.00
6J Kerry Collins JSY 10.00 25.00
7F Terrell Davis FB 20.00 50.00
7J Terrell Davis JSY 20.00 50.00
7P Terrell Davis Pants 20.00 50.00
7S Terrell Davis Shoes 20.00 50.00
8F Jim Druckenmiller FB 12.50 30.00
8J Jim Druckenmiller JSY 15.00 30.00
9F Warrick Dunn FB 15.00 40.00
9J Warrick Dunn JSY 15.00 40.00
9P Warrick Dunn Pants 15.00 40.00
9S Warrick Dunn Shoes 15.00 40.00
10F John Elway FB 40.00 100.00
10J John Elway JSY 40.00 100.00
10P John Elway Pants 40.00 100.00
10S John Elway Shoes 40.00 100.00
11F Brett Favre FB 40.00 100.00
11J Brett Favre JSY 40.00 100.00
12F Eddie George FB 15.00 40.00
12J Eddie George JSY 15.00 40.00
12P Eddie George Pants 15.00 40.00
12S Eddie George Shoes 15.00 40.00
13F Terry Glenn FB 12.50 30.00
13J Terry Glenn JSY 15.00 40.00
14F Leeland McElroy FB 10.00 25.00
15F Adrian Murrell FB 10.00 25.00
15J Adrian Murrell JSY 10.00 25.00
15P Adrian Murrell Pants 10.00 25.00
15S Adrian Murrell Shoes 10.00 25.00
16F Carl Pickens FB 12.50 30.00
16J Carl Pickens JSY 15.00 30.00
17F Kordell Stewart FB 15.00 40.00
17J Kordell Stewart JSY 15.00 40.00
18F Danny Wuerffel FB 15.00 40.00
18J Danny Wuerffel JSY 15.00 40.00

1998 Collector's Edge First Place

The 1998 Collector's Edge First Place set was issued in one series with a total of 250 standard size cards. Packs retailed for $4.99 each. The fronts feature large color action shots. The featured player's name, team name, and team position are found along the bottom of the card, printed in gold foil, with the First Place logo in the upper left corner. A number of cards list the incorrect player's position on the front, but no corrected versions have ever been reported. The checklist cards were numbered CK1, CK2, etc. and are listed after the base player cards. There were two different team logos for each checklist card.

COMPLETE SET (250) 35.00 60.00
1 Karim Abdul-Jabbar .30 .75
2 Flozell Adams RC .25 .60
3 Troy Aikman .60 1.50
4 Robert Smith .30 .75
5 Stephen Alexander RC .30 .75
6 Harold Shaw RC .25 .60
7 Marcus Allen .30 .75
8 Terry Allen .30 .75
9 Mike Alstott .30 .75
10 Jamal Anderson .30 .75
11 Reidel Anthony .20 .50
12 Jamie Asher .10 .30
13 Darnell Autry .10 .30
14 Phil Savoy RC .30 .75
15 Jon Ritchie RC .30 .75
16 Tony Banks .20 .50
18 Pat Barnes .10 .30
19 Charlie Batch RC .50 1.25
20 Mikhael Ricks RC .30 .75
21 Jerome Bettis .30 .75
22 Tim Biakabutuka .20 .50
23 Roosevelt Blackmon RC .25 .60
24 Jeff Blake .20 .50
25 Drew Bledsoe .50 1.25
26 Tony Boselli .10 .30
27 Peter Boulware .10 .30
28 Tony Brackens .10 .30
29 Corey Bradford RC .50 1.25
30 Michael Pittman RC .60 1.50
31 Keith Brooking RC .50 1.25
32 Robert Brooks .20 .50
33 Derrick Brooks .30 .75
34 Ken Oxendine RC .25 .60
35 R.W. McQuarters RC .30 .75
36 Tim Brown .30 .75
37 Chad Brown .10 .30
38 Isaac Bruce .30 .75
39 Mark Brunell .30 .75
40 Chris Canty .10 .30
41 Mark Carrier .10 .30
42 Rae Carruth .10 .30
43 Ki-Jana Carter .10 .30
44 Cris Carter UER .30 .75
45 Larry Centers .10 .30
46 Corey Chavous RC .50 1.25
47 Mark Chmura .20 .50
48 Cameron Cleeland RC .25 .60
49 Dexter Coakley .10 .30
50 Ben Coates .20 .50
51 Jonathan Linton RC .30 .75
52 Todd Collins .10 .30
53 Kerry Collins .20 .50
54 Tebucky Jones RC .25 .60
55 Curtis Conway .20 .50
56 Sam Cowart RC .30 .75
57 Bryan Cox .10 .30
58 Randall Cunningham .30 .75
59 Terrell Davis .30 .75
60 Troy Davis .10 .30
61 Pat Johnson RC .30 .75
62 Trent Dilfer .30 .75
63 Vonnie Holliday RC .30 .75
64 Corey Dillon .30 .75
65 Hugh Douglas .10 .30
66 Jim Druckenmiller .10 .30
67 Warrick Dunn .30 .75
68 Robert Edwards RC .30 .75
69 Greg Ellis RC .25 .60
70 John Elway 1.25 3.00
71 Bert Emanuel .20 .50
72 Bobby Engram .20 .50
73 Curtis Enis RC .25 .60
74 Marshall Faulk .40 1.00
75 Brett Favre 1.25 3.00
76 Doug Flutie .30 .75
77 Glenn Foley .20 .50
78 Antonio Freeman .30 .75
79 Gus Frerotte .10 .30
80 John Friesz .10 .30
81 Irving Fryar .20 .50
82 Joey Galloway .20 .50
83 Rich Gannon .30 .75
84 Charlie Garner .20 .50
85 Jeff George .20 .50
86 Eddie George .30 .75
87 Sean Gilbert .10 .30
88 Terry Glenn .30 .75
89 Aaron Glenn .10 .30
90 Tony Gonzalez .30 .75
91 Jeff Graham .10 .30
92 Elvis Grbac .20 .50
93 Jacquez Green RC .30 .75
94 Kevin Greene .20 .50
95 Brian Griese UER RC 1.00 2.50
96 Byron Hanspard .10 .30
97 Jim Harbaugh .20 .50
98 Kevin Hardy .10 .30
99 Walt Harris .10 .30
100 Marvin Harrison .30 .75
101 Rodney Harrison .20 .50
102 Jeff Hartings .30 .75
103 Ken Harvey .10 .30
104 Garrison Hearst .30 .75
105 Ike Hilliard .20 .50
106 Jeff Hostetler .10 .30
107 Bobby Hoying .20 .50
108 Michael Jackson .10 .30
109 Anthony Johnson .10 .30
110 Brad Johnson .30 .75
111 Keyshawn Johnson .30 .75
112 Charles Johnson .10 .30
113 Daryl Johnston .20 .50
114 Chris Jones .10 .30
115 George Jones .10 .30
116 Donald Hayes RC .30 .75
117 Danny Kanell .20 .50
118 Napoleon Kaufman .30 .75
119 Cortez Kennedy .10 .30
120 Eddie Kennison .20 .50
121 Levon Kirkland .10 .30
122 Jon Kitna .30 .75
123 Erik Kramer .10 .30
124 David LaFleur .10 .30
125 Lamar Lathon .10 .30
126 Ty Law .20 .50
127 Ryan Leaf RC .50 1.25
128 Dorsey Levens .30 .75
129 Ray Lewis .30 .75
130 Darryll Lewis .10 .30
131 Matt Hasselbeck RC 8.00 20.00
132 Greg Lloyd .10 .30
133 Kevin Lockett .10 .30
134 Keith Lyle .10 .30
135 Peyton Manning RC 8.00 20.00
136 Dan Marino 1.25 3.00
137 Wayne Martin .10 .30
138 Ahman Green RC 1.25 3.00
139 Tony Martin .20 .50
140 E.G. Green RC .30 .75
141 Derrick Mayes .20 .50
142 Ed McCaffrey .20 .50
143 Keenan McCardell .20 .50
144 O.J. McDuffie .20 .50
145 Leeland McElroy .10 .30
146 Willie McGinest .10 .30
147 Chester McGlockton .10 .30
148 Steve McNair .30 .75
149 Natrone Means .20 .50
150 Eric Metcalf .10 .30
151 Anthony Miller .10 .30
152 Rick Mirer .10 .30
153 Scott Mitchell .20 .50
154 John Mobley .10 .30
155 Warren Moon .30 .75
156 Herman Moore .20 .50
157 Randy Moss RC 4.00 10.00
158 Eric Moulds .30 .75
159 Muhsin Muhammad .20 .50
160 Adrian Murrell .20 .50
161 Marcus Nash RC .25 .60
162 Hardy Nickerson .10 .30
163 Ken Norton .10 .30
164 Neil O'Donnell .20 .50
165 Terrell Owens .30 .75
166 Orlando Pace .10 .30
167 Jammi German RC .25 .60
168 Erric Pegram .10 .30
169 Jason Peter RC .25 .60
170 Carl Pickens .20 .50
171 Jake Plummer .30 .75
172 John Randle .20 .50
174 Jake Reed .20 .50
175 Errict Rhett .20 .50
176 Simeon Rice .20 .50
177 Jerry Rice .60 1.50
178 Andre Rison .20 .50
179 Darrell Russell .10 .30
180 Rashaan Salaam .10 .30
181 Deion Sanders .30 .75
182 Barry Sanders 1.00 2.50
183 Chris Sanders .10 .30
184 Warren Sapp .20 .50
185 Junior Seau .30 .75
186 Jason Sehorn .20 .50
187 Shannon Sharpe .20 .50
188 Sedrick Shaw .10 .30
189 Heath Shuler .10 .30
190 Chris Floyd RC .25 .60
191 Terry Fair RC .30 .75
192 Kevin Dyson RC .50 1.25
193 Torrance Small .10 .30
194 Antowain Smith .30 .75
195 Bruce Smith .20 .50
196 Tarik Smith RC .30 .75
197 Emmitt Smith 1.00 2.50
198 Neil Smith .20 .50
199 Jimmy Smith .20 .50
200 Chris Spielman .10 .30
201 Danny Wuerffel .20 .50
202 Irving Spikes .10 .30
203 Shawn Springs .10 .30
204 Duane Starks RC .25 .60
205 Kordell Stewart .30 .75
206 J.J. Stokes .20 .50
207 Eric Swann .10 .30
208 Steve Tasker .10 .30
209 Tim Dwight RC .50 1.25
210 Jason Taylor .20 .50
211 Vinny Testaverde .20 .50
212 Thurman Thomas .30 .75
213 Broderick Thomas .10 .30
214 Derrick Thomas .30 .75
215 Zach Thomas .30 .75
216 Germane Crowell RC .30 .75
217 Amani Toomer .20 .50
218 Tamarick Vanover .10 .30
219 Ross Verba .10 .30
220 Andre Wadsworth RC .30 .75
221 Ray Zellars .10 .30
222 Chris Warren .20 .50
223 Steve Young .40 1.00
224 Tyrone Wheatley .20 .50
225 Reggie White .30 .75
226 John Avery RC .30 .75
227 Charles Woodson RC 1.25 3.00
228 Takeo Spikes RC .50 1.25
229 Bryant Young .10 .30
230 Tavian Banks RC .20 .50
231 Fred Beasley RC .25 .60
232 Chris Ruhman RC .25 .60
CK1A Broncos Logo CL .02 .10
CK1B Steelers Logo CL .02 .10
CK2A 49ers Logo CL .02 .10
CK2B Panthers Logo CL .02 .10
CK3A Giants Logo CL .02 .10
CK3B Packers Logo CL .02 .10
CK4A Colts Logo CL .02 .10
CK4B Dolphins Logo CL .02 .10
CK5A Chargers Logo CL .02 .10
CK5B Vikings Logo Cl .02 .10
CK6A Patriots Logo Cl .02 .10
CK6B Raiders Logo CL .02 .10
CK7A Buccaneers Logo CL .02 .10
CK7B Cowboys Logo CL .02 .10
CK8A Bills Logo CL .02 .10
CK8B Lions Logo CL .02 .10
CK9A Chiefs Logo CL .02 .10
CK9B Seahawks Logo CL .02 .10

1998 Collector's Edge First Place 50-Point

COMPLETE SET (250) 150.00 300.00
*50-POINT STARS: 2X TO 4X BASIC CARDS
*50-POINT RCs: .8X TO 2X
STATED ODDS 1:1
131 Matt Hasselbeck 25.00 60.00

1998 Collector's Edge First Place 50-Point Silver

*VETS/125: 12X TO 30X BASIC CARDS
*ROOKIES/125: 3X TO 8X BASIC CARDS
STATED ODDS 1:24
131 Matt Hasselbeck 100.00 200.00

1998 Collector's Edge First Place Gold One-of-One

NOT PRICED DUE TO SCARCITY

1998 Collector's Edge First Place Game Gear Jersey

Randomly inserted in packs at a rate of one in 480, this two card set is an insert to the Collector's Edge First Place base set. The fronts feature an actual swatch from the jerseys presented at the NFL Draft Day Ceremonies. The cardfronts show the player's holding up the jersey presented to them at the Draft. Both player's cards were also produced without the jersey swatches and issued as promos. We've numbered those below as P1 and P2.

COMPLETE SET (2) 30.00 80.00
STATED ODDS 1:480
1 Peyton Manning 20.00 50.00
2 Ryan Leaf 10.00 25.00
P1 Peyton Manning Promo 2.50 6.00
P2 Ryan Leaf Promo .75 2.00

1998 Collector's Edge First Place Ryan Leaf

Collector's Edge included 5-different Ryan Leaf cards in packs of 1998 First Place. Each differs only from the photo on the cardfront and the cardbacks are unnumbered. The gold foil bordered version was inserted into First Place packs. A silver foil bordered version and a plain non-foil version appeared on the market after Collector's Edge ceased producing football cards. Note that the "First Place" logo does not appear on the cards but that they first appeared as inserts into that product.

COMPLETE SET (5) 1.25 3.00
COMMON CARD (1-5) .30 .75
*GOLDS: .4X TO 1X BASIC INSERTS
*SILVERS: .4X TO 1X BASIC INSERTS

1998 Collector's Edge First Place Peyton Manning

Collector's Edge included 5-different Peyton Manning cards in packs of 1998 First Place. Each differs only from the photo on the cardfront and the cardbacks are unnumbered. The gold foil bordered version was inserted into First Place packs. A silver foil bordered version and a plain non-foil version appeared on the market after Collector's Edge ceased producing football cards. Note that the "First Place" logo does not appear on the cards but that they first appeared as inserts into that product.

COMPLETE SET (5) 8.00 20.00
COMMON CARD (1-5) 2.00 5.00
*GOLDS: .5X TO 1.2X BASIC INSERTS
*SILVERS: .5X TO 1.2X BASIC INSERTS

1999 Collector's Edge First Place Peyton Manning Game Gear Promos

PM1 Peyton Manning 3.00 8.00

1998 Collector's Edge First Place Markers

Randomly inserted in packs at a rate of one in 24, this 30-card set is an insert to the Collector's Edge First Place base set. The fronts feature color action shots and a special embossed foil icon recognizes the featured player's draft pick number.

COMPLETE SET (30) 50.00 100.00
STATED ODDS 1:24
1 Michael Pittman 1.25 3.00
2 Andre Wadsworth .60 1.50
3 Keith Brooking 1.00 2.50
4 Pat Johnson .60 1.50
5 Jonathan Linton .60 1.50
6 Donald Hayes .60 1.50
7 Mark Chmura .40 1.00
8 Terry Allen .60 1.50
9 Brian Griese 2.00 5.00
10 Marcus Nash .50 1.25
11 Germane Crowell .60 1.50
12 Roosevelt Blackmon .50 1.25
13 Peyton Manning 10.00 30.00
14 Tavian Banks .40 1.00
15 Fred Taylor 3.00 8.00
16 Jim Druckenmiller .25 .60
17 John Avery .60 1.50
18 Randy Moss 8.00 20.00
19 Robert Edwards .60 1.50
20 Cameron Cleeland .50 1.25
21 Joe Jurevicius 1.00 2.50
22 Charles Woodson 2.50 6.00
23 Terry Allen .60 1.50
24 Ryan Leaf 1.00 2.50
25 Chris Ruhman .50 1.25
26 Ahman Green 2.50 6.00
27 Jerome Pathon 1.00 2.50
28 Jacquez Green .60 1.50
29 Kevin Dyson 1.00 2.50
30 Skip Hicks 1.00 2.50

1998 Collector's Edge First Place Pro Signature Authentics

Randomly inserted in packs at a rate of one in 600, these cards were issued via mail redemption cards in Collector's Edge First Place. The fronts feature an up-close color photo with an authentic signature of the player. A Jumbo sized Peyton Manning card was also produced and distributed primarily as a distributor promo.

STATED ODDS 1:600
1 Jim Druckenmiller
2 Eddie George
3 Ryan Leaf/35 50.00 120.00
4 Peyton Manning/50 75.00 150.00
5 Peyton Manning Jumbo 75.00 150.00
6 Peyton Manning Commemorative 50.00 100.00
7 Emmitt Smith/50 75.00 125.00

1998 Collector's Edge First Place Record Setters

These cards were issued by Collector's Edge as promos and inserts into special retail packs in PSA graded form. Each is essentially a parallel of the player's base First Place card with the silver foil text "Record Setter" on the cardfronts highlighting a Record Setting performance or other career highlight for the featured player.

59 Terrell Davis .25 .60
(Super Bowl 33 Champs)
70 John Elway 1.00 2.50
(50,000-yards Passing)
135A Peyton Manning 2.00 5.00
(Record Setter)
135B Peyton Manning 2.00 5.00
(1998 Top Rookie)
136 Dan Marino 1.00 2.50
(400-TD Passes)
157A Randy Moss .75 2.00
(Rookie Record Setter)
157B Randy Moss .75 2.00
(Rookie of the Year)

1998 Collector's Edge First Place Rookie Ink

Randomly inserted in packs at a rate of one in 24, this 31-card set is an insert to the Collector's Edge First Place base set. The fronts feature color action shots with autographs from the top 1998 Rookies. Each card is enhanced with silver foil. The backs offer a certificate of authenticity. A Red Ink parallel set was also randomly seeded with each card numbered of 45 signed. Some cards were issued via mail redemption inserts.

BLUE INK STATED ODDS 1:24
*RED INK/40-50: 1X TO 2.5X BASIC AU
RED INK PRINT RUN 40-50
1 Terry Allen 6.00 15.00
2 Mike Alstott 7.50 20.00
3 Reidel Anthony 6.00 15.00
4 Justin Armour 4.00 10.00
5 Tavian Banks 4.00 10.00
6 Tiki Barber 12.00 30.00
7 Charlie Batch 7.50 20.00
8 Mark Bruener 4.00 10.00
9 Cris Carter 10.00 25.00
10 Stephen Davis 7.50 20.00
11 Jim Druckenmiller 4.00 10.00
12 Tim Dwight 7.50 20.00
13 Ahman Green 12.00 30.00
14 Jacquez Green 6.00 15.00
15 Kevin Greene 6.00 15.00
16 Brian Griese 7.50 20.00
17 Marvin Harrison 15.00 40.00
18 Skip Hicks 6.00 15.00
19 Robert Holcombe 6.00 15.00
20 Joe Jurevicius 7.50 20.00
21 Fred Lane 4.00 10.00
22 Ryan Leaf 6.00 15.00
23A Peyton Manning Blue 125.00 200.00
23B Peyton Manning Black 125.00 200.00
24 Derrick Mayes 6.00 15.00
25 Randy Moss 60.00 120.00
26 Adrian Murrell 4.00 10.00
27 Marcus Nash 4.00 10.00
28 Jeremy Newberry 4.00 10.00
29 Terrell Owens 15.00 40.00
30 Fred Taylor 7.50 20.00
31 Hines Ward 30.00 80.00

1998 Collector's Edge First Place Successors

Randomly inserted in packs at a rate of one in 8, this 25-card set is an insert to the Collector's Edge First Place base set. The fronts feature color action photo shots in the foreground with a shadowed image of a football in the background. Each card is mirror silver with gold foil.

COMPLETE SET (25) 25.00 60.00
STATED ODDS 1:8
1 Troy Aikman 1.50 4.00
2 Jerome Bettis .75 2.00
3 Drew Bledsoe 1.25 3.00
4 Tim Brown .75 2.00
5 Mark Brunell .75 2.00
6 Cris Carter .75 2.00
7 Terrell Davis .75 2.00
8 Robert Edwards .25 .60
9 John Elway 3.00 8.00
10 Brett Favre 3.00 8.00
11 Eddie George .75 2.00
12 Brian Griese .75 2.00
14 Ryan Leaf .40 1.00
15 Dorsey Levens .75 2.00
16 Peyton Manning 5.00 12.00
17 Dan Marino 3.00 8.00
18 Jim Druckenmiller .30 .75
19 Herman Moore .50 1.25
20 Randy Moss 3.00 8.00
21 Jake Plummer .75 2.00
22 Barry Sanders 2.50 6.00
23 Emmitt Smith 2.50 6.00
24 Rod Smith .50 1.25
25 Fred Taylor 1.00 2.50

1998 Collector's Edge First Place Triple Threat

Randomly inserted in packs, this multiple level chase set features a color facial shot in the foreground with a color body action shot in the background. Gold odds, 1:35; Silver odds, 1:24; and Bronze odds 1:12.

COMPLETE SET (40) 75.00 150.00
1-15/26-30 BRONZE STATED ODDS 1:12
16-25 SILVER STATED ODDS 1:24
31-40 GOLD STATED ODDS 1:36
1 Robert Brooks 1.00 2.50
2 Troy Aikman 3.00 8.00
3 Randy Moss 5.00 12.00
4 Tim Brown 1.50 4.00
5 Brad Johnson 1.50 4.00
6 Kevin Dyson 1.50 4.00
7 Mark Chmura 1.00 2.50
8 Joey Galloway 1.00 2.50
9 Eddie George 1.50 4.00
10 Napoleon Kaufman 1.50 4.00
11 Dan Marino 6.00 15.00
12 Ed McCaffrey 1.00 2.50
13 Herman Moore 1.00 2.50
14 Carl Pickens 1.00 2.50
15 Emmitt Smith 5.00 12.00
16 Drew Bledsoe 2.50 6.00
17 Keith Brooking 1.50 4.00
18 Mark Brunell 1.50 4.00
19 Terrell Davis 1.50 4.00
20 Antonio Freeman 1.50 4.00
21 Peyton Manning 8.00 20.00
22 Jerry Rice 3.00 8.00
23 Terry Allen 1.50 4.00
24 Danny Wuerffel 1.00 2.50
25 Jerome Bettis 1.50 4.00
26 Fred Taylor 1.25 3.00
27 Andre Wadsworth 1.00 2.50
28 Charles Woodson 1.50 4.00
29 Steve Young 2.00 5.00
30 Mark Chmura 1.00 2.50
31 Cris Carter 2.00 5.00
32 Jim Druckenmiller 2.00 5.00
33 Warrick Dunn 1.50 4.00
34 John Elway 5.00 12.00
35 Brett Favre 7.50 20.00
36 Ryan Leaf 2.00 5.00
37 Dorsey Levens 2.00 5.00
38 Terrell Owens 2.00 5.00
39 Barry Sanders 6.00 15.00
40 Kordell Stewart 2.00 5.00

1998 Collector's Edge First Place Triumph

Randomly inserted in packs at a rate of one in 12, this 25-card set is an insert to the Collector's Edge First Place product. The clear acetate card fronts feature a large action shot in the foreground with a head shot in the background. The cards were not numbered and are checklisted below in alphabetical order.

COMPLETE SET (25) 40.00 80.00
STATED ODDS 1:12
1 Troy Aikman 2.00 5.00
2 Jerome Bettis 1.00 2.50
3 Drew Bledsoe 1.50 4.00
4 Tim Brown 1.00 2.50
5 Mark Brunell 1.00 2.50
6 Cris Carter 1.00 2.50
7 Terrell Davis 1.00 2.50
8 Jim Druckenmiller .40 1.00
9 Robert Edwards .30 .75
10 John Elway 4.00 10.00
11 Brett Favre 4.00 10.00
12 Eddie George 1.00 2.50
13 Brian Griese 1.00 2.50
14 Napoleon Kaufman 1.00 2.50
15 Ryan Leaf .50 1.25
16 Dorsey Levens 1.00 2.50
17 Peyton Manning 6.00 15.00
18 Dan Marino 4.00 10.00
19 Herman Moore .60 1.50
20 Randy Moss 4.00 10.00
21 Jake Plummer 1.00 2.50
22 Barry Sanders 3.00 8.00
23 Emmitt Smith 3.00 8.00
24 Rod Smith .60 1.50
25 Fred Taylor 1.00 2.50

1999 Collector's Edge First Place Previews

These preview cards were issued to promote the 1999 Collector's Edge First Place product. Each card is essentially a parallel of the base card, but printed with gold foil instead of silver along with the word "preview" printed in black on the cardbacks.

COMPLETE SET 3.00 8.00
CB Champ Bailey .30 .75
CM Cade McNown .20 .50
DB David Boston .25 .60
DC Daunte Culpepper 1.00 2.50
EJ Edgerrin James 1.00 2.50
TC Tim Couch .30 .75
TH Torry Holt .60 1.50
CMC Chris McAlister .20 .50

1999 Collector's Edge First Place

Released as a 200-card set, the 1999 Collector's Edge First Place set is comprised of 148 veteran cards, two checklists, and 50 short-printed rookies. Base cards are printinted on thick 20 point card stock in full bleed color. This set was packaged in 24-pack boxes containing 12-cards per pack and carried a suggested retail of $3.99. A late addition #201 Kurt Warner card numbered of 500 was included in packs. The card was released later as an unnumbered Promo version through Shop at Home.

COMPLETE SET (200) 20.00 50.00
1 Adrian Murrell .20 .50
2 Rob Moore .20 .50
3 Jake Plummer .20 .50
4 Simeon Rice .20 .50
5 Frank Sanders .20 .50
6 Jamal Anderson .25 .60
7 Chris Calloway .20 .50
8 Chris Chandler .25 .60
9 Tim Dwight .25 .60
10 Terance Mathis .20 .50
11 Jessie Tuggle .20 .50
12 Tony Banks .25 .60
13 Priest Holmes .20 .50
14 Jermaine Lewis .20 .50
15 Scott Mitchell .20 .50
16 Doug Flutie .30 .75
17 Eric Moulds .20 .50
18 Andre Reed .30 .75
19 Antowain Smith .20 .50
20 Bruce Smith .25 .60
21 Thurman Thomas .25 .60
22 Steve Beuerlein .25 .60
23 Tim Biakabutuka .25 .60
24 Kevin Greene .30 .75
25 Muhsin Muhammad .20 .50
26 Edgar Bennett .25 .60
27 Curtis Conway .25 .60
28 Bobby Engram .20 .50
30 Erik Kramer .25 .60
31 Jeff Blake .25 .60
32 Corey Dillon .20 .50
33 Carl Pickens .25 .60
34 Darnay Scott .20 .50
35 Takeo Spikes .20 .50
36 Ty Detmer .20 .50
37 Terry Kirby .20 .50
38 Leslie Shepherd .20 .50
39 Chris Spielman .25 .60
40 Troy Aikman .40 1.00
41 Michael Irvin .30 .75
42 Rocket Ismail .25 .60
43 Ernie Mills .20 .50
44 Deion Sanders .25 .60
45 Emmitt Smith .50 1.25
46 Chris Warren .25 .60
47 Bubba Brister .20 .50
48 Terrell Davis .25 .60
49 Brian Griese .20 .50
50 Ed McCaffrey .25 .60
51 Shannon Sharpe .25 .60
52 Rod Smith .25 .60
53 Charlie Batch .20 .50
54 Terry Fair .20 .50
55 Herman Moore .25 .60
56 Johnnie Morton .25 .60
57 Barry Sanders .50 1.25
58 Santana Dotson .20 .50
59 Brett Favre .60 1.50
60 Mark Chmura .20 .50
61 Antonio Freeman .25 .60
62 Dorsey Levens .25 .60
63 Derrick Mayes .20 .50
64 Marvin Harrison .25 .60
65 Peyton Manning 1.00 2.50
66 Jerome Pathon .20 .50
67 Mark Brunell .25 .60
68 Keenan McCardell .25 .60
69 Jimmy Smith .25 .60
70 Fred Taylor .20 .50
71 Derrick Alexander WR .20 .50
72 Kimble Anders .20 .50
73 Elvis Grbac .20 .50
74 Warren Moon .30 .75
75 Byron Bam Morris .20 .50
76 Andre Rison .25 .60
77 Karim Abdul-Jabbar .20 .50
78 Dan Marino .60 1.50
79 Tony Martin .25 .60
80 O.J. McDuffie .25 .60
81 Zach Thomas .25 .60
82 Cris Carter .30 .75
83 Randall Cunningham .25 .60
84 Jeff George .20 .50
85 Randy Moss .25 .60
86 Jake Reed .25 .60
87 Robert Smith .20 .50
88 Drew Bledsoe .25 .60
89 Ben Coates .25 .60
90 Terry Glenn .25 .60
91 Ty Law .30 .75
92 Shawn Jefferson .20 .50
93 Cameron Cleeland .20 .50
94 Andre Hastings .20 .50
95 Billy Joe Hobert .20 .50
96 Eddie Kennison .25 .60
97 Gary Brown .20 .50
98 Kerry Collins .20 .50
99 Kent Graham .20 .50
100 Ike Hilliard .20 .50
101 Joe Jurevicius .20 .50
102 Wayne Chrebet .20 .50
103 Aaron Glenn .20 .50
104 Keyshawn Johnson .25 .60
105 Mo Lewis .20 .50
106 Curtis Martin .25 .60
107 Vinny Testaverde .20 .50
108 Tim Brown .30 .75
109 Rich Gannon .25 .60
110 James Jett .20 .50
111 Napoleon Kaufman .20 .50
112 Charles Woodson .30 .75
113 Koy Detmer .20 .50
114 Charles Johnson .20 .50
115 Duce Staley .20 .50
116 Jerome Bettis .30 .75
117 Courtney Hawkins .20 .50
118 Levon Kirkland .20 .50
119 Kordell Stewart .20 .50
120 Isaac Bruce .30 .75
121 Marshall Faulk .25 .60
122 Trent Green .20 .50
123 Amp Lee .20 .50
124 Jim Harbaugh .25 .60
125 Bryan Still .20 .50
126 Freddie Jones .20 .50
127 Mikhael Ricks .20 .50
128 Natrone Means .25 .60
129 Junior Seau .25 .60
130 Lawrence Phillips .25 .60
131 Terrell Owens .25 .60
132 Jerry Rice .75 2.00
133 J.J. Stokes .20 .50
134 Steve Young .40 1.00
135 Joey Galloway .25 .60
136 Jon Kitna .20 .50
137 Ricky Watters .25 .60
138 Mike Alstott .20 .50
139 Reidel Anthony .20 .50
140 Trent Dilfer .20 .50
141 Warrick Dunn .20 .50
142 Kevin Dyson .20 .50
143 Eddie George .25 .60
144 Steve McNair .25 .60
145 Frank Wycheck .25 .60
146 Skip Hicks .20 .50
147 Brad Johnson .25 .60
148 Michael Westbrook .20 .50
149 Checklist Card .10 .30
150 Checklist Card .10 .30
151 David Boston RC .30 .75
152 Patrick Kerney RC .30 .75
153 Chris McAlister RC .30 .75
154 Peerless Price RC .30 .75
155 Antoine Winfield RC .30 .75
156 D'Wayne Bates RC .30 .75
157 Cade McNown RC .30 .75
158 Akili Smith RC .30 .75
159 Rahim Abdullah RC .30 .75
160 Tim Couch RC .40 1.00
161 Kevin Johnson RC .40 1.00
162 Ebenezer Ekuban RC .30 .75
163 Dat Nguyen RC .50 1.25
164 Al Wilson RC .50 1.25
165 Chris Claiborne RC .30 .75
166 Sedrick Irvin RC .30 .75
167 Antuan Edwards RC .30 .75
168 Aaron Brooks RC .40 1.00
169 De'Mond Parker RC .30 .75
170 Edgerrin James RC .50 1.25
171 Fernando Bryant RC .30 .75
172 Mike Cloud RC .30 .75
173 John Tait RC .30 .75
174 Cecil Collins RC .30 .75
175 James Johnson RC .30 .75
176 Rob Konrad RC .30 .75
177 Daunte Culpepper RC .50 1.25
178 Jim Kleinsasser RC .50 1.25
179 Brock Huard RC .30 .75
180 Michael Bishop RC .40 1.00
181 Kevin Faulk RC .30 .75
182 Andy Katzenmoyer RC .40 1.00
183 Ricky Williams RC .50 1.25
184 Joe Montgomery RC .30 .75
186 Troy Edwards RC .30 .75
187 Amos Zereoue RC .30 .75
188 Joe Germaine RC .40 1.00
189 Torry Holt RC .60 1.50
190 Jermaine Fazande RC .30 .75
191 Reggie McGrew RC .30 .75
192 Karsten Bailey RC .30 .75
193 Lamar King RC .30 .75
194 Autry Denson RC .30 .75
195 Martin Gramatica RC .30 .75
196 Shaun King RC .30 .75
197 Darnell McDonald RC .30 .75
198 Anthony McFarland RC .40 1.00
199 Jevon Kearse RC .40 1.00
200 Champ Bailey RC .60 1.50
201 Kurt Warner/500 RC 40.00 80.00
201PG Kurt Warner Promo Gold 5.00 12.00
201PS Kurt Warner Promo Silver 5.00 12.00

1999 Collector's Edge First Place Galvanized

COMPLETE SET (200) 200.00 400.00
*1-150 VETS/500: 2X TO 5X BASIC CARDS
1-150 VETERAN PRINT RUN 500
*151-200 ROOKIES/100: 2.5X TO 6X
151-200 ROOKIE PRINT RUN 100

1999 Collector's Edge First Place Gold Ingot

COMPLETE SET (200) 40.00 80.00
*1-150 VETS: .8X TO 2X BASIC CARDS
*151-200 ROOKIES: .6X TO 1.5X
ONE GOLD INGOT PER PACK

1999 Collector's Edge First Place HoloGold

*1-150 VETS/50: 10X TO 25X BASIC CARDS
1-150 VETERAN PRINT RUN 50
*151-200 ROOKIES/10: 15X TO 40X
151-200 ROOKIE PRINT RUN 10

1999 Collector's Edge First Place Adrenalin

Randomly inserted in packs, this 20-card set features 20 high impact NFL players printed on clear vinyl card-stock. Each card is numbered out of 1000 and card backs carry an "A" prefix.

COMPLETE SET (20) 50.00 100.00
STATED PRINT RUN 1000 SERIAL #'d SETS
A1 Jake Plummer 2.00 5.00
A2 Jamal Anderson 2.00 5.00
A3 Eric Moulds 2.00 5.00
A4 Emmitt Smith 4.00 10.00
A5 Terrell Davis 2.00 5.00
A6 Barry Sanders 6.00 15.00
A7 Brett Favre 6.00 15.00
A8 Antonio Freeman 2.00 5.00
A9 Peyton Manning 5.00 12.00
A10 Mark Brunell 2.00 5.00
A11 Fred Taylor 2.00 5.00
A12 Dan Marino 6.00 15.00
A13 Cris Carter 2.00 5.00
A14 Randy Moss 4.00 10.00
A15 Keyshawn Johnson 2.00 5.00
A16 Curtis Martin 2.00 5.00
A17 Jerome Bettis 2.00 5.00
A18 Terrell Owens 2.00 5.00
A19 Joey Galloway 2.00 5.00
A20 Eddie George 2.00 5.00

1999 Collector's Edge First Place Excalibur

Cards from this set were distributed across three brands of 1999 Collector's Edge football products: Odyssey, First Place and Masters. The 9-cards inserted into First Place were randomly seeded at the rate of 1:24 packs. Note that the Favre card was inserted in both First Place and Masters and that no #23 Jake Plummer was released as a single card through packs. However, a 25-card uncut sheet was later released as a wrapper redemption at Edge events that did include the Jake Plummer card. We've priced the uncut sheet below. Some copies of the Jake Plummer card did surface after Edge ceased its card operations.

COMPLETE SET (9) 25.00 50.00
STATED ODDS 1:24
X2 Torry Holt 2.50 6.00
X5 Edgerrin James 4.00 10.00
X6 Brett Favre 5.00 12.00
X13 Peyton Manning 4.00 10.00
X17 Randy Moss 3.00 8.00
X19 Terrell Davis 1.50 4.00
X20 Mark Brunell 1.50 4.00
X22 Eddie George 1.50 4.00
X24 Doug Flutie 1.50 4.00
S1 Uncut Sheet 15.00 40.00

1999 Collector's Edge First Place Future Legends

Randomly inserted in packs at the rate of one in six, this 20-card set features some of the hottest rookies on holographic foil card stock. Card backs carry an "FL" prefix.

COMPLETE SET (20) 15.00 40.00
STATED ODDS 1:6
FL1 Tim Couch .60 1.50
FL2 Donovan McNabb 3.00 8.00
FL3 Akili Smith .60 1.50
FL4 Edgerrin James 2.50 6.00
FL5 Ricky Williams 1.25 3.00
FL6 Torry Holt 1.50 4.00
FL7 Champ Bailey .75 2.00
FL8 David Boston .60 1.50
FL9 Daunte Culpepper 2.50 6.00
FL10 Cade McNown .60 1.50
FL11 Troy Edwards .60 1.50
FL12 Chris Claiborne .40 1.00
FL13 Jevon Kearse .75 2.00
FL14 Shaun King .60 1.50
FL15 Kevin Faulk .60 1.50
FL16 James Johnson .60 1.50
FL17 Peerless Price .60 1.50
FL18 Kevin Johnson .60 1.50
FL19 Brock Huard .60 1.50
FL20 Joe Germaine .60 1.50

1999 Collector's Edge First Place Loud and Proud

Randomly inserted in packs at one in 12, this 20-card set showcases top stars of the NFL with intense action shots. Cards fronts are all holo-foil, while card backs carry an "LP" prefix.

COMPLETE SET (20) 25.00 50.00
STATED ODDS 1:12
LP1 Jamal Anderson 1.00 2.50
LP2 Emmitt Smith 2.00 5.00
LP3 Terrell Davis 1.00 2.50
LP4 Barry Sanders 3.00 8.00
LP5 Fred Taylor 1.00 2.50
LP6 Randy Moss 2.50 6.00
LP7 Antonio Freeman 1.00 2.50
LP8 Curtis Martin 1.00 2.50
LP9 Terrell Owens 1.00 2.50
LP10 Eddie George 1.00 2.50
LP11 Dan Marino 3.00 8.00
LP12 Brett Favre 3.00 8.00
LP13 Jerry Rice 2.00 5.00
LP14 Steve Young 1.25 3.00
LP15 Doug Flutie 1.00 2.50
LP16 Jake Plummer .60 1.50
LP17 Troy Aikman 2.00 5.00
LP18 Mark Brunell 1.00 2.50
LP19 Jon Kitna 1.00 2.50
LP20 Charlie Batch 1.00 2.50

1999 Collector's Edge First Place Pro Signature Authentics

Randomly inserted in packs at the rate of one in 24, this set

or purple ink autographs were the base set, blue ink autographs were hand serial numbered out of 40, and red ink autographs were hand sequentially numbered out of 10. Some were issued via mail redemption cards in packs. The unnumbered cards are listed alphabetically below.
STATED ODDS 1:24
*BLUE AU/40: 1X TO 2.5X BLACK AU
1 Rahim Abdullah 3.00 8.00
2 Kimble Anders 4.00 10.00
3 Dre Bly 3.00 8.00
4 David Boston 4.00 10.00
5 Cuncho Brown 3.00 8.00
6 Gary Brown purple/450 4.00 10.00
7 Ray Buchanan 3.00 8.00
8 Tim Couch 5.00 12.00
9 Autry Denson 3.00 8.00
10 Jared DeVries 3.00 8.00
11 Bobby Engram 4.00 10.00
12 Terry Fair 3.00 8.00
13 Kevin Faulk 4.00 10.00
14 Joey Galloway 4.00 10.00
15 Rich Gannon 5.00 12.00
16 Marvin Harrison 5.00 12.00
17 Andre Hastings 3.00 8.00
18 Courtney Hawkins 3.00 8.00
19 Brock Huard 5.00 12.00
20 Edgerrin James 10.00 25.00
22 Chris McAlister 4.00 10.00
23 Keenan McCardell 5.00 12.00
24 Donovan McNabb 15.00 40.00
25 Eric Moulds 5.00 12.00
26 Adrian Murrell 3.00 8.00
27 Dat Nguyen purple 4.00 10.00
28 Andre Reed 5.00 12.00
29 Frank Sanders 4.00 10.00
30 Jimmy Smith 5.00 12.00
31 Akili Smith 4.00 10.00
32 Duce Staley 5.00 12.00
33 Craig Yeast 4.00 10.00

1999 Collector's Edge First Place Rookie Game Gear

Randomly seeded in packs, this 10-card set features top rookies with swatches of game-used memorabilia coupled with the players signature. Each hobby pack version of the cards was sequentially numbered to 500. A retail pack Hologold version of six cards was produced without the serial numbering. Also, a "Preview" version of some cards was also produced with each card in this version missing the serial numbering and containing the "Preview" title.
STATED PRINT RUN 500 SERIAL #'d SETS
*HOLOGOLD: .15X TO .4X BASIC INSERTS
*PREVIEWS: .2X TO .5X BASIC INSERTS
RG1 Tim Couch 5.00 12.00
RG2 Donovan McNabb 10.00 25.00
RG3 Akili Smith 5.00 12.00
RG4 Daunte Culpepper 6.00 15.00
RG5 Ricky Williams 6.00 15.00
RG6 Kevin Johnson 5.00 12.00
RG7 Cade McNown 5.00 12.00
RG8 Torry Holt 7.50 20.00
RG9 Champ Bailey 5.00 12.00
RG10 David Boston 5.00 12.00

1999 Collector's Edge First Place Successors

Randomly inserted in packs at the rate of one in 12, this 15-card set doubles top rookies and top veterans of the same position on each card. Card fronts are all holofoil, and feature a silhouette of the veteran in the background and a full color action photo of the rookie in the foreground. Card backs carry an "S" prefix.
COMPLETE SET (15) 30.00 60.00
STATED ODDS 1.12
S1 D.Boston 1.00 2.50
C.Carter
S2 P.Price 1.25 3.00
E.Moulds
S3 C.McNown 3.00 8.00
B.Favre
S4 A.Smith 1.00 2.50
C.Batch
S5 T.Couch 4.00 10.00
P.Manning
S6 K.Johnson 1.00 2.50
J.Galloway
S7 E.James 4.00 10.00
E.Smith
S8 J.Johnson 1.00 2.50
C.Martin
S9 D.Culpeppor 4.00 10.00
D.Marino
S10 K.Faulk 3.00 8.00
B.Sanders
S11 R.Williams 1.50 4.00
M.Faulk
S12 D.McNabb 3.00 8.00
S.Young
S13 T.Edwards 1.00 2.50
K.Johnson
S14 T.Holt 2.50 6.00
J.Rice
S15 S.King 1.00 2.50
J.Plummer

1999 Collector's Edge Fury Previews

This set was released as a Preview of the 1999 Collector's Edge Fury base set. Each card is essentially a parallel version of the base set card with the player's initials as the card number along with the word "preview" on the cardbacks.
COMPLETE SET (10) 6.00 15.00
BF Brett Favre 1.20 3.00
CC Cris Carter .40 1.00
DM Dan Marino 1.20 3.00
JA Jamal Anderson .40 1.00
JB Jerome Bettis .40 1.00
PM Peyton Manning 1.20 3.00
RE Robert Edwards .25 .60
RM Randy Moss 1.20 3.00
TD Terrell Davis .80 2.00
WD Warrick Dunn .40 1.00

1999 Collector's Edge Fury

The 1999 Collector's Edge Fury set was issued in one series for a total of 200 cards. The fronts feature color action photos of NFL stars and rookies appearing for the first time in their NFL uniforms. The backs carry player information and career statistics.
COMPLETE SET (200) 15.00 40.00
1 Checklist Card 1 .10 .30
2 Checklist Card 2 .10 .30
3 Karim Abdul-Jabbar .20 .50
4 Troy Aikman .40 1.00
5 Derrick Alexander WR .20 .50
6 Mike Alstott .20 .50
7 Jamal Anderson .25 .60
8 Reidel Anthony .20 .50
9 Tiki Barber .25 .60
10 Charlie Batch .20 .50
11 Edgar Bennett .25 .60
12 Jerome Bettis .30 .75
13 Steve Beuerlein .25 .60
14 Tim Biakabutuka .25 .60
15 Jeff Blake .25 .60
16 Drew Bledsoe .25 .60
17 Bubby Brister .20 .50
18 Robert Brooks .25 .60
19 Gary Brown .20 .50
20 Tim Brown .30 .75
21 Isaac Bruce .30 .75
22 Mark Brunell .25 .60
23 Chris Calloway .20 .50
24 Cris Carter .30 .75
25 Larry Centers .20 .50
26 Chris Chandler .25 .60
27 Wayne Chrebet .20 .60
28 Cam Cleeland .20 .50
29 Kerry Collins .20 .50
30 Curtis Conway .25 .60
31 Germane Crowell .20 .50
32 Randall Cunningham .25 .60
33 Terrell Davis .25 .60
34 Koy Detmer .20 .50
35 Ty Detmer .20 .50
36 Trent Dilfer .20 .50
37 Corey Dillon .20 .50
38 Warrick Dunn .20 .50
39 Tim Dwight .25 .60
40 Kevin Dyson .20 .50
41 John Elway .50 1.25
42 Bobby Engram .20 .50
43 Curtis Enis .20 .50
44 Terry Fair .20 .50
45 Marshall Faulk .25 .60
46 Brett Favre 1.50 4.00
47 Doug Flutie .30 .75
48 Antonio Freeman .25 .60
49 Joey Galloway .25 .60
50 Rich Gannon .25 .60
51 Eddie George .25 .60
52 Jeff George .20 .50
53 Terry Glenn .25 .60
54 Elvis Grbac .20 .50
55 Ahman Green .25 .60
56 Jacquez Green .20 .50
57 Trent Green .20 .50
58 Kevin Greene .30 .75
59 Brian Griese .20 .50
60 Az-Zahir Hakim .20 .50
61 Jim Harbaugh .25 .60
62 Marvin Harrison .25 .60
63 Courtney Hawkins .20 .50
64 Garrison Hearst .20 .50
65 Ike Hilliard .20 .50
66 Billy Joe Hobert .20 .50
67 Priest Holmes .20 .50
68 Michael Irvin .30 .75
69 Rocket Ismail .25 .60
70 Shawn Jefferson .20 .50
71 James Jett .20 .50
72 Brad Johnson .25 .60
73 Charles Johnson .20 .50
74 Keyshawn Johnson .25 .60
75 Pat Johnson .20 .50
76 Joe Jurevicius .20 .50
77 Napoleon Kaufman .20 .50
78 Eddie Kennison .25 .60
79 Terry Kirby .20 .50
80 Jon Kitna .20 .50
81 Erik Kramer .25 .60
82 Fred Lane .20 .50
83 Ty Law .30 .75
84 Ryan Leaf .25 .60
85 Amp Lee .20 .50
86 Dorsey Levens .25 .60
87 Jermaine Lewis .20 .50
88 Sam Madison .20 .50
89 Peyton Manning 1.00 2.50
90 Dan Marino .60 1.50
91 Curtis Martin .25 .60
92 Tony Martin .25 .60
93 Terance Mathis .20 .50
94 Ed McCaffrey .25 .60
95 Keenan McCardell .25 .60
96 O.J. McDuffie .25 .60
97 Steve McNair .25 .60
98 Natrone Means .25 .60
99 Herman Moore .25 .60
100 Rob Moore .20 .50
101 Byron Bam Morris .20 .50
102 Johnnie Morton .25 .60
103 Randy Moss .25 .60
104 Eric Moulds .20 .50
105 Muhsin Muhammad .20 .50
106 Adrian Murrell .20 .50
107 Terrell Owens .25 .60
108 Jerome Pathon .20 .50
109 Carl Pickens .25 .60
110 Jake Plummer .20 .50
111 Andre Reed .30 .75
112 Jake Reed .25 .60
113 Jerry Rice .75 2.00
114 Mikhael Ricks .20 .50
115 Andre Rison .25 .60
116 Barry Sanders .50 1.25
117 Deion Sanders .25 .60
118 Frank Sanders .20 .50
119 O.J. Santiago .20 .50
120 Darnay Scott .20 .50
121 Junior Seau .25 .60
122 Shannon Sharpe .25 .60
123 Leslie Shepherd .20 .50
124 Antowain Smith .20 .50
125 Bruce Smith .25 .60
126 Emmitt Smith .50 1.25
127 Jimmy Smith .25 .60
128 Robert Smith .20 .50
129 Rod Smith .25 .60
130 Chris Spielman .25 .60
131 Takeo Spikes .20 .50
132 Duce Staley .20 .50
133 Kordell Stewart .20 .50
134 Bryan Still .20 .50
135 J.J. Stokes .20 .50
136 Fred Taylor .20 .50
137 Vinny Testaverde .20 .50
138 Yancey Thigpen .20 .50
139 Thurman Thomas .25 .60
140 Zach Thomas .25 .60
141 Amani Toomer .20 .50
142 Hines Ward .25 .60
143 Chris Warren .25 .60
144 Ricky Watters .25 .60
145 Michael Westbrook .20 .50
146 Alvis Whitted .20 .50
147 Charles Woodson .30 .75
148 Rod Woodson .30 .75
149 Frank Wycheck .25 .60
150 Steve Young .40 1.00
151 Rahim Abdullah RC .30 .75
152 Champ Bailey RC .60 1.50
153 D'Wayne Bates RC .30 .75
154 Michael Bishop RC .40 1.00
155 Dre Bly RC .50 1.25
156 David Boston RC .30 .75
157 Fernando Bryant RC .30 .75
158 Chris Claiborne RC .30 .75
159 Mike Cloud RC .30 .75
160 Cecil Collins RC .30 .75
161 Tim Couch RC .40 1.00
162 Daunte Culpepper RC .50 1.25
163 Antuan Edwards RC .30 .75
164 Troy Edwards RC .30 .75
165 Ebenezer Ekuban RC .30 .75
166 Kevin Faulk RC .30 .75
167 Joe Germaine RC .40 1.00
168 Aaron Gibson RC .30 .75
169 Martin Gramatica RC .30 .75
170 Torry Holt RC .60 1.50
171 Brock Huard RC .30 .75
172 Sedrick Irvin RC .30 .75
173 Edgerrin James RC .50 1.25
174 James Johnson RC .30 .75
175 Kevin Johnson RC .40 1.00
176 Andy Katzenmoyer RC .40 1.00
177 Jevon Kearse RC .40 1.00
178 Patrick Kerney RC .30 .75
179 Lamar King RC .30 .75
180 Shaun King RC .30 .75
181 Jim Kleinsasser RC .50 1.25
182 Rob Konrad RC .30 .75
183 Chris McAlister RC .30 .75
184 Anthony McFarland RC .40 1.00
185 Karsten Bailey RC .30 .75
186 Donovan McNabb RC 2.50 6.00
187 Cade McNown RC .30 .75
188 Joe Montgomery RC .30 .75
189 Dat Nguyen RC .50 1.25
190 Luke Petitgout RC .30 .75
191 Peerless Price RC .30 .75
192 Akili Smith RC .30 .75
193 Matt Stinchcomb RC .30 .75
194 John Tait RC .30 .75
195 Jermaine Fazande RC .30 .75
196 Ricky Williams RC .50 1.25
197 Al Wilson RC .50 1.25
198 Antoine Winfield RC .30 .75
199 Damien Woody RC .30 .75
200 Amos Zereoue RC .30 .75

1999 Collector's Edge Fury Galvanized

COMPLETE SET (200) 200.00 400.00
*1-150 VETS/500: 2X TO 5X BASIC CARDS
1-150 VETERAN PRINT RUN 500
*151-200 ROOKIES/100: 2.5X TO 6X
151-200 ROOKIE PRINT RUN 100
*PREVIEW VETS: .3X TO .8X BASIC CARDS
*PREVIEW ROOKIES: .2X TO .5X BASIC RC

1999 Collector's Edge Fury Gold Ingot

COMPLETE SET (200) 50.00 100.00
*1-150 VETS: .8X TO 2X BASIC CARDS
*151-200 ROOKIES: .6X TO 1.5X
ONE PER PACK

1999 Collector's Edge Fury HoloGold

*1-150 VETS/50: 10X TO 25X BASIC CARDS
1-150 VETERAN PRINT RUN 50
*151-200 ROOKIES/10: 15X TO 40X
151-200 ROOKIE PRINT RUN 10

1999 Collector's Edge Fury Extreme Team

Randomly inserted into packs at the rate of one in 24, this 10-card set features color action photos of the game's biggest stars printed on micro-etched gold holographic foil board.
COMPLETE SET (10) 25.00 60.00
STATED ODDS 1:24
E1 Keyshawn Johnson 2.00 5.00
E2 Emmitt Smith 4.00 10.00
E3 John Elway 6.00 15.00
E4 Doug Flutie 2.00 5.00
E5 Jamal Anderson 2.00 5.00
E6 Brett Favre 6.00 15.00
E7 Peyton Manning 6.00 15.00
E8 Fred Taylor 2.00 5.00
E9 Dan Marino 6.00 15.00
E10 Randy Moss 5.00 12.00

1999 Collector's Edge Fury Fast and Furious

Randomly inserted into packs, this 25-card set features color action photos of some of the biggest stars in football printed on plastic card stock with foil stamping. Each card is sequentially numbered out of 500.
COMPLETE SET (25) 40.00 100.00
STATED PRINT RUN 500 SERIAL #'d SETS
1 Jake Plummer 1.25 3.00
2 Jamal Anderson 2.00 5.00
3 Eric Moulds 2.00 5.00
4 Curtis Enis .75 2.00
5 Emmitt Smith 4.00 10.00
6 Deion Sanders 2.00 5.00
7 Terrell Davis 2.00 5.00
8 Barry Sanders 6.00 15.00
9 Herman Moore 1.25 3.00
10 Charlie Batch 2.00 5.00
11 Marshall Faulk 2.50 6.00
12 Mark Brunell 2.00 5.00
13 Fred Taylor 2.00 5.00
14 Randy Moss 5.00 12.00
15 Cris Carter 2.00 5.00
16 Robert Edwards .75 2.00
17 Keyshawn Johnson 2.00 5.00
18 Curtis Martin 2.00 5.00
19 Charles Woodson 2.00 5.00
20 Jerome Bettis 2.00 5.00
21 Kordell Stewart 1.25 3.00
22 Steve Young 2.50 6.00
23 Jerry Rice 4.00 10.00
24 Warrick Dunn 2.00 5.00
25 Eddie George 2.00 5.00

1999 Collector's Edge Fury Forerunners

Randomly inserted into packs at the rate of one in eight, this 15-card set features action color photos of some of the most powerful and talented running backs printed on holographic foil board with foil stamping.
COMPLETE SET (15) 20.00 50.00
STATED ODDS 1:8
F1 Jamal Anderson 1.50 4.00
F2 Curtis Enis .60 1.50
F3 Corey Dillon 1.50 4.00
F4 Emmitt Smith 3.00 8.00
F5 Barry Sanders 5.00 12.00
F6 Terrell Davis 1.50 4.00
F7 Marshall Faulk 2.00 5.00
F8 Fred Taylor 1.50 4.00
F9 Robert Smith 1.50 4.00
F10 Curtis Martin 1.50 4.00
F11 Jerome Bettis 1.50 4.00
F12 Garrison Hearst 1.00 2.50
F13 Warrick Dunn 1.50 4.00
F14 Eddie George 1.50 4.00
F15 Ricky Watters 1.00 2.50

1999 Collector's Edge Fury Game Ball

Randomly inserted into packs at the rate of one in 24, this 43-card set features action color photos of some of the biggest stars in the league printed on cards with an actual piece of a game-used football embedded in the card.
COMPLETE SET (43) 300.00 600.00
STATED ODDS 1:24
AF Antonio Freeman 6.00 15.00
AM Adrian Murrell 3.00 8.00
AS Antowain Smith 6.00 15.00
BF Brett Favre 20.00 50.00
BS Barry Sanders 20.00 50.00
CB Charlie Batch 6.00 15.00
CC Cris Carter 6.00 15.00
CD Corey Dillon 6.00 15.00
CE Curtis Enis 3.00 8.00
CM Curtis Martin 6.00 15.00
CP Carl Pickens 3.00 8.00
DL Dorsey Levens 6.00 15.00
DS Deion Sanders 6.00 15.00
EG Eddie George 6.00 15.00
ES Emmitt Smith 12.50 30.00
FT Fred Taylor 6.00 15.00
GH Garrison Hearst 3.00 8.00
HM Herman Moore 6.00 15.00
JB Jerome Bettis 6.00 15.00
JE John Elway 20.00 50.00
JG Joey Galloway 6.00 15.00
JP Jake Plummer 6.00 15.00
JR Jerry Rice 12.50 30.00
KS Kordell Stewart 6.00 15.00
MA Mike Alstott 6.00 15.00
MB Mark Brunell 6.00 15.00
MF Marshall Faulk 10.00 25.00
MI Michael Irvin 6.00 15.00
NK Napoleon Kaufman 6.00 15.00
NM Natrone Means 3.00 8.00
PM Peyton Manning 15.00 40.00
RJ Rob Johnson 3.00 8.00
RL Ryan Leaf 6.00 15.00
RM Randy Moss 12.50 30.00
RS Rod Smith 0.00 0.00
SM Steve McNair 6.00 15.00
SS Shannon Sharpe 3.00 8.00
SY Steve Young 7.50 20.00
TA Troy Aikman 12.50 30.00
TD Terrell Davis 6.00 15.00
TO Terrell Owens 6.00 15.00
WD Warrick Dunn 6.00 15.00
WM Warren Moon 6.00 15.00

1999 Collector's Edge Fury Heir Force

Randomly inserted into packs at the rate of one in six, this 20-card set features color action photos of top rookies printed on holographic foil board with foil stamping.
COMPLETE SET (20) 20.00 50.00
STATED ODDS 1:6
HF1 Rahim Abdullah .50 1.25
HF2 Champ Bailey .75 2.00
HF3 D'Wayne Bates .50 1.25
HF4 Michael Bishop .60 1.50
HF5 David Boston .60 1.50
HF6 Chris Claiborne .50 1.25
HF7 Tim Couch .60 1.50
HF8 Daunte Culpepper 2.50 6.00
HF9 Kevin Faulk .60 1.50
HF10 Torry Holt 1.50 4.00
HF11 Brock Huard .60 1.50
HF12 Edgerrin James 2.50 6.00
HF13 Andy Katzenmoyer .60 1.50
HF14 Shaun King .60 1.50
HF15 Rob Konrad .60 1.50
HF16 Donovan McNabb 3.00 8.00
HF17 Cade McNown .60 1.50
HF18 Peerless Price .60 1.50
HF19 Akili Smith .50 1.25
HF20 Ricky Williams 1.25 3.00

1999 Collector's Edge Fury Xplosive

Randomly inserted into packs at the rate of one in 12, this 20-card set features color action photos of top stars printed on micro-etched holofoil cards with foil stamping.
COMPLETE SET (20) 40.00 100.00
STATED ODDS 1:12
1 Jake Plummer 1.25 3.00
2 Doug Flutie 2.00 5.00
3 Eric Moulds 2.00 5.00
4 Troy Aikman 4.00 10.00
5 John Elway 6.00 15.00
6 Charlie Batch 2.00 5.00
7 Herman Moore 1.25 3.00
8 Brett Favre 6.00 15.00
9 Antonio Freeman 2.00 5.00
10 Peyton Manning 6.00 15.00
11 Mark Brunell 2.00 5.00
12 Dan Marino 6.00 15.00
13 Randy Moss 5.00 12.00
14 Drew Bledsoe 2.50 6.00
15 Keyshawn Johnson 2.00 5.00
16 Vinny Testaverde 1.25 3.00
17 Kordell Stewart 1.25 3.00
18 Terrell Owens 2.00 5.00
19 Jerry Rice 4.00 10.00
20 Steve Young 2.50 6.00

1997 Collector's Edge Masters Promos

COMPLETE SET (3) 1.25 3.00

1997 Collector's Edge Masters

The 1997 Collector's Edge Masters set was issued in one series totaling 270 cards and was distributed in six-card packs with a suggested retail price of $3.49. The set contains color photos of 240 top players in the NFL printed on metalized card stock, for the hobby version, with silver texture or regular white paper stock, for the retail version, plus 30 team flag cards which were inserted randomly at the rate of one every three packs. A collector could send in the Flag Card for either Green Bay or New England plus one Flag Card for each opponent beaten by these teams during the regular and post-season (one Flag Card per game) and receive a foil stamped limited edition team set of the Packers or the Patriots. The card wrappers carried the rules and details for this limited offer.
COMPLETE SET (270) 15.00 40.00
1 Cardinals Flag .20 .50
2 Larry Centers .25 .60
3 Rob Moore .25 .60
4 Frank Sanders .25 .60
5 Eric Swann .15 .40
6 Falcons Flag .20 .50
7 Morten Andersen UER .15 .40
8 Bert Emanuel .25 .60
9 Jeff George .25 .60
10 Craig Heyward .15 .40
11 Terance Mathis .25 .60
12 Clay Matthews .15 .40
13 Eric Metcalf .25 .60
14 Ravens Flag .20 .50
15 Rob Burnett .15 .40
16 Leroy Hoard .15 .40
17 Ernest Hunter .15 .40
18 Michael Jackson .25 .60
19 Stevon Moore .15 .40
20 Anthony Pleasant .15 .40
21 Vinny Testaverde .25 .60
22 Eric Zeier .25 .60
23 Bills Flag .20 .50
24 Todd Collins .15 .40
25 Russell Copeland .15 .40
26 Quinn Early .15 .40
27 Jim Kelly .40 1.00
28 Bryce Paup .15 .40
29 Andre Reed .25 .60
30 Bruce Smith .25 .60
31 Panthers Flag .20 .50
32 Steve Beuerlein .25 .60
33 Mark Carrier WR .15 .40
34 Kerry Collins .40 1.00
35 Willie Green .15 .40
36 Kevin Greene .25 .60
37 Eric Guliford .15 .40
38 Brett Maxie .15 .40
39 Tim McKyer .15 .40
40 Derrick Moore .15 .40
41 Bears Flag .20 .50
42 Curtis Conway .25 .60
43 Bryan Cox .15 .40
44 Jim Flanigan .15 .40
45 Robert Green .15 .40
46 Erik Kramer .15 .40
47 Dave Krieg .15 .40
48 Rashaan Salaam .15 .40
49 Alonzo Spellman .15 .40
50 Donnell Woolford .15 .40
51 Chris Zorich .15 .40
52 Bengals Flag .20 .50
53 Eric Bieniemy .15 .40
54 Jeff Blake .25 .60
55 Ki-Jana Carter .15 .40
56 John Copeland .15 .40
57 Garrison Hearst .25 .60
58 Tony McGee .15 .40
59 Carl Pickens .25 .60
60 Darnay Scott .25 .60
61 Bracy Walker .15 .40
62 Dan Wilkinson .15 .40
63 Cowboys Flag .20 .50
64 Troy Aikman .75 2.00
65 Bill Bates .25 .60
66 Shante Carver .15 .40
67 Michael Irvin .40 1.00
68 Daryl Johnston .25 .60
69 Jay Novacek .15 .40
70 Deion Sanders .40 1.00
71 Emmitt Smith 1.50 3.00
72 Herschel Walker .25 .60
73 Sherman Williams .15 .40
74 Broncos Flag .20 .50
75 Terrell Davis .50 1.25
76 John Elway 1.50 4.00
77 Ed McCaffrey .25 .60
78 Anthony Miller .15 .40
79 Michael Dean Perry .15 .40
80 Shannon Sharpe .25 .60
81 Mike Sherrard .15 .40
82 Lions Flag .20 .50
83 Scott Mitchell .25 .60
84 Glyn Milburn .15 .40
85 Herman Moore .25 .60
86 Johnnie Morton .25 .60
87 Brett Perriman .15 .40
88 Barry Sanders 1.25 3.00
89 Tracy Scroggins .15 .40
90 Packers Flag .20 .50
91 Edgar Bennett .25 .60
92 Robert Brooks .25 .60
93 Santana Dotson .15 .40
94 Brett Favre 2.00 4.00
95 Dorsey Levens .40 1.00
96 Craig Newsome .15 .40
97 Wayne Simmons .15 .40
98 Reggie White .40 1.00
99 Oilers Flag .20 .50
100 Chris Chandler .25 .60
101 Anthony Cook .15 .40
102 Willie Davis .15 .40
103 Mel Gray .15 .40
104 Ronnie Harmon .15 .40
105 Darryll Lewis .15 .40
106 Steve McNair .50 1.25
107 Todd McNair .15 .40
108 Rodney Thomas .15 .40
109 Colts Flag .20 .50
110 Trev Alberts .15 .40
111 Tony Bennett .15 .40
112 Quentin Coryatt .15 .40
113 Sean Dawkins .15 .40
114 Ken Dilger .15 .40
115 Marshall Faulk .50 1.25
116 Jim Harbaugh UER .25 .60
117 Ronald Humphrey .15 .40
118 Floyd Turner .15 .40
119 Jaguars Flag .20 .50
120 Tony Boselli .15 .40
121 Mark Brunell .50 1.25
122 Willie Jackson .15 .40
123 Jeff Lageman .15 .40
124 Natrone Means .25 .60
125 Andre Rison .25 .60
126 James O.Stewart .25 .60
127 Cedric Tillman .15 .40
128 Chiefs Flag .20 .50
129 Marcus Allen .40 1.00
130 Kimble Anders .25 .60
131 Steve Bono .25 .60
132 Dale Carter .15 .40
133 Lake Dawson .15 .40
134 Dan Saleaumua .15 .40
135 Neil Smith .25 .60
136 Derrick Thomas .40 1.00
137 Tamarick Vanover .25 .60
138 Dolphins Flag .20 .50
139 Fred Barnett .15 .40
140 Steve Emtman .15 .40
141 Eric Green .15 .40
142 Dan Marino 1.50 4.00
143 O.J. McDuffie .25 .60
144 Bernie Parmalee .15 .40
145 Vikings Flag .20 .50
146 Cris Carter .40 1.00
147 Jack Del Rio .15 .40
148 Qadry Ismail .25 .60
149 Amp Lee .15 .40
150 Warren Moon .40 1.00
151 John Randle .25 .60
152 Jake Reed .25 .60
153 Robert Smith .25 .60
154 Patriots Flag .20 .50
155 Drew Bledsoe .50 1.25
156 Vincent Brisby .15 .40
157 Willie Clay .15 .40
158 Ben Coates .25 .60
159 Curtis Martin .50 1.25
160 Dave Meggett .15 .40
161 Will Moore .15 .40
162 Chris Slade .15 .40
163 Saints Flag .20 .50
164 Mario Bates .15 .40
165 Jim Everett .15 .40
166 Michael Haynes .15 .40
167 Tyrone Hughes .15 .40
168 Haywood Jeffires .15 .40
169 Wayne Martin .15 .40
170 Renaldo Turnbull .15 .40
171 Giants Flag .20 .50
172 Dave Brown .15 .40
173 Chris Calloway .15 .40
174 Rodney Hampton .25 .60
175 Michael Strahan .25 .60
176 Tyrone Wheatley .25 .60
177 Jets Flag .20 .50
178 Kyle Brady .15 .40
179 Wayne Chrebet .40 1.00
180 Hugh Douglas .15 .40
181 Jeff Graham .15 .40
182 Adrian Murrell .25 .60
183 Neil O'Donnell .25 .60
184 Raiders Flag .20 .50
185 Tim Brown .40 1.00
186 Aundray Bruce .15 .40
187 Andrew Glover .15 .40
188 Jeff Hostetler .15 .40
189 Napoleon Kaufman .40 1.00
190 Terry McDaniel .15 .40
191 Chester McGlockton .15 .40
192 Pat Swilling .15 .40
193 Harvey Williams .15 .40
194 Eagles Flag .20 .50
195 Randall Cunningham .40 1.00
196 Irving Fryar .25 .60
197 William Fuller .15 .40
198 Charlie Garner .25 .60
199 Andy Harmon .15 .40
200 Rodney Peete .15 .40
201 Mark Seay .15 .40
202 Troy Vincent .15 .40
203 Ricky Watters .25 .60
204 Calvin Williams .15 .40
205 Steelers Flag .20 .50
206 Jerome Bettis .40 1.00
207 Chad Brown .15 .40
208 Greg Lloyd .15 .40
209 Byron Bam Morris .15 .40
210 Erric Pegram .15 .40
211 Kordell Stewart .40 1.00
212 Yancey Thigpen .25 .60
213 Rod Woodson .25 .60
214 Chargers Flag .20 .50
215 Darren Bennett .15 .40
216 Marco Coleman .15 .40
217 Stan Humphries .25 .60
218 Tony Martin .25 .60
219 Junior Seau .40 1.00
220 49ers Flag .20 .50
221 Chris Doleman .15 .40
222 William Floyd .25 .60
223 Merton Hanks .15 .40
224 Brent Jones .15 .40
225 Terry Kirby .25 .60
226 Derek Loville .15 .40
227 Ken Norton Jr. .15 .40
228 Gary Plummer .15 .40
229 Jerry Rice .75 2.00
230 J.J. Stokes .25 .60
231 Dana Stubblefield .15 .40
232 John Taylor .15 .40
233 Bryant Young .15 .40
234 Steve Young .60 1.50
235 Seahawks Flag .20 .50
236 Brian Blades .15 .40
237 Joey Galloway .25 .60
238 Carlton Gray .15 .40
239 Cortez Kennedy .15 .40
240 Rick Mirer .15 .40
241 Chris Warren .25 .60
242 Rams Flag .20 .50
243 Isaac Bruce .40 1.00
244 Troy Drayton .15 .40
245 D'Marco Farr .15 .40
246 Harold Green .15 .40
247 Chris Miller .15 .40
248 Leslie O'Neal .15 .40
249 Roman Phifer .15 .40
250 Buccaneers Flag .20 .50
251 Trent Dilfer .40 1.00
252 Alvin Harper .15 .40
253 Jackie Harris .15 .40
254 John Lynch .25 .60
255 Hardy Nickerson .15 .40
256 Errict Rhett .15 .40
257 Warren Sapp .25 .60
258 Todd Scott .15 .40
259 Charles Wilson UER .15 .40
260 Redskins Flag .20 .50
261 Terry Allen .40 1.00
262 Bill Brooks .15 .40
263 Henry Ellard .15 .40
264 Gus Frerotte .15 .40
265 Sean Gilbert .15 .40
266 Ken Harvey .15 .40
267 Brian Mitchell .15 .40
268 Heath Shuler .15 .40
269 James Washington .15 .40
270 Michael Westbrook .25 .60

1997 Collector's Edge Masters Retail

COMPLETE SET (270) 15.00 40.00
*RETAIL: .4X TO 1X BASIC CARDS

1997 Collector's Edge Masters Crucibles

Randomly inserted in hobby packs only at a rate of one in six, this 25-card set features color photos of the top draft picks for the 1997 season. Only 3000 of each card were produced and are sequentially numbered.
COMPLETE SET (25) 30.00 60.00
STATED ODDS 1:6 HOBBY
STATED PRINT RUN 3000 SERIAL #'d SETS
1 Jake Plummer 2.50 6.00
2 Byron Hanspard .60 1.50
3 Peter Boulware 1.00 2.50
4 Jay Graham .60 1.50
5 Antowain Smith 1.50 4.00
6 Rae Carruth .40 1.00
7 Darnell Autry .60 1.50
8 Corey Dillon 2.50 6.00
9 Bryant Westbrook .40 1.00
10 Joey Kent 1.00 2.50
11 Kevin Lockett .60 1.50
12 Pat Barnes .60 1.50
13 Tony Gonzalez 2.50 6.00
14 Yatil Green .60 1.50
15 Danny Wuerffel 1.00 2.50
16 Troy Davis .60 1.50
17 Tiki Barber 4.00 10.00
18 Ike Hilliard 1.00 2.50
19 Leon Johnson .60 1.50
20 Darrell Russell .40 1.00
21 Jim Druckenmiller .60 1.50
22 Shawn Springs .60 1.50
23 Orlando Pace 1.00 2.50
24 Warrick Dunn 2.00 5.00
25 Reidel Anthony .60 1.50

1997 Collector's Edge Masters Night Games

Randomly inserted in packs at a rate of one in 20, this 25-card set features embossed color photos of the hottest players with foil printing that fit together to form a spectacular background.
COMPLETE SET (25) 125.00 250.00
STATED ODDS 1:20
STATED PRINT RUN 1500 SERIAL #'d SETS
*PRISM/250: .8X TO 2X BASIC INSERTS
PRISMS STATED ODDS 1:60
PRISMS PRINT RUN 250 SERIAL #'d SETS
1 Terry Glenn 3.00 8.00
2 Eddie George 3.00 8.00
3 Ricky Watters 2.00 5.00
4 Barry Sanders 10.00 25.00
5 Curtis Martin 4.00 10.00
6 Brett Favre 12.50 30.00
7 Emmitt Smith 10.00 25.00
8 John Elway 12.50 30.00
9 Keyshawn Johnson 3.00 8.00
10 Kordell Stewart 3.00 8.00
11 Vinny Testaverde 2.00 5.00
12 Kerry Collins 3.00 8.00
13 Terrell Davis 4.00 10.00
14 Karim Abdul-Jabbar 1.00 2.50
15 Drew Bledsoe 4.00 10.00
16 Antonio Freeman 2.00 5.00
17 Tony Banks 1.00 2.50
18 Jerry Rice 6.00 15.00
19 Mark Brunell 3.00 8.00
20 Mike Alstott 3.00 8.00
21 Napoleon Kaufman 1.00 2.50
22 Herman Moore 1.00 2.50
23 Terry Allen 2.00 5.00
24 Jerome Bettis 3.00 8.00
25 Dorsey Levens 1.00 2.50

1997 Collector's Edge Masters 1996 Rookies

Randomly inserted in retail packs only at a rate of one in eight, this 25-card set features color player photos of the top rookies in their team uniforms from the 1996 season with "96 Rookie Year" foil stamped in gold. Only 2000 sets were made and each card is sequentially numbered.
COMPLETE SET (25) 30.00 60.00
STATED ODDS 1:8 RETAIL
STATED PRINT RUN 2000 SERIAL #'d SETS
1 Simeon Rice 1.25 3.00
2 Jonathan Ogden .75 2.00
3 Eric Moulds 1.50 4.00
4 Tim Biakabutuka 1.25 3.00
5 Walt Harris .75 2.00
6 John Mobley .75 2.00
7 Stephen Davis 1.50 4.00
8 Derrick Mayes 1.25 3.00
9 Eddie George 2.00 5.00
10 Marvin Harrison 3.00 8.00
11 Kevin Hardy .75 2.00
12 Jerome Woods .75 2.00
13 Karim Abdul-Jabbar 1.50 4.00
14 Duane Clemons .75 2.00
15 Terry Glenn 1.50 4.00
16 Ricky Whittle .75 2.00
17 Amani Toomer 1.25 3.00
18 Keyshawn Johnson 1.50 4.00
19 Rickey Dudley 1.25 3.00
20 Bobby Hoying 1.25 3.00
21 Tony Banks 1.25 3.00
22 Bryan Still .75 2.00
23 Terrell Owens 3.00 8.00
24 Reggie Brown RBK .75 2.00
25 Mike Alstott 1.50 4.00

1997 Collector's Edge Masters Nitro

Each of these cards is essentially a parallel to its corresponding base Collector's Edge Masters card. The addition of a gold foil starburst logo was included at the bottom of the card front. They were randomly inserted in packs at a rate of one in eight.
COMPLETE SET (36) 40.00 80.00
STATED ODDS 1:8
2 Larry Centers 1.25 2.50
18 Michael Jackson 1.25 2.50
24 Todd Collins .75 1.50
30 Bruce Smith 1.25 2.50
34 Kerry Collins 2.00 4.00
36 Kevin Greene 1.25 2.50
59 Carl Pickens 1.25 2.50
64 Troy Aikman 4.00 8.00
71 Emmitt Smith 6.00 12.00
75 Terrell Davis 2.50 5.00
76 John Elway 8.00 15.00
85 Herman Moore 1.25 2.50
88 Barry Sanders 6.00 12.00
94 Brett Favre 8.00 15.00
98 Reggie White 2.00 4.00
106 Steve McNair 2.50 5.00
115 Jim Harbaugh 1.25 2.50
121 Mark Brunell 2.50 5.00
136 Derrick Thomas 2.00 4.00
137 Tamarick Vanover 1.25 2.50
142 Dan Marino 8.00 15.00
155 Drew Bledsoe 2.50 5.00
159 Curtis Martin 2.50 5.00
167 Tyrone Hughes .75 1.50
189 Napoleon Kaufman 2.00 4.00
203 Ricky Watters 1.25 2.50
206 Jerome Bettis 2.00 4.00
207 Chad Brown .75 1.50
211 Kordell Stewart 2.00 4.00
218 Tony Martin 1.25 2.50
229 Jerry Rice 4.00 8.00
234 Steve Young 3.00 6.00
237 Joey Galloway 1.25 2.50
243 Isaac Bruce 2.00 4.00
261 Terry Allen 2.00 4.00
264 Gus Frerotte .75 1.50

1997 Collector's Edge Masters Packers Super Bowl XXXI

This 25-card redemption set features color player photos of the Green Bay Packers championship team. They were released as prize cards for the Capture the Flag redemption program in 1997 Collector's Edge Masters. Only 5000-base sets (gold and silver foil card) were produced and each card was sequentially numbered. An all gold foil parallel set was issued as well with each card numbered of 1000 sets produced.
COMPLETE SET (25) 10.00 20.00
SET AVAILABLE VIA MAIL REDEMPTION
STATED PRINT RUN 5000 SERIAL #'d SETS
*GOLD FOILS: .6X TO 1.5X BASIC INSERTS
GOLDS PRINT RUN 1000 SERIAL #'d SETS
1 Edgar Bennett .25 .60
2 Mark Chmura .15 .40
3 Brett Favre 1.50 4.00
4 Dorsey Levens .40 1.00
5 Wayne Simmons .15 .40
6 Robert Brooks .25 .60
7 Sean Jones .15 .40
8 George Koonce .15 .40
9 Craig Newsome .15 .40
10 Reggie White .40 1.00
11 Desmond Howard .25 .60
12 Antonio Freeman .60 1.50
13 Brett Favre 1.50 4.00
14 Keith Jackson .25 .60
15 Andre Rison .25 .60
16 Eugene Robinson .15 .40
17 LeRoy Butler .15 .40
18 Don Beebe .25 .60
19 Derrick Mayes .15 .40
20 Gilbert Brown .15 .40
21 Santana Dotson .15 .40
22 Brett Favre 1.50 4.00
23 Reggie White .40 1.00
24 Desmond Howard .25 .60
25 Antonio Freeman .60 1.50

1997 Collector's Edge Masters Playoff Game Ball

Randomly inserted in packs at a rate of one in 72, this 19-card set features color images of two rival players printed on metallic card stock with an embedded medallion struck from an authentic NFL football used by the rivals in the 1996 playoffs. The backs carry the game notes. A Gold Logo parallel version of the regular set with gold foil stamping limited to 10 copies was also randomly inserted into packs. Collector's Edge later released a parallel version with a synthetic diamond embedded into each piece of game football through the Shop at Home network. A Holofoil version was released as well with each card being printed on Holofoil card stock instead of silver foil stock like the basic inserts. Finally, a Proof version (not yet priced) of the Holofoil cards was also printed minus the game ball swatch. The word "Proof" is printed on the otherwise blank cardbacks of this version.
COMPLETE SET (19) 300.00 600.00
STATED ODDS 1:72
*DIAMOND CARDS: .8X TO 2X BASIC INSERTS
*HOLOFOILS: .4X TO 1X BASIC INSERTS
*HOLOFOIL PROOFS: .2X TO .5X BASIC INSERTS
1 N.Means/T.Thomas 8.00 20.00
2 T.Boselli/B.Smith 6.00 15.00
3 J.Bettis/M.Faulk 10.00 25.00
4 K.Stewart/J.Harbaugh 5.00 12.00
5 N.Means/T.Davis 8.00 20.00
6 M.Brunell/J.Elway 20.00 50.00
7 C.Martin/J.Bettis 10.00 25.00
8 D.Bledsoe/M.Brunell 10.00 25.00
9 T.Glenn/K.McCardell 6.00 15.00
10 R.Watters/T.Kirby 5.00 12.00
11 K.Greene/R.White 6.00 15.00
12 J.Rice/I.Fryar 12.00 30.00
13 D.Levens/T.Kirby 5.00 12.00
14 B.Favre/S.Young 30.00 80.00
15 A.Rison/J.Rice 12.00 30.00
16 R.White/K.Norton Jr. 6.00 15.00
17 K.Collins/T.Aikman 12.00 30.00
18 K.Collins/B.Favre 25.00 60.00
19 M.Carrier/A.Freeman 5.00 12.00

1997 Collector's Edge Masters Radical Rivals

Randomly inserted in hobby packs only at the rate of one in 30, this 12-card set features color photos of two top NFL star rivals matched-up on a double thick metalized card. Only 1000 of each card were produced and are sequentially numbered.
COMPLETE SET (13) 100.00 200.00
STATED ODDS 1:30 HOBBY
STATED PRINT RUN 1000 SERIAL #'d SETS
1 E.Smith 12.50 30.00
E.George
2 B.Favre 12.50 30.00
K.Collins
3 J.Rice 10.00 25.00
A.Freeman

4 R.Watters 3.00 8.00
N.Kaufman
5 H.Moore 3.00 8.00
K.Johnson
6 D.Marino 12.50 30.00
J.Elway
7 J.Bettis 3.00 8.00
K.Abdul-Jabbar
8 I.Bruce 3.00 8.00
C.Pickens
9 B.Sanders 10.00 25.00
T.Allen
10 T.Glenn 5.00 12.00
J.Galloway
11 M.Brunell 6.00 15.00
S.Young
12 T.Davis 12.50 30.00
C.Martin
NNO Title Card CL .40 1.00

1997 Collector's Edge Masters Ripped

Randomly inserted in packs at a rate of one in 24, this 19-card set features 18 color player photos on cards 19-36 with the nineteenth card being an unnumbered checklist. This set was a completion of the 1996 Collector's Edge Ripped set, and the cards were numbered accordingly.

COMPLETE SET (19) 75.00 150.00
STATED ODDS 1:24 RET
19 Troy Aikman 6.00 15.00
20 Drew Bledsoe 4.00 10.00
21 Tim Brown 3.00 8.00
22 Mark Brunell 4.00 10.00
23 Cris Carter 3.00 8.00
24 Kerry Collins 3.00 8.00
25 Barry Sanders 10.00 25.00
26 Eddie George 3.00 8.00
27 Karim Abdul-Jabbar 3.00 8.00
28 Curtis Martin 4.00 10.00
29 Carl Pickens 2.00 5.00
30 Marshall Faulk 4.00 10.00
31 Rashaan Salaam 1.25 3.00
32 Deion Sanders 3.00 8.00
33 Emmitt Smith 10.00 25.00
34 Herman Moore 2.00 5.00
35 Ricky Watters 2.00 5.00
36 Terry Allen 3.00 8.00
NNO Checklist Card 1.25 3.00

1997 Collector's Edge Masters Super Bowl Game Ball

Randomly inserted in packs at a rate of one in 350, this six-card set features color photos printed on gold metallic stock with an embedded medallion struck from an authentic NFL football used by players in Super Bowl XXXI. Reportedly, only 250 of each card was produced. There was also a Silver Logo set, inserted randomly in packs that is distinguished by its silver foil stamping. Only one of these sets exist, and it is not priced due to its scarcity.

COMPLETE SET (6) 150.00 300.00
STATED ODDS 1:350 RETAIL
STATED PRINT RUN 250 SETS
*DIAMOND: .8X TO 2X BASIC INSERTS
1 B.Favre 40.00 100.00
D.Bledsoe
2 D.Levens 25.00 60.00
C.Martin
3 D.Howard 10.00 25.00
D.Meggett
4 A.Freeman 25.00 60.00
T.Glenn
5 K.Jackson 10.00 25.00
B.Coates
6 W.McGinest
R.White

1998 Collector's Edge Masters Previews

14 Priest Holmes GOLD 1.00 2.50
DB David Boston .40 1.00
66 Brett Favre 3.00 8.00
S124 Napoleon Kaufman .40 1.00
148 Jerry Rice 1.50 4.00
150 Steve Young .75 2.00
183 Peyton Manning 2.50 6.00
S171 Jamal Anderson .60 1.50
S189 Curtis Martin SM .75 2.00
S195 Jerry Rice SM 1.50 4.00

1998 Collector's Edge Masters

The 1998 Collector's Edge Masters set was issued in one series totalling 199-cards and distributed in three-card packs with a suggested retail price of $6.99. The fronts feature color action player photos printed on micro-etched silver foil and sequentially numbered to 5,000. Card number 28 was never released. Four different limited edition parallel sets were also produced.

COMPLETE SET (199) 75.00 200.00
1 Rob Moore .40 1.00
2 Adrian Murrell .40 1.00
3 Jake Plummer .60 1.50
4 Michael Pittman RC 1.50 3.00
5 Frank Sanders .40 1.00
6 Andre Wadsworth RC .75 2.00
7 Jamal Anderson .60 1.50
8 Chris Chandler .40 1.00
9 Tim Dwight RC 1.00 2.50
10 Tony Martin .40 1.00
11 Terance Mathis .40 1.00
12 Ken Oxendine RC .50 1.25
13 Jim Harbaugh .40 1.00
14 Priest Holmes RC 10.00 25.00
15 Michael Jackson .25 .60
16 Pat Johnson RC .75 2.00
17 Jermaine Lewis .40 1.00
18 Eric Zeier .40 1.00
19 Doug Flutie .60 1.50
20 Rob Johnson .40 1.00
21 Eric Moulds .60 1.50
22 Andre Reed .40 1.00
23 Antowain Smith .60 1.50
24 Bruce Smith .40 1.00
25 Thurman Thomas .60 1.50
26 Steve Beuerlein .40 1.00
27 Kevin Greene .40 1.00
29 Rocket Ismail .25 .60
30 Fred Lane .25 .60
31 Muhsin Muhammad .40 1.00
32 Edgar Bennett .25 .60
33 Curtis Conway .40 1.00
34 Bobby Engram .40 1.00
35 Curtis Enis RC .50 1.25
36 Erik Kramer .25 .60
37 Chris Penn .25 .60
38 Jeff Blake .40 1.00
39 Corey Dillon .60 1.50
40 Neil O'Donnell .40 1.00
41 Carl Pickens .40 1.00
42 Darnay Scott .40 1.00
43 Damon Gibson RC .50 1.25
44 Troy Aikman 1.25 3.00
45 Billy Davis .25 .60
46 Michael Irvin .60 1.50
47 Ernie Mills .25 .60
48 Deion Sanders .60 1.50
49 Emmitt Smith 2.00 5.00
50 Chris Warren .40 1.00
51 Bubby Brister .25 .60
52 Terrell Davis .60 1.50
53 John Elway 2.50 6.00
54 Brian Griese RC 2.00 5.00
55 Ed McCaffrey .40 1.00
56 Marcus Nash RC .50 1.25
57 Shannon Sharpe .40 1.00
58 Rod Smith .40 1.00
59 Charlie Batch RC 1.00 2.50
60 Germane Crowell RC .75 2.00
61 Scott Mitchell .40 1.00
62 Johnnie Morton .40 1.00
63 Herman Moore .40 1.00
64 Barry Sanders 2.00 5.00
65 Robert Brooks .40 1.00
66 Brett Favre 2.50 6.00
67 Antonio Freeman .60 1.50
68 Raymont Harris .25 .60
69 Dorsey Levens .60 1.50
70 Reggie White .60 1.50
71 Marshall Faulk .75 2.00
72 Marvin Harrison .60 1.50
73 Peyton Manning RC 10.00 25.00
74 Jerome Pathon RC 1.00 2.50
75 Tavian Banks RC .75 2.00
76 Mark Brunell .60 1.50
77 Keenan McCardell .40 1.00
78 Jimmy Smith .40 1.00
79 Fred Taylor RC 1.50 4.00
80 Derrick Alexander .40 1.00
81 Donnell Bennett .25 .60
82 Rich Gannon .60 1.50
83 Elvis Grbac .40 1.00
84 Andre Rison .40 1.00
85 Rashaan Shehee RC .75 2.00
86 Karim Abdul-Jabbar .60 1.50
87 John Avery RC .75 2.00
88 Oronde Gadsden RC 1.00 2.50
89 Dan Marino 2.50 6.00
90 O.J. McDuffie .40 1.00
91 Zach Thomas .60 1.50
92 Cris Carter .60 1.50
93 Randall Cunningham .60 1.50
94 Brad Johnson .60 1.50
95 Randy Moss RC 6.00 15.00
96 Jake Reed .40 1.00
97 Robert Smith .60 1.50
98 Drew Bledsoe 1.00 2.50
99 Ben Coates .40 1.00
100 Robert Edwards RC .75 2.00
101 Terry Glenn .60 1.50
102 Shawn Jefferson .25 .60
103 Ty Law .40 1.00
104 Cameron Cleeland RC .50 1.25
105 Kerry Collins .40 1.00
106 Sean Dawkins .25 .60
107 Andre Hastings .25 .60
108 Lamar Smith .40 1.00
109 Danny Wuerffel .40 1.00
110 Gary Brown .25 .60
111 Chris Calloway .25 .60
112 Ike Hilliard .40 1.00
113 Joe Jurevicius RC 1.00 2.50
114 Danny Kanell .40 1.00
115 Wayne Chrebet .60 1.50
116 Glenn Foley .40 1.00
117 Keyshawn Johnson .60 1.50
118 Leon Johnson .25 .60
119 Curtis Martin .60 1.50
120 Vinny Testaverde .40 1.00
121 Tim Brown .60 1.50
122 Jeff George .40 1.00
123 James Jett .40 1.00
124 Napoleon Kaufman .60 1.50
125 Charles Woodson RC 1.25 3.00
126 Irving Fryar .40 1.00
127 Jeff Graham .25 .60
128 Bobby Hoying .40 1.00
129 Duce Staley .75 2.00
130 Jerome Bettis .60 1.50
131 Chris Fuamatu-Ma'afala RC .75 2.00
132 Courtney Hawkins .25 .60
133 Charles Johnson .25 .60
134 Kordell Stewart .60 1.50
135 Hines Ward RC 5.00 10.00
136 Tony Banks .40 1.00
137 Isaac Bruce .60 1.50
138 Robert Holcombe RC .75 2.00
139 Eddie Kennison .40 1.00
140 Ryan Leaf RC 1.00 2.50
141 Natrone Means .40 1.00
142 Mikhael Ricks RC .75 2.00
143 Junior Seau .60 1.50
144 Bryan Still .25 .60
145 Garrison Hearst .60 1.50
146 R.W. McQuarters RC .75 2.00
147 Terrell Owens .60 1.50
148 Jerry Rice 1.25 3.00
149 J.J. Stokes .40 1.00
150 Steve Young .75 2.00
151 Joey Galloway .40 1.00
152 Ahman Green RC 2.50 6.00
153 Warren Moon .60 1.50
154 Shawn Springs .25 .60
155 Ricky Watters .40 1.00
156 Mike Alstott .60 1.50
157 Reidel Anthony .40 1.00
158 Trent Dilfer .60 1.50
159 Warrick Dunn .60 1.50
160 Jacquez Green RC .75 2.00
161 Kevin Dyson RC 1.00 2.50
162 Eddie George .60 1.50
163 Steve McNair .60 1.50
164 Yancey Thigpen .25 .60
165 Frank Wycheck .25 .60
166 Terry Allen .60 1.50
167 Gus Frerotte .25 .60
168 Trent Green .60 1.50
169 Skip Hicks RC .75 2.00
170 Michael Westbrook .40 1.00
171 Jamal Anderson SM .60 1.50
172 Carl Pickens SM .40 1.00
173 Deion Sanders SM .60 1.50
174 Emmitt Smith SM 1.25 3.00
175 Terrell Davis SM .60 1.50
176 John Elway SM 1.50 4.00
177 Charlie Batch SM 1.00 2.50
178 Herman Moore SM .40 1.00
179 Barry Sanders SM 1.25 3.00
180 Brett Favre SM 1.50 4.00
181 Antonio Freeman SM .40 1.00
182 Marshall Faulk SM .75 2.00
183 Peyton Manning SM 8.00 20.00
184 Mark Brunell SM .60 1.50
185 Dan Marino SM 1.50 4.00
186 Randy Moss SM 5.00 12.00
187 Drew Bledsoe SM .60 1.50
188 Robert Edwards SM .40 1.00
189 Curtis Martin SM .60 1.50
190 Charles Woodson SM 1.00 2.50
191 Jerome Bettis SM .60 1.50
192 Robert Holcombe SM .40 1.00
193 Ryan Leaf SM 1.00 2.50
194 Natrone Means SM .40 1.00
195 Jerry Rice SM .75 2.00
196 Steve Young SM .60 1.50
197 Warrick Dunn SM .60 1.50
198 Eddie George SM .40 1.00
199 Peyton Manning CL 4.00 10.00
200 Ryan Leaf CL .60 1.50

1998 Collector's Edge Masters 50-point

COMPLETE SET (199) 250.00 400.00
*50-POINT: .5X TO 1.2X BASIC CARD
ONE PER PACK
STATED PRINT RUN 3000 SER.#'d SETS

1998 Collector's Edge Masters 50-point Gold

COMPLETE SET (199) 750.00 1500.00
*50-PNT GOLD VETS: 4X TO 10X BAS.CARD
*50-POINT GOLD ROOKIES: .8X TO 2X
STATED ODDS 1:20
STATED PRINT RUN 150 SERIAL #'d SETS

1998 Collector's Edge Masters Gold Redemption 500

COMP.FACT SET (199) 150.00 300.00
*VETS: 1.5X TO 4X BASIC CARDS
*ROOKIES: .5X TO 1.2X BASIC CARDS
ISSUED VIA MAIL EXCH IN SET FORM
STATED PRINT RUN 500 SER.#'d SETS

1998 Collector's Edge Masters Gold Redemption 100

COMP. FACT SET (199) 400.00 800.00
*VETS: 2.5X TO 6X BASIC CARDS
*ROOKIES: .8X TO 2X BASIC CARDS
STATED PRINT RUN 100 SER.#'d SETS

1998 Collector's Edge Masters HoloGold

STATED ODDS 1:300
STATED PRINT RUN 10 SERIAL #'d SETS
NOT PRICED DUE TO SCARCITY

1998 Collector's Edge Masters Legends

Randomly inserted in packs at the rate of one in eight, this 30-card set features color action photos of top stars printed using dot matrix hologram technology and accentuated with a blend of the pictured player's team colors. Each card is sequentially numbered to 2,500.

COMPLETE SET (30) 30.00 80.00
STATED ODDS 1:8
STATED PRINT RUN 2500 SERIAL #'d SETS
ML1 Jake Plummer 1.25 3.00
ML2 Doug Flutie 1.25 3.00
ML3 Corey Dillon 1.25 3.00
ML4 Carl Pickens .75 2.00
ML5 Troy Aikman 2.50 6.00
ML6 Deion Sanders 1.25 3.00
ML7 Emmitt Smith 4.00 10.00
ML8 Terrell Davis 1.25 3.00
ML9 John Elway 5.00 12.00
ML10 Herman Moore .75 2.00
ML11 Barry Sanders 4.00 10.00
ML12 Brett Favre 5.00 12.00
ML13 Antonio Freeman 1.25 3.00
ML14 Marshall Faulk 1.50 4.00
ML15 Mark Brunell 1.25 3.00
ML16 Dan Marino 5.00 12.00
ML17 Cris Carter 1.25 3.00
ML18 Drew Bledsoe 2.00 5.00
ML19 Keyshawn Johnson 1.25 3.00
ML20 Curtis Martin 1.25 3.00
ML21 Napoleon Kaufman 1.25 3.00
ML22 Jerome Bettis 1.25 3.00
ML23 Kordell Stewart 1.25 3.00
ML24 Natrone Means .75 2.00
ML25 Jerry Rice 2.50 6.00
ML26 Steve Young 1.50 4.00
ML27 Joey Galloway .75 2.00
ML28 Warrick Dunn 1.25 3.00
ML29 Eddie George 1.25 3.00
ML30 Terry Allen 1.25 3.00

1998 Collector's Edge Masters Main Event

Randomly inserted in packs at the rate of one in 16, this 20-card set features color action photos of top players during big games or game defining moments during the 1998 regular season. Each card is sequentially numbered to 2,000.

COMPLETE SET (20) 60.00 120.00
STATED ODDS 1:16
STATED PRINT RUN 2000 SERIAL #'d SETS
ME1 Troy Aikman 3.00 8.00
ME2 Jamal Anderson 1.50 4.00
ME3 Charlie Batch 1.00 2.50
ME4 Jerome Bettis 1.50 4.00
ME5 Mark Brunell 1.50 4.00
ME6 Terrell Davis 1.50 4.00
ME7 Warrick Dunn 1.50 4.00
ME8 Robert Edwards .75 2.00
ME9 John Elway 6.00 15.00
ME10 Brett Favre 6.00 15.00
ME11 Doug Flutie 1.50 4.00
ME12 Eddie George 1.50 4.00
ME13 Dan Marino 6.00 15.00
ME14 Curtis Martin 1.50 4.00
ME15 Randy Moss 6.00 15.00
ME16 Carl Pickens 1.00 2.50
ME17 Jake Plummer 1.50 4.00
ME18 Barry Sanders 5.00 12.00
ME19 Emmitt Smith 5.00 12.00
ME20 Fred Taylor 1.50 4.00

1998 Collector's Edge Masters Rookie Masters

Randomly inserted in packs at the rate of one in eight, this 30-card set features color action photos of top rookies in the NFL printed on prismatic foil stock. Each card is sequentially numbered to 2,500. Cards labeled as "Preview" were also produced of many of the cards in this set.

COMPLETE SET (30) 50.00 100.00
STATED ODDS 1:8
STATED PRINT RUN 2500 SERIAL #'d SETS
*PREVIEWS: .15X TO .4X BASIC INSERTS
RM1 Peyton Manning 10.00 25.00
RM2 Ryan Leaf 1.00 2.50
RM3 Charlie Batch 1.00 2.50
RM4 Brian Griese 2.00 5.00
RM5 Randy Moss 6.00 15.00
RM6 Jacquez Green .75 2.00
RM7 Kevin Dyson 1.00 2.50
RM8 Mikhael Ricks .75 2.00
RM9 Jerome Pathon 1.00 2.50
RM10 Joe Jurevicius 1.00 2.50
RM11 Germane Crowell .75 2.00
RM12 Tim Dwight 1.00 2.50
RM13 Pat Johnson .75 2.00
RM14 Hines Ward 4.00 10.00
RM15 Marcus Nash .50 1.25
RM16 Damon Gibson .50 1.25
RM17 Robert Edwards .75 2.00
RM18 Robert Holcombe .75 2.00
RM19 Tavian Banks .75 2.00
RM20 Fred Taylor 1.50 4.00
RM21 Skip Hicks .75 2.00
RM22 Curtis Enis .50 1.25
RM23 Ahman Green 2.50 6.00
RM24 John Avery .75 2.00
RM25 Chris Fuamatu-Ma'afala .75 2.00
RM26 Rashaan Shehee .75 2.00
RM27 Cameron Cleeland .50 1.25
RM28 Charles Woodson 1.25 3.00
RM29 R.W. McQuarters .75 2.00
RM30 Andre Wadsworth .75 2.00

1998 Collector's Edge Masters Sentinels

Randomly inserted in packs at the rate of one in 120, this 10-card set features color action photos of top NFL stars printed on clear vinyl technology-driven cards with foil stamping. Every card in the set is sequentially numbered to 500.

COMPLETE SET (10) 50.00 120.00
STATED ODDS 1:120
STATED PRINT RUN 500 SERIAL #'d SETS
S1 John Elway 10.00 30.00
S2 Brett Favre 10.00 30.00
S3 Barry Sanders 8.00 25.00
S4 Terrell Davis 2.50 6.00
S5 Dan Marino 10.00 30.00
S6 Emmitt Smith 8.00 25.00
S7 Randy Moss 10.00 25.00
S8 Peyton Manning 20.00 50.00
S9 Robert Edwards 1.50 4.00
S10 Fred Taylor 2.50 6.00

1998 Collector's Edge Masters Super Masters

Randomly inserted in packs at the rate of one in ten, this set features color action photos of current and retired Super Bowl stars printed on prismatic holoboard stock. Some retired players signed a limited number of cards with most being issued via mail redemption cards. Reportedly, Starr and Unitas signed just 50-cards each initially, but an additional 100-signed and serial numbered Unitas promo cards appeared on the market later on. Joe Namath (card #SM26) was not issued in packs but versions of the card stamped "media sample" on the back were made available at a later date. Some additional cards and players were also released after Edge ceased card operations. Each card issued in packs for the set was sequentially numbered to 2000.

STATED ODDS 1:10
UNSIGNED PRINT RUN 2000 SER.#'d SETS
SM1 Terrell Davis 1.25 3.00
SM2 John Elway 4.00 10.00
SM3 Shannon Sharpe 1.00 2.50
SM4 Rod Smith .75 2.00
SM5 Brett Favre 5.00 12.00
SM6 Antonio Freeman 1.25 3.00
SM7 Robert Brooks .75 2.00
SM8 Edgar Bennett .75 2.00
SM9 Reggie White 1.25 3.00
SM10 Troy Aikman 2.50 6.00
SM11 Michael Irvin 1.25 3.00
SM12 Deion Sanders 1.25 3.00
SM13 Emmitt Smith 4.00 10.00
SM14 Steve Young 1.50 4.00
SM15 Jerry Rice 2.50 6.00
SM16 Bart Starr 3.00 8.00
SM16AU Bart Starr AU/50* 100.00 175.00
SM17 Johnny Unitas 3.00 8.00
SM17AU John Unitas AU/50* 125.00 225.00
SM17P John Unitas AU/100 125.00 200.00
SM20 Drew Pearson UER 1.00 2.50
SM20 Larry Csonka 1.25 3.00
SM20AU Drew Pearson AU 7.50 20.00
SM21 John Riggins 1.25 3.00
SM22 Marcus Allen 1.25 3.00
SM23 Dwight Clark 1.00 2.50
SM23AU Dwight Clark AU 7.50 20.00
SM24 Phil Simms 1.25 3.00
SM25 Art Monk 1.00 2.50
SM26 Joe Namath 2.50 6.00
SM26S Joe Namath Sample 8.00 20.00
SM27 Len Dawson 1.25 3.00
SM27AU Len Dawson AU 12.00 30.00
SM28 Lynn Swann 1.50 4.00
SM29 John Stallworth 1.00 2.50
SM29AU John Stallworth AU 15.00 30.00
SM30 Butch Johnson AU 6.00 15.00
SM31 Roger Craig 1.00 2.50
SM31AU Roger Craig AU 7.50 20.00
SM32 Jack Ham 1.00 2.50
SM32AU Jack Ham AU 20.00 40.00

1998 Collector's Edge Masters Super Masters Previews

These card were issued to preview the Super Masters insert set from 1998 CE Masters. Each card is a basic insert with the word "Preview" printed within the white panel on the card's back.

SM17 Johnny Unitas 3.00 8.00
SM31 Roger Craig 1.25 3.00
SM32 Jack Ham Mill.Coll. 1.25 3.00

1999 Collector's Edge Masters Previews

Cards from this set are essentially a parallel version to the player's corresponding base card. The cardbacks contain the word "preview" and each was released primarily to dealers and distributors.

COMPLETE SET (15) 20.00 35.00
AB Aaron Brooks 2.50 6.00
AS Akili Smith .40 1.00
CB Champ Bailey .60 1.50
CM Cade McNown .60 1.50
DB David Boston 1.25 3.00
EJ Edgerrin James 2.50 6.00
JJ J.J. Johnson .60 1.50
KJ Kevin Johnson .75 2.00
KW Kurt Warner 3.00 8.00
OG Olandis Gary .75 2.00
PJ Patrick Jeffers .75 2.00
PP Peerless Price 1.00 2.50
TC Tim Couch 2.00 5.00
TE Troy Edwards .75 2.00
TH Torry Holt 1.00 2.50

1999 Collector's Edge Masters

Released as a 200-card set, 1999 Collector's Edge Masters features micro-etched holographic foil cards where each veteran base card is sequentially numbered to 5000. The 1999 Draft Picks cards were serial numbered of 5000 or 2000. Each pack contained three cards and carried a suggested retail price of $5.59. Retail boxes contained one PSA graded Collector's Edge Oddessy card.

COMPLETE SET (200) 300.00 500.00
1 David Boston RC .60 1.50
2 Mac Cody RC .60 1.50
3 Chris Greisen RC .60 1.50
4 Joel Makovicka RC .60 1.50
5 Adrian Murrell .25 .60
6 Jake Plummer .25 .60
7 Frank Sanders .25 .60
8 Jamal Anderson .30 .75
9 Chris Chandler .30 .75
10 Reginald Kelly RC .60 1.50
11 Patrick Kerney RC .60 1.50
12 Terance Mathis .25 .60
13 Jeff Paulk RC .60 1.50
14 Stoney Case .25 .60
15 Qadry Ismail .25 .60
16 Chris McAlister RC .60 1.50
17 Errict Rhett .25 .60
18 Brandon Stokley RC .75 2.00
19 Doug Flutie .40 1.00
20 Kamil Loud RC .60 1.50
21 Eric Moulds .25 .60
22 Peerless Price RC .60 1.50
23 Andre Reed .40 1.00
24 Antowain Smith .25 .60
25 Antoine Winfield RC .60 1.50
26 Steve Beuerlein .30 .75
27 Tim Biakabutuka .30 .75
28 Dameyune Craig RC 1.00 2.50
29 Patrick Jeffers RC 1.00 2.50
30 Muhsin Muhammad .25 .60
31 D'Wayne Bates RC .60 1.50
32 Marty Booker RC .60 1.50
33 Bobby Engram .25 .60
34 Curtis Enis .25 .60
35 Ty Hallock RC .60 1.50
36 Shane Matthews .25 .60
37 Cade McNown RC .60 1.50
38 Marcus Robinson .30 .75
39 Scott Covington RC .60 1.50
40 Corey Dillon .25 .60
41 Damon Griffin RC 1.00 2.50
42 Carl Pickens .30 .75
43 Darnay Scott .25 .60
44 Akili Smith RC .60 1.50
45 Craig Yeast RC .60 1.50
46 Darrin Chiaverini RC .60 1.50
47 Tim Couch RC .75 2.00
48 Phil Dawson RC .75 2.00
49 Kevin Johnson RC .75 2.00
50 Terry Kirby .25 .60
51 Wali Rainer RC .60 1.50
52 Troy Aikman .50 1.25
53 Ebenezer Ekuban RC .60 1.50
54 Michael Irvin .40 1.00
55 Rocket Ismail .30 .75
56 Wane McGarity RC .60 1.50
57 Dat Nguyen RC 1.00 2.50
58 Deion Sanders .30 .75
59 Emmitt Smith .60 1.50
60 Byron Chamberlain RC .75 2.00
61 Andre Cooper RC .60 1.50
62 Terrell Davis .30 .75
63 Olandis Gary RC 1.00 2.50
64 Brian Griese .25 .60
65 Ed McCaffrey .30 .75
66 Travis McGriff RC .60 1.50
67 Shannon Sharpe .30 .75
68 Rod Smith .30 .75
69 Al Wilson RC 1.00 2.50
70 Charlie Batch .25 .60
71 Chris Claiborne RC .60 1.50
72 Germane Crowell .25 .60
73 Greg Hill .25 .60
74 Sedrick Irvin RC .60 1.50
75 Herman Moore .30 .75
76 Johnnie Morton .30 .75
77 Barry Sanders .60 1.50
78 Aaron Brooks RC .75 2.00
79 Antuan Edwards RC .60 1.50
80 Brett Favre .75 2.00
81 Antonio Freeman .30 .75
82 Dorsey Levens .30 .75
83 Bill Schroeder .30 .75
84 E.G. Green .25 .60
85 Marvin Harrison .30 .75
86 Edgerrin James RC 1.00 2.50
87 Peyton Manning 1.25 3.00
88 Mark Brunell .30 .75
89 Jay Fiedler/5000 RC .60 1.50
90 Keenan McCardell .30 .75
91 Jimmy Smith .30 .75
92 James Stewart .25 .60
93 Fred Taylor .25 .60
94 Derrick Alexander WR .25 .60
95 Mike Cloud RC .60 1.50
96 Elvis Grbac .25 .60
97 Byron Bam Morris .25 .60
98 Andre Rison .30 .75
99 Cecil Collins RC .60 1.50
100 Damon Huard .25 .60
101 James Johnson RC .60 1.50
102 Rob Konrad RC .60 1.50
103 Dan Marino .75 2.00
104 O.J. McDuffie .30 .75
105 Cris Carter .40 1.00
106 Daunte Culpepper RC 1.00 2.50
107 Randall Cunningham .30 .75
108 Jeff George .25 .60
109 Jim Kleinsasser RC 1.00 2.50
110 Randy Moss .30 .75
111 Robert Smith .25 .60
112 Terry Allen .30 .75
113 Michael Bishop RC .75 2.00
114 Drew Bledsoe .30 .75
115 Kevin Faulk RC .60 1.50
116 Terry Glenn .30 .75
117 Andy Katzenmoyer RC .75 2.00
118 Billy Joe Hobert .25 .60
119 Eddie Kennison .30 .75
120 Ricky Williams RC 1.00 2.50
121 Tiki Barber .30 .75
122 Sean Bennett RC .60 1.50
123 Gary Brown .25 .60
124 Kent Graham .25 .60
125 Ike Hilliard .25 .60
126 Joe Montgomery RC .60 1.50
127 Amani Toomer .25 .60
128 Wayne Chrebet .25 .60
129 Keyshawn Johnson .30 .75
130 Curtis Martin .30 .75
131 Ray Lucas/5000 RC .50 1.25
132 Vinny Testaverde .25 .60
133 Tim Brown .40 1.00
134 Tony Bryant RC .60 1.50
135 Scott Dreisbach RC .60 1.50
136 Rich Gannon .30 .75
137 Tyrone Wheatley .30 .75
138 Charles Woodson .40 1.00
139 Na Brown RC .60 1.50
140 Charles Johnson .25 .60
141 Cecil Martin RC .60 1.50
142 Donovan McNabb RC 5.00 12.00
143 Doug Pederson .25 .60
144 Duce Staley .25 .60
145 Jerome Bettis .40 1.00
146 Kris Brown RC 1.00 2.50
147 Troy Edwards RC .60 1.50
148 Kordell Stewart .25 .60
149 Hines Ward .30 .75
150 Amos Zereoue RC .60 1.50
151 Dre Bly RC 1.00 2.50
152 Isaac Bruce .40 1.00
153 Marshall Faulk .30 .75
154 Joe Germaine RC .75 2.00
155 Az-Zahir Hakim .25 .60
156 Torry Holt RC 1.25 3.00
157 Kurt Warner RC 6.00 15.00
158 Justin Watson RC .60 1.50
159 Jermaine Fazande RC .60 1.50
160 Jeff Graham .25 .60
161 Jim Harbaugh .30 .75
162 Steve Heiden RC .60 1.50
163 Erik Kramer .30 .75
164 Natrone Means .30 .75
165 Mikhael Ricks .25 .60
166 Junior Seau .30 .75
167 Jeff Garcia RC 3.00 8.00
168 Charlie Garner .30 .75
169 Terry Jackson RC .60 1.50
170 Terrell Owens .30 .75
171 Jerry Rice 1.00 2.50
172 Steve Young .50 1.25
173 Karsten Bailey RC .60 1.50
174 Joey Galloway .30 .75
175 Brock Huard RC .60 1.50
176 Jon Kitna .25 .60
177 Derrick Mayes .25 .60
178 Charlie Rogers RC .60 1.50
179 Ricky Watters .30 .75
180 Rabih Abdullah RC .60 1.50
181 Mike Alstott .25 .60
182 Reidel Anthony .25 .60
183 Trent Dilfer .25 .60
184 Warrick Dunn .25 .60
185 Martin Gramatica RC .60 1.50
186 Shaun King RC .60 1.50
187 Darnell McDonald RC .60 1.50
188 Yo Murphy RC .60 1.50
189 Kevin Daft RC .60 1.50
190 Kevin Dyson .25 .60
191 Eddie George .30 .75
192 Jevon Kearse RC .75 2.00
193 Steve McNair .30 .75
194 Yancey Thigpen .25 .60
195 Champ Bailey RC 1.25 3.00
196 Albert Connell .25 .60
197 Stephen Davis .25 .60
198 Skip Hicks .25 .60
199 Brad Johnson .30 .75
200 Michael Westbrook .25 .60

1999 Collector's Edge Masters Galvanized

*VETERANS: 1.2X TO 3X BASIC CARDS
*ROOKIES: .5X TO 1.2X BASIC RC/2000
*ROOKIES: .8X TO 2X BASIC RC/5000
STATED PRINT RUN 1000 SERIAL #'d SETS

1999 Collector's Edge Masters HoloGold

*VETERANS/25: 12X TO 30X BASIC CARDS
*ROOKIES/25: 5X TO 12X BASIC RC/2000
*ROOKIES/25: 8X TO 20X BASIC RC/5000
HOLOGOLD STATED PRINT RUN 25

1999 Collector's Edge Masters HoloSilver

COMPLETE SET (200) 125.00 250.00
*VETERANS: .6X TO 1.5X BASIC CARDS
*ROOKIES: .25X TO .6X BASIC RC/2000
*ROOKIES: .4X TO 1X BASIC RC/5000
HOLOSILVER STATED PRINT RUN 3500

1999 Collector's Edge Masters Excalibur

Cards from the Excalibur set were distributed across three brands of 1999 Collector's Edge football products: Odyssey, First Place and Masters. The 8-cards inserted into Masters were each serial numbered of 5000. Note that the Favre card was inserted in both First Place and Masters and that no #23 Jake Plummer was released as a single card through packs. However, a 25-card uncut sheet was later released as a wrapper redemption at Edge events that did include the Jake Plummer card. We've priced the uncut sheet within the First Place listings. Some copies of the Jake Plummer card did surface after Edge ceased its card operations.

COMPLETE SET (8) 15.00 40.00
STATED PRINT RUN 5000 SER.#'d SETS
X3 Dan Marino 2.50 6.00
X6 Brett Favre 2.50 6.00
X7 Barry Sanders 2.00 5.00
X10 Champ Bailey 1.50 4.00
X12 Akili Smith .75 2.00
X14 Tim Couch 1.00 2.50
X18 Steve Young 1.50 4.00
X25 Curtis Martin 1.00 2.50

1999 Collector's Edge Masters Legends

Randomly inserted in packs, this 20-card set features top players on an all vinyl set with gold foil stamping. Each card is sequentially numbered to 1000.

COMPLETE SET (20) 75.00 150.00
STATED PRINT RUN 1000 SER.#'d SETS
ML1 Doug Flutie 2.00 5.00
ML2 Troy Aikman 2.50 6.00
ML3 Emmitt Smith 3.00 8.00
ML4 Terrell Davis 1.50 4.00
ML5 Charlie Batch 1.25 3.00
ML6 Barry Sanders 3.00 8.00
ML7 Brett Favre 4.00 10.00
ML8 Antonio Freeman 1.50 4.00
ML9 Peyton Manning 6.00 15.00
ML10 Mark Brunell 1.50 4.00
ML11 Fred Taylor 1.25 3.00
ML12 Dan Marino 4.00 10.00
ML13 Randy Moss 1.50 4.00
ML14 Drew Bledsoe 1.50 4.00
ML15 Kurt Warner 6.00 15.00
ML16 Marshall Faulk 1.50 4.00
ML17 Steve Young 2.50 6.00
ML18 Jerry Rice 5.00 12.00
ML19 Jon Kitna 1.25 3.00
ML20 Eddie George 1.50 4.00

1999 Collector's Edge Masters Main Event

Randomly inserted in packs, this 10-card set features dual-player key matchups from the 1999 season. Cards are printed on clear plastic and are sequentially numbered to 1000.

COMPLETE SET (10) 25.00 50.00
STATED PRINT RUN 1000 SER.#'d SETS
ME1 R.Moss 1.25 3.00
J.Anderson
ME2 M.Brunell 1.25 3.00
E.George
ME3 T.Davis 1.25 3.00
C.Collins
ME4 R.Ismail 1.25 3.00
S.Davis
ME5 T.Edwards 1.25 3.00
Kev.Johnson
ME6 A.Freeman 1.25 3.00
C.Batch
ME7 T.Glenn 1.25 3.00
M.Harrison
ME8 Key.Johnson 1.50 4.00
D.Flutie
ME9 C.McNown 1.50 4.00
R.Williams
ME10 S.Young 2.00 5.00
M.Faulk

1999 Collector's Edge Masters Majestic

Randomly inserted in packs, this 30-card set features NFL stars on a clear vinyl foil stamped card stock. Each card is sequentially numbered to 3000.

COMPLETE SET (30) 50.00 100.00
STATED PRINT RUN 3000 SER. #'d SETS
M1 Jake Plummer .75 2.00
M2 David Boston .75 2.00
M3 Doug Flutie 1.25 3.00
M4 Eric Moulds .75 2.00
M5 Peerless Price .75 2.00
M6 Tim Biakabutuka 1.00 2.50
M7 Troy Aikman 1.50 4.00
M8 Olandis Gary 1.25 3.00
M9 Brian Griese .75 2.00
M10 Charlie Batch .75 2.00
M11 Antonio Freeman 1.00 2.50
M12 Peyton Manning 4.00 10.00
M13 Edgerrin James 1.25 3.00
M14 Marvin Harrison 1.00 2.50
M15 Fred Taylor .75 2.00
M16 Daunte Culpepper 1.25 3.00
M17 Terry Glenn 1.00 2.50
M18 Keyshawn Johnson 1.00 2.50
M19 Curtis Martin 1.00 2.50
M20 Donovan McNabb 2.50 6.00
M21 Kordell Stewart .75 2.00
M22 Torry Holt 1.50 4.00
M23 Marshall Faulk 1.00 2.50
M24 Kurt Warner 4.00 10.00
M25 Jerry Rice 3.00 8.00
M26 Jon Kitna .75 2.00
M27 Eddie George 1.00 2.50
M28 Champ Bailey 1.50 4.00
M29 Brad Johnson 1.00 2.50
M30 Stephen Davis .75 2.00

1999 Collector's Edge Masters Pro Signature Authentics

The Pro Signatures Authentic cards were randomly inserted in packs of 1999 Collector's Edge Masters. Each was serial numbered of 500-cards. The Peyton Manning card was also released as a mail redemption card for the remainder of the1998 Rookie Ink trade cards. This second version was numbered of 445 on the cardback in blue ink but signed in black ink. The Kurt Warner card was also randomly inserted and hand numbered of 500.

COMPLETE SET (2) 125.00 250.00
STATED PRINT RUN 500 SER.#'d SETS
MANNING 1B ISSUED AS MAIL REDEMP.
1A Peyton Manning/500 40.00 80.00
1B Peyton Manning/445 40.00 80.00
1C Peyton Manning/40 100.00 175.00
2 Kurt Warner/500 50.00 100.00
1E Peyton Manning/1000 40.00 80.00

1999 Collector's Edge Masters Quest

Randomly inserted in packs, this 20-card set players on superbowl XXXIV contending teams. Cards are printed on vinyl and are highlighted with gold foil stamping. Each card is sequentially numbered to 3000.

COMPLETE SET (20) 20.00 40.00
STATED PRINT RUN 3000 SER.#'d SETS
Q1 Jake Plummer .75 2.00
Q2 Eric Moulds .75 2.00
Q3 Curtis Enis .75 2.00
Q4 Emmitt Smith 2.00 5.00
Q5 Brian Griese .75 2.00
Q6 Dorsey Levens 1.00 2.50
Q7 Marvin Harrison 1.00 2.50
Q8 Mark Brunell 1.00 2.50
Q9 Fred Taylor .75 2.00
Q10 Cris Carter 1.25 3.00
Q11 Terry Glenn 1.00 2.50
Q12 Keyshawn Johnson 1.00 2.50
Q13 Isaac Bruce 1.25 3.00
Q14 Terrell Owens 1.00 2.50
Q15 Jon Kitna .75 2.00
Q16 Natrone Means 1.00 2.50
Q17 Warrick Dunn .75 2.00
Q18 Steve McNair 1.00 2.50
Q19 Brad Johnson 1.00 2.50
Q20 Stephen Davis .75 2.00

1999 Collector's Edge Masters Rookie Masters

Randomly inserted in packs, this 30-card set features top draft picks on a holographic gold foil stamped card stock. Each card is sequentially numbered to 3000.

COMPLETE SET (30) 40.00 80.00
STATED PRINT RUN 3000 SER.#'d SETS
RM1 David Boston .75 2.00
RM2 Chris McAlister .75 2.00
RM3 Peerless Price .75 2.00
RM4 D'Wayne Bates .75 2.00
RM5 Cade McNown .75 2.00
RM6 Akili Smith .75 2.00
RM7 Tim Couch 1.00 2.50
RM8 Kevin Johnson 1.00 2.50
RM9 Wane McGarity .75 2.00
RM10 Chris Claiborne .75 2.00
RM11 Sedrick Irvin .75 2.00
RM12 Edgerrin James 1.25 3.00
RM13 Mike Cloud .75 2.00
RM14 Cecil Collins .75 2.00
RM15 James Johnson .75 2.00
RM16 Rob Konrad .75 2.00
RM17 Daunte Culpepper 1.25 3.00
RM18 Kevin Faulk .75 2.00
RM19 Andy Katzenmoyer 1.00 2.50
RM20 Ricky Williams 1.25 3.00
RM21 Donovan McNabb 2.50 6.00
RM22 Troy Edwards .75 2.00
RM23 Amos Zereoue .50 1.25
RM24 Joe Germaine 1.00 2.50
RM25 Torry Holt 1.50 4.00
RM26 Karsten Bailey .75 2.00
RM27 Brock Huard .75 2.00
RM28 Shaun King .75 2.00
RM29 Jevon Kearse 1.00 2.50
RM30 Champ Bailey 1.50 4.00

1999 Collector's Edge Masters Sentinels

Randomly inserted in packs, this 20-card set features 10 veterans and 10 rookies on a clear vinyl card stock with gold foil stamping. Each card is sequentially numbered to 500.

COMPLETE SET (20) 125.00 250.00
STATED PRINT RUN 500 SER.#'d SETS
S1 Troy Aikman 4.00 10.00
S2 Emmitt Smith 5.00 12.00
S3 Terrell Davis 2.50 6.00
S4 Barry Sanders 5.00 12.00
S5 Brett Favre 6.00 15.00
S6 Peyton Manning 10.00 25.00
S7 Dan Marino 6.00 15.00
S8 Randy Moss 2.50 6.00
S9 Drew Bledsoe 2.50 6.00
S10 Isaac Bruce 3.00 8.00
S11 Kurt Warner 10.00 25.00
S12 David Boston 1.50 4.00
S13 Cade McNown 1.50 4.00
S14 Akili Smith 1.50 4.00
S15 Tim Couch 2.00 5.00
S16 Edgerrin James 2.50 6.00
S17 Ricky Williams 2.50 6.00
S18 Donovan McNabb 5.00 12.00
S19 Troy Edwards 1.50 4.00
S20 Torry Holt 3.00 8.00
S18P Donovan McNabb PREVIEW 2.00 5.00

2000 Collector's Edge Masters

Released as a 250-card set, Masters features a base card printed on Dot Matrix Hologram card stock divided up into 200 veteran player cards and 50 rookie cards. Veteran cards are sequentially numbered to 2000 and rookies are sequentially numbered to 1000. Masters was packaged in 20-pack boxes with packs containing three cards and carried a suggested retial price of $5.99. Each hobby box contained one PSA 9 or 10 rookie card.

COMP.SET w/o SP's (200) 10.00 25.00
201-250 ROOKIE PRINT RUN 1000
1 David Boston .40 1.00
2 Michael Pittman .40 1.00
3 Jake Plummer .40 1.00
4 Frank Sanders .40 1.00
5 Jamal Anderson .50 1.25
6 Chris Chandler .50 1.25
7 Tim Dwight .50 1.25
8 Shawn Jefferson .40 1.00
9 Terance Mathis .40 1.00
10 Tony Banks .40 1.00
11 Trent Dilfer .40 1.00
12 Priest Holmes .40 1.00
13 Qadry Ismail .40 1.00
14 Jermaine Lewis .40 1.00
15 Shannon Sharpe .50 1.25
16 Doug Flutie .50 1.25
17 Rob Johnson .50 1.25
18 Jeremy McDaniel .40 1.00
19 Eric Moulds .40 1.00
20 Peerless Price .50 1.25
21 Antowain Smith .50 1.25
22 Steve Beuerlein .50 1.25
23 Tim Biakabutuka .50 1.25
24 Dialleo Burks RC .40 1.00
25 Dameyune Craig .40 1.00
26 Donald Hayes .40 1.00
27 Patrick Jeffers .40 1.00
28 Muhsin Muhammad .40 1.00
29 Reggie White .60 1.50
30 Bobby Engram .40 1.00
31 Curtis Enis .40 1.00
32 Eddie Kennison .40 1.00
33 Cade McNown .40 1.00
34 Marcus Robinson .50 1.25
35 Corey Dillon .40 1.00

36 James Hundon .40 1.00
37 Scott Mitchell .40 1.00
38 Tony McGee .40 1.00
39 Akili Smith .40 1.00
40 Craig Yeast .40 1.00
41 Darrin Chiaverini .40 1.00
42 Tim Couch .50 1.25
43 Kevin Johnson .40 1.00
44 Errict Rhett .50 1.25
45 Troy Aikman .75 2.00
46 Randall Cunningham .50 1.25
47 Joey Galloway .50 1.25
48 Rocket Ismail .50 1.25
49 James McKnight .40 1.00
50 Dat Nguyen .40 1.00
51 Emmitt Smith 1.00 2.50
52 Chris Warren .40 1.00
53 Robert Brooks .50 1.25
54 Terrell Davis .50 1.25
55 Gus Frerotte .40 1.00
56 Olandis Gary .50 1.25
57 Brian Griese .40 1.00
58 Ed McCaffrey .50 1.25
59 Rod Smith .50 1.25
60 Charlie Batch .40 1.00
61 Germane Crowell .40 1.00
62 Sedrick Irvin .40 1.00
63 Herman Moore .40 1.00
64 Johnnie Morton .50 1.25
65 James Stewart .40 1.00
66 Corey Bradford .40 1.00
67 Brett Favre 1.25 3.00
68 Antonio Freeman .50 1.25
69 Matt Hasselbeck .40 1.00
70 Dorsey Levens .50 1.25
71 Bill Schroeder .50 1.25
72 Ken Dilger .40 1.00
73 E.G. Green .40 1.00
74 Marvin Harrison .50 1.25
75 Edgerrin James .50 1.25
76 Peyton Manning 1.50 4.00
77 Jerome Pathon .40 1.00
78 Terrence Wilkins .40 1.00
79 Kyle Brady .40 1.00
80 Mark Brunell .50 1.25
81 Kevin Hardy .40 1.00
82 Stacey Mack .40 1.00
83 Keenan McCardell .50 1.25
84 Jimmy Smith .50 1.25
85 Fred Taylor .40 1.00
86 Derrick Alexander .40 1.00
87 Mike Cloud .40 1.00
88 Tony Gonzalez .50 1.25
89 Elvis Grbac .40 1.00
90 Kevin Lockett .40 1.00
91 Tony Richardson RC .40 1.00
92 Jay Fiedler .50 1.25
93 Oronde Gadsden .50 1.25
94 Damon Huard .40 1.00
95 Rob Konrad .40 1.00
96 James Johnson .40 1.00
97 Tony Martin .50 1.25
98 O.J. McDuffie .50 1.25
99 Lamar Smith .40 1.00
100 Thurman Thomas .50 1.25
101 Todd Bouman .40 1.00
102 Bubby Brister .40 1.00
103 Cris Carter .60 1.50
104 Daunte Culpepper .50 1.25
105 Matthew Hatchette .40 1.00
106 Randy Moss .50 1.25
107 Robert Smith .40 1.00
108 Moe Williams .40 1.00
109 Michael Bishop .40 1.00
110 Drew Bledsoe .50 1.25
111 Troy Brown .40 1.00
112 Kevin Faulk .40 1.00
113 Terry Glenn .50 1.25
114 Andy Katzenmoyer .40 1.00
115 Tony Simmons .40 1.00
116 Jeff Blake .50 1.25
117 Aaron Brooks .40 1.00
118 Jake Delhomme RC .50 1.25
119 Joe Horn .50 1.25
120 Jake Reed .50 1.25
121 Ricky Williams .50 1.25
122 Tiki Barber .50 1.25
123 Kerry Collins .40 1.00
124 Ike Hilliard .40 1.00
125 Amani Toomer .40 1.00
126 Wayne Chrebet .40 1.00
127 Ray Lucas .40 1.00
128 Curtis Martin .50 1.25
129 Vinny Testaverde .40 1.00
130 Dedric Ward .40 1.00
131 Tim Brown .60 1.50
132 Rickey Dudley .40 1.00
133 Rich Gannon .50 1.25
134 James Jett .50 1.25
135 Napoleon Kaufman .50 1.25
136 Tyrone Wheatley .40 1.00
137 Charles Woodson .60 1.50
138 Charles Johnson .40 1.00
139 Donovan McNabb .50 1.25
140 Torrance Small .40 1.00
141 Duce Staley .40 1.00
142 Jerome Bettis .60 1.50
143 Troy Edwards .40 1.00
144 Kent Graham .40 1.00
145 Richard Huntley .40 1.00
146 Kordell Stewart .40 1.00
147 Amos Zereoue .40 1.00
148 Isaac Bruce .60 1.50
149 Kevin Carter .40 1.00
150 Marshall Faulk .50 1.25
151 Trent Green .40 1.00
152 Az-Zahir Hakim .40 1.00
153 Robert Holcombe .40 1.00
154 Torry Holt .50 1.25
155 Kurt Warner 1.00 2.50
156 Kenny Bynum .40 1.00
157 Robert Chancey .40 1.00
158 Curtis Conway .50 1.25
159 Jermaine Fazande .40 1.00
160 Jeff Graham .40 1.00
161 Jim Harbaugh .50 1.25
162 Ryan Leaf .50 1.25
163 Junior Seau .50 1.25
164 Jeff Garcia .40 1.00
165 Charlie Garner .50 1.25
166 Terrell Owens .50 1.25
167 Jerry Rice 1.50 4.00
168 J.J. Stokes .50 1.25
169 Karsten Bailey .40 1.00
170 Sean Dawkins .40 1.00
171 Brock Huard .40 1.00
172 Jon Kitna .40 1.00
173 Derrick Mayes .40 1.00
174 Ricky Watters .50 1.25
175 Rabih Abdullah .40 1.00
176 Mike Alstott .40 1.00
177 Reidel Anthony .40 1.00
178 Warrick Dunn .40 1.00
179 Jacquez Green .40 1.00
180 Keyshawn Johnson .50 1.25
181 Shaun King .40 1.00
182 Warren Sapp .50 1.25
183 Kevin Dyson .50 1.25
184 Eddie George .50 1.25
185 Jevon Kearse .40 1.00
186 Steve McNair .50 1.25
187 Neil O'Donnell .40 1.00
188 Carl Pickens .50 1.25
189 Yancey Thigpen .40 1.00
190 Frank Wycheck .50 1.25
191 Champ Bailey .50 1.25
192 Larry Centers .40 1.00
193 Albert Connell .40 1.00
194 Stephen Davis .40 1.00
195 Jeff George .50 1.25
196 Brad Johnson .50 1.25
197 Deion Sanders .50 1.25
198 Bruce Smith .50 1.25
199 James Thrash .50 1.25
200 Michael Westbrook .40 1.00
201 Thomas Jones RC 1.50 4.00
202 Jamal Lewis RC 2.00 5.00
203 Chris Redman RC 1.25 3.00
204 Travis Taylor RC 1.25 3.00
205 Avion Black RC 1.25 3.00
206 Kwame Cavil RC 1.25 3.00
207 Sammy Morris RC 1.25 3.00
208 Brian Urlacher RC 6.00 15.00
209 Dez White RC 1.25 3.00
210 Ron Dugans RC 1.25 3.00
211 Danny Farmer RC 1.25 3.00
212 Curtis Keaton RC 1.25 3.00
213 Peter Warrick RC 1.25 3.00
214 Courtney Brown RC 1.50 4.00
215 JaJuan Dawson RC 1.25 3.00
216 Dennis Northcutt RC 1.25 3.00
217 Travis Prentice RC 1.25 3.00
218 Spergon Wynn RC 1.25 3.00
219 Michael Wiley RC 1.25 3.00
220 Mike Anderson RC 1.25 3.00
221 Chris Cole RC 1.50 4.00
222 Deltha O'Neal RC 1.25 3.00
223 Reuben Droughns RC 1.25 3.00
224 Bubba Franks RC 1.25 3.00
225 Charles Lee RC 1.25 3.00
226 Rob Morris RC 1.50 4.00
227 R.Jay Soward RC 1.25 3.00
228 Shyrone Stith RC 1.25 3.00
229 Frank Moreau RC 1.25 3.00
230 Sylvester Morris RC 1.25 3.00
231 J.R. Redmond RC 1.25 3.00
232 Chad Morton RC 1.50 4.00
233 Ron Dayne RC 2.00 5.00
234 Ron Dixon RC 1.25 3.00
235 Anthony Becht RC 1.25 3.00
236 Laveranues Coles RC 1.50 4.00
237 Chad Pennington RC 1.50 4.00
238 Sebastian Janikowski RC 2.00 5.00
239 Jerry Porter RC 2.00 5.00
240 Todd Pinkston RC 1.25 3.00
241 Gari Scott RC 1.25 3.00
242 Corey Simon RC 1.50 4.00
243 Plaxico Burress RC 1.50 4.00
244 Tee Martin RC 1.25 3.00
245 Trung Canidate RC 1.25 3.00
246 Trevor Gaylor RC 1.25 3.00
247 Giovanni Carmazzi RC 1.25 3.00
248 Tim Rattay RC 1.50 4.00
249 Shaun Alexander RC 2.00 5.00
250 Joe Hamilton RC 1.25 3.00

2000 Collector's Edge Masters HoloGold

*VETS 1-200: 3X TO 8X BASIC CARDS
*ROOKIES 201-250: 1X TO 2.5X
HOLOGOLD PRINT RUN 50 SER.#'d SETS

2000 Collector's Edge Masters HoloSilver

*VETS 1-200: 1.5X TO 4X BASIC CARDS
*ROOKIES 201-250: .5X TO 1.2X
HOLOSILVER PRINT RUN 1000 SER.#'d SETS

2000 Collector's Edge Masters Retail

*VETS 1-200: .1X TO .3X BASIC CARDS
*ROOKIES 201-250: .1X TO .25X

2000 Collector's Edge Masters Domain

Randomly inserted in packs, this 20-card set features player action photography on an all rainbow foil card stock with gold foil highlights. Each card is sequentially numbered to 5000.

COMPLETE SET (20) 10.00 25.00
STATED PRINT RUN 5000 SER.#'d SETS
D1 Qadry Ismail .50 1.25
D2 Muhsin Muhammad .50 1.25
D3 Marcus Robinson .60 1.50
D4 Akili Smith .50 1.25
D5 Tim Couch .60 1.50
D6 Kevin Johnson .50 1.25
D7 Troy Aikman 1.00 2.50
D8 Brian Griese .50 1.25
D9 James Stewart .50 1.25
D10 Dorsey Levens .60 1.50
D11 Marvin Harrison .60 1.50
D12 Cris Carter .75 2.00
D13 Daunte Culpepper .60 1.50
D14 Donovan McNabb .60 1.50
D15 Duce Staley .50 1.25
D16 Isaac Bruce .75 2.00
D17 Torry Holt .60 1.50
D18 Kurt Warner 1.25 3.00
D19 Jeff Garcia .50 1.25
D20 Jerry Rice 2.00 5.00

2000 Collector's Edge Masters Future Masters Gold

Randomly inserted in packs, this 30-card set features a rainbow holofoil card stock with this year's top Rooikes in action and gold foil highlights. Each card is sequentially numbered to 2000.

COMPLETE SET (30) 25.00 60.00
GOLD PRINT RUN 2000 SER.#'d SETS
*SILVER/3000: .3X TO .8X GOLD/2000
SILVER PRINT RUN 3000 SER.#'d SETS
FM1 Thomas Jones .75 2.00
FM2 Jamal Lewis 1.00 2.50
FM3 Chris Redman .60 1.50
FM4 Travis Taylor .60 1.50
FM5 Brian Urlacher 3.00 8.00
FM6 Dez White .60 1.50
FM7 Ron Dugans .60 1.50
FM8 Danny Farmer .60 1.50
FM9 Curtis Keaton .60 1.50
FM10 Peter Warrick .60 1.50
FM11 Courtney Brown .75 2.00
FM12 JaJuan Dawson .60 1.50
FM13 Dennis Northcutt .60 1.50
FM14 Travis Prentice .60 1.50
FM15 Spergon Wynn .60 1.50
FM16 Reuben Droughns .60 1.50
FM17 R.Jay Soward .60 1.50
FM18 J.R. Redmond .60 1.50
FM19 Ron Dayne 1.00 2.50
FM20 Anthony Becht .60 1.50
FM21 Laveranues Coles .75 2.00
FM22 Chad Pennington .75 2.00
FM23 Jerry Porter 1.00 2.50
FM24 Todd Pinkston .60 1.50
FM25 Plaxico Burress .75 2.00
FM26 Tee Martin .60 1.50
FM27 Trung Canidate .60 1.50
FM28 Giovanni Carmazzi .60 1.50
FM29 Tim Rattay .75 2.00
FM30 Joe Hamilton .60 1.50

2000 Collector's Edge Masters GameGear Leatherbacks

Randomly inserted in packs, this 10-card set features action player photos on the front which is all foil, and the back of the card is composed completely of a game used football. Each card is sequentially numbered to 12.

STATED PRINT RUN 12 SER.#'d SETS
DC Daunte Culpepper 25.00 60.00
KW Kurt Warner 60.00 150.00
PM Peyton Manning 125.00 250.00
PW Peter Warrick 20.00 50.00
RM Randy Moss 125.00 250.00
TC Tim Couch 25.00 60.00

2000 Collector's Edge Masters Hasta La Vista Gold

Randomly inserted in packs, this 20-card set features action photography on an all yellow and orange foil card with gold foil highlights. Cards are sequentially numbered to 2000.

COMPLETE SET (20) 20.00 50.00
GOLD STATED PRINT RUN 2000
*SILVER/3000: .3X TO .8X GOLD/2000
H1 Eric Moulds .60 1.50
H2 Cade McNown .60 1.50
H3 Emmitt Smith 1.50 4.00
H4 Terrell Davis .75 2.00
H5 Charlie Batch .60 1.50
H6 Marvin Harrison .75 2.00
H7 Edgerrin James .75 2.00
H8 Peyton Manning 2.50 6.00
H9 Mark Brunell .75 2.00
H10 Fred Taylor .60 1.50
H11 Daunte Culpepper .75 2.00
H12 Torry Holt .75 2.00
H13 Marshall Faulk .75 2.00
H14 Kurt Warner 1.50 4.00
H15 Ryan Leaf .75 2.00
H16 Keyshawn Johnson .75 2.00
H17 Shaun King .60 1.50
H18 Steve McNair .75 2.00
H19 Stephen Davis .60 1.50
H20 Brad Johnson .75 2.00

2000 Collector's Edge Masters K-Klub

Randomly inserted in packs, this 50-card set feautures an all vinyl card design with player action photography and gold foil highlights. Each card is sequentially numbered to 3000.

COMPLETE SET (50) 25.00 60.00
STATED PRINT RUN 3000 SER.#'d SETS
K1 David Boston .50 1.25
K2 Frank Sanders .50 1.25
K3 Jamal Anderson .60 1.50
K4 Terance Mathis .50 1.25
K5 Qadry Ismail .50 1.25
K6 Eric Moulds .50 1.25
K7 Antowain Smith .60 1.50
K8 Patrick Jeffers .50 1.25
K9 Muhsin Muhammad .50 1.25
K10 Curtis Enis .50 1.25
K11 Marcus Robinson .60 1.50
K12 Corey Dillon .50 1.25
K13 Kevin Johnson .50 1.25
K14 Joey Galloway .60 1.50
K15 Rocket Ismail .60 1.50
K16 Emmitt Smith 1.25 3.00
K17 Olandis Gary .60 1.50
K18 Ed McCaffrey .60 1.50
K19 Germane Crowell .50 1.25
K20 Herman Moore .50 1.25
K21 Antonio Freeman .60 1.50
K22 Dorsey Levens .60 1.50
K23 Marvin Harrison .60 1.50
K24 Edgerrin James .60 1.50
K25 Keenan McCardell .60 1.50
K26 Jimmy Smith .60 1.50
K27 Fred Taylor .50 1.25
K28 Cris Carter .75 2.00
K29 Randy Moss .60 1.50
K30 Robert Smith .50 1.25
K31 Terry Glenn .60 1.50
K32 Ricky Williams .60 1.50
K33 Curtis Martin .60 1.50
K34 Tim Brown .75 2.00
K35 Duce Staley .50 1.25
K36 Jerome Bettis .75 2.00
K37 Isaac Bruce .75 2.00
K38 Marshall Faulk .60 1.50
K39 Torry Holt .60 1.50
K40 Charlie Garner .60 1.50
K41 Terrell Owens .60 1.50
K42 Ricky Watters .60 1.50
K43 Warrick Dunn .50 1.25
K44 Keyshawn Johnson .60 1.50
K45 Kevin Dyson .60 1.50
K46 Eddie George .60 1.50
K47 Carl Pickens .60 1.50
K48 Albert Connell .50 1.25
K49 Stephen Davis .50 1.25
K50 Michael Westbrook .50 1.25

2000 Collector's Edge Masters Legends

Randomly seeded in packs, this 30-card set features features a foil dot matrix card stock with a background matrix hologram and gold foil highlights. Each card is sequentially numbered to 5000.

COMPLETE SET (30) 15.00 40.00
STATED PRINT RUN 5000 SER.#'d SETS
ML1 Jake Plummer .40 1.00
ML2 Eric Moulds .40 1.00
ML3 Cade McNown .40 1.00
ML4 Marcus Robinson .50 1.25
ML5 Akili Smith .40 1.00
ML6 Tim Couch .50 1.25
ML7 Troy Aikman .75 2.00
ML8 Emmitt Smith 1.00 2.50
ML9 Terrell Davis .50 1.25
ML10 Brett Favre 1.25 3.00
ML11 Antonio Freeman .50 1.25
ML12 Dorsey Levens .50 1.25
ML13 Mark Brunell .50 1.25
ML14 Fred Taylor .40 1.00
ML15 Cris Carter .60 1.50
ML16 Randy Moss .50 1.25
ML17 Drew Bledsoe .50 1.25
ML18 Curtis Martin .50 1.25
ML19 Donovan McNabb .50 1.25
ML20 Ricky Williams .50 1.25
ML21 Jerome Bettis .60 1.50
ML22 Isaac Bruce .60 1.50
ML23 Marshall Faulk .50 1.25
ML24 Jerry Rice 1.50 4.00
ML25 Jon Kitna .40 1.00
ML26 Keyshawn Johnson .50 1.25
ML27 Shaun King .40 1.00
ML28 Steve McNair .50 1.25
ML29 Stephen Davis .40 1.00
ML30 Brad Johnson .50 1.25

2000 Collector's Edge Masters Majestic

Randomly seeded in packs, this 30-card set features a rainbow holographic foil card stock with full color action photography and gold foil highlights. Each card is sequentially numbered to 5000.

COMPLETE SET (30) 15.00 40.00
STATED PRINT RUN 5000 SER.#'d SETS
M1 Thomas Jones .50 1.25
M2 Jamal Lewis .60 1.50
M3 Travis Taylor .40 1.00
M4 Brian Urlacher 2.00 5.00
M5 Dez White .40 1.00
M6 Danny Farmer .40 1.00
M7 Curtis Keaton .40 1.00
M8 Peter Warrick .40 1.00
M9 Courtney Brown .50 1.25
M10 JaJuan Dawson .40 1.00
M11 Spergon Wynn .40 1.00
M12 Michael Wiley .40 1.00
M13 Reuben Droughns .40 1.00
M14 Bubba Franks .40 1.00
M15 Rob Morris .50 1.25
M16 Sylvester Morris .40 1.00
M17 Ron Dayne .60 1.50
M18 Ron Dixon .40 1.00
M19 Anthony Becht .40 1.00
M20 Chad Pennington .50 1.25
M21 Sebastian Janikowski .60 1.50
M22 Todd Pinkston .40 1.00
M23 Corey Simon .50 1.25
M24 Plaxico Burress .50 1.25
M25 Tee Martin .40 1.00
M26 Trevor Gaylor .40 1.00
M27 Giovanni Carmazzi .40 1.00
M28 Tim Rattay .50 1.25
M29 Shaun Alexander .60 1.50
M30 Joe Hamilton .40 1.00

2000 Collector's Edge Masters Rookie Ink

Randomly inserted in packs, this four card set features autographed cards with full color player action photography and a whited out box along the right side of the card where the autograph appears. Each card is hand numbered. A Blue Ink (40-sets) parallel and Red Ink (9-10 sets) parallel were also randomly inserted in packs. An unsigned and un-serial numbered Shaun Alexander card appeared on the market after Collector's Edge ceased card operations. It was never issued signed originally and did not appear in packs. The cards were printed with gold foil highlights on the front.

*BLUE INK/40: 1X TO 2.5X BLACK
BLUE INK PRINT RUN 40 SER.#'d SETS
UNPRICED RED INK PRINT RUN 9-10
CK Curtis Keaton Gold/1130 6.00 15.00
CR Chris Redman/450 6.00 15.00
LC Laveranues Coles/475 8.00 20.00
SA Shaun Alexander Gold No AU 3.00 8.00
TP Travis Prentice Gold/800 6.00 15.00

2000 Collector's Edge Masters Rookie Masters

Randomly inserted in packs, this 30-card set features top 2000 rookies with the same card design as the Master Legends. Each card was sequentially numbered to 2000.

COMPLETE SET (30) 30.00 80.00
STATED PRINT RUN 2000 SER.#'d SETS
*PREVIEWS: .4X TO 1X BASIC INSERTS
MR1 Thomas Jones .75 2.00
MR2 Jamal Lewis 1.00 2.50
MR3 Chris Redman .60 1.50
MR4 Travis Taylor .60 1.50
MR5 Dez White .60 1.50
MR6 Ron Dugans .60 1.50
MR7 Curtis Keaton .60 1.50
MR8 Peter Warrick .60 1.50
MR9 Brian Urlacher 3.00 8.00
MR10 JaJuan Dawson .60 1.50
MR11 Dennis Northcutt .60 1.50
MR12 Travis Prentice .60 1.50
MR13 Spergon Wynn .60 1.50
MR14 Reuben Droughns .60 1.50
MR15 Bubba Franks .60 1.50
MR16 Sylvester Morris .60 1.50
MR17 J.R. Redmond .60 1.50
MR18 Ron Dayne 1.00 2.50
MR19 Anthony Becht .60 1.50
MR20 Laveranues Coles .75 2.00
MR21 Chad Pennington .75 2.00
MR22 Jerry Porter 1.00 2.50
MR23 Todd Pinkston .60 1.50
MR24 Plaxico Burress .75 2.00
MR25 Tee Martin .60 1.50
MR26 Trung Canidate .60 1.50
MR27 Giovanni Carmazzi .60 1.50
MR28 Tim Rattay .75 2.00
MR29 Shaun Alexander 1.00 2.50
MR30 Joe Hamilton .60 1.50

2000 Collector's Edge Masters Sentinel Rookies Gold

Randomly inserted in packs, this 30 card set features top 2000 rookies on an all vinyl card stock with gold foil highlights. Each card is sequentially numbered to 1000.

COMPLETE SET (30) 40.00 100.00
STATED PRINT RUN 1000 SER.#'d SETS
*SILVER/2000: .25X TO .6X GOLD/1000
RS1 Thomas Jones 1.00 2.50
RS2 Jamal Lewis 1.25 3.00
RS3 Chris Redman .75 2.00
RS4 Travis Taylor .75 2.00
RS5 Ron Dugans .75 2.00
RS6 Peter Warrick .75 2.00
RS7 Courtney Brown 1.00 2.50
RS8 Dennis Northcutt .75 2.00
RS9 Travis Prentice .75 2.00
RS10 Bubba Franks .75 2.00
RS11 R.Jay Soward .75 2.00
RS12 Sylvester Morris .75 2.00
RS13 J.R. Redmond .75 2.00
RS14 Ron Dayne 1.25 3.00
RS15 Laveranues Coles 1.00 2.50
RS16 Chad Pennington 1.00 2.50
RS17 Jerry Porter 1.25 3.00
RS18 Plaxico Burress 1.00 2.50
RS19 Trung Canidate .75 2.00
RS20 Shaun Alexander 1.25 3.00
RS21 Mike Anderson .75 2.00
RS22 Danny Farmer .75 2.00
RS23 Brian Urlacher 4.00 10.00
RS24 Michael Wiley .75 2.00
RS25 Rob Morris 1.00 2.50
RS26 Corey Simon 1.00 2.50
RS27 Sebastian Janikowski 1.25 3.00
RS28 Sammy Morris .75 2.00
RS29 Keith Bulluck 1.00 2.50
RS30 Frank Moreau .75 2.00

2000 Collector's Edge Masters Sentinels Gold

Randomly inserted in packs, this 20-card set features a clear vinyl card stock with player action photograpy and gold foil highlights. Each card is sequentially numbered to 1000.

COMPLETE SET (20) 30.00 80.00
GOLD PRINT RUN 1000 SER.#'d SETS
*SILVER/2000: .25X TO .6X GOLD/1000
S1 Jake Plummer .75 2.00
S2 Eric Moulds .75 2.00
S3 Cade McNown .75 2.00
S4 Akili Smith .75 2.00
S5 Tim Couch 1.00 2.50
S6 Kevin Johnson .75 2.00
S7 Troy Aikman 1.50 4.00
S8 Terrell Davis 1.00 2.50
S9 Brett Favre 2.50 6.00
S10 Edgerrin James 1.00 2.50
S11 Peyton Manning 3.00 8.00
S12 Daunte Culpepper 1.00 2.50
S13 Randy Moss 1.00 2.50
S14 Curtis Martin 1.00 2.50
S15 Donovan McNabb 1.00 2.50
S16 Ricky Williams 1.00 2.50
S17 Kurt Warner 2.00 5.00
S18 Jon Kitna .75 2.00
S19 Eddie George 1.00 2.50
S20 Brad Johnson 1.00 2.50

1999 Collector's Edge Millennium Collection Advantage

COMPLETE SET (190) 15.00 30.00
*VETERANS 1-190: .2X TO .5X BASIC ADVANT.
*ROOKIES 151-188 : .12X TO .3X BASIC ADVANT.
*BLUE FOILS: .4X TO 1X REDS

1999 Collector's Edge Millennium Collection First Place

*VETERANS 1-150 : .2X TO .5X BASIC ADVANT.
*ROOKIES 151-200 : .1X TO .3X BASIC ADVANT.
*BLUE FOILS: .4X TO 1X REDS

1999 Collector's Edge Millennium Collection Fury

*VETERANS 1-150: .2X TO .5X BASIC FURY
*ROOKIES 151-200: .12X TO .3X BASIC FURY
*BLUE FOILS: .4X TO 1X REDS

1999 Collector's Edge Millennium Collection Odyssey

*1-150 VETERANS: .2X TO .5X BASIC ODYSSEY
*1-150 ROOKIES: .15X TO .4X BASIC ODYSSEY
*151-170 2Q: .1X TO .3X BASIC ODYSSEY 2Q
*171-185 3Q: .08X TO .25X BASIC ODYSSEY 3Q
*186-195 4Q: .06X TO .15X BASIC ODYSSEY 4Q
*BLUE FOILS: .4X TO 1X REDS

1999 Collector's Edge Millennium Collection Triumph

COMPLETE SET (180) 15.00 30.00
*VETERANS: .2X TO .5X BASIC TRIUMPH
*ROOKIES: .12X TO .3X BASIC TRIUMPH
*BLUE FOILS: .4X TO 1X REDS

1998 Collector's Edge Odyssey Previews

This set was released as a Preview of the 1999 Collector's Edge Odyssey base set. Each card is essentially a parallel version of the base set card with the player's initials as the card number along with the word "preview" on the cardfronts.

COMPLETE SET (33) 25.00 60.00
202 Curtis Enis .40 1.00
206 Emmitt Smith 3Q 1.50 4.00
207 John Elway 3Q 2.50 6.00
208 Terrell Davis 3Q 1.00 2.50
209 Barry Sanders 3Q 1.50 4.00
210 Brett Favre 3Q 2.50 6.00
211 Antonio Freeman .40 1.00
212 Peyton Manning 2.50 6.00
213 Mark Brunell .60 1.50
215 Dan Marino 3Q 2.50 6.00
217 Drew Bledsoe 3Q .75 2.00
219 Curtis Martin .75 2.00
221 Jerome Bettis 3Q .60 1.50
224 Jerry Rice 3Q 1.25 3.00
225 Steve Young 3Q .75 2.00
226 Warren Moon 3Q .60 1.50
227 Trent Dilfer .60 1.50
229 Steve McNair 3Q .60 1.50
230 Eddie George 3Q .60 1.50
231 Curtis Enis 4Q .40 1.00
232 Carl Pickens 4Q .40 1.00
233 Troy Aikman 4Q 1.25 3.00
234 Emmitt Smith 4Q 1.50 4.00
235 John Elway 4Q 2.50 6.00
236 Terrell Davis 4Q 1.00 2.50
237 Barry Sanders 4Q 1.50 4.00
238 Brett Favre 4Q 2.50 6.00
239 Peyton Manning 4Q 2.50 6.00
240 Fred Taylor 4Q 1.25 3.00
241 Dan Marino 4Q 2.50 6.00
242 Randy Moss 4Q 2.00 5.00
243 Drew Bledsoe 4Q .75 2.00
244 Kordell Stewart 4Q .60 1.50
245 Jerome Bettis 4Q .60 1.50
246 Ryan Leaf 4Q .40 1.00
247 Jerry Rice 4Q 1.25 3.00
248 Steve Young 4Q .75 2.00
249 Warren Moon 4Q .60 1.50
250 Eddie George 4Q .60 1.50

1998 Collector's Edge Odyssey

This 250-card set was distributed in eight-card packs with a suggested retail price of $4.99 and features color action photos of 150 different players. The set is divided into four quarters with the 50 best players pictured on the 2nd Quarter cards. The 30 best of these are on the 3rd Quarter cards, and the 20 best of these are pictured on the 4th Quarter cards. A player that is listed in more than one quarter has a different picture on each of his cards. Cards #1-150 makeup the 1st Quarter which consists of all the players. Cards 151-200 are the 2nd Quarter cards and are shortprinted with an insertion rate of 1:2 packs. Cards 201-230 are the 3rd Quarter cards and are shortprinted even further with an insertion rate of 1:7 packs. Cards 231-250 are shortprinted even further and are available 1:24 packs.

COMPLETE SET (250) 200.00 400.00
1 Terance Mathis .12 .30
2 Tony Martin .15 .40
3 Chris Chandler .15 .40
4 Jamal Anderson .15 .40
5 Jake Plummer .12 .30
6 Adrian Murrell .12 .30
7 Rob Moore .12 .30
8 Frank Sanders .12 .30
9 Larry Centers .12 .30
10 Andre Wadsworth RC .40 1.00
11 Jim Harbaugh .20 .50
12 Errict Rhett .15 .40
13 Jermaine Lewis .12 .30
14 Michael Jackson .12 .30
15 Eric Zeier .12 .30
16 Rob Johnson .15 .40
17 Antowain Smith .15 .40
18 Andre Reed .20 .50
19 Bruce Smith .15 .40
20 Doug Flutie .20 .50
21 Thurman Thomas .15 .40
22 Kerry Collins .12 .30
23 Fred Lane .12 .30
24 Muhsin Muhammad .12 .30
25 Rae Carruth .12 .30
26 Rocket Ismail .15 .40
27 Kevin Greene .20 .50
28 Curtis Enis RC .30 .75
29 Curtis Conway .15 .40
30 Erik Kramer .12 .30
31 Edgar Bennett .15 .40
32 Neil O'Donnell .15 .40
33 Jeff Blake .15 .40
34 Carl Pickens .15 .40
35 Corey Dillon .12 .30
36 Troy Aikman .25 .60
37 Jason Garrett RC .40 1.00
38 Emmitt Smith .30 .75
39 Deion Sanders .15 .40
40 Michael Irvin .20 .50
41 Chris Warren .15 .40
42 John Elway .30 .75
43 Terrell Davis .15 .40
44 Shannon Sharpe .15 .40
45 Rod Smith WR .15 .40
46 Marcus Nash RC .25 .60
47 Brian Griese RC .50 1.25
48 Barry Sanders .30 .75
49 Herman Moore .15 .40
50 Scott Mitchell .15 .40
51 Johnnie Morton .15 .40
52 Rashaan Shehee RC .25 .60
53 Charlie Batch RC .40 1.00
54 Brett Favre .40 1.00
55 Dorsey Levens .15 .40
56 Antonio Freeman .20 .50
57 Reggie White .20 .50
58 Robert Brooks .15 .40
59 Raymont Harris .12 .30
60 Peyton Manning RC 6.00 15.00
61 Marshall Faulk .15 .40
62 Jerome Pathon RC .30 .75
63 Marvin Harrison .15 .40
64 Mark Brunell .15 .40
65 Fred Taylor RC .50 1.25
66 Jimmy Smith .15 .40
67 James Stewart .12 .30
68 Keenan McCardell .15 .40
69 Andre Rison .15 .40
70 Elvis Grbac .15 .40
71 Donnell Bennett .12 .30
72 Rich Gannon .15 .40
73 Derrick Thomas .20 .50
74 Dan Marino .40 1.00
75 Karim Abdul-Jabbar UER .12 .30
76 John Avery UER RC .30 .75
77 O.J. McDuffie .15 .40
78 Oronde Gadsden RC .30 .75
79 Zach Thomas .15 .40
80 Randy Moss RC 2.00 5.00
81 Cris Carter .20 .50
82 Jake Reed .15 .40
83 Robert Smith .12 .30
84 Brad Johnson .15 .40
85 Drew Bledsoe .15 .40
86 Robert Edwards RC .30 .75
87 Terry Glenn .15 .40
88 Troy Brown .12 .30
89 Shawn Jefferson .12 .30
90 Danny Wuerffel .15 .40
91 Dana Stubblefield .12 .30
92 Derrick Alexander .15 .40
93 Ray Zellars .12 .30
94 Andre Hastings .12 .30
95 Danny Kanell .12 .30
96 Tiki Barber .15 .40
97 Ike Hilliard .12 .30
98 Charles Way .12 .30
99 Chris Calloway .15 .40
100 Curtis Martin .15 .40
101 Glenn Foley .12 .30
102 Vinny Testaverde .12 .30
103 Keyshawn Johnson .15 .40
104 Wayne Chrebet .12 .30
105 Leon Johnson .12 .30
106 Jeff George .15 .40
107 Charles Woodson RC 1.00 2.50
108 Tim Brown .20 .50
109 James Jett .12 .30
110 Napoleon Kaufman .12 .30
111 Charlie Garner .15 .40
112 Bobby Hoying .15 .40
113 Duce Staley .12 .30
114 Irving Fryar .15 .40
115 Kordell Stewart .12 .30
116 Jerome Bettis .20 .50
117 Charles Johnson .12 .30
118 Randall Cunningham .15 .40
119 Courtney Hawkins .12 .30
120 Tony Banks .15 .40
121 Isaac Bruce .20 .50
122 Robert Holcombe RC .25 .60
123 Eddie Kennison .12 .30
124 Ryan Leaf RC .30 .75
125 Mikhael Ricks RC .30 .75
126 Natrone Means .15 .40
127 Junior Seau .15 .40
128 Jerry Rice .50 1.25
129 Terrell Owens .15 .40
130 Garrison Hearst .12 .30
131 Steve Young .25 .60
132 J.J. Stokes .15 .40
133 Warren Moon .20 .50
134 Joey Galloway .15 .40
135 Ricky Watters .15 .40
136 Ahman Green RC .50 1.25
137 Trent Dilfer .15 .40
138 Mike Alstott .12 .30
139 Warrick Dunn .12 .30
140 Reidel Anthony .12 .30
141 Jacquez Green RC .30 .75
142 Steve McNair .15 .40
143 Eddie George .15 .40
144 Yancey Thigpen .12 .30
145 Kevin Dyson RC .30 .75
146 Trent Green .12 .30
147 Gus Frerotte .12 .30
148 Terry Allen .15 .40
149 Michael Westbrook .15 .40
150 Jim Druckenmiller .12 .30
151 Jake Plummer 2Q .20 .50
152 Adrian Murrell 2Q .20 .50
153 Rob Johnson 2Q .25 .60
154 Antowain Smith 2Q .40 1.00
155 Kerry Collins 2Q .20 .50
156 Curtis Enis 2Q .40 1.00
157 Carl Pickens 2Q .25 .60
158 Corey Dillon 2Q .20 .50
159 Troy Aikman 2Q .40 1.00
160 Emmitt Smith 2Q .50 1.25
161 Deion Sanders 2Q .25 .60
162 Michael Irvin 2Q .30 .75
163 John Elway 2Q .50 1.25
164 Terrell Davis 2Q .25 .60
165 Shannon Sharpe 2Q .25 .60
166 Rod Smith 2Q .25 .60
167 Barry Sanders 2Q .50 1.25
168 Herman Moore 2Q .25 .60
169 Brett Favre 2Q .60 1.50
170 Dorsey Levens 2Q .25 .60
171 Antonio Freeman 2Q .30 .75
172 Peyton Manning 2Q 5.00 12.00
173 Marshall Faulk 2Q .25 .60
174 Mark Brunell 2Q .25 .60
175 Fred Taylor 2Q .60 1.50
176 Dan Marino 2Q .60 1.50
177 Randy Moss 2Q 2.50 6.00
178 Cris Carter 2Q .30 .75
179 Drew Bledsoe 2Q .25 .60
180 Robert Edwards 2Q .40 1.00
181 Curtis Martin 2Q .25 .60
182 Napoleon Kaufman 2Q .20 .50
183 Kordell Stewart 2Q .20 .50
184 Jerome Bettis 2Q .30 .75
185 Tony Banks 2Q .25 .60
186 Isaac Bruce 2Q .30 .75
187 Ryan Leaf 2Q .40 1.00
188 Natrone Means 2Q .25 .60
189 Jerry Rice 2Q .75 2.00
190 Terrell Owens 2Q .25 .60
191 Garrison Hearst 2Q .20 .50
192 Steve Young 2Q .40 1.00
193 Warren Moon 2Q .30 .75
194 Joey Galloway 2Q .25 .60
195 Trent Dilfer 2Q .25 .60
196 Mike Alstott 2Q .20 .50
197 Warrick Dunn 2Q .20 .50
198 Steve McNair 2Q .25 .60
199 Eddie George 2Q .25 .60
200 Terry Allen 2Q .25 .60
201 Jake Plummer 3Q .25 .60
202 Curtis Enis 3Q .50 1.25
203 Carl Pickens 3Q .30 .75
204 Corey Dillon 3Q .25 .60
205 Troy Aikman 3Q .50 1.25
206 Emmitt Smith 3Q .60 1.50
207 John Elway 3Q .60 1.50
208 Terrell Davis 3Q .30 .75
209 Barry Sanders 3Q .60 1.50
210 Brett Favre 3Q .75 2.00
211 Antonio Freeman 3Q .40 1.00
212 Peyton Manning 3Q 6.00 15.00
213 Mark Brunell 3Q .30 .75
214 Fred Taylor 3Q .75 2.00
215 Dan Marino 3Q .75 2.00
216 Randy Moss 3Q 3.00 8.00
217 Drew Bledsoe 3Q .30 .75
218 Robert Edwards 3Q .50 1.25
219 Curtis Martin 3Q .30 .75
220 Kordell Stewart 3Q .25 .60
221 Jerome Bettis 3Q .40 1.00
222 Tony Banks 3Q .30 .75
223 Ryan Leaf 3Q .50 1.25
224 Jerry Rice 3Q 1.00 2.50
225 Steve Young 3Q .50 1.25
226 Warren Moon 3Q .40 1.00
227 Trent Dilfer 3Q .30 .75
228 Warrick Dunn 3Q .25 .60
229 Steve McNair 3Q .30 .75
230 Eddie George 3Q .30 .75
231 Curtis Enis 4Q 1.00 2.50
232 Carl Pickens 4Q .75 2.00
233 Troy Aikman 4Q 1.25 3.00
234 Emmitt Smith 4Q 1.50 4.00
235 John Elway 4Q 1.50 4.00
236 Terrell Davis 4Q .75 2.00
237 Barry Sanders 4Q 1.50 4.00
238 Brett Favre 4Q 2.00 5.00
239 Peyton Manning 4Q 12.00 30.00
240 Fred Taylor 4Q 1.50 4.00
241 Dan Marino 4Q 2.00 5.00
242 Randy Moss 4Q 6.00 15.00
243 Drew Bledsoe 4Q .75 2.00
244 Kordell Stewart 4Q .60 1.50
245 Jerome Bettis 4Q 1.00 2.50
246 Ryan Leaf 4Q 1.00 2.50
247 Jerry Rice 4Q 2.50 6.00
248 Steve Young 4Q 1.25 3.00
249 Warren Moon 4Q 1.00 2.50
250 Eddie George 4Q .75 2.00

1998 Collector's Edge Odyssey Level 1 Galvanized

COMPLETE SET (250) 300.00 600.00
*VETS 1-150: 1.2X TO 3X BASIC CARDS
*ROOKIES 1-150: .6X TO 1.5X
GALVANIZED 1-150 STATED ODDS 1:3
*VETS 151-200: 1.5X TO 4X BASIC CARDS
*ROOKIES 151-200: .8X TO 2X
GALVANIZED 151-200 STATED ODDS 1:15
*VETS 201-230: 1.2X TO 3X BASIC CARDS
*ROOKIES 201-230: .6X TO 1.5X
GALVANIZED 201-230 STATED ODDS 1:29
*VETS 231-250: .8X TO 2X BASIC CARDS
*ROOKIES 231-250: .4X TO 1X
GALVANIZED 231-250 STATED ODDS 1:59

1998 Collector's Edge Odyssey Level 2 HoloGold

*VETS 1-150: 15X TO 40X BASIC CARDS
*ROOKIES 1-150: 3X TO 8X
HOLO.GOLD 1-150 STATED ODDS 1:34
HOLO.GOLD 1-150 PRINT RUN 150 SETS
*VETS 151-200: 10X TO 25X BASIC CARDS
*ROOKIES 151-200: 3X TO 8X
HOLO.GOLD 151-200 STATED ODDS 1:307
HOLO.GOLD 151-200 PRINT RUN 50 SETS
*VETS 201-230: 12X TO 30X BASIC CARDS
*ROOKIES 201-230: 4X TO 10X
HOLO.GOLD 201-230 STATED ODDS 1:840
HOLO.GOLD 201-230 PRINT RUN 30 SETS
*VETS 231-250: 6X TO 15X BASIC CARDS
*ROOKIES 231-250: 2X TO 5X
HOLO.GOLD 231-250 STATED ODDS 1:1920
HOLO.GOLD 231-250 PRINT RUN 20 SETS

1998 Collector's Edge Odyssey Double Edge

Randomly inserted in packs at the rate of one in 15, this 12-card set features color action photos of 12 top veteran stars paired with 12 top rookies printed on double-sided cards. Only one side of the card was printed with etched foil technology with cards numbered as "A" featuring the veteran printed with foil and "B" with the rookie player printed in foil.

COMPLETE SET (12) 25.00 60.00
STATED ODDS 1:15
1A J.Rice F/R.Moss 7.50 15.00
1B J.Rice/R.Moss F 7.50 15.00
2A B.Favre F/R.Leaf 5.00 12.00
2B B.Favre/R.Leaf F 5.00 12.00
3A D.Marino F/B.Hoying 5.00 12.00
3B D.Marino/B.Hoying F 5.00 12.00
4A D.Sanders F/C.Woodson 2.00 5.00
4B D.Sanders/C.Woodson F 2.00 5.00
5A T.Davis F/C.Enis 2.00 5.00
5B T.Davis/C.Enis F 2.00 5.00
6A B.Sanders F/F.Taylor 3.00 8.00
6B B.Sanders/F.Taylor F 3.00 8.00
7A E.Smith F/R.Edwards 4.00 10.00
7B E.Smith/R.Edwards F 4.00 10.00
8A J.Elway F/B.Griese 5.00 12.00
8B J.Elway/B.Griese F 5.00 12.00
9A R.White F/A.Wadsworth 1.50 4.00
9B R.White/A.Wadsworth F 1.50 4.00
10A D.Bledsoe F/C.Batch 2.00 5.00
10B D.Bledsoe/C.Batch F 2.00 5.00
11A D.Flutie F/G.Foley 1.50 4.00
11B D.Flutie/G.Foley F 1.50 4.00
12A N.Kaufman F/W.Dunn 1.25 3.00
12B N.Kaufman/W.Dunn F 1.25 3.00

1998 Collector's Edge Odyssey Game Ball

Redemption cards from this set were inserted into 1998 Collectors Edge Odyssey packs at a rate of one every 360 packs. The cards were exchangeable for an actual Game Ball card of the featured player including a diamond shaped swatch of football. The cardfronts include a color photo of the player against a silver holofoil background which includes a pattern of the team's logo. The words " Edge Authentic NFL Game Ball" and the Odyssey logo appear at the bottom of the card.

STATED ODDS 1:360
BS Barry Sanders 10.00 25.00
CB Charlie Batch 5.00 12.00
CC Cris Carter 6.00 15.00
ES Emmitt Smith 10.00 25.00
FT Fred Taylor 5.00 12.00
HM Herman Moore 4.00 10.00
JE John Elway 12.00 30.00
MB Mark Brunell 5.00 12.00
PM Peyton Manning 12.00 30.00
RM Randy Moss 6.00 15.00
TA Troy Aikman 8.00 20.00
TD Terrell Davis 6.00 15.00

1998 Collector's Edge Odyssey Leading Edge

Randomly inserted in packs at the rate of one in seven, this 30-card set features color player portraits with a small action photo of some of the NFL's top stars printed on foil cards.

COMPLETE SET (30) 20.00 50.00
STATED ODDS 1:7
1 Jake Plummer .30 .75
2 Rob Johnson .40 1.00
3 Curtis Enis .40 1.00
4 Carl Pickens .40 1.00
5 Troy Aikman .60 1.50
6 Emmitt Smith .75 2.00
7 John Elway .75 2.00
8 Terrell Davis .40 1.00
9 Shannon Sharpe .40 1.00
10 Barry Sanders .75 2.00
11 Brett Favre 1.00 2.50
12 Antonio Freeman .50 1.25
13 Peyton Manning 6.00 15.00
14 Marshall Faulk .40 1.00
15 Mark Brunell .40 1.00
16 Dan Marino 1.00 2.50
17 Randy Moss 3.00 8.00

18 Cris Carter .50 1.25
19 Robert Edwards .40 1.00
20 Curtis Martin .40 1.00
21 Ryan Leaf .40 1.00
22 Terrell Owens .40 1.00
23 Garrison Hearst .30 .75
24 Steve Young .60 1.50
25 Joey Galloway .40 1.00
26 Mike Alstott .30 .75
27 Warrick Dunn .30 .75
28 Eddie George .40 1.00
29 Kevin Dyson .40 1.00
30 Terry Allen .40 1.00

1998 Collector's Edge Odyssey Prodigies Autographs

Randomly inserted in packs at the rate of one in 24, this set features unnumbered borderless color action photos of top rookies and stars with the player's signature on the bottom half. John Elway and Terrell Davis cards were inserted in Collector's Edge Masters packs. A limited red ink parallel version of this set was also produced with each card being numbered between 10-80. Lastly, a few additional players appeared later in unsigned form, such as Charles Woodson and Troy Aikman, apparently after Collector's Edge ceased its card operations.

STATED ODDS 1:24
*RED INK/50-80: .8X TO 2X BASIC AUT
RED INK PRINT RUN 10-80
ELWAY/T.DAVIS INSERTED IN 1998 MASTERS
1 Tavian Banks 6.00 15.00
2 Charlie Batch 7.50 20.00
3 Blaine Bishop 6.00 15.00
4 Robert Brooks 7.50 20.00
5 Tim Brown 15.00 40.00
6 Mark Brunell 7.50 20.00
7 Wayne Chrebet 7.50 20.00
8 Terrell Davis Blue/40 25.00 60.00
9 Jim Druckenmiller 4.00 10.00
10 Robert Edwards 6.00 15.00
11 John Elway Blue/40 50.00 120.00
12 Doug Flutie 15.00 40.00
13 Glenn Foley 4.00 10.00
14 Oronde Gadsden 6.00 15.00
15 Joey Galloway 6.00 15.00
16 Garrison Hearst 7.50 20.00
17 Robert Holcombe 6.00 15.00
18 Joey Kent 6.00 15.00
19 Jon Kitna 7.50 20.00
20 Ryan Leaf 7.50 20.00
21 Peyton Manning 40.00 100.00
22 Herman Moore 7.50 20.00
23 Randy Moss 40.00 80.00
24 Terrell Owens 15.00 30.00
25 Mikhael Ricks 6.00 15.00
26 Antowain Smith 7.50 20.00
27 Emmitt Smith 50.00 100.00
28 Robert Smith 7.50 20.00
29 Rod Smith 7.50 20.00
30 J.J. Stokes 6.00 15.00
31 Fred Taylor 7.50 20.00
32 Derrick Thomas 40.00 80.00
33 Chris Warren 6.00 15.00
34 Eric Zeier 6.00 15.00

1998 Collector's Edge Odyssey Prodigies Unsigned

1 Troy Aikman 2.50 6.00
2 Jerry Rice 2.50 6.00
3 Barry Sanders 3.00 8.00
4 Charles Woodson 4.00 10.00

1998 Collector's Edge Odyssey Super Limited Edge

Randomly inserted in packs at the rate of one in 99, this 12-card set features color photos of some of the game's most collectible superstars.

COMPLETE SET (12) 50.00 120.00
STATED ODDS 1:99
1 Emmitt Smith 4.00 10.00
2 Deion Sanders 2.00 5.00
3 John Elway 4.00 10.00
4 Brett Favre 5.00 12.00
5 Antonio Freeman 2.50 6.00
6 Peyton Manning 12.00 30.00
7 Mark Brunell 2.00 5.00
8 Dan Marino 5.00 12.00
9 Randy Moss 6.00 15.00
10 Joey Galloway 2.00 5.00
11 Mike Alstott 1.50 4.00
12 Eddie George 2.00 5.00

1999 Collector's Edge Odyssey Previews

Cards from this set are essentially a parallel version to the player's corresponding base card. The cardbacks contain the word "preview" and each was released primarily to dealers and distributors.

DC Daunte Culpepper 1Q 2.00 5.00
EJ Edgerrin James 1Q 2.00 5.00
PM Peyton Manning 3Q 2.00 5.00
AS Akili Smith 1Q .60 1.50
DB David Boston 1Q .40 1.00
TE Troy Edwards 1Q .40 1.00
KF Kevin Faulk 1Q .60 1.50

1999 Collector's Edge Odyssey

Released as a 193-card set, 1999 Collector's Edge Odyssey features First through Fourth Quarter cards. First Quarter cards, 1-150, feature both rookies and veterans, Second Quarter cards, 151-170, are found one in four packs and feature top prospects, Third Quarter cards, 171-185, are found one in eight packs and feature veteran stars, and Fourth Quarter cards, 186-195, are found one in 24 packs and feature the 10 top prospects from the 1999 NFL draft. The cards are also distinguishable by the foil stamp along the bottom of the card front which relays what "Quarter" the card belongs to. Note that card numbers 21 and 55 were not released in packs

COMPLETE SET (193) 50.00 120.00
COMP.SET w/o SP's (148) 20.00 40.00
1 Checklist Card .10 .30
2 Checklist Card .10 .30
3 David Boston RC .25 .60
4 Rob Moore .20 .50
5 Adrian Murrell .20 .50
6 Jake Plummer .20 .50
7 Frank Sanders .20 .50
8 Jamal Anderson .25 .60
9 Chris Calloway .20 .50
10 Chris Chandler .25 .60
11 Tim Dwight .25 .60
12 Terance Mathis .20 .50
13 Tony Banks .25 .60
14 Priest Holmes .20 .50
15 Jermaine Lewis .20 .50
16 Chris McAlister RC .25 .60
17 Scott Mitchell .20 .50
18 Doug Flutie .30 .75
19 Eric Moulds .20 .50
20 Peerless Price RC .25 .60
21 A.Smith 30.00 80.00
A.Reed SP
22 Antowain Smith .20 .50
23 Antoine Winfield RC .25 .60
24 Steve Beuerlein .25 .60
25 Tim Biakabutuka .25 .60
26 Rae Carruth .20 .50
27 Muhsin Muhammad .20 .50
28 D'Wayne Bates RC .25 .60
29 Bobby Engram .20 .50
30 Curtis Enis .20 .50
31 Shane Matthews .20 .50
32 Cade McNown RC .25 .60
33 Jeff Blake .25 .60
34 Corey Dillon .20 .50
35 Carl Pickens .25 .60
36 Darnay Scott .20 .50
37 Akili Smith RC .25 .60
38 Tim Couch RC .30 .75
39 Kevin Johnson RC .30 .75
40 Terry Kirby .20 .50
41 Leslie Shepherd .20 .50
42 Troy Aikman .40 1.00
43 Michael Irvin .30 .75
44 Rocket Ismail .25 .60
45 Deion Sanders .25 .60
46 Emmitt Smith .50 1.25
47 Bubby Brister .20 .50
48 Terrell Davis .25 .60
49 Brian Griese .20 .50
50 Ed McCaffrey .25 .60
51 Shannon Sharpe .25 .60
52 Rod Smith .25 .60
53 Charlie Batch .20 .50
54 Chris Claiborne RC .25 .60
56 Herman Moore .25 .60
57 Johnnie Morton .25 .60
58 Ron Rivers .20 .50
59 Brett Favre .60 1.50
60 Mark Chmura .20 .50
61 Antonio Freeman .25 .60
62 Dorsey Levens .25 .60
63 E.G. Green .20 .50
64 Marvin Harrison .25 .60
65 Edgerrin James RC .40 1.00
66 Peyton Manning 1.00 2.50
67 Mark Brunell .25 .60
68 Keenan McCardell .25 .60
69 Jimmy Smith .25 .60
70 Fred Taylor .20 .50
71 Derrick Alexander WR .20 .50
72 Kimble Anders .20 .50
73 Mike Cloud RC .25 .60
74 Elvis Grbac .20 .50
75 Andre Rison .25 .60
76 Karim Abdul-Jabbar .20 .50
77 Cecil Collins RC .25 .60
78 James Johnson RC .25 .60
79 Rob Konrad RC .25 .60
80 Dan Marino .60 1.50
81 O.J. McDuffie .25 .60
82 Cris Carter .30 .75
83 Daunte Culpepper RC .40 1.00
84 Randall Cunningham .25 .60
85 Randy Moss .25 .60
86 Jake Reed .25 .60
87 Robert Smith .20 .50
88 Terry Allen .25 .60
89 Drew Bledsoe .25 .60
90 Ben Coates .25 .60
91 Kevin Faulk RC .25 .60
92 Terry Glenn .25 .60
93 Andy Katzenmoyer RC .30 .75
94 Cameron Cleeland .20 .50
95 Billy Joe Hobert .20 .50
96 Eddie Kennison .25 .60
97 Ricky Williams RC .40 1.00
98 Sean Bennett RC .25 .60
99 Gary Brown .20 .50
100 Kerry Collins .20 .50
101 Kent Graham .20 .50
102 Ike Hilliard .20 .50
103 Wayne Chrebet .20 .50
104 Keyshawn Johnson .25 .60
105 Curtis Martin .25 .60
106 Rick Mirer .25 .60
107 Tim Brown .30 .75
108 Rich Gannon .25 .60
109 Napoleon Kaufman .20 .50
110 Charles Woodson .30 .75
111 Charles Johnson .20 .50
112 Donovan McNabb RC 2.00 5.00
113 Doug Pederson .20 .50
114 Duce Staley .20 .50
115 Jerome Bettis .30 .75
116 Troy Edwards RC .25 .60
117 Kordell Stewart .20 .50
118 Amos Zereoue RC .25 .60
119 Isaac Bruce .30 .75
120 Marshall Faulk .25 .60
121 Joe Germaine RC .30 .75
122 Torry Holt RC .50 1.25
123 Kurt Warner RC 2.50 6.00
124 Jim Harbaugh .25 .60
125 Erik Kramer .25 .60
126 Natrone Means .25 .60
127 Junior Seau .25 .60
128 Terrell Owens .25 .60
129 Lawrence Phillips .25 .60
130 Jerry Rice .75 2.00
131 J.J. Stokes .20 .50
132 Steve Young .40 1.00
133 Karsten Bailey RC .25 .60
134 Joey Galloway .25 .60
135 Brock Huard RC .25 .60
136 Jon Kitna .20 .50
137 Ricky Watters .25 .60
138 Reidel Anthony .20 .50
139 Trent Dilfer .20 .50
140 Warrick Dunn .20 .50
141 Shaun King RC .25 .60
142 Jevon Kearse RC .30 .75
143 Kevin Dyson .20 .50
144 Eddie George .25 .60
145 Steve McNair .25 .60
146 Champ Bailey RC .50 1.25
147 Stephen Davis .20 .50
148 Skip Hicks .20 .50
149 Brad Johnson .25 .60
150 Michael Westbrook .20 .50
151 Chris McAlister 2Q .30 .75
152 Peerless Price 2Q .30 .75
153 Antoine Winfield 2Q .30 .75
154 D'Wayne Bates 2Q .30 .75
155 Kevin Johnson 2Q .40 1.00
156 Chris Claiborne 2Q .30 .75
157 Sedrick Irvin 2Q .30 .75
158 Mike Cloud 2Q .30 .75
159 Cecil Collins 2Q .30 .75
160 James Johnson 2Q .30 .75
161 Rob Konrad 2Q .30 .75
162 Daunte Culpepper 2Q .50 1.25
163 Andy Katzenmoyer 2Q .40 1.00
164 Amos Zereoue 2Q .30 .75
165 Joe Germaine 2Q .40 1.00
166 Karsten Bailey 2Q .30 .75
167 Brock Huard 2Q .30 .75
168 Shaun King 2Q .30 .75
169 Jevon Kearse 2Q .40 1.00
170 Champ Bailey 2Q .60 1.50
171 Jake Plummer 3Q .40 1.00
172 Doug Flutie 3Q .60 1.50
173 Troy Aikman 3Q .75 2.00
174 Emmitt Smith 3Q 1.00 2.50
175 Terrell Davis 3Q .50 1.25
176 Barry Sanders 3Q 1.00 2.50
177 Brett Favre 3Q 1.25 3.00
178 Peyton Manning 3Q 2.00 5.00
179 Mark Brunell 3Q .50 1.25
180 Fred Taylor 3Q .40 1.00
181 Dan Marino 3Q 1.25 3.00
182 Randy Moss 3Q .50 1.25
183 Drew Bledsoe 3Q .50 1.25
184 Jerry Rice 3Q 1.50 4.00
185 Steve Young 3Q .75 2.00
186 David Boston 4Q .60 1.50
187 Cade McNown 4Q .60 1.60
188 Akili Smith 4Q .60 1.50
189 Tim Couch 4Q .75 2.00
190 Edgerrin James 4Q 1.00 2.50
191 Kevin Faulk 4Q .60 1.50
192 Ricky Williams 4Q 1.00 2.50
193 Donovan McNabb 4Q 5.00 12.00
194 Troy Edwards 4Q .60 1.50
195 Torry Holt 4Q 1.25 3.00

1999 Collector's Edge Odyssey Two Minute Warning

*151-170 2Q/600: 1X TO 2.5X BASIC CARDS
151-170 SECOND QUARTER PRINT RUN 600
*171-185 3Q/300: 1.2X TO 3X BASIC CARDS
171-185 THIRD QUARTER PRINT RUN 300
*186-195 4Q/100: 1.5X TO 4X BASIC CARDS
186-195 FOURTH QUARTER PRINT RUN 100

1999 Collector's Edge Odyssey Overtime

*151-170 ROOKIES: 8X TO 20X HI COL.
151-170 STATED PRINT RUN 60 SER.#'d SETS
*171-185 STARS: 8X TO 20X HI COL.
171-185 STATED PRINT RUN 30 SER.#'d SETS
*186-195 ROOKIES: 8X TO 20X HI COL.
186-195 STATED PRINT RUN 10 SER.#'d SETS

1999 Collector's Edge Odyssey Cut 'n' Ripped

Randomly inserted in packs at the rate of one in 12, this 15-card set features top prospects displaying their muscles. Card backs carry a "CR" prefix.

COMPLETE SET (15) 10.00 20.00
STATED ODDS 1:12
CR1 Chris McAlister .30 .75
CR2 Kevin Johnson .40 1.00
CR3 Chris Claiborne .30 .75
CR4 Sedrick Irvin .30 .75
CR5 Edgerrin James .50 1.25
CR6 Mike Cloud .30 .75
CR7 James Johnson .30 .75
CR8 Rob Konrad .30 .75
CR9 Daunte Culpepper .50 1.25
CR10 Andy Katzenmoyer .40 1.00
CR11 Amos Zereoue .30 .75
CR12 Torry Holt .60 1.50
CR13 Shaun King .30 .75
CR14 Jevon Kearse .40 1.00
CR15 Champ Bailey .60 1.50

1999 Collector's Edge Odyssey Cutting Edge

Randomly inserted in packs at the rate of one in 18, this 10-card set spotlights top NFL quarterbacks. Card backs carry a "CE" prefix.

COMPLETE SET (10) 15.00 30.00
STATED ODDS 1:18
CE1 Akili Smith .60 1.50
CE2 Tim Couch .75 2.00
CE3 Brian Griese .60 1.50
CE4 Charlie Batch .60 1.50
CE5 Brett Favre 2.00 5.00
CE6 Peyton Manning 3.00 8.00
CE7 Mark Brunell .75 2.00
CE8 Dan Marino 2.00 5.00
CE9 Drew Bledsoe .75 2.00
CE10 Steve Young 1.25 3.00

1999 Collector's Edge Odyssey Excalibur

Cards from the Excalibur set were distributed across three brands of 1999 Collector's Edge football products: Odyssey, First Place and Masters. The 8-cards inserted into Odyssey were randomly inserted at the rate of 1:24 packs. Note that the Favre card was inserted in both First Place and Masters and that no #23 Jake Plummer was released as a single card through packs. However, a 25-card uncut sheet was later released as a wrapper redemption at Edge events that did include the Jake Plummer card. We've priced the uncut sheet within the First Place listings. Some copies of the Jake Plummer card did surface after Edge ceased its card operations.

COMPLETE SET (8) 15.00 30.00
STATED ODDS 1:24
X1 David Boston 1.00 2.50
X4 Cade McNown 1.00 2.50
X8 Troy Edwards 1.00 2.50
X9 Daunte Culpepper 1.50 4.00
X11 Ricky Williams 1.50 4.00
X15 Donovan McNabb 3.00 8.00
X16 Troy Aikman 2.00 5.00
X21 Emmitt Smith 2.50 6.00
X23 Jake Plummer 1.00 2.50

1999 Collector's Edge Odyssey End Zone

Randomly inserted in packs at the rate of one in nine, this 20-card set features NFL quarterbacks, receivers, and running backs that know how to make their way into the endzone. Card backs carry an "EZ" prefix.

COMPLETE SET (20) 15.00 30.00
STATED ODDS 1:9
EZ1 Jamal Anderson .75 2.00
EZ2 Priest Holmes .60 1.50
EZ3 Doug Flutie 1.00 2.50
EZ4 Eric Moulds .60 1.50
EZ5 Charlie Batch .60 1.50
EZ6 Barry Sanders 1.50 4.00
EZ7 Antonio Freeman .75 2.00
EZ8 Fred Taylor .60 1.50
EZ9 Cris Carter 1.00 2.50
EZ10 Randy Moss .75 2.00
EZ11 Keyshawn Johnson .75 2.00
EZ12 Curtis Martin .75 2.00
EZ13 Vinny Testaverde .60 1.50
EZ14 Kordell Stewart .60 1.50
EZ15 Jerry Rice 2.50 6.00
EZ16 Terrell Owens .75 2.00
EZ17 Jon Kitna .60 1.50
EZ18 Warrick Dunn .60 1.50
EZ19 Eddie George .75 2.00
EZ20 Steve McNair .75 2.00

1999 Collector's Edge Odyssey GameGear

Randomly seeded in packs at the rate of one in 360, this 8-card set features NFL players coupled with a swatch of a game used football. Card backs carry a "GG" prefix along with hand serial numbering. A Hologold version of each card (not serial numbered) surfaced in the hobby after Collector's Edge ceased operations. The Hologold cards were not inserted into packs.

STATED ODDS 1:360
GG1 Terrell Davis/500 4.00 10.00
GG1B Terrell Davis/172 4.00 10.00
GG2 Curtis Enis/338 2.50 6.00
GG3 Marshall Faulk/247 4.00 10.00
GG4 Brian Griese/500 4.00 10.00
GG5 Skip Hicks/315 2.50 6.00
GG6 Randy Moss/415 4.00 10.00
GG7 Lawrence Phillips/406 3.00 8.00
GG8 Fred Taylor/85 6.00 15.00
PM Peyton Manning 6.00 15.00

1999 Collector's Edge Odyssey GameGear Hologold

These cards are a Hologold parallel version of each basic GameGear insert card (not serial numbered). They surfaced in the hobby after Collector's Edge ceased operations. The Hologold cards were not inserted into packs. Each card except Peyton Manning was produced in two versions differentiated by the card number on the back.

COMPLETE SET (8) 15.00 30.00
INSERTED IN SPECIAL RETAIL PACKS
BG Brian Griese 1.25 3.00
CE Curtis Enis 1.25 3.00
FT Fred Taylor 1.25 3.00
GG1 Terrell Davis 1.25 3.00
GG2 Curtis Enis 1.25 3.00
GG3 Marshall Faulk 1.25 3.00
GG4 Brian Griese 1.25 3.00
GG5 Skip Hicks 1.25 3.00
GG6 Randy Moss 3.00 8.00
GG7 Lawrence Phillips 1.25 3.00
GG8 Fred Taylor 1.25 3.00
LP Lawrence Phillips 1.25 3.00
MF Marshall Faulk 1.25 3.00
PM Peyton Manning 5.00 12.00
RM Randy Moss 4.00 10.00
SH Skip Hicks 1.25 3.00
TD Terrell Davis 1.25 3.00

1999 Collector's Edge Odyssey Old School

Randomly inserted in packs at the rate of one in eight, this 25-card set sports cards of top 1999 NFL Draft choices where the players dressed up in vintage football equipment. Cards were shot in black and white, and then hand-colored to appear "vintage." Card backs carry an "OS" prefix.

COMPLETE SET (25) 25.00 50.00
STATED ODDS 1:8
OS1 David Boston .40 1.00
OS2 Chris McAlister .40 1.00
OS3 Peerless Price .40 1.00
OS4 D'Wayne Bates .40 1.00
OS5 Cade McNown .40 1.00
OS6 Akili Smith .40 1.00
OS7 Tim Couch .50 1.25
OS8 Kevin Johnson .50 1.25
OS9 Chris Claiborne .40 1.00
OS10 Sedrick Irvin .40 1.00
OS11 Edgerrin James .60 1.50
OS12 Mike Cloud .40 1.00
OS13 James Johnson .40 1.00
OS14 Rob Konrad .40 1.00
OS15 Daunte Culpepper .60 1.50
OS16 Kevin Faulk .40 1.00
OS17 Donovan McNabb 1.25 3.00
OS18 Troy Edwards .40 1.00
OS19 Amos Zereoue .40 1.00
OS20 Joe Germaine .50 1.25
OS21 Torry Holt .75 2.00
OS22 Karsten Bailey .40 1.00
OS23 Shaun King .40 1.00
OS24 Jevon Kearse .50 1.25
OS25 Champ Bailey .75 2.00

1999 Collector's Edge Odyssey Pro Signature Authentics

Randomly inserted in packs at the rate of one in 36, this set features authentic autographs from top rookies with each card signed in black ink. The cards look identical to the First Place Pro Signatures except that each player's card was machine serial numbered on the cardbacks as noted below. Blue Ink (hand serial numbered to 40) and red Ink (hand serial numbered to 10) were also produced for some cards in this set.

STATED ODDS 1:36
MACHINE SERIAL #'d 111-2435
*BLUE INK/40: 1X TO 2.5X BLACK INK
BLUE INK STATED PRINT RUN 40
UNPRICED RED INK PRINT RUN 10
1 D'Wayne Bates/1450 3.00 8.00
2 Michael Bishop/2200 4.00 10.00
3 Chris Claiborne/1120 3.00 8.00
4 Daunte Culpepper/450 12.00 30.00
5 Jared DeVries/290 4.00 10.00
6 Jeff Garcia/2110 10.00 25.00
7 Martin Gramatica/1950 4.00 10.00
8 Torry Holt/1115 10.00 25.00
9 Brock Huard/350 6.00 15.00
10 Sedrick Irvin/1240 3.00 8.00
11 Edgerrin James/435 10.00 25.00
12 Kevin Johnson/1920 3.00 8.00
13 Shaun King/920 4.00 10.00
14 Rob Konrad/1420 4.00 10.00
15 Darnell McDonald/2435 3.00 8.00
16 Peerless Price/825 6.00 15.00
17 Akili Smith/111 20.00 50.00
18 Ricky Williams/230 12.50 30.00
19 Amos Zereoue/1450 4.00 10.00

1999 Collector's Edge Odyssey Super Limited Edge

Randomly inserted in packs, this 30-card set features top NFL veterans on an insert card that is sequentially numbered to 1000.

COMPLETE SET (30) 50.00 100.00
STATED PRINT RUN 1000 SER.#'d SETS
SLE1 Jake Plummer 1.00 2.50
SLE2 Jamal Anderson 1.25 3.00
SLE3 Doug Flutie 1.50 4.00
SLE4 Eric Moulds 1.00 2.50
SLE5 Troy Aikman 2.00 5.00
SLE6 Emmitt Smith 2.50 6.00
SLE7 Terrell Davis 1.25 3.00
SLE8 Charlie Batch 1.00 2.50
SLE9 Herman Moore 1.25 3.00
SLE10 Barry Sanders 2.50 6.00
SLE11 Brett Favre 3.00 8.00
SLE12 Antonio Freeman 1.25 3.00
SLE13 Dorsey Levens 1.25 3.00
SLE14 Peyton Manning 5.00 12.00
SLE15 Mark Brunell 1.25 3.00
SLE16 Fred Taylor 1.00 2.50
SLE17 Dan Marino 3.00 8.00
SLE18 Cris Carter 1.50 4.00
SLE19 Randall Cunningham 1.25 3.00
SLE20 Randy Moss 1.25 3.00
SLE21 Drew Bledsoe 1.25 3.00
SLE22 Ricky Williams 1.50 4.00
SLE23 Keyshawn Johnson 1.25 3.00
SLE24 Curtis Martin 1.25 3.00
SLE25 Jerome Bettis 1.50 4.00
SLE26 Jerry Rice 4.00 10.00
SLE27 Terrell Owens 1.25 3.00
SLE28 Jon Kitna 1.00 2.50
SLE29 Eddie George 1.25 3.00
SLE30 Steve Young 2.00 5.00

2000 Collector's Edge Odyssey Previews

This set was released as a Preview to the 2000 Collector's Edge Odyssey base set. Each card is essentially a parallel version of the base set card along with the phrase "Preview XXX/999" on the cardbacks.

COMPLETE SET (16) 12.50 30.00
101 Thomas Jones .40 1.00
104 Jamal Lewis .50 1.25
105 Chris Redman .30 .75
106 Travis Taylor .30 .75
110 Brian Urlacher 1.50 4.00
111 Dez White .30 .75
112 Ron Dugans .30 .75
113 Curtis Keaton .30 .75
114 Peter Warrick .30 .75
115 Courtney Brown .40 1.00
117 Dennis Northcutt .30 .75
118 Travis Prentice .30 .75
124 Reuben Droughns .30 .75
125 Bubba Franks .30 .75
129 R.Jay Soward .30 .75
132 Sylvester Morris .30 .75
134 J.R. Redmond .30 .75
138 Ron Dayne .50 1.25
139 Anthony Becht .30 .75
140 Laveranues Coles .40 1.00
142 Chad Pennington .40 1.00
144 Jerry Porter .50 1.25
145 Todd Pinkston .30 .75
148 Plaxico Burress .40 1.00
149 Danny Farmer .30 .75
150 Tee Martin .30 .75
151 Trung Canidate .30 .75
153 Giovanni Carmazzi .30 .75
157 Shaun Alexander .50 1.25
158 Joe Hamilton .30 .75

2000 Collector's Edge Odyssey

Released in early October 2000, Collector's Edge Odyssey features a 190-card base set comprised of 100 veteran cards, 60 rookie cards (numbers 101-160) sequentially numbered to 999, 10 Survivors cards (numbers 161-170) sequentially numbered to 2500, and 20 Last Man Standing cards (numbers 171-190) sequentially numbered to 2500. Base cards feature green and purple foil borders and gold foil highlights. Odyssey was packaged in 20-pack boxes with each pack containing five cards and carried a suggested retail price of $4.99.

COMPLETE SET (190) 250.00 400.00
COMP.SET w/o SP's (100) 6.00 15.00
1 David Boston .20 .50
2 Jake Plummer .20 .50
3 Frank Sanders .20 .50
4 Jamal Anderson .25 .60
5 Chris Chandler .25 .60
6 Terance Mathis .20 .50
7 Tony Banks .20 .50
8 Qadry Ismail .20 .50
9 Doug Flutie .25 .60
10 Rob Johnson .25 .60
11 Eric Moulds .20 .50
12 Peerless Price .25 .60
13 Antowain Smith .25 .60
14 Steve Beuerlein .25 .60
15 Tim Biakabutuka .25 .60
16 Muhsin Muhammad .20 .50
17 Curtis Enis .20 .50
18 Cade McNown .20 .50
19 Marcus Robinson .25 .60
20 Corey Dillon .20 .50
21 Akili Smith .20 .50
22 Tim Couch .25 .60
23 Kevin Johnson .20 .50
24 Errict Rhett .25 .60
25 Troy Aikman .40 1.00
26 Joey Galloway .25 .60
27 Rocket Ismail .25 .60
28 Emmitt Smith .50 1.25
29 Terrell Davis .25 .60
30 Olandis Gary .25 .60
31 Brian Griese .20 .50
32 Ed McCaffrey .25 .60
33 Charlie Batch .20 .50
34 Germane Crowell .20 .50
35 Herman Moore .20 .50
36 James Stewart .20 .50
37 Brett Favre .60 1.50
38 Antonio Freeman .25 .60
39 Dorsey Levens .25 .60
40 Marvin Harrison .25 .60
41 Edgerrin James .25 .60
42 Peyton Manning .75 2.00
43 Terrence Wilkins .20 .50
44 Mark Brunell .25 .60
45 Keenan McCardell .25 .60
46 Jimmy Smith .25 .60
47 Fred Taylor .20 .50
48 Mike Cloud .20 .50
49 Tony Gonzalez .25 .60
50 Elvis Grbac .20 .50
51 Damon Huard .20 .50
52 James Johnson .20 .50
53 Tony Martin .25 .60
54 Cris Carter .30 .75
55 Daunte Culpepper .25 .60
56 Randy Moss .25 .60
57 Robert Smith .20 .50
58 Drew Bledsoe .25 .60
59 Terry Glenn .25 .60
60 Jeff Blake .25 .60
61 Ricky Williams .25 .60
62 Kerry Collins .20 .50
63 Ike Hilliard .20 .50
64 Amani Toomer .20 .50
65 Wayne Chrebet .20 .50
66 Curtis Martin .25 .60
67 Vinny Testaverde .20 .50
68 Tim Brown .30 .75
69 Rich Gannon .25 .60
70 Donovan McNabb .25 .60
71 Duce Staley .20 .50
72 Jerome Bettis .30 .75
73 Troy Edwards .20 .50
74 Kordell Stewart .20 .50
75 Isaac Bruce .30 .75
76 Marshall Faulk .25 .60
77 Torry Holt .25 .60
78 Kurt Warner .50 1.25
79 Jermaine Fazande .20 .50
80 Jim Harbaugh .25 .60
81 Jeff Garcia .20 .50
82 Charlie Garner .25 .60
83 Terrell Owens .25 .60
84 Jerry Rice .75 2.00
85 Jon Kitna .20 .50
86 Derrick Mayes .20 .50
87 Ricky Watters .25 .60
88 Mike Alstott .20 .50
89 Warrick Dunn .20 .50
90 Keyshawn Johnson .25 .60
91 Shaun King .20 .50
92 Kevin Dyson .25 .60
93 Eddie George .25 .60
94 Jevon Kearse .20 .50
95 Steve McNair .25 .60
96 Carl Pickens .25 .60
97 Champ Bailey .25 .60
98 Stephen Davis .20 .50
99 Brad Johnson .25 .60
100 Michael Westbrook .20 .50
101 Thomas Jones RC 2.50 6.00
102 Doug Johnson RC 2.00 5.00
103 Mareno Philyaw RC 2.00 5.00
104 Jamal Lewis RC 3.00 8.00
105 Chris Redman RC 2.00 5.00
106 Travis Taylor RC 2.00 5.00
107 Kwame Cavil RC 2.00 5.00
108 Sammy Morris RC 2.00 5.00
109 Frank Murphy RC 2.00 5.00
110 Brian Urlacher RC 10.00 25.00
111 Dez White RC 2.00 5.00
112 Ron Dugans RC 2.00 5.00
113 Curtis Keaton RC 2.00 5.00
114 Peter Warrick RC 2.00 5.00
115 Courtney Brown RC 2.50 6.00
116 JaJuan Dawson RC 2.00 5.00
117 Dennis Northcutt RC 2.00 5.00
118 Travis Prentice RC 2.00 5.00
119 Michael Wiley RC 2.00 5.00
120 Mike Anderson RC 2.00 5.00
121 Chris Cole RC 2.50 6.00
122 Jarious Jackson RC 2.50 6.00
123 Deltha O'Neal RC 2.00 5.00
124 Reuben Droughns RC 2.00 5.00
125 Bubba Franks RC 2.00 5.00
126 Anthony Lucas RC 2.00 5.00
127 Rondell Mealey RC 2.00 5.00
128 Rob Morris RC 2.50 6.00
129 R.Jay Soward RC 2.00 5.00
130 Shyrone Stith RC 2.00 5.00
131 Frank Moreau RC 2.00 5.00
132 Sylvester Morris RC 2.00 5.00
133 Doug Chapman RC 2.00 5.00
134 J.R. Redmond RC 2.00 5.00
135 Marc Bulger RC 2.50 6.00
136 Sherrod Gideon RC 2.00 5.00
137 Terrelle Smith RC 2.00 5.00
138 Ron Dayne RC 3.00 8.00
139 Anthony Becht RC 2.00 5.00
140 Laveranues Coles RC 2.50 6.00
141 Shaun Ellis RC 2.50 6.00
142 Chad Pennington RC 2.50 6.00
143 Sebastian Janikowski RC 3.00 8.00
144 Jerry Porter RC 3.00 8.00
145 Todd Pinkston RC 2.00 5.00
146 Gari Scott RC 2.00 5.00
147 Corey Simon RC 2.50 6.00
148 Plaxico Burress RC 2.50 6.00
149 Danny Farmer RC 2.00 5.00
150 Tee Martin RC 2.00 5.00
151 Trung Canidate RC 2.00 5.00
152 Trevor Gaylor RC 2.00 5.00
153 Giovanni Carmazzi RC 2.00 5.00
154 John Engelberger RC 2.00 5.00
155 Ahmed Plummer RC 2.00 5.00
156 Tim Rattay RC 2.50 6.00
157 Shaun Alexander RC 3.00 8.00
158 Joe Hamilton RC 2.00 5.00
159 Keith Bulluck RC 2.50 6.00
160 Todd Husak RC 2.00 5.00
161 Cade McNown SV .40 1.00
162 Tim Couch SV .50 1.25
163 Terrell Davis SV .50 1.25
164 Brett Favre SV 1.25 3.00
165 Edgerrin James SV .50 1.25
166 Peyton Manning SV 1.50 4.00
167 Daunte Culpepper SV .50 1.25
168 Randy Moss SV .50 1.25
169 Ricky Williams SV .50 1.25
170 Kurt Warner SV 1.00 2.50
171 Cade McNown LV .40 1.00
172 Akili Smith LV .40 1.00
173 Tim Couch LV .50 1.25
174 Troy Aikman LV .75 2.00
175 Emmitt Smith LV 1.00 2.50
176 Terrell Davis LV .50 1.25
177 Brett Favre LV 1.25 3.00
178 Edgerrin James LV .50 1.25
179 Peyton Manning LV 1.50 4.00
180 Mark Brunell LV .50 1.25
181 Daunte Culpepper LV .50 1.25
182 Randy Moss LV .50 1.25
183 Drew Bledsoe LV .50 1.25
184 Ricky Williams LV .50 1.25
185 Donovan McNabb LV .50 1.25
186 Torry Holt LV .50 1.25
187 Kurt Warner LV 1.00 2.50
188 Shaun King LV .40 1.00
189 Eddie George LV .50 1.25
190 Steve McNair LV .50 1.25

2000 Collector's Edge Odyssey Hologold Rookies

*ROOKIES 101-160: .4X TO 1X BASIC CARDS
HOLOGOLD ROOKIE PRINT RUN 500

2000 Collector's Edge Odyssey Retail

*VETS 1-100: .4X TO 1X HOBBY
*ROOKIES 101-160: .08X TO .2X HOBBY
*SV/LS 161-190: .2X TO .5X HOBBY

2000 Collector's Edge Odyssey GameGear Jerseybacks

Randomly inserted in packs, this set features top 2000 draft picks on a card where the back is a swatch of an authentic jersey worn by the player at the 2000 rookie photo shoot. Each card is sequentially numbered to 20. We've included pricing on only the cards that have been confirmed.

STATED PRINT RUN 20 SER.#'d SETS
AB Anthony Becht 5.00 12.00
BF Bubba Franks 5.00 12.00
BU Brian Urlacher 25.00 60.00
CK Curtis Keaton 5.00 12.00
CP Chad Pennington 6.00 15.00
CR Chris Redman 5.00 12.00
CS Corey Simon 6.00 15.00
DF Danny Farmer 5.00 12.00
DN Dennis Northcutt 5.00 12.00
DW Dez White 5.00 12.00
JH Joe Hamilton 5.00 12.00
JL Jamal Lewis 8.00 20.00
JP Jerry Porter 8.00 20.00
JR J.R. Redmond 5.00 12.00
LC Laveranues Coles 6.00 15.00
PB Plaxico Burress 6.00 15.00
PW Peter Warrick 5.00 12.00
RD Ron Dayne 8.00 20.00
RD Reuben Droughns 5.00 12.00
RD Ron Dugans 5.00 12.00
RS R.Jay Soward 5.00 12.00
SA Shaun Alexander 8.00 20.00
SM Sylvester Morris 5.00 12.00
TC Trung Canidate 5.00 12.00
TJ Thomas Jones 6.00 15.00
TM Tee Martin 5.00 12.00
TP Todd Pinkston 5.00 12.00
TP Travis Prentice 5.00 12.00
TT Travis Taylor 5.00 12.00

2000 Collector's Edge Odyssey GameGear Leatherbacks

Randomly inserted in packs, this 30-card set feaures full leather back cards of footballs used by the featured rookie at the 2000 rookie photo shoot. Each card is sequentially numbered to 12.

STATED PRINT RUN 12 SER.#'d SETS
AB Anthony Becht 6.00 15.00
BF Bubba Franks 6.00 15.00
BU Brian Urlacher 30.00 80.00
CB Courtney Brown 8.00 20.00
CK Curtis Keaton 6.00 15.00
CP Chad Pennington 8.00 20.00
CR Chris Redman 6.00 15.00
CS Corey Simon 8.00 20.00
DF Danny Farmer 6.00 15.00
DN Dennis Northcutt 6.00 15.00
DW Dez White 6.00 15.00
JH Joe Hamilton 6.00 15.00
JL Jamal Lewis 10.00 25.00
JP Jerry Porter 10.00 25.00
JR J.R. Redmond 6.00 15.00
LC Laveranues Coles 8.00 20.00
PB Plaxico Burress 8.00 20.00
PW Peter Warrick 6.00 15.00
RD1 Ron Dayne 10.00 25.00
RD2 Reuben Droughns 6.00 15.00
RD3 Ron Dugans 6.00 15.00
RS R.Jay Soward 6.00 15.00
SA Shaun Alexander 10.00 25.00
SM Sylvester Morris 6.00 15.00
TC Trung Canidate 6.00 15.00
TJ Thomas Jones 8.00 20.00
TM Tee Martin 6.00 15.00
TP Todd Pinkston 6.00 15.00
TP Travis Prentice 6.00 15.00
TT Travis Taylor 6.00 15.00

2000 Collector's Edge Odyssey Old School

Randomly inserted in Hobby packs at the rate of one in six and Retial packs at the rate of one in eight, this 30-card set features top 2000 draft picks wearing vintage football equipment.

COMPLETE SET (30) 12.00 30.00
STATED ODDS 1:6 HOB, 1:8 RET
OS1 Thomas Jones .30 .75
OS2 Jamal Lewis .40 1.00
OS3 Chris Redman .25 .60
OS4 Travis Taylor .25 .60
OS5 Brian Urlacher 1.25 3.00
OS6 Dez White .25 .60
OS7 Ron Dugans .25 .60
OS8 Curtis Keaton .25 .60
OS9 Peter Warrick .25 .60
OS10 Courtney Brown .30 .75
OS11 Dennis Northcutt .25 .60
OS12 Travis Prentice .25 .60
OS13 Reuben Droughns .25 .60
OS14 Bubba Franks .25 .60
OS15 R.Jay Soward .25 .60
OS16 Sylvester Morris .25 .60
OS17 J.R. Redmond .25 .60
OS18 Ron Dayne .40 1.00
OS19 Anthony Becht .25 .60
OS20 Laveranues Coles .30 .75
OS21 Chad Pennington .30 .75
OS22 Jerry Porter .40 1.00
OS23 Todd Pinkston .25 .60
OS24 Corey Simon .30 .75
OS25 Plaxico Burress .30 .75
OS26 Danny Farmer .25 .60
OS27 Tee Martin .25 .60
OS28 Trung Canidate .25 .60
OS29 Shaun Alexander .40 1.00
OS30 Joe Hamilton .25 .60

2000 Collector's Edge Odyssey Restaurant Quality

Randomly inserted in Hobby packs at the rate of one in 20 and Retail packs at the rate of one in 29, this 10-card set features top 2000 draft picks on a foil boad card stock with dot matrix printing and gold foil accents.

COMPLETE SET (10) 6.00 15.00
STATED ODDS 1:20 HOB, 1:29 RET
RQ1 Thomas Jones .40 1.00
RQ2 Jamal Lewis .50 1.25
RQ3 Travis Taylor .30 .75
RQ4 Peter Warrick .30 .75
RQ5 Bubba Franks .30 .75
RQ6 Sylvester Morris .30 .75
RQ7 Ron Dayne .50 1.25
RQ8 Chad Pennington .40 1.00
RQ9 Plaxico Burress .40 1.00
RQ10 Shaun Alexander .50 1.25

2000 Collector's Edge Odyssey Ripped

This set appeared on the secondary market years after Edge ceased football card operations. Each features a 2000 rookie in a pose taken during a workout or lifting weights.

R1 Thomas Jones .25 .60
R2 Jamal Lewis .30 .75
R3 Brian Urlacher 1.00 2.50
R4 Dez White .20 .50
R5 Curtis Keaton .20 .50
R6 Peter Warrick .20 .50
R7 Courtney Brown .25 .60
R8 Travis Prentice .20 .50
R9 Reuben Droughns .20 .50
R10 Bubba Franks .20 .50
R11 J.R. Redmond .20 .50
R12 Ron Dayne .30 .75
R13 Anthony Becht .20 .50
R14 Laveranues Coles .25 .60
R15 Chad Pennington .25 .60
R16 Jerry Porter .30 .75
R17 Plaxico Burress .25 .60
R18 Tee Martin .20 .50
R19 Trung Canidate .20 .50
R20 Shaun Alexander .30 .75

2000 Collector's Edge Odyssey Rookie Ink

Randomly inserted in Hobby packs at the rate of one in 99 and Retail packs at the rate of one in 150, this 12-card set features top draft picks and their authentic autographs. Each card was printed with either gold or silver foil on the fronts and also authenticated by PSA-DNA. They were also hand serial numbered on the backs.

STATED ODDS 1:99 HOB, 1:150 RET
BU Brian Urlacher Gold/795 20.00 50.00
CP Chad Pennington Gold/510 8.00 20.00
CR Chris Redman/475 6.00 15.00
DN Dennis Northcutt Gold/800 5.00 12.00
JL Jamal Lewis/540 10.00 25.00
JR J.R. Redmond/1610 5.00 12.00
LC Laveranues Coles Silver/1400 6.00 15.00
PB Plaxico Burress Gold/505 8.00 20.00
RD Ron Dayne/440 10.00 25.00
SM Sylvester Morris Gold/540 6.00 15.00
TJ Thomas Jones Gold/465 8.00 20.00
TP Todd Pinkston Silver/1035 5.00 12.00

2000 Collector's Edge Odyssey Tight

Randomly inserted in Hobby packs at the rate of one in 10, this 30-card set features full color action photography on a foil board card stock with gold foil highlights.

COMPLETE SET (30) 15.00 40.00
STATED ODDS 1:10 HOBBY
T1 Thomas Jones .40 1.00
T2 Jamal Lewis .50 1.25
T3 Chris Redman .30 .75
T4 Travis Taylor .30 .75
T5 Brian Urlacher 1.50 4.00
T6 Dez White .30 .75
T7 Ron Dugans .30 .75
T8 Curtis Keaton .30 .75
T9 Peter Warrick .30 .75
T10 Courtney Brown .40 1.00
T11 Dennis Northcutt .30 .75
T12 Travis Prentice .30 .75
T13 Reuben Droughns .30 .75
T14 Bubba Franks .30 .75
T15 R.Jay Soward .30 .75
T16 Sylvester Morris .30 .75
T17 J.R. Redmond .30 .75
T18 Ron Dayne .50 1.25
T19 Anthony Becht .30 .75
T20 Laveranues Coles .40 1.00
T21 Chad Pennington .40 1.00
T22 Jerry Porter .50 1.25
T23 Todd Pinkston .30 .75
T24 Corey Simon .40 1.00
T25 Plaxico Burress .40 1.00
T26 Danny Farmer .30 .75
T27 Tee Martin .30 .75
T28 Trung Canidate .30 .75
T29 Shaun Alexander .50 1.25
T30 Joe Hamilton .30 .75

2000 Collector's Edge Odyssey Wasssuppp

Randomly inserted in Hobby packs at the rate of one in 10 and Retail packs at the rate of one in 14, this 20-card set features top rookies on holographic foil board with gold full highlights.

COMPLETE SET (20) 10.00 25.00
STATED ODDS 1:10 HOB, 1:14 RET

W1 Thomas Jones .30 .75
W2 Jamal Lewis .40 1.00
W3 Travis Taylor .25 .60
W4 Ron Dugans .25 .60
W5 Peter Warrick .25 .60
W6 Dez White .25 .60
W7 Dennis Northcutt .25 .60
W8 Travis Prentice .25 .60
W9 Bubba Franks .25 .60
W10 R.Jay Soward .25 .60
W11 Sylvester Morris .25 .60
W12 J.R. Redmond .25 .60
W13 Ron Dayne .40 1.00
W14 Laveranues Coles .30 .75
W15 Chad Pennington .30 .75
W16 Jerry Porter .40 1.00
W17 Todd Pinkston .25 .60
W18 Plaxico Burress .30 .75
W19 Danny Farmer .25 .60
W20 Shaun Alexander .40 1.00

2000 Collector's Edge Awards Promos

R9 Kurt Warner 1.50 4.00
EJ Edgerrin James 1.00 2.50
KW Kurt Warner 1.50 4.00

1996 CE President's Reserve Promos

This six-card set was issued to preview the 1996 Collector's Edge President's Reserve series. The Promo set contains one card from each of the President's Reserve base and insert sets. The fronts feature color action player photos on various backgrounds while the backs carry player information and the word "Promo." The cards are virtually all numbered 1 and, therefore checklisted below in alphabetical order.

1 J.Blake .50 1.25
E.Rhett
2 D.Butkus 1.20 3.00
S.Bono
3 Philadelphia Eagles Candidates .20 .50
4 Rashaan Salaam .40 1.00
5 Junior Seau .30 .75
6 Michael Westbrook .50 1.25

1996 CE President's Reserve

The 1996 Collector's Edge President's Reserve set was issued in two series of 200 cards, for a total of 400 cards. A collector could preorder a box (either series) from a dealer for $149.95. Card fronts have a clear plastic background with the card and player's name in gold foil. Card backs contain statistical and biographical information. Reportedly, a total of 20,000 of each card was produced.

COMPLETE SET (400) 30.00 60.00
COMP.SERIES 1 (200) 15.00 30.00
COMP.SERIES 2 (200) 15.00 30.00
1 Larry Centers .20 .50
2 Frank Sanders .20 .50
3 Clyde Simmons .08 .25
4 Eric Swann .20 .50
5 Morten Andersen .08 .25
6 Lester Archambeau .08 .25
7 J.J. Birden .08 .25
8 Bert Emanuel .20 .50
9 Jumpy Geathers .08 .25
10 Jeff George .20 .50
11 Craig Heyward .08 .25
12 Bill Brooks .08 .25
13 Steve Christie .08 .25
14 Todd Collins .20 .50
15 Darick Holmes .08 .25
16 Andre Reed .20 .50
17 Bryce Paup .20 .50
18 Bruce Smith .40 1.00
19 Blake Brockermeyer .08 .25
20 Mark Carrier .08 .25
21 Kerry Collins .40 1.00
22 Darion Conner .08 .25
23 Eric Guliford .08 .25
24 Lamar Lathon .08 .25
25 Derrick Moore .08 .25
26 Frank Reich .08 .25
27 Kevin Butler .08 .25
28 Tony Carter RC .08 .25
29 Curtis Conway .40 1.00
30 Robert Green .08 .25
31 Jay Leeuwenburg RC .08 .25
32 Alonzo Spellman .08 .25
33 Chris Zorich .08 .25
34 Eric Bieniemy .08 .25
35 Jeff Blake .40 1.00
36 Tony McGee .08 .25
37 Carl Pickens .20 .50
38 Rob Burnett .08 .25
39 Earnest Byner .08 .25
40 Michael Jackson .20 .50
41 Antonio Langham .08 .25
42 Anthony Pleasant .08 .25
43 Vinny Testaverde .20 .50
44 Troy Aikman 1.25 2.50
45 Larry Allen .08 .25
46 Bill Bates .20 .50
47 Chris Boniol .08 .25
48 Charles Haley .20 .50
49 Michael Irvin .40 1.00
50 Robert Jones .08 .25
51 Leon Lett .08 .25
52 Russell Maryland .08 .25
53 Nate Newton .08 .25
54 Deion Sanders .60 1.50
55 Sherman Williams .08 .25
56 Darren Woodson .20 .50
57 Aaron Craver .08 .25
58 Terrell Davis .75 2.00
59 Jason Elam .20 .50
60 Simon Fletcher .08 .25
61 Anthony Miller .20 .50
62 Shannon Sharpe .20 .50
63 Tracy Scroggins .08 .25
64 Antonio London .08 .25
65 Scott Mitchell .20 .50
66 Johnnie Morton .20 .50
67 Barry Sanders 1.50 4.00
68 Edgar Bennett .20 .50
69 Mark Chmura .20 .50
70 Brett Favre 2.50 5.00
71 Mark Ingram .08 .25
72 Dorsey Levens .40 1.00
73 Wayne Simmons .08 .25
74 Gary Brown .08 .25
75 Anthony Cook .08 .25
76 Al Del Greco .08 .25
77 Haywood Jeffires .08 .25
78 Steve McNair .75 2.00
79 Rodney Thomas .08 .25
80 Trev Alberts .08 .25
81 Quentin Coryatt .08 .25
82 Ken Dilger .20 .50
83 Jim Harbaugh .20 .50
84 Floyd Turner .08 .25
85 Lamont Warren .08 .25
86 Steve Beuerlein .20 .50
87 Mark Brunell .60 1.50
88 Eugene Chung .08 .25
89 Jeff Lageman .08 .25
90 Willie Jackson .20 .50
91 Kimble Anders .08 .25
92 Steve Bono .20 .50
93 Derrick Thomas .40 1.00
94 Willie Davis .20 .50
95 Greg Hill .20 .50
96 Neil Smith .20 .50
97 Tamarick Vanover .40 1.00
98 James Hasty .08 .25
99 Gary Clark .08 .25
100 Marco Coleman .08 .25
101 Steve Emtman .08 .25
102 Irving Fryar .20 .50
103 Randal Hill .08 .25
104 Terry Kirby .20 .50
105 Dan Marino 2.00 5.00
106 Cris Carter .40 1.00
107 Jack Del Rio .08 .25
108 David Palmer .20 .50
109 Jake Reed .20 .50
110 Robert Smith .20 .50
111 Korey Stringer .15 .40
112 Orlando Thomas .08 .25
113 Drew Bledsoe .60 1.50
114 Vincent Brisby .08 .25
115 Ted Johnson RC .40 1.00
116 Curtis Martin .75 2.00
117 Chris Slade .08 .25
118 Jim Dombrowski .08 .25
119 William Roaf .08 .25
120 Quinn Early .08 .25
121 Wesley Walls .20 .50
122 Wayne Martin .08 .25
123 Irv Smith .08 .25
124 Torrance Small .08 .25
125 Dave Brown .20 .50
126 Chris Calloway .08 .25
127 Jumbo Elliott .08 .25
128 Rodney Hampton .20 .50
129 Tyrone Wheatley .20 .50
130 Kyle Brady .20 .50
131 Hugh Douglas .20 .50
132 Todd Scott .08 .25
133 Adrian Murrell. .20 .50
134 Wayne Chrebet .60 1.50
135 Aundray Bruce .08 .25
136 Andrew Glover .08 .25
137 Daryl Hobbs RC .08 .25
138 Napoleon Kaufman .40 1.00
139 Chester McGlockton .08 .25
140 Rob Fredrickson .08 .25
141 Guy McIntyre .08 .25
142 Bobby Taylor .20 .50
143 Fred Barnett .20 .50
144 William Fuller .08 .25
145 Rodney Peete .08 .25
146 Daniel Stubbs .08 .25
147 Charlie Garner .20 .50
148 Myron Bell .08 .25
149 Rod Woodson .20 .50
150 Charles Johnson .20 .50
151 Ernie Mills .08 .25
152 Levon Kirkland .08 .25
153 Carnell Lake .08 .25
154 Kevin Greene .20 .50
155 Neil O'Donnell .20 .50
156 Erric Pegram .20 .50
157 Ray Seals .08 .25
158 Willie Williams .08 .25
159 Kordell Stewart .40 1.00
160 Yancey Thigpen .20 .50
161 Darren Bennett .20 .50
162 Andre Coleman .08 .25
163 Aaron Hayden RC .40 1.00
164 Tony Martin .20 .50
165 Chris Mims .08 .25
166 Shawn Lee .08 .25
167 Junior Seau .40 1.00
168 Merton Hanks .08 .25
169 Rickey Jackson .08 .25
170 Derek Loville .08 .25
171 Gary Plummer .08 .25
172 J.J. Stokes .40 1.00
173 John Taylor .08 .25
174 Bryant Young .20 .50
175 Antonio Edwards RC .20 .50
176 Jocy Galloway .40 1.00
177 Carlton Gray .08 .25
178 Rick Mirer .20 .50
179 Winston Moss .08 .25
180 Jerome Bettis .40 1.00
181 Troy Drayton .08 .25
182 Wayne Gandy .08 .25
183 Sean Gilbert .08 .25
184 Jessie Hester .08 .25
185 Sean Landeta .08 .25
186 Roman Phifer .08 .25
187 Alberto White .08 .25
188 Santana Dotson .08 .25
189 Jerry Ellison RC .08 .25
190 Jackie Harris .08 .25
191 Courtney Hawkins .08 .25
192 Horace Copeland .08 .25
193 Hardy Nickerson .08 .25
194 Warren Sapp .08 .25
195 Terry Allen .20 .50
196 Henry Ellard .20 .50
197 Gus Frerotte .20 .50
198 John Gesek .08 .25
199 Jim Lachey .08 .25
200 Brian Mitchell .08 .25
201 Garrison Hearst .20 .50
202 Dave Krieg .08 .25
203 Rob Moore .20 .50
204 Aeneas Williams .08 .25
205 Chris Doleman .08 .25
206 Terance Mathis .08 .25
207 Clay Matthews .20 .50
208 Eric Metcalf .20 .50
209 Jessie Tuggle .08 .25
210 Cornelius Bennett .20 .50
211 Ruben Brown .08 .25
212 Russell Copeland .08 .25
213 Phil Hansen .08 .25
214 Jim Kelly .40 1.00
215 Don Beebe .08 .25
216 Willie Green .08 .25
217 Howard Griffith .08 .25
218 John Kasay .08 .25
219 Brett Maxie .08 .25
220 Tim McKyer .08 .25
221 Sam Mills .20 .50
222 Jim Flanigan .08 .25
223 Jeff Graham .08 .25
224 Erik Kramer .08 .25
225 Rashaan Salaam .20 .50
226 Steve Walsh .08 .25
227 Donnell Woolford .08 .25
228 Ki-Jana Carter .20 .50
229 John Copeland .08 .25
230 Harold Green .08 .25
231 Doug Pelfrey .08 .25
232 Darnay Scott .20 .50
233 Bracy Walker RC .08 .25
234 Dan Wilkinson .08 .25
235 Leroy Hoard .08 .25
236 Ernest Hunter UER .08 .25
237 Keenan McCardell .40 1.00
238 Stevon Moore .08 .25
239 Andre Rison .20 .50
240 Eric Zeier .20 .50
241 Larry Brown .08 .25
242 Shante Carver .08 .25
243 Chad Hennings .20 .50
244 John Jett .08 .25
245 Daryl Johnston .20 .50
246 Derek Kennard .08 .25
247 Brock Marion .08 .25
248 Jay Novacek .20 .50
249 Emmitt Smith 2.00 4.00
250 Tony Tolbert .08 .25
251 Mark Tuinei .08 .25
252 Erik Williams .08 .25
253 Kevin Williams .08 .25
254 John Elway 2.00 5.00
255 Ed McCaffrey .20 .50
256 Glyn Milburn .08 .25
257 Michael Dean Perry .08 .25
258 Mike Pritchard .08 .25
259 Willie Clay .08 .25
260 Jason Hanson .08 .25
261 Herman Moore .20 .50
262 Brett Perriman .20 .50
263 Lomas Brown .08 .25
264 Chris Spielman .20 .50
265 Henry Thomas .08 .25
266 Robert Brooks .40 1.00
267 Sean Jones .08 .25
268 John Jurkovic .08 .25
269 Anthony Morgan .08 .25
270 Craig Newsome .08 .25
271 Reggie White .40 1.00
272 Chris Chandler .20 .50
273 Mel Gray .08 .25
274 Darryll Lewis .08 .25
275 Bruce Matthews .08 .25
276 Todd McNair .08 .25
277 Chris Sanders .20 .50
278 Mark Stepnoski .08 .25
279 Ashley Ambrose .08 .25
280 Tony Bennett .08 .25
281 Zack Crockett .08 .25
282 Sean Dawkins .08 .25
283 Marshall Faulk .50 1.25
284 Ronald Humphrey .08 .25
285 Tony Siragusa .08 .25
286 Roosevelt Potts .08 .25
287 Bryan Barker .08 .25
288 Tony Boselli .20 .50
289 Keith Goganious .08 .25
290 Desmond Howard .20 .50
291 Don Davey .08 .25
292 Corey Mayfield .08 .25
293 James O. Stewart .20 .50
294 Cedric Tillman .08 .25
295 Marcus Allen .40 1.00
296 Dale Carter .08 .25
297 Lake Dawson .20 .50
298 Darren Mickell .08 .25
299 Dan Saleaumua .08 .25
300 Webster Slaughter .08 .25
301 Keith Cash .08 .25
302 Bryan Cox .08 .25
303 Jeff Cross .08 .25
304 Eric Green .08 .25
305 O.J. McDuffie .20 .50
306 Bernie Parmalee .08 .25
307 Billy Milner .08 .25
308 Pete Stoyanovich .08 .25
309 Troy Vincent .08 .25
310 Qadry Ismail .20 .50
311 Amp Lee .08 .25
312 Warren Moon .20 .50
313 Scottie Graham .08 .25
314 John Randle .20 .50
315 Fuad Reveiz .08 .25
316 Broderick Thomas .08 .25
317 Ben Coates .20 .50
318 Willie McGinest .08 .25
319 Dave Meggett .08 .25
320 Will Moore .08 .25
321 Dave Wohlabaugh RC .08 .25
322 Mario Bates .20 .50
323 Jim Everett .08 .25
324 Tyrone Hughes .08 .25
325 Vaughn Dunbar .08 .25
326 Renaldo Turnbull .08 .25
327 Michael Haynes .20 .50
328 Mike Sherrard .08 .25
329 Michael Strahan .20 .50
330 Herschel Walker .20 .50
331 Charles Wilson .08 .25
332 Otis Smith RC .20 .50
333 Mo Lewis .08 .25
334 Marvin Washington .08 .25
335 Tim Brown .40 1.00
336 Greg Skrepenak .08 .25
337 Kevin Gogan .08 .25
338 Jeff Hostetler .20 .50
339 Terry McDaniel .08 .25
340 Anthony Smith .08 .25
341 Pat Swilling .08 .25
342 Harvey Williams .08 .25
343 Tom Hutton RC .08 .25
344 Mike Mamula .08 .25
345 Randall Cunningham .40 1.00
346 Ricky Watters .20 .50
347 Andy Harmon .08 .25
348 William Thomas .08 .25
349 Calvin Williams .40 1.00
350 Mark Bruener .08 .25
351 Dermontti Dawson .20 .50
352 Greg Lloyd .20 .50
353 Norm Johnson .08 .25
354 Byron Bam Morris .08 .25
355 Thomas Newberry .08 .25
356 Darren Perry .08 .25
357 Rohn Stark .08 .25
358 Joel Steed .08 .25
359 Brendan Stai UER .08 .25
360 Justin Strzelczyk RC .08 .25
361 Leon Searcy .08 .25
362 Chad Brown .20 .50
363 John Carney .08 .25
364 Rodney Culver .20 .50
365 Ronnie Harmon .08 .25
366 Stan Humphries .20 .50
367 Leslie O'Neal .08 .25
368 Natrone Means .20 .50
369 Mark Seay .08 .25
370 William Floyd .20 .50
371 Brent Jones .08 .25
372 Tim McDonald .08 .25
373 Ken Norton, Jr. .20 .50
374 Jerry Rice 1.25 2.50
375 Dana Stubblefield .20 .50
376 Steve Young .75 2.00
377 Brian Blades .20 .50
378 Cortez Kennedy .20 .50
379 Michael Sinclair .08 .25
380 Lamar Smith .40 1.00
381 Chris Warren .20 .50
382 Johnny Bailey .08 .25
383 Isaac Bruce .40 1.00
384 Kevin Carter .20 .50
385 Shane Conlan .08 .25
386 D'Marco Farr .08 .25
387 Todd Kinchen .08 .25
388 Chris Miller .08 .25
389 Lonnie Marts .08 .25
390 Trent Dilfer .20 .50
391 Alvin Harper .08 .25
392 John Lynch .40 1.00
393 Errict Rhett .20 .50
394 Darnell Stephens RC .08 .25
395 Ken Harvey .08 .25
396 Eddie Murray .08 .25
397 Heath Shuler .20 .50
398 Matt Turk RC .08 .25
399 Michael Westbrook .40 1.00
400 James Washington .08 .25

1996 CE President's Reserve Air Force One

Randomly inserted in packs at a rate of one in 16, this 38-card set featured the most potent long ball threats in the game. Opalescent accents highlight both sides of these two-way-view plastic cards. Each card is individually numbered out of 2,500. Jumbo versions of these cards were issued as well (numbered of 1300). They were inserted one per box. Another parallel set was released at a later date and sold in complete set form with each card numbered of 300. However, the card serial numbering on this version began with the prefix "CS."

COMPLETE SET (38) 100.00 200.00
COMP.SERIES 1 (19) 50.00 100.00
COMP.SERIES 2 (19) 50.00 100.00
1-18: STATED ODDS 1:16 SER.1 PACKS
19-36: STATED ODDS 1:16 SER.2 PACKS
STATED PRINT RUN 2500 SERIAL #'d SETS
*JUMBOS: .2X TO .5X BASIC INSERTS
JUMBOS: ONE PER BOX
STATED PRINT RUN 1300 SERIAL #'d SETS
*CS/300 CARDS: .4X TO 1X BASIC INSERTS
1 Brett Favre 12.50 25.00
2 Neil O'Donnell 1.25 2.50
3 Steve Young 5.00 10.00
4 Dan Marino 12.50 25.00
5 Kerry Collins 2.50 5.00
6 Scott Mitchell 1.25 2.50
7 Deion Sanders 4.00 8.00
8 Michael Irvin 2.50 5.00
9 Tim Brown 2.50 5.00
10 Joey Galloway 2.50 5.00
11 Robert Brooks 2.50 5.00
12 Tony Martin 1.25 2.50
13 Michael Westbrook 2.50 5.00
14 Eric Metcalf 1.25 2.50
15 Vincent Brisby .60 1.25
16 Anthony Miller 1.25 2.50
17 J.J. Stokes 2.50 5.00
18 Kordell Stewart 2.50 5.00
19 Troy Aikman 6.00 12.00
20 Drew Bledsoe 4.00 8.00
21 Jeff Blake 2.50 5.00
22 John Elway 12.50 25.00
23 Jim Harbaugh 1.25 2.50
24 Erik Kramer .60 1.25
25 Herman Moore 1.25 2.50
26 Carl Pickens 1.25 2.50
27 Michael Irvin 2.50 5.00
28 Jerry Rice 6.00 12.00
29 Isaac Bruce 2.50 5.00
30 Yancey Thigpen 1.25 2.50
31 Brett Perriman 1.25 2.50
32 Ben Coates 1.25 2.50
33 Jay Novacek 1.25 2.50
34 Tamarick Vanover 2.50 5.00
35 Terrell Davis 5.00 10.00
36 Jeff Graham .60 1.25
NNO Checklist (1-18) .60 1.25
NNO Checklist (19-36) .60 1.25

1996 CE President's Reserve Candidates Long Shots

This set could be assembled via a mail redemption. Collector's Edge produced an exchange card for each team featuring that team's helmet logo and randomly inserted them into series one packs. The trade card could be sent-in (before the expiration date of 3/31/97) for another card featuring a "long shot" rookie from that team.

COMPLETE SET (30) 40.00 80.00
SER.1 TRADE CARDS STATED ODDS 1:4
LS1 Leeland McElroy .50 1.25
LS2 Richard Huntley .75 2.00
LS3 Ray Lewis 5.00 12.00
LS4 Eric Moulds 2.00 5.00
LS5 Muhsin Muhammad 2.00 5.00
LS6 Bobby Engram .75 2.00
LS7 Marco Battaglia .50 1.25
LS8 Stepfret Williams .50 1.25
LS9 Jeff Lewis .75 2.00
LS10 Ryan Stewart .50 1.25
LS11 Derrick Mayes 1.25 3.00
LS12 Mike Archie .75 2.00
LS13 Scott Slutzker .50 1.25
LS14 Kevin Hardy .75 2.00
LS15 Reggie Tongue .50 1.25
LS16 Zach Thomas 1.25 3.00
LS17 Duane Clemons .50 1.25
LS18 Tedy Bruschi 3.00 8.00
LS19 Ricky Whittle .50 1.25
LS20 Amani Toomer 1.25 3.00
LS21 Alex Van Dyke .75 2.00
LS22 Lance Johnstone .75 2.00
LS23 Bobby Hoying 1.25 3.00
LS24 Jahine Arnold .75 2.00
LS25 Tony Banks 1.25 3.00
LS26 Charlie Jones .75 2.00
LS27 Terrell Owens 4.00 8.00
LS28 Reggie Brown RBK .50 1.25
LS29 Mike Alstott 1.50 4.00
LS30 Stephen Davis 2.50 6.00

1996 CE President's Reserve Candidates Top Picks

This set could be assembled via a mail redemption. Collector's Edge produced an exchange card for each team featuring that team's helmet logo and randomly inserted them into series two packs. The trade card could be sent-in (before the expiration date of 3/31/97) for another card featuring a "top early pick" of that team from the 1996 NFL Draft. These prize cards were printed on white paper stock not plastic like the inserted cards. Collector's Edge actually had eight of the trade cards ready when packaging began for the series two product and inserted those eight player's cards directly into packs instead of the helmet redemption card. We've noted those eight below.

COMPLETE SET (30) 40.00 80.00
SER.2 TRADE CARDS STATED ODDS 1:4
1 Simeon Rice 1.50 4.00
2 Shannon Brown .50 1.25
3 Willie Anderson .50 1.25
4 Tim Biakabutuka 1.25 3.00
5 Eric Moulds 2.00 5.00
6 Kavika Pittman .50 1.25
7 Jonathan Ogden 2.00 5.00
8 Reggie Brown LB .50 1.25
9 John Mobley .50 1.25
10 John Michels .50 1.25
11 Walt Harris .50 1.25
12 Eddie George 2.00 5.00
13 Marvin Harrison 4.00 8.00
14 Kevin Hardy .75 2.00
15 Jerome Woods .50 1.25
16 Duane Clemons .50 1.25
17 Daryl Gardener .50 1.25
18 Terry Glenn 2.00 5.00
19 Alex Molden .50 1.25
20 Cedric Jones .50 1.25
21 Rickey Dudley 1.25 3.00
22 Keyshawn Johnson 1.50 4.00
23 Jermane Mayberry .50 1.25
24 Jamain Stephens .50 1.25
25 Lawrence Phillips 1.25 3.00
26 Bryan Still .75 2.00
27 Israel Ifeanyi .75 2.00
28 Pete Kendall .50 1.25
29 Regan Upshaw .50 1.25
30 Andre Johnson .50 1.25

1996 CE President's Reserve Honor Guard

Collector's Edge released these cards as part of a President's Reserve wrapper redemption offer. The offer allowed the collector to send in 16-wrappers for a Jumbo Running Mates card or 64-wrappers for a Jumbo Running Mates Gold card. One Honor Guard card was mailed out with each redemption. The offer expired March 31, 1997. Each card is individually numbered of 1000. Some Honor Guard complete sets were also released as a bonus item for purchasing a case of Edge Masters product from Shop at Home.

COMPLETE SET (30) 50.00 120.00
EACH CARD NUMBERED OF 1000
HG1 Troy Aikman 5.00 12.00
HG2 Michael Irvin 2.00 5.00
HG3 Emmitt Smith 8.00 20.00
HG4 Brett Favre 10.00 25.00
HG5 Steve Young 4.00 10.00
HG6 Tim Brown 2.00 5.00
HG7 Errict Rhett 1.00 2.50
HG8 Curtis Martin 4.00 10.00
HG9 Carl Pickens 1.00 2.50
HG10 Herman Moore 1.00 2.50
HG11 Robert Brooks 2.00 5.00
HG12 Michael Westbrook 2.00 5.00
HG13 Leon Lett .50 1.25
HG14 Russell Maryland .50 1.25
HG15 Eric Swann 1.00 2.50
HG16 John Elway 10.00 25.00
HG17 Barry Sanders 8.00 20.00
HG18 Dan Marino 10.00 25.00
HG19 Drew Bledsoe 3.00 8.00
HG20 Jerry Rice 5.00 12.00
HG21 Deion Sanders 3.00 8.00
HG22 Rashaan Salaam 1.00 2.50
HG23 Marshall Faulk 2.50 6.00
HG24 Napoleon Kaufman 2.00 5.00
HG25 Ki-Jana Carter 1.00 2.50
HG26 Cris Carter 2.00 5.00
HG27 Joey Galloway 2.00 5.00
HG28 Eric Metcalf 1.00 2.50
HG29 Derrick Thomas 2.00 5.00
HG30 Bruce Smith 2.00 5.00

1996 CE President's Reserve New Regime

Randomly inserted in packs at a rate of one in five, this 26-card set highlights 1995's top rookies. These die cut cards are individually numbered out of 12,000.

COMPLETE SET (26) 25.00 50.00
COMP.SERIES 1 (13) 12.50 25.00
COMP.SERIES 2 (13) 12.50 25.00
1-12: STATED ODDS 1:5 SER.1 PACKS
13-24: STATED ODDS 1:5 SER.2 PACKS
STATED PRINT RUN 12,000 SERIAL #'d SETS
1 Tamarick Vanover .75 2.00
2 Kerry Collins .75 2.00
3 J.J. Stokes .75 2.00
4 Napoleon Kaufman .75 2.00
5 Steve McNair 1.50 4.00
6 Todd Collins .40 1.00
7 Frank Sanders .40 1.00
8 Warren Sapp .20 .50
9 Tony Boselli .40 1.00
10 Curtis Martin 1.50 4.00
11 Ki-Jana Carter .40 1.00
12 Zack Crockett .20 .50
13 Joey Galloway .75 2.00
14 Terrell Davis 1.50 4.00
15 Chris Sanders .40 1.00
16 Rashaan Salaam .40 1.00
17 Michael Westbrook .75 2.00
18 Hugh Douglas .40 1.00
19 Eric Zeier .40 1.00
20 Kordell Stewart .75 2.00
21 Ted Johnson .75 2.00
22 Ken Dilger .40 1.00
23 Darick Holmes .20 .50
24 Wayne Chrebet 1.25 3.00
NNO Checklist (1-12) .20 .50
NNO Checklist (13-24) .20 .50

1996 CE President's Reserve Running Mates

Randomly inserted in packs at a rate of one in 33, this 24-card set features teammates of quarterbacks and running backs on double-front cards printed on silver holofoil stock. The cards are individually numbered out of 2000. Gold parallel versions of both series were inserted into packs as well. Reportedly, only 10 of each series one Gold cards were numbered and inserted into packs and 100 of each series two card inserted in Gold form. Jumbo versions of all 24-cards were also produced and released via a mail order wrapper redemption. The large cards measure approximately 8" by 10" and were individually numbered of 2000 for the silver version and 200 for the gold version. Each silver version card was available in exchange for 16 President's Reserve wrappers, with the gold cards exchanged for 64 wrappers. Finally, another Gold version (with an added cheklist card) minus the card serial numbering surfaced after Edge ceased football card operations.

COMPLETE SET (24) 125.00 250.00
COMP.SERIES 1 (12) 60.00 125.00
COMP.SERIES 2 (12) 60.00 125.00
1-12: STATED ODDS 1:33 SER.1 PACKS
13-24: STATED ODDS 1:33 SER.2 PACKS
STATED PRINT RUN 2000 SERIAL #'d SETS
*GOLD/10: 3X TO 8X SILVER/2000
*GOLD/100: 1X TO 2.5X SILVER/2000
*JUMBO SILVER/2000: .25X TO .5X
JUMBO SILVER PRINT RUN 2000 SER.#'d SETS
*JUMBO GOLD/200: .6X TO 1.5X
JUMBO GOLD PRINT RUN 200 SER.#'d SETS
RM1 E.Smith 10.00 25.00
T.Aikman
RM2 M.Faulk 4.00 10.00
J.Harbaugh
RM3 T.Davis 10.00 25.00
J.Elway
RM4 Humphries 3.00 8.00
N.Means
RM5 R.Salaam 3.00 8.00
E.Kramer
RM6 C.Miller 4.00 10.00
J.Bettis
RM7 E.Rhett 3.00 8.00
T.Dilfer
RM8 J.George 2.50 6.00
Heyward
RM9 G.Frerotte 3.00 8.00
T.Allen
RM10 C.Martin 5.00 12.00
D.Bledsoe
RM11 J.Blake 3.00 8.00
Ki.Carter
RM12 R.Mirer 3.00 8.00
C.Warren
RM13 B.Favre 10.00 25.00
E.Bennett
RM14 N.O'Donnell 2.50 6.00
B.Morris
RM15 B.Sanders 8.00 20.00
S.Mitchell
RM16 S.Young 6.00 15.00
D.Loville
RM17 W.Moon 2.50 6.00
R.Smith
RM18 H.Shuler 3.00 8.00
B.Mitchell
RM19 R.Peete 3.00 8.00
R.Watters
RM20 K.Collins 3.00 8.00
D.Moore
RM21 D.Marino 10.00 25.00
T.Kirby
RM22 S.Bono 4.00 10.00
M.Allen
RM23 J.Kelly 4.00 10.00
D.Holmes
RM24 K.Stewart 4.00 10.00
E.Pegram

1996 CE President's Reserve Tanned Rested Ready

Randomly inserted in packs at a rate of one in eight, this 27-card set features NFL stars in action shots from the February 1996 Pro Bowl. The player's photos are showcased in front of a palm tree. The backs have necessary player information and are individually numbered out of 7,500. Cards 1-12 were issued in the first series and Cards 13-25 were included in second series packs.

COMPLETE SET (27) 40.00 80.00
COMP.SERIES 1 (13) 25.00 50.00
COMP.SERIES 2 (14) 15.00 30.00
1-12: STATED ODDS 1:8 SER.1 PACKS
13-25: STATED ODDS 1:8 SER.2 PACKS
1 Jeff Blake 1.50 3.00
2 Warren Moon .75 1.50
3 Brett Favre 8.00 15.00
4 Steve Young 3.00 6.00
5 Emmitt Smith 6.00 12.00
6 Ricky Watters .75 1.50
7 Michael Irvin 1.50 3.00
8 Carl Pickens .75 1.50
9 Tim Brown 1.50 3.00
10 Anthony Miller .75 1.50
11 Darren Bennett .75 1.50
12 Yancey Thigpen .75 1.50
13 Bryce Paup .75 1.50
14 Jim Harbaugh .75 1.50
15 Barry Sanders 6.00 12.00
16 Herman Moore .75 1.50
17 Cris Carter 1.50 3.00
18 Chris Warren .75 1.50
19 Marshall Faulk 2.00 4.00
20 Curtis Martin 3.00 6.00
21 Ben Coates .75 1.50
22 Brent Jones .30 .75
23 Shannon Sharpe .75 1.50
24 Brian Mitchell .30 .75
25 Ken Harvey .30 .75
NNO Checklist (1-12) .30 .75
NNO Checklist (13-25) .30 .75

1996 CE President's Reserve TimeWarp

Randomly inserted in packs at a rate of one in 64, this 12-card insert standard-size set features two players per card. One of the players is still active, while the other is a retired superstar. The backs are individually numbered out of 2000. A parallel version of card #4 was released later through the Shop at Home network. The card is 5-times thicker than the base card and includes a Ruby embedded into the cardfront. Finally several cards made their way into the secondary market after Collector's Edge folded. Each of those is unnumbered but listed below at the end of the 12-card set listing.

COMPLETE SET (12) 30.00 80.00
1-6: RAND.INS. IN SERIES 1 PACKS
7-12: RAND.INS. IN SERIES 2 PACKS
1 J.Kemp 2.00 5.00
G.Lloyd
2 M.Faulk 3.00 8.00
Jurgensen
3 F.Tarkenton 2.50 6.00
Paup
4 Emmitt Smith 8.00 20.00
Staubach
4R E.Smith 60.00 100.00
Staubach Ruby
5 Curtis Martin 4.00 10.00
Lambert
6 Brett Favre 8.00 20.00
Youngblood
7 F.Tarkenton 3.00 8.00
R. White
8 A.Donovan 2.00 5.00
S.Bono
9 Troy Aikman 5.00 12.00
B.Mitchell
10 Kordell Stewart 2.50 6.00
Csonka
11 Deion Sanders 4.00 10.00
Butkus
12 Dan Marino 8.00 20.00
D.Jones
NNO W.Payton 5.00 12.00
R.White
NNO J.Namath 6.00 15.00
E.Smith

1998 CE Supreme Season Review Markers Previews

COMPLETE SET (30) 30.00 60.00
*PREVIEWS: .1X TO .2X BASIC INSERTS

1998 CE Supreme Season Review

The 200-card set of the 1998 Collector's Edge Supreme Season Review was distributed in six-card packs with a suggested retail price of $3.99 and feature borderless color action player photos. The set includes 170-player cards with 30-redemption cards for top draft picks from each team. The draft pick redemption cards expired March 31, 1999. The draft pick prize cards were numbered as part of the base set with a letter suffix attached to the card number.

COMPLETE SET (200) 30.00 60.00
COMP.SET w/o SPs (200) 10.00 25.00
1 Larry Centers .20 .50
2 Jake Plummer .20 .50
3 Simeon Rice .25 .60
4 Cardinals Draft Pick .02 .10
4A Andre Wadsworth RC .60 1.50
4B Michael Pittman RC .60 1.50
5 Jamal Anderson .25 .60
6 Bert Emanuel .25 .60
7 Byron Hanspard .20 .50
8 Falcons Draft Pick .02 .10
8A Jammi German RC .40 1.00
8B Keith Brooking RC .60 1.50
9 Derrick Alexander WR .25 .60
10 Peter Boulware .20 .50
11 Michael Jackson .20 .50
12 Ray Lewis .30 .75
13 Vinny Testaverde .20 .50
14 Ravens Draft Pick .02 .10
14A Duane Starks RC .40 1.00
14B Pat Johnson RC .50 1.25
15 Todd Collins .25 .60
16 Jim Kelly .30 .75
17 Andre Reed .30 .75
18 Antowain Smith .25 .60
19 Bruce Smith .25 .60
20 Thurman Thomas .25 .60
21 Bills Draft Pick .02 .10
21A Jonathan Linton RC .50 1.25
22 Tim Biakabutuka .25 .60
23 Rae Carruth .20 .50
24 Kerry Collins .20 .50
25 Anthony Johnson .25 .60
26 Lamar Lathon .20 .50
27 Panthers Draft Pick .02 .10
27A Jason Peter RC .40 1.00
27B Donald Hayes RC .40 1.00
28 Curtis Conway .25 .60
29 Bryan Cox .25 .60
30 Bobby Engram .20 .50
31 Erik Kramer .20 .50
32 Rick Mirer .25 .60
33 Rashaan Salaam .25 .60
34 Bears Draft Pick .02 .10
34A Curtis Enis RC .50 1.25
35 Jeff Blake .25 .60
36 Ki-Jana Carter .25 .60
37 Corey Dillon .20 .50
38 Carl Pickens .25 .60
39 Bengals Draft Pick .02 .10
39A Takeo Spikes RC .50 1.25
39B Brian Simmons RC .40 1.00
40 Troy Aikman .40 1.00
41 Daryl Johnston .30 .75
42 David LaFleur .20 .50
43 Anthony Miller .20 .50
44 Deion Sanders .25 .60
45 Emmitt Smith .50 1.25
46 Broderick Thomas .20 .50
47 Cowboys Draft Pick .02 .10
47A Greg Ellis RC .50 1.25
48 Terrell Davis .25 .60
49 John Elway .50 1.25
50 Ed McCaffrey .25 .60
51 John Mobley .20 .50
52 Bill Romanowski .25 .60
53 Shannon Sharpe .25 .60
54 Neil Smith .25 .60
55 Rod Smith WR .25 .60
56 Maa Tanuvasa .20 .50
57 Broncos Draft Pick .02 .10
57A Marcus Nash RC .40 1.00
57B Brian Griese RC .75 2.00
58 Scott Mitchell .25 .60
59 Herman Moore .25 .60
60 Barry Sanders .50 1.25
61 Lions Draft Pick .02 .10
61A Jamaal Alexander RC .40 1.00
61B Chris Liwienski RC .40 1.00
61C Terry Fair RC .50 1.25
61D Germane Crowell RC .40 1.00
61E Charlie Batch RC .60 1.50
62 Robert Brooks .25 .60
63 Mark Chmura .20 .50
64 Brett Favre .60 1.50
65 Antonio Freeman .30 .75
66 Dorsey Levens .25 .60
67 Derrick Mayes .25 .60
68 Ross Verba .20 .50
69 Reggie White .30 .75
70 Packers Draft Pick .02 .10
70A Vonnie Holliday RC .50 1.25
70B Roosevelt Blackmon RC .40 1.00
71 Marshall Faulk .25 .60
72 Jim Harbaugh .30 .75
73 Marvin Harrison .25 .60
74 Colts Draft Pick .02 .10
74A E.G. Green RC .50 1.25
74B Peyton Manning RC 6.00 15.00
75 Tony Brackens .20 .50
76 Mark Brunell .25 .60
77 Rob Johnson .25 .60
78 Keenan McCardell .25 .60
79 Natrone Means .25 .60
80 Jimmy Smith .25 .60
81 Jaguars Draft Pick .02 .10
81A Tavian Banks RC .50 1.25
82 Marcus Allen .30 .75
83 Tony Gonzalez .25 .60
84 Elvis Grbac .25 .60
85 Derrick Thomas .30 .75
86 Tamarick Vanover .20 .50
87 Chiefs Draft Pick .02 .10
87A Rashaan Shehee RC .40 1.00
88 Karim Abdul-Jabbar .20 .50
89 Fred Barnett .25 .60
90 Dan Marino .60 1.50
91 O.J. McDuffie .25 .60
92 Brett Perriman .25 .60
93 Irving Spikes .20 .50
94 Zach Thomas .25 .60
95 Dolphins Draft Pick .02 .10
95A John Avery RC .50 1.25
96 Cris Carter .30 .75
97 Brad Johnson .25 .60
98 John Randle .30 .75
99 Jake Reed .25 .60
100 Robert Smith .20 .50
101 Vikings Draft Pick .02 .10
101A Randy Moss RC 3.00 8.00
102 Drew Bledsoe .25 .60
103 Chris Canty .20 .50
104 Ben Coates .25 .60
105 Terry Glenn .25 .60
106 Curtis Martin .25 .60
107 Willie McGinest .20 .50
108 Sedrick Shaw .20 .50
109 Patriots Draft Pick .02 .10
109A Chris Floyd RC .40 1.00
109B Tebucky Jones RC .40 1.00
109C Harold Shaw RC .50 1.25
110 Mario Bates .20 .50
111 Heath Shuler .25 .60
112 Danny Wuerffel .25 .60
113 Saints Draft Pick .02 .10
113A Cameron Cleeland RC .50 1.25
114 Ray Zellars .20 .50
115 Tiki Barber .25 .60
116 Dave Brown .25 .60
117 Ike Hilliard .20 .50
118 Danny Kanell .20 .50
119 Jason Sehorn .25 .60
120 Amani Toomer .20 .50
121 Giants Draft Pick .02 .10
121A Shaun Williams RC .50 1.25
121B Joe Jurevicius RC .60 1.50
121C Brian Alford RC .40 1.00
122 Wayne Chrebet .20 .50
123 Hugh Douglas .20 .50
124 Jeff Graham .20 .50
125 Keyshawn Johnson .25 .60
126 Adrian Murrell .20 .50
127 Neil O'Donnell .25 .60
128 Jets Draft Pick .02 .10
128A Scott Frost RC .40 1.00
129 Tim Brown .30 .75
130 Jeff George .25 .60
131 Desmond Howard .25 .60
132 Napoleon Kaufman .20 .50
133 Darrell Russell .20 .50
134 Raiders Draft Pick .02 .10
134A Charles Woodson RC 1.50 4.00
135 Ty Detmer .20 .50
136 Irving Fryar .25 .60
137 Bobby Hoying .25 .60
138 Chris T. Jones .20 .50
139 Ricky Watters .25 .60
140 Eagles Draft Pick .02 .10
140A Allen Rossum RC .50 1.25
141 Jerome Bettis .30 .75
142 Charles Johnson .20 .50
143 George Jones .20 .50
144 Greg Lloyd .25 .60
145 Kordell Stewart .20 .50
146 Yancey Thigpen .20 .50
147 Steelers Draft Pick .02 .10
147A Chris Fuamatu-Ma'afala RC .50 1.25
148 Stan Humphries .25 .60
149 Tony Martin .25 .60
150 Eric Metcalf .25 .60
151 Junior Seau .25 .60
152 Chargers Draft Pick .02 .10
152A Ryan Leaf RC .50 1.25
153 Jim Druckenmiller .20 .50
154 William Floyd .20 .50
155 Kevin Greene .30 .75
156 Garrison Hearst .20 .50
157 Ken Norton .20 .50
158 Terrell Owens .25 .60
159 Jerry Rice .75 2.00
160 J.J. Stokes .25 .60
161 Dana Stubblefield .20 .50
162 Rod Woodson .30 .75
163 Bryant Young .25 .60
164 Steve Young .40 1.00
165 49ers Draft Pick .02 .10
165A Fred Beasley RC .40 1.00
165B R.W. McQuarters RC .60 1.50
165C Chris Ruhman RC .40 1.00
166 Steve Broussard .20 .50
167 Chad Brown .20 .50
168 Joey Galloway .25 .60
169 Jon Kitna .20 .50
170 Warren Moon .30 .75
171 Chris Warren .25 .60
172 Seahawks Draft Pick .02 .10
172A Ahman Green RC .75 2.00
173 Tony Banks .25 .60
174 Isaac Bruce .30 .75
175 Eddie Kennison .20 .50
176 Keith Lyle .20 .50
177 Lawrence Phillips .25 .60

178 Rams Draft Pick .02 .10
178A Robert Holcombe RC .40 1.00
179 Mike Alstott .20 .50
180 Reidel Anthony .20 .50
181 Trent Dilfer .25 .60
182 Warrick Dunn .20 .50
183 Hardy Nickerson .20 .50
184 Errict Rhett .25 .60
185 Warren Sapp .25 .60
186 Bucs Draft Pick .02 .10
186A Jacquez Green RC .50 1.25
187 Eddie George .25 .60
188 Darryll Lewis .20 .50
189 Steve McNair .25 .60
190 Chris Sanders .20 .50
191 Oilers Draft Pick .02 .10
191A Kevin Dyson RC .50 1.25
192 Terry Allen .25 .60
193 Jamie Asher .20 .50
194 Stephen Davis .20 .50
195 Gus Frerotte .20 .50
196 Sean Gilbert .20 .50
197 Ken Harvey .20 .50
198 Jeff Hostetler .25 .60
199 Michael Westbrook .25 .60
200 Redskins Draft Pick .02 .10
200A Stephen Alexander RC .50 1.25
200B Mike Sellers RC .50 1.25

1998 CE Supreme Season Review Gold Ingot

COMPLETE SET (200) 200.00 400.00
*VETS: 1.2X TO 3X BASIC CARDS
*ROOKIES: .6X TO 1.5X BASIC CARDS
STATED ODDS 1:1

1998 CE Supreme Season Review Personal Collection

STATED ODDS 1:4000
STATED PRINT RUN 1 SET

1998 CE Supreme Season Review Silver Holofoil

*SILVER: .5X TO 1.2X BASIC CARDS
74B Peyton Manning 8.00 20.00

1998 CE Supreme Season Review Markers

Randomly inserted in packs at the rate of one in 24, this 30-card set features borderless color player photos highlighted with special embossed foil and commemorates each player's outstanding achievements.

COMPLETE SET (30) 125.00 250.00
STATED ODDS 1:24
1 Jamal Anderson 4.00 10.00
2 Corey Dillon 4.00 10.00
3 Emmitt Smith 10.00 25.00
4 Terrell Davis 4.00 10.00
5 John Elway 12.50 30.00
6 Rod Smith 2.50 6.00
7 Herman Moore 2.50 6.00
8 Barry Sanders 10.00 25.00
9 Robert Brooks 2.50 6.00
10 Brett Favre 12.50 30.00
11 Antonio Freeman 4.00 10.00
12 Dorsey Levens 4.00 10.00
13 Marshall Faulk 5.00 12.00
14 Mark Brunell 4.00 10.00
15 Karim Abdul-Jabbar 4.00 10.00
16 Dan Marino 12.50 30.00
17 Cris Carter 4.00 10.00
18 Drew Bledsoe 5.00 12.00
19 Curtis Martin 4.00 10.00
20 Adrian Murrell 2.50 6.00
21 Tim Brown 4.00 10.00
22 Jeff George 2.50 6.00
23 Napoleon Kaufman 4.00 10.00
24 Jerome Bettis 4.00 10.00
25 Kordell Stewart 4.00 10.00
26 Yancey Thigpen 1.50 4.00
27 Garrison Hearst 4.00 10.00
28 Steve Young 4.00 10.00
29 Joey Galloway 2.50 6.00
30 Eddie George 4.00 10.00

1998 CE Supreme Season Review Pro-Signature Authentic

Randomly inserted in packs at the rate of one in 2300, this set features color player photos printed on 50-point, silver holofoil card stock with rainbow holofoil embossing and the hand-written autograph by the featured player. A Rookie Redemption card was inserted in packs and was exchangeable for either the Ryan Leaf or Peyton Manning signed cards with each being hand serial numbered of 500. The Emmitt Smith card was randomly inserted in 1998 Edge Masters packs. The backs contain a statement of authenticity. Reportedly, just 50 of each card were signed except for the Leaf and Manning.

OVERALL STATED ODDS 1:2300
VETERANS STATED PRINT RUN 50
ROOKIE REDEMPTION ODDS 1:800
EMMITT SMITH INSERTED IN 98 CE MASTERS
DH Desmond Howard 60.00 150.00
ES Emmitt Smith 150.00 300.00
JR Jerry Rice 125.00 250.00
MA Marcus Allen 60.00 150.00
PM Peyton Manning/500 60.00 120.00
RL Ryan Leaf/500 25.00 60.00
TA Troy Aikman 125.00 250.00
TD Terrell Davis 60.00 150.00
NNO Rookie Redemption .40 1.00

1998 CE Supreme Season Review T3 Previews

This set was released to promote the T3 insert in 1998 Edge Supreme Season Review. The cards are identical to the base insert set with the word "Preview" stamped on the cardfronts. Reportedly, card #18 was not released in the Preview card version.

COMPLETE SET (29) 40.00 100.00
*PROMO CARDS: X TO X BASE INSERT

1998 CE Supreme Season Review T3

Randomly inserted in packs, this 30-card set features color player photos of top players in different positions printed on mirror card stock with a gold-etched "Edge" foil stamp. Each position has different colored foil highlights and different insertion rates: 1:36 QB, 1:24 RB, and 1:12 WR.

COMPLETE SET (30) 100.00 200.00
STATED ODDS 1:36 QB/1:24 RB/1:12 WR
1 Rae Carruth 1.00 2.50
2 Carl Pickens 1.25 3.00
3 Troy Aikman 5.00 12.00
4 Emmitt Smith 5.00 12.00
5 Terrell Davis 1.50 4.00
6 John Elway 12.50 25.00
7 Herman Moore 1.25 3.00
8 Barry Sanders 10.00 20.00
9 Robert Brooks 1.25 3.00
10 Brett Favre 12.50 25.00
11 Antonio Freeman 1.50 4.00
12 Dorsey Levens 1.50 4.00
13 Rob Johnson 2.00 5.00
14 Jerry Rice 4.00 8.00
15 Dan Marino 12.50 25.00
16 Cris Carter 1.50 4.00
17 Drew Bledsoe 5.00 10.00
18 Curtis Martin 1.50 4.00
19 Adrian Murrell 1.50 4.00
20 Tim Brown 1.50 4.00
21 Napoleon Kaufman 1.50 4.00
22 Jerome Bettis 1.50 4.00
23 Kordell Stewart 2.00 5.00
24 Joey Galloway 1.25 3.00
25 Jim Druckenmiller 2.00 5.00
26 Terrell Owens 1.50 4.00
27 Jake Plummer 1.50 4.00
28 Warrick Dunn 1.50 4.00
29 Eddie George 1.50 4.00
30 Steve McNair 2.00 5.00

1999 Collector's Edge Supreme Previews

These cards were released as a preview to the 1999 Edge Supreme card release. Each is very similar to its base set counterpart except for the card number on back and "Preview" printed on the cardbacks.

COMPLETE SET (10) 6.00 15.00
BS Barry Sanders 1.60 4.00
CB Charlie Batch .80 2.00
ES Emmitt Smith 1.20 3.00
JA Jamal Anderson .40 1.00
KJ Keyshawn Johnson .40 1.00
MB Mark Brunell .80 2.00
PM Peyton Manning 2.00 5.00
RE Robert Edwards .40 1.00
RM Randy Moss 2.00 5.00
TD Terrell Davis 1.20 3.00

1999 Collector's Edge Supreme Draft Previews

These cards were released as preview or promo cards at various Collector's Edge functions in exchange for product wrappers or through the mail via various redemption cards. Each is essentially identical to the base Supreme card for the player except for the card numbering which is the player's initials in this Preview set. There are two versions of the Couch card with either a 1st Pick or 2nd Pick foil notation on the cardfront.

COMPLETE SET (6) 6.00 15.00
CB Champ Bailey .40 1.00
CC Chris Claiborne .30 .75
DC Daunte Culpepper 1.00 2.50
RW Ricky Williams 2.00 5.00
TC1 Tim Couch 1st Pick 2.00 5.00
TC2 Tim Couch 2nd Pick 2.00 5.00
TH Torry Holt .80 2.00

1999 Collector's Edge Supreme

The 1999 Collector's Edge Supreme set was issued in one series totalling 170-cards. The set features action player photos printed with high definition color and clarity on UV coated, silver foil stamped card stock. The backs carry the player's complete 1998 statistics. Forty short printed rookie cards from the 1999 NFL draft are included in the set along with mail redemption cards for each draft pick including #166. Card #166 Michael Wiley was released in very early packs only and quickly withdrawn with the #166 redemption card exchangeable for an Edgerrin James card.

COMPLETE SET (170) 25.00 60.00
1 Randy Moss CL .15 .40
2 Peyton Manning CL .60 1.50
3 Rob Moore .20 .50
4 Adrian Murrell .20 .50
5 Jake Plummer .20 .50
6 Andre Wadsworth .20 .50
7 Jamal Anderson .25 .60
8 Chris Chandler .25 .60
9 Tony Martin .25 .60
10 Terence Mathis .20 .50
11 Jim Harbaugh .25 .60
12 Priest Holmes .20 .50
13 Jermaine Lewis .20 .50
14 Eric Zeier .20 .50
15 Doug Flutie .30 .75
16 Eric Moulds .20 .50
17 Andre Reed .30 .75
18 Antowain Smith .20 .50
19 Steve Beuerlein .25 .60
20 Kevin Greene .30 .75
21 Rocket Ismail .25 .60
22 Fred Lane .20 .50
23 Edgar Bennett .25 .60
24 Curtis Conway .25 .60
25 Curtis Enis .20 .50
26 Erik Kramer .25 .60
27 Corey Dillon .20 .50
28 Neil O'Donnell .25 .60
29 Carl Pickens .25 .60
30 Darnay Scott .20 .50
31 Troy Aikman .40 1.00
32 Michael Irvin .30 .75
33 Deion Sanders .25 .60
34 Emmitt Smith .50 1.25
35 Chris Warren .25 .60
36 Terrell Davis .25 .60
37 John Elway .50 1.25
38 Ed McCaffrey .25 .60
39 Shannon Sharpe .25 .60
40 Rod Smith .25 .60
41 Charlie Batch .20 .50
42 Herman Moore .25 .60
43 Johnnie Morton .25 .60
44 Barry Sanders .50 1.25
45 Robert Brooks .25 .60
46 Brett Favre 1.50 4.00
47 Antonio Freeman .25 .60
48 Darick Holmes .20 .50
49 Dorsey Levens .25 .60
50 Reggie White .30 .75
51 Marshall Faulk .25 .60
52 Marvin Harrison .25 .60
53 Peyton Manning 1.00 2.50
54 Jerome Pathon .20 .50
55 Tavian Banks .20 .50
56 Mark Brunell .25 .60
57 Keenan McCardell .25 .60
58 Fred Taylor .20 .50
59 Derrick Alexander .20 .50
60 Donnell Bennett .20 .50
61 Rich Gannon .25 .60
62 Andre Rison .25 .60
63 Karim Abdul-Jabbar .20 .50
64 John Avery .20 .50
65 Oronde Gadsden .20 .50
66 Dan Marino .60 1.50
67 O.J. McDuffie .25 .60
68 Cris Carter .30 .75
69 Randall Cunningham .25 .60
70 Brad Johnson .25 .60
71 Randy Moss .25 .60
72 Jake Reed .25 .60
73 Robert Smith .20 .50
74 Drew Bledsoe .25 .60
75 Ben Coates .25 .60
76 Robert Edwards .20 .50
77 Terry Glenn .25 .60
78 Cameron Cleeland .20 .50
79 Kerry Collins .20 .50
80 Sean Dawkins .20 .50
81 Lamar Smith .20 .50
82 Gary Brown .20 .50
83 Chris Calloway .20 .50
84 Danny Kanell .20 .50
85 Ike Hilliard .20 .50
86 Wayne Chrebet .20 .50
87 Keyshawn Johnson .25 .60
88 Curtis Martin .25 .60
89 Vinny Testaverde .20 .50
90 Tim Brown .30 .75
91 Jeff George .20 .50
92 Napoleon Kaufman .20 .50
93 Charles Woodson .30 .75
94 Irving Fryar .25 .60
95 Bobby Hoying .20 .50
96 Duce Staley .20 .50
97 Jerome Bettis .30 .75
98 Courtney Hawkins .20 .50
99 Charles Johnson .20 .50
100 Kordell Stewart .20 .50
101 Hines Ward .25 .60
102 Tony Banks .25 .60
103 Isaac Bruce .30 .75
104 Robert Holcombe .20 .50
105 Ryan Leaf .25 .60
106 Natrone Means .25 .60
107 Mikhael Ricks .20 .50
108 Junior Seau .25 .60
109 Garrison Hearst .20 .50
110 Terrell Owens .25 .60
111 Jerry Rice .75 2.00
112 J.J. Stokes .20 .50
113 Steve Young .40 1.00
114 Joey Galloway .25 .60
115 Jon Kitna .20 .50
116 Warren Moon .30 .75
117 Ricky Watters .25 .60
118 Mike Alstott .20 .50
119 Reidel Anthony .20 .50
120 Warrick Dunn .20 .50
121 Trent Dilfer .20 .50
122 Jacquez Green .20 .50
123 Kevin Dyson .20 .50
124 Eddie George .25 .60
125 Steve McNair .25 .60
126 Frank Wycheck .25 .60
127 Terry Allen .25 .60
128 Trent Green .20 .50
129 Skip Hicks .20 .50
130 Michael Westbrook .20 .50
131 Rahim Abdullah RC .40 1.00
132 Champ Bailey RC .75 2.00
133 Marlon Barnes RC .40 1.00
134 D'Wayne Bates RC .40 1.00
135 Michael Bishop RC .50 1.25
136 Dre Bly RC .60 1.50
137 David Boston RC .40 1.00
138 Cuncho Brown UER RC .40 1.00
139 Na Brown RC .40 1.00
140 Tony Bryant RC .40 1.00
141 Tim Couch ERR RC 25.00 50.00
141TC Tim Couch COR RC 1.00 2.50
142 Chris Claiborne RC .40 1.00
143 Daunte Culpepper RC .60 1.50
144 Jared DeVries RC .40 1.00
145 Troy Edwards UER RC .40 1.00
146 Kris Farris RC .40 1.00
147 Kevin Faulk RC .40 1.00
148 Joe Germaine RC .50 1.25
149 Aaron Gibson RC .40 1.00
150 Torry Holt RC .75 2.00
151 Brock Huard RC .40 1.00
152 Sedrick Irvin RC .40 1.00
153 James Johnson RC .40 1.00
154 Kevin Johnson RC .50 1.25
155 Andy Katzenmoyer RC .50 1.25
156 Jevon Kearse RC .50 1.25
157 Shaun King RC .40 1.00
158 Rob Konrad RC .40 1.00
159 Chris McAlister RC .40 1.00
160 Darnell McDonald RC .40 1.00
161 Donovan McNabb RC 2.50 6.00
162 Cade McNown RC .40 1.00
163 Peerless Price RC .40 1.00
164 Akili Smith RC .40 1.00
165 Matt Stinchcomb RC .40 1.00
166A Michael Wiley SP 30.00 80.00
166B Edgerrin James RC 1.50 4.00
167 Ricky Williams RC .60 1.50
168 Antoine Winfield RC .40 1.00
169 Craig Yeast RC .40 1.00
170 Amos Zereoue RC .40 1.00

1999 Collector's Edge Supreme Galvanized

COMPLETE SET (167) 400.00 800.00
*VETS 3-130: 2.5X TO 6X BASIC CARDS
*ROOKIES 131-170: 1.5X TO 4X BASIC CARDS
*ROOKIE #141: .5X TO 1.2X BASIC CARD
STATED PRINT RUN 500 SER.#'d SETS
166A Michael Wiley pink 12.00 30.00
166B Edgerrin James ERR 50.00 100.00

1999 Collector's Edge Supreme Gold Ingot

*VETS 3-130: .8X TO 2X BASIC CARDS
*ROOKIES 131-170: .5X TO 1.2X BASIC CARDS
ONE PER PACK
141 Tim Couch ERR 20.00 50.00
166B Edgerrin James ERR 10.00 25.00

1999 Collector's Edge Supreme Future

Randomly inserted in packs at the rate of one in 24, this 10-card set features color photos of some of 1999 hottest draft picks printed on micro-etched foil board with foil stamping.

COMPLETE SET (10) 30.00 60.00
STATED ODDS 1:24
SF1 Ricky Williams 2.00 5.00
SF2 Tim Couch 1.50 4.00
SF3 Daunte Culpepper 3.00 8.00
SF4 Torry Holt 2.50 6.00
SF5 Edgerrin James 4.00 10.00
SF6 Brock Huard 1.50 4.00
SF7 Donovan McNabb 5.00 12.00
SF8 Joe Germaine 1.50 4.00
SF9 Cade McNown 1.50 4.00
SF10 Michael Bishop 1.50 4.00

1999 Collector's Edge Supreme Homecoming

Randomly inserted in packs at the rate of one in 12, this 20-card set features color and black-and-white photos of top draft picks paired with NFL stars from the same college printed on foil cards.

COMPLETE SET (20) 30.00 60.00
STATED ODDS 1:12
H1 R.Williams / P.Holmes 2.50 6.00
H2 A.Katzenmoyer / E.George 1.00 2.50
H3 D.Culpepper / S.Jefferson 2.50 6.00
H4 T.Holt / E.Kramer 2.00 5.00
H5 E.James / V.Testaverde 3.00 8.00
H6 C.Claiborne / J.Seau 1.00 2.50
H7 B.Huard / M.Brunell 1.00 2.50
H8 C.Bailey / T.Davis 1.00 2.50
H9 D.McNabb / R.Moore 4.00 10.00
H10 D.Boston / J.Galloway 1.00 2.50
H11 C.McNown / T.Aikman 3.00 8.00
H12 K.Faulk / F.Kennison 1.00 2.50
H13 S.Irvin / A.Rison 1.00 2.50
H14 R.Konrad / D.Johnston .60 1.50
H15 A.Zereoue / A.Murrell 1.00 2.50
H16 P.Price / P.Manning 3.00 8.00
H17 K.Johnson / M.Harrison 1.25 3.00
H18 J.Kearse / E.Smith 1.50 4.00
H19 A.Winfield / S.Springs .60 1.50
H20 T.Bryant / A.Wadsworth .60 1.50

1999 Collector's Edge Supreme Markers

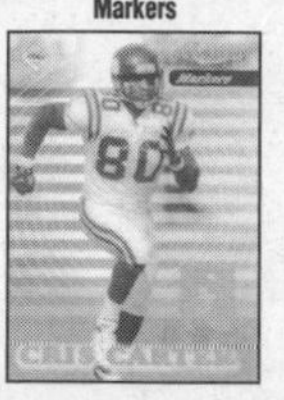

Randomly inserted in packs at the rate of one in 24, this 15-card set features color photos of NFL stars with record-setting perfomances and milestones reached in the 1998 season printed on clear vinyl stock with foil stamping. The cards are serial-numbered to 5000.

COMPLETE SET (15) 35.00 70.00
STATED PRINT RUN 5000 SERIAL #'d SETS
M1 Terrell Davis 1.25 3.00
M2 John Elway 4.00 10.00
M3 Dan Marino 4.00 10.00
M4 Peyton Manning 4.00 10.00
M5 Barry Sanders 4.00 10.00
M6 Emmitt Smith 2.50 6.00
M7 Randy Moss 4.00 10.00
M8 Jake Plummer .75 2.00
M9 Cris Carter 1.25 3.00
M10 Brett Favre 4.00 10.00
M11 Drew Bledsoe 1.50 4.00
M12 Charlie Batch 1.25 3.00
M13 Curtis Martin 1.25 3.00
M14 Mark Brunell 1.25 3.00
M15 Jamal Anderson 1.25 3.00

1999 Collector's Edge Supreme PSA Series

COMPLETE SET (10) 40.00 80.00
1/2/8/9 ANNOUNCED PRINT RUN 100
3/4/10 ANNOUNCED PRINT RUN 2000
5/6/7 ANNOUNCED PRINT RUN 700
1 Champ Bailey/100* 5.00 12.00
2 David Boston/100* 3.00 8.00
3 Tim Couch/2000* 1.50 4.00
4 Daunte Culpepper/2000* 2.50 6.00
5 Troy Edwards/700* 2.00 5.00
6 Torry Holt/700* 4.00 10.00
7 Edgerrin James/700* 5.00 12.00
8 Donovan McNabb/100* 10.00 25.00
9 Akili Smith/100* 3.00 8.00
10 Ricky Williams/2000* 2.00 5.00

1999 Collector's Edge Supreme Route XXXIII

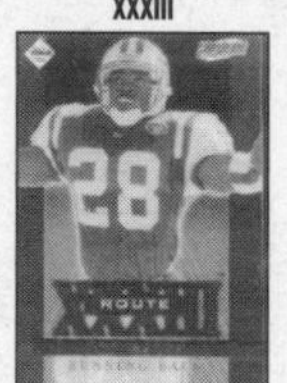

Randomly inserted into packs, this 10-card set features color photos of top players who played in the 1998 playoffs. Only 1,000 of each card was produced and sequentially numbered.

COMPLETE SET (10) 25.00 50.00
STATED PRINT RUN 1000 SERIAL #'d SETS
R1 Randy Moss 5.00 12.00
R2 Jamal Anderson 1.50 4.00
R3 Jake Plummer 1.00 2.50
R4 Steve Young 2.00 5.00
R5 Fred Taylor 1.50 4.00
R6 Dan Marino 5.00 12.00
R7 Keyshawn Johnson 1.50 4.00
R8 Curtis Martin 1.50 4.00
R9 John Elway 5.00 12.00
R10 Terrell Davis 1.50 4.00

1999 Collector's Edge Supreme Supremacy

Randomly inserted into packs, this five-card set features color Super Bowl photos of stars from Super Bowl XXXIII printed on foil board with foil stamping. Each card is numbered to 500.

COMPLETE SET (5) 15.00 30.00
STATED PRINT RUN 500 SERIAL #'d SETS
P2 Terrell Davis PREVIEW .75 2.00
S1 John Elway 7.50 20.00
S2 Terrell Davis 1.50 4.00
S3 Ed McCaffrey 1.50 4.00
S4 Jamal Anderson 1.50 4.00
S5 Chris Chandler 1.50 4.00

1999 Collector's Edge Supreme T3

This 30-card tiered, fractured insert set features color photos of ten of the NFL's top wide receivers, ten top running backs, and ten top quarterbacks. The wide receivers' photos are printed on foil board with bronze foil stamping and seeded in packs at the rate of one in eight. The running backs' photos are printed on foil board with silver foil stamping and seeded in packs at the rate of one in 12. The quarterbacks' photos are pinted on foil board with gold foil stamping and seeded at the rate of one in 24.

COMPLETE SET (30) 50.00 100.00
QB STATED ODDS 1:24
RB STATED ODDS 1:12
T1 Doug Flutie 1.50 4.00
T2 Troy Aikman 3.00 8.00
T3 John Elway 5.00 12.00
T4 Jake Plummer 1.50 4.00
T5 Brett Favre 5.00 12.00
T6 Mark Brunell 1.50 4.00
T7 Peyton Manning 5.00 12.00
T8 Dan Marino 5.00 12.00
T9 Drew Bledsoe 2.00 5.00
T10 Steve Young 2.00 5.00
T11 Jamal Anderson .75 2.00
T12 Emmitt Smith 2.00 5.00
T13 Terrell Davis 1.50 4.00
T14 Barry Sanders 3.00 8.00
T15 Robert Smith .50 1.25
T16 Robert Edwards .50 1.25
T17 Curtis Martin .75 2.00
T18 Jerome Bettis .75 2.00
T19 Fred Taylor 1.50 4.00
T20 Eddie George .75 2.00
T21 Michael Irvin .60 1.50
T22 Eric Moulds .60 1.50
T23 Herman Moore .60 1.50
T24 Reidel Anthony .40 1.00
T25 Randy Moss 2.00 5.00
T26 Cris Carter 1.50 4.00
T27 Keyshawn Johnson .60 1.50
T28 Jacquez Green .40 1.00
T29 Jerry Rice 1.25 3.00
T30 Terrell Owens .60 1.50

2000 Collector's Edge Supreme Previews

This set was issued to preview the 2000 Collector's Edge Supreme release. Each card is essentially a parallel version of the base Supreme card with the word "Preview" on the cardbacks and the player's initials as the card number.

COMPLETE SET (7) 6.00 15.00
EG Eddie George .40 1.00
EJ Edgerrin James .40 1.00
KW Kurt Warner .75 2.00
MB Mark Brunell .40 1.00
MF Marshall Faulk .40 1.00
PM Peyton Manning 1.25 3.00
SD Stephen Davis .30 .75

2000 Collector's Edge Supreme

Released as a 190-card set, 2000 Collector's Edge Supreme is composed of 150 veteran cards and 40 short-printed rookie cards, which were sequentially numbered to 2000. Several of the rookies were released as redemption cards with an expiration date of 3/31/2001. Supreme was packaged in 24-pack boxes containing 10 cards each, and carried a suggested retail price of $2.99. Card number 151 was initially intended to be LaVar Arrington who was pulled from production and, reportedly, never released in packs. Instead it was replaced by a redemption card that ultimately turned out to be redeemable for Sylvester Morris. However, a number of copies of the Arrington card made their way into the secondary market years later. Also, card #171 Bill Burke (and the HoloGold parallel) surfaced after Edge ceased football card operations.

COMPLETE SET (190) 15.00 30.00
COMP.FACT.SET (190) 20.00 40.00
COMP.SET w/o SP's (150) 7.50 20.00
151-190 ROOKIE PRINT RUN 2000
1 David Boston .15 .40
2 Adrian Murrell .15 .40
3 Michael Pittman .15 .40
4 Jake Plummer .15 .40
5 Frank Sanders .15 .40
6 Jamal Anderson .20 .50
7 Chris Chandler .20 .50
8 Terance Mathis .15 .40
9 Justin Armour .15 .40
10 Tony Banks .15 .40
11 Qadry Ismail .15 .40
12 Errict Rhett .20 .50
13 Doug Flutie .20 .50
14 Eric Moulds .15 .40
15 Peerless Price .20 .50
16 Andre Reed .25 .60
17 Antowain Smith .20 .50
18 Steve Beuerlein .20 .50
19 Tim Biakabutuka .20 .50
20 Muhsin Muhammad .15 .40
21 Wesley Walls .15 .40
22 Bobby Engram .15 .40
23 Curtis Enis .15 .40
24 Shane Matthews .15 .40
25 Cade McNown .15 .40
26 Jim Miller .15 .40
27 Marcus Robinson .20 .50
28 Corey Dillon .15 .40
29 Carl Pickens .20 .50
30 Darnay Scott .20 .50
31 Akili Smith .15 .40
32 Karim Abdul-Jabbar .15 .40
33 Tim Couch .20 .50
34 Kevin Johnson .15 .40
35 Troy Aikman .30 .75
36 Michael Irvin .25 .60
37 Rocket Ismail .20 .50
38 Deion Sanders .20 .50
39 Emmitt Smith .40 1.00
40 Terrell Davis .20 .50
41 Olandis Gary .20 .50
42 Brian Griese .15 .40
43 Ed McCaffrey .20 .50
44 Rod Smith .20 .50
45 Charlie Batch .15 .40
46 Germane Crowell .15 .40
47 Greg Hill .15 .40
48 Sedrick Irvin .15 .40
49 Herman Moore .15 .40
50 Johnnie Morton .20 .50
51 Corey Bradford .15 .40
52 Brett Favre .50 1.25
53 Antonio Freeman .20 .50
54 Dorsey Levens .20 .50
55 Bill Schroeder .20 .50
56 E.G. Green .15 .40
57 Marvin Harrison .20 .50
58 Edgerrin James .20 .50
59 Peyton Manning .60 1.50
60 Terrence Wilkins .15 .40
61 Mark Brunell .20 .50
62 Keenan McCardell .20 .50
63 Jimmy Smith .20 .50
64 James Stewart .15 .40
65 Fred Taylor .15 .40
66 Derrick Alexander .15 .40
67 Donnell Bennett .15 .40
68 Mike Cloud .15 .40
69 Tony Gonzalez .20 .50
70 Elvis Grbac .15 .40
71 Damon Huard .15 .40
72 James Johnson .15 .40
73 Rob Konrad .15 .40
74 Dan Marino .50 1.25
75 Tony Martin .20 .50
76 O.J. McDuffie .20 .50
77 Cris Carter .25 .60
78 Daunte Culpepper .20 .50
79 Jeff George .20 .50
80 Randy Moss .20 .50
81 Robert Smith .15 .40
82 Terry Allen .20 .50
83 Drew Bledsoe .20 .50
84 Kevin Faulk .15 .40
85 Terry Glenn .20 .50
86 Shawn Jefferson .15 .40
87 Billy Joe Hobert .15 .40
88 Eddie Kennison .15 .40
89 Billy Joe Tolliver .15 .40
90 Ricky Williams .20 .50
91 Tiki Barber .20 .50
92 Gary Brown .15 .40
93 Kent Graham .15 .40
94 Ike Hilliard .15 .40
95 Amani Toomer .15 .40
96 Wayne Chrebet .15 .40
97 Keyshawn Johnson .20 .50
98 Ray Lucas .15 .40
99 Curtis Martin .20 .50
100 Vinny Testaverde .15 .40
101 Tim Brown .25 .60
102 Rich Gannon .20 .50
103 James Jett .20 .50
104 Napoleon Kaufman .20 .50
105 Tyrone Wheatley .15 .40
106 Charles Johnson .15 .40
107 Donovan McNabb .20 .50
108 Duce Staley .15 .40
109 Jerome Bettis .25 .60
110 Troy Edwards .15 .40
111 Kordell Stewart .15 .40
112 Hines Ward .20 .50
113 Isaac Bruce .25 .60
114 Marshall Faulk .20 .50
115 Az-Zahir Hakim .15 .40
116 Torry Holt .20 .50
117 Kurt Warner .40 1.00
118 Jeff Graham .15 .40
119 Jim Harbaugh .20 .50
120 Freddie Jones .15 .40
121 Natrone Means .20 .50
122 Junior Seau .20 .50
123 Jeff Garcia .15 .40
124 Charlie Garner .20 .50
125 Terrell Owens .20 .50
126 Jerry Rice .60 1.50
127 Steve Young .30 .75
128 Sean Dawkins .15 .40
129 Joey Galloway .20 .50
130 Jon Kitna .15 .40
131 Derrick Mayes .15 .40
132 Ricky Watters .20 .50
133 Mike Alstott .15 .40
134 Reidel Anthony .15 .40
135 Trent Dilfer .15 .40
136 Warrick Dunn .15 .40
137 Jacquez Green .15 .40
138 Shaun King .15 .40
139 Kevin Dyson .20 .50
140 Eddie George .20 .50
141 Jevon Kearse .15 .40
142 Steve McNair .20 .50
143 Yancey Thigpen .15 .40
144 Champ Bailey .20 .50
145 Albert Connell .15 .40
146 Stephen Davis .15 .40
147 Brad Johnson .20 .50
148 Michael Westbrook .15 .40
149 Checklist .15 .40
150 Checklist .15 .40
151 Sylvester Morris RC 1.00 2.50
151B LaVar Arrington SP 2.00 5.00
152 Peter Warrick RC 1.00 2.50
153 Chad Pennington RC 1.25 3.00
154 Courtney Brown RC 1.00 2.50
155 Thomas Jones RC 1.25 3.00
156 Chris Redman RC 1.00 2.50
157 R.Jay Soward RC 1.00 2.50
158 Jamal Lewis RC 1.50 4.00
159 Shaun Alexander RC 1.50 4.00
160 Travis Taylor RC 1.00 2.50
161 Ron Dayne RC 1.50 4.00
162 Travis Prentice RC 1.00 2.50
163 Plaxico Burress RC 1.25 3.00
164 J.R. Redmond RC 1.00 2.50
165 Sherrod Gideon RC 1.00 2.50
166 Dez White RC 1.00 2.50
167 Chafie Fields RC 1.00 2.50
168 Brandon Short RC 1.00 2.50
169 Reuben Droughns RC 1.00 2.50
170 Trung Canidate RC 1.00 2.50
171 Keith Bulluck RC 1.25 3.00
171B Bill Burke 2.50 6.00
172 Doug Johnson RC 1.00 2.50
173 Shyrone Stith RC 1.00 2.50
174 Michael Wiley RC 1.00 2.50
175 Bubba Franks RC 1.00 2.50
176 Tom Brady RC 100.00 200.00
177 Anthony Lucas RC 1.00 2.50
178 Danny Farmer RC 1.00 2.50
179 Rob Morris RC 1.25 3.00
180 Dennis Northcutt RC 1.00 2.50
181 Troy Walters RC 1.00 2.50
182 Giovanni Carmazzi RC 1.00 2.50
183 Tee Martin RC 1.00 2.50
184 Joe Hamilton RC 1.00 2.50
185 Tim Rattay RC 1.25 3.00
186 Sebastian Janikowski RC 1.50 4.00
187 Na'il Diggs RC 1.00 2.50
188 Todd Husak RC 1.00 2.50
189 Jerry Porter RC 1.50 4.00
190 Brian Urlacher RC 5.00 12.00
59A P.Manning AUTO/300 50.00 100.00

2000 Collector's Edge Supreme Hologold

*1-150 VETS: 4X TO 10X BASIC CARDS
1-150 VETERAN PRINT RUN 200
*151-290 ROOKIE/20: 2X TO 5X
151-190 ROOKIE PRINT RUN 20
*151-290 ROOKIE NOT #'d: .8X TO 2X
59 Peyton Manning AUTO/200 50.00 100.00
176 Tom Brady 300.00 600.00

2000 Collector's Edge Supreme EdgeTech

Randomly inserted in packs, this set features veterans and rookies on a rainbow holographic foil card enhanced with gold foil highlights. Each card is hand numbered to 100. Card number ET49 LaVar Arrington was pulled from production and, reportedly, never released in packs. However, a small number of non-serial numbered copies made their way into the secondary market years later. Finally a non-serial numbered Preview version was also issued to promote the set.

COMPLETE SET (50) 300.00 600.00
STATED PRINT RUN 100 SER.#'d SETS
*PREVIEWS: .2X TO .5X BASIC INSERTS
ET1 Doug Flutie 3.00 8.00
ET2 Cade McNown 2.50 6.00
ET3 Akili Smith 2.50 6.00
ET4 Tim Couch 3.00 8.00
ET5 Kevin Johnson 2.50 6.00
ET6 Troy Aikman 5.00 12.00
ET7 Emmitt Smith 6.00 15.00
ET8 Terrell Davis 3.00 8.00
ET9 Brett Favre 8.00 20.00
ET10 Marvin Harrison 3.00 8.00
ET11 Edgerrin James 3.00 8.00
ET12 Peyton Manning 10.00 25.00
ET12AU Peyton Manning AUTO 90.00 150.00
ET13 Mark Brunell 3.00 8.00
ET14 Dan Marino 8.00 20.00
ET15 Randy Moss 3.00 8.00
ET16 Drew Bledsoe 3.00 8.00
ET17 Ricky Williams 3.00 8.00
ET18 Keyshawn Johnson 3.00 8.00
ET19 Curtis Martin 3.00 8.00
ET20 Donovan McNabb 3.00 8.00
ET21 Marshall Faulk 3.00 8.00
ET22 Torry Holt 3.00 8.00
ET23 Kurt Warner 6.00 15.00
ET24 Jerry Rice 10.00 25.00
ET25 Steve Young 5.00 12.00
ET26 Jon Kitna 2.50 6.00
ET27 Shaun King 2.50 6.00
ET28 Eddie George 3.00 8.00
ET29 Stephen Davis 2.50 6.00
ET30 Brad Johnson 3.00 8.00
ET31 Chad Pennington 2.00 5.00
ET32 Chris Redman 2.50 6.00
ET33 Tim Rattay 3.00 8.00
ET34 Tee Martin 2.50 6.00
ET35 Thomas Jones 2.50 6.00
ET36 Ron Dayne 4.00 10.00
ET37 Jamal Lewis 2.50 6.00
ET38 J.R. Redmond 2.50 6.00
ET39 Travis Prentice 2.50 6.00
ET40 Shaun Alexander 2.50 6.00
ET41 Michael Wiley 2.50 6.00
ET42 Shyrone Stith 2.50 6.00
ET43 Peter Warrick 2.50 6.00
ET44 Plaxico Burress 2.50 6.00
ET45 Travis Taylor 2.50 6.00
ET46 Jerry Porter 4.00 10.00
ET47 R.Jay Soward 2.50 6.00
ET48 Dez White 2.50 6.00
ET49 LaVar Arrington SP 5.00 12.00
ET50 Courtney Brown 3.00 8.00

2000 Collector's Edge Supreme Future

Randomly inserted in packs, this set features top rated rookies from the 2000 draft. Base cards feature action shots against a rainbow holofoil background with each sequentially numbered to 100. Card #SF10 was released after Collector's Edge ceased football card operations.

STATED PRINT RUN 100 SER.#'d SETS
SF1 Peter Warrick 1.50 4.00
SF2 Plaxico Burress 2.00 5.00
SF3 R.Jay Soward 1.50 4.00
SF4 Ron Dayne 2.50 6.00
SF5 Thomas Jones 2.00 5.00
SF6 Shaun Alexander 2.50 6.00
SF7 Chad Pennington 2.00 5.00
SF8 Chris Redman 1.50 4.00
SF9 Travis Prentice 1.50 4.00
SF10 Lavar Arrington SP 3.00 8.00

2000 Collector's Edge Supreme Monday Knights

Randomly inserted in packs at the rate of one in eight, this 20-card set features top NFL Performers on an all-foil insert card. Card backs carry an "MK" prefix.

COMPLETE SET (20) 10.00 25.00
STATED ODDS 1:8
MK1 Jake Plummer .40 1.00
MK2 Doug Flutie .50 1.25
MK3 Cade McNown .40 1.00
MK4 Akili Smith .40 1.00
MK5 Tim Couch .50 1.25
MK6 Kevin Johnson .40 1.00
MK7 Troy Aikman .75 2.00
MK8 Emmitt Smith 1.00 2.50
MK9 Terrell Davis .50 1.25
MK10 Charlie Batch .40 1.00
MK11 Brett Favre 1.25 3.00
MK12 Cris Carter .60 1.50
MK13 Drew Bledsoe .50 1.25
MK14 Ricky Williams .50 1.25
MK15 Curtis Martin .50 1.25
MK16 Jerry Rice 1.50 4.00
MK17 Jon Kitna .40 1.00
MK18 Shaun King .40 1.00
MK19 Eddie George .50 1.25
MK20 Brad Johnson .50 1.25

2000 Collector's Edge Supreme Pro Signature Authentics

Randomly inserted in packs at the rate of one in 197, this set features authentic autographs on the cardfronts with the standard Pro Signatures Authentic card design. Each is hand serial numbered on the back and includes a PSA/DNA authentication sticker. Note that these cards carry a 1999 copyright date on the backs as well as the Edge '99 logo on the fronts but most, if not all, were inserted into 2000 Edge Supreme packs. Additional cards were likely given away as promos and redemptions through the mail as well as appearing on the market after Edge ceased their card operations.

STATED ODDS 1:197
STATED PRINT RUN 10-1450
PM Peyton Manning/1000 Black 40.00 80.00
TC Tim Couch/650 Black 8.00 20.00
CM1 Cade McNown/650 Black 6.00 15.00
CM2 Cade McNown/325 Red 8.00 20.00
DM1 D.McDonald/230 Black 5.00 12.00
DM2 D.McDonald/40 Blue 8.00 20.00
JJ1 James Johnson/1450 Black 5.00 12.00
JJ2 James Johnson/42 Blue 8.00 20.00
RM1 Randy Moss/150 Blue 40.00 80.00
RM2 Randy Moss/150 Blue 40.00 80.00
RW1 Ricky Williams/230 Black 15.00 40.00
RW2 Ricky Williams/39 Blue 25.00 60.00

2000 Collector's Edge Supreme Update

Randomly inserted in packs of 2000 Collector's Edge EG, redemption cards carrying an expiration date of 12/31/2000 were to be exchanged for the PSA graded 8, 9 or 10 card of the redemption card's featured player. The prize cards (listed below) were an "Updated" version of the player's 2000 Edge Supreme card featuring the player in his NFL uniform. A few players in the base set were replaced in this Update set, most importantly Tom Brady was switched for Corey Simon. Some of the same graded cards were later released one per box in 2000 Collector's Edge T3 special retail boxes. While most of the cards were originally issued in PSA graded form, many can be found out of the holders as "raw" cards. All 40 cards were later issued as part of a 190-card factory set.

COMPLETE SET (40) 20.00 50.00
*ROOKIE U151-U190: .08X TO .25X BASIC RC
ALL 40 ISSUED IN SUPREME FACT.SET

2000 Collector's Edge Supreme Perfect Ten

Redemption cards for this set were randomly inserted in packs of 2000 Collector's Edge Supreme. The redemption cards were to be sent in for a PSA10 graded card of the featured player. Reportedly, only 100 of each redemption card was inserted in packs and the expiration date was 3/31/2001. Quantities of ungraded Perfect Ten cards surfaced later (along with a previously unissued LaVar Arrington) after Collector's Edge ceased operation in early 2001.

COMPLETE SET (10) 50.00 120.00
ANNOUNCED EXCH CARD PRINT RUN 100
1 Peter Warrick .75 2.00
2 Plaxico Burress 1.00 2.50
3 R.Jay Soward .75 2.00
4 Ron Dayne 1.25 3.00
5 Thomas Jones 1.00 2.50
6 Shaun Alexander 1.25 3.00
7 Chad Pennington 1.00 2.50
8 Chris Redman .75 2.00
9 Travis Prentice .75 2.00
10 LaVar Arrington 1.50 4.00

2000 Collector's Edge Supreme Route XXXIV

Randomly seeded in packs at the rate of one in 16, this 10-card set features action shots against a blue foil background. Cards also contain gold foil highlights and backs carry an "R" prefix.

COMPLETE SET (10) 7.50 20.00
STATED ODDS 1:16
R1 Peyton Manning 1.50 4.00
R2 Edgerrin James .50 1.25
R3 Warrick Dunn .40 1.00
R4 Dan Marino 1.25 3.00
R5 Steve McNair .50 1.25
R6 Mark Brunell .50 1.25
R7 Kurt Warner 1.00 2.50
R8 Marshall Faulk .50 1.25
R9 Randy Moss .50 1.25
R10 Stephen Davis .40 1.00

2000 Collector's Edge Supreme Team

Randomly inserted in packs at the rate of one in eight, this 20-card set features top players, by position, for both the NFC and AFC. Each card features a micro-etched foil background and card backs carry an "ST" prefix.

COMPLETE SET (20) 12.50 30.00
STATED ODDS 1:8
ST1 Peyton Manning 1.50 4.00
ST2 Kurt Warner 1.00 2.50
ST3 Tim Couch .50 1.25
ST4 Cade McNown .40 1.00
ST5 Akili Smith .40 1.00
ST6 Donovan McNabb .50 1.25
ST7 Edgerrin James .50 1.25
ST8 Stephen Davis .40 1.00
ST9 Mark Brunell .50 1.25
ST10 Brett Favre 1.25 3.00
ST11 Marvin Harrison .50 1.25
ST12 Isaac Bruce .60 1.50
ST13 Terrell Davis .50 1.25
ST14 Ricky Williams .50 1.25
ST15 Keyshawn Johnson .50 1.25
ST16 Randy Moss .50 1.25

ST17 Kevin Johnson .40 1.00
ST18 Torry Holt .50 1.25
ST19 Dan Marino 1.25 3.00
ST20 Troy Aikman .75 2.00

2000 Collector's Edge T3 Previews

These cards were issued to preview the 2000 Collector's Edge T3 football set. Each is essentially a parallel to it's base set card but has been numbered according to the player's initials. Each is marked on the backs "Preview XXX/999." Two parallels of the Preview cards were also produced: HoloPlatinum numbered of 500 and HoloRed numbered of 50.

COMPLETE SET (34) 30.00 60.00
*HOLOPLATINUM/500: .5X TO 1.2X BASIC PREVIEWS
*HOLORED/50: 1.2X TO 3X BASIC PREVIEWS
AB Anthony Becht .50 1.25
BU Brian Urlacher 2.50 6.00
CB Courtney Brown .60 1.50
CC Chris Cole .60 1.50
CP Chad Pennington .60 1.50
CR Chris Redman .50 1.25
DF Danny Farmer .50 1.25
DJ Doug Johnson .50 1.25
DN Dennis Northcutt .50 1.25
JA John Abraham .75 2.00
JH Joe Hamilton .50 1.25
JJ Jarious Jackson .60 1.50
JL Jamal Lewis .75 2.00
JP Jerry Porter .75 2.00
JR J.R. Redmond .50 1.25
KB Keith Bulluck .60 1.50
MW Michael Wiley .50 1.25
NN Tim Rattay .60 1.50
PB Plaxico Burress .60 1.50
PM Peyton Manning 2.00 5.00
RDA Ron Dayne .75 2.00
RDR Reuben Droughns .50 1.25
RDU Ron Dugans .50 1.25
RJS R.Jay Soward .50 1.25
RS R.Jay Soward .50 1.25
SA Shaun Alexander .75 2.00
SE Shaun Ellis .60 1.50
SM Sylvester Morris .50 1.25
TH Todd Husak .50 1.25
TJ Thomas Jones .60 1.50
TM Tee Martin .50 1.25
TP Travis Prentice .50 1.25
TT Travis Taylor .50 1.25
TW Troy Walters .50 1.25

2000 Collector's Edge T3

This 225-card set features enhanced gold foil printing on the front of white card stock. The left side of the card has a yellow border with blue spots. Prospect cards, 151-225, are sequentially numbered to 999. T3 was packaged in 20-pack boxes with packs containing five cards each.

COMP.SET w/o SP's (150) 12.50 30.00
151-225 ROOKIE PRINT RUN 999
1 David Boston .20 .50
2 Rob Moore .20 .50
3 Michael Pittman .20 .50
4 Jake Plummer .20 .50
5 Frank Sanders .20 .50
6 Jamal Anderson .25 .60
7 Chris Chandler .25 .60
8 Tim Dwight .25 .60
9 Shawn Jefferson .20 .50
10 Terance Mathis .20 .50
11 Tony Banks .20 .50
12 Priest Holmes .20 .50
13 Qadry Ismail .20 .50
14 Shannon Sharpe .25 .60
15 Doug Flutie .25 .60
16 Rob Johnson .25 .60
17 Eric Moulds .20 .50
18 Peerless Price .25 .60
19 Antowain Smith .25 .60
20 Steve Beuerlein .25 .60
21 Tim Biakabutuka .25 .60
22 Muhsin Muhammad .20 .50
23 Patrick Jeffers .20 .50
24 Wesley Walls .20 .50
25 Bobby Engram .20 .50
26 Curtis Enis .20 .50
27 Cade McNown .20 .50
28 Marcus Robinson .25 .60
29 Corey Dillon .20 .50
30 Carl Pickens .25 .60
31 Darnay Scott .25 .60
32 Akili Smith .20 .50
33 Tim Couch .25 .60
34 Kevin Johnson .20 .50
35 Errict Rhett .25 .60
36 Troy Aikman .40 1.00
37 Joey Galloway .25 .60
38 Rocket Ismail .25 .60
39 Emmitt Smith .50 1.25
40 Chris Warren .20 .50
41 Terrell Davis .25 .60
42 Olandis Gary .25 .60
43 Brian Griese .20 .50
44 Ed McCaffrey .25 .60
45 Rod Smith .25 .60
46 Charlie Batch .20 .50
47 Germane Crowell .20 .50
48 Sedrick Irvin .20 .50
49 Herman Moore .20 .50
50 Johnnie Morton .25 .60
51 James Stewart .20 .50
52 Brett Favre .60 1.50
53 Antonio Freeman .25 .60
54 Dorsey Levens .25 .60
55 Bill Schroeder .25 .60
56 Ken Dilger .20 .50
57 Marvin Harrison .25 .60
58 Edgerrin James .25 .60
59 Peyton Manning .75 2.00
60 Terrence Wilkins .20 .50
61 Mark Brunell .25 .60
62 Keenan McCardell .25 .60
63 Jimmy Smith .25 .60
64 Fred Taylor .20 .50
65 Derrick Alexander .20 .50
66 Donnell Bennett .20 .50
67 Mike Cloud .20 .50
68 Tony Gonzalez .25 .60
69 Elvis Grbac .20 .50
70 Tony Richardson RC .20 .50
71 Damon Huard .20 .50
72 James Johnson .20 .50
73 Rob Konrad .20 .50
74 Tony Martin .25 .60
75 O.J. McDuffie .25 .60
76 Cris Carter .30 .75
77 Daunte Culpepper .25 .60
78 Randy Moss .25 .60
79 Robert Smith .20 .50
80 Drew Bledsoe .25 .60
81 Kevin Faulk .20 .50
82 Terry Glenn .25 .60
83 Willie McGinest .25 .60
84 Tony Simmons .20 .50
85 Jeff Blake .25 .60
86 Jake Reed .25 .60
87 Ricky Williams .25 .60
88 Kerry Collins .20 .50
89 Ike Hilliard .20 .50
90 Joe Montgomery .20 .50
91 Amani Toomer .20 .50
92 Wayne Chrebet .20 .50
93 Ray Lucas .20 .50
94 Curtis Martin .25 .60
95 Vinny Testaverde .20 .50
96 Tim Brown .30 .75
97 Rich Gannon .25 .60
98 James Jett .25 .60
99 Napoleon Kaufman .25 .60
100 Tyrone Wheatley .20 .50
101 Charles Woodson .30 .75
102 Charles Johnson .20 .50
103 Donovan McNabb .25 .60
104 Duce Staley .20 .50
105 Jerome Bettis .30 .75
106 Troy Edwards .20 .50
107 Kent Graham .20 .50
108 Kordell Stewart .20 .50
109 Hines Ward .25 .60
110 Isaac Bruce .30 .75
111 Kevin Carter .20 .50
112 Marshall Faulk .25 .60
113 Trent Green .20 .50
114 Az-Zahir Hakim .20 .50
115 Torry Holt .25 .60
116 Kurt Warner .50 1.25
117 Curtis Conway .25 .60
118 Jermaine Fazande .20 .50
119 Jeff Graham .20 .50
120 Jim Harbaugh .25 .60
121 Junior Seau .25 .60
122 Jeff Garcia .20 .50
123 Charlie Garner .25 .60
124 Garrison Hearst .20 .50
125 Terrell Owens .25 .60
126 Jerry Rice .75 2.00
127 Steve Young .40 1.00
128 Sean Dawkins .20 .50
129 Jon Kitna .20 .50
130 Derrick Mayes .20 .50
131 Ricky Watters .25 .60
132 Mike Alstott .20 .50
133 Warrick Dunn .20 .50
134 Jacquez Green .20 .50
135 Keyshawn Johnson .25 .60
136 Shaun King .20 .50
137 Warren Sapp .25 .60
138 Kevin Dyson .25 .60
139 Eddie George .25 .60
140 Jevon Kearse .20 .50
141 Steve McNair .25 .60
142 Yancey Thigpen .20 .50
143 Frank Wycheck .25 .60
144 Champ Bailey .25 .60
145 Larry Centers .20 .50
146 Albert Connell .20 .50
147 Stephen Davis .20 .50
148 Jeff George .25 .60
149 Brad Johnson .25 .60
150 Michael Westbrook .20 .50
151 Thomas Jones RC 2.00 5.00
152 Doug Johnson RC 1.50 4.00
153 Mareno Philyaw RC 1.50 4.00
154 Jamal Lewis RC 2.50 6.00
155 Chris Redman RC 1.50 4.00
156 Travis Taylor RC 1.50 4.00
157 Kwame Cavil RC 1.50 4.00
158 Sammy Morris RC 1.50 4.00
159 Deon Grant RC 1.50 4.00
160 Frank Murphy RC 1.50 4.00
161 Brian Urlacher RC 8.00 20.00
162 Dez White RC 1.50 4.00
163 Ron Dugans RC 1.50 4.00
164 Curtis Keaton RC 1.50 4.00
165 Peter Warrick RC 1.50 4.00
166 Courtney Brown RC 2.00 5.00
167 JaJuan Dawson RC 1.50 4.00
168 Dennis Northcutt RC 1.50 4.00
169 Travis Prentice RC 1.50 4.00
170 Michael Wiley RC 1.50 4.00
171 Mike Anderson RC 1.50 4.00
172 Chris Cole RC 2.00 5.00
173 Jarious Jackson RC 2.00 5.00
174 Deltha O'Neal RC 1.50 4.00
175 Reuben Droughns RC 1.50 4.00
176 Na'il Diggs RC 1.50 4.00
177 Bubba Franks RC 1.50 4.00
178 Anthony Lucas RC 1.50 4.00
179 Rondell Mealey RC 1.50 4.00
180 Dan Kendra RC 1.50 4.00
181 Rob Morris RC 2.00 5.00
182 R.Jay Soward RC 1.50 4.00
183 Shyrone Stith RC 1.50 4.00
184 William Bartee RC 1.50 4.00
185 Frank Moreau RC 1.50 4.00
186 Sylvester Morris RC 1.50 4.00
187 Deon Dyer RC 1.50 4.00
188 Quinton Spotwood RC 1.50 4.00
189 Doug Chapman RC 1.50 4.00
190 Troy Walters RC 1.50 4.00
191 J.R. Redmond RC 1.50 4.00
192 Marc Bulger RC 2.00 5.00
193 Sherrod Gideon RC 1.50 4.00
194 Darren Howard RC 1.50 4.00
195 Chad Morton RC 2.00 5.00
196 Terrelle Smith RC 1.50 4.00
197 Ron Dayne RC 2.50 6.00
198 John Abraham RC 2.50 6.00
199 Anthony Becht RC 1.50 4.00
200 Laveranues Coles RC 2.00 5.00
201 Shaun Ellis RC 2.00 5.00
202 Chad Pennington RC 2.00 5.00
203 Sebastian Janikowski RC 2.50 6.00
204 Jerry Porter RC 2.50 6.00
205 Todd Pinkston RC 1.50 4.00
206 Corey Simon RC 2.00 5.00
207 Plaxico Burress RC 2.00 5.00
208 Danny Farmer RC 1.50 4.00
209 Tee Martin RC 1.50 4.00
210 Hank Poteat RC 1.50 4.00
211 Trung Canidate RC 1.50 4.00
212 Jacoby Shepherd RC 1.50 4.00
213 Trevor Gaylor RC 1.50 4.00
214 Giovanni Carmazzi RC 1.50 4.00
215 John Engelberger RC 1.50 4.00
216 Chafie Fields RC 1.50 4.00
217 Julian Peterson RC 2.50 6.00
218 Ahmed Plummer RC 1.50 4.00
219 Tim Rattay RC 2.00 5.00
220 Shaun Alexander RC 2.50 6.00
221 Joe Hamilton RC 1.50 4.00
222 Keith Bulluck RC 2.00 5.00
223 Erron Kinney RC 1.50 4.00
224 Todd Husak RC 1.50 4.00
225 Chris Samuels RC 2.50 6.00

2000 Collector's Edge T3 HoloPlatinum

*VETS 1-150: 2X TO 5X BASIC CARDS
*ROOKIE 151-225: .25X TO .6X
PLATINUM PRINT RUN 500 SER.#'d SETS

2000 Collector's Edge T3 HoloRed

*VETS 1-150: 6X TO 15X BASIC CARDS
*ROOKIES 151-225: .8X TO 2X
RED PRINT RUN 50 SER.#'d SETS

2000 Collector's Edge T3 Retail

COMPLETE SET (225) 40.00 80.00
*RET.VETS 1-150: .3X TO .8X HOBBY
*RET.ROOKIE 151-225: .08X TO .2X HOB

2000 Collector's Edge T3 Adrenaline

Randomly inserted in packs at the rate of one in 10, this 20-cards set features full color action photography set against a foil colored background.

COMPLETE SET (20) 10.00 25.00
STATED ODDS 1:10
A1 Doug Flutie .50 1.25
A2 Troy Aikman .75 2.00
A3 Emmitt Smith 1.00 2.50
A4 Terrell Davis .50 1.25
A5 Brett Favre 1.25 3.00
A6 Mark Brunell .50 1.25
A7 Fred Taylor .40 1.00
A8 Daunte Culpepper .50 1.25
A9 Drew Bledsoe .50 1.25
A10 Donovan McNabb .50 1.25
A11 Troy Edwards .40 1.00
A12 Isaac Bruce .60 1.50
A13 Marshall Faulk .50 1.25
A14 Jerry Rice 1.50 4.00
A15 Jon Kitna .40 1.00
A16 Shaun King .40 1.00
A17 Keyshawn Johnson .50 1.25
A18 Eddie George .50 1.25
A19 Steve McNair .50 1.25
A20 Stephen Davis .40 1.00

2000 Collector's Edge T3 EdgeQuest

Randomly seeded in packs, this 25-card set features top receivers, running backs and quarterbacks. Base cards are all foil and contain gold foil highlights. Each card is sequentially numbered to 1000.

COMPLETE SET (25) 30.00 60.00
STATED PRINT RUN 1000 SER.#'d SETS
EQ1 Marcus Robinson .75 2.00
EQ2 Kevin Johnson .60 1.50
EQ3 Randy Moss .75 2.00
EQ4 Troy Edwards .60 1.50
EQ5 Torry Holt .75 2.00
EQ6 Keyshawn Johnson .75 2.00
EQ7 Emmitt Smith 1.50 4.00
EQ8 Terrell Davis .75 2.00
EQ9 Edgerrin James .75 2.00
EQ10 Fred Taylor .60 1.50
EQ11 Ricky Williams .75 2.00
EQ12 Curtis Martin .75 2.00
EQ13 Marshall Faulk .75 2.00
EQ14 Eddie George .75 2.00
EQ15 Stephen Davis .60 1.50
EQ16 Cade McNown .60 1.50
EQ17 Akili Smith .60 1.50
EQ18 Tim Couch .75 2.00
EQ19 Brett Favre 2.00 5.00
EQ20 Peyton Manning 2.50 6.00
EQ21 Daunte Culpepper .75 2.00
EQ22 Donovan McNabb .75 2.00
EQ23 Kurt Warner 1.50 4.00
EQ24 Jon Kitna .60 1.50
EQ25 Shaun King .60 1.50
EQ14PG Eddie George Gold Preview 1.25 3.00
EQ14PS Eddie George Silver Preview 1.25 3.00

2000 Collector's Edge T3 Future Legends

Randomly inserted in packs at the rate of one in 10, this 20-card set features top young stars on an all holographic card stock.

COMPLETE SET (20) 6.00 15.00
STATED ODDS 1:10
FL1 Thomas Jones .40 1.00
FL2 Jamal Lewis .50 1.25
FL3 Travis Taylor .30 .75
FL4 Peter Warrick .30 .75
FL5 Ron Dayne .50 1.25
FL6 Chad Pennington .40 1.00
FL7 Plaxico Burress .40 1.00
FL8 Bubba Franks .30 .75
FL9 Shaun Alexander .50 1.25
FL10 Sylvester Morris .30 .75
FL11 Laveranues Coles .40 1.00
FL12 Jerry Porter .50 1.25
FL13 Todd Pinkston .30 .75
FL14 Dennis Northcutt .30 .75
FL15 Travis Prentice .30 .75
FL16 R.Jay Soward .30 .75
FL17 Chris Redman .30 .75
FL18 Trung Canidate .30 .75
FL19 Dez White .30 .75
FL20 J.R. Redmond .30 .75

2000 Collector's Edge T3 JerseyBacks

Randomly inserted in packs, this 10-card set is printed on actual game worn jerseys which make up the full card back. Each card is sequentially numbered to 20.

STATED PRINT RUN 20 SER.#'d SETS
CP Chad Pennington 20.00 50.00
JL Jamal Lewis 25.00 60.00
PB Plaxico Burress 20.00 50.00
PW Peter Warrick 15.00 40.00
RD Ron Dayne 25.00 60.00
RS R.Jay Soward
SA Shaun Alexander 50.00 120.00
SM Sylvester Morris 15.00 40.00
TJ Thomas Jones 20.00 50.00
TT Travis Taylor 15.00 40.00

2000 Collector's Edge T3 LeatherBacks

Randomly inserted in packs, this 20-card set includes a full cardback printed on swatches of game used footballs. Each card was sequentially numbered to 12.

STATED PRINT RUN 12 SER.#'d SETS
AS Akili Smith 20.00 50.00
BF Brett Favre 100.00 200.00
CM Cade McNown
DM Donovan McNabb 40.00 100.00
EG Eddie George 25.00 60.00
EJ Edgerrin James 25.00 60.00
ES Emmitt Smith 75.00 150.00
JK Jon Kitna 20.00 50.00
KW Kurt Warner 40.00 100.00
MR Marcus Robinson 25.00 60.00
PM Peyton Manning 100.00 200.00
RM Randy Moss 50.00 120.00
RW Ricky Williams 25.00 60.00
SD Stephen Davis 20.00 50.00
SK Shaun King 20.00 50.00
SM Steve McNair 25.00 60.00
TA Troy Aikman 40.00 100.00
TC Tim Couch 25.00 60.00
TD Terrell Davis 25.00 60.00
TH Torry Holt 25.00 60.00

2000 Collector's Edge T3 Heir Force

Randomly inserted in packs, this 30-card set features 2000 Draft Picks in their new jerseys set against a sky background. Cards contain gold foil highlights and are sequentially numbered to 1000.

COMPLETE SET (30) 40.00 80.00
STATED PRINT RUN 1000 SER.#'d SETS
HF1 Thomas Jones .50 1.25
HF2 Jamal Lewis .60 1.50
HF3 Chris Redman .40 1.00
HF4 Travis Taylor .40 1.00
HF5 Brian Urlacher 2.00 5.00
HF6 Dez White .40 1.00
HF7 Ron Dugans .40 1.00
HF8 Curtis Keaton .40 1.00
HF9 Peter Warrick .40 1.00
HF10 Courtney Brown .50 1.25
HF11 Dennis Northcutt .40 1.00
HF12 Travis Prentice .60 1.50
HF13 Reuben Droughns .40 1.00
HF14 Bubba Franks .40 1.00
HF15 R.Jay Soward .40 1.00
HF16 Sylvester Morris .40 1.00
HF17 J.R. Redmond .40 1.00
HF18 Ron Dayne .60 1.50
HF19 Anthony Becht .40 1.00
HF20 Laveranues Coles .50 1.25
HF21 Chad Pennington .50 1.25
HF22 Jerry Porter .60 1.50
HF23 Todd Pinkston .40 1.00
HF24 Corey Simon .50 1.25
HF25 Plaxico Burress .50 1.25
HF26 Danny Farmer .40 1.00
HF27 Tee Martin .40 1.00
HF28 Trung Canidate .40 1.00
HF29 Shaun Alexander .60 1.50
HF30 Joe Hamilton .40 1.00

2000 Collector's Edge T3 Overture

Randomly inserted in packs at the rate of one in 20, this 10-card set features all holographic foil cards with gold foil highlights.

COMPLETE SET (10) 10.00 20.00
STATED ODDS 1:20
O1 Cade McNown .40 1.00
O2 Akili Smith .40 1.00
O3 Tim Couch .50 1.25
O4 Edgerrin James .50 1.25
O5 Peyton Manning 1.50 4.00
O6 Daunte Culpepper .50 1.25
O7 Randy Moss .50 1.25
O8 Ricky Williams .50 1.25
O9 Torry Holt .50 1.25
O10 Kurt Warner 1.00 2.50

2000 Collector's Edge T3 Rookie Excalibur

Randomly inserted in packs, this 20-card set features players on a colored foil background with gold foil highlights. Each card is sequentially numbered to 1000.

COMPLETE SET (20) 30.00 60.00
STATED PRINT RUN 1000 SER.#'d SETS
RE1 Thomas Jones .75 2.00
RE2 Jamal Lewis 1.00 2.50
RE3 Chris Redman .60 1.50
RE4 Travis Taylor .60 1.50
RE5 Dez White .60 1.50
RE6 Peter Warrick .60 1.50
RE7 Dennis Northcutt .60 1.50
RE8 Travis Prentice .60 1.50
RE9 R.Jay Soward .60 1.50
RE10 Sylvester Morris .60 1.50
RE11 Ron Dayne 1.00 2.50
RE12 Chad Pennington .75 2.00
RE13 Laveranues Coles .75 2.00
RE14 Jerry Porter 1.00 2.50
RE15 Todd Pinkston .60 1.50
RE16 Plaxico Burress .75 2.00
RE17 Trung Canidate .60 1.50
RE18 Bubba Franks .60 1.50
RE19 Shaun Alexander 1.00 2.50
RE20 J.R. Redmond .60 1.50

2000 Collector's Edge T3 Rookie Ink

Randomly inserted in packs at the rate of one in 99, this 9-card set features top rookie autographs. Each card features action photography and an "autograph box" along the right side of the card. The cards were printed with either gold or silver foil highlights on the front. Unsigned and un-serial numbered cards of several players (Travis Taylor, J.R. Redmond and Peter Warrick) appeared on the market after Collector's Edge ceased card operations.

OVERALL STATED ODDS 1:99
BLACK INK PRINT RUN 440-1610
*BLUE/24-40: .8X TO 2X BLACK INK
BLUE INK PRINT RUN 24-40
UNPRICED RED INK PRINT RUN 10
CP Chad Pennington Silver/470 5.00 12.00
CR Chris Redman Silver/470 4.00 10.00
GC Giovanni Carmazzi Silver/1455 4.00 10.00
JL Jamal Lewis Silver/485 6.00 15.00
JR1 J.R. Redmond Gold/1610 4.00 10.00
PB Plaxico Burress Silver/440 5.00 12.00
RS R.Jay Soward Silver/1350 4.00 10.00
SM Sylvester Morris Silver/1000 4.00 10.00
TJ Thomas Jones Silver/915 5.00 12.00
PW Peter Warrick No AU 2.00 5.00
TT Travis Taylor Silver No AU 1.50 4.00
JR2 J.R. Redmond Silver No AU

1999 Collector's Edge Triumph Previews

Released early in the year, this set previews the card stock and design of the 1999 Collector's Edge Triumph set. The card numbers feature the player's initials and the word "preview" is printed on the cardbacks.

COMPLETE SET (39) 15.00 30.00
AD Autry Denson .30 .75
AK Andy Katzenmoyer .50 1.25
AS Akili Smith 1.00 2.50
AW Antoine Winfield .30 .75
AZ Amos Zereoue .50 1.25
BH Brock Huard .30 .75
CC2 Cecil Collins .50 1.25
CC1 Chris Claiborne .30 .75
CM2 Cade McNown .75 2.00
CM1 Chris McAlister .50 1.25
DB David Boston .75 2.00
DC Daunte Culpepper 2.50 6.00
DM Donovan McNabb 1.50 4.00
DN Dat Nguyen .50 1.25
EE Ebeneezer Ekuban .50 1.25
EJ Edgerrin James 2.50 6.00
JF Jermaine Fazande .50 1.25
JG Joe Germaine .50 1.25
JJ James Johnson .50 1.25
JM Joe Montgomery .50 1.25
KB Karsten Bailey .30 .75
KF Kevin Faulk .60 1.50
KJ Kevin Johnson .50 1.25
LP Larry Parker .30 .75
MC Mike Cloud .30 .75
MG Martin Gramatica .30 .75
PK Patrick Kerney .50 1.25
PP Peerless Price .50 1.25
RK Rob Konrad .30 .75
RW Ricky Williams 1.00 2.50
SI Sedrick Irvin .30 .75
SK Shaun King .50 1.25
TC Tim Couch 1.50 4.00
TE Troy Edwards .75 2.00
TH Torry Holt 1.00 2.50
CB1 Champ Bailey .60 1.50
CB2 Cuncho Brown .30 .75
DWB D'Wayne Bates .30 .75
JKE Jevon Kearse .75 2.00

1999 Collector's Edge Triumph

Released as a 180-card set, 1999 Collector's Edge Triumph features a single football team in each pack. Packs contain a shortprinted quarterback, a shortprinted rookie, a running back, two receivers, a defensive player, and a kicker.

COMPLETE SET (180) 20.00 50.00
1 Jamal Anderson .25 .60
2 Jerome Bettis .30 .75
3 Terrell Davis .25 .60
4 Corey Dillon .20 .50
5 Warrick Dunn .20 .50
6 Marshall Faulk .25 .60
7 Eddie George .25 .60
8 Garrison Hearst .20 .50
9 Skip Hicks .20 .50
10 Napoleon Kaufman .20 .50
11 Dorsey Levens .25 .60
12 Curtis Martin .25 .60
13 Natrone Means .25 .60
14 Adrian Murrell .20 .50
15 Barry Sanders .50 1.25
16 Antowain Smith .20 .50
17 Emmitt Smith .50 1.25
18 Robert Smith .20 .50
19 Fred Taylor .20 .50
20 Ricky Watters .25 .60
21 Cameron Cleeland .20 .50
22 Ben Coates .25 .60
23 Shannon Sharpe .25 .60
24 Frank Wycheck .25 .60
25 Derrick Alexander WR .20 .50
26 Reidel Anthony .20 .50
27 Robert Brooks .25 .60
28 Tim Brown .30 .75
29 Cris Carter .30 .75
30 Wayne Chrebet .20 .50
31 Curtis Conway .25 .60
32 Tim Dwight .25 .60
33 Kevin Dyson .20 .50
34 Antonio Freeman .25 .60
35 Joey Galloway .25 .60
36 Terry Glenn .25 .60
37 Marvin Harrison .25 .60
38 Ike Hilliard .20 .50
39 Michael Irvin .30 .75
40 Keyshawn Johnson .25 .60
41 Jermaine Lewis .20 .50
42 Terance Mathis .20 .50
43 Ed McCaffrey .25 .60
44 Keenan McCardell .25 .60
45 O.J. McDuffie .25 .60
46 Herman Moore .25 .60
47 Rob Moore .20 .50
48 Randy Moss .25 .60
49 Eric Moulds .20 .50
50 Muhsin Muhammad .20 .50
51 Terrell Owens .25 .60
52 Jerome Pathon .20 .50
53 Carl Pickens .25 .60
54 Andre Reed .30 .75
55 Jake Reed .25 .60
56 Jerry Rice .75 2.00
57 Andre Rison .25 .60
58 Jimmy Smith .25 .60
59 Rod Smith WR .25 .60
60 Michael Westbrook .20 .50
61 Morten Andersen .20 .50
62 Gary Anderson .20 .50
63 Doug Brien .20 .50
64 Chris Boniol .20 .50
65 John Carney .20 .50
66 Steve Christie .20 .50
67 Richie Cunningham .20 .50
68 Brad Daluiso .20 .50
69 AL Del Greco .20 .50
70 Jason Elam .20 .50
71 John Hall .20 .50
72 Jason Hanson .20 .50
73 Mike Hollis .20 .50
74 Norm Johnson .20 .50
75 Olindo Mare .20 .50
76 Doug Pelfrey .20 .50
77 Wade Richey .20 .50
78 Pete Stoyanovich .20 .50
79 Mike Vanderjagt .20 .50
80 Adam Vinatieri .20 .50
81 Ray Buchanan .20 .50
82 Jim Flanigan .20 .50
83 Darrell Green .30 .75
84 Kevin Greene .30 .75
85 Ty Law .30 .75
86 Ken Norton Jr. .20 .50
87 John Randle .30 .75
88 Bill Romanowski .25 .60
89 Deion Sanders .25 .60
90 Junior Seau .25 .60
91 Michael Sinclair .20 .50
92 Bruce Smith .25 .60
93 Takeo Spikes .20 .50
94 Michael Strahan .25 .60
95 Derrick Thomas .30 .75
96 Zach Thomas .25 .60
97 Andre Wadsworth .20 .50
98 Charles Woodson .30 .75
99 Checklist Card .10 .30
100 Checklist Card .10 .30
101 Troy Aikman .40 1.00
102 Tony Banks .25 .60
103 Charlie Batch .20 .50
104 Steve Beuerlein .25 .60
105 Jeff Blake .25 .60
106 Drew Bledsoe .25 .60
107 Bubby Brister .20 .50
108 Mark Brunell .25 .60
109 Chris Chandler .25 .60
110 Kerry Collins .20 .50
111 Randall Cunningham .25 .60
112 Koy Detmer .20 .50
113 Ty Detmer .20 .50
114 Trent Dilfer .20 .50
115 John Elway .50 1.25
116 Brett Favre .60 1.50
117 Doug Flutie .30 .75
118 Rich Gannon .25 .60
119 Jeff Garcia RC 2.00 5.00
120 Jeff George .20 .50
121 Jon Kitna .20 .50
122 Elvis Grbac .20 .50
123 Brian Griese .20 .50
124 Trent Green .20 .50
125 Jim Harbaugh .25 .60
126 Billy Joe Hobert .20 .50
127 Brad Johnson .25 .60
128 Rob Johnson .25 .60
129 Jon Kitna .20 .50
130 Erik Kramer .25 .60
131 Ryan Leaf .25 .60
132 Peyton Manning 1.00 2.50
133 Dan Marino .60 1.50
134 Steve McNair .25 .60
135 Scott Mitchell .20 .50
136 Warren Moon .30 .75
137 Jake Plummer .20 .50
138 Kordell Stewart .20 .50
139 Vinny Testaverde .20 .50
140 Steve Young .40 1.00
141 Champ Bailey RC .60 1.50
142 Karsten Bailey RC .30 .75
143 D'Wayne Bates RC .30 .75
144 David Boston RC .30 .75
145 Cuncho Brown RC .30 .75
146 Dat Nguyen RC .50 1.25
147 Chris Claiborne RC .30 .75
148 Mike Cloud RC .30 .75
149 Cecil Collins RC .30 .75
150 Tim Couch RC .40 1.00
151 Daunte Culpepper RC .50 1.25
152 Autry Denson RC .30 .75
153 Troy Edwards RC .30 .75
154 Ebenezer Ekuban RC .30 .75
155 Kevin Faulk RC .30 .75
156 Jermaine Fazande RC .30 .75
157 Joe Germaine RC .40 1.00
158 Martin Gramatica RC .30 .75
159 Torry Holt RC .60 1.50
160 Brock Huard RC .30 .75
161 Sedrick Irvin RC .30 .75
162 Edgerrin James RC .50 1.25
163 James Johnson RC .30 .75
164 Kevin Johnson RC .40 1.00
165 Andy Katzenmoyer RC .40 1.00
166 Jevon Kearse RC .40 1.00
167 Patrick Kerney RC .30 .75
168 Shaun King RC .30 .75
169 Jim Kleinsasser RC .50 1.25
170 Rob Konrad RC .30 .75
171 Chris McAlister RC .30 .75
172 Donovan McNabb RC 2.50 6.00
173 Cade McNown RC .30 .75
174 Joe Montgomery RC .30 .75
175 Peerless Price RC .30 .75
176 Akili Smith RC .30 .75
177 Ricky Williams RC .50 1.25
178 Larry Parker RC .40 1.00
179 Antoine Winfield RC .30 .75
180 Amos Zereoue RC .30 .75

1999 Collector's Edge Triumph Galvanized

*VETS 1-140: 2X TO 5X BASIC CARDS
*ROOKIES 141-180: 1.5X TO 4X BASIC CARDS
STATED PRINT RUN 500 SER.#'d SETS

1999 Collector's Edge Triumph Commissioner's Choice

Randomly inserted in packs at the rate of one in 15, this 10-card set showcases top NFL rookies. Card backs carry a "CC" prefix.

COMPLETE SET (10) 25.00 50.00
STATED ODDS 1:15
*GOLD/500: .8X TO 2X BASIC INSERTS
CC1 Tim Couch .75 2.00
CC2 Donovan McNabb 2.00 5.00
CC3 Cade McNown .60 1.50
CC4 Daunte Culpepper 1.00 2.50
CC5 Akili Smith .60 1.50
CC6 Ricky Williams 1.00 2.50
CC7 Edgerrin James 1.00 2.50
CC8 Torry Holt 1.25 3.00
CC9 David Boston .60 1.50
CC10 Champ Bailey 1.25 3.00

1999 Collector's Edge Triumph Fantasy Team

Randomly inserted in packs at the rate of one in 10, this 10-card set features top NFL stars. Card backs carry a "FT" prefix.

COMPLETE SET (10) 20.00 40.00
STATED ODDS 1:10
FT1 Terrell Davis .60 1.50
FT2 John Elway 1.25 3.00
FT3 Brett Favre 1.50 4.00
FT4 Peyton Manning 2.50 6.00
FT5 Dan Marino 1.50 4.00
FT6 Randy Moss .60 1.50
FT7 Jake Plummer .50 1.25
FT8 Barry Sanders 1.25 3.00
FT9 Emmitt Smith 1.25 3.00
FT10 Fred Taylor .50 1.25

1999 Collector's Edge Triumph Future Fantasy Team

Randomly seeded in packs at the rate of one in six, this 20-card set features top rookies with bright NFL futures. Card backs carry an "FFT" prefix.

COMPLETE SET (20) 20.00 40.00
STATED ODDS 1:6
FFT1 Champ Bailey .60 1.50
FFT2 D'Wayne Bates .30 .75
FFT3 David Boston .60 1.50
FFT4 Tim Couch .60 1.50
FFT5 Daunte Culpepper 2.00 5.00
FFT6 Troy Edwards .50 1.25
FFT7 Kevin Faulk .60 1.50
FFT8 Torry Holt 1.25 3.00
FFT9 Brock Huard .60 1.50
FFT10 Sedrick Irvin .30 .75
FFT11 Edgerrin James 2.00 5.00
FFT12 James Johnson .50 1.25
FFT13 Kevin Johnson .60 1.50
FFT14 Rob Konrad .50 1.25
FFT15 Donovan McNabb 2.50 6.00
FFT16 Cade McNown .50 1.25
FFT17 Peerless Price .60 1.50
FFT18 Akili Smith .50 1.25
FFT19 Ricky Williams 1.00 2.50
FFT20 Amos Zereoue .60 1.50

1999 Collector's Edge Triumph Heir Supply

Randomly inserted in packs at the rate of one in three, this 15-card set focuses on top rookies expected to lead their teams into the future. Card backs carry an "HS" prefix.

COMPLETE SET (15) 12.50 30.00
STATED ODDS 1:3
HS1 Ricky Williams .50 1.25
HS2 Tim Couch .40 1.00
HS3 Cade McNown .30 .75
HS4 Donovan McNabb 1.00 2.50
HS5 Akili Smith .30 .75
HS6 Daunte Culpepper .50 1.25
HS7 Torry Holt .60 1.50
HS8 Edgerrin James .50 1.25
HS9 David Boston .30 .75
HS10 Troy Edwards .30 .75
HS11 Peerless Price .30 .75
HS12 Champ Bailey .60 1.50
HS13 D'Wayne Bates .30 .75
HS14 Kevin Faulk .30 .75
HS15 Amos Zereoue .30 .75

1999 Collector's Edge Triumph K-Klub Y3K

Randomly inserted in packs, this 50-card set features top offensive threats. Each card is sequentially numbered to 1000. Card backs carry a "KK" prefix.

COMPLETE SET (50) 60.00 120.00
*PREVIEWS: .4X TO 1X BASIC INSERTS
STATED PRINT RUN 1000 SER.#'d SETS
KK1 Karim Abdul-Jabbar 1.00 2.50
KK2 Jamal Anderson 1.25 3.00
KK3 Jerome Bettis 1.50 4.00
KK4 Isaac Bruce 1.50 4.00
KK5 Cris Carter 1.50 4.00
KK6 Terrell Davis 1.25 3.00
KK7 Corey Dillon 1.00 2.50
KK8 Warrick Dunn 1.00 2.50
KK9 Curtis Enis 1.00 2.50
KK10 Marshall Faulk 1.25 3.00
KK11 Antonio Freeman 1.25 3.00
KK12 Joey Galloway 1.25 3.00
KK13 Eddie George 1.25 3.00
KK14 Terry Glenn 1.25 3.00
KK15 Garrison Hearst 1.00 2.50
KK16 Keyshawn Johnson 1.25 3.00
KK17 Napoleon Kaufman 1.00 2.50
KK18 Curtis Martin 1.25 3.00
KK19 Rob Moore 1.00 2.50
KK20 Herman Moore 1.25 3.00
KK21 Eric Moulds 1.00 2.50
KK22 Randy Moss 1.25 3.00
KK23 Adrian Murrell 1.00 2.50
KK24 Carl Pickens 1.25 3.00
KK25 Jerry Rice 4.00 10.00
KK26 Barry Sanders 2.50 6.00
KK27 Antowain Smith 1.00 2.50
KK28 Emmitt Smith 2.50 6.00
KK29 Fred Taylor 1.00 2.50
KK30 Ricky Watters 1.25 3.00
KK31 Troy Aikman 2.00 5.00
KK32 Charlie Batch 1.00 2.50
KK33 Drew Bledsoe 1.25 3.00
KK34 Mark Brunell 1.25 3.00
KK35 Chris Chandler 1.25 3.00
KK36 Randall Cunningham 1.25 3.00
KK37 Trent Dilfer 1.00 2.50
KK38 John Elway 2.50 6.00
KK39 Brett Favre 3.00 8.00
KK40 Doug Flutie 1.50 4.00
KK41 Brad Johnson 1.25 3.00
KK42 Jon Kitna 1.00 2.50
KK43 Ryan Leaf 1.25 3.00
KK44 Peyton Manning 5.00 12.00
KK45 Dan Marino 3.00 8.00
KK46 Steve McNair 1.25 3.00
KK47 Jake Plummer 1.00 2.50
KK48 Kordell Stewart 1.00 2.50
KK49 Vinny Testaverde 1.00 2.50
KK50 Steve Young 2.00 5.00

1999 Collector's Edge Triumph Pack Warriors

Randomly inserted in packs at one in four, this 15-card set features running backs, quarterbacks, and receivers. Card backs carry a "PW" prefix.

COMPLETE SET (15) 15.00 30.00
STATED ODDS 1:4
PW1 Jamal Anderson .50 1.25
PW2 Jake Plummer .40 1.00
PW3 Emmitt Smith 1.00 2.50
PW4 Troy Aikman .75 2.00
PW5 Terrell Davis .50 1.25
PW6 John Elway 1.00 2.50
PW7 Barry Sanders 1.00 2.50
PW8 Brett Favre 1.25 3.00
PW9 Peyton Manning 2.00 5.00
PW10 Dan Marino 1.25 3.00
PW11 Randy Moss .50 1.25
PW12 Keyshawn Johnson .50 1.25
PW13 Fred Taylor .40 1.00
PW14 Jerry Rice 1.50 4.00
PW15 Jerome Bettis .60 1.50

1999 Collector's Edge Triumph Signed, Sealed, Delivered

Randomly inserted in packs at the rate of one in 32, this 39-card set features authentic autographs from some of the NFL's top prospects. Each base autograph was reportedly signed in black ink. Blue ink and red ink variations were also produced with each of those version beings hand serial numbered on the cardbacks. A few single cards from this set have been seen minus the autograph on the front so beware of forgeries. These were likely released after old card inventory was liquidated.

STATED ODDS 1:32
*BLUE AU/40-50: 1X TO 2.5X BLACK AU
BLUE INK AUTO PRINT RUN 40-50
UNPRICED RED INK PRINT RUN 10
AD Autry Denson 3.00 8.00
AS Akili Smith 3.00 8.00
AW Antoine Winfield 5.00 12.00
AZ Amos Zereoue 3.00 8.00
BH Brock Huard 5.00 12.00
CB Cuncho Brown 2.50 6.00
CB1 Champ Bailey 7.50 20.00
CC Chris Claiborne 2.50 6.00
CC1 Cecil Collins 2.50 6.00
CM Chris McAlister 3.00 8.00
CMN Cade McNown 3.00 8.00
DB David Boston 5.00 12.00
DC Daunte Culpepper 7.50 20.00
DM Donovan McNabb 20.00 40.00
DN Dat Nguyen 5.00 12.00
EE Ebenezer Ekuban 3.00 8.00
EJ Edgerrin James 10.00 25.00
JF Jermaine Fazande 3.00 8.00
JG Joe Germaine 3.00 8.00
JJ James Johnson 3.00 8.00
JK Jevon Kearse 6.00 15.00
JK1 Jim Kleinsasser 5.00 12.00
JM Joe Montgomery 3.00 8.00
KB Karsten Bailey 3.00 8.00
KF Kevin Faulk 5.00 12.00
KJ Kevin Johnson 3.00 8.00
LP Larry Parker 3.00 8.00
MC Mike Cloud 3.00 8.00
MG Martin Gramatica 2.50 6.00
PK Patrick Kerney 3.00 8.00
PP Peerless Price 5.00 12.00
RK Rob Konrad 5.00 12.00
RW Ricky Williams 10.00 25.00
SI Sedrick Irvin 2.50 6.00
SK Shaun King 3.00 8.00
TC Tim Couch 5.00 12.00
TE Troy Edwards 3.00 8.00
TH Torry Holt 10.00 25.00
DWB D'Wayne Bates 3.00 8.00

1948 Colts Matchbooks

These standard sized (1 1/2" by 4 1/2") matchbooks were thought to have been released during the 1948 season. Each was printed in blue ink with a player head shot on gray card stock. Complete covers with matches intact are valued at approximately 1 1/2 times the prices listed below.

COMPLETE SET (10) 800.00 1200.00
1 Dick Barwegan 90.00 150.00
2 Lamar Davis 75.00 125.00
3 Spiro Dellerba 75.00 125.00
4 Lou Gambino 75.00 125.00
5 Rex Grossman 75.00 125.00
6 Jake Leicht 75.00 125.00
7 Charlie O'Rourke 75.00 125.00
8 Y.A. Tittle 250.00 500.00
9 Sam Vacanti 75.00 125.00
10 Herman Wedemeyer 90.00 150.00

1949 Colts Silber's Bakery

This rare set of cards was issued by Silber's Bakery only in the Baltimore area in 1949 and featured members of the AAFC Baltimore Colts including future Hall of Famer Y.A. Tittle. Each card measures roughly 2 1/4" by 3 1/4" and features a black and white photo on the front with basic vital statistics for the player below the image. "Silber's Trading Cards" appears above the photo. The cardbacks include brief rules to a contest using a letter printed on the cards to spell SILBER'S in exchange for various prizes. The team's home game schedule is also included on the backs. Any additions to this list are appreciated.

1 Dick Barwegan 800.00 1200.00
2 Hub Bechtol 600.00 1000.00
3 Ernie Blandin 600.00 1000.00
4 Lamar Davis 600.00 1000.00
5 Barry French 600.00 1000.00
6 Lou Gambino 600.00 1000.00
7 Dub Garrett 600.00 1000.00
8 Rex Grossman 600.00 1000.00
9 Johnny Mellus 600.00 1000.00
10 Bus Mertes 600.00 1000.00
11 John North 600.00 1000.00
12 Charlie O'Rouke 600.00 1000.00
13 Paul Page 600.00 1000.00
14 Bob Pfohl 600.00 1000.00
15 Billy Stone 600.00 1000.00
16 Y.A. Tittle 2000.00 3500.00
17 Sam Vacanti 600.00 1000.00
18 Win Williams 600.00 1000.00

1957 Colts Team Issue

These photos were issued around 1957 by the Baltimore Colts. Each features a black and white player photo with the player's name and team name in a white box near the picture. They measure approximately 8" by 10 1/4" and are blankbacked and unnumbered. Any additions to this list are welcomed.

COMPLETE SET (7) 50.00 100.00
1 Alan Ameche 10.00 20.00
2 L.G. Dupre 7.50 15.00
3 Bill Pellington 7.50 15.00
4 Bert Rechichar 7.50 15.00
5 George Shaw 7.50 15.00
6 Art Spinney 7.50 15.00
7 Carl Taseff 7.50 15.00

1958-60 Colts Team Issue

This set of photos was likely issued over a number of years by the Baltimore Colts. Each card features a black and white player photo with just the player's name and team name below the picture. They measure approximately 8" by 10 1/4" and are blankbacked and unnumbered. There are two known Johnny Unitas photo variations. Any additions to this list are welcomed.

COMPLETE SET (41)	400.00	700.00
1 Alan Ameche	10.00	20.00
2 Raymond Berry	18.00	30.00
3 Ordell Braase	7.50	15.00
4 Ray Brown	7.50	15.00
5 Milt Davis	7.50	15.00
6 Art DeCarlo	7.50	15.00
7 Art Donovan	15.00	25.00
8 L.G. Dupre	7.50	15.00
9 Weeb Ewbank CO	10.00	20.00
10 Alex Hawkins	7.50	15.00
11 Don Joyce	7.50	15.00
12 Ray Krouse	7.50	15.00
13 Harold Lewis	7.50	15.00
14 Gene Lipscomb	10.00	20.00
15 Gino Marchetti	15.00	25.00
16 Marv Matuszak	7.50	15.00
17 Lenny Moore	18.00	30.00
18 Jim Mutscheller	7.50	15.00
19 Steve Myhra	7.50	15.00
20 Andy Nelson	7.50	15.00
21 Buzz Nutter	7.50	15.00
22 Jim Parker	15.00	25.00
23 Bill Pellington	7.50	15.00
24 Sherman Plunkett	7.50	15.00
25 George Preas	7.50	15.00
26 Billy Pricer	7.50	15.00
27 Palmer Pyle	7.50	15.00
28 Bert Rechichar	7.50	15.00
29 Jerry Richardson	7.50	15.00
30 Johnny Sample	7.50	15.00
31 Alex Sandusky	7.50	15.00
32 Dave Sherer	7.50	15.00
33 Don Shinnick	7.50	15.00
34 Jackie Simpson	7.50	15.00
35 Art Spinney	7.50	15.00
36 Dick Szymanski	7.50	15.00
37 Carl Taseff	7.50	15.00
38A Johnny Unitas	40.00	75.00
38B Johnny Unitas	40.00	75.00
39 Jim Welch	7.50	15.00
40 1958 Team Picture	30.00	50.00

1960 Colts Jay Publishing

This 12-card photo set features 5" by 7" black-and-white photos of Baltimore Colts players. The photos show players in traditional posed action shots and were originally packaged 12 to a set. Sets sold primarily through Jay Publishing's Pro Football Yearbook in 1960 and originally sold for 25-cents. The backs are blank. The cards are unnumbered and checklisted below in alphabetical order.

COMPLETE SET (12)	75.00	135.00
1 Alan Ameche	6.00	12.00
2 Raymond Berry	7.50	15.00
3 Art Donovan	6.00	12.00
4 Don Joyce	5.00	10.00
5 Gene Lipscomb	6.00	12.00
6 Gino Marchetti	6.00	12.00
7 Lenny Moore	7.50	15.00
8 Jim Mutscheller	5.00	10.00
9 Steve Myhra	5.00	10.00
10 Jim Parker	6.00	12.00
11 Bill Pellington	5.00	10.00
12 Johnny Unitas	15.00	30.00

1961 Colts Jay Publishing

This 12-card set features (approximately) 5" by 7" black-and-white player photos. The photos show players in traditional poses with the quarterback preparing to throw, the runner heading downfield, and the defenseman ready for the tackle. These cards were packaged 12 to a packet and originally sold for 25 cents. The backs are blank. The cards are unnumbered and checklisted below in alphabetical order.

COMPLETE SET (12)	75.00	135.00
1 Raymond Berry	7.50	15.00
2 Art Donovan	6.00	12.00
3 Weeb Ewbank CO	6.00	12.00
4 Alex Hawkins	5.00	10.00
5 Gino Marchetti	6.00	12.00
6 Lenny Moore	7.50	15.00
7 Jim Mutscheller	5.00	10.00
8 Steve Myhra	5.00	10.00
9 Jimmy Orr	5.00	10.00
10 Jim Parker	6.00	12.00
11 Joe Perry	7.50	15.00
12 Johnny Unitas	15.00	30.00

1963-64 Colts Team Issue

These large photo cards were produced and distributed by the Baltimore Colts. Each photo measures approximately 7 7/8" by 10 1/4" and is black-and-white, blank backed, and printed on glossy heavy paper stock. The player's name appears in bold lettering below the photo with the team name and player's position, height, weight, and college below that. Except for size, these cards are virtually identical to the 1967 and 1968 sets with differences in the photos or text noted below on like players. The cards are unnumbered and checklisted below in alphabetical order. Any additions to this list are appreciated.

COMPLETE SET (34)	250.00	450.00
1 Raymond Berry	12.50	25.00
2 Jackie Burkett	7.50	15.00
3 Jim Colvin	7.50	15.00
4 Gary Cuozzo	10.00	20.00
5 Wiley Feagin	7.50	15.00
6 Tom Gilburg	7.50	15.00
7 Wendell Harris	7.50	15.00
8 Alex Hawkins	7.50	15.00
9 Jerry Hill	7.50	15.00
10 J.W. Lockett	7.50	15.00
11 Tony Lorick	7.50	15.00
12 Lenny Lyles	7.50	15.00
13 Dee Mackey	7.50	15.00
14 John Mackey	10.00	20.00
15 Butch Maples	7.50	15.00
16 Lou Michaels	7.50	15.00
17 Fred Miller	7.50	15.00
18 Lenny Moore	12.50	25.00
19 Andy Nelson	7.50	15.00
20 Jimmy Orr	7.50	15.00
21 Bill Pellington	7.50	15.00
22 Palmer Pyle	7.50	15.00
23 Alex Sandusky	7.50	15.00
24 Don Shinnick	7.50	15.00
25 Don Shula CO	18.00	30.00
26 Billy Ray Smith	7.50	15.00
27 Steve Stonebreaker	7.50	15.00
28 Dick Szymanski	7.50	15.00
29 Don Thompson	7.50	15.00
30 Johnny Unitas	25.00	40.00
31 Bob Vogel	7.50	15.00
32 Jim Welch	7.50	15.00
33 Butch Wilson	7.50	15.00
34 1963 Coaching Staff	10.00	20.00
35 1964 Coaching Staff	10.00	20.00

1965 Colts Team Issue

These large photos were produced and distributed by the Baltimore Colts. Each photo measures approximately 7 7/8" by 10" and is black-and-white, blank backed, and printed on heavy glossy stock. The player's name appears in bold lettering below the photo with the team name and player's position, height, weight, and college below that. Except for the slightly smaller size, these photos are virtually identical to the 1963-64 set and exactly the same format as the 1967 and 1968 sets. However, there are noticable differences from one year to the next in terms of the photos or text featured below each photo. We've made note of key changes below on like players from 1965-1968. The cards are unnumbered and checklisted below in alphabetical order.

COMPLETE SET (18)	125.00	250.00
1 Raymond Berry	10.00	20.00
2 Bob Boyd	6.00	12.00
3 Gary Cuozzo	7.50	15.00
4 Dennis Gaubatz	6.00	12.00
5 Jerry Hill	6.00	12.00
7 Tony Lorick	6.00	12.00
8 John Mackey	7.50	15.00
9 Fred Miller	6.00	12.00
10 Lenny Moore	10.00	20.00
11 Jimmy Orr	6.00	12.00
12 Jim Parker	7.50	15.00
14 Willie Richardson	6.00	12.00
15 Don Shinnick	6.00	12.00
16 Steve Stonebreaker	6.00	12.00
17 Johnny Unitas	25.00	40.00
18 Bob Vogel	6.00	12.00

1967 Colts Johnny Pro

These 41 die-cut punchouts were issued (six or seven per page) in an album which itself measured approximately 11" by 14". Each punchout is approximately 4 1/8" tall and 2 7/8" wide at its base. A stand came with each punchout, and by inserting the punchout in it, the player stood upright. Each punchout consisted of a color player photo against a green grass background. The player's jersey number, name, and position are printed in a white box toward the bottom. The punchouts are unnumbered and checklisted below in alphabetical order.

COMPLETE SET (41)	500.00	850.00
1 Sam Ball	7.50	15.00
2 Raymond Berry	25.00	50.00
3 Bob Boyd DB	7.50	15.00
4 Ordell Braase	7.50	15.00
5 Barry Brown	7.50	15.00
6 Bill Curry	12.50	25.00
7 Mike Curtis	12.50	25.00
8 Norman Davis	7.50	15.00
9 Jim Detwiler	7.50	15.00
10 Dennis Gaubatz	7.50	15.00
11 Alvin Haymond	7.50	15.00
12 Jerry Hill	7.50	15.00
13 Roy Hilton	10.00	20.00
14 David Lee	7.50	15.00
15 Jerry Logan	10.00	20.00
16 Tony Lorick	10.00	20.00
17 Lenny Lyles	10.00	20.00
18 John Mackey	17.50	35.00
19 Tom Matte	12.50	25.00
20 Lou Michaels	10.00	20.00
21 Fred Miller	7.50	15.00
22 Lenny Moore	25.00	50.00
23 Jimmy Orr	10.00	20.00
24 Jim Parker	17.50	35.00
25 Ray Perkins	10.00	20.00
26 Glenn Ressler	7.50	15.00
27 Willie Richardson	10.00	20.00
28 Don Shinnick	7.50	15.00
29 Billy Ray Smith	10.00	20.00
30 Bubba Smith	20.00	40.00
31 Charlie Stukes	7.50	15.00
32 Andy Stynchula	7.50	15.00
33 Dan Sullivan	7.50	15.00
34 Dick Szymanski	7.50	15.00
35 Johnny Unitas	50.00	100.00
36 Bob Vogel	10.00	20.00
37 Rick Volk	10.00	20.00
38 Bob Wade	7.50	15.00
39 Jim Ward	7.50	15.00
40 Jim Welch	7.50	15.00
41 Butch Wilson	7.50	15.00

1967 Colts Team Issue

These large photos were produced and distributed by the Baltimore Colts in 1967. Each photo measures approximately 7 7/8" by 10" (with a few measuring a slightly larger 10 1/4") and is black-and-white, blank backed, and printed on heavy glossy stock. The player's name appears in bold lettering below the photo with the team name and player's position, height, weight, and college below that. Except for the slightly smaller size on most, these photos are virtually identical to the 1963-64 set and exactly the same format as the 1965 and 1968 sets. However, there are noticable differences from one year to the next in terms of the photos or text featured below each photo. We've made note of key changes below on like players from 1965-1968. The cards are unnumbered and checklisted below in alphabetical order.

COMPLETE SET (44)	200.00	400.00
1 Bob Baldwin	6.00	12.00
2 Sam Ball	6.00	12.00
3 Raymond Berry	10.00	20.00
4 Bob Boyd	6.00	12.00
5 Jackie Burkett	6.00	12.00
6 Gary Cuozzo	6.00	12.00
7 Bill Curry	6.00	12.00
8 Mike Curtis	7.50	15.00
9 Norman Davis	6.00	12.00
10 Jim Detwiler	6.00	12.00
11 Dennis Gaubatz	6.00	12.00
12 Alvin Haymond	6.00	12.00
13 Jerry Hill	6.00	12.00
14 Roy Hilton	6.00	12.00
15 David Lee	6.00	12.00
16 Jerry Logan	6.00	12.00
17 Tony Lorick	6.00	12.00
18 Lenny Lyles	6.00	12.00
19 John Mackey	7.50	15.00
20 Tom Matte	7.50	15.00
21 Dale Memmelaar	6.00	12.00
22 Lou Michaels	6.00	12.00
23 Fred Miller	6.00	12.00
24 Lenny Moore	10.00	20.00
25 Jimmy Orr	6.00	12.00
26 Jim Parker	7.50	15.00
27 Ray Perkins	6.00	12.00
28 Glenn Ressler	6.00	12.00
29 Alex Sandusky	6.00	12.00
30 Willie Richardson	6.00	12.00
31 Don Shinnick	6.00	12.00
32 Don Shula CO	15.00	25.00
33 Billy Ray Smith	6.00	12.00
34 Bubba Smith	7.50	15.00
35 Andy Stynchula	6.00	12.00
36 Dan Sullivan	6.00	12.00
37 Dick Szymanski	6.00	12.00
38 Johnny Unitas	18.00	30.00
39 Bob Vogel	6.00	12.00
40 Rick Volk	6.00	12.00
41 Jim Ward	6.00	12.00
42 Jim Welch	6.00	12.00
43 Butch Wilson	6.00	12.00
44 1967 Coaches	7.50	15.00
Arns		
Shula		
Noll		
Biel		
Sand		
Rutl		
McCa		

1968 Colts Team Issue

These large photos were produced and distributed by the Baltimore Colts in 1968. Each photo measures approximately 8" by 10" and is black-and-white, blank backed, and printed on heavy glossy stock. The player's name appears in bold lettering below the photo with the team name and player's position, height, weight, and college below that. Except for the smaller size, these cards are virtually identical to the 1963-64 set and almost exactly the same format as the 1965 and 1967 sets. However, there are noticable differences from one year to the next in terms of the photos or text featured below each photo. We've made note of key changes below on like players from 1965-1968. The cards are unnumbered and checklisted below in alphabetical order.

COMPLETE SET (30)	200.00	350.00
1 Don Alley	6.00	12.00
2 Ordell Braase	6.00	12.00
3 Timmy Brown	6.00	12.00
4 Terry Cole	6.00	12.00
5 Mike Curtis	7.50	15.00
6 Bill Curry	6.00	12.00
7 Dennis Gaubatz	6.00	12.00
8 Alex Hawkins	6.00	12.00
9 Jerry Hill	6.00	12.00
10 Cornelius Johnson	6.00	12.00
11 Lenny Lyles	6.00	12.00
12 John Mackey	7.50	15.00
13 Tom Matte	7.50	15.00
14 Lou Michaels	6.00	12.00
15 Fred Miller	6.00	12.00
16 Earl Morrall	7.50	15.00
17 Preston Pearson	7.50	15.00
18 Ron Porter	6.00	12.00
19 Willie Richardson	6.00	12.00
20 Don Shinnick	6.00	12.00
21 Billy Ray Smith	6.00	12.00
22 Bubba Smith	7.50	15.00
23 Charlie Stukes	6.00	12.00
24 Dick Szymanski	6.00	12.00
25 Bob Vogel	6.00	12.00
26 Rick Volk	6.00	12.00
27 Jim Ward	6.00	12.00
28 John Williams T	6.00	12.00
29 Coaching Staff	7.50	15.00
30 Team Photo	10.00	20.00

1969-70 Colts Team Issue

This set of photos issued by the Colts measure roughly 8" by 10" and feature black and white player images with vital statistics below the photo. Each is blankbacked and features much of the same information as the 1967 and 1968 sets, but presented in much larger text. The player's name can be found with two different sized letters. Unless noted below, all these photos feature a player name with letters that are 3/16" tall. The small names feature letters only 1/8" tall. Any additions to this list are appreciated.

COMPLETE SET (29)	200.00	350.00
1 Ocie Austin	6.00	12.00
2 Sam Ball	6.00	12.00
3 Terry Cole	6.00	12.00
4 Tom Curtis	6.00	12.00
5 Jim Duncan	6.00	12.00
6 Speedy Duncan	6.00	12.00
7 Perry Lee Dunn	6.00	12.00
8 Bob Grant	6.00	12.00
9 Sam Havrilak	6.00	12.00
10 Ted Hendricks	7.50	15.00
11 Jerry Hill	6.00	12.00
12 Ron Kostelnik	6.00	12.00
13 Lenny Lyles	6.00	12.00
14 Tom Matte	7.50	15.00
15 Tom Maxwell	6.00	12.00
16 Lou Michaels	6.00	12.00
17 Fred Miller	6.00	12.00
18 Tom Mitchell	6.00	12.00
19 Earl Morrall	7.50	15.00
20 Jimmy Orr	6.00	12.00
21 Ray Perkins	6.00	12.00
22 Billy Ray Smith	6.00	12.00
23 Bubba Smith	7.50	15.00
24 Charlie Stukes	6.00	12.00
25 Dan Sullivan	6.00	12.00
26A Johnny Unitas Action	15.00	30.00
26B Johnny Unitas Portrait	15.00	30.00
27 Bob Vogel	6.00	12.00
28 Rick Volk	6.00	12.00
29 John Williams	6.00	12.00

1971 Colts Baltimore Sunday Sun Posters

These oversized (roughly 14 1/4" by 21 1/2") posters were to be cut from weekly issues of the Baltimore Sunday Sun newspaper in 1971. Each was printed in color and features typical newsprint pages on the backs. Any additions to this list are appreciated.

COMPLETE SET (17)	100.00	200.00
1 Norm Bulaich	5.00	10.00
2 Mike Curtis	6.00	12.00
3 Jim Duncan	5.00	10.00
4 Ted Hendricks	10.00	20.00
5 Roy Hilton	5.00	10.00
6 Eddie Hinton	5.00	10.00
7 Jerry Logan	5.00	10.00
8 John Mackey	7.50	15.00
9 Tom Matte	6.00	12.00
10 Tom Mitchell	5.00	10.00
11 Earl Morrall	7.50	15.00
12 Jim O'Brien	5.00	10.00
13 Bubba Smith	7.50	15.00
14 Charlie Stukes	5.00	10.00
15 Dan Sullivan	5.00	10.00
16 Bob Vogel	5.00	10.00
17 Rick Volk	5.00	10.00

1971 Colts Jewel Foods

These six color photos are thought to have been released by Jewel Foods in Baltimore. Each measures approximately 7" by 8 3/4" and includes the player's name and team name below the photo. They are blankbacked and unnumbered.

COMPLETE SET (6)	30.00	60.00
1 Norm Bulaich	2.50	5.00
2 Mike Curtis	5.00	10.00
3 Ted Hendricks	6.00	12.00
4 Tom Matte	5.00	10.00
5 Bubba Smith	6.00	12.00
6 Johnny Unitas	12.50	25.00

1971 Colts Team Issue

This set of photos was issued by the Baltimore Colts in 1971. Each photo measures 8" by 10" and includes a black and white player photo on the front with the player's name (printed in large or small letters) and team name below the photo. The photos are blank backed, unnumbered and checklisted below in alphabetical order. Photos in this set are very similar to the 1973 Colts photos except for the smaller font size (measures roughly 1 3/8') used in the team name. They are identical in design to the 1974 set except this year features all players in action photos unless noted below.

COMPLETE SET (10)	50.00	100.00
1 Karl Douglas	5.00	10.00
2 Ted Hendricks	7.50	15.00
3 Lonnie Hepburn	5.00	10.00
4 Dennis Nelson	5.00	10.00
5 Billy Newsome	5.00	10.00
6 Don Nottingham	5.00	10.00
7 Charlie Pittman	5.00	10.00
8A Bubba Smith	7.50	15.00
8B Bubba Smith	7.50	15.00
9 Rick Volk	5.00	10.00

1972 Colts Team Issue

This set of photos was issued by the Baltimore Colts around 1972. Many of these Colts team issue photos were issued over a period of years as players were added to the roster or left the team, therefore the year of issue is an estimate. Each photo in this group is of one of two distinctly different designs or formats. The first style measures 8" by 10" and includes a black and white player photo on the front. Below the photo are: the player's jersey number to the far right, followed by his name and team name printed in large letters. The second style features only the player's name and team name below the photo in small letters resembling that of typewriter type. All of the photos are blank backed, unnumbered and checklisted below in alphabetical order.

COMPLETE SET (20)	100.00	175.00
1 Dick Amman	5.00	10.00
2 Jim Bailey	5.00	10.00
3 Mike Curtis	6.00	12.00
4 Marty Domres	5.00	10.00
5 Glenn Doughty	5.00	10.00
6 Tom Drougas	5.00	10.00
7 Randy Edmunds	5.00	10.00
8 Chuck Hinton	5.00	10.00
9 Cornelius Johnson	5.00	10.00
10 Bruce Laird	5.00	10.00
11 Don McCauley	5.00	10.00
12 Ken Mendenhall	5.00	10.00
13 Jack Mildren	5.00	10.00
14 Lydell Mitchell	6.00	12.00
15 Nelson Munsey	5.00	10.00
16 Dennis Nelson	5.00	10.00
17 Billy Newsome	5.00	10.00
18 Cotton Speyrer	5.00	10.00
19 Dan Sullivan	5.00	10.00
20 Rick Volk	6.00	12.00

1973 Colts McDonald's

These 11" by 14" color posters were sponsored by and distributed through McDonald's stores. Each includes an artist's rendering of one or two Colts players along with the year and the "McDonald's Superstars Collector's Series" notation below the picture.

COMPLETE SET (4)	50.00	80.00
1 Raymond Chester	10.00	15.00
2 Mike Curtis	12.00	20.00
3 Ted Hendricks	15.00	25.00
Rick Volk		
4 Bert Jones	15.00	25.00

1973 Colts Team Issue B&W

This set of photos was issued by the Baltimore Colts in 1973. Each photo measures 8" by 10" and includes a black and white player photo on the front with the player's name and team below the photo. The photos are blank backed, unnumbered and checklisted below in alphabetical order. Photos in this set are very similar to the 1974 Colts photos except for the larger font size (measures roughly 2') used in the team name.

COMPLETE SET (28)	100.00	175.00
1 Dick Amman	4.00	8.00
2 Mike Barnes	4.00	8.00
3 Stan Cherry	4.00	8.00
4 Raymond Chester	5.00	10.00
5 Larry Christoff	4.00	8.00
6 Elmer Collett	4.00	8.00
7 Glenn Doughty	4.00	8.00
8 Tom Drougas	4.00	8.00
9 Joe Ehrmann	4.00	8.00
10 Hubert Ginn	4.00	8.00
11 Brian Herosian	4.00	8.00
12 Fred Hoaglin	4.00	8.00
13 George Hunt	4.00	8.00
14 Bert Jones	6.00	12.00
15 Mike Kaczmarek	4.00	8.00
16 Ed Mooney	4.00	8.00
17 Nelson Munsey	4.00	8.00
18 Dan Neal	4.00	8.00
19 Ray Oldham	4.00	8.00
20 Bill Olds	4.00	8.00
21 Gery Palmer	4.00	8.00
22 Tom Pierantozzi	4.00	8.00
23 Joe Schmiesing	4.00	8.00
24 Howard Schnellenberger CO	5.00	10.00
25 Ollie Smith	4.00	8.00
26 David Taylor T	4.00	8.00
27 Stan White LB	4.00	8.00
28 Bill Windauer	4.00	8.00

1973 Colts Team Issue Color

The NFLPA worked with many teams in 1973 to issued photo packs to be sold at stadium concession stands. Each measures approximately 7" by 8-5/8" and features a color player photo with a blank back. A small sheet with a player checklist was included in each 6-photo pack. Any additions to this list are appreciated.

1 Norm Bulaich	2.50	5.00
2 Mike Curtis	3.00	6.00
3 Ted Hendricks	4.00	8.00
4 Tom Matte	3.00	6.00
5 Bubba Smith	4.00	8.00

1974 Colts Team Issue

This set of photos was issued by the Baltimore Colts in 1974. Each photo measures 8" by 10" and includes a black and white player photo on the front with the player's name (printed in large letters) and team name below the photo. The players name is oriented to the far left unless noted below. The photos are blank backed, unnumbered and checklisted below in alphabetical order. Photos in this set are very similar to the 1973 Colts photos except for the smaller font size (measures roughly 1 3/8') used in the team name. The photos with the name to the far left are also identical in design to the 1971 set except this year features all players in portrait photos -- no action shots.

COMPLETE SET (34)	125.00	250.00
1 John Andrews	4.00	8.00
2 Jim Bailey	4.00	8.00
3 Mike Barnes	4.00	8.00
4 Tim Berra	4.00	8.00
5 Tony Bertuca	4.00	8.00
6 Roger Carr	5.00	10.00
7 Fred Cook	4.00	8.00
8 Mike Curtis	5.00	10.00
9 Dan Dickel	4.00	8.00
10 Glenn Doughty	4.00	8.00
11 John Dutton	5.00	10.00
12 Joe Ehrmann	4.00	8.00
13 Randy Hall	4.00	8.00
14 Ted Hendricks	6.00	12.00
15 Bert Jones	6.00	12.00
16 Rex Kern	4.00	8.00
17 Bruce Laird	4.00	8.00
18 Toni Linhart	4.00	8.00
19 Tom MacLeod	4.00	8.00
20 Ted Marchibroda CO	5.00	10.00
21 Jack Mildren	4.00	8.00
22 Nelson Munsey	4.00	8.00
23 Doug Nettles	4.00	8.00
24 Ray Oldham	4.00	8.00
25 Bill Olds	4.00	8.00
26 Joe Orduna	4.00	8.00
27 Robert Pratt	4.00	8.00
28 Danny Rhodes	4.00	8.00
29 Tim Rudnick	4.00	8.00
30 Freddie Scott	5.00	10.00
31 Dave Simonson	4.00	8.00
32 Bob Van Duyne	4.00	8.00
33 Steve Williams	4.00	8.00
34 Bill Windauer	4.00	8.00

1976 Colts Team Issue 5x7

This set of photos was issued by the Baltimore Colts in 1976. Each photo measures approximately 5" by 7". The fronts feature a black and white photo with player's name (on the left in large capital letters) and team name (on the right in slightly smaller letters) below the photo. The photos are blank backed, unnumbered and checklisted below in alphabetical order.

COMPLETE SET (12)	15.00	30.00
1 Roger Carr	2.00	4.00
2 Raymond Chester	2.00	4.00
3 Jim Cheyunski	1.50	3.00
4 Elmer Collett	1.50	3.00
5 Fred Cook	1.50	3.00
6 John Dutton	2.00	4.00
7 Joe Ehrmann	1.50	3.00
8 Bert Jones	2.50	5.00
9 Bruce Laird	1.50	3.00
10 Roosevelt Leaks	2.00	4.00
11 Lydell Mitchell	2.00	4.00
12 Lloyd Mumphord	1.50	3.00

1976 Colts Team Issue 8x10

This set of photos was issued by the Baltimore Colts in 1976. Each photo measures 8" by 10" and includes a black and white player photo on the front with the player's name (printed in bold letters) and team name below the photo. The players name is oriented to the far left and the team name to the far right. The photos are blank backed, unnumbered and checklisted below in alphabetical order. The photo style used in this set is nearly identical to the 1974 Colts photos except for the slightly different font style and size used in the player and team name. All of the photos are close-up portrait shots.

COMPLETE SET (44)	150.00	300.00
1 Mike Barnes	4.00	8.00
2 Tim Baylor	4.00	8.00
3 Forrest Blue	4.00	8.00
4 Roger Carr	5.00	10.00
5 Raymond Chester	5.00	10.00
6 Jim Cheyunski	4.00	8.00
7 Elmer Collett	4.00	8.00
8 Fred Cook	4.00	8.00
9 Dan Dickel	4.00	8.00
10 Glenn Doughty	4.00	8.00
11 John Dutton	5.00	10.00
12 Joe Ehrmann	4.00	8.00
13 Ron Fernandes	4.00	8.00
14 Randy Hall	4.00	8.00
15 Ken Huff	4.00	8.00
16 Bert Jones	6.00	12.00
17 Jimmie Kennedy	4.00	8.00
18 Mike Kirkland	4.00	8.00
19 Bruce Laird	4.00	8.00
20 Roosevelt Leaks	5.00	10.00
21 David Lee	4.00	8.00
22 Ron Lee	4.00	8.00
23 Toni Linhart	4.00	8.00
24 Derrel Luce	4.00	8.00
25 Ted Marchibroda CO	5.00	10.00
26 Don McCauley	4.00	8.00
27 Ken Mendenhall	4.00	8.00
28 Lydell Mitchell	5.00	10.00
29 Lloyd Mumphord	4.00	8.00
30 Nelson Munsey	4.00	8.00
31 Doug Nettles	4.00	8.00
32 Ken Novak	4.00	8.00
33 Ray Oldham	4.00	8.00
34 Robert Pratt	4.00	8.00
35 Freddie Scott	5.00	10.00
36 Sanders Shiver	4.00	8.00
37 Ed Simonini	4.00	8.00
38 Howard Stevens	4.00	8.00
39 David Taylor	4.00	8.00
40 Ricky Thompson	4.00	8.00
41 Bill Troup	4.00	8.00
42 Bob Van Duyne	4.00	8.00
43 Jackie Wallace	4.00	8.00
44 Stan White	4.00	8.00

1977 Colts Book Covers

These book covers were sponsored by Amoco and feature a member of the Baltimore Colts on the front in a black and white photo. The Colts team photo and schedule is printed on the back side once the cover is folded. Each measures roughly 13" by 20".

COMPLETE SET (5)	25.00	50.00
1 Glenn Doughty	4.00	10.00
2 Joe Ehrmann	4.00	10.00
3 Bert Jones	6.00	15.00
4 Ted Marchibroda CO	4.00	10.00
5 Lydell Mitchell	5.00	12.00

1977 Colts Team Issue

This set of photos was issued by the Baltimore Colts in 1977. Each photo measures approximately 5" by 7". The fronts feature a black and white photo with player's name (on the left) and team name (on the right) below the photo in small letters. The date "8/77" is also include just below the team name. The photos are blank backed, unnumbered and checklisted below in alphabetical order.

COMPLETE SET (12)	30.00	60.00
1 Mack Alston	3.00	6.00
2 Mike Barnes	3.00	6.00
3 Lyle Blackwood	3.00	6.00
4 Bert Jones	5.00	10.00
5 Ed Khayat CO	3.00	6.00
6 George Kunz	3.00	6.00
7 Darrell Luce	3.00	6.00
8 Ted Marchibroda CO	4.00	8.00
9 Robert Pratt	3.00	6.00
10 Norm Thompson	3.00	6.00
11 Bob Van Duyne	3.00	6.00
12 Stan White	3.00	6.00

1978-81 Colts Team Issue

This set of photos was issued by the Baltimore Colts. Each photo measures approximately 5" by 7". The fronts display player portrait photos with player name, postion, and team below the photo. The photos are blank backed, unnumbered and checklisted below in alphabetical order. This set listings is likely comprised of photos issued over a number of years. Any additions or confirmed variations on player photos or text styles are appreciated.

1 Mack Alston	2.00	5.00
2 Kim Anderson	2.00	5.00
3 Ron Baker	2.00	5.00
4 Mike Barnes	2.00	5.00
5 Tim Baylor	2.00	5.00
6 Lyle Blackwood	2.00	5.00
7 Mike Bragg	2.00	5.00
8 Larry Braziel	2.00	5.00
9 Randy Burke	2.00	5.00
10 Raymond Butler	2.50	6.00
11 Roger Carr	2.50	6.00
12 Fred Cook	2.00	5.00
13 Brian DeRoo	2.00	5.00
14 Curtis Dickey	2.50	6.00
15 Zachary Dixon	2.00	5.00
16 Ray Donaldson	2.00	5.00
17 Glenn Doughty	2.00	5.00
18 Joe Ehrmann	2.00	5.00
19 Greg Fields	2.00	5.00
20 Ron Fernandes	2.00	5.00
21 Chris Foote	2.00	5.00
22 Cleveland Franklin	2.00	5.00
23 Mike Garrett	2.50	6.00
24 Nesby Glasgow	2.00	5.00
25 Bubba Green	2.00	5.00
26 Wade Griffin	2.00	5.00
27 Lee Gross	2.00	5.00
28 Don Hardeman	2.00	5.00
29 Dwight Harrison	2.00	5.00
30 Jeff Hart	2.00	5.00
31 Derrick Hatchett	2.00	5.00
32 Dallas Hickman	2.00	5.00
33 Ken Huff	2.00	5.00
34 Marshall Johnson	2.00	5.00
35 Bert Jones	3.00	8.00
36 Ricky Jones	2.00	5.00
37 Barry Krauss	2.00	5.00
38 George Kunz	2.00	5.00
39 Bruce Laird	2.00	5.00
40 Greg Landry	3.00	8.00
41 Roosevelt Leaks	2.50	6.00
42 David Lee	2.00	5.00
43 Ron Lee FB	2.00	5.00
44 Toni Linhart	2.00	5.00
45 Derrel Luce	2.00	5.00
46 Reese McCall	2.00	5.00
47 Don McCauley	2.00	5.00
48 Randy McMillan	2.00	5.00
49 Ken Mendenhall	2.00	5.00
50 Steve Mike-Mayer	2.00	5.00
51 Jim Moore	2.00	5.00
52 Don Morrison	2.00	5.00
53 Lloyd Mumphord	2.00	5.00
54 Doug Nettles	2.00	5.00
55 Calvin O'Neal	2.00	5.00
56 Herb Orvis	2.00	5.00
57 Mike Ozdowski	2.00	5.00
58 Reggie Pinkney	2.00	5.00
59 Robert Pratt	2.00	5.00
60 Dave Rowe	2.00	5.00
61 Tim Sherwin	2.00	5.00
62A Sanders Shiver ERR	2.00	5.00
62B Sanders Shiver COR	2.00	5.00
63 David Shula	2.50	6.00
64 Mike Siani	2.00	5.00
65 Ed Simonini	2.00	5.00
66 Marvin Sims	2.00	5.00
67 Ed Smith	2.00	5.00
68 Hosea Taylor	2.00	5.00
69 Donnell Thompson	2.00	5.00
70 Norm Thompson	2.00	5.00
71 Bill Troup	2.00	5.00
72 Randy Van Diver	2.00	5.00
73 Bob Van Duyne	2.00	5.00
74 Joe Washington	2.50	6.00
75 Stan White	2.00	5.00
76 Mike Wood	2.00	5.00
77 Mike Woods	2.00	5.00
78 Steve Zabel	2.00	5.00

1981 Colts Coke Photos

This set of photos was sponsored by Coca-Cola with each measuring approximately 5" by 6 3/4". The fronts display color action player photos with white borders. Player identification is given below the photo between the Colts' helmet on the left and the Coke logo on the right. The photos are unnumbered and checklisted below in alphabetical order.

COMPLETE SET (24)	50.00	100.00
1 Mike Barnes	2.00	5.00
2 Larry Braziel	2.00	5.00
3 Randy Burke	2.00	5.00
4 Raymond Butler	2.50	6.00
5 Roger Carr	2.50	6.00
6 Curtis Dickey	2.50	6.00
7 Zachary Dixon	2.00	5.00
8 Nesby Glasgow	2.00	5.00
9 Bubba Green	2.00	5.00
10 Ken Huff	2.00	5.00
11 Ricky Jones	2.00	5.00
12 Greg Landry	3.00	8.00
13 Reese McCall	2.00	5.00
14 Randy McMillan	2.00	5.00
15 Jim Moore	2.00	5.00
16 Mike Ozdowski	2.00	5.00
17 Reggie Pinkney	2.00	5.00
18 Tim Sherwin	2.00	5.00
19 Sanders Shiver	2.00	5.00
20 Ed Simonini	2.00	5.00
21 Marvin Sims	2.00	5.00
22 Donnell Thompson	2.00	5.00
23 Randy Van Diver	2.00	5.00
24 Mike Wood	2.00	5.00

1985 Colts Kroger

This set of photos was sponsored by Kroger. Each photo measures approximately 5 1/2" by 8 1/2". The fronts display color action player photos with white borders. Player identification is given below the photo between the Colts' helmet on the left and the Kroger logo on the right. In navy blue print on a white background, the backs carry biographical information, the NFL logo, and the Kroger emblem. The photos are unnumbered and checklisted below in alphabetical order.

COMPLETE SET (33)	60.00	120.00
1 Dave Ahrens	1.50	4.00
2 Raul Allegre	1.50	4.00
3 Karl Baldischwiler	1.50	4.00
4 Pat Beach	1.50	4.00
5 Albert Bentley	2.00	5.00
6 Duane Bickett	2.00	5.00
7 Matt Bouza	1.50	4.00
8 Willie Broughton	1.50	4.00
9 Johnie Cooks	1.50	4.00
10 Eugene Daniel	2.00	5.00
11 Preston Davis	1.50	4.00
12 Ray Donaldson	1.50	4.00
13 Rod Dowhower	1.50	4.00
14 Owen Gill	1.50	4.00
15 Nesby Glasgow	1.50	4.00
16 Chris Hinton	1.50	4.00
17 Lamonte Hunley	1.50	4.00
18 Matt Kofler	1.50	4.00
19 Barry Krauss	1.50	4.00
20 Orlando Lowry	1.50	4.00
21 Robbie Martin	1.50	4.00
22 Randy McMillan	1.50	4.00
23 Cliff Odom	1.50	4.00
24 Tate Randle	1.50	4.00
25 Tim Sherwin	1.50	4.00
26 Byron Smith	1.50	4.00
27 Ron Solt	1.50	4.00
28 Rohn Stark	1.50	4.00
29 Donnell Thompson	1.50	4.00
30 Ben Utt	1.50	4.00
31 Brad White	1.50	4.00
32 George Wonsley	1.50	4.00
33 Anthony Young	1.50	4.00

1988 Colts Kroger

This set of photos was sponsored by Kroger and the Indianapolis Colts and very closely resembles the 1985 Colts Kroger issue. Each photo measures approximately 5 1/2" by 8 1/2" and features a black and white action photo, as opposed to color for the 1985 release. Player identification is given below the photo between the Colts' helmet on the left and the Kroger logo on the right. The black and white printed backs carry a short biographical section, the NFL logo, and the Kroger emblem. The photos are unnumbered and checklisted below in alphabetical order.

COMPLETE SET (26)	50.00	100.00
1 O'Brien Alston	1.50	4.00
2 Harvey Armstrong	1.50	4.00
3 Brian Baldinger	1.50	4.00
4 Michael Ball	1.50	4.00
5 John Baylor	1.50	4.00
6 Albert Bentley	2.00	5.00
7 Mark Boyer (blankbacked)	1.50	4.00
8 John Brandes	1.50	4.00
9 Bill Brooks	1.50	4.00
10 Donnie Dee	1.50	4.00
11 Eric Dickerson	4.00	10.00
12 Randy Dixon	1.50	4.00
13 Ray Donaldson	1.50	4.00
14 Chris Goode	1.50	4.00
15 Jon Hand	1.50	4.00
16 Jeff Herrod	1.50	4.00
17 Chris Hinton	1.50	4.00
18 Gary Hogeboom	1.50	4.00
19 Barry Krauss	1.50	4.00
20 Orlando Lowry	1.50	4.00
21 Rohn Stark	1.50	4.00
22 Craig Swoope	1.50	4.00
23 Jack Trudeau	1.50	4.00
24 Ben Utt	1.50	4.00
25 Clarence Verdin	1.50	4.00
26 Fredd Young	2.00	5.00

1988 Colts Police

The 1988 Police Indianapolis Colts set contains eight numbered cards measuring approximately 2 5/8" by 4 1/8". There are seven player cards and one coach card. The backs have one "Colts Tip" and one "Crime Tip."

COMPLETE SET (8)	3.00	8.00
1 Eric Dickerson	1.00	2.50
2 Barry Krauss	.40	1.00
3 Bill Brooks	.50	1.25
4 Duane Bickett	.40	1.00
5 Chris Hinton	.40	1.00
6 Eugene Daniel	.30	.75
7 Jack Trudeau	.50	1.25
8 Ron Meyer CO	.40	1.00

1989 Colts Police

The 1989 Police Indianapolis Colts set contains nine numbered cards measuring approximately 2 5/8" by 4 1/8". The fronts have white borders and color action photos; the horizontally-oriented backs have safety tips. These cards were printed on very thin stock. The set was also sponsored by Louis Rich Co. and WTHR-TV-13. According to sources, at least 50,000 sets were given away. One card was given to young persons each week during the season.

COMPLETE SET (9)	3.00	8.00
1 Colts Team Card	.25	.60
2 Dean Biasucci	.25	.60
3 Andre Rison	1.00	2.50
4 Chris Chandler	.75	2.00
5 O'Brien Alston	.25	.60
6 Ray Donaldson	.20	.50
7 Donnell Thompson	.25	.60
8 Fredd Young	.25	.60
9 Eric Dickerson	.60	1.50

1990 Colts Police

This eight-card set features members of the 1990 Indianapolis Colts. The cards in the set measure approximately 2 5/8" by 4 1/8" and have full-color action shots of the featured players on the front along with safety and crime-prevention tips on the back. The set was sponsored by Region Central Indiana Crime Stoppers, Louis Rich, and Station 13 WTHR.

COMPLETE SET (8)	2.00	5.00
1 Harvey Armstrong	.25	.60
2 Pat Beach	.25	.60
3 Albert Bentley	.30	.75
4 Kevin Call	.25	.60
5 Jeff George	1.20	3.00
6 Mike Prior	.25	.60
7 Rohn Stark	.30	.75
8 Clarence Verdin	.30	.75

1991 Colts Police

Sponsored by 13 WTHR and Coke, this eight-card measure 2 5/8" by 4 1/4". The fronts feature color action player photos inside white borders. The player's name, team name, and two logos occupy the lower white border. The backs carry biography, a Colts Quiz feature (with four questions and their answers), an anti-drug or alcohol message, and sponsor logos. The cards are numbered in the lower right corner; a message encourages the holder to contact his local police officer to collect the other cards in the set.

COMPLETE SET (8)	2.80	7.00
1 Jeff George	1.00	2.50
2 Jack Trudeau	.40	1.00
3 Jeff Herrod	.30	.75
4 Eric Dickerson	.60	1.50
5 Bill Brooks	.50	1.25
6 Jon Hand	.40	1.00
7 Keith Taylor	.30	.75
8 Randy Dixon	.30	.75

1994 Colts NIE

The set of cards measures standard size and were issued by the team with sponsorship from the NIE (Newspaper in Education) group: the Indianapolis Star and Indianapolis News. Each unnumbered card includes a color player photo on the front against a tectured border with a brief player bio printed in blue on the back.

COMPLETE SET (12)	7.50	15.00
1 Ray Buchanan	.60	1.50
2 Quentin Coryatt	.60	1.50
3 Eugene Daniel	.60	1.50
4 Sean Dawkins	.60	1.50
5 Marshall Faulk	1.50	4.00
6 Stephen Grant	.50	1.25
7 Derwin Gray	.50	1.25
8 Kirk Lowdermilk	.50	1.25
9 Roosevelt Potts	.50	1.25
10 Joe Staysniak	.50	1.25
11 Floyd Turner	.50	1.25
12 Will Wolford	.50	1.25

2005 Colts Activa Medallions

COMPLETE SET (22)	30.00	60.00
1 Raheem Brock	1.25	3.00
2 Dallas Clark	1.25	3.00
3 Ryan Diem	1.25	3.00
4 Dwight Freeney	1.25	3.00
5 Tarik Glenn	1.25	3.00
6 Nick Harper	1.25	3.00
7 Marvin Harrison	1.50	4.00
8 Edgerrin James	1.50	4.00
9 Cato June	1.25	3.00
10 Peyton Manning	2.00	5.00
11 Robert Mathis	1.25	3.00
12 Rob Morris	1.25	3.00
13 Montae Reagor	1.25	3.00
14 Dominic Rhodes	1.25	3.00
15 Bob Sanders	1.50	4.00
16 Jeff Saturday	1.25	3.00
17 Brandon Stokley	1.25	3.00
18 David Thornton	1.25	3.00
19 Mike Vanderjagt	1.25	3.00
20 Reggie Wayne	1.25	3.00
21 Josh Williams	1.25	3.00
22 Colts Logo	1.00	2.50

2006 Colts Score Indianapolis Star Jumbos

This set was produced by Donruss/Playoff with their Score brand and distributed by the Colts one card at a time at 2006 home games. One card was distributed at each home game starting August 20th and going through December. The over-sized cards measure 5x7 and feature an advertisement for the Indianapolis Star newspaper.

COMPLETE SET (10)	20.00	40.00
1 Jeff Saturday	1.25	3.00
2 Bob Sanders	2.00	5.00
3 Marvin Harrison	2.00	5.00
4 Reggie Wayne	2.00	5.00
5 Peyton Manning	6.00	15.00
6 Brandon Stokley	1.50	4.00
7 Dominic Rhodes	1.50	4.00
8 Dwight Freeney	1.50	4.00
9 Mike Doss	1.50	4.00
10 Dallas Clark	1.50	4.00

2006 Colts Topps

COMPLETE SET (12)	3.00	6.00
IND1 Peyton Manning	1.00	2.50
IND2 Dwight Freeney	.25	.60
IND3 Reggie Wayne	.30	.75
IND4 Bob Sanders	.30	.75
IND5 Dallas Clark	.25	.60
IND6 Dominic Rhodes	.25	.60
IND7 Cato June	.30	.75
IND8 Brandon Stokley	.25	.60
IND9 Marvin Harrison	.30	.75
IND10 Adam Vinatieri	.25	.60
IND11 Joseph Addai	.25	.60
IND12 Bryan Fletcher	.25	.60

2007 Colts Donruss Indianapolis Star Jumbos

COMPLETE SET (10)	15.00	30.00
1 Dallas Clark	1.25	3.00
2 Anthony Gonzalez	2.50	6.00
3 Marvin Harrison	2.50	6.00
4 Dwight Freeney	1.50	4.00
5 Tony Dungy CO	1.50	4.00
6 Peyton Manning	4.00	10.00
7 Reggie Wayne	1.50	4.00

8 Joseph Addai 2.50 6.00
9 Bob Sanders 1.50 4.00
10 Adam Vinatieri 1.50 4.00

2007 Colts Topps

COMPLETE SET (12) 3.00 6.00
1 Peyton Manning 1.50 4.00
2 Joseph Addai .40 1.00
3 Marvin Harrison .50 1.25
4 Dwight Freeney .40 1.00
5 Dallas Clark .50 1.25
6 Reggie Wayne .50 1.25
7 Adam Vinatieri .40 1.00
8 Ben Utecht .40 1.00
9 Bob Sanders .50 1.25
10 Robert Mathis .40 1.00
11 Anthony Gonzalez .40 1.00
12 Gary Brackett .40 1.00

2007 Colts Upper Deck Super Bowl XLI

COMPLETE SET (50) 10.00 20.00
1 Joseph Addai .50 1.25
2 Antoine Bethea .20 .50
3 Rocky Boiman .20 .50
4 Gary Brackett .20 .50
5 Raheem Brock .20 .50
6 Dallas Clark .20 .50
7 Jason David .20 .50
8 Ryan Diem .20 .50
9 Bryan Fletcher .20 .50
10 Dwight Freeney .30 .75
11 Gilbert Gardner .20 .50
12 Matt Giordano .20 .50
13 Tarik Glenn .20 .50
14 Nick Harper .20 .50
15 Marvin Harrison .40 1.00
16 Kelvin Hayden .20 .50
17 Marlin Jackson .20 .50
18 Cato June .20 .50
19 Ryan Lilja .20 .50
20 Peyton Manning .60 1.50
21 Robert Mathis .20 .50
22 Anthony McFarland .20 .50
23 Aaron Moorehead .20 .50
24 Rob Morris .20 .50
25 Darrell Reid .20 .50
26 Dominic Rhodes .30 .75
27 Bob Sanders .30 .75
28 Jeff Saturday .20 .50
29 Bo Schobel .20 .50
30 Jake Scott .20 .50
31 Hunter Smith .25 .60
32 Charlie Johnson .20 .50
33 Jim Sorgi .30 .75
34 John Standeford .20 .50
35 Josh Thomas .20 .50
36 Matt Ulrich .20 .50
37 Ben Utecht .20 .50
38 Adam Vinatieri .30 .75
39 Reggie Wayne .30 .75
40 Terrence Wilkins .20 .50
MM1 Reggie Wayne MM .30 .75
MM2 Kelvin Hayden MM .20 .50
MM3 Bob Sanders MM .30 .75
MM4 Dominic Rhodes MM .30 .75
NNO Jumbo Team Photo .50 1.25
SH1 Peyton Manning SH .60 1.50
SH2 Reggie Wayne SH .30 .75
SH3 Adam Vinatieri SH .30 .75
SH4 Joseph Addai SH .50 1.25
SH5 Marvin Harrison SH .40 1.00
MVP1 Peyton Manning MVP 1.00 2.50

2008 Colts Topps

COMPLETE SET (12) 2.50 5.00
1 Peyton Manning 1.50 4.00
2 Reggie Wayne .50 1.25
3 Joseph Addai .40 1.00
4 Dallas Clark .40 1.00
5 Bob Sanders .50 1.25
6 Kenton Keith .40 1.00
7 Antoine Bethea .40 1.00
8 Anthony Gonzalez .40 1.00
9 Marvin Harrison .50 1.25
10 Gary Brackett .40 1.00
11 Mike Hart .40 1.00
12 Dwight Freeney .40 1.00

1959 Comet Sweets Olympic Achievements

Celebrating various Olympic events, ceremonies, and their history, this 25-card set was issued by Comet Sweets. The cards are printed on thin cardboard stock and measure 1 7/16" by 2 9/16". Inside white borders, the fronts display water color paintings of various Olympic events. Some cards are horizontally oriented; others are vertically oriented. The set title "Olympic Achievements" appears at the top on the backs, with a discussion of the event below. This set is the first series; the cards are numbered "X to 25."

COMPLETE SET (25) 30.00 60.00
18 Football 1.50 3.00

1995 Connecticut Coyotes AFL

The Connecticut Coyotes released this set of 5-cards at their final home game of the 1995 Arena Football League season. The cardfronts feature a full bleed color photo while the unnumbered backs include player information. Reportedly, 5000 sets were produced.

COMPLETE SET (5) 3.20 8.00
1 Rick Buffington CO .80 2.00
2 Mike Hold .80 2.00
3 Merv Mosley .80 2.00
4 Tyrone Thurman .80 2.00
5 Team Photo .80 2.00

2005 Corpus Christi Hammerheads NIFL

COMPLETE SET (25) 6.00 12.00
1 Terrance Bennett .30 .75
2 Shomari Buchanan .30 .75
3 Chris Chambers .30 .75
4 Martin Dossett .30 .75
5 Brian Gaines .30 .75
6 Devin Green .30 .75
7 Mike Green .30 .75
8 Carl Greenwood .30 .75
9 Matt Hardison .30 .75
10 Chris Harrington .30 .75
11 Jonathan Hayhurst Asst.CO .30 .75
12 Anthony Hood .30 .75
13 Estus Hood .30 .75
14 Chester Jones Jr. .30 .75
15 David Lose .30 .75
16 LeDaniel Marshall .30 .75
17 Hershall McCurn .30 .75
18 Jason McKinley CO .30 .75
19 Eddie Miller .30 .75
20 Oscar Moreno .30 .75
21 Roy Salas .30 .75
22 Fred Wallace .30 .75
23 Derrick Watson .30 .75
24 Robert Watson .30 .75
25 Hank-Hammerhead (Mascot) .30 .75

1993-94 Costacos Brothers Poster Cards

COMPLETE SET (18) 10.00 20.00
1 Troy Aikman 1.25 3.00
2 Troy Aikman 1.25 3.00
Silver Bullet
8 Michael Irvin .20 .50
Playmaker
12 Rick Mirer .20 .50
Natural Wonder
16 Jerry Rice .75 2.00
Speed of Light
17 Emmitt Smith 1.25 3.00
Catch 22

1994 Costacos Brothers Poster Cards NFL

Produced by Costacos Brothers, Inc., this set of twelve 4 1/4" by 6 1/4" poster cards was sold in a cello-wrapped glossy cardboard sleeve that pictured the entire set on its front. A silver foil seal on the back carries the set serial number out of 25,000 produced. Inside white borders, the front pictures highlight in a unique style the player's nickname, reputation, or image. The horizontal backs have a postcard design, with a light gray team logo in the middle.

COMPLETE SET (12) 6.00 15.00
1 Troy Aikman .60 1.50
2 Barry Sanders 1.20 3.00
3 Steve Young .50 1.25
4 Rick Mirer .20 .50
5 John Elway 1.20 3.00
6 Dan Marino 1.20 3.00
7 Drew Bledsoe .60 1.50
8 Emmitt Smith 1.00 2.50
9 Warren Moon .30 .75
10 Jerry Rice .60 1.50
11 Michael Irvin .30 .75
12 Jim Kelly .30 .75

1960 Cowboys Team Sheets

This set of press photo sheets was released to publicize players signed early to the first Cowboys' team. Each sheet includes four black and white photos, measures roughly 8 1/2" X 11" and is blankbacked. Some of these player images were also issued as separate 8 x 10 photos as well.

COMPLETE SET (10) 150.00 250.00
1 T.Braatz 15.00 25.00
L.G.Dupre
J.Patera
B.Butler DB
2 G.Babb 15.00 25.00
D.Putnam
N.Borden
D.Heinrich
3 F.Clarke 15.00 25.00
D.Sherer
D.McIlhenny
B.Bradfute
4 M.Falls 15.00 25.00
D.Bishop
P.Dickson
B.Bercich
5 Bob Fry/Jim Doran/Fred Dugan/Fred Cone/Don Heinrich
15.00 25.00
6 W.Hansen 15.00 25.00
W.Kowalczyk
D.Klein
J.Houser
7 D.Healy 15.00 25.00
D.Bielski
B.Herchman
J.Tubbs
8 Meredith 35.00 60.00
Gonzaga
Guy
Frankhouser
9 Hussman 20.00 35.00
Mathews
LeBaron
Cronin
10 Lewis 18.00 30.00
Howton
Connelly
Mooty

1960-62 Cowboys Team Issue 5x7

Those team issued photos feature black and white player images taken of just head-and-shoulders. Each measures approximately 5" by 7" and was printed on glossy photographic paper stock. Most feature four white borders around the player image but some were created with just one white border at the bottom: noted below. Each photo is a portrait with the player wearing a blue early 1960s era stars-on-the-shoulder Cowboys jersey. The white border at the bottom contains just the player's name and team name printed in all capital letters. These cards are blankbacked and unnumbered. Any additions to the below list are appreciated.

COMPLETE SET (22) 125.00 250.00
1 Dick Bielski 6.00 12.00
2 Frank Clarke 7.50 15.00
3 Donnie Davis 6.00 12.00
4 Jim Doran 6.00 12.00
5 Ken Frost 6.00 12.00
6 Bob Fry 6.00 12.00
7 Mike Gaechter 6.00 12.00
8 John Gonzaga 6.00 12.00
9 Don Healy 6.00 12.00
10 Bill Herchman 6.00 12.00
11 Billy Howton 7.50 15.00
12 Lynn Hoyem 6.00 12.00
13 Walt Kowalczyk 6.00 12.00
14 Eddie LeBaron 7.50 15.00
15 Bob Lilly 12.50 25.00
16 Don McIlhenny 6.00 12.00
17 Don Meredith 18.00 30.00
18 Don Perkins 7.50 15.00
19 Duane Putnam 6.00 12.00
20 Guy Reese 6.00 12.00
21 Lorenzo Stanford 6.00 12.00
22 Don Talbert 6.00 12.00

1960-63 Cowboys Team Issue 8x10

The Dallas Cowboys issued these black-and-white photos and all feature the player wearing the original stars-on-the-sleeves blue jersey. Each measures 8" by 10" and was printed on glossy stock with white borders. Each photo features a posed action shot with the border below the photo containing just the player's name and team name. The type style and size may vary slightly on some photos, and some players have more than one pose, so this may indicate that they were released over a period of years. The photos are blankbacked and unnumbered. Any additions to the below list are appreciated.

1 Gene Babb 7.50 15.00
2 Bob Bercich 7.50 15.00
3A Dick Bielski 7.50 15.00
3B Dick Bielski 7.50 15.00
4 Don Bishop 7.50 15.00
5 Nate Borden 7.50 15.00
6 Amos Bullocks 7.50 15.00
7A Frank Clarke 10.00 20.00
7B Frank Clarke 10.00 20.00
8 Mike Connelly 7.50 15.00
9 Andy Cvercko 7.50 15.00
10 Gerry DeLucca 7.50 15.00
11 Jim Doran 7.50 15.00
12 L.G. Dupre 7.50 15.00
13 Ken Frost 7.50 15.00
14 Don Healy 7.50 15.00
15 Don Heinrich 7.50 15.00
16 Bill Herchman 7.50 15.00
17 John Houser 7.50 15.00
18A Billy Howton 10.00 20.00
18B Billy Howton 10.00 20.00
18C Billy Howton 10.00 20.00
19 Lee Roy Jordan 12.50 25.00
20A Eddie LeBaron 10.00 20.00
20B Eddie LeBaron 10.00 20.00
20C Eddie LeBaron 10.00 20.00
20D Eddie LeBaron 10.00 20.00
20E Eddie LeBaron portrait 10.00 20.00
21 Bob Lilly portrait 15.00 30.00
22 Warren Livingston 7.50 15.00
23 J.W. Lockett 7.50 15.00
24 Amos Marsh 7.50 15.00
25A Don Meredith 25.00 40.00
25B Don Meredith 25.00 40.00
25C Don Meredith 25.00 40.00
25D Don Meredith 25.00 40.00
26 Dick Nolan 7.50 15.00
27 Don Perkins 10.00 20.00
28 Larry Stephens 7.50 15.00
29A Jerry Tubbs 7.50 15.00
29B Jerry Tubbs 7.50 15.00
29C Jerry Tubbs 7.50 15.00

1961 Cowboys Team Issue 7x9

These team issued photos feature black-and-white player images taken of just head-and-shoulders. They were most likely issued as set in "photo pack" style but that has yet to be confirmed. Each measures approximately 7 1/2" by 9 1/2" and was printed on thin matte finish paper stock. They have four wide white borders and the bottom contains just the player's name and team name, unless noted below. These photos are blankbacked and unnumbered. They look very similar to the 1962 7x9 set but feature a much wider white border around the photos as well as unique images.

COMPLETE SET (8) 75.00 125.00
1 Dick Bielski 6.00 12.00
2 Frank Clarke 7.50 15.00
3 Billy Howton 7.50 15.00
4 Eddie LeBaron 7.50 15.00
5 Bob Lilly 10.00 20.00
6 Amos Marsh 6.00 12.00
7 Don Meredith 20.00 35.00
8 Jerry Tubbs 6.00 12.00

1961-62 Cowboys Team Issue 5x6

These team issued photos feature black-and-white player portraits taken of just head-and-shoulders. Each measures approximately 5" by 6 1/2" and was printed on thin matte-finish paper stock with four white borders. The bottom border contains just the player's name and team name with both oriented near the outside edges of the player images. This style, very similar to the Jay Publishing issues of the period, would be used by the Cowboys well into the 1980s. The photos are blankbacked and unnumbered.

COMPLETE SET (6) 40.00 80.00
1 L.G. Dupre 6.00 12.00
2 Don Healy 6.00 12.00
3 Eddie LeBaron 7.50 15.00
4 Don McIlhenny 6.00 12.00
5 Don Meredith 18.00 30.00
6 Jerry Tubbs 6.00 12.00

1962 Cowboys Team Issue 7x9 Photo Pack

These team issued photos feature black-and-white player images taken of just head-and-shoulders. They were issued as set in "photo pack" style. Each measures approximately 7 1/2" by 9 1/2" and was printed on thin matte finish paper stock. They have four white borders and the bottom contains just the player's name and team name, unless noted below. These cards are blankbacked and unnumbered. They look very similar to the 1961 7x9 set but feature a much thinner white border around the photos.

COMPLETE SET (10) 75.00 150.00
1 Don Bishop 6.00 12.00
2 Frank Clarke 7.50 15.00
3 Mike Gaechter 6.00 12.00
4 Sonny Gibbs 6.00 12.00
5 Billy Howton 7.50 15.00
6 Eddie LeBaron 7.50 15.00
7 Amos Marsh 6.00 12.00
8 Don Meredith 20.00 35.00
9 Don Perkins 7.50 15.00
10 Jerry Tubbs 6.00 12.00

1962-63 Cowboys Team Issue Sepia

These photos were issued by the Cowboys most likely over the course of the 1962 and 1963 seasons. Each features a sepia-toned posed action photo, measures approximately 4 7/8" by 6 1/2" and was printed on thin paper stock. A wide border at the bottom contains the player's name, position spelled out, and team name. The photos are blankbacked and unnumbered. Any additions to the below list are appreciated.

COMPLETE SET (17) 125.00 250.00
1 Bob Bercich 7.50 15.00
2 Mike Connelly 7.50 15.00
3 L.G. Dupre 7.50 15.00
4 Sonny Gibbs 7.50 15.00
5 Don Healy 7.50 15.00
6 Bill Herchman 7.50 15.00
7 Eddie LeBaron 10.00 20.00
8 Bob Lilly 15.00 30.00
9 Don Meredith 25.00 40.00
10 Bobby Plummer 7.50 15.00
11 Guy Reese Action 7.50 15.00
12 Guy Reese Port 7.50 15.00
13 Ray Schoenke 7.50 15.00
14 Jim Ray Smith 7.50 15.00
15 Don Talbert 7.50 15.00
(college photo)
16 Jerry Tubbs 7.50 15.00
17 Team Photo 12.50 25.00

1963-64 Cowboys Team Issue 7x9

These team issued photos feature black-and-white player images taken of just head-and-shoulders. They may have been issued as a set in "photo pack" style but that has not been confirmed. Each measures approximately 7 1/2" by 9 1/2" and was printed on glossy stock. They have four white borders and the bottom contains the player's name, position initals, and team name. These cards are blankbacked and unnumbered. They look very similar to the 1962 7x9 set with the thinner white border but these also include the player's position on every photo. The Clarke and Tubbs photos are virtually identical to the 1962 issue except for this position addition.

1 Frank Clarke 7.50 15.00
2 Buddy Dial 6.00 12.00
3 Cornell Green 6.00 12.00
4 Lee Roy Jordan 7.50 15.00
5 Tommy McDonald 7.50 15.00
6 Don Perkins 7.50 15.00
7 Jerry Tubbs 6.00 12.00

1964-66 Cowboys Team Issue 5x7

These team issued photos feature black-and-white images with roughly the player's chest up to his head in view. The player's are wearing the new solid white or solid blue 1964 era Cowboys jersey unless noted below. Each photo measures approximately 5" by 7" and was printed on glossy photographic paper stock with four white borders unless noted below. The bottom border contains just the player's name and team name. These cards are blankbacked and unnumbered. Any additions to the below list are appreciated.

COMPLETE SET (31) 200.00 350.00
1 George Andrie 6.00 12.00
2 Don Bishop 6.00 12.00
3 Jim Boeke 6.00 12.00
4 Frank Clarke 7.50 15.00
5 Jim Colvin 6.00 12.00
6 Dick Daniels 6.00 12.00
7 Austin Denney 6.00 12.00
(wearing t-shirt)
8A Buddy Dial 7.50 15.00
8B Buddy Dial 7.50 15.00
8C Buddy Dial 7.50 15.00
9 Leon Donohue 6.00 12.00
10 Lee Folkins 6.00 12.00
11 Cornell Green 7.50 15.00
12 Bob Hayes 15.00 25.00
13 Harold Hays 6.00 12.00
14 Chuck Howley 7.50 15.00
15 Jake Kupp 6.00 12.00
16 Tom Landry CO 15.00 25.00
17 Obert Logan 6.00 12.00
18 Billy Lothridge 6.00 12.00
19 Don Meredith 20.00 35.00
20 Ralph Neely 6.00 12.00
21 Don Perkins 7.50 15.00
22 Dan Reeves 10.00 20.00
23 Mel Renfro 10.00 20.00
24 Jerry Rhome 6.00 12.00
25 Ray Schoenke 6.00 12.00
26 Jim Ray Smith 6.00 12.00
27 Willie Townes 6.00 12.00
28 Danny Villanueva 6.00 12.00
29 Malcolm Walker 6.00 12.00

1965 Cowboys Team Issue 5x6

This team-issued set features black-and-white head-to-foot posed action player photos with white borders. Each photo measures approximately 5 1/2" by 6 1/2" but the exact width is known to vary due to inconsistent cutting. The player's name and team name appear below the image. Most players appear in their white jersey, but a few have been found with the road blue as noted below. The photos were printed on thick card stock with a dull matte finish and have unnumbered blankbacks.

COMPLETE SET (43) 300.00 500.00
1 George Andrie 6.00 12.00
2 Don Bishop 6.00 12.00
3 Jim Boeke 6.00 12.00
4A Frank Clarke Blue 7.50 15.00
4B Frank Clarke Wht 7.50 15.00
5 Jim Colvin 6.00 12.00
6 Mike Connelly 6.00 12.00
7 Buddy Dial 7.50 15.00
8 Leon Donohue Blue 6.00 12.00
9 Perry Lee Dunn 6.00 12.00
10A Dave Edwards Blue 6.00 12.00
10B Dave Edwards Wht 6.00 12.00
11 Mike Gaechter 6.00 12.00
12 Pete Gent 6.00 12.00
13 Cornell Green 6.00 12.00
14 Bob Hayes 12.50 25.00
15 Harold Hays 6.00 12.00
16 Chuck Howley 10.00 20.00
17 Joe Bob Isbell 6.00 12.00
18 Mitch Johnson Blue 6.00 12.00
19 Lee Roy Jordan 10.00 20.00
20 Jake Kupp 6.00 12.00
21 Bob Lilly 12.50 25.00
22 Tony Liscio 6.00 12.00
23 Warren Livingston 6.00 12.00
24 Obert Logan Blue 6.00 12.00
25 Dave Manders 6.00 12.00
26A Don Meredith Blue 18.00 30.00
26B Don Meredith Wht 18.00 30.00
27 Craig Morton Blue 10.00 20.00
28 Ralph Neely Blue 6.00 12.00
29 Pettis Norman 6.00 12.00
30 Don Perkins 7.50 15.00
31 Jethro Pugh Blue 6.00 12.00
32 Dan Reeves Blue 10.00 20.00
33 Mel Renfro 10.00 20.00
34 Jerry Rhome Blue 6.00 12.00
35 Colin Ridgway Blue 6.00 12.00
36 J.D. Smith Blue 6.00 12.00
37 Larry Stephens 6.00 12.00
38 Jim Stiger 6.00 12.00
39 Don Talbert Blue 6.00 12.00
40 Jerry Tubbs 6.00 12.00
41 Danny Villanueva Blue 6.00 12.00
42 Russell Wayt Blue 6.00 12.00
43 Maury Youmans 6.00 12.00

1965-66 Cowboys Team Issue 5-1/4x7 Position

These team issued photos feature black-and-white images with roughly the player's chest up to his head in view. The player's are pictured wearing the solid white Cowboys jersey unless noted below. Each photo measures approximately 5 1/4" by 7" and was printed on matte-finish paper stock with four white borders. The bottom border contains the player's name, position intials, and team name in all caps. These photos are blankbacked and unnumbered. Any additions to the below list are appreciated.

1 Frank Clarke 7.50 15.00
2 Buddy Dial 6.00 12.00
3 Lee Roy Jordan 7.50 15.00
4 Bob Lilly 10.00 20.00
5 Ralph Neely 6.00 12.00
6 Pettis Norman 6.00 12.00
7 Don Perkins 7.50 15.00
8 Jerry Tubbs 6.00 12.00

1966-67 Cowboys Team Issue 5x7

These team issued photos feature black-and-white images, measure approximately 5" by 7" and were printed on matte-finish thin paper stock with four white borders. The bottom border contains the player's name, position spelled out, and team name in uppre and lower case letters - making these unique to most Cowboys issues of the era. These photos are blankbacked and unnumbered. Any additions to the below list are appreciated.

1 George Andrie 6.00 12.00
2 Frank Clarke 7.50 15.00
3 Pete Gent 6.00 12.00
4 Bob Hayes 10.00 20.00
5 Lee Roy Jordan 7.50 15.00
6 Bob Lilly 10.00 20.00
7 Dave Manders 6.00 12.00
8 Don Meredith 18.00 30.00
9 Mel Renfro 7.50 15.00

1966-67 Cowboys Team Issue 8x10

The Dallas Cowboys issued these black-and-white player photos printed on glossy photographic paper. Each measures 8" by 10" and was printed on glossy stock with white borders. Each player photo is a posed action shot head-to-foot and features the player in the blue jersey unless noted below. The border below the photo contains just the player's name and team name in all caps. The type style and size varies slightly on some photos so this may indicate that they were released over a period of years. The photos are blankbacked and unnumbered but can often be found with a photographer's imprint on the backs along with a date. Any additions to the below list are appreciated.

COMPLETE SET (33) 300.00 500.00
1 George Andrie Wht 7.50 15.00
2 Don Bishop 7.50 15.00
3 Phil Clark Wht 7.50 15.00
4 Frank Clarke Wht 10.00 20.00
5 Buddy Dial 7.50 15.00
6 Ron East Wht 7.50 15.00
7 Walt Garrison 7.50 15.00
8 Bob Hayes 15.00 30.00
9 Harold Hays 7.50 15.00
10 Chuck Howley 10.00 20.00
11 Mitch Johnson 7.50 15.00
12 Lee Roy Jordan 10.00 20.00
13 Jake Kupp 7.50 15.00
14 Bob Lilly 15.00 25.00
15 Don Meredith 25.00 40.00
16 Craig Morton Wht 10.00 20.00
17 Ralph Neely 7.50 15.00
18 John Niland 7.50 15.00
19 Pettis Norman 7.50 15.00
20 Brig Owens 7.50 15.00
21 Don Perkins 10.00 20.00
22 Jethro Pugh Wht 7.50 15.00
23 Dan Reeves 10.00 20.00
24 Mel Renfro 10.00 20.00
25A Jerry Rhome Blue 7.50 15.00
25B Jerry Rhome Wht 7.50 15.00
26 Ernie Stautner ACO 10.00 20.00
27 Don Talbert 7.50 15.00
28 Willie Townes 7.50 15.00
29 Malcolm Walker 7.50 15.00
30 A.D. Whitfield 7.50 15.00
31 John Wilbur 7.50 15.00
32 Rayfield Wright Wht 10.00 20.00
33 Maury Youmans 7.50 15.00

1968 Cowboys Team Issue 8x10

The Dallas Cowboys issued these black-and-white player photos printed on glossy photographic paper stock. Each measures 8" by 10" and was printed with four white borders with the player's image as a posed action shot. The border below the photo contains the player's name, his position initials, and team name. The type style and size varies slightly on some photos so this may indicate that they were released over a period of years. The photos are blankbacked and unnumbered. Any additions to the below list are appreciated.

1 Raymond Berry ACO 10.00 20.00
2 Larry Cole 7.50 15.00
3 Dennis Homan 7.50 15.00
4 Tom Landry CO 15.00 25.00
5 Obert Logan 7.50 15.00
6 David McDaniels 7.50 15.00
7 Blaine Nye 7.50 15.00
8 Ron Widby 7.50 15.00

1969 Cowboys Tasco Prints

Tasco Associates produced this set of small Dallas Cowboys posters. The fronts feature a color artist's rendering of the player along with the player's name and position. The backs are blank. The prints measure approximately 11 1/2" by 16."

1 Chuck Howley 12.50 25.00
2 Bob Lilly 15.00 30.00
3 Ralph Neely 10.00 20.00
5 Dan Reeves 12.50 25.00
6 Mel Renfro 12.50 25.00

1969 Cowboys Team Issue 5x6

These team-issued photos feature black-and-white posed action player photos with white borders. Each measures approximately 5" by 6 1/2" and are virtually identical in style to the 1970 and 1971 listings. We've noted specific differences below (identified by the poses) for players that appear in more than one of the sets. Many of these photos were issued for more than one year but we've cataloged them just one time within the set listing that seems to fit best in terms of the pose style and the years the players were on the roster. A wide white border at the bottom contains only the player's name and team name. These cards are printed on thin card stock, have blankbacks and are unnumbered.

COMPLETE SET (25) 150.00 300.00
1 George Andrie 6.00 12.00
2 Craig Baynham 6.00 12.00
3 Ron East 6.00 12.00
4 Walt Garrison 6.00 12.00
5 Pete Gent 6.00 12.00
6 Bob Hayes 12.50 25.00
7 Chuck Howley 7.50 15.00
8 Lee Roy Jordan 7.50 15.00
9 Bob Lilly 12.50 25.00
10 Tony Liscio 6.00 12.00
11 Dave Manders 6.00 12.00
12 Don Meredith 20.00 35.00
13 Craig Morton 7.50 15.00
14 Ralph Neely 6.00 12.00
15 John Niland 6.00 12.00
16 Pettis Norman 6.00 12.00
17 Don Perkins 7.50 15.00
18A Dan Reeves 10.00 20.00
18B Dan Reeves 10.00 20.00
19 Mel Renfro 7.50 15.00
20 Lance Rentzel 6.00 12.00
21A Roger Staubach 25.00 40.00
21B Roger Staubach 25.00 40.00
22 Malcolm Walker 6.00 12.00
23 Ron Widby 6.00 12.00
24 John Wilbur 6.00 12.00
25 Rayfield Wright 7.50 15.00
(wearing jersey #85)

1969-72 Cowboys Team Issue 5x7

These team-issued photos feature black-and-white player images with white borders on four sides, unless otherwise noted below. Each photo measures approximately 5" by 7" and was printed on glossy photographic paper stock. Each photo is a portrait showing the player wearing a white jersey with just half of his jersey number showing. A thick white border at the bottom contains only the player's name and team name except for a few that also include initials for the player's position. They were issued over a period of years and feature a variety of type styles and type sizes for the lettering within the bottom border. We've noted differences in the player The photos are blankbacked and unnumbered.

1 Margene Adkins 6.00 12.00
2 George Andrie 6.00 12.00
3 Bob Asher 6.00 12.00
4 Mike Clark 6.00 12.00
5 Phil Clark 6.00 12.00
6 Ralph Coleman 6.00 12.00
7 Mike Ditka 10.00 20.00
8 Ron East 6.00 12.00
9 John Fitzgerald 6.00 12.00
10 Richmond Flowers 6.00 12.00
11 Walt Garrison 7.50 15.00
12 Cornell Green 6.00 15.00
13 Halvor Hagen 6.00 12.00
14A Bob Hayes 10.00 20.00
14B Bob Hayes 10.00 20.00
15A Calvin Hill 7.50 15.00
15B Calvin Hill 7.50 15.00
16 Dennis Homan 6.00 12.00
17 Mike Johnson 6.00 12.00
18A Lee Roy Jordan 7.50 15.00
18B Lee Roy Jordan 7.50 15.00
19 Tom Landry CO 12.50 25.00
20 D.D. Lewis 6.00 12.00
21 Bob Lilly 12.50 25.00
22 Dave Manders 6.00 12.00
23A Craig Morton 7.50 15.00
23B Craig Morton 7.50 15.00
24A Ralph Neely 6.00 12.00
24B Ralph Neely 6.00 12.00
25A John Niland 6.00 12.00
25B John Niland 6.00 12.00
26 Pettis Norman 6.00 12.00
27 Blaine Nye 6.00 12.00
28 Billy Parks 6.00 12.00
29 Dan Reeves 7.50 15.00
30A Mel Renfro 7.50 15.00
30B Mel Renfro 7.50 15.00
31 Lance Rentzel 6.00 12.00
32 Reggie Rucker 6.00 12.00
33 Les Shy 6.00 12.00
34 Tody Smith 6.00 12.00
35A Roger Staubach 20.00 35.00
35B Roger Staubach 20.00 35.00
35C Roger Staubach 20.00 35.00
35D Roger Staubach 20.00 35.00
36 Ernie Stautner ACO 6.00 12.00
37 Tom Stincic 6.00 12.00
38 Bill Thomas 6.00 12.00
39 Duane Thomas 6.00 12.00
40 Isaac Thomas 6.00 12.00
41 Willie Townes 6.00 12.00
42 Mark Washington 6.00 12.00
43 Claxton Welch 6.00 12.00
44 Fred Whittingham 6.00 12.00
45 Ron Widby 6.00 12.00
46A Rayfield Wright 7.50 15.00
46B Rayfield Wright 7.50 15.00

1970 Cowboys Team Issue 5x6

These team-issued photos feature black-and-white posed action player photos with white borders. Each measures approximately 5" by 6 1/2" and are virtually identical in style to the 1969 and 1971 listings. We've noted specific differences below (identified by the poses) for players that appear in more than one of the sets. Many of these photos were issued for more than one year but we've cataloged them just one time within the set listing that seems to fit best in terms of the pose style and the years the players were on the roster. A wide white border at the bottom contains only the player's name and team name. These cards are printed on thin card stock, have blankbacks and are unnumbered.

COMPLETE SET (30) 200.00 350.00
1 Herb Adderley 7.50 15.00
2 Margene Adkins 6.00 12.00
3 George Andrie 6.00 12.00
4 Bob Asher 6.00 12.00
5 Mike Clark 6.00 12.00
6 Mike Ditka 6.00 12.00
7 Dave Edwards 6.00 12.00
8 Walt Garrison 6.00 12.00
9 Cornell Green 6.00 12.00
10 Cliff Harris 7.50 15.00
11 Bob Hayes 10.00 20.00
12 Calvin Hill 7.50 15.00
13 Chuck Howley 7.50 15.00
14 Lee Roy Jordan 7.50 15.00
15 D.D. Lewis 6.00 12.00
16 Bob Lilly 10.00 20.00
17 Craig Morton 7.50 15.00
18 Ralph Neely 6.00 12.00
19 John Niland 6.00 12.00
20 Blaine Nye 6.00 12.00
21 Jethro Pugh 6.00 12.00
22 Dan Reeves 7.50 15.00
23 Mel Renfro 10.00 20.00
24 Roger Staubach 25.00 40.00
25 Duane Thomas 6.00 12.00
26 Pat Toomay 6.00 12.00
27 Mark Washington 6.00 12.00
28 Claxton Welch 6.00 12.00
29 Ron Widby 6.00 12.00
30 Rayfield Wright 7.50 15.00
(wearing jersey #70)

1970 Cowboys Team Issue 8x10

The Dallas Cowboys issued these black-and-white player photos, measuring 8" by 10," and printed on glossy stock with white borders. Each player photo is a posed action shot. The border below the photo contains just the player's name and team name. The type style and size varies slightly on some photos so this may indicate that they were released over a period of years. The photos are blankbacked and unnumbered. Any additions to the below list are appreciated.

1 Ron East 7.50 15.00
2 Halvor Hagen 7.50 15.00
3 Calvin Hill 10.00 20.00
4 Bob Lilly 12.50 25.00
(left foot off of the ground)
5 Blaine Nye 7.50 15.00
6 Tom Stincic 7.50 15.00

1971 Cowboys Team Issue 5x6

These team-issued photos feature black-and-white posed action player photos with white borders. Each measures approximately 5" by 6 1/2" and are virtually identical in style to the 1969 and 1970 listings. We've noted specific differences below (identified by the poses) for players that appear in more than one of the sets. Many of these photos were issued for more than one year but we've cataloged them just one time within the set listing that seems to fit best in terms of the pose style and the years the players were on the roster. A wide white border at the bottom contains only the player's name and team name. These cards are printed on thin card stock, have blankbacks and are unnumbered.

COMPLETE SET (23) 150.00 300.00
1 Lance Alworth 7.50 15.00
2 George Andrie 6.00 12.00
(cutting right, right foot raised)
3 Larry Cole 6.00 12.00
4 Mike Ditka 10.00 20.00
(with mustache)
5 John Fitzgerald 6.00 12.00
6 Toni Fritsch 6.00 12.00
7 Forrest Gregg 7.50 15.00
8 Bill Gregory 6.00 12.00
9 Bob Hayes 7.50 15.00
(white jersey; football in hands)
10 Chuck Howley 7.50 15.00
(white jersey; right foot raised)
11 Lee Roy Jordan 7.50 15.00
(white jersey; no clouds in background)
12 Tom Landry CO 12.50 25.00
13 D.D. Lewis 6.00 12.00
(with mustache)
14 Dave Manders 6.00 12.00
(both feet on ground)
15 John Niland 6.00 12.00
(white jersey; running to his left)
16 Gloster Richardson 6.00 12.00
17 Tody Smith 6.00 12.00
18 Don Talbert 6.00 12.00
19 Isaac Thomas 6.00 12.00
20 Pat Toomay 6.00 12.00
(right foot raised)
21 Billy Truax 6.00 12.00
22 Rodney Wallace 6.00 12.00
23 Charlie Waters 6.00 12.00

1972 Cowboys Team Issue 4x5-1/2

These team issued photos feature black-and-white posed action player photos with white borders. Many of the photos are identical to the larger sized pictures from 1971, but this series measures approximately 4 1/4" by 5 1/2" and was likely issued over a period of years. Each features the player's facsimile autograph on the front with a white border at the bottom containing the player's name and team name. These cards are printed on thin card stock and have unnumbered blank backs. They closely resemble the 1975-76 Team Issue set so we've noted differences below on players common to both sets.

COMPLETE SET (43) 200.00 400.00
1 Herb Adderley 6.00 12.00
2 Lance Alworth 7.50 15.00
3 George Andrie 5.00 10.00
4 John Babinecz 5.00 10.00
5 Benny Barnes 5.00 10.00
6 Marv Bateman 5.00 10.00
7 Larry Cole 5.00 10.00
(cutting to his right)
8 Jack Concannon 5.00 10.00
9 Mike Ditka 7.50 15.00
10 Dave Edwards 5.00 10.00
11 John Fitzgerald 5.00 10.00
12 Toni Fritsch 5.00 10.00
13 Jean Fugett 5.00 10.00
14 Walt Garrison 5.00 10.00
15 Cornell Green 6.00 12.00
16 Bill Gregory 5.00 10.00
17 Cliff Harris 6.00 12.00
(no mustache)
18 Bob Hayes 7.50 15.00
19 Calvin Hill 6.00 12.00
20 Chuck Howley 6.00 12.00
21 Lee Roy Jordan 6.00 12.00
(left foot raised)
22 Mike Keller 5.00 10.00
23 Tom Landry CO 10.00 20.00
24 D.D. Lewis 5.00 10.00
(with mustache)
25 Bob Lilly 10.00 20.00
26 Dave Manders 5.00 10.00
27 Mike Montgomery 5.00 10.00
28 Craig Morton 6.00 12.00
29 Ralph Neely 5.00 10.00
30 Robert Newhouse 5.00 10.00
31 John Niland 5.00 10.00
32 Blaine Nye 5.00 10.00
33 Billy Parks 5.00 10.00
34 Jethro Pugh 5.00 10.00
(left foot raised)
35 Dan Reeves 6.00 12.00
36 Mel Renfro 6.00 12.00
(left foot raised)
37 Roger Staubach 15.00 30.00
(jersey #12 on shoulder)
38 Pat Toomay 5.00 10.00
39 Billy Truax 5.00 10.00
40 Rodney Wallace 5.00 10.00
41 Mark Washington 5.00 10.00
42 Charlie Waters 6.00 12.00
(left foot raised)
43 Rayfield Wright 6.00 12.00
(charging forward)

1973 Cowboys McDonald's

This set of photos was sponsored by McDonald's. Each photo measures approximately 8" by 10" and features a posed color close-up photo bordered in white. The player's name and team name are printed in black in the bottom white border. The top portion of the back has biographical information, career summary, and career statistics. The bottom portion carries the Cowboys 1973 game schedule. The photos are unnumbered and are checklisted below alphabetically.

COMPLETE SET (4) 45.00 90.00
1 Walt Garrison 5.00 10.00
2 Calvin Hill 7.50 15.00
3 Bob Lilly 12.50 25.00
4 Roger Staubach 25.00 50.00

1973 Cowboys Team Issue 4x5-1/2

These team issued photos feature black-and-white posed player photos with white borders. Each photo measures approximately 4 1/4" by 5 1/2" and features the player's name and team name below the player image. Every player is shown in his white jersey and the images were cropped to show no more than half of the jersey number. Some images were also used to create the 5x7-1/2 version. Each photo was printed on thin paper stock, has a blankback and was not numbered. We've listed all known subjects; any additions to this list are appreciated.

COMPLETE SET (15) 60.00 120.00
1 Jim Arneson 4.00 8.00
2 Rodrigo Barnes 4.00 8.00
3 Marv Bateman 4.00 8.00
4 Jack Concannon 4.00 8.00
5 Billy Joe Dupree 5.00 10.00
6 Harvey Martin 5.00 10.00
7 Robert Newhouse 4.00 8.00
8 Billy Parks 4.00 8.00
9 Drew Pearson 7.50 15.00
10 Cyril Pinder 4.00 8.00
11 Golden Richards 4.00 8.00
12 Larry Robinson 4.00 8.00
13 Otto Stowe 4.00 8.00
14 Les Strayhorn 4.00 8.00
15 Bruce Walton 4.00 8.00

1973 Cowboys Team Issue 5x7-1/2

These team-issued photos feature black-and-white player pictures with a blank back. Each measures approximately 5 1/8" by 7 1/2" and was printed on glossy stock. A thick (3/8") white border surrounds the photo with the player's name and team name below. They are nearly identical to our list for 1974-76 except for the slightly larger overall size and different player photos. The 1973 photos typically show the player waist up with his full jersey number in view while the 1974-76 photos were taken more close-up. Any additions to the below list are appreciated.

COMPLETE SET (24) 75.00 150.00
1 Jim Arneson 4.00 8.00
2 John Babinecz 4.00 8.00
3 Gil Brandt PD 4.00 8.00
4 Larry Cole 4.00 8.00
5 Billy Joe DuPree 5.00 10.00
6 Walt Garrison 4.00 8.00
7 Bob Hayes 6.00 12.00
8 Calvin Hill 5.00 10.00
9 Ed Hughes ACO 4.00 8.00
10 Lee Roy Jordan 5.00 10.00
11 Tom Landry CO 7.50 15.00
12 Dave Manders 4.00 8.00
13 Harvey Martin 5.00 10.00
14 Robert Newhouse 4.00 8.00
15 John Niland 4.00 8.00
16 Blaine Nye 4.00 8.00
17 Jethro Pugh 4.00 8.00
18 Mel Renfro 6.00 12.00
19 John Smith 4.00 8.00
20 Otto Stowe 4.00 8.00
21 Pat Toomay 4.00 8.00
22 Bruce Walton 4.00 8.00
23 Charlie Waters 5.00 10.00
24 Rayfield Wright 5.00 10.00

1974-76 Cowboys Team Issue 5x7

These team-issued photos feature black-and-white player pictures with a blank back. Each measures approximately 5" by 7" and was printed on glossy photo paper stock. A thick (3/8") white border surrounds the photo with the player's name and team name below. They closely resemble the 1973 set but are generally cropped more closely with only a partial jersey number showing versus the 1973 photos. These were likely issued over a number of years as many variations can be found in the photos, but the text size is very close to the same on all of the photos. Any additions to the below list are appreciated.

1 Jim Arneson 4.00 8.00
2A Benny Barnes 4.00 8.00
(slight smile)
2B Benny Barnes 4.00 8.00
(no smile)
3 Bob Breunig 4.00 8.00
4 Warren Capone 4.00 8.00
5A Larry Cole 4.00 8.00
(jersey number barely shows)
5B Larry Cole 4.00 8.00
(half of jersey number shows)
6 Kyle Davis 4.00 8.00
7A Doug Dennison 4.00 8.00
(Jersey # to the right)
7B Doug Dennison 4.00 8.00
(Jersey # to the left)
8 Mike Ditka ACO 6.00 12.00
9 Pat Donovan 4.00 8.00
10A Billy Joe DuPree 5.00 10.00
(slight smile)
10B Billy Joe DuPree 5.00 10.00
(no smile)
11A Dave Edwards 4.00 8.00
(jersey # barely shows)
11B Dave Edwards 4.00 8.00
(half of jersey # shows)
12A John Fitzgerald 4.00 8.00
(jersey # barely shows)
12B John Fitzgerald 4.00 8.00
(half of jersey # shows)
13 Toni Fritsch 4.00 8.00
14A Jean Fugett 4.00 8.00
(smiling)
14B Jean Fugett 4.00 8.00
(not smiling)
15A Walt Garrison 4.00 8.00
(facing straight)
15B Walt Garrison 4.00 8.00
(looking slightly to his left)
16A Cornell Green 4.00 8.00
(4 on shoulder visible)
16B Cornell Green 4.00 8.00
(4 on shoulder not visible)
17A Bill Gregory 4.00 8.00
(1/2 of jersey number shows)
17B Bill Gregory 4.00 8.00
(1/3 of jersey number shows)
18A Cliff Harris 5.00 10.00
18B Cliff Harris 5.00 10.00
19 Bob Hayes 6.00 12.00
20 Thomas Henderson 5.00 10.00
21 Efren Herrera 4.00 8.00
22 Calvin Hill 5.00 10.00
23 Mitch Hoopes 4.00 8.00
24 Bill Houston 4.00 8.00
25 Percy Howard 4.00 8.00
26A Ron Howard 4.00 8.00
(smiling)

26B Ron Howard 4.00 8.00
(not smiling)
27 Randy Hughes 4.00 8.00
28 Ken Hutcherson 4.00 8.00
29 Ed Too Tall Jones 5.00 10.00
30A Lee Roy Jordan 5.00 10.00
(half of jersey # shows)
30B Lee Roy Jordan 5.00 10.00
(3/4 of jersey # shows)
31 Gene Killian 4.00 8.00
32 Burton Lawless 4.00 8.00
33A D.D. Lewis 4.00 8.00
(no mustache)
33B D.D. Lewis 4.00 8.00
(with mustache)
34 Bob Lilly 7.50 15.00
35 Clint Longley 4.00 8.00
36 Dave Manders 4.00 8.00
37A Harvey Martin 5.00 10.00
37B Harvey Martin 5.00 10.00
38 Dennis Morgan 4.00 8.00
39A Ralph Neely 4.00 8.00
(facing slightly to his right)
39B Ralph Neely 4.00 8.00
(facing slightly to his left)
40A Robert Newhouse 5.00 10.00
(half of jersey # shows)
40B Robert Newhouse 5.00 10.00
(jersey # not visible)
41A Blaine Nye/(smiling) 4.00 8.00
41B Blaine Nye/(slight smile) 4.00 8.00
42 Drew Pearson 6.00 12.00
43A Cal Peterson 4.00 8.00
(name listed Calvin)
43B Cal Peterson 4.00 8.00
(name listed Cal)
44A Jethro Pugh 4.00 8.00
44B Jethro Pugh 4.00 8.00
45 Dan Reeves ACO 5.00 10.00
46A Mel Renfro 5.00 10.00
46B Mel Renfro 5.00 10.00
47A Golden Richards 4.00 8.00
(looking to his right)
47B Golden Richards 4.00 8.00
(facing straight)
48 Herb Scott 4.00 8.00
49 Ron Sellers 4.00 8.00
50A Roger Staubach 12.50 25.00
50B Roger Staubach 12.50 25.00
51 Les Strayhorn 4.00 8.00
52 Pat Toomay 4.00 8.00
53 Louie Walker 4.00 8.00
54A Bruce Walton 4.00 8.00
(half jersey # visible)
54B Bruce Walton 4.00 8.00
(full jersey # visible)
55A Mark Washington 4.00 8.00
(not smiling)
55B Mark Washington 4.00 8.00
(smiling)
56A Charlie Waters 5.00 10.00
(no shoulder #'s visible)
56B Charlie Waters 5.00 10.00
(1 on shoulder visible)
57 Randy White 7.50 15.00
58 Rollie Woolsey 4.00 8.00
59 Rayfield Wright 5.00 10.00
60A Charlie Young 4.00 8.00
(half jersey # shows)
60B Charlie Young 4.00 8.00
(jersey # shows slightly)

1975-76 Cowboys Team Issue 4x5-1/2

This team issued photo set features black-and-white posed action player photos with white borders. Each photo measures approximately 4 1/2" by 5 1/2" and features a facsimile autograph on the front unless noted below. A wider (1/2") white border at the bottom contains the player's name and team. These cards are printed on thin card stock and have unnumbered blank backs. They closely resemble the 1972 Team Issue set so we've noted differences below on players common to both sets.

COMPLETE SET (28) 100.00 200.00
1 Benny Barnes 4.00 8.00
(no facsimile)
2 Bob Breunig 4.00 8.00
3 Larry Cole 4.00 8.00
(charging forward)
4 Kyle Davis 4.00 8.00
5 Pat Donovan 4.00 8.00
6 Cliff Harris 5.00 10.00
(with mustache; no facsimile)
7 Thomas Henderson 5.00 10.00
8 Efren Herrera 4.00 8.00
9 Mitch Hoopes 4.00 8.00
10 Ed Too Tall Jones 5.00 10.00
11 Lee Roy Jordan 5.00 10.00
(right foot raised)
12 Scott Laidlaw 4.00 8.00
13 Burton Lawless 4.00 8.00
14 D.D. Lewis 4.00 8.00
(no mustache)
15 Clint Longley 4.00 8.00
16 Harvey Martin 5.00 10.00
(no facsimile)
17 Robert Newhouse 4.00 8.00
(no facsimile)
18 Drew Pearson 5.00 10.00
(no facsimile)
19 Preston Pearson 5.00 10.00
20 Jethro Pugh 4.00 8.00
(right foot raised)
21 Mel Renfro 6.00 12.00
(right foot raised)
22 Golden Richards 4.00 8.00
23 Herb Scott 4.00 8.00
24 Roger Staubach 10.00 20.00
(no jersey number on shoulder)
25 Charlie Waters 4.00 8.00
(right foot raised)
26 Randy White 7.50 15.00
27 Rayfield Wright 5.00 10.00
(cutting to his left)
28 Charles Young 4.00 8.00

1976-78 Cowboys Team Issue 8x10

These photos were released by the Cowboys for player appearances and fan mail requests from roughly 1976-78. Each measures approximately 8" by 10" and fetures a black and white player photo. The player's name and team name appear immediately below the photo with slightly different font size and style used on the text for some of the photos. Many players were issued in more than one pose with some featuring only slight differences. Each is unnumbered and checklisted below alphabetically.

1A Bob Breunig 5.00 10.00
1B Bob Breunig 5.00 10.00
1C Bob Breunig 5.00 10.00
1D Bob Breunig 5.00 10.00
2 Glenn Carano 5.00 10.00
3 Larry Cole 5.00 10.00
(left foot off of the ground)
4 Jim Cooper 5.00 10.00
5A Doug Dennison 5.00 10.00
5B Doug Dennison 5.00 10.00
6 Pat Donovan 5.00 10.00
7 Tony Dorsett 10.00 20.00
8 Billy Joe DuPree 5.00 10.00
9 Jim Eidson 5.00 10.00
10 John Fitzgerald 5.00 10.00
11A Bill Gregory 5.00 10.00
11B Bill Gregory 5.00 10.00
12A Cliff Harris 6.00 12.00
12B Cliff Harris 6.00 12.00
12C Cliff Harris 6.00 12.00
13 Mike Hegman 5.00 10.00
14A Thomas Henderson 6.00 12.00
14B Thomas Henderson 6.00 12.00
14C Thomas Henderson 6.00 12.00
15A Efren Herrera 5.00 10.00
15B Efren Herrera 5.00 10.00
16A Tony Hill 6.00 12.00
16B Tony Hill 6.00 12.00
17 Randy Hughes 5.00 10.00
18A Bruce Huther 5.00 10.00
18B Bruce Huther 5.00 10.00
19 Jim Jensen 5.00 10.00
20A Butch Johnson 5.00 10.00
20B Butch Johnson 5.00 10.00
21A Ed Too Tall Jones 6.00 12.00
21B Ed Too Tall Jones 6.00 12.00
21C Ed Too Tall Jones 6.00 12.00
21D Ed Too Tall Jones 6.00 12.00
22 Lee Roy Jordan 6.00 12.00
23A Aaron Kyle 5.00 10.00
23B Aaron Kyle 5.00 10.00
24 Scott Laidlaw 5.00 10.00
25 Burton Lawless 5.00 10.00
26A D.D. Lewis 5.00 10.00
26B D.D. Lewis 5.00 10.00
27A Harvey Martin 6.00 12.00
27B Harvey Martin 5.00 10.00
28A Ralph Neely 5.00 10.00
28B Ralph Neely 5.00 10.00
29A Robert Newhouse 5.00 10.00
29B Robert Newhouse 5.00 10.00
30 Blaine Nye 5.00 10.00
31A Drew Pearson 6.00 12.00
31B Drew Pearson 6.00 12.00
31C Drew Pearson 6.00 12.00
32A Preston Pearson 6.00 12.00
32B Preston Pearson 6.00 12.00
33A Jethro Pugh 5.00 10.00
33B Jethro Pugh 5.00 10.00
33C Jethro Pugh 5.00 10.00
34 Tom Rafferty 5.00 10.00
35 Tom Randall 5.00 10.00
36A Mel Renfro 7.50 15.00
36B Mel Renfro 7.50 15.00
37A Golden Richards 5.00 10.00
37B Golden Richards 5.00 10.00
38 Jay Saldi 5.00 10.00
39 Rafael Septien 5.00 10.00
40A Roger Staubach 10.00 20.00
40B Roger Staubach 10.00 20.00
41A Mark Washington 5.00 10.00
41B Mark Washington 5.00 10.00
42A Charlie Waters 6.00 12.00
42B Charlie Waters 6.00 12.00
43A Randy White 10.00 20.00
43B Randy White 10.00 20.00
44 Rayfield Wright 6.00 12.00
45 Charlie Young 5.00 10.00

1977 Cowboys Burger King Glasses

Burger King restaurants in conjunction with Dr. Pepper released this set of 6-drinking glasses during the 1977 NFL season in Dallas area stores. Each features a black and white photo of a Cowboys player with his name and team name below the picture. This set can be differentiated from the 1978 Burger King due to the row of stars that encircle the glass, as well as the different player selection.

COMPLETE SET (6) 25.00 50.00
1 Billy Joe DuPree 5.00 10.00
2 Efren Herrera 3.75 7.50
3 Harvey Martin 6.00 12.00
4 Drew Pearson 6.00 12.00
5 Charlie Waters 5.00 10.00
6 Randy White 7.50 15.00

1978 Cowboys Burger King Glasses

Burger King restaurants in conjunction with Dr. Pepper released this set of 6-drinking glasses during the 1978 NFL season in Dallas area stores. Each features a black and white photo of a Cowboys player with his name and team name below the picture.

COMPLETE SET (6) 20.00 40.00
1 Bob Breunig 3.00 6.00
2 Pat Donovan 3.00 6.00
3 Cliff Harris 4.00 8.00
4 D.D. Lewis 4.00 8.00
5 Robert Newhouse 4.00 8.00
6 Golden Richards 3.00 6.00

1978 Cowboys Team Sheets

These 8" by 10" sheets were issued primarily to media outlets in need of player photos. Each sheet includes small photos for 8-players (except for the final sheet) with the player's name and position below each image. The "Dallas Cowboys" name is at the top of each sheet. The backs are blank

COMPLETE SET (6) 40.00 80.00
1 Sheet 1 5.00 10.00
2 Sheet 2 10.00 20.00
3 Sheet 3 6.00 12.00
4 Sheet 4 6.00 12.00
5 Sheet 5 12.50 25.00
6 Sheet 6 7.50 15.00

1979 Cowboys Police

The 1979 Dallas Cowboy Police set consists of 15 cards sponsored by the Kiwanis Clubs, the Dallas Cowboys Weekly (the official fan newspaper), and the local law enforcement agency. The cards measure approximately 2 5/8" by 4 1/8". The cards are unnumbered but have been numbered in the checklist below by the player's uniform number which appears on the fronts of the cards. The backs contain "Cowboys Tips" which draw analogies between action on the football field and law abiding action in real life. D.D. Lewis replaced Thomas (Hollywood) Henderson midway through the season; hence, both of these cards are available in lesser quantities than the other cards in this set.

COMPLETE SET (15) 10.00 20.00
12 Roger Staubach 4.00 8.00
33 Tony Dorsett 2.50 5.00
41 Charlie Waters .50 1.00
43 Cliff Harris .50 1.00
44 Robert Newhouse .25 .50
50 D.D. Lewis SP 1.50 3.00
53 Bob Breunig .25 .50
54 Randy White 1.25 2.50
56 Thomas Henderson SP 1.50 3.00
67 Pat Donovan .25 .50
79 Harvey Martin .50 1.00
80 Tony Hill .50 1.00
88 Drew Pearson .60 1.50
89 Billy Joe DuPree .50 1.00
NNO Tom Landry CO 2.00 4.00

1979 Cowboys Team Issue Bios

These photos were released by the Cowboys for player appearances and fan mail requests. This style and format was used for a number of years (from roughly 1979-1985) so we've included descriptions below to differentiate players released in more than one year. Each measures approximately 4" by 5 1/2" and was printed on thick paper stock. The white-bordered fronts display black-and-white player photos. The player's name and jersey number appear immediately below the photo with his position, height, weight, and college below that. The Cowboys helmet logo on included on the left. The backs are blank are unnumbered.

COMPLETE SET (53) 250.00 400.00
1 Benny Barnes 4.00 8.00
2 Larry Bethea 4.00 8.00
3 Alois Blackwell 4.00 8.00
4 Bob Breunig 4.00 8.00
(running to his left)
6 Guy Brown 4.00 8.00
7 Glenn Carano 4.00 8.00
(right foot raised)
8 Larry Cole 4.00 8.00
8 Jim Cooper 4.00 8.00
(no mustache; offensive tackle)
10 Doug Cosbie 4.00 8.00
(football in hands)
11 Anthony Dickerson 4.00 8.00
(left leg straight)
12 Pat Donovan 4.00 8.00
(jersey #7 obscured)
13 Tony Dorsett 7.50 15.00
(football in right hand)
14 Billy Joe Dupree 5.00 10.00
15 John Dutton 4.00 8.00
(cutting to his left slightly)
16 John Fitzgerald 4.00 8.00
(snapping the ball)
17 Andy Frederick 4.00 8.00
18 Richard Grimmett 4.00 8.00
19 Cliff Harris 5.00 10.00
20 Mike Hegman 4.00 8.00
(left hand at left shoulder)
21 Thomas Henderson 5.00 10.00
22 Tony Hill 5.00 10.00
(football up by shoulder)
23 Randy Hughes 4.00 8.00
24 Bruce Huther 4.00 8.00
25 Butch Johnson 4.00 8.00
(football up near head)
26 Ed Too Tall Jones 5.00 10.00
(cutting to his right)
29 Tom Landry CO 6.00 12.00
(star next to helmet logo)
31 D.D. Lewis 4.00 8.00
33 Harvey Martin 5.00 10.00
(jersey #7 partially obscured)
34 Aaron Mitchell 4.00 8.00
35 Robert Newhouse 5.00 10.00
(football in left arm)
36 Drew Pearson 6.00 12.00
(jersey #8 obscured; weight:183)
37 Preston Pearson 5.00 10.00
38 Tom Rafferty 4.00 8.00
39 Jay Saldi 4.00 8.00
40 Tex Schramm GM 5.00 10.00
41 Herb Scott 4.00 8.00
42 Rafael Septien 4.00 8.00
(right foot at left knee)
43 Robert Shaw 4.00 8.00
44 Ron Springs 4.00 8.00
(right foot at left knee)
45 Dave Stalls 4.00 8.00
46 Roger Staubach 15.00 25.00
47 Bruce Thornton 4.00 8.00
48 Dennis Thurman 4.00 8.00
(left leg raised)
49 Charlie Waters 5.00 10.00
50 Danny White 6.00 12.00
(feet planted)
51 Randy White 7.50 15.00
(running to his right)
52 Steve Wilson 4.00 8.00
(wearing jersey #81)

1979 Cowboys Team Sheets

These 8" by 10" sheets were issued primarily to media outlets in need of player photos. Each sheet includes small photos for 8-players with the player's jersey number, name and position below each image. The "Dallas Cowboys" name is at the top of each sheet. The backs are blank

COMPLETE SET (6) 40.00 80.00
1 Larry Bethea 5.00 10.00
Benny Barnes
Alois Blackwell
Bob Breunig
Larry Brinson
Guy Brown
Glenn Carano
Larry Cole
2 Jim Cooper 7.50 15.00
Doug Cosbie
Pat Donovan
Tony Dorsett
Billy Joe Dupree
John Fitzgerald
Andy Frederick
Richard Grimmett
3 Cliff Harris 5.00 10.00
Mike Hegman
Thomas Henderson
Tony Hill
Randy Hughes
Bruce Huther
Butch Johnson
Aaron Kyle
4 Scott Laidlaw 6.00 12.00
Burton Lawless
D.D. Lewis
Wade Manning
Harvey Martin
Aaron Mitchell
Robert Newhouse
Drew Pearson
5 Preston Pearson 5.00 10.00
Tom Rafferty
Jay Saldi
Herb Scott
Rafael Septien
Robert Shaw
Ron Springs
Dave Stalls
6 Roger Staubach 12.50 25.00
Bruce Thornton
Dennis Thurman
Charlie Waters
Danny White
Randy White
Steve Wilson
Rayfield Wright

1979-80 Cowboys Team Issue 4x5-1/2

These team issued photos feature black-and-white posed action player photos with white borders. Each photo measures approximately 4 1/4" by 5 1/2" and features the player's name and team name below the player image. Every player is shown in his white jersey and each photo was printed on thin paper matte-finish stock, has a blankback and was not numbered. We've listed all known subjects; any additions to this list are appreciated.

1 Tony Dorsett 6.00 12.00
2 Billy Joe DuPree 4.00 8.00
3 James Jones 4.00 8.00
4 D.D. Lewis 4.00 8.00
5 Drew Pearson 5.00 10.00
6 Roger Staubach 10.00 20.00
7 Danny White 6.00 12.00
8 Randy White 6.00 12.00

1980 Cowboys McDonald's

These cards were issued two per box on three different Happy Meal type boxes numbered "Super Box I" through "Super Box III." The individual cards, meant to be cut from the boxes, are unnumbered and blankbacked. We've listed prices for single cards, neatly cut from the box, below alphabetically according to the box on which the player appears. Complete Happy Meal Boxes carry a premium of 1.5X to 2X the prices listed below.

COMPLETE SET (6) 125.00 200.00
1 Chuck Howley 10.00 25.00
2 Don Perkins 10.00 25.00
3 Bob Lilly 12.00 30.00
4 Don Meredith 15.00 40.00
5 Walt Garrison 8.00 20.00
6 Roger Staubach 50.00 100.00

1980 Cowboys Police

Quite similar to the 1979 set, the 1980 Dallas Cowboys police set is unnumbered other than the player's uniform number (as is listed in the checklist below). The cards in this 14-card set measure approximately 2 5/8" by 4 1/8". The sponsors are the same as those of the 1979 issue and the section entitled "Cowboys Tips" is contained on the back. The Kiwanis and Cowboys helmet logos appear on the fronts of the cards.

COMPLETE SET (14) 6.00 12.00
1 Rafael Septien .40 1.00
11 Danny White 1.00 2.50
25 Aaron Kyle .25 .60
26 Preston Pearson .60 1.50
31 Benny Barnes .40 1.00
35 Scott Laidlaw .25 .60
42 Randy Hughes .25 .60
62 John Fitzgerald .40 1.00
63 Larry Cole .40 1.00
64 Tom Rafferty .40 1.00
68 Herb Scott .25 .60
70 Rayfield Wright .40 1.00
78 John Dutton .40 1.00
87 Jay Saldi .40 1.00

1980 Cowboys Team Issue

These photos were released by the Cowboys for player appearances and fan mail requests. This style and format was used for a number of years (from roughly 1979-1985) so we've included descriptions below to differentiate players released in more than one year. Each measures approximately 4" by 5 1/2" and was printed on thick paper stock. The white-bordered fronts display black-and-white player photos. The player's name and jersey number appear immediately below the photo with his position, height, weight, and college below that. The Cowboys helmet logo on included on the left. The backs are blank are unnumbered.

COMPLETE SET (27) 100.00 200.00
1 Bob Breunig 3.00 8.00
2 Glenn Carano 3.00 8.00
3 Dextor Clinkscale 3.00 8.00
4 Jim Cooper 3.00 8.00
5 Doug Cosbie 3.00 8.00
6 Anthony Dickerson 3.00 8.00
7 Pat Donovan 3.00 8.00
8 Tony Dorsett 6.00 15.00
9 John Dutton 3.00 8.00
12 Tony Hill 4.00 10.00
10 John Fitzgerald 3.00 8.00
(charging forward)
11 Mike Hegman 3.00 8.00
(left hand on jersey #5)
13 Gary Hogeboom 3.00 8.00
14 Butch Johnson 3.00 8.00
16 James Jones 3.00 8.00
15 Ed Too Tall Jones 4.00 10.00
17 Tom Landry CO 5.00 12.00
18 Harvey Martin 4.00 10.00
19 Robert Newhouse 3.00 8.00
20 Timmy Newsome 3.00 8.00
21 Drew Pearson 4.00 10.00
22 Kurt Petersen 3.00 8.00
23 Bill Roe 3.00 8.00
24 Rafael Septien 3.00 8.00
25 Roland Solomon 3.00 8.00
26 Ron Springs 3.00 8.00
27 Dennis Thurman 3.00 8.00
28 Norm Wells 3.00 8.00
29 Danny White 5.00 12.00
30 Randy White 6.00 15.00
31 Steve Wilson 3.00 8.00
(wearing jersey #45)

1980 Cowboys Team Sheets

These 8" by 10" sheets were issued primarily to media outlets in need of player photos. Each sheet includes small photos for 8-players with the player's jersey number, name and position below each image. "The Dallas Cowboys Football Club" is printed at the top of each sheet and the backs are blank

COMPLETE SET (7) 40.00 80.00
1 Benny Barnes 4.00 10.00
Larry Bethea
Bob Breunig
Guy Brown
Glenn Carano
Dextor Clinkscale
Larry Cole
Jim Cooper
2 Doug Cosbie 6.00 15.00
Anthony Dickerson
Pat Donovan
Tony Dorsett
Billy Joe Dupree
John Dutton
John Fitzgerald
Andy Frederick
3 Mike Hegman 5.00 12.00
Tony Hill
Gary Hogeboom
Randy Hughes
Eric Hurt
Bruce Huther
Butch Johnson
Ed Jones
4 James Jones 5.00 12.00
Aaron Kyle
D.D. Lewis
Harvey Martin
Aaron Mitchell
Robert Newhouse
Timmy Newsome
Drew Pearson
5 Preston Pearson 4.00 10.00
Kurt Petersen
Tom Rafferty
Bill Roe
Jay Saldi
Herb Scott
Rafael Septien
Robert Shaw
6 Roland Soloman 6.00 15.00
Ron Springs
Bruce Thornton
Dennis Thurman
Charlie Waters
Norm Wells
Danny White
Randy White
Steve Wilson
7 Coaching Staff 6.00 15.00
Tom Landry
Ermal Allen
Mike Ditka
Al Lavan
Jim Myers
Dan Reeves
Gene Stallings
Ernie Stautner
Jerry Tubbs
Bob Ward

1981 Cowboys Police

The 1981 Dallas Cowboys set of 14 cards is quite similar to oots of the previous two years. Since the cards are unnumbered, except for uniform number, the players have been listed by uniform number in the checklist below. The cards measure approximately 2 5/8" by 4 1/8". The set is sponsored by the Kiwanis Club, the local law enforcement agency, and the Dallas Cowboys Weekly. Appearing on the back along with a Cowboys helmet logo are "Cowboys Tips". A Kiwanis logo and Cowboys helmet logo appear on the front.

COMPLETE SET (14) 5.00 12.00
18 Glenn Carano .40 1.00
20 Ron Springs .40 1.00
23 James Jones COW .25 .60
26 Michael Downs .40 1.00
32 Dennis Thurman .40 1.00
45 Steve Wilson DB .25 .60
51 Anthony Dickerson .25 .60
52 Robert Shaw .25 .60
58 Mike Hegman .40 1.00
59 Guy Brown .25 .60
61 Jim Cooper .25 .60
72 Ed Too Tall Jones 1.00 2.50
84 Doug Cosbie .50 1.25
86 Butch Johnson .50 1.25

1981 Cowboys Thousand Oaks Police

This 14-card set was issued in Thousand Oaks, California, where the Cowboys conduct their summer pre-season workouts. These unnumbered cards measure approximately 2 5/8" by 4 1/8". Similar to other Cowboys sets, the distinguishing factors of this set are the Thousand Oaks Kiwanis Club and Thousand Oaks Police Department names printed on the backs in the place where other sets had the Kiwanis Club and law enforcement agency printed. The 14 players in this set are different from those in the regular set above. The cards are listed below by uniform number.

COMPLETE SET (14) 20.00 50.00
11 Danny White 1.25 3.00
31 Benny Barnes .60 1.50
33 Tony Dorsett 4.00 10.00
41 Charlie Waters 1.25 3.00
42 Randy Hughes .60 1.50
44 Robert Newhouse 1.00 2.50
54 Randy White 2.50 6.00
55 D.D. Lewis .60 1.50
78 John Dutton .60 1.50
79 Harvey Martin 1.00 2.50
80 Tony Hill 1.00 2.50
88 Drew Pearson 2.00 5.00
89 Billy Joe DuPree 1.00 2.50
NNO Tom Landry CO 3.00 8.00

1982 Cowboys Carrollton Park

The 1982 Carrollton Park Mall Cowboys set contains six photo cards in black and white with the words "Carrollton Park Mall" in blue at the bottom of the card front. The cards measure approximately 3" by 4". The backs contain the 1982 Cowboys schedule and brief career statistics of the player portrayed. The cards are numbered on the back and the set is available as an uncut sheet with no difference in value.

COMPLETE SET (6) 3.00 8.00
1 Roger Staubach 1.25 3.00
2 Danny White .30 .75
3 Tony Dorsett .60 1.50
4 Randy White .40 1.00
5 Charlie Waters .20 .50
6 Billy Joe DuPree .20 .50

1983 Cowboys Marketcom

In 1983 Marketcom issued a separate team set for the Cowboys. These 5 1/2" by 8 1/2" cards feature a large full color picture of each player with a white border. Similar to the 1982 regular 48-card issue, the Cowboys cards have the player's name on front at top and a facsimile autograph on the picture. The cards are unnumbered and the cardbacks carry biographical information, player profile, and statistics. The lower right corner of the card back indicates "St. Louis - Marketcom."

COMPLETE SET (10) 35.00 60.00
1 Bob Breunig 2.00 5.00
2 Pat Donovan 2.00 5.00
3 Tony Dorsett 8.00 20.00
4 Michael Downs 2.00 5.00
5 Butch Johnson 2.00 5.00
6 Harvey Martin 2.50 6.00
7 Timmy Newsome 2.00 5.00
8 Drew Pearson 3.00 8.00
9 Danny White 3.00 8.00
10 Randy White 4.00 10.00

1983 Cowboys Police

This unnumbered set of 28 cards was sponsored by the Kiwannis Club, Law Enforcement Agency, and the Dallas Cowboys Weekly. Cards are approximately 2 5/8" by 4 1/8" and have a white border around the photo on the front of the cards. The backs each contain a safety tip. Cards are listed in the checklist below in uniform number order. Four cheerleaders are included in the set and are so indicated by CHEER.

COMPLETE SET (28) 6.00 15.00
1 Rafael Septien .20 .50
11 Danny White .40 1.00
20 Ron Springs .20 .50
24 Everson Walls .20 .50
26 Michael Downs .12 .30
30 Timmy Newsome .12 .30
32 Dennis Thurman .20 .50
33 Tony Dorsett 1.00 2.50
47 Dextor Clinkscale .12 .30
53 Bob Breunig .20 .50
54 Randy White .75 2.00
65 Kurt Petersen .12 .30
67 Pat Donovan .12 .30
70 Howard Richards .12 .30
72 Ed Too Tall Jones .60 1.50
78 John Dutton .20 .50
79 Harvey Martin .20 .50
80 Tony Hill .20 .50
83 Doug Donley .12 .30
84 Doug Cosbie .20 .50
86 Butch Johnson .20 .50
88 Drew Pearson .60 1.50
89 Billy Joe DuPree .20 .50
NNO Tom Landry CO .75 2.00
NNO Melinda May CHEER .12 .30
NNO Dana Presley CHEER .12 .30
NNO Judy Trammell CHEER .12 .30
NNO Toni Washington CHEER .12 .30

1983-84 Cowboys Team Issue

These photos were released by the Cowboys for player appearances and fan mail requests. This style and format was used for a number of years (from roughly 1979-1985) so we've included descriptions below to differentiate players released in more than one year. Each measures approximately 4" by 5 1/2" and was printed on thick paper stock. The white-bordered fronts display black-and-white player photos. The player's name and jersey number appear immediately below the photo with his position, height, weight, and college below that. The Cowboys helmet logo on included on the left. The backs are blank are unnumbered.

COMPLETE SET (34) 100.00 200.00
1 Brian Baldinger 3.00 6.00
2 Bill Bates 4.00 8.00
3 Bob Breunig 3.00 6.00
(running to his right; weight: 227)
4 Dextor Clinkscale 3.00 6.00
(jersey #'s visible)
5 Fred Cornwell 3.00 6.00
6 Doug Cosbie 3.00 6.00
(football in air; left hand over jersey #8)
7 Anthony Dickerson 3.00 6.00
8A Doug Donley 3.00 6.00
(left hand down at waist)
8B Doug Donley 3.00 6.00
(left hand up at neck)
9A Tony Dorsett 6.00 12.00
(ball in left hand; right knee up at waist)
9B Tony Dorsett 6.00 12.00
(ball in right hand; cutting to his right)
10A Michael Downs 3.00 6.00
(right arm down by side)
10B Michael Downs 3.00 6.00
(right arm fully extended)
11 Ron Fellows 3.00 6.00
12 Rod Hill 3.00 6.00
13 Gary Hogeboom 3.00 6.00
14 Jim Jeffcoat 3.00 6.00
15 Ed Jones 4.00 8.00
16 Eugene Lockhart 3.00 6.00
17 Harvey Martin 4.00 8.00
(jersey #7 fully visible; weight: 255)
18 Timmy Newsome 3.00 6.00
(feet far apart)
19 Drew Pearson 4.00 8.00
(jersey #8 fully visible; Weight: 190)
20 Kurt Petersen 3.00 6.00
(clear sky in background)
21 Phil Pozderac 3.00 6.00
22 Mike Renfro 3.00 6.00
23 Howard Richards 3.00 6.00
24 Jeff Rohrer 3.00 6.00
25 Chris Schultz 3.00 6.00
26 Rafael Septien 3.00 6.00
(right foot waist high; left heel on ground)
27A Don Smerek 3.00 6.00
(charging forward)
27B Don Smerek 3.00 6.00
(cutting to his left slightly)
28 Danny Spradlin 3.00 6.00
29 Ron Springs 3.00 6.00
(wrist bands on elbows)
30 Mark Tuinei 4.00 8.00
31A Everson Walls 4.00 8.00
(jersey #'s half visible)
31B Everson Walls 4.00 8.00
(jersey #'s obscured)
32 John Warren 3.00 6.00
33 Danny White 5.00 10.00
(dropping back; jersey #'s hidden)
34 Randy White 5.00 10.00

1984 Cowboys Team Sheets

These 8" by 10" sheets were issued primarily to the media for use as player images for print. Each features 8-players or coaches with the player's jersey number, name, and position beneath his picture. The sheets are blankbacked and unnumbered.

COMPLETE SET (8) 20.00 50.00
1 Vince Albritton 2.50 6.00
Gary Allen
Dowe Aughtman
Brian
2 Dextor Clinkscale 3.00 8.00
Jim Cooper
Fred Cornwell
Doug
3 Michael Downs 2.00 5.00
John Dutton
Ron Fellows
Norm Gran
4 John Hunt 2.50 6.00
Jim Jeffcoat
Ed Too Tall Jones
Eugene
5 Kirk Phillips 2.00 5.00
Phil Pozderac
Tom Rafferty
Mike R
6 Victor Scott 2.00 5.00
Rafael Septien
Dom Smerek
Waddell
7 Everson Walls 4.00 10.00
Danny White
Randy White
Tom Landr
8 Dick Nolan 2.00 5.00
Jim Shofner
Gene Stallings
Ernie Sta

1985-86 Cowboys Frito Lay

The Cowboys Frito Lay photos were issued over a number of years in the mid 1980s. The cards measure approximately 4" by 5 1/2" and are printed on photographic quality paper stock. The white-bordered fronts display black-and-white player photos with the Cowboys helmet logo below the image in the lower left corner. The player's jersey number and name appear below the photo with his position, vital stats and college noted below that. The Frito Lay logo in the lower right corner rounds out the front. The backs are blank and unnumbered. Roger Staubach is included in the set even though he retired in 1979.

COMPLETE SET (53) 200.00 400.00
1 Vince Albritton 4.00 8.00
2 Brian Baldinger 4.00 8.00
3 Gordon Banks 4.00 8.00
4A Bill Bates 5.00 10.00
5 Dextor Clinkscale 4.00 8.00
6 Reggie Collier 4.00 8.00
7 Jim Cooper 4.00 8.00
8 Fred Cornwell 4.00 8.00
9 Doug Cosbie 4.00 8.00
10 Steve DeOssie 4.00 8.00
11A Tony Dorsett 10.00 20.00
12 Michael Downs 4.00 8.00
13 John Dutton 4.00 8.00
14 Ricky Easmon 4.00 8.00
15 Ron Fellows 4.00 8.00
16 Leon Gonzalez 4.00 8.00
17 Mike Hegman 4.00 8.00
18 Gary Hogeboom 4.00 8.00
19 Jim Jeffcoat 4.00 8.00
20 Ed Too Tall Jones 7.50 15.00
21 James Jones 4.00 8.00
22 Crawford Ker 4.00 8.00
23 Tom Landry CO 10.00 20.00
24 Robert Lavette 4.00 8.00
25 Eugene Lockhart 4.00 8.00
26 Timmy Newsome 4.00 8.00
27 Drew Pearson ACO 6.00 12.00
28 Steve Pelluer 4.00 8.00
29 Jesse Penn 4.00 8.00
30 Kurt Petersen 4.00 8.00
31 Karl Powe 4.00 8.00
32 Phil Pozderac UER 4.00 8.00
33 Tom Rafferty 4.00 8.00
34 Mike Renfro 4.00 8.00
35 Howard Richards 4.00 8.00
36 Jeff Rohrer 4.00 8.00
37 Mike Saxon 4.00 8.00
38 Victor Scott 4.00 8.00
39 Rafael Septien 4.00 8.00
40 Don Smerek 4.00 8.00
41 Roger Staubach 20.00 40.00
42 Broderick Thompson 4.00 8.00
43 Dennis Thurman 4.00 8.00
44 Glen Titensor 4.00 8.00
45 Mark Tuinei 5.00 10.00
46 Herschel Walker 7.50 15.00
47A Everson Walls 5.00 10.00
47B Everson Walls 5.00 10.00
48A Danny White 6.00 12.00
49 Randy White 7.50 15.00
50 John Williams 4.00 8.00
51 1985 Team Photo 5.00 10.00
52 1986 Team Photo 5.00 10.00
53 Valley Ranch Offices 4.00 8.00

1987 Cowboys Ace Fact Pack

This 33-card set measures approximately 2 1/4" by 3 5/8". This set, which was printed in West Germany (by Ace Fact Pack) for release in Great Britain, has rounded corners and a playing type card back. There were 22 players in this set which we have checklisted alphabetically.

COMPLETE SET (33) 100.00 200.00
1 Bill Bates 3.00 8.00
2 Doug Cosbie 2.00 5.00
3 Tony Dorsett 20.00 50.00
4 Michael Downs 1.25 3.00
5 John Dutton 2.00 5.00
6 Ron Fellows 1.25 3.00
7 Mike Hegman 1.25 3.00
8 Tony Hill 2.00 5.00
9 Jim Jeffcoat 2.00 5.00
10 Ed Too Tall Jones 6.00 15.00
11 Crawford Ker 1.25 3.00
12 Eugene Lockhart 1.25 3.00
13 Phil Pozderac 1.25 3.00
14 Tom Rafferty 1.25 3.00
15 Jeff Rohrer 1.25 3.00
16 Mike Sherrard 2.00 5.00
17 Glen Titensor 1.25 3.00
18 Mark Tuinei 2.00 5.00
19 Herschel Walker 8.00 20.00
20 Everson Walls 1.25 3.00
21 Danny White 5.00 12.00
22 Randy White 8.00 20.00
23 Cowboys Helmet 1.25 3.00
24 Cowboys Information 1.25 3.00
25 Cowboys Uniform 1.25 3.00
26 Game Record Holders 1.25 3.00
27 Season Record Holders 1.25 3.00
28 Career Record Holders 1.25 3.00
29 Record 1967-86 1.25 3.00
30 1986 Team Statistics 1.25 3.00
31 All-Time Greats 1.25 3.00
32 Roll of Honour 1.25 3.00
33 Texas Stadium 1.25 3.00

1974 Cowboys Team Issue 8x10

The Dallas Cowboys issued these black-and-white player photos, measuring 8" by 10," and printed on glossy stock with white borders. Each player photo is a posed action shot. The border below the photo contains just the player's name and team name. The type style and size varies slightly on some photos so this may indicate that they were released over a period of years. The photos are blankbacked and unnumbered. Any additions to the below list are appreciated.

1 Larry Cole 6.00 12.00
(right foot off of the ground)
2 Bob Hayes 7.50 15.00
3 Ron Howard 6.00 12.00
4 Cornell Green 6.00 12.00
5 Bob Lilly 10.00 20.00
6 Ralph Neely 6.00 12.00
7 Mel Renfro 7.50 15.00

1990 Cowboys Team Issue

The Cowboys issued these 5" by 7" black and white photos in 1990. Each includes a portrait or action shot of the featured player with his name and team name below the photo in all capital letters. The photo backs are blank.

COMPLETE SET (10) 25.00 50.00
1 Troy Aikman 7.50 15.00
2 Darren Benson 2.50 5.00
3 Louis Cheek 2.50 5.00
4 Dean Hamel 2.50 5.00
5 Issiac Holt 2.50 5.00
6 Babe Laufenberg 2.50 5.00
7 Eugene Lockhart 2.50 5.00
8 Randy Shannon 2.50 5.00
9 Derrick Shepard 2.50 5.00
10 Stan Smagala 2.50 5.00

1993 Cowboys Taco Bell Cups

These cups were issued at Dallas area Taco Bell restaurants during the 1993 season. Each cup contains 2 players on each side, and caricatures the players featured.

1 Bill Bates .80 2.00
Alvin Harper
2 Jay Novacek 1.60 4.00
Emmitt Smith

1994 Cowboys Pro Line Live Kroger Stickers

Each vertical strip measures 2 1/2" by 12" and features three stickers. Each of the three stickers are roughly 3 5/8" in height; a white tab at the top of the strip carries the week the stickers were available and the price (99 cents). The fronts display the same design as the 1994 Pro Line series, with full-bleed color action photos. The backs of the strips, which peel off, contain two different $1.00 Fuji film coupons and an official entry form to enter a sweepstakes for a team poster. The strips are numbered below by weeks.

COMPLETE SET (7) 2.40 6.00
1 Troy Aikman .60 1.50
2 Emmitt Smith 1.00 2.50
3 Michael Irvin .30 .75
4 Daryl Johnston .30 .75
5 Nate Newton .20 .50
6 Russell Maryland .20 .50
7 Alvin Harper .20 .50

1997 Cowboys Collector's Choice

Upper Deck released several team sets in 1997 in a blister pack wrapper. Each of the 14-cards in this set are very similar to the base Collector's Choice cards except for the card numbering on the cardback. A cover/checklist card was added featuring the team helmet.

COMPLETE SET (14) 1.50 4.00
DA1 Deion Sanders .20 .50
DA2 Jim Schwantz .02 .10
DA3 Michael Irvin .10 .30
DA4 Herschel Walker .07 .20
DA5 Emmitt Smith .60 1.50
DA6 Troy Aikman .40 1.00
DA7 Eric Bjornson .02 .10
DA8 David LaFleur .02 .10
DA9 Antonio Anderson .02 .10
DA10 Daryl Johnston .07 .20
DA11 Tony Tolbert .02 .10
DA12 Brock Marion .02 .10
DA13 Anthony Miller .07 .20
DA14 Checklist .20 .50
(Troy Aikman on back)

1997 Cowboys Score

This 15-card set of the Dallas Cowboys was distributed in five-card packs with a suggested retail price of $1.99. The fronts feature color action player photos with white borders and the player's name and team logo printed in team color foil at the bottom. The backs carry player information and career statistics. Platinum Team parallel cards were randomly seeded in packs featuring all foil cardfronts.

COMPLETE SET (15) 3.20 8.00
*PLATINUM TEAMS: 1X TO 2X
1 Emmitt Smith 1.20 3.00
2 Troy Aikman .80 2.00
3 Darren Woodson .15 .40
4 Michael Irvin .30 .75
5 Sherman Williams .08 .25
6 Daryl Johnston .15 .40
7 Deion Sanders .50 1.25
8 Kevin Williams .08 .25
9 Jim Schwantz .08 .25
10 Darrin Smith .08 .25
11 Kevin Smith .08 .25
12 Billy Davis .08 .25

13 Herschel Walker .15 .40
14 Fred Strickland .08 .25
15 Tony Tolbert .08 .25
PC1 Emmitt Smith PC 4.00 10.00

2005 Cowboys Activa Medallions

COMPLETE SET (22) 30.00 60.00
1 Troy Aikman 1.50 4.00
2 Tony Dorsett 1.50 4.00
3 Charles Haley 1.25 3.00
4 Cliff Harris 1.25 3.00
5 Chuck Howley 1.25 3.00
6 Michael Irvin 1.50 4.00
7 Daryl Johnston 1.25 3.00
8 Lee Roy Jordan 1.25 3.00
9 Bob Lilly 1.25 3.00
10 Harvey Martin 1.25 3.00
11 Don Meredith 1.50 4.00
12 Jay Novacek 1.25 3.00
13 Drew Pearson 1.25 3.00
14 Don Perkins 1.25 3.00
15 Mel Renfro 1.25 3.00
16 Emmitt Smith 2.00 5.00
17 Roger Staubach 1.50 4.00
18 Charlie Waters 1.25 3.00
19 Randy White 1.50 4.00
20 Darren Woodson 1.25 3.00
21 Rayfield Wright 1.25 3.00
22 Cowboys Logo 1.00 2.50

2006 Cowboys Donruss Thanksgiving Classic

COMPLETE SET (8) 4.00 10.00
DL1 Terry Glenn .60 1.50
DL2 Julius Jones .50 1.25
DL3 Roy Williams S .50 1.25
DL4 Jason Witten .60 1.50
DL5 Terrell Owens .60 1.50
DL6 Tony Dorsett 1.25 3.00
NNO DeMarcus Ware .60 1.50
NNO Cover Card CL .20 .50

2006 Cowboys Topps

COMPLETE SET (12) 3.00 6.00
DAL1 Drew Bledsoe .30 .75
DAL2 Roy Williams S .25 .60
DAL3 Julius Jones .25 .60
DAL4 Marion Barber .30 .75
DAL5 Terry Glenn .30 .75
DAL6 Jason Witten .30 .75
DAL7 DeMarcus Ware .30 .75
DAL8 Terence Newman .25 .60
DAL9 Terrell Owens .30 .75
DAL10 Mike Vanderjagt .25 .60
DAL11 Bobby Carpenter .25 .60
DAL12 Anthony Fasano .25 .60

2007 Cowboys Donruss Rowdy Rookies

This set of 6-cards was issued for the official kid's fan club of the Cowboys - Rowdy Rookies. Each includes the club's logo on the front.

COMPLETE SET (6) 4.00 10.00
1 Tony Romo 1.00 2.50
2 Terry Glenn .60 1.50
3 Jason Witten .60 1.50
4 DeMarcus Ware .60 1.50
5 Roy Williams S .50 1.25
6 Terence Newman .50 1.25

2007 Cowboys Donruss Thanksgiving Classic

COMPLETE SET (5) 4.00 8.00
1 Tony Romo 1.00 2.50
2 Terry Glenn .60 1.50
3 Roy Williams S .50 1.25
4 Troy Aikman 1.25 3.00
NNO Roy Williams S .50 1.25
Salvation Army

2007 Cowboys Topps

COMPLETE SET (12) 3.00 6.00
1 Marion Barber .50 1.25
2 Roy Williams S .40 1.00
3 Tony Romo .75 2.00
4 Julius Jones .40 1.00
5 DeMarcus Ware .50 1.25
6 Jason Witten .50 1.25
7 Terence Newman .40 1.00
8 Terrell Owens .50 1.25
9 Patrick Crayton .40 1.00
10 Bradie James .40 1.00
11 Terry Glenn .50 1.25
12 Anthony Spencer .50 1.25

2008 Cowboys Donruss Rowdy Rookies

This set of 6-cards was issued for the official kid's fan club of the Cowboys - Rowdy Rookies. Each includes the club's logo on the front.

COMPLETE SET (6) 5.00 10.00
1 Tony Romo .60 1.50
2 Terrell Owens .60 1.50
3 Marion Barber .50 1.25
4 Terence Newman .50 1.25
5 DeMarcus Ware .60 1.50
6 Jason Witten .60 1.50

2008 Cowboys Donruss Thanksgiving Classic

Many fans who attended the 2008 Thanksgiving game in Dallas were treated to this complete set. Donruss reported that more than 120,000 cards were given away to fans at both the Dallas and Philadelphia games. Each team set also included one card from the NFL Network broadcasters set.

COMPLETE SET (6) 6.00 12.00
1 Tony Romo .60 1.50
2 DeMarcus Ware .60 1.50
3 Terrell Owens .60 1.50
4 Randy White .75 2.00
5 Felix Jones .25 .60
NNO Marion Barber .50 1.25
Salvation Army

2008 Cowboys Merrick Mint Quarters

COMPLETE SET (12) 60.00 120.00
1 Marion Barber 5.00 10.00
2 Patrick Crayton 5.00 10.00
3 Leonard Davis 5.00 10.00
4 Adam Jones 5.00 10.00
5 Terence Newman 5.00 10.00
6 Terrell Owens 5.00 10.00
7 Tony Romo 6.00 12.00
8 Tony Romo half dollar 7.50 15.00
9 Zach Thomas 5.00 10.00
10 DeMarcus Ware 6.00 12.00
11 Roy Williams S 5.00 10.00
12 Jason Witten 6.00 12.00

2008 Cowboys Topps

COMPLETE SET (12) 3.00 6.00
1 Terrell Owens .50 1.25
2 DeMarcus Ware .50 1.25
3 Tony Romo .50 1.25
4 Marion Barber .40 1.00
5 Jason Witten .50 1.25
6 Ken Hamlin .40 1.00
7 Roy Williams S .40 1.00
8 Greg Ellis .40 1.00
9 Anthony Henry .40 1.00
10 Terence Newman .40 1.00
11 Patrick Crayton .50 1.25
12 Felix Jones .40 1.00

2011 Cowboys Panini Super Bowl XLV

This set was sold exclusively at the 2011 Super Bowl Card Show in Dallas. The cards feature the Super Bowl XLV logo on the fronts and the backs are numbered.

COMPLETE SET (10) 8.00 20.00
SB1 Miles Austin .75 2.00
SB2 Marion Barber .75 2.00
SB3 Dez Bryant 1.25 3.00
SB4 Tashard Choice .75 2.00
SB5 Felix Jones .75 2.00
SB6 Jay Ratliff 1.00 2.50
SB7 Tony Romo 1.00 2.50
SB8 DeMarcus Ware 1.00 2.50
SB9 Jason Witten 1.00 2.50
SB10 Mat McBriar .75 2.00

1994 CPC/Enviromint Medallions

To commemorate Joe Montana's career, Chicagoland Processing Corporation/Enviromint issued a silver medallion, a silver collector card and a gold medallion. Each one-troy ounce medallion is stamped with Montana's likeness, his team name, and his jersey number on the front while the words "Player of the Decade 1980's" are stamped on the reverse. Each 3.5 ounce silver collector card is stamped with a collage of Montana in both 49ers and Chiefs uniforms on the front. Its back carries team logos and the words "All-Time NFL Leader in QB Rating" and "Athlete of the Decade 1980's." The medallions and the card each have their own serial number. The production figures are as follows: silver medallion (7,000); silver collector card (10,000); silver medallion and card set (500); and gold medallion (100). Except for the serial number, the collectibles are unnumbered.

1 Joe Montana 24.00 60.00
Silver medallion
2 Joe Montana 24.00 60.00
Silver card
3 Joe Montana 50.00 125.00
Gold overlay medallion
4 Joe Montana 50.00 125.00
Gold overlay medallion

1976 Crane Discs

The 1976 Crane football disc set of 30 cards contains a black and white photo of the player surrounded by a colored border. These circular cards measure 3 3/8" in diameter. The word Crane completes the circle of the border. The backs contain a Crane (Potato Chips) advertisement and the letters MSA, signifying Michael Schechter Associates. A recently discovered version of the discs was apparently inserted into potato chip packages as several players have been found printed without the "National Football League Players" notation around the small football logo on the fronts. Known discs from this version also feature food product stains as would be expected. Franco Harris can only be found in this "product inserted" version of the discs. None of the second version of the discs are considered part of the complete set price below due to their scarcity. Any additions to the checklist of this version of the discs is appreciated. These discs were also available as a complete set via a mail-in offer on the potato chip wrappers; consequently they are commonly found in nice condition. Of these, there are 12 discs that were produced in shorter supply than the other 18 and are noted by SP in the checklist below. These extras found their way into the hobby when Crane sold their leftovers to a major midwestern dealer. Since the cards are unnumbered, they are ordered below alphabetically. The discs can also be found with the sponsor Saga Philadelphia School District on the cardback. The Saga discs are much more difficult to find and are listed as a separate release.

COMPLETE SET (30) 12.50 25.00
1 Ken Anderson .30 .60
2 Otis Armstrong .20 .40
3 Steve Bartkowski .20 .40
4 Terry Bradshaw 1.50 3.00
5 John Brockington SP .18 .35
6 Doug Buffone .13 .25
7 Wally Chambers .13 .25
8 Isaac Curtis SP .25 .50
9 Chuck Foreman .20 .40
10 Roman Gabriel SP .25 .50
11 Mel Gray .20 .40
12 Joe Greene .50 1.00
13 Franco Harris SP 7.50 15.00
14 James Harris SP .18 .35
15 Jim Hart .20 .40
16 Billy Kilmer .20 .40
17 Greg Landry SP .25 .50
18 Ed Marinaro SP .25 .50
19 Lawrence McCutcheon SP .25 .50
20 Terry Metcalf .20 .40
21 Lydell Mitchell SP .25 .50
22 Jim Otis .13 .25
23 Alan Page .30 .60
24 Walter Payton SP 7.50 15.00
25A Greg Pruitt SP .25 .50
25B Greg Pruitt SP 2.50 5.00
26 Charlie Sanders SP .30 .75
27 Ron Shanklin SP .18 .35
28 Roger Staubach 2.00 4.00
29 Jan Stenerud .20 .40
30 Charley Taylor .30 .60
31 Roger Wehrli .20 .50

1997 Crown Pro Stickers

COMPLETE SET (12) 8.00 20.00
R1 Tony Banks .40 1.00
R2 Keyshawn Johnson .60 1.50
R3 Joey Galloway .60 1.50
R4 Terry Glenn .60 1.50
R5 Eddie George .60 1.50
R6 Emmitt Smith 1.50 4.00
R7 Dan Marino 1.50 4.00
R8 Barry Sanders 1.25 3.00
R9 Kerry Collins .50 1.25
R10 Drew Bledsoe .60 1.50
R11 Tim Brown .60 1.50
R12 Brett Favre 2.00 5.00

1999 Crown Pro Key Chains

This set was issued by Crown Pro and distributed primarily through mass retailers. Each package contained a small player statue with an attached key ring. A small (1 1/8" by 2") Dog Tag was also included with the statue. The prices below are for complete unopened packages.

COMPLETE SET (6) 8.00 20.00
1 Troy Aikman 1.20 3.00
2 Terrell Davis 1.20 3.00
3 Brett Favre 1.60 4.00
4 Peyton Manning 1.60 4.00
5 Dan Marino 1.60 4.00
6 Randy Moss 1.60 4.00

1999 Crown Pro Self Inking Stampers

This set was issued by Crown Pro and distributed primarily through mass retailers. Each package contained a small player statue with a self inking stamp at the base of the statue. A standard sized (2 1/2" by 3 1/2") Pro Stamp was also included with the statue. The prices below are for complete unopened packages.

COMPLETE SET (9) 16.00 40.00
1 Troy Aikman 1.60 4.00
2 Terrell Davis 1.60 4.00
3 John Elway 2.00 5.00
4 Brett Favre 2.00 5.00
5 Peyton Manning 2.00 5.00
6 Dan Marino 2.00 5.00
7 Randy Moss 2.00 5.00
8 Barry Sanders 2.00 5.00
9 Steve Young 1.60 4.00

1995 Crown Royale

This set is actually a spin-off of the popular Gold Crown Die Cuts insert from the regular Pacific product. It contains 144 cards and was issued in four card packs. Some boxes of Crown Royale also contained one instant win card redeemable for a trip to Super Bowl XXX.

COMPLETE SET (144) 12.00 30.00
1 Lake Dawson .20 .50
2 Steve Beuerlein .20 .50
3 Jake Reed .20 .50
4 Jim Everett .08 .25
5 Sean Dawkins .20 .50
6 Jeff Hostetler .20 .50
7 Marshall Faulk 1.25 3.00
8 Jeff Blake RC .75 2.00
9 Dave Brown .20 .50
10 Frank Reich .08 .25
11 Rocket Ismail .20 .50
12 Jerry Jones OWN 8.00 25.00
13 Dan Marino 1.25 3.00
14 Ricky Watters .20 .50
15 Herman Moore .40 1.00
16 Daryl Johnston .20 .50
17 Craig Erickson .08 .25
18 Alexander Wright .08 .25
19 Reggie White .40 1.00
20 Andre Rison .20 .50
21 Fred Barnett .20 .50
22 Tyrone Wheatley RC 1.25 3.00
23 Charles Johnson .20 .50
24 Rashaan Salaam RC .20 .50
25 Mark Brunell .60 1.50
26 Derek Loville .08 .25
27 Garrison Hearst .40 1.00
28 Ken Norton Jr. .20 .50
29 Kerry Collins RC 1.50 4.00
30 Isaac Bruce .60 1.50
31 Andre Reed .20 .50
32 Leon Lett .08 .25
33 Deion Sanders .60 1.50
34 Terance Mathis .20 .50
35 Tim Bowens .08 .25
36 Shannon Sharpe .20 .50
37 Quinn Early .20 .50
38 Jerry Rice 1.00 2.50
39 Bruce Smith .40 1.00
40 Drew Bledsoe .60 1.50
41 Alvin Harper .08 .25
42 Jim Kelly .40 1.00
43 Napoleon Kaufman RC 1.25 3.00
44 Errict Rhett .20 .50
45 Henry Ellard .20 .50
46 Barry Sanders 1.50 4.00
47 Vincent Brisby .08 .25
48 Chris Zorich .08 .25
49 Zack Crockett RC .20 .50
50 Haywood Jeffires .08 .25
51 Byron Bam Morris .08 .25
52 John Kasay .08 .25
53 Scott Mitchell .20 .50
54 Boomer Esiason .20 .50
55 Eric Metcalf .20 .50
56 Kevin Greene .20 .50
57 Courtney Hawkins .08 .25
58 Adrian Murrell .08 .25
59 Larry Centers .20 .50
60 Leroy Hoard .08 .25
61 Lorenzo White .08 .25
62 Chris Spielman .20 .50
63 Carl Pickens .20 .50
64 Steve Young .75 2.00
65 Trent Dilfer .40 1.00
66 Erik Kramer .08 .25
67 Cortez Kennedy .20 .50
68 Ray Childress .08 .25
69 Rick Mirer .20 .50
70 Kevin Williams WR .20 .50
71 Joey Galloway RC 1.50 4.00
72 Dan Wilkinson .20 .50
73 Antonio Freeman RC 1.25 3.00
74 Curtis Conway .40 1.00
75 Troy Aikman 1.00 2.50
76 Natrone Means .20 .50
77 Jeff George .20 .50
78 Curtis Martin RC 3.00 8.00
79 William Floyd .20 .50
80 Anthony Miller .20 .50
81 Greg Hill .20 .50
82 Craig Heyward .20 .50
83 Brian Mitchell .08 .25
84 Anthony Carter .20 .50
85 Jerome Bettis .40 1.00
86 Jim Harbaugh .20 .50
87 Harvey Williams .08 .25
88 Tony Martin .20 .50
89 Rob Moore .20 .50
90 Neil O'Donnell .20 .50
91 Cris Carter .40 1.00
92 Warren Sapp RC 1.50 4.00
93 Terry Allen .20 .50
94 Michael Irvin .40 1.00
95 Heath Shuler .20 .50
96 Cornelius Bennett .20 .50
97 Randy Baldwin .08 .25
98 Vince Workman .08 .25
99 Irving Fryar .20 .50
100 Randall Cunningham .40 1.00
101 James O. Stewart RC 1.25 3.00
102 Stan Humphries .20 .50
103 Mario Bates .20 .50
104 Ben Coates .20 .50
105 Charlie Garner .40 1.00
106 Todd Collins RC 1.25 3.00
107 Tim Brown .40 1.00
108 Edgar Bennett .20 .50
109 J.J. Stokes RC .40 1.00
110 Michael Timpson .08 .25
111 Junior Seau .40 1.00
112 Bernie Parmalee .20 .50
113 Willie McGinest .20 .50
114 David Dunn RC .08 .25
115 Kyle Brady RC .40 1.00
116 Vinny Testaverde .20 .50
117 Ernest Givins .08 .25
118 Eric Zeier RC .40 1.00
119 Michael Jackson .20 .50
120 Chad May RC .08 .25
121 Dave Krieg .08 .25
122 Rodney Hampton .20 .50
123 Darnay Scott .20 .50
124 Chris Miller .08 .25
125 Emmitt Smith 1.50 4.00
126 Steve McNair RC 3.00 8.00
127 Warren Moon .20 .50
128 Robert Brooks .40 1.00
129 Bert Emanuel .40 1.00
130 John Elway 2.00 5.00
131 Chris Warren .20 .50
132 Herschel Walker .20 .50
133 Terry Kirby .20 .50
134 Michael Westbrook RC .40 1.00
135 Kordell Stewart RC 1.50 4.00
136 Terrell Davis RC 2.50 6.00
137 Desmond Howard .20 .50
138 Rodney Thomas RC .20 .50
139 Brett Favre 2.00 5.00
140 Ray Zellars RC .20 .50
141 Marcus Allen .40 1.00
142 Gus Frerotte .20 .50
143 Steve Bono .20 .50
144 Aaron Craver .08 .25
P144 Natrone Means Promo Jumbo .75 2.00

1995 Crown Royale Blue Holofoil

COMPLETE SET (144) 200.00 400.00
*STARS: 2.5X TO 6X BASIC CARDS
*RCs: 1.5X TO 4X BASIC CARDS
STATED ODDS 4:25 RETAIL

1995 Crown Royale Copper

COMPLETE SET (144) 150.00 300.00
*STARS: 2X TO 5X BASIC CARDS
*RCs: 1X TO 2.5X BASIC CARDS
STATED ODDS 4:25 HOBBY

1995 Crown Royale Cramer's Choice Jumbos

This oversized version was made due to the tremendous response to the regular sized insert set that was randomly inserted in the 1995 Pacific product. This six card set was randomly inserted as a chiptopper in boxes of Crown Royale at a rate of one in every 16 boxes. Cards are numbered with a "CC" prefix.

COMPLETE SET (6) 25.00 60.00
STATED ODDS 1:16 BOXES
CC1 Rashaan Salaam 1.25 3.00
CC2 Emmitt Smith 10.00 25.00
CC3 Marshall Faulk 8.00 20.00
CC4 Jerry Rice 6.00 15.00
CC5 Deion Sanders 4.00 10.00
CC6 Steve Young 5.00 12.00

1995 Crown Royale Pride of the NFL

This 36 card set was randomly inserted in packs at a rate of three in 25 packs and features some of the NFL's greatest players. Cards are numbered with a "PN" prefix.

COMPLETE SET (36) 30.00 80.00
STATED ODDS 3:25
PN1 Jim Kelly .75 2.00
PN2 Kerry Collins 2.00 5.00
PN3 Darnay Scott .40 1.00
PN4 Jeff Blake 1.00 2.50
PN5 Terry Allen .40 1.00
PN6 Emmitt Smith 3.00 8.00
PN7 Michael Irvin .75 2.00
PN8 Troy Aikman 2.00 5.00
PN9 John Elway 4.00 10.00
PN10 Napoleon Kaufman 1.50 4.00
PN11 Barry Sanders 3.00 8.00
PN12 Brett Favre 4.00 10.00
PN13 Michael Westbrook .50 1.25
PN14 Marcus Allen .75 2.00
PN15 Tim Brown .75 2.00
PN16 Bernie Parmalee .40 1.00
PN17 Dan Marino 4.00 10.00
PN18 Cris Carter .75 2.00
PN19 Drew Bledsoe 1.25 3.00
PN20 Mario Bates .40 1.00
PN21 Rodney Hampton .40 1.00
PN22 Ben Coates .40 1.00
PN23 Charles Johnson .40 1.00
PN24 Byron Bam Morris .20 .50
PN25 Stan Humphries .40 1.00
PN26 Rashaan Salaam .25 .60
PN27 Jerry Rice 2.00 5.00
PN28 Ricky Watters .40 1.00
PN29 Steve Young 1.50 4.00
PN30 Natrone Means .40 1.00
PN31 William Floyd .40 1.00
PN32 Chris Warren .40 1.00
PN33 Rick Mirer .40 1.00
PN34 Jerome Bettis .75 2.00
PN35 Errict Rhett .40 1.00
PN36 Heath Shuler .40 1.00

1995 Crown Royale Pro Bowl Die Cuts

This 20 card set was randomly inserted into packs at a rate of one in 25 packs and features the top players selected to the 1995 Pro Bowl. Cards are numbered with a "PB" prefix. Cards are also condition sensitive due to the complex die cut design.

COMPLETE SET (20) 50.00 120.00
STATED ODDS 1:25
PB1 Drew Bledsoe 2.00 5.00
PB2 Ben Coates 1.00 2.50
PB3 John Elway 10.00 25.00
PB4 Marshall Faulk 4.00 10.00
PB5 Dan Marino 10.00 25.00
PB6 Natrone Means 1.00 2.50
PB7 Junior Seau 2.00 5.00
PB8 Chris Warren 1.00 2.50
PB9 Rod Woodson 1.50 4.00
PB10 Tim Brown 2.00 5.00
PB11 Troy Aikman 5.00 12.00
PB12 Jerome Bettis 2.00 5.00
PB13 Michael Irvin 2.00 5.00
PB14 Jerry Rice 5.00 12.00
PB15 Barry Sanders 8.00 20.00
PB16 Deion Sanders 3.00 8.00
PB17 Emmitt Smith 8.00 20.00
PB18 Steve Young 4.00 10.00
PB19 Reggie White 2.00 5.00
PB20 Cris Carter 2.00 5.00

1996 Crown Royale

The 1996 Pacific Crown Royale set was issued in one series totalling 144 cards and was distributed in five-card packs. The set features color player images on an etched die cut gold crown background with the player's name and position printed at the bottom beside the team logo.

COMPLETE SET (144) 15.00 40.00
1 Dan Marino 2.00 5.00
2 Frank Sanders .25 .60
3 Bobby Engram RC .40 1.00
4 Cornelius Bennett .15 .40
5 Steve Bono .15 .40
6 Aaron Hayden RC .15 .40
7 Leroy Hoard .15 .40
8 Brett Perriman .15 .40
9 Irv Smith .15 .40
10 Jim Kelly .40 1.00
11 Rodney Thomas .15 .40
12 Eric Bieniemy .15 .40
13 Darnay Scott .25 .60
14 Ki-Jana Carter .25 .60
15 Kerry Collins .40 1.00
16 Shannon Sharpe .25 .60
17 Michael Westbrook .40 1.00
18 Steve McNair .75 2.00
19 Tony Banks RC .75 2.00
20 Rashaan Salaam .25 .60
21 Terrell Fletcher .15 .40
22 Michael Timpson .15 .40
23 Bobby Hoying RC .40 1.00
24 Quinn Early .15 .40
25 Warren Moon .25 .60
26 Tommy Vardell .15 .40
27 Marvin Harrison RC 6.00 12.00
28 Lake Dawson .15 .40
29 Karim Abdul-Jabbar RC .75 2.00
30 Chris Warren .25 .60
31 Heath Shuler .25 .60
32 Bert Emanuel .25 .60
33 Howard Griffith RC .25 .60
34 Alex Van Dyke RC .25 .60
35 Isaac Bruce .40 1.00
36 Mark Brunell .60 1.50
37 Winslow Oliver RC .25 .60
38 O.J. McDuffie .25 .60
39 Terrell Owens RC 6.00 12.00
40 Jerry Rice 1.00 2.50
41 Henry Ellard .15 .40
42 Chris Sanders .25 .60
43 Craig Heyward .15 .40
44 Eddie Kennison RC .75 2.00
45 Terrell Davis .75 2.00
46 Rodney Hampton .25 .60
47 Bryan Still RC .25 .60
48 Tim Brown .40 1.00
49 Keyshawn Johnson RC 2.50 6.00
50 Barry Sanders 1.50 4.00
51 Terry Allen .25 .60
52 Sean Dawkins .15 .40
53 Bryce Paup .15 .40
54 Brett Favre 2.00 5.00
55 Deion Sanders .60 1.50
56 Kevin Hardy RC .75 2.00
57 Kevin Williams .15 .40
58 Jeff George .25 .60
59 Tim Biakabutuka RC .75 2.00
60 Drew Bledsoe .60 1.50
61 Michael Jackson .25 .60
62 James O. Stewart .25 .60
63 Mario Bates .25 .60
64 Daryl Johnston .25 .60
65 Herman Moore .25 .60
66 Ben Coates .25 .60
67 Terry Glenn RC 2.50 6.00
68 Robert Smith .25 .60
69 Irving Fryar .25 .60
70 Napoleon Kaufman .40 1.00
71 Rickey Dudley RC .75 2.00
72 Bernie Parmalee .15 .40
73 Kyle Brady .15 .40
74 Neil O'Donnell .25 .60
75 Lawrence Phillips RC .75 2.00
76 Hardy Nickerson .15 .40
77 John Elway 2.00 5.00
78 Pete Mitchell .25 .60
79 Jason Dunn RC .50 1.25
80 Reggie White .40 1.00
81 J.J. Stokes .40 1.00
82 Jake Reed .25 .60
83 Yancey Thigpen .25 .60
84 Jonathan Ogden RC 1.50 4.00
85 Larry Centers .25 .60
86 Scott Mitchell .25 .60
87 Eric Zeier .15 .40
88 Anthony Miller .25 .60
89 Brian Blades .15 .40
90 Cris Carter .40 1.00
91 Kordell Stewart .40 1.00
92 Charles Way RC .50 1.25
93 Jeff Hostetler .15 .40
94 Brad Johnson .75 2.00
95 Marcus Allen .40 1.00
96 Errict Rhett .25 .60
97 Stan Humphries .25 .60
98 Michael Haynes .15 .40
99 Curtis Martin .75 2.00
100 Troy Aikman .75 2.50
101 Earnest Byner .15 .40
102 Vincent Brisby .15 .40
103 Zack Crockett .15 .40
104 Haywood Jeffires .15 .40
105 Joey Galloway .40 1.00
106 Carl Pickens .25 .60
107 Leeland McElroy RC .50 1.25
108 Adrian Murrell .25 .60
109 Joe Horn RC 5.00 10.00
110 Steve Young .75 2.00
111 Andre Rison .25 .60
112 Jim Everett .15 .40
113 Jamie Asher RC .50 1.25
114 Steve Walsh .15 .40
115 Robert Brooks .40 1.00
116 Eric Moulds RC 3.00 8.00
117 Edgar Bennett .25 .60
118 Greg Lloyd .25 .60
119 Jerris McPhail RC .25 .60
120 Marshall Faulk .60 1.50
121 Dave Brown .15 .40
122 Harvey Williams .15 .40
123 Trent Dilfer .40 1.00
124 Eddie George RC 3.00 8.00
125 Jeff Blake .40 1.00
126 Mark Chmura .25 .60
127 Boomer Esiason .25 .60
128 Jim Harbaugh .25 .60
129 Bryan Cox .15 .40
130 Ricky Watters .25 .60
131 Amani Toomer RC 2.50 6.00
132 Jim Miller .40 1.00
133 Cortez Kennedy .15 .40
134 Courtney Hawkins .15 .40
135 Junior Seau .40 1.00
136 Tamarick Vanover .25 .60
137 Jerome Bettis .40 1.00
138 Chris Calloway .15 .40
139 Rick Mirer .25 .60
140 Thurman Thomas .40 1.00
141 Sheddrick Wilson RC .25 .60
142 Charlie Garner .25 .60
143 Erik Kramer .15 .40
144 Emmitt Smith 1.50 4.00

1996 Crown Royale Blue

COMPLETE SET (144) 200.00 400.00
*STARS: 1.5X TO 4X BASIC CARDS
*RCs: 1X TO 2.5X BASIC CARDS
STATED ODDS 4:25 HOBBY

1996 Crown Royale Silver

COMPLETE SET (144) 250.00 500.00
*STARS: 2X TO 5X BASIC CARDS
*RCs: 1.2X TO 3X BASIC CARDS
STATED ODDS 4:25 RETAIL

1996 Crown Royale Cramer's Choice Jumbos

This 10-card serial-numbered set measuring approximately 4" by 5 1/2" is die cut in the shape of a trophy with a color player image on a silver foil background. The bottom of the card has a brown marble border with gold foil printing. Some cards were randomly seeded in boxes, while others were issued via a mail redemption (with an expiration date of 12/31/1996). Redemption cards for the players below containing an * were seeded at the rate of 1:385, the same insertion rate as the inserts.

COMPLETE SET (10) 125.00 300.00
STATED ODDS 1:385
1 John Elway 15.00 40.00
2 Brett Favre 15.00 40.00
3 Keyshawn Johnson 20.00 50.00
4 Dan Marino 15.00 40.00
5 Curtis Martin 6.00 15.00
6 Jerry Rice 8.00 20.00
7 Barry Sanders 12.50 30.00
8 Emmitt Smith 12.50 30.00
9 Kordell Stewart 3.00 8.00
10 Reggie White 3.00 8.00

1996 Crown Royale Field Force

Randomly inserted in packs at a rate of one in 49, this 20-card set features color player images on a football field background and printed in a new Etch-Tech design with explosive graphics.

COMPLETE SET (20) 100.00 250.00
STATED ODDS 1:49
1 Troy Aikman 4.00 10.00
2 Karim Abdul-Jabbar 2.00 5.00
3 Jeff Blake 1.50 4.00
4 Drew Bledsoe 2.50 6.00
5 Lawrence Phillips 2.00 5.00
6 Kerry Collins 1.50 4.00
7 Terrell Davis 3.00 8.00
8 John Elway 8.00 20.00
9 Brett Favre 8.00 20.00
10 Eddie George 8.00 20.00
11 Dan Marino 8.00 20.00
12 Curtis Martin 3.00 8.00
13 Jerry Rice 4.00 10.00
14 Rashaan Salaam 1.00 2.50
15 Barry Sanders 6.00 15.00
16 Deion Sanders 2.50 6.00
17 Emmitt Smith 6.00 15.00
18 Kordell Stewart 1.50 4.00
19 Chris Warren 1.00 2.50
20 Steve Young 3.00 8.00

1996 Crown Royale NFL Regime

Inserted one in every pack, this 110-card set features color action player photos inside a crown-shaped border of some of the league's old and new unsung heroes of the game.

COMPLETE SET (110) 12.50 25.00
ONE PER PACK
1 Steve Young .40 1.00
2 Jamir Miller .05 .15
3 Tyrone Brown .05 .15
4 Chris Shelling .05 .15
5 Warren Moon .07 .20
6 Shane Bonham .05 .15
7 Gary Brown T .05 .15
8 Chris Chandler .07 .20
9 Bradford Banta .05 .15
10 John Elway 1.00 2.50
11 Tom McManus .05 .15
12 Alfred Jackson CB .05 .15
13 Jay Barker .05 .15
14 Kirk Botkin .05 .15
15 Jim Kelly .15 .40
16 Lou Benfatti .05 .15
17 Billy Joe Hobert .07 .20
18 John Jackson .05 .15
19 Torin Dorn .05 .15
20 Drew Bledsoe .30 .75
21 Gale Gilbert .05 .15
22 James Atkins .05 .15
23 John Lynch .15 .40
24 James Jenkins .05 .15
25 Kerry Collins .15 .40
26 Eric Swann .05 .15
27 Dan Stryzinski .05 .15
28 Mike Groh .05 .15
29 Tim Tindale .05 .15
30 Kordell Stewart .30 .75
31 Frank Garcia C .05 .15
32 Mill Coleman .05 .15
33 Bracy Walker .05 .15
34 Ryan McNeil .05 .15
35 Rodney Hampton .07 .20
36 John Mobley .05 .15
37 Derek Russell .05 .15
38 Jeff George .07 .20
39 Steve Morrison .05 .15
40 Rashaan Salaam .07 .20
41 Ryan Christopherson .05 .15
42 Darren Anderson .05 .15
43 Ronnie Williams .05 .15
44 Scottie Graham .05 .15
45 Thurman Thomas .15 .40
46 Corwin Brown .05 .15
47 Lee DeRamus .05 .15
48 Ray Agnew .05 .15
49 Erik Howard .05 .15
50 Emmitt Smith .75 2.00
51 Dan Land .05 .15
52 Vinny Testaverde .07 .20
53 Myron Bell .05 .15
54 Keith Lyle .05 .15
55 Aaron Hayden .05 .15
56 Jeff Brohm .05 .15
57 Ronnie Harris .05 .15
58 Trent Dilfer .15 .40
59 Browning Nagle .05 .15
60 Jeff Blake .15 .40
61 Rich Owens .05 .15
62 Anthony Edwards .05 .15
63 Orlando Brown .05 .15
64 Matthew Campbell .05 .15
65 Ricky Watters .07 .20
66 Travis Hannah .05 .15
67 Melvin Tuten .05 .15
68 Aaron Taylor .05 .15
69 Dale Hellestrae .05 .15
70 Marshall Faulk .20 .50
71 Gary Anderson .05 .15
72 David Williams .05 .15
73 Jim Harbaugh .07 .20
74 Ray Hall .05 .15
75 Dan Marino 1.00 2.50
76 Chris Mims .05 .15
77 Matt Blundin .05 .15
78 Roy Barker .05 .15
79 John Burke .05 .15
80 Troy Aikman .50 1.25
81 Ed King .05 .15
82 Stan White .05 .15
83 Vance Joseph .05 .15
84 David Klingler .05 .15
85 Terrell Davis .40 1.00
86 Bobby Hoying .15 .40
87 Lethon Flowers .05 .15
88 Dwayne White .05 .15
89 Vaughn Parker .05 .15
90 Jerry Rice .50 1.25
91 Casey Weldon .05 .15
92 Rick Mirer .07 .20
93 Jim Pyne .05 .15
94 Matt Turk .05 .15
95 Marcus Allen .15 .40
96 Rob Moore .07 .20
97 Ruben Brown .05 .15
98 Zach Thomas .30 .75
99 Carwell Gardner .05 .15
100 Barry Sanders .75 2.00
101 Ben Coleman .05 .15
102 Steve Rhem .05 .15
103 Everett McIver .05 .15
104 Cole Ford .05 .15
105 Dave Krieg .05 .15
106 Anthony Parker .05 .15
107 Michael Brandon .05 .15
108 Michael McCrary .05 .15
109 Chad Fann .05 .15
110 Brett Favre 1.00 2.50

1996 Crown Royale Pro Bowl Die Cuts

Randomly inserted in packs at a rate of one in 25, this 20-card set features color images of last year's Pro Bowl players on a die cut pineapple shaped background.

COMPLETE SET (20) 30.00 80.00
STATED ODDS 1:25
1 Jeff Blake 1.25 3.00
2 Mark Chmura .75 2.00
3 Marshall Faulk 2.00 5.00
4 Brett Favre 6.00 15.00
5 Charles Haley .50 1.25
6 Merton Hanks .50 1.25
7 Greg Lloyd .75 2.00
8 Dan Marino 6.00 15.00
9 Curtis Martin 2.50 6.00
10 Anthony Miller .75 2.00
11 Herman Moore .75 2.00
12 Bryce Paup .50 1.25
13 Jerry Rice 3.00 8.00
14 Barry Sanders 5.00 12.00
15 Junior Seau 1.25 3.00
16 Emmitt Smith 5.00 12.00
17 Yancey Thigpen .75 2.00
18 Chris Warren .75 2.00
19 Ricky Watters .75 2.00
20 Steve Young 2.50 6.00

1996 Crown Royale Triple Crown Die Cuts

Randomly inserted in packs at a rate of one in 73, this 10-card set honors players who have led the league in a least three different categories. The serial-numbered set features color player images on a gold die cut triple crown background.

COMPLETE SET (10) 40.00 100.00
STATED ODDS 1:73
1 Troy Aikman 3.00 8.00
2 John Elway 6.00 15.00
3 Brett Favre 6.00 15.00
4 Keyshawn Johnson 4.00 10.00
5 Dan Marino 6.00 15.00
6 Curtis Martin 2.50 6.00
7 Jerry Rice 3.00 8.00
8 Barry Sanders 5.00 12.00
9 Emmitt Smith 5.00 12.00
10 Steve Young 2.50 6.00

1997 Crown Royale

This hobby exclusive set was issued in one series totalling 144-cards and was distributed in four-card packs. The set features color action player images printed on double-foiled double-etched cards with a die-cut gold crown background. The backs carry a paragraph about the player.

COMPLETE SET (144) 30.00 80.00
1 Larry Centers .30 .75
2 Kent Graham .20 .50
3 LeShon Johnson .20 .50
4 Leeland McElroy .20 .50
5 Jake Plummer RC 3.00 8.00
6 Jamal Anderson .50 1.25
7 Chris Chandler .30 .75
8 Byron Hanspard RC .30 .75
9 O.J. Santiago RC .30 .75
10 Derrick Alexander WR .30 .75
11 Jay Graham RC .30 .75
12 Michael Jackson .30 .75
13 Vinny Testaverde .30 .75
14 Todd Collins .20 .50
15 Jay Riemersma RC .20 .50
16 Antowain Smith RC 2.00 5.00
17 Steve Tasker .20 .50
18 Thurman Thomas .50 1.25
19 Rae Carruth RC .20 .50
20 Kerry Collins .50 1.25
21 Anthony Johnson .20 .50
22 Fred Lane RC .30 .75
23 Muhsin Muhammad .30 .75
24 Wesley Walls .30 .75
25 Darnell Autry RC .30 .75
26 Raymont Harris .20 .50
27 Erik Kramer .20 .50
28 Rick Mirer .20 .50
29 Rashaan Salaam .20 .50
30 Jeff Blake .30 .75
31 Ki-Jana Carter .20 .50
32 Corey Dillon RC 3.00 8.00
33 Carl Pickens .30 .75
34 Troy Aikman 1.00 2.50
35 Michael Irvin .50 1.25
36 Daryl Johnston .30 .75
37 David LaFleur RC .50 1.25
38 Deion Sanders .50 1.25
39 Emmitt Smith 1.50 4.00
40 Terrell Davis .60 1.50
41 John Elway 2.00 5.00
42 Ed McCaffrey .30 .75
43 Shannon Sharpe .30 .75
44 Neil Smith .30 .75
45 Scott Mitchell .30 .75
46 Herman Moore .30 .75
47 Johnnie Morton .30 .75
48 Barry Sanders 1.50 4.00
49 Robert Brooks .30 .75
50 Mark Chmura .30 .75
51 Brett Favre 2.00 5.00
52 Antonio Freeman .50 1.25
53 Dorsey Levens .50 1.25
54 Reggie White .50 1.25
55 Ken Dilger .20 .50
56 Marshall Faulk .60 1.50
57 Jim Harbaugh .30 .75
58 Marvin Harrison .50 1.25
59 Mark Brunell .60 1.50
60 Rob Johnson .50 1.25
61 Keenan McCardell .30 .75
62 Natrone Means .30 .75
63 Jimmy Smith .30 .75
64 Marcus Allen .50 1.25
65 Tony Gonzalez RC 3.00 8.00
66 Elvis Grbac .30 .75
67 Greg Hill .20 .50
68 Tamarick Vanover .30 .75
69 Karim Abdul-Jabbar .30 .75
70 Fred Barnett .20 .50
71 Dan Marino 2.00 5.00
72 O.J. McDuffie .30 .75
73 Jerris McPhail .20 .50
74 Cris Carter .50 1.25
75 Randall Cunningham .50 1.25
76 Brad Johnson .50 1.25
77 Jake Reed .30 .75
78 Robert Smith .30 .75
79 Drew Bledsoe .60 1.50
80 Ben Coates .30 .75
81 Terry Glenn .50 1.25
82 Curtis Martin .60 1.50
83 Troy Davis RC .30 .75
84 Heath Shuler .20 .50
85 Irv Smith .20 .50
86 Danny Wuerffel RC .50 1.25
87 Tiki Barber RC 5.00 12.00
88 Dave Brown .20 .50
89 Rodney Hampton .30 .75
90 Ike Hilliard RC 1.25 3.00
91 Amani Toomer .30 .75
92 Wayne Chrebet .50 1.25
93 Keyshawn Johnson .50 1.25
94 Adrian Murrell .30 .75
95 Neil O'Donnell .30 .75
96 Dedric Ward RC .30 .75
97 Tim Brown .50 1.25
98 Jeff George .30 .75
99 Desmond Howard .30 .75
100 Napoleon Kaufman .50 1.25
101 Ty Detmer .30 .75
102 Irving Fryar .30 .75
103 Bobby Hoying .30 .75
104 Ricky Watters .30 .75
105 Jerome Bettis .50 1.25
106 Will Blackwell RC .30 .75
107 Charles Johnson .30 .75
108 George Jones RC .30 .75
109 Kordell Stewart .50 1.25
110 Tony Banks .30 .75
111 Isaac Bruce .50 1.25
112 Eddie Kennison .30 .75
113 Lawrence Phillips .20 .50
114 Jim Everett .20 .50
115 Stan Humphries .30 .75
116 Freddie Jones .30 .75
117 Tony Martin .30 .75
118 Junior Seau .50 1.25
119 Jim Druckenmiller RC .30 .75
120 Garrison Hearst .30 .75
121 Brent Jones .20 .50
122 Terrell Owens .60 1.50
123 Jerry Rice 1.00 2.50
124 Steve Young .60 1.50
125 Chad Brown .20 .50
126 Joey Galloway .30 .75
127 Jon Kitna RC 5.00 10.00
128 Warren Moon .50 1.25
129 Chris Warren .30 .75
130 Mike Alstott .50 1.25
131 Reidel Anthony RC .50 1.25
132 Trent Dilfer .50 1.25
133 Warrick Dunn RC 2.50 6.00
134 Karl Williams RC .30 .75
135 Willie Davis .20 .50
136 Eddie George .50 1.25
137 Joey Kent RC .50 1.25
138 Steve McNair .60 1.50
139 Chris Sanders .20 .50
140 Terry Allen .50 1.25
141 Jamie Asher .20 .50
142 Stephen Davis .50 1.25
143 Henry Ellard .20 .50
144 Gus Frerotte .20 .50
S1 Mark Brunell Sample .40 1.00

1997 Crown Royale Blue Holofoil

*STARS: 6X TO 15X HI COL.
*ROOKIES: 2.5X TO 6X HI
STATED ODDS 1:25

1997 Crown Royale Gold Holofoil

*STARS: 2X TO 5X HI COL.
*ROOKIES: 1X TO 2.5X BASIC CARDS
STATED ODDS 4:25

1997 Crown Royale Silver
*SILVER STARS: 2X TO 4X HI COL.
*SILVER RCs: 1X TO 2X
SILVERS INSERTED IN SPECIAL RETAIL

1997 Crown Royale Cel-Fusion
Randomly inserted in packs at the rate of one in 49, this 20-card set features a color action player image printed on a trading card fused with a die-cut cel shaped like a football.
COMPLETE SET (20) 50.00 120.00
STATED ODDS 1:49
1 Antowain Smith 4.00 10.00
2 Troy Aikman 4.00 10.00
3 Emmitt Smith 6.00 15.00
4 Terrell Davis 2.50 6.00
5 John Elway 8.00 20.00
6 Barry Sanders 6.00 15.00
7 Brett Favre 8.00 20.00
8 Mark Brunell 2.50 6.00
9 Elvis Grbac 1.25 3.00
10 Karim Abdul-Jabbar 1.25 3.00
11 Dan Marino 8.00 20.00
12 Drew Bledsoe 2.50 6.00
13 Curtis Martin 2.50 6.00
14 Danny Wuerffel 1.00 2.50
15 Tiki Barber 10.00 25.00
16 Jeff George 1.25 3.00
17 Kordell Stewart 2.00 5.00
18 Tony Banks 1.25 3.00
19 Jerry Rice 4.00 10.00
20 Steve Young 2.50 6.00

1997 Crown Royale Chalk Talk
Randomly inserted in packs at the rate of one in 73, this set includes 20-cards. Each features a color player image on a chalk-board styled format of a football play printed on a laser-cut card.
COMPLETE SET (20) 50.00 120.00
STATED ODDS 1:73
1 Kerry Collins 2.00 5.00
2 Troy Aikman 4.00 10.00
3 Emmitt Smith 6.00 15.00
4 Terrell Davis 2.50 6.00
5 John Elway 8.00 20.00
6 Barry Sanders 6.00 15.00
7 Brett Favre 8.00 20.00
8 Mark Brunell 2.00 5.00
9 Marcus Allen 2.00 5.00
10 Dan Marino 8.00 20.00
11 Drew Bledsoe 2.50 6.00
12 Curtis Martin 2.50 6.00
13 Troy Davis .50 1.25
14 Napoleon Kaufman 1.00 2.50
15 Jerome Bettis 2.00 5.00
16 Jim Druckenmiller .50 1.25
17 Jerry Rice 4.00 10.00
18 Steve Young 2.50 6.00
19 Warrick Dunn 4.00 10.00
20 Eddie George 2.00 5.00

1997 Crown Royale Cramer's Choice Jumbos
Inserted one per box, this 10-card set features a color action player image on a large (4" by 5-1/2") die-cut silver foil trophy-shaped card. A Purple foil version of each card numbered of only 10-produced was also randomly seeded in boxes. Each of these cards was signed by Pacific Trading Cards President Michael Cramer. Finally a second purple version appeared on the market years later minus the serial numbering and Cramer signature.
COMPLETE SET (10) 25.00 60.00
ONE PER BOX
PURPLES/10 TOO SCARCE TO PRICE
*UNNUM.PURPLE: .6X TO 1.5X BASIC INSERTS
1 Deion Sanders 1.25 3.00
2 Emmitt Smith 4.00 10.00
3 Terrell Davis 1.50 4.00
4 John Elway 5.00 12.00
5 Barry Sanders 4.00 10.00
6 Brett Favre 5.00 12.00
7 Mark Brunell 1.25 3.00
8 Drew Bledsoe 1.50 4.00
9 Jim Druckenmiller .75 2.00
10 Eddie George 1.25 3.00

1997 Crown Royale Firestone on Football
Randomly inserted in packs at the rate of one in 25, this 21-card set features color action player images with etched-foil design backgrounds. Roy Firestone selected these players to appear in the set, and the backs display his unique insight into their lives as football's superheroes. Roy Firestone himself appears on card #21 with a future Hall of Fame QB offering his thoughts.
COMPLETE SET (21) 30.00 80.00
STATED ODDS 1:25
1 Kerry Collins 2.00 5.00
2 Troy Aikman 4.00 10.00
3 Deion Sanders 2.00 5.00
4 Emmitt Smith 6.00 15.00
5 Terrell Davis 2.50 6.00
6 John Elway 8.00 20.00
7 Barry Sanders 6.00 15.00
8 Brett Favre 8.00 20.00
9 Reggie White 2.00 5.00
10 Mark Brunell 2.00 5.00
11 Marcus Allen 2.00 5.00
12 Dan Marino 8.00 20.00
13 Drew Bledsoe 2.50 6.00
14 Terry Glenn 2.00 5.00
15 Curtis Martin 2.50 6.00
16 Jerome Bettis 2.00 5.00
17 Jerry Rice 4.00 10.00
18 Steve Young 2.50 6.00
19 Eddie George 2.00 5.00
20 Gus Frerotte .75 2.00
21 Roy Firestone .75 2.00

1997 Crown Royale Pro Bowl Die Cuts
Randomly inserted in packs at the rate of one in 25, this 20-card set features color images of players from the Pro Bowl. Each card is printed on a colorful foiled die-cut card with surfboards as the background.
COMPLETE SET (20) 40.00 100.00
STATED ODDS 1:25
1 Kerry Collins 1.50 4.00
2 Troy Aikman 3.00 8.00
3 Deion Sanders 1.50 4.00
4 Terrell Davis 2.00 5.00
5 John Elway 6.00 15.00
6 Shannon Sharpe 1.00 2.50
7 Barry Sanders 5.00 12.00
8 Brett Favre 6.00 15.00
9 Reggie White 1.50 4.00
10 Mark Brunell 1.50 4.00
11 Derrick Thomas 1.50 4.00
12 Drew Bledsoe 2.00 5.00
13 Ben Coates 1.00 2.50
14 Curtis Martin 2.00 5.00
15 Jerome Bettis 1.50 4.00
16 Isaac Bruce 1.50 4.00
17 Jerry Rice 3.00 8.00
18 Steve Young 2.00 5.00
19 Terry Allen 1.50 4.00
20 Gus Frerotte .60 1.50

1998 Crown Royale
The 1998 Pacific Crown Royale was issued in one series totalling 144 cards and distributed in six-card packs with a suggested retail price of $5.99. The set features color action player images printed on double-foiled, double-etched, all die-cut crown-shaped cards.
COMPLETE SET (144) 40.00 100.00
1 Larry Centers .20 .50
2 Rob Moore .30 .75
3 Adrian Murrell .30 .75
4 Jake Plummer .50 1.25
5 Jamal Anderson .50 1.25
6 Chris Chandler .30 .75
7 Tim Dwight RC 1.25 3.00
8 Tony Martin .30 .75
9 Jay Graham .20 .50
10 Pat Johnson RC 1.00 2.50
11 Jermaine Lewis .30 .75
12 Eric Zeier .30 .75
13 Rob Johnson .30 .75
14 Eric Moulds .50 1.25
15 Antowain Smith .50 1.25
16 Bruce Smith .30 .75
17 Steve Beuerlein .30 .75
18 Anthony Johnson .20 .50
19 Fred Lane .20 .50
20 Muhsin Muhammad .30 .75
21 Curtis Conway .30 .75
22 Curtis Enis RC .60 1.50
23 Erik Kramer .20 .50
24 Tony Parrish RC 1.25 3.00
25 Corey Dillon .50 1.25
26 Neil O'Donnell .30 .75
27 Carl Pickens .30 .75
28 Takeo Spikes RC 1.25 3.00
29 Troy Aikman 1.00 2.50
30 Michael Irvin .50 1.25
31 Deion Sanders .50 1.25
32 Emmitt Smith 1.50 4.00
33 Chris Warren .30 .75
34 Terrell Davis .50 1.25
35 John Elway 2.00 5.00
36 Brian Griese RC 2.50 6.00
37 Ed McCaffrey .30 .75
38 Shannon Sharpe .30 .75
39 Rod Smith WR .30 .75
40 Charlie Batch RC 1.25 3.00
41 Herman Moore .30 .75
42 Johnnie Morton .30 .75
43 Barry Sanders 1.50 4.00
44 Bryant Westbrook .20 .50
45 Robert Brooks .30 .75
46 Brett Favre 2.00 5.00
47 Antonio Freeman .50 1.25
48 Raymont Harris .20 .50
49 Vonnie Holliday RC 1.00 2.50
50 Reggie White .50 1.25
51 Marshall Faulk .60 1.50
52 E.G. Green RC 1.00 2.50
53 Marvin Harrison .50 1.25
54 Peyton Manning RC 10.00 25.00
55 Jerome Pathon RC 1.25 3.00
56 Tavian Banks RC .30 .75
57 Mark Brunell .50 1.25
58 Keenan McCardell .30 .75
59 Jimmy Smith .30 .75
60 Fred Taylor RC 2.00 5.00
61 Derrick Alexander WR .30 .75
62 Tony Gonzalez .50 1.25
63 Elvis Grbac .30 .75
64 Andre Rison .30 .75
65 Rashaan Shehee RC 1.00 2.50
66 Derrick Thomas .50 1.25
67 Karim Abdul-Jabbar .50 1.25
68 John Avery RC 1.00 2.50
69 Oronde Gadsden RC 1.25 3.00
70 Dan Marino 2.00 5.00
71 O.J. McDuffie .30 .75
72 Cris Carter .50 1.25
73 Randall Cunningham .50 1.25
74 Brad Johnson .50 1.25
75 Randy Moss RC 5.00 12.00
76 John Randle .30 .75
77 Jake Reed .30 .75
78 Robert Smith .50 1.25
79 Drew Bledsoe .75 2.00
80 Robert Edwards RC 1.00 2.50
81 Terry Glenn .50 1.25
82 Tebucky Jones RC .60 1.50
83 Tony Simmons RC 1.00 2.50
84 Mark Fields .20 .50
85 Andre Hastings .20 .50
86 Danny Wuerffel .30 .75
87 Ray Zellars .20 .50
88 Tiki Barber .50 1.25
89 Ike Hilliard .30 .75
90 Joe Jurevicius RC 1.25 3.00
91 Danny Kanell .30 .75
92 Wayne Chrebet .50 1.25
93 Glenn Foley .30 .75
94 Keyshawn Johnson .50 1.25
95 Leon Johnson .20 .50
96 Curtis Martin .50 1.25
97 Tim Brown .50 1.25
98 Jeff George .30 .75
99 Napoleon Kaufman .50 1.25
100 Jon Ritchie RC 1.00 2.50
101 Charles Woodson RC 2.50 6.00
102 Irving Fryar .30 .75
103 Bobby Hoying .30 .75
104 Allen Rossum RC .60 1.50
105 Duce Staley .60 1.50
106 Jerome Bettis .50 1.25
107 Chris Fuamatu-Ma'afala RC 1.00 2.50
108 Charles Johnson .20 .50
109 Levon Kirkland .20 .50
110 Kordell Stewart .50 1.25
111 Hines Ward RC 5.00 10.00
112 Tony Banks .30 .75
113 Tony Horne RC .60 1.50
114 Eddie Kennison .30 .75
115 Amp Lee .20 .50
116 Freddie Jones .20 .50
117 Ryan Leaf RC 1.25 3.00
118 Natrone Means .30 .75
119 Mikhael Ricks RC 1.00 2.50
120 Bryan Still .20 .50
121 Marc Edwards .20 .50
122 Garrison Hearst .50 1.25
123 Terrell Owens .50 1.25
124 Jerry Rice 1.00 2.50
125 J.J. Stokes .30 .75
126 Steve Young .60 1.50
127 Joey Galloway .30 .75
128 Ahman Green RC 2.50 6.00
129 Warren Moon .50 1.25
130 Ricky Watters .30 .75
131 Mike Alstott .50 1.25
132 Trent Dilfer .50 1.25
133 Warrick Dunn .50 1.25
134 Jacquez Green RC 1.00 2.50
135 Warren Sapp .30 .75
136 Kevin Dyson RC 1.25 3.00
137 Eddie George .50 1.25
138 Steve McNair .50 1.25
139 Yancey Thigpen .20 .50
140 Stephen Alexander RC 1.00 2.50
141 Terry Allen .50 1.25
142 Trent Green .60 1.50
143 Skip Hicks RC 1.00 2.50
144 Michael Westbrook .30 .75

1998 Crown Royale Limited Series
*VETS: 5X TO 12X BASIC CARDS
*ROOKIES: 2X TO 5X BASIC CARDS
STATED PRINT RUN 99 SER.#'d SETS

1998 Crown Royale Cramer's Choice Jumbos
Inserted one per box, this 10-card set features a color action player image on a large die-cut silver and gold foil trophy-shaped card. The player's chosen to be honored were selected by Pacific President/CEO, Michael Cramer. Six parallels with varying foil colors and number of sets were also produced. They are: Dark Blue, 35 serial-numbered sets; Green, 30 serial-numbered sets; Red, 25 serial-numbered sets; Light Blue, 20 serial-numbered sets; Gold, 10 serial-numbered sets; and Purple, 1 set signed by Michael Cramer.
COMPLETE SET (10) 60.00 120.00
OVERALL STATED ODDS 1 PER BOX
*DARK BLUES: 4X TO 10X BASIC INSERTS
DARK BLUE PRINT RUN 35 SERIAL #'d SETS
*GOLDS: 8X TO 20X BASIC INSERTS
GOLD PRINT RUN 10 SERIAL #'d SETS
*GREENS: 4X TO 10X BASIC INSERTS
GREEN PRINT RUN 30 SERIAL #'d SETS
*LIGHT BLUE: 5X TO 12X BASIC INSERTS
LIGHT BLUE PRINT RUN 20 SERIAL #'d SETS
*REDS: 5X TO 12X BASIC INSERTS
RED PRINT RUN 25 SERIAL #'d SETS
1 Terrell Davis 1.50 4.00
2 John Elway 6.00 15.00
3 Barry Sanders 5.00 12.00
4 Brett Favre 6.00 15.00
5 Peyton Manning 10.00 25.00
6 Mark Brunell 1.50 4.00
7 Dan Marino 6.00 15.00
8 Randy Moss 5.00 12.00
9 Jerry Rice 3.00 8.00
10 Warrick Dunn 1.50 4.00

1998 Crown Royale Living Legends
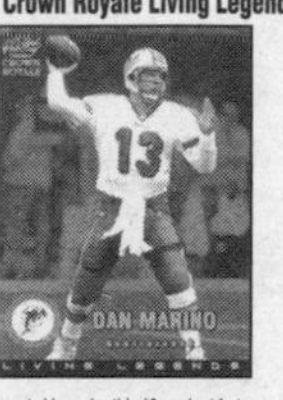

Randomly inserted in packs, this 10-card set features color action player images over a black-and-white background player photo. Only 375 serial-numbered sets were printed.
COMPLETE SET (10) 100.00 200.00
STATED PRINT RUN 375 SERIAL #'d SETS
1 Troy Aikman 5.00 12.00
2 Emmitt Smith 8.00 20.00
3 Terrell Davis 2.50 6.00
4 John Elway 10.00 25.00
5 Barry Sanders 8.00 20.00
6 Brett Favre 10.00 25.00
7 Mark Brunell 2.50 6.00
8 Dan Marino 10.00 25.00
9 Drew Bledsoe 4.00 10.00
10 Jerry Rice 5.00 12.00

1998 Crown Royale Master Performers
Randomly inserted in hobby packs only at the rate of two in 25, this 20-card set features color action player photos printed on fully foiled and etched cards with a gold oval design background.
COMPLETE SET (20) 40.00 80.00
STATED ODDS 2:25 HOBBY
1 Corey Dillon .75 2.00
2 Troy Aikman 1.50 4.00
3 Emmitt Smith 2.50 6.00
4 Terrell Davis .75 2.00
5 John Elway 3.00 8.00
6 Charlie Batch .50 1.25
7 Barry Sanders 2.50 6.00
8 Brett Favre 3.00 8.00
9 Peyton Manning 6.00 15.00
10 Mark Brunell .75 2.00
11 Fred Taylor 1.25 3.00
12 Dan Marino 3.00 8.00
13 Randy Moss 4.00 10.00
14 Drew Bledsoe 1.25 3.00
15 Curtis Martin .75 2.00
16 Kordell Stewart .75 2.00
17 Ryan Leaf .50 1.25
18 Jerry Rice 1.50 4.00
19 Steve Young 1.00 2.50
20 Warrick Dunn .75 2.00

1998 Crown Royale Pillars of the Game
Inserted one in every hobby pack, this 25-card hobby only set features color action player images with a pillar in the background printed on holographic gold foil cards which serve as the bottom card in every pack.
COMPLETE SET (25) 12.50 30.00
STATED ODDS 1:1 HOBBY
1 Antowain Smith .15 .40
2 Corey Dillon .15 .40
3 Troy Aikman .30 .75
4 Emmitt Smith .40 1.25
5 Terrell Davis .15 .40
6 John Elway .50 1.50
7 Charlie Batch .05 .15
8 Barry Sanders .40 1.25
9 Brett Favre .50 1.50
10 Antonio Freeman .08 .25
11 Peyton Manning 3.00 8.00
12 Mark Brunell .15 .40
13 Dan Marino .50 1.50
14 Randy Moss 2.00 5.00
15 Drew Bledsoe .25 .60
16 Curtis Martin .15 .40
17 Napoleon Kaufman .08 .25
18 Jerome Bettis .15 .40
19 Kordell Stewart .15 .40
20 Ryan Leaf .05 .15
21 Jerry Rice .30 .75
22 Steve Young .20 .50
23 Ricky Watters .08 .25
24 Eddie George .08 .25
25 Warrick Dunn .15 .40

1998 Crown Royale Pivotal Players
Inserted one per pack, this 25-card set featues action color images on a unique background and printed on holographic silver foil cards.
COMPLETE SET (25) 12.50 30.00
STATED ODDS 1:1 HOBBY
1 Jake Plummer .15 .40
2 Antowain Smith .15 .40
3 Corey Dillon .15 .40
4 Troy Aikman .30 .75
5 Deion Sanders .15 .40
6 Emmitt Smith .40 1.25
7 Terrell Davis .15 .40
8 John Elway .50 1.50
9 Charlie Batch .40 1.00
10 Barry Sanders .40 1.25
11 Brett Favre .50 1.50
12 Peyton Manning 3.00 8.00
13 Mark Brunell .15 .40
14 Fred Taylor .50 1.50
15 Dan Marino .50 1.50
16 Randy Moss 2.00 5.00
17 Drew Bledsoe .25 .60
18 Curtis Martin .15 .40
19 Napoleon Kaufman .15 .40
20 Jerome Bettis .15 .40
21 Kordell Stewart .15 .40
22 Ryan Leaf .40 1.00
23 Jerry Rice .30 .75
24 Eddie George .15 .40
25 Warrick Dunn .15 .40

1998 Crown Royale Rookie Paydirt
Randomly inserted in packs at the rate of one in 25, this 20-card set features color action photos with of top rookies printed on fully foiled and etched cards.
COMPLETE SET (20) 75.00 150.00
STATED ODDS 1:25 HOBBY
1 Curtis Enis .60 1.50
2 Marcus Nash .60 1.50
3 Charlie Batch 1.50 4.00
4 Vonnie Holliday 1.25 3.00
5 E.G. Green .60 1.50
6 Peyton Manning 12.00 30.00
7 Jerome Pathon 1.50 4.00
8 Tavian Banks .60 1.50
9 Fred Taylor 2.50 6.00
10 Rashaan Shehee .60 1.50
11 John Avery .60 1.50
12 Randy Moss 8.00 20.00
13 Robert Edwards 1.25 3.00
14 Charles Woodson 3.00 8.00
15 Hines Ward 5.00 12.00
16 Ryan Leaf 1.25 3.00
17 Mikhael Ricks .60 1.50
18 Ahman Green 3.00 8.00
19 Jacquez Green 1.25 3.00
20 Kevin Dyson 1.25 3.00

1999 Crown Royale
Released as a 144-card set, 1999 Crown Royale football features "crown" die-cut cards where veteran crowns where backgrounds are highlighted with silver foil and crown borders are highlighted with gold foil, and prospect crowns where backgrounds are highlighted with gold foil and crown borders are highlighted with silver foil. Crown Royale was packaged in 24-pack boxes with packs containing six cards and carried a suggested retail price of $5.99.
COMPLETE SET (144) 50.00 120.00
1 David Boston RC .50 1.25
2 Chris Greisen RC .50 1.25
3 Rob Moore .25 .60
4 Jake Plummer .25 .60
5 Frank Sanders .25 .60
6 Jamal Anderson .30 .75
7 Chris Chandler .30 .75
8 Tim Dwight .30 .75
9 Byron Hanspard .25 .60
10 Stoney Case .25 .60
11 Priest Holmes .25 .60
12 Jermaine Lewis .25 .60
13 Chris McAlister RC .50 1.25
14 Brandon Stokley RC .60 1.50
15 Doug Flutie .40 1.00
16 Eric Moulds .25 .60
17 Peerless Price RC .50 1.25
18 Antowain Smith .25 .60
19 Steve Beuerlein .30 .75
20 Tim Biakabutuka .30 .75
21 Muhsin Muhammad .25 .60
22 Curtis Conway .30 .75
23 Curtis Enis .25 .60
24 Shane Matthews .25 .60
25 Cade McNown RC .50 1.25
26 Marcus Robinson .30 .75
27 Jeff Blake .30 .75
28 Scott Covington RC .50 1.25
29 Corey Dillon .25 .60
30 Damon Griffin RC .75 2.00
31 Carl Pickens .30 .75
32 Akili Smith RC .50 1.25
33 Tim Couch RC .60 1.50
34 Kevin Johnson RC .60 1.50
35 Terry Kirby .25 .60
36 Leslie Shepherd .25 .60
37 Troy Aikman .50 1.25
38 Rocket Ismail .30 .75
39 Wane McGarity RC .50 1.25
40 Deion Sanders .30 .75
41 Emmitt Smith .60 1.50
42 Terrell Davis .30 .75
43 Brian Griese .25 .60
44 Ed McCaffrey .30 .75
45 Shannon Sharpe .30 .75
46 Rod Smith .30 .75
47 Charlie Batch .25 .60
48 Germane Crowell .25 .60
49 Sedrick Irvin RC .50 1.25
50 Herman Moore .30 .75
51 Barry Sanders .60 1.50
52 Brett Favre .75 2.00
53 Antonio Freeman .30 .75
54 Matt Hasselbeck .25 .60
55 Dorsey Levens .30 .75
56 Basil Mitchell RC .50 1.25
57 E.G. Green .25 .60
58 Marvin Harrison .30 .75
59 Edgerrin James RC .75 2.00
60 Peyton Manning 1.25 3.00
61 Terrence Wilkins RC .60 1.50
62 Mark Brunell .30 .75
63 Keenan McCardell .30 .75
64 Jimmy Smith .30 .75
65 Fred Taylor .25 .60
66 Derrick Alexander WR .25 .60
67 Elvis Grbac .25 .60
68 Warren Moon .40 1.00
69 Larry Parker RC .60 1.50
70 Andre Rison .30 .75
71 Cecil Collins RC .50 1.25
72 Damon Huard .25 .60
73 James Johnson RC .50 1.25
74 Rob Konrad RC .50 1.25
75 Dan Marino .75 2.00
76 O.J. McDuffie .30 .75
77 Cris Carter .40 1.00
78 Daunte Culpepper RC .75 2.00
79 Randall Cunningham .30 .75
80 Randy Moss UER .30 .75
81 Robert Smith .25 .60
82 Michael Bishop RC .60 1.50
83 Drew Bledsoe .30 .75
84 Ben Coates .30 .75
85 Kevin Faulk RC .50 1.25
86 Terry Glenn .30 .75
87 Billy Joe Hobert .25 .60
88 Eddie Kennison .30 .75
89 Keith Poole .25 .60
90 Ricky Williams RC .75 2.00
91 Sean Bennett RC .50 1.25
92 Kerry Collins .25 .60
93 Pete Mitchell .25 .60
94 Amani Toomer .25 .60
95 Wayne Chrebet .25 .60
96 Keyshawn Johnson .30 .75
97 Curtis Martin .30 .75
98 Tim Brown .40 1.00
99 Scott Dreisbach RC .50 1.25
100 Rich Gannon .30 .75
101 Napoleon Kaufman .25 .60
102 Tyrone Wheatley .30 .75
103 Duce Staley .25 .60
104 Charles Johnson .25 .60
105 Donovan McNabb RC 4.00 10.00
106 Torrance Small .25 .60
107 Jed Weaver RC .50 1.25
108 Jerome Bettis .40 1.00
109 Troy Edwards RC .50 1.25
110 Kordell Stewart .25 .60
111 Amos Zereoue RC .50 1.25
112 Isaac Bruce .40 1.00
113 Marshall Faulk .30 .75
114 Joe Germaine RC .60 1.50
115 Torry Holt RC 1.00 2.50
116 Kurt Warner RC 5.00 12.00
117 Jim Harbaugh .30 .75
118 Erik Kramer .30 .75
119 Natrone Means .30 .75
120 Junior Seau .30 .75
121 Jeff Garcia RC 3.00 8.00
122 Terrell Owens .30 .75
123 Jerry Rice 1.00 2.50
124 J.J. Stokes .25 .60
125 Steve Young .50 1.25
126 Sean Dawkins .25 .60
127 Brock Huard RC .50 1.25
128 Jon Kitna .25 .60
129 Derrick Mayes .25 .60
130 Charlie Rogers RC .50 1.25
131 Ricky Watters .30 .75
132 Mike Alstott .25 .60
133 Trent Dilfer .25 .60
134 Warrick Dunn .25 .60
135 Eric Zeier .25 .60
136 Kevin Daft RC .50 1.25
137 Kevin Dyson .25 .60
138 Eddie George .30 .75
139 Steve McNair .30 .75
140 Neil O'Donnell .30 .75
141 Champ Bailey RC 1.00 2.50
142 Albert Connell .25 .60
143 Stephen Davis .25 .60
144 Brad Johnson .30 .75

1999 Crown Royale Limited Series
*VETERANS: 2.5X TO 6X BASIC CARDS
*ROOKIES: 1.2X TO 3X BASIC CARDS
STATED PRINT RUN 99 SER.#'d SETS

1999 Crown Royale Premiere Date
*VETERANS: 3X TO 8X BASIC CARDS
*ROOKIES: 1.5X TO 4X BASIC CARDS
PREMIERE DATE/68 ODDS 1:25

1999 Crown Royale Card Supials
Randomly inserted in packs at the rate of two in 25, this 20-card set actually features two cards with each pull. Base cards, which are standard size, feature a cut in the back where a mini, 1/4 size, card supial of the same format is inserted. Combined players out of packs may not be the same.
COMPLETE SET (20) 50.00 100.00
*SMALL CARDS: .3X TO .8X LARGE
STATED ODDS 2:25
1 Cade McNown .60 1.50
2 Tim Couch .75 2.00
3 Troy Aikman 2.00 5.00
4 Emmitt Smith 2.50 6.00
5 Barry Sanders 3.00 8.00
6 Brett Favre 3.00 8.00
7 Edgerrin James 2.50 6.00
8 Peyton Manning 3.00 8.00
9 Mark Brunell .75 2.00
10 Fred Taylor .75 2.00
11 Damon Huard .75 2.00
12 Dan Marino 3.00 8.00
13 Randy Moss 2.50 6.00
14 Drew Bledsoe 1.25 3.00
15 Ricky Williams 1.25 3.00
16 Jerome Bettis .75 2.00
17 Kurt Warner 4.00 10.00
18 Terrell Owens .75 2.00
19 Jerry Rice 2.50 6.00
20 Jon Kitna .75 2.00

1999 Crown Royale Century 21
Randomly inserted in packs, this 10-card set features player on an all-foil card front set next to a foil-etching of their team's logo. Each card is sequentially numbered to 375.
COMPLETE SET (10) 50.00 100.00
STATED PRINT RUN 375 SER.#'d SETS
1 Jake Plummer 1.00 2.50
2 Tim Couch 1.00 2.50
3 Terrell Davis 1.50 4.00
4 Peyton Manning 6.00 15.00
5 Mark Brunell 1.50 4.00
6 Fred Taylor 1.50 4.00
7 Randy Moss 5.00 12.00
8 Drew Bledsoe 2.50 6.00
9 Ricky Williams 2.00 5.00
10 Kurt Warner 10.00 25.00

1999 Crown Royale Cramer's Choice Jumbos
Randomly inserted at one per box, this 10-card set features top players hand-picked by Michael Cramer himself. Each card is die-cut into a triangle and features rainbow holofoil. Six parallels, all of different color and serial number were released also.
COMPLETE SET (10) 30.00 60.00
OVERALL STATED ODDS ONE PER BOX
*DARK BLUE/35: 2X TO 5X BASIC INSERTS
*GOLD/10: 6X TO 15X BASIC INSERTS
*GREEN/30: 2X TO 5X BASIC INSERTS
*LIGHT BLUE/20: 3X TO 8X BASIC INSERTS
UNPRICED PURPLE PRINT RUN 1
*RED/25: 2.5X TO 6X BASIC INSERTS
1 Cade McNown 1.50 4.00
2 Tim Couch 2.50 6.00
3 Emmitt Smith 5.00 12.00
4 Edgerrin James 3.00 8.00
5 Mark Brunell 1.50 4.00
6 Fred Taylor 1.50 4.00
7 Randy Moss 3.00 8.00
8 Kurt Warner 4.00 10.00
9 Jon Kitna 1.50 4.00
10 Eddie George 1.50 4.00

1999 Crown Royale Franchise Glory
Randomly inserted in packs at the rate of one in one, this 25-card set features a blend of veterans and rising stars who have or are expected to be a franchise player for their team. Action player photos are set against a flag backdrop and "fireworks" highlights.
COMPLETE SET (25) 20.00 40.00
ONE PER PACK
1 Doug Flutie .40 1.00
2 Corey Dillon .40 1.00
3 Troy Aikman 1.00 2.50
4 Emmitt Smith 1.25 3.00
5 Terrell Davis .40 1.00
6 Herman Moore .25 .60
7 Barry Sanders 1.50 4.00
8 Brett Favre 1.50 4.00
9 Antonio Freeman .40 1.00
10 Peyton Manning 1.50 4.00
11 Mark Brunell .40 1.00
12 Fred Taylor .40 1.00
13 Dan Marino 1.50 4.00
14 Randy Moss 1.25 3.00
15 Drew Bledsoe .60 1.50
16 Keyshawn Johnson .40 1.00
17 Jerome Bettis .40 1.00
18 Marshall Faulk .60 1.50
19 Kurt Warner 5.00 12.00
20 Terrell Owens .40 1.00
21 Jerry Rice 1.25 3.00
22 Steve Young .60 1.50
23 Warrick Dunn .40 1.00
24 Eddie George .40 1.00
25 Brad Johnson .40 1.00

1999 Crown Royale Franchise Glory Super Bowl XXXIV
COMPLETE SET (25) 160.00 400.00
*SUPER BOWL CARDS: 4X TO 10X BASIC INSERTS

1999 Crown Royale Gold Crown Die Cuts
Randomly inserted in packs, this 6-card set features double-etched gold foil cards. Each card is sequentially numbered to 976.
COMPLETE SET (6) 30.00 60.00
STATED PRINT RUN 976 SER.#'d SETS
1 Tim Couch 1.25 3.00
2 Troy Aikman 3.00 8.00
3 Emmitt Smith 4.00 10.00
4 Damon Huard 1.25 3.00
5 Randy Moss 4.00 10.00
6 Kurt Warner 6.00 15.00

1999 Crown Royale Rookie Gold
Randomly inserted in packs at the rate of one in one, this 25-card set features top draft picks with player photos set on a gold base card. A die-cut parallel of this set was released also.
COMPLETE SET (25) 25.00 50.00
ONE PER PACK
*DIE CUT/10: 15X TO 40X BASIC INSERTS
1 David Boston .50 1.25
2 Brandon Stokley .60 1.50
3 Cade McNown .40 1.00
4 Akili Smith .40 1.00
5 Tim Couch .50 1.25
6 Kevin Johnson .50 1.25
7 Wane McGarity .25 .60
8 Edgerrin James 1.50 4.00
9 Terrence Wilkins .40 1.00
10 Cecil Collins .25 .60
11 Rob Konrad .40 1.00
12 James Johnson .40 1.00
13 Daunte Culpepper 1.50 4.00
14 Michael Bishop .50 1.25
15 Kevin Faulk .50 1.25
16 Ricky Williams .75 2.00
17 Scott Dreisbach .40 1.00
18 Donovan McNabb 2.00 5.00
19 Troy Edwards .40 1.00
20 Amos Zereoue .50 1.25
21 Joe Germaine .40 1.00
22 Torry Holt 1.25 3.00
23 Brock Huard .50 1.25
24 Charlie Rogers .25 .60
25 Champ Bailey .60 1.50

1999 Crown Royale Test of Time
Randomly inserted in packs at the rate of one in 25, this 10-card set features NFL players who have withstood the test of time. Cards are die cut in the form of stop watches.
COMPLETE SET (10) 30.00 60.00
STATED ODDS 1:25
1 Tim Couch 1.25 3.00
2 Emmitt Smith 3.00 8.00
3 Terrell Davis 1.00 2.50
4 Barry Sanders 4.00 10.00
5 Brett Favre 4.00 10.00
6 Antonio Freeman 1.00 2.50
7 Edgerrin James 4.00 10.00
8 Mark Brunell 1.00 2.50
9 Dan Marino 4.00 10.00
10 Jerry Rice 3.00 8.00

2000 Crown Royale
Crown Royale was released as a 144-card die cut base set with 36 short printed draft pick cards. Hobby versions feature a gold crown with silver background for veterans, and a silver crown with gold background for rookies. The retail version features a burgandy background with gold and silver foil on the crown die cut.
COMPLETE SET (144) 40.00 100.00
1 Rob Moore .25 .60
2 Jake Plummer .25 .60
3 Frank Sanders .25 .60
4 Jamal Anderson .30 .75
5 Chris Chandler .30 .75
6 Tim Dwight .30 .75
7 Tony Banks .25 .60
8 Priest Holmes .25 .60
9 Qadry Ismail .25 .60
10 Doug Flutie .30 .75
11 Rob Johnson .30 .75
12 Eric Moulds .25 .60
13 Peerless Price .30 .75
14 Steve Beuerlein .30 .75
15 Patrick Jeffers .25 .60
16 Muhsin Muhammad .25 .60
17 Curtis Enis .25 .60
18 Cade McNown .25 .60
19 Marcus Robinson .30 .75
20 Corey Dillon .25 .60
21 Darnay Scott .30 .75
22 Akili Smith .25 .60
23 Karim Abdul-Jabbar .25 .60
24 Tim Couch .30 .75
25 Kevin Johnson .25 .60
26 Troy Aikman .50 1.25
27 Joey Galloway .30 .75
28 Emmitt Smith .60 1.50
29 Terrell Davis .30 .75
30 Olandis Gary .30 .75
31 Brian Griese .25 .60
32 Ed McCaffrey .30 .75
33 Charlie Batch .25 .60
34 Herman Moore .25 .60
35 Barry Sanders .60 1.50
36 James Stewart .25 .60
37 Brett Favre .75 2.00
38 Antonio Freeman .30 .75
39 Dorsey Levens .30 .75
40 Marvin Harrison .30 .75
41 Edgerrin James .30 .75
42 Peyton Manning 1.00 2.50
43 Mark Brunell .30 .75
44 Keenan McCardell .30 .75
45 Jimmy Smith .30 .75
46 Fred Taylor .25 .60
47 Derrick Alexander .25 .60
48 Tony Gonzalez .30 .75
49 Elvis Grbac .25 .60
50 Damon Huard .25 .60
51 James Johnson .25 .60
52 Dan Marino .75 2.00
53 O.J. McDuffie .30 .75
54 Cris Carter .40 1.00
55 Daunte Culpepper .30 .75
56 Jeff George .30 .75
57 Randy Moss .30 .75
58 Robert Smith .25 .60
59 Drew Bledsoe .30 .75
60 Terry Glenn .30 .75
61 Lawyer Milloy .25 .60
62 Jeff Blake .30 .75
63 Keith Poole .25 .60
64 Ricky Williams .30 .75
65 Kerry Collins .25 .60
66 Ike Hilliard .25 .60
67 Amani Toomer .25 .60
68 Wayne Chrebet .25 .60
69 Keyshawn Johnson .30 .75
70 Ray Lucas .25 .60
71 Curtis Martin .30 .75
72 Vinny Testaverde .25 .60
73 Tim Brown .40 1.00
74 Rich Gannon .30 .75
75 Napoleon Kaufman .30 .75
76 Tyrone Wheatley .25 .60
77 Donovan McNabb .30 .75
78 Torrance Small .25 .60
79 Duce Staley .25 .60
80 Jerome Bettis .40 1.00
81 Troy Edwards .25 .60
82 Kordell Stewart .25 .60
83 Isaac Bruce .40 1.00
84 Marshall Faulk .30 .75
85 Torry Holt .30 .75
86 Kurt Warner .60 1.50
87 Jim Harbaugh .30 .75
88 Jermaine Fazande .25 .60
89 Junior Seau .30 .75
90 Charlie Garner .30 .75
91 Terrell Owens .30 .75
92 Jerry Rice 1.00 2.50
93 Steve Young .50 1.25
94 Sean Dawkins .25 .60
95 Jon Kitna .25 .60
96 Derrick Mayes .25 .60
97 Ricky Watters .30 .75
98 Mike Alstott .25 .60
99 Warrick Dunn .25 .60
100 Jacquez Green .25 .60
101 Shaun King .25 .60
102 Kevin Dyson .30 .75
103 Eddie George .30 .75
104 Jevon Kearse .25 .60
105 Steve McNair .30 .75
106 Stephen Davis .25 .60
107 Brad Johnson .30 .75
108 Michael Westbrook .25 .60
109 Shaun Alexander RC 1.00 2.50
110 Tom Brady RC 100.00 200.00
111 Marc Bulger RC .75 2.00
112 Plaxico Burress RC .75 2.00
113 Giovanni Carmazzi RC .60 1.50
114 Kwame Cavil RC .60 1.50
115 Chris Cole RC .75 2.00
116 Chris Coleman RC .60 1.50
117 Laveranues Coles RC .75 2.00
118 Ron Dayne RC 1.00 2.50
119 Reuben Droughns RC .60 1.50
120 Ron Dugans RC .60 1.50
121 Danny Farmer RC .60 1.50
122 Chafie Fields RC .60 1.50
123 Joe Hamilton RC .60 1.50
124 Todd Husak RC .60 1.50
125 Darrell Jackson RC .60 1.50
126 Thomas Jones RC .75 2.00
127 Jamal Lewis RC 1.00 2.50
128 Tee Martin RC .60 1.50
129 Rondell Mealey RC .60 1.50
130 Sylvester Morris RC .60 1.50
131 Chad Morton RC .75 2.00
132 Dennis Northcutt RC .60 1.50
133 Chad Pennington RC .75 2.00
134 Travis Prentice RC .60 1.50
135 Tim Rattay RC .75 2.00
136 Chris Redman RC .60 1.50
137 J.R. Redmond RC .60 1.50
138 R.Jay Soward RC .60 1.50
139 Shyrone Stith RC .60 1.50
140 Travis Taylor RC .60 1.50
141 Troy Walters RC .60 1.50
142 Peter Warrick RC .60 1.50
143 Dez White RC .60 1.50
144 Michael Wiley RC .60 1.50
S1 Jon Kitna Sample .60 1.50

2000 Crown Royale Draft Picks 499
*ROOKIES/499: .8X TO 2X BASE RC
STATED PRINT RUN 499 SER.#'d SETS
110 Tom Brady 125.00 250.00

2000 Crown Royale Limited Series
*VETS 1-108: 4X TO 10X BASIC CARDS
*ROOKIES 109-144: 1.5X TO 4X
STATED PRINT RUN 144 SER.#'d SETS
110 Tom Brady 150.00 300.00

2000 Crown Royale Premiere Date
*VETS 1-108: 4X TO 10X BASIC CARDS
*ROOKIES 109-144: 1.5X TO 4X
STATED PRINT RUN 145 SER.#'d SETS
110 Tom Brady 150.00 300.00

2000 Crown Royale Retail
COMPLETE SET (144) 60.00 120.00
*RETAIL CARDS: .4X TO 1X HOBBY
110 Tom Brady RC 60.00 125.00

2000 Crown Royale Cramer's Choice Jumbos
Randomly inserted at one per box, this 10-card set features top players hand-picked by Michael Cramer himself. Each card is die-cut into a triangle and features rainbow holofoil. Six parallels, all of different color and serial number were released also. Some additional parallels hit the market at a later date missing the serial numbering on the fronts.
COMPLETE SET (10) 12.50 30.00
STATED ODDS ONE PER HOBBY BOX
*DARK BLUE/35: 2.5X TO 6X BASIC INSERT
DARK BLUE PRINT RUN 35 SER.#'d SETS
*GOLD/10: 6X TO 15X BASIC INSERTS
GOLD PRINT RUN 10 SER.#'d SETS
*GREEN/30: 2.5X TO 6X BASIC INSERT
GREEN PRINT RUN 30 SER.#'d SETS
*LIGHT BLUE/20: 3X TO 8X BASIC INSERT
LIGHT BLUE PRINT RUN 20 SER.#'d SETS
UNPRICED PURPLE PRINT RUN 1
*RED/25: 3X TO 8X BASIC INSERT
RED PRINT RUN 25 SER.#'d SETS
1 Tim Couch 1.00 2.50
2 Emmitt Smith 2.00 5.00
3 Edgerrin James 1.00 2.50
4 Damon Huard .75 2.00
5 Randy Moss 1.00 2.50
6 Kurt Warner 2.00 5.00
7 Jon Kitna .75 2.00
8 Eddie George 1.00 2.50
9 Chad Pennington .75 2.00
10 Peter Warrick .75 2.00

2000 Crown Royale Fifth Anniversary Jumbos
Randomly inserted at six in 10 boxes, this 6-card jumbo set features the card designs of Crown Royale from 1995-2000. Card number one begins with 1995 and moves to card number six which is the 2000 design.
COMPLETE SET (6) 7.50 20.00
STATED ODDS 6:10 BOXES
1 Terrell Davis 1.00 2.50
2 Eddie George 1.00 2.50
3 Jon Kitna .75 2.00
4 Randy Moss 1.00 2.50
5 Kurt Warner 2.00 5.00
6 Peter Warrick .75 2.00

2000 Crown Royale First and Ten
Randomly inserted in Hobby packs, this 10-card set focuses on top yard-gainers. Each card features an action shot set against a football field background and a first down marker. These cards are sequentially numbered to 375. A retail version of each card was also produced minus the serial numbering.
COMPLETE SET (10) 30.00 60.00
STATED PRINT RUN 375 SER.#'d SETS
*RETAIL: .1X TO .3X BASIC INSERTS
1 Tim Couch 1.25 3.00
2 Troy Aikman 2.00 5.00
3 Emmitt Smith 2.50 6.00
4 Terrell Davis 1.25 3.00
5 Brett Favre 3.00 8.00
6 Edgerrin James 1.25 3.00
7 Peyton Manning 4.00 10.00
8 Randy Moss 1.25 3.00
9 Kurt Warner 2.50 6.00
10 Jerry Rice 4.00 10.00

2000 Crown Royale Game Worn Jerseys
Randomly inserted in packs, this 9-card set features a swatch of a game worn jersey coupled with an action photo of the featured player.
COMPLETE SET (9) 60.00 150.00
1 Eric Moulds 2.50 6.00
2 Brett Favre 8.00 20.00
3 Antonio Freeman 3.00 8.00
4 Ricky Williams 3.00 8.00
5 Tiki Barber 3.00 8.00
6 Charles Woodson 4.00 10.00
7 Isaac Bruce 4.00 10.00
8 Kurt Warner 6.00 15.00
9 Tim Couch 3.00 8.00

2000 Crown Royale In the Pocket
Randomly inserted in packs at the rate of two in 25, this 20-card set features a card with a circular cut through the right front of the card where a mini card is fitted behind the clear

foil cell. Mini versions may not match the larger versions out of packs.
COMPLETE SET (20) 40.00 80.00
STATED ODDS 2:25
*MINI: .25X TO .6X BASIC INSERTS
1 Tim Couch .75 2.00
2 Troy Aikman 1.25 3.00
3 Emmitt Smith 1.50 4.00
4 Charlie Batch .60 1.50
5 Edgerrin James .75 2.00
6 Peyton Manning 2.50 6.00
7 Mark Brunell .75 2.00
8 Randy Moss .75 2.00
9 Drew Bledsoe .75 2.00
10 Donovan McNabb .75 2.00
11 Kurt Warner 1.50 4.00
12 Jon Kitna .60 1.50
13 Eddie George .75 2.00
14 Steve McNair .75 2.00
15 Brad Johnson .75 2.00
16 Plaxico Burress .75 2.00
17 Ron Dayne 1.00 2.50
18 Thomas Jones .75 2.00
19 Chad Pennington .75 2.00
20 Peter Warrick .60 1.50

2000 Crown Royale In Your Face

Randomly inserted in Hobby at one in one pack and Retail at one in two packs, this 25-card set features close up portrait photos of NFL players with gold foil highlights.
COMPLETE SET (25) 7.50 20.00
STATED ODDS 1:1H/1:2R
*RAINBOW/20: 15X TO 40X BASIC INSERTS
RAINBOW PRINT RUN 20 SER.#'d SETS
RAINBOW FOUND ONLY IN HOBBY PACKS
1 Jake Plummer .20 .50
2 Cade McNown .20 .50
3 Marcus Robinson .25 .60
4 Corey Dillon .20 .50
5 Tim Couch .25 .60
6 Emmitt Smith .50 1.25
7 Terrell Davis .25 .60
8 Barry Sanders .50 1.25
9 Marvin Harrison .25 .60
10 Edgerrin James .25 .60
11 Mark Brunell .25 .60
12 Fred Taylor .20 .50
13 Dan Marino .60 1.50
14 Randy Moss .25 .60
15 Drew Bledsoe .25 .60
16 Ricky Williams .25 .60
17 Curtis Martin .25 .60
18 Isaac Bruce .30 .75
19 Marshall Faulk .25 .60
20 Kurt Warner .50 1.25
21 Jerry Rice .40 1.00
22 Jon Kitna .20 .50
23 Shaun King .20 .50
24 Eddie George .25 .60
25 Stephen Davis .20 .50

2000 Crown Royale Productions

Randomly inserted in packs at the rate of one in 25, this 20-card set features silhouette player photos on a die cut card shaped like a film reel and film cels.
COMPLETE SET (20) 20.00 50.00
STATED ODDS 1:25
1 Cade McNown .60 1.50
2 Tim Couch .75 2.00
3 Emmitt Smith 2.00 5.00
4 Olandis Gary .75 2.00
5 Barry Sanders 1.50 4.00
6 Brett Favre 2.00 5.00
7 Edgerrin James .75 2.00
8 Peyton Manning 2.50 6.00
9 Fred Taylor .60 1.50
10 Damon Huard .60 1.50
11 Dan Marino 2.00 5.00
12 Randy Moss .75 2.00
13 Drew Bledsoe .75 2.00
14 Ricky Williams .75 2.00
15 Marshall Faulk .75 2.00
16 Kurt Warner 1.50 4.00
17 Jerry Rice 2.50 6.00
18 Shaun King .60 1.50
19 Eddie George .75 2.00
20 Stephen Davis .60 1.50

2000 Crown Royale Rookie Autographs

Randomly inserted in packs, this 36-card set features authentic autographs. Cards from this set were inserted in both hobby and retail packs. Travis Taylor was also inserted in 2001 Crown Royale packs. Note that several players were short printed and Pacific later announced their print runs.
PACIFIC ANNOUNCED SOME PRINT RUNS
109 Shaun Alexander 12.00 30.00
110 Tom Brady 700.00 1200.00
111 Marc Bulger 6.00 15.00
112 Plaxico Burress 6.00 15.00
113 Giovanni Carmazzi 5.00 12.00
114 Kwame Cavil 5.00 12.00
115 Chris Cole 6.00 15.00
116 Chris Coleman 5.00 12.00
117 Laveranues Coles 6.00 15.00
118 Ron Dayne/100* 12.00 30.00
119 Reuben Droughns 5.00 12.00
120 Ron Dugans 5.00 12.00
121 Danny Farmer 5.00 12.00
122 Chafie Fields 5.00 12.00
123 Joe Hamilton 5.00 12.00
124 Todd Husak 5.00 12.00
125 Darrell Jackson 5.00 12.00
126 Thomas Jones 6.00 15.00
127 Jamal Lewis 8.00 20.00
128 Tee Martin 5.00 12.00
129 Rondell Mealey 5.00 12.00
130 Sylvester Morris 5.00 12.00
131 Chad Morton 6.00 15.00
132 Dennis Northcutt 5.00 12.00
133 Chad Pennington/100* 6.00 15.00
134 Travis Prentice 5.00 12.00
135 Tim Rattay 6.00 15.00
136 Chris Redman/100* 5.00 12.00
137 J.R. Redmond 5.00 12.00
138 R.Jay Soward 5.00 12.00
139 Shyrone Stith 5.00 12.00
140 Travis Taylor 5.00 12.00
141 Troy Walters
142 Peter Warrick/100* 5.00 12.00
143 Dez White 5.00 12.00
144 Michael Wiley 5.00 12.00

2000 Crown Royale Rookie Royalty

Randomly inserted in Hobby at one per pack and Retail at one in two, this 25-card set features top draft picks on a blue foil, laser etched card.
COMPLETE SET (25) 20.00 40.00
STATED ODDS 1:1H/1:2R
UNPRICED HOBBY DIE CUT PRINT RUN 1
1 Shaun Alexander .40 1.00
2 Tom Brady 25.00 50.00
3 Plaxico Burress .30 .75
4 Ron Dayne .40 1.00
5 Reuben Droughns .25 .60
6 Danny Farmer .25 .60
7 Chafie Fields .25 .60
8 Joe Hamilton .25 .60
9 Todd Husak .25 .60
10 Thomas Jones .30 .75
11 Jamal Lewis .40 1.00
12 Tee Martin .25 .60
13 Sylvester Morris .25 .60
14 Dennis Northcutt .25 .60
15 Chad Pennington .30 .75
16 Travis Prentice .25 .60
17 Tim Rattay .30 .75
18 Chris Redman .25 .60
19 J.R. Redmond .25 .60
20 R.Jay Soward .25 .60
21 Shyrone Stith .25 .60
22 Travis Taylor .25 .60
23 Troy Walters .25 .60
24 Peter Warrick .25 .60
25 Dez White .25 .60

2001 Crown Royale

Crown Royale was released as a 218-card die cut base set with 72 serial numbered draft pick cards. Hobby versions feature a gold crown with silver background for veterans, and a gold crown with gold background for rookies. The print runs for rookies varies for different positions, QB's are numbered to 500, RB's are numbered to 750, WR's are numbered to 1000, and all others are numbered to 1750. The Exchange card expired on December 31, 2001.
COMP.SET w/o SP's (144) 10.00 25.00
1 David Boston .20 .50
2 Thomas Jones .20 .50
3 Rob Moore .20 .50
4 Michael Pittman .25 .60
5 Jake Plummer .20 .50
6 Jamal Anderson .25 .60
7 Chris Chandler .25 .60
8 Tim Dwight .25 .60
9 Shawn Jefferson .20 .50
10 Doug Johnson .20 .50
11 Terance Mathis .20 .50
12 Tony Banks .20 .50
13 Trent Dilfer .20 .50
14 Elvis Grbac .25 .60
15 Priest Holmes .20 .50
16 Qadry Ismail .20 .50
17 Jamal Lewis .30 .75
18 Ray Lewis .30 .75
19 Shannon Sharpe .25 .60
20 Shawn Bryson .20 .50
21 Rob Johnson .25 .60
22 Eric Moulds .20 .50
23 Peerless Price .20 .50
24 Antowain Smith .25 .60
25 Steve Beuerlein .25 .60
26 Tim Biakabutuka .20 .50
27 Patrick Jeffers .20 .50
28 Muhsin Muhammad .20 .50
29 James Allen .20 .50
30 Bobby Engram .20 .50
31 Cade McNown .25 .60
32 Marcus Robinson .25 .60
33 Brian Urlacher .40 1.00
34 Corey Dillon .20 .50
35 Jon Kitna .20 .50
36 Akili Smith .20 .50
37 Peter Warrick .20 .50
38 Tim Couch .20 .50
39 Kevin Johnson .20 .50
40 Travis Prentice .20 .50
41 Troy Aikman .40 1.00
42 Rocket Ismail .25 .60
43 Emmitt Smith .50 1.25
44 Mike Anderson .20 .50
45 Terrell Davis .25 .60
46 Olandis Gary .20 .50
47 Brian Griese .20 .50
48 Ed McCaffrey .25 .60
49 Rod Smith .25 .60
50 Charlie Batch .20 .50
51 Herman Moore .20 .50
52 Johnnie Morton .25 .60
53 James Stewart .20 .50
54 Brett Favre .60 1.50
55 Antonio Freeman .30 .75
56 Ahman Green .25 .60
57 Dorsey Levens .25 .60
58 Bill Schroeder .25 .60
59 Marvin Harrison .25 .60
60 Edgerrin James .25 .60
61 Peyton Manning .75 2.00
62 Jerome Pathon .20 .50
63 Mark Brunell .25 .60
64 Keenan McCardell .25 .60
65 Jimmy Smith .25 .60
66 Fred Taylor .20 .50
67 Derrick Alexander .20 .50
68 Tony Gonzalez .25 .60
69 Sylvester Morris .20 .50
70 Tony Richardson .20 .50
71 Jay Fiedler .25 .60
72 Oronde Gadsden .20 .50
73 Tony Martin .25 .60
74 James McKnight .20 .50
75 Lamar Smith .25 .60
76 Cris Carter .30 .75
77 Daunte Culpepper .25 .60
78 Randy Moss .25 .60
79 Robert Smith .20 .50
80 Drew Bledsoe .25 .60
81 Troy Brown .20 .50
82 Kevin Faulk .20 .50
83 Terry Glenn .25 .60
84 J.R. Redmond .20 .50
85 Jeff Blake .25 .60
86 Aaron Brooks .20 .50
87 Joe Horn .20 .50
88 Ricky Williams .25 .60
89 Tiki Barber .25 .60
90 Kerry Collins .20 .50
91 Ron Dayne .25 .60
92 Ike Hilliard .20 .50
93 Amani Toomer .20 .50
94 Wayne Chrebet .20 .50
95 Curtis Martin .25 .60
96 Chad Pennington .20 .50
97 Vinny Testaverde .20 .50
98 Dedric Ward .20 .50
99 Tim Brown .30 .75
100 Rich Gannon .25 .60
101 Napoleon Kaufman .20 .50
102 Andre Rison .25 .60
103 Tyrone Wheatley .25 .60
104 Charles Johnson .20 .50
105 Donovan McNabb .25 .60
106 Torrance Small .20 .50
107 Duce Staley .20 .50
108 Jerome Bettis .30 .75
109 Plaxico Burress .20 .50
110 Kordell Stewart .20 .50
111 Hines Ward .25 .60
112 Isaac Bruce .30 .75
113 Marshall Faulk .25 .60
114 Trent Green .20 .50
115 Az-Zahir Hakim .20 .50
116 Torry Holt .25 .60
117 Kurt Warner .50 1.25
118 Curtis Conway .25 .60
119 Doug Flutie .25 .60
120 Jeff Graham .20 .50
121 Junior Seau .25 .60
122 Jeff Garcia .20 .50
123 Charlie Garner .25 .60
124 Terrell Owens .25 .60
125 Jerry Rice .60 1.50
126 Shaun Alexander .20 .50
127 Darrell Jackson .25 .60
128 Ricky Watters .25 .60
129 Mike Alstott .20 .50
130 Warrick Dunn .20 .50
131 Brad Johnson .25 .60
132 Keyshawn Johnson .25 .60
133 Shaun King .20 .50
134 Ryan Leaf .20 .50
135 Warren Sapp .25 .60
136 Kevin Dyson .20 .50
137 Eddie George .30 .75
138 Jevon Kearse .20 .50
139 Derrick Mason .20 .50
140 Steve McNair .25 .60
141 Stephen Davis .20 .50
142 Jeff George .25 .60
143 Deion Sanders .25 .60
144 Michael Westbrook .20 .50
145 A.Thomas AU/250 RC 10.00 25.00
146 Michael Vick AU/250 RC 30.00 80.00
147 Chris Chambers AU/250 RC 15.00 40.00
148 M.Bennett AU/250 RC 8.00 20.00
149 Chris Weinke AU/250 RC 8.00 20.00
150 Drew Brees AU/250 RC 400.00 800.00
151 L.Tomlinson AU/250 RC 40.00 100.00
152 M.Tuiasosopo AU/250 RC 8.00 20.00
153 David Terrell AU/250 RC 8.00 20.00
154 Rod Gardner AU/250 RC 8.00 20.00
155 Dan Alexander/1750 RC 2.00 5.00
156 Brian Allen/1750 RC 1.50 4.00
157 David Allen/750 RC 1.50 4.00
158 Will Allen/1750 RC 2.50 6.00
159 Scotty Anderson/1000 RC 2.50 6.00
160 Adam Archuleta/1750 RC 2.00 5.00
161 Jeff Backus/1750 RC 1.50 4.00
162 Alex Bannister/1000 RC 2.50 6.00
163 Kevan Barlow/750 RC 4.00 10.00
164 Gary Baxter/1750 RC 1.50 4.00
165 Josh Booty/500 RC 5.00 12.00
166 Larry Casher/1750 RC 1.50 4.00
167 Tay Cody/1750 RC 1.50 4.00
168 Jarrod Cooper/1750 RC 2.00 5.00
169 Ennis Davis/1750 RC 1.50 4.00
170 Leonard Davis/1750 RC 2.50 6.00
171 Tony Dixon/1750 RC 1.50 4.00
172 Tony Driver/1750 RC 2.00 5.00
173 Heath Evans/1750 RC 2.00 5.00
174 Jamar Fletcher/1750 RC 1.50 4.00
175 Derrick Gibson/1750 RC 1.50 4.00
176 M.Greenwood/1750 RC 1.50 4.00
177 E.Hartwell/1750 RC 1.50 4.00
178 Tim Hasselbeck/500 RC 5.00 12.00
179 Todd Heap/1750 RC 2.00 5.00
180 Travis Henry/750 RC 4.00 10.00
181 Josh Heupel/500 RC 6.00 15.00
182 Sedrick Hodge/1750 RC 1.50 4.00
183 Jabari Holloway/1750 RC 1.50 4.00
184 Willie Howard/1750 RC 1.50 4.00
185 Steve Hutchinson/1750 RC 30.00 60.00
186 James Jackson/750 RC 3.00 8.00
187 Chad Johnson/1000 RC 4.00 10.00
188 Rudi Johnson/750 RC 5.00 12.00
189 LaMont Jordan/750 RC 5.00 12.00
190 Ben Leard/500 RC 4.00 10.00
191 Alex Lincoln/1750 RC 1.50 4.00
192 Torrance Marshall/1750 RC 1.50 4.00
193 Deuce McAllister/750 RC 5.00 12.00
194 Jason McKinley/500 RC 4.00 10.00
195 Mike McMahon/500 RC 5.00 12.00
196 Snoop Minnis/1000 RC 2.50 6.00
197 Travis Minor/750 RC 4.00 10.00
198 Freddie Mitchell/1000 RC 2.50 6.00
199 Zeke Moreno/1750 RC 2.00 5.00
200 Quincy Morgan/1000 RC 3.00 8.00
201 Santana Moss/1000 RC 4.00 10.00
202 Bobby Newcombe/1000 RC 3.00 8.00
203 Moran Norris/1750 RC 1.50 4.00
204 Tommy Polley/1750 RC 1.50 4.00
205 Ken-Yon Rambo/1000 RC 2.50 6.00
206 Koren Robinson/1000 RC 3.00 8.00
207 Sage Rosenfels/500 RC 5.00 12.00
208 John Schlecht/1750 RC 1.50 4.00
209 Brandon Spoon/1750 RC 2.00 5.00
210 Michael Stone/1750 RC 1.50 4.00
211 Marcus Stroud/1750 RC 2.00 5.00
212 Vinny Sutherland/1000 RC 2.50 6.00
213 Joe Tafoya/1750 RC 1.50 4.00
214 Clevan Thomas/1750 RC 1.50 4.00
215 Ja'Mar Toombs/1750 RC 1.50 4.00
216 Fred Wakefield/1750 RC 1.50 4.00
217 Reggie Wayne/1000 RC 5.00 12.00
218 Reggie White/750 RC 3.00 8.00

2001 Crown Royale Limited Series

*VETS: 10X TO 25X BASIC CARDS
STATED PRINT RUN 25 SER.#'d SETS

2001 Crown Royale Platinum Blue

*VETS: 5X TO 12X BASIC CARDS
STATED PRINT RUN 75 SER.#'d SETS

2001 Crown Royale Premiere Date

*VETS/99: 5X TO 12X BASIC CARDS
STATED PRINT RUN 99 SER.#'d SETS

2001 Crown Royale Retail

COMPLETE SET (144) 10.00 25.00
*RETAIL VETS: .4X TO 1X HOBBY

2001 Crown Royale 21st Century Rookies

This 25 card insert set was available in both hobby and retail packs. There was one in every hobby pack and one in every two retail packs. It featured the top draft picks from the 2001 NFL Draft. These cards have a green background and are highlighted with a gold-foil stamp across the base of the card with the word rookies printed repeatedly.
COMPLETE SET (25) 12.50 30.00
STATED ODDS 1:1 HOB, 1:2 RET
1 Kevan Barlow .50 1.25
2 Michael Bennett .50 1.25
3 Josh Booty .50 1.25
4 Drew Brees 5.00 12.00
5 Chris Chambers .40 1.00
6 Rod Gardner .50 1.25
7 Tim Hasselbeck .50 1.25
8 Todd Heap .50 1.25
9 Travis Henry .50 1.25
10 Chad Johnson .60 1.50
11 Rudi Johnson .60 1.50
12 LaMont Jordan .60 1.50
13 Ben Leard .40 1.00
14 Deuce McAllister .60 1.50
15 Mike McMahon .50 1.25
16 Freddie Mitchell .40 1.00
17 Quincy Morgan .50 1.25
18 Sage Rosenfels .50 1.25
19 David Terrell .50 1.25
20 Anthony Thomas .60 1.50
21 LaDainian Tomlinson 2.00 5.00
22 Marques Tuiasosopo .50 1.25
23 Michael Vick 1.00 2.50
24 Reggie Wayne .75 2.00
25 Chris Weinke .50 1.25

2001 Crown Royale Coming Soon

This 10-card insert set featured the hottest draft picks from the 2001 NFL Draft. This set design featured the player in front of a clear blue sky for the background. These were serial numbered to 500 of each player.
COMPLETE SET (10) 20.00 50.00
STATED PRINT RUN 500 SER.#'d SETS
1 Drew Brees 12.00 30.00
2 Chris Chambers 1.00 2.50
3 Rod Gardner 1.25 3.00
4 Travis Henry 1.25 3.00
5 Deuce McAllister 1.50 4.00
6 David Terrell 1.25 3.00
7 Anthony Thomas 1.50 4.00
8 LaDainian Tomlinson 5.00 12.00
9 Michael Vick 2.50 6.00
10 Chris Weinke 1.25 3.00

2001 Crown Royale Cramers Choice Jumbos Footballs

Inserted one per hobby box, this 10-card set features top NFL stars with an authentic swatch of game used football attached to each cardfront. The cardfront was also enhanced by a silver prism background.
COMPLETE SET (10) 60.00 120.00
ONE PER HOBBY BOX
1 Jamal Lewis 5.00 12.00
2 Corey Dillon 3.00 8.00
3 Peter Warrick 3.00 8.00
4 Brett Favre 10.00 25.00
5 Fred Taylor 3.00 8.00
6 Daunte Culpepper 4.00 10.00
7 Randy Moss 4.00 10.00
8 Ricky Williams 4.00 10.00
9 Marshall Faulk 4.00 10.00
10 Kurt Warner 8.00 20.00

2001 Crown Royale Cramers Choice Jumbos Jerseys

Inserted one per hobby box, cards from this set features an authentic swatch of a game used jersey instead of a football as is with the base inserts. Card #1 Jamal Lewis was not produced in the jersey version. According to Pacific officials, the jersey version was printed in much smaller quantities (150-cards of each player, except for only 50-Favre cards) than the football swatch cards.
STATED PRINT RUN 50-150
2 Corey Dillon/150 5.00 12.00
3 Peter Warrick/150 5.00 12.00
4 Brett Favre/50 20.00 50.00
5 Fred Taylor/150 5.00 12.00
6 Daunte Culpepper/150 6.00 15.00
7 Randy Moss/150 6.00 15.00
8 Ricky Williams/150 6.00 15.00
9 Marshall Faulk/150 6.00 15.00
10 Kurt Warner/150 12.00 30.00

2001 Crown Royale Crown Rookies

Issued one per special retail pack, 10-card set features some of the hottest players selected at the 2001 NFL Draft. This set featured silver foil stamping and green boarders. These cards were serial numbered to 2500 for each player.
ONE PER SPECIAL RETAIL PACK
STATED PRINT RUN 2500 SER.#'d SETS
1 Kevan Barlow .50 1.25
2 Drew Brees 5.00 12.00
3 Travis Henry .50 1.25
4 Chad Johnson .60 1.50
5 Freddie Mitchell .40 1.00
6 Sage Rosenfels .50 1.25
7 Anthony Thomas .60 1.50
8 LaDainian Tomlinson 2.00 5.00
9 Marques Tuiasosopo .50 1.25
10 Chris Weinke .50 1.25

2001 Crown Royale Game Worn Jerseys

Randomly inserted into packs, this 15-card set features a swatch of a game worn jersey, coupled with an action photo of the featured player. Please note the stated print runs vary from player to player.
STATED PRINT RUN 276-523
1 Thomas Jones/277 4.00 10.00
2 Rob Johnson/277 5.00 12.00
3 Thurman Thomas/276 5.00 12.00
4 Corey Dillon/277 4.00 10.00
5 Peter Warrick/277 4.00 10.00
6 Brett Favre/277 12.00 30.00
7 Jay Fiedler/521 4.00 10.00
8 Lamar Smith/506 4.00 10.00
9 Aaron Brooks/523 3.00 8.00
10 Joe Horn/522 3.00 8.00
11 Ricky Williams/519 4.00 10.00
12 Marshall Faulk/277 5.00 12.00
13 Az-Zahir Hakim/519 3.00 8.00
14 Torry Holt/523 4.00 10.00
15 Kurt Warner/277 10.00 25.00

2001 Crown Royale Jewels of the Crown

This 25-card set was available in hobby and retail packs. The stated odds were one in every hobby pack and one in every two retail packs. The card design features the player's team color for the border and an action photo of the player.
COMPLETE SET (25) 5.00 12.00
STATED ODDS 1:1 HOB,1:2 RET
1 Trent Dilfer .20 .50
2 Brian Urlacher .40 1.00
3 Corey Dillon .20 .50
4 Peter Warrick .20 .50
5 Tim Couch .20 .50
6 Emmitt Smith .50 1.25
7 Mike Anderson .20 .50
8 Brian Griese .20 .50
9 Marvin Harrison .25 .60
10 Edgerrin James .25 .60
11 Mark Brunell .25 .60
12 Fred Taylor .20 .50
13 Daunte Culpepper .25 .60
14 Randy Moss .25 .60
15 Drew Bledsoe .25 .60
16 Ron Dayne .25 .60
17 Curtis Martin .25 .60
18 Rich Gannon .25 .60
19 Jerome Bettis .30 .75
20 Marshall Faulk .25 .60
21 Kurt Warner .50 1.25
22 Jeff Garcia .20 .50
23 Eddie George .30 .75
24 Steve McNair .25 .60
25 Stephen Davis .20 .50

2001 Crown Royale Landmarks

This 10-card set was randomly inserted into packs. These cards were serial numbered to 99 for each player. The card featured the player in an action pose with a scenic background.
COMPLETE SET (10) 40.00 100.00
STATED PRINT RUN 99 SER.#'d SETS
1 Emmitt Smith 6.00 15.00
2 Brian Griese 2.50 6.00
3 Edgerrin James 3.00 8.00
4 Brett Favre 8.00 20.00
5 Peyton Manning 10.00 25.00
6 Ricky Williams 3.00 8.00
7 Marshall Faulk 3.00 8.00
8 Kurt Warner 6.00 15.00
9 Jerry Rice 8.00 20.00
10 Eddie George 4.00 10.00

2001 Crown Royale Living Legends

This 20-card set was randomly inserted into packs. These cards were serial numbered to 950 for each player. The card design features the player in an action pose with a picture of his face in the background along with an action photo.
COMPLETE SET (20) 20.00 50.00
STATED PRINT RUN 950 SER.#'d SETS
1 Tim Couch .75 2.00
2 Troy Aikman 1.50 4.00
3 Emmitt Smith 2.00 5.00
4 Terrell Davis 1.00 2.50
5 Brian Griese .75 2.00
6 Brett Favre 2.50 6.00
7 Edgerrin James 1.00 2.50
8 Mark Brunell 1.00 2.50
9 Daunte Culpepper 1.00 2.50
10 Cris Carter 1.25 3.00
11 Randy Moss 1.00 2.50
12 Drew Bledsoe 1.00 2.50
13 Ricky Williams 1.00 2.50
14 Marshall Faulk 1.00 2.50
15 Kurt Warner 2.00 5.00
16 Junior Seau 1.00 2.50
17 Jerry Rice 2.50 6.00
18 Eddie George 1.25 3.00
19 Steve McNair 1.00 2.50
20 Stephen Davis .75 2.00

2001 Crown Royale Now Playing

This 20-card insert set featured the hottest superstars from the 2001 NFL. This set design featured the player in front of a clear blue sky for the background. These were serial numbered to 1000 of each player.
COMPLETE SET (20) 20.00 50.00
STATED PRINT RUN 1000 SER.#'d SETS
1 Peter Warrick .75 2.00
2 Tim Couch .75 2.00
3 Troy Aikman 1.50 4.00
4 Emmitt Smith 2.00 5.00
5 Terrell Davis 1.00 2.50
6 Brian Griese .75 2.00
7 Edgerrin James 1.00 2.50
8 Mark Brunell 1.00 2.50
9 Daunte Culpepper 1.00 2.50
10 Randy Moss 1.00 2.50
11 Drew Bledsoe 1.00 2.50
12 Ricky Williams 1.00 2.50
13 Ron Dayne 1.00 2.50
14 Donovan McNabb 1.00 2.50
15 Marshall Faulk 1.00 2.50
16 Kurt Warner 2.00 5.00
17 Jeff Garcia .75 2.00
18 Jerry Rice 2.50 6.00
19 Eddie George 1.25 3.00
20 Steve McNair 1.00 2.50

2001 Crown Royale Pro Bowl Honors

This 20-card set features 20 of the player from the 2001 Pro-Bowl. The cards were randomly inserted into packs and serial numbered to 850 for each player. The set design has a photo of the player in his Pro-Bowl jersey with the Pro-Bowl logo for the backdrop.
COMPLETE SET (20) 15.00 40.00
STATED PRINT RUN 850 SER.#'d SETS
1 Eric Moulds .75 2.00
2 Corey Dillon .75 2.00
3 Brian Griese .75 2.00
4 Marvin Harrison 1.00 2.50
5 Peyton Manning 3.00 8.00
6 Edgerrin James 1.00 2.50
7 Jimmy Smith 1.00 2.50
8 Tony Gonzalez 1.00 2.50
9 Elvis Grbac 1.00 2.50
10 Cris Carter 1.25 3.00
11 Daunte Culpepper 1.00 2.50
12 Randy Moss 1.00 2.50
13 Rich Gannon 1.00 2.50
14 Marshall Faulk 1.00 2.50
15 Torry Holt 1.00 2.50
16 Kurt Warner 2.00 5.00
17 Jeff Garcia .75 2.00
18 Terrell Owens 1.00 2.50
19 Warrick Dunn .75 2.00
20 Eddie George 1.25 3.00

2001 Crown Royale Rookie Jumbos

This 25-card jumbo set was issued as a hobby only box topper. Each card was individually serial numbered to 499 for each player. The set design was the same as the rookies from the base set except bigger.
COMPLETE SET (25) 40.00 100.00
STATED PRINT RUN 499 SER.#'d SETS
1 Dan Alexander 1.50 4.00
2 Alex Bannister 1.25 3.00
3 Kevan Barlow 1.50 4.00
4 Michael Bennett 1.50 4.00
5 Drew Brees 15.00 40.00
6 Chris Chambers 1.25 3.00
7 Rod Gardner 1.50 4.00
8 Travis Henry 1.50 4.00
9 Chad Johnson 2.00 5.00
10 Rudi Johnson 2.00 5.00
11 LaMont Jordan 2.00 5.00
12 Ben Leard 1.25 3.00
13 Deuce McAllister 2.00 5.00
14 Mike McMahon 1.50 4.00
15 Freddie Mitchell 1.25 3.00
16 Quincy Morgan 1.50 4.00
17 Koren Robinson 1.50 4.00
18 Sage Rosenfels 1.50 4.00
19 David Terrell 1.50 4.00
20 Anthony Thomas 2.00 5.00
21 LaDainian Tomlinson 6.00 15.00
22 Marques Tuiasosopo 1.50 4.00
23 Michael Vick 3.00 8.00
24 Reggie Wayne 2.50 6.00
25 Chris Weinke 1.50 4.00

2001 Crown Royale Rookie Royalty

Randomly inserted in Hobby at one per pack and Retail at one in two, this 20-card set features top draft picks on a gold foil, laser etched card. The cards were serial numbered to 1250 of each player.
COMPLETE SET (20) 20.00 50.00
STATED PRINT RUN 1250 SER. #'d SETS
1 Alex Bannister .60 1.50
2 Kevan Barlow .75 2.00
3 Michael Bennett .75 2.00
4 Drew Brees 8.00 20.00
5 Rod Gardner .75 2.00
6 Travis Henry .75 2.00
7 Chad Johnson 1.00 2.50
8 Rudi Johnson 1.00 2.50
9 Mike McMahon .75 2.00
10 Freddie Mitchell .60 1.50
11 Quincy Morgan .75 2.00
12 Koren Robinson .75 2.00
13 Sage Rosenfels .75 2.00
14 David Terrell .75 2.00
15 Anthony Thomas 1.00 2.50
16 LaDainian Tomlinson 3.00 8.00
17 Marques Tuiasosopo .75 2.00
18 Michael Vick 1.50 4.00
19 Reggie Wayne 1.25 3.00
20 Chris Weinke .75 2.00

2001 Crown Royale Rookie Signatures

Cards from this set were randomly inserted into both hobby and retail packs. They were inserted into hobby packs at a rate of one per box. The cards feature 31 skip-numbered players from the 2001 NFL Draft. The set design included a color photo of the player in an action pose with a black and white photo of his face in the background. Most cards were serial numbered to 500, but there were a few players with a shorter print run as noted below. The exchange expiration date was 12/31/2001.
PRINT RUN 500 UNLESS NOTED BELOW
1 Scotty Anderson/500 4.00 10.00
2 Alex Bannister/500 4.00 10.00
3 Kevan Barlow/500 5.00 12.00
4 Michael Bennett/100 8.00 20.00
5 Josh Booty/500 5.00 12.00
6 Drew Brees/100 600.00 1200.00
7 Chris Chambers/250 5.00 12.00
8 Heath Evans/500 5.00 12.00
11 Tim Hasselbeck/500 5.00 12.00
12 Todd Heap/500 5.00 12.00
15 James Jackson/500 4.00 10.00
16 Chad Johnson/500 15.00 40.00
17 Rudi Johnson/500 6.00 15.00
18 Ben Leard/500 4.00 10.00
19 Jason McKinley/500 4.00 10.00
20 Mike McMahon/500 5.00 12.00
21 Snoop Minnis/500 4.00 10.00
22 Freddie Mitchell/500 4.00 10.00
23 Quincy Morgan/500 5.00 12.00
24 Bobby Newcombe/500 5.00 12.00
25 Moran Norris/500 4.00 10.00
26 Sage Rosenfels/500 5.00 12.00
27 Vinny Sutherland/500 4.00 10.00
28 David Terrell/250 6.00 15.00
29 Anthony Thomas/250 8.00 20.00
30 LaDainian Tomlinson/100 40.00 100.00
32 Marques Tuiasosopo/250 6.00 15.00
33 Michael Vick/100 50.00 120.00
34 Reggie Wayne/500 12.00 30.00
35 Chris Weinke/100 8.00 20.00
36 Reggie White/500 4.00 10.00

2002 Crown Royale

Released in August 2002, this 216-card set includes 144 veterans and 72 rookies. The S.R.P. per hobby pack is $5.99. The rookies were inserted one per hobby pack or at a stated rate of one in four retail packs.
COMPLETE SET (216) 100.00 200.00
COMP.SET w/o RCs (144) 20.00 50.00
145-216 ROOKIE ODDS 1:1 H, 1:4 R
1 David Boston .25 .60
2 Thomas Jones .25 .60
3 Jake Plummer .25 .60
4 Frank Sanders .25 .60
5 Jamal Anderson .30 .75
6 Warrick Dunn .25 .60
7 Brian Finneran .25 .60
8 Shawn Jefferson .25 .60
9 Michael Vick .30 .75
10 Jeff Blake .30 .75
11 Jamal Lewis .30 .75
12 Ray Lewis .40 1.00
13 Chris Redman .25 .60
14 Travis Taylor .25 .60
15 Drew Bledsoe .30 .75
16 Travis Henry .25 .60
17 Eric Moulds .25 .60
18 Peerless Price .25 .60
19 Isaac Byrd .25 .60
20 Muhsin Muhammad .25 .60
21 Lamar Smith .25 .60
22 Chris Weinke .25 .60
23 Marty Booker .25 .60
24 Jim Miller .25 .60
25 Marcus Robinson .30 .75
26 Anthony Thomas .30 .75
27 Brian Urlacher .40 1.00
28 Corey Dillon .25 .60
29 Gus Frerotte .25 .60
30 Jon Kitna .25 .60
31 Darnay Scott .30 .75
32 Peter Warrick .25 .60
33 Tim Couch .25 .60
34 James Jackson .25 .60
35 Kevin Johnson .25 .60
36 Quincy Morgan .25 .60
37 Quincy Carter .25 .60
38 Joey Galloway .30 .75
39 Rocket Ismail .30 .75
40 Emmitt Smith .60 1.50
41 Mike Anderson .25 .60
42 Terrell Davis .30 .75
43 Brian Griese .25 .60
44 Ed McCaffrey .30 .75
45 Rod Smith .30 .75
46 Germane Crowell .25 .60
47 Az-Zahir Hakim .25 .60
48 Mike McMahon .25 .60
49 Bill Schroeder .25 .60
50 Brett Favre .75 2.00
51 Bubba Franks .25 .60
52 Antonio Freeman .40 1.00
53 Terry Glenn .30 .75
54 Ahman Green .30 .75
55 James Allen .25 .60
56 Corey Bradford .25 .60
57 Kent Graham .25 .60
58 Jermaine Lewis .25 .60
59 Marvin Harrison .30 .75
60 Edgerrin James .30 .75
61 Peyton Manning 1.00 2.50
62 Dominic Rhodes .25 .60
63 Reggie Wayne .30 .75
64 Mark Brunell .30 .75
65 Patrick Johnson .25 .60
66 Jimmy Smith .30 .75
67 Fred Taylor .25 .60
68 Tony Gonzalez .30 .75
69 Trent Green .25 .60
70 Priest Holmes .25 .60
71 Johnnie Morton .30 .75
72 Chris Chambers .25 .60
73 Jay Fiedler .30 .75
74 James McKnight .25 .60
75 Ricky Williams .30 .75
76 Derrick Alexander .25 .60
77 Michael Bennett .25 .60
78 Daunte Culpepper .30 .75
79 Randy Moss .30 .75
80 Tom Brady 2.00 5.00
81 Troy Brown .25 .60
82 Kevin Faulk .25 .60
83 David Patten .25 .60
84 Antowain Smith .30 .75
85 Aaron Brooks .25 .60
86 Joe Horn .25 .60
87 Deuce McAllister .30 .75
88 Jerome Pathon .25 .60
89 Tiki Barber .30 .75
90 Kerry Collins .25 .60
91 Ron Dayne .30 .75
92 Ike Hilliard .25 .60
93 Michael Strahan .30 .75
94 Amani Toomer .25 .60
95 Wayne Chrebet .25 .60
96 Laveranues Coles .30 .75
97 Curtis Martin .30 .75
98 Vinny Testaverde .25 .60
99 Tim Brown .40 1.00
100 Rich Gannon .30 .75
101 Charlie Garner .30 .75
102 Jerry Rice .75 2.00
103 Tyrone Wheatley .30 .75
104 Charles Woodson .40 1.00
105 Donovan McNabb .30 .75
106 Todd Pinkston .25 .60
107 Duce Staley .25 .60
108 James Thrash .30 .75
109 Jerome Bettis .40 1.00
110 Plaxico Burress .25 .60
111 Kordell Stewart .25 .60
112 Hines Ward .30 .75
113 Isaac Bruce .40 1.00
114 Marshall Faulk .30 .75
115 Torry Holt .30 .75
116 Kurt Warner .30 .75
117 Drew Brees .75 2.00
118 Curtis Conway .30 .75
119 Tim Dwight .25 .60
120 Doug Flutie .30 .75
121 Junior Seau .30 .75
122 LaDainian Tomlinson .40 1.00
123 Jeff Garcia .25 .60
124 Garrison Hearst .25 .60
125 Terrell Owens .30 .75
126 J.J. Stokes .25 .60
127 Shaun Alexander .25 .60
128 Trent Dilfer .25 .60
129 Darrell Jackson .30 .75
130 Koren Robinson .25 .60
131 Mike Alstott .25 .60
132 Brad Johnson .30 .75
133 Keyshawn Johnson .30 .75
134 Keenan McCardell .30 .75
135 Michael Pittman .30 .75
136 Warren Sapp .30 .75
137 Kevin Dyson .30 .75
138 Eddie George .30 .75
139 Derrick Mason .25 .60
140 Steve McNair .30 .75
141 Stephen Davis .25 .60
142 Rod Gardner .25 .60
143 Jacquez Green .25 .60
144 Shane Matthews .25 .60
145 Jason McAddley RC 1.00 2.50
146 Josh McCown RC 1.25 3.00
147 Josh Scobey RC 1.00 2.50
148 T.J. Duckett RC .75 2.00
149 Kahlil Hill RC .75 2.00
150 Kurt Kittner RC .75 2.00
151 Ron Johnson RC 1.00 2.50
152 Tellis Redmon RC .75 2.00
153 Chester Taylor RC 1.25 3.00
154 Josh Reed RC 1.00 2.50
155 Randy Fasani RC .75 2.00
156 DeShaun Foster RC 1.25 3.00
157 Julius Peppers RC 2.00 5.00
158 Adrian Peterson RC 1.00 2.50
159 Andre Davis RC .75 2.00
160 William Green RC 1.00 2.50
161 Antonio Bryant RC 1.25 3.00
162 Woody Dantzler RC 1.00 2.50
163 Ennis Haywood RC .75 2.00
164 Chad Hutchinson RC .75 2.00
165 Jamar Martin RC 1.00 2.50
166 Roy Williams RC .75 2.00
167 Herb Haygood RC .75 2.00
168 Ashley Lelie RC .75 2.00
169 Clinton Portis RC 1.25 3.00
170 Eddie Drummond RC .75 2.00
171 Joey Harrington RC .75 2.00
172 Luke Staley RC .75 2.00
173 Craig Nall RC 1.00 2.50
174 Javon Walker RC 1.25 3.00
175 Jarrod Baxter RC .75 2.00
176 David Carr RC .75 2.00
177 Delvon Flowers RC .75 2.00
178 Jabar Gaffney RC .75 2.00
179 Jonathan Wells RC 1.00 2.50
180 David Garrard RC 1.00 2.50
181 John Henderson RC 1.00 2.50
182 Omar Easy RC 1.00 2.50
183 Leonard Henry RC .75 2.00
184 Atrews Bell RC .75 2.00
185 Deion Branch RC 1.25 3.00
186 Rohan Davey RC 1.25 3.00
187 Daniel Graham RC 1.00 2.50
188 Antwoine Womack RC .75 2.00
189 J.T. O'Sullivan RC 1.00 2.50
190 Donte Stallworth RC 1.25 3.00
191 Tim Carter RC 1.00 2.50
192 Daryl Jones RC .75 2.00
193 Jeremy Shockey RC 1.25 3.00
194 Ronald Curry RC .75 2.00
195 Napoleon Harris RC 1.00 2.50
196 Larry Ned RC .75 2.00
197 Freddie Milons RC .75 2.00
198 Lito Sheppard RC 1.25 3.00
199 Brian Westbrook RC 1.50 4.00
200 Lee Mays RC .75 2.00
201 Antwaan Randle El RC 1.00 2.50
202 Eric Crouch RC 1.25 3.00
203 Lamar Gordon RC 1.00 2.50
204 Robert Thomas RC .75 2.00
205 Seth Burford RC .75 2.00
206 Reche Caldwell RC 1.00 2.50
207 Quentin Jammer RC 1.25 3.00
208 Brandon Doman RC .75 2.00
209 Maurice Morris RC 1.00 2.50
210 Jerramy Stevens RC 1.25 3.00
211 Travis Stephens RC .75 2.00
212 Marquise Walker RC .75 2.00
213 Jake Schifino RC .75 2.00
214 Ladell Betts RC 1.25 3.00
215 Patrick Ramsey RC 1.00 2.50
216 Cliff Russell RC .75 2.00

2002 Crown Royale Blue

*BLUE VETS/175: 3X TO 8X BASIC CARDS
1-144 VETERAN/175 ODDS 1:15 HOB/RET
1-144 VETERAN PRINT RUN 175
*BLUE ROOKIES/99: 2X TO 5X
145-216 ROOKIE/99 ODDS 1:25 HOB
145-216 ROOKIE PRINT RUN 99

2002 Crown Royale Red

COMPLETE SET (144) 40.00 100.00
*RED VETS: 1X TO 2.5X BASIC CARDS
RED/525 ODDS 1:3 HOBBY
STATED PRINT RUN 525 SER.#'d SETS

2002 Crown Royale Crowning Glory

This 20-card insert set is randomly inserted in hobby packs only at a rate of 1:25 for card #'s 1-10. It is randomly inserted in retail packs only at a rate of 1:25 for card #'s 11-20.
COMPLETE SET (20) 40.00 100.00
1-10 STATED ODDS 1:25 HOBBY
11-20 STATED ODDS 1:25 RETAIL
1 T.J. Duckett 1.00 2.50
2 DeShaun Foster 1.50 4.00
3 William Green 1.25 3.00
4 Ashley Lelie 1.00 2.50
5 Clinton Portis 1.50 4.00
6 Joey Harrington 1.00 2.50
7 David Carr 1.00 2.50
8 Jabar Gaffney 1.00 2.50
9 Donte Stallworth 1.50 4.00
10 Patrick Ramsey 1.25 3.00
11 Michael Vick 1.50 4.00
12 Anthony Thomas 1.50 4.00
13 Emmitt Smith 3.00 8.00
14 Brett Favre 4.00 10.00
15 Peyton Manning 5.00 12.00
16 Randy Moss 1.50 4.00
17 Tom Brady 10.00 25.00
18 Jerry Rice 4.00 10.00
19 Kurt Warner 1.50 4.00
20 LaDainian Tomlinson 2.00 5.00

2002 Crown Royale Legendary Heroes

This 10-card insert set is serially numbered of 80 and was inserted in packs at a stated rate of 1:392.
LEG. HERO/80 ODDS 1:392 HOB, 1:968 RET
STATED PRINT RUN 80 SER.#'d SETS
1 Emmitt Smith 10.00 25.00
2 Terrell Davis 5.00 12.00
3 Brett Favre 12.00 30.00
4 Peyton Manning 15.00 40.00
5 Ricky Williams 5.00 12.00
6 Randy Moss 5.00 12.00
7 Jerry Rice 12.00 30.00
8 Donovan McNabb 5.00 12.00
9 Marshall Faulk 5.00 12.00
10 Kurt Warner 5.00 12.00

2002 Crown Royale Majestic Motion

This 10-card insert set was inserted into packs at a stated rate of 1:25.
COMPLETE SET (10) 25.00 60.00
STATED ODDS 1:25 HOB, 1:49 RET
1 Michael Vick 1.50 4.00
2 Anthony Thomas 1.50 4.00
3 Emmitt Smith 3.00 8.00
4 Brett Favre 4.00 10.00
5 Peyton Manning 5.00 12.00
6 Randy Moss 1.50 4.00
7 Jerry Rice 4.00 10.00
8 Marshall Faulk 1.50 4.00
9 Kurt Warner 1.50 4.00
10 LaDainian Tomlinson 2.00 5.00

2002 Crown Royale Pro Bowl Honors
This 20-card insert set was inserted into packs at a stated rate of 1:6.
COMPLETE SET (20) 15.00 40.00
STATED ODDS 1:6 HOB, 1:13 RET
1 Brian Urlacher 1.25 3.00
2 Corey Dillon .60 1.50
3 Emmitt Smith 2.00 5.00
4 Terrell Davis .75 2.00
5 Ahman Green .75 2.00
6 Marvin Harrison .75 2.00
7 Edgerrin James .75 2.00
8 Peyton Manning 2.50 6.00
9 Daunte Culpepper .75 2.00
10 Randy Moss .75 2.00
11 Tom Brady 5.00 12.00
12 Curtis Martin .75 2.00
13 Rich Gannon .75 2.00
14 Jerry Rice 2.00 5.00
15 Donovan McNabb .75 2.00
16 Kordell Stewart .60 1.50
17 Marshall Faulk .75 2.00
18 Kurt Warner .75 2.00
19 Junior Seau .75 2.00
20 Eddie George .75 2.00

2002 Crown Royale Sunday Soldiers
This 20-card insert set was inserted into packs at a stated rate of 1:15.
COMPLETE SET (20) 30.00 80.00
STATED ODDS 1:15 HOB, 1:25 RET
1 T.J. Duckett 1.25 3.00
2 Michael Vick 1.50 4.00
3 Drew Bledsoe 1.50 4.00
4 DeShaun Foster 2.00 5.00
5 William Green 1.50 4.00
6 Emmitt Smith 3.00 8.00
7 Ashley Lelie 1.25 3.00
8 Joey Harrington 1.25 3.00
9 Brett Favre 4.00 10.00
10 David Carr 1.25 3.00
11 Peyton Manning 5.00 12.00
12 Randy Moss 1.50 4.00
13 Tom Brady 10.00 25.00
14 Donte Stallworth 2.00 5.00
15 Donovan McNabb 1.50 4.00
16 Marshall Faulk 1.50 4.00
17 Kurt Warner 1.50 4.00
18 LaDainian Tomlinson 2.00 5.00
19 Shaun Alexander 1.25 3.00
20 Patrick Ramsey 1.50 4.00

2002 Crown Royale Triple Threads Jerseys
This 40-card insert set features jersey cards containing three swatches. These cards were inserted at a rate of 2:25 and Pacific later announced the print runs. There is also a gold parallel of this set with each card serial numbered to 25.
STATED ODDS 2:25 HOB, 1:97 RET
*GOLD/25: .8X TO 2X BASIC TRIPLE
GOLD SERIAL #'d TO 25
1 Boston/Jones/Plummer/535 3.00 8.00
2 Jenkins/Mitch/Sanders/1079 3.00 8.00
3 Lewis/Redman/Taylor/326 5.00 12.00
4 Germany/Moulds/Price/256 3.00 8.00
5 Bryson/Morris/Riemer./731 3.00 8.00
6 Miller/Terrell/Urlacher/216 5.00 12.00
7 Housh/C.Johnson/Warr/480 3.00 8.00
8 Dawson/Northcutt/White/606 3.00 8.00
9 M.Ander/McCaff/R.Smith/100 4.00 10.00
10 S.Ander/Crowell/Howard/956 4.00 10.00
11 Brunell/J.Smith/Taylor/355 4.00 10.00
12 Blaylock/T.Green/Richard/776 3.00 8.00
13 R.Ander/Pennin/Testav/500 3.00 8.00
14 T.Brown/Jett/Jordan/1265 5.00 12.00
15 C.Lewis/Ce.Martin/Pinks/728 3.00 8.00
16 Bruener/Ward/Zereoue/900 4.00 10.00
17 Fuamatu/Kreider/Martin/1063 3.00 8.00
18 Flutie/Jenkins/Seau/1043 4.00 10.00
19 C.Bailey/S.Davis/McCant/1640 4.00 10.00
20 T.Davis/E.James/R.Will/215 4.00 10.00
21 Culpep/Brady/McNabb/281 12.00 30.00
22 Dillon/Alexander/George/983 4.00 10.00
23 E.Smith/Faulk/Tomlins/820 8.00 20.00
24 Vick/Weinke/Brees/246 10.00 25.00
25 Favre/Manning/Warner/480 15.00 40.00
26 A.Green/C.Martin/Bettis/727 5.00 12.00
27 Bledsoe/Couch/Griese/716 4.00 10.00
28 Brooks/Stewart/McNair/1217 4.00 10.00
29 Moss/Rice/Bruce/886 10.00 25.00
30 Harrison/Carter/Owens/361 5.00 12.00
31 J.Anders/Christn/Kelly/650 4.00 10.00
32 Gallo/Hamb/Woodson/730 4.00 10.00
33 Hasselbeck/Miii/Strong/606 3.00 8.00
34 Gilmore/Greisen/Jackson/486 3.00 8.00
35 Heap/Redman/Stokley/606 3.00 8.00
36 Hayes/Pass/An.Smith/892 4.00 10.00
37 D.Alexand/Bates/Walsh/544 3.00 8.00
38 E.Smith/A.Green/R.Will/232 8.00 20.00
39 Favre/Brunell/McNabb/558 10.00 25.00
40 Brees/Thomas/Weinke/554 10.00 25.00

2010 Crown Royale
201-235 ROOKIE AU PRINT RUN 199-499
1 Chris Wells .40 1.00
2 Larry Fitzgerald .50 1.25
3 Steve Breaston .40 1.00
4 Matt Ryan .50 1.25
5 Michael Turner .40 1.00
6 Roddy White .40 1.00
7 Anquan Boldin .40 1.00
8 Joe Flacco .50 1.25
9 Ray Rice .40 1.00
10 Lee Evans .50 1.25
11 Marshawn Lynch .50 1.25
12 Ryan Fitzpatrick .40 1.00
13 DeAngelo Williams .40 1.00
14 Matt Moore .40 1.00
15 Steve Smith .50 1.25
16 Devin Hester .50 1.25
17 Jay Cutler .40 1.00
18 Matt Forte .40 1.00
19 Carson Palmer .50 1.25
20 Cedric Benson .40 1.00
21 Chad Ochocinco .40 1.00
22 Terrell Owens .50 1.25
23 Jake Delhomme .40 1.00
24 Josh Cribbs .40 1.00
25 Mohamed Massaquoi .50 1.25
26 Felix Jones .40 1.00
27 Jason Witten .50 1.25
28 Miles Austin .40 1.00
29 Tony Romo .50 1.25
30 Eddie Royal .40 1.00
31 Knowshon Moreno .40 1.00
32 Kyle Orton .40 1.00
33 Brandon Pettigrew .40 1.00
34 Calvin Johnson .60 1.50
35 Matthew Stafford .50 1.25
36 Aaron Rodgers 1.25 3.00
37 Greg Jennings .40 1.00
38 Ryan Grant .50 1.25
39 Andre Johnson .50 1.25
40 Matt Schaub .40 1.00
41 Steve Slaton .40 1.00
42 Dallas Clark .40 1.00
43 Peyton Manning 1.50 4.00
44 Reggie Wayne .50 1.25
45 David Garrard .40 1.00
46 Maurice Jones-Drew .40 1.00
47 Mike Sims-Walker .40 1.00
48 Dwayne Bowe .50 1.25
49 Jamaal Charles .50 1.25
50 Matt Cassel .40 1.00
51 Brandon Marshall .50 1.25
52 Chad Henne .50 1.25
53 Ronnie Brown .40 1.00
54 Adrian Peterson .60 1.50
55 Brett Favre 1.25 3.00
56 Percy Harvin .40 1.00
57 Sidney Rice .40 1.00
58 Randy Moss .50 1.25
59 Tom Brady 1.50 4.00
60 Wes Welker .50 1.25
61 Drew Brees .60 1.50
62 Marques Colston .40 1.00
63 Pierre Thomas .40 1.00
64 Brandon Jacobs .40 1.00
65 Eli Manning .50 1.25
66 Steve Smith USC .40 1.00
67 Braylon Edwards .40 1.00
68 LaDainian Tomlinson .60 1.50
69 Mark Sanchez .40 1.00
70 Shonn Greene .40 1.00
71 Darren McFadden .40 1.00
72 Jason Campbell .40 1.00
73 Louis Murphy .40 1.00
74 DeSean Jackson .50 1.25
75 Kevin Kolb .40 1.00
76 LeSean McCoy .60 1.50
77 Ben Roethlisberger .60 1.50
78 Rashard Mendenhall .40 1.00
79 Troy Polamalu .60 1.50
80 Antonio Gates .50 1.25
81 Darren Sproles .50 1.25
82 Philip Rivers .60 1.50
83 Frank Gore .50 1.25
84 Michael Crabtree .40 1.00
85 Vernon Davis .40 1.00
86 Julius Jones .40 1.00
87 Matt Hasselbeck .40 1.00
88 T.J. Houshmandzadeh .40 1.00
89 Donnie Avery .40 1.00
90 James Laurinaitis .50 1.25
91 Steven Jackson .40 1.00
92 Cadillac Williams .40 1.00
93 Josh Freeman .50 1.25
94 Kellen Winslow Jr. .40 1.00
95 Chris Johnson .40 1.00
96 Kenny Britt .40 1.00
97 Vince Young .40 1.00
98 Chris Cooley .40 1.00
99 Clinton Portis .40 1.00
100 Donovan McNabb .50 1.25
101 Aaron Hernandez RC 1.00 2.50
102 Amari Spievey RC 1.00 2.50
103 Andrew Quarless RC 1.00 2.50
104 Anthony Davis RC 1.25 3.00
105 Anthony Dixon RC 1.00 2.50
106 Anthony McCoy RC 1.00 2.50
107 Antonio Brown RC 6.00 15.00
108 Blair White RC 1.00 2.50
109 Stephen Williams RC 1.50 4.00
110 Brandon Graham RC 1.25 3.00
111 Brandon Spikes RC 1.00 2.50
112 Brian Price RC 1.00 2.50
113 Bryan Bulaga RC 1.00 2.50
114 Carlos Dunlap RC 1.00 2.50
115 Carlton Mitchell RC 1.00 2.50
116 Chad Jones RC 1.00 2.50
117 Keith Toston RC 1.50 4.00
118 Chris Cook RC 1.00 2.50
119 Victor Cruz RC 2.00 5.00
120 Corey Wootton RC 1.00 2.50
121 Dan LeFevour RC 1.00 2.50
122 Dan Williams RC 1.00 2.50
123 Daryl Washington RC 1.00 2.50
124 David Gettis RC 1.00 2.50
125 David Reed RC 1.00 2.50
126 Deji Karim RC 1.25 3.00
127 Dennis Pitta RC 1.00 2.50
128 Derrick Morgan RC 1.00 2.50
129 Devin McCourty RC 1.25 3.00
130 Dezmon Briscoe RC 1.00 2.50
131 Dominique Franks RC 1.00 2.50
132 Michael Hoomanawanui RC 1.50 4.00
133 Earl Thomas RC 2.50 6.00
134 Ed Dickson RC 1.00 2.50
135 Everson Griffen RC 1.00 2.50
136 Johnathan Haggerty RC 1.25 3.00
137 Garrett Graham RC 1.00 2.50
138 Jacoby Ford RC 1.00 2.50
139 James Starks RC 1.25 3.00
140 Jared Odrick RC 1.25 3.00
141 Jarrett Brown RC 1.00 2.50
142 Jason Pierre-Paul RC 1.50 4.00
143 Jason Worilds RC 1.00 2.50
144 Javier Arenas RC 1.00 2.50
145 Jeremy Williams RC 1.00 2.50
146 Jermaine Cunningham RC 1.00 2.50
147 Jerome Murphy RC 1.25 3.00
148 Jerry Hughes RC 1.00 2.50
149 Matt Willis RC 1.50 4.00
150 Jimmy Graham RC 2.50 6.00
151 Joe Haden RC 1.50 4.00
152 Joe Webb RC 1.00 2.50
153 John Conner RC 1.00 2.50
154 John Skelton RC 1.25 3.00
155 Joique Bell RC 1.00 2.50
156 Jonathan Crompton RC 1.00 2.50
157 Kareem Jackson RC 1.00 2.50
158 Kerry Meier RC 1.25 3.00
159 Koa Misi RC 1.25 3.00
160 Kyle Williams RC 1.50 4.00
161 Kyle Wilson RC 1.00 2.50
162 Lamarr Houston RC 1.25 3.00
163 LeGarrette Blount RC 2.00 5.00
164 Brody Eldridge RC 1.50 4.00
165 Linval Joseph RC 1.00 2.50
166 Lonyae Miller RC 1.25 3.00
167 Major Wright RC 1.00 2.50
168 Marc Mariani RC 1.50 4.00
169 Maurkice Pouncey RC 1.25 3.00
170 Mike Iupati RC 1.50 4.00
171 Mike Neal RC 1.50 4.00
172 Morgan Burnett RC 1.25 3.00
173 Myron Lewis RC 1.25 3.00
174 Nate Allen RC 1.50 4.00
175 NaVorro Bowman RC 2.00 5.00
176 Pat Angerer RC 1.00 2.50
177 Patrick Robinson RC 1.25 3.00
178 Perrish Cox RC 1.25 3.00
179 Ricky Sapp RC 1.00 2.50
180 Riley Cooper RC 1.00 2.50
181 Russell Okung RC 1.00 2.50
182 Rusty Smith RC 1.50 4.00
183 Sean Canfield RC 1.00 2.50
184 Sean Lee RC 2.00 5.00
185 Sean Weatherspoon RC 1.00 2.50
186 Sergio Kindle RC 1.00 2.50
187 Seyi Ajirotutu RC 1.00 2.50
188 Tervaris Johnson RC 1.25 3.00
189 T.J. Ward RC 1.50 4.00
190 Taylor Mays RC 1.00 2.50
191 Chris Ivory RC 2.50 6.00
192 Terrence Cody RC 1.00 2.50
193 Thaddeus Lewis RC 1.25 3.00
194 Tony Moeaki RC 1.25 3.00
195 Tony Pike RC 1.00 2.50
196 Torell Troup RC 1.00 2.50
197 Trent Williams RC 1.25 3.00
198 Max Hall RC 1.50 4.00
199 Tyson Alualu RC 1.00 2.50
200 Zac Robinson RC 1.25 3.00
201 A.Edwards AU/499 RC 4.00 10.00
202 C.J. Spiller AU/299 RC 4.00 10.00
203 D.Thomas AU/399 RC 12.00 30.00
204 E.Sanders AU/499 RC 5.00 12.00
205 Gerald McCoy AU/199 RC 4.00 10.00
206 J.Gresham AU/499 RC 3.00 8.00
207 J.Dwyer AU/499 RC 3.00 8.00
208 Ryan Mathews AU/299 RC 4.00 10.00
209 Mardy Gilyard AU/499 RC 3.00 8.00
210 Mike Williams AU/499 RC 3.00 8.00
211 Tim Tebow AU/299 RC 25.00 60.00
212 Toby Gerhart AU/449 RC 3.00 8.00
213 R.McClain AU/499 RC 3.00 8.00
214 Montario Hardesty AU/499 RC 3.00 8.00
215 Ben Tate AU/499 RC 3.00 8.00
216 D.Williams AU/449 RC 3.00 8.00
217 Eric Berry AU/499 RC 5.00 12.00
218 Marcus Easley AU/499 RC 3.00 8.00
219 Jahvid Best AU/299 RC 4.00 10.00
220 Joe McKnight AU/499 RC 3.00 8.00
221 Jordan Shipley AU/499 RC 3.00 8.00
222 Eric Decker AU/499 RC 4.00 10.00
223 Brandon LaFell AU/499 RC 5.00 12.00
224 Golden Tate AU/299 RC 5.00 12.00
225 Colt McCoy AU/299 RC 5.00 12.00
226 Sam Bradford AU/299 RC 5.00 12.00
227 Dez Bryant AU/299 RC 25.00 60.00
228 Jimmy Clausen AU/299 RC 4.00 10.00
229 Arrelious Benn AU/399 RC 3.00 8.00
230 Rob Gronkowski AU/499 RC 40.00 80.00
231 Mike Kafka AU/499 RC 4.00 10.00
232 Taylor Price AU/499 RC 3.00 8.00
233 Andre Roberts AU/499 RC 4.00 10.00
234 N.Suh AU/399 RC 6.00 15.00
235 D.McCluster AU/499 RC 4.00 10.00

2010 Crown Royale Blue
*VETS: 2X TO 5X BASIC CARDS
*ROOKIES: .8X TO 2X BASIC CARDS
BLUE PRINT RUN 100 SER.#'d SETS

2010 Crown Royale Gold
*VETS: 4X TO 10X BASIC CARDS
*ROOKIES: 1.5X TO 4X BASIC CARDS
GOLD PRINT RUN 25 SER.#'d SETS

2010 Crown Royale All Pros
1 Austin Collie 1.25 3.00
2 Chris Wells 1.25 3.00
3 Brent Celek 1.25 3.00
4 Chris Cooley 1.25 3.00
5 DeSean Jackson 1.50 4.00
6 Donald Driver 1.50 4.00
7 Heath Miller 1.25 3.00
8 Jeremy Maclin 1.25 3.00
9 Joe Flacco 1.50 4.00
10 Jonathan Stewart 1.25 3.00
11 Knowshon Moreno 1.25 3.00
12 LeSean McCoy 2.00 5.00
13 Marques Colston 1.25 3.00
14 Miles Austin 1.25 3.00
15 Percy Harvin 1.25 3.00
16 Rashard Mendenhall 1.25 3.00
17 Santana Moss 1.50 4.00
18 Vince Young 1.25 3.00
19 Vincent Jackson 1.25 3.00
20 Ed Reed 1.50 4.00
21 Greg Olsen 1.50 4.00
22 Joseph Addai 1.25 3.00
23 Ronnie Brown 1.25 3.00
24 Jamaal Charles 1.50 4.00
25 Derrick Mason 1.25 3.00

2010 Crown Royale All Pros Materials
STATED PRINT RUN 80-299
*PRIME/50: .6X TO 1.5X BASIC JSY/160-299
*PRIME/15-25: .8X TO 2X BASIC JSY/160-299
*PRIME/50: .5X TO 1.2X BASIC JSY/80
PRIME STATED PRINT RUN 5-50
2 Chris Wells/250 2.50 6.00
3 Brent Celek/299 3.00 8.00
4 Chris Cooley/250 4.00 10.00
6 Donald Driver/80 4.00 10.00
7 Heath Miller/299 2.50 6.00
8 Jeremy Maclin/299 2.50 6.00
9 Joe Flacco/299 3.00 8.00
10 Jonathan Stewart/299 2.50 6.00
11 Knowshon Moreno/220 2.50 6.00
12 LeSean McCoy/299 4.00 10.00
13 Marques Colston/299 2.50 6.00
15 Percy Harvin/299 2.50 6.00
16 Rashard Mendenhall/299 4.00 10.00
17 Santana Moss/299 3.00 8.00
18 Vince Young/299 2.50 6.00
19 Vincent Jackson/299 2.50 6.00
20 Ed Reed/299 4.00 10.00
21 Greg Olsen/299 3.00 8.00
22 Joseph Addai/299 2.50 6.00
23 Ronnie Brown/160 2.50 6.00
24 Jamaal Charles/299 3.00 8.00
25 Derrick Mason/299 2.50 6.00

2010 Crown Royale Autographs Blue
101-200 STATED PRINT RUN 50
201-235 STATED PRINT RUN 25-50
*101-200 BSE AU/199-249: .3X TO .8X BLU/50
*101-200 BASE AU/99: .4X TO 1X BLU AU/50
EXCH EXPIRATION: 4/27/2012
101 Aaron Hernandez 10.00 25.00
105 Anthony Dixon 5.00 12.00
106 Anthony McCoy 5.00 12.00
107 Antonio Brown 50.00 100.00
108 Blair White 5.00 12.00
110 Brandon Graham 6.00 15.00
111 Brandon Spikes 5.00 12.00
113 Bryan Bulaga 5.00 12.00
114 Carlos Dunlap 5.00 12.00
115 Carlton Mitchell 5.00 12.00
116 Chad Jones 5.00 12.00
118 Chris Cook 5.00 12.00
120 Corey Wootton 5.00 12.00
121 Dan LeFevour 5.00 12.00
123 Daryl Washington 5.00 12.00
124 David Gettis 5.00 12.00
128 Derrick Morgan 5.00 12.00
129 Devin McCourty 6.00 15.00
130 Dezmon Briscoe 5.00 12.00
131 Dominique Franks 5.00 12.00
133 Earl Thomas 12.00 30.00
134 Ed Dickson 5.00 12.00
135 Everson Griffen 5.00 12.00
137 Garrett Graham 5.00 12.00
138 Jacoby Ford 5.00 12.00
139 James Starks 6.00 15.00
141 Jarrett Brown 5.00 12.00
142 Jason Pierre-Paul 8.00 20.00
143 Jason Worilds 5.00 12.00
145 Jeremy Williams 5.00 12.00
148 Jerry Hughes 5.00 12.00
150 Jimmy Graham 20.00 40.00
151 Joe Haden 8.00 20.00
154 John Skelton 6.00 15.00
155 Joique Bell 5.00 12.00
156 Jonathan Crompton 5.00 12.00
157 Kareem Jackson 6.00 12.00
161 Kyle Wilson 5.00 12.00
163 LeGarrette Blount 10.00 25.00
166 Lonyae Miller 6.00 15.00
172 Morgan Burnett 6.00 15.00
174 Nate Allen 8.00 20.00
175 NaVorro Bowman 10.00 25.00
177 Patrick Robinson 6.00 15.00
178 Perrish Cox 6.00 15.00
179 Ricky Sapp 5.00 12.00
180 Riley Cooper 5.00 12.00
181 Russell Okung 5.00 12.00
183 Sean Canfield 5.00 12.00
184 Sean Lee 10.00 25.00
185 Sean Weatherspoon 5.00 12.00
186 Sergio Kindle 5.00 12.00
187 Seyi Ajirotutu 5.00 12.00
190 Taylor Mays 5.00 12.00
195 Tony Pike 5.00 12.00
197 Trent Williams 6.00 15.00
200 Zac Robinson 6.00 15.00
201 Armanti Edwards/50 6.00 15.00
202 C.J. Spiller/25 8.00 20.00
203 Demaryius Thomas/50 12.00 30.00
204 Emmanuel Sanders/50 8.00 20.00
205 Gerald McCoy/50 5.00 12.00
206 Jermaine Gresham/50 5.00 12.00
207 Jonathan Dwyer/50 5.00 12.00
208 Ryan Mathews/25 8.00 20.00
209 Mardy Gilyard/50 5.00 12.00
210 Mike Williams/50 5.00 12.00
211 Tim Tebow/25 40.00 100.00
212 Toby Gerhart/50 8.00 20.00
213 Rolando McClain/50 5.00 12.00
214 Montario Hardesty/50 5.00 12.00
215 Ben Tate/50 5.00 12.00
216 Damian Williams/50 5.00 12.00
217 Eric Berry/50 8.00 20.00
218 Marcus Easley/50 5.00 12.00
219 Jahvid Best/25 8.00 20.00
220 Joe McKnight/50 5.00 12.00
221 Jordan Shipley/50 5.00 12.00
222 Eric Decker/50 6.00 15.00
223 Brandon LaFell/50 8.00 20.00
224 Golden Tate/50 6.00 15.00
225 Colt McCoy/25 10.00 25.00
226 Sam Bradford/25 10.00 25.00
227 Dez Bryant/25 50.00 120.00
228 Jimmy Clausen/25 8.00 20.00
229 Arrelious Benn/50 5.00 12.00
230 Rob Gronkowski/50 30.00 60.00
231 Mike Kafka/50 6.00 15.00
232 Taylor Price/50 5.00 12.00
233 Andre Roberts/50 6.00 15.00
234 Ndamukong Suh/50 10.00 25.00
235 Dexter McCluster/50 6.00 15.00

2010 Crown Royale Autographs Gold
1-100 VETERAN PRINT RUN 1-25
*GOLD ROOKIE/25: .5X TO 1.2X BLUE AU/50
101-235 ROOKIE PRINT RUN 10-25
EXCH EXPIRATION: 4/27/2012
8 Joe Flacco/15
9 Ray Rice/25 10.00 25.00
17 Jay Cutler/15 10.00 25.00
20 Cedric Benson/25 10.00 25.00
24 Josh Cribbs/15
26 Felix Jones/15 10.00 25.00
32 Kyle Orton/15 10.00 25.00
35 Matthew Stafford/15 30.00 80.00
38 Ryan Grant/25 15.00 40.00
43 Peyton Manning/25 100.00 175.00
48 Dwayne Bowe/20 12.00 30.00
49 Jamaal Charles/15 12.00 30.00
53 Ronnie Brown/25 15.00 40.00
56 Percy Harvin/25
65 Eli Manning/15 40.00 80.00
67 Braylon Edwards/15 10.00 25.00
69 Mark Sanchez/25 30.00 60.00
70 Shonn Greene/25 10.00 25.00
73 Louis Murphy/25 10.00 25.00
74 DeSean Jackson/20 15.00 40.00
75 Kevin Kolb/25 10.00 25.00
76 LeSean McCoy/15 15.00 40.00
78 Rashard Mendenhall/25 10.00 25.00
81 Darren Sproles/20 12.00 30.00
84 Michael Crabtree/25 10.00 25.00
96 Kenny Britt/20 10.00 25.00
98 Chris Cooley/20 30.00 60.00
100 Donovan McNabb/15

2010 Crown Royale Kings of the NFL
1 Peyton Manning 5.00 12.00
2 Adrian Peterson 2.00 5.00
3 Aaron Rodgers 4.00 10.00
4 Ben Roethlisberger 2.00 5.00
5 Calvin Johnson 2.00 5.00
6 Cadillac Williams 1.25 3.00
7 Chris Johnson 1.25 3.00
8 Frank Gore 1.50 4.00
9 Matt Ryan 1.50 4.00
10 Wes Welker 1.50 4.00
11 Ryan Grant 1.50 4.00
12 Matt Schaub 1.25 3.00
13 Vernon Davis 1.25 3.00
14 Greg Jennings 1.25 3.00
15 Lee Evans 1.50 4.00
16 Devery Henderson 1.25 3.00
17 Brandon Jacobs 1.25 3.00
18 Dallas Clark 1.25 3.00
19 Josh Cribbs 1.25 3.00
20 Matt Forte 1.25 3.00
21 Mark Sanchez 1.25 3.00
22 Roddy White 1.25 3.00
23 Pierre Thomas 1.25 3.00
24 Ray Rice 1.25 3.00
25 Sidney Rice 1.25 3.00

2010 Crown Royale Kings of the NFL Materials
STATED PRINT RUN 10-299
1 Peyton Manning/299 10.00 25.00
2 Adrian Peterson/299 4.00 10.00
4 Ben Roethlisberger/299 4.00 10.00
5 Calvin Johnson/290 4.00 10.00
6 Cadillac Williams/200 2.50 6.00
7 Chris Johnson/299 2.50 6.00
8 Frank Gore/299 3.00 8.00
9 Matt Ryan/299 3.00 8.00
10 Wes Welker/299 3.00 8.00
13 Vernon Davis/299 2.50 6.00
14 Greg Jennings/175 2.50 6.00
15 Lee Evans/299 3.00 8.00
16 Devery Henderson/299 2.50 6.00
18 Dallas Clark/299 2.50 6.00
19 Josh Cribbs/10
20 Matt Forte/299 2.50 6.00
21 Mark Sanchez/299 2.50 6.00
22 Roddy White/245 2.50 6.00
24 Ray Rice/299 2.50 6.00
25 Sidney Rice/299 2.50 6.00

2010 Crown Royale Kings of the NFL Materials Prime
*PRIME/50: .6X TO 1.5X BASIC JSY/175-299
*PRIME/15: .8X TO 2X BASIC JSY/175
PRIME PRINT RUN 15-50
17 Brandon Jacobs/50 4.00 10.00

2010 Crown Royale Kings of the NFL Materials Autographs
STATED PRINT RUN 15-25
1 Peyton Manning/20 60.00 120.00
2 Adrian Peterson/25 75.00 150.00
4 Ben Roethlisberger/20 60.00 120.00
5 Calvin Johnson/25 30.00 80.00
6 Cadillac Williams/25
8 Frank Gore/25 15.00 40.00
9 Matt Ryan/25 30.00 60.00
13 Vernon Davis/25 12.00 30.00
15 Lee Evans/20 15.00 40.00
16 Devery Henderson/15
18 Dallas Clark/25 20.00 50.00
19 Josh Cribbs/25
20 Matt Forte/25 12.00 30.00
21 Mark Sanchez/25 30.00 80.00
22 Roddy White/25 12.00 30.00
24 Ray Rice/25 12.00 30.00
25 Sidney Rice/25 12.00 30.00

2010 Crown Royale Living Legends
1 Barry Sanders 4.00 10.00
2 Bruce Smith 2.00 5.00
3 Charley Taylor 1.50 4.00
4 Charlie Joiner 1.50 4.00
5 Chuck Bednarik 2.00 5.00
6 Daryle Lamonica 1.50 4.00
7 Deacon Jones 2.00 5.00
8 Del Shofner 1.50 4.00
9 Joe Namath 3.00 8.00
10 Floyd Little 1.50 4.00
11 Frank Gifford 2.00 5.00
12 Henry Ellard 1.50 4.00
13 Jim Brown 3.00 8.00
14 Jim Otto 1.50 4.00
15 Jimmy Orr 1.50 4.00
16 Joe Greene 2.50 6.00
17 Joe Montana 8.00 20.00
18 John Elway 4.00 10.00
19 John Randle 2.00 5.00
20 Ozzie Newsome 2.00 5.00
21 Paul Warfield 2.00 5.00
22 Pete Retzlaff 1.50 4.00
23 Rickey Jackson 1.50 4.00
24 Sonny Jurgensen 2.00 5.00
25 Willie Lanier 1.50 4.00

2010 Crown Royale Living Legends Materials
STATED PRINT RUN 49-299
*PRIME/50: .6X TO 1.5X BASIC JSY/190-299
*PRIME/25: .8X TO 2X BASIC JSY/190-299
1 Barry Sanders/190 10.00 25.00
2 Bruce Smith/299 5.00 12.00
3 Charley Taylor/299 4.00 10.00
4 Charlie Joiner/299 4.00 10.00
5 Chuck Bednarik/230 5.00 12.00
6 Daryle Lamonica/299 4.00 10.00
7 Deacon Jones/299 5.00 12.00
9 Joe Namath/299 8.00 20.00
11 Frank Gifford/219 5.00 12.00
12 Henry Ellard/299 4.00 10.00
13 Jim Brown/49 10.00 25.00
14 Jim Otto/299 4.00 10.00
16 Joe Greene/299 6.00 15.00
17 Joe Montana/299 20.00 50.00
18 John Elway/299 10.00 25.00
19 John Randle/299 5.00 12.00
20 Ozzie Newsome/266 5.00 12.00
21 Paul Warfield/299 5.00 12.00
23 Rickey Jackson/299 4.00 10.00
24 Sonny Jurgensen/299 5.00 12.00
25 Willie Lanier/299 4.00 10.00

2010 Crown Royale Majestic
1 Alan Page 2.00 5.00
2 Alex Karras 2.00 5.00
3 Andre Reed 2.00 5.00
4 Archie Manning 2.00 5.00
5 Billy Howton 1.50 4.00
6 Boyd Dowler 1.50 4.00
7 Charley Trippi 1.50 4.00
8 Dante Lavelli 1.50 4.00
9 Dave Casper 1.50 4.00
10 Forrest Gregg 1.50 4.00
11 Fred Williamson 1.50 4.00
12 Harlon Hill 1.50 4.00
13 Howie Long 2.50 6.00
14 Jan Stenerud 1.50 4.00
15 Joe Klecko 1.50 4.00
16 Johnny Morris 1.50 4.00
17 Kellen Winslow 2.00 5.00
18 Larry Little 1.50 4.00
19 Lee Roy Selmon 1.50 4.00
20 Lem Barney 1.50 4.00
21 Len Dawson 2.50 6.00
22 Lenny Moore 1.50 4.00
23 Leroy Kelly 2.00 5.00
24 Lydell Mitchell 1.50 4.00
25 Mike Alstott 1.50 4.00
26 Mike Curtis 1.50 4.00
27 Paul Krause 1.50 4.00
28 Phil Simms 2.00 5.00
29 Raymond Berry 2.00 5.00
30 Rick Casares 1.50 4.00
31 Ron Mix 1.50 4.00
32 Sammy Baugh 2.50 6.00
33 Tiki Barber 2.00 5.00
34 Tom Rathman 1.50 4.00
35 Walter Payton 5.00 12.00
36 Wayne Chrebet 1.50 4.00
37 Willie Brown 1.50 4.00
38 Willie Davis 1.50 4.00
39 Willie Wood 1.50 4.00
40 Y.A. Tittle 2.50 6.00

2010 Crown Royale Majestic Materials
STATED PRINT RUN 25-299
1 Alan Page/299 5.00 12.00
2 Alex Karras/299 5.00 12.00
3 Andre Reed/40 6.00 15.00
4 Archie Manning/135 6.00 15.00
9 Dave Casper/165 4.00 10.00
10 Forrest Gregg/299 4.00 10.00
13 Howie Long/201 6.00 15.00
14 Jan Stenerud/43 5.00 12.00
15 Joe Klecko/299 4.00 10.00
18 Larry Little/299 4.00 10.00
19 Lee Roy Selmon/299 4.00 10.00
20 Lem Barney/200 4.00 10.00
21 Len Dawson/299 6.00 15.00
22 Lenny Moore/299 4.00 10.00
23 Leroy Kelly/25 8.00 20.00
28 Phil Simms/299 5.00 12.00
29 Raymond Berry/299 5.00 12.00
31 Ron Mix/95 5.00 12.00
32 Sammy Baugh/299 10.00 25.00
33 Tiki Barber/299 5.00 12.00
34 Tom Rathman/299 5.00 12.00
35 Walter Payton/299 12.00 30.00
36 Wayne Chrebet/115 5.00 12.00
37 Willie Brown/299 4.00 10.00
40 Y.A. Tittle/299 6.00 15.00

2010 Crown Royale Majestic Materials Prime
PRIME PRINT RUN 1-50
3 Andre Reed/25 6.00 15.00
13 Howie Long/25 8.00 20.00
18 Larry Little/25 5.00 12.00
19 Lee Roy Selmon/25 5.00 12.00
21 Len Dawson/25 8.00 20.00
25 Mike Alstott/30 4.00 10.00
29 Raymond Berry/25 6.00 15.00
31 Ron Mix/25 5.00 12.00
33 Tiki Barber/50 5.00 12.00
34 Tom Rathman/25 6.00 15.00
35 Walter Payton/25 15.00 40.00
36 Wayne Chrebet/50 4.00 10.00
40 Y.A. Tittle/25 8.00 20.00

2010 Crown Royale Rookie Die Cut Material Autographs
STATED PRINT RUN 50 SER.#'d SETS
EXCH EXPIRATION: 4/27/2012
1 Andre Roberts 8.00 20.00
2 Armanti Edwards 8.00 20.00
3 Arrelious Benn 6.00 15.00
4 Ben Tate 6.00 15.00
5 Brandon LaFell 10.00 25.00
6 C.J. Spiller 6.00 15.00
7 Colt McCoy 8.00 20.00
8 Damian Williams 6.00 15.00
9 Demaryius Thomas 15.00 40.00
10 Dexter McCluster 8.00 20.00
11 Dez Bryant 40.00 80.00
12 Emmanuel Sanders 10.00 25.00
13 Eric Berry 10.00 25.00
14 Eric Decker 8.00 20.00
15 Gerald McCoy 6.00 15.00
16 Golden Tate 8.00 20.00
17 Jahvid Best 6.00 15.00
18 Jermaine Gresham 6.00 15.00
19 Jimmy Clausen 6.00 15.00
20 Joe McKnight 6.00 15.00
21 Jonathan Dwyer 6.00 15.00
22 Jordan Shipley 6.00 15.00
23 Marcus Easley 6.00 15.00
24 Mardy Gilyard 6.00 15.00
25 Mike Kafka 8.00 20.00
26 Mike Williams 6.00 15.00
27 Montario Hardesty 6.00 15.00
28 Ndamukong Suh 12.00 30.00
29 Rob Gronkowski 30.00 60.00
30 Rolando McClain 6.00 15.00
31 Ryan Mathews 6.00 15.00
32 Sam Bradford 8.00 20.00
33 Taylor Price 6.00 15.00
34 Tim Tebow 30.00 80.00
35 Toby Gerhart 6.00 15.00

2010 Crown Royale Rookie Royalty
1 Armanti Edwards 1.25 3.00
2 Brandon LaFell 1.50 4.00
3 Toby Gerhart 1.00 2.50
4 Andre Roberts 1.25 3.00
5 Golden Tate 1.25 3.00
6 Emmanuel Sanders 1.50 4.00
7 Jimmy Clausen 1.00 2.50
8 Mardy Gilyard 1.00 2.50
9 Joe McKnight 1.00 2.50
10 Mike Kafka 1.25 3.00
11 Tim Tebow 3.00 8.00
12 Taylor Price 1.00 2.50
13 Rob Gronkowski 3.00 8.00
14 Mike Williams 1.00 2.50
15 Colt McCoy 1.25 3.00
16 Arrelious Benn 1.00 2.50
17 Damian Williams 1.00 2.50
18 Jermaine Gresham 1.00 2.50
19 Jahvid Best 1.00 2.50
20 Sam Bradford 1.25 3.00
21 Ndamukong Suh 2.00 5.00
22 C.J. Spiller 1.00 2.50
23 Demaryius Thomas 2.50 6.00
24 Dez Bryant 2.50 6.00
25 Jonathan Dwyer 1.00 2.50
26 Montario Hardesty 1.00 2.50
27 Ryan Mathews 1.00 2.50
28 Marcus Easley 1.00 2.50
29 Ben Tate 1.00 2.50
30 Jordan Shipley 1.00 2.50
31 Dexter McCluster 1.25 3.00
32 Eric Berry 1.50 4.00
33 Eric Decker 1.25 3.00
34 Rolando McClain 1.00 2.50
35 Gerald McCoy 1.00 2.50

2010 Crown Royale Rookie Royalty Autographs
STATED PRINT RUN 10-25
EXCH EXPIRATION: 4/27/2012
1 Armanti Edwards/25 6.00 15.00
2 Brandon LaFell/25 8.00 20.00
3 Toby Gerhart/25 5.00 12.00
4 Andre Roberts/25 6.00 15.00
5 Golden Tate/10
6 Emmanuel Sanders/25 8.00 20.00
7 Jimmy Clausen/10
8 Mardy Gilyard/25 5.00 12.00
9 Joe McKnight/25 5.00 12.00
10 Mike Kafka/25 6.00 15.00
11 Tim Tebow/10
12 Taylor Price/25 5.00 12.00
13 Rob Gronkowski/25 30.00 60.00
14 Mike Williams/25 5.00 12.00
15 Colt McCoy/10
16 Arrelious Benn/25 5.00 12.00
17 Damian Williams/25 5.00 12.00
18 Jermaine Gresham/25 5.00 12.00
19 Jahvid Best/10
21 Ndamukong Suh/25 10.00 25.00
22 C.J. Spiller/10
23 Demaryius Thomas/25 12.00 30.00
24 Dez Bryant/10
25 Jonathan Dwyer/25 5.00 12.00
26 Montario Hardesty/25 5.00 12.00
27 Ryan Mathews/10
28 Marcus Easley/25 5.00 12.00
29 Ben Tate/25 5.00 12.00
30 Jordan Shipley/25 5.00 12.00
31 Dexter McCluster/25 6.00 15.00
32 Eric Berry/25 8.00 20.00
33 Eric Decker/25 6.00 15.00
34 Rolando McClain/25 5.00 12.00
35 Gerald McCoy/25 5.00 12.00

2010 Crown Royale Rookie Royalty Materials
STATED PRINT RUN 299 SER.#'d SETS
*PRIME/50: .8X TO 2X BASIC JSY/299
1 Armanti Edwards 2.00 5.00
2 Brandon LaFell 2.50 6.00
3 Toby Gerhart 1.50 4.00
4 Andre Roberts 2.00 5.00
5 Golden Tate 2.00 5.00
6 Emmanuel Sanders 2.50 6.00
7 Jimmy Clausen 1.50 4.00
8 Mardy Gilyard 1.50 4.00
9 Joe McKnight 1.50 4.00
10 Mike Kafka 2.00 5.00
11 Tim Tebow 5.00 12.00
12 Taylor Price 1.50 4.00
13 Rob Gronkowski 5.00 12.00
14 Mike Williams 1.50 4.00
15 Colt McCoy 2.00 5.00
16 Arrelious Benn 1.50 4.00
17 Damian Williams 1.50 4.00
18 Jermaine Gresham 1.50 4.00
19 Jahvid Best 1.50 4.00
20 Sam Bradford 2.00 5.00
21 Ndamukong Suh 3.00 8.00
22 C.J. Spiller 1.50 4.00
23 Demaryius Thomas 4.00 10.00
24 Dez Bryant 4.00 10.00
25 Jonathan Dwyer 1.50 4.00
26 Montario Hardesty 1.50 4.00
27 Ryan Mathews 1.50 4.00
28 Marcus Easley 1.50 4.00
29 Ben Tate 1.50 4.00
30 Jordan Shipley 1.50 4.00
31 Dexter McCluster 2.00 5.00
32 Eric Berry 2.50 6.00
33 Eric Decker 2.00 5.00
34 Rolando McClain 1.50 4.00
35 Gerald McCoy 1.50 4.00

2010 Crown Royale Rookie Royalty Materials Autographs
STATED PRINT RUN 25-50
*PRIME/25: .5X TO 1.2X BASIC JSY AU/50
EXCH EXPIRATION. 4/27/2012
1 Armanti Edwards/50 6.00 15.00
2 Brandon LaFell/50 8.00 20.00
3 Toby Gerhart/50 5.00 12.00
4 Andre Roberts/50 6.00 15.00
5 Golden Tate/50 6.00 15.00
6 Emmanuel Sanders/50 8.00 20.00
7 Jimmy Clausen/25 6.00 15.00
8 Mardy Gilyard/50 5.00 12.00
9 Joe McKnight/50 5.00 12.00
10 Mike Kafka/50 6.00 15.00
11 Tim Tebow/25 30.00 80.00
12 Taylor Price/50 5.00 12.00
13 Rob Gronkowski/50 30.00 60.00
14 Mike Williams/50 5.00 12.00
15 Colt McCoy/25 8.00 20.00
16 Arrelious Benn/50 5.00 12.00
17 Damian Williams/50 5.00 12.00
18 Jermaine Gresham/50 5.00 12.00
19 Jahvid Best/50 5.00 12.00
20 Sam Bradford/25 8.00 20.00
21 Ndamukong Suh/50 10.00 25.00
22 C.J. Spiller/25 6.00 15.00
23 Demaryius Thomas/50 12.00 30.00
24 Dez Bryant/50 40.00 80.00
25 Jonathan Dwyer/50 5.00 12.00
26 Montario Hardesty/50 5.00 12.00
27 Ryan Mathews/50 5.00 12.00
28 Marcus Easley/50 5.00 12.00
29 Ben Tate/50 5.00 12.00
30 Jordan Shipley/50 5.00 12.00
31 Dexter McCluster/50 6.00 15.00
32 Eric Berry/50 8.00 20.00
33 Eric Decker/50 6.00 15.00
34 Rolando McClain/50 5.00 12.00
35 Gerald McCoy/50 5.00 12.00

2010 Crown Royale Royalty
1 Brett Favre 4.00 10.00
2 Tom Brady 5.00 12.00
3 Larry Fitzgerald 1.50 4.00
4 Randy Moss 1.50 4.00
5 Reggie Wayne 1.50 4.00
6 Tony Romo 1.50 4.00
7 DeAngelo Williams 1.25 3.00
8 Drew Brees 2.00 5.00
9 Antonio Gates 1.50 4.00
10 Maurice Jones-Drew 1.25 3.00
11 Steve Smith 1.50 4.00
12 Tony Gonzalez 1.50 4.00
13 Ray Lewis 2.00 5.00
14 Troy Polamalu 2.00 5.00
15 Brian Urlacher 2.00 5.00
16 Steven Jackson 1.25 3.00
17 Jason Witten 1.50 4.00
18 Hines Ward 1.50 4.00
19 Eli Manning 1.50 4.00
20 Michael Turner 1.25 3.00
21 Chad Ochocinco 1.25 3.00
22 Andre Johnson 1.50 4.00
23 Carson Palmer 1.50 4.00
24 Darrelle Revis 1.25 3.00
25 Philip Rivers 2.00 5.00

2010 Crown Royale Royalty Materials
STATED PRINT RUN 245-299
1 Brett Favre/299 8.00 20.00
2 Tom Brady/299 10.00 25.00
3 Larry Fitzgerald/299 3.00 8.00
4 Randy Moss/299 3.00 8.00
5 Reggie Wayne/299 3.00 8.00
6 Tony Romo/299 3.00 8.00
7 DeAngelo Williams/290 2.50 6.00
9 Antonio Gates/299 3.00 8.00
10 Maurice Jones-Drew/299 2.50 6.00
12 Tony Gonzalez/270 3.00 8.00
13 Ray Lewis/299 4.00 10.00
14 Troy Polamalu/299 4.00 10.00
15 Brian Urlacher/299 4.00 10.00
16 Steven Jackson/290 2.50 6.00
17 Jason Witten/299 3.00 8.00
18 Hines Ward/299 3.00 8.00
19 Eli Manning/299 3.00 8.00
21 Chad Ochocinco/299 2.50 6.00
22 Andre Johnson/245 3.00 8.00
23 Carson Palmer/299 3.00 8.00
24 Darrelle Revis/290 2.50 6.00
25 Philip Rivers/299 4.00 10.00

2010 Crown Royale Royalty Materials Prime
*PRIME/40-50: .6X TO 1.5X BASIC JSY
*PRIME/15: .8X TO 2X BASIC JSY
PRIME STATED PRINT RUN 15-50
11 Steve Smith/50 5.00 12.00

2010 Crown Royale Royalty Materials Autographs
STATED PRINT RUN 5-25
EXCH EXPIRATION: 4/27/2012
1 Brett Favre/20 100.00 200.00
2 Tom Brady/20 125.00 250.00
5 Reggie Wayne/25 15.00 40.00
6 Tony Romo/25 40.00 80.00
7 DeAngelo Williams/25 12.00 30.00
9 Antonio Gates/20 15.00 40.00
10 Maurice Jones-Drew/25 12.00 30.00
11 Steve Smith/5
12 Tony Gonzalez/25 15.00 40.00
14 Troy Polamalu/25 50.00 100.00
17 Jason Witten/25 15.00 40.00
19 Eli Manning/25 40.00 80.00
21 Chad Ochocinco/20 12.00 30.00
22 Andre Johnson/25 15.00 40.00
23 Carson Palmer/20 15.00 40.00
25 Philip Rivers/25 20.00 50.00

2010 Crown Royale The Zone
RAMDON INSERTS IN PACKS
1 Bernard Berrian 1.25 3.00
2 Braylon Edwards 1.25 3.00
3 Darren Sproles 1.50 4.00
4 Darren McFadden 1.25 3.00
5 Clinton Portis 1.25 3.00
6 Devin Hester 1.50 4.00
7 Dustin Keller 1.25 3.00
8 Johnny Knox 1.25 3.00
9 Jerricho Cotchery 1.25 3.00
10 Ladell Betts 1.25 3.00
11 Laurence Maroney 1.25 3.00
12 Marion Barber 1.50 4.00
13 Matthew Stafford 1.50 4.00
14 Michael Crabtree 1.25 3.00
15 Reggie Bush 1.25 3.00
16 Robert Meachem 1.25 3.00
17 Shonn Greene 1.25 3.00
18 T.J. Houshmandzadeh 1.25 3.00
19 Visanthe Shiancoe 1.50 4.00
20 Felix Jones 1.25 3.00
21 Matt Hasselbeck 1.25 3.00
22 Owen Daniels 1.25 3.00
23 Steve Smith USC 1.25 3.00
24 Todd Heap 1.25 3.00
25 Pierre Garcon 1.50 4.00

2010 Crown Royale The Zone Materials Prime
STATED PRINT RUN 15-50
1 Bernard Berrian/50 4.00 10.00
2 Braylon Edwards/50 4.00 10.00
3 Darren Sproles/50 5.00 12.00
4 Darren McFadden/50 4.00 10.00
5 Clinton Portis/50 4.00 10.00
6 Devin Hester/50 5.00 12.00
7 Dustin Keller/50 4.00 10.00
8 Johnny Knox/50 4.00 10.00
9 Jerricho Cotchery/50 4.00 10.00
10 Ladell Betts/50 4.00 10.00
11 Laurence Maroney/50 4.00 10.00
12 Marion Barber/50 5.00 12.00
13 Matthew Stafford/50 5.00 12.00
15 Reggie Bush/50 4.00 10.00
16 Robert Meachem/50 4.00 10.00

19 Visanthe Shiancoe/50 5.00 12.00
20 Felix Jones/50 4.00 10.00
21 Matt Hasselbeck/40 4.00 10.00
22 Owen Daniels/50 4.00 10.00
23 Steve Smith USC/20 5.00 12.00
24 Todd Heap/15 5.00 12.00

2011 Crown Royale

101-200 ROOKIES ONE PER HOBBY PACK
201-236 JSY AU RC PRINT RUN 199-299
EXCH EXPIRATION: 4/26/2013
1 Aaron Rodgers 1.25 3.00
2 Adrian Peterson .75 2.00
3 Ahmad Bradshaw .50 1.25
4 Andre Johnson .60 1.50
5 Anquan Boldin .50 1.25
6 Antonio Gates .50 1.25
7 Arian Foster .50 1.25
8 Beanie Wells .50 1.25
9 Ben Roethlisberger .75 2.00
10 Brandon Lloyd .50 1.25
11 Braylon Edwards .50 1.25
12 Calvin Johnson .75 2.00
13 Carson Palmer .60 1.50
14 Cedric Benson .50 1.25
15 Chad Henne .60 1.50
16 Chad Ochocinco .50 1.25
17 Chris Cooley .50 1.25
18 Chris Johnson .50 1.25
19 Colt McCoy .50 1.25
20 Danny Amendola .60 1.50
21 Danny Woodhead .60 1.50
22 Darren McFadden .50 1.25
23 David Garrard .50 1.25
24 Davone Bess .50 1.25
25 DeSean Jackson .60 1.50
26 Devin Hester .60 1.50
27 Donald Driver .60 1.50
28 Donovan McNabb .60 1.50
29 Drew Brees .75 2.00
30 Dwayne Bowe .60 1.50
31 Eli Manning .60 1.50
32 Felix Jones .50 1.25
33 Frank Gore .60 1.50
34 Greg Jennings .50 1.25
35 Hakeem Nicks .50 1.25
36 Jahvid Best .50 1.25
37 Jamaal Charles .60 1.50
38 Jason Witten .60 1.50
39 Jay Cutler .50 1.25
40 Jeremy Maclin .50 1.25
41 Joe Flacco .60 1.50
42 John Carlson .50 1.25
43 Johnny Knox .50 1.25
44 Jonathan Stewart .50 1.25
45 Josh Cribbs .50 1.25
46 Josh Freeman .60 1.50
47 Justin Forsett .60 1.50
48 Bo Scaife .50 1.25
49 Knowshon Moreno .50 1.25
50 LaDainian Tomlinson .75 2.00
51 Larry Fitzgerald .60 1.50
52 Lee Evans .60 1.50
53 LeGarrette Blount .60 1.50
54 LeSean McCoy .75 2.00
55 Marcedes Lewis .50 1.25
56 Mario Manningham .50 1.25
57 Mark Sanchez .50 1.25
58 Marques Colston .50 1.25
59 Matt Cassel .50 1.25
60 Matt Forte .50 1.25
61 Matt Ryan .60 1.50
62 Matt Schaub .50 1.25
63 Matthew Stafford .60 1.50
64 Maurice Jones-Drew .50 1.25
65 Michael Crabtree .50 1.25
66 Michael Turner .50 1.25
67 Michael Vick .60 1.50
68 Mike Goodson .50 1.25
69 Mike Tolbert .50 1.25
70 Mike Wallace .50 1.25
71 Mike Williams USC .50 1.25
72 Mike Williams .60 1.50
73 Miles Austin .50 1.25
74 Nate Washington .50 1.25
75 Nnamdi Asomugha .50 1.25
76 Percy Harvin .50 1.25
77 Peyton Hillis .50 1.25
78 Peyton Manning 1.50 4.00
79 Philip Rivers .75 2.00
80 Pierre Garcon .60 1.50
81 Rashard Mendenhall .50 1.25
82 Ray Rice .50 1.25
83 Reggie Bush .50 1.25
84 Reggie Wayne .60 1.50
85 Roddy White .50 1.25
86 Ronnie Brown .60 1.50
87 Ryan Fitzpatrick .50 1.25
88 Ryan Torain .50 1.25
89 Sam Bradford .50 1.25
90 Sidney Rice .50 1.25
91 Steve Breaston .50 1.25
92 Steve Johnson .50 1.25
93 Steve Smith .60 1.50
94 Steven Jackson .50 1.25
95 Tim Tebow .75 2.00
96 Tom Brady 2.00 5.00
97 Tony Romo .60 1.50
98 Vernon Davis .50 1.25
99 Wes Welker .60 1.50
100 Zach Miller .50 1.25
101 Aaron Williams RC 1.25 3.00
102 Adrian Clayborn RC 1.25 3.00
103 Ahmad Black RC 1.50 4.00
104 Akeem Ayers RC 1.25 3.00
105 Aldon Smith RC 1.25 3.00
106 Aldrick Robinson RC 1.50 4.00
107 Allen Bradford RC 1.25 3.00
108 Anthony Allen RC 1.25 3.00
109 Anthony Castonzo RC 1.25 3.00
110 Baron Batch RC 1.50 4.00
111 Brandon Harris RC 1.25 3.00
112 Brooks Reed RC 1.50 4.00
113 Bruce Carter RC 1.25 3.00
114 Cameron Heyward RC 1.50 4.00
115 Cameron Jordan RC 1.50 4.00
116 Cecil Shorts RC 1.25 3.00
117 Chris Culliver RC 1.25 3.00
118 Corey Liuget RC 1.25 3.00
119 D.J. Williams RC 1.25 3.00
120 Da'Quan Bowers RC 1.25 3.00
121 Da'Rel Scott RC 1.25 3.00
122 Daniel Hardy RC 1.50 4.00
123 Danny Watkins RC 1.25 3.00
124 David Ausberry RC 1.25 3.00
125 DeMarco Sampson RC 1.25 3.00
126 DeMarcus Van Dyke RC 1.50 4.00
127 Denarius Moore RC 1.25 3.00
128 Derek Sherrod RC 1.25 3.00
129 Dion Lewis RC 1.50 4.00
130 Dontay Moch RC 1.25 3.00
131 Dwayne Harris RC 1.25 3.00
132 Evan Royster RC 1.25 3.00
133 Gabe Carimi RC 1.50 4.00
134 Greg Jones RC 1.50 4.00
135 Greg McElroy RC 2.00 5.00
136 Greg Salas RC 1.25 3.00
137 J.J. Watt RC 6.00 15.00
138 Jabaal Sheard RC 1.25 3.00
139 Jacquizz Rodgers RC 1.25 3.00
140 Jaiquawn Jarrett RC 1.25 3.00
141 James Carpenter RC 1.50 4.00
142 Jarvis Jenkins RC 1.25 3.00
143 Jay Finley RC 1.50 4.00
144 Jeremy Kerley RC 2.00 5.00
145 Jimmy Smith RC 1.25 3.00
146 Johnny White RC 1.25 3.00
147 Jonas Mouton RC 1.50 4.00
148 Jordan Cameron RC 1.50 4.00
149 Julius Thomas RC 1.50 4.00
150 Jurrell Casey RC 1.25 3.00
151 Justin Houston RC 1.50 4.00
152 Kealoha Pilares RC 1.25 3.00
153 Kelvin Sheppard RC 1.25 3.00
154 Kris Durham RC 1.25 3.00
155 Lance Kendricks RC 1.25 3.00
156 Lee Smith RC 1.50 4.00
157 Luke Stocker RC 1.25 3.00
158 Marcus Cannon RC 1.25 3.00
159 Marcus Gilbert RC 2.00 5.00
160 Marcus Gilchrist RC 1.25 3.00
161 Martez Wilson RC 1.25 3.00
162 Marvin Austin RC 1.25 3.00
163 Mason Foster RC 1.25 3.00
164 Mike Pouncey RC 2.00 5.00
165 Muhammad Wilkerson RC 1.25 3.00
166 Nate Irving RC 1.50 4.00
167 Nate Solder RC 1.25 3.00
168 Nathan Enderle RC 1.25 3.00
169 Nick Fairley RC 1.25 3.00
170 Niles Paul RC 1.25 3.00
171 Orlando Franklin RC 1.50 4.00
172 Owen Marecic RC 1.25 3.00
173 Patrick Peterson RC 2.50 6.00
174 Phil Taylor RC 1.25 3.00
175 Prince Amukamara RC 1.25 3.00
176 Quinton Carter RC 1.25 3.00
177 Rahim Moore RC 1.25 3.00
178 Ras-I Dowling RC 1.25 3.00
179 Richard Gordon RC 1.25 3.00
180 Ricky Stanzi RC 1.25 3.00
181 Robert Housler RC 1.25 3.00
182 Robert Quinn RC 1.25 3.00
183 Rodney Hudson RC 1.25 3.00
184 Ronald Johnson RC 1.25 3.00
185 Roy Helu RC 1.25 3.00
186 Ryan Kerrigan RC 1.50 4.00
187 Ryan Whalen RC 1.25 3.00
188 Scotty McKnight RC 1.25 3.00
189 Shane Bannon RC 1.25 3.00
190 Stanley Havili RC 1.25 3.00
191 Stefen Wisniewski RC 2.00 5.00
192 Stephen Burton RC 1.25 3.00
193 Stephen Paea RC 1.25 3.00
194 T.J. Yates RC 1.25 3.00
195 Tandon Doss RC 1.25 3.00
196 Terrell McClain RC 1.50 4.00
197 Tyler Sash RC 1.25 3.00
198 Tyrod Taylor RC 2.50 6.00
199 Tyron Smith RC 1.50 4.00
200 Virgil Green RC 1.25 3.00
201 Greg Little JSY AU/299 RC 15.00 40.00
202 Kaepernick JSY AU/299 RC 10.00 25.00
203 T.Jones JSY AU/299 RC 6.00 15.00
204 K.Hunter JSY AU/299 RC 6.00 15.00
205 C.Ponder JSY AU/199 RC 6.00 15.00
206 R.Mallett JSY AU/199 RC 6.00 15.00
207 R.Cobb JSY AU/299 RC 10.00 25.00
208 K.Rudolph JSY AU/299 RC 6.00 15.00
209 J.Jernigan JSY AU/299 RC 6.00 15.00
210 Andy Dalton JSY AU/299 RC 15.00 40.00
211 Torrey Smith JSY AU/299 RC 6.00 15.00
212 T.Young JSY AU/299 RC 15.00 40.00
213 D.Carter JSY AU/299 RC 6.00 15.00
214 Von Miller JSY AU/299 RC 20.00 50.00
215 S.Vereen JSY AU/299 RC 8.00 20.00
216 Alex Green JSY AU/299 RC 6.00 15.00
217 Mark Ingram JSY AU/199 RC 10.00 25.00
218 Murray JSY AU/299 RC EX 12.00 30.00
219 J.Todman JSY AU/299 RC 6.00 15.00
220 Julio Jones JSY AU/299 RC 50.00 100.00
221 Hankerson JSY AU/299 RC 6.00 15.00
222 J.Harper JSY AU/299 RC 6.00 15.00
223 V.Brown JSY AU/299 RC 6.00 15.00
224 D.Thomas JSY AU/299 RC 6.00 15.00
225 Dareus JSY AU/299 RC EXCH
226 J.Locker JSY AU/199 RC 6.00 15.00
227 B.Gabbert JSY AU/199 RC 6.00 15.00
228 C.Newton JSY AU/199 RC 60.00 120.00
229 Bilal Powell JSY AU/299 RC 8.00 20.00
230 Clyde Gates JSY AU/299 RC 6.00 15.00
231 R.Williams JSY AU/299 RC 6.00 15.00
232 M.Leshoure JSY AU/299 RC 15.00 40.00
233 Ridley JSY AU/299 RC 6.00 15.00
234 Baldwin JSY AU/299 RC 15.00 40.00
235 Austin Pettis JSY AU/299 RC 6.00 15.00
236 A.J. Green JSY AU/199 RC 40.00 100.00

2011 Crown Royale Blue

*1-100 VETS/100: 2X TO 5X BASIC CARDS
*101-200 ROOK/100: .6X TO 1.5X BASIC CARDS
BLUE PRINT RUN 100 SER.#'d SETS

2011 Crown Royale Gold

*1-100 VETS/25: 4X TO 10X BASIC CARDS
*101-200 ROOK/25: 1.2X TO 3X BASIC CARDS
GOLD PRINT RUN 25 SER.#'d SETS

2011 Crown Royale All Pros

1 Arian Foster 1.25 3.00
2 Jamaal Charles 1.50 4.00
3 Roddy White 1.25 3.00
4 Reggie Wayne 1.50 4.00
5 Devin Hester 1.50 4.00
6 Tom Brady 5.00 12.00
7 Julius Peppers 1.50 4.00
8 Haloti Ngata 1.25 3.00
9 Ndamukong Suh 1.50 4.00
10 Clay Matthews 2.00 5.00
11 James Harrison 1.50 4.00
12 Patrick Willis 1.50 4.00
13 Jerod Mayo 1.25 3.00
14 Nnamdi Asomugha 1.25 3.00
15 Darrelle Revis 1.25 3.00
16 Ed Reed 1.50 4.00
17 Troy Polamalu 2.00 5.00
18 Shane Lechler 1.25 3.00
19 Billy Cundiff 1.25 3.00
20 Vonta Leach 1.25 3.00

2011 Crown Royale All Pros Materials

STATED PRINT RUN 75-299
*PRIME/50: .6X TO 1.5X JSY/199-299
*PRIME/50: .5X TO 1.2X JSY/75-99
1 Arian Foster/99 3.00 8.00
2 Jamaal Charles/75 4.00 10.00
3 Roddy White/199 2.50 6.00
4 Reggie Wayne/299 3.00 8.00
5 Devin Hester/99 4.00 10.00
6 Tom Brady/99 12.00 30.00
7 Julius Peppers/99 5.00 12.00
9 Ndamukong Suh/299 3.00 8.00
10 Clay Matthews/299 6.00 15.00
11 James Harrison/299 6.00 15.00
12 Patrick Willis/299 3.00 8.00
15 Darrelle Revis/299 2.50 6.00
16 Ed Reed/299 3.00 8.00
17 Troy Polamalu/99 5.00 12.00

2011 Crown Royale All Pros Materials Autographs

STATED PRINT RUN 5-25
1 Arian Foster/15 15.00 40.00
10 Clay Matthews/25 30.00 60.00
12 Patrick Willis/25 15.00 40.00
15 Darrelle Revis/25 15.00 40.00

2011 Crown Royale Autographs Gold

UNPRICED GOLD VET AU PRINT RUN 1
ROOKIE PRINT RUN 299-499
*ROOKIE BLUE/50: .6X TO 1.5X GOLD/499
*ROOKIE BLUE/50: .5X TO 1.2X GOLD/299
101 Aaron Williams/499 3.00 8.00
102 Adrian Clayborn/499 6.00 15.00
103 Ahmad Black/499 5.00 12.00
104 Akeem Ayers/499 3.00 8.00
105 Aldon Smith/499 3.00 8.00
106 Aldrick Robinson/499 4.00 10.00
107 Allen Bradford/499 3.00 8.00
108 Anthony Allen/499 3.00 8.00
109 Anthony Castonzo/499 3.00 8.00
111 Brandon Harris/499 3.00 8.00
114 Cameron Heyward/499 4.00 10.00
115 Cameron Jordan/499 4.00 10.00
116 Cecil Shorts/499 3.00 8.00
118 Corey Liuget/499 3.00 8.00
119 D.J. Williams/499 3.00 8.00
120 Da'Quan Bowers/499 3.00 8.00
121 Da'Rel Scott/499 3.00 8.00
127 Denarius Moore/499 8.00 20.00
129 Dion Lewis/499 4.00 10.00
131 Dwayne Harris/499 3.00 8.00
132 Evan Royster/499 6.00 15.00
134 Greg Jones/499 4.00 10.00
135 Greg McElroy/499 5.00 12.00
136 Greg Salas/499 3.00 8.00
137 J.J. Watt/499 50.00 100.00
139 Jacquizz Rodgers/499 3.00 8.00
144 Jeremy Kerley/499 5.00 12.00
145 Jimmy Smith/499 3.00 8.00
146 Johnny White/499 3.00 8.00
148 Jordan Cameron/499 4.00 10.00
149 Julius Thomas/499 4.00 10.00
151 Justin Houston/499 3.00 8.00
152 Kealoha Pilares/499 3.00 8.00
154 Kris Durham/499 3.00 8.00
155 Lance Kendricks/499 3.00 8.00
157 Luke Stocker/499 3.00 8.00
158 Marcus Cannon/499 3.00 8.00
161 Martez Wilson/499 3.00 8.00
168 Nathan Enderle/499 3.00 8.00
170 Niles Paul/499 3.00 8.00
172 Owen Marecic/499 EXCH 3.00 8.00
174 Phil Taylor/499 5.00 12.00
175 Prince Amukamara/499 6.00 15.00
176 Quinton Carter/499 3.00 8.00
177 Rahim Moore/499 3.00 8.00
180 Ricky Stanzi/299 4.00 10.00
181 Robert Housler/499 3.00 8.00
184 Ronald Johnson/499 3.00 8.00
185 Roy Helu/499 3.00 8.00
186 Ryan Kerrigan/499 8.00 20.00
187 Ryan Whalen/499 3.00 8.00
188 Scotty McKnight/499 3.00 8.00
189 Shane Bannon/499 3.00 8.00
190 Stanley Havili/499 3.00 8.00
192 Stephen Burton/499 3.00 8.00
193 Stephen Paea/499 3.00 8.00
194 T.J. Yates/499 3.00 8.00
195 Tandon Doss/499 3.00 8.00
197 Tyler Sash/499 3.00 8.00
198 Tyrod Taylor/499 6.00 15.00
199 Tyron Smith/499 4.00 10.00

2011 Crown Royale Calling All Captains

1 Tony Gonzalez 1.50 4.00
2 Ray Lewis 2.00 5.00
3 Ryan Fitzpatrick 1.25 3.00
4 Steve Smith 1.50 4.00
5 Dhani Jones 1.25 3.00
6 Jason Witten 1.50 4.00
7 Brandon Lloyd 1.25 3.00
8 Calvin Johnson 2.00 5.00
9 Greg Jennings 1.25 3.00
10 Matt Schaub 1.25 3.00
11 Maurice Jones-Drew 1.25 3.00
12 David Garrard 1.25 3.00
13 Adrian Peterson 2.00 5.00
14 Will Smith 1.25 3.00
15 Mark Sanchez 1.25 3.00
16 Peyton Manning 4.00 10.00
17 Asante Samuel 1.25 3.00
18 Antonio Gates 1.25 3.00
19 Vernon Davis 1.25 3.00
20 Steven Jackson 1.25 3.00
21 Josh Freeman 1.50 4.00
22 Tom Brady 5.00 12.00
23 London Fletcher 1.50 4.00
24 Hines Ward 1.50 4.00

2011 Crown Royale Calling All Captains Materials

STATED PRINT RUN 99-299
1 Tony Gonzalez/299 3.00 8.00
2 Ray Lewis/299 4.00 10.00
3 Ryan Fitzpatrick/299 2.50 6.00
6 Jason Witten/299 4.00 10.00
8 Calvin Johnson/299 5.00 12.00
10 Matt Schaub/299 2.50 6.00
11 Maurice Jones-Drew/99 3.00 8.00
12 David Garrard/299 2.50 6.00
13 Adrian Peterson/299 4.00 10.00
14 Will Smith/200 2.50 6.00
15 Mark Sanchez/299 2.50 6.00
16 Peyton Manning/299 8.00 20.00
18 Antonio Gates/299 2.50 6.00
19 Vernon Davis/299 2.50 6.00
20 Steven Jackson/299 2.50 6.00
22 Tom Brady/99 12.00 30.00
24 Hines Ward/299 4.00 10.00

2011 Crown Royale Calling All Captains Materials Prime

STATED PRINT RUN 8-50
1 Tony Gonzalez/50 5.00 12.00
2 Ray Lewis/50 6.00 15.00
3 Ryan Fitzpatrick/50 4.00 10.00
4 Steve Smith/50 5.00 12.00
6 Jason Witten/50 6.00 15.00
7 Brandon Lloyd/50 4.00 10.00
8 Calvin Johnson/50 8.00 20.00
11 Maurice Jones-Drew/50 4.00 10.00
12 David Garrard/50 4.00 10.00
13 Adrian Peterson/50 6.00 15.00
15 Mark Sanchez/50 4.00 10.00
17 Asante Samuel/50 4.00 10.00
18 Antonio Gates/50 4.00 10.00
19 Vernon Davis/50 4.00 10.00
20 Steven Jackson/50 4.00 10.00
23 London Fletcher/50 6.00 15.00

2011 Crown Royale Calling All Captains Materials Autographs

STATED PRINT RUN 5-15
4 Steve Smith/15
6 Jason Witten/15 15.00 40.00
10 Matt Schaub/15 10.00 25.00
12 David Garrard/15 12.00 30.00
23 London Fletcher/15 25.00 50.00

2011 Crown Royale Crown Jewel Rookies

1 Christian Ponder 1.25 3.00
2 Julio Jones 4.00 10.00
3 Jerrel Jernigan 1.25 3.00
4 Kyle Rudolph 1.25 3.00
5 Greg Little 1.50 4.00
6 Clyde Gates 1.25 3.00
7 Cam Newton 6.00 15.00
8 Shane Vereen 1.50 4.00
9 Titus Young 1.25 3.00
10 Mikel Leshoure 1.25 3.00
11 Ryan Mallett 1.25 3.00
12 DeMarco Murray 2.50 6.00
13 Colin Kaepernick 2.00 5.00
14 Ryan Williams 1.25 3.00
15 Daniel Thomas 1.25 3.00
16 Bilal Powell 1.50 4.00
17 Stevan Ridley 1.25 3.00
18 Andy Dalton 2.50 6.00
19 Torrey Smith 1.25 3.00
20 Taiwan Jones 1.25 3.00
21 Von Miller 2.00 5.00
22 Vincent Brown 1.25 3.00
23 Mark Ingram 2.00 5.00
24 Jake Locker 1.25 3.00
25 Blaine Gabbert 1.25 3.00
26 A.J. Green 3.00 8.00
27 Randall Cobb 2.00 5.00
28 Leonard Hankerson 1.25 3.00
29 Delone Carter 1.25 3.00
30 Alex Green 1.25 3.00
31 Marcell Dareus 1.25 3.00
32 Jamie Harper 1.25 3.00
33 Kendall Hunter 1.25 3.00
34 Jonathan Baldwin 1.25 3.00
35 Jordan Todman 1.25 3.00
36 Austin Pettis 1.25 3.00

2011 Crown Royale Crown Jewel Rookies Autographs Sapphire

AUTO STATED PRINT RUN 1-25
1 Christian Ponder/25 6.00 15.00
2 Julio Jones/25 60.00 125.00
3 Jerrel Jernigan/25
4 Kyle Rudolph/25 6.00 15.00
5 Greg Little/25 8.00 20.00
6 Clyde Gates/25 6.00 15.00
8 Shane Vereen/25 8.00 20.00
9 Titus Young/25 6.00 15.00
10 Mikel Leshoure/25 6.00 15.00
11 Ryan Mallett/25 15.00 40.00
12 DeMarco Murray/25 12.00 30.00
13 Colin Kaepernick/25 10.00 25.00
14 Ryan Williams/25 15.00 40.00
15 Daniel Thomas/25 6.00 15.00
18 Andy Dalton/25 15.00 40.00
19 Torrey Smith/25 6.00 15.00
21 Von Miller/25 15.00 40.00
22 Vincent Brown/25 6.00 15.00
23 Mark Ingram/25 10.00 25.00
24 Jake Locker/25 6.00 15.00
25 Blaine Gabbert/25 6.00 15.00
26 A.J. Green/25 30.00 60.00
27 Randall Cobb/25 10.00 25.00
28 Leonard Hankerson/25 6.00 15.00
31 Marcell Dareus/25 6.00 15.00
32 Jamie Harper/25 6.00 15.00
33 Kendall Hunter/25 6.00 15.00
34 Jonathan Baldwin/25 6.00 15.00
35 Jordan Todman/25 6.00 15.00

2011 Crown Royale Jersey Number Materials

STATED PRINT RUN 50 SER.#'d SETS
1 Adrian Peterson 6.00 15.00
2 Pierre Thomas
3 Jeremy Maclin 4.00 10.00
4 Ray Rice 4.00 10.00
5 DeAngelo Hall 4.00 10.00
6 Matt Cassel 4.00 10.00
7 Marques Colston 4.00 10.00
8 Philip Rivers 6.00 15.00
9 Devin Hester 5.00 12.00
10 Ben Roethlisberger 6.00 15.00
11 C.J. Spiller 4.00 10.00
12 Anquan Boldin 4.00 10.00
13 Steven Jackson 4.00 10.00
14 Tom Brady 15.00 40.00
15 Patrick Willis 5.00 12.00
16 Louis Murphy 4.00 10.00
17 Julius Peppers 6.00 15.00
18 Shonn Greene 4.00 10.00
19 Vernon Davis 4.00 10.00
20 Brent Celek 4.00 10.00

2011 Crown Royale Kings of the NFL

1 Aaron Rodgers 2.50 6.00
2 Reggie Wayne 1.25 3.00
3 Wes Welker 1.25 3.00
4 DeSean Jackson 1.25 3.00
5 Larry Fitzgerald 1.25 3.00
6 Calvin Johnson 1.50 4.00
7 Greg Jennings 1.00 2.50
8 Chris Johnson 1.00 2.50
9 Tom Brady 4.00 10.00
10 Mark Sanchez 1.00 2.50
11 Arian Foster 1.00 2.50
12 Adrian Peterson 1.50 4.00
13 Matt Ryan 1.25 3.00
14 Brandon Lloyd 1.00 2.50
15 LeSean McCoy 1.50 4.00
16 Hines Ward 1.25 3.00
17 Roddy White 1.00 2.50
18 Peyton Manning 3.00 8.00
19 Brian Urlacher 1.50 4.00
20 Michael Turner 1.00 2.50

2011 Crown Royale Kings of the NFL Materials

STATED PRINT RUN 99-299
1 Aaron Rodgers/299 10.00 25.00
2 Reggie Wayne/299 3.00 8.00
3 Wes Welker/99 4.00 10.00
4 DeSean Jackson/299 3.00 8.00
5 Larry Fitzgerald/99 4.00 10.00
6 Calvin Johnson/299 4.00 10.00
8 Chris Johnson/299 2.50 6.00
9 Tom Brady/99 12.00 30.00
10 Mark Sanchez/299 2.50 6.00
11 Arian Foster/299 2.50 6.00
12 Adrian Peterson/299 4.00 10.00
13 Matt Ryan/299 3.00 8.00
15 LeSean McCoy/299 4.00 10.00
16 Hines Ward/299 4.00 10.00
17 Roddy White/199 2.50 6.00
18 Peyton Manning/299 8.00 20.00
19 Brian Urlacher/299 4.00 10.00
20 Michael Turner/99 3.00 8.00

2011 Crown Royale Kings of the NFL Materials Prime

STATED PRINT RUN 5-50
1 Aaron Rodgers/50 15.00 40.00
2 Reggie Wayne/50 4.00 10.00
3 Wes Welker/50 4.00 10.00
4 DeSean Jackson/50 4.00 10.00
5 Larry Fitzgerald/50 4.00 10.00
6 Calvin Johnson/50 5.00 12.00
8 Chris Johnson/50 3.00 8.00
10 Mark Sanchez/50 3.00 8.00
12 Adrian Peterson/50 5.00 12.00
13 Matt Ryan/50 4.00 10.00
14 Brandon Lloyd/50 3.00 8.00
15 LeSean McCoy/50 5.00 12.00
16 Hines Ward/50 5.00 12.00
17 Roddy White/50 3.00 8.00
19 Brian Urlacher/50 5.00 12.00
20 Michael Turner/50 3.00 8.00

2011 Crown Royale Kings of the NFL Materials Autographs

AUTO STATED PRINT RUN 5-25
1 Aaron Rodgers/20 200.00 350.00
4 DeSean Jackson/25 12.00 30.00
5 Larry Fitzgerald/20
10 Mark Sanchez/15 15.00 40.00
11 Arian Foster/15 20.00 50.00
13 Matt Ryan/20 25.00 50.00
15 LeSean McCoy/20 15.00 40.00
18 Peyton Manning/15 75.00 150.00
20 Michael Turner/20

2011 Crown Royale Knights of the Gridiron

*GOLD/100: .6X TO 1.5X BASIC INSERTS
*BLACK/25: 1.5X TO 4X BASIC INSERTS
1 Jared Allen 1.50 4.00
2 Clay Matthews 2.50 6.00
3 Brian Cushing 1.50 4.00
4 Jerod Mayo 1.50 4.00
5 Brian Urlacher 2.50 6.00
6 Charles Woodson 2.50 6.00
7 Nnamdi Asomugha 1.50 4.00
8 Dhani Jones 1.50 4.00
9 Patrick Willis 2.00 5.00
10 Darrelle Revis 1.50 4.00

2011 Crown Royale Living Legends

1 Alex Karras 2.00 5.00
2 Art Monk 2.50 6.00
3 Bart Starr 4.00 10.00
4 Billy Howton 1.50 4.00
5 Bobby Bell 1.50 4.00
6 Boomer Esiason 2.00 5.00
7 Boyd Dowler 1.50 4.00
8 Charley Trippi 1.50 4.00
9 Craig James 1.50 4.00
10 Deacon Jones 2.00 5.00
11 Doug Flutie 2.00 5.00
12 Doug Williams 2.00 5.00
13 Dub Jones 1.50 4.00
14 Frank Gifford 2.00 5.00
15 Harlon Hill 1.50 4.00
16 Jack Lambert 2.50 6.00
17 Ozzie Newsome 2.00 5.00
18 Sterling Sharpe 2.00 5.00
19 Wayne Chrebet 1.50 4.00
20 Willie Brown 1.50 4.00

2011 Crown Royale Living Legends Autographs

AUTO STATED PRINT RUN 1-25
1 Alex Karras/25 10.00 25.00
4 Billy Howton/25
5 Bobby Bell/25 8.00 20.00
7 Boyd Dowler/25 10.00 25.00
8 Charley Trippi/25 8.00 20.00
13 Dub Jones/25 8.00 20.00
15 Harlon Hill/25
17 Ozzie Newsome/25
20 Willie Brown/25 8.00 20.00

2011 Crown Royale Living Legends Materials Prime

PRIME PRINT RUN 25 SER.#'d SETS
*BASE JSY/199-299: .2X TO .5X PRIME/25
*BASE JSY/99: .25X TO .6X PRIME/25
1 Alex Karras 10.00 25.00
3 Bart Starr 15.00 40.00
6 Boomer Esiason 10.00 25.00
11 Doug Flutie 10.00 25.00
16 Jack Lambert 12.00 30.00
17 Ozzie Newsome 10.00 25.00
18 Sterling Sharpe 10.00 25.00
19 Wayne Chrebet 8.00 20.00
20 Willie Brown 8.00 20.00

2011 Crown Royale Living Legends Materials Autographs

STATED PRINT RUN 20-25
*PRIME/15: .6X TO 1.5X BASIC JSY AU/20-25
1 Alex Karras/25 12.00 30.00
3 Bart Starr/20 60.00 120.00
6 Boomer Esiason/25 15.00 40.00
9 Craig James/25 12.00 30.00
11 Doug Flutie/25 15.00 40.00
16 Jack Lambert/25 30.00 60.00
17 Ozzie Newsome/25 12.00 30.00
18 Sterling Sharpe/25 12.00 30.00
19 Wayne Chrebet/25 10.00 25.00
20 Willie Brown/25 10.00 25.00

2011 Crown Royale Majestic

1 Johnny Knox 1.25 3.00
2 Andre Johnson 1.50 4.00
3 Josh Freeman 1.50 4.00
4 Danny Woodhead 1.50 4.00
5 Tim Tebow 2.00 5.00
6 Michael Vick 1.50 4.00
7 Visanthe Shiancoe 1.50 4.00
8 Eli Manning 1.50 4.00
9 Heath Miller 1.25 3.00
10 Peyton Hillis 1.25 3.00
11 Maurice Jones-Drew 1.25 3.00
12 Shonn Greene 1.25 3.00
13 DeMarcus Ware 1.50 4.00
14 Miles Austin 1.25 3.00
15 Drew Brees 2.00 5.00
16 Bo Scaife 1.25 3.00
17 Joe Flacco 1.50 4.00
18 Jamaal Charles 1.50 4.00
19 Jay Cutler 1.25 3.00
20 Ryan Mathews 1.50 4.00

2011 Crown Royale Majestic Materials

STATED PRINT RUN 50-299
*PRIME/50: .6X TO 1.5X BASIC JSY/199-299
*PRIME/50: .5X TO 1.2X BASIC JSY/75-99
*PRIME/25: .6X TO 1.5X BASIC JSY/50
1 Johnny Knox 3.00 8.00
2 Andre Johnson 3.00 8.00
3 Josh Freeman 3.00 8.00
4 Danny Woodhead 3.00 8.00
5 Tim Tebow 5.00 12.00
6 Michael Vick 3.00 8.00
7 Visanthe Shiancoe 3.00 8.00
8 Eli Manning 4.00 10.00
9 Heath Miller 2.50 6.00
10 Peyton Hillis 2.50 6.00
11 Maurice Jones-Drew 3.00 8.00
12 Shonn Greene 2.50 6.00
13 DeMarcus Ware 3.00 8.00
14 Miles Austin 2.50 6.00
15 Drew Brees 4.00 10.00
16 Bo Scaife 2.50 6.00
17 Joe Flacco 3.00 8.00
18 Jamaal Charles 4.00 10.00
19 Jay Cutler 2.50 6.00
20 Ryan Mathews 3.00 8.00

2011 Crown Royale Majestic Materials Autographs

JSY AU STATED PRINT RUN 10-25
1 Johnny Knox /25 10.00 25.00
5 Tim Tebow/15 40.00 100.00
9 Heath Miller/25 12.00 30.00
10 Peyton Hillis/20 15.00 40.00
11 Maurice Jones-Drew/15 15.00 40.00
12 Shonn Greene/20 15.00 40.00
14 Miles Austin/20 25.00 50.00
15 Drew Brees/20 50.00 100.00
16 Bo Scaife/20 10.00 25.00
17 Joe Flacco/15 25.00 50.00
19 Jay Cutler/15 15.00 40.00
20 Ryan Mathews/25 12.00 30.00

2011 Crown Royale Net Fusion

1 Sebastian Janikowski 8.00 20.00
2 David Akers 6.00 15.00
3 Billy Cundiff 6.00 15.00
4 Robbie Gould 20.00 50.00
5 Adam Vinatieri 6.00 15.00
6 Jay Feely 6.00 15.00
7 Rob Bironas 8.00 20.00
8 Nate Kaeding 6.00 15.00
9 Mason Crosby 8.00 20.00
10 Josh Scobee 6.00 15.00
11 Garrett Hartley 6.00 15.00
12 Ryan Succop 6.00 15.00
13 Nick Folk 6.00 15.00
14 Neil Rackers 6.00 15.00
15 Stephen Gostkowski 12.00 30.00
16 Olindo Mare 6.00 15.00
17 David Buehler 6.00 15.00
18 Ryan Longwell 6.00 15.00
19 Matt Prater 20.00 50.00
20 Graham Gano 6.00 15.00

2011 Crown Royale Player Die Cut Materials

STATED PRINT RUN 3-100
1 David Harris/100 4.00 10.00
2 Dallas Clark/100 4.00 10.00
3 Tony Romo/100 5.00 12.00
4 Ahmad Bradshaw/16 8.00 20.00
5 Troy Polamalu/49 8.00 20.00
6 Vincent Jackson/100 4.00 10.00
7 Frank Gore/100 5.00 12.00
8 Felix Jones/100 4.00 10.00
9 Darren McFadden/49
10 Jonathan Stewart/25 6.00 15.00
12 Tashard Choice/100 4.00 10.00
13 James Laurinaitis/49
14 Chris Cooley/100 4.00 10.00
15 Santana Moss/25 8.00 20.00
16 Malcom Floyd/25 6.00 15.00
17 LaDainian Tomlinson/100 6.00 15.00
18 Michael Vick/100 5.00 12.00
19 Matt Schaub/100 4.00 10.00
20 LaRon Landry/100 4.00 10.00

2011 Crown Royale Player Die Cut Materials Autographs

STATED PRINT RUN 5-25
EXCH EXPIRATION: 4/26/2013
1 David Harris/15 10.00 25.00
2 Dallas Clark/25
3 Tony Romo/20 30.00 60.00
6 Vincent Jackson/25 10.00 25.00
7 Frank Gore/25 15.00 40.00
13 James Laurinaitis/25 10.00 25.00
14 Chris Cooley/20 10.00 25.00
16 Malcom Floyd/25 10.00 25.00
17 LaDainian Tomlinson/20 25.00 50.00

2011 Crown Royale Rookie Die Cut Material Autographs Blue

*BLUE AU/50: .5X TO 1.2X JSY AU/299
*BLUE AU/50: .4X TO 1X JSY AU/199
BLUE JSY AU PRINT RUN 50
202 Colin Kaepernick 12.00 30.00
210 Andy Dalton 15.00 40.00
228 Cam Newton 100.00 250.00

2011 Crown Royale Rookie Royalty

1 Jamie Harper .75 2.00
2 Ryan Williams .75 2.00
3 Titus Young .75 2.00
4 Mark Ingram 1.25 3.00
5 Greg Little 1.00 2.50
6 Torrey Smith .75 2.00
7 Marcell Dareus .75 2.00
8 Mikel Leshoure .75 2.00
9 Jake Locker .75 2.00
10 Leonard Hankerson .75 2.00
11 Christian Ponder .75 2.00
12 Julio Jones 2.50 6.00
13 Andy Dalton 1.50 4.00
14 Kendall Hunter .75 2.00
15 Colin Kaepernick 1.25 3.00
16 Austin Pettis .75 2.00
17 Delone Carter .75 2.00
18 Clyde Gates .75 2.00
19 Stevan Ridley .75 2.00
20 Jonathan Baldwin .75 2.00
21 Shane Vereen 1.00 2.50
22 Jordan Todman .75 2.00
23 Daniel Thomas .75 2.00
24 Blaine Gabbert .75 2.00
25 Taiwan Jones .75 2.00
26 Vincent Brown .75 2.00
27 Cam Newton 4.00 10.00
28 Randall Cobb 1.25 3.00
29 DeMarco Murray 1.50 4.00
30 Bilal Powell 1.00 2.50
31 A.J. Green 2.00 5.00
32 Kyle Rudolph .75 2.00
33 Jerrel Jernigan .75 2.00
34 Von Miller 1.25 3.00
35 Alex Green .75 2.00
36 Ryan Mallett .75 2.00

2011 Crown Royale Rookie Royalty Materials

STATED PRINT RUN 299 SER.#'d SETS
*PRIME/50: .8X TO 2X BASIC JSY/299
1 Jamie Harper 1.50 4.00
2 Ryan Williams 1.50 4.00
3 Titus Young 1.50 4.00
4 Mark Ingram 2.50 6.00
5 Greg Little 2.00 5.00
6 Torrey Smith 1.50 4.00
7 Marcell Dareus 1.50 4.00
8 Mikel Leshoure 1.50 4.00
9 Jake Locker 1.50 4.00
10 Leonard Hankerson 1.50 4.00
11 Christian Ponder 1.50 4.00
12 Julio Jones 5.00 12.00
13 Andy Dalton 3.00 8.00
14 Kendall Hunter 1.50 4.00
15 Colin Kaepernick 2.50 6.00
16 Austin Pettis 1.50 4.00
17 Delone Carter 1.50 4.00
18 Clyde Gates 1.50 4.00
19 Stevan Ridley 1.50 4.00
20 Jonathan Baldwin 1.50 4.00
21 Shane Vereen 2.00 5.00
22 Jordan Todman 1.50 4.00
23 Daniel Thomas 1.50 4.00
24 Blaine Gabbert 1.50 4.00
25 Taiwan Jones 1.50 4.00
26 Vincent Brown 1.50 4.00
27 Cam Newton 8.00 20.00
28 Randall Cobb 2.50 6.00
29 DeMarco Murray 3.00 8.00
30 Bilal Powell 2.00 5.00
31 A.J. Green 4.00 10.00
32 Kyle Rudolph 1.50 4.00
33 Jerrel Jernigan 1.50 4.00
34 Von Miller 2.50 6.00
35 Alex Green 1.50 4.00
36 Ryan Mallett 1.50 4.00

2011 Crown Royale Rookie Royalty Materials Autographs

JSY AUTO PRINT RUN 25-100
*PRIME AU/25: .6X TO 1.5X JSY AU/100
*PRIME AU/25: .5X TO 1.2X JSY AU/50
EXCH EXPIRATION: 4/26/2013
1 Jamie Harper/100 5.00 12.00
2 Ryan Williams/100 5.00 12.00
3 Titus Young/100 12.00 30.00
4 Mark Ingram/50 10.00 25.00
5 Greg Little/100 6.00 15.00
6 Torrey Smith/100 5.00 12.00
7 Marcell Dareus/100 EXCH
8 Mikel Leshoure/100 10.00 25.00
9 Jake Locker/50 6.00 15.00
10 Leonard Hankerson/100 5.00 12.00
11 Christian Ponder/50 6.00 15.00
12 Julio Jones/100 30.00 80.00
13 Andy Dalton/100 12.00 30.00
14 Kendall Hunter/100 5.00 12.00
15 Colin Kaepernick/100 8.00 20.00
16 Austin Pettis/100 5.00 12.00
17 Delone Carter/100 5.00 12.00
18 Clyde Gates/100 5.00 12.00
19 Stevan Ridley/100 5.00 12.00
20 Jonathan Baldwin/100 10.00 25.00
21 Shane Vereen/100 6.00 15.00
22 Jordan Todman/100 5.00 12.00
23 Daniel Thomas/100 5.00 12.00
24 Blaine Gabbert/50 6.00 15.00
25 Taiwan Jones/100 12.00 30.00
26 Vincent Brown/100 5.00 12.00
27 Cam Newton/25 100.00 200.00
28 Randall Cobb/100 8.00 20.00
29 DeMarco Murray/100 10.00 25.00
30 Bilal Powell/100 6.00 15.00
31 A.J. Green/50 40.00 80.00
32 Kyle Rudolph/100 5.00 12.00
33 Jerrel Jernigan/100 5.00 12.00
34 Von Miller/100 12.00 30.00
35 Alex Green/100 5.00 12.00
36 Ryan Mallett/50 6.00 15.00

2011 Crown Royale Royalty

1 Keith Jackson 1.50 4.00
2 Jan Stenerud 1.50 4.00
3 Forrest Gregg 1.50 4.00
4 Don Meredith 2.50 6.00
5 Richard Dent 1.50 4.00
6 Franco Harris 2.50 6.00
7 Fran Tarkenton 2.50 6.00
8 Steve Bartkowski 2.00 5.00
9 Bob Lilly 2.00 5.00
10 George Blanda 2.00 5.00
11 Dick Butkus 3.00 8.00
12 Mark Carrier 1.50 4.00
13 John Hadl 1.50 4.00
14 John Fuqua 1.50 4.00
15 John Brodie 1.50 4.00
16 Fred Biletnikoff 2.50 6.00
17 Emmitt Smith 4.00 10.00
18 Dan Marino 5.00 12.00
19 Ken Anderson 2.00 5.00
20 Bernie Kosar 2.00 5.00

2011 Crown Royale Royalty Materials

STATED PRINT RUN 99-299
*PRIME/25: .8X TO 2X BASIC JSY/299
*PRIME/25: .6X TO 1.5X BASIC JSY/99
1 Keith Jackson/99 5.00 12.00
2 Jan Stenerud/299 4.00 10.00
3 Forrest Gregg/99 5.00 12.00
4 Don Meredith/99 15.00 40.00
5 Richard Dent/299 4.00 10.00
6 Franco Harris/99 8.00 20.00
7 Fran Tarkenton/99 8.00 20.00
8 Steve Bartkowski/299 5.00 12.00
9 Bob Lilly/99 6.00 15.00
10 George Blanda/299 6.00 15.00
11 Dick Butkus/99 10.00 25.00
12 Mark Carrier/299 4.00 10.00
13 John Hadl/299 4.00 10.00
14 John Fuqua/99 8.00 20.00
15 John Brodie/99
16 Fred Biletnikoff/299 6.00 15.00
17 Emmitt Smith/99 10.00 25.00
18 Dan Marino/299 10.00 25.00
19 Ken Anderson/99 6.00 15.00
20 Bernie Kosar/299 6.00 15.00

2011 Crown Royale Royalty Materials Autographs

STATED PRINT RUN 20-25
EXCH EXPIRATION: 4/26/2013
1 Keith Jackson/25 12.00 30.00
2 Jan Stenerud/25 20.00 50.00
3 Forrest Gregg/25 12.00 30.00
5 Richard Dent/25 12.00 30.00
6 Franco Harris/25 30.00 60.00
7 Fran Tarkenton/25 20.00 50.00
8 Steve Bartkowski/25 15.00 40.00
9 Bob Lilly/25 25.00 60.00
11 Dick Butkus/25 30.00 60.00
12 Mark Carrier/25 20.00 50.00
13 John Hadl/25 EXCH 12.00 30.00
14 John Fuqua/25 12.00 30.00
15 John Brodie/25 30.00 60.00
16 Fred Biletnikoff/25 20.00 50.00
17 Emmitt Smith/20 90.00 150.00
18 Dan Marino/25 75.00 150.00
19 Ken Anderson/25 EXCH 15.00 40.00
20 Bernie Kosar/25 15.00 40.00

2011 Crown Royale The Zone

1 Darren McFadden 1.25 3.00
2 Lee Evans 1.50 4.00
3 Jahvid Best 1.25 3.00
4 Jacoby Ford 1.50 4.00
5 Michael Crabtree 1.25 3.00
6 Percy Harvin 1.25 3.00
7 Matt Forte 1.25 3.00
8 Steve Smith 1.50 4.00
9 DeAngelo Williams 1.25 3.00
10 Braylon Edwards 1.25 3.00
11 Colt McCoy 1.25 3.00
12 Rashard Mendenhall 1.25 3.00
13 Santonio Holmes 1.25 3.00
14 Mike Wallace 1.25 3.00
15 Sam Bradford 1.25 3.00
16 Felix Jones 1.25 3.00
17 Knowshon Moreno 1.25 3.00
18 Dwayne Bowe 1.50 4.00
19 Antonio Gates 1.25 3.00
20 Mike Thomas 1.50 4.00

2011 Crown Royale The Zone Materials

STATED PRINT RUN 94-299
*PRIME/50: .6X TO 1.5X BASIC JSY/199-299
*PRIME/50: .5X TO 1.2X BASIC JSY/94-99
*PRIME/25: .6X TO 1.5X BASIC JSY/99
1 Darren McFadden/99 3.00 8.00
2 Lee Evans/299 3.00 8.00
3 Jahvid Best/99 3.00 8.00
4 Jacoby Ford/299 3.00 8.00
5 Michael Crabtree/199 2.50 6.00
6 Percy Harvin/99 3.00 8.00
7 Matt Forte/99 3.00 8.00
8 Steve Smith/299 3.00 8.00
9 DeAngelo Williams/299 2.50 6.00
11 Colt McCoy/299 2.50 6.00

12 Rashard Mendenhall/99 3.00 8.00
13 Santonio Holmes/99 3.00 8.00
14 Mike Wallace/99 3.00 8.00
15 Sam Bradford/99 3.00 8.00
16 Felix Jones/299 2.50 6.00
17 Knowshon Moreno/299 2.50 6.00
18 Dwayne Bowe/94 4.00 10.00
19 Antonio Gates/299 2.50 6.00
20 Mike Thomas/99 4.00 10.00

2011 Crown Royale The Zone Materials Autographs

STATED PRINT RUN 10-25
EXCH EXPIRATION: 4/26/2013
1 Darren McFadden/25 12.00 30.00
2 Lee Evans/20 12.00 30.00
3 Jahvid Best/25 10.00 25.00
4 Jacoby Ford/25
5 Michael Crabtree/20 10.00 25.00
6 Percy Harvin/20 15.00 40.00
7 Matt Forte/20
9 DeAngelo Williams/25 10.00 25.00
11 Colt McCoy/25 10.00 25.00
12 Rashard Mendenhall/20 10.00 25.00
13 Santonio Holmes/25 10.00 25.00
14 Mike Wallace/20 10.00 25.00
15 Sam Bradford/20 10.00 25.00
16 Felix Jones/20 10.00 25.00
17 Knowshon Moreno/20 10.00 25.00
18 Dwayne Bowe/25 12.00 30.00

2012 Crown Royale

EXCH EXPIRATION: 7/4/2014
1 Aaron Rodgers 1.25 3.00
2 Greg Jennings .50 1.25
3 Jordy Nelson .60 1.50
4 Charles Woodson .75 2.00
5 Jermichael Finley .50 1.25
6 Joe Flacco .60 1.50
7 Anquan Boldin .50 1.25
8 Ray Rice .50 1.25
9 Torrey Smith .50 1.25
10 Ray Lewis .75 2.00
11 Andy Dalton .60 1.50
12 A.J. Green .75 2.00
13 BenJarvus Green-Ellis .60 1.50
14 Jermaine Gresham .50 1.25
15 Greg Little .50 1.25
16 Josh Cribbs .50 1.25
17 Mohamed Massaquoi .50 1.25
18 D'Qwell Jackson .50 1.25
19 Ben Roethlisberger .75 2.00
20 Mike Wallace .50 1.25
21 Isaac Redman .75 2.00
22 Troy Polamalu .75 2.00
23 Antonio Brown .75 2.00
24 Matt Schaub .50 1.25
25 Andre Johnson .60 1.50
26 Arian Foster .60 1.50
27 Owen Daniels .50 1.25
28 J.J. Watt .75 2.00
29 Reggie Wayne .60 1.50
30 Austin Collie .50 1.25
31 Donald Brown .50 1.25
32 Delone Carter .50 1.25
33 Blaine Gabbert .50 1.25
34 Marcedes Lewis .50 1.25
35 Maurice Jones-Drew .50 1.25
36 Paul Posluszny .50 1.25
37 Laurent Robinson .50 1.25
38 Chris Johnson .50 1.25
39 Kenny Britt .50 1.25
40 Jake Locker .75 2.00
41 Jared Cook .50 1.25
42 Ryan Fitzpatrick .50 1.25
43 Steve Johnson .60 1.50
44 C.J. Spiller .50 1.25
45 Fred Jackson .60 1.50
46 Mario Williams .50 1.25
47 Reggie Bush .50 1.25
48 Davone Bess .50 1.25
49 Daniel Thomas .50 1.25
50 Karlos Dansby .50 1.25
51 Anthony Fasano .50 1.25
52 Tom Brady 2.00 5.00
53 Rob Gronkowski .75 2.00
54 Wes Welker .60 1.50
55 Aaron Hernandez .60 1.50
56 Brandon Lloyd .50 1.25
57 Mark Sanchez .50 1.25
58 Shonn Greene .50 1.25
59 Tim Tebow .75 2.00
60 Darrelle Revis .50 1.25
61 Santonio Holmes .50 1.25
62 Peyton Manning 1.50 4.00
63 Willis McGahee .50 1.25
64 Demaryius Thomas .75 2.00
65 Eric Decker .50 1.25
66 Von Miller .60 1.50
67 Matthew Stafford .60 1.50
68 Ndamukong Suh .60 1.50
69 Calvin Johnson .75 2.00
70 Brandon Pettigrew .50 1.25
71 Jay Cutler .50 1.25
72 Brandon Marshall .60 1.50
73 Matt Forte .50 1.25
74 Devin Hester .60 1.50
75 Julius Peppers .60 1.50
76 Cam Newton .75 2.00
77 Brandon LaFell .50 1.25
78 Greg Olsen .60 1.50
79 Steve Smith .60 1.50
80 DeAngelo Williams .50 1.25
81 Larry Fitzgerald .60 1.50
82 Kevin Kolb .50 1.25
83 Early Doucet .50 1.25
84 Patrick Peterson .50 1.25
85 Beanie Wells .50 1.25
86 Matt Ryan .60 1.50
87 Michael Turner .50 1.25
88 Roddy White .50 1.25
89 Tony Gonzalez .60 1.50
90 Julio Jones .75 2.00
91 Christian Ponder .50 1.25
92 Percy Harvin .50 1.25
93 Adrian Peterson .75 2.00
94 Jared Allen .50 1.25
95 Toby Gerhart .50 1.25
96 Drew Brees .75 2.00
97 Marques Colston .50 1.25
98 Darren Sproles .60 1.50
99 Mark Ingram .60 1.50
100 Jimmy Graham .75 2.00
101 Eli Manning .60 1.50
102 Jason Pierre-Paul .50 1.25
103 Ahmad Bradshaw .50 1.25
104 Hakeem Nicks .50 1.25
105 Victor Cruz .60 1.50
106 Darren McFadden .50 1.25
107 Darrius Heyward-Bey .50 1.25
108 Carson Palmer .60 1.50
109 Denarius Moore .50 1.25
110 Michael Vick .60 1.50
111 LeSean McCoy .75 2.00
112 DeSean Jackson .60 1.50
113 Brent Celek .50 1.25
114 Jeremy Maclin .50 1.25
115 Philip Rivers .75 2.00
116 Antonio Gates .60 1.50
117 Malcom Floyd .50 1.25
118 Ryan Mathews .60 1.50
119 Robert Meachem .50 1.25
120 Alex Smith .60 1.50
121 Frank Gore .60 1.50
122 Michael Crabtree .50 1.25
123 Randy Moss .60 1.50
124 Vernon Davis .50 1.25
125 Tony Romo .60 1.50
126 DeMarco Murray .60 1.50
127 DeMarcus Ware .75 2.00
128 Jason Witten .60 1.50
129 Miles Austin .50 1.25
130 Marshawn Lynch .60 1.50
131 Matt Flynn .50 1.25
132 Sidney Rice .50 1.25
133 Golden Tate .50 1.25
134 Sam Bradford .50 1.25
135 Steven Jackson .50 1.25
136 Steve Smith .60 1.50
137 Lance Kendricks .50 1.25
138 Dallas Clark .50 1.25
139 Josh Freeman .60 1.50
140 LeGarrette Blount .60 1.50
141 Vincent Jackson .50 1.25
142 Santana Moss .60 1.50
143 Pierre Garcon .60 1.50
144 Roy Helu .50 1.25
145 Fred Davis .50 1.25
146 Matt Cassel .50 1.25
147 Jamaal Charles .60 1.50
148 Dwayne Bowe .60 1.50
149 Peyton Hillis .50 1.25
150 Tamba Hali .50 1.25
151 Alfred Morris RC 1.25 3.00
152 Adrien Robinson RC 1.25 3.00
153 Andre Branch RC 1.25 3.00
154 B.J. Coleman RC 1.25 3.00
155 B.J. Cunningham RC 1.25 3.00
156 Bobby Rainey RC 1.25 3.00
157 Bobby Wagner RC 2.00 5.00
158 Brandon Taylor RC 1.25 3.00
159 Brandon Hardin RC 1.50 4.00
160 Bruce Irvin RC 1.50 4.00
161 Bryce Brown RC 1.25 3.00
162 Case Keenum RC 2.50 6.00
163 Casey Hayward RC 1.25 3.00
164 Chandler Harnish RC 1.25 3.00
165 Chandler Jones RC 1.25 3.00
166 Chris Polk RC 1.25 3.00
167 Chris Rainey RC 1.25 3.00
168 Cory Harkey RC 1.50 4.00
169 Coty Sensabaugh RC 1.50 4.00
170 Courtney Upshaw RC 1.50 4.00
171 Cyrus Gray RC 1.25 3.00
172 Dan Herron RC 1.25 3.00
173 Danny Coale RC 1.25 3.00
174 David DeCastro RC 1.25 3.00
175 Davin Meggett RC 1.25 3.00
176 Deangelo Peterson RC 1.25 3.00
177 Demario Davis RC 1.25 3.00
178 Derek Wolfe RC 1.50 4.00
179 Devon Still RC 1.50 4.00
180 Devon Wylie RC 1.25 3.00
181 Dont'a Hightower RC 2.00 5.00
182 Dontari Poe RC 1.25 3.00
183 Dre Kirkpatrick RC 1.25 3.00
184 Bill Bentley RC 1.50 4.00
185 Jeff Demps RC 1.50 4.00
186 Josh Cooper RC 1.50 4.00
187 Fletcher Cox RC 2.00 5.00
188 George Iloka RC 1.25 3.00
189 Gerell Robinson RC 1.25 3.00
190 Rod Streater RC 2.00 5.00
191 Harrison Smith RC 1.25 3.00
192 Jamell Fleming RC 1.25 3.00
193 James Hanna RC 1.25 3.00
194 Janoris Jenkins RC 1.50 4.00
195 Jared Crick RC 1.25 3.00
196 Jeff Fuller RC 1.25 3.00
197 Jerel Worthy RC 1.25 3.00
198 Jonathan Martin RC 1.25 3.00
199 Josh Robinson RC 2.00 5.00
200 Juron Criner RC 1.25 3.00
201 Kellen Moore RC 1.50 4.00
202 Kendall Reyes RC 1.25 3.00
203 Keshawn Martin RC 1.50 4.00
204 Kevin Zeitler RC 1.25 3.00
205 Kirk Cousins RC 5.00 12.00
206 Ladarius Green RC 1.25 3.00
207 LaVon Brazill RC 2.00 5.00
208 Lavonte David RC 2.00 5.00
209 Luke Kuechly RC 3.00 8.00
210 Marc Tyler RC 1.25 3.00
211 Mark Barron RC 1.25 3.00
212 Marquis Maze RC 1.25 3.00
213 Marvin Jones RC 1.25 3.00
214 Marvin McNutt RC 1.25 3.00
215 Matt Kalil RC 1.25 3.00
216 Melvin Ingram RC 1.25 3.00
217 Michael Brockers RC 1.25 3.00
218 Michael Smith RC 1.50 4.00
219 Mike Martin RC 1.50 4.00
220 Morris Claiborne RC 1.25 3.00
221 Mychal Kendricks RC 2.00 5.00
222 Najee Goode RC 1.25 3.00
223 Nick Perry RC 1.50 4.00
224 Olivier Vernon RC 2.00 5.00
225 Omar Bolden RC 1.50 4.00
226 Orson Charles RC 1.25 3.00
227 Quinton Coples RC 1.25 3.00
228 Rhett Ellison RC 1.50 4.00
229 Riley Reiff RC 1.25 3.00
230 Rishard Matthews RC 1.25 3.00
231 Ronnell Lewis RC 1.25 3.00
232 Ryan Lindley RC 1.25 3.00
233 Sean Spence RC 1.50 4.00
234 Shea McClellin RC 1.50 4.00
235 Stephon Gilmore RC 1.50 4.00
236 T.Y. Hilton RC 2.50 6.00
237 Tauren Poole RC 1.25 3.00
238 Tavon Wilson RC 1.50 4.00
239 Terrance Ganaway RC 1.50 4.00
240 Tyrone Crawford RC 1.25 3.00
241 Vick Ballard RC 1.50 4.00
242 Vinny Curry RC 1.50 4.00
243 Vontaze Burfict RC 1.50 4.00
244 Whitney Mercilus RC 1.25 3.00
245 Josh Gordon RC 3.00 8.00
246 Brandon Bolden RC 1.25 3.00
247 Tim Benford RC 1.25 3.00
248 Tommy Streeter RC 1.25 3.00
249 Travis Benjamin RC 1.25 3.00
250 Trumaine Johnson RC 1.25 3.00
251 A.J. Jenkins JSY AU/349 RC 5.00 12.00
252 A.Jeffery JSY AU/349 RC 12.00 30.00
253 A.Luck JSY AU/249 RC 75.00 150.00
254 Bernard Pierce JSY AU/349 RC 5.00 12.00
255 B.Weeden JSY AU/249 RC 5.00 12.00
256 Brian Quick JSY AU/349 RC 5.00 12.00
257 B.Osweiler JSY AU/349 RC 5.00 12.00
258 Chris Givens JSY AU/349 RC 5.00 12.00
259 Coby Fleener JSY AU/349 RC 5.00 12.00
260 David Wilson JSY AU/249 RC 5.00 12.00
261 DeVier Posey JSY AU/349 RC 5.00 12.00
262 D.Martin JSY AU/249 RC 8.00 20.00
263 Dwayne Allen JSY AU/249 RC 5.00 12.00
264 Isaiah Pead JSY AU/249 RC 5.00 12.00
265 Jarius Wright JSY AU/349 RC 5.00 12.00
266 Joe Adams JSY AU/349 RC 5.00 12.00
267 J.Blackmon JSY AU/249 RC 5.00 12.00
268 K.Wright JSY AU/249 RC EX 5.00 12.00
269 L.Miller JSY AU/249 RC 8.00 20.00
270 L.James JSY AU/349 RC EX 5.00 12.00
271 Michael Egnew JSY AU/349 RC 5.00 12.00
272 M.Floyd JSY AU/249 RC 5.00 12.00
273 M.Sanu JSY AU/249 RC 8.00 20.00
274 N.Foles JSY AU/349 RC 15.00 40.00
275 Nick Toon JSY AU/349 RC 5.00 12.00
276 R.Griffin III JSY AU/249 RC 6.00 15.00
277 Robert Turbin JSY AU/349 RC 5.00 12.00
278 Ronnie Hillman JSY AU/349 RC 5.00 12.00
279 R.Randle JSY AU/349 RC 5.00 12.00
280 R.Wilson JSY AU/349 RC EX 50.00 100.00
281 Ryan Broyles JSY AU/349 RC 5.00 12.00
282 R.Tannehill JSY AU/249 RC 8.00 20.00
283 Stephen Hill JSY AU/249 RC 5.00 12.00
284 T.J. Graham JSY AU/349 RC 5.00 12.00
285 Richardson JSY AU/249 RC 5.00 12.00

2012 Crown Royale Bronze

*VETS: 1.2X TO 3X BASIC CARDS
*ROOKIES: .5X TO 1.2X BASIC CARDS
RANDOM INSERTS IN RETAIL PACKS

2012 Crown Royale Gold Holofoil

*VETS/99: 1.5X TO 4X BASIC CARDS
*ROOKIES/99: .6X TO 1.5X BASIC CARDS
*ROOK.JSY AU/99: .5X TO 1.2X JSY AU RC
253 Andrew Luck JSY AU 100.00 200.00
280 Russell Wilson JSY AU 75.00 150.00

2012 Crown Royale Green Holofoil

*VETS/49: 2X TO 5X BASIC CARDS
*ROOKIES/49: .8X TO 2X BASIC CARDS
*ROOK.JSY AU/49: .6X TO 1.5X JSY AU RC
253 Andrew Luck JSY AU 125.00 250.00

2012 Crown Royale Purple

*VETS/25: 3X TO 8X BASIC CARDS
*ROOKIES/25: 1X TO 2.5X BASIC RC
*ROOK.JSY AU/25: .8X TO 2X JSY AU RC
253 Andrew Luck JSY AU 150.00 300.00
274 Nick Foles JSY AU 40.00 100.00
280 Russell Wilson JSY AU 100.00 200.00

2012 Crown Royale Retail

*VETS: .1X TO .3X BASIC CARDS
*ROOKIES: .3X TO .8X BASIC RC
251 A.J. Jenkins JSY RC 1.50 4.00
252 Alshon Jeffery JSY RC 3.00 8.00
253 Andrew Luck JSY RC 15.00 40.00
254 Bernard Pierce JSY RC 1.50 4.00
255 Brandon Weeden JSY RC 1.50 4.00
256 Brian Quick JSY RC 1.50 4.00
257 Brock Osweiler JSY RC 1.50 4.00
258 Chris Givens JSY RC 1.50 4.00
259 Coby Fleener JSY RC 1.50 4.00
260 David Wilson JSY RC 1.50 4.00
261 DeVier Posey JSY RC 1.50 4.00
262 Doug Martin JSY RC 2.50 6.00
263 Dwayne Allen JSY RC 1.50 4.00
264 Isaiah Pead JSY RC 1.50 4.00
265 Jarius Wright JSY RC 1.50 4.00
266 Joe Adams JSY RC 1.50 4.00
267 Justin Blackmon JSY RC 1.50 4.00
268 Kendall Wright JSY RC 1.50 4.00
269 Lamar Miller JSY RC 2.50 6.00
270 LaMichael James JSY RC 1.50 4.00
271 Michael Egnew JSY RC 1.50 4.00
272 Michael Floyd JSY RC 1.50 4.00
273 Mohamed Sanu JSY RC 2.50 6.00
274 Nick Foles JSY RC 4.00 10.00
275 Nick Toon JSY RC 1.50 4.00
277 Robert Turbin JSY RC 1.50 4.00
278 Ronnie Hillman JSY RC 1.50 4.00
279 Rueben Randle JSY RC 1.50 4.00
280 Russell Wilson JSY RC 12.00 30.00
281 Ryan Broyles JSY RC 1.50 4.00
282 Ryan Tannehill JSY RC 2.50 6.00
283 Stephen Hill JSY RC 1.50 4.00
284 T.J. Graham JSY RC 1.50 4.00
285 Trent Richardson JSY RC 1.50 4.00

2012 Crown Royale Silver Holofoil

*VETS/149: 1.2X TO 3X BASIC CARDS
*ROOKIES/149: .5X TO 1.2X BASIC CARDS
*ROOK.JSY AU/149: .5X TO 1.2X JSY AU RC
253 Andrew Luck JSY AU 75.00 150.00
280 Russell Wilson JSY AU 75.00 150.00

2012 Crown Royale Crowning Glory Materials

1 Eli Manning/99 3.00 8.00
2 Adrian Peterson/99 4.00 10.00
3 Arian Foster/99 3.00 8.00
4 Drew Brees/99 4.00 10.00
5 Dwayne Bowe/99 3.00 8.00
6 Greg Jennings/99 2.50 6.00
7 Jay Cutler/99 2.50 6.00
8 Larry Fitzgerald/99 3.00 8.00
10 Matthew Stafford/25 5.00 12.00
11 Maurice Jones-Drew/30 4.00 10.00
12 Roddy White/99 2.50 6.00
14 Philip Rivers/99 4.00 10.00
15 Santana Moss/99 3.00 8.00
16 Steven Jackson/99 2.50 6.00
17 Tom Brady/99 10.00 25.00
18 Vernon Davis/99 2.50 6.00
19 Mike Wallace/99 2.50 6.00
20 Ray Rice/99 2.50 6.00
21 Steve Smith/99 3.00 8.00
22 Chris Johnson/99 2.50 6.00
23 Christian Ponder/99 2.50 6.00
24 Darren Sproles/99 3.00 8.00
25 Mark Sanchez/99 2.50 6.00
26 Wes Welker/99 3.00 8.00
27 Darren McFadden/99 2.50 6.00
28 DeAngelo Williams/99 2.50 6.00
30 Tony Romo/99 3.00 8.00

2012 Crown Royale Crowning Glory Materials Prime

1 Eli Manning/49 5.00 12.00
2 Adrian Peterson/49 6.00 15.00
3 Arian Foster/49 5.00 12.00
5 Dwayne Bowe/49 5.00 12.00
8 Larry Fitzgerald/19 6.00 15.00
12 Roddy White/49 4.00 10.00
14 Philip Rivers/49 6.00 15.00
15 Santana Moss/49 5.00 12.00
16 Steven Jackson/49 4.00 10.00
17 Tom Brady/49 15.00 40.00
18 Vernon Davis/49 4.00 10.00
19 Mike Wallace/49 4.00 10.00
20 Ray Rice/49 4.00 10.00
21 Steve Smith/49 5.00 12.00
23 Christian Ponder/49 4.00 10.00
24 Darren Sproles/49 5.00 12.00
25 Mark Sanchez/49 4.00 10.00
26 Wes Welker/49 5.00 12.00
27 Darren McFadden/49 4.00 10.00
30 Tony Romo/49 5.00 12.00

2012 Crown Royale Field Force

*BLUE/25: 1.2X TO 3X BASIC INSERTS
*GREEN/10: 1.5X TO 4X BASIC INSERTS
*RED/100: .6X TO 1.5X BASIC INSERTS
1 Ed Reed 1.25 3.00
2 D'Qwell Jackson 1.00 2.50
3 James Harrison 1.25 3.00
4 J.J. Watt 1.50 4.00
5 Robert Mathis 1.00 2.50
6 Paul Posluszny 1.00 2.50
7 Mario Williams 1.00 2.50
8 Karlos Dansby 1.00 2.50
9 Jerod Mayo 1.00 2.50
10 Darrelle Revis 1.00 2.50
11 Elvis Dumervil 1.00 2.50
12 Tamba Hali 1.00 2.50
13 Takeo Spikes 1.00 2.50
14 Lance Briggs 1.25 3.00
15 Kyle Vanden Bosch 1.00 2.50
16 Clay Matthews 1.50 4.00
17 Jared Allen 1.00 2.50
18 Jon Beason 1.00 2.50
19 DeMarcus Ware 1.50 4.00
20 Jason Pierre-Paul 1.00 2.50
21 Nnamdi Asomugha 1.00 2.50
22 London Fletcher 1.25 3.00
23 Aldon Smith 1.00 2.50
24 James Laurinaitis 1.00 2.50
25 Patrick Peterson 1.00 2.50

2012 Crown Royale Legendary Silhouette Material Autographs

*PRIME/15-25: .8X TO 2X JSY AU/75-99
*PRIME/15-25: .6X TO 1.5X JSY AU/38-53
*PRIME/15-25: .5X TO 1.2X JSY AU/25
EXCH EXPIRATION: 7/4/2014
1 John Elway/40 90.00 150.00
2 Joe Namath/40 75.00 150.00
3 Bo Jackson/25 60.00 100.00
4 Jim McMahon/33 15.00 40.00
5 Randall Cunningham/49 20.00 50.00
6 Bobby Mitchell/75 EXCH 12.00 30.00
7 Boomer Esiason/49 20.00 50.00
8 Doug Flutie/49 15.00 40.00
9 Cris Carter/40 40.00 80.00
10 Willie Brown/99 10.00 25.00
11 Curtis Martin/25 40.00 80.00
12 Joe Montana/25 100.00 175.00
13 Rocket Ismail/49 15.00 40.00
14 Ed Too Tall Jones/38 12.00 30.00
15 Paul Hornung/75 15.00 40.00
16 Lee Roy Selmon/99 10.00 25.00
17 Sterling Sharpe/53 15.00 40.00
18 Bernie Kosar/49 15.00 40.00
19 Jim Plunkett/99 15.00 40.00
20 Ronnie Lott/49 15.00 40.00
21 Eric Dickerson/49 15.00 40.00
22 Alan Page/49 EXCH 20.00 50.00
23 Mark Duper/49 12.00 30.00
24 Emmitt Smith/22 100.00 175.00
25 Barry Sanders/20 100.00 175.00
26 Dan Marino/25 100.00 175.00
27 Jerry Rice/25 75.00 150.00
28 Jim Kelly/40 20.00 50.00
29 Lawrence Taylor/25 40.00 80.00
30 Kurt Warner/40 40.00 80.00

2012 Crown Royale Majestic Motion

*BLUE/25: 1.2X TO 3X BASIC INSERTS
*GREEN/10: 1.5X TO 4X BASIC INSERTS
*RED/100: .6X TO 1.5X BASIC INSERTS
1 Torrey Smith 1.00 2.50
2 A.J. Green 1.50 4.00
3 Antonio Brown 1.50 4.00
4 Andre Johnson 1.25 3.00
5 Donald Brown 1.00 2.50
6 Laurent Robinson 1.00 2.50
7 Kenny Britt 1.00 2.50
8 C.J. Spiller 1.00 2.50
9 Reggie Bush 1.00 2.50
10 Wes Welker 1.25 3.00
11 Shonn Greene 1.00 2.50
12 Demaryius Thomas 1.50 4.00
13 Dwayne Bowe 1.25 3.00
14 Darren McFadden 1.00 2.50
15 Robert Meachem 1.00 2.50
16 Matt Forte 1.00 2.50
17 Jordy Nelson 1.25 3.00
18 Roddy White 1.00 2.50
19 Steve Smith 1.25 3.00
20 Marques Colston 1.00 2.50
21 DeMarco Murray 1.25 3.00
22 Hakeem Nicks 1.00 2.50
23 LeSean McCoy 1.50 4.00
24 Pierre Garcon 1.25 3.00
25 Sidney Rice 1.00 2.50

2012 Crown Royale NFL Regime

*BLUE/25: 1.2X TO 3X BASIC INSERTS
*GREEN/10: 1.5X TO 4X BASIC INSERTS
*RED/100: .6X TO 1.5X BASIC INSERTS
1 Ray Rice 1.00 2.50
2 Mike Wallace 1.00 2.50
3 Arian Foster 1.25 3.00
4 Maurice Jones-Drew 1.00 2.50
5 Chris Johnson 1.00 2.50
6 Fred Jackson 1.25 3.00
7 Tom Brady 4.00 10.00
8 Peyton Manning 3.00 8.00
9 Jamaal Charles 1.25 3.00
10 Philip Rivers 1.50 4.00
11 Jay Cutler 1.00 2.50
12 Calvin Johnson 1.50 4.00
13 Aaron Rodgers 2.50 6.00
14 Adrian Peterson 1.50 4.00
15 Michael Turner 1.00 2.50
16 Drew Brees 1.50 4.00
17 Vincent Jackson 1.00 2.50
18 Tony Romo 1.25 3.00
19 Michael Vick 1.25 3.00
20 Santana Moss 1.25 3.00
21 Larry Fitzgerald 1.25 3.00
22 Randy Moss 1.25 3.00
23 Marshawn Lynch 1.25 3.00
24 Eli Manning 1.25 3.00
25 Steven Jackson 1.00 2.50

2012 Crown Royale Panini's Choice Autographs Gold

1 Michael Turner/15 8.00 20.00
2 Andre Rison/25 20.00 40.00
3 Vinny Testaverde/25 8.00 20.00
4 D.D. Lewis/25 8.00 20.00
6 Kellen Winslow/25 12.00 30.00
9 Adrian Peterson/15 90.00 150.00
10 Ahmad Bradshaw/25 12.00 30.00
11 Alex Smith/15 12.00 30.00
12 Andy Dalton/15 10.00 25.00
13 Aaron Hernandez/15 12.00 30.00
14 Antonio Gates/15 10.00 25.00
15 C.J. Spiller/25 12.00 30.00
16 BenJarvus Green-Ellis/25 15.00 40.00
17 Brandon Jacobs/25 8.00 20.00
18 Brandon LaFell/25 8.00 20.00
19 Brandon Lloyd/25 12.00 30.00
20 Cam Newton/25 40.00 80.00
21 Charles Woodson/15 100.00 175.00
22 Jerod Mayo/25 8.00 20.00
23 Jon Beason/25 8.00 20.00
24 Josh Cribbs/25 8.00 20.00
25 Kevin Kolb/25 8.00 20.00
26 LeGarrette Blount/25 10.00 25.00
27 DeMarcus Ware/25 12.00 30.00
28 London Fletcher/25 12.00 30.00
29 Mario Williams/25 10.00 25.00
30 Eli Manning/15 10.00 25.00
32 Marshawn Lynch/15 20.00 40.00
33 Fred Davis/25 10.00 25.00
34 Fred Jackson/15 12.00 30.00
35 Greg Jennings/15 8.00 20.00
36 Greg Little/25 8.00 20.00
37 Mark Ingram/25 10.00 25.00
38 Matt Cassel/25 8.00 20.00
39 Jason Witten/15 30.00 60.00
40 Matt Flynn/25 8.00 20.00
41 Matthew Stafford/15 25.00 50.00
42 Jermaine Gresham/25 8.00 20.00
43 Jermichael Finley/25 8.00 20.00
44 Brandon Pettigrew/25 8.00 20.00
45 Joe Flacco/15 25.00 50.00
46 Jordy Nelson/15 12.00 30.00
47 Josh Freeman/25 12.00 30.00
48 Derrick Johnson/25 8.00 20.00
49 Mike Williams/15 10.00 25.00
50 Jason Pierre-Paul/25 12.00 30.00
51 LeSean McCoy/15 12.00 30.00
52 Matt Forte/25 8.00 20.00
53 Matt Schaub/25 8.00 20.00
54 Greg Olsen/25 10.00 25.00
55 Jonathan Baldwin/25 8.00 20.00
56 Heath Miller/25 12.00 30.00
57 Kevin Walter/25 8.00 20.00
58 Robert Mathis/25 8.00 20.00
60 Knowshon Moreno/25 8.00 20.00
61 Pierre Garcon/25 10.00 25.00
62 Felix Jones/25 8.00 20.00
67 Torrey Smith/25 12.00 30.00
68 Brent Celek/25 8.00 20.00
69 Vincent Jackson/15 8.00 20.00
70 Steve Johnson/15 10.00 25.00

2012 Crown Royale Pivotal Players

*BLUE/25: 1.2X TO 3X BASIC INSERTS
*GREEN/10: 1.5X TO 4X BASIC INSERTS
*RED/100: .6X TO 1.5X BASIC INSERTS
1 Anquan Boldin 1.00 2.50
2 Andy Dalton 1.25 3.00
3 Greg Little 1.00 2.50
4 Ben Roethlisberger 1.50 4.00
5 Matt Schaub 1.00 2.50
6 Reggie Wayne 1.25 3.00
7 Chris Johnson 1.00 2.50
8 Aaron Hernandez 1.25 3.00
9 Santonio Holmes 1.00 2.50
10 Willis McGahee 1.00 2.50
11 Matt Cassel 1.00 2.50
12 Carson Palmer 1.25 3.00
13 Antonio Gates 1.25 3.00
14 Brandon Marshall 1.25 3.00
15 Matthew Stafford 1.25 3.00
16 Jermichael Finley 1.00 2.50
17 Percy Harvin 1.00 2.50
18 Tony Gonzalez 1.25 3.00
19 Cam Newton 1.50 4.00
20 Mark Ingram 1.25 3.00
21 Mike Williams 1.25 3.00
22 Dez Bryant 1.50 4.00
23 Victor Cruz 1.25 3.00
24 DeSean Jackson 1.25 3.00
25 Alex Smith 1.25 3.00

2012 Crown Royale Rookie Paydirt Materials

*GRN PRIME/49: .6X TO 1.5X BASIC JSY/149
*BRONZE RET: .4X TO 1X BASIC JSY/149
1 A.J. Jenkins 1.50 4.00
2 Alshon Jeffery 3.00 8.00
3 Andrew Luck 15.00 30.00
4 Bernard Pierce 1.50 4.00
5 Brandon Weeden 1.50 4.00
6 Brian Quick 1.50 4.00
7 Brock Osweiler 1.50 4.00
8 Chris Givens 1.50 4.00
9 Coby Fleener 1.50 4.00
10 David Wilson 1.50 4.00
11 DeVier Posey 1.50 4.00
12 Doug Martin 2.50 6.00
13 Dwayne Allen 1.50 4.00
14 Isaiah Pead 1.50 4.00
15 Jarius Wright 1.50 4.00
16 Joe Adams 1.50 4.00
17 Justin Blackmon 1.50 4.00
18 Kendall Wright 1.50 4.00
19 Lamar Miller 2.50 6.00
20 LaMichael James 1.50 4.00
21 Michael Egnew 1.50 4.00
22 Michael Floyd 1.50 4.00
23 Mohamed Sanu 2.50 6.00
24 Nick Foles 4.00 10.00
25 Nick Toon 1.50 4.00
26 Robert Griffin III 2.00 5.00
27 Robert Turbin 1.50 4.00
28 Ronnie Hillman 1.50 4.00
29 Rueben Randle 1.50 4.00
30 Russell Wilson 10.00 25.00
31 Ryan Broyles 1.50 4.00
32 Ryan Tannehill 2.50 6.00
33 Stephen Hill 1.50 4.00
34 T.J. Graham 1.50 4.00
35 Trent Richardson 1.50 4.00

2012 Crown Royale Rookie Royalty Materials

*ROYALTY/149: .4X TO 1X PAYDIRT/149
*BRONZE RET: .4X TO 1X BASIC JSY/149
*GRN PRIME/49: .6X TO 1.5X BASIC JSY/149

2012 Crown Royale Rookie Signatures

*GREEN/49: .6X TO 1.5X BASIC AU/245
*GREEN/49: .5X TO 1.2X BASIC AU/88-99
*PURPLE/25: .8X TO 2X BASIC AU/245
*PURPLE/25: .6X TO 1.5X BASIC AU/88-99
1 Alfred Morris/99 3.00 8.00
2 Adrien Robinson/99 3.00 8.00
3 Andre Branch/245 2.50 6.00
4 B.J. Coleman/99 3.00 8.00
5 B.J. Cunningham/245 2.50 6.00
6 Bobby Rainey/245 2.50 6.00
7 Bobby Wagner/245 4.00 10.00
8 Brandon Taylor/245 2.50 6.00
9 Brandon Hardin/245 3.00 8.00
10 Bruce Irvin/245 3.00 8.00
11 Bryce Brown/99 3.00 8.00
12 Case Keenum/245 15.00 40.00
13 Casey Hayward/245 2.50 6.00
14 Chandler Harnish/99 3.00 8.00
15 Chandler Jones/99 3.00 8.00
16 Chris Polk/245 2.50 6.00
17 Chris Rainey/99 3.00 8.00
18 Cory Harkey/245 3.00 8.00
19 Coty Sensabaugh/245 3.00 8.00
20 Courtney Upshaw/245 3.00 8.00
21 Cyrus Gray/245 2.50 6.00
22 Dan Herron/245 2.50 6.00
23 Danny Coale/245 2.50 6.00
24 David DeCastro/245 2.50 6.00
25 Davin Meggett/245 2.50 6.00
26 Deangelo Peterson/245 2.50 6.00
27 Demario Davis/245 2.50 6.00
28 Derek Wolfe/99 EXCH 8.00 20.00
29 Devon Still/245 3.00 8.00
30 Devon Wylie/99 3.00 8.00
31 Dont'a Hightower/245 4.00 10.00
32 Dontari Poe/99 3.00 8.00
33 Dre Kirkpatrick/99 3.00 8.00
34 Bill Bentley/245 3.00 8.00
35 Jeff Demps/99 4.00 10.00
36 Josh Cooper/99 4.00 10.00
37 Fletcher Cox/245 4.00 10.00
38 George Iloka/245 2.50 6.00
39 Gerell Robinson/245 2.50 6.00
40 Rod Streater/99 5.00 12.00
41 Harrison Smith/245 5.00 12.00
42 Jamell Fleming/245 2.50 6.00
43 James Hanna/245 2.50 6.00
44 Janoris Jenkins/245 3.00 8.00
45 Jared Crick/99 3.00 8.00
46 Jeff Fuller/245 2.50 6.00
47 Jerel Worthy/99 3.00 8.00
48 Jonathan Martin/245 2.50 6.00
49 Josh Robinson/245 4.00 10.00
50 Juron Criner/245 2.50 6.00
51 Kellen Moore/245 3.00 8.00
52 Kendall Reyes/245 2.50 6.00
53 Keshawn Martin/99 4.00 10.00
54 Kevin Zeitler/245 2.50 6.00
55 Kirk Cousins/245 10.00 25.00
56 Ladarius Green/245 5.00 12.00
57 LaVon Brazill/245 4.00 10.00
58 Lavonte David/88 6.00 15.00
59 Luke Kuechly/245 15.00 40.00
60 Marc Tyler/245 2.50 6.00
61 Mark Barron/99 3.00 8.00
62 Marquis Maze/245 2.50 6.00
63 Marvin Jones/245 2.50 6.00
64 Marvin McNutt/245 2.50 6.00
65 Matt Kalil/99 3.00 8.00
66 Melvin Ingram/99 3.00 8.00
67 Michael Brockers/99 3.00 8.00
68 Michael Smith/99 4.00 10.00
69 Mike Martin/245 3.00 8.00
70 Morris Claiborne/66 3.00 8.00
71 Mychal Kendricks/245 4.00 10.00
72 Najee Goode/245 2.50 6.00
73 Nick Perry/99 4.00 10.00
74 Olivier Vernon/245 4.00 10.00
75 Omar Bolden/245 3.00 8.00
76 Orson Charles/245 2.50 6.00
77 Quinton Coples/245 2.50 6.00
78 Rhett Ellison/245 3.00 8.00
79 Riley Reiff/245 2.50 6.00
80 Rishard Matthews/245 2.50 6.00
81 Ronnell Lewis/99 3.00 8.00
82 Ryan Lindley/99 3.00 8.00
83 Sean Spence/245 3.00 8.00
84 Shea McClellin/99 4.00 10.00
85 Stephon Gilmore/99 4.00 10.00
86 T.Y. Hilton/99 6.00 15.00
87 Tauren Poole/245 2.50 6.00
88 Tavon Wilson/245 3.00 8.00
89 Terrance Ganaway/245 3.00 8.00
90 Tyrone Crawford/245 2.50 6.00
91 Vick Ballard/99 4.00 10.00
92 Vinny Curry/245 3.00 8.00
93 Vontaze Burfict/245 3.00 8.00
94 Whitney Mercilus/245 2.50 6.00
95 Josh Gordon/245 6.00 15.00
96 Brandon Bolden/99 8.00 20.00
97 Tim Benford/245 2.50 6.00
98 Tommy Streeter/99 3.00 8.00
99 Travis Benjamin 2.50 6.00
100 Trumaine Johnson/245 2.50 6.00

2012 Crown Royale Rookie Signatures Silver Holofoil

*SLVR HOLO/149: .4X TO 1X BASIC AU/245
*SLVR HOLO/149: .3X TO .8X BASIC AU/88
*SLVR HOLO/120: .4X TO 1X BASIC AU/99
*SLVR HOLO/49: .5X TO 1.2X BASIC AU/66
*SLVR HOLO/25: .8X TO 2X BASIC AU/245
*SLVR HOLO/25: .6X TO 1.5X BASIC AU/99
1 Alfred Morris/25 5.00 12.00

2012 Crown Royale Sunday Soldiers Materials

1 Patrick Willis/99 3.00 8.00
2 Michael Turner/99 2.50 6.00
3 Ray Lewis/99 5.00 12.00
4 Troy Polamalu/99 4.00 10.00
5 Andre Johnson/99 3.00 8.00
7 Marcedes Lewis/99 2.50 6.00
9 Wes Welker/99 3.00 8.00
10 Shonn Greene/99 2.50 6.00
11 Von Miller/99 3.00 8.00
12 Jamaal Charles/99 3.00 8.00
13 Ryan Mathews/99 3.00 8.00
14 Matt Forte/99 2.50 6.00
15 Nnamdi Asomugha/99 2.50 6.00
16 Aaron Rodgers/40 10.00 25.00
17 Percy Harvin/99 2.50 6.00
18 Jonathan Stewart/99 2.50 6.00
19 Marques Colston/99 2.50 6.00
20 Matt Cassel/99 2.50 6.00
21 Antonio Gates/99 3.00 8.00
22 Ahmad Bradshaw/99 2.50 6.00
23 Jeremy Maclin/99 2.50 6.00
24 Brian Orakpo/99 3.00 8.00
25 Will Smith/99 2.50 6.00
26 Zach Miller/99 2.50 6.00
27 Sam Bradford/99 2.50 6.00
28 Vonta Leach/99 2.50 6.00
29 Reggie Bush/99 2.50 6.00
30 Arian Foster/99 3.00 8.00

2012 Crown Royale Sunday Soldiers Materials Prime

2 Michael Turner/49 4.00 10.00
3 Ray Lewis/49 8.00 20.00
4 Troy Polamalu/49 6.00 15.00
9 Wes Welker/49 5.00 12.00
10 Shonn Greene/49 4.00 10.00
11 Von Miller/49 5.00 12.00
12 Jamaal Charles/49 5.00 12.00
13 Ryan Mathews/25 6.00 15.00
14 Matt Forte/49 4.00 10.00
15 Nnamdi Asomugha/25 5.00 12.00
17 Percy Harvin/49 4.00 10.00
18 Jonathan Stewart/49 4.00 10.00
19 Marques Colston/49 4.00 10.00
20 Matt Cassel/49 4.00 10.00
21 Antonio Gates/49 5.00 12.00
22 Ahmad Bradshaw/49 4.00 10.00
23 Jeremy Maclin/16 5.00 12.00
24 Brian Orakpo/49 5.00 12.00
25 Will Smith/49 4.00 10.00
27 Sam Bradford/49 4.00 10.00
30 Arian Foster/49 5.00 12.00

2013 Crown Royale

HOBBY PRINTED WITH SILVER FOIL
EXCH EXPIRATION: 8/12/2015
1 A.J. Green .60 1.50
2 Aaron Rodgers 1.00 2.50
3 Adrian Peterson .60 1.50
4 Alex Smith .50 1.25
5 Alfred Morris .40 1.00
6 Andre Johnson .40 1.00
7 Andrew Luck 1.00 2.50
8 Andy Dalton .50 1.25
9 Anquan Boldin .40 1.00
10 Antonio Brown .60 1.50
11 Antonio Gates .50 1.25
12 Arian Foster .50 1.25
13 Ben Roethlisberger .60 1.50
14 BenJarvus Green-Ellis .50 1.25
15 Brandon Marshall .50 1.25
16 Brandon Weeden .40 1.00
17 C.J. Spiller .40 1.00
18 Calvin Johnson .60 1.50
19 Cam Newton .60 1.50
20 Carson Palmer .50 1.25
21 Cecil Shorts .40 1.00
22 Charles Woodson .60 1.50
23 Chris Givens .40 1.00
24 Chris Ivory .50 1.25
25 Chris Johnson .40 1.00
26 Clay Matthews .60 1.50
27 Colin Kaepernick .50 1.25
28 Danny Amendola .50 1.25
29 Darren McFadden .50 1.25
30 David Wilson .40 1.00
31 DeMarco Murray .50 1.25
32 Demaryius Thomas .50 1.25
33 DeSean Jackson .50 1.25
34 Dez Bryant .60 1.50
35 Doug Martin .50 1.25
36 Drew Brees .60 1.50
37 Dwayne Bowe .50 1.25
38 Eli Manning .50 1.25
39 Frank Gore .50 1.25
40 Fred Jackson .50 1.25
41 Greg Jennings .40 1.00
42 J.J. Watt .50 1.25
43 Jamaal Charles .50 1.25
44 Jason Witten .50 1.25
45 Jay Cutler .40 1.00
46 Jeremy Kerley .40 1.00
47 Jimmy Graham .60 1.50
48 Joe Flacco .50 1.25
49 Darrelle Revis .40 1.00
50 Josh Gordon .40 1.00
51 Julio Jones .60 1.50
52 Justin Blackmon .40 1.00
53 Kendall Wright .40 1.00
54 Kyle Rudolph .40 1.00
55 Lamar Miller .40 1.00
56 Larry Fitzgerald .50 1.25
57 LeSean McCoy .60 1.50
58 London Fletcher .50 1.25
59 Luke Kuechly .50 1.25
60 Malcom Floyd .40 1.00
61 Marques Colston .40 1.00
62 Marshawn Lynch .50 1.25
63 Matt Forte .40 1.00
64 Matt Ryan .50 1.25
65 Matt Schaub .40 1.00
66 Matthew Stafford .50 1.25
67 Maurice Jones-Drew .40 1.00
68 Michael Floyd .40 1.00
69 Michael Vick .50 1.25
70 Mike Wallace .40 1.00
71 Percy Harvin .40 1.00
72 Peyton Manning 3.00 8.00
73 Philip Rivers .60 1.50
74 Randall Cobb .50 1.25
75 Ray Rice .40 1.00
76 Reggie Bush .40 1.00
77 Reggie Wayne .50 1.25
78 Richard Sherman .60 1.50
79 Rob Gronkowski .60 1.50
80 Robert Griffin III .40 1.00
81 Roddy White .40 1.00
82 Russell Wilson 1.25 3.00
83 Ryan Tannehill .50 1.25
84 Sam Bradford .40 1.00
85 Santonio Holmes .40 1.00
86 Stevan Ridley .40 1.00
87 Steve Smith .50 1.25
88 Steve Johnson .50 1.25
89 T.Y. Hilton .50 1.25
90 Terrelle Pryor .50 1.25
91 Tom Brady 1.50 4.00
92 Tony Romo .75 2.00
93 Torrey Smith .40 1.00
94 Trent Richardson .40 1.00
95 Troy Polamalu .60 1.50
96 Vernon Davis .40 1.00
97 Victor Cruz .50 1.25
98 Vincent Jackson .40 1.00
99 Von Miller .50 1.25
100 Wes Welker .50 1.25
101 Aaron Mellette RC .75 2.00
102 Ace Sanders RC .75 2.00
103 Alan Bonner RC .75 2.00
104 Alec Ogletree RC .75 2.00
105 Alex Okafor RC .75 2.00
106 Arthur Brown RC .75 2.00
107 Barkevious Mingo RC .75 2.00
108 Benny Cunningham RC 1.25 3.00
109 B.J. Daniels RC 1.25 3.00
110 Bjoern Werner RC .75 2.00
111 Brad Sorensen RC .75 2.00
112 Brice Butler RC .75 2.00
113 Blidi Wreh-Wilson RC 1.00 2.50
114 C.J. Anderson RC 1.50 4.00
115 Caleb Sturgis RC 1.25 3.00
116 Chance Warmack RC .75 2.00
117 Chris Gragg RC .75 2.00
118 Chris Harper RC .75 2.00
119 Chris Thompson RC .75 2.00
120 Cierre Wood RC .75 2.00
121 Cobi Hamilton RC .75 2.00
122 Corey Fuller RC .75 2.00
123 Cornellius Carradine RC .75 2.00
124 D.J. Hayden RC .75 2.00
125 Damontre Moore RC .75 2.00
126 Da'Rick Rogers RC .75 2.00
127 Darius Slay RC .75 2.00
128 Datone Jones RC .75 2.00
129 David Amerson RC .75 2.00
130 Dee Milliner RC .75 2.00
131 Dennis Johnson RC .75 2.00
132 Desmond Trufant RC .75 2.00
133 Dion Sims RC .75 2.00
134 D.J. Swearinger RC .75 2.00
135 D.J. Fluker RC .75 2.00
136 Dustin Hopkins RC .75 2.00
137 Earl Wolff RC 1.25 3.00
138 Eric Fisher RC .75 2.00
139 Eric Reid RC 1.00 2.50
140 Ezekiel Ansah RC .75 2.00
141 Jack Doyle RC .75 2.00
142 Jamar Taylor RC .75 2.00
143 Jamie Collins RC .75 2.00
144 Jaron Brown RC .75 2.00
145 Jarvis Jones RC .75 2.00
146 Jawan Jamison RC .75 2.00
147 Jeff Tuel RC .75 2.00
148 Johnthan Banks RC .75 2.00
149 Jon Bostic RC .75 2.00
150 Johnathan Cyprien RC .75 2.00
151 Jordan Poyer RC .75 2.00
152 Josh Boyce RC .75 2.00
153 Justin Brown RC 1.25 3.00
154 Kawann Short RC .75 2.00
155 Kenbrell Thompkins RC 1.25 3.00
156 Kenjon Barner RC .75 2.00
157 Kenny Vaccaro RC .75 2.00
158 Kevin Minter RC .75 2.00
159 Khiry Robinson RC 1.25 3.00
160 Kiko Alonso RC 1.00 2.50
161 Latavius Murray RC 1.00 2.50
162 Levine Toilolo RC 1.00 2.50
163 Luke Joeckel RC .75 2.00
164 Luke Willson RC 1.25 3.00
165 Margus Hunt RC .75 2.00
166 Marlon Brown RC 1.25 3.00
167 Marquess Wilson RC 1.25 3.00
168 Matt Elam RC .75 2.00
169 Matt McGloin RC 2.50 6.00
170 Matt Scott RC .75 2.00
171 Matt Simms RC 1.00 2.50
172 Michael Cox RC 1.00 2.50
173 Michael Ford RC 1.25 3.00
174 Mike James RC 1.25 3.00
175 Mychal Rivera RC .75 2.00
176 Nick Kasa RC .75 2.00
177 Nick Moody RC 1.00 2.50
178 Onterio McCalebb RC 1.00 2.50
179 Phillip Thomas RC .75 2.00
180 Ray Graham RC .75 2.00
181 Rex Burkhead RC 1.00 2.50
182 Robert Alford RC .75 2.00
183 Rodney Smith RC .75 2.00
184 Russell Shepard RC .75 2.00
185 Ryan Griffin RC .75 2.00
186 Ryan Griffin TE RC .75 2.00
187 Ryan Spadola RC 1.00 2.50
188 Sam Montgomery RC .75 2.00
189 Sheldon Richardson RC .75 2.00
190 Sio Moore RC .75 2.00
191 Spencer Ware RC .75 2.00
192 Tavarres King RC .75 2.00
193 Theo Riddick RC .75 2.00
194 Travis Kelce RC 2.00 5.00
195 Tyler Bray RC .75 2.00
196 Tyrann Mathieu RC 1.25 3.00
197 Xavier Rhodes RC .75 2.00
198 Zac Dysert RC 2.00 5.00
199 Zac Stacy RC .75 2.00
200 Zach Sudfeld RC .75 2.00
201 Aaron Dobson JSY AU RC 5.00 12.00
202 Andre Ellington JSY AU RC 10.00 25.00
203 Christine Michael JSY AU RC 5.00 12.00
204 C.Patterson JSY AU RC 5.00 12.00
205 DeAndre Hopkins JSY AU RC 10.00 25.00
206 Denard Robinson JSY AU RC 5.00 12.00
207 Dion Jordan JSY AU RC 5.00 12.00
208 Eddie Lacy JSY AU RC 5.00 12.00
209 EJ Manuel JSY AU RC 12.00 30.00
210 Gavin Escobar JSY AU RC 6.00 15.00
211 Geno Smith JSY AU RC 5.00 12.00
212 Giovani Bernard JSY AU RC 5.00 12.00
213 J.Franklin JSY AU RC 5.00 12.00
214 J.Reed JSY AU RC EXCH 8.00 20.00
215 Joseph Randle JSY AU RC 5.00 12.00

216 Justin Hunter JSY AU RC 10.00 25.00
217 Keenan Allen JSY AU RC 12.00 30.00
218 Kenny Stills JSY AU RC 6.00 15.00
219 Knile Davis JSY AU RC 5.00 12.00
220 Landry Jones JSY AU RC 5.00 12.00
221 Le'Veon Bell JSY AU RC 25.00 50.00
222 Manti Te'o JSY AU RC 6.00 15.00
223 Marcus Lattimore JSY AU RC 5.00 12.00
224 Markus Wheaton JSY AU RC 5.00 12.00
225 M.Goodwin JSY AU RC 5.00 12.00
226 Matt Barkley JSY AU RC 5.00 12.00
227 Mike Gillislee JSY AU RC 5.00 12.00
228 Mike Glennon JSY AU RC 5.00 12.00
229 Montee Ball JSY AU RC 5.00 12.00
230 Quinton Patton JSY AU RC 5.00 12.00
231 Robert Woods JSY AU RC 8.00 20.00
232 Ryan Nassib JSY AU RC 5.00 12.00
233 Stedman Bailey JSY AU RC 5.00 12.00
234 Stepfan Taylor JSY AU RC 5.00 12.00
235 Tavon Austin JSY AU RC 6.00 15.00
236 T.Williams JSY AU RC 5.00 12.00
237 Tyler Eifert JSY AU RC 5.00 12.00
238 Tyler Wilson JSY AU RC 6.00 15.00
239 Vance McDonald JSY AU RC 6.00 15.00
240 Zach Ertz JSY AU RC 10.00 25.00

2013 Crown Royale Bronze Holofoil

*1-100 VETS/299: 1.2X TO 3X BASIC CARDS
*101-200 ROOKIES/299: .6X TO 1.5X BASIC RC

2013 Crown Royale Gold

*1-100 VETS/99: 2X TO 5X BASIC CARDS
*101-200 ROOKIES/99: 1X TO 2.5X BASIC RC
*201-240 RK.JSY AU/49: .5X TO 1.2X JSY AU/299

2013 Crown Royale Gold Holofoil

*1-100 VETS/25: 3X TO 8X BASIC CARDS
*101-200 ROOKIES/25: 1.5X TO 4X BASIC RC

2013 Crown Royale Green

*1-100 VETS/10: 4X TO 10X BASIC CARDS
*101-200 ROOKIES/10: 2X TO 5X BASIC RC
*201-240 RK.JSY AU/25: .8X TO 2X JSY AU/299

2013 Crown Royale Red

*1-100 VETS/99: 2X TO 5X BASIC CARDS
*101-200 ROOKIES/99: 1X TO 2.5X BASIC RC

2013 Crown Royale Red Holofoil

*1-100 VETS/25: 3X TO 8X BASIC CARDS
*101-200 ROOKIES/25: 1.5X TO 4X BASIC RC

2013 Crown Royale Silver Holofoil

*1-100 VETS/299: 1.2X TO 3X BASIC CARDS
*101-200 ROOKIES/299: .6X TO 1.5X BASIC RC

2013 Crown Royale All Pros Materials

*PRIME/30-49: .8X TO 2X JSY/195-299
*PRIME/15-25: 1X TO 2.5X JSY/195-299
1 Andy Dalton/299 2.50 6.00
2 Brandon Browner/299 4.00 10.00
3 C.J. Spiller/195 2.00 5.00
4 Charles Woodson/299 4.00 10.00
5 Doug Martin/299 2.50 6.00
6 J.J. Watt/299 8.00 20.00
7 Jamaal Charles/299 2.50 6.00
8 Julio Jones/299 3.00 8.00
9 Kam Chancellor/299 6.00 15.00
10 Kyle Rudolph/299 2.00 5.00
11 Marshawn Lynch/299 2.50 6.00
12 Matt Schaub/299 2.00 5.00
13 Maurice Jones-Drew/299 2.00 5.00
14 Ndamukong Suh/299 2.50 6.00
15 Patrick Peterson/299 2.00 5.00
16 Peyton Manning/299 12.00 30.00
17 Philip Rivers/299 3.00 8.00
18 Roddy White/299 2.00 5.00
19 Russell Wilson/299 8.00 20.00
20 Von Miller/299 2.50 6.00

2013 Crown Royale Crown Jewels

*GOLD/25: 1.2X TO 3X BASIC INSERTS
1 A.J. Green 1.50 4.00
2 Aaron Rodgers 2.50 6.00
3 Adrian Peterson 1.50 4.00
4 Andre Johnson 1.00 2.50
5 Andrew Luck 2.50 6.00
6 Calvin Johnson 1.50 4.00
7 Cam Newton 1.50 4.00
8 Colin Kaepernick 1.25 3.00
9 Doug Martin 1.25 3.00
10 Drew Brees 1.50 4.00
11 Eli Manning 1.25 3.00
12 Joe Flacco 1.25 3.00
13 Larry Fitzgerald 1.25 3.00
14 LeSean McCoy 1.50 4.00
15 Matt Ryan 1.25 3.00
16 Peyton Manning 10.00 25.00
17 Robert Griffin III 1.00 2.50
18 Russell Wilson 4.00 10.00
19 Tom Brady 4.00 10.00
20 Tony Romo 1.25 3.00

2013 Crown Royale Crown Royale Signatures Silver

EXCH EXPRATION: 8/12/2015
*GOLD VETS/15: .4X TO 1X SILVER AU/25
*GOLD ROOKIES/25: .5X TO 1.2X SILVER AU/49
1 A.J. Green EXCH 15.00 30.00
3 Adrian Peterson EXCH 60.00 120.00
4 Andrew Luck EXCH 40.00 80.00
6 Colin Kaepernick EXCH 15.00 40.00
201 Aaron Dobson 4.00 10.00
202 Andre Ellington 4.00 10.00
203 Christine Michael 8.00 20.00
204 Cordarrelle Patterson 4.00 10.00
205 DeAndre Hopkins 10.00 25.00
206 Denard Robinson 4.00 10.00
207 Dion Jordan 4.00 10.00
208 Eddie Lacy 4.00 10.00
209 EJ Manuel 4.00 10.00
210 Gavin Escobar 4.00 10.00
211 Geno Smith 4.00 10.00
212 Giovani Bernard 4.00 10.00
213 Johnathan Franklin 4.00 10.00
214 Jordan Reed 6.00 15.00
215 Joseph Randle 4.00 10.00
216 Justin Hunter 8.00 20.00
217 Keenan Allen 15.00 40.00
218 Kenny Stills 4.00 10.00
219 Knile Davis 4.00 10.00
220 Landry Jones 4.00 10.00
221 Le'Veon Bell 15.00 40.00
222 Manti Te'o 5.00 12.00
223 Marcus Lattimore 4.00 10.00
224 Markus Wheaton 4.00 10.00
225 Marquise Goodwin 4.00 10.00
226 Matt Barkley 4.00 10.00
227 Mike Gillislee 4.00 10.00
228 Mike Glennon
229 Montee Ball 4.00 10.00
230 Quinton Patton 4.00 10.00
231 Robert Woods 6.00 15.00
232 Ryan Nassib 4.00 10.00
233 Stedman Bailey 4.00 10.00
234 Stepfan Taylor 4.00 10.00
235 Tavon Austin 5.00 12.00
236 Terrance Williams 4.00 10.00
237 Tyler Eifert 4.00 10.00
238 Tyler Wilson 4.00 10.00
239 Vance McDonald 5.00 12.00
240 Zach Ertz 8.00 20.00

2013 Crown Royale Heirs to the Throne Combos Materials

*PRIME/25: .8X TO 2X BASIC JSY/299
*RETAIL/99: .5X TO 1.2X BASIC JSY/299
1 Robert Woods 2.50 6.00
2 Gavin Escobar 1.50 4.00
3 Le'Veon Bell 5.00 12.00
4 Vance McDonald 2.00 5.00
5 Montee Ball 1.50 4.00
6 Aaron Dobson 1.50 4.00
7 Eddie Lacy 1.50 4.00
8 Christine Michael 1.50 4.00
9 Mike Glennon 1.50 4.00
10 Terrance Williams 1.50 4.00

2013 Crown Royale Heirs to the Throne Materials

*PRIME/25: .8X TO 2X JSY/199-299
*PRIME/25: .6X TO 1.5X JSY/99
*RETAIL/149-299: .4X TO 1X JSY/299
*RETAIL/299: .5X TO 1.3X JSY/99
*RETAIL/125: .5X TO 1.3X JSY/299
*RETAIL/49: .6X TO 1.5X JSY/199-299
*RETAIL/49: .5X TO 1.2X JSY/99
*RETAIL/25: .8X TO 2X JSY/299
*RETAIL/25: .6X TO 1.5X JSY/99
1 Aaron Dobson/99 2.00 5.00
2 Andre Ellington/299 1.50 4.00
3 Christine Michael/299 1.50 4.00
4 Cordarrelle Patterson/299 1.50 4.00
5 DeAndre Hopkins/299 4.00 10.00
6 Denard Robinson/299 1.50 4.00
7 Dion Jordan/299 1.50 4.00
8 Eddie Lacy/199 1.50 4.00
9 EJ Manuel/299 3.00 8.00
10 Gavin Escobar/299 1.50 4.00
11 Geno Smith/299 1.50 4.00
12 Giovani Bernard/299 1.50 4.00
13 Johnathan Franklin/299 1.50 4.00
14 Jordan Reed/299 2.50 6.00
15 Joseph Randle/299 1.50 4.00
16 Justin Hunter/299 1.50 4.00
17 Keenan Allen/299 4.00 10.00
18 Kenny Stills/299 1.50 4.00
19 Knile Davis/299 1.50 4.00
20 Landry Jones/299 1.50 4.00
21 Le'Veon Bell/299 4.00 10.00
22 Manti Te'o/299 2.00 5.00
23 Marcus Lattimore/299 1.50 4.00
24 Markus Wheaton/299 1.50 4.00
25 Marquise Goodwin/99 2.00 5.00
26 Matt Barkley/299 3.00 8.00
27 Mike Gillislee/299 1.50 4.00
28 Mike Glennon/299 4.00 10.00
29 Montee Ball/299 1.50 4.00
30 Quinton Patton/299 1.50 4.00
31 Robert Woods/299 2.50 6.00
32 Ryan Nassib/299 1.50 4.00
33 Stedman Bailey/299 1.50 4.00
34 Stepfan Taylor/299 1.50 4.00
35 Tavon Austin/299 2.00 5.00
36 Terrance Williams/299 1.50 4.00
37 Tyler Eifert/299 1.50 4.00
38 Tyler Wilson/299 1.50 4.00
39 Vance McDonald/299 2.00 5.00
40 Zach Ertz/99 4.00 10.00

2013 Crown Royale Heirs to the Throne Trios Materials

*PRIME/25: .8X TO 2X BASIC JSY/299
*RETAIL/99: .5X TO 1.2X BASIC JSY/299
1 Tavon Austin 2.00 5.00
2 EJ Manuel 4.00 10.00
3 Tyler Eifert 1.50 4.00
4 DeAndre Hopkins 4.00 10.00
5 Cordarrelle Patterson 1.50 4.00
6 Justin Hunter 1.50 4.00
7 Zach Ertz 3.00 8.00
8 Giovani Bernard 1.50 4.00
9 Manti Te'o 2.00 5.00
10 Geno Smith 1.50 4.00

2013 Crown Royale Knights of the Gridiron Materials

*PRIME/25: 1X TO 2.5X JSY/299
*PRIME/25: .8X TO 2X BASIC JSY/95
*PRIME/25: .5X TO 1.2X BASIC JSY/20
1 Adrian Peterson/299 3.00 8.00
2 Alfred Morris/20 4.00 10.00
3 Andrew Luck/299 5.00 12.00
4 Cam Newton/299 3.00 8.00
5 Colin Kaepernick/299 2.50 6.00
6 Doug Martin/299 2.50 6.00
7 Peyton Manning/200 6.00 15.00
8 Ray Rice/299 2.00 5.00
9 Robert Griffin III/299 2.00 5.00
10 Russell Wilson/95 8.00 20.00

2013 Crown Royale Legendary Silhouette Material Autographs

1 Deion Sanders 30.00 60.00
2 Earl Campbell
3 Jim Brown
4 Marcus Allen 15.00 40.00
5 Marshall Faulk 30.00 60.00
6 Raymond Berry
7 Roger Staubach 50.00 100.00
8 Terry Bradshaw 50.00 100.00
9 Tony Dorsett 15.00 40.00
10 Troy Aikman

2013 Crown Royale Panini's Choice Autographs Silver

*SILVER/25: .4X TO 1X CROWN AU/25
*SILVER/49: .4X TO 1X CROWN AU/49
*GOLD/15: .4X TO 1X SILVER/25
*GOLD/25: .5X TO 1.2X SILVER/49

2013 Crown Royale Pillars of the Game Materials

*PRIME/20-25: 1X TO 2.5X JSY/275-299
*PRIME/25: .8X TO 2X JSY/99
1 Adrian Peterson/299 3.00 8.00
2 Andre Johnson/299 2.00 5.00
3 Andrew Luck/299 5.00 12.00
4 Antonio Gates/299 2.50 6.00
5 Cam Newton/299 3.00 8.00
6 Champ Bailey/299 2.50 6.00
7 Colin Kaepernick/299 2.50 6.00
8 Drew Brees/299 3.00 8.00
9 Jason Witten/299 2.50 6.00
10 Joe Flacco/299 2.50 6.00
11 Julius Peppers/299 2.50 6.00
12 Larry Fitzgerald/299 2.50 6.00
13 London Fletcher/299 2.50 6.00
14 Matt Ryan/299 2.50 6.00
15 Peyton Manning/299 12.00 30.00
16 Reggie Wayne/275 2.50 6.00
17 Robert Griffin III/299 2.00 5.00
18 Russell Wilson/99 8.00 20.00
19 Santana Moss/299 2.50 6.00
20 Tom Brady/299 6.00 15.00

2013 Crown Royale Pivotal Players

*GOLD/25: 1.2X TO 3X BASIC INSERTS
1 A.J. Green 1.50 4.00
2 Adrian Peterson 1.50 4.00
3 Alfred Morris 1.00 2.50
4 Andrew Luck 2.50 6.00
5 Anquan Boldin 1.00 2.50
6 Brandon Marshall 1.25 3.00
7 C.J. Spiller 1.00 2.50
8 Clay Matthews 1.50 4.00
9 Colin Kaepernick 1.25 3.00
10 Dez Bryant 1.50 4.00
11 J.J. Watt 1.25 3.00
12 Jamaal Charles 1.25 3.00
13 Julio Jones 1.50 4.00
14 Larry Fitzgerald 1.25 3.00
15 Ray Rice 1.00 2.50
16 Rob Gronkowski 1.50 4.00
17 Robert Griffin III 1.00 2.50
18 Russell Wilson 3.00 8.00
19 Victor Cruz 1.25 3.00
20 Wes Welker 1.25 3.00

2013 Crown Royale Retail

*1-100 VETS: .15X TO .4X HOBBY
*101-200 ROOKIES: .3X TO .8X HOBBY

2013 Crown Royale Rookie Panini's Choice

*GOLD/25: 1X TO 2.5X BASIC INSERTS
1 Aaron Dobson 1.00 2.50
2 Andre Ellington 1.00 2.50
3 Christine Michael 1.00 2.50
4 Cordarrelle Patterson 1.00 2.50
5 DeAndre Hopkins 2.50 6.00
6 Denard Robinson 1.00 2.50
7 Dion Jordan 1.00 2.50
8 Eddie Lacy 1.00 2.50
9 EJ Manuel 1.00 2.50
10 Gavin Escobar 1.00 2.50
11 Geno Smith 1.00 2.50
12 Giovani Bernard 1.00 2.50
13 Johnathan Franklin 1.00 2.50
14 Jordan Reed 1.50 4.00
15 Joseph Randle 1.00 2.50
16 Justin Hunter 1.00 2.50
17 Keenan Allen 2.00 5.00
18 Kenny Stills 1.00 2.50
19 Knile Davis 1.00 2.50
20 Landry Jones 1.00 2.50
21 Le'Veon Bell 3.00 8.00
22 Manti Te'o 1.25 3.00
23 Marcus Lattimore 1.00 2.50
24 Markus Wheaton 1.00 2.50
25 Marquise Goodwin 1.00 2.50
26 Matt Barkley .50 1.25
27 Mike Gillislee 1.00 2.50
28 Mike Glennon 1.00 2.50
29 Montee Ball 1.00 2.50
30 Quinton Patton 1.00 2.50
31 Robert Woods 1.50 4.00
32 Ryan Nassib 1.00 2.50
33 Stedman Bailey 1.00 2.50
34 Stepfan Taylor 1.00 2.50
35 Tavon Austin 1.25 3.00
36 Terrance Williams 1.00 2.50
37 Tyler Eifert 1.00 2.50
38 Tyler Wilson 1.00 2.50
39 Vance McDonald 1.25 3.00
40 Zach Ertz 2.00 5.00

2013 Crown Royale Rookie Royalty Materials

*PRIME/49: .8X TO 2X BASIC JSY/299
*PRIME/49: .6X TO 1.5X BASIC JSY/99
*PRIME/49: .5X TO 1.2X BASIC JSY/25
1 Aaron Dobson/25 2.50 6.00
2 Andre Ellington/299 1.50 4.00
3 Christine Michael/99 2.00 5.00
4 Cordarrelle Patterson/299 1.50 4.00
5 DeAndre Hopkins/25 6.00 15.00
6 Denard Robinson/299 1.50 4.00
7 Dion Jordan/299 1.50 4.00
8 Eddie Lacy/25 2.50 6.00
9 EJ Manuel/99 4.00 10.00
10 Gavin Escobar/99 2.00 5.00
11 Geno Smith/249 1.50 4.00
12 Giovani Bernard/99 2.00 5.00
13 Johnathan Franklin/99 2.00 5.00
14 Jordan Reed/99 2.50 6.00
15 Joseph Randle/99 2.00 5.00
16 Justin Hunter/99 2.00 5.00
17 Keenan Allen/99 5.00 12.00
18 Kenny Stills/299 1.50 4.00
19 Knile Davis/99 2.00 5.00
20 Landry Jones/299 1.50 4.00
21 Le'Veon Bell/99 5.00 12.00
22 Manti Te'o/299 2.00 5.00
23 Marcus Lattimore/299 1.50 4.00
24 Markus Wheaton/299 1.50 4.00
25 Marquise Goodwin/25 2.50 6.00
26 Matt Barkley/99 2.00 5.00
27 Mike Gillislee/299 1.50 4.00
28 Mike Glennon/99 2.00 5.00
29 Montee Ball/299 1.50 4.00
30 Quinton Patton/99 2.00 5.00
31 Robert Woods/25 4.00 10.00
32 Ryan Nassib/299 1.50 4.00
33 Stedman Bailey/99 2.00 5.00
34 Stepfan Taylor/299 1.50 4.00
35 Tavon Austin/99 2.50 6.00
36 Terrance Williams/99 2.00 5.00
37 Tyler Eifert/99 2.00 5.00
38 Tyler Wilson/99 2.00 5.00
39 Vance McDonald/99 2.50 6.00
40 Zach Ertz/25 5.00 12.00

2013 Crown Royale Rookie Signatures Bronze Holofoil

*BASE AU/200-250: .3X TO .8X BRNZ HOL/99
*BASE AU/75-150: .4X TO 1X BRNZ HOLO/99
*BASE AU/25-35: .6X TO 1.5X BRNZ HOLO/99
*BRNZ/75-150: .4X TO 1X BRNZ HOLO/99
*BRNZ/50: .5X TO 1.2X BRNZE HOLO/99
*BRNZ/25: .6X TO 1.5X BRNZE HOLO/99
*GOLD/49: .5X TO 1.2X BRNZE HOLO/99
*GLD HOLO/25: .6X TO 1.5X BRNZ HOL/99
*RED/49: .5X TO 1.2X BRNZE HOLO/99
*RED/24: .6X TO 1.5X BRNZE HOLO/99
*SLVR HOLO/99: .4X TO 1X BRNZ HOLO/99
101 Aaron Mellette/99 2.50 6.00
102 Ace Sanders/99 2.50 6.00
103 Alan Bonner/99 2.50 6.00
104 Alec Ogletree/99 2.50 6.00
105 Alex Okafor/99 2.50 6.00
106 Arthur Brown/99 2.50 6.00
107 Barkevious Mingo/99 2.50 6.00
108 Benny Cunningham/99 4.00 10.00
109 B.J. Daniels/99 4.00 10.00
110 Bjoern Werner/99 2.50 6.00
111 Brad Sorensen/99 2.50 6.00
112 Brice Butler/99 2.50 6.00
113 Blidi Wreh-Wilson/99 3.00 8.00
114 C.J. Anderson/99 5.00 12.00
115 Caleb Sturgis/99 4.00 10.00
116 Chance Warmack/99 2.50 6.00
117 Chris Gragg/99 2.50 6.00
118 Chris Harper/99 2.50 6.00
119 Chris Thompson/99 2.50 6.00
120 Cierre Wood/99 2.50 6.00
121 Cobi Hamilton/99 2.50 6.00
122 Corey Fuller/99 2.50 6.00
123 Cornellius Carradine/99 2.50 6.00
124 D.J. Hayden/99 2.50 6.00
125 Damontre Moore/99 2.50 6.00
126 Da'Rick Rogers/99 2.50 6.00
127 Darius Slay/99 2.50 6.00
128 Datone Jones/99 2.50 6.00
129 David Amerson/99 2.50 6.00
130 Dee Milliner/99 2.50 6.00
131 Dennis Johnson/99 2.50 6.00
132 Desmond Trufant/99 2.50 6.00
133 Dion Sims/99 2.50 6.00
134 D.J. Swearinger/99 2.50 6.00
135 D.J. Fluker/99 2.50 6.00
136 Dustin Hopkins/99 2.50 6.00
137 Earl Wolff/99 4.00 10.00
138 Eric Fisher/81 2.50 6.00
139 Eric Reid/99 8.00 20.00
140 Ezekiel Ansah/99 2.50 6.00
141 Jack Doyle/99 2.50 6.00
142 Jamar Taylor/99 2.50 6.00
143 Jamie Collins/99 2.50 6.00
144 Jaron Brown/99 2.50 6.00
145 Jarvis Jones/99 2.50 6.00
146 Jawan Jamison/99 2.50 6.00
147 Jeff Tuel/99 2.50 6.00
148 Johnthan Banks/99 2.50 6.00
149 Jon Bostic/99 8.00 20.00
150 Johnathan Cyprien/99 2.50 6.00
151 Kerwynn Williams/99 2.50 6.00
152 Josh Boyce/99 2.50 6.00
153 Justin Brown/99 4.00 10.00
154 Kawann Short/99 2.50 6.00
155 Kenbrell Thompkins/99 4.00 10.00
156 Kenjon Barner/99 2.50 6.00
157 Kenny Vaccaro/99 2.50 6.00
158 Kevin Minter/99 2.50 6.00
159 Khiry Robinson/99 4.00 10.00
160 Kiko Alonso/99 3.00 8.00
161 Latavius Murray/99 12.50 25.00
162 Levine Toilolo/99 3.00 8.00
163 Luke Joeckel/99 2.50 6.00
164 Luke Willson/99 4.00 10.00
165 Margus Hunt/99 2.50 6.00
166 Marlon Brown/99 4.00 10.00
167 Marquess Wilson/99 4.00 10.00
168 Matt Elam/99 2.50 6.00
169 Matt McGloin/99 8.00 20.00
170 Skye Dawson/99 3.00 8.00
171 Matt Simms/99 3.00 8.00
172 Michael Cox/99 3.00 8.00
173 Michael Ford/99 4.00 10.00
174 Mike James/99 4.00 10.00
175 Mychal Rivera/99 2.50 6.00
176 Nick Kasa/99 2.50 6.00
177 Nick Moody/99 3.00 8.00
178 Joseph Fauria/99 2.50 6.00
179 Phillip Thomas/99 2.50 6.00
180 Ray Graham/99 2.50 6.00
181 Rex Burkhead/99 3.00 8.00
182 Robert Alford/99 2.50 6.00
183 Rodney Smith/99 2.50 6.00
184 Russell Shepard/99 2.50 6.00
185 Ryan Griffin/99 2.50 6.00
186 Ryan Griffin TE/99 2.50 6.00
187 Ryan Spadola/99 3.00 8.00
188 Sam Montgomery/99 2.50 6.00
189 Timothy Wright/99 3.00 8.00
190 Sio Moore/99 2.50 6.00
191 Spencer Ware/99 2.50 6.00
192 Tavarres King/99 2.50 6.00
193 Ryan Otten/99 2.50 6.00
194 Travis Kelce/99 15.00 40.00
195 Tyler Bray/99 2.50 6.00
196 Tyrann Mathieu/99 4.00 10.00
197 Xavier Rhodes/99 2.50 6.00
198 Zac Dysert/99 2.50 6.00
199 Zac Stacy/99 2.50 6.00
200 Zach Sudfeld/99 2.50 6.00

2013 Crown Royale Silhouette Material Autographs

EXCH EXPIRATION: 8/12/2015
*GOLD/25: .5X TO 1.2X BASIC AU/49
*GOLD/15: .4X TO 1X BASIC AU/18-25
1 Adrian Peterson/25 EXCH 60.00 120.00
3 Antonio Gates/49 EXCH
5 Colin Kaepernick/25 EXCH 30.00 60.00
7 Drew Brees/20 EXCH 75.00 150.00
10 Jamaal Charles/49 EXCH 15.00 40.00
12 LeSean McCoy/49 EXCH 20.00 50.00
15 Peyton Manning/18 EXCH 150.00 250.00

2013 Crown Royale Rookie Silhouettes Retail

*PRIME/49-99: 1X TO 2.5X JSY/149-299
*PRIME/49-99: .8X TO 2X JSY/49-99
*PRIME/99: .6X TO 1.5X JSY/25
*PRIME/25: 1.2X TO 3X JSY/299
*PRIME/25: .8X TO 2X JSY/49
*PRIME/25: .6X TO 1.5X JSY/25
1 Aaron Dobson/25 2.50 6.00
2 Andre Ellington/299 1.50 4.00
3 Christine Michael/99 2.00 5.00
4 Cordarrelle Patterson/299 1.50 4.00
5 DeAndre Hopkins/25 6.00 15.00
6 Denard Robinson/299 1.50 4.00
7 Dion Jordan/299 1.50 4.00
8 Eddie Lacy/25 2.50 6.00
9 EJ Manuel/99 4.00 10.00
10 Gavin Escobar/99 2.00 5.00
11 Geno Smith/299 1.50 4.00
12 Giovani Bernard/249 1.50 4.00
13 Johnathan Franklin/299 1.50 4.00
14 Jordan Reed/299 2.50 6.00
15 Joseph Randle/249 1.50 4.00
16 Justin Hunter/25 2.50 6.00
17 Keenan Allen/99 5.00 12.00
18 Kenny Stills/299 1.50 4.00
19 Knile Davis/149 1.50 4.00
20 Landry Jones/299 1.50 4.00
21 Le'Veon Bell/25 6.00 15.00
22 Manti Te'o/299 2.00 5.00
23 Marcus Lattimore/299 1.50 4.00
24 Markus Wheaton/299 1.50 4.00
25 Marquise Goodwin/49 2.00 5.00
26 Matt Barkley/49 2.00 5.00
27 Mike Gillislee/299 1.50 4.00
28 Mike Glennon/199 1.50 4.00
29 Montee Ball/299 1.50 4.00
30 Quinton Patton/299 1.50 4.00
31 Robert Woods/49 3.00 8.00
32 Ryan Nassib/299 1.50 4.00
33 Stedman Bailey/299 1.50 4.00
34 Stepfan Taylor/299 1.50 4.00
35 Tavon Austin/99 2.50 6.00
36 Terrance Williams/99 2.00 5.00
37 Tyler Eifert/25 2.50 6.00
38 Tyler Wilson/199 1.50 4.00
39 Vance McDonald/99 2.50 6.00
40 Zach Ertz/49 4.00 10.00

2013 Crown Royale Test of Time

*GOLD/25: 1.2X TO 3X BASIC INSERTS
1 Tony Gonzalez 1.50 4.00
2 Charles Woodson 2.00 5.00
3 London Fletcher 1.50 4.00
4 Peyton Manning 10.00 25.00
5 Champ Bailey 1.50 4.00
6 Tom Brady 5.00 12.00
7 Drew Brees 2.00 5.00
8 Reggie Wayne 1.50 4.00
9 Santana Moss 1.50 4.00
10 Steve Smith 1.50 4.00
11 Dwight Freeney 1.50 4.00
12 Ed Reed 1.50 4.00
13 Julius Peppers 1.50 4.00
14 Michael Vick 1.50 4.00
15 Andre Johnson 1.25 3.00
16 Anquan Boldin 1.25 3.00
17 Antonio Gates 1.50 4.00
18 Jason Witten 1.50 4.00
19 Tony Romo 1.50 4.00
20 Troy Polamalu 2.00 5.00

2014 Crown Royale

EXCH EXPIRATION: 5/26/2016
1 LeSean McCoy .60 1.50
2 Jamaal Charles .50 1.25
3 Adrian Peterson .60 1.50
4 Matt Forte .40 1.00
5 Eddie Lacy .40 1.00
6 Jimmy Graham .60 1.50
7 Calvin Johnson .60 1.50
8 Marshawn Lynch .50 1.25
9 Dez Bryant .60 1.50
10 DeMarco Murray .50 1.25
11 Demaryius Thomas .50 1.25
12 Montee Ball .40 1.00
13 Julio Jones .60 1.50
14 A.J. Green .00 1.50
15 Brandon Marshall .40 1.00
16 Rob Gronkowski .60 1.50
17 Arian Foster .50 1.25
18 Jordy Nelson .50 1.25
19 Giovani Bernard .40 1.00
20 Zac Stacy .40 1.00
21 Le'Veon Bell .50 1.25
22 Doug Martin .50 1.25
23 Peyton Manning 1.25 3.00
24 Alshon Jeffery .50 1.25
25 Keenan Allen .50 1.25
26 Antonio Brown .60 1.50
27 J.J. Watt .60 1.50
28 C.J. Spiller .40 1.00
29 Alfred Morris .40 1.00
30 Andre Johnson .50 1.25
31 Randall Cobb .50 1.25
32 Aaron Rodgers 1.25 3.00
33 Drew Brees .60 1.50
34 Russell Wilson 1.00 2.50
35 Vincent Jackson .40 1.00
36 Larry Fitzgerald .50 1.25
37 Andre Ellington .40 1.00
38 Toby Gerhart .40 1.00
39 Ryan Mathews .50 1.25
40 Richard Sherman .60 1.50
41 Matthew Stafford .50 1.25
42 Frank Gore .50 1.25
43 Jordan Cameron .40 1.00
44 Vernon Davis .40 1.00
45 Torrey Smith .40 1.00
46 Victor Cruz .50 1.25
47 Wes Welker .50 1.25
48 Joique Bell .40 1.00
49 Reggie Bush .40 1.00
50 Carson Palmer .50 1.25
51 Trent Richardson .40 1.00
52 Roddy White .40 1.00
53 Cordarrelle Patterson .40 1.00
54 Percy Harvin .40 1.00
55 Michael Floyd .40 1.00
56 DeSean Jackson .50 1.25
57 Michael Crabtree .40 1.00
58 Marques Colston .40 1.00
59 Jason Witten .50 1.25
60 Steven Jackson .40 1.00
61 Rashad Jennings .40 1.00
62 Lamar Miller .40 1.00
63 Ben Tate .40 1.00
64 Stevan Ridley .40 1.00
65 Chris Johnson .40 1.00
66 Andrew Luck .75 2.00
67 Cam Newton .60 1.50
68 T.Y. Hilton .50 1.25
69 Julian Edelman .60 1.50
70 Mike Wallace .40 1.00
71 Kendall Wright .40 1.00
72 Jeremy Maclin .40 1.00
73 Jay Cutler .40 1.00
74 Eli Manning .50 1.25
75 Eric Decker .40 1.00
76 Matt Ryan .50 1.25
77 Tony Romo .50 1.25
78 Nick Foles .50 1.25
79 Pierre Thomas .40 1.00
80 Fred Jackson .50 1.25
81 Bernard Pierce .40 1.00
82 Philip Rivers .60 1.50
83 Colin Kaepernick .50 1.25
84 Joe Flacco .50 1.25
85 Greg Olsen .50 1.25
86 Clay Matthews .60 1.50
87 Tom Brady 1.50 4.00
88 Robert Griffin III .40 1.00
89 Rueben Randle .40 1.00
90 Andy Dalton .50 1.25
91 Cecil Shorts III .40 1.00
92 DeAndre Hopkins .50 1.25
93 Riley Cooper .50 1.25
94 Maurice Jones-Drew .40 1.00
95 Darren McFadden .40 1.00
96 Geno Smith .40 1.00
97 Alex Smith .50 1.25
98 Ben Roethlisberger .60 1.50
99 Reggie Wayne .50 1.25
100 Sam Bradford .40 1.00
101 Allen Hurns RC 1.00 2.50
102 Isaiah Crowell RC 1.00 2.50
103 Keith Wenning RC 1.00 2.50
104 Devin Street RC .75 2.00
105 Arthur Lynch RC .75 2.00
106 Trent Murphy RC .75 2.00
107 Robert Herron RC .75 2.00
108 L'Damian Washington RC 1.00 2.50
109 Ahmad Dixon RC .75 2.00
110 Scott Crichton RC .75 2.00
111 Marion Grice RC .75 2.00
112 Chris Borland RC .75 2.00
113 Lache Seastrunk RC .75 2.00
114 David Fales RC .75 2.00
115 Kony Ealy RC 1.00 2.50
116 Chris Smith RC .75 2.00
117 James Wright RC 1.00 2.50
118 Silas Redd RC 1.00 2.50
119 Crockett Gillmore RC 1.00 2.50
120 Timmy Jernigan RC .75 2.00
121 Ryan Grant RC .75 2.00
122 Kyle Fuller RC .75 2.00
123 Alfred Blue RC .75 2.00
124 Stephen Morris RC .75 2.00
125 Deone Bucannon RC .75 2.00
126 Michael Sam RC .75 2.00
127 Jerick McKinnon RC 1.00 2.50
128 Darqueze Dennard RC 1.00 2.50
129 Preston Brown RC .75 2.00
130 Telvin Smith RC .75 2.00
131 John Brown RC 1.25 3.00
132 Michael Campanaro RC .75 2.00
133 Troy Niklas RC .75 2.00
134 Jackson Jeffcoat RC 1.00 2.50
135 Jeff Janis RC .75 2.00
136 Martavis Bryant RC 1.00 2.50
137 Bruce Ellington RC .75 2.00
138 Brandon Coleman RC .75 2.00
139 Taylor Lewan RC .75 2.00
140 Kevin Norwood RC .75 2.00
141 Ted Bolser RC 1.00 2.50
142 Ha Ha Clinton-Dix RC 1.00 2.50
143 Lorenzo Taliaferro RC .75 2.00
144 Anthony Barr RC .75 2.00
145 Quincy Enunwa RC 1.25 3.00
146 Zach Mettenberger RC .75 2.00
147 James White RC 1.50 4.00
148 Tyler Gaffney RC .75 2.00
149 Shayne Skov RC .75 2.00
150 Kyle Van Noy RC 1.00 2.50
151 Bradley Roby RC .75 2.00
152 Damien Williams RC .75 2.00
153 Antonio Andrews RC .75 2.00
154 Storm Johnson RC .75 2.00
155 Jake Matthews RC .75 2.00
156 Ryan Shazier RC 1.25 3.00
157 Asa Watson RC .75 2.00
158 Philly Brown RC 1.00 2.50
159 C.J. Mosley RC 1.00 2.50
160 Jace Amaro RC .75 2.00
161 Shaq Evans RC .75 2.00
162 Calvin Pryor RC .75 2.00
163 Jason Verrett RC .75 2.00
164 Marcus Smith RC .75 2.00
165 Greg Robinson RC .75 2.00
166 Jimmie Ward RC 1.00 2.50
167 Jared Abbrederis RC .75 2.00
168 James Wilder Jr. RC 1.00 2.50
169 Jalen Saunders RC .75 2.00
170 Stephon Tuitt RC 1.25 3.00
171 Ra'Shede Hageman RC .75 2.00
172 Pierre Desir RC .75 2.00
173 Ja'Wuan James RC .75 2.00
174 Marcus Roberson RC 1.00 2.50
175 Ed Reynolds RC .75 2.00
176 Richard Rodgers RC 1.25 3.00
177 Ray Agnew RC .75 2.00
178 Rajion Neal RC .75 2.00
179 DeMarcus Lawrence RC 1.00 2.50
180 Trevor Reilly RC .75 2.00
181 Garrett Gilbert RC .75 2.00
182 Rob Blanchflower RC .75 2.00
183 Taylor Gabriel RC 1.00 2.50
184 Tevin Reese RC .75 2.00
185 C.J. Fiedorowicz RC .75 2.00
186 Zack Martin RC 1.00 2.50
187 Matt Hazel RC .75 2.00
188 Walter Powell RC .75 2.00
189 Justin Gilbert RC .75 2.00
190 Josh Huff RC 1.00 2.50
191 Lamarcus Joyner RC 1.00 2.50
192 Dominique Easley RC .75 2.00
193 Orleans Darkwa RC 1.25 3.00
194 Aaron Donald RC 2.00 5.00
195 Dustin Vaughan RC .75 2.00
196 Gator Hoskins RC 1.00 2.50
197 Henry Josey RC .75 2.00
198 Albert Wilson RC 1.00 2.50
199 Corey Washington RC 1.25 3.00
200 Cody Parkey RC 1.00 2.50
201 J.Manziel JSY AU/299 RC 12.00 30.00
202 T.Bridgewater JSY AU/299 RC 8.00 20.00
203 Blake Bortles JSY AU/299 RC 6.00 15.00
204 S.Watkins JSY AU/299 RC 8.00 20.00
205 Mike Evans JSY AU/299 RC 12.00 30.00
206 K.Benjamin JSY AU/175 RC 8.00 20.00
207 B.Sankey JSY AU/199 RC 5.00 12.00
208 Tre Mason JSY AU/175 RC 5.00 12.00
209 Jeremy Hill JSY AU/199 RC 6.00 15.00
210 Tom Savage JSY AU/99 RC 5.00 12.00
211 T.West JSY AU/299 RC 5.00 12.00
212 Tajh Boyd JSY AU/99 RC 5.00 12.00
213 P.Richardson JSY AU/99 RC 6.00 15.00
214 O.Beckham JSY AU/299 RC 40.00 100.00
215 Marqise Lee JSY AU/99 RC 6.00 15.00
216 Logan Thomas JSY AU/99 RC 5.00 12.00
217 Khalil Mack JSY AU/299 RC 20.00 50.00
218 Ka'Deem Carey JSY AU/99 RC 5.00 12.00
219 J.Matthews JSY AU/299 RC 8.00 20.00
220 J.Garoppolo JSY AU/175 RC 75.00 150.00
221 Jarvis Landry JSY AU/299 RC 12.00 30.00
222 J.Clowney JSY AU/99 RC EX 6.00 15.00
223 Eric Ebron JSY AU/149 RC
224 Dri Archer JSY AU/299 RC 5.00 12.00
225 Donte Moncrief JSY AU/299 RC 5.00 12.00
226 D.Freeman JSY AU/249 RC 8.00 20.00
227 Derek Carr JSY AU/149 RC 40.00 100.00
228 D.Thomas JSY AU/299 RC
229 D.Adams JSY AU/299 RC EX 15.00 40.00
230 Jace Amaro JSY AU/199 RC 5.00 12.00
231 Cody Latimer JSY AU/299 RC 6.00 15.00
232 Charles Sims JSY AU/99 RC 5.00 12.00
233 C.Hyde JSY AU/199 RC EX 6.00 15.00
234 Brandin Cooks JSY AU/199 RC 8.00 20.00
235 Seferian-Jnkns JSY AU/149 RC 5.00 12.00
236 Asa Watson JSY AU/299 RC 5.00 12.00
237 Andre Williams JSY AU/99 RC 5.00 12.00
238 Allen Robinson JSY AU/99 RC 12.00 30.00
239 A.J. McCarron JSY AU/149 RC 5.00 12.00
240 Aaron Murray JSY AU/99 RC 5.00 12.00

2014 Crown Royale Gold

*1-100 VETS/99: 2X TO 5X BASIC CARDS
*101-200 ROOKIES/99: 1X TO 2.5X BASIC RC
*ROOK.JSY AU/35-49: .5X TO 1.2X JSY AU RC
EXCH EXPIRATION: 5/26/2016
220 Jimmy Garoppolo JSY AU/49 100.00 200.00

2014 Crown Royale Gold Holofoil

*1-100 VETS/25: 3X TO 8X BASIC CARDS
*101-200 ROOKIES/25: 1.5X TO 4X BASIC RC

2014 Crown Royale Purple

*1-100 VETS/10: 5X TO 12X BASIC CARDS
*101-200 ROOKIES/10: 2.5X TO 6X BASIC RC
*201-240 RK.JSY AU/25: .8X TO 2X JSY AU/299
220 Jimmy Garoppolo JSY AU 200.00 300.00

2014 Crown Royale Retail Blue Holofoil

*1-100 VETS/199: 1.2X TO 3X BASIC CARDS
*101-200 ROOKIES/199: .6X TO 1.5X BASIC RC

2014 Crown Royale Retail Bronze

*1-100 VETS: 1X TO 2.5X BASIC CARDS
*101-200 ROOKIES: .5X TO 1.2X BASIC RC

2014 Crown Royale Retail Pink

*1-100 VETS/10: 5X TO 12X BASIC CARDS
*101-200 ROOKIES/10: 2.5X TO 6X BASIC RC

2014 Crown Royale Retail Red

*1-100 VETS/99: 2X TO 5X BASIC CARDS
*101-200 ROOKIES/99: 1X TO 2.5X BASIC RC

2014 Crown Royale Retail Red Holofoil

*1-100 VETS/25: 3X TO 8X BASIC CARDS
*101-200 ROOKIES/25: 1.5X TO 4X BASIC RC

2014 Crown Royale Retail Rookies Jersey Number

*ROOKIES/70-99: 1X TO 2.5X BASIC CARDS
*ROOKIES/31-54 1.2X TO 3X BASIC CARDS
*ROOKIES/14-30: 1.5X TO 4X BASIC CARDS

2014 Crown Royale Rookies Premiere Date

*PREM.DATE/14: 2.5X TO 6X BASIC RC

2014 Crown Royale Silver Holofoil

*1-100 VETS/199: 1.2X TO 3X BASIC CARDS
*101-200 ROOKIES/199: .6X TO 1.5X BASIC RC
127 Jerick McKinnon 1.50 4.00

2014 Crown Royale Air to the Throne

*RED: .5X TO 1.2X BASIC INSERTS
*BLUE: .6X TO 1.5X BASIC INSERTS
AT1 P.Manning/J.Manziel 3.00 8.00
AT2 P.Manning/J.Manziel 3.00 8.00

2014 Crown Royale All Pro Materials

*PRIME/99: .8X TO 2X BASIC JSY/470-499
1 Antonio Brown/476 5.00 12.00
2 Dez Bryant/499 5.00 12.00
3 Larry Fitzgerald/499 2.00 5.00
4 Matt Forte/499 1.50 4.00
5 A.J. Green/499 2.50 6.00
6 Eddie Lacy/499 1.50 4.00
7 LeSean McCoy/499 2.50 6.00
8 Alex Smith/499 2.00 5.00
9 J.J. Watt/499 8.00 20.00
10 Cordarrelle Patterson/499 1.50 4.00
11 Ndamukong Suh/499 2.00 5.00
12 Vontaze Burfict/499 1.50 4.00
13 Derrick Johnson/499 1.50 4.00
14 Patrick Peterson/499 1.50 4.00
15 Eric Reid/499 2.00 5.00
16 Darrelle Revis/499 1.50 4.00
17 Tim Jennings/470 1.50 4.00
18 Gerald McCoy/499 1.50 4.00
19 Brian Orakpo/499 2.50 6.00
20 Cameron Wake/474 1.50 4.00
21 Dexter McCluster/499 2.00 5.00
22 Mike Tolbert/499 2.00 5.00
23 T.J. Ward/499 1.50 4.00
24 Eric Weddle/499 4.00 10.00
25 Paul Posluszny/499 1.50 4.00

2014 Crown Royale Crown Jewels

*RED: .5X TO 1.2X BASIC INSERTS
*GREEN: .6X TO 1.5X BASIC INSERTS
CJ1 Brett Favre 2.00 5.00
CJ2 Peyton Manning 2.00 5.00
CJ3 Tom Brady 2.50 6.00
CJ4 Emmitt Smith 1.50 4.00
CJ5 Adrian Peterson 1.00 2.50
CJ6 Calvin Johnson 1.00 2.50
CJ7 Steve Young 1.25 3.00
CJ8 Johnny Manziel .60 1.50
CJ9 Blake Bortles .50 1.25
CJ10 Teddy Bridgewater .60 1.50

2014 Crown Royale Crown Signatures

11 Len Dawson/25 10.00 25.00
16 Paul Warfield/25 8.00 20.00
17 Carl Eller/25 6.00 15.00
18 Jackie Smith/25 6.00 15.00
19 Paul Hornung/25
20 Kellen Winslow/25 8.00 20.00
21 Randy White/25 8.00 20.00
22 Ozzie Newsome/20 8.00 20.00
23 Jackie Slater/25 6.00 15.00
28 Jamaal Charles/25 6.00 15.00
29 Michael Floyd/20 5.00 12.00
31 Manti Te'o/20 6.00 15.00
32 Terrance Williams/20 5.00 12.00
33 Trent Dilfer/25 6.00 15.00
34 Torrey Smith/20 5.00 12.00
35 Joseph Randle/20 5.00 12.00
36 Barkevious Mingo/25 5.00 12.00
37 Gavin Escobar/25 5.00 12.00
38 Joseph Fauria/20 5.00 12.00
39 Jarrett Boykin/25 5.00 12.00
40 Jeremy Kerley/25 5.00 12.00
41 Mike James/20 5.00 12.00
42 Luke Kuechly/20 15.00 40.00
43 Jordan Poyer/25 5.00 12.00
44 Timothy Wright/20 5.00 12.00
45 Bryce Brown/25 5.00 12.00
46 Brandon Flowers/25 5.00 12.00
57 A.J. Green/25 8.00 20.00
58 Antonio Gates/25 5.00 12.00
59 Darren Sproles/20 6.00 15.00
60 C.J. Spiller/25 5.00 12.00
61 Hakeem Nicks/25
62 DeMarcus Ware/25
63 Mike Glennon/15 8.00 20.00
64 Jordy Nelson/25 15.00 40.00
65 Danny Amendola/20 6.00 15.00
67 Giovani Bernard/25 5.00 12.00
68 Cordarrelle Patterson/20 5.00 12.00
70 Earl Thomas/20 12.00 30.00
71 Keenan Allen/25 6.00 15.00
72 Eddie Lacy/25 5.00 12.00
73 Cameron Wake/20 25.00 50.00
75 James Laurinaitis/20 6.00 15.00
76 Robert Woods/20 6.00 15.00
77 T.Y. Hilton/25 8.00 20.00
78 Nick Foles/25 6.00 15.00
79 Kiko Alonso/20 5.00 12.00
80 Aaron Dobson/20 5.00 12.00
81 Kenny Stills/25 5.00 12.00
82 Zach Ertz/20 6.00 15.00
84 Ben Tate/20 5.00 12.00
85 Robert Mathis/20 5.00 12.00
87 Alshon Jeffery/25
88 Jordan Cameron/20 5.00 12.00
89 Andre Ellington/20 5.00 12.00
90 Zac Stacy/25 5.00 12.00
92 Knile Davis/25 5.00 12.00
95 Randall Cobb/20
96 Cecil Shorts III/20 5.00 12.00
97 Kenbrell Thompkins/25 5.00 12.00
100 Scott Chandler/20 5.00 12.00

2014 Crown Royale Crown Signatures Retail Bronze

36 Barkevious Mingo/75 4.00 10.00
37 Gavin Escobar/75 4.00 10.00
38 Joseph Fauria/75 4.00 10.00
39 Jarrett Boykin/99 4.00 10.00
40 Jeremy Kerley/99 4.00 10.00
41 Mike James/99 4.00 10.00
43 Jordan Poyer/99 4.00 10.00
44 Timothy Wright/75 4.00 10.00
45 Bryce Brown/99 4.00 10.00
46 Brandon Flowers/75 4.00 10.00
92 Knile Davis/75 4.00 10.00
97 Kenbrell Thompkins/75 4.00 10.00
100 Scott Chandler/75 4.00 10.00

2014 Crown Royale Crown Signatures Silver Holofoil

*SILVER/15: .5X TO 1.2X BASIC AU/20-25
*SILVER/20: .4X TO 1X BASIC AU/20-25
*SILVER/35: .5X TO 1.2X BASIC AU/75

2014 Crown Royale Dual Rookie Silhouettes

*PRIME/25: .6X TO 1.5X DUAL JSY/99
DSAE D.Adams/E.Ebron
DSCL K.Carey/M.Lee 2.00 5.00
DSMM A.McCarron/T.Mason 1.50 4.00
DSTC D.Thomas/B.Cooks 2.50 6.00
DSBIG A.Robinson/C.Latimer 2.50 6.00
DSCIN J.Hill/A.McCarron 2.00 5.00
DSCLE J.Manziel/T.West 2.50 6.00
DSCLM S.Watkins/T.Boyd 2.50 6.00
DSFSU D.Freeman/K.Benjamin 2.50 6.00
DSHOU T.Savage/J.Clowney 2.00 5.00
DSJAC M.Lee/B.Bortles 2.00 5.00
DSKCC A.Murray/D.Thomas 1.50 4.00
DSMIA J.Landry/O.Beckham Jr. 4.00 10.00
DSNYG A.Williams/O.Beckham Jr. 4.00 10.00
DSOAK D.Carr/K.Mack 8.00 20.00
DSQB1 T.Bridgewater/B.Bortles 2.50 6.00
DSQB2 J.Garoppolo/L.Thomas 12.00 30.00
DSRB1 C.Hyde/J.Hill 2.00 5.00
DSRD1 S.Watkins/T.Bridgewater 2.50 6.00
DSTAM J.Manziel/M.Evans 4.00 10.00
DSTBB C.Sims/M.Evans 4.00 10.00
DSWAS A.Sfrn-Jnkns/B.Snky 1.50 4.00
DSWR1 D.Archer/J.Matthews 2.50 6.00
DSWR2 J.Matthews/K.Benjamin 2.50 6.00
DSWR3 D.Moncrief/P.Richardson 2.00 5.00

2014 Crown Royale Heirs to the Throne Materials

*PRIME/99: .6X TO 1.5X BASIC JSY/499
HTAM A.J. McCarron 1.25 3.00
HTBB Blake Bortles 1.50 4.00
HTBC Brandin Cooks 2.00 5.00
HTBG Jimmy Garoppolo 10.00 25.00
HTBS Bishop Sankey 1.25 3.00
HTCH Carlos Hyde 1.50 4.00
HTDC Derek Carr 8.00 20.00
HTJF Johnny Manziel 2.00 5.00
HTJH Jeremy Hill 1.50 4.00
HTKB Kelvin Benjamin 2.00 5.00
HTME Mike Evans 3.00 8.00
HTOB Odell Beckham Jr. 6.00 15.00
HTSW Sammy Watkins 2.00 5.00
HTTB Teddy Bridgewater 2.00 5.00
HTTM Tre Mason 1.25 3.00

2014 Crown Royale Heirs to the Throne Materials Combos

*PRIME/99: .6X TO 1.5X BASIC JSY/399
HTCBC K.Benjamin/B.Cooks 2.50 6.00
HTCBG J.Garoppolo/T.Bridgewater 12.00 30.00
HTCMB B.Bortles/J.Manziel 2.50 6.00
HTCSM B.Sankey/T.Mason 1.50 4.00
HTCWE M.Evans/S.Watkins 4.00 10.00

2014 Crown Royale Heirs to the Throne Materials Trios

*PRIME/99: .6X TO 1.5X BASIC JSY/399
*PRIME/25-49: .75X TO 2X BASIC JSY/399
*PRIME/25-49: .5X TO 1.2X BASIC JSY/99
HTCWR1 Rbnsn/Evns/Mtthws/399 4.00 10.00
HTCWR2 Bnjmn/Cks/Wtkns/399 2.50 6.00
HTTQB1 Brtls/Mnzl/Brdgwtr/399 2.50 6.00
HTTRB1 Wllms/Hyde/Frmn/399 2.50 6.00
HTTSEC Shw/Ebrn/Clwny/99 3.00 8.00

2014 Crown Royale Jumbo Silhouettes

*PRIME/25: .6X TO 1.5X BASIC JSY/99
JSAM A.J. McCarron 1.50 4.00
JSAMU Aaron Murray 1.50 4.00
JSAR Allen Robinson 2.50 6.00
JSAW Andre Williams 1.50 4.00
JSBB Blake Bortles 2.00 5.00
JSBC Brandin Cooks 2.50 6.00
JSBS Bishop Sankey 1.50 4.00
JSCH Carlos Hyde 2.00 5.00
JSCL Cody Latimer 2.00 5.00
JSDA Davante Adams 2.50 6.00
JSDC Derek Carr 10.00 25.00
JSJC Jadeveon Clowney 2.00 5.00
JSJG Jimmy Garoppolo 12.00 30.00
JSJH Jeremy Hill 2.00 5.00
JSJM Johnny Manziel 2.50 6.00
JSJMA Jordan Matthews 2.50 6.00
JSKB Kelvin Benjamin 2.50 6.00
JSKC Ka'Deem Carey 1.50 4.00
JSME Mike Evans 4.00 10.00
JSOB Odell Beckham Jr. 4.00 10.00
JSPR Paul Richardson 2.00 5.00
JSSW Sammy Watkins 2.50 6.00
JSTB Teddy Bridgewater 2.50 6.00
JSTM Tre Mason 1.50 4.00
JSTS Tom Savage 1.50 4.00

2014 Crown Royale Knights and Squires

*RED: .5X TO 1.2X BASIC INSERTS
*GREEN: .6X TO 1.5X BASIC INSERTS
KS1 C.Kaepernick/J.Montana 8.00 20.00
KS2 B.Favre/J.Manziel 1.50 4.00
KS3 A.Luck/P.Manning 4.00 10.00
KS4 C.Johnson/M.Evans 1.25 3.00
KS5 B.Rthlsbrgr/T.Brdgwtr .75 2.00
KS6 B.Bortles/A.Rodgers 1.50 4.00
KS7 B.Marshall/J.Matthews .75 2.00
KS8 D.Ware/J.Clowney .60 1.50
KS9 A.Peterson/J.Hill .75 2.00
KS10 J.Garoppolo/T.Brady 4.00 10.00
KS11 B.Sankey/C.Johnson .50 1.25
KS12 E.Ebron/J.Graham .75 2.00
KS13 J.Amaro/J.Witten .60 1.50
KS14 J.Gilbert/R.Sherman .75 2.00
KS15 S.Watkins/S.Johnson .75 2.00
KS16 C.Matthews/K.Mack 2.00 5.00

2014 Crown Royale Knights of the Round Table Materials

*PRIME/99: .8X TO 2X BASIC JSY/399
*PRIME/99: .6X TO 1.5X BASIC JSY/149-199
*PRIME/49: 1X TO 2.5X BASIC JSY/399
*PRIME/45: .8X TO 2X BASIC JSY/199
*PRIME/50: .6X TO 1.5X BASIC JSY/99
KRAG A.J. Green/399 2.50 6.00
KRCJ C.J. Spiller/399 1.50 4.00
KRCK Colin Kaepernick/99 3.00 8.00
KRCN Cam Newton/399 2.50 6.00
KRDB Drew Brees/399 2.50 6.00
KRDM Darren McFadden/399 1.50 4.00
KRDT Demaryius Thomas/399 2.00 5.00
KREM Eli Manning/399 2.00 5.00
KRJC Jamaal Charles/399 2.00 5.00
KRJF Joe Flacco/199 2.50 6.00
KRJG Josh Gordon/399 1.50 4.00
KRJR Jerry Rice/249 6.00 15.00
KRJY Jay Cutler/399 1.50 4.00
KRKW Kurt Warner/199 5.00 12.00
KRLM LeSean McCoy/149 3.00 8.00
KRMR Matt Ryan/399 2.00 5.00
KRPM Peyton Manning/199 10.00 25.00
KRSB Sam Bradford/399 1.50 4.00
KRSJ Steve Johnson/399 2.00 5.00
KRTB Tom Brady/99 10.00 25.00

2014 Crown Royale Master Craftsmen

*RED: .5X TO 1.2X BASIC INSERTS
*GREEN: .6X TO 1.5X BASIC INSERTS
MC1 Peyton Manning 3.00 8.00
MC2 Drew Brees 1.50 4.00
MC3 Aaron Rodgers 3.00 8.00
MC4 Adrian Peterson 1.50 4.00
MC5 Marshawn Lynch 1.25 3.00
MC6 Jamaal Charles 1.25 3.00
MC7 Calvin Johnson 1.50 4.00
MC8 Brandon Marshall 1.00 2.50
MC9 A.J. Green 1.50 4.00
MC10 Jimmy Graham 1.50 4.00
MC11 J.J. Watt 1.50 4.00
MC12 Ndamukong Suh 1.25 3.00
MC13 Clay Matthews 1.50 4.00
MC14 Aldon Smith 1.00 2.50
MC15 Richard Sherman 1.50 4.00
MC16 Darrelle Revis 1.00 2.50

2014 Crown Royale Panini's Choice

*RED: .5X TO 1.2X BASIC INSERTS
*GREEN: .6X TO 1.5X BASIC INSERTS
PC1 Johnny Manziel 1.00 2.50
PC2 Teddy Bridgewater 1.00 2.50
PC3 Blake Bortles .75 2.00
PC4 Sammy Watkins 1.00 2.50
PC5 Mike Evans 1.50 4.00
PC6 Kelvin Benjamin 1.00 2.50
PC7 Odell Beckham Jr. 1.50 4.00
PC8 Brandin Cooks 1.00 2.50
PC9 Jeremy Hill .75 2.00
PC10 Tre Mason .60 1.50
PC11 Jimmy Garoppolo 5.00 12.00
PC12 Tom Savage .60 1.50
PC13 Bishop Sankey .60 1.50
PC14 Terrance West .60 1.50
PC15 Paul Richardson .75 2.00
PC16 Marqise Lee .75 2.00
PC17 Jordan Matthews 1.00 2.50
PC18 Ka'Deem Carey .60 1.50
PC19 Jadeveon Clowney .75 2.00
PC20 Derek Carr 4.00 10.00
PC21 Cody Latimer .75 2.00
PC22 Carlos Hyde .75 2.00
PC23 Eric Ebron .75 2.00
PC24 Jace Amaro .60 1.50
PC25 De'Anthony Thomas .60 1.50
PC26 Jarvis Landry 1.25 3.00
PC27 James White 1.25 3.00
PC28 Zach Mettenberger .60 1.50
PC29 Aaron Murray .60 1.50
PC30 A.J. McCarron .60 1.50
PC31 Davante Adams 1.00 2.50
PC32 Andre Williams .60 1.50

2014 Crown Royale Rookie Royalty Materials

*PRIME/75-99: .6X TO 1.5X BASIC JSY/499
*PRIME/25-49: .8X TO 2X BASIC JSY/499
*PRIME/25: .5X TO 1.2X BASIC JSY/99
RR1 Aaron Murray/499 1.25 3.00
RR2 A.J. McCarron/499 1.25 3.00
RR3 Allen Robinson/499 2.00 5.00
RR4 Andre Williams/499 1.25 3.00
RR5 Asa Watson/499 1.25 3.00
RR6 Austin Seferian-Jenkins/499 1.25 3.00
RR7 Brandin Cooks/499 2.00 5.00
RR8 Carlos Hyde/499 1.50 4.00
RR9 Charles Sims/499 1.25 3.00
RR10 Cody Latimer/499 1.50 4.00
RR11 Jace Amaro/99 2.00 5.00
RR12 Tajh Boyd/499 1.25 3.00
RR13 Paul Richardson/499 1.50 4.00
RR14 Odell Beckham Jr./499 8.00 25.00
RR15 Marqise Lee/499 1.50 4.00
RR16 Logan Thomas/499 1.25 3.00
RR17 Khalil Mack/499 5.00 12.00
RR18 Ka'Deem Carey/499 1.25 3.00
RR19 Jordan Matthews/499 2.00 5.00
RR20 Jimmy Garoppolo/499 10.00 25.00
RR21 Jarvis Landry/499 2.50 6.00
RR22 Jadeveon Clowney/499 1.50 4.00
RR23 Eric Ebron/499 1.50 4.00
RR24 Dri Archer/499 1.25 3.00
RR25 Donte Moncrief/499 1.25 3.00
RR26 Devonta Freeman/499 2.00 5.00
RR27 Derek Carr/499 8.00 20.00
RR28 De'Anthony Thomas/499 1.25 3.00
RR29 Davante Adams/499 2.00 5.00
RR30 Terrance West/499 1.25 3.00
RR31 Tom Savage/499 1.25 3.00
RR32 Jeremy Hill/499 1.50 4.00
RR33 Tre Mason/499 1.25 3.00
RR34 Bishop Sankey/499 1.25 3.00
RR35 Kelvin Benjamin/499 2.00 5.00
RR36 Mike Evans/499 3.00 8.00
RR37 Sammy Watkins/499 2.00 5.00
RR38 Blake Bortles/499 1.50 4.00
RR39 Teddy Bridgewater/499 2.00 5.00
RR40 Johnny Manziel/499 2.00 5.00

2014 Crown Royale Rookie Signatures

SAA Antonio Andrews/149 3.00 8.00
SAB Anthony Barr/50 5.00 12.00
SABL Alfred Blue/149 3.00 8.00
SAD Ahmad Dixon/99 4.00 10.00
SAH Allen Hurns/50 6.00 15.00
SAL Arthur Lynch/99 4.00 10.00
SAM A.J. McCarron/49 5.00 12.00
SAN Andre Williams/50 5.00 12.00
SAW Asa Watson/299 3.00 8.00
SBB Blake Bortles/25 8.00 20.00
SBC Brandon Coleman/75 4.00 10.00
SBO Branden Oliver/99 6.00 15.00
SCB Chris Borland/50 5.00 12.00
SCF C.J. Fiedorowicz/299 3.00 8.00
SCH Cody Hoffman/99 4.00 10.00
SCM C.J. Mosley/50 8.00 20.00
SCR Cyril Richardson/99 4.00 10.00
SCS Chris Smith/99 4.00 10.00
SDB Deone Bucannon/99 4.00 10.00
SDD Darqueze Dennard/75 5.00 12.00
SDE Dominique Easley/99 4.00 10.00
SDF David Fales/35 5.00 12.00
SDS Devin Street/299 3.00 8.00
SDY David Yankey/99 4.00 10.00
SER Ed Reynolds/299 3.00 8.00
SGG Garrett Gilbert/299 3.00 8.00
SGR Greg Robinson/99 4.00 10.00
SHA Ha Ha Clinton-Dix/50 6.00 15.00
SIC Isaiah Crowell/299 4.00 10.00
SJA Jared Abbrederis/50 5.00 12.00
SJAM Jace Amaro/299 3.00 8.00
SJB John Brown/299 5.00 12.00
SJF Johnny Manziel/25 10.00 25.00
SJH Jeremy Hill/299 4.00 10.00
SJJ Jeff Janis/299 3.00 8.00
SJL Jordan Lynch/99 5.00 12.00
SJM Jake Matthews/50 6.00 15.00
SJO Jordan Matthews/299 5.00 12.00
SJV Jason Verrett/99 4.00 10.00
SJW Jimmie Ward/299 4.00 10.00
SJW James White/99
SJWI James Wilder Jr./299 4.00 10.00
SKB Kelvin Benjamin/99 6.00 15.00
SKC Ka'Deem Carey/50 5.00 12.00
SKE Kony Ealy/50 6.00 15.00
SKF Kyle Fuller/99 4.00 10.00
SKN Kevin Norwood/299 3.00 8.00
SKV Kyle Van Noy/50 6.00 15.00
SKW Keith Wenning/299 4.00 10.00
SLJ Lamarcus Joyner/99 5.00 12.00
SLS Lache Seastrunk/25 6.00 15.00
SLT Lorenzo Taliaferro/99 5.00 12.00
SLW L'Damian Washington/99 5.00 12.00
SMCA Michael Campanaro/299 3.00 8.00
SMC Jerick McKinnon/299 4.00 10.00
SMD Mike Davis/75 4.00 10.00
SME Mike Evans/299 8.00 20.00
SMG Marion Grice/299 3.00 8.00
SMH Matt Hazel/299 3.00 8.00
SMR Marcus Roberson/99 5.00 12.00
SMS Michael Sam/75 4.00 10.00
SMSM Marcus Smith/50 5.00 12.00
SPB Preston Brown/149 3.00 8.00
SPD Pierre Desir/149 3.00 8.00
SQE Quincy Enunwa/299 5.00 12.00
SRH Ra'Shede Hageman/50 5.00 12.00
SRHE Robert Herron/75 4.00 10.00
SRN Rajion Neal/299 3.00 8.00
SRR Richard Rodgers/299 5.00 12.00
SRRO Rashad Ross/299 3.00 8.00
SRS Ryan Shazier/50 8.00 20.00
SSC Scott Crichton/99 4.00 10.00
SSS Shayne Skov/75 4.00 10.00
SSW Sammy Watkins/299 5.00 12.00
STB Teddy Bridgewater/35 8.00 20.00
STG Tyler Gaffney/50 5.00 12.00
STJ Timmy Jernigan/99 4.00 10.00
STL Taylor Lewan/99 4.00 10.00
STM Trent Murphy/75 4.00 10.00
STN Troy Niklas/50 5.00 12.00
STR Tevin Reese/50 5.00 12.00
STRE Trevor Reilly/50 5.00 12.00
STS Telvin Smith/99 4.00 10.00
STSW Travis Swanson/50 5.00 12.00
STW Terrance West/99 4.00 10.00
SXS Xavier Su'A-Filo/99 5.00 12.00
SYS Yawin Smallwood/99 4.00 10.00

2014 Crown Royale Rookie Silhouettes

*BLUE/49: .5X TO 1.2X BASIC JSY/99-199
*RED/25: .6X TO 1.5X BASIC JSY/99-199
201 Johnny Manziel/99 3.00 8.00
202 Teddy Bridgewater/99 3.00 8.00
203 Blake Bortles/199 2.50 6.00
204 Sammy Watkins/199 3.00 8.00
205 Mike Evans/199 5.00 12.00
206 Kelvin Benjamin/199 3.00 8.00
207 Bishop Sankey/199 2.00 5.00
208 Tre Mason/199 2.00 5.00
209 Jeremy Hill/199 2.50 6.00
210 Tom Savage/199 2.00 5.00
211 Terrance West/199 2.00 5.00
212 Tajh Boyd/199 2.00 5.00
213 Paul Richardson/199 2.50 6.00
214 Odell Beckham Jr./199 12.00 30.00
215 Marqise Lee/199 2.50 6.00
216 Logan Thomas/199 2.00 5.00
217 Khalil Mack/199 8.00 20.00
218 Ka'Deem Carey/199 2.00 5.00
219 Jordan Matthews/199 3.00 8.00
220 Jimmy Garoppolo/199 15.00 40.00
221 Jarvis Landry/199 4.00 10.00
222 Jadeveon Clowney/199 2.50 6.00
223 Eric Ebron/199 2.50 6.00
224 Dri Archer/100 2.00 5.00
225 Donte Moncrief/199 2.00 5.00
226 Devonta Freeman/199 3.00 8.00
227 Derek Carr/199 12.00 30.00
228 De'Anthony Thomas/199 2.00 5.00
229 Davante Adams/199 3.00 8.00
230 Jace Amaro/199 2.00 5.00
231 Cody Latimer/199 2.50 6.00
232 Charles Sims/199 2.00 5.00
233 Carlos Hyde/199 2.50 6.00
234 Brandin Cooks/199 3.00 8.00
235 Austin Seferian-Jenkins/199 2.00 5.00
236 Asa Watson/199 2.00 5.00
237 Andre Williams/199 2.00 5.00
238 Allen Robinson/199 3.00 8.00
239 A.J. McCarron/199 2.00 5.00
240 Aaron Murray/199 2.00 5.00

2014 Crown Royale Silhouette Material Autographs

SICS C.J. Spiller/15
SIDB Dez Bryant/20 50.00 100.00
SIDBO Dwayne Bowe/15 8.00 20.00
SIJC Jay Cutler/15
SIJF Joe Flacco/15 25.00 50.00
SIML Marshawn Lynch/15 40.00 80.00
SIPM Peyton Manning/18 150.00 300.00

2014 Crown Royale The King's Court

*RED: .5X TO 1.2X BASIC INSERTS
*GREEN: .6X TO 1.5X BASIC INSERTS
KC1 Thomas/Manning/Welker 2.00 5.00
KC2 Harvin/Wilson/Lynch 1.50 4.00
KC3 Boldin/Kaepernick/Gore .75 2.00
KC4 Jeffery/Marshall/Cutler .75 2.00
KC5 Witten/Bryant/Romo 1.00 2.50
KC6 Rivers/Mathews/Allen 1.00 2.50
KC7 Newton/Williams/Benjamin 1.00 2.50
KC8 Manziel/Gordon/West 1.00 2.50
KC9 Peterson/Bridgewater/Patterson 1.00 2.50
KC10 Richardson/Luck/Nicks 1.25 3.00
KC11 Green/Dalton/Bernard 1.00 2.50
KC12 Nelson/Rodgers/Lacy 2.00 5.00
KC13 Stafford/Johnson/Ebron 1.00 2.50
KC14 Morris/Jackson/Griffin III .75 2.00
KC15 Edelman/Brady/Gronkowski 2.50 6.00
KC16 Manuel/Spiller/Watkins 1.00 2.50
KC17 Martin/McCown/Evans 1.50 4.00
KC18 Robinson/Bortles/Lee 1.00 2.50
KC19 Flacco/Smith/Smith .75 2.00
KC20 Cooks/Brees/Graham 1.00 2.50
KC21 Roethlisberger/Bell/Brown 1.00 2.50
KC22 Manning/Cruz/Beckham Jr. 1.50 4.00
KC23 Smith/Thomas/Charles .75 2.00
KC24 Bradford/Austin/Mason .60 1.50

2015 Crown Royale

1 DeSean Jackson .50 1.25
2 Tavon Austin .40 1.00
3 Tony Romo .50 1.25
4 Nick Foles .50 1.25
5 Jared Cook .40 1.00
6 Ndamukong Suh .50 1.25
7 Devin Hester .50 1.25
8 Marshawn Lynch .50 1.25
9 Sammy Watkins .50 1.25
10 Marqise Lee .40 1.00
11 Anquan Boldin .40 1.00
12 Delanie Walker .40 1.00
13 Gerald McCoy .40 1.00
14 Jason Witten .50 1.25
15 Calvin Johnson .60 1.50
16 Larry Fitzgerald .50 1.25
17 Travis Kelce .60 1.50
18 Sam Bradford .40 1.00
19 Jordan Matthews .50 1.25
20 Dez Bryant .60 1.50
21 Emmanuel Sanders .50 1.25
22 Colin Kaepernick .50 1.25
23 Brandon Marshall .40 1.00
24 Julius Thomas .40 1.00
25 Peyton Manning 1.25 3.00
26 Blake Bortles .40 1.00
27 Isaiah Crowell .40 1.00
28 Julio Jones .60 1.50
29 Frank Gore .50 1.25
30 Martavis Bryant .40 1.00
31 Victor Cruz .50 1.25
32 Ben Roethlisberger .60 1.50
33 Tom Brady 1.50 4.00
34 Carson Palmer .50 1.25
35 Jordy Nelson .50 1.25
36 Latavius Murray .40 1.00
37 DeAndre Hopkins .50 1.25
38 Darrelle Revis .40 1.00
39 Philip Rivers .60 1.50
40 Joe Flacco .50 1.25
41 Steve Smith Sr. .50 1.25
42 Arian Foster .50 1.25
43 Justin Forsett .50 1.25
44 Jamaal Charles .50 1.25
45 Joseph Randle .40 1.00
46 Andy Dalton .50 1.25
47 Kendall Wright .40 1.00
48 Alex Smith .50 1.25
49 Tyrod Taylor .50 1.25
50 Mike Evans .50 1.25
51 Rob Gronkowski .60 1.50
52 Drew Brees .60 1.50
53 Josh McCown .50 1.25
54 Le'Veon Bell .50 1.25
55 Michael Crabtree .40 1.00
56 Jeremy Hill .40 1.00
57 Matthew Stafford .50 1.25
58 Demaryius Thomas .50 1.25
59 Randall Cobb .50 1.25
60 Devonta Freeman .50 1.25
61 Jordan Reed .40 1.00
62 Mark Ingram .50 1.25
63 Eddie Lacy .40 1.00
64 Alshon Jeffery .50 1.25
65 Matt Ryan .50 1.25
66 A.J. Green .60 1.50
67 Derek Carr .60 1.50
68 DeMarco Murray .50 1.25
69 Ryan Mallett .50 1.25
70 Cam Newton .60 1.50
71 T.Y. Hilton .50 1.25
72 Russell Wilson .75 2.00
73 Ryan Tannehill .50 1.25
74 Charles Woodson .60 1.50
75 Adrian Peterson .60 1.50
76 Aaron Rodgers 1.25 3.00
77 Marques Colston .40 1.00
78 Antonio Gates .40 1.00
79 Odell Beckham Jr. .60 1.50
80 Bishop Sankey .40 1.00
81 Jimmy Graham .60 1.50
82 Antonio Brown .60 1.50
83 Alfred Morris .40 1.00
84 Doug Martin .50 1.25
85 Teddy Bridgewater .50 1.25
86 Greg Olsen .50 1.25
87 LeGarrette Blount .50 1.25
88 Keenan Allen .50 1.25
89 LeSean McCoy .60 1.50
90 Chris Ivory .50 1.25
91 Matt Forte .40 1.00
92 Golden Tate .40 1.00
93 Jay Cutler .40 1.00
94 Patrick Peterson .40 1.00
95 Kelvin Benjamin .50 1.25
96 Vernon Davis .40 1.00
97 Eli Manning .50 1.25
98 Jarvis Landry .50 1.25
99 Jeremy Maclin .40 1.00
100 Andrew Luck .75 2.00
101 Tyler Kroft RC 1.00 2.50
102 James O'Shaughnessy RC .75 2.00
103 Malcom Brown RC .75 2.00
104 Senquez Golson RC .75 2.00
105 Trey Williams RC 1.00 2.50
106 Shakim Phillips RC .75 2.00
107 Randy Gregory RC .75 2.00
108 Hau'oli Kikaha RC 1.00 2.50
109 Carl Davis RC 1.00 2.50
110 Nate Orchard RC .75 2.00
111 Eric Kendricks RC .75 2.00
112 Kyle Emanuel RC 1.00 2.50
113 Zach Zenner RC 1.50 4.00
114 Dominique Brown RC .75 2.00
115 Jarryd Hayne RC 1.25 3.00
116 Eric Tomlinson RC 1.00 2.50
117 Jake Ryan RC 1.25 3.00
118 Quandre Diggs RC .75 2.00
119 Duron Carter RC 1.00 2.50
120 Kevin Johnson RC .75 2.00
121 Nick Marshall RC 1.25 3.00
122 Ramik Wilson RC 1.00 2.50
123 Nick Boyle RC .75 2.00
124 Jaxon Shipley RC .75 2.00
125 Doran Grant RC 1.25 3.00
126 Terrell Watson RC 1.25 3.00
127 Cameron Meredith RC 1.25 3.00
128 Charcandrick West RC 1.00 2.50
129 Kurtis Drummond RC 1.00 2.50
130 Derron Smith RC .75 2.00
131 Trevor Siemian RC 2.00 5.00
132 Frank Clark RC .75 2.00
133 Terrence Magee RC 1.25 3.00
134 Quinten Rollins RC 1.50 4.00
135 Dreamius Smith RC 2.00 5.00
136 Malcolm Brown RC 1.00 2.50
137 Geoff Swaim RC 1.00 2.50
138 Chris Harper RC 1.00 2.50
139 Xavier Cooper RC .75 2.00
140 Geremy Davis RC 1.00 2.50
141 Arik Armstead AU/299 RC 3.00 8.00
142 Bud Dupree AU/149 RC 4.00 10.00
143 Danny Shelton AU/149 RC 3.00 8.00
144 Marcus Peters AU/149 RC 5.00 12.00
146 Shaq Thompson AU/299 RC 4.00 10.00
147 Trae Waynes AU/149 RC 3.00 8.00
148 Vic Beasley Jr. AU/149 RC 4.00 10.00
149 Stephone Anthony AU/100 RC 4.00 10.00
150 Benardrick McKinney AU/299 RC 3.00 8.00
152 Eddie Goldman AU/299 RC 3.00 8.00
153 Jalen Collins AU/299 RC 3.00 8.00
154 Landon Collins AU/149 RC 4.00 10.00
155 Markus Golden AU/299 RC 3.00 8.00
156 Eric Rowe AU/100 RC 4.00 10.00
157 Ronald Darby AU/299 RC 3.00 8.00
158 Clive Walford AU/299 RC 3.00 8.00
159 Danielle Hunter AU/299 RC 4.00 10.00
160 P.J. Williams AU/200 RC 4.00 10.00
161 Josh Harper AU/299 RC 3.00 8.00
162 Mario Edwards Jr. AU/49 RC 5.00 12.00
163 Paul Dawson AU/299 RC 4.00 10.00
165 Josh Shaw AU/125 RC 5.00 12.00
166 Cameron Artis-Payne AU/149 RC 3.00 8.00
167 Jesse James AU/249 RC 4.00 10.00
168 Gus Johnson AU/299 RC 5.00 12.00
169 Thomas Rawls AU/299 RC 8.00 20.00
171 MyCole Pruitt AU/299 RC 3.00 8.00
172 Tony Lippett AU/149 RC 3.00 8.00
173 Austin Hill AU/299 RC 3.00 8.00
175 Josh Robinson AU/299 RC 3.00 8.00
176 Nick O'Leary AU/299 RC 3.00 8.00
177 Darren Waller AU/299 RC 4.00 10.00
178 Dezmin Lewis AU/299 RC 3.00 8.00
179 Tre McBride AU/299 RC 3.00 8.00
180 Ben Koyack AU/299 RC 5.00 12.00
181 Mario Alford AU/100 RC 4.00 10.00
182 D'Joun Smith AU/299 RC 5.00 12.00
183 Da'Ron Brown AU/299 RC 3.00 8.00
184 Kenny Hilliard AU/299 RC 3.00 8.00
185 Antwan Goodley AU/299 RC 3.00 8.00
186 DaVaris Daniels AU/99 RC 4.00 10.00
187 Dres Anderson AU/299 RC 3.00 8.00
188 Jordan Taylor AU/225 RC 4.00 10.00
189 Taylor Heinicke AU/199 RC 5.00 12.00
190 Titus Davis AU/299 RC 4.00 10.00
191 Trey Williams AU/299 RC 4.00 10.00
192 DeAndrew White AU/99 RC 6.00 15.00
193 Rannell Hall AU/49 RC 5.00 12.00
194 Marcus Murphy AU/299 RC 3.00 8.00
195 Damarious Randall AU/299 RC 4.00 10.00
196 DeAndre Smelter AU/299 RC 3.00 8.00
197 Byron Jones AU/299 RC 5.00 12.00
198 E.J. Bibbs AU/299 RC 4.00 10.00
199 Owamagbe Odighizuwa AU/299 RC 4.00 10.00
200 Blake Bell AU/299 RC 5.00 12.00
201 Amari Cooper JSY AU/199 RC 15.00 40.00
202 Ameer Abdullah JSY AU/299 RC 8.00 20.00
203 Breshad Perriman JSY AU/299 RC 5.00 12.00
204 Brett Hundley JSY AU/299 RC 5.00 12.00
205 Bryce Petty JSY AU/299 RC 5.00 12.00
209 David Johnson JSY AU/299 RC 12.00 30.00
210 DeVante Parker JSY AU/299 RC 8.00 20.00
211 Devin Funchess JSY AU/299 RC 8.00 20.00
212 Devin Smith JSY AU/299 RC 5.00 12.00
214 Duke Johnson JSY AU/299 RC 8.00 20.00
215 Garrett Grayson JSY AU/199 RC 5.00 12.00
216 Jaelen Strong JSY AU/299 RC 6.00 15.00
217 Jameis Winston JSY AU/299 RC 12.00 30.00
218 Jamison Crowder JSY AU/299 RC 6.00 15.00
220 Jeremy Langford JSY AU/299 RC 5.00 12.00
221 Justin Hardy JSY AU/299 RC 5.00 12.00
223 Kevin White JSY AU/299 RC 6.00 15.00
225 Marcus Mariota JSY AU/299 RC 20.00 50.00
226 Matt Jones JSY AU/299 RC 5.00 12.00
227 Maxx Williams JSY AU/299 RC 5.00 12.00
228 Melvin Gordon JSY AU/299 RC 12.00 30.00
229 Mike Davis JSY AU/299 RC 5.00 12.00
230 Nelson Agholor JSY AU/299 RC 6.00 15.00
232 Rashad Greene JSY AU/299 RC 5.00 12.00
233 Sammie Coates JSY AU/299 RC 6.00 15.00
234 Sean Mannion JSY AU/299 RC 5.00 12.00
235 Stefon Diggs JSY AU/299 RC EXCH 12.00 30.00
236 T.J. Yeldon JSY AU/299 RC 5.00 12.00
238 Todd Gurley JSY AU/299 RC EXCH 20.00 50.00
239 Ty Montgomery JSY AU/299 RC 5.00 12.00
240 Tyler Lockett JSY AU/299 RC 8.00 20.00
241 Vince Mayle JSY AU/299 RC 6.00 15.00

2015 Crown Royale Gold Holofoil

*1-100 VETS/25: 3X TO 8X BASIC CARDS

2015 Crown Royale Premier Date

*ROOKIES: 2X TO 5X BASIC CARDS
*ROOK AU/15: 1X TO 2.5X BASIC CARDS/125-299
*ROOK AU/15: .8X TO 2X BASIC CARDS/99-100

2015 Crown Royale Purple

*ROOKIES: 1.5X TO 4X BASIC CARDS
*ROOK AU/25: .8X TO 2X BASIC AU/125-299
*ROOK AU/25: .6X TO 1.5X BASIC AU/100
*ROOK AU/20: ..8X TO 2X BASIC AU/99-100
*ROOK AU/15: .6X TO 1.5X BASIC AU/49
*ROOK JSY AU/25: .8X TO 2X BASIC JSY AU/299
*ROOK JSY AU/15: 1X TO 2.5X BASIC JSY AU/199

2015 Crown Royale Retail Bronze

*VETS(1-100): 1X TO 2.5X BASIC CARDS
*ROOK (101-140): .5X TO 1.2X BASIC CARDS
*ROOK AU/125-299: .4X TO 1X BASIC AU/149-299
*ROOK AU/75-99: .4X TO 1X BASIC AU/100
*ROOK AU/75-99: .5X TO 1.2X BASIC AU/125-299
*ROOK AU/49-60: .6X TO 1.5X BASIC AU/125-149
*ROOK AU/50: .6X TO 1.5X BASIC AU/149-299
*ROOK AU/99: .5X TO 1.2X BASIC AU/99
*ROOK AU/25: .5X TO 1.2X BASIC AU/49

2015 Crown Royale Retail Jersey Number

*ROOKIES/71-99: 1X TO 2.5X BASIC CARDS
*ROOKIES/31-58: 1.2X TO 3X BASIC CARDS
*ROOKIES/26-30: 1.5X TO 4X BASIC CARDS
*ROOKIES/15-24: 2X TO 5X BASIC CARDS
*ROOK AU/71-99: .5X TO 1.2X BASIC AU/125-299
*ROOK AU/31-58: .6X TO 1.5X BASIC AU/125-299
*ROOK AU/26-30: .8X TO 2X BASIC AU/125-299
*ROOK AU/15-24: 1X TO 2.5X BASIC AU/125-299
*ROOK AU/15-24: .8X TO 2X BASIC AU/100
*ROOK AU/15-24 .6X TO 1.5X BASIC AU/49

2015 Crown Royale Retail Pewter

*VETS: 1.2X TO 3X BASIC CARDS

2015 Crown Royale Retail Red

*VETS/99 (1-100): 2X TO 5X BASIC CARDS
*ROOK/199 (101-140): .8X TO 2X BASIC CARDS
*ROOK AU/99: .5X TO 1.2X BASIC AU/149-299
*ROOK AU/25: .8X TO 2X BASIC AU/149-299
*ROOK AU/99: .5X TO 1.2X BASIC AU/149-299

2015 Crown Royale Retail Red Holofoil

*VETS/25: 3X TO 8X BASIC CARDS

2015 Crown Royale Retail Team Name

*ROOKIES/99: 1X TO 2.5X BASIC CARDS
*ROOK AU/25: .8X TO 2X BASIC AU/149-299
*ROOK AU/25: .6X TO 1.5X BASIC AU/100
*ROOK AU/15: .6X TO 1.5X BASIC AU/49
*ROOK AU/20: 1X TO 2.5X BASIC AU/199

2015 Crown Royale Silver Holofoil

*VETS: 1.2X TO 3X BASIC CARDS
*ROOKIES: .6X TO 1.5X BASIC RC
*ROOK AU/75-99: .5X TO 1.2X BASIC AU
*ROOK AU/75-99: .4X TO 1X BASIC AU/100
*ROOK AU/75-99: .5X TO 1.2X BASIC AU

2015 Crown Royale All Pro Materials

*BRONZE/49: .6X TO 1.5X BASIC JSY/199-299
*BRONZE/49: .5X TO 1.2X BASIC JSY/99
*BRONZE/25: .5X TO 1.2X BASIC JSY/49
PBMAB Antoine Bethea/249 1.25 3.00
PBMAD Andy Dalton/275 1.50 4.00
PBMAT Aqib Talib/299 1.25 3.00
PBMDH Devin Hester/249 1.50 4.00
PBMDJ D'Qwell Jackson/299 1.25 3.00
PBMDS Darren Sproles/199 1.50 4.00
PBMES Emmanuel Sanders
PBMJF Justin Forsett/99 2.00 5.00
PBMJJ J.J. Watt/99 2.50 6.00
PBMJN Jordy Nelson/99 2.00 5.00
PBMJW Jason Witten/25 3.00 8.00
PBMLK Luke Kuechly/99 2.00 5.00
PBMLT Lawrence Timmons/299 1.25 3.00
PBMMB Martellus Bennett/299 1.25 3.00
PBMMD Marcell Dareus/299 1.25 3.00
PBMMI Mark Ingram/49 2.50 6.00
PBMNM Nick Mangold/299 1.25 3.00
PBMOBJ Odell Beckham Jr./49 3.00 8.00
PBMRC Randall Cobb
PBMSS Sam Shields/299 1.25 3.00
PBMTH Tamba Hali/299 1.25 3.00
PBMTR Tony Romo
PBMTY T.Y. Hilton/25 3.00 8.00
PBMVM Von Miller/199 1.50 4.00
PGMMS Matthew Stafford

2015 Crown Royale Crown Signatures

*GOLD: .5X TO 1.2X BASIC AU
6 Donte Moncrief/50 5.00 12.00
10 John Brown/50 5.00 12.00
14 Latavius Murray/75 3.00 8.00

2015 Crown Royale Crowning Achievements Jerseys

*GOLD/99: .5X TO 1.2X BASIC JSY/134-199
*GOLD/40: .6X TO 1.5X BASIC JSY/134-199
*GOLD/28: .4X TO 1X BASIC JSY/25
CAAB Antonio Brown/199 3.00 8.00
CAAG Ahman Green/45 4.00 10.00
CABG Bob Griese/175 3.00 8.00
CABJ Bo Jackson/199 4.00 10.00
CACC Cris Carter/199 3.00 8.00
CACJ Calvin Johnson/199 3.00 8.00
CAED Eric Dickerson/199 2.50 6.00
CAFB Fred Biletnikoff/99 4.00 10.00
CAJE John Elway/199 5.00 12.00
CAJM Joe Montana/199 8.00 20.00
CAJN Joe Namath/150 6.00 15.00
CAJT Joe Theismann/199 3.00 8.00
CAJW Jason Witten/199 2.50 6.00
CAKW Kurt Warner/199 2.50 6.00
CALC Larry Csonka/199 2.50 6.00
CALT Lawrence Taylor/199 3.00 8.00
CAMF Marshall Faulk/28 4.00 10.00
CAMR Matt Ryan/199 2.50 6.00
CAON Ozzie Newsome/199 2.50 6.00
CAPM Peyton Manning/199 6.00 15.00
CARW2 Randy White/199 2.50 6.00
CASL Steve Largent/199 3.00 8.00
CATA Troy Aikman/199 4.00 10.00
CATB1 Tom Brady/199 8.00 20.00
CATD Terrell Davis/50 4.00 10.00
CAWP Walter Payton/134 12.00 30.00

2015 Crown Royale Dual Rookie Silhouettes

*GOLD/25: .6X TO 1.5X BASIC JSY/99
DSAADJ D.Johnson/A.Abdullah 4.00 10.00
DSACKW A.Cooper/K.White 5.00 12.00
DSACTY Amari Cooper/T.J. Yeldon 5.00 12.00
DSBPBA B.Perriman/B.Allen 1.50 4.00
DSBPDS B.Petty/D.Smith 1.50 4.00
DSCCTG C.Conley/T.Gurley 6.00 15.00
DSDFDS D.Funchess/D.Smith 2.50 6.00
DSDFJS D.Funchess/J.Strong 2.50 6.00
DSDJPD P.Dorsett/D.Johnson 2.50 6.00
DSDPJA D.Parker/J.Ajayi 2.50 6.00
DSGGSM G.Grayson/S.Mannion 1.50 4.00
DSJCMJ J.Crowder/M.Jones 2.00 5.00
DSJHTC J.Hardy/T.Coleman 2.00 5.00
DSJLKW K.White/J.Langford 4.00 10.00
DSJWMM M.Mariota/J.Winston 8.00 20.00
DSLWNA L.Williams/N.Agholor 2.00 5.00
DSMGTG T.Gurley/M.Gordon 6.00 15.00
DSMMDGB D.Beckham/M.Mariota 6.00 15.00
DSMWDC D.Cobb/M.Williams 1.50 4.00
DSNABP B.Perriman/N.Agholor 2.00 5.00
DSPDDP P.Dorsett/D.Parker 2.50 6.00
DSRGJW J.Winston/R.Greene 6.00 15.00
DSSCVM S.Coates/V.Mayle 2.00 5.00
DSTLSD S.Diggs/T.Lockett 4.00 10.00
DSTYBH Brett Hundley/Ty Montgomery 1.50 4.00

2015 Crown Royale Heirs to the Throne Materials

*BRONZE/99: .6X TO 1.5X BASIC JSY/499
*SILVER/25: 1X TO 2.5X BASIC JSY/499
HTAA Ameer Abdullah 2.00 5.00
HTAC Amari Cooper 4.00 10.00
HTBP Breshad Perriman 1.25 3.00
HTDC David Cobb 1.25 3.00
HTDJ Duke Johnson 2.00 5.00
HTDP DeVante Parker 2.00 5.00
HTJW Jameis Winston 4.00 10.00
HTKW Kevin White 1.50 4.00
HTMG Melvin Gordon 3.00 8.00
HTMM Marcus Mariota 5.00 12.00
HTNA Nelson Agholor 1.50 4.00
HTPD Phillip Dorsett 1.25 3.00
HTTC Tevin Coleman 1.50 4.00
HTTG Todd Gurley 5.00 12.00
HTTL Tyler Lockett 2.00 5.00

2015 Crown Royale Heirs to the Throne Materials Combos

*GOLD/25: .6X TO 1.5X BASIC JSY/99
HTBCGG B.Cooks/G.Grayson 2.00 5.00
HTBOMG B.Olivor/M.Gordon 4.00 10.00
HTBPDS B.Petty/D.Smith 1.50 4.00
HTBSMM B.Sankey/M.Mariota 6.00 15.00
HTDCAC D.Carr/A.Cooper 5.00 12.00
HTDFTC D.Freeman/T.Coleman 2.00 5.00
HTJMDJ J.Manziel/D.Johnson 2.50 6.00
HTKWJL K.White/J.Langford 2.00 5.00
HTMEJW J.Winston/M.Evans 6.00 15.00
HTTGTM T.Gurley/T.Mason 6.00 15.00

2015 Crown Royale Heirs to the Throne Materials Trios

*GOLD/25: .6X TO 1.5X BASIC JSY/99
1 Amari Cooper 4.00 10.00
Derek Carr
Khalil Mack
2 Tavon Austin 4.00 10.00
Todd Gurley
Tre Mason
3 Jordan Reed 2.00 5.00
Matt Jones
Jamison Crowder
4 Jameis Winston 6.00 15.00
Austin Seferian-Jenkins
Mike Evans
5 Marcus Mariota 6.00 15.00
Bishop Sankey
Dorial Green-Beckham
6 Jeremy Langford 2.00 5.00
Alshon Jeffery
Kevin White
7 Jay Ajayi 2.50 6.00
DeVante Parker
Jarvis Landry
8 Brett Hundley 2.00 5.00
Ty Montgomery
Davante Adams
9 Breshad Perriman 2.00 5.00
Buck Allen
Maxx Williams
10 Duke Johnson 2.50 6.00
Isaiah Crowell
Johnny Manziel

2015 Crown Royale Jumbo Silhouettes

*GOLD/25: .6X TO 1.5X BASIC JSY/99
JSAA Ameer Abdullah 2.50 6.00
JSAC Amari Cooper 5.00 12.00
JSBP1 Breshad Perriman 1.50 4.00
JSBP2 Bryce Petty 1.50 4.00
JSCC Chris Conley 1.50 4.00
JSDC David Cobb 1.50 4.00
JSDF Devin Funchess 2.50 6.00
JSDGB Dorial Green-Beckham 1.50 4.00
JSDJ Duke Johnson 2.50 6.00
JSDP DeVante Parker 2.50 6.00
JSJW Jameis Winston 6.00 15.00
JSKW Kevin White 2.00 5.00
JSLW Leonard Williams 1.50 4.00
JSMG Melvin Gordon 4.00 10.00
JSMM Marcus Mariota 6.00 15.00
JSMW Maxx Williams 1.50 4.00
JSNA Nelson Agholor 2.00 5.00
JSPD Phillip Dorsett 1.50 4.00
JSRG Rashad Greene 1.50 4.00
JSSC Sammie Coates 2.00 5.00
JSSD Stefon Diggs 4.00 10.00
JSTC Tevin Coleman 2.00 5.00
JSTG Todd Gurley 6.00 15.00
JSTL Tyler Lockett 2.50 6.00
JSTY T.J. Yeldon 1.50 4.00

2015 Crown Royale Knights of the Round Table Materials

*BRONZE/49: .6X TO 1.5X BASIC JSY/145-299
*BRONZE/49: .5X TO 1.2X BASIC JSY/95-108
KRAJ A.J. Green/277 3.00 8.00
KRAJ2 Alshon Jeffery/299 2.50 6.00
KRAL Andrew Luck/99 5.00 12.00
KRAP Adrian Peterson
KRBF Brett Favre/299 6.00 15.00
KRBS Barry Sanders/95 12.00 30.00
KRCN Cam Newton/299 2.50 6.00
KRDB Drew Brees/53
KRDM Dan Marino/145 10.00 25.00
KREM Eli Manning/99 3.00 8.00
KRES Emmanuel Sanders/299 2.50 6.00
KRJE Julian Edelman/299 3.00 8.00
KRJF Joe Flacco/299 2.50 6.00
KRJJ Julio Jones/299 3.00 8.00
KRKW Kurt Warner/124
KRRT Ryan Tannehill/299 2.50 6.00
KRRW Russell Wilson
KRSY Steve Young/299 4.00 10.00
KRTR Tony Romo/299 2.50 6.00
KRWP Walter Payton/108 15.00 40.00

2015 Crown Royale Men at Arms

*RED: .5X TO 1.2X BASIC INSERTS
*GREEN: .6X TO 1.5X BASIC INSERTS
*BLUE: .8X TO 2X BASIC INSERT
MA1 Aaron Rodgers 2.00 5.00
MA2 Ben Roethlisberger 1.00 2.50
MA3 Tom Brady 2.50 6.00
MA4 Andrew Luck 1.25 3.00
MA5 Tony Romo .75 2.00
MA6 Joe Flacco .75 2.00
MA7 Philip Rivers 1.00 2.50
MA8 Peyton Manning 2.00 5.00
MA9 Russell Wilson 1.25 3.00
MA10 Matt Ryan .75 2.00
MA11 Carson Palmer .75 2.00
MA12 Drew Brees 1.00 2.50
MA13 Matthew Stafford .75 2.00
MA14 Ryan Tannehill .75 2.00
MA15 Colin Kaepernick .75 2.00
MA16 Andy Dalton .75 2.00
MA17 Cam Newton 1.00 2.50
MA18 Jay Cutler .60 1.50
MA19 Teddy Bridgewater .75 2.00
MA20 Alex Smith .75 2.00

2015 Crown Royale Pink Ribbons

*RED: .5X TO 1.2X BASIC INSERTS
*GREEN: .6X TO 1.5X BASIC INSERTS
*BLUE: .8X TO 2X BASIC INSERT
PR1 Russell Wilson 1.25 3.00
PR2 Dez Bryant 1.00 2.50
PR3 Victor Cruz .75 2.00
PR4 J.J. Watt 1.00 2.50
PR5 Eric Decker .60 1.50
PR6 Charles Woodson 1.00 2.50
PR7 Ben Roethlisberger 1.00 2.50
PR8 Tom Brady 2.50 6.00
PR9 Matthew Stafford .75 2.00
PR10 Colin Kaepernick .75 2.00
PR11 Larry Fitzgerald .75 2.00
PR12 Cam Newton 1.00 2.50
PR13 Arian Foster .75 2.00
PR14 Clay Matthews 1.00 2.50
PR15 Julio Jones 1.00 2.50
PR16 Demaryius Thomas .75 2.00
PR17 Mario Williams .60 1.50
PR18 Drew Brees 1.00 2.50
PR19 Andrew Luck 1.25 3.00
PR20 Alshon Jeffery .75 2.00

2015 Crown Royale Pro Bowl

*RED: .5X TO 1.2X BASIC INSERTS
*GREEN: .6X TO 1.5X BASIC INSERTS
*BLUE: .8X TO 2X BASIC INSERTS
PB1 Drew Brees 1.00 2.50
PB2 Andrew Luck 1.25 3.00
PB3 Patrick Peterson .60 1.50
PB4 Jamaal Charles .75 2.00
PB5 Justin Forsett .75 2.00
PB6 T.Y. Hilton .75 2.00
PB7 Antonio Brown 1.00 2.50
PB8 A.J. Green 1.00 2.50
PB9 Jordy Nelson .75 2.00
PB10 J.J. Watt 1.00 2.50
PB11 Matt Ryan .75 2.00
PB12 Tony Romo .75 2.00
PB13 Matthew Stafford .75 2.00
PB14 C.J. Anderson .75 2.00
PB15 DeMarco Murray .75 2.00
PB16 Emmanuel Sanders .75 2.00
PB17 Odell Beckham Jr. 1.00 2.50
PB18 Golden Tate .60 1.50
PB19 Jason Witten .75 2.00
PB20 Joe Haden .60 1.50

2015 Crown Royale Regal Rookies

*RED: .5X TO 1.2X BASIC INSERTS
*GREEN: .6X TO 1.5X BASIC INSERTS
*BLUE: .8X TO 2X BASIC INSERTS
RR1 Amari Cooper 1.25 3.00
RR2 Ameer Abdullah .60 1.50
RR3 Breshad Perriman .40 1.00
RR4 Bryce Petty .40 1.00
RR5 Chris Conley .40 1.00
RR6 David Cobb .40 1.00
RR7 DeVante Parker .60 1.50
RR8 Devin Funchess .60 1.50
RR9 Duke Johnson .60 1.50
RR10 Garrett Grayson .40 1.00
RR11 Jameis Winston 1.00 2.50
RR12 Kevin White .50 1.25
RR13 Marcus Mariota 1.50 4.00
RR14 Melvin Gordon 1.00 2.50
RR15 Nelson Agholor .50 1.25
RR16 Phillip Dorsett .40 1.00
RR17 Sammie Coates .50 1.25
RR18 T.J. Yeldon .40 1.00
RR19 Tevin Coleman .50 1.25
RR20 Tyler Lockett .60 1.50

2015 Crown Royale Rookie Royalty Materials

*BRONZE/199: .5X TO 1.2X BASIC JSY/499
*SILVER/25: .8X TO 2X BASIC JSY/499
RRMAA Ameer Abdullah 2.00 5.00
RRMAC Amari Cooper 4.00 10.00
RRMBA Buck Allen 1.50 4.00
RRMBH Brett Hundley 1.25 3.00
RRMBP1 Breshad Perriman 1.25 3.00
RRMBP2 Bryce Petty 1.25 3.00
RRMCC Chris Conley 1.25 3.00
RRMDC David Cobb 1.25 3.00
RRMDF Devin Funchess 2.00 5.00
RRMDGB Dorial Green-Beckham 1.25 3.00
RRMDJ David Johnson 3.00 8.00
RRMDP DeVante Parker 2.00 5.00
RRMDS Devin Smith 1.25 3.00
RRMDU Duke Johnson 2.00 5.00
RRMGG Garrett Grayson 1.25 3.00
RRMJA Jay Ajayi 2.00 5.00
RRMJC Jamison Crowder 1.50 4.00
RRMJH Justin Hardy 1.25 3.00
RRMJL Jeremy Langford 1.25 3.00
RRMJS Jaelen Strong 1.50 4.00
RRMJW Jameis Winston 5.00 12.00
RRMKA Karlos Williams 1.25 3.00
RRMKW Kevin White 1.50 4.00
RRMLW Leonard Williams 1.25 3.00
RRMMD Mike Davis 1.25 3.00
RRMMG Melvin Gordon 3.00 8.00
RRMMJ Matt Jones 1.25 3.00
RRMMM Marcus Mariota 5.00 12.00
RRMMW Maxx Williams 1.25 3.00
RRMNA Nelson Agholor 1.50 4.00
RRMPD Phillip Dorsett 1.25 3.00
RRMRG Rashad Greene 1.25 3.00
RRMSC Sammie Coates 1.50 4.00
RRMSD Stefon Diggs 3.00 8.00
RRMSM Sean Mannion 1.25 3.00
RRMTC Tevin Coleman 1.50 4.00
RRMTG Todd Gurley 5.00 12.00
RRMTL Tyler Lockett 2.00 5.00
RRMTM Ty Montgomery 1.25 3.00
RRMTY T.J. Yeldon 1.25 3.00

2015 Crown Royale Rookie Royalty Signatures

RRSAA Ameer Abdullah/150 5.00 12.00
RRSBB Blake Bell/199 5.00 12.00
RRSBD Bud Dupree/199 4.00 10.00
RRSBJ Byron Jones/199 5.00 12.00
RRSBP Bryce Petty/99 4.00 10.00
RRSCAP Cameron Artis-Payne/199 3.00 8.00
RRSCC Chris Conley/199 3.00 8.00
RRSCW Clive Walford/199 3.00 8.00
RRSDA Danny Shelton/199 3.00 8.00
RRSDC David Cobb/199 3.00 8.00
RRSDF Devin Funchess/150 5.00 12.00
RRSDGB Dorial Green-Beckham/140
RRSDJ David Johnson/199 20.00 40.00
RRSDR Damarious Randall/199 4.00 10.00
RRSDS Devin Smith/99 4.00 10.00
RRSER Eric Rowe/25 6.00 15.00
RRSJH Justin Hardy/199 3.00 8.00
RRSJN J.J. Nelson/75
RRSJR Josh Robinson/199 3.00 8.00
RRSJS Jaelen Strong/125 4.00 10.00
RRSJW Jameis Winston/99 10.00 25.00
DDSKA Kwon Alexander/199 4.00 10.00
RRSKB Kenny Bell/199 5.00 12.00
RRSKJ Kevin Johnson/199 3.00 8.00
RRSMD Mike Davis/199 3.00 8.00
RRSMG Melvin Gordon/110 8.00 20.00
RRSMM Marcus Mariota/99 15.00 40.00
RRSMP Marcus Peters/199 5.00 12.00
RRSNA Nelson Agholor/99
RRSNO Nick O'Leary/99 4.00 10.00
RRSSC Sammie Coates/199 4.00 10.00
RRSSM Sean Mannion/199 3.00 8.00
RRSST Shaq Thompson/199 4.00 10.00
RRSTK Tyler Kroft/199 4.00 10.00
RRSTL Tyler Lockett/199 5.00 12.00
RRSTM Ty Montgomery/199 3.00 8.00
RRSTO Tony Lippett/199 3.00 8.00
RRSTW Trae Waynes/199 3.00 8.00
RRSVB Vic Beasley Jr./199 4.00 10.00

2015 Crown Royale Rookie Royalty Signatures Purple

*PURPLE/25: .8X TO 2X BASIC AU/110-199
*PURPLE/25: .6X TO 1.5X BASIC AU/75-99
*PURPLE/15: .5X TO 1.2X BASIC AU/25

2015 Crown Royale Rookie Royalty Signatures Retail Bronze

*BRONZE/99: .5X TO 1.2X BASIC AU/110-199
*BRONZE/95: .4X TO 1X BASIC AU/75-99
*BRONZE/49: .6X TO 1.5X BASIC AU/110-199
*BRONZE/25: .8X TO 2X BASIC AU/110-199
*BRONZE/25: .4X TO 1X BASIC AU/25
*BRONZE/15: .8X TO 2X BASIC AU/75-99

2015 Crown Royale Rookie Royalty Signatures Retail Red

*RETAIL RED/25: .8X TO 2X BASIC AU/110-199
*RETAIL RED/15: .8X TO 2X BASIC AU/75-99

2015 Crown Royale Rookie Silhouettes

*GOLD/49: .6X TO 1.5X BASIC JSY/299
*PURPLE/25: .8X TO 2X BASIC JSY/299
201 Amari Cooper 5.00 12.00
202 Ameer Abdullah 2.50 6.00
203 Breshad Perriman 1.50 4.00
204 Brett Hundley 1.50 4.00
205 Bryce Petty 1.50 4.00
206 Buck Allen 2.00 5.00
207 Chris Conley 1.50 4.00
208 David Cobb 1.50 4.00
209 David Johnson 4.00 10.00
210 DeVante Parker 2.50 6.00
211 Devin Funchess 2.50 6.00
212 Devin Smith 1.50 4.00
213 Dorial Green-Beckham 1.50 4.00
214 Duke Johnson 2.50 6.00

215 Garrett Grayson 1.50 4.00
216 Jaelen Strong 2.00 5.00
217 Jameis Winston 6.00 15.00
218 Jamison Crowder 2.00 5.00
219 Jay Ajayi 2.50 6.00
220 Jeremy Langford 1.50 4.00
221 Justin Hardy 1.50 4.00
222 Karlos Williams 1.50 4.00
223 Kevin White 2.00 5.00
224 Leonard Williams 1.50 4.00
225 Marcus Mariota 6.00 15.00
226 Matt Jones 1.50 4.00
227 Maxx Williams 1.50 4.00
228 Melvin Gordon 4.00 10.00
229 Mike Davis 1.50 4.00
230 Nelson Agholor 2.00 5.00
231 Phillip Dorsett 1.50 4.00
232 Rashad Greene 1.50 4.00
233 Sammie Coates 2.00 5.00
234 Sean Mannion 1.50 4.00
235 Stefon Diggs 4.00 10.00
236 T.J. Yeldon 1.50 4.00
237 Tevin Coleman 2.00 5.00
238 Todd Gurley 6.00 15.00
239 Ty Montgomery 1.50 4.00
240 Tyler Lockett 2.50 6.00
241 Vince Mayle 2.00 5.00

2015 Crown Royale Sovereign Signatures

*BRONZE/25: .5X TO 1.2X BASIC AU/50
*BRONZE/15: .6X TO 1.5X BASIC AU/50
*GOLD/25: .5X TO 1.2X BASIC AU/50
5 Fred Biletnikoff 6.00 15.00
8 Jim Kiick 4.00 10.00

2015 Crown Royale The King's Court

*GREEN: .6X TO 1.5X BASIC INSERTS
*RED: .5X TO 1.2X BASIC INSERTS
*BLUE: .75X TO 2X BASIC INSERTS
KC1 Rdgrs/Lcy/Nlsn 2.00 5.00
KC2 Sndrs/Mnng/Thms 2.00 5.00
KC3 Brwn/Rthlsbrgr/Bll 1.00 2.50
KC4 Brynt/Wttn/Rmo 1.00 2.50
KC5 Lck/Jhnsn/Hltn 1.25 3.00
KC6 Jnes/Ryn/Whte 1.00 2.50
KC7 Ftzgrld/Ellngtn/Plmr .75 2.00
KC8 Flcco/Frstt/Smth .75 2.00
KC9 Nwtn/Fnchss/Olsn 1.00 2.50
KC10 Jffry/Frte/Ctlr .75 2.00
KC11 Grn/Dltn/Hll 1.00 2.50
KC12 Abdllh/Jhnsn/Sttfrd 1.00 2.50
KC13 Smth/Chrls/Mcln .75 2.00
KC14 Mllr/Tnnhll/Prkr 1.00 2.50
KC15 Ingrm/Clstn/Brs 1.00 2.50
KC16 Mnng/Bckhm/Crz 1.00 2.50
KC17 Rvrs/Gtes/Grdn 1.50 4.00
KC18 Lnch/Wlsn/Lcktt 1.25 3.00
KC19 Snky/Wrght/Mrta 2.50 6.00
KC20 Wnstn/Jnkns/Evns 2.50 6.00

2016 Crown Royale

1 LeSean McCoy .60 1.50
2 Darrelle Revis .40 1.00
3 A.J. Green .60 1.50
4 Antonio Gates .40 1.00
5 Ameer Abdullah .40 1.00
6 Jameis Winston .60 1.50
7 T.Y. Hilton .50 1.25
8 Jeremy Maclin .40 1.00
9 Carson Palmer .50 1.25
10 Rob Gronkowski .60 1.50
11 Sammy Watkins .60 1.50
12 Amari Cooper .60 1.50
13 Robert Griffin III .40 1.00
14 Philip Rivers .60 1.50
15 Matthew Stafford .50 1.25
16 Doug Martin .50 1.25
17 Andrew Luck .75 2.00
18 Todd Gurley II .60 1.50
19 Larry Fitzgerald .50 1.25
20 Julian Edelman .60 1.50
21 Cam Newton .60 1.50
22 Derek Carr .60 1.50
23 Gary Barnidge .40 1.00
24 Blaine Gabbert .40 1.00
25 Aaron Rodgers 1.25 3.00
26 Mike Evans .50 1.25
27 Frank Gore .50 1.25
28 Kenny Britt .40 1.00
29 Matt Ryan .50 1.25
30 Drew Brees .60 1.50
31 Greg Olsen .50 1.25
32 Jordan Matthews .50 1.25
33 Jason Witten .50 1.25
34 Carlos Hyde .40 1.00
35 Jordy Nelson .50 1.25
36 Marcus Mariota .60 1.50
37 Blake Bortles .40 1.00
38 Ryan Tannehill .50 1.25
39 Devonta Freeman .50 1.25
40 Brandin Cooks .50 1.25
41 Jay Cutler .40 1.00
42 Ryan Mathews .50 1.25
43 Tony Romo .50 1.25
44 Darren Sproles .50 1.25
45 Randall Cobb .50 1.25
46 DeMarco Murray .50 1.25
47 Allen Hurns .40 1.00
48 Jarvis Landry .50 1.25
49 Julio Jones .60 1.50
50 Odell Beckham Jr. .60 1.50
51 Jeremy Langford .50 1.25
52 Antonio Brown .60 1.50
53 Dez Bryant .60 1.50
54 Russell Wilson .75 2.00
55 DeAndre Hopkins .50 1.25
56 Jordan Reed .40 1.00
57 Allen Robinson .50 1.25
58 Teddy Bridgewater .50 1.25
59 Joe Flacco .50 1.25
60 Eli Manning .50 1.25
61 Alshon Jeffery .50 1.25
62 Ben Roethlisberger .60 1.50
63 Demaryius Thomas .50 1.25
64 Thomas Rawls .40 1.00
65 J.J. Watt .60 1.50
66 Pierre Garcon .50 1.25
67 Alex Smith .50 1.25
68 Adrian Peterson .60 1.50
69 Justin Forsett .50 1.25
70 Matt Forte .40 1.00
71 Andy Dalton .50 1.25
72 Le'Veon Bell .50 1.25
73 Von Miller .50 1.25
74 Richard Sherman .60 1.50
75 Lamar Miller .40 1.00
76 Kirk Cousins .60 1.50
77 Jamaal Charles .50 1.25
78 Tom Brady 1.50 4.00
79 Tyrod Taylor .50 1.25
80 Brandon Marshall .40 1.00
81 Tyler Boyd RC .75 2.00
82 Josh Doctson RC .75 2.00
83 Moritz Bohringer RC .60 1.50
84 Paxton Lynch RC .60 1.50
85 Connor Cook RC .75 2.00
86 Jared Goff RC 4.00 10.00
87 Michael Thomas RC 1.25 3.00
88 Joey Bosa RC 1.25 3.00
89 C.J. Prosise RC .60 1.50
90 Corey Coleman RC 1.00 2.50
91 Braxton Miller RC .60 1.50
92 Laquon Treadwell RC .75 2.00
93 Dak Prescott RC 3.00 8.00
94 Derrick Henry RC 1.50 4.00
95 Cardale Jones RC .60 1.50
96 Carson Wentz RC 6.00 15.00
97 Christian Hackenberg RC .60 1.50
98 Ezekiel Elliott RC 3.00 8.00
99 Paul Perkins RC .60 1.50
100 Will Fuller RC 1.00 2.50

2016 Crown Royale Bronze

*VETS/249: 1X TO 2.5X BASIC CARDS
*ROOKIES/249: .6X TO 1.5X BASIC CARDS

2016 Crown Royale Holo Gold

*VETS/149: 1.2X TO 3X BASIC CARDS
*ROOKIES/149: .8X TO 2X BASIC CARDS

2016 Crown Royale Holo Light Blue

*VETS/99: 1.2X TO 3X BASIC CARDS
*ROOKIES/99: .8X TO 2X BASIC CARDS

2016 Crown Royale Holo Platinum

*VETS/49: 1.5X TO 4X BASIC CARDS
*ROOKIES/49: 1X TO 2.5X BASIC CARDS
93 Dak Prescott 25.00 50.00
98 Ezekiel Elliott 25.00 50.00

2016 Crown Royale Pink

*VETS/199: 1X TO 2.5X BASIC CARDS
*ROOKIES/199: .6X TO 1.5X BASIC CARDS

2016 Crown Royale Jumbo Rookie Silhouette Jerseys

*PINK/250: .5X TO 1.2X BASIC JSY
*PLATINUM/50: .6X TO 1.5X BASIC JSY
1 Demarcus Robinson 1.50 4.00
2 Michael Thomas 3.00 8.00
3 Trevor Davis 1.50 4.00
4 Tyler Boyd 2.00 5.00
5 Alex Collins 2.00 5.00
6 Jared Goff 5.00 12.00
7 Kenneth Dixon 1.50 4.00
8 Corey Coleman 2.50 6.00
9 Leonte Carroo 1.50 4.00
10 Paxton Lynch 1.50 4.00
11 Jonathan Williams 2.00 5.00
12 Tyler Ervin 1.50 4.00
13 Christian Hackenberg 1.50 4.00
14 Braxton Miller 1.50 4.00
15 Jordan Howard 3.00 8.00
16 Carson Wentz 6.00 15.00
17 DeAndre Washington 1.50 4.00
18 Will Fuller 2.50 6.00
19 Chris Moore 2.00 5.00
20 Derrick Henry 4.00 10.00
21 Keenan Reynolds 2.00 5.00
22 C.J. Prosise 1.50 4.00
23 Wendell Smallwood 1.50 4.00
24 Cody Kessler 1.50 4.00
25 Pharoh Cooper 1.50 4.00
26 Joey Bosa 3.00 8.00
27 Devontae Booker 2.00 5.00
28 Josh Doctson 2.00 5.00
29 Kenyan Drake 2.50 6.00
30 Connor Cook 2.00 5.00
31 Kevin Hogan 2.00 5.00
32 Paul Perkins 1.50 4.00
33 Moritz Bohringer 1.50 4.00
34 Sterling Shepard 2.00 5.00
35 Dak Prescott 8.00 20.00
36 Ezekiel Elliott 8.00 20.00
37 Hunter Henry 2.00 5.00
38 Laquon Treadwell 2.00 5.00
39 Ricardo Louis 1.50 4.00
40 Cardale Jones 1.50 4.00

2016 Crown Royale Rookie Autographs

1 Jared Goff 50.00 100.00
2 Carson Wentz 50.00 100.00
3 Derrick Henry
4 Paxton Lynch 2.50 6.00
5 Ezekiel Elliott 50.00 100.00
6 Connor Cook 3.00 8.00
7 Laquon Treadwell 3.00 8.00
8 Corey Coleman 4.00 10.00
9 Cardale Jones 2.50 6.00
10 Michael Thomas 5.00 12.00
11 Will Fuller 4.00 10.00
12 Josh Doctson 3.00 8.00
13 Christian Hackenberg 2.50 6.00
14 C.J. Prosise 2.50 6.00
15 Tyler Boyd 3.00 8.00
16 Paul Perkins 2.50 6.00
17 Joey Bosa 5.00 12.00
18 Braxton Miller 2.50 6.00
19 Cody Kessler 2.50 6.00
20 Scooby Wright III 2.50 6.00
21 Maurice Canady 2.50 6.00
22 Jalen Mills 3.00 8.00
23 Adolphus Washington 2.50 6.00
24 Kenny Clark 2.50 6.00
25 Emmanuel Ogbah 3.00 8.00
26 Chris Jones 2.50 6.00
27 Su'a Cravens 2.50 6.00
28 Sean Davis 2.50 6.00
29 Adam Gotsis 2.50 6.00
30 Carl Nassib 2.50 6.00
32 Bronson Kaufusi 2.50 6.00
33 Cody Core 2.50 6.00
34 Daryl Worley 2.50 6.00
35 Austin Hooper 2.50 6.00
36 Andrew Billings 3.00 8.00
37 Deion Jones 2.50 6.00
39 Nick Vannett 2.50 6.00
40 Kyler Fackrell 3.00 8.00
41 Joshua Perry 2.50 6.00
42 Tyler Higbee 2.50 6.00
44 Blake Martinez 3.00 8.00
45 Tajae Sharpe 3.00 8.00
47 Derek Watt 4.00 10.00
49 Charone Peake 2.50 6.00
50 Keith Marshall 2.50 6.00
51 Kei'Varae Russell 2.50 6.00
52 Cyrus Jones 2.50 6.00
54 Miles Killebrew 2.50 6.00
55 D.J. White 2.50 6.00
56 Kendall Fuller 3.00 8.00
57 Kevon Seymour 2.50 6.00
58 Demarcus Ayers 2.50 6.00

2016 Crown Royale Rookie Autographs Pink

*PINK/200-250: .5X TO 1.2X BASIC AU
*PINK/50: .8X TO 2X BASIC AU

2016 Crown Royale Rookie Autographs Platinum

*PLATINUM/50: .8X TO 2X BASIC AU

2017 Crown Royale

1 Joe Flacco .50 1.25
2 Terrell Suggs .40 1.00
3 A.J. Green .60 1.50
4 Andy Dalton .50 1.25
5 Jeremy Hill .40 1.00
6 Isaiah Crowell .40 1.00
7 Corey Coleman .40 1.00
8 Ben Roethlisberger .60 1.50
9 Le'Veon Bell .50 1.25
10 Antonio Brown .60 1.50
11 Mike Glennon .50 1.25
12 Jordan Howard .60 1.50
13 Leonard Floyd .40 1.00
14 Matthew Stafford .50 1.25
15 Golden Tate III .40 1.00
16 Aaron Rodgers 1.25 3.00
17 Jordy Nelson .50 1.25
18 Clay Matthews .50 1.25
19 Sam Bradford .40 1.00
20 Kyle Rudolph .40 1.00
21 J.J. Watt .60 1.50
22 DeAndre Hopkins .50 1.25
23 Lamar Miller .40 1.00
24 Andrew Luck .75 2.00
25 Frank Gore .50 1.25
26 T.Y. Hilton .50 1.25
27 Blake Bortles .40 1.00
28 Allen Robinson .50 1.25
29 T.J. Yeldon .40 1.00
30 Marcus Mariota .60 1.50
31 Delanie Walker .40 1.00
32 DeMarco Murray .50 1.25
33 Tyrod Taylor .50 1.25
34 LeSean McCoy .60 1.50
35 Sammy Watkins .60 1.50
36 Jay Cutler .40 1.00
37 Jarvis Landry .50 1.25
38 Jay Ajayi .50 1.25
39 Tom Brady 1.50 4.00
40 Rob Gronkowski .60 1.50
41 James White .50 1.25
42 Julian Edelman .60 1.50
43 Eric Decker .40 1.00
44 Matt Forte .40 1.00
45 Josh McCown .40 1.00
46 Von Miller .50 1.25
47 Demaryius Thomas .50 1.25
48 Devontae Booker .40 1.00
49 Alex Smith .50 1.25
50 Tyreek Hill .60 1.50
51 Travis Kelce .60 1.50
52 Eric Berry .50 1.25
53 Philip Rivers .60 1.50
54 Joey Bosa .60 1.50
55 Melvin Gordon .50 1.25
56 Antonio Gates .40 1.00
57 Derek Carr .60 1.50
58 Khalil Mack .60 1.50
59 Amari Cooper .60 1.50
60 Marshawn Lynch .50 1.25
61 Dak Prescott .60 1.50
62 Ezekiel Elliott .75 2.00
63 Jason Witten .50 1.25
64 Dez Bryant .60 1.50
65 Eli Manning .50 1.25
66 Odell Beckham Jr. .60 1.50
67 Brandon Marshall .40 1.00
68 Carson Wentz .75 2.00
69 Jordan Matthews .40 1.00
70 Alshon Jeffery .50 1.25
71 Kirk Cousins .60 1.50
72 Josh Norman .40 1.00
73 David Johnson .60 1.50
74 Larry Fitzgerald .50 1.25
75 Aaron Donald .60 1.50
76 Todd Gurley II .60 1.50
77 Carlos Hyde .40 1.00
78 Russell Wilson .75 2.00
79 Richard Sherman .60 1.50
80 Tyler Lockett .50 1.25
81 Myles Garrett RC 2.00 5.00
82 Mitchell Trubisky RC 3.00 8.00
83 Deshaun Watson RC 4.00 10.00
84 Patrick Mahomes II RC 12.00 30.00
85 Corey Davis RC 1.00 2.50
86 Mike Williams RC 1.00 2.50
87 Leonard Fournette RC 2.00 5.00
88 Christian McCaffrey RC 1.50 4.00
89 Dalvin Cook RC 1.50 4.00
90 Jamal Adams RC .60 1.50
91 John Ross III RC .75 2.00
92 O.J. Howard RC .75 2.00
93 Jabrill Peppers RC 1.00 2.50
94 Taco Charlton RC .60 1.50
95 David Njoku RC .75 2.00
96 T.J. Watt RC 2.00 5.00
97 Solomon Thomas RC .60 1.50
98 Marshon Lattimore RC .75 2.00
99 Haason Reddick RC .60 1.50
100 Derek Barnett RC .75 2.00

2017 Crown Royale Bronze

*VETS/299: 1X TO 2.5X BASIC CARDS
*ROOKIES/299: .6X TO 1.5X BASIC CARDS

2017 Crown Royale Light Blue

*VETS/99: 1.2X TO 3X BASIC CARDS
*ROOKIES/99: .8X TO 2X BASIC CARDS

2017 Crown Royale Pink

*VETS/249: 1X TO 2.5X BASIC CARDS
*ROOKIES/249: .6X TO 1.5X BASIC CARDS

2017 Crown Royale Platinum

*VETS/49: 1.5X TO 4X BASIC CARDS
*ROOKIES/49: 1X TO 2.5X BASIC CARDS

2017 Crown Royale Jumbo Rookie Silhouette Jerseys

*PINK/250: .5X TO 1.2X BASIC JSY
*PLATINUM/50: .8X TO 2X BASIC JSY
1 Nathan Peterman 2.00 5.00
2 Zay Jones 2.00 5.00
3 Christian McCaffrey 3.00 8.00
4 Curtis Samuel 2.00 5.00
5 Mitchell Trubisky 5.00 12.00
6 Joe Mixon 3.00 8.00
7 John Ross III 2.00 5.00
8 DeShone Kizer 1.50 4.00
9 Carlos Henderson 1.50 4.00
10 Kenny Golladay 2.50 6.00
11 Jamaal Williams 1.50 4.00
12 Deshaun Watson 6.00 15.00
13 D'Onta Foreman 2.00 5.00
14 Marlon Mack 2.50 6.00
15 Dede Westbrook 1.50 4.00
16 Leonard Fournette 5.00 12.00
17 Kareem Hunt 3.00 8.00
18 Patrick Mahomes II 20.00 50.00
19 Mike Williams 2.50 6.00
20 Cooper Kupp 2.50 6.00
21 Josh Reynolds 1.50 4.00
22 Dalvin Cook 3.00 8.00
23 Alvin Kamara 6.00 15.00
24 Davis Webb 1.50 4.00
25 Evan Engram 2.00 5.00
26 Wayne Gallman 2.00 5.00
27 ArDarius Stewart 1.50 4.00
28 Mack Hollins 1.50 4.00
29 James Conner 3.00 8.00
30 JuJu Smith-Schuster 3.00 8.00
31 R. Joshua Dobbs 2.00 5.00
32 C.J. Beathard 1.50 4.00
33 Joe Williams 1.50 4.00
34 Amara Darboh 1.50 4.00
35 Chris Godwin 2.00 5.00
36 Jeremy McNichols 1.50 4.00
37 O.J. Howard 2.00 5.00
38 Corey Davis 2.50 6.00
39 Taywan Taylor 1.50 4.00
40 Samaje Perine 1.50 4.00

1986 DairyPak Cartons

This set of 24 numbered cards was issued as the side panel on half-gallon cartons of various brands of milk all over the country. Depending on the sponsoring milk company, the cards can be found in a large number of printing colors including: black, blue/red, brown, green, olive green, lime green, dark blue, lavender, light blue, aqua, orange, pink, purple, red, salmon or yellow. The actual pictures of the players on the cards are in black and white. Each player's card also contains a facsimile autograph above or to the side of his head. The prices listed below are for cards cut from the carton. Complete carton prices are 50 percent greater than the prices listed below. The cards, when cut on the dotted line, measure approximately 3 1/4" by 4 7/16". The set was only licensed by the NFL Players Association and hence team logos are not shown, i.e., the players are pictured without helmets. The bottom of the panel details an offer to receive a 24" by 32" poster (featuring the card fronts of the 24 NFL Superstars featured in this set) for 1.95 and two proofs-of-purchase. The Lofton card was supposedly withdrawn at some time during the promotion; however there does not appear to be any drastic shortage of Lofton cards needed for complete sets.
COMPLETE SET (24) 40.00 80.00
1 Joe Montana 8.00 20.00
2 Marcus Allen 1.25 3.00
3 Art Monk 1.00 2.50
4 Mike Quick .75 2.00
5 John Elway 6.00 15.00
6 Eric Hipple .60 1.50
7 Louis Lipps .75 2.00
8 Dan Fouts 1.25 3.00
9 Phil Simms 1.00 2.50
10 Mike Rozier .60 1.50
11 Greg Bell .60 1.50
12 Ottis Anderson 1.00 2.50
13 Dave Krieg .75 2.00
14 Anthony Carter .75 2.00
15 Freeman McNeil .75 2.00
16 Doug Cosbie .60 1.50
17 James Lofton 1.25 3.00
18 Dan Marino 6.00 15.00
19 James Wilder .60 1.50
20 Cris Collinsworth UER .75 2.00
21 Eric Dickerson 1.25 3.00
22 Walter Payton 8.00 20.00
23 Ozzie Newsome 1.00 2.50
24 Chris Hinton .60 1.50

2007 Dallas Desperados AFL Donruss

This set was produced by Donruss and issued at a regular season Desperados game in 2007.
COMPLETE SET (15) 5.00 10.00
ANNOUNCED PRINT RUN 5000 SETS
1 Clint Dolezel .50 1.25
2 Will Pettis .40 1.00
3 Colston Weatherington .30 .75
4 Devin Wyman .30 .75
5 Duke Pettijohn .30 .75
6 Marcus Nash .50 1.25
7 Jeff Chase .30 .75
8 Terrance Dotsy .30 .75
9 Josh White .30 .75
10 Bobby Keyes .30 .75
11 Jermaine Jones .30 .75
12 Rickie Simpkins .30 .75
13 Will McClay CO .30 .75
PL1 Clint Dolezel .50 1.25
PL2 Will Pettis .40 1.00

2008 Dallas Desperados AFL Donruss

This set was produced by Donruss, sponsored by Pepsi, and issued at a regular season Desperados game in 2008.
D1 Clint Dolezel .50 1.25
D2 Colston Weatherington .30 .75
D3 Jermaine Jones .30 .75
D4 Rickie Simpkins .30 .75
D5 Bobby Keyes .30 .75
D6 Josh White .30 .75
D7 Andrae Thurman .30 .75
D8 Duke Pettijohn .30 .75
D9 Marcus Nash .50 1.25
D10 Jeff Chase .30 .75
D11 Terrance Dotsy .30 .75
D12 Will Pettis .40 1.00
D16 Anthony Armctong 1.00 2.50

1999 Danbury Mint 22K Gold

The Danbury Mint issued these 22K Gold cards in 1999. Each card was produced with an all-gold foil cardfront and back and carried an initial retail sales price of $9.99. An album complete with matching plastic pages was issued for the set as well.
1 Troy Aikman 5.00 12.00
2 Morten Andersen 2.50 6.00
3 Jamal Anderson 3.00 8.00
4 Jessie Armstead 3.00 8.00
5 Drew Bledsoe 4.00 10.00
6 Tony Boselli 2.50 6.00
7 Tim Brown 4.00 10.00
8 Mark Brunell 3.00 8.00
9 Cris Carter 4.00 10.00
10 Ben Coates 2.50 6.00
11 Randall Cunningham 3.00 8.00
12 Terrell Davis 4.00 10.00
13 Dermontti Dawson 2.50 6.00
14 Corey Dillon 4.00 10.00
15 John Elway 7.50 20.00
16 Marshall Faulk 4.00 10.00
17 Brett Favre 7.50 20.00
18 Eddie George 3.00 8.00
19 Darrell Green 3.00 8.00
20 Michael Irvin 4.00 10.00
21 Cortez Kennedy 2.50 6.00
22 Levon Kirkland 2.50 6.00
23 Peyton Manning 6.00 15.00
24 Dan Marino 7.50 20.00
25 Curtis Martin 4.00 10.00
26 Bruce Matthews 2.50 6.00
27 Herman Moore 3.00 8.00
28 Randy Moss 5.00 12.00
29 Hardy Nickerson 2.50 6.00
30 Jonathan Ogden 2.50 6.00
31 Carl Pickens 3.00 8.00
32 Jake Plummer 3.00 8.00
33 Jerry Rice 6.00 15.00
34 Willie Roaf 2.50 6.00
35 Barry Sanders 7.50 20.00
36 Warren Sapp 3.00 8.00
37 Junior Seau 4.00 10.00
38 Bruce Smith 4.00 10.00
39 Emmitt Smith 6.00 15.00
40 Michael Strahan 3.00 8.00
41 Dana Stubblefield 2.50 6.00
42 Dave Szott 2.50 6.00
43 Bobby Taylor 2.50 6.00
44 Derrick Thomas 4.00 10.00
45 Zach Thomas 4.00 10.00
46 Wesley Walls 2.50 6.00
47 Reggie White 4.00 10.00
48 Aeneas Williams 2.50 6.00
49 Rod Woodson 3.00 8.00
50 Steve Young 5.00 12.00

1999-01 Danbury Mint 22K Gold Legends

The Danbury Mint issued these 22K Gold cards at the rate of 2-per month from 1999-2001. Each card was produced with an all-gold foil cardfront and back and carried an initial retail sales price of $9.99. The cards are sealed individually in clear plastic holders. There is no year designations on the cards and the copyright line simply reads "ISM-MBI." Complete sets could have been purchased for $599.99 and an album complete with matching plastic sheets was issued for the set as well.
COMPLETE SET (50) 150.00 400.00
1 Jerry Kramer 3.00 8.00
2 Matt Snell 3.00 8.00
3 Franco Harris 6.00 15.00
4 Jim Hart 2.50 6.00
5 Paul Krause 2.50 6.00
6 Otto Graham 4.00 10.00
7 Bert Jones 2.50 6.00
8 Joe Jacoby 2.50 6.00
9 Billy Kilmer 2.50 6.00
10 Ben Davidson 2.50 6.00
11 Bart Starr 7.50 20.00
12 Garo Yepremian 2.50 6.00
13 Floyd Little 2.50 6.00
14 Andre Tippett 2.50 6.00
15 Gale Sayers 6.00 15.00
16 Ken Riley 2.50 6.00
17 Bob Lilly 4.00 10.00
18 Lee Roy Jordan 3.00 8.00
19 Chuck Bednarik 4.00 10.00
20 Steve Bartkowski 3.00 8.00
21 Dan Hampton 3.00 8.00
22 Paul Hornung 5.00 12.00
23 Kyle Rote 2.50 6.00
24 Carl Eller 3.00 8.00
25 Joe Ferguson 2.50 6.00
26 Daryle Lamonica 3.00 8.00
27 James Lofton 3.00 8.00
28 Y.A. Tittle 4.00 10.00
29 Bobby Bell 3.00 8.00
30 Len Dawson 5.00 12.00
31 John Stallworth 4.00 10.00
32 Steve Largent 4.00 10.00
33 Mike Singletary 4.00 10.00
34 Tommy Nobis 3.00 8.00
35 Lenny Moore 3.00 8.00
36 John Hadl 3.00 8.00
37 Harry Carson 3.00 8.00
38 Joe Washington 2.50 6.00
39 Drew Pearson 3.00 8.00
40 Ron Jaworski 3.00 8.00
41 Mark Moseley 2.50 6.00
42 John Mackey 2.50 6.00
43 Jan Stenerud 2.50 6.00
44 Jim Plunkett 3.00 8.00
45 Jim Taylor 4.00 10.00
46 George Blanda 5.00 12.00
47 Tom Matte 3.00 8.00
48 Harold Carmichael 3.00 8.00
49 Jackie Smith 2.50 6.00
50 Ottis Anderson 2.50 6.00

2001-02 Danbury Mint 22K Gold Super Bowl XXXVI

This set was issued by the Danbury Mint in a special binder with each card within a plastic holder mounted to a page. It commemorates the Patriots Super Bowl win following the 2001 season.
COMPLETE SET (8) 40.00 80.00
1 Drew Bledsoe 4.00 10.00
2 Tom Brady 15.00 30.00
3 Troy Brown 2.50 6.00
4 Tedy Bruschi 3.00 8.00
5 Ty Law 2.50 6.00
6 Lawyer Milloy 2.50 6.00
7 Antowain Smith 2.50 6.00
8 Adam Vinatieri 4.00 10.00

1970 Dayton Daily News

Each of these "bubble gum-less cards" are actually a cut-out photo from The Dayton Daily News newspaper. Each card measures approximately 3 1/2" by 4" when properly cut. The checklist below is incomplete, any additions to it would be appreciated.
1 Herb Adderley 5.00 10.00
2 Virgil Carter 2.50 5.00
4 Gary Cuozzo 3.00 6.00
6 Ken Dyer 2.50 5.00
7 Walt Garrison 3.00 6.00
8 Bob Hayes 4.00 8.00
9 Bob Lilly 6.00 12.00
13 Joe Morrison 3.00 6.00
14 Craig Morton 4.00 8.00
16 Bart Starr 15.00 30.00
17 Fran Tarkenton 10.00 20.00
161 Bill Bergey 3.00 6.00
172 Don Cockroft UER 2.50 5.00
174 John DeMarie 2.50 5.00
176A Dale Lindsey ERR 2.50 5.00
176B Dale Lindsey COR 2.50 5.00
182 Fred Hoaglin 2.50 5.00
190 Mike Howell 2.50 5.00
191 Al Jenkins 2.50 5.00
194 Milt Morin 2.50 5.00
200 Donny Anderson 3.00 6.00
201 Fred Carr 2.50 5.00
209 Pete Case 2.50 5.00
214 Tucker Frederickson 3.00 6.00
217 Mike Wilson G 2.50 5.00
220 Bill Munson 3.00 6.00
221 Bennie McRae 2.50 5.00
224 Bubba Smith 4.00 8.00
226 John Brodie 4.00 8.00
229 Ken Willard 3.00 6.00
234 John Mackey 5.00 10.00
236 Mike Curtis 3.00 6.00
241 Earl Morrall 3.00 6.00
242 Jim O'Brien 2.50 5.00

1971-72 Dell Photos

Measuring approximately 8 1/4" by 10 3/4", the 1971-72 Dell Pro Football Guide features a center insert that unfolds to display 48 color player photos that are framed by black and yellow border stripes. Each picture measures approximately 1 3/4" by 3" and is not perforated. The player's name and team name are printed beneath the picture. The backs have various color action shots that are framed by a black-and-white film type pattern. Biographies on the NFL stars featured on the insert are found throughout the guide. The uncut set still in the book brings up to a 25 percent premium over the complete set price. The pictures are unnumbered and checklisted below in alphabetical order.
COMPLETE SET (48) 40.00 80.00
1 Dan Abramowicz .40 1.00
2 Herb Adderley 1.00 2.00
3 Lem Barney .60 1.50
4 Bobby Bell .60 1.50
5 George Blanda 2.00 4.00
6 Terry Bradshaw 5.00 10.00
7 John Brodie 1.00 2.00
8 Larry Brown .50 1.25
9 Dick Butkus 4.00 8.00
10 Fred Carr .40 1.00
11 Virgil Carter .40 1.00
12 Mike Curtis .50 1.25
13 Len Dawson 1.25 3.00
14 Carl Eller .60 1.50
15 Mel Farr .40 1.00
16 Roman Gabriel .60 1.50
17 Gary Garrison .40 1.00
18 Dick Gordon .40 1.00
19 Bob Griese 3.00 6.00
20 Bob Hayes 1.00 2.00
21 Rich Jackson .40 1.00
22 Charley Johnson .50 1.25
23 Ron Johnson .40 1.00
24 Deacon Jones .60 1.50
25 Sonny Jurgensen 1.00 2.00
26 Leroy Kelly 1.00 2.00
27 Daryle Lamonica .60 1.50
28 MacArthur Lane .40 1.00
29 Willie Lanier .60 1.50
30 Bob Lilly 1.00 2.50
31 Floyd Little .50 1.25
32 Mike Lucci .40 1.00
33 Don Maynard 1.00 2.50
34 Joe Namath 5.00 10.00
35 Tommy Nobis .60 1.50
36 Merlin Olsen 1.00 2.00
37 Alan Page 1.00 2.00
38 Gerry Philbin .40 1.00
39 Jim Plunkett .60 1.50
40 Tim Rossovich .40 1.00
41 Gale Sayers 4.00 8.00
42 Dennis Shaw .40 1.00
43 O.J. Simpson 3.00 8.00
44 Fran Tarkenton 2.00 5.00
45 Johnny Unitas 5.00 12.00
46 Paul Warfield 1.25 3.00
47 Gene Washington 49er .50 1.25
48 Larry Wilson .60 1.50

1995 Destiny Tom Landry Phone Cards

This set of phone cards was released to highlight the career of Tom Landry. Each color card follows the typical phone card style and size and includes the card number on the front. Each was also numbered of 2000 sets produced.
COMPLETE SET (5) 14.00 35.00
COMMON CARD (1-5) 3.20 8.00

1996 Destiny Telecom Men of Destiny Phone Cards

*GOLD/1000: .6X TO 1.5X BASIC CARD
1 Boomer Esiason 1.25 3.00
2 Seth Joyner 1.00 2.50
3 Clyde Simmons 1.00 2.50
4 Cornelius Bennett 1.25 3.00
5 Bobby Hebert 1.00 2.50
6 Eric Metcalf 1.00 2.50
7 Earnest Byner 1.00 2.50
8 Leroy Hoard 1.00 2.50
9 Vinny Testaverde 1.25 3.00
10 Jim Kelly 2.00 5.00
11 Bruce Smith 1.50 4.00
12 Thurman Thomas 1.50 4.00
13 Steve Beuerlein 1.00 2.50
14 Mark Carrier 1.00 2.50
15 Eric Davis 1.00 2.50
16 Kerry Collins 1.25 3.00
17 Bryan Cox 1.00 2.50
18 Erik Kramer 1.00 2.50
19 Rashaan Salaam 1.00 2.50
20 Jeff Blake 1.25 3.00
21 Carl Pickens 1.25 3.00
22 Darnay Scott 1.00 2.50
23 Troy Aikman 3.00 8.00
24 Charles Haley 1.50 4.00
25 Michael Irvin 2.00 5.00
26 Deion Sanders 2.50 6.00
27 Emmitt Smith 5.00 12.00
28 Herschel Walker 1.50 4.00
29 Terrell Davis 2.00 5.00
30 John Elway 5.00 12.00
31 Mike Pritchard .75 2.00
32 Shannon Sharpe 1.25 3.00
33 Reggie Brown .75 2.00
34 Barry Sanders 5.00 12.00
35 Robert Brooks 1.25 3.00
36 Brett Favre 6.00 15.00
37 Anthony Morgan .75 2.00
38 Reggie White 1.50 4.00
39 Mel Gray 1.00 2.50
40 Steve McNair 1.25 3.00
41 Rodney Thomas 1.00 2.50
42 Sean Dawkins 1.00 2.50
43 Marshall Faulk 1.50 4.00
44 Jim Harbaugh 1.25 3.00
45 Mark Brunell 1.25 3.00
46 Natrone Means 1.00 2.50
47 Andre Rison 1.25 3.00
48 Marcus Allen 1.50 4.00
49 Steve Bono 1.00 2.50
50 Derrick Thomas 2.00 5.00
51 Karim Abdul-Jabbar 1.00 2.50
52 Dan Marino 6.00 15.00
53 O.J. McDuffie 1.00 2.50
54 Cris Carter 1.50 4.00
55 Qadry Ismail 1.00 2.50
56 Warren Moon 1.25 3.00
57 Robert Smith 1.00 2.50
58 Drew Bledsoe 1.25 3.00
59 Shawn Jefferson .75 2.00
60 Eric Allen 1.00 2.50
61 Jim Everett 1.00 2.50
62 Michael Haynes 1.00 2.50
63 Dave Brown 1.00 2.50
64 Rodney Hampton 1.00 2.50
65 Mike Sherrard .75 2.00
66 Jeff Graham 1.00 2.50
67 Keyshawn Johnson 1.00 2.50
68 Neil O'Donnell 1.00 2.50
69 Tim Brown 1.25 3.00
70 Jeff Hostetler 1.00 2.50
71 Napoleon Kaufman 1.00 2.50
72 Harvey Williams .75 2.00
73 Ty Detmer 1.00 2.50
74 Irving Fryar 1.00 2.50
75 Rodney Peete 1.00 2.50
76 Ricky Watters 1.00 2.50
77 Kordell Stewart 1.00 2.50
78 Mike Tomczak 1.00 2.50
79 Rod Woodson 1.25 3.00
80 Isaac Bruce 1.25 3.00
81 Steve Walsh .75 2.00
82 Aaron Hayden .75 2.00
83 Stan Humphries 1.00 2.50
84 Junior Seau 1.25 3.00
85 Elvis Grbac 1.00 2.50
86 Brent Jones 1.00 2.50
87 Ken Norton .75 2.00
88 Jerry Rice 4.00 10.00
89 J.J. Stokes 1.00 2.50
90 Steve Young 2.00 5.00
91 Brian Blades 1.00 2.50
92 Joey Galloway 1.25 3.00
93 Rick Mirer 1.00 2.50
94 Steve Smith .75 2.00
95 Horace Copeland .75 2.00
96 Trent Dilfer 1.25 3.00
97 Alvin Harper 1.00 2.50
98 Terry Allen 1.00 2.50
99 Gus Frerotte 1.00 2.50
100 Michael Westbrook 1.00 2.50

1933 Diamond Matchbooks Silver

Diamond Match Co. produced their first football matchbook set in 1933. Many covers appear with both a green and pink background on the text area surrounded by a silver border, although a few cards appear in only one color. This set is clearly the most difficult to complete of all the football Diamond Matchbooks. Each cover measures approximately 1 1/2" by 4 1/2" (when completely folded out) and is priced below as unfolded with the matches removed. Complete covers with matches intact sometimes sell for as much as 1-1/2 ttimes the prices listed below. Although the covers are not numbered, we've assigned numbers alphabetically with the white bordered All-American Seal leading off and the color variations listed with a G (green) and P (pink) suffix. Several covers are thought to be much more difficult to find; we've labeled those as SP below.
1 All-American Board Seal 30.00 60.00
2G Gene Alford 40.00 75.00
2P Gene Alford 40.00 75.00
3G Marger Apsit 40.00 75.00
3P Marger Apsit 40.00 75.00
4G Red Badgro 75.00 125.00
4P Red Badgro 75.00 125.00
5G Cliff Battles 100.00 175.00
5P Cliff Battles 100.00 175.00
6P Maury Bodenger 40.00 75.00
7P Jim Bowdoin 40.00 75.00
8G John Boylan 40.00 75.00
8P John Boylan 40.00 75.00
9G Hank Bruder 60.00 100.00
9P Hank Bruder 60.00 100.00
10G Carl Brumbaugh 40.00 75.00
10P Carl Brumbaugh 40.00 75.00
11P Bill Buckler 40.00 75.00
12G Jerome Buckley 40.00 75.00
12P Jerome Buckley 40.00 75.00
13G Dale Burnett 40.00 75.00
13P Dale Burnett 40.00 75.00
14P Ernie Caddel 60.00 100.00
15G1 Chris Cagle OFB 60.00 100.00
15G2 Chris Cagle WFB 75.00 150.00
15P Chris Cagle 60.00 100.00
16G Glen Campbell 40.00 75.00
16P Glen Campbell 40.00 75.00
17G John Cannella 40.00 75.00
18P Zuck Carlson 40.00 75.00
19P George Christensen 75.00 125.00
20G Stu Clancy 40.00 75.00
21G Paul(Rip) Collins 40.00 75.00
21P Paul(Rip) Collins 40.00 75.00
22P Jack Connell 40.00 75.00
23P George Corbett 40.00 75.00
24G Orien Crow 40.00 75.00
24P Orien Crow 40.00 75.00
25G Ed Danowski 40.00 75.00
25P Ed Danowski 40.00 75.00
26G Sylvester(Red) Davis 40.00 75.00
26P Sylvester(Red) Davis 40.00 75.00
27G Johnny Dell Isola 60.00 100.00
27P Johnny Dell Isola 60.00 100.00
28P John Doehring 40.00 75.00
29G Turk Edwards 175.00 300.00
29P Turk Edwards 175.00 300.00
30G Earl Elser 40.00 75.00
30P Earl Elser 40.00 75.00
31G Ox Emerson 60.00 100.00
31P Ox Emerson 60.00 100.00
32G Tiny Feather SP 75.00 125.00
33G Ray Flaherty 75.00 125.00
33P Ray Flaherty 75.00 125.00
34G Ike Frankian 40.00 75.00
34P Ike Frankian 40.00 75.00
35G Red Grange 300.00 500.00
35P Red Grange 300.00 500.00
36G Len Grant 40.00 75.00
37G Ace Gutowsky 75.00 125.00
37P Ace Gutowsky 75.00 125.00
38G Mel Hein 300.00 500.00
39P Arnie Herber 600.00 1000.00
40G Bill Hewitt 350.00 600.00
40P Bill Hewitt 350.00 600.00
41G Herman Hickman 60.00 100.00
41P Herman Hickman 60.00 100.00
42G Clarke Hinkle 350.00 600.00
42P Clarke Hinkle 350.00 600.00
43G Cal Hubbard 600.00 1000.00
43P Cal Hubbard 600.00 1000.00
44G George Hurley 40.00 75.00
44P George Hurley 40.00 75.00
45P Herman Hussey SP 75.00 125.00
46G Cecil (Tex) Irvin 40.00 75.00
47G Luke Johnsos 75.00 125.00
47P Luke Johnsos 75.00 125.00
48G Bruce Jones 40.00 75.00
48P Bruce Jones 40.00 75.00
49G Potsy Jones 40.00 75.00
50P Thacker Kaye SP 75.00 125.00
51G Shipwreck Kelly 60.00 100.00
51P Shipwreck Kelly 60.00 100.00
52P Joe Doc Kopcha 60.00 100.00
53G Joe Kurth 90.00 150.00
53P Joe Kurth 90.00 150.00
54G Milo Lubratevich 40.00 75.00
54P Milo Lubratevich 40.00 75.00
55G Father Lumpkin 60.00 100.00
55P Father Lumpkin 60.00 100.00
56G Jim MacMurdo 40.00 75.00
56P Jim MacMurdo 40.00 75.00
57P Joe Maniaci 40.00 75.00
58G Jack McBride 40.00 75.00
59G Ookie Miller 40.00 75.00
59P Ookie Miller 40.00 75.00
60P Buster Mitchell 40.00 75.00
61P Keith Molesworth 40.00 75.00
62P Bob Monnett 90.00 150.00
63G Hap Moran 40.00 75.00
63P Hap Moran 40.00 75.00
64G Bill Morgan 40.00 75.00
65P Maynard Morrison SP 75.00 125.00
66P Mathew Murray 40.00 75.00
67G Jim Musick 40.00 75.00
67P Jim Musick 40.00 75.00
68P Bronko Nagurski SP 600.00 1000.00
69P Dick Nesbitt 40.00 75.00
70G Harry Newman 60.00 100.00
71G1 Bill Owen ERR 75.00 125.00
71G2 Bill Owen COR 40.00 75.00
72G Steve Owen SP 150.00 250.00
73P Andy Pavlicovic 60.00 100.00
74P Bert Pearson 40.00 75.00
75G William Pendergast 40.00 75.00
75P William Pendergast 40.00 75.00
76P Jerry Pepper 40.00 75.00
77P Stan Piawlock 40.00 75.00
78G Erny Pinckert 60.00 100.00
78P Erny Pinckert 60.00 100.00
79G Glenn Presnell 40.00 75.00
79P Glenn Presnell 40.00 75.00
80P Jess Quatse 90.00 150.00
81G Hank Reese 40.00 75.00
82G Dick Richards 40.00 75.00
82P Dick Richards 40.00 75.00
83P Tony Sarausky 40.00 75.00
84G Elmer Schaake 40.00 75.00
84P Elmer Schaake 40.00 75.00
85G John Schneller 40.00 75.00
85P John Schneller 40.00 75.00
86P Johnny Sisk 40.00 75.00
87G Mike Steponovich 40.00 75.00
87P Mike Steponovich 40.00 75.00
88G Ken Strong 250.00 400.00
89P Charles Tackwell 60.00 100.00
90G Harry Thayer 40.00 75.00
90P Harry Thayer 40.00 75.00
91P Walt Uzdavinis 40.00 75.00
92P John Welch 40.00 75.00

93P William Whalen	40.00	75.00
94G Mule Wilson	60.00	100.00
94P Mule Wilson	60.00	100.00
95G Frank Babe Wright	40.00	75.00
95P Frank Babe Wright	40.00	75.00

1934 Diamond Matchbooks

The 1934 Diamond Matchbook set is the first of many issues from the company printed with colorful borders. Four border colors were used for this set: blue, green, red, and tan. Many players appear with three border color variations, while some only appear with one, two or four different border colors. We've noted below known border colors for each matchbook. It is thought that a complete checklist with all color variations is still unknown. A Tan colored Bronko Nagurski matchbook was recently discovered as was a Green Clarke Hinkle. There is no player position included nor picture frame border shown on the player photo. The text printing is in black ink and each cover measures approximately 1 1/2" by 4 1/2" when completely unfolded. The set is very similar in appearance to the 1935 issues, but can be distinguished by the single lined manufacturer's identification "The Diamond Match Co., N.Y.C." Complete covers with matches intact sometimes sell for as much as 1-1/2 ttimes the prices listed below. Although the covers are not numbered, we've assigned numbers alphabetically. Several covers are thought to be much more difficult to find, we've labeled those as SP below.

1 Arvo Antilla G/R/T	18.00	30.00
2 Red Badgro B/G/R/T	35.00	60.00
3 Norbert Bartell R SP	150.00	300.00
4 Cliff Battles G/R/T	50.00	80.00
5 Chuck Bennis B/G/R/T	18.00	30.00
6 Jack Beynon G/R/T	18.00	30.00
7 Maury Bodenger G/R/T (misspelled Morry)	18.00	30.00
8 John Bond G/R/T	18.00	30.00
9 John Brown G/R/T	18.00	30.00
10 Carl Brumbaugh R/T SP	150.00	300.00
11 Dale Burnett B/G/R/T	18.00	30.00
12 Ernie Caddel R SP	50.00	100.00
13 Chris Red Cagle G SP	50.00	100.00
14 Glen Campbell G/R/T	18.00	30.00
15 John Cannella G/R/T	18.00	30.00
16 Joe Carter T SP	150.00	300.00
17 Les Caywood B SP	50.00	100.00
18 George Buck Chapman G/R/T	18.00	30.00
19 Frank Christensen G	18.00	30.00
20 Stu Clancy G/R/T	18.00	30.00
21 Myers Algy Clark B/G/R/T	18.00	30.00
22 Paul Rip Collins G/R/T	18.00	30.00
23 Jack Connell G/R/T SP	50.00	100.00
24 Orien Crow G/R/T	18.00	30.00
25 Lone Star Dietz CO G/R/T SP	50.00	100.00
26 John Doehring T SP	150.00	300.00
27 Jimmie Downey T SP	150.00	300.00
28 Turk Edwards B/G/R/T	50.00	80.00
29 Ox Emerson R	20.00	35.00
30 Tiny Feather B/G/R/T	18.00	30.00
31 Ray Flaherty G/R/T	35.00	60.00
32 Frank Froschauer G/R/T	18.00	30.00
33 Chuck Galbreath G/R/T	18.00	30.00
34 Red Gragg G/R/T	18.00	30.00
35 Red Grange G/R/T SP	800.00	1200.00
36 Cy Grant G/R/T	18.00	30.00
37 Leonard Grant B/G/R/T	18.00	30.00
38 Ross Grant B	18.00	30.00
39 Jack Griffith B/G/R	18.00	30.00
40 Ed Gryboski G/R/T	18.00	30.00
41 Ace Gutowsky G/R/T	25.00	40.00
42 Swede Hanson G/R/T	18.00	30.00
43 Mel Hein G/R/T	35.00	60.00
44 Warren Heller G/R/T	18.00	30.00
45 Bill Hewitt R SP	500.00	800.00
46 Clarke Hinkle G SP	500.00	800.00
47 Cecil Tex Irvin G/R/T	18.00	30.00
48 Frank Johnson G/R/T	18.00	30.00
49 Jack Johnson G	18.00	30.00
50 Robert Jones G SP	150.00	300.00
51 Potsy Jones B/G/R/T	18.00	30.00
52 Carl Jorgensen G/R SP	150.00	300.00
53 John Karcis G/R/T	18.00	30.00
54 Eddie Kawal G/R SP	50.00	100.00
55 Shipwreck Kelly G SP	150.00	300.00
56 George Kenneally T SP	150.00	300.00
57 Walt Kiesling G/R SP	1000.00	1500.00
58 Jack Knapper T SP	150.00	300.00
59 Frank Knox R SP	50.00	100.00
60 Joe Doc Kopcha G/R SP	150.00	300.00
61 Joe Kresky T SP	150.00	300.00
62 Joe Laws G/R SP	150.00	300.00
63 Russ Lay G/R/T	18.00	30.00
64 Hilary Biff Lee B/G/R/T	18.00	30.00
65 Gil LeFebvre B/G/R/T	18.00	30.00
66 Jim Leonard G/R/T	18.00	30.00
67 Les Lindberg B/G/R/T	18.00	30.00
68 John Lipski T	18.00	30.00
69 Milo Lubratevich G/T	18.00	30.00
70 Father Lumpkin G/R SP	50.00	100.00
71 Link Lyman T SP	500.00	800.00
72 Jim MacMurdo T	18.00	30.00
73 Ed Matesic R SP	150.00	300.00
74 Dave McCollough B/G/R/T	18.00	30.00
75 John McKnight G/R/T	18.00	30.00
76 Johnny Blood McNally G/R/T	250.00	400.00
77 Al Minot G/R/T	18.00	30.00
78 Keith Molesworth SP	35.00	60.00
79 Jim Mooney B/G/R/T	18.00	30.00
80 Leroy Moorehead G/R/T	18.00	30.00
81 Bill Morgan G/R/T	18.00	30.00
82 Bob Moser R/T SP	50.00	100.00
83 Lee Mulleneaux B	18.00	30.00
84 George Munday G/R/T	18.00	30.00
85 George Musso R/T SP	1000.00	1500.00
86 Bronko Nagurski T SP	500.00	800.00
87 Harry Newman G	20.00	35.00
88 Al Norgard G SP	150.00	300.00
89 John Oehler G/R/T	18.00	30.00
90 Charlie Opper G/R/T	18.00	30.00
91 Bill Owen G/R/T	18.00	30.00
92 Steve Owen G/R/T	35.00	60.00
93 Bert Pearson T SP	150.00	300.00
94 Tom Perkinson B/G/R/T	18.00	30.00
95 Mace Pike R SP	35.00	60.00
96 Joe Pilconis R SP	150.00	300.00
97 Lew Pope B	18.00	30.00
98 Crain Portman G/R/T	18.00	30.00
99 Glenn Presnell B/G/R/T	18.00	30.00
100 Jess Quatse G/R/T SP	50.00	100.00
101 Clare Randolph G/T SP	50.00	100.00
102 Hank Reese G/R/T	18.00	30.00
103 Paul Riblett B/R/T SP	150.00	300.00
104 Dick Richards G SP	150.00	300.00
105 Jack Roberts G/R/T	18.00	30.00
106 John Lee Rogers B/G/R/T	18.00	30.00
107 Gene Ronzani G/R SP	150.00	300.00
108 Bob Rowe R SP	35.00	60.00
109 John Schneller T SP	35.00	60.00
110 Adolph Schwammel G SP	150.00	300.00
111 Earl Red Seick T SP	150.00	300.00
112 Allen Shi G/R/T	18.00	30.00
113 Ben Smith G/R/T	18.00	30.00
114 Ken Strong G/R/T	60.00	100.00
115 Elmer Taber R T SP	50.00	100.00
116 Charles Tackwell B	18.00	30.00
117 Ray Tesser G/R/T	18.00	30.00
118 John Thomason G/R/T	18.00	30.00
119 Charlie Turbyville G/R/T (misspelled Turbeyville)	18.00	30.00
120 Claude Urevig R SP	50.00	100.00
121 John Harp Vaughan G/R/T	18.00	30.00
122 Henry Wagnon G/R/T	18.00	30.00
123 John West G/R/T	18.00	30.00
124 Lee Woodruff G/R/T	18.00	30.00
125 Jim Zyntell G/R/T	18.00	30.00

1934 Diamond Matchbooks College Rivals

Diamond Match Co. produced this set issued in 1934. Each cover features a top college rivalry with a short write-up about the latest games between the two teams. The covers contain a single line manufacturer's identification "The Diamond Match Co. N.Y.C." This set is very similar to the 1935 issue, but can be distinguished by the last line of type in the text as indicated below. Each of the twelve unnumbered covers was produced with either a black or tan colored border. Some collectors attempt to assemble a complete 24-card set with all variations. Complete covers with matches intact sometimes sell for as much as 1-1/2 times the prices listed below.

COMPLETE SET (12)	175.00	300.00
1 Alabama vs. Fordham SP	75.00	125.00
2 Army vs. Navy	12.50	25.00
3 Fordham vs. St. Mary's	10.00	20.00
4 Georgia vs. Georgia Tech	10.00	20.00
5 Holy Cross vs. Boston College	10.00	20.00
6 Lafayette vs. Lehigh	10.00	20.00
7 Michigan vs. Ohio State	12.50	25.00
8 Notre Dame vs. Army	12.50	25.00
9 Penn vs. Cornell	10.00	20.00
10 USC vs. Notre Dame	12.50	25.00
11 Yale vs. Harvard	10.00	20.00
12 Yale vs. Princeton	10.00	20.00

1935 Diamond Matchbooks

The 1935 Diamond Matchbook set is very similar in design to the 1934 set, but can be distinguished by the double lined manufacturer's identification "Made in U.S.A./The Diamond Match Co., N.Y.C." Only three border colors were used for this set: green, red, and tan and each player appears with only one border color. There is no player position included nor picture frame border shown on the player photo. The text printing is in black ink and each cover measures approximately 1 1/2" by 4 1/2" when completely unfolded. Complete covers with matches intact sometimes sell for as much as 1-1/2 ttimes the prices listed below. Although the covers are not numbered, we've assigned numbers alphabetically.

1 Alf Anderson	15.00	25.00
2 Alec Ashford	15.00	25.00
3 Gene Augusterfer SP	30.00	60.00
4 Red Badgro	20.00	35.00
5 Cliff Battles	35.00	60.00
6 Harry Benson	15.00	25.00
7 Tony Blazine	15.00	25.00
8 John Bond	15.00	25.00
9 Maurice (Mule) Bray	15.00	25.00
10 Dale Burnett	15.00	25.00
11 Charles(Cocky) Bush	15.00	25.00
12 Ernie Caddel	18.00	30.00
13 Zuck Carlson	15.00	25.00
14 Joe Carter	15.00	25.00
15 Cy Casper	15.00	25.00
16 Paul Causey	15.00	25.00
17 Frank Christensen	15.00	25.00
18 Stu Clancy	15.00	25.00
19 Dutch Clark	90.00	150.00
20 Paul(Rip) Collins	15.00	25.00
21 Dave Cook	15.00	25.00
22 Fred Crawford	15.00	25.00
23 Paul Cuba	15.00	25.00
24 Harry Ebding	15.00	25.00
25 Turk Edwards	35.00	60.00
26 Marvin(Swede) Ellstrom	15.00	25.00
27 Beattie Feathers	25.00	40.00
28 Ray Flaherty	20.00	35.00
29 John Gildea	15.00	25.00
30 Tom Graham	15.00	25.00
31 Len Grant	15.00	25.00
32 Maurice Green	15.00	25.00
33 Norman Greeney	15.00	25.00
34 Ace Gutowsky	18.00	30.00
35 Julius Hall	15.00	25.00
36 Swede Hanson	15.00	25.00
37 Charles Harold	15.00	25.00
38 Tom Haywood	15.00	25.00
39 Mel Hein	75.00	125.00
40 Bill Hewitt	90.00	150.00
41 Cecil(Tex) Irvin	15.00	25.00
42 Frank Johnson	15.00	25.00
43 Jack Johnson	15.00	25.00
44 Luke Johnsos	18.00	30.00
45 Potsy Jones	15.00	25.00
46 Carl Jorgensen	25.00	40.00
47 George Kenneally	15.00	25.00
48 Roger(Reds) Kirkman	15.00	25.00
49 Frank Knox	15.00	25.00
50 Joe Doc Kopcha	18.00	30.00
51 Rick Lackman	15.00	25.00
52 Jim Leonard	15.00	25.00
53 Joe(Hunk) Malkovich	15.00	25.00
54 Ed Manske	15.00	25.00
55 Bernie Masterson	18.00	30.00
56 James McMillen	15.00	25.00
57 Mike Mikulak	15.00	25.00
58 Ookie Miller	15.00	25.00
59 Milford(Dub) Miller	15.00	25.00
60 Al Minot	15.00	25.00
61 Buster Mitchell	15.00	25.00
62 Bill Morgan	15.00	25.00
63 George Musso	35.00	60.00
64 Harry Newman	18.00	30.00
65 Al Nichelini	15.00	25.00
66 Bill(Red) Owen	15.00	25.00
67 Steve Owen	20.00	35.00
68 Max Padlow	15.00	25.00
69 Hal Pangle	15.00	25.00
70 Melvin(Swede) Pittman	15.00	25.00
71 William(Red) Pollock	15.00	25.00
72 Glenn Presnell	15.00	25.00
73 George(Mousie) Rado	15.00	25.00
74 Clare Randolph	15.00	25.00
75 Hank Reese	15.00	25.00
76 Ray Richards	15.00	25.00
77 Doug Russell	15.00	25.00
78 Sandy Sandberg	15.00	25.00
79 Phil Sarboe	15.00	25.00
80 Big John Schneller	15.00	25.00
81 Michael Sebastian	15.00	25.00
82 Allen Shi	15.00	25.00
83 Johnny Sisk	15.00	25.00
84 James(Red) Stacy	15.00	25.00
85 Ed Storm	15.00	25.00
86 Ken Strong	35.00	60.00
87 Art Strutt	15.00	25.00
88 Frank Sullivan	15.00	25.00
89 Charles Treadaway	15.00	25.00
90 John Turley	15.00	25.00
91 Claude Urevig	15.00	25.00
92 Charles(Pug) Vaughan	15.00	25.00
93 Izzy Weinstock	15.00	25.00
94 Henry Wiesenbaugh	15.00	25.00
95 Joe Zeller	15.00	25.00
96 Vince Zizak	15.00	25.00

1935 Diamond Matchbooks College Rivals

Diamond Match Co. produced this set issued in 1935. Each cover features a top college rivalry with a short write-up about the latest games between the two teams. The covers contain either a single line or a double line manufacturer's identification "Made in U.S.A./The Diamond Match Co. N.Y.C." This set is very similar to the 1934 issue but can be distinguished by the last line of type in the text as indicated below. Each of the unnumbered covers was produced with three versions. The manufacturer's name can be found as a single line with either a black or a tan colored border and the covers can be found in tan with a double lined manufacturer's name. Some collectors attempt to assemble a complete 36-book set with all variations. Complete covers with matches intact sometimes sell for as much as 1-1/2 times the prices listed below.

COMPLETE SET (11)	125.00	200.00
1 Alabama vs. Fordham	20.00	40.00
2 Army vs. Navy	12.50	25.00
3 Fordham vs. St. Mary's	10.00	20.00
4 Georgia vs. Georgia Tech	10.00	20.00
5 Holy Cross vs. Boston College	10.00	20.00
6 Lafayette vs. Lehigh	10.00	20.00
7 Michigan vs. Ohio State	12.50	25.00
8 Notre Dame vs. Army	12.50	25.00
9 Penn vs. Cornell	10.00	20.00
10 USC vs. Notre Dame	12.50	25.00
11 Yale vs. Harvard	10.00	20.00
12 Yale vs. Princeton	10.00	20.00

1936 Diamond Matchbooks

The Diamond Match Co. produced these matchbook covers featuring players of the Chicago Bears and Philadelphia Eagles. They measure approximately 1 1/2" by 4 1/2" (when completely folded out). We've listed below the players alphabetically by team with the Bears first. Each of the covers was produced with either black or brown ink on the text. Three border colors (green, red and tan) were used on the covers, but each player appears with only one border color in black ink and one border color in brown ink. The only exception is Ray Nolting who appears with two border colors with both black and brown ink versions. A picture frame design is included on the left and right sides of the player photo. Don Jackson's and all of the Bears' players' positions are included before the bio. Some collectors consider these two or more separate issues due to the variations and assemble "sets" with either the brown or black printing. Since no price differences are seen between variations and the text and photos are identical for each version, we've listed them together. With all variations, a total of 96-covers were produced. A few of the players are included in the 1937 set as well with only slight differences between the two issues. For those players, we've included the first or last lines of text to help identify the year. Complete covers with matches intact sometimes sell for as much as 1-1/2 ttimes the prices listed below.

COMPLETE SET (47)	500.00	800.00
1 Carl Brumbaugh	10.00	20.00
2 Zuck Carlson	10.00	20.00
3 George Corbett	10.00	20.00
4 John Doehring	10.00	20.00
5 Beattie Feathers	12.50	25.00
6 Dan Fortmann	12.50	25.00
7 George Grosvenor	10.00	20.00
8 Bill Hewitt	18.00	30.00
9 Luke Johnsos	10.00	20.00
10 William Karr	10.00	20.00
11 Eddie Kawal	10.00	20.00
12 Jack Manders	10.00	20.00
13 Bernie Masterson	10.00	20.00
14 Eddie Michaels	10.00	20.00
15 Ookie Miller	10.00	20.00
16 Keith Molesworth	10.00	20.00
17 George Musso	12.50	25.00
18 Bronko Nagurski	150.00	250.00
19 Ray Nolting	10.00	20.00
20 Vernon Oech	10.00	20.00
21 William(Red) Pollock	10.00	20.00
22 Gene Ronzani	10.00	20.00
23 Ted Rosequist	10.00	20.00
24 Johnny Sisk	10.00	20.00
25 Joe Stydahar	12.50	25.00
26 Frank Sullivan	10.00	20.00
27 Russell Thompson	10.00	20.00
28 Milt Trost	10.00	20.00
29 Joe Zeller	10.00	20.00
30 Bill Brian	7.50	15.00
31 Art Buss	7.50	15.00
32 Joe Carter	7.50	15.00
33 Swede Hanson	7.50	15.00
34 Don Jackson	7.50	15.00
35 John Kusko	7.50	15.00
36 Jim Leonard	7.50	15.00
37 Jim MacMurdo	7.50	15.00
38 Ed Manske	7.50	15.00
39 Forrest McPherson	7.50	15.00
40 George Mulligan	7.50	15.00
41 Joe Pilconis	7.50	15.00
42 Hank Reese	7.50	15.00
43 Jim Russell	7.50	15.00
44 Dave Smukler	7.50	15.00
45 Pete Stevens	7.50	15.00
46 John Thomason	7.50	15.00
47 Vince Zizak	7.50	15.00

1937 Diamond Matchbooks

The Diamond Match Co. produced these matchbook covers featuring players of the Chicago Bears. They measure approximately 1 1/2" by 4 1/2" (when completely folded out). The covers look very similar to the 1936 set, but use a slightly smaller print type. Each of the 24-covers was produced with either black or brown ink on the text. Three border colors (green, red and tan) were used on the covers, with all three used for each of the brown ink varieties. Only one border color was used for each cover printed in black ink. Similar to the 1936 issue, a picture frame design is included on the left and right sides of the player photo. Some collectors consider these two separate issues due to the variations and assemble "sets" with either the brown or black printing. Since no price differences are seen between variations and the text and photos are identical for each version, we've listed them together. With all variations, a total of 96-covers were produced. Several of the players are included in the 1936 set as well with only slight differences between the two issues. For those players, we've included the first or last lines of text to help identify the year. Complete covers with matches intact sometimes sell for as much as 1-1/2 ttimes the prices listed below. Although the covers are not numbered, we've assigned numbers alphabetically.

COMPLETE SET (24)	200.00	350.00
1 Frank Bausch	7.50	15.00
2 Delbert Bjork	7.50	15.00
3 William(Red) Conkright	7.50	15.00
4 George Corbett	7.50	15.00
5 John Doehring	7.50	15.00
6 Beattie Feathers	10.00	20.00
7 Dan Fortmann	10.00	20.00
8 Sam Francis	7.50	15.00
9 Henry Hammond	7.50	15.00
10 William Karr	7.50	15.00
11 Jack Manders	7.50	15.00
12 Ed Manske	7.50	15.00
13 Bernie Masterson	7.50	15.00
14 Keith Molesworth	7.50	15.00
15 George Musso	10.00	20.00
16 Ray Nolting	7.50	15.00
17 Richard Plasman	7.50	15.00
18 Gene Ronzani	7.50	15.00
19 Joe Stydahar	10.00	20.00
20 Frank Sullivan	7.50	15.00
21 Russell Thompson	7.50	15.00
22 Milt Trost	7.50	15.00
23 George Wilson	7.50	15.00
24 Joe Zeller	7.50	15.00

1938 Diamond Matchbooks

Diamond Match Co. again produced a matchcover set for 1938 featuring players from the Bears and Lions. They measure approximately 1 1/2" by 4 1/2" (when completely folded out). The overall border color is silver with the bio background color being red for the Bears (1-12) and blue for the Lions (13-24). The Lions players seem to be much tougher to find than the Bears. We've assigned card numbers below alphabetically by the two teams included. There are no known variations. Complete covers with matches intact sometimes sell for as much as 1-1/2 ttimes the prices listed below.

COMPLETE SET (24)	600.00	1000.00
1 Delbert Bjork	15.00	25.00
2 Raymond Buivid	15.00	25.00
3 Gary Famiglietti	15.00	25.00
4 Dan Fortmann	20.00	35.00
5 Bert Johnson	15.00	25.00
6 Jack Manders	15.00	25.00
7 Joe Maniaci	15.00	25.00
8 Lester McDonald	15.00	25.00
9 Frank Sullivan	15.00	25.00
10 Robert Swisher	15.00	25.00
11 Russell Thompson	15.00	25.00
12 Gust Zarnas	15.00	25.00
13 Ernie Caddel	35.00	60.00
14 Lloyd Cardwell	30.00	50.00
15 Dutch Clark	175.00	300.00
16 Jack Johnson	30.00	50.00
17 Ed Klewicki	30.00	50.00
18 James McDonald	30.00	50.00
19 James(Monk) Moscrip	30.00	50.00
20 Maurice (Babe) Patt	30.00	50.00
21 Bob Reynolds	30.00	50.00
22 Kent Ryan	30.00	50.00
23 Fred Vanzo	30.00	50.00
24 Alex Wojciechowicz	125.00	200.00

1992 Diamond Stickers

Produced by Diamond Publishing Inc., the first series of NFL Superstar stickers consists of 160 stickers, each measuring approximately 1 15/16" by 2 15/16". The stickers were sold in six-sticker packets and could be pasted in a 36-page sticker album. Fight hundred autographed stickers were randomly inserted throughout the packs; apparently, each of the featured stars (Mark Carrier, Cornelius Bennett, Chris Miller, and Rob Moore) signed 200 each. The fronts feature action color player photos framed by a team-color coded inner border and a white outer border. The team name appears in the team's accent color within the top border. The horizontally oriented backs are white with purple print and carry biographical and statistical information. The stickers are numbered on the back and checklisted alphabetically according to teams in the AFC and NFC.

COMPLETE SET (160)	15.00	40.00
1 Super Bowl XXVI logo	.10	.30
2 Super Bowl XXVI logo	.10	.30
3 Jim Kelly	.30	.75
4 Thurman Thomas	.20	.50
5 Andre Reed	.15	.40
6 James Lofton	.15	.40
7 Cornelius Bennett	.10	.30
8 Boomer Esiason	.15	.40
9 Harold Green	.07	.20
10 Anthony Munoz	.15	.40
11 Mitchell Price	.07	.20
12 Lewis Billups	.07	.20
13 Bernie Kosar	.10	.30
14 Eric Metcalf	.10	.30
15 Michael Dean Perry	.10	.30
16 Van Waiters	.07	.20
17 Brian Brennan	.07	.20
18 John Elway	1.50	4.00
19 Gaston Green	.07	.20
20 Vance Johnson	.08	.25
21 Dennis Smith	.07	.20
22 Clarence Kay	.07	.20
23 Warren Moon	.15	.40
24 Haywood Jeffires	.10	.30
25 Cris Dishman	.07	.20
26 Bubba McDowell	.07	.20
27 Ray Childress	.15	.40
28 Eric Dickerson	.15	.40
29 Jessie Hester	.07	.20
30 Clarence Verdin	.07	.20
31 Bill Brooks	.10	.30
32 Albert Bentley	.07	.20
33 Christian Okoye	.10	.30
34 Derrick Thomas	.15	.40
35 Dino Hackett	.07	.20
36 Deron Cherry	.07	.20
37 Bill Maas	.07	.20
38 Todd Marinovich	.07	.20
39 Roger Craig	.15	.40
40 Greg Townsend	.07	.20
41 Ronnie Lott	.20	.50
42 Howie Long	.15	.40
43 Dan Marino	1.50	4.00
44 Mark Clayton	.10	.30
45 Sammie Smith	.07	.20
46 Jim Jensen	.07	.20
47 Reggie Roby	.07	.20
48 Brent Williams	.07	.20
49 Andre Tippett	.15	.40
50 John Stephens	.07	.20
51 Johnny Rembert	.07	.20
52 Irving Fryar	.10	.30
53 Ken O'Brien	.08	.25
54 Al Toon	.10	.30
55 Brad Baxter	.08	.25
56 James Hasty	.07	.20
57 Rob Moore	.10	.30
58 Neil O'Donnell	.10	.30
59 Bubby Brister	.10	.30
60 Louis Lipps	.07	.20
61 Merril Hoge	.08	.25
62 Gary Anderson K	.08	.25
63 John Friesz	.08	.25
64 Junior Seau	.15	.40
65 Leslie O'Neal	.08	.25
66 Rod Bernstine	.07	.20
67 Burt Grossman	.07	.20
68 Brian Blades	.08	.25
69 Cortez Kennedy	.10	.30
70 David Wyman	.07	.20
71 John L. Williams	.07	.20
72 Robert Blackmon	.07	.20
73 Checklist 33-48	.10	.30
74 Checklist 49-64	.07	.20
75 Jerry Rice	.75	2.00
76 Jay Novacek	.15	.40
77 Mark Rypien	.10	.30
78 P.Swilling D.Thomas	.20	.50
79 Deion Sanders	.50	1.25
80 Mel Gray	.07	.20
81 Earnest Byner	.08	.25
82 Eric Allen	.08	.25
83 Mike Singletary	.20	.50
84 Andre Rison	.15	.40
85 Checklist 65-80	.08	.25
86 Checklist 81-96	.07	.20
87 Chris Miller	.10	.30
88 Andre Rison	.15	.40
89 Deion Sanders	.50	1.25
90 Michael Haynes	.07	.20
91 Tim Green	.07	.20
92 Jim Harbaugh	.15	.40
93 Mark Carrier DB	.07	.20
94 Mike Singletary	.20	.50
95 William Perry	.10	.30
96 Donnell Woolford	.07	.20
97 Troy Aikman	.75	2.00
98 Michael Irvin	.30	.75
99 Russell Maryland	.08	.25
100 Jay Novacek	.15	.40
101 Ken Norton Jr.	.08	.25
102 Mel Gray	.07	.20
103 Bennie Blades	.07	.20
104 Rodney Peete	.08	.25
105 Brett Perriman	.08	.25
106 William White	.07	.20
107 Vai Sikahema	.07	.20
108 Vince Workman	.07	.20
109 Jeff Query	.07	.20
110 Sterling Sharpe	.15	.40
111 Tony Mandarich	.07	.20
112 Jim Everett	.10	.30
113 Flipper Anderson	.08	.25
114 Robert Delpino	.07	.20
115 Darryl Henley	.07	.20
116 Henry Ellard	.10	.30
117 Wade Wilson	.08	.25
118 Anthony Carter	.10	.30
119 Chris Doleman	.10	.30
120 Cris Carter	.20	.50
121 Henry Thomas	.07	.20
122 Steve Walsh	.08	.25
123 Pat Swilling	.10	.30
124 Dalton Hilliard	.07	.20
125 Floyd Turner	.07	.20
126 Craig Heyward	.10	.30
127 Jeff Hostetler	.10	.30
128 Phil Simms	.20	.50
129 Lawrence Taylor	.20	.50
130 Mark Ingram	.08	.25
131 Leonard Marshall	.08	.25
132 Randall Cunningham	.15	.40
133 Eric Allen	.08	.25
134 Keith Byars	.08	.25
135 Fred Barnett	.10	.30
136 Wes Hopkins	.07	.20
137 Ernie Jones	.07	.20
138 Johnny Johnson	.07	.20
139 Anthony Thompson	.07	.20
140 Timm Rosenbach	.07	.20
141 Randal Hill	.07	.20
142 Steve Young	.60	1.50
143 Jerry Rice	.75	2.00
144 Tom Rathman	.08	.25
145 Charles Haley	.15	.40
146 John Taylor	.15	.40
147 Vinny Testaverde	.15	.40
148 Gary Anderson RB	.08	.25
149 Broderick Thomas	.07	.20
150 Mark Carrier WR	.10	.30
151 Ian Beckles	.07	.20
152 Mark Rypien	.10	.30
153 Earnest Byner	.08	.25
154 Gary Clark	.10	.30
155 Monte Coleman	.07	.20
156 Ricky Ervins	.07	.20
157 Earnest Byner	.08	.25
158 Jim Kelly	.30	.75
159 Checklist 129-144	.07	.20
160 Mark Rypien	.10	.30

1938 Dixie Lids Small

This unnumbered set of lids is actually a combined sport and non-sport set with 24 different lids. The lids are found in more than one size, approximately 2 11/16" in diameter as well as 2 5/16" in diameter. The catalog designation is F7-1. The 1938 lids are distinguished from the 1937 Dixie Lids by the fact that the 1938 lids are printed in blue ink whereas the 1938 lids are printed in black or wine-colored ink. In the checklist below only the sports subjects are checklisted; non-sport subjects (celebrities) included in this 24 card set are Don Ameche, Annabella, Gene Autry, Warner Baxter, William Boyd, Bobby Breen, Gary Cooper, Alice Fay, Sonja Henie, Tommy Kelly, June Lang, Colonel Tim McCoy, Tyrone Power, Tex Ritter, Simone Simon, Bob Steele, The Three Musquiteers and Jane Withers.

COMPLETE SPORT SET (6)	250.00	500.00
*LARGE: .6X TO 1.5X SMALL		
1 Sam Baugh	75.00	125.00
6 Bronko Nagurski	90.00	150.00

1938 Dixie Premiums

This is a parallel issue to the lids -- an attractive "premium" large picture of each of the subjects in the Dixie Lids set. The premiums are printed on thick stock and feature a large color drawing on the front; each unnumbered premium measures approximately 8" X 10". The 1938 premiums are distinguished from the 1937 Dixie Lid premiums by the fact that the 1938 premiums contain a light green border whereas the 1937 premiums have a darker green border completely around the photo. Also, on the reverse, the 1938 premiums have a single gray sline line at the top leading to the player's name in script. Again, we have only checklisted the sports personalities.

COMPLETE SET (6)	375.00	750.00
1 Sam Baugh	150.00	250.00
6 Bronko Nagurski	150.00	250.00

1999 Doak Walker Award Banquet

This set of three cards was released to attendees of the 1998 Dr.Pepper Doak Walker Award Banquet in January 1999. Each card features a photo of the player on the cardfront and career highlights on the back. The unnumbered cards are listed alphabetically below.

COMPLETE SET (3)	14.00	35.00
1 Gale Sayers	2.40	6.00
2 Doak Walker	2.40	6.00
3 Ricky Williams	10.00	25.00

1992 Dog Tags

Produced by Chris Martin Enterprises, Inc., this boxed set consists of 81 dog tags. Made of durable plastic, each tag measures approximately 2 1/8" by 3 3/8" and, with its rounded corners, resembles a credit card. The set subdivides into three groups: team tags (1-28), regular player tags (29-76), and rookie tags (R1-R5). The cards are numbered on both sides. Tag number 42 (Emmitt Smith) was also issued as a promo, stamped "PROMO TAG" on its back. Also produced was a Chris Martin dog tag that was personally autographed.

COMPLETE SET (81)	40.00	100.00
1 Atlanta Falcons	.20	.50
2 Buffalo Bills	.20	.50
3 Chicago Bears	.20	.50
4 Cincinnati Bengals	.20	.50
5 Cleveland Browns	.20	.50
6 Dallas Cowboys	.30	.75
7 Denver Broncos	.20	.50
8 Detroit Lions	.20	.50
9 Green Bay Packers	.20	.50
10 Houston Oilers	.20	.50
11 Indianapolis Colts	.20	.50
12 Kansas City Chiefs	.20	.50
13 Los Angeles Raiders	.30	.75
14 Los Angeles Rams	.20	.50
15 Miami Dolphins	.30	.75
16 Minnesota Vikings	.20	.50
17 New England Patriots	.20	.50
18 New Orleans Saints	.20	.50
19 New York Giants	.20	.50
20 New York Jets	.20	.50
21 Philadelphia Eagles	.20	.50
22 Phoenix Cardinals	.20	.50
23 Pittsburgh Steelers	.20	.50
24 San Diego Chargers	.20	.50
25 San Francisco 49ers	.20	.50
26 Seattle Seahawks	.20	.50
27 Tampa Bay Buccaneers	.20	.50
28 Washington Redskins	.20	.50
29 Chris Martin	.30	.75
30 Dan Marino	4.80	12.00
31 Chris Miller	.40	1.00
32 Deion Sanders	1.20	3.00
33 Jim Kelly	.60	1.50
34 Thurman Thomas	.60	1.50
35 Jim Harbaugh	.60	1.50
36 Mike Singletary	.40	1.00
37 Boomer Esiason	.40	1.00
38 Anthony Munoz	.60	1.50
39 Bernie Kosar	.40	1.00
40 Troy Aikman	2.40	6.00
41 Michael Irvin	.60	1.50
42 Emmitt Smith	4.80	12.00
43 John Elway	4.80	12.00
44 Rodney Peete	.40	1.00
45 Sterling Sharpe	.40	1.00
46 Haywood Jeffires	.40	1.00
47 Warren Moon	.60	1.50
48 Jeff George	.40	1.00
49 Christian Okoye	.40	1.00
50 Derrick Thomas	.60	1.50
51 Howie Long	.60	1.50
52 Ronnie Lott	.40	1.00
53 Jim Everett	.40	1.00
54 Mark Clayton	.40	1.00
55 Anthony Carter	.40	1.00
56 Chris Doleman	.40	1.00
57 Andre Tippett	.30	.75
58 Pat Swilling	.40	1.00
59 Jeff Hostetler	.40	1.00
60 Lawrence Taylor	.60	1.50
61 Rob Moore	.40	1.00
62 Ken O'Brien	.30	.75
63 Keith Byars	.40	1.00
64 Randall Cunningham	.60	1.50
65 Johnny Johnson	.30	.75
66 Timm Rosenbach	.40	1.00
67 Bubby Brister	.40	1.00
68 John Friesz	.40	1.00
69 Jerry Rice	2.40	6.00
70 Steve Young	2.00	5.00
71 Dan McGwire	.40	1.00
72 Broderick Thomas	.30	.75
73 Vinny Testaverde	.40	1.00
74 Gary Clark	.40	1.00
75 Mark Rypien	.40	1.00
76 Neil Smith	.40	1.00
R1 Dale Carter	.40	1.00
R2 Steve Emtman	.40	1.00
R3 David Klingler	.40	1.00
R4 Tommy Maddox	.40	1.00
R5 Vaughn Dunbar	.40	1.00
29AU Chris Martin AU	4.00	10.00
P1 Chris Martin Promo	.40	1.00
P2 Emmitt Smith Promo	2.40	6.00

1993 Dog Tags

Produced by Chris Martin Enterprises, Inc., this set of "Dog Tags Plus" consists of 110 individual player tags and 28 team tags. Two tags, numbers 48 and 138, were not produced. The dog tags were originally distributed in random assortments but later as complete team sets. The only two teams not included in the team set packaging were the Atlanta Falcons and the Los Angeles Raiders. There were also 25,000 sequentially numbered Joe Montana limited edition bonus tags. The collector could obtain one of these Montana tags through a mail-in offer for 5.00 and three proofs of purchase. Reportedly 50,000 of each base set tag were produced, with each one sequentially numbered. Autographed tags were randomly inserted throughout the cases. The players with randomly-inserted autograph tags were Dale Carter, Chris Martin, Emmitt Smith, and Harvey Williams. Also collectors could enter a contest to win a seven-point diamond tag and a 14K gold bead chain. Made of durable plastic, each tag measures approximately 2 1/8" by 3 3/8" and, with its rounded corners, resembles a credit card. After team logo tags (1-28), the set is arranged alphabetically within teams.

COMPLETE SET (138)	50.00	125.00
1 Atlanta Falcons	.20	.50
2 Buffalo Bills	.20	.50
3 Chicago Bears	.20	.50
4 Cincinnati Bengals	.20	.50
5 Cleveland Browns	.20	.50
6 Dallas Cowboys	.30	.75
7 Denver Broncos	.20	.50
8 Detroit Lions	.20	.50
9 Green Bay Packers	.20	.50
10 Houston Oilers	.20	.50
11 Indianapolis Colts	.20	.50
12 Kansas City Chiefs	.20	.50
13 Los Angeles Raiders	.30	.75
14 Los Angeles Rams	.20	.50
15 Miami Dolphins	.30	.75
16 Minnesota Vikings	.20	.50
17 New England Patriots	.20	.50
18 New Orleans Saints	.20	.50
19 New York Giants	.20	.50
20 New York Jets	.20	.50
21 Philadelphia Eagles	.20	.50
22 Phoenix Cardinals	.20	.50
23 Pittsburgh Steelers	.20	.50
24 San Diego Chargers	.20	.50
25 San Francisco 49ers	.20	.50
26 Seattle Seahawks	.20	.50
27 Tampa Bay Buccaneers	.20	.50
28 Washington Redskins	.20	.50
29 Steve Broussard	.30	.75
30 Chris Miller	.30	.75
31 Andre Rison	.60	1.50
32 Deion Sanders	1.20	3.00
33 Cornelius Bennett	.40	1.00
34 Jim Kelly	.60	1.50
35 Bruce Smith	.60	1.50
36 Thurman Thomas	.60	1.50
37 Neal Anderson	.30	.75
38 Mark Carrier DB	.30	.75
39 Jim Harbaugh	.60	1.50
40 Alonzo Spellman	.30	.75
41 David Fulcher	.30	.75
42 Harold Green	.30	.75
43 David Klingler	.30	.75
44 Carl Pickens	.40	1.00
45 Bernie Kosar	.30	.75
46 Clay Matthews	.40	1.00
47 Eric Metcalf	.40	1.00
49 Troy Aikman	2.00	5.00
50 Michael Irvin	.60	1.50
51 Russell Maryland	.40	1.00
52 Emmitt Smith	3.20	8.00
53 Steve Atwater	.30	.75
54 John Elway	4.00	10.00
55 Tommy Maddox	.60	1.50
56 Shannon Sharpe	.60	1.50
57 Herman Moore	.60	1.50
58 Rodney Peete	.40	1.00
59 Barry Sanders	4.00	10.00
60 Andre Ware	.40	1.00
61 Terrell Buckley	.30	.75
62 Brett Favre	4.80	12.00
63 Sterling Sharpe	.40	1.00
64 Reggie White	.60	1.50
65 Ray Childress	.40	1.00
66 Haywood Jeffires	.40	1.00
67 Warren Moon	.60	1.50
68 Lorenzo White	.30	.75
69 Duane Bickett	.30	.75
70 Quentin Coryatt	.40	1.00
71 Steve Emtman	.30	.75
72 Jeff George	.60	1.50
73 Dale Carter	.40	1.00
74 Neil Smith	.40	1.00
75 Derrick Thomas	.60	1.50
76 Harvey Williams	.40	1.00
77 Eric Dickerson	.40	1.00
78 Howie Long	.60	1.50
79 Todd Marinovich	.30	.75
80 Alexander Wright	.30	.75
81 Flipper Anderson	.30	.75
82 Jim Everett	.30	.75
83 Cleveland Gary	.30	.75
84 Chris Martin	.30	.75
85 Irving Fryar	.40	1.00
86 Keith Jackson	.40	1.00
87 Dan Marino	4.00	10.00
88 Louis Oliver	.30	.75
89 Terry Allen	.60	1.50
90 Anthony Carter	.30	.75
91 Chris Doleman	.40	1.00
92 Rich Gannon	.60	1.50
93 Eugene Chung	.30	.75
94 Marv Cook	.30	.75
95 Leonard Russell	.40	1.00
96 Andre Tippett	.30	.75
97 Morten Andersen	.30	.75
98 Vaughn Dunbar	.30	.75
99 Rickey Jackson	.30	.75
100 Sam Mills	.30	.75
101 Derek Brown TE	.30	.75
102 Lawrence Taylor	.60	1.50
103 Rodney Hampton	.40	1.00
104 Phil Simms	.40	1.00
105 Johnny Mitchell	.40	1.00
106 Rob Moore	.40	1.00
107 Blair Thomas	.30	.75
108 Browning Nagle	.30	.75
109 Eric Allen	.30	.75
110 Fred Barnett	.40	1.00
111 Randall Cunningham	.60	1.50
112 Herschel Walker	.40	1.00
113 Chris Chandler	.40	1.00
114 Randal Hill	.30	.75
115 Ricky Proehl	.30	.75
116 Eric Swann	.40	1.00
117 Barry Foster	.40	1.00
118 Eric Green	.30	.75
119 Neil O'Donnell	.40	1.00
120 Rod Woodson	.40	1.00
121 Marion Butts	.40	1.00
122 Stan Humphries	.40	1.00
123 Anthony Miller	.40	1.00
124 Junior Seau	.60	1.50
125 Amp Lee	.30	.75
126 Jerry Rice	2.00	5.00
127 Ricky Watters	.40	1.00
128 Steve Young	1.60	4.00
129 Brian Blades	.40	1.00
130 Cortez Kennedy	.40	1.00
131 Dan McGwire	.30	.75
132 John L. Williams	.30	.75
133 Reggie Cobb	.30	.75
134 Steve DeBerg	.40	1.00
135 Keith McCants	.30	.75
136 Broderick Thomas	.30	.75
137 Earnest Byner	.30	.75
139 Mark Rypien	.30	.75
140 Ricky Sanders	.30	.75
LE1 Joe Montana Bonus	3.20	8.00
P1 Chris Martin Promo	.20	.50
P2 Super Bowl XXVII Promo	.75	2.00

1967 Dolphins Royal Castle

This 27-card set was issued by Royal Castle, a south Florida hamburger stand, at a rate of two new cards every week during the season. These unnumbered cards measure approximately 3" by 4 3/8". The front features a black and white (almost sepia-toned) posed photo of the player enframed by an orange border, with the player's signature below the photo. Biographical information is given on the back (including player's nickname where appropriate), along with the logos for the Miami Dolphins and Royal Castle. This set features a card of Bob Griese during his rookie season. There may be a 28th card of George Wilson Jr., but it has never been substantiated. There are 17-cards that are easier than the others; rather than calling these double prints, the other ten cards are marked as SP's in the checklist below.

COMPLETE SET (27)	4500.00	7000.00
1 Joe Auer SP	175.00	300.00
2 Tom Beier	75.00	125.00
3 Mel Branch	75.00	125.00
4 Jon Brittenum	75.00	125.00
5 George Chesser	75.00	125.00
6 Edward Cooke	75.00	125.00
7 Frank Emanuel SP	175.00	300.00
8 Tom Erlandson SP	175.00	300.00
9 Norm Evans SP	200.00	350.00
10 Bob Griese SP	1800.00	3000.00
11 Abner Haynes SP	250.00	400.00
12 Jerry Hopkins SP	175.00	300.00
13 Frank Jackson	75.00	125.00
14 Billy Joe	75.00	125.00
15 Wahoo McDaniel	150.00	250.00
16 Robert Neff	75.00	125.00
17 Billy Neighbors	75.00	125.00
18 Rick Norton	75.00	125.00
19 Bob Petrich	75.00	125.00
20 Jim Riley	75.00	125.00
21 John Stofa SP	175.00	300.00
22 Laverne Torczon	75.00	125.00
23 Howard Twilley	75.00	125.00
24 Jim Warren SP	175.00	300.00
25 Dick Westmoreland	75.00	125.00
26 Maxie Williams	75.00	125.00
27 George Wilson Sr. SP	200.00	350.00

1970 Dolphins Team Issue

The Miami Dolphins likely issued this series of player photos over a two or three year period around 1970. The format is the same for each photo with only subtle differences in the type (size and style) and player position (some spelled out and others initials only). Each of these black-and-white photos measures approximately 5" by 7" and is blankbacked and unnumbered.

COMPLETE SET (12)	60.00	120.00
1 Dean Brown	6.00	12.00
2 Frank Cornish DT	6.00	12.00
3 Ted Davis	6.00	12.00
4 Norm Evans	6.00	12.00
5 Hubert Ginn	6.00	12.00
6 Mike Kolen	6.00	12.00
7 Bob Kuechenberg	7.50	15.00
8 Stan Mitchell	6.00	12.00
9 Lloyd Mumphord	6.00	12.00
10 Dick Palmer	6.00	12.00
11 Barry Pryor	6.00	12.00
12 Bill Stanfill	6.00	12.00

1970-71 Dolphins Team Issue

The Miami Dolphins likely issued this series of player photos over a two or three year period around 1970. The format is the same for each photo with only subtle differences in the type (size and style) and player position (some are included while others are not). Each of these black-and-white photos measures approximately 8" by 10" and is blankbacked and unnumbered.

COMPLETE SET (22)	125.00	250.00
1 Dick Anderson	6.00	12.00
2 Dick Anderson	6.00	12.00
3 Nick Buoniconti	7.50	15.00
4 Larry Csonka	10.00	18.00
5 Manny Fernandez	6.00	12.00
6 Tom Goode	6.00	12.00
7 Bob Griese	12.00	20.00
8 Jimmy Hines	6.00	12.00
9 Jim Kiick	7.50	15.00
10 Mike Kolen	6.00	12.00
11 Larry Little	7.50	15.00

12 Bob Matheson 6.00 12.00
13 Mercury Morris 7.50 15.00
14 Bob Petrella 6.00 12.00
15 Larry Seiple 6.00 12.00
16 Don Shula CO 12.00 20.00
18 Otto Stowe 6.00 12.00
19 Howard Twilley 6.00 12.00
20 Paul Warfield 7.50 15.00
21 Paul Warfield 7.50 15.00
22 Garo Yepremian 6.00 12.00

1972 Dolphins Glasses

This set of player glasses was thought to have been issued in 1972. Each features a color artist's rendition of a Dolphins player against a background of white. The reverse includes a short bio of the player. The glasses stand roughly 5 1/2" tall with a diameter of 2 3/4."

COMPLETE SET (8) 50.00 100.00
1 Larry Csonka 15.00 25.00
2 Larry Little 6.00 12.00
2 Jim Kiick 6.00 12.00
2 Nick Buoniconti 7.50 15.00
3 Bob Griese 15.00 25.00
4 Mercury Morris 6.00 12.00
5 Paul Warfield 10.00 20.00
6 Manny Fernandez 6.00 12.00

1972 Dolphins Koole Frozen Cups

This set of plastic cups was sponsored by Koole Frozen Foods and Coca-Cola. Each looks very similar to the 1972 7-11 cups with a color artist's rendering of the featured player along with a cup number of 20 in the set. Each cup measures roughly 5 1/4" tall with a diameter at the top of 3 1/4."

COMPLETE SET (20) 100.00 200.00
1 Dick Anderson 6.00 12.00
2 Nick Buoniconti 7.50 15.00
3 Bob Griese 15.00 25.00
4 Bob Kuechenberg 6.00 12.00
5 Bill Stanfill 4.00 8.00
6 Jake Scott 6.00 12.00
7 Manny Fernandez 6.00 12.00
8 Earl Morrall 7.50 15.00
9 Larry Csonka 15.00 25.00
10 Jim Kiick 7.50 15.00
11 Bob Heinz 4.00 8.00
12 Jim Langer 7.50 15.00
13 Bob Matheson 4.00 8.00
14 Vern Den Herder 4.00 8.00
15 Larry Little 7.50 15.00
16 Curtis Johnson 4.00 8.00
17 Mercury Morris 6.00 12.00
18 Paul Warfield 12.00 20.00
19 Marv Fleming 6.00 12.00
20 Lloyd Mumphord 4.00 8.00

1972 Dolphins Team Issue

These large (approximately 8 1/2" by 11") black and white photos were issued by the Dolphins around 1972. Each features the player's name, position initals and team name below the photo with a facsimile autograph on the image.

COMPLETE SET (12) 60.00 120.00
1 Dick Anderson 5.00 10.00
2 Marlin Briscoe 5.00 10.00
3 Nick Buoniconti 6.00 12.00
4 Larry Csonka 7.50 15.00
5 Manny Fernandez 5.00 10.00
6 Bob Griese 10.00 20.00
7 Jim Kiick 6.00 12.00
8 Larry Little 6.00 12.00
9 Earl Morrall 5.00 10.00
10 Mercury Morris 6.00 12.00
11 Don Shula CO 10.00 20.00
12 Garo Yepremian 5.00 10.00

1972 Dolphins Team Issue Color

These color photos, issued in 1972, measure roughly 8 3/8" by 10 1/2" and feature a player photo surrounded by a white border with the player's name and position in the upper border. The photo backs include a detailed player bio and statistics as well as the name "Dolphins Graphics, Miami Florida" at the bottom.

COMPLETE SET (6) 40.00 80.00
1 Nick Buoniconti 7.50 15.00
2 Larry Csonka 10.00 20.00
3 Manny Fernandez 5.00 10.00
4 Bob Griese 12.50 25.00
5 Jim Kiick 6.00 12.00
6 Paul Warfield 10.00 20.00

1974 Dolphins All-Pro Graphics

Each of these ten photos measures approximately 8 1/4" by 10 3/4". The fronts feature color action photos bordered in white. The player's name, position, and team name appear in the top border, while the copyright year (1974) and the manufacturer "All Pro Graphics, Inc." are printed in the bottom white border at the left. It is reported that several of these photos do not have the tagline in the lower left corner. The backs are blank. The photos are unnumbered and checklisted below in alphabetical order.

COMPLETE SET (10) 62.50 125.00
1 Dick Anderson 6.00 12.00
2 Nick Buoniconti 7.50 15.00
3 Larry Csonka 10.00 20.00
4 Manny Fernandez 4.00 8.00
5 Bob Griese 12.50 25.00
6 Jim Kiick 6.00 12.00
7 Earl Morrall 7.50 15.00
8 Mercury Morris 6.00 12.00
9 Jake Scott 5.00 10.00
10 Garo Yepremian 4.00 8.00

1974 Dolphins Team Issue

The Miami Dolphins likely issued this series of player photos over a two or three year period around 1974. The format is the same for each photo with only subtle differences in the type size and style. The photos are similar to the 1970 release but feature a distinctly different type style. Each of these black-and-white photos measures approximately 5" by 7" and is blankbacked and unnumbered.

COMPLETE SET (21) 75.00 150.00
1 Charlie Babb 4.00 8.00
2 Mel Baker 4.00 8.00
3 Bruce Bannon 4.00 8.00
4 Randy Crowder 4.00 8.00
5 Norm Evans 4.00 8.00
6 Hubert Ginn 4.00 8.00
7 Irv Goode 4.00 8.00
8 Bob Heinz 4.00 8.00
9 Curtis Johnson 4.00 8.00
10 Bob Kuechenberg 5.00 10.00
11 Nat Moore 5.00 10.00
12 Wayne Moore 4.00 8.00
13 Lloyd Mumphord 4.00 8.00
14 Ed Newman 4.00 8.00
15 Don Reese 4.00 8.00
16 Larry Seiple 4.00 8.00
17 Bill Stanfill 5.00 10.00
18 Henry Stuckey 4.00 8.00
19 Doug Swift 4.00 8.00
20 Jeris White 4.00 8.00
21 Tom Wickert 4.00 8.00

1976 Dolphins McDonald's

This set of photos was sponsored by McDonald's. Each photo measures approximately 8" by 10" and features a posed color close-up photo bordered in white. The player's name and team name are printed in black below the player's photo with the Dolphin's 1976 regular season schedule below it. The top portion of the back has a black and white photo and biographical information on the player. The bottom portion carries an ad for McDonald's. The photos are unnumbered and are checklisted below alphabetically.

COMPLETE SET (4) 15.00 30.00
1 Dick Anderson 5.00 10.00
2 Vern Den Herder 4.00 8.00
3 Nat Moore 5.00 10.00
4 Don Nottingham 4.00 8.00

1980 Dolphins Police

The 1980 Miami Dolphins set contains 16 unnumbered cards, which have been listed by player uniform number in the checklist below. The cards measure approximately 2 5/8" by 4 1/8". The set was sponsored by the Kiwanis Club, the local law enforcement agency, and the Miami Dolphins. The backs contain "Dolphins Tips" and the Miami Dolphins logo. The backs are printed in black with blue accent on white card stock. The fronts contain the Kiwanis logo, but not the Dolphins logo as in the following year. The card of Larry Little is reportedly more difficult to obtain than other cards in this set.

COMPLETE SET (16) 50.00 100.00
5 Uwe Von Schamann 1.25 3.00
10 Don Strock 2.50 6.00
12 Bob Griese 6.00 15.00
22 Tony Nathan 2.50 6.00
24 Delvin Williams 2.50 6.00
25 Tim Foley 1.50 4.00
50 Larry Gordon 1.25 3.00
58 Kim Bokamper 1.25 3.00
64 Ed Newman 1.25 3.00
66 Larry Little SP 8.00 20.00
67 Bob Kuechenberg 2.50 6.00
73 Bob Baumhower 1.50 4.00
77 A.J. Duhe 2.50 6.00
82 Duriel Harris 1.50 4.00
89 Nat Moore 2.50 6.00
NNO Don Shula CO 6.00 15.00

1981 Dolphins Police

The 1981 Miami Dolphins police set consists of 16 numbered cards. The cards measure approximately 2 5/8" by 4 1/8". Player uniform numbers also appear on the fronts of the cards, as does a Kiwanis and blue Dolphins logo. The set is sponsored by the local Kiwanis Club, the local law enforcement agency, and the Dolphins. The backs feature the Dolphins logo and "Dolphins Tips". Card backs are printed in black with gold and blue accent on thin white card stock.

COMPLETE SET (16) 8.00 20.00
1 Duriel Harris .60 1.50
2 Bob Kuechenberg .60 1.50
3 Don Bessillieu .40 1.00
4 Gerald Small .40 1.00
5 David Woodley .60 1.50
6 Don McNeal .40 1.00
7 Nat Moore .75 2.00
8 A.J. Duhe .60 1.50
9 Glenn Blackwood .40 1.00
10 Don Strock .75 2.00
11 Doug Betters .40 1.00
12 George Roberts .40 1.00
13 Bob Baumhower .60 1.50
14 Kim Bokamper .40 1.00
15 Tony Nathan .75 2.00
16 Don Shula CO 2.50 6.00

1981 Dolphins Team Issue

The Dolphins likely issued this series of player photos over a period of years in the early 1980s. The format is the same for each photo with only subtle differences in the type size and style. Each photo features a black and white game action shot of the player and measures approximately 5" by 7." The photos are also blankbacked and unnumbered.

COMPLETE SET (16) 25.00 50.00
1 Bill Barnett 1.25 3.00
2 Glenn Blackwood 1.25 3.00
3 Bob Brudzinski 1.25 3.00
4 A.J. Duhe 1.50 4.00
5 Nick Giaquinto 1.25 3.00
6 Bruce Hardy 1.25 3.00
7 Jim Jensen 1.25 3.00
8 Mike Kozlowski 1.25 3.00
9 Bob Kuechenberg 1.50 4.00
10 Eric Laakso 1.25 3.00
11A Don McNeal 1.25 3.00
11B Don McNeal 1.25 3.00
12 Tom Orosz 1.25 3.00
13 Steve Potter 1.25 3.00
14 Steve Shull 1.25 3.00
15 Tommy Vigorito 1.25 3.00
16 David Woodley 1.50 4.00

1982 Dolphins Police

The 1982 Miami Dolphins set of 16 numbered cards is one of the most attractive of the police sets. The cards measure approximately 2 5/8" by 4 1/8". The orange and greenish-blue frame line on the front contains the player's number and name. The Kiwanis logo is also contained on the front. The backs are printed in black, orange, greenish-blue, and blue ink and feature "Dolphins Tips," the Dolphins logo, and the Kiwanis logo. The set is sponsored by the Kiwanis Club, the local law enforcement agency, and the Dolphins. Shula and Von Schamann are supposedly a little tougher to find than the other cards in the set.

COMPLETE SET (16) 12.00 30.00
1 Don Shula CO SP 4.00 10.00
2 Uwe Von Schamann SP 1.50 4.00
3 Jimmy Cefalo .60 1.50
4 Andra Franklin .60 1.50
5 Larry Gordon .40 1.00
6 Nat Moore .75 2.00
7 Bob Baumhower .60 1.50
8 A.J. Duhe .60 1.50
9 Tony Nathan .75 2.00
10 Glenn Blackwood .40 1.00
11 Don Strock .75 2.00
12 David Woodley .60 1.50
13 Kim Bokamper .40 1.00
14 Bob Kuechenberg .60 1.50
15 Duriel Harris .60 1.50
16 Ed Newman .40 1.00

1983 Dolphins Police

This numbered set of 16 cards features the Miami Dolphins. Cards measure approximately 2 5/8" by 4 1/8". The cards are numbered on the back in the bottom right corner. The cards look very similar to the 1982 Police Dolphins set. Card backs feature black print with orange and aquamarine accent on white card stock. The cards were sponsored by Kiwanis, Law Enforcement Agencies, Burger King, and the Miami Dolphins. The Burger King and Kiwanis logos both appear on the fronts of the cards.

COMPLETE SET (16) 7.50 15.00
1 Earnie Rhone .40 1.00
2 Andra Franklin .40 1.00
3 Eric Laakso .40 1.00
4 Joe Rose .40 1.00
5 David Woodley .50 1.25
6 Uwe Von Schamann .40 1.00
7 Eddie Hill .40 1.00
8 Bruce Hardy .40 1.00
9 Woody Bennett .40 1.00
10 Fulton Walker .40 1.00
11 Lyle Blackwood .40 1.00
12 A.J. Duhe .50 1.25
13 Don Shula CO 1.50 4.00
14 Duriel Harris .50 1.25
15 Bob Brudzinski .40 1.00
16 Bob Baumhower .40 1.00

1984 Dolphins Police

This unnumbered 17-card set features the Miami Dolphins. The Mark Clayton card was added to the set after the first sixteen cards had been distributed. Cards measure approximately 2 5/8" by 4 1/8". Cards are listed below alphabetically by player's name. The Dan Marino card is noteworthy in that it features Marino during his rookie year for cards. Cards are known to exist with the glossy sheen on the back due to a printing error. It is unknown what percent of the print run was reversed in that fashion.

COMPLETE SET (17) 20.00 40.00
1 Bob Baumhower .30 .75
2 Doug Betters .30 .75
3 Glenn Blackwood .20 .50
4 Kim Bokamper .20 .50
5 Dolfan Denny (Mascot) .20 .50
6 A.J. Duhe .30 .75
7 Mark Duper .75 2.00
8 Jim Jensen .30 .75
9 Dan Marino 10.00 25.00
10 Don McNeal .20 .50
11 Nat Moore .40 1.00
12 Tony Nathan .40 1.00
13 Ed Newman .20 .50
14 Don Shula CO 1.25 3.00
15 Dwight Stephenson .30 .75
16 Fulton Walker .20 .50
17 Mark Clayton SP 1.50 4.00

1985 Dolphins Police

This 16-card set is numbered on the back. The card backs are printed in black ink on white card stock. Cards measure 2 5/8" by 4 1/8". The set was sponsored by Kiwanis, Hospital Corporation of America, the Dolphins, and area law enforcement agencies. Uniform numbers are printed on the card front above the player's name. Cards are known to exist with the glossy sheen on the back due to a printing error. It is unknown what percent of the print run was reversed in that fashion.

COMPLETE SET (16) 10.00 25.00
1 William Judson .15 .40
2 Fulton Walker .20 .50
3 Mark Clayton .60 1.50
4 Lyle Blackwood and .20 .50
5 Dan Marino 6.00 15.00
6 Reggie Roby .30 .75
7 Doug Betters .20 .50
8 Jay Brophy .15 .40
9 Dolfan Denny (Mascot) .15 .40
10 Kim Bokamper .15 .40
11 Mark Duper .50 1.25
12 Nat Moore .30 .75
13 Mike Kozlowski .15 .40
14 Don Shula CO .60 1.50
15 Don McNeal .15 .40
16 Tony Nathan .30 .75

1985 Dolphins Posters

These small posters (measuring roughly 18" by 25") feature a color photo of a Dolphins' player on the front with a facsimile autograph and a blank back. Each was sponsored by Eckerd Drug and Kodak and includes a strip of coupons at the bottom. The title "Dolphins 20 Years" appears below each photo.

COMPLETE SET (9) 75.00 125.00
1 Reggie Roby 4.00 10.00
2 Tony Nathan 4.00 10.00
3 Don Shula 8.00 20.00
4 Bob Baumhower 5.00 12.00
5 L.Blackwood 4.00 10.00
G.Blackwood
6 Mark Duper 6.00 15.00
7 Dan Marino 20.00 40.00
8 Mark Clayton 6.00 15.00
9 Doug Betters 4.00 10.00

1986 Dolphins Police

This 16-card set is numbered on the card backs, which are printed in black ink on white card stock. Cards measure approximately 2 5/8" by 4 1/8". The set was sponsored by Kiwanis, Anon Anew, the Dolphins, and area law enforcement agencies. Uniform numbers are printed on the front of the card.

COMPLETE SET (16) 6.00 15.00
1 Dwight Stephenson .30 .75
2 Bob Baumhower .20 .50
3 Dolfan Denny (Mascot) .15 .40
4 Don Shula CO .60 1.50
5 Dan Marino 3.00 8.00
6 Tony Nathan .30 .75
7 Mark Duper .50 1.25
8 John Offerdahl .40 1.00
9 Fuad Reveiz .15 .40
10 Hugh Green .20 .50
11 Lorenzo Hampton .20 .50
12 Mark Clayton .60 1.50
13 Nat Moore .30 .75
14 Bob Brudzinski .15 .40
15 Reggie Roby .20 .50
16 T.J. Turner .20 .50

1987 Dolphins Ace Fact Pack

This 33-card set measures approximately 2 1/4" by 3 5/8". The set was printed in West Germany (by Ace Fact Pack) for release in Great Britain. This set features members of the Miami Dolphins and the set has rounded corners on the front and a design for Ace (looks like a playing card) on the back. We have checklisted the set in alphabetical order.

COMPLETE SET (33) 250.00 500.00
1 Bob Baumhower 2.50 6.00
2 Woody Bennett 2.00 5.00
3 Doug Betters 2.50 6.00
4 Glenn Blackwood 2.50 6.00
5 Bud Brown 2.00 5.00
6 Bob Brudzinski 2.00 5.00
7 Mark Clayton 4.00 10.00
8 Mark Duper 4.00 10.00
9 Roy Foster 2.00 5.00
10 Jon Giesler 2.00 5.00
11 Hugh Green 2.50 6.00
12 Lorenzo Hampton 2.00 5.00
13 Bruce Hardy 2.00 5.00
14 William Judson 2.00 5.00
15 Greg Koch 2.00 5.00
16 Paul Lankford 2.00 5.00
17 George Little 2.00 5.00
18 Dan Marino 200.00 350.00
19 John Offerdahl 2.50 6.00
20 Dwight Stephenson 2.50 6.00
21 Don Strock 2.50 6.00
22 T.J. Turner 2.00 5.00
23 Dolphins Helmet 2.00 5.00
24 Dolphins Information 2.00 5.00
25 Dolphins Uniform 2.00 5.00
26 Game Record Holders 2.00 5.00
27 Season Record Holders 2.00 5.00
28 Career Record Holders 2.00 5.00
29 Record 1967-86 2.00 5.00
30 1986 Team Statistics 2.00 5.00
31 All-Time Greats 2.00 5.00
32 Roll of Honour 2.00 5.00
33 Joe Robbie Stadium 2.00 5.00

1987 Dolphins Holsum

This 22-card set features players of the Miami Dolphins; cards were available only in Holsum Bread packages. The set was co-produced by Mike Schechter Associates on behalf of the NFL Players Association. The cards are standard size, 2 1/2" by 3 1/2", and are done in full color. Card fronts have a color photo within a green border and the backs are printed in black ink on white card stock.

COMPLETE SET (22) 60.00 120.00
1 Bob Baumhower 1.50 4.00
2 Mark Brown 1.50 4.00
3 Mark Clayton 2.00 5.00
4 Mark Duper 2.00 5.00
5 Roy Foster 1.50 4.00
6 Hugh Green 1.50 4.00
7 Lorenzo Hampton 1.50 4.00
8 William Judson 1.50 4.00
9 George Little 1.50 4.00
10 Dan Marino 15.00 40.00
11 Nat Moore 1.50 4.00
12 Tony Nathan 1.50 4.00
13 John Offerdahl 1.50 4.00
14 James Pruitt 1.50 4.00
15 Fuad Reveiz 1.50 4.00
16 Dwight Stephenson 2.50 6.00
17 Glenn Blackwood 1.50 4.00
18 Bruce Hardy 1.50 4.00
19 Reggie Roby 1.50 4.00
20 Bob Brudzinski 1.50 4.00
21 Ron Jaworski 1.50 4.00
22 T.J. Turner 1.50 4.00

1987 Dolphins Police

This 16-card set is numbered on the back and measures approximately 2 5/8" by 4 1/8". The set was sponsored by Kiwanis, Children's Center of Fair Oaks Hospital at Boca/Delray, the Dolphins, and area law enforcement agencies. Uniform numbers are printed on the front of the card. Reportedly approximately three million cards were produced for this promotion. The Dwight Stephenson card is considered more difficult to find than the other cards in the set.

COMPLETE SET (16) 25.00 40.00
1 Joe Robbie OWN .50 1.25
2 Glenn Blackwood .50 1.25
3 Mark Duper .60 1.50
4 Fuad Reveiz .50 1.25
5 Dolfan Denny (Mascot) .50 1.25
6 Dwight Stephenson SP 2.50 6.00
7 Hugh Green .60 1.50
8 Larry Csonka 1.00 2.50
9 Bud Brown .50 1.25
10 Don Shula CO 1.00 2.50
11 T.J. Turner .50 1.25
12 Reggie Roby .50 1.25
13 Dan Marino 8.00 20.00
14 John Offerdahl .50 1.25
15 Bruce Hardy .50 1.25
16 Lorenzo Hampton .50 1.25

1988 Dolphins Holsum

This 12-card set features players of the Miami Dolphins; cards were available only in Holsum Bread packages. The set was co-produced by Mike Schechter Associates on behalf of the NFL Players Association. The cards are standard size, 2 1/2" by 3 1/2", and are done in full color. Card fronts have a color photo within a green border and the backs are printed in black ink on white card stock.

COMPLETE SET (12) 15.00 30.00
1 Mark Clayton 1.25 3.00
2 Dwight Stephenson 1.50 4.00
3 Mark Duper 1.25 3.00
4 John Offerdahl .75 2.00
5 Dan Marino 6.00 15.00
6 T.J. Turner .60 1.50
7 Lorenzo Hampton .60 1.50
8 Bruce Hardy .60 1.50
9 Fuad Reveiz .60 1.50
10 Reggie Roby .60 1.50
11 William Judson .60 1.50
12 Bob Brudzinski .60 1.50

1995 Dolphins Chevron Pin Cards

Chevron released these 8-cards as a promotion throughout the 1995 season. The cards themselves are unnumbered, but have been arranged below in accordance with the checklist printed on each cardback. A lapel pin was included with and attached to each card in the lower right hand corner. Each card measures approximately 3" by 5" and includes a color photo on front and text on back along with a checklist.

COMPLETE SET (8) 8.00 20.00
1 Miami Dolphins .80 2.00
2 Dan Marino 4.00 10.00
3 Bryan Cox .80 2.00
4 Troy Vincent .80 2.00
5 Irving Fryar 1.20 3.00
6 Eric Green .80 2.00
7 Team '95 1.20 3.00
8 Hall of Famers 1.60 4.00

1996 Dolphins AT&T

This set was issued in 1996 on a large perforated sheet. Each card when separated measures roughly 2 1/2" by 3" and includes a color photo of the player along with the AT&T sponsor logo on the cardfronts. The cardbacks feature the typical player statistics and bio.

COMPLETE SET (24) 15.00 30.00
1 Karim Abdul-Jabbar .50 1.25
2 Trace Armstrong .40 1.00
3 Fred Barnett .50 1.25
4 Tim Bowens .40 1.00
5 James Brown .40 1.00
6 Terrell Buckley .50 1.25
7 Troy Drayton .40 1.00
8 Daryl Gardener .40 1.00
9 Chris Gray .40 1.00
10 Dwight Hollier .40 1.00
11 Calvin Jackson .40 1.00
12 Jimmy Johnson CO .40 1.00
13 John Kidd .40 1.00
14 Dan Marino 2.50 6.00
15 O.J. McDuffie .50 1.25
16 Louis Oliver .40 1.00
17 Stanley Pritchett .40 1.00
18 Tim Ruddy .40 1.00
19 Keith Sims .40 1.00
20 Chris Singleton .40 1.00
21 Daniel Stubbs .40 1.00
22 Zach Thomas .75 2.00
23 Richmond Webb .40 1.00
24 Shawn Wooden .40 1.00

1996 Dolphins Miami Subs Cards/Coins

The Miami Dolphins, in conjunction with Miami Subs Restaurants, produced this 9-card and 9-coin set commemorating the 1972 Super Bowl VII team and the present Miami Dolphins. The card fronts feature color action player photos with the player's name printed diagonally on the right side on the card. The backs display the complete 9-card checklist and individual card numbers. We've listed the cards below using a "CA" prefix. The coin fronts feature a player likeness with the player's name and jersey number. The backs display the Dolphins team logo. The coins are unnumbered but have been listed below alphabetically using a "CO" prefix. A cardboard holder featuring Dan Marino, Bernie Kosar, Jimmy Johnson, Fred Barnett, and Mark Clayton was produced to house the set.

COMP.CARD/COIN SET (18) 15.00 30.00
COMPLETE CARD SET (9) 10.00 18.00
COMPLETE COIN SET (9) 5.00 12.00
CA1 Dan Marino 3.00 8.00
CA2 Larry Csonka 1.00 2.50
CA3 Pete Stoyanovich .60 1.50
CA4 Paul Warfield 1.00 2.50
CA5 Bernie Kosar .60 1.50
CA6 Mark Clayton .60 1.50
CA7 Fred Barnett .60 1.50
CA8 Nat Moore .75 2.00
CA9 Don Shula 1.50 4.00
George Allen
CO1 Fred Barnett .40 1.00
CO2 Mark Clayton .40 1.00
CO3 Larry Csonka .60 1.50
CO4 Bernie Kosar .40 1.00
CO5 Dan Marino 2.00 5.00
CO6 Nat Moore .50 1.25
CO7 Pete Stoyanovich .40 1.00
CO8 Paul Warfield .60 1.50
CO9 Super Bowl VII Trophy .50 1.25
NNO Display Holder .60 1.50

1997 Dolphins Collector's Choice

Upper Deck released several team sets in 1997 in a blister pack wrapper. Each of the 14-cards in this set are very similar to the base Collector's Choice cards except for the card numbering on the cardback. A cover/checklist card was added featuring the team helmet.

COMPLETE SET (14) 1.50 4.00
MI1 Karim Abdul-Jabbar .10 .30
MI2 O.J. McDuffie .07 .20
MI3 Troy Drayton .02 .10
MI4 Zach Thomas .20 .50
MI5 Irving Spikes .02 .10
MI6 Shane Burton .07 .20
MI7 Stanley Pritchett .02 .10
MI8 Yatil Green .10 .30
MI9 Dan Marino .75 2.00
MI10 Jerris McPhail .02 .10
MI11 Daryl Gardener .02 .10
MI12 Fred Barnett .07 .20
MI13 Terrell Buckley .02 .10
MI14 Checklist .30 .75
(Dan Marino on back)

1997 Dolphins NCL

This set was issued in 1997 on a large perforated sheet. Each card when separated measures roughly 2 1/2" by 3" and includes a color photo of the player along with the NCL (Norwegian Cruise Lines) sponsor logo on the cardfronts. The cardbacks feature the typical player statistics and bio. A second version was also produced, perhaps initially as an uncut sheet, that is missing the glossy surface on the front of the cards and also missing the perforated edges.

COMPLETE SET (24) 15.00 30.00
*NON-GLOSSY: .4X TO 1X GLOSSY VERSION
1 Karim Abdul-Jabbar .50 1.25
2 Trace Armstrong .40 1.00
3 Tim Bowens .50 1.25
4 James Brown .40 1.00
5 Terrell Buckley .50 1.25
6 Troy Drayton .40 1.00
7 Daryl Gardener .40 1.00
8 Anthony Harris .40 1.00
9 Calvin Jackson .40 1.00
10 Jimmy Johnson CO .50 1.25
11 Olindo Mare .40 1.00
12 Dan Marino 3.00 6.00
13 O.J. McDuffie .50 1.25
14 Everett McIver .40 1.00
15 Stanley Pritchett .40 1.00
16 Derrick Rodgers .40 1.00
17 Tim Ruddy .40 1.00
18 Keith Sims .40 1.00
19 Jason Taylor .75 2.00
20 George Teague .40 1.00
21 Lamar Thomas .40 1.00
22 Zach Thomas .75 2.00
23 Richmond Webb .50 1.25
24 Shawn Wooden .40 1.00

1997 Dolphins Score

This 15-card set of the Miami Dolphins was distributed in five-card packs with a suggested retail price of $1.99. The fronts feature color action player photos with white borders and the player's name and team logo printed in team color foil at the bottom. The backs carry player information and career statistics. Platinum Team parallel cards were randomly seeded in packs featuring all foil cardfronts.

COMPLETE SET (15) 3.20 8.00
*PLATINUM TEAMS: 1X TO 2X
1 Dan Marino 1.60 4.00
2 Troy Drayton .08 .25
3 O.J. McDuffie .15 .40
4 Karim Abdul-Jabbar .30 .75
5 Terrell Buckley .08 .25
6 Stanley Pritchett .08 .25
7 Jerris McPhail .08 .25
8 Fred Barnett .15 .40
9 Zach Thomas .15 .40
10 Daryl Gardener .08 .25
11 Tim Bowens .08 .25
12 Shawn Wooden .08 .25
13 Richmond Webb .08 .25
14 Lamar Thomas .08 .25
15 Craig Erickson .08 .25

1999 Dolphins NCL

This set was issued in 1999 on a large perforated sheet. Each card when separated measures roughly 2 1/2" by 3" and includes a color photo of the player along with the NCL (Norwegian Cruise Lines) sponsor logo on the cardfronts. The cardbacks feature the typical player statistics and bio.

COMPLETE SET (24) 15.00 30.00
1 Tim Bowens .40 1.00
2 James Brown .40 1.00
3 Terrell Buckley .50 1.25
4 Cecel Collins .40 1.00
5 Mark Dixon .40 1.00
6 Kevin Donnalley .40 1.00
7 Troy Drayton .40 1.00
8 Daryl Gardener .40 1.00
9 Calvin Jackson .40 1.00
10 Jimmy Johnson CO .50 1.25
11 Robert Jones LB .40 1.00
12 Rob Konrad .40 1.00
13 Sam Madison .50 1.25
14 Olindo Mare .40 1.00
15 Dan Marino 3.00 6.00
16 Brock Marion .40 1.00
17 Tony Martin .50 1.25
18 O.J. McDuffie .50 1.25
19 Kenny Mixon .40 1.00
20 Derrick Rodgers .40 1.00
21 Tim Ruddy .40 1.00
22 Jason Taylor .50 1.25
23 Zach Thomas .75 2.00
24 Richmond Webb .50 1.25

2000 Dolphins NCL

This set was issued in 2000 on a large perforated sheet. Each card when separated measures roughly 2 1/2" by 3" and includes a color photo of the player along with the NCL (Norwegian Cruise Lines) sponsor logo on the cardfronts. The cardbacks feature the typical player statistics and bio.

COMPLETE SET (30) 12.50 25.00
1 Trace Armstrong .40 1.00
2 Tim Bowens .40 1.00
3 Mark Dixon .40 1.00
4 Kevin Donnalley .40 1.00
5 Jay Fiedler .50 1.25
6 Oronde Gadsden .40 1.00
7 Daryl Gardener .40 1.00
8 Hunter Goodwin .40 1.00
9 Larry Izzo .40 1.00
10 Robert Jones .40 1.00
11 Rob Konrad .40 1.00
12 Sam Madison .40 1.00
13 Olindo Mare .40 1.00
14 Brock Marion .40 1.00
15 Tony Martin .50 1.25
16 O.J. McDuffie .50 1.25
17 Kenny Mixon .40 1.00
18 Derrick Rodgers .40 1.00
19 Tim Ruddy .40 1.00
20 Brent Smith .40 1.00
21 Lamar Smith .40 1.00
22 Patrick Surtain .40 1.00
23 Jason Taylor .60 1.50
24 Thurman Thomas .75 2.00
25 Zach Thomas .60 1.50
26 Matt Turk .40 1.00
27 Todd Wade .40 1.00
28 Brian Walker .40 1.00
29 Dave Wannstedt CO .40 1.00
30 Richmond Webb .40 1.00

2001 Dolphins Bookmarks

This set of bookmarks was issued in the Miami area by local libraries. Each card measures roughly 2" by 8" and features a color image of the player on the front and vital statistics, two more photos, and reading public service notes on the back.

COMPLETE SET (3) 4.00 8.00
1 Sam Madison .75 2.00
2 O.J. McDuffie 1.25 3.00
3 Zach Thomas 1.50 4.00

2001 Dolphins NCL

This set was issued in 2001 as six different 5-card perforated sheets stapled together as a booklet. Each card when separated measures roughly 2 1/2" by 3" and includes a color photo of the player along with his name and team name below the photo. The NCL (Norwegian Cruise Lines) sponsor logo appears on the unnumbered cardbacks as well as player statistics and a brief bio.

COMPLETE SET (30) 10.00 20.00
1 Tim Bowens .30 .75
2 Lorenzo Bromell .30 .75
3 Nick Buoniconti .60 1.50
4 Chris Chambers .40 1.00
5 Mark Dixon .30 .75
6 Deon Dyer .30 .75
7 Jay Fiedler .50 1.25
8 Spencer Folau .30 .75
9 Oronde Gadsden .30 .75
10 Daryl Gardener .30 .75
11 Hunter Goodwin .30 .75
12 Morlon Greenwood .30 .75
13 Rob Konrad .30 .75
14 Sam Madison .30 .75
15 Olindo Mare .30 .75
16 Brock Marion .30 .75
17 James McKnight .30 .75
18 Kenny Mixon .30 .75
19 Tom Perry .30 .75
20 Derrick Rodgers .30 .75
21 Tim Ruddy .30 .75
22 Twan Russell .30 .75
23 Lamar Smith .30 .75
24 Patrick Surtain .30 .75
25 Jason Taylor .50 1.25
26 Zach Thomas .60 1.50
27 Matt Turk .30 .75
28 Todd Wade .30 .75
29 Brian Walker .30 .75
30 Dave Wannstedt CO .30 .75

2005 Dolphins Greats DHL

This set, sponsored by DHL, was distributed at a Dolphins home game during the 2005 season. Each unnumbered card measures standard size but features rounded corners similar to a standard playing card. The set includes 40 of the greatest Dolphins players in history to celebrate the team's 40th season.

COMPLETE SET (40) 12.50 25.00
1 Dick Anderson .30 .75
2 Trace Armstrong .30 .75
3 Bob Baumhower .30 .75
4 Kim Bokamper .30 .75
5 Tim Bowens .30 .75
6 Nick Buoniconti .40 1.00
7 Mark Clayton .40 1.00
8 Bryan Cox .30 .75
9 Larry Csonka .50 1.25
10 A.J. Duhe .30 .75
11 Mark Duper .40 1.00
12 Manny Fernandez .30 .75
13 Bob Griese .60 1.50
14 Larry Izzo .30 .75
15 Keith Jackson .30 .75
16 Jim Kiick .40 1.00
17 Bob Kuechenberg .30 .75
18 Jim Langer .40 1.00
19 Larry Little .40 1.00
20 Sam Madison .30 .75
21 Olindo Mare .30 .75
22 Dan Marino 2.00 5.00
23 Brock Marion .30 .75
24 O.J. McDuffie .30 .75
25 Nat Moore .30 .75
26 Mercury Morris .40 1.00
27 John Offerdahl .30 .75
28 Reggie Roby .30 .75
29 Tim Ruddy .30 .75
30 Jake Scott .30 .75
31 Keith Sims .30 .75
32 Dwight Stephenson .30 .75
33 Pete Stoyanovich .30 .75
34 Patrick Surtain .30 .75
35 Jason Taylor .30 .75
36 Zach Thomas .50 1.25
37 Paul Warfield .50 1.25
38 Richmond Webb .30 .75
39 Ricky Williams .40 1.00
40 Garo Yepremian .30 .75

2006 Dolphins Topps

COMPLETE SET (12) 3.00 6.00
MIA1 Jason Taylor .30 .75
MIA2 Chris Chambers .25 .60
MIA3 Zach Thomas .30 .75
MIA4 Randy McMichael .25 .60
MIA5 Ronnie Brown .30 .75
MIA6 Marty Booker .25 .60
MIA7 Travis Minor .25 .60
MIA8 Kevin Carter .25 .60
MIA9 Travis Daniels .25 .60
MIA10 Daunte Culpepper .30 .75
MIA11 Jason Allen .30 .75
MIA12 Derek Hagan .30 .75

2007 Dolphins Donruss Playoff Super Bowl XLI Card Show

These cards were issued via a wrapper redemption program at the Donruss booth at the 2007 Super Bowl XLI Card Show in Miami. Each card features the Super Bowl XLI logo on the front and was issued one card at a time in exchange for the collector opening three packs of 2006 Topps football products at the booth.

SB9 Dan Marino 2.50 6.00
SB10 Chris Chambers .60 1.50
SB11 Jason Taylor .50 1.25
SB12 Marty Booker .50 1.25

2007 Dolphins Topps

COMPLETE SET (12) 2.50 5.00
1 Jason Taylor .50 1.25
2 Ronnie Brown .40 1.00
3 Chris Chambers .40 1.00
4 Zach Thomas .50 1.25
5 David Martin .40 1.00
6 Marty Booker .40 1.00
7 Derek Hagan .40 1.00
8 Joey Porter .40 1.00
9 Daunte Culpepper .50 1.25
10 Channing Crowder .40 1.00
11 Ted Ginn Jr. .50 1.25
12 John Beck .40 1.00

2007 Dolphins Topps Super Bowl XLI Card Show

These cards were issued via a wrapper redemption program at the Topps booth at the 2007 Super Bowl XLI Card Show in Miami. Each card features the Super Bowl XLI logo on the front and was issued one card at a time in exchange for the collector opening three packs of 2006 Topps football products at the booth.

1 Dan Marino 2.50 6.00
2 Zach Thomas .50 1.25
3 Ronnie Brown .75 2.00
4 Joey Harrington .50 1.25

2007 Dolphins Upper Deck Super Bowl XLI Card Show

These cards were issued via a wrapper redemption program at the Upper Deck booth at the 2007 Super Bowl XLI Card Show in Miami. Each card was serial numbered to 2006 and features the Super Bowl XLI logo on the front.

5 Dan Marino 2.50 6.00
6 Bob Griese .75 2.00
7 Wes Welker .50 1.25
8 Jason Allen .50 1.25

2008 Dolphins Topps

COMPLETE SET (12) 2.50 5.00
1 Josh McCown .40 1.00
2 John Beck .40 1.00
3 Ted Ginn Jr. .40 1.00
4 Ronnie Brown .40 1.00
5 Jason Taylor .50 1.25
6 Derek Hagan .40 1.00
7 David Martin .40 1.00
8 Channing Crowder .40 1.00
9 Joey Porter .40 1.00
10 Lorenzo Booker .40 1.00
11 Chad Henne .50 1.25
12 Jake Long .60 1.50

1991 Domino's Quarterbacks

This 50-card NFL quarterback set was produced by Upper Deck and sponsored by Domino's Pizza in conjunction with Coca-Cola and NFL Properties. These standard-size cards were part of a national promotion that was kicked off during the August 3, 1991, "NBC Sportsworld" telecast of "NFL Quarterback Challenge". The cards were distributed through the 5,000 Domino's restaurants across the country. During August, or while supplies lasted, customers who ordered the Domino's Pizza NFL Kick-off Deal received two medium cheese pizzas, four cans of Coke, Diet Coke, or Coke Classic, and one free foil pack with four NFL Quarterback cards, all for 9.99. The first 32 cards in the set were active quarterbacks arranged in alphabetical order by teams. Cards 33-46 feature retired quarterbacks in alphabetical order by player name and cards 47-49 depict quarterback duos from the same team but different eras.

COMPLETE SET (50) 2.40 6.00
1 Chris Miller .02 .10
2 Jim Kelly .08 .25
3 Jim Harbaugh .08 .25
4 Boomer Esiason .05 .15
5 Bernie Kosar .05 .15
6 Troy Aikman .20 .50
7 John Elway .40 1.00
8 Rodney Peete .02 .10
9 Andre Ware .02 .10
10 Anthony Dilweg .02 .10
11 Warren Moon .08 .25
12 Jeff George .05 .15
13 Jim Everett .02 .10
14 Jay Schroeder .02 .10
15 Wade Wilson .02 .10
16 Dan Marino .40 1.00
17 Phil Simms .05 .15
18 Jeff Hostetler .02 .10
19 Ken O'Brien .02 .10
20 Timm Rosenbach .02 .10
21 Bubby Brister .02 .10
22 Steve DeBerg .05 .15
23 Randall Cunningham .08 .25
24 Steve Walsh .02 .10
25 Billy Joe Tolliver .02 .10
26 Steve Young .15 .40
27 Dave Krieg .02 .10
28 Dan McGwire .02 .10
29 Vinny Testaverde .05 .15
30 Stan Humphries .02 .10
31 Mark Rypien .02 .10
32 Terry Bradshaw .20 .50
33 John Brodie .05 .15
34 Len Dawson .05 .15
35 Dan Fouts .05 .15
36 Otto Graham .15 .40
37 Bob Griese .08 .25
38 Sonny Jurgensen .08 .25
39 Daryle Lamonica .05 .15
40 Archie Manning .05 .15
41 Jim Plunkett .05 .15
42 Bart Starr .20 .50
43 Roger Staubach .20 .50
44 Joe Theismann .08 .25
45 Y.A. Tittle .08 .25
46 Johnny Unitas .20 .50
47 Cowboy Gunslingers .20 .50
48 Cajun Connection .15 .40
49 Marino .30 .75
Griese Duo
50 Checklist Card .02 .10

1996 Donruss

The 1996 Donruss set was issued in one series totalling 240 cards. The only subset included was Rookies (208-237). The fronts feature color action player photos. The backs carry a small player photo with biographical information and career statistics.

COMPLETE SET (240) 7.50 20.00
1 Barry Sanders .60 1.50
2 Flipper Anderson .02 .10
3 Ben Coates .07 .20
4 Rob Johnson .15 .40
5 Rodney Hampton .07 .20
6 Desmond Howard .07 .20
7 Craig Heyward .02 .10
8 Alvin Harper .02 .10
9 Todd Collins .07 .20
10 Ken Norton Jr. .02 .10
11 Stan Humphries .07 .20
12 Aeneas Williams .02 .10
13 Jeff Hostetler .02 .10
14 Frank Sanders .07 .20
15 J.J. Birden .02 .10
16 Bryce Paup .02 .10
17 Bill Brooks .02 .10
18 Kevin Williams .02 .10
19 Boomer Esiason .07 .20
20 O.J. McDuffie .07 .20
21 Eric Swann .02 .10
22 Neil Smith .07 .20
23 Charlie Garner .07 .20
24 Greg Lloyd .07 .20
25 Willie Jackson .07 .20
26 Shawn Jefferson .02 .10
27 Rodney Peete .02 .10
28 Michael Westbrook .15 .40
29 J.J. Stokes .15 .40
30 Troy Aikman .40 1.00
31 Sean Dawkins .02 .10
32 Larry Centers .07 .20
33 Herschel Walker .07 .20
34 Stoney Case .02 .10
35 Kevin Greene .07 .20
36 Quinn Early .02 .10
37 Fred Barnett .02 .10
38 Andre Coleman .02 .10
39 Mark Chmura .07 .20
40 Adrian Murrell .07 .20
41 Roosevelt Potts .02 .10
42 Jay Novacek .02 .10
43 Derrick Alexander .07 .20
44 Ken Dilger .07 .20
45 Rob Moore .07 .20
46 Cris Carter .15 .40
47 Jeff Blake .15 .40
48 Derek Loville .02 .10
49 Tyrone Wheatley .07 .20
50 Terrell Fletcher .02 .10
51 Sherman Williams .02 .10
52 Justin Armour .02 .10
53 Kordell Stewart .15 .40
54 Tim Brown .15 .40
55 Kevin Carter .02 .10
56 Andre Rison .07 .20
57 James O.Stewart .07 .20
58 Brent Jones .02 .10
59 Erik Kramer .02 .10
60 Floyd Turner .02 .10
61 Ricky Watters .07 .20
62 Hardy Nickerson .02 .10
63 Aaron Craver .02 .10
64 Dave Krieg .02 .10
65 Warren Moon .07 .20
66 Wayne Chrebet .20 .50
67 Napoleon Kaufman .15 .40
68 Terance Mathis .02 .10
69 Chad May .02 .10
70 Andre Reed .07 .20
71 Reggie White .15 .40
72 Brett Favre .75 2.00
73 Chris Zorich .02 .10
74 Kerry Collins .15 .40
75 Herman Moore .07 .20
76 Yancey Thigpen .07 .20

77 Glenn Foley .07 .20
78 Quentin Coryatt .02 .10
79 Terry Kirby .07 .20
80 Edgar Bennett .07 .20
81 Mark Brunell .25 .60
82 Heath Shuler .07 .20
83 Gus Frerotte .07 .20
84 Deion Sanders .25 .60
85 Calvin Williams .02 .10
86 Junior Seau .15 .40
87 Jim Kelly .15 .40
88 Daryl Johnston .07 .20
89 Irving Fryar .07 .20
90 Brian Blades .02 .10
91 Willie Davis .02 .10
92 Jerome Bettis .15 .40
93 Marcus Allen .15 .40
94 Jeff Graham .02 .10
95 Rick Mirer .07 .20
96 Harvey Williams .02 .10
97 Steve Atwater .02 .10
98 Carl Pickens .07 .20
99 Darick Holmes .02 .10
100 Bruce Smith .07 .20
101 Vinny Testaverde .07 .20
102 Thurman Thomas .15 .40
103 Drew Bledsoe .25 .60
104 Bernie Parmalee .02 .10
105 Greg Hill .07 .20
106 Steve McNair .30 .75
107 Andre Hastings .02 .10
108 Eric Metcalf .02 .10
109 Kimble Anders .07 .20
110 Steve Tasker .02 .10
111 Mark Carrier WR .02 .10
112 Jerry Rice .40 1.00
113 Joey Galloway .15 .40
114 Robert Smith .07 .20
115 Hugh Douglas .07 .20
116 Willie McGinest .02 .10
117 Terrell Davis .30 .75
118 Cortez Kennedy .02 .10
119 Marshall Faulk .20 .50
120 Michael Haynes .02 .10
121 Isaac Bruce .15 .40
122 Brian Mitchell .02 .10
123 Bryan Cox .02 .10
124 Tamarick Vanover .07 .20
125 William Floyd .07 .20
126 Chris Chandler .07 .20
127 Carnell Lake .02 .10
128 Aaron Bailey .02 .10
129 Darnay Scott .07 .20
130 Darren Woodson .07 .20
131 Ernie Mills .02 .10
132 Charles Haley .07 .20
133 Rocket Ismail .02 .10
134 Bert Emanuel .07 .20
135 Lake Dawson .02 .10
136 Jake Reed .07 .20
137 Dave Brown .02 .10
138 Steve Bono .02 .10
139 Terry Allen .07 .20
140 Errict Rhett .07 .20
141 Rod Woodson .07 .20
142 Charles Johnson .02 .10
143 Emmitt Smith .60 1.50
144 Ki-Jana Carter .07 .20
145 Garrison Hearst .07 .20
146 Rashaan Salaam .07 .20
147 Tony Boselli .02 .10
148 Derrick Thomas .15 .40
149 Mark Seay .02 .10
150 Derrick Alexander .02 .10
151 Christian Fauria .02 .10
152 Aaron Hayden .02 .10
153 Chris Warren .07 .20
154 Dave Meggett .02 .10
155 Jeff George .07 .20
156 Jackie Harris .02 .10
157 Michael Irvin .15 .40
158 Scott Mitchell .07 .20
159 Trent Dilfer .15 .40
160 Kyle Brady .02 .10
161 Dan Marino .75 2.00
162 Curtis Martin .30 .75
163 Mario Bates .07 .20
164 Erric Pegram .02 .10
165 Eric Zeier .02 .10
166 Rodney Thomas .02 .10
167 Neil O'Donnell .07 .20
168 Warren Sapp .02 .10
169 Jim Harbaugh .07 .20
170 Henry Ellard .02 .10
171 Anthony Miller .07 .20
172 Derrick Moore .02 .10
173 John Elway .75 2.00
174 Vincent Brisby .02 .10
175 Antonio Freeman .15 .40
176 Chris Sanders .07 .20
177 Steve Young .30 .75
178 Shannon Sharpe .07 .20
179 Brett Perriman .02 .10
180 Orlando Thomas .02 .10
181 Eric Bjornson .02 .10
182 Natrone Means .07 .20
183 Jim Everett .02 .10
184 Curtis Conway .15 .40
185 Robert Brooks .15 .40
186 Tony Martin .07 .20
187 Mark Carrier DB .02 .10
188 LeShon Johnson .02 .10
189 Bernie Kosar .02 .10
190 Ray Zellars .02 .10
191 Steve Walsh .02 .10
192 Craig Erickson .02 .10
193 Tommy Maddox .15 .40
194 Leslie O'Neal .02 .10
195 Harold Green .02 .10
196 Steve Beuerlein .07 .20
197 Ronald Moore .02 .10
198 Leslie Shepherd .02 .10
199 Leroy Hoard .02 .10
200 Michael Jackson .07 .20
201 Will Moore .02 .10
202 Ricky Ervins .02 .10
203 Keith Jennings .02 .10
204 Eric Green .02 .10
205 Mark Rypien .02 .10
206 Torrance Small .02 .10
207 Sean Gilbert .02 .10
208 Mike Alstott RC .40 1.00
209 Willie Anderson RC .02 .10
210 Alex Molden RC .02 .10
211 Jonathan Ogden RC .50 1.25
212 Stepfret Williams RC .07 .20
213 Jeff Lewis RC .07 .20
214 Regan Upshaw RC .02 .10
215 Daryl Gardener RC .02 .10
216 Danny Kanell RC .15 .40
217 John Mobley RC .02 .10
218 Reggie Brown LB RC .02 .10
219 Muhsin Muhammad RC .40 1.00
220 Kevin Hardy RC .15 .40
221 Stanley Pritchett RC .07 .20
222 Cedric Jones RC .02 .10
223 Marco Battaglia RC .02 .10
224 Duane Clemons RC .02 .10
225 Jerald Moore RC .07 .20
226 Simeon Rice RC .40 1.00
227 Chris Darkins RC .02 .10
228 Bobby Hoying RC .15 .40
229 Stephen Davis RC .60 1.50
230 Walt Harris RC .02 .10
231 Jermane Mayberry RC .02 .10
232 Tony Brackens RC .15 .40
233 Eric Moulds RC .50 1.25
234 Alex Van Dyke RC .07 .20
235 Marvin Harrison RC 1.00 2.50
236 Rickey Dudley RC .15 .40
237 Terrell Owens RC 1.00 2.50
238 Jerry Rice CL .15 .40
239 Dan Marino CL .15 .40
240 Emmitt Smith CL .15 .40

1996 Donruss Press Proofs

COMPLETE SET (240) 125.00 250.00
*STARS: 5X TO 12X BASIC CARDS
*RCs: 2.5X TO 6X BASIC CARDS
STATED ODDS 1:5
ANNOUNCED PRINT RUN 2000 SETS

1996 Donruss Elite

This 20-card set was issued in both a gold and silver version and features color player photos in silver or gold borders. The backs carry another player photo with a paragraph about the player on either a gold or silver background. Only 10,000 of each silver card was produced and only 2,000 of each gold card. Each card is sequentially numbered.

COMPLETE SET (20) 40.00 100.00
STAT.PRINT RUN 10,000 SER.#'d SETS
*GOLD STARS: .8X TO 2X SILVERS
GOLD STAT.PRINT RUN 2000 SER.#'d SETS
1 Emmitt Smith 4.00 10.00
2 Barry Sanders 5.00 12.00
3 Marshall Faulk 1.50 4.00
4 Curtis Martin 2.50 6.00
5 Junior Seau 1.25 3.00
6 Troy Aikman 3.00 8.00
7 Steve Young 2.50 6.00
8 Dan Marino 6.00 15.00
9 Brett Favre 6.00 15.00
10 John Elway 6.00 15.00
11 Kerry Collins 1.25 3.00
12 Drew Bledsoe 2.00 5.00
13 Jerry Rice 3.00 8.00
14 Keyshawn Johnson 1.50 4.00
15 Deion Sanders 2.00 5.00
16 Isaac Bruce 1.25 3.00
17 Rashaan Salaam .60 1.50
18 Tim Biakabutuka .75 2.00
19 Lawrence Phillips .75 2.00
20 Robert Brooks 1.25 3.00

1996 Donruss Hit List

Randomly inserted in packs, this 20-card set features color action player photos on a silver foil background. The die cut cards feature team colored borders on two sides. Only 10,000 of each card was produced.

COMPLETE SET (20) 40.00 100.00
STATED PRINT RUN 10,000 SERIAL #'d SETS
*PROMOS: .4X TO 1X BASIC INSERTS
1 Bruce Smith .50 1.25
2 Barry Sanders 4.00 10.00
3 Kevin Hardy 1.00 2.50
4 Greg Lloyd .50 1.25
5 Brett Favre 5.00 12.00
6 Emmitt Smith 4.00 10.00
7 Kerry Collins 1.00 2.50
8 Ken Norton Jr. .25 .60
9 Steve Atwater .25 .60
10 Curtis Martin 2.00 5.00
11 Chris Warren .50 1.25
12 Steve Young 2.00 5.00
13 Marshall Faulk 1.25 3.00
14 Junior Seau 1.00 2.50
15 Lawrence Phillips 2.50 6.00
16 Troy Aikman 2.50 6.00
17 Jerry Rice 2.50 6.00
18 Dan Marino 5.00 12.00
19 Reggie White 1.00 2.50
20 John Elway 5.00 12.00

1996 Donruss Rated Rookies

Randomly inserted in packs, this 10-card set features color player action images on a green background. The backs carry a small player portrait with player information.

COMPLETE SET (10) 10.00 25.00
1 Keyshawn Johnson 1.25 3.00
2 Terry Glenn 1.25 3.00
3 Tim Biakabutuka 1.25 3.00
4 Bobby Engram .75 2.00
5 Leeland McElroy .75 2.00
6 Eddie George 1.50 4.00
7 Lawrence Phillips 1.25 3.00
8 Derrick Mayes .75 2.00
9 Karim Abdul-Jabbar 1.25 3.00
10 Eddie Kennison

1996 Donruss Stop Action

Inserted in jumbo (magazine) packs only, this set features color action player with a film strip border design. The backs carry player information. Only 4000 of this set was printed and are sequentially numbered.

COMPLETE SET (10) 25.00 60.00
STATED PRINT RUN 4000 SERIAL #'d SETS
RANDOM INSERTS IN JUMBO PACKS
1 Deion Sanders 2.00 5.00
2 Troy Aikman 3.00 8.00
3 Brett Favre 6.00 15.00
4 Steve Young 2.50 6.00
5 Joey Galloway 1.25 3.00
6 Dan Marino 6.00 15.00
7 Jerry Rice 3.00 8.00
8 Emmitt Smith 5.00 12.00
9 Isaac Bruce 1.25 3.00
10 Barry Sanders 5.00 12.00

1996 Donruss What If?

Randomly inserted in hobby packs only, this 10-card set features color player photos on the Donruss card design of the individual year that is stated on each card. The backs carry another player photo on a star burst design along side information about the player. Only 5000 of each card was produced.

COMPLETE SET (10) 25.00 60.00
RANDOM INSERTS IN HOBBY PACKS
STATED PRINT RUN 5000 SERIAL #'d SETS
1 Troy Aikman 3.00 8.00
2 Jerry Rice 3.00 8.00
3 Barry Sanders 5.00 12.00
4 Drew Bledsoe 2.00 5.00
5 Deion Sanders 2.00 5.00
6 Brett Favre 6.00 15.00
7 Dan Marino 6.00 15.00
8 Steve Young 2.50 6.00
9 Emmitt Smith 5.00 12.00
10 John Elway 6.00 15.00

1996 Donruss Will To Win

Randomly inserted in retail packs only, this 10-card set features a color player image on a brown-and-black background with copper foil highlights. The backs carry another player photo and a paragraph about the player. Only 5000 of this set was produced.

COMPLETE SET (10) 30.00 80.00
RANDOM INSERTS IN RETAIL PACKS
STATED PRINT RUN 5000 SERIAL #'d SETS
1 Emmitt Smith 5.00 12.00
2 Brett Favre 6.00 15.00
3 Curtis Martin 2.50 6.00
4 Jerry Rice 3.00 8.00
5 Barry Sanders 5.00 12.00
6 Errict Rhett .60 1.50
7 Troy Aikman 3.00 8.00
8 Dan Marino 6.00 15.00
9 Steve Young 2.50 6.00
10 John Elway 6.00 15.00

1997 Donruss

The 1997 Donruss set was issued in one series totaling 230 cards.The cards were distributed in 10-card hobby packs with a suggested retail price of $1.99 and 14-card blister packs with a suggested retail of $2.99. Blister packs also contained one ad/cover promo card as listed below. Cardfronts feature color action player photos with foil treatment, while the backs carry player information.

COMPLETE SET (230) 7.50 20.00
1 Dan Marino .75 2.00
2 Brett Favre .75 2.00
3 Emmitt Smith .60 1.50
4 Eddie George .20 .50
5 Karim Abdul-Jabbar .10 .30
6 Terrell Davis .25 .60
7 Curtis Martin .25 .60
8 Drew Bledsoe .25 .60
9 Jerry Rice .40 1.00
10 Troy Aikman .40 1.00
11 Barry Sanders .60 1.50
12 Mark Brunell .25 .60
13 Kerry Collins .20 .50
14 Steve Young .25 .60
15 Kordell Stewart .20 .50
16 Eddie Kennison .10 .30
17 Terry Glenn .20 .50
18 John Elway .75 2.00
19 Joey Galloway .10 .30
20 Deion Sanders .20 .50
21 Keyshawn Johnson .20 .50
22 Lawrence Phillips .07 .20
23 Ricky Watters .10 .30
24 Marvin Harrison .20 .50
25 Bobby Engram .10 .30
26 Marshall Faulk .25 .60
27 Carl Pickens .10 .30
28 Isaac Bruce .20 .50
29 Herman Moore .10 .30
30 Jerome Bettis .20 .50
31 Rashaan Salaam .07 .20
32 Errict Rhett .07 .20
33 Tim Biakabutuka .10 .30
34 Robert Brooks .10 .30
35 Antonio Freeman .20 .50
36 Steve McNair .25 .60
37 Jeff Blake .10 .30
38 Tony Banks .10 .30
39 Terrell Owens .25 .60
40 Eric Moulds .20 .50
41 Leeland McElroy .07 .20
42 Chris Sanders .07 .20
43 Thurman Thomas .20 .50
44 Bruce Smith .10 .30
45 Reggie White .20 .50
46 Chris Warren .10 .30
47 J.J. Stokes .10 .30
48 Ben Coates .10 .30
49 Tim Brown .20 .50
50 Marcus Allen .20 .50
51 Michael Irvin .20 .50
52 William Floyd .10 .30
53 Ken Dilger .07 .20
54 Bobby Taylor .07 .20
55 Keenan McCardell .10 .30
56 Raymont Harris .07 .20
57 Keith Byars .07 .20
58 O.J. McDuffie .10 .30
59 Robert Smith .10 .30
60 Bert Emanuel .10 .30
61 Rick Mirer .07 .20
62 Vinny Testaverde .10 .30
63 Kyle Brady .07 .20
64 Mark Bruener .07 .20
65 Neil O'Donnell .10 .30
66 Anthony Johnson .07 .20
67 Ken Norton .07 .20
68 Warren Sapp .10 .30
69 Amani Toomer .10 .30
70 Simeon Rice .10 .30
71 Kevin Hardy .07 .20
72 Junior Seau .20 .50
73 Neil Smith .10 .30
74 LeShon Johnson .07 .20
75 Quinn Early .07 .20
76 Andre Reed .10 .30
77 Jake Reed .10 .30
78 Elvis Grbac .10 .30
79 Tyrone Wheatley .10 .30
80 Adrian Murrell .10 .30
81 Fred Barnett .07 .20
82 Darrell Green .10 .30
83 Stan Humphries .10 .30
84 Troy Drayton .07 .20
85 Steve Atwater .07 .20
86 Quentin Coryatt .07 .20
87 Dan Wilkinson .07 .20
88 Scott Mitchell .10 .30
89 Willie McGinest .07 .20
90 Kevin Smith .07 .20
91 Gus Frerotte .07 .20
92 Byron Bam Morris .07 .20
93 Darick Holmes .07 .20
94 Zach Thomas .20 .50
95 Tom Carter .07 .20
96 Cortez Kennedy .07 .20
97 Kevin Williams .07 .20
98 Michael Haynes .07 .20
99 Lamont Warren .07 .20
100 Jeff Graham .07 .20
101 Alex Van Dyke .07 .20
102 Jim Everett .07 .20
103 Chris Chandler .10 .30
104 Qadry Ismail .10 .30
105 Ray Zellars .07 .20
106 Chris T. Jones .07 .20
107 Charlie Garner .10 .30
108 Bobby Hoying .10 .30
109 Mark Chmura .10 .30
110 Cris Carter .20 .50
111 Darnay Scott .10 .30
112 Anthony Miller .07 .20
113 Desmond Howard .10 .30
114 Terance Mathis .10 .30
115 Rodney Hampton .10 .30
116 Napoleon Kaufman .20 .50
117 Jim Harbaugh .10 .30
118 Shannon Sharpe .10 .30
119 Irving Fryar .10 .30
120 Garrison Hearst .10 .30
121 Terry Allen .20 .50
122 Larry Centers .10 .30
123 Sean Dawkins .07 .20
124 Jeff George .10 .30
125 Tony Martin .10 .30
126 Mike Alstott .20 .50
127 Rickey Dudley .10 .30
128 Kevin Carter .07 .20
129 Derrick Alexander WR .10 .30
130 Greg Lloyd .07 .20
131 Bryce Paup .07 .20
132 Derrick Thomas .20 .50
133 Greg Hill .07 .20
134 Jamal Anderson .20 .50
135 Curtis Conway .10 .30
136 Frank Sanders .10 .30
137 Brett Perriman .07 .20
138 Edgar Bennett .10 .30
139 Wayne Chrebet .20 .50
140 Natrone Means .10 .30
141 Eric Metcalf .10 .30
142 Trent Dilfer .20 .50
143 Terry Kirby .10 .30
144 Johnnie Morton .10 .30
145 Dale Carter .07 .20
146 Michael Westbrook .10 .30
147 Stanley Pritchett .07 .20
148 Todd Collins .07 .20
149 Tamarick Vanover .10 .30
150 Kevin Greene .10 .30
151 Lamar Lathon .07 .20
152 Muhsin Muhammad .10 .30
153 Dorsey Levens .20 .50
154 Rod Woodson .10 .30
155 Brent Jones .07 .20
156 Michael Jackson .10 .30
157 Shawn Jefferson .07 .20
158 Kimble Anders .10 .30
159 Sean Gilbert .07 .20
160 Carnell Lake .07 .20
161 Darren Woodson .07 .20
162 Dave Meggett .07 .20
163 Henry Ellard .07 .20
164 Eric Swann .07 .20
165 Tony Boselli .07 .20
166 Daryl Johnston .10 .30
167 Willie Jackson .07 .20
168 Wesley Walls .10 .30
169 Mario Bates .07 .20
170 Lake Dawson .07 .20
171 Mike Mamula .07 .20
172 Ed McCaffrey .10 .30
173 Tony Brackens .07 .20
174 Craig Heyward .07 .20
175 Harvey Williams .07 .20
176 Dave Brown .07 .20
177 Aaron Glenn .07 .20
178 Jeff Hostetler .07 .20
179 Alvin Harper .07 .20
180 Ty Detmer .10 .30
181 James Jett .10 .30
182 James O.Stewart .10 .30
183 Warren Moon .20 .50
184 Herschel Walker .10 .30
185 Ki-Jana Carter .07 .20
186 Leslie O'Neal .07 .20
187 Danny Kanell .07 .20
188 Eric Bjornson .07 .20
189 Alex Molden .07 .20
190 Bryant Young .07 .20
191 Merton Hanks .07 .20
192 Heath Shuler .07 .20
193 Brian Blades .07 .20
194 Steve Bono .10 .30
195 Wayne Simmons .07 .20
196 Warrick Dunn RC .60 1.50
197 Peter Boulware RC .20 .50
198 David LaFleur RC .07 .20
199 Shawn Springs RC .10 .30
200 Reidel Anthony RC .20 .50
201 Jim Druckenmiller RC .10 .30
202 Orlando Pace RC .20 .50
203 Yatil Green RC .10 .30
204 Bryant Westbrook RC .07 .20
205 Tiki Barber RC 1.25 3.00
206 James Farrior RC .20 .50
207 Rae Carruth RC .07 .20
208 Danny Wuerffel RC .20 .50
209 Corey Dillon RC .75 2.00
210 Ike Hilliard RC .30 .75
211 Tony Gonzalez RC .75 2.00
212 Antowain Smith RC .50 1.25
213 Pat Barnes RC .20 .50
214 Troy Davis RC .10 .30
215 Byron Hanspard RC .10 .30
216 Joey Kent RC .20 .50
217 Jake Plummer RC .75 2.00
218 Kenny Holmes RC .20 .50
219 Darnell Autry RC .10 .30
220 Darrell Russell RC .07 .20
221 Walter Jones RC .30 .75
222 Dwayne Rudd RC .20 .50
223 Tom Knight RC .07 .20
224 Kevin Lockett RC .10 .30
225 Will Blackwell RC .10 .30
226 Dan Marino CL .15 .40
227 Brett Favre CL .15 .40
228 Emmitt Smith CL .20 .50
229 Barry Sanders CL .20 .50
230 Jerry Rice CL .08 .25
P1 Drew Bledsoe Promo .40 1.00
P2 Mark Brunell Promo .40 1.00
P3 Barry Sanders Promo .60 1.50

1997 Donruss Press Proofs Gold Die Cuts

COMPLETE SET (230) 200.00 400.00
*STARS: 8X TO 20X BASIC CARDS
*RCs: 5X TO 12X BASIC CARDS
GOLD STATED PRINT RUN 500 SETS

1997 Donruss Press Proofs Silver

COMPLETE SET (230) 75.00 150.00
*STARS: 3X TO 8X BASIC CARDS
*RCs: 2.5X TO 6X BASIC CARDS
STATED PRINT RUN 1500 SER.#'d SETS

1997 Donruss Elite

Randomly inserted in packs, this 20-card set features color action player photos with silver foil borders. Only 5000 of each card were produced and sequentially numbered. A Gold parallel set was also produced and numbered of 2000 sets made.

COMPLETE SET (20) 40.00 100.00
SILVER STATED PRINT RUN 5000 #'d SETS
*GOLD CARDS: .8X TO 2X SILVERS
GOLD STATED PRINT RUN 2000 #'d SETS
1 Emmitt Smith 5.00 12.00
2 Dan Marino 6.00 15.00
3 Brett Favre 6.00 15.00
4 Curtis Martin 2.00 5.00
5 Terrell Davis 2.00 5.00
6 Barry Sanders 5.00 12.00
7 Drew Bledsoe 2.00 5.00
8 Mark Brunell 2.00 5.00
9 Troy Aikman 3.00 8.00
10 Jerry Rice 3.00 8.00
11 Steve McNair 2.00 5.00
12 Kerry Collins 1.50 4.00
13 John Elway 6.00 15.00
14 Eddie George 1.50 4.00
15 Karim Abdul-Jabbar 1.00 2.50
16 Kordell Stewart 1.50 4.00
17 Jerome Bettis 1.50 4.00
18 Terry Glenn 1.50 4.00
19 Errict Rhett .60 1.50
20 Carl Pickens 1.00 2.50

1997 Donruss Legends of the Fall

Randomly inserted in packs, this 10-card set features art work of the NFL's top superstars by artist Dan Gardiner. The first 500 of these exclusive illustrations were printed directly on actual canvas. Only 10,000 of each card were produced and were sequentially numbered.

COMPLETE SET (10) 30.00 80.00
STATED PRINT RUN 10,000 #'d SETS
*CANVAS CARDS: .6X TO 1.5X BASIC INSERTS
CANVAS PRINT RUN FIRST 500 SETS
1 Troy Aikman 3.00 8.00
2 Barry Sanders 5.00 12.00
3 John Elway 6.00 15.00
4 Dan Marino 6.00 15.00
5 Emmitt Smith 5.00 12.00
6 Jerry Rice 3.00 8.00
7 Deion Sanders 1.50 4.00
8 Brett Favre 6.00 15.00
9 Marcus Allen 1.50 4.00
10 Steve Young 2.00 5.00

1997 Donruss Passing Grade

Randomly inserted in hobby packs only, this 16-card set features color photos of top quarterbacks with a unique card-within-a-card design with red-foil stamping. Each player was issued with both a football shaped die-cut card inside an outer envelope style card assembled together. We've listed below the outer envelope as card #A and the die cut football shaped card as #B. Only 3,000 of each card were produced and sequentially numbered.

COMPLETE SET (16) 60.00 120.00
*FOOTBALL DC: .4X TO 1X OUTER ENVELOPE
STATED PRINT RUN 3000 #'d SETS
RANDOM INSERTS IN HOBBY PACKS
1A Steve Young 2.00 5.00
2A Drew Bledsoe 1.50 4.00
3A Mark Brunell 1.50 4.00
4A Kerry Collins 1.50 4.00
5A Steve McNair 1.50 4.00
6A John Elway 5.00 12.00
7A Ty Detmer 1.25 3.00
8A Jeff Blake 1.25 3.00
9A Dan Marino 5.00 12.00
10A Kordell Stewart 1.50 4.00
11A Tony Banks 1.25 3.00
12A Brett Favre 5.00 12.00
13A Gus Frerotte 1.00 2.50
14A Troy Aikman 2.50 6.00
15A Jeff George 1.25 3.00
16A Brad Johnson 1.25 3.00

1997 Donruss Rated Rookies

Randomly inserted in packs, this 10-card set features color player photos of outstanding rookies printed with micro-etch holofoil stamping. A much tougher gold holofoil parallel set entitled Medalists was also produced and randomly inserted into packs.

COMPLETE SET (10) 20.00 40.00
*MEDALISTS: 1.2X TO 3X BASIC INSERTS
*PRESS PROOF: 1.5X TO 4X BASIC INSERTS
1 Ike Hilliard 1.50 4.00
2 Warrick Dunn 2.50 6.00
3 Yatil Green .60 1.50
4 Jim Druckenmiller .60 1.50
5 Rae Carruth .50 1.25
6 Antowain Smith 1.50 4.00
7 Tiki Barber 5.00 12.00
8 Byron Hanspard .60 1.50
9 Reidel Anthony 1.00 2.50
10 Jake Plummer 3.00 8.00

1997 Donruss Zoning Commission

Randomly inserted in retail packs only, this 20-card set features color player photos of top scoring players and are printed on micro-etched, full holographic foil card stock with gold foil stamping. Only 5,000 of each card were produced and are sequentially numbered.

COMPLETE SET (20) 60.00 120.00
RANDOM INSERTS IN RETAIL PACKS
STATED PRINT RUN 5000 #'d SETS
1 Brett Favre 6.00 15.00
2 Jerry Rice 3.00 8.00
3 Jerome Bettis 1.50 4.00
4 Troy Aikman 3.00 8.00
5 Drew Bledsoe 2.00 5.00
6 Natrone Means 1.00 2.50
7 Steve Young 2.00 5.00
8 John Elway 6.00 15.00
9 Barry Sanders 5.00 12.00
10 Emmitt Smith 5.00 12.00
11 Curtis Martin 2.00 5.00
12 Terry Allen 1.50 4.00
13 Dan Marino 6.00 15.00
14 Mark Brunell 2.00 5.00
15 Terry Glenn 1.50 4.00
16 Herman Moore 1.00 2.50
17 Ricky Watters 1.00 2.50
18 Terrell Davis 2.00 5.00
19 Isaac Bruce 1.50 4.00
20 Curtis Conway 1.00 2.50

1998 Donruss Elite Promos

These cards were released in 1998 as a preview to the Donruss product which was never printed due to the bankruptcy of Pinnacle Brands. Each card was serial numbered of 2500 but it is unknown how many cards actually made it out into the secondary market.

1 Brett Favre 3.00 8.00
6 Drew Bledsoe 1.25 3.00
7 Troy Aikman 2.00 5.00
13 Steve McNair 1.25 3.00
15 Steve Young 1.50 4.00
16 Terry Glenn 1.00 2.50
17 Deion Sanders 1.25 3.00
20 Jake Plummer 1.00 2.50

1999 Donruss

Released as a 200-card set, the 1999 Donruss set features 150 veteran cards and a 50-card rookie subset inserted at one in four packs. Two parallel sets were released also, each numbered to a specifc season stat, or a career stat. Donurss was packaged in 24-pack boxes containing seven cards each.

COMPLETE SET (200) 40.00 100.00
COMP.SET w/o SP's (150) 10.00 20.00
1 Jake Plummer .15 .40
2 Rob Moore .15 .40
3 Adrian Murrell .15 .40
4 Frank Sanders .15 .40
5 Jamal Anderson .20 .50
6 Tim Dwight .20 .50
7 Terance Mathis .15 .40
8 Chris Chandler .20 .50
9 Byron Hanspard .15 .40
10 Priest Holmes .15 .40
11 Jermaine Lewis .15 .40
12 Errict Rhett .15 .40
13 Doug Flutie .25 .60
14 Eric Moulds .15 .40
15 Antowain Smith .15 .40
16 Thurman Thomas .20 .50
17 Andre Reed .25 .60
18 Bruce Smith .20 .50
19 Tim Biakabutuka .20 .50
20 Rae Carruth UER .15 .40
21 Muhsin Muhammad .15 .40
22 Curtis Enis .15 .40
23 Curtis Conway .20 .50
24 Bobby Engram .15 .40
25 Corey Dillon .15 .40
26 Carl Pickens .20 .50
27 Jeff Blake .20 .50
28 Darnay Scott .15 .40
29 Ty Detmer .15 .40
30 Leslie Shepherd .15 .40
31 Emmitt Smith .40 1.00
32 Troy Aikman .30 .75
33 Michael Irvin .25 .60
34 Deion Sanders .20 .50
35 Rocket Ismail .20 .50
36 John Elway .40 1.00
37 Terrell Davis .20 .50
38 Ed McCaffrey .20 .50
39 Shannon Sharpe .20 .50
40 Rod Smith .20 .50
41 Bubby Brister .15 .40
42 Brian Griese .15 .40
43 Barry Sanders .40 1.00
44 Charlie Batch .15 .40
45 Herman Moore .20 .50
46 Germane Crowell .15 .40
47 Johnnie Morton .20 .50
48 Ron Rivers .15 .40
49 Brett Favre .50 1.25
50 Antonio Freeman .20 .50
51 Dorsey Levens .20 .50
52 Mark Chmura .15 .40
53 Corey Bradford .20 .50
54 Bill Schroeder .20 .50
55 Peyton Manning ERR .75 2.00
56 Marvin Harrison .20 .50
57 E.G. Green .15 .40
58 Fred Taylor .15 .40
59 Mark Brunell .20 .50
60 Tavian Banks .15 .40
61 Jimmy Smith .20 .50
62 Keenan McCardell .20 .50
63 Warren Moon .25 .60
64 Derrick Alexander WR .15 .40
65 Byron Bam Morris .15 .40
66 Elvis Grbac .15 .40
67 Andre Rison .20 .50
68 Dan Marino .50 1.25
69 Karim Abdul-Jabbar .15 .40
70 O.J. McDuffie .20 .50
71 Tony Martin .20 .50
72 Randy Moss .20 .50
73 Cris Carter .25 .60
74 Randall Cunningham .20 .50
75 Robert Smith .15 .40
76 Jeff George .15 .40
77 Jake Reed .20 .50
78 Terry Allen .20 .50
79 Drew Bledsoe .20 .50
80 Terry Glenn .20 .50
81 Ben Coates .20 .50
82 Tony Simmons .15 .40
83 Cam Cleeland .15 .40
84 Eddie Kennison .20 .50
85 Kerry Collins .15 .40
86 Ike Hilliard .15 .40
87 Gary Brown .15 .40
88 Joe Jurevicius .15 .40
89 Kent Graham .15 .40
90 Wayne Chrebet .15 .40
91 Keyshawn Johnson .20 .50
92 Curtis Martin .20 .50
93 Vinny Testaverde .15 .40
94 Tim Brown .25 .60
95 Napoleon Kaufman .15 .40
96 Charles Woodson .25 .60
97 Tyrone Wheatley .20 .50
98 Rich Gannon .20 .50
99 Charles Johnson .15 .40
100 Duce Staley .15 .40
101 Kordell Stewart .15 .40
102 Jerome Bettis .25 .60
103 Hines Ward .20 .50
104 Ryan Leaf .20 .50
105 Natrone Means .20 .50
106 Jim Harbaugh .20 .50
107 Junior Seau .20 .50
108 Mikhael Ricks .15 .40
109 Jerry Rice .60 1.50
110 Steve Young .30 .75
111 Garrison Hearst .15 .40
112 Terrell Owens .20 .50
113 Lawrence Phillips .20 .50
114 J.J. Stokes .15 .40
115 Sean Dawkins .15 .40
116 Derrick Mayes .15 .40
117 Joey Galloway .20 .50
118 Jon Kitna .15 .40
119 Ahman Green .20 .50
120 Ricky Watters .20 .50
121 Isaac Bruce .25 .60
122 Marshall Faulk .20 .50
123 Az-Zahir Hakim .15 .40
124 Warrick Dunn .15 .40
125 Mike Alstott .15 .40
126 Trent Dilfer .15 .40
127 Reidel Anthony .15 .40
128 Jacquez Green .15 .40
129 Warren Sapp .20 .50
130 Eddie George .20 .50
131 Steve McNair .20 .50
132 Kevin Dyson .15 .40
133 Yancey Thigpen .15 .40
134 Frank Wycheck .20 .50
135 Stephen Davis .15 .40
136 Brad Johnson .20 .50
137 Skip Hicks .15 .40
138 Michael Westbrook .15 .40
139 Darrell Green .25 .60
140 Albert Connell .15 .40
141 Tim Couch RC .50 1.25
142 Donovan McNabb RC 3.00 8.00
143 Akili Smith RC .40 1.00
144 Edgerrin James RC .60 1.50
145 Ricky Williams RC .60 1.50
146 Torry Holt RC .75 2.00
147 Champ Bailey RC .75 2.00
148 David Boston RC .40 1.00
149 Andy Katzenmoyer RC .50 1.25
150 Chris McAlister RC .40 1.00
151 Daunte Culpepper RC .60 1.50
152 Cade McNown RC .40 1.00
153 Troy Edwards RC .40 1.00
154 Kevin Johnson RC .50 1.25
155 James Johnson RC .40 1.00
156 Rob Konrad RC .40 1.00
157 Jim Kleinsasser RC .60 1.50
158 Kevin Faulk RC .40 1.00
159 Joe Montgomery RC .40 1.00
160 Shaun King RC .40 1.00
161 Peerless Price RC .40 1.00
162 Mike Cloud RC .40 1.00
163 Jermaine Fazande RC .40 1.00
164 D'Wayne Bates RC .40 1.00
165 Brock Huard RC .40 1.00
166 Marty Booker RC .40 1.00
167 Karsten Bailey RC .40 1.00
168 Shawn Bryson RC .40 1.00
169 Jeff Paulk RC .40 1.00
170 Travis McGriff RC .40 1.00
171 Amos Zereoue RC .40 1.00
172 Craig Yeast RC .40 1.00
173 Joe Germaine RC .50 1.25
174 Dameane Douglas RC .40 1.00
175 Brandon Stokley RC .50 1.25
176 Larry Parker RC .50 1.25
177 Joel Makovicka RC .40 1.00
178 Wane McGarity RC .40 1.00
179 Na Brown RC .40 1.00
180 Cecil Collins RC .40 1.00
181 Nick Williams RC .40 1.00
182 Charlie Rogers RC .40 1.00
183 Darrin Chiaverini RC .40 1.00
184 Terry Jackson RC .40 1.00
185 De'Mond Parker RC .40 1.00
186 Sedrick Irvin RC .40 1.00
187 MarTay Jenkins RC .50 1.25
188 Kurt Warner RC 4.00 10.00
189 Michael Bishop RC UER .50 1.25
190 Sean Bennett RC .40 1.00
191 Jamal Anderson CL .15 .40
192 Eric Moulds CL .12 .30
193 Terrell Davis CL .15 .40
194 John Elway CL .40 1.00
195 Barry Sanders CL .40 1.00
196 Peyton Manning CL .40 1.00
197 Fred Taylor CL .12 .30
198 Dan Marino CL .40 1.00
199 Randy Moss CL .15 .40
200 Terrell Owens CL .15 .40

1999 Donruss Stat Line Career

*STARS/400-589: 5X TO 12X BASIC CARDS
*ROOKIES/400-589: .8X TO 2X BASIC CARDS
*STARS/300-399: 4X TO 10X BASIC CARDS
*ROOKIES/300-399: 1.2X TO 3X BASIC CARDS
*STARS/200-299: 5X TO 12X BASIC CARDS
*ROOKIES/200-299: 1.5X TO 4X BASIC CARDS
*STARS/140-199: 8X TO 20X BASIC CARDS
*ROOKIES/140-199: 2X TO 5X BASIC CARDS
*STARS/100-139: 10X TO 25X BASIC CARDS
*ROOKIES/100-139: 2.5X TO 6X BASIC CARDS
*STARS/70-99: 15X TO 40X BASIC CARDS
*ROOKIES/70-99: 3X TO 8X BASIC CARDS
*STARS/45-69: 20X TO 50X BASIC CARDS
*STARS/30-44: 25X TO 60X BASIC
*STARS/20-29: 30X TO 80X BASIC
*STARS/10-19: 50X TO 100X BASIC

1999 Donruss Stat Line Season

*ROOKIES/200-299: 1.5X TO 4X BASIC CARDS
*ROOKIES/140-199: 2X TO 5X BASIC CARDS
*ROOKIES/100-139: 2.5X TO 6X BASIC CARDS
*ROOKIES/70-99: 3X TO 8X BASIC CARDS
*STARS/45-69: 20X TO 50X BASIC CARDS
*ROOKIES/45-69: 4X TO 10X BASIC CARDS
*STARS/30-44: 30X TO 80X BASIC CARDS
*ROOKIES/30-44: 5X TO 12X BASIC CARDS
*STARS/20-29: 40X TO 100X BASIC CARDS
*STARS/10-19: 50X TO 120X BASIC CARDS
*ROOKIES/10-19: 8X TO 20X BASIC CARDS

1999 Donruss All-Time Gridiron Kings

Randomly inserted in packs, this 5-card set features five of the NFL's legends. Card fronts feature a "painted" player portrait and are sequentially numbered to 1000. The first 500 serial numbers of each card were printed on a canvas card stock and were autographed by the respective player. Card backs carry an "AGK" prefix.

COMPLETE SET (5) 30.00 60.00
STATED PRINT RUN 1000 SER.#'d SETS
FIRST 500 CARDS SIGNED ON CANVAS STOCK
AGK1 Bart Starr 7.50 20.00
AGK2 Johnny Unitas 7.50 20.00
AGK3 Earl Campbell 5.00 12.00
AGK4 Walter Payton 10.00 25.00
AGK5 Jim Brown 7.50 20.00

1999 Donruss All-Time Gridiron Kings Autographs

Randomly inserted in packs, this 5-card set consists of the first 500 serial numbered All-Time Gridiron Kings set cards. Each card is printed on canvas card-stock and contains an authentic autograph of the featured player. Some cards were issued via a mail redemption.

FIRST 500 CARDS SIGNED ON CANVAS STOCK
AGK1 Bart Starr 75.00 125.00
AGK2 Johnny Unitas 150.00 250.00
AGK3 Earl Campbell 30.00 60.00
AGK4 Walter Payton 300.00 600.00
AGK5 Jim Brown 50.00 100.00

1999 Donruss Elite Insert

Randomly inserted in 1999 Donruss packs, this 20-card set previews the Donruss Elite set to be released later in the season. Card backs carry an "EL" prefix, and cards are sequentially numbered to 2500.

COMPLETE SET (20) 40.00 80.00
STATED PRINT RUN 2500 SER.#'d SETS
EL1 Cris Carter 1.25 3.00
EL2 Jerry Rice 3.00 8.00
EL3 Mark Brunell 1.00 2.50
EL4 Brett Favre 2.50 6.00
EL5 Keyshawn Johnson 1.00 2.50
EL6 Eddie George 1.00 2.50
EL7 John Elway 2.00 5.00
EL8 Troy Aikman 1.50 4.00
EL9 Marshall Faulk 1.00 2.50
EL10 Antonio Freeman 1.00 2.50
EL11 Drew Bledsoe 1.00 2.50
EL12 Steve Young 1.50 4.00
EL13 Dan Marino 2.50 6.00
EL14 Emmitt Smith 2.00 5.00
EL15 Fred Taylor .75 2.00
EL16 Jake Plummer .75 2.00
EL17 Terrell Davis 1.00 2.50
EL18 Peyton Manning 4.00 10.00
EL19 Randy Moss 1.00 2.50
EL20 Barry Sanders 2.00 5.00

1999 Donruss Executive Producers

Randomly inserted in packs, this 45-card insert set is broken down into three subsets. Running backs appear on a blue background card, wide receivers appear on a green background card, and Quarterbacks appear on a red background card. Each card is sequentially numbered to to a player-specific statistic from the 1998 season.

COMPLETE SET (45) 50.00 100.00
EP1 Dan Marino/3497 2.50 6.00
EP2 John Elway/2806 3.00 8.00
EP3 Kordell Stewart/2560 .60 1.50
EP4 Troy Aikman/2330 2.00 5.00
EP5 Steve Young/4170 1.00 2.50
EP6 Doug Flutie/2711 .75 2.00
EP7 Drew Bledsoe/3633 1.00 2.50
EP8 Jon Kitna/1177 .75 2.00
EP9 Steve McNair/3228 .75 2.00
EP10 Mark Brunell/2601 .75 2.00
EP11 Randall Cunningham/3704 .75 2.00
EP12 Jake Plummer/3737 .60 1.50
EP13 Charlie Batch/2178 .75 2.00
EP14 Peyton Manning/3739 2.00 5.00
EP15 Brett Favre/4212 3.00 8.00
EP16 Terrell Davis/2008 1.25 3.00
EP17 Fred Taylor/1223 1.25 3.00
EP18 Eddie George/1294 .75 2.00
EP19 Corey Dillon/1130 1.00 2.50
EP20 Jamal Anderson/1846 1.00 2.50
EP21 Curtis Martin/1287 1.00 2.50
EP22 Dorsey Levens/378 1.25 3.00
EP23 Karim Abdul-Jabbar/960 1.00 2.50
EP24 Curtis Enis/497 1.00 2.50
EP25 Mike Alstott/846 1.00 2.50
EP26 Natrone Means/883 1.00 2.50
EP27 Jerome Bettis/1185 1.00 2.50
EP28 Warrick Dunn/1026 1.00 2.50
EP29 Emmitt Smith/1332 2.50 6.00
EP30 Barry Sanders/1491 4.00 10.00
EP31 Jerry Rice/1157 2.50 6.00
EP32 Randy Moss/1313 2.50 6.00
EP33 Keyshawn Johnson/1131 1.00 2.50
EP34 Isaac Bruce/457 1.25 3.00
EP35 Antonio Freeman/1424 1.00 2.50
EP36 Eric Moulds/1368 1.00 2.50
EP37 Tim Dwight/94 2.50 6.00
EP38 Herman Moore/983 1.00 2.50
EP39 Tim Brown/1012 1.00 2.50
EP40 Marshall Faulk/1319 1.50 4.00
EP41 Terry Glenn/792 1.00 2.50
EP42 Joey Galloway/1047 1.00 2.50
EP43 Carl Pickens/1023 .75 2.00
EP44 Terrell Owens/1097 1.00 2.50
EP45 Cris Carter/1011 1.00 2.50

1999 Donruss Fan Club Gold

Randomly inserted in packs, this 20-card set focuses on players that are fan favorites. Each card is sequentially numbered out of 5000, and contains information about the Donruss web site for an interactive trivia game. The cardfronts for the hobby version were printed with gold foil highlights. A retail version was also produced and printed with silver foil on the front and no serial numbering on the back.

COMPLETE SET (20) 25.00 50.00
GOLD PRINT RUN 5000 SER.#'d SETS
*SILVER: .3X TO .8X GOLD
SILVERS INSERTED IN RETAIL PACKS
FC1 Troy Aikman 1.25 3.00
FC2 Ricky Williams 1.00 2.50
FC3 Jerry Rice 2.50 6.00
FC4 Brett Favre 2.00 5.00
FC5 Terrell Davis .75 2.00
FC6 Doug Flutie 1.00 2.50

FC7 John Elway 1.50 4.00
FC8 Steve Young 1.25 3.00
FC9 Steve McNair .75 2.00
FC10 Kordell Stewart .60 1.50
FC11 Drew Bledsoe .75 2.00
FC12 Donovan McNabb 2.00 5.00
FC13 Dan Marino 2.00 5.00
FC14 Cade McNown .60 1.50
FC15 Vinny Testaverde .60 1.50
FC16 Jake Plummer .60 1.50
FC17 Randall Cunningham .75 2.00
FC18 Peyton Manning 3.00 8.00
FC19 Keyshawn Johnson .75 2.00
FC20 Barry Sanders 1.50 4.00

1999 Donruss Gridiron Kings

Randomly inserted in packs, this 20-card set features player "paintings" on a card highlighted with silver foil. Each card is sequentially numbered to 5000 where the first 500 of each card were printed on a canvas card-stock. Card backs carry a "GK" prefix.

COMPLETE SET (20) 50.00 100.00
STATED PRINT RUN 5000 SER.#'d SETS
CANVAS/500: 1X TO 2.5X BASIC INSERTS
GK1 Randy Moss 1.25 3.00
GK2 Fred Taylor 1.00 2.50
GK3 Doug Flutie 1.50 4.00
GK4 Brett Favre 3.00 8.00
GK5 Mark Brunell 1.25 3.00
GK6 Troy Aikman 2.00 5.00
GK7 John Elway 2.50 6.00
GK8 Jerry Rice 4.00 10.00
GK9 Drew Bledsoe 1.25 3.00
GK10 Eddie George 1.25 3.00
GK11 Randall Cunningham 1.25 3.00
GK12 Emmitt Smith 2.50 6.00
GK13 Dan Marino 3.00 8.00
GK14 Jake Plummer 1.00 2.50
GK15 Jamal Anderson 1.25 3.00
GK16 Terrell Davis 1.25 3.00
GK17 Steve Young 2.00 5.00
GK18 Peyton Manning 5.00 12.00
GK19 Jerome Bettis 1.50 4.00
GK20 Barry Sanders 2.50 6.00

1999 Donruss Private Signings

Randomly inserted in packs at the rate of one in 174, this set features authentic autographs of then current NFL stars. Donruss announced print runs on these inserts. Each card carries a copyright date of 1998, but includes a foil stamp on the front that reads "Authentic Signature 1999." Additional autographs, missing this 1999 stamp, surfaced at a later date and are cataloged as 1998 Donruss Private Signings. Some cards were available in redemption form only with an expiration date of 5/1/2000. The unnumbered cards are listed below alphabetically. Reportedly, Jake Plummer never signed cards for the set.

1 Mike Alstott/600* 12.00 30.00
2 Jerome Bettis/500* 30.00 60.00
3 Tim Brown/500* 12.00 30.00
4 Isaac Bruce/500* 12.00 30.00
5 Cris Carter/600* 12.00 30.00
6 Randall Cunningham/150* 12.00 30.00
7 Terrell Davis/475* 12.00 30.00
8 Corey Dillon/500* 8.00 20.00
9 Curtis Enis/500* 6.00 15.00
10 Doug Flutie/275* 12.00 30.00
11 Antonio Freeman/500* 12.00 30.00
12 Eddie George/300* 12.00 30.00
13 Brian Griese/1500* 12.00 30.00
14 Skip Hicks/500* 6.00 15.00
15 Priest Holmes/500* 3.00 8.00
16 Natrone Means/500* 7.50 20.00
17 Randy Moss/250* 40.00 80.00
18 Eric Moulds/800* 12.00 30.00
19 Terrell Owens/500* 20.00 40.00
20 Jerry Rice/50* 75.00 150.00
21 Barry Sanders/50* 100.00 200.00
22 Neil Smith/350* 6.00 15.00
23 Duce Staley/500* 12.00 30.00
24 Kordell Stewart/300* 8.00 20.00
25 Fred Taylor/175* 12.00 30.00
26 Vinny Testaverde/500* 8.00 20.00
27 Derrick Thomas/350* 75.00 125.00
28 Thurman Thomas/500* 15.00 40.00
29 Wesley Walls/500* 6.00 15.00
30 Ricky Williams/150* 12.00 30.00
31 Steve Young/150* 40.00 80.00

1999 Donruss Rated Rookies

Randomly seeded in packs, this 20-card set showcases the top rookies form the 1999 draft on a card with silver foil highlights. Each card is sequentially numbered out of 5000 and a parallel of this insert set was released also. Card backs carry an "RR" prefix.

COMPLETE SET (20) 40.00 80.00
STATED PRINT RUN 5000 SER.#'d SETS
MEDALIST/250: 1X TO 2.5X BASIC INSERTS
RR1 Tim Couch .75 2.00
RR2 Peerless Price .60 1.50
RR3 Ricky Williams 1.00 2.50
RR4 Torry Holt 1.25 3.00
RR5 Champ Bailey 1.25 3.00
RR6 Rob Konrad .60 1.50
RR7 Donovan McNabb 2.00 5.00
RR8 Edgerrin James 1.00 2.50
RR9 David Boston .60 1.50
RR10 Akili Smith .60 1.50
RR11 Cecil Collins .60 1.50
RR12 Troy Edwards .60 1.50
RR13 Daunte Culpepper 1.00 2.50
RR14 Kevin Faulk .60 1.50
RR15 Kevin Johnson .75 2.00
RR16 Cade McNown .60 1.50
RR17 Shaun King .60 1.50
RR18 Brock Huard .60 1.50
RR19 James Johnson .60 1.50
RR20 Sedrick Irvin .60 1.50

1999 Donruss Rookie Gridiron Kings

Randomly inserted in packs, this 10-card set features player "paintings" on a card highlighted with silver foil. Each card is sequentially numbered to 5000 where the first 500 of each card were printed on a canvas card-stock. Card backs carry a "RGK" prefix.

COMPLETE SET (10) 30.00 60.00
STATED PRINT RUN 5000 SER.#'d SETS
CANVAS/500: 1X TO 2.5X BASIC INSERTS
RGK1 Ricky Williams 1.25 3.00
RGK2 Donovan McNabb 2.50 6.00
RGK3 Daunte Culpepper 1.25 3.00
RGK4 Edgerrin James 1.25 3.00
RGK5 David Boston .75 2.00
RGK6 Champ Bailey 1.50 4.00
RGK7 Torry Holt 1.50 4.00
RGK8 Cade McNown .75 2.00
RGK9 Akili Smith .75 2.00
RGK10 Tim Couch 1.00 2.50

1999 Donruss Zoning Commission

Randomly inserted in packs, this 25-card set NFL stars who always seem to find their way into the end zone. Each card is sequentially numbered out of 1000. A parallel version of this set was released also.

COMPLETE SET (25) 30.00 60.00
STATED PRINT RUN 1000 SER.#'d SETS
1 Eric Moulds .60 1.50
2 Steve Young 1.25 3.00
3 Brad Johnson .75 2.00
4 Peyton Manning 3.00 8.00
5 Randy Moss .75 2.00
6 Brett Favre 2.00 5.00
7 Emmitt Smith 1.50 4.00
8 Mark Brunell .75 2.00
9 Keyshawn Johnson .75 2.00
10 Dan Marino 2.00 5.00
11 Eddie George .75 2.00
12 Drew Bledsoe .75 2.00
13 Terrell Davis .75 2.00
14 Terrell Owens .75 2.00
15 Barry Sanders 1.50 4.00
16 Curtis Martin .75 2.00
17 John Elway 1.50 4.00
18 Jake Plummer .60 1.50
19 Jerry Rice 2.50 6.00
20 Fred Taylor .60 1.50
21 Antonio Freeman .75 2.00
22 Marshall Faulk .75 2.00
23 Dorsey Levens .75 2.00
24 Steve McNair .75 2.00
25 Cris Carter 1.00 2.50

1999 Donruss Zoning Commission Red

2 Steve Young/36 20.00 50.00
4 Peyton Manning/26 60.00 150.00
6 Brett Favre/31 60.00 150.00
8 Mark Brunell/20 30.00 80.00
10 Dan Marino/23 60.00 150.00
12 Drew Bledsoe/20 30.00 80.00
13 Terrell Davis/21 30.00 80.00
17 John Elway/22 75.00 200.00

2000 Donruss

Released in early October, Donruss features a 250-card base set comprised of 150 veteran cards and 100 rookie cards. Each shortprinted rookie card is sequentially numbered to 1325. Donruss was packaged differently for both Hobby and Retail. Retail boxes contained 24 packs of seven cards each and carried a suggested retail price of $1.99, and Hobby boxes contained 18 packs of 16 cards each and carried a suggested retail price of $3.99.

COMPLETE SET (250) 150.00 400.00
COMP.SET w/o RC's (150) 7.50 20.00
151-250 ROOKIE PRINT RUN 1325
1 Jake Plummer .12 .30
2 Frank Sanders .12 .30
3 Rob Moore .12 .30
4 David Boston .12 .30
5 Tim Dwight .15 .40
6 Jamal Anderson .15 .40
7 Chris Chandler .15 .40
8 Terance Mathis .12 .30
9 Tony Banks .12 .30
10 Jermaine Lewis .12 .30
11 Shannon Sharpe .15 .40
12 Trent Dilfer .12 .30
13 Qadry Ismail .12 .30
14 Eric Moulds .12 .30
15 Doug Flutie .15 .40
16 Antowain Smith .15 .40
17 Jonathan Linton .12 .30
18 Peerless Price .15 .40
19 Rob Johnson .15 .40
20 Natrone Means .15 .40
21 Muhsin Muhammad .12 .30
22 Wesley Walls .12 .30
23 Tim Biakabutuka .15 .40
24 Steve Beuerlein .15 .40
25 Patrick Jeffers .12 .30
26 Curtis Enis .12 .30
27 Cade McNown .12 .30
28 Bobby Engram .12 .30
29 Marcus Robinson .15 .40
30 Marty Booker .12 .30
31 Corey Dillon .12 .30
32 Darnay Scott .15 .40
33 Carl Pickens .15 .40
34 Akili Smith .12 .30
35 Michael Basnight .12 .30
36 Tim Couch .15 .40
37 Kevin Johnson .12 .30
38 Karim Abdul-Jabbar .12 .30
39 Errict Rhett .15 .40
40 Darrin Chiaverini .12 .30
41 Emmitt Smith .30 .75
42 Troy Aikman .25 .60
43 Joey Galloway .15 .40
44 Randall Cunningham .15 .40
45 Michael Irvin .20 .50
46 Rocket Ismail .15 .40
47 Jason Tucker .12 .30
48 Terrell Davis .15 .40
49 John Elway .30 .75
50 Olandis Gary .15 .40
51 Ed McCaffrey .15 .40
52 Rod Smith .15 .40
53 Brian Griese .12 .30
54 Charlie Batch .12 .30
55 Barry Sanders .30 .75
56 Herman Moore .12 .30
57 Johnnie Morton .15 .40
58 Germane Crowell .12 .30
59 James Stewart .12 .30
60 Brett Favre .40 1.00
61 Dorsey Levens .15 .40
62 Antonio Freeman .15 .40
63 Corey Bradford .12 .30
64 Bill Schroeder .15 .40
65 E.G. Green .12 .30
66 Peyton Manning .50 1.25
67 Edgerrin James .15 .40
68 Marvin Harrison .15 .40
69 Terrence Wilkins .12 .30
70 Mark Brunell .15 .40
71 Fred Taylor .12 .30
72 Keenan McCardell .15 .40
73 Jimmy Smith .15 .40
74 Warren Moon .20 .50
75 Elvis Grbac .12 .30
76 Tony Gonzalez .15 .40
77 Dan Marino .40 1.00
78 O.J. McDuffie .15 .40
79 Tony Martin .15 .40
80 James Johnson .12 .30
81 Thurman Thomas .15 .40
82 Randy Moss .15 .40
83 Daunte Culpepper .15 .40
84 Cris Carter .20 .50
85 Robert Smith .12 .30
86 John Randle .20 .50
87 Drew Bledsoe .15 .40
88 Terry Glenn .15 .40
89 Kevin Faulk .12 .30
90 Ricky Williams .15 .40
91 Jeff Blake .15 .40
92 Jake Reed .15 .40
93 Amani Toomer .12 .30
94 Kerry Collins .12 .30
95 Tiki Barber .15 .40
96 Ike Hilliard .12 .30
97 Curtis Martin .15 .40
98 Vinny Testaverde .12 .30
99 Wayne Chrebet .12 .30
100 Ray Lucas .12 .30
101 Charles Woodson .20 .50
102 Napoleon Kaufman .15 .40
103 Tim Brown .20 .50
104 Tyrone Wheatley .12 .30
105 Rich Gannon .15 .40
106 Duce Staley .12 .30
107 Donovan McNabb .15 .40
108 Amos Zereoue .12 .30
109 Kordell Stewart .12 .30
110 Jerome Bettis .20 .50
111 Troy Edwards .12 .30
112 Ryan Leaf .15 .40
113 Junior Seau .15 .40
114 Jim Harbaugh .15 .40
115 Jermaine Fazande .12 .30
116 Curtis Conway .15 .40
117 Steve Young .25 .60
118 Jerry Rice .50 1.25
119 Terrell Owens .15 .40
120 Charlie Garner .15 .40
121 Jeff Garcia .12 .30
122 Jon Kitna .12 .30
123 Derrick Mayes .12 .30
124 Ricky Watters .15 .40
125 Kurt Warner .30 .75
126 Marshall Faulk .15 .40
127 Torry Holt .15 .40
128 Az-Zahir Hakim .12 .30
129 Isaac Bruce .20 .50
130 Mike Alstott .12 .30
131 Warrick Dunn .12 .30
132 Shaun King .12 .30
133 Keyshawn Johnson .15 .40
134 Jacquez Green .12 .30
135 Reidel Anthony .12 .30
136 Warren Sapp .15 .40
137 Eddie George .15 .40
138 Steve McNair .15 .40
139 Yancey Thigpen .12 .30
140 Kevin Dyson .15 .40
141 Frank Wycheck .15 .40
142 Jevon Kearse .12 .30
143 Stephen Davis .12 .30
144 Skip Hicks .12 .30
145 Brad Johnson .15 .40
146 Bruce Smith .15 .40
147 Michael Westbrook .12 .30
148 Albert Connell .12 .30
149 Jeff George .15 .40
150 Deion Sanders .15 .40
151 Courtney Brown RC 2.00 5.00
152 Corey Simon RC 2.00 5.00
153 Brian Urlacher RC 8.00 20.00
154 Shaun Ellis RC 2.00 5.00
155 John Abraham RC 2.50 6.00
156 Deltha O'Neal RC 1.50 4.00
157 Ahmed Plummer RC 1.50 4.00
158 Chris Hovan RC 2.00 5.00
159 Rob Morris RC 2.00 5.00
160 Keith Bulluck RC 2.00 5.00
161 Darren Howard RC 1.50 4.00
162 John Engelberger RC 1.50 4.00
163 Raynoch Thompson RC 1.50 4.00
164 Cornelius Griffin RC 1.50 4.00
165 William Bartee RC 1.50 4.00
166 Fred Robbins RC 1.50 4.00
167 Micheal Boireau RC 1.50 4.00
168 Brandon Short RC 1.50 4.00
169 Jacoby Shepherd RC 1.50 4.00
170 Peter Warrick RC 1.50 4.00
171 Jamal Lewis RC 2.50 6.00
172 Thomas Jones RC 2.00 5.00
173 Plaxico Burress RC 2.00 5.00
174 Travis Taylor RC 1.50 4.00
175 Ron Dayne RC 2.50 6.00
176 Bubba Franks RC 1.50 4.00
177 Sebastian Janikowski RC 2.50 6.00
178 Chad Pennington RC 2.00 5.00
179 Shaun Alexander RC 2.50 6.00
180 Sylvester Morris RC 1.50 4.00
181 Anthony Becht RC 1.50 4.00
182 R.Jay Soward RC 1.50 4.00
183 Trung Canidate RC 1.50 4.00
184 Dennis Northcutt RC 1.50 4.00
185 Todd Pinkston RC 1.50 4.00
186 Jerry Porter RC 2.50 6.00
187 Travis Prentice RC 1.50 4.00
188 Giovanni Carmazzi RC 1.50 4.00
189 Ron Dugans RC 1.50 4.00
190 Erron Kinney RC 1.50 4.00
191 Dez White RC 1.50 4.00
192 Chris Cole RC 2.00 5.00
193 Ron Dixon RC 1.50 4.00
194 Chris Redman RC 1.50 4.00
195 J.R. Redmond RC 1.50 4.00
196 Laveranues Coles RC 2.00 5.00
197 JaJuan Dawson RC 1.50 4.00
198 Darrell Jackson RC 1.50 4.00
199 Reuben Droughns RC 1.50 4.00
200 Doug Chapman RC 1.50 4.00
201 Terrelle Smith RC 1.50 4.00
202 Curtis Keaton RC 1.50 4.00
203 Gari Scott RC 1.50 4.00
204 Danny Farmer RC 1.50 4.00
205 Hank Poteat RC 1.50 4.00
206 Ben Kelly RC 1.50 4.00
207 Corey Moore RC 1.50 4.00
208 Na'il Diggs RC 1.50 4.00
209 Aaron Shea RC 2.00 5.00
210 Trevor Gaylor RC 1.50 4.00
211 Julian Peterson RC 2.50 6.00
212 Frank Moreau RC 1.50 4.00
213 Deon Dyer RC 1.50 4.00
214 Avion Black RC 1.50 4.00
215 Paul Smith RC 1.50 4.00
216 Michael Wiley RC 1.50 4.00
217 Dante Hall RC 1.50 4.00
218 Mike Brown RC 1.50 4.00
219 Sammy Morris RC 1.50 4.00
220 Billy Volek RC 2.50 6.00
221 Tee Martin RC 1.50 4.00
222 Troy Walters RC 1.50 4.00
223 Chad Morton RC 2.00 5.00
224 Erik Flowers RC 1.50 4.00
225 Ronney Jenkins RC 1.50 4.00
226 Thomas Hamner RC 1.50 4.00
227 Mareno Philyaw RC 1.50 4.00
228 James Williams RC 1.50 4.00
229 Mike Anderson RC 1.50 4.00
230 Tom Brady RC 250.00 400.00
231 Mike Green RC 2.00 5.00
232 Todd Husak RC 1.50 4.00
233 Tim Rattay RC 2.00 5.00
234 Jarious Jackson RC 2.00 5.00
235 Joe Hamilton RC 1.50 4.00
236 Shyrone Stith RC 1.50 4.00
237 Rondell Mealey RC 1.50 4.00
238 Demario Brown RC 1.50 4.00
239 Chris Coleman RC 1.50 4.00
240 Dwayne Goodrich RC 1.50 4.00
241 Drew Haddad RC 1.50 4.00
242 Doug Johnson RC 1.50 4.00
243 Windrell Hayes RC 1.50 4.00
244 Charles Lee RC 1.50 4.00
245 Kevin McDougal RC 1.50 4.00
246 Spergon Wynn RC 1.50 4.00
247 Shockmain Davis RC 1.50 4.00
248 Jamel White RC 1.50 4.00
249 Bashir Yamini RC 1.50 4.00
250 Kwame Cavil RC 1.50 4.00
NNO Kurt Warner Promo

2000 Donruss Stat Line Career

*VETS/200-300: 5X TO 12X BASIC CARDS
*ROOKIES/200-300: .4X TO 1X
*VETS/140-199: 6X TO 15X BASIC CARDS
*ROOKIES/140-199: .5X TO 1.2X
*VETS/100-139: 8X TO 20X BASIC CARDS
*ROOKIES/100-139: .6X TO 1.5X
*VETS/70-99: 10X TO 25X BASIC CARDS
*ROOKIES/70-99: .8X TO 2X
*VETS/40-69: 12X TO 30X BASIC CARDS
*ROOKIES/40-69: 1X TO 2.5X
*VETS/30-39: 15X TO 40X BASIC CARDS
*ROOKIES/30-39: 1.2X TO 3X
*VETS/20-29: 20X TO 50X BASIC
*ROOKIES/20-29: 1.5X TO 4X
*ROOKIES/10-19: 2X TO 5X
CAREER/2-300 ODDS 1:25 HOB, 1:48 RET
CARDS SER.#'d TO A CAREER STAT
230 Tom Brady/214 300.00 500.00

2000 Donruss Stat Line Season

*VETS/70-99: 10X TO 25X BASIC CARDS
*ROOKIES/70-99: .8X TO 2X
*VETS/40-69: 12X TO 30X BASIC CARDS
*ROOKIES/40-69: 1X TO 2.5X
*VETS/30-39: 15X TO 40X BASIC CARDS
*ROOKIES/30-39: 1.2X TO 3X
*VETS/20-29: 20X TO 50X BASIC CARDS
*ROOKIES/20-29: 1.5X TO 4X
*VETS/10-19: 25X TO 60X BASIC CARDS
*ROOKIES/10-19: 2X TO 5X
SEASON/1-99 ODDS 1:192 H, 1:396 R
230 Tom Brady/20 1000.00 2000.00

2000 Donruss All-Time Gridiron Kings

Randomly inserted in Hobby packs, this 10-card set features original art of the NFL's all-time greatest. Each card is sequentially numbered to 2500.

COMPLETE SET (10) 12.50 30.00
STATED PRINT RUN 2500 SER.#'d SETS
1 Joe Montana 4.00 10.00
2 Terry Bradshaw 3.00 8.00
3 Fran Tarkenton 1.25 3.00
4 Dan Fouts 1.00 2.50
5 Sammy Baugh 1.25 3.00
6 Eric Dickerson 1.00 2.50
7 Bob Griese 1.25 3.00
8 Ken Stabler 1.50 4.00
9 Joe Namath 2.50 6.00
10 Lawrence Taylor 1.25 3.00

2000 Donruss All-Time Gridiron Kings Studio Autographs

Randomly inserted in Hobby packs, this set parallels the base All-Time Gridiron Kings set enhanced with authentic player autographs. Each card is sequentially numbered to 250. Some cards were issued through exchange redemptions that carried an expiration date of 10/31/2001 and Dan Fouts never signed cards for the set. Instead, his redemption card was exchanged for a 1997 Leaf Dan Fouts autogrpahed card.

STAT.PRINT RUN 250 SER.#'d SETS
1 Joe Montana 40.00 100.00
2 Terry Bradshaw 30.00 80.00
3 Fran Tarkenton 20.00 50.00
5 Sammy Baugh 50.00 100.00
6 Eric Dickerson 15.00 40.00
7 Bob Griese 15.00 40.00
8 Ken Stabler 15.00 40.00
9 Joe Namath 50.00 100.00
10 Lawrence Taylor 20.00 50.00

2000 Donruss Dominators

Randomly inserted in packs, this 60-card set features the most dominating players in the game on a card with a black border along the left side and gold foil highlights. Each card is sequentially numbered to 5000.

COMPLETE SET (60) 12.50 30.00
STATED PRINT RUN 5000 SER.#'d SETS
1 Jake Plummer .25 .60
2 Tim Couch .30 .75
3 Emmitt Smith .60 1.50
4 Troy Aikman .50 1.25
5 John Elway .60 1.50
6 Terrell Davis .30 .75
7 Charlie Batch .25 .60
8 Barry Sanders .60 1.50
9 Brett Favre .75 2.00
10 Peyton Manning 1.00 2.50
11 Edgerrin James .30 .75
12 Mark Brunell .30 .75
13 Fred Taylor .25 .60
14 Dan Marino .75 2.00
15 Randy Moss .30 .75
16 Drew Bledsoe .30 .75
17 Ricky Williams .30 .75
18 Jerry Rice 1.00 2.50
19 Steve Young .50 1.25
20 Kurt Warner .60 1.50
21 Eddie George .30 .75
22 Jamal Anderson .30 .75
23 Eric Moulds .25 .60
24 Cade McNown .25 .60
25 Corey Dillon .25 .60
26 Kevin Johnson .25 .60
27 Joey Galloway .30 .75
28 Olandis Gary .30 .75
29 Dorsey Levens .30 .75
30 Antonio Freeman .30 .75
31 Marvin Harrison .30 .75
32 Daunte Culpepper .30 .75
33 Cris Carter .40 1.00
34 Robert Smith .25 .60
35 Curtis Martin .30 .75
36 Tim Brown .40 1.00
37 Duce Staley .25 .60
38 Donovan McNabb .30 .75
39 Jerome Bettis .40 1.00
40 Terrell Owens .30 .75
41 Jon Kitna .25 .60
42 Marshall Faulk .30 .75
43 Warrick Dunn .25 .60
44 Shaun King .25 .60
45 Keyshawn Johnson .30 .75
46 Steve McNair .30 .75
47 Stephen Davis .25 .60
48 Brad Johnson .30 .75
49 Muhsin Muhammad .25 .60
50 Marcus Robinson .30 .75
51 Akili Smith .25 .60
52 Brian Griese .25 .60
53 Germane Crowell .25 .60
54 Jimmy Smith .30 .75
55 Ricky Watters .30 .75
56 Isaac Bruce .40 1.00
57 Warren Sapp .30 .75
58 Jevon Kearse .25 .60
59 Michael Westbrook .25 .60
60 Ed McCaffrey .30 .75

2000 Donruss Elite Series

Randomly inserted in packs, this 40-card set features base design with three borders along the left right and bottom. Cards are enhanced with red foil highlights and are sequentially numbered to 2500.

COMPLETE SET (40) 25.00 60.00
STATED PRINT RUN 2500 SER.#'d SETS
ES1 Jake Plummer .50 1.25
ES2 Emmitt Smith 1.25 3.00
ES3 Tim Couch .60 1.50
ES4 Troy Aikman 1.00 2.50
ES5 John Elway 1.25 3.00
ES6 Terrell Davis .60 1.50
ES7 Barry Sanders 1.25 3.00
ES8 Brett Favre 1.50 4.00
ES9 Peyton Manning 2.00 5.00
ES10 Mark Brunell .60 1.50
ES11 Edgerrin James .60 1.50
ES12 Fred Taylor .50 1.25
ES13 Dan Marino 1.50 4.00
ES14 Randy Moss .60 1.50
ES15 Drew Bledsoe .60 1.50
ES16 Ricky Williams .60 1.50
ES17 Jerry Rice 2.00 5.00
ES18 Steve Young 1.00 2.50
ES19 Kurt Warner 1.25 3.00
ES20 Eddie George .60 1.50
ES21 Deion Sanders .60 1.50
ES22 Cade McNown .50 1.25
ES23 Joey Galloway .60 1.50
ES24 Dorsey Levens .60 1.50
ES25 Antonio Freeman .60 1.50
ES26 Marvin Harrison .60 1.50
ES27 Daunte Culpepper .60 1.50
ES28 Cris Carter .75 2.00
ES29 Curtis Martin .60 1.50
ES30 Tim Brown .75 2.00
ES31 Donovan McNabb .60 1.50
ES32 Jerome Bettis .75 2.00
ES33 Marshall Faulk .60 1.50
ES34 Jon Kitna .50 1.25
ES35 Keyshawn Johnson .60 1.50
ES36 Steve McNair .60 1.50
ES37 Stephen Davis .50 1.25
ES38 Jimmy Smith .60 1.50
ES39 Brad Johnson .60 1.50
ES40 Isaac Bruce .75 2.00

2000 Donruss Gridiron Kings

Randomly inserted in packs, this 10-card set features original artwork of some of the NFL's top players. Each card is sequentially numbered to 2500.

COMPLETE SET (10) 12.50 30.00
STATED PRINT RUN 2500 SER.#'d SETS
*STUDIO/250: 1.2X TO 3X BASIC INSERTS
STUDIO PRINT RUN 250 SER.#'d SETS
GK1 Emmitt Smith 1.50 4.00
GK2 John Elway 1.50 4.00
GK3 Barry Sanders 1.50 4.00
GK4 Brett Favre 2.00 5.00
GK5 Peyton Manning 2.50 6.00
GK6 Dan Marino 2.00 5.00
GK7 Randy Moss .75 2.00
GK8 Jerry Rice 2.50 6.00
GK9 Steve Young 1.25 3.00
GK10 Kurt Warner 1.50 4.00

2000 Donruss Gridiron Kings Studio Autographs

Randomly inserted in packs, this 10-card set is comprised of the first 50 serial numbered copies of the Gridiron Kings Studio set. Each card contains an authentic player autograph. Some cards were issued through exchange redemptions that carried an expiration date of 10/31/2001. Randy Moss signed just 19-cards for the set instead of 50 with each serial numbered of 19 in silver foil on the cardbacks.

STATED PRINT RUN 19-50
GK1 Emmitt Smith 100.00 200.00
GK2 John Elway 75.00 150.00
GK3 Barry Sanders 75.00 150.00
GK4 Brett Favre 125.00 250.00
GK5 Peyton Manning 75.00 150.00
GK6 Dan Marino 150.00 300.00
GK7 Randy Moss/19 100.00 200.00
GK8 Jerry Rice 75.00 150.00
GK9 Steve Young 30.00 80.00
GK10 Kurt Warner 25.00 60.00

2000 Donruss Jersey King Autographs

Randomly inserted in packs, this 10-card set features original artwork, a swatch of game worn jersey in the shape of a crown, and an authentic player autograph. Each card is sequentially numbered to 50. Some cards were issued through exchange redemptions that carried an expiration date of 10/31/2001.

STATED PRINT RUN 50 SER.#'d SETS
1 John Elway 100.00 200.00
2 Barry Sanders 75.00 150.00
3 Dan Marino 125.00 250.00
4 Jerry Rice 125.00 250.00
5 Kurt Warner 50.00 125.00
6 Joe Montana 100.00 200.00
7 Terry Bradshaw 75.00 150.00
8 Fran Tarkenton 30.00 80.00
9 Eric Dickerson 25.00 60.00
10 Joe Namath 60.00 120.00

2000 Donruss Rated Rookies

Randomly inserted in packs, this 40-card set features the top rated rookies from the 2000 crop. Each card has a gold background, is enhanced with silver foil highlights, and is sequentially numbered to 2500.

COMPLETE SET (40) 25.00 60.00
STATED PRINT RUN 2500 SER.#'d SETS
*MEDALIST/100: 1.2X TO 3X BASIC INSERTS
MEDALIST PRINT RUN 100 SER.#'d SETS
1 Peter Warrick .50 1.25
2 Jamal Lewis .75 2.00
3 Thomas Jones .60 1.50
4 Plaxico Burress .60 1.50
5 Travis Taylor .50 1.25
6 Ron Dayne .75 2.00
7 Bubba Franks .50 1.25
8 Chad Pennington .60 1.50
9 Shaun Alexander .75 2.00
10 Sylvester Morris .50 1.25
11 R.Jay Soward .50 1.25
12 Trung Canidate .50 1.25
13 Dennis Northcutt .50 1.25
14 Todd Pinkston .50 1.25
15 Jerry Porter .75 2.00
16 Travis Prentice .50 1.25
17 Giovanni Carmazzi .50 1.25
18 Ron Dugans .50 1.25
19 Dez White .50 1.25
20 Chris Cole .60 1.50
21 Ron Dixon .50 1.25
22 Chris Redman .50 1.25
23 J.R. Redmond .50 1.25
24 Laveranues Coles .60 1.50
25 JaJuan Dawson .50 1.25
26 Darrell Jackson .50 1.25
27 Reuben Droughns .50 1.25
28 Doug Chapman .50 1.25
29 Curtis Keaton .50 1.25
30 Gari Scott .50 1.25
31 Danny Farmer .50 1.25
32 Trevor Gaylor .50 1.25
33 Anthony Becht .50 1.25
34 Frank Moreau .50 1.25
35 Avion Black .50 1.25
36 Michael Wiley .50 1.25
37 Dante Hall .50 1.25
38 Tim Rattay .60 1.50
39 Tee Martin .50 1.25
40 Courtney Brown .60 1.50

2000 Donruss Rookie Gridiron Kings

Randomly inserted in Hobby packs, this 10-card set features original artwork of top rookies from the 2000 draft. Each card is sequentially numbered to 2500.

COMPLETE SET (10) 10.00 25.00
STATED PRINT RUN 2500 SER.#'d SETS
*STUDIO/250: 1.2X TO 3X BASIC INSERTS
STUDIO PRINT RUN 250 SER.#'d SETS
1 Peter Warrick .30 .75
2 Jamal Lewis .50 1.25
3 Thomas Jones .40 1.00
4 Plaxico Burress .40 1.00
5 Travis Taylor .30 .75
6 Ron Dayne .50 1.25
7 Chad Pennington .40 1.00
8 Shaun Alexander .50 1.25
9 Sylvester Morris .30 .75
10 Chris Redman .30 .75

2000 Donruss Rookie Gridiron Kings Studio Autographs

Randomly inserted in packs, this 10-card set is comprised of the first 50 serial #'d copies of the Rookie Gridiron Kings Studio Set. Each card includes an authentic player autograph. Some cards were issued through exchange redemptions that carried an expiration date of 10/31/2001.

ANNOUNCED PRINT RUN 50 SETS
1 Peter Warrick 10.00 25.00
2 Jamal Lewis 15.00 40.00
3 Thomas Jones 12.00 30.00
4 Plaxico Burress 12.00 30.00
5 Travis Taylor 10.00 25.00
6 Ron Dayne 12.00 30.00
7 Chad Pennington 12.00 30.00
8 Shaun Alexander 15.00 40.00
10 Chris Redman 10.00 25.00

2000 Donruss Signature Series Red

Randomly inserted in packs, this set features a red backdrop and an authentic player autograph. Although the cards are not serial numbered, print runs were announced by Playoff and noted below. Some cards were issued through exchange redemptions that carried an expiration date of 10/31/2001.

PLAYOFF ANNC'D PRINT RUNS 25-750
1 Troy Aikman/25* 50.00 100.00
2 Tony Banks/325* 3.00 8.00
3 Jeff Blake/125* 5.00 12.00
4 Drew Bledsoe/35* 20.00 50.00
5 Isaac Bruce/25* 15.00 40.00
6 Trung Canidate/75* 6.00 15.00
7 Giovanni Carmazzi/175* 4.00 10.00
8 Kwame Cavil/375* 3.00 8.00
9 Doug Chapman/375* 4.00 10.00
10 Trevor Gaylor
11 Kerry Collins/125* 7.50 20.00
12 Albert Connell/750* 3.00 8.00
13 Tim Couch/25* 15.00 40.00
14 Germane Crowell/350* 3.00 8.00
16 Reuben Droughns/375* 6.00 15.00
17 Ron Dugans/175* 4.00 10.00
18 Tim Dwight/350* 5.00 12.00
19 Troy Edwards/350* 3.00 8.00
20 Danny Farmer/175* 5.00 12.00
21 Kevin Faulk/750* 3.00 8.00
22 Marshall Faulk/25* 25.00 60.00
23 Jermaine Fazande/750* 3.00 8.00
24 Antonio Freeman/175* 6.00 15.00
26 Olandis Gary/350* 5.00 12.00
28 Eddie George/25* 15.00 40.00
29 Marvin Harrison/75* 15.00 40.00
30 Torry Holt/75* 12.50 30.00
32 Edgerrin James/25* 25.00 60.00
33 Patrick Jeffers/750* 3.00 8.00
34 Brad Johnson/25* 15.00 40.00
35 Kevin Johnson/350* 4.00 10.00
37 Tee Martin/275* 5.00 12.00
38 Derrick Mayes/750* 3.00 8.00
39 Cade McNown/75* 6.00 15.00
40 Sylvester Morris/125* 5.00 12.00
41 Randy Moss/75* 40.00 80.00
42 Eric Moulds/100* 7.50 20.00
43 Dennis Northcutt/175* 5.00 12.00
44 Todd Pinkston/175* 5.00 12.00
45 Jake Plummer/25* 15.00 40.00
46 Jerry Porter/175* 6.00 15.00
47 Travis Prentice/175* 5.00 12.00
48 Tim Rattay/375* 5.00 12.00
49 J.R. Redmond/175* 5.00 12.00
50 Corey Simon/175* 6.00 15.00
51 Akili Smith/75* 6.00 15.00
52 Antowain Smith/75* 7.50 20.00
53 Jimmy Smith/75* 7.50 20.00
55 Shyrone Stith/175* 4.00 10.00
56 Fred Taylor/75* 7.50 20.00
57 Thurman Thomas/75* 15.00 40.00
58 Kurt Warner/75* 25.00 50.00
59 Ricky Williams/25* 20.00 50.00
60 Tyrone Wheatley/350* 4.00 10.00

2000 Donruss Signature Series Blue

Randomly inserted in packs, this 37-card set parallels the base Signature Series Red set with blue color in the background. Stated print run for the set was 100-serial numbered cards. Some were issued through exchange redemptions that carried an expiration date of 10/31/2001.

STATED PRINT RUN 100 SER.#'d SETS
2 Tony Banks 6.00 15.00
3 Jeff Blake
7 Giovanni Carmazzi 6.00 15.00
8 Kwame Cavil 6.00 15.00
9 Doug Chapman 6.00 15.00
11 Kerry Collins 6.00 15.00
12 Albert Connell 6.00 15.00
14 Germane Crowell 6.00 15.00
16 Reuben Droughns 6.00 15.00
17 Ron Dugans 6.00 15.00
18 Tim Dwight 8.00 20.00
19 Troy Edwards 6.00 15.00
20 Danny Farmer 6.00 15.00
21 Kevin Faulk 6.00 15.00
23 Jermaine Fazande 6.00 15.00
24 Antonio Freeman 8.00 20.00
26 Olandis Gary 8.00 20.00
33 Patrick Jeffers 6.00 15.00
35 Kevin Johnson 6.00 15.00
37 Tee Martin 6.00 15.00
38 Derrick Mayes 6.00 15.00
40 Sylvester Morris 6.00 15.00
43 Dennis Northcutt 6.00 15.00
44 Todd Pinkston 6.00 15.00
46 Jerry Porter 10.00 25.00
47 Travis Prentice 6.00 15.00
48 Tim Rattay 8.00 20.00
49 J.R. Redmond 6.00 15.00
50 Corey Simon 8.00 20.00
55 Shyrone Stith 6.00 15.00
60 Tyrone Wheatley 6.00 15.00

2000 Donruss Signature Series Gold

Randomly inserted in packs, this 60-card set parallels the base Signature Series Red set with Gold backgrounds instead of red. Each card was serial numbered of 25. Some cards were issued through exchange redemptions that carried an expiration date of 10/31/2001.

STATED PRINT RUN 25 SER.#'d SETS
1 Troy Aikman 50.00 100.00
2 Tony Banks 10.00 25.00
3 Jeff Blake 12.00 30.00
4 Drew Bledsoe
5 Isaac Bruce 15.00 40.00
6 Trung Canidate 10.00 25.00
7 Giovanni Carmazzi 10.00 25.00
8 Kwame Cavil 10.00 25.00
9 Doug Chapman 10.00 25.00
11 Kerry Collins 10.00 25.00
12 Albert Connell 10.00 25.00
13 Tim Couch 12.00 30.00
14 Germane Crowell 10.00 25.00
16 Reuben Droughns 10.00 25.00
17 Ron Dugans
18 Tim Dwight 12.00 30.00
19 Troy Edwards 10.00 25.00
20 Kevin Faulk 10.00 25.00
21 Danny Farmer
22 Marshall Faulk 20.00 50.00
23 Jermaine Fazande
24 Antonio Freeman 12.00 30.00
26 Olandis Gary 12.00 30.00
28 Eddie George 12.00 30.00
29 Marvin Harrison 12.00 30.00
30 Torry Holt 12.00 30.00
32 Edgerrin James
33 Patrick Jeffers 10.00 25.00
34 Brad Johnson 12.00 30.00
35 Kevin Johnson 10.00 25.00
37 Tee Martin 10.00 25.00
38 Derrick Mayes 10.00 25.00
39 Cade McNown 10.00 25.00
40 Sylvester Morris 10.00 25.00
41 Randy Moss 50.00 100.00
42 Eric Moulds 10.00 25.00
43 Dennis Northcutt 10.00 25.00
44 Todd Pinkston 10.00 25.00
45 Jake Plummer 10.00 25.00
46 Jerry Porter 15.00 40.00
47 Travis Prentice
48 Tim Rattay 12.00 30.00
49 J.R. Redmond 10.00 25.00
50 Corey Simon 12.00 30.00
51 Akili Smith 10.00 25.00
52 Antowain Smith 12.00 30.00
53 Jimmy Smith 12.00 30.00
55 Shyrone Stith 10.00 25.00
56 Fred Taylor 10.00 25.00
57 Thurman Thomas 12.00 30.00
58 Kurt Warner 40.00 80.00
59 Ricky Williams 12.00 30.00
60 Tyrone Wheatley 10.00 25.00

2000 Donruss Zoning Commission

Randomly inserted in packs, this 60-card set features a die cut card stock and full color action photography. Each card is sequentially numbered to 1000.

COMPLETE SET (60) 30.00 80.00
STATED PRINT RUN 1000 SER.#'d SETS
*RED/41: 4X TO 10X BASIC INSERTS
*RED/22-26: 5X TO 12X BASIC INSERTS
*RED/11-19: 6X TO 15X BASIC INSERTS
RED STATED PRINT RUN 8-41
1 Jake Plummer .60 1.50
2 Tim Couch .75 2.00
3 Emmitt Smith 1.50 4.00
4 Troy Aikman 1.25 3.00
5 Charlie Batch .60 1.50
6 Brett Favre 2.00 5.00
7 Peyton Manning 2.50 6.00
8 Edgerrin James .75 2.00
9 Mark Brunell .75 2.00
10 Fred Taylor .60 1.50
11 Dan Marino 2.00 5.00
12 Randy Moss .75 2.00
13 Drew Bledsoe .75 2.00
14 Ricky Williams .75 2.00
15 Jerry Rice 2.50 6.00
16 Steve Young 1.25 3.00
17 Kurt Warner 1.50 4.00
18 Eddie George .75 2.00
19 Eric Moulds .60 1.50
20 Doug Flutie .75 2.00
21 Antowain Smith .75 2.00
22 Cade McNown .60 1.50
23 Corey Dillon .60 1.50
24 Kevin Johnson .60 1.50
25 Joey Galloway .75 2.00
26 Olandis Gary .75 2.00
27 Dorsey Levens .75 2.00
28 Antonio Freeman .75 2.00
29 Marvin Harrison .75 2.00
30 Cris Carter 1.00 2.50
31 Robert Smith .60 1.50
32 Curtis Martin .75 2.00
33 Tim Brown 1.00 2.50
34 Duce Staley .60 1.50
35 Donovan McNabb .75 2.00
36 Kordell Stewart .60 1.50
37 Jerome Bettis 1.00 2.50
38 Terrell Owens .75 2.00
39 Jon Kitna .60 1.50
40 Marshall Faulk .75 2.00
41 Torry Holt .75 2.00
42 Mike Alstott .60 1.50
43 Shaun King .60 1.50
44 Keyshawn Johnson .75 2.00
45 Steve McNair .75 2.00
46 Stephen Davis .60 1.50
47 Brad Johnson .75 2.00
48 Qadry Ismail .60 1.50
49 Muhsin Muhammad .60 1.50
50 Patrick Jeffers .60 1.50
51 Marcus Robinson .75 2.00
52 Akili Smith .60 1.50
53 Germane Crowell .60 1.50
54 James Stewart .60 1.50
55 Jimmy Smith .75 2.00
56 Amani Toomer .60 1.50
57 Charlie Garner .75 2.00
58 Isaac Bruce 1.00 2.50
59 Albert Connell .60 1.50
60 Jeff George .75 2.00

2002 Donruss Samples

*SILVER SAMPLES: 1X TO 2.5X BASIC CARDS
*GOLD SAMPLES: 1.5X TO 4X BASIC CARDS

2002 Donruss

Released in August 2002, this 300-card set includes 200 veterans and 100 rookies. Pack SRP was $2.99. Boxes contained 24 packs of 5 cards.

COMPLETE SET (300) 60.00 120.00
COMP.SET w/o SP's (200) 7.50 20.00
1 Jake Plummer .12 .30
2 David Boston .12 .30
3 MarTay Jenkins .12 .30
4 Thomas Jones .12 .30
5 Frank Sanders .12 .30
6 Shawn Jefferson .12 .30
7 Alge Crumpler .15 .40
8 Michael Vick .15 .40
9 Jamal Anderson .15 .40
10 Warrick Dunn .12 .30
11 Peter Boulware .12 .30
12 Jamal Lewis .15 .40
13 Jeff Blake .15 .40
14 Travis Taylor .12 .30
15 Ray Lewis .20 .50
16 Todd Heap .12 .30
17 Nate Clements .12 .30
18 Alex Van Pelt .12 .30
19 Reggie Germany .12 .30
20 Larry Centers .12 .30
21 Eric Moulds .12 .30
22 Travis Henry .12 .30
23 Wesley Walls .15 .40
24 Steve Smith .20 .50
25 Lamar Smith .12 .30
26 Patrick Jeffers .15 .40
27 Chris Weinke .12 .30
28 Muhsin Muhammad .12 .30
29 Marcus Robinson .15 .40
30 Jim Miller .12 .30
31 Anthony Thomas .15 .40
32 David Terrell .12 .30
33 Brian Urlacher .20 .50
34 Marty Booker .12 .30
35 Darnay Scott .15 .40
36 Jon Kitna .12 .30
37 Chad Johnson .12 .30
38 T.J. Houshmandzadeh .12 .30
39 Corey Dillon .12 .30
40 Peter Warrick .12 .30
41 Gerard Warren .12 .30
42 Anthony Henry .12 .30
43 Quincy Morgan .12 .30
44 JaJuan Dawson .12 .30
45 Tim Couch .12 .30
46 Kevin Johnson .12 .30
47 James Jackson .12 .30
48 La'Roi Glover .12 .30
49 Anthony Wright .12 .30
50 Rocket Ismail .15 .40
51 Troy Hambrick .12 .30
52 Emmitt Smith .30 .75
53 Quincy Carter .12 .30
54 Joey Galloway .15 .40
55 Shannon Sharpe .15 .40
56 Kevin Kasper .12 .30
57 Olandis Gary .15 .40

58 Brian Griese .12 .30
59 Rod Smith .15 .40
60 Terrell Davis .15 .40
61 Ed McCaffrey .15 .40
62 Mike Anderson .12 .30
63 Bill Schroeder .12 .30
64 Scotty Anderson .12 .30
65 Mike McMahon .12 .30
66 James Stewart .12 .30
67 Az-Zahir Hakim .12 .30
68 Germane Crowell .12 .30
69 Kabeer Gbaja-Biamila .12 .30
70 LeRoy Butler .15 .40
71 Antonio Freeman .20 .50
72 Bubba Franks .12 .30
73 Brett Favre .40 1.00
74 Ahman Green .15 .40
75 Terry Glenn .15 .40
76 Jamie Sharper .15 .40
77 Tony Simmons .12 .30
78 James Allen .12 .30
79 Terrence Wilkins .12 .30
80 Dominic Rhodes .12 .30
81 Qadry Ismail .12 .30
82 Peyton Manning .50 1.25
83 Edgerrin James .15 .40
84 Marvin Harrison .15 .40
85 Reggie Wayne .15 .40
86 Fred Taylor .12 .30
87 Elvis Joseph .12 .30
88 Mark Brunell .15 .40
89 Keenan McCardell .15 .40
90 Jimmy Smith .15 .40
91 Kyle Brady .12 .30
92 Derrick Alexander .12 .30
93 Johnnie Morton .15 .40
94 Trent Green .12 .30
95 Priest Holmes .12 .30
96 Tony Gonzalez .15 .40
97 Snoop Minnis .12 .30
98 Travis Minor .12 .30
99 Oronde Gadsden .12 .30
100 Jay Fiedler .15 .40
101 Chris Chambers .12 .30
102 Ricky Williams .15 .40
103 Zach Thomas .15 .40
104 Byron Chamberlain .12 .30
105 Todd Bouman .12 .30
106 Daunte Culpepper .15 .40
107 Michael Bennett .12 .30
108 Randy Moss .15 .40
109 Cris Carter .20 .50
110 David Patten .12 .30
111 Donald Hayes .12 .30
112 Tom Brady 1.00 2.50
113 Antowain Smith .15 .40
114 Troy Brown .12 .30
115 Drew Bledsoe .15 .40
116 Bryan Cox .15 .40
117 Boo Williams .12 .30
118 Aaron Brooks .12 .30
119 Deuce McAllister .15 .40
120 Joe Horn .12 .30
121 Amani Toomer .12 .30
122 Ron Dayne .15 .40
123 Kerry Collins .12 .30
124 Ike Hilliard .12 .30
125 Tiki Barber .15 .40
126 Michael Strahan .15 .40
127 Chad Pennington .12 .30
128 Santana Moss .15 .40
129 LaMont Jordan .15 .40
130 Curtis Martin .15 .40
131 Wayne Chrebet .12 .30
132 Laveranues Coles .15 .40
133 Vinny Testaverde .12 .30
134 Charles Woodson .20 .50
135 Tyrone Wheatley .15 .40
136 Jerry Porter .12 .30
137 Rich Gannon .15 .40
138 Charlie Garner .15 .40
139 Tim Brown .20 .50
140 Jerry Rice .40 1.00
141 James Thrash .15 .40
142 Todd Pinkston .12 .30
143 A.J. Feeley .12 .30
144 Donovan McNabb .15 .40
145 Duce Staley .12 .30
146 Freddie Mitchell .12 .30
147 Correll Buckhalter .12 .30
148 Casey Hampton .12 .30
149 Hines Ward .15 .40
150 Chris Fuamatu-Ma'afala .12 .30
151 Jerome Bettis .20 .50
152 Kordell Stewart .12 .30
153 Plaxico Burress .12 .30
154 Kendrell Bell .12 .30
155 Trevor Gaylor .12 .30
156 Curtis Conway .15 .40
157 Doug Flutie .15 .40
158 Drew Brees .40 1.00
159 LaDainian Tomlinson .20 .50
160 Junior Seau .15 .40
161 Bryant Young .12 .30
162 Andre Carter .12 .30
163 Eric Johnson .12 .30
164 Jeff Garcia .12 .30
165 Garrison Hearst .12 .30
166 Terrell Owens .15 .40
167 Kevan Barlow .12 .30
168 Levon Kirkland .12 .30
169 Ricky Watters .15 .40
170 Trent Dilfer .12 .30
171 Shaun Alexander .12 .30
172 Koren Robinson .12 .30
173 Darrell Jackson .15 .40
174 Adam Archuleta .12 .30
175 Aeneas Williams .12 .30
176 Trung Canidate .12 .30
177 Kurt Warner .15 .40
178 Marshall Faulk .15 .40
179 Torry Holt .15 .40
180 Isaac Bruce .20 .50
181 John Lynch .15 .40
182 Joe Jurevicius .12 .30
183 Brad Johnson .15 .40
184 Rob Johnson .15 .40
185 Keyshawn Johnson .15 .40
186 Mike Alstott .12 .30
187 Warren Sapp .15 .40
188 Drew Bennett .15 .40
189 Frank Wycheck .12 .30
190 Kevin Dyson .15 .40
191 Steve McNair .15 .40
192 Eddie George .15 .40
193 Jevon Kearse .12 .30
194 Derrick Mason .12 .30
195 Champ Bailey .15 .40
196 Darrell Green .20 .50
197 Bruce Smith .15 .40
198 Jacquez Green .12 .30
199 Stephen Davis .12 .30
200 Rod Gardner .12 .30
201 David Carr RC .60 1.50
202 Joey Harrington RC .60 1.50
203 Patrick Ramsey RC .75 2.00
204 Kurt Kittner RC .60 1.50
205 Rohan Davey RC 1.00 2.50
206 Josh McCown RC 1.00 2.50
207 David Garrard RC .75 2.00
208 Randy Fasani RC .60 1.50
209 Atrews Bell RC .60 1.50
210 Brandon Doman RC .60 1.50
211 Eric Crouch RC 1.00 2.50
212 Woody Dantzler RC .75 2.00
213 Chad Hutchinson RC .60 1.50
214 Zak Kustok RC .60 1.50
215 Ronald Curry RC .60 1.50
216 William Green RC .75 2.00
217 T.J. Duckett RC .60 1.50
218 Clinton Portis RC 1.00 2.50
219 DeShaun Foster RC 1.00 2.50
220 Lamar Gordon RC .75 2.00
221 Jonathan Wells RC .75 2.00
222 Adrian Peterson RC .75 2.00
223 Ladell Betts RC 1.00 2.50
224 Maurice Morris RC .75 2.00
225 Brian Westbrook RC 1.25 3.00
226 Luke Staley RC .60 1.50
227 Travis Stephens RC .60 1.50
228 Craig Nall RC .75 2.00
229 Chester Taylor RC 1.00 2.50
230 Ken Simonton RC .60 1.50
231 Verron Haynes RC .60 1.50
232 Tellis Redmon RC .60 1.50
233 J.T. O'Sullivan RC .75 2.00
234 Major Applewhite RC 1.00 2.50
235 Ricky Williams RC .75 2.00
236 James Mungro RC 1.00 2.50
237 Josh Scobey RC .75 2.00
238 Najeh Davenport RC .60 1.50
239 Dicenzo Miller RC .60 1.50
240 Ennis Haywood RC .60 1.50
241 Jabar Gaffney RC .60 1.50
242 Antonio Bryant RC 1.00 2.50
243 Donte Stallworth RC 1.00 2.50
244 Josh Reed RC .75 2.00
245 Ashley Lelie RC .60 1.50
246 Reche Caldwell RC .75 2.00
247 Marquise Walker RC .60 1.50
248 Javon Walker RC 1.00 2.50
249 Andre Davis RC .60 1.50
250 Antwaan Randle El RC .75 2.00
251 Kelly Campbell RC .75 2.00
252 Cliff Russell RC .60 1.50
253 Kahlil Hill RC .60 1.50
254 Ron Johnson RC .75 2.00
255 Deion Branch RC 1.00 2.50
256 Brian Poli-Dixon RC .60 1.50
257 Freddie Milons RC .60 1.50
258 Lee Mays RC .60 1.50
259 Tim Carter RC .75 2.00
260 Terry Charles RC .60 1.50
261 Jamar Martin RC .75 2.00
262 Jason McAddley RC .75 2.00
263 Chris Hope RC 1.00 2.50
264 Howard Green RC .60 1.50
265 Jeremy Shockey RC 1.00 2.50
266 Daniel Graham RC .75 2.00
267 Eddie Freeman RC .60 1.50
268 Julius Peppers RC 1.50 4.00
269 Kalimba Edwards RC .75 2.00
270 Dwight Freeney RC 1.25 3.00
271 Dennis Johnson RC .60 1.50
272 Alex Brown RC 1.00 2.50
273 Bryan Thomas RC .60 1.50
274 Bryan Fletcher RC .60 1.50
275 Will Overstreet RC .60 1.50
276 Ryan Denney RC .60 1.50
277 Charles Grant RC 1.00 2.50
278 John Henderson RC .75 2.00
279 Albert Haynesworth RC 1.00 2.50
280 Wendell Bryant RC .60 1.50
281 Ryan Sims RC 1.00 2.50
282 Anthony Weaver RC .60 1.50
283 Larry Tripplett RC .60 1.50
284 Alan Harper RC .60 1.50
285 Napoleon Harris RC .75 2.00
286 Robert Thomas RC .60 1.50
287 Levar Fisher RC .60 1.50
288 Andra Davis RC .60 1.50
289 Quentin Jammer RC 1.00 2.50
290 Phillip Buchanon RC 1.00 2.50
291 Keyuo Craver RC .60 1.50
292 Lito Sheppard RC 1.00 2.50
293 Rocky Calmus RC .75 2.00
294 Mike Rumph RC .60 1.50
295 Mike Echols RC .60 1.50
296 Joseph Jefferson RC .60 1.50
297 Roy Williams RC .60 1.50
298 Ed Reed RC 4.00 10.00
299 Michael Lewis RC .75 2.00
300 Eddie Drummond RC .60 1.50

2002 Donruss Stat Line Career

*STARS/300-430: 3X TO 8X
*ROOKIES/300-430: .6X TO 1.5X
*STARS/200-299: 4X TO 10X
*ROOKIES/200-299: .8X TO 2X
*STARS/150-199: 5X TO 12X
*ROOKIES/150-199: 1X TO 2.5X
*VETS/101-149: 6X TO 15X
*ROOKIES/101-149: 1.2X TO 3X
*VETS/70-99: 10X TO 25X
*ROOKIES/70-99: 2X TO 5X
*VETS/45-69: 12X TO 30X
*ROOKIES/45-69: 2.5X TO 6X
*VETS/30-44: 20X TO 50X
*ROOKIES/30-44: 4X TO 10X
*ROOKIES/20-29: 5X TO 12X
*ROOKIES/10-19: 6X TO 15X
CAREER STATED PRINT RUN 17-430

2002 Donruss Stat Line Season

*ROOKIES/379: .6X TO 1.5X
*VETS/150-196: 5X TO 12X
*ROOKIES/150-196: 1X TO 2.5X
*VETS/101-149: 6X TO 15X
*ROOKIES/101-149: 1.2X TO 3X
*VETS/70-99: 10X TO 25X
*ROOKIES/70-99: 2X TO 5X
*VETS/45-69: 12X TO 30X
*ROOKIES/45-69: 2.5X TO 6X
*VETS/30-44: 20X TO 50X
*ROOKIES/30-44: 4X TO 10X
*VETS/20-29: 25X TO 60X
*ROOKIES/20-29: 5X TO 12X
*VETS/10-19: 30X TO 80X
*ROOKIES/10-19: 6X TO 15X
SEASON STATED PRINT RUN 3-379
SERIAL #'d UNDER 10 NOT PRICED

2002 Donruss All-Time Gridiron Kings

This 10-card insert set is sequentially #'d to 2000, and features some of the NFL's greatest heroes. There is also a Studio Series parallel set that is numbered to 250.

COMPLETE SET (10) 15.00 40.00
STATED PRINT RUN 2000 SER.#'d SETS
*STUDIO/250: 1X TO 2.5X BASIC INSERTS
STUDIO PRINT RUN 250 SER.#'d SETS
AT1 Dan Marino 3.00 8.00
AT2 Jim Kelly 1.50 4.00
AT3 Earl Campbell 1.50 4.00
AT4 John Elway 2.50 6.00
AT5 Dick Butkus 2.00 5.00
AT6 Troy Aikman 2.00 5.00
AT7 Barry Sanders 2.50 6.00
AT8 Roger Staubach 2.00 5.00
AT9 John Riggins 1.25 3.00
AT10 Steve Young 2.00 5.00

2002 Donruss Elite Series

This 20-card insert set is seqentially #'d to 1500. There is also a parallel version which features authentic autographs, and are sequentially #'d to 50.

COMPLETE SET (20) 20.00 50.00
STATED PRINT RUN 1500 SER.#'d SETS
ES1 Brett Favre 2.50 6.00
ES2 Kordell Stewart .75 2.00
ES3 Jevon Kearse .75 2.00
ES4 Ahman Green 1.00 2.50
ES5 Anthony Thomas 1.00 2.50
ES6 Cris Carter 1.25 3.00
ES7 Tim Brown 1.25 3.00
ES8 Ray Lewis 1.25 3.00
ES9 Aaron Brooks .75 2.00
ES10 Isaac Bruce 1.25 3.00
ES11 Chris Chambers .75 2.00
ES12 David Boston .75 2.00
ES13 Jimmy Smith 1.00 2.50
ES14 Brian Urlacher 1.25 3.00
ES15 Edgerrin James 1.00 2.50
ES16 Dan Marino 2.50 6.00
ES17 Barry Sanders 2.00 5.00
ES18 Steve Young 1.50 4.00
ES19 Troy Aikman 1.50 4.00
ES20 Thurman Thomas 1.00 2.50

2002 Donruss Elite Series Autographs

This 20-card insert set is a parallel to Elite Series. It is sequentially #'d to 50 and features authentic autographs.

STATED PRINT RUN 50 SER.#'d SETS
ES1 Brett Favre 100.00 175.00
ES2 Kordell Stewart 10.00 25.00
ES3 Jevon Kearse 10.00 25.00
ES4 Ahman Green 12.00 30.00
ES5 Anthony Thomas 12.00 30.00
ES6 Cris Carter 25.00 50.00
ES7 Tim Brown 25.00 50.00
ES8 Ray Lewis 50.00 100.00
ES9 Aaron Brooks 10.00 25.00
ES10 Isaac Bruce 15.00 40.00
ES11 Chris Chambers 10.00 25.00
ES12 David Boston 10.00 25.00
ES13 Jimmy Smith 12.00 30.00
ES14 Brian Urlacher 40.00 80.00
ES15 Edgerrin James 12.00 30.00
ES16 Dan Marino 75.00 150.00
ES17 Barry Sanders 60.00 120.00
ES18 Steve Young 40.00 80.00
ES19 Troy Aikman 50.00 100.00
ES20 Thurman Thomas 12.00 30.00

2002 Donruss Executive Producers

This 20-card insert set is sequentially #'d to 1000, and features 20 of the NFL's most productive performers.

COMPLETE SET (20) 30.00 80.00
STATED PRINT RUN 1000 SER.#'d SETS
EP1 Randy Moss 1.25 3.00
EP2 Emmitt Smith 2.50 6.00
EP3 Kurt Warner 1.25 3.00
EP4 Jerry Rice 3.00 8.00
EP5 Edgerrin James 1.25 3.00
EP6 Anthony Thomas 1.25 3.00
EP7 Jerome Bettis 1.50 4.00
EP8 Daunte Culpepper 1.25 3.00
EP9 Brian Griese 1.00 2.50
EP10 Steve McNair 1.25 3.00
EP11 Marshall Faulk 1.25 3.00
EP12 Ahman Green 1.25 3.00
EP13 Peyton Manning 4.00 10.00
EP14 Shaun Alexander 1.00 2.50
EP15 Donovan McNabb 1.25 3.00
EP16 Jeff Garcia 1.00 2.50
EP17 Eddie George 1.25 3.00
EP18 Tim Brown 1.50 4.00
EP19 Brett Favre 3.00 8.00
EP20 Curtis Martin 1.25 3.00

2002 Donruss Gridiron Kings Inserts

This 20-card insert set is sequentially #'d to 2000. Each card features an artists rendition of the player. There is also a Studio Series parallel which is serial #'d to 250.

COMPLETE SET (20) 25.00 60.00
STATED PRINT RUN 2000 SER.#'d SETS
*STUDIO/250: 1X TO 2.5X BASIC INSERT
STUDIO PRINT RUN 250 SER.#'d SETS
GK1 Emmitt Smith 2.00 5.00
GK2 Jerome Bettis 1.25 3.00
GK3 Jerry Rice 2.50 6.00
GK4 Brett Favre 2.50 6.00
GK5 Tom Brady 6.00 15.00
GK6 Anthony Thomas 1.00 2.50
GK7 Kurt Warner 1.00 2.50
GK8 Daunte Culpepper 1.00 2.50
GK9 Brian Griese .75 2.00
GK10 Cris Carter 1.25 3.00
GK11 Peyton Manning 3.00 8.00
GK12 Donovan McNabb 1.00 2.50
GK13 LaDainian Tomlinson 1.25 3.00
GK14 Eddie George 1.00 2.50
GK15 Edgerrin James 1.00 2.50
GK16 Randy Moss 1.00 2.50
GK17 Tim Brown 1.25 3.00
GK18 Brian Urlacher 1.25 3.00
GK19 Marshall Faulk 1.00 2.50
GK20 Michael Vick 1.00 2.50

2002 Donruss Jersey Kings

This 20-card insert set includes a single-swatch of game-worn jersey. Each card is sequentially #'d to 125.

STATED PRINT RUN 125 SER.#'d SETS
*STUDIO/25: .8X TO 2X BASIC JSY/125
STUDIO PRINT RUN 25 SER.#'d SETS
JK1 Emmitt Smith 10.00 25.00
JK2 Jerome Bettis 6.00 15.00
JK3 Jerry Rice 12.00 30.00
JK4 Brett Favre 12.00 30.00
JK5 Tom Brady 30.00 80.00
JK6 Anthony Thomas 5.00 12.00
JK7 Kurt Warner 5.00 12.00
JK8 Daunte Culpepper 5.00 12.00
JK9 Brian Griese 4.00 10.00
JK10 Cris Carter 6.00 15.00
JK11 Peyton Manning 15.00 40.00
JK12 Donovan McNabb 5.00 12.00
JK13 LaDainian Tomlinson 6.00 15.00
JK14 Eddie George 5.00 12.00
JK15 Edgerrin James 5.00 12.00
JK16 Randy Moss 5.00 12.00
JK17 Tim Brown 6.00 15.00
JK18 Brian Urlacher 6.00 15.00
JK19 Marshall Faulk 5.00 12.00
JK20 Michael Vick 5.00 12.00

2002 Donruss Leather Kings

This 20-card insert set features a single-swatch of game-used football and is sequentially #'d to 250. There is also a Studio Series parallel that is #'d to 25.

STATED PRINT RUN 250 SER.#'d SETS
*STUDIO/25: 1.2X TO 3X BASIC JSY/250
STUDIO PRINT RUN 25 SER.#'d SETS
LK1 Emmitt Smith 10.00 25.00
LK2 Jerome Bettis 6.00 15.00
LK3 Jerry Rice 12.00 30.00
LK4 Brett Favre 12.00 30.00
LK5 Tom Brady 30.00 80.00
LK6 Anthony Thomas 5.00 12.00
LK7 Kurt Warner 5.00 12.00
LK8 Daunte Culpepper 5.00 12.00
LK9 Brian Griese 4.00 10.00
LK10 Cris Carter 6.00 15.00
LK11 Peyton Manning 15.00 40.00
LK12 Donovan McNabb 5.00 12.00
LK13 LaDainian Tomlinson 6.00 15.00
LK14 Eddie George 5.00 12.00
LK15 Edgerrin James 5.00 12.00
LK16 Randy Moss 5.00 12.00
LK17 Tim Brown 6.00 15.00
LK18 Brian Urlacher 6.00 15.00
LK19 Marshall Faulk 5.00 12.00
LK20 Michael Vick 5.00 12.00

2002 Donruss Private Signings

This 50-card insert set is inserted into packs at a rate of 1:160. Each card features an authentic autograph of many of todays top players. Some cards were issued in packs via mail redemption cards that carried an expiration date of 5/21/2004. In 2005, Donruss/Playoff made an announcement of print runs for many older autographed sets including this one. Those announced print runs are included below. Finally, Javon Walker was redeemed without an autograph with the card stamped "NO AUTOGRAPH" on the front.

STATED ODDS 1:160
PS1 Adrian Peterson 5.00 12.00
PS2 Alex Brown 6.00 15.00
PS3 Andra Davis 4.00 10.00
PS4 Andre Davis 4.00 10.00
PS5 Andre Lott 4.00 10.00
PS6 Antonio Bryant 6.00 15.00
PS7 Brian Poli-Dixon 4.00 10.00
PS8 Bryant McKinnie 4.00 10.00
PS9 Chad Hutchinson 4.00 10.00
PS10 Chester Taylor 10.00 25.00
PS11 Clinton Portis/50* 10.00 25.00
PS12 Cortlen Johnson 4.00 10.00
PS13 Damien Anderson 4.00 10.00
PS14 David Carr/50* 6.00 15.00
PS15 David Garrard 10.00 25.00
PS16 Demontray Carter 4.00 10.00
PS17 Dwight Freeney 8.00 20.00
PS18 Ed Reed 40.00 80.00
PS19 Eric Crouch/63* 10.00 25.00
PS20 Freddie Milons 4.00 10.00
PS21 Javon Walker NO AUTO 6.00 15.00
PS22 Ron Johnson 5.00 12.00
PS23 Jerramy Stevens/50* 10.00 25.00
PS24 Joey Harrington/75* 6.00 15.00
PS25 Josh Reed/50* 8.00 20.00
PS26 Julius Peppers/15*
PS27 Kalimba Edwards 5.00 12.00
PS28 Kelly Campbell 5.00 12.00
PS29 Ken Simonton 4.00 10.00
PS30 Keyuo Craver
PS31 Kurt Kittner/50* 6.00 15.00
PS32 Lito Sheppard 6.00 15.00
PS33 Luke Staley 4.00 10.00
PS34 Maurice Morris 5.00 12.00
PS35 Najeh Davenport 4.00 10.00
PS36 Quentin Jammer 6.00 15.00
PS37 Reche Caldwell/50* 8.00 20.00
PS38 Rocky Calmus 5.00 12.00
PS39 Tavon Mason 4.00 10.00
PS40 Woody Dantzler/25* 12.00 30.00
PS41 John Riggins/100* 20.00 50.00
PS42 Deuce McAllister/50* 8.00 20.00
PS43 Drew Brees/50* 40.00 80.00
PS44 Edgerrin James/27* 15.00 40.00
PS45 Emmitt Smith/25* 125.00 250.00
PS46 Kurt Warner/35* 25.00 50.00
PS47 Marshall Faulk/50* 15.00 40.00
PS48 Quincy Carter/50* 6.00 15.00
PS49 Tim Brown/50* 15.00 40.00
PS50 Brett Favre/25* 150.00 250.00

2002 Donruss Rookie Year Materials

This 10-card insert set includes a single-swatch of game-worn jersey from each players rookie season and is sequentially #'d to 100.

STATED PRINT RUN 100 SER.#'d SETS
RY1 John Riggins 15.00 40.00
RY2 Joe Montana 30.00 80.00
RY3 Randy Moss 8.00 20.00
RY4 Ricky Williams 8.00 20.00
RY5 Tim Couch 6.00 15.00
RY6 Peyton Manning 25.00 60.00
RY7 Mark Brunell 8.00 20.00
RY8 Keyshawn Johnson 8.00 20.00
RY9 LaDainian Tomlinson 10.00 25.00
RY10 Michael Vick 8.00 20.00

2002 Donruss Rookie Year Materials Numbers

This set is a parallel of the Rookie Year Materials set. Each card is sequentially #'d to the players jersey number.

STATED PRINT RUN 2-84
SERIAL #'d UNDER 25 NOT PRICED
RY1 John Riggins/44 25.00 60.00
RY3 Randy Moss/84 15.00 40.00
RY4 Ricky Williams/34 20.00 50.00
RY9 LaDainian Tomlinson/21 25.00 60.00

2002 Donruss Zoning Commission

This 8-card insert set is sequentially #'d to 500, and features some of the NFL's top scoring machines.

COMPLETE SET (8) 15.00 40.00
STATED PRINT RUN 500 SER.#'d SETS
ZC1 Marshall Faulk 2.00 5.00
ZC2 Terrell Owens 2.00 5.00
ZC3 Shaun Alexander 1.50 4.00
ZC4 Marvin Harrison 2.00 5.00
ZC5 Antowain Smith 2.00 5.00
ZC6 Kurt Warner 2.00 5.00
ZC7 Jeff Garcia 1.50 4.00
ZC8 Brett Favre 5.00 12.00

2003 Donruss AFL Star Standouts

These cards were issued in one 9-card panel that included one cover/advertising card in the middle. Each features a star Arena Football League player with a typical all-color cardback. The cards are commonly found in uncut sheet form but can be separated at the perforations.

COMPLETE SET (9) 4.00 8.00
1 Greg Hopkins .40 1.00
2 Aaron Garcia .50 1.25
3 Jay Gruden .75 2.00
4 Chris Jackson .40 1.00
5 Jim Kubiak .50 1.25
6 Freddie Solomon .50 1.25
7 Clevan Thomas .40 1.00
8 Hunkie Cooper .40 1.00
NNO Cover Card .40 1.00

2006 Donruss Frito Lay

These cards were issued four at a time in specially marked packages of Frito Lay products in January 2007. Each card was produced in the design of the 2006 Score set but included a Donruss logo at the top of the card along with a Frito Lay logo. Two partial parallel sets were also issued with the cards featuring either a Doritos or Cheetos Brand logo on the front. The Doritos version is slightly tougher to find than the base Frito Lay with the Cheetos version being the most difficult to pull.

COMPLETE SET (28) 25.00 50.00
1 Brett Favre 1.50 4.00
2 Ben Roethlisberger 1.00 2.50
3 Peyton Manning 2.00 5.00
4 LaDainian Tomlinson .75 2.00
5 Larry Johnson .50 1.25
6 Tom Brady 2.50 6.00
7 Shaun Alexander .50 1.25
8 Ronnie Brown .60 1.50
9 Eli Manning .60 1.50
10 Cadillac Williams .60 1.50
11 Michael Vick .60 1.50
12 Brian Urlacher .75 2.00
13 Carson Palmer .60 1.50
14 Roy Williams S .50 1.25
15 Troy Polamalu .75 2.00
16 Donovan McNabb .60 1.50
17 Clinton Portis .50 1.25
18 DeAngelo Williams .50 1.25
19 A.J. Hawk .50 1.25
20 Laurence Maroney .40 1.00
21 Greg Jennings .60 1.50
22 Matt Leinart .40 1.00
23 Jay Cutler .50 1.25
24 Reggie Bush .60 1.50
25 Vince Young .40 1.00
CL1 Leinart/Bush CL .40 1.00
CL2 Clemens/Washington CL .25 .60
CL3 M.Drew/M.Lewis CL .40 1.00

2006 Donruss Frito Lay Cheetos

COMPLETE SET (16) 30.00 60.00
*CHEETOS: .6X TO 1.5X FRITO LAY
CL5 White .60 1.50
Leinart
Bush CL

2006 Donruss Frito Lay Doritos

COMPLETE SET (16) 25.00 50.00
*DORITOS: .5X TO 1.2X FRITO LAY
CL4 Leinart .30 .75
V.Young CL

2006 Donruss Playoff Orlando Auto Auction Association

COMPLETE SET (11) 15.00 30.00
H03 Jason White 1.50 4.00
H51 Dick Kazmaier 1.50 4.00
H58 Pete Dawkins 1.50 4.00
H60 Joe Bellino 1.50 4.00
H67 Gary Beban 1.50 4.00
H72 Johnny Rodgers 2.00 5.00
H74 Archie Griffin 2.00 5.00
H76 Tony Dorsett 2.50 6.00
H78 Billy Sims 2.00 5.00
H92 Gino Torretta 1.50 4.00
H96 Danny Wuerffel 1.50 4.00

2006 Donruss Pop Warner

COMPLETE SET (6) 3.00 8.00
1 Reggie Bush .40 1.00
2 Matt Leinart .25 .60
3 Donovan McNabb .40 1.00
4 LaDainian Tomlinson .50 1.25
5 Larry Fitzgerald .40 1.00
6 Marcus Allen .50 1.25

2006 Donruss Thanksgiving Classic Beckett Inserts

COMPLETE SET (6) 6.00 12.00
DN1 Jay Cutler .40 1.00
DN2 Mike Bell .30 .75
MI1 Ronnie Brown .40 1.00
NO1 Reggie Bush .50 1.25
TB1 Cadillac Williams .40 1.00
TN1 Vince Young .30 .75

2006 Donruss Tom Landry

This single card was given away at the event of the memorial of the Texas State Cemetery in the name of Tom Landry.

NNO Tom Landry 2.00 5.00

2007 Donruss Frito Lay

COMPLETE SET (25) 20.00 40.00
1 Adrian Peterson 1.50 4.00
2 Brady Quinn .50 1.25
3 Calvin Johnson 1.50 4.00
4 Gaines Adams .60 1.50
5 Marshawn Lynch 1.00 2.50
6 Ted Ginn .60 1.50
7 JaMarcus Russell .50 1.25
8 Donald Driver .40 1.00
9 Champ Bailey .40 1.00
10 DeAngelo Hall .30 .75
11 Frank Gore .40 1.00
12 Jonathan Vilma .30 .75
13 Larry Johnson .30 .75
14 Drew Brees .50 1.25
15 Torry Holt .40 1.00
16 Vince Young .30 .75
17 Antonio Gates .50 1.25
18 Andre Johnson .40 1.00
19 Anquan Boldin .30 .75
20 Carson Palmer .40 1.00
21 Maurice Jones-Drew .30 .75
22 Michael Strahan .40 1.00
23 Shaun Alexander .30 .75
24 Steve Smith .40 1.00
25 Tedy Bruschi .40 1.00
C1 Brian Westbrook .50 1.25
C2 Steve McNair .60 1.50
D1 Tony Romo 1.00 2.50
D2 Marvin Harrison .60 1.50
D3 LaRon Landry .75 2.00
L1 Devin Hester .60 1.50
L2 Hines Ward .60 1.50

2007 Donruss London Game

Many fans who attended the 2007 international game in London were treated to this complete set. The set features three cards from each of the two teams that matched up.

COMPLETE SET (6) 6.00 12.00
1 Eli Manning .75 2.00
2 Jason Taylor .75 2.00
3 Jeremy Shockey .60 1.50
4 Ronnie Brown .60 1.50
5 Steve Smith USC .40 1.00
6 Ted Ginn .50 1.25

2007 Donruss National Convention

COMPLETE SET (7) 15.00 40.00
1 JaMarcus Russell .60 1.50
2 Calvin Johnson 2.00 5.00
3 Joe Thomas 1.00 2.50
4 Adrian Peterson 2.00 5.00
5 Ted Ginn Jr. .75 2.00
6 Troy Smith .60 1.50
7 Brady Quinn .60 1.50

2007 Donruss Pepsi National Convention

This set was issued at the 2007 National Sports Collector's Convention in Cleveland. Collectors who presented a special coupon at the Donruss Playoff booth at the event received a complete set. Each card features the Pepsi logo on the fornt.

COMPLETE SET (6) 5.00 12.00
1 Brady Quinn .30 .75
2 Torry Holt .40 1.00
3 Adrian Peterson 1.00 2.50
4 Calvin Johnson 1.00 2.50
5 Tony Romo .60 1.50
6 Dwayne Jarrett .40 1.00

2007 Donruss Playoff Award Winner Promos

These cards were issued at the 2007 Super Bowl XLI Card Show in Miami and feature players who won 2006 NFL season awards. Each card, except Reggie Bush, was issued one card at a time in exchange for the collector opening three packs of 2006 Donruss Playoff football products at their card show booth. The Reggie Bush card was issued as part of the wrapper redemption program at the Beckett Media booth.

MVPLT LaDainian Tomlinson 1.00 2.50
CPOYCP Chad Pennington .60 1.50
DPOYJT Jason Taylor .50 1.25
DROYDR DeMeco Ryans .60 1.50
OPOYLT LaDainian Tomlinson 1.00 2.50
OROYVY Vince Young 3.00 8.00
SPEDRB Reggie Bush 5.00 12.00

2007 Donruss Thanksgiving Classic NFL Network

COMPLETE SET (4) 2.50 6.00
1 Rich Eisen .60 1.50
2 Marshall Faulk .75 2.00
3 Steve Mariucci .60 1.50
4 Deion Sanders .75 2.00

2008 Donruss London Game

Many fans who attended the 2008 international game in London were treated to this complete set. The set features three cards from each of the two teams that matched up.

COMPLETE SET (6) 6.00 12.00
1 Reggie Bush .50 1.25
2 Drew Brees .75 2.00
3 Sedrick Ellis .50 1.25
4 LaDainian Tomlinson .75 2.00
5 Shawne Merriman .50 1.25
6 Antoine Cason .60 1.50

2008 Donruss National Convention VIP Crown

V1 Darren McFadden .75 2.00
V2 Matt Forte 1.25 3.00
V3 Matt Ryan 2.50 6.00
V4 Jonathan Stewart 1.25 3.00
V5 Joe Flacco 1.50 4.00
V6 Felix Jones .75 2.00

2008 Donruss National Convention VIP Crown Autographs

RANDOM INSERTS IN 2009 LIMITED PACKS
V3 Matt Ryan 100.00 200.00

2008 Donruss Playoff Award Winner Promos

Cards from this set were issued at the 2008 NFL Experience Super Bowl Card Show in Glendale Arizona. Most were released as complete sets for winners of the "Spin the Wheel" game at the Donruss Playoff booth at the show. The Greg Ellis card was short-printed and the Adrian Peterson RB foil card was released at the Beckett booth at the show.

COMPLETE SET (7) 5.00 12.00
AP Adrian Peterson OROY .60 1.50
BS Bob Sanders DPOY .50 1.25
GE Greg Ellis CPOY SP .40 1.00
PW Patrick Willis DROY .50 1.25
TB1 Tom Brady MVP 2.00 5.00
TB2 Tom Brady OPOY 2.00 5.00
APRB Adrian Peterson RB foil .60 1.50
NE16 Tom Brady 2.00 5.00
Wes Welker
Randy Moss

2008 Donruss Playoff Silver Signatures

Cards from this set were issued via mail as replacement cards for various unfulfilled redemptions from Donruss Playoff football products. The company also released some for promotional purposes at shows. Each features a sticker autograph of the featured player. Although the cards are not serial numbered, Donruss Playoff did announce print runs for most of the cards.

AJ Andre Johnson/104* 6.00 15.00
AM Art Monk/122* 20.00 40.00
APJ Adam Jones/185* 5.00 12.00
AR Andre Reed/160* 12.00 30.00
AR2 Antrel Rolle/168* 5.00 12.00
AY Ashton Youboty/54* 5.00 12.00
CB Cedric Benson/64* 5.00 12.00
CH Chris Henry/146* 6.00 15.00
CR Carlos Rogers/548* 5.00 12.00
DB Derrick Brooks/577* 5.00 12.00
DM Dan Marino/64* 100.00 200.00
DS2 Don Shula/40* 15.00 30.00
HE Herman Edwards/628* 10.00 25.00
JA Jared Allen 30.00 60.00
JE John Elway 60.00 120.00
JK Jevon Kearse/261* 5.00 12.00
JL Johnny Lujack/230* 12.00 30.00
JP Joe Perry 8.00 20.00
JT2 Joe Theismann/1050* 8.00 20.00
KJ Kevin Jones/42* 5.00 12.00
KS Ken Stabler 12.00 30.00
LB Lance Briggs/825* 10.00 25.00
LS Lee Roy Selmon/34* 12.00 30.00
MG Mark Gastineau 8.00 20.00
PD Pete Dawkins/47* 10.00 25.00
RB Reggie Brown/37* 5.00 12.00
TB Terry Bradshaw/31* 50.00 100.00
TJ Tarvaris Jackson/101* 5.00 12.00
TR Tony Romo/10*

2008 Donruss Pop Warner

This set was issued at the 2008 Pop Warner Super Bowl. Each card features the Pop Warner logo at the top.

COMPLETE SET (6) 6.00 12.00
1 Darren McFadden .20 .50
2 Matt Ryan .60 1.50
3 Felix Jones .20 .50
4 Peyton Manning 1.50 4.00
5 Adrian Peterson .60 1.50
6 Devin Hester .50 1.25

2008 Donruss 7-11 EA Sports Madden

COMPLETE SET (10) 15.00 40.00
1 Tony Romo 1.00 2.50
2 Peyton Manning 3.00 8.00
3 Vince Young .75 2.00
4 LaDainian Tomlinson 1.25 3.00
5 Adrian Peterson 1.25 3.00
6 Ben Roethlisberger 1.25 3.00
7 Darren McFadden .75 2.00
8 Matt Ryan 2.50 6.00
9 Maurice Jones-Drew .75 2.00
10 Matt Hasselbeck .75 2.00

2008 Donruss Thanksgiving Classic NFL Network

Cards from this set were issued one per team set with either the Dallas Cowboys or Philadelphia Eagles Thanksgiving day sets. Each features an NFL Network commentator on the front and a brief NFL Network schedule on the back.

COMPLETE SET (7) 3.00 8.00
1 Terrell Davis .60 1.50
2 Rich Eisen .40 1.00
3 Marshall Faulk .60 1.50
4 Steve Mariucci .40 1.00
5 Deion Sanders .60 1.50
6 Warren Sapp .50 1.25
7 Rod Woodson .50 1.25

2008 Donruss Toronto Game

Many fans who attended the 2008 international game in Toronto were treated to this complete set. The set features three cards from each of the two teams that matched up.

COMPLETE SET (6) 4.00 8.00
1 Marshawn Lynch .60 1.50
2 Lee Evans .60 1.50
3 James Hardy .25 .60
4 Ronnie Brown .50 1.25
5 Ted Ginn .50 1.25
6 Chad Henne .30 .75

2009 Donruss Draft NFL Patch Promos

Cards from this set were released at the Hawaii Trade Conference Mainland Edition in April 2009. Each includes a manufactured swatch featuring an NFL logo.

CW Chris Wells SP 2.50 6.00
MC Michael Crabtree 4.00 10.00
MS1 Mark Sanchez 2.50 6.00
MS2 Matthew Stafford 12.00 30.00

2009 Donruss Draft Team Logo Promos

Cards from this promo set were issued at the NFL Draft in April 2009. Each features a sticker of the player's new NFL team helmet logo attached to the cardfront.

CW Chris Wells 6.00 15.00
JM Jeremy Maclin 8.00 20.00
KM Knowshon Moreno 6.00 15.00
MC Michael Crabtree 10.00 25.00
PH Percy Harvin 6.00 15.00
MS1 Mark Sanchez 6.00 15.00
MS2 Matthew Stafford 30.00 80.00

2009 Donruss NFL Draft Rookie Helmet Autographs

1 Matthew Stafford 40.00 100.00
2 Mark Sanchez 30.00 80.00
3 Chris Wells 12.00 30.00
4 Percy Harvin 8.00 20.00
5 Jeremy Maclin 12.00 30.00
6 Knowshon Moreno 6.00 15.00
7 Michael Crabtree 12.00 30.00

2009 Donruss Playoff Award Winner Promos

This set was issued at the Donruss/Playoff booth during the 2009 Super Bowl Card Show in Tampa, Florida. Single cards were given to collectors as prizes for a spin-the-wheel contest. The features former Super Bowl MVP Award winners and top 2008 NFL rookies.

COMPLETE SET (12) 7.50 15.00
SBAP Adrian Peterson .60 1.50
SBBF Brett Favre Jets 1.25 3.00
SBCJ Chris Johnson .40 1.00
SBDJ Dexter Jackson SBMVP .40 1.00
SBDM Darren McFadden .60 1.50
SBEM Eli Manning SBMVP .50 1.25
SBHW Hines Ward SBMVP .50 1.25
SBMR Matt Ryan .50 1.25
SBPM Peyton Manning SBMVP 1.50 4.00
SBRL Ray Lewis SBMVP .60 1.50
SBTB Tom Brady SBMVP 2.00 5.00
OROYMR Matt Ryan ROY .50 1.25

2009 Donruss Pro Bowl Promos

As part of their sponsorship of the 2009 NFL Pro Bowl, Donruss created this set of 10-cards issued around that weekend's events.

COMPLETE SET (10) 6.00 15.00
AJ Andre Johnson .60 1.50
AP Adrian Peterson .75 2.00
CJ Chris Johnson .50 1.25
DB Drew Brees .75 2.00
JF Joe Flacco .60 1.50
LF Larry Fitzgerald .60 1.50
LT LaDainian Tomlinson .75 2.00
MF Matt Forte .50 1.25
MR Matt Ryan .60 1.50
PM Peyton Manning 2.00 5.00

2009 Donruss Super Bowl XLIII Jersey Promos

Cards from this set were issued at the Donruss/Playoff booth during the 2009 Super Bowl Card Show in Tampa, Florida. A single card was given to any collector that purchased a Score Super Bowl XLIII Glossy factory set at the booth during the show.

AP Adrian Peterson 10.00 25.00
DM Darren McFadden 10.00 25.00
FJ Felix Jones 6.00 15.00
JA Joseph Addai 6.00 15.00
LT LaDainian Tomlinson 10.00 25.00
PR Philip Rivers 10.00 25.00
RM Rashard Mendenhall 6.00 15.00
RM Randy Moss 8.00 20.00
TB Tom Brady 30.00 80.00
TO Terrell Owens 8.00 20.00

2009 Donruss Super Bowl XLIII VIP Promos

COMPLETE SET (11) 12.00 30.00
AP Adrian Peterson 1.00 2.50
BF Brett Favre 2.00 5.00
CJ Chris Johnson .60 1.50
DJ Dexter Jackson .60 1.50
DM Darren McFadden 1.00 2.50
EM Eli Manning .75 2.00
HW Hines Ward .75 2.00
MR Matt Ryan .75 2.00
PM Peyton Manning 2.50 6.00
RL Ray Lewis 1.00 2.50
TB Tom Brady 3.00 8.00

2015 Donruss

1 Colin Kaepernick .30 .75
2 Jay Cutler .25 .60
3 Andy Dalton .30 .75
4 Matt Cassel .25 .60
5 Peyton Manning .75 2.00
6 Johnny Manziel .30 .75
7 Mike Glennon .30 .75
8 Carson Palmer .30 .75
9 Philip Rivers .40 1.00
10 Alex Smith .30 .75
11 Andrew Luck .50 1.25
12 Tony Romo .30 .75
13 Ryan Tannehill .30 .75
14 Sam Bradford .25 .60
15 Matt Ryan .30 .75
16 Eli Manning .30 .75
17 Blake Bortles .25 .60
18 Geno Smith .25 .60
19 Matthew Stafford .30 .75
20 Aaron Rodgers .75 2.00
21 Cam Newton .40 1.00
22 Tom Brady 1.00 2.50
23 Derek Carr .40 1.00
24 Nick Foles .30 .75
25 Joe Flacco .30 .75
26 Robert Griffin III .25 .60
27 Drew Brees .40 1.00
28 Russell Wilson .50 1.25
29 Ben Roethlisberger .40 1.00
30 Brian Hoyer .25 .60
31 Zach Mettenberger .25 .60
32 Teddy Bridgewater .30 .75
33 Carlos Hyde .25 .60
34 Matt Forte .25 .60
35 Jeremy Hill .25 .60
36 LeSean McCoy .40 1.00
37 C.J. Anderson .30 .75
38 Terrance West .25 .60
39 Doug Martin .30 .75
40 Andre Ellington .25 .60
41 Danny Woodhead .30 .75
42 Jamaal Charles .30 .75
43 Frank Gore .30 .75
44 Darren McFadden .25 .60
45 Lamar Miller .25 .60
46 DeMarco Murray .30 .75
47 Devonta Freeman .30 .75
48 Rashad Jennings .25 .60
49 Denard Robinson .25 .60
50 Stevan Ridley .25 .60
51 Joique Bell .25 .60
52 Eddie Lacy .25 .60
53 Jonathan Stewart .25 .60
54 LeGarrette Blount .30 .75
55 Latavius Murray .25 .60
56 Tre Mason .30 .75
57 Justin Forsett .30 .75
58 Alfred Morris .25 .60
59 Mark Ingram .30 .75
60 Marshawn Lynch .30 .75
61 Le'Veon Bell .30 .75
62 Arian Foster .30 .75
63 Bishop Sankey .25 .60
64 Adrian Peterson .40 1.00
65 Torrey Smith .25 .60
66 Alshon Jeffery .30 .75
67 A.J. Green .40 1.00
68 Sammy Watkins .30 .75
69 Demaryius Thomas .30 .75
70 Dwayne Bowe .30 .75
71 Mike Evans .30 .75
72 Larry Fitzgerald .30 .75

73 Keenan Allen .30 .75
74 Jeremy Maclin .25 .60
75 T.Y. Hilton .30 .75
76 Dez Bryant .40 1.00
77 Greg Jennings .25 .60
78 Jordan Matthews .30 .75
79 Julio Jones .40 1.00
80 Odell Beckham Jr. .40 1.00
81 Marqise Lee .25 .60
82 Brandon Marshall .25 .60
83 Calvin Johnson .40 1.00
84 Jordy Nelson .30 .75
85 Kelvin Benjamin .30 .75
86 Julian Edelman .40 1.00
87 Michael Crabtree .25 .60
88 Tavon Austin .25 .60
89 Steve Smith .30 .75
90 DeSean Jackson .30 .75
91 Marques Colston .25 .60
92 Doug Baldwin .30 .75
93 Antonio Brown .40 1.00
94 DeAndre Hopkins .30 .75
95 Kendall Wright .25 .60
96 Mike Wallace .25 .60
97 Vernon Davis .25 .60
98 Martellus Bennett .25 .60
99 Tyler Eifert .30 .75
100 Robert Woods .30 .75
101 Emmanuel Sanders .30 .75
102 Taylor Gabriel .25 .60
103 Vincent Jackson .25 .60
104 Michael Floyd .25 .60
105 Antonio Gates .25 .60
106 Travis Kelce .40 1.00
107 Andre Johnson .30 .75
108 Jason Witten .30 .75
109 Jordan Cameron .25 .60
110 Brent Celek .25 .60
111 Roddy White .25 .60
112 Victor Cruz .30 .75
113 Julius Thomas .25 .60
114 Eric Decker .25 .60
115 Golden Tate .25 .60
116 Randall Cobb .30 .75
117 Greg Olsen .30 .75
118 Rob Gronkowski .40 1.00
119 Charles Woodson .40 1.00
120 Stedman Bailey .25 .60
121 Marlon Brown .25 .60
122 Pierre Garcon .30 .75
123 Brandin Cooks .30 .75
124 Jimmy Graham .40 1.00
125 Martavis Bryant .25 .60
126 Cecil Shorts III .25 .60
127 Delanie Walker .25 .60
128 Cordarrelle Patterson .25 .60
129 Justin Smith .25 .60
130 Kyle Fuller .25 .60
131 Geno Atkins .25 .60
132 Mario Williams .25 .60
133 Von Miller .30 .75
134 Joe Haden .25 .60
135 Gerald McCoy .25 .60
136 Patrick Peterson .25 .60
137 Brandon Flowers .25 .60
138 Justin Houston .25 .60
139 D'Qwell Jackson .25 .60
140 Anthony Hitchens .25 .60
141 Ndamukong Suh .30 .75
142 Kiko Alonso .25 .60
143 Desmond Trufant .25 .60
144 Jason Pierre-Paul .25 .60
145 Paul Posluszny .25 .60
146 Darrelle Revis .25 .60
147 Haloti Ngata .25 .60
148 Clay Matthews .40 1.00
149 Luke Kuechly .30 .75
150 Devin McCourty .25 .60
151 Khalil Mack .40 1.00
152 Robert Quinn .30 .75
153 Terrell Suggs .25 .60
154 DeAngelo Hall .30 .75
155 Anthony Spencer .25 .60
156 Richard Sherman .40 1.00
157 James Harrison .30 .75
158 J.J. Watt .40 1.00
159 Brian Orakpo .25 .60
160 Anthony Barr .25 .60
161 Joe Montana 1.00 2.50
162 Bo Jackson .50 1.25
163 Brett Favre .75 2.00
164 Jerry Rice .60 1.50
165 Barry Sanders .60 1.50
166 John Elway .60 1.50
167 Emmitt Smith .60 1.50
168 LaDainian Tomlinson .30 .75
169 Marshall Faulk .30 .75
170 Dan Marino .75 2.00
171 Lawrence Taylor .40 1.00
172 Joe Namath .50 1.25
173 Tim Brown .40 1.00
174 Kurt Warner .30 .75
175 Terry Bradshaw .50 1.25
176 Cris Carter .40 1.00
177 Brian Urlacher .40 1.00
178 Deion Sanders .30 .75
179 Earl Campbell .40 1.00
180 Gale Sayers .40 1.00
181 Jerome Bettis .40 1.00
182 Jim Kelly .40 1.00
183 Steve Young .50 1.25
184 Michael Irvin .40 1.00
185 Terrell Davis .30 .75
186 Byron Jones RC .60 1.50
187 Dante Fowler Jr. RC .60 1.50
188 Vic Beasley RC .50 1.25
189 Trae Waynes RC .40 1.00
190 Malcom Brown RC .40 1.00
191 Stephone Anthony RC .40 1.00
192 Damarious Randall RC .50 1.25
193 Shaq Thompson RC .50 1.25
194 Shane Ray RC .40 1.00
195 Bud Dupree RC .50 1.25
196 Marcus Peters RC .60 1.50
197 Brandon Scherff RC .60 1.50
198 Landon Collins RC .50 1.25
199 Ronald Darby RC .40 1.00
200 Randy Gregory RC .40 1.00
201 Jameis Winston RR RC 1.00 2.50
202 Marcus Mariota RR RC 1.50 4.00
203 Amari Cooper RR RC 1.25 3.00
204 Leonard Williams RR RC .40 1.00
205 Kevin White RR RC .50 1.25
206 Todd Gurley RR RC 1.50 4.00
207 DeVante Parker RR RC .60 1.50
208 Melvin Gordon RR RC 1.00 2.50
209 Nelson Agholor RR RC .50 1.25
210 Breshad Perriman RR RC .40 1.00
211 Phillip Dorsett RR RC .40 1.00
212 T.J. Yeldon RR RC .40 1.00
213 Devin Smith RR RC .40 1.00
214 Dorial Green-Beckham RR RC .40 1.00
215 Devin Funchess RR RC .60 1.50
216 Ameer Abdullah RR RC .60 1.50
217 Maxx Williams RR RC .40 1.00
218 Tyler Lockett RR RC .60 1.50
219 Jaelen Strong RR RC .50 1.25
220 Tevin Coleman RR RC .50 1.25
221 Garrett Grayson RR RC .40 1.00
222 Chris Conley RR RC .40 1.00
223 Duke Johnson RR RC .60 1.50
224 David Johnson RR RC 1.00 2.50
225 Sammie Coates RR RC .50 1.25
226 Sean Mannion RR RC .40 1.00
227 Ty Montgomery RR RC .40 1.00
228 Matt Jones RR RC .40 1.00
229 Bryce Petty RR RC .40 1.00
230 Jamison Crowder RR RC .50 1.25
231 Jeremy Langford RR RC .40 1.00
232 Justin Hardy RR RC .40 1.00
233 Vince Mayle RR RC .50 1.25
234 Buck Allen RR RC .50 1.25
235 Mike Davis RR RC .40 1.00
236 David Cobb RR RC .40 1.00
237 Rashad Greene RR RC .40 1.00
238 Stefon Diggs RR RC 1.00 2.50
239 Brett Hundley RR RC .40 1.00
240 Jay Ajayi RR RC .60 1.50
241 Joe Montana CLS 1.25 3.00
242 Dan Marino CLS 1.00 2.50
243 Brett Favre CLS 1.00 2.50
244 Emmitt Smith CLS .75 2.00
245 Barry Sanders CLS .75 2.00
246 Jerry Rice CLS .75 2.00
247 Steve Largent CLS .50 1.25
248 Aaron Rodgers CLS 1.00 2.50
249 Tom Brady CLS 1.25 3.00
250 Peyton Manning CLS 1.00 2.50
251 Dez Bryant CLS .50 1.25
252 Calvin Johnson CLS .50 1.25
253 DeMarco Murray CLS .40 1.00
254 Marshawn Lynch CLS .40 1.00
255 Jameis Winston CLS .75 2.00
256 Marcus Mariota CLS 1.25 3.00
257 Amari Cooper CLS 1.00 2.50
258 Todd Gurley CLS 1.25 3.00
259 Melvin Gordon CLS .75 2.00
260 Kevin White CLS .40 1.00
261 Colin Kaepernick GK .60 1.50
262 Matt Forte GK .50 1.25
263 A.J. Green GK .75 2.00
264 Sammy Watkins GK .60 1.50
265 Peyton Manning GK 1.50 4.00
266 Barkevious Mingo GK .50 1.25
267 Gerald McCoy GK .50 1.25
268 Larry Fitzgerald GK .60 1.50
269 Philip Rivers GK .75 2.00
270 Jamaal Charles GK .60 1.50
271 Andrew Luck GK 1.00 2.50
272 Tony Romo GK .60 1.50
273 Ryan Tannehill GK .60 1.50
274 Sam Bradford GK .50 1.25
275 Matt Ryan GK .60 1.50
276 Odell Beckham Jr. GK .75 2.00
277 Paul Posluszny GK .50 1.25
278 Eric Decker GK .50 1.25
279 Calvin Johnson GK .75 2.00
280 Aaron Rodgers GK 1.50 4.00
281 Cam Newton GK .75 2.00
282 Tom Brady GK 2.00 5.00
283 Derek Carr GK .75 2.00
284 James Laurinaitis GK .60 1.50
285 Joe Flacco GK .60 1.50
286 Robert Griffin III GK .50 1.25
287 Drew Brees GK .75 2.00
288 Russell Wilson GK 1.00 2.50
289 Ben Roethlisberger GK .75 2.00
290 J.J. Watt GK .75 2.00
291 Kendall Wright GK .50 1.25
292 Teddy Bridgewater GK .60 1.50
293 Earl Campbell GL .75 2.00
294 Franco Harris GL .75 2.00
295 Gale Sayers GL .75 2.00
296 Joe Namath GL 1.00 2.50
297 Larry Csonka GL .60 1.50
298 Len Dawson GL .75 2.00
299 Paul Hornung GL .75 2.00
300 Eric Dickerson GL .60 1.50

2015 Donruss Holo Back

*HOLO: .5X TO 1.2X BASIC CARDS

2015 Donruss Press Proofs Blue

*BLUE/99: 1.5X TO 4X BASIC CARDS(1-185)
*BLUE/99: 1X TO 2.5X BASIC CARDS(186-240)
*BLUE/99: 1.2X TO 3X BASIC CARDS(241-260)
*BLUE/99: .8X TO 2X BASIC CARDS(1-185)

2015 Donruss Press Proofs Purple

*PURPLE/199: 1X TO 2.5X BASIC CARDS(1-185)
*PURPLE/199: .6X TO 1.5X BASIC CARDS(186-240)
*PURPLE/199: .8X TO 2X BASIC CARDS(241-260)
*PURPLE/199: .5X TO 1.2X BASIC CARDS(261-300)
202 Marcus Mariota RR 15.00 40.00

2015 Donruss Press Proofs Silver

*SILVER/25: 3X TO 8X BASIC CARDS(1-185)
*SILVER/25: 2X TO 5X BASIC CARDS(186-240)
*SILVER/25: 2.5X TO 6X BASIC CARDS(241-260)
*SILVER/25: 1.5X TO 4X BASIC CARDS(261-300)

2015 Donruss Red

*RED: .6X TO 1.5X BASIC CARDS

2015 Donruss Stat Line Career

*SEAS/300-729: .8X TO 2X BASIC CARDS(1-185)
*SEAS/150-297: 1X TO 2.5X BASIC CARDS
*SEAS/100-148: 1.2X TO 3X BASIC CARDS
*SEAS/79-99: 1.5X TO 4X BASIC CARDS
*SEAS/50-74: 2X TO 5X BASIC CARDS
*SEAS/27-49: 2.5X TO 6X BASIC CARDS
*SEAS/300-729: .5X TO 1.2X BASIC CARDS(186-240)
*SEAS/150-297: .6X TO 1.5X BASIC CARDS
*SEAS/100-148: .8X TO 2X BASIC CARDS
*SEAS/79-99: 1X TO 2.5X BASIC CARDS
*SEAS/50-74: 1.2X TO 3X BASIC CARDS
*SEAS/27-49: 1.5X TO 4X BASIC CARDS
*SEAS/300-729: .6X TO 1.5X BASIC CARDS(241-260)
*SEAS/150-297: .8X TO 2X BASIC CARDS
*SEAS/100-148: 1X TO 2.5X BASIC CARDS
*SEAS/300-729: .4X TO 1X BASIC CARDS(261-300)
*SEAS/150-297: .5X TO 1.2X BASIC CARDS
*SEAS/100-148: .6 TO 1.5X BASIC CARDS
*SEAS/79-99: .8X TO 2X BASIC CARDS
*SEAS/50-74: 1X TO 2.5X BASIC CARDS
*SEAS/27-49: 1.2X TO 3X BASIC CARDS

2015 Donruss Stat Line Season

*SEAS/301-703: .8X TO 2X BASIC CARDS(1-185)
*SEAS/151-295: 1X TO 2.5X BASIC CARDS
*SEAS/101-150: 1.2X TO 3X BASIC CARDS
*SEAS/75-99: 1.5X TO 4X BASIC CARDS
*SEAS/50-73: 2X TO 5X BASIC CARDS
*SEAS/30-47: 2.5X TO 6X BASIC CARDS
*SEAS/16-24: 3X TO 8X BASIC CARDS
*SEAS/301-703: .5X TO 1.2X BASIC CARDS(186-240)
*SEAS/151-295: .6X TO 1.5X BASIC CARDS
*SEAS/101-150: .8X TO 2X BASIC CARDS
*SEAS/75-99: 1X TO 2.5X BASIC CARDS
*SEAS/50-73: 1.2X TO 3X BASIC CARDS
*SEAS/30-47: 1.5X TO 4X BASIC CARDS
*SEAS/16-24: 2X TO 5X BASIC CARDS
*SEAS/301-703: .6X TO 1.5X BASIC CARDS(241-260)
*SEAS/151-295: .8X TO 2X BASIC CARDS
*SEAS/101-150: 1X TO 2.5X BASIC CARDS
*SEAS/301-703: .4X TO 1X BASIC CARDS(261-300)
*SEAS/151-295: .5X TO 1.2X BASIC CARDS
*SEAS/101-150: .6 TO 1.5X BASIC CARDS
*SEAS/75-99: .8X TO 2X BASIC CARDS
*SEAS/50-73: 1X TO 2.5X BASIC CARDS
*SEAS/30-47: 1.2X TO 3X BASIC CARDS

2015 Donruss Stat Line Years

*YEAR/20: 3X TO 8X BASIC CARDS(1-185)
*YEAR/15-19: 4X TO 10X BASIC CARDS
*YEAR/20: 2.5X TO 6X BASIC CARDS(241-260)
*YEAR/15-19: 3X TO 8X BASIC CARDS
*YEAR/20: 2X TO 5X BASIC CARDS(261-300)
*YEAR/15-19: 1.5X TO 4X BASIC CARDS

2015 Donruss Dominator

1 Aaron Rodgers 3.00 8.00
2 Antonio Brown 1.50 4.00
3 Larry Fitzgerald 1.25 3.00
4 Teddy Bridgewater 1.25 3.00
5 Steve Smith 1.25 3.00
6 Julio Jones 1.50 4.00
7 Peyton Manning 3.00 8.00
8 Sammy Watkins 1.25 3.00
9 Colin Kaepernick 1.25 3.00
10 Alfred Morris 1.00 2.50
11 Kendall Wright 1.00 2.50
12 Cam Newton 1.50 4.00
13 Rob Gronkowski 1.50 4.00
14 Tony Romo 1.25 3.00
15 Joe Haden 1.00 2.50
16 Marshawn Lynch 1.25 3.00
17 Blake Bortles 1.00 2.50
18 Jamaal Charles 1.25 3.00
19 Drew Brees 1.50 4.00
20 DeMarco Murray 1.25 3.00
21 Antonio Gates 1.00 2.50
22 Alshon Jeffery 1.25 3.00
23 Andrew Luck 2.00 5.00
24 Demaryius Thomas 1.25 3.00
25 Mike Evans 1.25 3.00
26 Tom Brady 4.00 10.00
27 Jordy Nelson 1.25 3.00
28 Ryan Tannehill 1.25 3.00
29 Russell Wilson 2.00 5.00
30 Odell Beckham Jr. 1.50 4.00
31 A.J. Green 1.50 4.00
32 Calvin Johnson 1.50 4.00
33 Arian Foster 1.25 3.00
34 Matt Forte 1.00 2.50
35 Aaron Donald 1.50 4.00
36 Le'Veon Bell 1.25 3.00
37 Derek Carr 1.50 4.00
38 Dez Bryant 1.50 4.00
39 Matt Ryan 1.25 3.00
40 Eric Decker 1.00 2.50

2015 Donruss Dominator Autographs

DAAB Anquan Boldin/150 6.00 15.00
DAAG Antonio Gates/150 6.00 15.00
DADB Drew Brees/25 25.00 50.00
DADT Demaryius Thomas/100 8.00 20.00
DAEL Eddie Lacy/150 6.00 15.00
DAJJ J.J. Watt/25 30.00 60.00
DALK Luke Kuechly/100 20.00 40.00
DAML Marshawn Lynch/100 25.00 50.00
DAMS Matthew Stafford/50 20.00 40.00
DAVC Victor Cruz/150 8.00 20.00

2015 Donruss Elite Inserts

1 Larry Fitzgerald .50 1.25
2 Cam Newton .60 1.50
3 Calvin Johnson .60 1.50
4 Peyton Manning 1.25 3.00
5 Dez Bryant .60 1.50
6 Russell Wilson .75 2.00
7 Arian Foster .50 1.25
8 Aaron Rodgers 1.25 3.00
9 Blake Bortles .40 1.00
10 Drew Brees .60 1.50
11 DeSean Jackson .50 1.25
12 Derek Carr .60 1.50
13 Tre Mason .50 1.25
14 Andrew Luck .75 2.00
15 Matt Forte .40 1.00
16 Philip Rivers .60 1.50
17 Eli Manning .50 1.25
18 A.J. Green .60 1.50
19 Colin Kaepernick .50 1.25
20 Jordy Nelson .50 1.25
21 Jamaal Charles .50 1.25
22 Matthew Stafford .50 1.25
23 Kendall Wright .40 1.00
24 Demaryius Thomas .50 1.25
25 Julio Jones .60 1.50
26 Ryan Tannehill .50 1.25
27 DeMarco Murray .50 1.25
28 Matt Ryan .50 1.25
29 Mike Evans .50 1.25
30 Ben Roethlisberger .60 1.50
31 Teddy Bridgewater .50 1.25
32 Tom Brady 1.50 4.00
33 Marshawn Lynch .50 1.25
34 Brandon Marshall .40 1.00
35 Tony Romo .50 1.25
36 Le'Veon Bell .50 1.25
37 Rob Gronkowski .60 1.50
38 LeSean McCoy .60 1.50
39 Isaiah Crowell .40 1.00
40 Joe Flacco .50 1.25
41 Jay Ajayi .40 1.00
42 Brett Hundley .25 .60
43 Stefon Diggs .60 1.50
44 Rashad Greene .25 .60
45 David Cobb .25 .60
46 Mike Davis .25 .60
47 Buck Allen .30 .75
48 Vince Mayle .30 .75
49 Justin Hardy .25 .60
50 Jeremy Langford .25 .60
51 Jamison Crowder .30 .75
52 Bryce Petty .25 .60
53 Matt Jones .25 .60
54 Ty Montgomery .25 .60
55 Sean Mannion .25 .60
56 Sammie Coates .30 .75
57 David Johnson .60 1.50
58 Duke Johnson .40 1.00
59 Chris Conley .25 .60
60 Garrett Grayson .25 .60
61 Tevin Coleman .30 .75
62 Jaelen Strong .30 .75
63 Tyler Lockett .40 1.00
64 Maxx Williams .25 .60
65 Ameer Abdullah .40 1.00
66 Devin Funchess .40 1.00
67 Dorial Green-Beckham .25 .60
68 Devin Smith .25 .60
69 T.J. Yeldon .25 .60
70 Phillip Dorsett .25 .60
71 Breshad Perriman .25 .60
72 Nelson Agholor .30 .75
73 Melvin Gordon .60 1.50
74 DeVante Parker .40 1.00
75 Todd Gurley 1.00 2.50
76 Kevin White .30 .75
77 Leonard Williams .25 .60
78 Amari Cooper .75 2.00
79 Marcus Mariota 1.00 2.50
80 Jameis Winston .60 1.50

2015 Donruss Elite Inserts New Breed Jerseys

*PRIME/49: .6X TO 1.5X BASIC JSY
NBAA Ameer Abdullah 2.00 5.00
NBAC Amari Cooper 4.00 10.00
NBBA Buck Allen 1.50 4.00
NBBH Brett Hundley 1.25 3.00
NBBRP Breshad Perriman 1.25 3.00
NBBYP Bryce Petty 1.25 3.00
NBCC Chris Conley 1.25 3.00
NBDC David Cobb 1.25 3.00
NBDF Devin Funchess 2.00 5.00
NBDGB Dorial Green-Beckham 1.25 3.00
NBDJ David Johnson 3.00 8.00
NBDS Devin Smith 1.25 3.00
NBDUJ Duke Johnson 2.00 5.00
NBDVP DeVante Parker 2.00 5.00
NBGG Garrett Grayson 1.25 3.00
NBJA Jay Ajayi 2.00 5.00
NBJC Jamison Crowder 1.50 4.00
NBJH Justin Hardy 1.25 3.00
NBJL Jeremy Langford 1.25 3.00
NBJS Jaelen Strong 1.50 4.00
NBJW Jameis Winston 3.00 8.00
NBKW Kevin White 1.50 4.00
NBLW Leonard Williams 1.25 3.00
NBMD Mike Davis 1.25 3.00
NBMG Melvin Gordon 3.00 8.00
NBMJ Matt Jones 1.25 3.00
NBMM Marcus Mariota 5.00 12.00
NBMW Maxx Williams 1.25 3.00
NBNA Nelson Agholor 1.50 4.00
NBPD Phillip Dorsett 1.25 3.00
NBRG Rashad Greene 1.25 3.00
NBSC Sammie Coates 1.50 4.00
NBSD Stefon Diggs 3.00 8.00
NBSM Sean Mannion 1.25 3.00
NBTC Tevin Coleman 1.50 4.00
NBTG Todd Gurley 4.00 10.00
NBTL Tyler Lockett 2.00 5.00
NBTM Ty Montgomery 1.25 3.00
NBTY T.J. Yeldon 1.25 3.00
NBVM Vince Mayle 1.50 4.00

2015 Donruss Elite Inserts New Breed Jerseys Autographs

NBAAA Ameer Abdullah 4.00 10.00
NBAAC Amari Cooper 30.00 60.00
NBABRP Breshad Perriman 2.50 6.00
NBABYP Bryce Petty 2.50 6.00
NBADF Devin Funchess 4.00 10.00
NBADJ David Johnson 10.00 25.00
NBADVP DeVante Parker 4.00 10.00
NBAJA Jay Ajayi 4.00 10.00
NBAJS Jaelen Strong
NBAJW Jameis Winston 6.00 15.00
NBAKW Kevin White 3.00 8.00
NBAMG Melvin Gordon 6.00 15.00
NBAMM Marcus Mariota 25.00 50.00
NBANA Nelson Agholor 3.00 8.00
NBAPD Phillip Dorsett 2.50 6.00
NBASC Sammie Coates 3.00 8.00
NBATC Tevin Coleman 3.00 8.00
NBATG Todd Gurley 8.00 20.00
NBATY T.J. Yeldon 2.50 6.00

2015 Donruss Elite Inserts New Breed Jerseys Prime Autographs

*PRIME/25: .8X TO 2X JSY AU
NBADGB Dorial Green-Beckham/25 5.00 12.00
NBAJW Jameis Winston/25 12.00 30.00
NBAMM Marcus Mariota/25 40.00 80.00

2015 Donruss Elite Inserts Passing the Torch

1 O.Beckham Jr./V.Cruz .60 1.50
2 B.Perriman/S.Smith .50 1.25
3 D.Brees/G.Grayson .60 1.50
4 A.Cooper/T.Brown 1.25 3.00
5 T.Brady/J.Garoppolo 1.50 4.00
6 P.Dorsett/R.Wayne .50 1.25
7 L.Tomlinson/M.Gordon 1.00 2.50
8 M.Faulk/T.Gurley 1.50 4.00
9 R.Gregory/R.White .50 1.25
10 F.Taylor/T.Yeldon .40 1.00

2015 Donruss Elite Inserts Passing the Torch Autographs

PTBAL B.Perriman/S.Smith/25
PTGBP T.Montgomery/R.Cobb/25
PTMIN F.Tarkenton/T.Bridgewater/25 25.00 50.00
PTNOS G.Grayson/D.Brees/25 75.00 150.00
PTNYJ D.Smith/E.Decker/25 20.00 40.00
PTPIT A.Brown/S.Coates/25 25.00 50.00
PTSTL M.Faulk/T.Gurley/25 75.00 150.00

2015 Donruss Elite Inserts Passing the Torch Jerseys

PTMATL R.White/J.Hardy 2.00 5.00
PTMBAL T.Suggs/C.Mosley 3.00 8.00
PTMCAR K.Benjamin/D.Funchess 2.00 5.00
PTMDAL D.Murray/J.Randle 2.50 6.00
PTMDET A.Abdullah/B.Sanders 10.00 25.00
PTMFAL D.Freeman/T.Coleman 1.50 4.00
PTMGBP B.Favre/B.Hundley 10.00 25.00
PTMIND P.Dorsett/T.Hilton 2.50 6.00
PTMJAC F.Taylor/T.Yeldon 1.25 3.00
PTMMIN F.Tarkenton/T.Bridgewater 3.00 8.00
PTMNEP J.Garoppolo/T.Brady 10.00 25.00
PTMNOS D.Brees/G.Grayson 2.00 5.00
PTMNYG O.Beckham Jr./V.Cruz 3.00 8.00
PTMNYJ L.Williams/S.Richardson 1.25 3.00
PTMPHI B.Celek/Z.Ertz 2.50 6.00
PTMPIT A.Brown/S.Coates 3.00 8.00
PTMSAN C.Hyde/M.Davis 2.00 5.00
PTMSDC L.Tomlinson/M.Gordon 3.00 8.00
PTMSLR T.Gurley/M.Faulk 5.00 12.00
PTMWAS J.Crowder/D.Jackson 2.50 6.00

2015 Donruss Elite Inserts Rookie Signatures

ERSAA Arik Armstead 2.50 6.00
ERSBD Bud Dupree 3.00 8.00
ERSBH Brett Hundley 2.50 6.00
ERSBW Bo Wallace 2.50 6.00
ERSCAP Cameron Artis-Payne 2.50 6.00
ERSCC Chris Conley 2.50 6.00
ERSCW Clive Walford 2.50 6.00
ERSDC David Cobb 2.50 6.00
ERSDES Devin Smith 2.50 6.00
ERSDGR Deontay Greenberry 2.50 6.00
ERSDS Danny Shelton 2.50 6.00
ERSEG Eddie Goldman 2.50 6.00
ERSEK Eric Kendricks 2.50 6.00
ERSJH Justin Hardy 2.50 6.00
ERSJJ Jesse James 3.00 8.00
ERSJL Jeremy Langford 2.50 6.00
ERSKB Kenny Bell 4.00 10.00
ERSLC Landon Collins 3.00 8.00
ERSMB1 Malcolm Brown 3.00 8.00
ERSMB2 Malcom Brown 2.50 6.00
ERSMD Mike Davis 2.50 6.00
ERSMJ Matt Jones 2.50 6.00
ERSMP Marcus Peters 4.00 10.00
ERSNOL Nick O'Leary 2.50 6.00
ERSOO Owamagbe Odighizuwa 3.00 8.00
ERSPJW P.J. Williams 3.00 8.00
ERSRGE Rashad Greene 2.50 6.00
ERSSM Sean Mannion 2.50 6.00
ERSSR Shane Ray 2.50 6.00
ERSST Shaq Thompson 3.00 8.00
ERSTM Ty Montgomery 2.50 6.00
ERSTYL Tyler Lockett 4.00 10.00
ERSVM Vince Mayle 3.00 8.00

2015 Donruss Elite Inserts Throwback Threads

*PRIME/17-25: 1.2X TO 3X BASIC JSY
TTBG Bob Griese 3.00 8.00
TTBU Brian Urlacher 3.00 8.00
TTCB Champ Bailey 2.50 6.00
TTCM Curtis Martin 2.50 6.00
TTCS Larry Csonka 5.00 12.00
TTDCL Dwight Clark 2.50 6.00
TTEC Earl Campbell 3.00 8.00
TTED Eric Dickerson 2.50 6.00
TTJK Jim Kelly 3.00 8.00
TTJR John Riggins 2.50 6.00
TTLDT LaDainian Tomlinson 2.50 6.00
TTMA Marcus Allen 3.00 8.00
TTMS Michael Strahan 2.50 6.00
TTON Ozzie Newsome 2.50 6.00
TTRL Ronnie Lott 2.50 6.00
TTRW Rod Woodson 2.50 6.00
TTRWH Randy White 2.50 6.00
TTSL Steve Largent 3.00 8.00
TTTB Tim Brown 3.00 8.00
TTTT Thurman Thomas 2.50 6.00

2015 Donruss Elite Series

1 Tom Brady 2.00 5.00
2 Andrew Luck 1.00 2.50
3 DeMarco Murray .60 1.50
4 Julio Jones .75 2.00
5 Antonio Brown .75 2.00
6 Dez Bryant .75 2.00
7 Aaron Rodgers 1.50 4.00
8 Marshawn Lynch .60 1.50
9 Drew Brees .75 2.00
10 J.J. Watt .75 2.00

2015 Donruss Elite Series Signatures

1 Marques Colston 6.00 15.00
2 Giovani Bernard 6.00 15.00
3 Ryan Tannehill 8.00 20.00
4 Percy Harvin
5 Jason Witten 20.00 40.00
6 DeMarcus Ware 8.00 20.00
7 Joe Flacco
8 Nick Foles 8.00 20.00
9 Colin Kaepernick 8.00 20.00
10 Matt Ryan 12.00 30.00

2015 Donruss Rookie Threads

*PRIME/49: .6X TO 1.5X BASIC JSY
DRTAA Ameer Abdullah 2.00 5.00
DRTAC Amari Cooper 4.00 10.00
DRTBA Buck Allen 1.50 4.00
DRTBH Brett Hundley 1.25 3.00
DRTBRP Breshad Perriman 1.25 3.00
DRTBYP Bryce Petty 1.25 3.00
DRTCC Chris Conley 1.25 3.00
DRTDC David Cobb 1.25 3.00
DRTDF Devin Funchess 2.00 5.00
DRTDGB Dorial Green-Beckham 1.25 3.00
DRTDJ David Johnson 4.00 10.00
DRTDS Devin Smith 1.25 3.00
DRTDUJ Duke Johnson 2.00 5.00
DRTDVP DeVante Parker 2.00 5.00
DRTGG Garrett Grayson 1.25 3.00
DRTJA Jay Ajayi 2.00 5.00
DRTJC Jamison Crowder 1.50 4.00
DRTJH Justin Hardy 1.25 3.00
DRTJL Jeremy Langford 1.25 3.00
DRTJS Jaelen Strong 1.50 4.00
DRTJW Jameis Winston 3.00 8.00
DRTKW Kevin White 1.50 4.00
DRTLW Leonard Williams 1.25 3.00
DRTMD Mike Davis 1.25 3.00
DRTMG Melvin Gordon 3.00 8.00
DRTMJ Matt Jones 1.25 3.00
DRTMM Marcus Mariota 5.00 12.00
DRTMW Maxx Williams 1.25 3.00
DRTNA Nelson Agholor 1.50 4.00
DRTPD Phillip Dorsett 1.25 3.00
DRTRGE Rashad Greene 1.25 3.00
DRTSC Sammie Coates 1.50 4.00
DRTSD Stefon Diggs 3.00 8.00
DRTSM Sean Mannion 1.25 3.00
DRTTC Tevin Coleman 1.50 4.00
DRTTG Todd Gurley 4.00 10.00
DRTTJY T.J. Yeldon 1.25 3.00
DRTTL Tyler Lockett 2.00 5.00
DRTTM Ty Montgomery 1.25 3.00
DRTVM Vince Mayle 1.50 4.00

2015 Donruss Rookie Throwbacks '84

1 Rob Gronkowski 1.00 2.50
2 T.J. Yeldon .60 1.50
3 Matthew Stafford .75 2.00
4 DeMarco Murray .75 2.00
5 Dorial Green-Beckham .60 1.50
6 Demaryius Thomas .75 2.00
7 Drew Brees 1.00 2.50
8 Devin Funchess 1.00 2.50
9 Adrian Peterson 1.00 2.50
10 Antonio Brown 1.00 2.50
11 Phillip Dorsett .60 1.50
12 Russell Wilson 1.25 3.00
13 Eli Manning .75 2.00
14 Larry Fitzgerald .75 2.00
15 Breshad Perriman .60 1.50
16 Dez Bryant 1.00 2.50

2015 Donruss Rookie Throwbacks '85

1 Ben Roethlisberger 1.50 4.00
2 Tony Romo 1.25 3.00
3 Jameis Winston 1.50 4.00
4 Matt Ryan 1.25 3.00
5 A.J. Green 1.50 4.00
6 Calvin Johnson 1.50 4.00
7 Amari Cooper 2.00 5.00
8 T.Y. Hilton 1.25 3.00
9 Cam Newton 1.50 4.00
10 Todd Gurley 2.50 6.00
11 Jamaal Charles 1.25 3.00
12 Philip Rivers 1.50 4.00
13 Devin Smith .60 1.50
14 Jordy Nelson 1.25 3.00
15 Bishop Sankey 1.00 2.50
16 DeVante Parker 1.00 2.50

2015 Donruss Rookie Throwbacks '85 Autographs

1 Cam Newton/20 20.00 40.00
2 Ben Roethlisberger/20 30.00 60.00
3 Peyton Manning/15 100.00 200.00
4 Jamaal Charles/25 15.00 30.00
5 Tony Romo/15 30.00 80.00
6 Carson Palmer/25 8.00 20.00
7 Richard Sherman/25 40.00 80.00
8 Vincent Jackson/25 6.00 15.00

2015 Donruss Signature Series Insert

DSSAC Adrian Clayborn 3.00 8.00
DSSAD Aaron Dobson 3.00 8.00
DSSADA Andy Dalton 4.00 10.00
DSSAF Arian Foster 4.00 10.00
DSSAH Allen Hurns 3.00 8.00
DSSAR Adrien Robinson 3.00 8.00
DSSAS Alex Smith 12.00 30.00
DSSASJ Austin Seferian-Jenkins 3.00 8.00
DSSAW Andre Williams 3.00 8.00
DSSBB Bryce Brown 3.00 8.00
DSSBF Brandon Flowers 3.00 8.00
DSSBLF Brandon LaFell 3.00 8.00
DSSBM Barkevious Mingo 3.00 8.00
DSSBO Branden Oliver 4.00 10.00
DSSCC Charles Clay 3.00 8.00
DSSCK Case Keenum 4.00 10.00
DSSCOS Connor Shaw 3.00 8.00
DSSCS Charles Sims 3.00 8.00
DSSDAH DeAndre Hopkins 6.00 15.00
DSSDW Danny Woodhead 4.00 10.00
DSSET Earl Thomas 6.00 15.00
DSSGE Gavin Escobar 3.00 8.00
DSSJA Jared Abbrederis 3.00 8.00
DSSJB John Brown 4.00 10.00
DSSJF Joseph Fauria 3.00 8.00
DSSJH Justin Hunter 3.00 8.00
DSSJL James Laurinaitis 4.00 10.00
DSSJR Joseph Randle 3.00 8.00
DSSJUF Justin Forsett 4.00 10.00
DSSKDC Ka'Deem Carey 3.00 8.00
DSSMB Montee Ball 3.00 8.00
DSSNT Nick Toon 3.00 8.00
DSSPP Patrick Peterson 3.00 8.00
DSSRS Rod Streater 3.00 8.00
DSSRW Robert Woods 4.00 10.00
DSSSL Sean Lee 6.00 15.00
DSSTN Troy Niklas 3.00 8.00
DSSTW Timothy Wright 3.00 8.00
DSSVMD Vance McDonald 3.00 8.00
DSSZM Zach Mettenberger 3.00 8.00

2015 Donruss The Rookies

1 David Johnson 1.50 4.00
2 Tevin Coleman .75 2.00
3 Karlos Williams .60 1.50
4 Breshad Perriman .60 1.50
5 Maxx Williams .60 1.50
6 Tyler Kroft .75 2.00
7 Devin Funchess 1.00 2.50
8 Kevin White .75 2.00
9 Duke Johnson 1.00 2.50
10 Randy Gregory .60 1.50
11 Shane Ray .60 1.50
12 Ameer Abdullah 1.00 2.50
13 Ty Montgomery .60 1.50
14 Brett Hundley .60 1.50
15 Jaelen Strong .75 2.00
16 Phillip Dorsett .60 1.50
17 T.J. Yeldon .60 1.50
18 Chris Conley .60 1.50
19 DeVante Parker 1.00 2.50
20 Jay Ajayi 1.00 2.50
21 Stefon Diggs 1.50 4.00
22 Malcom Brown .60 1.50
23 Garrett Grayson .60 1.50
24 Landon Collins .75 2.00
25 Leonard Williams .60 1.50
26 Devin Smith .60 1.50
27 Amari Cooper 2.00 5.00
28 Clive Walford .60 1.50
29 Nelson Agholor .75 2.00
30 Sammie Coates .75 2.00
31 Melvin Gordon 1.50 4.00
32 Mike Davis .60 1.50
33 Tyler Lockett 1.00 2.50
34 Todd Gurley 2.50 6.00
35 Jameis Winston 1.50 4.00
36 Kenny Bell 1.00 2.50
37 Marcus Mariota 2.50 6.00
38 Dorial Green-Beckham .60 1.50
39 Matt Jones .60 1.50
40 Jamison Crowder .75 2.00

2015 Donruss The Rookies Autographs

1 Marcus Mariota/25 30.00 60.00
3 Devin Funchess/250 4.00 10.00
4 Jameis Winston/25 12.00 30.00
6 Devin Smith/250 2.50 6.00
7 Sammie Coates/250 3.00 8.00
8 Phillip Dorsett/110 3.00 8.00
9 Duke Johnson/250 4.00 10.00

2015 Donruss Threads

*PRIME/25: .8X TO 2X BASIC JSY
DROS Orlando Scandrick 2.00 5.00
DTADA Andy Dalton 2.50 6.00
DTAG Antonio Gates 2.00 5.00
DTAJG A.J. Green 3.00 8.00
DTAW Andre Williams 2.00 5.00
DTBB Blake Bortles 2.00 5.00
DTBC Brandin Cooks 2.50 6.00
DTBO Branden Oliver 2.50 6.00
DTBSA Bishop Sankey 2.00 5.00
DTCBE Cole Beasley 5.00 12.00
DTCH Carlos Hyde 2.00 5.00
DTCL Cody Latimer 2.00 5.00
DTCN Cam Newton 3.00 8.00
DTCS Charles Sims 2.00 5.00
DTDA Davante Adams 2.50 6.00
DTDAH DeAngelo Hall 2.50 6.00
DTDAT De'Anthony Thomas 2.00 5.00
DTDCA Derek Carr 3.00 8.00
DTDR Denard Robinson 2.00 5.00
DTDR Allen Robinson 2.50 6.00
DTDS Dion Sims 2.00 5.00
DTDSJ DeSean Jackson 2.50 6.00
DTEE Eric Ebron 2.00 5.00
DTGB Giovani Bernard 2.00 5.00
DTJCH Jamaal Charles 2.50 6.00
DTJCL Jadeveon Clowney 2.00 5.00
DTJG Jimmy Garoppolo 4.00 10.00
DTJH Jeremy Hill 2.00 5.00
DTJHA Joe Haden 2.00 5.00
DTJHO Justin Houston 2.00 5.00
DTJHU Justin Hunter 2.00 5.00
DTJL Jarvis Landry 2.50 6.00
DTJM Jordan Matthews 2.50 6.00
DTJR Jordan Reed 2.00 5.00
DTJYM Johnny Manziel 2.50 6.00
DTKB Kelvin Benjamin 2.50 6.00
DTKD Knile Davis 2.00 5.00
DTLM Lamar Miller 2.00 5.00
DTLSM LeSean McCoy 3.00 8.00
DTMAF Malcom Floyd 2.00 5.00
DTMBA Montee Ball 2.00 5.00
DTMBE Martellus Bennett 2.00 5.00
DTMC Marques Colston 2.00 5.00
DTME Mike Evans 2.50 6.00
DTMF Michael Floyd 2.00 5.00
DTML Marqise Lee 2.00 5.00
DTOBJ Odell Beckham Jr. 3.00 8.00
DTPHR Philip Rivers 3.00 8.00
DTPM Peyton Manning 10.00 25.00
DTPPE Patrick Peterson 2.00 5.00
DTPPO Paul Posluszny 2.00 5.00
DTRMC Rolando McClain 2.00 5.00
DTRQ Robert Quinn 2.50 6.00
DTRT Ryan Tannehill 2.50 6.00
DTRW Robert Woods 2.50 6.00
DTSW Sammy Watkins 2.50 6.00
DTTB Teddy Bridgewater 2.50 6.00
DTTH Tamba Hali 2.00 5.00
DTTM Tre Mason 2.50 6.00

2016 Donruss

1 Carson Palmer .30 .75
2 Larry Fitzgerald .30 .75
3 David Johnson .40 1.00
4 Chris Johnson .25 .60
5 John Brown .30 .75
6 Michael Floyd .25 .60
7 Tyrann Mathieu .30 .75
8 Patrick Peterson .25 .60
9 Kurt Warner .30 .75
10 Chandler Jones .25 .60
11 Matt Ryan .30 .75
12 Devonta Freeman .30 .75
13 Tevin Coleman .30 .75
14 Julio Jones .40 1.00
15 Jacob Tamme .25 .60
16 Mohamed Sanu .25 .60
17 Paul Worrilow .25 .60
18 Desmond Trufant .25 .60
19 Warrick Dunn .25 .60
20 Joe Flacco .30 .75
21 Eric Weddle .25 .60
22 Justin Forsett .30 .75
23 Steve Smith Sr. .30 .75
24 Kamar Aiken .25 .60
25 Jimmy Smith .25 .60
26 Terrell Suggs .25 .60
27 Elvis Dumervil .25 .60
28 Ray Lewis .40 1.00
29 Buck Allen .25 .60
30 Tyrod Taylor .30 .75
31 LeSean McCoy .40 1.00
32 Karlos Williams .25 .60
33 Sammy Watkins .40 1.00
34 Robert Woods .30 .75
35 Charles Clay .25 .60
36 Stephon Gilmore .25 .60
37 Corey Graham .25 .60
38 Jim Kelly .40 1.00
39 Cam Newton .40 1.00
40 Jonathan Stewart .25 .60
41 Ted Ginn Jr. .25 .60
42 Kelvin Benjamin .30 .75
43 Greg Olsen .30 .75
44 Devin Funchess .25 .60
45 Luke Kuechly .30 .75
46 Thomas Davis .25 .60
47 Josh Norman .25 .60
48 Kevin Greene .40 1.00
49 Jay Cutler .25 .60
50 Jeremy Langford .30 .75
51 Alshon Jeffery .30 .75
52 Kevin White .25 .60
53 Marquess Wilson .25 .60
54 Lamarr Houston .25 .60
55 Gale Sayers .40 1.00
56 Zach Miller .25 .60
57 Eddie Royal .25 .60
58 Andy Dalton .30 .75
59 Adam Jones .25 .60
60 Jeremy Hill .25 .60
61 Giovani Bernard .25 .60
62 A.J. Green .40 1.00
63 Tyler Eifert .30 .75
64 Carlos Dunlap .25 .60
65 Geno Atkins .25 .60
66 Ickey Woods .25 .60
67 Josh McCown .25 .60
68 Robert Griffin III .25 .60
69 Duke Johnson .25 .60
70 Gary Barnidge .25 .60
71 Joe Thomas .25 .60
72 Isaiah Crowell .25 .60
73 Joe Haden .25 .60
74 Ozzie Newsome .30 .75
75 Brian Hartline .25 .60
76 Tony Romo .30 .75
77 Darren McFadden .25 .60
78 Terrance Williams .25 .60
79 Jason Witten .30 .75
80 Dez Bryant .40 1.00
81 Cole Beasley .40 1.00
82 Sean Lee .30 .75
83 Alfred Morris .25 .60
84 Dan Bailey .25 .60
85 Emmitt Smith .60 1.50
86 C.J. Anderson .30 .75
87 Demaryius Thomas .30 .75
88 Emmanuel Sanders .40 1.00
89 Von Miller .30 .75
90 DeMarcus Ware .30 .75
91 Brandon Marshall .25 .60
92 John Elway .60 1.50
93 Chris Harris .25 .60
94 Aqib Talib .25 .60
95 Marvin Jones .25 .60
96 Matthew Stafford .30 .75
97 Ameer Abdullah .25 .60
98 Golden Tate III .25 .60
99 Eric Ebron .25 .60
100 Theo Riddick .25 .60
101 Ezekiel Ansah .25 .60
102 Haloti Ngata .25 .60
103 Barry Sanders .60 1.50
104 Aaron Rodgers .75 2.00
105 Eddie Lacy .25 .60
106 James Starks .25 .60
107 Randall Cobb .30 .75
108 Jordy Nelson .30 .75
109 John Kuhn .25 .60
110 Richard Rodgers .30 .75
111 Clay Matthews .40 1.00
112 Julius Peppers .30 .75
113 Brett Favre .75 2.00
114 Earl Campbell .40 1.00
115 Brock Osweiler .25 .60
116 Cecil Shorts III .25 .60
117 Vince Wilfork .25 .60
118 DeAndre Hopkins .30 .75
119 Jadeveon Clowney .25 .60
120 Brian Cushing .25 .60
121 J.J. Watt .40 1.00
122 Whitney Mercilus .25 .60
123 Lamar Miller .25 .60
124 Andrew Luck .50 1.25
125 Frank Gore .30 .75
126 Donte Moncrief .30 .75
127 T.Y. Hilton .30 .75
128 D'Qwell Jackson .25 .60
129 Phillip Dorsett .25 .60
130 Robert Mathis .25 .60
131 Pat McAfee .30 .75
132 Peyton Manning .75 2.00
133 Blake Bortles .25 .60
134 T.J. Yeldon .25 .60
135 Denard Robinson .25 .60
136 Allen Robinson .30 .75
137 Julius Thomas .25 .60
138 Allen Hurns .25 .60
139 Paul Posluszny .25 .60
140 Johnathan Cyprien .25 .60
141 Fred Taylor .25 .00
142 Chris Ivory .30 .75
143 Alex Smith .30 .75
144 Jamaal Charles .30 .75
145 Charcandrick West .25 .60
146 Jeremy Maclin .25 .60
147 Travis Kelce .40 1.00
148 Derrick Johnson .25 .60
149 Eric Berry .30 .75
150 Marcus Peters .25 .60
151 Len Dawson .40 1.00
152 Robert Quinn .30 .75
153 Case Keenum .30 .75
154 Todd Gurley II .40 1.00
155 Alec Ogletree .25 .60
156 Tavon Austin .25 .60
157 Kenny Britt .25 .60
158 Aaron Donald .40 1.00
159 Mark Barron .25 .60
160 Eric Dickerson .30 .75
161 Ryan Tannehill .30 .75
162 Jay Ajayi .30 .75
163 Jarvis Landry .30 .75
164 DeVante Parker .30 .75
165 Reshad Jones .25 .60
166 Ndamukong Suh .30 .75
167 Dan Marino .75 2.00
168 Mario Williams .25 .60
169 Cameron Wake .25 .60
170 Teddy Bridgewater .30 .75
171 Adrian Peterson .40 1.00
172 Jerick McKinnon .25 .60
173 Stefon Diggs .30 .75
174 Kyle Rudolph .25 .60
175 Anthony Barr .25 .60
176 Everson Griffen .25 .60
177 Harrison Smith .25 .60
178 Fran Tarkenton .40 1.00
179 Martellus Bennett .25 .60
180 Tom Brady 1.00 2.50
181 Dion Lewis .25 .60
182 Rob Gronkowski .40 1.00
183 Julian Edelman .40 1.00
184 Danny Amendola .30 .75
185 Jamie Collins .25 .60
186 Stephen Gostkowski .30 .75
187 Steve Grogan .25 .60
188 Malcolm Butler .40 1.00
189 Drew Brees .40 1.00
190 Mark Ingram .30 .75
191 Brandin Cooks .30 .75
192 Willie Snead .30 .75
193 Coby Fleener .25 .60
194 Kenny Vaccaro .25 .60
195 Delvin Breaux RC .30 .75
196 Cameron Jordan .25 .60
197 Archie Manning .30 .75
198 Olivier Vernon .25 .60
199 Eli Manning .30 .75
200 Rashad Jennings .25 .60
201 Victor Cruz .30 .75
202 Dominique Rodgers-Cromartie .25 .60
203 Odell Beckham Jr. .40 1.00
204 Shane Vereen .30 .75
205 Rueben Randle .25 .60

206 Landon Collins .25 .60
207 Lawrence Taylor .40 1.00
208 Matt Forte .25 .60
209 Ryan Fitzpatrick .25 .60
210 Nick Mangold .25 .60
211 Brandon Marshall .25 .60
212 Eric Decker .25 .60
213 David Harris .25 .60
214 Muhammad Wilkerson .25 .60
215 Darrelle Revis .25 .60
216 Joe Namath .50 1.25
217 Derek Carr .40 1.00
218 Latavius Murray .25 .60
219 Amari Cooper .40 1.00
220 Michael Crabtree .25 .60
221 Seth Roberts .30 .75
222 Khalil Mack .40 1.00
223 Malcolm Smith .40 1.00
224 Sebastian Janikowski .25 .60
225 Bo Jackson .50 1.25
226 Malcolm Jenkins .30 .75
227 Sam Bradford .25 .60
228 Ryan Mathews .30 .75
229 Darren Sproles .30 .75
230 Jordan Matthews .30 .75
231 Zach Ertz .30 .75
232 Brent Celek .25 .60
233 Fletcher Cox .25 .60
234 Ron Jaworski .30 .75
235 Ben Roethlisberger .40 1.00
236 DeAngelo Williams .25 .60
237 Le'Veon Bell .30 .75
238 Antonio Brown .40 1.00
239 Markus Wheaton .25 .60
240 Cameron Heyward .25 .60
241 Ryan Shazier .25 .60
242 James Harrison .30 .75
243 Lawrence Timmons .30 .75
244 Terry Bradshaw .50 1.25
245 Travis Benjamin .25 .60
246 Philip Rivers .40 1.00
247 Melvin Gordon .30 .75
248 Danny Woodhead .30 .75
249 Keenan Allen .30 .75
250 Antonio Gates .25 .60
251 Steve Johnson .30 .75
252 Melvin Ingram .25 .60
253 LaDainian Tomlinson .30 .75
254 Eric Reid .30 .75
255 Colin Kaepernick .30 .75
256 Blaine Gabbert .25 .60
257 Carlos Hyde .25 .60
258 Shaun Draughn RC .30 .75
259 Torrey Smith .25 .60
260 Ahmad Brooks .25 .60
261 NaVorro Bowman .30 .75
262 Joe Montana 1.00 2.50
263 Russell Wilson .50 1.25
264 Thomas Rawls .25 .60
265 Kam Chancellor .40 1.00
266 Doug Baldwin .30 .75
267 Tyler Lockett .30 .75
268 Jermaine Kearse .25 .60
269 Jimmy Graham .40 1.00
270 Richard Sherman .40 1.00
271 Michael Bennett RC .25 .60
272 Steve Largent .40 1.00
273 Jameis Winston .40 1.00
274 Doug Martin .30 .75
275 Brent Grimes .25 .60
276 Mike Evans .30 .75
277 Austin Seferian-Jenkins .25 .60
278 Vincent Jackson .25 .60
279 Gerald McCoy .25 .60
280 Kwon Alexander .25 .60
281 Warren Sapp .30 .75
282 Rishard Matthews .25 .60
283 DeMarco Murray .30 .75
284 Marcus Mariota .40 1.00
285 Kendall Wright .25 .60
286 Delanie Walker .25 .60
287 Dorial Green-Beckham .25 .60
288 Jurrell Casey .25 .60
289 Brian Orakpo .25 .60
290 Avery Williamson .25 .60
291 Eddie George .30 .75
292 Kirk Cousins .40 1.00
293 Matt Jones .30 .75
294 Jordan Reed .25 .60
295 DeSean Jackson .30 .75
296 Jamison Crowder .25 .60
297 Ryan Kerrigan .25 .60
298 Pierre Garcon .30 .75
299 John Riggins .30 .75
300 Bashaud Breeland .25 .60
301 Adam Gotsis RC .40 1.00
302 Adolphus Washington RC .40 1.00
303 Artie Burns RC .50 1.25
304 A'Shawn Robinson RC .40 1.00
305 Austin Johnson RC .40 1.00
306 Bronson Kaufusi RC .40 1.00
307 Carl Nassib RC .40 1.00
308 Charles Tapper RC .50 1.25
309 Chris Jones RC .40 1.00
310 Cyrus Jones RC .40 1.00
311 Darron Lee RC .40 1.00
312 DeForest Buckner RC .40 1.00
313 Deion Jones RC .40 1.00
314 Derek Watt RC .60 1.50
315 Emmanuel Ogbah RC .50 1.25
316 Eric Murray RC .40 1.00
317 Glenn Gronkowski RC .40 1.00
318 Jake Rudock RC .40 1.00
319 James Bradberry RC .50 1.25
320 Jarran Reed RC .40 1.00
321 Jihad Ward RC .40 1.00
322 Jonathan Bullard RC .40 1.00
323 Kamalei Correa RC .40 1.00
324 Karl Joseph RC .40 1.00
325 Keanu Neal RC .40 1.00
326 KeiVarae Russell RC .40 1.00
327 Kendall Fuller RC .50 1.25
328 Kenny Clark RC .40 1.00
329 Kevin Dodd RC .40 1.00
330 Leonard Floyd RC .50 1.25
331 Mackensie Alexander RC .40 1.00
332 Maliek Collins RC .40 1.00
333 Moritz Bohringer RC .40 1.00
334 Noah Spence RC .40 1.00
335 Reggie Ragland RC .40 1.00
336 Robert Nkemdiche RC .50 1.25
337 Roberto Aguayo RC .40 1.00
338 Sean Davis RC .40 1.00
339 Shaq Lawson RC .40 1.00
340 Sheldon Rankins RC .50 1.25
341 Shilique Calhoun RC .40 1.00
342 Su'a Cravens RC .40 1.00
343 T.J. Green RC .60 1.50
344 Vernon Butler RC .40 1.00
345 Vernon Hargreaves III RC .60 1.50
346 Vonn Bell RC .50 1.25
347 Will Redmond RC .60 1.50
348 William Jackson III RC .50 1.25
349 Xavien Howard RC .50 1.25
350 Yannick Ngakoue RC .60 1.50
351 Alex Collins RR RC .50 1.25
352 Austin Hooper RR RC .40 1.00
353 Braxton Miller RR RC .40 1.00
354 C.J. Prosise RR RC .40 1.00
355 Cardale Jones RR RC .40 1.00
356 Carson Wentz RR RC 4.00 10.00
357 Chris Moore RR RC .50 1.25
358 Christian Hackenberg RR RC .40 1.00
359 Cody Kessler RR RC .40 1.00
360 Connor Cook RR RC .50 1.25
361 Corey Coleman RR RC .60 1.50
362 Dak Prescott RR RC 2.00 5.00
363 DeAndre Washington RR RC .40 1.00
364 Demarcus Robinson RR RC .40 1.00
365 Derrick Henry RR RC 1.00 2.50
366 Devontae Booker RR RC .50 1.25
367 Eli Apple RR RC .50 1.25
368 Ezekiel Elliott RR RC 2.00 5.00
369 Hunter Henry RR RC .50 1.25
370 Jacoby Brissett RR RC .50 1.25
371 Jalen Ramsey RR RC .60 1.50
372 Jared Goff RR RC 2.50 6.00
373 Jaylon Smith RR RC .40 1.00
374 Jeff Driskel RR RC .40 1.00
375 Joey Bosa RR RC .75 2.00
376 Jonathan Williams RR RC .50 1.25
377 Jordan Howard RR RC 1.00 2.50
378 Josh Doctson RR RC .50 1.25
379 Keenan Reynolds RR RC .50 1.25
380 Kenneth Dixon RR RC .40 1.00
381 Kenyan Drake RR RC .60 1.50
382 Kevin Hogan RR RC .50 1.25
383 Laquon Treadwell RR RC .50 1.25
384 Leonte Carroo RR RC .40 1.00
385 Malcolm Mitchell RR RC .40 1.00
386 Michael Thomas RR RC .75 2.00
387 Myles Jack RR RC .50 1.25
388 Nick Vannett RR RC .40 1.00
389 Paul Perkins RR RC .40 1.00
390 Paxton Lynch RR RC .40 1.00
391 Pharoh Cooper RR RC .40 1.00
392 Rashard Higgins RR RC .40 1.00
393 Ricardo Louis RR RC .40 1.00
394 Sterling Shepard RR RC .50 1.25
395 Tajae Sharpe RR RC .50 1.25
396 Trevor Davis RR RC .40 1.00
397 Tyler Boyd RR RC .50 1.25
398 Tyler Ervin RR RC .40 1.00
399 Wendell Smallwood RR RC .40 1.00
400 Will Fuller RR RC .60 1.50

2016 Donruss Aqueous Test
*VETS: 1.5X TO 4X BASIC CARDS
*ROOKIES: 1X TO 2.5X BASIC CARDS

2016 Donruss Press Proofs Blue
*VETS: .6X TO 1.5X BASIC CARDS
*ROOKIES: .6X TO 1.5X BASIC CARDS

2016 Donruss Press Proofs Gold
*VETS/50: 2X TO 5X BASIC CARDS
*ROOKIES/50: 1.25X TO 3X BASIC CARDS

2016 Donruss Press Proofs Gold Die Cut
*VETS/25: 2.5X TO 6X BASIC CARDS
*ROOKIES/25: 1.5X TO 4X BASIC CARDS

2016 Donruss Press Proofs Green
*VETS: 1X TO 2.5X BASIC CARDS
*ROOKIES: .8X TO 2X BASIC CARDS

2016 Donruss Press Proofs Red
*VETS: 1X TO 2.5X BASIC CARDS
*ROOKIES: .8X TO 2X BASIC CARDS

2016 Donruss Press Proofs Silver
*VETS/100: 1.5X TO 4X BASIC CARDS
*ROOKIES/100: 1X TO 2.5X BASIC CARDS

2016 Donruss Press Proofs Silver Die Cut
*VETS/75: 1.5X TO 4X BASIC CARDS
*ROOKIES/75: 1X TO 2.5X BASIC CARDS

2016 Donruss Stat Line Season
*VETS/200-400: 1X TO 2.5X BASIC CARDS
*VETS/100-199: 1.2X TO 3X BASIC CARDS
*VETS/61-99: 1.5X TO 4X BASIC CARDS
*VETS/35-60: 2X TO 5X BASIC CARDS
*VETS/25-34: 2.5X TO 6X BASIC CARDS
*VETS/15-24: 3X TO 86X BASIC CARDS
*ROOKIES/200-400: .6X TO 1.5X BASIC CARDS
*ROOKIES/100-198: .8X TO 2X BASIC CARDS
*ROOKIES/61-98: 1X TO 2.5X BASIC CARDS
*ROOKIES/35-60: 1.2X TO 3X BASIC CARDS
*ROOKIES/26-34: 1.5X TO 4X BASIC CARDS
*ROOKIES/15-24: 2X TO 5X BASIC CARDS
356 Carson Wentz/294 RR 10.00 25.00
362 Dak Prescott/316 RR 10.00 25.00
368 Ezekiel Elliott/289 RR 10.00 25.00

2016 Donruss 1987 Classics
*HOLO/100: 1.5X TO 4X BASIC INSERTS
1 Jerry Rice 1.00 2.50
2 Eric Dickerson .50 1.25
3 Warren Moon .60 1.50
4 Bruce Smith .50 1.25
5 Mike Singletary .60 1.50
6 Ronnie Lott .50 1.25
7 Joe Montana 1.50 4.00
8 John Elway 1.00 2.50
9 Steve Largent .60 1.50
10 Lawrence Taylor .60 1.50
11 Darrell Green .50 1.25
12 Randall Cunningham .50 1.25
13 Marcus Allen .50 1.25
14 Jim Kelly .60 1.50
15 Dan Marino 1.25 3.00
16 Charles Haley .60 1.50
17 Jim McMahon .50 1.25
18 Andre Reed .50 1.25
19 Bo Jackson .75 2.00
20 Tony Dorsett .60 1.50

2016 Donruss All Pros
*HOLO/100: 1.5X TO 4X BASIC INSERTS
1 Cam Newton .60 1.50
2 Adrian Peterson .60 1.50
3 Doug Martin .50 1.25
4 Mike Tolbert .40 1.00
5 Rob Gronkowski .60 1.50
6 Antonio Brown .60 1.50
7 Julio Jones .60 1.50
8 J.J. Watt .60 1.50
9 Khalil Mack .60 1.50
10 Aaron Donald .60 1.50
11 Geno Atkins .40 1.00
12 Von Miller .50 1.25
13 Tyrann Mathieu .50 1.25
14 Luke Kuechly .50 1.25
15 NaVorro Bowman .50 1.25
16 Patrick Peterson .40 1.00
17 Josh Norman .40 1.00
18 Eric Berry .50 1.25
19 Tyler Lockett .50 1.25
20 Stephen Gostkowski .50 1.25

2016 Donruss All Time Gridiron Kings
*STUDIO/250: .6X TO 1.5X BASIC INSERTS
1 Troy Aikman .75 2.00
2 Brett Favre 1.25 3.00
3 Jack Ham .50 1.25
4 Charles Woodson .60 1.50
5 Edgerrin James .50 1.25
6 Marshall Faulk .50 1.25
7 Jerome Bettis .60 1.50
8 Charles Haley .60 1.50
9 Steve Young .75 2.00
10 Jim Plunkett .50 1.25
11 Joe Montana 1.50 4.00
12 Darrell Green .50 1.25
13 Joe Namath .75 2.00
14 Eddie George .50 1.25
15 Emmitt Smith 1.00 2.50
16 Joe Greene .60 1.50
17 Barry Sanders 1.00 2.50
18 Ron Jaworski .50 1.25
19 Andre Reed .50 1.25
20 Earl Campbell .60 1.50
21 Lawrence Taylor .60 1.50
22 Franco Harris .60 1.50
23 Tim Brown .60 1.50
24 Ed Reed .50 1.25
25 Jerry Rice 1.00 2.50
26 Peyton Manning 1.25 3.00
27 Dan Marino 1.25 3.00
28 Warren Moon .60 1.50
29 Hines Ward .50 1.25
30 Eric Dickerson .50 1.25

2016 Donruss Canton Kings Jerseys
*STUDIO/25: .6X TO 1.5X BASIC JSY
1 Barry Sanders 5.00 12.00
2 Dan Marino 8.00 20.00
3 Earl Campbell 3.00 8.00
4 Jerome Bettis 3.00 8.00
5 Jerry Rice 5.00 12.00
6 Joe Namath 8.00 20.00
7 John Elway 5.00 12.00
8 Junior Seau 2.50 6.00
9 Larry Csonka 2.50 6.00
11 Len Dawson 3.00 8.00
12 Marcus Allen 2.50 6.00
13 Marshall Faulk 2.50 6.00
14 Marvin Harrison 2.50 6.00
15 Roger Staubach 4.00 10.00
16 Ronnie Lott 2.50 6.00
17 Steve Young 4.00 10.00
18 Thurman Thomas 2.50 6.00
19 Tony Dorsett 3.00 8.00
20 Warren Moon 3.00 8.00

2016 Donruss Changing Stripes Jerseys
*PRIME/25: .6X TO 1.5X BASIC JSY
1 Amari Cooper 3.00 8.00
2 Andrew Luck 4.00 10.00
3 Odell Beckham Jr. 3.00 8.00
4 Darren McFadden 2.00 5.00
5 DeMarcus Ware 2.50 6.00
6 Derek Carr 3.00 8.00
7 DeSean Jackson 2.50 6.00
8 Emmanuel Sanders 3.00 8.00
9 Eric Decker 2.00 5.00
10 Jameis Winston 3.00 8.00
11 Jeremy Maclin 2.00 5.00
12 Jimmy Graham 3.00 8.00
13 Joe Montana 15.00 40.00
14 Kevin White 2.00 5.00
15 LeSean McCoy 3.00 8.00
16 Marcus Allen 2.50 6.00
17 Marcus Mariota 8.00 20.00
18 Sam Bradford 2.00 5.00
19 T.J. Yeldon 2.00 5.00
20 Todd Gurley 3.00 8.00

2016 Donruss Dominators
1 Dez Bryant 1.00 2.50
2 Eli Manning .75 2.00
3 Zach Ertz .75 2.00
4 Jordan Reed .60 1.50
5 Patrick Peterson .60 1.50
6 NaVorro Bowman .75 2.00
7 Russell Wilson 1.25 3.00
8 Todd Gurley 1.00 2.50
9 Jeremy Langford .75 2.00
10 Matthew Stafford .75 2.00
11 Aaron Rodgers 2.00 5.00
12 Adrian Peterson 1.00 2.50
13 Matt Ryan .75 2.00
14 Cam Newton 1.00 2.50
15 Drew Brees 1.00 2.50
16 Doug Martin .75 2.00
17 Sammy Watkins 1.00 2.50
18 Jarvis Landry .75 2.00
19 Tom Brady 2.50 6.00
20 Brandon Marshall .60 1.50
21 Peyton Manning 2.00 5.00
22 Travis Kelce 1.00 2.50
23 Amari Cooper 1.00 2.50
24 Philip Rivers 1.00 2.50
25 Joe Flacco .75 2.00
26 Andy Dalton .75 2.00
27 Gary Barnidge .60 1.50
28 Antonio Brown 1.00 2.50
29 DeAndre Hopkins .75 2.00
30 J.J. Watt 1.00 2.50
31 Andrew Luck 1.25 3.00
32 T.J. Yeldon .60 1.50
33 Marcus Mariota 1.00 2.50
34 Greg Olsen .75 2.00
35 Kirk Cousins 1.00 2.50
36 Clay Matthews 1.00 2.50
37 Rob Gronkowski 1.00 2.50
38 Tyler Lockett .75 2.00
39 Jason Witten .75 2.00
40 Derek Carr 1.00 2.50

2016 Donruss Dominators Autographs
2 Antonio Brown/15 30.00 60.00
5 Patrick Peterson/100 4.00 10.00
6 Clay Matthews/25 EXCH 20.00 50.00
7 DeAndre Hopkins/75 12.00 30.00
8 Zach Ertz/100 5.00 12.00
9 Derek Carr/50 25.00 50.00
10 Travis Kelce/100 6.00 15.00

2016 Donruss Elite Series
1 Blake Bortles .60 1.50
2 Demaryius Thomas .75 2.00
3 Derek Carr 1.00 2.50
4 Eli Manning .75 2.00
5 Jordy Nelson .75 2.00
6 Darrelle Revis .60 1.50
7 Russell Wilson 1.25 3.00
8 Devonta Freeman .75 2.00
9 Adrian Peterson 1.00 2.50
10 Matthew Stafford .75 2.00
11 Antonio Brown 1.00 2.50
12 Allen Robinson .75 2.00
13 Doug Baldwin .75 2.00
14 Sammy Watkins 1.00 2.50
15 Ben Roethlisberger 1.00 2.50
16 Steve Smith Sr. .75 2.00
17 Jeremy Maclin .60 1.50
18 Tony Romo .75 2.00
19 Jameis Winston 1.00 2.50
20 Antonio Gates .60 1.50

2016 Donruss Elite Series Autographs
3 Derek Carr/25 25.00 60.00
4 Eli Manning/10 50.00 100.00
5 Jordy Nelson/50 15.00 40.00
6 Darrelle Revis/25 15.00 40.00
8 Devonta Freeman/50 6.00 15.00
10 Matthew Stafford/25 25.00 50.00
11 Antonio Brown/25 30.00 60.00
13 Doug Baldwin/20 25.00 50.00
16 Steve Smith Sr./25 15.00 40.00
20 Antonio Gates/25 6.00 15.00

2016 Donruss Elite Series Rookies
1 Jared Goff 4.00 10.00
2 Carson Wentz 6.00 15.00
3 Paxton Lynch .60 1.50
4 Ezekiel Elliott 3.00 8.00
5 Derrick Henry 1.50 4.00
6 C.J. Prosise .60 1.50
7 Laquon Treadwell .75 2.00
8 Josh Doctson .75 2.00
9 Will Fuller 1.00 2.50
10 Corey Coleman 1.00 2.50
11 Sterling Shepard .75 2.00
12 Hunter Henry .75 2.00
13 Joey Bosa 1.25 3.00
14 DeForest Buckner .60 1.50
15 A'Shawn Robinson .60 1.50
16 Myles Jack .75 2.00
17 Reggie Ragland .60 1.50
18 Jalen Ramsey 1.00 2.50
19 Vernon Hargreaves III 1.00 2.50
20 Moritz Bohringer .60 1.50

2016 Donruss Elite Series Rookies Autographs
1 Jared Goff/25 60.00 125.00
2 Carson Wentz/25 60.00 125.00
3 Paxton Lynch/25 6.00 15.00
4 Ezekiel Elliott/50 EXCH 75.00 150.00
5 Derrick Henry/25 40.00 80.00
6 C.J. Prosise/50 5.00 12.00
7 Laquon Treadwell/30 8.00 20.00
8 Josh Doctson/50 6.00 15.00
9 Will Fuller/50 8.00 20.00
10 Corey Coleman/50 8.00 20.00
11 Sterling Shepard/75 5.00 12.00
12 Hunter Henry/50 6.00 15.00
13 Joey Bosa/50 10.00 25.00
14 DeForest Buckner/50 5.00 12.00
15 A'Shawn Robinson/50 5.00 12.00
16 Myles Jack/75 5.00 12.00
17 Reggie Ragland/75 4.00 10.00
18 Jalen Ramsey/50 8.00 20.00
19 Vernon Hargreaves III/50 8.00 20.00
20 Moritz Bohringer/75 10.00 25.00

2016 Donruss Fans of the Game
*HOLO/100: .6X TO 1.5X BASIC INSERTS
1 Daisy Ridley 2.00 5.00
2 Al Pacino 2.00 5.00
3 Megan Fox 2.00 5.00
4 Skylar Astin 2.00 5.00
5 Daniella Monet 2.00 5.00
6 Marisa Miller 2.00 5.00
7 Darryl McDaniels 2.00 5.00

2016 Donruss Fans of the Game Autographs
1 Daisy Ridley SP 100.00 200.00
2 Al Pacino SP 30.00 80.00
3 Megan Fox SP 50.00 100.00
4 Skylar Astin 6.00 15.00
5 Daniella Monet 15.00 40.00
6 Marisa Miller 10.00 25.00
7 Darryl McDaniels 8.00 20.00

2016 Donruss Gridiron Kings
*STUDIO/250: 1X TO 2.5X BASIC INSERTS
1 Tony Romo .50 1.25
2 Odell Beckham Jr. .60 1.50
3 Tom Brady 1.50 4.00
4 Cam Newton .60 1.50
5 Marcus Mariota .60 1.50
6 Aaron Rodgers 1.25 3.00
7 Jeremy Maclin .40 1.00
8 Julio Jones .60 1.50
9 Andrew Luck .75 2.00
10 Philip Rivers .60 1.50
11 Ben Roethlisberger .60 1.50
12 Kirk Cousins .60 1.50
13 Blake Bortles .40 1.00
14 Rob Gronkowski .60 1.50
15 Todd Gurley .60 1.50
16 Russell Wilson .75 2.00
17 Clay Matthews .60 1.50
18 Le'Veon Bell .50 1.25
19 NaVorro Bowman .50 1.25
20 Dez Bryant .60 1.50
21 Adrian Peterson .60 1.50
22 DeMarco Murray .50 1.25
23 Matthew Stafford .50 1.25
24 Brandon Marshall .40 1.00
25 A.J. Green .60 1.50
26 Sammy Watkins .60 1.50
27 Luke Kuechly .50 1.25
28 Joe Flacco .50 1.25
29 Drew Brees .60 1.50
30 J.J. Watt .60 1.50
31 Devonta Freeman .50 1.25
32 Travis Benjamin .40 1.00
33 Ryan Tannehill .50 1.25
34 Larry Fitzgerald .50 1.25
35 Jay Cutler .40 1.00
36 Allen Robinson .50 1.25
37 Teddy Bridgewater .50 1.25
38 Von Miller .50 1.25
39 Amari Cooper .60 1.50
40 Jameis Winston .60 1.50

2016 Donruss Gridiron Kings Autographs
2 Marcus Mariota/16 60.00 125.00
4 Andrew Luck/15 50.00 100.00
5 Philip Rivers/15 15.00 40.00
6 Kirk Cousins/25 20.00 50.00
7 Blake Bortles/25 15.00 40.00
9 Clay Matthews/50 EXCH 20.00 50.00
10 Dez Bryant/25 EXCH 30.00 60.00
11 Matthew Stafford/15 15.00 40.00
12 A.J. Green/30 12.00 30.00
14 Luke Kuechly/50 15.00 40.00
15 Drew Brees/15 50.00 100.00
17 Teddy Bridgewater/25 12.00 30.00
18 Von Miller/25 15.00 40.00
19 Amari Cooper/25 EXCH 20.00 50.00
20 Jameis Winston/15 40.00 80.00

2016 Donruss Jersey Kings
*STUDIO/25: .6X TO 1.5X BASIC JSY
1 A.J. Green 3.00 8.00
2 Aaron Rodgers 6.00 15.00
3 Adrian Peterson 3.00 8.00
4 Andrew Luck 4.00 10.00
5 Antonio Brown 3.00 8.00
6 Ben Roethlisberger 6.00 15.00
7 Blake Bortles 2.00 5.00
8 Cam Newton 3.00 8.00
9 Darrelle Revis 2.00 5.00
10 Jameis Winston 3.00 8.00
11 DeMarcus Ware 2.50 6.00
12 Dez Bryant 3.00 8.00
13 Drew Brees 3.00 8.00
14 Eli Manning 2.50 6.00
15 Eric Berry 2.50 6.00
16 Giovani Bernard 2.00 5.00
17 J.J. Watt 3.00 8.00
18 Jarvis Landry 2.50 6.00
19 Jay Cutler 2.00 5.00
20 Jeremy Hill 2.00 5.00
21 Joe Flacco 2.50 6.00
22 Jonathan Stewart 2.00 5.00
23 Jordan Reed 2.00 5.00
24 Julian Edelman 3.00 8.00
25 Julio Jones 3.00 8.00
26 Khalil Mack 3.00 8.00
27 Kirk Cousins 3.00 8.00
28 Marcus Mariota 3.00 8.00
29 Larry Fitzgerald 2.50 6.00
30 Mark Ingram 2.50 6.00
31 Matt Ryan 2.50 6.00
32 Odell Beckham Jr. 3.00 8.00
33 Peyton Manning 6.00 15.00
34 Philip Rivers 3.00 8.00
35 Russell Wilson 4.00 10.00
36 Ryan Tannehill 2.50 6.00
37 Sam Bradford 2.00 5.00
38 T.Y. Hilton 2.50 6.00
39 Tom Brady 8.00 20.00
40 Tony Romo 2.50 6.00

2016 Donruss Leather Kings
1 Amari Cooper 3.00 8.00
2 Andrew Luck 4.00 10.00
3 David Johnson 3.00 8.00
4 Jameis Winston 3.00 8.00
5 Todd Gurley 3.00 8.00
6 Tyler Lockett 2.50 6.00
7 Marcus Mariota 3.00 8.00
8 Odell Beckham Jr. 3.00 8.00
9 Russell Wilson 4.00 10.00
10 Tom Brady 8.00 20.00

2016 Donruss Legends of the Fall
*HOLO/100: 1.5X TO 4X BASIC INSERTS
1 Joe Namath .75 2.00
2 Adam Vinatieri .50 1.25
3 Eli Manning .50 1.25
4 Terry Bradshaw .75 2.00
5 Tom Brady 1.50 4.00
6 Roger Staubach .75 2.00
7 John Elway 1.00 2.50
8 Drew Brees .60 1.50
9 Joe Montana 1.50 4.00
10 Marcus Allen .50 1.25
11 James Harrison .50 1.25
12 Franco Harris .60 1.50
13 Peyton Manning 1.25 3.00
14 Brett Favre 1.25 3.00
15 Emmitt Smith 1.00 2.50
16 Thurman Thomas .50 1.25
17 Terrell Davis .50 1.25
18 Jerry Rice 1.00 2.50
19 Michael Irvin .60 1.50
20 Larry Fitzgerald .50 1.25
21 Ray Lewis .60 1.50
22 Russell Wilson .75 2.00
23 Kurt Warner .50 1.25
24 Steve Young .75 2.00

2016 Donruss Passing the Torch Jerseys
*PRIME/25: .8X TO 2X BASIC JSY
1 A.Abdullah/B.Sanders 8.00 20.00
2 D.Funchess/S.Smith 2.50 6.00
3 K.Williams/L.McCoy 3.00 8.00
4 D.Moncrief/M.Harrison 2.50 6.00
5 J.Ajayi/L.Miller 2.50 6.00
6 C.Carter/S.Diggs 3.00 8.00
7 L.Tmlnsn/M.Grdn 2.50 6.00
8 J.Crowder/P.Garcon 2.50 6.00
9 M.Ingram/R.Williams 2.50 6.00
10 D.McFadden/D.Murray 2.50 6.00
11 G.Bernard/J.Hill 2.00 5.00
12 D.Martin/W.Dunn 2.50 6.00
13 M.Faulk/T.Gurley 3.00 8.00
14 A.Boldin/B.Perriman 2.00 5.00
15 J.Jones/R.White 3.00 8.00
16 D.Parker/J.Landry 2.50 6.00
17 D.Freeman/S.Jackson 2.50 6.00
18 D.Johnson/I.Crowell 2.00 5.00
19 J.Matthews/N.Agholor 2.50 6.00
20 D.Ware/V.Miller 2.50 6.00

2016 Donruss Peyton Manning Top Targets
*HOLO/100: 1X TO 2.5X BASIC INSERTS
1 M.Harrison/P.Manning 1.50 4.00
2 P.Manning/R.Wayne 1.50 4.00
3 D.Clark/P.Manning 1.50 4.00
4 D.Thomas/P.Manning 1.50 4.00
5 E.James/P.Manning 1.50 4.00
6 E.Decker/P.Manning 1.50 4.00
7 E.Sanders/P.Manning 1.50 4.00
8 P.Manning/W.Welker 1.50 4.00
9 J.Thomas/P.Manning 1.50 4.00
10 P.Manning/P.Garcon 1.50 4.00

2016 Donruss Peyton Manning Top Targets Dual Autographs
1 M.Harrison/P.Manning EXCH 75.00 150.00
2 P.Manning/R.Wayne 75.00 150.00
3 D.Clark/P.Manning 75.00 150.00
4 D.Thomas/P.Manning 75.00 150.00
5 E.James/P.Manning 75.00 150.00

2016 Donruss Peyton Manning Tribute
*HOLO/100: 1X TO 2.5X BASIC INSERTS

2016 Donruss Peyton Manning Tribute Autographs
1 Peyton Manning 60.00 125.00
2 Peyton Manning 60.00 125.00
3 Peyton Manning 60.00 125.00
4 Peyton Manning 60.00 125.00
5 Peyton Manning 60.00 125.00

2016 Donruss Pro Bowl Kings Jerseys
*STUDIO/25: .8X TO 2X BASIC JSY
1 Andy Dalton 2.50 6.00
2 Golden Tate III 2.00 5.00
3 Bob Lilly 2.50 6.00
4 Charles Woodson 3.00 8.00
5 Dan Marino 6.00 15.00
6 DeMarcus Ware 2.50 6.00
7 Dwight Freeney 2.00 5.00
8 Eddie George 2.50 6.00
9 Emmanuel Sanders 3.00 8.00
10 Eric Weddle 2.00 5.00
11 Antonio Brown 3.00 8.00
12 J.J. Watt 3.00 8.00
13 Jason Witten 2.50 6.00
14 Jordy Nelson 2.50 6.00
15 Julio Jones 3.00 8.00
16 Kam Chancellor 3.00 8.00
17 Kurt Warner 2.50 6.00
18 Larry Fitzgerald 2.50 6.00
19 LeSean McCoy 3.00 8.00
20 Matthew Stafford 2.50 6.00
21 Maurice Jones-Drew 2.00 5.00
22 Maurkice Pouncey 2.00 5.00
23 Odell Beckham Jr. 3.00 8.00
24 Philip Rivers 3.00 8.00
25 Ryan Kerrigan 2.00 5.00
26 Ryan Mathews 2.50 6.00
27 Sebastian Janikowski 2.00 5.00
28 Tony Dorsett 3.00 8.00
29 Tony Romo 2.50 6.00
30 Tyron Smith 2.00 5.00

2016 Donruss Production Line Hits
*HOLO/100: 1.5X TO 4X BASIC INSERTS
1 J.J. Watt .60 1.50
2 NaVorro Bowman .50 1.25
3 Lavonte David .40 1.00
4 Reshad Jones .40 1.00
5 Paul Posluszny .40 1.00
6 Khalil Mack .60 1.50
7 Ezekiel Ansah .40 1.00
8 Carlos Dunlap .40 1.00
9 Von Miller .50 1.25
10 Sean Lee .50 1.25

2016 Donruss Production Line Touchdowns
*HOLO/100: 1.5X TO 4X BASIC INSERTS
1 Devonta Freeman .50 1.25
2 Adrian Peterson .60 1.50
3 DeAngelo Williams .40 1.00
4 Todd Gurley .60 1.50
5 Doug Baldwin .50 1.25
6 Brandon Marshall .40 1.00
7 Allen Robinson .50 1.25
8 Odell Beckham Jr. .60 1.50
9 Tyler Eifert .50 1.25
10 Rob Gronkowski .60 1.50
11 Jordan Reed .40 1.00
12 Tom Brady 1.50 4.00
13 Blake Bortles .40 1.00
14 Eli Manning .50 1.25
15 Cam Newton .60 1.50

2016 Donruss Production Line Yards
*HOLO/100: 1.5X TO 4X BASIC INSERTS
1 Adrian Peterson .60 1.50
2 Doug Martin .50 1.25
3 Todd Gurley .60 1.50
4 Darren McFadden .40 1.00
5 Chris Ivory .50 1.25
6 Julio Jones .60 1.50
7 Antonio Brown .60 1.50
8 DeAndre Hopkins .50 1.25
9 Brandon Marshall .40 1.00
10 Odell Beckham Jr. .60 1.50
11 Drew Brees .60 1.50
12 Philip Rivers .60 1.50
13 Tom Brady 1.50 4.00
14 Carson Palmer .50 1.25
15 Matt Ryan .50 1.25

2016 Donruss Rookie Phenom Jersey Autographs
1 Derrick Henry 10.00 25.00
2 Ezekiel Elliott 75.00 150.00
4 Devontae Booker 8.00 20.00
5 Kenyan Drake 6.00 15.00
6 Keenan Reynolds 5.00 12.00
7 Josh Doctson 5.00 12.00
8 Sterling Shepard 5.00 12.00
9 Tyler Boyd 12.00 30.00
10 Trevor Davis 4.00 10.00
11 Braxton Miller 4.00 10.00
12 Michael Thomas 8.00 20.00
13 Leonte Carroo 4.00 10.00
14 Moritz Bohringer 8.00 20.00
15 Jared Goff
16 Carson Wentz 50.00 100.00
17 Dak Prescott 30.00 60.00
18 DeAndre Washington 4.00 10.00
19 Cody Kessler 4.00 10.00
20 Joey Bosa 8.00 20.00

2016 Donruss Rookie Phenom Jerseys
1 Kenneth Dixon 1.25 3.00
2 Chris Moore 1.50 4.00
3 Keenan Reynolds 1.50 4.00
4 Cardale Jones 1.25 3.00
5 Jonathan Williams 1.50 4.00
6 Jordan Howard 3.00 8.00
7 Tyler Boyd 1.50 4.00
8 Cody Kessler 1.25 3.00
9 Corey Coleman 2.00 5.00
10 Ricardo Louis 1.25 3.00
11 Dak Prescott 6.00 15.00
12 Ezekiel Elliott 8.00 20.00
13 Paxton Lynch 1.25 3.00
14 Devontae Booker 1.50 4.00
15 Trevor Davis 1.25 3.00
16 Tyler Ervin 1.25 3.00
17 Braxton Miller 1.25 3.00
18 Will Fuller 2.00 5.00
19 Kevin Hogan 1.50 4.00
20 Demarcus Robinson 1.25 3.00
21 Jared Goff 8.00 20.00
22 Pharoh Cooper 1.25 3.00
23 Kenyan Drake 2.00 5.00
24 Leonte Carroo 1.25 3.00
25 Laquon Treadwell 1.50 4.00
26 DeAndre Washington 1.25 3.00
27 Hunter Henry 1.50 4.00
28 Michael Thomas 2.50 6.00
29 Paul Perkins 1.25 3.00
30 Sterling Shepard 1.50 4.00
31 Christian Hackenberg 1.25 3.00
32 Connor Cook 1.50 4.00
33 Carson Wentz 6.00 15.00
34 Wendell Smallwood 1.25 3.00
35 Joey Bosa 4.00 10.00
36 Moritz Bohringer 1.25 3.00
37 Alex Collins 1.50 4.00
38 C.J. Prosise 1.25 3.00
39 Derrick Henry 3.00 8.00
40 Josh Doctson 1.50 4.00

2016 Donruss Rookie Threads
1 Joey Bosa 2.50 6.00
2 Cardale Jones 1.25 3.00
3 Carson Wentz 6.00 15.00
4 Christian Hackenberg 1.25 3.00
5 Cody Kessler 1.25 3.00
6 Connor Cook 1.50 4.00
7 Dak Prescott 6.00 15.00
8 DeAndre Washington 1.25 3.00
9 Jared Goff 8.00 20.00
10 Kevin Hogan 1.50 4.00
11 Paxton Lynch 1.25 3.00
12 Alex Collins 1.50 4.00
13 C.J. Prosise 1.25 3.00
14 Derrick Henry 5.00 12.00
15 Devontae Booker 1.50 4.00
16 Ezekiel Elliott 8.00 20.00
17 Jonathan Williams 1.50 4.00
18 Jordan Howard 3.00 8.00
19 Kenneth Dixon 1.25 3.00
20 Kenyan Drake 2.00 5.00
21 Paul Perkins 1.25 3.00
22 Tyler Ervin 1.25 3.00
23 Wendell Smallwood 1.25 3.00
24 Hunter Henry 1.50 4.00
25 Braxton Miller 1.25 3.00
26 Chris Moore 1.50 4.00
27 Corey Coleman 2.00 5.00
28 Demarcus Robinson 1.25 3.00
29 Josh Doctson 1.50 4.00
30 Keenan Reynolds 1.50 4.00
31 Laquon Treadwell 1.50 4.00
32 Leonte Carroo 1.25 3.00
33 Moritz Bohringer 1.25 3.00
34 Michael Thomas 2.50 6.00
35 Pharoh Cooper 1.25 3.00
36 Ricardo Louis 1.25 3.00
37 Sterling Shepard 1.50 4.00
38 Trevor Davis 1.25 3.00
39 Tyler Boyd 1.50 4.00
40 Will Fuller 2.00 5.00

2016 Donruss Signature Marks
1 Daniel Braverman/25 6.00 15.00
2 Brandon Doughty/100 4.00 10.00
3 Wendell Smallwood/100 4.00 10.00
4 Kendall Fuller/25 8.00 20.00
5 Devontae Booker/50 6.00 15.00
6 Cody Kessler/50 5.00 12.00
7 Su'a Cravens/50 5.00 12.00
8 Tajae Sharpe/50 6.00 15.00
9 Myles Jack/50 6.00 15.00
10 Paul Perkins/50 5.00 12.00
11 Thomas Duarte/100 4.00 10.00
12 Josh Doctson/50 6.00 15.00
13 Kolby Listenbee/50 5.00 12.00
14 Kevin Dodd/35 5.00 12.00
15 Austin Hooper/50 5.00 12.00
16 Pharoh Cooper/50 5.00 12.00
17 Thomas Rawls/100 4.00 10.00
18 Russell Wilson/25 30.00 80.00
19 Leonte Carroo/50 5.00 12.00
20 Jerome Bettis/50 25.00 50.00
21 Antonio Brown/50 25.00 50.00
22 Terry Bradshaw/25 50.00 100.00
23 Zach Ertz/100 5.00 12.00
24 DeForest Buckner/50
25 Laquon Treadwell/50 30.00
26 Robert Nkemdiche/25 8.00 20.00
27 Emmanuel Ogbah/100 5.00 12.00
28 Sterling Shepard/50 6.00 15.00
29 Braxton Miller/50 5.00 12.00
30 Cardale Jones/25 25.00
32 Eli Apple/50 6.00 15.00
33 Ezekiel Elliott/25 75.00 150.00
34 Joey Bosa/25 12.00 30.00
35 Michael Thomas/50 10.00 25.00
36 Vonn Bell/100 5.00 12.00
37 Jaylon Smith/100 4.00 10.00
38 Will Fuller/50 8.00 20.00
39 Carson Wentz/25 60.00 150.00
40 Joe Namath/50 50.00 100.00
41 Drew Brees/25 25.00 50.00
42 Troy Brown/75 4.00 10.00
43 John Hannah/100 4.00 10.00
44 Jacoby Brissett/100 5.00 12.00
45 Keenan Reynolds/75 5.00 12.00
46 Dak Prescott/50 40.00 80.00
47 Adrian Peterson/25 EXCH 40.00 80.00
48 Aaron Burbridge/50 5.00 12.00
49 Connor Cook/50 6.00 15.00
52 Dan Marino/25 50.00 100.00
53 Paxton Lynch/50 5.00 12.00
54 Jeff Driskel/50 5.00 12.00
55 Eric Dickerson/50 15.00 40.00
56 Bo Jackson/50 40.00 80.00
57 Glenn Gronkowski/50 5.00 12.00
59 Blake Bortles/50 12.00 30.00
61 Marvin Harrison/50 EXCH 15.00 40.00
62 Jordan Howard/50 12.00 30.00
63 Brock Osweiler/50 5.00 12.00
64 Earl Campbell/25 15.00 40.00
65 Don Majkowski/100 12.00 30.00
66 Brett Favre/25 60.00 120.00
68 Jalen Ramsey/25 10.00 25.00
69 Demarcus Robinson/100 4.00 10.00
70 Kelvin Taylor/50 5.00 12.00
71 Vernon Hargreaves III/100 6.00 15.00
73 Jeremy Cash/25 8.00 20.00
74 Matthew Stafford/25 12.00 30.00
75 Darren McFadden/50 5.00 12.00
76 Rashard Higgins/50 5.00 12.00
77 Ozzie Newsome/50 6.00 15.00
78 Jayron Kearse/50 5.00 12.00
79 Mackensie Alexander/25 6.00 15.00
82 Jared Goff/25 50.00 100.00
83 Kenny Lawler/50 8.00 20.00
84 Trevor Davis/100 4.00 10.00
86 Corey Coleman/25 10.00 25.00
87 Ray Lewis/25 50.00 100.00
89 Cody Core/100 4.00 10.00
90 Alex Collins/40 6.00 15.00
91 Brandon Allen/100 4.00 10.00
92 Hunter Henry/100 5.00 12.00
93 Jonathan Williams/50 6.00 15.00
94 John Brown/50 6.00 15.00
95 A'Shawn Robinson/50 5.00 12.00
96 Derrick Henry/25 50.00 100.00
98 Kenyan Drake/50 8.00 20.00
99 Reggie Ragland/50 5.00 12.00
100 Moritz Bohringer/100 8.00 20.00

2016 Donruss Sophomore Swatches
*PRIME/25: .8X TO 2X BASIC JSY
1 Marcus Mariota 3.00 8.00
2 Jameis Winston 3.00 8.00
3 Ameer Abdullah 2.00 5.00
4 Buck Allen 2.00 5.00
5 Melvin Gordon 2.50 6.00
6 Todd Gurley 3.00 8.00
7 David Johnson 3.00 8.00
8 Matt Jones 2.50 6.00
9 Jeremy Langford 2.50 6.00
10 Karlos Williams 2.00 5.00
11 T.J. Yeldon 2.00 5.00
12 Sammie Coates 2.00 5.00
13 Amari Cooper 3.00 8.00
14 Jamison Crowder 2.00 5.00
15 Stefon Diggs 2.50 6.00
16 Phillip Dorsett 2.00 5.00
17 Devin Funchess 2.00 5.00
18 Dorial Green-Beckham 2.00 5.00
19 Tyler Lockett 2.50 6.00
20 Kevin White 2.00 5.00

2016 Donruss The Legends Series
1 Troy Aikman 1.25 3.00
2 Brett Favre 2.00 5.00
3 Kurt Warner .75 2.00
4 Barry Sanders 1.50 4.00
5 Emmitt Smith 1.50 4.00
6 Bo Jackson 1.25 3.00
7 Steve Largent 1.00 2.50
8 Fred Biletnikoff 1.00 2.50
9 Rod Woodson .75 2.00
10 Ray Lewis 1.00 2.50

2016 Donruss The Rookies
1 Jared Goff 4.00 10.00
2 Carson Wentz 6.00 15.00
3 Paxton Lynch .60 1.50
4 Christian Hackenberg .60 1.50
5 Cody Kessler .60 1.50
6 Connor Cook .75 2.00
7 Dak Prescott 5.00 12.00
8 Cardale Jones .60 1.50
9 Jacoby Brissett .75 2.00
10 Ezekiel Elliott 20.00 40.00
11 Derrick Henry 1.50 4.00
12 Kenyan Drake 1.00 2.50
13 C.J. Prosise .60 1.50
14 Tyler Ervin .60 1.50
15 Kenneth Dixon .60 1.50
16 Devontae Booker .75 2.00
17 Paul Perkins .60 1.50
18 Jordan Howard 1.50 4.00
19 Corey Coleman 1.00 2.50
20 Josh Doctson .75 2.00
21 Will Fuller 1.00 2.50
22 Laquon Treadwell .75 2.00
23 Sterling Shepard .75 2.00
24 Michael Thomas 1.25 3.00
25 Tyler Boyd .75 2.00
26 Braxton Miller .60 1.50
27 Leonte Carroo .60 1.50
28 Chris Moore .75 2.00
29 Malcolm Mitchell .60 1.50
30 Tajae Sharpe .75 2.00
31 Joey Bosa 1.25 3.00
32 Jalen Ramsey 1.00 2.50
33 DeForest Buckner .60 1.50
34 Sheldon Rankins .75 2.00
35 Myles Jack .75 2.00
36 Vernon Hargreaves III 1.00 2.50
37 Eli Apple .75 2.00
38 Jaylon Smith .60 1.50
39 Shaq Lawson .60 1.50
40 Darron Lee .60 1.50

2016 Donruss The Rookies Autographs
1 Ezekiel Elliott/100 EXCH 100.00 200.00
2 Jared Goff/50 40.00 80.00
3 Laquon Treadwell/100 5.00 12.00
4 Corey Coleman/150 5.00 12.00
5 Derrick Henry/50 12.00 30.00
6 Carson Wentz/50 75.00 125.00
7 Braxton Miller/100 4.00 10.00
8 Kenyan Drake/150 5.00 12.00
9 Will Fuller/150
10 Paxton Lynch/85 8.00 20.00

2016 Donruss Threads
*PRIME/25: .8X TO 2X BASIC JSY
1 Alex Smith 2.50 6.00
2 Allen Robinson 2.50 6.00
3 Amari Cooper 3.00 8.00
4 Andy Dalton 2.50 6.00
5 Brandin Cooks 2.50 6.00
6 Buck Allen 2.00 5.00
7 C.J. Anderson 2.50 6.00
8 Cam Newton 3.00 8.00
9 Carlos Hyde 2.00 5.00
10 Cole Beasley 3.00 8.00

11 Colin Kaepernick 2.50 6.00
12 Darren McFadden 2.00 5.00
13 Davante Adams 2.00 5.00
14 Larry Fitzgerald 2.50 6.00
15 Denard Robinson 2.00 5.00
16 Devin Funchess 2.00 5.00
17 Devonta Freeman 2.50 6.00
18 Dorial Green-Beckham 2.00 5.00
19 Earl Thomas III 2.50 6.00
20 Emmanuel Sanders 3.00 8.00
21 Geno Atkins 2.00 5.00
22 Jameis Winston 3.00 8.00
23 Jamison Crowder 2.00 5.00
24 Jeremy Langford 2.50 6.00
25 Jerry Hughes 2.00 5.00
26 Joe Haden 2.00 5.00
27 Terrance Williams 2.00 5.00
28 Junior Seau 2.50 6.00
29 Kelvin Benjamin 2.50 6.00
30 LeSean McCoy 3.00 8.00
31 Marcus Mariota 3.00 8.00
32 Ronnie Hillman 2.00 5.00
33 Ryan Kerrigan 2.00 5.00
34 Sammie Coates 2.00 5.00
35 Sammy Watkins 3.00 8.00
36 Stefon Diggs 2.50 6.00
37 T.J. Yeldon 2.00 5.00
38 Teddy Bridgewater 2.50 6.00
39 Tyler Eifert 2.50 6.00
40 Von Miller 2.50 6.00

2017 Donruss

1 J.J. Watt .40 1.00
2 Josh McCown .25 .60
3 Cameron Meredith .25 .60
4 Richard Sherman .40 1.00
5 C.J. Anderson .30 .75
6 Dan Fouts .30 .75
7 Ted Ginn Jr. .25 .60
8 Cody Kessler .25 .60
9 Mohamed Sanu .25 .60
10 Eli Manning .30 .75
11 Steve Smith .30 .75
12 DeAndre Washington .25 .60
13 Golden Tate III .25 .60
14 Ryan Tannehill .30 .75
15 Jalen Ramsey .25 .60
16 Michael Thomas .40 1.00
17 Tedy Bruschi .40 1.00
18 Antonio Brown .40 1.00
19 Cameron Brate .25 .60
20 A.J. Green .40 1.00
21 Larry Fitzgerald .30 .75
22 Joe Flacco .30 .75
23 Phil Simms .30 .75
24 Lorenzo Alexander .25 .60
25 Rob Gronkowski .40 1.00
26 Joe Haden .25 .60
27 Martellus Bennett .25 .60
28 Haloti Ngata .25 .60
29 Charles Sims .25 .60
30 Desmond Trufant .25 .60
31 Calvin Johnson .40 1.00
32 Bruce Smith .30 .75
33 Julian Edelman .40 1.00
34 Ben Roethlisberger .40 1.00
35 Cam Newton .40 1.00
36 Josh Norman .25 .60
37 Tyrann Mathieu .30 .75
38 Demaryius Thomas .30 .75
39 Dak Prescott .40 1.00
40 Frank Gore .30 .75
41 Theo Riddick .25 .60
42 Jason Pierre-Paul .25 .60
43 Terrell Suggs .25 .60
44 Allen Robinson .30 .75
45 Jared Goff .40 1.00
46 Xavier Rhodes .25 .60
47 Greg Olsen .30 .75
48 Julio Jones .40 1.00
49 Kwon Alexander .25 .60
50 Leonard Williams .25 .60
51 Robert Woods .30 .75
52 Jurrell Casey .25 .60
53 Ryan Shazier .25 .60
54 DeForest Buckner .25 .60
55 Eric Ebron .25 .60
56 Hunter Henry .25 .60
57 Marvin Jones Jr. .25 .60
58 Geno Atkins .25 .60
59 Aqib Talib .25 .60
60 Randy Moss .30 .75
61 Chris Hogan .25 .60
62 Alshon Jeffery .30 .75
63 Will Fuller V .25 .60
64 Tom Brady 1.00 2.50
65 Terrelle Pryor .25 .60
66 Chris Harris .25 .60
67 Carson Palmer .30 .75
68 Sam Bradford .25 .60
69 Danny Amendola .30 .75
70 Aaron Donald .40 1.00
71 Robby Anderson .25 .60
72 Ty Montgomery .25 .60
73 Kyle Long .25 .60
74 Giovani Bernard .25 .60
75 Janoris Jenkins .25 .60
76 David Johnson .40 1.00
77 Davante Adams .30 .75
78 Jamie Collins .25 .60
79 Carson Wentz .50 1.25
80 Mark Ingram .30 .75
81 Kenny Britt .25 .60
82 Jeremy Hill .25 .60
83 Eric Berry .30 .75
84 Navorro Bowman .30 .75
85 Cameron Wake .25 .60
86 Robert Kelley .25 .60
87 Matt Forte .25 .60
88 Marcell Dareus .25 .60
89 Carlos Dunlap .25 .60
90 Terrance Williams .25 .60
91 Quincy Enunwa .25 .60
92 Jimmy Graham .40 1.00
93 Darren Sproles .30 .75
94 Jonathan Stewart .25 .60
95 Patrick Peterson .25 .60
96 Troy Aikman .50 1.25
97 Bilal Powell .25 .60
98 Christian Okoye .25 .60
99 Terrance West .25 .60
100 Jordan Howard .40 1.00
101 Willie Roaf .25 .60
102 Cordarrelle Patterson .25 .60
103 Clay Matthews .30 .75
104 Keenan Allen .30 .75
105 Jay Ajayi .30 .75
106 J.J. Nelson .25 .60
107 Vic Beasley Jr. .25 .60
108 Marquise Goodwin .25 .60
109 Corey Coleman .25 .60
110 Tevin Coleman .30 .75
111 Adam Thielen .40 1.00
112 Latavius Murray .25 .60
113 Pierre Garcon .30 .75
114 Ezekiel Elliott .50 1.25
115 Emmanuel Sanders .40 1.00
116 Matthew Stafford .30 .75
117 Landon Collins .25 .60
118 Paul Hornung .40 1.00
119 Russell Wilson .50 1.25
120 Devonta Freeman .30 .75
121 Ha Ha Clinton-Dix .25 .60
122 Zach Ertz .30 .75
123 Deion Sanders .30 .75
124 Spencer Ware .25 .60
125 Jeremy Kerley .25 .60
126 Kamar Aiken .25 .60
127 Markus Wheaton .25 .60
128 Tyrell Williams .25 .60
129 Travis Kelce .40 1.00
130 Luke Kuechly .30 .75
131 Coby Fleener .25 .60
132 Kevin White .25 .60
133 Derek Carr .40 1.00
134 Torrey Smith .25 .60
135 Gerald McCoy .25 .60
136 Vontae Davis .25 .60
137 Thomas Davis .25 .60
138 Tavon Austin .25 .60
139 Jameis Winston .30 .75
140 Tajae Sharpe .25 .60
141 Trevor Siemian .25 .60
142 Jordan Matthews .25 .60
143 T.J. Yeldon .25 .60
144 Dan Marino .75 2.00
145 Brandon LaFell .25 .60
146 Jarvis Landry .30 .75
147 John Kuhn .25 .60
148 Charles Clay .25 .60
149 Melvin Gordon .30 .75
150 Cameron Jordan .25 .60
151 Devin Funchess .25 .60
152 Amari Cooper .40 1.00
153 DeSean Jackson .30 .75
154 Joey Bosa .40 1.00
155 Thomas Rawls .25 .60
156 Jesse James .25 .60
157 Marqise Lee .25 .60
158 LeSean McCoy .40 1.00
159 Julius Thomas .25 .60
160 Andrew Luck .50 1.25
161 Jordan Reed .25 .60
162 Jim Zorn .25 .60
163 Ed Reed .30 .75
164 Von Miller .30 .75
165 Rishard Matthews .25 .60
166 John Brown .30 .75
167 Boomer Esiason .30 .75
168 Brandon Marshall .25 .60
169 Jerick McKinnon .25 .60
170 Melvin Ingram .25 .60
171 Blake Bortles .25 .60
172 Austin Hooper .25 .60
173 Damon Harrison RC .25 .60
174 Allen Hurns .25 .60
175 Cole Beasley .40 1.00
176 Zach Brown .25 .60
177 Eli Rogers .25 .60
178 Ameer Abdullah .25 .60
179 James Harrison .30 .75
180 Paul Perkins .25 .60
181 Eddie Lacy .25 .60
182 C.J. Fiedorowicz .25 .60
183 Michael Crabtree .25 .60
184 Rich Gannon .25 .60
185 T.Y. Hilton .30 .75
186 Anthony Barr .25 .60
187 Franco Harris .40 1.00
188 Philip Rivers .40 1.00
189 C.J. Mosley .30 .75
190 Tyreek Hill .40 1.00
191 Mark Brunell .30 .75
192 Casey Hayward .25 .60
193 James White .30 .75
194 Chandler Jones .25 .60
195 Doug Martin .30 .75
196 Jamison Crowder .25 .60
197 Jadeveon Clowney .25 .60
198 Joe Theismann .40 1.00
199 A.J. Bouye RC .25 .60
200 Drew Brees .40 1.00
201 Randall Cobb .30 .75
202 Tyrod Taylor .30 .75
203 Jim Brown .50 1.25
204 Paul Posluszny .25 .60
205 Todd Gurley II .40 1.00
206 Joe Namath .50 1.25
207 Erik Walden .25 .60
208 Alfred Morris .25 .60
209 Jalen Richard .25 .60
210 Brian Cushing .25 .60
211 Sammy Watkins .40 1.00
212 Dee Ford .25 .60
213 Eddie George .30 .75
214 Marcus Mariota .40 1.00
215 Ryan Korrigan .25 .60
216 Doug Baldwin .30 .75
217 Peyton Manning .75 2.00
218 Kenny Stills .25 .60
219 Matt Ryan .30 .75
220 Josh Doctson .25 .60
221 Tyler Eifert .30 .75
222 Marcus Peters .25 .60
223 Brian Orakpo .25 .60
224 Alec Ogletree .25 .60
225 Mike Evans .30 .75
226 Donte Moncrief .30 .75
227 Carlos Hyde .25 .60
228 Jeremy Langford .30 .75
229 Johnny Unitas .60 1.50
230 Mike Glennon .30 .75
231 Derrick Henry .30 .75
232 Muhammad Wilkerson .25 .60
233 Brian Hoyer .25 .60
234 Kyle Juszczyk .25 .60
235 Julius Peppers .30 .75
236 Whitney Mercilus .25 .60
237 Walter Payton .75 2.00
238 Dennis Pitta .25 .60
239 Andy Dalton .30 .75
240 Dwayne Allen .25 .60
241 Marshawn Lynch .30 .75
242 Ottis Anderson .25 .60
243 Jack Doyle .25 .60
244 Brian Quick .25 .60
245 Dez Bryant .40 1.00
246 Sterling Shepard .30 .75
247 Odell Beckham Jr. .40 1.00
248 Dontrelle Inman RC .25 .60
249 Fletcher Cox .25 .60
250 Eric Decker .25 .60
251 Aaron Rodgers .75 2.00
252 Jeremy Maclin .25 .60
253 Jordy Nelson .30 .75
254 Danny Woodhead .30 .75
255 Derrick Brooks .25 .60
256 Le'Veon Bell .30 .75
257 Mark Barron .25 .60
258 Marshall Faulk .30 .75
259 Leonard Floyd .25 .60
260 Kelvin Benjamin .30 .75
261 Sean Lee .30 .75
262 Reggie White .40 1.00
263 Ndamukong Suh .30 .75
264 Cliff Avril .25 .60
265 Ezekiel Ansah .25 .60
266 Delanie Walker .25 .60
267 Willie Snead .30 .75
268 Brandin Cooks .30 .75
269 Khalil Mack .40 1.00
270 Duke Johnson .25 .60
271 Lamar Miller .25 .60
272 Jerry Rice .60 1.50
273 DeAndre Hopkins .30 .75
274 Adam Vinatieri .25 .60
275 Philly Brown .25 .60
276 Cameron Heyward .25 .60
277 Jason Witten .30 .75
278 Ryan Mathews .30 .75
279 Isaiah Crowell .25 .60
280 Devontae Booker .25 .60
281 DeMarco Murray .30 .75
282 DeVante Parker .30 .75
283 Tom Savage .25 .60
284 Harrison Smith .25 .60
285 Stefon Diggs .30 .75
286 Mike Wallace .25 .60
287 Bobby Wagner .25 .60
288 Kirk Cousins .40 1.00
289 Alex Smith .30 .75
290 Tony Romo .30 .75
291 Dontari Poe .25 .60
292 Adrian Peterson .40 1.00
293 Jerrell Freeman .25 .60
294 Jared Cook .25 .60
295 Jamaal Charles .30 .75
296 David Harris .25 .60
297 Eric Reid .30 .75
298 Joe Thomas .25 .60
299 Dont'a Hightower .25 .60
300 Martavis Bryant .25 .60
301 Josh Reynolds RR RC .40 1.00
302 Marlon Mack RR RC .60 1.50
303 ArDarius Stewart RR RC .40 1.00
304 DeShone Kizer RR RC .40 1.00
305 Chris Godwin RR RC .50 1.25
306 Samaje Perine RR RC .40 1.00
307 Amara Darboh RR RC .40 1.00
308 Joe Williams RR RC .40 1.00
309 Zay Jones RR RC .50 1.25
310 Brian Hill RR RC .40 1.00
311 Mack Hollins RR RC .40 1.00
312 Donnel Pumphrey RR RC .50 1.25
313 Chad Hansen RR RC .40 1.00
314 David Njoku RR RC .50 1.25
315 Taywan Taylor RR RC .40 1.00
316 Corey Davis RR RC .60 1.50
317 Jamaal Williams RR RC .40 1.00
318 Christian McCaffrey RR RC 1.00 2.50
319 Leonard Fournette RR RC 1.25 3.00
320 C.J. Beathard RR RC .40 1.00
321 Josh Malone RR RC .40 1.00
322 James Conner RR RC .75 2.00
323 Brad Kaaya RR RC .40 1.00
324 Mike Williams RR RC .60 1.50
325 Kenny Golladay RR RC .60 1.50
326 JuJu Smith-Schuster RR RC 1.00 2.50
327 Patrick Mahomes II RR RC 10.00 25.00
328 Mitchell Trubisky RR RC 2.00 5.00
329 Cooper Kupp RR RC .60 1.50
330 Evan Engram RR RC .50 1.25
331 R. Joshua Dobbs RR RC .50 1.25
332 Kareem Hunt RR RC .75 2.00
333 Shelton Gibson RR RC .40 1.00
334 Nathan Peterman RR RC .50 1.25
335 Joe Mixon RR RC .75 2.00
336 Carlos Henderson RR RC .40 1.00
337 Dede Westbrook RR RC .40 1.00
338 Wayne Gallman RR RC .50 1.25
339 Ryan Switzer RR RC .50 1.25
340 D'Onta Foreman RR RC .50 1.25
341 Noah Brown RR RC .50 1.25
342 O.J. Howard RR RC .50 1.25
343 Dalvin Cook RR RC 1.00 2.50
344 John Ross III RR RC .50 1.25
345 Deshaun Watson RR RC 2.50 6.00
346 Curtis Samuel RR RC .50 1.25
347 Malachi Dupre RR RC .40 1.00
348 Davis Webb RR RC .40 1.00
349 Alvin Kamara RR RC 1.50 4.00
350 Jeremy McNichols RR RC .40 1.00
351 Sidney Jones RC .40 1.00
352 Tre'Davious White RC .40 1.00
353 Zach Cunningham RC .50 1.25
354 Adam Shaheen RC .40 1.00
355 Jordan Leggett RC .40 1.00
356 Myles Garrett RC 1.25 3.00
357 Bucky Hodges RC .40 1.00
358 Derek Barnett RC .50 1.25
359 Matthew Dayes RC .40 1.00
360 Jarrad Davis RC .50 1.25
361 Quincy Wilson RC .40 1.00
362 Taco Charlton RC .40 1.00
363 Chidobe Awuzie RC .50 1.25
364 Chad Williams RC .40 1.00
365 Jeremy Sprinkle RC .40 1.00
366 Solomon Thomas RC .40 1.00
367 Robert Davis RC .40 1.00
368 Malik Hooker RC .40 1.00
369 Chad Kelly RC .40 1.00
370 Charles Harris RC .40 1.00
371 DeMarcus Walker RC .40 1.00
372 T.J. Watt RC 1.25 3.00
373 Dawuane Smoot RC .40 1.00
374 Jonnu Smith RC .40 1.00
375 Trent Taylor RC .50 1.25
376 Jamal Adams RC .40 1.00
377 Stacy Coley RC .40 1.00
378 Marlon Humphrey RC .40 1.00
379 Kevin King RC .50 1.25
380 Gareon Conley RC .40 1.00
381 Raekwon McMillan RC .40 1.00
382 Reuben Foster RC .40 1.00
383 Jordan Willis RC .40 1.00
384 Tarik Cohen RC .75 2.00
385 Aaron Jones RC 1.00 2.50
386 Marshon Lattimore RC .50 1.25
387 Isaiah Ford RC .40 1.00
388 Jonathan Allen RC .50 1.25
389 Malik McDowell RC .40 1.00
390 Jabrill Peppers RC .60 1.50
391 Obi Melifonwu RC .40 1.00
392 Gerald Everett RC .40 1.00
393 Chris Wormley RC .40 1.00
394 Jake Butt RC .50 1.25
395 Elijah McGuire RC .40 1.00
396 Haason Reddick RC .40 1.00
397 Elijah Hood RC .40 1.00
398 Adoree' Jackson RC .50 1.25
399 Budda Baker RC .40 1.00
400 Takkarist McKinley RC .40 1.00

2017 Donruss Aqueous Test

*VETS: 2X TO 5X BASIC CARDS
*ROOKIES: 1X TO 2.5X BASIC CARDS
327 Patrick Mahomes II RR 30.00 80.00

2017 Donruss Press Proofs Blue

*VETS: .6X TO 1.5X BASIC CARDS
*ROOKIES: .6X TO 1.5X BASIC CARDS

2017 Donruss Press Proofs Bronze

*VETS: 1X TO 2.5X BASIC CARDS
*ROOKIES: .8X TO 2X BASIC CARDS

2017 Donruss Press Proofs Gold

*VETS/50: 2X TO 5X BASIC CARDS
*ROOKIES/50: 1.25X TO 3X BASIC CARDS

2017 Donruss Press Proofs Gold Die Cut

*VETS/25: 2.5X TO 6X BASIC CARDS
*ROOKIES/25: 1.5X TO 4X BASIC CARDS

2017 Donruss Press Proofs Green

*VETS: 1X TO 2.5X BASIC CARDS
*ROOKIES: .8X TO 2X BASIC CARDS

2017 Donruss Press Proofs Red

*VETS: 1X TO 2.5X BASIC CARDS
*ROOKIES: .8X TO 2X BASIC CARDS

2017 Donruss Press Proofs Silver

*VETS/100: 1.5X TO 4X BASIC CARDS
*ROOKIES/100: 1X TO 2.5X BASIC CARDS

2017 Donruss Press Proofs Silver Die Cut

*VETS/75: 1.5X TO 4X BASIC CARDS
*ROOKIES/75: 1X TO 2.5X BASIC CARDS

2017 Donruss Jersey Number

*VETS/73-99: 1.5X TO 4X BASIC CARDS
*VETS/35-59: 2X TO 5X BASIC CARDS
*VETS/25-34: 2.5X TO 6X BASIC CARDS
*VETS/15-24: 3X TO 86X BASIC CARDS
*ROOKIES/73-99: 1X TO 2.5X BASIC CARDS
*ROOKIES/35-59: 1.2X TO 3X BASIC CARDS
*ROOKIES/25-34: 1.5X TO 4X BASIC CARDS
*ROOKIES/15-24: 2X TO 5X BASIC CARDS
327 Patrick Mahomes II RR/15 200.00 400.00

2017 Donruss Season Stat Line

*VETS/210-400: 1X TO 2.5X BASIC CARDS
*VETS/100-190: 1.2X TO 3X BASIC CARDS
*VETS/61-98: 1.5X TO 4X BASIC CARDS
*VETS/35-60: 2X TO 5X BASIC CARDS
*VETS/26-34: 2.5X TO 6X BASIC CARDS
*VETS/15-24: 3X TO 86X BASIC CARDS
*ROOKIES/100-198: .8X TO 2X BASIC CARDS
*ROOKIES/61-98: 1X TO 2.5X BASIC CARDS
*ROOKIES/35-60: 1.2X TO 3X BASIC CARDS
*ROOKIES/26-34: 1.5X TO 4X BASIC CARDS
*ROOKIES/15-24: 2X TO 5X BASIC CARDS
327 Patrick Mahomes II RR/41 100.00 200.00

2017 Donruss '81 Tribute

*HOLO/100: 1.5X TO 4X BASIC INSERTS
1 DeMarco Murray .50 1.25
2 Todd Gurley II .60 1.50
3 Drew Brees .60 1.50
4 Larry Fitzgerald .50 1.25
5 Carson Wentz .75 2.00
6 Jordan Howard .60 1.50
7 Antonio Brown .60 1.50
8 Ezekiel Elliott .75 2.00
9 Richard Sherman .60 1.50
10 Aaron Rodgers 1.25 3.00
11 Khalil Mack .60 1.50
12 Jarvis Landry .50 1.25
13 Odell Beckham Jr. .60 1.50
14 Julio Jones .60 1.50
15 Ben Roethlisberger .60 1.50
16 A.J. Green .60 1.50
17 Philip Rivers .60 1.50
18 Von Miller .50 1.25
19 Jameis Winston .50 1.25
20 J.J. Watt .60 1.50
21 Kirk Cousins .60 1.50
22 Adrian Peterson .60 1.50
23 Derek Carr .60 1.50
24 Matt Ryan .50 1.25
25 Le'Veon Bell .50 1.25
26 Dak Prescott .60 1.50
27 Russell Wilson .75 2.00
28 Matthew Stafford .50 1.25
29 Marcus Mariota .60 1.50
30 Andrew Luck .75 2.00
31 Devonta Freeman .50 1.25
32 Tom Brady 1.50 4.00
33 Amari Cooper .60 1.50
34 Cam Newton .60 1.50
35 David Johnson .60 1.50

2017 Donruss '81 Tribute Autographs

1 DeMarco Murray/25 8.00 20.00
2 Todd Gurley II/25 15.00 40.00
8 Ezekiel Elliott/25 50.00 100.00
9 Richard Sherman/25 15.00 40.00
16 A.J. Green/25 10.00 25.00
21 Kirk Cousins/49 8.00 20.00
23 Derek Carr/25 40.00 80.00
25 Le'Veon Bell/25 15.00 40.00
31 Devonta Freeman/25 8.00 20.00
35 David Johnson/25 10.00 25.00

2017 Donruss All Time Gridiron Kings

*STUDIO/100: 1.5X TO 4X BASIC INSERTS
1 Bruce Smith .50 1.25
2 Marvin Harrison .50 1.25
3 Deion Sanders .50 1.25
4 Ray Lewis .60 1.50
5 Emmitt Smith 1.00 2.50
6 Terrell Davis .50 1.25
7 Jerry Rice 1.00 2.50
8 Joe Namath .75 2.00
9 Barry Sanders 1.00 2.50
10 Kevin Greene .50 1.25
11 Curtis Martin .50 1.25
12 Michael Irvin .60 1.50
13 Dick Butkus .75 2.00
14 Roger Staubach .75 2.00
15 Eric Dickerson .60 1.50
16 Terry Bradshaw 1.00 2.50
17 Jim Kelly .60 1.50
18 John Elway 1.00 2.50
19 Bo Jackson .75 2.00
20 Kurt Warner .50 1.25
21 Dan Fouts .50 1.25
22 Michael Strahan .50 1.25
23 Ed Reed .50 1.25
24 Randy Moss .50 1.25
25 Franco Harris .60 1.50
26 Tony Dorsett .60 1.50
27 Joe Greene .60 1.50
28 John Riggins .50 1.25
29 Brett Favre 1.25 3.00
30 Marshall Faulk .50 1.25
31 Dan Marino 1.25 3.00
32 Peyton Manning 1.25 3.00
33 Eddie George .50 1.25
34 Steve Young .75 2.00
35 Jerome Bettis .60 1.50
36 Troy Aikman .75 2.00
37 Joe Montana 1.50 4.00
38 John Stallworth .50 1.25
39 Brian Urlacher .60 1.50
40 Lance Alworth .50 1.25

2017 Donruss Award Winning Autographs

1 Priest Holmes 6.00 15.00

2017 Donruss Canton Kings Jerseys

*STUDIO/25: .6X TO 1.5X BASIC JSY/99
1 Steve Young 5.00 12.00
2 Bobby Layne 3.00 8.00
3 Tony Dorsett 4.00 10.00
4 Joe Montana 10.00 25.00
5 John Elway 6.00 15.00
6 Barry Sanders 6.00 15.00
7 Len Dawson 4.00 10.00
8 Bob Griese 4.00 10.00
9 Fred Biletnikoff 4.00 10.00
10 Johnny Unitas 10.00 25.00
11 Tom Landry 15.00 40.00
12 Jerry Rice 6.00 15.00
13 Walter Payton 8.00 20.00
14 Joe Namath 10.00 25.00
15 Larry Csonka 3.00 8.00
16 Eric Dickerson 4.00 10.00
17 Mike Ditka 4.00 10.00
18 Bob Lilly 3.00 8.00
19 Roger Staubach 5.00 12.00
20 Earl Campbell 4.00 10.00

2017 Donruss Dominators Autographs

3 Devonta Freeman/25 6.00 15.00
11 DeMarco Murray/25 6.00 15.00
15 Tyreek Hill/25 15.00 40.00
18 LeSean McCoy/25 10.00 25.00
21 David Johnson/25 20.00 40.00
23 Mike Evans/25 6.00 15.00
25 Derek Carr/25 30.00 60.00
27 Le'Veon Bell/25 12.00 30.00
30 Ezekiel Elliott/25 40.00 80.00
33 Jordy Nelson/25 15.00 40.00

2017 Donruss Fans of the Game Autographs

1 Joey Belladonna 20.00 20.00
2 Genevieve Morton 6.00 15.00
3 Chris Berman 20.00 20.00
5 Dick Vitale 20.00 20.00

2017 Donruss Ground Force Autographs

3 Curtis Martin/25 6.00 15.00
4 LaDainian Tomlinson/25 20.00 50.00
5 Jerome Bettis/25 20.00 50.00
6 Ezekiel Elliott/25 40.00 80.00
8 DeMarco Murray/25 6.00 15.00
10 Le'Veon Bell/25 15.00 40.00
11 LeSean McCoy/25 10.00 25.00
12 David Johnson/25 12.00 30.00
13 Devonta Freeman/25 12.00 30.00
14 Todd Gurley II/25 15.00 40.00
16 Leonard Fournette/25 25.00 50.00
17 Dalvin Cook/49 10.00 25.00
18 Christian McCaffrey/49 40.00 80.00
19 Alvin Kamara/49 15.00 40.00
20 D'Onta Foreman/49 5.00 12.00

2017 Donruss Highlights

*STUDIO/100: 1.25X TO 3X BASIC INSERTS
1 Frank Gore .60 1.50
2 Tom Brady 2.00 5.00
3 Eli Manning .60 1.50
4 Dak Prescott .75 2.00
5 Adam Vinatieri .50 1.25
6 Philip Rivers .75 2.00
7 Drew Brees .75 2.00
8 Larry Fitzgerald .60 1.50
9 Tom Brady 2.00 5.00
10 Larry Fitzgerald .60 1.50
11 Julius Peppers .60 1.50
12 Tom Brady 2.00 5.00
13 LeGarrette Blount .60 1.50
14 Tom Brady 2.00 5.00
15 Marcus Mariota .75 2.00
16 Le'Veon Bell .60 1.50
17 Matt Ryan .60 1.50
18 David Johnson .75 2.00
19 Kirk Cousins .75 2.00
20 Aaron Rodgers 1.50 4.00

2017 Donruss Inducted

*HOLO/99: 1.25X TO 3X BASIC INSERTS
1 Morten Andersen .75 2.00
2 Terrell Davis 1.00 2.50
3 LaDainian Tomlinson 1.00 2.50
4 Kurt Warner 1.00 2.50

2017 Donruss Inducted Autographs

1 Morten Andersen/99 8.00 20.00
2 Terrell Davis/25 15.00 40.00
3 LaDainian Tomlinson/25 20.00 50.00
4 Kurt Warner/25 25.00 50.00

2017 Donruss Leather Kings

*STUDIO/25: .6X TO 1.5X BASIC BALL/99
1 Tom Brady 10.00 25.00
2 Jordan Reed 2.50 6.00
3 Doug Martin 3.00 8.00
4 Alshon Jeffery 3.00 8.00
5 Andrew Luck 5.00 12.00
6 Russell Wilson 5.00 12.00
7 Davante Adams 3.00 8.00
8 Brandin Cooks 3.00 8.00
9 Odell Beckham Jr. 4.00 10.00
10 Le'Veon Bell 3.00 8.00

2017 Donruss Legends of the Fall

*HOLO/100: 1.5X TO 4X BASIC INSERTS
1 Ray Lewis .60 1.50
2 Franco Harris .60 1.50
3 Steve Young .75 2.00
4 Marshawn Lynch .50 1.25
5 Hines Ward .50 1.25
6 Tom Brady 1.50 4.00
7 Von Miller .50 1.25
8 Brett Favre 1.25 3.00
9 Aaron Rodgers 1.25 3.00
10 John Elway 1.00 2.50
11 Kurt Warner .50 1.25
12 Marcus Allen .50 1.25
13 Len Dawson .60 1.50
14 Jerry Rice 1.00 2.50
15 John Stallworth .50 1.25
16 Peyton Manning 1.25 3.00
17 Eli Manning .50 1.25
18 Joe Montana 1.50 4.00
19 Drew Brees .60 1.50
20 Emmitt Smith 1.00 2.50
21 Terrell Davis .50 1.25
22 John Riggins .50 1.25
23 Joe Namath .75 2.00
24 Michael Irvin .60 1.50
25 Doug Williams .50 1.25
26 Troy Aikman .75 2.00

2017 Donruss Pro Bowl Kings Jerseys

*STUDIO/25: .6X TO 1.5X BASIC JSY/99
1 Ryan Mathews 3.00 8.00
2 Drew Brees 4.00 10.00
3 Matthew Slater 2.50 6.00
4 Golden Tate III 2.50 6.00
5 John Kuhn 2.50 6.00
6 Andy Dalton 3.00 8.00
7 Mario Williams 2.50 6.00
8 Cameron Wake 2.50 6.00
9 Rod Woodson 3.00 8.00
10 DeMarcus Ware 3.00 8.00
11 Tony Dorsett 4.00 10.00
12 Dwight Freeney 2.50 6.00
13 Richie Incognito 2.50 6.00
14 Joe Haden 2.50 6.00
15 Justin Houston 2.50 6.00
16 C.J. Anderson 3.00 8.00
17 Odell Beckham Jr. 4.00 10.00
18 Clay Matthews 3.00 8.00
19 Tamba Hali 2.50 6.00
20 Dontari Poe 2.50 6.00
21 Aaron Donald 4.00 10.00
22 Gerald McCoy 2.50 6.00
23 Johnny Hekker 2.50 6.00
24 Joe Thomas 2.50 6.00
25 LeSean McCoy 4.00 10.00
26 C.J. Mosley 3.00 8.00
27 Patrick Peterson 2.50 6.00
28 DeMarco Murray 3.00 8.00
29 Ryan Kerrigan 2.50 6.00
30 Doug Martin 3.00 8.00

2017 Donruss Production Line Sacks

*HOLO/100: .75X TO 2X BASIC INSERTS
1 Vic Beasley Jr. .75 2.00
2 Von Miller 1.00 2.50
3 Lorenzo Alexander .75 2.00
4 Markus Golden .75 2.00
5 Danielle Hunter .75 2.00
6 Cliff Avril .75 2.00
7 Cameron Wake .75 2.00
8 Erik Walden .75 2.00
9 Khalil Mack 1.25 3.00
10 Joey Bosa 1.25 3.00

2017 Donruss Production Line Touchdowns

*HOLO/100: .75X TO 2X BASIC INSERTS
1 Aaron Rodgers 2.50 6.00
2 Matt Ryan 1.00 2.50
3 Drew Brees 1.25 3.00
4 Philip Rivers 1.25 3.00
5 Andrew Luck 1.50 4.00
6 LeGarrette Blount 1.00 2.50
7 David Johnson 1.25 3.00
8 Ezekiel Elliott 1.50 4.00
9 LeSean McCoy 1.25 3.00
10 Devonta Freeman 1.00 2.50
11 Jordy Nelson 1.00 2.50
12 Davante Adams 1.00 2.50
13 Antonio Brown 1.25 3.00
14 Mike Evans 1.00 2.50
15 Odell Beckham Jr. 1.25 3.00

2017 Donruss Rookie Gridiron Kings Autographs

1 Nathan Peterman/49 6.00 15.00
3 C.J. Beathard/49 5.00 12.00
4 O.J. Howard/49 6.00 15.00
5 Davis Webb/49 5.00 12.00
8 Corey Davis/25 10.00 25.00
9 D'Onta Foreman/49 6.00 15.00
10 Christian McCaffrey/25 15.00 40.00
11 Alvin Kamara/49 20.00 50.00
13 Samaje Perine/49 5.00 12.00
14 R. Joshua Dobbs/49 6.00 15.00
15 Dalvin Cook/25 15.00 40.00
17 JuJu Smith-Schuster/25 25.00 50.00
18 Mike Williams/25 10.00 25.00
19 Dede Westbrook/49 5.00 12.00
20 John Ross III/25 8.00 20.00

2017 Donruss Rookie Phenom Jersey Autographs

1 Mitchell Trubisky 40.00 80.00
2 Leonard Fournette 15.00 40.00
3 Corey Davis 6.00 15.00
4 Mike Williams 6.00 15.00
5 Christian McCaffrey 40.00 80.00
6 John Ross III 5.00 12.00
7 Patrick Mahomes II 250.00 400.00
8 Deshaun Watson 50.00 100.00
9 O.J. Howard 5.00 12.00
10 Evan Engram 5.00 12.00
11 Zay Jones 5.00 12.00
12 Curtis Samuel 5.00 12.00
13 Dalvin Cook 30.00 60.00
14 Joe Mixon 8.00 20.00
15 DeShone Kizer 4.00 10.00
16 JuJu Smith-Schuster 15.00 40.00
17 Alvin Kamara 15.00 40.00
18 D'Onta Foreman 5.00 12.00
19 Dede Westbrook 4.00 10.00
20 Samaje Perine 4.00 10.00

2017 Donruss Rookie Phenom Jersey Autographs Prime

*PRIME/25: .6X TO 1.5X BASIC JSY AU/99
1 Mitchell Trubisky 60.00 125.00
2 Leonard Fournette 20.00 50.00
5 Christian McCaffrey 75.00 150.00
7 Patrick Mahomes II 125.00 250.00
8 Deshaun Watson 75.00 150.00

2017 Donruss Rookie Phenom Jerseys

*PRIME/25: 1X TO 2.5X BASIC JSY
*BLUE: .4X TO 1X BASIC JSY
*RED: .4X TO 1X BASIC JSY
1 Mitchell Trubisky 4.00 10.00
2 Leonard Fournette 5.00 12.00
3 Corey Davis 2.00 5.00
4 Mike Williams 2.00 5.00
5 Christian McCaffrey 4.00 10.00
6 John Ross III 1.50 4.00
7 Patrick Mahomes II 15.00 40.00
8 Deshaun Watson 6.00 15.00
9 O.J. Howard 1.50 4.00
10 Evan Engram 1.50 4.00
11 Zay Jones 1.50 4.00
12 Curtis Samuel 1.50 4.00
13 Dalvin Cook 4.00 10.00
14 Joe Mixon 3.00 8.00
15 DeShone Kizer 1.25 3.00
16 JuJu Smith-Schuster 3.00 8.00
17 Alvin Kamara 3.00 8.00
18 Cooper Kupp 2.00 5.00
19 Taywan Taylor 1.25 3.00
20 ArDarius Stewart 1.25 3.00
21 Carlos Henderson 1.25 3.00
22 Chris Godwin 1.50 4.00
23 Kareem Hunt 2.50 6.00
24 Davis Webb 1.25 3.00
25 D'Onta Foreman 1.50 4.00
26 Kenny Golladay 2.00 5.00
27 C.J. Beathard 1.25 3.00
28 James Conner 2.50 6.00
29 Amara Darboh 1.25 3.00
30 Dede Westbrook 1.25 3.00
31 Samaje Perine 1.25 3.00
32 Josh Reynolds 1.25 3.00
33 Mack Hollins 1.25 3.00
34 Joe Williams 1.25 3.00
35 Nathan Peterman 1.50 4.00
36 Jeremy McNichols 1.25 3.00
37 Jamaal Williams 1.25 3.00
38 R. Joshua Dobbs 1.50 4.00
39 Wayne Gallman 1.50 4.00
40 Marlon Mack 2.00 5.00

2017 Donruss Salute to Service

*HOLO/100: 1.25X TO 3X BASIC INSERTS
1 Darren Woodson .60 1.50
2 Drew Brees .75 2.00
3 Roger Staubach 1.00 2.50
4 Steve Smith .60 1.50
5 Alejandro Villanueva 10.00 25.00
6 Joe Thomas .50 1.25
7 Jermaine Kearse .50 1.25
8 Golden Tate III .50 1.25
9 Deone Bucannon .50 1.25
10 Blake Bortles .50 1.25
11 Rocky Bleier .60 1.50
12 Eric Decker .50 1.25
13 Vincent Jackson .50 1.25
14 Joe Cardona .50 1.25
15 Garrett Celek .50 1.25
16 DeMarcus Ware .60 1.50
17 Richie Incognito .50 1.25
18 Brian Cushing .50 1.25
19 Jerrell Freeman .50 1.25
20 Derrick Johnson .50 1.25

2017 Donruss Signature Marks

1 Jim Kelly 6.00 15.00
2 Derrick Henry 5.00 12.00
3 Torrey Smith 4.00 10.00
4 Bill Parcells 10.00 25.00
5 John Elway 10.00 25.00
6 Paul Hornung 6.00 15.00
7 Roger Staubach 25.00 50.00
8 Marvin Jones 4.00 10.00
9 Brian Urlacher 15.00 40.00
10 DeAndre Washington 4.00 10.00
11 Kurt Warner 25.00 50.00
12 Michael Thomas 6.00 15.00
13 Isaiah Crowell 4.00 10.00
14 Vernon Hargreaves III 4.00 10.00
15 Peyton Manning 75.00 150.00
16 Jaylon Smith 4.00 10.00
17 John Riggins 8.00 20.00
18 Jimmy Garoppolo 30.00 60.00
19 Michael Strahan
20 Kenneth Dixon 4.00 10.00
21 Dan Fouts
22 Tyler Boyd 4.00 10.00
23 Emmitt Smith
24 Artie Burns 4.00 10.00
25 Michael Irvin
26 Myles Jack 4.00 10.00
27 Troy Aikman
28 Y.A. Tittle 10.00 25.00
29 Tony Dorsett 12.00 30.00
30 Alex Collins 4.00 10.00
31 Ed Reed 15.00 40.00
32 Corey Coleman 4.00 10.00
33 Brett Favre
34 Desmond Trufant 4.00 10.00
35 Dan Marino
36 Reggie Ragland 4.00 10.00
37 Steve Young
38 Blake Bortles 4.00 10.00
39 Jerome Bettis 30.00 60.00
40 Wendell Smallwood 4.00 10.00
41 Calvin Johnson
42 Torry Holt 5.00 12.00
43 Aaron Rodgers 200.00 300.00
44 Kony Ealy 4.00 10.00
45 Joe Namath 40.00 80.00
46 Darron Lee 4.00 10.00
47 Reggie Wayne 5.00 12.00
48 Andrew Luck
49 Ray Lewis
50 Gilbert Brown 4.00 10.00
52 Laquon Treadwell 4.00 10.00
53 Terry Bradshaw
54 Robert Nkemdiche 4.00 10.00
55 Barry Sanders
56 Randy Moss
57 Marshall Faulk 15.00 40.00
58 Joe Montana
59 Lance Briggs 5.00 12.00
60 Chris Ivory 5.00 12.00
61 Deion Sanders
62 John Brown 5.00 12.00
63 Jerry Rice 25.00
64 Glenn Gronkowski 4.00 10.00
65 Deshaun Watson 40.00 80.00
66 Leonard Fournette 30.00 60.00
67 Mitchell Trubisky 40.00 80.00
68 DeShone Kizer 3.00 8.00
69 Dalvin Cook 25.00 50.00
70 Mike Williams 5.00 12.00
71 Brad Kaaya 3.00 8.00
72 Christian McCaffrey 30.00 60.00
73 Corey Davis 5.00 12.00
74 JuJu Smith-Schuster 8.00 20.00
75 Patrick Mahomes II 150.00 300.00
76 D'Onta Foreman 4.00 10.00
77 Dede Westbrook 3.00 8.00
78 John Ross III 4.00 10.00
79 O.J. Howard 4.00 10.00
80 Alvin Kamara 12.00 30.00
81 Curtis Samuel 4.00 10.00
82 Davis Webb 3.00 8.00
83 Isaiah Ford 3.00 8.00
84 Jerod Evans 4.00 10.00
85 Samaje Perine 3.00 8.00
86 Amara Darboh 3.00 8.00
87 Brian Hill 3.00 8.00
88 Carlos Henderson 3.00 8.00
89 Corey Clement 4.00 10.00
90 Elijah Hood 3.00 8.00
91 Jeremy McNichols 3.00 8.00
92 Malachi Dupre 3.00 8.00
93 Matthew Dayes 3.00 8.00
94 Wayne Gallman 4.00 10.00
95 Chad Kelly 3.00 8.00
96 Evan Engram 4.00 10.00
97 ArDarius Stewart 3.00 8.00
98 Artavis Scott 3.00 8.00
100 Chad Hansen 3.00 8.00

2017 Donruss Signature Marks Blue

*BLUE/25: .6X TO 1.5X BASIC AU
*BLUE/25: .8X TO 2X ROOK AU
75 Patrick Mahomes II/25 250.00 500.00

2017 Donruss Sophomore Swatches

*PRIME/25: .6X TO 1.5X BASIC JSY/99
1 Dak Prescott 4.00 10.00
2 Corey Coleman 2.50 6.00
3 Josh Doctson 2.50 6.00
4 Jared Goff 4.00 10.00
5 C.J. Prosise 2.50 6.00
6 Derrick Henry 3.00 8.00
7 Joey Bosa 4.00 10.00
8 Paxton Lynch 2.50 6.00
9 Sterling Shepard 3.00 8.00
10 Connor Cook 2.50 6.00
11 Hunter Henry 2.50 6.00
12 Michael Thomas 4.00 10.00
13 Will Fuller V 2.50 6.00
14 Carson Wentz 5.00 12.00
15 Tyler Boyd 2.50 6.00
16 Tyreek Hill 4.00 10.00
17 Cody Kessler 2.50 6.00
18 Ezekiel Elliott 5.00 12.00
19 Jordan Howard 4.00 10.00
20 Laquon Treadwell 2.50 6.00

2017 Donruss Team Heroes

1 Steve Largent .75 2.00
2 Emmitt Smith 1.25 3.00
3 Lawrence Taylor .75 2.00
4 Terry Bradshaw 1.25 3.00
5 Dan Marino 1.50 4.00
6 Tom Brady 2.00 5.00
7 Jim Kelly .75 2.00
8 Ben Roethlisberger .75 2.00
9 Jim Brown 1.00 2.50
10 Matt Ryan .60 1.50
11 Hines Ward .60 1.50
12 Larry Fitzgerald .60 1.50
13 Ray Lewis .75 2.00
14 Richard Sherman .75 2.00
15 John Elway 1.25 3.00
16 Eli Manning .60 1.50
17 Barry Sanders 1.25 3.00
18 Philip Rivers .75 2.00
19 Marvin Harrison .60 1.50
20 Aaron Rodgers 1.50 4.00

2017 Donruss Team Heroes Autographs

1 Steve Largent/25 10.00 25.00
3 Lawrence Taylor/25 20.00 50.00
11 Hines Ward/25 20.00 50.00
14 Richard Sherman/25 10.00 25.00

2017 Donruss The Elite Series

1 Odell Beckham Jr. .60 1.50
2 Richard Sherman .60 1.50
3 Philip Rivers .60 1.50
4 Jordy Nelson .50 1.25
5 Adrian Peterson .60 1.50
6 Julio Jones .60 1.50
7 Russell Wilson .75 2.00
8 J.J. Watt .60 1.50
9 Marcus Mariota .60 1.50
10 Matt Ryan .50 1.25
11 Tom Brady 1.50 4.00
12 Ezekiel Elliott .75 2.00
13 A.J. Green .60 1.50
14 Eli Manning .50 1.25
15 T.Y. Hilton .50 1.25
16 Antonio Brown .60 1.50
17 Dak Prescott .60 1.50
18 Drew Brees .60 1.50
19 Matthew Stafford .50 1.25
20 Le'Veon Bell .60 1.50
21 Joe Flacco .50 1.25
22 Andrew Luck .75 2.00
23 Aaron Rodgers 1.25 3.00
24 Amari Cooper .60 1.50
25 Ben Roethlisberger .60 1.50
26 Jameis Winston .50 1.25
27 David Johnson .60 1.50
28 Derek Carr .60 1.50
29 Todd Gurley II .60 1.50
30 Cam Newton .60 1.50

2017 Donruss The Elite Series Autographs
4 Jordy Nelson/25 15.00 40.00
12 Ezekiel Elliott/25 50.00 100.00
13 A.J. Green/25 12.00 30.00
20 Le'Veon Bell/25
27 David Johnson/25 15.00 40.00
28 Derek Carr/25 30.00 60.00
29 Todd Gurley II/25 12.00 30.00

2017 Donruss The Elite Series Rookies
1 Mitchell Trubisky 2.50 6.00
2 Leonard Fournette 1.50 4.00
3 Corey Davis .75 2.00
4 Mike Williams .75 2.00
5 Christian McCaffrey 1.25 3.00
6 John Ross III .60 1.50
7 Patrick Mahomes II 15.00 40.00
8 Deshaun Watson 3.00 8.00
9 O.J. Howard .60 1.50
10 Evan Engram .60 1.50
11 Zay Jones .60 1.50
12 Curtis Samuel .60 1.50
13 Dalvin Cook 1.25 3.00
14 Joe Mixon 1.00 2.50
15 DeShone Kizer .50 1.25
16 JuJu Smith-Schuster 1.25 3.00
17 Alvin Kamara 2.00 5.00
18 Cooper Kupp .75 2.00
19 Taywan Taylor .50 1.25
20 ArDarius Stewart .50 1.25
21 Carlos Henderson .50 1.25
22 Chris Godwin .60 1.50
23 Kareem Hunt 1.00 2.50
24 Davis Webb .50 1.25
25 D'Onta Foreman .60 1.50
26 Kenny Golladay .75 2.00
27 C.J. Beathard .50 1.25
28 James Conner 1.00 2.50
29 Amara Darboh .50 1.25
30 Dede Westbrook .50 1.25

2017 Donruss The Elite Series Rookies Autographs
3 Corey Davis/25 10.00 25.00
4 Mike Williams/25 6.00 15.00
5 Christian McCaffrey/25 50.00 100.00
6 John Ross III/25 25.00 50.00
9 O.J. Howard/49 12.00 30.00
10 Evan Engram/99 3.00 8.00
11 Zay Jones/49 4.00 10.00
12 Curtis Samuel/49 4.00 10.00
13 Dalvin Cook/25 50.00 100.00
14 Joe Mixon/99 5.00 12.00
16 JuJu Smith-Schuster/25 10.00 25.00
17 Alvin Kamara/49 12.00 30.00
18 Cooper Kupp/99 8.00 20.00
20 ArDarius Stewart/99 2.50 6.00
21 Carlos Henderson/99 2.50 6.00
22 Chris Godwin/399 2.50 6.00
23 Kareem Hunt/99 15.00 40.00
24 Davis Webb/499 2.00 5.00
25 D'Onta Foreman/49 10.00 25.00
26 Kenny Golladay/99 4.00 10.00
27 C.J. Beathard/49 12.00 30.00
29 Amara Darboh/499 2.00 5.00
30 Dede Westbrook/49 3.00 8.00

2017 Donruss The Legends Series
1 Michael Strahan .60 1.50
2 Peyton Manning 1.50 4.00
3 Jerome Bettis .75 2.00
4 Barry Sanders 1.25 3.00
5 Roger Staubach 1.00 2.50
6 Joe Montana 2.00 5.00
7 Troy Aikman 1.00 2.50
8 Emmitt Smith 1.25 3.00
9 Steve Young 1.00 2.50
10 John Elway 1.25 3.00
11 Tony Dorsett .75 2.00
12 Dan Marino 1.50 4.00
13 Dick Butkus 1.00 2.50
14 Deion Sanders .60 1.50
15 John Riggins .60 1.50
16 Brett Favre 1.50 4.00
17 Marshall Faulk .60 1.50
18 Terry Bradshaw 1.25 3.00
19 Brian Urlacher .75 2.00
20 Jerry Rice 1.25 3.00

2017 Donruss The Rookies
1 Mitchell Trubisky 3.00 8.00
2 Leonard Fournette 2.00 5.00
3 Corey Davis 1.00 2.50
4 Mike Williams 1.00 2.50
5 Christian McCaffrey 1.50 4.00
6 John Ross III .75 2.00
7 Patrick Mahomes II 15.00 40.00
8 Deshaun Watson 4.00 10.00
9 O.J. Howard .75 2.00
10 Evan Engram .75 2.00
11 Zay Jones .75 2.00
12 Curtis Samuel .75 2.00
13 Dalvin Cook 1.50 4.00
14 Joe Mixon 1.25 3.00
15 DeShone Kizer .60 1.50
16 JuJu Smith-Schuster 1.50 4.00
17 Alvin Kamara 2.50 6.00
18 Cooper Kupp 1.00 2.50
19 Taywan Taylor .60 1.50
20 ArDarius Stewart .60 1.50
21 Carlos Henderson .60 1.50
22 Chris Godwin .75 2.00
23 Kareem Hunt 1.25 3.00
24 Davis Webb .60 1.50
25 D'Onta Foreman .75 2.00
26 Kenny Golladay 1.00 2.50
27 C.J. Beathard .60 1.50
28 James Conner 1.25 3.00
29 Amara Darboh .60 1.50
30 Dede Westbrook .60 1.50
31 Samaje Perine .60 1.50
32 Josh Reynolds .60 1.50
33 Mack Hollins .60 1.50
34 Joe Williams .60 1.50
35 Nathan Peterman .75 2.00
36 Jeremy McNichols .60 1.50
37 Jamaal Williams .60 1.50
38 R. Joshua Dobbs .75 2.00
39 Wayne Gallman .75 2.00
40 Marlon Mack 1.00 2.50

2017 Donruss The Rookies Autographs
3 Corey Davis/25 12.00 30.00
4 Mike Williams/25 6.00 15.00
5 Christian McCaffrey/25 100.00 200.00
6 John Ross III/25 5.00 12.00
9 O.J. Howard/49 4.00 10.00
10 Evan Engram/499 2.50 6.00
11 Zay Jones/49 4.00 10.00
12 Curtis Samuel/49 4.00 10.00
13 Dalvin Cook/25 40.00 80.00
14 Joe Mixon/99 5.00 12.00
16 JuJu Smith-Schuster/25 10.00 25.00
17 Alvin Kamara/49 12.00 30.00
18 Cooper Kupp/499 3.00 8.00
20 ArDarius Stewart/499 2.00 5.00
21 Carlos Henderson/499 2.00 5.00
22 Chris Godwin/499 2.50 6.00
23 Kareem Hunt/277 12.00 30.00
24 Davis Webb/499 2.00 5.00
25 D'Onta Foreman/49 4.00 10.00
26 Kenny Golladay/499 3.00 8.00
27 C.J. Beathard/49 15.00 40.00
29 Amara Darboh/499 2.00 5.00
30 Dede Westbrook/49 3.00 8.00
31 Samaje Perine/499 2.00 5.00
32 Josh Reynolds/499 2.00 5.00
33 Mack Hollins/499 2.00 5.00
34 Joe Williams/499 2.00 5.00
35 Nathan Peterman/49 4.00 10.00
36 Jeremy McNichols/499 2.00 5.00
37 Jamaal Williams/99 2.50 6.00
38 R. Joshua Dobbs/99 3.00 8.00
39 Wayne Gallman/99 3.00 8.00
40 Marlon Mack/499 3.00 8.00

2017 Donruss Threads
1 Dan Marino/25 12.00 30.00
2 John Elway/25 10.00 25.00
3 Matthew Stafford/99 3.00 8.00
4 Aaron Rodgers/25 12.00 30.00
5 Tony Romo/49 4.00 10.00
6 Brett Favre/25 12.00 30.00
7 Ndamukong Suh/99 3.00 8.00
8 Champ Bailey/99 3.00 8.00
9 Earl Thomas III/99 3.00 8.00
10 Eric Berry/99 3.00 8.00
11 Maurice Jones-Drew/99 2.50 6.00
12 Kenny Stills/99 2.50 6.00
13 Peyton Manning/49 8.00 20.00
14 Adrian Peterson/49 5.00 12.00
15 Thomas Rawls/99 2.50 6.00
16 Byron Jones/99 2.50 6.00
17 Alfred Morris/99 2.50 6.00
18 Dontari Poe/99 2.50 6.00
19 Jerry Rice/25 10.00 25.00
20 Geno Atkins/99 2.50 6.00
21 John Riggins/49 4.00 10.00
22 LeSean McCoy/99 4.00 10.00
23 Philip Rivers/99 4.00 10.00
24 Alex Smith/99 3.00 8.00
25 Emmanuel Sanders/99 4.00 10.00
26 Cam Newton/25 6.00 15.00
27 Aqib Talib/99 2.50 6.00
28 Ed Reed/49 4.00 10.00
29 Marcus Allen/49 4.00 10.00
30 Joe Flacco/99 3.00 8.00
31 Paul Hornung/49 5.00 12.00
32 Matt Ryan/49 4.00 10.00
33 Cole Beasley/99 4.00 10.00
34 Andy Dalton/99 3.00 8.00
35 DeMarcus Ware/99 3.00 8.00
36 Cameron Wake/99 2.50 6.00
37 Lamar Miller/99 2.50 6.00
38 Eli Manning/49 4.00 10.00
39 Antonio Gates/99 2.50 6.00
40 Joe Montana/25 15.00 40.00

2017 Donruss Top Targets
*HOLO/100: 1.5X TO 4X BASIC INSERTS
1 Larry Fitzgerald .50 1.25
2 Antonio Brown .60 1.50
3 Odell Beckham Jr. .60 1.50
4 Julian Edelman .60 1.50
5 Jordy Nelson .50 1.25
6 Mike Evans .50 1.25
7 Doug Baldwin .50 1.25
8 Jarvis Landry .50 1.25
9 Michael Thomas .60 1.50
10 T.Y. Hilton .50 1.25
11 Golden Tate III .40 1.00
12 Demaryius Thomas .50 1.25
13 Michael Crabtree .40 1.00
14 Dennis Pitta .40 1.00
15 Travis Kelce .60 1.50
16 Stefon Diggs .50 1.25
17 Amari Cooper .60 1.50
18 Julio Jones .60 1.50
19 Kyle Rudolph .40 1.00
20 David Johnson .60 1.50
21 Greg Olsen .50 1.25
22 Pierre Garcon .50 1.25
23 Emmanuel Sanders .60 1.50
24 Brandin Cooks .50 1.25
25 Zach Ertz .50 1.25
26 DeAndre Hopkins .50 1.25
27 Terrelle Pryor .40 1.00
28 Davante Adams .50 1.25
29 Cole Beasley .60 1.50
30 Le'Veon Bell .50 1.25

2017 Donruss Top Targets Autographs
5 Jordy Nelson/25 15.00 40.00
6 Mike Evans/25 8.00 20.00
7 Doug Baldwin/25 8.00 20.00
9 Michael Thomas/49 8.00 20.00
11 Golden Tate III/25 6.00 15.00
12 Demaryius Thomas/25 8.00 20.00
20 David Johnson/25 10.00 25.00
21 Greg Olsen/25 8.00 20.00
23 Emmanuel Sanders/49 8.00 20.00
24 Brandin Cooks/49 12.00 30.00
25 Zach Ertz/34 6.00 15.00
30 Le'Veon Bell/25 8.00 20.00

2017 Donruss Up Tempo
*HOLO/100: 1.25X TO 3X BASIC INSERTS
1 Emmanuel Sanders .75 2.00
2 Tyreek Hill .75 2.00
3 Dak Prescott .75 2.00
4 DeMarco Murray .60 1.50
5 Odell Beckham Jr. .75 2.00
6 Sterling Shepard .60 1.50
7 Russell Wilson 1.00 2.50
8 David Johnson .75 2.00
9 Le'Veon Bell .60 1.50
10 Eric Berry .60 1.50
11 Amari Cooper .75 2.00
12 Julio Jones .75 2.00
13 Will Fuller V .50 1.25
14 T.Y. Hilton .60 1.50
15 Ezekiel Elliott 1.00 2.50
16 Vic Beasley Jr. .50 1.25
17 Von Miller .60 1.50
18 Khalil Mack .75 2.00
19 Patrick Peterson .50 1.25
20 Richard Sherman .75 2.00

2018 Donruss
1 David Johnson .40 1.00
2 Larry Fitzgerald .30 .75
3 Chandler Jones .25 .60
4 Haason Reddick .25 .60
5 Deone Bucannon .25 .60
6 J.J. Nelson .25 .60
7 Patrick Peterson .25 .60
8 Tyrann Mathieu .30 .75
9 Kurt Warner .30 .75
10 Julio Jones .40 1.00
11 Alex Mack .25 .60
12 Matt Ryan .30 .75
13 Devonta Freeman .30 .75
14 Mohamed Sanu .25 .60
15 Vic Beasley Jr. .25 .60
16 Keanu Neal .25 .60
17 Desmond Trufant .25 .60
18 Deion Sanders .30 .75
19 Joe Flacco .30 .75
20 Terrell Suggs .25 .60
21 Jimmy Smith .25 .60
22 Alex Collins .25 .60
23 C.J. Mosley .30 .75
24 Jared Cook .25 .60
25 Eric Weddle .25 .60
26 Justin Tucker .25 .60
27 Jonathan Ogden .30 .75
28 Tyrod Taylor .30 .75
29 LeSean McCoy .40 1.00
30 Kelvin Benjamin .30 .75
31 Charles Clay .25 .60
32 Thurman Thomas .30 .75
33 Tre'Davious White .25 .60
34 Zay Jones .25 .60
35 Jordan Matthews .25 .60
36 A.J. McCarron .25 .60
37 Cam Newton .40 1.00
38 Luke Kuechly .30 .75
39 Greg Olsen .30 .75
40 Christian McCaffrey .40 1.00
41 Devin Funchess .25 .60
42 Thomas Davis .25 .60
43 Kawann Short .25 .60
44 Julius Peppers .30 .75
45 Mario Addison RC .25 .60
46 Mitchell Trubisky .40 1.00
47 Jordan Howard .40 1.00
48 Kyle Long .25 .60
49 Leonard Floyd .25 .60
50 Tarik Cohen .30 .75
51 Adam Shaheen .40 1.00
52 Cameron Meredith .25 .60
53 Eddie Jackson .25 .60
54 Teddy Bridgewater .30 .75
55 Andy Dalton .30 .75
56 A.J. Green .40 1.00
57 Ken Anderson .25 .60
58 Giovani Bernard .25 .60
59 Geno Atkins .25 .60
60 Joe Mixon .30 .75
61 Tyler Eifert .30 .75
62 Carlos Dunlap .25 .60
63 Carl Lawson .25 .60
64 Alex Smith .30 .75
65 Nathan Peterman .25 .60
66 Jabrill Peppers .25 .60
67 Duke Johnson .25 .60
68 David Njoku .25 .60
69 Josh Gordon .25 .60
70 Chris Hogan .25 .60
71 Joe Thomas .25 .60
72 Myles Garrett .40 1.00
73 Brian Urlacher .40 1.00
74 Ozzie Newsome .30 .75
75 Dak Prescott .40 1.00
76 Ezekiel Elliott .50 1.25
77 Zack Martin .25 .60
78 Jason Witten .30 .75
79 Sean Lee .30 .75
80 Tony Dorsett .40 1.00
81 Dan Bailey .25 .60
82 Travis Frederick .25 .60
83 DeMarcus Lawrence .25 .60
84 Peyton Manning .75 2.00
85 Von Miller .30 .75
86 Aqib Talib .25 .60
87 Demaryius Thomas .30 .75
88 Emmanuel Sanders .40 1.00
89 Chris Harris Jr. .25 .60
90 Devontae Booker .25 .60
91 Darian Stewart .25 .60
92 Brandon Marshall .25 .60
93 Brandon McManus .25 .60
94 Matthew Stafford .30 .75
95 Golden Tate III .25 .60
96 Ezekiel Ansah .25 .60
97 Darius Slay .25 .60
98 Ameer Abdullah .25 .60
99 Kenny Golladay .25 .60
100 Marvin Jones Jr. .25 .60
101 Jarrad Davis .25 .60
102 Barry Sanders .60 1.50
103 Aaron Rodgers .75 2.00
104 Jordy Nelson .30 .75
105 Aaron Jones .30 .75
106 Ha Ha Clinton-Dix .25 .60
107 Clay Matthews .30 .75
108 Randall Cobb .30 .75
109 Davante Adams .30 .75
110 Brett Favre .75 2.00
111 Ty Montgomery .25 .60
112 Tony Gonzalez .30 .75
113 J.J. Watt .40 1.00
114 Deshaun Watson .50 1.25
115 DeAndre Hopkins .30 .75
116 Will Fuller V .25 .60
117 D'Onta Foreman .25 .60
118 Jadeveon Clowney .25 .60
119 Lamar Miller .25 .60
120 Zach Cunningham .25 .60
121 Andrew Luck .50 1.25
122 Jacoby Brissett .25 .60
123 T.Y. Hilton .30 .75
124 Marlon Mack .25 .60
125 Jack Doyle .25 .60
126 Malik Hooker .25 .60
127 Antonio Morrison .25 .60
128 Adam Vinatieri .25 .60
129 Blake Bortles .25 .60
130 Leonard Fournette .40 1.00
131 Allen Robinson .30 .75
132 Jalen Ramsey .30 .75
133 Calais Campbell .25 .60
134 A.J. Bouye .25 .60
135 Marqise Lee .25 .60
136 Myles Jack .25 .60
137 Mark Brunell .25 .60
138 Patrick Mahomes II 1.50 4.00
139 Tyreek Hill .40 1.00
140 Kareem Hunt .30 .75
141 Travis Kelce .40 1.00
142 Eric Berry .30 .75
143 Justin Houston .25 .60
144 Marcus Peters .25 .60
145 Daniel Sorensen .25 .60
146 Eric Fisher .25 .60
147 Jared Goff .40 1.00
148 Todd Gurley II .40 1.00
149 Robert Woods .30 .75
150 Aaron Donald .40 1.00
151 Sammy Watkins .40 1.00
152 Cooper Kupp .30 .75
153 Alec Ogletree .25 .60
154 Johnny Hekker .25 .60
155 Marshall Faulk .30 .75
156 Joey Bosa .40 1.00
157 Keenan Allen .30 .75
158 Melvin Gordon .30 .75
159 Philip Rivers .40 1.00
160 Tyrell Williams .25 .60
161 Mike Williams .25 .60
162 Hunter Henry .25 .60
163 LaDainian Tomlinson .30 .75
164 Ryan Tannehill .30 .75
165 Jarvis Landry .30 .75
166 DeVante Parker .30 .75
167 Kenyan Drake .25 .60
168 Jason Taylor .30 .75
169 Reshad Jones .25 .60
170 Cameron Wake .25 .60
171 Robert Quinn .25 .60
172 Kenny Stills .25 .60
173 Stefon Diggs .30 .75
174 Adam Thielen .40 1.00
175 Case Keenum .30 .75
176 Cris Carter .40 1.00
177 Sam Bradford .25 .60
178 Anthony Barr .25 .60
179 Dalvin Cook .30 .75
180 Everson Griffen .25 .60
181 Xavier Rhodes .25 .60
182 Harrison Smith .40 1.00
183 Tom Brady 1.00 2.50
184 Brandin Cooks .30 .75
185 Rob Gronkowski .40 1.00
186 Julian Edelman .40 1.00
187 Devin McCourty .25 .60
188 Stephon Gilmore .25 .60
189 Malcolm Butler .40 1.00
190 James White .30 .75
191 Danny Amendola .30 .75
192 Drew Bledsoe .30 .75
193 Drew Brees .40 1.00
194 Michael Thomas .40 1.00
195 Mark Ingram .30 .75
196 Alvin Kamara .30 .75
197 Marshon Lattimore .25 .60
198 Ted Ginn Jr. .25 .60
199 Marcus Williams .25 .60
200 Archie Manning .30 .75
201 Brandon Graham .25 .60
202 Odell Beckham Jr. .40 1.00
203 Eli Manning .30 .75
204 Landon Collins .25 .60
205 Evan Engram .25 .60
206 Olivier Vernon .25 .60
207 Wayne Gallman .25 .60
208 Sterling Shepard .30 .75
209 Lawrence Taylor .40 1.00
210 Josh McCown .25 .60
211 Robby Anderson .25 .60
212 Jermaine Kearse .25 .60
213 Jamal Adams .30 .75
214 Bilal Powell .25 .60
215 Joe Klecko .25 .60
216 Leonard Williams .25 .60
217 Derek Carr .40 1.00
218 Michael Crabtree .25 .60
219 Amari Cooper .40 1.00
220 Marshawn Lynch .30 .75
221 Khalil Mack .40 1.00
222 Rodney Hudson .25 .60
223 Kelechi Osemele .25 .60
224 Bo Jackson .50 1.25
225 Doug Martin .30 .75
226 Bruce Irvin .25 .60
227 Carson Wentz .50 1.25
228 Nick Foles .30 .75
229 Jerry Rice .60 1.50
230 Alshon Jeffery .30 .75
231 Jay Ajayi .30 .75
232 Fletcher Cox .25 .60
233 Zach Ertz .30 .75
234 Ron Jaworski .30 .75
235 Mike Alstott .25 .60
236 LeGarrette Blount .30 .75
237 Nelson Agholor .25 .60
238 Ben Roethlisberger .40 1.00
239 Antonio Brown .40 1.00
240 Le'Veon Bell .30 .75
241 Terry Bradshaw .60 1.50
242 David DeCastro .25 .60
243 Maurkice Pouncey .25 .60
244 Ryan Shazier .25 .60
245 Alejandro Villanueva .30 .75
246 JuJu Smith-Schuster .40 1.00
247 T.J. Watt .30 .75
248 Kyle Juszczyk .25 .60
249 Jimmy Garoppolo .50 1.25
250 Carlos Hyde .25 .60
251 Marquise Goodwin .25 .60
252 George Kittle .25 .60
253 Pierre Garcon .30 .75
254 Jerick McKinnon .25 .60
255 Kirk Cousins .40 1.00
256 DeForest Buckner .25 .60
257 Russell Wilson .50 1.25
258 Richard Sherman .40 1.00
259 Jimmy Graham .40 1.00
260 Earl Thomas III .30 .75
261 Bobby Wagner .25 .60
262 Doug Baldwin .30 .75
263 Chris Carson .30 .75
264 Tyler Lockett .30 .75
265 Frank Clark .25 .60
266 Jameis Winston .30 .75
267 Mike Evans .30 .75
268 Gerald McCoy .25 .60
269 Cameron Brate .25 .60
270 DeSean Jackson .30 .75
271 Kwon Alexander .25 .60
272 Jason Pierre-Paul .25 .60
273 O.J. Howard .25 .60
274 Jacquizz Rodgers .25 .60
275 Earl Campbell .40 1.00
276 Brett Kern RC .25 .60
277 Jurrell Casey .25 .60
278 Marcus Mariota .40 1.00
279 Derrick Henry .40 1.00
280 Dion Lewis .25 .60
281 Delanie Walker .25 .60
282 Corey Davis .30 .75
283 Kevin Byard .25 .60
284 Brian Orakpo .25 .60
285 Ryan Kerrigan .25 .60
286 Brandon Scherff .25 .60
287 Walter Jones .25 .60
288 Samaje Perine .25 .60
289 Jamison Crowder .25 .60
290 Josh Norman .25 .60
291 Vernon Davis .25 .60
292 Chris Thompson .25 .60
293 Josh Doctson .25 .60
294 Joe Theismann .40 1.00
295 Frank Gore .30 .75
296 Casey Hayward .25 .60
297 Cameron Jordan .25 .60
298 Damon Harrison .25 .60
299 Isaiah Crowell .25 .60
300 John Elway .60 1.50
301 Sam Darnold RR RC 2.50 6.00
302 Josh Rosen RR RC 1.25 3.00
303 Baker Mayfield RR RC 5.00 12.00
304 Josh Allen RR RC 1.50 4.00
305 Mason Rudolph RR RC 1.00 2.50
306 Saquon Barkley RR RC 3.00 8.00
307 Derrius Guice RR RC .75 2.00
308 Nick Chubb RR RC 1.25 3.00
309 Ronald Jones II RR RC .40 1.00
310 Sony Michel RR RC 1.25 3.00
311 Calvin Ridley RR RC 1.00 2.50
312 Courtland Sutton RR RC .60 1.50
313 Christian Kirk RR RC .60 1.50
314 Anthony Miller RR RC .60 1.50
315 D.J. Chark RR RC .50 1.25
316 D.J. Moore RR RC .75 2.00
317 Lamar Jackson RR RC 2.50 6.00
318 Rashaad Penny RR RC .60 1.50
319 Bradley Chubb RR RC .60 1.50
320 Kerryon Johnson RR RC .60 1.50
321 Dante Pettis RR RC .60 1.50
322 James Washington RR RC .75 2.00
323 Royce Freeman RR RC .50 1.25
324 Michael Gallup RR RC .75 2.00
325 Tre'Quan Smith RR RC .60 1.50
326 Keke Coutee RR RC .50 1.25
327 Nyheim Hines RR RC .50 1.25
328 Kyle Lauletta RR RC .60 1.50
329 Mark Walton RR RC .50 1.25
330 Kalen Ballage RR RC .50 1.25
331 Jaleel Scott RR RC .40 1.00
332 J'Mon Moore RR RC .40 1.00
333 Daurice Fountain RR RC .50 1.25
334 Jaylen Samuels RR RC .50 1.25
335 Mike White RR RC .50 1.25
336 Marquez Valdes-Scantling RR RC .50 1.25
337 Mike Gesicki RR RC .50 1.25
338 DaeSean Hamilton RR RC .50 1.25
339 Hayden Hurst RR RC .50 1.25
340 Ito Smith RR RC .50 1.25
341 Antonio Callaway RR RC .50 1.25
342 Braxton Berrios RR RC .40 1.00
343 Equanimeous St. Brown RR RC .60 1.50
344 Bo Scarbrough RR RC .50 1.25
345 John Kelly RR RC .50 1.25
346 Shaquem Griffin RR RC .60 1.50
347 Dallas Goedert RR RC .50 1.25
348 Denzel Ward RR RC 1.00 2.50
349 Jordan Lasley RR RC .40 1.00
350 Ian Thomas RR RC .40 1.00
351 Quenton Nelson RC .60 1.50
352 Mike McGlinchey RC .75 2.00
353 Minkah Fitzpatrick RC .75 2.00
354 Vita Vea RC .60 1.50
355 Daron Payne RC .60 1.50
356 Marcus Davenport RC .75 2.00
357 Tremaine Edmunds RC .75 2.00
358 Derwin James RC .75 2.00
359 Jaire Alexander RC .60 1.50
360 Leighton Vander Esch RC 1.25 3.00
361 Rashaan Evans RC .60 1.50
362 Terrell Edmunds RC 1.25 3.00
363 Taven Bryan RC .40 1.00
364 Mike Hughes RC .60 1.50
365 Darius Leonard RC 1.00 2.50
366 Harold Landry RC .40 1.00
367 Joshua Jackson RC .75 2.00
368 Breeland Speaks RC .50 1.25
369 Uchenna Nwosu RC .60 1.50
370 Kemoko Turay RC .50 1.25
371 M.J. Stewart RC .40 1.00
372 Jessie Bates RC .60 1.50
373 Donte Jackson RC .60 1.50
374 Duke Dawson RC .40 1.00
375 P.J. Hall RC .50 1.25
376 Isaiah Oliver RC .40 1.00
377 Carlton Davis RC .50 1.25
378 Tyquan Lewis RC .50 1.25
379 Troy Fumagalli RC .50 1.25
380 Tyler Conklin RC .40 1.00
381 Jordan Wilkins RC .50 1.25
382 Luke Falk RC .50 1.25
383 Tanner Lee RC .50 1.25
384 Christopher Herndon IV RC .40 1.00
385 Durham Smythe RC .40 1.00
386 Chase Edmonds RC .40 1.00
387 Dalton Schultz RC .50 1.25
388 Jordan Akins RC .40 1.00
389 Danny Etling RC .50 1.25
390 Alex McGough RC .50 1.25
391 Javon Wims RC .40 1.00
392 Derrick Nnadi RC .40 1.00
393 Da'Shawn Hand RC .40 1.00
394 Micah Kiser RC .40 1.00
395 Marcell Ateman RC .50 1.25
396 Avonte Maddox RC .50 1.25
397 Josh Sweat RC .50 1.25
398 Dylan Cantrell RC .40 1.00
399 Daniel Carlson RC .40 1.00
400 Trenton Cannon RC .50 1.25

2018 Donruss Aqueous Test
*VETS: 2X TO 5X BASIC CARDS
*ROOKIES: 1X TO 2.5X BASIC CARDS
303 Baker Mayfield RR 15.00 40.00
306 Saquon Barkley RR 12.00 30.00

2018 Donruss Press Proof Blue
*VETS: .6X TO 1.5X BASIC CARDS
*ROOKIES: .6X TO 1.5X BASIC CARDS
303 Baker Mayfield RR 10.00 25.00
306 Saquon Barkley RR 8.00 20.00

2018 Donruss Press Proof Gold
*VETS/50: 2X TO 5X BASIC CARDS
*ROOKIES/50: 1.25X TO 3X BASIC CARDS
303 Baker Mayfield RR 25.00 60.00
306 Saquon Barkley RR 25.00 50.00

2018 Donruss Press Proof Gold Die Cut
*VETS/25: 2.5X TO 6X BASIC CARDS
*ROOKIES/25: 1.5X TO 4X BASIC CARDS
303 Baker Mayfield RR 30.00 80.00
306 Saquon Barkley RR 30.00 80.00

2018 Donruss Press Proof Green
*VETS: 1X TO 2.5X BASIC CARDS
*ROOKIES: .8X TO 2X BASIC CARDS
306 Saquon Barkley RR 10.00 25.00

2018 Donruss Press Proof Red
*VETS: 1X TO 2.5X BASIC CARDS
*ROOKIES: .8X TO 2X BASIC CARDS
303 Baker Mayfield RR 12.00 30.00
306 Saquon Barkley RR 10.00 25.00

2018 Donruss Press Proof Silver
*VETS/100: 1.5X TO 4X BASIC CARDS
*ROOKIES/100: 1X TO 2.5X BASIC CARDS
303 Baker Mayfield RR 15.00 40.00
306 Saquon Barkley RR 12.00 30.00

2018 Donruss Press Proof Silver Die Cut
*VETS/75: 1.5X TO 4X BASIC CARDS
303 Baker Mayfield RR 25.00 60.00
306 Saquon Barkley RR 12.00 30.00

2018 Donruss Season Stat Line
*VETS/132-400: 1.2X TO 3X BASIC CARDS
*VETS/65-125: 1.5X TO 4X BASIC CARDS
*VETS/35-64: 2X TO 5X BASIC CARDS
*VETS/26-34: 2.5X TO 6X BASIC CARDS
*VETS/15-23: 3X TO 8X BASIC CARDS
*ROOK/132-400: .8X TO 2X BASIC CARDS
*ROOK/65-125: 1X TO 2.5X BASIC CARDS
*ROOK/35-64: 1.2X TO 3X BASIC CARDS
*ROOK/26-34: 1.5X TO 4X BASIC CARDS
*ROOK/15-23: 2X TO 5X BASIC CARDS
306 Saquon Barkley/99 RR 12.00 30.00

2018 Donruss '88 Tribute
*HOLO/100: 1.5X TO 4X BASIC INSERTS
1 Aaron Rodgers 1.25 3.00
2 Carson Wentz .75 2.00
3 Jameis Winston .50 1.25
4 Deshaun Watson .75 2.00
5 Alvin Kamara .50 1.25
6 Todd Gurley II .60 1.50
7 Tyreek Hill .60 1.50
8 Matt Ryan .50 1.25
9 A.J. Green .60 1.50
10 Jalen Ramsey .50 1.25
11 Matthew Stafford .50 1.25
12 Melvin Gordon .50 1.25
13 Derek Carr .60 1.50
14 Russell Wilson .75 2.00
15 Rob Gronkowski .60 1.50

2018 Donruss '88 Tribute Autographs
5 Alvin Kamara/25 15.00 40.00
7 Tyreek Hill/25 10.00 25.00
12 Melvin Gordon/25 8.00 20.00

2018 Donruss '98 Tribute
*HOLO/100: 1.5X TO 4X BASIC INSERTS
1 Tom Brady 1.50 4.00
2 Odell Beckham Jr. .60 1.50
3 Antonio Brown .60 1.50
4 Jordan Howard .60 1.50
5 Ezekiel Elliott .75 2.00
6 Jared Goff .60 1.50
7 Jimmy Garoppolo .75 2.00
8 Julio Jones .60 1.50
9 Adam Thielen .60 1.50
10 Larry Fitzgerald .50 1.25
11 Drew Brees .60 1.50
12 Marcus Mariota .60 1.50
13 Khalil Mack .60 1.50
14 Von Miller .50 1.25
15 Cam Newton .60 1.50

2018 Donruss '98 Tribute Autographs
9 Adam Thielen/25 30.00 60.00

2018 Donruss All Pro Kings
*STUDIO/25: .6X TO 1.5X BASIC INSERTS/125
1 Ty Law 2.50 6.00
2 Travis Kelce 2.50 6.00
3 Tony Romo 2.00 5.00
4 Tony Gonzalez 2.00 5.00
5 Terrell Suggs 1.50 4.00
6 Ricky Williams 2.00 5.00
7 Jeremy Shockey 1.50 4.00
8 Richard Sherman 2.50 6.00
9 Mike Evans 2.00 5.00
10 Matt Ryan 2.00 5.00
11 Luke Kuechly 2.00 5.00
12 Jordy Nelson 2.00 5.00
13 Jason Witten 2.00 5.00
14 Hines Ward 2.00 5.00
15 Greg Olsen 2.00 5.00
16 Fred Taylor 1.50 4.00
17 Frank Gore 2.00 5.00
18 Edgerrin James 2.00 5.00
19 Earl Thomas III 2.00 5.00
20 Clinton Portis 1.50 4.00
21 Clay Matthews 2.00 5.00
22 Charles Woodson 2.50 6.00
23 Antonio Brown 2.50 6.00
24 A.J. Green 2.50 6.00
25 Cameron Wake 1.50 4.00
26 Calais Campbell 1.50 4.00
27 Dan Marino 5.00 12.00
28 Ezekiel Elliott 3.00 8.00
29 Geno Atkins 1.50 4.00
30 Joe Thomas 1.50 4.00

2018 Donruss All Time Gridiron Kings
*STUDIO/100: 1.5X TO 4X BASIC INSERTS
1 LaVar Arrington .40 1.00
2 Peyton Manning 1.25 3.00
3 Emmitt Smith 1.00 2.50
4 Troy Aikman .75 2.00
5 Michael Irvin .60 1.50
6 Brian Urlacher .60 1.50
7 Dick Butkus .75 2.00
8 John Elway 1.00 2.50
9 Warren Sapp .50 1.25
10 Randy Moss .50 1.25
11 John Lynch .50 1.25
12 Brian Dawkins .60 1.50
13 Thurman Thomas .50 1.25
14 Charles Woodson .60 1.50
15 Larry Little .40 1.00
16 Joe Theismann .60 1.50
17 Barry Sanders 1.00 2.50
18 Curtis Martin .50 1.25
19 Roger Staubach .75 2.00
20 Tony Dorsett .60 1.50
21 Mike Singletary .60 1.50
22 Steve Largent .60 1.50
23 Edgerrin James .50 1.25
24 Terry Bradshaw 1.00 2.50
25 Franco Harris .60 1.50
26 Ozzie Newsome .50 1.25
27 Terrell Davis .50 1.25
28 Jerome Bettis .60 1.50
29 Ty Law .60 1.50
30 Brian Bosworth .50 1.25
31 Shaun Alexander .40 1.00
32 LaDainian Tomlinson .50 1.25
33 Jim Kelly .60 1.50
34 Jason Taylor .50 1.25
35 Howie Long .60 1.50
36 Willis McGahee .40 1.00
37 Carl Eller .40 1.00
38 Deion Sanders .50 1.25
39 Joe Greene .60 1.50
40 Eric Dickerson .60 1.50

2018 Donruss Champ is Here
*HOLO/100: 1.5X TO 4X BASIC INSERTS
1 Nick Foles .50 1.25
2 Jay Ajayi .50 1.25
3 Corey Clement .40 1.00
4 Zach Ertz .50 1.25
5 Brandon Graham .40 1.00
6 Nelson Agholor .40 1.00
7 LeGarrette Blount .50 1.25
8 Trey Burton .40 1.00
9 Alshon Jeffery .50 1.25
10 Torrey Smith .40 1.00
11 Chris Long .40 1.00
12 Jalen Mills .40 1.00
13 Corey Graham .40 1.00
14 Rodney McLeod .40 1.00
15 Fletcher Cox .40 1.00
16 Jake Elliott .50 1.25
17 Derek Barnett .40 1.00
18 Mychal Kendricks .40 1.00
19 Lane Johnson .40 1.00
20 Jason Kelce .40 1.00

2018 Donruss Changing Stripes Jerseys
*PRIME/25: .6X TO 1.5X BASIC JSY/99
*PRIME/15: .4X TO 1X BASIC JSY/20
1 Matt Forte 2.50 6.00
2 Jerome Bettis 4.00 10.00
3 Kenny Stills 2.50 6.00
4 Kiko Alonso 2.50 6.00
5 Kurt Warner 3.00 8.00
6 LaDainian Tomlinson 3.00 8.00
7 Lamar Miller 2.50 6.00
8 LeSean McCoy 4.00 10.00
9 Marcus Allen 4.00 10.00
10 Marshall Faulk 3.00 8.00
11 Marshawn Lynch 3.00 8.00
12 Maurice Jones-Drew 2.50 6.00
13 Michael Vick 3.00 8.00
14 Champ Bailey 3.00 8.00
15 Rich Gannon 3.00 8.00
16 Ricky Williams 3.00 8.00
17 Warren Moon 4.00 10.00
18 Deion Sanders/20 6.00 15.00
19 Alshon Jeffery 3.00 8.00
20 Brett Favre 8.00 20.00

2018 Donruss Dominators
1 Russell Wilson .75 2.00
2 Todd Gurley II .60 1.50
3 Alvin Kamara .50 1.25
4 Leonard Fournette .60 1.50
5 Deshaun Watson .75 2.00
6 Carson Wentz .75 2.00
7 Jared Goff .60 1.50
8 Le'Veon Bell .50 1.25
9 Antonio Brown .60 1.50
10 Tom Brady 1.50 4.00
11 Cam Newton .60 1.50
12 Ezekiel Elliott .75 2.00
13 Matthew Stafford .50 1.25
14 Drew Brees .60 1.50
15 Kareem Hunt .50 1.25
16 Melvin Gordon .50 1.25
17 Keenan Allen .50 1.25
18 Jordan Howard .60 1.50
19 Larry Fitzgerald .50 1.25
20 Matt Ryan .50 1.25
21 Julio Jones .60 1.50
22 Marcus Mariota .60 1.50
23 Derek Carr .60 1.50
24 Khalil Mack .60 1.50
25 J.J. Watt .60 1.50
26 Rob Gronkowski .60 1.50
27 Travis Kelce .60 1.50
28 Chandler Jones .40 1.00
29 Calais Campbell .40 1.00
30 DeMarcus Lawrence .40 1.00
31 Kevin Byard .40 1.00
32 A.J. Bouye .40 1.00
33 Jalen Ramsey .50 1.25
34 Luke Kuechly .50 1.25
35 Bobby Wagner .40 1.00
36 Aaron Donald .60 1.50
37 Joey Bosa .60 1.50
38 Julius Peppers .50 1.25
39 Cameron Wake .40 1.00
40 Terrell Suggs .40 1.00

2018 Donruss Dominators Autographs
3 Alvin Kamara/25 15.00 40.00
15 Kareem Hunt/25 8.00 20.00
16 Melvin Gordon/25 8.00 20.00
27 Travis Kelce/25 10.00 25.00
28 Chandler Jones/25 6.00 15.00
31 Kevin Byard/25 12.00 30.00
34 Luke Kuechly/25 EXCH 12.00 30.00
36 Aaron Donald/25 10.00 25.00
37 Joey Bosa/25 10.00 25.00
40 Terrell Suggs/25 6.00 15.00

2018 Donruss Fans of the Game Autographs
1 James Caan 12.00 30.00
2 Chris Evans 50.00 100.00
3 Matthew Berry 6.00 15.00
4 Drea de Matteo 6.00 15.00
5 Chloe Kim 25.00 50.00

2018 Donruss Glory
*HOLO/100: 1.5X TO 4X BASIC INSERTS
1 Alejandro Villanueva .50 1.25
2 Roger Staubach .75 2.00
3 Drew Brees .60 1.50
4 Derek Carr .60 1.50
5 Larry Fitzgerald .50 1.25
6 Doug Baldwin .50 1.25
7 Delanie Walker .40 1.00
8 J.J. Watt .60 1.50
9 Joe Thomas .40 1.00
10 Jarvis Landry .50 1.25

2018 Donruss Gridiron Kings
*STUDIO/100: 1.5X TO 4X BASIC INSERTS
1 Tom Brady 1.50 4.00
2 Larry Fitzgerald .50 1.25
3 Matt Ryan .50 1.25
4 Julio Jones .60 1.50
5 Joe Flacco .50 1.25
6 LeSean McCoy .60 1.50
7 Luke Kuechly .50 1.25
8 Cam Newton .60 1.50
9 Jordan Howard .60 1.50
10 A.J. Green .60 1.50
11 Myles Garrett .60 1.50
12 Dak Prescott .60 1.50
13 Jason Witten .50 1.25
14 Von Miller .50 1.25
15 Matthew Stafford .50 1.25
16 Aaron Rodgers 1.25 3.00
17 Doug Baldwin .50 1.25
18 J.J. Watt .60 1.50
19 Andrew Luck .75 2.00
20 Blake Bortles .40 1.00
21 Tyreek Hill .60 1.50
22 Keenan Allen .50 1.25
23 Kenyan Drake .40 1.00
24 Adam Thielen .60 1.50
25 Alvin Kamara .50 1.25
26 Odell Beckham Jr. .60 1.50
27 Jamal Adams .50 1.25
28 Derek Carr .60 1.50
29 Khalil Mack .60 1.50
30 Carson Wentz .75 2.00
31 Fletcher Cox .40 1.00
32 Antonio Brown .60 1.50
33 Le'Veon Bell .50 1.25
34 Jimmy Garoppolo .75 2.00
35 Russell Wilson .75 2.00
36 Jameis Winston .50 1.25
37 Mike Evans .50 1.25
38 Marcus Mariota .60 1.50
39 Alex Smith .50 1.25
40 Josh Norman .40 1.00

2018 Donruss Gridiron Kings Autographs
6 LeSean McCoy/25 10.00 25.00
7 Luke Kuechly/25 EXCH 12.00 30.00
9 Jordan Howard/25 10.00 25.00
17 Doug Baldwin/25
21 Tyreek Hill/25 10.00 25.00
23 Kenyan Drake/25 6.00 15.00
24 Adam Thielen/25 30.00 60.00
25 Alvin Kamara/25 15.00 40.00
27 Jamal Adams/25 8.00 20.00
31 Fletcher Cox/25 6.00 15.00
39 Alex Smith/25 20.00 50.00

2018 Donruss Ground Force
*HOLO/100: 1.5X TO 4X BASIC INSERTS
1 Kareem Hunt .50 1.25
2 Alvin Kamara .50 1.25
3 Jordan Howard .60 1.50
4 Dalvin Cook .50 1.25
5 Leonard Fournette .60 1.50
6 Ezekiel Elliott .75 2.00
7 David Johnson .60 1.50
8 LeSean McCoy .60 1.50
9 Christian McCaffrey .60 1.50
10 Devontae Booker .40 1.00
11 Le'Veon Bell .50 1.25
12 Frank Gore .50 1.25
13 Melvin Gordon .50 1.25
14 Todd Gurley II .60 1.50
15 Kenyan Drake .40 1.00
16 Mark Ingram .50 1.25
17 Jay Ajayi .50 1.25
18 Carlos Hyde .40 1.00
19 Derrick Henry .60 1.50
20 Samaje Perine .40 1.00

2018 Donruss Ground Force Autographs
1 Kareem Hunt/49 6.00 15.00
2 Alvin Kamara/25 15.00 40.00
3 Jordan Howard/49 8.00 20.00
5 Leonard Fournette/25
7 David Johnson/49 10.00 25.00
8 LeSean McCoy/25 10.00 25.00
9 Christian McCaffrey/25 10.00 25.00
12 Frank Gore/25 8.00 20.00
13 Melvin Gordon/25 8.00 20.00
15 Kenyan Drake/49 5.00 12.00
16 Mark Ingram/25
18 Carlos Hyde/49 5.00 12.00
19 DeMarco Murray/49 6.00 15.00

2018 Donruss Highlights
*HOLO/100: 1.5X TO 4X BASIC INSERTS
1 Chandler Jones .40 1.00
2 Adrian Clayborn .40 1.00
3 Christian McCaffrey .60 1.50
4 Kareem Hunt .50 1.25
5 Alvin Kamara .50 1.25
6 Drew Brees .60 1.50
7 Tom Brady 1.50 4.00
8 Antonio Brown .60 1.50
9 Calais Campbell .40 1.00
10 Myles Garrett .60 1.50
11 Deshaun Watson .75 2.00
12 Kareem Hunt .50 1.25
13 Case Keenum .50 1.25
14 Todd Gurley II .60 1.50
15 Tom Brady 1.50 4.00

16 JuJu Smith-Schuster .60 1.50
17 Carson Wentz .75 2.00
18 DeAndre Hopkins .50 1.25
19 DeMarcus Lawrence .40 1.00
20 Le'Veon Bell .50 1.25

2018 Donruss Inducted

*HOLO/100: 1.5X TO 4X BASIC INSERTS
1 Brian Urlacher .60 1.50
2 Brian Dawkins .60 1.50
3 Randy Moss .50 1.25
5 Jerry Kramer .40 1.00

2018 Donruss Inducted Autographs

2 Brian Dawkins/49 40.00 80.00
5 Jerry Kramer/99 25.00 50.00

2018 Donruss Jersey Kings

*STUDIO/25: .6X TO 1.5X BASIC JSY/150
1 Aaron Rodgers 8.00 20.00
2 Todd Gurley II 4.00 10.00
3 Dak Prescott 4.00 10.00
4 Leonard Fournette 4.00 10.00
5 Blake Bortles 2.50 6.00
6 Matthew Stafford 3.00 8.00
7 David Johnson 4.00 10.00
8 Matt Ryan 3.00 8.00
9 Joe Flacco 3.00 8.00
10 LeSean McCoy 4.00 10.00
11 Luke Kuechly 3.00 8.00
12 Christian McCaffrey 4.00 10.00
13 Jordan Howard 4.00 10.00
14 Mitchell Trubisky 4.00 10.00
15 Jadeveon Clowney 2.50 6.00
16 Andrew Luck 5.00 12.00
17 Kareem Hunt 3.00 8.00
18 Patrick Mahomes II 10.00 25.00
19 Joey Bosa 4.00 10.00
20 Melvin Gordon 3.00 8.00
21 Jared Goff 4.00 10.00
22 Stefon Diggs 3.00 8.00
23 Dalvin Cook 3.00 8.00
24 Kenyan Drake 2.50 6.00
25 Alvin Kamara 3.00 8.00
26 Evan Engram 2.50 6.00
27 Khalil Mack 4.00 10.00
28 Carson Wentz 5.00 12.00
29 Antonio Brown 4.00 10.00
30 JuJu Smith-Schuster 4.00 10.00
31 Ben Roethlisberger 4.00 10.00
32 Russell Wilson 5.00 12.00
33 Doug Baldwin 3.00 8.00
34 Jameis Winston 3.00 8.00
35 O.J. Howard 2.50 6.00
36 DeMarco Murray 3.00 8.00
37 Marcus Mariota 4.00 10.00
38 Samaje Perine 2.50 6.00
39 Deshaun Watson 5.00 12.00
40 Odell Beckham Jr. 4.00 10.00

2018 Donruss Leather Kings

*STUDIO/25: .6X TO 1.5X BASIC BALL/99
*STUDIO/25: .5X TO 1.2X BASIC BALL/49
1 Andrew Luck 5.00 12.00
2 Joe Montana 10.00 25.00
3 Carlos Hyde/25 4.00 10.00
4 Carson Wentz 5.00 12.00
5 Dak Prescott 4.00 10.00
6 Jameis Winston 3.00 8.00
7 Jay Ajayi 3.00 8.00
8 Jimmy Garoppolo 12.00 30.00
10 Tom Brady/49 15.00 40.00

2018 Donruss Legends of the Fall

*HOLO/100: 1.5X TO 4X BASIC INSERTS
1 Brian Dawkins .60 1.50
2 Jason Taylor .50 1.25
3 Brian Urlacher .60 1.50
4 Randy Moss .50 1.25
5 Peyton Manning 1.25 3.00
6 Michael Strahan .50 1.25
7 Tony Gonzalez .50 1.25
8 Curtis Martin .50 1.25
9 Charles Woodson .60 1.50
10 Jerry Rice 1.00 2.50
11 Terrell Davis .50 1.25
12 Dick Butkus .75 2.00
13 Bruce Smith .50 1.25
14 Hines Ward .50 1.25
15 Tim Brown .60 1.50
16 Michael Irvin .60 1.50
17 Cris Carter .60 1.50
18 Joe Theismann .60 1.50
19 Jonathan Ogden .50 1.25
20 Emmitt Smith 1.00 2.50

2018 Donruss Legends of the Fall Autographs

1 Brian Dawkins/25 40.00 100.00
7 Tony Gonzalez/25
8 Curtis Martin/25 8.00 20.00
12 Dick Butkus/25 15.00 40.00
13 Bruce Smith/25 12.00 30.00
14 Hines Ward/25 12.00 30.00
15 Tim Brown/25 10.00 25.00
18 Joe Theismann/25 10.00 25.00

2018 Donruss Matthew Berry's Fantasy Life

1 Aaron Rodgers 1.25 3.00
2 Tom Brady 1.50 4.00
3 Russell Wilson .75 2.00
4 Deshaun Watson .75 2.00
5 Carson Wentz .75 2.00
6 Le'Veon Bell .50 1.25
7 Todd Gurley II .60 1.50
8 David Johnson .60 1.50
9 Ezekiel Elliott .75 2.00
10 Kareem Hunt .50 1.25
11 Antonio Brown .60 1.50
12 DeAndre Hopkins .50 1.25
13 Michael Thomas .60 1.50
14 Rob Gronkowski .60 1.50
15 Travis Kelce .60 1.50
16 Saquon Barkley 3.00 8.00
17 Derrius Guice .75 2.00
18 Rashaad Penny .60 1.50
19 Sony Michel 1.25 3.00
20 Royce Freeman .50 1.25

2018 Donruss Matthew Berry's Fantasy Life Autographs

7 Todd Gurley II/25 10.00 25.00
8 David Johnson/25 10.00 25.00
9 Ezekiel Elliott/25
10 Kareem Hunt/25 8.00 20.00
11 Antonio Brown/25 30.00 60.00
14 Rob Gronkowski/25 12.00 30.00
15 Travis Kelce/49 8.00 20.00
16 Saquon Barkley/49 150.00 250.00
17 Derrius Guice/49 10.00 25.00
18 Rashaad Penny/49 8.00 20.00
19 Sony Michel/49 15.00 40.00
20 Royce Freeman/49 6.00 15.00

2018 Donruss MVP

*HOLO/100: 1.5X TO 4X BASIC INSERTS
1 Tom Brady 1.50 4.00
2 Matt Ryan .50 1.25
3 Cam Newton .60 1.50
4 Aaron Rodgers 1.25 3.00
5 Peyton Manning 1.25 3.00
6 Adrian Peterson .60 1.50
7 LaDainian Tomlinson .50 1.25
8 Rich Gannon .50 1.25
9 Kurt Warner .50 1.25
10 Marshall Faulk .50 1.25
11 Terrell Davis .50 1.25
12 Barry Sanders 1.00 2.50
13 Brett Favre 1.25 3.00
14 Steve Young .75 2.00
15 Emmitt Smith 1.00 2.50
16 Thurman Thomas .50 1.25
17 Joe Montana 1.50 4.00
18 John Elway 1.00 2.50
19 Lawrence Taylor .60 1.50
20 Marcus Allen .60 1.50
21 Dan Marino 1.25 3.00
22 Joe Theismann .60 1.50
23 Earl Campbell .60 1.50
24 Terry Bradshaw 1.00 2.50
25 Fran Tarkenton .60 1.50

2018 Donruss Passing the Torch Jerseys

1 B.Chubb/V.Miller 5.00 12.00
2 J.Namath/S.Darnold 20.00 50.00
3 J.Kelly/J.Allen 12.00 30.00
4 J.Rosen/K.Warner 12.00 30.00
5 C.Ridley/J.Jones 8.00 20.00
6 M.Lynch/R.Penny 5.00 12.00
7 J.Flacco/L.Jackson 12.00 30.00
8 C.Martin/S.Michel 10.00 25.00
9 C.Sutton/D.Thomas 5.00 12.00
10 A.Abdullah/K.Johnson 5.00 12.00
11 C.Kirk/L.Fitzgerald 5.00 12.00
12 C.Portis/D.Guice 6.00 15.00
13 H.Ward/J.Washington 6.00 15.00
14 R.Freeman/T.Davis 4.00 10.00
15 B.Rthlsbrgr/M.Rudolph 8.00 20.00
16 E.Manning/K.Lauletta 5.00 12.00
17 M.White/T.Romo 4.00 10.00
18 D.Chark/M.Lee 4.00 10.00
19 D.Bryant/M.Gallup 6.00 15.00
20 F.Gore/N.Hines 4.00 10.00

2018 Donruss Rookie Gridiron Kings

*STUDIO/100: 1.2X TO 3X BASIC INSERTS
1 Sam Darnold 3.00 8.00
2 Josh Rosen 1.50 4.00
3 Baker Mayfield 5.00 12.00
4 Josh Allen 2.00 5.00
5 Mason Rudolph 1.25 3.00
6 Saquon Barkley 4.00 10.00
7 Derrius Guice 1.00 2.50
8 Nick Chubb 1.50 4.00
9 Ronald Jones II .50 1.25
10 Sony Michel 1.50 4.00
11 Calvin Ridley 1.25 3.00
12 Courtland Sutton .75 2.00
13 Christian Kirk .75 2.00
14 Anthony Miller .75 2.00
15 D.J. Chark .60 1.50
16 D.J. Moore 1.00 2.50
17 Lamar Jackson 3.00 8.00
18 Rashaad Penny .75 2.00
19 Bradley Chubb .75 2.00
20 Kerryon Johnson .75 2.00

2018 Donruss Rookie Gridiron Kings Autographs

5 Mason Rudolph/49 12.00 30.00
7 Derrius Guice/49 10.00 25.00
8 Nick Chubb/49 15.00 40.00
9 Ronald Jones II/49 5.00 12.00
10 Sony Michel/49 15.00 40.00
11 Calvin Ridley/49 12.00 30.00
12 Courtland Sutton/49 8.00 20.00
13 Christian Kirk/49 8.00 20.00
14 Anthony Miller/49 8.00 20.00
15 D.J. Chark/49 EXCH 6.00 15.00
16 D.J. Moore/49 10.00 25.00
18 Rashaad Penny/49 EXCH 8.00 20.00
19 Bradley Chubb/49 8.00 20.00
20 Kerryon Johnson/49 8.00 20.00

2018 Donruss Rookie Phenom Jersey Autographs

COMMON CARD/99 6.00 15.00
1 Sam Darnold/49 50.00 100.00
2 Josh Rosen/49 15.00 40.00
3 Baker Mayfield/49 60.00 125.00
4 Josh Allen/49 40.00 80.00
5 Mason Rudolph/99 10.00 25.00
6 Saquon Barkley/49 90.00 150.00
7 Derrius Guice/99 8.00 20.00
8 Nick Chubb/99 12.00 30.00
9 Ronald Jones II/99 4.00 10.00
10 Sony Michel/99 12.00 30.00
11 Calvin Ridley/99 10.00 25.00
12 Courtland Sutton/99 6.00 15.00
13 Christian Kirk/99 6.00 15.00
14 Anthony Miller/99 6.00 15.00
15 D.J. Chark/99 EXCH 5.00 12.00
16 D.J. Moore/99 8.00 20.00
17 Lamar Jackson/15
18 Rashaad Penny/99 EXCH 6.00 15.00
19 Bradley Chubb/99 6.00 15.00
20 Kerryon Johnson/99 10.00 25.00

2018 Donruss Rookie Phenom Jersey Autographs Prime

6 Saquon Barkley 100.00 200.00

2018 Donruss Rookie Threads

*BLUE: .4X TO 1X BASIC JSY
*ORANGE: .4X TO 1X BASIC JSY
*PRIME/25: 1X TO 2.5X BASIC JSY
*RED: .4X TO 1X BASIC INSERTS
1 Sam Darnold 5.00 12.00
2 Josh Rosen 5.00 12.00
3 Baker Mayfield 6.00 15.00
4 Josh Allen 4.00 10.00
5 Mason Rudolph 3.00 8.00
6 Saquon Barkley 6.00 15.00
7 Derrius Guice 2.50 6.00
8 Nick Chubb 4.00 10.00
9 Ronald Jones II 1.25 3.00
10 Sony Michel 3.00 8.00
11 Calvin Ridley 3.00 8.00
12 Courtland Sutton 2.00 5.00
13 Christian Kirk 2.00 5.00
14 Anthony Miller 2.00 5.00
15 D.J. Chark 1.50 4.00
16 D.J. Moore 2.50 6.00
17 Lamar Jackson 5.00 12.00
18 Rashaad Penny 2.00 5.00
19 Bradley Chubb 2.00 5.00
20 Kerryon Johnson 2.00 5.00
21 Dante Pettis 2.00 5.00
22 James Washington 2.50 6.00
23 Royce Freeman 1.50 4.00
24 Michael Gallup 2.50 6.00
25 Tre'Quan Smith 2.00 5.00
26 Keke Coutee 1.50 4.00
27 Nyheim Hines 1.50 4.00
28 Kyle Lauletta 2.00 5.00
29 Mark Walton 1.50 4.00
30 Kalen Ballage 1.50 4.00
31 Jaleel Scott 1.25 3.00
32 J'Mon Moore 1.25 3.00
33 Daurice Fountain 1.50 4.00
34 Jaylen Samuels 1.50 4.00
35 Mike White 1.50 4.00
36 M.VldsScntlng 1.50 4.00
37 Mike Gesicki 1.50 4.00
38 DaeSean Hamilton 1.50 4.00
39 Hayden Hurst 1.50 4.00
40 Ito Smith 1.50 4.00

2018 Donruss Signature Marks

1 Aaron Donald 6.00 15.00
2 Adam Thielen 15.00 40.00
3 Alex Collins 4.00 10.00
4 Alex Smith 12.00 30.00
5 Allen Robinson 5.00 12.00
6 Alvin Kamara 10.00 25.00
7 Andre Reed
8 Antonio Brown 25.00 50.00
9 Blake Bortles 4.00 10.00
10 C.J. Mosley 5.00 12.00
11 Cameron Heyward 4.00 10.00
12 Chandler Jones 4.00 10.00
13 Charlie Joiner 4.00 10.00
14 Chris Doleman 8.00 20.00
15 Corey Coleman 4.00 10.00
16 Corey Davis 5.00 12.00
17 Curtis Martin 5.00 12.00
18 David Johnson 8.00 20.00
19 Dede Westbrook 4.00 10.00
20 Deion Sanders 25.00 50.00
21 Deshaun Watson
22 Devin Hester 6.00 15.00
23 D'Onta Foreman 4.00 10.00
24 Earl Campbell
25 Edgerrin James 5.00 12.00
26 Melvin Ingram 4.00 10.00
27 Eric Dickerson 6.00 15.00
28 Ezekiel Elliott
29 Fletcher Cox 4.00 10.00
30 Greg Olsen 5.00 12.00
31 Harrison Smith 15.00 40.00
32 J.D. McKissic 4.00 10.00
33 Jamal Adams 5.00 12.00
34 James Harrison 10.00 25.00
35 Jared Goff 30.00 60.00
36 Jeff Garcia 4.00 10.00
37 Jerick McKinnon 4.00 10.00
38 Jermaine Kearse 4.00 10.00
39 Jimmy Garoppolo 40.00 80.00
40 Joe Klecko 4.00 10.00
41 Joe Mixon 5.00 12.00
42 Joe Montana 75.00 150.00
43 Joe Namath
44 Joe Theismann 6.00 15.00
45 Jonathan Stewart 4.00 10.00
46 JuJu Smith-Schuster 10.00 25.00
47 Justin Tucker 10.00 25.00
48 Ken Anderson 10.00 25.00
49 LaVar Arrington 4.00 10.00
50 LeGarrette Blount 5.00 12.00
51 Leonard Fournette 10.00 25.00
52 Lynn Dickey 8.00 20.00
53 Malik Hooker 4.00 10.00
54 Marcus Peters 4.00 10.00
55 Mark Gastineau 4.00 10.00
56 Marquette King 4.00 10.00
57 Marshall Faulk 8.00 20.00
58 Marshon Lattimore 8.00 20.00
59 Mike Alstott 8.00 20.00
60 Mitchell Trubisky 30.00 60.00
61 Nelson Agholor 4.00 10.00
62 O.J. Howard 4.00 10.00
63 Ottis Anderson
64 Patrick Mahomes II 10.00 25.00
65 Terrell Suggs 4.00 10.00
66 Ricky Williams 5.00 12.00
67 Stephon Gilmore 4.00 10.00
68 Sterling Shepard 5.00 12.00
69 Tony Romo
70 Vinny Testaverde 4.00 10.00
71 Josh Rosen 10.00 25.00
72 Sam Darnold 25.00 50.00
73 Luke Falk 4.00 10.00
74 Baker Mayfield 100.00 200.00
75 Josh Allen 30.00 60.00
76 Mason Rudolph 8.00 20.00
77 Saquon Barkley 60.00 125.00
78 Derrius Guice 6.00 15.00
79 Nick Chubb 10.00 25.00
80 Sony Michel 10.00 25.00
81 Ronald Jones II 3.00 8.00
82 Calvin Ridley 8.00 20.00
83 Courtland Sutton 5.00 12.00
84 Christian Kirk 5.00 12.00
85 Anthony Miller 5.00 12.00
87 D.J. Moore 6.00 15.00
89 Mike White 4.00 10.00
90 Simmie Cobbs Jr. 5.00 12.00
91 Royce Freeman 4.00 10.00
92 Kerryon Johnson 5.00 12.00
94 Kalen Ballage 4.00 10.00
95 Nyheim Hines 4.00 10.00
96 Bo Scarbrough 4.00 10.00
97 Deontay Burnett 4.00 10.00
98 Marcell Ateman 4.00 10.00
99 Dallas Goedert 4.00 10.00
100 Bradley Chubb 5.00 12.00

2018 Donruss Snow Days

*HOLO/100: 1.5X TO 4X BASIC INSERTS
1 Matthew Stafford .50 1.25
2 Joe Namath .75 2.00
3 Nick Foles .50 1.25
4 JuJu Smith-Schuster .60 1.50
5 Tom Brady 1.50 4.00
6 Brian Urlacher .60 1.50
7 Le'Veon Bell .50 1.25
8 Antonio Brown .60 1.50
9 Brett Favre 1.25 3.00
10 Aaron Rodgers 1.25 3.00
11 Jabrill Peppers .40 1.00
12 Troy Aikman .75 2.00
13 Myles Garrett .60 1.50
14 Marlon Mack .40 1.00
15 Clay Matthews .50 1.25
16 DeAndre Hopkins .50 1.25
17 Frank Gore .50 1.25
18 Jordan Howard .60 1.50
19 Von Miller .50 1.25
20 Chuck Foreman .40 1.00

2018 Donruss Snow Days Autographs

3 Nick Foles/25 8.00 20.00
4 JuJu Smith-Schuster/49 8.00 20.00
12 Troy Aikman/10
14 Marlon Mack/49 5.00 12.00
15 Clay Matthews/10
17 Frank Gore/25 8.00 20.00
18 Jordan Howard/49 8.00 20.00

2018 Donruss Sophomore Swatches

*PRIME/25: .6X TO 1.5X BASIC JSY/150
1 T.J. Watt 3.00 8.00
2 Jabrill Peppers 2.50 6.00
3 Ryan Switzer 2.50 6.00
4 Mitchell Trubisky 4.00 10.00
5 Deshaun Watson 5.00 12.00
6 Kareem Hunt 3.00 8.00
7 Patrick Mahomes II 10.00 25.00
8 Leonard Fournette 4.00 10.00
9 JuJu Smith-Schuster 4.00 10.00
10 Christian McCaffrey 4.00 10.00
11 Dalvin Cook 3.00 8.00
12 Mike Williams 2.50 6.00
13 Corey Davis 3.00 8.00
14 Evan Engram 2.50 6.00
15 O.J. Howard 2.50 6.00
16 Alvin Kamara 3.00 8.00
17 Joe Mixon 3.00 8.00
18 Samaje Perine 2.50 6.00
19 Kenny Golladay 2.50 6.00
20 Cooper Kupp 3.00 8.00

2018 Donruss Team Heroes

1 Tom Brady 1.50 4.00
2 Antonio Brown .60 1.50
3 Alvin Kamara .50 1.25
4 Deshaun Watson .75 2.00
5 Carson Wentz .75 2.00
6 Julio Jones .60 1.50
7 Kareem Hunt .50 1.25
8 Jimmy Garoppolo .75 2.00
9 Aaron Rodgers 1.25 3.00
10 A.J. Green .60 1.50
11 Tyreek Hill .60 1.50
12 Khalil Mack .60 1.50
13 Odell Beckham Jr. .60 1.50
14 Adam Thielen .60 1.50
15 Jordan Howard .60 1.50
16 Larry Fitzgerald .50 1.25
17 Jared Goff .60 1.50
18 Jalen Ramsey .50 1.25
19 Jason Witten .50 1.25
20 Matthew Stafford .50 1.25

2018 Donruss The Elite Series

1 Leonard Fournette .60 1.50
2 Alvin Kamara .50 1.25
3 Deshaun Watson .75 2.00
4 Andrew Luck .75 2.00
5 Jameis Winston .50 1.25
6 Ben Roethlisberger .60 1.50
7 Ezekiel Elliott .75 2.00
8 Dak Prescott .60 1.50
9 Matt Ryan .50 1.25
10 Julio Jones .60 1.50
11 Derek Carr .60 1.50
12 Carson Wentz .75 2.00
13 Jared Goff .60 1.50
14 Todd Gurley II .60 1.50
15 Jordan Howard .60 1.50
16 Christian McCaffrey .60 1.50
17 Adam Thielen .60 1.50
18 Jimmy Garoppolo .75 2.00
19 Von Miller .50 1.25
20 Antonio Brown .60 1.50
21 Aaron Rodgers 1.25 3.00
22 Odell Beckham Jr. .60 1.50
23 Drew Brees .60 1.50
24 Tom Brady 1.50 4.00
25 Rob Gronkowski .60 1.50
26 Travis Kelce .60 1.50
27 Joe Thomas .40 1.00
28 Vic Beasley Jr. .40 1.00
29 Fletcher Cox .40 1.00
30 Larry Fitzgerald .50 1.25

2018 Donruss The Elite Series Autographs

2 Alvin Kamara 15.00 40.00
15 Jordan Howard 10.00 25.00
16 Christian McCaffrey 10.00 25.00
17 Adam Thielen 30.00 60.00
26 Travis Kelce 10.00 25.00
28 Vic Beasley Jr.
29 Fletcher Cox 6.00 15.00

2018 Donruss The Elite Series Rookies Autographs

5 Mason Rudolph/49 12.00 30.00
7 Derrius Guice/49 10.00 25.00
8 Nick Chubb/49 15.00 40.00
9 Ronald Jones II/99 6.00 15.00
10 Sony Michel/49 15.00 40.00
11 Calvin Ridley/49 12.00 30.00
12 Courtland Sutton/49 8.00 20.00
13 Christian Kirk/49 8.00 20.00
14 Anthony Miller/99 10.00 25.00
15 D.J. Chark/99 EXCH 8.00 20.00
16 D.J. Moore/99 12.00 30.00
18 Rashaad Penny/99 EXCH 10.00 25.00
19 Bradley Chubb/99 10.00 25.00
20 Kerryon Johnson/99 10.00 25.00
21 Dante Pettis/99 10.00 25.00
22 James Washington/99 12.00 30.00
23 Royce Freeman/99 8.00 20.00
24 Michael Gallup/99 12.00 30.00
25 Tre'Quan Smith/99 10.00 25.00
26 Keke Coutee/99 8.00 20.00
27 Nyheim Hines/99 8.00 20.00
28 Kyle Lauletta/99
29 Mark Walton/99
30 Kalen Ballage/99 8.00 20.00

2018 Donruss The Legends Series

1 Peyton Manning 1.25 3.00
2 Deion Sanders .50 1.25
3 Brian Urlacher .60 1.50
4 Bruce Smith .50 1.25
5 Eric Dickerson .60 1.50
6 Rod Woodson .60 1.50
7 Dan Marino 1.25 3.00
8 Terry Bradshaw 1.00 2.50
9 Steve Young .75 2.00
10 Michael Strahan .50 1.25
11 Marshall Faulk .50 1.25
12 Michael Irvin .60 1.50
13 Tony Gonzalez .50 1.25
14 Randy Moss .50 1.25
15 Joe Namath .75 2.00
16 Jonathan Ogden .50 1.25
17 John Lynch .50 1.25
18 Shaun Alexander .40 1.00
19 Mike Alstott .40 1.00
20 Bo Jackson .75 2.00

2018 Donruss The Rookies

1 Sam Darnold 3.00 8.00
2 Josh Rosen 1.50 4.00
3 Baker Mayfield 5.00 12.00
4 Josh Allen 2.00 5.00
5 Mason Rudolph 1.25 3.00
6 Saquon Barkley 4.00 10.00
7 Derrius Guice 1.00 2.50
8 Nick Chubb 1.50 4.00
9 Ronald Jones II .50 1.25
10 Sony Michel 1.50 4.00
11 Calvin Ridley 1.25 3.00
12 Courtland Sutton .75 2.00
13 Christian Kirk .75 2.00
14 Anthony Miller .75 2.00
15 D.J. Chark .60 1.50
16 D.J. Moore 1.00 2.50
17 Lamar Jackson 3.00 8.00
18 Rashaad Penny .75 2.00
19 Bradley Chubb .75 2.00
20 Kerryon Johnson .75 2.00
21 Dante Pettis .75 2.00
22 James Washington 1.00 2.50
23 Royce Freeman .60 1.50
24 Michael Gallup 1.00 2.50
25 Tre'Quan Smith .75 2.00
26 Keke Coutee .60 1.50
27 Nyheim Hines .60 1.50
28 Kyle Lauletta .75 2.00
29 Mark Walton .60 1.50
30 Kalen Ballage .60 1.50
31 Jaleel Scott .50 1.25
32 J'Mon Moore .50 1.25
33 Daurice Fountain .60 1.50
34 Jaylen Samuels .60 1.50
35 Mike White .60 1.50
36 Marquez Valdes-Scantling .60 1.50
37 Mike Gesicki .60 1.50
38 DaeSean Hamilton .60 1.50
39 Hayden Hurst .60 1.50
40 Ito Smith .60 1.50

2018 Donruss The Rookies Autographs

5 Mason Rudolph/49 12.00 30.00
7 Derrius Guice/25 12.00 30.00
8 Nick Chubb/49 15.00 40.00
9 Ronald Jones II/499 3.00 8.00
10 Sony Michel/49 15.00 40.00
11 Calvin Ridley/25 15.00 40.00
12 Courtland Sutton/49 8.00 20.00
13 Christian Kirk/49 8.00 20.00
14 Anthony Miller/199 5.00 12.00
16 D.J. Moore/49 10.00 25.00
18 Rashaad Penny/299 EXCH 5.00 12.00
19 Bradley Chubb/299 5.00 12.00
20 Kerryon Johnson/499 5.00 12.00
21 Dante Pettis/499 5.00 12.00
22 James Washington/499 6.00 15.00
23 Royce Freeman/499 4.00 10.00
24 Michael Gallup/499 6.00 15.00
25 Tre'Quan Smith/499 5.00 12.00
26 Keke Coutee/499 4.00 10.00
27 Nyheim Hines/499 4.00 10.00
30 Kalen Ballage/499 4.00 10.00
31 Jaleel Scott/499 3.00 8.00
32 J'Mon Moore/499 3.00 8.00
33 Daurice Fountain/499 4.00 10.00
35 Mike White/499 4.00 10.00
36 M.VldsScntlng/499 4.00 10.00
37 Mike Gesicki/499 4.00 10.00
38 DaeSean Hamilton/499 4.00 10.00
39 Hayden Hurst/499 4.00 10.00
40 Ito Smith/299 4.00 10.00

2018 Donruss Threads

1 Andrew Luck 5.00 12.00
2 Allen Robinson 3.00 8.00
3 Corey Coleman 2.50 6.00
4 D'Onta Foreman 2.50 6.00
5 Dak Prescott 4.00 10.00
6 Ezekiel Elliott 5.00 12.00
7 Dalvin Cook 3.00 8.00
8 David Johnson 4.00 10.00
9 Derrick Henry 4.00 10.00
10 Hunter Henry 2.50 6.00
11 Joey Bosa 4.00 10.00
12 Jared Goff 4.00 10.00
13 Jordan Howard 4.00 10.00
14 Todd Gurley II 4.00 10.00
15 Kenyan Drake 2.50 6.00
16 Khalil Mack 4.00 10.00
17 Michael Thomas 4.00 10.00
18 Patrick Mahomes II 10.00 25.00
19 Wayne Gallman 2.50 6.00
20 Sterling Shepard 3.00 8.00
21 Will Fuller V 2.50 6.00
22 Adam Vinatieri 2.50 6.00
23 A.J. McCarron 2.50 6.00
24 Alshon Jeffery 3.00 8.00
25 Amari Cooper 4.00 10.00
26 Ameer Abdullah 2.50 6.00
27 Andy Dalton 3.00 8.00
28 Antonio Gates 2.50 6.00
29 Blake Bortles 2.50 6.00
30 Brandin Cooks 3.00 8.00
31 Clay Matthews 3.00 8.00
32 DeAndre Hopkins 3.00 8.00
33 Demaryius Thomas 3.00 8.00
34 Derek Carr 4.00 10.00
35 Jarvis Landry 3.00 8.00
36 Devonta Freeman 3.00 8.00
37 Duke Johnson 2.50 6.00
38 Fletcher Cox 2.50 6.00
39 Golden Tate III 2.50 6.00
40 Josh Gordon 2.50 6.00

2018 Donruss Walter Payton NFL Man of the Year

*HOLO/100: 1.5X TO 4X BASIC INSERTS
1 J.J. Watt .60 1.50
2 Larry Fitzgerald .50 1.25
3 Eli Manning .50 1.25
4 Jason Witten .50 1.25
5 Kurt Warner .50 1.25
6 Jason Taylor .50 1.25
7 LaDainian Tomlinson .50 1.25
8 Drew Brees .60 1.50
9 Peyton Manning 1.25 3.00
10 Warrick Dunn .40 1.00
11 Jerome Bettis .60 1.50
12 Derrick Brooks .40 1.00
13 Cris Carter .60 1.50
14 Dan Marino 1.25 3.00
15 Troy Aikman .75 2.00
16 John Elway 1.00 2.50
17 Mike Singletary .60 1.50
18 Warren Moon .60 1.50
19 Steve Largent .60 1.50
20 Joe Theismann .60 1.50
21 Joe Greene .60 1.50
22 Roger Staubach .75 2.00
23 Franco Harris .60 1.50
24 Ken Anderson .40 1.00
25 Len Dawson .60 1.50

2001 Donruss Classics

This 200 card set was issued in six-card packs with an SRP of $11.99 per pack. There was 18 packs issued per box. The first 100 cards featured NFL veterans while the final 100 cards featured 2001 NFL rookies or NFL legends. Cards numbered 101 through 150 were issued at a stated print run of 475 sets while the legends were issued at a stated print run of 1425 sets.

COMP.SET w/o SPs (100) 7.50 20.00
1 David Boston .20 .50
2 Jake Plummer .20 .50
3 Thomas Jones .20 .50
4 Jamal Anderson .25 .60
5 Chris Redman .30 .75
6 Elvis Grbac .25 .60
7 Jamal Lewis .30 .75
8 Qadry Ismail .20 .50
9 Ray Lewis .30 .75
10 Shannon Sharpe .25 .60
11 Travis Taylor .20 .50
12 Eric Moulds .20 .50
13 Rob Johnson .25 .60
14 Muhsin Muhammad .20 .50
15 Brian Urlacher .40 1.00
16 Cade McNown .25 .60
17 Marcus Robinson .25 .60
18 Akili Smith .20 .50
19 Corey Dillon .20 .50
20 Peter Warrick .20 .50
21 Courtney Brown .20 .50
22 Tim Couch .20 .50
23 Emmitt Smith .50 1.25
24 Brian Griese .20 .50
25 Ed McCaffery .25 .60
26 Olandis Gary .20 .50
27 Mike Anderson .20 .50
28 Rod Smith .25 .60
29 Terrell Davis .25 .60
30 Charlie Batch .20 .50
31 James Stewart .20 .50
32 Ahman Green .25 .60
33 Antonio Freeman .30 .75
34 Brett Favre .60 1.50
35 Edgerrin James .25 .60
36 Marvin Harrison .25 .60
37 Peyton Manning .75 2.00
38 Fred Taylor .20 .50
39 Jimmy Smith .25 .60
40 Keenan McCardell .25 .60
41 Mark Brunell .25 .60
42 Sylvester Morris .20 .50
43 Tony Gonzalez .25 .60
44 Zach Thomas .25 .60
45 Jay Fiedler .25 .60
46 Lamar Smith .25 .60
47 Cris Carter .30 .75
48 Daunte Culpepper .25 .60
49 Randy Moss .25 .60
50 Drew Bledsoe .25 .60
51 Terry Glenn .25 .60
52 Aaron Brooks .20 .50
53 Joe Horn .20 .50
54 Ricky Williams .25 .60
55 Amani Toomer .20 .50
56 Ike Hilliard .20 .50
57 Kerry Collins .20 .50
58 Ron Dayne .25 .60
59 Tiki Barber .25 .60
60 Chad Pennington .20 .50
61 Curtis Martin .25 .60
62 Laveranues Coles .25 .60
63 Vinny Testaverde .20 .50
64 Wayne Chrebet .20 .50
65 Charles Woodson .30 .75
66 Rich Gannon .25 .60
67 Tim Brown .30 .75
68 Tyrone Wheatley .25 .60
69 Corey Simon .20 .50
70 Donovan McNabb .25 .60
71 Duce Staley .20 .50
72 Jerome Bettis .30 .75
73 Plaxico Burress .20 .50
74 Doug Flutie .25 .60
75 Junior Seau .25 .60
76 Jeff Garcia .20 .50
77 Jerry Rice .60 1.50
78 Giovanni Carmazzi .20 .50
79 Terrell Owens .25 .60
80 Darrell Jackson .25 .60
81 Ricky Watters .25 .60
82 Shaun Alexander .20 .50
83 Isaac Bruce .30 .75
84 Kurt Warner .50 1.25
85 Marshall Faulk .25 .60
86 Torry Holt .25 .60
87 Brad Johnson .25 .60
88 Keyshawn Johnson .25 .60
89 Mike Alstott .20 .50
90 Shaun King .20 .50
91 Warren Sapp .25 .60
92 Warrick Dunn .20 .50
93 Eddie George .30 .75
94 Jevon Kearse .20 .50
95 Steve McNair .25 .60
96 Jeff George .25 .60
97 Stephen Davis .20 .50
98 Charlie Garner .25 .60
99 Trent Dilfer .20 .50
100 Troy Aikman .40 1.00
101 Michael Vick RC 4.00 10.00
102 Drew Brees RC 20.00 50.00
103 Chris Weinke RC 2.00 5.00
104 Mike McMahon RC 2.00 5.00
105 Jesse Palmer RC 2.00 5.00
106 Quincy Carter RC 2.00 5.00
107 Josh Heupel RC 2.50 6.00
108 Tim Hasselbeck RC 2.00 5.00
109 LaDainian Tomlinson RC 8.00 20.00
110 Deuce McAllister RC 2.50 6.00
111 Michael Bennett RC 2.00 5.00
112 Anthony Thomas RC 2.50 6.00
113 LaMont Jordan RC 2.50 6.00
114 Travis Henry RC 2.00 5.00
115 Kevan Barlow RC 2.00 5.00
116 Travis Minor RC 2.00 5.00
117 Rudi Johnson RC 2.50 6.00
118 David Allen RC 1.50 4.00
119 Heath Evans RC 2.00 5.00
120 Moran Norris RC 1.50 4.00
121 David Terrell RC 2.00 5.00
122 Koren Robinson RC 2.00 5.00
123 Rod Gardner RC 2.00 5.00
124 Santana Moss RC 2.50 6.00
125 Freddie Mitchell RC 1.50 4.00
126 Reggie Wayne RC 3.00 8.00
127 Quincy Morgan RC 2.00 5.00
128 Chad Johnson RC 2.50 6.00
129 Robert Ferguson RC 2.50 6.00
130 Chris Chambers RC 1.50 4.00
131 Snoop Minnis RC 1.50 4.00
132 Eddie Berlin RC 1.50 4.00
133 Alex Bannister RC 1.50 4.00
134 Todd Heap RC 2.00 5.00
135 Alge Crumpler RC 2.50 6.00
136 Justin Smith RC 3.00 8.00
137 Andre Carter RC 2.00 5.00
138 Jamal Reynolds RC 1.50 4.00
139 Richard Seymour RC 2.50 6.00
140 Marcus Stroud RC 2.00 5.00
141 Casey Hampton RC 2.50 6.00
142 Gerard Warren RC 2.00 5.00
143 Torrance Marshall RC 1.50 4.00
144 Brian Allen RC 1.50 4.00
145 Morlon Greenwood RC 1.50 4.00
146 Keith Adams RC 1.50 4.00
147 Will Allen RC 2.50 6.00
148 Nate Clements RC 2.00 5.00
149 Adam Archuleta RC 2.00 5.00
150 Hakim Akbar RC 1.50 4.00
151 James Lofton .50 1.25
152 Jim Kelly .75 2.00
153 Gale Sayers .75 2.00
154 Mike Singletary .75 2.00
155 Boomer Esiason .60 1.50
156 Charlie Joiner .50 1.25
157 Ken Anderson .60 1.50
158 Y.A. Tittle .75 2.00
159 Jim Brown 1.00 2.50
160 Otto Graham .60 1.50
161 Ozzie Newsome .60 1.50
162 Drew Pearson .60 1.50
163 Lance Alworth .60 1.50
164 Roger Staubach 1.00 2.50
165 Tony Dorsett .75 2.00
166 John Elway 1.25 3.00
167 Barry Sanders 1.25 3.00
168 Bart Starr 1.50 4.00
169 Paul Hornung .75 2.00
170 Earl Campbell .75 2.00
171 Warren Moon .75 2.00
172 Johnny Unitas 1.50 4.00
173 Deacon Jones .60 1.50
174 Eric Dickerson .60 1.50
175 Bob Griese .75 2.00
176 Dan Marino 1.50 4.00
177 Larry Csonka .75 2.00
178 Paul Warfield .60 1.50
179 Fran Tarkenton .75 2.00
180 Archie Manning .60 1.50
181 Frank Gifford .75 2.00
182 Lawrence Taylor .75 2.00
183 Dan Fouts .60 1.50
184 Don Maynard .60 1.50
185 Joe Namath 1.25 3.00
186 Fred Biletnikoff .75 2.00
187 Marcus Allen .75 2.00
188 Jim Plunkett .60 1.50
189 Franco Harris .75 2.00
190 Terry Bradshaw 1.00 2.50
191 Joe Montana 2.50 6.00
192 Roger Craig .60 1.50
193 Steve Young 1.00 2.50
194 Dwight Clark .60 1.50
195 Steve Largent .75 2.00
196 Art Monk .75 2.00
197 Charley Taylor .50 1.25
198 Joe Theismann .75 2.00
199 Sammy Baugh .75 2.00
200 Sonny Jurgensen .75 2.00

2001 Donruss Classics Significant Signatures

All rookie and retired players from the base set (cards #101-200) were issued in this signed version of the basic issue cards. Stated odds for the cards was 1:18 packs and a few players were initially issued via exchange cards in packs. Those carried an expiration date of May 1, 2003. In 2005, Donruss/Playoff made an announcement of print runs for many older autographed sets including this one. Those announced print runs are included below.

STATED ODDS 1:18
ANNOUNCED PRINT RUNS LISTED BELOW
101 Michael Vick/25* 150.00 300.00
102 Drew Brees/30* 250.00 400.00
103 Chris Weinke/30* 12.00 30.00
104 Mike McMahon/125* 6.00 15.00
105 Jesse Palmer/150* 6.00 15.00
106 Quincy Carter/50* 8.00 20.00
107 Josh Heupel/100* 8.00 20.00
108 Tim Hasselbeck/150* 6.00 15.00
109 LaDainian Tomlinson/50* 125.00 250.00
110 Deuce McAllister/25* 15.00 40.00
111 Michael Bennett/30* 12.00 30.00
112 Anthony Thomas/50* 10.00 25.00
113 LaMont Jordan/50* 10.00 25.00
114 Travis Henry/100* 6.00 15.00
115 Kevan Barlow/125* 6.00 15.00
116 Travis Minor/150* 6.00 15.00
117 Rudi Johnson/75* 10.00 25.00
118 David Allen/150* 5.00 12.00
119 Heath Evans/150* 6.00 15.00
120 Moran Norris/150* 5.00 12.00
121 David Terrell/25* 12.00 30.00
122 Koren Robinson/25* 12.00 30.00
123 Rod Gardner/25* 12.00 30.00
124 Santana Moss/30* 25.00 50.00
125 Freddie Mitchell/30* 10.00 25.00
126 Reggie Wayne/30* 20.00 50.00
127 Quincy Morgan/75* 8.00 20.00
128 Chad Johnson/75* 10.00 25.00
129 Robert Ferguson/85* 8.00 20.00
130 Chris Chambers/75* 6.00 15.00
131 Snoop Minnis/100* 5.00 12.00
132 Eddie Berlin/190* 5.00 12.00
133 Alex Bannister/100* 5.00 12.00
134 Todd Heap/100* 6.00 15.00
135 Alge Crumpler/200* 8.00 20.00
136 Justin Smith/75* 12.00 30.00
137 Andre Carter/50* 8.00 20.00
138 Jamal Reynolds/55* 6.00 15.00
139 Richard Seymour No Auto 5.00 12.00
140 Marcus Stroud/200* 6.00 15.00
141 Casey Hampton No Auto 5.00 12.00
142 Gerard Warren/50* 8.00 20.00
143 Torrance Marshall 5.00 12.00
144 Brian Allen 5.00 12.00
145 Morlon Greenwood 5.00 12.00
146 Keith Adams No Auto 3.00 8.00
147 Will Allen/150* 8.00 20.00
148 Nate Clements No Auto 4.00 10.00
149 Adam Archuleta No Auto 4.00 10.00
150 Hakim Akbar 5.00 12.00
151 James Lofton 8.00 20.00
152 Jim Kelly/175* 20.00 50.00
153 Gale Sayers/175* 30.00 50.00
154 Mike Singletary 12.00 30.00
155 Boomer Esiason/100* 10.00 25.00
156 Charlie Joiner 8.00 20.00
157 Ken Anderson 10.00 25.00
158 Y.A. Tittle 20.00 40.00
159 Jim Brown 40.00 80.00
160 Otto Graham 30.00 80.00
161 Ozzie Newsome 10.00 25.00
162 Drew Pearson 10.00 25.00
163 Lance Alworth/100* 30.00 60.00
164 Roger Staubach/50* 60.00 120.00
165 Tony Dorsett/100* 30.00 60.00
166 John Elway/50* 100.00 200.00
167 Barry Sanders/75* 60.00 120.00
168 Bart Starr/125* 75.00 150.00
169 Paul Hornung 12.00 30.00
170 Earl Campbell/100* 20.00 40.00
171 Warren Moon/142* 15.00 40.00
172 Johnny Unitas/125* 200.00 350.00
173 Deacon Jones 12.00 30.00
174 Eric Dickerson/100* 15.00 40.00
175 Bob Griese 12.00 30.00
176 Dan Marino/50* 100.00 200.00
177 Larry Csonka 25.00 50.00
178 Paul Warfield 10.00 25.00
179 Fran Tarkenton 12.00 30.00
180 Archie Manning 10.00 25.00
181 Frank Gifford 30.00 60.00
182 Lawrence Taylor/50* 25.00 50.00
183 Dan Fouts 15.00 40.00
184 Don Maynard 10.00 25.00
185 Joe Namath 50.00 100.00
186 Fred Biletnikoff 12.00 30.00
187 Marcus Allen/50* 25.00 50.00
188 Jim Plunkett 10.00 25.00
189 Franco Harris 30.00 60.00
190 Terry Bradshaw/150* 50.00 100.00
191 Joe Montana 60.00 120.00
192 Roger Craig 10.00 25.00
193 Steve Young/75* 35.00 60.00
194 Dwight Clark 10.00 25.00
195 Steve Largent 12.00 30.00
196 Art Monk 15.00 40.00
197 Charley Taylor 8.00 20.00
198 Joe Theismann/100* 12.00 30.00
199 Sammy Baugh/100* 100.00 200.00
200 Sonny Jurgensen/100* 12.00 30.00

2001 Donruss Classics Timeless Tributes

*VET 1-100: 5X TO 12X BASIC CARDS
*ROOKIES 101-150: .8X TO 2X
*LEGENDS 151-200: 2X TO 5X
STATED PRINT RUN 100 SER.#'d SETS
153 Gale Sayers 4.00 10.00

2001 Donruss Classics Classic Combos

Randomly inserted in packs, these cards featured either two or four equipment pieces. The two player cards had a stated print run of 100 cards while the four player cards had a stated print run of 25 cards. A few cards used Helmet swatches and those are noted with a HEL suffix. In addition, a few of these cards were signed by the player(s) on the card and those were also limited to 25 cards. Finally, some were issued via exchange cards that expired on 5/31/2003.

DUALS PRINT RUN 100 SERIAL #'d SETS
QUADS PRINT RUN 25 SERIAL #'d SETS
1 W.Payton/G.Sayers/75 12.00 30.00
1A W.Payton/G.Sayers AU/25 60.00 125.00
2 McNown/McMahon AU 25.00 60.00
3 Staubach JER/Dorsett HEL 5.00 12.00
4 T.Aikman/E.Smith 6.00 15.00
5 T.Bradshaw/F.Harris 5.00 12.00
6 Greene H AU/Ham H AU 25.00 60.00
7 J.Montana/J.Rice 12.00 30.00
8 S.Young/T.Owens 5.00 12.00
9 J.Kelly/T.Thomas 3.00 8.00
10 D.Flutie/E.Moulds 3.00 8.00
11 Namath J/Maynard H/75 8.00 20.00
11A Namath J AU/Maynard H/25 50.00 100.00
12 V.Testaverde/C.Martin 3.00 8.00
13A D.Jones/F.Dryer AU/100 3.00 8.00
13B Jones AU/Dryer AU/100 50.00 100.00
14 K.Warner/I.Bruce 6.00 15.00
15 Montana H/M.Allen JER 12.00 30.00
16 T.Gonzalez/Syl.Morris 3.00 8.00
17 P.Simms J AU/L.Taylor H 4.00 10.00

18 K.Collins/R.Dayne 3.00 8.00
19 J.Plunkett/G.Blanda 3.00 8.00
20 Stabler AU/Lamonica AU 75.00 150.00
21 Campbell HEL/Moon JER 4.00 10.00
22 E.George JER/McNair HEL 4.00 10.00
23 D.Marino/J.Elway 8.00 20.00
25 B.Sanders/E.Dickerson 6.00 15.00
26 M.Faulk/T.Davis 3.00 8.00
27 P.Manning/E.James 10.00 25.00
28 M.Brunell/F.Taylor 3.00 8.00
29 D.Culpepper/R.Moss 3.00 8.00
30 B.Favre/A.Freeman 8.00 20.00
31 Pytn/Syrs/McNwn/McMa 15.00 40.00
32 Staub/Drsett H/Aikmn/Emmitt 10.00 25.00
33 Brds/Hrris/Grne H/J.Ham 8.00 20.00
34 Montana/Rice/Young/Owens 20.00 50.00
35 Kelly/Thomas/Flutie/Molds
36 Namath/Mynrd H/Testa/Martin 10.00 25.00
37 Jones/Wmr/Bruce/Dryer 10.00 25.00
38 Montan/Alln/Gnzlz/Morris 20.00 50.00
39 Simms/LT HEL/Coll/Dayne 6.00 15.00
40 Plunkett/Blanda/Stab/Lam 8.00 20.00
41 Camp H/Moon/Grge/McNr H 6.00 15.00
43 B.Sndrs/Dkrsn/M.Flk/T.Dvs 5.00 12.00
44 Mnning/James/Brnll/Tylr 15.00 40.00
45 Culp/R.Mss/Favre/Frman 12.00 30.00

2001 Donruss Classics Hash Marks

Issued at a rate of one per box, these 25 cards feature a mix of the best players of yesterday as well as some current players and include a piece of game-used turf swatch.
STATED ODDS ONE PER BOX
HM1 Jamal Lewis 3.00 8.00
HM2 Jim Kelly 3.00 8.00
HM3 Archie Griffin 2.00 5.00
HM4 Walter Payton 8.00 20.00
HM5 Emmitt Smith 5.00 12.00
HM6 Troy Aikman 4.00 10.00
HM7 John Elway 5.00 12.00
HM8 Barry Sanders 5.00 12.00
HM9 Bart Starr 6.00 15.00
HM10 Brett Favre 6.00 15.00
HM11 Reggie White 3.00 8.00
HM12 Edgerrin James 2.50 6.00
HM13 Dan Marino 6.00 15.00
HM14 Fran Tarkenton 3.00 8.00
HM15 Cris Carter 3.00 8.00
HM16 Cris Collinsworth 2.00 5.00
HM17 Fred Biletnikoff 3.00 8.00
HM18 George Blanda 2.50 6.00
HM19 Donovan McNabb 2.50 6.00
HM20 Jerry Rice 6.00 15.00
HM21 Steve Young 4.00 10.00
HM22 Steve Largent 3.00 8.00
HM23 Marshall Faulk 2.50 6.00
HM24 Eddie George 3.00 8.00
HM25 Joe Theismann 3.00 8.00

2001 Donruss Classics Hash Marks Autographs

This parallel to the Hash Mark insert set was randomly inserted in packs. These cards feature the players signature along with the piece of game-used turf swatch. The exchange cards had an expiration date of May 1, 2003. In 2005, Donruss/Playoff made an announcement of print runs for many older autographed sets including this one. Those announced print runs are included below.
ANNOUNCED PRINT RUNS BELOW
HM2 Jim Kelly/25* 60.00 120.00
HM3 Archie Griffin/100* 10.00 25.00
HM7 John Elway/25* 75.00 150.00
HM8 Barry Sanders/25* 60.00 120.00
HM9 Bart Starr/25* 60.00 120.00
HM14 Fran Tarkenton/25* 40.00 80.00
HM16 Cris Collinsworth/100* 10.00 25.00
HM18 George Blanda/100* 25.00 50.00

2001 Donruss Classics Stadium Stars

Issued at a rate of one in 18 packs, these 24 cards feature a mix of active and retired players and also include a swatch of a stadium seat taken from some of football's most heralded venues.
STATED ODDS 1:18
SS1 Johnny Unitas 10.00 25.00
SS2 Raymond Berry 5.00 12.00
SS3 Jamal Lewis 5.00 12.00
SS4 Ray Lewis 5.00 12.00
SS5 Eddie George 5.00 12.00
SS6 Jim Brown 8.00 20.00
SS7 Ozzie Newsome 5.00 12.00
SS8 Paul Warfield 5.00 12.00
SS9 Tim Couch 3.00 8.00
SS10 John Elway 12.50 30.00
SS11 Rocky Bleier 5.00 12.00
SS13 Jack Lambert 10.00 25.00
SS14 John Stallworth 6.00 15.00
SS15 Bernie Kosar 5.00 12.00
SS16 Jerome Bettis 8.00 20.00
SS17 Emmitt Smith 8.00 20.00
SS18 Troy Aikman 8.00 20.00
SS19 Barry Sanders 10.00 25.00
SS20 Brett Favre 12.50 30.00
SS21 Donovan McNabb 4.00 10.00
SS22 Corey Dillon 3.00 8.00
SS23 Jerry Rice 10.00 25.00
SS24 Steve Young 8.00 20.00
SS25 Dan Marino 12.50 30.00

2001 Donruss Classics Stadium Stars Autograph

This quasi-parallel to the Stadium Stars insert set was randomly inserted in packs. These cards feature the players signature along with the piece of a stadium seat. A few of the cards in this set were originally issued as exchange cards in packs with an expiration date of 5/1/2003. In 2005, Donruss/Playoff made an announcement of print runs for many older autographed sets including this one. Those announced print runs are included below.
ANNOUNCED PRINT RUNS BELOW
SS1 Johnny Unitas/25* 200.00 350.00
SS2 Raymond Berry/200* 12.50 30.00
SS6 Jim Brown/25* 60.00 120.00
SS7 Ozzie Newsome/75* 10.00 25.00
SS8 Paul Warfield/25* 20.00 40.00
SS11 Rocky Bleier/100* 30.00 80.00
SS13 Jack Lambert/100* 75.00 150.00
SS14 John Stallworth/200* 20.00 50.00
SS24 Steve Young/25* 50.00 100.00

2001 Donruss Classics Team Colors

Issued at a rate of one in 18 packs, these 50 cards feature one, three, or six swatches of game-worn jerseys and/or pants.
STATED ODDS 1:18
TC1 John Elway Pants 6.00 15.00
TC2 Brian Griese 2.50 6.00
TC3 Terrell Davis 3.00 8.00
TC4 Olandis Gary 2.50 6.00
TC5 Rod Smith P 3.00 8.00
TC6 Ed McCaffrey 3.00 8.00
TC7 Ald/Rom/Mob/Try/Smt/Pry P 10.00 25.00
TC8 Neil/Zimmran/Schlereth Pants 8.00 20.00
TC9 Kurt Warner Pants 6.00 15.00
TC10 Marshall Faulk Pants 3.00 8.00
TC11 Isaac Bruce Pants 4.00 10.00
TC12 L.Fltchr/M.Jns/Lyght Pants 8.00 20.00
TC13 A.Hakim/I.Bruce/T.Holt 12.00 30.00
TC14 M.Faulk/J.Watson/Holcmb 15.00 30.00
TC15 Eddie George Pants 4.00 10.00
TC16 Eddie George 4.00 10.00
TC17 Jevon Kearse Pants 2.50 6.00
TC18 Jevon Kearse 2.50 6.00
TC19 Steve McNair 3.00 8.00
TC20 Brett Favre 8.00 20.00
TC21 Antonio Freeman 4.00 10.00
TC22 Dorsey Levens 3.00 8.00
TC23 LeRoy Butler 3.00 8.00
TC24 Daunte Culpepper 3.00 8.00
TC25 Warren Moon 4.00 10.00
TC26 R.Moss/C.Carter/J.Reed 15.00 30.00
TC27 Mark Brunell 3.00 8.00
TC28 Fred Taylor 2.50 6.00
TC29 J.Smith/McCardell/Soward 8.00 20.00
TC30 Hardy Nickerson 2.50 6.00
TC31 Tony Boselli 3.00 8.00
TC32 Troy Aikman 5.00 12.00
TC33 Emmitt Smith 6.00 15.00
TC34 Daryl Johnston 4.00 10.00
TC35 Deion Sanders 3.00 8.00
TC36 Bill Bates 2.50 6.00
TC37 Michael Irvin 4.00 10.00
TC38 Barry Sanders 6.00 15.00
TC39 Sedrick Irvin 2.50 6.00
TC40 Charlie Batch 2.50 6.00
TC41 Herman Moore 2.50 6.00
TC42 Johnnie Morton 3.00 8.00
TC43 Donovan McNabb 3.00 8.00
TC44 Irving Fryar 3.00 8.00
TC45 Charles Johnson 2.50 6.00
TC46 Duce Staley 2.50 6.00
TC47 Curtis Martin 3.00 8.00
TC48 Bryan Cox 3.00 8.00
TC49 Vinny Testaverde 2.50 6.00
TC50 Lucas/Key.Jhnsn/Chrbt 8.00 20.00

2001 Donruss Classics Team Colors Autographs

This quasi-parallel to the Team Colors insert set was randomly inserted in packs. These cards feature the players signature along with either a swatch of game-worn jersey or pant. A few of the cards in this set were issued as exchange cards that carried an expiration date of 5/1/2003. In 2005, Donruss/Playoff made an announcement of print runs for many older autographed sets including this one. Those announced print runs are included below.
ANNOUNCED PRINT RUNS 25-100
TC9 Kurt Warner/25* 30.00 80.00
TC25 Warren Moon/25* 40.00 80.00
TC34 Daryl Johnston/100* 15.00 40.00
TC36 Bill Bates/100* 15.00 40.00
TC44 Irving Fryar/100* 10.00 25.00

2001 Donruss Classics Timeless Treasures

Issued at a rate of one in 340, these five cards feature players along with a memorabilia item from a famous event in football history.
STATED ODDS 1:340
1 Mike Anderson FB SP 20.00 12.00
2 John Fuqua JSY 10.00 12.00
3 Corey Dillon JSY 12.50 12.00
4 Jamal Lewis PYLON 10.00 15.00
5 Drew Bledsoe JSY SP 25.00 15.00

2001 Donruss Classics Chicago Collection

NOT PRICED DUE TO SCARCITY

2002 Donruss Classics Samples

*SILVER SAMPLES: 1X TO 2.5X BASIC CARDS
*GOLD SAMPLES: 1.5X TO 4X BASIC CARDS

2002 Donruss Classics

Released in July 2002. The set contains 100 veterans, 50 rookies, and 49 retired players. The retired players and the rookies are sequentially #'d to 1000. Some cards were issued only via redemption. The EXCH expiration date is 2/1/2004. Boxes included 9 packs of 6 cards.
COMP.SET w/o SP's (100) 7.50 20.00
151-200 ROOKIE PRINT RUN 1000
1 David Boston .20 .50
2 Jake Plummer .20 .50
3 Jamal Anderson .25 .60
4 Michael Vick .25 .60
5 Chris Weinke .20 .50
6 Muhsin Muhammad .20 .50
7 Steve Smith .30 .75
8 Anthony Thomas .25 .60
9 David Terrell .20 .50
10 Brian Urlacher .30 .75
11 Marty Booker .20 .50
12 Quincy Carter .20 .50
13 Emmitt Smith .50 1.25
14 Mike McMahon .20 .50
15 James Stewart .20 .50
16 Brett Favre .60 1.50
17 Ahman Green .25 .60
18 Antonio Freeman .30 .75
19 Michael Bennett .20 .50
20 Randy Moss .25 .60
21 Cris Carter .30 .75
22 Daunte Culpepper .25 .60
23 Aaron Brooks .20 .50
24 Ricky Williams .25 .60
25 Deuce McAllister .25 .60
26 Kerry Collins .20 .50
27 Michael Strahan .25 .60
28 Donovan McNabb .25 .60
29 Duce Staley .20 .50
30 Freddie Mitchell .20 .50
31 Correll Buckhalter .20 .50
32 Jeff Garcia .20 .50
33 Terrell Owens .25 .60
34 Garrison Hearst .20 .50
35 Marshall Faulk .25 .60
36 Isaac Bruce .30 .75
37 Kurt Warner .25 .60
38 Torry Holt .25 .60
39 Brad Johnson .25 .60
40 Keyshawn Johnson .25 .60
41 Mike Alstott .20 .50
42 Warrick Dunn .20 .50
43 Stephen Davis .20 .50
44 Rod Gardner .20 .50
45 Bruce Smith .25 .60
46 Elvis Grbac .20 .50
47 Ray Lewis .30 .75
48 Jamal Lewis .25 .60
49 Rob Johnson .25 .60
50 Eric Moulds .20 .50
51 Travis Henry .20 .50
52 Corey Dillon .20 .50
53 Peter Warrick .20 .50
54 Tim Couch .20 .50
55 James Jackson .20 .50
56 Kevin Johnson .20 .50
57 Brian Griese .20 .50
58 Terrell Davis .25 .60
59 Rod Smith .25 .60
60 Mike Anderson .20 .50
61 Peyton Manning .75 2.00
62 Marvin Harrison .25 .60
63 Edgerrin James .25 .60
64 Dominic Rhodes .20 .50
65 Mark Brunell .25 .60
66 Fred Taylor .20 .50
67 Jimmy Smith .25 .60
68 Tony Gonzalez .25 .60
69 Trent Green .20 .50
70 Priest Holmes .20 .50
71 Snoop Minnis .20 .50
72 Jay Fiedler .25 .60
73 Lamar Smith .20 .50
74 Chris Chambers .20 .50
75 Tom Brady 1.50 4.00
76 Drew Bledsoe .25 .60
77 Antowain Smith .25 .60
78 Troy Brown .20 .50
79 Vinny Testaverde .20 .50
80 Curtis Martin .25 .60
81 Wayne Chrebet .20 .50
82 Laveranues Coles .25 .60
83 Tim Brown .30 .75
84 Jerry Rice .60 1.50
85 Rich Gannon .25 .60
86 Charlie Garner .25 .60
87 Kordell Stewart .20 .50
88 Jerome Bettis .30 .75
89 Kendrell Bell .20 .50
90 Plaxico Burress .20 .50
91 Drew Brees .60 1.50
92 LaDainian Tomlinson .30 .75
93 Doug Flutie .25 .60
94 Shaun Alexander .20 .50
95 Matt Hasselbeck .20 .50
96 Koren Robinson .20 .50
97 Steve McNair .25 .60
98 Eddie George .25 .60
99 Derrick Mason .20 .50
100 Jevon Kearse .20 .50
101 Joe Montana 4.00 10.00
102 Joe Namath 2.00 5.00
103 Warren Moon 1.25 3.00
104 Dan Marino 2.50 6.00
105 Steve Bartkowski 1.00 2.50
106 John Elway 2.00 5.00
107 Troy Aikman 1.50 4.00
108 Steve Young 1.50 4.00
109 Terry Bradshaw 1.50 4.00
110 Bart Starr 2.50 6.00
111 Bert Jones .75 2.00
112 Craig Morton 1.00 2.50
113 Bob Griese 1.25 3.00
114 Dan Fouts 1.00 2.50
115 Phil Simms 1.00 2.50
116 Jim McMahon 1.25 3.00
117 Joe Theismann 1.25 3.00
118 Ken Stabler 1.50 4.00
119 Johnny Unitas 2.00 5.00
120 Roger Staubach 1.50 4.00
121 Len Dawson 1.25 3.00
122 Tony Dorsett 1.25 3.00
123 Gale Sayers 1.25 3.00
124 Jim Kelly 1.25 3.00
125 Herschel Walker 1.25 3.00
126 John Riggins 1.00 2.50
127 Eric Dickerson 1.00 2.50
128 Franco Harris 1.25 3.00
129 Earl Campbell 1.25 3.00
130 Thurman Thomas 1.00 2.50
131 Barry Sanders 2.00 5.00
132 Marcus Allen 1.25 3.00
134 Natrone Means .75 2.00
135 Steve Largent 1.25 3.00
136 Don Maynard 1.00 2.50
137 Henry Ellard .75 2.00
138 Sterling Sharpe 1.00 2.50
139 Art Monk 1.25 3.00
140 Andre Reed 1.00 2.50
141 Raymond Berry 1.00 2.50
142 Ozzie Newsome 1.00 2.50
143 William Perry 1.00 2.50
144 Deacon Jones 1.00 2.50
145 Howie Long 1.25 3.00
146 L.C. Greenwood .75 2.00
147 Ronnie Lott 1.00 2.50
148 Dick Butkus 1.50 4.00
149 Fran Tarkenton 1.25 3.00
150 Mike Singletary 1.25 3.00
151 David Carr RC 1.25 3.00
152 Joey Harrington RC 1.25 3.00
153 Patrick Ramsey RC 1.50 4.00
154 Kurt Kittner RC 1.25 3.00
155 DeShaun Foster RC 2.00 5.00
156 William Green RC 1.50 4.00
157 Clinton Portis RC 2.00 5.00
158 T.J. Duckett RC 1.25 3.00
159 Cliff Russell RC 1.25 3.00
160 Antonio Bryant RC 2.00 5.00
161 Donte Stallworth RC 2.00 5.00
162 Reche Caldwell RC 1.50 4.00
163 Jabar Gaffney RC 1.25 3.00
164 Ashley Lelie RC 1.25 3.00
165 Andre Davis RC 1.25 3.00
166 Josh Reed RC 1.50 4.00
167 Ron Johnson RC 1.50 4.00
168 Kelly Campbell RC 1.50 4.00
169 Javon Walker RC 2.00 5.00
170 Antwaan Randle El RC 1.50 4.00
171 Marquise Walker RC 1.25 3.00
172 Jeremy Shockey RC 2.00 5.00
173 Jerramy Stevens RC 2.00 5.00
174 Daniel Graham RC 1.50 4.00
175 Julius Peppers RC 3.00 8.00
176 Kalimba Edwards RC 1.50 4.00
177 Alex Brown RC 2.00 5.00
178 Will Overstreet RC 1.25 3.00
179 Dwight Freeney RC 2.50 6.00
180 John Henderson RC 1.50 4.00
181 Ryan Sims RC 2.00 5.00
182 Albert Haynesworth RC 2.00 5.00
183 Wendell Bryant RC 1.25 3.00
184 Anthony Weaver RC 1.25 3.00
185 Napoleon Harris RC 1.50 4.00
186 Robert Thomas RC 1.25 3.00
187 Quentin Jammer RC 2.00 5.00
188 Ed Reed RC 8.00 20.00
189 Roy Williams RC 1.25 3.00
190 Phillip Buchanon RC 2.00 5.00
191 Lito Sheppard RC 2.00 5.00
192 Mike Rumph RC 1.25 3.00
193 Keyuo Craver RC 1.25 3.00
194 Randy Fasani RC 1.25 3.00
195 Rohan Davey RC 2.00 5.00
196 Chad Hutchinson RC 1.25 3.00
197 Eric Crouch RC 2.00 5.00
198 Lamar Gordon RC 1.50 4.00
199 Brian Westbrook RC 2.50 6.00
200 Adrian Peterson RC 1.50 4.00

2002 Donruss Classics Timeless Tributes

*VETS 1-100: 4X TO 10X BASIC CARDS
1-100 VETERAN PRINT RUN 150
*LEGENDS 101-150: 2X TO 5X
*ROOKIES 151-200: .8X TO 2X
101-200 PRINT RUN 100
123 Gale Sayers 6.00 15.00

2002 Donruss Classics Classic Materials

Set contains one, two, or three swatches of game-used material on each card with each sequentially numbered to varying quantities from 50 to 350.
STATED PRINT RUN 50-350
CM1 Bart Starr/50 30.00 80.00
CM2 William Perry HEL/100 10.00 25.00
CM3 L.C. Greenwood Shoe/100 8.00 20.00
CM4 Len Dawson HEL/100 12.00 30.00
CM5 Terry Bradshaw/100 15.00 40.00
CM6 Bob Griese/100 12.00 30.00
CM7 Ken Stabler/150 12.00 30.00
CM8 Steve Largent/250 8.00 20.00
CM9 Earl Campbell/150 10.00 25.00
CM10 Warren Moon/300 8.00 20.00
CM11 Fran Tarkenton/250 8.00 20.00
CM12 Barry Sanders/100 20.00 50.00
CM13 Dan Marino/250 15.00 40.00
CM14 John Elway/250 12.00 30.00
CM15 Marcus Allen/300 8.00 20.00
CM16 Ozzie Newsome/300 6.00 15.00
CM17 Howie Long/300 12.00 30.00
CM18 Deacon Jones/300 6.00 15.00
CM19 Jerry Rice/250 15.00 40.00
CM20 Bert Jones/300 5.00 12.00
CM21 B.Favre/S.Sharpe/100 30.00 80.00
CM22 J.Unitas/R.Berry/100 40.00 100.00
CM23 E.Smith/H.Walker/100 30.00 80.00
CM24 Montana/Young/100 40.00 100.00
CM25 Theismann/Monk/100 20.00 50.00
CM26 Namath/Maynard/100 30.00 80.00
CM27 Dickerson/Ellard/100 10.00 25.00
CM28 J.Kelly/A.Reed/100 20.00 50.00
CM29 Payton/Sayers/Thom/50 50.00 120.00
CM30 Staub/Mort/Aikman/50 40.00 100.00
CM31 Butk/Sing/Urlach/50 125.00 250.00

2002 Donruss Classics Classic Materials Autographs

This set parallels the Classic Materials set, with each card featuring an authentic signature. Cards are sequentially numbered. Some cards were issued only via redemption. The exchange expiration date was 2/1/2004.
STATED PRINT RUN 10-25
CM2 William Perry/25 30.00 80.00
CM3 L.C. Greenwood/25 25.00 60.00
CM7 Ken Stabler/25 40.00 100.00
CM10 Warren Moon/25 40.00 100.00
CM12 Barry Sanders/25 100.00 200.00
CM13 Dan Marino/25 125.00 250.00
CM18 Deacon Jones/25 30.00 80.00
CM19 Jerry Rice/25 125.00 250.00
CM20 Bert Jones/50 15.00 40.00

2002 Donruss Classics Classic Pigskin

Set features one swatch of game-used Super Bowl football sequentially numbered to 250. There was also a parallel "Doubles" version serial numbered to just 25.
STATED PRINT RUN 250 SER.#'d SETS
*DOUBLE/25: 1.2X TO 3X BASIC INSERTS
DOUBLES PRINT RUN 25 SER.#'d SETS
CP1 Jerry Rice 15.00 40.00
CP2 Joe Montana 15.00 40.00
CP3 Troy Aikman 10.00 25.00
CP4 Emmitt Smith 12.00 30.00
CP5 Ray Lewis 8.00 20.00
CP6 Jamal Lewis 6.00 15.00

2002 Donruss Classics New Millennium Classics Jerseys

Set features one swatch of game-worn jersey sequentially #'d to 400 or 500.
STATED PRINT RUN 400-500
NM1 Ahman Green/400 5.00 12.00
NM2 Brian Griese/400 4.00 10.00
NM3 Chris Chambers/400 4.00 10.00
NM4 Curtis Martin/400 5.00 12.00
NM5 Daunte Culpepper/400 5.00 12.00
NM6 Edgerrin James/400 5.00 12.00
NM7 Emmitt Smith/400 10.00 25.00
NM8 Kurt Warner/400 5.00 12.00
NM9 Marshall Faulk/400 5.00 12.00
NM10 Randy Moss/400 5.00 12.00
NM11 Antonio Freeman/500 6.00 15.00
NM12 Charles Woodson/500 6.00 15.00
NM13 Corey Dillon/400 4.00 10.00
NM14 Cris Carter/400 6.00 15.00
NM15 David Boston/400 4.00 10.00
NM16 Donovan McNabb/400 5.00 12.00
NM17 Drew Bledsoe/400 5.00 12.00
NM18 Champ Bailey/500 5.00 12.00
NM19 Eric Moulds/400 4.00 10.00
NM20 Germane Crowell/500 4.00 10.00
NM21 Jake Plummer/400 4.00 10.00
NM22 Jeff Garcia/400 4.00 10.00
NM23 Jerome Bettis/500 6.00 15.00
NM24 Jevon Kearse/500 4.00 10.00
NM25 Keyshawn Johnson/400 5.00 12.00
NM26 Kordell Stewart/500 4.00 10.00
NM27 Warren Sapp/400 5.00 12.00
NM28 Marvin Harrison/500 5.00 12.00
NM29 Zach Thomas/400 5.00 12.00
NM30 Rod Smith/500 5.00 12.00
NM31 Steve McNair/400 5.00 12.00
NM32 Terrell Owens/400 5.00 12.00

2002 Donruss Classics Past and Present Jerseys

Features one or two swatches of game-worn jersey sequentially #'d to 400 for singles and 100 for doubles. Some cards were issued only via redemption. The EXCH expiration date is 2/1/2004.
SINGLES PRINT RUN 400 SER.#'d SETS
PP1 Donovan McNabb 5.00 12.00
PP2 Kurt Warner 5.00 12.00
PP3 Mark Brunell 5.00 12.00
PP4 Jeff Garcia 4.00 10.00
PP5 Brett Favre 12.00 30.00
PP6 LaDainian Tomlinson 6.00 15.00
PP7 Jamal Anderson 5.00 12.00
PP8 Mike Anderson 4.00 10.00
PP9 Terrell Davis 5.00 12.00
PP10 Ricky Watters 5.00 12.00
PP11 Stephen Davis 4.00 10.00
PP12 Eddie George 5.00 12.00
PP13 Marshall Faulk 5.00 12.00
PP14 Edgerrin James 5.00 12.00
PP15 Jerome Bettis 6.00 15.00
PP16 Emmitt Smith 10.00 25.00
PP18 Tony Dorsett 12.00 30.00
PP19 Thurman Thomas 6.00 15.00
PP20 Marcus Allen 10.00 25.00
PP21 E.Campbell/F.Harris 20.00 50.00
PP22 E.Dickerson/B.Sanders 20.00 50.00
PP23 G.Sayer/J.Riggins 50.00 120.00
PP24 D.Marino/J.Elway 30.00 80.00
PP25 T.Aikman/S.Young 12.00 30.00

2002 Donruss Classics Past and Present Jersey Autographs

This set parallels the Past and Present set, but each card is autographed. Marshall Faulk was issued only via redemption. The EXCH expiration date was 2/1/2004.
STATED PRINT RUN 25 SER.#'d SETS
PP7 Jamal Anderson 15.00 40.00
PP8 Mike Anderson 12.00 30.00
PP9 Terrell Davis 15.00 40.00
PP10 Ricky Watters
PP11 Stephen Davis
PP13 Marshall Faulk 15.00 40.00
PP14 Edgerrin James 15.00 40.00

2002 Donruss Classics Significant Signatures

This set is a partial parallel to the base Donruss Classics set with each card featuring an authentic autograph. The set is sequentially #'d to varying quantities. Some cards were issued only via redemption. The EXCH expiration date is 2/1/2004. Some players did not sign for the set and the cards were issued with "no autograph" printed on the fronts as noted below.
STATED PRINT RUN 20-250
1 David Boston/50 8.00 20.00
5 Chris Weinke/100 6.00 15.00
8 Anthony Thomas/150 8.00 20.00
9 David Terrell/100 6.00 15.00
10 Brian Urlacher/224 12.00 30.00
12 Quincy Carter/250 6.00 15.00
14 Mike McMahon/250 6.00 15.00
16 Brett Favre/25 175.00 300.00
17 Ahman Green/50 40.00 80.00
19 Michael Bennett/150 6.00 15.00
22 Daunte Culpepper/50 10.00 25.00
23 Aaron Brooks/150 6.00 15.00
24 Ricky Williams/35 20.00 50.00
25 Deuce McAllister/150 8.00 20.00
26 Kerry Collins/142 10.00 25.00
27 Michael Strahan/50 15.00 40.00
31 Correll Buckhalter/250 6.00 15.00
32 Jeff Garcia/25 12.00 30.00
33 Terrell Owens/100 15.00 40.00
35 Marshall Faulk/25 15.00 40.00
36 Isaac Bruce/125 10.00 25.00
37 Kurt Warner/40 30.00 80.00
38 Torry Holt/150 8.00 20.00
43 Stephen Davis/100 12.50 30.00
44 Rod Gardner/25 12.00 30.00
46 Elvis Grbac/75 8.00 20.00
47 Ray Lewis/100 30.00 60.00
48 Jamal Lewis/100 15.00 40.00
50 Eric Moulds/150 6.00 15.00
51 Travis Henry No Auto/100 7.50 20.00
53 Peter Warrick/100 7.50 20.00
55 James Jackson/200 6.00 15.00
58 Terrell Davis/50 12.00 30.00
60 Mike Anderson/75 8.00 20.00
62 Marvin Harrison/75 25.00 50.00
63 Edgerrin James/50 10.00 25.00
65 Mark Brunell/75 10.00 25.00
67 Jimmy Smith/150 8.00 20.00
68 Tony Gonzalez/75 10.00 25.00
71 Snoop Minnis No Auto/200 6.00 15.00
74 Chris Chambers/75 8.00 20.00
76 Drew Bledsoe/75 30.00 60.00
79 Vinny Testaverde/100 12.50 30.00
82 Laveranues Coles/200 8.00 20.00
83 Tim Brown/75 25.00 50.00
87 Kordell Stewart/50 8.00 20.00
91 Drew Brees/150 30.00 60.00
96 Koren Robinson/200 6.00 15.00
100 Jevon Kearse/100 7.50 20.00
101 Joe Montana/100 75.00 150.00
102 Joe Namath/50 60.00 120.00
104 Dan Marino/25 175.00 300.00
105 Steve Bartkowski/97 8.00 20.00
106 John Elway/25 125.00 250.00
107 Troy Aikman/40 75.00 125.00
108 Steve Young/50 40.00 80.00
109 Terry Bradshaw/78 60.00 120.00
110 Bart Starr/40 90.00 150.00
111 Bert Jones/243 6.00 15.00
112 Craig Morton/250 8.00 20.00
113 Bob Griese/50 30.00 50.00
114 Dan Fouts/25 15.00 40.00
115 Phil Simms/50 30.00 60.00
116 Jim McMahon/66 15.00 40.00
117 Joe Theismann/93 15.00 40.00
118 Ken Stabler/63 15.00 40.00
119 Johnny Unitas/75 175.00 300.00
120 Roger Staubach/55 50.00 100.00
121 Len Dawson/50 25.00 50.00
122 Tony Dorsett/50 25.00 50.00
123 Gale Sayers/25 40.00 100.00
125 Herschel Walker/50 20.00 40.00
126 John Riggins/125 25.00 60.00
127 Eric Dickerson/25 15.00 40.00
128 Franco Harris/25 20.00 50.00
129 Earl Campbell/50 25.00 50.00
130 Thurman Thomas/150 15.00 40.00
131 Barry Sanders/50 75.00 150.00
132 Marcus Allen/25 20.00 50.00
134 Natrone Means/170 6.00 15.00
135 Steve Largent/20 50.00 100.00
136 Don Maynard/112 8.00 20.00
137 Henry Ellard/20 12.00 30.00
138 Sterling Sharpe/116 12.50 30.00
139 Art Monk/25 30.00 60.00
140 Andre Reed/117 7.50 20.00
141 Raymond Berry/68 12.00 30.00
142 Ozzie Newsome/43 12.00 30.00
143 William Perry/75 12.00 30.00
144 Deacon Jones/50 12.00 30.00
145 Howie Long/25 60.00 120.00
146 L.C. Greenwood/75 25.00 60.00
147 Ronnie Lott/75 20.00 40.00
148 Dick Butkus/24 75.00 150.00
149 Fran Tarkenton/50 30.00 60.00
150 Mike Singletary/50 15.00 40.00
151 David Carr/50 8.00 20.00
152 Joey Harrington/50 8.00 20.00
156 William Green/43 12.00 30.00
157 Clinton Portis/150 10.00 25.00
160 Antonio Bryant/100 12.50 30.00
161 Donte Stallworth/33 40.00 100.00
164 Ashley Lelie/100 12.50 30.00
165 Andre Davis/150 6.00 15.00
166 Josh Reed/75 10.00 25.00
168 Kelly Campbell/250 8.00 20.00
176 Kalimba Edwards/250 8.00 20.00
177 Alex Brown/250 10.00 25.00
181 Ryan Sims/250 No Auto 10.00 25.00
186 Robert Thomas/250 6.00 15.00
189 Roy Williams/150 6.00 15.00
192 Mike Rumph/200 6.00 15.00
200 Adrian Peterson/200 8.00 20.00

2002 Donruss Classics Timeless Treasures

Randomly inserted into packs, this six-card set features one swatch of game-used material sequentially #'d to varying quanitites. A highlight of this set was a card featuring game-used pieces from Jim Thorpe. This was the first card to feature game-used Jim Thorpe memorabilia.
STATED PRINT RUN 25-375
TT1 Red Grange HEL/25 200.00 350.00
TT2 Jim Thorpe/100 60.00 120.00
TT3 Brett Favre/375 12.00 30.00
TT4 Terrell Davis/375 6.00 15.00
TT5 Barry Sanders/300 12.00 30.00
TT6 Jerry Rice/375 12.00 30.00

2003 Donruss Classics Samples

*SAMPLES: .8X TO 2X BASIC CARDS

2003 Donruss Classics Samples Gold

*GOLD: .8X TO 2X SILVER SAMPLES

2003 Donruss Classics

Released in July of 2003, this set consists of 250 cards, including 100 veterans, 50 retired players, and 100 rookies. The retired players were serial numbered to 1000, and the rookies were serial numbered to 900. Please note that several rookies were issued in packs as exchange cards with an expiration date of 1/7/2005. Please note that the EXCH cards are listed with a quantity of 100, due to Playoff destroying the remainder of the print run. Boxes contained two 9-pack mini-boxes. Pack SRP was $6.
COMP.SET w/o SP's (100) 7.50 20.00
151-250 ROOKIE PRINT RUN 100-900
1 Jake Plummer .20 .50
2 Marcel Shipp .20 .50
3 David Boston .20 .50
4 Michael Vick .25 .60
5 T.J. Duckett .20 .50
6 Warrick Dunn .20 .50
7 Ray Lewis .30 .75
8 Jamal Lewis .25 .60
9 Todd Heap .20 .50
10 Drew Bledsoe .25 .60
11 Travis Henry .20 .50
12 Peerless Price .20 .50
13 Eric Moulds .20 .50
14 Julius Peppers .30 .75
15 Steve Smith .30 .75
16 Lamar Smith .25 .60
17 Anthony Thomas .25 .60
18 Marty Booker .20 .50
19 Brian Urlacher .30 .75
20 Corey Dillon .20 .50
21 Chad Johnson .20 .50
22 Tim Couch .20 .50
23 William Green .20 .50
24 Quincy Morgan .20 .50
25 Chad Hutchinson .20 .50
26 Emmitt Smith .50 1.25
27 Antonio Bryant .20 .50
28 Roy Williams .20 .50
29 Brian Griese .20 .50
30 Clinton Portis .20 .50
31 Rod Smith .25 .60
32 Ashley Lelie .20 .50
33 Joey Harrington .20 .50
34 James Stewart .20 .50
35 Bill Schroeder .20 .50
36 Brett Favre .60 1.50
37 Ahman Green .25 .60
38 Donald Driver .25 .60
39 David Carr .20 .50
40 Jonathan Wells .20 .50
41 Corey Bradford .20 .50
42 Peyton Manning .75 2.00
43 Edgerrin James .25 .60
44 Marvin Harrison .25 .60
45 Mark Brunell .25 .60
46 Fred Taylor .20 .50
47 Jimmy Smith .25 .60
48 Trent Green .20 .50
49 Priest Holmes .20 .50
50 Tony Gonzalez .25 .60
51 Ricky Williams .25 .60
52 Chris Chambers .20 .50
53 Zach Thomas .25 .60
54 Daunte Culpepper .25 .60
55 Michael Bennett .20 .50
56 Randy Moss .25 .60
57 Tom Brady 1.25 3.00
58 Antowain Smith .25 .60
59 Troy Brown .20 .50
60 Aaron Brooks .20 .50
61 Deuce McAllister .25 .60
62 Donte Stallworth .20 .50
63 Kerry Collins .20 .50
64 Jeremy Shockey .20 .50
65 Amani Toomer .20 .50
66 Chad Pennington .20 .50
67 Curtis Martin .25 .60
68 Laveranues Coles .20 .50
69 Rich Gannon .25 .60
70 Charlie Garner .25 .60
71 Jerry Rice .60 1.50
72 Tim Brown .30 .75
73 Donovan McNabb .25 .60
74 Duce Staley .20 .50
75 Todd Pinkston .20 .50
76 Tommy Maddox .20 .50
77 Jerome Bettis .30 .75
78 Plaxico Burress .20 .50
79 Hines Ward .25 .60
80 Drew Brees .30 .75
81 LaDainian Tomlinson .30 .75
82 Junior Seau .25 .60
83 Jeff Garcia .20 .50
84 Garrison Hearst .20 .50
85 Terrell Owens .25 .60
86 Matt Hasselbeck .20 .50
87 Shaun Alexander .20 .50
88 Koren Robinson .25 .60
89 Kurt Warner .25 .60
90 Marshall Faulk .25 .60
91 Isaac Bruce .30 .75
92 Brad Johnson .25 .60
93 Mike Alstott .20 .50
94 Keyshawn Johnson .30 .75
95 Steve McNair .25 .60
96 Eddie George .25 .60
97 Derrick Mason .20 .50
98 Patrick Ramsey .25 .60
99 Stephen Davis .20 .50
100 Rod Gardner .20 .50
101 Archie Manning 1.00 2.50
102 Bo Jackson 1.50 4.00
103 Bob Griese 1.25 3.00
104 Bob Lilly 1.00 2.50
105 Craig James 1.00 2.50
106 Cliff Branch .75 2.00
107 Dan Fouts 1.00 2.50
108 Daryl Johnston 1.00 2.50
109 Daryle Lamonica .75 2.00
110 Dick Butkus 1.50 4.00
111 Don Maynard 1.00 2.50
112 Ed Too Tall Jones .75 2.00
113 Franco Harris 1.50 4.00
114 Frank Gifford 1.25 3.00
115 Fred Biletnikoff 1.25 3.00
116 Gale Sayers 1.25 3.00
117 George Blanda 1.00 2.50
118 Herman Edwards 1.00 2.50
119 Herschel Walker 1.00 2.50
120 Jack Ham 1.00 2.50
121 Jack Tatum .75 2.00
122 Jack Youngblood .75 2.00
123 James Lofton .75 2.00
124 Jay Novacek 1.00 2.50
125 Jim Brown 1.50 4.00
126 Jim McMahon/100* 20.00 40.00
127 Jim Plunkett 1.00 2.50
129 Joe Greene 1.25 3.00
130 Joe Montana 4.00 10.00
131 John Riggins 1.00 2.50
132 John Stallworth 1.00 2.50
133 John Taylor/100* 2.00 5.00
134 Ken Stabler 1.50 4.00
135 L.C. Greenwood .75 2.00
136 Lance Alworth 1.00 2.50
137 Mel Blount 1.00 2.50
138 Mike Ditka/100* 3.00 8.00
139 Paul Hornung 1.25 3.00
140 Randy White 1.00 2.50
141 Raymond Berry 1.00 2.50
142 Roger Craig 1.00 2.50
143 Roger Staubach 1.50 4.00
144 Ron Jaworski 1.00 2.50
145 Sammy Baugh 1.25 3.00
146 Sonny Jurgenson 1.00 2.50
147 Steve Young 1.50 4.00
148 Ted Hendricks 1.00 2.50
149 Thurman Thomas 1.25 3.00
150 Tom Jackson/100* 2.00 5.00
151 Brian St.Pierre RC 1.25 3.00
152 Byron Leftwich RC 1.50 4.00
153 Carson Palmer RC 2.50 6.00
154 Chris Simms RC 1.25 3.00
155 Dave Ragone RC 1.25 3.00
156 Ken Dorsey RC 1.50 4.00
157 Kliff Kingsbury RC 2.00 5.00
158 Kyle Boller RC 1.25 3.00
159 Rex Grossman RC 1.50 4.00
160 Seneca Wallace RC 1.50 4.00
161 Jason Gesser RC 1.50 4.00
162 Artose Pinner RC 1.25 3.00
163 Avon Cobourne RC 1.25 3.00
164 Cecil Sapp RC 1.25 3.00
165 Chris Brown RC 1.25 3.00
166 Derek Watson RC 1.25 3.00
167 Domanick Davis RC 1.50 4.00
168 Dwone Hicks RC 1.25 3.00
169 Earnest Graham RC 2.00 5.00
170 Justin Fargas RC 2.00 5.00
171 Larry Johnson RC 1.50 4.00
172 Lee Suggs RC 1.25 3.00
173 Musa Smith RC 1.25 3.00
174 Onterrio Smith RC 1.25 3.00
175 Quentin Griffin RC 1.50 4.00
176 Willis McGahee RC 1.50 4.00
177 Sultan McCullough RC 1.25 3.00
178 LaBrandon Toefield RC 1.25 3.00
179 B.J. Askew RC 1.50 4.00
180 Andre Johnson RC 3.00 8.00
181 Anquan Boldin RC 2.00 5.00
182 Arnaz Battle RC 2.00 5.00
183 Bethel Johnson RC 1.25 3.00
184 Billy McMullen RC 1.25 3.00
185 Bobby Wade RC 1.50 4.00
186 Brandon Lloyd RC 2.00 5.00
187 Bryant Johnson RC 2.00 5.00
188 Charles Rogers RC 1.50 4.00
189 Doug Gabriel RC 1.50 4.00
190 Justin Gage RC 1.50 4.00
191 Kareem Kelly RC 1.25 3.00
192 Kelley Washington RC 1.25 3.00
193 Kevin Curtis RC 1.25 3.00
194 Nate Burleson RC 1.50 4.00
195 Sam Aiken RC 1.50 4.00
196 Shaun McDonald RC 1.50 4.00
197 Talman Gardner RC 1.25 3.00
198 Taylor Jacobs RC 1.25 3.00
199 Terrence Edwards RC 1.25 3.00
200 Tyrone Calico RC 1.25 3.00
201 Walter Young RC 1.25 3.00
202 Ryan Hoag/100 RC 4.00 10.00
203 Paul Arnold RC 1.25 3.00
204 Bennie Joppru RC 1.25 3.00
205 Dallas Clark RC 2.00 5.00
206 George Wrighster RC 1.25 3.00
207 Jason Witten RC 5.00 12.00
208 Mike Pinkard RC 1.25 3.00
209 Robert Johnson RC 1.25 3.00
210 Teyo Johnson RC 1.50 4.00
211 Calvin Pace RC 1.25 3.00
212 Chris Kelsay RC 1.50 4.00
213 Cory Redding RC 1.50 4.00
214 DeWayne Robertson RC 1.50 4.00
215 DeWayne White RC 1.25 3.00
216 Jerome McDougle RC 1.25 3.00
217 Kenny Peterson RC 1.50 4.00
218 Kindal Moorehead RC 1.50 4.00
219 Michael Haynes RC 1.25 3.00
220 Terrell Suggs RC 1.50 4.00
221 Tully Banta-Cain RC 2.00 5.00
222 Jimmy Kennedy RC 1.50 4.00
223 Johnathan Sullivan RC 1.25 3.00
224 Kevin Williams RC 2.00 5.00
225 Nick Eason/100 RC 4.00 10.00
226 Rien Long RC 1.25 3.00
227 Ty Warren RC 1.50 4.00
228 William Joseph RC 1.25 3.00
229 Boss Bailey RC 1.50 4.00
230 Bradie James RC 2.00 5.00
231 Victor Hobson RC 1.25 3.00
232 Clifton Smith RC 1.25 3.00
233 E.J. Henderson/100 RC 5.00 12.00
234 Gerald Hayes/100 RC 5.00 12.00
235 LaMarcus McDonald RC 1.25 3.00
236 Nick Barnett RC 2.00 5.00
237 Terry Pierce RC 1.25 3.00
238 Andre Woolfolk RC 1.25 3.00
239 Dennis Weathersby RC 1.25 3.00
240 Drayton Florence RC 2.00 5.00
241 Eugene Wilson RC 2.00 5.00
242 Marcus Trufant RC 1.50 4.00
243 Rashean Mathis RC 1.25 3.00
244 Ricky Manning RC 1.50 4.00
245 Sammy Davis/100 RC 5.00 12.00
246 Terence Newman RC 2.00 5.00
247 Julian Battle RC 1.50 4.00
248 Ken Hamlin RC 2.00 5.00
249 Mike Doss RC 2.00 5.00
250 Troy Polamalu RC 15.00 25.00

2003 Donruss Classics Timeless Tributes

*VETS 1-100: 4X TO 10X BASIC CARDS
*LEGENDS 101-150: 1.5X TO 4X BASE/1000
*LEGENDS 101-150: .8X TO 2X BASE/100
1-149 PRINT RUN 150 SER.#'d SETS
*ROOKIES 151-250: .8X TO 2X
150-250 PRINT RUN 100 SER. #'d SETS
250 Troy Polamalu 40.00 100.00

2003 Donruss Classics Classic Pigskin

Randomly inserted into packs, this set features swatches of game used Super Bowl football. Each card is serial numbered to 250. There is also a Pigskin Doubles set, featuring swatches of game used Super Bowl footballs and a piece from the laces with each card numbered to 25.
STATED PRINT RUN 250 SER.#'d SETS
*DOUBLE/25: .8X TO 2X SINGLE FB
PS1 Marcus Allen 4.00 10.00
PS2 John Elway 6.00 15.00
PS3 Jim Kelly 4.00 10.00
PS4 Emmitt Smith 6.00 15.00
PS5 Trent Dilfer 2.50 6.00
PS6 Tom Brady 15.00 40.00

2003 Donruss Classics Classic Materials

Randomly inserted into packs, this set game worn jersey swatches, with each card serial numbered to various quantities. Please note that several cards were issued in packs as exchange cards with an expiration date of 1/7/2005.
STATED PRINT RUN 10-400
SER.#'d TO 10 TOO SCARCE TO PRICE
CM1 Alan Page/100 4.00 10.00
CM2 Andre Reed/400 3.00 8.00
CM3 Art Monk/400 6.00 15.00
CM4 Bart Starr/50 50.00 80.00
CM5 Earl Campbell/300 4.00 10.00
CM6 Eric Dickerson/400 3.00 8.00
CM7 Irving Fryar/400 2.50 6.00
CM8 Jim Kelly/400 4.00 10.00
CM9 Larry Csonka/100 6.00 15.00
CM11 Marcus Allen/400 4.00 10.00
CM12 Ray Nitschke/75 30.00 50.00
CM13 Terry Bradshaw/300 5.00 12.00
CM14 Tony Dorsett/100 6.00 15.00
CM15 Troy Aikman/300 5.00 12.00
CM16 Barry Sanders/200 12.00 30.00
CM17 Craig James/400 3.00 8.00
CM18 Dan Fouts/300 3.00 8.00
CM19 Dan Marino/400 8.00 20.00
CM20 Daryl Johnston/400 3.00 8.00
CM21 Frank Gifford/100 6.00 15.00
CM22 Steve Young/400 5.00 12.00
CM23 Herman Edwards/400 3.00 8.00
CM24 Jack Youngblood/100 4.00 10.00
CM25 Jim Brown/50 30.00 80.00
CM26 Warren Moon/400 4.00 10.00
CM27 Jimmy Johnson/400 3.00 8.00
CM28 Randy White/125 5.00 12.00
CM29 Ron Jaworski/100 5.00 12.00
CM30 Cris Carter/400 4.00 10.00
CM31 D.Butkus/W.Payton/100 60.00 120.00
CM32 McMahon/Sayers/100 25.00 50.00
CM33 E.Campbell/W.Moon/100 10.00 25.00
CM34 F.Harris/Bradshaw/100 30.00 80.00
CM35 Lamonica/Biletnik/100 20.00 50.00
CM36 Hendricks/Tatum/100 20.00 50.00
CM37 Aikman/Novacek/100 25.00 50.00
CM38 Staubach/Dorsett/100 20.00 50.00
CM39 J.Unitas/R.Berry/100 30.00 80.00
CM40 P.Manning/E.James/100 15.00 40.00

2003 Donruss Classics Classic Materials Autographs

Randomly inserted into packs, this set features game worn jersey swatches, along with authentic player autographs. Cards are serial numbered to various quantities. Please note that several cards were issued in packs as exchange cards

with an expiration date of 1/7/2005.
STATED PRINT RUN 50-100
CM1 Alan Page/100 30.00 60.00
CM2 Andre Reed/50 15.00 40.00
CM3 Art Monk/50 40.00 80.00
CM4 Bart Starr/50 100.00 250.00
CM5 Earl Campbell/50 30.00 60.00
CM6 Eric Dickerson/50 40.00 80.00
CM7 Irving Fryar/100 15.00 40.00
CM8 Jim Kelly/50 40.00 100.00
CM9 Larry Csonka/65 30.00 60.00
CM10 Leonard Marshall/100 15.00 40.00
CM11 Marcus Allen/50 35.00 60.00
CM13 Terry Bradshaw/50 100.00 175.00
CM14 Tony Dorsett/50 40.00 80.00
CM15 Troy Aikman/75 75.00 150.00

2003 Donruss Classics Dress Code Jerseys

Randomly inserted into packs, this set features game worn jersey swatches. Each card is serial numbered to 550.
STATED PRINT RUN 550 SER.#'d SETS
DC1 Dennis Northcutt 2.50 6.00
DC2 Jason Taylor 3.00 8.00
DC3 Donovan McNabb 3.00 8.00
DC4 Jerome Bettis 4.00 10.00
DC5 Joey Harrington 2.50 6.00
DC6 Duce Staley 2.50 6.00
DC7 Keyshawn Johnson 4.00 10.00
DC8 Kurt Warner 3.00 8.00
DC9 Santana Moss 3.00 8.00
DC10 Marvin Harrison 3.00 8.00
DC11 Michael Strahan 3.00 8.00
DC12 Mike Alstott 2.50 6.00
DC13 Rod Gardner 2.50 6.00
DC14 Rod Smith 3.00 8.00
DC15 Stephen Davis 2.50 6.00
DC16 Charles Woodson 4.00 10.00
DC17 Eric Moulds 2.50 6.00
DC18 Jeff Garcia 2.50 6.00
DC19 Anthony Thomas 3.00 8.00

2003 Donruss Classics Membership

Randomly inserted into packs, this set highlights past and present NFL superstars. Each card is serial numbered to 1500. Please note that card M11 was issued in packs as an exchange card with an expiration date of 1/7/2005.
STATED PRINT RUN 1500 SER.#'d SETS
M1 Warren Moon 1.00 2.50
M2 Dan Marino 2.00 5.00
M3 John Elway 1.50 4.00
M4 Jerry Rice 2.00 5.00
M5 Cris Carter 1.00 2.50
M6 Tim Brown 1.00 2.50
M7 Emmitt Smith 1.50 4.00
M8 John Riggins .75 2.00
M9 Priest Holmes .60 1.50
M10 Lawrence Taylor 1.00 2.50
M11 Reggie White 1.00 2.50
M12 Bruce Smith .75 2.00
M13 Jerry Rice 2.00 5.00
M14 Emmitt Smith 1.50 4.00
M15 Marcus Allen 1.00 2.50
M16 Walter Payton 3.00 8.00
M17 Emmitt Smith 1.50 4.00
M18 Barry Sanders 1.50 4.00
M19 Eric Dickerson .75 2.00
M20 Tony Dorsett 1.00 2.50

2003 Donruss Classics Membership VIP Jerseys

Randomly inserted into packs, each card features swatches of game worn jersey. Each card is serial numbered to various quantities. Please note that card M11 was issued in packs as an exchange card with an expiration date of 1/7/2005.
STATED PRINT RUN 75-400
M1 Warren Moon/400 4.00 10.00
M2 Dan Marino/250 8.00 20.00
M3 John Elway/250 6.00 15.00
M4 Jerry Rice/250 8.00 20.00
M5 Cris Carter/200 4.00 10.00
M6 Tim Brown/200 4.00 10.00
M7 Emmitt Smith/75 8.00 20.00
M8 John Riggins/100 6.00 15.00
M9 Priest Holmes/300 2.50 6.00
M10 Lawrence Taylor/200 4.00 10.00
M11 Reggie White/300 4.00 10.00
M12 Bruce Smith/400 3.00 8.00
M13 Jerry Rice/75 12.00 30.00
M14 Emmitt Smith/100 8.00 20.00
M15 Marcus Allen/150 4.00 10.00
M16 Walter Payton/100 25.00 60.00
M17 Emmitt Smith/250 6.00 15.00
M19 Eric Dickerson/250 3.00 8.00
M20 Tony Dorsett/100 5.00 12.00

2003 Donruss Classics Membership VIP Jerseys Autographs

Randomly inserted into packs, this set features game worn jersey swatches and authentic player autographs. Each player signed the first 50 serial numbered cards in the Membership VIP set except John Elway who signed only 15-cards. Please note that cards M1 and M11 were issued in packs as exchange cards with an expiration date of 1/7/2005.
PLAYOFF ANNOUNCED PRINT RUNS BELOW
M1 Warren Moon/50* 15.00 40.00
M2 Dan Marino/50* 75.00 150.00
M3 John Elway/15* 150.00 300.00
M10 Lawrence Taylor/50* 30.00 80.00
M11 Reggie White/50* 150.00 250.00
M18 Barry Sanders/50 100.00 200.00

2003 Donruss Classics Significant Signatures

Randomly inserted into packs, this semi-parallel set features player autographs on foil stickers. Each card is serial numbered to various quantities. Please note that several cards were issued in packs as exchange cards with an expiration date of 1/7/2005.
STATED PRINT RUN 15-300
4 Michael Vick/25 50.00 100.00
8 Jamal Lewis/25 15.00 40.00
13 Eric Moulds/50 10.00 25.00
17 Anthony Thomas/25 15.00 40.00
18 Marty Booker/50 10.00 25.00
19 Brian Urlacher/25 40.00 100.00
20 Corey Dillon No Auto 6.00 15.00
30 Clinton Portis/25 12.00 30.00
31 Rod Smith/50 12.00 30.00
33 Joey Harrington/25 12.00 30.00
36 Brett Favre/15 125.00 250.00
37 Ahman Green/25 15.00 40.00
38 Donald Driver/50 25.00 50.00
39 David Carr/15 12.00 30.00
44 Marvin Harrison/25 15.00 40.00
47 Jimmy Smith/50 12.00 30.00
49 Priest Holmes/25 12.00 30.00
52 Chris Chambers/25 12.00 30.00
53 Zach Thomas/25 15.00 40.00
56 Randy Moss/25 40.00 80.00
58 Antowain Smith/50 12.00 30.00
66 Chad Pennington/25 12.00 30.00
68 Laveranues Coles/50 10.00 25.00
76 Tommy Maddox/50 10.00 25.00
83 Jeff Garcia/25 12.00 30.00
84 Garrison Hearst/25 12.00 30.00
85 Terrell Owens/25 15.00 40.00
89 Kurt Warner/50 25.00 50.00
91 Isaac Bruce/25 20.00 50.00
93 Mike Alstott/25 12.00 30.00
95 Steve McNair/25 15.00 40.00
97 Derrick Mason/25 12.00 30.00
101 Archie Manning/150 10.00 25.00
102 Bo Jackson/100 40.00 80.00
103 Bob Griese/100 12.00 30.00
104 Bob Lilly/200 10.00 25.00
105 Craig James/200 10.00 25.00
106 Cliff Branch/200 8.00 20.00
107 Dan Fouts/100 20.00 40.00
108 Daryl Johnston/200 20.00 40.00
109 Daryle Lamonica/150 8.00 20.00
110 Dick Butkus/100 50.00 80.00
111 Don Maynard/100 10.00 25.00
112 Ed Too Tall Jones/200 8.00 20.00
113 Franco Harris/100 20.00 40.00
114 Frank Gifford/100 20.00 50.00
115 Fred Biletnikoff/100 15.00 40.00
116 Gale Sayers/100 30.00 60.00
117 George Blanda/100 20.00 40.00
118 Herman Edwards/150 10.00 25.00
119 Herschel Walker/200 15.00 40.00
120 Jack Ham/150 15.00 30.00
121 Jack Tatum/150 40.00 80.00
122 Jack Youngblood/150 8.00 20.00
123 James Lofton/100 8.00 20.00
124 Jay Novacek/200 30.00 80.00
125 Jim Brown/250 30.00 60.00
127 Jim Plunkett/200 10.00 25.00
128 Jimmy Johnson/100 30.00 60.00
129 Joe Greene/100 25.00 50.00
130 Joe Montana/200 50.00 120.00
131 John Riggins/200 20.00 50.00
132 John Stallworth/250 15.00 40.00
133 John Taylor/250 10.00 25.00
134 Ken Stabler/150 20.00 50.00
135 L.C. Greenwood/150 15.00 40.00
136 Lance Alworth/150 20.00 50.00
137 Mel Blount/253 10.00 25.00
138 Mike Ditka/100 20.00 50.00
139 Paul Hornung/200 15.00 40.00
140 Randy White/200 10.00 25.00
141 Raymond Berry/150 10.00 25.00
142 Roger Craig/150 10.00 25.00
143 Roger Staubach/117 40.00 80.00
144 Ron Jaworski/150 10.00 25.00
145 Sammy Baugh/200 60.00 120.00
146 Sonny Jurgenson/150 10.00 25.00
147 Steve Young/100 40.00 80.00
148 Ted Hendricks/150 10.00 25.00
150 Tom Jackson/250 10.00 25.00
152 Byron Leftwich/100 15.00 40.00
153 Carson Palmer/100 25.00 60.00
154 Chris Simms/125 12.00 30.00
155 Dave Ragone/200 6.00 15.00
164 Cecil Sapp/225 6.00 15.00
176 Willis McGahee/125 30.00 60.00
189 Doug Gabriel/250 8.00 20.00
190 Justin Gage/220 8.00 20.00
204 Bennie Joppru/200 6.00 15.00
210 Teyo Johnson/250 8.00 20.00
214 DeW Robertson/250 No AU 4.00 10.00
215 DeWayne White/250 6.00 15.00
216 Jerome McDougle/250 6.00 15.00
217 Ken Peterson/300 No AU 4.00 10.00
223 John Sullivan/300 No AU 3.00 8.00
224 Kevin Williams/250 10.00 25.00
226 Rien Long/250 6.00 15.00
228 William Joseph/250 6.00 15.00
233 E.J. Henderson/200 8.00 20.00
239 Dennis Weathersby/250 6.00 15.00
242 Marcus Trufant/250 8.00 20.00
246 Terence Newman/250 10.00 25.00
249 Mike Doss/200 10.00 25.00

2003 Donruss Classics Timeless Triples Jerseys

Randomly inserted into packs, this set features three swatches of memorabilia. Each card is serial numbered to 50, 100, or 150.
STATED PRINT RUN 50-150
TT1 Doak/Thorpe/Grange/50 200.00 400.00
TT2 Kelly/Thurman/Reed/150 20.00 50.00
TT3 Aikman/Emmitt/Moose/100 30.00 80.00
TT4 Montana/Taylor/Rice/150 30.00 80.00
TT5 Marino/Griese/Fiedler/100 40.00 100.00
TT6 Davis/Anderson/Portis/50 15.00 40.00
TT7 Bilet/Rice/Brown/100 20.00 50.00
TT8 Warner/Faulk/Bruce/100 12.00 30.00
TT9 Greene/Blount/Green/100 25.00 60.00
TT10 McNair/George/Mason/100 12.00 30.00

2004 Donruss Classics

Donruss Classics initially released in mid-July 2004. The base set consists of 250-cards including 50-Legends subset cards serial numbered to 2000 and 100-rookies with print runs ranging from 500 to 1850. Hobby boxes contained 18-packs of 6-cards and carried an S.R.P. of $5.99 per pack. Three parallel sets and a variety of inserts can be found seeded in hobby and retail packs highlighted by the Timeless Triples Jerseys inserts and the multi-tiered Significant Signatures autograph inserts.
COMP.SET w/o SP's (100) 7.50 20.00
151-175 RC PRINT RUN 1850 SER.#'d SETS
176-200 RC PRINT RUN 1250 SER.#'d SETS
201-225 RC PRINT RUN 925 SER.#'d SETS
226-250 RC PRINT RUN 500 SER.#'d SETS
1 Anquan Boldin .20 .50
2 Emmitt Smith .50 1.25
3 Michael Vick .25 .60
4 Peerless Price .20 .50
5 Warrick Dunn .20 .50
6 Jamal Lewis .25 .60
7 Kyle Boller .20 .50
8 Terrell Suggs .20 .50
9 Todd Heap .20 .50
10 Drew Bledsoe .25 .60
11 Travis Henry .20 .50
12 DeShaun Foster .25 .60
13 Jake Delhomme .20 .50
14 Stephen Davis .20 .50
15 Steve Smith .30 .75
16 Anthony Thomas .25 .60
17 Brian Urlacher .30 .75
18 Rex Grossman .20 .50
19 Chad Johnson .20 .50
20 Carson Palmer .25 .60
21 Rudi Johnson .20 .50
22 Andre Davis .20 .50
23 Lee Suggs .25 .60
24 Quincy Carter .20 .50
25 Roy Williams S .20 .50
26 Clinton Portis .20 .50
27 Jake Plummer .20 .50
28 Rod Smith .25 .60
29 Charles Rogers .20 .50
30 Joey Harrington .20 .50
31 Ahman Green .25 .60
32 Brett Favre .60 1.50
33 Javon Walker .20 .50
34 Andre Johnson .25 .60
35 David Carr .20 .50
36 Domanick Davis .20 .50
37 Edgerrin James .25 .60
38 Marvin Harrison .25 .60
39 Peyton Manning .75 2.00
40 Reggie Wayne .25 .60
41 Byron Leftwich .20 .50
42 Fred Taylor .20 .50
43 Jimmy Smith .25 .60
44 Priest Holmes .20 .50
45 Dante Hall .20 .50
46 Tony Gonzalez .25 .60
47 Trent Green .20 .50
48 Chris Chambers .20 .50
49 Ricky Williams .25 .60
50 Zach Thomas .25 .60
51 Daunte Culpepper .25 .60
52 Michael Bennett .20 .50
53 Randy Moss .25 .60
54 Deion Branch .20 .50
55 Adam Vinatieri .20 .50
56 Tedy Bruschi .25 .60
57 Tom Brady 1.25 3.00
58 Aaron Brooks .20 .50
59 Deuce McAllister .25 .60
60 Donte' Stallworth .20 .50
61 Joe Horn .20 .50
62 Jeremy Shockey .20 .50
63 Kerry Collins .20 .50
64 Michael Strahan .25 .60
65 Tiki Barber .25 .60
66 Chad Pennington .20 .50
67 Curtis Martin .25 .60
68 Santana Moss .25 .60
69 Jerry Rice .60 1.50
70 Charles Woodson .30 .75
71 Rod Woodson .25 .60
72 Tim Brown .30 .75
73 Brian Westbrook .20 .50
74 Correll Buckhalter .20 .50
75 Donovan McNabb .25 .60
76 Antwaan Randle El .20 .50
77 Hines Ward .25 .60
78 Kendrell Bell .20 .50
79 David Boston .20 .50
80 Drew Brees .30 .75
81 LaDainian Tomlinson .30 .75
82 Jeff Garcia .20 .50
83 Kevan Barlow .20 .50
84 Terrell Owens .25 .60
85 Koren Robinson .20 .50
86 Matt Hasselbeck .20 .50
87 Shaun Alexander .20 .50
88 Isaac Bruce .30 .75
89 Marc Bulger .20 .50
90 Marshall Faulk .25 .60
91 Torry Holt .25 .60
92 Brad Johnson .25 .60
93 Keenan McCardell .20 .50
94 Keyshawn Johnson .25 .60
95 Derrick Mason .20 .50
96 Eddie George .25 .60
97 Steve McNair .25 .60
98 LaVar Arrington .20 .50
99 Laveranues Coles .20 .50
100 Patrick Ramsey .25 .60
101 Archie Manning .60 1.50
102 Bart Starr 2.00 5.00
103 Bo Jackson 1.00 2.50
104 Bob Griese .75 2.00
105 Christian Okoye .50 1.25
106 Daryl Johnston .60 1.50
107 Deacon Jones .60 1.50
108 Deion Sanders .60 1.50
109 Dick Butkus 1.00 2.50
110 Lynn Swann 1.00 2.50
111 Don Maynard .60 1.50
112 Don Shula .75 2.00
113 Franco Harris 1.00 2.50
114 Fred Biletnikoff .75 2.00
115 Gale Sayers .75 2.00
116 George Blanda .75 2.00
117 Herman Edwards .60 1.50
118 Herschel Walker .75 2.00
119 Jack Lambert 1.00 2.50
120 James Lofton .50 1.25
121 Jim Plunkett .60 1.50
122 Jim Thorpe .75 2.00
123 Joe Greene .75 2.00
124 John Riggins .60 1.50
125 L.C. Greenwood .50 1.25
126 Larry Csonka .75 2.00
127 Leroy Kelly .60 1.50
128 Walter Payton 3.00 8.00
129 Marcus Allen .75 2.00
130 Mark Bavaro .50 1.25
131 Mel Blount .60 1.50
132 Michael Irvin .75 2.00
133 Mike Ditka .75 2.00
134 Mike Singletary .75 2.00
135 Ozzie Newsome .60 1.50
136 Paul Hornung .75 2.00
137 Paul Warfield .60 1.50
138 Randall Cunningham .60 1.50
139 Ray Nitschke .75 2.00
140 Reggie White .75 2.00
141 Richard Dent .50 1.25
142 Sammy Baugh .75 2.00
143 Sonny Jurgensen .60 1.50
144 Sterling Sharpe .60 1.50
145 Steve Largent .75 2.00
146 Terrell Davis .60 1.50
147 Terry Bradshaw 1.00 2.50
148 Thurman Thomas .60 1.50
149 Tony Dorsett .75 2.00
150 Warren Moon .75 2.00
151 John Navarre RC 1.00 2.50
152 Derek Abney RC 1.00 2.50
153 Ryan Dinwiddie RC 1.00 2.50
154 Bruce Perry/100 RC 7.50 20.00
155 Adimchinobe Echemandu RC 1.25 3.00
156 Troy Fleming RC 1.00 2.50
157 Brandon Miree RC 1.00 2.50
158 Jarrett Payton RC 1.25 3.00
159 Ben Hartsock RC 1.00 2.50
160 Chris Cooley RC 1.25 3.00
161 Derrick Ward RC 1.50 4.00
162 Triandos Luke RC 1.00 2.50
163 Clarence Moore RC 1.00 2.50
164 D.J. Hackett RC 1.00 2.50
165 Mark Jones RC 1.00 2.50
166 Sloan Thomas RC 1.25 3.00
167 Jamaar Taylor RC 1.00 2.50
168 Casey Bramlet RC 1.00 2.50
169 Drew Carter RC 1.25 3.00
170 Antwan Odom RC 1.00 2.50
171 Marquise Hill RC 1.00 2.50
172 Ricardo Colclough RC 1.00 2.50
173 Keith Smith RC 1.00 2.50
174 Joey Thomas RC 1.00 2.50
175 Stuart Schweigert RC 1.25 3.00
176 Cody Pickett RC 1.25 3.00
177 B.J. Symons RC 1.25 3.00
178 Matt Mauck RC 1.25 3.00
179 Bradlee Van Pelt RC 1.50 4.00
180 Jim Sorgi RC 1.50 4.00
181 Ernest Wilford RC 1.50 4.00
182 Bernard Berrian RC 1.25 3.00
183 Darius Watts RC 1.25 3.00
184 Derrick Hamilton RC 1.25 3.00
185 Jerricho Cotchery RC 1.50 4.00
186 Jeris McIntyre RC 1.25 3.00
187 Carlos Francis RC 1.25 3.00
188 Maurice Mann RC 1.25 3.00
189 Randy Starks RC 1.25 3.00
190 Darnell Dockett RC 2.00 5.00
191 Marcus Tubbs RC 1.25 3.00
192 Daryl Smith RC 1.25 3.00
193 Karlos Dansby RC 1.50 4.00
194 Michael Boulware RC 2.00 5.00
195 Teddy Lehman RC 1.25 3.00
196 Will Poole RC 2.00 5.00
197 Derrick Strait RC 1.25 3.00
198 Ahmad Carroll RC 1.25 3.00
199 Jeremy LeSueur RC 1.25 3.00
200 Bob Sanders RC 2.50 6.00
201 J.P. Losman RC 1.25 3.00
202 Matt Schaub RC 1.25 3.00
203 Josh Harris RC 1.25 3.00
204 Luke McCown RC 1.25 3.00
205 Quincy Wilson RC 1.25 3.00
206 Michael Turner RC 1.25 3.00
207 Mewelde Moore RC 1.50 4.00
208 Cedric Cobbs RC 1.25 3.00
209 Ben Watson RC 1.50 4.00
210 Michael Jenkins RC 1.25 3.00
211 Devery Henderson RC 1.25 3.00
212 Johnnie Morant RC 1.25 3.00
213 Keary Colbert RC 1.25 3.00
214 Devard Darling RC 1.25 3.00
215 P.K. Sam RC 1.25 3.00
216 Samie Parker RC 1.25 3.00
217 Jason Babin RC 2.00 5.00
218 Tommie Harris RC 1.50 4.00
219 Vince Wilfork RC 2.00 5.00
220 Jonathan Vilma RC 1.50 4.00
221 D.J. Williams RC 2.00 5.00
222 Chris Gamble RC 1.25 3.00
223 Matt Ware RC 2.00 5.00
224 Shawntae Spencer RC 1.25 3.00
225 Sean Jones RC 1.25 3.00
226 Drew Henson RC 1.50 4.00
227 Ben Roethlisberger RC 12.00 30.00
228 Eli Manning RC 12.00 30.00
229 Philip Rivers RC 5.00 12.00
230 Steven Jackson RC 2.50 6.00
231 Kevin Jones RC 2.00 5.00
232 Chris Perry RC 1.50 4.00
233 Greg Jones RC 1.50 4.00
234 Tatum Bell RC 1.50 4.00
235 Jeff Smoker RC 2.00 5.00
236 Julius Jones RC 1.50 4.00
237 Kellen Winslow RC 1.50 4.00
238 Ben Troupe RC 1.50 4.00
239 Larry Fitzgerald RC 6.00 15.00
240 Craig Krenzel RC 1.50 4.00
241 Roy Williams RC 1.50 4.00
242 Reggie Williams RC 1.50 4.00
243 Michael Clayton RC 2.00 5.00
244 Lee Evans RC 2.50 6.00
245 Rashaun Woods RC 1.50 4.00
246 Kenechi Udeze RC 2.00 5.00
247 Will Smith RC 2.00 5.00
248 DeAngelo Hall RC 2.50 6.00
249 Dunta Robinson RC 1.50 4.00
250 Sean Taylor RC 10.00 25.00

2004 Donruss Classics Timeless Tributes Green

*STARS 1-100: 8X TO 20X BASE CARD HI
*LEGENDS 101-150: 2.5X TO 6X BASIC CARDS
*ROOKIES 151-175: 1.5X TO 4X BASE CARD HI
*ROOKIES 176-200: 1.2X TO 3X BASE CARD HI
*ROOKIES 201-225: 1.2X TO 3X BASE CARD HI
*ROOKIES 226-250: 1X TO 2.5X BASE CARD HI
STATED PRINT RUN 50 SER.#'d SETS
UNPRICED PLATINUM PRINT RUN 1 SET

2004 Donruss Classics Timeless Tributes Platinum

UNPRICED PLATINUM PRINT RUN 1 SET

2004 Donruss Classics Timeless Tributes Red

*STARS 1-100: 4X TO 10X BAIC CARDS
*LEGENDS 101-150: 1.2X TO 3X
*ROOKIES 151-175: 1X TO 2.5X BASIC CARD
*ROOKIES 176-200: .8X TO 2X
*ROOKIES 201-225: .8X TO 2X
*ROOKIES 226-250: .6X TO 1.5X
STATED PRINT RUN 100 SER.#'d SETS

2004 Donruss Classics Classic

C1-C30 PRINT RUN 1000 SER.#'d SETS
C31-C45 PRINT RUN 750 SER.#'d SETS
C46-C50 PRINT RUN 500 SER.#'d SETS
C1 Barry Sanders 1.50 4.00
C2 Bart Starr 2.50 6.00
C3 Bob Griese 1.00 2.50
C4 Dan Marino 2.00 5.00
C5 Doak Walker 1.00 2.50
C6 Don Shula 1.00 2.50
C7 Emmitt Smith 1.50 4.00
C8 Franco Harris 1.25 3.00
C9 Jerry Rice 2.00 5.00
C10 Jim Brown 1.25 3.00
C11 Jim Kelly 1.00 2.50
C12 Jim Thorpe 1.00 2.50
C13 Joe Montana 3.00 8.00
C14 Joe Namath 1.50 4.00
C15 John Elway 1.50 4.00
C16 John Riggins .75 2.00
C17 Johnny Unitas 2.50 6.00
C19 Lawrence Taylor 1.00 2.50
C20 Mark Bavaro .60 1.50
C21 Michael Irvin 1.00 2.50
C22 Mike Singletary 1.00 2.50
C23 Paul Warfield .75 2.00
C24 Ray Nitschke 1.00 2.50
C25 Roger Staubach 1.25 3.00
C26 Terrell Davis .75 2.00
C27 Terry Bradshaw 1.25 3.00
C28 Tom Brady 4.00 10.00
C29 Troy Aikman 1.25 3.00
C30 Walter Payton 5.00 12.00
C31 B.Starr/R.Nitschke 3.00 8.00
C32 Bo.Griese/D.Marino 2.50 6.00
C33 W.Payton/M.Singletary 5.00 12.00
C34 D.Walker/B.Sanders 2.00 5.00
C35 D.Shula/J.Unitas 3.00 8.00
C36 R.Staubach/T.Aikman 1.50 4.00
C37 M.Irvin/E.Smith 2.00 5.00
C38 J.Montana/J.Rice 4.00 10.00
C39 J.Brown/P.Warfield 1.50 4.00
C40 J.Kelly/T.Thomas 1.25 3.00
C41 J.Namath/J.Riggins 2.00 5.00
C42 J.Elway/T.Davis 2.00 5.00
C43 L.Taylor/M.Bavaro 1.25 3.00
C44 T.Bradshaw/F.Harris 1.50 4.00
C45 D.Walker/J.Thorpe 2.50 6.00
C46 Marino/Elway/Kelly 6.00 15.00
C47 Unitas/Namath/Starr 5.00 12.00
C48 Payton/B.Sand/E.Smith 7.50 20.00
C49 Thorpe/D.Walker/J.Brown 5.00 12.00
C50 Aikman/Montana/Brady 7.50 20.00

2004 Donruss Classics Classic Materials

C1-C30 PRINT RUN 150 SER.#'d SETS
C31-C45 PRINT RUN 75 SER.#'d SETS
C46-C50 PRINT RUN 25 SER.#'d SETS
C1 Barry Sanders 6.00 15.00
C2 Bart Starr 12.50 30.00
C3 Bob Griese 4.00 10.00
C4 Dan Marino 15.00 40.00
C5 Doak Walker 10.00 25.00
C6 Don Shula 4.00 10.00
C7 Emmitt Smith 6.00 15.00
C8 Franco Harris 5.00 12.00
C9 Jerry Rice 8.00 20.00
C10 Jim Brown 5.00 12.00
C11 Jim Kelly 4.00 10.00
C12 Jim Thorpe 40.00 100.00
C13 Joe Montana 12.00 30.00
C14 Joe Namath 6.00 15.00
C15 John Elway 6.00 15.00
C16 John Riggins 3.00 8.00
C17 Johnny Unitas 15.00 30.00
C18 Larry Csonka 4.00 10.00
C19 Lawrence Taylor 4.00 10.00
C20 Mark Bavaro 2.50 6.00
C21 Michael Irvin 4.00 10.00
C22 Mike Singletary 4.00 10.00
C23 Paul Warfield 3.00 8.00
C24 Ray Nitschke 15.00 30.00
C25 Roger Staubach 12.50 30.00
C26 Terrell Davis 3.00 8.00
C27 Terry Bradshaw 12.50 30.00
C28 Tom Brady 15.00 40.00
C29 Troy Aikman 5.00 12.00
C30 Walter Payton 15.00 40.00
C31 B.Starr/R.Nitschke 15.00 40.00
C32 Bo.Griese/D.Marino 40.00 80.00
C33 W.Payton/M.Singletary 30.00 80.00
C34 D.Walker/B.Sanders 25.00 50.00
C35 D.Shula/J.Unitas 25.00 50.00
C36 R.Staubach/T.Aikman 25.00 50.00
C37 M.Irvin/E.Smith 20.00 50.00
C38 J.Montana/J.Rice 40.00 100.00
C39 J.Brown/P.Warfield 15.00 40.00
C40 J.Kelly/T.Thomas 15.00 40.00
C41 J.Namath/J.Riggins 25.00 60.00
C42 J.Elway/T.Davis 20.00 50.00
C43 L.Taylor/M.Bavaro 20.00 50.00
C44 T.Bradshaw/F.Harris 25.00 50.00
C45 D.Walker/Thorpe 75.00 150.00
C46 Marino/Elway/Kelly 20.00 50.00
C47 Unitas/Namath/Starr 40.00 80.00
C48 Payton/Sanders/Smith 60.00 125.00
C49 Thorpe/D.Walker/J.Brown 125.00 200.00
C50 Aikman/Montana/Brady 50.00 120.00

2004 Donruss Classics Classic Pigskin

SINGLES PRINT RUN 250 SER.#'d SETS
*DOUBLE/25: 1.2X TO 3X BASIC INSERT/250
DOUBLES PRINT RUN 25 SER.#'d SETS
CP1 Roger Staubach 12.00 30.00
CP2 Lawrence Taylor 10.00 25.00
CP3 Joe Montana 15.00 40.00
CP4 Emmitt Smith 15.00 30.00
CP5 Troy Aikman 10.00 25.00
CP6 Tom Brady 15.00 40.00

2004 Donruss Classics Dress Code Jerseys

STATED PRINT RUN 250 SER.#'d SETS
DC1 Aaron Brooks 2.00 5.00
DC2 Ahman Green 2.50 6.00
DC3 Brian Urlacher 3.00 8.00
DC4 Byron Leftwich 2.00 5.00
DC5 Chad Johnson 2.00 5.00
DC6 Chris Chambers 2.00 5.00
DC7 Curtis Martin 2.50 6.00
DC8 Daunte Culpepper 2.50 6.00
DC9 David Carr 2.00 5.00
DC10 Donovan McNabb 2.50 6.00
DC11 Drew Bledsoe 2.50 6.00
DC12 Drew Brees 3.00 8.00
DC13 Eddie George 2.50 6.00
DC14 Isaac Bruce 3.00 8.00
DC15 Jake Plummer 2.00 5.00
DC16 Jeff Garcia 2.00 5.00
DC17 Jerome Bettis 3.00 8.00
DC18 Jevon Kearse 2.00 5.00
DC19 Joey Harrington 2.00 5.00
DC20 Kurt Warner 2.50 6.00
DC21 LaVar Arrington 2.00 5.00
DC22 Laveranues Coles 2.00 5.00
DC23 Marc Bulger 2.00 5.00
DC24 Stephen Davis 2.00 5.00
DC25 Torrell Owens 2.50 6.00

2004 Donruss Classics Legendary Players

STATED PRINT RUN 1000 SER.#'d SETS
LP1 Barry Sanders 1.00 2.50
LP2 Bart Starr 1.50 4.00
LP3 Bruce Smith .50 1.25
LP4 Dan Marino 1.25 3.00
LP5 Deion Sanders .50 1.25
LP6 Earl Campbell .60 1.50
LP7 Franco Harris .75 2.00
LP8 Fred Biletnikoff .60 1.50
LP9 Jim Brown .75 2.00
LP10 Joe Montana 2.00 5.00
LP11 Joe Namath 1.00 2.50
LP12 Johnny Unitas 1.50 4.00
LP14 Lawrence Taylor .60 1.50
LP15 Mark Bavaro .40 1.00
LP16 Mike Singletary .60 1.50
LP17 Ozzie Newsome .50 1.25
LP18 Sterling Sharpe .50 1.25
LP19 Steve Largent .60 1.50
LP20 Terry Bradshaw .75 2.00
LP21 Thurman Thomas .50 1.25
LP22 Walter Payton 2.50 6.00
LP23 Warren Moon .60 1.50
LP24 Jim Thorpe .60 1.50
LP25 Reggie White .60 1.50

2004 Donruss Classics Legendary Players Jerseys

STATED PRINT RUN 100 SER.#'d SETS
LP1 Barry Sanders 6.00 15.00
LP2 Bart Starr 10.00 25.00
LP3 Bruce Smith 3.00 8.00
LP4 Dan Marino 8.00 20.00
LP5 Deion Sanders 3.00 8.00
LP6 Earl Campbell 4.00 10.00
LP7 Franco Harris 5.00 12.00
LP8 Fred Biletnikoff 4.00 10.00
LP9 Jim Brown 5.00 12.00
LP10 Joe Montana 15.00 40.00
LP11 Joe Namath 10.00 25.00
LP12 Johnny Unitas 10.00 25.00
LP13 Larry Csonka 4.00 10.00
LP14 Lawrence Taylor 4.00 10.00
LP15 Mark Bavaro 2.50 6.00
LP16 Mike Singletary 4.00 10.00
LP17 Ozzie Newsome 3.00 8.00
LP18 Sterling Sharpe 3.00 8.00
LP19 Steve Largent 4.00 10.00
LP20 Terry Bradshaw 5.00 12.00
LP21 Thurman Thomas 3.00 8.00
LP22 Walter Payton 15.00 40.00
LP23 Warren Moon 4.00 10.00
LP24 Jim Thorpe 30.00 150.00
LP25 Reggie White 4.00 10.00

2004 Donruss Classics Membership

STATED PRINT RUN 1000 SER.#'d SETS
M1 Anquan Boldin .40 1.00
M2 Barry Sanders 1.00 2.50
M3 Brett Favre 1.25 3.00
M4 Chad Pennington .40 1.00
M5 Clinton Portis .40 1.00
M6 Dan Marino 1.25 3.00
M7 Earl Campbell .60 1.50
M8 Jamal Lewis .50 1.25
M9 Jim Brown .75 2.00
M10 Jim Kelly .60 1.50
M11 Joe Montana 2.00 5.00
M12 Joe Namath 1.00 2.50
M13 John Elway 1.00 2.50
M14 Johnny Unitas 1.50 4.00
M15 LaDainian Tomlinson .60 1.50
M16 Lawrence Taylor .60 1.50
M17 Marcus Allen .60 1.50
M18 Marshall Faulk .50 1.25
M19 Michael Vick .50 1.25
M20 Peyton Manning 1.50 4.00
M21 Ricky Williams .50 1.25
M22 Roger Staubach .75 2.00
M23 Steve McNair .50 1.25
M24 Tom Brady 2.50 6.00
M25 Troy Aikman .75 2.00

2004 Donruss Classics Membership VIP Jerseys

STATED PRINT RUN 250 SER.#'d SETS
M1 Anquan Boldin 2.00 5.00
M2 Barry Sanders 5.00 12.00
M3 Brett Favre 6.00 15.00
M4 Chad Pennington 2.00 5.00
M5 Clinton Portis 2.00 5.00
M6 Dan Marino 6.00 15.00
M7 Earl Campbell 3.00 8.00
M8 Jamal Lewis 2.50 6.00
M9 Jim Brown 4.00 10.00
M10 Jim Kelly 3.00 8.00
M11 Joe Montana 10.00 25.00
M12 Joe Namath 5.00 12.00
M13 John Elway 5.00 12.00
M14 Johnny Unitas 10.00 25.00
M15 LaDainian Tomlinson 3.00 8.00
M16 Lawrence Taylor 3.00 8.00
M17 Marcus Allen 3.00 8.00
M18 Marshall Faulk 2.50 6.00
M19 Michael Vick 2.50 6.00
M20 Peyton Manning 8.00 20.00
M21 Ricky Williams 2.50 6.00
M22 Roger Staubach 4.00 10.00
M23 Steve McNair 2.50 6.00
M24 Tom Brady 15.00 40.00
M25 Troy Aikman 4.00 10.00

2004 Donruss Classics Membership VIP Jerseys Autographs

FIRST 25 JERSEY CARDS SIGNED
M2 Barry Sanders 75.00 150.00
M6 Dan Marino 100.00 200.00
M7 Earl Campbell 30.00 60.00
M9 Jim Brown 50.00 100.00
M10 Jim Kelly 40.00 80.00
M11 Joe Montana 100.00 200.00
M12 Joe Namath 75.00 150.00
M13 John Elway 100.00 200.00
M16 Lawrence Taylor 40.00 80.00
M22 Roger Staubach 50.00 100.00
M25 Troy Aikman 50.00 100.00

2004 Donruss Classics Sideline Generals

STATED PRINT RUN 2000 SER.#'d SETS
SG1 Switzer/J.Johnson 2.50 6.00
SG2 B.Walsh/Belichick 2.00 5.00
SG3 C.Noll/B.Cowher 3.00 8.00
SG4 D.Shula/T.Dungy 1.25 3.00
SG5 D.Vermeil/A.Reid 1.25 3.00

2004 Donruss Classics Sideline Generals Autographs

STATED PRINT RUN 250 SER.#'d SETS
SG1 Switzer/J.Johnson 40.00 80.00
SG2 B.Walsh/Belichick 200.00 400.00
SG3 C.Noll/B.Cowher 125.00 225.00
SG4 D.Shula/T.Dungy 40.00 80.00
SG5 D.Vermeil/A.Reid 25.00 50.00

2004 Donruss Classics Significant Signatures Green

*GREEN: .2X TO .5X PLATINUM
STATED PRINT RUN 75 SER.#'d SETS
110 Lynn Swann 150.00 300.00
140 Reggie White 150.00 250.00
142 Sammy Baugh No Auto 15.00 40.00

2004 Donruss Classics Significant Signatures Platinum

STATED PRINT RUN 25 SER.#'d SETS
1 Anquan Boldin 12.00 30.00
3 Michael Vick 50.00 80.00
6 Jamal Lewis 15.00 40.00
7 Kyle Boller 12.00 30.00
9 Todd Heap 12.00 30.00
13 Jake Delhomme 12.00 30.00
14 Stephen Davis 12.00 30.00
15 Steve Smith 20.00 50.00
17 Brian Urlacher 20.00 50.00
18 Rex Grossman 12.00 30.00
19 Chad Johnson 12.00 30.00
21 Rudi Johnson 12.00 30.00
25 Roy Williams S 12.00 30.00
30 Joey Harrington 12.00 30.00
32 Brett Favre 125.00 250.00
33 Javon Walker 12.00 30.00
35 David Carr 12.00 30.00
36 Domanick Davis 12.00 30.00
43 Jimmy Smith 15.00 40.00
44 Priest Holmes 12.00 30.00
45 Dante Hall 12.00 30.00
48 Chris Chambers 12.00 30.00
55 Adam Vinatieri 12.00 30.00
57 Tom Brady 175.00 300.00
58 Aaron Brooks 12.00 30.00
59 Deuce McAllister 15.00 40.00
61 Joe Horn
64 Michael Strahan 15.00 40.00
65 Tiki Barber 25.00 60.00
66 Chad Pennington 12.00 30.00
68 Santana Moss 15.00 40.00
75 Donovan McNabb 40.00 100.00
76 Antwaan Randle El 12.00 30.00
77 Hines Ward 15.00 40.00
78 Kendrell Bell 12.00 30.00
86 Matt Hasselbeck 12.00 30.00
87 Shaun Alexander 12.00 30.00
91 Torry Holt 15.00 40.00
94 Keyshawn Johnson 15.00 40.00
95 Derrick Mason 12.00 30.00
96 Eddie George 20.00 50.00
97 Steve McNair 15.00 40.00
99 Laveranues Coles 12.00 30.00
100 Patrick Ramsey 15.00 40.00
101 Archie Manning 20.00 50.00
102 Bart Starr 100.00 200.00
103 Bo Jackson 30.00 80.00
104 Bob Griese 25.00 60.00
105 Christian Okoye 15.00 40.00
106 Daryl Johnston 30.00 80.00
107 Deacon Jones 20.00 50.00
108 Deion Sanders 40.00 100.00
109 Dick Butkus 30.00 80.00
110 Lynn Swann 200.00 400.00
111 Don Maynard 20.00 50.00
112 Don Shula 25.00 60.00
113 Franco Harris 30.00 80.00
114 Fred Biletnikoff 25.00 60.00
115 Gale Sayers 25.00 60.00
116 George Blanda 40.00 80.00
117 Herman Edwards 20.00 50.00
118 Herschel Walker 25.00 60.00
119 Jack Lambert 50.00 100.00
120 James Lofton 15.00 40.00
121 Jim Plunkett 20.00 50.00
123 Joe Greene 25.00 60.00
124 John Riggins 20.00 50.00
125 L.C. Greenwood 15.00 40.00
127 Leroy Kelly 20.00 50.00
129 Marcus Allen 25.00 60.00
130 Mark Bavaro 15.00 40.00
131 Mel Blount 20.00 50.00
132 Michael Irvin 30.00 80.00
133 Mike Ditka 25.00 60.00
134 Mike Singletary 20.00 50.00
135 Ozzie Newsome 20.00 50.00
136 Paul Hornung 25.00 60.00
137 Paul Warfield 20.00 50.00
138 Randall Cunningham 20.00 50.00
140 Reggie White 175.00 300.00
141 Richard Dent 15.00 40.00
142 Sammy Baugh No Auto 25.00 50.00
143 Sonny Jurgensen 20.00 50.00
144 Sterling Sharpe 20.00 50.00
145 Steve Largent 25.00 60.00
146 Terrell Davis 20.00 50.00
147 Terry Bradshaw 75.00 150.00
148 Thurman Thomas 20.00 50.00
149 Tony Dorsett 25.00 60.00
150 Warren Moon 25.00 60.00
164 D.J. Hackett 10.00 25.00
172 Ricardo Colclough 10.00 25.00
181 Ernest Wilford 12.00 30.00
182 Bernard Berrian 10.00 25.00
183 Darius Watts 10.00 25.00
184 Derrick Hamilton 10.00 25.00
185 Jerricho Cotchery 12.00 30.00
198 Ahmad Carroll 10.00 25.00
201 J.P. Losman 10.00 25.00
202 Matt Schaub 10.00 25.00
203 Josh Harris 10.00 25.00
204 Luke McCown 10.00 25.00
205 Quincy Wilson 10.00 25.00
206 Michael Turner 10.00 25.00
207 Mewelde Moore 12.00 30.00
208 Cedric Cobbs 10.00 25.00
209 Ben Watson 12.00 30.00
210 Michael Jenkins 10.00 25.00
211 Devery Henderson 10.00 25.00
212 Johnnie Morant 10.00 25.00
213 Keary Colbert 10.00 25.00
214 Devard Darling 10.00 25.00
215 P.K. Sam 10.00 25.00
216 Samie Parker 10.00 25.00
218 Tommie Harris 12.00 30.00
219 Vince Wilfork 15.00 40.00
220 Jonathan Vilma 12.00 30.00
222 Chris Gamble 10.00 25.00
225 Sean Jones 10.00 25.00
226 Drew Henson 10.00 25.00
227 Ben Roethlisberger 200.00 350.00
228 Eli Manning 200.00 350.00
229 Philip Rivers 60.00 150.00
230 Steven Jackson 15.00 40.00
231 Kevin Jones 12.00 30.00
232 Chris Perry 10.00 25.00
233 Greg Jones 10.00 25.00
234 Tatum Bell 10.00 25.00
236 Julius Jones 10.00 25.00
238 Ben Troupe 10.00 25.00
241 Roy Williams WR 10.00 25.00
242 Reggie Williams 10.00 25.00
243 Michael Clayton 12.00 30.00
244 Lee Evans 15.00 40.00
245 Rashaun Woods 10.00 25.00
246 Kenechi Udeze 12.00 30.00
247 Will Smith
248 DeAngelo Hall 15.00 40.00
249 Dunta Robinson 10.00 25.00

2004 Donruss Classics Significant Signatures Red

PLAYOFF ANNOUNCED PRINT RUNS BELOW
7 Kyle Boller/50* 10.00 25.00
9 Todd Heap/50* 12.00 25.00
15 Steve Smith 12.00 30.00
21 Rudi Johnson 8.00 20.00
33 Javon Walker/50* 12.00 30.00
36 Domanick Davis 12.00 25.00
45 Dante Hall/25* 12.00 30.00
48 Chris Chambers/25* 12.50 30.00
55 Adam Vinatieri/75* 20.00 40.00
68 Santana Moss 10.00 25.00
95 Derrick Mason/90* 8.00 20.00
99 Laveranues Coles/25* 12.00 30.00
101 Archie Manning/75* 12.00 30.00
103 Bo Jackson/50* 50.00 120.00
105 Christian Okoye 10.00 25.00
106 Daryl Johnston 12.00 30.00
107 Deacon Jones 10.00 25.00
110 Lynn Swann/62* 150.00 300.00
111 Don Maynard 8.00 20.00
114 Fred Biletnikoff 12.00 30.00
116 George Blanda/84* 25.00 50.00
117 Herman Edwards 12.00 30.00
118 Herschel Walker 12.00 30.00
120 James Lofton 8.00 20.00
121 Jim Plunkett 10.00 25.00
123 Joe Greene/75* 25.00 50.00
124 John Riggins 12.00 30.00
125 L.C. Greenwood 10.00 25.00
127 Leroy Kelly 10.00 25.00
130 Mark Bavaro/50* 12.00 30.00
131 Mel Blount 12.00 30.00
133 Mike Ditka/75 20.00 40.00
136 Paul Hornung 12.00 30.00
137 Paul Warfield 10.00 25.00
138 Randall Cunningham 10.00 25.00
141 Richard Dent/50* 10.00 25.00
142 Sammy Baugh No Auto 12.00 30.00
143 Sonny Jurgensen 10.00 25.00
144 Sterling Sharpe/66* 20.00 40.00
145 Steve Largent/75* 12.00 30.00
148 Thurman Thomas 12.00 30.00
150 Warren Moon/50* 15.00 40.00
164 D.J. Hackett 6.00 15.00
182 Bernard Berrian 6.00 15.00
184 Derrick Hamilton 6.00 15.00
185 Jerricho Cotchery 8.00 20.00
207 Mewelde Moore 8.00 20.00
208 Cedric Cobbs 6.00 15.00
211 Devery Henderson/75* 12.00 30.00
212 Johnnie Morant 6.00 15.00
213 Keary Colbert 6.00 15.00
215 P.K. Sam 6.00 15.00
233 Greg Jones/75* 10.00 25.00

2004 Donruss Classics Team Colors Jerseys Away

AWAY PRINT RUN 150 SER.#'d SETS
*HOME/75: .6X TO 1.5X AWAY JSY/150
HOME PRINT RUN 75 SER.#'d SETS
*PRIME/25: 1.2X TO 3X AWAY JSY/150
PRIME PRINT RUN 25 SER.#'d SETS
TC1 Anquan Boldin 2.00 5.00
TC2 Barry Sanders 5.00 12.00
TC3 Brian Urlacher 3.00 8.00
TC4 Daunte Culpepper 2.50 6.00
TC5 Deuce McAllister 2.50 6.00
TC6 Donovan McNabb 2.50 6.00
TC7 Drew Bledsoe 2.50 6.00
TC8 Earl Campbell 3.00 8.00
TC9 Edgerrin James 2.50 6.00
TC10 Jeremy Shockey 2.00 5.00
TC11 Jerry Rice 6.00 15.00
TC12 Jim Kelly 3.00 8.00
TC13 Brett Favre 6.00 15.00
TC14 John Elway 5.00 12.00
TC15 Kurt Warner 2.50 6.00
TC16 LaDainian Tomlinson 3.00 8.00
TC17 Marshall Faulk 2.50 6.00
TC18 Marvin Harrison 2.50 6.00
TC19 Peyton Manning 8.00 20.00
TC20 Plaxico Burress 2.00 5.00
TC21 Priest Holmes 2.00 5.00
TC22 Randy Moss 2.50 6.00
TC23 Steve McNair 2.50 6.00
TC24 Torry Holt 2.50 6.00
TC25 Walter Payton 12.00 30.00

2004 Donruss Classics Timeless Triples Jerseys

STATED PRINT RUN 100 SER.#'d SETS
UNPRICED PRIME SER.#'d TO 10
TT1 Biletnikoff/Plunkett/M.Allen 10.00 25.00
TT2 Butkus/Payton/Singletary 40.00 100.00

TT3 Bradshaw/Harris/Swann 12.00 30.00
TT4 Starr/Nitschke/Favre 25.00 60.00
TT5 Griese/Csonka/Marino 20.00 50.00
TT6 Shula/Unitas/Manning 25.00 60.00
TT7 Montana/Rice/Owens 30.00 80.00
TT8 Aikman/Emmitt/Irvin 15.00 40.00
TT9 Brown/Warfield/Kelly 12.00 30.00
TT10 Namath/Riggins/Maynard 15.00 40.00
TT11 Elway/Davis/Smith 15.00 40.00
TT12 Kelly/Bruce/Thomas 10.00 25.00
TT13 Greene/Greenwood/Blount 10.00 25.00
TT14 Staubach/Doresett/Deion 12.00 30.00

2005 Donruss Classics

This 250-card set was released in August, 2005. The set was issued in the hobby in five-card packs with an $6 SRP which came 18 packs to a box. Cards numbered 1-100 feature active veterans basically in team alphabetical order while cards numbered 101-150 feature retired greats also in team alphabetica order and cards 151-250 feature 2005 rookies In the rookie section, cards numbered 226-250 were all signed by the player as well. Cards numbered 101-150 have a stated print run of 1000 serial numbered sets, cards numbered 151-175 have a stated print run of 1999 serial numbered sets, cards numbered 176-200 have a stated print rut of 1499 serial numbered sets, cards numbered 201-225 have a stated print run of 999 serial numbered sets and the signed rookie cards (226-250) have a stated print run of 499 serial numbered sets.

COMP.SET w/o SP's (100) 7.50 20.00
101-150 LEG PRINT RUN 1000 SER.#'d SETS
151-175 PRINT RUN 1999 SER.#'d SETS
176-200 PRINT RUN 1499 SER.#'d SETS
201-225 PRINT RUN 999 SER.#'d SETS
226-250 AU PRINT RUN 499 SER.#'d SETS
1 Kurt Warner .25 .60
2 Josh McCown .25 .60
3 Larry Fitzgerald .30 .75
4 Alge Crumpler .25 .60
5 Michael Vick .25 .60
6 Warrick Dunn .20 .50
7 Todd Heap .20 .50
8 Jamal Lewis .25 .60
9 Kyle Boller .20 .50
10 Drew Bledsoe .25 .60
11 Lee Evans .25 .60
12 Willis McGahee .20 .50
13 Steve Smith .30 .75
14 Jake Delhomme .20 .50
15 Muhsin Muhammad .20 .50
16 Brian Urlacher .30 .75
17 Rex Grossman .20 .50
18 Thomas Jones .20 .50
19 Carson Palmer .25 .60
20 Chad Johnson .20 .50
21 Rudi Johnson .20 .50
22 Antonio Bryant .20 .50
23 Kellen Winslow Jr. .20 .50
24 Lee Suggs .20 .50
25 Julius Jones .20 .50
26 Keyshawn Johnson .25 .60
27 Roy Williams S .20 .50
28 Jake Plummer .20 .50
29 Rod Smith .25 .60
30 Tatum Bell .20 .50
31 Joey Harrington .20 .50
32 Kevin Jones .20 .50
33 Roy Williams WR .20 .50
34 Ahman Green .25 .60
35 Brett Favre .60 1.50
36 Javon Walker .20 .50
37 Andre Johnson .25 .60
38 David Carr .20 .50
39 Domanick Davis .20 .50
40 Edgerrin James .25 .60
41 Marvin Harrison .25 .60
42 Peyton Manning .75 2.00
43 Reggie Wayne .25 .60
44 Byron Leftwich .20 .50
45 Fred Taylor .20 .50
46 Jimmy Smith .25 .60
47 Priest Holmes .20 .50
48 Tony Gonzalez .25 .60
49 Trent Green .20 .50
50 A.J. Feeley .20 .50
51 Chris Chambers .20 .50
52 Zach Thomas .25 .60
53 Daunte Culpepper .25 .60
54 Michael Bennett .20 .50
55 Randy Moss .25 .60
56 Corey Dillon .20 .50
57 David Givens .20 .50
58 Tom Brady 1.25 3.00
59 Aaron Brooks .20 .50
60 Deuce McAllister .25 .60
61 Joe Horn .20 .50
62 Eli Manning .50 1.25
63 Jeremy Shockey .20 .50
64 Tiki Barber .25 .60
65 Chad Pennington .20 .50
66 Curtis Martin .25 .60
67 Santana Moss .25 .60
68 Jerry Porter .20 .50
69 Kerry Collins .20 .50
70 J.P. Losman .20 .50
71 Brian Westbrook .20 .50
72 Donovan McNabb .25 .60
73 Terrell Owens .25 .60
74 Ben Roethlisberger .50 1.25
75 Duce Staley .20 .50
76 Hines Ward .25 .60
77 Jerome Bettis .30 .75
78 Antonio Gates .30 .75
79 Drew Brees .30 .75
80 LaDainian Tomlinson .30 .75
81 Brandon Lloyd .20 .50
82 Kevan Barlow .20 .50
83 Laveranues Coles .20 .50
84 Darrell Jackson .20 .50
85 Jerry Rice .60 1.50
86 Matt Hasselbeck .20 .50
87 Shaun Alexander .20 .50
88 Isaac Bruce .30 .75
89 Marc Bulger .20 .50
90 Steven Jackson .20 .50
91 Torry Holt .25 .60
92 Brian Griese .20 .50
93 Michael Clayton .20 .50
94 Mike Alstott .20 .50
95 Chris Brown .20 .50
96 Drew Bennett .25 .60
97 Steve McNair .25 .60
98 Clinton Portis .20 .50
99 LaVar Arrington .20 .50
100 Patrick Ramsey .25 .60
101 Don Shula 1.50 4.00
102 James Lofton 1.00 2.50
103 Thurman Thomas 1.25 3.00
104 Gale Sayers 1.50 4.00
105 Mike Singletary 1.50 4.00
106 Boomer Esiason 1.25 3.00
107 Cris Collinsworth 1.25 3.00
108 Ickey Woods 1.00 2.50
109 Jim Brown 2.00 5.00
110 Leroy Kelly 1.25 3.00
111 Ozzie Newsome 1.25 3.00
112 Paul Warfield 1.25 3.00
113 Deion Sanders 1.25 3.00
114 Herschel Walker 1.50 4.00
115 Mike Ditka 1.50 4.00
116 Michael Irvin 1.50 4.00
117 Roger Staubach 2.00 5.00
118 Tony Dorsett 1.50 4.00
119 Troy Aikman 2.00 5.00
120 John Elway 2.50 6.00
121 Barry Sanders 2.50 6.00
122 Bart Starr 2.50 6.00
123 Paul Hornung 1.50 4.00
124 Sterling Sharpe 1.25 3.00
125 Warren Moon 1.50 4.00
126 Christian Okoye 1.00 2.50
127 Marcus Allen 1.50 4.00
128 Deacon Jones 1.25 3.00
129 Bob Griese 1.50 4.00
130 Dan Marino 3.00 8.00
131 Fran Tarkenton 1.50 4.00
132 Y.A. Tittle 1.50 4.00
133 Don Maynard 1.25 3.00
134 Joe Namath 2.50 6.00
135 Jim Plunkett 1.25 3.00
136 Bo Jackson 2.00 5.00
137 Herman Edwards 1.00 2.50
138 Randall Cunningham 1.25 3.00
139 Franco Harris 1.50 4.00
140 Jack Lambert 1.50 4.00
141 Joe Greene 1.50 4.00
142 L.C. Greenwood 1.00 2.50
143 Terry Bradshaw 2.00 5.00
144 Dan Fouts 1.25 3.00
145 Joe Montana 5.00 12.00
146 John Taylor 1.25 3.00
147 Roger Craig 1.50 4.00
148 Steve Young 2.00 5.00
149 Steve Largent 1.50 4.00
150 Sonny Jurgensen 1.25 3.00
151 Adam Jones RC 1.25 3.00
152 Antrel Rolle RC 2.00 5.00
153 Carlos Rogers RC 2.00 5.00
154 DeMarcus Ware RC 4.00 10.00
155 Shawne Merriman RC 2.00 5.00
156 Thomas Davis RC 1.25 3.00
157 Derrick Johnson RC 1.50 4.00
158 Travis Johnson RC 1.25 3.00
159 David Pollack RC 1.25 3.00
160 Erasmus James RC 1.25 3.00
161 Marcus Spears RC 1.25 3.00
162 Fabian Washington RC 1.25 3.00
163 Luis Castillo RC 1.50 4.00
164 Marlin Jackson RC 1.25 3.00
165 Mike Patterson RC 1.25 3.00
166 Brodney Pool RC 1.50 4.00
167 Barrett Ruud RC 1.50 4.00
168 Shaun Cody RC 1.50 4.00
169 Stanford Routt RC 1.50 4.00
170 Josh Bullocks RC 1.50 4.00
171 Kevin Burnett RC 1.50 4.00
172 Corey Webster RC 1.50 4.00
173 Lofa Tatupu RC 1.50 4.00
174 Justin Miller RC 1.25 3.00
175 Odell Thurman RC 2.00 5.00
176 Heath Miller RC 3.00 8.00
177 Vernand Morency RC 1.50 4.00
178 Ryan Moats RC 1.50 4.00
179 Courtney Roby RC 1.50 4.00
180 Alex Smith TE RC 1.50 4.00
181 Kevin Everett RC 2.50 6.00
182 Brandon Jones RC 2.00 5.00
183 Maurice Clarett 1.50 4.00
184 Marion Barber RC 1.50 4.00
185 Brandon Jacobs RC 2.00 5.00
186 Matt Cassel RC 1.50 4.00
187 Stefan LeFors RC 1.50 4.00
188 Alvin Pearman RC 1.50 4.00
189 James Kilian RC 1.50 4.00
190 Airese Currie RC 1.50 4.00
191 Damien Nash RC 2.00 5.00
192 Dan Orlovsky RC 1.50 4.00
193 Larry Brackins RC 1.50 4.00
194 Rasheed Marshall RC 2.00 5.00
195 Marcus Maxwell RC 1.50 4.00
196 LeRon McCoy RC 1.50 4.00
197 Harry Williams RC 2.00 5.00
198 Noah Herron RC 1.50 4.00
199 Tab Perry RC 1.50 4.00
200 Chad Owens RC 1.50 4.00
201 Alex Smith QB RC 6.00 15.00
202 Ronnie Brown RC 2.00 5.00
203 Braylon Edwards RC 1.50 4.00
204 Cedric Benson RC 1.50 4.00
205 Cadillac Williams RC 1.50 4.00
206 Troy Williamson RC 1.50 4.00
207 Mike Williams 2.00 5.00
208 Matt Jones RC 1.50 4.00
209 Mark Clayton RC 1.50 4.00
210 Aaron Rodgers RC 25.00 50.00
211 Jason Campbell RC 1.50 4.00
212 Roddy White RC 2.50 6.00
213 Reggie Brown RC 1.50 4.00
214 Mark Bradley RC 1.50 4.00
215 J.J. Arrington RC 2.00 5.00
216 Eric Shelton RC 1.50 4.00
217 Roscoe Parrish RC 1.50 4.00
218 Terrence Murphy RC 1.50 4.00
219 Vincent Jackson RC 2.50 6.00
220 Frank Gore RC 3.00 8.00
221 Charlie Frye RC 1.50 4.00
222 Andrew Walter RC 1.50 4.00
223 David Greene RC 1.50 4.00
224 Kyle Orton RC 1.50 4.00
225 Ciatrick Fason RC 1.50 4.00
226 Cedric Houston AU RC 6.00 15.00
227 Dante Ridgeway AU RC 4.00 10.00
228 Craig Bragg AU RC 4.00 10.00
229 Deandra Cobb AU RC 4.00 10.00
230 Derek Anderson AU RC 5.00 12.00
231 Paris Warren AU RC 5.00 12.00
232 Lionel Gates AU RC 4.00 10.00
233 Anthony Davis AU RC 4.00 10.00
234 Ryan Fitzpatrick AU RC 6.00 15.00
235 J.R. Russell AU RC 4.00 10.00
236 Dan Cody AU RC 4.00 10.00
237 Bryant McFadden AU RC 5.00 12.00
238 Adrian McPherson AU RC 4.00 10.00
239 Chris Henry AU RC 5.00 12.00
240 Craphonso Thorpe AU RC 4.00 10.00
241 Darren Sproles AU RC 6.00 15.00
242 Fred Gibson AU RC 4.00 10.00
243 Jerome Mathis AU RC 6.00 15.00
244 Josh Davis AU RC 4.00 10.00
245 Kay-Jay Harris AU RC 4.00 10.00
246 Matt Roth AU RC 4.00 10.00
247 Roydell Williams AU RC 5.00 12.00
248 Steve Savoy AU RC 4.00 10.00
249 T.A. McLendon AU RC 4.00 10.00
250 Taylor Stubblefield AU RC 4.00 10.00

2005 Donruss Classics Timeless Tributes Bronze

*VETERANS 1-100: 4X TO 10X BASIC CARDS
*LEGENDS 101-150: 1X TO 2.5X
*ROOKIES 201-225: .6X TO 1.5X
COMMON ROOKIE 226-250 2.50 6.00
ROOKIE SEMISTARS 226-250 3.00 8.00
ROOKIE UNL.STARS 226-250 4.00 10.00
STATED PRINT RUN 100 SER.#'d SETS
230 Derek Anderson 3.00 8.00

2005 Donruss Classics Timeless Tributes Gold

*VETERANS 1-100: 10X TO 25X BASIC CARDS
*LEGENDS 101-150: 2X TO 5X BASIC CARDS
*ROOKIES 201-225: 2X TO 5X BASIC RC
COMMON ROOKIE 226-250 8.00 20.00
ROOKIE SEMISTARS 226-250 10.00 25.00
ROOKIE UNL.STARS 226-250 12.50 30.00
STATED PRINT RUN 25 SER.#'d SETS

2005 Donruss Classics Timeless Tributes Platinum

UNPRICED PLATINUM SER.#'d OF 10

2005 Donruss Classics Timeless Tributes Silver

*VETERANS 1-100: 6X TO 15X BASIC CARDS
*LEGENDS 101-150: 1.2X TO 3X
*ROOKIES 201-225: 1X TO 2.5X BASIC CARDS
COMMON ROOKIE 226-250 4.00 10.00
ROOKIE SEMISTARS 226-250 5.00 12.00
ROOKIE UNL.STARS 226-250 6.00 15.00
STATED PRINT RUN 50 SER.#'d SETS
230 Derek Anderson 5.00 12.00

2005 Donruss Classics Classic Combos Bronze

BRONZE PRINT RUN 500 SER.#'d SETS
*GOLD/100: .8X TO 2X BRONZE/500
*SILVER/250: .5X TO 1.2X BRONZE/500
1 J.Brown/B.Sanders 3.00 8.00
2 M.Ditka/W.Payton 5.00 12.00
3 E.Campbell/B.Jackson 2.50 6.00
4 G.Sayers/T.Davis 2.00 5.00
5 Bo.Griese/D.Marino 4.00 10.00
6 J.Montana/J.Elway 6.00 15.00
7 B.Starr/T.Bradshaw 3.00 8.00
8 R.Staubach/T.Aikman 2.50 6.00
9 J.Namath/J.Kelly 3.00 8.00
10 S.Young/M.Vick 2.50 6.00
11 D.Maynard/S.Largent 2.00 5.00
12 J.Rice/M.Irvin 4.00 10.00

2005 Donruss Classics Classic Combos Jerseys

STATED PRINT RUN 75 SER.#'d SETS
*PRIME/15: 1X TO 2.5X BASIC DUAL/75
1 J.Brown/B.Sanders 10.00 25.00
2 M.Ditka/W.Payton 15.00 40.00
3 E.Campbell/B.Jackson 8.00 20.00
4 G.Sayers/T.Davis 6.00 15.00
5 Bo.Griese/D.Marino 12.00 30.00
6 J.Montana/J.Elway 20.00 50.00
7 B.Starr/T.Bradshaw 10.00 25.00
8 R.Staubach/T.Aikman 8.00 20.00
9 J.Namath/J.Kelly 10.00 25.00
10 S.Young/M.Vick 8.00 20.00
11 D.Maynard/S.Largent 6.00 15.00
12 J.Rice/M.Irvin 12.00 30.00

2005 Donruss Classics Classic Pigskin

STATED PRINT RUN 250 SER.#'d SETS
*DOUBLE/25: .8X TO 2X BASIC INSERT
1 Bart Starr 25.00 60.00
2 John Elway 20.00 50.00
3 Bob Griese 12.00 30.00
4 Tony Dorsett 12.00 30.00
5 Walter Payton 60.00 125.00
6 Joe Montana 20.00 50.00

2005 Donruss Classics Classic Quads Bronze

BRONZE PRINT RUN 100 SER.#'d SETS
*GOLD/25: .8X TO 2X BRONZE/100
*SILVER/50: .5X TO 1.2X BRONZE/100
1 Thrpe/Brwn/Paytn/B.Snds 10.00 25.00
2 Campbell/Allen/Bo/Davis 5.00 12.00
3 Brdshw/Mntana/Aikmn/Brdy 15.00 40.00
4 Starr/Namath/Elway/Favre 8.00 20.00
5 Marino/P.Mann/Young/Vick 10.00 25.00
6 Staubach/Griese/Rice/Irvin 8.00 20.00

2005 Donruss Classics Classic Quads Jerseys

STATED PRINT RUN 25 SER.#'d SETS
UNPRICED PRIME PRINT RUN 5
1 Thrpe/Brwn/Paytn/Sndrs 300.00 400.00
2 Campbell/Allen/Bo/Davis 40.00 100.00
3 Brdshw/Mntana/Aikmn/Brdy 75.00 150.00
4 Starr/Namath/Elway/Favre 75.00 150.00
5 Marino/P.Mann/Young/Vick 75.00 150.00
6 Staubach/Griese/Rice/Irvin 50.00 100.00

2005 Donruss Classics Classic Singles Bronze

BRONZE PRINT RUN 1000 SER.#'d SETS
*GOLD/250: .8X TO 2X BRONZE/1000
*SILVER/500: .5X TO 1.2X BRONZE/1000
SILVER PRINT RUN 500 SER.#'d SETS
1 Barry Sanders 2.50 6.00
2 Bo Jackson 2.00 5.00
3 Bob Griese 1.50 4.00
4 Brett Favre 2.50 6.00
5 Dan Marino 3.00 8.00
6 Deion Sanders 1.25 3.00
7 Don Maynard 1.25 3.00
8 Earl Campbell 1.50 4.00
9 Gale Sayers 1.50 4.00
10 Jerry Rice 2.50 6.00
11 Jim Kelly 1.50 4.00
12 Joe Montana 5.00 12.00
13 Joe Namath 2.50 6.00
14 John Elway 2.50 6.00
15 Michael Irvin 1.50 4.00
16 Mike Ditka 1.50 4.00
17 Randall Cunningham 1.25 3.00
18 Roger Staubach 2.00 5.00
19 Steve Largent 1.50 4.00
20 Steve Young 2.00 5.00
21 Terrell Davis 1.25 3.00
22 Terry Bradshaw 2.00 5.00
23 Troy Aikman 2.00 5.00
24 Walter Payton 4.00 10.00

2005 Donruss Classics Classic Singles Jerseys

STATED PRINT RUN 150 SER.#'d SETS
*PRIME/25: 1X TO 2.5X BASIC JSY/150
PRIME PRINT RUN 25 SER.#'d SETS
CS1 Barry Sanders 8.00 20.00
CS2 Bo Jackson 8.00 20.00
CS3 Bob Griese 5.00 12.00
CS4 Brett Favre 8.00 20.00
CS5 Dan Marino 10.00 25.00
CS6 Deion Sanders 4.00 10.00
CS7 Don Maynard 4.00 10.00
CS8 Earl Campbell 5.00 12.00
CS9 Gale Sayers 5.00 12.00
CS10 Jerry Rice 8.00 20.00
CS11 Jim Kelly 5.00 12.00
CS12 Joe Montana 15.00 40.00
CS13 Joe Namath 8.00 20.00
CS14 John Elway 8.00 20.00
CS15 Michael Irvin 5.00 12.00
CS16 Mike Ditka 6.00 15.00
CS17 Randall Cunningham 4.00 10.00
CS18 Roger Staubach 6.00 15.00
CS19 Steve Largent 5.00 12.00
CS20 Steve Young 6.00 15.00
CS21 Terrell Davis 4.00 10.00
CS22 Terry Bradshaw 6.00 15.00
CS23 Troy Aikman 6.00 15.00
CS24 Walter Payton 12.00 30.00

2005 Donruss Classics Classic Triples Bronze

BRONZE PRINT RUN 250 SER.#'d SETS
*GOLD/75: .8X TO 2X BRONZE/250
*SILVER/150: .5X TO 1.2X BRONZE/250
1 Brown/Payton/Sanders 8.00 20.00
2 Campbell/Allen/Bo 4.00 10.00
3 Bradshaw/Montana/Brady 12.00 30.00
4 Starr/Elway/Favre 6.00 15.00
5 Namath/Marino/P.Manning 8.00 20.00
6 Staubach/Griese/Aikman 4.00 10.00
7 Young/Cunningham/Vick 4.00 10.00
8 Largent/Rice/Irvin 6.00 15.00

2005 Donruss Classics Classic Triples Jerseys

STATED PRINT RUN 50 SER.#'d SETS
UNPRICED PRIME PRINT RUN 10
1 Brown/Payton/Sanders 50.00 120.00
2 Campbell/Allen/Bo 20.00 50.00
3 Bradshaw/Montana/Brady 50.00 100.00
4 Starr/Elway/Favre 50.00 100.00
5 Namath/Marino/P.Manning 40.00 100.00
6 Staubach/Griese/Aikman 20.00 50.00
7 Young/Cunningham/Vick 20.00 50.00
8 Largent/Rice/Irvin 25.00 60.00

2005 Donruss Classics Dress Code Jerseys

STATED PRINT RUN 250 SER.#'d SETS
*PRIME/25: 1.2X TO 3X BASIC JSY/250
1 Alex Smith QB 8.00 20.00
2 Adam Jones 2.50 6.00
3 Andrew Walter 2.00 5.00
4 Braylon Edwards 2.00 5.00
5 Cadillac Williams 2.00 5.00
6 Carlos Rogers 3.00 8.00
7 Charlie Frye 2.00 5.00
8 Clatrick Fason 2.00 5.00
9 Eric Shelton 2.00 5.00
10 Frank Gore 4.00 10.00
11 J.J. Arrington 2.50 6.00
12 Jason Campbell 2.00 5.00
13 Kyle Orton 2.00 5.00
14 Mark Bradley 2.00 5.00
15 Mark Clayton 2.00 5.00
16 Maurice Clarett 2.50 6.00
17 Matt Jones 2.00 5.00
18 Reggie Brown 2.00 5.00
19 Roddy White 3.00 8.00
20 Ronnie Brown 2.50 6.00
21 Roscoe Parrish 2.00 5.00
22 Stefan LeFors 2.00 5.00
23 Terrence Murphy 2.00 5.00
24 Troy Williamson 2.00 5.00
25 Vincent Jackson 3.00 8.00

2005 Donruss Classics Legendary Players Bronze

BRONZE PRINT RUN 1000 SER.#'d SETS
*GOLD/250: .8X TO 2X BRONZE/1000
*SILVER/500: .5X TO 1.2X BRONZE/1000
L1 Barry Sanders 2.50 6.00
L2 Bart Starr 2.50 6.00
L3 Bo Jackson 2.00 5.00
L4 Bob Griese 1.50 4.00
L5 Boomer Esiason 1.25 3.00
L6 Brett Favre 2.50 6.00
L7 Dan Marino 3.00 8.00
L8 Deacon Jones 1.25 3.00
L9 Deion Sanders 1.00 2.50
L10 Don Maynard 1.25 3.00
L11 Don Meredith 1.50 4.00
L12 Gale Sayers 1.50 4.00
L13 Jerry Rice 2.50 6.00
L14 Jim Brown 2.00 5.00
L15 Jim Kelly 1.50 4.00
L16 Jim Thorpe 2.00 5.00
L17 Joe Greene 1.50 4.00
L18 Joe Montana 5.00 12.00
L19 Joe Namath 2.50 6.00
L20 John Elway 2.50 6.00
L21 Jack Lambert 1.50 4.00
L22 Michael Irvin 1.50 4.00
L23 Randall Cunningham 1.25 3.00
L24 Sterling Sharpe 1.25 3.00
L25 Steve Largent 1.50 4.00
L26 Steve Young 2.00 5.00
L27 Troy Aikman 2.00 5.00
L28 Walter Payton 4.00 10.00
L29 Lawrence Taylor 1.50 4.00
L30 Mike Ditka 1.50 4.00

2005 Donruss Classics Legendary Players Jerseys

STATED PRINT RUN 150 SER.#'d SETS
*PRIME/25: 1X TO 2.5X BASIC JSY/150
1 Barry Sanders 10.00 25.00
2 Bart Starr 10.00 25.00
3 Bo Jackson 8.00 20.00
4 Bob Griese 6.00 15.00
5 Boomer Esiason 5.00 12.00
6 Brett Favre 10.00 25.00
7 Dan Marino 10.00 25.00
8 Deacon Jones 5.00 12.00
9 Deion Sanders 4.00 10.00
10 Don Maynard 5.00 12.00
11 Don Meredith 12.00 30.00
12 Gale Sayers 6.00 15.00
13 Jerry Rice 10.00 25.00
14 Jim Brown 8.00 20.00
15 Jim Kelly 6.00 15.00
16 Jim Thorpe 60.00 120.00
17 Joe Greene 6.00 15.00
18 Joe Montana 20.00 50.00
19 Joe Namath 10.00 25.00
20 John Elway 10.00 25.00
21 Jack Lambert 6.00 15.00
22 Michael Irvin 6.00 15.00
23 Randall Cunningham 5.00 12.00
24 Sterling Sharpe 5.00 12.00
25 Steve Largent 6.00 15.00
26 Steve Young 8.00 20.00
27 Troy Aikman 8.00 20.00
28 Walter Payton 15.00 40.00
29 Lawrence Taylor 6.00 15.00
30 Mike Ditka 6.00 15.00

2005 Donruss Classics Membership Bronze

BRONZE PRINT RUN 1000 SER.#'d SETS
*GOLD/250: .8X TO 2X BRONZE/1000
*SILVER/500: .5X TO 1.2X BRONZE/1000
MS1 Barry Sanders 2.50 6.00
MS2 Ben Roethlisberger 2.00 5.00
MS3 Brett Favre 2.50 6.00
MS4 Brian Urlacher 1.25 3.00
MS5 Dan Marino 3.00 8.00
MS6 Daunte Culpepper 1.00 2.50
MS7 Deion Sanders 1.25 3.00
MS8 Donovan McNabb 1.00 2.50
MS9 Earl Campbell 1.50 4.00
MS10 Gale Sayers 1.50 4.00
MS11 Jamal Lewis 1.00 2.50
MS12 Jerry Rice 2.50 6.00
MS13 Jim Kelly 1.50 4.00
MS14 Joe Montana 5.00 12.00
MS15 Joe Namath 2.50 6.00
MS16 John Elway 2.50 6.00
MS17 LaDainian Tomlinson 1.25 3.00
MS18 Lawrence Taylor 1.50 4.00
MS19 Marshall Faulk 1.00 2.50
MS20 Marvin Harrison 1.00 2.50
MS21 Michael Irvin 1.50 4.00
MS22 Michael Strahan 1.00 2.50
MS23 Michael Vick 1.00 2.50
MS24 Peyton Manning 3.00 8.00
MS25 Randall Cunningham 1.25 3.00
MS26 Randy Moss 1.00 2.50
MS27 Steve Young 2.00 5.00
MS28 Terrell Davis 1.25 3.00
MS29 Troy Aikman 2.00 5.00
MS30 Walter Payton 4.00 10.00

2005 Donruss Classics Membership VIP Jerseys

STATED PRINT RUN 150 SER.#'d SETS
*PRIME/25: 1X TO 2.5X BASIC JSY/150
MS1 Barry Sanders 8.00 20.00
MS2 Ben Roethlisberger 6.00 15.00
MS3 Brett Favre 8.00 20.00
4 Brian Urlacher 4.00 10.00
MS5 Dan Marino 10.00 25.00
MS6 Daunte Culpepper 3.00 8.00
MS7 Deion Sanders 4.00 10.00
MS8 Donovan McNabb 3.00 8.00
MS9 Earl Campbell 5.00 12.00
MS10 Gale Sayers 5.00 12.00
MS11 Jamal Lewis 3.00 8.00
MS12 Jerry Rice 8.00 20.00
MS13 Jim Kelly 5.00 12.00
MS14 Joe Montana 15.00 40.00
MS15 Joe Namath 8.00 20.00
MS16 John Elway 8.00 20.00
MS17 LaDainian Tomlinson 4.00 10.00
MS18 Lawrence Taylor 5.00 12.00
MS19 Marshall Faulk 3.00 8.00
MS20 Marvin Harrison 3.00 8.00
MS21 Michael Irvin 5.00 12.00
MS22 Michael Strahan 3.00 8.00
MS23 Michael Vick 3.00 8.00
MS24 Peyton Manning 10.00 25.00
MS25 Randall Cunningham 4.00 10.00
MS26 Randy Moss 3.00 8.00
MS27 Steve Young 6.00 15.00
MS28 Terrell Davis 4.00 10.00
MS29 Troy Aikman 6.00 15.00
MS30 Walter Payton 12.00 30.00

2005 Donruss Classics Past and Present Bronze

BRONZE PRINT RUN 1000 SER.#'d SETS
*GOLD/250: .8X TO 2X BRONZE/1000
*SILVER/500: .5X TO 1.2X BRONZE/1000
PP1 J.Kelly/D.Bledsoe 1.50 4.00
PP2 T.Thomas/W.McGahee 1.25 3.00
PP3 G.Sayers/W.Payton 4.00 10.00
PP4 M.Singletary/B.Urlacher 1.50 4.00
PP5 Collinsworth/Ch.Johnson 1.25 3.00
PP6 J.Brown/J.Lewis 2.00 5.00
PP7 T.Dorsett/Ju.Jones 1.50 4.00
PP8 M.Irvin/Key.Johnson 1.50 4.00
PP9 J.Elway/J.Plummer 2.50 6.00
PP10 B.Sanders/Kev.Jones 2.50 6.00
PP11 B.Starr/B.Favre 3.00 8.00
PP12 E.Campbell/Ch.Brown 1.50 4.00
PP13 W.Moon/S.McNair 1.50 4.00
PP14 Bo.Griese/D.Marino 3.00 8.00
PP15 F.Tarkenton/Culpepper 1.50 4.00
PP16 D.Bledsoe/T.Brady 5.00 12.00
PP17 C.Martin/C.Dillon 1.00 2.50
PP18 F.Tarkenton/E.Manning 2.50 6.00
PP19 J.Namath/C.Pennington 2.50 6.00
PP20 Cunningham/McNabb 1.25 3.00
PP21 Bradshaw/Roethlisberger 2.50 6.00
PP22 F.Harris/J.Bettis 1.50 4.00
PP23 S.Largent/D.Jackson 1.50 4.00
PP24 M.Faulk/S.Jackson 1.00 2.50

2005 Donruss Classics Past and Present Jerseys

STATED PRINT RUN 50 SER.#'d SETS
UNPRICED PRIME PRINT RUN 10
1 J.Kelly/D.Bledsoe 5.00 12.00
2 T.Thomas/W.McGahee 4.00 10.00
3 G.Sayers/W.Payton 40.00 100.00
4 M.Singletary/B.Urlacher 5.00 12.00
5 Collinsworth/Ch.Johnson 4.00 10.00
6 J.Brown/Ja.Lewis 6.00 15.00
7 T.Dorsett/Ju.Jones 5.00 12.00
8 M.Irvin/Key.Johnson 5.00 12.00
9 J.Elway/J.Plummer 8.00 20.00
10 B.Sanders/Kev.Jones 8.00 20.00
11 B.Starr/B.Favre 20.00 50.00
12 E.Campbell/Ch.Brown 5.00 12.00
13 W.Moon/S.McNair 5.00 12.00
14 Bo.Griese/D.Marino 20.00 50.00
15 F.Tarkenton/Culpepper 5.00 12.00
16 D.Bledsoe/T.Brady 20.00 50.00
17 C.Martin/C.Dillon 4.00 10.00
18 F.Tarkenton/E.Manning 8.00 20.00
19 J.Namath/Pennington 8.00 20.00
20 Cunningham/McNabb 4.00 10.00
21 Bradshaw/Roethlisberger 8.00 20.00
22 F.Harris/J.Bettis 5.00 12.00
23 S.Largent/D.Jackson 5.00 12.00
24 M.Faulk/S.Jackson 4.00 10.00

2005 Donruss Classics Significant Signatures Bronze

BRONZE STATED PRINT RUN 15-150
CARDS SER.#'d UNDER 25 NOT PRICED
4 Alge Crumpler/75 8.00 20.00
5 Michael Vick/25 40.00 80.00
7 Todd Heap/75 6.00 15.00
9 Kyle Boller/75 6.00 15.00
10 Drew Bledsoe/25 12.00 30.00
11 Lee Evans/75 8.00 20.00
12 Willis McGahee/50 6.00 15.00
13 Steve Smith/75 10.00 25.00
14 Jake Delhomme/15 10.00 25.00
16 Brian Urlacher/15 15.00 40.00
17 Rex Grossman/75 6.00 15.00
19 Carson Palmer/15 12.00 30.00
20 Chad Johnson/75 10.00 25.00
21 Rudi Johnson/100 5.00 12.00
25 Julius Jones/25 10.00 25.00
26 Keyshawn Johnson/25 12.00 30.00
27 Roy Williams S/50 6.00 15.00
30 Tatum Bell/100 5.00 12.00
31 Joey Harrington/15 10.00 25.00
33 Roy Williams WR/15 10.00 25.00
34 Ahman Green/15 12.00 30.00
35 Brett Favre/15 100.00 200.00
37 Andre Johnson/50 8.00 20.00
38 David Carr/15 10.00 25.00
39 Domanick Davis/75 6.00 15.00
41 Marvin Harrison/15 12.00 30.00
42 Peyton Manning/15 75.00 150.00
43 Reggie Wayne/25 12.00 30.00
44 Byron Leftwich/15 10.00 25.00
46 Jimmy Smith/50 8.00 20.00
47 Priest Holmes/15 10.00 25.00
49 Trent Green/15 10.00 25.00
51 Chris Chambers/50 6.00 15.00
56 Corey Dillon/25 10.00 25.00
58 Tom Brady/15 125.00 250.00
59 Aaron Brooks/25 10.00 25.00
60 Deuce McAllister/25 12.00 30.00
61 Joe Horn/50 6.00 15.00
62 Eli Manning/25 75.00 135.00
64 Tiki Barber/25 25.00 50.00
65 Chad Pennington/15 10.00 25.00
70 J.P. Losman/100 5.00 12.00
71 Brian Westbrook/50 6.00 15.00
72 Donovan McNabb/15 30.00 60.00
74 Ben Roethlisberger/15 75.00 150.00
75 Duce Staley/75 6.00 15.00
76 Hines Ward/75 25.00 50.00
78 Antonio Gates/100 8.00 20.00
83 Laveranues Coles/75 6.00 15.00
84 Darrell Jackson/75 6.00 15.00
85 Jerry Rice/15 100.00 175.00
86 Matt Hasselbeck/50 6.00 15.00
90 Steven Jackson/50 6.00 15.00
93 Michael Clayton/75 6.00 15.00
95 Chris Brown/75 6.00 15.00
98 Clinton Portis/25 10.00 25.00
100 Patrick Ramsey/25 12.00 30.00
101 Don Shula/25 20.00 50.00
102 James Lofton/100 6.00 15.00
103 Thurman Thomas/75 10.00 25.00
104 Gale Sayers/15 30.00 60.00
105 Mike Singletary/50 12.00 30.00
106 Boomer Esiason/50 12.00 30.00
107 Cris Collinsworth/50 10.00 25.00
108 Ickey Woods/150 6.00 15.00
109 Jim Brown/15 50.00 100.00
110 Leroy Kelly/100 10.00 25.00
111 Ozzie Newsome/75 10.00 25.00
112 Paul Warfield/50 8.00 20.00
113 Deion Sanders/15 EXCH
114 Herschel Walker/100 12.00 30.00
115 Mike Ditka/50 30.00 60.00
116 Michael Irvin/25 20.00 50.00
117 Roger Staubach/15 25.00 60.00
118 Tony Dorsett/15 20.00 50.00
119 Troy Aikman/15 40.00 80.00
120 John Elway/15 100.00 200.00
121 Barry Sanders/15 75.00 150.00
122 Bart Starr/15 100.00 175.00
123 Paul Hornung/100 10.00 25.00
124 Sterling Sharpe/25 15.00 40.00
125 Warren Moon/25 20.00 50.00
126 Christian Okoye/150 6.00 15.00
127 Marcus Allen/25 30.00 60.00
128 Deacon Jones/100 8.00 20.00
129 Bob Griese/50 15.00 30.00
130 Dan Marino/15 100.00 200.00
131 Fran Tarkenton/50 15.00 30.00
132 Y.A. Tittle/75 15.00 40.00
133 Don Maynard/75 10.00 25.00
134 Joe Namath/15 50.00 100.00
135 Jim Plunkett/100 8.00 20.00
136 Bo Jackson/50 40.00 80.00
137 Herman Edwards/100 6.00 15.00
138 Randall Cunningham/50 12.50 30.00
139 Franco Harris/25 20.00 50.00
140 Jack Lambert/25 25.00 50.00
141 Joe Greene/50 12.00 30.00
142 L.C. Greenwood/100 10.00 25.00
143 Terry Bradshaw/15 50.00 100.00
144 Dan Fouts/15 15.00 40.00
145 Joe Montana/15 100.00 200.00
146 John Taylor/100 6.00 15.00
147 Roger Craig/50 12.00 30.00
148 Steve Young/15 40.00 80.00
149 Steve Largent/50 15.00 40.00
150 Sonny Jurgensen/50 10.00 25.00
151 Adam Jones/25 10.00 25.00
155 Shawne Merriman/75 10.00 25.00
157 Derrick Johnson/75 8.00 20.00
159 David Pollack/50 6.00 15.00
176 Heath Miller/75 15.00 40.00
178 Ryan Moats/75 6.00 15.00
179 Courtney Roby/25 10.00 25.00
183 Maurice Clarett/15 10.00 25.00
184 Marion Barber/75 6.00 15.00
201 Alex Smith QB/15 50.00 100.00
202 Ronnie Brown/75 8.00 20.00
203 Braylon Edwards/25 10.00 25.00
204 Cedric Benson/15 10.00 25.00
205 Cadillac Williams/15 10.00 25.00
206 Troy Williamson/15 10.00 25.00
207 Mike Williams/15 12.00 30.00
208 Matt Jones/15 10.00 25.00
209 Mark Clayton/25 10.00 25.00
210 Aaron Rodgers/25 300.00 450.00
211 Jason Campbell/15 10.00 25.00
212 Roddy White/15 15.00 40.00
213 Reggie Brown/25 10.00 25.00
214 Mark Bradley/75 6.00 15.00
215 J.J. Arrington/15 12.00 30.00
216 Eric Shelton/75 6.00 15.00
217 Roscoe Parrish/75 6.00 15.00
218 Terrence Murphy/75 6.00 15.00
219 Vincent Jackson/75 10.00 25.00
220 Frank Gore/75 20.00 50.00
221 Charlie Frye/50 6.00 15.00
222 Andrew Walter/15 10.00 25.00
223 David Greene/75 6.00 15.00
224 Kyle Orton/75 6.00 15.00
225 Clatrick Fason/75 6.00 15.00

2005 Donruss Classics Significant Signatures Gold

*GOLD/15-25: .6X TO 1.5X BRONZE AU
GOLD STATED PRINT RUN
CARDS SER.#'d UNDER 15 NOT PRICED

2005 Donruss Classics Significant Signatures Platinum

*PLATINUM/25: 1X TO 2.5X BRONZE
PLATINUM STATED PRINT RUN 1-25
CARDS SER.#'d UNDER 25 NOT PRICED

2005 Donruss Classics Significant Signatures Silver

*SILVER/50-100: .5X TO 1.2X BRONZE AU
*SILVER/25: .6X TO 1.5X BRONZE AU
SILVER STATED PRINT RUN 10-100
CARDS SER.#'d UNDER 25 NOT PRICED
212 Roddy White/50 12.00 30.00

2005 Donruss Classics Stadium Stars Goal Line Bronze

BRONZE PRINT RUN 750 SER.#'d SETS
*GOLD/250: .6X TO 1.5X BRONZE/750
*SILVER/500: .4X TO 1X BRONZE/750
1 Michael Vick 1.25 3.00
2 Jamal Lewis 1.25 3.00
3 Kyle Boller 1.00 2.50
4 Drew Bledsoe 1.25 3.00
5 Lee Evans 1.25 3.00
6 Jake Delhomme 1.00 2.50
7 Julius Peppers 1.25 3.00
8 Brian Urlacher 1.50 4.00
9 Carson Palmer 1.25 3.00
10 Jeff Garcia 1.00 2.50
11 Julius Jones 1.00 2.50
12 Joey Harrington 1.00 2.50
13 Andre Johnson 1.25 3.00
14 David Carr 1.00 2.50
15 Domanick Davis 1.00 2.50
16 Marvin Harrison 1.25 3.00
17 Peyton Manning 4.00 10.00
18 Byron Leftwich 1.00 2.50
19 Tony Gonzalez 1.25 3.00
20 Junior Seau 1.25 3.00
21 Jason Taylor 1.25 3.00
22 Michael Bennett 1.00 2.50
23 Aaron Brooks 1.00 2.50
24 Larry Fitzgerald 1.50 4.00
25 Eli Manning 2.50 6.00
26 Jeremy Shockey 1.00 2.50
27 Michael Strahan 1.25 3.00
28 Chad Pennington 1.00 2.50
29 Justin McCareins 1.00 2.50
30 John Abraham 1.00 2.50
31 Charles Woodson 1.50 4.00
32 Brian Westbrook 1.00 2.50
33 Donovan McNabb 1.25 3.00
34 Freddie Mitchell 1.00 2.50
35 Ben Roethlisberger 2.50 6.00
36 Duce Staley 1.00 2.50
37 Hines Ward 1.25 3.00
38 Koren Robinson 1.00 2.50
39 Matt Hasselbeck 1.00 2.50
40 Isaac Bruce 1.50 4.00
41 Marc Bulger 1.00 2.50
42 Torry Holt 1.25 3.00
43 Steven Jackson 1.00 2.50
44 Mike Alstott 1.00 2.50
45 Chris Brown 1.00 2.50
46 Derrick Mason 1.00 2.50
47 Drew Bennett 1.25 3.00
48 LaVar Arrington 1.00 2.50
49 Patrick Ramsey 1.25 3.00
50 Rod Gardner 1.00 2.50

2005 Donruss Classics Stadium Stars 30 Yard Line Jerseys

30-YARD PRINT RUN 199 SER.#'d SETS
*40-YARD/150: .4X TO 1X 30-YRD/199
*50-YARD/25: 1X TO 2.5X 30-YRD/199
1 Michael Vick 3.00 8.00
2 Jamal Lewis 3.00 8.00
3 Kyle Boller 2.50 6.00
4 Drew Bledsoe 3.00 8.00
5 Lee Evans 3.00 8.00
6 Jake Delhomme 2.50 6.00
7 Julius Peppers 3.00 8.00
8 Brian Urlacher 4.00 10.00
9 Carson Palmer 3.00 8.00
10 Jeff Garcia 2.50 6.00
11 Julius Jones 2.50 6.00
12 Joey Harrington 2.50 6.00
13 Andre Johnson 3.00 8.00
14 David Carr 2.50 6.00
15 Domanick Davis 2.50 6.00
16 Marvin Harrison 3.00 8.00
17 Peyton Manning 10.00 25.00
18 Byron Leftwich 2.50 6.00
19 Tony Gonzalez 3.00 8.00
20 Junior Seau 3.00 8.00
21 Jason Taylor 3.00 8.00
22 Michael Bennett 2.50 6.00
23 Aaron Brooks 2.50 6.00
24 Larry Fitzgerald 4.00 10.00
25 Eli Manning 6.00 15.00
26 Jeremy Shockey 2.50 6.00
27 Michael Strahan 3.00 8.00
28 Chad Pennington 2.50 6.00
29 Justin McCareins 2.50 6.00
30 John Abraham 2.50 6.00
31 Charles Woodson 4.00 10.00
32 Brian Westbrook 2.50 6.00
33 Donovan McNabb 3.00 8.00
34 Freddie Mitchell 2.50 6.00
35 Ben Roethlisberger 6.00 15.00
36 Duce Staley 2.50 6.00
37 Hines Ward 3.00 8.00
38 Koren Robinson 2.50 6.00
39 Matt Hasselbeck 2.50 6.00
40 Isaac Bruce 4.00 10.00
41 Marc Bulger 2.50 6.00
42 Torry Holt 3.00 8.00
43 Steven Jackson 2.50 6.00
44 Mike Alstott 2.50 6.00
45 Chris Brown 2.50 6.00
46 Derrick Mason 2.50 6.00
47 Drew Bennett 3.00 8.00
48 LaVar Arrington 2.50 6.00
49 Patrick Ramsey 3.00 8.00
50 Rod Gardner 2.50 6.00

2005 Donruss Classics Team Colors Bronze

BRONZE PRINT RUN 1000 SER.#'d SETS
*GOLD/250: .8X TO 2X BRONZE/1000
*SILVER/500: .5X TO 1.2X BRONZE/1000
TC1 Aaron Brooks .75 2.00
TC2 Dan Marino 3.00 8.00
TC3 David Carr .75 2.00
TC4 Deion Sanders 1.25 3.00
TC5 Donovan McNabb 1.00 2.50
TC6 Hines Ward 1.00 2.50
TC7 Jake Delhomme .75 2.00
TC8 Jerry Rice 2.50 6.00
TC9 John Elway 2.50 6.00
TC10 Marc Bulger .75 2.00
TC11 Matt Hasselbeck .75 2.00
TC12 Michael Irvin 1.50 4.00
TC13 Peyton Manning 3.00 8.00
TC14 Michael Vick 1.00 2.50
TC15 Steve Young 2.00 5.00
TC16 Tony Gonzalez 1.00 2.50
TC17 Torry Holt 1.00 2.50
TC18 Troy Aikman 2.00 5.00
TC19 Walter Payton 4.00 10.00
TC20 Isaac Bruce 1.25 3.00
TC21 Anquan Boldin .75 2.00
TC22 Larry Fitzgerald 1.25 3.00
TC23 Stephen Davis .75 2.00
TC24 Drew Bledsoe 1.00 2.50
TC25 LaDainian Tomlinson 1.25 3.00

2005 Donruss Classics Team Colors Jerseys Away

AWAY PRINT RUN 199 SER.#'d SETS
*HOME/99: .5X TO 1.2X AWAY JSY/199
*PRIME/25: 1X TO 2.5X AWAY JSY/199
1 Aaron Brooks 2.00 5.00
2 Dan Marino 6.00 15.00
3 David Carr 2.00 5.00
4 Deion Sanders 2.50 6.00
5 Donovan McNabb 2.50 6.00
6 Hines Ward 2.50 6.00
7 Jake Delhomme 2.00 5.00
8 Jerry Rice 6.00 15.00
9 John Elway 5.00 12.00
10 Marc Bulger 2.00 5.00
11 Matt Hasselbeck 2.00 5.00
12 Michael Irvin 3.00 8.00
13 Peyton Manning 8.00 20.00
14 Michael Vick 2.50 6.00
15 Steve Young 4.00 10.00
16 Tony Gonzalez 2.50 6.00
17 Torry Holt 2.50 6.00
18 Troy Aikman 4.00 10.00
19 Walter Payton 8.00 20.00
20 Isaac Bruce 3.00 8.00
21 Anquan Boldin 2.00 5.00
22 Larry Fitzgerald 3.00 8.00
23 Stephen Davis 2.00 5.00
24 Drew Bledsoe 2.50 6.00
25 LaDainian Tomlinson 3.00 8.00

2005 Donruss Classics Timeless Triples Bronze

BRONZE PRINT RUN 1000 SER.#'d SETS
*GOLD/250: .8X TO 2X BRONZE/1000
*SILVER/500: .5X TO 1.2X BRONZE/1000
1 J.Kelly/T.Thomas/Bledsoe 1.50 4.00
2 Payton/Sayers/Dent 4.00 10.00
3 J.Brown/Warfield/L.Kelly 2.00 5.00
4 Staubach/Aikman/Irvin 2.00 5.00
5 Campbell/Moon/McNair 1.50 4.00
6 Unitas/P.Manning/Shula 4.00 10.00
7 Namath/Maynard/Penning 2.50 6.00
8 Tarkenton/Eli/L.Taylor 2.50 6.00
9 Rice/Bo/M.Allen 3.00 8.00
10 Montana/M.Allen/Holmes 5.00 12.00

2005 Donruss Classics Timeless Triples Jerseys

STATED PRINT RUN 100 SER.#'d SETS
UNPRICED PRIME PRINT RUN 10
1 J.Kelly/T.Thomas/Bledsoe 10.00 25.00
2 Payton/Sayers/Dent 25.00 60.00
3 J.Brown/Warfield/L.Kelly 12.00 30.00
4 Staubach/Aikman/Irvin 12.00 30.00
5 Campbell/Moon/McNair 10.00 25.00
6 Unitas/P.Manning/Shula 25.00 60.00

7 Namath/Maynard/Penning 15.00 40.00
8 Tarkenton/Eli/Taylor 15.00 40.00
9 J.Rice/Bo/M.Allen 20.00 50.00
10 Montana/M.Allen/Holmes 30.00 80.00

2006 Donruss Classics

This 274-card set was released in July, 2006. Cards numbered 1-100 feature veterans in alphabetical team order, while cards numbered 101-160 are rookies printed to different serial numbering, cards 161-225 feature signed rookies (again to differing serial numbering) and the set concludes with retired greats (226-274) most of which were sequenced in first name alphabetical order. All the retired greats were issued to a stated print run of 1000 serial numbered copies.

COMP.SET w/o SP's (100) 7.50 20.00
LEGEND PRINT RUN 1000 SER.#'d SETS
1 Anquan Boldin .20 .50
2 Kurt Warner .25 .60
3 Larry Fitzgerald .25 .60
4 Marcel Shipp .20 .50
5 Alge Crumpler .25 .60
6 Michael Vick .25 .60
7 Warrick Dunn .20 .50
8 Jamal Lewis .25 .60
9 Kyle Boller .20 .50
10 Eric Moulds .20 .50
11 J.P. Losman .25 .60
12 Willis McGahee .20 .50
13 Jake Delhomme .20 .50
14 Stephen Davis .20 .50
15 Steve Smith .30 .75
16 Cedric Benson .20 .50
17 Kyle Orton .20 .50
18 Muhsin Muhammad .20 .50
19 Thomas Jones .20 .50
20 Carson Palmer .25 .60
21 Chad Johnson .20 .50
22 Rudi Johnson .20 .50
23 T.J. Houshmandzadeh .20 .50
24 Braylon Edwards .20 .50
25 Reuben Droughns .25 .60
26 Trent Dilfer .20 .50
27 Drew Bledsoe .25 .60
28 Julius Jones .20 .50
29 Keyshawn Johnson .25 .60
30 Terry Glenn .25 .60
31 Ashley Lelie .20 .50
32 Jake Plummer .20 .50
33 Tatum Bell .20 .50
34 Joey Harrington .20 .50
35 Kevin Jones .20 .50
36 Roy Williams WR .20 .50
37 Aaron Rodgers .75 2.00
38 Brett Favre .60 1.50
39 Samkon Gado .20 .50
40 Andre Johnson .25 .60
41 David Carr .20 .50
42 Domanick Davis .20 .50
43 Edgerrin James .25 .60
44 Marvin Harrison .25 .60
45 Peyton Manning .75 2.00
46 Reggie Wayne .25 .60
47 Byron Leftwich .20 .50
48 Fred Taylor .20 .50
49 Jimmy Smith .25 .60
50 Matt Jones .20 .50
51 Larry Johnson .20 .50
52 Tony Gonzalez .25 .60
53 Trent Green .20 .50
54 Chris Chambers .20 .50
55 Ricky Williams .20 .50
56 Ronnie Brown .25 .60
57 Daunte Culpepper .25 .60
58 Mewelde Moore .20 .50
59 Nate Burleson .20 .50
60 Corey Dillon .20 .50
61 Deion Branch .20 .50
62 Tom Brady 1.00 2.50
63 Aaron Brooks .20 .50
64 Deuce McAllister .25 .60
65 Donte Stallworth .20 .50
66 Eli Manning .25 .60
67 Plaxico Burress .20 .50
68 Tiki Barber .25 .60
69 Chad Pennington .20 .50
70 Curtis Martin .25 .60
71 Laveranues Coles .20 .50
72 Kerry Collins .20 .50
73 LaMont Jordan .25 .60
74 Randy Moss .25 .60
75 Brian Westbrook .20 .50
76 Donovan McNabb .25 .60
77 Reggie Brown .20 .50
78 Ben Roethlisberger .40 1.00
79 Hines Ward .25 .60
80 Willie Parker .25 .60
81 Antonio Gates .30 .75
82 Drew Brees .30 .75
83 LaDainian Tomlinson .30 .75
84 Alex Smith QB .25 .60
85 Frank Gore .25 .60
86 Darrell Jackson .25 .60
87 Matt Hasselbeck .20 .50
88 Shaun Alexander .20 .50
89 Marc Bulger .20 .50
90 Steven Jackson .20 .50
91 Torry Holt .25 .60
92 Cadillac Williams .25 .60
93 Joey Galloway .25 .60
94 Michael Clayton .20 .50
95 Chris Brown .20 .50
96 Steve McNair .25 .60
97 Drew Bennett .25 .60
98 Clinton Portis .20 .50
99 Mark Brunell .25 .60
100 Santana Moss .25 .60
101 Brodie Croyle/999 RC 1.50 4.00
102 Omar Jacobs/1499 RC 1.50 4.00
103 Charlie Whitehurst/999 RC 1.50 4.00
104 Tarvaris Jackson/999 RC 1.50 4.00
105 Kellen Clemens/999 RC 1.50 4.00
106 Vince Young/599 RC 2.00 5.00
107 Reggie McNeal/1499 RC 1.50 4.00
108 Marcus Vick/1499 RC 1.50 4.00
109 DonTrell Moore/1499 RC 2.00 5.00
110 Willie Reid/1499 RC 2.00 5.00
111 Matt Leinart/599 RC 2.00 5.00
112 Jay Cutler/599 RC 2.50 6.00
113 Brad Smith/1499 RC 2.00 5.00
114 Joseph Addai/599 RC 2.00 5.00
115 DeAngelo Williams/599 RC 2.50 6.00
116 Laurence Maroney/599 RC 2.00 5.00
117 Jerious Norwood/999 RC 1.50 4.00
118 Claude Wroten/1499 RC 1.50 4.00
119 Antonio Cromartie/1499 RC 2.00 5.00
120 Maurice Drew/999 RC 2.50 6.00
121 Anwar Phillips/1499 RC 2.00 5.00
122 LenDale White/599 RC 2.00 5.00
123 Reggie Bush/599 RC 3.00 8.00
124 Cedric Humes/1499 RC 1.50 4.00
125 Jerome Harrison/1499 RC 1.50 4.00
126 Brian Calhoun/999 RC 1.50 4.00
127 Joe Klopfenstein/999 RC 1.50 4.00
128 Leonard Pope/1499 RC 2.50 6.00
129 Vernon Davis/599 RC 2.50 6.00
130 Anthony Fasano/999 RC 1.50 4.00
131 Marcedes Lewis/999 RC 1.50 4.00
132 Dominique Byrd/1499 RC 1.50 4.00
133 Derek Hagan/1499 RC 2.00 5.00
134 Pat Watkins/1499 RC 2.00 5.00
135 Todd Watkins/1499 RC 1.50 4.00
136 Jeremy Bloom/1499 RC 1.50 4.00
137 Chad Jackson/599 RC 2.00 5.00
138 Devin Hester/1499 RC 3.00 8.00
139 Sinorice Moss/599 RC 2.00 5.00
140 Jason Avant/1499 RC 1.50 4.00
141 Maurice Stovall/1499 RC 1.50 4.00
142 Santonio Holmes/599 RC 2.50 6.00
143 Travis Wilson/999 RC 1.50 4.00
144 Demetrius Williams/1499 RC 1.50 4.00
145 Bernard Pollard/1499 RC 2.00 5.00
146 Michael Robinson/1499 RC 1.50 4.00
147 Brandon Marshall/1499 RC 3.00 8.00
148 Greg Jennings/999 RC 2.50 6.00
149 Brandon Williams/1499 RC 1.50 4.00
150 Jonathan Orr/1499 RC 2.00 5.00
151 David Thomas/1499 RC 1.50 4.00
152 Skyler Green/1499 RC 1.50 4.00
153 Mario Williams/499 RC 3.00 8.00
154 Ernie Sims/999 RC 1.50 4.00
155 A.J. Hawk/599 RC 2.50 6.00
156 Donte Whitner/1499 RC 2.00 5.00
157 Michael Huff/999 RC 2.00 5.00
158 Leon Washington/1499 RC 1.50 4.00
159 P.J. Daniels/1499 RC 1.50 4.00
160 Cory Rodgers/1499 RC 1.50 4.00
161 Tony Scheffler AU/499 RC 8.00 20.00
162 Paul Pinegar AU/999 RC 3.00 8.00
163 D.J. Shockley AU/599 RC 5.00 12.00
164 Ben Obomanu AU/899 RC 4.00 10.00
165 Adam Jennings AU/599 RC 5.00 12.00
166 Brandon Kirsch AU/999 RC 4.00 10.00
167 Mike Bell AU/999 RC 3.00 8.00
168 De'Arrius Howard AU/999 RC 5.00 12.00
169 Martin Nance AU/999 RC 3.00 8.00
170 Miles Austin AU/999 RC 4.00 10.00
171 Wendell Mathis AU/999 RC 4.00 10.00
172 Gerald Riggs AU/995 RC 4.00 10.00
173 Hank Baskett AU/999 RC 3.00 8.00
174 Greg Lee AU/999 RC 3.00 8.00
175 Quinton Ganther AU/799 RC 3.00 8.00
176 Garrett Mills/1499 RC 2.00 5.00
177 Jeff Webb AU/599 RC 5.00 12.00
178 Delanie Walker AU/599 RC 8.00 20.00
179 D'Brick. Ferguson AU/599 RC 4.00 10.00
180 Mathias Kiwanuka AU/499 RC 6.00 15.00
181 Kamerion Wimbley AU/499 RC 5.00 12.00
182 Tamba Hali AU/499 RC 6.00 15.00
183 Brodrick Bunkley AU/499 RC 5.00 12.00
184 Gabe Watson/1499 RC 1.50 4.00
185 Haloti Ngata AU/499 RC 5.00 12.00
186 DeMeco Ryans AU/599 RC 5.00 12.00
187 A.J. Nicholson/1499 RC 1.50 4.00
188 Abdul Hodge AU/999 RC 5.00 12.00
189 Chad Greenway AU/499 RC 6.00 15.00
190 D'Qwell Jackson AU/599 RC 4.00 10.00
191 Manny Lawson AU/499 RC 5.00 12.00
192 Bobby Carpenter AU/499 RC 4.00 10.00
193 Jon Alston AU/999 RC 3.00 8.00
194 Thomas Howard AU/599 RC 4.00 10.00
195 Tye Hill AU/499 RC 4.00 10.00
196 Kelly Jennings AU/499 RC 5.00 12.00
197 Ashton Youboty AU/999 RC 3.00 8.00
198 Alan Zemaitis AU/999 RC 3.00 8.00
199 Johnathan Joseph AU/499 RC 5.00 12.00
200 Jimmy Williams AU/599 RC 4.00 10.00
201 Ko Simpson AU/999 RC 4.00 10.00
202 Jason Allen AU/499 RC 5.00 12.00
203 Darnell Bing AU/999 RC 4.00 10.00
204 Erik Meyer AU/999 RC 3.00 8.00
205 Bruce Gradkowski AU/499 RC 5.00 12.00
206 Darrell Hackney AU/999 RC 4.00 10.00
207 Derrick Ross AU/799 RC 4.00 10.00
208 Drew Olson AU/999 RC 3.00 8.00
209 Taurean Henderson AU/999 RC 3.00 8.00
210 Andre Hall AU/999 RC 4.00 10.00
211 D.Aromashodu AU/899 RC 6.00 15.00
212 Mike Hass AU/599 RC 4.00 10.00
213 Ingle Martin AU/499 RC 5.00 12.00
214 Marques Hagans AU/499 RC 4.00 10.00
215 Wali Lundy AU/499 RC 4.00 10.00
216 Domenik Hixon AU/499 RC 6.00 15.00
217 Ethan Kilmer AU/899 RC 4.00 10.00
218 Bennie Brazell/1499 RC 2.00 5.00
219 David Anderson/1499 RC 2.00 5.00
220 Marques Colston AU/770 RC 5.00 12.00
221 Kevin McMahan AU/999 RC 4.00 10.00
222 Anthony Mix/1499 RC 2.00 5.00
223 John McCargo AU/499 RC 4.00 10.00
224 Rocky McIntosh/1499 RC 1.50 4.00
225 Cedric Griffin AU/599 RC 5.00 12.00
226 Barry Sanders 2.50 6.00
227 Bart Starr 2.50 6.00
228 Bo Jackson 2.00 5.00
229 Bob Griese 1.50 4.00
230 Bobby Layne 1.25 3.00
231 Boomer Esiason 1.25 3.00
232 Bulldog Turner 1.25 3.00
233 Dan Marino 3.00 8.00
234 Deacon Jones 1.25 3.00
235 Derrick Thomas 2.00 5.00
236 Dick Butkus 2.00 5.00
237 Don Meredith 1.50 4.00
238 Eric Dickerson 1.25 3.00
239 Fran Tarkenton 1.50 4.00
240 Fred Biletnikoff 1.50 4.00
241 Gale Sayers 1.50 4.00
242 Harvey Martin 1.00 2.50
243 Herman Edwards 1.25 3.00
244 Jack Lambert 1.50 4.00
245 Jim Brown 2.00 5.00
246 Jim Kelly 1.50 4.00
247 Jim Plunkett 1.25 3.00
248 Jim Thorpe 2.00 5.00
249 Joe Montana 5.00 12.00
250 John Elway 2.50 6.00
251 John Riggins 1.25 3.00
252 Johnny Unitas 2.50 6.00
253 Len Dawson 1.50 4.00
254 Marcus Allen 1.50 4.00
255 Mike Singletary 1.50 4.00
256 Ozzie Newsome 1.25 3.00
257 Phil Simms 1.25 3.00
258 Ray Nitschke 1.50 4.00
259 Red Grange 2.00 5.00
260 Roger Staubach 2.00 5.00
261 Ronnie Lott 1.25 3.00
262 Steve Largent 1.50 4.00
263 Terry Bradshaw 2.00 5.00
264 Troy Aikman 2.00 5.00
265 Walter Payton 3.00 8.00
266 Bill Dudley 1.25 3.00
267 Joe Perry 1.25 3.00
268 Charley Trippi 1.00 2.50
269 Paul Lowe 1.00 2.50
270 Clem Daniels 1.00 2.50
271 Ken Kavanaugh 1.00 2.50
272 Andre Reed 1.25 3.00
273 Steve Van Buren 1.25 3.00
274 Jim Taylor 1.50 4.00

2006 Donruss Classics Timeless Tributes Bronze

*VETERANS: 4X TO 10X BASIC CARDS
COMMON ROOKIE 2.50 6.00
ROOKIE SEMISTARS 4.00 10.00
ROOKIE UNL.STARS 5.00 12.00
*LEGENDS: 1X TO 2.5X BASIC CARDS
STATED PRINT RUN 100 SER.#'d SETS
106 Vince Young 3.00 8.00
112 Jay Cutler 4.00 10.00
115 DeAngelo Williams 4.00 10.00
120 Maurice Drew 5.00 12.00
123 Reggie Bush 5.00 12.00
138 Devin Hester 6.00 15.00
142 Santonio Holmes 4.00 10.00
148 Greg Jennings 5.00 12.00
154 Ernie Sims 3.00 8.00
155 A.J. Hawk 4.00 10.00
220 Marques Colston 5.00 12.00

2006 Donruss Classics Timeless Tributes Gold

*VETERANS: 8X TO 20X BASIC CARDS
*ROOKIES: .6X TO 1.5X BRONZE ROOKIES
*LEGENDS: 2X TO 5X BASIC CARDS
GOLD PRINT RUN 25 SER.#'d SETS

2006 Donruss Classics Timeless Tributes Platinum

UNPRICED PLAT.PRINT RUN 10 SER.#'d SETS

2006 Donruss Classics Timeless Tributes Silver

*VETERANS: 6X TO 15X BASIC CARDS
*ROOKIES: .5X TO 1.2X BRONZE ROOKIES
*LEGENDS: 1.5X TO 4X BASIC CARDS
STATED PRINT RUN 50 SER.#'d SETS

2006 Donruss Classics Classic Combos Bronze

BRONZE PRINT RUN 500 SER.#'d SETS
*GOLD: .6X TO 1.5X BRONZE INSERTS
GOLD PRINT RUN 100 SER.#'d SETS
*PLATINUM: 1.2X TO 3X BRONZE INSERTS
PLATINUM PRINT RUN 25 SER.#'d SETS
*SILVER: .5X TO 1.2X BRONZE INSERTS
SILVER PRINT RUN 250 SER.#'d SETS
1 B.Sanders/G.Sayers 3.00 8.00
2 B.Griese/L.Dawson 2.00 5.00
3 D.Marino/J.Montana 6.00 15.00
4 D.Meredith/T.Aikman 2.50 6.00
5 D.Butkus/D.Jones 2.50 6.00
6 J.Brown/J.Thorpe 2.50 6.00
7 J.Lambert/H.Martin 2.00 5.00
8 J.Kelly/J.Elway 3.00 8.00
9 M.Singletary/B.Turner 2.00 5.00
10 J.Unitas/P.Manning 5.00 12.00
11 O.Newsome/S.Largent 2.00 5.00
12 E.Dickerson/W.Payton 4.00 10.00
13 B.Esiason/P.Simms 1.50 4.00
14 D.Walker/D.Clark 2.00 5.00
15 S.Young/Y.Tittle 2.50 6.00
16 J.Plunkett/F.Biletnikoff 2.00 5.00

2006 Donruss Classics Classic Combos Jerseys

STATED PRINT RUN 50-250
UNPRICED PRIME PRINT RUN 1-10
1 B.Sanders/G.Sayers/207 12.00 30.00
2 B.Griese/L.Dawson/163 8.00 20.00
3 D.Marino/J.Montana/250 12.00 30.00
4 D.Meredith/T.Aikman/50 20.00 50.00
5 D.Butkus/D.Jones/150 10.00 25.00
6 J.Brown/J.Thorpe/25 150.00 250.00
7 J.Lambert/H.Martin/250 6.00 15.00
8 J.Kelly/J.Elway/250 12.00 30.00
9 M.Singletary/C.Turner/163 10.00 25.00
10 J.Unitas/P.Manning/215 12.00 30.00
11 O.Newsome/S.Largent/163 6.00 15.00
12 E.Dickerson/W.Payton/163 15.00 40.00
13 B.Esiason/P.Simms/250 6.00 15.00
14 D.Walker/D.Clark/50 60.00 100.00
15 S.Young/Y.Tittle/215 10.00 25.00
16 J.Plunkett/F.Biletnikoff/215 6.00 15.00

2006 Donruss Classics Classic Pigskin

STATED PRINT RUN 250 SER.#'d SETS
*DOUBLES: 1X TO 2.5X BASIC INSERTS
DOUBLES PRINT RUN 25 SER.#'d SETS
1 Bart Starr 30.00 60.00
2 Andre Reed 6.00 15.00
3 Fred Biletnikoff 8.00 20.00
4 John Elway 12.00 30.00
5 Jim Kelly 10.00 25.00
6 Thurman Thomas 8.00 20.00

2006 Donruss Classics Classic Quads Bronze

BRONZE PRINT RUN 100 SER.#'d SETS
*GOLD: .6X TO 1.5X BRONZE INSERTS
GOLD PRINT RUN 25 SER.#'d SETS
UNPRICED PLATINUM PRINT RUN 10
*SILVER: .5X TO 1.2X BRONZE INSERTS
SILVER PRINT RUN 50 SER.#'d SETS
1 Starr/Unitas/Tittle/Meredith 10.00 25.00
2 Jones/Turner/Martin/Lambert 6.00 15.00
3 Brwn/Sndrs/Dckrsn/Pytn 10.00 25.00
4 Mont/Dwsn/P.Mann/Fvre 12.50 30.00
5 Kelly/Aikman/Elway/Marino 10.00 25.00
6 Esiason/Griese/Simms/Young 8.00 20.00
7 Lrgnt/Nwsm/Bilet/Ellard 8.00 20.00
8 Butkus/Single/Lott/Thomas 8.00 20.00

2006 Donruss Classics Classic Quads Materials

STATED PRINT RUN 50 SER.#'d SETS
UNPRICED PRIME PRINT RUN 1-5 SETS
2 Deadon/Bulldog/Martin/Lambert 15.00 40.00
3 Brwn/Sndrs/Dckrsn/Pytn 60.00 150.00
4 Mont/Dwsn/P.Mnn/Fvre 50.00 120.00
5 Kelly/Aikman/Elway/Marino 40.00 100.00
6 Esias/Griese/Simms/Young 30.00 80.00
7 Lrgnt/Nwsm/Bilet/Ellrd 20.00 50.00
8 Btks/Single/Lott/D.Thms 25.00 60.00

2006 Donruss Classics Classic Singles Bronze

BRONZE PRINT RUN 1000 SER.#'d SETS
*GOLD: .8X TO 2X BRONZE INSERTS
GOLD PRINT RUN 100 SER.#'d SETS
*PLATINUM: 1.2X TO 3X BRONZE INSERTS
PLATINUM PRINT RUN 25 SER.#'d SETS
*SILVER: .6X TO 1.5X BRONZE INSERTS
SILVER PRINT RUN 250 SER.#'d SETS
1 Barry Sanders 2.50 6.00
2 Bob Griese 1.50 4.00
3 Dan Marino 3.00 8.00
4 Eric Dickerson 1.25 3.00
5 Don Meredith 1.50 4.00
6 Herman Edwards 1.25 3.00
7 Jim Brown 2.00 5.00
8 Jack Lambert 1.50 4.00
9 Jim Kelly 1.50 4.00
10 Joe Montana 5.00 12.00
11 Jim Thorpe 2.00 5.00
12 John Elway 2.50 6.00
13 Peyton Manning 4.00 10.00
14 Marcus Allen 1.50 4.00
15 Len Dawson 1.50 4.00
16 Jim Plunkett 1.25 3.00
17 Mike Singletary 1.50 4.00
18 Ozzie Newsome 1.25 3.00
19 Ronnie Lott 1.25 3.00
20 Steve Largent 1.50 4.00
21 Walter Payton 3.00 8.00
22 Dick Butkus 2.00 5.00
23 Deacon Jones 1.25 3.00
24 Gale Sayers 1.50 4.00
25 Harvey Martin 1.00 2.50
26 Johnny Unitas 2.50 6.00
27 Troy Aikman 2.00 5.00
28 Ray Nitschke 1.50 4.00
29 Boomer Esiason 1.25 3.00
30 Phil Simms 1.25 3.00

2006 Donruss Classics Classic Singles Jerseys

STATED PRINT RUN 75-250 SETS
*PRIME/25: 1.2X TO 3X BASIC JERSEYS
PRIME STATED PRINT RUN 1-25
1 Barry Sanders/250 8.00 20.00
2 Bob Griese/189 4.00 10.00
3 Dan Marino/250 10.00 25.00
4 Eric Dickerson/250 4.00 10.00
5 Don Meredith/75 10.00 25.00
6 Herman Edwards/250 3.00 8.00
7 Jim Brown/175 6.00 15.00
8 Jack Lambert/250 5.00 12.00
9 Jim Kelly/250 5.00 12.00
10 Joe Montana/250 10.00 25.00
11 Jim Thorpe/100 60.00 120.00
12 John Elway/250 8.00 20.00
13 Peyton Manning/250 8.00 20.00
14 Marcus Allen/250 4.00 10.00
15 Len Dawson/250 4.00 10.00
16 Jim Plunkett/250 4.00 10.00
17 Mike Singletary/200 4.00 10.00
18 Ozzie Newsome/250 4.00 10.00
19 Ronnie Lott/250 4.00 10.00
20 Steve Largent/215 4.00 10.00
21 Walter Payton/163 10.00 25.00
22 Dick Butkus/250 6.00 15.00
23 Deacon Jones/250 4.00 10.00
24 Gale Sayers/250 6.00 15.00
25 Harvey Martin/250 5.00 12.00
26 Johnny Unitas/250 10.00 25.00
27 Troy Aikman/250 6.00 15.00
28 Ray Nitschke/250 6.00 15.00
29 Boomer Esiason/250 3.00 8.00
30 Phil Simms/250 4.00 10.00

2006 Donruss Classics Classic Triples Bronze

BRONZE PRINT RUN 250 SER.#'d SETS
*GOLD: .6X TO 1.5X BRONZE INSERTS
GOLD PRINT RUN 50 SER.#'d SETS
UNPRICED PLATINUM PRINT RUN 10 SE'TS
*SILVER: .5X TO 1.2X BRONZE INSERTS
SILVER PRINT RUN 100 SER.#'d SETS
1 Singletary/Turner/Butkus 5.00 12.00
2 Thorpe/Sayers/Payton 8.00 20.00
3 Thomas/Jones/Martin 4.00 10.00
4 Sanders/Dickerson/Allen 6.00 15.00
5 Young/Marino/Simms 8.00 20.00
6 Meredith/Montana/Unitas 8.00 20.00
7 Aikman/Kelly/Elway 6.00 15.00
8 Griese/Dawson/Starr 6.00 15.00
9 Biletnikoff/Largent/Newsome 4.00 10.00
10 Tittle/Manning/Plunkett 5.00 12.00

2006 Donruss Classics Classic Triples Materials

STATED PRINT RUN 100 SER.#'d SETS
UNPRICED PRIME PRINT RUN 1-10
1 Singletary 15.00 40.00
Turner
Butkus
2 Thorpe/Sayers/Payton/50 100.00 200.00
3 Thomas/Jones/Martin 25.00 60.00
4 Sanders/Dickerson/Allen 15.00 40.00
5 Young/Marino/Simms 25.00 60.00
6 Meredith/Montana/Unitas/25 75.00 125.00
7 Aikman/Kelly/Elway 15.00 40.00
8 Grises/Dawson/Starr/55 25.00 60.00
9 Biletnikoff/Largent/Newsome 15.00 40.00
10 Tittle/Manning/Plunkett 15.00 40.00

2006 Donruss Classics Legendary Players Bronze

BRONZE PRINT RUN 1000 SER.#'d SETS
*GOLD: .8X TO 2X BRONZE INSERTS
GOLD PRINT RUN 100 SER.#'d SETS
*PLATINUM: 1.2X TO 3X BRONZE INSERTS
PLATINUM PRINT RUN 25 SER.#'d SETS
*SILVER: .6X TO 1.5X BRONZE INSERTS
SILVER PRINT RUN 250 SER.#'d SETS
1 Barry Sanders 2.50 6.00
2 Bobby Layne 1.25 3.00
3 Bulldog Turner 1.25 3.00
4 Dan Marino 3.00 8.00
5 Y.A. Tittle 1.50 4.00
7 Yale Lary 1.00 2.50
8 Lance Alworth 1.25 3.00
9 John Elway 2.50 6.00
10 Troy Aikman 2.00 5.00
11 Daryle Lamonica 1.00 2.50
12 Henry Ellard 1.00 2.50
13 Jerry Rice 3.00 8.00
14 Fred Biletnikoff 1.50 4.00
15 Deacon Jones 1.25 3.00
16 Jim Brown 2.00 5.00
17 Joe Montana 5.00 12.00
18 Johnny Unitas 2.50 6.00
19 Roger Staubach 2.00 5.00
20 John Riggins 1.25 3.00
21 Steve Largent 1.50 4.00
22 Ozzie Newsome 1.25 3.00
23 Terry Bradshaw 2.00 5.00
24 Jim Plunkett 1.25 3.00
25 Gale Sayers 1.50 4.00
26 Phil Simms 1.25 3.00
27 Jack Lambert 1.50 4.00
28 Walter Payton 3.00 8.00
29 Ray Nitschke 1.50 4.00
30 Don Meredith 1.50 4.00

2006 Donruss Classics Legendary Players Jerseys

STATED PRINT RUN 50-250 SETS
*PRIME/25: 1.2X TO 3X BASIC JERSEYS
PRIME PRINT RUN 2-25 SETS
1 Barry Sanders/250 8.00 20.00
2 Bobby Layne/50 20.00 50.00
3 Bulldog Turner/250 5.00 12.00
4 Dan Marino/250 8.00 20.00
5 Y.A. Tittle/250 5.00 12.00
7 Yale Lary/250 5.00 12.00
8 Lance Alworth/250 6.00 15.00
9 John Elway/250 6.00 15.00
10 Troy Aikman/250 6.00 15.00
11 Daryle Lamonica/250 5.00 12.00
12 Henry Ellard/250 4.00 10.00
13 Jerry Rice/250 6.00 15.00
14 Fred Biletnikoff/250 5.00 12.00
15 Deacon Jones/250 4.00 10.00
16 Jim Brown/100 8.00 20.00
17 Joe Montana/250 10.00 25.00
18 Johnny Unitas/250 10.00 25.00
19 Roger Staubach/215 8.00 20.00
20 John Riggins/150 4.00 10.00
21 Steve Largent/215 4.00 10.00
22 Ozzie Newsome/175 4.00 10.00
23 Terry Bradshaw/189 8.00 20.00
24 Jim Plunkett/250 4.00 10.00
25 Gale Sayers/215 6.00 15.00
26 Phil Simms/250 4.00 10.00
27 Jack Lambert/250 6.00 15.00
28 Walter Payton/189 10.00 25.00
29 Ray Nitschke/250 8.00 20.00
30 Don Meredith/107 10.00 25.00

2006 Donruss Classics Membership Bronze

BRONZE PRINT RUN 1000 SER.#'d SETS
*GOLD: .8X TO 2X BRONZE INSERTS
GOLD PRINT RUN 100 SER.#'d SETS
*PLATINUM: 1.2X TO 3X BRONZE INSERTS
PLATINUM PRINT RUN 25 SER.#'d SETS
*SILVER: .6X TO 1.5X BRONZE INSERTS
SILVER PRINT RUN 250 SER.#'d SETS
1 Aaron Brooks .75 2.00
2 Alex Smith QB 1.00 2.50
3 Alge Crumpler 1.00 2.50
4 Ben Roethlisberger 1.50 4.00
5 Braylon Edwards .75 2.00
6 Cadillac Williams 1.00 2.50
7 Carson Palmer 1.00 2.50
8 Chad Pennington .75 2.00
9 Clinton Portis .75 2.00
10 Deuce McAllister 1.00 2.50
11 Edgerrin James 1.00 2.50
12 Jimmy Smith 1.00 2.50
13 Marvin Harrison 1.00 2.50
14 Michael Vick 1.00 2.50
15 Randy Moss 1.00 2.50
16 Ronnie Brown 1.00 2.50
17 T.J. Houshmandzadeh .75 2.00
18 Terrell Owens 1.00 2.50
19 Thomas Jones .75 2.00
20 Warrick Dunn .75 2.00

2006 Donruss Classics Membership VIP Jerseys

STATED PRINT RUN 250 SER.#'d SETS
*PRIME: 1X TO 2.5X BASIC JERSEYS
PRIME PRINT RUN 25 SER.#'d SETS
1 Aaron Brooks 3.00 8.00
2 Alex Smith QB 4.00 10.00
3 Alge Crumpler 2.50 6.00
4 Ben Roethlisberger 10.00 25.00
5 Braylon Edwards 4.00 10.00
6 Cadillac Williams 4.00 10.00
7 Carson Palmer 4.00 10.00
8 Chad Pennington 3.00 8.00
9 Clinton Portis 4.00 10.00
10 Deuce McAllister 3.00 8.00
11 Edgerrin James 4.00 10.00
12 Jimmy Smith 3.00 8.00
13 Marvin Harrison 4.00 10.00
14 Michael Vick 4.00 10.00
15 Randy Moss 4.00 10.00
16 Ronnie Brown 4.00 10.00
17 T.J. Houshmandzadeh 2.50 6.00
18 Terrell Owens 4.00 10.00
19 Thomas Jones 3.00 8.00
20 Warrick Dunn 3.00 8.00

2006 Donruss Classics Monday Night Heroes Bronze

BRONZE PRINT RUN 1000 SER.#'d SETS
*GOLD: .8X TO 2X BRONZE INSERTS
GOLD PRINT RUN 100 SER.#'d SETS
*PLATINUM: 1.2X TO 3X BRONZE INSERTS
PLATINUM PRINT RUN 25 SER.#'d SETS
*SILVER: .6X TO 1.5X BRONZE INSERTS
SILVER PRINT RUN 250 SER.#'d SETS
1 Antonio Gates 1.25 3.00
2 Antwaan Randle El .75 2.00
3 Ben Roethlisberger 1.50 4.00
4 Brian Westbrook .75 2.00
5 Cadillac Williams 1.00 2.50
6 Carson Palmer 1.00 2.50
7 Chad Johnson .75 2.00
8 Clinton Portis .75 2.00
9 Corey Dillon .75 2.00
10 Curtis Martin 1.00 2.50
11 Daunte Culpepper 1.00 2.50
12 Donovan McNabb 1.00 2.50
13 Drew Bledsoe 1.00 2.50
14 Drew Brees 1.25 3.00
15 Edgerrin James 1.00 2.50
16 Eli Manning 1.00 2.50
17 Jake Plummer .75 2.00
18 Jimmy Smith 1.00 2.50
19 Julius Jones .75 2.00
20 LaDainian Tomlinson 1.25 3.00
21 Marvin Harrison 1.00 2.50
22 Matt Hasselbeck .75 2.00
23 Michael Vick 1.00 2.50
24 Peyton Manning 3.00 8.00
25 Randy Moss 1.00 2.50
26 Willis McGahee .75 2.00
27 Shaun Alexander .75 2.00
28 Steven Jackson .75 2.00
29 Tom Brady 4.00 10.00
30 Trent Green .75 2.00

2006 Donruss Classics Monday Night Heroes Jerseys

STATED PRINT RUN 250 SER.#'d SETS
*PRIME: 1X TO 2.5X BASIC JERSEYS
PRIME PRINT RUN 25 SER.#'d SETS
1 Antonio Gates 4.00 10.00
2 Antwaan Randle El 3.00 8.00
3 Ben Roethlisberger 10.00 25.00
4 Brian Westbrook 3.00 8.00
5 Cadillac Williams 4.00 10.00
6 Carson Palmer 4.00 10.00
7 Chad Johnson 3.00 8.00
8 Clinton Portis 4.00 10.00
9 Corey Dillon 3.00 8.00
10 Curtis Martin 4.00 10.00
11 Daunte Culpepper 4.00 10.00
12 Donovan McNabb 4.00 10.00
13 Drew Bledsoe 4.00 10.00
14 Drew Brees 4.00 10.00
15 Edgerrin James 4.00 10.00
16 Eli Manning 6.00 15.00
17 Jake Plummer 3.00 8.00
18 Jimmy Smith/230 3.00 8.00
19 Julius Jones 4.00 10.00
20 LaDainian Tomlinson 4.00 10.00
21 Marvin Harrison 4.00 10.00
22 Matt Hasselbeck 4.00 10.00
23 Michael Vick 4.00 10.00
24 Peyton Manning 8.00 20.00
25 Randy Moss 4.00 10.00
26 Willis McGahee 3.00 8.00
27 Shaun Alexander 5.00 12.00
28 Steven Jackson 4.00 10.00
29 Tom Brady 6.00 15.00
30 Trent Green 3.00 8.00

2006 Donruss Classics Monday Night Heroes Jerseys Autographs

STATED PRINT RUN 5-25
UNPRICED PRIME AUTO PRINT RUN 5
1 Antonio Gates/25 10.00 25.00
16 Eli Manning/25 60.00 120.00
22 Matt Hasselbeck/25 30.00 60.00
28 Steven Jackson/25 10.00 25.00

2006 Donruss Classics Saturday Stars Bronze

BRONZE PRINT RUN 1000 SER.#'d SETS
*GOLD: .8X TO 2X BRONZE INSERTS
GOLD PRINT RUN 100 SER.#'d SETS
*PLATINUM: 1.2X TO 3X BRONZE INSERTS
PLATINUM PRINT RUN 25 SER.#'d SETS
*SILVER: .6X TO 1.5X BRONZE INSERTS
SILVER PRINT RUN 250 SER.#'d SETS
1 Cadillac Williams 1.00 2.50
2 Ronnie Brown 1.00 2.50
3 Mike Singletary 1.25 3.00
4 Fred Taylor .75 2.00
5 Jevon Kearse .75 2.00
6 Anquan Boldin .75 2.00
7 Laveranues Coles .75 2.00
8 Hines Ward 1.00 2.50
9 Michael Clayton .75 2.00
10 Clinton Portis .75 2.00
11 Edgerrin James 1.00 2.50
12 Jeremy Shockey .75 2.00
13 Kellen Winslow .75 2.00
14 Reggie Wayne 1.00 2.50
15 Sean Taylor 1.25 3.00
16 Willis McGahee .75 2.00
17 Braylon Edwards .75 2.00
18 Ahman Green 1.00 2.50
19 Barry Sanders 2.00 5.00
20 Curtis Martin 1.00 2.50
21 Dan Marino 2.50 6.00
22 Terry Bradshaw 1.50 4.00
23 Eric Dickerson 1.00 2.50
24 John Elway 2.00 5.00
25 Peyton Manning 3.00 8.00
26 Cedric Benson .75 2.00
27 Carson Palmer 1.00 2.50
28 Michael Vick 1.00 2.50
29 Drew Bledsoe 1.00 2.50
30 Lee Evans 1.00 2.50

2006 Donruss Classics Saturday Stars Autographs

STATED PRINT RUN 5-25
14 Reggie Wayne/25 15.00 30.00

2006 Donruss Classics Saturday Stars Jerseys

STATED PRINT RUN 18-250
*PRIME/16-28: 1X TO 2.5X BASIC JERSEYS
PRIME PRINT RUN 6-28
1 Cadillac Williams 5.00 12.00
2 Ronnie Brown 5.00 12.00
3 Mike Singletary/236 6.00 15.00
5 Jevon Kearse/88 4.00 10.00
6 Anquan Boldin/164 4.00 10.00
7 Laveranues Coles 4.00 10.00
8 Hines Ward 5.00 12.00
9 Michael Clayton 4.00 10.00
10 Clinton Portis/102 4.00 10.00
11 Edgerrin James 5.00 12.00
12 Jeremy Shockey/139 4.00 10.00
13 Kellen Winslow 4.00 10.00
14 Reggie Wayne 5.00 12.00
15 Sean Taylor 10.00 25.00
16 Willis McGahee 4.00 10.00
17 Braylon Edwards 4.00 10.00
18 Ahman Green 5.00 12.00
19 Barry Sanders 10.00 25.00
20 Curtis Martin 5.00 12.00
21 Dan Marino 12.00 30.00
22 Terry Bradshaw 8.00 20.00
23 Eric Dickerson 5.00 12.00
24 John Elway 10.00 25.00
25 Peyton Manning 15.00 40.00
26 Cedric Benson 4.00 10.00
27 Carson Palmer 5.00 12.00
28 Michael Vick 5.00 12.00
29 Drew Bledsoe 5.00 12.00
30 Lee Evans 5.00 12.00

2006 Donruss Classics Saturday Stars Jerseys Autographs

UNPRICED AUTO PRINT RUN 4-15
UNPRICED PRIME AU PRINT RUN 2-5

2006 Donruss Classics School Colors

ONE PER CASE
1 Vince Young 1.50 4.00
2 Reggie Bush 2.50 6.00
3 Matt Leinart 1.50 4.00
4 Jay Cutler 2.00 5.00
5 Laurence Maroney 1.50 4.00
6 DeAngelo Williams 2.00 5.00
7 Vernon Davis 2.00 5.00
8 Chad Jackson 1.50 4.00
9 Santonio Holmes 2.00 5.00
10 Sinorice Moss 1.50 4.00
11 Charlie Whitehurst 1.50 4.00
12 Erik Meyer 1.50 4.00
13 Joseph Addai 1.50 4.00
14 Brodie Croyle 1.50 4.00
15 Maurice Drew 2.50 6.00
16 Jerious Norwood 1.50 4.00
17 Demetrius Williams 1.50 4.00
18 Todd Watkins 1.50 4.00
19 Travis Wilson 1.50 4.00
20 Marcedes Lewis 1.50 4.00

2006 Donruss Classics School Colors Autographs

STATED PRINT RUN 25 SER.#'d SETS
1 Vince Young 12.00 30.00
2 Reggie Bush 20.00 50.00
3 Matt Leinart 40.00 100.00
4 Jay Cutler 15.00 40.00
5 Laurence Maroney 12.00 30.00
6 DeAngelo Williams 30.00 80.00
7 Vernon Davis 15.00 40.00
8 Chad Jackson 12.00 30.00
9 Santonio Holmes 50.00 100.00
10 Sinorice Moss 12.00 30.00
11 Charlie Whitehurst 12.00 30.00
12 Erik Meyer 12.00 30.00
13 Joseph Addai 12.00 30.00
14 Brodie Croyle 12.00 30.00
15 Maurice Drew 50.00 100.00
16 Jerious Norwood 12.00 30.00
17 Demetrius Williams 12.00 30.00
18 Todd Watkins 12.00 30.00
19 Travis Wilson 12.00 30.00
20 Marcedes Lewis 12.00 30.00

2006 Donruss Classics Significant Signatures Gold

ROOKIE PRINT RUN 100 SER.#'d SETS
LEGEND PRINT RUN 5-100
SERIAL #'d UNDER 25 NOT PRICED
101 Brodie Croyle 6.00 15.00
102 Omar Jacobs 6.00 15.00
103 Charlie Whitehurst 6.00 15.00
104 Tarvaris Jackson 6.00 15.00
105 Kellen Clemens 6.00 15.00
106 Vince Young 6.00 15.00
107 Reggie McNeal Â• 6.00 15.00
110 Willie Reid 8.00 20.00
111 Matt Leinart 6.00 15.00
112 Jay Cutler 8.00 20.00
113 Brad Smith 8.00 20.00
114 Joseph Addai 6.00 15.00
115 DeAngelo Williams 8.00 20.00
116 Laurence Maroney 6.00 15.00
117 Jerious Norwood 6.00 15.00
118 Claude Wroten 6.00 15.00
120 Maurice Drew 10.00 25.00
121 Anwar Phillips 8.00 20.00
122 LenDale White 6.00 15.00
123 Reggie Bush 10.00 25.00
124 Cedric Humes 6.00 15.00
126 Brian Calhoun 6.00 15.00
127 Joe Klopfenstein 6.00 15.00
128 Leonard Pope 10.00 25.00
129 Vernon Davis 8.00 20.00
130 Anthony Fasano 6.00 15.00
131 Marcedes Lewis 6.00 15.00
132 Dominique Byrd 6.00 15.00
133 Derek Hagan 8.00 20.00
134 Pat Watkins 8.00 20.00
135 Todd Watkins 6.00 15.00
136 Jeremy Bloom 6.00 15.00
137 Chad Jackson 6.00 15.00
138 Devin Hester 12.00 30.00
139 Sinorice Moss 6.00 15.00
140 Jason Avant 6.00 15.00
141 Maurice Stovall 6.00 15.00
142 Santonio Holmes 8.00 20.00
143 Travis Wilson 6.00 15.00
144 Demetrius Williams 6.00 15.00
145 Bernard Pollard 8.00 20.00
146 Michael Robinson 6.00 15.00
147 Brandon Marshall 12.00 30.00
148 Greg Jennings 10.00 25.00
149 Brandon Williams 6.00 15.00
150 Jonathan Orr 8.00 20.00
151 David Thomas 6.00 15.00
152 Skyler Green 6.00 15.00
153 Mario Williams 10.00 25.00
155 A.J. Hawk 8.00 20.00
156 Donte Whitner 8.00 20.00
157 Michael Huff 8.00 20.00
158 Leon Washington 6.00 15.00
159 P.J. Daniels 6.00 15.00
241 Gale Sayers/40 30.00 80.00
243 Herman Edwards/100 8.00 20.00
245 Jim Brown/32 50.00 100.00
251 John Riggins/44 25.00 50.00
255 Mike Singletary/50 15.00 40.00
256 Ozzie Newsome/50 8.00 20.00
266 Bill Dudley/100 25.00 50.00
267 Joe Perry/34 25.00 50.00
268 Charley Trippi/100 15.00 40.00
269 Paul Lowe/100 8.00 20.00
270 Clem Daniels/36 10.00 25.00
271 Ken Kavanaugh/100 12.00 30.00
272 Andre Reed/100 10.00 25.00
274 Jim Taylor/31 30.00 80.00

2006 Donruss Classics Significant Signatures Platinum

*PLAT/25: .6X TO 1.5X GOLD AUTOS
PLAT.ROOKIE PRINT RUN 25 SER.#'d SETS
PLATINUM LEGEND PRINT RUN 1-25
SERIAL #'d UNDER 25 NOT PRICED

2006 Donruss Classics Sunday's Best Bronze

BRONZE PRINT RUN 1000 SER.#'d SETS
*GOLD: .8X TO 2X BRONZE INSERTS
GOLD PRINT RUN 100 SER.#'d SETS
*PLATINUM: 1.2X TO 3X BRONZE INSERTS
PLATINUM PRINT RUN 25 SER.#'d SETS
*SILVER: .6X TO 1.5X BRONZE INSERTS
SILVER PRINT RUN 250 SER.#'d SETS
1 Willis McGahee .75 2.00
2 Alge Crumpler 1.00 2.50
3 Antonio Gates 1.25 3.00
4 Antwaan Randle El .75 2.00
5 Ben Roethlisberger 1.50 4.00
6 Warrick Dunn .75 2.00
7 Brian Westbrook .75 2.00
8 Cadillac Williams 1.00 2.50
9 Carson Palmer 1.00 2.50
10 Chad Johnson .75 2.00
11 Chad Pennington .75 2.00
12 Clinton Portis .75 2.00
13 Corey Dillon .75 2.00
14 Curtis Martin 1.00 2.50
15 Deion Branch .75 2.00
16 Deuce McAllister 1.00 2.50
17 Domanick Davis .75 2.00
18 Donovan McNabb 1.00 2.50
19 Drew Bledsoe 1.00 2.50
20 Drew Brees 1.25 3.00
21 Edgerrin James 1.00 2.50
22 Eli Manning 1.00 2.50
23 Jake Plummer .75 2.00
24 Jimmy Smith 1.00 2.50
25 Julius Jones .75 2.00
26 LaDainian Tomlinson 1.25 3.00
27 Marvin Harrison 1.00 2.50
28 Matt Hasselbeck .75 2.00
29 Michael Vick 1.00 2.50
30 Peyton Manning 3.00 8.00
31 Randy Moss 1.00 2.50
32 Ronnie Brown 1.00 2.50
33 Shaun Alexander .75 2.00
34 Steve Smith 1.25 3.00
35 Steven Jackson .75 2.00
36 T.J. Houshmandzadeh .75 2.00
37 Tatum Bell .75 2.00
38 Thomas Jones .75 2.00
39 Tom Brady 4.00 10.00
40 Trent Green .75 2.00

2006 Donruss Classics Sunday's Best Jerseys

STATED PRINT RUN 250 SER.#'d SETS
*PRIME: 1X TO 2.5X BASIC JERSEYS
PRIME PRINT RUN 25 SER.#'d SETS
1 Willis McGahee 2.50 6.00
2 Alge Crumpler 3.00 8.00
3 Antonio Gates 4.00 10.00
4 Antwaan Randle El 2.50 6.00
5 Ben Roethlisberger 5.00 12.00
6 Warrick Dunn 2.50 6.00
7 Brian Westbrook 2.50 6.00
8 Cadillac Williams 3.00 8.00
9 Carson Palmer 3.00 8.00
10 Chad Johnson 2.50 6.00
11 Chad Pennington 2.50 6.00
12 Clinton Portis 2.50 6.00
13 Corey Dillon 2.50 6.00
14 Curtis Martin 3.00 8.00
15 Deion Branch 2.50 6.00
16 Deuce McAllister 3.00 8.00
17 Domanick Davis 2.50 6.00
18 Donovan McNabb 3.00 8.00
19 Drew Bledsoe 3.00 8.00
20 Drew Brees 4.00 10.00
21 Edgerrin James 3.00 8.00
22 Eli Manning 3.00 8.00
23 Jake Plummer 2.50 6.00
24 Jimmy Smith 3.00 8.00
25 Julius Jones 2.50 6.00
26 LaDainian Tomlinson 4.00 10.00
27 Marvin Harrison 3.00 8.00
28 Matt Hasselbeck 2.50 6.00
29 Michael Vick 3.00 8.00
30 Peyton Manning 10.00 25.00
31 Randy Moss 3.00 8.00
32 Ronnie Brown 3.00 8.00
33 Shaun Alexander 2.50 6.00
34 Steve Smith 4.00 10.00
35 Steven Jackson 2.50 6.00
36 T.J. Houshmandzadeh 2.50 6.00
37 Tatum Bell 2.50 6.00
38 Thomas Jones 2.50 6.00
39 Tom Brady 12.00 30.00
40 Trent Green 2.50 6.00

2006 Donruss Classics Sunday's Best Jerseys Autographs

STATED PRINT RUN 10-25
UNPRICED PRIME PRINT RUN 5 SETS
2 Alge Crumpler/25 10.00 25.00
17 Domanick Davis/25 10.00 25.00
28 Matt Hasselbeck/25 30.00 60.00
32 Ronnie Brown/25 30.00 80.00

2006 Donruss Classics Timeless Triples Bronze

BRONZE PRINT RUN 1000 SER.#'d SETS
*GOLD: .8X TO 2X BRONZE INSERTS
GOLD PRINT RUN 100 SER.#'d SETS
*PLATINUM: 1.2X TO 3X BRONZE INSERTS
PLATINUM PRINT RUN 25 SER.#'d SETS
*SILVER: .6X TO 1.5X BRONZE INSERTS
SILVER PRINT RUN 250 SER.#'d SETS
1 Montana/Young/Smith QB 3.00 8.00
2 Dunn/Vick/Crumpler 1.50 4.00
3 Sayers/Payton/Benson 4.00 10.00
4 Esiason/Johnson/Palmer 1.50 4.00
5 Staubach/Aikman/Bledsoe 2.50 6.00
6 Layne/Lary/Sandoro 2.50 6.00

7 Allen/Holmes/Johnson 2.00 5.00
8 Thorpe/Clark/Grange 3.00 8.00
9 Tomlinson/Brees/Gates 2.00 5.00
10 Starr/Favre/Rodgers 4.00 10.00

2006 Donruss Classics Timeless Triples Materials

STATED PRINT RUN 100 SER.#'d SETS
UNPRICED PRIME PRINT RUN 10 SETS
1 Montana/Young/Smith QB 30.00 80.00
2 Dunn/Vick/Crumpler 10.00 25.00
3 Gayers/Payton/Benson 25.00 60.00
4 Esiason/Johnson/Palmer 10.00 25.00
5 Staubach/Aikman/Bledsoe 15.00 40.00
6 Laybe/Lary/Sanders/50 40.00 80.00
7 Allen/Holmes/Johnson 12.00 30.00
8 Thorpe/Clark/Grange/50 250.00 450.00
9 Tomlinson/Brees/Gates 10.00 25.00
10 Starr/Favre/Rodgers 40.00 80.00

2007 Donruss Classics

This 271-card set was released in July, 2007. The set was issued into the hobby five-card packs, with a $6 SRP, which came 18 packs to a box. Cards numbered 1-100 feature active veterans sequenced in their 2006 team alphabetical order, while cards numbered 101-150 feature retired greats in first name alphabetical order which were issued to a stated print run of 999 serial numbered copies. The set concludes with Rookie Cards from 151-275 of which cards numbered 221-275 were signed by the player. The cards between 151-220 were issued to stated print runs of between 599 and 1499 serial numbered cards while the cards between 221 and 275 were issued to stated print runs of between 499 and 999 serial numbered cards. Cards numbers 102, 107, 119 and 132 were not made for this set.

COMP.SET w/o SP's (100) 7.50 20.00
LEGEND PRINT RUN 999 SER.#'d SETS
ROOKIE PRINT RUN 499-1499
1 Anquan Boldin .20 .50
2 Edgerrin James .25 .60
3 Larry Fitzgerald .25 .60
4 Matt Leinart .20 .50
5 Alge Crumpler .25 .60
6 Michael Vick .25 .60
7 Warrick Dunn .20 .50
8 Todd Heap .20 .50
9 Mark Clayton .20 .50
10 Steve McNair .25 .60
11 J.P. Losman .20 .50
12 Lee Evans .25 .60
13 Willis McGahee .20 .50
14 DeAngelo Williams .20 .50
15 Jake Delhomme .20 .50
16 Steve Smith .25 .60
17 Brian Urlacher .30 .75
18 Muhsin Muhammad .20 .50
19 Rex Grossman .20 .50
20 Thomas Jones .20 .50
21 Carson Palmer .25 .60
22 Chad Johnson .20 .50
23 Rudi Johnson .20 .50
24 T.J. Houshmandzadeh .20 .50
25 Braylon Edwards .20 .50
26 Charlie Frye .25 .60
27 Julius Jones .20 .50
28 Terrell Owens .25 .60
29 Tony Romo .40 1.00
30 Javon Walker .25 .60
31 Jay Cutler .20 .50
32 Mike Bell .25 .60
33 Jon Kitna .20 .50
34 Kevin Jones .20 .50
35 Roy Williams WR .20 .50
36 Brett Favre .60 1.50
37 Donald Driver .25 .60
38 Ahman Green .25 .60
39 Andre Johnson .25 .60
40 Matt Schaub .20 .50
41 Eric Moulds .20 .50
42 Joseph Addai .20 .50
43 Marvin Harrison .25 .60
44 Peyton Manning .75 2.00
45 Reggie Wayne .25 .60
46 Byron Leftwich .20 .50
47 Fred Taylor .20 .50
48 Maurice Jones-Drew .20 .50
49 Larry Johnson .20 .50
50 Tony Gonzalez .25 .60
51 Trent Green .20 .50
52 Chris Chambers .20 .50
53 Daunte Culpepper .25 .60
54 Ronnie Brown .20 .50
55 Chester Taylor .20 .50
56 Tarvaris Jackson .20 .50
57 Travis Taylor .20 .50
58 Tom Brady 1.00 2.50
59 Corey Dillon .20 .50
60 Laurence Maroney .25 .60
61 Deuce McAllister .25 .60
62 Drew Brees .30 .75
63 Marques Colston .20 .50
64 Reggie Bush .20 .50
65 Eli Manning .25 .60
66 Jeremy Shockey .20 .50
67 Plaxico Burress .20 .50
68 Chad Pennington .20 .50
69 Laveranues Coles .20 .50
70 Leon Washington .20 .50
71 LaMont Jordan .25 .60
72 Michael Huff .25 .60
73 Randy Moss .25 .60
74 Brian Westbrook .20 .50
75 Donovan McNabb .25 .60
76 Reggie Brown .20 .50
77 Ben Roethlisberger .30 .75
78 Hines Ward .25 .60
79 Willie Parker .25 .60
80 Antonio Gates .30 .75
81 LaDainian Tomlinson .30 .75
82 Philip Rivers .30 .75
83 Alex Smith QB .25 .60
84 Frank Gore .25 .60
85 Vernon Davis .20 .50
86 Darrell Jackson .20 .50
87 Matt Hasselbeck .20 .50
88 Shaun Alexander .20 .50
89 Marc Bulger .20 .50
90 Steven Jackson .20 .50
91 Torry Holt .25 .60
92 Bruce Gradkowski .20 .50
93 Cadillac Williams .25 .60
94 Joey Galloway .25 .60
95 Drew Bennett .20 .50
96 Vince Young .20 .50
97 Travis Henry .25 .60
98 Clinton Portis .20 .50
99 Jason Campbell .20 .50
100 Santana Moss .25 .60
101 Archie Manning 1.50 4.00
103 Bill Bates 1.25 3.00
104 Bob Hayes 2.50 6.00
105 Bob Lilly 1.50 4.00
106 Bobby Mitchell 1.50 4.00
108 Charley Taylor 1.25 3.00
109 Charlie Joiner 1.25 3.00
110 Cliff Harris 1.25 3.00
111 Cris Collinsworth 1.50 4.00
112 Dan Fouts 1.50 4.00
113 Daryle Lamonica 1.25 3.00
114 Dave Casper 1.25 3.00
115 Don Maynard 1.60 4.00
116 Earl Campbell 2.00 5.00
117 Forrest Gregg 1.25 3.00
118 Franco Harris 2.00 5.00
120 Gale Sayers 2.00 5.00
121 Gene Upshaw 1.25 3.00
122 George Blanda 1.50 4.00
123 Hugh McElhenny 1.50 4.00
124 Jack Youngblood 1.50 4.00
125 Boyd Dowler 1.25 3.00
126 Jan Stenerud 1.25 3.00
127 Jim McMahon 2.50 6.00
128 Harlon Hill 1.25 3.00
129 Joe Namath 2.50 6.00
130 Joe Theismann 2.00 5.00
131 John Mackey 1.50 4.00
133 Kellen Winslow 1.25 3.00
134 Ken Stabler 2.50 6.00
135 Lenny Moore 1.25 3.00
136 Lou Groza 1.50 4.00
137 Mark Duper 1.25 3.00
138 Michael Irvin 2.00 5.00
139 Paul Warfield 1.50 4.00
140 Randall Cunningham 1.50 4.00
141 Roger Craig 1.50 4.00
142 Ron Mix 1.25 3.00
143 Roosevelt Brown 1.25 3.00
144 Roosevelt Grier 1.25 3.00
145 Sam Huff 1.50 4.00
146 Sammy Baugh 2.00 5.00
147 Sterling Sharpe 1.50 4.00
148 Tim Brown 2.00 5.00
149 Y.A. Tittle 2.00 5.00
150 Yale Lary 1.25 3.00
151 JaMarcus Russell/599 RC 2.50 6.00
152 Brady Quinn/599 RC 2.50 6.00
153 Kevin Kolb/1499 RC 2.00 5.00
154 John Beck/1499 RC 1.50 4.00
155 Drew Stanton/1499 RC 1.50 4.00
156 Trent Edwards/1499 RC 1.50 4.00
157 Isaiah Stanback/1499 RC 1.50 4.00
158 Troy Smith/1499 RC 1.50 4.00
159 Adrian Peterson/599 RC 8.00 20.00
160 Marshawn Lynch/599 RC 5.00 12.00
161 Kenny Irons/599 RC 2.50 6.00
162 Chris Henry/599 RC 2.50 6.00
163 Brian Leonard/599 RC 2.50 6.00
164 Brandon Jackson/599 RC 2.50 6.00
165 Lorenzo Booker/599 RC 3.00 8.00
166 Tony Hunt/599 RC 2.50 6.00
167 Garrett Wolfe/599 RC 2.50 6.00
168 Michael Bush/599 RC 2.50 6.00
169 Antonio Pittman/1499 RC 1.50 4.00
170 Kolby Smith/1499 RC 1.50 4.00
171 DeShawn Wynn/1499 RC 1.50 4.00
172 Calvin Johnson/599 RC 8.00 20.00
173 Ted Ginn Jr.RC/599 RC 3.00 8.00
174 Dwayne Bowe/599 RC 2.50 6.00
175 Robert Meachem/599 RC 3.00 8.00
176 Craig Buster Davis/599 RC 2.50 6.00
177 Anthony Gonzalez/599 RC 2.50 6.00
178 Sidney Rice/1499 RC 2.00 5.00
179 Dwayne Jarrett/1499 RC 2.00 5.00
180 Steve Smith USC/1499 RC 1.50 4.00
181 Jacoby Jones/1499 RC 1.50 4.00
182 Yamon Figurs/1499 RC 1.50 4.00
183 Laurent Robinson/1499 RC 2.50 6.00
184 Jason Hill/1499 RC 1.50 4.00
185 James Jones/1499 RC 1.50 4.00
186 Mike Walker/1499 RC 2.50 6.00
187 Paul Williams/1499 RC 1.50 4.00
188 Johnnie Lee Higgins/1499 RC 1.50 4.00
189 Chris Davis/1499 RC 1.50 4.00
190 Aundrae Allison/1499 RC 1.50 4.00
191 David Clowney/1499 RC 1.50 4.00
192 Courtney Taylor/1499 RC 1.50 4.00
193 Dallas Baker/1499 RC 1.50 4.00
194 Greg Olsen/1499 RC 2.50 6.00
195 Zach Miller/1499 RC 1.50 4.00
196 Amobi Okoye/1499 RC 2.00 5.00
197 Alan Branch/1499 RC 1.50 4.00
198 Gaines Adams/1499 RC 2.00 5.00
199 Jamaal Anderson/1499 RC 2.00 5.00
200 Adam Carriker/1499 RC 1.50 4.00
201 Jarvis Moss/1499 RC 1.50 4.00
202 Anthony Spencer/1499 RC 2.00 5.00
203 LaMarr Woodley/1499 RC 3.00 8.00
204 Tim Crowder/1499 RC 2.00 5.00
205 Victor Abiamiri/1499 RC 1.50 4.00
206 Patrick Willis/1499 RC 2.50 6.00
207 David Harris/1499 RC 1.50 4.00
208 Lawrence Timmons/1499 RC 2.50 6.00
209 Jon Beason/1499 RC 1.50 4.00
210 Paul Posluszny/1499 RC 1.50 4.00
211 Leon Hall/1499 RC 1.50 4.00
212 Aaron Ross/1499 RC 1.50 4.00
213 Chris Houston/1499 RC 1.50 4.00
214 Eric Wright/1499 RC 1.50 4.00
215 Josh Wilson/1499 RC 2.00 5.00
216 LaRon Landry/1499 RC 2.50 6.00
217 Michael Griffin/1499 RC 1.50 4.00
218 Reggie Nelson/1499 RC 1.50 4.00
219 Brandon Meriweather/1499 RC 2.00 5.00
220 Sabby Piscitelli/1499 RC 1.50 4.00
221 Jordan Palmer AU/499 RC 6.00 15.00
222 Jon Cornish AU/999 RC 4.00 10.00
223 Jared Zabransky AU/499 RC 5.00 12.00
224 Jarrett Hicks AU/999 RC 4.00 10.00
225 Kenneth Darby AU/499 RC 5.00 12.00
226 Steve Breaston AU/499 RC 5.00 12.00
227 Matt Spaeth AU/499 RC 8.00 20.00
228 Stewart Bradley AU/499 RC 5.00 12.00
229 Tymere Zimmerman AU/999 RC 3.00 8.00
230 Kenny Scott AU/999 RC 3.00 8.00
231 Chris Leak AU/499 RC 5.00 12.00
232 Ronnie McGill AU/999 RC 4.00 10.00
234 Syndric Steptoe AU/499 RC 6.00 15.00
235 Charles Johnson No AU 1.00 2.50
236 Chansi Stuckey AU/499 RC 6.00 15.00
237 Nate Ilaoa AU/499 RC 6.00 15.00
239 Aaron Fairooz AU/999 RC 4.00 10.00
240 Jeff Rowe AU/499 RC 5.00 12.00
241 Rhema McKnight AU/999 RC 3.00 8.00
242 Danny Ware AU/999 RC 5.00 12.00
243 Tyler Palko AU/999 RC 5.00 12.00
244 Syvelle Newton AU/999 RC 4.00 10.00
245 Michael Okwo AU/499 RC 6.00 15.00
246 Brandon Siler AU/999 RC 3.00 8.00
247 Ryan McBean AU/999 RC 5.00 12.00
248 Ray McDonald AU/499 RC 6.00 15.00
249 David Ball AU/999 RC 3.00 8.00
250 Alonzo Coleman AU/999 RC 4.00 10.00
251 H.B. Blades AU/999 RC 3.00 8.00
252 Thomas Clayton AU/499 RC 6.00 15.00
253 Darius Walker AU/499 RC 5.00 12.00
255 Dwayne Wright AU/499 RC 5.00 12.00
256 Rufus Alexander AU/999 RC 3.00 8.00
257 Gary Russell AU/999 RC 4.00 10.00
258 Aaron Rouse AU/499 RC 5.00 12.00
259 Joel Filani AU/499 RC 5.00 12.00
260 Zak DeOssie AU/999 RC 4.00 10.00
261 Scott Chandler AU/499 RC 8.00 20.00
263 Tim Shaw AU/999 RC 4.00 10.00
264 Jemalle Cornelius AU/999 RC 4.00 10.00
265 Ahmad Bradshaw AU/499 RC 8.00 20.00
266 Earl Everett AU/999 RC 3.00 8.00
267 D'Juan Woods AU/999 RC 3.00 8.00
268 Toby Korrodi AU/999 RC 4.00 10.00
269 Ryne Robinson AU/499 RC 6.00 15.00
270 Selvin Young AU/999 RC 3.00 8.00
271 Marcus McCauley AU/499 RC 5.00 12.00
272 Daymeion Hughes AU/499 RC 5.00 12.00
273 A.J. Davis AU/999 RC 3.00 8.00
274 David Irons AU/999 RC 3.00 8.00
275 Josh Gattis AU/999 RC 3.00 8.00

2007 Donruss Classics Timeless Tributes Bronze

*VETERANS 1-100: 4X TO 10X BASIC CARDS
*LEGENDS 101-150: 1X TO 2.5X BASIC CARDS
COMMON ROOKIE (151-275) 4.00 10.00
ROOKIE SEMISTARS 5.00 12.00
ROOKIE UNL.STARS 6.00 15.00
STATED PRINT RUN 100 SER.#'d SETS
151 JaMarcus Russell 4.00 10.00
152 Brady Quinn 4.00 10.00
153 Kevin Kolb 5.00 12.00
156 Trent Edwards 4.00 10.00
158 Troy Smith 4.00 10.00
159 Adrian Peterson 12.00 30.00
160 Marshawn Lynch 8.00 20.00
164 Brandon Jackson 4.00 10.00
168 Michael Bush 4.00 10.00
169 Antonio Pittman 4.00 10.00
170 Kolby Smith 4.00 10.00
171 DeShawn Wynn 4.00 10.00
172 Calvin Johnson 12.00 30.00
173 Ted Ginn Jr. 5.00 12.00
174 Dwayne Bowe 4.00 10.00
177 Anthony Gonzalez 4.00 10.00
178 Sidney Rice 5.00 12.00
180 Steve Smith USC 4.00 10.00
181 Jacoby Jones 4.00 10.00
194 Greg Olsen 6.00 15.00
199 Jamaal Anderson 5.00 12.00
200 Adam Carriker 4.00 10.00
206 Patrick Willis 6.00 15.00
208 Lawrence Timmons 6.00 15.00
210 Paul Posluszny 4.00 10.00
216 LaRon Landry 6.00 15.00
218 Reggie Nelson 4.00 10.00
223 Jared Zabransky 4.00 10.00
231 Chris Leak 4.00 10.00

2007 Donruss Classics Timeless Tributes Gold

*VETS 1-100: 8X TO 20X BASIC CARDS
*LEGENDS 101-150: 2X TO 5X BASIC CARDS
*ROOKIES: .6X TO 1.5X TRIBUTE BRONZE
STATED PRINT RUN 25 SER.#'d SETS

2007 Donruss Classics Timeless Tributes Platinum

*VETS 1-100: 12X TO 30X BASIC CARDS
*LEGENDS 101-150: 3X TO 8X BASIC CARDS
*ROOKIES: 1X TO 2.5X TRIBUTE BRONZE
STATED PRINT RUN 10 SER.#'d SETS

2007 Donruss Classics Timeless Tributes Silver

*VETS 1-100: 6X TO 15X BASIC CARDS
*LEGENDS 101-150: 1.5X TO 4X BASIC CARDS
*ROOKIES: .5X TO 1.2X TRIBUTE BRONZE
STATED PRINT RUN 50 SER.#'d SETS

2007 Donruss Classics Classic Combos Bronze

BRONZE PRINT RUN 1000 SER.#'d SETS
*GOLD/100: .8X TO 2X BRONZE/1000
GOLD PRINT RUN 100 SER.#'d SETS
*PLATINUM/25: 1.5X TO 4X BRONZE/1000
PLATINUM PRINT RUN 25 SER.#'d SETS
*SILVER/250: .6X TO 1.5X BRONZE/1000
SILVER PRINT RUN 250 SER.#'d SETS
1 D.Jones/Youngblood .75 2.00
2 J.McMahon/W.Payton 2.00 5.00
3 J.Montana/R.Craig 3.00 8.00
5 L.Dawson/J.Stenerud 1.00 2.50
7 D.Fouts/K.Winslow .75 2.00
8 T.Thomas/J.Kelly 1.00 2.50
9 J.Theismann/J.Riggins 1.00 2.50
10 D.Marino/M.Duper 2.00 5.00
11 T.Aikman/M.Irvin 1.25 3.00
12 T.Davis/J.Elway 1.50 4.00
13 R.Staubach/B.Hayes 1.25 3.00
14 J.Rice/S.Young 2.00 5.00
15 D.Maynard/J.Namath 1.25 3.00

2007 Donruss Classics Classic Combos Jerseys

STATED PRINT RUN 250 SER.#'d SETS
*PRIME/16-25: 1X TO 2.5X BASIC JSYs
PRIME PRINT RUN 16-25
1 D.Jones/Youngblood 4.00 10.00
2 J.McMahon/W.Payton 10.00 25.00
3 J.Montana/R.Craig 15.00 40.00
5 L.Dawson/J.Stenerud 5.00 12.00
7 D.Fouts/K.Winslow 4.00 10.00
8 T.Thomas/Kelly 5.00 12.00
9 J.Theismann/Riggins 5.00 12.00
10 D.Marino/M.Duper 10.00 25.00
11 T.Aikman/M.Irvin 6.00 15.00
12 T.Davis/J.Elway 8.00 20.00
13 R.Staubach/B.Hayes 6.00 15.00
14 J.Rice/S.Young 10.00 25.00
15 D.Maynard/J.Namath 6.00 15.00

2007 Donruss Classics Classic Quads Bronze

BRONZE PRINT RUN 250 SER.#'d SETS
*GOLD/25: .8X TO 2X BRONZE/250
GOLD PRINT RUN 25 SER.#'d SETS
*PLATINUM/10: 1.5X TO 4X BRONZE/250
PLATINUM PRINT RUN 10 SER.#'d SETS
*SILVER/50: .6X TO 1.5X BRONZE/250
SILVER PRINT RUN 50 SER.#'d SETS
1 Mont/Baugh/Graham/Unitas 8.00 20.00
2 Sayers/McMah/Payton/Single 5.00 12.00
3 Fouts/Mix/Winslow/Alworth 2.00 5.00
4 Aikm/Irvin/Hayes/Staubach 3.00 8.00
5 Unitas/Rice/Mont/Berry 8.00 20.00
6 Marino/Rice/Brown/Elway 5.00 12.00
7 Marino/Tark/Favre/Elway 5.00 12.00
8 Newsm/Groza/Brwn/Warf 3.00 8.00
10 Kelly/Irvin/Thomas/Aikman 3.00 8.00

2007 Donruss Classics Classic Quads Jerseys

STATED PRINT RUN 100 SER.#'d SETS
*PRIME/20-25: .8X TO 2X BASIC JSYs
PRIME PRINT RUN 5-25
1 Mont/Baugh/Graham/Unitas 75.00 150.00
2 Sayers/McMah/Payton/Single 40.00 100.00
3 Fouts/Mix/Winslow/Alworth 25.00 50.00
4 Aikm/Irvin/Hayes/Staubach 40.00 80.00
5 Unitas/Rice/Mont/Berry 50.00 100.00
6 Marino/Rice/Brown/Elway 25.00 60.00
7 Marino/Tark/Favre/Elway 20.00 50.00
8 New/Groza/Brwn/Warf/85 25.00 50.00
10 Kelly/Irvin/Thomas/Aikman 25.00 50.00

2007 Donruss Classics Classic Singles Bronze

BRONZE PRINT RUN 1000 SER.#'d SETS
*GOLD/100: .8X TO 2X BRONZE/1000
GOLD PRINT RUN 100 SER.#'d SETS
*PLATINUM/25: 1.2X TO 3X BRONZE/1000
PLATINUM PRINT RUN 25 SER.#'d SETS
*SILVER/250: .6X TO 1.5X BRONZE/1000
SILVER PRINT RUN 250 SER.#'d SETS
1 Bob Lilly .75 2.00
2 Charlie Joiner .60 1.50
3 Earl Campbell 1.00 2.50
5 Gale Sayers 1.00 2.50
6 Joe Theismann 1.00 2.50
7 Ken Stabler 1.25 3.00
8 Larry Csonka 1.00 2.50
9 Lawrence Taylor 1.00 2.50
10 Marcus Allen 1.00 2.50
11 Mike Singletary 1.00 2.50
12 Randall Cunningham .75 2.00
13 Thurman Thomas .75 2.00
14 Barry Sanders 1.50 4.00
15 Bo Jackson 1.25 3.00
16 Dan Marino 2.00 5.00
17 Deacon Jones .75 2.00
18 Fran Tarkenton 1.00 2.50
19 Jerry Rice 2.00 5.00
20 Jim Kelly 1.00 2.50
21 John Riggins .75 2.00
22 Len Dawson 1.00 2.50
23 Ronnie Lott .75 2.00
24 Steve Young 1.25 3.00
25 Terrell Davis .75 2.00
26 Troy Aikman 1.25 3.00
27 Walter Payton 2.00 5.00
28 Johnny Unitas 1.50 4.00
29 Lance Alworth .75 2.00
30 Lenny Moore .60 1.50

2007 Donruss Classics Classic Singles Jerseys

STATED PRINT RUN 250 SER.#'d SETS
*PRIME/25: .8X TO 2X BASIC JSY
PRIME PRINT RUN 2-25
*JSY.NUM./74-80: .5X TO 1.2X BASIC JSY
*JSY.NUM./39-56: .6X TO 1.5X BASIC JSY
*JSY.NUM./30-34: .8X TO 2X BASIC JSY
*JSY.NUM./16-24: 1X TO 2.5X BASIC JSY
JERSEY NUMBER PRINT RUN 7-80
1 Bob Lilly/250 3.00 8.00
2 Charlie Joiner/250 2.50 6.00
3 Earl Campbell/250 4.00 10.00
5 Gale Sayers/125 4.00 10.00
6 Joe Theismann/250 4.00 10.00
7 Ken Stabler/150 5.00 12.00
8 Larry Csonka/250 4.00 10.00
9 Lawrence Taylor/250 4.00 10.00
10 Marcus Allen/250 4.00 10.00
11 Mike Singletary/250 4.00 10.00
12 Randall Cunningham/250 3.00 8.00
13 Thurman Thomas/175 3.00 8.00
14 Barry Sanders/250 6.00 15.00
15 Bo Jackson/250 5.00 12.00
16 Dan Marino/250 8.00 20.00
17 Deacon Jones/120 3.00 8.00
18 Fran Tarkenton/250 4.00 10.00
19 Jerry Rice/250 8.00 20.00
20 Jim Kelly/250 4.00 10.00
21 John Riggins/250 3.00 8.00
22 Len Dawson/175 4.00 10.00
23 Ronnie Lott/250 3.00 8.00
24 Steve Young/250 5.00 12.00
25 Terrell Davis/175 3.00 8.00
26 Troy Aikman/250 5.00 12.00
27 Walter Payton/175 12.00 30.00
28 Johnny Unitas/175 6.00 15.00
29 Lance Alworth/175 3.00 8.00
30 Lenny Moore/250 2.50 6.00

2007 Donruss Classics Classic Triples Bronze

BRONZE PRINT RUN 500 SER.#'d SETS
*GOLD/50: .6X TO 1.5X BRONZE/500
GOLD PRINT RUN 50 SER.#'d SETS
*PLATINUM/10: 1X TO 2.5X BRONZE/500
PLATINUM PRINT RUN 10 SER.#'d SETS
*SILVER/250: .5X TO 1.2X BRONZE/500
SILVER PRINT RUN 250 SER.#'d SETS
1 J.Brown/Groza/Graham 2.50 6.00
2 Lilly/Hayes/Staubach 2.50 6.00
3 Montana/Rice/Craig 6.00 15.00
4 McMahon/Payton/Single 4.00 10.00
7 Fouts/Winslow/Alworth 1.50 4.00
8 Unitas/Berry/Moore 3.00 8.00
9 Aikman/Elway/S.Young 3.00 8.00
10 D.Jones/Yngblood/Lilly 1.50 4.00

2007 Donruss Classics Classic Triples Jerseys

STATED PRINT RUN 250 SER.#'d SETS
*PRIME/16-25: .8X TO 2X BASIC JSYs
PRIME PRINT RUN 2-25
1 J.Brown/Groza/Graham 8.00 20.00
2 Lilly/Hayes/Staubach 8.00 20.00
3 Montana/Rice/Craig 20.00 50.00
4 McMahon/Payton/Single 12.00 30.00
7 Fouts/Winslow/Alworth 5.00 12.00
8 Unitas/Berry/Moore 10.00 25.00
9 Aikman/Elway/S.Young 10.00 25.00
10 D.Jones/Yngblood/Lilly 5.00 12.00

2007 Donruss Classics Legendary Players Bronze

BRONZE PRINT RUN 1000 SER.#'d SETS
*GOLD/100: .8X TO 2X BRONZE/1000
GOLD PRINT RUN 100 SER.#'d SETS
*PLATINUM/25: 1.2X TO 3X BRONZE/1000
PLATINUM PRINT RUN 25 SER.#'d SETS
*SILVER/250: .6X TO 1.5X BRONZE/1000
SILVER PRINT RUN 250 SER.#'d SETS
2 Bill Bates .60 1.50
3 Bob Hayes 1.25 3.00
4 Cris Collinsworth .75 2.00
5 Dan Fouts .75 2.00
6 Forrest Gregg .60 1.50
7 Franco Harris 1.00 2.50
8 Jack Youngblood .75 2.00
9 Jan Stenerud .60 1.50
10 Jim McMahon 1.25 3.00
11 Joe Namath 1.25 3.00
12 John Hannah .60 1.50
14 Lou Groza .75 2.00
15 Mark Duper .60 1.50
16 Michael Irvin 1.00 2.50
17 Randall Cunningham .75 2.00
18 Roger Craig .75 2.00
19 Sterling Sharpe .75 2.00
20 Tim Brown 1.00 2.50
21 Sammy Baugh 1.00 2.50
22 Y.A. Tittle 1.00 2.50
23 Sam Huff .75 2.00
24 Ron Mix .60 1.50
25 Roosevelt Brown .60 1.50
26 Kellen Winslow .75 2.00
27 Joe Montana 3.00 8.00
28 John Elway 1.50 4.00
29 Jim Brown 1.25 3.00
30 Roger Staubach 1.25 3.00

2007 Donruss Classics Legendary Players Jerseys

STATED PRINT RUN 250 SER.#'d SETS
*PRIME/25: 1X TO 2.5X BASIC JSYs
PRIME PRINT RUN 25 SER.#'d SETS
*TEAM LOGO/70-88: .6X TO 1.5X BASIC JSYs
*TEAM LOGO/32-40: .8X TO 2X BASIC JSYs
*TEAM LOGO/22: 1X TO 2.5X BASIC JSYs
TEAM LOGO PRINT RUN 3-88
2 Bill Bates 2.00 5.00
3 Bob Hayes 4.00 10.00
4 Cris Collinsworth 2.50 6.00
5 Dan Fouts 2.50 6.00
6 Forrest Gregg 2.00 5.00
7 Franco Harris/185 3.00 8.00
8 Jack Youngblood 2.50 6.00
9 Jan Stenerud 2.00 5.00
10 Jim McMahon/175 4.00 10.00
11 Joe Namath/175 8.00 20.00
12 John Hannah 2.00 5.00
14 Lou Groza/175 2.50 6.00
15 Mark Duper 2.00 5.00
16 Michael Irvin 3.00 8.00
17 Randall Cunningham 2.50 6.00
18 Roger Craig/175 2.50 6.00
19 Sterling Sharpe 2.50 6.00
20 Tim Brown 3.00 8.00
21 Sammy Baugh/175 3.00 8.00
22 Y.A. Tittle 3.00 8.00
23 Sam Huff 2.50 6.00
24 Ron Mix 2.00 5.00
25 Roosevelt Brown 2.00 5.00
26 Kellen Winslow/175 2.50 6.00
27 Joe Montana 10.00 25.00
28 John Elway 5.00 12.00
29 Jim Brown 8.00 20.00
30 Roger Staubach/175 8.00 20.00

2007 Donruss Classics Membership Bronze

BRONZE PRINT RUN 1000 SER.#'d SETS
*GOLD/100: .6X TO 1.5X BRONZE/1000
GOLD PRINT RUN 100 SER.#'d SETS
*PLATINUM/25: 1.2X TO 3X BRONZE/1000
PLATINUM PRINT RUN 25 SER.#'d SETS
*SILVER/250: .5X TO 1.2X BRONZE/1000
SILVER PRINT RUN 250 SER.#'d SETS
1 Alex Smith QB .75 2.00
2 Leon Washington .60 1.50
3 Reggie Bush .60 1.50
4 Joseph Addai .60 1.50
5 Marques Colston .60 1.50
6 Cadillac Williams .75 2.00
7 Ronnie Brown .60 1.50
8 Vince Young .60 1.50
9 Laurence Maroney .75 2.00
10 Jerious Norwood .60 1.50
11 Mike Bell .75 2.00
12 Vernon Davis .60 1.50
13 Maurice Jones-Drew .60 1.50
14 Jay Cutler .60 1.50
15 DeAngelo Williams .60 1.50
16 Matt Leinart .60 1.50
17 Sinorice Moss .75 2.00
18 LenDale White .75 2.00
19 Devin Hester .75 2.00
20 Santonio Holmes .60 1.50

2007 Donruss Classics Membership VIP Jerseys

JERSEY PRINT RUN 170-250
*PRIME/20-25: 1X TO 2.5X BASIC JSYs
PRIME PRINT RUN 6-25
*TEAM LOGO/83-85: .6X TO 1.5X BASIC JSYs
*TEAM LOGO/32-39: .8X TO 2X BASIC JSYs
*TEAM LOGO/20-29: 1X TO 2.5X BASIC JSYs
TEAM LOGO PRINT RUN 6-85
1 Alex Smith QB 3.00 8.00
2 Leon Washington 2.50 6.00
3 Reggie Bush/170 2.50 6.00
4 Joseph Addai 2.50 6.00
5 Marques Colston 2.50 6.00
6 Cadillac Williams 3.00 8.00
7 Ronnie Brown 2.50 6.00
8 Vince Young 2.50 6.00
9 Laurence Maroney 3.00 8.00
10 Jerious Norwood 2.50 6.00
11 Mike Bell 3.00 8.00
12 Vernon Davis 2.50 6.00
13 Maurice Jones-Drew 2.50 6.00
14 Jay Cutler 2.50 6.00
15 DeAngelo Williams 2.50 6.00
16 Matt Leinart 2.50 6.00
17 Sinorice Moss 3.00 8.00
18 LenDale White 3.00 8.00
19 Devin Hester 3.00 8.00
20 Santonio Holmes 2.50 6.00

2007 Donruss Classics Monday Night Heroes Bronze

BRONZE PRINT RUN 1000 SER.#'d SETS
*GOLD/100: .6X TO 1.5X BRONZE/1000
GOLD PRINT RUN 100 SER.#'d SETS
*PLATINUM/25: 1.2X TO 3X BRONZE/1000
PLATINUM PRINT RUN 25 SER.#'d SETS
*SILVER/250: .5X TO 1.2X BRONZE/1000
SILVER PRINT RUN 250 SER.#'d SETS
1 Chester Taylor .60 1.50
2 Fred Taylor .60 1.50
3 Donovan McNabb .75 2.00
4 Greg Lewis .60 1.50
5 Brett Favre 2.00 5.00
6 Matt Leinart .60 1.50
7 Anquan Boldin .60 1.50
8 Eli Manning .75 2.00
9 Tony Romo 1.25 3.00
10 Terrell Owens .75 2.00
11 Tiki Barber .75 2.00
12 Plaxico Burress .60 1.50
13 Tom Brady 3.00 8.00
14 Ben Watson .60 1.50
15 Mewelde Moore .60 1.50
16 Deion Branch .60 1.50
17 Jake Delhomme .60 1.50
18 Steve Smith .75 2.00
19 Maurice Jones-Drew .60 1.50
20 Shaun Alexander .60 1.50
21 Donald Driver .75 2.00
22 Donte Stallworth .75 2.00
23 DeAngelo Williams .60 1.50
24 Steven Jackson .60 1.50
25 Marc Bulger .60 1.50
26 Thomas Jones .60 1.50
27 Peyton Manning 2.50 6.00
28 Marvin Harrison .75 2.00
29 Rudi Johnson .60 1.50
30 Brian Westbrook .60 1.50

2007 Donruss Classics Monday Night Heroes Jerseys

JERSEY STATED PRINT RUN 175-250
*PRIME/25: 1X TO 2.5X BASIC JSYs
PRIME PRINT RUN 25 SER.#'d SETS
UNPRICED PRIME AUTOS SER.#'d TO 10
*JSY.NUM/80-89: .6X TO 1.5X BASIC JSYs
*JSY.NUM/30-39: .8X TO 2X BASIC JSYs
*JSY.NUM/20-29: 1X TO 2.5X BASIC JSYs
JERSEY NUMBER PRINT RUN 4-89
1 Chester Taylor 2.50 6.00
2 Fred Taylor/240 2.50 6.00
3 Donovan McNabb 3.00 8.00
4 Greg Lewis 2.50 6.00
5 Brett Favre 8.00 20.00
6 Matt Leinart/200 2.50 6.00
7 Anquan Boldin 2.50 6.00
8 Eli Manning 3.00 8.00
9 Tony Romo 5.00 12.00
10 Terrell Owens 3.00 8.00
11 Tiki Barber 3.00 8.00
12 Plaxico Burress 2.50 6.00
13 Tom Brady 12.00 30.00
14 Ben Watson 2.50 6.00
15 Mewelde Moore 2.50 6.00
16 Deion Branch 2.50 6.00
17 Jake Delhomme 2.50 6.00
18 Steve Smith 3.00 8.00
19 Maurice Jones-Drew/225 2.50 6.00
20 Shaun Alexander 2.50 6.00
21 Donald Driver 3.00 8.00
22 Donte Stallworth 3.00 8.00
23 DeAngelo Williams 2.50 6.00
24 Steven Jackson/240 2.50 6.00
25 Marc Bulger 2.50 6.00
26 Thomas Jones 2.50 6.00
27 Peyton Manning 10.00 25.00
28 Marvin Harrison 3.00 8.00
29 Rudi Johnson 2.50 6.00
30 Brian Westbrook/175 2.50 6.00

2007 Donruss Classics Monday Night Heroes Jerseys Jersey Numbers Autographs

STATED PRINT RUN 4-39
1 Chester Taylor/29 8.00 20.00
2 Fred Taylor/28 12.50 25.00
11 Tiki Barber/21
23 DeAngelo Williams/34 20.00 40.00
24 Steven Jackson/39 20.00 40.00
29 Rudi Johnson/32
30 Brian Westbrook/36

2007 Donruss Classics Saturday Stars Bronze

BRONZE PRINT RUN 1000 SER.#'d SETS
*GOLD/100 .6X TO 1.5X BRONZE/1000
GOLD PRINT RUN 100 SER.#'d SETS
*PLATINUM/25: 1.2X TO 3X BRONZE/1000
PLATINUM PRINT RUN 25 SER.#'d SETS
*SILVER/250: .5X TO 1.2X BRONZE/1000
SILVER PRINT RUN 250 SER.#'d SETS
UNPRICED AUTO PRINT RUN 5
1 A.J. Hawk .60 1.50
2 Joseph Addai .60 1.50
3 Demetrius Williams .60 1.50
4 Marcedes Lewis .60 1.50
5 Jay Cutler .60 1.50
6 Matt Leinart .60 1.50
7 Reggie Bush .60 1.50
8 LenDale White .75 2.00
9 Laurence Maroney .75 2.00
10 Maurice Jones-Drew .60 1.50
11 Maurice Stovall .60 1.50
12 Travis Wilson .60 1.50
13 Mario Williams .75 2.00
14 Vince Young .60 1.50
15 Larry Fitzgerald .75 2.00
16 Dovory Henderson .60 1.50
17 Andre Johnson .75 2.00
18 Santana Moss .75 2.00
19 Roger Staubach 1.25 3.00
20 Lawrence Taylor 1.00 2.50
21 Thurman Thomas .75 2.00
22 Steven Jackson .60 1.50
23 Frank Gore .75 2.00
24 Roy Williams WR .60 1.50
25 Marcus Allen 1.00 2.50
26 Julius Jones .60 1.50
27 Larry Csonka 1.00 2.50
28 Antonio Bryant .60 1.50
29 Sinorice Moss .75 2.00
30 Tony Dorsett 1.00 2.50

2007 Donruss Classics Saturday Stars Jerseys

JERSEY PRINT RUN 150-250
*PRIME/25: 1X TO 2.5X BASIC JSYs
PRIME PRINT RUN 25 SER.#'d SETS
UNPRICED PRIME AUTO PRINT RUN 1-10
*JSY.NUM/80-98: .5X TO 1.2X BASIC JSY
*JSY.NUM/39-47: .6X TO 1.5X BASIC JSY
*JSY.NUM/19-22: 1X TO 2.5X BASIC JSY
*JSY.NUM/33-34: .8X TO 2X BASIC JSY
JERSEY NUMBERS PRINT RUN 1-98
1 A.J. Hawk 2.00 5.00
2 Joseph Addai 2.00 5.00
3 Demetrius Williams 2.00 5.00
4 Marcedes Lewis 2.00 5.00
5 Jay Cutler 2.00 5.00
6 Matt Leinart 2.00 5.00
7 Reggie Bush 2.00 5.00
8 LenDale White 2.50 6.00
9 Laurence Maroney 2.50 6.00
10 Maurice Jones-Drew 2.00 5.00
11 Maurice Stovall 2.00 5.00
12 Travis Wilson 2.00 5.00
13 Mario Williams 2.50 6.00
14 Vince Young 2.00 5.00
15 Larry Fitzgerald 2.50 6.00
16 Devery Henderson 2.00 5.00
17 Andre Johnson 2.50 6.00
18 Santana Moss/185 2.50 6.00
19 Roger Staubach 8.00 20.00
20 Lawrence Taylor 3.00 8.00
21 Thurman Thomas 2.50 6.00
22 Steven Jackson/150 2.00 5.00
23 Frank Gore 2.50 6.00
24 Roy Williams WR 2.00 5.00
25 Marcus Allen 6.00 15.00
26 Julius Jones 6.00 15.00
27 Larry Csonka 3.00 8.00
28 Antonio Bryant 2.00 5.00
29 Sinorice Moss 2.50 6.00
30 Tony Dorsett 3.00 8.00

2007 Donruss Classics Saturday Stars Jerseys Jersey Numbers Autographs

STATED PRINT RUN 1-34
8 LenDale White/21 12.00 30.00
22 Steven Jackson/34 15.00 40.00
25 Marcus Allen/33 25.00 50.00
30 Tony Dorsett/33 15.00 40.00

2007 Donruss Classics School Colors

1 Brady Quinn 2.00 5.00
2 JaMarcus Russell 2.00 5.00
3 Troy Smith 2.00 5.00
4 Adrian Peterson 6.00 15.00
5 Marshawn Lynch 4.00 10.00
6 Kenny Irons 2.00 5.00
7 Calvin Johnson 6.00 15.00
8 Ted Ginn Jr. 2.50 6.00
9 Dwayne Jarrett 2.50 6.00
10 Sidney Rice 2.50 6.00
11 Robert Meachem 2.50 6.00
12 Chris Leak 2.00 5.00
13 Craig Buster Davis 2.00 5.00
14 Darrelle Revis 2.50 6.00
15 Paul Posluszny 2.00 5.00
16 Reggie Nelson 2.00 5.00
17 Trent Edwards 2.00 5.00
18 Brandon Jackson 2.00 5.00
19 Paul Williams 2.00 5.00
20 Johnnie Lee Higgins 2.00 5.00
21 Jordan Palmer 2.50 6.00
22 Garrett Wolfe 2.00 5.00
23 Gary Russell 2.50 6.00
24 Steve Smith USC 2.00 5.00
25 Aaron Ross 2.00 5.00
26 Michael Bush 2.00 5.00
27 Tony Hunt 2.00 5.00
28 Drew Stanton 2.00 5.00
29 LaRon Landry 3.00 8.00
30 Lawrence Timmons 3.00 8.00

2007 Donruss Classics School Colors Autographs

STATED PRINT RUN 25 SER.#'d SETS
1 Brady Quinn 12.00 30.00
2 JaMarcus Russell 12.00 30.00
3 Troy Smith 12.00 30.00
4 Adrian Peterson 125.00 250.00
5 Marshawn Lynch 30.00 60.00
6 Kenny Irons 12.00 30.00
7 Calvin Johnson 75.00 150.00
8 Ted Ginn Jr. 15.00 40.00
9 Dwayne Jarrett 15.00 40.00
10 Sidney Rice 15.00 40.00
11 Robert Meachem 16.00 40.00
12 Chris Leak 12.00 30.00
13 Craig Buster Davis 12.00 30.00
14 Darrelle Revis 15.00 40.00
15 Paul Posluszny 12.00 30.00
16 Reggie Nelson 12.00 30.00
17 Trent Edwards 12.00 30.00
18 Brandon Jackson 12.00 30.00
19 Paul Williams 12.00 30.00
20 Johnnie Lee Higgins 12.00 30.00
21 Jordan Palmer 15.00 40.00
22 Garrett Wolfe 12.00 30.00
23 Gary Russell 15.00 40.00
24 Steve Smith USC 12.00 30.00
25 Aaron Ross 12.00 30.00
26 Michael Bush 12.00 30.00
27 Tony Hunt 12.00 30.00
28 Drew Stanton 12.00 30.00
29 LaRon Landry 20.00 50.00
30 Lawrence Timmons 20.00 50.00

2007 Donruss Classics Significant Signatures Gold

GOLD PRINT RUN 10-100
1 Anquan Boldin/25 12.00 30.00
10 Steve McNair/50 15.00 40.00
49 Larry Johnson/25 15.00 40.00
54 Ronnie Brown/25 15.00 40.00
90 Steven Jackson/100 15.00 30.00
103 Bill Bates/100 10.00 25.00
105 Bob Lilly/25 12.00 30.00
109 Charlie Joiner/25
110 Cliff Harris/100 12.00 30.00
112 Dan Fouts/100 20.00 40.00
113 Daryle Lamonica/25 15.00 40.00
114 Dave Casper/100 10.00 25.00
115 Don Maynard/25 12.00 30.00
120 Gale Sayers/25 30.00 60.00
123 Hugh McElhenny/100 12.50 30.00
124 Jack Youngblood/25 15.00 40.00
125 Boyd Dowler/100 15.00 40.00
127 Jim McMahon/50 25.00 50.00
128 Harlon Hill/100 12.50 30.00
131 John Mackey/100 12.50 30.00
135 Lenny Moore/25 15.00 40.00
139 Paul Warfield/75 12.00 30.00
141 Roger Craig/25 25.00 50.00
144 Rosey Grier/100 12.50 30.00
147 Sterling Sharpe/25
150 Yale Lary/25 12.00 30.00
151 JaMarcus Russell 12.00 30.00
152 Brady Quinn 8.00 20.00
153 Kevin Kolb 10.00 25.00
154 John Beck 8.00 20.00
155 Drew Stanton 8.00 20.00
156 Trent Edwards 8.00 20.00
157 Isaiah Stanback 8.00 20.00
158 Troy Smith 8.00 20.00
159 Adrian Peterson 100.00 200.00
160 Marshawn Lynch 20.00 50.00
161 Kenny Irons 8.00 20.00
162 Chris Henry 8.00 20.00
163 Brian Leonard 8.00 20.00
164 Brandon Jackson 8.00 20.00
165 Lorenzo Booker 10.00 25.00
166 Tony Hunt 8.00 20.00
167 Garrett Wolfe 8.00 20.00
168 Michael Bush 8.00 20.00
169 Antonio Pittman 8.00 20.00
170 Kolby Smith 8.00 20.00
171 DeShawn Wynn 8.00 20.00
172 Calvin Johnson 60.00 120.00
173 Ted Ginn Jr. 20.00 50.00
174 Dwayne Bowe 8.00 20.00
175 Robert Meachem 10.00 25.00
177 Anthony Gonzalez 8.00 20.00
178 Sidney Rice 10.00 25.00
179 Dwayne Jarrett 10.00 25.00
180 Steve Smith USC 8.00 20.00
181 Jacoby Jones 8.00 20.00
182 Yamon Figurs 8.00 20.00
183 Laurent Robinson 12.00 30.00
184 Jason Hill 8.00 20.00
185 James Jones 8.00 20.00
186 Mike Walker 12.00 30.00
187 Paul Williams 8.00 20.00
188 Johnnie Lee Higgins 8.00 20.00
189 Chris Davis 8.00 20.00
190 Aundrae Allison 8.00 20.00
191 David Clowney 8.00 20.00
193 Dallas Baker 8.00 20.00
194 Greg Olsen 12.00 30.00
195 Zach Miller 8.00 20.00
196 Amobi Okoye 10.00 25.00
198 Gaines Adams 10.00 25.00
199 Jamaal Anderson 10.00 25.00
200 Adam Carriker 8.00 20.00
202 Anthony Spencer 10.00 25.00
203 LaMarr Woodley 15.00 40.00
204 Tim Crowder 10.00 25.00
205 Victor Abiamiri 8.00 20.00
206 Patrick Willis 12.00 30.00
207 David Harris 8.00 20.00
208 Lawrence Timmons 12.00 30.00
209 Jon Beason 8.00 20.00
210 Paul Posluszny 8.00 20.00
211 Leon Hall 8.00 20.00
212 Aaron Ross 8.00 20.00
213 Chris Houston 8.00 20.00
215 Josh Wilson 10.00 25.00
216 LaRon Landry 12.00 30.00
217 Michael Griffin 8.00 20.00
218 Reggie Nelson 8.00 20.00
219 Brandon Meriweather 10.00 25.00
220 Sabby Piscitelli 8.00 20.00

2007 Donruss Classics Significant Signatures Platinum

*PLATINUM ROOKIES/25: .6X TO 1.5X GOLD
PLATINUM PRINT RUN 5-25
SER.#'d UNDER 25 NOT PRICED
151 JaMarcus Russell 40.00 100.00
152 Brady Quinn 12.00 30.00
159 Adrian Peterson 200.00 400.00
172 Calvin Johnson 100.00 200.00

2007 Donruss Classics Sunday's Best Bronze

BRONZE PRINT RUN 1000 SER.#'d SETS
*GOLD/100: .6X TO 1.5X BRONZE/1000
GOLD PRINT RUN 100 SER.#'d SETS
*PLATINUM/25: 1.2X TO 3X BRONZE/1000
PLATINUM PRINT RUN 25 SER.#'d SETS
*SILVER/250: .5X TO 1.2X BRONZE/1000
SILVER PRINT RUN 250 SER.#'d SETS
1 LaDainian Tomlinson 1.00 2.50
2 Drew Brees 1.00 2.50
3 Michael Vick .75 2.00
4 Frank Gore .75 2.00
5 Carson Palmer .75 2.00
6 Willie Parker .75 2.00
7 T.J. Houshmandzadeh .60 1.50
8 Alge Crumpler .75 2.00
9 Tony Gonzalez .75 2.00
10 Larry Fitzgerald .75 2.00
11 Roy Williams WR .60 1.50
12 Reggie Wayne .75 2.00
13 Muhsin Muhammad .60 1.50
14 Steve McNair .75 2.00
15 Larry Johnson .60 1.50
16 Mark Clayton .60 1.50
17 Philip Rivers 1.00 2.50
18 Deuce McAllister .75 2.00
19 Darrell Jackson .60 1.50
20 Tatum Bell .60 1.50
21 Joe Horn .60 1.60
22 Chris Chambers .60 1.50
23 Santana Moss .75 2.00
24 Laveranues Coles .60 1.50
25 Chad Pennington .60 1.50
26 Andre Johnson .75 2.00

27 Trent Green .60 1.50
28 Randy McMichael .60 1.50
29 Ben Roethlisberger 1.00 2.50
30 Rex Grossman .60 1.50
31 Torry Holt .75 2.00
32 Jerricho Cotchery .60 1.50
33 Matt Hasselbeck .60 1.50
34 Julius Jones .60 1.50
35 Todd Heap .60 1.50
36 Javon Walker .75 2.00
37 Willis McGahee .60 1.50
38 Chad Johnson .60 1.50
39 Hines Ward .75 2.00
40 Ahman Green .75 2.00

2007 Donruss Classics Sunday's Best Jerseys

JERSEY PRINT RUN 45-250
*PRIME/25: 1X TO 2.5X BASIC JSYs
PRIME PRINT RUN 25 SER.#'d SETS
UNPRICED PRIME AUTOS PRINT RUN 10
*JSY.NUM/80-89: .6X TO 1.5X BASIC JSYs
*JSY.NUM/30-39: .8X TO 2X BASIC JSYs
*JSY.NUM/21-27: 1X TO 2.5X BASIC JSYs
JERSEY NUMBERS PRINT RUN 7-89
1 LaDainian Tomlinson 4.00 10.00
2 Drew Brees 4.00 10.00
3 Michael Vick 3.00 8.00
4 Frank Gore/188 3.00 8.00
5 Carson Palmer 3.00 8.00
6 Willie Parker 3.00 8.00
7 T.J. Houshmandzadeh 2.50 6.00
8 Alge Crumpler 3.00 8.00
9 Tony Gonzalez 3.00 8.00
10 Larry Fitzgerald 3.00 8.00
11 Roy Williams WR 2.50 6.00
12 Reggie Wayne/180 3.00 8.00
13 Muhsin Muhammad 2.50 6.00
14 Steve McNair 3.00 8.00
15 Larry Johnson 2.50 6.00
16 Mark Clayton 2.50 6.00
17 Philip Rivers/240 4.00 10.00
18 Deuce McAllister 3.00 8.00
19 Darrell Jackson 2.50 6.00
20 Tatum Bell 2.50 6.00
21 Joe Horn 2.50 6.00
22 Chris Chambers 2.50 6.00
23 Santana Moss 3.00 8.00
24 Laveranues Coles 2.50 6.00
25 Chad Pennington 2.50 6.00
26 Andre Johnson 3.00 8.00
27 Trent Green 2.50 6.00
28 Randy McMichael/45 3.00 8.00
29 Ben Roethlisberger 4.00 10.00
30 Rex Grossman 2.50 6.00
31 Torry Holt 3.00 8.00
32 Jerricho Cotchery 2.50 6.00
33 Matt Hasselbeck 2.50 6.00
34 Julius Jones 2.50 6.00
35 Todd Heap 2.50 6.00
36 Javon Walker 3.00 8.00
37 Willis McGahee 2.50 6.00
38 Chad Johnson 2.50 6.00
39 Hines Ward 3.00 8.00
40 Ahman Green 3.00 8.00

2007 Donruss Classics Sunday's Best Jerseys Jersey Numbers Autographs

STATED PRINT RUN 7-89
1 LaDainian Tomlinson/21 50.00 100.00
4 Frank Gore/21
6 Willie Parker/39 20.00 40.00
7 T.J. Houshmandzadeh/84 12.00 30.00
15 Larry Johnson/27 20.00 50.00
18 Deuce McAllister/26
32 Jerricho Cotchery/89 10.00 25.00

2007 Donruss Classics Timeless Triples Bronze

BRONZE PRINT RUN 1000 SER.#'d SETS
*GOLD/100: .6X TO 1.5X BRONZE/1000
GOLD PRINT RUN 100 SER.#'d SETS
*PLATINUM/25: 1X TO 2.5X BRONZE/1000
PLATINUM PRINT RUN 25 SER.#'d SETS
*SILVER/250: .5X TO 1.2X BRONZE/1000
SILVER PRINT RUN 250 SER.#'d SETS
1 Owens/Romo/Glenn 2.50 6.00
2 Gates/Rivers/Tomlins 2.00 5.00
3 Walker/M.Bell/Cutler 1.50 4.00
4 Brees/McAlli/Bush 2.00 5.00
5 Parker/Ward/Roethlis 2.00 5.00
6 Housh/Palmer/C.Jhn 1.50 4.00
7 Driver/Favre/Hawk 4.00 10.00
8 Green/LJ/Gonzalez 1.50 4.00
9 Brady/Dillon/Maroney 6.00 15.00
10 P.Mann/Wayne/Hrrisn 5.00 12.00

2007 Donruss Classics Timeless Triples Jerseys

JERSEY PRINT RUN 250 SER.#'d SETS
*PRIME/25: .8X TO 2X BASIC JSYs
PRIME PRINT RUN 25 SER.#'d SETS
1 Owens/Romo/Glenn 15.00 40.00
2 Gates/Rivers/Tomlins 8.00 20.00
3 Walker/M.Bell/Cutler 5.00 12.00
4 Brees/McAlli/Bush 12.00 30.00
5 Parker/Ward/Roethlis 12.00 30.00
6 Housh/Palmer/C.Jhn 8.00 20.00
7 Driver/Favre/Hawk 12.00 30.00
8 Green/LJ/Gonzalez 8.00 20.00
9 Brady/Dillon/Maroney 10.00 25.00
10 P.Mann/Wayne/Hrrisn 10.00 25.00

2008 Donruss Classics

This set was released on July 2, 2008. The base set consists of 248 cards. Cards 1-100 feature veterans, cards 101-150 are Legends serial numbered of 999, and cards 151-250 are rookies. Most are standard rookie cards serial numbered to 999, while others are autographed rookie cards serial numbered from 375 to 499.

COMP.SET w/o SP's (100) 7.50 20.00
101-150 LEGEND PRINT RUN 999
UNSIGNED ROOKIE PRINT RUN 999
AU ROOKIE PRINT RUN 99-499
1 Edgerrin James .25 .60
2 Larry Fitzgerald .25 .60
3 Matt Leinart .20 .50
4 Warrick Dunn .20 .50
5 Roddy White .20 .50
6 Alge Crumpler .20 .50
7 Willis McGahee .20 .50
8 Mark Clayton .20 .50
9 Derrick Mason .20 .50
10 Trent Edwards .20 .50
11 Marshawn Lynch .25 .60
12 Lee Evans .25 .60
13 DeAngelo Williams .20 .50
14 DeShaun Foster .20 .50
15 Steve Smith .25 .60
16 Cedric Benson .20 .50
17 Bernard Berrian .20 .50
18 Greg Olsen .25 .60
19 Carson Palmer .25 .60
20 Chad Johnson .20 .50
21 T.J. Houshmandzadeh .20 .50
22 Rudi Johnson .20 .50
23 Brady Quinn .20 .50
24 Jamal Lewis .25 .60
25 Braylon Edwards .20 .50
26 Tony Romo .25 .60
27 Terrell Owens .25 .60
28 Jason Witten .25 .60
29 Marion Barber .20 .50
30 Jay Cutler .20 .50
31 Brandon Marshall .25 .60
32 Brandon Stokley .20 .50
33 Jon Kitna .20 .50
34 Roy Williams WR .20 .50
35 Shaun McDonald .20 .50
36 Aaron Rodgers .60 1.50
37 Greg Jennings .20 .50
38 Ryan Grant .25 .60
39 Matt Schaub .20 .50
40 Andre Johnson .25 .60
41 Kevin Walter .25 .60
42 Peyton Manning .75 2.00
43 Reggie Wayne .25 .60
44 Joseph Addai .20 .50
45 Dallas Clark .20 .50
46 David Garrard .20 .50
47 Fred Taylor .20 .50
48 Maurice Jones-Drew .20 .50
49 Larry Johnson .20 .50
50 Tony Gonzalez .25 .60
51 Dwayne Bowe .25 .60
52 Ronnie Brown .20 .50
53 Ted Ginn Jr. .20 .50
54 John Beck .20 .50
55 Tarvaris Jackson .20 .50
56 Adrian Peterson .30 .75
57 Chester Taylor .20 .50
58 Tom Brady 1.00 2.50
59 Randy Moss .25 .60
60 Wes Welker .25 .60
61 Laurence Maroney .25 .60
62 Drew Brees .30 .75
63 Marques Colston .20 .50
64 Reggie Bush .20 .50
65 Eli Manning .25 .60
66 Plaxico Burress .20 .50
67 Brandon Jacobs .20 .50
68 Kellen Clemens .20 .50
69 Jerricho Cotchery .20 .50
70 Thomas Jones .20 .50
71 Justin Fargas .20 .50
72 Jerry Porter .20 .50
73 JaMarcus Russell .20 .50
74 Donovan McNabb .25 .60
75 Brian Westbrook .20 .50
76 Kevin Curtis .20 .50
77 Ben Roethlisberger .30 .75
78 Willie Parker .25 .60
79 Hines Ward .25 .60
80 Philip Rivers .30 .75
81 LaDainian Tomlinson .30 .75
82 Antonio Gates .25 .60
83 Frank Gore .25 .60
84 Vernon Davis .20 .50
85 Devin Hester .25 .60
86 Matt Hasselbeck .20 .50
87 Julius Jones .20 .50
88 Deion Branch .20 .50
89 Marc Bulger .20 .50
90 Steven Jackson .20 .50
91 Torry Holt .25 .60
92 Jeff Garcia .20 .50
93 Earnest Graham .20 .50
94 Joey Galloway .25 .60
95 Vince Young .20 .50
96 LenDale White .20 .50
97 Roydell Williams .20 .50
98 Jason Campbell .20 .50
99 Chris Cooley .20 .50
100 Clinton Portis .20 .50
101 Jay Novacek 1.50 4.00
102 Knute Rockne 3.00 8.00
103 Tom Landry 2.50 6.00
104 Sammy Baugh 2.00 5.00
105 Willie Lanier 1.25 3.00
106 Ken Strong 1.25 3.00
107 Marion Motley 1.50 4.00
108 Tom Fears 1.25 3.00
109 Bob Waterfield 1.50 4.00
110 Hank Stram 1.50 4.00
111 Elroy Hirsch 1.50 4.00
112 Dick Lane 1.25 3.00
113 Jim Parker 1.25 3.00
114 Red Grange 2.50 6.00
115 Bobby Layne 1.50 4.00
116 Norm Van Brocklin 1.50 4.00
117 Michael Irvin 2.00 5.00
118 Steve Largent 2.00 5.00
119 Dick Butkus 2.50 6.00
120 Ray Nitschke 2.00 5.00
121 Lawrence Taylor 2.00 5.00
122 Bob Lilly 1.50 4.00
123 Mike Singletary 2.00 5.00
124 Y.A. Tittle 2.00 5.00
125 Steve Young 2.50 6.00
126 Tim Brown 2.00 5.00
127 Joe Greene 2.00 5.00
128 Paul Krause 1.25 3.00
129 Troy Aikman 2.50 6.00
130 Bo Jackson 2.50 6.00
131 George Blanda 1.50 4.00
132 Charlie Joiner 1.25 3.00
133 Walter Payton 4.00 10.00
134 Jack Youngblood 1.25 3.00
135 Ozzie Newsome 1.50 4.00
136 Dan Marino 4.00 10.00
137 John Elway 3.00 8.00
138 Joe Montana 6.00 15.00
139 Barry Sanders 3.00 8.00
140 Doak Walker 2.00 5.00
141 Lem Barney 1.25 3.00
142 Bert Bell 1.25 3.00
143 Bulldog Turner 1.50 4.00
144 Greasy Neale 1.25 3.00
145 Ernie Stautner 1.25 3.00
146 Frank Gatski 1.25 3.00
148 Leo Nomellini 1.25 3.00
150 Otto Graham 1.50 4.00
151 Brandon Flowers AU/499 RC 5.00 12.00
152 Tracy Porter AU/499 RC 5.00 12.00
153 Terrell Thomas RC 1.50 4.00
154 Chevis Jackson AU/375 RC 4.00 10.00
155 Reggie Smith AU/499 RC 4.00 10.00
156 Phillip Merling RC 1.50 4.00
157 Calais Campbell RC 2.00 5.00
158 Quentin Groves RC 2.00 5.00
159 Pat Sims RC 2.00 5.00
160 Dan Connor RC 1.50 4.00
161 Shawn Crable AU/436 RC 4.00 10.00
162 Xavier Adibi RC 1.50 4.00
163 Jerod Mayo RC 2.50 6.00
164 Jordon Dizon RC 1.50 4.00
165 Jake Long RC 2.50 6.00
166 Matt Ryan RC 5.00 12.00
167 Brian Brohm RC 1.50 4.00
168 Chad Henne RC 2.00 5.00
169 Dennis Dixon RC 1.50 4.00
170 Erik Ainge RC 1.50 4.00
171 Colt Brennan RC 2.00 5.00
172 Andre Woodson RC 1.50 4.00
173 Marcus Thomas RC 2.00 5.00
174 Darren McFadden RC 1.50 4.00
175 Jonathan Stewart RC 2.50 6.00
176 Felix Jones RC 1.50 4.00
177 Rashard Mendenhall RC 1.50 4.00
178 Tashard Choice RC 1.50 4.00
179 Ryan Torain AU/499 RC 5.00 12.00
180 Tim Hightower RC 2.00 5.00
181 Craig Steltz AU/499 RC 4.00 10.00
182 Caleb Campbell RC 2.50 6.00
183 Dustin Keller RC 2.00 5.00
184 John Carlson RC 1.50 4.00
185 Fred Davis RC 1.50 4.00
186 Martellus Bennett AU/499 RC 5.00 12.00
187 Donnie Avery RC 2.00 5.00
188 Devin Thomas RC 1.50 4.00
189 Jordy Nelson RC 5.00 12.00
190 James Hardy RC 1.50 4.00
191 Eddie Royal RC 1.50 4.00
192 Jerome Simpson RC 2.00 5.00
193 DeSean Jackson RC 3.00 8.00
194 Malcolm Kelly RC 1.50 4.00
195 Limas Sweed RC 1.50 4.00
196 Earl Bennett RC 2.50 6.00
197 Early Doucet RC 1.50 4.00
198 Harry Douglas RC 2.00 5.00
199 Mario Manningham RC 1.50 4.00
200 Andre Caldwell RC 1.50 4.00
201 Leodis McKelvin AU/499 RC 5.00 12.00
202 Antoine Cason AU/499 RC 5.00 12.00
203 D.Rodgers-Crom AU/499 RC 5.00 12.00
204 Aqib Talib RC 2.50 6.00
205 Mike Jenkins RC 1.50 4.00
206 Vernon Gholston AU/499 RC 4.00 10.00
207 Derrick Harvey AU/499 RC 4.00 10.00
208 L.Jackson AU/499 RC 4.00 10.00
209 Chris Long AU/499 RC 5.00 12.00
210 Kentwan Balmer AU/499 RC 4.00 10.00
211 Glenn Dorsey RC 1.50 4.00
212 Sedrick Ellis RC 1.50 4.00
213 Jacob Hester AU/499 RC 4.00 10.00
214 Owen Schmitt AU/499 RC 4.00 10.00
215 Peyton Hillis AU/499 RC 6.00 15.00
216 Kenny Phillips RC 1.50 4.00
217 Curtis Lofton AU/499 RC 5.00 12.00
218 Keith Rivers AU/499 RC 4.00 10.00
219 Joe Flacco AU/399 RC 8.00 20.00
220 Matt Flynn AU/499 RC 4.00 10.00
221 Kevin O'Connell AU/499 RC 4.00 10.00
222 John D.Booty AU/349 RC 4.00 10.00
223 Josh Johnson AU/399 RC 4.00 10.00
224 Matt Forte AU/499 RC 8.00 20.00
225 Thomas Brown AU/499 RC 4.00 10.00
226 C.Washington AU/499 RC 5.00 12.00
227 Justin Forsett AU/499 RC 5.00 12.00
228 Cory Boyd AU/499 RC 4.00 10.00
229 Allen Patrick AU/499 RC 4.00 10.00
230 Chris Johnson AU/499 RC 5.00 12.00
231 Ray Rice AU/499 RC 4.00 10.00
232 K.Smith AU/99 RC EXCH 12.00 30.00
233 Mike Hart AU/499 RC 4.00 10.00
234 Jamaal Charles AU/499 RC 6.00 15.00
235 Steve Slaton AU/99 RC 12.00 30.00
236 Brad Cottam AU/499 RC 4.00 10.00
237 Jermichael Finley AU/499 RC 10.00 25.00
238 Martin Rucker AU/499 RC 4.00 10.00
239 Jacob Tamme AU/499 RC 5.00 12.00
240 Kellen Davis AU/499 RC 4.00 10.00
241 Will Franklin AU/499 RC 5.00 12.00
242 Marcus Smith AU/499RC 5.00 12.00
243 Keenan Burton RC 1.50 4.00
244 Josh Morgan AU/499 RC 4.00 10.00
245 Kevin Robinson RC 1.50 4.00
246 Paul Hubbard AU/499 RC 4.00 10.00
247 Adrian Arrington RC 1.50 4.00
248 Marcus Monk AU/499 RC 5.00 12.00
249 Lavelle Hawkins AU/499 RC 5.00 12.00
250 Dexter Jackson AU/499 RC 6.00 15.00

2008 Donruss Classics Timeless Tributes Bronze

*VETS 1-100: 3X TO 8X BASIC CARDS
*LEGENDS 101-150: .6X TO 1.5X BASIC CARDS
COMMON ROOKIE (151-250) 2.00 5.00
ROOKIE SEMISTARS 2.50 6.00
ROOKIE UNL.STARS 3.00 8.00
STATED PRINT RUN 250 SER.#'d SETS
163 Jerod Mayo 3.00 8.00
165 Jake Long 3.00 8.00
166 Matt Ryan 6.00 15.00
167 Brian Brohm 2.00 5.00
168 Chad Henne 2.50 6.00
169 Dennis Dixon 2.00 5.00
170 Erik Ainge 2.00 5.00
171 Colt Brennan 2.50 6.00
172 Andre Woodson 2.00 5.00
174 Darren McFadden 2.00 5.00
175 Jonathan Stewart 3.00 8.00
176 Felix Jones 2.00 5.00
177 Rashard Mendenhall 2.00 5.00
180 Tim Hightower 2.50 6.00
188 Devin Thomas 2.00 5.00
189 Jordy Nelson 6.00 15.00
190 James Hardy 2.00 5.00
193 DeSean Jackson 4.00 10.00
194 Malcolm Kelly 2.00 5.00
195 Limas Sweed 2.00 5.00
197 Early Doucet 2.00 5.00
199 Mario Manningham 2.00 5.00
205 Mike Jenkins 2.00 5.00
206 Vernon Gholston 2.00 5.00
209 Chris Long 2.50 6.00
211 Glenn Dorsey 2.00 5.00
213 Jacob Hester 2.00 5.00
214 Owen Schmitt 2.00 5.00
215 Peyton Hillis 3.00 8.00
218 Keith Rivers 2.00 5.00
219 Joe Flacco 4.00 10.00
220 Matt Flynn 2.00 5.00
221 Kevin O'Connell 2.00 5.00
222 John David Booty 2.00 5.00
223 Josh Johnson 2.00 5.00
224 Matt Forte 3.00 8.00
230 Chris Johnson 2.50 6.00
231 Ray Rice 2.00 5.00
232 Kevin Smith 2.00 5.00
233 Mike Hart 2.00 5.00
234 Jamaal Charles 3.00 8.00
235 Steve Slaton 2.00 5.00
250 Dexter Jackson 3.00 8.00

2008 Donruss Classics Timeless Tributes Gold

*VETS 1-100: 5X TO 12X BASIC CARDS
*LEGENDS 101-150: 1X TO 2.5X BASIC CARDS
*ROOKIES: .6X TO 1.5X TRIBUTE BRONZE
STATED PRINT RUN 50 SER.#'d SETS

2008 Donruss Classics Timeless Tributes Platinum

*VETS 1-100: 10X TO 25X BASIC CARDS
*LEGENDS 101-150: 2X TO 5X BASIC CARDS
*ROOKIES: 1X TO 2.5X TRIBUTE BRONZE
STATED PRINT RUN 25 SER.#'d SETS

2008 Donruss Classics Timeless Tributes Silver

*VETS 1-100: 4X TO 10X BASIC CARDS
*LEGENDS 101-150: .8X TO 2X BASIC CARDS
*ROOKIES: .5X TO 1.2X TRIBUTE BRONZE
STATED PRINT RUN 100 SER.#'d SETS

2008 Donruss Classics Classic Combos

STATED PRINT RUN 1000 SER.#'d SETS
*SILVER/250: .6X TO 1.5X BASIC INSERTS
SILVER PRINT RUN 250 SER.#'d SETS
*GOLD/100: .8X TO 2X BASIC INSERTS
GOLD PRINT RUN 100 SER.#'d SETS
*PLATINUM/25: 1.5X TO 4X BASIC INSERTS
PLATINUM PRINT RUN 25 SER.#'d SETS
1 H.Stram/W.Lanier .75 2.00
2 T.Landry/R.Staubach 1.25 3.00
3 G.Upshaw/M.Olsen .60 1.50
4 E.Smith/M.Irvin 1.50 4.00
5 B.Layne/D.Lane .75 2.00
6 L.Kelly/J.Brown 1.25 3.00
7 J.Parker/R.Berry .75 2.00
8 E.Hirsch/T.Fears .75 2.00
9 T.Aikman/J.Novacek 1.25 3.00
10 J.Montana/J.Rice 3.00 8.00
11 S.Young/J.Elway 1.50 4.00
12 B.Lilly/J.Greene 1.00 2.50
13 D.Marino/J.Montana 3.00 8.00
14 H.Stram/T.Landry 1.25 3.00
15 J.Thorpe/S.Baugh 1.25 3.00

2008 Donruss Classics Classic Combos Jerseys

STATED PRINT RUN 10-250
*PRIME/25: 1X TO 2.5X BASIC JSY/250
PRIME PRINT RUN 4-25
SER.#'d UNDER 25 NOT PRICED
1 H.Stram/W.Lanier 8.00 20.00
2 T.Landry/R.Staubach 20.00 40.00
3 G.Upshaw/M.Olsen 6.00 15.00
4 E.Smith/M.Irvin 12.00 30.00
5 B.Layne/D.Lane 8.00 20.00
6 L.Kelly/J.Brown/85 12.00 30.00
7 J.Parker/R.Berry 6.00 15.00
8 E.Hirsch/T.Fears 6.00 15.00
9 T.Aikman/J.Novacek 10.00 25.00
10 J.Montana/J.Rice 12.00 30.00
11 S.Young/J.Elway 10.00 25.00
12 B.Lilly/J.Greene 6.00 15.00
13 D.Marino/J.Montana 15.00 40.00
14 H.Stram/T.Landry 12.00 30.00

2008 Donruss Classics Classic Cuts

STATED PRINT RUN 1-50
7 Tom Fears/15 50.00 100.00
8 Bob Waterfield/25 60.00 120.00
9 Hank Stram/25 50.00 120.00
10 Elroy Hirsch/15 50.00 100.00
16 Doak Walker/25 125.00 250.00
17 Bert Bell/50 50.00 100.00
20 Ernie Stautner/50 40.00 80.00
21 Frank Gatski/25 60.00 120.00
27 Otto Graham/15 60.00 120.00
28 Bulldog Turner/50 50.00 100.00
29 Pete Pihos/15 50.00 100.00
32 Walter Payton/34 200.00 400.00
33 Weeb Ewbank/50 40.00 80.00
34 Wellington Mara/17 75.00 150.00

2008 Donruss Classics Classic Quads

STATED PRINT RUN 1000 SER.#'d SETS
*SILVER/250: .6X TO 1.5X BASIC INSERTS
SILVER PRINT RUN 250 SER.#'d SETS
*GOLD/100: .8X TO 2X BASIC INSERTS
GOLD PRINT RUN 100 SER.#'d SETS
*PLATINUM/25: 1.5X TO 4X BASIC INSERTS
PLATINUM PRINT RUN 25 SER.#'d SETS
1 Aikman/Smith/Irvin/Novacek 1.50 4.00
2 Layne/Sanders/Walker/Barney 1.50 4.00
3 Johnson/Moss/Owens/Holt .75 2.00
4 Owens/Tomlin/Moss/Harrison 1.00 2.50
5 James/Taylor/Tomlinson/Dunn 1.00 2.50
6 Favre/Brady/Manning/Roeth 3.00 8.00
7 Sanders/Tomlin/Payton/Smith 2.00 5.00
8 Aikman/Elway/Marino/Young 2.00 5.00
9 Smith/Payton/Sanders/Dickrsn 2.00 5.00
10 Rice/Largent/Irvin/Brown 2.00 5.00

2008 Donruss Classics Classic Quads Jerseys

STATED PRINT RUN 100 SER.#'d SETS
*PRIME/25: .8X TO 2X BASIC QUAD/100
PRIME PRINT RUN 2-25
SER.#'d UNDER 25 NOT PRICED
1 Aikman/Smith/Irvin/Novacek 30.00 80.00
2 Layne/Sanders/Walker/Barney 25.00 60.00
3 Johnson/Moss/Owens/Holt 12.00 30.00
4 Owens/Tomlin/Moss/Harrison 12.00 30.00
5 James/Taylor/Tomlinson/Dunn 12.00 30.00
6 Favre/Brady/Manning/Roeth 40.00 100.00
7 Sanders/Tomlin/Payton/Smith 40.00 100.00
8 Aikman/Elway/Marino/Young 25.00 60.00
9 Smith/Payton/Sandrs/Dickrsn 50.00 120.00
10 Rice/Largent/Irvin/Brown 15.00 40.00

2008 Donruss Classics Classic Singles

STATED PRINT RUN 1000 SER.#'d SETS
*SILVER/250: .6X TO 1.5X BASIC INSERTS
SILVER PRINT RUN 250 SER.#'d SETS
*GOLD/100: .8X TO 2X BASIC INSERTS
GOLD PRINT RUN 100 SER.#'d SETS
*PLATINUM/25: 1.5X TO 4X BASIC INSERTS
PLATINUM PRINT RUN 25 SER.#'d SETS
1 Emmitt Smith 1.25 3.00
2 Joe Montana 2.50 6.00
3 John Elway 1.25 3.00
4 Dan Marino 1.50 4.00
5 Gene Upshaw .50 1.25
6 John Mackey .50 1.25
7 Knute Rockne 1.25 3.00
8 Tom Landry 1.00 2.50
9 Sammy Baugh .75 2.00
10 Willie Lanier .50 1.25
11 Ken Strong .50 1.25
12 Marion Motley .60 1.50
13 Tom Fears .50 1.25
14 Bob Waterfield .60 1.50
15 Hank Stram .60 1.50
16 Elroy Hirsch .60 1.50
17 Dick Lane .50 1.25
18 Jim Parker .50 1.25
19 Jim Thorpe 1.00 2.50
20 Bobby Layne .60 1.50
21 Norm Van Brocklin .60 1.50
22 Merlin Olsen .50 1.25
23 Jim Brown 1.00 2.50
24 Bob Lilly .60 1.50
25 Chuck Bednarik .60 1.50
26 Leroy Kelly .60 1.50
27 Raymond Berry .60 1.50
28 Roger Staubach 1.00 2.50
29 Dan Fouts .60 1.50
30 Eric Dickerson .60 1.50

2008 Donruss Classics Classic Singles Jerseys

STATED PRINT RUN 10-50
*PRIME/15-25: .6X TO 1.5X BASIC JSY/50
*PRIME/15-25: .5X TO 1.2X BASIC JSY/25
PRIME PRINT RUN 1-25
*JERSEY #'s/50-88: .4X TO 1X BASIC JSY/50
*JERSEY #'s/32-40: .5X TO 1.2X BASIC JSY/50
*JERSEY #'s/14-29: .6X TO 1.5X BASIC JSY/50
JERSEY NUMBERS PRINT RUN 1-88
*JERSEY #'s PRIME/25: .6X TO 1.5X BASIC JSY/50
JERSEY NUMBERS PRIME PRINT RUN 1-25
SERIAL #'d UNDER 20 NOT PRICED
1 Emmitt Smith 15.00 40.00
2 Joe Montana 30.00 80.00
3 John Elway 15.00 40.00
4 Dan Marino 20.00 50.00
5 Gene Upshaw 6.00 15.00
6 John Mackey 6.00 15.00
7 Knute Rockne Jkt 30.00 60.00
8 Tom Landry 20.00 50.00
9 Sammy Baugh 12.00 30.00
10 Willie Lanier 6.00 15.00
11 Ken Strong 6.00 15.00
12 Marion Motley 10.00 25.00
13 Tom Fears 6.00 15.00
14 Bob Waterfield 10.00 25.00
15 Hank Stram 8.00 20.00
16 Elroy Hirsch 8.00 20.00
17 Dick Lane 6.00 15.00
18 Jim Parker 6.00 15.00
20 Bobby Layne 8.00 20.00
21 Norm Van Brocklin 10.00 25.00
22 Merlin Olsen 6.00 15.00
23 Jim Brown 12.00 30.00
24 Bob Lilly 8.00 20.00
25 Chuck Bednarik 8.00 20.00
26 Leroy Kelly/25 10.00 25.00
27 Raymond Berry 8.00 20.00
28 Roger Staubach 12.00 30.00
29 Dan Fouts 8.00 20.00
30 Eric Dickerson 8.00 20.00

2008 Donruss Classics Classic Singles Jerseys Autographs

STATED PRINT RUN 10-25
2 Joe Montana/20 100.00 175.00
3 John Elway/15 60.00 120.00
4 Dan Marino/25 100.00 200.00
5 Gene Upshaw/25 10.00 25.00
6 John Mackey/25 10.00 25.00
23 Jim Brown/20 50.00 100.00
24 Bob Lilly/25 12.00 30.00
25 Chuck Bednarik/25 12.00 30.00
27 Raymond Berry/25 15.00 40.00
29 Dan Fouts/25 30.00 60.00

2008 Donruss Classics Classic Singles Jerseys Jersey Numbers Autographs

SERIAL #'d UNDER 15 NOT PRICED
JERSEY NUMBERS PRINT RUN 5-25
ANNC'D EXCH EXPIRATION: 1/2/2010
5 Gene Upshaw/15 30.00 60.00
6 John Mackey /15 15.00 40.00
27 Raymond Berry/25 15.00 40.00
29 Dan Fouts/25 25.00 60.00

2008 Donruss Classics Classic Singles Jerseys Jersey Numbers Prime Autographs

SERIAL #'d UNDER 25 NOT PRICED
JERSEY NUMBERS PRIME PRINT RUN 1-25
27 Raymond Berry/25 20.00 50.00

2008 Donruss Classics Classic Singles Jerseys Prime Autographs

PRIME PRINT RUN 5-25
SERIAL #'d UNDER 20 NOT PRICED
5 Gene Upshaw/20 12.00 30.00
6 John Mackey/20 12.00 30.00
27 Raymond Berry/25 20.00 50.00

2008 Donruss Classics Classic Triples

STATED PRINT RUN 1000 SER.#'d SETS
*SILVER/250: .6X TO 1.5X BASIC INSERTS
SILVER PRINT RUN 250 SER.#'d SETS
*GOLD/100: .8X TO 2X BASIC INSERTS
GOLD PRINT RUN 100 SER.#'d SETS
*PLATINUM/25: 1.5X TO 4X BASIC INSERTS
PLATINUM PRINT RUN 25 SER.#'d SETS
1 Rockne/Stram/Landry 1.50 4.00
2 Kelly/Brown/Motley 1.25 3.00
3 Lanier/Butkus/Nitschke 1.25 3.00
4 Lilly/Greene/Upshaw 1.00 2.50
5 Layne/Van Brocklin/Waterfield .75 2.00
6 Olsen/Greene/Youngblood 1.00 2.50
7 Bednarik/Motley/Lane .75 2.00
8 Thorpe/Baugh/Strong 1.25 3.00
9 Rice/Largent/Newsome 2.00 5.00
10 Montana/Aikman/Brady 3.00 8.00

2008 Donruss Classics Classic Triples Jerseys

STATED PRINT RUN 75-250
*PRIME/25: .8X TO 2X BASIC JSY/250
PRIME PRINT RUN 1-25
1 Rockne Jkt/Stram/Landry 25.00 60.00
2 Kelly/Brown/Motley/75 15.00 40.00
3 Lanier/Butkus/Nitschke 12.00 30.00
4 Lilly/Greene/Upshaw 6.00 15.00
5 Layne/Van Brocklin/Waterfield 10.00 25.00
6 Olsen/Greene/Youngblood 6.00 15.00
7 Bednarik/Motley/Lane 10.00 25.00
8 Thorpe/Baugh/Strong/100 50.00 100.00
9 Rice/Largent/Newsome 10.00 25.00
10 Montana/Aikman/Brady 15.00 40.00

2008 Donruss Classics Membership

STATED PRINT RUN 1000 SER.#'d SETS
*SILVER/250: .6X TO 1.5X BASIC INSERTS
SILVER PRINT RUN 250 SER.#'d SETS
*GOLD/100: .8X TO 2X BASIC INSERTS
GOLD PRINT RUN 100 SER.#'d SETS
*PLATINUM/25: 1.5X TO 4X BASIC INSERTS
PLATINUM PRINT RUN 25 SER.#'d SETS
1 Adrian Peterson .75 2.00
2 Wes Welker .60 1.50
3 Dwayne Bowe .60 1.50
4 Marshawn Lynch .60 1.50
5 Steven Jackson .50 1.25
6 Santana Moss .50 1.25
7 Braylon Edwards .50 1.25
8 Jason Witten .60 1.50
9 Derek Anderson .50 1.25
10 Marion Barber .50 1.25
11 Ryan Grant .60 1.50
12 David Garrard .50 1.25
13 Matt Schaub .50 1.25
14 Justin Fargas .50 1.25
15 LaRon Landry .60 1.50
16 Tarvaris Jackson .50 1.25
17 Roddy White .50 1.25
18 Brandon Marshall .60 1.50
19 Patrick Willis .60 1.50
20 Calvin Johnson .75 2.00

2008 Donruss Classics Membership VIP Jerseys

STATED PRINT RUN 250 SER.#'d SETS
*PRIME/25: 1X TO 2.5X BASIC JSY/250
PRIME PRINT RUN 25 SER.#'d SETS
*DIE CUT/100: .6X TO 1.5X BASIC JSY/250
DIE CUT PRINT RUN 100 SER.#'d SETS
*DC PRIME/25: 1.2X TO 3X BASIC JSY/250
DIE CUT PRIME PRINT RUN 25 SER.#'d SETS
1 Adrian Peterson 4.00 10.00
2 Wes Welker 3.00 8.00
3 Dwayne Bowe 3.00 8.00
4 Marshawn Lynch 3.00 8.00
5 Steven Jackson 2.50 6.00
6 Santana Moss 2.50 6.00
7 Braylon Edwards 2.50 6.00
8 Jason Witten 3.00 8.00
9 Derek Anderson 2.50 6.00
10 Marion Barber 2.50 6.00
11 Ryan Grant 3.00 8.00
12 David Garrard 2.50 6.00
13 Matt Schaub 2.50 6.00
14 Justin Fargas 2.50 6.00
15 LaRon Landry 3.00 8.00
16 Tarvaris Jackson 2.50 6.00
17 Roddy White 2.50 6.00
18 Brandon Marshall 3.00 8.00
19 Patrick Willis 3.00 8.00
20 Calvin Johnson 4.00 10.00

2008 Donruss Classics Monday Night Heroes

STATED PRINT RUN 1000 SER.#'d SETS
*SILVER/250: .6X TO 1.5X BASIC INSERTS
SILVER PRINT RUN 250 SER.#'d SETS
*GOLD/100: .8X TO 2X BASIC INSERTS
GOLD PRINT RUN 100 SER.#'d SETS
*PLATINUM/25: 1.5X TO 4X BASIC INSERTS
PLATINUM PRINT RUN 25 SER.#'d SETS
1 Carson Palmer .60 1.50
2 Chad Johnson .50 1.25
3 Edgerrin James .60 1.50
4 Donovan McNabb .60 1.50
5 Brian Westbrook .50 1.25
6 Tom Brady 2.50 6.00
7 Randy Moss .60 1.50
8 T.J. Houshmandzadeh .50 1.25
9 Brandon Jones .50 1.25
10 Jason Witten .60 1.50
11 Eli Manning .60 1.50
12 Plaxico Burress .50 1.25
13 Peyton Manning 2.00 5.00
14 Brett Favre 1.50 4.00
15 Jay Cutler .50 1.25
16 Ryan Grant .60 1.50
17 Greg Jennings .50 1.25
18 Ben Roethlisberger .75 2.00
19 Santonio Holmes .50 1.25
20 Matt Hasselbeck .50 1.25
21 Vince Young .50 1.25
22 Brandon Stokley .50 1.25
23 Hines Ward .60 1.50
24 Willis McGahee .50 1.25
25 Derrick Mason .50 1.25
26 Drew Brees .75 2.00
27 Tarvaris Jackson .50 1.25
28 Adrian Peterson .75 2.00
29 LaDainian Tomlinson .75 2.00
30 Brandon Marshall .60 1.50

2008 Donruss Classics Monday Night Heroes Jerseys

STATED PRINT RUN 210-250
*PRIME/25: 1X TO 2.5X BASIC JSY/210-250
PRIME PRINT RUN 25 SER.#'d SETS
*JSY #'s/81-86: .6X TO 1.5X BASIC JSY/210-250
*JSY #'s/32-36: .8X TO 2X BASIC JSY/210-250
*JSY #'s/21-28: 1X TO 2.5X BASIC JSY/210-250
JERSEY NUMBERS PRINT RUN 4-86
1 Carson Palmer 3.00 8.00
2 Chad Johnson 2.50 6.00
3 Edgerrin James 3.00 8.00
4 Donovan McNabb 3.00 8.00
5 Brian Westbrook 2.50 6.00
6 Tom Brady 12.00 30.00
7 Randy Moss 3.00 8.00
8 T.J. Houshmandzadeh 2.50 6.00
9 Brandon Jones 2.50 6.00
10 Jason Witten 3.00 8.00
11 Eli Manning 3.00 8.00
12 Plaxico Burress 2.50 6.00
13 Peyton Manning 10.00 25.00
14 Brett Favre 8.00 20.00
15 Jay Cutler 2.50 6.00
16 Ryan Grant 3.00 8.00
17 Greg Jennings 2.50 6.00
18 Ben Roethlisberger 4.00 10.00
19 Santonio Holmes 2.50 6.00
20 Matt Hasselbeck 2.50 6.00
21 Vince Young 2.50 6.00
22 Brandon Stokley 2.50 6.00
23 Hines Ward 3.00 8.00
24 Willis McGahee 2.50 6.00
25 Derrick Mason 2.50 6.00
26 Drew Brees 4.00 10.00
27 Tarvaris Jackson 2.50 6.00
28 Adrian Peterson/210 4.00 10.00
29 LaDainian Tomlinson 4.00 10.00
30 Brandon Marshall 3.00 8.00

2008 Donruss Classics Monday Night Heroes Jerseys Jersey Numbers Autographs

STATED PRINT RUN 4-25
2 Chad Johnson/25 12.00 30.00
5 Brian Westbrook/20 15.00 40.00
8 T.J. Houshmandzadeh/15 12.00 30.00
10 Jason Witten/20 25.00 50.00
17 Greg Jennings/20 12.00 30.00
18 Ben Roethlisberger/19 60.00 120.00
19 Santonio Holmes/15 15.00 40.00
26 Drew Brees/20 50.00 100.00
27 Tarvaris Jackson/15 12.00 30.00
28 Adrian Peterson/25 100.00 200.00
30 Brandon Marshall/25 15.00 40.00

2008 Donruss Classics Monday Night Heroes Jerseys Prime Autographs

PRIME PRINT RUN 1-20
SERIAL #'d UNDER 20 NOT PRICED
ANNC'D EXCH EXPIRATION: 1/2/2010
17 Greg Jennings/20 12.00 30.00
26 Drew Brees/15 30.00 80.00

2008 Donruss Classics Old School Colors

STATED PRINT RUN 1000 SER.#'d SETS
1 Dan Marino 2.00 5.00
2 Braylon Edwards .60 1.50
3 Roger Staubach 1.25 3.00
4 Thurman Thomas .75 2.00
5 Barry Sanders 1.50 4.00
6 Tony Dorsett 1.00 2.50
7 Eric Dickerson .75 2.00
8 John Elway 1.50 4.00
9 Peyton Manning 2.50 6.00
10 Carson Palmer .75 2.00
11 Steve Largent 1.00 2.50
12 Laveranues Coles .60 1.50
13 Willis McGahee .60 1.50
14 Fred Taylor .60 1.50
15 Mike Singletary 1.00 2.50
16 Reggie Wayne .75 2.00
17 Lawrence Taylor 1.00 2.50
18 Hines Ward .75 2.00
19 Roy Williams WR .60 1.50
20 Lee Evans .75 2.00
21 Reggie Williams .75 2.00
22 Andre Johnson .75 2.00
24 Marcus Allen 1.00 2.50
25 Kellen Winslow .60 1.50

2008 Donruss Classics Old School Colors Autographs

STATED PRINT RUN 4-25
SERIAL #'d UNDER 20 NOT PRICED
ANNC'D EXCH EXPIRATION: 1/2/2010
1 Dan Marino/20 125.00 200.00
2 Braylon Edwards/20 EXCH 20.00 40.00
4 Thurman Thomas/25 25.00 50.00
5 Barry Sanders/20 EXCH 60.00 120.00
6 Tony Dorsett/25 25.00 50.00
7 Eric Dickerson/25 25.00 50.00
11 Steve Largent/25 20.00 40.00
13 Willis McGahee/20 12.00 30.00
15 Mike Singletary/20 25.00 50.00
16 Reggie Wayne/20 EXCH 15.00 40.00
17 Lawrence Taylor/25 25.00 50.00
24 Marcus Allen/25 15.00 40.00

2008 Donruss Classics Old School Colors Jerseys

STATED PRINT RUN 40-100
*PRIME/25: .8X TO 2X BASIC JSY/40-100
PRIME PRINT RUN 25 SER.#'d SETS
1 Dan Marino/68 15.00 40.00
2 Braylon Edwards 5.00 12.00
3 Roger Staubach 12.00 30.00
4 Thurman Thomas 8.00 20.00
5 Barry Sanders 12.00 30.00
6 Tony Dorsett/66 10.00 25.00
7 Eric Dickerson 8.00 20.00
8 John Elway 15.00 40.00
9 Peyton Manning 15.00 40.00
10 Carson Palmer
11 Steve Largent 10.00 25.00
12 Laveranues Coles 5.00 12.00
13 Willis McGahee 5.00 12.00
15 Mike Singletary 10.00 25.00
17 Lawrence Taylor 10.00 25.00
18 Hines Ward 6.00 15.00
19 Roy Williams WR/66 5.00 12.00
20 Lee Evans 6.00 15.00
21 Reggie Williams 6.00 15.00
22 Andre Johnson/40 6.00 15.00
24 Marcus Allen 10.00 25.00
25 Kellen Winslow Jr. 6.00 15.00

2008 Donruss Classics Saturday Stars

STATED PRINT RUN 1000 SER.#'d SETS
*SILVER/250: .6X TO 1.5X BASIC INSERTS
SILVER PRINT RUN 250 SER.#'d SETS
*GOLD/100: .8X TO 2X BASIC INSERTS
GOLD PRINT RUN 100 SER.#'d SETS
*PLATINUM/25: 1.5X TO 4X BASIC INSERTS
PLATINUM PRINT RUN 25 SER.#'d SETS
1 Allen Patrick .50 1.25
2 Antoine Cason .60 1.50
3 Brian Brohm .50 1.25
4 Chad Henne .60 1.50
5 Chris Long .60 1.50
6 Colt Brennan .60 1.50
7 Dan Connor .50 1.25
8 Dennis Dixon .50 1.25
9 Early Doucet .50 1.25
10 Eddie Royal .50 1.25
11 Erik Ainge .50 1.25
12 DJ Hall .50 1.25
13 Glenn Dorsey .50 1.25
14 John David Booty .50 1.25
15 Keith Rivers .50 1.25
16 Kenny Phillips .50 1.25
17 Limas Sweed .50 1.25
18 Matt Ryan 1.50 4.00
19 Matt Flynn .50 1.25
20 Mike Hart .50 1.25
21 Malcolm Kelly .50 1.25
22 Mario Manningham .50 1.25
23 Adrian Arrington .50 1.25
24 Darren McFadden .50 1.25
25 DeSean Jackson 1.00 2.50
26 Felix Jones .50 1.25
27 Jamaal Charles .75 2.00
28 Jonathan Stewart .75 2.00
29 Rashard Mendenhall .50 1.25
30 Steve Slaton .50 1.25

2008 Donruss Classics Saturday Stars Autographs

STATED PRINT RUN 25 SER.#'d SETS
1 Allen Patrick 8.00 20.00
2 Antoine Cason 10.00 25.00
3 Brian Brohm 8.00 20.00
4 Chad Henne 10.00 25.00
5 Chris Long 10.00 25.00
6 Colt Brennan 10.00 25.00
7 Dan Connor 8.00 20.00
8 Dennis Dixon 8.00 20.00
9 Early Doucet 8.00 20.00
11 Erik Ainge 8.00 20.00
14 John David Booty 8.00 20.00
15 Keith Rivers 8.00 20.00
17 Limas Sweed 8.00 20.00
18 Matt Ryan 40.00 80.00
19 Matt Flynn 8.00 20.00
20 Mike Hart 8.00 20.00
21 Malcolm Kelly 8.00 20.00
22 Mario Manningham 8.00 20.00
23 Adrian Arrington 8.00 20.00
24 Darren McFadden 40.00 80.00
25 DeSean Jackson 15.00 40.00
26 Felix Jones 8.00 20.00
27 Jamaal Charles 12.00 30.00
28 Jonathan Stewart 12.00 30.00
29 Rashard Mendenhall 8.00 20.00
30 Steve Slaton 8.00 20.00

2008 Donruss Classics Saturday Stars Jerseys

STATED PRINT RUN 55-250
*PRIME/25: 1X TO 2.5X BASIC JSY/230-250
*PRIME/25: .8X TO 2X BASIC JSY/55
PRIME PRINT RUN 25 SER.#'d SETS
*JSY #'s/55-91: .5X TO 1.2X BASIC JSY/230-250
*JSY #'s/40: .6X TO 1.5X BASIC JSY/230-250
*JSY #'s/20 28: .8X TO 2X BASIC JSY/230-250
JERSEY NUMBERS PRINT RUN 1-91 SER.#'d SETS
UNPRICED JSY #'s AU PRINT RUN 10
UNPRICED PRIME AU PRINT RUN 5
1 Allen Patrick 2.50 6.00
2 Antoine Cason/230 3.00 8.00
3 Brian Brohm 2.50 6.00
4 Chad Henne 3.00 8.00
5 Chris Long 3.00 8.00
6 Colt Brennan 3.00 8.00
7 Dan Connor 2.50 6.00
8 Dennis Dixon 2.50 6.00
9 Early Doucet 2.50 6.00
10 Eddie Royal 2.50 6.00
11 Erik Ainge 2.50 6.00
12 DJ Hall 2.50 6.00
13 Glenn Dorsey 2.50 6.00
14 John David Booty 2.50 6.00
15 Keith Rivers 2.50 6.00
16 Kenny Phillips 2.50 6.00
17 Limas Sweed 2.50 6.00
18 Matt Ryan 10.00 25.00
19 Matt Flynn 2.50 6.00
20 Mike Hart 2.50 6.00
21 Malcolm Kelly 2.50 6.00
23 Adrian Arrington/55 3.00 8.00
24 Darren McFadden 2.50 6.00
25 DeSean Jackson 5.00 12.00
26 Felix Jones 2.50 6.00
27 Jamaal Charles 4.00 10.00
28 Jonathan Stewart 4.00 10.00
29 Rashard Mendenhall 2.50 6.00
30 Steve Slaton 2.50 6.00

2008 Donruss Classics School Colors

STATED PRINT RUN 1000 SER.#'d SETS
1 Ali Highsmith .50 1.25
2 Allen Patrick .50 1.25
3 Antoine Cason .60 1.50
4 Brian Brohm .50 1.25
5 Chad Henne .60 1.50
6 Chevis Jackson .50 1.25
7 Chris Long .60 1.50
8 Colt Brennan .60 1.50
9 DJ Hall .50 1.25
10 Dan Connor .50 1.25
11 Dennis Dixon .50 1.25
12 Early Doucet .50 1.25
13 Eddie Royal .50 1.25
14 Erik Ainge .50 1.25
15 Ernie Wheelwright .60 1.50
16 Fred Davis .50 1.25
17 Glenn Dorsey .50 1.25
18 Harry Douglas .60 1.50
19 Jamar Adams .50 1.25
20 John David Booty .50 1.25
21 Jonathan Hefney .50 1.25
22 Keith Rivers .50 1.25
23 Kenny Phillips .50 1.25
24 Lawrence Jackson .50 1.25
25 Limas Sweed .50 1.25
26 Marcus Monk .60 1.50
27 Matt Ryan 1.50 4.00
28 Matt Flynn .50 1.25
29 Mike Hart .50 1.25
30 Malcolm Kelly .50 1.25
31 Mario Manningham .50 1.25

32 Owen Schmitt .50 1.25
33 Quentin Groves .60 1.50
34 Robert Killebrew .60 1.50
35 Sedrick Ellis .50 1.25
36 Shawn Crable .50 1.25
37 Terrell Thomas .50 1.25
38 Xavier Adibi .50 1.25
39 Adrian Arrington .50 1.25
40 Aqib Talib .75 2.00
41 Brandon Flowers .60 1.50
42 Calais Campbell .60 1.50
43 Darren McFadden .50 1.25
44 DeSean Jackson 1.00 2.50
45 Felix Jones .50 1.25
46 Jamaal Charles .75 2.00
47 Jonathan Stewart .75 2.00
48 Rashard Mendenhall .50 1.25
49 Steve Slaton .50 1.25
50 Vernon Gholston .50 1.25

2008 Donruss Classics School Colors Autographs

STATED PRINT RUN 50 SER.#'d SETS
2 Allen Patrick 8.00 20.00
3 Antoine Cason 10.00 25.00
4 Brian Brohm 8.00 20.00
5 Chad Henne 10.00 25.00
6 Chevis Jackson 8.00 20.00
7 Chris Long 10.00 25.00
8 Colt Brennan 10.00 25.00
9 DJ Hall 8.00 20.00
10 Dan Connor 8.00 20.00
11 Dennis Dixon 8.00 20.00
14 Erik Ainge 8.00 20.00
15 Ernie Wheelwright 10.00 25.00
16 Fred Davis 8.00 20.00
17 Glenn Dorsey 8.00 20.00
18 Harry Douglas 10.00 25.00
19 Jamar Adams 8.00 20.00
20 John David Booty 8.00 20.00
22 Keith Rivers 8.00 20.00
24 Lawrence Jackson 8.00 20.00
25 Limas Sweed 8.00 20.00
26 Marcus Monk 10.00 25.00
27 Matt Ryan 40.00 100.00
28 Matt Flynn 8.00 20.00
29 Mike Hart 8.00 20.00
30 Malcolm Kelly 8.00 20.00
31 Mario Manningham 12.00 30.00
32 Owen Schmitt 8.00 20.00
33 Quentin Groves 10.00 25.00
34 Robert Killebrew 10.00 25.00
36 Shawn Crable 8.00 20.00
37 Terrell Thomas 8.00 20.00
38 Xavier Adibi 8.00 20.00
39 Adrian Arrington 8.00 20.00
41 Brandon Flowers 10.00 25.00
42 Calais Campbell 10.00 25.00
43 Darren McFadden 8.00 20.00
44 DeSean Jackson 15.00 40.00
45 Felix Jones 8.00 20.00
46 Jamaal Charles 15.00 40.00
47 Jonathan Stewart 20.00 50.00
48 Rashard Mendenhall 8.00 20.00
49 Steve Slaton 8.00 20.00
50 Vernon Gholston 8.00 20.00

2008 Donruss Classics School Colors Jerseys

STATED PRINT RUN 60-100
*PRIME/25: .8X TO 2X BASIC JSY/60-100
PRIME PRINT RUN 10-25
1 Ali Highsmith 3.00 8.00
2 Allen Patrick 3.00 8.00
3 Antoine Cason 4.00 10.00
4 Brian Brohm 3.00 8.00
5 Chad Henne 4.00 10.00
6 Chevis Jackson 3.00 8.00
7 Chris Long 4.00 10.00
8 Colt Brennan 4.00 10.00
9 DJ Hall 3.00 8.00
10 Dan Connor 3.00 8.00
11 Dennis Dixon 3.00 8.00
12 Early Doucet 3.00 8.00
13 Eddie Royal 3.00 8.00
14 Erik Ainge 10.00 25.00
15 Ernie Wheelwright 4.00 10.00
16 Fred Davis 3.00 8.00
17 Glenn Dorsey 3.00 8.00
18 Harry Douglas 4.00 10.00
19 Jamar Adams/94 3.00 8.00
20 John David Booty 3.00 8.00
21 Jonathan Hefney 3.00 8.00
22 Keith Rivers 3.00 8.00
23 Kenny Phillips 3.00 8.00
24 Lawrence Jackson 3.00 8.00
25 Limas Sweed 3.00 8.00
26 Marcus Monk 4.00 10.00
27 Matt Ryan 10.00 25.00
28 Matt Flynn 3.00 8.00
29 Mike Hart 3.00 8.00
30 Malcolm Kelly 3.00 8.00
31 Mario Manningham 3.00 8.00
32 Owen Schmitt 3.00 8.00
33 Quentin Groves/60 4.00 10.00
34 Robert Killebrew 4.00 10.00
35 Sedrick Ellis 3.00 8.00
36 Shawn Crable 3.00 8.00
37 Terrell Thomas 3.00 8.00
38 Xavier Adibi 3.00 8.00
39 Adrian Arrington 3.00 8.00
40 Aqib Talib 5.00 12.00
41 Brandon Flowers 4.00 10.00
42 Calais Campbell 4.00 10.00
43 Darren McFadden 3.00 8.00
44 DeSean Jackson 6.00 15.00
45 Felix Jones 3.00 8.00
46 Jamaal Charles 5.00 12.00
47 Jonathan Stewart 10.00 25.00
48 Rashard Mendenhall 3.00 8.00
49 Steve Slaton 3.00 8.00
50 Vernon Gholston 3.00 8.00

2008 Donruss Classics Significant Signatures Gold

STATED PRINT RUN 25-125
153 Terrell Thomas/125 5.00 12.00
157 Calais Campbell/125 6.00 15.00
158 Quentin Groves/125 6.00 15.00
159 Pat Sims/25 12.00 30.00
160 Dan Connor/125 5.00 12.00
162 Xavier Adibi/125 5.00 12.00
163 Jerod Mayo/125 8.00 20.00
164 Jordon Dizon/25 10.00 25.00
165 Jake Long/25 15.00 40.00
166 Matt Ryan/125 30.00 60.00
167 Brian Brohm/125 5.00 12.00
168 Chad Henne/125 6.00 15.00
169 Dennis Dixon/125 5.00 12.00
170 Erik Ainge/125 5.00 12.00
171 Colt Brennan/125 6.00 15.00
172 Andre Woodson/125 5.00 12.00
173 Marcus Thomas/50 10.00 25.00
174 Darren McFadden/125 5.00 12.00
175 Jonathan Stewart/125 8.00 20.00
176 Felix Jones/125 5.00 12.00
177 Rashard Mendenhall/125 5.00 12.00
178 Tashard Choice/125 5.00 12.00
180 Tim Hightower/50 10.00 25.00
182 Caleb Campbell/125 8.00 20.00
183 Dustin Keller/125 6.00 15.00
184 John Carlson/125 5.00 12.00
185 Fred Davis/125 5.00 12.00
187 Donnie Avery/125 6.00 15.00
188 Devin Thomas/125 5.00 12.00
189 Jordy Nelson/50 25.00 50.00
190 James Hardy/125 5.00 12.00
191 Eddie Royal/50 8.00 20.00
192 Jerome Simpson/125 6.00 15.00
193 DeSean Jackson/125 10.00 25.00
194 Malcolm Kelly/125 5.00 12.00
195 Limas Sweed/125 5.00 12.00
196 Earl Bennett/125 8.00 20.00
197 Early Doucet/50 8.00 20.00
198 Harry Douglas/50 10.00 25.00
199 Mario Manningham/125 10.00 25.00
200 Andre Caldwell/125 5.00 12.00
205 Mike Jenkins/50 8.00 20.00
211 Glenn Dorsey/25 10.00 25.00
245 Kevin Robinson/50 8.00 20.00
247 Adrian Arrington/25

2008 Donruss Classics Significant Signatures Platinum

*PLATINUM/25: .6X TO 1.5X GOLD AU/125
PLATINUM PRINT RUN 5-25
166 Matt Ryan/25 90.00 150.00
174 Darren McFadden/25 8.00 20.00
177 Rashard Mendenhall/25 8.00 20.00

2008 Donruss Classics Sunday's Best

STATED PRINT RUN 1000 SER.#'d SETS
*SILVER/250: .6X TO 1.5X BASIC INSERTS
SILVER PRINT RUN 250 SER.#'d SETS
*GOLD/100: .8X TO 2X BASIC INSERTS
GOLD PRINT RUN 100 SER.#'d SETS
*PLATINUM/25: 1.5X TO 4X BASIC INSERTS
PLATINUM PRINT RUN 25 SER.#'d SETS
1 Wes Welker .60 1.50
2 Jamal Lewis .60 1.50
3 Joseph Addai .50 1.25
4 Dwayne Bowe .60 1.50
5 Philip Rivers .75 2.00
6 Larry Fitzgerald .60 1.50
7 Larry Johnson .50 1.25
8 Willie Parker .60 1.50
9 Adrian Peterson .75 2.00
10 Terrell Owens .60 1.50
11 Reggie Wayne .60 1.50
12 Jason Campbell .50 1.25
13 Frank Gore .60 1.50
14 Antonio Gates .60 1.50
15 Braylon Edwards .50 1.25
16 Derek Anderson .50 1.25
17 Plaxico Burress .50 1.25
18 Steve Smith .60 1.50
19 Tony Gonzalez .60 1.50
20 Tom Brady 2.50 6.00
21 Peyton Manning 2.00 5.00
22 Laurence Maroney .60 1.50
23 Clinton Portis .50 1.25
24 Donald Driver .60 1.50
25 Marshawn Lynch .60 1.50
26 Brett Favre 1.50 4.00
27 Reggie Bush .50 1.25
28 Marion Barber .50 1.25
29 Vince Young .50 1.25
30 Steven Jackson .50 1.25
31 Ryan Grant .60 1.50
32 Marques Colston .50 1.25
33 Tony Romo .60 1.50
34 Torry Holt .60 1.50
35 Eli Manning .60 1.50
36 Matt Hasselbeck .50 1.25
37 Brandon Jacobs .50 1.25
38 Maurice Jones-Drew .50 1.25
39 Deion Branch .50 1.25
40 Devin Hester .60 1.50

2008 Donruss Classics Sunday's Best Jerseys

STATED PRINT RUN 250 SER.#'d SETS
*PRIME/25: 1X TO 2.5X BASIC JSY/250
PRIME PRINT RUN 25 SER.#'d SETS
*JERSEY #'s/80-89: .5X TO 1.2X BASIC INSERTS
*JERSEY #'s/31-39: .6X TO 1.5X BASIC INSERTS
*JERSEY #'s/21-29: .8X TO 2X BASIC INSERTS
JERSEY NUMBERS PRINT RUN 3-89
1 Wes Welker 3.00 8.00
2 Jamal Lewis 3.00 8.00
3 Joseph Addai 2.50 6.00
4 Dwayne Bowe 3.00 8.00
5 Philip Rivers 4.00 10.00
6 Larry Fitzgerald 3.00 8.00
7 Larry Johnson 2.50 6.00
8 Willie Parker 3.00 8.00
9 Adrian Peterson 4.00 10.00
10 Terrell Owens 3.00 8.00
11 Reggie Wayne 3.00 8.00
12 Jason Campbell 2.50 6.00
13 Frank Gore 3.00 8.00
14 Antonio Gates 3.00 8.00
15 Braylon Edwards 2.50 6.00
16 Derek Anderson 2.50 6.00
17 Plaxico Burress 2.50 6.00
18 Steve Smith 3.00 8.00
19 Tony Gonzalez 3.00 8.00
20 Tom Brady 12.00 30.00
21 Peyton Manning 10.00 25.00
22 Laurence Maroney 3.00 8.00
23 Clinton Portis 2.50 6.00
24 Donald Driver 3.00 8.00
25 Marshawn Lynch 3.00 8.00
26 Brett Favre 8.00 20.00
27 Reggie Bush 2.50 6.00
28 Marion Barber 2.50 6.00
29 Vince Young 2.50 6.00
30 Steven Jackson 2.50 6.00
31 Ryan Grant 3.00 8.00
32 Marques Colston 2.50 6.00
33 Tony Romo 3.00 8.00
34 Torry Holt 3.00 8.00
35 Eli Manning 3.00 8.00
36 Matt Hasselbeck 2.50 6.00
37 Brandon Jacobs 2.50 6.00
38 Maurice Jones-Drew 2.50 6.00
39 Deion Branch 2.50 6.00
40 Devin Hester 3.00 8.00

2008 Donruss Classics Sunday's Best Jerseys Jersey Numbers Autographs

STATED PRINT RUN 5-25
SERIAL #'d UNDER 20 NOT PRICED
7 Larry Johnson/25 12.00 30.00
9 Adrian Peterson/25 100.00 200.00
13 Frank Gore/15 15.00 40.00
24 Donald Driver/25 15.00 40.00
25 Marshawn Lynch/25 15.00 40.00
28 Marion Barber/15 15.00 40.00
32 Marques Colston/25 15.00 40.00
33 Tony Romo/20 50.00 100.00
37 Brandon Jacobs/20 15.00 40.00
38 Maurice Jones-Drew/20 15.00 40.00

2008 Donruss Classics Sunday's Best Jerseys Prime Autographs

PRIME PRINT RUN 1-25
7 Larry Johnson/25 20.00 50.00
9 Adrian Peterson/15 75.00 150.00
24 Donald Driver/15 30.00 60.00
25 Marshawn Lynch/20 20.00 50.00
32 Marques Colston/25 20.00 50.00
37 Brandon Jacobs/15 15.00 40.00

2008 Donruss Classics Team Colors

RANDOM INSERTS IN RETAIL PACKS
1 Darren McFadden 1.25 3.00
2 Felix Jones 1.25 3.00
3 Jonathan Stewart 2.00 5.00
4 Rashard Mendenhall 1.25 3.00
5 Matt Ryan 4.00 10.00
6 Brian Brohm 1.25 3.00
7 Chad Henne 1.50 4.00
8 Joe Flacco 2.50 6.00
9 Donnie Avery 1.50 4.00
10 Devin Thomas 1.25 3.00

2008 Donruss Classics Timeless Treasures

STATED PRINT RUN 1000 SER.#'d SETS
*SILVER/250: .6X TO 1.5X BASIC INSERTS
SILVER PRINT RUN 250 SER.#'d SETS
*GOLD/100: .8X TO 2X BASIC INSERTS
GOLD PRINT RUN 100 SER.#'d SETS
*PLATINUM/25: 1.5X TO 4X BASIC INSERTS
PLATINUM PRINT RUN 25 SER.#'d SETS
1 Y.A. Tittle 2.00 5.00
2 Tony Dorsett 2.00 5.00
3 Tom Landry 2.50 6.00
4 Knute Rockne 3.00 8.00
5 Peyton Manning 5.00 12.00
6 Paul Krause 1.25 3.00
7 Jim Brown 2.50 6.00
8 Hank Stram 1.50 4.00
9 John Elway 3.00 8.00
10 George Blanda 1.50 4.00
11 Emmitt Smith 3.00 8.00
12 Dan Marino 4.00 10.00
13 Charlie Joiner 1.25 3.00
14 Sammy Baugh 2.00 5.00
15 Bo Jackson 2.50 6.00

2008 Donruss Classics Timeless Treasures Cuts

STATED PRINT RUN 1-25
SERIAL #'d UNDER 25 NOT PRICED
8 Hank Stram/25 60.00 150.00
10 George Blanda/25 30.00 60.00

2008 Donruss Classics Timeless Treasures Material

STATED PRINT RUN 250 SER.#'d SETS
*PRIME/25: 1X TO 2.5X BASIC JSY/250
PRIME PRINT RUN 1-25
1 Y.A. Tittle 6.00 15.00
2 Tony Dorsett 6.00 15.00
3 Tom Landry 15.00 40.00
4 Knute Rockne Jkt 20.00 50.00
5 Peyton Manning 6.00 15.00
7 Jim Brown 8.00 20.00
8 Hank Stram 6.00 15.00
9 John Elway 10.00 25.00
10 George Blanda 6.00 15.00
11 Emmitt Smith 12.00 30.00
12 Dan Marino 12.00 30.00
13 Charlie Joiner 4.00 10.00
14 Sammy Baugh/100 10.00 25.00
15 Bo Jackson 8.00 20.00

2008 Donruss Classics Timeless Treasures Material Autographs

STATED PRINT RUN 10-25
SERIAL #'d UNDER 20 NOT PRICED
2 Tony Dorsett/25 30.00 60.00
7 Jim Brown/20 50.00 100.00
10 George Blanda/25 25.00 50.00
12 Dan Marino/25 75.00 150.00
13 Charlie Joiner/25 20.00 40.00
15 Bo Jackson/25 40.00 80.00

2008 Donruss Classics Timeless Treasures Material Prime Autographs

PRIME PRINT RUN 5-25 SER.#'d SETS
SERIAL #'d UNDER 25 NOT PRICED
2 Tony Dorsett/25 40.00 80.00
15 Bo Jackson/25 40.00 80.00

2009 Donruss Classics

COMP.SET w/o SP's (100) 7.50 20.00
101-150 LEGEND PRINT RUN 999
ROOKIE UNSIGNED PRINT RUN 999
ROOKIE AUTO PRINT RUN 299-999
1 Anquan Boldin .20 .50
2 Kurt Warner .25 .60
3 Larry Fitzgerald .25 .60
4 Steve Breaston .25 .60
5 Matt Ryan .25 .60
6 Michael Turner .20 .50
7 Roddy White .20 .50
8 Joe Flacco .25 .60
9 Willis McGahee .20 .50
10 Derrick Mason .20 .50
11 Lee Evans .25 .60
12 Marshawn Lynch .25 .60
13 DeAngelo Williams .20 .50
14 Jake Delhomme .20 .50
15 Jonathan Stewart .20 .50
16 Steve Smith .25 .60
17 Greg Olsen .25 .60
18 Kyle Orton .20 .50
19 Matt Forte .20 .50
20 Carson Palmer .25 .60
21 Chad Ochocinco .20 .50
22 T.J. Houshmandzadeh .20 .50
23 Brady Quinn .20 .50
24 Braylon Edwards .20 .50
25 Jamal Lewis .25 .60
26 Kellen Winslow Jr. .20 .50
27 Felix Jones .20 .50
28 Roy Williams WR .20 .50
29 Marion Barber .25 .60
30 Tony Romo .25 .60
31 Brandon Marshall .25 .60
32 Eddie Royal .20 .50
33 Jay Cutler .20 .50
34 Calvin Johnson .30 .75
35 Kevin Smith .20 .50
36 Aaron Rodgers .60 1.50
37 Donald Driver .25 .60
38 Ryan Grant .25 .60
39 Andre Johnson .25 .60
40 Matt Schaub .20 .50
41 Steve Slaton .20 .50
42 Anthony Gonzalez .20 .50
43 Joseph Addai .20 .50
44 Peyton Manning .75 2.00
45 Reggie Wayne .25 .60
46 David Garrard .20 .50
47 Maurice Jones-Drew .20 .50
48 Marcedes Lewis .20 .50
49 Dwayne Bowe .25 .60
50 Larry Johnson .20 .50
51 Chad Pennington .20 .50
52 Ronnie Brown .20 .50
53 Ricky Williams .25 .60
54 Adrian Peterson .30 .75
55 Bernard Berrian .20 .50
56 Chester Taylor .20 .50
57 Laurence Maroney .25 .60
58 Randy Moss .25 .60
59 Tom Brady 1.00 2.50
60 Drew Brees .30 .75
61 Marques Colston .20 .50
62 Reggie Bush .20 .50
63 Brandon Jacobs .20 .50
64 Kevin Boss .20 .50
65 Eli Manning .25 .60
66 Kellen Clemens .20 .50
67 Jerricho Cotchery .20 .50
68 Laveranues Coles .20 .50
69 Thomas Jones .20 .50
70 JaMarcus Russell .20 .50
71 Justin Fargas .20 .50
72 Darren McFadden .30 .75
73 Brian Westbrook .20 .50
74 Donovan McNabb .25 .60
75 Kevin Curtis .20 .50
76 Ben Roethlisberger .30 .75
77 Heath Miller .20 .50
78 Santonio Holmes .20 .50
79 Willie Parker .20 .50
80 Antonio Gates .25 .60
81 LaDainian Tomlinson .30 .75
82 Philip Rivers .30 .75
83 Frank Gore .25 .60
84 Isaac Bruce .30 .75
85 Deion Branch .20 .50
86 Julius Jones .20 .50
87 Matt Hasselbeck .20 .50
88 Marc Bulger .20 .50
89 Steven Jackson .20 .50
90 Donnie Avery .20 .50
91 Antonio Bryant .20 .50
92 Earnest Graham .20 .50
93 Derrick Ward .20 .50
94 Chris Johnson .20 .50
95 Justin Gage .20 .50
96 LenDale White .20 .50
97 Chris Cooley .20 .50
98 Clinton Portis .20 .50
99 Jason Campbell .20 .50
100 Santana Moss .25 .60
101 Alan Page 1.25 3.00
102 Andre Reed 1.50 4.00
103 Barry Sanders 3.00 8.00
104 Billy Sims 1.50 4.00
105 Bo Jackson 2.50 6.00
106 Bob Lilly 1.50 4.00
107 Bobby Layne 1.50 4.00
108 Carl Eller 1.25 3.00
109 Chuck Bednarik 1.50 4.00
110 Ace Parker 1.25 3.00
111 Cliff Harris 1.50 4.00
112 Danny White 1.50 4.00
113 Daryl Johnston 1.50 4.00
114 Dave Casper 1.25 3.00
115 Earl Campbell 2.00 5.00
116 Emmitt Smith 3.00 8.00
117 Eric Dickerson 1.50 4.00
118 Franco Harris 2.00 5.00
119 Gale Sayers 2.00 5.00
121 Jack Youngblood 1.25 3.00
122 Jay Novacek 1.50 4.00
123 Jerry Rice 4.00 10.00
124 Jim Brown 2.50 6.00
125 Jim Kelly 2.00 5.00
126 Jim McMahon 1.50 4.00
127 Joe Greene 2.00 5.00
128 Joe Montana 6.00 15.00
129 John Stallworth 1.50 4.00
130 Lawrence Taylor 2.00 5.00
131 Lou Groza 1.50 4.00
132 Marion Motley 1.50 4.00
133 Merlin Olsen 1.25 3.00
134 Michael Irvin 2.00 5.00
135 Mike Singletary 2.00 5.00
136 Phil Simms 1.50 4.00
137 Reggie White 2.00 5.00
138 Roger Craig 1.50 4.00
139 Roger Staubach 2.50 6.00
140 Sid Luckman 1.50 4.00
141 Steve Young 2.50 6.00
142 Ted Hendricks 1.25 3.00
143 Thurman Thomas 1.50 4.00
144 Tim Brown 2.00 5.00
145 Tom Landry 2.50 6.00
146 Tony Dorsett 2.00 5.00
147 Troy Aikman 2.50 6.00
148 Walter Payton 3.00 8.00
149 William Perry 1.25 3.00
150 Y.A. Tittle 2.00 5.00
151 Aaron Curry RC 2.00 5.00
152 Aaron Kelly AU/999 RC 3.00 8.00
153 Aaron Maybin RC 1.50 4.00
154 Alphonso Smith RC 1.25 3.00
155 Andre Brown AU/299 RC 5.00 12.00
156 Andre Smith RC 1.25 3.00
157 Arian Foster RC 3.00 8.00
158 Austin Collie AU/399 RC 4.00 10.00
159 B.J. Raji RC 1.50 4.00
160 Brandon Gibson AU/499 RC 5.00 12.00
161 Brandon Pettigrew RC 1.25 3.00
162 Brandon Tate AU/399 RC 5.00 12.00
163 Brian Cushing RC 1.25 3.00
164 Brian Hartline RC 2.00 5.00
165 Brian Orakpo RC 1.50 4.00
166 Brian Robiskie RC 1.25 3.00
167 Brooks Foster AU/399 RC 4.00 10.00
168 Cameron Morrah RC 1.25 3.00
169 Cedric Peerman AU/499 RC 4.00 10.00
170 Chase Coffman AU/299 RC 4.00 10.00
171 Chris Wells RC 1.25 3.00
172 Clay Matthews RC 5.00 12.00
173 Clint Sintim AU/299 RC 4.00 10.00
174 Cody Brown RC 1.25 3.00
175 Cornelius Ingram AU/399 RC 4.00 10.00
176 Darcel McBath RC 1.25 3.00
177 Darius Butler RC 1.50 4.00
178 Darius Passmore AU/999 RC 3.00 8.00
179 Darrius Heyward-Bey RC 2.00 5.00
180 Demetrius Byrd RC 1.50 4.00
181 Deon Butler AU/399 RC 4.00 10.00
182 Derrick Williams AU/299 RC 4.00 10.00
183 Devin Moore AU/999 RC 3.00 8.00
184 Dominique Edison AU/499 RC 4.00 10.00
185 Donald Brown RC 1.25 3.00
186 Eugene Monroe RC 1.25 3.00
187 Everette Brown RC 1.25 3.00
188 Gartrell Johnson RC 1.25 3.00
189 Glen Coffee RC 1.25 3.00
190 Graham Harrell AU/999 RC 8.00 20.00
191 Hakeem Nicks RC 1.50 4.00
192 Hunter Cantwell AU/999 RC 3.00 8.00
193 Ian Johnson RC 1.25 3.00
194 Jairus Byrd RC 2.00 5.00
195 James Casey AU/299 RC 5.00 12.00
196 James Davis RC 1.25 3.00
197 James Laurinaitis RC 1.25 3.00
198 Jared Cook AU/299 RC 5.00 12.00
199 Jarett Dillard AU/299 RC 4.00 10.00
200 Jason Smith RC 1.25 3.00
201 Javon Ringer RC 1.25 3.00
202 Jeremiah Johnson AU/999 RC 3.00 8.00
203 Jeremy Childs RC 1.25 3.00
204 Jeremy Maclin RC 1.50 4.00
205 John Parker Wilson AU/999 RC 3.00 8.00
206 Johnny Knox AU/399 RC 5.00 12.00
207 Josh Freeman RC 1.25 3.00
208 Juaquin Iglesias AU/399 RC 4.00 10.00
209 Kenny Britt RC 2.00 5.00
210 Kenny McKinley AU/399 RC 4.00 10.00
211 Kevin Ogletree AU/999 RC 4.00 10.00
212 Knowshon Moreno RC 1.25 3.00
213 Kory Sheets AU/999 RC 4.00 10.00
214 Larry English RC 1.50 4.00
215 LeSean McCoy RC 3.00 8.00
216 Louis Delmas RC 1.50 4.00
217 Louis Murphy RC 1.25 3.00
218 Malcolm Jenkins RC 1.25 3.00
219 Mark Sanchez RC 1.25 3.00
220 Matthew Stafford RC 6.00 15.00
221 Michael Crabtree RC 2.00 5.00
222 Michael Mitchell RC 1.25 3.00
223 Mike Goodson AU/299 RC 5.00 12.00
224 Mike Thomas AU/299 RC 4.00 10.00
225 Mike Wallace AU/299 RC 15.00 30.00
226 Mohamed Massaquoi RC 1.25 3.00
227 Nate Davis AU/299 RC 12.50 25.00
228 Nathan Brown AU/999 RC 4.00 10.00
229 Pat White RC 1.50 4.00
230 Patrick Chung RC 1.25 3.00
231 Patrick Turner AU/399 RC 4.00 10.00
232 Percy Harvin RC 1.25 3.00
233 Peria Jerry RC 1.25 3.00
234 Quan Cosby AU/999 RC 3.00 8.00
235 Quinten Lawrence RC 1.25 3.00
236 Quinn Johnson AU/699 RC 3.00 8.00
237 Ramses Barden AU/299 RC 4.00 10.00
238 Rashad Jennings AU/499 RC 5.00 12.00
239 Rey Maualuga AU/299 RC 6.00 15.00
240 Rhett Bomar AU/299 RC 4.00 10.00
241 Richard Quinn RC 1.50 4.00
242 Shawn Nelson AU/499 RC 4.00 10.00
243 Shonn Greene RC 1.25 3.00
244 Stephen McGee AU/299 RC 4.00 10.00
245 Tom Brandstater AU/299 RC 5.00 12.00
246 Tony Fiammetta AU/699 RC 3.00 8.00
247 Travis Beckum AU/499 RC 4.00 10.00
248 Tyrell Sutton AU/999 RC 3.00 8.00
249 Tyson Jackson RC 1.25 3.00
250 Vontae Davis RC 1.25 3.00

2009 Donruss Classics Timeless Tributes Gold

*VETS 1-100: 5X TO 12X BASIC CARDS
*LEGENDS 101-150: 1X TO 2.5X BASIC CARDS
*ROOKIES 151-250: .5X TO 1.2X TT SILVER
STATED PRINT RUN 50 SER.#'d SETS

2009 Donruss Classics Timeless Tributes Platinum

*VETS 1-100: 8X TO 20X BASIC CARDS
*LEGENDS 101-150: 1.5X TO 4X BASIC CARDS
*ROOKIES 151-250: .8X TO 2X TT SILVER
STATED PRINT RUN 25 SER.#'d SETS

2009 Donruss Classics Timeless Tributes Silver

*VETS 1-100: 4X TO 10X BASIC CARDS
*LEGENDS 101-150: .8X TO 2X BASIC CARDS
STATED PRINT RUN 100 SER.#'d SETS
151 Aaron Curry 2.50 6.00
152 Aaron Kelly 1.50 4.00
153 Aaron Maybin 2.00 5.00
154 Alphonso Smith 1.50 4.00
155 Andre Brown 2.00 5.00
156 Andre Smith 1.50 4.00
157 Arian Foster 4.00 10.00
158 Austin Collie 1.50 4.00
159 B.J. Raji 2.00 5.00
160 Brandon Gibson 2.00 5.00
161 Brandon Pettigrew 1.50 4.00
162 Brandon Tate 2.00 5.00
163 Brian Cushing 1.50 4.00
164 Brian Hartline 2.50 6.00
165 Brian Orakpo 2.00 5.00
166 Brian Robiskie 1.50 4.00
167 Brooks Foster 1.50 4.00
168 Cameron Morrah 1.50 4.00
169 Cedric Peerman 1.50 4.00
170 Chase Coffman 1.50 4.00
171 Chris Wells 1.50 4.00
172 Clay Matthews 6.00 15.00
173 Clint Sintim 1.50 4.00
174 Cody Brown 1.50 4.00
175 Cornelius Ingram 1.50 4.00
176 Darcel McBath 1.50 4.00
177 Darius Butler 2.00 5.00
178 Darius Passmore 1.50 4.00
179 Darrius Heyward-Bey 2.50 6.00
180 Demetrius Byrd 2.00 5.00
181 Deon Butler 1.50 4.00
182 Derrick Williams 1.50 4.00
183 Devin Moore 1.50 4.00
184 Dominique Edison 1.50 4.00
185 Donald Brown 1.50 4.00
186 Eugene Monroe 1.50 4.00
187 Everette Brown 1.50 4.00
188 Gartrell Johnson 1.50 4.00
189 Glen Coffee 1.50 4.00
190 Graham Harrell 1.50 4.00
191 Hakeem Nicks 2.00 5.00
192 Hunter Cantwell 1.50 4.00
193 Ian Johnson 1.50 4.00
194 Jairus Byrd 2.50 6.00
195 James Casey 2.00 5.00
196 James Davis 1.50 4.00
197 James Laurinaitis 1.50 4.00
198 Jared Cook 2.00 5.00
199 Jarett Dillard 1.50 4.00
200 Jason Smith 1.50 4.00
201 Javon Ringer 1.50 4.00
202 Jeremiah Johnson 1.50 4.00
203 Jeremy Childs 1.50 4.00
204 Jeremy Maclin 2.00 5.00
205 John Parker Wilson 1.50 4.00
206 Johnny Knox 2.00 5.00
207 Josh Freeman 1.50 4.00
208 Juaquin Iglesias 1.50 4.00
209 Kenny Britt 2.50 6.00
210 Kenny McKinley 1.50 4.00
211 Kevin Ogletree 2.00 5.00
212 Knowshon Moreno 1.50 4.00
213 Kory Sheets 2.00 5.00
214 Larry English 2.00 5.00
215 LeSean McCoy 4.00 10.00
216 Louis Delmas 2.00 5.00
217 Louis Murphy 1.50 4.00
218 Malcolm Jenkins 1.50 4.00
219 Mark Sanchez 1.50 4.00
220 Matthew Stafford 8.00 20.00
221 Michael Crabtree 2.50 6.00
222 Michael Mitchell 1.50 4.00
223 Mike Goodson 2.00 5.00
224 Mike Thomas 1.50 4.00
225 Mike Wallace 2.50 6.00
226 Mohamed Massaquoi 1.50 4.00
227 Nate Davis 1.50 4.00
228 Nathan Brown 2.00 5.00
229 Pat White 2.00 5.00
230 Patrick Chung 1.50 4.00
231 Patrick Turner 1.50 4.00
232 Percy Harvin 1.50 4.00
233 Peria Jerry 1.50 4.00
234 Quan Cosby 1.50 4.00
235 Quinten Lawrence 1.50 4.00
236 Quinn Johnson 1.50 4.00
237 Ramses Barden 1.50 4.00
238 Rashad Jennings 2.00 5.00
239 Rey Maualuga 2.50 6.00
240 Rhett Bomar 1.50 4.00
241 Richard Quinn 2.00 5.00
242 Shawn Nelson 1.50 4.00
243 Shonn Greene 1.50 4.00
244 Stephen McGee 1.50 4.00
245 Tom Brandstater 2.00 5.00
246 Tony Fiammetta 1.50 4.00
247 Travis Beckum 1.50 4.00
248 Tyrell Sutton 1.50 4.00
249 Tyson Jackson 1.50 4.00
250 Vontae Davis 1.50 4.00

2009 Donruss Classics Classic Combos

*GOLD/100: .8X TO 2X BASIC INSERTS
GOLD PRINT RUN 100 SER.#'d SETS
*PLATINUM/25: 1.2X TO 3X BASIC INSERTS
PLATINUM PRINT RUN 25 SER.#'d SETS
*SILVER/250: .6X TO 1.5X BASIC INSERTS
SILVER PRINT RUN 250
1 A.Page/C.Eller .75 2.00
2 Y.Tittle/S.Young 1.50 4.00
3 J.Brown/L.Groza 1.50 4.00
4 D.Casper/T.Brown 1.25 3.00
5 J.Youngblood/M.Olsen .75 2.00
6 E.Smith/D.Johnston 2.00 5.00
7 E.Dickerson/D.Jackson 1.50 4.00
8 P.Simms/L.Taylor 1.25 3.00
9 J.Stallworth/F.Harris 1.25 3.00
10 C.Bednarik/R.White 1.25 3.00
11 J.Montana/R.Craig 4.00 10.00
12 T.Landry/T.Dorsett 1.50 4.00
13 A.Reed/T.Thomas 1.00 2.50
14 C.Harris/B.Lilly 1.00 2.50
15 W.Payton/W.Perry 2.00 5.00

2009 Donruss Classics Classic Combos Jerseys

STATED PRINT RUN 30-50
*PRIME/25: .8X TO 2X DUAL JSY/25
PRIME PRINT RUN 5-25
1 A.Page/C.Eller 5.00 12.00
2 Y.Tittle/S.Young 10.00 25.00
3 J.Brown/L.Groza 10.00 25.00
4 D.Casper/T.Brown 8.00 20.00
5 J.Youngblood/M.Olsen 5.00 12.00
6 E.Smith/Johnston/30 15.00 40.00
7 E.Dickerson/B.Jackson 10.00 25.00
8 P.Simms/L.Taylor 8.00 20.00
9 J.Stallworth/F.Harris 8.00 20.00
10 C.Bednarik/R.White 8.00 20.00
11 J.Montana/R.Craig 25.00 60.00
12 T.Landry/T.Dorsett 15.00 30.00
13 A.Reed/T.Thomas 6.00 15.00
14 C.Harris/B.Lilly 8.00 20.00

2009 Donruss Classics Classic Cuts

STATED PRINT RUN 1-100
4 Arnie Weinmeister/27 40.00 80.00
14 Bill Willis/18 40.00 80.00
27 Ace Parker/55 25.00 60.00
28 Clark Shaughnessy/62 25.00 60.00
31 Bulldog Turner/23 50.00 100.00
34 Dante Lavelli/21 30.00 80.00
35 Dick Night Train Lane/21 50.00 100.00
45 Ernie Stautner/77 20.00 50.00
47 Frank Gatski/28 50.00 100.00
49 Gene Upshaw/20 20.00 50.00
51 George Connor/34 25.00 60.00
53 George McAfee/16 40.00 80.00
54 George Musso/15 40.00 80.00
56 Glenn Davis/23 40.00 80.00
57 Hank Stram/66 20.00 50.00
64 Jim Ringo/21 30.00 80.00
78 Lamar Hunt/17 60.00 120.00
84 Lou Groza/25 30.00 80.00
91 Red Badgro/46 25.00 60.00
92 Otto Graham/23 50.00 100.00
97 Pete Pihos/25 40.00 80.00
100 Ray Flaherty/18 50.00 100.00
106 Roosevelt Brown/100 15.00 40.00
107 Sammy Baugh/28 60.00 120.00
108 Sid Gillman/32 40.00 80.00
111 Steve Van Buren/14 60.00 120.00
114 Tom Fears/26 30.00 80.00
115 Tony Canadeo/55 25.00 60.00
117 Walter Payton/25 150.00 300.00
119 Weeb Ewbank/53 30.00 80.00

2009 Donruss Classics Classic Quads

*GOLD/100: .8X TO 2X BASIC INSERTS
GOLD PRINT RUN 100 SER.#'d SETS
*PLATINUM/25: 1.2X TO 3X BASIC INSERTS
PLATINUM PRINT RUN 25 SER.#'d SETS
*SILVER HOLO/250: .6X TO 1.5X BASIC INSERTS
SILVER HOLOFOIL PRINT RUN 250
1 Reed/Irvin/Rice/Brown 2.50 6.00
2 Montna/Craig/Rice/Yng 4.00 10.00
3 Sndrs/Cmpbll/Emmt/Paytn 2.00 5.00
5 Lckmn/McMhn/Syrs/Pytn 2.00 5.00
6 Lndry/Stabch/Lilly/Harris 1.50 4.00
7 Emmt/Irvin/Jhnstn/Novack 2.00 5.00
9 Dickrsn/Bo/Caspr/Hndrks 1.50 4.00
10 Olsen/Page/Eller/Yngbld .75 2.00

2009 Donruss Classics Classic Singles

*GOLD/100: .8X TO 2X BASIC INSERTS
GOLD PRINT RUN 100 SER.#'d SETS
*PLATINUM/25: 1.2X TO 3X BASIC INSERTS
PLATINUM PRINT RUN 25 SER.#'d SETS
*SILVER HOL/250: .6X TO 1.5X BASIC INSERTS
SILVER HOLOFOIL PRINT RUN 250
1 Alan Page .60 1.50
2 Andre Reed .75 2.00
3 Barry Sanders 1.50 4.00
4 Bo Jackson 1.25 3.00
5 Bob Lilly .75 2.00
6 Carl Eller .60 1.50
7 Chuck Bednarik .75 2.00
8 Daryl Johnston .75 2.00
9 Dave Casper .60 1.50
10 Emmitt Smith 1.50 4.00
11 Eric Dickerson .75 2.00
12 Franco Harris 1.00 2.50
13 Jack Youngblood .60 1.50
14 Jim Brown 1.25 3.00
15 Joe Montana 3.00 8.00
16 John Stallworth .75 2.00
17 Lawrence Taylor 1.00 2.50
18 Lou Groza .75 2.00
19 Merlin Olsen .60 1.50
20 Phil Simms .75 2.00
21 Reggie White 1.00 2.50
22 Roger Craig .75 2.00
23 Steve Young 1.25 3.00
24 Thurman Thomas .75 2.00
25 Tim Brown 1.00 2.50
26 Tom Landry 1.25 3.00
27 Tony Dorsett 1.00 2.50
28 Walter Payton 1.50 4.00
29 William Perry .60 1.50
30 Y.A. Tittle 1.00 2.50

2009 Donruss Classics Classic Singles Jerseys

STATED PRINT RUN 42-250
*PRIME/32-50: .8X TO 2X BASIC JSY/250
*PRIME/15-25: 1X TO 2.5X BASIC JSY/250
PRIME PRINT RUN 2-50
1 Alan Page 2.50 6.00
2 Andre Reed 3.00 8.00
3 Barry Sanders 6.00 15.00
4 Bo Jackson 5.00 12.00
5 Bob Lilly 3.00 8.00
6 Carl Eller 2.50 6.00
7 Chuck Bednarik 3.00 8.00
9 Dave Casper 2.50 6.00
10 Emmitt Smith 6.00 15.00
11 Eric Dickerson 3.00 8.00
12 Franco Harris 4.00 10.00
13 Jack Youngblood 2.50 6.00
14 Jim Brown 5.00 12.00
15 Joe Montana 12.00 30.00
16 John Stallworth 3.00 8.00
17 Lawrence Taylor 4.00 10.00
18 Lou Groza 3.00 8.00
19 Merlin Olsen 2.50 6.00
20 Phil Simms 3.00 8.00
21 Reggie White 8.00 20.00
22 Roger Craig 3.00 8.00
23 Steve Young 5.00 12.00
24 Thurman Thomas 3.00 8.00
25 Tim Brown 4.00 10.00
26 Tom Landry Jkt 15.00 30.00
27 Tony Dorsett 4.00 10.00
28 Walter Payton 6.00 15.00
30 Y.A. Tittle/42 6.00 15.00

2009 Donruss Classics Classic Singles Jerseys Autographs

STATED PRINT RUN 25 SER.#'d SETS
*PRIME/25: .5X TO 1.2X BASIC JSY AU/25
PRIME PRINT RUN 1-25
1 Alan Page 12.00 30.00
2 Andre Reed 15.00 40.00
3 Barry Sanders 75.00 135.00
4 Bo Jackson 50.00 100.00
5 Bob Lilly 15.00 40.00
6 Carl Eller 12.00 30.00
7 Chuck Bednarik 15.00 40.00
9 Dave Casper 15.00 40.00
10 Emmitt Smith 100.00 200.00
11 Eric Dickerson 25.00 50.00
12 Franco Harris 25.00 50.00
13 Jack Youngblood 15.00 40.00
14 Jim Brown 40.00 80.00
15 Joe Montana 75.00 150.00
16 John Stallworth 25.00 50.00
17 Lawrence Taylor 40.00 80.00
19 Merlin Olsen 20.00 50.00
20 Phil Simms 15.00 40.00
22 Roger Craig 15.00 40.00
23 Steve Young 40.00 80.00
24 Thurman Thomas 25.00 50.00
25 Tim Brown 20.00 50.00
27 Tony Dorsett 25.00 50.00
30 Y.A. Tittle 30.00 60.00

2009 Donruss Classics Classic Triples

*GOLD/100: .8X TO 2X BASIC INSERTS
GOLD PRINT RUN 100 SER.#'d SETS
*PLATINUM/25: 1.5X TO 4X BASIC INSERTS
PLATINUM PRINT RUN 25 SER.#'d SETS
*SILVER/250: .6X TO 1.5X BASIC INSERTS
SILVER PRINT RUN 250
1 Staubch/White/Aikmn 1.25 3.00
2 Kelly/Reed/Thomas 1.00 2.50
3 Greene/R.White/Yngbld 1.00 2.50
4 Smith/Irvin/Novacek 1.50 4.00
5 Montana/Rice/Craig 3.00 8.00
7 Brown/Groza/Motley 1.25 3.00
8 Luckman/Sayers/Payton 1.50 4.00
9 Layne/Sims/Sanders 1.50 4.00
10 Tittle/Montana/Young 3.00 8.00

2009 Donruss Classics Classic Triples Jerseys

STATED PRINT RUN 25 SER.#'d SETS
1 Staubch/White/Aikmn 15.00 40.00
2 Kelly/Reed/Thomas 12.00 30.00
3 Greene/R.White/Yngbld 12.00 30.00
4 Smith/Irvin/Novacek 25.00 60.00
5 Montana/Rice/Craig 40.00 100.00
7 Brown/Groza/Motley 15.00 40.00
8 Luckman/Sayers/Payton 20.00 50.00
9 Layne/Sims/Sanders 20.00 50.00
10 Tittle/Montana/Young 40.00 100.00

2009 Donruss Classics Dress Code

*GOLD/100: .8X TO 2X BASIC INSERTS
GOLD PRINT RUN 100 SER.#'d SETS
*PLATINUM/25: 1.5X TO 4X BASIC INSERTS
PLATINUM PRINT RUN 25 SER.#'d SETS
*SILVER/250: .6X TO 1.5X BASIC INSERTS
SILVER PRINT RUN 250
1 Antonio Gates .75 2.00
2 Ben Roethlisberger 1.00 2.50
3 Cadillac Williams .75 2.00
4 Chad Ochocinco .60 1.50
5 Deuce McAllister .75 2.00
6 Frank Gore .75 2.00
7 Jason Witten .75 2.00
8 Jerricho Cotchery .60 1.50
9 Joseph Addai .60 1.50
10 Justin McCareins .60 1.50
11 Kevin Curtis .60 1.50
12 Ladell Betts .60 1.50
13 Larry Johnson .60 1.50
14 Lee Evans .75 2.00
15 Marion Barber .75 2.00
16 Marques Colston .60 1.50
17 Matt Hasselbeck .60 1.50
18 Maurice Jones-Drew .60 1.50
19 Reggie Wayne .75 2.00
20 Steven Jackson .60 1.50
21 Tarvaris Jackson .75 2.00
22 T.J. Houshmandzadeh .60 1.50
23 Tony Gonzalez .75 2.00
24 Tony Romo .75 2.00
25 Vincent Jackson .60 1.50

2009 Donruss Classics Dress Code Jerseys

STATED PRINT RUN 15-299
*PRIME/50: .6X TO 1.5X BASE JSY/290-299
*PRIME/50: .8X TO 2X BASE JSY/80-108
*PRIME/50: 1X TO 2.5X BASE JSY/15
*PRIME/18-25: 1X TO 2.5X BASE JSY/290-299
PRIME PRINT RUN 18-50
1 Antonio Gates/299 3.00 8.00
2 Ben Roethlisberger/299 4.00 10.00
3 Cadillac Williams/299 3.00 8.00
4 Chad Ochocinco/299 2.50 6.00
5 Deuce McAllister/80 4.00 10.00
6 Frank Gore/299 3.00 8.00
7 Jason Witten/299 3.00 8.00
8 Jerricho Cotchery/299 2.50 6.00
9 Joseph Addai/299 2.50 6.00
10 Justin McCareins/299 2.50 6.00
11 Kevin Curtis/299 2.50 6.00
12 Ladell Betts/108 3.00 8.00
13 Larry Johnson/299 2.50 6.00
14 Lee Evans/299 3.00 8.00
15 Marion Barber/299 3.00 8.00
16 Marques Colston/299 2.50 6.00
17 Matt Hasselbeck/299 2.50 6.00
18 Maurice Jones-Drew/299 2.50 6.00
19 Reggie Wayne/299 3.00 8.00
20 Steven Jackson/299 2.50 6.00
21 Tarvaris Jackson/299 3.00 8.00
22 T.J. Houshmandzadeh/15 4.00 10.00
23 Tony Gonzalez/299 3.00 8.00
24 Tony Romo/299 3.00 8.00
25 Vincent Jackson/299 2.50 6.00

2009 Donruss Classics Dress Code Jerseys Autographs

STATED PRINT RUN 5-25
SERIAL #'d UNDER 15 NOT PRICED
5 Deuce McAllister/25 12.00 30.00
22 T.J. Houshmandzadeh/15 12.00 30.00

2009 Donruss Classics Dress Code Jerseys Prime Autographs

STATED PRINT RUN 5-25
5 Deuce McAllister/25 15.00 40.00
11 Kevin Curtis/25 15.00 40.00
13 Larry Johnson/25 15.00 40.00
16 Marques Colston/25 15.00 40.00
21 Tarvaris Jackson/25 15.00 40.00
25 Vincent Jackson/25 15.00 40.00

2009 Donruss Classics Membership

*GOLD/100: .8X TO 2X BASIC INSERTS
GOLD PRINT RUN 100 SER.#'d SETS
*PLATINUM/25: 1.2X TO 3X BASIC INSERTS
PLATINUM PRINT RUN 25 SER.#'d SETS
*SILVER/250: .6X TO 1.5X BASIC INSERTS
SILVER PRINT RUN 250
1 Aaron Rodgers 2.00 5.00
2 Chris Cooley .60 1.50

3 Chris Johnson .60 1.50
4 David Garrard .60 1.50
5 Derrick Ward .60 1.50
6 DeSean Jackson .75 2.00
7 Devin Hester .75 2.00
8 Dwayne Bowe .75 2.00
9 Earnest Graham .60 1.50
10 Eddie Royal .60 1.50
11 Heath Miller .60 1.50
12 Jason Campbell .60 1.50
13 Joe Flacco .75 2.00
14 Jonathan Stewart .60 1.50
15 Justin Fargas .60 1.50
16 Kellen Winslow Jr. .60 1.50
17 Leon Washington .60 1.50
18 Matt Forte .60 1.50
19 Matt Ryan .75 2.00
20 Michael Turner .60 1.50
21 Roddy White .60 1.50
22 Selvin Young .60 1.50
23 Kyle Orton .60 1.50
24 Trent Edwards .60 1.50
25 Vernon Davis .60 1.50

2009 Donruss Classics Membership VIP Jerseys

STATED PRINT RUN 285-299
*PRIME/30-50: .6X TO 1.5X BASIC JSY/285-299
*PRIME/25: 1X TO 2.5X BASIC JSY/299
PRIME PRINT RUN 25-50
1 Aaron Rodgers 8.00 20.00
2 Chris Cooley 2.50 6.00
4 David Garrard 2.50 6.00
7 Devin Hester 3.00 8.00
8 Dwayne Bowe 3.00 8.00
12 Jason Campbell 2.50 6.00
13 Joe Flacco 3.00 8.00
14 Jonathan Stewart 2.50 6.00
15 Justin Fargas 2.50 6.00
17 Leon Washington 2.50 6.00
19 Matt Ryan 3.00 8.00
20 Michael Turner 2.50 6.00
21 Roddy White 2.50 6.00
22 Selvin Young 2.50 6.00
24 Trent Edwards 2.50 6.00
25 Vernon Davis 2.50 6.00

2009 Donruss Classics Monday Night Heroes

*GOLD/100: .8X TO 2X BASIC INSERTS
GOLD PRINT RUN 100 SER.#'d SETS
*PLATINUM/25: 1.2X TO 3X BASIC INSERTS
PLATINUM PRINT RUN 25 SER.#'d SETS
*SILVER/250: .6X TO 1.5X BASIC INSERTS
SILVER PRINT RUN 250 SER.#'d SETS
1 Adrian Peterson 1.50 4.00
2 Jay Cutler 1.00 2.50
3 Tony Romo 1.25 3.00
4 Brian Westbrook 1.00 2.50
5 Brett Favre 3.00 8.00
6 Philip Rivers 1.50 4.00
7 Derrick Mason 1.00 2.50
8 Santonio Holmes 1.00 2.50
9 Drew Brees 1.50 4.00
10 Bernard Berrian 1.00 2.50
11 Derrick Ward 1.00 2.50
12 Braylon Edwards 1.00 2.50
13 Randy Moss 1.25 3.00
14 Wes Welker 1.25 3.00
15 Dallas Clark 1.00 2.50
16 LenDale White 1.00 2.50
17 Willie Parker 1.00 2.50
18 Clinton Portis 1.00 2.50
19 Kurt Warner 1.25 3.00
20 Anquan Boldin 1.00 2.50
21 Marshawn Lynch 1.25 3.00
22 Greg Jennings 1.00 2.50
23 Steve Slaton 1.00 2.50
24 Andre Johnson 1.25 3.00
25 DeAngelo Williams 1.00 2.50
26 Jonathan Stewart 1.00 2.50
27 Steve Smith 1.25 3.00
28 Donovan McNabb 1.25 3.00
29 Aaron Rodgers 3.00 8.00
30 Matt Forte 1.00 2.50

2009 Donruss Classics Monday Night Heroes Jerseys

JERSEY PRINT RUN 175-299
*PRIME/50: .6X TO 1.5X BASIC JSY/175-299
*PRIME/19-25: 1X TO 2.5X BASIC JSY/175-299
PRIME STATED PRINT RUN 19-50
1 Adrian Peterson/299 4.00 10.00
2 Jay Cutler/299 2.50 6.00
3 Tony Romo/299 3.00 8.00
4 Brian Westbrook/299 2.50 6.00
5 Brett Favre/250 8.00 20.00
6 Philip Rivers/299 4.00 10.00
7 Derrick Mason/299 2.50 6.00
8 Santonio Holmes/299 2.50 6.00
9 Drew Brees/299 4.00 10.00
10 Bernard Berrian/299 2.50 6.00
11 Derrick Ward/175 2.50 6.00
12 Braylon Edwards/299 2.50 6.00
13 Randy Moss/299 3.00 8.00
14 Wes Welker/299 3.00 8.00
15 Dallas Clark/299 2.50 6.00
16 LenDale White/299 2.50 6.00
17 Willie Parker/299 2.50 6.00
18 Clinton Portis/299 2.50 6.00
20 Anquan Boldin/294 2.50 6.00
21 Marshawn Lynch/299 3.00 8.00
22 Greg Jennings/299 2.50 6.00
23 Steve Slaton/299 2.50 6.00
24 Andre Johnson/299 3.00 8.00
25 DeAngelo Williams/299 2.50 6.00
26 Jonathan Stewart/299 2.50 6.00
27 Steve Smith/299 3.00 8.00
28 Donovan McNabb/299 3.00 8.00
29 Aaron Rodgers/299 8.00 20.00

2009 Donruss Classics Saturday Stars

*GOLD/100: .8X TO 2X BASIC INSERTS
GOLD PRINT RUN 100 SER.#'d SETS
*PLATINUM/25: 1.2X TO 3X BASIC INSRTS
PLATINUM PRINT RUN 25 SER.#'d SETS
*SILVER/250: .6X TO 1.5X BASIC INSERTS
SILVER PRINT RUN 250 SER.#'d SETS
1 Andre Smith .60 1.50
2 Nate Davis .60 1.50
3 Brandon Pettigrew .60 1.50
4 Brian Cushing .60 1.50
5 Brian Orakpo .75 2.00
6 Brian Robiskie .60 1.50
7 Chase Coffman .60 1.50
8 Chris Wells .60 1.50
9 Clint Sintim .60 1.50
10 Derrick Williams .60 1.50
11 Donald Brown .60 1.50
12 Graham Harrell .60 1.50
13 Hakeem Nicks .75 2.00
14 James Laurinaitis .60 1.50
15 Javon Ringer .60 1.50
16 Jeremiah Johnson .60 1.50
17 Jeremy Maclin .75 2.00
18 Juaquin Iglesias .60 1.50
19 Knowshon Moreno .60 1.50
20 LeSean McCoy 1.50 4.00
21 Louis Murphy .60 1.50
22 Malcolm Jenkins .60 1.50
23 Mark Sanchez .60 1.50
24 Matthew Stafford 3.00 8.00
25 Michael Crabtree 1.00 2.50
26 Pat White .75 2.00
27 Percy Harvin .60 1.50
28 Quan Cosby .60 1.50
29 Rey Maualuga 1.00 2.50
30 Shonn Greene .60 1.50

2009 Donruss Classics Saturday Stars Autographs

STATED PRINT RUN 25-100
2 Nate Davis/50 5.00 12.00
4 Brian Cushing/50 5.00 12.00
5 Brian Orakpo/50 6.00 15.00
6 Brian Robiskie/50 5.00 12.00
7 Chase Coffman/50 5.00 12.00
8 Chris Wells/50 5.00 12.00
9 Clint Sintim/100 5.00 12.00
10 Derrick Williams/50 5.00 12.00
11 Donald Brown/25 5.00 12.00
12 Graham Harrell/100 12.00 30.00
13 Hakeem Nicks/50 6.00 15.00
14 James Laurinaitis/50 5.00 12.00
16 Jeremiah Johnson/100 5.00 12.00
17 Jeremy Maclin/50 6.00 15.00
18 Juaquin Iglesias/50 5.00 12.00
19 Knowshon Moreno/50 5.00 12.00
20 LeSean McCoy/25 12.00 30.00
22 Malcolm Jenkins/100 5.00 12.00
23 Mark Sanchez/25 5.00 12.00
24 Matthew Stafford/25 40.00 100.00
25 Michael Crabtree/50 8.00 20.00
26 Pat White/50 6.00 15.00
27 Percy Harvin/50 5.00 12.00
28 Quan Cosby/100 5.00 12.00
29 Rey Maualuga/50 8.00 20.00
30 Shonn Greene/50 5.00 12.00

2009 Donruss Classics Saturday Stars Jerseys

JERSEY PRINT RUN 50-299
*PRIME/50: .8X TO 2X BASIC JSY/150-299
*PRIME/50: .5X TO 1.2X BASIC JSY/50
*PRIME/25: .8X TO 2X BASIC JSY/150-299
PRIME PRINT RUN 25-50
4 Brian Cushing/299 2.00 5.00
5 Brian Orakpo/50 3.00 8.00
10 Derrick Williams/200 2.00 5.00
11 Donald Brown/150 2.00 5.00
12 Graham Harrell/299 2.00 5.00
14 James Laurinaitis/299 2.00 5.00
16 Jeremiah Johnson/299 2.00 5.00
18 Juaquin Iglesias/299 2.00 5.00
20 LeSean McCoy/299 5.00 12.00
23 Mark Sanchez/299 2.00 5.00
24 Matthew Stafford/150 8.00 20.00
28 Quan Cosby/299 2.00 5.00
29 Rey Maualuga/299 3.00 8.00

2009 Donruss Classics Saturday Stars Jerseys Autographs

JSY AU PRINT RUN 25 SER.#'d SETS
4 Brian Cushing 6.00 15.00
5 Brian Orakpo 8.00 20.00
10 Derrick Williams 6.00 15.00
11 Donald Brown 6.00 15.00
12 Graham Harrell 15.00 40.00
14 James Laurinaitis 6.00 15.00
16 Jeremiah Johnson 6.00 15.00
18 Juaquin Iglesias 6.00 15.00
20 LeSean McCoy 15.00 40.00
23 Mark Sanchez 6.00 15.00
24 Matthew Stafford 50.00 120.00
28 Quan Cosby 6.00 15.00
29 Rey Maualuga 20.00 50.00

2009 Donruss Classics School Colors

1 Aaron Curry 1.25 3.00
2 Aaron Maybin 1.00 2.50
3 B.J. Raji 1.00 2.50
4 Mohamed Massaquoi .75 2.00
5 Brandon Pettigrew .75 2.00
6 Brian Cushing .75 2.00
7 Brian Orakpo 1.00 2.50
8 Brian Robiskie .75 2.00
9 Chase Coffman .75 2.00
10 Chris Wells .75 2.00
11 Clint Sintim .75 2.00
12 Darrius Heyward-Bey 1.25 3.00
13 Derrick Williams .75 2.00
14 Donald Brown .75 2.00
15 Hakeem Nicks 1.00 2.50
16 James Casey 1.00 2.50
17 James Laurinaitis .75 2.00
18 Javon Ringer .75 2.00
19 Jeremiah Johnson .75 2.00
20 Jeremy Maclin 1.00 2.50
21 Josh Freeman .75 2.00
22 Juaquin Iglesias .75 2.00
23 Kenny Britt 1.25 3.00
24 Knowshon Moreno .75 2.00
25 Larry English 1.00 2.50
26 LeSean McCoy 2.00 5.00
27 Malcolm Jenkins .75 2.00
28 Mark Sanchez .75 2.00
29 Matthew Stafford 4.00 10.00
30 Michael Crabtree 1.25 3.00
31 Nate Davis .75 2.00
32 Pat White 1.00 2.50
33 Percy Harvin .75 2.00
34 Rashad Jennings 1.00 2.50
35 Rey Maualuga 1.25 3.00
36 Shonn Greene .75 2.00

2009 Donruss Classics School Colors Autographs

1 Aaron Curry 10.00 25.00
5 Brandon Pettigrew 6.00 15.00
8 Brian Robiskie 6.00 15.00
10 Chris Wells 6.00 15.00
12 Darrius Heyward-Bey 10.00 25.00
13 Derrick Williams 6.00 15.00
14 Donald Brown 6.00 15.00
15 Hakeem Nicks 8.00 20.00
16 James Casey 8.00 20.00
18 Javon Ringer 6.00 15.00
20 Jeremy Maclin 8.00 20.00
21 Josh Freeman 6.00 15.00
22 Juaquin Iglesias 6.00 15.00
23 Kenny Britt 10.00 25.00
24 Knowshon Moreno 6.00 15.00
26 LeSean McCoy 15.00 40.00
28 Mark Sanchez 6.00 15.00
29 Matthew Stafford 40.00 100.00
30 Michael Crabtree 10.00 25.00
31 Nate Davis 6.00 15.00
32 Pat White 8.00 20.00
33 Percy Harvin 6.00 15.00
36 Shonn Greene 6.00 15.00

2009 Donruss Classics Significant Signatures Gold

32-90 VET PRINT RUN 10-20
*GOLD LEGEND/50-126: .3X TO .8X PLAT.AU/25
101-50 LEGEND PRINT RUN 26-126
*GOLD ROOKIE/250: .2X TO .5X PLAT.AU/25
151-250 ROOKIE PRINT RUN 150-250
32 Eddie Royal/20 10.00 25.00
35 Kevin Smith/20 10.00 25.00
42 Anthony Gonzalez/20 10.00 25.00
90 Donnie Avery/20 10.00 25.00
101 Alan Page/91 8.00 20.00
102 Andre Reed/75 10.00 25.00
103 Barry Sanders/26 60.00 120.00
104 Billy Sims/76 10.00 25.00
106 Bob Lilly/76 10.00 25.00
108 Carl Eller/95 8.00 20.00
109 Chuck Bednarik/101 10.00 25.00
110 Ace Parker/51 20.00 40.00
111 Cliff Harris/76 10.00 25.00
112 Danny White/51 12.00 30.00
113 Daryl Johnston/126 20.00 50.00
114 Dave Casper/101 8.00 20.00
115 Earl Campbell/51 12.00 30.00
116 Emmitt Smith/26 75.00 150.00
117 Eric Dickerson/51 12.00 30.00
118 Franco Harris/51 25.00 50.00
119 Gale Sayers/51 25.00 50.00
121 Jack Youngblood/76 10.00 25.00
122 Jay Novacek/126 15.00 40.00
123 Jerry Rice/26 75.00 150.00
124 Jim Brown/50 30.00 60.00
125 Jim Kelly/51 30.00 60.00
126 Jim McMahon/51 12.00 30.00
127 Joe Greene/51 25.00 50.00
128 Joe Montana/26 60.00 120.00
129 John Stallworth/51 15.00 40.00
130 Lawrence Taylor/50 20.00 40.00
133 Merlin Olsen/76 15.00 40.00
134 Michael Irvin/26 25.00 50.00
135 Mike Singletary/51 20.00 40.00
136 Phil Simms/51 15.00 30.00
138 Roger Craig/101 10.00 25.00
139 Roger Staubach/26 40.00 80.00
141 Steve Young/51 25.00 50.00
142 Ted Hendricks/51 8.00 20.00
143 Thurman Thomas/51 15.00 40.00
144 Tim Brown/66 20.00 40.00
146 Tony Dorsett/32 25.00 50.00
147 Troy Aikman/26 40.00 80.00
149 William Perry/126 8.00 20.00
150 Y.A. Tittle/59 12.00 30.00
151 Aaron Curry/250 6.00 15.00
159 B.J. Raji/250 5.00 12.00
163 Brian Cushing/250 4.00 10.00
165 Brian Orakpo/250 5.00 12.00
166 Brian Robiskie/250 4.00 10.00
171 Chris Wells/150 4.00 10.00
172 Clay Matthews/250 25.00 50.00
179 Darrius Heyward-Bey/250 6.00 15.00
185 Donald Brown/250 4.00 10.00
187 Everette Brown/250 4.00 10.00
191 Hakeem Nicks/250 5.00 12.00
197 James Laurinaitis/250 8.00 20.00
200 Jason Smith/250 4.00 10.00
204 Jeremy Maclin/250 5.00 12.00
207 Josh Freeman/250 4.00 10.00
212 Knowshon Moreno/150 4.00 10.00
214 Larry English/250 5.00 12.00
215 LeSean McCoy/250 10.00 25.00
218 Malcolm Jenkins/250 4.00 10.00
219 Mark Sanchez/250 4.00 10.00
220 Matthew Stafford/150 30.00 80.00
221 Michael Crabtree/250 6.00 15.00
226 Mohamed Massaquoi/250 8.00 20.00
229 Pat White/250 5.00 12.00
232 Percy Harvin/250 4.00 10.00
249 Tyson Jackson/250 4.00 10.00
250 Vontae Davis/250 4.00 10.00

2009 Donruss Classics Significant Signatures Platinum

101-150 LEGEND PRINT RUN 15-25
151-250 ROOKIE PRINT RUN 25
101 Alan Page/25 10.00 25.00
102 Andre Reed/25 12.00 30.00
103 Barry Sanders/15 75.00 150.00
104 Billy Sims/25 12.00 30.00
106 Bob Lilly/25 12.00 30.00
108 Carl Eller/25 10.00 25.00
109 Chuck Bednarik/25 12.00 30.00
110 Ace Parker/25 25.00 50.00
111 Cliff Harris/25 12.00 30.00
112 Danny White/25 15.00 40.00
113 Daryl Johnston/25 30.00 60.00
114 Dave Casper/25 10.00 25.00
115 Earl Campbell/25 15.00 40.00
116 Emmitt Smith/15 100.00 175.00
117 Eric Dickerson/25 15.00 40.00
118 Franco Harris/25 25.00 60.00
119 Gale Sayers/25 25.00 60.00
121 Jack Youngblood/25 12.00 30.00
122 Jay Novacek/25 20.00 50.00
123 Jerry Rice/15 90.00 150.00
124 Jim Brown/15 40.00 80.00
125 Jim Kelly/25 30.00 80.00
126 Jim McMahon/25 20.00 40.00
127 Joe Greene/25 25.00 60.00
128 Joe Montana/15 50.00 10.00
129 John Stallworth/25 20.00 50.00
130 Lawrence Taylor/15 25.00 50.00
133 Merlin Olsen/25 20.00 50.00
134 Michael Irvin/15 30.00 60.00
135 Mike Singletary/25 20.00 50.00
136 Phil Simms/25 15.00 40.00
138 Roger Craig/25 12.00 30.00
139 Roger Staubach/15 50.00 100.00
141 Steve Young/25 30.00 60.00
142 Ted Hendricks/25 10.00 25.00
143 Thurman Thomas/25 20.00 50.00
144 Tim Brown/25 20.00 50.00
146 Tony Dorsett/15 30.00 60.00
147 Troy Aikman/15 50.00 100.00
149 William Perry/25 10.00 25.00
150 Y.A. Tittle/25 15.00 40.00
151 Aaron Curry/25 12.00 30.00
152 Aaron Kelly/25 8.00 20.00
155 Andre Brown/25 10.00 25.00
158 Austin Collie/25 8.00 20.00
159 B.J. Raji/25 10.00 25.00
160 Brandon Gibson/25 10.00 25.00
162 Brandon Tate/25 10.00 25.00
163 Brian Cushing/25 8.00 20.00
165 Brian Orakpo/25 10.00 25.00
166 Brian Robiskie/25 8.00 20.00
167 Brooks Foster/25 8.00 20.00
169 Cedric Peerman/25 8.00 20.00
170 Chase Coffman/25 8.00 20.00
171 Chris Wells/25 8.00 20.00
172 Clay Matthews/25 40.00 80.00
173 Clint Sintim/25 8.00 20.00
175 Cornelius Ingram/25 8.00 20.00
178 Darius Passmore/25 8.00 20.00
179 Darrius Heyward-Bey/25 12.00 30.00
181 Deon Butler/25 8.00 20.00
182 Derrick Williams/25 8.00 20.00
183 Devin Moore/25 8.00 20.00
184 Dominique Edison/25 8.00 20.00
185 Donald Brown/25 8.00 20.00
187 Everette Brown/25 8.00 20.00
189 Glen Coffee/25 8.00 20.00
190 Graham Harrell/25 20.00 59.00
191 Hakeem Nicks/25 10.00 25.00
192 Hunter Cantwell/25 EXCH 8.00 20.00
195 James Casey/25 10.00 25.00
197 James Laurinaitis/25 15.00 40.00
198 Jared Cook/25 10.00 25.00
199 Jarett Dillard/25 8.00 20.00
200 Jason Smith/25 8.00 20.00
202 Jeremiah Johnson/25 8.00 20.00
204 Jeremy Maclin/25 10.00 25.00
205 John Parker Wilson/25 8.00 20.00
206 Johnny Knox/25 10.00 25.00
207 Josh Freeman/25 8.00 20.00
208 Juaquin Iglesias/25 8.00 20.00
210 Kenny McKinley/25 8.00 20.00
211 Kevin Ogletree/25 10.00 25.00
212 Knowshon Moreno/25 8.00 20.00
213 Kory Sheets/25 10.00 25.00
214 Larry English/25 10.00 25.00
215 LeSean McCoy/25 20.00 50.00
218 Malcolm Jenkins/25 8.00 20.00
219 Mark Sanchez/25 8.00 20.00
220 Matthew Stafford/25 60.00 150.00
221 Michael Crabtree/25 12.00 30.00
223 Mike Goodson/25 10.00 25.00
224 Mike Thomas/25 8.00 20.00
225 Mike Wallace/25 12.00 30.00
226 Mohamed Massaquoi/25 8.00 20.00
227 Nate Davis/25 8.00 20.00
228 Nathan Brown/25 10.00 25.00
229 Pat White/25 10.00 25.00
231 Patrick Turner/25 8.00 20.00
232 Percy Harvin/25 8.00 20.00
234 Quan Cosby/25 8.00 20.00
236 Quinn Johnson/25 8.00 20.00
237 Ramses Barden/25 8.00 20.00
238 Rashad Jennings/25 10.00 25.00
239 Rey Maualuga/25 12.00 30.00
240 Rhett Bomar/25 8.00 20.00
242 Shawn Nelson/25 8.00 20.00
243 Shonn Greene/25 8.00 20.00
244 Stephen McGee/25 8.00 20.00
245 Tom Brandstater/25 10.00 25.00
246 Tony Fiammetta/25 8.00 20.00
247 Travis Beckum/25 8.00 20.00
248 Tyrell Sutton/25 8.00 20.00
249 Tyson Jackson/25 8.00 20.00
250 Vontae Davis/25 8.00 20.00

2009 Donruss Classics Sunday's Best

*GOLD/100: .8X TO 2X BASIC INSERTS
GOLD PRINT RUN 100 SER.#'d SETS
*PLATINUM/25: 1.5X TO 4X BASIC INSERTS
PLATINUM PRINT RUN 25 SER.#'d SETS
*SILVER/250: .6X TO 1.5X BASIC INSERTS
SILVER PRINT RUN 250 SER.#'d SETS
1 Aaron Rodgers 3.00 8.00
2 Adrian Peterson 1.50 4.00
3 Andre Johnson 1.25 3.00
4 Anquan Boldin 1.00 2.50
5 Anthony Gonzalez 1.00 2.50
6 Ben Roethlisberger 1.50 4.00
7 Brandon Jacobs 1.00 2.50
8 Brandon Marshall 1.25 3.00
9 Braylon Edwards 1.00 2.50
10 Brian Westbrook 1.00 2.50
11 Calvin Johnson 1.50 4.00
12 Clinton Portis 1.00 2.50
13 Dallas Clark 1.00 2.50
14 DeAngelo Williams 1.00 2.50
15 Donald Driver 1.25 3.00
16 Drew Brees 1.50 4.00
17 Eli Manning 1.25 3.00
18 Greg Jennings 1.00 2.50
19 Hines Ward 1.25 3.00
20 Jake Delhomme 1.00 2.50
21 Jay Cutler 1.00 2.50
22 Joseph Addai 1.00 2.50
23 Kurt Warner 1.25 3.00
24 Larry Fitzgerald 1.25 3.00
25 Lee Evans 1.25 3.00
26 LenDale White 1.00 2.50
27 Marshawn Lynch 1.25 3.00
28 Marvin Harrison 1.25 3.00
29 Matt Schaub 1.00 2.50
30 Maurice Jones-Drew 1.00 2.50
31 Peyton Manning 4.00 10.00
32 Philip Rivers 1.50 4.00
33 Reggie Wayne 1.25 3.00
34 Ronnie Brown 1.00 2.50
35 Ryan Grant 1.25 3.00
36 Santonio Holmes 1.00 2.50
37 Terrell Owens 1.25 3.00
38 Torry Holt 1.25 3.00
39 Vincent Jackson 1.00 2.50
40 Willie Parker 1.00 2.50

2009 Donruss Classics Sunday's Best Jerseys

JERSEY PRINT RUN 288-299
*PRIME/50: .6X TO 1.5X BASIC JSY/288-299
*PRIME/20-25: 1X TO 2.5X BASIC JSY/288-299
PRIME JERSEY PRINT RUN 20-50
1 Aaron Rodgers 8.00 20.00
2 Adrian Peterson 4.00 10.00
3 Andre Johnson 3.00 8.00
4 Anquan Boldin 2.50 6.00
5 Anthony Gonzalez 2.50 6.00
6 Ben Roethlisberger 4.00 10.00
7 Brandon Jacobs 2.50 6.00
8 Brandon Marshall 3.00 8.00
9 Braylon Edwards 2.50 6.00
10 Brian Westbrook 2.50 6.00
11 Calvin Johnson 4.00 10.00
12 Clinton Portis 2.50 6.00
13 Dallas Clark 2.50 6.00
14 DeAngelo Williams 2.50 6.00
15 Donald Driver 3.00 8.00
16 Drew Brees 4.00 10.00
17 Eli Manning 3.00 8.00
18 Greg Jennings 2.50 6.00
19 Hines Ward 3.00 8.00
20 Jake Delhomme 2.50 6.00
21 Jay Cutler 2.50 6.00
22 Joseph Addai 2.50 6.00
24 Larry Fitzgerald 3.00 8.00
25 Lee Evans 3.00 8.00
26 LenDale White 2.50 6.00
27 Marshawn Lynch 3.00 8.00
29 Matt Schaub 2.50 6.00
30 Maurice Jones-Drew 2.50 6.00
31 Peyton Manning 10.00 25.00
32 Philip Rivers 4.00 10.00
33 Reggie Wayne/288 3.00 8.00
34 Ronnie Brown 2.50 6.00
35 Ryan Grant 3.00 8.00
36 Santonio Holmes 2.50 6.00
37 Terrell Owens 3.00 8.00
38 Torry Holt 3.00 8.00
39 Vincent Jackson 2.50 6.00
40 Willie Parker 2.50 6.00

2009 Donruss Classics Sunday's Best Jerseys Autographs

JERSEY AUTO PRINT RUN 5-25
5 Anthony Gonzalez/25

2009 Donruss Classics Team Colors

RANDOM INSERTS IN RETAIL PACKS
1 Aaron Curry 1.50 4.00
2 Andre Brown 1.25 3.00
3 Brandon Pettigrew 1.00 2.50
4 Tyson Jackson 1.00 2.50
5 Brian Robiskie 1.00 2.50
6 Chris Wells 1.00 2.50
7 Darrius Heyward-Bey 1.50 4.00
8 Deon Butler 1.00 2.50
9 Derrick Williams 1.00 2.50
10 Donald Brown 1.00 2.50
11 Glen Coffee 1.00 2.50
12 Hakeem Nicks 1.25 3.00
13 Jason Smith 1.00 2.50
14 Javon Ringer 1.00 2.50
15 Jeremy Maclin 1.25 3.00
16 Josh Freeman 1.00 2.50
17 Juaquin Iglesias 1.00 2.50
18 Kenny Britt 1.50 4.00
19 Knowshon Moreno 1.00 2.50
20 LeSean McCoy 2.50 6.00
21 Mark Sanchez 1.00 2.50
22 Matthew Stafford 5.00 12.00
23 Michael Crabtree 1.50 4.00
24 Mike Thomas 1.00 2.50
25 Mike Wallace 1.50 4.00
26 Mohamed Massaquoi 1.00 2.50
27 Nate Davis 1.00 2.50
28 Pat White 1.25 3.00
29 Patrick Turner 1.00 2.50
30 Percy Harvin 1.00 2.50
31 Ramses Barden 1.00 2.50
32 Rhett Bomar 1.00 2.50
33 Shonn Greene 1.00 2.50
34 Stephen McGee 1.00 2.50

2016 Donruss NFL Draft

1 Carson Wentz 3.00 8.00
2 Jared Goff 2.00 5.00
3 Joey Bosa .60 1.50
4 Laremy Tunsil .30 .75
5 Laquon Treadwell .40 1.00
6 Jalen Ramsey .50 1.25
7 Myles Jack .40 1.00
8 DeForest Buckner .30 .75
9 Corey Coleman .50 1.25
10 Derrick Henry .75 2.00

1999 Donruss Elite

The 1999 Donruss Elite set was issued in one series totalling 200 cards. The fronts feature action color player photos with player information on the backs. Cards 1-100 were printed on foil board and were inserted four cards per pack. Cards 101-200, which includes 40 short-printed rookies, were printed on micro-etched foil cards and inserted one per pack. Two die-cut parallel sets were produced. Donruss Elite Status cards were sequentially numbered to the featured player's jersey number, and the Donruss Elite Aspirations cards were sequentially numbered to the remaining number out of 100.

COMPLETE SET (200) 30.00 80.00
COMP.SET w/o SP's (160) 15.00 30.00
1 Warren Moon .40 1.00
2 Terry Allen UER .30 .75
3 Jeff George .25 .60
4 Brett Favre .75 2.00
5 Rob Moore .25 .60
6 Bubby Brister .25 .60
7 John Elway .60 1.50
8 Troy Aikman .50 1.25
9 Steve McNair .30 .75
10 Charlie Batch .25 .60
11 Elvis Grbac .25 .60
12 Trent Dilfer .25 .60
13 Kerry Collins .25 .60
14 Neil O'Donnell .30 .75
15 Tony Simmons .25 .60
16 Ryan Leaf .30 .75
17 Bobby Hoying .25 .60
18 Marvin Harrison .30 .75
19 Keyshawn Johnson .30 .75
20 Cris Carter .40 1.00
21 Deion Sanders .30 .75
22 Emmitt Smith UER .60 1.50
23 Antowain Smith .25 .60
24 Terry Fair .25 .60
25 Robert Holcombe .25 .60
26 Napoleon Kaufman .25 .60
27 Eddie George .30 .75
28 Corey Dillon .25 .60
29 Adrian Murrell .25 .60
30 Charles Way .25 .60
31 Amp Lee .25 .60
32 Ricky Watters .30 .75
33 Gary Brown .25 .60
34 Thurman Thomas .30 .75
35 Pat Johnson .25 .60
36 Jerome Bettis .40 1.00
37 Muhsin Muhammad .25 .60
38 Kimble Anders .25 .60
39 Curtis Enis .25 .60
40 Mike Alstott .25 .60
41 Charles Johnson .25 .60
42 Chris Warren .30 .75
43 Tony Banks .30 .75
44 Leroy Hoard .25 .60
45 Chris Fuamatu-Ma'afala .25 .60
46 Michael Irvin .40 1.00
47 Robert Edwards .25 .60
48 Hines Ward .30 .75
49 Trent Green .25 .60
50 Eric Zeier .25 .60
51 Sean Dawkins .25 .60
52 Yancey Thigpen .25 .60
53 Jacquez Green .25 .60
54 Zach Thomas .30 .75
55 Junior Seau .30 .75
56 Darnay Scott .25 .60
57 Kent Graham .25 .60
58 O.J. Santiago .25 .60
59 Tony Gonzalez .30 .75
60 Ty Detmer .25 .60
61 Albert Connell .25 .60
62 James Jett .25 .60
63 Bert Emanuel .30 .75
64 Derrick Alexander WR .25 .60
65 Wesley Walls .30 .75
66 Jake Reed .30 .75
67 Randall Cunningham .30 .75
68 Leslie Shepherd .25 .60
69 Mark Chmura .25 .60
70 Bobby Engram .25 .60
71 Rickey Dudley .25 .60
72 Darick Holmes .25 .60
73 Andre Reed .40 1.00
74 Az-Zahir Hakim .25 .60
75 Cameron Cleeland .25 .60
76 Lamar Thomas .25 .60
77 Oronde Gadsden .25 .60
78 Ben Coates .30 .75
79 Bruce Smith .30 .75
80 Jerry Rice 1.00 2.50
81 Tim Brown .40 1.00
82 Michael Westbrook .25 .60
83 J.J. Stokes .25 .60
84 Shannon Sharpe .30 .75
85 Reidel Anthony .25 .60
86 Antonio Freeman .30 .75
87 Keenan McCardell .30 .75
88 Terry Glenn .30 .75
89 Andre Rison .30 .75
90 Neil Smith .25 .60
91 Terrance Mathis .25 .60
92 Rocket Ismail .30 .75
93 Byron Bam Morris .25 .60
94 Ike Hilliard .25 .60
95 Eddie Kennison .30 .75
96 Tavian Banks .25 .60
97 Yatil Green .25 .60
98 Frank Wycheck .30 .75
99 Warren Sapp UER .30 .75
100 Germane Crowell .25 .60
101 Curtis Martin .60 1.50
102 John Avery .50 1.25
103 Eric Moulds .50 1.25
104 Randy Moss .60 1.50
105 Terrell Owens .60 1.50
106 Vinny Testaverde .50 1.25
107 Doug Flutie .75 2.00
108 Mark Brunell .60 1.50
109 Isaac Bruce UER .75 2.00
110 Kordell Stewart .50 1.25
111 Drew Bledsoe .60 1.50
112 Chris Chandler .60 1.50
113 Dan Marino 1.50 4.00
114 Brian Griese .50 1.25
115 Carl Pickens .60 1.50
116 Jake Plummer .50 1.25
117 Natrone Means .60 1.50
118 Peyton Manning 2.50 6.00
119 Garrison Hearst .50 1.25
120 Barry Sanders 1.25 3.00
121 Steve Young 1.00 2.50
122 Rashaan Shehee .50 1.25
123 Ed McCaffrey .60 1.50
124 Charles Woodson .75 2.00
125 Dorsey Levens .60 1.50
126 Robert Smith .50 1.25
127 Greg Hill .50 1.25
128 Fred Taylor .50 1.25
129 Marcus Nash .50 1.25
130 Terrell Davis .60 1.50
131 Ahman Green .60 1.50
132 Jamal Anderson .60 1.50
133 Karim Abdul-Jabbar .50 1.25
134 Jermaine Lewis .50 1.25
135 Jerome Pathon .50 1.25
136 Brad Johnson .60 1.50
137 Herman Moore .60 1.50
138 Tim Dwight .60 1.50
139 Johnnie Morton .60 1.50
140 Marshall Faulk .60 1.50
141 Frank Sanders .50 1.25
142 Kevin Dyson .50 1.25
143 Curtis Conway .60 1.50
144 Derrick Mayes .50 1.25
145 O.J. McDuffie .60 1.50
146 Joe Jurevicius .50 1.25
147 Jon Kitna .50 1.25
148 Joey Galloway .60 1.50
149 Jimmy Smith .60 1.50
150 Skip Hicks .50 1.25
151 Rod Smith .60 1.50
152 Duce Staley .50 1.25
153 James Stewart .50 1.25
154 Rob Johnson .60 1.50
155 Mikhael Ricks .50 1.25
156 Wayne Chrebet .50 1.25
157 Robert Brooks .60 1.50
158 Tim Biakabutuka .60 1.50
159 Priest Holmes .50 1.25
160 Warrick Dunn .50 1.25
161 Champ Bailey RC 1.50 4.00
162 D'Wayne Bates RC .75 2.00
163 Michael Bishop RC 1.00 2.50
164 David Boston RC .75 2.00
165 Na Brown RC .75 2.00
166 Chris Claiborne RC .75 2.00
167 Joe Montgomery RC .75 2.00
168 Mike Cloud RC .75 2.00
169 Travis McGriff RC .75 2.00
170 Tim Couch RC 1.00 2.50
171 Daunte Culpepper RC 1.25 3.00
172 Autry Denson RC .75 2.00
173 Jermaine Fazande RC .75 2.00
174 Troy Edwards RC .75 2.00
175 Kevin Faulk RC .75 2.00
176 Dee Miller UER RC .75 2.00
177 Brock Huard RC .75 2.00
178 Torry Holt RC 1.50 4.00
179 Sedrick Irvin RC .75 2.00
180 Edgerrin James RC 1.25 3.00
181 Joe Germaine RC 1.00 2.50
182 James Johnson RC .75 2.00
183 Kevin Johnson RC 1.00 2.50
184 Andy Katzenmoyer RC 1.00 2.50
185 Jevon Kearse RC 1.00 2.50
186 Shaun King RC .75 2.00
187 Rob Konrad RC .75 2.00
188 Jim Kleinsasser RC 1.25 3.00
189 Chris McAlister RC .75 2.00
190 Donovan McNabb RC 6.00 15.00
191 Cade McNown RC .75 2.00
192 De'Mond Parker RC .75 2.00
193 Craig Yeast RC .75 2.00
194 Shawn Bryson RC .75 2.00
195 Peerless Price RC .75 2.00
196 Darnell McDonald RC .75 2.00
197 Akili Smith RC .75 2.00
198 Tai Streets RC 1.00 2.50
199 Ricky Williams RC 1.25 3.00
200 Amos Zereoue RC .75 2.00

1999 Donruss Elite Aspirations

CARDS #'d UNDER 20 NOT PRICED
1 Warren Moon/99 5.00 12.00
2 Terry Allen/79 4.00 10.00
3 Jeff George/97 3.00 8.00
4 Brett Favre/96 25.00 60.00
6 Bubby Brister/94 3.00 8.00
7 John Elway/93 25.00 60.00
8 Troy Aikman/92 15.00 40.00
9 Steve McNair/91 5.00 12.00
10 Charlie Batch/90 5.00 12.00
11 Elvis Grbac/89 3.00 8.00
12 Trent Dilfer/88 3.00 8.00
13 Kerry Collins/87 3.00 8.00
14 Neil O'Donnell/88 3.00 8.00
16 Ryan Leaf/84 5.00 12.00
17 Bobby Hoying/93 3.00 8.00
19 Keyshawn Johnson/81 5.00 12.00
20 Cris Carter/20 20.00 50.00
21 Deion Sanders/79 7.50 20.00
22 Emmitt Smith/78 25.00 60.00
23 Antowain Smith/77 7.50 20.00
24 Terry Fair/77 2.50 6.00
25 Robert Holcombe/75 2.50 6.00
26 Napoleon Kaufman/74 7.50 20.00
27 Eddie George/73 7.50 20.00
28 Corey Dillon/72 7.50 20.00
29 Adrian Murrell/71 4.00 10.00
30 Charles Way/70 2.50 6.00
31 Amp Lee/69 2.50 6.00
32 Ricky Watters/68 4.00 10.00
33 Gary Brown/67 2.50 6.00
34 Thurman Thomas/66 7.50 20.00
36 Jerome Bettis/64 10.00 25.00
38 Kimble Anders/62 5.00 12.00
39 Curtis Enis/61 3.00 8.00
40 Mike Alstott/60 10.00 25.00
42 Chris Warren/58 3.00 8.00
43 Tony Banks/88 3.00 8.00
44 Leroy Hoard/56 3.00 8.00
45 Chris Fuamatu-Ma'afala/55 3.00 8.00
47 Robert Edwards/53 3.00 8.00
49 Trent Green/90 3.00 8.00
50 Eric Zeier/90 3.00 8.00
54 Zach Thomas/46 10.00 25.00
55 Junior Seau/45 10.00 25.00
57 Kent Graham/90 2.00 5.00
60 Ty Detmer/89 2.00 5.00
67 Randall Cunningham/93 5.00 12.00
72 Darick Holmes/78 2.50 6.00
79 Bruce Smith/22 20.00 50.00
80 Jerry Rice/20 75.00 150.00
93 Byron Bam Morris/61 3.00 8.00
96 Tavian Banks/78 2.50 6.00
101 Curtis Martin/72 7.50 20.00
102 John Avery/80 2.00 5.00
103 Eric Moulds/20 20.00 50.00
106 Vinny Testaverde/84 3.00 8.00
107 Doug Flutie/93 5.00 12.00
108 Mark Brunell/92 5.00 12.00
109 Isaac Bruce/20 20.00 50.00
110 Kordell Stewart/90 5.00 12.00
111 Drew Bledsoe/89 12.50 30.00
112 Chris Chandler/88 3.00 8.00
113 Dan Marino/87 25.00 60.00
114 Brian Griese/86 6.00 12.00
116 Jake Plummer/84 3.00 8.00
117 Natrone Means/80 3.00 8.00
118 Peyton Manning/82 25.00 60.00
119 Garrison Hearst/80 5.00 12.00
120 Barry Sanders/80 25.00 60.00
121 Steve Young/92 12.50 30.00
122 Rashaan Shehee/78 2.50 6.00
124 Charles Woodson/76 7.50 20.00
125 Dorsey Levens/75 7.50 20.00
126 Robert Smith/74 7.50 20.00
127 Greg Hill/73 2.50 6.00
128 Fred Taylor/72 7.50 20.00
130 Terrell Davis/70 7.50 20.00
131 Ahman Green/70 7.50 20.00
132 Jamal Anderson/68 7.50 20.00
133 Karim Abdul-Jabbar/67 4.00 10.00
136 Brad Johnson/86 5.00 12.00
140 Marshall Faulk/72 12.50 30.00
144 Derrick Mayes/20 20.00 50.00
147 Jon Kitna/93 5.00 12.00
150 Skip Hicks/80 2.00 5.00
151 Rod Smith/20 20.00 50.00
152 Duce Staley/78 7.50 20.00
153 James Stewart/67 4.00 10.00
154 Rob Johnson/89 3.00 8.00
155 Mikhael Ricks/90 2.00 5.00
156 Wayne Chrebet/20 20.00 50.00
158 Tim Biakabutuka/79 4.00 10.00
159 Priest Holmes/67 12.50 25.00
160 Warrick Dunn/72 7.50 20.00
161 Champ Bailey/96 7.50 20.00
162 D'Wayne Bates/95 5.00 12.00
163 Michael Bishop/93 5.00 12.00
164 David Boston/91 5.00 12.00
165 Na Brown/81 3.00 8.00
166 Chris Claiborne/45 3.00 8.00
167 Joe Montgomery/67 4.00 10.00
168 Mike Cloud/79 4.00 10.00
169 Travis McGriff/97 2.00 5.00
170 Tim Couch/98 5.00 12.00
171 Daunte Culpepper/92 25.00 60.00
172 Autry Denson/67 4.00 10.00
173 Jermaine Fazande/70 4.00 10.00
174 Troy Edwards/84 3.00 8.00
175 Kevin Faulk/97 5.00 12.00
176 Dee Miller/85 2.00 5.00
177 Brock Huard/93 5.00 12.00
179 Sedrick Irvin/67 12.50 25.00
180 Edgerrin James/95 25.00 60.90
181 Joe Germaine/93 3.00 8.00
182 James Johnson/78 4.00 10.00
183 Kevin Johnson/88 5.00 12.00
184 Andy Katzenmoyer/55 5.00 12.00
185 Jevon Kearse/58 12.00 30.00
186 Shaun King/90 3.00 8.00
187 Rob Konrad/56 10.00 25.00
188 Jim Kleinsasser/78 4.00 10.00
189 Chris McAlister/89 4.00 10.00
190 Donovan McNabb/95 20.00 50.00
191 Cade McNown/82 3.00 8.00
192 De'Mond Parker/67 2.50 6.00
193 Craig Yeast/97 5.00 12.00
194 Shawn Bryson/76 7.50 20.00
195 Peerless Price/63 7.50 20.00
196 Darnell McDonald/20 20.00 50.00
197 Akili Smith/89 2.00 5.00
199 Ricky Williams/66 15.00 40.00
200 Amos Zereoue/80 5.00 12.00

1999 Donruss Elite Status

CARDS #'d UNDER 20 NOT PRICED
2 Terry Allen/21 12.50 30.00
5 Rob Moore/85 3.00 8.00
15 Tony Simmons/81 2.00 5.00
18 Marvin Harrison/88 5.00 12.00
20 Cris Carter/80 5.00 12.00
21 Deion Sanders/21 20.00 50.00
22 Emmitt Smith/22 75.00 150.00
23 Antowain Smith/23 20.00 50.00
24 Terry Fair/23 6.00 15.00
25 Robert Holcombe/25 6.00 15.00
26 Napoleon Kaufman/26 20.00 50.00
27 Eddie George/27 25.00 60.00
28 Corey Dillon/28 20.00 50.00
29 Adrian Murrell/29 12.50 30.00
30 Charles Way/30 4.00 10.00
31 Amp Lee/31 4.00 10.00
32 Ricky Watters/32 7.50 20.00
33 Gary Brown/33 4.00 10.00
34 Thurman Thomas/34 15.00 40.00
35 Patrick Johnson/85 2.00 5.00
36 Jerome Bettis/36 15.00 40.00
37 Muhsin Muhammad/87 3.00 8.00
38 Kimble Anders/38 4.00 10.00
39 Curtis Enis/39 4.00 10.00
40 Mike Alstott/40 15.00 40.00
41 Charles Johnson/81 3.00 8.00
42 Chris Warren/42 4.00 10.00
44 Leroy Hoard/44 4.00 10.00
45 Chris Fuamatu-Ma'afala/45 3.00 8.00
46 Michael Irvin/88 5.00 12.00
47 Robert Edwards/47 3.00 8.00
48 Hines Ward/86 5.00 12.00
51 Sean Dawkins/86 2.00 5.00
52 Yancey Thigpen/82 2.00 5.00
53 Jacquez Green/81 2.00 5.00
54 Zach Thomas/54 10.00 25.00
55 Junior Seau/55 10.00 25.00
56 Darnay Scott/86 3.00 8.00
58 O.J. Santiago/88 2.00 5.00
59 Tony Gonzalez/88 5.00 12.00
61 Albert Connell/83 2.00 5.00
62 James Jett/82 3.00 8.00
63 Bert Emanuel/87 2.00 5.00
64 Derrick Alexander WR/82 3.00 8.00
65 Wesley Walls/85 3.00 8.00
66 Jake Reed/86 3.00 8.00
68 Leslie Shepherd/86 2.00 5.00
69 Mark Chmura/89 2.00 5.00
70 Bobby Engram/81 2.00 5.00
71 Rickey Dudley/83 2.00 5.00
72 Darick Holmes/22 6.00 15.00
73 Andre Reed/83 3.00 8.00
74 Az-Zahir Hakim/81 3.00 8.00
75 Cameron Cleeland/85 2.00 5.00
76 Lamar Thomas/85 2.00 5.00
77 Oronde Gadsden/86 2.00 5.00
78 Ben Coates/87 3.00 8.00
79 Bruce Smith/78 2.50 6.00
80 Jerry Rice/80 20.00 50.00
81 Tim Brown/81 5.00 12.00
82 Michael Westbrook/82 3.00 8.00
83 J.J. Stokes/83 3.00 8.00
84 Shannon Sharpe/84 3.00 8.00
85 Reidel Anthony/85 3.00 8.00
86 Antonio Freeman/86 5.00 12.00
87 Keenan McCardell/87 3.00 8.00
88 Terry Glenn/88 5.00 12.00
89 Andre Rison/89 3.00 8.00
90 Neil Smith/90 2.00 5.00
91 Terrance Mathis/81 3.00 8.00
92 Rocket Ismail/81 3.00 8.00
93 Byron Bam Morris/39 4.00 10.00
94 Ike Hilliard/88 3.00 8.00
95 Eddie Kennison/88 3.00 8.00
96 Tavian Banks/22 6.00 15.00
97 Yatil Green/87 2.00 5.00
98 Frank Wycheck/89 2.00 5.00
99 Warren Sapp/99 2.00 5.00
100 Germane Crowell/82 2.00 5.00
101 Curtis Martin/28 20.00 50.00
102 John Avery/20 6.00 15.00
103 Eric Moulds/80 5.00 12.00
104 Randy Moss/84 25.00 60.00
105 Terrell Owens/81 5.00 12.00
106 Isaac Bruce/80 5.00 12.00

115 Carl Pickens/81 3.00 8.00
117 Natrone Means/20 12.50 30.00
119 Garrison Hearst/20 20.00 50.00
120 Barry Sanders/20 125.00 250.00
122 Rashaan Shehee/22 6.00 15.00
123 Ed McCaffrey/87 3.00 8.00
124 Charles Woodson/24 20.00 50.00
125 Dorsey Levens/25 20.00 50.00
126 Robert Smith/26 20.00 50.00
127 Greg Hill/27 6.00 15.00
128 Fred Taylor/28 25.00 60.00
129 Marcus Nash/82 2.00 5.00
130 Terrell Davis/30 30.00 80.00
131 Ahman Green/30 15.00 40.00
132 Jamal Anderson/32 15.00 40.00
133 Karim Abdul-Jabbar/33 7.50 20.00
134 Jermaine Lewis/84 3.00 8.00
135 Jerome Pathon/86 2.00 5.00
137 Herman Moore/84 3.00 8.00
138 Tim Dwight/83 5.00 12.00
139 Johnnie Morton/87 3.00 8.00
140 Marshall Faulk/28 30.00 80.00
141 Frank Sanders/81 3.00 8.00
142 Kevin Dyson/87 3.00 8.00
143 Curtis Conway/83 3.00 8.00
144 Derrick Mayes/80 3.00 8.00
145 O.J. McDuffie/81 3.00 8.00
146 Joe Jurevicius/86 3.00 8.00
148 Joey Galloway/84 3.00 8.00
149 Jimmy Smith/82 3.00 8.00
150 Skip Hicks/20 6.00 15.00
151 Rod Smith/80 3.00 8.00
152 Duce Staley/22 20.00 50.00
153 James Stewart/33 7.50 20.00
156 Wayne Chrebet/80 5.00 12.00
157 Robert Brooks/87 3.00 8.00
158 Tim Biakabutuka/21 12.50 30.00
159 Priest Holmes/33 30.00 60.00
160 Warrick Dunn/28 20.00 50.00
166 Chris Claiborne/55 3.00 8.00
167 Joe Montgomery/33 7.50 20.00
168 Mike Cloud/21 12.50 30.00
172 Autry Denson/23 12.50 30.00
173 Jermaine Fazande/30 7.50 20.00
178 Torry Holt/81 12.50 30.00
179 Sedrick Irvin/33 20.00 50.00
182 James Johnson/22 12.50 30.00
184 Andy Katzenmoyer/45 12.50 30.00
185 Jevon Kearse/42 15.00 40.00
187 Rob Konrad/44 15.00 40.00
188 Jim Kleinsasser/82 5.00 12.00
192 De'Mond Parker/33 4.00 10.00
194 Shawn Bryson/24 20.00 50.00
195 Peerless Price/37 15.00 40.00
196 Darnell McDonald/80 7.50 20.00
198 Tai Streets/86 5.00 12.00
199 Ricky Williams/34 40.00 100.00
200 Amos Zereoue/20 20.00 50.00

1999 Donruss Elite Common Threads

Randomly inserted into packs, this 18-card set features color photos of top players printed on cards featuring pieces of game-used jerseys of two teammates. Each card is sequentially numbered to only 150, and players are featured individually and back to back with jersey swatches.

MULTI-COLORED SWATCHES: .6X TO 1.5X
STATED PRINT RUN 150 SERIAL #'d SETS
1 R.Moss/R.Cunningham 25.00 60.00
2 Randy Moss 25.00 60.00
3 Randall Cunningham 12.00 30.00
4 J.Elway/T.Davis 25.00 60.00
5 John Elway 30.00 80.00
6 Terrell Davis 15.00 40.00
7 J.Rice/S.Young 25.00 60.00
8 Jerry Rice 25.00 60.00
9 Steve Young 25.00 60.00
10 M.Brunell/F.Taylor 20.00 50.00
11 Mark Brunell 12.00 30.00
12 Fred Taylor 12.00 30.00
13 K.Stewart/J.Bettis 12.00 30.00
14 Kordell Stewart 12.00 30.00
15 Jerome Bettis 15.00 40.00
16 D.Marino/K.Jabbar 40.00 100.00
17 Dan Marino 40.00 100.00
18 Karim Abdul-Jabbar 10.00 25.00

1999 Donruss Elite Field of Vision

Randomly inserted into packs, this 36-card set features color photos of 12-top players printed on three cards each displaying the three sections of the football playing field: left, middle, and right. Each player's card is linked by his 1998 season total in passing, rushing or receiving yards. Each card is sequentially numbered (as noted below) to the amount of yards gained to the respective section of the playing field. A die-cut parallel version of this set was also produced highlighting the total number of completions, receptions or rushing attempts to each part of the playing field.

1A Dan Marino/1712 4.00 10.00
1B Dan Marino/834 6.00 15.00
1C Dan Marino/951 6.00 15.00
2A Emmitt Smith/640 5.00 12.00
2B Emmitt Smith/202 7.50 20.00
2C Emmitt Smith/490 5.00 12.00
3A Jake Plummer/1165 2.00 5.00
3B Jake Plummer/624 3.00 8.00
3C Jake Plummer/1948 2.00 5.00
4A Brett Favre/1409 4.00 10.00
4B Brett Favre/983 6.00 15.00
4C Brett Favre/1820 4.00 10.00
5A Fred Taylor/486 2.00 5.00
5B Fred Taylor/400 2.00 5.00
5C Fred Taylor/337 2.50 6.00
6A Drew Bledsoe/1355 2.00 5.00
6B Drew Bledsoe/689 3.00 8.00
6C Drew Bledsoe/1589 2.00 5.00
7A Terrell Davis/1283 2.00 5.00
7B Terrell Davis/306 4.00 10.00
7C Terrell Davis/419 3.00 8.00
8A Jerry Rice/611 4.00 10.00
8B Jerry Rice/234 7.50 20.00
8C Jerry Rice/312 6.00 15.00
9A Randy Moss/639 6.00 15.00
9B Randy Moss/16 50.00 120.00
9C Randy Moss/658 6.00 15.00
10A John Elway/1320 5.00 12.00
10B John Elway/615 6.00 15.00
10C John Elway/871 6.00 15.00
11A Peyton Manning/1141 5.00 12.00
11B Peyton Manning/1020 5.00 12.00
11C Peyton Manning/1578 4.00 10.00
12A Barry Sanders/556 6.00 15.00
12B Barry Sanders/373 7.50 20.00
12C Barry Sanders/562 6.00 15.00

1999 Donruss Elite Field of Vision Die Cuts

1A Dan Marino/164 15.00 40.00
1B Dan Marino/56 40.00 100.00
1C Dan Marino/90 25.00 60.00
2A Emmitt Smith/158 7.50 20.00
2B Emmitt Smith/64 25.00 60.00
2C Emmitt Smith/97 12.50 30.00
3A Jake Plummer/89 7.50 20.00
3B Jake Plummer/44 15.00 40.00
3C Jake Plummer/191 3.00 8.00
4A Brett Favre/112 20.00 50.00
4B Brett Favre/67 40.00 100.00
4C Brett Favre/168 15.00 40.00
5A Fred Taylor/103 7.50 20.00
5B Fred Taylor/79 10.00 25.00
6C Fred Taylor/82 10.00 25.00
6A Drew Bledsoe/90 7.50 20.00
6B Drew Bledsoe/48 12.50 30.00
6C Drew Bledsoe/125 3.00 8.00
7A Terrell Davis/217 4.00 10.00
7B Terrell Davis/66 10.00 25.00
7C Terrell Davis/109 5.00 12.00
8A Jerry Rice/50 25.00 60.00
8C Jerry Rice/21 60.00 120.00
9A Randy Moss/34 30.00 80.00
9C Randy Moss/33 30.00 80.00
10A John Elway/98 25.00 60.00
10B John Elway/35 50.00 120.00
10C John Elway/77 30.00 80.00
11A Peyton Manning/110 15.00 40.00
11B Peyton Manning/79 20.00 50.00
11C Peyton Manning/137 10.00 25.00
12A Barry Sanders/137 15.00 40.00
12B Barry Sanders/83 30.00 80.00
12C Barry Sanders/123 20.00 50.00

1999 Donruss Elite Passing the Torch

Randomly inserted into packs, this 18-card set features color action photos of 12 elite rookies, current stars, and NFL legends printed on holographic foil cards. The first 100 of the 1500 sequentially numbered cards were autographed separately or back-to-back by the featured player or players. The numbering scheme for cards #4-7 incorrectly included more than one player combination, thus cards #13-15 were never produced. The Ricky Williams card was produced in more than one version with differing team names being used. According to Playoff, the Saints team is the common version with the other versions being released by mistake only very early in the print run. It is thought that Rams, Bengals, Colts, Eagles, and Redskins variations were made. We've listed the known versions below.

COMPLETE SET (18) 75.00 150.00
TOTAL PRINT RUN 1500 SERIAL #'d SETS
FIRST 100-CARDS WERE SIGNED
1 J.Unitas/P.Manning 6.00 15.00
2 Johnny Unitas 4.00 10.00
3 Peyton Manning 6.00 15.00
4A W.Payton/B.Sanders 10.00 25.00
4B E.Smith/F.Taylor 5.00 12.00
5A Walter Payton 6.00 15.00
5B Emmitt Smith 4.00 10.00
6A Barry Sanders 7.50 15.00
6B Fred Taylor 2.00 5.00
7A Campbell/R.Will COR 6.00 15.00
7B Camp/Will ERR Rams 30.00 50.00
7C Camp/Will ERR 'skins 30.00 50.00
8 Earl Campbell 2.00 5.00
9A Ricky Williams COR 2.50 6.00
9B Ricky Williams ERR Rams 30.00 50.00
9C Ricky Williams ERR 'skins 30.00 50.00
10 J.Brown/T.Davis 3.00 8.00
11 Jim Brown 4.00 10.00
12 Terrell Davis 2.00 5.00
16 C.Carter/R.Moss 5.00 12.00
17 Cris Carter 2.00 5.00
18 Randy Moss 5.00 12.00

1999 Donruss Elite Passing the Torch Autographs

This 18-card set features the first 100 of each of the cards of the 1999 Donruss Elite Passing the Torch regular insert set. These 100 were autographed separately or back-to-back by the featured player or players. Some of the cards were issued via mail redemption cards with an expiration date of 5/1/2000.

FIRST 100-CARDS OF PRINT RUN SIGNED
1 J.Unitas/P.Manning 900.00 1500.00
2 Johnny Unitas 350.00 600.00
3 Peyton Manning 100.00 200.00
4A W.Payton/B.Sanders 1500.00 2500.00
4B E.Smith/F.Taylor 200.00 400.00
5A Walter Payton 600.00 900.00
5B Emmitt Smith 175.00 300.00
6A Barry Sanders 100.00 200.00
6B Fred Taylor 30.00 60.00
7 E.Campbell/R.Williams 60.00 120.00
8 Earl Campbell 50.00 100.00
9 Ricky Williams 30.00 60.00
10 J.Brown/T.Davis 125.00 250.00
11 Jim Brown 100.00 200.00
12 Terrell Davis 50.00 100.00
16 C.Carter/R.Moss 150.00 300.00
17 Cris Carter 60.00 120.00
18 Randy Moss 125.00 200.00

1999 Donruss Elite Power Formulas

Randomly inserted into packs, this 30-card set features color action photos of the NFL's most powerful players with statistical formulas behind their greatness displayed on the cardbacks. Each card is printed utilizing holographic technology and is sequentially numbered to 3500.

COMPLETE SET (30) 50.00 100.00
STATED PRINT RUN 3500 SERIAL #'d SETS
1 Randy Moss 3.00 8.00
2 Terrell Davis 1.25 3.00
3 Brett Favre 4.00 10.00
4 Dan Marino 4.00 10.00
5 Barry Sanders 4.00 10.00
6 Peyton Manning 4.00 10.00
7 John Elway 4.00 10.00
8 Fred Taylor 1.25 3.00
9 Emmitt Smith 2.50 6.00
10 Steve Young 1.50 4.00
11 Jerry Rice 2.50 6.00
12 Jake Plummer 1.25 3.00
13 Kordell Stewart 1.25 3.00
14 Mark Brunell 1.25 3.00
15 Drew Bledsoe 1.50 4.00
16 Eddie George 1.25 3.00
17 Troy Aikman 2.50 6.00
18 Warrick Dunn 1.25 3.00
19 Keyshawn Johnson 1.25 3.00
20 Jamal Anderson 1.25 3.00
21 Randall Cunningham 1.25 3.00
22 Doug Flutie 1.25 3.00
23 Jerome Bettis 1.25 3.00
24 Garrison Hearst 1.25 3.00
25 Curtis Martin 1.25 3.00
26 Corey Dillion 1.25 3.00
27 Antowain Smith 1.25 3.00
28 Antonio Freeman 1.25 3.00
29 Terrell Owens 1.25 3.00
30 Carl Pickens 1.25 3.00

1999 Donruss Elite Primary Colors Yellow

Randomly inserted into packs, this 40-card set features color action photos of some of football's finest players printed on yellow, blue, and red foil cards. The Yellow cards are numbered to 1875, Blue to 950, and Red to 25. Die-cut parallel versions of each of these three insert sets were also produced. The Yellow Die-Cut cards are numbed to 25, Blue to 50, and Red to 75. Each of the 40 pictured players have a total of 3,000 individually numbered cards.

COMPLETE SET (40) 75.00 150.00
YELLOW PRINT RUN 1875 SER.#'d SETS
*BLUE CARDS: .6X TO 1.5X YELLOW
BLUE PRINT RUN 950 SERIAL #'d SET
*RED STARS: 8X TO 20X YELLOWS
*RED ROOKIES: 5X TO 12X YELLOWS
RED PRINT RUN 25 SERIAL #'d SET
*BLUE DIE CUT STARS: 4X TO 10X YELL.
*BLUE DIE CUT ROOKIES: 3X TO 8X
BLUE DIE CUT PRINT RUN 50 SER.#'d SETS
*RED DIE CUT STARS: 4X TO 10X YELLOWS
*RED DIE CUT ROOKIES: 2.5X TO 6X
RED DIE CUT PRINT RUN 75 SER.#'d SETS
*YELLOW DIE CUT STARS: 6X TO 15X
*YELLOW DIE CUT ROOKIES: 4X TO 10X
YELLOW DIE CUT PRINT RUN 25 SER.#'d SETS
1 Herman Moore 1.25 3.00
2 Marshall Faulk 2.00 5.00
3 Dorsey Levens 1.25 3.00
4 Napoleon Kaufman 1.25 3.00
5 Jamal Anderson 1.25 3.00
6 Edgerrin James 4.00 10.00
7 Troy Aikman 2.50 6.00
8 Cris Carter 1.25 3.00
9 Eddie George 1.25 3.00
10 Donovan McNabb 5.00 12.00
11 Drew Bledsoe 1.50 4.00
12 Daunte Culpepper 4.00 10.00
13 Mark Brunell 1.25 3.00
14 Corey Dillon 1.25 3.00
15 Kordell Stewart 1.25 3.00
16 Curtis Martin 1.25 3.00
17 Jake Plummer 1.25 3.00
18 Charlie Batch 1.25 3.00
19 Jerry Rice 2.50 6.00
20 Antonio Freeman 1.25 3.00
21 Steve Young 1.50 4.00
22 Steve McNair 1.25 3.00
23 Emmitt Smith 2.50 6.00
24 Terrell Owens 1.25 3.00
25 Fred Taylor 1.25 3.00
26 Joey Galloway 1.25 3.00
27 John Elway 4.00 10.00
28 Ryan Leaf 1.25 3.00
29 Barry Sanders 4.00 10.00
30 Ricky Williams 2.00 5.00
31 Dan Marino 4.00 10.00
32 Tim Couch 1.25 3.00
33 Brett Favre 4.00 10.00
34 Eric Moulds 1.25 3.00
35 Peyton Manning 4.00 10.00
36 Deion Sanders 1.25 3.00
37 Terrell Davis 1.25 3.00
38 Tim Brown 1.25 3.00
39 Randy Moss 3.00 8.00
40 Mike Alstott 1.25 3.00

2000 Donruss Elite

Released as a 200-card set, 2000 Donruss Elite is comprised of 100 base cards, 25 short-printed veteran cards, and 75 prospect cards which are sequentially numbered to 2000 with the first 500 of each die-cut. Some Rookie Cards were issued via mail redemptions that carried an expiration date of 5/31/2001. Base cards are printed on foil board with red foil highlights. Elite was packaged in 18-pack boxes containing five cards each and carried a suggested retail price of $3.99.

COMPLETE SET (200) 300.00 500.00
COMP.SET w/o SP's (100) 6.00 15.00
126-200 ROOKIE PRINT RUN 2000
1 Jake Plummer .15 .40
2 David Boston .15 .40
3 Rob Moore .15 .40
4 Chris Chandler .20 .50
5 Tim Dwight .20 .50
6 Terance Mathis .15 .40
7 Jamal Anderson .20 .50
8 Priest Holmes .15 .40
9 Tony Banks .15 .40
10 Shannon Sharpe .20 .50
11 Qadry Ismail .15 .40
12 Eric Moulds .15 .40
13 Doug Flutie .20 .50
14 Antowain Smith .20 .50
15 Peerless Price .20 .50
16 Muhsin Muhammad .15 .40
17 Tim Biakabutuka .20 .50
18 Patrick Jeffers .15 .40
19 Steve Beuerlein .20 .50
20 Wesley Walls .15 .40
21 Curtis Enis .15 .40
22 Marcus Robinson .20 .50
23 Carl Pickens .20 .50
24 Corey Dillon .15 .40
25 Akili Smith .15 .40
26 Darnay Scott .20 .50
27 Kevin Johnson .15 .40
28 Errict Rhett .20 .50
29 Emmitt Smith .40 1.00
30 Deion Sanders .20 .50
31 Troy Aikman .30 .75
32 Joey Galloway .20 .50
33 Michael Irvin .25 .60
34 Rocket Ismail .20 .50
35 Jason Tucker .15 .40
36 Ed McCaffrey .20 .50
37 Rod Smith .20 .50
38 Brian Griese .15 .40
39 Terrell Davis .20 .50
40 Olandis Gary .20 .50
41 Charlie Batch .15 .40
42 Johnnie Morton .20 .50
43 Herman Moore .15 .40
44 James Stewart .15 .40
45 Dorsey Levens .20 .50
46 Antonio Freeman .20 .50
47 Brett Favre .50 1.25
48 Bill Schroeder .20 .50
49 Peyton Manning .60 1.50
50 Keenan McCardell .20 .50
51 Fred Taylor .15 .40
52 Jimmy Smith .20 .50
53 Elvis Grbac .15 .40
54 Tony Gonzalez .20 .50
55 Derrick Alexander .15 .40
56 Dan Marino .50 1.25
57 Tony Martin .20 .50
58 James Johnson .15 .40
59 Damon Huard .15 .40
60 Thurman Thomas .20 .50
61 Robert Smith .15 .40
62 Randall Cunningham .20 .50
63 Jeff George .20 .50
64 Terry Glenn .20 .50
65 Drew Bledsoe .20 .50
66 Jeff Blake .20 .50
67 Amani Toomer .15 .40
68 Kerry Collins .15 .40
69 Joe Montgomery .15 .40
70 Vinny Testaverde .15 .40
71 Ray Lucas .15 .40
72 Keyshawn Johnson .20 .50
73 Wayne Chrebet .15 .40
74 Napoleon Kaufman .20 .50
75 Tim Brown .25 .60
76 Rich Gannon .20 .50
77 Duce Staley .15 .40
78 Kordell Stewart .15 .40
79 Jerome Bettis .25 .60
80 Troy Edwards .15 .40
81 Natrone Means .20 .50
82 Curtis Conway .20 .50
83 Jim Harbaugh .20 .50
84 Junior Seau .20 .50
85 Jermaine Fazande .15 .40
86 Terrell Owens .20 .50
87 Charlie Garner .20 .50
88 Steve Young .30 .75
89 Jeff Garcia .15 .40
90 Derrick Mayes .15 .40
91 Ricky Watters .20 .50
92 Az-Zahir Hakim .15 .40
93 Torry Holt .20 .50
94 Warren Sapp .20 .50
95 Mike Alstott .15 .40
96 Warrick Dunn .15 .40
97 Kevin Dyson .20 .50
98 Bruce Smith .20 .50
99 Albert Connell .15 .40
100 Michael Westbrook .15 .40
101 Cade McNown .50 1.25
102 Tim Couch .60 1.50
103 John Elway 1.25 3.00
104 Barry Sanders 1.25 3.00
105 Germane Crowell .50 1.25
106 Marvin Harrison .60 1.50
107 Edgerrin James .60 1.50
108 Mark Brunell .60 1.50
109 Randy Moss .60 1.50
110 Cris Carter .75 2.00
111 Daunte Culpepper .60 1.50
112 Ricky Williams .60 1.50
113 Curtis Martin .60 1.50
114 Donovan McNabb .60 1.50
115 Jerry Rice 2.00 5.00
116 Jon Kitna .50 1.25
117 Isaac Bruce .75 2.00
118 Marshall Faulk .60 1.50
119 Kurt Warner 1.25 3.00
120 Shaun King .50 1.25
121 Eddie George .60 1.50
122 Steve McNair .60 1.50
123 Jevon Kearse .50 1.25
124 Stephen Davis .50 1.25
125 Brad Johnson .60 1.50
126 Mike Anderson RC 1.25 3.00
127 Peter Warrick RC 1.25 3.00
128 Courtney Brown RC 1.50 4.00
129 Plaxico Burress RC 1.50 4.00
130 Corey Simon RC 1.50 4.00
131 Thomas Jones RC 1.50 4.00
132 Travis Taylor RC 1.25 3.00
133 Shaun Alexander RC 2.00 5.00
134 Deon Grant RC 1.25 3.00
135 Chris Redman RC 1.25 3.00
136 Chad Pennington RC 1.50 4.00
137 Jamal Lewis RC 2.00 5.00
138 Brian Urlacher RC 6.00 15.00
139 Keith Bulluck RC 1.50 4.00
140 Bubba Franks RC 1.25 3.00
141 Dez White RC 1.25 3.00
142 Na'il Diggs RC 1.25 3.00
143 Ahmed Plummer RC 1.25 3.00
144 Ron Dayne RC 2.00 5.00
145 Shaun Ellis RC 1.50 4.00
146 Sylvester Morris RC 1.25 3.00
147 Deltha O'Neal RC 1.25 3.00
148 Raynoch Thompson RC 1.25 3.00
149 R.Jay Soward RC 1.25 3.00
150 Mario Edwards RC 1.25 3.00
151 John Engelberger RC 1.25 3.00
152 Dwayne Goodrich RC 1.25 3.00
153 Sherrod Gideon RC 1.25 3.00
154 John Abraham RC 2.00 5.00
155 Ben Kelly RC 1.25 3.00
156 Travis Prentice RC 1.25 3.00
157 Darrell Jackson RC 1.25 3.00
158 Giovanni Carmazzi RC 1.25 3.00
159 Anthony Lucas RC 1.25 3.00
160 Danny Farmer RC 1.25 3.00
161 Dennis Northcutt RC 1.25 3.00
162 Troy Walters RC 1.25 3.00
163 Laveranues Coles RC 1.50 4.00
164 Tee Martin RC 1.25 3.00
165 J.R. Redmond RC 1.25 3.00
166 Tim Rattay RC 1.50 4.00
167 Jerry Porter RC 2.00 5.00
168 Sebastian Janikowski RC 2.00 5.00
169 Michael Wiley RC 1.25 3.00
170 Reuben Droughns RC 1.25 3.00
171 Trung Canidate RC 1.25 3.00
172 Shyrone Stith RC 1.25 3.00
173 Chris Hovan RC 1.50 4.00
174 Brandon Short RC 1.25 3.00
175 Mark Roman RC 1.25 3.00
176 Trevor Gaylor RC 1.25 3.00
177 Chris Cole RC 1.50 4.00
178 Hank Poteat RC 1.25 3.00
179 Darren Howard RC 1.25 3.00
180 Rob Morris RC 1.50 4.00
181 Spergon Wynn RC 1.25 3.00
182 Marc Bulger RC 1.50 4.00
183 Tom Brady RC 200.00 400.00
184 Todd Husak RC 1.25 3.00
185 Gari Scott RC 1.25 3.00
186 Erron Kinney RC 1.25 3.00
187 Julian Peterson RC 2.00 5.00
188 Sammy Morris RC 1.25 3.00
189 Rondell Mealey RC 1.25 3.00
190 Doug Chapman RC 1.25 3.00
191 Ron Dugans RC 1.25 3.00
192 Deon Dyer RC 1.25 3.00
193 Fred Robbins RC 1.25 3.00
194 Ike Charlton RC 1.25 3.00
195 Mareno Philyaw RC 1.25 3.00
196 Thomas Hamner RC 1.25 3.00
197 Jarious Jackson RC 1.50 4.00
198 Anthony Becht RC 1.25 3.00
199 Joe Hamilton RC 1.25 3.00
200 Todd Pinkston RC 1.25 3.00

2000 Donruss Elite Aspirations

*VETS/70-99: 8X TO 20X BASE 1-100
*VETS/70-99: 2.5X TO 6X BASE 101-125
*ROOKIES/70-99: 1X TO 2.5X
*VETS/45-69: 10X TO 25X BASE 1-100
*VETS/45-69: 3X TO 8X BASE 101-125
*ROOKIE/45-69: 1.2X TO 3X BASIC CARD
*VETS/20-29: 20X TO 50X BASE 1-100
*VETS/20-29: 6X TO 15X BASE 101-125
*ROOKIE/20-29: 2.5X TO 6X BASIC CARD
*VETS/10-19: 25X TO 60X BASE 1-100
*VETS/10-19: 8X TO 20X BASE 101-125
*ROOKIE/10-19: 3X TO 8X BASIC CARD
STATED PRINT RUN 1-99
183 Tom Brady/90 900.00 1500.00

2000 Donruss Elite Rookie Die Cuts

*DIE CUTS: .6X TO 1.5X BASE RCs
FIRST 500 SER.#'d RC's WERE DIE CUT
183 Tom Brady 300.00 600.00

2000 Donruss Elite Status

*VETS/78-99: 8X TO 20X BASE 1-100
*VETS/78-99: 2.5X TO 6X BASE 101-125
*ROOKIES/78-99: 1X TO 2.5X
*VETS/40-55: 10X TO 25X BASE 1-100
*VETS/40-55: 3X TO 8X BASE 101-125
*ROOKIE/40-55: 1.2X TO 3X BASIC CARD
*VETS/30-39: 12X TO 30X BASE 1-100
*VETS/30-39: 4X TO 10X BASE 101-125
*ROOKIE/30-39: 1.5X TO 4X BASIC CARD
*VETS/20-29: 20X TO 50X BASE 1-100
*VETS/20-29: 6X TO 15X BASE 101-125
*ROOKIE/20-29: 2.5X TO 6X BASIC CARD
*VETS/10-19: 25X TO 60X BASE 1-100
*VETS/10-19: 8X TO 20X BASE 101-125
*ROOKIE/11-19: 3X TO 8X BASIC CARD
STATED PRINT RUN 1-99

2000 Donruss Elite Craftsmen

Randomly inserted in packs, this 40-card set features players on a blue foil card with embossed accents. Each card is sequentially numbered to 2500.

COMPLETE SET (40) 40.00 80.00
STATED PRINT RUN 2500 SER.#'d SETS
*MASTERS/50: 3X TO 8X BASIC INSERTS
MASTERS PRINT RUN 50 SER.#'d SETS
C1 Dan Marino 1.50 4.00
C2 Edgerrin James .60 1.50
C3 Peyton Manning 2.00 5.00
C4 Drew Bledsoe .60 1.50
C5 Doug Flutie .60 1.50
C6 Curtis Martin .60 1.50
C7 Eddie George .60 1.50
C8 Steve McNair .60 1.50
C9 Fred Taylor .50 1.25
C10 Mark Brunell .60 1.50
C11 Tim Couch .60 1.50
C12 Corey Dillon .50 1.25
C13 Terrell Davis .60 1.50
C14 Jon Kitna .50 1.25
C15 Emmitt Smith 1.25 3.00
C16 Troy Aikman 1.00 2.50
C17 Stephen Davis .50 1.25
C18 Brad Johnson .60 1.50
C19 Jake Plummer .50 1.25
C20 Brett Favre 1.50 4.00
C21 Barry Sanders 1.25 3.00
C22 Marshall Faulk .60 1.50
C23 Kurt Warner 1.25 3.00
C24 Ricky Williams .60 1.50
C25 Steve Young 1.00 2.50
C26 Randy Moss .60 1.50
C27 John Elway 1.25 3.00
C28 Jerry Rice 2.00 5.00
C29 Tim Brown .75 2.00
C30 Cris Carter .75 2.00
C31 Antonio Freeman .60 1.50
C32 Joey Galloway .60 1.50
C33 Terry Glenn .60 1.50
C34 Marvin Harrison .60 1.50
C35 Keyshawn Johnson .60 1.50
C36 Eric Moulds .50 1.25
C37 Isaac Bruce .75 2.00
C38 Peter Warrick .50 1.25
C39 Plaxico Burress .60 1.50
C40 Thomas Jones .60 1.50

2000 Donruss Elite Down and Distance

Randomly inserted in packs, this 48-card set features four versions of each player. Each card is serial numbered to the total number of yards gained in 1999 by each player on the specific featured down.

STATED PRINT RUN 2-1857
CARDS SER.#'d TO A 1999 SEASON STAT
1D1 Randy Moss/611 1.00 2.50
1D2 Randy Moss/493 1.00 2.50
1D3 Randy Moss/263 1.25 3.00
1D4 Randy Moss/46 2.50 6.00
2D1 Brett Favre/1386 2.00 5.00
2D2 Brett Favre/1543 2.00 5.00
2D3 Brett Favre/1139 2.00 5.00
2D4 Brett Favre/23 10.00 25.00
3D1 Dan Marino/1023 2.00 5.00
3D2 Dan Marino/855 2.50 6.00
3D3 Dan Marino/505 2.50 6.00
3D4 Dan Marino/65 4.00 10.00
4D1 Peyton Manning/1857 2.50 6.00
4D2 Peyton Manning/1219 2.50 6.00
4D3 Peyton Manning/1029 2.50 6.00
4D4 Peyton Manning/30 8.00 20.00
5D1 Emmitt Smith/832 2.00 5.00
5D2 Emmitt Smith/506 2.00 5.00
5D3 Emmitt Smith/55 3.00 8.00
6D1 Jerry Rice/391 3.00 8.00
6D2 Jerry Rice/238 4.00 10.00
6D3 Jerry Rice/176 4.00 10.00
6D4 Jerry Rice/25 12.00 30.00
7D1 Mark Brunell/1066 .75 2.00
7D2 Mark Brunell/1112 .75 2.00
7D3 Mark Brunell/878 1.00 2.50
8D1 Eddie George/716 1.00 2.50
8D2 Eddie George/487 1.00 2.50
8D3 Eddie George/98 1.50 4.00
9D1 Marshall Faulk/762 1.00 2.50
9D2 Marshall Faulk/512 1.00 2.50
9D3 Marshall Faulk/101 1.50 4.00
10D1 Kurt Warner/1682 1.50 4.00
10D2 Kurt Warner/1336 1.50 4.00
10D3 Kurt Warner/1307 1.50 4.00
10D4 Kurt Warner/28 8.00 20.00
11D1 Edgerrin James/894 1.00 2.50
11D2 Edgerrin James/531 1.00 2.50
11D3 Edgerrin James/126 1.25 3.00
12D1 Tim Couch/940 1.00 2.50
12D2 Tim Couch/908 1.00 2.50
12D3 Tim Couch/564 1.00 2.50
12D4 Tim Couch/35 2.50 6.00

2000 Donruss Elite Down and Distance Die Cuts

STATED PRINT RUN 1-220
1D1 Randy Moss/34 2.50 6.00
1D2 Randy Moss/30 2.50 6.00
1D3 Randy Moss/14 5.00 12.00
2D1 Brett Favre/133 3.00 8.00
2D2 Brett Favre/119 3.00 8.00
2D3 Brett Favre/88 4.00 10.00
3D1 Dan Marino/82 4.00 10.00
3D2 Dan Marino/77 4.00 10.00
3D3 Dan Marino/42 6.00 15.00
4D1 Peyton Manning/121 4.00 10.00
4D2 Peyton Manning/118 4.00 10.00
4D3 Peyton Manning/91 5.00 12.00
5D1 Emmitt Smith/175 2.50 6.00
5D2 Emmitt Smith/121 2.50 6.00
5D3 Emmitt Smith/29 8.00 20.00
6D1 Jerry Rice/24 12.00 30.00
6D2 Jerry Rice/24 12.00 30.00
6D3 Jerry Rice/16 15.00 40.00
7D1 Mark Brunell/81 1.50 4.00
7D2 Mark Brunell/100 1.50 4.00
7D3 Mark Brunell/77 1.50 4.00
8D1 Eddie George/171 1.25 3.00
8D2 Eddie George/119 1.25 3.00
8D3 Eddie George/29 4.00 10.00
9D1 Marshall Faulk/138 1.25 3.00
9D2 Marshall Faulk/94 1.50 4.00
9D3 Marshall Faulk/20 4.00 10.00
10D1 Kurt Warner/129 2.50 6.00
10D2 Kurt Warner/106 2.50 6.00
10D3 Kurt Warner/87 3.00 8.00
11D1 Edgerrin James/220 1.25 3.00
11D2 Edgerrin James/130 1.25 3.00
11D3 Edgerrin James/17 5.00 12.00
12D1 Tim Couch/83 1.50 4.00
12D2 Tim Couch/81 1.50 4.00
12D3 Tim Couch/56 1.50 4.00

2000 Donruss Elite Passing the Torch

Randomly seeded in packs, this 18-card set features single player cards, PT1-PT12, which are sequentially numbered to 1500 with the first 100 cards autographed, and double player cards, PT13-PT18, which are sequentially numbered to 500 with the first 50 cards autographed. Cards are printed on gold holographic foil.

COMPLETE SET (18) 100.00 200.00
PT1-PT12 STATED PRINT RUN 1500
PT1-PT12 FIRST 100 CARDS SIGNED
PT13-PT18 STATED PRINT RUN 500
PT13-PT18 FIRST 50 CARDS SIGNED
PT1 Jerry Rice 4.00 10.00
PT2 Randy Moss 1.25 3.00
PT3 Dan Marino 3.00 8.00
PT4 Kurt Warner 2.50 6.00
PT5 Joe Montana 5.00 12.00
PT6 Steve Young 2.00 5.00
PT7 Bart Starr 4.00 10.00
PT8 Brett Favre 3.00 8.00
PT9 Roger Staubach 2.00 5.00
PT10 Troy Aikman 2.00 5.00
PT11 Gale Sayers 1.50 4.00
PT12 Edgerrin James 1.25 3.00
PT13 J.Rice/R.Moss 6.00 15.00
PT14 D.Marino/K.Warner 5.00 12.00
PT15 J.Montana/S.Young 8.00 20.00
PT16 B.Starr/B.Favre 6.00 15.00
PT17 R.Staubach/T.Aikman 3.00 8.00
PT18 G.Sayers/E.James 2.50 6.00

2000 Donruss Elite Passing the Torch Autographs

Randomly inserted in packs, this 18-card set feaures autographed versions of the base Passing the Torch insert cards. The first 100 serial numbered cards of 1-12 are autographed, and the first 50 serial numbered cards of 13-18 are autographed. Card backs carry a "PT" prefix.

PT1-PT12 FIRST 100-CARDS SIGNED
PT13-PT18 FIRST 50-CARDS SIGNED
PT1 Jerry Rice 90.00 150.00
PT2 Randy Moss 50.00 100.00
PT3 Dan Marino 100.00 200.00
PT4 Kurt Warner 35.00 60.00
PT5 Joe Montana 100.00 200.00
PT6 Steve Young 50.00 100.00
PT7 Bart Starr 100.00 200.00
PT8 Brett Favre 125.00 250.00
PT9 Roger Staubach 50.00 100.00
PT10 Troy Aikman 60.00 120.00
PT11 Gale Sayers 40.00 80.00
PT12 Edgerrin James 20.00 50.00
PT13 J.Rice/R.Moss 500.00 800.00
PT14 D.Marino/K.Warner 125.00 250.00
PT15 J.Montana/S.Young 250.00 400.00
PT16 B.Starr/B.Favre 250.00 400.00
PT17 R.Staubach/T.Aikman 100.00 200.00
PT18 G.Sayers/E.James 100.00 200.00

2000 Donruss Elite Throwback Threads

Randomly inserted in packs, this set features swatches of authentic game worn jerseys. Single jersey cards, TT1-TT30, are sequentially numbered to 100, and dual jersey cards, TT30-TT45, are sequentially numbered to 50. Some players also signed all or a limited number of the jersey cards as noted below. Finally, some cards were released at a later date missing the serial numbering, those typically sell for a discount.

TT1-TT30 SINGLE JSY PRINT RUN 100
TT31-TT45 DUAL JSY PRINT RUN 50
TT1 Joe Namath AU/100 100.00 200.00
TT2 Dan Marino 20.00 50.00
TT3 Walter Payton 30.00 80.00
TT4 Barry Sanders 15.00 40.00
TT5 Joe Montana/50* 30.00 80.00
TT5A Joe Montana AU/50* 125.00 250.00
TT6 Steve Young 25.00 50.00
TT7 Eric Dickerson/50* 15.00 40.00
TT7A Eric Dickerson AU/50* 30.00 80.00
TT8 Edgerrin James 8.00 20.00
TT9 Johnny Unitas/75* 30.00 80.00
TT9A Johnny Unitas AU/25* 300.00 450.00
TT10 Peyton Manning 25.00 60.00
TT11 Bart Starr/75* 30.00 80.00
TT11A Bart Starr AU/25* 200.00 400.00
TT12 Brett Favre 20.00 50.00
TT13 Terry Bradshaw/50* 30.00 80.00
TT13A Terry Bradshaw AU/50* 125.00 250.00
TT14 Kurt Warner 15.00 40.00
TT15 Dan Fouts/50* 25.00 60.00
TT15A Dan Fouts AU/50* 50.00 100.00
TT16 Drew Bledsoe 8.00 20.00
TT17 Earl Campbell/75* 30.00 60.00
TT17A Earl Campbell AU/25* 75.00 150.00
TT18 Eddie George 8.00 20.00
TT19 Jim Brown 25.00 60.00
TT20 Terrell Davis 8.00 20.00
TT21 Marcus Allen 20.00 50.00
TT22 Emmitt Smith 15.00 40.00
TT23 Bob Griese/75* 25.00 50.00
TT23A Bob Griese AU/25* 60.00 120.00
TT24 Brian Griese 6.00 15.00
TT25 Roger Staubach AU/100 75.00 150.00
TT26 Troy Aikman 25.00 50.00
TT27 Ken Stabler/75* 25.00 60.00
TT27 Ken Stabler AU/25* 100.00 200.00
TT28 Jake Plummer 6.00 15.00
TT29 Fran Tarkenton/75* 25.00 50.00
TT29 Fran Tarkenton AU/25* 75.00 150.00
TT30 Mark Brunell 8.00 20.00
TT31 Namath AU/Marino AU 250.00 500.00
TT32 W.Payton/B.Sanders 60.00 120.00
TT33 J.Montana/S.Young 30.00 80.00
TT34 E.Dickerson/E.James 20.00 50.00
TT35 J.Unitas/P.Manning 40.00 100.00
TT36 B.Starr/B.Favre 60.00 120.00
TT37 T.Bradshaw/K.Warner 25.00 60.00
TT38 D.Fouts/D.Bledsoe 20.00 50.00
TT39 E.Campbell/E.George 20.00 50.00
TT40 J.Brown/T.Davis 25.00 60.00
TT41 M.Allen/E.Smith 30.00 80.00
TT42 B.Griese/Br.Griese 20.00 50.00
TT43 Staubach AU/Aikman AU 125.00 250.00
TT44 K.Stabler/J.Plummer 20.00 50.00
TT45 F.Tarkenton/M.Brunell 20.00 50.00

2000 Donruss Elite Turn of the Century

Randomly inserted in packs, this 60-card set identifies 60 stars, young and old, expected to carry the NFL into the 21st century. Each card is sequentially numbered to 1000 and card backs carry a "TC" prefix.

COMPLETE SET (60) 100.00 200.00
STATED PRINT RUN 1000 SER.#'d SETS
*GOLD DIE CUT/21: 4X TO 10X BASIC INSERTS
GOLD DIE CUT PRINT RUN 21
TC1 Dan Marino 2.00 5.00
TC2 Edgerrin James .75 2.00
TC3 Peyton Manning 2.50 6.00
TC4 Drew Bledsoe .75 2.00
TC5 Doug Flutie .75 2.00
TC6 Curtis Martin .75 2.00
TC7 Eddie George .75 2.00
TC8 Steve McNair .75 2.00
TC9 Fred Taylor .60 1.50
TC10 Mark Brunell .75 2.00
TC11 Tim Couch .75 2.00
TC12 Peter Warrick .60 1.50
TC13 Terrell Davis .75 2.00
TC14 Jon Kitna .60 1.50
TC15 Emmitt Smith 1.50 4.00
TC16 Troy Aikman 1.25 3.00
TC17 Stephen Davis .60 1.50
TC18 Brad Johnson .75 2.00
TC19 Jake Plummer .60 1.50
TC20 Brett Favre 2.00 5.00
TC21 Barry Sanders 1.50 4.00
TC22 Marshall Faulk .75 2.00
TC23 Kurt Warner 1.50 4.00
TC24 Ricky Williams .75 2.00
TC25 Steve Young 1.25 3.00
TC26 Randy Moss .75 2.00
TC27 John Elway 1.50 4.00
TC28 Jerry Rice 2.50 6.00
TC29 Plaxico Burress .75 2.00
TC30 Cris Carter 1.00 2.50
TC31 Antonio Freeman .75 2.00
TC32 Thomas Jones .75 2.00
TC33 Travis Taylor .60 1.50
TC34 Marvin Harrison .75 2.00
TC35 Keyshawn Johnson .75 2.00
TC36 Shaun Alexander 1.00 2.50
TC37 Isaac Bruce 1.00 2.50
TC38 Ricky Watters .75 2.00
TC39 Ron Dayne 1.00 2.50
TC40 Brian Griese .60 1.50
TC41 Charlie Batch .60 1.50
TC42 Jamal Lewis 1.00 2.50
TC43 Jamal Anderson .75 2.00
TC44 Dorsey Levens .75 2.00
TC45 Chris Redman .60 1.50
TC46 Robert Smith .60 1.50
TC47 Chad Pennington .75 2.00
TC48 Terrell Owens .75 2.00
TC49 Deion Sanders .75 2.00
TC50 Duce Staley .60 1.50
TC51 Dez White .60 1.50
TC52 Jimmy Smith .75 2.00
TC53 Cade McNown .60 1.50
TC54 Daunte Culpepper .75 2.00
TC55 Akili Smith .60 1.50
TC56 Torry Holt .75 2.00
TC57 Kevin Johnson .60 1.50
TC58 Shaun King .60 1.50
TC59 Olandis Gary .75 2.00
TC60 Donovan McNabb .75 2.00

2001 Donruss Elite

Released as a 200-card set, 2001 Donruss Elite is comprised of 100 base cards, 100 rookie cards which are sequentially numbered to 500 with the first 50 of each autographed. Please note that some of the Rookie Cards were short printed and some were issued as redemption cards to be mailed in. Base cards are printed on foil board with team color highlights foil highlights. Elite was packaged in 18-pack boxes containing five cards each and carried a suggested retail price of $3.99.

COMP.SET w/o SP's (100) 7.50 20.00
ROOKIE PRINT RUN 250-500
1 David Boston .15 .40
2 Jake Plummer .15 .40
3 Thomas Jones .15 .40
4 Jamal Anderson .20 .50
5 Chris Redman .25 .60
6 Jamal Lewis .25 .60
7 Shannon Sharpe .20 .50
8 Travis Taylor .15 .40
9 Trent Dilfer .15 .40
10 Doug Flutie .20 .50
11 Eric Moulds .15 .40
12 Rob Johnson .20 .50
13 Muhsin Muhammad .15 .40
14 Steve Beuerlein .20 .50
15 Brian Urlacher .30 .75
16 Cade McNown .20 .50
17 Marcus Robinson .20 .50
18 Akili Smith .15 .40
19 Corey Dillon .15 .40
20 Peter Warrick .15 .40
21 Kevin Johnson .15 .40
22 Tim Couch .15 .40
23 Emmitt Smith .40 1.00
24 Troy Aikman .30 .75
25 Brian Griese .15 .40
26 John Elway .40 1.00
27 Mike Anderson .15 .40
28 Rod Smith .20 .50
29 Terrell Davis .20 .50
30 Barry Sanders .40 1.00
31 Charlie Batch .15 .40
32 James Stewart .15 .40
33 Ahman Green .20 .50
34 Antonio Freeman .25 .60
35 Brett Favre .50 1.25
36 Edgerrin James .20 .50
37 Marvin Harrison .20 .50
38 Peyton Manning .60 1.50
39 Fred Taylor .15 .40
40 Jimmy Smith .20 .50
41 Keenan McCardell .20 .50
42 Mark Brunell .20 .50
43 Derrick Alexander .15 .40
44 Elvis Grbac .20 .50
45 Sylvester Morris .15 .40
46 Tony Gonzalez .20 .50
47 Dan Marino .50 1.25
48 Jay Fiedler .20 .50
49 Lamar Smith .20 .50
50 Oronde Gadsden .15 .40
51 Cris Carter .25 .60
52 Daunte Culpepper .20 .50
53 Randy Moss .20 .50
54 Robert Smith .15 .40
55 Drew Bledsoe .20 .50
56 Terry Glenn .20 .50
57 Aaron Brooks .15 .40
58 Joe Horn .15 .40
59 Ricky Williams .20 .50
60 Amani Toomer .15 .40
61 Ike Hilliard .15 .40
62 Kerry Collins .15 .40
63 Ron Dayne .20 .50
64 Tiki Barber .20 .50
65 Chad Pennington .15 .40
66 Curtis Martin .20 .50
67 Vinny Testaverde .15 .40
68 Wayne Chrebet .15 .40
69 Rich Gannon .20 .50
70 Tim Brown .25 .60
71 Tyrone Wheatley .20 .50
72 Donovan McNabb .20 .50
73 Jerome Bettis .25 .60
74 Plaxico Burress .15 .40
75 Junior Seau .20 .50
76 Charlie Garner .20 .50
77 Jeff Garcia .15 .40
78 Jerry Rice .50 1.25
79 Terrell Owens .20 .50
80 Darrell Jackson .20 .50
81 Ricky Watters .20 .50
82 Shaun Alexander .15 .40
83 Isaac Bruce .25 .60
84 Kurt Warner .40 1.00
85 Marshall Faulk .20 .50
86 Torry Holt .20 .50
87 Trent Green .15 .40
88 Keyshawn Johnson .20 .50
89 Shaun King .15 .40
90 Warren Sapp .20 .50
91 Warrick Dunn .15 .40
92 Eddie George .25 .60
93 Jevon Kearse .15 .40
94 Steve McNair .20 .50
95 Albert Connell .15 .40
96 Jeff George .20 .50
97 Brad Johnson .20 .50
98 Bruce Smith .20 .50
99 Michael Westbrook .15 .40
100 Stephen Davis .15 .40
101 Michael Vick RC 6.00 15.00
102 Drew Brees RC 75.00 150.00
103 Chris Weinke RC 3.00 8.00
104 Quincy Carter RC 3.00 8.00
105 Sage Rosenfels RC 3.00 8.00
106 Josh Heupel RC 4.00 10.00
107 Tony Driver RC 3.00 8.00
108 Ben Leard RC 2.50 6.00
109 Marques Tuiasosopo RC 3.00 8.00
110 Tim Hasselbeck RC 3.00 8.00
111 Mike McMahon RC 3.00 8.00
112 Deuce McAllister RC 4.00 10.00
113 LaMont Jordan RC 4.00 10.00
114 LaDainian Tomlinson RC 12.00 30.00
115 James Jackson RC 2.50 6.00
116 Anthony Thomas RC 4.00 10.00
117 Travis Henry RC 3.00 8.00
118 DeAngelo Evans RC 3.00 8.00
119 Travis Minor RC 3.00 8.00
120 Rudi Johnson RC 4.00 10.00
121 Michael Bennett RC 3.00 8.00
122 Kevan Barlow RC 3.00 8.00
123 Dan Alexander RC 3.00 8.00
124 David Allen RC 2.50 6.00
125 Correll Buckhalter RC 2.50 6.00
126 David Rivers RC 2.50 6.00
127 Reggie White RC 2.50 6.00
128 Moran Norris RC 2.50 6.00
129 Ja'Mar Toombs RC 2.50 6.00
130 Jason McKinley RC 2.50 6.00
131 Scotty Anderson RC 2.50 6.00
132 Dustin McClintock RC 3.00 8.00
133 Heath Evans RC 3.00 8.00
134 David Terrell RC 3.00 8.00
135 Santana Moss RC 4.00 10.00
136 Rod Gardner RC 3.00 8.00
137 Quincy Morgan RC 3.00 8.00
138 Freddie Mitchell RC 2.50 6.00
139 Boo Williams RC 2.50 6.00
140 Reggie Wayne RC 5.00 12.00
141 Ronney Daniels RC 2.50 6.00
142 Bobby Newcombe RC 3.00 8.00
143 Reggie Germany/250 RC 3.00 8.00
144 Jesse Palmer RC 3.00 8.00

Card	Low	High
145 Robert Ferguson RC	4.00	10.00
146 Ken-Yon Rambo RC	2.50	6.00
147 Alex Bannister RC	2.50	6.00
148 Koren Robinson RC	3.00	8.00
149 Chad Johnson RC	4.00	10.00
150 Chris Chambers RC	2.50	6.00
151 Javon Green RC	2.50	6.00
152 Snoop Minnis RC	2.50	6.00
153 Vinny Sutherland RC	2.50	6.00
154 Cedrick Wilson RC	3.00	8.00
155 John Capel/250 RC	3.00	8.00
156 T.J. Houshmandzadeh RC	3.00	8.00
157 Todd Heap RC	3.00	8.00
158 Alge Crumpler RC	4.00	10.00
159 Jabari Holloway RC	2.50	6.00
160 Marcellus Rivers RC	2.50	6.00
161 Rashon Burns RC	2.50	6.00
162 Tony Stewart RC	3.00	8.00
163 Jevaris Johnson RC	2.50	6.00
164 Jamal Reynolds RC	2.50	6.00
165 Andre Carter RC	3.00	8.00
166 David Warren RC	2.50	6.00
167 Justin Smith RC	5.00	12.00
168 Josh Booty RC	3.00	8.00
169 Karon Riley RC	2.50	6.00
170 Cedric Scott RC	2.50	6.00
171 Kenny Smith RC	2.50	6.00
172 Richard Seymour RC	4.00	10.00
173 Willie Howard RC	2.50	6.00
174 Markus Steele RC	2.50	6.00
175 Marcus Stroud RC	3.00	8.00
176 Damione Lewis RC	3.00	8.00
177 Casey Hampton RC	6.00	15.00
178 Ennis Davis RC	2.50	6.00
179 Gerard Warren RC	3.00	8.00
180 Tommy Polley RC	2.50	6.00
181 Kendrell Bell/250 RC	5.00	12.00
182 Dan Morgan RC	3.00	8.00
183 Morlon Greenwood RC	2.50	6.00
184 Quinton Caver/250	3.00	8.00
185 Keith Adams RC	2.50	6.00
186 Brian Allen RC	2.50	6.00
187 Carlos Polk RC	2.50	6.00
188 Torrance Marshall RC	2.50	6.00
189 Jamie Winborn RC	3.00	8.00
190 Jamar Fletcher RC	2.50	6.00
191 Ken Lucas RC	3.00	8.00
192 Fred Smoot RC	3.00	8.00
193 Nate Clements RC	3.00	8.00
194 Will Allen RC	4.00	10.00
195 W.Middlebrooks/250 RC	4.00	10.00
196 Gary Baxter RC	2.50	6.00
197 Derrick Gibson RC	2.50	6.00
198 Robert Carswell/250 RC	3.00	8.00
199 Hakim Akbar RC	2.50	6.00
200 Adam Archuleta RC	3.00	8.00

2001 Donruss Elite Aspirations

*VETS/70-99: 8X TO 20X BASIC CARDS
*ROOKIE/70-99: .3X TO .8X RC/500
*ROOKIE/70-99: .25X TO .6X RC/250
*VETS/45-69: 10X TO 25X BASIC CARDS
*ROOKIES/45-69: .4X TO 1X RC/500
*ROOKIES/45-69: .3X TO .8X RC/250
*ROOKIES/30-44: .5X TO 1.2X RC/500
*ROOKIES/30-44: .4X TO 1X RC/250
*VETS/20-29: 20X TO 50X BASIC CARDS
*ROOKIES/20-29: 1X TO 2.5X RC/500
*ROOKIES/20-29: .8X TO 2X RC/250
*VETS/10-19: 25X TO 60X BASIC CARDS
*ROOKIES/10-19: 1.2X TO 3X RC/500

Card	Low	High
101 Michael Vick/93	30.00	60.00
102 Drew Brees/85	250.00	500.00
114 LaDainian Tomlinson/95	25.00	60.00

2001 Donruss Elite Status

*VETS/70-99: 8X TO 20X BASIC CARDS
*ROOKIES/70-99: .3X TO .8X RC/500
*VETS/45-69: 10X TO 25X BASIC CARDS
*ROOKIES/45-69: .4X TO 1X RC/500
*VETS/30-44: 12X TO 30X BASIC CARDS
*ROOKIES/30-44: .5X TO 1.2X RC/500
*VETS/20-29: 20X TO 50X BASIC CARDS
*ROOKIES/20-29: 1X TO 2.5X RC/500
*STARS/10-19: 25X TO 60X BASIC CARDS
*ROOKIES/10-19: 1.2X TO 3X RC/500

Card	Low	High
102 Drew Brees/15	400.00	800.00
181 Kendrell Bell/37	5.00	12.00
195 Willie Middlebrooks/42	4.00	10.00

2001 Donruss Elite Turn of the Century Autographs

Randomly Inserted In packs, this 100-card set features the rookie crop of players expected to carry the NFL into the 21st century. Each card is sequentially numbered to 500 since they were to be considered a variation on the base RCs, but just the first 50 serial numbered cards were actually signed. Some cards were issued in packs as mail redemptions which carried an expiration date of May 1, 2003. Finally, several players did not ultimately sign for the set so those cards were either issued with "no autograph" printed on the fronts. The Michael Vick card was never officially issued and his exchange card was generally redeemed for signed cards of othe rplayers. However, some unsigned copies made their way to the market with the appropriate die cut shape and set name on the front.

STATED PRINT RUN 50 SER.#'d SETS

Card	Low	High
101 Michael Vick unsigned	30.00	80.00
102 Drew Brees	200.00	350.00
103 Chris Weinke	10.00	25.00
104 Quincy Carter	10.00	25.00
105 Sage Rosenfels	10.00	25.00
106 Josh Heupel	12.00	30.00
107 Tony Driver No Auto	6.00	15.00
108 Ben Leard	8.00	20.00
109 Marques Tuiasosopo	10.00	25.00
110 Tim Hasselbeck	10.00	25.00
111 Mike McMahon	10.00	25.00
112 Deuce McAllister	12.00	30.00
113 LaMont Jordan	12.00	30.00
114 LaDainian Tomlinson	60.00	120.00
115 James Jackson	8.00	20.00
116 Anthony Thomas	12.00	30.00
117 Travis Henry	10.00	25.00
118 DeAngelo Evans	10.00	25.00
119 Travis Minor	10.00	25.00
120 Rudi Johnson	12.00	30.00
121 Michael Bennett	10.00	25.00
122 Kevan Barlow	10.00	25.00
123 Dan Alexander	10.00	25.00
124 David Allen	8.00	20.00
125 Correll Buckhalter	8.00	20.00
126 David Rivers No Auto	5.00	12.00
127 Reggie White	8.00	20.00
128 Moran Norris	8.00	20.00
129 Ja'Mar Toombs No Auto	5.00	12.00
130 Jason McKinley No Auto	5.00	12.00
131 Scotty Anderson	8.00	20.00
132 Dustin McClintock No Auto	6.00	15.00
133 Heath Evans	10.00	25.00
134 David Terrell	10.00	25.00
135 Santana Moss	12.00	30.00
136 Rod Gardner	10.00	25.00
137 Quincy Morgan	10.00	25.00
138 Freddie Mitchell	8.00	20.00
139 Boo Williams	8.00	20.00
140 Reggie Wayne	50.00	100.00
141 Ronney Daniels	8.00	20.00
142 Bobby Newcombe	10.00	25.00
143 Reggie Germany	8.00	20.00
144 Jesse Palmer	10.00	25.00
145 Robert Ferguson	12.00	30.00
146 Ken-Yon Rambo	8.00	20.00
147 Alex Bannister	8.00	20.00
148 Koren Robinson	10.00	25.00
149 Chad Johnson	12.00	30.00
150 Chris Chambers	8.00	20.00
151 Javon Green	8.00	20.00
152 Snoop Minnis	8.00	20.00
153 Vinny Sutherland	8.00	20.00
154 Cedrick Wilson	10.00	25.00
155 John Capel No Auto	5.00	12.00
156 T.J. Houshmandzadeh	10.00	25.00
157 Todd Heap	10.00	25.00
158 Alge Crumpler	12.00	30.00
159 Jabari Holloway	8.00	20.00
160 Marcellus Rivers No Auto	5.00	12.00
161 Rashon Burns	8.00	20.00
162 Tony Stewart	10.00	25.00
163 Jevaris Johnson No Auto	5.00	12.00
164 Jamal Reynolds	8.00	20.00
165 Andre Carter	10.00	25.00
166 David Warren No Auto	5.00	12.00
167 Justin Smith	15.00	40.00
168 Josh Booty	10.00	25.00
169 Karon Riley	8.00	20.00
170 Cedric Scott	8.00	20.00
171 Kenny Smith	8.00	20.00
172 Richard Seymour No Auto	8.00	20.00
173 Willie Howard	8.00	20.00
174 Markus Steele	8.00	20.00
175 Marcus Stroud	10.00	25.00
176 Damione Lewis	10.00	25.00
177 Casey Hampton No Auto	8.00	20.00
178 Ennis Davis	8.00	20.00
179 Gerard Warren	10.00	25.00
180 Tommy Polley	8.00	20.00
181 Kendrell Bell	12.00	30.00
182 Dan Morgan	10.00	25.00
183 Morlon Greenwood	8.00	20.00
184 Quinton Caver No Auto	5.00	12.00
185 Keith Adams No Auto	5.00	12.00
186 Brian Allen	8.00	20.00
187 Carlos Polk	8.00	20.00
188 Torrance Marshall	8.00	20.00
189 Jamie Winborn	10.00	25.00
190 Jamar Fletcher No Auto	5.00	12.00
191 Ken Lucas	10.00	25.00
192 Fred Smoot No Auto	6.00	15.00
193 Nate Clements No Auto	6.00	15.00
194 Will Allen	12.00	30.00
195 Willie Middlebrooks No Auto	6.00	15.00
196 Gary Baxter	8.00	20.00
197 Derrick Gibson No Auto	5.00	12.00
198 Robert Carswell No Auto	5.00	12.00
199 Hakim Akbar	8.00	20.00
200 Adam Archuleta No Auto	6.00	15.00

2001 Donruss Elite Face To Face

This 45-card set was randomly inserted into packs, and carry a "FF" prefix. The single player cards, FF1-FF30, were serial numbered to 100, and had a piece of a game used face mask from the featured player. The dual player cards, FF31-FF45, were serial numbered to 50 and contained pieces of game used face masks from both featured players.

FF1-FF30 SINGLE MASK PRINT RUN 100
FF31-FF45 DUAL MASK PRINT RUN 50

Card	Low	High
FF1 John Elway	8.00	20.00
FF2 Dan Marino	10.00	25.00
FF3 Brett Favre	10.00	25.00
FF4 Barry Sanders	8.00	20.00
FF5 Marshall Faulk	4.00	10.00
FF6 Edgerrin James	4.00	10.00
FF7 Troy Aikman	6.00	15.00
FF8 Steve Young	6.00	15.00
FF9 Jamal Anderson	4.00	10.00
FF10 Terrell Davis	4.00	10.00
FF11 Tim Brown	5.00	12.00
FF12 Jerry Rice	10.00	25.00
FF13 Isaac Bruce	5.00	12.00
FF14 Torry Holt	4.00	10.00
FF15 Reggie White DE	5.00	12.00
FF16 Warren Sapp	4.00	10.00
FF17 Jerome Bettis	5.00	12.00
FF18 Fred Taylor	3.00	8.00
FF19 Ray Lewis	5.00	12.00
FF20 Eddie George	5.00	12.00
FF21 Ryan Leaf	3.00	8.00
FF22 Peyton Manning	12.00	30.00
FF23 Lawrence Taylor	5.00	12.00
FF24 Phil Simms	4.00	10.00
FF25 Joe Montana	15.00	40.00
FF26 Marcus Allen	5.00	12.00
FF27 Keyshawn Johnson	4.00	10.00
FF28 Wayne Chrebet	3.00	8.00
FF29 Shaun King	3.00	8.00
FF30 Donovan McNabb	4.00	10.00
FF31 D.Marino/J.Elway	20.00	50.00
FF32 B.Favro/B.Sanders	20.00	50.00
FF33 E.James/M.Faulk	8.00	20.00
FF34 T.Aikman/S.Young	12.00	30.00
FF35 J.Anderson/T.Davis	8.00	20.00
FF36 J.Rice/T.Brown	20.00	50.00
FF37 I.Bruce/T.Holt	10.00	25.00
FF38 R.White/W.Sapp	10.00	25.00
FF39 F.Taylor/J.Bettis	10.00	25.00
FF40 R.Lewis/E.George	10.00	25.00
FF41 P.Manning/R.Leaf	25.00	60.00
FF42 P.Simms/L.Taylor	10.00	25.00
FF43 J.Montana/M.Allen	30.00	80.00
FF44 W.Chrebet/K.Johnson	8.00	20.00
FF45 D.McNabb/S.King	8.00	20.00

2001 Donruss Elite Face To Face Autographs

This 13-card autograph set was randomly inserted into packs all as redemption cards. The cards featured a piece of game used face mask from the featured player or players and the print runs varied from player to player.

ANNOUNCED PRINT RUN 15-55

Card	Low	High
1 John Elway/55*	100.00	200.00
2 Dan Marino/35*	125.00	250.00
4 Barry Sanders/50*	125.00	200.00
8 Steve Young/35*	75.00	135.00
10 Terrell Davis/15*		
23 Lawrence Taylor/25*	75.00	125.00
31 J.Elway/D.Marino/15*		
33 E.James/M.Faulk/15*		
34 T.Aikman/S.Young/15*		
42 P.Simms/L.Taylor/15*		

2001 Donruss Elite Passing the Torch

Randomly seeded in packs, this 24-card set features single player cards, PT1-PT16, which are sequentially numbered to 1000, and double player cards, PT17-PT24, which are sequentially numbered to 500. Cards are printed on gold holographic foil and card backs carry a "PT" prefix. Several cards were released via a mail redemption card that carried an expiration date of 5/01/2003.

Card	Low	High
COMPLETE SET (24)	50.00	100.00

PT1-PT16 SINGLE PLAYER PRINT RUN 1000
PT17-PT24 DUAL PLAYER PRINT RUN 500

Card	Low	High
PT1 John Elway	1.25	3.00
PT2 Brian Griese	.50	1.25
PT3 Dick Butkus	1.00	2.50
PT4 Brian Urlacher	1.00	2.50
PT5 Fran Tarkenton	.75	2.00
PT6 Daunte Culpepper	.60	1.50
PT7 Jim Brown	1.00	2.50
PT8 Jamal Lewis	.75	2.00
PT9 Larry Csonka	.75	2.00
PT10 Ron Dayne	.60	1.50
PT11 Tony Dorsett	.75	2.00
PT12 Emmitt Smith	1.25	3.00
PT13 Eric Dickerson	.60	1.50
PT14 Marshall Faulk	.60	1.50
PT15 Joe Namath	1.25	3.00
PT16 Chad Pennington	.50	1.25
PT17 J.Elway/B.Griese	.75	2.00
PT18 B.Urlacher/D.Butkus	1.50	4.00
PT19 Tarkenton/Culpepper	1.25	3.00
PT20 J.Lewis/J.Brown	1.50	4.00
PT21 L.Csonka/R.Dayne	1.25	3.00
PT22 T.Dorsett/E.Smith	2.00	5.00
PT23 M.Faulk/E.Dickerson	1.00	2.50
PT24 J.Namath/C.Pennington	2.00	5.00

2001 Donruss Elite Passing the Torch Autographs

Randomly seeded in packs, this 24-card set features single player autographed cards, PT1-PT16, which are sequentially numbered to 100, and double player autographed cards, PT17-PT24, which are sequentially numbered to 50 . Cards are printed on gold holographic foil and card backs carry a "PT" prefix. Several cards were released via a mail redemption card that carried an expiration date of 5/01/2003.

PT1-PT16 SINGLE PRINT RUN 100
PT17-PT24 DUAL PRINT RUN 50

Card	Low	High
PT1 John Elway	90.00	150.00
PT2 Brian Griese	20.00	50.00
PT3 Dick Butkus	35.00	80.00
PT4 Brian Urlacher	30.00	80.00
PT5 Fran Tarkenton	25.00	60.00
PT6 Daunte Culpepper	15.00	40.00
PT7 Jim Brown	50.00	120.00
PT8 Jamal Lewis	15.00	40.00
PT9 Larry Csonka	30.00	80.00
PT10 Ron Dayne	15.00	40.00
PT11 Tony Dorsett	40.00	80.00
PT12 Emmitt Smith	150.00	225.00
PT13 Eric Dickerson	20.00	50.00
PT14 Marshall Faulk	40.00	80.00
PT15 Joe Namath	60.00	150.00
PT16 Chad Pennington	20.00	50.00
PT17 J.Elway/B.Griese	75.00	150.00
PT18 B.Urlacher/D.Butkus	125.00	200.00
PT19 Tarkenton/Culpepper	40.00	100.00
PT20 J.Lewis/J.Brown	75.00	135.00
PT21 L.Csonka/R.Dayne	40.00	100.00
PT22 T.Dorsett/E.Smith	150.00	250.00
PT23 M.Faulk/E.Dickerson	60.00	120.00
PT24 J.Namath/Pennington	75.00	150.00

2001 Donruss Elite Primary Colors

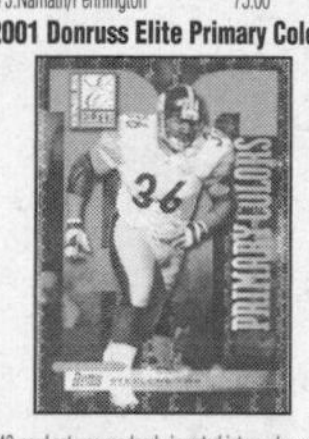

This 40-card set was randomly inserted into packs, and was serial numbered to 975. The cards contained a "PC" prefix and were the red variation and the base version of the set.

Card	Low	High
COMPLETE SET (40)	50.00	100.00

STATED PRINT RUN 975 SER.#'d SETS
*RED DIE CUT/25: 5X TO 12X
RED DIE CUT PRINT RUN 25
*BLUE/200: .8X TO 2X BASIC INSERTS
BLUE PRINT RUN 200
*BLUE DIE CUT/50: 3X TO 8X
BLUE DIE CUT PRINT RUN 50
*YELLOW/25: 4X TO 10X BASIC INSERTS
YELLOW PRINT RUN 25
*YELLOW DIE CUT/75: 2X TO 5X
YELLOW DIE CUT PRINT RUN 75

Card	Low	High
PC1 Peyton Manning	2.50	8.00
PC2 Edgerrin James	.75	2.00
PC3 Marvin Harrison	.75	2.00
PC4 Curtis Martin	.75	2.00
PC5 Eric Moulds	.60	1.50
PC6 Dan Marino	2.00	5.00
PC7 Drew Bledsoe	.75	2.00
PC8 Drew Brees	25.00	50.00
PC9 Jamal Lewis	1.00	2.50
PC10 Michael Vick	1.50	4.00
PC11 Eddie George	1.00	2.50
PC12 Steve McNair	.75	2.00
PC13 Jerome Bettis	1.00	2.50
PC14 Koren Robinson	.75	2.00
PC15 Mark Brunell	.75	2.00
PC16 Fred Taylor	.60	1.50
PC17 Michael Bennett	.75	2.00
PC18 David Terrell	.75	2.00
PC19 Brian Griese	.60	1.50
PC20 Mike Anderson	.60	1.50
PC21 John Elway	1.50	4.00
PC22 Terrell Owens	.75	2.00
PC23 Rudi Johnson	1.00	2.50
PC24 Jerry Rice	2.00	5.00
PC25 Ricky Williams	.75	2.00
PC26 Aaron Brooks	.60	1.50
PC27 Kurt Warner	1.50	4.00
PC28 Marshall Faulk	.75	2.00
PC29 Isaac Bruce	1.00	2.50
PC30 Brett Favre	2.00	5.00
PC31 Santana Moss	1.00	2.50
PC32 Daunte Culpepper	.75	2.00
PC33 Randy Moss	.75	2.00
PC34 Cris Carter	1.00	2.50
PC35 Barry Sanders	1.50	4.00
PC36 Emmitt Smith	1.50	4.00
PC37 Stephen Davis	.60	1.50
PC38 Ron Dayne	.75	2.00
PC39 Donovan McNabb	.75	2.00
PC40 Deuce McAllister	1.00	2.50

2001 Donruss Elite Prime Numbers

This 30-card set was randomly inserted into packs and featured 10 players with 3 versions of each player. Donruss took one amazing stat from each of the 10 players and broke that down by digit and serial numbered the cards to 3 different quantities. Please note the serial numbers are different for each player.

STATED PRINT RUN 1-400

Card	Low	High
PN1A Dan Marino/300	3.00	8.00
PN1B Dan Marino/80	6.00	15.00
PN2A John Elway/300	2.50	6.00
PN2B John Elway/40	8.00	20.00
PN3A Mike Anderson/200	1.50	4.00
PN3B Mike Anderson/50	3.00	8.00
PN4A Randy Moss/200	2.00	5.00
PN5A Daunte Culpepper/300	1.25	3.00
PN5B Daunte Culpepper/50	4.00	10.00
PN6A Kurt Warner/400	2.50	6.00
PN6B Kurt Warner/40	8.00	20.00
PN7A Jerry Rice/100	6.00	15.00
PN7B Jerry Rice/80	6.00	15.00
PN8A Edgerrin James/200	2.00	5.00
PN9A Peyton Manning/300	4.00	10.00
PN9B Peyton Manning/20	20.00	50.00
PN10A Brett Favre/100	6.00	15.00
PN10B Brett Favre/40	10.00	25.00

2001 Donruss Elite Prime Numbers Die Cuts

This 30-card set was randomly inserted into packs and featured 10 players with 3 versions of each player. Donruss took one amazing stat from each of the 10 players and broke that down by digit and serial numbered the cards to 3 different quantities, but they took this just one step further and made these the die-cut version and added a holo-foil board and with gold-foil highlights. Please note the serial numbers are different for each player.

STATED PRINT RUN 12-440

Card	Low	High
PN1A Dan Marino/85	6.00	15.00
PN1B Dan Marino/305	3.00	8.00
PN1C Dan Marino/380	3.00	8.00
PN2A John Elway/48	8.00	20.00
PN2B John Elway/308	2.50	6.00
PN2C John Elway/340	2.50	6.00
PN3A Mike Anderson/51	3.00	8.00
PN3B Mike Anderson/201	1.50	4.00
PN3C Mike Anderson/250	1.00	2.50
PN4A Randy Moss/12	6.00	15.00
PN4B Randy Moss/202	2.00	5.00
PN4C Randy Moss/210	2.00	5.00
PN5A Daunte Culpepper/57	4.00	10.00
PN5B Daunte Culpepper/307	1.25	3.00
PN5C Daunte Culpepper/350	1.25	3.00
PN6A Kurt Warner/41	8.00	20.00
PN6B Kurt Warner/401	2.50	6.00
PN6C Kurt Warner/440	2.50	6.00
PN7A Jerry Rice/87	6.00	15.00
PN7B Jerry Rice/107	6.00	15.00
PN7C Jerry Rice/180	5.00	12.00
PN8A Edgerrin James/19	6.00	15.00
PN8B Edgerrin James/209	2.00	5.00
PN8C Edgerrin James/210	2.00	5.00
PN9A Peyton Manning/26	20.00	50.00
PN9B Peyton Manning/306	4.00	10.00
PN9C Peyton Manning/320	4.00	10.00
PN10A Brett Favre/41	10.00	25.00
PN10B Brett Favre/101	6.00	15.00
PN10C Brett Favre/140	5.00	12.00

2001 Donruss Elite Throwback Threads

Randomly inserted in packs, this set features swatches of authentic game worn jerseys. Single jersey cards, TT1-TT30, are sequentially numbered to 100, and dual jersey cards, TT30-TT45, are sequentially numbered to 50.

TT1-TT30 SINGLE JSY PRINT RUN 100
TT31-TT45 DUAL JSY PRINT RUN 50

Card	Low	High
TT1 Art Monk	2.50	6.00
TT2 Joe Theismann	2.50	6.00
TT3 Jim Kelly	2.50	6.00
TT4 Thurman Thomas	2.00	5.00
TT5 Joe Namath	20.00	50.00
TT6 Don Maynard	2.00	5.00
TT7 Bob Griese	2.50	6.00
TT8 Larry Csonka	2.50	6.00
TT9 Joe Montana	15.00	40.00
TT10 Jerry Rice	5.00	12.00
TT11 Raymond Berry	2.00	5.00
TT12 Marvin Harrison	2.00	5.00
TT13 Warren Moon	2.50	6.00
TT14 Steve McNair	2.00	5.00
TT15 Terrell Davis	2.00	5.00
TT16 Mike Anderson	1.50	4.00
TT17 Frank Gifford	2.50	6.00
TT18 Ron Dayne	2.00	5.00
TT19 Walter Payton	20.00	50.00
TT20 Gale Sayers	2.50	6.00
TT21 Terry Bradshaw	3.00	8.00
TT22 Franco Harris	2.50	6.00
TT23 Troy Aikman	3.00	8.00
TT24 Emmitt Smith	4.00	10.00
TT25 Fran Tarkenton	2.50	6.00
TT26 Daunte Culpepper	2.00	5.00
TT27 John Elway	4.00	10.00
TT28 Brian Griese	1.50	4.00
TT29 Eric Dickerson	2.00	5.00
TT30 Marshall Faulk	2.00	5.00
TT31 J.Theismann/A.Monk	3.00	8.00
TT32 T.Thomas/J.Kelly	2.50	6.00
TT33 J.Namath/D.Maynard	5.00	12.00
TT34 B.Griese/L.Csonka	3.00	8.00
TT35 J.Montana/J.Rice	10.00	25.00
TT36 R.Berry/M.Harrison	2.50	6.00
TT37 W.Moon/S.McNair	3.00	8.00
TT38 T.Davis/M.Anderson	2.50	6.00
TT39 F.Gifford/R.Dayne	3.00	8.00
TT40 W.Payton/G.Sayers	0.00	20.00
TT41 T.Bradshaw/F.Harris	4.00	10.00
TT42 T.Aikman/E.Smith	5.00	12.00
TT43 F.Tarkenton/D.Culpepper	3.00	8.00
TT44 J.Elway/B.Griese	2.00	5.00
TT45 E.Dickerson/M.Faulk	2.50	6.00

2001 Donruss Elite Throwback Threads Autographs

Randomly inserted in packs, this 26-card set features swatches of authentic game worn jerseys and an autograph. Single jersey cards, TT1-TT30, are sequentially numbered to 100, and dual jersey cards, TT30-TT45, are sequentially numbered to 50. Please note that the announced print runs vary from player to player, and all players were initially issued as redemptions.

ANNOUNCED PRINT RUNS LISTED BELOW

Card	Low	High
TT1 Art Monk/25*	40.00	80.00
TT2 Joe Theismann/25*	40.00	80.00
TT3 Jim Kelly/39*	40.00	100.00
TT5 Joe Namath/25*	100.00	200.00
TT6 Don Maynard/25*	25.00	60.00
TT8 Larry Csonka/35*	40.00	80.00
TT9 Joe Montana/16*	100.00	225.00
TT11 Raymond Berry/15*		
TT12 Marvin Harrison/50*	20.00	50.00
TT13 Warren Moon/25*	40.00	80.00
TT16 Mike Anderson/50*	20.00	50.00
TT17 Frank Gifford/15*	30.00	60.00
TT20 Gale Sayers/15*	75.00	150.00
TT21 Terry Bradshaw/25*	100.00	200.00
TT23 Troy Aikman/25*	75.00	150.00
TT24 Emmitt Smith/15*	125.00	250.00
TT26 Daunte Culpepper/50*	25.00	60.00
TT27 John Elway/15*	125.00	250.00
TT33 Namath/Maynard/25*	125.00	200.00
TT34 B.Griese/L.Csonka/15*		
TT35 J.Montana/J.Rice/15*		
TT43 Trkntn/Clpper/15*		
TT44 B.Griese/J.Elway/15*		
TT45 Dickerson/M.Faulk/15*	40.00	80.00

2001 Donruss Elite Title Waves

This 30-card set was randomly inserted in packs, and was sequentially numbered to the year the featured player won one of five different titles. The first 100 were produced on holo-foil board.

Card	Low	High
COMPLETE SET (30)	20.00	50.00

*HOLOFOIL/100: 2.5X TO 6X BASIC INSERTS
HOLOFOIL PRINT RUN 100 SER.#'d SETS

Card	Low	High
TW1 Kurt Warner/1999	1.00	2.50
TW2 Dan Marino/1994	1.25	3.00
TW3 Brett Favre/1995	1.25	3.00
TW4 Peyton Manning/2000	1.50	4.00
TW5 John Elway/1996	1.00	2.50
TW6 Steve Young/1997	.75	2.00
TW7 Barry Sanders/1997	1.00	2.50
TW8 Emmitt Smith/1993	1.00	2.50
TW9 Terrell Davis/1998	.50	1.25
TW10 Edgerrin James/2000	.50	1.25
TW11 Stephen Davis/1999	.40	1.00
TW12 Curtis Martin/1995	.50	1.25
TW13 Marvin Harrison/1999	.50	1.25
TW14 Antonio Freeman/1998	.60	1.50
TW15 Jerry Rice/1995	1.25	3.00
TW16 Randy Moss/1999	.50	1.25
TW17 Tim Brown/1997	.60	1.50
TW18 Isaac Bruce/1996	.60	1.50
TW19 Ricky Williams/2000	.50	1.25
TW20 Peyton Manning/1999	1.50	4.00
TW21 Eddie George/2000	.60	1.50
TW22 Barry Sanders/1993	1.00	2.50
TW23 Daunte Culpepper/2000	.50	1.25
TW24 Dan Marino/1994	1.25	3.00
TW25 John Elway/1999	1.00	2.50
TW26 Marshall Faulk/2000	.50	1.25
TW27 Brett Favre/1997	1.25	3.00
TW28 Steve Young/1995	.75	2.00
TW29 Troy Aikman/1993	.75	2.00
TW30 Jerry Rice/1990	1.25	3.00

2001 Donruss Elite Chicago Collection

NOT PRICED DUE TO SCARCITY

2002 Donruss Elite Samples

*SILVER SAMPLE: .8X TO 2X BASIC CARDS
*GOLD SAMPLE: 1.5X TO 4X BASIC CARDS

2002 Donruss Elite

This 200-card set was released in June, 2002. The first 100-cards in this set feature veterans while cards #101-200 feature rookies. The rookie cards were sequentially numbered to 400.

Card	Low	High
COMP.SET w/o SP's (100)	7.50	20.00
1 Elvis Grbac	.15	.40
2 Jamal Lewis	.20	.50
3 Ray Lewis	.25	.60
4 Travis Henry	.15	.40
5 Eric Moulds	.15	.40
6 Corey Dillon	.15	.40
7 Peter Warrick	.15	.40
8 Tim Couch	.15	.40
9 James Jackson	.15	.40
10 Kevin Johnson	.15	.40
11 Mike Anderson	.15	.40
12 Terrell Davis	.20	.50
13 Brian Griese	.15	.40
14 Rod Smith	.20	.50
15 Marvin Harrison	.20	.50
16 Reggie Wayne	.20	.50
17 Dominic Rhodes	.15	.40
18 Edgerrin James	.20	.50
19 Mark Brunell	.20	.50
20 Keenan McCardell	.20	.50
21 Jimmy Smith	.20	.50
22 Tony Gonzalez	.20	.50
23 Trent Green	.15	.40
24 Priest Holmes	.15	.40
25 Snoop Minnis	.15	.40
26 Chris Chambers	.15	.40
27 Jay Fiedler	.20	.50
28 Travis Minor	.15	.40
29 Lamar Smith	.15	.40
30 Tom Brady	1.25	3.00
31 Troy Brown	.15	.40
32 Antowain Smith	.20	.50
33 Laveranues Coles	.20	.50
34 Curtis Martin	.20	.50
35 Vinny Testaverde	.15	.40
36 Wayne Chrebet	.15	.40
37 Tim Brown	.25	.60
38 Rich Gannon	.20	.50
39 Jerry Rice	.50	1.25
40 Charlie Garner	.20	.50
41 Jerome Bettis	.25	.60
42 Plaxico Burress	.15	.40
43 Kordell Stewart	.15	.40
44 Kendrell Bell	.15	.40
45 Doug Flutie	.20	.50
46 LaDainian Tomlinson	.25	.60
47 Junior Seau	.20	.50
48 Drew Brees	.50	1.25
49 Shaun Alexander	.15	.40
50 Koren Robinson	.15	.40
51 Ricky Watters	.20	.50
52 Eddie George	.20	.50
53 Derrick Mason	.15	.40
54 Steve McNair	.20.	.50
55 David Boston	.15	.40
56 Jake Plummer	.15	.40
57 Chris Chandler	.20	.50
58 Jamal Anderson	.20	.50
59 Michael Vick	.20	.50
60 Wesley Walls	.20	.50
61 Chris Weinke	.15	.40
62 David Terrell	.15	.40
63 Anthony Thomas	.20	.50
64 Brian Urlacher	.25	.60
65 Quincy Carter	.15	.40
66 Rocket Ismail	.20	.50
67 Emmitt Smith	.40	1.00
68 James Stewart	.15	.40
69 Germane Crowell	.15	.40
70 Mike McMahon	.15	.40
71 Brett Favre	.50	1.25
72 Ahman Green	.20	.50
73 Antonio Freeman	.25	.60
74 Michael Bennett	.15	.40
75 Cris Carter	.25	.60
76 Daunte Culpepper	.20	.50
77 Randy Moss	.20	.50
78 Aaron Brooks	.15	.40
79 Deuce McAllister	.20	.50
80 Ricky Williams	.20	.50
81 Kerry Collins	.15	.40
82 Ron Dayne	.20	.50
83 Amani Toomer	.15	.40
84 Correll Buckhalter	.15	.40
85 James Thrash	.20	.50
86 Freddie Mitchell	.15	.40
87 Duce Staley	.15	.40
88 Jeff Garcia	.15	.40
89 Garrison Hearst	.15	.40
90 Terrell Owens	.20	.50
91 Isaac Bruce	.25	.60
92 Marshall Faulk	.20	.50
93 Torry Holt	.20	.50
94 Kurt Warner	.20	.50
95 Mike Alstott	.15	.40
96 Brad Johnson	.20	.50
97 Keyshawn Johnson	.20	.50
98 Stephen Davis	.15	.40
99 Rod Gardner	.15	.40
100 Tony Banks	.15	.40
101 David Carr RC	3.00	8.00
102 Joey Harrington RC	3.00	8.00
103 Rohan Davey RC	5.00	12.00
104 Chad Hutchinson RC	3.00	8.00
105 Patrick Ramsey RC	4.00	10.00
106 Kurt Kittner RC	3.00	8.00
107 Eric Crouch RC	5.00	12.00
108 David Garrard RC	4.00	10.00
109 Ronald Curry RC	3.00	8.00
110 Zak Kustok RC	3.00	8.00
111 Woody Dantzler RC	4.00	10.00
112 Wes Pate RC	3.00	8.00
113 Brian Westbrook RC	6.00	15.00
114 Josh McCown RC	5.00	12.00
115 Travis Stephens RC	3.00	8.00
116 Luke Staley RC	3.00	8.00
117 William Green RC	4.00	10.00
118 Clinton Portis RC	5.00	12.00
119 DeShaun Foster RC	5.00	12.00
120 Verron Haynes RC	3.00	8.00
121 T.J. Duckett RC	3.00	8.00
122 Antwoine Womack RC	3.00	8.00
123 Leonard Henry RC	3.00	8.00
124 Lamar Gordon RC	4.00	10.00
125 Adrian Peterson RC	4.00	10.00
126 Chester Taylor RC	5.00	12.00
127 Damien Anderson RC	3.00	8.00
128 Maurice Morris RC	4.00	10.00
129 Ricky Williams RC	4.00	10.00
130 Terry Charles RC	3.00	8.00
131 Demontray Carter RC	3.00	8.00
132 Jason McAddley RC	4.00	10.00
133 Ladell Betts RC	5.00	12.00
134 Cortlen Johnson RC	3.00	8.00
135 James Mungro RC	5.00	12.00
136 Atrews Bell RC	3.00	8.00
137 Josh Scobey RC	4.00	10.00
138 Justin Peelle RC	3.00	8.00
139 Najeh Davenport RC	3.00	8.00
140 Josh Reed RC	4.00	10.00
141 Marquise Walker RC	3.00	8.00
142 Jabar Gaffney RC	3.00	8.00
143 Antwaan Randle El RC	4.00	10.00
144 Ashley Lelie RC	3.00	8.00
145 Tavon Mason RC	3.00	8.00
146 Antonio Bryant RC	5.00	12.00
147 Javon Walker RC	5.00	12.00
148 Kelly Campbell RC	4.00	10.00
149 Ron Johnson RC	4.00	10.00
150 Andre Davis RC	3.00	8.00
151 Cliff Russell RC	3.00	8.00
152 Reche Caldwell RC	4.00	10.00
153 Kyle Johnson RC	3.00	8.00
154 Freddie Milons RC	3.00	8.00
155 Brian Poli-Dixon RC	3.00	8.00
156 David Thornton RC	3.00	8.00
157 Bryan Thomas RC	3.00	8.00
158 Kahlil Hill RC	3.00	8.00
159 Deion Branch RC	5.00	12.00
160 Akin Ayodele RC	4.00	10.00
161 Donte Stallworth RC	5.00	12.00
162 Tim Carter RC	4.00	10.00
163 Kenyon Coleman RC	3.00	8.00
164 Jeremy Shockey RC	5.00	12.00
165 Eddie Freeman RC	3.00	8.00
166 Tracey Wistrom RC	4.00	10.00
167 Daniel Graham RC	4.00	10.00
168 Julius Peppers RC	8.00	20.00
169 Alex Brown RC	5.00	12.00
170 Dwight Freeney RC	6.00	15.00
171 Kalimba Edwards RC	4.00	10.00
172 Dennis Johnson RC	3.00	8.00
173 Travis Fisher RC	4.00	10.00
174 John Henderson RC	4.00	10.00
175 Anthony Weaver RC	3.00	8.00
176 Ryan Sims RC	5.00	12.00
177 Alan Harper RC	3.00	8.00
178 Larry Tripplett RC	3.00	8.00
179 Wendell Bryant RC	3.00	8.00
180 Albert Haynesworth RC	5.00	12.00
181 Levar Fisher RC	3.00	8.00
182 Andra Davis RC	3.00	8.00
183 Joseph Jefferson RC	3.00	8.00
184 Lamont Thompson RC	4.00	10.00
185 Robert Thomas RC	3.00	8.00
186 Michael Lewis RC	4.00	10.00
187 Rocky Calmus RC	4.00	10.00
188 Napoleon Harris RC	4.00	10.00
189 Lito Sheppard RC	5.00	12.00
190 Quentin Jammer RC	5.00	12.00
191 Roy Williams RC	3.00	8.00
192 Marques Anderson RC	4.00	10.00
193 Chris Hope RC	5.00	12.00
194 Raonall Smith RC	3.00	8.00
195 Mike Rumph RC	3.00	8.00
196 James Allen RC	3.00	8.00
197 Ed Reed RC	15.00	40.00
198 Mike Williams RC	3.00	8.00
199 Phillip Buchanon RC	5.00	12.00
200 Bryant McKinnie RC	3.00	8.00

2002 Donruss Elite Aspirations

*VETS/70-99: 8X TO 20X BASIC CARDS
*ROOKIES/70-99: .4X TO 1X
*VETS/45-69: 10X TO 25X
*ROOKIES/45-69: .5X TO 1.2X
*VETS/30-44: 15X TO 40X
*ROOKIES/30-44: .8X TO 2X
*VETS/20-29: 20X TO 50X
*ROOKIES/20-29: 1X TO 2.5X
*VETS/10-19: 25X TO 60X
*ROOKIES/10-19: 1.2X TO 3X
ASPIRATIONS PRINT RUN 1-98
SERIAL #'d UNDER 10 NOT PRICED

2002 Donruss Elite Status

*VETS/70-99: 8X TO 20X BASIC CARDS
*ROOKIES/70-99: .4X TO 1X
*VETS/45-69: 10X TO 25X
*ROOKIES/45-69: .5X TO 1.2X
*ROOKIES/30-44: .8X TO 2X
*VETS/20-29: 20X TO 50X
*ROOKIES/20-29: 1X TO 2.5X
*VETS/10-19: 25X TO 60X
*ROOKIES/10-19: 1.2X TO 3X
STATUS STATED PRINT RUN 2-99
SERIAL #'d UNDER 10 NOT PRICED

2002 Donruss Elite Turn of the Century Autographs

This 50-card parallel is composed of the first 50 serial numbered rookies, with each card featuring an authentic autograph. Many cards were issued via redemption with an expiration date of 1/1/2004.

STATED PRINT RUN 40 SER.#'d SETS
FIRST 40 CARDS OF PRINT RUN SIGNED

Card	Low	High
101 David Carr	10.00	25.00
102 Joey Harrington	10.00	25.00
103 Rohan Davey	15.00	40.00
106 Kurt Kittner	10.00	25.00
107 Eric Crouch	15.00	40.00
111 Woody Dantzler	12.00	30.00
115 Travis Stephens	10.00	25.00
116 Luke Staley	10.00	25.00
117 William Green	12.00	30.00
118 Clinton Portis	15.00	40.00
119 DeShaun Foster	15.00	40.00
121 T.J. Duckett	10.00	25.00
125 Adrian Peterson	12.00	30.00
127 Damien Anderson	10.00	25.00
128 Maurice Morris	12.00	30.00
131 Demontray Carter	10.00	25.00
134 Cortlen Johnson	10.00	25.00
139 Najeh Davenport	10.00	25.00
140 Josh Reed	12.00	30.00
141 Marquise Walker	10.00	25.00
142 Jabar Gaffney	10.00	25.00
143 Antwaan Randle El	12.00	30.00
144 Ashley Lelie	10.00	25.00
146 Antonio Bryant	15.00	40.00
147 Javon Walker	15.00	40.00
148 Kelly Campbell	12.00	30.00
149 Ron Johnson	12.00	30.00
150 Andre Davis	10.00	25.00
152 Reche Caldwell	12.00	30.00
154 Freddie Milons	10.00	25.00
155 Brian Poli-Dixon	10.00	25.00
161 Donte Stallworth	15.00	40.00
164 Jeremy Shockey	15.00	40.00
167 Daniel Graham	12.00	30.00
168 Julius Peppers	75.00	135.00
169 Alex Brown	15.00	40.00
170 Dwight Freeney	20.00	50.00
171 Kalimba Edwards	12.00	30.00
174 John Henderson	12.00	30.00
176 Ryan Sims No Auto	15.00	40.00
179 Wendell Bryant	10.00	25.00
181 Levar Fisher	10.00	25.00
182 Andra Davis	10.00	25.00
185 Robert Thomas	10.00	25.00
187 Rocky Calmus	12.00	30.00
189 Lito Sheppard	15.00	40.00
190 Quentin Jammer	15.00	40.00
191 Roy Williams	10.00	25.00
195 Mike Rumph	10.00	25.00
199 Phillip Buchanon No Auto	15.00	40.00

2002 Donruss Elite Back to the Future

This 24-card set features single player cards that are sequentially numbered to 800 with the double player cards being sequentially numbered to 400.

Card	Low	High
COMPLETE SET (24)	40.00	100.00

BF1-BF16 SINGLE PRINT RUN 800
BF17-BF24 DUAL PRINT RUN 400

Card	Low	High
BF1 Walter Payton	5.00	12.00
BF2 Anthony Thomas	1.00	2.50
BF3 Bernie Kosar	1.00	2.50
BF4 James Jackson	.75	2.00
BF5 Troy Aikman	1.50	4.00
BF6 Quincy Carter	.75	2.00
BF7 Steve Bartkowski	1.00	2.50
BF8 Michael Vick	1.00	2.50
BF9 Natrone Means	.75	2.00
BF10 LaDainian Tomlinson	1.25	3.00
BF11 Earl Campbell	1.25	3.00
BF12 Eddie George	1.00	2.50
BF13 Eric Dickerson	1.00	2.50
BF14 Edgerrin James	1.00	2.50
BF15 John Elway	2.00	5.00
BF16 Brian Griese	.75	2.00
BF17 W.Payton/A.Thomas	8.00	20.00
BF18 B.Kosar/J.Jackson	1.50	4.00
BF19 T.Aikman/Q.Carter	2.50	6.00
BF20 S.Bartkowski/M.Vick	1.50	4.00
BF21 N.Means/L.Tomlinson	2.00	5.00
BF22 E.Campbell/E.George	2.00	5.00
BF23 E.Dickerson/E.James	1.50	4.00
BF24 J.Elway/Br.Griese	3.00	8.00

2002 Donruss Elite Back to the Future Threads

This set is a parallel of the Back to the Future set, with the addition of a swatch of game used jersey.

BF1-BF16 SINGLES PRINT RUN 75
BF17-BF24 DUAL PRINT RUN 25

Card	Low	High
BF1 Walter Payton	50.00	120.00
BF2 Anthony Thomas	6.00	15.00
BF4 James Jackson	5.00	12.00
BF5 Troy Aikman	20.00	40.00
BF6 Quincy Carter	5.00	12.00
BF7 Steve Bartkowski	8.00	20.00
BF8 Michael Vick	6.00	15.00
BF9 Natrone Means	6.00	15.00
BF10 LaDainian Tomlinson	8.00	20.00
BF11 Earl Campbell	12.00	30.00
BF12 Eddie George	6.00	15.00
BF13 Eric Dickerson	8.00	20.00
BF14 Edgerrin James	6.00	15.00
BF15 John Elway	15.00	40.00
BF16 Brian Griese	5.00	12.00
BF17 W.Payton/A.Thomas	60.00	120.00
BF19 T.Aikman/Q.Carter	40.00	100.00
BF20 S.Bartkowski/M.Vick	20.00	50.00
BF21 N.Means/L.Tomlinson	25.00	60.00
BF22 E.Campbell/E.George	15.00	40.00
BF23 E.Dickerson/E.James	20.00	50.00
BF24 J.Elway/Br.Griese	100.00	200.00

2002 Donruss Elite College Ties

This 25-card insert focuses on NFL standouts and 2002 draftees who attended the same college. Each card is sequentially numbered to 1600.

Card	Low	High
COMPLETE SET (25)	20.00	50.00

STATED PRINT RUN 1600 SER.#'d SETS

Card	Low	High
CT1 D.Terrell/M.Walker	.60	1.50
CT2 T.Henry/T.Stephens	.60	1.50
CT3 T.Dilfer/D.Carr	.60	1.50
CT4 J.Kearse/A.Brown	1.00	2.50
CT5 A.Green/E.Crouch	1.00	2.50
CT6 E.James/C.Portis	1.00	2.50
CT7 P.Burress/T.Duckett	.60	1.50
CT8 S.Minnis/J.Walker	1.00	2.50
CT9 K.Dyson/C.Russell	.75	2.00
CT10 M.Vick/A.Davis	.75	2.00
CT11 C.Johnson/K.Simonton	.60	1.50
CT12 F.Mitchell/D.Foster	1.00	2.50
CT13 Q.Ismail/M.Harrison	.75	2.00
CT14 Q.Carter/K.Bell	.60	1.50
CT15 B.Griese/T.Brady	5.00	12.00
CT16 J.Bettis/T.Brown	1.00	2.50
CT17 E.George/C.Carter	1.00	2.50
CT18 M.Alstott/D.Brees	2.00	5.00
CT19 C.Martin/K.Barlow	.75	2.00
CT20 R.Williams/P.Holmes	.75	2.00
CT21 C.Garner/J.Lewis	.75	2.00
CT22 Key.Johnson/J.Seau	.75	2.00
CT23 M.Brunell/C.Dillon	.75	2.00
CT24 E.Smith/F.Taylor	1.50	4.00
CT25 E.James/J.Jackson	.75	2.00

2002 Donruss Elite Face to Face

This 15-card insert features two players and offers game-used facemask swatches. The card is highlighted by silver foil stamping and is sequentially numbered to 350.

STATED PRINT RUN 350 SER.#'d SETS

Card	Low	High
FF1 E.George/Z.Thomas	6.00	15.00
FF2 M.Irvin/D.Green	8.00	20.00
FF3 M.Anderson/J.Seau	6.00	15.00
FF4 J.Plummer/J.Sehorn	6.00	15.00
FF5 M.Brunell/J.Kearse	6.00	15.00
FF6 R.Moss/B.Favre	15.00	40.00
FF7 K.Collins/R.Lewis	8.00	20.00
FF8 S.McNair/K.Warner	6.00	15.00
FF9 J.Elway/S.Young	12.00	30.00
FF10 C.Carter/J.Rice	15.00	40.00
FF11 T.Couch/D.Culpepper	6.00	15.00
FF12 D.Marino/B.Sanders	15.00	40.00
FF13 M.Vick/L.Tomlinson	8.00	20.00
FF14 T.Aikman/W.Moon	10.00	25.00
FF15 C.Martin/L.Smith	6.00	15.00

2002 Donruss Elite Passing the Torch

This 24-card insert set focuses on football legends and rising stars. The cards are designed with no borders and set on double-sided holo-foil board. The singles are sequentially numbered to 800 with the doubles sequentially numbered to 400.

Card	Low	High
COMPLETE SET (24)	25.00	60.00

PT1-PT16 SINGLE PRINT RUN 800
PT17-PT24 DUAL PRINT RUN 400 SER.#'d SETS

Card	Low	High
PT1 Thurman Thomas	1.00	2.50
PT2 Travis Henry	.75	2.00
PT3 Gale Sayers	1.25	3.00
PT4 Anthony Thomas	1.00	2.50
PT5 Dan Fouts	1.00	2.50
PT6 Drew Brees	2.50	6.00
PT7 Bernie Kosar	1.00	2.50
PT8 Tim Couch	.75	2.00
PT9 Steve Young	1.50	4.00
PT10 Jeff Garcia	.75	2.00
PT11 Ricky Watters	1.00	2.50
PT12 Shaun Alexander	.75	2.00
PT13A Robert Smith	.75	2.00
PT13B Herschel Walker	1.25	3.00
PT14 Michael Bennett	.75	2.00
PT15 Jerry Rice	2.50	6.00
PT16 Terrell Owens	1.00	2.50
PT17 T.Thomas/T.Henry	1.50	4.00
PT18 G.Sayers/A.Thomas	2.00	5.00
PT19 D.Fouts/D.Brees	4.00	10.00
PT20 B.Kosar/T.Couch	1.50	4.00
PT21 S.Young/J.Garcia	2.50	6.00
PT22 R.Watters/S.Alexander	1.50	4.00
PT23A R.Smith/M.Bennett	1.25	3.00
PT23B H.Walker/M.Bennett	2.00	5.00
PT24 J.Rice/T.Owens	4.00	10.00

2002 Donruss Elite Passing the Torch Autographs

This set is a parallel of the Passing the Torch set, with the addition of authentic autographs. The single player cards are sequentially numbered to 100 with the double player cards sequentially numbered to 50.

PT1-PT16 SINGLE AU PRINT RUN 100
PT17-PT24 DUAL AU PRINT RUN 50

Card	Low	High
PT1 Thurman Thomas	12.00	30.00
PT2 Travis Henry	10.00	25.00
PT3 Gale Sayers	25.00	60.00
PT4 Anthony Thomas	12.00	30.00
PT5 Dan Fouts	12.00	30.00
PT6 Drew Brees	30.00	80.00
PT7 Bernie Kosar	12.00	30.00
PT8 Tim Couch	10.00	25.00
PT9 Steve Young	30.00	60.00
PT10 Jeff Garcia	10.00	25.00
PT11 Ricky Watters	12.00	30.00
PT12 Shaun Alexander	15.00	40.00

PT13 Herschel Walker 20.00 50.00
PT14 Michael Bennett 10.00 25.00
PT15 Jerry Rice 60.00 120.00
PT16 Terrell Owens 15.00 40.00
PT17 T.Thomas/T.Henry 25.00 60.00
PT18 G.Sayers/A.Thomas 30.00 80.00
PT19 D.Fouts/D.Brees 50.00 120.00
PT20 B.Kosar/T.Couch 25.00 60.00
PT21 S.Young/J.Garcia 50.00 120.00
PT22 Watters/Alexander 20.00 50.00
PT23 H.Walker/M.Bennett 30.00 80.00
PT24 J.Rice/T.Owens 75.00 150.00

2002 Donruss Elite Prime Numbers

This 10-card insert features football greats who share the same jersey numbers. The dual player cards are die-cut and set on metalized film board. Cards are sequentially numbered to 1600.

COMPLETE SET (10) 7.50 20.00
STATED PRINT RUN 1600 SER.#'d SETS
PN1 B.Urlacher/Z.Thomas 1.00 2.50
PN2 C.Weinke/J.Plummer .60 1.50
PN3 D.Brees/S.McNair 2.00 5.00
PN4 J.Garcia/K.Collins .60 1.50
PN5 E.Smith/D.Staley 1.50 4.00
PN6 E.George/R.Dayne .75 2.00
PN7 C.Martin/M.Faulk .75 2.00
PN8 R.Moss/C.Chambers .75 2.00
PN9 T.Brown/T.Owens 1.00 2.50
PN10 J.Rice/I.Bruce 2.00 5.00

2002 Donruss Elite Recollection Autographs

Randomly inserted into packs, this set features two cards bought back from the secondary market by Playoff, and signed by Jeff Garcia. Each card features a unique Recollection Collection embossed stamp.

STATED PRINT RUN 25-75
1 Jeff Garcia/25 40.00 80.00
2 Jeff Garcia/75 20.00 50.00

2002 Donruss Elite Throwback Threads

This 30-card insert set features one or two swatches of game-worn jerseys from retired legends and current stars. The singles are sequentially numbered to 75. The doubles are sequentially numbered to 25. A few cards were issued as exchange cards which could be redeemed until January 1, 2004.

TT1-TT20 SINGLES PRINT RUN 75
TT21-TT30 DUAL PRINT RUN 25
TT1 Jim Thorpe 100.00 200.00
TT2 Red Grange HEL 125.00 250.00
TT3 Bart Starr/50* 25.00 60.00
TT4 Brett Favre/50* 20.00 50.00
TT5 Joe Namath/50* 20.00 50.00
TT6 John Riggins/50* 15.00 40.00
TT7 Dan Marino/50* 25.00 60.00
TT8 Bob Griese/50* 12.50 30.00
TT9 Roger Staubach 15.00 40.00
TT10 Troy Aikman/50* 15.00 40.00
TT11 Bernie Kosar 12.50 30.00
TT12 Ozzie Newsome 10.00 25.00
TT13 John Elway 20.00 50.00
TT14 Craig Morton 10.00 25.00
TT15 Jim McMahon/50* 15.00 40.00
TT16 Walter Payton 25.00 60.00
TT17 Franco Harris 15.00 40.00
TT18 Jerome Bettis 25.00 50.00
TT19 Brian Urlacher 12.50 30.00
TT20 Dick Butkus 20.00 50.00
TT21 J.Thorpe/R.Grange HEL 400.00 800.00
TT22 B.Starr/B.Favre 50.00 100.00
TT23 J.Namath/J.Riggins 30.00 80.00
TT24 D.Marino/Bo.Griese 50.00 120.00
TT25 R.Staubach/T.Aikman 30.00 80.00
TT26 B.Kosar/O.Newsome 20.00 50.00
TT27 J.Elway/C.Morton 30.00 80.00
TT28 J.McMahon/W.Payton 60.00 120.00
TT29 F.Harris/J.Bettis 25.00 60.00
TT30 B.Urlacher/D.Butkus 25.00 60.00

2002 Donruss Elite Throwback Threads Autographs

This parallel to the basic Throwback Threads insert set features authentic autographs with each card sequentially numbered to 25. Only 8 of the 30-insert cards were produced in this signed version. Joe Namath was issued as an exchange card with an expiration date of Jan.1, 2004.

STATED PRINT RUN 25 SER.#'d SETS
TT3 Bart Starr 150.00 300.00
TT4 Brett Favre 200.00 400.00
TT5 Joe Namath 100.00 200.00
TT6 John Riggins 60.00 120.00
TT7 Dan Marino 150.00 300.00
TT8 Bob Griese 50.00 100.00
TT10 Troy Aikman 75.00 150.00
TT15 Jim McMahon 90.00 175.00

2003 Donruss Elite Samples

*SAMPLES: .8X TO 2X BASIC CARDS
*GOLD: .8X TO 2X SILVER

2003 Donruss Elite

Released in June 2003, this set is composed of 100 veterans and 100 rookies, which were serial numbered to 500. Each box contained 20 packs of 5 cards, and carried an SRP of $3. Please note that several cards were originally issued in packs as redemptions with an exchange deadline of 12/1/2004.

COMP.SET w/o SP's (100) 7.50 20.00
101-200 ROOKIE PRINT RUN 100-500
1 Jamal Lewis .20 .50
2 Ray Lewis .25 .60
3 Todd Heap .15 .40
4 Drew Bledsoe .20 .50
5 Travis Henry .15 .40
6 Eric Moulds .15 .40
7 Peerless Price .15 .40
8 Jon Kitna .15 .40
9 Corey Dillon .15 .40
10 Chad Johnson .15 .40
11 Tim Couch .15 .40
12 William Green .15 .40
13 Andre Davis .15 .40
14 Brian Griese .15 .40
15 Ashley Lelie .15 .40
16 Clinton Portis .15 .40
17 Rod Smith .20 .50
18 David Carr .15 .40
19 Jonathan Wells .15 .40
20 Jabar Gaffney .15 .40
21 Peyton Manning .60 1.50
22 Edgerrin James .20 .50
23 Marvin Harrison .20 .50
24 Mark Brunell .20 .50
25 Jimmy Smith .20 .50
26 Fred Taylor .15 .40
27 Priest Holmes .15 .40
28 Trent Green .15 .40
29 Tony Gonzalez .20 .50
30 Chris Chambers .15 .40
31 Zach Thomas .20 .50
32 Ricky Williams .20 .50
33 Tom Brady 1.00 2.50
34 Antowain Smith .20 .50
35 Troy Brown .15 .40
36 Chad Pennington .15 .40
37 Curtis Martin .20 .50
38 Laveranues Coles .15 .40
39 Tim Brown .25 .60
40 Rich Gannon .20 .50
41 Jerry Rice .50 1.25
42 Charlie Garner .20 .50
43 Antwaan Randle El .15 .40
44 Plaxico Burress .15 .40
45 Tommy Maddox .15 .40
46 Jerome Bettis .40 1.00
47 Drew Brees .25 .60
48 LaDainian Tomlinson .25 .60
49 Junior Seau .20 .50
50 Eddie George .20 .50
51 Steve McNair .20 .50
52 Derrick Mason .15 .40
53 David Boston .15 .40
54 Jake Plummer .15 .40
55 Marcel Shipp .15 .40
56 Michael Vick .20 .50
57 T.J. Duckett .15 .40
58 Warrick Dunn .15 .40
59 Julius Peppers .25 .60
60 Steve Smith .25 .60
61 Muhsin Muhammad .15 .40
62 Anthony Thomas .20 .50
63 Brian Urlacher .25 .60
64 Marty Booker .15 .40
65 Chad Hutchinson .15 .40
66 Antonio Bryant .15 .40
67 Emmitt Smith .40 1.00
68 Joey Harrington .15 .40
69 Germane Crowell .15 .40
70 James Stewart .15 .40
71 Brett Favre .50 1.25
72 Donald Driver .20 .50
73 Ahman Green .20 .50
74 Randy Moss .20 .50
75 Michael Bennett .15 .40
76 Daunte Culpepper .20 .50
77 Aaron Brooks .15 .40
78 Deuce McAllister .20 .50
79 Donte Stallworth .15 .40
80 Tiki Barber .20 .50
81 Jeremy Shockey .15 .40
82 Kerry Collins .15 .40
83 Donovan McNabb .20 .50
84 James Thrash .15 .40
85 Duce Staley .15 .40
86 Jeff Garcia .15 .40
87 Terrell Owens .20 .50
88 Garrison Hearst .15 .40
89 Shaun Alexander .15 .40
90 Darrell Jackson .20 .50
91 Koren Robinson .20 .50
92 Marshall Faulk .20 .50
93 Kurt Warner .20 .50
94 Isaac Bruce .25 .60
95 Keyshawn Johnson .25 .60
96 Brad Johnson .20 .50
97 Warren Sapp .20 .50
98 Patrick Ramsey .20 .50
99 Rod Gardner .15 .40
100 Stephen Davis .15 .40
101 Brian St.Pierre RC 2.50 6.00
102 Byron Leftwich RC 3.00 8.00
103 Carson Palmer RC 5.00 12.00
104 Chris Simms RC 2.50 6.00
105 Dave Ragone RC 2.50 6.00
106 Ken Dorsey RC 3.00 8.00
107 Kliff Kingsbury RC 4.00 10.00
108 Kyle Boller RC 2.50 6.00
109 Rex Grossman RC 3.00 8.00
110 Seneca Wallace RC 3.00 8.00
111 Jason Gesser RC 3.00 8.00
112 Artose Pinner RC 2.50 6.00
113 Avon Cobourne RC 2.50 6.00
114 Cecil Sapp RC 2.50 6.00
115 Chris Brown RC 2.50 6.00
116 Derek Watson RC 2.50 6.00
117 Domanick Davis RC 3.00 8.00
118 Dwone Hicks/100 RC 10.00 25.00
119 Earnest Graham RC 4.00 10.00
120 Justin Fargas RC 4.00 10.00
121 Larry Johnson RC 3.00 8.00
122 Lee Suggs RC 2.50 6.00
123 Musa Smith RC 2.50 6.00
124 Onterrio Smith RC 2.50 6.00
125 Quentin Griffin RC 3.00 8.00
126 Willis McGahee RC 3.00 8.00
127 Sultan McCullough RC 2.50 6.00
128 LaBrandon Toefield RC 2.50 6.00
129 B.J. Askew RC 3.00 8.00
130 Andre Johnson RC 6.00 15.00
131 Anquan Boldin RC 4.00 10.00
132 Arnaz Battle RC 4.00 10.00
133 Bethel Johnson RC 2.50 6.00
134 Billy McMullen RC 2.50 6.00
135 Bobby Wade RC 3.00 8.00
136 Brandon Lloyd RC 4.00 10.00
137 Bryant Johnson RC 4.00 10.00
138 Charles Rogers RC 3.00 8.00
139 Doug Gabriel RC 3.00 8.00
140 Justin Gage RC 3.00 8.00
141 Kareem Kelly RC 2.50 6.00
142 Kelley Washington RC 2.50 6.00
143 Kevin Curtis RC 2.50 6.00
144 Nate Burleson RC 3.00 8.00
145 Sam Aiken RC 3.00 8.00
146 Shaun McDonald RC 3.00 8.00
147 Talman Gardner RC 2.50 6.00
148 Taylor Jacobs RC 2.50 6.00
149 Terrence Edwards RC 2.50 6.00
150 Tyrone Calico RC 2.50 6.00
151 Walter Young RC 2.50 6.00
152 Ryan Hoag/100 RC 10.00 25.00
153 Paul Arnold/100 RC 10.00 25.00
154 Bennie Joppru RC 2.50 6.00
155 Dallas Clark RC 4.00 10.00
156 George Wrighster RC 2.50 6.00
157 Jason Witten RC 10.00 25.00
158 Mike Pinkard RC 2.50 6.00
159 Robert Johnson/100 RC 10.00 25.00
160 Teyo Johnson RC 3.00 8.00
161 Andrew Williams RC 2.50 6.00
162 Chris Kelsay RC 3.00 8.00
163 Cory Redding RC 3.00 8.00
164 DeWayne Robertson RC 3.00 8.00
165 DeWayne White RC 2.50 6.00
166 Jerome McDougle RC 2.50 6.00
167 Kenny Peterson RC 3.00 8.00
168 Kindal Moorehead RC 3.00 8.00
169 Michael Haynes RC 2.50 6.00
170 Terrell Suggs RC 3.00 8.00
171 Tully Banta-Cain RC 4.00 10.00
172 Jimmy Kennedy RC 3.00 8.00
173 Johnathan Sullivan RC 2.50 6.00
174 Kevin Williams RC 4.00 10.00
175 Nick Eason/100 RC 10.00 25.00
176 Rien Long RC 2.50 6.00
177 Ty Warren RC 3.00 8.00
178 William Joseph RC 2.50 6.00
179 Boss Bailey RC 3.00 8.00
180 Bradie James RC 4.00 10.00
181 Victor Hobson RC 2.50 6.00
182 Clifton Smith/100 RC 10.00 25.00
183 E.J. Henderson/100 RC 12.00 30.00
184 Gerald Hayes/100 RC 12.00 30.00
185 LaM McDonald/100 RC 10.00 25.00
186 Nick Barnett RC 4.00 10.00
187 Terry Pierce RC 2.50 6.00
188 Andre Woolfolk RC 2.50 6.00
189 Dennis Weathersby RC 2.50 6.00
190 Drayton Florence/100 RC 15.00 40.00
191 Eugene Wilson RC 4.00 10.00
192 Marcus Trufant RC 3.00 8.00
193 Rashean Mathis RC 2.50 6.00
194 Ricky Manning RC 3.00 8.00
195 Sammy Davis/100 RC 12.00 30.00
196 Terence Newman RC 4.00 10.00
197 Julian Battle RC 3.00 8.00
198 Ken Hamlin RC 4.00 10.00
199 Mike Doss RC 4.00 10.00
200 Troy Polamalu/100 RC 90.00 150.00

2003 Donruss Elite Aspiration

*VETS/70-99: 8X TO 20X BASIC CARD
*ROOKIES/70-99: .4X TO 1X SP/100 RC
*ROOKIES/70-99: .5X TO 1.2X
*VETS/45-69: 10X TO 25X
*ROOKIES/45-69: .4X TO 1X SP/100 RC
*ROOKIES/45-69: .6X TO 1.5X BASIC RC
*ROOKIES/30-44: .5X TO 1.2X SP/100 RC
*ROOKIES/30-44: .8X TO 2X
*VETS/20-29: 15X TO 40X
*ROOKIES/20-29: 1X TO 2.5X
*VETS/10-19: 20X TO 50X
*ROOKIES/10-19: 1.2X TO 3X
STATED PRINT RUN 1-98
UNPRICED GOLD ASPIRATIONS #'d OF 1
200 Troy Polamalu/57 90.00 150.00

2003 Donruss Elite Status

*VETS/70-99: 8X TO 20X BASIC CARD
*ROOKIES/70-99: .4X TO 1X SP/100 RC
*ROOKIES/70-99: .5X TO 1.2X
*VETS/45-69: 10X TO 25X
*ROOKIES/45-69: .4X TO 1X SP/100 RC
*ROOKIES/45-69: .6X TO 1.5X
*VETS/30-44: 12X TO 30X
*ROOKIES/30-44: .8X TO 2X
*VETS/20-29: 15X TO 40X
*ROOKIES/20-29: .6X TO 1.5X SP/100 RC
*ROOKIES/20-29: 1X TO 2.5X
*VETS/10-19: 20X TO 50X
*ROOKIES/10-19: 1.2X TO 3X
STATED PRINT RUN 2-99
200 Troy Polamalu/43 90.00 150.00

2003 Donruss Elite Turn of the Century Autographs

Randomly inserted into packs, this set consists of 50 cards, each signed by a 2003 rookie. Each card is serial numbered to 125. Please note that several players were issued in packs as exchange cards, with an expiration date of 12/1/2004.

STATED PRINT RUN 125 SER.#'d SETS
101 Brian St.Pierre 8.00 20.00
102 Byron Leftwich 10.00 25.00
103 Carson Palmer 30.00 80.00
104 Chris Simms 8.00 20.00
105 Dave Ragone 8.00 20.00
108 Kyle Boller 8.00 20.00
109 Rex Grossman 10.00 25.00
112 Artose Pinner 8.00 20.00
114 Cecil Sapp 8.00 20.00
115 Chris Brown 8.00 20.00
120 Justin Fargas 12.00 30.00
121 Larry Johnson 10.00 25.00
122 Lee Suggs 8.00 20.00
123 Musa Smith 8.00 20.00
124 Onterrio Smith 8.00 20.00
126 Willis McGahee 40.00 100.00
130 Andre Johnson 30.00 80.00
136 Brandon Lloyd 12.00 30.00
137 Bryant Johnson 12.00 30.00
138 Charles Rogers 10.00 25.00
139 Doug Gabriel 10.00 25.00
140 Justin Gage 10.00 25.00
142 Kelley Washington 8.00 20.00
143 Kevin Curtis 8.00 20.00
145 Sam Aiken 10.00 25.00
148 Taylor Jacobs 8.00 20.00
149 Terrence Edwards 8.00 20.00
150 Tyrone Calico 8.00 20.00
154 Bennie Joppru 8.00 20.00
155 Dallas Clark 12.00 30.00
157 Jason Witten 30.00 60.00
158 Mike Pinkard 8.00 20.00
160 Teyo Johnson 10.00 25.00
162 Chris Kelsay 10.00 25.00
164 DeWayne Robertson No AU 6.00 15.00
165 DeWayne White 8.00 20.00
166 Jerome McDougle 8.00 20.00
167 Kenny Peterson No AU 6.00 15.00
170 Terrell Suggs 20.00 50.00
172 Jimmy Kennedy 10.00 25.00
173 Johnathon Sullivan No AU 5.00 12.00
174 Kevin Williams 20.00 50.00
176 Rien Long 8.00 20.00
178 William Joseph 8.00 20.00
179 Boss Bailey 10.00 25.00
183 E.J. Henderson 10.00 25.00
189 Dennis Weathersby 8.00 20.00
192 Marcus Trufant 10.00 25.00
196 Terence Newman 12.00 30.00
199 Mike Doss 12.00 30.00

2003 Donruss Elite Back to the Future

This 18-card set features single player cards that are serial numbered to 1000 with the double player cards being serial numbered to 500.

BF1-BF12 PRINT RUN 1000
BF13-BF18 PRINT RUN 500
BF1 Drew Brees 1.50 4.00
BF2 Dan Fouts 1.25 3.00
BF3 Marvin Harrison 1.25 3.00
BF4 Raymond Berry 1.25 3.00
BF5 Rod Gardner 1.00 2.50
BF6 Art Monk 1.50 4.00
BF7 Daunte Culpepper 1.25 3.00
BF8 Warren Moon 1.50 4.00
BF9 Kerry Collins 1.00 2.50
BF10 Frank Gifford 1.50 4.00
BF11 Tom Brady 6.00 15.00
BF12 Drew Bledsoe 1.25 3.00
BF13 D.Brees/D.Fouts 2.00 5.00
BF14 M.Harrison/R.Berry 1.50 4.00
BF15 R.Gardner/A.Monk 2.00 5.00
BF16 D.Culpepper/W.Moon 2.00 5.00
BF17 K.Collins/F.Gifford 2.00 5.00
BF18 T.Brady/D.Bledsoe 8.00 20.00

2003 Donruss Elite Back to the Future Threads

This set is a parallel of the Back to the Future set, with the addition of a swatch of game used jersey. Cards 1-12 are serial numbered to 250, while cards 13-18 are serial numbered to 100.

1-12 PRINT RUN 250 SER.#'d SETS
13-18 PRINT RUN 100 SER.#'d SETS
BF1 Drew Brees 4.00 10.00
BF2 Dan Fouts 10.00 25.00
BF3 Marvin Harrison 3.00 8.00
BF4 Raymond Berry 3.00 8.00
BF5 Rod Gardner 2.50 6.00
BF6 Art Monk 4.00 10.00
BF7 Daunte Culpepper 3.00 8.00
BF8 Warren Moon 4.00 10.00
BF9 Kerry Collins 2.50 6.00
BF10 Frank Gifford 4.00 10.00
BF11 Tom Brady 15.00 40.00
BF12 Drew Bledsoe 3.00 8.00
BF13 D.Brees/D.Fouts 6.00 15.00
BF14 M.Harrison/R.Berry 5.00 12.00
BF15 R.Gardner/A.Monk 6.00 15.00
BF16 D.Culpepper/W.Moon 6.00 15.00
BF17 K.Collins/F.Gifford 6.00 15.00
BF18 T.Brady/D.Bledsoe 25.00 60.00

2003 Donruss Elite College Ties

This 25-card set focuses on NFL standouts and 2003 draftees who attended the same college. Each card is serial numbered to 2000.

COMPLETE SET (15) 15.00 40.00
STATED PRINT RUN 2000 SER.#'d SETS
CT1 Ric.Williams/C.Simms 1.00 2.50
CT2 C.Pennington/B.Leftwich .60 1.50
CT3 Key.Johnson/C.Palmer 1.00 2.50
CT4 D.Branch/D.Ragone .75 2.00
CT5 D.Bledsoe/J.Gesser 1.00 2.50
CT6 J.Shockey/K.Dorsey 1.00 2.50
CT7 M.Vick/L.Suggs 1.00 2.50
CT8 C.Portis/W.McGahee .60 1.50
CT9 E.Smith/R.Grossman 2.00 5.00
CT10 P.Burress/C.Rogers .75 2.00
CT11 S.Moss/A.Johnson 1.25 3.00
CT12 K.Collins/L.Johnson .60 1.50
CT13 D.Stallworth/K.Washington .75 2.00
CT14 W.Sapp/W.Joseph 1.00 2.50
CT15 N.Clements/M.Doss 1.25 3.00

2003 Donruss Elite Masks of Steel

Randomly inserted into packs, this set features pieces of game used face mask. Cards 1-25 were serial numbered to 400, cards 26-30 were serial numbered to 50, and cards 31-35 were serial numbered to 25.

MS1-MS25 PRINT RUN 350-400
MS26-MS30 PRINT RUN 50
MS31-MS35 PRINT RUN 25
MS1 Michael Vick 3.00 8.00
MS2 Marvin Harrison 3.00 8.00
MS3 Jeff Garcia 2.50 6.00
MS4 Eddie George 3.00 8.00
MS5 Tom Brady 15.00 40.00
MS6 Jerry Rice/350 8.00 20.00
MS7 Aaron Brooks 2.50 6.00
MS8 Chris Chambers 2.50 6.00
MS9 Kordell Stewart 2.50 6.00
MS10 Koren Robinson 3.00 8.00
MS11 Quincy Morgan 2.50 6.00
MS12 Deuce McAllister 3.00 8.00
MS13 LaDainian Tomlinson 4.00 10.00
MS14 Travis Henry 2.50 6.00
MS15 Mark Brunell 3.00 8.00
MS16 Quincy Carter 2.50 6.00
MS17 Chad Johnson 2.50 6.00
MS18 Chad Pennington 2.50 6.00
MS19 Drew Brees 4.00 10.00
MS20 Santana Moss 3.00 8.00
MS21 Kevan Barlow 2.50 6.00
MS22 Reggie Wayne 3.00 8.00
MS23 Anthony Thomas 3.00 8.00
MS24 Todd Heap 2.50 6.00
MS25 Michael Bennett 2.50 6.00
MS26 M.Vick/A.Brooks 8.00 20.00
MS27 E.George/A.Thomas 8.00 20.00
MS28 D.McAllister/T.Henry 8.00 20.00
MS29 J.Garcia/J.Rice 20.00 50.00
MS30 L.Tomlinson/D.Brees 10.00 25.00
MS31 Brees/Brunell/Q.Carter 15.00 40.00
MS32 Henry/Bennett/A.Thomas 12.00 30.00
MS33 J.Rice/Harrison/Chmbrs 30.00 80.00
MS34 George/McAllis/Tomlin 15.00 40.00
MS35 Vick/Brooks/Garcia 12.00 30.00

2003 Donruss Elite Passing the Torch

This 27-card insert set focuses on football legends and rising stars. The cards are designed with no borders and set on double-sided holo-foil board. The singles are serial numbered to 1000 with the doubles serial numbered to 500. Please note that cards 17, 18, and 29 were not released. Also note that cards #PT8 and PT24 were issued in packs as exchange cards with an expiration date of 12/1/2004.

COMPLETE SET (27) 30.00 80.00
PT1-PT20 PRINT RUN 1000
PT21-PT27 PRINT RUN 500
PT1 David Carr 1.00 2.50
PT2 Warren Moon 2.00 5.00
PT3 Patrick Ramsey 1.25 3.00
PT4 Joe Theismann 2.00 5.00
PT5 Clinton Portis 1.00 2.50
PT6 Terrell Davis 1.50 4.00
PT7 Roy Williams 1.00 2.50
PT8 Deion Sanders 1.50 4.00
PT9 Deuce McAllister 1.25 3.00
PT10 Ricky Williams 1.25 3.00
PT11 Drew Bledsoe 1.25 3.00
PT12 Jim Kelly 2.00 5.00
PT13 Jerome Bettis 1.50 4.00
PT14 Franco Harris 2.50 6.00
PT15 Priest Holmes 1.00 2.50
PT16 Marcus Allen 2.00 5.00
PT19 Kendrell Bell 1.00 2.50
PT20 Jack Lambert 2.00 5.00
PT21 D.Carr/W.Moon 2.50 6.00
PT22 P.Ramsey/J.Theisman 2.50 6.00
PT23 C.Portis/T.Davis 2.00 5.00
PT24 D.Sanders/Roy Williams 2.00 5.00
PT25 D.McAllister/Ric.Williams 2.00 5.00
PT26 D.Bledsoe/J.Kelly 2.00 5.00
PT27 J.Bettis/F.Harris 3.00 8.00
PT28 P.Holmes/M.Allen 2.50 6.00
PT30 K.Bell/J.Lambert 2.50 6.00

2003 Donruss Elite Passing the Torch Autographs

This set is a parallel of the Passing the Torch set, with the addition of authentic autographs. The single player cards are serial numbered to 100 with the double player cards serial numbered to 50. Please note that cards 17, 18, and 29 were not released. Also, please note that several cards were issued in packs as exchange cards, with an expiration date of 12/1/2004.

PT1-PT20 SINGLE AU PRINT RUN 100
PT21-PT30 DUAL AU PRINT RUN 50
PT1 David Carr 10.00 25.00
PT2 Warren Moon 20.00 50.00
PT3 Patrick Ramsey 12.00 30.00
PT4 Joe Theismann 20.00 50.00
PT5 Clinton Portis 10.00 25.00
PT6 Terrell Davis 15.00 40.00
PT7 Roy Williams 10.00 25.00
PT8 Deion Sanders 40.00 100.00
PT9 Deuce McAllister 10.00 25.00
PT10 Ricky Williams 12.00 30.00
PT11 Drew Bledsoe 12.00 30.00
PT12 Jim Kelly 30.00 80.00
PT13 Jerome Bettis 40.00 80.00
PT14 Franco Harris 25.00 60.00
PT15 Priest Holmes 10.00 25.00
PT16 Marcus Allen 20.00 50.00
PT19 Kendrell Bell 10.00 25.00
PT20 Jack Lambert 50.00 80.00
PT21 D.Carr/W.Moon 25.00 60.00
PT22 P.Ramsey/Theismann 40.00 100.00
PT23 C.Portis/T.Davis 30.00 80.00
PT24 D.Sanders/Ro.Williams 60.00 120.00
PT25 McAllister/Ri.William 30.00 80.00
PT26 D.Bledsoe/J.Kelly 40.00 100.00
PT27 J.Bettis/F.Harris 100.00 175.00
PT28 P.Holmes/M.Allen 40.00 100.00
PT30 K.Bell/J.Lambert 40.00 100.00

2003 Donruss Elite Prime Patches

Randomly inserted into packs, this 20-card set features game used jersey patch swatches. Each card is serial numbered to 50.

STATED PRINT RUN 50 SER.#'d SETS
PP1 Emmitt Smith 10.00 25.00
PP2 William Green 4.00 10.00
PP3 Travis Henry 4.00 10.00
PP4 Tim Brown 6.00 15.00
PP5 Steve McNair 5.00 12.00
PP6 Jerry Rice 12.00 30.00
PP7 Michael Vick 5.00 12.00
PP8 Jamal Lewis 5.00 12.00
PP9 Brett Favre 12.00 30.00
PP10 Randy Moss 5.00 12.00
PP11 Joey Harrington 4.00 10.00
PP12 Peyton Manning 15.00 40.00
PP13 Garrison Hearst 4.00 10.00
PP14 Junior Seau 5.00 12.00
PP15 Priest Holmes 4.00 10.00
PP16 Deuce McAllister 5.00 12.00
PP17 Terrell Owens 5.00 12.00
PP18 LaDainian Tomlinson 6.00 15.00
PP19 Donovan McNabb 5.00 12.00
PP20 Eddie George 5.00 12.00
PP7P Michael Vick Promo 5.00 12.00

2003 Donruss Elite Pro Bowl Standouts

Randomly inserted into packs, this set features members of the 2002 Pro Bowl squad. Each card is serial numbered to 2002.

COMPLETE SET (20) 15.00 40.00
STATED PRINT RUN 2002 SER.#'d SETS
PB1 Donovan McNabb 1.00 2.50
PB2 Mike Alstott .75 2.00
PB3 Jeff Garcia .75 2.00
PB4 Deuce McAllister 1.00 2.50
PB5 Michael Bennett .75 2.00
PB6 Marshall Faulk 1.00 2.50
PB7 Jeremy Shockey .75 2.00
PB8 Terrell Owens 1.00 2.50
PB9 Joe Horn .75 2.00
PB10 Brian Urlacher 1.25 3.00
PB11 Rich Gannon 1.00 2.50
PB12 Drew Bledsoe 1.00 2.50
PB13 Peyton Manning 3.00 8.00
PB14 Ricky Williams 1.00 2.50
PB15 Travis Henry .75 2.00
PB16 LaDainian Tomlinson 1.25 3.00
PB17 Marvin Harrison 1.00 2.50
PB18 Jerry Rice 2.50 6.00
PB19 Eric Moulds .75 2.00
PB20 Zach Thomas 1.00 2.50

2003 Donruss Elite Throwback Threads

This 30-card insert set features one or two swatches of game-worn jerseys from retired legends and current stars. The singles are serial numbered to 250. The doubles are serial numbered to 75.

TT1-TT30 SINGLE PRINT RUN 250
TT31-TT45 DUAL JSY PRINT RUN 75
TT1 Joe Montana 30.00 80.00
TT2 Jeff Garcia 5.00 12.00
TT3 Walter Payton 20.00 50.00
TT4 Red Grange 75.00 150.00
TT5 Jim Kelly 10.00 25.00
TT6 Thurman Thomas 10.00 25.00
TT7 Jim Brown 12.00 30.00
TT8 Jim Thorpe 50.00 120.00
TT9 Bob Griese 10.00 25.00
TT10 Larry Csonka 10.00 25.00
TT11 Barry Sanders 12.00 30.00
TT12 Doak Walker 20.00 50.00
TT13 Warren Moon 10.00 25.00
TT14 Earl Campbell 10.00 25.00
TT15 Eric Dickerson 8.00 20.00
TT16 Marshall Faulk 6.00 15.00
TT17 Joe Theismann 10.00 25.00
TT18 John Riggins 8.00 20.00
TT19 Fred Biletnikoff 10.00 25.00
TT20 Jerry Rice 15.00 40.00
TT21 Joe Greene 10.00 25.00
TT22 L.C. Greenwood 6.00 15.00
TT23 Sterling Sharpe 10.00 25.00
TT24 James Lofton 6.00 15.00
TT25 Tony Dorsett 10.00 25.00
TT26 Emmitt Smith 15.00 40.00
TT27 Bart Starr 15.00 40.00
TT28 Ray Nitschke 12.00 30.00
TT29 Sonny Jurgensen 8.00 20.00
TT30 Charley Taylor 6.00 15.00
TT31 J.Montana/J.Garcia 30.00 80.00
TT32 W.Payton/R.Grange 100.00 250.00
TT33 J.Kelly/T.Thomas 20.00 50.00
TT34 J.Brown/J.Thorpe 125.00 250.00
TT35 B.Griese/L.Csonka 20.00 50.00
TT36 B.Sanders/D.Walker 40.00 100.00
TT37 W.Moon/E.Campbell 12.00 30.00
TT38 E.Dickerson/M.Faulk 15.00 40.00
TT39 Theismann/J.Riggins 20.00 50.00
TT40 F.Biletnikoff/J.Rice 40.00 100.00
TT41 J.Greene/Greenwood 20.00 50.00
TT42 S.Sharpe/J.Lofton 20.00 50.00
TT43 T.Dorsett/E.Smith 30.00 80.00
TT44 B.Starr/R.Nitschke 50.00 120.00
TT45 Jurgensen/C.Taylor 12.00 30.00

2003 Donruss Elite Throwback Threads Autographs

This parallel to the basic Throwback Threads insert set features authentic autographs with each card serial numbered to 25. Please note that Larry Csonka and Sterling Sharpe were issued in packs as exchange cards with an expiration date of 12/1/2004.

STATED PRINT RUN 25 SER.#'d SETS
TT1 Joe Montana 175.00 300.00
TT7 Jim Brown 60.00 150.00
TT9 Bob Griese 30.00 80.00
TT10 Larry Csonka 30.00 80.00
TT11 Barry Sanders 100.00 200.00
TT14 Earl Campbell 30.00 80.00
TT18 John Riggins 25.00 60.00
TT23 Sterling Sharpe 30.00 80.00

2004 Donruss Elite

Donruss Elite was released in late June 2004. The base set consists of 200-cards including 100-veterans and 100-rookies. The rookie subset featured cards serial numbered to 500. Hobby boxes contained 20-packs of 5-cards each at an SRP of $5. Included in the product was an extensive selection of inserts and memorabilia sets highlighted by the Turn of the Century Autographs set and the very first Lynn Swann game-used memorabilia card in Throwback Threads.

COMP.SET w/o SP's (100) 7.50 20.00
ROOKIE PRINT RUN 500 SER.#'d SETS
1 Emmitt Smith .50 1.25
2 Anquan Boldin .20 .50
3 Michael Vick .25 .60
4 Peerless Price .20 .50
5 T.J. Duckett .20 .50
6 Warrick Dunn .20 .50
7 Jamal Lewis .25 .60
8 Kyle Boller .20 .50
9 Todd Heap .20 .50
10 Ray Lewis .30 .75
11 Drew Bledsoe .25 .60
12 Eric Moulds .20 .50
13 Travis Henry .20 .50
14 Jake Delhomme .20 .50
15 Stephen Davis .20 .50
16 Steve Smith .30 .75
17 Anthony Thomas .25 .60
18 Brian Urlacher .30 .75
19 Rex Grossman .20 .50
20 Chad Johnson .20 .50
21 Carson Palmer .25 .60
22 Rudi Johnson .20 .50
23 Peter Warrick .20 .50
24 Andre Davis .20 .50
25 Tim Couch .25 .60
26 Quincy Carter .20 .50
27 Roy Williams S .20 .50
28 Terence Newman .25 .60
29 Clinton Portis .20 .50
30 Jake Plummer .20 .50
31 Rod Smith .25 .60
32 Charles Rogers .20 .50
33 Joey Harrington .20 .50
34 Ahman Green .25 .60
35 Brett Favre .60 1.50
36 Javon Walker .20 .50
37 Andre Johnson .25 .60
38 David Carr .20 .50
39 Domanick Davis .20 .50
40 Edgerrin James .25 .60
41 Marvin Harrison .25 .60
42 Peyton Manning .75 2.00
43 Reggie Wayne .25 .60
44 Byron Leftwich .20 .50
45 Fred Taylor .20 .50
46 Jimmy Smith .25 .60
47 Priest Holmes .20 .50
48 Tony Gonzalez .25 .60
49 Trent Green .20 .50
50 Chris Chambers .20 .50
51 Ricky Williams .25 .60
52 Zach Thomas .25 .60
53 Daunte Culpepper .25 .60
54 Michael Bennett .20 .50
55 Moe Williams .20 .50
56 Randy Moss .25 .60
57 Deion Branch .20 .50
58 Tom Brady 1.25 3.00
59 Tedy Bruschi .25 .60
60 Aaron Brooks .20 .50
61 Deuce McAllister .25 .60
62 Joe Horn .20 .50
63 Jeremy Shockey .20 .50
64 Kerry Collins .20 .50
65 Michael Strahan .25 .60
66 Tiki Barber .25 .60
67 Chad Pennington .20 .50
68 Curtis Martin .25 .60
69 Santana Moss .25 .60
70 Jerry Porter .20 .50
71 Jerry Rice .60 1.50
72 Tim Brown .30 .75
73 Brian Westbrook .20 .50
74 Correll Buckhalter .20 .50
75 Donovan McNabb .25 .60
76 Hines Ward .25 .60
77 Kendrell Bell .20 .50
78 Plaxico Burress .20 .50
79 David Boston .20 .50
80 Drew Brees .30 .75
81 LaDainian Tomlinson .30 .75
82 Jeff Garcia .20 .50
83 Kevan Barlow .20 .50
84 Terrell Owens .25 .60
85 Koren Robinson .20 .50
86 Matt Hasselbeck .20 .50
87 Shaun Alexander .20 .50
88 Isaac Bruce .30 .75
89 Marc Bulger .20 .50
90 Marshall Faulk .25 .60
91 Torry Holt .25 .60
92 Brad Johnson .25 .60
93 Derrick Brooks .20 .50
94 Keenan McCardell .20 .50
95 Derrick Mason .20 .50
96 Eddie George .25 .60
97 Steve McNair .25 .60
98 Jevon Kearse .20 .50
99 Laveranues Coles .20 .50
100 Patrick Ramsey .25 .60
101 Adimchinobe Echemandu RC 2.50 6.00
102 Ahmad Carroll RC 2.00 5.00
103 Antwan Odom RC 2.00 5.00
104 B.J. Johnson RC 2.00 5.00
105 Ben Roethlisberger RC 20.00 50.00
106 Ben Troupe RC 2.00 5.00
107 Ben Watson RC 2.50 6.00
108 Bernard Berrian RC 2.00 5.00
109 Bob Sanders RC 4.00 10.00
110 Brandon Everage RC 2.00 5.00
111 Brandon Miree RC 2.00 5.00
112 Carlos Francis RC 2.00 5.00
113 Cedric Cobbs RC 2.00 5.00
114 Chad Lavalais RC 2.00 5.00
115 Chris Collins RC 2.00 5.00
116 Chris Gamble RC 2.00 5.00
117 Chris Perry RC 2.00 5.00
118 Cody Pickett RC 2.00 5.00
119 Craig Krenzel RC 2.00 5.00
120 D.J. Hackett RC 2.00 5.00
121 D.J. Williams RC 3.00 8.00
122 Darius Watts RC 2.00 5.00
123 Darnell Dockett RC 3.00 8.00
124 DeAngelo Hall RC 3.00 8.00
125 Derek Abney RC 2.00 5.00
126 Derrick Hamilton RC 2.00 5.00
127 Derrick Strait RC 2.00 5.00
128 Devard Darling RC 2.00 5.00
129 Devery Henderson RC 2.00 5.00
130 Dontarrious Thomas RC 2.50 6.00
131 Drew Henson RC 2.00 5.00
132 Dunta Robinson RC 2.00 5.00
133 Dwan Edwards RC 2.00 5.00
134 Eli Manning RC 15.00 40.00
135 Ernest Wilford RC 2.50 6.00
136 Fred Russell RC 2.50 6.00
137 Greg Jones RC 2.00 5.00
138 Igor Olshansky RC 2.50 6.00
139 J.P. Losman RC 2.00 5.00
140 Jared Lorenzen RC 2.50 6.00
141 Jarrett Payton RC 2.50 6.00
142 Jason Babin RC 3.00 8.00
143 Jason Fife RC 2.00 5.00
144 Jeff Smoker RC 2.50 6.00
145 Jeremy LeSueur RC 2.00 5.00
146 Jerricho Cotchery RC 2.50 6.00
147 John Navarre RC 2.00 5.00
148 John Standeford RC 2.00 5.00
149 Johnnie Morant RC 2.00 5.00
150 Jonathan Vilma RC 2.50 6.00
151 Josh Davis RC 2.50 6.00
152 Josh Harris RC 2.00 5.00
153 Julius Jones RC 2.00 5.00
154 Justin Jenkins RC 2.00 5.00
155 Karlos Dansby RC 2.50 6.00
156 Keary Colbert RC 2.00 5.00
157 Keith Smith RC 2.00 5.00
158 Keiwan Ratliff RC 2.00 5.00
159 Kellen Winslow RC 2.00 5.00
160 Kendrick Starling RC 2.00 5.00
161 Kenechi Udeze RC 2.50 6.00
162 Kevin Jones RC 2.50 6.00
163 Larry Fitzgerald RC 8.00 20.00
164 Lee Evans RC 3.00 8.00
165 Luke McCown RC 2.00 5.00
166 Marquise Hill RC 2.00 5.00
167 Matt Schaub RC 2.00 5.00
168 Matt Ware RC 3.00 8.00
169 Matt Mauck RC 2.00 5.00
170 Maurice Mann RC 2.00 5.00
171 Mewelde Moore RC 2.50 6.00
172 Michael Boulware RC 3.00 8.00
173 Michael Clayton RC 2.50 6.00
174 Michael Jenkins RC 2.00 5.00
175 Michael Turner RC 2.00 5.00
176 B.J. Symons RC 2.00 5.00
177 Nathan Vasher RC 3.00 8.00
178 P.K. Sam RC 2.00 5.00
179 Philip Rivers RC 6.00 15.00
180 Quincy Wilson RC 2.00 5.00
181 Ran Carthon RC 2.00 5.00
182 Randy Starks RC 2.00 5.00
183 Rashaun Woods RC 2.00 5.00
184 Reggie Williams RC 2.00 5.00
185 Ricardo Colclough RC 2.00 5.00
186 Robert Kent RC 2.00 5.00
187 Roy Williams RC 2.00 5.00
188 Samie Parker RC 2.00 5.00
189 Scott Rislov RC 2.00 5.00
190 Sean Jones RC 2.00 5.00
191 Sean Taylor RC 15.00 30.00
192 Steven Jackson RC 3.00 8.00
193 Stuart Schweigert RC 2.50 6.00
194 Tatum Bell RC 2.00 5.00
195 Teddy Lehman RC 2.00 5.00
196 Tommie Harris RC 2.50 6.00
197 Troy Fleming RC 2.00 5.00
198 Vince Wilfork RC 3.00 8.00
199 Will Poole RC 3.00 8.00
200 Will Smith RC 2.50 6.00

2004 Donruss Elite Aspirations

*VETS/70-99: 6X TO 15X BASIC CARDS
*ROOKIES/70-99: .6X TO 1.5X
*VETS/45-69: 8X TO 20X
*ROOKIES/45-69: .8X TO 2X
*ROOKIES/30-44: 1X TO 2.5X
*VETS/20-29: 12X TO 30X
*ROOKIES/20-29: 1.2X TO 3X
*VETS/10-19: 15X TO 40X
*ROOKIES/10-19: 1.5X TO 4X
STATED PRINT RUN 2-99

2004 Donruss Elite Status

*VETS/70-99: 6X TO 15X BASIC CARDS
*ROOKIES/70-99: .6X TO 1.5X
*VETS/45-69: 8X TO 20X
*ROOKIES/45-69: .8X TO 2X
*VETS/30-44: 6X TO 15X
*ROOKIES/30-44: 1X TO 2.5X
*VETS/20-29: 12X TO 30X
*ROOKIES/20-29: 1.2X TO 3X
*VETS/10-19: 15X TO 40X
*ROOKIES/10-19: 1.5X TO 4X
STATED PRINT RUN 1-98

2004 Donruss Elite Career Best

COMPLETE SET (15) 20.00 50.00
STATED PRINT RUN 1650 SER.#'d SETS
CB1 Barry Sanders 2.00 5.00
CB2 Brett Favre 2.50 6.00
CB3 Chad Pennington .75 2.00
CB4 Clinton Portis .75 2.00
CB5 Dan Marino 2.50 6.00
CB6 Priest Holmes .75 2.00
CB7 Deuce McAllister 1.00 2.50
CB8 Jerry Rice 2.50 6.00
CB9 John Elway 2.00 5.00
CB10 Marshall Faulk 1.00 2.50
CB11 Emmitt Smith 2.00 5.00
CB12 Marvin Harrison 1.00 2.50
CB13 Peyton Manning 3.00 8.00
CB14 Ricky Williams 1.00 2.50
CB15 Steve McNair 1.00 2.50

2004 Donruss Elite Career Best Jerseys

STATED PRINT RUN 250 SER. #'d SETS
*PRIME/25: 1.2X TO 3X BASIC JSY/250
PRIME PRINT RUN 25 SER. #'d SETS
*YEAR: .6X TO 1.5X BASIC JSY/250
YEAR STATED PRINT RUN 84-103
CB1 Barry Sanders 5.00 12.00
CB2 Brett Favre 6.00 15.00
CB3 Chad Pennington 2.00 5.00
CB4 Clinton Portis 2.00 5.00
CB5 Dan Marino 6.00 15.00
CB6 Priest Holmes 2.00 5.00
CB7 Deuce McAllister 2.50 6.00
CB8 Jerry Rice 6.00 15.00
CB9 John Elway 5.00 12.00
CB10 Marshall Faulk 2.50 6.00
CB11 Emmitt Smith 5.00 12.00
CB12 Marvin Harrison 2.50 6.00
CB13 Peyton Manning 8.00 20.00
CB14 Ricky Williams 2.50 6.00
CB15 Steve McNair 2.50 6.00

2004 Donruss Elite College Ties

COMPLETE SET (15) 15.00 40.00
STATED PRINT RUN 2000 SER.#'d SETS
CT1 D.McAllister/E.Manning 2.50 6.00
CT2 T.Holt/P.Rivers 1.00 2.50
CT3 P.Ramsey/J.P.Losman .75 2.00
CT4 C.Johnson/S.Jackson .50 1.25
CT5 M.Vick/K.Jones .75 2.00
CT6 Ri.Williams/Ro.Williams WR 1.00 3.00
CT7 C.Dillon/Reg.Williams .60 1.50
CT8 D.Davis/M.Clayton .75 2.00
CT9 J.Shockey/K.Winslow .60 1.50
CT10 A.Thomas/C.Perry .75 2.00
CT11 A.Bryant/L.Fitzgerald 1.25 3.00
CT12 E.George/M.Jenkins .75 2.00
CT13 W.Dunn/G.Jones .60 1.50
CT14 M.Bennett/L.Evans 1.00 2.50
CT15 J.Porter/Q.Wilson .60 1.50

2004 Donruss Elite Face to Face Face Masks

STATED PRINT RUN 125 SER.#'d SETS
FF1 J.Kelly/T.Aikman 5.00 12.00
FF2 B.Favre/R.Moss 8.00 20.00
FF3 R.Williams/D.McAllister 3.00 8.00
FF4 B.Urlacher/M.Bennett 4.00 10.00
FF5 J.Elway/D.Marino 8.00 20.00
FF6 Z.Thomas/T.Henry 3.00 8.00
FF7 P.Manning/C.Bailey 10.00 25.00
FF8 M.Faulk/S.Alexander 3.00 8.00
FF9 B.Sanders/M.Singletary 6.00 15.00
FF10 E.Smith/T.Owens 6.00 15.00
FF11 P.Holmes/R.Gannon 3.00 8.00
FF12 P.Manning/S.McNair 20.00 50.00
FF13 J.Shockey/T.Heap 2.50 6.00
FF14 C.Pennington/T.Brady 15.00 40.00
FF15 Ch.Johnson/M.Harrison 3.00 8.00
FF16 J.Garcia/M.Bulger 2.50 6.00
FF17 R.Lewis/E.George 4.00 10.00
FF18 T.Holt/K.Robinson 3.00 8.00
FF19 Jerry Rice Dual 8.00 20.00
FF20 M.Hasselbeck/A.Boldin 2.50 6.00
FF21 J.Plummer/T.Green 2.50 6.00
FF22 C.Chambers/S.Moss 3.00 8.00
FF23 P.Warrick/E.Reed 3.00 8.00
FF24 K.Faulk/C.Dillon 2.50 6.00
FF25 A.Green/D.Staley 3.00 8.00

2004 Donruss Elite Gridiron Gear Bronze

BRONZE STATED PRINT RUN 250
*GOLD/25: 1.2X TO 3X BRONZE/250
GOLD STATED PRINT RUN 25
*PLATINUM/10: 2X TO 5X BASIC INSERTS
PLATINUM PRINT RUN 10
*SILVER/150: .5X TO 1.2X BRONZE/250
SILVER STATED PRINT RUN 150
GG1 Ashley Lelie 2.00 5.00
GG2 Chris Chambers 2.00 5.00
GG3 Correll Buckhalter 2.00 5.00
GG4 Donovan McNabb 2.50 6.00
GG5 Drew Brees 3.00 8.00
GG6 Fred Taylor 2.00 5.00
GG7 Hines Ward 2.50 6.00
GG8 Isaac Bruce 3.00 8.00
GG9 Jeff Garcia 2.00 5.00
GG10 Jerome Bettis 3.00 8.00
GG11 Jevon Kearse 2.00 5.00
GG12 Jimmy Smith 2.50 6.00
GG13 Joey Harrington 2.00 5.00
GG14 Josh Reed 2.00 5.00
GG15 LaDainian Tomlinson 3.00 8.00
GG16 Marc Bulger 2.00 5.00
GG17 Steve McNair 2.50 6.00
GG18 Peyton Manning 8.00 20.00

GG19 Randy Moss 2.50 6.00
GG20 Santana Moss 2.50 6.00
GG21 Tim Brown 3.00 8.00
GG22 Dan Marino 6.00 15.00
GG23 John Elway 5.00 12.00
GG24 Barry Sanders 5.00 12.00
GG25 Troy Aikman 4.00 10.00

2004 Donruss Elite Lineage

COMPLETE SET (5) 8.00 20.00
STATED ODDS 1:24
L1 A.Brooks/M.Vick .75 2.00
L2 R.Barber/T.Barber .75 2.00
L3 Archie/Eli/P.Manning 5.00 12.00
L4 C.Johnson/Key.Johnson .75 2.00
L5 A.Dorsett/T.Dorsett 1.00 2.50

2004 Donruss Elite Lineage Autographs

STATED PRINT RUN 100 SER.#'d SETS
L1 A.Brooks/M.Vick 25.00 60.00
L2 R.Barber/T.Barber 25.00 60.00
L3 Archie/Eli/P.Manning 250.00 500.00
L4 C.Johnson/K.Johnson 20.00 50.00
L5 A.Dorsett/T.Dorsett 25.00 60.00

2004 Donruss Elite Passing the Torch

PT1-PT20 PRINT RUN 1000 SER.#'d SETS
PT21-PT30 PRINT RUN 500 SER.#'d SETS
PT1 Earl Campbell 1.50 4.00
PT2 Domanick Davis 1.00 2.50
PT3 Ricky Williams 1.25 3.00
PT4 Larry Csonka 1.50 4.00
PT5 John Elway 2.50 6.00
PT6 Jake Plummer 1.00 2.50
PT7 Mike Singletary 1.50 4.00
PT8 Brian Urlacher 1.50 4.00
PT9 Drew Bledsoe 1.25 3.00
PT10 Tom Brady 6.00 15.00
PT11 Paul Hornung 1.50 4.00
PT12 Ahman Green 1.25 3.00
PT13 Randall Cunningham 1.25 3.00
PT14 Donovan McNabb 1.25 3.00
PT15 Christian Okoye 1.00 2.50
PT16 Priest Holmes 1.00 2.50
PT17 Warren Moon 1.50 4.00
PT18 Steve McNair 1.25 3.00
PT19 Archie Manning 1.25 3.00
PT20 Eli Manning 3.00 8.00
PT21 D.Davis/E.Campbell 2.50 6.00
PT22 L.Csonka/Ri.Williams 2.50 6.00
PT23 J.Plummer/J.Elway 4.00 10.00
PT24 B.Urlacher/M.Singletary 2.50 6.00
PT25 D.Bledsoe/T.Brady 10.00 25.00
PT26 A.Green/P.Hornung 2.50 6.00
PT27 D.McNabb/Cunningham 2.00 5.00
PT28 C.Okoye/P.Holmes 1.50 4.00
PT29 S.McNair/W.Moon 2.50 6.00
PT30 A.Manning/E.Manning 5.00 12.00

2004 Donruss Elite Passing the Torch Autographs

PT1-PT20 PRINT RUN 100 SER.#'d SETS
PT21-PT30 PRINT RUN 50 SER.#'d SETS
PT1 Earl Campbell 20.00 50.00
PT2 Domanick Davis 12.00 30.00
PT3 Bob Griese 20.00 50.00
PT4 Larry Csonka 20.00 50.00
PT5 John Elway 50.00 120.00
PT6 Jake Plummer 12.00 30.00
PT7 Mike Singletary 20.00 50.00
PT8 Brian Urlacher 20.00 50.00
PT9 Drew Bledsoe 15.00 40.00
PT10 Tom Brady 150.00 250.00
PT11 Paul Hornung 20.00 50.00
PT12 Ahman Green 15.00 40.00
PT13 Randall Cunningham 15.00 40.00
PT14 Donovan McNabb 15.00 40.00
PT15 Christian Okoye 12.00 30.00
PT16 Priest Holmes 12.00 30.00
PT17 Warren Moon 20.00 50.00
PT18 Steve McNair 15.00 40.00
PT19 Archie Manning 15.00 40.00
PT20 Eli Manning 60.00 120.00
PT21 D.Davis/E.Campbell 30.00 80.00
PT22 L.Csonka/Bo.Griese 40.00 80.00
PT23 J.Plummer/J.Elway 100.00 200.00
PT24 B.Urlacher/M.Singletary 50.00 100.00
PT25 D.Bledsoe/T.Brady 150.00 250.00
PT26 A.Green/Hornung 30.00 80.00
PT27 D.McNabb/Cunningham 60.00 120.00
PT28 C.Okoye/P.Holmes 20.00 50.00
PT29 S.McNair/W.Moon 30.00 80.00
PT30 A.Manning/E.Manning 100.00 200.00

2004 Donruss Elite Series

STATED PRINT RUN 850 SER.#'d SETS
ES1 Aaron Brooks 1.00 2.50
ES2 Ahman Green 1.25 3.00
ES3 Anquan Boldin 1.00 2.50
ES4 Brett Favre 3.00 8.00
ES5 Brian Urlacher 1.50 4.00
ES6 Byron Leftwich 1.00 2.50
ES7 Chad Johnson 1.00 2.50
ES8 Chad Pennington 1.00 2.50
ES9 Chris Chambers 1.00 2.50
ES10 Clinton Portis 1.00 2.50
ES11 David Carr 1.00 2.50
ES12 Deuce McAllister 1.25 3.00
ES13 Drew Bledsoe 1.25 3.00
ES14 Edgerrin James 1.25 3.00
ES15 Jamal Lewis 1.25 3.00
ES16 Jerry Rice 3.00 8.00
ES17 Jimmy Smith 1.25 3.00
ES18 LaDainian Tomlinson 1.50 4.00
ES19 Michael Vick 1.25 3.00
ES20 Donovan McNabb 1.25 3.00
ES21 Peyton Manning 4.00 10.00
ES22 Priest Holmes 1.00 2.50
ES23 Randy Moss 1.25 3.00
ES24 Ricky Williams 1.25 3.00
ES25 Steve McNair 1.25 3.00
ES26 Terrell Owens 1.25 3.00
ES27 Tom Brady 6.00 15.00
ES28 Emmitt Smith 2.50 6.00
ES29 Daunte Culpepper 1.25 3.00
ES30 Joey Harrington 1.00 2.50

2004 Donruss Elite Series Jerseys Bronze

BRONZE PRINT RUN 250 SER.#'d SETS
*GOLD/25: 1X TO 2.5X BRONZE
GOLD PRINT RUN 25 SER.#'d SETS
*PLATINUM/10: 2X TO 5X BRONZE
PLATINUM PRINT RUN 10
*SILVER/150: .5X TO 1.2X BRONZE
SILVER PRINT RUN 150 SER.#'d SETS
ES1 Aaron Brooks 2.50 6.00
ES2 Ahman Green 3.00 8.00
ES3 Anquan Boldin 2.50 6.00
ES4 Brett Favre 8.00 20.00
ES5 Brian Urlacher 4.00 10.00
ES6 Byron Leftwich 2.50 6.00
ES7 Chad Johnson 2.50 6.00
ES8 Chad Pennington 2.50 6.00
ES9 Chris Chambers 2.50 6.00
ES10 Clinton Portis 2.50 6.00
ES11 David Carr 2.50 6.00
ES12 Deuce McAllister 3.00 8.00
ES13 Drew Bledsoe 3.00 8.00
ES14 Edgerrin James 3.00 8.00
ES15 Jamal Lewis 3.00 8.00
ES16 Jerry Rice 8.00 20.00
ES17 Jimmy Smith 3.00 8.00
ES18 LaDainian Tomlinson 4.00 10.00
ES19 Michael Vick 3.00 8.00
ES20 Donovan McNabb 3.00 8.00
ES21 Peyton Manning 10.00 25.00
ES22 Priest Holmes 2.50 6.00
ES23 Randy Moss 3.00 8.00
ES24 Ricky Williams 3.00 8.00
ES25 Steve McNair 3.00 8.00
ES26 Terrell Owens 3.00 8.00
ES27 Tom Brady 15.00 40.00
ES28 Emmitt Smith 8.00 20.00
ES29 Daunte Culpepper 3.00 8.00
ES30 Joey Harrington 2.50 6.00

2004 Donruss Elite Throwback Threads

TT1-TT30 PRINT RUN 150 SER. #'d SETS
TT31-TT45 PRINT RUN 75 SER. #'d SETS
TT1 Mark Bavaro 2.50 6.00
TT2 Jeremy Shockey 2.50 6.00
TT3 Tony Dorsett 4.00 10.00
TT4 Clinton Portis 2.50 6.00
TT5 Lynn Swann 12.00 30.00
TT6 Hines Ward 3.00 8.00
TT7 Larry Csonka 4.00 10.00
TT8 Ricky Williams 3.00 8.00
TT9 Troy Aikman 5.00 12.00
TT10 Quincy Carter 2.50 6.00
TT11 Jim Kelly 4.00 10.00
TT12 Drew Bledsoe 3.00 8.00
TT13 Mike Singletary 4.00 10.00
TT14 Brian Urlacher 4.00 10.00
TT15 Warren Moon 4.00 10.00
TT16 David Carr 2.50 6.00
TT17 Thurman Thomas 3.00 8.00
TT18 Travis Henry 2.50 6.00
TT19 Marcus Allen 4.00 10.00
TT20 Priest Holmes 2.50 6.00
TT21 Randall Cunningham 3.00 8.00
TT22 Donovan McNabb 3.00 8.00
TT23 Joe Namath 6.00 15.00
TT24 Chad Pennington 2.50 6.00
TT25 Jim Brown 5.00 12.00
TT26 Jamal Lewis 3.00 8.00
TT27 Walter Payton 15.00 40.00
TT28 LaDainian Tomlinson 4.00 10.00
TT29 Johnny Unitas 10.00 25.00
TT30 Peyton Manning 10.00 25.00
TT31 M.Bavaro/J.Shockey 3.00 8.00
TT32 T.Dorsett/C.Portis 5.00 12.00
TT33 L.Swann/H.Ward 12.00 30.00
TT34 L.Csonka/Ri.Williams 10.00 25.00
TT35 T.Aikman/Q.Carter 6.00 15.00
TT36 J.Kelly/D.Bledsoe 5.00 12.00
TT37 M.Singletary/B.Urlacher 5.00 12.00
TT38 W.Moon/D.Carr 5.00 12.00
TT39 T.Thomas/T.Henry 4.00 10.00
TT40 M.Allen/P.Holmes 5.00 12.00
TT41 Cunningham/McNabb 4.00 10.00
TT42 J.Namath/C.Pennington 8.00 20.00
TT43 J.Brown/J.Lewis 6.00 15.00
TT44 W.Payton/L.Tomlinson 12.00 30.00
TT45 J.Unitas/P.Manning 15.00 40.00

2004 Donruss Elite Throwback Threads Prime

*PRIME TT1-TT30: 1X TO 2.5X BASIC INSERTS
*PRIME TT31-TT45: .8X TO 2X
STATED PRINT RUN 25 SER.#'d SETS

2004 Donruss Elite Turn of the Century Autographs

STATED PRINT RUN 125 SER.#'d SETS
105 Ben Roethlisberger 100.00 200.00
108 Bernard Berrian 8.00 20.00
116 Chris Gamble 8.00 20.00
117 Chris Perry 8.00 20.00
120 D.J. Hackett 8.00 20.00
124 DeAngelo Hall 12.00 30.00
126 Derrick Hamilton 8.00 20.00
128 Devard Darling 8.00 20.00
129 Devery Henderson 8.00 20.00
131 Drew Henson 8.00 20.00
132 Dunta Robinson 8.00 20.00
134 Eli Manning 50.00 120.00
135 Ernest Wilford 10.00 25.00
137 Greg Jones 8.00 20.00
139 J.P. Losman 8.00 20.00
146 Jerricho Cotchery 10.00 25.00
149 Johnnie Morant 8.00 20.00
150 Jonathan Vilma 10.00 25.00
152 Josh Harris 8.00 20.00
153 Julius Jones 8.00 20.00
156 Keary Colbert 8.00 20.00
159 Kellen Winslow Jr. 8.00 20.00
162 Kevin Jones 10.00 25.00
163 Larry Fitzgerald 60.00 120.00
164 Lee Evans 12.00 30.00
165 Luke McCown 8.00 20.00
167 Matt Schaub 8.00 20.00
173 Michael Clayton 10.00 25.00
174 Michael Jenkins 8.00 20.00
175 Michael Turner 8.00 20.00
179 Philip Rivers 50.00 100.00
180 Quincy Wilson 8.00 20.00
183 Rashaun Woods 8.00 20.00
184 Reggie Williams 8.00 20.00
185 Ricardo Colclough 8.00 20.00
187 Roy Williams WR 8.00 20.00
188 Samie Parker 8.00 20.00
192 Steven Jackson 12.00 30.00
194 Tatum Bell 8.00 20.00
196 Tommie Harris 10.00 25.00
198 Vince Wilfork 12.00 30.00
200 Will Smith 10.00 25.00

2005 Donruss Elite

Donruss Elite was initially released in late-June 2005. The base set consists of 200-cards including 100-rookies serial numbered to 499. Hobby boxes contained 20-packs of 5-cards and carried an S.R.P. of $5 per pack. Three parallel sets and a variety of inserts can be found seeded in packs highlighted by the Turn of the Century Autographs and Passing the Torch Autographs inserts.

COMP.SET w/o SP's (100) 7.50 20.00
101-200 PRINT RUN 499 SER.#'d SETS
1 Kurt Warner .25 .60
2 Larry Fitzgerald .30 .75
3 Anquan Boldin .20 .50
4 Emmitt Smith .60 1.50
5 Michael Vick .25 .60
6 Warrick Dunn .20 .50
7 Alge Crumpler .25 .60
8 Jamal Lewis .25 .60
9 Kyle Boller .20 .50
10 Ray Lewis .30 .75
11 Drew Bledsoe .25 .60
12 Willis McGahee .20 .50
13 Travis Henry .20 .50
14 Eric Moulds .20 .50
15 Rex Grossman .20 .50
16 Brian Urlacher .30 .75
17 Thomas Jones .20 .50
18 Carson Palmer .25 .60
19 Rudi Johnson .20 .50
20 Chad Johnson .20 .50
21 J.P. Losman .20 .50
22 Lee Suggs .20 .50
23 Antonio Bryant .20 .50
24 Julius Jones .20 .50
25 Roy Williams S .20 .50
26 Keyshawn Johnson .25 .60
27 Jake Plummer .20 .50
28 Tatum Bell .20 .50
29 Rod Smith .25 .60
30 Joey Harrington .20 .50
31 Kevin Jones .20 .50
32 Roy Williams WR .20 .50
33 Brett Favre .60 1.50
34 Ahman Green .25 .60
35 Javon Walker .20 .50
36 David Carr .20 .50
37 Andre Johnson .25 .60
38 Domanick Davis .20 .50
39 Peyton Manning .75 2.00
40 Edgerrin James .25 .60
41 Brandon Stokley .20 .50
42 Reggie Wayne .25 .60
43 Marvin Harrison .25 .60
44 Byron Leftwich .20 .50
45 Jimmy Smith .25 .60
46 Fred Taylor .20 .50
47 Trent Green .20 .50
48 Priest Holmes .20 .50
49 Tony Gonzalez .25 .60
50 A.J. Feeley .20 .50
51 Chris Chambers .20 .50
52 Daunte Culpepper .25 .60
53 Randy Moss .25 .60
54 Onterrio Smith .20 .50
55 Corey Dillon .20 .50
56 Tom Brady 1.25 3.00
57 David Givens .20 .50
58 Aaron Brooks .20 .50
59 Deuce McAllister .25 .60
60 Joe Horn .20 .50
61 Eli Manning .50 1.25
62 Tiki Barber .25 .60
63 Jeremy Shockey .20 .50
64 Chad Pennington .20 .50
65 Curtis Martin .25 .60
66 Santana Moss .25 .60
67 Kerry Collins .20 .50
68 Jerry Porter .20 .50
69 Donovan McNabb .25 .60
70 Terrell Owens .25 .60
71 Brian Westbrook .20 .50
72 Ben Roethlisberger .50 1.25
73 Plaxico Burress .20 .50
74 Hines Ward .25 .60
75 Jerome Bettis .30 .75
76 Duce Staley .20 .50
77 Antonio Gates .30 .75
78 Drew Brees .30 .75
79 LaDainian Tomlinson .30 .75
80 Brandon Lloyd .20 .50
81 Kevan Barlow .20 .50
82 Matt Hasselbeck .20 .50
83 Shaun Alexander .20 .50
84 Darrell Jackson .20 .50
85 Jerry Rice .60 1.50
86 Marc Bulger .20 .50
87 Marshall Faulk .25 .60
88 Steven Jackson .20 .50
89 Isaac Bruce .30 .75
90 Torry Holt .25 .60
91 Michael Clayton .20 .50
92 Brian Griese .20 .50
93 Mike Alstott .20 .50
94 Steve McNair .25 .60
95 Derrick Mason .20 .50
96 Chris Brown .20 .50
97 Drew Bennett .25 .60
98 Patrick Ramsey .25 .60
99 Clinton Portis .20 .50
100 LaVar Arrington .20 .50
101 Aaron Rodgers RC 75.00 125.00
102 Adam Jones RC 2.50 6.00
103 Adrian McPherson RC 2.50 6.00
104A Alex Smith TE ERR RC 2.50 6.00
104B Alex Smith TE COR RC 2.50 6.00
105A Alex Smith QB ERR RC 10.00 25.00
105B Alex Smith QB COR RC 10.00 25.00
106 Alvin Pearman RC 2.50 6.00
107 Andrew Walter RC 2.50 6.00
108 Anthony Davis RC 2.50 6.00
109 Antrel Rolle RC 4.00 10.00
110 Anttaj Hawthorne RC 2.50 6.00
111 Brandon Browner RC 4.00 10.00
112 Brandon Jacobs RC 3.00 8.00
113 Braylon Edwards RC 2.50 6.00
114 Brock Berlin RC 2.50 6.00
115 Brandon Jones RC 3.00 8.00
116 Bryant McFadden RC 3.00 8.00
117 Carlos Rogers RC 4.00 10.00
118 Cadillac Williams RC 2.50 6.00
119 Cedric Benson RC 2.50 6.00
120 Cedric Houston RC 4.00 10.00
121 Channing Crowder RC 3.00 8.00
122 Charles Frederick RC 2.50 6.00
123 Charlie Frye RC 2.50 6.00
124 Chase Lyman RC 2.50 6.00
125 Chris Henry RC 3.00 8.00
126 Chris Rix RC 3.00 8.00
127 Ciatrick Fason RC 2.50 6.00
128 Corey Webster RC 3.00 8.00
129 Courtney Roby RC 2.50 6.00
130 Craig Bragg RC 2.50 6.00
131 Craphonso Thorpe RC 2.50 6.00
132 Damien Nash RC 3.00 8.00
133 Dan Cody RC 2.50 6.00
134 Dan Orlovsky RC 2.50 6.00
135 Dante Ridgeway RC 2.50 6.00
136 Darian Durant RC 2.50 6.00
137 Darren Sproles RC 4.00 10.00
138 Darryl Blackstock RC 2.50 6.00
139 David Greene RC 2.50 6.00
140 David Pollack RC 2.50 6.00
141 DeMarcus Ware RC 8.00 20.00
142 Derek Anderson RC 3.00 8.00
143 Derrick Johnson RC 3.00 8.00
144 Erasmus James RC 2.50 6.00
145 Eric Shelton RC 2.50 6.00
146 Ernest Shazor RC 3.00 8.00
147 Fabian Washington RC 2.50 6.00
148 Frank Gore UER RC 5.00 12.00
149 Fred Amey RC 3.00 8.00
150 Fred Gibson RC 2.50 6.00
151 Maurice Clarett 3.00 8.00
152 Gino Guidugli RC 2.50 6.00
153 Heath Miller RC 5.00 12.00
154 J.J. Arrington RC 3.00 8.00
155 J.R. Russell RC 2.50 6.00
156 Jason Campbell RC 2.50 6.00
157 Jason White RC 4.00 10.00
158 Jerome Mathis RC 4.00 10.00
159 Josh Bullocks RC 3.00 8.00
160 Josh Davis RC 2.50 6.00
161 Justin Miller RC 2.50 6.00
162 Justin Tuck RC 3.00 8.00
163 Kay-Jay Harris RC 2.50 6.00
164 Kevin Burnett RC 3.00 8.00
165 Kyle Orton RC 2.50 6.00
166 Larry Brackins RC 2.50 6.00
167 Marcus Spears RC 2.50 6.00
168 Marion Barber RC 2.50 6.00
169 Mark Bradley RC 2.50 6.00
170 Mark Clayton RC 2.50 6.00
171 Marlin Jackson RC 2.50 6.00
172 Matt Jones RC 2.50 6.00
173 Matt Roth RC 2.50 6.00
174 Mike Patterson RC 2.50 6.00
175 Mike Williams 3.00 8.00
176 Airese Currie RC 2.50 6.00
177 Reggie Brown RC 2.50 6.00
178 Roddy White RC 4.00 10.00
179 Ronnie Brown RC 3.00 8.00
180 Roscoe Parrish RC 2.50 6.00
181 Roydell Williams RC 3.00 8.00
182 Ryan Fitzpatrick RC 4.00 10.00
183 Rasheed Marshall RC 3.00 8.00
184 Ryan Moats RC 3.00 8.00
185 Shaun Cody RC 3.00 8.00
186 Shawne Merriman RC 4.00 10.00
187 Chad Owens RC 2.50 6.00
188 Stefan LeFors RC 2.50 6.00
189 Steve Savoy RC 2.50 6.00
190 T.A. McLendon RC 2.50 6.00
191 Tab Perry RC 2.50 6.00
192 Taylor Stubblefield RC 2.50 6.00
193 Terrence Murphy RC 2.50 6.00
194 Thomas Davis RC 2.50 6.00
195 Timmy Chang RC 2.50 6.00
196 Travis Johnson RC 2.50 6.00
197 Troy Williamson RC 2.50 6.00
198 Vernand Morency RC 2.50 6.00
199 Vincent Jackson RC 4.00 10.00
200 Walter Reyes RC 2.50 6.00

2005 Donruss Elite Aspirations

*VETS/70-99: 5X TO 12X BASIC CARDS
*ROOKIES/70-99: .6X TO 1.5X
*VETS/44-69: 6X TO 15X
*ROOKIES/44-69: .8X TO 2X
*VETS/20-29: 10X TO 25X
*ROOKIES/20-29: 1.2X TO 3X
STATED PRINT RUN 1-99
#'d UNDER 20 TOO SCARCE TO PRICE
101 Aaron Rodgers/92 125.00 200.00
105A Alex Smith QB ERR/89 15.00 40.00
105B Alex Smith QB COR/89 12.00 30.00

2005 Donruss Elite Status Gold

*VETS: 10X TO 25X BASIC CARDS
*ROOKIES: 1.2X TO 3X BASIC CARDS
STATED PRINT RUN 24 SER.#'d SETS
101 Aaron Rodgers 175.00 300.00

2005 Donruss Elite Status Red

*VETS/70-99: 5X TO 12X BASIC CARDS
*ROOKIES/70-99: .6X TO 1.5X
*VETS/45-69: 6X TO 15X
*ROOKIES/45-69: .8X TO 2X
*VETS/30-44: 8X TO 20X
*ROOKIES/30-44: 1X TO 2.5X
*VETS/20-29: 10X TO 25X
*ROOKIES/20-29: 1.2X TO 3X
STATED PRINT RUN 1-99
#'d/19 or LESS TOO SCARCE TO PRICE

2005 Donruss Elite Back to the Future Green

COMPLETE SET (15) 12.00 30.00
STATED PRINT RUN 1000 SER.#'d SETS
*BLUE/500: .5X TO 1.2X GREEN/1000
*RED/250: .6X TO 1.5X GREEN/1000
BF1 Cunningham/McNabb .75 2.00
BF2 D.Fouts/D.Brees 1.00 2.50
BF3 M.Allen/P.Holmes 1.00 2.50
BF4 St.Sharpe/J.Walker .75 2.00
BF5 S.Largent/D.Jackson 1.00 2.50
BF6 J.Bettis/D.Staley 1.00 2.50
BF7 M.Irvin/Key.Johnson 1.00 2.50
BF8 E.Moulds/L.Evans .75 2.00
BF9 J.Smith/Re.Williams .75 2.00
BF10 W.Payton/T.Jones 2.50 6.00
BF11 M.Faulk/S.Jackson .75 2.00
BF12 W.Moon/S.McNair 1.00 2.50
BF13 C.Martin/C.Dillon .75 2.00
BF14 Key.Johnson/Mi.Clayton .75 2.00
BF15 C.Dillon/R.Johnson .60 1.50

2005 Donruss Elite Back to the Future Jerseys

STATED PRINT RUN 100 SER.#'d SETS
UNPRICED PRIME PRINT RUN 10
BF1 Cunningham/McNabb 4.00 10.00
BF2 D.Fouts/D.Brees 5.00 12.00
BF3 M.Allen/P.Holmes 5.00 12.00
BF4 St.Sharpe/J.Walker 4.00 10.00
BF5 S.Largent/D.Jackson 5.00 12.00
BF6 J.Bettis/D.Staley 5.00 12.00
BF7 M.Irvin/Key.Johnson 5.00 12.00
BF8 E.Moulds/L.Evans 4.00 10.00
BF9 J.Smith/Re.Williams 4.00 10.00
BF10 W.Payton/T.Jones 12.00 30.00
BF11 M.Faulk/S.Jackson 4.00 10.00
BF12 W.Moon/S.McNair 5.00 12.00
BF13 C.Martin/C.Dillon 4.00 10.00
BF14 Key.Johnson/Mi.Clayton 4.00 10.00
BF15 C.Dillon/R.Johnson 3.00 8.00

2005 Donruss Elite Career Best Red

RED STATED PRINT RUN 1000
*BLACK/250: .6X TO 1.5X RED/1000
*GOLD/500: .5X TO 1.2X RED/1000
CB1 Andre Johnson .75 2.00
CB2 Barry Sanders 1.50 4.00
CB3 Ben Roethlisberger 1.50 4.00
CB4 Brett Favre 2.00 5.00
CB5 Brian Urlacher 1.00 2.50
CB6 Brian Westbrook .60 1.50
CB7 Byron Leftwich .60 1.50
CB8 Carson Palmer .75 2.00
CB9 Chad Johnson .60 1.50
CB10 Chad Pennington .60 1.50
CB11 Corey Dillon .60 1.50
CB12 Dan Marino 2.00 5.00
CB13 Daunte Culpepper .75 2.00
CB14 David Carr .60 1.50
CB15 Deuce McAllister .75 2.00
CB16 Donovan McNabb .75 2.00
CB17 Drew Bledsoe .75 2.00
CB18 Edgerrin James .75 2.00
CB19 Jake Delhomme .60 1.50
CB20 Jake Plummer .60 1.50
CB21 Jamal Lewis .75 2.00
CB22 Javon Walker .60 1.50
CB23 Jerry Rice 2.00 5.00
CB24 Joe Montana 3.00 8.00
CB25 Joey Harrington .60 1.50
CB26 John Elway 1.50 4.00
CB27 Julius Jones .60 1.50
CB28 Kevin Jones .60 1.50
CB29 LaDainian Tomlinson 1.00 2.50
CB30 Marc Bulger .60 1.50
CB31 Marshall Faulk .75 2.00
CB32 Marvin Harrison .75 2.00
CB33 Matt Hasselbeck .60 1.50
CB34 Michael Clayton .60 1.50
CB35 Michael Vick .75 2.00
CB36 Peyton Manning 2.50 6.00
CB37 Priest Holmes .60 1.50
CB38 Randy Moss .75 2.00
CB39 Larry Fitzgerald 1.00 2.50
CB40 Rudi Johnson .60 1.50
CB41 Shaun Alexander .60 1.50
CB42 Steve McNair .75 2.00
CB43 Steve Young 1.25 3.00
CB44 Terrell Owens .75 2.00
CB45 Tom Brady 4.00 10.00
CB46 Torry Holt .75 2.00
CB47 Trent Green .60 1.50
CB48 Troy Aikman 1.25 3.00
CB49 Walter Payton 2.50 6.00
CB50 Willis McGahee .60 1.60

2005 Donruss Elite Career Best Jerseys

STATED PRINT RUN 175 SER.#'d SETS
*YEAR/77-104: .5X TO 1.2X BASIC JSY/175
CB1 Andre Johnson 2.50 6.00
CB2 Barry Sanders 5.00 12.00
CB3 Ben Roethlisberger 5.00 12.00
CB4 Brett Favre 6.00 15.00
CB5 Brian Urlacher 3.00 8.00
CB6 Brian Westbrook 2.00 5.00
CB7 Byron Leftwich 2.00 5.00
CB8 Carson Palmer 2.50 6.00
CB9 Chad Johnson 2.00 5.00
CB10 Chad Pennington 2.00 5.00
CB11 Corey Dillon 2.00 5.00
CB12 Dan Marino 6.00 15.00
CB13 Daunte Culpepper 2.50 6.00
CB14 David Carr 2.00 5.00
CB15 Deuce McAllister 2.50 6.00
CB16 Donovan McNabb 2.50 6.00
CB17 Drew Bledsoe 2.50 6.00
CB18 Edgerrin James 2.50 6.00
CB19 Jake Delhomme 2.00 5.00
CB20 Jake Plummer 2.00 5.00
CB21 Jamal Lewis 2.50 6.00
CB22 Javon Walker 2.00 5.00
CB23 Jerry Rice 6.00 15.00
CB24 Joe Montana 10.00 25.00
CB25 Joey Harrington 2.00 5.00
CB26 John Elway 5.00 12.00
CB27 Julius Jones 2.50 6.00
CB28 Kevin Jones 2.00 5.00
CB29 LaDainian Tomlinson 3.00 8.00
CB30 Marc Bulger 2.00 5.00
CB31 Marshall Faulk 2.50 6.00
CB32 Marvin Harrison 2.50 6.00
CB33 Matt Hasselbeck 2.00 5.00
CB34 Michael Clayton 2.00 5.00
CB35 Michael Vick 2.50 6.00
CB36 Peyton Manning 8.00 20.00
CB37 Priest Holmes 2.00 5.00
CB38 Randy Moss 2.50 6.00
CB39 Larry Fitzgerald 3.00 8.00
CB40 Rudi Johnson 2.00 5.00
CB41 Shaun Alexander 2.00 5.00
CB42 Steve McNair 2.50 6.00
CB43 Steve Young 4.00 10.00
CB44 Terrell Owens 2.50 6.00
CB45 Tom Brady 12.00 30.00
CB46 Torry Holt 2.50 6.00
CB47 Trent Green 2.00 5.00
CB48 Troy Aikman 4.00 10.00
CB49 Walter Payton 12.00 30.00
CB50 Willis McGahee 2.00 5.00

2005 Donruss Elite College Ties

STATED ODDS 1:20
CT1 K.Boller/A.Rodgers 6.00 15.00
CT2 S.Smith/A.Smith QB 2.00 5.00
CT3 R.Williams WR/C.Benson .50 1.25
CT4 Bo Jackson/Ron.Brown 1.00 2.50
CT5 R.Johnson/C.Williams .50 1.25
CT6 T.Brady/B.Edwards 3.00 8.00
CT7 D.Robinson/T.Williamson .50 1.25
CT8 T.Bell/V.Morency .50 1.25
CT9 R.Grossman/C.Fason .50 1.25
CT10 C.Portis/R.Parrish .50 1.25

2005 Donruss Elite College Ties Autographs

STATED PRINT RUN 50 SER.#'d SETS
CT1 K.Boller/A.Rodgers 125.00 250.00
CT2 S.Smith/A.Smith QB 50.00 100.00
CT3 Williams WR/Benson 20.00 50.00
CT4 Bo Jackson/Ron.Brown 50.00 100.00
CT5 Ru.Johnson/C.Williams 40.00 80.00
CT6 T.Brady/B.Edwards 100.00 200.00
CT7 D.Robinson/T.Williamson 15.00 40.00
CT8 T.Bell AU/Morency No AU 15.00 40.00
CT9 R.Grossman/C.Fason 20.00 50.00
CT10 C.Portis/R.Parrish 20.00 50.00

2005 Donruss Elite Elite Teams Silver

SILVER STATED PRINT RUN 1000
*GOLD/250: .6X TO 1.5X SILVER/1000
*RED/500: .5X TO 1.2X SILVER/1000
ET1 Boldin/Fitz/McCown 1.00 2.50
ET2 Vick/Duckett/Price .75 2.00
ET3 Lewis/Boller/Heap .75 2.00
ET4 McGahee/Bled/Moulds .75 2.00
ET5 Delhomme/Smith/Davis .60 1.50
ET6 Palmer/Johnson/Johnson .75 2.00
ET7 Jones/Johnson/Will.S .75 2.00
ET8 Jones/Harring/Will.WR .60 1.50
ET9 Favre/Green/Walker 2.00 5.00
ET10 Carr/Davis/Johnson .75 2.00
ET11 Manning/Harrison/James 2.50 6.00
ET12 Leftwich/Taylor/Smith .75 2.00
ET13 Holmes/Green/Hall .60 1.50
ET14 Moss/Culpep/Bennett .75 2.00
ET15 Brady/Dillon/Law 4.00 10.00
ET16 McAll/Brooks/Stallworth .75 2.00
ET17 E.Mann/Shock/Toom 1.50 4.00
ET18 Pennington/Martin/Moss .75 2.00
ET19 McNabb/Owens/Westbr .75 2.00
ET20 Roeth/Burress/Staley 1.50 4.00
ET21 Alex/Hassel/Jackson .60 1.50
ET22 Bulger/Faulk/Bruce 1.00 2.50
ET23 Clayton/Alstott/Johnson .60 1.50
ET24 Brown/McNair/Mason .75 2.00
ET25 Portis/Arrington/Coles .75 2.00

2005 Donruss Elite Elite Teams Jerseys

STATED PRINT RUN 100 SER.#'d SETS
*PRIME/25: .8X TO 2X BASIC JSY/100
ET1 Boldin/Fitz/McCown 5.00 12.00
ET2 Vick/Duckett/Price 4.00 10.00
ET3 Lewis/Boller/Heap 4.00 10.00
ET4 McGahee/Bled/Moulds 4.00 10.00
ET5 Delhomme/Smith/Davis 3.00 8.00
ET6 Palmer/Johnson/Johnson 4.00 10.00
ET7 Jones/Johnson/Will.S 4.00 10.00
ET8 Jones/Harring/Will.WR 3.00 8.00
ET9 Favre/Green/Walker 10.00 25.00
ET10 Carr/Davis/Johnson 4.00 10.00
ET11 Manning/Harrison/James 12.00 30.00
ET12 Leftwich/Taylor/Smith 4.00 10.00
ET13 Holmes/Green/Hall 3.00 8.00
ET14 Moss/Culpep/Bennett 4.00 10.00
ET15 Brady/Dillon/Law 20.00 50.00
ET16 McAll/Brooks/Stallworth 4.00 10.00
ET17 E.Mann/Shock/Toom 8.00 20.00
ET18 Pennington/Martin/Moss 4.00 10.00
ET19 McNabb/Owens/Westb 4.00 10.00
ET20 Roeth/Burress/Staley 8.00 20.00
ET21 Alex/Hassel/Jackson 3.00 8.00
ET22 Bulger/Faulk/Bruce 5.00 12.00
ET23 Clayton/Alstott/Johnson 3.00 8.00
ET24 Brown/McNair/Mason 4.00 10.00
ET25 Portis/Arrington/Coles 3.00 8.00

2005 Donruss Elite Face 2 Face Gold

GOLD STATED PRINT RUN 1000
*BLACK/500: .5X TO 1.2X GOLD/1000
*RED/250: .6X TO 1.5X GOLD/1000
CB1 A.Johnson/A.Boldin .75 2.00
CB2 D.Carr/B.Leftwich .60 1.50
CB3 D.Culpepper/J.Harrington .75 2.00
CB4 T.Brady/C.Pennington 4.00 10.00
CB5 J.Elway/B.Favre 2.00 5.00
CB6 D.Marino/P.Manning 2.50 6.00
CB7 T.Aikman/D.McNabb 1.25 3.00
CB8 D.McAllister/S.Davis .75 2.00
CB9 R.Moss/A.Green .75 2.00
CB10 J.Lewis/K.Bell .75 2.00
CB11 P.Holmes/L.Tomlinson 1.00 2.50
CB12 H.Ward/C.Johnson .75 2.00
CB13 T.Holt/K.Robinson .75 2.00
CB14 M.Hasselbeck/M.Bulger .60 1.50
CB15 J.Rice/M.Harrison 2.00 5.00
CB16 M.Faulk/S.Alexander .75 2.00
CB17 R.Lewis/B.Urlacher 1.00 2.50
CB18 J.Shockey/T.Heap .60 1.50
CB19 J.Plummer/T.Green .60 1.50
CB20 B.Sanders/E.Smith 2.00 5.00
CB21 S.Moss/C.Chambers .75 2.00
CB22 T.Owens/J.Garcia .75 2.00
CB23 P.Manning/S.McNair 2.50 6.00
CB24 J.Delhomme/S.Smith .60 1.50
CB25 J.Montana/S.Young 3.00 8.00

2005 Donruss Elite Face 2 Face Jerseys

JERSEY STATED PRINT RUN 250
*FACEMASK/75-125: .6X TO 1.5X JSY/250
CB1 A.Johnson/A.Boldin 4.00 10.00
CB2 D.Carr/B.Leftwich 3.00 8.00
CB3 D.Culpepper/J.Harrington 4.00 10.00
CB4 T.Brady/C.Pennington 20.00 50.00
CB5 J.Elway/B.Favre 12.00 30.00
CB6 D.Marino/P.Manning 12.00 30.00
CB7 T.Aikman/D.McNabb 8.00 20.00
CB8 D.McAllister/S.Davis 4.00 10.00
CB9 R.Moss/A.Green 4.00 10.00
CB10 J.Lewis/K.Bell 4.00 10.00
CB11 P.Holmes/L.Tomlinson 5.00 12.00
CB12 H.Ward/C.Johnson 4.00 10.00
CB13 T.Holt/K.Robinson 4.00 10.00
CB14 M.Hasselbeck/M.Bulger 3.00 8.00
CB15 J.Rice/M.Harrison 10.00 25.00
CB16 M.Faulk/S.Alexander 4.00 10.00
CB17 R.Lewis/B.Urlacher 8.00 20.00
CB18 J.Shockey/T.Heap 3.00 8.00
CB19 J.Plummer/T.Green 3.00 8.00
CB20 B.Sanders/E.Smith 12.00 30.00
CB21 S.Moss/C.Chambers 4.00 10.00
CB22 T.Owens/J.Garcia 4.00 10.00
CB23 P.Manning/S.McNair 12.00 30.00
CB24 J.Delhomme/S.Smith 3.00 8.00
CB25 J.Montana/S.Young 20.00 50.00

2005 Donruss Elite Passing the Torch Red

RED PT1-PT20 PRINT RUN 1000
RED PT21-PT30 PRINT RUN 750
*BLUE: .6X TO 1.5X RED/750-1000
BLUE PT1-PT20 PRINT RUN 250
BLUE PT21-PT30 PRINT RUN 100
*GREEN: .5X TO 1.2X RED/750-1000
GREEN PT1-PT20 PRINT RUN 500
GREEN PT21-PT30 PRINT RUN 250
PT1 Eric Dickerson .75 2.00
PT2 Steven Jackson .60 1.50
PT3 Thurman Thomas .75 2.00
PT4 Willis McGahee .60 1.50
PT5 Len Dawson 1.00 2.50
PT6 Trent Green .60 1.50
PT7 Terry Bradshaw 1.25 3.00
PT8 Ben Roethlisberger 1.50 4.00
PT9 Terrell Davis .75 2.00
PT10 Tatum Bell .60 1.50
PT11 Boomer Esiason .75 2.00
PT12 Carson Palmer .75 2.00
PT13 Cris Collinsworth .75 2.00
PT14 Chad Johnson .60 1.50
PT15 John Riggins .75 2.00
PT16 Clinton Portis .60 1.50
PT17 Dan Marino 2.00 5.00
PT18 Peyton Manning 2.50 6.00
PT19 Joe Montana 3.00 8.00
PT20 Tom Brady 4.00 10.00
PT21 Dickerson/S.Jackson 1.00 2.50
PT22 T.Thomas/McGahee 1.00 2.50
PT23 L.Dawson/T.Green 1.25 3.00
PT24 Bradshaw/Roethlis 2.00 5.00
PT25 T.Davis/T.Bell 1.00 2.50
PT26 B.Esiason/C.Palmer 1.00 2.50
PT27 Collinsworth/Ch.Johnsn 1.00 2.50
PT28 J.Riggins/C.Portis 1.00 2.50
PT29 D.Marino/P.Manning 3.00 8.00
PT30 J.Montana/T.Brady 5.00 12.00

2005 Donruss Elite Passing the Torch Autographs

PT1-PT20 AUTO PRINT RUN 100
PT21-PT30 DUAL AU PRINT RUN 50
PT1 Eric Dickerson 15.00 40.00
PT2 Steven Jackson 10.00 25.00
PT3 Thurman Thomas 15.00 40.00
PT4 Willis McGahee 10.00 25.00
PT5 Len Dawson 20.00 50.00
PT6 Trent Green 10.00 25.00
PT7 Terry Bradshaw 50.00 100.00
PT8 Ben Roethlisberger 60.00 120.00
PT9 Terrell Davis 15.00 40.00
PT10 Tatum Bell 10.00 25.00
PT11 Boomer Esiason 15.00 40.00
PT12 Carson Palmer 12.00 30.00
PT13 Cris Collinsworth 15.00 40.00
PT14 Chad Johnson 8.00 20.00
PT15 John Riggins 15.00 40.00
PT16 Clinton Portis 10.00 25.00
PT17 Dan Marino 75.00 150.00
PT18 Peyton Manning 60.00 100.00
PT19 Joe Montana 75.00 150.00
PT20 Tom Brady 125.00 200.00
PT21 E.Dickerson/S.Jackson 25.00 60.00
PT22 T.Thomas/McGahee 25.00 60.00
PT23 L.Dawson/T.Green 20.00 50.00
PT24 Bradshaw/Roethlisberger 175.00 350.00
PT25 T.Davis/T.Bell 25.00 60.00
PT26 B.Esiason/C.Palmer 20.00 50.00
PT27 Collinswrth/Ch.Johnsn 25.00 60.00
PT28 J.Riggins/C.Portis 25.00 60.00
PT29 Marino/P.Manning 175.00 300.00
PT30 Montana/Brady 250.00 400.00

2005 Donruss Elite Series

COMPLETE SET (25) 25.00 60.00
STATED PRINT RUN 1000 SER.#'d SETS
ES1 Ben Roethlisberger 2.00 5.00
ES2 Brett Favre 2.50 6.00
ES3 Brian Urlacher 1.25 3.00
ES4 Byron Leftwich .75 2.00
ES5 Carson Palmer 1.00 2.50
ES6 Chad Pennington .75 2.00
ES7 Clinton Portis .75 2.00
ES8 Corey Dillon .75 2.00
ES9 Daunte Culpepper 1.00 2.50
ES10 David Carr .75 2.00
ES11 Donovan McNabb 1.00 2.50
ES12 Jerry Rice 2.50 6.00
ES13 Julius Jones .75 2.00
ES14 Kevin Jones .75 2.00
ES15 LaDainian Tomlinson 1.25 3.00
ES16 Marvin Harrison 1.00 2.50
ES17 Michael Vick 1.00 2.50
ES18 Peyton Manning 3.00 8.00
ES19 Priest Holmes .75 2.00
ES20 Randy Moss 1.00 2.50
ES21 Ray Lewis 1.25 3.00
ES22 Shaun Alexander .75 2.00
ES23 Terrell Owens 1.00 2.50
ES24 Tom Brady 5.00 12.00
ES25 Willis McGahee .75 2.00

2005 Donruss Elite Series Jerseys

STATED PRINT RUN 199 SER.#'d SETS
*PRIME/25: 1X TO 2.5X BASIC JSY/199
ES1 Ben Roethlisberger 5.00 12.00
ES2 Brett Favre 6.00 15.00
ES3 Brian Urlacher 3.00 8.00
ES4 Byron Leftwich 2.00 5.00
ES5 Carson Palmer 2.50 6.00
ES6 Chad Pennington 2.00 5.00
ES7 Clinton Portis 2.00 5.00
ES8 Corey Dillon 2.00 5.00
ES9 Daunte Culpepper 2.50 6.00
ES10 David Carr 2.00 5.00
ES11 Donovan McNabb 2.50 6.00
ES12 Jerry Rice 6.00 15.00
ES13 Julius Jones 2.00 5.00
ES14 Kevin Jones 2.00 5.00
ES15 LaDainian Tomlinson 3.00 8.00
ES16 Marvin Harrison 2.50 6.00
ES17 Michael Vick 2.50 6.00
ES18 Peyton Manning 8.00 20.00
ES19 Priest Holmes 2.00 5.00
ES20 Randy Moss 2.50 6.00
ES21 Ray Lewis 3.00 8.00
ES22 Shaun Alexander 2.00 5.00
ES23 Terrell Owens 2.50 6.00
ES24 Tom Brady 12.00 30.00
ES25 Willis McGahee 2.00 5.00

2005 Donruss Elite Throwback Threads

TT1-TT30 STATED PRINT RUN 150
TT31-TT45 STATED PRINT RUN 75
*PRIME TT1-TT30: .8X TO 2X BASIC JSY
PRIME TT1-TT30 PRINT RUN 25
UNPRICED PRIME TT31-TT45 PRINT RUN 10
TT1 Joe Montana 49ers 12.00 30.00
TT2 Tom Brady 15.00 40.00
TT3 Joe Montana Chiefs 12.00 30.00
TT4 Trent Green 2.50 6.00
TT5 Joe Namath 6.00 15.00
TT6 Chad Pennington 2.50 6.00
TT7 John Elway 6.00 15.00
TT8 Jake Plummer 2.50 6.00
TT9 John Riggins 3.00 8.00
TT10 Clinton Portis 2.50 6.00
TT11 Tony Dorsett 4.00 10.00
TT12 Julius Jones 2.50 6.00
TT13 Thurman Thomas 3.00 8.00
TT14 Willis McGahee 2.50 6.00
TT15 Terry Bradshaw 5.00 12.00
TT16 Ben Roethlisberger 6.00 15.00
TT17 Fran Tarkenton Vikings 4.00 10.00
TT18 Daunte Culpepper 3.00 8.00
TT19 Dan Marino 8.00 20.00
TT20 Peyton Manning 10.00 25.00
TT21 Barry Sanders 6.00 15.00
TT22 Kevin Jones 2.50 6.00
TT23 Fran Tarkenton Giants 4.00 10.00
TT24 Eli Manning 6.00 15.00
TT25 Steve Young 5.00 12.00
TT26 Michael Vick 3.00 8.00
TT27 Earl Campbell 4.00 10.00
TT28 Domanick Davis 2.50 6.00
TT29 Boomer Esiason 3.00 8.00
TT30 Carson Palmer 3.00 8.00
TT31 J.Montana/T.Brady 30.00 80.00
TT32 J.Montana/T.Green 30.00 60.00
TT33 J.Namath/Pennington 12.50 30.00
TT34 J.Elway/J.Plummer 20.00 50.00
TT35 J.Riggins/C.Portis 15.00 40.00
TT36 T.Dorsett/J.Jones 10.00 25.00
TT37 T.Thomas/W.McGahee 10.00 25.00
TT38 Bradshaw/Roethlisberger 40.00 100.00
TT39 Tarkenton/Culpepper 10.00 25.00
TT40 D.Marino/P.Manning 30.00 80.00
TT41 B.Sanders/K.Jones 25.00 60.00
TT42 F.Tarkenton/E.Manning 12.50 30.00
TT43 S.Young/M.Vick 12.50 30.00
TT44 E.Campbell/D.Davis 7.50 20.00
TT45 B.Esiason/C.Palmer 10.00 25.00

2005 Donruss Elite Turn of the Century Autographs

STATED PRINT RUN 125 SER.#'d SETS
101 Aaron Rodgers 200.00 400.00
102 Adam Jones 8.00 20.00
103 Adrian McPherson 8.00 20.00
105 Alex Smith QB ERR 25.00 60.00
108 Anthony Davis 8.00 20.00
109 Antrel Rolle 12.00 30.00
113 Braylon Edwards 8.00 20.00
116 Bryant McFadden 10.00 25.00
117 Carlos Rogers 12.00 30.00
118 Cadillac Williams 8.00 20.00
119 Cedric Benson 8.00 20.00
123 Charlie Frye 8.00 20.00
127 Ciatrick Fason 8.00 20.00
129 Courtney Roby 8.00 20.00
130 Craig Bragg 8.00 20.00
131 Craphonso Thorpe 8.00 20.00
133 Dan Cody 8.00 20.00
139 David Greene 8.00 20.00
140 David Pollack 8.00 20.00
143 Derrick Johnson 10.00 25.00
145 Eric Shelton 8.00 20.00
148 Frank Gore 15.00 40.00
151 Maurice Clarett 8.00 20.00
153 Heath Miller 15.00 40.00
154 J.J. Arrington 10.00 25.00
156 Jason Campbell 8.00 20.00
157 Jason White 12.00 30.00
158 Jerome Mathis 12.00 30.00
160 Josh Davis 8.00 20.00
163 Kay-Jay Harris 8.00 20.00
165 Kyle Orton 8.00 20.00
168 Marion Barber 8.00 20.00
169 Mark Bradley 8.00 20.00
170 Mark Clayton 8.00 20.00
172 Matt Jones 8.00 20.00
175 Mike Williams 10.00 25.00
177 Reggie Brown 8.00 20.00
178 Roddy White 12.00 30.00
179 Ronnie Brown 10.00 25.00
180 Roscoe Parrish 8.00 20.00
184 Ryan Moats 8.00 20.00
186 Shawne Merriman 12.00 30.00
188 Stefan LeFors 8.00 20.00
189 Steve Savoy 8.00 20.00
192 Taylor Stubblefield 8.00 20.00
193 Terrence Murphy 8.00 20.00
196 Travis Johnson 8.00 20.00
197 Troy Williamson 8.00 20.00
198 Vernand Morency 8.00 20.00
199 Vincent Jackson 12.00 30.00

2006 Donruss Elite

This 225-card set was released in June, 2008. The set was issued into the hobby in five-card packs, with an $5 SRP, which came 20 packs to a box. The first 100 cards in this set are veterans sequenced in team alphabetical order while cards numbered 101-225 feature rookies sequenced in first name order. The Rookie Cards were all printed to a stated print run of 599 serial numbered sets.

COMP.SET w/o RC's (100) 7.50 20.00
ROOKIE PRINT RUN 599 SER.#'d SETS
1 Anquan Boldin .25 .60
2 Kurt Warner .30 .75
3 Larry Fitzgerald .30 .75
4 Marcel Shipp .25 .60
5 Alge Crumpler .30 .75
6 Michael Vick .30 .75
7 Warrick Dunn .25 .60
8 Derrick Mason .25 .60
9 Jamal Lewis .30 .75

10 Kyle Boller .25 .60
11 J.P. Losman .30 .75
12 Lee Evans .30 .75
13 Willis McGahee .25 .60
14 Jake Delhomme .25 .60
15 Stephen Davis .25 .60
16 Steve Smith .40 1.00
17 Cedric Benson .25 .60
18 Kyle Orton .25 .60
19 Thomas Jones .25 .60
20 Carson Palmer .30 .75
21 Chad Johnson .25 .60
22 Rudi Johnson .25 .60
23 Braylon Edwards .25 .60
24 Reuben Droughns .30 .75
25 Trent Dilfer .25 .60
26 Drew Bledsoe .30 .75
27 Julius Jones .25 .60
28 Keyshawn Johnson .30 .75
29 Jake Plummer .25 .60
30 Rod Smith .30 .75
31 Tatum Bell .25 .60
32 Joey Harrington .25 .60
33 Kevin Jones .25 .60
34 Roy Williams WR .25 .60
35 Aaron Rodgers 1.00 2.50
36 Brett Favre .75 2.00
37 Ahman Green .30 .75
38 Andre Johnson .30 .75
39 David Carr .25 .60
40 Domanick Davis .25 .60
41 Edgerrin James .30 .75
42 Marvin Harrison .30 .75
43 Peyton Manning 1.00 2.50
44 Byron Leftwich .25 .60
45 Fred Taylor .25 .60
46 Jimmy Smith .30 .75
47 Matt Jones .25 .60
48 Larry Johnson .25 .60
49 Tony Gonzalez .30 .75
50 Trent Green .25 .60
51 Chris Chambers .25 .60
52 Ricky Williams .25 .60
53 Ronnie Brown .30 .75
54 Randy McMichael .25 .60
55 Daunte Culpepper .30 .75
56 Mewelde Moore .25 .60
57 Nate Burleson .25 .60
58 Corey Dillon .25 .60
59 Deion Branch .25 .60
60 Tom Brady 1.25 3.00
61 Aaron Brooks .25 .60
62 Deuce McAllister .30 .75
63 Donte Stallworth .25 .60
64 Eli Manning .30 .75
65 Jeremy Shockey .25 .60
66 Plaxico Burress .25 .60
67 Tiki Barber .30 .75
68 Chad Pennington .25 .60
69 Curtis Martin .30 .75
70 Laveranues Coles .25 .60
71 Kerry Collins .25 .60
72 LaMont Jordan .30 .75
73 Randy Moss .30 .75
74 Donovan McNabb .30 .75
75 Reggie Brown .25 .60
76 Brian Westbrook .25 .60
77 Ben Roethlisberger .50 1.25
78 Duce Staley .25 .60
79 Hines Ward .30 .75
80 Antonio Gates .40 1.00
81 Drew Brees .40 1.00
82 LaDainian Tomlinson .40 1.00
83 Alex Smith QB .30 .75
84 Kevan Barlow .25 .60
85 Brandon Lloyd .25 .60
86 Darrell Jackson .30 .75
87 Matt Hasselbeck .25 .60
88 Shaun Alexander .25 .60
89 Marc Bulger .25 .60
90 Steven Jackson .25 .60
91 Torry Holt .30 .75
92 Cadillac Williams .30 .75
93 Joey Galloway .30 .75
94 Michael Clayton .25 .60
95 Chris Brown .25 .60
96 Drew Bennett .30 .75
97 Steve McNair .30 .75
98 Clinton Portis .25 .60
99 Mark Brunell .30 .75
100 Santana Moss .30 .75
101 A.J. Hawk RC 4.00 10.00
102 Abdul Hodge RC 3.00 8.00
103 Adam Jennings RC 4.00 10.00
104 Alan Zemaitis RC 3.00 8.00
105 Andre Hall RC 4.00 10.00
106 Anthony Fasano RC 3.00 8.00
107 Anthony Mix RC 4.00 10.00
108 Ashton Youboty RC 3.00 8.00
109 Miles Austin RC 4.00 10.00
110 Barrick Nealy RC 4.00 10.00
111 Ben Obomanu RC 4.00 10.00
112 Bobby Carpenter RC 3.00 8.00
113 Brad Smith RC 4.00 10.00
114 Brandon Kirsch RC 4.00 10.00
115 Brandon Marshall RC 6.00 15.00
116 Brandon Williams RC 5.00 12.00
117 Brett Elliott RC 5.00 12.00
118 Brian Calhoun RC 3.00 8.00
119 Brodie Croyle RC 3.00 8.00
120 Brodrick Bunkley RC 4.00 10.00
121 Bruce Gradkowski RC 4.00 10.00
122 Cedric Griffin RC 4.00 10.00
123 Cedric Humes RC 3.00 8.00
124 Chad Greenway RC 5.00 12.00
125 Chad Jackson RC 3.00 8.00
126 Charlie Whitehurst RC 3.00 8.00
127 Cory Rodgers RC 3.00 8.00
128 D.J. Shockley RC 4.00 10.00
129 Darnell Bing RC 4.00 10.00
130 Darrell Hackney RC 4.00 10.00
131 David Thomas RC 3.00 8.00
132 D'Brickashaw Ferguson RC 3.00 8.00
133 DeAngelo Williams RC 4.00 10.00
134 De'Arrius Howard RC 5.00 12.00
135 Dee Webb RC 4.00 10.00
136 Delanie Walker RC 6.00 15.00
137 DeMeco Ryans RC 4.00 10.00
138 Demetrius Williams RC 3.00 8.00
139 Derek Hagan RC 4.00 10.00
140 Derrick Ross RC 4.00 10.00
141 Devin Aromashodu RC 3.00 8.00
142 Devin Hester RC 6.00 15.00
143 Dominique Byrd RC 3.00 8.00
144 Donte Whitner RC 4.00 10.00
145 DonTrell Moore RC 4.00 10.00
146 D'Qwell Jackson RC 3.00 8.00
147 Drew Olson RC 3.00 8.00
148 Eric Winston RC 3.00 8.00
149 Erik Meyer RC 3.00 8.00
150 Ernie Sims RC 3.00 8.00
151 Gabe Watson RC 3.00 8.00
152 Gerald Riggs RC 4.00 10.00
153 Ryan Gilbert RC 4.00 10.00
154 Greg Jennings RC 5.00 12.00
155 Greg Lee RC 3.00 8.00
156 Haloti Ngata RC 4.00 10.00
157 Hank Baskett RC 0.00 0.00
158 Ingle Martin RC 4.00 10.00
159 Jason Allen RC 4.00 10.00
160 Jason Avant RC 3.00 8.00
161 Jason Carter RC 4.00 10.00
162 Jay Cutler RC 4.00 10.00
163 Jeff King RC 4.00 10.00
164 Jeff Webb RC 4.00 10.00
165 Jeremy Bloom RC 3.00 8.00
166 Jerious Norwood RC 3.00 8.00
167 Jerome Harrison RC 3.00 8.00
168 Jimmy Williams RC 3.00 8.00
169 Joe Klopfenstein RC 3.00 8.00
170 Jon Alston RC 3.00 8.00
171 Johnathan Joseph RC 4.00 10.00
172 Jonathan Orr RC 4.00 10.00
173 Joseph Addai RC 3.00 8.00
174 Kai Parham RC 5.00 12.00
175 Kamerion Wimbley RC 4.00 10.00
176 Kellen Clemens RC 3.00 8.00
177 Kelly Jennings RC 4.00 10.00
178 Kent Smith RC 5.00 12.00
179 Ko Simpson RC 4.00 10.00
180 Laurence Maroney RC 3.00 8.00
181 Lawrence Vickers RC 4.00 10.00
182 LenDale White RC 3.00 8.00
183 Leon Washington RC 3.00 8.00
184 Leonard Pope RC 5.00 12.00
185 Manny Lawson RC 4.00 10.00
186 Marcedes Lewis RC 3.00 8.00
107 Marcus Vick RC 3.00 8.00
188 Mario Williams RC 5.00 12.00
189 Marques Colston RC 5.00 12.00
190 Martin Nance RC 3.00 8.00
191 Mathias Kiwanuka RC 5.00 12.00
192 Matt Leinart RC 3.00 8.00
193 Maurice Drew RC 5.00 12.00
194 Maurice Stovall RC 3.00 8.00
195 Michael Huff RC 4.00 10.00
196 Michael Robinson RC 3.00 8.00
197 Mike Bell RC 3.00 8.00
198 Mike Hass RC 3.00 8.00
199 Omar Jacobs RC 3.00 8.00
200 Owen Daniels RC 5.00 12.00
201 P.J. Daniels RC 3.00 8.00
202 Paul Pinegar RC 3.00 8.00
203 Quinton Ganther RC 3.00 8.00
204 Reggie Bush RC 5.00 12.00
205 Reggie McNeal RC 3.00 8.00
206 Rodrique Wright RC 3.00 8.00
207 Santonio Holmes RC 4.00 10.00
208 Sinorice Moss RC 3.00 8.00
209 Skyler Green RC 3.00 8.00
210 Tamba Hali RC 5.00 12.00
211 Tarvaris Jackson RC 3.00 8.00
212 Taurean Henderson RC 3.00 8.00
213 Terrence Whitehead RC 4.00 10.00
214 Tim Day RC 4.00 10.00
215 Todd Watkins RC 3.00 8.00
216 Tony Scheffler RC 5.00 12.00
217 Travis Lulay RC 4.00 10.00
218 Travis Wilson RC 3.00 8.00
219 Tye Hill RC 3.00 8.00
220 Vernon Davis RC 4.00 10.00
221 Vince Young RC 3.00 8.00
222 Wali Lundy RC 3.00 8.00
223 Wendell Mathis RC 4.00 10.00
224 Willie Reid RC 4.00 10.00
225 Winston Justice RC 4.00 10.00

2006 Donruss Elite Aspirations

*VETS/70-99: 5X TO 12X BASIC CARDS
*ROOKIES/70-99: .6X TO 1.5X BAS.CARDS
*VETS/45-69: 6X TO 15X BASIC CARDS
*ROOKIES/45-69: .8X TO 2X BAS.CARDS
*ROOKIES/30-44: 1X TO 2.5X BAS.CARDS
*VETS/20-29: 10X TO 25X BASIC CARDS
*ROOKIES/20-29: 1.2X TO 3X BAS.CARDS
SER.#'d UNDER 20 NOT PRICED

2006 Donruss Elite Status

*VETS/70-99: 5X TO 12X BASIC CARDS
*ROOKIES/70-99: .6X TO 1.5X BAS.CARDS
*VETS/45-69: 6X TO 15X BASIC CARDS
*ROOKIES/45-69: .8X TO 2X BAS.CARDS
*VETS/30-44: 8X TO 20X BASIC CARDS
*ROOKIES/30-44: 1X TO 2.5X BAS.CARDS
*VETS/20-29: 10X TO 25X BASIC CARDS
*ROOKIES/20-29: 1.2X TO 3X BAS.CARDS
SER.#'d UNDER 20 NOT PRICED

2006 Donruss Elite Status Gold

*VETERANS: 10X TO 25X BASIC CARDS
*ROOKIES: 1.2X TO 3X BASIC CARDS
STATED PRINT RUN 24 SER.#'d SETS

2006 Donruss Elite Back to the Future Green

GREEN PRINT RUN 1000 SER.#'d SETS
*BLUE: .5X TO 1.2X GREEN
BLUE PRINT RUN 500 SER.#'d SETS
*RED: .6X TO 1.5X GREEN
RED PRINT RUN 250 SER.#'d SETS
1 J.Plummer/J.McCown 1.00 2.50
2 A.Reed/L.Evans 1.00 2.50
3 S.Smith/K.Colbert 1.50 4.00
4 G.Sayers/T.Jones 2.00 5.00
5 L.Dawson/T.Green 1.50 4.00
6 B.Sanders/K.Jones 2.50 6.00
7 B.Griese/J.Fiedler 1.00 2.50
8 B.Esiason/C.Palmer 1.50 4.00
9 R.Moss/N.Burleson 1.50 4.00
10 T.Bradshaw/B.Roethlisberger 3.00 8.00
11 M.Allen/L.Jordan 1.50 4.00
12 J.Elway/J.Plummer 2.50 6.00
13 R.Staubach/D.Bledsoe 2.50 6.00
14 J.Bettis/W.Parker 1.50 4.00
15 D.Marino/R.Brown 3.00 8.00
16 M.Singletary/B.Urlacher 1.50 4.00
17 D.Jones/F.Tarkenton 1.50 4.00
18 E.Campbell/C.Brown 1.50 4.00
19 D.Sanders/R.Williams 1.50 4.00
20 I.Woods/R.Johnson 1.00 2.50
21 K.Warner/M.Bulger 1.00 2.50
22 P.Holmes/L.Johnson 1.50 4.00
23 M.Brunell/B.Leftwich 1.00 2.50
24 M.Faulk/E.James 1.50 4.00
25 R.Williams/D.McAllister 1.00 2.50

2006 Donruss Elite Back to the Future Jerseys

STATED PRINT RUN 299 SER.#'d SETS
*PRIME: 1X TO 2.5X BASIC INSERTS
PRIME PRINT RUN 25 SER.#'d SETS
1 J.Plummer/J.McCown 4.00 10.00
2 A.Reed/L.Evans 4.00 10.00
3 S.Smith/K.Colbert 4.00 10.00
4 G.Sayers/T.Jones 8.00 20.00
5 L.Dawson/T.Green 5.00 12.00
6 B.Sanders/K.Jones 10.00 25.00
7 B.Griese/J.Fiedler 4.00 10.00
8 B.Esiason/C.Palmer 6.00 15.00
9 R.Moss/N.Burleson 4.00 10.00
10 T.Bradshaw/B.Roethlisberger 15.00 40.00
11 M.Allen/L.Jordan 6.00 15.00
12 J.Elway/J.Plummer 10.00 25.00
13 R.Staubach/D.Bledsoe 8.00 20.00
14 J.Bettis/W.Parker 12.50 30.00
15 D.Marino/R.Brown 12.50 30.00
16 M.Singletary/B.Urlacher 8.00 20.00
17 D.Jones/F.Tarkenton 5.00 12.00
18 E.Campbell/C.Brown 5.00 12.00
19 D.Sanders/R.Williams 5.00 12.00
20 I.Woods/R.Johnson 4.00 10.00
21 K.Warner/M.Bulger 4.00 10.00
22 P.Holmes/L.Johnson 6.00 15.00
23 M.Brunell/B.Leftwich 4.00 10.00
24 M.Faulk/E.James 5.00 12.00
25 R.Williams/D.McAllister 4.00 10.00

2006 Donruss Elite Chain Reaction Gold

GOLD PRINT RUN 1000 SER.#'d SETS
*BLACK: .5X TO 1.2X GOLD INSERTS
BLACK PRINT RUN 500 SER.#'d SETS
*RED: .6X TO 1.5X GOLD INSERTS
RED PRINT RUN 250 SER.#'d SETS
1 Darrell Jackson 1.00 2.50
2 Aaron Brooks .75 2.00
3 Daunte Culpepper 1.00 2.50
4 Joey Harrington .75 2.00
5 David Carr .75 2.00
6 Steve McNair 1.00 2.50
7 Matt Hasselbeck .75 2.00
8 Jake Plummer .75 2.00
9 Byron Leftwich .75 2.00
10 Randy Moss 1.00 2.50
11 Hines Ward 1.00 2.50
12 Chris Chambers .75 2.00
13 Anquan Boldin .75 2.00
14 Rod Smith 1.00 2.50
15 Shaun Alexander .75 2.00
16 Michael Vick 1.00 2.50
17 Ronnie Brown 1.00 2.50
18 Domanick Davis .75 2.00
19 Priest Holmes .75 2.00
20 Matt Jones .75 2.00
21 Brett Favre 2.50 6.00
22 Willie Parker 1.00 2.50
23 Fred Taylor .75 2.00
24 Edgerrin James 1.00 2.50
25 Steve Smith 1.25 3.00

2006 Donruss Elite Chain Reaction Jerseys

STATED PRINT RUN 299 SER.#'d SETS
*PRIME: .6X TO 1.5X BASIC INSERTS
PRIME PRINT RUN 99 SER.#'d SETS
1 Darrell Jackson 2.50 6.00
2 Aaron Brooks/54 4.00 10.00
3 Daunte Culpepper 4.00 10.00
4 Joey Harrington 3.00 8.00
5 David Carr 3.00 8.00
6 Steve McNair 4.00 10.00
7 Matt Hasselbeck 3.00 8.00
8 Jake Plummer 4.00 10.00
9 Byron Leftwich 3.00 8.00
10 Randy Moss 4.00 10.00
11 Hines Ward 4.00 10.00
12 Chris Chambers 3.00 8.00
13 Anquan Boldin 3.00 8.00
14 Rod Smith 3.00 8.00
15 Shaun Alexander 5.00 12.00
16 Michael Vick 4.00 10.00
17 Ronnie Brown/200 4.00 10.00
18 Domanick Davis 2.50 6.00
19 Priest Holmes 3.00 8.00
20 Matt Jones 2.50 6.00
21 Brett Favre 10.00 25.00
22 Willie Parker/200 5.00 12.00
23 Fred Taylor 3.00 8.00
24 Edgerrin James 4.00 10.00
25 Steve Smith 4.00 10.00

2006 Donruss Elite College Ties Green

GREEN PRINT RUN 1000 SER.#'d SETS
*BLACK: .6X TO 1.5X GREEN INSERTS
BLACK PRINT RUN 250 SER.#'d SETS
*GOLD: .5X TO 1.2X GREEN INSERTS
GOLD PRINT RUN 500 SER.#'d SETS
1 C.Palmer/M.Leinart 2.00 5.00
2 P.Manning/G.Riggs 2.50 6.00
3 A.Boldin/L.Washington 1.50 4.00
4 R.Staubach/J.Bellino 2.00 5.00
5 D.Bledsoe/J.Harrison 1.50 4.00
6 J.Jones/A.Fasano 1.50 4.00
7 B.Edwards/J.Avant 1.50 4.00
8 M.Leinart/R.Bush 2.00 5.00
9 C.Benson/V.Young 3.00 8.00
10 M.Vick/M.Vick 1.50 4.00
11 Matt Leinart 2.00 5.00
12 Gerald Riggs 1.00 2.50
13 Leon Washington 1.50 4.00
14 Maurice Drew 2.00 5.00
15 Jerome Harrison 1.00 2.50
16 Anthony Fasano 1.00 2.50
17 Jason Avant 1.00 2.50
18 Reggie Bush 2.00 5.00
19 Vince Young 3.00 8.00
20 Marcus Vick 1.50 4.00

2006 Donruss Elite College Ties Autographs

STATED PRINT RUN 25-50 SER.#'d SETS
1 Palmer/Leinart/50 20.00 50.00
2 P.Manning/G.Riggs/30 75.00 150.00
3 A.Boldin/L.Washington/25 25.00 50.00
4 R.Staubach/J.Bellino/25 100.00 200.00
6 J.Jones/A.Fasano/50 20.00 50.00
7 B.Edwards/J.Avant/50 30.00 80.00
8 M.Leinart/R.Bush/50 20.00 50.00
9 C.Benson/V.Young/50 15.00 40.00
11 Matt Leinart/25 20.00 50.00
12 Gerald Riggs/25 20.00 40.00
13 Leon Washington/25 20.00 40.00
14 Maurice Drew/25 40.00 100.00
15 Jerome Harrison/25 20.00 50.00
16 Anthony Fasano/25 20.00 50.00
17 Jason Avant/25 20.00 40.00
18 Reggie Bush/25 25.00 60.00
19 Vince Young/25 15.00 40.00

2006 Donruss Elite College Ties Jerseys

PRINT RUN 17-250 SER.#'d SETS
1 C.Palmer/M.Leinart/250 8.00 20.00
2 P.Manning/G.Riggs/250 10.00 25.00
3 A.Boldin/L.Washington/250 6.00 15.00
4 R.Staubach/J.Bellino/200 10.00 25.00
6 J.Jones/A.Fasano/49 12.50 30.00
7 B.Edwards/J.Avant/250 8.00 20.00
8 M.Leinart/R.Bush/250 4.00 10.00
9 C.Benson/V.Young/250 8.00 20.00
10 Mi.Vick/Mar.Vick/225 6.00 15.00
11 Matt Leinart/100 6.00 15.00
18 Reggie Bush/100 4.00 10.00

2006 Donruss Elite College Ties Jerseys Prime

*PRIME/99: .6X TO 1.5X BASIC INSERTS
*PRIME/25-50: .8X TO 2X BASIC INSERTS
PRIME PRINT RUN 5-99 SER.#'d SETS
5 D.Bledsoe/J.Harrison/99 15.00 40.00

2006 Donruss Elite Elite Teams Black

BLACK PRINT RUN 1000 SER.#'d SETS
*GOLD: .6X TO 1.5X BLACK INSERTS
GOLD PRINT RUN 250 SER.#'d SETS
*RED: .5X TO 1.2X BLACK INSERTS
RED PRINT RUN 500 SER.#'d SETS
1 Crumpler/Vick/Dunn 1.00 2.50
2 Evans/Losman/McGahee 1.00 2.50
3 Davis/Delhomme/Smith 1.25 3.00
4 Benson/Orton/Jones .75 2.00
5 Johnson/Palmer/Johnson 1.00 2.50
6 Johnson/Bledsoe/Jones 1.00 2.50
7 Lelie/Plummer/Bell .75 2.00
8 Green/Favre/Ferguson 2.50 6.00
9 Wayne/Manning/James 4.00 10.00
10 Smith/Leftwich/Jones 1.00 2.50
11 Johnson/Green/Gonzalez 1.00 2.50
12 Williamson/Culpepper/Burleson 1.00 2.50
13 Dillon/Brady/Branch 4.00 10.00
14 McAllister/Brooks/Horn 1.00 2.50
15 Burress/Manning/Barber 1.00 2.50
16 Martin/Pennington/Coles 1.00 2.50
17 Moss/Collins/Jordan 1.00 2.50
18 Westbrook/McNabb/Brown 1.00 2.50
19 Ward/Roethlisberger/Parker 3.00 8.00
20 Gates/Brees/Tomlinson 1.25 3.00
21 Lloyd/Smith/Barlow 1.00 2.50
22 Jackson/Hasselbeck/Alexander 1.00 2.50
23 Jackson/Bulger/Holt 1.00 2.50
24 Williams/Clayton/Alstott 1.00 2.50
25 Brown/McNair/Jones 1.00 2.50

2006 Donruss Elite Elite Teams Jerseys

STATED PRINT RUN 99 SER.#'d SETS
*PRIME/25: .8X TO 2X BASIC JSY/99
PRIME PRINT RUN 25 SER.#'d SETS
1 Crumpler/Vick/Dunn 8.00 20.00
2 Evans/Losman/McGahee 8.00 20.00
3 Davis/Delhomme/Smith 10.00 25.00
4 Benson/Orton/Jones 6.00 15.00
5 Johnson/Palmer/Johnson 8.00 20.00
6 Johnson/Bledsoe/Jones 8.00 20.00
7 Lelie/Plummer/Bell 6.00 15.00
8 Green/Favre/Ferguson 15.00 40.00
9 Wayne/Manning/James 25.00 60.00
10 Smith/Leftwich/Jones 8.00 20.00
11 Johnson/Green/Gonzalez 8.00 20.00
12 Williamson/Culpepper/Burleson 8.00 20.00
13 Dillon/Brady/Branch 30.00 80.00
14 McAllister/Brooks/Horn 8.00 20.00
15 Burress/Manning/Barber 8.00 20.00
16 Martin/Pennington/Coles 8.00 20.00
17 Moss/Collins/Jordan 8.00 20.00
18 Westbrook/McNabb/Brown 8.00 20.00
19 Ward/Roethlisberger/Parker 12.00 30.00
20 Gates/Brees/Tomlinson 10.00 25.00
21 Lloyd/Smith/Barlow 8.00 20.00
22 Jackson/Hasselbeck/Alexander 8.00 20.00
23 Jackson/Bulger/Holt 8.00 20.00
24 Williams/Clayton/Alstott 8.00 20.00
25 Brown/McNair/Jones 8.00 20.00

2006 Donruss Elite Passing the Torch Red

RED PRINT RUN 1000 SER.#'d SETS
*BLUE: .6X TO 1.5X RED INSERTS
BLUE PRINT RUN 250 SER.#'d SETS
*GREEN: .5X TO 1.2X RED INSERTS
GREEN PRINT RUN 500 SER.#'d SETS
1 Alex Smith QB 1.50 4.00
2 Steve Young 2.00 5.00
3 Braylon Edwards 1.50 4.00
4 Paul Warfield 1.50 4.00
5 Cedric Benson 1.50 4.00
6 Gale Sayers 1.50 4.00
7 Eli Manning 2.00 5.00
8 Phil Simms 1.50 4.00
9 Willie Parker 1.50 4.00
10 Jerome Bettis 1.50 4.00
11 Julius Jones 1.50 4.00
12 Tony Dorsett 1.50 4.00
13 Kevin Jones 1.50 4.00
14 Barry Sanders 2.50 6.00
15 LaMont Jordan 1.00 2.50
16 Bo Jackson 1.50 4.00
17 Nate Burleson 1.00 2.50
18 Cris Carter 1.50 4.00
19 Antonio Gates 1.50 4.00
20 Lance Alworth 1.00 2.50
21 A.Smith QB/S.Young 2.00 5.00
22 B.Edwards/P.Warfield 1.50 4.00
23 C.Benson/G.Sayers 1.50 4.00
24 E.Manning/P.Simms 2.00 5.00
25 W.Parker/J.Bettis 1.50 4.00
26 J.Jones/T.Dorsett 1.50 4.00
27 K.Jones/B.Sanders 2.50 6.00
28 L.Jordan/B.Jackson 1.50 4.00
29 N.Burleson/C.Carter 1.50 4.00
30 A.Gates/L.Alworth 1.50 4.00

2006 Donruss Elite Passing the Torch Autographs

STATED PRINT RUN 49-99
1 Alex Smith QB/99 15.00 40.00
2 Steve Young/49 40.00 80.00
3 Braylon Edwards/99 12.00 30.00
4 Paul Warfield/99 10.00 25.00
5 Cedric Benson/99 12.00 30.00
6 Gale Sayers/49 25.00 50.00
7 Eli Manning/49 50.00 100.00
8 Phil Simms/99 15.00 40.00
9 Willie Parker/99 10.00 25.00
10 Jerome Bettis/49 30.00 60.00
11 Julius Jones/49 10.00 25.00
12 Tony Dorsett/49 25.00 50.00
13 Kevin Jones/99 8.00 20.00
14 Barry Sanders/49 60.00 120.00
15 LaMont Jordan/99 10.00 25.00
16 Bo Jackson/99 40.00 80.00
17 Nate Burleson/99 8.00 20.00
18 Cris Carter/99 12.00 30.00
19 Antonio Gates/99 12.00 30.00
20 Lance Alworth/99 15.00 40.00
21 Smith QB/Young/49 50.00 100.00
22 Edwards/Warfield/49 25.00 60.00
23 Benson/Sayers/49 30.00 80.00
24 Eli/P.Simms/49 50.00 120.00
25 Parker/Bettis/49 50.00 120.00
26 J.Jones/T.Dorsett/49 30.00 80.00
27 K.Jns/B.Sndrs/49 50.00 120.00
28 L.Jordan/Bo/49 40.00 100.00
29 Burleson/C.Cart/49 30.00 80.00
30 A.Gates/L.Alworth/49 30.00 80.00

2006 Donruss Elite Prime Targets Gold

GOLD PRINT RUN 1000 SER.#'d SETS
*BLACK: .5X TO 1.2X GOLD INSERTS
BLACK PRINT RUN 500 SER.#'d SETS
*RED: .6X TO 1.5X GOLD INSERTS
RED PRINT RUN 250 SER.#'d SETS
1 LaDainian Tomlinson 1.25 3.00
2 Shaun Alexander .75 2.00
3 Edgerrin James 1.00 2.50
4 Steven Jackson .75 2.00
5 Stephen Davis .75 2.00
6 Steve Smith 1.25 3.00
7 Marvin Harrison 1.00 2.50
8 Antonio Gates 1.25 3.00
9 Chad Johnson .75 2.00
10 Larry Fitzgerald 1.00 2.50

2006 Donruss Elite Prime Targets Jerseys

STATED PRINT RUN 299 SER.#'d SETS
*PRIME: .6X TO 1.5X BASIC INSERTS
PRIME PRINT RUN 50 SER.#'d SETS
1 LaDainian Tomlinson 4.00 10.00
2 Shaun Alexander 4.00 10.00
3 Edgerrin James 4.00 10.00
4 Steven Jackson 4.00 10.00
5 Stephen Davis 3.00 8.00
6 Steve Smith 4.00 10.00
7 Marvin Harrison 4.00 10.00
8 Antonio Gates 4.00 10.00
9 Chad Johnson 3.00 8.00
10 Larry Fitzgerald 3.00 8.00

2006 Donruss Elite Series Gold

GOLD PRINT RUN 1000 SER.#'d SETS
*BLACK: .5X TO 1.2X GOLD INSERTS
BLACK PRINT RUN 500 SER.#'d SETS
*RED: .6X TO 1.5X GOLD INSERTS
RED PRINT RUN 250 SER.#'d SETS
1 Aaron Brooks .75 2.00
2 Kyle Orton .75 2.00
3 Michael Vick 1.00 2.50
4 Troy Williamson .75 2.00
5 Jason Campbell .75 2.00
6 Antonio Gates 1.25 3.00
7 Jerry Porter .75 2.00
8 Amani Toomer .75 2.00
9 Andre Johnson 1.00 2.50
9AU Andre Johnson AU/25 12.50 30.00
10 Alex Smith QB 1.00 2.50
11 Aaron Rodgers 3.00 8.00
12 Bethel Johnson .75 2.00
13 Brandon Lloyd .75 2.00
14 Bryant Johnson .75 2.00
15 Cedric Benson .75 2.00
16 Clinton Portis .75 2.00
17 Torry Holt 1.00 2.50
18 Chad Johnson .75 2.00
19 Tom Brady 4.00 10.00
20 Warrick Dunn .75 2.00
21 Willis McGahee .75 2.00
22 Kevin Jones .75 2.00
23 Corey Dillon .75 2.00
24 LaMont Jordan 1.00 2.50
25 Steven Jackson .75 2.00

2006 Donruss Elite Series Jerseys

STATED PRINT RUN 299 SER.#'d SETS
*PRIME: .6X TO 1.5X BASIC INSERTS
PRIME PRINT RUN 50 SER.#'d SETS
1 Aaron Brooks/54 4.00 10.00
2 Kyle Orton 3.00 8.00
3 Michael Vick 3.00 8.00
4 Troy Williamson 2.50 6.00
5 Jason Campbell 3.00 8.00
6 Antonio Gates 4.00 10.00
7 Jerry Porter 3.00 8.00
8 Amani Toomer 3.00 8.00
9 Andre Johnson 2.50 6.00
10 Alex Smith QB 4.00 10.00
11 Aaron Rodgers 15.00 40.00
12 Bethel Johnson/150 2.50 6.00
13 Brandon Lloyd 2.50 6.00
14 Bryant Johnson 2.50 6.00
15 Cedric Benson 4.00 10.00
16 Clinton Portis 4.00 10.00
17 Torry Holt 3.00 8.00
18 Chad Johnson 3.00 8.00
19 Tom Brady 6.00 15.00
20 Warrick Dunn 3.00 8.00
21 Willis McGahee 3.00 8.00
22 Kevin Jones 4.00 10.00
23 Corey Dillon 3.00 8.00
24 LaMont Jordan 3.00 8.00
25 Steven Jackson 4.00 10.00

2006 Donruss Elite Status Autographs Gold

STATED PRINT RUN 24 SER.#'d SETS
UNPRICED BLACK AUs SER.#'d TO 1
101 A.J. Hawk 15.00 40.00
102 Abdul Hodge 12.00 30.00
103 Adam Jennings 15.00 40.00
104 Alan Zemaitis 12.00 30.00
105 Andre Hall 15.00 40.00
106 Anthony Fasano 12.00 30.00
109 Miles Austin 15.00 40.00
111 Ben Obomanu 15.00 40.00
112 Bobby Carpenter 12.00 30.00
113 Brad Smith 15.00 40.00
114 Brandon Kirsch 15.00 40.00
115 Brandon Marshall 25.00 60.00
116 Brandon Williams 12.00 30.00
118 Brian Calhoun 12.00 30.00
121 Bruce Gradkowski 15.00 40.00
123 Cedric Humes 12.00 30.00
124 Chad Greenway 20.00 50.00
125 Chad Jackson 12.00 30.00
126 Charlie Whitehurst 12.00 30.00
128 D.J. Shockley 15.00 40.00
129 Darnell Bing 15.00 40.00
132 D'Brickashaw Ferguson 12.00 30.00
133 DeAngelo Williams 50.00 120.00
136 Delanie Walker 25.00 60.00
137 DeMeco Ryans 15.00 40.00
138 Demetrius Williams 12.00 30.00
139 Derek Hagan 15.00 40.00
140 Derrick Ross 15.00 40.00
141 Devin Aromashodu 12.00 30.00
143 Dominique Byrd 12.00 30.00
146 D'Qwell Jackson 12.00 30.00
147 Drew Olson 12.00 30.00
149 Erik Meyer 12.00 30.00
152 Gerald Riggs 15.00 40.00
154 Greg Jennings 20.00 50.00
155 Greg Lee 12.00 30.00
156 Haloti Ngata 15.00 40.00
157 Hank Baskett 12.00 30.00
160 Jason Avant 12.00 30.00
162 Jay Cutler 15.00 40.00
164 Jeff Webb 15.00 40.00
166 Jerious Norwood 12.00 30.00
168 Jimmy Williams 12.00 30.00
169 Joe Klopfenstein 12.00 30.00
170 Jon Alston 12.00 30.00
172 Jonathan Orr 15.00 40.00
173 Joseph Addai 12.00 30.00
175 Kamerion Wimbley 15.00 40.00
176 Kellen Clemens 12.00 30.00
177 Kelly Jennings 15.00 40.00
179 Ko Simpson 15.00 40.00
180 Laurence Maroney 12.00 30.00
182 LenDale White 12.00 30.00
183 Leon Washington 40.00 80.00
184 Leonard Pope 20.00 50.00
186 Marcedes Lewis 12.00 30.00
188 Mario Williams 20.00 50.00
190 Martin Nance 12.00 30.00
192 Matt Leinart 50.00 120.00
193 Maurice Drew 20.00 50.00
194 Maurice Stovall 12.00 30.00
195 Michael Huff 15.00 40.00
196 Michael Robinson 12.00 30.00
198 Mike Hass 12.00 30.00
199 Omar Jacobs 12.00 30.00
202 Paul Pinegar 12.00 30.00
203 Quinton Ganther 12.00 30.00
204 Reggie Bush 20.00 50.00
205 Reggie McNeal 12.00 30.00
207 Santonio Holmes 40.00 100.00
208 Sinorice Moss 12.00 30.00
209 Skyler Green 12.00 30.00
210 Tamba Hali 20.00 50.00
211 Tarvaris Jackson 12.00 30.00
215 Todd Watkins 12.00 30.00
218 Travis Wilson 12.00 30.00
219 Tye Hill 12.00 30.00
220 Vernon Davis 15.00 40.00
221 Vince Young 12.00 30.00
223 Wendell Mathis 15.00 40.00

2006 Donruss Elite Throwback Threads

STATED PRINT RUN 20-249 SER.#'d SETS
*PRIME/30: .8X TO 2X BASIC INSERTS
PRIME PRINT RUN 5-30 SER.#'d SETS
1 Johnny Unitas 12.50 30.00
2 Peyton Manning 8.00 20.00
3 Don Meredith 8.00 20.00
4 Troy Aikman 6.00 15.00
5 Bobby Layne 12.00 30.00
6 Barry Sanders 10.00 25.00
7 Joe Montana 12.50 30.00
8 Alex Smith QB 5.00 12.00
9 Fred Biletnikoff 6.00 15.00
10 Randy Moss 4.00 10.00
11 Walter Payton 12.50 30.00
12 Cedric Benson 4.00 10.00
13 Ozzie Newsome 3.00 8.00
14 Braylon Edwards 4.00 10.00
15 Jim Brown/100 8.00 20.00
16 Reuben Droughns 3.00 8.00
17 Steve Largent 4.00 10.00
18 Darrell Jackson 3.00 8.00
19 Jim Kelly 5.00 12.00
20 J.P. Losman 3.00 8.00
21 Marcus Allen 4.00 10.00
22 Larry Johnson 5.00 12.00
23 Ronnie Lott 4.00 10.00
24 Lawrence Taylor 4.00 10.00
25 Red Grange/75 75.00 150.00
26 Ray Nitschke 10.00 25.00
28 Curtis Martin 4.00 10.00
29 Herschel Walker 4.00 10.00
30 Daunte Culpepper 4.00 10.00
31 J.Unitas/P.Manning/249 20.00 40.00
32 D.Meredith/T.Aikman/162 20.00 40.00
33 B.Layne/B.Sanders/149 20.00 40.00
34 J.Montana/A.Smith QB/249 20.00 40.00
35 F.Biletnikoff/R.Moss/249 8.00 20.00
36 W.Payton/C.Benson/162 20.00 40.00
37 O.Newsome/B.Edwards/249 6.00 15.00
38 J.Brown/R.Droughns/162 8.00 20.00
39 S.Largent/D.Jackson/162 6.00 15.00
40 J.Kelly/J.Losman/249 8.00 20.00
41 M.Allen/L.Johnson/200 10.00 25.00
42 R.Lott/L.Taylor/249 8.00 20.00
43 R.Grange/R.Nitschke/25 125.00 225.00
44 J.Riggins/C.Martin/44 8.00 20.00
45 H.Walker/D.Culpepper/248 8.00 20.00

2006 Donruss Elite Throwback Threads Autographs

NOT PRICED DUE TO SCARCITY
UNPRICED PRIME PRINT RUN 1-5 SETS

2006 Donruss Elite Turn of the Century Autographs

STATED PRINT RUN 50-100
101 A.J. Hawk/50 10.00 25.00
102 Abdul Hodge 8.00 20.00
103 Adam Jennings 10.00 25.00
104 Alan Zemaitis 8.00 20.00
105 Andre Hall 10.00 25.00
106 Anthony Fasano 8.00 20.00
109 Miles Austin 10.00 25.00
111 Ben Obomanu 10.00 25.00
112 Bobby Carpenter/50 8.00 20.00
113 Brad Smith 10.00 25.00
114 Brandon Kirsch 10.00 25.00
115 Brandon Marshall 15.00 40.00
116 Brandon Williams 8.00 20.00
118 Brian Calhoun 8.00 20.00
121 Bruce Gradkowski 10.00 25.00
123 Cedric Humes 8.00 20.00
124 Chad Greenway/50 12.00 30.00
125 Chad Jackson 8.00 20.00
126 Charlie Whitehurst 8.00 20.00
128 D.J. Shockley 10.00 25.00
129 Darnell Bing 10.00 25.00
132 D'Brickashaw Ferguson 8.00 20.00
133 DeAngelo Williams 10.00 25.00
136 Delanie Walker 15.00 40.00
137 DeMeco Ryans 10.00 25.00
138 Demetrius Williams 8.00 20.00
139 Derek Hagan 10.00 25.00
140 Derrick Ross 10.00 25.00
141 Devin Aromashodu 8.00 20.00
143 Dominique Byrd 8.00 20.00
146 D'Qwell Jackson 8.00 20.00
147 Drew Olson 8.00 20.00
149 Erik Meyer 8.00 20.00
152 Gerald Riggs 10.00 25.00
154 Greg Jennings 12.00 30.00
155 Greg Lee 8.00 20.00
156 Haloti Ngata 10.00 25.00
157 Hank Baskett 8.00 20.00
160 Jason Avant 8.00 20.00
162 Jay Cutler 10.00 25.00
164 Jeff Webb 10.00 25.00
166 Jerious Norwood 8.00 20.00
168 Jimmy Williams 8.00 20.00
169 Joe Klopfenstein 8.00 20.00
170 Jon Alston 8.00 20.00
172 Jonathan Orr 10.00 25.00
173 Joseph Addai 8.00 20.00
175 Kamerion Wimbley/50 10.00 25.00
176 Kellen Clemens 8.00 20.00
177 Kelly Jennings/50 10.00 25.00
179 Ko Simpson 10.00 25.00
180 Laurence Maroney 8.00 20.00
182 LenDale White 8.00 20.00
183 Leon Washington 8.00 20.00
184 Leonard Pope 12.00 30.00
186 Marcedes Lewis 8.00 20.00
188 Mario Williams/50 12.00 30.00
190 Martin Nance
192 Matt Leinart 8.00 20.00
193 Maurice Drew 20.00 50.00
194 Maurice Stovall 8.00 20.00
195 Michael Huff/50 10.00 25.00
196 Michael Robinson 8.00 20.00
198 Mike Hass 8.00 20.00
199 Omar Jacobs 8.00 20.00
202 Paul Pinegar 8.00 20.00
203 Quinton Ganther 8.00 20.00
204 Reggie Bush 12.00 30.00
205 Reggie McNeal 8.00 20.00
207 Santonio Holmes 10.00 25.00
208 Sinorice Moss 8.00 20.00
209 Skyler Green 8.00 20.00
210 Tamba Hali/50 12.00 30.00
211 Tarvaris Jackson/50 8.00 20.00
215 Todd Watkins 8.00 20.00
218 Travis Wilson 8.00 20.00
219 Tye Hill/50 8.00 20.00
220 Vernon Davis 10.00 25.00
221 Vince Young 8.00 20.00
223 Wendell Mathis 10.00 25.00

2006 Donruss Elite Zoning Commission Gold

GOLD PRINT RUN 1000 SER.#'d SETS
*BLACK: .5X TO 1.2X GOLD INSERTS
BLACK PRINT RUN 500 SER.#'d SETS
*RED: .6X TO 1.5X GOLD INSERTS
RED PRINT RUN 250 SER.#'d SETS
1 Tom Brady 4.00 10.00
2 Donovan McNabb 1.00 2.50
3 Brett Favre 2.50 6.00
4 Carson Palmer 1.00 2.50
5 Peyton Manning 3.00 8.00
6 Drew Brees 1.25 3.00
7 Drew Bledsoe 1.00 2.50
8 Eli Manning 1.00 2.50
9 Trent Green 0.75 2.00
10 Kerry Collins 0.75 2.00
11 Jake Delhomme 0.75 2.00
12 Marc Bulger 0.75 2.00
13 Ben Roethlisberger 1.50 4.00
14 Michael Vick 1.00 2.50
15 Steve Smith 1.25 3.00
16 Santana Moss 1.00 2.50
17 Chad Johnson 0.75 2.00
18 Terrell Owens 1.00 2.50
19 Plaxico Burress 0.75 2.00
20 Torry Holt 1.00 2.50
21 Reggie Wayne 1.00 2.50
22 Jeremy Shockey 0.75 2.00
23 Jimmy Smith 1.00 2.50
24 Donte Stallworth 0.75 2.00
25 Alge Crumpler 1.00 2.50
26 Deion Branch 0.75 2.00
27 Keyshawn Johnson 1.00 2.50
28 Warrick Dunn 0.75 2.00
29 Willis McGahee 0.75 2.00
30 Tiki Barber 1.00 2.50
31 Clinton Portis 0.75 2.00
32 Rudi Johnson 0.75 2.00
33 Cadillac Williams 1.00 2.50
34 Thomas Jones 0.75 2.00
35 Larry Johnson 0.75 2.00
36 Kevin Jones 0.75 2.00
37 Corey Dillon 0.75 2.00
38 Julius Jones 0.75 2.00
39 Brian Westbrook 0.75 2.00
40 Curtis Martin 1.00 2.50

2006 Donruss Elite Zoning Commission Jerseys

STATED PRINT RUN 399 SER.#'d SETS
*PRIME: .6X TO 1.5X BASIC INSERTS
PRIME PRINT RUN 50 SER.#'d SETS
1 Tom Brady 6.00 15.00
2 Donovan McNabb 4.00 10.00
3 Brett Favre 10.00 25.00
4 Carson Palmer 4.00 10.00
5 Peyton Manning 6.00 15.00
6 Drew Brees 4.00 10.00
7 Drew Bledsoe 4.00 10.00
8 Eli Manning 5.00 12.00
9 Trent Green 3.00 8.00
10 Kerry Collins 3.00 8.00
11 Jake Delhomme 3.00 8.00
12 Marc Bulger 3.00 8.00
13 Ben Roethlisberger 8.00 20.00
14 Michael Vick 4.00 10.00
15 Steve Smith 4.00 10.00
16 Santana Moss 3.00 8.00
17 Chad Johnson 3.00 8.00
18 Terrell Owens 4.00 10.00
19 Plaxico Burress 3.00 8.00
20 Torry Holt 3.00 8.00
21 Reggie Wayne 3.00 8.00
22 Jeremy Shockey 4.00 10.00
23 Jimmy Smith 3.00 8.00
24 Donte Stallworth 3.00 8.00
25 Alge Crumpler 2.50 6.00
26 Deion Branch 2.50 6.00
27 Keyshawn Johnson/54 4.00 10.00
28 Warrick Dunn 3.00 8.00
29 Willis McGahee 3.00 8.00
30 Tiki Barber 4.00 10.00
31 Clinton Portis 4.00 10.00
32 Rudi Johnson 3.00 8.00
33 Cadillac Williams/321 4.00 10.00
34 Thomas Jones 3.00 8.00
35 Larry Johnson 4.00 10.00
36 Kevin Jones 4.00 10.00
37 Corey Dillon 3.00 8.00
38 Julius Jones 4.00 10.00
39 Brian Westbrook 3.00 8.00
40 Curtis Martin 4.00 10.00

2007 Donruss Elite

This 200-card set was released in June, 2007. The set was issued into the hobby in five-card packs, with a $5 SRP, which came 20 packs to a box. Cards numbered 1-100 feature veterans in their 2006 team alphabetical order while cards 101-200 feature 2007 NFL rookies. Those Rookie Cards were issued to a stated print run of 599 serial numbered sets.

COMP.SET w/o RC's (100) 7.50 20.00
ROOKIE PRINT RUN 599 SER.#'d SETS
1 Anquan Boldin .25 .60
2 Edgerrin James .30 .75
3 Matt Leinart .25 .60
4 Alge Crumpler .30 .75
5 Michael Vick .30 .75
6 Jerious Norwood .25 .60
7 Warrick Dunn .25 .60
8 Jamal Lewis .30 .75
9 Mark Clayton .25 .60
10 Steve McNair .30 .75
11 J.P. Losman .25 .60
12 Lee Evans .30 .75
13 Willis McGahee .25 .60
14 DeAngelo Williams .25 .60
15 Jake Delhomme .25 .60
16 Steve Smith .30 .75
17 Bernard Berrian .25 .60
18 Rex Grossman .25 .60
19 Thomas Jones .25 .60
20 Carson Palmer .30 .75
21 Chad Johnson .25 .60
22 Rudi Johnson .25 .60
23 T.J. Houshmandzadeh .25 .60
24 Braylon Edwards .25 .60
25 Charlie Frye .30 .75
26 Reuben Droughns .30 .75
27 Julius Jones .25 .60
28 Terrell Owens .30 .75
29 Tony Romo .50 1.25
30 Javon Walker .30 .75
31 Jay Cutler .25 .60
32 Mike Bell .30 .75
33 Jon Kitna .25 .60
34 Kevin Jones .25 .60
35 Roy Williams WR .25 .60
36 Brett Favre .75 2.00
37 Donald Driver .30 .75

38 Ahman Green .30 .75
39 Andre Johnson .30 .75
40 Matt Schaub .25 .60
41 Wali Lundy .25 .60
42 Joseph Addai .25 .60
43 Marvin Harrison .30 .75
44 Peyton Manning 1.00 2.50
45 Reggie Wayne .30 .75
46 Byron Leftwich .25 .60
47 Fred Taylor .25 .60
48 Maurice Jones-Drew .25 .60
49 Larry Johnson .25 .60
50 Tony Gonzalez .30 .75
51 Trent Green .25 .60
52 Chris Chambers .25 .60
53 Daunte Culpepper .30 .75
54 Ronnie Brown .25 .60
55 Chester Taylor .25 .60
56 Tarvaris Jackson .25 .60
57 Travis Taylor .25 .60
58 Tom Brady 1.25 3.00
59 Corey Dillon .25 .60
60 Laurence Maroney .30 .75
61 Deuce McAllister .30 .75
62 Drew Brees .40 1.00
63 Marques Colston .25 .60
64 Reggie Bush .25 .60
65 Brandon Jacobs .25 .60
66 Eli Manning .30 .75
67 Jeremy Shockey .25 .60
68 Chad Pennington .25 .60
69 Laveranues Coles .25 .60
70 Leon Washington .25 .60
71 Ronald Curry .25 .60
72 LaMont Jordan .30 .75
73 Randy Moss .30 .75
74 Brian Westbrook .25 .60
75 Donovan McNabb .30 .75
76 Reggie Brown .25 .60
77 Ben Roethlisberger .40 1.00
78 Hines Ward .30 .75
79 Willie Parker .30 .75
80 Antonio Gates .40 1.00
81 LaDainian Tomlinson .40 1.00
82 Philip Rivers .40 1.00
83 Alex Smith QB .30 .75
84 Frank Gore .30 .75
85 Vernon Davis .25 .60
86 Darrell Jackson .25 .60
87 Matt Hasselbeck .25 .60
88 Shaun Alexander .25 .60
89 Marc Bulger .25 .60
90 Steven Jackson .25 .60
91 Torry Holt .30 .75
92 Chris Simms .25 .60
93 Cadillac Williams .30 .75
94 Joey Galloway .30 .75
95 Drew Bennett .25 .60
96 LenDale White .30 .75
97 Vince Young .25 .60
98 Clinton Portis .25 .60
99 Jason Campbell .25 .60
100 Santana Moss .30 .75
101 A.J. Davis RC 2.50 6.00
102 Aaron Ross RC 2.50 6.00
103 Aaron Rouse RC 2.50 6.00
104 Adam Carriker RC 2.50 6.00
105 Adrian Peterson RC 8.00 20.00
106 Ahmad Bradshaw RC 4.00 10.00
107 Alan Branch RC 2.50 6.00
108 Amobi Okoye RC 3.00 8.00
109 Anthony Gonzalez RC 2.50 6.00
110 Anthony Spencer RC 3.00 8.00
111 Antonio Pittman RC 2.50 6.00
112 Aundrae Allison RC 2.50 6.00
113 Brady Quinn RC 2.50 6.00
114 Brandon Jackson RC 2.50 6.00
115 Brandon Meriweather RC 3.00 8.00
116 Brandon Siler RC 2.50 6.00
117 Brian Leonard RC 2.50 6.00
118 Calvin Johnson RC 8.00 20.00
119 Chansi Stuckey RC 3.00 8.00
120 Chris Davis RC 2.50 6.00
121 Chris Henry RC 2.50 6.00
122 Chris Houston RC 2.50 6.00
123 Chris Leak RC 2.50 6.00
124 Courtney Taylor RC 2.50 6.00
125 Craig Buster Davis RC 2.50 6.00
126 Dallas Baker RC 2.50 6.00
127 Darius Walker RC 2.50 6.00
128 Darrelle Revis RC 3.00 8.00
129 David Ball RC 2.50 6.00
130 David Clowney RC 2.50 6.00
131 David Harris RC 2.50 6.00
132 DeShawn Wynn RC 2.50 6.00
133 D'Juan Woods RC 2.50 6.00
134 Drew Stanton RC 2.50 6.00
135 Dwayne Bowe RC 2.50 6.00
136 Dwayne Jarrett RC 3.00 8.00
137 Dwayne Wright RC 2.50 6.00
138 Eric Weddle RC 3.00 8.00
139 Gaines Adams RC 3.00 8.00
140 Garrett Wolfe RC 2.50 6.00
141 Gary Russell RC 3.00 8.00
142 Greg Olsen RC 4.00 10.00
143 H.B. Blades RC 2.50 6.00
144 Isaiah Stanback RC 2.50 6.00
145 Jacoby Jones RC 2.50 6.00
146 Jamaal Anderson RC 3.00 8.00
147 JaMarcus Russell RC 2.50 6.00
148 James Jones RC 2.50 6.00
149 Jared Zabransky RC 2.50 6.00
150 Jarrett Hicks RC 3.00 8.00
151 Jarvis Moss RC 2.50 6.00
152 Jason Hill RC 2.50 6.00
153 Jason Snelling RC 2.50 6.00
154 Jeff Rowe RC 2.50 6.00
155 Joel Filani RC 2.50 6.00
156 John Beck RC 2.50 6.00
157 Johnnie Lee Higgins RC 2.50 6.00
158 Jon Beason RC 2.50 6.00
159 Jon Cornish RC 3.00 8.00
160 Jonathan Wade RC 2.50 6.00
161 Jordan Kent RC 3.00 8.00
162 Jordan Palmer RC 3.00 8.00
163 Kenneth Darby RC 2.50 6.00
164 Kenny Irons RC 2.50 6.00
165 Kevin Kolb RC 3.00 8.00
166 Kolby Smith RC 2.50 6.00
167 LaRon Landry RC 4.00 10.00
168 Laurent Robinson RC 4.00 10.00
169 Lawrence Timmons RC 4.00 10.00
170 Leon Hall RC 2.50 6.00
171 Lorenzo Booker RC 3.00 8.00
172 Marshawn Lynch RC 5.00 12.00
173 Matt Trannon RC 2.50 6.00
174 Michael Bush RC 2.50 6.00
175 Michael Griffin RC 2.50 6.00
176 Mike Walker RC 4.00 10.00
177 Nate Ilaoa RC 3.00 8.00
178 Patrick Willis RC 4.00 10.00
179 Paul Posluszny RC 2.50 6.00
180 Paul Williams RC 2.50 6.00
181 Reggie Nelson RC 2.50 6.00
182 Rhema McKnight RC 2.50 6.00
183 Robert Meachem RC 3.00 8.00
184 Rufus Alexander RC 2.50 6.00
185 Ryan Moore RC 3.00 8.00
186 Selvin Young RC 2.50 6.00
187 Sidney Rice RC 3.00 8.00
188 Steve Breaston RC 2.50 6.00
189 Steve Smith USC RC 2.50 6.00
190 Syvelle Newton RC 3.00 8.00
191 DeMarcus Tank Tyler RC 2.50 6.00
192 Ted Ginn Jr. RC 3.00 8.00
193 Tony Hunt RC 2.50 6.00
194 Trent Edwards RC 2.50 6.00
195 Troy Smith RC 2.50 6.00
196 Tyler Palko RC 4.00 10.00
197 Tymere Zimmerman RC 2.50 6.00
198 Yamon Figurs RC 2.50 6.00
199 Zac Taylor RC 3.00 8.00
200 Zach Miller RC 2.50 6.00

2007 Donruss Elite Aspirations

*VETS/70-99: 5X TO 12X BASIC CARDS
*ROOKIES/70-99: .6X TO 1.5X BASIC CARDS
*VETS/45-69: 6X TO 15X BASIC CARDS
*ROOKIES/45-69: .8X TO 2X BASIC CARDS
*VETS/20-29: 10X TO 25X BASIC CARDS
*ROOKIES/20-29: 1.2X TO 3X BASIC CARDS
*VETS/10-19: 12X TO 30X BASIC CARDS
*ROOKIES/10-19: 1.5X TO 4X BASIC CARDS
SERIAL #'d UNDER 20 NOT PRICED
STATED PRINT RUN 6-99 SER.#'d SETS

2007 Donruss Elite Status

*VETS/70-99: 5X TO 12X BASIC CARDS
*ROOKIES/70-99: .6X TO 1.5X BASIC CARDS
*ROOKIES/45-69: .8X TO 2X BASIC CARDS
*VETS/30-44: 8X TO 20X BASIC CARDS
*ROOKIES/30-44: 1X TO 2.5X BASIC CARDS
*VETS/20-29: 10X TO 25X BASIC CARDS
*ROOKIES/20-29: 1.2X TO 3X BASIC CARDS
*VETS/10-19: 12X TO 30X BASIC CARDS
*ROOKIES/10-19: 1.5X TO 4X BASIC CARDS
STATED PRINT RUN 1-93
SERIAL #'d UNDER 20 NOT PRICED

2007 Donruss Elite Status Gold

*VETS 1-100: 10X TO 25X BASIC CARDS
*ROOKIES 101-200: 1.2X TO 3X BASIC CARDS
STATED PRINT RUN 24 SER.#'d SETS

2007 Donruss Elite Back to the Future Green

GREEN PRINT RUN 800 SER.#'d SETS
*BLUE/400: .6X TO 1.2X GREEN/800
BLUE PRINT RUN 400 SER.#'d SETS
*RED/200: .6X TO 1.5X GREEN/800
RED PRINT RUN 200 SER.#'d SETS
1 H.Ward/S.Holmes .75 2.00
2 F.Taylor/Jones-Drew .60 1.50
3 W.Dunn/J.Norwood .60 1.50
4 S.McNair/V.Young .75 2.00
5 T.Aikman/T.Romo 1.25 3.00
6 D.Fouts/P.Rivers 1.00 2.50
7 J.Elway/J.Cutler 1.50 4.00
8 E.Dickerson/J.Addai .75 2.00
10 G.Sayers/R.Bush 1.00 2.50
11 J.Brown/L.Tomlinson 1.25 3.00
12 L.Taylor/S.Merriman 1.00 2.50
13 M.Leinart/S.Young 1.25 3.00
14 T.Brown/M.Colston 1.00 2.50
15 B.Urlacher/A.Hawk 1.00 2.50
16 R.Craig/F.Gore .75 2.00
17 R.Cunningham/M.Vick .75 2.00
18 M.Irvin/T.Owens 1.00 2.50
19 M.Allen/S.Jackson 1.00 2.50
20 D.Casper/T.Gonzalez .75 2.00
21 J.Rice/M.Harrison 2.00 5.00
22 R.Smith/B.Marshall .75 2.00
23 M.Duper/C.Chambers .60 1.50
24 B.Bates/R.Williams S .60 1.50
25 J.Theismann/J.Campbell 1.00 2.50

2007 Donruss Elite Back to the Future Jerseys

STATED PRINT RUN 46-299
*PRIME/25: .8X TO 2X JSY/150-299
*PRIME/25: .5X TO 1.2X JSY/46
PRIME PRINT RUN 25 SER.#'d SETS
1 H.Ward/S.Holmes 4.00 10.00
2 F.Taylor/Jones-Drew 3.00 8.00
3 W.Dunn/J.Norwood 3.00 8.00
4 S.McNair/V.Young 4.00 10.00
5 T.Aikman/T.Romo/150 6.00 15.00
6 D.Fouts/P.Rivers 5.00 12.00
7 J.Elway/J.Cutler 12.00 30.00
8 E.Dickerson/J.Addai 6.00 15.00
10 G.Sayers/R.Bush 12.00 30.00
11 J.Brown/L.Tomlinson 8.00 20.00
12 L.Taylor/S.Merriman/150 5.00 12.00
13 M.Leinart/S.Young 8.00 20.00
14 T.Brown/M.Colston/150 5.00 12.00
15 B.Urlacher/A.Hawk 5.00 12.00
16 R.Craig/F.Gore 4.00 10.00
17 R.Cunningham/M.Vick 4.00 10.00
18 M.Irvin/T.Owens/150 5.00 12.00
19 M.Allen/S.Jackson 5.00 12.00
20 D.Casper/T.Gonzalez 4.00 10.00
21 J.Rice/M.Harrison 8.00 20.00
22 R.Smith/B.Marshall/150 4.00 10.00
23 M.Duper/C.Chambers 3.00 8.00
24 B.Bates/R.Williams S 3.00 8.00
25 J.Theismann/J.Campbell/46 8.00 20.00

2007 Donruss Elite Chain Reaction Gold

GOLD PRINT RUN 1000 SER.#'d SETS
*BLACK/400: .5X TO 1.2X GOLD/1000
BLACK PRINT RUN 400 SER.#'d SETS
*RED/200: .6X TO 1.5X GOLD/1000
RED PRINT RUN 200 SER.#'d SETS
1 Plaxico Burress .75 2.00
2 Chris Henry .75 2.00
3 Antonio Gates 1.25 3.00
4 Lee Evans 1.00 2.50
5 Reggie Brown .75 2.00
6 Marques Colston .75 2.00
7 Alge Crumpler 1.00 2.50
8 Jeremy Shockey .75 2.00
9 Roy Williams WR .75 2.00
10 Andre Johnson 1.00 2.50
11 Laveranues Coles .75 2.00
12 Terry Glenn 1.00 2.50
13 LaDainian Tomlinson 1.25 3.00
14 Larry Johnson .75 2.00
15 Rudi Johnson .75 2.00
16 Edgerrin James 1.00 2.50
17 Jamal Lewis 1.00 2.50
18 Willis McGahee .75 2.00
19 Drew Brees 1.25 3.00
20 Peyton Manning 3.00 8.00
21 Donovan McNabb 1.00 2.50
22 Carson Palmer 1.00 2.50
23 Tom Brady 4.00 10.00
24 Marc Bulger .75 2.00
25 Philip Rivers 1.25 3.00

2007 Donruss Elite Chain Reaction Jerseys

STATED PRINT RUN 150 SER.#'d SETS
*PRIME/99: .5X TO 1.2X BASIC JSY/150
*PRIME/30: .8X TO 2X BASIC JSY/150
PRIME PRINT RUN 30-99
1 Plaxico Burress 2.00 5.00
2 Chris Henry 2.00 5.00
3 Antonio Gates 3.00 8.00
4 Lee Evans 2.50 6.00
5 Reggie Brown 2.00 5.00
6 Marques Colston 2.00 5.00
7 Alge Crumpler 2.50 6.00
8 Jeremy Shockey 2.00 5.00
9 Roy Williams WR 2.00 5.00
10 Andre Johnson 2.50 6.00
11 Laveranues Coles 2.00 5.00
12 Terry Glenn 2.50 6.00
13 LaDainian Tomlinson 3.00 8.00
14 Larry Johnson 2.00 5.00
15 Rudi Johnson 2.00 5.00
16 Edgerrin James 2.50 6.00
17 Jamal Lewis 2.50 6.00
18 Willis McGahee 2.00 5.00
19 Drew Brees 3.00 8.00
20 Peyton Manning 8.00 20.00
21 Donovan McNabb 2.50 6.00
22 Carson Palmer 2.50 6.00
23 Tom Brady 10.00 25.00
24 Marc Bulger 2.00 5.00
25 Philip Rivers 3.00 8.00

2007 Donruss Elite College Ties Green

GREEN PRINT RUN 800 SER.#'d SETS
*GOLD/400: .5X TO 1.2X GREEN/800
GOLD PRINT RUN 400 SER.#'d SETS
*BLACK/200: .6X TO 1.5X GREEN/800
BLACK PRINT RUN 200 SER.#'d SETS
1 C.Williams/K.Irons 1.50 4.00
2 R.Williams S/A.Peterson 4.00 10.00
3 D.Hagan/Z.Miller 1.25 3.00
4 M.Leinart/S.Smith USC 1.00 2.50
5 M.Stovall/B.Quinn 3.00 8.00
6 J.Addai/D.Bowe 1.00 2.50
7 M.Clayton/C.Davis 1.50 4.00
8 R.Meachem/J.Swain 1.25 3.00
9 R.Bush/D.Jarrett 3.00 8.00
10 A.Green/Z.Taylor 3.00 8.00
11 D.Henderson/J.Russell 1.00 2.50
12 A.Hawk/T.Smith 2.50 6.00
13 F.Gore/T.Moss 1.50 4.00
14 T.Barber/J.Snelling 1.50 4.00
15 R.Brown/C.Taylor 1.25 3.00
16 A.Boldin/L.Booker 1.50 4.00
17 C.Benson/S.Young 1.00 2.50
18 M.Bush/A.Okoye 2.00 5.00
19 A.Rodgers/M.Lynch 4.00 10.00
20 L.Johnson/P.Posluszny 2.50 6.00

2007 Donruss Elite College Ties Autographs

STATED PRINT RUN 10-25
SERIAL #'d UNDER 25 NOT PRICED
1 C.Williams/K.Irons AU/25 15.00 40.00
2 R.Will S/Peterson AU/10 100.00 200.00
3 D.Hagan/Z.Miller AU/25 15.00 40.00
6 J.Addai/D.Bowe AU/25 15.00 40.00
8 R.Meachem/J.Swain/25
9 R.Bush/D.Jarrett/10 40.00 80.00
12 A.Hawk/T.Smith AU/25 30.00 80.00
17 C.Benson AU/S.Young AU/25 20.00 50.00
18 M.Bush AU/A.Okoye AU/25 30.00 80.00
19 A.Rodgers/M.Lynch AU/25 60.00 120.00
20 L.John AU/Posluszny AU/25 30.00 60.00

2007 Donruss Elite College Ties Jerseys

STATED PRINT RUN 120-250
*PRIME/50-99: .6X TO 1.5X BASIC JSYs
*PRIME/25-35: .8X TO 2X BASIC JSYs
PRIME PRINT RUN 25-99
1 C.Williams/K.Irons/250 6.00 15.00
2 R.Will S/Peterson/200 25.00 60.00
3 D.Hagan/Z.Miller/120 5.00 12.00
4 Leinart/S.Smith USC/250 8.00 20.00
5 M.Stovall/B.Quinn/250 12.00 30.00
6 J.Addai/D.Bowe/250 4.00 10.00
7 M.Clayton/C.Davis/250 6.00 15.00
8 R.Meachem/J.Swain/250 10.00 25.00
9 R.Bush/D.Jarrett/250 12.00 30.00
10 A.Green/Z.Taylor/120 12.00 30.00
11 Henderson/Russell/250 4.00 10.00
12 A.Hawk/T.Smith/120 10.00 25.00
13 F.Gore/T.Moss/120 5.00 12.00
15 R.Brown/C.Taylor/250 5.00 12.00
16 A.Boldin/L.Booker/120 5.00 12.00
17 C.Benson/S.Young/120 4.00 10.00

2007 Donruss Elite Passing the Torch Red

RED PRINT RUN 800 SER.#'d SETS
*GREEN/400: .5X TO 1.2X RED/800
GREEN PRINT RUN 400 SER.#'d SETS
*BLUE/200: .6X TO 1.5X RED/800
BLUE PRINT RUN 200 SER.#'d SETS
1 Steve McNair .60 1.50
2 Vince Young .60 1.50
3 Troy Aikman 1.25 3.00
4 Tony Romo 1.00 2.50
5 Dan Fouts .60 1.50
6 Philip Rivers 1.00 2.50
7 Archie Manning .60 1.50
8 Drew Brees .75 2.00
9 Curtis Martin .60 1.50
10 Leon Washington .60 1.50
11 Corey Dillon .50 1.25
12 Laurence Maroney .60 1.50
13 John Elway 1.50 4.00
14 Jay Cutler .50 1.25
15 Eric Dickerson .75 2.00
16 Joseph Addai .60 1.50
17 Terrell Davis .60 1.50
18 Mike Bell .60 1.50
19 Sterling Sharpe .60 1.50
20 Greg Jennings .60 1.50
21 S.McNair/V.Young .75 2.00
22 T.Aikman/T.Romo 1.00 2.50
23 D.Fouts/P.Rivers 1.00 2.50
24 A.Manning/D.Brees 1.00 2.50
25 C.Martin/L.Washington .75 2.00
26 C.Dillon/L.Maroney .75 2.00
27 J.Elway/J.Cutler 1.25 3.00
28 E.Dickerson/J.Addai .60 1.50
29 T.Davis/M.Bell .75 2.00
30 S.Sharpe/G.Jennings .75 2.00

2007 Donruss Elite Passing the Torch Autographs

1-20 SINGLE AU STATED PRINT RUN 99
21-30 DUAL AU STATED PRINT RUN 49
1 Steve McNair 15.00 40.00
2 Vince Young 10.00 25.00
3 Troy Aikman 30.00 60.00
4 Tony Romo 30.00 60.00
5 Dan Fouts 25.00 50.00
6 Philip Rivers 15.00 40.00
8 Drew Brees 30.00 60.00
9 Curtis Martin 25.00 60.00
10 Leon Washington 12.00 30.00
11 Corey Dillon 10.00 25.00
12 Laurence Maroney 12.00 30.00
13 John Elway 40.00 80.00
14 Jay Cutler 20.00 50.00
15 Eric Dickerson 15.00 40.00
16 Joseph Addai 12.00 30.00
17 Terrell Davis 15.00 40.00
18 Mike Bell 10.00 25.00
19 Sterling Sharpe 15.00 40.00
20 Greg Jennings 15.00 40.00
21 S.McNair/V.Young 40.00 100.00
22 T.Aikman/T.Romo 75.00 150.00
23 D.Fouts/P.Rivers 20.00 50.00
24 A.Manning/D.Brees 75.00 150.00
25 C.Martin/Washington 30.00 60.00
27 J.Elway/J.Cutler 40.00 80.00
28 E.Dickerson/J.Addai 40.00 80.00
29 T.Davis/M.Bell 20.00 40.00
30 S.Sharpe/G.Jennings 50.00 100.00

2007 Donruss Elite Prime Targets Gold

GOLD PRINT RUN 1000 SER.#'d SETS
*BLACK/400: .5X TO 1.2X GOLD/1000
BLACK PRINT RUN 400 SER.#'d SETS
*RED/200: .6X TO 1.5X GOLD/1000
RED PRINT RUN 200 SER.#'d SETS
1 Reggie Bush .50 1.25
2 Terrell Owens .60 1.50
3 LaDainian Tomlinson .75 2.00
4 Chad Johnson .50 1.25
5 Steven Jackson .50 1.25
6 Maurice Jones-Drew .50 1.25
7 Marvin Harrison .60 1.50
8 Donald Driver .60 1.50
9 Darrell Jackson .50 1.25
10 Torry Holt .60 1.50

2007 Donruss Elite Prime Targets Jerseys

STATED PRINT RUN 175-299
*PRIME/50: .6X TO 1.5X BASIC JSYs
PRIME PRINT RUN 50 SER.#'d SETS
1 Reggie Bush 2.00 5.00
2 Terrell Owens/175 2.50 6.00
3 LaDainian Tomlinson/250 3.00 8.00
4 Chad Johnson 2.00 5.00
5 Steven Jackson 2.00 5.00
6 Maurice Jones-Drew 2.00 5.00
7 Marvin Harrison 2.50 6.00
8 Donald Driver 2.50 6.00
9 Darrell Jackson 2.00 5.00
10 Torry Holt 2.50 6.00

2007 Donruss Elite Series Gold

GOLD PRINT RUN 1000 SER.#'d SETS
*BLACK/400: .5X TO 1.2X GOLD/1000
BLACK PRINT RUN 400 SER.#'d SETS
*RED/200: .6X TO 1.5X GOLD/1000
RED PRINT RUN 200 SER.#'d SETS
1 Hines Ward .60 1.50
2 Peyton Manning 2.00 5.00
3 Drew Brees .75 2.00
4 Vince Young .50 1.25
5 Reggie Bush .50 1.25
6 Matt Leinart .50 1.25
7 Maurice Jones-Drew .50 1.25
8 Joseph Addai .50 1.25
9 Tony Romo 1.00 2.50
10 Philip Rivers .75 2.00
11 LaDainian Tomlinson .75 2.00
12 Vernon Davis .50 1.25
13 Frank Gore .60 1.50
14 Willie Parker .60 1.50
15 Steven Jackson .50 1.25
16 Cadillac Williams .60 1.50
17 Ronnie Brown .50 1.25
18 Chris Chambers .50 1.25
19 Larry Fitzgerald .60 1.50
20 Mark Clayton .50 1.25
21 Braylon Edwards .50 1.25
22 Matt Hasselbeck .50 1.25
23 J.P. Losman .50 1.25
24 Thomas Jones .50 1.25
25 Shaun Alexander .50 1.25

2007 Donruss Elite Series Autographs

UNPRICED AUTO PRINT RUN 1-10

2007 Donruss Elite Series Jerseys

STATED PRINT RUN 30-299
*PRIME/99: .5X TO 1.2X JSY/150-299
*PRIME/99: .25X TO .6X JSY/30
*PRIME/50: .6X TO 1.5X JSY/150-199

PRIME PRINT RUN 25-99
1 Hines Ward/30 5.00 12.00
2 Peyton Manning/170 8.00 20.00
3 Drew Brees/175 3.00 8.00
4 Vince Young/175 2.00 5.00
5 Reggie Bush/175 2.00 5.00
6 Matt Leinart/175 2.00 5.00
7 Maurice Jones-Drew/175 2.00 5.00
8 Joseph Addai/175 2.00 5.00
9 Tony Romo/150 4.00 10.00
10 Philip Rivers/175 3.00 8.00
11 LaDainian Tomlinson/175 3.00 8.00
12 Vernon Davis/175 2.00 5.00
13 Frank Gore/115 2.50 6.00
14 Willie Parker/175 2.50 6.00
15 Steven Jackson/175 2.00 5.00
16 Cadillac Williams/175 2.50 6.00
17 Ronnie Brown/299 2.00 5.00
18 Chris Chambers/299 2.00 5.00
19 Larry Fitzgerald/299 2.50 6.00
20 Mark Clayton/299 2.00 5.00
21 Braylon Edwards/175 2.00 5.00
22 Matt Hasselbeck/299 2.00 5.00
23 J.P. Losman/299 2.00 5.00
24 Thomas Jones/299 2.00 5.00
25 Shaun Alexander/175 2.00 5.00

2007 Donruss Elite Status Autographs Gold

GOLD PRINT RUN 24 SER.#'d SETS
UNPRICED BLACK PRINT RUN 1
101 A.J. Davis 12.00 30.00
102 Aaron Ross 12.00 30.00
103 Aaron Rouse 12.00 30.00
104 Adam Carriker 12.00 30.00
105 Adrian Peterson 250.00 450.00
106 Ahmad Bradshaw 20.00 50.00
108 Amobi Okoye 15.00 40.00
109 Anthony Gonzalez 12.00 30.00
110 Anthony Spencer 15.00 40.00
111 Antonio Pittman 12.00 30.00
112 Aundrae Allison 12.00 30.00
113 Brady Quinn 30.00 80.00
114 Brandon Jackson 12.00 30.00
116 Brandon Siler 12.00 30.00
117 Brian Leonard 12.00 30.00
118 Calvin Johnson 150.00 250.00
119 Chansi Stuckey 15.00 40.00
120 Chris Davis 12.00 30.00
121 Chris Henry 12.00 30.00
122 Chris Houston 12.00 30.00
123 Chris Leak 10.00 25.00
124 Courtney Taylor 12.00 30.00
126 Dallas Baker 12.00 30.00
127 Darius Walker 12.00 30.00
128 Darrelle Revis 15.00 40.00
129 David Ball 12.00 30.00
130 David Clowney 12.00 30.00
131 David Harris 12.00 30.00
132 DeShawn Wynn 12.00 30.00
133 D'Juan Woods 12.00 30.00
134 Drew Stanton 12.00 30.00
135 Dwayne Bowe 12.00 30.00
136 Dwayne Jarrett 15.00 40.00
137 Dwayne Wright 12.00 30.00
139 Gaines Adams 15.00 40.00
140 Garrett Wolfe 12.00 30.00
141 Gary Russell 15.00 40.00
142 Greg Olsen 20.00 50.00
143 H.B. Blades 12.00 30.00
144 Isaiah Stanback 12.00 30.00
146 Jamaal Anderson 15.00 40.00
147 JaMarcus Russell 12.00 30.00
148 James Jones 12.00 30.00
149 Jared Zabransky 12.00 30.00
150 Jarrett Hicks 15.00 40.00
151 Jarvis Moss 12.00 30.00
152 Jason Hill 12.00 30.00
153 Jason Snelling 12.00 30.00
154 Jeff Rowe 12.00 30.00
155 Joel Filani 12.00 30.00
156 John Beck 12.00 30.00
157 Johnnie Lee Higgins 12.00 30.00
158 Jon Beason 12.00 30.00
159 Jon Cornish 15.00 40.00
162 Jordan Palmer 15.00 40.00
163 Kenneth Darby 12.00 30.00
164 Kenny Irons 12.00 30.00
165 Kevin Kolb 15.00 40.00
166 Kolby Smith 12.00 30.00
167 LaRon Landry 20.00 50.00
168 Laurent Robinson 20.00 50.00
169 Lawrence Timmons 20.00 50.00
170 Leon Hall 12.00 30.00
171 Lorenzo Booker 15.00 40.00
172 Marshawn Lynch 25.00 60.00
174 Michael Bush 12.00 30.00
175 Michael Griffin 12.00 30.00
176 Mike Walker 20.00 50.00
177 Nate Ilaoa 15.00 40.00
178 Patrick Willis 20.00 50.00
179 Paul Posluszny 12.00 30.00
180 Paul Williams 12.00 30.00
181 Reggie Nelson 12.00 30.00
182 Rhema McKnight 12.00 30.00
183 Robert Meachem 15.00 40.00
184 Rufus Alexander 12.00 30.00
186 Selvin Young 12.00 30.00
187 Sidney Rice 15.00 40.00
188 Steve Breaston 12.00 30.00
189 Steve Smith USC 12.00 30.00
190 Syvelle Newton 15.00 40.00
192 Ted Ginn Jr. 15.00 40.00
193 Tony Hunt 12.00 30.00
194 Trent Edwards 12.00 30.00
195 Troy Smith 12.00 30.00
196 Tyler Palko 20.00 50.00
197 Tymere Zimmerman 12.00 30.00
198 Yamon Figurs 12.00 30.00
200 Zach Miller 12.00 30.00

2007 Donruss Elite Teams Black

BLACK PRINT RUN 800 SER.#'d SETS
*RED/400: .5X TO 1.2X BLACK/800
RED PRINT RUN 400 SER.#'d SETS
*GOLD/200: .6X TO 1.5X BLACK/800
GOLD PRINT RUN 200 SER.#'d SETS
1 Leinart/James/Boldin .75 2.00
2 Vick/Crumpler/Norwood .75 2.00
3 McNair/Mason/Clayton .75 2.00
4 Losman/McGahee/Evans .75 2.00
5 Delhomme/Smith/Williams .75 2.00
6 Grossman/Berrian/Benson .60 1.50
7 Palmer/Johnson/Houshmandzadeh .75 2.00
8 Romo/Jones/Owens 1.25 3.00
9 Cutler/Bell/Walker .75 2.00
10 Favre/Hawk/Driver 2.00 5.00
11 Manning/Harrison/Addai 2.50 6.00
12 Leftwich/Taylor/J-Drew .60 1.50
13 Brady/Dillon/Maroney 3.00 8.00
14 Brees/McAllister/Bush 1.00 2.50
15 Manning/Shockey/Jacobs .75 2.00
16 McNabb/Westbrook/Stallworth .75 2.00
17 Roethlisberger/Parker/Ward 1.00 2.50
18 Rivers/Tomlinson/Gates 1.00 2.50
19 Smith QB/Gore/Davis .75 2.00
20 Hasselbeck/Alexander/Jackson .60 1.50
21 Bulger/Jackson/Holt .75 2.00
22 Young/Jones/White .75 2.00
23 Campbell/Portis/Moss .75 2.00
24 Green/Johnson/Gonzalez .75 2.00
25 Pennington/Washington/Coles .60 1.50

2007 Donruss Elite Teams Jerseys

STATED PRINT RUN 50-99
*PRIME/25: .8X TO 2X BASIC JSY
PRIME PRINT RUN 25 SER.#'d SETS
1 Leinart/James/Boldin 8.00 20.00
2 Vick/Crumpler/Norwood 8.00 20.00
3 McNair/Mason/Clayton 8.00 20.00
4 Losman/McGahee/Evans 8.00 20.00
5 Delhomme/Smith/Williams 8.00 20.00
6 Grossman/Berrian/Benson 6.00 15.00
7 Palmer/Johnson/Houshmandzadeh 8.00 20.00
8 Romo/Jones/Owens/50 12.00 30.00
9 Cutler/Bell/Walker 8.00 20.00
10 Favre/Hawk/Driver 20.00 50.00
11 Manning/Harrison/Addai 25.00 60.00
12 Leftwich/Taylor/J-Drew 6.00 15.00
13 Brady/Dillon/Maroney 30.00 80.00
14 Brees/McAllister/Bush 10.00 25.00
15 Manning/Shockey/Jacobs 8.00 20.00
16 McNabb/Westbrook/Stallworth 8.00 20.00
17 Roethlisberger/Parker/Ward 10.00 25.00
18 Rivers/Tomlinson/Gates 10.00 25.00
19 Smith QB/Gore/Davis 8.00 20.00
20 Hasselbeck/Alexander/Jackson 6.00 15.00
21 Bulger/Jackson/Holt 8.00 20.00
22 Young/Jones/White 8.00 20.00
23 Campbell/Portis/Moss/50 8.00 20.00
24 Green/Johnson/Gonzalez 8.00 20.00
25 Pennington/Washington/Coles 6.00 15.00

2007 Donruss Elite Throwback Threads

1-30 PRINT RUN 175-249
31-45 PRINT RUN 100 SER.#'d SETS
*PRIME/20-30: .8X TO 2X BASIC JSYs
PRIME PRINT RUN 6-30
1 Joe Namath/175 6.00 15.00
2 Chad Pennington 2.00 5.00
3 Ozzie Newsome 2.50 6.00
4 Kellen Winslow/245 2.00 5.00
5 Dick Butkus 4.00 10.00
6 Brian Urlacher 3.00 8.00
7 Cris Collinsworth 2.50 6.00
8 Chad Johnson 2.00 5.00
9 Barry Sanders 5.00 12.00
10 Reggie Bush 2.00 5.00
11 Earl Campbell 3.00 8.00
12 Jamal Lewis 2.50 6.00
13 Dan Marino 6.00 15.00
14 Daunte Culpepper 2.50 6.00
16 Terry Glenn 2.50 6.00
17 Roger Staubach 4.00 10.00
18 Tony Romo/175 4.00 10.00
19 Gale Sayers 3.00 8.00
20 Devin Hester 2.50 6.00
21 Warren Moon 3.00 8.00
22 Vince Young 2.00 5.00
23 Jim Brown 6.00 15.00
24 LaDainian Tomlinson 3.00 8.00
25 Dan Fouts 2.50 6.00
26 Philip Rivers 3.00 8.00
27 Tom Brady 10.00 25.00
28 Matt Leinart 2.00 5.00
29 Jim McMahon 4.00 10.00
30 Rex Grossman 2.00 5.00
31 J.Namath/C.Pennington 10.00 25.00
32 O.Newsome/K.Winslow 4.00 10.00
33 D.Butkus/B.Urlacher 6.00 15.00
34 C.Collinsworth/C.Johnson 4.00 10.00
35 B.Sanders/R.Bush 8.00 20.00
36 E.Campbell/J.Lewis 5.00 12.00
37 D.Marino/D.Culpepper 10.00 25.00
39 R.Staubach/T.Romo 6.00 15.00
40 G.Sayers/D.Hester 5.00 12.00
41 W.Moon 5.00 12.00
V.Young
42 J.Brown/L.Tomlinson 6.00 15.00
43 D.Fouts/P.Rivers 5.00 12.00
44 T.Brady/M.Leinart 15.00 40.00
45 J.McMahon/R.Grossman 6.00 15.00

2007 Donruss Elite Throwback Threads Autographs

UNPRICED AUTO PRINT RUN 1-10
UNPRICED AU PRIME PRINT RUN 1-5

2007 Donruss Elite Turn of the Century Autographs

STATED PRINT RUN 50-100
101 A.J. Davis/100 8.00 20.00
103 Aaron Rouse/100 8.00 20.00
104 Adam Carriker/100 8.00 20.00
105 Adrian Peterson/100 125.00 200.00
106 Ahmad Bradshaw/100 12.00 30.00
108 Amobi Okoye/50 12.00 30.00
109 Anthony Gonzalez/100 8.00 20.00
111 Antonio Pittman/50 10.00 25.00
112 Aundrae Allison/50 10.00 25.00
113 Brady Quinn/100 8.00 20.00
114 Brandon Jackson/100 8.00 20.00
115 Brandon Meriweather/50 12.00 30.00
116 Brandon Siler/100 8.00 20.00
117 Brian Leonard/100 8.00 20.00
118 Calvin Johnson/100 60.00 120.00
119 Chansi Stuckey/100 10.00 25.00
120 Chris Davis/50 10.00 25.00
121 Chris Henry/100 8.00 20.00
122 Chris Houston/50 10.00 25.00
123 Chris Leak/50 10.00 25.00
124 Courtney Taylor/50 10.00 25.00
126 Dallas Baker/100 8.00 20.00
127 Darius Walker/100 8.00 20.00
128 Darrelle Revis/50 12.00 30.00
129 David Ball/100 8.00 20.00
130 David Clowney/100 8.00 20.00
131 David Harris/100 8.00 20.00
132 DeShawn Wynn/100 8.00 20.00
133 D'Juan Woods/100 8.00 20.00
134 Drew Stanton/100 12.00 30.00
135 Dwayne Bowe/100 8.00 20.00
136 Dwayne Jarrett/100 10.00 25.00
137 Dwayne Wright/50 10.00 25.00
139 Gaines Adams/100 10.00 25.00
140 Garrett Wolfe/50 10.00 25.00
142 Greg Olsen/100 12.00 30.00
144 Isaiah Stanback/50 10.00 25.00
145 Jacoby Jones/50 10.00 25.00
146 Jamaal Anderson/50 12.00 30.00
147 JaMarcus Russell/100 8.00 20.00
148 James Jones/50 15.00 40.00
149 Jared Zabransky/100 8.00 20.00
152 Jason Hill/100 8.00 20.00
153 Jason Snelling/50 10.00 25.00
154 Jeff Rowe/100 8.00 20.00
155 Joel Filani/100 8.00 20.00
156 John Beck/100 8.00 20.00
157 Johnnie Lee Higgins/50 10.00 25.00
158 Jon Beason/100 8.00 20.00
159 Jon Cornish/100 10.00 25.00
162 Jordan Palmer/50 EXCH 12.00 30.00
163 Kenneth Darby/100 8.00 20.00
164 Kenny Irons/100 8.00 20.00
165 Kevin Kolb/100 10.00 25.00
166 Kolby Smith/100 8.00 20.00
167 LaRon Landry/100 12.00 30.00
168 Laurent Robinson/50 15.00 40.00
169 Lawrence Timmons/100 12.00 30.00
170 Leon Hall/100 8.00 20.00
171 Lorenzo Booker/100 10.00 25.00
172 Marshawn Lynch/100 20.00 40.00
174 Michael Bush/50 10.00 25.00
175 Michael Griffin/50 10.00 25.00
176 Mike Walker/100 12.00 30.00
177 Nate Ilaoa/50 12.00 30.00
178 Patrick Willis/50 15.00 40.00
179 Paul Posluszny/50 10.00 25.00
180 Paul Williams/100 8.00 20.00
181 Reggie Nelson/100 8.00 20.00
182 Rhema McKnight/50 10.00 25.00
183 Robert Meachem/100 10.00 25.00
184 Rufus Alexander/100 8.00 20.00
186 Selvin Young/50 10.00 25.00
187 Sidney Rice/100 10.00 25.00
188 Steve Breaston/50 10.00 25.00
189 Steve Smith USC/100 8.00 20.00
190 Syvelle Newton/50 12.00 30.00
192 Ted Ginn Jr./100 10.00 25.00
193 Tony Hunt/50 10.00 25.00
194 Trent Edwards/50 10.00 25.00
195 Troy Smith/50 10.00 25.00
196 Tyler Palko/100 12.00 30.00
197 Tymere Zimmerman/100 8.00 20.00
198 Yamon Figurs/100 8.00 20.00
200 Zach Miller/50 10.00 25.00

2007 Donruss Elite Zoning Commission Gold

GOLD PRINT RUN 1000 SER.#'d SETS
*BLACK/400: .5X TO 1.2X GOLD/1000
BLACK PRINT RUN 400 SER.#'d SETS
*RED/200: .6X TO 1.5X GOLD/1000
RED PRINT RUN 200 SER.#'d SETS
1 Vince Young .50 1.25
2 Drew Brees .75 2.00
3 Peyton Manning 2.00 5.00
4 Matt Leinart .50 1.25
5 Jay Cutler .50 1.25
6 Carson Palmer .60 1.50
7 Marc Bulger .50 1.25
8 Jon Kitna .50 1.25
9 Tom Brady 2.50 6.00
10 Philip Rivers .75 2.00
11 Michael Vick .60 1.50
12 Eli Manning .60 1.50
13 Rex Grossman .50 1.25
14 Steve McNair .60 1.50
15 Tony Romo 1.00 2.50
16 Chad Johnson .50 1.25
17 Marvin Harrison .60 1.50
18 Reggie Wayne .60 1.50
19 Roy Williams WR .50 1.25
20 Anquan Boldin .50 1.25
21 Donald Driver .60 1.50
22 Torry Holt .60 1.50
23 Steve Smith .60 1.50
24 Javon Walker .60 1.50
25 T.J. Houshmandzadeh .50 1.25
26 Tony Gonzalez .60 1.50
27 LaDainian Tomlinson .75 2.00
28 Larry Johnson .50 1.25
29 Frank Gore .60 1.50
30 Tiki Barber .60 1.50
31 Steven Jackson .50 1.25
32 Willie Parker .60 1.50
33 Brian Westbrook .50 1.25
34 Rudi Johnson .50 1.25
35 Chester Taylor .50 1.25
36 Joseph Addai .50 1.25
37 Deuce McAllister .60 1.50
38 Julius Jones .50 1.25
39 Ahman Green .60 1.50
40 Thomas Jones .50 1.25

2007 Donruss Elite Zoning Commission Jerseys

STATED PRINT RUN 150-175
*PRIME/50: .6X TO 1.5X BASIC JSY
PRIME PRINT RUN 50 SER.#'d SETS
1 Vince Young 2.00 5.00
2 Drew Brees 3.00 8.00
3 Peyton Manning 8.00 20.00
4 Matt Leinart 2.00 5.00
5 Jay Cutler 2.00 5.00
6 Carson Palmer 2.50 6.00
7 Marc Bulger 2.00 5.00
8 Jon Kitna/150 2.00 5.00
9 Tom Brady 10.00 25.00
10 Philip Rivers 3.00 8.00
11 Michael Vick 2.50 6.00
12 Eli Manning 2.50 6.00
13 Rex Grossman 2.00 5.00
14 Steve McNair 2.50 6.00
15 Tony Romo/150 4.00 10.00
16 Chad Johnson 2.00 5.00
17 Marvin Harrison 2.50 6.00
18 Reggie Wayne 2.50 6.00
19 Roy Williams WR 2.00 5.00
20 Anquan Boldin 2.00 5.00
21 Donald Driver 2.50 6.00
22 Torry Holt 2.50 6.00
23 Steve Smith 2.50 6.00
24 Javon Walker 2.50 6.00
25 T.J. Houshmandzadeh 2.00 5.00
26 Tony Gonzalez 2.50 6.00
27 LaDainian Tomlinson 3.00 8.00
28 Larry Johnson/170 2.00 5.00
29 Frank Gore 2.50 6.00
30 Tiki Barber 2.50 6.00
31 Steven Jackson 2.00 5.00
32 Willie Parker 2.50 6.00
33 Brian Westbrook 2.00 5.00
34 Rudi Johnson 2.00 5.00
35 Chester Taylor 2.00 5.00
36 Joseph Addai 2.00 5.00
37 Deuce McAllister 2.50 6.00
38 Julius Jones 2.00 5.00
39 Ahman Green 2.50 6.00
40 Thomas Jones 2.00 5.00

2007 Donruss Elite National Convention

COMPLETE SET (20) 40.00 80.00
STATED PRINT RUN 599 SER.#'d SETS
*STATUS GOLD/25: 1.2X TO 3X
*STATUS RED/50: .8X TO 2X
UNPRICED AUTO PRINT RUN 6-10
PHOTOS ARE UPDATED NFL IMAGES
105 Adrian Peterson 3.00 8.00
109 Anthony Gonzalez 1.00 2.50
113 Brady Quinn 1.00 2.50
114 Brandon Jackson 1.00 2.50
118 Calvin Johnson 3.00 8.00
121 Chris Henry 1.00 2.50
134 Drew Stanton 1.00 2.50
135 Dwayne Bowe 1.00 2.50
136 Dwayne Jarrett 1.25 3.00
142 Greg Olsen 1.50 4.00
147 JaMarcus Russell 1.00 2.50
156 John Beck 1.00 2.50
164 Kenny Irons 1.00 2.50
165 Kevin Kolb 1.25 3.00
172 Marshawn Lynch 2.00 5.00
174 Michael Bush 1.00 2.50
183 Robert Meachem 1.25 3.00
189 Steve Smith USC 1.00 2.50
192 Ted Ginn Jr. 1.25 3.00
195 Troy Smith 1.00 2.50

2008 Donruss Elite

This set was released on June 11, 2008. The base set consists of 200 cards. Cards 1-100 feature veterans, and cards 101-200 are rookies serial numbered of 199, 249, 299, and 999. The rookies serial numbered of 199, 249, and 299 are autographed.

COMP.SET w/o RC's (100) 7.50 20.00
ROOKIE PRINT RUN 199-999
1 Anquan Boldin .25 .60
2 Edgerrin James .30 .75
3 Larry Fitzgerald .30 .75
4 Matt Leinart .25 .60
5 Alge Crumpler .25 .60
6 Warrick Dunn .25 .60
7 Roddy White .25 .60
8 Willis McGahee .25 .60
9 Todd Heap .25 .60
10 Derrick Mason .25 .60
11 Marshawn Lynch .30 .75
12 Trent Edwards .25 .60
13 Lee Evans .30 .75
14 Steve Smith .30 .75
15 DeShaun Foster .25 .60
16 DeAngelo Williams .25 .60
17 Cedric Benson .25 .60
18 Bernard Berrian .25 .60
19 Devin Hester .30 .75
20 Carson Palmer .30 .75
21 T.J. Houshmandzadeh .25 .60
22 Chad Johnson .25 .60
23 Jamal Lewis .30 .75
24 Braylon Edwards .25 .60
25 Kellen Winslow .25 .60
26 Tony Romo .30 .75
27 Terrell Owens .30 .75
28 Jason Witten .30 .75
29 Jay Cutler .25 .60
30 Travis Henry .25 .60
31 Brandon Marshall .30 .75
32 Jon Kitna .25 .60
33 Roy Williams WR .25 .60
34 Calvin Johnson .40 1.00
35 Brett Favre .75 2.00
36 Greg Jennings .25 .60
37 Ryan Grant .30 .75
38 Matt Schaub .25 .60
39 Ahman Green .30 .75
40 Andre Johnson .30 .75
41 Peyton Manning 1.00 2.50
42 Reggie Wayne .30 .75
43 Marvin Harrison .30 .75
44 Joseph Addai .25 .60
45 David Garrard .25 .60
46 Fred Taylor .25 .60
47 Reggie Williams .30 .75
48 Larry Johnson .25 .60
49 Tony Gonzalez .30 .75
50 Dwayne Bowe .30 .75
51 Derek Hagan .25 .60
52 Ronnie Brown .25 .60
53 Ted Ginn Jr. .25 .60
54 Tarvaris Jackson .25 .60
55 Chester Taylor .25 .60
56 Adrian Peterson .40 1.00
57 Tom Brady 1.25 3.00
58 Laurence Maroney .30 .75
59 Randy Moss .30 .75
60 Wes Welker .30 .75
61 Drew Brees .40 1.00
62 Reggie Bush .25 .60
63 Marques Colston .25 .60
64 Eli Manning .30 .75
65 Brandon Jacobs .25 .60
66 Plaxico Burress .25 .60
67 Thomas Jones .25 .60
68 Jerricho Cotchery .25 .60
69 Laveranues Coles .25 .60
70 JaMarcus Russell .25 .60
71 Justin Fargas .25 .60
72 Jerry Porter .25 .60
73 Donovan McNabb .30 .75
74 Brian Westbrook .25 .60
75 Kevin Curtis .25 .60
76 Ben Roethlisberger .40 1.00
77 Willie Parker .30 .75
78 Santonio Holmes .25 .60
79 Hines Ward .30 .75
80 Philip Rivers .40 1.00
81 LaDainian Tomlinson .40 1.00
82 Antonio Gates .30 .75
83 Frank Gore .30 .75
84 Arnaz Battle .25 .60
85 Vernon Davis .25 .60
86 Matt Hasselbeck .25 .60
87 Shaun Alexander .25 .60
88 Deion Branch .25 .60
89 Marc Bulger .25 .60
90 Torry Holt .30 .75
91 Steven Jackson .25 .60
92 Jeff Garcia .25 .60
93 Joey Galloway .30 .75
94 Earnest Graham .25 .60
95 Vince Young .25 .60
96 LenDale White .25 .60
97 Roydell Williams .25 .60
98 Clinton Portis .25 .60
99 Chris Cooley .25 .60
100 Santana Moss .25 .60

101 Matt Ryan AU/199 RC 50.00 100.00
102 Brian Brohm AU/199 RC 5.00 12.00
103 Chad Henne AU/199 RC 6.00 15.00
104 Andre Woodson AU/249 RC 5.00 12.00
105 Joe Flacco AU/299 RC 10.00 25.00
106 John David Booty/999 RC 1.50 4.00
107 Josh Johnson/999 RC 1.50 4.00
108 Erik Ainge AU/299 RC 5.00 12.00
109 Colt Brennan AU/249 RC 6.00 15.00
110 Dennis Dixon AU/299 RC 5.00 12.00
111 Kevin O'Connell/999 RC 1.50 4.00
112 Matt Flynn/999 RC 1.50 4.00
113 Bernard Morris/999 RC 2.00 5.00
114 Sam Keller/999 RC 1.50 4.00
115 Paul Smith/999 RC 1.50 4.00
116 Darren McFadden AU/199 RC 5.00 12.00
117 Jonathan Stewart AU/199 RC 12.00 30.00
118 R.Mendenhall AU/199 RC 5.00 12.00
119 Felix Jones AU/199 RC 5.00 12.00
120 Chris Johnson/999 RC 2.00 5.00
121 Jamaal Charles/999 RC 2.50 6.00
122 Ray Rice/999 RC 1.50 4.00
123 Steve Slaton/999 RC 1.50 4.00
124 Mike Hart/999 RC 1.50 4.00
125 Matt Forte AU/299 RC 15.00 40.00
126 Tashard Choice AU/299 RC 5.00 12.00
127 Kevin Smith/999 RC 1.50 4.00
128 Allen Patrick/999 RC 1.50 4.00
129 Thomas Brown/999 RC 1.50 4.00
130 Justin Forsett AU/299 RC 6.00 15.00
131 Cory Boyd AU/299 RC 5.00 12.00
132 Dantrell Savage/999 RC 2.00 5.00
133 Kalvin McRae/999 RC 1.50 4.00
134 Darrell Strong AU/299 RC 6.00 15.00
135 Owen Schmitt AU/299 RC 5.00 12.00
136 Peyton Hillis AU/299 RC 8.00 20.00
137 Jacob Hester AU/299 RC 5.00 12.00
138 Fred Davis/999 RC 1.50 4.00
139 Martellus Bennett AU/299 RC 6.00 15.00
140 John Carlson AU/299 RC 5.00 12.00
141 Martin Rucker/999 RC 1.50 4.00
142 Brad Cottam AU/299 RC 5.00 12.00
143 Jermichael Finley/999 RC 1.50 4.00
144 Jacob Tamme/999 RC 2.00 5.00
145 Dustin Keller AU/299 RC 6.00 15.00
146 Kellen Davis/999 RC 1.50 4.00
147 DeSean Jackson AU/249 RC 10.00 25.00
148 James Hardy AU/299 RC 5.00 12.00
149 Malcolm Kelly AU/249 RC 5.00 12.00
150 Early Doucet AU/199 RC 5.00 12.00
151 Limas Sweed AU/249 RC 5.00 12.00
152 Andre Caldwell AU/299 RC 5.00 12.00
153 Mario Manningham AU/299 RC 5.00 12.00
154 Devin Thomas AU/299 RC 5.00 12.00
155 Donnie Avery AU/299 RC 6.00 15.00
156 Earl Bennett AU/299 RC 8.00 20.00
157 Eddie Royal AU/249 RC 5.00 12.00
158 Lavelle Hawkins AU/299 RC 6.00 15.00
159 DJ Hall/999 RC 1.50 4.00
160 Adarius Bowman/999 RC 2.00 5.00
161 Jordy Nelson AU/249 RC 15.00 40.00
162 Harry Douglas AU/299 RC 6.00 15.00
163 Jerome Simpson AU/299 RC 6.00 15.00
164 Dorien Bryant/999 RC 2.00 5.00
165 Will Franklin/999 RC 2.00 5.00
166 Keenan Burton/999 RC 1.50 4.00
167 Kevin Robinson/999 RC 1.50 4.00
168 Paul Hubbard AU/299 RC 5.00 12.00
169 Davone Bess/999 RC 2.00 5.00
170 Adrian Arrington/999 RC 1.50 4.00
171 Dexter Jackson AU/299 RC 8.00 20.00
172 Ryan Grice-Mullen/999 RC 1.50 4.00
173 Darius Reynaud/999 RC 1.50 4.00
174 Josh Morgan AU/299 RC 5.00 12.00
175 Anthony Alridge/999 RC 1.50 4.00
176 Jason Rivers/999 RC 1.50 4.00
177 Marcus Smith AU/299 RC 6.00 15.00
178 Mark Bradford/999 RC 1.50 4.00
179 Marcus Monk AU/299 RC 6.00 15.00
180 Chris Long/999 RC 2.00 5.00
181 Vernon Gholston/999 RC 1.50 4.00
182 Derrick Harvey/999 RC 1.50 4.00
183 Glenn Dorsey/999 RC 1.50 4.00
184 Sedrick Ellis/999 RC 1.50 4.00
185 Dan Connor AU/299 RC 5.00 12.00
186 Curtis Lofton/999 RC 2.00 5.00
187 Keith Rivers AU/299 RC 5.00 12.00
188 Xavier Adibi/999 RC 1.50 4.00
189 Ali Highsmith/999 RC 1.50 4.00
190 Quentin Groves AU/299 RC 6.00 15.00
191 Erin Henderson/999 RC 2.00 5.00
192 Mike Jenkins/999 RC 1.50 4.00
193 Antoine Cason AU/299 RC 6.00 15.00
194 D.Rodgers-Cromartie/999 RC 2.00 5.00
195 Leodis McKelvin/999 RC 2.00 5.00
196 Aqib Talib/999 RC 2.50 6.00
197 Reggie Smith/999 RC 1.50 4.00
198 Tracy Porter AU/299 RC 6.00 15.00
199 Terrell Thomas AU/299 RC 5.00 12.00
200 Kenny Phillips/999 RC 1.50 4.00

2008 Donruss Elite 10th Anniversary

*VETS/10: 8X TO 20X BASIC CARDS
STATED PRINT RUN 10 SER.#'d SETS

2008 Donruss Elite Aspirations

*VETS/70-98: 4X TO 10X BASIC CARDS
*VETS/53-69: 5X TO 12X BASIC CARDS
*VETS/20: 8X TO 20X BASIC CARDS
*VETS/10-19: 10X TO 25X BASIC CARDS
COMMON ROOKIE/72-99 2.50 6.00
ROOKIE SEMIS/72-99 3.00 8.00
ROOKIE UNL.STAR/72-99 4.00 10.00
COMMON ROOKIE/45-66 5.00 12.00
COMMON ROOKIE/20-28 6.00 15.00
COMMON ROOKIE/10-19 8.00 20.00
ROOKIE SEMIS/10-19 10.00 25.00
ROOKIE UNL.STAR/10-19 12.00 30.00
STATED PRINT RUN 9-99
101 Matt Ryan/88 8.00 20.00
102 Brian Brohm/88 2.50 6.00
103 Chad Henne/93 3.00 8.00
104 Andre Woodson/97 2.50 6.00
105 Joe Flacco/95 5.00 12.00
106 John David Booty/90 2.50 6.00
107 Josh Johnson/89 2.50 6.00
108 Erik Ainge/90 2.50 6.00
109 Colt Brennan/85 3.00 8.00
110 Dennis Dixon/90 2.50 6.00
111 Kevin O'Connell/93 2.50 6.00
112 Matt Flynn/85 2.50 6.00
116 Darren McFadden/95 2.50 6.00
117 Jonathan Stewart/72 4.00 10.00
118 Rashard Mendenhall/95 2.50 6.00
119 Felix Jones/75 2.50 6.00
120 Chris Johnson/95 3.00 8.00
121 Jamaal Charles/75 4.00 10.00
122 Ray Rice/73 2.50 6.00
123 Steve Slaton/90 2.50 6.00
124 Mike Hart/80 2.50 6.00
125 Matt Forte/75 4.00 10.00
127 Kevin Smith/76 2.50 6.00
135 Owen Schmitt/65 3.00 8.00
136 Peyton Hillis/78 4.00 10.00
137 Jacob Hester/82 2.50 6.00
139 Martellus Bennett/87 3.00 8.00
147 DeSean Jackson/99 5.00 12.00
148 James Hardy/18 8.00 20.00
149 Malcolm Kelly/96 2.50 6.00
150 Early Doucet/91 2.50 6.00
151 Limas Sweed/96 2.50 6.00
153 Mario Manningham/14 8.00 20.00
154 Devin Thomas/95 2.50 6.00
161 Jordy Nelson/73 8.00 20.00
169 Davone Bess/93 3.00 8.00
171 Dexter Jackson/98 4.00 10.00
174 Josh Morgan/98 2.50 6.00
181 Vernon Gholston/50 3.00 8.00
183 Glenn Dorsey/28 5.00 12.00
187 Keith Rivers/45 3.00 8.00
192 Mike Jenkins/96 2.50 6.00

2008 Donruss Elite Status

*VETS/80-89: 4X TO 10X BASIC CARDS
*VETS/30-47: 6X TO 15X BASIC CARDS
*VETS/20-29: 8X TO 20X BASIC CARDS
*VETS/10-19: 10X TO 25X BASIC CARDS
COMMON ROOKIE/72-91 2.50 6.00
ROOKIE SEMIS/72-91 3.00 8.00
ROOKIE UNL.STAR/72-91 4.00 10.00
COMMON ROOKIE/49-55 5.00 12.00
COMMON ROOKIE/34-45 6.00 15.00
COMMON ROOKIE/20-29 5.00 12.00
ROOKIE SEMIS/20-29 6.00 15.00
ROOKIE UNL.STAR/20-29 8.00 20.00
COMMON ROOKIE/10-19 10.00 25.00
ROOKIE UNL.STAR/10-19 12.00 30.00
STATED PRINT RUN 1-91
101 Matt Ryan/12 25.00 60.00
102 Brian Brohm/12 8.00 20.00
106 John David Booty/10 8.00 20.00
107 Josh Johnson/11 8.00 20.00
108 Erik Ainge/10 8.00 20.00
109 Colt Brennan/15 10.00 25.00
110 Dennis Dixon/10 8.00 20.00
112 Matt Flynn/15 8.00 20.00
117 Jonathan Stewart/28 8.00 20.00
119 Felix Jones/25 5.00 12.00
121 Jamaal Charles/25 8.00 20.00
122 Ray Rice/27 5.00 12.00
123 Steve Slaton/10 8.00 20.00
124 Mike Hart/20 5.00 12.00
125 Matt Forte/25 8.00 20.00
127 Kevin Smith/24 5.00 12.00
135 Owen Schmitt/35 4.00 10.00
136 Peyton Hillis/22 8.00 20.00
137 Jacob Hester/18 8.00 20.00
139 Martellus Bennett/13 10.00 25.00
148 James Hardy/82 2.50 6.00
153 Mario Manningham/86 2.50 6.00
161 Jordy Nelson/27 15.00 40.00
180 Chris Long/91 3.00 8.00
181 Vernon Gholston/50 3.00 8.00
183 Glenn Dorsey/72 2.50 6.00
187 Keith Rivers/55 3.00 8.00

2008 Donruss Elite Status Gold

*VETS 1-100: 6X TO 15X BASIC CARDS
COMMON ROOKIE (101-200) 5.00 12.00
ROOKIE SEMISTARS 6.00 15.00
ROOKIE UNL.STARS 8.00 20.00
GOLD PRINT RUN 24 SER.#'d SETS
101 Matt Ryan 15.00 40.00
102 Brian Brohm 5.00 12.00
103 Chad Henne 6.00 15.00
104 Andre Woodson 5.00 12.00
105 Joe Flacco 10.00 25.00
106 John David Booty 5.00 12.00
107 Josh Johnson 5.00 12.00
108 Erik Ainge 5.00 12.00
109 Colt Brennan 6.00 15.00
110 Dennis Dixon 5.00 12.00
111 Kevin O'Connell 5.00 12.00
112 Matt Flynn 5.00 12.00
116 Darren McFadden 5.00 12.00
117 Jonathan Stewart 8.00 20.00
118 Rashard Mendenhall 5.00 12.00
119 Felix Jones 5.00 12.00
120 Chris Johnson 6.00 15.00
121 Jamaal Charles 8.00 20.00
122 Ray Rice 5.00 12.00
123 Steve Slaton 5.00 12.00
124 Mike Hart 5.00 12.00
125 Matt Forte 8.00 20.00
127 Kevin Smith 5.00 12.00
136 Peyton Hillis 8.00 20.00
139 Martellus Bennett 6.00 15.00
147 DeSean Jackson 10.00 25.00
148 James Hardy 5.00 12.00
149 Malcolm Kelly 5.00 12.00
150 Early Doucet 5.00 12.00
151 Limas Sweed 5.00 12.00
153 Mario Manningham 5.00 12.00
154 Devin Thomas 5.00 12.00
161 Jordy Nelson 15.00 40.00
169 Davone Bess 6.00 15.00
171 Dexter Jackson 8.00 20.00
174 Josh Morgan 5.00 12.00
180 Chris Long 6.00 15.00
181 Vernon Gholston 5.00 12.00
183 Glenn Dorsey 5.00 12.00
187 Keith Rivers 5.00 12.00
192 Mike Jenkins 5.00 12.00

2008 Donruss Elite Chain Reaction Gold

GOLD PRINT RUN 800 SER.#'d SETS
*BLACK/400: .5X TO 1.2X GOLD/800
BLACK PRINT RUN 400 SER.#'d SETS
*RED/200: .6X TO 1.5X GOLD/800
RED PRINT RUN 200 SER.#'d SETS
1 Adrian Peterson .75 2.00
2 Willie Parker .60 1.50
3 Brian Westbrook .50 1.25
4 Marshawn Lynch .60 1.50
5 Willis McGahee .50 1.25
6 Brandon Jacobs .50 1.25
7 Joseph Addai .50 1.25
8 Marvin Harrison .60 1.50
9 Tom Brady 2.50 6.00
10 Tony Romo .60 1.50
11 Peyton Manning 2.00 5.00
12 Brett Favre 1.50 4.00
13 Carson Palmer .60 1.50
14 Jay Cutler .50 1.25
15 Donovan McNabb .60 1.50
16 Marion Barber .50 1.25
17 Reggie Bush .50 1.25
18 Roy Williams WR .50 1.25
19 Hines Ward .60 1.50
20 Dwayne Bowe .60 1.50
21 Anthony Gonzalez .50 1.25
22 Ted Ginn Jr. .50 1.25
23 Larry Johnson .50 1.25
24 Maurice Jones-Drew .50 1.25
25 Donald Driver .60 1.50

2008 Donruss Elite Chain Reaction Jerseys

STATED PRINT RUN 199 SER.#'d SETS
*PRIME/50: .6X TO 1.5X BASIC JSY/199
PRIME PRINT RUN 50 SER.#'d SETS
1 Adrian Peterson 3.00 8.00
2 Willie Parker 2.50 6.00
3 Brian Westbrook 2.00 5.00
4 Marshawn Lynch 2.50 6.00
5 Willis McGahee 2.00 5.00
6 Brandon Jacobs 2.00 5.00
7 Joseph Addai 2.00 5.00
8 Marvin Harrison 2.50 6.00
9 Tom Brady 10.00 25.00
10 Tony Romo 2.50 6.00
11 Peyton Manning 8.00 20.00
12 Brett Favre 6.00 15.00
13 Carson Palmer 2.50 6.00
14 Jay Cutler 2.00 5.00
15 Donovan McNabb 2.50 6.00
16 Marion Barber 2.00 5.00
17 Reggie Bush 2.00 5.00
18 Roy Williams WR 2.00 5.00
19 Hines Ward 2.50 6.00
20 Dwayne Bowe 2.50 6.00
21 Anthony Gonzalez 2.00 5.00
22 Ted Ginn Jr. 2.00 5.00
23 Larry Johnson 2.00 5.00
24 Maurice Jones-Drew 2.00 5.00
25 Donald Driver 2.50 6.00

2008 Donruss Elite College Ties Autographs

STATED PRINT RUN 50 SER.#'d SETS
1 Simeon Castille 5.00 12.00
2 Chris Long 6.00 15.00
4 Antoine Cason 6.00 15.00
5 Marcus Monk 6.00 15.00
6 Quentin Groves 6.00 15.00
7 Matt Ryan 30.00 60.00
8 DeSean Jackson 10.00 25.00
9 Colt Brennan 6.00 15.00
10 Rashard Mendenhall 5.00 12.00
13 Vernon Gholston 5.00 12.00
14 Dan Connor 5.00 12.00
15 Robert Killebrew 6.00 15.00
17 Darren McFadden 5.00 12.00
18 Early Doucet 5.00 12.00
19 Mario Manningham 5.00 12.00
20 Malcolm Kelly 5.00 12.00
21 Jonathan Stewart 12.00 30.00
22 Brian Brohm 5.00 12.00
23 Chad Henne 6.00 15.00
24 Steve Slaton 5.00 12.00
25 Mike Hart 5.00 12.00

2008 Donruss Elite College Ties Green

GREEN PRINT RUN 800 SER.#'d SETS
*GOLD/400: .5X TO 1.2X GREEN/800
GOLD PRINT RUN 400 SER.#'d SETS
*BLACK/200: .6X TO 1.5X GREEN/800
BLACK PRINT RUN 200 SER.#'d SETS
1 Simeon Castille .50 1.25
2 Chris Long .60 1.50
3 DJ Hall .50 1.25
4 Antoine Cason .60 1.50
5 Marcus Monk .60 1.50
6 Quentin Groves .60 1.50
7 Matt Ryan 1.50 4.00
8 DeSean Jackson 1.00 2.50
9 Colt Brennan .60 1.50
10 Rashard Mendenhall .50 1.25
11 Aqib Talib .75 2.00
12 Ernie Wheelwright .60 1.50
13 Vernon Gholston .50 1.25
14 Dan Connor .50 1.25
15 Robert Killebrew .60 1.50
16 Xavier Adibi .50 1.25
17 Darren McFadden .50 1.25
18 Early Doucet .50 1.25
19 Mario Manningham .50 1.25
20 Malcolm Kelly .50 1.25
21 Jonathan Stewart .75 2.00
22 Brian Brohm .50 1.25
23 Chad Henne .60 1.50
24 Steve Slaton .50 1.25
25 Mike Hart .50 1.25

2008 Donruss Elite College Ties Jerseys

STATED PRINT RUN 150 SER.#'d SETS
*PRIME/50: .8X TO 2X BASIC JSY/150
*PRIME/25: 1X TO 2.5X BASIC JSY/150
PRIME PRINT RUN 25-50
1 Simeon Castille 4.00 10.00
2 Chris Long 3.00 8.00
3 DJ Hall 4.00 10.00
4 Antoine Cason 3.00 8.00
5 Marcus Monk 4.00 10.00
6 Quentin Groves 3.00 8.00
7 Matt Ryan 10.00 25.00
8 DeSean Jackson 5.00 12.00
9 Colt Brennan 3.00 8.00
10 Rashard Mendenhall 2.50 6.00
11 Aqib Talib 4.00 10.00
12 Ernie Wheelwright 3.00 8.00
13 Vernon Gholston 4.00 10.00
14 Dan Connor 4.00 10.00
15 Robert Killebrew 3.00 8.00
16 Xavier Adibi 3.00 8.00
17 Darren McFadden 2.50 6.00
18 Early Doucet 4.00 10.00
19 Mario Manningham 2.50 6.00
20 Malcolm Kelly 6.00 15.00
21 Jonathan Stewart 6.00 15.00
22 Brian Brohm 2.50 6.00
23 Chad Henne 3.00 8.00
24 Steve Slaton 2.50 6.00
25 Mike Hart 6.00 15.00

2008 Donruss Elite College Ties Combos Autographs

STATED PRINT RUN 50 SER.#'d SETS
2 M.Kelly/A.Patrick 10.00 25.00
3 J.Stewart/D.Dixon 20.00 50.00
4 McFadden/F.Jones 6.00 15.00
5 B.Brohm/H.Douglas 6.00 15.00
6 M.Hart/C.Henne 8.00 20.00
9 M.Flynn/E.Doucet 6.00 15.00
10 S.Slaton/O.Schmitt 6.00 15.00
11 S.Crable/J.Adams 10.00 25.00
12 J.Charles/L.Sweed 15.00 40.00
13 E.Royal/B.Flowers 8.00 20.00
16 K.Rivers/T.Thomas 15.00 40.00

2008 Donruss Elite College Ties Combos Green

GREEN PRINT RUN 800 SER.#'d SETS
*GOLD/400: .5X TO 1.2X GREEN/800
GOLD PRINT RUN 400 SER.#'d SETS
*BLACK/200: .6X TO 1.5X GREEN/800
BLACK PRINT RUN 200 SER.#'d SETS
1 E.Ainge/J.Hefney .50 1.25
2 M.Kelly/A.Patrick .50 1.25
3 J.Stewart/D.Dixon .75 2.00
4 D.McFadden/F.Jones .50 1.25
5 B.Brohm/H.Douglas .60 1.50
6 M.Hart/C.Henne .60 1.50
7 S.Ellis/L.Jackson .50 1.25
8 K.Phillips/C.Campbell .60 1.50
9 M.Flynn/E.Doucet .50 1.25
10 S.Slaton/O.Schmitt .50 1.25
11 S.Crable/J.Adams .50 1.25
12 J.Charles/L.Sweed .75 2.00
13 E.Royal/B.Flowers .60 1.50
14 A.Highsmith/C.Steltz .50 1.25
15 J.Booty/F.Davis .50 1.25
16 K.Rivers/T.Thomas .50 1.25
17 M.Manningham/A.Arrington .50 1.25
18 C.Jackson/G.Dorsey .50 1.25
19 D.Hall/S.Castille .50 1.25
20 Q.Groves/R.Brown .60 1.50

2008 Donruss Elite College Ties Combos Jerseys

STATED PRINT RUN 100 SER.#'d SETS
*PRIME/25: .6X TO 1.5X BASIC JSY/100
PRIME PRINT RUN 25 SER.#'d SETS
1 E.Ainge/J.Hefney 10.00 25.00
2 M.Kelly/A.Patrick 10.00 25.00
3 J.Stewart/D.Dixon 10.00 25.00
4 D.McFadden/F.Jones 4.00 10.00
5 B.Brohm/H.Douglas 4.00 10.00
6 M.Hart/C.Henne 5.00 12.00
7 S.Ellis/L.Jackson 5.00 12.00
8 K.Phillips/C.Campbell 5.00 12.00
9 M.Flynn/E.Doucet 4.00 10.00
10 S.Slaton/O.Schmitt 4.00 10.00
11 S.Crable/J.Adams 5.00 12.00
12 J.Charles/L.Sweed 6.00 15.00
13 E.Royal/B.Flowers 5.00 12.00
14 A.Highsmith/C.Steltz 5.00 12.00
15 J.Booty/F.Davis 4.00 10.00
16 K.Rivers/T.Thomas 5.00 12.00
17 M.Manningham/A.Arrington 8.00 20.00
18 C.Jackson/G.Dorsey 5.00 12.00
19 D.Hall/S.Castille 5.00 12.00
20 Q.Groves/R.Brown 5.00 12.00

2008 Donruss Elite National Convention

COMPLETE SET (20) 20.00 50.00
ASPIRATIONS/50: .6X TO 1.5X BASE/499
ASPIRATIONS/50: .5X TO 1.2X BASE/299
STATUS GOLD/25: 1.2X TO 3X BASE/499
STATUS GOLD/25: 1X TO 2.5X BASE/299
STATUS RED/50: .6X TO 1.5X BASE/499
STATUS RED/50: .5X TO 1.2X BASE/299
UNPRICED AUTO PRINT RUN 5-10
101 Matt Ryan/499 2.00 5.00
102 Brian Brohm/499 .60 1.50
103 Chad Henne/499 .75 2.00
105 Joe Flacco/499 1.25 3.00
116 Darren McFadden/499 .60 1.50
117 Jonathan Stewart/499 1.00 2.50
118 Rashard Mendenhall/499 .60 1.50
119 Felix Jones/499 .60 1.50
120 Chris Johnson/499 .75 2.00
121 Jamaal Charles/499 1.00 2.50
125 Matt Forte/499 1.00 2.50
148 James Hardy/499 .60 1.50
149 Malcom Kelly/499 .60 1.50
151 Limas Sweed/499 .60 1.50
153 Mario Manningham/499 .60 1.50
154 Devin Thomas/299 .75 2.00
155 Donnie Avery/299 1.00 2.50
157 Eddie Royal/299 .75 2.00
161 Jordy Nelson/299 2.50 6.00
201 Jake Long/499 1.00 2.50

2008 Donruss Elite Passing the Torch Autographs

STATED PRINT RUN 25 SER.#'d SETS
1 Sayers/Hester/10 250.00 400.00
2 E.Smith/M.Barber 125.00 250.00
3 B.Sanders/Peterson 250.00 500.00
4 T.Thomas/M.Lynch 50.00 100.00
5 J.Kelly/T.Edwards 60.00 120.00
7 Tarkenton/T.Jackson 30.00 60.00
8 R.Craig/F.Gore 40.00 80.00
9 D.Ryans/P.Willis 50.00 100.00
10 E.Campbell/L.White 40.00 80.00
11 D.Marino/B.Favre 250.00 450.00
12 F.Gifford/E.Manning 60.00 120.00
14 J.Rice/C.Johnson 150.00 250.00
15 D.Casper/Z.Miller 25.00 50.00

2008 Donruss Elite Passing the Torch Red

RED PRINT RUN 800 SER.#'d SETS
*GREEN/400: .5X TO 1.2X RED/800
GREEN PRINT RUN 400 SER.#'d SETS
*BLUE/200: .6X TO 1.5X RED/800
BLUE PRINT RUN 200 SER.#'d SETS
1 G.Sayers/D.Hester 2.00 5.00
2 E.Smith/M.Barber 2.50 6.00
3 B.Sanders/A.Peterson 2.50 6.00
4 T.Thomas/M.Lynch 1.25 3.00
5 J.Kelly/T.Edwards 1.50 4.00
6 F.Harris/W.Parker 1.50 4.00
7 F.Tarkenton/T.Jackson 1.50 4.00
8 R.Craig/F.Gore 1.25 3.00
9 D.Ryans/P.Willis 1.25 3.00
10 E.Campbell/L.White 1.50 4.00
11 D.Marino/B.Favre 3.00 8.00
12 F.Gifford/E.Manning 1.50 4.00
13 J.Novacek/J.Witten 1.25 3.00
14 J.Rice/C.Johnson 3.00 8.00
15 D.Casper/Z.Miller 1.00 2.50

2008 Donruss Elite Prime Targets Gold

GOLD PRINT RUN 800 SER.#'d SETS
*BLACK/400: .5X TO 1.2X GOLD/800
BLACK PRINT RUN 400 SER.#'d SETS
*RED/200: .6X TO 1.5X GOLD/800
RED PRINT RUN 200 SER.#'d SETS
1 Terrell Owens .60 1.50
2 Randy Moss .60 1.50
3 Chad Johnson .50 1.25
4 Reggie Wayne .60 1.50
5 Larry Fitzgerald .60 1.50
6 Braylon Edwards .50 1.25
7 Torry Holt .60 1.50
8 Brandon Marshall .60 1.50
9 Joey Galloway .60 1.50
10 T.J. Houshmandzadeh .50 1.25
11 Jason Witten .60 1.50
12 Tony Gonzalez .60 1.50
13 Greg Jennings .50 1.25
14 Plaxico Burress .50 1.25
15 Antonio Gates .60 1.50
16 Marques Colston .50 1.25
17 Lee Evans .60 1.50
18 Steve Smith .60 1.50
19 Calvin Johnson .75 2.00
20 Dwayne Bowe .60 1.50
21 Santonio Holmes .50 1.25
22 Andre Johnson .60 1.50
23 Jeremy Shockey .50 1.25
24 Bernard Berrian .50 1.25
25 Jerricho Cotchery .50 1.25

2008 Donruss Elite Prime Targets Jerseys

STATED PRINT RUN 199 SER.#'d SETS
*PRIME/50: .6X TO 1.5X BASIC JSY/199
PRIME PRINT RUN 50 SER.#'d SETS
1 Terrell Owens 3.00 8.00
2 Randy Moss 3.00 8.00
3 Chad Johnson 2.50 6.00
4 Reggie Wayne 3.00 8.00
5 Larry Fitzgerald 3.00 8.00
6 Braylon Edwards 2.50 6.00
7 Torry Holt 3.00 8.00
8 Brandon Marshall 3.00 8.00
9 Joey Galloway 3.00 8.00
10 T.J. Houshmandzadeh 2.50 6.00
11 Jason Witten 3.00 8.00
12 Tony Gonzalez 3.00 8.00
13 Greg Jennings 2.50 6.00
14 Plaxico Burress 2.50 6.00
15 Antonio Gates 3.00 8.00
16 Marques Colston 2.50 6.00
17 Lee Evans 3.00 8.00
18 Steve Smith 3.00 8.00
19 Calvin Johnson 4.00 10.00
20 Dwayne Bowe 3.00 8.00
21 Santonio Holmes 2.50 6.00
22 Andre Johnson 3.00 8.00
23 Jeremy Shockey 2.50 6.00
24 Bernard Berrian 2.50 6.00
25 Jerricho Cotchery 2.50 6.00

2008 Donruss Elite Stars Red

RED PRINT RUN 800 SER.#'d SETS
*GOLD/400: .5X TO 1.2X RED/800
GOLD PRINT RUN 400 SER.#'d SETS
*BLACK/200: .6X TO 1.5X RED/800
BLACK PRINT RUN 200 SER.#'d SETS
1 Brett Favre 1.50 4.00
2 T.J. Houshmandzadeh .50 1.25
3 Reggie Wayne .60 1.50
4 Warrick Dunn .50 1.25
5 Matt Hasselbeck .50 1.25
6 Terrell Owens .60 1.50
7 Drew Brees .75 2.00
8 Eli Manning .60 1.50
9 Ben Roethlisberger .75 2.00
10 Vince Young .50 1.25
11 Peyton Manning 2.00 5.00
12 Wes Welker .60 1.50
13 Derrick Mason .50 1.25
14 Jerry Porter .50 1.25
15 Donald Driver .60 1.50
16 Derek Anderson .50 1.25
17 Jay Cutler .50 1.25
18 Philip Rivers .75 2.00
19 Donovan McNabb .60 1.50
20 Derrick Ward .50 1.25
21 LaDainian Tomlinson .75 2.00
22 Adrian Peterson .75 2.00
23 Frank Gore .60 1.50
24 Tom Brady 2.50 6.00
25 Tony Romo .60 1.50

2008 Donruss Elite Stars Jerseys Silver

SILVER PRINT RUN 199 SER.#'d SETS
*GOLD/100: .5X TO 1.2X SLVR JSY/199
GOLD PRINT RUN 100 SER.#'d SETS
*BLACK PRIME/50: .6X TO 1.5X SLVR/199
BLACK PRIME PRINT RUN 50 SER.#'d SETS
1 Brett Favre 8.00 20.00
2 T.J. Houshmandzadeh 2.50 6.00
3 Reggie Wayne 3.00 8.00
4 Warrick Dunn 2.50 6.00
5 Matt Hasselbeck 2.50 6.00
6 Terrell Owens 3.00 8.00
7 Drew Brees 4.00 10.00
8 Eli Manning 3.00 8.00
9 Ben Roethlisberger 4.00 10.00
10 Vince Young 2.50 6.00
11 Peyton Manning 10.00 25.00
12 Wes Welker 3.00 8.00
13 Derrick Mason 2.50 6.00
14 Jerry Porter 2.50 6.00
15 Donald Driver 3.00 8.00
16 Derek Anderson 2.50 6.00
17 Jay Cutler 2.50 6.00
18 Philip Rivers 4.00 10.00
19 Donovan McNabb 3.00 8.00
20 Derrick Ward 2.50 6.00
21 LaDainian Tomlinson 4.00 10.00
22 Adrian Peterson 4.00 10.00
23 Frank Gore 3.00 8.00
24 Tom Brady 12.00 30.00
25 Tony Romo 3.00 8.00

2008 Donruss Elite Status Autographs Gold

COMMON CARD 12.00 30.00
SEMISTARS 15.00 40.00
UNLISTED STARS 20.00 50.00
GOLD PRINT RUN 24 SER.#'d SETS
UNPRICED AUTO BLACK PRINT RUN 1
101 Matt Ryan 100.00 200.00
102 Brian Brohm 12.00 30.00
103 Chad Henne 15.00 40.00
105 Joe Flacco 25.00 60.00
106 John David Booty 12.00 30.00
109 Colt Brennan 15.00 40.00
111 Kevin O'Connell 12.00 30.00
112 Matt Flynn 12.00 30.00
116 Darren McFadden 12.00 30.00
117 Jonathan Stewart 20.00 50.00
118 Rashard Mendenhall 12.00 30.00
119 Felix Jones 12.00 30.00
120 Chris Johnson 15.00 40.00
121 Jamaal Charles 20.00 50.00
122 Ray Rice 12.00 30.00
123 Steve Slaton 12.00 30.00
124 Mike Hart 12.00 30.00
125 Matt Forte 25.00 60.00
126 Tashard Choice 12.00 30.00
136 Peyton Hillis 20.00 50.00
147 DeSean Jackson 25.00 60.00
151 Limas Sweed 12.00 30.00
155 Donnie Avery 15.00 40.00
157 Eddie Royal 12.00 30.00
161 Jordy Nelson 40.00 80.00
169 Davone Bess 15.00 40.00
180 Chris Long 15.00 40.00

2008 Donruss Elite Teams Black

BLACK PRINT RUN 800 SER.#'d SETS
*RED/400: .5X TO 1.2X BLACK/800TS
RED PRINT RUN 400 SER.#'d SETS
*GOLD/200: .6X TO 1.5X BLACK/800TS
GOLD PRINT RUN 200 SER.#'d SETS
1 Romo/Owens/Witten .75 2.00
2 Brady/Moss/Maroney 3.00 8.00
3 Palmer/Johnson/Housh .75 2.00
4 Roeth/Parker/Ward 1.00 2.50
5 Warner/Fitzger/Boldin .75 2.00
6 Edwards/Lynch/Evans .75 2.00
7 Favre/Jennings/Grant 2.00 5.00
8 Manning/Wyne/Addai 2.50 6.00
9 Jcksn/Peterson/Taylor 1.00 2.50
10 Eli/Jacobs/Burress .75 2.00
11 Anderson/Edwards/Wins .60 1.50
12 Kitna/Will.WR/Johnson 1.00 2.50
13 Garrard/Taylor/Jones .60 1.50
14 Johnson/Gonzal/Bowe .75 2.00
15 Brees/Bush/Colston 1.00 2.50
16 Jones/Cotchery/Coles .60 1.50
17 McNabb/Wstbrk/Curtis .75 2.00
18 Rivers/Tomlinson/Gates 1.00 2.50
19 Hassel/Alxndr/Branch .60 1.50
20 Bulger/Jackson/Holt .75 2.00
21 Young/White/Jones .60 1.50
22 Campbell/Portis/Cooley .60 1.50
23 McGahee/Mason/Lewis 1.00 2.50
24 Foster/Smith/Williams .75 2.00
25 Benson/Berrian/Hester .75 2.00

2008 Donruss Elite Teams Jerseys

STATED PRINT RUN 199 SER.#'d SETS
*PRIME/50: .6X TO 1.5X BASIC JSY/199
PRIME PRINT RUN 50 SER.#'d SETS
1 Romo/Owens/Witten 12.00 30.00
2 Brady/Moss/Maroney 12.00 30.00
3 Palmer/Johnson/Housh 6.00 15.00
4 Roeth/Parker/Ward 12.00 30.00
5 Warner/Fitzger/Boldin 6.00 15.00
6 Edwards/Lynch/Evans 6.00 15.00
7 Favre/Jennings/Grant 15.00 40.00
8 Manning/Wayne/Addai 12.00 30.00
9 Jcksn/Petersn/Taylor 12.00 30.00
10 Eli/Jacobs/Burress 8.00 20.00
11 Anderson/Edwards/Wins 6.00 15.00
12 Kitna/Will.WR/Johnson 5.00 12.00
13 Garrard/Taylor/Jones 6.00 15.00
14 Johnson/Gonzal/Bowe 6.00 15.00
15 Brees/Bush/Colston 10.00 25.00
16 Jones/Cotchery/Coles 5.00 12.00
17 McNabb/Wstbrk/Curtis 6.00 15.00
18 Rivers/Tomlinson/Gates 8.00 20.00
19 Hassel/Alexndr/Branch 5.00 12.00
20 Bulger/Jackson/Holt 5.00 12.00
21 Young/White/Jones 6.00 15.00
22 Campbell/Portis/Cooley 6.00 15.00
23 McGahee/Mason/Lewis 5.00 12.00
24 Foster/Smith/Willms/190 5.00 12.00
25 Benson/Berrian/Hester 8.00 20.00

2008 Donruss Elite Throwback Threads

STATED PRINT RUN 199 SER.#'d SETS
*PRIME/50: .6X TO 1.5X BASIC JSY/199
*PRIME/20-30: .8X TO 2X BASIC JSY/199
PRIME PRINT RUN 50 SER.#'d SETS
UNPRICED AUTO PRINT RUN 4-10
UNPRICED PRIME AUTO PRINT RUN 2-5
1 Emmitt Smith 10.00 25.00
2 Marion Barber 2.50 6.00
3 Barry Sanders 10.00 25.00
4 Adrian Peterson 4.00 10.00
5 Thurman Thomas 5.00 12.00
6 Marshawn Lynch 3.00 8.00
7 Jim Kelly 6.00 15.00
8 Trent Edwards 2.50 6.00
9 Franco Harris 6.00 15.00
10 Willie Parker 3.00 8.00
11 Fran Tarkenton 6.00 15.00
12 Tarvaris Jackson 2.50 6.00
13 Roger Craig 5.00 12.00
14 Frank Gore 3.00 8.00
15 Earl Campbell 6.00 15.00
16 LenDale White 2.50 6.00
17 Dan Marino 12.00 30.00
18 Brett Favre 8.00 20.00
19 Lawrence Taylor 6.00 15.00
20 Shawne Merriman 2.50 6.00
21 Archie Manning 5.00 12.00
22 Peyton Manning 10.00 25.00
23 Elroy Hirsch 6.00 15.00
24 Torry Holt 3.00 8.00
25 Tom Landry 20.00 40.00
26 Hank Stram 6.00 15.00
27 Frank Gifford 6.00 15.00
28 Eli Manning 5.00 12.00
29 Ken Strong 5.00 12.00
30 Sid Luckman 8.00 20.00
31 E.Smith/M.Barber 12.00 30.00
32 B.Sanders/A.Peterson 20.00 40.00
33 T.Thomas/M.Lynch 6.00 15.00
34 J.Kelly/T.Edwards 8.00 20.00
35 F.Harris/W.Parker 8.00 20.00
36 F.Tarkenton/T.Jackson 6.00 15.00
37 R.Craig/F.Gore 5.00 12.00
38 E.Campbell/L.White 6.00 15.00
39 D.Marino/B.Favre 25.00 60.00
40 L.Taylor/S.Merriman 8.00 20.00
41 A.Manning/P.Manning 15.00 40.00
42 E.Hirsch/T.Holt 10.00 25.00
43 T.Landry/H.Stram 20.00 50.00
44 F.Gifford/E.Manning 8.00 20.00
45 K.Strong/S.Luckman 10.00 25.00

2008 Donruss Elite Throwback Threads Autographs

UNPRICED AUTO PRINT RUN 4-10
UNPRICED PRIME AUTO PRINT RUN 2-5

2008 Donruss Elite Turn of the Century Autographs

COMMON CARD 6.00 15.00
SEMISTARS 8.00 20.00
UNLISTED STARS 10.00 25.00
STATED PRINT RUN 10-100
SERIAL #'d TO 10 NOT PRICED
105 Joe Flacco/50 12.00 30.00
106 John David Booty/100 6.00 15.00
107 Josh Johnson/100 6.00 15.00
108 Erik Ainge/50 6.00 15.00
110 Dennis Dixon/50 6.00 15.00
111 Kevin O'Connell/100 6.00 15.00
112 Matt Flynn/100 6.00 15.00
113 Bernard Morris/50 8.00 20.00
114 Sam Keller/50 6.00 15.00
115 Paul Smith/100 6.00 15.00
120 Chris Johnson/100 8.00 20.00
121 Jamaal Charles/100 10.00 25.00
122 Ray Rice/100 6.00 15.00
123 Steve Slaton/100 6.00 15.00
124 Mike Hart/100 6.00 15.00
125 Matt Forte/50 30.00 80.00
126 Tashard Choice/50 6.00 15.00
128 Allen Patrick/100 6.00 15.00
130 Justin Forsett/50 8.00 20.00
131 Cory Boyd/50 6.00 15.00
132 Dantrell Savage/50 8.00 20.00
133 Kalvin McRae/100 6.00 15.00
134 Darrell Strong/50 8.00 20.00
135 Owen Schmitt/50 6.00 15.00
136 Peyton Hillis/50 10.00 25.00
137 Jacob Hester/50 6.00 15.00
139 Martellus Bennett/50 8.00 20.00
140 John Carlson/50 6.00 15.00
141 Martin Rucker/100 6.00 15.00
142 Brad Cottam/50 6.00 15.00
143 Jermichael Finley/100 6.00 15.00
144 Jacob Tamme/100 8.00 20.00
145 Dustin Keller/50 8.00 20.00
146 Kellen Davis/100 6.00 15.00
148 James Hardy/50 6.00 15.00
152 Andre Caldwell/50 6.00 15.00
153 Mario Manningham/50 6.00 15.00
154 Devin Thomas/50 6.00 15.00
155 Donnie Avery/50 8.00 20.00
156 Earl Bennett/50 10.00 25.00
157 Eddie Royal/50 6.00 15.00
158 Lavelle Hawkins/50 8.00 20.00
159 DJ Hall/50 6.00 15.00
160 Adarius Bowman/100 8.00 20.00
161 Jordy Nelson/50 25.00 50.00
162 Harry Douglas/50 8.00 20.00
163 Jerome Simpson/50 8.00 20.00
164 Dorien Bryant/100 8.00 20.00
165 Will Franklin/100 8.00 20.00
168 Paul Hubbard/50 6.00 15.00
169 Davone Bess/100 8.00 20.00
171 Dexter Jackson/50 10.00 25.00
173 Darius Reynaud/100 6.00 15.00
174 Josh Morgan/50 6.00 15.00
175 Anthony Alridge/100 6.00 15.00
177 Marcus Smith/50 8.00 20.00
178 Mark Bradford/100 6.00 15.00
179 Marcus Monk/50 8.00 20.00
180 Chris Long/100 8.00 20.00
181 Vernon Gholston/100 6.00 15.00
182 Derrick Harvey/100 6.00 15.00
185 Dan Connor/50 6.00 15.00
186 Curtis Lofton/100 8.00 20.00
187 Keith Rivers/50 6.00 15.00
190 Quentin Groves/50 8.00 20.00
191 Erin Henderson/100 8.00 20.00
193 Antoine Cason/50 8.00 20.00
194 Dominique Rodgers-Cromartie/100 8.00 20.00
195 Leodis McKelvin/100 8.00 20.00
198 Tracy Porter/50 8.00 20.00
199 Terrell Thomas/50 6.00 15.00

2008 Donruss Elite Zoning Commission Gold

GOLD PRINT RUN 800 SER.#'d SETS
*BLACK/400: .5X TO 1.2X GOLD/800
BLACK PRINT RUN 400 SER.#'d SETS
*RED/200: .6X TO 1.5X GOLD/800
RED PRINT RUN 200 SER.#'d SETS
1 Plaxico Burress .50 1.25
2 Peyton Manning 2.00 5.00
3 Carson Palmer .60 1.50
4 Joseph Addai .50 1.25
5 Ted Ginn Jr. .50 1.25
6 Steve Smith USC .60 1.50
7 Sidney Rice .50 1.25
8 Vince Young .50 1.25
9 Chester Taylor .50 1.25
10 Marion Barber .50 1.25
11 Rudi Johnson .50 1.25
12 LenDale White .50 1.25
13 Deion Branch .50 1.25
14 Laurence Maroney .60 1.50
15 Tedy Bruschi .60 1.50
16 Kevin Jones .50 1.25
17 Fred Taylor .50 1.25
18 Clinton Portis .50 1.25
19 Zach Thomas .60 1.50
20 Shaun Alexander .50 1.25
21 Thomas Jones .50 1.25
22 DeShaun Foster .50 1.25
23 Ed Reed .60 1.50
24 Jason Witten .60 1.50
25 Deuce McAllister .60 1.50
26 Edgerrin James .60 1.50
27 Jon Kitna .50 1.25
28 Kevin Curtis .50 1.25
29 Brian Urlacher .75 2.00
30 Brandon Marshall .60 1.50
31 Marc Bulger .50 1.25
32 Jamal Lewis .60 1.50
33 Darrelle Revis .50 1.25
34 Jeremy Shockey .50 1.25
35 Santonio Holmes .50 1.25
36 Steven Jackson .50 1.25
37 Laveranues Coles .50 1.25
38 Ronnie Brown .50 1.25
39 Cadillac Williams .60 1.50
40 Antonio Gates .60 1.50

2008 Donruss Elite Zoning Commission Jerseys

STATED PRINT RUN 45-299
*PRIME/50: .6X TO 1.5X BASIC JSY/299
*PRIME/50: .5X TO 1.2X BASIC JSY/45-71
PRIME PRINT RUN 50 SER.#'d SETS
1 Plaxico Burress 2.50 6.00
2 Peyton Manning 10.00 25.00
3 Carson Palmer 3.00 8.00
4 Joseph Addai 2.50 6.00
5 Ted Ginn Jr. 2.50 6.00
6 Steve Smith USC 3.00 8.00
7 Sidney Rice 2.50 6.00
8 Vince Young 2.50 6.00
9 Chester Taylor 2.50 6.00
10 Marion Barber 2.50 6.00
11 Rudi Johnson 2.50 6.00
12 LenDale White 2.50 6.00
13 Deion Branch 2.50 6.00
14 Laurence Maroney 3.00 8.00
15 Tedy Bruschi 3.00 8.00
16 Kevin Jones 2.50 6.00
17 Fred Taylor 2.50 6.00
18 Clinton Portis 2.50 6.00
19 Zach Thomas 3.00 8.00
20 Shaun Alexander 2.50 6.00
21 Thomas Jones 2.50 6.00
22 DeShaun Foster/45 3.00 8.00
23 Ed Reed 3.00 8.00
24 Jason Witten 3.00 8.00
25 Deuce McAllister 3.00 8.00
26 Edgerrin James 3.00 8.00
27 Jon Kitna 2.50 6.00
28 Kevin Curtis 2.50 6.00
29 Brian Urlacher 4.00 10.00
30 Brandon Marshall 3.00 8.00
31 Marc Bulger 2.50 6.00
32 Jamal Lewis 3.00 8.00
33 Darrelle Revis 2.50 6.00
34 Jeremy Shockey 2.50 6.00
35 Santonio Holmes 2.50 6.00
36 Steven Jackson 2.50 6.00
37 Laveranues Coles 2.50 6.00
38 Ronnie Brown 2.50 6.00
39 Cadillac Williams/71 4.00 10.00
40 Antonio Gates 3.00 8.00

2009 Donruss Elite

COMP.SET w/o RC's (100) 7.50 20.00
ROOKIE AUTO PRINT RUN 299-999
200-250 INSERTED IN RETAIL PACKS
1 Kurt Warner .30 .75
2 Larry Fitzgerald .30 .75
3 Anquan Boldin .25 .60
4 Tim Hightower .25 .60
5 Roddy White .25 .60
6 Michael Turner .25 .60
7 Matt Ryan .30 .75
8 Willis McGahee .25 .60
9 Joe Flacco .30 .75
10 Trent Edwards .25 .60
11 Marshawn Lynch .30 .75
12 Lee Evans .30 .75
13 Steve Smith .30 .75
14 DeAngelo Williams .25 .60
15 Jake Delhomme .25 .60
16 Jonathan Stewart .25 .60
17 Devin Hester .30 .75
18 Kyle Orton .25 .60
19 Matt Forte .25 .60
20 Carson Palmer .30 .75
21 Chad Ochocinco .25 .60
22 T.J. Houshmandzadeh .25 .60
23 Brady Quinn .25 .60
24 Jamal Lewis .30 .75
25 Kellen Winslow .25 .60
26 Braylon Edwards .25 .60
27 Tony Romo .30 .75
28 Terrell Owens .30 .75
29 Marion Barber .30 .75
30 Jason Witten .30 .75
31 Jay Cutler .25 .60
32 Brandon Marshall .30 .75
33 Eddie Royal .25 .60
34 Calvin Johnson .40 1.00
35 Kevin Smith .25 .60
36 Aaron Rodgers .75 2.00
37 Ryan Grant .30 .75
38 Greg Jennings .25 .60
39 Matt Schaub .25 .60
40 Andre Johnson .30 .75
41 Steve Slaton .25 .60
42 Peyton Manning 1.00 2.50
43 Joseph Addai .25 .60
44 Reggie Wayne .30 .75
45 Dallas Clark .25 .60
46 David Garrard .25 .60
47 Marcedes Lewis .25 .60
48 Maurice Jones-Drew .25 .60
49 Larry Johnson .25 .60
50 Dwayne Bowe .30 .75
51 Chad Pennington .25 .60
52 Ronnie Brown .25 .60
53 Greg Camarillo .30 .75
54 Bernard Berrian .25 .60
55 Adrian Peterson .40 1.00
56 Chester Taylor .25 .60
57 Tom Brady 1.25 3.00
58 Randy Moss .30 .75
59 Wes Welker .30 .75
60 Drew Brees .40 1.00
61 Reggie Bush .25 .60
62 Jeremy Shockey .25 .60
63 Eli Manning .30 .75
64 Amani Toomer .25 .60
65 Brandon Jacobs .25 .60
66 Kellen Clemens .25 .60
67 Jerricho Cotchery .25 .60
68 Laveranues Coles .25 .60
69 Thomas Jones .25 .60
70 JaMarcus Russell .25 .60
71 Justin Fargas .25 .60
72 Zach Miller .25 .60
73 Donovan McNabb .30 .75
74 Brian Westbrook .25 .60
75 DeSean Jackson .30 .75
76 Ben Roethlisberger .40 1.00
77 Willie Parker .25 .60
78 Hines Ward .30 .75
79 Heath Miller .25 .60
80 Philip Rivers .40 1.00
81 LaDainian Tomlinson .40 1.00
82 Vincent Jackson .25 .60
83 Frank Gore .30 .75
84 Isaac Bruce .40 1.00
85 Matt Hasselbeck .25 .60
86 Deion Branch .25 .60
87 John Carlson .30 .75
88 Marc Bulger .25 .60
89 Steven Jackson .25 .60
90 Donnie Avery .25 .60
91 Derrick Ward .25 .60
92 Earnest Graham .25 .60
93 Antonio Bryant .25 .60

94 Kerry Collins .25 .60
95 Justin Gage .25 .60
96 Chris Johnson .25 .60
97 Jason Campbell .25 .60
98 Clinton Portis .25 .60
99 Santana Moss .30 .75
100 Chris Cooley .25 .60
101 Aaron Curry RC 2.50 6.00
102 Aaron Kelly AU/999 RC 3.00 8.00
103 Aaron Maybin RC 2.00 5.00
104 Alphonso Smith RC 1.50 4.00
105 Andre Brown AU/299 RC 5.00 12.00
106 Arian Foster RC 4.00 10.00
107 Austin Collie AU/299 RC 4.00 10.00
108 B.J. Raji RC 2.00 5.00
109 Brandon Gibson AU/499 RC 4.00 10.00
110 Brandon Pettigrew RC 1.50 4.00
111 Brandon Tate AU/299 RC 5.00 12.00
112 Brian Cushing AU/299 RC 4.00 10.00
113 Brian Hartline RC 2.50 6.00
114 Brian Orakpo AU/299 RC 5.00 12.00
115 Brian Robiskie RC 1.50 4.00
116 Brooks Foster AU/499 RC 3.00 8.00
117 Cameron Morrah RC 1.50 4.00
118 Cedric Peerman AU/499 RC 3.00 8.00
119 Chase Coffman AU/299 RC 4.00 10.00
120 Chip Vaughn RC 1.50 4.00
121 Chris Wells RC 1.50 4.00
122 Clay Matthews AU/299 RC 30.00 60.00
123 Clint Sintim AU/299 RC 4.00 10.00
124 Connor Barwin RC 2.00 5.00
125 Cornelius Ingram AU/499 RC 3.00 8.00
126 D.J. Moore RC 2.00 5.00
127 Darius Passmore RC 1.50 4.00
128 Darrius Heyward-Bey RC 2.50 6.00
129 Demetrius Byrd RC 2.00 5.00
130 Deon Butler AU/299 RC 4.00 10.00
131 Derrick Williams RC 1.50 4.00
132 Devin Moore AU/999 RC 3.00 8.00
133 Dominique Edison AU/499 RC 3.00 8.00
134 Donald Brown RC 1.50 4.00
135 Everette Brown AU/299 RC 4.00 10.00
136 Glen Coffee RC 1.50 4.00
137 Graham Harrell AU/999 RC 6.00 15.00
138 Hakeem Nicks RC 2.00 5.00
139 Hunter Cantwell RC 1.50 4.00
140 Ian Johnson RC 1.50 4.00
141 James Casey AU/499 RC 4.00 10.00
142 James Davis RC 1.50 4.00
143 James Laurinaitis AU/299 RC 6.00 15.00
144 Jared Cook AU/299 RC 5.00 12.00
145 Jarett Dillard RC 1.50 4.00
146 Javon Ringer RC 1.50 4.00
147 Jeremiah Johnson AU/999 RC 3.00 8.00
148 Jeremy Childs RC 1.50 4.00
149 Jeremy Maclin RC 2.00 5.00
150 John Parker Wilson AU/999 RC 3.00 8.00
151 Johnny Knox AU/499 RC 4.00 10.00
152 Josh Freeman RC 1.50 4.00
153 Juaquin Iglesias RC 1.50 4.00
154 Kenny Britt RC 2.50 6.00
155 Kenny McKinley AU/499 RC 3.00 8.00
156 Kevin Ogletree AU/999 RC 4.00 10.00
157 Knowshon Moreno RC 1.50 4.00
158 Kory Sheets AU/999 RC 4.00 10.00
159 Larry English AU/299 RC 5.00 12.00
160 LeSean McCoy RC 4.00 10.00
161 Louis Delmas RC 2.00 5.00
162 Louis Murphy RC 1.50 4.00
163 Malcolm Jenkins RC 1.50 4.00
164 Mark Sanchez RC 1.50 4.00
165 Matthew Stafford RC 8.00 20.00
166 Bear Pascoe RC 2.00 5.00
167 Michael Crabtree RC 2.50 6.00
168 Michael Johnson RC 1.50 4.00
169 Mike Goodson AU/299 RC 5.00 12.00
170 Mike Thomas RC 1.50 4.00
171 Mike Wallace RC 2.50 6.00
172 Mohamed Massaquoi RC 1.50 4.00
173 Nate Davis AU/299 RC 4.00 10.00
174 Nathan Brown AU/999 RC 4.00 10.00
175 P.J. Hill AU/999 RC 3.00 8.00
176 Pat White RC 2.00 5.00
177 Patrick Chung RC 1.50 4.00
178 Patrick Turner AU/299 RC 4.00 10.00
179 Percy Harvin RC 1.50 4.00
180 Peria Jerry RC 1.50 4.00
181 Quan Cosby AU/999 RC 3.00 8.00
182 Quinn Johnson AU/499 RC 3.00 8.00
183 Ramses Barden AU/299 RC 4.00 10.00
184 Rashad Jennings AU/499 RC 4.00 10.00
185 Rashad Johnson RC 1.50 4.00
186 Rey Maualuga RC 2.50 6.00
187 Rhett Bomar RC 1.50 4.00
188 Gartrell Johnson RC 1.50 4.00
189 Sammie Stroughter RC 1.50 4.00
190 Sean Smith RC 1.50 4.00
191 Shawn Nelson AU/499 RC 3.00 8.00
192 Shonn Greene RC 1.50 4.00
193 Stephen McGee RC 1.50 4.00
194 Tom Brandstater AU/299 RC 5.00 12.00
195 Tony Fiammetta AU/499 RC 3.00 8.00
196 Travis Beckum AU/299 RC 4.00 10.00
197 Tyrell Sutton RC 1.50 4.00
198 Tyson Jackson RC 1.50 4.00
199 Vontae Davis AU/299 RC 4.00 10.00
200 William Moore RC 1.50 4.00
201 Andre Smith RC 1.00 2.50
202 Asher Allen RC 1.00 2.50
203 Brandon Underwood RC 1.00 2.50
204 Alex Mack RC 1.00 2.50
205 Captain Munnerlyn RC 1.25 3.00
206 Chris Clemons RC 1.00 2.50
207 Cody Brown RC 1.00 2.50
208 Coye Francies RC 1.00 2.50
209 Eric Wood RC 1.00 2.50
210 Darcel McBath RC 1.00 2.50
211 Darius Butler RC 1.25 3.00
212 Darry Beckwith RC 1.00 2.50
213 David Bruton RC 1.00 2.50
214 Sherrod Martin RC 1.00 2.50
215 Eben Britton RC 1.25 3.00
216 Richard Quinn RC 1.25 3.00
217 Eugene Monroe RC 1.00 2.50
218 Evander Hood RC 1.50 4.00
219 Fili Moala RC 1.00 2.50
220 Duke Robinson RC 1.00 2.50
221 Gerald McRath RC 1.25 3.00
222 Herman Johnson RC 1.25 3.00
223 Jairus Byrd RC 1.50 4.00
224 Jamon Meredith RC 1.00 2.50
225 Jarron Gilbert RC 1.25 3.00
226 Jason Phillips RC 1.25 3.00
227 Jason Smith RC 1.00 2.50
228 Jason Williams RC 1.25 3.00
229 Jasper Brinkley RC 1.25 3.00
230 Anthony Hill RC 1.00 2.50
231 Kaluka Maiava RC 1.00 2.50
232 Keenan Lewis RC 1.50 4.00
233 Kraig Urbik RC 1.25 3.00
234 Lawrence Sidbury RC 1.00 2.50
235 Marcus Freeman RC 1.00 2.50
236 Michael Hamlin RC 1.00 2.50
237 Michael Oher RC 1.50 4.00
238 Mike Mickens RC 1.00 2.50
239 Nic Harris RC 1.25 3.00
240 Paul Kruger RC 1.50 4.00
241 Phil Loadholt RC 1.25 3.00
242 Robert Ayers RC 1.00 2.50
243 Ron Brace RC 1.25 3.00
244 Scott McKillop RC 1.00 2.50
245 Sen'Derrick Marks RC 1.00 2.50
246 Troy Kropog RC 1.00 2.50
247 Tyrone McKenzie RC 1.25 3.00
248 Victor Harris RC 1.25 3.00
249 William Beatty RC 1.00 2.50
250 Zack Follett RC 1.00 2.50

2009 Donruss Elite Aspirations

*VETS/70-99: 4X TO 10X BASIC CARDS
*VETS/46-69: 5X TO 12X BASIC CARDS
*VETS/20-29: 8X TO 20X BASIC CARDS
*VETS/10-19: 10X TO 25X BASIC CARDS
*ROOK/70-99: .2X TO .5X STATUS GOLD
*ROOK/46-69: .25X TO .6X STATUS GOLD
*ROOK/30-45: .3X TO .8X STATUS GOLD
*ROOK/20-29: .4X TO 1X STATUS GOLD
*ROOK/10-19: .6X TO 1.5X STATUS GOLD
STATED PRINT RUN 1-99
SERIAL #'d UNDER 10 NOT PRICED

2009 Donruss Elite Retail

COMPLETE SET (100) 7.50 20.00
*VETS: .4X TO 1X BASIC CARDS
RETAIL PRINTED ON WHITE STOCK

2009 Donruss Elite Status

*VETS/70-99: 4X TO 10X BASIC CARDS
*ROOK/70-99: .2X TO .5X STATUS GOLD
*VETS/46-69: 5X TO 12X BASIC CARDS
*ROOK/46-69: .25X TO .6X STATUS GOLD
*VETS/30-45: 6X TO 15X BASIC CARDS
*ROOK/30-45: .3X TO .8X STATUS GOLD
*VETS/20-29: 8X TO 20X BASIC CARDS
*ROOK/20-29: .4X TO 1X STATUS GOLD
*VETS/10-19: 10X TO 25X BASIC CARDS
*ROOK/10-19: .6X TO 1.5X STATUS GOLD
STATED PRINT RUN 1-99
SERIAL #'d UNDER 10 NOT PRICED

2009 Donruss Elite Status Gold

*VETS: 8X TO 20X BASIC CARDS
COMMON ROOKIE 5.00 12.00
ROOKIE SEMISTARS 6.00 15.00
ROOKIE UNL.STARS 8.00 20.00
STATED PRINT RUN 24 SER.#'d SETS
101 Aaron Curry 8.00 20.00
103 Aaron Maybin 6.00 15.00
108 B.J. Raji 6.00 15.00
110 Brandon Pettigrew 5.00 12.00
111 Brandon Tate 6.00 15.00
112 Brian Cushing 5.00 12.00
114 Brian Orakpo 6.00 15.00
115 Brian Robiskie 5.00 12.00
121 Chris Wells 5.00 12.00
122 Clay Matthews 20.00 50.00
128 Darrius Heyward-Bey 8.00 20.00
131 Derrick Williams 5.00 12.00
134 Donald Brown 5.00 12.00
136 Glen Coffee 5.00 12.00
137 Graham Harrell 5.00 12.00
138 Hakeem Nicks 6.00 15.00
143 James Laurinaitis 10.00 25.00
149 Jeremy Maclin 6.00 15.00
152 Josh Freeman 5.00 12.00
153 Juaquin Iglesias 5.00 12.00
154 Kenny Britt 8.00 20.00
157 Knowshon Moreno 5.00 12.00
160 LeSean McCoy 12.00 30.00
163 Malcolm Jenkins 5.00 12.00
164 Mark Sanchez 5.00 12.00
165 Matthew Stafford 25.00 60.00
167 Michael Crabtree 8.00 20.00
172 Mohamed Massaquoi 5.00 12.00
173 Nate Davis 5.00 12.00
176 Pat White 6.00 15.00
179 Percy Harvin 5.00 12.00
182 Quinn Johnson 5.00 12.00
186 Rey Maualuga 8.00 20.00
192 Shonn Greene 5.00 12.00

2009 Donruss Elite Chain Reaction Gold

GOLD PRINT RUN 899 SER.#'d SETS
*BLACK/399: .5X TO 1.2X GOLD/899
BLACK PRINT RUN 399 SER.#'d SETS
*RED/199: .6X TO 1.5X GOLD/899
RED PRINT RUN 199 SER.#'d SETS
1 Ryan Grant 1.00 2.50
2 Willie Parker .75 2.00
3 Chris Johnson .75 2.00
4 Ricky Williams 1.00 2.50
5 Steven Jackson .75 2.00
6 Santana Moss 1.00 2.50
7 T.J. Houshmandzadeh .75 2.00
8 Steve Slaton .75 2.00
9 DeSean Jackson 1.00 2.50
10 Anthony Gonzalez .75 2.00
11 Derrick Mason .75 2.00
12 Bernard Berrian .75 2.00
13 Devin Hester 1.00 2.50
14 Laveranues Coles .75 2.00
15 Justin Gage .75 2.00
16 Laurence Maroney 1.00 2.50
17 Kevin Curtis .75 2.00
18 Vernon Davis .75 2.00
19 Brandon Jacobs .75 2.00
20 Chris Cooley .75 2.00
21 Antonio Gates 1.00 2.50
22 Thomas Jones .75 2.00
23 Marion Barber 1.00 2.50
24 Reggie Bush .75 2.00
25 Larry Johnson .75 2.00

2009 Donruss Elite Chain Reaction Jerseys

STATED PRINT RUN 175-299
*PRIME/33-50: .8X TO 2X BASIC JSY
PRIME PRINT RUN 33-50
1 Ryan Grant/299 2.50 6.00
2 Willie Parker/299 2.00 5.00
3 Chris Johnson/299 2.00 5.00
4 Ricky Williams/299 2.50 6.00
5 Steven Jackson/299 2.00 5.00
6 Santana Moss/299 2.50 6.00
7 T.J. Houshmandzadeh/175 2.00 5.00
8 Steve Slaton/299 2.00 5.00
9 DeSean Jackson/299 2.50 6.00
10 Anthony Gonzalez/299 2.00 5.00
11 Derrick Mason/299 2.00 5.00
12 Bernard Berrian/299 2.00 5.00
13 Devin Hester/299 2.50 6.00
14 Laveranues Coles/299 2.00 5.00
15 Justin Gage/299 2.00 5.00
16 Laurence Maroney/299 2.50 6.00
17 Kevin Curtis/299 2.00 5.00
18 Vernon Davis/299 2.00 5.00
19 Brandon Jacobs/299 2.00 5.00
20 Chris Cooley/299 2.00 5.00
21 Antonio Gates/299 2.50 6.00
22 Thomas Jones/299 2.00 5.00
23 Marion Barber/299 2.50 6.00
24 Reggie Bush/299 2.00 5.00
25 Larry Johnson/299 2.00 5.00

2009 Donruss Elite College Ties Green

GREEN PRINT RUN 899 SER.#'d SETS
*BLACK/199: .6X TO 1.5X GREEN/899
BLACK PRINT RUN 199 SER.#'d SETS
*GOLD/399: .5X TO 1.2X GREEN/899
GOLD PRINT RUN 399 SER.#'d SETS
1 Brandon Pettigrew .50 1.25
2 Brian Robiskie .50 1.25
3 Chase Coffman .50 1.25
4 Chris Wells .50 1.25
5 Darrius Heyward-Bey .75 2.00
6 Derrick Williams .50 1.25
7 Donald Brown .50 1.25
8 Hakeem Nicks .60 1.50
9 Javon Ringer .50 1.25
10 Jeremy Maclin .60 1.50
11 Josh Freeman .50 1.25
12 Juaquin Iglesias .50 1.25
13 Kenny Britt .75 2.00
14 Knowshon Moreno .50 1.25
15 LeSean McCoy 1.25 3.00
16 Mark Sanchez .50 1.25
17 Matthew Stafford 2.50 6.00
18 Michael Crabtree .75 2.00
19 Mohamed Massaquoi .50 1.25
20 Nate Davis .50 1.25
21 Pat White .60 1.50
22 Percy Harvin .50 1.25
23 Rashad Jennings .60 1.50
24 Rhett Bomar .50 1.25
25 Shonn Greene .50 1.25

2009 Donruss Elite College Ties Autographs

STATED PRINT RUN 50 SER.#'d SETS
1 Brandon Pettigrew 5.00 12.00
3 Chase Coffman 5.00 12.00
4 Chris Wells 5.00 12.00
5 Darrius Heyward-Bey 8.00 20.00
6 Derrick Williams 5.00 12.00
7 Donald Brown 5.00 12.00
8 Hakeem Nicks 6.00 15.00
9 Javon Ringer 5.00 12.00
10 Jeremy Maclin 6.00 15.00
11 Josh Freeman 5.00 12.00
12 Juaquin Iglesias 5.00 12.00
13 Kenny Britt 8.00 20.00
14 Knowshon Moreno 5.00 12.00
15 LeSean McCoy 12.00 30.00
16 Mark Sanchez 5.00 12.00
17 Matthew Stafford 40.00 100.00
18 Michael Crabtree 8.00 20.00
19 Mohamed Massaquoi 5.00 12.00
20 Nate Davis 5.00 12.00
21 Pat White 6.00 15.00
22 Percy Harvin 5.00 12.00
23 Rashad Jennings 6.00 15.00
24 Rhett Bomar 5.00 12.00
25 Shonn Greene 5.00 12.00

2009 Donruss Elite College Ties Combos Green

GREEN PRINT RUN 899 SER.#'d SETS
*BLACK/199: .6X TO 1.5X GREEN/899
BLACK PRINT RUN 199 SER.#'d SETS
*GOLD/399: .5X TO 1.2X GREEN/899
GOLD PRINT RUN 399 SER.#'d SETS
1 G.Coffee/J.Wilson .50 1.25
2 A.Kelly/J.Davis .50 1.25
3 L.Murphy/P.Harvin .50 1.25
4 Pascoe/Brandstater .60 1.50
5 K.Moreno/M.stafford 2.50 6.00
6 D.Byrd/Q.Johnson .60 1.50
7 C.Coffman/J.Maclin .60 1.50
8 B.Tate/H.Nicks .60 1.50
9 M.Jenkins/C.Wells .50 1.25
10 Laurinaitis/B.Robiskie .50 1.25
11 A.Maybin/D.Williams .60 1.50
12 G.Orton/K.Sheets .60 1.50
13 J.Casey/J.Dillard .60 1.50
14 J.Cook/K.McKinley .60 1.50
15 B.Orakpo/Q.Cosby .60 1.50
16 M.Crabtree/G.Harrell .75 2.00
17 M.Sanchez/P.Turner .50 1.25
18 Maualuga/B.Cushing .50 1.25
19 C.Peerman/K.Ogletree .60 1.50
20 P.Hill/T.Beckum .50 1.25
21 J.Ringer/D.Thomas .50 1.25
22 S.Greene/D.Clark .50 1.25
23 Heyward-Bey/L.Jordan .75 2.00
24 J.Freeman/J.Nelson .60 1.50
25 K.Britt/R.Rice .75 2.00

2009 Donruss Elite College Ties Combos Autographs

STATED PRINT RUN 50 SER.#'d SETS
1 G.Coffee/J.Wilson 25.00 50.00
5 K.Moreno/M.stafford 30.00 80.00
7 C.Coffman/J.Maclin 15.00 40.00
8 B.Tate/H.Nicks 8.00 20.00
9 M.Jenkins/C.Wells 15.00 40.00
14 J.Cook/K.McKinley 12.00 30.00
15 B.Orakpo/Q.Cosby 12.00 30.00
16 M.Crabtree/G.Harrell 10.00 25.00
17 M.Sanchez/P.Turner 6.00 15.00
18 Maualuga/B.Cushing 6.00 15.00
19 C.Peerman/K.Ogletree 8.00 20.00
21 J.Ringer/D.Thomas 6.00 15.00
22 S.Greene/D.Clark 15.00 40.00
23 Heyward-Bey/L.Jordan 12.00 30.00
24 J.Freeman/J.Nelson 15.00 40.00
25 K.Britt/R.Rice 10.00 25.00

2009 Donruss Elite Passing the Torch Red

RED PRINT RUN 999 SER.#'d SETS
*BLUE/199: .6X TO 1.5X RED/999
BLUE PRINT RUN 199 SER.#'d SETS
*GREEN/499: .5X TO 1.2X RED/999
GREEN PRINT RUN 499 SER.#'d SETS
1 G.Sayers/M.Forte 1.50 4.00
2 B.Sanders/K.Smith 2.50 6.00
3 J.Namath/B.Favre 3.00 8.00
4 B.Jackson/McFadden 2.00 5.00
5 T.Dorsett/F.Jones 1.50 4.00
6 D.Maynard/D.Keller 1.25 3.00
7 M.Allen/J.Charles 1.50 4.00
8 E.Campbell/C.Johnson 1.50 4.00
9 M.Irvin/A.Johnson 1.50 4.00
10 R.Berry/R.Wayne 1.25 3.00
11 A.Reed/L.Evans 1.25 3.00
12 R.Craig/F.Gore 1.25 3.00
13 J.Stallworth/S.Holmes 1.25 3.00
14 T.Barber/B.Jacobs 1.25 3.00
15 J.Mackey/D.Clark 1.00 2.50

2009 Donruss Elite Passing the Torch Autographs

STATED PRINT RUN 25 SER.#'d SETS
1 Sayers/M.Forte 40.00 80.00
2 B.Sanders/K.Smith 75.00 150.00
3 J.Namath/B.Favre 200.00 350.00
4 B.Jackson/McFadden 75.00 150.00
5 T.Dorsett/F.Jones 50.00 100.00
6 D.Maynard/D.Keller 25.00 50.00
7 M.Allen/J.Charles 30.00 60.00
8 Campbell/C.Johnson 30.00 60.00
9 Irvin/A.Johnson 50.00 100.00
10 R.Berry/R.Wayne 30.00 60.00
11 A.Reed/L.Evans
12 R.Craig/F.Gore 30.00 60.00
13 J.Stallworth/S.Holmes 40.00 80.00
14 T.Barber/B.Jacobs 25.00 60.00
15 J.Mackey/D.Clark 20.00 60.00

2009 Donruss Elite Prime Targets Gold

GOLD PRINT RUN 899 SER.#'d SETS
*BLACK/399: .5X TO 1.2X GOLD/899
BLACK PRINT RUN 399 SER.#'d SETS
*RED/199: .6X TO 1.5X GOLD/899
RED PRINT RUN 199 SER.#'d SETS
1 Andre Johnson 1.00 2.50
2 Roddy White .75 2.00
3 Calvin Johnson 1.25 3.00
4 Anquan Boldin .75 2.00
5 Reggie Wayne 1.00 2.50
6 Lee Evans 1.00 2.50
7 Dwayne Bowe 1.00 2.50
8 Hines Ward 1.00 2.50
9 Braylon Edwards .75 2.00
10 Torry Holt 1.00 2.50
11 Donald Driver 1.00 2.50
12 Marques Colston .75 2.00
13 Eddie Royal .75 2.00
14 Justin McCareins .75 2.00
15 Tony Gonzalez 1.00 2.50
16 Dallas Clark .75 2.00
17 Adrian Peterson 1.25 3.00
18 Brian Westbrook .75 2.00
19 Maurice Jones-Drew .75 2.00
20 Marshawn Lynch 1.00 2.50
21 LaDainian Tomlinson 1.25 3.00
22 Derrick Ward .75 2.00
23 Joseph Addai .75 2.00
24 Randy Moss 1.00 2.50
25 Jason Witten 1.00 2.50

2009 Donruss Elite Prime Targets Jerseys

JERSEY PRINT RUN 150-299
*PRIME/50: .8X TO 2X BASIC JSY/260-299
*PRIME/50: .6X TO 1.5X BASIC JSY/150
PRIME PRINT RUN 50 SER.#'d SETS
1 Andre Johnson/299 2.50 6.00
2 Roddy White/299 2.00 5.00
3 Calvin Johnson/299 3.00 8.00
4 Anquan Boldin/299 2.00 5.00
5 Reggie Wayne/150 3.00 8.00
6 Lee Evans/299 2.50 6.00
7 Dwayne Bowe/299 2.50 6.00
8 Hines Ward/299 2.50 6.00
9 Braylon Edwards/299 2.00 5.00
10 Torry Holt/299 2.50 6.00
11 Donald Driver/299 2.50 6.00
12 Marques Colston/299 2.00 5.00
13 Eddie Royal/299 2.00 5.00
14 Justin McCareins/299 2.00 5.00
15 Tony Gonzalez/299 2.50 6.00
16 Dallas Clark/299 2.00 5.00
17 Adrian Peterson/299 3.00 8.00
18 Brian Westbrook/299 2.00 5.00
19 Maurice Jones-Drew/299 2.00 5.00
20 Marshawn Lynch/299 2.50 6.00
21 LaDainian Tomlinson/299 3.00 8.00
22 Derrick Ward/260 2.00 5.00
23 Joseph Addai/299 2.00 5.00
24 Randy Moss/299 2.50 6.00
25 Jason Witten/299 2.50 6.00

2009 Donruss Elite Series Red

RED PRINT RUN 999 SER.#'d SETS
*BLUE/199: .6X TO 1.5X RED/999
BLUE PRINT RUN 199 SER.#'d SETS
*GREEN/499: .5X TO 1.2X RED/999
GREEN PRINT RUN 499 SER.#'d SETS
1 LaDainian Tomlinson 1.25 3.00
2 Peyton Manning 3.00 8.00
3 Jake Delhomme .75 2.00
4 Tom Brady 4.00 10.00
5 Donovan McNabb 1.00 2.50
6 Ray Lewis 1.25 3.00
7 Vincent Jackson .75 2.00
8 Jason Campbell .75 2.00
9 Kellen Winslow .75 2.00
10 Kyle Orton .75 2.00
11 Joe Flacco 1.00 2.50
12 Correll Buckhalter .75 2.00
13 Matt Ryan 1.00 2.50
14 Aaron Rodgers 2.50 6.00
15 Bob Sanders 1.00 2.50
16 Deuce McAllister 1.00 2.50
17 Joey Galloway 1.00 2.50
18 Roddy White .75 2.00
19 Jonathan Stewart .75 2.00
20 Matt Hasselbeck .75 2.00
21 Jamal Lewis 1.00 2.50
22 Willis McGahee .75 2.00
23 Marc Bulger .75 2.00
24 Warrick Dunn .75 2.00
25 Leon Washington .75 2.00
26 Matt Schaub .75 2.00
27 Justin Fargas .75 2.00
28 David Garrard .75 2.00
29 Jeff Garcia .75 2.00
30 Trent Edwards .75 2.00
31 DeMeco Ryans 1.00 2.50
32 Fred Taylor .75 2.00
33 Chester Taylor .75 2.00
34 Patrick Willis 1.00 2.50
35 Tony Romo 1.00 2.50

2009 Donruss Elite Series Jerseys

JERSEY PRINT RUN 5-299
*PRIME/35-50: .8X TO 2X BASIC JSY/299
*PRIME/35-50: .6X TO 1.5X BASIC JSY/150
PRIME PRINT RUN 1-50
1 LaDainian Tomlinson/299 3.00 8.00
2 Peyton Manning/299 8.00 20.00
4 Tom Brady/299 10.00 25.00
5 Donovan McNabb/299 2.50 6.00
6 Ray Lewis/299 3.00 8.00
7 Vincent Jackson/299 2.00 5.00
8 Jason Campbell/299 2.00 5.00
9 Kellen Winslow/299 2.00 5.00
11 Joe Flacco/299 2.50 6.00
12 Correll Buckhalter/299 2.00 5.00
15 Bob Sanders/299 2.50 6.00
16 Deuce McAllister/299 2.50 6.00
17 Joey Galloway/299 2.50 6.00
18 Roddy White/150 2.50 6.00
19 Jonathan Stewart/299 2.00 5.00
20 Matt Hasselbeck/299 2.00 5.00
21 Jamal Lewis/299 2.50 6.00
22 Willis McGahee/299 2.00 5.00
23 Marc Bulger/299 2.00 5.00
25 Leon Washington/299 2.00 5.00
26 Matt Schaub/299 2.00 5.00
27 Justin Fargas/299 2.00 5.00
28 David Garrard/299 2.00 5.00
29 Jeff Garcia/299 2.00 5.00
30 Trent Edwards/299 2.00 5.00
31 DeMeco Ryans/299 2.50 6.00
32 Fred Taylor/299 2.00 5.00
33 Chester Taylor/299 2.00 5.00
34 Patrick Willis/299 2.50 6.00
35 Tony Romo/299 2.50 6.00

2009 Donruss Elite Stars Gold

GOLD PRINT RUN 899 SER.#'d SETS
*BLACK/399: .5X TO 1.2X GOLD/899
BLACK PRINT RUN 399 SER.#'d SETS
*RED/199: .6X TO 1.5X GOLD/899
RED PRINT RUN 199 SER.#'d SETS
1 Drew Brees 1.25 3.00
2 Jay Cutler .75 2.00
3 Peyton Manning 3.00 8.00
4 Philip Rivers 1.25 3.00
5 Brandon Jacobs .75 2.00
6 Frank Gore 1.00 2.50
7 Terrell Owens 1.00 2.50
8 Brian Westbrook .75 2.00
9 Tony Romo 1.00 2.50
10 Maurice Jones-Drew .75 2.00
11 Adrian Peterson 1.25 3.00
12 Brett Favre 2.50 6.00
13 LaDainian Tomlinson 1.25 3.00
14 DeAngelo Williams .75 2.00
15 Eli Manning 1.00 2.50
16 Anquan Boldin .75 2.00
17 Clinton Portis .75 2.00
18 Brian Urlacher 1.25 3.00
19 Greg Jennings .75 2.00
20 Randy Moss 1.00 2.50
21 Steve Smith 1.00 2.50
22 Tom Brady 4.00 10.00
23 T.J. Houshmandzadeh .75 2.00
24 Ben Roethlisberger 1.25 3.00
25 Reggie Wayne 1.00 2.50

2009 Donruss Elite Stars Jerseys Gold

JERSEY PRINT RUN 100-299
*PRIME/40-50: .8X TO 2X BASIC JSY/299
*PRIME/40-50: .6X TO 1.5X BASIC JSY/100-150
PRIME PRINT RUN 40-50
1 Drew Brees/299 3.00 8.00
2 Jay Cutler/299 2.00 5.00
3 Peyton Manning/299 8.00 20.00
4 Philip Rivers/299 3.00 8.00
5 Brandon Jacobs/299 2.00 5.00
6 Frank Gore/299 2.50 6.00
7 Terrell Owens/299 2.50 6.00
8 Brian Westbrook/299 2.00 5.00
9 Tony Romo/299 2.50 6.00
10 Maurice Jones-Drew/299 2.00 5.00
11 Adrian Peterson/299 3.00 8.00
12 Brett Favre/299 6.00 15.00
13 LaDainian Tomlinson/299 3.00 8.00
14 DeAngelo Williams/299 2.00 5.00
15 Eli Manning/299 2.50 6.00
16 Anquan Boldin/299 2.00 5.00
17 Clinton Portis/100 2.50 6.00
18 Brian Urlacher/299 3.00 8.00
19 Greg Jennings/299 2.00 5.00
20 Randy Moss/299 2.50 6.00
21 Steve Smith/299 2.50 6.00
22 Tom Brady/299 10.00 25.00
23 T.J. Houshmandzadeh/150 2.50 6.00
24 Ben Roethlisberger/299 3.00 8.00
25 Reggie Wayne/299 2.50 6.00

2009 Donruss Elite Status Autographs Gold

GOLD PRINT RUN 24 SER.#'d SETS
101 Aaron Curry 15.00 40.00
102 Aaron Kelly 10.00 25.00
105 Andre Brown 12.00 30.00
107 Austin Collie 10.00 25.00
108 B.J. Raji 12.00 30.00
109 Brandon Gibson 12.00 30.00
110 Brandon Pettigrew 10.00 25.00
111 Brandon Tate 12.00 30.00
112 Brian Cushing 10.00 25.00
114 Brian Orakpo 12.00 30.00
115 Brian Robiskie 10.00 25.00
116 Brooks Foster 10.00 25.00
118 Cedric Peerman 10.00 25.00
119 Chase Coffman 10.00 25.00
121 Chris Wells 10.00 25.00
122 Clay Matthews 60.00 120.00
123 Clint Sintim 10.00 25.00
125 Cornelius Ingram 10.00 25.00
128 Darrius Heyward-Bey 15.00 40.00
130 Deon Butler 10.00 25.00
131 Derrick Williams 10.00 25.00
132 Devin Moore 10.00 25.00
133 Dominique Edison 10.00 25.00
134 Donald Brown 10.00 25.00
135 Everette Brown 10.00 25.00
136 Glen Coffee 10.00 25.00
137 Graham Harrell 25.00 60.00
138 Hakeem Nicks 12.00 30.00
141 James Casey 12.00 30.00
143 James Laurinaitis 20.00 50.00
144 Jared Cook 12.00 30.00
146 Javon Ringer 10.00 25.00
147 Jeremiah Johnson 10.00 25.00
149 Jeremy Maclin 12.00 30.00
150 John Parker Wilson 10.00 25.00
151 Johnny Knox 12.00 30.00
152 Josh Freeman 10.00 25.00
153 Juaquin Iglesias 10.00 25.00
154 Kenny Britt 15.00 40.00
155 Kenny McKinley 10.00 25.00
156 Kevin Ogletree 12.00 30.00
157 Knowshon Moreno 10.00 25.00
158 Kory Sheets 12.00 30.00
159 Larry English 12.00 30.00
160 LeSean McCoy 25.00 60.00
163 Malcolm Jenkins 10.00 25.00
164 Mark Sanchez 50.00 120.00
165 Matthew Stafford 125.00 200.00
167 Michael Crabtree 15.00 40.00
169 Mike Goodson 12.00 30.00
170 Mike Thomas 10.00 25.00
171 Mike Wallace 15.00 40.00
172 Mohamed Massaquoi 10.00 25.00
173 Nate Davis 10.00 25.00
174 Nathan Brown 12.00 30.00
175 P.J. Hill 10.00 25.00
176 Pat White 12.00 30.00
178 Patrick Turner 10.00 25.00
179 Percy Harvin 10.00 25.00
181 Quan Cosby 10.00 25.00
182 Quinn Johnson 10.00 25.00
183 Ramses Barden 10.00 25.00
184 Rashad Jennings 12.00 30.00
186 Rey Maualuga 15.00 40.00
187 Rhett Bomar 10.00 25.00
191 Shawn Nelson 10.00 25.00
192 Shonn Greene 10.00 25.00
193 Stephen McGee 10.00 25.00
194 Tom Brandstater 12.00 30.00
195 Tony Fiammetta 10.00 25.00
196 Travis Beckum 10.00 25.00
198 Tyson Jackson 10.00 25.00
199 Vontae Davis 10.00 25.00

2009 Donruss Elite Throwback Threads

DUAL JERSEY PRINT RUN 30-299
1 Willis McGahee/65
3 Jamal Lewis/130 5.00 12.00
5 Deion Branch/299 3.00 8.00
6 Terrell Owens/299 4.00 10.00
7 Randy Moss/299 4.00 10.00
8 Laveranues Coles/299 3.00 8.00
9 Thomas Jones/299 3.00 8.00
10 Clinton Portis/299 3.00 8.00
11 Warrick Dunn/30 5.00 12.00
12 Drew Brees/299 5.00 12.00
13 Edgerrin James/299 4.00 10.00
14 Santana Moss/299 4.00 10.00
15 Jeff Garcia/285 3.00 8.00
16 Alge Crumpler/299 3.00 8.00
17 Doucet/J.Russell/299 5.00 12.00
18 B.Brohm/M.Bush/299 4.00 10.00
19 B.Quinn/J.Jones/100 12.00 30.00
20 Benson/J.Charles/280 5.00 12.00
21 J.Booty/M.Leinart/299 4.00 10.00
22 G.Sayers/M.Forte/140 8.00 20.00
23 J.Namath/B.Favre/100 15.00 40.00
24 Dickerson/McFad/250 6.00 15.00
25 Campbell/L.White/200 6.00 15.00
26 Deion Sanders/299 8.00 20.00
28 Devery Henderson/299 3.00 8.00
29 Frank Gore/214 4.00 10.00
30 Reggie Williams/149
31 Lee Evans/200 4.00 10.00
32 Jay Cutler/275 3.00 8.00
33 Carson Palmer/299 4.00 10.00
34 Matt Leinart/299 3.00 8.00
35 Reggie Bush/299 3.00 8.00
36 Willis McGahee/299 3.00 8.00
37 Jeremy Shockey/299 3.00 8.00
38 Cadillac Williams/50
39 Peyton Manning/180 12.00 30.00
40 Larry Fitzgerald/299 4.00 10.00
41 Mario Williams/299 4.00 10.00
42 Kellen Winslow/275 3.00 8.00
43 Braylon Edwards/299 3.00 8.00
44 Ronnie Brown/130 4.00 10.00
45 Jevon Kearse/299 3.00 8.00
46 Anquan Boldin/299 3.00 8.00
47 Felix Jones/299 6.00 15.00
48 Vince Young/80 4.00 10.00
49 Adrian Peterson/299 15.00 30.00
50 Dwayne Bowe/299 4.00 10.00

2009 Donruss Elite Throwback Threads Prime

*PRIME/35-50: .8X TO 2X BASE JSY/214-299
*PRIME/20-29: 1X TO 2.5X BASE JSY/214-299
*PRIME/45-50: .6X TO 1.5X BASE JSY/65-180
*PRIME/45-50: .5X TO 1.2X BASE JSY/30-50
PRIME PRINT RUN 1-50
SERIAL #'d UNDER 20 NOT PRICED
2 Michael Turner/45 6.00 15.00

2009 Donruss Elite Throwback Threads Autographs

STATED PRINT RUN 5-25
SERIAL #'d UNDER 15 NOT PRICED
12 Drew Brees/25 50.00 100.00
18 B.Brohm/M.Bush/25 15.00 40.00
20 Benson/J.Charles/25 25.00 60.00
21 J.Booty/Leinart/25 12.00 30.00
22 Sayers/M.Forte/25 50.00 100.00
23 Namath/Favre/25 150.00 300.00
24 Dickerson/McFad/25 40.00 80.00
25 Campbell/L.White/25 30.00 80.00
26 Deion Sanders/25 60.00 120.00
27 Eddie Royal/25 15.00 40.00
28 Devery Henderson/15 15.00 40.00
29 Frank Gore/25 15.00 40.00
34 Matt Leinart/25 25.00 50.00
38 Cadillac Williams/25 15.00 40.00
39 Peyton Manning/25 100.00 175.00
43 Braylon Edwards/25 15.00 40.00
44 Ronnie Brown/25 15.00 40.00
49 Adrian Peterson/25 75.00 150.00

2009 Donruss Elite Turn of the Century Autographs

STATED PRINT RUN 25-250
101 Aaron Curry/250 8.00 20.00
108 B.J. Raji/250 6.00 15.00
110 Brandon Pettigrew/25 10.00 25.00
115 Brian Robiskie/75 6.00 15.00
121 Chris Wells/200 5.00 12.00
128 Darrius Heyward-Bey/200 8.00 20.00
131 Derrick Williams/25 10.00 25.00
134 Donald Brown/200 5.00 12.00
136 Glen Coffee/50 6.00 15.00
138 Hakeem Nicks/200 6.00 15.00
146 Javon Ringer/25 10.00 25.00
149 Jeremy Maclin/200 6.00 15.00
152 Josh Freeman/200 5.00 12.00
153 Juaquin Iglesias/200 5.00 12.00
154 Kenny Britt/25 15.00 40.00
157 Knowshon Moreno/200 5.00 12.00
160 LeSean McCoy/200 12.00 30.00
163 Malcolm Jenkins/250 5.00 12.00
164 Mark Sanchez/250 12.00 30.00
165 Matthew Stafford/200 25.00 60.00
167 Michael Crabtree/250 8.00 20.00
170 Mike Thomas/250 5.00 12.00
171 Mike Wallace/100 10.00 25.00
172 Mohamed Massaquoi/200 5.00 12.00
176 Pat White/200 6.00 15.00
179 Percy Harvin/200 5.00 12.00
186 Rey Maualuga/250 8.00 20.00
187 Rhett Bomar/50 6.00 15.00
192 Shonn Greene/25 10.00 25.00
193 Stephen McGee/50 6.00 15.00
198 Tyson Jackson/250 5.00 12.00

2009 Donruss Elite Zoning Commission Gold

GOLD PRINT RUN 899 SER.#'d SETS
*BLACK/399: .5X TO 1.2X GOLD/899
BLACK PRINT RUN 399 SER.#'d SETS
*RED/199: .6X TO 1.5X GOLD/899
RED PRINT RUN 199 SER.#'d SETS
1 Larry Fitzgerald 1.00 2.50
2 Greg Jennings .75 2.00
3 Brandon Marshall 1.00 2.50
4 Steve Smith 1.00 2.50
5 Wes Welker 1.00 2.50
6 Jerricho Cotchery .75 2.00
7 Santonio Holmes .75 2.00
8 Randy Moss 1.00 2.50
9 Vincent Jackson .75 2.00
10 Marvin Harrison 1.00 2.50
11 Chad Ochocinco .75 2.00
12 Amani Toomer .75 2.00
13 Terrell Owens 1.00 2.50
14 Justin Gage .75 2.00
15 Reggie Brown .75 2.00
16 Patrick Crayton .75 2.00
17 Josh Reed .75 2.00
18 Selvin Young .75 2.00
19 Clinton Portis .75 2.00
20 Michael Turner .75 2.00
21 DeAngelo Williams .75 2.00
22 Frank Gore 1.00 2.50
23 Ronnie Brown .75 2.00
24 Matt Forte .75 2.00
25 LenDale White .75 2.00

2009 Donruss Elite Zoning Commission Jerseys

JERSEY PRINT RUN 20-299
*PRIME/41-50: .8X TO 2X BASE JSY/260-299
*PRIME/50: .6X TO 1.5X BASE JSY/99-100
*PRIME/50: .5X TO 1.2X BASE JSY/20
PRIME STATED PRINT RUN 41-50
1 Larry Fitzgerald/299 2.50 6.00
2 Greg Jennings/260 2.00 5.00
3 Brandon Marshall/299 2.50 6.00
4 Steve Smith/299 2.50 6.00
5 Wes Welker/299 2.50 6.00
6 Jerricho Cotchery/299 2.00 5.00
7 Santonio Holmes/299 2.00 5.00
8 Randy Moss/299 2.50 6.00
9 Vincent Jackson/299 2.00 5.00
11 Chad Ochocinco/299 2.00 5.00
12 Amani Toomer/299 2.00 5.00
13 Terrell Owens/299 2.50 6.00
14 Justin Gage/299 2.00 5.00
15 Reggie Brown/299 2.00 5.00
16 Patrick Crayton/299 2.00 5.00
17 Josh Reed/299 2.00 5.00
18 Selvin Young/299 2.00 5.00
19 Clinton Portis/99 2.50 6.00
20 Michael Turner/100 2.50 6.00
21 DeAngelo Williams/299 2.00 5.00
22 Frank Gore/299 2.50 6.00
23 Ronnie Brown/20 3.00 8.00
24 Matt Forte/299 2.00 5.00
25 LenDale White/299 2.00 5.00

2009 Donruss Elite National Convention

STATED PRINT RUN 499-999
*ASPIR.RED/50: .6X TO 1.5X BASIC CARD/999
*ASPIR.RED/50: .5X TO 1.2X BASIC CARD/499
*STATUS BLUE/50: .6X TO 1.5X BASIC CARD/999
*STATUS BLUE/50: .5X TO 1.2X BASIC CARD/499
*STATUS GOLD/25: .8X TO 2X BASIC CARD/999
*STATUS GOLD/25: .6X TO 1.5X BASIC CARD/499
101 Aaron Curry/999 1.00 2.50
110 Brandon Pettigrew/999 .60 1.50
115 Brian Robiskie/999 .60 1.50
121 Chris Wells/999 .60 1.50
128 Darrius Heyward-Bey/499 1.25 3.00
134 Donald Brown/999 .60 1.50
136 Glen Coffee/499 .75 2.00
138 Hakeem Nicks/999 .75 2.00
149 Jeremy Maclin/999 .75 2.00
152 Josh Freeman/999 .60 1.50
154 Kenny Britt/999 1.00 2.50
157 Knowshon Moreno/999 .60 1.50
160 LeSean McCoy/499 2.00 5.00
163 Malcolm Jenkins/499 .75 2.00
164 Mark Sanchez/999 .60 1.50
165 Matthew Stafford/999 3.00 8.00
167 Michael Crabtree/499 1.25 3.00
171 Mike Wallace/999 1.00 2.50
172 Mohamed Massaquoi/999 .60 1.50
179 Percy Harvin/999 .60 1.50
227 Jason Smith/499 .75 2.00

2009 Donruss Elite National Convention Insert Promos

STATED PRINT RUN 499 SER.#'d SETS
*BLUE/50: .5X TO 1.2X BASIC CARD/499
*GOLD/25: .6X TO 1.5X BASIC CARD/499
*RED/50: .5X TO 1.2X BASIC CARD/499
KM Knowshon Moreno ZC .60 1.50
MC Michael Crabtree PT 1.00 2.50
CBW Chris Wells CR .60 1.50
DHB Darrius Heyward-Bey PT 1.00 2.50
MS1 Matthew Stafford ES 3.00 8.00
MS2 Mark Sanchez ES .60 1.50

2009 Donruss Elite National Convention Insert Promos Autographs

NOT PRICED DUE TO SCARCITY

2010 Donruss Elite

COMP.SET w/o RC's (100) 7.50 20.00
101-200 ROOKIE PRINT RUN 999
1 Anquan Boldin .20 .50
2 Chris Wells .20 .50
3 Larry Fitzgerald .25 .60
4 Matt Ryan .25 .60
5 Michael Turner .20 .50
6 Roddy White .20 .50
7 Joe Flacco .25 .60
8 Ray Rice .20 .50
9 Todd Heap .20 .50
10 Lee Evans .25 .60
11 Marshawn Lynch .25 .60
12 Ryan Fitzpatrick .20 .50
13 DeAngelo Williams .20 .50
14 Jonathan Stewart .20 .50
15 Steve Smith .25 .60
16 Greg Olsen .25 .60
17 Jay Cutler .20 .50
18 Matt Forte .20 .50
19 Carson Palmer .25 .60
20 Cedric Benson .20 .50
21 Chad Ochocinco .20 .50
22 Jake Delhomme .20 .50
23 Jerome Harrison .20 .50
24 Josh Cribbs .20 .50
25 Jason Witten .25 .60
26 Marion Barber .25 .60
27 Miles Austin .20 .50
28 Tony Romo .25 .60
29 Brandon Marshall .25 .60
30 Knowshon Moreno .20 .50
31 Kyle Orton .20 .50
32 Calvin Johnson .30 .75
33 Kevin Smith .20 .50
34 Matthew Stafford .25 .60
35 Aaron Rodgers .60 1.50
36 Greg Jennings .20 .50
37 Ryan Grant .25 .60
38 Andre Johnson .25 .60
39 Matt Schaub .20 .50
40 Steve Slaton .20 .50
41 Dallas Clark .20 .50
42 Pierre Garcon .25 .60
43 Peyton Manning .75 2.00
44 Reggie Wayne .25 .60
45 David Garrard .20 .50
46 Maurice Jones-Drew .20 .50
47 Mike Sims-Walker .20 .50
48 Dwayne Bowe .25 .60
49 Jamaal Charles .25 .60
50 Matt Cassel .20 .50
51 Chad Henne .25 .60
52 Davone Bess .20 .50
53 Ronnie Brown .20 .50
54 Adrian Peterson .30 .75
55 Brett Favre .60 1.50
56 Sidney Rice .20 .50
57 Visanthe Shiancoe .25 .60
58 Laurence Maroney .20 .50
59 Tom Brady .75 2.00
60 Wes Welker .25 .60
61 Devery Henderson .20 .50
62 Drew Brees .30 .75
63 Pierre Thomas .20 .50
64 Brandon Jacobs .20 .50
65 Eli Manning .25 .60
66 Steve Smith USC .20 .50
67 Mark Sanchez .20 .50
68 Shonn Greene .20 .50
69 Jerricho Cotchery .20 .50
70 Chaz Schilens .20 .50
71 Darren McFadden .20 .50
72 Zach Miller .20 .50
73 Brent Celek .20 .50
74 DeSean Jackson .25 .60
75 Kevin Kolb .20 .50
76 Ben Roethlisberger .30 .75
77 Rashard Mendenhall .20 .50
78 Santonio Holmes .20 .50
79 Antonio Gates .25 .60
80 Darren Sproles .25 .60
81 Philip Rivers .30 .75
82 Vincent Jackson .20 .50
83 Frank Gore .25 .60
84 Michael Crabtree .20 .50
85 Vernon Davis .20 .50
86 Julius Jones .20 .50
87 Nate Burleson .20 .50
88 T.J. Houshmandzadeh .20 .50
89 Donnie Avery .20 .50
90 Kyle Boller .20 .50
91 Steven Jackson .20 .50
92 Cadillac Williams .20 .50
93 Josh Freeman .25 .60
94 Kellen Winslow Jr. .20 .50
95 Bo Scaife .20 .50
96 Chris Johnson .20 .50
97 Vince Young .20 .50
98 Chris Cooley .20 .50
99 Clinton Portis .20 .50
100 Donovan McNabb .25 .60
101 Kareem Jackson RC 1.50 4.00
102 Rolando McClain RC 1.50 4.00
103 Rob Gronkowski RC 5.00 12.00
104 Chris McGaha RC 1.50 4.00
105 Ben Tate RC 1.50 4.00
106 David Gettis RC 1.50 4.00
107 Kyle Wilson RC 1.50 4.00
108 Freddie Barnes RC 1.50 4.00
109 James Starks RC 2.00 5.00
110 Jahvid Best RC 1.50 4.00
111 Antonio Brown RC 12.00 30.00

112 Dan LeFevour RC 1.50 4.00
113 Mardy Gilyard RC 1.50 4.00
114 Tony Pike RC 1.50 4.00
115 Andre Roberts RC 2.00 5.00
116 C.J. Spiller RC 1.50 4.00
117 Jacoby Ford RC 1.50 4.00
118 Ricky Sapp RC 1.50 4.00
119 Andre Dixon RC 2.50 6.00
120 Marcus Easley RC 1.50 4.00
121 Aaron Hernandez RC 1.50 4.00
122 Brandon Spikes RC 1.50 4.00
123 Carlos Dunlap RC 1.50 4.00
124 Joe Haden RC 2.50 6.00
125 Riley Cooper RC 1.50 4.00
126 Tim Tebow RC 5.00 12.00
127 Patrick Robinson RC 2.00 5.00
128 John Skelton RC 2.00 5.00
129 Lonyae Miller RC 2.00 5.00
130 Ryan Mathews RC 1.50 4.00
131 Seyi Ajirotutu RC 1.50 4.00
132 Demaryius Thomas RC 4.00 10.00
133 Derrick Morgan RC 1.50 4.00
134 Jonathan Dwyer RC 1.50 4.00
135 Morgan Burnett RC 2.00 5.00
136 Arrelious Benn RC 1.50 4.00
137 Bryan Bulaga RC 1.50 4.00
138 Dezmon Briscoe RC 1.50 4.00
139 Brandon LaFell RC 2.50 6.00
140 Chad Jones RC 1.50 4.00
141 Charles Scott RC 1.50 4.00
142 Jimmy Graham RC 4.00 10.00
143 Brandon Graham RC 2.00 5.00
144 Blair White RC 1.50 4.00
145 Eric Decker RC 2.00 5.00
146 Dexter McCluster RC 2.00 5.00
147 Jevan Snead RC 1.50 4.00
148 Shay Hodge RC 1.50 4.00
149 Anthony Dixon RC 1.50 4.00
150 Armanti Edwards RC 2.00 5.00
151 Sean Weatherspoon RC 1.50 4.00
152 Ndamukong Suh RC 3.00 8.00
153 Pat Paschall RC 1.50 4.00
154 Corey Wootton RC 1.50 4.00
155 Mike Kafka RC 2.00 5.00
156 Golden Tate RC 2.00 5.00
157 Jimmy Clausen RC 1.50 4.00
158 Taylor Price RC 1.50 4.00
159 Emmanual Sanders RC 2.50 6.00
160 Dominique Franks RC 1.50 4.00
161 Gerald McCoy RC 1.50 4.00
162 Jermaine Gresham RC 1.50 4.00
163 Sam Bradford RC 2.00 5.00
164 Trent Williams RC 2.00 5.00
165 Dez Bryant RC 10.00 25.00
166 Perrish Cox RC 2.00 5.00
167 Russell Okung RC 1.50 4.00
168 Zac Robinson RC 2.00 5.00
169 Ed Dickson RC 1.50 4.00
170 LeGarrette Blount RC 3.00 8.00
171 Sean Canfield RC 1.50 4.00
172 NaVorro Bowman RC 5.00 12.00
173 Sean Lee RC 3.00 8.00
174 Devin McCourty RC 2.00 5.00
175 Carlton Mitchell RC 1.50 4.00
176 Jason Pierre-Paul RC 2.50 6.00
177 Nate Allen RC 2.50 6.00
178 Anthony McCoy RC 1.50 4.00
179 Damian Williams RC 1.50 4.00
180 Everson Griffen RC 1.50 4.00
181 Joe McKnight RC 1.50 4.00
182 Taylor Mays RC 1.50 4.00
183 Toby Gerhart RC 1.50 4.00
184 Mike Williams RC 1.50 4.00
185 Daryl Washington RC 1.50 4.00
186 Jerry Hughes RC 1.50 4.00
187 Eric Berry RC 2.50 6.00
188 Jonathan Crompton RC 1.50 4.00
189 Montario Hardesty RC 1.50 4.00
190 Colt McCoy RC 2.00 5.00
191 Earl Thomas RC 4.00 10.00
192 Jordan Shipley RC 1.50 4.00
193 Sergio Kindle RC 1.50 4.00
194 Andre Anderson RC 1.50 4.00
195 Jeremy Williams RC 1.50 4.00
196 Chris Cook RC 1.50 4.00
197 Jason Worilds RC 1.50 4.00
198 Joique Bell RC 1.50 4.00
199 Jarrett Brown RC 1.50 4.00
200 Garrett Graham RC 1.50 4.00

2010 Donruss Elite Aspirations

*VETS/70-99: 5X TO 12X BASIC CARDS
*ROOK/70-99: .6X TO 1.5X BASIC CARDS
*VETS/46-69: 6X TO 15X BASIC CARDS
*ROOK/46-69: .8X TO 2X BASIC CARDS
*VETS/30-45: 8X TO 20X BASIC CARDS
*ROOK/30-45: 1X TO 2.5X BASIC CARDS
*VETS/20-29: 10X TO 25X BASIC CARDS
*ROOK/20-29: 1.2X TO 3X BASIC CARDS
*VETS/10-19: 12X TO 30X BASIC CARDS
*ROOK/10-19: 2X TO 5X BASIC CARDS
STATED PRINT RUN 1-99

2010 Donruss Elite Status

*VETS/70-99: 5X TO 12X BASIC CARDS
*ROOK/70-99: .6X TO 1.5X BASIC CARDS
*VETS/46-69: 6X TO 15X BASIC CARDS
*ROOK/46-69: .8X TO 2X BASIC CARDS
*VETS/30-45: 8X TO 20X BASIC CARDS
*ROOK/30-45: 1X TO 2.5X BASIC CARDS
*VETS/20-29: 10X TO 25X BASIC CARDS
*ROOK/20-29: 1.2X TO 3X BASIC CARDS
*VETS/10-19: 12X TO 30X BASIC CARDS
*ROOK/10-19: 2X TO 5X BASIC CARDS
STATED PRINT RUN 1-99

2010 Donruss Elite Status Black

*VETS 1-100: 10X TO 25X BASIC CARDS
*ROOKIES 101-200: 1.2X TO 3X BASIC CARDS
STATUS PRINT RUN 24 SER.#'d SETS

2010 Donruss Elite Aspirations Autographs

7-67 VETERAN PRINT RUN 10-24
102-200 ROOKIE PRINT RUN 49
7 Joe Flacco/10
31 Kyle Orton/15
39 Matt Schaub/15
48 Dwayne Bowe/15
59 Tom Brady/10
67 Mark Sanchez/24 25.00 60.00
102 Rolando McClain/49 6.00 15.00
103 Rob Gronkowski/49 40.00 80.00
104 Chris McGaha/49 6.00 15.00
105 Ben Tate/49 6.00 15.00
106 David Gettis/49 6.00 15.00
108 Freddie Barnes/49 6.00 15.00
109 James Starks/49 8.00 20.00
110 Jahvid Best/49 6.00 15.00
111 Antonio Brown/49 30.00 80.00
112 Dan LeFevour/49 6.00 15.00
114 Tony Pike/49 6.00 15.00
115 Andre Roberts/49 8.00 20.00
116 C.J. Spiller/49 6.00 15.00
117 Jacoby Ford/49 6.00 15.00
120 Marcus Easley/49 6.00 15.00
121 Aaron Hernandez/49 6.00 15.00
124 Joe Haden/49 10.00 25.00
125 Riley Cooper/49 12.00 30.00
126 Tim Tebow/49 30.00 80.00
127 Patrick Robinson/49 8.00 20.00
129 Lonyae Miller/49 8.00 20.00
130 Ryan Mathews/49 6.00 15.00
131 Seyi Ajirotutu/49 6.00 15.00
132 Demaryius Thomas/49 15.00 40.00
133 Derrick Morgan/49 6.00 15.00
134 Jonathan Dwyer/49 6.00 15.00
135 Morgan Burnett/49 8.00 20.00
136 Arrelious Benn/49 6.00 15.00
137 Bryan Bulaga/49 6.00 15.00
138 Dezmon Briscoe/49 6.00 15.00
139 Brandon LaFell/49 10.00 25.00
140 Chad Jones/49 6.00 15.00
141 Charles Scott/49 6.00 15.00
143 Brandon Graham/49 8.00 20.00
144 Blair White/49 6.00 15.00
145 Eric Decker/49 8.00 20.00
146 Dexter McCluster/49 8.00 20.00
147 Jevan Snead/49 6.00 15.00
148 Shay Hodge/49 6.00 15.00
150 Armanti Edwards/49 8.00 20.00
151 Sean Weatherspoon/49 6.00 15.00
152 Ndamukong Suh/49 12.00 30.00
153 Pat Paschall/49 6.00 15.00
154 Corey Wootton/49 6.00 15.00
155 Mike Kafka/49 8.00 20.00
156 Golden Tate/49 8.00 20.00
157 Jimmy Clausen/49 6.00 15.00
158 Taylor Price/49 6.00 15.00
159 Emmanuel Sanders/49 10.00 25.00
160 Dominique Franks/49 6.00 15.00
161 Gerald McCoy/49 6.00 15.00
162 Jermaine Gresham/49 6.00 15.00
163 Sam Bradford/49 8.00 20.00
165 Dez Bryant/49 40.00 100.00
166 Perrish Cox/49 8.00 20.00
168 Zac Robinson/49 8.00 20.00
169 Ed Dickson/49 6.00 15.00
170 LeGarrette Blount/49 12.00 30.00
171 Sean Canfield/49 6.00 15.00
173 Sean Lee/49 15.00 30.00
174 Devin McCourty/49 8.00 20.00
175 Carlton Mitchell/49 6.00 15.00
176 Jason Pierre-Paul/49 10.00 25.00
177 Nate Allen/49 10.00 25.00
178 Anthony McCoy/49 6.00 15.00
179 Damian Williams/49 6.00 15.00
180 Everson Griffen/49 6.00 15.00
182 Taylor Mays/49 6.00 15.00
183 Toby Gerhart/49 6.00 15.00
186 Jerry Hughes/49 6.00 15.00
188 Jonathan Crompton/49 6.00 15.00
189 Montario Hardesty/49 6.00 15.00
190 Colt McCoy/49 8.00 20.00
191 Earl Thomas/49 15.00 40.00
192 Jordan Shipley/49 6.00 15.00
193 Sergio Kindle/49 6.00 15.00
194 Andre Anderson/49 6.00 15.00
195 Jeremy Williams/49 6.00 15.00
196 Chris Cook/49 6.00 15.00
197 Jason Worilds/49 6.00 15.00
198 Joique Bell/49 6.00 15.00
199 Jarrett Brown/49 6.00 15.00
200 Garrett Graham/49 6.00 15.00

2010 Donruss Elite Chain Reaction Gold

GOLD PRINT RUN 999 SER.#'d SETS
*BLACK/99: .8X TO 2X GOLD/999
*RED/49: 1X TO 2.5X GOLD/999
1 Aaron Rodgers 2.50 6.00
2 Josh Cribbs .75 2.00
3 Austin Collie .75 2.00
4 Ben Roethlisberger 1.25 3.00
5 Brandon Jacobs .75 2.00
6 Calvin Johnson 1.25 3.00
7 Cadillac Williams .75 2.00
8 Carson Palmer 1.00 2.50
9 Chris Johnson .75 2.00
10 Donald Driver 1.00 2.50
11 Donovan McNabb 1.00 2.50
12 Drew Brees 1.25 3.00
13 Eli Manning 1.00 2.50
14 Hines Ward 1.00 2.50
15 Joe Flacco 1.00 2.50
16 Percy Harvin .75 2.00
17 Peyton Manning 3.00 8.00
18 Pierre Garcon 1.00 2.50
19 Rashard Mendenhall .75 2.00
20 Steve Smith 1.00 2.50

2010 Donruss Elite Chain Reaction Jerseys

STATED PRINT RUN 196-299
*PRIME/50: .8X TO 2X BASIC JSY
1 Aaron Rodgers/299 6.00 15.00
2 Josh Cribbs/299 2.00 5.00
4 Ben Roethlisberger/299 3.00 8.00
5 Brandon Jacobs/299 2.00 5.00
6 Calvin Johnson/299 3.00 8.00
7 Cadillac Williams/299 2.00 5.00
8 Carson Palmer/299 2.50 6.00
10 Donald Driver/196 2.50 6.00
11 Donovan McNabb/299 2.50 6.00
12 Drew Brees/299 3.00 8.00
13 Eli Manning/299 2.50 6.00
14 Hines Ward/299 2.50 6.00
15 Joe Flacco/299 2.50 6.00
16 Percy Harvin/299 2.00 5.00
17 Peyton Manning/299 8.00 20.00
19 Rashard Mendenhall/299 2.00 5.00
20 Steve Smith/299 2.50 6.00

2010 Donruss Elite Down and Distance Jerseys

STATED PRINT RUN 3-299
1 Aaron Rodgers/299 6.00 15.00
2 Calvin Johnson/299 3.00 8.00
3 Antonio Gates/299 2.50 6.00
4 Anthony Gonzalez/299 2.00 5.00
6 Chris Cooley/299 2.00 5.00
7 LaDainian Tomlinson/299 3.00 8.00
8 Jonathan Stewart/299 2.00 5.00
9 Frank Gore/299 2.50 6.00
10 Jason Witten/299 2.50 6.00
11 Justin Gage/299 2.00 5.00
13 Jamaal Charles/299 2.50 6.00
14 Vernon Davis/299 2.00 5.00
16 Ryan Grant/299 2.50 6.00
17 Hakeem Nicks/299 2.50 6.00
19 Antwaan Randle El/225 2.00 5.00
20 Leon Washington/3
21 Ben Roethlisberger/299 3.00 8.00
22 Marques Colston/299 2.00 5.00
23 Eli Manning/299 2.50 6.00
24 Ben Watson/200 2.00 5.00
25 Rashard Mendenhall/299 2.00 5.00
26 Sidney Rice/34 5.00 12.00
27 Reggie Wayne/299 2.50 6.00
29 Randy Moss/299 2.50 6.00
30 Steven Jackson/299 2.00 5.00
31 Santonio Holmes/55 3.00 8.00
32 Marion Barber/299 2.50 6.00
33 Mike Wallace/299 2.00 5.00
34 Vincent Jackson/299 2.00 5.00
35 Cadillac Williams/299 2.00 5.00
36 Owen Daniels/299 2.00 5.00
37 Philip Rivers/299 3.00 8.00
38 Patrick Crayton/299 2.00 5.00
39 Dallas Clark/299 2.00 5.00
40 Donald Driver/299 2.50 6.00
41 Matt Forte/299 2.00 5.00
42 Muhsin Muhammad/299 2.00 5.00
43 Adrian Peterson/299 3.00 8.00
44 Darren Sproles/299 2.50 6.00
45 Larry Fitzgerald/299 2.50 6.00
46 Steve Smith/299 2.50 6.00
47 Todd Heap/299 2.00 5.00
48 Steve Slaton/299 2.00 5.00
49 Peyton Manning/200 8.00 20.00
50 Wes Welker/299 2.50 6.00

2010 Donruss Elite Down and Distance Jerseys Red Zone Prime

*PRIME/50: .8X TO 2X BASIC JSY/200-299
*PRIME/50: .5X TO 1.2X BASIC JSY/34-55
*PRIME/15: 1.2X TO 3X BASIC JSY/299
PRIME PRINT RUN 15-50
12 Miles Austin/50 4.00 10.00

2010 Donruss Elite Down and Distance Jerseys Autographs

STATED PRINT RUN 5-25
3 Antonio Gates/10
21 Ben Roethlisberger/5
23 Eli Manning/10
33 Mike Wallace/25 20.00 40.00
34 Vincent Jackson/10
41 Matt Forte/10
46 Steve Smith/10

2010 Donruss Elite Passing the Torch Red

RED PRINT RUN 999 SER.#'d SETS
*BLUE/49: 1X TO 2.5X RED/999
*GREEN/99: .8X TO 2X RED/999
1 J.Namath/M.Sanchez 2.00 5.00
2 B.Favre/F.Tarkenton 3.00 8.00
3 B.Jones/V.Davis 1.25 3.00
4 D.Ware/E.Jones 1.25 3.00
5 J.Charles/P.Holmes 1.25 3.00
6 C.Carter/S.Rice 1.50 4.00
7 K.Moreno/T.Davis 1.25 3.00
8 E.Smith/F.Jones 2.50 6.00
9 J.Taylor/M.Crabtree 2.00 5.00
10 C.Martin/S.Greene 1.50 4.00
11 B.Celek/P.Retzlaff 1.00 2.50
12 D.Revis/D.Sanders 1.25 3.00
13 S.Largent/W.Welker 1.50 4.00
14 J.Lambert/J.Harrison 2.00 5.00
15 M.Irvin/M.Austin 1.50 4.00

2010 Donruss Elite Passing the Torch Autographs

STATED PRINT RUN 25 SER.#'d SETS
EXCH EXPIRATION: 12/16/2011
1 J.Namath/M.Sanchez 75.00 150.00
2 B.Favre/F.Tarkenton 150.00 300.00
3 B.Jones/V.Davis 30.00 60.00
4 D.Ware/E.Jones 40.00 80.00
5 J.Charles/P.Holmes 40.00 80.00
7 K.Moreno/T.Davis 60.00 120.00
8 E.Smith/F.Jones 100.00 200.00
9 J.Taylor/M.Crabtree 40.00 80.00
10 C.Martin/S.Greene 40.00 80.00
11 B.Celek/P.Retzlaff 15.00 40.00
12 D.Revis/D.Sanders 60.00 120.00

2010 Donruss Elite Prime Targets Gold

GOLD PRINT RUN 999 SER.#'d SETS
*BLACK/99: .8X TO 2X GOLD/999
*RED/49: 1X TO 2.5X GOLD/999
1 Adrian Peterson 1.25 3.00
2 Andre Johnson 1.00 2.50
3 Antonio Gates 1.00 2.50
4 Brandon Marshall 1.00 2.50
5 Chris Johnson .75 2.00
6 Dallas Clark .75 2.00
7 DeSean Jackson 1.00 2.50
8 Frank Gore 1.00 2.50
9 Jamaal Charles 1.00 2.50
10 Larry Fitzgerald 1.00 2.50
11 Miles Austin .75 2.00
12 Randy Moss 1.00 2.50
13 Darren Sproles 1.00 2.50
14 Reggie Wayne 1.00 2.50
15 Ricky Williams 1.00 2.50
16 Ryan Grant 1.00 2.50
17 Sidney Rice .75 2.00
18 DeAngelo Williams .75 2.00
19 Vincent Jackson .75 2.00
20 Wes Welker 1.00 2.50

2010 Donruss Elite Prime Targets Jerseys

STATED PRINT RUN 299 SER.#'d SETS
1 Adrian Peterson 3.00 8.00
2 Andre Johnson 2.50 6.00
3 Antonio Gates 2.50 6.00
4 Brandon Marshall 2.50 6.00
6 Dallas Clark 2.00 5.00
8 Frank Gore 2.50 6.00
9 Jamaal Charles 2.50 6.00
10 Larry Fitzgerald 2.50 6.00
12 Randy Moss 2.50 6.00
13 Darren Sproles 2.50 6.00
14 Reggie Wayne 2.50 6.00
15 Ricky Williams 2.50 6.00
16 Ryan Grant 2.50 6.00
17 Sidney Rice 3.00 8.00
18 DeAngelo Williams 2.00 5.00
19 Vincent Jackson 2.00 5.00
20 Wes Welker 2.50 6.00

2010 Donruss Elite Prime Targets Jerseys Prime

*PRIME/50: .8X TO 2X BASIC JSY/299
PRIME PRINT RUN 2-50
5 Chris Johnson/50 4.00 10.00

2010 Donruss Elite Rookie NFL Shield

NLF SHIELD PRINT RUN 999 SER.#'d SETS
*TEAM LOGO/999: .4X TO 1X NFL SHIELD/999
1 Andre Roberts 1.00 2.50
2 Armanti Edwards 1.00 2.50
3 Arrelious Benn .75 2.00
4 Ben Tate .75 2.00
5 Brandon LaFell 1.25 3.00
6 C.J. Spiller .75 2.00
7 Colt McCoy 1.00 2.50
8 Damian Williams .75 2.00
9 Demaryius Thomas 2.00 5.00
10 Dexter McCluster 1.00 2.50
11 Dez Bryant 2.00 5.00
12 Emmanuel Sanders 1.25 3.00
13 Eric Berry 1.25 3.00
14 Eric Decker 1.00 2.50
15 Gerald McCoy .75 2.00
16 Golden Tate 1.00 2.50
17 Jahvid Best .75 2.00
18 Jermaine Gresham .75 2.00
19 Jimmy Clausen .75 2.00
20 Joe McKnight .75 2.00
21 Jonathan Dwyer .75 2.00
22 Jordan Shipley .75 2.00
23 Marcus Easley .75 2.00
24 Mardy Gilyard .75 2.00
25 Mike Kafka 1.00 2.50
26 Mike Williams .75 2.00
27 Montario Hardesty .75 2.00
28 Ndamukong Suh 1.50 4.00
29 Rob Gronkowski 2.50 6.00
30 Rolando McClain .75 2.00
31 Ryan Mathews .75 2.00
32 Sam Bradford 1.00 2.50
33 Taylor Price .75 2.00
34 Tim Tebow 2.50 6.00
35 Toby Gerhart .75 2.00

2010 Donruss Elite Rookie NFL Shield Autographs

1 Andre Roberts 5.00 12.00
2 Armanti Edwards 5.00 12.00
3 Arrelious Benn 4.00 10.00
4 Ben Tate 4.00 10.00
5 Brandon LaFell 6.00 15.00
6 C.J. Spiller 4.00 10.00
7 Colt McCoy 5.00 12.00
8 Damian Williams 4.00 10.00
9 Demaryius Thomas 10.00 25.00
10 Dexter McCluster 5.00 12.00
11 Dez Bryant 30.00 60.00
12 Emmanuel Sanders 6.00 15.00
13 Eric Berry 12.00 30.00
14 Eric Decker 5.00 12.00
15 Gerald McCoy 4.00 10.00
16 Golden Tate 5.00 12.00
17 Jahvid Best 4.00 10.00
18 Jermaine Gresham 4.00 10.00
19 Jimmy Clausen 4.00 10.00
20 Joe McKnight 4.00 10.00
21 Jonathan Dwyer 4.00 10.00
22 Jordan Shipley 4.00 10.00
23 Marcus Easley 4.00 10.00
24 Mardy Gilyard 4.00 10.00
25 Mike Kafka 5.00 12.00
26 Mike Williams 4.00 10.00
27 Montario Hardesty 4.00 10.00
28 Ndamukong Suh 12.00 30.00
29 Rob Gronkowski 20.00 40.00
30 Rolando McClain 4.00 10.00
31 Ryan Mathews 4.00 10.00
32 Sam Bradford 5.00 12.00
33 Taylor Price 4.00 10.00
34 Tim Tebow 30.00 60.00
35 Toby Gerhart 4.00 10.00

2010 Donruss Elite Rookie NFL Team Logo Autographs

1 Andre Roberts 5.00 12.00
2 Armanti Edwards 6.00 15.00
3 Arrelious Benn 4.00 10.00
4 Ben Tate 4.00 10.00
5 Brandon LaFell 8.00 20.00
6 C.J. Spiller 4.00 10.00
7 Colt McCoy 5.00 12.00
8 Damian Williams 4.00 10.00
9 Demaryius Thomas 10.00 25.00
10 Dexter McCluster 5.00 12.00
11 Dez Bryant 40.00 80.00
12 Emmanuel Sanders 6.00 15.00
13 Eric Berry 12.00 30.00
14 Eric Decker 5.00 12.00
15 Gerald McCoy 4.00 10.00
16 Golden Tate 5.00 12.00
17 Jahvid Best 4.00 10.00
18 Jermaine Gresham 4.00 10.00
19 Jimmy Clausen 4.00 10.00
20 Joe McKnight 4.00 10.00
21 Jonathan Dwyer 4.00 10.00
22 Jordan Shipley 4.00 10.00
23 Marcus Easley 4.00 10.00
24 Mardy Gilyard 4.00 10.00
25 Mike Kafka 5.00 12.00
26 Mike Williams 4.00 10.00
27 Montario Hardesty 4.00 10.00
28 Ndamukong Suh 20.00 50.00
29 Rob Gronkowski 25.00 50.00
30 Rolando McClain 4.00 10.00
31 Ryan Mathews 4.00 10.00
32 Sam Bradford 5.00 12.00
33 Taylor Price 4.00 10.00
34 Tim Tebow 30.00 60.00
35 Toby Gerhart 4.00 10.00

2010 Donruss Elite Series Red

RED PRINT RUN 999 SER.#'d SETS
*BLUE/49: 1X TO 2.5X RED/999
*GREEN/99: .8X TO 2X RED/999
1 Adrian Peterson 1.25 3.00
2 Andre Johnson 1.00 2.50
3 Ben Roethlisberger 1.25 3.00
4 Bob Sanders 1.00 2.50
5 Brian Urlacher 1.25 3.00
6 Calvin Johnson 1.25 3.00
7 Dallas Clark .75 2.00
8 Darrelle Revis .75 2.00
9 Ed Reed 1.00 2.50
10 Felix Jones .75 2.00
11 Greg Jennings .75 2.00
12 Jason Witten 1.00 2.50
13 Jay Cutler .75 2.00
14 Joseph Addai .75 2.00
15 LaDainian Tomlinson 1.25 3.00
16 LaRon Landry .75 2.00
17 Marshawn Lynch 1.00 2.50
18 Patrick Willis 1.00 2.50
19 Philip Rivers 1.25 3.00
20 Pierre Thomas .75 2.00
21 Ray Lewis 1.25 3.00
22 Sidney Rice .75 2.00
23 Terrell Suggs .75 2.00
24 Vince Young .75 2.00
25 Willis McGahee .75 2.00

2010 Donruss Elite Series Jerseys

STATED PRINT RUN 38-299
*PRIME/50: .8X TO 2X BASIC JSY/216-299
*PRIME/34: .5X TO 1.2X BASIC JSY/38
*PRIME/25: 1X TO 2.5X BASIC JSY/299
1 Adrian Peterson/299 3.00 8.00
2 Andre Johnson/299 2.50 6.00
3 Ben Roethlisberger/299 3.00 8.00
4 Bob Sanders/299 2.50 6.00
5 Brian Urlacher/299 3.00 8.00
6 Calvin Johnson/299 3.00 8.00
7 Dallas Clark/299 2.00 5.00
8 Darrelle Revis/299 3.00 6.00
9 Ed Reed/299 2.50 6.00
10 Felix Jones/299 2.00 5.00
11 Greg Jennings/299 2.00 5.00
12 Jason Witten/299 2.50 6.00
13 Jay Cutler/39 3.00 8.00
14 Joseph Addai/299 2.00 5.00
15 LaDainian Tomlinson/299 3.00 8.00
16 LaRon Landry/299 2.00 5.00
17 Marshawn Lynch/299 2.50 6.00
18 Patrick Willis/38 4.00 10.00
19 Philip Rivers/299 3.00 8.00
21 Ray Lewis/299 4.00 10.00
22 Sidney Rice/216 3.00 8.00
23 Terrell Suggs/299 2.00 5.00
24 Vince Young/299 2.00 5.00
25 Willis McGahee/299 2.00 5.00

2010 Donruss Elite Stars Gold

GOLD PRINT RUN 999 SER.#'d SETS
*BLACK/99: .8X TO 2X GOLD/999
*RED/49: 1X TO 2.5X GOLD/999
1 Bernard Berrian .75 2.00
2 Brian Westbrook .75 2.00
3 Chris Cooley .75 2.00
4 David Garrard .75 2.00
5 DeAngelo Williams .75 2.00
6 Devery Henderson .75 2.00
7 Devin Hester 1.00 2.50
8 Jerricho Cotchery .75 2.00
9 Marion Barber 1.00 2.50
10 Laurence Maroney .75 2.00
11 Mark Sanchez .75 2.00
12 Matt Forte .75 2.00
13 Matt Ryan 1.00 2.50
14 Michael Turner .75 2.00
15 Nate Burleson .75 2.00
16 Reggie Bush .75 2.00
17 Ronnie Brown .75 2.00
18 T.J. Houshmandzadeh .75 2.00
19 Tony Gonzalez 1.00 2.50
20 Torry Holt 1.00 2.50

2010 Donruss Elite Stars Jerseys Gold

STATED PRINT RUN 100-299
*PRIME/50: .8X TO 2X BASIC JSY/261-299
*PRIME/50: .6X TO 1.5X BASIC JSY/100
1 Bernard Berrian/299 2.00 5.00
2 Brian Westbrook/299 2.00 5.00
3 Chris Cooley/299 2.00 5.00
4 David Garrard/299 2.00 5.00
5 DeAngelo Williams/299 2.00 5.00
6 Devery Henderson/299 2.00 5.00
7 Devin Hester/299 2.50 6.00
8 Jerricho Cotchery/299 2.00 5.00
9 Marion Barber/299 2.50 6.00
10 Laurence Maroney/299 2.00 5.00
11 Mark Sanchez/299 2.00 5.00
12 Matt Forte/299 2.00 5.00
13 Matt Ryan/299 2.50 6.00
14 Michael Turner/261 2.00 5.00
15 Nate Burleson/299 2.00 5.00
16 Reggie Bush/299 2.00 5.00
17 Ronnie Brown/299 2.00 5.00
19 Tony Gonzalez/299 2.50 6.00
20 Torry Holt/100 3.00 8.00

2010 Donruss Elite Status Autographs

102-200 ROOKIE PRINT RUN 24
7 Joe Flacco/5
13 DeAngelo Williams/15 10.00 25.00
15 Steve Smith/5
18 Matt Forte/5
28 Tony Romo/5
31 Kyle Orton/5
39 Matt Schaub/10
48 Dwayne Bowe/5
59 Tom Brady/5
67 Mark Sanchez/10
102 Rolando McClain/24 10.00 25.00
103 Rob Gronkowski/24 50.00 100.00
104 Chris McGaha/24 10.00 25.00
105 Ben Tate/24 10.00 25.00
106 David Gettis/24 10.00 25.00
108 Freddie Barnes/24 10.00 25.00
109 James Starks/24 12.00 30.00
110 Jahvid Best/24 10.00 25.00
111 Antonio Brown/24 80.00 200.00
112 Dan LeFevour/24 10.00 25.00
114 Tony Pike/24 10.00 25.00
115 Andre Roberts/24 12.00 30.00
116 C.J. Spiller/24 10.00 25.00
117 Jacoby Ford/24 10.00 25.00
120 Marcus Easley/24 10.00 25.00
121 Aaron Hernandez/24 10.00 25.00
123 Carlos Dunlap/24 10.00 25.00
124 Joe Haden/24 15.00 40.00
125 Riley Cooper/24 10.00 25.00
126 Tim Tebow/24 75.00 150.00
127 Patrick Robinson/24 12.00 30.00
129 Lonyae Miller/24 12.00 30.00
130 Ryan Mathews/24 10.00 25.00
131 Seyi Ajirotutu/24 10.00 25.00
132 Demaryius Thomas/24 25.00 60.00
133 Derrick Morgan/24 10.00 25.00
134 Jonathan Dwyer/24 10.00 25.00
135 Morgan Burnett/24 12.00 30.00
136 Arrelious Benn/24 10.00 25.00
137 Bryan Bulaga/24 10.00 25.00
138 Dezmon Briscoe/24 10.00 25.00
139 Brandon LaFell/24 15.00 40.00
140 Chad Jones/24 10.00 25.00
141 Charles Scott/24 10.00 25.00
143 Brandon Graham/24 12.00 30.00
144 Blair White/24 10.00 25.00
145 Eric Decker/24 12.00 30.00
146 Dexter McCluster/24 12.00 30.00
147 Jevan Snead/24 10.00 25.00
148 Shay Hodge/24 10.00 25.00
150 Armanti Edwards/24 12.00 30.00
151 Sean Weatherspoon/24 10.00 25.00
152 Ndamukong Suh/24 60.00 120.00
153 Pat Paschall/24 10.00 25.00
154 Corey Wootton/24 10.00 25.00
155 Mike Kafka/24 12.00 30.00
156 Golden Tate/24 12.00 30.00
157 Jimmy Clausen/24 10.00 25.00
158 Taylor Price/24 10.00 25.00
159 Emmanuel Sanders/24 15.00 40.00
160 Dominique Franks/24 10.00 25.00
161 Gerald McCoy/24 10.00 25.00
162 Jermaine Gresham/24 10.00 25.00
163 Sam Bradford/24 12.00 30.00
165 Dez Bryant/24 75.00 150.00
166 Perrish Cox/24 12.00 30.00
168 Zac Robinson/24 12.00 30.00
169 Ed Dickson/24 10.00 25.00
170 LeGarrette Blount/24 20.00 50.00
171 Sean Canfield/24 10.00 25.00
173 Sean Lee/24 25.00 50.00
174 Devin McCourty/24 12.00 30.00
175 Carlton Mitchell/24 10.00 25.00
176 Jason Pierre-Paul/24 15.00 40.00
177 Nate Allen/24 15.00 40.00
178 Anthony McCoy/24 10.00 25.00
179 Damian Williams/24 10.00 25.00
180 Everson Griffen/24 10.00 25.00
182 Taylor Mays/24 10.00 25.00
183 Toby Gerhart/24 10.00 25.00
186 Jerry Hughes/24 10.00 25.00
188 Jonathan Crompton/24 10.00 25.00
189 Montario Hardesty/24 10.00 25.00
190 Colt McCoy/24 12.00 30.00
191 Earl Thomas/24 25.00 60.00
192 Jordan Shipley/24 10.00 25.00
193 Sergio Kindle/24 10.00 25.00
194 Andre Anderson/24 10.00 25.00
195 Jeremy Williams/24 10.00 25.00
196 Chris Cook/24 10.00 25.00
197 Jason Worilds/24 10.00 25.00
198 Joique Bell/24 10.00 25.00
199 Jarrett Brown/24 10.00 25.00
200 Garrett Graham/24 10.00 25.00

2010 Donruss Elite Super Bowl XLIV

STATED PRINT RUN 999 SER.#'d SETS
1 Garrett Hartley 1.50 4.00
2 Reggie Bush 1.50 4.00
3 Darren Sharper 1.50 4.00
4 Robert Meachem 1.50 4.00
5 Tracy Porter 1.50 4.00
6 Drew Brees 2.50 6.00
7 Devery Henderson 1.50 4.00
8 Pierre Thomas 1.50 4.00
9 Jeremy Shockey 1.50 4.00
10 Marques Colston 1.50 4.00

2010 Donruss Elite Super Bowl XLIV Autographs

STATED PRINT RUN 4-44
4 Robert Meachem/7
5 Tracy Porter/8
6 Drew Brees/7
7 Devery Henderson/44 15.00 30.00
8 Pierre Thomas/4
10 Marques Colston/5

2010 Donruss Elite Super Bowl XLIV Materials

STATED PRINT RUN 264-299
*PRIME/44: .8X TO 2X BASIC JSY/264-299
2 Reggie Bush/299 6.00 15.00
6 Drew Brees/299 8.00 20.00
7 Devery Henderson/299 5.00 12.00
9 Jeremy Shockey/264 5.00 12.00
10 Marques Colston/299 5.00 12.00

2010 Donruss Elite Throwback Threads

1-10 SINGLE PRINT RUN 200-299
11-20 DUAL PRINT RUN 50-150
1 Deion Sanders/299 5.00 12.00
2 Cris Carter/299 6.00 15.00
3 Rod Woodson/299 5.00 12.00
4 Brent Jones/299 4.00 10.00
5 Brett Favre/299 6.00 15.00
7 Bernie Kosar/299 5.00 12.00
8 Harvey Martin/200 6.00 15.00
9 John Taylor/299 4.00 10.00
10 Curtis Martin/299 5.00 12.00
11 D.Ware/H.Martin/150 6.00 15.00
12 Ricky Williams Dual/150 6.00 15.00
14 D.Revis/D.Sanders/150 10.00 25.00
15 B.Jones/V.Davis/150 5.00 12.00
16 R.Woodson/T.Polamalu/150 8.00 20.00
17 J.Charles/P.Holmes/80 6.00 15.00
18 E.Smith/F.Jones/150 15.00 40.00
19 Drew Brees Dual/50 8.00 20.00
20 C.Carter/S.Rice/150 8.00 20.00

2010 Donruss Elite Throwback Threads Prime

*PRIME 1-10: .6X TO 1.5X BASIC JSY/200-299
1-10 PRIME SINGLE PRINT RUN 10-50
*PRIME 11-20: .6X TO 1.5X BASIC DUAL/50-150
11-20 PRIME DUAL PRINT RUN 2-25
6 Priest Holmes/50 6.00 15.00

2010 Donruss Elite Throwback Threads Autographs

1 Deion Sanders/15 40.00 80.00

2010 Donruss Elite Turn of the Century Autographs

STATED PRINT RUN 199-499
102 Rolando McClain/399 4.00 10.00
103 Rob Gronkowski/299 30.00 60.00
104 Chris McGaha/400 4.00 10.00
105 Ben Tate/399 4.00 10.00
106 David Gettis/499 4.00 10.00
108 Freddie Barnes/499 4.00 10.00
109 James Starks/499 5.00 12.00
110 Jahvid Best/249 5.00 12.00
111 Antonio Brown/499 40.00 80.00
112 Dan LeFevour/499 4.00 10.00
114 Tony Pike/499 4.00 10.00
115 Andre Roberts/399 5.00 12.00
116 C.J. Spiller/199 5.00 12.00
117 Jacoby Ford/499 4.00 10.00
120 Marcus Easley/399 4.00 10.00
121 Aaron Hernandez/399 4.00 10.00
123 Carlos Dunlap/299 5.00 12.00
124 Joe Haden/399 8.00 20.00
125 Riley Cooper/499 4.00 10.00
126 Tim Tebow/199 30.00 80.00
127 Patrick Robinson/399 5.00 12.00
129 Lonyae Miller/499 5.00 12.00
130 Ryan Mathews/199 5.00 12.00
131 Seyi Ajirotutu/499 4.00 10.00
132 Demaryius Thomas/249 12.00 30.00
133 Derrick Morgan/499 4.00 10.00
134 Jonathan Dwyer/399 4.00 10.00
135 Morgan Burnett/399 5.00 12.00
136 Arrelious Benn/299 5.00 12.00
137 Bryan Bulaga/399 4.00 10.00
138 Dezmon Briscoe/499 4.00 10.00
139 Brandon LaFell/399 6.00 15.00
140 Chad Jones/499 4.00 10.00
141 Charles Scott/499 4.00 10.00
143 Brandon Graham/499 5.00 12.00
144 Blair White/499 4.00 10.00
145 Eric Decker/399 8.00 20.00
146 Dexter McCluster/299 6.00 15.00
147 Jevan Snead/399 4.00 10.00
148 Shay Hodge/499 4.00 10.00
150 Armanti Edwards/399 5.00 12.00
151 Sean Weatherspoon/499 4.00 10.00
152 Ndamukong Suh/399 15.00 40.00
153 Pat Paschall/499 4.00 10.00
154 Corey Wootton/399 4.00 10.00
155 Mike Kafka/299 6.00 15.00
156 Golden Tate/249 6.00 15.00
157 Jimmy Clausen/249 5.00 12.00
158 Taylor Price/399 4.00 10.00
159 Emmanuel Sanders/399 8.00 20.00
160 Dominique Franks/499 4.00 10.00
161 Gerald McCoy/399 4.00 10.00
162 Jermaine Gresham/299 5.00 12.00
163 Sam Bradford/199 6.00 15.00
165 Dez Bryant/249 40.00 80.00
166 Perrish Cox/499 5.00 12.00
168 Zac Robinson/499 5.00 12.00
169 Ed Dickson/399 4.00 10.00
170 LeGarrette Blount/499 8.00 20.00
171 Sean Canfield/499 4.00 10.00
173 Sean Lee/399 8.00 20.00
174 Devin McCourty/499 5.00 12.00
175 Carlton Mitchell/499 4.00 10.00
176 Jason Pierre-Paul/399 6.00 15.00
177 Nate Allen/499 6.00 15.00
178 Anthony McCoy/399 4.00 10.00
179 Damian Williams/299 5.00 12.00
180 Everson Griffen/399 4.00 10.00
182 Taylor Mays/399 4.00 10.00
183 Toby Gerhart/299 5.00 12.00
186 Jerry Hughes/399 4.00 10.00
188 Jonathan Crompton/399 4.00 10.00
189 Montario Hardesty/299 5.00 12.00
190 Colt McCoy/249 6.00 15.00
191 Earl Thomas/399 10.00 25.00
192 Jordan Shipley/299 5.00 12.00
193 Sergio Kindle/499 4.00 10.00
194 Andre Anderson/499 4.00 10.00
195 Jeremy Williams/499 4.00 10.00
196 Chris Cook/499 4.00 10.00
197 Jason Worilds/499 4.00 10.00
198 Joique Bell/499 4.00 10.00
199 Jarrett Brown/399 4.00 10.00
200 Garrett Graham/499 4.00 10.00

2010 Donruss Elite Zoning Commission Gold

GOLD PRINT RUN 999 SER.#'d SETS
*BLACK/99: .8X TO 2X GOLD/999
*RED/49: 1X TO 2.5X GOLD/999
1 Brent Celek .75 2.00
2 Chad Ochocinco .75 2.00
3 Drew Brees 1.25 3.00
4 Frank Gore 1.00 2.50
5 Greg Jennings .75 2.00
6 Heath Miller .75 2.00
7 Jason Witten 1.00 2.50
8 Lee Evans 1.00 2.50
9 Marques Colston .75 2.00
10 Matt Schaub .75 2.00
11 Maurice Jones-Drew .75 2.00
12 Mike Sims-Walker .75 2.00
13 Philip Rivers 1.25 3.00
14 Ray Rice .75 2.00
15 Santonio Holmes .75 2.00
16 Steven Jackson .75 2.00
17 Tom Brady 3.00 8.00
18 Tony Romo 1.00 2.50
19 Vernon Davis .75 2.00
20 Visanthe Shiancoe 1.00 2.50

2010 Donruss Elite Zoning Commission Jerseys

STATED PRINT RUN 135-299
*PRIME/50: .8X TO 2X BASIC JSY/237-299
*PRIME/50: .6X TO 1.5X BASIC JSY/135
2 Chad Ochocinco/299 2.00 5.00
3 Drew Brees/299 3.00 8.00
4 Frank Gore/299 2.50 6.00
5 Greg Jennings/299 2.00 5.00
6 Heath Miller/299 2.00 5.00
7 Jason Witten/299 2.50 6.00
8 Lee Evans/237 2.50 6.00
9 Marques Colston/299 2.00 5.00
10 Matt Schaub/299 2.00 5.00
11 Maurice Jones-Drew/299 2.00 5.00
13 Philip Rivers/299 3.00 8.00
15 Santonio Holmes/135 2.50 6.00
16 Steven Jackson/299 2.00 5.00
17 Tom Brady/299 8.00 20.00
18 Tony Romo/299 2.50 6.00
19 Vernon Davis/299 2.00 5.00
20 Visanthe Shiancoe/299 3.00 8.00

2010 Donruss Elite National Convention

ANNOUNCED PRINT RUN 499 SETS
1 Aaron Rodgers 1.50 4.00
2 Adrian Peterson 1.50 4.00
3 Brett Favre 6.00 15.00
4 Chris Johnson 1.25 3.00
5 C.J. Spiller 2.50 6.00
6 Colt McCoy 5.00 12.00
7 Dez Bryant 6.00 15.00
8 Drew Brees 1.25 3.00
9 Jahvid Best 3.00 8.00
10 Jimmy Clausen 3.00 8.00
11 Joe Flacco 1.25 3.00
12 Larry Fitzgerald 1.25 3.00
13 Mark Sanchez 1.50 4.00
14 Peyton Manning 1.50 4.00
15 Ray Rice 1.25 3.00
16 Ryan Matthews UER 2.50 6.00
17 Sam Bradford 4.00 10.00
18 Tim Tebow 5.00 12.00
19 Tom Brady 1.50 4.00
20 Tony Romo 1.25 3.00

2010 Donruss Elite National Convention Aspirations

*ASPIRATIONS: .8X TO 2X BASIC CARDS
ANNOUNCED PRINT RUN 50

2010 Donruss Elite National Convention Status

*STATUS: .8X TO 2X BASIC CARDS
ANNOUNCED PRINT RUN 25

2010 Donruss Elite National Convention Autographs

STATED PRINT RUN 1-25
5 C.J. Spiller/25 20.00 50.00
10 Jimmy Clausen/25 30.00 80.00
15 Ray Rice/20 25.00 50.00
16 Ryan Matthews/25 UER 20.00 50.00
(last name misspelled on front)
17 Sam Bradford/25 30.00 60.00

2011 Donruss Elite

COMP.SET w/o RC's (100) 8.00 20.00
101-200 ROOKIE PRINT RUN 999
BF INSERTS IN BLACK FRIDAY PACKS
UNPRICED PRINT PLATE #'d TO 1
1 Chris Wells .20 .50
2 Larry Fitzgerald .25 .60
3 Steve Breaston .20 .50
4 Matt Ryan .25 .60
5 Michael Turner .20 .50
6 Roddy White .20 .50
7 Anquan Boldin .20 .50
8 Joe Flacco .25 .60
9 Ray Rice .20 .50
10 Fred Jackson .20 .50
11 Ryan Fitzpatrick .20 .50
12 Steve Johnson .20 .50
13 DeAngelo Williams .20 .50
14 Jonathan Stewart .20 .50
15 Steve Smith .25 .60
16 Devin Hester .25 .60
17 Jay Cutler .25 .60
18 Johnny Knox .20 .50
19 Matt Forte .20 .50
20 Carson Palmer .25 .60
21 Cedric Benson .20 .50
22 Chad Johnson .20 .50
23 Colt McCoy .20 .50
24 Josh Cribbs .20 .50
25 Peyton Hillis .20 .50
26 Felix Jones .20 .50
27 Jason Witten .25 .60
28 Miles Austin .20 .50
29 Tony Romo .25 .60
30 Brandon Lloyd .20 .50
31 Knowshon Moreno .20 .50
32 Tim Tebow .30 .75
33 Calvin Johnson .30 .75
34 Jahvid Best .20 .50
35 Matthew Stafford .25 .60
36 Aaron Rodgers .60 1.50
37 Donald Driver .25 .60
38 Greg Jennings .20 .50
39 Andre Johnson .25 .60
40 Arian Foster .20 .50
41 Matt Schaub .20 .50
42 Peyton Manning .60 1.50
43 Pierre Garcon .25 .60
44 Reggie Wayne .25 .60
45 David Garrard .20 .50
46 Marcedes Lewis .20 .50
47 Maurice Jones-Drew .20 .50
48 Dwayne Bowe .25 .60
49 Jamaal Charles .25 .60
50 Matt Cassel .20 .50
51 Brandon Marshall .25 .60
52 Chad Henne .25 .60
53 Ronnie Brown .25 .60
54 Adrian Peterson .30 .75
55 Percy Harvin .20 .50
56 Tarvaris Jackson .20 .50
57 Tom Brady .75 2.00
58 Danny Woodhead .25 .60
59 Wes Welker .25 .60
60 Drew Brees .30 .75
61 Marques Colston .20 .50
62 Reggie Bush .20 .50
63 Ahmad Bradshaw .20 .50
64 Eli Manning .25 .60
65 Hakeem Nicks .20 .50
66 Mario Manningham .20 .50
67 Braylon Edwards .20 .50
68 LaDainian Tomlinson .30 .75
69 Mark Sanchez .25 .60
70 Darren McFadden .20 .50
71 Jason Campbell .20 .50
72 Zach Miller .20 .50
73 DeSean Jackson .25 .60
74 Jeremy Maclin .20 .50
75 LeSean McCoy .30 .75
76 Michael Vick .25 .60
77 Ben Roethlisberger .30 .75
78 Mike Wallace .25 .60
79 Rashard Mendenhall .20 .50
80 Antonio Gates .20 .50
81 Mike Tolbert .20 .50
82 Philip Rivers .30 .75
83 Frank Gore .25 .60
84 Michael Crabtree .20 .50
85 Vernon Davis .20 .50
86 John Carlson .20 .50
87 Justin Forsett .25 .60
88 Mike Williams .20 .50
89 Danny Amendola .25 .60
90 Sam Bradford .30 .75
91 Steven Jackson .20 .50
92 Josh Freeman .25 .60

93 LeGarrette Blount .25 .60
94 Mike Williams .25 .60
95 Chris Johnson .20 .50
96 Kenny Britt .20 .50
97 Nate Washington .20 .50
98 Chris Cooley .20 .50
99 Donovan McNabb .25 .60
100 Ryan Torain .20 .50
101 A.J. Green RC 4.00 10.00
102 Aaron Williams RC 1.50 4.00
103 Adrian Clayborn RC 1.50 4.00
104 Ahmad Black RC 2.00 5.00
105 Akeem Ayers RC 1.50 4.00
106 Aldon Smith RC 1.50 4.00
106B Aldon Smith BF .75 2.00
107 Alex Green RC 1.50 4.00
108 Andy Dalton RC 3.00 8.00
109 Austin Pettis RC 1.50 4.00
110 Bilal Powell RC 2.00 5.00
111 Blaine Gabbert RC 1.50 4.00
112 Brandon Harris RC 1.50 4.00
113 Brooks Reed RC 2.00 5.00
114 Bruce Carter RC 1.50 4.00
115 Cam Newton RC 8.00 20.00
115B Cam Newton BF UER 4.00 10.00
116 Cameron Heyward RC 2.00 5.00
117 Cameron Jordan RC 2.00 5.00
118 Cecil Shorts RC 1.50 4.00
119 Christian Ponder RC 1.50 4.00
120 Colin Kaepernick RC 2.50 6.00
121 Colin McCarthy RC 2.00 5.00
122 Corey Liuget RC 1.50 4.00
123 Tyron Smith RC 2.00 5.00
123B Tyron Smith BF 1.00 2.50
124 Curtis Brown RC 1.50 4.00
125 D.J. Williams RC 1.50 4.00
126 Daniel Thomas RC 1.50 4.00
127 Da'Quan Bowers RC 1.50 4.00
128 Darvin Adams RC 1.50 4.00
129 Davon House RC 1.50 4.00
130 Jordan Cameron RC 2.00 5.00
131 DeAndre McDaniel RC 1.50 4.00
132 Delone Carter RC 1.50 4.00
133 DeMarco Murray RC 3.00 8.00
134 Denarius Moore RC 1.50 4.00
135 Derrick Locke RC 2.00 5.00
136 Dion Lewis RC 2.00 5.00
137 Drake Nevis RC 1.50 4.00
138 Dwayne Harris RC 1.50 4.00
139 Edmond Gates RC 1.50 4.00
140 Evan Royster RC 1.50 4.00
141 Greg Jones RC 2.00 5.00
142 Greg Little RC 2.00 5.00
143 Greg McElroy RC 2.50 6.00
143B Greg McElroy BF 1.25 3.00
144 Greg Salas RC 1.50 4.00
145 J.J. Watt RC 8.00 20.00
145B J.J. Watt BF 4.00 10.00
146 Jabaal Sheard RC 1.50 4.00
147 Jacquizz Rodgers RC 1.50 4.00
147B Jacquizz Rodgers BF .75 2.00
148 Jake Locker RC 1.50 4.00
149 Jamie Harper RC 1.50 4.00
150 Jeremy Kerley RC 2.50 6.00
151 Jerrel Jernigan RC 1.50 4.00
152 Jimmy Smith RC 1.50 4.00
153 John Clay RC 2.50 6.00
154 Jonathan Baldwin RC 1.50 4.00
155 Jordan Todman RC 1.50 4.00
156 Roy Helu RC 1.50 4.00
156B Roy Helu BF .75 2.00
157 Julio Jones RC 5.00 12.00
158 Justin Houston RC 2.00 5.00
159 Kendall Hunter RC 1.50 4.00
160 Kyle Rudolph RC 1.50 4.00
161 Lance Kendricks RC 1.50 4.00
162 Leonard Hankerson RC 1.50 4.00
163 Luke Stocker RC 1.50 4.00
164 Marcell Dareus RC 1.50 4.00
165 Mark Ingram RC 2.50 6.00
165B Mark Ingram BF 1.25 3.00
166 Martez Wilson RC 1.50 4.00
167 Mike Pouncey RC 2.50 6.00
168 Mikel Leshoure RC 1.50 4.00
169 Nick Fairley RC 1.50 4.00
169B Nick Fairley BF .75 2.00
170 Niles Paul RC 1.50 4.00
170B Niles Paul BF .75 2.00
171 Muhammad Wilkerson RC 1.50 4.00
172 Owen Marecic RC 1.50 4.00
173 Pat Devlin RC 2.50 6.00
174 Patrick Peterson RC 3.00 8.00
174B Patrick Peterson BF 1.50 4.00
175 Phil Taylor RC 1.50 4.00
176 Prince Amukamara RC 1.50 4.00
177 Quan Sturdivant RC 2.00 5.00
178 Quinton Carter RC 1.50 4.00
179 Rahim Moore RC 1.50 4.00
180 Randall Cobb RC 2.50 6.00
181 Ricky Stanzi RC 1.50 4.00
181B Ricky Stanzi BF .75 2.00
182 Rob Housler RC 1.50 4.00
183 Robert Quinn RC 1.50 4.00
184 Ronald Johnson RC 1.50 4.00
185 Ryan Kerrigan RC 2.00 5.00
186 Ryan Mallett RC 1.50 4.00
187 Ryan Whalen RC 1.50 4.00
188 Ryan Williams RC 1.50 4.00
189 Shane Vereen RC 2.00 5.00
190 Stanley Havili RC 1.50 4.00
191 Stephen Paea RC 1.50 4.00
192 Stevan Ridley RC 1.50 4.00
193 Taiwan Jones RC 1.50 4.00
194 Tandon Doss RC 1.50 4.00
195 Ras-I Dowling RC 1.50 4.00
196 Titus Young RC 1.50 4.00
197 Torrey Smith RC 1.50 4.00
198 Tyler Sash RC 1.50 4.00
199 Vincent Brown RC 1.50 4.00
200 Von Miller RC 2.50 6.00
201 Terrelle Pryor BF 1.25 3.00

2011 Donruss Elite Aspirations

*VETS/71-99: 5X TO 12X BASIC CARDS
*ROOKIES/71-99: .6X TO 1.5X BASIC CARDS
*VETS/46-69: 6X TO 15X BASIC CARDS
*ROOKIES/46-69: .8X TO 2X BASIC CARDS
*ROOKIES/30-45: 1X TO 2.5X BASIC CARDS
*VETS/20: 10X TO 25X BASIC CARDS
*ROOKIES/20: 1.2X TO 3X BASIC CARDS
*VETS/10-19: 12X TO 30X BASIC CARDS
*ROOKIES/10-19: 1.5X TO 4X BASIC CARDS
STATED PRINT RUN 1-99

2011 Donruss Elite Status

*VETS/70-99: 5X TO 12X BASIC CARDS
*ROOKIES/70-99: .6X TO 1.5X BASIC CARDS
*VETS/46-57: 6X TO 15X BASIC CARDS
*ROOKIES/46-57: .8X TO 2X BASIC CARDS
*VETS/31-45: 8X TO 20X BASIC CARDS
*ROOKIES/31-45: 1X TO 2.5X BASIC CARDS
*VETS/20-29: 10X TO 25X BASIC CARDS
*ROOKIES/20-29: 1.2X TO 3X BASIC CARDS
*VETS/10-19: 12X TO 30X BASIC CARDS
*ROOKIES/10-19: 1.5X TO 4X BASIC CARDS
STATED PRINT RUN 1-99

2011 Donruss Elite Status Black

*VETS 1-100: 10X TO 25X BASIC CARDS
*ROOKIES 101-200: 1.2X TO 3X
STATED PRINT RUN 24 SER.#'d SETS

2011 Donruss Elite Aspirations Autographs

1-100 VETERAN PRINT RUN 5-25
ROOKIE STATED PRINT RUN 49
SERIAL #'d UNDER 16 NOT PRICED
5 Michael Turner/17 15.00 40.00
14 Jonathan Stewart/25 12.00 30.00
23 Colt McCoy/25 12.00 30.00
24 Josh Cribbs/25 12.00 30.00
37 Donald Driver/25 15.00 40.00
43 Pierre Garcon/16 20.00 50.00
55 Percy Harvin/25 12.00 30.00
69 Mark Sanchez/25 15.00 40.00
74 Jeremy Maclin/25 12.00 30.00
81 Mike Tolbert/25 12.00 30.00
90 Sam Bradford/25 12.00 30.00
94 Mike Williams/25 15.00 40.00
101 A.J. Green 20.00 50.00
102 Aaron Williams 8.00 20.00
103 Adrian Clayborn 6.00 15.00
104 Ahmad Black 8.00 20.00
105 Akeem Ayers 6.00 15.00
106 Aldon Smith 6.00 15.00
107 Alex Green 6.00 15.00
108 Andy Dalton 12.00 30.00
109 Austin Pettis 6.00 15.00
110 Bilal Powell 8.00 20.00
111 Blaine Gabbert 6.00 15.00
112 Brandon Harris 6.00 15.00
115 Cam Newton 50.00 100.00
116 Cameron Heyward 8.00 20.00
117 Cameron Jordan 8.00 20.00
118 Cecil Shorts 6.00 15.00
119 Christian Ponder 6.00 15.00
120 Colin Kaepernick 10.00 25.00
122 Corey Liuget 8.00 20.00
125 D.J. Williams 6.00 15.00
126 Daniel Thomas 6.00 15.00
127 Da'Quan Bowers 6.00 15.00
131 DeAndre McDaniel 6.00 15.00
132 Delone Carter 6.00 15.00
133 DeMarco Murray 12.00 30.00
134 Denarius Moore 25.00 60.00
135 Derrick Locke 8.00 20.00
136 Dion Lewis 8.00 20.00
138 Dwayne Harris 6.00 15.00
139 Edmond Gates 6.00 15.00
140 Evan Royster 6.00 15.00
141 Greg Jones 8.00 20.00
142 Greg Little 8.00 20.00
144 Greg Salas 6.00 15.00
145 J.J. Watt 60.00 120.00
148 Jake Locker 6.00 15.00
149 Jamie Harper 6.00 15.00
150 Jeremy Kerley 10.00 25.00
151 Jerrel Jernigan 6.00 15.00
152 Jimmy Smith 6.00 15.00
153 John Clay 8.00 20.00
154 Jonathan Baldwin 6.00 15.00
155 Jordan Todman 6.00 15.00
157 Julio Jones 40.00 80.00
159 Kendall Hunter 6.00 15.00
160 Kyle Rudolph 6.00 15.00
161 Lance Kendricks 6.00 15.00
162 Leonard Hankerson 6.00 15.00
163 Luke Stocker 6.00 15.00
164 Marcell Dareus 6.00 15.00
165 Mark Ingram 10.00 25.00
166 Martez Wilson 8.00 20.00
168 Mikel Leshoure 6.00 15.00
170 Niles Paul 6.00 15.00
173 Pat Devlin 8.00 20.00
175 Phil Taylor 6.00 15.00
176 Prince Amukamara 6.00 15.00
178 Quinton Carter 6.00 15.00
179 Rahim Moore 6.00 15.00
180 Randall Cobb 10.00 25.00
181 Ricky Stanzi 6.00 15.00
184 Ronald Johnson 8.00 20.00
185 Ryan Kerrigan 8.00 20.00
186 Ryan Mallett 12.00 30.00
187 Ryan Whalen 6.00 15.00
188 Ryan Williams 20.00 50.00
189 Shane Vereen 8.00 20.00
190 Stanley Havili 6.00 15.00
191 Stephen Paea 6.00 15.00
192 Stevan Ridley 6.00 15.00
193 Taiwan Jones 6.00 15.00
194 Tandon Doss 6.00 15.00
196 Titus Young 6.00 15.00
197 Torrey Smith 6.00 15.00
198 Tyler Sash 6.00 15.00
199 Vincent Brown 6.00 15.00
200 Von Miller 15.00 40.00

2011 Donruss Elite Craftsmen Gold

GOLD PRINT RUN 999 SER.#'d SETS
*BLACK/99: .8X TO 2X GOLD/999
*RED/49: 1X TO 2.5X GOLD/999
1 Aaron Rodgers 2.00 5.00
2 Andre Johnson 1.00 2.50
3 Antonio Gates .75 2.00
4 Braylon Edwards .75 2.00
5 Calvin Johnson 1.25 3.00
6 Carson Palmer 1.00 2.50
7 Darren McFadden .75 2.00
8 David Garrard .75 2.00
9 Devery Henderson .75 2.00
10 Devin Hester 1.00 2.50
11 Drew Brees 1.25 3.00
12 Heath Miller .75 2.00
13 Jamaal Charles 1.00 2.50
14 Jason Witten 1.00 2.50
15 Jeremy Maclin .75 2.00
16 Joe Flacco 1.00 2.50
17 Lee Evans 1.00 2.50
18 Matt Schaub .75 2.00
19 Michael Turner .75 2.00
20 Mike Wallace .75 2.00
21 Peyton Manning 2.50 6.00
22 Sam Bradford .75 2.00
23 Santonio Holmes .75 2.00
24 Steven Jackson .75 2.00
25 Vincent Jackson .75 2.00
26 Andy Dalton BF .60 1.50

2011 Donruss Elite Craftsmen Jerseys

STATED PRINT RUN 299 SER.#'d SETS
*PRIME/50: .8X TO 2X BASIC JSY/299
1 Aaron Rodgers 5.00 12.00
2 Andre Johnson 2.50 6.00
3 Antonio Gates 2.00 5.00
4 Braylon Edwards 2.00 5.00
5 Calvin Johnson 3.00 8.00
6 Carson Palmer 2.50 6.00
7 Darren McFadden 2.00 5.00
8 David Garrard 2.00 5.00
9 Devery Henderson 2.00 5.00
10 Devin Hester 2.50 6.00
11 Drew Brees 3.00 8.00
12 Heath Miller 2.00 5.00
13 Jamaal Charles 2.50 6.00
14 Jason Witten 3.00 8.00
15 Jeremy Maclin 2.00 5.00
16 Joe Flacco 2.50 6.00
17 Lee Evans 2.50 6.00
18 Matt Schaub 2.00 5.00
19 Michael Turner 2.00 5.00
20 Mike Wallace 2.00 5.00
21 Peyton Manning 6.00 15.00
22 Sam Bradford 2.00 5.00
23 Santonio Holmes 2.00 5.00
24 Steven Jackson 2.00 5.00
25 Vincent Jackson 2.00 5.00

2011 Donruss Elite Down and Distance Black Friday

INSERTED IN BLACK FRIDAY PACKS
52 Julio Jones .60 1.50
53 A.J. Green .50 1.25

2011 Donruss Elite Down and Distance Jerseys

STATED PRINT RUN 30-299
*PRIME/35-50: .8X TO 2X BASIC JSY/214-299
*PRIME/40: .4X TO 1X BASIC JSY/30
2 Chris Wells/299 2.00 5.00
3 Bernard Berrian/299 2.00 5.00
4 Bo Scaife/225 2.00 5.00
5 Brandon Jacobs/299 2.00 5.00
6 Brandon Marshall/299 2.50 6.00
7 Cadillac Williams/299 2.00 5.00
8 Dallas Clark/299 2.00 5.00
9 Darren Sproles/299 2.50 6.00
10 Donald Driver/299 2.50 6.00
11 Dustin Keller/299 2.50 6.00
12 Eddie Royal/299 2.00 5.00
13 Felix Jones/299 2.00 5.00
14 Frank Gore/299 2.50 6.00
15 Greg Olsen/299 2.50 6.00
16 James Jones/30 4.00 10.00
17 Jeremy Shockey/299 2.00 5.00
18 Johnny Knox/299 2.00 5.00
19 Jonathan Stewart/299 2.00 5.00
20 Joseph Addai/299 2.00 5.00
21 Kenny Britt/275 2.00 5.00
22 Kevin Boss/299 2.00 5.00
23 Louis Murphy/299 2.00 5.00
24 Malcom Floyd/299 2.00 5.00
25 Marion Barber/299 2.00 5.00
26 Matt Cassel/299 2.00 5.00
27 Matthew Stafford/299 2.50 6.00
28 Mike Sims-Walker/299 2.50 6.00
29 Sam Hurd/299 2.00 5.00
30 Miles Austin/299 3.00 8.00
31 Willis McGahee/299 2.00 5.00
32 Nate Washington/299 2.00 5.00
33 Owen Daniels/299 2.00 5.00
34 Pierre Garcon/299 2.50 6.00
35 Randy Moss/299 2.50 6.00
36 Robert Meachem/214 2.00 5.00
37 Ronnie Brown/299 2.50 6.00
38 Ryan Fitzpatrick/299 2.00 5.00
40 Ryan Mathews/299 2.50 6.00
41 Santana Moss/299 2.50 6.00
42 Shonn Greene/299 2.00 5.00
43 Sidney Rice/299 2.00 5.00
44 Steve Smith/299 2.50 6.00
45 Tarvaris Jackson/299 2.00 5.00
46 Tashard Choice/299 2.00 5.00
47 Todd Heap/299 2.00 5.00
48 Tony Gonzalez/299 2.50 6.00
49 Wes Welker/299 3.00 8.00

2011 Donruss Elite Down and Distance Jerseys Autographs

JERSEY AUTO PRINT RUN 6-25
UNPRICED PRIME AU PRINT RUN 9-10
3 Bernard Berrian/25 12.00 30.00
8 Dallas Clark/25 12.00 30.00
16 James Jones/15 12.00 30.00
19 Jonathan Stewart/25 12.00 30.00
22 Kevin Boss/25 12.00 30.00
23 Louis Murphy/19 12.00 30.00
40 Ryan Mathews/25 15.00 40.00
42 Shonn Greene/25 12.00 30.00

2011 Donruss Elite Hit List Gold

STATED PRINT RUN 999 SER.#'d SETS
*BLACK/99: .8X TO 2X GOLD/999
*RED/49: 1X TO 2.5X GOLD/999
1 Barrett Ruud .75 2.00
2 Brian Cushing .75 2.00
3 Brian Urlacher 1.25 3.00
4 Chad Greenway 1.00 2.50
5 Clay Matthews 1.25 3.00
6 Curtis Lofton .75 2.00
7 Darrelle Revis .75 2.00
8 DeMarcus Ware 1.00 2.50
9 Dwight Freeney .75 2.00
10 Ed Reed 1.00 2.50
11 James Harrison 1.00 2.50
12 James Laurinaitis .75 2.00
13 Jared Allen .75 2.00
14 Jerod Mayo .75 2.00
15 Jon Beason .75 2.00
16 Julius Peppers 1.00 2.50
17 LaRon Landry .75 2.00
18 London Fletcher 1.00 2.50
19 Ndamukong Suh 1.00 2.50
20 Patrick Willis 1.00 2.50
21 Ray Lewis 1.25 3.00
22 Stephen Tulloch .75 2.00
23 Tamba Hali .75 2.00
24 Troy Polamalu 1.25 3.00
25 Asante Samuel .75 2.00
26 Von Miller BF .50 1.25

2011 Donruss Elite Hit List Jerseys

STATED PRINT RUN 299 SER.#'d SETS
*PRIME/50: .8X TO 2X BASIC JSY/299
1 Barrett Ruud 2.50 6.00
3 Brian Urlacher 4.00 10.00
4 Chad Greenway 3.00 8.00
5 Clay Matthews 6.00 15.00
7 Darrelle Revis 2.50 6.00
8 DeMarcus Ware 3.00 8.00
9 Dwight Freeney 2.50 6.00
10 Ed Reed 3.00 8.00
11 James Harrison 4.00 10.00
12 James Laurinaitis 2.50 6.00
13 Jared Allen 2.50 6.00
15 Jon Beason 2.50 6.00
17 LaRon Landry 2.50 6.00
18 London Fletcher 3.00 8.00
20 Patrick Willis 3.00 8.00
21 Ray Lewis 4.00 10.00
23 Tamba Hali 3.00 8.00
24 Troy Polamalu 4.00 10.00
25 Asante Samuel 2.50 6.00

2011 Donruss Elite Legends of the Fall Gold

GOLD PRINT RUN 999 SER.#'d SETS
*BLACK/99: .8X TO 2X GOLD/999
*RED/49: 1X TO 2.5X GOLD/999
1 Adrian Peterson 1.25 3.00
2 Ben Roethlisberger 1.25 3.00
3 Chad Johnson .75 2.00
4 Chris Johnson .75 2.00
5 DeSean Jackson 1.00 2.50
6 Donovan McNabb 1.00 2.50
7 Dwayne Bowe 1.00 2.50
8 Eli Manning 1.00 2.50
9 Greg Jennings .75 2.00
10 Jay Cutler .75 2.00
11 LaDainian Tomlinson 1.25 3.00
12 Larry Fitzgerald 1.00 2.50
13 LeSean McCoy 1.25 3.00
14 Mark Sanchez .75 2.00
15 Matt Ryan 1.00 2.50
16 Maurice Jones-Drew .75 2.00
17 Michael Vick 1.00 2.50
18 Percy Harvin .75 2.00
19 Philip Rivers 1.25 3.00
20 Ray Rice .75 2.00
21 Roddy White .75 2.00
22 Reggie Wayne 1.00 2.50
23 Tony Romo 1.00 2.50
24 Tom Brady 3.00 8.00
25 Vernon Davis .75 2.00

2011 Donruss Elite Legends of the Fall Jerseys

STATED PRINT RUN 76-299
*PRIME/50: .8X TO 2X BASIC JSY/299
*PRIME/50: .6X TO 1.5X BASIC JSY/76
1 Adrian Peterson/299 3.00 8.00
3 Chad Johnson/299 2.00 5.00
4 Chris Johnson/299 2.00 5.00
5 DeSean Jackson/299 2.50 6.00
6 Donovan McNabb/299 2.50 6.00
7 Dwayne Bowe/299 2.50 6.00
8 Eli Manning/299 2.50 6.00
9 Greg Jennings/76 2.50 6.00
10 Jay Cutler/299 2.00 5.00
11 LaDainian Tomlinson/299 3.00 8.00
12 Larry Fitzgerald/299 2.50 6.00
13 LeSean McCoy/299 3.00 8.00
14 Mark Sanchez/299 2.00 5.00
15 Matt Ryan/299 2.50 6.00
16 Maurice Jones-Drew/299 2.00 5.00
17 Michael Vick/299 2.50 6.00
18 Percy Harvin/299 2.00 5.00
19 Philip Rivers/299 3.00 8.00
20 Ray Rice/299 3.00 8.00
21 Roddy White/299 2.00 5.00
22 Reggie Wayne/299 2.50 6.00
23 Tony Romo/299 2.50 6.00
24 Tom Brady/299 8.00 20.00
25 Vernon Davis/299 2.00 5.00

2011 Donruss Elite New Breed Jersey

STATED PRINT RUN 299 SER.#'d SETS
*PRIME/50: .8X TO 2X BASIC JSY/299
1 A.J. Green 4.00 10.00
2 Alex Green 1.50 4.00
3 Andy Dalton 3.00 8.00
4 Austin Pettis 1.50 4.00
5 Bilal Powell 2.00 5.00
6 Blaine Gabbert 1.50 4.00
7 Cam Newton 8.00 20.00
8 Christian Ponder 1.50 4.00
9 Colin Kaepernick 2.50 6.00
10 Daniel Thomas 1.50 4.00
11 Delone Carter 1.50 4.00
12 DeMarco Murray 3.00 8.00
13 Greg Little 2.00 5.00
14 Jake Locker 1.50 4.00
15 Jamie Harper 1.50 4.00
16 Jerrel Jernigan 1.50 4.00
17 Jonathan Baldwin 1.50 4.00
18 Jordan Todman 1.50 4.00
19 Julio Jones 5.00 12.00
20 Kendall Hunter 1.50 4.00
21 Kyle Rudolph 1.50 4.00
22 Leonard Hankerson 1.50 4.00
23 Marcell Dareus 1.50 4.00
24 Mark Ingram 2.50 6.00
25 Mikel Leshoure 1.50 4.00
26 Randall Cobb 2.50 6.00
27 Ryan Mallett 1.50 4.00
28 Ryan Williams 1.50 4.00
29 Shane Vereen 2.00 5.00
30 Stevan Ridley 1.50 4.00
31 Taiwan Jones 1.50 4.00
32 Titus Young 1.50 4.00
33 Torrey Smith 1.50 4.00
34 Vincent Brown 1.50 4.00
35 Von Miller 2.50 6.00
36 Edmond Gates 1.50 4.00

2011 Donruss Elite New Breed Jersey Autographs

STATED PRINT RUN 25 SER.#'d SETS
UNPRICED PRIME AU PRINT RUN 10
1 A.J. Green 40.00 80.00
2 Alex Green 8.00 20.00
3 Andy Dalton 15.00 40.00
4 Austin Pettis 8.00 20.00
5 Bilal Powell 10.00 25.00
6 Blaine Gabbert 8.00 20.00
7 Cam Newton 75.00 150.00
8 Christian Ponder 8.00 20.00
9 Colin Kaepernick 12.00 30.00
10 Daniel Thomas 8.00 20.00
11 Delone Carter 8.00 20.00
12 DeMarco Murray 15.00 40.00
13 Greg Little 10.00 25.00
14 Jake Locker 8.00 20.00
15 Jamie Harper 8.00 20.00
16 Jerrel Jernigan 8.00 20.00
17 Jonathan Baldwin 8.00 20.00
18 Jordan Todman 8.00 20.00
19 Julio Jones 40.00 80.00
20 Kendall Hunter 8.00 20.00
21 Kyle Rudolph 8.00 20.00
22 Leonard Hankerson 8.00 20.00
23 Marcell Dareus 8.00 20.00
24 Mark Ingram 12.00 30.00
25 Mikel Leshoure 8.00 20.00
26 Randall Cobb 12.00 30.00
27 Ryan Mallett 15.00 40.00
28 Ryan Williams 8.00 20.00
29 Shane Vereen 10.00 25.00
30 Stevan Ridley 8.00 20.00
31 Taiwan Jones 8.00 20.00
32 Titus Young 8.00 20.00
33 Torrey Smith 8.00 20.00
34 Vincent Brown 8.00 20.00
35 Von Miller 20.00 50.00
36 Edmond Gates 8.00 20.00

2011 Donruss Elite Passing the Torch Autographs

STATED PRINT RUN 19-25
EXCH EXPIRATION: 12/22/2012
1 P.Mann/Bradford/25 125.00 250.00
2 Tomlin/Mathws/25 60.00 120.00
3 Elway/Tebow/25 150.00 300.00
4 M.Irvin/Bryant/25 75.00 150.00
5 T.Gonzalez/Moeaki/25 50.00 100.00
6 K.Johnson/M.Will/25 40.00 80.00
7 Cunningham/Vick/25 40.00 100.00
8 Harris/Mendnhll/25 40.00 80.00
9 Holmes/Foster/25 50.00 100.00
10 Harvin/Bradford/25 40.00 100.00
11 Starr/Namath/25 125.00 250.00
12 S.HolmesE.Manning/25 50.00 100.00
13 Brees/Rodgers/25 200.00 350.00
14 Martin/Tomlinson/25 50.00 100.00
15 M.Ingram/C.Newton/25 25.00 50.00

2011 Donruss Elite Power Formulas Gold

STATED PRINT RUN 999 SER.#'d SETS
*BLACK/99: .8X TO 2X GOLD/999
*RED/49: 1X TO 2.5X GOLD/999
1 Ahmad Bradshaw .75 2.00
2 Anquan Boldin .75 2.00
3 Anthony Gonzalez .75 2.00
4 Arian Foster .75 2.00
5 Brent Celek .75 2.00
6 C.J. Spiller .75 2.00
7 Chad Henne 1.00 2.50
8 Chris Cooley .75 2.00
9 DeAngelo Williams .75 2.00
10 Dez Bryant 1.25 3.00
11 Hakeem Nicks .75 2.00
12 Hines Ward 1.00 2.50
13 Jahvid Best .75 2.00
14 Josh Cribbs .75 2.00
15 Josh Freeman 1.00 2.50
16 Knowshon Moreno .75 2.00
17 Marques Colston .75 2.00
18 Matt Forte .75 2.00
19 Michael Crabtree .75 2.00
20 Mike Williams 1.00 2.50
21 Rashard Mendenhall .75 2.00
22 Reggie Bush .75 2.00
23 Rob Gronkowski 1.25 3.00
24 Tim Tebow 1.25 3.00
25 Visanthe Shiancoe 1.00 2.50
26 Mark Ingram BF .50 1.25
27 Cam Newton BF 1.50 4.00

2011 Donruss Elite Power Formulas Jerseys Prime

PRIME PRINT RUN 50 SER.#'d SETS
*BASE JSY/299: .2X TO .5X PRIME/50
1 Ahmad Bradshaw 4.00 10.00
2 Anquan Boldin 4.00 10.00
3 Anthony Gonzalez 4.00 10.00
4 Arian Foster 4.00 10.00
5 Brent Celek 4.00 10.00
6 C.J. Spiller 4.00 10.00
7 Chad Henne 5.00 12.00
8 Chris Cooley 4.00 10.00
9 DeAngelo Williams 4.00 10.00
10 Dez Bryant 6.00 15.00
11 Hakeem Nicks 4.00 10.00
12 Hines Ward 6.00 15.00
13 Jahvid Best 4.00 10.00
14 Josh Cribbs 4.00 10.00
15 Josh Freeman 5.00 12.00
16 Knowshon Moreno 4.00 10.00
17 Marques Colston 4.00 10.00
18 Matt Forte 4.00 10.00
19 Michael Crabtree 4.00 10.00
21 Rashard Mendenhall 4.00 10.00
22 Reggie Bush 4.00 10.00
24 Tim Tebow 6.00 15.00
25 Visanthe Shiancoe 5.00 12.00

2011 Donruss Elite Rookie NFL Shield

STATED PRINT RUN 999 SER.#'d SETS
*TEAM LOGO/999: .4X TO 1X NFL SHIELD/999
1 A.J. Green 2.00 5.00
2 Austin Pettis .75 2.00
3 Greg Little 1.00 2.50
4 Jerrel Jernigan .75 2.00
5 Jonathan Baldwin .75 2.00
6 Julio Jones 2.50 6.00
7 Leonard Hankerson .75 2.00
8 Randall Cobb 1.25 3.00
9 Titus Young .75 2.00
10 Torrey Smith .75 2.00
11 Vincent Brown .75 2.00
12 Von Miller 1.25 3.00
13 Marcell Dareus .75 2.00
14 Alex Green .75 2.00
15 Bilal Powell 1.00 2.50
16 Daniel Thomas .75 2.00
17 Delone Carter .75 2.00
18 DeMarco Murray 1.50 4.00
19 Jamie Harper .75 2.00
20 Jordan Todman .75 2.00
21 Kendall Hunter .75 2.00
22 Mark Ingram 1.25 3.00
23 Mikel Leshoure .75 2.00
24 Ryan Williams .75 2.00
25 Shane Vereen 1.00 2.50
26 Stevan Ridley .75 2.00
27 Taiwan Jones .75 2.00
28 Andy Dalton 1.50 4.00
29 Blaine Gabbert .75 2.00
30 Cam Newton 4.00 10.00
31 Christian Ponder .75 2.00
32 Colin Kaepernick 1.25 3.00
33 Jake Locker .75 2.00
34 Kyle Rudolph .75 2.00
35 Ryan Mallett .75 2.00
36 Edmond Gates .75 2.00

2011 Donruss Elite Rookie NFL Shield Autographs

RANDOM INSERTS IN PACKS
1 A.J. Green 20.00 50.00
2 Austin Pettis 4.00 10.00
3 Greg Little 5.00 12.00
4 Jerrel Jernigan 4.00 10.00
5 Jonathan Baldwin 8.00 20.00
6 Julio Jones 25.00 50.00
7 Leonard Hankerson 4.00 10.00
8 Randall Cobb 6.00 15.00
9 Titus Young 4.00 10.00
10 Torrey Smith 4.00 10.00
11 Vincent Brown 6.00 15.00
12 Von Miller 10.00 25.00
13 Marcell Dareus 4.00 10.00
14 Alex Green 15.00 30.00
15 Bilal Powell 5.00 12.00
16 Daniel Thomas 4.00 10.00
17 Delone Carter 4.00 10.00
18 DeMarco Murray 8.00 20.00
19 Jamie Harper 4.00 10.00
20 Jordan Todman 4.00 10.00
21 Kendall Hunter 4.00 10.00
22 Mark Ingram 6.00 15.00
23 Mikel Leshoure 4.00 10.00
24 Ryan Williams 4.00 10.00
25 Shane Vereen 5.00 12.00
26 Stevan Ridley 4.00 10.00
27 Taiwan Jones 4.00 10.00
28 Andy Dalton 8.00 20.00
29 Blaine Gabbert 4.00 10.00
30 Edmund Gates 4.00 10.00
31 Christian Ponder 4.00 10.00
32 Colin Kaepernick 6.00 15.00
33 Jake Locker 4.00 10.00
34 Kyle Rudolph 4.00 10.00
35 Ryan Mallett 10.00 25.00
36 Cam Newton 30.00 80.00

2011 Donruss Elite Rookie NFL Team Logo Autographs

RANDOM INSERTS IN PACKS
1 A.J. Green 20.00 50.00
2 Austin Pettis 4.00 10.00
3 Greg Little 5.00 12.00
4 Jerrel Jernigan 4.00 10.00
5 Jonathan Baldwin 8.00 20.00
6 Julio Jones 25.00 50.00
7 Leonard Hankerson 4.00 10.00
8 Randall Cobb 6.00 15.00
9 Titus Young 4.00 10.00
10 Torrey Smith 4.00 10.00
11 Vincent Brown 6.00 15.00
12 Von Miller 10.00 25.00
13 Marcell Dareus 4.00 10.00
14 Alex Green 15.00 30.00
15 Bilal Powell 5.00 12.00
16 Daniel Thomas 4.00 10.00
17 Delone Carter 4.00 10.00
18 DeMarco Murray 8.00 20.00
19 Jamie Harper 4.00 10.00
20 Jordan Todman 4.00 10.00
21 Kendall Hunter 4.00 10.00
22 Mark Ingram 6.00 15.00
23 Mikel Leshoure 4.00 10.00
24 Ryan Williams 4.00 10.00
25 Shane Vereen 5.00 12.00
26 Stevan Ridley 4.00 10.00
27 Taiwan Jones 4.00 10.00
28 Andy Dalton 8.00 20.00
29 Blaine Gabbert 4.00 10.00
30 Cam Newton 30.00 80.00
31 Christian Ponder 4.00 10.00
32 Colin Kaepernick 6.00 15.00
33 Jake Locker 4.00 10.00
34 Kyle Rudolph 4.00 10.00
35 Ryan Mallett 10.00 25.00
36 Edmond Gates 4.00 10.00

2011 Donruss Elite Status Autographs

UNPRICED VET PRINT RUN 3-10
*ROOKIES/24: .6X TO 1.5X ASPIR.AU/49
101-200 ROOKIE PRINT RUN 24
UNPRICED STATUS BLACK PRINT RUN 1
108 Andy Dalton 20.00 50.00
111 Blaine Gabbert 10.00 25.00
115 Cam Newton 75.00 150.00
119 Christian Ponder 10.00 25.00
120 Colin Kaepernick 15.00 40.00
148 Jake Locker 10.00 25.00
157 Julio Jones 50.00 100.00
165 Mark Ingram 15.00 40.00

2011 Donruss Elite Throwback Threads

STATED PRINT RUN 66-99
*PRIME/25: .8X TO 2X BASIC JSY/66-99
1 O.Graham/S.Baugh/99 20.00 50.00
2 D.Sanders/B.Jackson/99 15.00 40.00
3 Cunningham/M.Vick/99 10.00 25.00
4 J.Montana/T.Brady/99 30.00 60.00
5 J.Plunkett/M.Allen/99 12.00 30.00
6 D.White/E.Jones/99 8.00 20.00
7 R.Berry/L.Moore /99 10.00 25.00
8 E.Smith/E.Dickerson/99 15.00 40.00
9 R.Dent/J.McMahon/99 10.00 25.00
10 B.Griese/P.Warfield/66 10.00 25.00
11 P.Hornung/F.Gregg/99 12.00 30.00
12 D.Marino/M.Duper/99 15.00 40.00
13 G.Blanda/J.Stenerud/99 10.00 25.00
14 B.Esiason/J.Kelly/99 12.00 30.00
15 J.Greene/R.Staubach/99 12.00 30.00

2011 Donruss Elite Throwback Threads Autographs

DUAL AU STATED PRINT RUN 3-25
UNPRICED PRIME AU PRINT RUN 10
2 D.Sndrs/Jacksn/25 90.00 150.00
3 Cunningham/Vick/25 75.00 150.00
4 Montana/Brady/25 EXCH
5 Plunkett/M.Allen/25 40.00 100.00
6 D.White/E.Jones/25 40.00 100.00
7 Berry/L.Moore/25 30.00 80.00
8 E.Smith/Dickerson/25 125.00 200.00
9 Dent/McMahon/25 60.00 120.00
10 Griese/Warfield/25 40.00 100.00
11 Hornung/F.Gregg/25 40.00 100.00
12 Marino/Duper/25 125.00 250.00
14 Esiason/J.Kelly/25 40.00 100.00
15 Greene/Stbch/25 EXCH 60.00 120.00

2011 Donruss Elite Turn of the Century Autographs

STATED PRINT RUN 14-499
UNPRICED PRINT PLATE #'d TO 1
101 A.J. Green/199 25.00 60.00
102 Aaron Williams/499 5.00 12.00
103 Adrian Clayborn/499 4.00 10.00
104 Ahmad Black/499 5.00 12.00
105 Akeem Ayers/499 4.00 10.00
106 Aldon Smith/499 4.00 10.00
107 Alex Green/499 4.00 10.00
108 Andy Dalton/199 10.00 25.00
109 Austin Pettis/499 4.00 10.00
110 Bilal Powell/399 5.00 12.00
111 Blaine Gabbert/199 5.00 12.00
112 Brandon Harris/499 5.00 12.00
115 Cam Newton/199 40.00 100.00
116 Cameron Heyward/499 5.00 12.00
117 Cameron Jordan/499 5.00 12.00
118 Cecil Shorts/499 4.00 10.00
119 Christian Ponder/199 5.00 12.00
120 Colin Kaepernick/199 8.00 20.00
122 Corey Liuget/499 5.00 12.00
125 D.J. Williams/299 5.00 12.00
126 Daniel Thomas/299 5.00 12.00
127 Da'Quan Bowers/299 5.00 12.00
131 DeAndre McDaniel/499 5.00 12.00
132 Delone Carter/299 5.00 12.00
133 DeMarco Murray/299 10.00 25.00
135 Derrick Locke/199 6.00 15.00
136 Dion Lewis/499 5.00 12.00
138 Dwayne Harris/499 4.00 10.00
139 Edmond Gates/299 6.00 15.00
140 Evan Royster/499 4.00 10.00
141 Greg Jones/499 5.00 12.00
142 Greg Little/299 8.00 20.00
144 Greg Salas/499 4.00 10.00
145 J.J. Watt/499 40.00 80.00
148 Jake Locker/199 5.00 12.00
149 Jamie Harper/299 6.00 15.00
150 Jeremy Kerley/499 6.00 15.00
151 Jerrel Jernigan/299 6.00 15.00
152 Jimmy Smith/499 5.00 12.00
153 John Clay/499 5.00 12.00
154 Jonathan Baldwin/299 5.00 12.00
155 Jordan Todman/299 6.00 15.00
157 Julio Jones/199 20.00 50.00
159 Kendall Hunter/299 5.00 12.00
160 Kyle Rudolph/299 5.00 12.00
161 Lance Kendricks/499 5.00 12.00
162 Leonard Hankerson/299 5.00 12.00
163 Luke Stocker/499 5.00 12.00
164 Marcell Dareus/499 4.00 10.00
165 Mark Ingram/199 8.00 20.00
166 Martez Wilson/499 5.00 12.00
168 Mikel Leshoure/299 5.00 12.00
170 Niles Paul/499 4.00 10.00
173 Pat Devlin/14
175 Phil Taylor/499 4.00 10.00
176 Prince Amukamara/399 4.00 10.00
178 Quinton Carter/499 4.00 10.00
179 Rahim Moore/499 4.00 10.00
180 Randall Cobb/299 8.00 20.00
181 Ricky Stanzi/299 5.00 12.00
184 Ronald Johnson/499 4.00 10.00
185 Ryan Kerrigan/499 5.00 12.00
186 Ryan Mallett/199 15.00 40.00
187 Ryan Whalen/499 4.00 10.00
188 Ryan Williams/299 5.00 12.00
189 Shane Vereen/299 6.00 15.00
190 Stanley Havili/499 4.00 10.00
191 Stephen Paea/499 4.00 10.00
192 Stevan Ridley/399 4.00 10.00
193 Taiwan Jones/499 4.00 10.00
194 Tandon Doss/499 5.00 12.00
196 Titus Young/299 5.00 12.00
197 Torrey Smith/299 5.00 12.00
198 Tyler Sash/499 4.00 10.00
199 Vincent Brown/99 6.00 15.00
200 Von Miller/299 12.00 30.00

2011 Donruss Elite National Convention

ANNOUNCED PRINT RUN 500 SETS
*BLUE/10: 2X TO 5X BASIC CARDS
*RED/25: 1.5X TO 4X BASIC CARDS
1 Aaron Rodgers 1.50 4.00
2 Adrian Peterson 1.50 4.00
3 Peyton Manning 2.00 5.00
4 Sam Bradford 1.50 4.00
5 Tim Tebow 1.50 4.00
6 Tom Brady 1.50 4.00
7 Terrelle Pryor 3.00 8.00

2011 Donruss Elite National Convention VIP

*BLUE/10: 2X TO 5X BASIC CARDS
*RED/25: 1.5X TO 4X BASIC CARDS
VIP1 Cam Newton 2.50 6.00
VIP2 Mark Ingram .75 2.00
VIP3 Terrelle Pryor 3.00 8.00
VIP4 A.J. Green 1.25 3.00
VIP5 Jake Locker .50 1.25
VIP6 Blaine Gabbert .50 1.25

2007 Donruss Elite Extra Edition

COMPLETE SET (142)
COMP.SET w/o AU's (92) 8.00 20.00
COMMON CARD (1-92) .20 .50
COMMON AU (92-142) 4.00 10.00
OVERALL AUTO/MEM ODDS 1:5
AU PRINT RUNS B/WN 374-999 COPIES PER
EXCHANGE DEADLINE 07/01/2009
66 Ara Parseghian .20 .50
70 Frank Broyles .20 .50
74 Steve Spurrier .20 .50
75 Tom Osborne .20 .50
76 Vince Dooley .20 .50
82 Clint Dolezel .20 .50

2007 Donruss Elite Extra Edition Aspirations

*ASP 1-92: 3X TO 8X BASIC
OVERALL INSERT ODDS 1:4
STATED PRINT RUN 100 SER.#'d SETS

2007 Donruss Elite Extra Edition Status

*STATUS 1-92: 4X TO 10X BASIC
OVERALL INSERT ODDS 1:4
STATED PRINT RUN 50 SER.#'d SETS

2007 Donruss Elite Extra Edition Collegiate Patches

OVERALL AUTO/MEM ODDS 1:5
PRINT RUNS B/WN 25-250 COPIES PER
NO PRICING ON QTY 25 OR LESS
2 Ara Parseghian/250 15.00 40.00
4 Burt Reynolds/25
8 Frank Broyles/250 6.00 15.00
15 Ron Howard/25
16 Steve Spurrier/100
17 Tom Osborne/249 20.00 50.00
18 Vince Dooley/250 6.00 15.00
24 Steve Spurrier/100

2007 Donruss Elite Extra Edition School Colors

OVERALL INSERT ODDS 1:4
STATED PRINT RUN 1500 SER.#'d SETS
12 Steve Spurrier .75 2.00
13 Tom Osborne .75 2.00
18 Ara Parseghian .75 2.00
20 Frank Broyles .75 2.00
24 Vince Dooley .75 2.00
27 Burt Reynolds .75 2.00
28 Ron Howard .75 2.00

2007 Donruss Elite Extra Edition School Colors Autographs

OVERALL AUTO/MEM ODDS 1:5
PRINT RUNS B/WN 10-50 COPIES PER
NO PRICING ON QTY 25 OR LESS
EXCHANGE DEADLINE 07/01/2009
12 Steve Spurrier/25 12.50 30.00
13 Tom Osborne/25
18 Ara Parseghian/25 12.50 30.00
20 Frank Broyles/25 10.00 25.00
24 Vince Dooley/25
27 Burt Reynolds/10
28 Ron Howard/10

2007 Donruss Elite Extra Edition Signature Aspirations

OVERALL AU/MEM ODDS 1:5
PRINT RUNS B/WN 5-100 COPIES PER
NO PRICING ON QTY 25 OR LESS
EXCHANGE DEADLINE 07/01/2007
66 Ara Parseghian/100 12.50 30.00
70 Frank Broyles/100 5.00 12.00
74 Steve Spurrier/25
75 Tom Osborne/100 12.50 30.00
76 Vince Dooley/50 10.00 25.00
82 Clint Dolezel/100 4.00 10.00

2007 Donruss Elite Extra Edition Signature Status

OVERALL AU/MEM ODDS 1:5
PRINT RUNS B/WN 1-50 COPIES PER
NO PRICING ON QTY 25 OR LESS
EXCHANGE DEADLINE 07/01/2007
66 Ara Parseghian/50 20.00 50.00
70 Frank Broyles/50 8.00 20.00
74 Steve Spurrier/10
75 Tom Osborne/50 20.00 50.00
76 Vince Dooley/25
82 Clint Dolezel/50 6.00 15.00

2007 Donruss Elite Extra Edition Signature Turn of the Century

OVERALL AU/MEM ODDS 1:5
PRINT RUNS B/WN 10-500 COPIES PER
NO PRICING ON QTY 25 OR LESS
EXCHANGE DEADLINE 07/01/2007
66 Ara Parseghian/69 10.00 25.00
70 Frank Broyles/69 6.00 15.00
74 Steve Spurrier/59 30.00 60.00
75 Tom Osborne/320 10.00 25.00
76 Vince Dooley/91 6.00 15.00
82 Clint Dolezel/243 4.00 10.00

2007 Donruss Elite Extra Edition Throwback Threads

OVERALL AUTO/MEM ODDS 1:5
PRINT RUNS B/WN 44-500 COPIES PER
5 Clint Dolezel/500 3.00 8.00
8 Vince Dooley/500 3.00 8.00
20 Steve Spurrier/500 4.00 10.00

2007 Donruss Elite Extra Edition Throwback Threads Prime

*PRIME: .75X TO 2X BASIC
OVERALL AUTO/MEM ODDS 1:5
PRINT RUNS B/WN 3-50 COPIES PER
NO PRICING ON QTY 25 OR LESS
8 Vince Dooley/7

2007 Donruss Elite Extra Edition Throwback Threads Autographs

OVERALL AUTO/MEM ODDS 1:5
PRINT RUNS B/WN 50-100 COPIES PER
EXCHANGE DEADLINE 07/01/2009
5 Clint Dolezel/100 6.00 15.00
8 Vince Dooley/50 10.00 25.00
20 Steve Spurrier/50 30.00 60.00

2005 Donruss Gridiron Gear

This 150-card set was relased in February, 2007. This set was issued in the hobby through five-card packs which came 18 packs to a box. Cards numbered 1-100 feature veterans sequenced in first name alphabetical order while cards numbered 101-150 feature rookies. The rookie cards were all issued to a stated print run of 399 serial numbered sets.

COMP.SET w/o RC's (100) 10.00 25.00
101-150 PRINT RUN 399 SER.#'d SETS
1 Aaron Brooks .25 .60
2 Ahman Green .30 .75
3 Alge Crumpler .30 .75
4 Amani Toomer .25 .60
5 Andre Johnson .30 .75
6 Anquan Boldin .25 .60
7 Antonio Gates .40 1.00
8 Antwaan Randle El .25 .60

9 Ashley Lelie .25 .60
10 Barry Sanders 1.50 4.00
11 Ben Roethlisberger .60 1.50
12 Bob Griese 1.00 2.50
13 Brandon Lloyd .25 .60
14 Brett Favre .75 2.00
15 Brian Urlacher .40 1.00
16 Brian Westbrook .25 .60
17 Byron Leftwich .25 .60
18 Carson Palmer .30 .75
19 Chad Johnson .25 .60
20 Chad Pennington .25 .60
21 Champ Bailey .30 .75
22 Chris Brown .25 .60
23 Chris Chambers .25 .60
24 Clinton Portis .25 .60
25 Corey Dillon .25 .60
26 Curtis Martin .30 .75
27 Daunte Culpepper .30 .75
28 David Carr .25 .60
29 Deion Sanders .30 .75
30 Derrick Brooks .25 .60
31 Deuce McAllister .30 .75
32 Domanick Davis .25 .60
33 Don Maynard .75 2.00
34 Donovan McNabb .30 .75
35 Drew Bledsoe .30 .75
36 Drew Brees .50 1.25
37 Edgerrin James .30 .75
38 Eli Manning .60 1.50
39 Eric Moulds .25 .60
40 Fred Taylor .25 .60
41 Hines Ward .30 .75
42 Ickey Woods .60 1.50
43 Isaac Bruce .40 1.00
44 J.P. Losman .25 .60
45 Jake Delhomme .25 .60
46 Jake Plummer .25 .60
47 Jamal Lewis .30 .75
48 Javon Walker .25 .60
49 Jeremy Shockey .25 .60
50 Jerome Bettis .40 1.00
51 Jerry Porter .25 .60
52 Jevon Kearse .25 .60
53 Jimmy Smith .30 .75
54 Joe Namath 1.50 4.00
55 Joey Harrington .25 .60
56 Josh McCown .30 .75
57 Josh Reed .25 .60
58 Julius Jones .25 .60
59 Julius Peppers .30 .75
60 Keary Colbert .25 .60
61 Kerry Collins .25 .60
62 Kevin Jones .25 .60
63 Kyle Boller .25 .60
64 LaDainian Tomlinson .40 1.00
65 LaMont Jordan .30 .75
66 Larry Fitzgerald .40 1.00
67 Lee Evans .30 .75
68 Marc Bulger .25 .60
69 Marvin Harrison .30 .75
70 Matt Hasselbeck .25 .60
71 Michael Clayton .25 .60
72 Michael Vick .30 .75
73 Mike Alstott .25 .60
74 Muhsin Muhammad .25 .60
75 Nate Burleson .25 .60
76 Peyton Manning 1.00 2.50
77 Plaxico Burress .25 .60
78 Priest Holmes .25 .60
79 Randy Moss .30 .75
80 Ray Lewis .40 1.00
81 Reggie Wayne .30 .75
82 Rex Grossman .25 .60
83 Rod Smith .30 .75
84 Roy Williams S .25 .60
85 Roy Williams WR .25 .60
86 Rudi Johnson .25 .60
87 Shaun Alexander .25 .60
88 Sonny Jurgensen .75 2.00
89 Stephen Davis .25 .60
90 Steve McNair .30 .75
91 Steve Smith .40 1.00
92 Steven Jackson .25 .60
93 Terrell Owens .30 .75
94 Tiki Barber .30 .75
95 Todd Heap .25 .60
96 Tom Brady .60 1.50
97 Tony Gonzalez .30 .75
98 Torry Holt .30 .75
99 Trent Green .25 .60
100 Willis McGahee .25 .60
101 Alex Smith QB RC 5.00 12.00
102 Ronnie Brown RC 1.50 4.00
103 Braylon Edwards RC 1.25 3.00
104 Cedric Benson RC 1.25 3.00
105 Cadillac Williams RC 1.25 3.00
106 Adam Jones RC 1.25 3.00
107 Troy Williamson RC 1.25 3.00
108 Mike Williams 1.50 4.00
109 Derrick Johnson RC 1.50 4.00
110 Demarcus Ware RC 5.00 12.00
111 Matt Jones RC 1.25 3.00
112 Mark Clayton RC 1.25 3.00
113 Aaron Rodgers RC 30.00 60.00
114 Jason Campbell RC 1.25 3.00
115 Roddy White RC 2.00 5.00
116 Heath Miller RC 2.50 6.00
117 Reggie Brown RC 1.25 3.00
118 Mark Bradley RC 1.25 3.00
119 J.J. Arrington RC 1.50 4.00
120 Odell Thurman RC 2.00 5.00
121 Roscoe Parrish RC 1.25 3.00
122 Terrence Murphy RC 1.25 3.00
123 Vincent Jackson RC 2.00 5.00
124 Frank Gore RC 2.50 6.00
125 Charlie Frye RC 1.25 3.00
126 Courtney Roby RC 1.25 3.00
127 Andrew Walter RC 1.25 3.00
128 Vernand Morency RC 1.25 3.00
129 Ryan Moats RC 1.50 4.00
130 Chris Henry RC 1.50 4.00
131 David Greene RC 1.25 3.00
132 Brandon Jones RC 1.50 4.00
133 Kyle Orton RC 1.25 3.00
134 Marion Barber RC 1.25 3.00
135 Brandon Jacobs RC 1.50 4.00
136 Ciatrick Fason RC 1.25 3.00
137 Lofa Tatupu RC 1.50 4.00
138 Stefan LeFors RC 1.25 3.00
139 Alvin Pearman RC 1.25 3.00
140 Darren Sproles RC 2.00 5.00
141 Samkon Gado RC 2.00 5.00
142 Antrel Rolle RC 2.00 5.00
143 Maurice Clarett 1.50 4.00
144 Adrian McPherson RC 1.25 3.00
145 Eric Shelton RC 1.25 3.00
146 Bo Scaife RC 1.50 4.00
147 Carlos Rogers RC 2.00 5.00
148 Otis Amey RC 1.50 4.00
149 Alex Smith TE RC 1.25 3.00
150 Jerome Mathis RC 2.00 5.00

2005 Donruss Gridiron Gear Gold Holofoil

*VETS: 3X TO 8X BASIC CARDS
*RETIRED: 2X TO 5X BASIC CARDS
*ROOKIES: .6X TO 1.5X BASIC CARDS
STATED PRINT RUN 100 SER.#'d SETS

2005 Donruss Gridiron Gear Platinum Holofoil

*VETS: 8X TO 20X BASIC CARDS
*RETIRED: 5X TO 12X BASIC CARDS
*ROOKIES: 1X TO 2.5X BASIC CARDS
STATED PRINT RUN 25 SER.#'d SETS
113 Aaron Rodgers 100.00 175.00

2005 Donruss Gridiron Gear Silver Holofoil

*VETS: 2X TO 5X BASIC CARDS
*RETIRED: 1.2X TO 3X BASIC CARDS
STATED PRINT RUN 250 SER.#'d SETS

2005 Donruss Gridiron Gear Autographs Silver

SILVER STATED PRINT RUN 1-250
#'d UNDER 20 NOT PRICED DUE TO SCARCITY
UNPRICED PLATINUM PRINT RUN 1-10
1 Aaron Brooks/49 6.00 15.00
3 Alge Crumpler/80 6.00 15.00
6 Anquan Boldin/46 6.00 15.00
11 Ben Roethlisberger/23 100.00 200.00
30 Derrick Brooks/250 4.00 10.00
31 Deuce McAllister/26 10.00 25.00
32 Domanick Davis/250 4.00 10.00
38 Eli Manning/71 40.00 80.00
44 J.P. Losman/61 5.00 12.00
45 Jake Delhomme/100 8.00 20.00
52 Jevon Kearse/250 4.00 10.00
54 Joe Namath/67 30.00 60.00
58 Julius Jones/50 8.00 20.00
60 Keary Colbert/125 4.00 10.00
63 Kyle Boller/33 8.00 20.00
65 LaMont Jordan/250 5.00 12.00
67 Lee Evans/62 6.00 15.00
69 Marvin Harrison/28 10.00 25.00
70 Matt Hasselbeck/45 10.00 25.00
75 Nate Burleson/51 5.00 12.00
81 Reggie Wayne/30 10.00 25.00
82 Rex Grossman/63 8.00 20.00
84 Roy Williams S/75 8.00 20.00
86 Rudi Johnson/40 6.00 15.00
88 Sonny Jurgensen/63 8.00 20.00
91 Steve Smith/50 8.00 20.00
94 Tiki Barber/72 15.00 30.00
95 Todd Heap/79 5.00 12.00
99 Trent Green/56 5.00 12.00

2005 Donruss Gridiron Gear Autographs Gold Holofoil

STATED PRINT RUN 25 SER.#'d SETS
1 Aaron Brooks 8.00 20.00
3 Alge Crumpler 10.00 25.00
5 Andre Johnson 15.00 40.00
6 Anquan Boldin 8.00 20.00
7 Antonio Gates 12.00 30.00
11 Ben Roethlisberger 100.00 200.00
15 Brian Urlacher 25.00 50.00
17 Byron Leftwich 8.00 20.00
22 Chris Brown 8.00 20.00
28 David Carr 8.00 20.00
29 Deion Sanders 30.00 60.00
30 Derrick Brooks 15.00 40.00
32 Domanick Davis 8.00 20.00
33 Don Maynard 10.00 25.00
35 Drew Bledsoe 10.00 25.00
38 Eli Manning 50.00 100.00
41 Hines Ward 35.00 60.00
44 J.P. Losman 8.00 20.00
45 Jake Delhomme 8.00 20.00
52 Jevon Kearse 8.00 20.00
53 Jimmy Smith 10.00 25.00
54 Joe Namath 40.00 80.00
58 Julius Jones 8.00 20.00
60 Keary Colbert 8.00 20.00
61 Kerry Collins 8.00 20.00
63 Kyle Boller 8.00 20.00
65 LaMont Jordan 10.00 25.00
67 Lee Evans 10.00 25.00
69 Marvin Harrison 10.00 25.00
70 Matt Hasselbeck 15.00 40.00
71 Michael Clayton 8.00 20.00
75 Nate Burleson 8.00 20.00
76 Peyton Manning 60.00 100.00
81 Reggie Wayne 10.00 25.00
82 Rex Grossman 12.00 30.00
84 Roy Williams S 8.00 20.00
85 Roy Williams WR 8.00 20.00
86 Rudi Johnson 8.00 20.00
87 Shaun Alexander 15.00 40.00
88 Sonny Jurgensen 10.00 25.00
91 Steve Smith 12.00 30.00
94 Tiki Barber 20.00 50.00
95 Todd Heap 8.00 20.00
99 Trent Green 8.00 20.00
100 Willis McGahee 8.00 20.00

2005 Donruss Gridiron Gear Autographs Silver Holofoil

PRINT RUN 100 SER.#'d SETS UNLESS NOTED
5 Andre Johnson/100 12.00 30.00
6 Anquan Boldin/100 6.00 15.00
30 Derrick Brooks/100 6.00 15.00
31 Deuce McAllister/31 10.00 25.00
32 Domanick Davis/100 6.00 15.00
33 Don Maynard/100 8.00 20.00
45 Jake Delhomme/50 10.00 25.00
52 Jevon Kearse/100 6.00 15.00
53 Jimmy Smith/100 8.00 20.00
60 Keary Colbert/100 6.00 15.00
65 LaMont Jordan/100 8.00 20.00
67 Lee Evans/100 8.00 20.00
84 Roy Williams S/100 6.00 15.00
87 Shaun Alexander/100 12.00 30.00
95 Todd Heap/100 6.00 15.00

2005 Donruss Gridiron Gear Jerseys

STATED PRINT RUN 1-150
SERIAL #'d UNDER 10 NOT PRICED
3 Alge Crumpler 3.00 8.00
4 Amani Toomer 2.50 6.00
5 Andre Johnson/50 4.00 10.00
6 Anquan Boldin 2.50 6.00
8 Antwaan Randle El/80 3.00 8.00
9 Ashley Lelie/55 3.00 8.00
11 Ben Roethlisberger 6.00 15.00
12 Bob Griese 4.00 10.00
13 Brandon Lloyd 2.50 6.00
14 Brett Favre 8.00 20.00
15 Brian Urlacher/65 5.00 12.00
16 Brian Westbrook 2.50 6.00
17 Byron Leftwich 2.50 6.00
18 Carson Palmer 3.00 8.00
20 Chad Pennington 2.50 6.00
21 Champ Bailey/15 10.00 25.00
24 Clinton Portis/15 6.00 15.00
25 Corey Dillon 2.50 6.00
26 Curtis Martin 3.00 8.00
27 Daunte Culpepper/35 6.00 15.00
28 David Carr 2.50 6.00
29 Deion Sanders 5.00 12.00
30 Derrick Brooks 5.00 12.00
31 Deuce McAllister 3.00 8.00
33 Don Maynard 3.00 8.00
34 Donovan McNabb/85 4.00 10.00
35 Drew Bledsoe 3.00 8.00
36 Drew Brees 4.00 10.00
38 Eli Manning 6.00 15.00
41 Hines Ward/75 6.00 15.00
42 Ickey Woods 3.00 8.00
43 Isaac Bruce 4.00 10.00
44 J.P. Losman 2.50 6.00
45 Jake Delhomme/120 2.50 6.00
46 Jake Plummer 2.50 6.00
47 Jamal Lewis 3.00 8.00
48 Javon Walker/35 5.00 12.00
50 Jerome Bettis 8.00 20.00
51 Jerry Porter 2.50 6.00
52 Jevon Kearse 2.50 6.00
53 Jimmy Smith/11 8.00 20.00
54 Joe Namath/50 15.00 30.00
55 Joey Harrington 2.50 6.00
56 Josh McCown 3.00 8.00
57 Josh Reed 2.50 6.00
58 Julius Jones 2.50 6.00
59 Julius Peppers 3.00 8.00
60 Keary Colbert 2.50 6.00
62 Kevin Jones/31 5.00 12.00
63 Kyle Boller 2.50 6.00
64 LaDainian Tomlinson 4.00 10.00
66 Larry Fitzgerald 4.00 10.00
67 Lee Evans 3.00 8.00
68 Marc Bulger 2.50 6.00
69 Marvin Harrison 3.00 8.00
70 Matt Hasselbeck/107 2.50 6.00
71 Michael Clayton/93 3.00 8.00
72 Michael Vick 5.00 12.00
73 Mike Alstott/90 3.00 8.00
75 Nate Burleson 2.50 6.00
76 Peyton Manning/100 10.00 25.00
78 Priest Holmes 2.50 6.00
79 Randy Moss 3.00 8.00
80 Ray Lewis/21 15.00 30.00
81 Reggie Wayne 3.00 8.00
82 Rex Grossman 2.50 6.00
84 Roy Williams S/45 3.00 8.00
85 Roy Williams WR/75 3.00 8.00
86 Rudi Johnson/26 5.00 12.00
87 Shaun Alexander/100 2.50 6.00
88 Sonny Jurgensen/55 6.00 15.00
90 Steve McNair/17 8.00 20.00
92 Steven Jackson 2.50 6.00
94 Tiki Barber/13 8.00 20.00
95 Todd Heap 2.50 6.00
96 Tom Brady 15.00 40.00
97 Tony Gonzalez 3.00 8.00
98 Torry Holt 3.00 8.00
99 Trent Green/25 5.00 12.00
100 Willis McGahee/69 3.00 8.00
101 Alex Smith QB 8.00 20.00
102 Ronnie Brown 2.50 6.00
103 Braylon Edwards 2.00 5.00
105 Cadillac Williams 2.00 5.00
106 Adam Jones 2.00 5.00
107 Troy Williamson 2.00 5.00
111 Matt Jones 2.00 5.00
112 Mark Clayton 2.00 5.00
114 Jason Campbell 2.00 5.00
115 Roddy White 3.00 8.00
117 Reggie Brown 2.00 5.00
118 Mark Bradley 2.00 5.00
119 J.J. Arrington 2.50 6.00
121 Roscoe Parrish 2.00 5.00
122 Terrence Murphy 2.00 5.00
123 Vincent Jackson 3.00 8.00
124 Frank Gore 4.00 10.00
125 Charlie Frye 2.00 5.00
126 Courtney Roby 2.00 5.00
127 Andrew Walter 2.00 5.00
128 Vernand Morency 2.00 5.00
129 Ryan Moats 2.00 5.00
133 Kyle Orton 2.00 5.00
136 Ciatrick Fason 2.00 5.00
138 Stefan LeFors 2.00 5.00
142 Antrel Rolle 3.00 8.00
143 Maurice Clarett 2.00 5.00
145 Eric Shelton 2.00 5.00
147 Carlos Rogers 3.00 8.00

2005 Donruss Gridiron Gear Jerseys Name Plate

*ROOKIES/50: .8X TO 2X BASIC JSY/150
*ROOKIES/31: 1X TO 2.5X BASIC JSY/150
NAME PLATE PRINT RUN 1-60
SERIAL #'d UNDER 10 NOT PRICED
3 Alge Crumpler/20 10.00 25.00
4 Amani Toomer/40 6.00 15.00
5 Andre Johnson/10 12.00 30.00
6 Anquan Boldin/50 6.00 15.00
8 Antwaan Randle El/60 6.00 15.00
9 Ashley Lelie/19 10.00 25.00
10 Barry Sanders/20 60.00 100.00
11 Ben Roethlisberger/30 30.00 80.00
12 Bob Griese/10 15.00 40.00
13 Brandon Lloyd/15 10.00 25.00
15 Brian Urlacher/50 10.00 25.00
17 Byron Leftwich/24 8.00 20.00
19 Chad Johnson/35 8.00 20.00
20 Chad Pennington/24 8.00 20.00
21 Champ Bailey/15 12.00 30.00
22 Chris Brown/19 10.00 25.00
23 Chris Chambers/50 6.00 15.00
24 Clinton Portis/10 10.00 25.00
25 Corey Dillon/20 8.00 20.00
26 Curtis Martin/50 8.00 20.00
27 Daunte Culpepper/38 10.00 25.00
28 David Carr/11 10.00 25.00
29 Deion Sanders/35 10.00 25.00
31 Deuce McAllister/50 8.00 20.00
32 Domanick Davis/33 8.00 20.00
33 Don Maynard/25 12.00 30.00
35 Drew Bledsoe/17 12.00 30.00
37 Edgerrin James/25 10.00 25.00
38 Eli Manning/25 20.00 50.00
40 Fred Taylor/19 10.00 25.00
44 J.P. Losman/21 8.00 20.00
45 Jake Delhomme/43 6.00 15.00
46 Jake Plummer/50 6.00 15.00
47 Jamal Lewis/50 8.00 20.00
52 Jevon Kearse/29 8.00 20.00
53 Jimmy Smith/50 8.00 20.00
56 Josh McCown/13 12.00 30.00
58 Julius Jones/15 10.00 25.00
59 Julius Peppers/50 8.00 20.00
62 Kevin Jones/26 8.00 20.00
63 Kyle Boller/36 8.00 20.00
64 LaDainian Tomlinson/50 10.00 25.00
66 Larry Fitzgerald/21 12.00 30.00
67 Lee Evans/12 12.00 30.00
69 Marvin Harrison/50 8.00 20.00
73 Mike Alstott/16 10.00 25.00
76 Peyton Manning/50 25.00 60.00
78 Priest Holmes/20 8.00 20.00
79 Randy Moss/12 12.00 30.00
80 Ray Lewis/30 12.00 30.00
81 Reggie Wayne/25 10.00 25.00
82 Rex Grossman/50 6.00 15.00
83 Rod Smith/36 10.00 25.00
84 Roy Williams S/50 6.00 15.00
86 Rudi Johnson/50 6.00 15.00
87 Shaun Alexander/50 6.00 15.00
89 Stephen Davis/14 10.00 25.00
92 Steven Jackson/28 8.00 20.00
95 Todd Heap/21 8.00 20.00
96 Tom Brady/34 50.00 125.00
98 Torry Holt/21 10.00 25.00
100 Willis McGahee/18 10.00 25.00

2005 Donruss Gridiron Gear Jerseys Numbers

*ROOKIES/100: .6X TO 1.5X BASIC JSY/150
STATED PRINT RUN 1-100
SERIAL #'d UNDER 10 NOT PRICED
2 Ahman Green/50 8.00 20.00
3 Alge Crumpler/50 8.00 20.00
4 Amani Toomer/50 6.00 15.00
5 Andre Johnson/50 8.00 20.00
6 Anquan Boldin/50 6.00 15.00
7 Antonio Gates/50 10.00 25.00
8 Antwaan Randle El/50 6.00 15.00
9 Ashley Lelie/50 6.00 15.00
10 Barry Sanders/50 15.00 40.00
12 Bob Griese/25 15.00 40.00
13 Brandon Lloyd/50 6.00 15.00
15 Brian Urlacher/50 10.00 25.00
16 Brian Westbrook/50 6.00 15.00
17 Byron Leftwich/46 6.00 15.00
19 Chad Johnson/50 6.00 15.00
21 Champ Bailey/50 8.00 20.00
22 Chris Brown/40 6.00 15.00
23 Chris Chambers/50 6.00 15.00
24 Clinton Portis/50 6.00 15.00
25 Corey Dillon/50 6.00 15.00
26 Curtis Martin/50 8.00 20.00
27 Daunte Culpepper/50 8.00 20.00
28 David Carr/50 6.00 15.00
29 Deion Sanders/50 8.00 20.00
30 Derrick Brooks/50 10.00 25.00
31 Deuce McAllister/50 8.00 20.00
33 Don Maynard/50 10.00 25.00
35 Drew Bledsoe/40 8.00 20.00
36 Drew Brees/50 10.00 25.00
37 Edgerrin James/50 8.00 20.00
38 Eli Manning/50 15.00 40.00
39 Eric Moulds/50 6.00 15.00
40 Fred Taylor/50 6.00 15.00
41 Hines Ward/50 8.00 20.00
42 Ickey Woods/50 8.00 20.00
43 Isaac Bruce/50 10.00 25.00
44 J.P. Losman/12 10.00 25.00
45 Jake Delhomme/27 8.00 20.00
46 Jake Plummer/50 6.00 15.00
47 Jamal Lewis/50 8.00 20.00
48 Javon Walker/50 6.00 15.00
49 Jeremy Shockey/50 6.00 15.00
50 Jerome Bettis/50 15.00 40.00
51 Jerry Porter/50 6.00 15.00
52 Jevon Kearse/50 6.00 15.00
53 Jimmy Smith/50 8.00 20.00
56 Josh McCown/50 8.00 20.00
57 Josh Reed/50 6.00 15.00
58 Julius Jones/30 8.00 20.00
59 Julius Peppers/50 8.00 20.00
60 Keary Colbert/50 6.00 15.00
62 Kevin Jones/35 8.00 20.00
63 Kyle Boller/41 6.00 15.00
64 LaDainian Tomlinson/50 10.00 25.00
66 Larry Fitzgerald/50 10.00 25.00
67 Lee Evans/50 8.00 20.00
69 Marvin Harrison/50 8.00 20.00
70 Matt Hasselbeck/25 8.00 20.00
71 Michael Clayton/50 6.00 15.00
72 Michael Vick/10 20.00 50.00
73 Mike Alstott/23 8.00 20.00
75 Nate Burleson/50 6.00 15.00
76 Peyton Manning/50 25.00 60.00
78 Priest Holmes/50 6.00 15.00
79 Randy Moss/50 8.00 20.00
80 Ray Lewis/42 10.00 25.00
82 Rex Grossman/28 8.00 20.00
83 Rod Smith/32 10.00 25.00
84 Roy Williams S/25 8.00 20.00
86 Rudi Johnson/50 6.00 15.00
87 Shaun Alexander/50 6.00 15.00
89 Stephen Davis/50 6.00 15.00
91 Steve Smith/50 10.00 25.00
92 Steven Jackson/33 8.00 20.00
94 Tiki Barber/11 12.00 30.00
95 Todd Heap/50 6.00 15.00
96 Tom Brady/50 40.00 100.00
97 Tony Gonzalez/50 8.00 20.00
98 Torry Holt/50 8.00 20.00
99 Trent Green/50 6.00 15.00

2005 Donruss Gridiron Gear Jerseys Team Logo

*ROOKIES/20-25: 1.5X TO 4X BASIC JSY/150
*ROOKIES/14-18: 2X TO 5X BASIC JSY/150
STATED PRINT RUN 1-25
SERIAL #'d UNDER 10 NOT PRICED
8 Antwaan Randle El/15 12.00 30.00
19 Chad Johnson/25 10.00 25.00
22 Chris Brown/12 12.00 30.00
23 Chris Chambers/25 10.00 25.00
25 Corey Dillon/20 10.00 25.00
26 Curtis Martin/10 15.00 40.00
29 Deion Sanders/25 25.00 60.00
31 Deuce McAllister/25 12.00 30.00
40 Fred Taylor/25 10.00 25.00
45 Jake Delhomme/25 10.00 25.00
50 Jerome Bettis/23 50.00 120.00
52 Jevon Kearse/25 10.00 25.00
59 Julius Peppers/25 12.00 30.00
60 Keary Colbert/15 12.00 30.00
63 Kyle Boller/25 10.00 25.00
73 Mike Alstott/22 10.00 25.00
75 Nate Burleson/13 12.00 30.00
86 Rudi Johnson/13 12.00 30.00
89 Stephen Davis/14 12.00 30.00
95 Todd Heap/18 12.00 30.00
96 Tom Brady/17 80.00 200.00
98 Torry Holt/25 12.00 30.00

2005 Donruss Gridiron Gear Next Generation Gold

COMPLETE SET (10) 6.00 15.00
STATED PRINT RUN 1000 SER.#'d SETS
*GOLD HOLO/100: .8X TO 2X GOLD/1000
*PLAT.HOLO/25: 1.2X TO 3X GOLD/1000
*SILVER HOLO/250: .5X TO 1.2X GOLD/1000
1 Andre Johnson 1.00 2.50
2 Bryant Johnson .75 2.00
3 Charles Rogers .75 2.00
4 Darius Watts .75 2.00
5 Josh McCown 1.00 2.50
6 Keary Colbert .75 2.00
7 Larry Fitzgerald 1.25 3.00
8 Michael Clayton .75 2.00
9 Nate Burleson .75 2.00
10 Reggie Williams .75 2.00

2005 Donruss Gridiron Gear Next Generation Autographs

SERIAL #'d UNDER 20 NOT PRICED
1 Andre Johnson/50 12.00 30.00
6 Keary Colbert/50 6.00 15.00

2005 Donruss Gridiron Gear Next Generation Jersey Autographs

COMMON CARD/15-35 8.00 20.00
UNL.STARS/15-35 12.00 30.00
SERIAL #'d UNDER 20 NOT PRICED
UNPRICED TEAM LOGO AU PRINT RUN 1-2
UNPRICED DBL PATCH AU PRINT RUN 1-10
UNPRICED NAME PLATE AU PRINT RUN 1-2
*JSY NUMB AU/25: .4X TO 1X AU/35
6 Keary Colbert/35 8.00 20.00
8 Michael Clayton/15 12.00 30.00

2005 Donruss Gridiron Gear Next Generation Jerseys

STATED PRINT RUN 90-150
*DBL PATCH/30-50: .8X TO 2X JSY/90-150
*DBL PATCH/17-25: 1X TO 2.5X JSY/90-150
*JUMBO/56-100: .6X TO 1.5X JSY/90-150
*JUMBO/10-21: 1X TO 2.5X JSY/90-150
*JUM.PTCH/44-50: 1X TO 2.5X JSY/90-150
*JUM.PTCH/21-29: 1.2X TO 3X JSY/90-150
*NAME PLATE/35-50: .8X TO 2X JSY/90-150
*NAME PLATE/10-25: 1.2X TO 3X JSY/90-150
*JSY NO/50-100: .8X TO 2X JSY/90-150
*JSY NO/11: 1.2X TO 3X JSY/90-150
UNPRICED TEAM LOGO PRINT RUN 1-10
1 Andre Johnson/150 2.50 6.00
2 Bryant Johnson/150 2.00 5.00
3 Charles Rogers/90 2.00 5.00
4 Darius Watts/150 2.00 5.00
5 Josh McCown/150 2.50 6.00
6 Keary Colbert/150 2.00 5.00
7 Larry Fitzgerald/150 3.00 8.00
8 Michael Clayton/100 2.00 5.00
9 Nate Burleson/150 2.00 5.00
10 Reggie Williams/150 2.00 5.00

2005 Donruss Gridiron Gear Past and Present Gold

COMPLETE SET (20) 20.00 50.00
STATED PRINT RUN 750 SER.#'d SETS
*GOLD HOLOFOIL: .8X TO 2X BASIC CARDS
GOLD HOLOFOIL PRINT RUN 100 SER.#'d SETS
*PLATINUM HOLO: 1.2X TO 3X BASIC CARDS
PLATINUM HOLOFOIL PRINT RUN 25 SETS
*SILVER HOLO: .5X TO 1.2X BASIC CARDS
SILVER HOLOFOIL PRINT RUN 250 SETS
1 Aaron Brooks .60 1.50
2 Ahman Green .75 2.00
3 Carson Palmer .75 2.00
4 Clinton Portis .60 1.50
5 Corey Dillon .60 1.50
6 Curtis Martin .75 2.00
7 DeShaun Foster .75 2.00
8 Duce Staley .60 1.50
9 Hines Ward .75 2.00
10 Jake Plummer .60 1.50
11 Jeremy Shockey .60 1.50
12 Jerome Bettis 1.00 2.50
13 Jevon Kearse .60 1.50
14 Julius Jones .60 1.50
15 Marshall Faulk .75 2.00
16 Ricky Williams .75 2.00
17 Roy Williams S .60 1.50
18 Stephen Davis .60 1.50
19 Steven Jackson .60 1.50
20 Terrell Owens .75 2.00

2005 Donruss Gridiron Gear Past and Present Autographs

AUTO STATED PRINT RUN 2-250
SERIAL #'d UNDER 24 NOT PRICED
1 Aaron Brooks/25 10.00 25.00
8 Duce Staley/24 10.00 25.00
13 Jevon Kearse/250 5.00 12.00
14 Julius Jones/25 10.00 25.00

2005 Donruss Gridiron Gear Past and Present Jerseys Double

STATED PRINT RUN 5-75
SERIAL #'d UNDER 15 NOT PRICED
*DBL NME PLTE/15-25: 1X TO 2.5X DBL/75
1 Aaron Brooks/75 3.00 8.00
2 Ahman Green/15 6.00 15.00
3 Carson Palmer/75 4.00 10.00
4 Clinton Portis/75 3.00 8.00
5 Corey Dillon/75 3.00 8.00
6 Curtis Martin/75 4.00 10.00
8 Duce Staley/75 3.00 8.00
10 Jake Plummer/75 3.00 8.00
13 Jevon Kearse/75 3.00 8.00
14 Julius Jones/50 3.00 8.00
15 Marshall Faulk/65 4.00 10.00
16 Ricky Williams/75 4.00 10.00
17 Roy Williams S/26 5.00 12.00
18 Stephen Davis/75 3.00 8.00
19 Steven Jackson/40 4.00 10.00
20 Terrell Owens/30 5.00 12.00

2005 Donruss Gridiron Gear Past and Present Jerseys Jumbo Swatch

STATED PRINT RUN 3-100
SERIAL #'d UNDER 20 NOT PRICED
1 Aaron Brooks/30 5.00 12.00
3 Carson Palmer/67 5.00 12.00
5 Corey Dillon/35 5.00 12.00
6 Curtis Martin/30 6.00 15.00
8 Duce Staley/100 4.00 10.00
9 Hines Ward/100 5.00 12.00
10 Jake Plummer/100 4.00 10.00
12 Jerome Bettis/100 6.00 15.00
14 Julius Jones/40 5.00 12.00
15 Marshall Faulk/27 8.00 20.00
16 Ricky Williams/100 5.00 12.00
17 Roy Williams S/23 6.00 15.00
18 Stephen Davis/100 4.00 10.00
19 Steven Jackson/30 5.00 12.00

2005 Donruss Gridiron Gear Past and Present Jerseys Jumbo Swatch Prime

STATED PRINT RUN 6-50
#'d UNDER 20 NOT PRICED DUE TO SCARCITY
2 Ahman Green/48 8.00 20.00
5 Corey Dillon/50 6.00 15.00
6 Curtis Martin/50 8.00 20.00
7 DeShaun Foster/50 8.00 20.00
8 Duce Staley/50 6.00 15.00
9 Hines Ward/50 8.00 20.00
10 Jake Plummer/23 10.00 25.00
11 Jeremy Shockey/50 6.00 15.00
12 Jerome Bettis/46 10.00 25.00
13 Jevon Kearse/50 6.00 15.00
14 Julius Jones/29 10.00 25.00
16 Ricky Williams/50 8.00 20.00
17 Roy Williams S/50 6.00 15.00
18 Stephen Davis/50 6.00 15.00
19 Steven Jackson/20 10.00 25.00

2005 Donruss Gridiron Gear Past and Present Jerseys Name Plate Single

STATED PRINT RUN 1-50
SERIAL #'d UNDER 15 NOT PRICED
2 Ahman Green/25 10.00 25.00
3 Carson Palmer/20 10.00 25.00
4 Clinton Portis/25 8.00 20.00
5 Corey Dillon/50 6.00 15.00
6 Curtis Martin/28 10.00 25.00
8 Duce Staley/35 6.00 15.00
9 Hines Ward/50 8.00 20.00
10 Jake Plummer/50 6.00 15.00
11 Jeremy Shockey/31 6.00 15.00
12 Jerome Bettis/50 10.00 25.00
13 Jevon Kearse/36 6.00 15.00
16 Ricky Williams/50 8.00 20.00
17 Roy Williams S/19 8.00 20.00
18 Stephen Davis/18 8.00 20.00
20 Terrell Owens/15 10.00 25.00

2005 Donruss Gridiron Gear Past and Present Jerseys Name Plate Single Autographs

STATED PRINT RUN 5-25
SERIAL #'d UNDER 20 NOT PRICED
1 Aaron Brooks/25 12.00 30.00
14 Julius Jones/21 12.00 30.00
19 Steven Jackson/24 12.00 30.00

2005 Donruss Gridiron Gear Past and Present Jerseys Numbers Single

PRINT RUN 100 SER.#'d SETS UNLESS NOTED
#'d UNDER 20 NOT PRICED DUE TO SCARCITY
*DOUBLE/30-50: .6X TO 1.5X SNGL/100
*DOUBLE/25: .8X TO 2X SNGL/100
*DOUBLE/22-25: .6X TO 1.5X SNGL/40-50
*DOUBLE/15-25: .5X TO 1.2X SNGL/20-25
1 Aaron Brooks/20 6.00 15.00
2 Ahman Green/30 6.00 15.00
3 Carson Palmer/40 6.00 15.00
4 Clinton Portis/100 4.00 10.00
5 Corey Dillon/100 4.00 10.00
6 Curtis Martin/100 5.00 12.00
7 DeShaun Foster/100 5.00 12.00
8 Duce Staley/100 4.00 10.00
9 Hines Ward/100 5.00 12.00
10 Jake Plummer/100 4.00 10.00
11 Jeremy Shockey/93 4.00 10.00
12 Jerome Bettis/100 15.00 40.00
13 Jevon Kearse/89 4.00 10.00
14 Julius Jones/50 5.00 12.00
15 Marshall Faulk/100 5.00 12.00
16 Ricky Williams/100 5.00 12.00
17 Roy Williams S/25 6.00 15.00
18 Stephen Davis/100 4.00 10.00
19 Steven Jackson/20 6.00 15.00

2005 Donruss Gridiron Gear Past and Present Jerseys Numbers Single Autographs

STATED PRINT RUN 2-50
SERIAL #'d UNDER 25 NOT PRICED
1 Aaron Brooks/50 10.00 25.00
2 Ahman Green/25 15.00 40.00
9 Hines Ward/45 40.00 100.00
17 Roy Williams S/25 12.00 30.00

2005 Donruss Gridiron Gear Past and Present Jerseys Single

SERIAL #'d UNDER 20 NOT PRICED
1 Aaron Brooks/50 2.50 6.00
2 Ahman Green/35 4.00 10.00
3 Carson Palmer/150 2.50 6.00
4 Clinton Portis/15 4.00 10.00
5 Corey Dillon/150 2.00 5.00
6 Curtis Martin/150 2.50 6.00
8 Duce Staley/85 2.50 6.00
9 Hines Ward/150 2.50 6.00
10 Jake Plummer/150 2.00 5.00
12 Jerome Bettis/150 3.00 8.00
13 Jevon Kearse/150 2.00 5.00
14 Julius Jones/22 4.00 10.00
15 Marshall Faulk/150 2.50 6.00
16 Ricky Williams/150 2.50 6.00
17 Roy Williams S/30 3.00 8.00
18 Stephen Davis/150 2.00 5.00
19 Steven Jackson/55 2.50 6.00
20 Terrell Owens/25 5.00 12.00

2005 Donruss Gridiron Gear Past and Present Jerseys Single Autographs

STATED PRINT RUN 1-50
*DBL JSY AU/25: .5X TO 1.2X JSY AU/50
UNPRICED JSY NUM AU PRINT RUN 1-10
UNPRICED NME PLTE DBL PRINT RUN 1-15
UNPRICED TM LOGO DBL PRINT RUN 1-5
UNPRICED TM LOGO SINGL PRINT RUN 1-10
SERIAL #'d UNDER 20 NOT PRICED
1 Aaron Brooks/50 8.00 20.00
9 Hines Ward/50 40.00 80.00
13 Jevon Kearse/50 10.00 25.00
17 Roy Williams S/50 12.00 30.00
19 Steven Jackson/50 12.00 30.00

2005 Donruss Gridiron Gear Past and Present Jerseys Team Logo Single

TEAM LOGO SINGLE PRINT RUN 1-25
SERIAL #'d UNDER 15 NOT PRICED
*TEAM LOGO DBL/15: .5X TO 1.2X SNGL
5 Corey Dillon/25 6.00 15.00
6 Curtis Martin/25 8.00 20.00
7 DeShaun Foster/16 8.00 20.00
8 Duce Staley/25 6.00 15.00
13 Jevon Kearse/25 6.00 15.00
16 Ricky Williams/25 8.00 20.00
18 Stephen Davis/16 6.00 15.00
19 Steven Jackson/15 6.00 15.00
20 Terrell Owens/20 8.00 20.00

2005 Donruss Gridiron Gear Performers Gold

GOLD STATED PRINT RUN 500
*GOLD HOLO/100: .8X TO 2X GOLD/500
*PLATINUM/25: 1.2X TO 3X GOLD/500
*SILVER HOLO/250: .5X TO 1.2X GOLD/500
1 Tatum Bell 1.00 2.50
2 Antonio Gates 1.50 4.00
3 Barry Sanders 2.50 6.00
4 Brett Favre 3.00 8.00
5 Brian Westbrook 1.00 2.50
6 Chad Johnson 1.00 2.50
7 Chris Chambers 1.00 2.50
8 Corey Simon 1.00 2.50
9 Deion Branch 1.00 2.50
10 Deion Sanders 1.25 3.00
11 Deuce McAllister 1.25 3.00
12 Donte Stallworth 1.00 2.50
13 Doug Flutie 1.25 3.00
14 Drew Bledsoe 1.25 3.00
15 Drew Brees 1.50 4.00
16 Earl Campbell 1.50 4.00
17 Eddie George 1.25 3.00
18 Edgerrin James 1.25 3.00
19 Eric Moulds 1.00 2.50
20 Fred Taylor 1.00 2.50
21 Andre Johnson 1.25 3.00
22 Ickey Woods 1.00 2.50
23 Isaac Bruce 1.50 4.00
24 Javon Walker 1.00 2.50
25 Jerry Rice 3.00 8.00
26 Joey Harrington 1.00 2.50
27 John Taylor 1.00 2.50
28 Junior Seau 1.25 3.00
29 Ken Stabler 2.00 5.00
30 L.C. Greenwood 1.00 2.50
31 LaDainian Tomlinson 1.50 4.00
32 Larry Fitzgerald 1.50 4.00
33 Leroy Kelly 1.25 3.00
34 Mark Brunell 1.25 3.00
35 Michael Vick 1.25 3.00
36 Mike Singletary 1.50 4.00
37 Paul Warfield 1.25 3.00
38 Peyton Manning 4.00 10.00
39 Plaxico Burress 1.00 2.50
40 Randy Moss 1.25 3.00
41 Jake Plummer 1.00 2.50
42 Ricky Williams 1.25 3.00
43 Roger Craig 1.50 4.00
44 Shaun Alexander 1.00 2.50
45 Steve Smith 1.50 4.00
46 Terence Newman 1.00 2.50
47 Tom Brady 6.00 15.00
48 Tony Gonzalez 1.25 3.00
49 Warren Sapp 1.25 3.00
50 Willis McGahee 1.00 2.50

2005 Donruss Gridiron Gear Performers Autographs

STATED PRINT RUN 1-250
1 Tatum Bell/90 12.50 30.00
3 Barry Sanders/25 75.00 150.00
9 Deion Branch/14 12.00 30.00
16 Earl Campbell/25 15.00 40.00
21 Andre Johnson/25 15.00 40.00
27 John Taylor/89 8.00 20.00
29 Ken Stabler/250 15.00 40.00
35 Michael Vick/40 20.00 50.00
43 Roger Craig/98 12.50 30.00
44 Shaun Alexander/25 15.00 40.00
45 Steve Smith/15 15.00 40.00

2005 Donruss Gridiron Gear Performers Jersey Autographs

STATED PRINT RUN 1-50
*DBL PATCH/22-25: .6X TO 1.5X JSY AU
*TEAM LOGO/25: .6X TO 1.5X JSY AU
2 Antonio Gates/50 15.00 40.00
6 Chad Johnson/50 10.00 25.00
9 Deion Branch/50 10.00 25.00
16 Earl Campbell/50 15.00 40.00
26 Joey Harrington/20 12.00 30.00
27 John Taylor/30 12.00 30.00
30 L.C. Greenwood/16 12.00 30.00
35 Michael Vick/50 30.00 80.00
36 Mike Singletary/50 15.00 40.00
43 Roger Craig/15 20.00 50.00
44 Shaun Alexander/50 15.00 40.00
46 Terence Newman/25 12.00 30.00
50 Willis McGahee/50 10.00 25.00

2005 Donruss Gridiron Gear Performers Jerseys

STATED PRINT RUN 1-150
*JUMBO/50-100: .6X TO 1.5X JSY
*JUMBO/30-41: .8X TO 2X JSY
*JUMBO/20-25: 1X TO 2.5X JSY
1 Tatum Bell/150 2.00 5.00
2 Antonio Gates/80 4.00 10.00
4 Brett Favre/150 6.00 15.00
5 Brian Westbrook/150 2.00 5.00
6 Chad Johnson/50 3.00 8.00
7 Chris Chambers/25 5.00 12.00
8 Corey Simon/150 2.00 5.00
9 Deion Branch/70 2.50 6.00
10 Deion Sanders/150 2.50 6.00
11 Deuce McAllister/150 2.50 6.00
12 Donte Stallworth/120 2.00 5.00
13 Doug Flutie/150 2.50 6.00
14 Drew Bledsoe/150 2.50 6.00
15 Drew Brees/150 3.00 8.00
16 Earl Campbell/150 3.00 8.00
17 Eddie George/22 6.00 15.00
18 Edgerrin James/15 6.00 15.00
22 Ickey Woods/150 2.00 5.00
23 Isaac Bruce/150 3.00 8.00
24 Javon Walker/150 2.00 5.00
25 Jerry Rice/150 6.00 15.00
26 Joey Harrington/150 2.00 5.00
27 John Taylor/100 2.50 6.00
28 Junior Seau/150 2.50 6.00
30 L.C. Greenwood/100 2.50 6.00
31 LaDainian Tomlinson/150 3.00 8.00
32 Larry Fitzgerald/150 3.00 8.00
33 Leroy Kelly/75 3.00 8.00
34 Mark Brunell/150 2.50 6.00
35 Michael Vick/150 2.50 6.00
36 Mike Singletary/75 4.00 10.00
37 Paul Warfield/25 6.00 15.00
38 Peyton Manning/150 8.00 20.00
40 Randy Moss/150 2.50 6.00
41 Jake Plummer/150 2.00 5.00
42 Ricky Williams/150 2.50 6.00
43 Roger Craig/150 3.00 8.00
44 Shaun Alexander/75 2.50 6.00
46 Terence Newman/125 2.00 5.00
47 Tom Brady/150 12.00 30.00
48 Tony Gonzalez/150 2.50 6.00
49 Warren Sapp/118 2.50 6.00
50 Willis McGahee/125 2.00 5.00

2005 Donruss Gridiron Gear Performers Jerseys Jumbo Swatch Prime

STATED PRINT RUN 2-50
2 Antonio Gates/27 10.00 25.00
3 Barry Sanders/20 20.00 50.00
4 Brett Favre/42 15.00 40.00
5 Brian Westbrook/50 5.00 12.00
6 Chad Johnson/50 5.00 12.00
7 Chris Chambers/50 5.00 12.00
8 Corey Simon/50 5.00 12.00
11 Deuce McAllister/50 6.00 15.00
12 Donte Stallworth/50 5.00 12.00
13 Doug Flutie/33 6.00 15.00
15 Drew Brees/50 8.00 20.00
17 Eddie George/23 10.00 25.00
18 Edgerrin James/50 6.00 15.00
19 Eric Moulds/38 5.00 12.00
20 Fred Taylor/50 5.00 12.00
22 Ickey Woods/20 8.00 20.00
23 Isaac Bruce/50 8.00 20.00
24 Javon Walker/50 5.00 12.00
25 Jerry Rice/50 15.00 40.00
26 Joey Harrington/50 5.00 12.00
27 John Taylor/25 6.00 15.00
28 Junior Seau/50 6.00 15.00
31 LaDainian Tomlinson/15 12.00 30.00
34 Mark Brunell/27 8.00 20.00
36 Mike Singletary/25 10.00 25.00
38 Peyton Manning/50 20.00 50.00
39 Plaxico Burress/16 8.00 20.00
40 Randy Moss/50 6.00 15.00
41 Jake Plummer/41 5.00 12.00
42 Ricky Williams/50 6.00 15.00
44 Shaun Alexander/28 6.00 15.00
45 Steve Smith/15 12.00 30.00
46 Terence Newman/46 5.00 12.00
48 Tony Gonzalez/50 6.00 15.00
49 Warren Sapp/50 6.00 15.00
50 Willis McGahee/50 5.00 12.00

2005 Donruss Gridiron Gear Performers Jerseys Name Plate

STATED PRINT RUN 1-50
3 Barry Sanders/50 15.00 40.00
5 Brian Westbrook/50 6.00 15.00
6 Chad Johnson/50 6.00 15.00
7 Chris Chambers/50 6.00 15.00
8 Corey Simon/50 6.00 15.00
10 Deion Sanders/20 10.00 25.00
11 Deuce McAllister/50 8.00 20.00
12 Donte Stallworth/29 8.00 20.00
13 Doug Flutie/25 10.00 25.00
14 Drew Bledsoe/16 10.00 25.00
15 Drew Brees/19 12.00 30.00
16 Earl Campbell/25 12.00 30.00
17 Eddie George/45 8.00 20.00
18 Edgerrin James/50 8.00 20.00
19 Eric Moulds/48 6.00 15.00
20 Fred Taylor/50 6.00 15.00
22 Ickey Woods/36 6.00 15.00
23 Isaac Bruce/50 10.00 25.00
24 Javon Walker/45 6.00 15.00
25 Jerry Rice/50 20.00 50.00
26 Joey Harrington/50 6.00 15.00
31 LaDainian Tomlinson/26 12.00 30.00
34 Mark Brunell/50 8.00 20.00
38 Peyton Manning/25 25.00 60.00
40 Randy Moss/36 8.00 20.00
41 Jake Plummer/16 8.00 20.00
42 Ricky Williams/48 8.00 20.00
44 Shaun Alexander/25 8.00 20.00
46 Terence Newman/35 6.00 15.00
47 Tom Brady/23 25.00 60.00
48 Tony Gonzalez/36 8.00 20.00
49 Warren Sapp/20 10.00 25.00

2005 Donruss Gridiron Gear Performers Jerseys Numbers

STATED PRINT RUN 1-100
2 Antonio Gates/100 8.00 20.00
3 Barry Sanders/100 12.00 30.00
4 Brett Favre/80 15.00 40.00
5 Brian Westbrook/100 5.00 12.00
6 Chad Johnson/100 5.00 12.00
7 Chris Chambers/100 5.00 12.00
8 Corey Simon/100 5.00 12.00
9 Deion Branch/55 6.00 15.00
10 Deion Sanders/100 6.00 15.00
11 Deuce McAllister/100 6.00 15.00
12 Donte Stallworth/100 5.00 12.00
13 Doug Flutie/80 6.00 15.00
14 Drew Bledsoe/15 10.00 25.00
15 Drew Brees/100 8.00 20.00
16 Earl Campbell/100 8.00 20.00
17 Eddie George/100 6.00 15.00
18 Edgerrin James/100 6.00 15.00
19 Eric Moulds/100 5.00 12.00
20 Fred Taylor/100 5.00 12.00
21 Andre Johnson/20 10.00 25.00

22 Ickey Woods/100 5.00 12.00
23 Isaac Bruce/100 8.00 20.00
24 Javon Walker/100 5.00 12.00
25 Jerry Rice/100 15.00 40.00
26 Joey Harrington/25 8.00 20.00
27 John Taylor/25 8.00 20.00
28 Junior Seau/100 6.00 15.00
31 LaDainian Tomlinson/100 8.00 20.00
32 Larry Fitzgerald/100 8.00 20.00
34 Mark Brunell/100 6.00 15.00
36 Mike Singletary/50 10.00 25.00
37 Paul Warfield/50 8.00 20.00
38 Peyton Manning/50 25.00 60.00
39 Plaxico Burress/26 8.00 20.00
40 Randy Moss/100 6.00 15.00
41 Jake Plummer/99 5.00 12.00
42 Ricky Williams/100 6.00 15.00
43 Roger Craig/73 10.00 25.00
44 Shaun Alexander/37 6.00 15.00
45 Steve Smith/35 10.00 25.00
46 Terence Newman/75 5.00 12.00
47 Tom Brady/64 40.00 100.00
48 Tony Gonzalez/100 6.00 15.00
49 Warren Sapp/100 6.00 15.00

2005 Donruss Gridiron Gear Performers Jerseys Numbers Autographs

STATED PRINT RUN 1-50
*NAME PLATE/25: .4X TO 1X JSY NUM/25
*NAME PLATE/25: .5X TO 1.2X JSY NUM/50
2 Antonio Gates/50 20.00 50.00
3 Barry Sanders/25 125.00 200.00
6 Chad Johnson/50 20.00 50.00
9 Deion Branch/50 15.00 40.00
16 Earl Campbell/25 30.00 80.00
21 Andre Johnson/25 15.00 40.00
26 Joey Harrington/25 15.00 40.00
35 Michael Vick/25 50.00 100.00
43 Roger Craig/35 25.00 60.00
44 Shaun Alexander/25 20.00 50.00
46 Terence Newman/25 15.00 40.00
50 Willis McGahee/25 20.00 50.00

2005 Donruss Gridiron Gear Performers Jerseys Patch Double

STATED PRINT RUN 1-50
3 Barry Sanders/50 12.00 30.00
4 Brett Favre/25 20.00 50.00
7 Chris Chambers/50 5.00 12.00
8 Corey Simon/50 5.00 12.00
11 Deuce McAllister/50 6.00 15.00
16 Earl Campbell/25 10.00 25.00
17 Eddie George/25 8.00 20.00
18 Edgerrin James/25 8.00 20.00
19 Eric Moulds/30 6.00 15.00
20 Fred Taylor/50 5.00 12.00
23 Isaac Bruce/25 10.00 25.00
25 Jerry Rice/15 25.00 60.00
28 Junior Seau/28 8.00 20.00
31 LaDainian Tomlinson/50 8.00 20.00
32 Larry Fitzgerald/50 8.00 20.00
34 Mark Brunell/50 6.00 15.00
36 Mike Singletary/30 10.00 25.00
38 Peyton Manning/25 25.00 60.00
39 Plaxico Burress/50 5.00 12.00
40 Randy Moss/50 6.00 15.00
42 Ricky Williams/50 6.00 15.00
44 Shaun Alexander/15 8.00 20.00
48 Tony Gonzalez/50 6.00 15.00
49 Warren Sapp/30 8.00 20.00

2005 Donruss Gridiron Gear Performers Jerseys Team Logo

STATED PRINT RUN 2-25
5 Brian Westbrook/25 8.00 20.00
6 Chad Johnson/25 8.00 20.00
7 Chris Chambers/25 8.00 20.00
8 Corey Simon/25 8.00 20.00
11 Deuce McAllister/25 10.00 25.00
12 Donte Stallworth/20 8.00 20.00
14 Drew Bledsoe/25 10.00 25.00
17 Eddie George/25 10.00 25.00
20 Fred Taylor/25 8.00 20.00
28 Junior Seau/16 10.00 25.00
34 Mark Brunell/25 10.00 25.00
40 Randy Moss/17 10.00 25.00
42 Ricky Williams/25 10.00 25.00
47 Tom Brady/24 50.00 125.00
49 Warren Sapp/25 10.00 25.00

2005 Donruss Gridiron Gear Pro Bowl Squad Gold

COMPLETE SET (5) 8.00 20.00
GOLD STATED PRINT RUN 1000
*GOLD HOLO/100: .6X TO 1.5X GOLD/1000
*PLATINUM/25: 1X TO 2.5X GOLD/1000
*SILVER HOLO/250.: .5X TO 1.2X GOLD/1000
1 Daunte Culpepper 1.25 3.00
2 Fran Tarkenton 1.50 4.00
3 Jamal Lewis 1.25 3.00
4 Jeff Garcia 1.00 2.50
5 Tom Brady 6.00 15.00

2005 Donruss Gridiron Gear Pro Bowl Squad Jerseys

STATED PRINT RUN 100 SER.#'d SETS
*DBL PATCH/19-25: 1.2X TO 3X JSY/100
*NAME PLATE/15-22: 1.2X TO 3X JSY/100
*JSY NUM/100: .6X TO 1.5X JSY/100
*JSY NUM/42: .8X TO 2X JSY/100
*TEAM LOGO/15-18: 1.2X TO 3X JSY/100
1 Daunte Culpepper 4.00 10.00
2 Fran Tarkenton 5.00 12.00
3 Jamal Lewis 4.00 10.00
4 Jeff Garcia 3.00 8.00
5 Tom Brady 20.00 50.00

2005 Donruss Gridiron Gear Rookie Jerseys Jumbo Swatch

STATED PRINT RUN 52-150
*PRIME/75: 1X TO 2.5X BASIC JSY/52-150
101 Alex Smith QB/139 10.00 25.00
102 Ronnie Brown/150 3.00 8.00
103 Braylon Edwards/150 2.50 6.00
105 Cadillac Williams/150 2.50 6.00
106 Adam Jones/150 3.00 8.00
107 Troy Williamson/150 2.50 6.00
111 Matt Jones/150 2.50 6.00
112 Mark Clayton/150 2.50 6.00
114 Jason Campbell/150 2.50 6.00
115 Roddy White/150 4.00 10.00
118 Mark Bradley/150 2.50 6.00
121 Roscoe Parrish/150 2.50 6.00
122 Terrence Murphy/150 2.50 6.00
123 Vincent Jackson/150 4.00 10.00
124 Frank Gore/92 5.00 12.00
125 Charlie Frye/150 2.50 6.00
126 Courtney Roby/150 2.50 6.00
127 Andrew Walter/150 2.50 6.00
128 Vernand Morency/150 2.50 6.00
129 Ryan Moats/150 3.00 8.00
133 Kyle Orton/52 2.50 6.00
136 Ciatrick Fason/150 2.50 6.00
138 Stefan LeFors/150 2.50 6.00
142 Antrel Rolle/150 4.00 10.00
143 Maurice Clarett/150 3.00 8.00
145 Eric Shelton/150 2.50 6.00
147 Carlos Rogers/150 4.00 10.00

2005 Donruss Gridiron Gear Triplets Gold

STATED PRINT RUN 1000 SER.#'d SETS
*GOLD HOLO/100: .6X TO 1.5X GOLD/1000
*PLATINUM/25: 1X TO 2.5X GOLD/1000
*SILVER HOLO/250: .5X TO 1.2X GOLD/1000
1 Glenn/Abraham/Vilma 1.25 3.00
2 Toomer/Hilliard/Dayne 1.25 3.00
3 Randle El/Ward/Bettis 2.00 5.00
4 Seymour/Givens/Branch 1.25 3.00
5 Leftwich/Taylor/Smith 1.50 4.00
6 Brown/Bennett/Kearse 1.50 4.00
7 Chambers/Taylor/Seau 1.50 4.00
8 McNabb/Buck/Staley 1.50 4.00
9 Hall/Gonz/Green 1.50 4.00
10 Brooks/Clay/Alstott 1.25 3.00
11 McAll/Stall/Horn 1.50 4.00
12 Driver/Walker/Ferg 1.50 4.00
13 Brees/Seau/LT 2.00 5.00
14 Moulds/Reed/Evans 1.50 4.00
15 John/Bled/Will S 1.50 4.00

2005 Donruss Gridiron Gear Triplets Jerseys

STATED PRINT RUN 25-100
*NME PLTE/41-50: 1X TO 2.5X JSY/55-100
*JSY NUM/50-100: .8X TO 2X JSY/55-100
*JSY NUM/100: .5X TO 1.2X JSY/25
*JSY NUM/17-25: 1.2X TO 3X JSY/55-100
*JSY NUM/25: 1X TO 2.5X JSY/33
*TEAM LOGO/25: 1.2X TO 3X JSY/100
1 Glenn/Abraham/Vilma/100 5.00 12.00
2 Toomer/Hilliard/Dayne/100 5.00 12.00
3 Randle El/Ward/Bettis/100 15.00 40.00
4 Seymour/Givens/Branch/100 5.00 12.00
5 Leftwich/Taylor/Smith/100 6.00 15.00
6 Brown/Bennett/Kearse/55 6.00 15.00
7 Chambers/Taylor/Seau/100 6.00 15.00
8 McNabb/Buck/Staley/33 8.00 20.00
9 Hall/Gonz/Green/25 10.00 25.00
10 Brooks/Clay/Alstott/100 5.00 12.00
11 McAll/Stall/Horn/100 6.00 15.00
12 Driver/Walker/Ferg/75 6.00 15.00
13 Brees/Seau/LT/100 8.00 20.00
14 Moulds/Reed/Evans/100 6.00 15.00
15 John/Bled/Will S/100 6.00 15.00

2006 Donruss Gridiron Gear

This 231-card set was released in October, 2006. The set is broken down into veterans in team alphabetical order (1-100) and 2006 rookies (101-231). Within the rookies, cards numbered 101-200 were issued to a stated print run of 599 serial numbered sets and cards numbered 201-231 were issued to a stated production run of 50 sets and those cards also featured a player-worn swatch.

COMP.SET w/o RC's (100) 10.00 25.00
ROOKIE PRINT RUN 599 SER.#'d SETS
201-231 ANNOUNCED PRINT RUN 50
201-231 JSY RCs FEATURE JUMBO SWATCH
1 Edgerrin James .30 .75
2 Kurt Warner .30 .75
3 Larry Fitzgerald .30 .75
4 Alge Crumpler .30 .75
5 Michael Vick .30 .75
6 Warrick Dunn .25 .60
7 Jamal Lewis .30 .75
8 Mike Anderson .25 .60
9 Neil Rackers .25 .60
10 Derrick Mason .25 .60
11 J.P. Losman .30 .75
12 Lee Evans .30 .75
13 Willis McGahee .25 .60
14 DeShaun Foster .30 .75
15 Jake Delhomme .25 .60
16 Josh Brown .25 .60
17 Steve Smith .40 1.00
18 Cedric Benson .25 .60
19 Rex Grossman .25 .60
20 Shayne Graham .25 .60
21 Carson Palmer .30 .75
22 Chad Johnson .25 .60
23 Rudi Johnson .25 .60
24 T.J. Houshmandzadeh .25 .60
25 Charlie Frye .30 .75
26 Lance Briggs .30 .75
27 Reuben Droughns .30 .75
28 Drew Bledsoe .30 .75
29 Julius Jones .25 .60
30 Terrell Owens .30 .75
31 Terry Glenn .30 .75
32 Jake Plummer .25 .60
33 Rod Smith .30 .75
34 Tatum Bell .25 .60
35 Robert Mathis .25 .60
36 Kevin Jones .25 .60
37 Roy Williams WR .25 .60
38 Ahman Green .30 .75
39 Brett Favre .75 2.00
40 Scottie Vines .25 .60
41 Samkon Gado .25 .60
42 Andre Johnson .30 .75
43 David Carr .25 .60
44 Domanick Davis .25 .60
45 Marvin Harrison .30 .75
46 Peyton Manning 1.00 2.50
47 Reggie Wayne .30 .75
48 Byron Leftwich .25 .60
49 Fred Taylor .25 .60
50 Jimmy Smith .30 .75
51 Matt Jones .25 .60
52 Larry Johnson .25 .60
53 Tony Gonzalez .30 .75
54 Trent Green .25 .60
55 Chris Chambers .25 .60
56 Daunte Culpepper .30 .75
57 Ronnie Brown .30 .75
58 Robert Pollard .25 .60
59 Mewelde Moore .25 .60
60 Chester Taylor .30 .75
61 Corey Dillon .25 .60
62 Deion Branch .25 .60
63 Tom Brady 1.25 3.00
64 Deuce McAllister .30 .75
65 Drew Brees .40 1.00
66 Donte Stallworth .25 .60
67 Eli Manning .30 .75
68 Jeremy Shockey .25 .60
69 Plaxico Burress .25 .60
70 Tiki Barber .30 .75
71 Chad Pennington .25 .60
72 Curtis Martin .30 .75
73 Laveranues Coles .25 .60
74 LaMont Jordan .30 .75
75 Randy Moss .30 .75
76 Aaron Brooks .25 .60
77 Brian Westbrook .25 .60
78 Donovan McNabb .30 .75
79 Jabar Gaffney .25 .60
80 Ben Roethlisberger .50 1.25
81 Hines Ward .30 .75
82 Willie Parker .30 .75
83 Antonio Gates .40 1.00
84 LaDainian Tomlinson .40 1.00
85 Philip Rivers .40 1.00
86 Alex Smith QB .30 .75
87 Edell Shepherd RC .25 .60
88 Kevan Barlow .25 .60
89 Darrell Jackson .30 .75
90 Matt Hasselbeck .25 .60
91 Shaun Alexander .25 .60
92 Marc Bulger .25 .60
93 Torry Holt .30 .75
94 Steven Jackson .25 .60
95 Chris Simms .25 .60
96 Cadillac Williams .30 .75
97 Joey Galloway .30 .75
98 Chris Brown .25 .60
99 Clinton Portis .25 .60
100 Santana Moss .30 .75
101 A.J. Nicholson RC 1.25 3.00
102 Abdul Hodge RC 1.25 3.00
103 Adam Jennings RC 1.50 4.00
104 Andre Hall RC 1.50 4.00
105 Anthony Fasano RC 1.25 3.00
106 Anthony Mix RC 1.50 4.00
107 Anthony Smith RC 2.00 5.00
108 Antonio Cromartie RC 1.50 4.00
109 Ashton Youboty RC 1.25 3.00
110 Ben Obomanu RC 1.50 4.00
111 Bennie Brazell RC 1.50 4.00
112 Bernard Pollard RC 1.50 4.00
113 Bobby Carpenter RC 1.25 3.00
114 Brad Smith RC 1.50 4.00
115 Brodie Croyle RC 1.25 3.00
116 Brodrick Bunkley RC 1.50 4.00
117 Bruce Gradkowski RC 1.50 4.00
118 Calvin Lowry RC 2.00 5.00
119 Cedric Griffin RC 1.50 4.00
120 Cedric Humes RC 1.25 3.00
121 Chad Greenway RC 2.00 5.00
122 Claude Wroten RC 1.25 3.00
123 Cory Rodgers RC 1.25 3.00
124 D.J. Shockley RC 1.50 4.00
125 Danieal Manning RC 2.00 5.00
126 Daniel Bullocks RC 1.25 3.00
127 Darryl Tapp RC 1.50 4.00
128 David Anderson RC 1.50 4.00
129 David Kirtman RC 1.50 4.00
130 David Pittman RC 1.50 4.00
131 David Thomas RC 1.25 3.00
132 Dawan Landry RC 2.00 5.00
133 D'Brickashaw Ferguson RC 1.25 3.00
134 Delanie Walker RC 2.50 6.00
135 DeMario Minter RC 1.50 4.00
136 DeMeco Ryans RC 1.50 4.00
137 Derrick Ross RC 1.50 4.00
138 Devin Aromashodu RC 1.25 3.00
139 Devin Hester RC 2.50 6.00
140 Domenik Hixon RC 2.00 5.00
141 Dominique Byrd RC 1.25 3.00
142 Donte Whitner RC 1.50 4.00
143 D'Qwell Jackson RC 1.25 3.00
144 Dusty Dvoracek RC 2.00 5.00
145 Erik Meyer RC 1.25 3.00
146 Ernie Sims RC 1.25 3.00
147 Ethan Kilmer RC 1.50 4.00
148 Gabe Watson RC 1.25 3.00
149 Garrett Mills RC 1.50 4.00
150 Greg Blue RC 1.50 4.00
151 Greg Jennings RC 2.00 5.00
152 Greg Lee RC 1.25 3.00
153 Haloti Ngata RC 1.50 4.00
154 Ingle Martin RC 1.50 4.00
155 Jai Lewis RC 1.50 4.00
156 Jason Allen RC 1.50 4.00
157 Jay Cutler RC 1.50 4.00
158 Jeffrey Webb RC 1.50 4.00
159 Jeremy Bloom RC 1.25 3.00
160 Jerome Harrison RC 1.25 3.00
161 Jimmy Williams RC 1.25 3.00
162 John David Washington RC 1.25 3.00
163 John McCargo RC 1.25 3.00
164 Johnathan Joseph RC 1.50 4.00
165 Jon Alston RC 1.25 3.00
166 Jonathan Orr RC 1.50 4.00
167 Joseph Addai RC 1.25 3.00
168 Kamerion Wimbley RC 1.50 4.00
169 Kelly Jennings RC 1.50 4.00
170 Ko Simpson RC 1.50 4.00
171 Leonard Pope RC 2.00 5.00
172 Manny Lawson RC 1.50 4.00
173 Marcus Maxey RC 1.50 4.00
174 Marcus Vick RC 1.25 3.00
175 Marques Hagans RC 1.25 3.00
176 Martin Nance RC 1.25 3.00
177 Mathias Kiwanuka RC 2.00 5.00
178 Mike Bell RC 1.25 3.00
179 Mike Hass RC 1.25 3.00
180 Nate Salley RC 1.50 4.00
181 Owen Daniels RC 2.00 5.00
182 P.J. Daniels RC 1.25 3.00
183 Pat Watkins RC 1.50 4.00
184 Paul Pinegar RC 1.25 3.00
185 Quinton Ganther RC 1.25 3.00
186 Reggie McNeal RC 1.25 3.00
187 Richard Marshall RC 1.50 4.00
188 Rocky McIntosh RC 1.25 3.00
189 Roman Harper RC 1.50 4.00
190 Skyler Green RC 1.25 3.00
191 Tamba Hali RC 2.00 5.00
192 Thomas Howard RC 1.25 3.00
193 Tim Jennings RC 2.00 5.00
194 Todd Watkins RC 1.25 3.00
195 Tony Scheffler RC 2.00 5.00
196 Tye Hill RC 1.25 3.00
197 Wali Lundy RC 1.25 3.00
198 Wendell Mathis RC 1.50 4.00
199 Will Blackmon RC 1.25 3.00
200 Willie Reid RC 1.50 4.00
201 Brian Calhoun JSY RC 2.00 5.00
202 Joe Klopfenstein JSY RC 2.00 5.00
203 Travis Wilson JSY RC 2.00 5.00
204 Charlie Whitehurst JSY RC 2.00 5.00
205 DeAngelo Williams JSY RC 2.50 6.00
206 Maurice Stovall JSY RC 2.00 5.00
207 A.J. Hawk JSY RC 2.50 6.00
208 Kellen Clemens JSY RC 2.00 5.00
209 Leon Washington JSY RC 2.00 5.00
210 Sinorice Moss JSY RC 2.00 5.00
211 Demetrius Williams JSY RC 2.00 5.00
212 Jerious Norwood JSY RC 2.00 5.00
213 Santonio Holmes JSY RC 2.50 6.00
214 Omar Jacobs JSY RC 2.00 5.00
215 Brandon Marshall JSY RC 4.00 10.00
216 Jason Avant JSY RC 2.00 5.00
217 Derek Hagan JSY RC 2.50 6.00
218 Brandon Williams JSY RC 2.00 5.00
219 Vernon Davis JSY RC 2.50 6.00
220 Michael Robinson JSY RC 2.00 5.00
221 Matt Leinart JSY RC 2.00 5.00
222 Reggie Bush JSY RC 3.00 8.00
223 LenDale White JSY RC 2.00 5.00
224 Vince Young JSY RC 2.00 5.00
225 Maurice Drew JSY RC 3.00 8.00
226 Marcedes Lewis JSY RC 2.00 5.00
227 Mario Williams JSY RC 3.00 8.00
228 Michael Huff JSY RC 2.50 6.00
229 Tarvaris Jackson JSY RC 2.00 5.00
230 Laurence Maroney JSY RC 2.00 5.00
231 Chad Jackson JSY RC 2.00 5.00

2006 Donruss Gridiron Gear Gold Holofoil

*VETERANS: 1.5X TO 4X BASIC CARDS
RANDOM INSERTS IN RETAIL PACKS

2006 Donruss Gridiron Gear Gold Holofoil O's

*VETS 1-100: 2.5X TO 6X BASIC CARDS
*ROOKIES 101-200: .6X TO 1.5X BASIC CARDS
RANDOM INSERTS IN RETAIL PACKS
STATED PRINT RUN 100 SER.#'d SETS

2006 Donruss Gridiron Gear Gold Holofoil X's

*VETS 1-100: 2.5X TO 6X BASIC CARDS
*ROOKIES 101-200: .6X TO 1.5X BASIC CARDS
RANDOM INSERTS IN HOBBY PACKS
STATED PRINT RUN 100 SER.#'d SETS

2006 Donruss Gridiron Gear Platinum Holofoil

*VETERANS: 4X TO 10X BASIC CARDS
RANDOM INSERTS IN RETAIL PACKS

2006 Donruss Gridiron Gear Platinum Holofoil O's

*VETS 1-100: 6X TO 15X BASIC CARDS
*ROOKIES 101-200: 1X TO 2.5X BASIC CARDS
RANDOM INSERTS IN RETAIL PACKS
STATED PRINT RUN 25 SER.#'d SETS

2006 Donruss Gridiron Gear Platinum Holofoil X's

*VETS 1-100: 6X TO 15X BASIC CARDS
*ROOKIES 101-200: 1X TO 2.5X BASIC CARDS
RANDOM INSERTS IN HOBBY PACKS
STATED PRINT RUN 25 SER.#'d SETS

2006 Donruss Gridiron Gear Retail

*ROOKIES 101-200: .4X TO 1X BASIC CARDS
STATED PRINT RUN 599 SER.#'d SETS

2006 Donruss Gridiron Gear Silver Holofoil

*VETERANS: 1X TO 2.5X BASIC CARDS
RANDOM INSERTS IN RETAIL PACKS

2006 Donruss Gridiron Gear Silver Holofoil O's

*VETS 1-100: 1.5X TO 4X BASIC CARDS
RANDOM INSERTS IN RETAIL PACKS
STATED PRINT RUN 250 SER.#'d SETS

2006 Donruss Gridiron Gear Silver Holofoil X's

*VETS 1-100: 1.5X TO 4X BASIC CARDS
RANDOM INSERTS IN HOBBY PACKS
STATED PRINT RUN 250 SER.#'d SETS

2006 Donruss Gridiron Gear Autographs Gold Holofoil

STATED PRINT RUN 5-250 SER.#'d SETS
SERIAL #'d UNDER 25 NOT PRICED
1 Edgerrin James/25 10.00 25.00
3 Larry Fitzgerald/35 25.00 50.00
9 Neil Rackers/100 5.00 12.00
12 Lee Evans/35 8.00 20.00
13 Willis McGahee/35 6.00 15.00
15 Jake Delhomme/35 6.00 15.00
16 Josh Brown/100 5.00 12.00
20 Shayne Graham/100 5.00 12.00
25 Charlie Frye/25 10.00 25.00
26 Lance Briggs/100 30.00 60.00
34 Tatum Bell/50 6.00 15.00
35 Robert Mathis/100 5.00 12.00
37 Roy Williams WR/25 8.00 20.00
40 Scottie Vines/100 5.00 12.00
41 Samkon Gado/25 8.00 20.00
46 Peyton Manning/20 60.00 120.00
48 Byron Leftwich/50 6.00 15.00
50 Jimmy Smith/35 8.00 20.00
51 Matt Jones/50 6.00 15.00
52 Larry Johnson/25 8.00 20.00
55 Chris Chambers/25 8.00 20.00
57 Ronnie Brown/25 10.00 25.00
58 Robert Pollard/100 5.00 12.00
74 LaMont Jordan/35 8.00 20.00
78 Donovan McNabb/25 25.00 60.00
82 Willie Parker/75 6.00 15.00
84 LaDainian Tomlinson/25 30.00 80.00
87 Edell Shepherd/100 5.00 12.00
89 Darrell Jackson/35 8.00 20.00
90 Matt Hasselbeck/35 6.00 15.00
93 Torry Holt/25 10.00 25.00
94 Steven Jackson/25 8.00 20.00
98 Chris Brown/25 8.00 20.00
99 Clinton Portis/25 8.00 20.00
101 A.J. Nicholson/225 4.00 10.00
102 Abdul Hodge/250 4.00 10.00
103 Adam Jennings/250 5.00 12.00
104 Andre Hall/70 6.00 15.00
105 Anthony Fasano/75 5.00 12.00
106 Anthony Mix/250 5.00 12.00
108 Antonio Cromartie/100 6.00 15.00
109 Ashton Youboty/208 4.00 10.00
110 Ben Obomanu/165 5.00 12.00
111 Bennie Brazell/250 5.00 12.00
112 Bernard Pollard/250 5.00 12.00
113 Bobby Carpenter/175 4.00 10.00
114 Brad Smith/250 5.00 12.00
115 Brodie Croyle/225 4.00 10.00
116 Brodrick Bunkley/75 6.00 15.00
117 Bruce Gradkowski/75 6.00 15.00
119 Cedric Griffin/250 5.00 12.00
120 Cedric Humes/175 4.00 10.00
121 Chad Greenway/250 6.00 15.00
122 Claude Wroten/250 4.00 10.00
123 Cory Rodgers/250 4.00 10.00
124 D.J. Shockley/75 6.00 15.00
128 David Anderson/250 5.00 12.00
131 David Thomas/250 4.00 10.00
133 D'Brickashaw Ferguson/250 4.00 10.00
134 Delanie Walker/250 8.00 20.00
136 DeMeco Ryans/125 6.00 15.00
139 Devin Hester/100 10.00 25.00
140 Domenik Hixon/250 6.00 15.00
141 Dominique Byrd/75 5.00 12.00
142 Donte Whitner/250 5.00 12.00
143 D'Qwell Jackson/25 6.00 15.00
145 Erik Meyer/250 4.00 10.00
147 Ethan Kilmer/250 5.00 12.00
148 Gabe Watson/175 4.00 10.00
149 Garrett Mills/250 5.00 12.00
151 Greg Jennings/100 8.00 20.00
152 Greg Lee/30 6.00 15.00
153 Haloti Ngata/225 5.00 12.00
154 Ingle Martin/75 6.00 15.00
156 Jason Allen/250 5.00 12.00
157 Jay Cutler/225 5.00 12.00
158 Jeffrey Webb/250 5.00 12.00
160 Jerome Harrison/75 5.00 12.00
161 Jimmy Williams/250 4.00 10.00
163 John McCargo/250 4.00 10.00
164 Johnathan Joseph/25 8.00 20.00
165 Jon Alston/219 4.00 10.00
166 Jonathan Orr/250 5.00 12.00
167 Joseph Addai/225 4.00 10.00
168 Kamerion Wimbley/25 8.00 20.00
169 Kelly Jennings/75 6.00 15.00
170 Ko Simpson/250 5.00 12.00
171 Leonard Pope/75 8.00 20.00
172 Manny Lawson/250 5.00 12.00
175 Marques Hagans/250 4.00 10.00
176 Martin Nance/30 6.00 15.00
177 Mathias Kiwanuka/25 10.00 25.00
178 Mike Bell/94 5.00 12.00
179 Mike Hass/250 4.00 10.00
181 Owen Daniels/81 8.00 20.00
182 P.J. Daniels/75 5.00 12.00
183 Pat Watkins/250 5.00 12.00
184 Paul Pinegar/219 4.00 10.00
185 Quinton Ganther/250 4.00 10.00
186 Reggie McNeal/75 5.00 12.00
188 Rocky McIntosh/250 4.00 10.00
190 Skyler Green/250 4.00 10.00
191 Tamba Hali/175 6.00 15.00
192 Thomas Howard/219 4.00 10.00
194 Todd Watkins/250 4.00 10.00
195 Tony Scheffler/250 6.00 15.00
196 Tye Hill/100 5.00 12.00
197 Wali Lundy/250 4.00 10.00
198 Wendell Mathis/70 6.00 15.00
200 Willie Reid/250 5.00 12.00

2006 Donruss Gridiron Gear Autographs Platinum Holofoil

*VETERANS/25: .8X TO 2X GOLD/100
*ROOKIES/25: .4X TO 1X GOLD/25-35
*ROOKIES/25: .6X TO 1.5X GOLD/165-250
*ROOKIES/25: .5X TO 1.2X GOLD/70-125
PLATINUM PRINT RUN 1-25 SER.#'d SETS
SERIAL #'d UNDER NOT PRICED
26 Lance Briggs/25 40.00 80.00
139 Devin Hester/25 12.00 30.00
157 Jay Cutler/25 40.00 80.00
167 Joseph Addai/25 15.00 40.00

2006 Donruss Gridiron Gear Jerseys

STATED PRINT RUN 89-250
*O's/50: .5X TO 1.2X BASIC INSERTS
O's PRINT RUN 50 SER.#'d SETS
*PRIME/25: .8X TO 2X BASIC INSERTS
PRIME PRINT RUN 25 SER.#'d SETS
*X's/86-100: .5X TO 1.2X BASIC INSERTS
*X's/25-60: .6X TO 1.5X BASIC INSERTS
X's PRINT RUN 25-100 SER.#'d SETS
*RETAIL: .4X TO 1X BASIC INSERTS
RETAIL PRINTED ON WHITE STOCK
1 Edgerrin James/89 3.00 8.00
3 Larry Fitzgerald/250 3.00 8.00
4 Alge Crumpler/125 3.00 8.00
5 Michael Vick/250 3.00 8.00
6 Warrick Dunn/125 2.50 6.00
7 Jamal Lewis/250 3.00 8.00
11 J.P. Losman/150 3.00 8.00
12 Lee Evans/125 3.00 8.00
13 Willis McGahee/97 2.50 6.00
14 DeShaun Foster/125 3.00 8.00
15 Jake Delhomme/125 2.50 6.00
17 Steve Smith/125 4.00 10.00
18 Cedric Benson/100 2.50 6.00
19 Rex Grossman/97 2.50 6.00
21 Carson Palmer/125 3.00 8.00
22 Chad Johnson/125 2.50 6.00
23 Rudi Johnson/250 2.50 6.00
24 T.J. Houshmandzadeh/125 2.50 6.00
25 Charlie Frye/125 3.00 8.00
27 Reuben Droughns/125 3.00 8.00
28 Drew Bledsoe/150 3.00 8.00
29 Julius Jones/125 2.50 6.00
31 Terry Glenn/125 3.00 8.00
32 Jake Plummer/250 2.50 6.00
33 Rod Smith/100 3.00 8.00
34 Tatum Bell/125 2.50 6.00
36 Kevin Jones/125 2.50 6.00
37 Roy Williams WR/150 2.50 6.00
38 Ahman Green/125 3.00 8.00
39 Brett Favre/125 8.00 20.00
41 Samkon Gado/100 2.50 6.00
42 Andre Johnson/125 3.00 8.00
43 David Carr/250 2.50 6.00
44 Domanick Davis/150 2.50 6.00
45 Marvin Harrison/125 3.00 8.00
46 Peyton Manning/125 10.00 25.00
47 Reggie Wayne/250 3.00 8.00
48 Byron Leftwich/250 2.50 6.00
49 Fred Taylor/150 2.50 6.00
50 Jimmy Smith/125 3.00 8.00
51 Matt Jones/125 2.50 6.00
52 Larry Johnson/125 2.50 6.00
53 Tony Gonzalez/125 3.00 8.00
54 Trent Green/200 2.50 6.00
55 Chris Chambers/125 2.50 6.00
56 Daunte Culpepper/250 3.00 8.00
57 Ronnie Brown/125 3.00 8.00
59 Mewelde Moore/125 2.50 6.00
61 Corey Dillon/125 2.50 6.00
62 Deion Branch/125 2.50 6.00
63 Tom Brady/200 12.00 30.00
64 Deuce McAllister/250 3.00 8.00
66 Donte Stallworth/125 2.50 6.00
67 Eli Manning/125 3.00 8.00
68 Jeremy Shockey/250 2.50 6.00
69 Plaxico Burress/150 2.50 6.00
70 Tiki Barber/150 3.00 8.00
71 Chad Pennington/250 2.50 6.00
72 Curtis Martin/125 3.00 8.00
73 Laveranues Coles/125 2.50 6.00
74 LaMont Jordan/130 3.00 8.00
75 Randy Moss/125 3.00 8.00
77 Brian Westbrook/125 2.50 6.00
78 Donovan McNabb/250 3.00 8.00
80 Ben Roethlisberger/125 5.00 12.00
81 Hines Ward/125 3.00 8.00
82 Willie Parker/125 3.00 8.00
83 Antonio Gates/125 4.00 10.00
84 LaDainian Tomlinson/125 4.00 10.00
85 Philip Rivers/125 4.00 10.00
86 Alex Smith QB/125 3.00 8.00
88 Kevan Barlow/250 2.50 6.00
89 Darrell Jackson/125 3.00 8.00
90 Matt Hasselbeck/125 2.50 6.00
91 Shaun Alexander/100 2.50 6.00
92 Marc Bulger/150 2.50 6.00
93 Torry Holt/125 3.00 8.00
94 Steven Jackson/125 2.50 6.00
95 Chris Simms/150 2.50 6.00
96 Cadillac Williams/125 3.00 8.00
97 Joey Galloway/150 3.00 8.00
98 Chris Brown/250 2.50 6.00
99 Clinton Portis/200 2.50 6.00
100 Santana Moss/100 3.00 8.00

2006 Donruss Gridiron Gear Next Generation Gold

GOLD PRINT RUN 500 SER.#'d SETS
*RED: .4X TO 1X GOLD/500
*SILVER/250: .5X TO 1.2X GOLD/500
SILVER PRINT RUN 250 SER.#'d SETS
*HOLOGOLD/100: .6X TO 1.5X GOLD/500
HOLOGOLD PRINT RUN 100 SER.#'d SETS
*PLATINUM/25: 1X TO 2.5X GOLD/500
PLATINUM PRINT RUN 25 SER.#'d SETS
1 Alex Smith QB 1.00 2.50
2 Braylon Edwards .75 2.00
3 Cadillac Williams 1.00 2.50
4 Cedric Benson .75 2.00
5 Charlie Frye 1.00 2.50
6 Dallas Clark .75 2.00
7 Matt Jones .75 2.00
8 Philip Rivers 1.25 3.00
9 Samkon Gado .75 2.00
10 Willie Parker 1.00 2.50
11 Anquan Boldin .75 2.00
12 Antonio Gates 1.25 3.00
13 Chris Brown .75 2.00
14 Eli Manning 1.00 2.50
15 Julius Jones .75 2.00
16 Kevin Jones .75 2.00
17 Larry Fitzgerald 1.00 2.50
18 Lee Evans 1.00 2.50
19 Mark Clayton .75 2.00
20 Reggie Brown .75 2.00
21 Ronnie Brown 1.00 2.50
22 Roy Williams WR .75 2.00
23 Steven Jackson .75 2.00
24 T.J. Houshmandzadeh .75 2.00
25 Willis McGahee .75 2.00

2006 Donruss Gridiron Gear Next Generation Autographs

STATED PRINT RUN 5-50 SER.#'d SETS
SERIAL #'d UNDER 25 NOT PRICED
6 Dallas Clark/35 10.00 25.00
7 Matt Jones/25
10 Willie Parker/40 12.00 30.00
17 Larry Fitzgerald/25 25.00 50.00
19 Mark Clayton/50 10.00 25.00

2006 Donruss Gridiron Gear Next Generation Jerseys

STATED PRINT RUN 150-250
*COMBO PRIME/25-50: .8X TO 2X
*JUMBO/25-50: .6X TO 1.5X BASIC INSERTS
*JUMBO PRIME/15-25: 1X TO 2.5X
*PRIME/25-50: .8X TO 2X BASIC INSERTS
COMBO JSY AUTOS/1-10 NOT PRICED
PRIME AUTOS/1-10 NOT PRICED
1 Alex Smith QB/200 3.00 8.00
2 Braylon Edwards/250 2.50 6.00
3 Cadillac Williams/200 3.00 8.00
4 Cedric Benson/200 2.50 6.00
5 Charlie Frye/200 3.00 8.00
6 Dallas Clark/200 2.50 6.00
7 Matt Jones/200 2.50 6.00
8 Philip Rivers/200 4.00 10.00
9 Samkon Gado/150 2.50 6.00
10 Willie Parker/200 3.00 8.00
11 Anquan Boldin/250 2.50 6.00
12 Antonio Gates/250 4.00 10.00
13 Chris Brown/250 2.50 6.00
14 Eli Manning/250 3.00 8.00
15 Julius Jones/250 2.50 6.00
16 Kevin Jones/250 2.50 6.00
17 Larry Fitzgerald/250 3.00 8.00
18 Lee Evans/250 3.00 8.00
19 Mark Clayton/150 2.50 6.00
20 Reggie Brown/250 2.50 6.00
21 Ronnie Brown/250 3.00 8.00
22 Roy Williams WR/250 2.50 6.00
23 Steven Jackson/250 2.50 6.00
24 T.J. Houshmandzadeh/250 2.50 6.00
25 Willis McGahee/250 2.50 6.00

2006 Donruss Gridiron Gear Next Generation Jerseys Autographs

STATED PRINT RUN 2-40
17 Larry Fitzgerald/20 25.00 50.00

2006 Donruss Gridiron Gear Performers Gold

GOLD PRINT RUN 500 SER.#'d SETS
*RED: .3X TO .8X GOLD/500
*SILVER/250: .5X TO 1.2X GOLD/500
SILVER PRINT RUN 250 SER.#'d SETS
*HOLOGOLD/100: .6X TO 1.5X GOLD/500
HOLOGOLD PRINT RUN 100 SER.#'d SETS
*PLATINUM/25: 1X TO 2.5X GOLD/500
PLATINUM PRINT RUN 25 SER.#'d SETS
1 Jim Otto 1.00 2.50
2 Paul Warfield 1.25 3.00
3 Craig Morton 1.00 2.50
4 Paul Krause 1.00 2.50
5 Joe Greene 1.50 4.00
6 Thurman Thomas 1.25 3.00
7 Lee Roy Selmon 1.00 2.50
8 Lester Hayes 1.00 2.50
9 Ozzie Newsome 1.25 3.00
10 Jim Plunkett 1.25 3.00
11 Mark Gastineau 1.00 2.50
12 Henry Ellard 1.00 2.50
13 Boomer Esiason 1.25 3.00
14 Herschel Walker 1.25 3.00
15 Eric Dickerson 1.25 3.00
16 Dan Marino 3.00 8.00
17 Barry Sanders 2.50 6.00
18 Jim Kelly 2.00 5.00
19 Julius Peppers .75 2.00
20 Tedy Bruschi 1.25 3.00
21 T.J. Houshmandzadeh .75 2.00
22 Rudi Johnson .75 2.00
23 Steve Smith 1.25 3.00
24 Peyton Manning 2.00 5.00
25 Brett Favre 2.50 6.00
26 Torry Holt .75 2.00
27 Donovan McNabb 1.25 3.00
28 Marc Bulger .75 2.00
29 Alge Crumpler .75 2.00
30 Larry Johnson 1.25 3.00
31 Nate Burleson .75 2.00
32 Charlie Frye 1.25 3.00
33 Carson Palmer 1.25 3.00
34 Samkon Gado 1.25 3.00
35 Javon Walker .75 2.00
36 Tiki Barber 1.25 3.00
37 Reuben Droughns .75 2.00
38 Darrell Jackson .75 2.00
39 Chris Chambers .75 2.00
40 Ben Roethlisberger 2.50 6.00
41 Dallas Clark .75 2.00
42 Reggie Brown .75 2.00
43 LaDainian Tomlinson 1.25 3.00
44 Shaun Alexander 1.25 3.00
45 Marvin Harrison 1.25 3.00
46 Robert Ferguson .75 2.00
47 Michael Vick 1.25 3.00
48 Clinton Portis 1.25 3.00
49 Curtis Martin 1.25 3.00
50 Philip Rivers 1.25 3.00

2006 Donruss Gridiron Gear Performers Autographs

STATED PRINT RUN 1-250 SER.#'d SETS
SERIAL #'d UNDER 25 NOT PRICED
1 Jim Otto/35 10.00 25.00
3 Craig Morton/25 10.00 25.00
4 Paul Krause/50 8.00 20.00
5 Joe Greene/25
6 Thurman Thomas/35 12.00 30.00
7 Lee Roy Selmon/40 12.00 30.00
8 Lester Hayes/250 8.00 20.00
9 Ozzie Newsome/40 8.00 20.00
10 Jim Plunkett/35 10.00 25.00
11 Mark Gastineau/35 10.00 25.00
13 Boomer Esiason/35 15.00 40.00
14 Herschel Walker/35 15.00 40.00
18 Jim Kelly/25 20.00 50.00
20 Tedy Bruschi/250 25.00 50.00
28 Marc Bulger/45 10.00 25.00
38 Darrell Jackson/25 10.00 25.00
41 Dallas Clark/25 10.00 25.00
43 LaDainian Tomlinson/25 50.00 100.00
44 Shaun Alexander/25 25.00 50.00

2006 Donruss Gridiron Gear Performers Jerseys

STATED PRINT RUN 43-200 SER.#'d SETS
*COMBOS/25-50: .5X TO 1.2X BASIC INSERTS
COMBO AUTOS/1-10 NOT PRICED
*COMBO PRM/15-25: .8X TO 2X BASIC INSERTS
COMBO PRIME AUTOS/1-25 NOT PRICED
*JUMBO SWATCH/25-30: .6X TO 1.5X BASIC INSERTS
UNPRICED JUMBO PRIME PRINT RUN 10
*PRIME/25: .8X TO 2X BASIC INSERTS
PRIME AUTOS/1-25 NOT PRICED
*RED: .4X TO 1X BASIC INSERTS
1 Jim Otto/100 4.00 10.00
2 Paul Warfield/100 4.00 10.00
3 Craig Morton/100 3.00 8.00
4 Paul Krause/200 3.00 8.00
5 Joe Greene/43 6.00 15.00
6 Thurman Thomas/100 4.00 10.00
7 Lee Roy Selmon/200 4.00 10.00
9 Ozzie Newsome/100 4.00 10.00
10 Jim Plunkett/150 3.00 8.00
11 Mark Gastineau/100 4.00 10.00
12 Henry Ellard/200 3.00 8.00
13 Boomer Esiason/200 3.00 8.00
14 Herschel Walker/75 3.00 8.00
15 Eric Dickerson/100 3.00 8.00
16 Dan Marino/100 10.00 25.00
17 Barry Sanders/100 8.00 20.00
18 Jim Kelly/100 5.00 12.00
21 T.J. Houshmandzadeh/100 3.00 8.00
22 Rudi Johnson/100 3.00 8.00
23 Steve Smith/100 4.00 10.00
24 Peyton Manning/100 6.00 15.00
25 Brett Favre/100 8.00 20.00
26 Torry Holt/100 3.00 8.00
27 Donovan McNabb/100 4.00 10.00
28 Marc Bulger/100 3.00 8.00
29 Alge Crumpler/100 3.00 8.00
30 Larry Johnson/100 4.00 10.00
32 Charlie Frye/100 4.00 10.00
33 Carson Palmer/94 4.00 10.00
34 Samkon Gado/100 4.00 10.00
35 Javon Walker/100 3.00 8.00
36 Tiki Barber/100 4.00 10.00
37 Reuben Droughns/100 2.50 6.00
38 Darrell Jackson/100 3.00 8.00
39 Chris Chambers/100 3.00 8.00
40 Ben Roethlisberger/100 8.00 20.00
41 Dallas Clark/100 2.50 6.00
42 Reggie Brown/100 2.50 6.00
43 LaDainian Tomlinson/100 4.00 10.00
44 Shaun Alexander/100 4.00 10.00
45 Marvin Harrison/100 4.00 10.00
46 Robert Ferguson/100 2.50 6.00
47 Michael Vick/100 4.00 10.00
48 Clinton Portis/100 4.00 10.00
49 Curtis Martin/100 4.00 10.00
50 Philip Rivers/100 4.00 10.00

2006 Donruss Gridiron Gear Performers Jerseys Autographs

STATED PRINT RUN 1-30
SERIAL #'d UNDER 15 NOT PRICED
1 Jim Otto/25 12.00 30.00
4 Paul Krause/30 10.00 25.00
7 Lee Roy Selmon/25 25.00 50.00
9 Ozzie Newsome/25 10.00 25.00
10 Jim Plunkett/25 12.00 30.00
11 Mark Gastineau/25 12.00 30.00
18 Jim Kelly/25 25.00 60.00
28 Marc Bulger/25 12.00 30.00
43 LaDainian Tomlinson/15 25.00 50.00

2006 Donruss Gridiron Gear Plates and Patches

STATED PRINT RUN 25-100 SER.#'d SETS
1 Tom Brady/100 12.00 30.00
2 LaDainian Tomlinson/47 10.00 25.00
3 Hines Ward/50 10.00 25.00
4 Matt Hasselbeck/50 8.00 20.00
5 Willis McGahee/100 8.00 20.00
6 Carson Palmer/50 10.00 25.00
7 Shaun Alexander/25 10.00 25.00
8 Ben Roethlisberger/25 20.00 50.00
9 Steve Smith/50 8.00 20.00
10 Tiki Barber/50 8.00 20.00
11 Peyton Manning/50 15.00 40.00
12 Torry Holt/90 6.00 15.00
13 Michael Vick/80 8.00 20.00
14 Ahman Green/100 6.00 15.00

2006 Donruss Gridiron Gear Playbook Gold

GOLD PRINT RUN 500 SER.#'d SETS
*RED: .3X TO .8X GOLD/500
*SILVER/250: .5X TO 1.2X GOLD/500
SILVER PRINT RUN 250 SER.#'d SETS
*HOLOGOLD/100: .6X TO 1.5X GOLD/500
HOLOGOLD PRINT RUN 100 SER.#'d SETS
*PLATINUM/25: 1X TO 2.5X GOLD/500
PLATINUM PRINT RUN 25 SER.#'d SETS
1 Steve Smith 1.25 3.00
2 Chad Johnson .75 2.00
3 Julius Jones .75 2.00
4 Brett Favre 2.50 6.00
5 Peyton Manning 3.00 8.00
6 Marvin Harrison 1.00 2.50
7 Larry Johnson .75 2.00
8 Tiki Barber 1.00 2.50
9 Ben Roethlisberger 1.50 4.00
10 Antonio Gates 1.25 3.00
11 Carson Palmer 1.00 2.50
12 Shaun Alexander .75 2.00
13 Hines Ward 1.00 2.50
14 Donte Stallworth .75 2.00
15 Anquan Boldin .75 2.00
16 Curtis Martin 1.00 2.50
17 Willis McGahee .75 2.00
18 Clinton Portis .75 2.00
19 Donovan McNabb 1.00 2.50
20 Tom Brady 4.00 10.00
21 Tatum Bell .75 2.00
22 Tony Gonzalez 1.00 2.50
23 Michael Vick 1.00 2.50
24 Byron Leftwich .75 2.00
25 Randy Moss 1.00 2.50

2006 Donruss Gridiron Gear Playbook Jerseys O's

O's PRINT RUN 250 SER.#'d SETS
*X's/250: .4X TO 1X O's JERSEYS
*PATCHES/25: 1X TO 2.5X JSY O's
1 Steve Smith 3.00 8.00
2 Chad Johnson 2.00 5.00
3 Julius Jones 2.00 5.00
4 Brett Favre 6.00 15.00
5 Peyton Manning 8.00 20.00
6 Marvin Harrison 2.50 6.00
7 Larry Johnson 2.00 5.00
8 Tiki Barber 2.50 6.00
9 Ben Roethlisberger 4.00 10.00
10 Antonio Gates 3.00 8.00
11 Carson Palmer 2.50 6.00
12 Shaun Alexander 2.00 5.00
13 Hines Ward 2.50 6.00
14 Donte Stallworth 2.00 5.00
15 Anquan Boldin 2.00 5.00
16 Curtis Martin 2.50 6.00
17 Willis McGahee 2.00 5.00
18 Clinton Portis 2.00 5.00
19 Donovan McNabb 2.50 6.00
20 Tom Brady 10.00 25.00
21 Tatum Bell 2.00 5.00
22 Tony Gonzalez 2.50 6.00
23 Michael Vick 2.50 6.00
24 Byron Leftwich 2.00 5.00
25 Randy Moss 2.50 6.00

2006 Donruss Gridiron Gear Player Timeline Gold

GOLD PRINT RUN 500 SER.#'d SETS
*RED: .3X TO .8X GOLD/500
*SILVER/250: .5X TO 1.2X GOLD/500
SILVER PRINT RUN 250 SER.#'d SETS
*HOLOGOLD/100: .6X TO 1.5X GOLD/500
HOLOGOLD PRINT RUN 100 SER.#'d SETS
*PLATINUM/25: 1X TO 2.5X GOLD/500
PLATINUM PRINT RUN 25 SER.#'d SETS
1 Barry Sanders 2.50 6.00
2 Ronnie Brown 1.00 2.50
3 Laveranues Coles .75 2.00
4 Lee Evans 1.00 2.50
5 Andre Johnson 1.00 2.50
6 Drew Bledsoe 1.00 2.50
7 Santana Moss 1.00 2.50
8 Willis McGahee .75 2.00

9 Braylon Edwards	.75	2.00
10 Ahman Green	1.00	2.50
11 Julius Jones	.75	2.00
12 Roy Williams S	.75	2.00
13 Thurman Thomas	1.25	3.00
14 Dan Marino	3.00	8.00
15 Tony Dorsett	1.50	4.00
16 Joe Greene	1.50	4.00
17 Eric Dickerson	1.25	3.00
18 Lawrence Taylor	1.50	4.00
19 Kevin Jones	.75	2.00
20 Peyton Manning	3.00	8.00
21 Cadillac Williams	1.00	2.50
22 Mike Hass	.50	1.25
23 Joseph Addai	.50	1.25
24 Mario Williams	.75	2.00
25 Demetrius Williams	.50	1.25
26 Marcedes Lewis	.50	1.25
27 Sinorice Moss	.50	1.25
28 Jay Cutler	.60	1.50
29 LenDale White	.50	1.25
30 A.J. Hawk	.60	1.50
31 Laurence Maroney	.50	1.25
32 Maurice Drew	.75	2.00
33 Maurice Stovall	.50	1.25
34 Travis Wilson	.50	1.25
35 Curtis Martin	1.00	2.50
36 Jeremy Shockey	.75	2.00
37 Paul Warfield	1.25	3.00
38 Michael Clayton	.75	2.00
39 Roy Williams WR	.75	2.00
40 Deion Sanders	1.00	2.50

2006 Donruss Gridiron Gear Player Timeline Autographs

STATED PRINT RUN 5-50 SER.#'d SETS

4 Lee Evans/20	10.00	25.00
13 Thurman Thomas/25	15.00	40.00
15 Tony Dorsett/20	25.00	50.00
16 Joe Greene/25		
17 Eric Dickerson/25	15.00	40.00
18 Lawrence Taylor/50	20.00	50.00
24 Mario Williams/25	12.00	30.00
25 Demetrius Williams/25	10.00	25.00
26 Marcedes Lewis/35	8.00	20.00
27 Sinorice Moss/25	10.00	25.00
28 Jay Cutler/35	15.00	40.00
29 LenDale White/30	10.00	25.00
30 A.J. Hawk/30	30.00	80.00
31 Laurence Maroney/35	12.00	30.00
32 Maurice Drew/30	25.00	60.00
33 Maurice Stovall/35	6.00	15.00
34 Travis Wilson/35	6.00	15.00
39 Roy Williams WR/25	10.00	25.00
40 Deion Sanders/50	20.00	50.00

2006 Donruss Gridiron Gear Player Timeline Jerseys

STATED PRINT RUN 75-250 SER.#'d SETS

*COMBOS/75-100: .5X TO 1.2X BASIC JSYs

*COMBOS/40-59: .6X TO 1.5X BASIC JSYs

*COMBO PRIME/37-50: .8X TO 2X

*JUMBO SWATCH/25-50: .6X TO 1.5X

*PRIME/25-50: .8X TO 2X BASIC JSYs

*JUMBO SWATCH PRIME/25: 1X TO 2.5X

*RED: .4X TO 1X BASIC JSYs

1 Barry Sanders/100	10.00	25.00
2 Ronnie Brown/250	3.00	8.00
3 Laveranues Coles/139	2.50	6.00
4 Lee Evans/250	3.00	8.00
5 Andre Johnson/200	3.00	8.00
6 Drew Bledsoe/175	3.00	8.00
7 Santana Moss/200	3.00	8.00
8 Willis McGahee/250	2.50	6.00
9 Braylon Edwards/200	2.50	6.00
10 Ahman Green/200	3.00	8.00
11 Julius Jones/200	2.50	6.00
12 Roy Williams S/200	2.50	6.00
13 Thurman Thomas/250	5.00	12.00
14 Dan Marino/150	12.00	30.00
15 Tony Dorsett/250	6.00	15.00
16 Joe Greene/250	6.00	15.00
17 Eric Dickerson/150	5.00	12.00
18 Lawrence Taylor/200	6.00	15.00
19 Kevin Jones/200	2.50	6.00
20 Peyton Manning/150	10.00	25.00
21 Cadillac Williams/200	3.00	8.00
22 Mike Hass/250	1.25	3.00
23 Joseph Addai/250	1.25	3.00
24 Mario Williams/250	2.00	5.00
25 Demetrius Williams/250	1.25	3.00
26 Marcedes Lewis/250	1.25	3.00
27 Sinorice Moss/250	1.25	3.00
28 Jay Cutler/250	1.50	4.00
29 LenDale White/250	1.25	3.00
30 A.J. Hawk/250	4.00	10.00
31 Laurence Maroney/250	1.25	3.00
32 Maurice Drew/250	2.00	5.00
33 Maurice Stovall/250	1.25	3.00
34 Travis Wilson/250	1.25	3.00
35 Curtis Martin/75	3.00	8.00
36 Jeremy Shockey/250	2.50	6.00
37 Paul Warfield/75	5.00	12.00
38 Michael Clayton/250	2.50	6.00
39 Roy Williams WR/250	2.50	6.00
40 Deion Sanders/250	3.00	8.00

2006 Donruss Gridiron Gear Player Timeline Jerseys Autographs

STATED PRINT RUN 1-50

UNPRICED JSY COMBO AU PRINT RUN 1-20

UNPRICED COMBO PRIME PRINT RUN 1-15

UNPRICED PRIME PRINT RUN 1-25

16 Joe Greene/25	30.00	60.00
18 Lawrence Taylor/30	30.00	60.00
20 Peyton Manning/25	75.00	135.00
23 Joseph Addai/25	8.00	20.00
24 Mario Williams/20	15.00	40.00
26 Marcedes Lewis/25	8.00	20.00
28 Jay Cutler/25	10.00	25.00
29 LenDale White/25	8.00	20.00
30 A.J. Hawk/25	15.00	40.00
31 Laurence Maroney/25		
32 Maurice Drew/25	25.00	60.00
33 Maurice Stovall/30	8.00	20.00
34 Travis Wilson/30	8.00	20.00
40 Deion Sanders/50	30.00	60.00

2006 Donruss Gridiron Gear Rivals Gold

GOLD PRINT RUN 500 SER.#'d SETS

*RED: .3X TO .8X GOLD/500

*SILVER/250: .5X TO 1.2X GOLD/500

SILVER PRINT RUN 250 SER.#'d SETS

*HOLOGOLD/100: .6X TO 1.5X GOLD/500

HOLOGOLD PRINT RUN 100 SER.#'d SETS

*PLATINUM/25: 1X TO 2.5X GOLD/500

PLATINUM PRINT RUN 25 SER.#'d SETS

1 L.Taylor/J.Theismann	1.25	3.00
2 P.Mann/Roethlisberger	3.00	8.00
3 C.Martis/S.Alexander	1.00	2.50
4 Y.Tittle/Y.Lary	1.25	3.00
5 D.Marino/J.Kelly	2.50	6.00
6 W.Payton/T.Dorsett	2.50	6.00
7 B.Sanders/T.Thomas	2.00	5.00
8 C.Portis/R.Williams S	.75	2.00
9 B.Urlacher/A.Green	1.25	3.00
10 T.Glenn/S.Moss	1.00	2.50
11 D.Lamonica/L.Alworth	1.00	2.50
12 P.Warfield/C.Branch	1.00	2.50
13 L.Tomlinson/L.Johnson	1.25	3.00
14 J.Jones/T.Jones	.75	2.00
15 C.Johnson/T.Polamalu	1.25	3.00

2006 Donruss Gridiron Gear Rivals Jerseys

STATED PRINT RUN 100 SER.#'d SETS

*PRIME/25-30: .8X TO 2X BASIC JSYs

PRIME PRINT RUN 10-30 SER.#'d SETS

1 L.Taylor/J.Theismann	8.00	20.00
2 P.Mann/Roethlisberger	10.00	25.00
3 C.Martis/S.Alexander	6.00	15.00
4 Y.Tittle/Y.Lary	8.00	20.00
5 D.Marino/J.Kelly	12.00	30.00
6 W.Payton/T.Dorsett	15.00	40.00
7 B.Sanders/T.Thomas	12.00	30.00
8 C.Portis/R.Williams S	6.00	15.00
9 B.Urlacher/A.Green	6.00	15.00
10 T.Glenn/S.Moss	6.00	15.00
11 D.Lamonica/L.Alworth	8.00	20.00
12 P.Warfield/C.Branch	8.00	20.00
13 L.Tomlinson/L.Johnson	8.00	20.00
14 J.Jones/T.Jones	6.00	15.00
15 C.Johnson/T.Polamalu	8.00	20.00

2006 Donruss Gridiron Gear Rookie Jerseys

*SINGLES/50: .3X TO .8X BASIC RCs

STATED PRINT RUN 50 SER.#'d SETS

2006 Donruss Gridiron Gear Rookie Jerseys Combos

*COMBOS/50: .4X TO 1X BASIC RCs

STATED PRINT RUN 50 SER.#'d SETS

2006 Donruss Gridiron Gear Rookie Jerseys Combos Prime

*COMBO PRIME/50: .6X TO 1.5X BASIC RCs

PRIME PRINT RUN 50 SER.#'d SETS

2006 Donruss Gridiron Gear Rookie Jerseys Jumbo Swatch Prime

*JUMBO PRIME: .5X TO 1.2X BASIC RCs

PRIME/150 ANNOUNCED PRINT RUN 50

2006 Donruss Gridiron Gear Rookie Jerseys Prime

*PRIME/50: .4X TO 1X BASIC RCs

PRIME PRINT RUN 50 SER.#'d SETS

2006 Donruss Gridiron Gear Rookie Jerseys Retail Red

*RETAIL/50: .3X TO .8X BASIC RCs

RETAIL PRINT RUN 50 SER.#'d SETS

2006 Donruss Gridiron Gear Rookie Jerseys Trios

*TRIOS/50: .6X TO 1.5X BASIC RCs

STATED PRINT RUN 50 SER.#'d SETS

2006 Donruss Gridiron Gear Rookie Jerseys Trios Prime

*TRIO PRIME/50: .8X TO 2X BASIC RCs

TRIO PRIME PRINT RUN 50 SER.#'d SETS

2006 Donruss Gridiron Gear Rookie Jerseys Autographs

AUTO PRINT RUN 50 SER.#'d SETS

*COMBO AU/50: .4X TO 1X BASIC INSERTS

*PRIME: .5X TO 1.2X BASIC INSERTS

*COMBO PRIME AU/50: .5X TO 1.2X

201 Brian Calhoun	6.00	15.00
202 Joe Klopfenstein	6.00	15.00
203 Travis Wilson	6.00	15.00
204 Charlie Whitehurst	6.00	15.00
205 DeAngelo Williams	8.00	20.00
206 Maurice Stovall	6.00	15.00
207 A.J. Hawk	8.00	20.00
208 Kellen Clemens	6.00	15.00
209 Leon Washington	6.00	15.00
210 Sinorice Moss	6.00	15.00
211 Demetrius Williams	6.00	15.00
212 Jerious Norwood	6.00	15.00
213 Santonio Holmes	8.00	20.00
214 Omar Jacobs	6.00	15.00
215 Brandon Marshall	12.00	30.00
216 Jason Avant	6.00	15.00
217 Derek Hagan	8.00	20.00
218 Brandon Williams	6.00	15.00
219 Vernon Davis	8.00	20.00
220 Michael Robinson	6.00	15.00
221 Matt Leinart	6.00	15.00
222 Reggie Bush	10.00	25.00
223 LenDale White	6.00	15.00
224 Vince Young	6.00	15.00
225 Maurice Drew	10.00	25.00
226 Marcedes Lewis	6.00	15.00
227 Mario Williams	10.00	25.00
228 Michael Huff	8.00	20.00
229 Tarvaris Jackson	6.00	15.00
230 Laurence Maroney	6.00	15.00
231 Chad Jackson	6.00	15.00

2006 Donruss Gridiron Gear Rookie Jerseys Jumbo Swatch Autographs

AUTO/150 ANNOUNCED PRINT RUN 50

201 Brian Calhoun	8.00	20.00
202 Joe Klopfenstein	8.00	20.00
203 Travis Wilson	8.00	20.00
204 Charlie Whitehurst	8.00	20.00
205 DeAngelo Williams	10.00	25.00
206 Maurice Stovall	8.00	20.00
207 A.J. Hawk	10.00	25.00
208 Kellen Clemens	8.00	20.00
209 Leon Washington	8.00	20.00
210 Sinorice Moss	8.00	20.00
211 Demetrius Williams	8.00	20.00
212 Jerious Norwood	8.00	20.00
213 Santonio Holmes	10.00	25.00
214 Omar Jacobs	8.00	20.00
215 Brandon Marshall	15.00	40.00
216 Jason Avant	8.00	20.00
217 Derek Hagan	10.00	25.00
218 Brandon Williams	8.00	20.00
219 Vernon Davis	10.00	25.00
220 Michael Robinson	8.00	20.00
221 Matt Leinart	8.00	20.00
222 Reggie Bush	12.00	30.00
223 LenDale White	8.00	20.00
224 Vince Young	8.00	20.00
225 Maurice Drew	12.00	30.00
226 Marcedes Lewis	8.00	20.00
227 Mario Williams	12.00	30.00
228 Michael Huff	10.00	25.00
229 Tarvaris Jackson	8.00	20.00
230 Laurence Maroney	8.00	20.00
231 Chad Jackson	8.00	20.00

2007 Donruss Gridiron Gear

This 234-card set was released in October, 2007. The set was issued into the hobby in five-card packs, with a $6 SRP, which came 18 packs to a box. The set is divided into veterans (1-100) and 2007 NFL rookies (101-234). Within the Rookie Card grouping there are two subsets: Cards numbered 101-200 were issued to a stated print run of 599 serial numbered sets and cards numbered 201-234 which were signed by the player were issued to a stated print run of 100 serial numbered sets.

COMP.SET w/o RC's (100)	10.00	25.00
101-200 ROOKIE PRINT RUN 599		
201-234 AU ROOKIE PRINT RUN 100		
1 Tony Romo	.50	1.25
2 Julius Jones	.25	.60
3 Terrell Owens	.30	.75
4 Eli Manning	.30	.75
5 Plaxico Burress	.25	.60
6 Jeremy Shockey	.25	.60
7 Brandon Jacobs	.25	.60
8 Donovan McNabb	.30	.75
9 Brian Westbrook	.25	.60
10 Reggie Brown	.25	.60
11 Jason Campbell	.25	.60
12 Clinton Portis	.25	.60
13 Santana Moss	.30	.75
14 Rex Grossman	.25	.60
15 Cedric Benson	.25	.60
16 Muhsin Muhammad	.25	.60
17 Jon Kitna	.25	.60
18 Roy Williams WR	.25	.60
19 Tatum Bell	.25	.60
20 Brett Favre	.75	2.00
21 Donald Driver	.30	.75
22 Greg Jennings	.25	.60
23 Tarvaris Jackson	.25	.60
24 Chester Taylor	.25	.60
25 Joe Horn	.25	.60
26 Warrick Dunn	.25	.60
27 Alge Crumpler	.30	.75
28 Jake Delhomme	.25	.60
29 Steve Smith	.30	.75
30 DeAngelo Williams	.25	.60
31 Drew Brees	.40	1.00
32 Deuce McAllister	.30	.75
33 Reggie Bush	.25	.60
34 Jeff Garcia	.25	.60
35 Cadillac Williams	.30	.75
36 Joey Galloway	.30	.75
37 Matt Leinart	.25	.60
38 Edgerrin James	.30	.75
39 Anquan Boldin	.25	.60
40 Larry Fitzgerald	.30	.75
41 Marc Bulger	.25	.60
42 Steven Jackson	.25	.60
43 Torry Holt	.30	.75
44 Alex Smith QB	.30	.75
45 Frank Gore	.30	.75
46 Vernon Davis	.25	.60
47 Darrell Jackson	.25	.60
48 Matt Hasselbeck	.25	.60
49 Shaun Alexander	.25	.60
50 Deion Branch	.25	.60
51 J.P. Losman	.25	.60
52 Lee Evans	.30	.75
53 Josh Reed	.25	.60
54 Trent Green	.25	.60
55 Ronnie Brown	.25	.60
56 Chris Chambers	.25	.60
57 Tom Brady	1.25	3.00
58 Laurence Maroney	.30	.75
59 Randy Moss	.30	.75
60 Chad Pennington	.25	.60
61 Laveranues Coles	.25	.60
62 Leon Washington	.25	.60
63 Steve McNair	.30	.75
64 Willis McGahee	.25	.60
65 Mark Clayton	.25	.60
66 Carson Palmer	.30	.75
67 Rudi Johnson	.25	.60
68 Chad Johnson	.25	.60
69 T.J. Houshmandzadeh	.25	.60
70 Charlie Frye	.30	.75
71 Braylon Edwards	.25	.60
72 Jamal Lewis	.30	.75
73 Ben Roethlisberger	.40	1.00
74 Willie Parker	.30	.75
75 Hines Ward	.30	.75
76 Ahman Green	.30	.75
77 Andre Johnson	.30	.75
78 Matt Schaub	.25	.60
79 Peyton Manning	1.00	2.50
80 Joseph Addai	.25	.60
81 Marvin Harrison	.30	.75
82 Reggie Wayne	.30	.75
83 Byron Leftwich	.25	.60
84 Fred Taylor	.25	.60
85 Maurice Jones-Drew	.25	.60
86 Vince Young	.25	.60
87 LenDale White	.30	.75
88 Brandon Jones	.25	.60
89 Jay Cutler	.25	.60
90 Javon Walker	.30	.75
91 Mike Bell	.30	.75
92 Larry Johnson	.25	.60
93 Tony Gonzalez	.30	.75
94 Brodie Croyle	.30	.75
95 Andrew Walter	.25	.60
96 LaMont Jordan	.30	.75
97 Philip Rivers	.40	1.00
98 LaDainian Tomlinson	.40	1.00
99 Vincent Jackson	.25	.60
100 Antonio Gates	.40	1.00
101 A.J. Davis RC	1.50	4.00
102 Aaron Ross RC	1.50	4.00
103 Aaron Rouse RC	1.50	4.00
104 Adam Carriker RC	1.50	4.00
105 Ahmad Bradshaw RC	2.50	6.00
106 Alan Branch RC	1.50	4.00
107 Alonzo Coleman RC	2.00	5.00
108 Amobi Okoye RC	2.00	5.00
109 Anthony Spencer RC	2.00	5.00
110 Aundrae Allison RC	1.50	4.00
111 Ben Patrick RC	2.00	5.00
112 Brandon Meriweather RC	2.00	5.00
113 Buster Davis RC	2.00	5.00
114 Chansi Stuckey RC	2.00	5.00
115 Charles Johnson RC	1.50	4.00
116 Chris Davis RC	1.50	4.00
117 Chris Houston RC	1.50	4.00
118 Chris Leak RC	1.50	4.00
119 Courtney Taylor RC	1.50	4.00
120 Craig Buster Davis RC	1.50	4.00
121 Dallas Baker RC	1.50	4.00
122 Dan Bazuin RC	2.00	5.00
123 Darius Walker RC	1.50	4.00
124 Darrelle Revis RC	2.00	5.00
125 David Ball RC	1.50	4.00
126 David Clowney RC	1.50	4.00
127 David Harris RC	1.50	4.00
128 David Irons RC	1.50	4.00
129 Daymeion Hughes RC	1.50	4.00
130 DeShawn Wynn RC	1.50	4.00
131 Dwayne Wright RC	1.50	4.00
132 Earl Everett RC	1.50	4.00
133 Eric Frampton RC	2.00	5.00
134 Eric Weddle RC	2.00	5.00
135 Eric Wright RC	1.50	4.00
136 Fred Bennett RC	1.50	4.00
137 Zak DeOssie RC	2.00	5.00
138 Gary Russell RC	2.00	5.00
139 H.B. Blades RC	1.50	4.00
140 Ikaika Alama-Francis RC	2.50	6.00
141 Isaiah Stanback RC	1.50	4.00
142 Jacoby Jones RC	1.50	4.00
143 Jamaal Anderson RC	2.00	5.00
144 James Jones RC	1.50	4.00
145 Jared Zabransky RC	1.50	4.00
146 Jarrett Hicks RC	2.00	5.00
147 Jarvis Moss RC	1.50	4.00
148 Jason Snelling RC	1.50	4.00
149 Jeff Rowe RC	1.50	4.00
150 Joel Filani RC	1.50	4.00
151 Jon Beason RC	1.50	4.00
152 Jonathan Wade RC	1.50	4.00
153 Jordan Kent RC	2.00	5.00
154 Jordan Palmer RC	2.00	5.00
155 Josh Gattis RC	1.50	4.00
156 Josh Wilson RC	2.00	5.00
157 Kenneth Darby RC	1.50	4.00
158 Kenny Scott RC	1.50	4.00
159 Kolby Smith RC	1.50	4.00
160 LaMarr Woodley RC	3.00	8.00
161 LaRon Landry RC	2.50	6.00
162 Laurent Robinson RC	2.50	6.00
163 Lawrence Timmons RC	2.50	6.00
164 Legedu Naanee RC	2.00	5.00
165 Leon Hall RC	1.50	4.00
166 Levi Brown RC	1.50	4.00
167 Marcus McCauley RC	1.50	4.00
168 Matt Spaeth RC	2.50	6.00
169 Michael Griffin RC	1.50	4.00
170 Michael Okwo RC	2.00	5.00
171 Mike Walker RC	2.50	6.00
172 Nate Ilaoa RC	2.00	5.00
173 Paul Posluszny RC	1.50	4.00
174 Quentin Moses RC	1.50	4.00
175 Ray McDonald RC	2.00	5.00
176 Reggie Ball RC	2.00	5.00
177 Reggie Nelson RC	1.50	4.00
178 Rhema McKnight RC	1.50	4.00
179 Jerard Rabb RC	2.00	5.00
180 Roy Hall RC	2.50	6.00
181 Rufus Alexander RC	1.50	4.00
182 Ryan McBean RC	2.50	6.00
183 Ryne Robinson RC	2.00	5.00
184 Sabby Piscitelli RC	1.50	4.00
185 Scott Chandler RC	2.50	6.00
186 Selvin Young RC	1.50	4.00
187 Steve Breaston RC	1.50	4.00
188 Stewart Bradley RC	1.50	4.00
189 Syndric Steptoe RC	2.00	5.00
190 Mason Crosby RC	2.00	5.00
191 Demarcus Tank Tyler RC	1.50	4.00
192 Thomas Clayton RC	2.00	5.00
193 Tim Crowder RC	2.00	5.00
194 Tim Shaw RC	2.00	5.00
195 Toby Korrodi RC	2.00	5.00
196 Tyler Palko RC	2.50	6.00
197 Tyler Thigpen RC	2.50	6.00
198 Daniel Sepulveda RC	2.00	5.00
199 Victor Abiamiri RC	1.50	4.00
200 Zach Miller RC	1.50	4.00
201 Marshawn Lynch AU RC	20.00	40.00
202 Yamon Figurs AU RC	8.00	20.00
203 Joe Thomas AU RC	12.00	30.00
204 Brandon Jackson AU RC	8.00	20.00
205 Steve Smith USC AU RC	8.00	20.00
206 Ted Ginn AU RC	10.00	25.00
207 Dwayne Bowe AU RC	8.00	20.00
208 Anthony Gonzalez AU RC	8.00	20.00
209 Sidney Rice AU RC	10.00	25.00
210 Chris Henry RB AU RC	8.00	20.00
211 Trent Edwards AU RC	8.00	20.00
212 Calvin Johnson AU RC	60.00	120.00
213 Greg Olsen AU RC	12.00	30.00
214 Antonio Pittman AU RC	8.00	20.00
215 Kevin Kolb AU RC	10.00	25.00
216 Adrian Peterson AU RC	125.00	250.00
217 Brian Leonard AU RC	8.00	20.00
218 Patrick Willis AU RC	12.00	30.00
219 Jason Hill AU RC	8.00	20.00
220 Robert Meachem AU RC	10.00	25.00
221 Michael Bush AU RC	8.00	20.00
222 Tony Hunt AU RC	8.00	20.00
223 Garrett Wolfe AU RC	8.00	20.00
224 Paul Williams AU RC	8.00	20.00
225 Brady Quinn AU RC	8.00	20.00
226 Gaines Adams AU RC	10.00	25.00
227 JaMarcus Russell AU RC	8.00	20.00
228 Dwayne Jarrett AU RC	10.00	25.00
229 Johnnie Lee Higgins AU RC	8.00	20.00
230 Drew Stanton AU RC	8.00	20.00
231 Troy Smith AU RC	8.00	20.00
232 Lorenzo Booker AU RC	10.00	25.00
233 Kenny Irons AU RC	8.00	20.00
234 John Beck AU RC	8.00	20.00

2007 Donruss Gridiron Gear Gold Holofoil

*VETS 1-100: 1.5X TO 4X BASIC CARDS

STATED PRINT RUN 200 SER.#'d SETS

2007 Donruss Gridiron Gear Gold Holofoil O's

*VETS 1-100: 2.5X TO 6X BASIC CARDS

*ROOKIES 101-200: .6X TO 1.5X BASIC CARDS

STATED PRINT RUN 100 SER.#'d SETS

2007 Donruss Gridiron Gear Gold Holofoil X's

*VETS 1-100: 2.5X TO 6X BASIC CARDS

*ROOKIES 101-200: .6X TO 1.5X BASIC CARDS

STATED PRINT RUN 100 SER.#'d SETS

2007 Donruss Gridiron Gear Platinum Holofoil

*VETS 1-100: 3X TO 8X BASIC CARDS

STATED PRINT RUN 50 SER.#'d SETS

2007 Donruss Gridiron Gear Platinum Holofoil O's

*VETS 1-100: 5X TO 12X BASIC CARDS

*ROOKIES 101-200: 1X TO 2.5X BASIC CARDS

STATED PRINT RUN 25 SER.#'d SETS

2007 Donruss Gridiron Gear Platinum Holofoil X's

*VETS 1-100: 5X TO 12X BASIC CARDS

*ROOKIES 101-200: 1X TO 2.5X BASIC CARDS

STATED PRINT RUN 25 SER.#'d SETS

2007 Donruss Gridiron Gear Red Holofoil

*VETS 1-100: .8X TO 2X BASIC CARDS

2007 Donruss Gridiron Gear Silver Holofoil

*VETS 1-100: 1X TO 2.5X BASIC CARDS

2007 Donruss Gridiron Gear Silver Holofoil O's

*VETS 1-100: 1.5X TO 4X BASIC CARDS

STATED PRINT RUN 250 SER.#'d SETS

2007 Donruss Gridiron Gear Silver Holofoil X's

*VETS 1-100: 1.5X TO 4X BASIC CARDS

STATED PRINT RUN 250 SER.#'d SETS

2007 Donruss Gridiron Gear Autographs Gold Holofoil

GOLD HOLOFOIL PRINT RUN 5-250

SERIAL #'d UNDER 25 NOT PRICED

102 Aaron Ross/250	2.50	6.00
104 Adam Carriker/100	3.00	8.00
108 Amobi Okoye/100	4.00	10.00
111 Ben Patrick/250	3.00	8.00
112 Brandon Meriweather/250	3.00	8.00
114 Chansi Stuckey/100	4.00	10.00
116 Chris Davis/100	3.00	8.00
118 Chris Leak/100	3.00	8.00
119 Courtney Taylor/100	3.00	8.00
122 Dan Bazuin/250	3.00	8.00
123 Darius Walker/250	2.50	6.00
124 Darrelle Revis/100	4.00	10.00
126 David Clowney/100	3.00	8.00
127 David Harris/250	2.50	6.00
130 DeShawn Wynn/100	3.00	8.00
131 Dwayne Wright/100	3.00	8.00
133 Eric Frampton/250	3.00	8.00
136 Fred Bennett/250	2.50	6.00
141 Isaiah Stanback/100	3.00	8.00
142 Jacoby Jones/100	3.00	8.00
143 Jamaal Anderson/100	4.00	10.00
144 James Jones/100	3.00	8.00
148 Jason Snelling/250	2.50	6.00
149 Jeff Rowe/100	3.00	8.00
150 Joel Filani/100	3.00	8.00
159 Kolby Smith/100	3.00	8.00
160 LaMarr Woodley/250	8.00	20.00
161 LaRon Landry/100	5.00	12.00
162 Laurent Robinson/100	5.00	12.00
163 Lawrence Timmons/100	5.00	12.00
165 Leon Hall/100	3.00	8.00
166 Levi Brown/250	2.50	6.00
169 Michael Griffin/250	2.50	6.00
173 Paul Posluszny/100	3.00	8.00
174 Quentin Moses/250	2.50	6.00
175 Ray McDonald/250	3.00	8.00
176 Reggie Ball/250	3.00	8.00
177 Reggie Nelson/100	3.00	8.00
184 Sabby Piscitelli/250	2.50	6.00
185 Scott Chandler/100	5.00	12.00
193 Tim Crowder/250	3.00	8.00
199 Victor Abiamiri/250	2.50	6.00
200 Zach Miller/100	3.00	8.00

2007 Donruss Gridiron Gear Autographs Platinum Holofoil

102 Aaron Ross/25	5.00	12.00
103 Aaron Rouse/25	5.00	12.00
104 Adam Carriker/25	5.00	12.00
105 Ahmad Bradshaw/25	8.00	20.00
108 Amobi Okoye/25	6.00	15.00
109 Anthony Spencer/25	6.00	15.00
111 Ben Patrick/25	6.00	15.00
112 Brandon Meriweather/25	6.00	15.00
114 Chansi Stuckey/25	6.00	15.00
116 Chris Davis/25	5.00	12.00
117 Chris Houston/25	5.00	12.00
118 Chris Leak/25	5.00	12.00
119 Courtney Taylor/25	5.00	12.00
121 Dallas Baker/25	5.00	12.00
122 Dan Bazuin/25	6.00	15.00
123 Darius Walker/25	5.00	12.00
124 Darrelle Revis/25	6.00	15.00
126 David Clowney/25	5.00	12.00
127 David Harris/25	5.00	12.00
128 David Irons/25	5.00	12.00
129 Daymeion Hughes/25	5.00	12.00
130 DeShawn Wynn/25	5.00	12.00
131 Dwayne Wright/25	5.00	12.00
132 Earl Everett/25	5.00	12.00
133 Eric Frampton/25	6.00	15.00
136 Fred Bennett/25	5.00	12.00
139 H.B. Blades/25	5.00	12.00
140 Ikaika Alama-Francis/25	8.00	20.00
141 Isaiah Stanback/25	5.00	12.00
142 Jacoby Jones/25	5.00	12.00
143 Jamaal Anderson/25	6.00	15.00
144 James Jones/25	5.00	12.00
145 Jared Zabransky/25	5.00	12.00
146 Jarrett Hicks/25	6.00	15.00
148 Jason Snelling/25	5.00	12.00
149 Jeff Rowe/25	5.00	12.00
150 Joel Filani/25	5.00	12.00
151 Jon Beason/25	5.00	12.00
152 Jonathan Wade/25	5.00	12.00
153 Jordan Kent/25	6.00	15.00
154 Jordan Palmer/25	6.00	15.00
155 Josh Gattis/25	5.00	12.00
156 Josh Wilson/25	6.00	15.00
157 Kenneth Darby/25	5.00	12.00
158 Kenny Scott/25	5.00	12.00
159 Kolby Smith/25	15.00	40.00
160 LaMarr Woodley/25	15.00	40.00
161 LaRon Landry/25	8.00	20.00
162 Laurent Robinson/25	8.00	20.00
163 Lawrence Timmons/25	8.00	20.00
165 Leon Hall/25	5.00	12.00
166 Levi Brown/25	5.00	12.00
167 Marcus McCauley/25	5.00	12.00
168 Matt Spaeth/25	8.00	20.00
169 Michael Griffin/25	5.00	12.00
170 Michael Okwo/25	6.00	15.00
171 Mike Walker/25	8.00	20.00
172 Nate Ilaoa/25	6.00	15.00
173 Paul Posluszny/25	5.00	12.00
174 Quentin Moses/25	5.00	12.00
175 Ray McDonald/25	6.00	15.00
176 Reggie Ball/25	6.00	15.00
177 Reggie Nelson/25	5.00	12.00
178 Rhema McKnight/25	5.00	12.00
182 Ryan McBean/25	8.00	20.00
183 Ryne Robinson/25	6.00	15.00
184 Sabby Piscitelli/25	5.00	12.00
185 Scott Chandler/25	8.00	20.00
186 Selvin Young/25	20.00	50.00
188 Stewart Bradley/25	5.00	12.00
193 Tim Crowder/25	6.00	15.00
194 Tim Shaw/25	6.00	15.00
195 Toby Korrodi/25	6.00	15.00
196 Tyler Palko/25	8.00	20.00
199 Victor Abiamiri/25	5.00	12.00
200 Zach Miller/25	5.00	12.00

2007 Donruss Gridiron Gear EA Sports Madden

1 Peyton Manning	2.00	5.00
2 Jason Elam	.50	1.25
3 Patrick Willis	.75	2.00
4 LaRon Landry	.75	2.00
5 Ray Lewis	.75	2.00
6 JaMarcus Russell	.50	1.25
7 Adam Vinatieri	.50	1.25
8 Alan Faneca	.50	1.25
9 LaDainian Tomlinson	.75	2.00
10 Jason Taylor	.60	1.50
11 Reggie Bush	.50	1.25
12 Marcus McNeill	.50	1.25
13 Marvin Harrison	.60	1.50
14 Shaun Alexander	.50	1.25
15 Shawne Merriman	.50	1.25
16 Champ Bailey	.60	1.50
17 Chad Johnson	.50	1.25
18 Chris McAlister	.50	1.25
19 Ty Law	.75	2.00
20 Brian Urlacher	.75	2.00
21 Tom Brady	2.50	6.00
22 Troy Polamalu	.75	2.00
23 Calvin Johnson	1.50	4.00
24 Dwayne Jarrett	.60	1.50
25 Ted Ginn Jr.	.60	1.50
26 Yamon Figurs	.50	1.25
27 Vince Young	.50	1.25
28 Larry Johnson	.50	1.25

2007 Donruss Gridiron Gear Jerseys O's

O's PRINT RUN 100 SER.#'d SETS

*X's/100-175: .4X TO 1X O's JSYs

X's PRINT RUN 100-175

*PRIME/50: .6X TO 1.5X X's JSYs

PRIME PRINT RUN 50 SER.#'d SETS

1 Tony Romo	5.00	12.00
2 Julius Jones	2.50	6.00
3 Terrell Owens	3.00	8.00
4 Eli Manning	3.00	8.00
5 Plaxico Burress	2.50	6.00
6 Jeremy Shockey	2.50	6.00
7 Brandon Jacobs	2.50	6.00
8 Donovan McNabb	3.00	8.00
9 Brian Westbrook	2.50	6.00
10 Reggie Brown	2.50	6.00
11 Jason Campbell	2.50	6.00
12 Clinton Portis	2.50	6.00
13 Santana Moss	3.00	8.00
14 Rex Grossman	2.50	6.00
15 Cedric Benson	2.50	6.00
16 Muhsin Muhammad	2.50	6.00
17 Jon Kitna	2.50	6.00
18 Roy Williams WR	2.50	6.00
20 Brett Favre	8.00	20.00
21 Donald Driver	3.00	8.00
22 Greg Jennings	2.50	6.00
23 Tarvaris Jackson	2.50	6.00
24 Chester Taylor	2.50	6.00
26 Warrick Dunn	2.50	6.00
27 Alge Crumpler	3.00	8.00
28 Jake Delhomme	2.50	6.00
29 Steve Smith	3.00	8.00
30 DeAngelo Williams	2.50	6.00
31 Drew Brees	4.00	10.00
32 Deuce McAllister	3.00	8.00
33 Reggie Bush	2.50	6.00
34 Jeff Garcia	2.50	6.00
35 Cadillac Williams	3.00	8.00
36 Joey Galloway	3.00	8.00
37 Matt Leinart	2.50	6.00
38 Edgerrin James	3.00	8.00
39 Anquan Boldin	2.50	6.00
40 Larry Fitzgerald	3.00	8.00
41 Marc Bulger	2.50	6.00
42 Steven Jackson	2.50	6.00
43 Torry Holt	3.00	8.00
44 Alex Smith QB	3.00	8.00
45 Frank Gore	3.00	8.00
46 Vernon Davis	2.50	6.00
48 Matt Hasselbeck	2.50	6.00
49 Shaun Alexander	2.50	6.00
50 Deion Branch	2.50	6.00
51 J.P. Losman	2.50	6.00
52 Lee Evans	3.00	8.00
53 Josh Reed	2.50	6.00
54 Trent Green	2.50	6.00
55 Ronnie Brown	2.50	6.00
56 Chris Chambers	2.50	6.00
57 Tom Brady	12.00	30.00
58 Laurence Maroney	3.00	8.00
59 Randy Moss	3.00	8.00
60 Chad Pennington	2.50	6.00
61 Laveranues Coles	2.50	6.00
62 Leon Washington	2.50	6.00
63 Steve McNair	3.00	8.00
65 Mark Clayton/66	2.50	6.00
66 Carson Palmer	3.00	8.00
67 Rudi Johnson	2.50	6.00
68 Chad Johnson	2.50	6.00
69 T.J. Houshmandzadeh	2.50	6.00
70 Charlie Frye	3.00	8.00
71 Braylon Edwards	2.50	6.00
72 Jamal Lewis	3.00	8.00
73 Ben Roethlisberger	4.00	10.00
74 Willie Parker	3.00	8.00
75 Hines Ward	3.00	8.00
77 Andre Johnson	3.00	8.00
79 Peyton Manning	10.00	25.00
80 Joseph Addai	2.50	6.00
81 Marvin Harrison	3.00	8.00
82 Reggie Wayne	3.00	8.00
83 Byron Leftwich	2.50	6.00
84 Fred Taylor	2.50	6.00
85 Maurice Jones-Drew	2.50	6.00
86 Vince Young	2.50	6.00
87 LenDale White	3.00	8.00
88 Brandon Jones	2.50	6.00
89 Jay Cutler	2.50	6.00
90 Javon Walker	3.00	8.00
91 Mike Bell	3.00	8.00
92 Larry Johnson	2.50	6.00
93 Tony Gonzalez	3.00	8.00
94 Brodie Croyle	3.00	8.00
96 LaMont Jordan	3.00	8.00
97 Philip Rivers	4.00	10.00
98 LaDainian Tomlinson	4.00	10.00
99 Vincent Jackson	2.50	6.00
100 Antonio Gates	4.00	10.00

2007 Donruss Gridiron Gear Next Generation Gold

GOLD PRINT RUN 500 SER.#'d SETS

*RED: .3X TO .8X GOLD/500

*SILVER/250: .5X TO 1.2X GOLD/500

SILVER PRINT RUN 250 SER.#'d SETS

*GOLD HOLO/100: .6X TO 1.5X GOLD/500

GOLD HOLOFOIL PRINT RUN 100 SER.#'d SETS

*PLATINUM/25: 1X TO 2.5X GOLD/500

PLATINUM PRINT RUN 25 SER.#'d SETS

1 Aaron Rodgers	2.00	5.00
2 A.J. Hawk	.50	1.25
3 Anthony Fasano	.50	1.25
4 Bernard Berrian	.50	1.25
5 Brandon Jacobs	.50	1.25
6 Brandon Marshall	.60	1.50
7 Brodie Croyle	.60	1.50
8 DeAngelo Williams	.50	1.25
9 DeMeco Ryans	.60	1.50
10 Demetrius Williams	.50	1.25
11 Devin Hester	.60	1.50
12 Frank Gore	.60	1.50
13 Hank Baskett	.60	1.50
14 Jay Cutler	.50	1.25
15 Jerricho Cotchery	.50	1.25
16 Jerious Norwood	.50	1.25
17 Joseph Addai	.50	1.25
18 Ladell Betts	.50	1.25
19 LenDale White	.60	1.50
20 Marion Barber	.60	1.50
21 Marques Colston	.50	1.25
22 Matt Leinart	.50	1.25
23 Michael Turner	.50	1.25
24 Mike Furrey	.60	1.50
25 Mike Bell	.60	1.50
26 Reggie Bush	.50	1.25
27 Santonio Holmes	.50	1.25
28 Shawne Merriman	.50	1.25
29 Vince Young	.50	1.25
30 Vincent Jackson	.50	1.25
31 Maurice Jones-Drew	.50	1.25
32 Greg Jennings	.50	1.25
33 Devery Henderson	.50	1.25
34 Chester Taylor	.50	1.25
35 Patrick Crayton	.50	1.25
36 Tony Romo	1.00	2.50
37 Vernon Davis	.50	1.25
38 Todd Heap	.50	1.25
39 Reggie Williams	.60	1.50
40 Nate Burleson	.50	1.25

2007 Donruss Gridiron Gear Next Generation Autographs

STATED PRINT RUN 25 SER.#'d SETS

UNPRICED JSY AUTO PRINT RUN 6-13

UNPRICED JSY COMBO AUTO PRINT RUN 3-5

UNPRICED JSY PRIME AUTO PRINT RUN 5

13 Hank Baskett	6.00	15.00
15 Jerricho Cotchery	5.00	12.00
27 Santonio Holmes	5.00	12.00
32 Greg Jennings	5.00	12.00

2007 Donruss Gridiron Gear Next Generation Jerseys

STATED PRINT RUN 77-250

*COMBO PRIME/50: .6X TO 1.5X BASIC JSY

COMBO PRIME PRINT RUN 50

*JUMBO/32-50: .6X TO 1.5X BASIC JSYs

JUMBO SWATCH PRINT RUN 32-50

*JUMBO PRIME/15-25: 1X TO 2.5X BASIC JSYs

JUMBO PRIME PRINT RUN 2-25

*PRIME/50: .6X TO 1.5X BASIC JSY

*PRIME/25: .8X TO 2X BASIC JSY

PRIME PRINT RUN 25-50

1 Aaron Rodgers	8.00	20.00
2 A.J. Hawk	2.00	5.00
3 Anthony Fasano	2.00	5.00
4 Bernard Berrian	2.00	5.00
5 Brandon Jacobs	2.00	5.00
6 Brandon Marshall/77	2.50	6.00
7 Brodie Croyle	2.50	6.00
8 DeAngelo Williams	2.00	5.00
9 DeMeco Ryans	2.50	6.00
10 Demetrius Williams	2.00	5.00
11 Devin Hester	2.50	6.00
12 Frank Gore	2.50	6.00
13 Hank Baskett	2.50	6.00
14 Jay Cutler	2.00	5.00
15 Jerricho Cotchery	2.00	5.00
16 Jerious Norwood	2.00	5.00
17 Joseph Addai	2.00	5.00
18 Ladell Betts	2.00	5.00
19 LenDale White	2.50	6.00
20 Marion Barber	2.50	6.00
21 Marques Colston	2.00	5.00
22 Matt Leinart	2.00	5.00
23 Michael Turner	2.00	5.00
24 Mike Furrey	2.50	6.00
25 Mike Bell	2.50	6.00
26 Reggie Bush	2.00	5.00
27 Santonio Holmes	2.00	5.00
28 Shawne Merriman	2.00	5.00
29 Vince Young	2.00	5.00
30 Vincent Jackson	2.00	5.00
31 Maurice Jones-Drew	2.00	5.00
32 Greg Jennings	2.00	5.00
33 Devery Henderson	2.00	5.00
34 Chester Taylor	2.00	5.00
35 Patrick Crayton	2.00	5.00
36 Tony Romo	4.00	10.00
37 Vernon Davis	2.00	5.00
38 Todd Heap	2.00	5.00
39 Reggie Williams	2.50	6.00
40 Nate Burleson	2.00	5.00

2007 Donruss Gridiron Gear NFL Gridiron Rookie Signatures

STATED PRINT RUN 25-30

1 John Beck/26	8.00	20.00
2 Kenny Irons/30	8.00	20.00
3 Lorenzo Booker/25	10.00	25.00
4 Troy Smith/25	8.00	20.00
5 Drew Stanton/30	8.00	20.00
6 Johnnie Lee Higgins/25	8.00	20.00
7 Dwayne Jarrett/30	10.00	25.00
8 JaMarcus Russell/25	8.00	20.00
9 Gaines Adams/25	10.00	25.00
10 Brady Quinn/30	8.00	20.00
11 Paul Williams/25	8.00	20.00
12 Garrett Wolfe/30	8.00	20.00
13 Tony Hunt/30	8.00	20.00
14 Michael Bush/25	8.00	20.00
15 Robert Meachem/25	10.00	25.00
16 Jason Hill/25	8.00	20.00
17 Patrick Willis/25	12.00	30.00
18 Brian Leonard/30	8.00	20.00
19 Adrian Peterson/30	150.00	300.00
20 Kevin Kolb/25	10.00	25.00
21 Antonio Pittman/25	8.00	20.00
22 Greg Olsen/25	12.00	30.00
23 Calvin Johnson/30	50.00	120.00
24 Trent Edwards/30	8.00	20.00
25 Chris Henry RB/30	8.00	20.00
26 Sidney Rice/25	10.00	25.00
27 Anthony Gonzalez/30	8.00	20.00
28 Dwayne Bowe/25	8.00	20.00
29 Ted Ginn Jr./25	10.00	25.00
30 Steve Smith USC/25	8.00	20.00
31 Brandon Jackson/25	8.00	20.00
32 Joe Thomas/30	12.00	30.00
33 Yamon Figurs/30	8.00	20.00
34 Marshawn Lynch/30	15.00	40.00

2007 Donruss Gridiron Gear NFL Teams Veteran Signatures

STATED PRINT RUN 6-32

SERIAL #'d UNDER 22 NOT PRICED

1 Andre Johnson/22	12.50	25.00
2 Ben Roethlisberger	50.00	100.00
3 Brett Favre	125.00	200.00
5 Eli Manning	50.00	80.00
6 Donovan McNabb		
7 Drew Brees	40.00	80.00
8 LaDainian Tomlinson	30.00	80.00
9 Larry Johnson	25.00	50.00
10 Marvin Harrison	20.00	40.00
12 Maurice Jones-Drew	12.50	25.00
13 A.J. Hawk	20.00	40.00
14 Cedric Benson	20.00	40.00
15 Peyton Manning	75.00	150.00
16 Reggie Bush	20.00	50.00
17 Reggie Wayne	15.00	40.00
18 Rex Grossman	12.50	25.00
19 Ronnie Brown	20.00	40.00
20 Cadillac Williams	20.00	40.00
22 Rudi Johnson	12.50	25.00
23 Steve Smith	20.00	40.00
24 Steven Jackson	20.00	40.00
26 T.J. Houshmandzadeh	12.50	25.00
28 Torry Holt	20.00	40.00
29 Vince Young	15.00	40.00
30 Willie Parker	25.00	50.00
31 Willis McGahee	12.50	25.00
32 Jay Cutler	10.00	25.00

2007 Donruss Gridiron Gear NFL Teams Rookie Signatures

STATED PRINT RUN 30 SER.#'d SETS

1 John Beck	8.00	20.00
2 Kenny Irons	8.00	20.00
3 Lorenzo Booker	10.00	25.00
4 Troy Smith	8.00	20.00
5 Drew Stanton	8.00	20.00
6 Johnnie Lee Higgins	8.00	20.00
7 Dwayne Jarrett	10.00	25.00
8 JaMarcus Russell	8.00	20.00
9 Gaines Adams	10.00	25.00
10 Brady Quinn	8.00	20.00
11 Paul Williams	8.00	20.00
12 Garrett Wolfe	8.00	20.00
13 Tony Hunt	8.00	20.00
14 Michael Bush	8.00	20.00
15 Robert Meachem	10.00	25.00
16 Jason Hill	8.00	20.00
17 Patrick Willis	12.00	30.00
18 Brian Leonard	8.00	20.00
19 Adrian Peterson	150.00	300.00
20 Kevin Kolb	10.00	25.00
21 Antonio Pittman	8.00	20.00
22 Greg Olsen	12.00	30.00
23 Calvin Johnson	50.00	120.00
24 Trent Edwards	8.00	20.00
26 Sidney Rice	10.00	25.00
27 Anthony Gonzalez	8.00	20.00
28 Dwayne Bowe	8.00	20.00
29 Ted Ginn Jr.	10.00	25.00
30 Steve Smith USC	8.00	20.00
32 Joe Thomas	12.00	30.00
33 Yamon Figurs	8.00	20.00
34 Marshawn Lynch	15.00	40.00

2007 Donruss Gridiron Gear Performers Gold

GOLD PRINT RUN 500 SER.#'d SETS

*RED: .3X TO .8X GOLD/500

*SILVER/250: .5X TO 1.2X GOLD/500

SILVER PRINT RUN 250 SER.#'d SETS

*GOLD HOLO/100: .6X TO 1.5X GOLD/500

GOLD HOLOFOIL PRINT RUN 100 SER.#'d SETS

*PLATINUM/25: 1X TO 2.5X GOLD/500

PLATINUM PRINT RUN 25 SER.#'d SETS

1 Alan Page	.60	1.50
2 Archie Manning	.75	2.00
3 Barry Sanders	1.50	4.00
4 Bart Starr	1.50	4.00
5 Bill Bates	.60	1.50
6 Billy Howton	.60	1.50
7 Bob Griese	1.00	2.50
8 Boyd Dowler	.60	1.50
9 Charley Taylor	.60	1.50

10 Chuck Bednarik .75 2.00
11 Cris Collinsworth .75 2.00
12 Dan Marino 2.00 5.00
13 Dante Lavelli .60 1.50
14 Daryle Lamonica .60 1.50
15 Deacon Jones .75 2.00
16 Eric Dickerson .75 2.00
17 Fred Biletnikoff 1.00 2.50
18 Gale Sayers 1.00 2.50
19 Harlon Hill .60 1.50
20 Jack Youngblood .75 2.00
21 Jethro Pugh .60 1.50
22 Jimmy Orr .60 1.50
23 Joe Namath 1.25 3.00
24 Johnny Morris .60 1.50
25 Larry Little .60 1.50
26 Lydell Mitchell .60 1.50
27 Merlin Olsen .60 1.50
28 Rick Casares .60 1.50
29 Rosey Grier .60 1.50
30 Sonny Jurgensen .75 2.00
31 Sterling Sharpe .75 2.00
32 Steve Largent 1.00 2.50
33 Tony Dorsett 1.00 2.50
34 Willie Brown .60 1.50
35 Willie Lanier .60 1.50
36 Yale Lary .60 1.50
37 Marvin Harrison .75 2.00
38 Matt Hasselbeck .60 1.50
39 J.P. Losman .60 1.50
40 Carson Palmer .75 2.00
41 Steve McNair .75 2.00
42 Lee Evans .75 2.00
43 Donald Driver .75 2.00
44 Hines Ward .75 2.00
45 Antonio Gates 1.00 2.50
46 Frank Gore .75 2.00
47 Rudi Johnson .60 1.50
48 Fred Taylor .60 1.50
49 Joseph Addai .60 1.50
50 Larry Fitzgerald .75 2.00

2007 Donruss Gridiron Gear Performers Autographs

STATED PRINT RUN 75-250 SER.#'d SETS
22 Jimmy Orr/250 5.00 12.00
27 Merlin Olsen/75 15.00 30.00

2007 Donruss Gridiron Gear Performers Jerseys

STATED PRINT RUN 90-250
*COMBOS/50-100: .5X TO 1.2X BASIC JSYs
COMBOS PRINT RUN 50-100
*COMBO PRIME/25-50: .8X TO 2X BASIC JSYs
COMBOS PRIME PRINT RUN 5-50
*JUM.SWATCH/19-50: .8X TO 2X BASIC JSYs
JUMBO SWATCH PRINT RUN 19-50
*JUMBO PRIME/15-25: 1.2X TO 3X BASIC JSYs
JUMBO SWATCH PRIME PRINT RUN 10-25
*PRIME/25-50: .6X TO 1.5X BASIC JSYs
PRIME PRINT RUN 5-50
3 Barry Sanders/240 10.00 25.00
4 Bart Starr 10.00 25.00
5 Bill Bates/150 4.00 10.00
7 Bob Griese/150 6.00 15.00
9 Charley Taylor/150 4.00 10.00
11 Cris Collinsworth/150 5.00 12.00
12 Dan Marino 12.00 30.00
14 Daryle Lamonica/150 4.00 10.00
15 Deacon Jones/150 5.00 12.00
16 Eric Dickerson 5.00 12.00
17 Fred Biletnikoff 6.00 15.00
18 Gale Sayers 6.00 15.00
20 Jack Youngblood 5.00 12.00
23 Joe Namath 6.00 15.00
25 Larry Little 4.00 10.00
27 Merlin Olsen 4.00 10.00
30 Sonny Jurgensen/90 5.00 12.00
31 Sterling Sharpe 5.00 12.00
32 Steve Largent 6.00 15.00
33 Tony Dorsett 6.00 15.00
34 Willie Brown 4.00 10.00
36 Yale Lary/235 4.00 10.00
37 Marvin Harrison 3.00 8.00
38 Matt Hasselbeck 2.50 6.00
39 J.P. Losman 2.50 6.00
40 Carson Palmer 3.00 8.00
41 Steve McNair 3.00 8.00
42 Lee Evans 3.00 8.00
43 Donald Driver 3.00 8.00
44 Hines Ward 3.00 8.00
45 Antonio Gates 4.00 10.00
46 Frank Gore 3.00 8.00
47 Rudi Johnson 2.50 6.00
48 Fred Taylor 2.50 6.00
49 Joseph Addai 2.50 6.00
50 Larry Fitzgerald 3.00 8.00

2007 Donruss Gridiron Gear Performers Jerseys Autographs

STATED PRINT RUN 10-25
*JSY COMBO AUTO/25: .5X TO 1.2X JSY AU/25
JSY COMBO AUTO PRINT RUN 3-25
UNPRICED JSY COMBO PRIME PRINT RUN 5
UNPRICED PRIME AUTO PRINT RUN 5-15
SERIAL #'d UNDER 25 NOT PRICED
27 Merlin Olsen/25 15.00 40.00

2007 Donruss Gridiron Gear Plates and Patches

STATED PRINT RUN 100 SER.#'d SETS
1 Donovan McNabb 6.00 15.00
2 Tom Brady 20.00 50.00
3 Peyton Manning 15.00 40.00
4 LaDainian Tomlinson 8.00 20.00
5 Tony Romo 25.00 60.00
6 Shaun Alexander 5.00 12.00
7 Carson Palmer 6.00 15.00
8 Vince Young 5.00 12.00
9 Reggie Bush 5.00 12.00
10 Terrell Owens 6.00 15.00

2007 Donruss Gridiron Gear Playbook Gold

GOLD PRINT RUN 500 SER.#'d SETS
*RED: .3X TO .8X GOLD/500
*SILVER/250: .5X TO 1.2X GOLD/500
SILVER PRINT RUN 250 SER.#'d SETS
*GOLD HOLO/100: .6X TO 1.5X GOLD/500
GOLD HOLOFOIL PRINT RUN 100 SER.#'d SETS
*PLATINUM/25: 1X TO 2.5X GOLD/500
PLATINUM PRINT RUN 25 SER.#'d SETS
1 Eli Manning .75 2.00
2 Chad Pennington .60 1.50
3 Drew Brees 1.00 2.50
4 Marc Bulger .60 1.50
5 Brett Favre 2.00 5.00
6 Ben Roethlisberger 1.00 2.50
7 Philip Rivers 1.00 2.50
8 Matt Leinart .60 1.50
9 Reggie Wayne .75 2.00
10 Chad Johnson .60 1.50
11 Roy Williams WR .60 1.50
12 Anquan Boldin .60 1.50
13 Torry Holt .75 2.00
14 Andre Johnson .75 2.00
15 T.J. Houshmandzadeh .60 1.50
16 Larry Johnson .60 1.50
17 Steven Jackson .60 1.50
18 Willie Parker .75 2.00
19 Brian Westbrook .60 1.50
20 Edgerrin James .75 2.00
21 Warrick Dunn .60 1.50
22 Julius Jones .60 1.50
23 Deuce McAllister .75 2.00
24 Ronnie Brown .60 1.50
25 Cadillac Williams .75 2.00

2007 Donruss Gridiron Gear Playbook Jerseys X's

X's PRINT RUN 250 SER.#'d SETS
*O's: .4X TO 1X X's JSYs
O's PRINT RUN 250 SER.#'d SETS
*PATCH/25: .8X TO 2X X's JSYs
PATCH PRINT RUN 25 SER.#'d SETS
1 Eli Manning 3.00 8.00
2 Chad Pennington 2.50 6.00
3 Drew Brees 4.00 10.00
4 Marc Bulger 2.50 6.00
5 Brett Favre 8.00 20.00
6 Ben Roethlisberger 4.00 10.00
7 Philip Rivers 4.00 10.00
8 Matt Leinart 2.50 6.00
9 Reggie Wayne 3.00 8.00
10 Chad Johnson 2.50 6.00
11 Roy Williams WR 2.50 6.00
12 Anquan Boldin 2.50 6.00
13 Torry Holt 3.00 8.00
14 Andre Johnson 3.00 8.00
15 T.J. Houshmandzadeh 2.50 6.00
16 Larry Johnson 2.50 6.00
17 Steven Jackson 2.50 6.00
18 Willie Parker 3.00 8.00
19 Brian Westbrook 2.50 6.00
20 Edgerrin James 3.00 8.00
21 Warrick Dunn 2.50 6.00
22 Julius Jones 2.50 6.00
23 Deuce McAllister 3.00 8.00
24 Ronnie Brown 2.50 6.00
25 Cadillac Williams 3.00 8.00

2007 Donruss Gridiron Gear Player Timeline Gold

GOLD PRINT RUN 500 SER.#'d SETS
*RED: .3X TO .8X GOLD/500
*SILVER/250: .5X TO 1.2X GOLD/500
SILVER PRINT RUN 250 SER.#'d SETS
*GOLD HOLO/100: .6X TO 1.5X GOLD/500
GOLD HOLOFOIL PRINT RUN 100 SER.#'d SETS
*PLATINUM/25: 1X TO 2.5X GOLD/500
PLATINUM PRINT RUN 25 SER.#'d SETS
1 Carson Palmer .75 2.00
2 Larry Fitzgerald .75 2.00
3 Cedric Benson .60 1.50
4 Reggie Williams .75 2.00
5 Matt Leinart .60 1.50
6 Reggie Bush .60 1.50
7 Vince Young .60 1.50
8 Devery Henderson .60 1.50
9 Frank Gore .75 2.00
10 Kenny Irons .60 1.50
11 Dwayne Jarrett .75 2.00
12 Steve Smith USC .60 1.50
13 Greg Olsen 1.00 2.50
14 Brady Quinn .60 1.50
15 Adrian Peterson 2.00 5.00
16 JaMarcus Russell .60 1.50
17 Dwayne Bowe .60 1.50
18 Johnnie Lee Higgins .60 1.50
19 Robert Meachem .75 2.00
20 Michael Bush .60 1.50
21 Steven Jackson .60 1.50
22 Steve McNair .75 2.00
23 Terrell Owens .75 2.00
24 Edgerrin James .75 2.00
25 Deion Branch .60 1.50

2007 Donruss Gridiron Gear Player Timeline Autographs

STATED PRINT RUN 7-100
3 Cedric Benson/100 8.00 20.00
6 Reggie Bush/25 40.00 100.00
8 Devery Henderson/100 6.00 15.00
9 Frank Gore/50 8.00 20.00
10 Kenny Irons/25 10.00 25.00
11 Dwayne Jarrett/25 10.00 25.00
12 Steve Smith USC/25 8.00 20.00
13 Greg Olsen/25 12.00 30.00
15 Adrian Peterson/28 150.00 250.00
16 JaMarcus Russell/18 10.00 25.00
17 Dwayne Bowe/25 8.00 20.00
18 Johnnie Lee Higgins/25 8.00 20.00
19 Robert Meachem/25 10.00 25.00
20 Michael Bush/25 10.00 25.00
21 Steven Jackson/50 10.00 25.00

2007 Donruss Gridiron Gear Player Timeline Jerseys

STATED PRINT RUN 50-250
*COMBOS/80-100: .5X TO 1.2X BASIC JSYs
*COMBOS/30: .8X TO 2X BASIC JSYs
COMBOS PRINT RUN 30-100
*CMBO PRIME/50: .6X TO 1.5X BASIC JSY
*CMBO PRIME/25: .8X TO 2X BASIC JSY
COMBOS PRIME PRINT RUN 5-50
*JUM.SWATCH/40-50: .6X TO 1.5X BASIC JSY
JUMBO SWATCH PRIME PRINT RUN 40-50
*JUMBO PRIME/15-25: .8X TO 2X BASIC JSY
JUMBO SWATCH PRIME PRINT RUN 5-25
*PRIME/50: .6X TO 1.5X BASIC JSY
*PRIME/25: .8X TO 2X BASIC JSY
PRIME PRINT RUN 10-50
1 Carson Palmer 2.50 6.00
2 Larry Fitzgerald 2.50 6.00
3 Cedric Benson 2.00 5.00
4 Reggie Williams 2.50 6.00
5 Matt Leinart 2.00 5.00
6 Reggie Bush 2.00 5.00
7 Vince Young 2.00 5.00
8 Devery Henderson 2.00 5.00
9 Frank Gore 2.50 6.00
10 Kenny Irons 2.00 5.00
11 Dwayne Jarrett 2.50 6.00
12 Steve Smith USC 2.00 5.00
13 Greg Olsen 3.00 8.00
14 Brady Quinn 2.00 5.00
15 Adrian Peterson 6.00 15.00
16 JaMarcus Russell 2.00 5.00
17 Dwayne Bowe 2.00 5.00
18 Johnnie Lee Higgins 2.00 5.00
19 Robert Meachem 2.50 6.00
20 Michael Bush 2.00 5.00
21 Steven Jackson 2.00 5.00
22 Steve McNair 2.50 6.00
23 Terrell Owens/50 2.50 6.00
24 Edgerrin James 2.50 6.00
25 Deion Branch 2.00 5.00

2007 Donruss Gridiron Gear Player Timeline Jerseys Autographs

STATED PRINT RUN 5-25 SER.#'d SETS
*COMBO/25: .5X TO 1.2X BASIC JSY AUTO/25
COMBO JSY AUTO PRINT RUN 5-25
*CMBO PRIM/25: .5X TO 1.2X BSC.JSY AU/25
COMBO JSY PRIME PRINT RUN 1-25
*PRIME/20-25: .5X TO 1.2X BASIC JSY AU/25
PRIME PRINT RUN 2-25
3 Cedric Benson/25 10.00 25.00
8 Devery Henderson/25 10.00 25.00
9 Frank Gore/25 15.00 40.00
10 Kenny Irons/25 12.00 30.00
11 Dwayne Jarrett/25 10.00 25.00
12 Steve Smith USC/25 8.00 20.00
13 Greg Olsen/25 15.00 40.00
14 Brady Quinn/25 20.00 50.00
16 JaMarcus Russell/25 15.00 40.00
21 Steven Jackson/25 15.00 40.00

2007 Donruss Gridiron Gear Rivals Gold

GOLD PRINT RUN 500 SER.#'d SETS
*RED: .3X TO .8X GOLD/500
*SILVER/250: .5X TO 1.2X GOLD/500
SILVER PRINT RUN 250 SER.#'d SETS
*GOLD HOLO/100: .6X TO 1.5X GOLD/500
GOLD HOLOFOIL PRINT RUN 100 SER.#'d SETS
*PLATINUM/25: 1X TO 2.5X GOLD/500
PLATINUM PRINT RUN 25 SER.#'d SETS
1 P.Manning/B.Urlacher 2.50 6.00
2 D.McNabb/T.Owens .75 2.00
3 Tomlinson/Alexander 1.00 2.50
4 T.Holt/A.Boldin .75 2.00
5 M.Harrison/C.Johnson .75 2.00
6 B.Favre/R.Grossman 2.00 5.00
7 R.Williams S/R.Will.WR .60 1.50
8 V.Young/M.Leinart .60 1.50
9 M.Hasselbeck/T.Romo 1.25 3.00
10 C.Palmer/Roethlisberger 1.00 2.50
11 C.Portis/J.Jones .60 1.50
12 L.Johnson/L.Jordan .75 2.00
13 B.Edwards/H.Ward .75 2.00
14 R.Wayne/R.Lewis 1.00 2.50
15 E.Manning/C.Pennington .75 2.00
16 T.Brady/P.Rivers 3.00 8.00

2007 Donruss Gridiron Gear Rivals Jerseys

STATED PRINT RUN 100 SER.#'d SETS
*PRIME/25: .8X TO 2X BASIC JSYs
PRIME PRINT RUN 25 SER.#'d SETS
1 P.Manning/B.Urlacher 10.00 25.00
2 D.McNabb/T.Owens 3.00 8.00
3 Tomlinson/Alexander 4.00 10.00
4 T.Holt/A.Boldin 3.00 8.00
5 M.Harrison/C.Johnson 3.00 8.00
6 B.Favre/R.Grossman 8.00 20.00
7 R.Williams S/R.Will.WR 2.50 6.00
8 V.Young/M.Leinart 2.50 6.00
9 M.Hasselbeck/T.Romo 5.00 12.00
10 C.Palmer/Roethlisberger 4.00 10.00
11 C.Portis/J.Jones 2.50 6.00
12 L.Johnson/L.Jordan 3.00 8.00
13 B.Edwards/H.Ward 3.00 8.00
14 R.Wayne/R.Lewis 4.00 10.00
15 E.Manning/C.Pennington 3.00 8.00
16 T.Brady/P.Rivers 12.00 30.00

2007 Donruss Gridiron Gear Rookie Jerseys

STATED PRINT RUN 50 SER.#'d SETS
*COMBOS/50: .5X TO 1.2X BASIC JSYs
COMBOS PRINT RUN 50 SER.#'d SETS
*CMBO PRIME/25-50: .6X TO 1.5X BASIC JSY
COMBOS PRIME PRINT RUN 25-50
*JUMBO SWATCH/50: .6X TO 1.5X BASIC JSYs
JUMBO SWATCH PRINT RUN 50
*JUMBO PRIME/50: 1X TO 2.5X BASIC JSYs
JUMBO SWATCH PRIME PRINT RUN 2-50
*PRIME/50: .6X TO 1.5X BASIC JSYs
PRIME PRINT RUN 10-50
*RETAIL RED/50: .4X TO 1X BASIC JSYs
RETAIL RED PRINT RUN 50
*TRIOS/50: .8X TO 2X BASIC JSYs
TRIOS PRINT RUN 50
*TRIOS PRIME/25-50: 1.2X TO 3X BASIC JSYs
TRIOS PRIME PRINT RUN 25-50
201 Marshawn Lynch 3.00 8.00
202 Yamon Figurs 1.50 4.00
203 Joe Thomas 2.50 6.00
204 Brandon Jackson 1.50 4.00
205 Steve Smith USC 1.50 4.00
206 Ted Ginn Jr. 2.00 5.00
207 Dwayne Bowe 1.50 4.00
208 Anthony Gonzalez 1.50 4.00
209 Sidney Rice 2.00 5.00
210 Chris Henry RB 1.50 4.00
211 Trent Edwards 1.50 4.00
212 Calvin Johnson 5.00 12.00
213 Greg Olsen 2.50 6.00
214 Antonio Pittman 1.50 4.00
215 Kevin Kolb 2.00 5.00
216 Adrian Peterson 5.00 12.00
217 Brian Leonard 1.50 4.00
218 Patrick Willis 2.50 6.00
219 Jason Hill 1.50 4.00
220 Robert Meachem 2.00 5.00
221 Michael Bush 1.50 4.00
222 Tony Hunt 1.50 4.00
223 Garrett Wolfe 1.50 4.00
224 Paul Williams 1.50 4.00
225 Brady Quinn 1.50 4.00
226 Gaines Adams 2.00 5.00
227 JaMarcus Russell 1.50 4.00
228 Dwayne Jarrett 2.00 5.00
229 Johnnie Lee Higgins 1.50 4.00
230 Drew Stanton 1.50 4.00
231 Troy Smith 1.50 4.00
232 Lorenzo Booker 2.00 5.00
233 Kenny Irons 1.50 4.00
234 John Beck 1.50 4.00

2007 Donruss Gridiron Gear Rookie Jerseys Combos Prime Autographs

*COMBO PRIME AU/50: .4X TO 1X BASE RC/100
COMBOS PRIME AUTO PRINT RUN 10-50

2007 Donruss Gridiron Gear Rookie Jerseys Prime Autographs

*JSY PRIME AU/50: .4X TO 1X BASE RC/100
JERSEY PRIME AUTO PRINT RUN 5-50

2007 Donruss Gridiron Gear Rookie Jerseys Trios Prime Autographs

*TRIOS PRIME/50: .5X TO 1.2X BASE RC/100
TRIOS PRIME PRINT RUN 10-50
216 Adrian Peterson 150.00 300.00

2007 Donruss Gridiron Gear Retail

*RETAIL ROOKIE: .4X TO 1X BASIC CARDS
STATED PRINT RUN 599 SER.#'d SETS
RETAIL PRINTED ON WHITE CARD STOCK

2008 Donruss Gridiron Gear

COMP.SET w/o RC's (100) 7.50 20.00
101-200 ROOKIE PRINT RUN 999
ROOKIE AUTO PRINT RUN 100
1 Matt Leinart .25 .60
2 Larry Fitzgerald .30 .75
3 Anquan Boldin .25 .60
4 Edgerrin James .30 .75
5 Jerious Norwood .25 .60
6 Roddy White .25 .60
7 Michael Turner .25 .60
8 Willis McGahee .25 .60
9 Derrick Mason .25 .60
10 Mark Clayton .25 .60
11 Trent Edwards .25 .60
12 Marshawn Lynch .30 .75
13 Lee Evans .30 .75
14 Steve Smith .30 .75
15 DeAngelo Williams .25 .60
16 Jake Delhomme .25 .60
17 Brian Urlacher .40 1.00
18 Devin Hester .30 .75
19 Rex Grossman .25 .60
20 Carson Palmer .30 .75
21 T.J. Houshmandzadeh .25 .60
22 Rudi Johnson .25 .60
23 Derek Anderson .25 .60
24 Kellen Winslow .25 .60
25 Braylon Edwards .25 .60
26 Tony Romo .30 .75
27 Terrell Owens .30 .75
28 Marion Barber .25 .60
29 Jason Witten .30 .75
30 Jay Cutler .25 .60
31 Selvin Young .25 .60
32 Brandon Marshall .30 .75
33 Jon Kitna .25 .60
34 Roy Williams WR .25 .60
35 Calvin Johnson .40 1.00
36 Aaron Rodgers .75 2.00
37 Ryan Grant .30 .75
38 Greg Jennings .25 .60
39 Matt Schaub .25 .60
40 Ahman Green .30 .75
41 Andre Johnson .30 .75
42 Peyton Manning 1.00 2.50
43 Joseph Addai .25 .60
44 Reggie Wayne .30 .75
45 Anthony Gonzalez .25 .60
46 David Garrard .25 .60
47 Fred Taylor .25 .60
48 Maurice Jones-Drew .25 .60
49 Brodie Croyle .30 .75
50 Larry Johnson .25 .60
51 Tony Gonzalez .30 .75
52 John Beck .25 .60
53 Ronnie Brown .25 .60
54 Ted Ginn Jr. .25 .60
55 Tarvaris Jackson .25 .60
56 Adrian Peterson .40 1.00
57 Chester Taylor .25 .60
58 Tom Brady 1.25 3.00
59 Randy Moss .30 .75
60 Laurence Maroney .30 .75
61 Drew Brees .40 1.00
62 Reggie Bush .25 .60
63 Marques Colston .25 .60
64 Eli Manning .30 .75
65 Plaxico Burress .25 .60
66 Brandon Jacobs .25 .60
67 Brett Favre 2.00 5.00
68 Jerricho Cotchery .25 .60
69 Laveranues Coles .25 .60
70 JaMarcus Russell .25 .60
71 Justin Fargas .25 .60
72 Zach Miller .25 .60
73 Donovan McNabb .30 .75
74 Brian Westbrook .25 .60
75 Kevin Curtis .25 .60
76 Ben Roethlisberger .40 1.00
77 Willie Parker .30 .75
78 Hines Ward .30 .75
79 Santonio Holmes .25 .60
80 Philip Rivers .40 1.00
81 LaDainian Tomlinson .40 1.00
82 Antonio Gates .30 .75
83 Alex Smith QB .30 .75
84 Frank Gore .30 .75
85 Vernon Davis .25 .60
86 Matt Hasselbeck .25 .60
87 Deion Branch .25 .60
88 Julius Jones .25 .60
89 Marc Bulger .25 .60
90 Steven Jackson .25 .60
91 Torry Holt .30 .75
92 Jeff Garcia .25 .60
93 Cadillac Williams .30 .75
94 Joey Galloway .30 .75
95 Vince Young .25 .60
96 LenDale White .25 .60
97 Roydell Williams .25 .60
98 Jason Campbell .25 .60
99 Clinton Portis .25 .60
100 Chris Cooley .25 .60
101 Adrian Arrington RC 1.25 3.00
102 Alex Brink RC 1.50 4.00
103 Ali Highsmith RC 1.25 3.00
104 Allen Patrick RC 1.25 3.00
105 Andre Woodson RC 1.25 3.00
106 Anthony Alridge RC 1.25 3.00
107 Antoine Cason RC 1.50 4.00
108 Aqib Talib RC 2.00 5.00
109 Arman Shields RC 1.50 4.00
110 Brad Cottam RC 1.25 3.00
111 Brandon Flowers RC 1.50 4.00
112 Calais Campbell RC 1.50 4.00
113 Caleb Campbell RC 2.00 5.00
114 Chauncey Washington RC 1.50 4.00
115 Chevis Jackson RC 1.25 3.00
116 Colt Brennan RC 1.50 4.00
117 Cory Boyd RC 1.25 3.00
118 Craig Steltz RC 1.25 3.00
119 Curtis Lofton RC 1.50 4.00
120 DJ Hall RC 1.25 3.00
121 Dan Connor RC 1.25 3.00
122 Dantrell Savage RC 1.50 4.00
123 Darius Reynaud RC 1.25 3.00
124 Darrell Strong RC 1.50 4.00
125 David Vobora RC 1.25 3.00
126 Davone Bess RC 1.50 4.00
127 Dennis Dixon RC 1.25 3.00
128 Derrick Harvey RC 1.25 3.00
129 D.Rodgers-Cromartie RC 1.50 4.00
130 Erik Ainge RC 1.25 3.00
131 Erin Henderson RC 1.50 4.00
132 Ernie Wheelwright RC 1.50 4.00
133 Fred Davis RC 1.25 3.00
134 Joe Jon Finley RC 1.25 3.00
135 Jacob Hester RC 1.25 3.00
136 Jacob Tamme RC 1.50 4.00
137 Jalen Parmele RC 1.50 4.00
138 Jamar Adams RC 1.25 3.00
139 Jason Rivers RC 1.25 3.00
140 Jaymar Johnson RC 1.25 3.00
141 Jed Collins RC 1.50 4.00
142 Jerod Mayo RC 2.00 5.00
143 Jermichael Finley RC 1.25 3.00
144 Jerome Felton RC 1.25 3.00
145 John Carlson RC 1.25 3.00
146 Jonathan Hefney RC 1.25 3.00
147 Jordon Dizon RC 1.25 3.00
148 Josh Johnson RC 1.25 3.00
149 Josh Morgan RC 1.25 3.00
150 Justin Forsett RC 1.50 4.00
151 Justin Harper RC 1.25 3.00
152 Kalvin McRae RC 1.25 3.00
153 Keenan Burton RC 1.25 3.00
154 Keith Rivers RC 1.25 3.00
155 Kellen Davis RC 1.25 3.00
156 Kenneth Moore RC 1.25 3.00
157 Kenny Phillips RC 1.25 3.00
158 Kentwan Balmer RC 1.25 3.00
159 Kevin Robinson RC 1.25 3.00
160 Lavelle Hawkins RC 1.50 4.00
161 Lawrence Jackson RC 1.25 3.00
162 Leodis McKelvin RC 1.50 4.00
163 Marcus Monk RC 1.50 4.00
164 Marcus Smith RC 1.50 4.00
165 Marcus Thomas RC 1.50 4.00
166 Marcus Henry RC 1.25 3.00
167 Mario Urrutia RC 1.25 3.00
168 Mark Bradford RC 1.25 3.00
169 Martellus Bennett RC 1.50 4.00
170 Martin Rucker RC 1.25 3.00
171 Matt Flynn RC 1.25 3.00
172 Mike Hart RC 1.25 3.00
173 Mike Jenkins RC 1.25 3.00
174 Owen Schmitt RC 1.25 3.00
175 Pat Sims RC 1.50 4.00
176 Patrick Lee RC 1.25 3.00
177 Paul Hubbard RC 1.25 3.00
178 Paul Smith RC 1.25 3.00
179 Peyton Hillis RC 2.00 5.00
180 Phillip Merling RC 1.25 3.00
181 Pierre Garcon RC 2.50 6.00
182 Quentin Groves RC 1.50 4.00
183 Reggie Smith RC 1.25 3.00
184 Ryan Grice-Mullen RC 1.25 3.00
185 Ryan Torain RC 1.50 4.00
186 Sam Keller RC 1.25 3.00
187 Sedrick Ellis RC 1.25 3.00
188 Shawn Crable RC 1.25 3.00
189 Simeon Castille RC 1.25 3.00
190 Steve Johnson RC 2.50 6.00
191 Tashard Choice RC 1.25 3.00
192 Terrell Thomas RC 1.25 3.00
193 Terrence Wheatley RC 1.25 3.00
194 Thomas Brown RC 1.25 3.00
195 Tim Hightower RC 1.50 4.00
196 Tracy Porter RC 1.50 4.00
197 Vernon Gholston RC 1.25 3.00
198 Will Franklin RC 1.50 4.00
199 Xavier Adibi RC 1.25 3.00
200 Xavier Omon RC 1.25 3.00
201 Andre Caldwell JSY AU RC 6.00 15.00
202 Brian Brohm JSY AU RC 6.00 15.00
203 Chad Henne JSY AU RC 8.00 20.00
204 Chris Johnson JSY AU RC 8.00 20.00
205 D.McFadden JSY AU RC 6.00 15.00
206 D.Jackson JSY AU RC 12.00 30.00
207 Devin Thomas JSY AU RC 6.00 15.00
208 Dexter Jackson JSY AU RC 10.00 25.00
209 Donnie Avery JSY AU RC 8.00 20.00
210 Dustin Keller JSY AU RC 8.00 20.00
211 Earl Bennett JSY AU RC 10.00 25.00
212 Early Doucet JSY AU RC 6.00 15.00
213 Eddie Royal JSY AU RC 6.00 15.00
214 Felix Jones JSY AU RC 6.00 15.00
215 Glenn Dorsey JSY AU RC 6.00 15.00
216 Harry Douglas JSY AU RC 8.00 20.00
217 Jamaal Charles JSY AU RC 10.00 25.00
218 James Hardy JSY AU RC 6.00 15.00
219 Jerome Simpson JSY AU RC 8.00 20.00
220 Joe Flacco JSY AU RC 12.00 30.00
221 John David Booty JSY AU RC 6.00 15.00
222 Jonathan Stewart JSY AU RC 10.00 25.00
223 Jordy Nelson JSY AU RC 20.00 40.00
224 Kevin O'Connell JSY AU RC 6.00 15.00
225 Kevin Smith JSY AU RC 6.00 15.00
226 Limas Sweed JSY AU RC 6.00 15.00
227 Malcolm Kelly JSY AU RC 6.00 15.00
228 Mario Manningham JSY AU RC 6.00 15.00
229 Matt Forte JSY AU RC 20.00 50.00
230 Matt Ryan JSY AU RC 40.00 100.00
231 Rashard Mendenhall JSY AU RC 6.00 15.00
232 Ray Rice JSY AU RC 6.00 15.00
233 Steve Slaton JSY AU RC 6.00 15.00
234 Jake Long JSY AU RC 10.00 25.00

2008 Donruss Gridiron Gear Gold Holofoil

*VETS 1-100: 1.5X TO 4X BASIC CARDS
STATED PRINT RUN 200 SER.#'d SETS
67 Brett Favre 3.00 8.00

2008 Donruss Gridiron Gear Gold Holofoil O's

*VETS 1-100: 2.5X TO 6X BASIC CARDS
*ROOKIES 101-200: .6X TO 1.5X BASIC CARDS
STATED PRINT RUN 100 SER.#'d SETS
67 Brett Favre 5.00 12.00

2008 Donruss Gridiron Gear Gold Holofoil X's

*VETS 1-100: 2.5X TO 6X BASIC CARDS
*ROOKIES 101-200: .6X TO 1.5X BASIC CARDS
STATED PRINT RUN 100 SER.#'d SETS
67 Brett Favre 5.00 12.00

2008 Donruss Gridiron Gear Platinum Holofoil

*VETS 1-100: 3X TO 8X BASIC CARDS
STATED PRINT RUN 50 SER.#'d SETS

2008 Donruss Gridiron Gear Platinum Holofoil O's

*VETS 1-100: 5X TO 12X BASIC CARDS
*ROOKIES 101-200: 1X TO 2.5X BASIC CARDS
STATED PRINT RUN 25 SER.#'d SETS

2008 Donruss Gridiron Gear Platinum Holofoil X's

*VETS 1-100: 5X TO 12X BASIC CARDS
*ROOKIES 101-200: 1X TO 2.5X BASIC CARDS
STATED PRINT RUN 25 SER.#'d SETS

2008 Donruss Gridiron Gear Red Holofoil

*VETS 1-100: .8X TO 2X BASIC CARDS
67 Brett Favre 2.50 6.00

2008 Donruss Gridiron Gear Retail

*VETERANS 1-100: .3X TO .8X BASIC CARDS
*ROOKIES 101-200: .4X TO 1X BASIC CARDS
ROOKIES PRINT RUN 999 SER.#'d SETS

2008 Donruss Gridiron Gear Silver Holofoil

*VETS 1-100: 1X TO 2.5X BASIC CARDS
67 Brett Favre 2.00 5.00

2008 Donruss Gridiron Gear Silver Holofoil O's

*VETS: 1.5X TO 4X BASIC CARDS
STATED PRINT RUN 250 SER.#'d SETS
67 Brett Favre 3.00 8.00

2008 Donruss Gridiron Gear Silver Holofoil X's

*VETS: 1.5X TO 4X BASIC CARDS
STATED PRINT RUN 250 SER.#'d SETS
67 Brett Favre 3.00 8.00

2008 Donruss Gridiron Gear Autographs Gold Holofoil

STATED PRINT RUN 5-250
*PLATINUM/25: .6X TO 1.5X GOLD/250
*PLATINUM/25: .5X TO 1.2X GOLD/50-100
*PLATINUM/25: .4X TO 1X GOLD/25-35
PLATINUM HOLOFOIL PRINT RUN 1-25
101 Adrian Arrington 3.00 8.00
103 Ali Highsmith 3.00 8.00
104 Allen Patrick/100 4.00 10.00
105 Andre Woodson/100 4.00 10.00
106 Anthony Alridge/25 5.00 12.00
107 Antoine Cason/100 5.00 12.00
108 Aqib Talib/100 6.00 15.00
110 Brad Cottam/100 4.00 10.00
112 Calais Campbell 4.00 10.00
113 Caleb Campbell/100 6.00 15.00
116 Colt Brennan/100 6.00 15.00
117 Cory Boyd 3.00 8.00
119 Curtis Lofton 4.00 10.00
121 Dan Connor 3.00 8.00
122 Dantrell Savage 4.00 10.00
123 Darius Reynaud 3.00 8.00
124 Darrell Strong/35 6.00 15.00
126 Davone Bess 4.00 10.00
127 Dennis Dixon/100 8.00 20.00
128 Derrick Harvey 3.00 8.00
129 Dominique Rodgers-Cromartie 4.00 10.00
130 Erik Ainge 3.00 8.00
131 Erin Henderson 4.00 10.00
133 Fred Davis 3.00 8.00
135 Jacob Hester/100 4.00 10.00
136 Jacob Tamme 4.00 10.00
139 Jason Rivers 3.00 8.00
142 Jerod Mayo 5.00 12.00
143 Jermichael Finley 3.00 8.00
145 John Carlson 3.00 8.00
147 Jordon Dizon/26 5.00 12.00
148 Josh Johnson 3.00 8.00
149 Josh Morgan/25 5.00 12.00
150 Justin Forsett/25 6.00 15.00
153 Keenan Burton 3.00 8.00
154 Keith Rivers 3.00 8.00
155 Kellen Davis 3.00 8.00
157 Kenny Phillips 3.00 8.00
158 Kentwan Balmer 3.00 8.00
159 Kevin Robinson/25 5.00 12.00
160 Lavelle Hawkins 4.00 10.00
161 Lawrence Jackson 3.00 8.00
162 Leodis McKelvin 4.00 10.00
164 Marcus Smith/50 5.00 12.00
165 Marcus Thomas/25 6.00 15.00
168 Mark Bradford 3.00 8.00
169 Martellus Bennett 4.00 10.00
170 Martin Rucker 3.00 8.00
171 Matt Flynn 3.00 8.00
172 Mike Hart/100 4.00 10.00
173 Mike Jenkins 3.00 8.00
175 Pat Sims 4.00 10.00
178 Paul Smith 3.00 8.00
179 Peyton Hillis/25 8.00 20.00
180 Phillip Merling 3.00 8.00
183 Reggie Smith 3.00 8.00
184 Ryan Grice-Mullen 3.00 8.00
185 Ryan Torain/25 6.00 15.00
186 Sam Keller 3.00 8.00
187 Sedrick Ellis 3.00 8.00
191 Tashard Choice/100 4.00 10.00
192 Terrell Thomas 3.00 8.00
194 Thomas Brown/25 5.00 12.00
195 Tim Hightower/25 15.00 40.00
197 Vernon Gholston 3.00 8.00
198 Will Franklin/25 6.00 15.00
199 Xavier Adibi 3.00 8.00

2008 Donruss Gridiron Gear Jerseys

BASIC JERSEY PRINT RUN 32-250
*O/92-100: .5X TO 1.2X BASIC JSY/145-250
*O/92-100: .4X TO 1X BASIC JSY/80-125
*O/92-100: .3X TO .8X BASIC JSY/80-125
*O/27-34: .6X TO 1.5X BASIC JSY/250
O's PRINT RUN 15-100
*X/98-100: .5X TO 1.2X BASIC JSY/145-250
*X/98-100: .4X TO 1X BASIC JSY/80-125
*X/98-100: .3X TO .8X BASIC JSY/32-65
X's PRINT RUN 100 SER.#'d SETS
1 Matt Leinart 2.00 5.00
2 Larry Fitzgerald 2.50 6.00
3 Anquan Boldin 2.00 5.00
4 Edgerrin James/125 3.00 8.00
8 Willis McGahee/80 2.50 6.00
10 Mark Clayton/240 2.00 5.00
11 Trent Edwards 2.00 5.00
12 Marshawn Lynch 2.50 6.00
13 Lee Evans/50 4.00 10.00
14 Steve Smith/58 4.00 10.00
17 Brian Urlacher 3.00 8.00
18 Devin Hester 2.50 6.00
19 Rex Grossman 2.00 5.00
20 Carson Palmer 2.50 6.00
21 T.J. Houshmandzadeh 2.00 5.00
22 Rudi Johnson 2.00 5.00
23 Derek Anderson 2.00 5.00
25 Braylon Edwards 2.00 5.00
26 Tony Romo 2.50 6.00
27 Terrell Owens 2.50 6.00
28 Marion Barber 2.00 5.00
29 Jason Witten 2.50 6.00
30 Jay Cutler 2.00 5.00
32 Brandon Marshall 2.50 6.00
33 Jon Kitna/160 2.00 5.00
34 Roy Williams WR 2.00 5.00
36 Aaron Rodgers/100 10.00 25.00
37 Ryan Grant 2.50 6.00
38 Greg Jennings 2.00 5.00
41 Andre Johnson 2.50 6.00
42 Peyton Manning 10.00 20.00
43 Joseph Addai 2.00 5.00
44 Reggie Wayne 2.50 6.00
46 David Garrard/90 2.50 6.00
47 Fred Taylor 2.00 5.00
48 Maurice Jones-Drew 2.00 5.00
49 Brodie Croyle 2.50 6.00
50 Larry Johnson/145 2.00 5.00
51 Tony Gonzalez 2.50 6.00
53 Ronnie Brown 2.00 5.00
55 Tarvaris Jackson/200 2.00 5.00
56 Adrian Peterson 3.00 8.00
57 Chester Taylor 2.00 5.00
58 Tom Brady 10.00 25.00
59 Randy Moss 2.50 6.00
60 Laurence Maroney 2.50 6.00
61 Drew Brees/51 5.00 12.00
62 Reggie Bush/35 3.00 8.00
63 Marques Colston 2.00 5.00
64 Eli Manning 2.50 6.00
65 Plaxico Burress 2.00 5.00
66 Brandon Jacobs/32 3.00 8.00
68 Jerricho Cotchery/65 3.00 8.00
73 Donovan McNabb/45 4.00 10.00
74 Brian Westbrook 2.00 5.00
76 Ben Roethlisberger 3.00 8.00
77 Willie Parker 2.50 6.00
78 Hines Ward/83 3.00 8.00
79 Santonio Holmes 2.00 5.00
80 Philip Rivers/125 4.00 10.00
81 LaDainian Tomlinson 3.00 8.00
82 Antonio Gates 2.50 6.00
83 Alex Smith QB/230 2.50 6.00
84 Frank Gore 2.50 6.00
85 Vernon Davis/35 3.00 8.00
86 Matt Hasselbeck 2.00 5.00
88 Julius Jones 2.00 5.00
89 Marc Bulger 2.00 5.00
90 Steven Jackson 2.00 5.00
91 Torry Holt 2.50 6.00
92 Jeff Garcia 2.00 5.00
93 Cadillac Williams/230 2.50 6.00
95 Vince Young/240 2.00 5.00
96 LenDale White 2.00 5.00
97 Roydell Williams 2.00 5.00
98 Jason Campbell 2.00 5.00
99 Clinton Portis 2.00 5.00
100 Chris Cooley/110 2.50 6.00

2008 Donruss Gridiron Gear Jerseys Prime

PRIME PRINT RUN 2-50
2 Larry Fitzgerald 5.00 12.00
3 Anquan Boldin 4.00 10.00
4 Edgerrin James 5.00 12.00
8 Willis McGahee 4.00 10.00
10 Mark Clayton 4.00 10.00
11 Trent Edwards/40 4.00 10.00
12 Marshawn Lynch 5.00 12.00
13 Lee Evans 5.00 12.00
14 Steve Smith 5.00 12.00
16 Jake Delhomme 4.00 10.00
17 Brian Urlacher 6.00 15.00
19 Rex Grossman 4.00 10.00
20 Carson Palmer 5.00 12.00
21 T.J. Houshmandzadeh 4.00 10.00
22 Rudi Johnson 4.00 10.00
23 Derek Anderson 4.00 10.00
25 Braylon Edwards 4.00 10.00
26 Tony Romo 5.00 12.00
27 Terrell Owens 5.00 12.00
28 Marion Barber 4.00 10.00
29 Jason Witten 5.00 12.00
30 Jay Cutler 4.00 10.00
33 Jon Kitna 4.00 10.00
34 Roy Williams WR 4.00 10.00
35 Calvin Johnson 6.00 15.00
36 Aaron Rodgers 15.00 40.00
37 Ryan Grant/19 5.00 12.00
38 Greg Jennings 4.00 10.00
41 Andre Johnson 5.00 12.00
42 Peyton Manning/56 20.00 40.00
43 Joseph Addai 4.00 10.00
44 Reggie Wayne 5.00 12.00
45 Anthony Gonzalez 4.00 10.00
46 David Garrard 4.00 10.00
47 Fred Taylor 4.00 10.00
48 Maurice Jones-Drew 4.00 10.00
49 Brodie Croyle/25 5.00 12.00
50 Larry Johnson 4.00 10.00
51 Tony Gonzalez 5.00 12.00
53 Ronnie Brown 4.00 10.00
54 Ted Ginn Jr. 4.00 10.00
56 Adrian Peterson 6.00 15.00
57 Chester Taylor/45 4.00 10.00
58 Tom Brady 20.00 50.00
59 Randy Moss 5.00 12.00
60 Laurence Maroney 5.00 12.00
61 Drew Brees 6.00 15.00
62 Reggie Bush 4.00 10.00
63 Marques Colston 4.00 10.00
64 Eli Manning/25 5.00 12.00
65 Plaxico Burress 4.00 10.00
66 Brandon Jacobs 4.00 10.00
68 Jerricho Cotchery/45 4.00 10.00
69 Laveranues Coles 4.00 10.00
73 Donovan McNabb 5.00 12.00
74 Brian Westbrook 4.00 10.00
76 Ben Roethlisberger 6.00 15.00
77 Willie Parker 5.00 12.00
78 Hines Ward 5.00 12.00
79 Santonio Holmes 4.00 10.00
80 Philip Rivers/36 6.00 15.00
81 LaDainian Tomlinson 6.00 15.00
82 Antonio Gates 5.00 12.00
83 Alex Smith QB 5.00 12.00
84 Frank Gore 5.00 12.00
85 Vernon Davis 4.00 10.00
86 Matt Hasselbeck 4.00 10.00
87 Deion Branch 4.00 10.00
89 Marc Bulger 4.00 10.00
90 Steven Jackson 4.00 10.00
91 Torry Holt 5.00 12.00
92 Jeff Garcia/40 4.00 10.00
93 Cadillac Williams 5.00 12.00
95 Vince Young 4.00 10.00
96 LenDale White/45 4.00 10.00
97 Roydell Williams 4.00 10.00
98 Jason Campbell 4.00 10.00
99 Clinton Portis 4.00 10.00
100 Chris Cooley/25 4.00 10.00

2008 Donruss Gridiron Gear Next Generation Gold

GOLD PRINT RUN 500 SER.#'d SETS
*RED: .3X TO .8X GOLD/500
*SILVER/250: .5X TO 1.2X GOLD/500
SILVER PRINT RUN 250 SER.#'d SETS
*GOLD HOLO/100: .6X TO 1.5X GOLD/500
GOLD HOLO.PRINT RUN 100 SER.#'d SETS
*PLATINUM/25: 1X TO 2.5X GOLD/500
PLATINUM PRINT RUN 25 SER.#'d SETS
1 James Hardy .50 1.25
2 Malcolm Kelly .50 1.25
3 Jake Long .75 2.00
4 Matt Ryan 1.50 4.00
5 Dexter Jackson .75 2.00
6 Jerome Simpson .60 1.50
7 Jordy Nelson 1.50 4.00
8 Kevin O'Connell .50 1.25
9 Chad Henne .60 1.50
10 Mario Manningham .50 1.25
11 Jonathan Stewart .75 2.00
12 Devin Thomas .50 1.25
13 Limas Sweed .50 1.25
14 Kevin Smith .50 1.25
15 Glenn Dorsey .50 1.25
16 Darren McFadden .50 1.25
17 Dustin Keller .60 1.50
18 Earl Bennett .75 2.00
19 Joe Flacco 1.00 2.50
20 Ray Rice .50 1.25
21 Steve Slaton .50 1.25
22 Eddie Royal .50 1.25
23 Early Doucet .50 1.25
24 John David Booty .50 1.25
25 Jamaal Charles .75 2.00
26 Matt Forte .75 2.00
27 Felix Jones .50 1.25
28 Rashard Mendenhall .50 1.25
29 Chris Johnson .60 1.50
30 DeSean Jackson 1.00 2.50
31 Brian Brohm .50 1.25
32 Andre Caldwell .75 2.00
33 Donnie Avery .60 1.50
34 Harry Douglas .60 1.50
35 Calvin Johnson 1.25 3.00
36 Anthony Gonzalez .75 2.00
37 Zach Miller .75 2.00
38 James Jones .75 2.00
39 Ryan Grant 1.00 2.50
40 Kenny Watson .75 2.00

2008 Donruss Gridiron Gear Next Generation Jerseys

STATED PRINT RUN 250 SER.#'d SETS
*PRIME/50: .8X TO 2X BASIC JSY/250
PRIME PRINT RUN 2-50
*COMBO PRIME/20-50: .8X TO 2X JSY/250
COMBO PRIME PRINT RUN 10-50
*JUMBO/19-50: .6X TO 1.5X BASIC JSY/250
JUMBO SWATCH PRINT RUN 19-50
*JUMBO PRIME/25: .8X TO 2X BASIC JSY/250
JUMBO PRIME PRINT RUN 1-25
1 James Hardy 1.50 4.00
2 Malcolm Kelly 1.50 4.00
3 Jake Long 2.50 6.00
4 Matt Ryan 5.00 12.00
5 Dexter Jackson 2.50 6.00
6 Jerome Simpson 2.00 5.00
7 Jordy Nelson 5.00 12.00
8 Kevin O'Connell 1.50 4.00
9 Chad Henne 2.00 5.00
10 Mario Manningham 1.50 4.00
11 Jonathan Stewart 2.50 6.00
12 Devin Thomas 1.50 4.00
13 Limas Sweed 1.50 4.00
14 Kevin Smith 1.50 4.00
15 Glenn Dorsey 1.50 4.00
16 Darren McFadden 1.50 4.00
17 Dustin Keller 2.00 5.00
18 Earl Bennett 2.50 6.00
19 Joe Flacco 3.00 8.00
20 Ray Rice 1.50 4.00
21 Steve Slaton 1.50 4.00
22 Eddie Royal 1.50 4.00
23 Early Doucet 1.50 4.00
24 John David Booty 1.50 4.00
25 Jamaal Charles 2.50 6.00
26 Matt Forte 2.50 6.00
27 Felix Jones 1.50 4.00
28 Rashard Mendenhall 1.50 4.00
29 Chris Johnson 2.00 5.00
30 DeSean Jackson 3.00 8.00
31 Brian Brohm 1.50 4.00
32 Andre Caldwell 1.50 4.00
33 Donnie Avery 2.00 5.00
34 Harry Douglas 2.00 5.00
38 James Jones 2.00 5.00
39 Ryan Grant 2.50 6.00

2008 Donruss Gridiron Gear Next Generation Jerseys Autographs

STATED PRINT RUN 50 SER.#'d SETS
*PRIME/25: .5X TO 1.2X BASIC JSY AU/50
PRIME PRINT RUN 1-25

1 James Hardy 4.00 10.00
2 Malcolm Kelly 4.00 10.00
3 Jake Long 6.00 15.00
4 Matt Ryan 40.00 80.00
5 Dexter Jackson 6.00 15.00
6 Jerome Simpson 5.00 12.00
7 Jordy Nelson 12.00 30.00
8 Kevin O'Connell 4.00 10.00
9 Chad Henne 5.00 12.00
10 Mario Manningham 4.00 10.00
11 Jonathan Stewart 6.00 15.00
12 Devin Thomas 4.00 10.00
13 Limas Sweed 4.00 10.00
14 Kevin Smith
16 Darren McFadden 4.00 10.00
17 Dustin Keller 5.00 12.00
18 Earl Bennett 6.00 15.00
19 Joe Flacco 8.00 20.00
20 Ray Rice 4.00 10.00
21 Steve Slaton 4.00 10.00
22 Eddie Royal 4.00 10.00
23 Early Doucet 4.00 10.00
24 John David Booty 4.00 10.00
25 Jamaal Charles 6.00 15.00
26 Matt Forte 25.00 50.00
27 Felix Jones 4.00 10.00
28 Rashard Mendenhall 4.00 10.00
29 Chris Johnson 5.00 12.00
30 DeSean Jackson 12.00 30.00
31 Brian Brohm 4.00 10.00
32 Andre Caldwell 4.00 10.00
33 Donnie Avery 5.00 12.00
38 James Jones/25 6.00 15.00
39 Ryan Grant/25 25.00 50.00

2008 Donruss Gridiron Gear NFL Gridiron Rookie Signatures
STATED PRINT RUN 40 SER.#'d SETS
1 Chris Johnson 6.00 15.00
2 Darren McFadden 5.00 12.00
3 DeSean Jackson 10.00 25.00
4 Eddie Royal 5.00 12.00
5 Dustin Keller 6.00 15.00
6 Jamaal Charles 8.00 20.00
7 Jerome Simpson 6.00 15.00
8 John David Booty 5.00 12.00
9 Jordy Nelson 15.00 40.00
10 Kevin Smith 5.00 12.00
11 Malcolm Kelly 5.00 12.00
12 Matt Forte 15.00 40.00
13 Rashard Mendenhall 5.00 12.00
14 Steve Slaton 5.00 12.00
15 Dexter Jackson 8.00 20.00
16 Andre Caldwell 5.00 12.00
17 Joe Flacco 10.00 25.00
18 Brian Brohm 5.00 12.00
19 Felix Jones 5.00 12.00
20 Limas Sweed 5.00 12.00
21 Early Doucet 5.00 12.00
22 Donnie Avery 6.00 15.00
23 Chad Henne 6.00 15.00
24 Glenn Dorsey 5.00 12.00
25 Jonathan Stewart 8.00 20.00
26 Ray Rice 5.00 12.00
27 Matt Ryan 25.00 60.00
28 Mario Manningham 5.00 12.00
29 Kevin O'Connell 5.00 12.00
30 James Hardy 5.00 12.00
31 Devin Thomas 5.00 12.00
32 Harry Douglas 6.00 15.00
33 Jake Long 8.00 20.00
34 Earl Bennett 8.00 20.00

2008 Donruss Gridiron Gear NFL Teams Rookie Signatures
STATED PRINT RUN 30 SER.#'d SETS
1 Devin Thomas 5.00 12.00
2 Dexter Jackson 8.00 20.00
3 Donnie Avery 6.00 15.00
4 Dustin Keller 6.00 15.00
5 Earl Bennett 8.00 20.00
7 Eddie Royal 5.00 12.00
8 Felix Jones 5.00 12.00
9 Glenn Dorsey EXCH
10 Andre Caldwell 5.00 12.00
11 Brian Brohm 5.00 12.00
12 Chad Henne 6.00 15.00
13 Chris Johnson 6.00 15.00
14 Darren McFadden 5.00 12.00
15 Jamaal Charles 8.00 20.00
16 James Hardy 5.00 12.00
17 Jerome Simpson 6.00 15.00
18 Mario Manningham 5.00 12.00
19 Matt Forte 25.00 60.00
20 Matt Ryan 60.00 120.00
21 Rashard Mendenhall 5.00 12.00
22 Ray Rice 5.00 12.00
23 Steve Slaton 5.00 12.00
24 Jake Long 8.00 20.00
25 Chris Long 6.00 15.00
26 John David Booty 5.00 12.00
27 Jonathan Stewart 8.00 20.00
28 Jordy Nelson 15.00 40.00
29 Kevin O'Connell 5.00 12.00
30 Kevin Smith 5.00 12.00
31 Limas Sweed 5.00 12.00
32 Malcolm Kelly 5.00 12.00
33 Joe Flacco 10.00 25.00
34 Harry Douglas EXCH
35 DeSean Jackson 20.00 50.00

2008 Donruss Gridiron Gear NFL Teams Veteran Signatures
STATED PRINT RUN 25 SER.#'d SETS
1 Peyton Manning 60.00 120.00
2 Ben Roethlisberger 60.00 120.00
3 Braylon Edwards 8.00 20.00
4 Donald Driver 10.00 25.00
5 Frank Gore 10.00 25.00
7 Reggie Wayne 12.00 30.00
8 Roddy White 8.00 20.00
9 T.J. Houshmandzadeh 8.00 20.00
10 Trent Edwards 8.00 20.00
11 Vincent Jackson 8.00 20.00
12 Willie Parker 10.00 25.00
13 Ryan Grant 20.00 40.00
14 Tony Romo 40.00 100.00
15 Brandon Jacobs 8.00 20.00
16 Josh Cribbs 20.00 40.00
17 DeAngelo Williams 8.00 20.00
18 Drew Brees 40.00 80.00
19 Greg Lewis 8.00 20.00
21 Justin Fargas 8.00 20.00
22 Larry Johnson 8.00 20.00
23 Ladell Betts 8.00 20.00
24 Marques Colston 8.00 20.00
25 Patrick Willis 10.00 25.00
26 Santonio Holmes 8.00 20.00
27 Selvin Young 8.00 20.00
28 Sidney Rice 8.00 20.00
29 Wes Welker 25.00 60.00
30 Zach Miller 8.00 20.00
31 Adrian Peterson 90.00 150.00

2008 Donruss Gridiron Gear Performers Gold
GOLD PRINT RUN 500 SER.#'d SETS
*RED: .3X TO .8X GOLD/500
*SILVER/250: .5X TO 1.2X GOLD/500
SILVER PRINT RUN 250 SER.#'d SETS
*GOLD HOLO/100: .6X TO 1.5X GOLD/500
GOLD HOLO PRINT RUN 100 SER.#'d SETS
*PLATINUM/25: 1X TO 2.5X GOLD/500
PLATINUM PRINT RUN 25 SER.#'d SETS
1 Alex Karras 1.00 2.50
2 Barry Sanders 2.00 5.00
3 Bert Jones .75 2.00
4 Bill Dudley .75 2.00
5 Billy Howton .75 2.00
6 Dante Lavelli .75 2.00
7 Bob Griese 1.25 3.00
8 Brett Favre 2.50 6.00
9 Carl Eller .75 2.00
10 Charley Trippi .75 2.00
11 Cliff Harris .75 2.00
12 Dan Marino 2.50 6.00
13 Danny White .75 2.00
14 Daryl Johnston 1.00 2.50
15 Daryle Lamonica 1.00 2.50
16 Del Shofner .75 2.00
17 Don Perkins .75 2.00
18 Fred Dryer .75 2.00
19 Fred Williamson .75 2.00
20 Gary Collins .75 2.00
21 Cris Collinsworth 1.00 2.50
22 Jan Stenerud .75 2.00
23 Joe Montana 4.00 10.00
24 John Riggins 1.00 2.50
25 Ken Stabler 1.25 3.00
26 Lance Alworth 1.00 2.50
27 Len Dawson 1.25 3.00
28 Lenny Moore .75 2.00
29 Leroy Kelly 1.00 2.50
30 Lydell Mitchell .75 2.00
31 Marcus Allen 1.25 3.00
32 Mark Duper .75 2.00
33 Mike Curtis .75 2.00
34 Ozzie Newsome 1.00 2.50
35 Paul Warfield 1.00 2.50
36 Pete Retzlaff .75 2.00
37 Randall Cunningham 1.00 2.50
38 Raymond Berry 1.00 2.50
39 Reggie White 1.25 3.00
40 Rosey Grier .75 2.00
41 Sammy Baugh 1.25 3.00
42 Steve Young 1.50 4.00
43 Ted Hendricks .75 2.00
44 Tommy McDonald 1.00 2.50
45 Troy Aikman 1.50 4.00
46 William Perry .75 2.00
47 Willie Davis .75 2.00
48 Willie Wood .75 2.00
49 Y.A. Tittle 1.25 3.00
50 Yale Lary .75 2.00

2008 Donruss Gridiron Gear Performers Autographs
STATED PRINT RUN 1-250
SERIAL #'d TO 1 NOT PRICED
1 Alex Karras/25 12.00 30.00
3 Bert Jones/50 8.00 20.00
4 Bill Dudley/96 8.00 20.00
5 Billy Howton/250 8.00 20.00
6 Dante Lavelli/50 8.00 20.00
10 Charley Trippi/100 8.00 20.00
15 Daryle Lamonica/50 10.00 25.00
16 Del Shofner/250 8.00 20.00
17 Don Perkins/100 8.00 20.00
19 Fred Williamson/100 20.00 40.00
20 Gary Collins/175 8.00 20.00
21 Cris Collinsworth/25 12.00 30.00
22 Jan Stenerud/100 8.00 20.00
28 Lenny Moore/100 8.00 20.00
29 Leroy Kelly/100 10.00 25.00
30 Lydell Mitchell/250 8.00 20.00
33 Mike Curtis/100 8.00 20.00
34 Ozzie Newsome/25 12.00 30.00
36 Pete Retzlaff/100 8.00 20.00
37 Randall Cunningham/75 15.00 40.00
38 Raymond Berry/100 10.00 25.00
40 Rosey Grier/75 8.00 20.00
44 Tommy McDonald/25 12.00 30.00
46 William Perry/150 8.00 20.00
47 Willie Davis/100 12.00 30.00
48 Willie Wood/100 12.00 30.00
50 Yale Lary/50 8.00 20.00

2008 Donruss Gridiron Gear Performers Jerseys
STATED PRINT RUN 250 SER.#'d SETS
*PRIME/50: .6X TO 1.5X BASIC JSY
*PRIME/15-25: .8X TO 2X BASIC JSY
PRIME PRINT RUN 5-50
1 Alex Karras 2.50 6.00
3 Bert Jones 2.00 5.00
8 Brett Favre 6.00 15.00
11 Cliff Harris/240 2.00 5.00
12 Dan Marino 6.00 15.00
13 Danny White 2.00 5.00
15 Daryle Lamonica/175 2.50 6.00
18 Fred Dryer 2.00 5.00
21 Cris Collinsworth/150 2.50 6.00
23 Joe Montana 10.00 25.00
24 John Riggins 2.50 6.00
25 Ken Stabler/90 3.00 8.00
28 Lenny Moore 2.00 5.00
31 Marcus Allen 3.00 8.00
32 Mark Duper/145 2.00 5.00
34 Ozzie Newsome 2.50 6.00
35 Paul Warfield 2.50 6.00
38 Raymond Berry 2.50 6.00
39 Reggie White 6.00 15.00
40 Rosey Grier 2.00 5.00
41 Sammy Baugh 8.00 20.00
42 Steve Young 4.00 10.00
43 Ted Hendricks 2.00 5.00
44 Tommy McDonald 2.50 6.00
45 Troy Aikman 4.00 10.00

2008 Donruss Gridiron Gear Performers Jerseys Autographs
STATED PRINT RUN 2-50
*PRIME/25: .6X TO 1.5X BASE JSY/50
*PRIME/25: .5X TO 1.2X BASE JSY/25
PRIME PRINT RUN 2-25
SERIAL #'d UNDER 25 NOT PRICED
1 Alex Karras/50 12.00 30.00
2 Barry Sanders/25 60.00 120.00
3 Bert Jones/25 12.00 30.00
7 Bob Griese/50 15.00 40.00
11 Cliff Harris/50 10.00 25.00
13 Danny White/25 15.00 40.00
15 Daryle Lamonica/25 15.00 40.00
18 Fred Dryer/25 12.00 30.00
23 Joe Montana/25 60.00 120.00
24 John Riggins/50 15.00 40.00
25 Ken Stabler/25 20.00 50.00
28 Lenny Moore/50 10.00 25.00
31 Marcus Allen/25 20.00 50.00
32 Mark Duper/25 12.00 30.00
34 Ozzie Newsome/25 15.00 40.00
35 Paul Warfield/25 15.00 40.00
37 Randall Cunningham/25 40.00 80.00
38 Raymond Berry/50 12.00 30.00
40 Rosey Grier/50 10.00 25.00
42 Steve Young/25 30.00 80.00
43 Ted Hendricks/25 12.00 30.00
44 Tommy McDonald/25 15.00 40.00

2008 Donruss Gridiron Gear Performers Jerseys Combos
*COMBOS/50-100: .5X TO 1.2X BASIC JSY
COMBOS PRINT RUN 1-100
*COMBO PRIME/50: .6X TO 1.5X BASIC JSY
*COMBO PRIME/25-30: .8X TO 2X BASIC JSY
COMBO PRIME PRINT RUN 5-50

2008 Donruss Gridiron Gear Performers Jerseys Combos Autographs
STATED PRINT RUN 10-25
*PRIME/15-25: .4X TO 1X JSY COMBO/25
PRIME PRINT RUN 1-25
1 Alex Karras 15.00 40.00
2 Barry Sanders/15 60.00 120.00
3 Bert Jones 12.00 30.00
7 Bob Griese 20.00 50.00
8 Brett Favre/15 125.00 200.00
11 Cliff Harris 12.00 30.00
13 Danny White 12.00 30.00
14 Daryl Johnston 20.00 50.00
15 Daryle Lamonica 15.00 40.00
18 Fred Dryer 12.00 30.00
23 Joe Montana/19 60.00 120.00
24 John Riggins 20.00 50.00
25 Ken Stabler 20.00 50.00
28 Lenny Moore 12.00 30.00
31 Marcus Allen 20.00 50.00
32 Mark Duper 12.00 30.00
34 Ozzie Newsome 15.00 40.00
37 Randall Cunningham 40.00 80.00
38 Raymond Berry 15.00 40.00
40 Rosey Grier 12.00 30.00
42 Steve Young 40.00 80.00
43 Ted Hendricks/15 15.00 40.00
44 Tommy McDonald 15.00 40.00
49 Y.A. Tittle 20.00 50.00

2008 Donruss Gridiron Gear Performers Jerseys Jumbo Swatch
*JUMBO/50: .6X TO 1.5X BASIC JSY
*JUMBO/15-25: .8X TO 2X BASIC JSY
JUMBO PRINT RUN 5-50
*JUMBO PRIME/25: 1X TO 2.5X BASIC JSY
JUMBO PRIME PRINT RUN 1-25

2008 Donruss Gridiron Gear Plates and Patches
STATED PRINT RUN 100 SER.#'d SETS
1 Adrian Peterson 6.00 15.00
2 Marshawn Lynch 5.00 12.00
3 Antonio Gates 5.00 12.00
4 Fred Taylor 4.00 10.00
5 Tony Romo 5.00 12.00
6 Joseph Addai 4.00 10.00
7 Tony Gonzalez 5.00 12.00
8 Torry Holt 5.00 12.00
9 Brandon Jacobs 4.00 10.00
10 Brian Westbrook 4.00 10.00
11 Randy Moss 5.00 12.00
12 Marques Colston 4.00 10.00
13 Willis McGahee 4.00 10.00
14 Reggie Wayne 5.00 12.00
15 Clinton Portis 4.00 10.00

2008 Donruss Gridiron Gear Plates and Patches Autographs
STATED PRINT RUN 25 SER.#'d SETS
1 Adrian Peterson 60.00 120.00
4 Fred Taylor 12.00 30.00
5 Tony Romo 75.00 150.00
9 Brandon Jacobs 12.00 30.00
10 Brian Westbrook 12.00 30.00
12 Marques Colston 12.00 30.00
14 Reggie Wayne 15.00 40.00

2008 Donruss Gridiron Gear Playbook Gold
GOLD PRINT RUN 500 SER.#'d SETS
*RED: .3X TO .8X GOLD/500
*SILVER/250: .5X TO 1.2X GOLD/500
SILVER PRINT RUN 250 SER.#'d SETS
*GOLD HOLO/100: .6X TO 1.5X GOLD/500
GOLD HOLO PRINT RUN 100 SER.#'d SETS
*PLATINUM/25: 1X TO 2.5X GOLD/500
PLATINUM PRINT RUN 25 SER.#'d SETS
1 Adrian Peterson .75 2.00
2 Peyton Manning 2.00 5.00
3 Tom Brady 2.50 6.00
4 Tony Romo .60 1.50
5 Carson Palmer .60 1.50
6 Torry Holt .60 1.50
7 David Garrard .50 1.25
8 Braylon Edwards .50 1.25
9 Eli Manning .60 1.50
10 Willie Parker .60 1.50
11 T.J. Houshmandzadeh .50 1.25
12 Jay Cutler .50 1.25
13 Steve Smith .60 1.50
14 Larry Fitzgerald .60 1.50
15 Plaxico Burress .50 1.25
16 Greg Jennings .50 1.25
17 Ben Roethlisberger .75 2.00
18 Reggie Wayne .60 1.50
19 LaDainian Tomlinson .75 2.00
20 Santonio Holmes .50 1.25
21 Philip Rivers .75 2.00
22 Marshawn Lynch .60 1.50
23 Brian Westbrook .50 1.25
24 Maurice Jones-Drew .50 1.25
25 Edgerrin James .60 1.50

2008 Donruss Gridiron Gear Playbook Jerseys O's
O's PRINT RUN 125-250
*X's/90-250: .4X TO 1X O'S/125-250
X's STATED PRINT RUN 9-250
*PATCH/25: .8X TO 2X O'S/125-250
PATCHES STATED PRINT RUN 25
1 Adrian Peterson 3.00 8.00
2 Peyton Manning 8.00 20.00
3 Tom Brady 10.00 25.00
4 Tony Romo 2.50 6.00
5 Carson Palmer 2.50 6.00
6 Torry Holt 2.50 6.00
7 David Garrard 2.00 5.00
8 Braylon Edwards 2.00 5.00
9 Eli Manning 2.50 6.00
10 Willie Parker 2.50 6.00
11 T.J. Houshmandzadeh 2.00 5.00
12 Jay Cutler 2.00 5.00
13 Steve Smith 2.50 6.00
14 Larry Fitzgerald 2.50 6.00
15 Plaxico Burress 2.00 5.00
16 Greg Jennings 2.00 5.00
17 Ben Roethlisberger 3.00 8.00
18 Reggie Wayne 2.50 6.00
19 LaDainian Tomlinson 3.00 8.00
20 Santonio Holmes 2.00 5.00
21 Philip Rivers 3.00 8.00
22 Marshawn Lynch 2.50 6.00
23 Brian Westbrook/125 2.00 5.00
24 Maurice Jones-Drew 2.00 5.00
25 Edgerrin James 2.50 6.00

2008 Donruss Gridiron Gear Player Timeline Gold
GOLD PRINT RUN 500 SER.#'d SETS
*RED: .3X TO .8X GOLD/500
*SILVER/250: .5X TO 1.2X GOLD/500
SILVER PRINT RUN 250 SER.#'d SETS
*GOLD HOLO/100: .6X TO 1.5X GOLD/500
GOLD HOLO PRINT RUN 100 SER.#'d SETS
*PLATINUM/25: 1X TO 2.5X GOLD/500
PLATINUM PRINT RUN 25 SER.#'d SETS
1 Reggie White .75 2.00
2 Joe Montana 2.50 6.00
3 Warren Moon .75 2.00
4 John Riggins .60 1.50
5 Randy Moss .60 1.50
6 Julius Jones .50 1.25
7 Isaac Bruce .75 2.00
8 Alge Crumpler .50 1.25
9 Bernard Berrian .50 1.25
10 Clinton Portis .50 1.25
11 Brandon Stokley .50 1.25
12 Zach Thomas .60 1.50
13 Santana Moss .50 1.25
14 Ahman Green .60 1.50
15 Jamal Lewis .60 1.50
16 Plaxico Burress .50 1.25
17 Derrick Mason .50 1.25
18 Nate Burleson .50 1.25
19 DeShaun Foster .50 1.25
20 Michael Turner .50 1.25
21 Warrick Dunn .50 1.25
22 Jeff Garcia .50 1.25
23 Drew Brees .75 2.00
24 Darren McFadden .50 1.25
25 Willis McGahee .50 1.25

2008 Donruss Gridiron Gear Player Timeline Autographs
STATED PRINT RUN 1-100
4 John Riggins/25 15.00 40.00
9 Bernard Berrian/53 8.00 20.00
17 Derrick Mason/100 8.00 20.00
20 Michael Turner/25 8.00 20.00

2008 Donruss Gridiron Gear Player Timeline Jerseys Prime
PRIME PRINT RUN 25-50
*BASIC JSY/70-250: .2X TO .5X PRIME/25-50
*BASIC JSY/25: .3X TO .8X PRIME/25-50
BASIC JERSEY PRINT RUN 2-250
*COMBO JSY/60-100: .3X TO .8X PRIME/25-50
*COMBO JSY/20-30: .4X TO 1X PRIME/25-50
COMBO JERSEY PRINT RUN 10-100
*COMBO JSY PRIME/25-50: .4X TO 1X PRIME
COMBO JERSEY PRIME PRINT RUN 1-50
*JUMBO JSY/25-50: .3X TO .8X PRIME
JUMBO JERSEY PRINT RUN 10-50
*JUMBO PRIME/20-25: .5X TO 1.2X PRIME
JUMBO PRIME PRINT RUN 12-25
1 Reggie White/25 12.00 30.00
2 Joe Montana 25.00 60.00
3 Warren Moon 8.00 20.00
4 John Riggins/25 6.00 15.00
5 Randy Moss 5.00 12.00
6 Julius Jones 4.00 10.00
7 Isaac Bruce 6.00 15.00
8 Alge Crumpler 4.00 10.00
9 Bernard Berrian 4.00 10.00
10 Clinton Portis/30 4.00 10.00
11 Brandon Stokley/25 4.00 10.00
12 Zach Thomas 5.00 12.00
13 Santana Moss 4.00 10.00
14 Ahman Green 5.00 12.00
15 Jamal Lewis 5.00 12.00
16 Plaxico Burress 4.00 10.00
17 Derrick Mason 4.00 10.00
18 Nate Burleson 4.00 10.00
19 DeShaun Foster 4.00 10.00
20 Michael Turner 4.00 10.00
21 Warrick Dunn 4.00 10.00
22 Jeff Garcia 4.00 10.00
23 Drew Brees 6.00 15.00
24 Darren McFadden 2.00 5.00
25 Willis McGahee 4.00 10.00

2008 Donruss Gridiron Gear Player Timeline Jerseys Autographs
BASIC JSY AUTO PRINT RUN 10-50
*PRIME/15-25: .5X TO 1.2X BASIC JSY AU
PRIME PRINT RUN 3-25
*JSY COMBO AU/20-25: .4X TO 1X
JSY COMBO AUTO PRINT RUN 5-25
UNPRICED COMBO AU PRIME PRINT RUN 15-20
SERIAL #'d UNDER 25 NOT PRICED
2 Joe Montana/15 75.00 150.00
4 John Riggins/50 15.00 40.00
9 Bernard Berrian/25 12.00 30.00
17 Derrick Mason/25 12.00 30.00
20 Michael Turner/50 10.00 25.00
24 Darren McFadden/25 6.00 15.00

2008 Donruss Gridiron Gear Rivals Gold
GOLD PRINT RUN 500 SER.#'d SETS
*RED: .3X TO .8X GOLD/500
*SILVER/250: .5X TO 1.2X GOLD/500
SILVER PRINT RUN 250 SER.#'d SETS
*GOLD HOLO/100: .6X TO 1.5X GOLD/500
GOLD HOLO PRINT RUN 100 SER.#'d SETS
*PLATINUM/25: 1X TO 2.5X GOLD/500
PLATINUM PRINT RUN 25 SER.#'d SETS
1 R.Moss/T.Owens .75 2.00
2 P.Manning/T.Brady 3.00 8.00
3 E.Manning/T.Romo .75 2.00
4 L.Maroney/S.Merriman .75 2.00
5 C.Palmer/R.Lewis 1.00 2.50
6 T.Aikman/S.Young 1.25 3.00
7 B.Favre/M.Strahan 2.00 5.00
8 T.Houshmandzadeh/B.Edwards .60 1.50
9 C.Portis/M.Barber .60 1.50
10 J.Cutler/T.Gonzalez .75 2.00

2008 Donruss Gridiron Gear Rivals Jerseys
STATED PRINT RUN 10-100
*PRIME/25: .8X TO 2X BASIC DUAL
PRIME PRINT RUN 2-25
1 R.Moss/T.Owens 4.00 10.00
3 E.Manning/T.Romo/65 4.00 10.00
4 L.Maroney/S.Merriman 4.00 10.00
5 C.Palmer/R.Lewis/50 5.00 12.00
6 T.Aikman/S.Young 10.00 25.00
7 B.Favre/M.Strahan 10.00 25.00
8 T.Houshmandzadeh/B.Edwards 3.00 8.00
9 C.Portis/M.Barber 3.00 8.00
10 J.Cutler/T.Gonzalez 4.00 10.00

2008 Donruss Gridiron Gear Rookie Gridiron Gems Jerseys
BASIC JSY PRINT RUN 50 SER.#'d SETS
*COMBO/50: .5X TO 1.2X BASIC JSY/50
*COMBO PRIME/25: .6X TO 1.5X BASIC JSY/50
*JUMBO/50: .5X TO 1.2X BASIC JSY/50
*JUMBO PRIME/25: .8X TO 2X BASIC JSY/50
*PRIME/50: .5X TO 1.2X BASIC JSY/50
*RETAIL RED/50: .4X TO 1X BASIC JSY/50
*TRIOS/50: .6X TO 1.5X BASIC JSY/50
*TRIOS PRIME/25: .8X TO 2X BASIC JSY/50
201 Andre Caldwell 1.50 4.00
202 Brian Brohm 1.50 4.00
203 Chad Henne 2.00 5.00
204 Chris Johnson 2.00 5.00
205 Darren McFadden 1.50 4.00
206 DeSean Jackson 3.00 8.00
207 Devin Thomas 1.50 4.00
208 Dexter Jackson 2.50 6.00
209 Donnie Avery 2.00 5.00
210 Dustin Keller 2.00 5.00
211 Earl Bennett 2.50 6.00
212 Early Doucet 1.50 4.00
213 Eddie Royal 1.50 4.00
214 Felix Jones 1.50 4.00
215 Glenn Dorsey 1.50 4.00
216 Harry Douglas 2.00 5.00
217 Jamaal Charles 2.50 6.00
218 James Hardy 1.50 4.00
219 Jerome Simpson 2.00 5.00
220 Joe Flacco 3.00 8.00
221 John David Booty 1.50 4.00
222 Jonathan Stewart 2.50 6.00
223 Jordy Nelson 5.00 12.00
224 Kevin O'Connell 1.50 4.00
225 Kevin Smith 1.50 4.00
226 Limas Sweed 1.50 4.00
227 Malcolm Kelly 1.50 4.00
228 Mario Manningham 1.50 4.00
229 Matt Forte 5.00 12.00
230 Matt Ryan 8.00 20.00
231 Rashard Mendenhall 1.50 4.00
232 Ray Rice 1.50 4.00
233 Steve Slaton 1.50 4.00
234 Jake Long 2.50 6.00

2008 Donruss Gridiron Gear Rookie Gridiron Gems Jerseys Autographs Prime
*PRIME JSY AU/50: .4X TO 1X BASE JSY AU
STATED PRINT RUN 50 SER.#'d SETS

2008 Donruss Gridiron Gear Rookie Gridiron Gems Jerseys Combos Autographs Prime
*PRIME JSY AU/50: .4X TO 1X BASE JSY AU
STATED PRINT RUN 50 SER.#'d SETS

2008 Donruss Gridiron Gear Rookie Gridiron Gems Jerseys Trios Autographs Prime
*TRIO JSY AU/50: .5X TO 1.2X BASE JSY AU
STATED PRINT RUN 50 SER.#'d SETS

2009 Donruss Gridiron Gear
COMP.SET w/o RC's (100) 10.00 25.00
101-200 ROOKIE PRINT RUN 999
201-234 ROOKIE AU PRINT RUN 98-100
1 Aaron Rodgers .60 1.50
2 Adrian Peterson .30 .75
3 Andre Johnson .25 .60
4 Anthony Gonzalez .20 .50
5 Antonio Bryant .20 .50
6 Antonio Gates .25 .60
7 Ben Roethlisberger .30 .75
8 Bernard Berrian .20 .50
9 Brady Quinn .20 .50
10 Brandon Jacobs .20 .50
11 Brandon Marshall .25 .60
12 Braylon Edwards .20 .50
13 Brian Urlacher .30 .75
14 Brian Westbrook .20 .50
15 Calvin Johnson .30 .75
16 Carson Palmer .25 .60
17 Chad Ochocinco .20 .50
18 Chad Pennington .20 .50
19 Chris Cooley .20 .50
20 Chris Johnson .20 .50
21 Clinton Portis .20 .50
22 Darren McFadden .30 .75
23 Daunte Culpepper .25 .60
24 David Garrard .20 .50
25 DeAngelo Williams .20 .50
26 Derrick Ward .20 .50
27 DeSean Jackson .25 .60
28 Donnie Avery .20 .50
29 Donovan McNabb .25 .60
30 Drew Brees .30 .75
31 Dwayne Bowe .25 .60
32 Eddie Royal .20 .50
33 Eli Manning .25 .60
34 Frank Gore .25 .60
35 Greg Olsen .25 .60
36 Greg Jennings .20 .50
37 Jake Delhomme .20 .50
38 Jamal Lewis .25 .60
39 JaMarcus Russell .20 .50
40 Jason Campbell .20 .50
41 Jason Witten .25 .60
42 Jay Cutler .20 .50
43 Jerricho Cotchery .20 .50
44 Joe Flacco .25 .60
45 Joseph Addai .20 .50
46 Josh Morgan .20 .50
47 Julius Jones .20 .50
48 Kellen Winslow Jr. .20 .50
49 Kerry Collins .20 .50
50 Kevin Boss .20 .50
51 Kevin Smith .20 .50
52 Kurt Warner .25 .60
53 Kyle Orton .20 .50
54 LaDainian Tomlinson .30 .75
55 Larry Fitzgerald .25 .60
56 Larry Johnson .20 .50
57 Laurence Maroney .25 .60
58 Laveranues Coles .20 .50
59 Lee Evans .25 .60
60 LenDale White .20 .50
61 Leon Washington .20 .50
62 Marc Bulger .20 .50
63 Marion Barber .25 .60
64 Marques Colston .20 .50
65 Marshawn Lynch .25 .60
66 Matt Cassel .20 .50
67 Matt Forte .20 .50
68 Matt Hasselbeck .20 .50
69 Matt Ryan .25 .60
70 Matt Schaub .20 .50
71 Maurice Jones-Drew .20 .50
72 Michael Turner .20 .50
73 Peyton Manning .75 2.00
74 Philip Rivers .30 .75
75 Randy Moss .25 .60
76 Ray Rice .20 .50
77 Reggie Bush .20 .50
78 Reggie Wayne .25 .60
79 Ricky Williams .25 .60
80 Roddy White .20 .50
81 Ronnie Brown .20 .50
82 Ryan Grant .25 .60
83 Santonio Holmes .20 .50
84 Steve Breaston .25 .60
85 Steve Slaton .20 .50
86 Steve Smith .25 .60
87 Steven Jackson .20 .50
88 T.J. Houshmandzadeh .20 .50
89 Brett Favre 5.00 12.00
90 Terrell Owens .25 .60
91 Tom Brady 1.00 2.50
92 Tony Gonzalez .25 .60
93 Tony Romo .25 .60
94 Torry Holt .25 .60
95 Vernon Davis .20 .50
96 Vincent Jackson .20 .50
97 Wes Welker .25 .60
98 Willie Parker .20 .50
99 Willis McGahee .20 .50
100 Zach Miller .20 .50
101 Aaron Brown RC 1.50 4.00
102 Aaron Kelly RC 1.25 3.00
103 Aaron Maybin RC 1.50 4.00
104 Alex Mack RC 1.25 3.00
105 Alphonso Smith RC 1.25 3.00
106 Andre Smith RC 1.25 3.00
107 Anthony Hill RC 1.25 3.00
108 Arian Foster RC 3.00 8.00
109 Austin Collie RC 1.25 3.00
110 B.J. Raji RC 1.50 4.00
111 Bear Pascoe RC 1.50 4.00
112 Bernard Scott RC 2.00 5.00
113 Bradley Fletcher RC 1.25 3.00
114 Brandon Gibson RC 1.50 4.00
115 Brandon Tate RC 1.50 4.00
116 Brian Cushing RC 1.25 3.00
117 Brian Hartline RC 2.00 5.00
118 Brian Orakpo RC 1.50 4.00
119 Brooks Foster RC 1.25 3.00
120 Cameron Morrah RC 1.25 3.00
121 Cedric Peerman RC 1.25 3.00
122 Chase Coffman RC 1.25 3.00
123 Chase Daniel RC 1.50 4.00
124 Chris Ogbonnaya RC 1.50 4.00
125 Clay Matthews RC 5.00 12.00
126 Clint Sintim RC 1.25 3.00
127 Cody Brown RC 1.25 3.00
128 Connor Barwin RC 1.50 4.00
129 Cornelius Ingram RC 1.25 3.00
130 Curtis Painter RC 1.25 3.00
131 Dan Gronkowski RC 1.25 3.00
132 Darcel McBath RC 1.25 3.00
133 Darius Butler RC 1.50 4.00
134 David Johnson RC 1.50 4.00
135 David Veikune RC 1.50 4.00
136 Davon Drew RC 1.25 3.00
137 DeAndre Levy RC 1.50 4.00
138 Demetrius Byrd RC 1.50 4.00
139 Derek Cox RC 2.00 5.00
140 Devin Moore RC 1.25 3.00
141 Dominique Edison RC 1.25 3.00
142 Eddie Williams RC 1.50 4.00
143 Eric Wood RC 1.25 3.00
144 Eugene Monroe RC 1.25 3.00
145 Evander Hood RC 2.00 5.00
146 Everette Brown RC 1.25 3.00
147 Frank Summers RC 2.00 5.00
148 Fui Vakapuna RC 1.50 4.00
149 Gartrell Johnson RC 1.25 3.00
150 Hunter Cantwell RC 1.25 3.00
151 James Casey RC 1.50 4.00
152 James Davis RC 1.25 3.00
153 James Laurinaitis RC 1.25 3.00
154 Jared Cook RC 1.50 4.00
155 Jarett Dillard RC 1.25 3.00
156 Jairus Byrd RC 2.00 5.00
157 Jason Williams RC 1.50 4.00
158 Javarris Williams RC 1.50 4.00
159 Jeremy Childs RC 1.25 3.00
160 John Nalbone RC 1.25 3.00
161 John Phillips RC 2.00 5.00
162 Johnny Knox RC 1.50 4.00
163 Julian Edelman RC 6.00 15.00
164 Keith Null RC 1.50 4.00
165 Kenny McKinley RC 1.25 3.00
166 Kevin Ogletree RC 1.50 4.00
167 Kory Sheets RC 1.50 4.00
168 Lardarius Webb RC 2.00 5.00
169 Larry English RC 1.50 4.00
170 Louis Delmas RC 1.50 4.00
171 Louis Murphy RC 1.25 3.00
172 Malcolm Jenkins RC 1.25 3.00
173 Manuel Johnson RC 1.25 3.00
174 Marko Mitchell RC 1.25 3.00
175 Michael Mitchell RC 1.25 3.00
176 Michael Oher RC 2.00 5.00
177 Mike Goodson RC 1.50 4.00
178 Mike Teel RC 1.25 3.00
179 P.J. Hill RC 1.25 3.00
180 Patrick Chung RC 1.25 3.00
181 Peria Jerry RC 1.25 3.00
182 Quan Cosby RC 1.25 3.00
183 Quinn Johnson RC 1.25 3.00
184 Quinten Lawrence RC 1.25 3.00
185 Rashad Jennings RC 1.50 4.00
186 Rey Maualuga RC 2.00 5.00
187 Richard Quinn RC 1.50 4.00
188 Robert Ayers RC 1.25 3.00
189 Ron Brace RC 1.50 4.00
190 Sammie Stroughter RC 1.25 3.00
191 Sean Smith RC 1.25 3.00
192 Shawn Nelson RC 1.25 3.00
193 Sherrod Martin RC 1.25 3.00
194 Tiquan Underwood RC 1.25 3.00
195 Tom Brandstater RC 1.50 4.00
196 Tony Fiammetta RC 1.25 3.00
197 Travis Beckum RC 1.25 3.00
198 Tyrell Sutton RC 1.25 3.00
199 Vontae Davis RC 1.25 3.00
200 William Moore RC 1.25 3.00
201 Mark Sanchez JSY AU RC 12.00 30.00
202 Chris Wells JSY AU RC 5.00 12.00
203 M.Stafford JSY AU RC 30.00 80.00
204 Donald Brown JSY AU RC 6.00 15.00
205 Hakeem Nicks JSY AU RC 8.00 20.00
206 M.Crabtree JSY AU RC 10.00 25.00
207 B.Pettigrew JSY AU RC 6.00 15.00
208 Ramses Barden JSY AU RC 6.00 15.00
209 Kenny Britt JSY AU RC 10.00 25.00
210 Deon Butler JSY AU RC 6.00 15.00
211 J.Iglesias JSY AU RC 6.00 15.00
212 Jeremy Maclin JSY AU RC 8.00 20.00
213 Glen Coffee JSY AU/99 RC 6.00 15.00
214 Jason Smith JSY AU RC 6.00 15.00
215 Patrick Turner JSY AU RC 6.00 15.00
216 K.Moreno JSY AU RC 6.00 15.00
217 M.Massaquoi JSY AU RC 6.00 15.00
218 Shonn Greene JSY AU RC 6.00 15.00
219 Nate Davis JSY AU RC 6.00 15.00
220 LeSean McCoy JSY AU RC 15.00 40.00
221 Pat White JSY AU RC 8.00 20.00
222 Percy Harvin JSY AU RC 6.00 15.00
223 Tyson Jackson JSY AU RC 6.00 15.00
224 Javon Ringer JSY AU RC 6.00 15.00
225 Mike Wallace JSY AU RC 10.00 25.00
226 Josh Freeman JSY AU/98 RC 6.00 15.00
227 Stephen McGee JSY AU RC 6.00 15.00
228 Mike Thomas JSY AU RC 6.00 15.00
229 Brian Robiskie JSY AU RC 6.00 15.00
230 Aaron Curry JSY AU RC 10.00 25.00
231 Andre Brown JSY AU RC 8.00 20.00
232 Derrick Williams JSY AU RC 6.00 15.00
233 D.Heyward-Bey JSY AU RC 10.00 25.00
234 Rhett Bomar JSY AU RC 6.00 15.00

2009 Donruss Gridiron Gear Gold O's
*VETS 1-100: 3X TO 8X BASIC CARDS
*ROOKIES 101-200: .6X TO 1.5X BASIC CARDS
STATED PRINT RUN 100 SER.#'d SETS
89 Brett Favre 12.00 30.00

2009 Donruss Gridiron Gear Gold X's
*VETS 1-100: 3X TO 8X BASIC CARDS
*ROOKIES 101-200: .6X TO 1.5X BASIC CARDS
STATED PRINT RUN 100 SER.#'d SETS
89 Brett Favre 12.00 30.00

2009 Donruss Gridiron Gear Platinum O's
*VETS 1-100: 6X TO 15X BASIC CARDS
*ROOKIES 101-200: 1X TO 2.5X BASIC CARDS
STATED PRINT RUN 25 SER.#'d SETS
89 Brett Favre 25.00 60.00

2009 Donruss Gridiron Gear Platinum X's
*VETS 1-100: 6X TO 15X BASIC CARDS
*ROOKIES 101-200: 1X TO 2.5X BASIC CARDS
STATED PRINT RUN 25 SER.#'d SETS
89 Brett Favre 25.00 60.00

2009 Donruss Gridiron Gear Silver O's
*VETS 1-100: 2X TO 5X BASIC CARDS
*ROOKIES 101-200: .4X TO 1X BASIC CARDS
STATED PRINT RUN 250 SER.#'d SETS
89 Brett Favre 8.00 20.00

2009 Donruss Gridiron Gear Silver X's
*VETS 1-100: 2X TO 5X BASIC CARDS
*ROOKIES 101-200: .4X TO 1X BASIC CARDS
STATED PRINT RUN 250 SER.#'d SETS
89 Brett Favre 8.00 20.00

2009 Donruss Gridiron Gear Autographs Gold
VET STATED PRINT RUN 4-75
ROOKIE STATED PRINT RUN 25-250
30 Drew Brees/50 40.00 80.00
59 Lee Evans/50 6.00 15.00
67 Matt Forte/50 5.00 12.00
69 Matt Ryan/25 40.00 80.00
82 Ryan Grant/75 8.00 20.00
85 Steve Slaton/40 5.00 12.00
102 Aaron Kelly/250 3.00 8.00
103 Aaron Maybin/25 6.00 15.00
109 Austin Collie/100 3.00 8.00
110 B.J. Raji/100 4.00 10.00
114 Brandon Gibson/100 4.00 10.00
115 Brandon Tate/100 4.00 10.00
116 Brian Cushing/100 3.00 8.00
118 Brian Orakpo/100 4.00 10.00
119 Brooks Foster/100 3.00 8.00
120 Cameron Morrah/100 3.00 8.00
121 Cedric Peerman/100 3.00 8.00
122 Chase Coffman/100 3.00 8.00
125 Clay Matthews/100 30.00 60.00
126 Clint Sintim/100 3.00 8.00
129 Cornelius Ingram/100 3.00 8.00
138 Demetrius Byrd/100 4.00 10.00
140 Devin Moore/25 5.00 12.00
141 Dominique Edison/250 3.00 8.00
146 Everette Brown/100 3.00 8.00
150 Hunter Cantwell/100 3.00 0.00
151 James Casey/100 4.00 10.00
153 James Laurinaitis/100 3.00 8.00
154 Jared Cook/100 4.00 10.00
155 Jarett Dillard/100 3.00 8.00
162 Johnny Knox/250 4.00 10.00
165 Kenny McKinley/100 3.00 8.00
166 Kevin Ogletree/25 6.00 15.00
169 Larry English/100 4.00 10.00
171 Louis Murphy/100 3.00 8.00
172 Malcolm Jenkins/100 3.00 8.00
177 Mike Goodson/100 No AU 1.50 4.00
179 P.J. Hill/100 3.00 8.00
182 Quan Cosby/25 5.00 12.00
183 Quinn Johnson/100 3.00 8.00
185 Rashad Jennings/100 4.00 10.00
186 Rey Maualuga/100 5.00 12.00
192 Shawn Nelson No AU/100 2.00 5.00
195 Tom Brandstater/100 4.00 10.00
196 Tony Fiammetta/100 3.00 8.00
197 Travis Beckum/250 3.00 8.00
198 Tyrell Sutton/25 5.00 12.00
199 Vontae Davis/100 3.00 8.00

2009 Donruss Gridiron Gear Autographs Platinum
STATED PRINT RUN 1-25
SER.#'d UNDER 16 NOT PRICED
30 Drew Brees/25 50.00 100.00
59 Lee Evans/25 8.00 20.00
67 Matt Forte/25 6.00 15.00
76 Ray Rice/16 6.00 15.00
82 Ryan Grant/25 10.00 25.00
85 Steve Slaton/25 6.00 15.00
102 Aaron Kelly/25 5.00 12.00
109 Austin Collie/25 5.00 12.00
110 B.J. Raji/25 6.00 15.00
114 Brandon Gibson/25 6.00 15.00
115 Brandon Tate/25 6.00 15.00
116 Brian Cushing/25 5.00 12.00
118 Brian Orakpo/25 6.00 15.00
119 Brooks Foster/25 5.00 12.00
120 Cameron Morrah/25 5.00 12.00
121 Cedric Peerman/25 5.00 12.00
122 Chase Coffman/25 5.00 12.00
125 Clay Matthews/25 50.00 100.00
126 Clint Sintim/25 5.00 12.00
129 Cornelius Ingram/25 5.00 12.00
138 Demetrius Byrd/25 6.00 15.00
141 Dominique Edison/25 5.00 12.00
146 Everette Brown/25 5.00 12.00
150 Hunter Cantwell/25 5.00 12.00
151 James Casey/25 6.00 15.00
153 James Laurinaitis/25 5.00 12.00
154 Jared Cook/25 6.00 15.00
155 Jarett Dillard/25 5.00 12.00
162 Johnny Knox/25 6.00 15.00
165 Kenny McKinley/25 5.00 12.00
169 Larry English/25 6.00 15.00
171 Louis Murphy/25 5.00 12.00
172 Malcolm Jenkins/25 5.00 12.00
177 Mike Goodson/25 No AU 2.50 6.00
179 P.J. Hill/25 5.00 12.00
183 Quinn Johnson/25 5.00 12.00
185 Rashad Jennings/25 6.00 15.00
186 Rey Maualuga/25 8.00 20.00
192 Shawn Nelson No AU/25 3.00 8.00
195 Tom Brandstater/25 6.00 15.00
196 Tony Fiammetta/25 5.00 12.00
197 Travis Beckum/25 5.00 12.00
199 Vontae Davis/25 5.00 12.00

2009 Donruss Gridiron Gear Jerseys
STATED PRINT RUN 9-250
8 Bernard Berrian/60 2.50 6.00
16 Carson Palmer/250 2.50 6.00
29 Donovan McNabb/250 2.50 6.00
30 Drew Brees/250 3.00 8.00
31 Dwayne Bowe/90 3.00 8.00
34 Frank Gore/225 2.50 6.00
39 JaMarcus Russell/210 2.00 5.00
40 Jason Campbell/40 3.00 8.00
42 Jay Cutler/250 2.00 5.00
59 Lee Evans/35 4.00 10.00
62 Marc Bulger/250 2.00 5.00
65 Marshawn Lynch/225 2.50 6.00
73 Peyton Manning/250 8.00 20.00
79 Ricky Williams/250 2.50 6.00
100 Zach Miller/45 3.00 8.00

2009 Donruss Gridiron Gear Jerseys Prime
PRIME PRINT RUN 1-50
SERIAL #'d UNDER 30 NOT PRICED
6 Antonio Gates/50 5.00 12.00
9 Brady Quinn/45 4.00 10.00
12 Braylon Edwards/30 4.00 10.00
14 Brian Westbrook/50 4.00 10.00
17 Chad Ochocinco/50 4.00 10.00
19 Chris Cooley/50 4.00 10.00
21 Clinton Portis/50 4.00 10.00
25 DeAngelo Williams/50 4.00 10.00
31 Dwayne Bowe/30 5.00 12.00
34 Frank Gore/50 5.00 12.00
40 Jason Campbell/30 4.00 10.00
56 Larry Johnson/50 4.00 10.00
57 Laurence Maroney/50 5.00 12.00
59 Lee Evans/35 5.00 12.00
62 Marc Bulger/50 4.00 10.00
63 Marion Barber/50 5.00 12.00
65 Marshawn Lynch/50 5.00 12.00
68 Matt Hasselbeck/50 4.00 10.00
71 Maurice Jones-Drew/50 4.00 10.00
79 Ricky Williams/50 5.00 12.00
81 Ronnie Brown/50 4.00 10.00
82 Ryan Grant/50 5.00 12.00
83 Santonio Holmes/50 4.00 10.00
86 Steve Smith/50 5.00 12.00
87 Steven Jackson/50 4.00 10.00
91 Tom Brady/50 20.00 50.00
96 Vincent Jackson/50 4.00 10.00
98 Willie Parker/50 4.00 10.00

2009 Donruss Gridiron Gear Jerseys X's
X's HOBBY PRINT RUN 2-100
*RET.O's/80-100: .4X TO 1X HOB X's
*RET.O's/40-65: .5X TO 1.2X HOB X's
*RET.O's/19-30: .6X TO 1.5X HOB X's
O's RETAIL PRINT RUN 10-100

7 Ben Roethlisberger/100 4.00 10.00
8 Bernard Berrian/100 2.50 6.00
10 Brandon Jacobs/100 2.50 6.00
11 Brandon Marshall/100 3.00 8.00
12 Braylon Edwards/100 2.50 6.00
16 Carson Palmer/100 3.00 8.00
25 DeAngelo Williams/100 2.50 6.00
29 Donovan McNabb/100 3.00 8.00
30 Drew Brees/100 4.00 10.00
31 Dwayne Bowe/100 3.00 8.00
34 Frank Gore/100 3.00 8.00
35 Greg Olsen/100 3.00 8.00
36 Greg Jennings/100 2.50 6.00
39 JaMarcus Russell/100 2.50 6.00
40 Jason Campbell/100 2.50 6.00
42 Jay Cutler/100 2.50 6.00
45 Joseph Addai/100 2.50 6.00
54 LaDainian Tomlinson/25 6.00 15.00
56 Larry Johnson/100 2.50 6.00
59 Lee Evans/100 3.00 8.00
60 LenDale White/100 2.50 6.00
61 Leon Washington/100 2.50 6.00
62 Marc Bulger/100 2.50 6.00
65 Marshawn Lynch/100 3.00 8.00
69 Matt Ryan/100 3.00 8.00
73 Peyton Manning/100 10.00 25.00
74 Philip Rivers/65 5.00 12.00
75 Randy Moss/90 3.00 8.00
78 Reggie Wayne/100 3.00 8.00
79 Ricky Williams/100 3.00 8.00
99 Willis McGahee/55 3.00 8.00

2009 Donruss Gridiron Gear Next Generation

*GOLD/100: .6X TO 1.5X BASIC INSERTS
*PLATINUM/25: .8X TO 2X BASIC INSERTS
*SILVER/250: .5X TO 1.2X BASIC INSERTS
1 Matthew Stafford 2.50 6.00
2 Mark Sanchez .50 1.25
3 Michael Crabtree .75 2.00
4 LeSean McCoy 1.25 3.00
5 Donald Brown .50 1.25
6 Kenny Britt .75 2.00
7 Josh Freeman .50 1.25
8 Deon Butler .50 1.25
9 Juaquin Iglesias .50 1.25
10 Ramses Barden .50 1.25
11 Patrick Turner .50 1.25
12 Knowshon Moreno .50 1.25
13 Pat White .60 1.50
14 Hakeem Nicks .60 1.50
15 Jason Smith .50 1.25
16 Darrius Heyward-Bey .75 2.00
17 Mike Thomas .50 1.25
18 Nate Davis .50 1.25
19 Mohamed Massaquoi .50 1.25
20 Aaron Curry .75 2.00
21 Percy Harvin .50 1.25
22 Tyson Jackson .50 1.25
23 Mike Wallace .75 2.00
24 Javon Ringer .50 1.25
25 Glen Coffee .50 1.25
26 Chris Wells .50 1.25
27 Brandon Pettigrew .50 1.25
28 Rhett Bomar .50 1.25
29 Shonn Greene .50 1.25
30 Brian Robiskie .50 1.25
31 Derrick Williams .50 1.25
32 Jeremy Maclin .60 1.50
33 Andre Brown .60 1.50
34 Stephen McGee .50 1.25

2009 Donruss Gridiron Gear Next Generation Jerseys

STATED PRINT RUN 250 SER.#'d SETS
*COMBOS PRIME/50: .8X TO 2X BASIC JSY
*JUMBO PRIME/25: 1X TO 2.5X BASIC JSY
*PRIME/50: .6X TO 1.5X BASIC JSY
1 Matthew Stafford 6.00 15.00
2 Mark Sanchez 1.25 3.00
3 Michael Crabtree 2.00 5.00
4 LeSean McCoy 3.00 8.00
5 Donald Brown 1.25 3.00
6 Kenny Britt 2.00 5.00
7 Josh Freeman 1.25 3.00
8 Deon Butler 1.25 3.00
9 Juaquin Iglesias 1.25 3.00
10 Ramses Barden 1.25 3.00
11 Patrick Turner 1.25 3.00
12 Knowshon Moreno 1.25 3.00
13 Pat White 1.50 4.00
14 Hakeem Nicks 1.50 4.00
15 Jason Smith 1.25 3.00
16 Darrius Heyward-Bey 2.00 5.00
17 Mike Thomas 1.25 3.00
18 Nate Davis 1.25 3.00
19 Mohamed Massaquoi 1.25 3.00
20 Aaron Curry 2.00 5.00
21 Percy Harvin 1.25 3.00
22 Tyson Jackson 1.25 3.00
23 Mike Wallace 2.00 5.00
24 Javon Ringer 1.25 3.00
25 Glen Coffee 1.25 3.00
26 Chris Wells 1.25 3.00
27 Brandon Pettigrew 1.25 3.00
28 Rhett Bomar 1.25 3.00
29 Shonn Greene 1.25 3.00
30 Brian Robiskie 1.25 3.00
31 Derrick Williams 1.25 3.00
32 Jeremy Maclin 1.50 4.00
33 Andre Brown 1.50 4.00
34 Stephen McGee 1.25 3.00

2009 Donruss Gridiron Gear Next Generation Jerseys Combos Autographs Prime

STATED PRINT RUN 25 SER.#'d SETS
1 Matthew Stafford 50.00 120.00
2 Mark Sanchez 40.00 80.00
3 Michael Crabtree 8.00 20.00
4 LeSean McCoy 12.00 30.00
5 Donald Brown 5.00 12.00
6 Kenny Britt 8.00 20.00
7 Josh Freeman 5.00 12.00
8 Deon Butler 5.00 12.00
9 Juaquin Iglesias 5.00 12.00
10 Ramses Barden 5.00 12.00
11 Patrick Turner 5.00 12.00
12 Knowshon Moreno 5.00 12.00
13 Pat White 6.00 15.00
14 Hakeem Nicks 6.00 15.00
15 Jason Smith 5.00 12.00
16 Darrius Heyward-Bey 8.00 20.00
17 Mike Thomas 5.00 12.00
18 Nate Davis 5.00 12.00
19 Mohamed Massaquoi 5.00 12.00
20 Aaron Curry 8.00 20.00
21 Percy Harvin 5.00 12.00
22 Tyson Jackson 5.00 12.00
23 Mike Wallace 8.00 20.00
24 Javon Ringer 5.00 12.00
25 Glen Coffee 5.00 12.00
26 Chris Wells 5.00 12.00
27 Brandon Pettigrew 5.00 12.00
28 Rhett Bomar 5.00 12.00
29 Shonn Greene 5.00 12.00
30 Brian Robiskie 5.00 12.00
31 Derrick Williams 5.00 12.00
32 Jeremy Maclin 6.00 15.00
33 Andre Brown 6.00 15.00
34 Stephen McGee 5.00 12.00

2009 Donruss Gridiron Gear Next Generation Materials Combos

STATED PRINT RUN 250 SER.#'d SETS
*PRIME/25: .6X TO 1.5X BASIC COMBO
1 Heyward-Bey/Nicks 2.50 6.00
2 S.Greene/J.Ringer 1.50 4.00
3 B.Robiskie/D.Williams 1.50 4.00
4 J.Maclin/B.Pettigrew 2.00 5.00
5 D.Brown/L.McCoy 4.00 10.00
6 M.Thomas/P.Turner 1.50 4.00
7 P.Harvin/M.Massaquoi 1.50 4.00
8 M.Crabtree/J.Iglesias 2.50 6.00
9 D.Brown/S.Greene 1.50 4.00
10 A.Brown/A.Curry 2.50 6.00

2009 Donruss Gridiron Gear Next Generation Materials Triple

STATED PRINT RUN 250 SER.#'d SETS
*PRIME/25: .6X TO 1.5X BASIC TRIPLE
1 Staffrd/Sanchez/Frman 8.00 20.00
2 Jackson/Curry/Smith 2.50 6.00
3 Moreno/Brown/Wells 1.50 4.00
4 McCoy/Greene/Coffee 4.00 10.00
5 Hywrd/Crabtr/Maclin 2.50 6.00
6 White/McGee/Bomar 1.50 4.00
7 Petti/Robis/Massa 1.50 4.00
8 Harvin/Nicks/Britt 2.50 6.00
9 Williams/Wallace/Barden 2.50 6.00
10 Thomas/Turner/Sanchez 6.00 15.00

2009 Donruss Gridiron Gear NFL Gridiron Rookie Signatures

*GRIDIRON/42-45: .5X TO 1.2X TEAMS AU/50
STATED PRINT RUN 42-45

2009 Donruss Gridiron Gear NFL Teams Rookie Signatures

STATED PRINT RUN 50 SER.#'d SETS
1 Glen Coffee 5.00 12.00
2 Michael Crabtree 8.00 20.00
3 Nate Davis 5.00 12.00
4 Javon Ringer 5.00 12.00
5 Kenny Britt 8.00 20.00
6 Mike Wallace 8.00 20.00
7 Jeremy Maclin 5.00 12.00
8 LeSean McCoy 12.00 30.00
9 Donald Brown 5.00 12.00
10 Mike Thomas 5.00 12.00
11 Tyson Jackson 5.00 12.00
12 Josh Freeman 5.00 12.00
13 Darrius Heyward-Bey 8.00 20.00
14 Aaron Curry 8.00 20.00
15 Deon Butler 5.00 12.00
16 Jason Smith 5.00 12.00
17 Juaquin Iglesias 5.00 12.00
18 Stephen McGee 5.00 12.00
19 Andre Brown 6.00 15.00
20 Hakeem Nicks 6.00 15.00
21 Ramses Barden 5.00 12.00
22 Rhett Bomar 5.00 12.00
23 Percy Harvin 5.00 12.00
24 Pat White 6.00 15.00
25 Patrick Turner 5.00 12.00
26 Chris Wells 5.00 12.00
27 Mark Sanchez 5.00 12.00
28 Shonn Greene 5.00 12.00
29 Brian Robiskie 5.00 12.00
30 Mohamed Massaquoi 5.00 12.00
31 Brandon Pettigrew 5.00 12.00
32 Derrick Williams 5.00 12.00
33 Matthew Stafford 30.00 80.00
34 Knowshon Moreno 5.00 12.00

2009 Donruss Gridiron Gear NFL Teams Veteran Signatures

STATED PRINT RUN 25-500
1 Yale Lary/75 10.00 25.00
2 Pete Retzlaff/74 8.00 20.00
3 Lee Roy Selmon/100 15.00 40.00
4 Don Perkins/125 12.00 30.00
5 Willie Lanier/150 8.00 20.00
6 Willie Davis/98 15.00 40.00
7 Mark Gastineau/102 8.00 20.00
8 Lydell Mitchell/200 8.00 20.00
9 Joe Klecko/119 8.00 20.00
10 Archie Manning/175 15.00 40.00
11 Fred Williamson/123 10.00 25.00
12 Dan Marino/100 50.00 100.00
13 Gene Upshaw/150 12.00 30.00
14 Cliff Harris/137 10.00 25.00
15 Chuck Bednarik/25 40.00 80.00
16 Mark Duper/162 10.00 25.00
17 Dan Fouts/150 25.00 50.00
18 Charlie Joiner/200 8.00 20.00
19 Deacon Jones/140 10.00 25.00
20 Don Maynard/200 8.00 20.00
21 Jethro Pugh/250 8.00 20.00
22 Billy Howton/250 8.00 20.00
23 Darrell Green/250 15.00 40.00
24 Charley Taylor/250 8.00 20.00
25 Willie Brown/350 8.00 20.00
26 Larry Little/367 6.00 15.00
27 Lem Barney/400 8.00 20.00
28 Paul Krause/450 8.00 20.00
29 Rick Casares/500 6.00 15.00
30 Joe Namath/50 50.00 100.00
31 Jim Brown/100 30.00 60.00

2009 Donruss Gridiron Gear Performers

*GOLD/100: .6X TO 1.5X BASIC INSERTS
*PLATINUM/25: .8X TO 2X BASIC INSERTS
*SILVER/250: .5X TO 1.2X BASIC INSERTS
1 Knowshon Moreno .50 1.25
2 Matthew Stafford 2.50 6.00
3 Derrick Williams .50 1.25
4 Brandon Pettigrew .50 1.25
5 Mohamed Massaquoi .50 1.25
6 Brian Robiskie .50 1.25
7 Shonn Greene .50 1.25
8 Mark Sanchez .50 1.25
9 Chris Wells .50 1.25
10 Patrick Turner .50 1.25
11 Pat White .60 1.50
12 Glen Coffee .50 1.25
13 Michael Crabtree .75 2.00
14 Nate Davis .50 1.25
15 Javon Ringer .50 1.25
16 Kenny Britt .75 2.00
17 Mike Wallace .75 2.00
18 Jeremy Maclin .60 1.50
19 LeSean McCoy 1.25 3.00
20 Donald Brown .50 1.25
21 Mike Thomas .50 1.25
22 Tyson Jackson .50 1.25
23 Josh Freeman .50 1.25
24 Percy Harvin .50 1.25
25 Ramses Barden .50 1.25
26 Andre Brown .60 1.50
27 Juaquin Iglesias .50 1.25
28 Deon Butler .50 1.25
29 Darrius Heyward-Bey .75 2.00
30 Aaron Curry .75 2.00
31 Jason Smith .50 1.25
32 Stephen McGee .50 1.25
33 Hakeem Nicks .60 1.50
34 Rhett Bomar .50 1.25

2009 Donruss Gridiron Gear Performers Jerseys

STATED PRINT RUN 250 SER.#'d SETS
*COMBOS/100: .5X TO 1.2X BASIC JSY
*COMBOS PRIME/50: .8X TO 2X BASIC JSY
*JUMBO PRIME/25: 1X TO 2.5X BASIC JSY
*PRIME/50: .6X TO 1.5X BASIC JSY
1 Knowshon Moreno 1.25 3.00
2 Matthew Stafford 6.00 15.00
3 Derrick Williams 1.25 3.00
4 Brandon Pettigrew 1.25 3.00
5 Mohamed Massaquoi 1.25 3.00
6 Brian Robiskie 1.25 3.00
7 Shonn Greene 1.25 3.00
8 Mark Sanchez 8.00 20.00
9 Chris Wells 1.25 3.00
10 Patrick Turner 1.25 3.00
11 Pat White 1.50 4.00
12 Glen Coffee 1.25 3.00
13 Michael Crabtree 2.00 5.00
14 Nate Davis 1.25 3.00
15 Javon Ringer 1.25 3.00
16 Kenny Britt 2.00 5.00
17 Mike Wallace 2.00 5.00
18 Jeremy Maclin 1.50 4.00
19 LeSean McCoy 3.00 8.00
20 Donald Brown 1.25 3.00
21 Mike Thomas 1.25 3.00
22 Tyson Jackson 1.25 3.00
23 Josh Freeman 1.25 3.00
24 Percy Harvin 1.25 3.00
25 Ramses Barden 1.25 3.00
26 Andre Brown 1.50 4.00
27 Juaquin Iglesias 1.25 3.00
28 Deon Butler 1.25 3.00
29 Darrius Heyward-Bey 2.00 5.00
30 Aaron Curry 2.00 5.00
31 Jason Smith 1.25 3.00
32 Stephen McGee 1.25 3.00
33 Hakeem Nicks 1.50 4.00
34 Rhett Bomar 1.25 3.00

2009 Donruss Gridiron Gear Performers Materials Combos Autographs Prime

COMBO PRIME AU PRINT RUN 25
1 Knowshon Moreno 5.00 12.00
2 Matthew Stafford 50.00 100.00
3 Derrick Williams EXCH 5.00 12.00
4 Brandon Pettigrew 5.00 12.00
5 Mohamed Massaquoi 5.00 12.00
6 Brian Robiskie 5.00 12.00
7 Shonn Greene 5.00 12.00
8 Mark Sanchez 30.00 80.00
9 Chris Wells 5.00 12.00
10 Patrick Turner 5.00 12.00
11 Pat White 6.00 15.00
12 Glen Coffee 5.00 12.00
13 Michael Crabtree 8.00 20.00
14 Nate Davis 5.00 12.00
15 Javon Ringer 5.00 12.00
16 Kenny Britt 8.00 20.00
17 Mike Wallace 8.00 20.00
18 Jeremy Maclin 6.00 15.00
19 LeSean McCoy 12.00 30.00
20 Donald Brown 5.00 12.00
21 Mike Thomas 5.00 12.00
22 Tyson Jackson 5.00 12.00
23 Josh Freeman 5.00 12.00
24 Percy Harvin 5.00 12.00
25 Ramses Barden 5.00 12.00
26 Andre Brown 6.00 15.00
27 Juaquin Iglesias 5.00 12.00
28 Deon Butler 5.00 12.00
29 Darrius Heyward-Bey 8.00 20.00
30 Aaron Curry 8.00 20.00
31 Jason Smith 5.00 12.00
32 Stephen McGee 5.00 12.00
33 Hakeem Nicks 6.00 15.00
34 Rhett Bomar 5.00 12.00

2009 Donruss Gridiron Gear Plates and Patches

STATED PRINT RUN 35-100
1 Andre Johnson/100 5.00 12.00
2 Antonio Gates/100 5.00 12.00
3 Brian Westbrook/100 4.00 10.00
6 Chad Ochocinco/100 4.00 10.00
8 Frank Gore/100 5.00 12.00
10 Jason Campbell/100 4.00 10.00
11 Lee Evans/35 6.00 15.00
13 Maurice Jones-Drew/100 4.00 10.00
15 Steve Smith/100 5.00 12.00

2009 Donruss Gridiron Gear Plates and Patches Autographs

STATED PRINT RUN 25 SER.#'d SETS
1 Andre Johnson 20.00 50.00
11 Lee Evans 12.00 30.00

2009 Donruss Gridiron Gear Playbook

*GOLD/100: .6X TO 1.5X BASIC INSERTS
*PLATINUM/25: .8X TO 2X BASIC INSERTS
*SILVER/250: .5X TO 1.2X BASIC INSERTS
1 DeAngelo Williams .50 1.25
2 Willie Parker .50 1.25
3 Philip Rivers .75 2.00
4 Joseph Addai .50 1.25
5 Aaron Rodgers 1.50 4.00
6 LaDainian Tomlinson .75 2.00
7 Tony Romo .60 1.50
8 Reggie Bush .50 1.25
9 Michael Turner .50 1.25
10 Adrian Peterson .75 2.00
11 Clinton Portis .50 1.25
12 Matt Hasselbeck .50 1.25
13 Matt Ryan .60 1.50
14 Wes Welker .60 1.50
15 Anthony Gonzalez .50 1.25
16 Larry Fitzgerald .60 1.50
17 Peyton Manning 2.00 5.00
18 Randy Moss .60 1.50
19 Ben Roethlisberger .75 2.00
20 Kurt Warner .60 1.50
21 Drew Brees .75 2.00
22 Marion Barber .60 1.50
23 Steven Jackson .50 1.25
24 Santonio Holmes .50 1.25
25 Maurice Jones-Drew .50 1.25

2009 Donruss Gridiron Gear Playbook Jerseys Patch

STATED PRINT RUN 8-50
1 DeAngelo Williams/50 4.00 10.00
2 Willie Parker/50 4.00 10.00
5 Aaron Rodgers/20 15.00 40.00
10 Adrian Peterson/50 6.00 15.00
11 Clinton Portis/50 4.00 10.00
15 Anthony Gonzalez/25 5.00 12.00
19 Ben Roethlisberger/20 8.00 20.00
22 Marion Barber/50 5.00 12.00
23 Steven Jackson/50 4.00 10.00
24 Santonio Holmes/50 4.00 10.00
25 Maurice Jones-Drew/50 4.00 10.00

2009 Donruss Gridiron Gear Playbook Jerseys X's

STATED PRINT RUN 40-250
*RET.O's/195-250: .4X TO 1X HOB X's/250
4 Joseph Addai/250 2.00 5.00
10 Adrian Peterson/40 5.00 12.00
13 Matt Ryan/225 2.50 6.00
17 Peyton Manning/250 8.00 20.00
21 Drew Brees/250 3.00 8.00

2009 Donruss Gridiron Gear Player Timeline

*GOLD/100: .6X TO 1.5X BASIC INSERTS
*PLATINUM/25: .8X TO 2X BASIC INSERTS
*SILVER/250: .5X TO 1.2X BASIC INSERTS
1 Jimmy Orr .50 1.25
2 Steve Largent .75 2.00
3 Antoine Cason .50 1.25
4 Brandon Meriweather .50 1.25
5 Chad Henne .60 1.50
6 DeSean Jackson .60 1.50
7 Early Doucet .60 1.50
8 Jamaal Charles .60 1.50
9 Malcolm Kelly .50 1.25
10 Vernon Gholston .50 1.25
11 Limas Sweed .60 1.50
12 Aqib Talib .50 1.25
13 LaRon Landry .50 1.25
14 Laveranues Coles .50 1.25
15 Terrell Owens .60 1.50
16 Kellen Winslow Jr. .50 1.25
17 Roy Williams WR .50 1.25
18 Torry Holt .60 1.50
19 Cedric Benson .50 1.25
20 Joe Namath 1.00 2.50
21 Jim Brown 1.00 2.50
22 Jay Cutler .50 1.25
23 Kyle Orton .50 1.25
24 Tony Gonzalez .60 1.50
25 Thomas Jones .50 1.25

2009 Donruss Gridiron Gear Player Timeline Autographs

STATED PRINT RUN 3-250
1 Jimmy Orr/250 4.00 10.00
2 Steve Largent/22 15.00 40.00
3 Antoine Cason/250 4.00 10.00
4 Brandon Meriweather/77 5.00 12.00
6 DeSean Jackson/100 5.00 12.00
7 Early Doucet/114 5.00 12.00
11 Limas Sweed/250 5.00 12.00
13 LaRon Landry/250 4.00 10.00
20 Joe Namath/50 40.00 80.00
21 Jim Brown/32 50.00 100.00

2009 Donruss Gridiron Gear Player Timeline Jerseys

STATED PRINT RUN 1-250
2 Steve Largent/250 5.00 12.00
3 Antoine Cason/55 2.50 6.00
4 Brandon Meriweather/200 2.00 5.00
5 Chad Henne/250 2.50 6.00
6 DeSean Jackson/20 5.00 12.00
8 Jamaal Charles/250 2.50 6.00
9 Malcolm Kelly/250 2.00 5.00
11 Limas Sweed/250 2.50 6.00
12 Aqib Talib/250 2.00 5.00
13 LaRon Landry/250 2.00 5.00
14 Laveranues Coles/250 2.00 5.00
15 Terrell Owens/250 2.50 6.00
17 Roy Williams WR/250 2.00 5.00
18 Torry Holt/250 2.50 6.00
19 Cedric Benson/250 2.00 5.00
21 Jim Brown/25 10.00 25.00
22 Jay Cutler/250 2.00 5.00
23 Kyle Orton/250 2.00 5.00
24 Tony Gonzalez/65 3.00 8.00
25 Thomas Jones/250 2.00 5.00

2009 Donruss Gridiron Gear Player Timeline Jerseys Jumbo Swatch

STATED PRINT RUN 1-50
2 Steve Largent/50 8.00 20.00
3 Antoine Cason/50 3.00 8.00
4 Brandon Meriweather/50 3.00 8.00
5 Chad Henne/50 4.00 10.00
7 Early Doucet/50 4.00 10.00
8 Jamaal Charles/50 4.00 10.00
9 Malcolm Kelly/50 3.00 8.00
11 Limas Sweed/50 4.00 10.00
12 Aqib Talib/50 3.00 8.00
13 LaRon Landry/50 3.00 8.00
14 Laveranues Coles/50 3.00 8.00
15 Terrell Owens/45 4.00 10.00
17 Roy Williams WR/25 4.00 10.00
18 Torry Holt/50 4.00 10.00
19 Cedric Benson/50 3.00 8.00
22 Jay Cutler/50 3.00 8.00
23 Kyle Orton/50 3.00 8.00
24 Tony Gonzalez/50 4.00 10.00
25 Thomas Jones/50 3.00 8.00

2009 Donruss Gridiron Gear Player Timeline Jerseys Jumbo Swatch Prime

STATED PRINT RUN 1-25
2 Steve Largent/25 12.00 30.00
4 Brandon Meriweather/25 5.00 12.00
8 Jamaal Charles/25 6.00 15.00
11 Limas Sweed/25 6.00 15.00
12 Aqib Talib/25 5.00 12.00
14 Laveranues Coles/25 5.00 12.00
15 Terrell Owens/25 6.00 15.00
16 Kellen Winslow Jr./25 5.00 12.00
17 Roy Williams WR/25 5.00 12.00
18 Torry Holt/25 6.00 15.00
19 Cedric Benson/25 5.00 12.00
23 Kyle Orton/25 5.00 12.00
24 Tony Gonzalez/25 6.00 15.00
25 Thomas Jones/25 5.00 12.00

2009 Donruss Gridiron Gear Player Timeline Jerseys Prime

STATED PRINT RUN 1-50
2 Steve Largent/50 8.00 20.00
4 Brandon Meriweather/40 3.00 8.00
7 Early Doucet/20 5.00 12.00
8 Jamaal Charles/50 4.00 10.00
9 Malcolm Kelly/30 3.00 8.00
10 Vernon Gholston /50 3.00 8.00
11 Limas Sweed/50 4.00 10.00
12 Aqib Talib/50 3.00 8.00
14 Laveranues Coles/50 3.00 8.00
15 Terrell Owens/50 4.00 10.00
16 Kellen Winslow Jr./50 3.00 8.00
17 Roy Williams WR/50 3.00 8.00
18 Torry Holt/50 4.00 10.00
19 Cedric Benson/50 3.00 8.00
23 Kyle Orton/50 3.00 8.00
24 Tony Gonzalez/50 4.00 10.00
25 Thomas Jones/50 3.00 8.00

2009 Donruss Gridiron Gear Player Timeline Jerseys Autographs

STATED PRINT RUN 5-50
2 Steve Largent/25
3 Antoine Cason/50 6.00 15.00
4 Brandon Meriweather/50 6.00 15.00
5 Chad Henne/25 10.00 25.00
6 DeSean Jackson/25 10.00 25.00
7 Early Doucet/50 8.00 20.00
11 Limas Sweed/50 8.00 20.00
13 LaRon Landry/50 6.00 15.00

2009 Donruss Gridiron Gear Player Timeline Jerseys Autographs Prime

STATED PRINT RUN 5-30
3 Antoine Cason/25 10.00 25.00
4 Brandon Meriweather/25 10.00 25.00
5 Chad Henne/22 12.00 30.00
7 Early Doucet/25 12.00 30.00
10 Vernon Gholston /30 10.00 25.00
11 Limas Sweed/25 12.00 30.00
13 LaRon Landry/25 10.00 25.00
21 Jim Brown/25 40.00 80.00

2009 Donruss Gridiron Gear Rivals

*GOLD/100: .6X TO 1.5X BASIC INSERTS
*PLATINUM/25: .8X TO 2X BASIC INSERTS
*SILVER/250: .5X TO 1.2X BASIC INSERTS
1 R.Brown/M.Lynch .60 1.50
2 R.Moss/T.Jones .60 1.50
3 R.Grant/B.Urlacher .75 2.00
4 D.McNabb/E.Manning .60 1.50
5 H.Ward/L.White .60 1.50
6 T.Newman/C.Portis .50 1.25
7 G.Jennings/A.Peterson .75 2.00
8 P.Manning/T.Brady 2.50 6.00
9 J.Witten/B.Jacobs .60 1.50
10 W.Parker/R.Lewis .75 2.00

2009 Donruss Gridiron Gear Rivals Jerseys

STATED PRINT RUN 5-250
2 R.Moss/T.Jones 5.00 12.00
8 P.Manning/T.Brady 20.00 50.00

2009 Donruss Gridiron Gear Rivals Jerseys Prime

STATED PRINT RUN 1-50
1 R.Brown/M.Lynch/50 8.00 20.00
6 T.Newman/C.Portis/50 6.00 15.00
8 P.Manning/T.Brady/45 25.00 60.00

2009 Donruss Gridiron Gear Rookie Gridiron Gems Jerseys Prime

STATED PRINT RUN 50 SER.#'d SETS
*COMBO PRM/50: .6X TO 1.5X PRIME/50
*JUMBO PRM/50: .6X TO 1.5X PRIME/50
*JSY TRIO/50: .5X TO 1.2X PRIME/50
*PRIME TRIO/50: .6X TO 1.5X PRIME/50
*RETAIL/50: .4X TO 1X PRIME/50
201 Mark Sanchez 1.25 3.00
202 Chris Wells 1.25 3.00
203 Matthew Stafford 6.00 15.00
204 Donald Brown 1.25 3.00
205 Hakeem Nicks 1.50 4.00
206 Michael Crabtree 2.00 5.00
207 Brandon Pettigrew 1.25 3.00
208 Ramses Barden 1.25 3.00
209 Kenny Britt 2.00 5.00
210 Deon Butler 1.25 3.00
211 Juaquin Iglesias 1.25 3.00
212 Jeremy Maclin 1.50 4.00
213 Glen Coffee 1.25 3.00
214 Jason Smith 1.25 3.00
215 Patrick Turner 1.25 3.00
216 Knowshon Moreno 1.25 3.00
217 Mohamed Massaquoi 1.25 3.00
218 Shonn Greene 1.25 3.00
219 Nate Davis 1.25 3.00
220 LeSean McCoy 3.00 8.00
221 Pat White 1.50 4.00
222 Percy Harvin 1.25 3.00
223 Tyson Jackson 1.25 3.00
224 Javon Ringer 1.25 3.00
225 Mike Wallace 2.00 5.00
226 Josh Freeman 1.25 3.00
227 Stephen McGee 1.25 3.00
228 Mike Thomas 1.25 3.00
229 Brian Robiskie 1.25 3.00
230 Aaron Curry 2.00 5.00
231 Andre Brown 1.50 4.00
232 Derrick Williams 1.25 3.00
233 Darrius Heyward-Bey 2.00 5.00
234 Rhett Bomar 1.25 3.00

2009 Donruss Gridiron Gear Rookie Gridiron Gems Jerseys Trios Autographs Prime

*TRIO AU/25: .5X TO 1.2X BASIC JSY AU
STATED PRINT RUN 25 SER.#'d SETS

2003 Donruss Kickoff Magazine

Cards from this set were issued in 8-card sheets in two different issues of Kickoff magazine. They were produced by Donruss/Playoff and came perforated on each sheet.
COMPLETE SET (16) 5.00 10.00
1 Marcellus Wiley .20 .50
2 Sam Adams .20 .50
3 Eddie George .30 .75
4 Jeff Garcia .40 1.00
5 Keith Brooking .20 .50
6 Drew Bledsoe .50 1.25
7 Edgerrin James .50 1.25
8 Zach Thomas .40 1.00
9 Shaun O'Hara .20 .50
10 Tiki Barber .30 .75
11 Ronde Barber .30 .75
12 Ricky Williams .60 1.50
13 Hines Ward .40 1.00
14 Eddie Mason .20 .50
15 Billy Conaty .20 .50
16 Gerald McBurrows .20 .50

2016 Donruss Optic

1 Carson Palmer .30 .75
2 Larry Fitzgerald .30 .75
3 David Johnson .40 1.00
4 Matt Ryan .30 .75
5 Devonta Freeman .30 .75
6 Julio Jones .40 1.00
7 Joe Flacco .30 .75
8 Justin Forsett .30 .75
9 Steve Smith Sr. .30 .75
10 Tyrod Taylor .30 .75
11 LeSean McCoy .40 1.00
12 Sammy Watkins .40 1.00
13 Cam Newton .40 1.00
14 Jonathan Stewart .25 .60
15 Kelvin Benjamin .30 .75
16 Greg Olsen .30 .75
17 Jay Cutler .25 .60
18 Jeremy Langford .30 .75
19 Alshon Jeffery .30 .75
20 Andy Dalton .30 .75
21 Jeremy Hill .25 .60
22 A.J. Green .40 1.00
23 Robert Griffin III .25 .60
24 Duke Johnson .25 .60
25 Gary Barnidge .25 .60
26 Tony Romo .30 .75
27 Jason Witten .30 .75
28 Dez Bryant .40 1.00
29 C.J. Anderson .30 .75
30 Demaryius Thomas .30 .75
31 Emmanuel Sanders .40 1.00
32 Von Miller .30 .75
33 Matthew Stafford .30 .75
34 Ameer Abdullah .25 .60
35 Golden Tate III .25 .60
36 Aaron Rodgers .75 2.00
37 Eddie Lacy .25 .60
38 Randall Cobb .30 .75
39 Jordy Nelson .30 .75
40 Brock Osweiler .25 .60
41 DeAndre Hopkins .30 .75
42 J.J. Watt .40 1.00
43 Lamar Miller .25 .60
44 Andrew Luck .50 1.25
45 Frank Gore .30 .75
46 T.Y. Hilton .30 .75
47 Blake Bortles .25 .60
48 Allen Robinson .30 .75
49 Chris Ivory .30 .75
50 Alex Smith .30 .75
51 Jamaal Charles .30 .75
52 Jeremy Maclin .25 .60
53 Todd Gurley II .40 1.00
54 Tavon Austin .25 .60
55 Aaron Donald .40 1.00
56 Ryan Tannehill .30 .75
57 Jarvis Landry .30 .75
58 DeVante Parker .30 .75
59 Teddy Bridgewater .30 .75
60 Adrian Peterson .40 1.00
61 Stefon Diggs .30 .75
62 Tom Brady 1.00 2.50
63 Rob Gronkowski .40 1.00
64 Julian Edelman .40 1.00
65 Drew Brees .40 1.00
66 Mark Ingram .30 .75
67 Brandin Cooks .30 .75
68 Eli Manning .30 .75
69 Victor Cruz .30 .75
70 Odell Beckham Jr. .40 1.00
71 Matt Forte .25 .60
72 Brandon Marshall .25 .60
73 Eric Decker .25 .60
74 Derek Carr .40 1.00
75 Latavius Murray .25 .60
76 Amari Cooper .40 1.00
77 Sam Bradford .25 .60
78 Ryan Mathews .30 .75
79 Jordan Matthews .30 .75
80 Ben Roethlisberger .40 1.00
81 Le'Veon Bell .30 .75
82 Antonio Brown .40 1.00
83 Philip Rivers .40 1.00
84 Melvin Gordon .30 .75
85 Keenan Allen .30 .75
86 Blaine Gabbert .25 .60
87 Carlos Hyde .25 .60
88 Torrey Smith .25 .60
89 Russell Wilson .50 1.25
90 Thomas Rawls .25 .60
91 Doug Baldwin .30 .75
92 Jameis Winston .40 1.00
93 Doug Martin .30 .75
94 Mike Evans .30 .75
95 DeMarco Murray .30 .75
96 Marcus Mariota .40 1.00
97 Dorial Green-Beckham .25 .60
98 Kirk Cousins .40 1.00
99 Matt Jones .30 .75
100 Jordan Reed .25 .60
101 Adam Gotsis RC .40 1.00
102 Adolphus Washington RC .40 1.00
103 Artie Burns RC .50 1.25
104 A'Shawn Robinson RC .40 1.00
105 Austin Johnson RC .40 1.00
106 Bronson Kaufusi RC .40 1.00
107 Carl Nassib RC .40 1.00
108 Charles Tapper RC .50 1.25
109 Chris Jones RC .40 1.00
110 Cody Core RC .40 1.00
111 Darron Lee RC .40 1.00
112 DeForest Buckner RC .40 1.00
113 Deion Jones RC .40 1.00
114 Derek Watt RC .60 1.50
115 Emmanuel Ogbah RC .50 1.25
116 Eric Murray RC .40 1.00
117 Tyreek Hill RC 1.50 4.00
118 Jake Rudock RC .40 1.00
119 James Bradberry RC .50 1.25
120 Jarran Reed RC .40 1.00
121 Jihad Ward RC .40 1.00
122 Jonathan Bullard RC .40 1.00
123 Kamalei Correa RC .40 1.00
124 Karl Joseph RC .40 1.00
125 Keanu Neal RC .40 1.00
126 Kei'Varae Russell RC .40 1.00
127 Kendall Fuller RC .50 1.25
128 Kenny Clark RC .40 1.00
129 Kevin Dodd RC .40 1.00
130 Nate Sudfeld RC .40 1.00
131 Mackensie Alexander RC .40 1.00
132 Maliek Collins RC .40 1.00
133 Eli Apple RC .50 1.25
134 Noah Spence RC .40 1.00
135 Reggie Ragland RC .40 1.00
136 Robert Nkemdiche RC .50 1.25
137 Roberto Aguayo RC .40 1.00
138 Sean Davis RC .40 1.00
139 Kelvin Taylor RC .40 1.00
140 Sheldon Rankins RC .50 1.25
141 Shilique Calhoun RC .40 1.00
142 Su'a Cravens RC .40 1.00
143 T.J. Green RC .60 1.50
144 Vernon Butler RC .40 1.00
145 Vernon Hargreaves III RC .60 1.50
146 Vonn Bell RC .50 1.25
147 Will Redmond RC .60 1.50
148 William Jackson III RC .50 1.25
149 Xavien Howard RC .50 1.25
150 Yannick Ngakoue RC .60 1.50
151 Alex Collins RR RC .50 1.25
152 Austin Hooper RR RC .40 1.00
153 Braxton Miller RR RC .40 1.00
154 C.J. Prosise RR RC .40 1.00
155 Cardale Jones RR RC .40 1.00
156 Carson Wentz RR RC 4.00 10.00
157 Chris Moore RR RC .50 1.25
158 Christian Hackenberg RR RC .40 1.00
159 Cody Kessler RR RC .40 1.00
160 Connor Cook RR RC .50 1.25
161 Corey Coleman RR RC .60 1.50
162 Dak Prescott RR RC 4.00 10.00
163 DeAndre Washington RR RC .40 1.00
164 Demarcus Robinson RR RC .40 1.00
165 Derrick Henry RR RC 1.00 2.50
166 Devontae Booker RR RC .50 1.25
167 Moritz Bohringer RR RC .40 1.00
168 Ezekiel Elliott RR RC 4.00 10.00
169 Hunter Henry RR RC .50 1.25
170 Jacoby Brissett RR RC .50 1.25
171 Jalen Ramsey RR RC .60 1.50
172 Jared Goff RR RC 2.50 6.00
173 Jaylon Smith RR RC .40 1.00
174 Jeff Driskel RR RC .40 1.00
175 Joey Bosa RR RC .75 2.00
176 Jonathan Williams RR RC .50 1.25
177 Jordan Howard RR RC 1.00 2.50
178 Josh Doctson RR RC .50 1.25
179 Keenan Reynolds RR RC .50 1.25
180 Kenneth Dixon RR RC .40 1.00
181 Kenyan Drake RR RC .60 1.50
182 Kevin Hogan RR RC .50 1.25
183 Laquon Treadwell RR RC .50 1.25
184 Leonte Carroo RR RC .40 1.00
185 Malcolm Mitchell RR RC .40 1.00
186 Michael Thomas RR RC .75 2.00
187 Myles Jack RR RC .50 1.25
188 Nick Vannett RR RC .40 1.00
189 Paul Perkins RR RC .40 1.00
190 Paxton Lynch RR RC .40 1.00
191 Pharoh Cooper RR RC .40 1.00
192 Rashard Higgins RR RC .40 1.00
193 Ricardo Louis RR RC .40 1.00
194 Sterling Shepard RR RC .50 1.25
195 Tajae Sharpe RR RC .50 1.25
196 Trevor Davis RR RC .40 1.00
197 Tyler Boyd RR RC .50 1.25
198 Tyler Ervin RR RC .40 1.00
199 Wendell Smallwood RR RC .40 1.00
200 Will Fuller V RR RC .60 1.50

2016 Donruss Optic Aqua

*AQUA VET/299: 1.2X TO 3X BASIC VET
*AQUA RC/299: .75X TO 2X BASIC RR

2016 Donruss Optic Black

*BLACK VET/25: 3X TO 8X BASIC VET
*BLACK RC/25: 2X TO 5X BASIC RC
162 Dak Prescott RR 40.00 100.00
168 Ezekiel Elliott RR 90.00 150.00

2016 Donruss Optic Blue

*BLUE VET/199: 1.5X TO 4X BASIC VET
*BLUE RC: 1X TO 2.5X BASIC RC

2016 Donruss Optic Bronze

*BRONZE: .6X TO 1.5X BASIC ROOKIES

2016 Donruss Optic Carolina Blue

*CAR.BLU VET/50: 2.5X TO 6X BASIC VET
*CAR.BLU RC/50: 1.5X TO 4X BASIC RC

2016 Donruss Optic Holo

*HOLO VET: .75X TO 2X BASIC VET
*HOLO RC: .5X TO 1.2X BASIC RR
168 Ezekiel Elliott RR 15.00 40.00

2016 Donruss Optic Orange

*ORANGE VET/199: 1.5X TO 4X BASIC VET
*ORANGE RC: 1X TO 2.5X BASIC RR

2016 Donruss Optic Red

*RED VET/99: 2X TO 5X BASIC VET
*RED RC/99: 1.2X TO 3X BASIC RC
156 Carson Wentz RR 15.00 40.00
162 Dak Prescott RR 15.00 40.00
168 Ezekiel Elliott RR 50.00 100.00

2016 Donruss Optic Red and Yellow

*ROOKIES: .6X TO 1.5X BASIC CARDS

2016 Donruss Optic Dual Rookie Autographs

1 C.Wentz/J.Goff 100.00 200.00
2 D.Henry/E.Elliott 100.00 200.00
3 D.Booker/P.Lynch 10.00 25.00
4 C.Jones/C.Hcknbrg 8.00 20.00
5 B.Miller/W.Fuller 12.00 30.00
6 A.Collins/C.Prosise 10.00 25.00
7 J.Doctson/L.Treadwell 10.00 25.00
8 C.Wentz/D.Prescott
9 P.Perkins/S.Shepard 10.00 25.00
10 C.Kessler/C.Coleman 12.00 30.00

2016 Donruss Optic Fans of the Game

*BLUE/149: 1X TO 2.5X BASIC INSERTS
*RED/99: 1.2X TO 3X BASIC INSERTS
1 Daisy Ridley 1.00 2.50
2 Al Pacino 1.00 2.50
3 Megan Fox 1.00 2.50
4 Skylar Astin 1.00 2.50
5 Daniella Monet 1.00 2.50
6 Marisa Miller 1.00 2.50
7 Darryl McDaniels 1.00 2.50

2016 Donruss Optic Gridiron Kings

*BLUE/149: 1X TO 2.5X BASIC INSERTS
*RED/99: 1.2X TO 3X BASIC INSERTS
1 Tony Romo .50 1.25
2 Odell Beckham Jr. .60 1.50
3 Tom Brady 1.50 4.00
4 Cam Newton .60 1.50
5 Marcus Mariota .60 1.50
6 Aaron Rodgers 1.25 3.00
7 Jeremy Maclin .40 1.00
8 Julio Jones .60 1.50
9 Andrew Luck .75 2.00
10 Philip Rivers .60 1.50
11 Ben Roethlisberger .60 1.50
12 Kirk Cousins .60 1.50
13 Blake Bortles .40 1.00
14 Rob Gronkowski .60 1.50
15 Todd Gurley II .60 1.50
16 Russell Wilson .75 2.00
17 Clay Matthews .60 1.50
18 Le'Veon Bell .50 1.25
19 Navorro Bowman .50 1.25
20 Dez Bryant .60 1.50
21 Adrian Peterson .60 1.50
22 DeMarco Murray .50 1.25
23 Matthew Stafford .50 1.25
24 Brandon Marshall .40 1.00
25 A.J. Green .60 1.50
26 Sammy Watkins .60 1.50
27 Luke Kuechly .50 1.25
28 Joe Flacco .50 1.25
29 Drew Brees .60 1.50
30 J.J. Watt .60 1.50
31 Devonta Freeman .50 1.25
32 Travis Benjamin .40 1.00
33 Ryan Tannehill .50 1.25
34 Larry Fitzgerald .50 1.25
35 Jay Cutler .40 1.00
36 Allen Robinson .50 1.25
37 Teddy Bridgewater .50 1.25
38 Von Miller .50 1.25
39 Amari Cooper .60 1.50
40 Jameis Winston .60 1.50

2016 Donruss Optic Inducted

*BLUE/149: 1X TO 2.5X BASIC INSERTS
*RED/99: 1.2X TO 3X BASIC INSERTS
1 Brett Favre 1.25 3.00
2 Marvin Harrison .50 1.25
3 Kevin Greene .60 1.50
4 Ken Stabler .60 1.50

2016 Donruss Optic Legends of the Fall

*BLUE/149: 1X TO 2.5X BASIC INSERTS
*RED/99: 1.2X TO 3X BASIC INSERTS
1 Joe Namath .75 2.00
2 Adam Vinatieri .50 1.25
3 Eli Manning .50 1.25
4 Terry Bradshaw .75 2.00
5 Tom Brady 1.50 4.00
6 Roger Staubach .75 2.00
7 John Elway 1.00 2.50
8 Drew Brees .60 1.50
9 Kellen Winslow .50 1.25
10 Marcus Allen .50 1.25
11 James Harrison .50 1.25
12 Franco Harris .60 1.50
13 Peyton Manning 1.25 3.00
14 Brett Favre 1.25 3.00
15 Emmitt Smith 1.00 2.50
16 Thurman Thomas .50 1.25
17 Terrell Davis .50 1.25
18 Jerry Rice 1.00 2.50
19 Michael Irvin .60 1.50
20 Larry Fitzgerald .50 1.25
21 Ray Lewis .60 1.50
22 Russell Wilson .75 2.00
23 Kurt Warner .50 1.25
24 Steve Young .75 2.00

2016 Donruss Optic Peyton Manning Top Targets

*BLUE/149: 1X TO 2.5X BASIC INSERTS
*RED/99: 1.2X TO 3X BASIC INSERTS
1 M.Harrison/P.Manning 1.25 3.00
2 P.Manning/R.Wayne 1.25 3.00
3 D.Clark/P.Manning 1.25 3.00
4 D.Thomas/P.Manning 1.25 3.00
5 E.James/P.Manning 1.25 3.00
6 P.Manning/E.Decker 1.25 3.00
7 P.Manning/E.Sanders 1.25 3.00
8 P.Manning/W.Welker 1.25 3.00
9 J.Thomas/P.Manning 1.25 3.00
10 P.Manning/P.Garcon 1.25 3.00

2016 Donruss Optic Peyton Manning Tribute
*BLUE/149: 1X TO 2.5X BASIC INSERTS
*RED/99: 1.2X TO 3X BASIC INSERTS
1 Peyton Manning 1.25 3.00
2 Peyton Manning 1.25 3.00
3 Peyton Manning 1.25 3.00
4 Peyton Manning 1.25 3.00
5 Peyton Manning 1.25 3.00
6 Peyton Manning 1.25 3.00
7 Peyton Manning 1.25 3.00
8 Peyton Manning 1.25 3.00
9 Peyton Manning 1.25 3.00
10 Peyton Manning 1.25 3.00
11 Peyton Manning 1.25 3.00
12 Peyton Manning 1.25 3.00
13 Peyton Manning 1.25 3.00
14 Peyton Manning 1.25 3.00
15 Peyton Manning 1.25 3.00
16 Peyton Manning 1.25 3.00
17 Peyton Manning 1.25 3.00
18 Peyton Manning 1.25 3.00

2016 Donruss Optic Prototypes
*BLUE/149: 1X TO 2.5X BASIC INSERTS
*RED/99: 1.2X TO 3X BASIC INSERTS
1 A.J. Green .60 1.50
2 Amari Cooper .60 1.50
3 Andrew Luck .75 2.00
4 Ben Roethlisberger .60 1.50
5 Blake Bortles .40 1.00
6 Carson Palmer .50 1.25
7 DeAndre Hopkins .50 1.25
8 Demaryius Thomas .50 1.25
9 Derek Carr .60 1.50
10 Jamaal Charles .50 1.25
11 Jameis Winston .60 1.50
12 Joe Flacco .50 1.25
13 Jordan Matthews .50 1.25
14 Larry Fitzgerald .50 1.25
15 Le'Veon Bell .50 1.25
16 Marcus Mariota .60 1.50
17 Odell Beckham Jr. .60 1.50
18 Philip Rivers .60 1.50
19 Rob Gronkowski .60 1.50
20 Todd Gurley II .60 1.50
21 Von Miller .50 1.25
22 Alshon Jeffery .50 1.25
23 Aaron Donald .60 1.50
24 Matthew Stafford .50 1.25
25 Tony Romo .50 1.25
26 Kirk Cousins .60 1.50
27 Mark Ingram .50 1.25
28 Eli Manning .50 1.25
29 Jarvis Landry .50 1.25
30 David Johnson .60 1.50
31 Joe Haden .40 1.00
32 Matt Ryan .50 1.25
33 LeSean McCoy .60 1.50

2016 Donruss Optic Rated Rookies Autographs
152 Austin Hooper 3.00 8.00
153 Braxton Miller 3.00 8.00
154 C.J. Prosise 3.00 8.00
155 Cardale Jones 3.00 8.00
156 Carson Wentz 100.00 200.00
157 Chris Moore 4.00 10.00
158 Christian Hackenberg 3.00 8.00
159 Cody Kessler 3.00 8.00
160 Connor Cook 4.00 10.00
161 Corey Coleman 5.00 12.00
162 Dak Prescott 6.00 125.00
163 DeAndre Washington 3.00 8.00
164 Demarcus Robinson 3.00 8.00
165 Derrick Henry 8.00 20.00
166 Devontae Booker 4.00 10.00
167 Moritz Bohringer 3.00 8.00
168 Ezekiel Elliott 90.00 150.00
169 Hunter Henry 4.00 10.00
170 Jacoby Brissett 4.00 10.00
171 Jalen Ramsey 5.00 12.00
172 Jared Goff 60.00 125.00
173 Jaylon Smith 3.00 8.00
174 Jeff Driskel 3.00 8.00
175 Joey Bosa 6.00 15.00
176 Jonathan Williams 4.00 10.00
177 Jordan Howard 15.00 40.00
178 Josh Doctson 4.00 10.00
179 Keenan Reynolds 4.00 10.00
180 Kenneth Dixon 3.00 8.00
181 Kenyan Drake 5.00 12.00
182 Kevin Hogan 4.00 10.00
183 Laquon Treadwell 4.00 10.00
184 Leonte Carroo 3.00 8.00
185 Malcolm Mitchell 3.00 8.00
186 Michael Thomas 6.00 15.00
188 Nick Vannett 3.00 8.00
189 Paul Perkins 3.00 8.00
190 Paxton Lynch 3.00 8.00
191 Pharoh Cooper 3.00 8.00
192 Rashard Higgins 3.00 8.00
194 Sterling Shepard 4.00 10.00
195 Tajae Sharpe 4.00 10.00
196 Trevor Davis 3.00 8.00
197 Tyler Boyd 4.00 10.00
198 Tyler Ervin 3.00 8.00
199 Wendell Smallwood 3.00 8.00
200 Will Fuller V 5.00 12.00

2016 Donruss Optic Rated Rookies Autographs Black
*BLACK/25: .75X TO 2X BASIC AU/150
156 Carson Wentz 300.00 600.00
162 Dak Prescott 150.00 300.00
168 Ezekiel Elliott 200.00 400.00
172 Jared Goff 200.00 400.00

2016 Donruss Optic Rated Rookies Autographs Blue
*BLUE/75: .6X TO 1.5X BASIC AU/75
156 Carson Wentz 200.00 400.00
162 Dak Prescott 100.00 200.00
168 Ezekiel Elliott 150.00 300.00
172 Jared Goff 100.00 200.00

2016 Donruss Optic Rated Rookies Autographs Holo
*HOLO/99: .5X TO 1.2X BASIC AU/150
156 Carson Wentz 150.00 300.00
162 Dak Prescott 75.00 150.00
168 Ezekiel Elliott 150.00 300.00
172 Jared Goff 150.00 300.00

2016 Donruss Optic Rated Rookies Autographs Red
*RED/50: .6X TO 1.5X BASIC AU/150
156 Carson Wentz 200.00 400.00
162 Dak Prescott 150.00 250.00
168 Ezekiel Elliott 200.00 400.00
172 Jared Goff 200.00 400.00

2016 Donruss Optic Rookie Patch Autograph
1 Alex Collins 10.00 25.00
2 Braxton Miller 8.00 20.00
3 C.J. Prosise 8.00 20.00
4 Cardale Jones 8.00 20.00
5 Carson Wentz 200.00 400.00
6 Chris Moore 10.00 25.00
7 Christian Hackenberg 8.00 20.00
8 Cody Kessler 8.00 20.00
9 Connor Cook 10.00 25.00
10 Corey Coleman 12.00 30.00
11 Dak Prescott 125.00 250.00
12 DeAndre Washington 8.00 20.00
13 Demarcus Robinson 8.00 20.00
14 Derrick Henry 20.00 50.00
15 Devontae Booker 10.00 25.00
16 Ezekiel Elliott 150.00 300.00
17 Hunter Henry 25.00 50.00
18 Jared Goff 100.00 200.00
19 Joey Bosa 15.00 40.00
20 Jonathan Williams 10.00 25.00
21 Jordan Howard 20.00 50.00
22 Josh Doctson 10.00 25.00
23 Keenan Reynolds 10.00 25.00
24 Kenneth Dixon 8.00 20.00
25 Kenyan Drake 12.00 30.00
27 Laquon Treadwell 10.00 25.00
28 Leonte Carroo 8.00 20.00
29 Michael Thomas 30.00 60.00
30 Moritz Bohringer 8.00 20.00
31 Paul Perkins 8.00 20.00
32 Paxton Lynch 8.00 20.00
33 Pharoh Cooper 8.00 20.00
34 Ricardo Louis 8.00 20.00
35 Sterling Shepard 10.00 25.00
36 Trevor Davis 8.00 20.00
37 Tyler Boyd 10.00 25.00
38 Tyler Ervin 8.00 20.00
39 Wendell Smallwood 8.00 20.00
40 Will Fuller V 12.00 30.00

2016 Donruss Optic Rookie Signatures
*BASE AU/150: .3X TO .8X HOLO AU/99
117 Tyreek Hill 25.00 50.00

2016 Donruss Optic Rookie Signatures Black
*BLACK/25: .6X TO 1.5X BASIC AU/99

2016 Donruss Optic Rookie Signatures Blue
*BLUE/75: .4X TO 1X HOLO AU/99

2016 Donruss Optic Rookie Signatures Red
*RED/50: .5X TO 1.2X HOLO AU/99
117 Tyreek Hill 30.00 80.00

2016 Donruss Optic Rookie Threads
*B&G: .3X TO .8X BASIC JSY/150-175
*BRONZE: .3X TO .8X BASIC JSY/150-175
*PINK: .3X TO .8X BASIC JSY/150-175
*PRIME/50: .6X TO 1.5X BASIC JSY/150-175
1 Alex Collins/175 2.50 6.00
2 Braxton Miller/175 2.00 5.00
3 C.J. Prosise/175 2.00 5.00
4 Cardale Jones/175 2.00 5.00
5 Carson Wentz/150 8.00 20.00
6 Chris Moore/175 2.50 6.00
7 Christian Hackenberg/175 2.00 5.00
8 Cody Kessler/175 2.00 5.00
9 Connor Cook/175 2.50 6.00
10 Corey Coleman/175 3.00 8.00
11 Dak Prescott/150 10.00 25.00
12 DeAndre Washington/175 2.00 5.00
13 Demarcus Robinson/175 2.00 5.00
14 Derrick Henry/150 5.00 12.00
15 Devontae Booker/175 2.50 6.00
16 Ezekiel Elliott/150 10.00 25.00
17 Hunter Henry/175 2.50 6.00
18 Jared Goff/150 6.00 15.00
19 Joey Bosa/150 4.00 10.00
20 Jonathan Williams/175 2.50 6.00
21 Jordan Howard/175 4.00 10.00
22 Josh Doctson/175 2.50 6.00
23 Keenan Reynolds/175 2.50 6.00
24 Kenneth Dixon/175 2.00 5.00
25 Kenyan Drake/175 3.00 8.00
26 Kevin Hogan/175 2.50 6.00
27 Laquon Treadwell/175 2.50 6.00
28 Leonte Carroo/175 2.00 5.00
29 Michael Thomas/175 4.00 10.00
30 Moritz Bohringer/175 2.00 5.00
31 Paul Perkins/175 2.00 5.00
32 Paxton Lynch/150 2.00 5.00
33 Pharoh Cooper/175 2.00 5.00
34 Ricardo Louis/175 2.00 5.00
35 Sterling Shepard/150 2.50 6.00
36 Trevor Davis/175 2.00 5.00
37 Tyler Boyd/175 2.50 6.00
38 Tyler Ervin/175 2.00 5.00
39 Wendell Smallwood/175 2.00 5.00
40 Will Fuller V/150 3.00 8.00

2016 Donruss Optic The Elite Series Autographs
1 Blake Bortles/20 6.00 15.00
2 Demaryius Thomas/20 8.00 20.00
3 Derek Carr/20
4 Eli Manning/20 25.00 50.00
5 Jordy Nelson/20 8.00 20.00
8 Devonta Freeman/20 8.00 20.00
10 Matthew Stafford/20 40.00 80.00
11 Antonio Brown/20 30.00 60.00
12 Allen Robinson/20 8.00 20.00
13 Doug Baldwin/20 8.00 20.00
14 Sammy Watkins/20 10.00 25.00
16 Steve Smith Sr./20 8.00 20.00
17 Jeremy Maclin/20 6.00 15.00
19 Jameis Winston/20 25.00 50.00
20 Antonio Gates/20 6.00 15.00
21 David Johnson/20 10.00 25.00
22 Ryan Tannehill/20 8.00 20.00
23 A.J. Green/20 10.00 25.00

2016 Donruss Optic The Legends Series Autographs
1 Troy Aikman/20 40.00 80.00
3 Kurt Warner/20 25.00 50.00
6 Bo Jackson/20 30.00 60.00
7 Steve Largent/20 10.00 25.00
8 Fred Biletnikoff/20 10.00 25.00
9 Rod Woodson/20 8.00 20.00
10 Ray Lewis/20 40.00 80.00
12 Ed Reed/20 25.00 50.00
13 Andre Reed/20 8.00 20.00
14 Randall Cunningham/20 25.00 50.00

2016 Donruss Optic The Rookies
1 Jared Goff 2.50 6.00
2 Carson Wentz 4.00 10.00
3 Paxton Lynch .40 1.00
4 Christian Hackenberg .40 1.00
5 Cody Kessler .40 1.00
6 Connor Cook .50 1.25
7 Dak Prescott 6.00 15.00
8 Cardale Jones .40 1.00
9 Jacoby Brissett .50 1.25
10 Ezekiel Elliott 8.00 20.00
11 Derrick Henry 1.00 2.50
12 Kenyan Drake .60 1.50
13 C.J. Prosise .40 1.00
14 Tyler Ervin .40 1.00
15 Kenneth Dixon .40 1.00
16 Devontae Booker .50 1.25
17 Paul Perkins .40 1.00
18 Jordan Howard 1.00 2.50
19 Corey Coleman .60 1.50
20 Josh Doctson .50 1.25
21 Will Fuller V .60 1.50
22 Laquon Treadwell .50 1.25
23 Sterling Shepard .50 1.25
24 Michael Thomas .75 2.00
25 Tyler Boyd .50 1.25
26 Braxton Miller .40 1.00
27 Leonte Carroo .40 1.00
28 Chris Moore .50 1.25
29 Malcolm Mitchell .40 1.00
30 Tajae Sharpe .50 1.25
31 Joey Bosa .75 2.00
32 Jalen Ramsey .60 1.50
33 DeForest Buckner .40 1.00
34 Sheldon Rankins .50 1.25
35 Myles Jack .50 1.25
36 Vernon Hargreaves III .60 1.50
37 Eli Apple .50 1.25
38 Jaylon Smith .40 1.00
39 Shaq Lawson .40 1.00
40 Darron Lee .40 1.00

2016 Donruss Optic The Rookies Blue
*BLUE/149: 1X TO 2.5X BASIC INSERTS

2016 Donruss Optic The Rookies Red
*RED/99: 1.2X TO 3X BASIC INSERTS
7 Dak Prescott 30.00 60.00
10 Ezekiel Elliott 40.00 100.00

2016 Donruss Optic Threads
1 Allen Robinson/100 2.50 6.00
2 Amari Cooper/100 3.00 8.00
3 Brandin Cooks/100 2.50 6.00
4 Carlos Hyde/100 2.00 5.00
5 Larry Fitzgerald/100 2.50 6.00
6 Denard Robinson/100 2.00 5.00
7 Devin Funchess/100 2.00 5.00
8 Devonta Freeman/100 2.50 6.00
9 Dorial Green-Beckham/100 2.00 5.00
10 Earl Thomas III/100 2.50 6.00
11 Geno Atkins/100 2.00 5.00
12 Jameis Winston/100 3.00 8.00
13 Jeremy Langford/100 2.50 6.00
14 Joe Haden/100 2.00 5.00
15 Junior Seau/50 3.00 8.00
16 Kelvin Benjamin/100 2.50 6.00
17 Sammy Watkins/100 3.00 8.00
18 Stefon Diggs/100 2.50 6.00
19 T.J. Yeldon/100 2.00 5.00
20 Von Miller/50 3.00 8.00

2016 Donruss Optic Triple Rookie Autographs
1 Lnch/Wntz/Gff 175.00 350.00
2 Drke/Hnry/Ellt 75.00 150.00
3 Clmn/Dctsn/Fllr 15.00 40.00
4 Shprd/Trdwll/Thms 20.00 50.00
5 Jns/Prsctt/Brsstt 75.00 150.00

2016 Donruss Optic X-Factor
*BLUE/149: 1X TO 2.5X BASIC INSERTS
*RED/99: 1.2X TO 3X BASIC INSERTS
1 Aaron Rodgers 1.25 3.00
2 Adrian Peterson .60 1.50
3 Antonio Brown .60 1.50
4 Barry Sanders 1.00 2.50
5 Cam Newton .60 1.50
6 Carson Wentz 4.00 10.00
7 Dan Marino 1.25 3.00
8 Doug Martin .50 1.25
9 Drew Brees .60 1.50
10 Emmitt Smith 1.00 2.50
11 J.J. Watt .60 1.50
12 Jared Goff 2.50 6.00
13 Jerry Rice 1.00 2.50
14 Todd Gurley II .60 1.50
15 John Elway 1.00 2.50
16 Julio Jones .60 1.50
17 Roger Staubach .75 2.00
18 Russell Wilson .75 2.00
19 Terry Bradshaw .75 2.00
20 Tom Brady 1.50 4.00

2017 Donruss Optic
1 Tom Brady 1.00 2.50
2 Eli Manning .30 .75
3 Lamar Miller .25 .60
4 Carson Wentz .50 1.25
5 Melvin Gordon .30 .75
6 Russell Wilson .50 1.25
7 Mike Wallace .25 .60
8 Alex Smith .30 .75
9 A.J. Green .40 1.00
10 Sam Bradford .25 .60
11 Emmanuel Sanders .40 1.00
12 Isaiah Crowell .25 .60
13 Robby Anderson .25 .60
14 Clay Matthews .30 .75
15 Le'Veon Bell .30 .75
16 Allen Robinson .30 .75
17 Jameis Winston .30 .75
18 Julio Jones .40 1.00
19 Tavon Austin .25 .60
20 Greg Olsen .30 .75
21 Von Miller .30 .75
22 Jordan Matthews .25 .60
23 Terrelle Pryor Sr. .25 .60
24 LeSean McCoy .40 1.00
25 DeAndre Hopkins .30 .75
26 Eddie Lacy .25 .60
27 Mike Evans .30 .75
28 Latavius Murray .25 .60
29 Jeremy Hill .25 .60
30 Brandon Marshall .25 .60
31 Todd Gurley II .40 1.00
32 Kelvin Benjamin .30 .75
33 Brandin Cooks .30 .75
34 Dak Prescott .40 1.00
35 DeMarco Murray .30 .75
36 Randall Cobb .30 .75
37 Blake Bortles .25 .60
38 Devonta Freeman .30 .75
39 DeSean Jackson .30 .75
40 Pierre Garcon .30 .75
41 Jordan Reed .25 .60
42 Carlos Hyde .25 .60
43 Aaron Rodgers .75 2.00
44 Matt Ryan .30 .75
45 Allen Hurns .25 .60
46 Jerrell Freeman .25 .60
47 Marcus Mariota .40 1.00
48 Derek Carr .40 1.00
49 Ezekiel Elliott .50 1.25
50 Amari Cooper .40 1.00
51 Tyrod Taylor .30 .75
52 Joey Bosa .40 1.00
53 Andy Dalton .30 .75
54 Stefon Diggs .30 .75
55 Golden Tate III .25 .60
56 Odell Beckham Jr. .40 1.00
57 Alshon Jeffery .30 .75
58 Kirk Cousins .40 1.00
59 Larry Fitzgerald .30 .75
60 Frank Gore .30 .75
61 Dez Bryant .40 1.00
62 Drew Brees .40 1.00
63 Jordy Nelson .30 .75
64 Marshawn Lynch .30 .75
65 Travis Kelce .40 1.00
66 Joe Flacco .30 .75
67 Brian Hoyer .25 .60
68 Ryan Tannehill .30 .75
69 Jordan Howard .40 1.00
70 Michael Thomas .40 1.00
71 Josh McCown .25 .60
72 Doug Baldwin .30 .75
73 Antonio Brown .40 1.00
74 Andrew Luck .50 1.25
75 J.J. Watt .40 1.00
76 Philip Rivers .40 1.00
77 Tajae Sharpe .25 .60
78 Jamie Collins .25 .60
79 Rob Gronkowski .40 1.00
80 Marvin Jones Jr. .25 .60
81 Demaryius Thomas .30 .75
82 Adrian Peterson .40 1.00
83 Carson Palmer .30 .75
84 Khalil Mack .40 1.00
85 Tyreek Hill .40 1.00
86 Terrell Suggs .25 .60
87 Richard Sherman .40 1.00
88 Jay Ajayi .30 .75
89 Mike Glennon .30 .75
90 Jarvis Landry .30 .75
91 Matt Forte .25 .60
92 Corey Coleman .25 .60
93 Ben Roethlisberger .40 1.00
94 Matthew Stafford .30 .75
95 David Johnson .40 1.00
96 T.Y. Hilton .30 .75
97 Jared Goff .40 1.00
98 Sammy Watkins .40 1.00
99 Julian Edelman .40 1.00
100 Cam Newton .40 1.00
101 Sidney Jones RC .40 1.00
102 Tre'Davious White RC .40 1.00
103 Zach Cunningham RC .50 1.25
104 Adam Shaheen RC .40 1.00
105 Jordan Leggett RC .40 1.00
106 Myles Garrett RC 1.25 3.00
107 Bucky Hodges RC .40 1.00
108 Derek Barnett RC .50 1.25
109 Matthew Dayes RC .40 1.00
110 Jarrad Davis RC .50 1.25
111 Quincy Wilson RC .40 1.00
112 Taco Charlton RC .40 1.00
113 Chidobe Awuzie RC .50 1.25
114 Chad Williams RC .40 1.00
115 Jeremy Sprinkle RC .40 1.00
116 Solomon Thomas RC .40 1.00
117 Robert Davis RC .40 1.00
118 Malik Hooker RC .40 1.00
119 Chad Kelly RC .40 1.00
120 Charles Harris RC .40 1.00
121 DeMarcus Walker RC .40 1.00
122 T.J. Watt RC 1.25 3.00
123 Dawuane Smoot RC .40 1.00
124 Jonnu Smith RC .40 1.00
125 Trent Taylor RC .50 1.25
126 Jamal Adams RC .40 1.00
127 Stacy Coley RC .40 1.00
128 Marlon Humphrey RC .40 1.00
129 Kevin King RC .50 1.25
130 Gareon Conley RC .40 1.00
131 Raekwon McMillan RC .40 1.00
132 Reuben Foster RC .40 1.00
133 Jordan Willis RC .40 1.00
134 Tarik Cohen RC .75 2.00
135 Aaron Jones RC 1.00 2.50
136 Marshon Lattimore RC .50 1.25
137 Isaiah Ford RC .40 1.00
138 Jonathan Allen RC .50 1.25
139 Malik McDowell RC .40 1.00
140 Jabrill Peppers RC .60 1.50
141 Obi Melifonwu RC .40 1.00
142 Gerald Everett RC .40 1.00
143 Chris Wormley RC .40 1.00
144 Jake Butt RC .50 1.25
145 Elijah McGuire RC .40 1.00
146 Haason Reddick RC .40 1.00
147 Elijah Hood RC .40 1.00
148 Adoree' Jackson RC .50 1.25
149 Budda Baker RC .40 1.00
150 Takkarist McKinley RC .40 1.00
151 Josh Reynolds RR RC .40 1.00
152 Marlon Mack RR RC .60 1.50
153 ArDarius Stewart RR RC .40 1.00
154 DeShone Kizer RR RC .40 1.00
155 Chris Godwin RR RC .50 1.25
156 Samaje Perine RR RC .40 1.00
157 Amara Darboh RR RC .40 1.00
158 Joe Williams RR RC .50 1.25
159 Zay Jones RR RC .40 1.00
160 Brian Hill RR RC .40 1.00
161 Mack Hollins RR RC .40 1.00
162 Donnel Pumphrey RR RC .50 1.25
163 Chad Hansen RR RC .40 1.00
164 David Njoku RR RC .50 1.25
165 Taywan Taylor RR RC .40 1.00
166 Corey Davis RR RC .60 1.50
167 Jamaal Williams RR RC .40 1.00
168 Christian McCaffrey RR RC 1.00 2.50
169 Leonard Fournette RR RC 1.25 3.00
170 C.J. Beathard RR RC .40 1.00
171 Josh Malone RR RC .40 1.00
172 James Conner RR RC .75 2.00
173 Brad Kaaya RR RC .40 1.00
174 Mike Williams RR RC .60 1.50
175 Kenny Golladay RR RC .60 1.50
176 JuJu Smith-Schuster RR RC 1.00 2.50
177 Patrick Mahomes II RR RC 20.00 50.00
178 Mitchell Trubisky RR RC 2.00 5.00
179 Cooper Kupp RR RC .60 1.50
180 Evan Engram RR RC .50 1.25
181 R. Joshua Dobbs RR RC .50 1.25
182 Kareem Hunt RR RC .75 2.00
183 Shelton Gibson RR RC .40 1.00
184 Nathan Peterman RR RC .50 1.25
185 Joe Mixon RR RC .75 2.00
186 Carlos Henderson RR RC .40 1.00
187 Dede Westbrook RR RC .40 1.00
188 Wayne Gallman RR RC .50 1.25
189 Ryan Switzer RR RC .50 1.25
190 D'Onta Foreman RR RC .50 1.25
191 Noah Brown RR RC .50 1.25
192 O.J. Howard RR RC .50 1.25
193 Dalvin Cook RR RC 1.00 2.50
194 John Ross III RR RC .50 1.25
195 Deshaun Watson RR RC 2.50 6.00
196 Curtis Samuel RR RC .50 1.25
197 Malachi Dupre RR RC .40 1.00
198 Davis Webb RR RC .40 1.00
199 Alvin Kamara RR RC 1.50 4.00
200 Jeremy McNichols RR RC .40 1.00

2017 Donruss Optic Aqua
*AQUA VET/299: 1.2X TO 3X BASIC VET
*AQUA RC/299: .75X TO 2X BASIC RR
177 Patrick Mahomes II RR 50.00 100.00

2017 Donruss Optic Black
*BLACK VET/25: 3X TO 8X BASIC VET
*BLACK RC/25: 2X TO 5X BASIC RC
177 Patrick Mahomes II RR 200.00 400.00

2017 Donruss Optic Blue
*BLUE VET/199: 1.5X TO 4X BASIC VET
*BLUE RC: 1X TO 2.5X BASIC RC
177 Patrick Mahomes II RR 75.00 150.00

2017 Donruss Optic Holo
*HOLO VET: .75X TO 2X BASIC VET
*HOLO RC: .5X TO 1.2X BASIC RR
177 Patrick Mahomes II RR 40.00 80.00

2017 Donruss Optic Lime
*ROOKIES: .8X TO 2X BASIC CARDS
177 Patrick Mahomes II RR 60.00 125.00

2017 Donruss Optic Orange
*ORANGE VET/199: 1.5X TO 4X BASIC VET
*ORANGE RC: 1X TO 2.5X BASIC RR
177 Patrick Mahomes II RR 75.00 150.00

2017 Donruss Optic Pink
*ROOKIES: .6X TO 1.5X BASIC CARDS
177 Patrick Mahomes II RR 40.00 80.00

2017 Donruss Optic Purple
*PURPLE VETS/50: 2.5X TO 6X BASIC CARDS
*PURPLE RC/50: 1.5X TO 4X BASIC CARDS
177 Patrick Mahomes II RR 100.00 200.00

2017 Donruss Optic Red
*RED VET/99: 2X TO 5X BASIC VET
*RED RC/99: 1.2X TO 3X BASIC RC
177 Patrick Mahomes II RR 75.00 150.00

2017 Donruss Optic '81 Tribute
*BLUE/149: .75X TO 2X BASIC INSERTS
*RED/99: 1X TO 2.5X BASIC INSERTS
1 DeMarco Murray .60 1.50
2 Todd Gurley II .75 2.00
3 Drew Brees .75 2.00
4 Larry Fitzgerald .60 1.50
5 Carson Wentz 1.00 2.50
6 Jordan Howard .75 2.00
7 Antonio Brown .75 2.00
8 Ezekiel Elliott 1.00 2.50
9 Richard Sherman .75 2.00
10 Aaron Rodgers 1.50 4.00
11 Khalil Mack .75 2.00
12 Jarvis Landry .60 1.50
13 Odell Beckham Jr. .75 2.00
14 Julio Jones .75 2.00
15 Ben Roethlisberger .75 2.00
16 A.J. Green .75 2.00
17 Philip Rivers .75 2.00
18 Von Miller .60 1.50
19 Jameis Winston .60 1.50
20 J.J. Watt .75 2.00
21 Kirk Cousins .75 2.00
22 Adrian Peterson .75 2.00
23 Derek Carr .75 2.00
24 Matt Ryan .60 1.50
25 Le'Veon Bell .60 1.50
26 Dak Prescott .75 2.00
27 Russell Wilson 1.00 2.50
28 Matthew Stafford .60 1.50
29 Marcus Mariota .75 2.00
30 Andrew Luck 1.00 2.50
31 Devonta Freeman .60 1.50
32 Tom Brady 2.00 5.00
33 Amari Cooper .75 2.00
34 Cam Newton .75 2.00
35 David Johnson .75 2.00

2017 Donruss Optic AKA
*BLUE/149: .75X TO 2X BASIC INSERTS
*RED/99: 1X TO 2.5X BASIC INSERTS
1 Roger Staubach 1.00 2.50
2 Jameis Winston .60 1.50
3 Travis Kelce .75 2.00
4 Joe Namath 1.00 2.50
5 Marshawn Lynch .60 1.50
6 Cam Newton .75 2.00
7 Randy White .60 1.50
8 Ezekiel Elliott 1.00 2.50
9 Terry Bradshaw 1.25 3.00
10 Jerome Bettis .75 2.00
11 Tyrann Mathieu .60 1.50
12 Christian Okoye .50 1.25
13 Ed Reed .60 1.50
14 Gale Sayers .75 2.00
15 Tom Brady 2.00 5.00
16 Jerry Rice 1.25 3.00
17 Walter Payton 1.50 4.00
18 Deion Sanders .60 1.50
19 Peyton Manning 1.50 4.00
20 Rob Gronkowski .75 2.00
21 J.J. Watt .75 2.00
22 Joe Montana 2.00 5.00
23 Ben Roethlisberger .75 2.00
24 Le'Veon Bell .60 1.50
25 Lance Alworth .60 1.50
26 Red Grange 1.00 2.50
27 Mitchell Trubisky 2.50 6.00
28 John Ross III .60 1.50
29 Jabrill Peppers .75 2.00
30 Patrick Mahomes II 25.00 60.00

2017 Donruss Optic Fans of the Game
*BLUE/149: .75X TO 2X BASIC INSERTS
*RED/99: 1X TO 2.5X BASIC INSERTS
1 Joey Belladonna .75 2.00
2 Genevieve Morton .75 2.00
3 Chris Berman .75 2.00
4 Dick Vitale .75 2.00

2017 Donruss Optic Gridiron Kings
*BLUE/149: .75X TO 2X BASIC INSERTS
*RED/99: 1X TO 2.5X BASIC INSERTS
1 Jordy Nelson .60 1.50
2 Antonio Brown .75 2.00
3 Ben Roethlisberger .75 2.00
4 David Johnson .75 2.00
5 Marcus Mariota .75 2.00
6 Derek Carr .75 2.00
7 Odell Beckham Jr. .75 2.00
8 Richard Sherman .75 2.00
9 Philip Rivers .75 2.00
10 Eli Manning .60 1.50
11 Adrian Peterson .75 2.00
12 Jordan Howard .75 2.00
13 J.J. Watt .75 2.00
14 Matthew Stafford .60 1.50
15 Matt Ryan .60 1.50
16 Tom Brady 2.00 5.00
17 Ezekiel Elliott 1.00 2.50
18 A.J. Green .75 2.00
19 Amari Cooper .75 2.00
20 Jameis Winston .60 1.50
21 Russell Wilson 1.00 2.50
22 Mike Evans .60 1.50
23 Devonta Freeman .60 1.50
24 Le'Veon Bell .60 1.50
25 Carson Wentz 1.00 2.50
26 DeMarco Murray .60 1.50
27 Julio Jones .75 2.00
28 Von Miller .60 1.50
29 Dak Prescott .75 2.00
30 Drew Brees .75 2.00
31 Todd Gurley II .75 2.00
32 Cam Newton .75 2.00
33 Joe Flacco .60 1.50
34 Andrew Luck 1.00 2.50
35 Aaron Rodgers 1.50 4.00
36 Tyreek Hill .75 2.00
37 Michael Thomas .75 2.00

2017 Donruss Optic Illusions
*BLUE/149: .75X TO 2X BASIC INSERTS
*RED/99: 1X TO 2.5X BASIC INSERTS
1 Jim Kelly / Nathan Peterman .75 2.00
2 O.J. Howard / Ozzie Newsome .60 1.50
3 Kareem Hunt / Priest Holmes 1.00 2.50
4 Andre Reed / Zay Jones .60 1.50
5 Chuck Foreman / Dalvin Cook 1.25 3.00
6 Jim McMahon / Mitchell Trubisky 2.50 6.00
7 DeShone Kizer / Joe Montana 2.00 5.00
8 Mike Williams / Lance Alworth .75 2.00
9 Alvin Kamara / Darren Sproles 2.00 5.00
10 A.J. Green / John Ross III .75 2.00
11 Ben Roethlisberger / R. Joshua Dobbs .75 2.00
12 Myles Garrett / Von Miller 1.50 4.00
13 Evan Engram / Mark Bavaro .60 1.50
14 Curtis Samuel / Steve Smith Sr. .60 1.50
15 Joe Mixon / Adrian Peterson 1.00 2.50
16 Fred Taylor / Leonard Fournette 1.50 4.00
17 Antonio Brown / JuJu Smith-Schuster 1.25 3.00
18 Christian McCaffrey / Ed McCaffrey 1.25 3.00
19 D'Onta Foreman / Ricky Williams .60 1.50
20 Len Dawson / Patrick Mahomes II 10.00 25.00
21 Cam Newton / Deshaun Watson 3.00 8.00
22 Eli Manning / Davis Webb .60 1.50
23 James Conner / Jerome Bettis 1.00 2.50
24 Dez Bryant / Corey Davis .75 2.00
25 Mike Evans / Chris Godwin .60 1.50
26 Anquan Boldin / Kenny Golladay .75 2.00
27 J.J. Watt / T.J. Watt 1.50 4.00
28 Ezekiel Elliott / Emmitt Smith 1.25 3.00
29 Jimmy Garoppolo / Tom Brady 2.00 5.00
30 Joe Montana / Steve Young 2.00 5.00

2017 Donruss Optic Inducted
*BLUE/149: .75X TO 2X BASIC INSERTS
*RED/99: 1X TO 2.5X BASIC INSERTS
1 Morten Andersen .50 1.25
2 Terrell Davis .60 1.50
3 LaDainian Tomlinson .60 1.50
4 Kurt Warner .60 1.50

2017 Donruss Optic Rated Rookies Autographs
151 Josh Reynolds/150 3.00 8.00
152 Marlon Mack/99 6.00 15.00
153 ArDarius Stewart/150 3.00 8.00
154 DeShone Kizer/150 3.00 8.00
155 Chris Godwin/150 4.00 10.00
156 Samaje Perine/150 3.00 8.00
157 Amara Darboh/150 3.00 8.00
158 Joe Williams/150 3.00 8.00
159 Zay Jones/150 4.00 10.00
161 Mack Hollins/150 3.00 8.00
162 Donnel Pumphrey/150 4.00 10.00
163 Chad Hansen/150 3.00 8.00
164 David Njoku/150 4.00 10.00
165 Taywan Taylor/150 3.00 8.00
166 Corey Davis/150 5.00 12.00
167 Jamaal Williams/125 3.00 8.00
168 Christian McCaffrey/150 30.00 60.00
169 Leonard Fournette/150 10.00 25.00
170 C.J. Beathard/150 3.00 8.00
171 Josh Malone/150 3.00 8.00
172 James Conner/150 12.00 30.00
173 Brad Kaaya/150 3.00 8.00
174 Mike Williams/150 5.00 12.00
175 Kenny Golladay/150 5.00 12.00
176 JuJu Smith-Schuster/150 30.00 60.00
177 Patrick Mahomes II/150 250.00 400.00
178 Mitchell Trubisky/150 60.00 125.00
179 Cooper Kupp/150 EXCH 12.00 30.00
180 Evan Engram/150 4.00 10.00
181 R. Joshua Dobbs/150 4.00 10.00
182 Kareem Hunt/150 12.00 30.00
183 Shelton Gibson/150 3.00 8.00
184 Nathan Peterman/150 4.00 10.00
185 Joe Mixon/99 12.00 30.00
186 Carlos Henderson/150 3.00 8.00
187 Dede Westbrook/150 3.00 8.00
188 Wayne Gallman/150 4.00 10.00
189 Ryan Switzer/150 4.00 10.00
190 D'Onta Foreman/150 4.00 10.00
191 Noah Brown/150
192 O.J. Howard/150 4.00 10.00
193 Dalvin Cook/150 25.00 50.00
194 John Ross III/150 4.00 10.00
195 Deshaun Watson/150 EXCH 75.00 150.00
196 Curtis Samuel/150 4.00 10.00
197 Malachi Dupre/150 3.00 8.00
198 Davis Webb/150 10.00 25.00
199 Alvin Kamara/150 30.00 60.00
200 Jeremy McNichols/150 3.00 8.00

2017 Donruss Optic Rated Rookies Autographs Black
*BLACK/25: .8X TO 2X BASIC AU/150
*BLACK/15: .8X TO 2X BASIC AU/99
176 JuJu Smith-Schuster/25 100.00 200.00
177 Patrick Mahomes II/25 600.00 1000.00
178 Mitchell Trubisky/25 100.00 200.00
195 Deshaun Watson/25 EXCH 150.00 250.00
199 Alvin Kamara/25 100.00 200.00

2017 Donruss Optic Rated Rookies Autographs Blue
*BLUE/75: .5X TO 1.2X BASIC AU/125-150
*BLUE/49: .5X TO 1.2X BASIC AU/99
176 JuJu Smith-Schuster/75 60.00 125.00
177 Patrick Mahomes II/75 300.00 500.00
178 Mitchell Trubisky/75 60.00 125.00
195 Deshaun Watson/75 EXCH 75.00 150.00
199 Alvin Kamara/75 50.00 100.00

2017 Donruss Optic Rated Rookies Autographs Holo
*HOLO/99: .5X TO 1.2X BASIC AU/125-150
*HOLO/79: .4X TO 1X BASIC AU/99
176 JuJu Smith-Schuster/99 60.00 125.00
177 Patrick Mahomes II/99 300.00 500.00
178 Mitchell Trubisky/99 60.00 125.00
195 Deshaun Watson/99 75.00 150.00
199 Alvin Kamara/99 50.00 100.00

2017 Donruss Optic Rated Rookies Autographs Purple
*PURPLE/35: .6X TO 1.5X BASIC AU/125-150
*PURPLE/20: .8X TO 2X BASIC AU/99
176 JuJu Smith-Schuster/35 75.00 150.00
177 Patrick Mahomes II/35 350.00 600.00
178 Mitchell Trubisky/35 75.00 150.00
195 Deshaun Watson/35 200.00 300.00
199 Alvin Kamara/35 60.00 125.00

2017 Donruss Optic Rated Rookies Autographs Red
*RED/50: .6X TO 1.5X BASIC AU/125-150
*RED/30: .6X TO 1.5X BASIC AU/99
176 JuJu Smith-Schuster/50 75.00 150.00
177 Patrick Mahomes II/50 350.00 600.00
178 Mitchell Trubisky/50 75.00 150.00
195 Deshaun Watson/50 200.00 300.00
199 Alvin Kamara/50 60.00 125.00

2017 Donruss Optic Rookie Autographs
101 Sidney Jones 2.50 6.00
102 Tre'Davious White 2.50 6.00
104 Adam Shaheen 2.50 6.00
105 Jordan Leggett 2.50 6.00
109 Matthew Dayes 2.50 6.00
110 Jarrad Davis 3.00 8.00
111 Quincy Wilson 2.50 6.00
112 Taco Charlton 2.50 6.00
113 Chidobe Awuzie 3.00 8.00
114 Chad Williams 2.50 6.00
115 Jeremy Sprinkle 2.50 6.00
116 Solomon Thomas 2.50 6.00
117 Robert Davis 2.50 6.00
118 Malik Hooker 2.50 6.00
119 Chad Kelly 2.50 6.00
120 Charles Harris 2.50 6.00
121 DeMarcus Walker 2.50 6.00
122 T.J. Watt 8.00 20.00
123 Dawuane Smoot 2.50 6.00
124 Jonnu Smith 2.50 6.00
125 Trent Taylor 3.00 8.00
126 Jamal Adams 2.50 6.00
127 Stacy Coley 2.50 6.00
128 Marlon Humphrey 2.50 6.00
131 Raekwon McMillan 2.50 6.00
133 Jordan Willis 2.50 6.00
134 Tarik Cohen 5.00 12.00
135 Aaron Jones 8.00 20.00
136 Marshon Lattimore 3.00 8.00
137 Isaiah Ford 2.50 6.00
138 Jonathan Allen 3.00 8.00
140 Jabrill Peppers 4.00 10.00
141 Obi Melifonwu 2.50 6.00
142 Gerald Everett 2.50 6.00
143 Chris Wormley 2.50 6.00
144 Jake Butt 3.00 8.00
145 Elijah McGuire 2.50 6.00
146 Haason Reddick 2.50 6.00
147 Elijah Hood 2.50 6.00
149 Budda Baker 2.50 6.00

2017 Donruss Optic Rookie Autographs Black
*BLACK/25: 1X TO 2.5X BASIC AU
*BLACK/15: 1.2X TO 3X BASIC AU

2017 Donruss Optic Rookie Autographs Blue
*BLUE/75: .6X TO 1.5X BASIC AU
*BLUE/49: .8X TO 2X BASIC AU
*BLUE/25: 1X TO 2.5X BASIC AU

2017 Donruss Optic Rookie Autographs Bronze
*BRONZE: .5X TO 1.2X BASIC AU

2017 Donruss Optic Rookie Autographs Holo
*HOLO/79-99: .6X TO 1.5X BASIC AU
*HOLO/30: 1X TO 2.5X BASIC AU

2017 Donruss Optic Rookie Autographs Red
*RED/50: .8X TO 2X BASIC AU
*RED/30: 1X TO 2.5X BASIC AU
*RED/20: 1.2X TO 3X BASIC AU

2017 Donruss Optic Rookie Dual Autographs
1 C.Godwin / O.Howard 10.00 25.00
2 D.Foreman / D.Watson
3 T.Taylor / C.Davis 12.00 30.00
4 D.Wstbrk / L.Fournette 25.00 60.00
5 K.Hunt / P.Mahomes
6 N.Peterman / Z.Jones 10.00 25.00
7 D.Webb / E.Engram 10.00 25.00
8 C.McCaffrey / C.Samuel 40.00 80.00
9 J.SmthSchstr / J.Conner 20.00 50.00
10 J.Mixon / J.Ross 15.00 40.00

2017 Donruss Optic Rookie Gridiron Kings
*BLUE/149: .75X TO 2X BASIC INSERTS
*RED/99: 1X TO 2.5X BASIC INSERTS
1 Nathan Peterman .60 1.50
2 Patrick Mahomes II 12.00 30.00
3 C.J. Beathard .50 1.25
4 O.J. Howard .60 1.50
5 Davis Webb .50 1.25
6 Mitchell Trubisky 2.50 6.00
7 DeShone Kizer .50 1.25
8 Corey Davis .75 2.00
9 D'Onta Foreman .60 1.50
10 Christian McCaffrey 1.25 3.00
11 Alvin Kamara 2.00 5.00
12 Deshaun Watson 5.00 12.00
13 Samaje Perine .50 1.25
14 R. Joshua Dobbs .60 1.50
15 Dalvin Cook 1.25 3.00
16 Leonard Fournette 1.50 4.00
17 JuJu Smith-Schuster 1.25 3.00
18 Mike Williams .75 2.00
19 Dede Westbrook .50 1.25
20 John Ross III .60 1.50

2017 Donruss Optic Rookie Patch Autographs
1 Mitchell Trubisky 100.00 200.00
2 Leonard Fournette 50.00 100.00
3 Corey Davis 20.00 50.00
4 Mike Williams 20.00 50.00
5 Christian McCaffrey 60.00 125.00
6 John Ross III 15.00 40.00
7 Patrick Mahomes II 400.00 800.00
8 Deshaun Watson 250.00 400.00
9 O.J. Howard 15.00 40.00
10 Evan Engram 15.00 40.00
11 Zay Jones 15.00 40.00
13 Dalvin Cook
14 Joe Mixon 25.00 60.00
15 DeShone Kizer 12.00 30.00
16 JuJu Smith-Schuster 50.00 100.00
17 Alvin Kamara
18 Cooper Kupp 20.00 50.00
19 Taywan Taylor 12.00 30.00
20 ArDarius Stewart 12.00 30.00
21 Carlos Henderson 12.00 30.00
22 Chris Godwin 15.00 40.00
23 Kareem Hunt 30.00 80.00
24 Davis Webb 12.00 30.00
25 D'Onta Foreman 15.00 40.00
26 Kenny Golladay 20.00 50.00
27 C.J. Beathard 12.00 30.00
29 Amara Darboh 12.00 30.00
30 Dede Westbrook 12.00 30.00
31 Samaje Perine 12.00 30.00
32 Josh Reynolds 12.00 30.00
33 Mack Hollins 12.00 30.00
34 Joe Williams 12.00 30.00
35 Nathan Peterman 15.00 40.00
36 Ryan Switzer 15.00 40.00
38 R. Joshua Dobbs 15.00 40.00

2017 Donruss Optic Rookie Phenom Jerseys
*PRIME/25: .8X TO 2X BASIC JSY
1 Mitchell Trubisky 6.00 15.00
2 Leonard Fournette 6.00 15.00
3 Corey Davis 3.00 8.00
4 Mike Williams 3.00 8.00
5 Christian McCaffrey 6.00 15.00
6 John Ross III 2.50 6.00
7 Patrick Mahomes II 25.00 50.00
8 Deshaun Watson 8.00 20.00
9 O.J. Howard 2.50 6.00
10 Evan Engram 2.50 6.00
11 Zay Jones 2.50 6.00
12 Curtis Samuel 2.50 6.00
13 Dalvin Cook 4.00 10.00
14 Joe Mixon 4.00 10.00
15 DeShone Kizer 2.00 5.00
16 JuJu Smith-Schuster 4.00 10.00
17 Alvin Kamara 6.00 15.00
18 Cooper Kupp 3.00 8.00
19 Taywan Taylor 2.00 5.00
20 ArDarius Stewart 2.00 5.00
21 Carlos Henderson 2.00 5.00
22 Chris Godwin 2.50 6.00
23 Kareem Hunt 4.00 10.00
24 Davis Webb 2.00 5.00
25 D'Onta Foreman 2.50 6.00
26 Kenny Golladay 3.00 8.00
27 C.J. Beathard 2.00 5.00
28 R. Joshua Dobbs 2.50 6.00

29 Amara Darboh	2.00	5.00
30 Dede Westbrook	2.00	5.00

2017 Donruss Optic Rookie Threads

*PRIME/25: .8X TO 2X BASIC JSY

1 Mitchell Trubisky	6.00	15.00
2 Leonard Fournette	6.00	15.00
3 Corey Davis	3.00	8.00
4 Mike Williams	3.00	8.00
5 Christian McCaffrey	6.00	15.00
6 John Ross III	2.50	6.00
7 Patrick Mahomes II	15.00	40.00
8 Deshaun Watson	8.00	20.00
9 O.J. Howard	2.50	6.00
10 Evan Engram	2.50	6.00
11 Zay Jones	2.50	6.00
12 Curtis Samuel	2.50	6.00
13 Dalvin Cook	4.00	10.00
14 Joe Mixon	4.00	10.00
15 DeShone Kizer	2.00	5.00
16 JuJu Smith-Schuster	4.00	10.00
17 Alvin Kamara	6.00	15.00
18 Cooper Kupp	3.00	8.00
19 Taywan Taylor	2.00	5.00
20 ArDarius Stewart	2.00	5.00
21 Carlos Henderson	2.00	5.00
22 Chris Godwin	2.50	6.00
23 Kareem Hunt	4.00	10.00
24 Davis Webb	2.00	5.00
25 D'Onta Foreman	2.50	6.00
26 Kenny Golladay	3.00	8.00
27 C.J. Beathard	2.00	5.00
28 James Conner	4.00	10.00
29 Amara Darboh	2.00	5.00
30 Dede Westbrook	2.00	5.00
31 Samaje Perine	2.00	5.00
32 Josh Reynolds	2.00	5.00
33 R. Joshua Dobbs	2.50	6.00
34 Joe Williams	2.00	5.00
35 Nathan Peterman	2.50	6.00

2017 Donruss Optic Rookie Triple Autographs

1 Chsn/Hnt/Mhms	100.00	200.00
2 Trbsky/Wtsn/Mhms	250.00	400.00
3 Wbb/Engrm/Gllmn	30.00	60.00
4 Ck/McCffry/Frntte	100.00	200.00
5 SmthSchstr/Cnr/Dbbs	40.00	80.00

2017 Donruss Optic The Elite Series Autographs

3 Jordy Nelson/20	25.00	50.00
9 Ezekiel Elliott/20		
10 A.J. Green/20	12.00	30.00
21 David Johnson/20	12.00	30.00
22 Derek Carr/20	40.00	80.00
25 Deshaun Watson/20	100.00	200.00
26 Mitchell Trubisky/20	75.00	150.00
27 Leonard Fournette/20	25.00	60.00
28 Dalvin Cook/20	40.00	80.00
29 Christian McCaffrey/20	60.00	125.00
30 Patrick Mahomes II/20	300.00	600.00

2017 Donruss Optic The Rookies

*BLUE/149: .75X TO 2X BASIC INSERTS
*RED/99: 1X TO 2.5X BASIC INSERTS

1 Mitchell Trubisky	2.50	6.00
2 Leonard Fournette	1.50	4.00
3 Corey Davis	.75	2.00
4 Mike Williams	.75	2.00
5 Christian McCaffrey	1.25	3.00
6 John Ross III	.60	1.50
7 Patrick Mahomes II	15.00	40.00
8 Deshaun Watson	6.00	15.00
9 O.J. Howard	.60	1.50
10 Evan Engram	.60	1.50
11 Zay Jones	.60	1.50
12 Curtis Samuel	.60	1.50
13 Dalvin Cook	1.25	3.00
14 Joe Mixon	1.00	2.50
15 DeShone Kizer	.50	1.25
16 JuJu Smith-Schuster	1.25	3.00
17 Alvin Kamara	2.00	5.00
18 Cooper Kupp	.75	2.00
19 Taywan Taylor	.50	1.25
20 ArDarius Stewart	.50	1.25
21 Carlos Henderson	.50	1.25
22 Chris Godwin	.60	1.50
23 Kareem Hunt	1.00	2.50
24 Davis Webb	.50	1.25
25 D'Onta Foreman	.60	1.50
26 Kenny Golladay	.75	2.00
27 C.J. Beathard	.50	1.25
28 James Conner	1.00	2.50
29 Amara Darboh	.50	1.25
30 Dede Westbrook	.50	1.25
31 Samaje Perine	.50	1.25
32 Josh Reynolds	.50	1.25
33 Mack Hollins	.50	1.25
34 Joe Williams	.50	1.25
35 Nathan Peterman	.60	1.50
36 Jeremy McNichols	.50	1.25
37 Jamaal Williams	.50	1.25
38 R. Joshua Dobbs	.60	1.50
39 Wayne Gallman	.60	1.50
40 Marlon Mack	.75	2.00

2018 Donruss Optic

1 David Johnson	.40	1.00
2 Larry Fitzgerald	.30	.75
3 Patrick Peterson	.25	.60
4 Matt Ryan	.30	.75
5 Julio Jones	.40	1.00
6 Devonta Freeman	.30	.75
7 Vic Beasley Jr.	.25	.60
8 Mohamed Sanu	.25	.60
9 Joe Flacco	.30	.75
10 Terrell Suggs	.25	.60
11 Alex Collins	.25	.60
12 LeSean McCoy	.40	1.00
13 Charles Clay	.25	.60
14 Kelvin Benjamin	.30	.75
15 Cam Newton	.40	1.00
16 Christian McCaffrey	.40	1.00
17 Greg Olsen	.30	.75
18 Mitchell Trubisky	.40	1.00
19 Jordan Howard	.40	1.00
20 Khalil Mack	.40	1.00
21 Andy Dalton	.30	.75
22 A.J. Green	.40	1.00
23 Joe Mixon	.30	.75
24 Jabrill Peppers	.25	.60
25 Carlos Hyde	.25	.60
26 Myles Garrett	.40	1.00
27 Dak Prescott	.40	1.00
28 Ezekiel Elliott	.50	1.25
29 Sean Lee	.30	.75
30 Emmanuel Sanders	.40	1.00
31 Von Miller	.30	.75
32 Demaryius Thomas	.30	.75
33 Devontae Booker	.25	.60
34 Matthew Stafford	.30	.75
35 Golden Tate III	.25	.60
36 Marvin Jones Jr.	.25	.60
37 Aaron Rodgers	.75	2.00
38 Clay Matthews	.30	.75
39 Davante Adams	.30	.75
40 Deshaun Watson	.50	1.25
41 DeAndre Hopkins	.30	.75
42 J.J. Watt	.40	1.00
43 Andrew Luck	.50	1.25
44 T.Y. Hilton	.30	.75
45 Marlon Mack	.25	.60
46 Blake Bortles	.25	.60
47 Leonard Fournette	.40	1.00
48 Calais Campbell	.25	.60
49 Patrick Mahomes II	1.25	3.00
50 Kareem Hunt	.30	.75
51 Tyreek Hill	.40	1.00
52 Jared Goff	.40	1.00
53 Todd Gurley II	.40	1.00
54 Aaron Donald	.40	1.00
55 Sammy Watkins	.40	1.00
56 Philip Rivers	.40	1.00
57 Melvin Gordon	.30	.75
58 Keenan Allen	.30	.75
59 DeVante Parker	.30	.75
60 Cameron Wake	.25	.60
61 Kenyan Drake	.25	.60
62 Kirk Cousins	.40	1.00
63 Dalvin Cook	.30	.75
64 Adam Thielen	.40	1.00
65 Tom Brady	1.00	2.50
66 James White	.30	.75
67 Rob Gronkowski	.40	1.00
68 Drew Brees	.40	1.00
69 Alvin Kamara	.30	.75
70 Michael Thomas	.40	1.00
71 Eli Manning	.30	.75
72 Odell Beckham Jr.	.40	1.00
73 Landon Collins	.25	.60
74 Robby Anderson	.25	.60
75 Bilal Powell	.25	.60
76 Leonard Williams	.25	.60
77 Derek Carr	.40	1.00
78 Marshawn Lynch	.30	.75
79 Amari Cooper	.40	1.00
80 Carson Wentz	.50	1.25
81 Jay Ajayi	.30	.75
82 Nelson Agholor	.25	.60
83 Ben Roethlisberger	.40	1.00
84 Le'Veon Bell	.30	.75
85 Antonio Brown	.40	1.00
86 Jimmy Garoppolo	.50	1.25
87 Jerick McKinnon	.25	.60
88 Marquise Goodwin	.25	.60
89 Russell Wilson	.50	1.25
90 Doug Baldwin	.30	.75
91 Earl Thomas III	.30	.75
92 Jameis Winston	.30	.75
93 Mike Evans	.30	.75
94 O.J. Howard	.25	.60
95 Marcus Mariota	.40	1.00
96 Derrick Henry	.40	1.00
97 Dion Lewis	.25	.60
98 Alex Smith	.30	.75
99 Josh Norman	.25	.60
100 Jamison Crowder	.25	.60
101 Quenton Nelson RC	.60	1.50
102 Jordan Thomas RC	.50	1.25
103 Minkah Fitzpatrick RC	.75	2.00
104 Vita Vea RC	.60	1.50
105 Daron Payne RC	.60	1.50
106 Marcus Davenport RC	.75	2.00
107 Tremaine Edmunds RC	.75	2.00
108 Derwin James RC	.75	2.00
109 Jaire Alexander RC	.60	1.50
110 Logan Woodside RC	.60	1.50
111 Justin Jackson RC	.50	1.25
112 Justin Watson RC	.50	1.25
113 Damion Ratley RC	.50	1.25
114 Ray-Ray McCloud RC	.40	1.00
115 Leighton Vander Esch RC	1.25	3.00
116 Cedrick Wilson Jr. RC	.40	1.00
117 Richie James RC	.40	1.00
118 Auden Tate RC	.40	1.00
119 Austin Proehl RC	.40	1.00
120 Trey Quinn RC	.40	1.00
121 Mark Andrews RC	.60	1.50
122 Mike Hughes RC	.60	1.50
123 Malik Jefferson RC	.50	1.25
124 Ryan Izzo RC	.40	1.00
125 David Williams RC	.50	1.25
126 Simmie Cobbs Jr. RC	.60	1.50
127 Deon Cain RC	.50	1.25
128 Boston Scott RC	.50	1.25
129 Troy Fumagalli RC	.50	1.25
130 Tyler Conklin RC	.40	1.00
131 Jordan Wilkins RC	.50	1.25
132 Luke Falk RC	.50	1.25
133 Tanner Lee RC	.50	1.25
134 Christopher Herndon IV RC	.40	1.00
135 Durham Smythe RC	.40	1.00
136 Chase Edmonds RC	.40	1.00
137 Dalton Schultz RC	.50	1.25
138 Jake Wieneke RC	.50	1.25
139 Danny Etling RC	.50	1.25
140 Equanimeous St. Brown RC	.60	1.50
141 Jordan Akins RC	.40	1.00
142 Devonte Boyd RC	.40	1.00
143 Jester Weah RC	.40	1.00
144 Deontay Burnett RC	.50	1.25
145 Marcell Ateman RC	.50	1.25
146 Josh Adams RC	.75	2.00
147 Avonte Maddox RC	.50	1.25
148 Dylan Cantrell RC	.40	1.00
149 Kurt Benkert RC	.50	1.25
150 DaeSean Hamilton RR RC	.50	1.25
151 Sam Darnold RR RC	2.50	6.00
152 Josh Rosen RR RC	1.25	3.00
153 Baker Mayfield RR RC	10.00	25.00
154 Josh Allen RR RC	1.50	4.00
155 Mason Rudolph RR RC	1.00	2.50
156 Saquon Barkley RR RC	5.00	12.00
157 Derrius Guice RR RC	.75	2.00
158 Nick Chubb RR RC	1.25	3.00
159 Ronald Jones II RR RC	.40	1.00
160 Sony Michel RR RC	1.25	3.00
161 Calvin Ridley RR RC	1.00	2.50
162 Courtland Sutton RR RC	.60	1.50
163 Christian Kirk RR RC	.60	1.50
164 Anthony Miller RR RC	.60	1.50
165 D.J. Chark Jr. RR RC	.50	1.25
166 D.J. Moore RR RC	.75	2.00
167 Lamar Jackson RR RC	2.50	6.00
168 Rashaad Penny RR RC	.60	1.50
169 Bradley Chubb RR RC	.60	1.50
170 Kerryon Johnson RR RC	.60	1.50
171 Dante Pettis RR RC	.60	1.50
172 James Washington RR RC	.75	2.00
173 Royce Freeman RR RC	.50	1.25
174 Michael Gallup RR RC	.75	2.00
175 Tre'Quan Smith RR RC	.60	1.50
176 Keke Coutee RR RC	.50	1.25
177 Nyheim Hines RR RC	.50	1.25
178 Kyle Lauletta RR RC	.60	1.50
179 Mark Walton RR RC	.50	1.25
180 Kalen Ballage RR RC	.50	1.25
181 Jaleel Scott RR RC	.40	1.00
182 J'Mon Moore RR RC	.40	1.00
183 Daurice Fountain RR RC	.50	1.25
184 Jaylen Samuels RR RC	.50	1.25
185 Mike White RR RC	.50	1.25
186 Marquez Valdes-Scantling RR RC	.50	1.25
187 Mike Gesicki RR RC	.50	1.25
188 Ito Smith RR RC	.50	1.25
189 Hayden Hurst RR RC	.50	1.25
190 Ian Thomas RR RC	.40	1.00
191 Antonio Callaway RR RC	.50	1.25
192 Braxton Berrios RR RC	.40	1.00
193 Alex McGough RR RC	.50	1.25
194 Bo Scarbrough RR RC	.50	1.25
195 John Kelly RR RC	.50	1.25
196 Shaquem Griffin RR RC	.60	1.50
197 Dallas Goedert RR RC	.50	1.25
198 Denzel Ward RR RC	1.00	2.50
199 Jordan Lasley RR RC	.40	1.00

2018 Donruss Optic Aqua

*AQUA VET/299: 1.2X TO 3X BASIC VET
*AQUA RC/299: .75X TO 2X BASIC RR

153 Baker Mayfield RR	20.00	50.00
156 Saquon Barkley RR	15.00	40.00

2018 Donruss Optic Black Velocity

*BLACK VET/25: 3X TO 8X BASIC VET
*BLACK RC/25: 2X TO 5X BASIC RC

153 Baker Mayfield RR	100.00	200.00
156 Saquon Barkley RR	150.00	300.00

2018 Donruss Optic Blue

*BLUE VET/199: 1.5X TO 4X BASIC VET
*BLUE RC: 1X TO 2.5X BASIC RC

153 Baker Mayfield RR	30.00	60.00
156 Saquon Barkley RR	15.00	40.00

2018 Donruss Optic Bronze

*ROOKIES: .6X TO 1.5X BASIC CARDS

153 Baker Mayfield RR	40.00	80.00

2018 Donruss Optic Green Velocity

*ROOKIES: .6X TO 1.5X BASIC CARDS

153 Baker Mayfield RR	30.00	60.00

2018 Donruss Optic Holo

153 Baker Mayfield RR	20.00	50.00
156 Saquon Barkley RR	12.00	30.00

2018 Donruss Optic Orange

*ORANGE VET/199: 1.5X TO 4X BASIC VET
*ORANGE RC: 1X TO 2.5X BASIC RR

153 Baker Mayfield RR	30.00	60.00
156 Saquon Barkley RR	15.00	40.00

2018 Donruss Optic Pink

*ROOKIES: .6X TO 1.5X BASIC CARDS

153 Baker Mayfield RR	25.00	50.00

2018 Donruss Optic Purple

*PURPLE VETS/50: 2.5X TO 6X BASIC CARDS
*PURPLE RC/50: 1.5X TO 4X BASIC CARDS

153 Baker Mayfield RR	50.00	100.00
156 Saquon Barkley RR	60.00	125.00

2018 Donruss Optic Purple Stars

*PUR. STAR VET/25: 3X TO 8X BASIC VET
*PUR. STAR RC/25: 2X TO 5X BASIC RC

153 Baker Mayfield RR	100.00	200.00
156 Saquon Barkley RR	150.00	300.00

2018 Donruss Optic Red

*RED VET/99: 2X TO 5X BASIC VET
*RED RC/99: 1.2X TO 3X BASIC RC

153 Baker Mayfield RR	25.00	60.00
156 Saquon Barkley RR	60.00	125.00
157 Derrius Guice RR	2.50	6.00

2018 Donruss Optic Red and Yellow

*ROOKIES: .6X TO 1.5X BASIC CARDS

153 Baker Mayfield RR	25.00	50.00

2018 Donruss Optic Teal Velocity

*ROOKIES: .6X TO 1.5X BASIC CARDS

153 Baker Mayfield RR	50.00	100.00
156 Saquon Barkley RR	30.00	60.00

2018 Donruss Optic '88 Tribute

1 Aaron Rodgers	1.50	4.00
2 Carson Wentz	1.00	2.50
3 Jameis Winston	.60	1.50
4 Deshaun Watson	1.00	2.50
5 Alvin Kamara	.60	1.50
6 Todd Gurley II	.75	2.00
7 Tyreek Hill	.75	2.00
8 Matt Ryan	.60	1.50
9 A.J. Green	.75	2.00
10 Jalen Ramsey	.60	1.50
11 Matthew Stafford	.60	1.50
12 Melvin Gordon	.60	1.50
13 Derek Carr	.75	2.00
14 Russell Wilson	1.00	2.50
15 Rob Gronkowski	.75	2.00

2018 Donruss Optic '98 Tribute

1 Tom Brady	2.00	5.00
2 Odell Beckham Jr.	.75	2.00
3 Antonio Brown	.75	2.00
4 Jordan Howard	.75	2.00
5 Ezekiel Elliott	1.00	2.50
6 Jared Goff	.75	2.00
7 Jimmy Garoppolo	1.00	2.50
8 Julio Jones	.75	2.00
9 Adam Thielen	.75	2.00
10 Larry Fitzgerald	.60	1.50
11 Drew Brees	.75	2.00
12 Marcus Mariota	.75	2.00
13 Khalil Mack	.75	2.00
14 Von Miller	.60	1.50
15 Cam Newton	.75	2.00

2018 Donruss Optic Downtown

1 Tom Brady	25.00	60.00
2 Drew Brees	10.00	25.00
3 Deshaun Watson	12.00	30.00
4 Antonio Brown	10.00	25.00
5 Aaron Rodgers	20.00	50.00
6 Russell Wilson	12.00	30.00
7 Ezekiel Elliott	12.00	30.00
8 Jimmy Garoppolo	12.00	30.00
9 Cam Newton	10.00	25.00
10 Carson Wentz	12.00	30.00
11 Sam Darnold	25.00	60.00
12 Baker Mayfield	60.00	125.00
13 Josh Rosen	12.00	30.00
14 Josh Allen	15.00	40.00
15 Saquon Barkley	30.00	80.00
16 Lamar Jackson	25.00	60.00
17 Bradley Chubb	6.00	15.00
18 Anthony Miller	6.00	15.00
19 Calvin Ridley	10.00	25.00
20 Ronald Jones II	4.00	10.00

2018 Donruss Optic Elite Series

1 Leonard Fournette	.75	2.00
2 Deshaun Watson	1.00	2.50
3 Andrew Luck	1.00	2.50
4 Jameis Winston	.60	1.50
5 Ben Roethlisberger	.75	2.00
6 Ezekiel Elliott	1.00	2.50
7 Dak Prescott	.75	2.00
8 Matt Ryan	.60	1.50
9 Derek Carr	.75	2.00
10 Carson Wentz	1.00	2.50
11 Jared Goff	.75	2.00
12 Todd Gurley II	.75	2.00
13 Christian McCaffrey	.75	2.00
14 Adam Thielen	.75	2.00
15 Jimmy Garoppolo	1.00	2.50
16 Von Miller	.60	1.50
17 Antonio Brown	.75	2.00
18 Aaron Rodgers	1.50	4.00
19 Odell Beckham Jr.	.75	2.00
20 Drew Brees	.75	2.00
21 Tom Brady	2.00	5.00
22 Rob Gronkowski	.75	2.00
23 Travis Kelce	.75	2.00
24 Vic Beasley Jr.	.50	1.25
25 Fletcher Cox	.50	1.25

2018 Donruss Optic Elite Series Autographs

24 Vic Beasley Jr./50	6.00	15.00
25 Fletcher Cox/50	6.00	15.00

2018 Donruss Optic Explosive

1 Le'Veon Bell	1.00	2.50
2 Antonio Brown	1.25	3.00
3 Ezekiel Elliott	1.50	4.00
4 Odell Beckham Jr.	1.25	3.00
5 Todd Gurley II	1.25	3.00
6 Julio Jones	1.25	3.00
7 Saquon Barkley	12.00	30.00
8 Tyreek Hill	1.25	3.00
9 Alvin Kamara	1.00	2.50
10 Michael Thomas	1.25	3.00
11 A.J. Green	1.25	3.00
12 Stefon Diggs	1.00	2.50
13 DeAndre Hopkins	1.00	2.50
14 Devonta Freeman	1.00	2.50
15 Rob Gronkowski	1.25	3.00

2018 Donruss Optic Fans of the Game

1 James Caan	.75	2.00
2 Chris Evans	.75	2.00
3 Matthew Berry	.75	2.00
4 Drea de Matteo	.75	2.00
5 Chloe Kim	.75	2.00

2018 Donruss Optic Fans of the Game Autographs

1 James Caan		
2 Chris Evans	100.00	200.00
3 Matthew Berry		
4 Drea de Matteo	12.00	30.00
5 Chloe Kim	50.00	100.00

2018 Donruss Optic Illusions

1 Tom Brady	3.00	8.00
2 Cam Newton	1.25	3.00
3 Ezekiel Elliott	1.50	4.00
4 Deshaun Watson	1.50	4.00
5 Odell Beckham Jr.	1.25	3.00
6 Jordan Howard	1.25	3.00
7 Jalen Ramsey	1.00	2.50
8 Julio Jones	1.25	3.00
9 Le'Veon Bell	1.00	2.50
10 Carson Wentz	1.50	4.00
11 Travis Kelce	1.25	3.00
12 Drew Brees	1.25	3.00
13 Aaron Rodgers	2.50	6.00
14 Ben Roethlisberger	1.25	3.00
15 Todd Gurley II	1.25	3.00
16 Von Miller	1.00	2.50
17 David Johnson	1.25	3.00
18 Matt Ryan	1.00	2.50
19 A.J. Green	1.25	3.00
20 Jared Goff	1.25	3.00

2018 Donruss Optic Legends Series

1 Peyton Manning	2.50	6.00
2 Deion Sanders	1.00	2.50
3 Brian Urlacher	1.25	3.00
4 Bruce Smith	1.00	2.50
5 Eric Dickerson	1.25	3.00
6 Rod Woodson	1.25	3.00
7 Dan Marino	2.50	6.00
8 Terry Bradshaw	2.00	5.00
9 Steve Young	1.50	4.00
10 Michael Strahan	1.00	2.50
11 Marshall Faulk	1.00	2.50
12 Michael Irvin	1.25	3.00
13 Tony Gonzalez	1.00	2.50
14 Randy Moss	1.00	2.50
15 Joe Namath	1.50	4.00
16 Jonathan Ogden	1.00	2.50
17 John Lynch	1.00	2.50
18 Shaun Alexander	.75	2.00
19 Mike Alstott	.75	2.00
20 Bo Jackson	1.50	4.00

2018 Donruss Optic MVP

1 Tom Brady	3.00	8.00
2 Matt Ryan	1.00	2.50
3 Cam Newton	1.25	3.00
4 Aaron Rodgers	2.50	6.00
5 Peyton Manning	2.50	6.00
6 Adrian Peterson	1.25	3.00
7 LaDainian Tomlinson	1.00	2.50
8 Rich Gannon	1.00	2.50
9 Kurt Warner	1.00	2.50
10 Marshall Faulk	1.00	2.50
11 Terrell Davis	1.00	2.50
12 Barry Sanders	2.00	5.00
13 Brett Favre	2.50	6.00
14 Steve Young	1.50	4.00
15 Emmitt Smith	2.00	5.00
16 Thurman Thomas	1.00	2.50
17 Joe Montana	3.00	8.00
18 John Elway	2.00	5.00
19 Lawrence Taylor	1.25	3.00
20 Marcus Allen	1.25	3.00
21 Dan Marino	2.50	6.00
22 Joe Theismann	1.25	3.00
23 Earl Campbell	1.25	3.00
24 Terry Bradshaw	2.00	5.00
25 Fran Tarkenton	1.25	3.00

2018 Donruss Optic Rated Rookies Autographs

150 DaeSean Hamilton/125	5.00	12.00
151 Sam Darnold/50	100.00	200.00
152 Josh Rosen/125	25.00	50.00
153 Baker Mayfield/125	125.00	250.00
154 Josh Allen/150	50.00	100.00
155 Mason Rudolph/85	15.00	40.00
156 Saquon Barkley/150	100.00	200.00
157 Derrius Guice/25	40.00	80.00
158 Nick Chubb/110	25.00	60.00
159 Ronald Jones II/125	4.00	10.00
160 Sony Michel/85	15.00	40.00
161 Calvin Ridley/50	25.00	50.00
162 Courtland Sutton/25	10.00	25.00
163 Christian Kirk/25	10.00	25.00
164 Anthony Miller/110	6.00	15.00
165 D.J. Chark Jr./75	5.00	12.00
166 D.J. Moore/50	12.00	30.00
167 Lamar Jackson/50	100.00	200.00
168 Rashaad Penny/40	8.00	20.00
169 Bradley Chubb/25 EXCH	15.00	40.00
170 Kerryon Johnson/50 EXCH	20.00	50.00
171 Dante Pettis/85	10.00	25.00
172 James Washington/85	8.00	20.00
173 Royce Freeman/125	5.00	12.00
174 Michael Gallup/75 EXCH	12.00	30.00
175 Tre'Quan Smith/125	6.00	15.00
176 Keke Coutee/125	5.00	12.00
177 Nyheim Hines/125	5.00	12.00
178 Kyle Lauletta/125	6.00	15.00
179 Mark Walton/50	6.00	15.00
180 Kalen Ballage/75 EXCH	5.00	12.00
181 Jaleel Scott/125	4.00	10.00
182 J'Mon Moore/125	4.00	10.00
183 Daurice Fountain/125	5.00	12.00
184 Jaylen Samuels/125	8.00	20.00
185 Mike White/125	5.00	12.00
186 Marquez Valdes-Scantling/150	8.00	20.00
187 Mike Gesicki/125	5.00	12.00
188 Ito Smith/125	5.00	12.00
189 Hayden Hurst/25	8.00	20.00
190 Ian Thomas/125	4.00	10.00
192 Braxton Berrios/125	4.00	10.00
193 Alex McGough/50	6.00	15.00
194 Bo Scarbrough/125	5.00	12.00
195 John Kelly/150	4.00	10.00
196 Shaquem Griffin/125	6.00	15.00
197 Dallas Goedert/125	5.00	12.00
198 Denzel Ward/125 EXCH	10.00	25.00
199 Jordan Lasley/150	3.00	8.00

2018 Donruss Optic Rated Rookies Autographs Black Velocity

*BL VEL/25: .8X TO 2X BASIC AU/150
*BL VEL/25: .6X TO 1.5X BASIC AU/75-125
*BL VEL/25: .5X TO 1.2X BASIC AU/40-50
*BL VEL/25: .4X TO 1X BASIC AU/25

153 Baker Mayfield	250.00	500.00
156 Saquon Barkley	300.00	600.00
167 Lamar Jackson	125.00	250.00

2018 Donruss Optic Rated Rookies Autographs Blue

*BLUE/75: .5X TO 1.2X BASIC AU/150
*BLUE/75: .4X TO 1X BASIC AU/75-125
*BLUE/75: .3X TO .8X BASIC AU/40-50
*BLUE/75: X TO X BASIC AU/25

153 Baker Mayfield	225.00	350.00
156 Saquon Barkley	125.00	250.00

2018 Donruss Optic Rated Rookies Autographs Holo

*HOLO/99: .5X TO 1.2X BASIC AU/150
*HOLO/99: .4X TO 1X BASIC AU/75-125
*HOLO/99: .3X TO .8X BASIC AU/40-50
*HOLO/99: X TO X BASIC AU/25

153 Baker Mayfield	225.00	350.00
156 Saquon Barkley	125.00	250.00
167 Lamar Jackson	75.00	150.00

2018 Donruss Optic Rated Rookies Autographs Purple

*PURPLE/35: .6X TO 1.5X BASIC AU/150
*PURPLE/35: .5X TO 1.2X BASIC AU/75-125
*PURPLE/35: .4X TO 1X BASIC AU/40-50
*PURPLE/35: .3X TO .8X BASIC AU/25

153 Baker Mayfield	250.00	400.00
156 Saquon Barkley	300.00	500.00
167 Lamar Jackson	100.00	200.00

2018 Donruss Optic Rated Rookies Autographs Purple Stars

*PUR STAR/50: .6X TO 1.5X BASIC AU/150
*PUR STAR/50: .5X TO 1.2X BASIC AU/75-125
*PUR STAR/50: .4X TO 1X BASIC AU/40-50
*PUR STAR/50: .3X TO .8X BASIC AU/25

153 Baker Mayfield	250.00	400.00
156 Saquon Barkley	300.00	500.00
167 Lamar Jackson	100.00	200.00

2018 Donruss Optic Rated Rookies Autographs Red

*RED/50: .6X TO 1.5X BASIC AU/150
*RED/50: .5X TO 1.2X BASIC AU/75-125
*RED/50: .4X TO 1X BASIC AU/40-50
*RED/50: .3X TO .8X BASIC AU/25

153 Baker Mayfield	250.00	400.00
156 Saquon Barkley	300.00	500.00
167 Lamar Jackson	100.00	200.00

2018 Donruss Optic Rookie Autographs

101 Quenton Nelson/50	8.00	20.00
102 Jordan Thomas/150	4.00	10.00
103 Minkah Fitzpatrick/150	6.00	15.00
104 Vita Vea/50		
107 Tremaine Edmunds/50	10.00	25.00
108 Derwin James/50 EXCH	25.00	60.00
109 Jaire Alexander/50	8.00	20.00
111 Justin Jackson/50	6.00	15.00
112 Justin Watson/150	4.00	10.00
113 Damion Ratley/50	6.00	15.00
114 Ray-Ray McCloud/50	5.00	12.00
116 Cedrick Wilson Jr./50	5.00	12.00
117 Richie James/50	5.00	12.00
118 Auden Tate/50	5.00	12.00
120 Trey Quinn/50	5.00	12.00
121 Mark Andrews/50	8.00	20.00
122 Mike Hughes/50	8.00	20.00
123 Malik Jefferson/50	6.00	15.00
124 Ryan Izzo/150	3.00	8.00
127 Deon Cain/150	4.00	10.00
128 Boston Scott/50	6.00	15.00
132 Luke Falk/150	4.00	10.00
133 Tanner Lee/50	6.00	15.00
134 Christopher Herndon IV/25	6.00	15.00
135 Durham Smythe/150	3.00	8.00
136 Chase Edmonds/150	3.00	8.00
137 Dalton Schultz/150	4.00	10.00
138 Jake Wieneke/50	6.00	15.00
139 Danny Etling/150	4.00	10.00
144 Deontay Burnett/150	4.00	10.00
145 Marcell Ateman/150	4.00	10.00
147 Avonte Maddox/150	4.00	10.00
148 Dylan Cantrell/150	3.00	8.00
149 Kurt Benkert/150	4.00	10.00

2018 Donruss Optic Rookie Autographs Black Velocity

*BL VEL/25: .8X TO 2X BASIC AU/150
*BL VEL/25: .5X TO 1.2X BASIC AU/50
*BL VEL/25: .4X TO 1X BASIC AU/25

2018 Donruss Optic Rookie Autographs Blue

*BLUE/75: .5X TO 1.2X BASIC AU/150
*BLUE/75: .3X TO .8X BASIC AU/40-50
*BLUE/75: X TO X BASIC AU/25

2018 Donruss Optic Rookie Autographs Holo

*HOLO/99: .5X TO 1.2X BASIC AU/150
*HOLO/99: .3X TO .8X BASIC AU/50
*HOLO/99: X TO X BASIC AU/25

2018 Donruss Optic Rookie Autographs Purple

*PURPLE/35: .6X TO 1.5X BASIC AU/150
*PURPLE/35: .4X TO 1X BASIC AU/50
*PURPLE/35: .3X TO .8X BASIC AU/25

2018 Donruss Optic Rookie Autographs Purple Stars

*PUR STAR/50: .6X TO 1.5X BASIC AU/150
*PUR STAR/50: .4X TO 1X BASIC AU/50
*PUR STAR/50: .3X TO .8X BASIC AU/25

2018 Donruss Optic Rookie Autographs Red

*RED/50: .6X TO 1.5X BASIC AU/150
*RED/50: .4X TO 1X BASIC AU/50
*RED/50: .3X TO .8X BASIC AU/25

2018 Donruss Optic Rookie Dual Autographs

5 N.Chubb/S.Michel/15	75.00	150.00
6 D.Hamilton/C.Sutton/25	10.00	25.00
7 R.Jones II/R.Freeman/25	8.00	20.00
9 K.Johnson/R.Jones II/25	15.00	40.00
10 K.Coutee/T.Smith/25	10.00	25.00
11 D.Fountain/N.Hines/25	8.00	20.00
12 J.Samuels/K.Ballage/25	8.00	20.00

2018 Donruss Optic Rookie Elite Series

1 Sam Darnold	5.00	12.00
2 Josh Rosen	2.50	6.00
3 Baker Mayfield	8.00	20.00
4 Josh Allen	3.00	8.00
5 Mason Rudolph	2.00	5.00
6 Saquon Barkley	6.00	15.00
7 Nick Chubb	2.50	6.00
8 Ronald Jones II	.75	2.00
9 Sony Michel	2.50	6.00
10 Courtland Sutton	1.25	3.00
11 Anthony Miller	1.25	3.00
12 D.J. Moore	1.50	4.00
13 Rashaad Penny	1.25	3.00
14 Kerryon Johnson	1.25	3.00
15 Dante Pettis	1.25	3.00
16 James Washington	1.50	4.00
17 Royce Freeman	1.00	2.50
18 Tre'Quan Smith	1.25	3.00
19 Keke Coutee	1.00	2.50
20 Nyheim Hines	1.00	2.50

2018 Donruss Optic Rookie Elite Series Autographs Purple Stars

*ELITE/25: .5X TO 1.2X PURPLE AU/50
*ELITE/15: .6X TO 1.5X PURPLE AU/50

1 Sam Darnold	30.00	80.00
2 Josh Rosen	15.00	40.00
3 Baker Mayfield	100.00	200.00
4 Josh Allen	50.00	100.00
5 Mason Rudolph	12.00	30.00
6 Saquon Barkley EXCH	125.00	250.00
7 Nick Chubb	15.00	40.00
8 Ronald Jones II	5.00	12.00
9 Sony Michel	15.00	40.00
10 Courtland Sutton	8.00	20.00
11 Anthony Miller	8.00	20.00
12 D.J. Moore	10.00	25.00
13 Rashaad Penny	8.00	20.00
14 Kerryon Johnson	8.00	20.00
15 Dante Pettis	8.00	20.00
16 James Washington	10.00	25.00
17 Royce Freeman	6.00	15.00
18 Tre'Quan Smith	8.00	20.00
19 Keke Coutee EXCH	6.00	15.00
20 Nyheim Hines	6.00	15.00

2018 Donruss Optic Rookie Patch Autographs

1 Sam Darnold	75.00	150.00
2 Josh Rosen	25.00	60.00
3 Baker Mayfield	150.00	300.00
4 Josh Allen	60.00	125.00
5 Mason Rudolph	20.00	50.00
6 Saquon Barkley EXCH	150.00	300.00
7 Derrius Guice EXCH	15.00	40.00
8 Nick Chubb	25.00	60.00
9 Ronald Jones II	8.00	20.00
10 Sony Michel	25.00	60.00
11 Calvin Ridley	20.00	50.00
12 Courtland Sutton	12.00	30.00
13 Christian Kirk	12.00	30.00
14 Anthony Miller	12.00	30.00
15 D.J. Chark Jr.	10.00	25.00
16 D.J. Moore	15.00	40.00
18 Rashaad Penny	12.00	30.00
19 Bradley Chubb EXCH	12.00	30.00
20 Kerryon Johnson	12.00	30.00
21 Dante Pettis EXCH	15.00	40.00
22 James Washington	15.00	40.00
23 Royce Freeman	10.00	25.00
24 Michael Gallup	15.00	40.00
25 Tre'Quan Smith	12.00	30.00
26 Keke Coutee	10.00	25.00
27 Nyheim Hines	10.00	25.00
28 Kyle Lauletta	12.00	30.00
29 Mark Walton	10.00	25.00
30 Kalen Ballage	10.00	25.00
31 Jaleel Scott	8.00	20.00
32 J'Mon Moore	8.00	20.00
33 Daurice Fountain	10.00	25.00
34 Jaylen Samuels	10.00	25.00
35 Mike White	10.00	25.00
36 Marquez Valdes-Scantling	10.00	25.00
37 Mike Gesicki	10.00	25.00
38 DaeSean Hamilton	10.00	25.00
39 Hayden Hurst	10.00	25.00
40 Ito Smith	10.00	25.00

2018 Donruss Optic Rookie Phenoms Jerseys

*HORO: .5X TO 1.2X BASIC JSY
*HOR R&Y: .5X TO 1.2X BASIC JSY
*R&Y: .5X TO 1.2X BASIC JSY
*PRIME/50: .6X TO 1.5X BASIC JSY

1 DaeSean Hamilton	2.50	6.00
2 Sam Darnold	8.00	20.00
3 Josh Rosen	5.00	12.00
4 Baker Mayfield	8.00	20.00
5 Josh Allen	5.00	12.00
6 Mason Rudolph	4.00	10.00
7 Saquon Barkley	10.00	25.00
8 Derrius Guice	4.00	10.00
9 Nick Chubb	4.00	10.00
10 Ronald Jones II	2.00	5.00
11 Sony Michel	4.00	10.00
12 Calvin Ridley	4.00	10.00
13 Courtland Sutton	3.00	8.00
14 Christian Kirk	3.00	8.00
15 Anthony Miller	3.00	8.00
16 D.J. Chark Jr.	2.50	6.00
17 D.J. Moore	4.00	10.00
18 Lamar Jackson	8.00	20.00
19 Rashaad Penny	3.00	8.00
20 Bradley Chubb	3.00	8.00
21 Michael Gallup	4.00	10.00
22 Tre'Quan Smith	3.00	8.00
23 Keke Coutee	2.50	6.00
24 Nyheim Hines	2.50	6.00
25 Mark Walton	2.50	6.00
26 Kalen Ballage	2.50	6.00
27 Jaleel Scott	2.00	5.00
28 J'Mon Moore	2.00	5.00
29 Daurice Fountain	2.50	6.00
30 Jaylen Samuels	2.50	6.00
31 Mike White	2.50	6.00
32 Mike Gesicki	2.50	6.00
33 Hayden Hurst	2.50	6.00

2018 Donruss Optic Rookie Threads

*PRIME/50: .6X TO 1.5X BASIC JSY
*R&Y: .5X TO 1.2X BASIC JSY

1 DaeSean Hamilton	2.50	6.00
2 Sam Darnold	8.00	20.00
3 Josh Rosen	5.00	12.00
4 Baker Mayfield	8.00	20.00
5 Josh Allen	5.00	12.00
6 Mason Rudolph	4.00	10.00
7 Saquon Barkley	10.00	25.00
8 Derrius Guice	4.00	10.00
9 Ronald Jones II	2.00	5.00
10 Sony Michel	4.00	10.00
11 Calvin Ridley	4.00	10.00
12 Courtland Sutton	3.00	8.00
13 Christian Kirk	3.00	8.00
14 D.J. Chark Jr.	2.50	6.00
15 Lamar Jackson	8.00	20.00
16 Rashaad Penny	3.00	8.00
17 Bradley Chubb	3.00	8.00
18 Kerryon Johnson	3.00	8.00
19 Dante Pettis	3.00	8.00
20 James Washington	4.00	10.00
21 Royce Freeman	2.50	6.00
22 Tre'Quan Smith	3.00	8.00
23 Kyle Lauletta	3.00	8.00
24 Mark Walton	2.50	6.00
25 Kalen Ballage	2.50	6.00
26 Jaleel Scott	2.00	5.00
27 J'Mon Moore	2.00	5.00
28 Daurice Fountain	2.50	6.00
29 Jaylen Samuels	2.50	6.00
30 Mike White	2.50	6.00
31 Marquez Valdes-Scantling	2.50	6.00
32 Mike Gesicki	2.50	6.00
33 Ito Smith	2.50	6.00
34 Hayden Hurst	2.50	6.00

2018 Donruss Optic Rookie Triple Autographs

3 Chbb/Brkly/Mchl/15	225.00	350.00
5 Sttn/Frmn/Chbb/15		
6 Wshngtn/Rdlph/Smls/15	40.00	80.00
8 Jhnsn/Pnny/Hns/25	40.00	80.00

2018 Donruss Optic The Champ is Here

1 Nick Foles	1.00	2.50
2 Jay Ajayi	1.00	2.50
3 Corey Clement	.75	2.00
4 Zach Ertz	1.00	2.50
5 Brandon Graham	.75	2.00
6 Nelson Agholor	.75	2.00
7 LeGarrette Blount	1.00	2.50
8 Trey Burton	.75	2.00
9 Alshon Jeffery	1.00	2.50
10 Torrey Smith	.75	2.00
11 Chris Long	.75	2.00
12 Jalen Mills	.75	2.00
13 Corey Graham	.75	2.00
14 Rodney McLeod	.75	2.00
15 Fletcher Cox	.75	2.00
16 Jake Elliott	1.00	2.50
17 Derek Barnett	.75	2.00
18 Mychal Kendricks	.75	2.00
19 Lane Johnson	.75	2.00
20 Jason Kelce	.75	2.00

2007 Donruss Playoff Authentic Signatures

JT Joe Theismann	10.00	25.00

1997 Donruss Preferred

The 1997 Donruss Preferred set was issued in one series totalling 150 cards. The fronts feature color player photos on all-foil, micro-etched card stock with micro-etched borders. The set is divided into 80 bronze (5:1 insert odds), 40 silver (1:5), 20 gold (1:17), and 10 platinum cards (1:48) cards. The set contains the topical subset: National Treasure (118-147).

COMPLETE SET (150)	150.00	300.00
COMP.BRONZE SET (80)	10.00	25.00
1 Emmitt Smith P	7.50	20.00
2 Steve Young G	3.00	8.00
3 Cris Carter S	2.50	6.00
4 Tim Biakabutuka B	.25	.60
5 Brett Favre P	10.00	25.00
6 Troy Aikman G	4.00	10.00
7 Eddie Kennison S	1.50	4.00
8 Ben Coates B	.25	.60
9 Dan Marino P	10.00	25.00
10 Deion Sanders G	2.50	6.00
11 Curtis Conway S	1.50	4.00
12 Jeff George B	.25	.60
13 Barry Sanders P	7.50	20.00
14 Kerry Collins G	2.50	6.00
15 Marvin Harrison S	2.50	6.00
16 Bobby Engram B	.25	.60
17 Jerry Rice P	5.00	12.00
18 Kordell Stewart G	2.50	6.00
19 Tony Banks S	2.50	6.00
20 Jim Harbaugh B	.25	.60
21 Mark Brunell P	2.50	6.00
22 Steve McNair G	3.00	8.00
23 Terrell Owens S	3.00	8.00
24 Raymont Harris B	.15	.40
25 Curtis Martin P	3.00	8.00
26 Karim Abdul-Jabbar G	2.50	6.00
27 Joey Galloway S	1.50	4.00
28 Bobby Hoying B	.25	.60
29 Terrell Davis P	3.00	8.00
30 Terry Glenn G	1.50	4.00
31 Antonio Freeman S	2.50	6.00
32 Brad Johnson B	.40	1.00
33 Drew Bledsoe P	2.50	6.00
34 John Elway G	8.00	20.00
35 Herman Moore G	1.50	4.00
36 Robert Brooks S	1.50	4.00
37 Rod Smith B	.40	1.00
38 Eddie George P	2.50	6.00
39 Keyshawn Johnson G	2.50	6.00
40 Greg Hill S	1.00	2.50
41 Scott Mitchell B	.25	.60
42 Muhsin Muhammad B	.25	.60
43 Isaac Bruce G	2.50	6.00
44 Jeff Blake S	1.50	4.00
45 Neil O'Donnell B	.25	.60
46 Jimmy Smith B	.25	.60
47 Jerome Bettis G	2.50	6.00
48 Terry Allen S	1.50	4.00
49 Andre Reed B	.25	.60
50 Frank Sanders B	.25	.60
51 Tim Brown G	2.50	6.00
52 Thurman Thomas S	1.50	4.00
53 Heath Shuler B	.15	.40
54 Vinny Testaverde B	.25	.60
55 Marcus Allen S	2.50	6.00
56 Napoleon Kaufman B	.40	1.00
57 Derrick Alexander WR B	.25	.60
58 Carl Pickens G	1.50	4.00
59 Marshall Faulk S	3.00	8.00
60 Mike Alstott B	.40	1.00
61 Jamal Anderson B	.40	1.00
62 Ricky Watters G	1.50	4.00
63 Dorsey Levens S	2.50	6.00
64 Todd Collins B	.15	.40
65 Trent Dilfer B	.40	1.00
66 Natrone Means S	1.50	4.00
67 Gus Frerotte B	.15	.40
68 Irving Fryar B	.25	.60
69 Adrian Murrell S	1.50	4.00
70 Rodney Hampton B	.25	.60
71 Garrison Hearst B	.25	.60
72 Reggie White S	2.50	6.00
73 Anthony Johnson B	.15	.40
74 Tony Martin B	.25	.60
75 Chris Sanders S	1.00	2.50
76 O.J. McDuffie B	.25	.60
77 Leeland McElroy B	.15	.40
78 Ki-Jana Carter S	1.50	4.00
79 Anthony Miller B	.15	.40
80 Johnnie Morton B	.25	.60
81 Robert Smith S	.25	.60
82 Brett Perriman B	.15	.40
83 Errict Rhett B	.15	.40
84 Michael Irvin S	1.50	4.00
85 Darnay Scott B	.25	.60
86 Shannon Sharpe B	.25	.60
87 Lawrence Phillips S	1.50	4.00
88 Bruce Smith B	.25	.60
89 James O.Stewart B	.25	.60
90 J.J. Stokes B	.25	.60
91 Chris Warren B	.25	.60
92 Daryl Johnston B	.25	.60
93 Andre Rison B	.25	.60
94 Rashaan Salaam B	.15	.40
95 Amani Toomer B	.25	.60
96 Warrick Dunn G RC	6.00	15.00
97 Tiki Barber RC S	6.00	15.00
98 Peter Boulware B RC	.40	1.00
99 Ike Hilliard RC G	4.00	10.00
100 Antowain Smith S RC	4.00	10.00
101 Yatil Green S RC	1.50	4.00
102 Tony Gonzalez B RC	3.00	8.00
103 Reidel Anthony G RC	2.50	6.00
104 Troy Davis S RC	1.50	4.00
105 Rae Carruth S RC	1.00	2.50
106 David LaFleur RC B	.15	.40
107 Jim Druckenmiller G RC	1.50	4.00
108 Joey Kent S RC	1.50	4.00
109 Byron Hanspard S RC	1.50	4.00
110 Darrell Russell B RC	.15	.40
111 Danny Wuerffel S RC	2.50	6.00
112 Jake Plummer S RC	4.00	10.00
113 Jay Graham B RC	.25	.60
114 Corey Dillon S RC	4.00	10.00
115 Orlando Pace B RC	.40	1.00
116 Pat Barnes S RC	1.50	4.00
117 Shawn Springs B RC	.25	.60
118 Troy Aikman NT B	.75	2.00
119 Drew Bledsoe NT B	.40	1.00
120 Mark Brunell NT B	.40	1.00
121 Kerry Collins NT B	.40	1.00
122 Terrell Davis NT B	.50	1.25
123 Jerome Bettis NT B	.40	1.00
124 Brett Favre NT B	2.00	4.00
125 Eddie George NT B	.40	1.00
126 Terry Glenn NT B	.40	1.00
127 Karim Abdul-Jabbar NT B	.25	.60
128 Keyshawn Johnson NT B	.40	1.00
129 Dan Marino NT B	2.00	4.00
130 Curtis Martin NT B	.50	1.25
131 Natrone Means NT B	.25	.60
132 Herman Moore NT S	1.50	4.00
133 Jerry Rice NT B	.75	2.00
134 Barry Sanders NT B	1.25	3.00
135 Deion Sanders NT B	.40	1.00
136 Emmitt Smith NT B	1.50	3.00
137 Kordell Stewart NT B	.40	1.00

138 Steve Young NT B .50 1.25
139 Carl Pickens NT S 1.50 4.00
140 Isaac Bruce NT S 2.50 6.00
141 Steve McNair NT S 2.00 5.00
142 John Elway NT S 5.00 10.00
143 Cris Carter NT B .25 .60
144 Tim Brown NT B .25 .60
145 Ricky Watters NT B .15 .40
146 Robert Brooks NT B .25 .60
147 Jeff Blake NT B .25 .60
148 Tiki Barber CL B .60 1.50
149 Jim Druckenmiller CL B .15 .40
150 Warrick Dunn CL B .50 1.25

1997 Donruss Preferred Cut To The Chase

COMP.BRONZE SET (80) 150.00 300.00
*BRONZE STARS: 2X TO 5X HI COL.
*BRONZE RCs: 2X TO 4X
BRONZE STATED ODDS 1:7
*SILVER STARS: 1X TO 2.5X HI COL.
*SILVER RCs: 1.25X TO 2.5X
SILVER STATED ODDS 1:63
*GOLD STARS: .6X TO 1.5X HI COL.
*GOLD RCs: .8X TO 2X
GOLD STATED ODDS 1:189
*PLATINUM STARS: .6X TO 1.5X HI COL.
PLATINUM STATED ODDS 1:756

1997 Donruss Preferred Chain Reaction

This 24-card set features color player photos printed on die-cut, plastic card stock with holographic foil treatments. Two cards can be placed side-by-side to connect superstar teammates. The cards are sequentially numbered to 3,000.
COMPLETE SET (24) 100.00 200.00
STATED PRINT RUN 3000 SERIAL #'d SETS
1A Dan Marino 8.00 20.00
1B Karim Abdul-Jabbar 2.00 5.00
2A Troy Aikman 4.00 10.00
2B Emmitt Smith 6.00 15.00
3A Steve McNair 3.00 8.00
3B Eddie George 2.50 6.00
4A Brett Favre 10.00 25.00
4B Robert Brooks 2.00 5.00
5A John Elway 8.00 20.00
5B Terrell Davis 3.00 8.00
6A Drew Bledsoe 3.00 8.00
6B Curtis Martin 3.00 8.00
7A Steve Young 4.00 10.00
7B Jerry Rice 5.00 12.00
8A Mark Brunell 3.00 8.00
8B Natrone Means 2.00 5.00
9A Barry Sanders 6.00 15.00
9B Herman Moore 2.50 6.00
10A Kordell Stewart 2.50 6.00
10B Jerome Bettis 3.00 8.00
11A Jeff Blake 2.00 5.00
11B Carl Pickens 2.50 6.00
12A Lawrence Phillips 2.00 5.00
12B Isaac Bruce 2.50 6.00

1997 Donruss Preferred Double-Wide Tins

These tins, featuring two players on each tin, were issued by Donruss only to their retail outlets. The prices below refer to opened tins.
COMPLETE SET (12) 5.00 12.00
1 E.Smith .40 1.50
T.Davis
2 T.Aikman .40 1.00
K.Collins
3 H.Moore .20 .50
C.Pickens
4 B.Favre .75 2.00
M.Brunell
5 D.Sanders .40 1.00
K.Stewart
6 B.Sanders .60 1.50
K.Abdul-Jabbar
7 J.Rice .40 1.00
T.Glenn
8 D.Marino .75 2.00
D.Bledsoe
9 J.Elway .75 2.00
S.Young
10 C.Martin .40 1.00
W.Dunn
11 E.George .40 1.00
T.Brown
12 K.Johnson .20 .50
I.Hilliard

1997 Donruss Preferred Precious Metals

This 15-card set is a partial parallel version of the base set. The player photos are printed on cards that contain one gram (roughly .032 troy ounce) of actual .999 silver, gold, or platinum. It was announced that no more than 100 of each card was produced.
ANNOUNCED PRINT RUN 100 SETS
ONE GRAM (.032 Troy Oz) METAL PER CARD
1 Drew Bledsoe Plat 50.00 100.00
2 Curtis Martin Plat. 50.00 100.00
3 Troy Aikman Gold 60.00 120.00
4 Eddie George Plat 40.00 80.00
5 Warrick Dunn Gold 50.00 100.00
6 Brett Favre Plat 100.00 200.00
7 John Elway Gold 75.00 150.00
8 Barry Sanders Plat 75.00 150.00
9 Emmitt Smith Plat 75.00 150.00
10 Terrell Davis Plat 50.00 100.00
11 Mark Brunell 40.00 80.00
12 Jerry Rice Plat 60.00 120.00
13 Dan Marino Plat 100.00 200.00
14 Terry Glenn 40.00 80.00
15 Tiki Barber 50.00 100.00

1997 Donruss Preferred Staremasters

This 24-card set features up-close face photos of top players printed on all-foil card stock accented with holographic foil stamping. Each card is sequentially numbered out of 1,500.
COMPLETE SET (24) 100.00 250.00
STATED PRINT RUN 1500 SERIAL #'d SETS
1 Tim Brown 2.00 5.00
2 Mark Brunell 4.00 10.00
3 Kerry Collins 3.00 8.00
4 Brett Favre 12.50 30.00
5 Eddie George 3.00 8.00
6 Terry Glenn 3.00 8.00
7 Dan Marino 12.50 30.00
8 Curtis Martin 4.00 10.00
9 Jerry Rice 6.00 15.00
10 Barry Sanders 10.00 25.00
11 Deion Sanders 3.00 8.00
12 Emmitt Smith 10.00 25.00
13 Drew Bledsoe 4.00 10.00
14 Troy Aikman 6.00 15.00
15 Tiki Barber 5.00 12.00
16 Terrell Davis 4.00 10.00
17 Karim Abdul-Jabbar 2.00 5.00
18 Warrick Dunn 5.00 12.00
19 John Elway 15.00 40.00
20 Yatil Green 2.00 5.00
21 Ike Hilliard 2.00 5.00
22 Kordell Stewart 3.00 8.00
23 Ricky Watters 1.25 3.00
24 Steve Young 4.00 10.00

1997 Donruss Preferred Tins

Each tin box of Donruss Preferred features one of 24 different players pictured on the lid with blue accents. Only 1200 of each of these tins were produced.
COMP.BLUE PACK SET (24) 10.00 20.00
COMP.SILVER PACK SET (24) 100.00 200.00
*SILVER PACK TINS: 5X TO 10X BLUES
STATED PRINT RUN 1200 SETS
*BLUE BOX TINS: 3X TO 6X BLUE PACKS
STATED PRINT RUN 1200 SETS
*GOLD PACK TINS: 10X TO 20X BLUE PACKS
STATED PRINT RUN 300 SETS
*GOLD BOX TINS: 8X TO 16X BLUE PACKS
STATED PRINT RUN 300 SETS
1 Mark Brunell .25 .60
2 Karim Abdul-Jabbar .10 .30
3 Terry Glenn .20 .50
4 Brett Favre .75 2.00
5 Troy Aikman .40 1.00
6 Eddie George .20 .50
7 John Elway .75 2.00
8 Steve Young .25 .60
9 Terrell Davis .25 .60
10 Kordell Stewart .20 .50
11 Drew Bledsoe .25 .60
12 Kerry Collins .20 .50
13 Dan Marino .75 2.00
14 Tim Brown .10 .30
15 Carl Pickens .20 .50
16 Warrick Dunn .25 .60
17 Herman Moore .20 .50
18 Curtis Martin .25 .60
19 Ike Hilliard .20 .50
20 Barry Sanders .60 1.50
21 Deion Sanders .20 .50
22 Emmitt Smith .60 1.50
23 Keyshawn Johnson .20 .50
24 Jerry Rice .40 1.00

1999 Donruss Preferred QBC

Released as a 120-card set, 1999 Donruss Preferred QBC features only members of the Quarterback Club and is divided up into four tiers. Tier one, Bronze, are found three in every pack, tier two, Silver, are found one per pack, tier three, Gold, are found one in four, and tier four, Platinum, are found one in eight. Base cards feature action photos and a "fleck" foil border.
COMPLETE SET (120) 75.00 150.00
COMP.BRONZE SET (45) 12.50 25.00
1 Troy Aikman B .40 1.00
2 Tony Banks B .25 .60
3 Jeff Blake B .25 .60
4 Drew Bledsoe B .25 .60
5 Bubby Brister B .20 .50
6 Chris Chandler B .25 .60
7 Kerry Collins B .20 .50
8 Randall Cunningham B .25 .60
9 Terrell Davis B .25 .60
10 Trent Dilfer B .20 .50
11 John Elway B .50 1.25
12 Boomer Esiason B .30 .75
13 Jim Everett B .20 .50
14 Brett Favre B .60 1.50
15 Doug Flutie B .30 .75
16 Gus Frerotte B .20 .50
17 Jeff George B .20 .50
18 Elvis Grbac B .20 .50
19 Jim Harbaugh B .25 .60
20 Michael Irvin B .30 .75
21 Brad Johnson B .25 .60
22 Keyshawn Johnson B .25 .60
23 Danny Kanell B .20 .50
24 Jim Kelly B .30 .75
25 Bernie Kosar B .25 .60
26 Erik Kramer B .25 .60
27 Ryan Leaf B .25 .60
28 Peyton Manning B 1.00 2.50
29 Dan Marino B .60 1.50
30 Donovan McNabb B RC .75 2.00
31 Steve McNair B .25 .60
32 Cade McNown B RC .25 .60
33 Scott Mitchell B .20 .50
34 Warren Moon B .30 .75
35 Neil O'Donnell B .25 .60
36 Jake Plummer B .20 .50
37 Jerry Rice B .75 2.00
38 Barry Sanders B .50 1.25
39 Junior Seau B .25 .60
40 Phil Simms B .30 .75
41 Kordell Stewart B .20 .50
42 Vinny Testaverde B .20 .50
43 Ricky Williams B RC .40 1.00
44 Steve Young B .40 1.00
45 Marino .60 1.50
Favre
Elway B
46 Troy Aikman S .50 1.25
47 Tony Banks S .30 .75
48 Drew Bledsoe S .30 .75
49 Bubby Brister S .25 .60
50 Chris Chandler S .30 .75
51 Kerry Collins S .25 .60
52 Randall Cunningham S .30 .75
53 Terrell Davis S .30 .75
54 Trent Dilfer S .25 .60
55 John Elway S .60 1.50
56 Boomer Esiason S .40 1.00
57 Brett Favre S .75 2.00
58 Doug Flutie S .40 1.00
59 Elvis Grbac S .25 .60
60 Jim Harbaugh S .30 .75
61 Michael Irvin S .40 1.00
62 Brad Johnson S .30 .75
63 Keyshawn Johnson S .30 .75
64 Jim Kelly S .40 1.00
65 Ryan Leaf S .30 .75
66 Peyton Manning S 1.25 3.00
67 Dan Marino S .75 2.00
68 Donovan McNabb S 1.00 2.50
69 Steve McNair S .30 .75
70 Cade McNown S .30 .75
71 Warren Moon S .40 1.00
72 Jake Plummer S .25 .60
73 Jerry Rice S 1.00 2.50
74 Barry Sanders S .60 1.50
75 Junior Seau S .30 .75
76 Phil Simms S .40 1.00
77 Kordell Stewart S .25 .60
78 Vinny Testaverde S .25 .60
79 Ricky Williams S .50 1.25
80 Steve Young S .50 1.25
81 Troy Aikman G 1.00 2.50
82 Drew Bledsoe G .60 1.50
83 Bubby Brister G .50 1.25
84 Chris Chandler G .60 1.50
85 Randall Cunningham G .60 1.50
86 Terrell Davis G .60 1.50
87 John Elway G 1.25 3.00
88 Brett Favre G 1.50 4.00
89 Doug Flutie G .75 2.00
90 Brad Johnson G .60 1.50
91 Keyshawn Johnson G .60 1.50
92 Ryan Leaf G .60 1.50
93 Peyton Manning G 2.50 6.00
94 Dan Marino G 1.50 4.00
95 Donovan McNabb G 2.00 5.00
96 Steve McNair G .60 1.50
97 Cade McNown G .60 1.50
98 Warren Moon G .75 2.00
99 Jake Plummer G .50 1.25
100 Jerry Rice G 2.00 5.00
101 Barry Sanders G 1.25 3.00
102 Kordell Stewart G .50 1.25
103 Vinny Testaverde G .50 1.25
104 Ricky Williams G 1.00 2.50
105 Steve Young G 1.00 2.50
106 Troy Aikman P 1.50 4.00
107 Drew Bledsoe P 1.00 2.50
108 Terrell Davis P 1.00 2.50
109 John Elway P 2.00 5.00
110 Brett Favre P 2.50 6.00
111 Keyshawn Johnson P 1.00 2.50
112 Peyton Manning P 4.00 10.00
113 Dan Marino P 2.50 6.00
114 Donovan McNabb P 3.00 8.00
115 Cade McNown P 1.00 2.50
116 Jake Plummer P .75 2.00
117 Jerry Rice P 3.00 8.00
118 Barry Sanders P 2.00 5.00
119 Kordell Stewart P .75 2.00
120 Ricky Williams P 1.50 4.00

1999 Donruss Preferred QBC Power

*POWER BRONZE STARS: 2X TO 5X HI COL.
*POWER BRONZE RCs: 1.2X TO 3X
POWER BRONZE PRINT RUN 500 SER.#'d SETS
*POWER SILVER STARS: 2X TO 5X HI COL.
*POWER SILVER ROOKIES: 1.2X TO 3X
POWER SILVER PRINT RUN 300 SER.#'d SETS
*POWER GOLD STARS: 2.5X TO 6X HI COL.
*POWER GOLD ROOKIES: 1.2X TO 3X
POWER GOLD PRINT RUN 150 SER.#'d SETS
*POWER PLATINUM STARS: 3X TO 8X HI COL.
*POWER PLATINUM ROOKIES: 1.5X TO 4X
POWER PLAT.PRINT RUN 50 SER.#'d SETS

1999 Donruss Preferred QBC Autographs

Randomly inserted in packs, this 15-card set features top players and rookies coupled with an authentic autograph. Some cards were issued via mail redemptions that carried an expiration date of 5/1/2000.
1 Steve Young 15.00 40.00
2 Ricky Williams 15.00 40.00
3 Jerry Rice 60.00 100.00
4 Jake Plummer 12.50 30.00
5 Peyton Manning 50.00 100.00
6 Michael Irvin 15.00 40.00
7 Dan Marino 60.00 120.00
8 Randall Cunningham 15.00 40.00
9 Troy Aikman 40.00 80.00
10 Terrell Davis 15.00 40.00
11 Vinny Testaverde 12.50 30.00
12 Chris Chandler 10.00 25.00
13 Kordell Stewart 10.00 25.00
14 Bubby Brister 8.00 20.00
15 Steve McNair 15.00 40.00

1999 Donruss Preferred QBC Chain Reaction

Randomly inserted in packs, this 20-card set features die-cut cards shaped on one side like a down marker. Card stock is colored holofoil and A and B versions combine together to form a "jumbo" card. Each card is sequentially numbered to 5000.
COMPLETE SET (20) 30.00 60.00
STATED PRINT RUN 5000 SERIAL #'d SETS
1A Terrell Davis 1.00 2.50
1B Ricky Williams 1.25 3.00
2A Donovan McNabb 3.00 8.00
2B Cade McNown .50 1.25
3A Brett Favre 3.00 8.00
3B Barry Sanders 3.00 8.00
4A Jerry Rice 2.00 5.00
4B Steve Young 1.25 3.00
5A John Elway 3.00 8.00
5B Chris Chandler .60 1.50
6A Dan Marino 3.00 8.00
6B Drew Bledsoe 1.25 3.00
7A Keyshawn Johnson 1.00 2.50
7B Vinny Testaverde .60 1.50
8A Warren Moon 1.00 2.50
8B Steve McNair 1.00 2.50
9A Jake Plummer .60 1.50
9B Kordell Stewart .60 1.50
10A Troy Aikman 2.00 5.00
10B Peyton Manning 3.00 8.00

1999 Donruss Preferred QBC Hard Hats

Randomly seeded in packs, this 30-card set features top players on a clear plastic die-cut card shaped like a helmet. Each card is sequentially numbered to 3000.
COMPLETE SET (30) 60.00 120.00
STATED PRINT RUN 3000 SER.#'d SETS
1 Brett Favre 6.00 15.00
2 Keyshawn Johnson 2.00 5.00
3 John Elway 6.00 15.00
4 Drew Bledsoe 2.50 6.00
5 Chris Chandler 1.25 3.00
6 Terrell Davis 2.00 5.00
7 Ryan Leaf 2.00 5.00
8 Ricky Williams 2.00 5.00
9 Cade McNown .75 2.00
10 Barry Sanders 6.00 15.00
11 Donovan McNabb 5.00 12.00
12 Peyton Manning 6.00 15.00
13 Troy Aikman 4.00 10.00
14 Steve Young 2.50 6.00
15 Vinny Testaverde 1.25 3.00
16 Dan Marino 6.00 15.00
17 Steve McNair 2.00 5.00
18 Kordell Stewart 1.25 3.00
19 Michael Irvin 1.25 3.00
20 Jake Plummer 1.25 3.00
21 Jerry Rice 4.00 10.00
22 Brad Johnson 2.00 5.00
23 Phil Simms .75 2.00
24 Jim Kelly .75 2.00
25 Trent Dilfer 1.25 3.00
26 Kerry Collins 1.25 3.00
27 Warren Moon 2.00 5.00
28 Bubby Brister .75 2.00
29 Randall Cunningham 2.00 5.00
30 Doug Flutie 2.00 5.00

1999 Donruss Preferred QBC Materials

Randomly inserted in packs, this 21-card set features swatches of game-used jerseys, shoes, and helmets. Jersey and shoe cards are numbered out of 300 and Helmet cards are numbered out of 120.
JERSEY PRINT RUN 300 SER. #'d SETS
SHOE PRINT RUN 300 SER. #'d SETS
HELMET PRINT RUN 120 SER. #'d SETS
1 Dan Marino J 25.00 60.00
2 John Elway J 20.00 50.00
3 Drew Bledsoe J 10.00 25.00
4 Jake Plummer J 8.00 20.00
5A Doug Flutie White 10.00 25.00
5H Doug Flutie Blue 10.00 25.00
6 Peyton Manning J 25.00 60.00
7A Jerry Rice White/150 30.00 80.00
7H Jerry Rice Red 20.00 50.00
8 Brett Favre J 25.00 60.00
9 Jim Kelly J 12.00 30.00
10 Barry Sanders J 20.00 50.00
11 Keyshawn Johnson S 8.00 20.00
12 Brett Favre S 25.00 60.00
13 John Elway S 20.00 50.00
14 Troy Aikman S 15.00 40.00
15 Terrell Davis S 10.00 25.00
16 Dan Marino H 40.00 100.00
17 Troy Aikman H 25.00 60.00
18 Brett Favre H 40.00 100.00
19 Jerry Rice H 30.00 80.00
20 Terrell Davis H 15.00 40.00

1999 Donruss Preferred QBC National Treasures

Randomly inserted in packs, this 44-card set features action photos set on a green background with a National Treasures logo in the bottom right corner. Each card is sequentially numbered to 2000.
COMPLETE SET (44) 75.00 150.00
STATED PRINT RUN 2000 SERIAL #'d SETS
1 Jake Plummer 1.25 3.00
2 Chris Chandler 1.25 3.00
3 Danny Kanell .75 2.00
4 Tony Banks 1.25 3.00
5 Scott Mitchell .75 2.00
6 Doug Flutie 2.00 5.00
7 Jim Kelly .75 2.00
8 Erik Kramer .75 2.00
9 Cade McNown 1.00 2.50
10 Jeff Blake 1.25 3.00
11 Boomer Esiason .75 2.00
12 Bernie Kosar .75 2.00
13 Troy Aikman 4.00 10.00
14 Michael Irvin 1.25 3.00
15 Bubby Brister .75 2.00
16 Terrell Davis 2.00 5.00
17 John Elway 6.00 15.00
18 Gus Frerotte .75 2.00
19 Barry Sanders 6.00 15.00
20 Brett Favre 6.00 15.00
21 Peyton Manning 6.00 15.00
22 Elvis Grbac 1.25 3.00
23 Warren Moon 2.00 5.00
24 Dan Marino 6.00 15.00
25 Randall Cunningham 2.00 5.00
26 Jeff George 1.25 3.00
27 Drew Bledsoe 2.50 6.00
28 Ricky Williams 2.50 6.00
29 Kerry Collins 1.25 3.00
30 Phil Simms .75 2.00
31 Keyshawn Johnson 2.00 5.00
32 Vinny Testaverde 1.25 3.00
33 Donovan McNabb 6.00 15.00
34 Kordell Stewart 1.25 3.00
35 Jim Harbaugh 1.25 3.00
36 Ryan Leaf 2.00 5.00
37 Junior Seau 2.00 5.00
38 Jerry Rice 4.00 10.00
39 Steve Young 2.50 6.00
40 Jim Everett .75 2.00
41 Trent Dilfer 1.25 3.00
42 Steve McNair 2.00 5.00
43 Brad Johnson 2.00 5.00
44 Neil O'Donnell 1.25 3.00

1999 Donruss Preferred QBC Passing Grade

Randomly inserted in packs, this 20-card set features die-cut yellow cards with a pull-out football containing stats. Each card is sequentially numbered to 1500.
COMPLETE SET (20) 75.00 150.00
STATED PRINT RUN 1500 SERIAL #'d SETS
1 Steve Young 3.00 8.00
2 Dan Marino 8.00 20.00
3 Kordell Stewart 1.50 4.00
4 Trent Dilfer 1.50 4.00
5 Doug Flutie 2.50 6.00
6 Vinny Testaverde 1.50 4.00
7 Donovan McNabb 6.00 15.00
8 Brad Johnson 2.50 6.00
9 Troy Aikman 5.00 12.00
10 Brett Favre 8.00 20.00
11 Steve McNair 2.50 6.00
12 Peyton Manning 8.00 20.00
13 John Elway 8.00 20.00
14 Chris Chandler 1.50 4.00
15 Randall Cunningham 2.50 6.00
16 Cade McNown 1.00 2.50
17 Ryan Leaf 2.50 6.00
18 Drew Bledsoe 3.00 8.00
19 Jake Plummer 1.50 4.00
20 Warren Moon 2.50 6.00

1999 Donruss Preferred QBC Precious Metals

Randomly inserted in packs, this 30-card set is printed on one gram (roughly .032 troy ounce) of actual .999 silver, gold, or platinum. Each card is numbered out of 25.
STATED PRINT RUN 25 SER.#'d SETS
1 Troy Aikman G 50.00 120.00
2 Drew Bledsoe G 40.00 100.00
3 Terrell Davis G 30.00 80.00
4 John Elway P 75.00 200.00
5 Brett Favre P 75.00 200.00
6 Keyshawn Johnson G 25.00 60.00
7 Peyton Manning G 60.00 150.00
8 Dan Marino P 75.00 200.00
9 Donovan McNabb G 75.00 150.00
10 Cade McNown G 20.00 50.00
11 Jake Plummer G 25.00 60.00
12 Jerry Rice P 60.00 150.00
13 Barry Sanders P 60.00 150.00
14 Kordell Stewart G 20.00 50.00
15 Ricky Williams P 30.00 80.00
16 Bubby Brister S 20.00 50.00
17 Chris Chandler S 20.00 50.00
18 Randall Cunningham S 30.00 80.00
19 Doug Flutie S 30.00 80.00
20 Brad Johnson S 25.00 60.00
21 Ryan Leaf S 20.00 50.00
22 Steve McNair S 30.00 80.00
23 Warren Moon S 30.00 80.00
24 Vinny Testaverde S 20.00 50.00
25 Steve Young S 40.00 100.00
26 Kerry Collins S 20.00 50.00
27 Trent Dilfer S 20.00 50.00
28 Boomer Esiason S 30.00 80.00
29 Jim Kelly S 30.00 80.00
30 Phil Simms S 30.00 80.00

1999 Donruss Preferred QBC Staremasters

Randomly seeded in packs, this 20-card set features close up photos of the respective player's eyes. Each card is sequentially numbered out of 1000.
COMPLETE SET (20) 100.00 200.00
STATED PRINT RUN 1000 SERIAL #'d SETS
1 Jake Plummer 1.50 4.00
2 Doug Flutie 2.50 6.00
3 Cade McNown 1.00 2.50
4 Troy Aikman 5.00 12.00
5 Michael Irvin 1.50 4.00
6 Terrell Davis 2.50 6.00
7 John Elway 8.00 20.00
8 Barry Sanders 8.00 20.00
9 Brett Favre 8.00 20.00
10 Peyton Manning 8.00 20.00
11 Dan Marino 8.00 20.00
12 Randall Cunningham 2.50 6.00
13 Drew Bledsoe 3.00 8.00
14 Ricky Williams 2.50 6.00
15 Keyshawn Johnson 2.50 6.00
16 Donovan McNabb 6.00 15.00
17 Kordell Stewart 1.50 4.00
18 Ryan Leaf 2.50 6.00
19 Steve Young 3.00 8.00
20 Jerry Rice 5.00 12.00

1999 Donruss Preferred QBC X-Ponential Power

Randomly inserted in packs, this 20-card set features top players on an all foil card die-cut in the shape of half of an "X". When combined, the A and B cards form a jumbo complete "X" card. Each card is sequentially numbered to 2500.
COMPLETE SET (20) 75.00 150.00
STATED PRINT RUN 2500 SERIAL #'d SETS
1A Troy Aikman 3.00 8.00
1B Cade McNown 1.00 2.50
2A Kordell Stewart 1.00 2.50
2B Steve McNair 1.50 4.00
3A Donovan McNabb 6.00 15.00
3B Ricky Williams 2.50 6.00
4A Barry Sanders 5.00 12.00
4B Terrell Davis 1.50 4.00
5A Dan Marino 5.00 12.00
5B Peyton Manning 5.00 12.00
6A Jerry Rice 3.00 8.00
6B Keyshawn Johnson 1.50 4.00
7A Doug Flutie 1.50 4.00
7B Jim Kelly .60 1.50
8A Brett Favre 5.00 12.00
8B Steve Young 2.00 5.00
9A Drew Bledsoe 2.00 5.00
9B Ryan Leaf 1.50 4.00
10A John Elway 5.00 12.00
10B Jake Plummer 1.00 2.50

2000 Donruss Preferred

Released as a 103-card set, Donruss Preferred cards feature the members of the NFL's Quarterback Club. Base cards are white bordered on the top and feature player action photography centered on an orange, red, or purple border on the left and right sides of the card with silver foil highlights. Preferred was packaged in 10-pack boxes with four cards plus one Beckett Grading Services graded card per pack and carried a suggested retail price of $18.99.
COMPLETE SET (103) 8.00 20.00
1 Jake Plummer .12 .30
2 Chris Chandler .15 .40
3 Trent Dilfer .12 .30
4 Doug Flutie .15 .40
5 Cade McNown .12 .30
6 Michael Irvin .20 .50
7 Troy Aikman .25 .60
8 Terrell Davis .15 .40
9 John Elway .30 .75
10 Brett Favre .40 1.00
11 Peyton Manning .50 1.25
12 Warren Moon .20 .50
13 Randall Cunningham .15 .40
14 Drew Bledsoe .15 .40
15 Ricky Williams .15 .40
16 Kerry Collins .12 .30
17 Vinny Testaverde .12 .30
18 Donovan McNabb .15 .40
19 Jim Harbaugh .15 .40
20 Jerry Rice .50 1.25
21 Steve Young .25 .60
22 Keyshawn Johnson .15 .40
23 Neil O'Donnell .12 .30
24 Steve McNair .15 .40
25 Brad Johnson .15 .40
26 Jeff George .15 .40
27 Dan Marino .40 1.00
28 Jim Kelly .20 .50
29 Barry Sanders .30 .75
30 Phil Simms .20 .50
31 Gus Frerotte .12 .30
32 Elvis Grbac .12 .30
33 Jeff Blake .15 .40
34 Kordell Stewart .12 .30
35 Tony Banks .12 .30
36 Doug Flutie C .15 .40
37 Cade McNown C .12 .30
38 Troy Aikman C .25 .60
39 Terrell Davis C .15 .40
40 John Elway C .30 .75
41 Brett Favre C .40 1.00
42 Peyton Manning C .50 1.25
43 Drew Bledsoe C .15 .40
44 Ricky Williams C .15 .40
45 Kerry Collins C .12 .30
46 Vinny Testaverde C .12 .30
47 Donovan McNabb C .15 .40
48 Kordell Stewart C .12 .30
49 Ryan Leaf C .15 .40
50 Jerry Rice C .50 1.25
51 Steve Young C .25 .60
52 Keyshawn Johnson C .15 .40
53 Steve McNair C .15 .40
54 Jeff George C .15 .40
55 Dan Marino C .40 1.00
56 Jim Kelly C .20 .50
57 Barry Sanders C .30 .75
58 Bernie Kosar C .15 .40
59 Chris Chandler C .15 .40
60 Jim Everett C .15 .40
61 Jake Plummer HS .12 .30
62 Cade McNown HS .12 .30
63 Troy Aikman HS .25 .60
64 Ricky Williams HS .15 .40
65 Donovan McNabb HS .15 .40
66 Steve Young HS .25 .60
67 Brad Johnson HS .15 .40
68 Kerry Collins HS .12 .30
69 Ryan Leaf HS .15 .40
70 Drew Bledsoe HS .15 .40
71 Jake Plummer PS .12 .30
72 Chris Chandler PS .15 .40
73 Michael Irvin PS .20 .50
74 Troy Aikman PS .25 .60
75 Terrell Davis PS .15 .40
76 John Elway PS .30 .75
77 Brett Favre PS .40 1.00
78 Peyton Manning PS .50 1.25
79 Drew Bledsoe PS .15 .40
80 Junior Seau PS .15 .40
81 Jerry Rice PS .50 1.25
82 Steve Young PS .25 .60
83 Keyshawn Johnson PS .15 .40
84 Steve McNair PS .15 .40
85 Brad Johnson PS .15 .40
86 Dan Marino PS .40 1.00
87 Jim Kelly PS .20 .50
88 Barry Sanders PS .30 .75
89 Phil Simms PS .20 .50
90 Boomer Esiason PS .20 .50
91 Jake Plummer OF .12 .30
92 Chris Chandler OF .15 .40
93 Bubby Brister OF .12 .30
94 Cade McNown OF .12 .30
95 Jim Harbaugh OF .15 .40
96 Peyton Manning OF .50 1.25
97 Donovan McNabb OF .15 .40
98 Jim Kelly OF .20 .50
99 Brad Johnson OF .15 .40
100 Kordell Stewart OF .12 .30
101 Rob Johnson SP .40 1.00
102 Jevon Kearse SP .30 .75
103 Rich Gannon SP .40 1.00

2000 Donruss Preferred Power

*VETS 1-20: 2X TO 5X BASIC CARDS
1-20 VETERAN PRINT RUN 750
*VETS 21-40: 2.5X TO 6X BASIC CARDS
21-40 VETERAN PRINT RUN 500
*VETS 41-60: 3X TO 8X BASIC CARDS
41-60 VETERAN PRINT RUN 300
*VETS 61-80: 5X TO 12X BASIC CARDS
61-80 VETERAN PRINT RUN 150
*VETS 81-100: 10X TO 25X BASIC CARD
*VETS 101-103: 4X TO 10X BASIC CARD
81-103 VETERAN PRINT RUN 50

2000 Donruss Preferred Lettermen

Randomly inserted in packs, this 97-card tiered set features a player action photo card with a letter centered along the bottom from the featured player's last name. A card tier exists for each letter in a player's name. The first letter is numbered out of 1000, the second letter is numbered out of 750, the third letter is numbered out of 500, the fourth letter is numbered out of 350, the fifth letter is numbered out of 250, and the sixth letter is numbered out of 125. These cards are inserted one in every nine packs.
STATED ODDS 1:9
STATED PRINT RUN 50-1000
LM1 Peyton Manning/1000 2.50 6.00
LM2 Peyton Manning/750 2.50 6.00
LM3 Peyton Manning/500 3.00 8.00
LM4 Peyton Manning/350 3.00 8.00
LM5 Peyton Manning/250 4.00 10.00
LM6 Peyton Manning/125 5.00 12.00
LM7 Peyton Manning/75 6.00 15.00
LM8 Dan Marino/1000 2.00 5.00
LM9 Dan Marino/750 2.00 5.00
LM10 Dan Marino/500 2.50 6.00
LM11 Dan Marino/350 2.50 6.00
LM12 Dan Marino/250 3.00 8.00
LM13 Dan Marino/125 4.00 10.00
LM14 John Elway/1000 1.50 4.00
LM15 John Elway/750 1.50 4.00
LM16 John Elway/500 2.00 5.00
LM17 John Elway/350 2.00 5.00
LM18 John Elway/250 2.50 6.00
LM19 Terrell Davis/1000 .75 2.00
LM20 Terrell Davis/750 .75 2.00
LM21 Terrell Davis/500 1.00 2.50
LM22 Terrell Davis/350 1.00 2.50
LM23 Terrell Davis/250 1.25 3.00
LM24 Jerry Rice/1000 2.50 6.00
LM25 Jerry Rice/750 2.50 6.00
LM26 Jerry Rice/500 3.00 8.00
LM27 Jerry Rice/350 3.00 8.00
LM28 Cade McNown/1000 .60 1.50
LM29 Cade McNown/750 .60 1.50
LM30 Cade McNown/500 .75 2.00
LM31 Cade McNown/350 .75 2.00
LM32 Cade McNown/250 1.00 2.50
LM33 Cade McNown/125 1.25 3.00
LM34 Ricky Williams/1000 .75 2.00
LM35 Ricky Williams/750 .75 2.00
LM36 Ricky Williams/500 1.00 2.50
LM37 Ricky Williams/350 1.00 2.50
LM38 Ricky Williams/250 1.25 3.00
LM39 Ricky Williams/125 1.50 4.00
LM40 Ricky Williams/75 2.00 5.00
LM41 Ricky Williams/50 2.00 5.00
LM42 Drew Bledsoe/1000 .75 2.00
LM43 Drew Bledsoe/750 .75 2.00
LM44 Drew Bledsoe/500 1.00 2.50
LM45 Drew Bledsoe/350 1.00 2.50
LM46 Drew Bledsoe/250 1.25 3.00
LM47 Drew Bledsoe/125 1.50 4.00
LM48 Drew Bledsoe/75 2.00 5.00
LM49 Steve McNair/1000 .75 2.00
LM50 Steve McNair/750 .75 2.00
LM51 Steve McNair/500 1.00 2.50
LM52 Steve McNair/350 1.00 2.50
LM53 Steve McNair/250 1.25 3.00
LM54 Steve McNair/125 1.50 4.00
LM55 Troy Aikman/1000 1.25 3.00
LM56 Troy Aikman/750 1.25 3.00
LM57 Troy Aikman/500 1.50 4.00
LM58 Troy Aikman/350 1.50 4.00
LM59 Troy Aikman/250 2.00 5.00
LM60 Troy Aikman/125 2.50 6.00
LM61 Jake Plummer/1000 .60 1.50
LM62 Jake Plummer/750 .60 1.50
LM63 Jake Plummer/500 .75 2.00
LM64 Jake Plummer/350 .75 2.00
LM65 Jake Plummer/250 1.00 2.50
LM66 Jake Plummer/125 1.25 3.00
LM67 Jake Plummer/75 1.50 4.00
LM68 Steve Young/1000 1.25 3.00
LM69 Steve Young/750 1.25 3.00
LM70 Steve Young/500 1.50 4.00
LM71 Steve Young/350 1.50 4.00
LM72 Steve Young/250 2.00 5.00
LM73 Barry Sanders/1000 1.50 4.00
LM74 Barry Sanders/750 1.50 4.00
LM75 Barry Sanders/500 2.00 5.00
LM76 Barry Sanders/350 2.00 5.00
LM77 Barry Sanders/250 3.00 8.00
LM78 Barry Sanders/125 4.00 10.00
LM79 Barry Sanders/75 8.00 20.00
LM80 Brett Favre/1000 2.00 5.00
LM81 Brett Favre/750 2.00 5.00
LM82 Brett Favre/500 2.50 6.00
LM83 Brett Favre/350 2.50 6.00
LM84 Brett Favre/250 3.00 8.00
LM85 Donovan McNabb/1000 .75 2.00
LM86 Donovan McNabb/750 .75 2.00
LM87 Donovan McNabb/500 1.00 2.50
LM88 Donovan McNabb/350 1.00 2.50
LM89 Donovan McNabb/250 1.25 3.00
LM90 Donovan McNabb/125 1.50 4.00
LM91 Brad Johnson/1000 .75 2.00
LM92 Brad Johnson/750 .75 2.00
LM93 Brad Johnson/500 1.00 2.50
LM94 Brad Johnson/350 1.00 2.50
LM95 Brad Johnson/250 1.25 3.00
LM96 Brad Johnson/125 1.50 4.00
LM97 Brad Johnson/75 2.00 5.00

2000 Donruss Preferred Materials

Randomly inserted in packs at the rate of one in 34, this 44-card set features full color photography coupled with a square swatch of game worn memorabilia. Each card is sequentially numbered. These cards were also shrinkwrapped separately within the card pack.
STATED ODDS 1:34
PM1 Jerry Rice H/125 10.00 25.00
PM2 John Elway H/125 12.00 30.00
PM3 Doug Flutie H/125 3.00 8.00
PM4 Barry Sanders H/125 6.00 15.00
PM5 Dan Marino P/250 6.00 15.00
PM6 Jerry Rice P/250 8.00 20.00
PM7 Steve McNair S/50 4.00 10.00
PM8 Keyshawn Johnson S/125 3.00 8.00
PM9 Peyton Manning S/125 10.00 25.00
PM10 Steve Young S/125 5.00 12.00
PM11 John Elway S/125 6.00 15.00
PM12 Dan Marino S/125 8.00 20.00
PM13 Warren Moon S/125 4.00 10.00
PM14 Kordell Stewart S/125 2.50 6.00
PM15 Brett Favre S/125 8.00 20.00
PM16 Barry Sanders S/125 6.00 15.00
PM17 R.Cunningham S/125 3.00 8.00
PM18 Bernie Kosar J/300 2.50 6.00
PM19 Boomer Esiason J/300 3.00 8.00
PM20 Brett Favre J/100 8.00 20.00
PM21 Barry Sanders J/200 5.00 12.00
PM22 Cade McNown J/300 2.00 5.00
PM23 Dan Marino J/300 6.00 15.00
PM24 Drew Bledsoe J/100 3.00 8.00
PM25 Doug Flutie J W/300 2.50 6.00
PM26 Doug Flutie J B/300 2.50 6.00
PM27 Donovan McNabb J/300 2.50 6.00
PM28 Jerry Rice J/300 8.00 20.00
PM29 Jim Harbaugh J/300 2.50 6.00
PM30 Jim Kelly J/300 3.00 8.00
PM31 John Elway J/100 6.00 15.00
PM32 Jake Plummer J/300 2.00 5.00
PM33 Junior Seau J/300 2.50 6.00
PM34 Kordell Stewart J/300 2.00 5.00
PM35 Phil Simms J/200 3.00 8.00
PM36 Peyton Manning J/100 10.00 25.00
PM37 R.Cunningham J/300 2.50 6.00
PM38 Ricky Williams J W/100 3.00 8.00
PM39 Ricky Williams J B/100 3.00 8.00
PM40 Steve McNair J/100 3.00 8.00
PM41 Steve Young J/300 4.00 10.00
PM42 Troy Aikman J/100 5.00 12.00
PM43 Vinny Testaverde J/300 2.00 5.00
PM44 Warren Moon J/300 3.00 8.00

2000 Donruss Preferred National Treasures

Randomly seeded in packs at the rate of one in eight, this 41-card set features a silver bordered card with a player action photo set against the American flag. A purple oval name box is centered along the bottom of the card and the Donruss Preferred logo is stamped on in silver foil. Cards are sequentially numbered to 1000
COMPLETE SET (41) 30.00 80.00
STATED ODDS 1:8
STATED PRINT RUN 1000 SER.#'d SETS
NT1 Warren Moon 1.25 3.00
NT2 Steve Young 1.50 4.00
NT3 Jeff Blake 1.00 2.50
NT4 Brett Favre 2.50 6.00
NT5 Donovan McNabb 1.00 2.50
NT6 Bubby Brister .75 2.00
NT7 John Elway 2.00 5.00
NT8 Troy Aikman 1.50 4.00
NT9 Steve McNair 1.00 2.50
NT10 Kordell Stewart .75 2.00
NT11 Drew Bledsoe 1.00 2.50
NT12 Chris Chandler 1.00 2.50
NT13 Dan Marino 2.50 6.00
NT14 Brad Johnson 1.00 2.50
NT15 Jim Kelly 1.25 3.00
NT16 Jake Plummer .75 2.00
NT17 Boomer Esiason 1.25 3.00
NT18 Peyton Manning 3.00 8.00
NT19 Keyshawn Johnson 1.00 2.50
NT20 Barry Sanders 2.00 5.00
NT21 Bernie Kosar 1.00 2.50
NT22 Cade McNown .75 2.00
NT23 Elvis Grbac .75 2.00
NT24 Junior Seau 1.00 2.50
NT25 Phil Simms 1.25 3.00
NT26 Jim Everett 1.00 2.50
NT27 Vinny Testaverde .75 2.00
NT28 Jerry Rice 3.00 8.00
NT29 Terrell Davis 1.00 2.50
NT30 Ryan Leaf 1.00 2.50
NT31 Neil O'Donnell .75 2.00
NT32 Ricky Williams 1.00 2.50
NT33 Michael Irvin 1.25 3.00
NT34 Jim Harbaugh 1.00 2.50
NT35 Jeff George 1.00 2.50
NT36 Gus Frerotte .75 2.00
NT37 Doug Flutie 1.00 2.50
NT38 Trent Dilfer .75 2.00
NT39 Randall Cunningham 1.00 2.50
NT40 Kerry Collins .75 2.00
NT41 Tony Banks .75 2.00

2000 Donruss Preferred Pass Time

Randomly inserted in packs at the rate of one in 31, this 20-card set features base cards with a centered player action photo set against a split background. The left side of the background is shaded to match the featured player's team colors while the right side is gray and displays a player stat. Each card is sequentially numbered to 500.
COMPLETE SET (20) 30.00 60.00
STATED ODDS 1:31
STATED PRINT RUN 500 SER.#'d SETS
PT1 John Elway 2.50 6.00
PT2 Jim Kelly 1.50 4.00
PT3 Steve McNair 1.25 3.00
PT4 Doug Flutie 1.25 3.00
PT5 Dan Marino 3.00 8.00
PT6 Brett Favre 3.00 8.00
PT7 Cade McNown 1.00 2.50
PT8 Elvis Grbac 1.00 2.50
PT9 Vinny Testaverde 1.00 2.50
PT10 Kordell Stewart 1.00 2.50
PT11 Donovan McNabb 1.25 3.00
PT12 Jake Plummer 1.00 2.50
PT13 Troy Aikman 2.00 5.00
PT14 Chris Chandler 1.25 3.00
PT15 Kerry Collins 1.00 2.50
PT16 Peyton Manning 4.00 10.00
PT17 Steve Young 2.00 5.00
PT18 Brad Johnson 1.25 3.00
PT19 Jeff Blake 1.25 3.00
PT20 Drew Bledsoe 1.25 3.00

2000 Donruss Preferred Pen Pals

Randomly inserted in packs overall at the rate of one in 43, this 96-card set features between one and four authentic player autographs on the card front. Some cards were issued via mail redemptions that carried an expiration date of 3/31/2002.
PP1-PP41 ANNC'D PRINT RUN 50
PP42-PP76 ANNC'D PRINT RUN 40
PP77-PP91 ANNC'D PRINT RUN 20
PP92-PP96 ANNC'D PRINT RUN 10
OVERALL STATED ODDS 1:43
PP1 Warren Moon 12.50 30.00
PP2 Steve Young 20.00 50.00
PP3 Jeff Blake 6.00 15.00
PP4 Brett Favre 75.00 150.00
PP5 Donovan McNabb 20.00 40.00
PP6 Bubby Brister 6.00 15.00
PP7 John Elway 50.00 100.00
PP8 Troy Aikman 40.00 80.00
PP9 Steve McNair 15.00 40.00
PP10 Kordell Stewart 7.50 20.00
PP11 Drew Bledsoe 30.00 60.00
PP12 Chris Chandler 6.00 15.00
PP13 Dan Marino 75.00 150.00
PP14 Brad Johnson 7.50 20.00
PP15 Jim Kelly 20.00 50.00
PP16 Jake Plummer 7.50 20.00
PP17 Boomer Esiason 7.50 20.00
PP18 Peyton Manning 40.00 80.00
PP19 Keyshawn Johnson 7.50 20.00
PP20 Barry Sanders 75.00 125.00
PP21 Bernie Kosar 7.50 20.00
PP22 Cade McNown 6.00 15.00
PP23 Elvis Grbac 6.00 15.00
PP24 Junior Seau 30.00 60.00
PP25 Phil Simms 20.00 40.00
PP26 Jim Everett 6.00 15.00
PP27 Vinny Testaverde 7.50 20.00
PP28 Jerry Rice 60.00 120.00
PP29 Terrell Davis 15.00 30.00
PP30 Ryan Leaf 6.00 15.00
PP31 Neil O'Donnell 6.00 15.00
PP32 Ricky Williams 12.50 30.00
PP33 Michael Irvin 15.00 30.00
PP34 Jim Harbaugh 15.00 30.00
PP35 Jeff George 6.00 15.00
PP36 Gus Frerotte 6.00 15.00
PP37 Doug Flutie 12.50 30.00
PP38 Trent Dilfer 6.00 15.00
PP39 Randall Cunningham 12.50 30.00
PP40 Kerry Collins 7.50 20.00
PP41 Tony Banks 6.00 15.00
PP42 J.Rice/S.Young 150.00 300.00
PP43 J.Kelly/D.Flutie 60.00 120.00
PP44 T.Aikman/M.Irvin 60.00 120.00
PP45 J.Blake/R.Williams 25.00 50.00
PP46 J.Elway/T.Davis 75.00 150.00
PP47 K.Johnson/V.Testaverde 25.00 50.00
PP48 W.Moon/E.Grbac 30.00 80.00
PP49 B.Brister/J.Elway 75.00 150.00
PP50 P.Manning/R.Leaf 60.00 120.00
PP51 S.Young/V.Testaverde 40.00 80.00
PP52 Leaf/Seau 30.00 60.00

PP53 J.Elway/D.Marino 300.00 500.00
PP54 J.Kelly/T.Aikman 75.00 150.00
PP55 J.Kelly/P.Simms 60.00 100.00
PP56 B.Favre/T.Aikman 150.00 350.00
PP57 J.Plummer/B.Johnson 25.00 50.00
PP58 B.Sanders/J.Rice 300.00 450.00
PP59 D.Marino/P.Manning 300.00 500.00
PP60 Simms/Collins 25.00 50.00
PP61 C.McNown/D.McNabb 35.00 60.00
PP62 T.Davis/R.Williams 50.00 120.00
PP63 P.Manning/J.Elway 200.00 350.00
PP64 T.Aikman/J.Plummer 40.00 80.00
PP65 S.McNair/D.McNabb 40.00 80.00
PP66 S.Young/C.McNown 25.00 50.00
PP67 B.Sanders/T.Davis 100.00 200.00
PP68 D.Bledsoe/R.Leaf 25.00 50.00
PP69 C.McNown/T.Aikman 40.00 80.00
PP70 Cunningham/Chandler 25.00 50.00
PP71 B.Favre/J.Rice 200.00 400.00
PP72 P.Manning/B.Johnson 75.00 150.00
PP73 J.Plummer/S.Young 25.00 50.00
PP74 B.Favre/J.Elway 200.00 400.00
PP75 S.McNair/K.Stewart 20.00 40.00
PP76 B.Sanders/R.Williams 100.00 175.00
PP77 Kelly/Esiason/Simms 90.00 150.00
PP78 Irvin/Rice/Johnson 150.00 300.00
PP79 Davis/Rice/Manning 250.00 400.00
PP81 Plummer/Aikmn/Johnsn 50.00 120.00
PP82 Will/McNabb/McNown 30.00 80.00
PP83 Aikmn/Bledsoe/Chandlr 75.00 150.00
PP84 Flutie/Plummer/Young 50.00 120.00
PP85 McNair/Cnning/McNbb 75.00 150.00
PP86 Elway/Aikman/Young 250.00 400.00
PP87 Willms/Favre/Davis 175.00 300.00
PP88 Marino/Sanders/Rice 400.00 600.00
PP89 Aikman/Chndlr/Sanders 175.00 300.00
PP90 Marino/Elway/Favre 500.00 800.00
PP91 Sanders/Willms/Davis 125.00 250.00
PP92 Mar/Elwy/Favr/Mann
PP93 Rice/Key./T.Davis/R.Will.
PP94 Aikman/Young/Rice/Irvin
PP95 McNr/McNab/Yng/McNw

2000 Donruss Preferred QB Challenge Materials

Randomly seeded in packs, this 16-card set features Quarterback Challenge worn jerseys, footballs and used towels. Jerseys are sequentially numbered out of 500, footballs are sequentially numbered to 250, and towels are sequentially numbered to 225. A full color action photo is centered between purple borders with the swatch of memorabilia in the lower right hand corner of the card front.

STATED PRINT RUN 220-500
CM1 Donovan McNabb J/500 4.00 10.00
CM2 Jake Plummer J/500 3.00 8.00
CM3 Cade McNown J/500 3.00 8.00
CM4 Tony Banks J/500 3.00 8.00
CM5 Peyton Manning F/250 15.00 40.00
CM6 Donovan McNabb F/250 5.00 12.00
CM7 Brad Johnson F/250 5.00 12.00
CM8 Chris Chandler F/250 5.00 12.00
CM9 Jake Plummer F/250 4.00 10.00
CM10 Cade McNown F/250 4.00 10.00
CM11 Donovan McNabb T/225 5.00 12.00
CM12 Chris Chandler T/225 5.00 12.00
CM13 Cade McNown T/225 4.00 10.00
CM14 Jake Plummer T/225 4.00 10.00
CM15 Peyton Manning T/225 15.00 40.00
CM16 Brad Johnson T/225 5.00 12.00

2000 Donruss Preferred Signatures

Randomly inserted in packs at the rate of one in 51, this 19-card set features a player action photo in the lower right hand corner with team name and logo in the lower left hand corner set against a team color background. Centered in gold foil along the top of the card is a lighter color box where the player's autograph appears. Playoff Inc. announced the print runs and we've noted those below.

STATED ODDS 1:51
PLAYOFF ANNC'D PRINT RUNS 20-450
PS1 Brett Favre/20* 125.00 250.00
PS2 Drew Bledsoe/20* 30.00 80.00
PS3 Peyton Manning/20* 75.00 200.00
PS4 Terrell Davis/20* 30.00 80.00
PS5 Cade McNown/300* 5.00 12.00
PS6 Donovan McNabb/20* 60.00 120.00
PS7 Brad Johnson/340* 8.00 20.00
PS8 Dan Marino/20* 125.00 250.00
PS9 John Elway/50* 75.00 150.00
PS10 Troy Aikman/20* 75.00 150.00
PS11 Jeff Blake/410* 6.00 15.00
PS12 Vinny Testaverde/350* 6.00 15.00
PS13 Steve Young/20* 50.00 100.00
PS14 Steve McNair/20* 50.00 100.00
PS15 Jake Plummer/280* 5.00 12.00
PS16 Jim Harbaugh/450* 10.00 25.00
PS17 Kordell Stewart/410* 5.00 12.00
PS18 Junior Seau/410* 25.00 50.00
PS19 Ricky Williams/20* 25.00 60.00
PS20 Rob Johnson/100* 10.00 25.00
PS21 Jevon Kearse/200* 6.00 15.00
PS22 Rich Gannon/200* 8.00 20.00

2000 Donruss Preferred Staremasters

Randomly inserted in packs at the rate of one in eight, this 20-card set features framed player action shots on an all foil card with the word "Staremaster" in gold foil along the top. Cards are sequentially numbered to 1500.

COMPLETE SET (20) 15.00 40.00
STATED ODDS 1:8
STATED PRINT RUN 1500 SER.#'d SETS
SM1 Steve Young 1.25 3.00
SM2 Brad Johnson .75 2.00
SM3 Brett Favre 2.00 5.00
SM4 Junior Seau .75 2.00
SM5 Donovan McNabb .75 2.00
SM6 Jake Plummer .60 1.50
SM7 John Elway 1.50 4.00
SM8 Peyton Manning 2.50 6.00
SM9 Troy Aikman 1.25 3.00
SM10 Keyshawn Johnson .75 2.00
SM11 Steve McNair .75 2.00
SM12 Barry Sanders 1.50 4.00
SM13 Kordell Stewart .60 1.50
SM14 Cade McNown .60 1.50
SM15 Drew Bledsoe .75 2.00
SM16 Ricky Williams .75 2.00
SM17 Doug Flutie .75 2.00
SM18 Jerry Rice 2.50 6.00
SM19 Dan Marino 2.00 5.00
SM20 Terrell Davis .75 2.00

2010 Donruss Rated Rookies

COMPLETE SET (100) 6.00 15.00
COMP.FACT.SET (101) 15.00 25.00
1 Aaron Hernandez .20 .50
2 Andre Roberts .25 .60
3 Andrew Quarless .20 .50
4 Anthony Dixon .20 .50
5 Anthony McCoy .20 .50
6 Antonio Brown 1.50 4.00
7 Armanti Edwards .25 .60
8 Arrelious Benn .20 .50
9 Ben Tate .20 .50
10 Brandon Graham .25 .60
11 Brandon LaFell .30 .75
12 Brandon Spikes .20 .50
13 Brody Eldridge .30 .75
14 Bryan Bulaga .20 .50
15 C.J. Spiller .20 .50
16 Carlton Mitchell .20 .50
17 Chris Cook .20 .50
18 Chris Ivory .50 1.25
19 Colt McCoy .25 .60
20 Corey Wootton .20 .50
21 Damian Williams .20 .50
22 Dan LeFevour .20 .50
23 David Gettis .20 .50
24 David Nelson .30 .75
25 David Reed .20 .50
26 Deji Karim .25 .60
27 Demaryius Thomas .50 1.25
28 Dennis Pitta .20 .50
29 Derrick Morgan .20 .50
30 Devin McCourty .25 .60
31 Dexter McCluster .25 .60
32 Dez Bryant .50 1.25
33 Donald Jones .30 .75
34 Earl Thomas .50 1.25
35 Ed Dickson .20 .50
36 Emmanuel Sanders .30 .75
37 Eric Berry .30 .75
38 Eric Decker .25 .60
39 Fendi Onobun .25 .60
40 Garrett Graham .20 .50
41 Gerald McCoy .20 .50
42 Golden Tate .25 .60
43 Jacoby Ford .20 .50
44 Jahvid Best .20 .50
45 Jason Pierre-Paul .30 .75
46 Jason Worilds .20 .50
47 Javier Arenas .20 .50
48 Jeremy Horne .25 .60
49 Jermaine Gresham .20 .50
50 Jerry Hughes .20 .50
51 Jimmy Clausen .20 .50
52 Jimmy Graham .50 1.25
53 Joe Haden .30 .75
54 Joe McKnight .20 .50
55 Joe Webb .20 .50
56 John Conner .20 .50
57 John Skelton .25 .60
58 Jonathan Dwyer .20 .50
59 Jordan Shipley .20 .50
60 Kareem Jackson .20 .50
61 Keiland Williams .25 .60
62 Keith Toston .30 .75
63 Kerry Meier .25 .60
64 Kyle Williams .30 .75
65 Marc Mariani .30 .75
66 Marcus Easley .20 .50
67 Mardy Gilyard .20 .50
68 Marlon Moore .30 .75
69 Max Hall .30 .75
70 Max Komar .30 .75
71 Michael Hoomanawanui .30 .75
72 Mickey Shuler .30 .75
73 Mike Kafka .25 .60
74 Mike Williams .20 .50
75 Montario Hardesty .20 .50
76 Morgan Burnett .25 .60
77 Nate Allen .30 .75
78 NaVorro Bowman .40 1.00
79 Ndamukong Suh .40 1.00
80 Patrick Robinson .25 .60
81 Perrish Cox .25 .60
82 Ricky Sapp .20 .50
83 Riley Cooper .20 .50
84 Rob Gronkowski .60 1.50
85 Roberto Wallace .25 .60
86 Rolando McClain .20 .50
87 Russell Okung .20 .50
88 Ryan Mathews .20 .50
89 Sam Bradford .25 .60
90 Sean Lee .40 1.00
91 Sean Weatherspoon .20 .50
92 Stephen Williams .30 .75
93 Taylor Mays .20 .50
94 Taylor Price .20 .50
95 Tim Tebow .60 1.50
96 Toby Gerhart .20 .50
97 Tony Moeaki .25 .60
98 Tony Pike .20 .50
99 Trent Williams .25 .60
100 Victor Cruz .40 1.00

2010 Donruss Rated Rookies Autographs

ONE AUTO PER FACTORY SET
EXCH EXPIRATION: 7/5/2012
1 Aaron Hernandez/125* 4.00 10.00
2 Andre Roberts/25* 10.00 25.00
3 Andrew Quarless 4.00 10.00
4 Anthony Dixon/25* 8.00 20.00
5 Anthony McCoy/125* 4.00 10.00
6 Antonio Brown/25* 30.00 60.00
7 Armanti Edwards/25* 10.00 25.00
8 Arrelious Benn/25* 8.00 20.00
9 Ben Tate/25* 8.00 20.00
10 Brandon Graham/25* 10.00 25.00
11 Brandon LaFell/25*
12 Brandon Spikes/125* 4.00 10.00
13 Brody Eldridge 6.00 15.00
14 Bryan Bulaga/125* 8.00 20.00
15 C.J. Spiller/25* 8.00 20.00
16 Carlton Mitchell/25* 8.00 20.00
17 Chris Cook/125* 4.00 10.00
18 Chris Ivory 6.00 15.00
19 Colt McCoy/25* 10.00 25.00
20 Corey Wootton/425* 4.00 10.00
21 Damian Williams/25* 8.00 20.00
22 Dan LeFevour/25* 8.00 20.00
23 David Gettis/125* 4.00 10.00
24 David Nelson 8.00 20.00
25 David Reed 4.00 10.00
26 Deji Karim 5.00 12.00
27 Demaryius Thomas/25* 20.00 50.00
28 Dennis Pitta 8.00 20.00
29 Derrick Morgan/25* 8.00 20.00
30 Devin McCourty/25* 10.00 25.00
32 Dez Bryant/25* 50.00 100.00
33 Donald Jones 6.00 15.00
34 Earl Thomas/125* 10.00 25.00
35 Ed Dickson 4.00 10.00
36 Emmanuel Sanders/25* 12.00 30.00
37 Eric Berry/25* 20.00 50.00
38 Eric Decker/25* 10.00 25.00
39 Fendi Onobun 4.00 10.00
40 Garrett Graham/25* 8.00 20.00
41 Gerald McCoy/25* 8.00 20.00
42 Golden Tate/25*
43 Jacoby Ford/125* 4.00 10.00
44 Jahvid Best/25* 8.00 20.00
45 Jason Pierre-Paul/125* 6.00 15.00
46 Jason Worilds/125* 5.00 12.00
47 Javier Arenas 4.00 10.00
48 Jeremy Horne 4.00 10.00
49 Jermaine Gresham/25* 15.00 40.00
50 Jerry Hughes 5.00 12.00
51 Jimmy Clausen/25* 8.00 20.00
52 Jimmy Graham/125* 15.00 40.00
53 Joe Haden/125* 6.00 15.00
54 Joe McKnight/25* 10.00 25.00
55 Joe Webb 4.00 10.00
56 John Conner 5.00 12.00
57 John Skelton/500* 5.00 12.00
59 Jordan Shipley/25* 8.00 20.00
60 Kareem Jackson/125* 5.00 12.00
61 Keiland Williams 5.00 12.00
62 Keith Toston 6.00 15.00
63 Kerry Meier 5.00 12.00
64 Kyle Williams 5.00 12.00
65 Marc Mariani 6.00 15.00
66 Marcus Easley/25* 8.00 20.00
67 Mardy Gilyard/25*
68 Marlon Moore 5.00 12.00
69 Max Hall/500* 6.00 15.00
70 Max Komar 6.00 15.00
71 Michael Hoomanawanui 5.00 12.00
72 Mickey Shuler 6.00 15.00
73 Mike Kafka/25* 10.00 25.00
74 Mike Williams/25*
75 Montario Hardesty/25* 8.00 20.00
76 Morgan Burnett/300* 5.00 12.00
77 Nate Allen/125* 6.00 15.00
78 NaVorro Bowman/125* 8.00 20.00
79 Ndamukong Suh/25* 15.00 40.00
80 Patrick Robinson/300* 5.00 12.00
81 Perrish Cox/250* 5.00 12.00
82 Ricky Sapp/125* 4.00 10.00
83 Riley Cooper/25* 8.00 20.00
84 Rob Gronkowski/25* 50.00 120.00
85 Roberto Wallace 5.00 12.00
86 Rolando McClain/25* 8.00 20.00
87 Russell Okung 4.00 10.00
88 Ryan Mathews/25* 8.00 20.00
89 Sam Bradford/25* 10.00 25.00
90 Sean Lee/125* 8.00 20.00
91 Sean Weatherspoon/25* 8.00 20.00
92 Stephen Williams 5.00 12.00
93 Taylor Mays/125* 4.00 10.00
94 Taylor Price/25* 8.00 20.00
95 Tim Tebow/25* 50.00 120.00
96 Toby Gerhart/25*
97 Tony Moeaki 5.00 12.00
98 Tony Pike/25* 8.00 20.00
99 Trent Williams/125* 5.00 12.00
100 Victor Cruz 8.00 20.00

2011 Donruss Rated Rookies National Convention

COMPLETE SET (10)
*RED/25: 1.5X TO 4X BASIC CARDS
RR1 Cam Newton 2.50 6.00
RR2 Jake Locker 1.25 3.00
RR3 Mark Ingram 1.25 3.00
RR4 Julio Jones 2.00 5.00
RR5 A.J. Green 2.00 5.00

1995 Donruss Red Zone

The 1995 Donruss Red Zone series consists of 336 cards. The standard-sized rounded-corner playing cards were distributed as part of a football game. The cards were available in both 80-card starter decks and 12-card booster packs. A Deluxe Double Deck Game Set was distributed as well that contained two 80-card decks and one 12-card pack. The red backs carry the game logo. The cards were unnumbered and are checklisted in alphabetical order within each team below. All cards were available in both issues, but some cards were printed in greater supply than others, and those are noted with the designation DP below. Conversely, there are cards that were produced in smaller quantities than the others, and those are listed with the designation SP below. A 98-card expansion Update set was released later in foil packs.

COMPLETE SET (336) 100.00 250.00
1 Michael Bankston .10 .30
2 Larry Centers .20 .50
3 Ben Coleman DP .01 .05
4 Ed Cunningham DP .01 .05
5 Garrison Hearst .60 1.50
6 Eric Hill .10 .30
7 Lorenzo Lynch DP .01 .05
8 Clyde Simmons DP .01 .05
9 Eric Swann .20 .50
10 Aeneas Williams SP .80 2.00
11 Chris Doleman .10 .30
12 Bert Emanuel DP .20 .50
13 Roman Fortin DP .01 .05
14 Jeff George SP 1.20 3.00
15 Craig Heyward DP .02 .10
16 D.J. Johnson SP .80 2.00
17 Terance Mathis SP 1.20 3.00
18 Clay Matthews DP .01 .05
19 Kevin Ross DP .01 .05
20 Jessie Tuggle DP .01 .05
21 Bob Whitfield SP .80 2.00
22 Cornelius Bennett SP .80 2.00
23 Russell Copeland DP .10 .30
24 John Fina SP .80 2.00
25 Carwell Gardner DP .01 .05
26 Henry Jones DP .01 .05
27 Jim Kelly SP 3.00 8.00
28 Mark Maddox DP .01 .05
29 Glenn Parker .10 .30
30 Andre Reed SP 1.20 3.00
31 Bruce Smith SP 1.20 3.00
32 Thomas Smith DP .01 .05
33 Joe Cain DP .01 .05
34 Mark Carrier DB .20 .50
35 Curtis Conway DP .20 .50
36 Al Fontenot DP .01 .05
37 Jeff Graham DP .02 .10
38 Raymont Harris DP .01 .05
39 Andy Heck .10 .30
40 Erik Kramer DP .02 .10
41 Vinson Smith .10 .30
42 Lewis Tillman DP .01 .05
43 Steve Walsh .10 .30
44 James Williams DP .01 .05
45 Donnell Woolford SP .80 2.00
46 Mike Brim DP .01 .05
47 Tony McGee DP .01 .05
48 Carl Pickens .30 .75
49 Keith Rucker DP .01 .05
50 Darnay Scott SP 1.20 3.00
51 Dan Wilkinson DP .02 .10
52 Darryl Williams DP .01 .05
53 Derrick Alexander WR .20 .50
54 Carl Banks DP .01 .05
55 Rob Burnett SP .80 2.00
56 Earnest Byner .10 .30
57 Steve Everitt DP .01 .05
58 Leroy Hoard SP .80 2.00
59 Michael Jackson DP .01 .05
60 Pepper Johnson .10 .30
61 Tony Jones .10 .30
62 Antonio Langham .10 .30
63 Anthony Pleasant DP .01 .05
64 Vinny Testaverde DP .02 .10
65 Eric Turner SP .80 2.00
66 Tommy Vardell .10 .30
67 Troy Aikman SP 5.00 12.00
68 Larry Brown .10 .30
69 Dixon Edwards DP .10 .30
70 Charles Haley SP .80 2.00
71 Michael Irvin SP 2.00 5.00
72 Daryl Johnston DP .02 .10
73 Leon Lett .10 .30
74 Nate Newton .10 .30
75 Jay Novacek SP .80 2.00
76 Darrin Smith .10 .30
77 Kevin Smith .10 .30
78 Tony Tolbert DP .01 .05
79 Mark Tuinei SP .80 2.00
80 Kevin Williams DP .02 .10
81 Darren Woodson .10 .30
82 Elijah Alexander .10 .30
83 Steve Atwater .10 .30
84 Rod Bernstine SP .80 2.00
85 Ray Crockett .10 .30
86 Shane Dronett DP .01 .05
87 John Elway SP 10.00 20.00
88 Simon Fletcher .10 .30
89 Brian Habib DP .01 .05
90 Glyn Milburn .10 .30
91 Anthony Miller SP .80 2.00
92 Mike Pritchard DP .02 .10
93 Shannon Sharpe .20 .50
94 Gary Zimmerman DP .01 .05
95 Bennie Blades .10 .30
96 Lomas Brown SP .80 2.00
97 Mike Johnson DP .01 .05
98 Robert Massey DP .01 .05
99 Scott Mitchell DP .02 .10
100 Herman Moore SP 1.20 3.00
101 Brett Perriman .20 .50
102 Barry Sanders SP 10.00 20.00
103 Tracy Scroggins DP .01 .05
104 Chris Spielman .10 .30
105 Doug Widell SP .80 2.00
106 Edgar Bennett SP 1.20 3.00
107 LeRoy Butler DP .01 .05
108 Harry Galbreath DP .01 .05
109 Sean Jones SP .80 2.00
110 George Koonce DP .01 .05
111 Anthony Morgan DP .01 .05
112 Ken Ruettgers DP .01 .05
113 Fred Strickland DP .01 .05
114 George Teague .10 .30
115 Reggie White SP 2.00 5.00
116 Micheal Barrow .10 .30
117 Blaine Bishop DP .01 .05
118 Gary Brown .10 .30
119 Ray Childress .10 .30
120 Kenny Davidson SP .80 2.00
121 Cris Dishman SP .80 2.00
122 Brad Hopkins SP .80 2.00
123 Haywood Jeffires DP .01 .05
124 Eddie Robinson DP .01 .05
125 Al Smith DP .01 .05
126 David Williams SP .80 2.00
127 Tony Bennett SP .80 2.00
128 Ray Buchanan SP .80 2.00
129 Quentin Coryatt DP .02 .10
130 Eugene Daniel DP .01 .05
131 Sean Dawkins DP .02 .10
132 Marshall Faulk SP 4.00 10.00
133 Jim Harbaugh .20 .50
134 Jeff Herrod DP .01 .05
135 Kirk Lowdermilk DP .01 .05
136 Tony Siragusa DP .01 .05
137 Floyd Turner DP .01 .05
138 Will Wolford SP .80 2.00
139 Marcus Allen .20 .50
140 Kimble Anders SP .80 2.00
141 Steve Bono DP .10 .30
142 Dale Carter DP .01 .05
143 Mark Collins DP .01 .05
144 Willie Davis .20 .50
145 Lake Dawson DP .02 .10
146 Tim Grunhard DP .01 .05
147 Greg Hill DP .02 .10
148 George Jamison DP .01 .05
149 Darren Mickell DP .01 .05
150 Will Shields DP .01 .05
151 Tracy Simien DP .01 .05
152 Neil Smith SP .80 2.00
153 Tim Bowens DP .01 .05
154 J.B. Brown DP .01 .05
155 Keith Byars .10 .30
156 Bryan Cox .10 .30
157 Jeff Cross .10 .30
158 Irving Fryar SP .80 2.00
159 Ron Heller .10 .30
160 Terry Kirby SP .80 2.00
161 Dan Marino SP 10.00 20.00
162 O.J. McDuffie .30 .75
163 Bernie Parmalee DP .02 .10
164 Chris Singleton DP .01 .05
165 Troy Vincent SP .80 2.00
166 Richmond Webb SP .80 2.00
167 Roy Barker DP .01 .05
168 Cris Carter DP .08 .25
169 Jack Del Rio SP .80 2.00
170 Chris Hinton DP .01 .05
171 Qadry Ismail .20 .50
172 Amp Lee .10 .30
173 Ed McDaniel .10 .30
174 Randall McDaniel DP .02 .10
175 Warren Moon SP 2.00 5.00
176 John Randle SP 1.20 3.00
177 Jake Reed DP .02 .10
178 Robert Smith DP .02 .10
179 Todd Steussie DP .01 .05
180 Dewayne Washington DP .01 .05
181 Bruce Armstrong DP .01 .05
182 Drew Bledsoe 1.00 2.50
183 Vincent Brisby DP .01 .05
184 Vincent Brown DP .01 .05
185 Ben Coates SP 1.20 3.00
186 Sam Gash DP .01 .05
187 Myron Guyton DP .01 .05
188 Maurice Hurst SP .80 2.00
189 Mike Jones DP .01 .05
190 Bob Kratch DP .01 .05
191 Chris Slade SP .80 2.00
192 Derek Brown .10 .30
193 Vince Buck DP .01 .05
194 Jim Dombrowski DP .01 .05
195 Quinn Early DP .02 .10
196 Jim Everett .20 .50
197 Michael Haynes DP .02 .10
198 Wayne Martin SP .80 2.00
199 Lorenzo Neal DP .01 .05
200 William Roaf SP .80 2.00
201 Irv Smith DP .01 .05
202 Jimmy Spencer DP .01 .05
203 Winfred Tubbs DP .01 .05
204 Renaldo Turnbull SP .80 2.00
205 Michael Brooks DP .01 .05
206 Dave Brown DP .02 .10
207 Chris Calloway .10 .30
208 Jesse Campbell DP .01 .05
209 Jumbo Elliott DP .01 .05
210 Keith Hamilton DP .01 .05
211 Rodney Hampton DP .02 .10
212 Corey Miller DP .01 .05
213 Doug Riesenberg DP .01 .05
214 Mike Sherrard .10 .30
215 Phillippi Sparks .10 .30
216 Michael Strahan DP .80 2.00
217 Richie Anderson DP .80 2.00
218 Brad Baxter DP .01 .05
219 Tony Casillas DP .01 .05
220 Roger Duffy .10 .30
221 Boomer Esiason DP .02 .10
222 Aaron Glenn DP .01 .05
223 Bobby Houston DP .01 .05
224 Mo Lewis SP .80 2.00
225 Siupeli Malamala DP .01 .05
226 Johnny Mitchell DP .01 .05
227 Eddie Anderson DP .01 .05
228 Jerry Ball DP .01 .05
229 Greg Biekert .10 .30
230 Tim Brown SP 2.00 5.00
231 Rob Fredrickson DP .01 .05
232 Nolan Harrison .10 .30
233 Jeff Hostetler DP .02 .10
234 Rocket Ismail SP 1.20 3.00
235 Terry McDaniel SP .80 2.00
236 Chester McGlockton SP .80 2.00
237 Don Mosebar .10 .30
238 Anthony Smith .10 .30
239 Harvey Williams DP .02 .10
240 Steve Wisniewski DP .01 .05
241 Fred Barnett .20 .50
242 Randall Cunningham .40 1.00
243 William Fuller SP .80 2.00
244 Charlie Garner .80 2.00
245 Vaughn Hebron DP .01 .05
246 Lester Holmes .10 .30
247 Greg Jackson SP .80 2.00
248 Bill Romanowski DP .01 .05
249 William Thomas SP .80 2.00
250 Bernard Williams .10 .30
251 Calvin Williams DP .01 .05
252 Michael Zordich SP .80 2.00
253 Chad Brown SP .80 2.00
254 Dermontti Dawson DP .02 .10
255 Kevin Greene SP 1.20 3.00
256 Charles Johnson .20 .50
257 Carnell Lake .10 .30
258 Greg Lloyd SP .80 2.00
259 Neil O'Donnell DP .10 .30
260 Ray Seals DP .01 .05
261 Leon Searcy SP .80 2.00
262 Yancey Thigpen DP .40 1.00
263 John L. Williams DP .01 .05
264 Rod Woodson SP .80 2.00
265 Stan Brock .10 .30
266 Courtney Hall .10 .30
267 Ronnie Harmon .10 .30
268 Dwayne Harper DP .01 .05
269 Rodney Harrison DP .40 1.00
270 Stan Humphries DP .20 .50
271 Shawn Jefferson .10 .30
272 Shawn Lee .10 .30
273 Tony Martin .20 .50
274 Natrone Means SP 1.20 3.00
275 Chris Mims SP .80 2.00
276 Leslie O'Neal SP .80 2.00
277 Junior Seau SP 1.20 3.00
278 Mark Seay DP .02 .10
279 Harry Swayne DP .01 .05
280 Eric Davis .10 .30
281 William Floyd .20 .50
282 Merton Hanks SP .80 2.00
283 Brent Jones .20 .50
284 Tim McDonald DP .01 .05
285 Ken Norton SP .80 2.00
286 Gary Plummer DP .01 .05
287 Jerry Rice SP 5.00 12.00
288 Dana Stubblefield SP .10 .30
289 John Taylor SP .80 2.00
290 Bryant Young DP .02 .10
291 Steve Young SP 4.00 10.00
292 Steve Wallace SP .80 2.00
293 Sam Adams DP .01 .05
294 Robert Blackmon DP .01 .05
295 Jeff Blackshear DP .01 .05
296 Brian Blades .20 .50
297 Howard Ballard SP .80 2.00
298 Cortez Kennedy DP .01 .05
299 Rick Mirer .20 .50
300 Eugene Robinson DP .01 .05
301 Chris Warren SP 1.20 3.00
302 Terry Wooden SP .80 2.00
303 Johnny Bailey .10 .30
304 Isaac Bruce DP .30 .75
305 Shane Conlan DP .01 .05
306 Troy Drayton DP .01 .05
307 Sean Gilbert DP .01 .05
308 Leo Goeas DP .01 .05
309 Jessie Hester .10 .30
310 Clarence Jones .10 .30
311 Todd Lyght .10 .30
312 Chris Miller DP .02 .10
313 Toby Wright DP .01 .05
314 Robert Young DP .01 .05
315 Eric Curry DP .01 .05
316 Trent Dilfer .20 .50
317 Thomas Everett DP .01 .05
318 Paul Gruber DP .01 .05
319 Jackie Harris DP .01 .05
320 Courtney Hawkins DP .01 .05
321 Lonnie Marts DP .01 .05
322 Tony Mayberry DP .01 .05
323 Martin Mayhew DP .01 .05
324 Hardy Nickerson DP .01 .05
325 Errict Rhett DP .30 .75
326 Reggie Brooks DP .01 .05
327 Tom Carter DP .01 .05
328 Henry Ellard SP .80 2.00
329 Darrell Green SP .80 2.00
330 Ken Harvey SP .80 2.00
331 James Jenkins DP .01 .05
332 Tim Johnson DP .01 .05
333 Jim Lachey .10 .30
334 Brian Mitchell .10 .30
335 Heath Shuler .30 .75
336 Tony Woods DP .01 .05

1995 Donruss Red Zone Update

This 98-card Update (expansion) set to the Red Zone release was distributed in foil pack form in late 1995. The cards essentially follow the design of the first series and include many of the star players not included in the first release. We've designated the short-printed cards below as SP. The Emmitt Smith, Brett Favre, Deion Sanders, and Kordell Stewart cards appear to be the most difficult to find.

COMPLETE SET (98) 75.00 150.00
1 Seth Joyner SP .50 1.25
2 Dave Krieg .40 1.00
3 Rob Moore .75 2.00
4 Frank Sanders SP 2.00 5.00
5 J.J. Birden .40 1.00
6 Moe Gardner .40 1.00
7 Eric Metcalf .40 1.00
8 Bill Brooks .40 1.00
9 Phil Hansen .40 1.00
10 Darick Holmes .50 1.25
11 Bryce Paup SP .50 1.25
12 Blake Brockermeyer .40 1.00
13 Mark Carrier WR SP .50 1.25
14 Kerry Collins 2.00 5.00
15 Mike Fox .40 1.00
16 Derrick Graham .40 1.00
17 Howard Griffith .40 1.00
18 Lamar Lathon .40 1.00
19 Bubba McDowell .40 1.00
20 Pete Metzelaars .40 1.00
21 Sam Mills .40 1.00
22 Derrick Moore .40 1.00
23 Rod Smith .40 1.00
24 Gerald Williams .40 1.00
25 Rashaan Salaam SP .75 2.00
26 Chris Zorich .40 1.00
27 Eric Bieniemy .40 1.00
28 Jeff Blake .75 2.00
29 Ki-Jana Carter SP .75 2.00
30 James Francis .40 1.00
31 Bruce Kozerski .40 1.00
32 Kevin Sargent SP .50 1.25
33 Steve Tovar .40 1.00
34 Andre Rison SP .75 2.00
35 Deion Sanders SP 3.20 8.00
36 Emmitt Smith SP 6.00 15.00
37 Terrell Davis 5.00 12.00
38 Michael Dean Perry .40 1.00
39 Ron Rivers .50 1.25
40 Henry Thomas SP .50 1.25
41 Robert Brooks .50 1.25
42 Mark Chmura .75 2.00
43 Brett Favre SP 8.00 20.00
44 Dorsey Levens .75 2.00
45 Chris Chandler .75 2.00
46 Chris Sanders .75 2.00
47 Rodney Thomas .40 1.00
48 Roosevelt Potts SP .50 1.25
49 Tony Boselli .40 1.00
50 Mark Brunell 1.60 4.00
51 Vinnie Clark SP .50 1.25
52 Don Davey .40 1.00
53 Vaughn Dunbar .40 1.00
54 Keith Goganious .40 1.00
55 Desmond Howard SP .75 2.00
56 Willie Jackson .50 1.25
57 Jeff Lageman .40 1.00
58 James O. Stewart 2.00 5.00
59 Mickey Washington .40 1.00
60 Dave Widell .40 1.00
61 James Williams .40 1.00
62 Keith Cash .40 1.00
63 Eric Green SP .50 1.25
64 Charles Mincy .40 1.00
65 Curtis Martin 4.00 10.00
66 Dave Meggett .40 1.00
67 Tim Roberts .40 1.00
68 Mario Bates .50 1.25
69 Rufus Porter .40 1.00
70 Tyrone Wheatley 1.60 4.00
71 Wayne Chrebet 2.40 6.00
72 Todd Scott .40 1.00
73 Marvin Washington .40 1.00
74 Napoleon Kaufman 2.40 6.00
75 Pat Swilling .40 1.00
76 Andy Harmon .40 1.00
77 Mike Mamula .40 1.00
78 Ricky Watters SP .75 2.00
79 Byron Bam Morris .40 1.00
80 Eric Pegram .40 1.00
81 Joel Steed .40 1.00
82 Kordell Stewart SP 4.00 10.00
83 Dennis Gibson .40 1.00
84 Derek Loville .40 1.00
85 Jesse Sapolu .40 1.00
86 Joey Galloway SP 4.00 10.00
87 Winston Moss .40 1.00
88 Steve Smith .40 1.00
89 Jerome Bettis 1.00 2.50
90 Carlos Jenkins .40 1.00
91 Jerry Ellison .40 1.00
92 Alvin Harper SP .50 1.25
93 Warren Sapp .40 1.00
94 Terry Allen SP .75 2.00
95 Gus Frerotte .50 1.25
96 Marvcus Patton .40 1.00
97 Ed Simmons .40 1.00
98 Michael Westbrook 1.20 3.00

2009 Donruss Rookies and Stars

COMP.SET w/o SP's (100) 8.00 20.00
116-200 ROOKIE PRINT RUN 999
201-234 ROOK.AU PRINT RUN 139-142
1 Kurt Warner .25 .60
2 Larry Fitzgerald .25 .60
3 Steve Breaston .25 .60
4 Matt Ryan .25 .60
5 Michael Turner .20 .50
6 Roddy White .20 .50
7 Derrick Mason .20 .50
8 Joe Flacco .25 .60
9 Willis McGahee .20 .50
10 Lee Evans .25 .60
11 Marshawn Lynch .25 .60
12 Trent Edwards .20 .50
13 DeAngelo Williams .20 .50
14 Jake Delhomme .20 .50
15 Jonathan Stewart .20 .50
16 Steve Smith .25 .60
17 Greg Olsen .25 .60
18 Kyle Orton .20 .50
19 Matt Forte .20 .50
20 Carson Palmer .25 .60
21 Chad Ochocinco .20 .50
22 T.J. Houshmandzadeh .20 .50
23 Brady Quinn .20 .50
24 Braylon Edwards .20 .50
25 Jamal Lewis .25 .60
26 Jason Witten .25 .60
27 Marion Barber .25 .60
28 Tony Romo .25 .60
29 Brandon Marshall .25 .60
30 Jay Cutler .20 .50
31 Eddie Royal .20 .50
32 Calvin Johnson .30 .75
33 Daunte Culpepper .25 .60
34 Kevin Smith .20 .50
35 Aaron Rodgers .60 1.50
36 Greg Jennings .20 .50
37 Ryan Grant .25 .60
38 Andre Johnson .25 .60
39 Matt Schaub .20 .50
40 Owen Daniels .20 .50
41 Steve Slaton .20 .50
42 Anthony Gonzalez .20 .50
43 Joseph Addai .20 .50
44 Peyton Manning .75 2.00
45 Reggie Wayne .25 .60
46 David Garrard .20 .50
47 Marcedes Lewis .20 .50
48 Maurice Jones-Drew .20 .50
49 Dwayne Bowe .25 .60
50 Larry Johnson .20 .50
51 Tony Gonzalez .25 .60
52 Chad Pennington .20 .50
53 Ricky Williams .25 .60
54 Ronnie Brown .20 .50
55 Adrian Peterson .30 .75
56 Bernard Berrian .20 .50
57 Tarvaris Jackson .25 .60
58 Laurence Maroney .25 .60
59 Tom Brady 1.00 2.50
60 Wes Welker .25 .60
61 Drew Brees .30 .75
62 Marques Colston .20 .50
63 Reggie Bush .20 .50
64 Brandon Jacobs .20 .50
65 Eli Manning .25 .60
66 Kevin Boss .20 .50
67 Thomas Jones .20 .50
68 Jerricho Cotchery .20 .50
69 Leon Washington .20 .50
70 Darren McFadden .30 .75
71 JaMarcus Russell .20 .50
72 Zach Miller .20 .50
73 Brian Westbrook .20 .50
74 DeSean Jackson .25 .60
75 Donovan McNabb .25 .60
76 Ben Roethlisberger .30 .75
77 Heath Miller .20 .50
78 Santonio Holmes .20 .50
79 Willie Parker .20 .50
80 LaDainian Tomlinson .30 .75
81 Philip Rivers .30 .75
82 Vincent Jackson .20 .50
83 Frank Gore .25 .60
84 Shaun Hill .20 .50
85 Vernon Davis .20 .50
86 John Carlson .25 .60
87 Julius Jones .20 .50
88 Matt Hasselbeck .20 .50
89 Marc Bulger .20 .50
90 Steven Jackson .20 .50
91 Torry Holt .25 .60
92 Antonio Bryant .20 .50
93 Cadillac Williams .25 .60
94 Kellen Winslow .20 .50
95 Chris Johnson .20 .50
96 Kerry Collins .20 .50
97 LenDale White .20 .50
98 Chris Cooley .20 .50
99 Clinton Portis .20 .50
100 Jason Campbell .20 .50
101 Santonio Holmes ELE 1.00 2.50
102 Willie Parker ELE 1.00 2.50
103 Kurt Warner ELE 1.25 3.00
104 Brian Westbrook ELE 1.00 2.50
105 Tim Hightower ELE 1.00 2.50
106 Donovan McNabb ELE 1.25 3.00
107 Wes Welker ELE 1.25 3.00
108 Randy Moss ELE 1.25 3.00
109 Philip Rivers ELE 1.50 4.00
110 Antonio Gates ELE 1.25 3.00
111 Thomas Jones ELE 1.00 2.50
112 Brandon Marshall ELE 1.25 3.00
113 Nate Burleson ELE 1.00 2.50
114 Leon Washington ELE 1.00 2.50
115 Brandon Jacobs ELE 1.00 2.50
116 Aaron Kelly RC 1.25 3.00
117 Aaron Maybin RC 1.50 4.00
118 Alphonso Smith RC 1.25 3.00
119 Andre Smith RC 1.25 3.00
120 Arian Foster RC 3.00 8.00
121 Asher Allen RC 1.25 3.00
122 Austin Collie RC 1.25 3.00
123 B.J. Raji RC 1.50 4.00
124 Bradley Fletcher RC 1.25 3.00
125 Brandon Gibson RC 1.50 4.00
126 Brian Cushing RC 1.25 3.00
127 Brian Hartline RC 2.00 5.00
128 Brian Orakpo RC 1.50 4.00
129 Brooks Foster RC 1.25 3.00
130 Cameron Morrah RC 1.25 3.00
131 Cedric Peerman RC 1.25 3.00
132 Chase Coffman RC 1.25 3.00
133 Chip Vaughn RC 1.25 3.00
134 Chris Owens RC 1.25 3.00
135 Clay Matthews RC 5.00 12.00
136 Clint Sintim RC 1.25 3.00
137 Cody Brown RC 1.25 3.00
138 Connor Barwin RC 1.50 4.00
139 Cornelius Ingram RC 1.25 3.00
140 Darcel McBath RC 1.25 3.00
141 Darius Butler RC 1.50 4.00
142 Darius Passmore RC 1.25 3.00
143 David Bruton RC 1.25 3.00
144 DeAndre Levy RC 1.50 4.00
145 Demetrius Byrd RC 1.50 4.00
146 Devin Moore RC 1.25 3.00
147 Dominique Edison RC 1.25 3.00
148 Eugene Monroe RC 1.25 3.00
149 Evander Hood RC 2.00 5.00
150 Everette Brown RC 1.25 3.00
151 Brandon Tate RC 1.50 4.00
152 Graham Harrell RC 1.25 3.00
153 Hunter Cantwell RC 1.25 3.00
154 Jairus Byrd RC 2.00 5.00
155 James Casey RC 1.50 4.00
156 James Laurinaitis RC 1.25 3.00
157 Jared Cook RC 1.50 4.00
158 Jarett Dillard RC 1.25 3.00
159 Jason Williams RC 1.50 4.00
160 Jeremiah Johnson RC 1.25 3.00
161 Jeremy Childs RC 1.25 3.00
162 Jerraud Powers RC 1.25 3.00
163 John Parker Wilson RC 1.25 3.00
164 Johnny Knox RC 1.50 4.00
165 Kaluka Maiava RC 1.25 3.00
166 Keenan Lewis RC 2.00 5.00
167 Kenny McKinley RC 1.25 3.00
168 Kevin Barnes RC 1.25 3.00
169 Kevin Ogletree RC 1.50 4.00
170 Kory Sheets RC 1.50 4.00
171 Lardarius Webb RC 2.00 5.00
172 Larry English RC 1.50 4.00
173 Louis Delmas RC 1.50 4.00
174 Louis Murphy RC 1.25 3.00
175 Malcolm Jenkins RC 1.25 3.00
176 Michael Mitchell RC 1.25 3.00
177 Mike Goodson RC 1.50 4.00
178 Nathan Brown RC 1.50 4.00
179 P.J. Hill RC 1.25 3.00
180 Patrick Chung RC 1.25 3.00
181 Peria Jerry RC 1.25 3.00
182 Quan Cosby RC 1.25 3.00
183 Quinn Johnson RC 1.25 3.00
184 Rashad Jennings RC 1.50 4.00
185 Rashad Johnson RC 1.25 3.00
186 Rey Maualuga RC 2.00 5.00
187 Richard Quinn RC 1.50 4.00
188 Robert Ayers RC 1.25 3.00
189 Ryan Mouton RC 1.25 3.00
190 Sean Smith RC 1.25 3.00
191 Sen'Derrick Marks RC 1.25 3.00
192 Shawn Nelson RC 1.25 3.00
193 Sherrod Martin RC 1.25 3.00
194 Tom Brandstater RC 1.50 4.00
195 Tony Fiammetta RC 1.25 3.00
196 Travis Beckum RC 1.25 3.00
197 Tyrell Sutton RC 1.25 3.00
198 Tyrone McKenzie RC 1.50 4.00
199 Vontae Davis RC 1.25 3.00
200 William Moore RC 1.25 3.00
201 Matthew Stafford AU RC 50.00 120.00
202 Jason Smith AU RC 6.00 15.00
203 Tyson Jackson AU RC 6.00 15.00
204 Aaron Curry AU RC 10.00 25.00
205 Mark Sanchez AU RC 25.00 60.00
206 Darrius Heyward-Bey AU RC 10.00 25.00
207 Michael Crabtree AU RC 10.00 25.00
208 Knowshon Moreno AU RC 6.00 15.00
209 Josh Freeman AU RC 6.00 15.00
210 Jeremy Maclin AU RC 8.00 20.00
211 Brandon Pettigrew AU RC 6.00 15.00
212 Percy Harvin AU RC 6.00 15.00
213 Donald Brown AU RC 6.00 15.00
214 Hakeem Nicks AU RC 8.00 20.00
215 Kenny Britt AU RC 10.00 25.00
216 Chris Wells AU RC 6.00 15.00
217 Brian Robiskie AU RC 6.00 15.00
218 Pat White AU RC 8.00 20.00
219 Mohamed Massaquoi AU RC 6.00 15.00
220 LeSean McCoy AU RC 15.00 40.00
221 Shonn Greene AU RC 6.00 15.00
222 Glen Coffee AU RC 6.00 15.00
223 Derrick Williams AU RC 6.00 15.00
224 Javon Ringer AU RC 6.00 15.00
225 Mike Wallace AU RC 10.00 25.00
226 Ramses Barden AU RC 6.00 15.00
227 Patrick Turner AU RC 6.00 15.00
228 Deon Butler AU RC 6.00 15.00
229 Juaquin Iglesias AU RC 6.00 15.00
230 Stephen McGee AU RC 6.00 15.00
231 Mike Thomas AU RC 6.00 15.00
232 Andre Brown AU RC 8.00 20.00
233 Rhett Bomar AU RC 6.00 15.00
234 Nate Davis AU RC 6.00 15.00

2009 Donruss Rookies and Stars Gold Retail

*VETS 1-100: .6X TO 1.5X BASIC R&S
*ELEM 101-115: .3X TO .8X BASIC R&S
*ROOKIES 116-200: .4X TO 1X BASIC R&S
RANDOM INSERTS IN RETAIL PACKS

2009 Donruss Rookies and Stars Longevity Parallel Gold

*VETS 1-100: 4X TO 10X BASIC CARDS
*ELEMENT 101-115: 1X TO 2.5X BASIC CARDS
*ROOKIE 116-200: 1X TO 2.5X BASIC CARDS
STATED PRINT RUN 49 SER.#'d SETS

2009 Donruss Rookies and Stars Longevity Parallel Platinum

*VETS 1-100: 5X TO 12X BASIC CARDS
*ELEMENT 101-115: 1.2X TO 3X BASIC CARDS
*ROOKIE 116-200: 1.2X TO 3X BASIC CARDS
STATED PRINT RUN 25 SER.#'d SETS

2009 Donruss Rookies and Stars Longevity Parallel Silver

*VETS 1-100: 2X TO 5X BASIC CARDS
*ELEMENT 101-115: .5X TO 1.2X BASIC CARDS
*ROOKIE 116-200: .6X TO 1.5X BASIC CARDS
STATED PRINT RUN 249 SER.#'d SETS

2009 Donruss Rookies and Stars Longevity Parallel Silver Holofoil

*VETS 1-100: 3X TO 8X BASIC CARDS
*ELEMENT 101-115: .8X TO 2X BASIC CARDS
*ROOKIE 116-200: .8X TO 2X BASIC CARDS
STATED PRINT RUN 99 SER.#'d SETS

2009 Donruss Rookies and Stars Autographs

STATED PRINT RUN 1-100
SERIAL #'d UNDER 20 NOT PRICED
12 Trent Edwards/30 6.00 15.00
15 Jonathan Stewart/25 8.00 20.00
22 T.J. Houshmandzadeh/25 8.00 20.00
34 Kevin Smith/100 5.00 12.00
36 Greg Jennings/20 10.00 25.00
41 Steve Slaton/100 5.00 12.00
42 Anthony Gonzalez/65 5.00 12.00
43 Joseph Addai/30 6.00 15.00
57 Tarvaris Jackson/25 10.00 25.00
62 Marques Colston/100 5.00 12.00
72 Zach Miller/100 5.00 12.00
74 DeSean Jackson/50 8.00 20.00
82 Vincent Jackson/50 5.00 12.00
83 Frank Gore/20 10.00 25.00
86 John Carlson/35 8.00 20.00

2009 Donruss Rookies and Stars Crosstraining

*BLACK/100: .6X TO 1.5X BASIC INSERTS
*GOLD/500: .5X TO 1.2X BASIC INSERTS
1 Matthew Stafford 2.00 5.00
2 Mark Sanchez .40 1.00
3 Josh Freeman .40 1.00
4 Pat White .50 1.25
5 Stephen McGee .40 1.00
6 Rhett Bomar .40 1.00
7 Nate Davis .40 1.00
8 Mike Thomas .40 1.00
9 Mohamed Massaquoi .40 1.00
10 Derrick Williams .40 1.00
11 Aaron Curry .60 1.50
12 Mike Wallace .60 1.50
13 Ramses Barden .40 1.00
14 Patrick Turner .40 1.00
15 Deon Butler .40 1.00
16 Juaquin Iglesias .40 1.00
17 Jeremy Maclin .50 1.25
18 Percy Harvin .40 1.00
19 Hakeem Nicks .50 1.25
20 Kenny Britt .60 1.50
21 Darrius Heyward-Bey .60 1.50
22 Michael Crabtree .60 1.50
23 Brian Robiskie .40 1.00
24 Brandon Pettigrew .40 1.00
25 Donald Brown .40 1.00
26 Chris Wells .40 1.00
27 Knowshon Moreno .40 1.00
28 LeSean McCoy 1.25 3.00
29 Shonn Greene .40 1.00
30 Glen Coffee .40 1.00
31 Andre Brown .50 1.25
32 Javon Ringer .40 1.00
33 Jason Smith .40 1.00
34 Tyson Jackson .40 1.00

2009 Donruss Rookies and Stars Crosstraining Materials

STATED PRINT RUN 299 SER.#'d SETS
*PRIME/50: .6X TO 1.5X BASIC JSY/299
1 Matthew Stafford 8.00 20.00
2 Mark Sanchez 1.50 4.00
3 Josh Freeman 1.50 4.00
4 Pat White 2.00 5.00
5 Stephen McGee 1.50 4.00
6 Rhett Bomar 1.50 4.00
7 Nate Davis 1.50 4.00
8 Mike Thomas 2.50 6.00
9 Mohamed Massaquoi 1.50 4.00
10 Derrick Williams 1.50 4.00
11 Aaron Curry 2.50 6.00
12 Mike Wallace 2.50 6.00
13 Ramses Barden 1.50 4.00
14 Patrick Turner 1.50 4.00
15 Deon Butler 1.50 4.00
16 Juaquin Iglesias 1.50 4.00
17 Jeremy Maclin 2.00 5.00
18 Percy Harvin 1.50 4.00
19 Hakeem Nicks 2.00 5.00
20 Kenny Britt 2.50 6.00
21 Darrius Heyward-Bey 2.50 6.00
22 Michael Crabtree 2.50 6.00
23 Brian Robiskie 1.50 4.00
24 Brandon Pettigrew 1.50 4.00
25 Donald Brown 1.50 4.00
26 Chris Wells 1.50 4.00
27 Knowshon Moreno 1.50 4.00
28 LeSean McCoy 4.00 10.00
29 Shonn Greene 1.50 4.00
30 Glen Coffee 1.50 4.00
31 Andre Brown 2.00 5.00
32 Javon Ringer 1.50 4.00
33 Jason Smith 1.50 4.00
34 Tyson Jackson 1.50 4.00

2009 Donruss Rookies and Stars Dress for Success Jerseys

STATED PRINT RUN 299 SER.#'d SETS
*PRIME/50: .6X TO 1.5X BASIC JSY/299
*LONG/100: .5X TO 1.2X BASIC JSY/299
1 Mohamed Massaquoi 1.25 3.00
2 Aaron Curry 2.00 5.00
3 Mark Sanchez 1.25 3.00
4 Stephen McGee 1.25 3.00
5 Deon Butler 1.25 3.00
6 Michael Crabtree 2.00 5.00
7 Kenny Britt 2.00 5.00
8 Tyson Jackson 1.25 3.00
9 Donald Brown 1.25 3.00
10 Nate Davis 1.25 3.00
11 Rhett Bomar 1.25 3.00
12 Javon Ringer 1.25 3.00
13 LeSean McCoy 3.00 8.00
14 Darrius Heyward-Bey 2.00 5.00
15 Glen Coffee 1.25 3.00
16 Josh Freeman 1.25 3.00
17 Hakeem Nicks 1.50 4.00
18 Shonn Greene 1.25 3.00
19 Chris Wells 1.25 3.00
20 Jeremy Maclin 1.50 4.00
21 Brian Robiskie 1.25 3.00
22 Matthew Stafford 6.00 15.00
23 Jason Smith 1.25 3.00
24 Percy Harvin 1.25 3.00
25 Patrick Turner 1.25 3.00
26 Pat White 1.50 4.00
27 Juaquin Iglesias 1.25 3.00
28 Mike Wallace 2.00 5.00
29 Derrick Williams 1.25 3.00
30 Mike Thomas 2.00 5.00
31 Brandon Pettigrew 1.25 3.00
32 Knowshon Moreno 1.25 3.00
33 Andre Brown 1.50 4.00
34 Ramses Barden 1.25 3.00

2009 Donruss Rookies and Stars Dress for Success Jerseys Autographs

STATED PRINT RUN 25-100
1 Mohamed Massaquoi/100 5.00 12.00
2 Aaron Curry/100 8.00 20.00
3 Mark Sanchez/25 40.00 100.00
4 Stephen McGee/100 5.00 12.00
5 Deon Butler/100 5.00 12.00
6 Michael Crabtree/100 8.00 20.00
7 Kenny Britt/25 12.00 30.00
8 Tyson Jackson/100 5.00 12.00
9 Donald Brown/100 5.00 12.00
10 Nate Davis/100 5.00 12.00
11 Rhett Bomar/100 5.00 12.00
12 Javon Ringer/100 5.00 12.00
13 LeSean McCoy/100 15.00 40.00
14 Darrius Heyward-Bey/100 8.00 20.00
15 Glen Coffee/100 5.00 12.00
16 Josh Freeman/100 5.00 12.00
17 Hakeem Nicks/100 6.00 15.00
18 Shonn Greene/25 EXCH 8.00 20.00
19 Chris Wells/100 5.00 12.00
20 Jeremy Maclin/100 6.00 15.00
21 Brian Robiskie/100 5.00 12.00
22 Matthew Stafford/15 75.00 150.00
23 Jason Smith/100 5.00 12.00
24 Percy Harvin/100 5.00 12.00
25 Patrick Turner/100 5.00 12.00
26 Pat White/50 8.00 20.00
27 Juaquin Iglesias/100 5.00 12.00
28 Mike Wallace/100 8.00 20.00
29 Derrick Williams/100 5.00 12.00
30 Mike Thomas/100 5.00 12.00
31 Brandon Pettigrew/25 8.00 20.00
32 Knowshon Moreno/100 5.00 12.00
33 Andre Brown/100 6.00 15.00
34 Ramses Barden/100 5.00 12.00

2009 Donruss Rookies and Stars Elements Materials Holofoil

HOLOFOIL PRINT RUN 30-50
*FOIL/80-100: .3X TO .8X HOLOFOIL/30-50
*BASE JSY/299: .25X TO .6X HOLO/30-50
*BASE JSY/75-135: .3X TO .8X HOLO/30-50

2009 Donruss Rookies and Stars Freshman Orientation Materials Jerseys

STATED PRINT RUN 299 SER.#'d SETS
*PRIME/50: .6X TO 1.5X BASIC JSY/299
*LONG/100: .5X TO 1.2X BASIC JSY/299
1 Jason Smith 1.25 3.00
2 Tyson Jackson 1.25 3.00
3 Aaron Curry 2.00 5.00
4 Knowshon Moreno 1.25 3.00
5 Donald Brown 1.25 3.00
6 Chris Wells 1.25 3.00
7 LeSean McCoy 3.00 8.00
8 Shonn Greene 1.25 3.00
9 Glen Coffee 1.25 3.00
10 Andre Brown 1.50 4.00
11 Mike Thomas 2.00 5.00
12 Derrick Williams 1.25 3.00
13 Javon Ringer 1.25 3.00
14 Mike Wallace 2.00 5.00
15 Ramses Barden 1.25 3.00
16 Patrick Turner 1.25 3.00
17 Deon Butler 1.25 3.00
18 Juaquin Iglesias 1.25 3.00
19 Brian Robiskie 1.25 3.00
20 Mohamed Massaquoi 1.25 3.00
21 Hakeem Nicks 1.50 4.00
22 Kenny Britt 2.00 5.00
23 Jeremy Maclin 1.50 4.00
24 Brandon Pettigrew 1.25 3.00
25 Percy Harvin 1.25 3.00
26 Darrius Heyward-Bey 2.00 5.00
27 Michael Crabtree 2.00 5.00
28 Josh Freeman 1.25 3.00
29 Mark Sanchez 1.25 3.00
30 Matthew Stafford 6.00 15.00
31 Pat White 1.50 4.00
32 Stephen McGee 1.25 3.00
33 Rhett Bomar 1.25 3.00
34 Nate Davis 1.25 3.00

2009 Donruss Rookies and Stars Freshman Orientation Materials Jerseys Autographs

STATED PRINT RUN 1-100
SERIAL #'d UNDER 25 NOT PRICED
1 Jason Smith/100 5.00 12.00
2 Tyson Jackson/100 5.00 12.00
3 Aaron Curry/100 8.00 20.00
4 Knowshon Moreno/100 5.00 12.00
5 Donald Brown/100 5.00 12.00
6 Chris Wells/100 5.00 12.00
7 LeSean McCoy/100 12.00 30.00
8 Shonn Greene/25 8.00 20.00
9 Glen Coffee/100 5.00 12.00
10 Andre Brown/100 6.00 15.00
11 Mike Thomas/100 5.00 12.00
12 Derrick Williams/100 5.00 12.00
13 Javon Ringer/100 5.00 12.00
14 Mike Wallace/100 8.00 20.00
15 Ramses Barden/100 5.00 12.00
16 Patrick Turner/100 5.00 12.00
17 Deon Butler/100 5.00 12.00
19 Brian Robiskie/100 5.00 12.00
20 Mohamed Massaquoi/100 5.00 12.00
21 Hakeem Nicks/100 6.00 15.00
22 Kenny Britt/25 12.00 30.00
23 Jeremy Maclin/100 6.00 15.00
24 Brandon Pettigrew/25 8.00 20.00
25 Percy Harvin/100 5.00 12.00
26 Darrius Heyward-Bey/100 8.00 20.00
27 Michael Crabtree/100 8.00 20.00
28 Josh Freeman/100 5.00 12.00
29 Mark Sanchez/25 30.00 80.00
30 Matthew Stafford/25 50.00 120.00
31 Pat White/50 8.00 20.00
32 Stephen McGee/100 5.00 12.00
33 Rhett Bomar/100 5.00 12.00
34 Nate Davis/100 5.00 12.00

2009 Donruss Rookies and Stars Gold Stars

*BLACK/50: .8X TO 2X BASIC INSERTS
*GOLD/500: .5X TO 1.2X BASIC INSERTS
*HOLOFOIL/100: .6X TO 1.5X BASIC INSERTS
1 Ben Roethlisberger .75 2.00
2 Wes Welker .60 1.50
3 Chris Johnson .50 1.25
4 Larry Johnson .50 1.25
5 Tony Romo .60 1.50
6 Matt Ryan .60 1.50
7 Tony Gonzalez .60 1.50
8 Marques Colston .50 1.25
9 Frank Gore .60 1.50
10 Marshawn Lynch .60 1.50
11 Brandon Marshall .60 1.50
12 Jake Delhomme .50 1.25
13 Maurice Jones-Drew .50 1.25
14 Antonio Gates .60 1.50
15 Joe Flacco .60 1.50
16 Willie Parker .50 1.25
17 Steve Smith .60 1.50
18 Torry Holt .60 1.50
19 Vincent Jackson .50 1.25
20 Lee Evans .60 1.50

2009 Donruss Rookies and Stars Gold Stars Autographs

STATED PRINT RUN 1-50
SERIAL #'d UNDER 15 NOT PRICED
4 Larry Johnson/25 8.00 20.00
6 Matt Ryan/15 40.00 80.00
8 Marques Colston/50 5.00 12.00
13 Maurice Jones-Drew/15 10.00 25.00
15 Joe Flacco/25 10.00 25.00
19 Vincent Jackson/50 5.00 12.00

2009 Donruss Rookies and Stars Gold Stars Materials Prime

PRIME JSY PRINT RUN 15-50
*BASE/299: .25X TO .6X PRIME/50
*BASE/299: .2X TO .5X PRIME/25
*BASE/100: .3X TO .8X PRIME/50
*BASE/100: .25X TO .6X PRIME/15-25
BASE JSY PRINT RUN 100-299
1 Ben Roethlisberger/50 6.00 15.00
2 Wes Welker/50 5.00 12.00
3 Chris Johnson/15 5.00 12.00
4 Larry Johnson/50 4.00 10.00
5 Tony Romo/50 5.00 12.00
6 Matt Ryan/25 6.00 15.00
8 Marques Colston/50 4.00 10.00
9 Frank Gore/50 5.00 12.00
10 Marshawn Lynch/50 5.00 12.00
11 Brandon Marshall/50 5.00 12.00
12 Jake Delhomme/25 5.00 12.00
13 Maurice Jones-Drew/50 4.00 10.00
14 Antonio Gates/50 5.00 12.00
15 Joe Flacco/25 6.00 15.00
16 Willie Parker/50 4.00 10.00
17 Steve Smith/50 5.00 12.00
19 Vincent Jackson/50 4.00 10.00
20 Lee Evans/50 5.00 12.00

2009 Donruss Rookies and Stars Materials Emerald Prime Longevity

STATED PRINT RUN 25-50
*BLACK PRM/25: .5X TO 1.2X EMERALD/50
*BLACK PRM/25: .4X TO 1X EMRLD/28-30
BLACK PRIME PRINT RUN 1-25
*GOLD RETAIL: .25X TO .6X EMERALD/50
*GOLD RETAIL: .2X TO .5X EMERALD/25
2 Larry Fitzgerald/50 5.00 12.00
4 Matt Ryan/50 5.00 12.00
5 Michael Turner/50 4.00 10.00
6 Roddy White/50 4.00 10.00
7 Derrick Mason/50 4.00 10.00
8 Joe Flacco/50 5.00 12.00
9 Willis McGahee/50 4.00 10.00
10 Lee Evans/50 5.00 12.00
11 Marshawn Lynch/50 5.00 12.00
12 Trent Edwards/50 4.00 10.00
13 DeAngelo Williams/50 4.00 10.00
14 Jake Delhomme/25 5.00 12.00
15 Jonathan Stewart/50 4.00 10.00
16 Steve Smith/50 5.00 12.00
17 Greg Olsen/50 5.00 12.00
20 Carson Palmer/50 5.00 12.00
21 Chad Ochocinco/50 4.00 10.00
23 Brady Quinn/50 4.00 10.00
24 Braylon Edwards/50 4.00 10.00
26 Jason Witten/50 5.00 12.00
27 Marion Barber/50 5.00 12.00
28 Tony Romo/25 6.00 15.00
29 Brandon Marshall/50 5.00 12.00
32 Calvin Johnson/50 6.00 15.00
33 Daunte Culpepper/50 5.00 12.00
35 Aaron Rodgers/50 12.00 30.00
36 Greg Jennings/50 4.00 10.00
37 Ryan Grant/50 5.00 12.00
38 Andre Johnson/50 5.00 12.00
41 Steve Slaton/50 4.00 10.00
42 Anthony Gonzalez/28 5.00 12.00
43 Joseph Addai/50 4.00 10.00
44 Peyton Manning/50 15.00 40.00
45 Reggie Wayne/50 5.00 12.00
46 David Garrard/50 4.00 10.00
48 Maurice Jones-Drew/50 4.00 10.00
49 Dwayne Bowe/50 5.00 12.00
50 Larry Johnson/50 4.00 10.00
53 Ricky Williams/50 5.00 12.00
54 Ronnie Brown/50 4.00 10.00
55 Adrian Peterson/50 6.00 15.00
56 Bernard Berrian/50 4.00 10.00
58 Laurence Maroney/50 5.00 12.00
59 Tom Brady/50 20.00 50.00
60 Wes Welker/50 5.00 12.00
61 Drew Brees/30 8.00 20.00
62 Marques Colston/50 4.00 10.00
63 Reggie Bush/50 4.00 10.00
64 Brandon Jacobs/50 4.00 10.00
65 Eli Manning/50 5.00 12.00
68 Jerricho Cotchery/50 4.00 10.00
69 Leon Washington/50 4.00 10.00
70 Darren McFadden/50 6.00 15.00
71 JaMarcus Russell/25 5.00 12.00
73 Brian Westbrook/50 4.00 10.00
75 Donovan McNabb/50 5.00 12.00
76 Ben Roethlisberger/50 6.00 15.00
78 Santonio Holmes/50 4.00 10.00
79 Willie Parker/50 4.00 10.00
80 LaDainian Tomlinson/50 6.00 15.00
81 Philip Rivers/50 6.00 15.00
82 Vincent Jackson/50 4.00 10.00
83 Frank Gore/50 5.00 12.00
85 Vernon Davis/50 4.00 10.00
88 Matt Hasselbeck/50 4.00 10.00
89 Marc Bulger/50 4.00 10.00
90 Steven Jackson/50 4.00 10.00
93 Cadillac Williams/50 5.00 12.00
95 Chris Johnson/25 5.00 12.00
97 LenDale White/50 4.00 10.00
98 Chris Cooley/50 4.00 10.00
99 Clinton Portis/50 4.00 10.00
100 Jason Campbell/50 4.00 10.00

2009 Donruss Rookies and Stars NFL Draft Patch Autographs

STATED PRINT RUN 88-100
1 Josh Freeman/100 6.00 15.00
2 Brian Cushing/100 6.00 15.00
3 LeSean McCoy/88 15.00 40.00
4 Malcolm Jenkins/100 6.00 15.00

2009 Donruss Rookies and Stars Prime Cuts Combos

PRIMT CUT COMBO PRINT RUN 30-50
*BASE PRM CUT/50: .3X TO .8X COMBO/50
1 Jay Cutler/30 5.00 12.00
2 Thomas Jones/50 5.00 12.00
3 Greg Jennings/50 5.00 12.00
4 Jason Witten/50 6.00 15.00
5 Steve Smith/50 6.00 15.00
6 Ronnie Brown/50 5.00 12.00
7 LaDainian Tomlinson/50 8.00 20.00
8 Eli Manning/50 6.00 15.00
9 Brian Westbrook/50 5.00 12.00
10 Braylon Edwards/50 5.00 12.00
11 Santonio Holmes/50 5.00 12.00
12 Marion Barber/50 6.00 15.00
13 Jason Campbell/50 5.00 12.00
14 Tom Brady/50 25.00 60.00
15 Reggie Wayne/50 6.00 15.00

2009 Donruss Rookies and Stars Rookie Autographs Holofoil

STATED PRINT RUN 83 250
116 Aaron Kelly/250 2.50 6.00
122 Austin Collie/150 2.50 6.00
123 B.J. Raji/100 6.00 15.00
125 Brandon Gibson/125 3.00 8.00
126 Brian Cushing/100 3.00 8.00
128 Brian Orakpo/100 4.00 10.00
129 Brooks Foster/150 2.50 6.00
130 Cameron Morrah/250 2.50 6.00
131 Cedric Peerman/100 3.00 8.00
132 Chase Coffman/125 2.50 6.00
135 Clay Matthews/100 25.00 50.00
136 Clint Sintim/100 3.00 8.00
139 Cornelius Ingram/125 2.50 6.00
142 Darius Passmore/250 2.50 6.00
146 Devin Moore/250 2.50 6.00
147 Dominique Edison/100 3.00 8.00
150 Everette Brown/250 2.50 6.00
151 Brandon Tate/125 3.00 8.00
152 Graham Harrell/250 6.00 15.00
153 Hunter Cantwell/250 2.50 6.00
155 James Casey/125 3.00 8.00
156 James Laurinaitis/125 2.50 6.00
157 Jared Cook/125 3.00 8.00
158 Jarett Dillard/125 2.50 6.00
163 John Parker Wilson/250 2.50 6.00
164 Johnny Knox/200 3.00 8.00
167 Kenny McKinley/125 2.50 6.00
169 Kevin Ogletree/250 3.00 8.00
170 Kory Sheets/250 3.00 8.00
175 Malcolm Jenkins/83 3.00 8.00
177 Mike Goodson/200 3.00 8.00
179 P.J. Hill/250 2.50 6.00
182 Quan Cosby/250 2.50 6.00
183 Quinn Johnson/250 2.50 6.00
184 Rashad Jennings/180 3.00 8.00
186 Rey Maualuga/100 5.00 12.00
192 Shawn Nelson/100 3.00 8.00
194 Tom Brandstater/100 4.00 10.00
195 Tony Fiammetta/250 2.50 6.00
196 Travis Beckum/125 2.50 6.00
199 Vontae Davis/150 2.50 6.00

2009 Donruss Rookies and Stars Rookie Patch Autographs Gold

*GOLD/25: .5X TO 1.2X BASE AU/139-142
GOLD PRINT RUN 25 SER.#'d SETS
201 Matthew Stafford 100.00 200.00
205 Mark Sanchez 40.00 100.00

2009 Donruss Rookies and Stars Rookie Jersey Jumbo Swatch

STATED PRINT RUN 50 SER.#'d SETS
*EMERALD/10: 1X TO 2.5X BASIC JSY/50
*GOLD/25: .6X TO 1.5X BASIC JSY/50
*LONGEVITY/50: .4X TO 1X BASIC JSY
201 Matthew Stafford 12.00 30.00
202 Jason Smith 2.50 6.00
203 Tyson Jackson 2.50 6.00
204 Aaron Curry 4.00 10.00
205 Mark Sanchez 2.50 6.00
206 Darrius Heyward-Bey 4.00 10.00
207 Michael Crabtree 4.00 10.00
208 Knowshon Moreno 2.50 6.00
209 Josh Freeman 2.50 6.00
210 Jeremy Maclin 3.00 8.00
211 Brandon Pettigrew 2.50 6.00
212 Percy Harvin 2.50 6.00
213 Donald Brown 2.50 6.00
214 Hakeem Nicks 3.00 8.00
215 Kenny Britt 4.00 10.00
216 Chris Wells 2.50 6.00
217 Brian Robiskie 2.50 6.00
218 Pat White 3.00 8.00
219 Mohamed Massaquoi 2.50 6.00
220 LeSean McCoy 6.00 15.00
221 Shonn Greene 2.50 6.00
222 Glen Coffee 2.50 6.00
223 Derrick Williams 2.50 6.00
224 Javon Ringer 2.50 6.00
225 Mike Wallace 4.00 10.00
226 Ramses Barden 2.50 6.00
227 Patrick Turner 2.50 6.00
228 Deon Butler 2.50 6.00
229 Juaquin Iglesias 2.50 6.00
230 Stephen McGee 2.50 6.00
231 Mike Thomas 2.50 6.00
232 Andre Brown 3.00 8.00
233 Rhett Bomar 2.50 6.00
234 Nate Davis 2.50 6.00

2009 Donruss Rookies and Stars Rookie Patch Autographs College

STATED PRINT RUN 19-70
201 Matthew Stafford/22 75.00 150.00
203 Tyson Jackson/20 8.00 20.00
204 Aaron Curry/20 12.00 30.00
205 Mark Sanchez/20 25.00 60.00
206 Darrius Heyward-Bey/19 12.00 30.00
207 Michael Crabtree/21 12.00 30.00
208 Knowshon Moreno/20 8.00 20.00
209 Josh Freeman/70 6.00 15.00
210 Jeremy Maclin/20 10.00 25.00
211 Brandon Pettigrew/20 8.00 20.00
212 Percy Harvin/19 8.00 20.00
213 Donald Brown/20 8.00 20.00
214 Hakeem Nicks/19 10.00 25.00
215 Kenny Britt/20 12.00 30.00
216 Chris Wells/19 40.00 80.00
217 Brian Robiskie/20 8.00 20.00
218 Pat White/20 10.00 25.00
219 Mohamed Massaquoi/20 8.00 20.00
220 LeSean McCoy/68 15.00 40.00
221 Shonn Greene/20 8.00 20.00
222 Glen Coffee/20 8.00 20.00
223 Derrick Williams/19 8.00 20.00
224 Javon Ringer/20 8.00 20.00
225 Mike Wallace/19 12.00 30.00
226 Ramses Barden/20 8.00 20.00
227 Patrick Turner/20 8.00 20.00
228 Deon Butler/20 8.00 20.00
229 Juaquin Iglesias/20 20.00 50.00
230 Stephen McGee/20 8.00 20.00
231 Mike Thomas/19 8.00 20.00
232 Andre Brown/19 10.00 25.00

2009 Donruss Rookies and Stars Statistical Standouts Materials Prime

PRIME PRINT RUN 25-50
*BASE JSY/240-299: .25X TO .6X PRIME/50
*BASE JSY/240-299: .2X TO .5X PRIME/25
*BASE JSY/95: .3X TO .8X PRIME/50
*BASE JSY/25: .3X TO .8X PRIME/25
BASE JSY PRINT RUN 25-299
1 Aaron Rodgers/50 10.00 25.00
2 Drew Brees/50 5.00 12.00
4 Peyton Manning/50 12.00 30.00
5 Philip Rivers/50 5.00 12.00
6 Brandon Jacobs/50 3.00 8.00
7 Clinton Portis/50 3.00 8.00
8 DeAngelo Williams/50 3.00 8.00
9 Michael Turner/25 4.00 10.00
10 Adrian Peterson/50 5.00 12.00
11 Andre Johnson/50 4.00 10.00
12 Calvin Johnson/50 5.00 12.00
13 Larry Fitzgerald/25 5.00 12.00
14 Randy Moss/50 4.00 10.00
15 Roddy White/50 3.00 8.00

2009 Donruss Rookies and Stars Statistical Standouts Materials Autographs

STATED PRINT RUN 1-25
SERIAL #'d UNDER 15 NOT PRICED
8 DeAngelo Williams/25 15.00 30.00
9 Michael Turner/15 20.00 40.00

2009 Donruss Rookies and Stars Studio Rookies

*BLACK/100: .6X TO 1.5X BASIC INSERTS
GOLD/500: .5X TO 1.2X BASIC INSERTS
1 Jason Smith .50 1.25
2 Tyson Jackson .50 1.25
3 Aaron Curry .75 2.00
4 Darrius Heyward-Bey .75 2.00
5 Michael Crabtree .75 2.00
6 Percy Harvin .50 1.25
7 Hakeem Nicks .60 1.50
8 Kenny Britt .75 2.00
9 Brian Robiskie .50 1.25
10 Derrick Williams .50 1.25
11 Jeremy Maclin .60 1.50
12 Mike Wallace .75 2.00
13 Ramses Barden .50 1.25
14 Patrick Turner .50 1.25
15 Deon Butler .50 1.25
16 Juaquin Iglesias .50 1.25
17 Mohamed Massaquoi .50 1.25
18 Mike Thomas .50 1.25
19 Andre Brown .60 1.50
20 LeSean McCoy 1.25 3.00
21 Shonn Greene .50 1.25
22 Glen Coffee .50 1.25
23 Chris Wells .50 1.25
24 Donald Brown .50 1.25
25 Knowshon Moreno .50 1.25
26 Javon Ringer .50 1.25
27 Brandon Pettigrew .50 1.25
28 Matthew Stafford 2.50 6.00
29 Pat White .60 1.50
30 Mark Sanchez .50 1.25
31 Josh Freeman .50 1.25
32 Rhett Bomar .50 1.25
33 Nate Davis .50 1.25
34 Stephen McGee .50 1.25

2009 Donruss Rookies and Stars Studio Rookies Materials

STATED PRINT RUN 299 SER.#'d SETS
*PRIME/50: .6X TO 1.5X BASIC JSY/299
PRIME PRINT RUN 50 SER.#'d SETS
1 Jason Smith 1.50 4.00
2 Tyson Jackson 1.50 4.00
3 Aaron Curry 2.50 6.00
4 Darrius Heyward-Bey 2.50 6.00
5 Michael Crabtree 2.50 6.00
6 Percy Harvin 1.50 4.00
7 Hakeem Nicks 2.00 5.00
8 Kenny Britt 2.50 6.00
9 Brian Robiskie 1.50 4.00
10 Derrick Williams 1.50 4.00
11 Jeremy Maclin 2.00 5.00
12 Mike Wallace 2.50 6.00
13 Ramses Barden 1.50 4.00
14 Patrick Turner 1.50 4.00
15 Deon Butler 1.50 4.00
16 Juaquin Iglesias 1.50 4.00
17 Mohamed Massaquoi 1.50 4.00
18 Mike Thomas 1.50 4.00
19 Andre Brown 2.00 5.00
20 LeSean McCoy 4.00 10.00
21 Shonn Greene 1.50 4.00
22 Glen Coffee 1.50 4.00
23 Chris Wells 1.50 4.00
24 Donald Brown 1.50 4.00
25 Knowshon Moreno 1.50 4.00
26 Javon Ringer 1.50 4.00
27 Brandon Pettigrew 1.50 4.00
28 Matthew Stafford 8.00 20.00
29 Pat White 2.00 5.00
30 Mark Sanchez 1.50 4.00
31 Josh Freeman 1.50 4.00
32 Rhett Bomar 1.50 4.00
33 Nate Davis 1.50 4.00
34 Stephen McGee 1.50 4.00

2009 Donruss Rookies and Stars Studio Rookies Combos

*BLACK/100: .6X TO 1.5X BASIC INSERTS
*GOLD/500: .5X TO 1.2X BASIC INSERTS
1 J.Maclin/L.McCoy 1.25 3.00
2 A.Curry/D.Butler .75 2.00
3 M.Crabtree/N.Davis .75 2.00
4 M.Stafford/B.Pettigrew 2.50 6.00
5 H.Nicks/R.Bomar .60 1.50
6 M.Sanchez/S.Greene .50 1.25
7 J.Ringer/K.Britt .75 2.00
8 P.Turner/P.White .60 1.50
9 Massaquoi/B.Robiskie .50 1.25
10 M.Stafford/M.Sanchez 2.50 6.00

2009 Donruss Rookies and Stars Studio Rookies Combos Materials

STATED PRINT RUN 299 SER.#'d SETS
*PRIME/50: .6X TO 1.5X DUAL JSY/299
1 J.Maclin/L.McCoy 4.00 10.00
2 A.Curry/D.Butler 2.50 6.00
3 M.Crabtree/N.Davis 2.50 6.00
4 M.Stafford/B.Pettigrew 8.00 20.00
5 H.Nicks/R.Bomar 2.00 5.00
6 M.Sanchez/S.Greene 1.50 4.00
7 J.Ringer/K.Britt 2.50 6.00
8 P.Turner/P.White 2.00 5.00
9 Massaquoi/B.Robiskie 1.50 4.00
10 M.Stafford/M.Sanchez 8.00 20.00

2009 Donruss Rookies and Stars Longevity

COMP.SET w/o RC's (100) 8.00 20.00
*VETS 1-100: .4X TO 1X BASIC R&S
*ELEM 101-115: .25X TO .6X BASIC R&S
*ROOKIES 116-200: .4X TO 1X BASIC R&S
116-200 ROOKIE PRINT RUN 999
201-234 UNPRICED AUTO PRINT RUN 10

2009 Donruss Rookies and Stars Longevity Emerald

*VETS 1-100: 5X TO 12X BASIC R&S
*ELEMENT 101-115: 1.2X TO 3X BASIC R&S
*ROOKIES 116-200: 1.2X TO 3X BASIC R&S
STATED PRINT RUN 25 SER.#'d SETS

2009 Donruss Rookies and Stars Longevity Ruby

*VETS 1-100: 2.5X TO 6X BASIC R&S
*ELEMENT 101-115: .6X TO 1.5X BASIC R&S
*ROOKIES 116-200: .6X TO 1.5X BASIC R&S
1-200 STATED PRINT RUN 150 SER.#'d SETS

2009 Donruss Rookies and Stars Longevity Sapphire

*VETS 1-100: 3X TO 8X BASIC R&S
*ELEMENT 101-115: .8X TO 2X BASIC R&S
*ROOKIES 116-200: .8X TO 2X BASIC R&S
1-200 STATED PRINT RUN 75

2009 Donruss Rookies and Stars Longevity Autographs

VET STATED PRINT RUN 5-100
34 Kevin Smith/100 6.00 15.00
41 Steve Slaton/100 8.00 20.00
42 Anthony Gonzalez/30 8.00 20.00
57 Tarvaris Jackson/25 10.00 25.00
62 Marques Colston/100 6.00 15.00
72 Zach Miller/30 8.00 20.00
74 DeSean Jackson/35 8.00 20.00
82 Vincent Jackson/20 8.00 20.00
86 John Carlson/27 8.00 20.00
116 Aaron Kelly/250 2.50 6.00
122 Austin Collie/150 2.50 6.00
123 B.J. Raji/100 4.00 10.00
125 Brandon Gibson/125 3.00 8.00
126 Brian Cushing/100 3.00 8.00
128 Brian Orakpo/100 4.00 10.00
129 Brooks Foster/150 2.50 6.00
130 Cameron Morrah/250 2.50 6.00
131 Cedric Peerman/100 3.00 8.00
132 Chase Coffman/125 2.50 6.00
135 Clay Matthews/100 30.00 60.00
136 Clint Sintim/100 3.00 8.00
139 Cornelius Ingram/125 2.50 6.00
142 Darius Passmore/250 2.50 6.00
146 Devin Moore/250 2.50 6.00
147 Dominique Edison/100 3.00 8.00
150 Everette Brown/250 2.50 6.00
151 Brandon Tate/125 3.00 8.00
152 Graham Harrell/250 6.00 15.00
153 Hunter Cantwell/250 2.50 6.00
155 James Casey/125 3.00 8.00
156 James Laurinaitis/125 2.50 6.00
157 Jared Cook/125 3.00 8.00
158 Jarett Dillard/125 2.50 6.00
163 John Parker Wilson/28 8.00 20.00
164 Johnny Knox/200 3.00 8.00
167 Kenny McKinley/125 2.50 6.00
169 Kevin Ogletree/250 3.00 8.00
170 Kory Sheets/250 3.00 8.00
172 Larry English/100 4.00 10.00
177 Mike Goodson/200 3.00 8.00
179 P.J. Hill/250 2.50 6.00
182 Quan Cosby/250 2.50 6.00
183 Quinn Johnson/250 2.50 6.00
186 Rey Maualuga/100 5.00 12.00
192 Shawn Nelson/100 3.00 8.00
194 Tom Brandstater/100 4.00 10.00
195 Tony Fiammetta/250 2.50 6.00
196 Travis Beckum/125 2.50 6.00
199 Vontae Davis/150 2.50 6.00

2009 Donruss Rookies and Stars Longevity Materials Sapphire

SAPPHIRE PRINT RUN 20-100
*RUBY JSY/155-299: .3X TO .8X SAPP/100
*RUBY JSY/70-115: .4X TO 1X SAPP/100
*RUBY JSY/70-115: .3X TO .8X SAPP/50
*RUBY JSY/40: .5X TO 1.2X SAPP/100
*RUBY JSY/25: .6X TO 1.5X SAPP/100
RUBY STATED PRINT RUN 25-299
2 Larry Fitzgerald/100 4.00 10.00
4 Matt Ryan/100 4.00 10.00
5 Michael Turner/75 3.00 8.00
6 Roddy White/100 3.00 8.00
7 Derrick Mason/100 3.00 8.00
8 Joe Flacco/100 4.00 10.00
9 Willis McGahee/100 3.00 8.00
10 Lee Evans/20 6.00 15.00
11 Marshawn Lynch/100 4.00 10.00
12 Trent Edwards/100 3.00 8.00
13 DeAngelo Williams/100 3.00 8.00
14 Jake Delhomme/50 4.00 10.00
15 Jonathan Stewart/35 5.00 12.00
16 Steve Smith/100 4.00 10.00
17 Greg Olsen/100 4.00 10.00
20 Carson Palmer/100 4.00 10.00
21 Chad Ochocinco/100 3.00 8.00
23 Brady Quinn/100 3.00 8.00
24 Braylon Edwards/100 3.00 8.00
26 Jason Witten/100 4.00 10.00
27 Marion Barber/100 4.00 10.00
28 Tony Romo/100 4.00 10.00
29 Brandon Marshall/100 4.00 10.00
32 Calvin Johnson/100 5.00 12.00
33 Daunte Culpepper/100 4.00 10.00
36 Greg Jennings/100 3.00 8.00
37 Ryan Grant/100 4.00 10.00
38 Andre Johnson/100 4.00 10.00
39 Matt Schaub/100 3.00 8.00
41 Steve Slaton/100 3.00 8.00
42 Anthony Gonzalez/100 3.00 8.00
43 Joseph Addai/100 3.00 8.00
44 Peyton Manning/100 12.00 30.00
46 David Garrard/100 3.00 8.00
48 Maurice Jones-Drew/100 3.00 8.00
49 Dwayne Bowe/100 4.00 10.00
50 Larry Johnson/100 3.00 8.00
52 Chad Pennington/100 3.00 8.00
53 Ricky Williams/100 4.00 10.00
54 Ronnie Brown/100 3.00 8.00
55 Adrian Peterson/100 5.00 12.00
56 Bernard Berrian/100 3.00 8.00
57 Tarvaris Jackson/100 4.00 10.00
58 Laurence Maroney/100 4.00 10.00
59 Tom Brady/100 15.00 40.00
60 Wes Welker/100 4.00 10.00
61 Drew Brees/100 5.00 12.00
62 Marques Colston/100 3.00 8.00
63 Reggie Bush/100 3.00 8.00
64 Brandon Jacobs/100 3.00 8.00
65 Eli Manning/100 4.00 10.00
68 Jerricho Cotchery/100 3.00 8.00
69 Leon Washington/100 3.00 8.00
70 Darren McFadden/100 5.00 12.00
71 JaMarcus Russell/50 4.00 10.00
73 Brian Westbrook/100 3.00 8.00
75 Donovan McNabb/100 4.00 10.00
76 Ben Roethlisberger/100 5.00 12.00
78 Santonio Holmes/100 3.00 8.00
79 Willie Parker/65 4.00 10.00
80 LaDainian Tomlinson/100 5.00 12.00
81 Philip Rivers/100 5.00 12.00
82 Vincent Jackson/100 3.00 8.00
83 Frank Gore/100 4.00 10.00
85 Vernon Davis/60 4.00 10.00
88 Matt Hasselbeck/100 3.00 8.00
89 Marc Bulger/100 3.00 8.00
90 Steven Jackson/100 3.00 8.00
93 Cadillac Williams/100 4.00 10.00
95 Chris Johnson/50 4.00 10.00
96 Kerry Collins/100 3.00 8.00
97 LenDale White/100 3.00 8.00
98 Chris Cooley/100 3.00 8.00
99 Clinton Portis/100 3.00 8.00
100 Jason Campbell/100 3.00 8.00

2015 Donruss Signature Series

1 Aaron Donald 4.00 10.00
2 Anthony Barr 2.50 6.00
3 Barkevious Mingo 2.50 6.00
4 Danny Lansanah 2.50 6.00
5 Darrin Reaves 2.50 6.00
6 Devin Street 2.50 6.00
7 Earl Wolff 2.50 6.00
8 Jerrell Freeman 2.50 6.00
9 Kerwynn Williams 2.50 6.00
10 Robert Herron 2.50 6.00
11 Shaq Evans 2.50 6.00
12 TJ Jones 2.50 6.00
13 Tommy Streeter 2.50 6.00
14 Travis Swanson 2.50 6.00
15 Kenbrell Thompkins 2.50 6.00
16 Alan Bonner 2.50 6.00
17 Bryce Brown 2.50 6.00
18 Christian Kirksey 2.50 6.00
19 Cobi Hamilton 2.50 6.00
20 Jarrett Boykin 2.50 6.00
21 Kony Ealy 2.50 6.00
22 Kyle Van Noy 2.50 6.00
23 Latavius Murray 2.50 6.00
24 Lorenzo Taliaferro 2.50 6.00
25 Michael Campanaro 2.50 6.00
26 Mike James 2.50 6.00
27 Rajion Neal 2.50 6.00
28 Pierre Desir 2.50 6.00
29 Evan Rodriguez 2.50 6.00
30 Benny Cunningham 3.00 8.00
31 Brandon Coleman 2.50 6.00
32 Crockett Gillmore 2.50 6.00
33 Damontre Moore 2.50 6.00
34 Jake Matthews 2.50 6.00
35 Rod Streater 2.50 6.00
36 Trevor Reilly 2.50 6.00
37 Ra'Shede Hageman 2.50 6.00
38 Sam Barrington RC 2.50 6.00
39 C.J. Fiedorowicz 2.50 6.00
40 Chris Smith 2.50 6.00
41 Connor Shaw 2.50 6.00
42 Cory Harkey 2.50 6.00
43 Ed Reynolds 2.50 6.00
44 Isaiah Burse 2.50 6.00
45 Isaiah Crowell 2.50 6.00
46 James Develin RC 4.00 10.00
47 Jimmie Ward 2.50 6.00
48 Scott Crichton 3.00 8.00
49 T.J. Carrie 2.50 6.00
50 Timothy Wright 2.50 6.00
51 Silas Redd 2.50 6.00
52 Adrien Robinson 2.50 6.00
53 D.J. Fluker 2.50 6.00
54 Chris Borland 4.00 10.00
55 Jeff Janis 2.50 6.00
56 Jordan Poyer 2.50 6.00
57 Darius Slay 2.50 6.00
58 Sio Moore 2.50 6.00
59 Orleans Darkwa 3.00 8.00
60 Keshawn Martin 2.50 6.00
61 Darqueze Dennard 2.50 6.00
62 Deone Bucannon 2.50 6.00
63 John Brown 3.00 8.00
64 Lamarcus Joyner 2.50 6.00
65 Louis Nix III 2.50 6.00
66 Marcus Smith 2.50 6.00
67 Scott Chandler 2.50 6.00
68 Travis Kelce 10.00 25.00
69 Troy Brown 2.50 6.00
70 Troy Niklas 2.50 6.00
71 Tyler Gaffney 2.50 6.00
72 Zack Martin 2.50 6.00
73 Albert Wilson 2.50 6.00
74 Brice Butler 2.50 6.00
75 Jerick McKinnon 2.50 6.00
76 Ben Tate 2.50 6.00
77 Joe Andruzzi 2.50 6.00
78 Brandon LaFell 2.50 6.00
79 Jim Kiick 2.50 6.00
80 Micah Hyde 3.00 8.00
81 Case Keenum 3.00 8.00
82 Robert Mathis 2.50 6.00
83 Ja'Wuan James 2.50 6.00
84 Austin Seferian-Jenkins 2.50 6.00
85 Brandon Flowers 2.50 6.00
86 Charles Haley 3.00 8.00
87 Joseph Fauria 2.50 6.00
88 Steve Grogan 2.50 6.00
89 Tom Savage 2.50 6.00
90 Xavier Rhodes 2.50 6.00
91 Jace Amaro 2.50 6.00
92 Kenny Stills 2.50 6.00
94 Charles Sims 2.50 6.00
95 Charlie Joiner 2.50 6.00
96 Chris Polk 2.50 6.00
97 Gavin Escobar 2.50 6.00
98 Harold Carmichael 2.50 6.00
99 Ron Mix 2.50 6.00
100 Austin Davis 3.00 8.00
101 C.J. Anderson 4.00 10.00
102 Emmanuel Sanders 4.00 10.00
104 Julius Thomas 3.00 8.00
105 Manti Te'o 4.00 10.00
106 Mike Quick 3.00 8.00
107 Mark Chmura
108 Dan Hampton 3.00 8.00
109 Eric Ebron 3.00 8.00
110 Willie McGinest 6.00 15.00
111 Aaron Dobson 3.00 8.00
112 Aeneas Williams 3.00 8.00
113 David Carr 3.00 8.00
114 David Fales 3.00 8.00
115 Derrick Brooks 12.00 30.00
116 Don Majkowski 8.00 20.00
117 Jan Stenerud 3.00 8.00
118 John Hannah 3.00 8.00
119 Justin Hunter 3.00 8.00
120 Malcolm Smith 8.00 20.00
121 Robert Brooks 8.00 20.00
122 Torry Holt 4.00 10.00
123 Trent Dilfer 4.00 10.00
124 Wilbert Montgomery 3.00 8.00
125 Bubba Franks 3.00 8.00
126 Janoris Jenkins 3.00 8.00
127 Danny Woodhead 4.00 10.00
128 Zach Mettenberger 3.00 8.00
129 Montee Ball 3.00 8.00
130 Andre Williams 3.00 8.00
132 Giovani Bernard 3.00 8.00
133 Mike Evans 4.00 10.00
134 Calvin Pryor 3.00 8.00
135 Michael Floyd 3.00 8.00
136 Mike Glennon 4.00 10.00
137 Stedman Bailey 3.00 8.00
138 Theo Riddick 3.00 8.00
139 DeAndre Hopkins 8.00 20.00
140 Tyler Eifert 4.00 10.00
141 Kenbrell Thompkins 3.00 8.00
142 Jarrett Boykin 3.00 8.00
143 Charles Haley 15.00 30.00
144 Daunte Culpepper 4.00 10.00
145 Malcolm Smith 3.00 8.00
146 Patrick Peterson
147 Ozzie Newsome 8.00 20.00
148 Marqise Lee 3.00 8.00
149 Kellen Winslow 12.00 30.00
150 Danny Amendola 4.00 10.00
151 Paul Warfield 6.00 15.00
152 Antonio Freeman 5.00 12.00
153 Roger Craig 12.00 30.00
154 Ronde Barber
155 Ryan Nassib 4.00 10.00
156 Steve Johnson 4.00 10.00
157 Torrey Smith 3.00 8.00
158 Cordarrelle Patterson 3.00 8.00
159 Hakeem Nicks 3.00 8.00
160 Sidney Rice 3.00 8.00
161 Derek Carr 15.00 30.00
162 Jimmy Garoppolo 6.00 15.00
163 Ricky Williams 8.00 20.00
164 Alshon Jeffery
165 Luke Kuechly
166 Vincent Jackson
167 Vance McDonald 3.00 8.00
168 Darren McFadden 3.00 8.00
169 DeSean Jackson
170 Greg Jennings
171 Jeremy Maclin 3.00 8.00
172 Von Miller 12.00 30.00
173 Warrick Dunn 8.00 20.00
174 Victor Cruz
175 Andy Dalton 8.00 20.00
176 Ronnie Brown 3.00 8.00
177 Dennis Pitta 3.00 8.00
178 Nick Toon 3.00 8.00
179 Champ Bailey
180 Darren Sproles
181 Knowshon Moreno 3.00 8.00
182 Matt Barkley 3.00 8.00
183 Matt Schaub 3.00 8.00
184 Raymond Berry
185 Ronnie Lott
186 D.J. Hayden 3.00 8.00
187 Brandon Flowers 3.00 8.00
188 Randy White
189 Demarvius Thomas

190 Randall Cobb 10.00 25.00
191 Roger Craig
192 Bob Lilly 4.00 10.00
193 James Lofton 3.00 8.00
194 Eddie Lacy 3.00 8.00
195 Doug Martin
196 Jackie Slater 3.00 8.00
197 Doug Flutie
198 Rod Woodson 10.00 25.00
199 Alex Smith 15.00 40.00
200 Clay Matthews 20.00 50.00
201 Antonio Brown 15.00 40.00
202 Antonio Gates
203 Arian Foster
204 Bill Parcells
205 Bo Jackson 40.00 80.00
206 Bob Griese
207 Carson Palmer 15.00 30.00
208 Dallas Clark
209 DeAngelo Williams
210 Devin Hester 6.00 15.00
211 Dez Bryant
212 Donald Driver
213 EJ Manuel
214 Eric Decker
215 Eric Dickerson 10.00 25.00
216 Forrest Gregg 10.00 25.00
217 Fran Tarkenton
218 Frank Gore
219 Fred Taylor
220 Jamaal Charles
221 Jason Witten 15.00 40.00
222 Jerome Bettis
223 Joe Theismann 8.00 20.00
224 LaDainian Tomlinson 25.00 50.00
225 Len Dawson 50.00 100.00
226 Matt Forte 10.00 25.00
227 Nick Foles
228 Teddy Bridgewater 12.00 30.00
229 Tim Brown
230 Warren Moon 12.00 30.00
231 Lawrence Taylor 25.00 50.00
232 Marcus Allen 15.00 40.00
233 Richard Sherman 30.00 60.00
234 Blake Bortles
235 Dick Butkus 25.00 50.00
236 Fred Biletnikoff 12.00 30.00
237 Jay Cutler
238 Joe Flacco
239 Branden Oliver 6.00 15.00
240 Earl Campbell 20.00 40.00
241 Harry Douglas 5.00 12.00
242 Curtis Martin 15.00 30.00
243 Matthew Stafford
244 Sam Bradford
245 Warren Sapp
246 Jim Kelly
247 Larry Csonka
248 Matt Ryan 15.00 30.00
249 Michael Strahan
250 Philip Rivers
251 Andrew Luck
252 Ryan Mallett
253 Jamar Taylor
254 Matt Elam
255 Brian Urlacher
256 Bruce Smith 20.00 40.00
257 Champ Bailey
258 Colin Kaepernick
259 Frank Gifford
260 Kurt Warner
261 Marshall Faulk
262 Mike Ditka
263 Rob Gronkowski 25.00 50.00
264 Ryan Tannehill 6.00 15.00
265 Steve Young
266 Tony Dorsett 25.00 50.00
267 Trent Dilfer
268 Wes Welker 10.00 25.00
269 Drew Brees
270 Tony Romo
271 Richard Rodgers
272 Deion Sanders 40.00 80.00
273 Eli Manning
274 John Riggins
275 Roger Staubach
276 Andrew Hawkins
277 Ben Roethlisberger
278 Alex Smith
279 Bill Parcells
280 Bill Parcells
281 Bill Parcells
282 Carson Palmer
283 Dan Marino
284 Darren McFadden
285 Darren Sproles
286 DeAngelo Williams
287 DeSean Jackson
288 Devin Hester
289 Eric Decker
290 Hakeem Nicks 5.00 12.00
291 Jeremy Maclin
292 Ricky Williams
293 Vincent Jackson
294 Warrick Dunn
295 Curtis Martin
296 Frank Gore
297 Nick Foles
298 Wes Welker 10.00 25.00
299 Vinny Testaverde
300 Antoine Bethea
301 Michael Irvin
302 Russell Wilson
303 Adrian Peterson
304 Joe Namath
305 Peyton Manning
306 Brett Favre
307 Joe Montana
308 John Elway
309 Emmitt Smith
310 Tom Brady
311 Aaron Rodgers
312 Peyton Manning
313 Vincent Jackson
314 Philip Rivers
315 Eli Manning
316 Mark Chmura
317 Ben Roethlisberger
318 Fred Taylor
319 Bubba Franks
320 Devin Hester
321 Brett Favre
322 Joe Theismann
323 Matthew Stafford
324 Tony Romo
325 Alex Smith
326 Michael Strahan
327 Doug Martin
328 Arian Foster
329 Donald Driver
330 DeSean Jackson
331 Victor Cruz
332 Drew Brees
333 Deion Sanders
334 Russell Wilson
335 Frank Gore
336 Kurt Warner
337 Patrick Peterson
338 Jamaal Charles
339 Andrew Luck
340 Tom Brady
341 Dez Bryant
342 Jason Witten
343 Jay Cutler
344 Adrian Peterson
345 Matt Ryan
346 LaDainian Tomlinson
347 Antonio Brown
348 James Lofton
349 Bruce Smith
350 Jan Stenerud
351 Raymond Berry
352 Troy Aikman
353 Aeneas Williams
354 Derrick Brooks
355 Michael Irvin
356 Deion Sanders
357 John Hannah
358 Michael Strahan
359 Dan Hampton
360 Larry Csonka
361 Tim Brown
362 Charlie Joiner
363 Joe Namath
364 Marcus Allen
365 Roger Staubach
366 Fred Biletnikoff
367 Curtis Martin
368 Joe Greene
369 Charles Haley
370 Paul Warfield
371 Ronnie Lott
372 Frank Gifford
373 Forrest Gregg
374 Kellen Winslow
375 Dick Butkus
376 Shannon Sharpe
377 Len Dawson
378 Jim Kelly
379 Tony Dorsett
380 Warren Moon 12.00 30.00
381 Ozzie Newsome
382 Rod Woodson
383 Randy White
384 Marshall Faulk
385 Jackie Slater
386 Eric Dickerson
387 Fran Tarkenton
388 Emmitt Smith
389 Mike Ditka
390 Earl Campbell
391 Dan Marino
392 Bob Lilly
393 John Riggins
394 Lawrence Taylor
395 Joe Montana
396 Bob Griese
397 John Elway
398 Steve Young
399 Jerome Bettis
400 Warren Sapp
401 Darren Waller RC 4.00 10.00
402 Blake Bell RC 5.00 12.00
403 Da'Ron Brown RC 3.00 8.00
404 Tyler Kroft RC 4.00 10.00
405 Dezmin Lewis RC 3.00 8.00
406 Eli Harold RC 3.00 8.00
407 Eric Rowe RC 3.00 8.00
408 Hau'oli Kikaha RC 4.00 10.00
410 J.J. Nelson RC 3.00 8.00
411 Josh Shaw RC 5.00 12.00
412 Kenny Hilliard RC 3.00 8.00
413 Mario Alford RC 3.00 8.00
414 MyCole Pruitt RC 3.00 8.00
415 Stephone Anthony RC 3.00 8.00
416 Titus Davis RC 4.00 10.00
417 Arik Armstead RC 3.00 8.00
418 Jesse James RC 4.00 10.00
419 Jordan Taylor RC 8.00 20.00
420 Kenny Bell RC 5.00 12.00
422 Kwon Alexander RC 4.00 10.00
423 Levi Norwood RC 3.00 8.00
424 P.J. Williams RC 4.00 10.00
425 Ronald Darby RC 3.00 8.00
426 Taylor Heinicke RC 5.00 12.00
427 Tre McBride RC 3.00 8.00
428 Mario Edwards Jr. RC 3.00 8.00
429 Markus Golden RC 3.00 8.00
430 Nick O'Leary RC 3.00 8.00
431 Antwan Goodley RC 3.00 8.00
432 Ben Koyack RC 5.00 12.00
433 Benardrick McKinney RC 3.00 8.00
434 Danielle Hunter RC 4.00 10.00
435 Denzel Perryman RC 3.00 8.00
436 Dres Anderson RC 3.00 8.00
437 Eddie Goldman RC 3.00 8.00
438 Eric Kendricks RC 3.00 8.00
439 Josh Robinson RC 3.00 8.00
440 Marcus Murphy RC 3.00 8.00
441 Nate Orchard RC 3.00 8.00
443 Terrence Magee RC 5.00 12.00
444 Trey Williams RC 4.00 10.00
445 Byron Jones RC 5.00 12.00
446 Clive Walford RC 3.00 8.00
447 Malcom Brown RC 3.00 8.00
448 Senquez Golson RC 3.00 8.00
449 Shaq Thompson RC 4.00 10.00
450 Bud Dupree RC 4.00 10.00
451 Danny Shelton RC 3.00 8.00
452 Marcus Peters RC 8.00 20.00
453 Brandon Scherff RC 5.00 12.00
454 Tony Lippett RC 3.00 8.00
455 Landon Collins RC 4.00 10.00
456 Trae Waynes RC 3.00 8.00
457 Vic Beasley Jr. RC 4.00 10.00
459 Cameron Artis-Payne RC 3.00 8.00
460 Sean Mannion JSY AU RC 4.00 10.00
461 Karlos Williams JSY AU RC 4.00 10.00
462 Vince Mayle JSY AU RC 5.00 12.00
463 Justin Hardy JSY AU RC 4.00 10.00
464 Jamison Crowder JSY AU RC 5.00 12.00
465 Chris Conley JSY AU RC 4.00 10.00
466 Phillip Dorsett JSY AU RC EXCH 4.00 10.00
467 Ty Montgomery JSY AU RC 4.00 10.00
468 Stefon Diggs JSY AU RC 10.00 25.00
469 Mike Davis JSY AU RC 4.00 10.00
470 Tyler Lockett JSY AU RC 6.00 15.00
471 Jeremy Langford JSY AU RC 4.00 10.00
472 Devin Smith JSY AU RC 4.00 10.00
473 Buck Allen JSY AU RC 5.00 12.00
474 Garrett Grayson JSY AU RC 4.00 10.00
475 David Johnson JSY AU RC 15.00 30.00
476 Leonard Williams JSY AU RC 4.00 10.00
477 Maxx Williams JSY AU RC 4.00 10.00
478 Rashad Greene JSY AU RC 4.00 10.00
479 Bryce Petty JSY AU RC 4.00 10.00
480 Matt Jones JSY AU RC 4.00 10.00
481 Sammie Coates JSY AU RC 5.00 12.00
482 David Cobb JSY AU RC 4.00 10.00
483 Duke Johnson JSY AU RC 6.00 15.00
484 T.J. Yeldon JSY AU RC 6.00 15.00
485 Dorial Green-Beckham JSY AU RC 4.00 10.00
486 Jay Ajayi JSY AU RC 6.00 15.00
487 DeVante Parker JSY AU RC 6.00 15.00
488 Devin Funchess JSY AU RC 6.00 15.00
489 Breshad Perriman JSY AU RC 4.00 10.00
490 Jaelen Strong JSY AU RC 5.00 12.00
491 Tevin Coleman JSY AU RC 5.00 12.00
492 Ameer Abdullah JSY AU RC 6.00 15.00
493 Nelson Agholor JSY AU RC 5.00 12.00
494 Todd Gurley JSY AU RC 40.00 80.00
495 Kevin White JSY AU RC 5.00 12.00
496 Amari Cooper JSY AU RC
497 Brett Hundley JSY AU RC 4.00 10.00
498 Melvin Gordon JSY AU RC 10.00 25.00
499 Marcus Mariota JSY AU RC 25.00 50.00
500 Jameis Winston JSY AU RC 10.00 25.00

2016 Donruss Signature Series

1 Jordan Richards 2.50 6.00
2 Kaelin Clay 2.50 6.00
3 Quandre Diggs 2.50 6.00
4 Terron Ward 2.50 6.00
5 Trevor Siemian 8.00 20.00
8 Arik Armstead 2.50 6.00
9 Mike Tolbert 2.50 6.00
11 Nate Orchard 2.50 6.00
13 Preston Brown 2.50 6.00
15 Cole Beasley 15.00 40.00
16 Preston Smith 3.00 8.00
17 Keith Mumphery 2.50 6.00
18 MyCole Pruitt 2.50 6.00
19 Tyler Murphy 2.50 6.00
20 Chris Smith 2.50 6.00
21 Cameron Heyward 2.50 6.00
22 Stephone Anthony 2.50 6.00
23 Jon Dorenbos 5.00 12.00
24 Cory Harkey 2.50 6.00
25 Kiko Alonso 2.50 6.00
26 Deone Bucannon 2.50 6.00
27 Mason Crosby 8.00 20.00
28 Morten Andersen 2.50 6.00
30 Christian Okoye 6.00 15.00
31 Haloti Ngata 2.50 6.00
32 Isaiah Burse 2.50 6.00
34 Kenny Bell 2.50 6.00
35 Matt Hazel 2.50 6.00
36 Paul Dawson 2.50 6.00
37 Earl Wolff 2.50 6.00
38 Rishard Matthews 2.50 6.00
39 TJ Jones 2.50 6.00
40 Geno Atkins 2.50 6.00
42 Anthony Harris 2.50 6.00
43 Jerrell Freeman 8.00 20.00
44 Brian Mitchell 2.50 6.00
46 Ed Reynolds 2.50 6.00
48 Eric Kendricks 2.50 6.00
49 Jimmie Ward 2.50 6.00
50 Muhammad Wilkerson 2.50 6.00
51 Steve Atwater 8.00 20.00
52 Cedric Ogbuehi 2.50 6.00
53 La'el Collins 2.50 6.00
54 Thomas Davis 2.50 6.00
56 Lorenzo Mauldin 2.50 6.00
57 Josh Shaw 2.50 6.00
58 Sean Mannion 2.50 6.00
63 Jim Kiick 2.50 6.00
64 David DeCastro 2.50 6.00
65 Travis Swanson 2.50 6.00
66 Steve Tasker 2.50 6.00
67 Brandon Coleman 2.50 6.00
69 Scott Crichton 2.50 6.00
70 Danny Shelton 2.50 6.00
72 Dexter Manley 8.00 20.00
74 Marvin Jones 2.50 6.00
75 Carl Davis 2.50 6.00
76 Rod Streater 2.50 6.00
77 Tony Lippett 2.50 6.00
78 Kenjon Barner 2.50 6.00
80 Trae Waynes 2.50 6.00
81 Marcus Smith 2.50 6.00
83 Quinten Rollins 3.00 8.00
85 Frank Clark 2.50 6.00
86 Andrus Peat 2.50 6.00
87 T.J. Carrie 2.50 6.00
88 Jalston Fowler 2.50 6.00
89 Trey Williams 2.50 6.00
90 Ernest Givins 2.50 6.00
91 Delvin Breaux 3.00 8.00
92 Taylor Heinicke 2.50 6.00
95 Eric Rowe 2.50 6.00
96 Ryan Kalil 2.50 6.00
97 Brandon McManus 2.50 6.00
98 Jackson Jeffcoat 2.50 6.00
99 Yannick Ngakoue 4.00 10.00
100 Dan Bailey 15.00 30.00
102 Adam Vinatieri
104 Ryan Fitzpatrick 6.00 15.00
106 Sebastian Janikowski 10.00 25.00
107 Chris Doleman 2.50 6.00
109 Brian Cushing 2.50 6.00
110 Joe Haden 2.50 6.00
111 Eric Berry 3.00 8.00
115 Mike Vrabel 2.50 6.00
116 Chris Ivory 3.00 8.00
118 Ryan Shazier 2.50 6.00
121 Aaron Donald 4.00 10.00
124 David Johnson 10.00 25.00
125 Mark Gastineau 25.00 50.00
127 Ickey Woods 8.00 20.00
129 Joe Thomas 10.00 25.00
130 Neil Smith 2.50 6.00
131 Jermaine Kearse 8.00 20.00
132 Matt Jones 8.00 20.00
134 Steve Grogan 2.50 6.00
135 Justin Forsett 3.00 8.00
136 John Hannah 2.50 6.00
137 Troy Brown 8.00 20.00
139 James White 3.00 8.00
140 Travis Benjamin 2.50 6.00
141 C.J. Anderson 3.00 8.00
142 John Brown
144 Kordell Stewart 3.00 8.00
145 Jeremy Langford 3.00 8.00
146 Charcandrick West 2.50 6.00
148 T.J. Yeldon 2.50 6.00
149 Charlie Joiner 2.50 6.00
150 Victor Cruz
151 Charles Haley 4.00 10.00
152 Devin Funchess 2.50 6.00
153 Josh Gordon 2.50 6.00
154 Phil McConkey 3.00 8.00
155 Thomas Rawls 2.50 6.00
156 Crockett Gillmore
157 Ameer Abdullah 2.50 6.00
158 Dick LeBeau 10.00 25.00
159 Bill Bates 2.50 6.00
160 Torry Holt 3.00 8.00
161 Tedy Bruschi
162 Chris Spielman 2.50 6.00
163 Russ Grimm 2.50 6.00
166 Randall Cunningham 15.00 40.00
167 Derrick Brooks 2.50 6.00
169 Zach Ertz 3.00 8.00
170 Ozzie Newsome 8.00 20.00
171 Willie McGinest 6.00 15.00
172 Derek Carr 30.00 60.00
173 Jordy Nelson 8.00 20.00
174 Travis Kelce 4.00 10.00
175 Brett Favre 60.00 125.00
176 Barry Sanders 50.00 100.00
177 Troy Aikman 40.00 80.00
178 Dan Marino 60.00 125.00
179 Jerry Rice 60.00 125.00
180 Doug Flutie 6.00 15.00
181 LaDainian Tomlinson 12.00 30.00
183 Warren Moon 8.00 20.00
185 Steve Largent 10.00 25.00
186 Ray Lewis 30.00 60.00
187 Ben Roethlisberger
189 Joe Flacco
190 Andrew Luck 25.00 50.00
191 Marcus Mariota 25.00 50.00
192 Bill Parcells 12.00 30.00
193 Richard Sherman 12.00 30.00
194 Joe Namath
195 Kevin Greene
196 J.J. Watt 30.00 60.00
197 Marshawn Lynch 15.00 40.00
198 Eric Dickerson 20.00 50.00
200 Fred Dryer 2.50 6.00
201 Artie Burns RC 4.00 10.00
202 Eli Apple RC 4.00 10.00
203 Jalen Ramsey RC 5.00 12.00
204 Vernon Hargreaves III RC 5.00 12.00
205 William Jackson III RC 4.00 10.00
207 Shaq Lawson RC 3.00 8.00
208 Kenny Clark RC 3.00 8.00
209 Robert Nkemdiche RC 4.00 10.00
210 Sheldon Rankins RC 4.00 10.00
213 Karl Joseph RC 3.00 8.00
214 Keanu Neal RC 3.00 8.00
216 James Bradberry RC 4.00 10.00
217 Mackensie Alexander RC 3.00 8.00
218 T.J. Green RC 5.00 12.00
219 Xavien Howard RC 4.00 10.00
220 Emmanuel Ogbah RC 4.00 10.00
221 Kevin Dodd RC 3.00 8.00
222 Adam Gotsis RC 3.00 8.00
223 A'Shawn Robinson RC 3.00 8.00
224 Austin Johnson RC 3.00 8.00
225 Chris Jones RC 3.00 8.00
226 Jarran Reed RC 3.00 8.00
228 Deion Jones RC 3.00 8.00
229 Jaylon Smith RC 3.00 8.00
231 Myles Jack RC 4.00 10.00
232 Noah Spence RC 3.00 8.00
233 Reggie Ragland RC 3.00 8.00
234 Su'a Cravens RC 3.00 8.00
235 Vonn Bell RC 4.00 10.00
236 KeiVarae Russell RC 3.00 8.00
237 Jacoby Brissett RC 4.00 10.00
238 Austin Hooper RC 3.00 8.00
239 Nick Vannett RC 3.00 8.00
241 Tyler Higbee RC 3.00 8.00
242 Malcolm Mitchell RC 3.00 8.00
243 Tyreek Hill RC 12.00 30.00
244 Jordan Payton RC 3.00 8.00
245 Rashard Higgins RC 3.00 8.00
246 Tajae Sharpe RC 4.00 10.00
247 Brandon Allen RC 3.00 8.00
248 Jake Rudock RC 3.00 8.00
249 Jeff Driskel RC 3.00 8.00
250 Nate Sudfeld RC 3.00 8.00
252 Jayron Kearse RC 3.00 8.00
253 Rico Gathers RC 3.00 8.00
254 Aaron Burbridge RC 3.00 8.00
255 Cody Core RC 3.00 8.00
256 Brandon Doughty RC 3.00 8.00
257 Keith Marshall RC 3.00 8.00
258 Kenny Lawler RC 5.00 12.00
259 Demarcus Ayers RC 3.00 8.00
260 Robert Kelley RC 5.00 12.00
261 Jared Goff JSY AU RC 25.00 60.00
262 Carson Wentz JSY AU RC 60.00 125.00
263 Joey Bosa JSY AU RC 8.00 20.00
264 Ezekiel Elliott JSY AU RC 50.00 100.00
265 Corey Coleman JSY AU RC 6.00 15.00
266 Will Fuller V JSY AU RC 6.00 15.00
267 Josh Doctson JSY AU RC 5.00 12.00
268 Laquon Treadwell JSY AU RC 5.00 12.00
269 Paxton Lynch JSY AU RC
271 Sterling Shepard JSY AU RC 5.00 12.00
272 Derrick Henry JSY AU RC 10.00 25.00
273 Michael Thomas JSY AU RC 8.00 20.00
274 Christian Hackenberg JSY AU RC 4.00 10.00
275 Tyler Boyd JSY AU RC 5.00 12.00
276 Kenyan Drake JSY AU RC 6.00 15.00
277 Braxton Miller JSY AU RC 4.00 10.00
278 Leonte Carroo JSY AU RC 4.00 10.00
279 C.J. Prosise JSY AU RC 4.00 10.00
280 Cody Kessler JSY AU RC 4.00 10.00
281 Connor Cook JSY AU RC 5.00 12.00
284 Pharoh Cooper JSY AU RC 4.00 10.00
285 Tyler Ervin JSY AU RC 4.00 10.00
287 Kenneth Dixon JSY AU RC 4.00 10.00
288 Dak Prescott JSY AU RC 30.00 60.00
289 Devontae Booker JSY AU RC 5.00 12.00
290 Cardale Jones JSY AU RC 4.00 10.00
292 Paul Perkins JSY AU RC 4.00 10.00
203 Jordan Howard JSY AU RC 10.00 25.00
296 Kevin Hogan JSY AU RC 5.00 12.00
297 Trevor Davis JSY AU RC 4.00 10.00
298 Alex Collins JSY AU RC 5.00 12.00
299 Moritz Bohringer JSY AU RC 4.00 10.00
300 Keenan Reynolds JSY AU RC 5.00 12.00

2016 Donruss Signature Series Gold

*VETS/25: 1X TO 2.5X BASIC AU
*VETS/15: 1.2X TO 3X BASIC AU
*RC AU/25: .8X TO 2X BASIC AU
*RC JSY AU/25: .8X TO 2X BASIC JSY AU
262 Carson Wentz JSY AU 125.00 250.00

2016 Donruss Signature Series Holo Gold

*RC AU/15: 1X TO 2.5X RC AU
*RC JSY AU/15: 1X TO 2.5X RC JSY AU
262 Carson Wentz JSY AU 150.00 300.00

2016 Donruss Signature Series Holo Silver

*VETS/35-50: .8X TO 2X BASIC AU
*VETS/25: 1X TO 2.5X BASIC AU
*VETS/15: 1.2X TO 3X BASIC AU
*RC AU/50: .6X TO 1.5X BASIC AU
*RC JSY AU/50: .6X TO 1.5X BASIC JSY AU
262 Carson Wentz JSY AU 75.00 150.00
264 Ezekiel Elliott JSY AU 75.00 150.00

2016 Donruss Signature Series Award Winning Signatures

*HOLO SILV/50: .8X TO 2X BASIC AU
*GOLD/25: 1X TO 2.5X BASIC AU
*HOLO GOLD/15: 1.2X TO 3X BASIC AU
1 Paul Hornung 6.00 15.00
2 Y.A. Tittle 6.00 15.00
3 Fran Tarkenton
4 Earl Campbell 20.00 50.00
5 Dan Marino
6 Marcus Allen 10.00 25.00
7 Lawrence Taylor 15.00 40.00
8 Boomer Esiason 5.00 12.00
9 Thurman Thomas 12.00 30.00
10 Steve Young
11 Brett Favre
12 Barry Sanders 50.00 100.00
13 Terrell Davis
14 Kurt Warner 15.00 40.00
15 Marshall Faulk
16 Joe Theismann 6.00 15.00
17 LaDainian Tomlinson
18 Aaron Rodgers 150.00 250.00

2016 Donruss Signature Series Elusive Ink

2 John Kuhn 6.00 15.00
3 Cole Beasley 25.00 50.00
4 Dan Bailey 12.00 30.00
6 Trevor Siemian 6.00 15.00
8 Mason Crosby 6.00 15.00
10 Rob Ninkovich 25.00 50.00
11 Muhammad Wilkerson 6.00 15.00
12 Nick Mangold 6.00 15.00
13 Geno Atkins 6.00 15.00
15 Brandon McManus 6.00 15.00
16 Philly Brown 6.00 15.00
17 Mike Tolbert 6.00 15.00
18 Ryan Kalil 6.00 15.00
23 Michael Bennett 15.00 40.00
24 Sebastian Janikowski 15.00 40.00
25 Delvin Breaux 8.00 20.00
26 Brett Keisel 15.00 40.00
27 Ed Reed 25.00 50.00
28 Jeff Saturday 12.00 30.00
30 Mike Vrabel 6.00 15.00
31 Tedy Bruschi 25.00 50.00
33 Ernest Givins 6.00 15.00
34 Neil Smith 6.00 15.00
35 Christian Okoye 6.00 15.00
36 Chris Doleman 6.00 15.00
37 Morten Andersen 6.00 15.00
38 Mark Schlereth 12.00 30.00
39 Steve Atwater 12.00 30.00
40 Steve Tasker 6.00 15.00
41 Dick LeBeau 12.00 30.00
44 Vance Johnson 20.00 40.00
45 Darren Woodson 12.00 30.00
46 Chris Spielman 6.00 15.00
47 Jim Zorn 12.00 30.00
48 Kabeer Gbaja-Biamila 6.00 15.00

2016 Donruss Signature Series Signature Pairs

3 P.Perkins/S.Shepard/50 6.00 15.00
6 J.Brissett/M.Mitchell/100 15.00 40.00
7 K.Drake/L.Carroo/100 6.00 15.00
9 A.Collins/C.Prosise/25 8.00 20.00
12 D.Robinson/T.Hill/100 15.00 40.00
15 C.Moore/K.Reynolds/100 5.00 12.00
16 L.Treadwell/M.Bohringer/15
18 C.Coleman/R.Louis/25 10.00 25.00
19 B.Miller/T.Ervin/100 4.00 10.00
20 M.Vrabel/T.Bruschi/25 8.00 20.00
21 A.Vinatieri/T.Brown/15 75.00 150.00
24 B.Bates/D.Woodson/25 30.00 60.00
25 J.Zorn/S.Largent/15
28 R.Ragland/S.Lawson/100 4.00 10.00
29 C.Core/T.Boyd/100 5.00 12.00
31 J.Ramsey/M.Jack/100 6.00 15.00
32 D.Walker/T.Sharpe/100 5.00 12.00
33 J.Kearse/M.Alexander/100 4.00 10.00
34 M.Thomas/S.Rankins/25 12.00 30.00
35 A.Burbridge/D.Buckner/100 4.00 10.00
36 J.Doctson/K.Marshall/25 8.00 20.00
39 C.Ivory/T.Yeldon/50 6.00 15.00
40 C.Okoye/N.Smith/100 4.00 10.00
41 D.Washington/K.Joseph/100 4.00 10.00
42 A.Hooper/K.Neal/100 4.00 10.00
44 R.Aguayo/S.Janikowski/25 6.00 15.00

2016 Donruss Signature Series Signature Prime

2 Alex Collins/25 15.00 40.00
4 Allen Hurns/25 12.00 30.00
6 Ameer Abdullah/25 12.00 30.00
12 Braxton Miller/25 12.00 30.00
13 Breshad Perriman/25 12.00 30.00
14 Brett Keisel/50 20.00 50.00
17 C.J. Prosise/15 15.00 40.00
21 Chris Moore/50 12.00 30.00
24 Cole Beasley/50 15.00 40.00
27 Dak Prescott/50
28 Dan Bailey/50 10.00 25.00
29 Danny Woodhead/15 20.00 50.00
30 Trevor Davis/50 10.00 25.00
32 Delanie Walker/25 12.00 30.00
38 Devontae Booker/50 12.00 30.00
48 Geno Atkins/25 12.00 30.00
50 Haloti Ngata/25 12.00 30.00
53 Hunter Henry/50 12.00 30.00
54 Jacoby Brissett/35 12.00 30.00
56 Jamison Crowder/15 15.00 40.00
58 Jarvis Landry/20 20.00 50.00
59 Jeff Saturday/50 10.00 25.00
61 Jeremy Langford/15 20.00 50.00
62 Joe Haden/25 12.00 30.00
64 Joe Thomas/50 10.00 25.00
65 Joey Bosa/25 25.00 60.00
66 John Kuhn/50 10.00 25.00
68 Jordan Howard/50 25.00 60.00
69 Jordan Matthews/15 20.00 50.00
70 Josh Doctson/15 20.00 50.00
72 Justin Hardy/50 10.00 25.00
73 Stefon Diggs/50 12.00 30.00
74 Keenan Reynolds/50 12.00 30.00
76 Kendall Wright/15 15.00 40.00
77 Kenyan Drake/50 15.00 40.00
78 Malcolm Mitchell/50 10.00 25.00
80 Leonte Carroo/50 10.00 25.00
84 Matt Jones/25 15.00 40.00
87 Michael Thomas/25 25.00 60.00
88 Mike Tolbert/45 10.00 25.00
89 Moritz Bohringer/50 10.00 25.00
91 Nick Mangold/50 10.00 25.00
92 Paul Perkins/50 10.00 25.00
94 Pharoh Cooper/50 10.00 25.00
96 Ryan Kalil/50 10.00 25.00
98 Tyler Boyd/35 12.00 30.00
99 Sterling Shepard/50 12.00 30.00
100 Wendell Smallwood/50 10.00 25.00

2016 Donruss Signature Series Team Trademarks

1 Andre Reed 5.00 12.00
2 Dan Marino 50.00 100.00
3 Tedy Bruschi 15.00 40.00
4 Nick Mangold 4.00 10.00
5 Ray Lewis
6 Boomer Esiason 12.00 30.00
7 Ozzie Newsome 5.00 12.00
8 Rod Woodson 15.00 40.00
9 DeAndre Hopkins 5.00 12.00
10 Peyton Manning
11 T.J. Yeldon 4.00 10.00
13 C.J. Anderson 5.00 12.00
14 Christian Okoye 4.00 10.00
15 Tim Brown
16 LaDainian Tomlinson 12.00 30.00
18 Y.A. Tittle 6.00 15.00
19 Ron Jaworski 5.00 12.00
20 Joe Theismann 10.00 25.00
21 Dan Hampton 4.00 10.00
22 Barry Sanders
23 Brett Favre 90.00 150.00
24 Carl Eller 4.00 10.00
25 Deion Sanders
26 Kevin Greene 6.00 15.00
27 Archie Manning 12.00 30.00
28 Derrick Brooks 4.00 10.00
29 David Johnson 6.00 15.00
30 Eric Dickerson
31 Jerry Rice 50.00 100.00
32 Steve Largent 10.00 25.00

2008 Donruss Sports Legends

This set was released on December 10, 2008. The base set consists of 144 cards and features cards of players from various sports.

COMPLETE SET (144) 40.00 100.00
2 Jim Brown .75 2.00
9 Joe Montana 1.25 3.00
16 John Elway 1.00 2.50
21 Troy Aikman .75 2.00
29 John Riggins .50 1.25
36 Frank Gifford .50 1.25
41 Roger Staubach .75 2.00
53 Steve Young .75 2.00
59 Earl Campbell .50 1.25
64 Jim Kelly .60 1.50
69 Lance Alworth .50 1.25
73 Dan Marino 1.25 3.00
78 Tony Dorsett .60 1.50
82 Vince Dooley .40 1.00
83 Bob Griese .50 1.25
88 Jim Taylor .50 1.25
96 Eric Dickerson .50 1.25
104 Dan Fouts .60 1.50
108 Michael Irvin .50 1.25
113 Dick Butkus .75 2.00
118 Gale Sayers .75 2.00
131 Lawrence Taylor .60 1.50
138 Raymond Berry .50 1.25
142 Lenny Moore .50 1.25
148 Knute Rockne 1.00 2.50

2008 Donruss Sports Legends Mirror Blue

*BLUE/100: 2X TO 5X BASIC CARDS
STATED PRINT RUN 100 SER.#'d SETS

2008 Donruss Sports Legends Mirror Gold

*GOLD/25: 3X TO 8X BASIC CARDS
STATED PRINT RUN 25 SER.#'d SETS

2008 Donruss Sports Legends Mirror Red

*RED/250: 1.5X TO 4X BASIC CARDS
STATED PRINT RUN 250 SER.#'d SETS

2008 Donruss Sports Legends Certified Cuts

STATED PRINT RUN 1-100
SERIAL #'d TO 1 NOT PRICED
2 Bo Schembechler/1

2008 Donruss Sports Legends Champions

SILVER PRINT RUN 1000 SER.#'d SETS
*GOLD/100: .6X TO 1.5X SILVER/1000
GOLD PRINT RUN 100 SER.#'d SETS
2 Joe Montana 3.00 8.00
5 John Riggins 1.50 4.00
8 Roger Staubach 2.00 5.00
12 John Elway 2.50 6.00

2008 Donruss Sports Legends Champions Materials

STATED PRINT RUN 10-250
2 Joe Montana Jsy/250 8.00 20.00
5 John Riggins Jsy/250 6.00 15.00
8 Roger Staubach Jsy/250 6.00 15.00
12 John Elway Jsy/250 6.00 15.00

2008 Donruss Sports Legends Champions Signatures

STATED PRINT RUN 1-100
SERIAL #'d UNDER 25 NOT PRICED

2008 Donruss Sports Legends College Heroes

SILVER PRINT RUN 1000 SER.#'d SETS
*GOLD/100: .6X TO 1.5X SILVER/1000
GOLD PRINT RUN 100 SER.#'d SETS
3 Adrian Peterson 3.00 8.00
4 Bo Jackson 2.00 5.00

2008 Donruss Sports Legends College Heroes Materials

STATED PRINT RUN 50-250
3 Adrian Peterson Jsy/250 8.00 20.00
4 Bo Jackson Jsy/250 8.00 20.00

2008 Donruss Sports Legends College Heroes Signatures

STATED PRINT RUN 25-100
3 Adrian Peterson/25 60.00 100.00
4 Bo Jackson/25 60.00 100.00

2008 Donruss Sports Legends Collegiate Legends Patch Autographs

STATED PRINT RUN 25-250
7 Steve Spurrier/75 30.00 60.00
12 Steve Spurrier/65 30.00 60.00
24 Bo Jackson/25 60.00 100.00
25 Deion Sanders/50 50.00 100.00

2008 Donruss Sports Legends Legends of the Game Combos

STATED PRINT RUN 25-100
UNPRICED PRIME PRINT RUN 1-10
1 Rockne Jkt/P.O'Brien/25 40.00 80.00
3 Montana Jsy/Rockne Jkt 30.00 60.00
5 D.Fouts Jsy/T.Gwynn Jsy 12.00 30.00
7 N.Ryan Jsy/T.Aikman Jsy 20.00 50.00
8 Campbell Jsy/Hayes Jsy 6.00 15.00
11 Ryan Jsy/Campbell Jsy 12.00 30.00
12 Mays Jsy/Montana Jsy/50 30.00 60.00
15 Ripken Jr. Bat/Berry Jsy 25.00 50.00

2008 Donruss Sports Legends Materials Mirror Blue

*MIRROR BLUE: .5X TO 1.2X MIRROR RED
MIRROR BLUE PRINT RUN 5-250
SERIAL #'d UNDER 15 NOT PRICED
29 John Riggins/25 6.00 15.00

2008 Donruss Sports Legends Materials Mirror Gold

*GOLD/25: .8X TO 2X MIRROR RED
GOLD PRINT RUN 1-25 SER.#'d SETS
SERIAL #'d UNDER 20 NOT PRICED
21 Troy Aikman/1
118 Gale Sayers/1
131 Lawrence Taylor/1

2008 Donruss Sports Legends Materials Mirror Red

MIRROR RED PRINT RUN 10-500
SERIAL #'d UNDER 25 NOT PRICED
*GOLD/25: .8X TO 2X MIRROR RED
UNPRICED MIRROR EMERALD PRINT RUN 1-5
UNPRICED MIRROR BLACK PRINT RUN 1
9 Joe Montana Jsy/100 8.00 20.00
16 John Elway Jsy/100 6.00 15.00
21 Troy Aikman Jsy/10
29 John Riggins Jsy/100 4.00 10.00
41 Roger Staubach Jsy/100 5.00 12.00
53 Steve Young Jsy/100 5.00 12.00
59 Earl Campbell Jsy/50 4.00 10.00
64 Jim Kelly Jsy/100 5.00 12.00
73 Dan Marino Jsy/100 8.00 20.00
78 Tony Dorsett Jsy/100 5.00 12.00
82 Vince Dooley Sweater/500 3.00 8.00
83 Bob Griese Jsy/50 5.00 12.00
96 Eric Dickerson Jsy/100 4.00 10.00
104 Dan Fouts Jsy/100 5.00 12.00
108 Michael Irvin Jsy/25 4.00 10.00
113 Dick Butkus Jsy/25 8.00 20.00
131 Lawrence Taylor Jsy/10
138 Raymond Berry Jsy/100 3.00 8.00
142 Lenny Moore Jsy/100 3.00 8.00
148 Knute Rockne Jkt/500 10.00 25.00

2008 Donruss Sports Legends Museum Collection

SILVER PRINT RUN 1000 SER.#'d SETS
*GOLD/100: .6X TO 1.5X SILVER/1000
GOLD PRINT RUN 100 SER.#'d SETS
2 Joe Montana 3.00 8.00
6 John Elway 2.50 6.00
8 Raymond Berry 1.25 3.00
10 Roger Staubach 2.00 5.00
14 Steve Young 2.00 5.00
15 Tony Dorsett 1.50 4.00
16 Knute Rockne 2.50 6.00
18 Dan Marino 3.00 8.00
20 Lenny Moore 1.25 3.00
24 Dan Fouts 1.50 4.00
26 Eric Dickerson 1.25 3.00

2008 Donruss Sports Legends Museum Collection Materials

STATED PRINT RUN 25-250
*PRIME/25: .6X TO 1.5X BASIC MATERIAL
PRIME PRINT RUN 1-25
SERIAL #'d UNDER 25 NOT PRICED
2 Joe Montana/100 10.00 25.00
6 John Elway/100 8.00 20.00
8 Raymond Berry/250 4.00 10.00
10 Roger Staubach/100 6.00 15.00
14 Steve Young/250 6.00 15.00
15 Tony Dorsett/250 6.00 15.00
16 Knute Rockne Jkt/250 12.00 30.00
18 Dan Marino/100 10.00 25.00
20 Lenny Moore/250 4.00 10.00
24 Dan Fouts/250 6.00 15.00
26 Eric Dickerson/250 5.00 12.00

2008 Donruss Sports Legends Museum Collection Signatures

STATED PRINT RUN 1-250
SERIAL #'d UNDER 25 NOT PRICED
2 Joe Montana/10
6 John Elway/10
8 Raymond Berry/10
10 Roger Staubach/10
14 Steve Young/10
15 Tony Dorsett/10
18 Dan Marino/10
20 Lenny Moore/10
24 Dan Fouts/10
26 Eric Dickerson/1

2008 Donruss Sports Legends Museum Collection Signatures Materials

STATED PRINT RUN 1-50
SERIAL #'d UNDER 25 NOT PRICED

2008 Donruss Sports Legends Museum Curator Collection Materials

STATED PRINT RUN 10-100
*PRIME/25: .6X TO 1.5X BASIC MATERIAL
PRIME PRINT RUN 1-25
SERIAL #'d UNDER 25 NOT PRICED
2 Joe Montana/10
6 John Elway/10
8 Raymond Berry/100 5.00 12.00
10 Roger Staubach/10
14 Steve Young/100 8.00 20.00
15 Tony Dorsett/100 8.00 20.00
16 Knute Rockne Jkt/100 15.00 40.00
18 Dan Marino/25 15.00 40.00
20 Lenny Moore/100 5.00 12.00
24 Dan Fouts/100 8.00 20.00
26 Eric Dickerson/100 6.00 15.00

2008 Donruss Sports Legends Museum Curator Collection Signatures Materials

STATED PRINT RUN 1-25
SERIAL #'d UNDER 25 NOT PRICED

2008 Donruss Sports Legends Signature Connection Combos

STATED PRINT RUN 25-100
2 Ripken/Riggins/25 150.00 250.00
3 D.Fouts/T.Gwynn/25 60.00 100.00
4 N.Ryan/T.Aikman/25 100.00 175.00
5 E.Hayes/E.Cmpbll/25 20.00 40.00
6 Sayers/L.Woodard/25 20.00 40.00
7 B.Feller/J.Brown/25 60.00 120.00
8 L.Alworth/Moncrief/10 90.00 150.00
10 J.Brown/M.Powell/25
11 Bo Jcksn/Deion/25 100.00 175.00
12 T.Aikman/B.Walton/25 60.00 100.00

2008 Donruss Sports Legends Signatures Mirror Blue

MIRROR BLUE PRINT RUN 2-250
SERIAL #'d UNDER 10 NOT PRICED
UNPRICED MIRROR EMERALD PRINT RUN 1-5
UNPRICED MIRROR BLACK PRINT RUN 1
2 Jim Brown/25
9 Joe Montana/25 75.00 150.00
16 John Elway/25 75.00 150.00
21 Troy Aikman/25 40.00 80.00
29 John Riggins/25 15.00 40.00
36 Frank Gifford/25 20.00 50.00
41 Roger Staubach/25
59 Earl Campbell/25
64 Jim Kelly/15 30.00 60.00
83 Bob Griese/25 12.00 30.00
88 Jim Taylor/15 30.00 60.00
104 Dan Fouts/25 15.00 40.00
108 Michael Irvin/25 15.00 40.00
113 Dick Butkus/15 50.00 100.00
131 Lawrence Taylor/25 15.00 40.00
142 Lenny Moore/25 10.00 25.00

2008 Donruss Sports Legends Signatures Mirror Gold

MIRROR GOLD PRINT RUN 4-25
SERIAL #'d UNDER 10 NOT PRICED
2 Jim Brown/10
9 Joe Montana/10 100.00 175.00
16 John Elway/10 100.00 175.00
21 Troy Aikman/10 50.00 100.00
29 John Riggins/10 20.00 50.00
36 Frank Gifford/10 25.00 60.00
41 Roger Staubach/10
53 Steve Young/10
59 Earl Campbell/10
64 Jim Kelly/10 30.00 80.00
69 Lance Alworth/10
73 Dan Marino/10
78 Tony Dorsett/25 15.00 40.00
83 Bob Griese/10 15.00 40.00
88 Jim Taylor/10 30.00 80.00
104 Dan Fouts/15 20.00 50.00
108 Michael Irvin/10 20.00 50.00
113 Dick Butkus/10 60.00 120.00
118 Gale Sayers/10
131 Lawrence Taylor/20 20.00 50.00
138 Raymond Berry/25 15.00 40.00
142 Lenny Moore/20 12.00 30.00

2008 Donruss Sports Legends Signatures Mirror Red

*MIRROR RED: .3X TO .8X MIRROR BLUE
MIRROR RED PRINT RUN 25-1370
36 Frank Gifford/25 20.00 50.00
83 Bob Griese/55 10.00 25.00
88 Jim Taylor/25 20.00 50.00
108 Michael Irvin/25 15.00 40.00
113 Dick Butkus/25 30.00 80.00
131 Lawrence Taylor/50 12.00 30.00
142 Lenny Moore/50 8.00 20.00

2006 Donruss Threads

This 285-card set was released in August, 2006. The set was issued into the hobby in five-card packs, with an $3.99 SRP, which came 24 packs to a box. Cards numbered 1-150 feature veterans; while cards numbered 151-285 all feature rookies. Cards numbered 151-225 were issued to a stated print run of 999 serial numbered sets while cards numbered 226-260 were all signed by the featured player and were issued to a stated print run of between 100 and 240 serial numbered copies.

COMP.SET w/o RC's (150) 10.00 25.00
151-225 ROOKIES SER. #'d TO 999
226-260 ROOKIE AU PRINT RUN 100-240
261-285 ROOK. AUs SER. #'d TO 999
1 Braylon Edwards .25 .60
2 Jason Witten .30 .75
3 Julius Jones .25 .60
4 Roy Williams S .25 .60
5 Terry Glenn .30 .75
6 Ashley Lelie .25 .60
7 Kevin Jones .25 .60
8 Mike Williams .25 .60
9 Roy Williams WR .25 .60
10 Aaron Rodgers 1.00 2.50
11 Tatum Bell .25 .60
12 Samkon Gado .25 .60
13 Corey Bradford .25 .60
14 Dallas Clark .25 .60
15 Matt Jones .25 .60
16 Larry Johnson .25 .60
17 Byron Leftwich .25 .60
18 Fred Taylor .25 .60
19 Anquan Boldin .25 .60
20 Kurt Warner .30 .75
21 Larry Fitzgerald .30 .75
22 Alge Crumpler .30 .75
23 Michael Vick .30 .75
24 Warrick Dunn .25 .60

25 Jamal Lewis .30 .75
26 Ray Lewis .40 1.00
27 Eric Moulds .25 .60
28 Josh Reed .25 .60
29 Lee Evans .30 .75
30 Steve Smith .40 1.00
31 Brian Urlacher .40 1.00
32 Thomas Jones .25 .60
33 Chad Johnson .25 .60
34 Rudi Johnson .25 .60
35 T.J. Houshmandzadeh .25 .60
36 Reuben Droughns .30 .75
37 Drew Bledsoe .30 .75
38 Keyshawn Johnson .30 .75
39 Jake Plummer .25 .60
40 Rod Smith .30 .75
41 Mike Anderson .25 .60
42 Joey Harrington .25 .60
43 Brett Favre .75 2.00
44 Donald Driver .30 .75
45 Javon Walker .30 .75
46 Andre Johnson .30 .75
47 David Carr .25 .60
48 Domanick Davis .25 .60
49 Edgerrin James .30 .75
50 Marvin Harrison .30 .75
51 Peyton Manning 1.00 2.50
52 Reggie Wayne .30 .75
53 Jimmy Smith .30 .75
54 Tony Gonzalez .30 .75
55 Trent Green .25 .60
56 Eddie Kennison .25 .60
57 Chris Chambers .25 .60
58 Zach Thomas .30 .75
59 Daunte Culpepper .30 .75
60 Corey Dillon .25 .60
61 Deion Branch .25 .60
62 Tedy Bruschi .30 .75
63 Tom Brady 1.25 3.00
64 Deuce McAllister .30 .75
65 Donte Stallworth .25 .60
66 Jeremy Shockey .25 .60
67 Tiki Barber .30 .75
68 Chad Pennington .25 .60
69 Curtis Martin .30 .75
70 Donovan McNabb .30 .75
71 Antwaan Randle El .25 .60
72 Hines Ward .30 .75
73 Antonio Gates .40 1.00
74 Drew Brees .40 1.00
75 Keenan McCardell .30 .75
76 LaDainian Tomlinson .40 1.00
77 Alex Smith QB .30 .75
78 Brandon Lloyd .25 .60
79 Frank Gore .30 .75
80 Kevan Barlow .25 .60
81 Darrell Jackson .30 .75
82 Joe Jurevicius .25 .60
83 Matt Hasselbeck .25 .60
84 Shaun Alexander .25 .60
85 Shaun McDonald .25 .60
86 Marc Bulger .25 .60
87 Steven Jackson .25 .60
88 Torry Holt .30 .75
89 Cadillac Williams .30 .75
90 Chris Simms .25 .60
91 Joey Galloway .30 .75
92 Michael Clayton .25 .60
93 Chris Brown .25 .60
94 Drew Bennett .30 .75
95 Steve McNair .30 .75
96 Tyrone Calico .25 .60
97 Clinton Portis .25 .60
98 David Patten .25 .60
99 Mark Brunell .30 .75
100 Santana Moss .30 .75
101 Randy McMichael .25 .60
102 Ronnie Brown .30 .75
103 Mewelde Moore .25 .60
104 Nate Burleson .25 .60
105 Troy Williamson .25 .60
106 David Givens .30 .75
107 Aaron Brooks .25 .60
108 Laveranues Coles .25 .60
109 Justin McCareins .25 .60
110 Kerry Collins .25 .60
111 LaMont Jordan .30 .75
112 Randy Moss .30 .75
113 Jerry Porter .25 .60
114 Brian Westbrook .25 .60
115 Plaxico Burress .25 .60
116 Joe Horn .25 .60
117 Eli Manning .30 .75
118 Reggie Brown .25 .60
119 Ryan Moats .25 .60
120 Ben Roethlisberger .50 1.25
121 Willie Parker .30 .75
122 Marcus Pollard .25 .60
123 Bubba Franks .25 .60
124 Jabar Gaffney .25 .60
125 Brandon Stokley .25 .60
126 Ernest Wilford .25 .60
127 Dante Hall .25 .60
128 Marty Booker .25 .60
129 Samie Parker .25 .60
130 J.J. Arrington .25 .60
131 Marcel Shipp .25 .60
132 Michael Jenkins .25 .60
133 T.J. Duckett .25 .60
134 Derrick Mason .25 .60
135 Kyle Boller .25 .60
136 Mark Clayton .25 .60
137 Willis McGahee .25 .60
138 DeShaun Foster .30 .75
139 Jake Delhomme .25 .60
140 Julius Peppers .30 .75
141 Keary Colbert .25 .60
142 Stephen Davis .25 .60
143 Todd Heap .25 .60
144 J.P. Losman .30 .75
145 Muhsin Muhammad .25 .60
146 Carson Palmer .30 .75
147 Cedric Benson .25 .60
148 Rex Grossman .25 .60
149 Charlie Frye .30 .75
150 Dennis Northcutt .25 .60
151 Mathias Kiwanuka RC 2.50 6.00
152 Ingle Martin RC 2.00 5.00
153 Reggie McNeal RC 1.50 4.00
154 Bruce Gradkowski RC 2.00 5.00
155 D.J. Shockley RC 2.00 5.00
156 Paul Pinegar RC 1.50 4.00
157 Brandon Kirsch RC 2.00 5.00
158 P.J. Daniels RC 1.50 4.00
159 Marques Hagans RC 1.50 4.00
160 Jerome Harrison RC 1.50 4.00
161 Wali Lundy RC 1.50 4.00
162 Cedric Humes RC 1.50 4.00
163 Quinton Ganther RC 1.50 4.00
164 Mike Bell RC 1.50 4.00
165 John David Washington RC 1.50 4.00
166 Anthony Fasano RC 1.50 4.00
167 Tony Scheffler RC 2.50 6.00
168 Leonard Pope RC 2.50 6.00
169 David Thomas RC 1.50 4.00
170 Dominique Byrd RC 1.50 4.00
171 Devin Hester RC 3.00 8.00
172 Willie Reid RC 2.00 5.00
173 Brad Smith RC 2.00 5.00
174 Cory Rodgers RC 1.50 4.00
175 Domenik Hixon RC 2.50 6.00
176 Jeremy Bloom RC 1.50 4.00
177 Jonathan Orr RC 2.00 5.00
178 Jeff Webb RC 2.00 5.00
179 Ethan Kilmer RC 2.00 5.00
180 Bennie Brazell RC 2.00 5.00
181 David Anderson RC 2.00 5.00
182 Kevin McMahan RC 2.00 5.00
183 Anthony Mix RC 2.00 5.00
184 D'Brickashaw Ferguson RC 1.50 4.00
185 Kamerion Wimbley RC 2.00 5.00
186 Tamba Hali RC 2.50 6.00
187 Haloti Ngata RC 2.00 5.00
188 Brodrick Bunkley RC 2.00 5.00
189 John McCargo RC 1.50 4.00
190 Claude Wroten RC 1.50 4.00
191 Gabe Watson RC 1.50 4.00
192 D'Qwell Jackson RC 1.50 4.00
193 Abdul Hodge RC 1.50 4.00
194 Ernie Sims RC 1.50 4.00
195 Chad Greenway RC 2.50 6.00
196 Bobby Carpenter RC 1.50 4.00
197 Manny Lawson RC 2.00 5.00
198 DeMeco Ryans RC 2.00 5.00
199 Rocky McIntosh RC 1.50 4.00
200 Thomas Howard RC 1.50 4.00
201 Jon Alston RC 1.50 4.00
202 A.J. Nicholson RC 1.50 4.00
203 Tye Hill RC 1.50 4.00
204 Antonio Cromartie RC 2.00 5.00
205 Johnathan Joseph RC 2.00 5.00
206 Kelly Jennings RC 2.00 5.00
207 Ashton Youboty RC 1.50 4.00
208 Alan Zemaitis RC 1.50 4.00
209 Jason Allen RC 2.00 5.00
210 Cedric Griffin RC 2.00 5.00
211 Ko Simpson RC 2.00 5.00
212 Pat Watkins RC 2.00 5.00
213 Donte Whitner RC 2.00 5.00
214 Bernard Pollard RC 2.00 5.00
215 Darnell Bing RC 2.00 5.00
216 Marcus Vick RC 1.50 4.00
217 Roman Harper RC 2.00 5.00
218 Anthony Smith RC 2.50 6.00
219 Daniel Bullocks RC 1.50 4.00
220 Eric Smith RC 2.00 5.00
221 Danieal Manning RC 2.50 6.00
222 Anthony Schlegel RC 2.00 5.00
223 Dusty Dvoracek RC 2.50 6.00
224 Darryl Tapp RC 2.00 5.00
225 Chris Gocong RC 2.00 5.00
226 Brandon Williams AU/240 RC 8.00 20.00
227 Michael Robinson AU/240 RC 8.00 20.00
228 Vernon Davis AU/100 RC 10.00 25.00
229 Brandon Marshall AU/240 RC 15.00 40.00
230 Travis Wilson AU/180 RC 8.00 20.00
231 Maurice Stovall AU/140 RC 8.00 20.00
232 Matt Leinart AU/140 RC 8.00 20.00
233 Ch.Whitehurst AU/200 RC 8.00 20.00
234 Derek Hagan AU/100 RC 10.00 25.00
235 Jason Avant AU/150 RC 8.00 20.00
236 Jerious Norwood AU/210 RC 8.00 20.00
237 Sinorice Moss AU/100 RC 8.00 20.00
238 Marcedes Lewis AU/100 RC 8.00 20.00
239 Maurice Drew AU/100 RC 12.00 30.00
240 Kellen Clemens AU/210 RC 8.00 20.00
241 Leon Washington AU/200 RC 8.00 20.00
242 Brian Calhoun AU/140 RC 8.00 20.00
243 A.J. Hawk AU/100 RC 10.00 25.00
244 DeAn.Williams AU/160 RC 10.00 25.00
245 Chad Jackson AU/140 RC 8.00 20.00
246 L.Maroney AU/140 RC 8.00 20.00
247 Michael Huff AU/100 RC 10.00 25.00
248 Joe Klopfenstein AU/240 RC 8.00 20.00
249 Dem.Williams AU/160 RC 8.00 20.00
250 Reggie Bush AU/100 RC 12.00 30.00
251 Omar Jacobs AU/120 RC 8.00 20.00
252 Santonio Holmes AU/120 RC 10.00 25.00
253 Mario Williams AU/160 RC 12.00 30.00
254 LenDale White AU/100 RC 8.00 20.00
255 Vince Young AU/100 RC 8.00 20.00
256 Tarvaris Jackson AU/210 RC 8.00 20.00
257 Jay Cutler AU/120 RC 10.00 25.00
258 Joseph Addai AU/100 RC 8.00 20.00
259 Brodie Croyle AU/120 RC 8.00 20.00
260 Greg Jennings AU/240 RC 12.00 30.00
261 Erik Meyer AU RC 3.00 8.00
262 Drew Olson AU RC 3.00 8.00
263 Darrell Hackney AU RC 4.00 10.00
264 Andre Hall AU RC 4.00 10.00
265 Taurean Henderson AU RC 3.00 8.00
266 Derrick Ross AU RC 4.00 10.00
267 De'Arrius Howard AU RC 5.00 12.00
268 Wendell Mathis AU RC 4.00 10.00
269 Gerald Riggs AU RC 4.00 10.00
270 Garrett Mills AU RC 4.00 10.00
271 Jai Lewis AU RC 4.00 10.00
272 Skyler Green AU RC 3.00 8.00
273 Mike Hass AU RC 3.00 8.00
274 Delanie Walker AU RC 6.00 15.00
275 Adam Jennings AU RC 4.00 10.00
276 Todd Watkins AU RC 3.00 8.00
277 Devin Aromashodu AU RC 3.00 8.00
278 Ben Obomanu AU RC 4.00 10.00
279 Marques Colston AU RC 5.00 12.00
280 Miles Austin AU RC 4.00 10.00
281 Martin Nance AU RC 3.00 8.00
282 Greg Lee AU RC 3.00 8.00
283 Hank Baskett AU RC 3.00 8.00
284 Jimmy Williams AU RC 3.00 8.00
285 Anwar Phillips AU RC 4.00 10.00

2006 Donruss Threads Bronze Holofoil

*VETERANS 1-150: 2X TO 5X BASIC CARDS
*ROOKIES 151-225: .5X TO 1.2X
STATED PRINT RUN 250 SER.#'d SETS

2006 Donruss Threads Gold Holofoil

*VETERANS 1-150: 4X TO 10X BASIC CARDS
*ROOKIES 151-225: 1X TO 2.5X BASIC CARDS
STATED PRINT RUN 50 SER.#'d SETS

2006 Donruss Threads Platinum Holofoil

*VETERANS 1-150: 6X TO 15X BASIC CARDS
*ROOKIES 151-225: 1.5X TO 4X BASIC CARDS
STATED PRINT RUN 25 SER.#'d SETS

2006 Donruss Threads Retail Blue

*VETERANS 1-150: 2X TO 5X BASIC CARDS
*ROOKIES 151-225: .5X TO 1.2X
STATED PRINT RUN 200 SER.#'d SETS

2006 Donruss Threads Retail Rookies

*ROOKIES: .4X TO 1X BASIC CARDS
RETAIL/999 PRINTED ON WHITE STOCK

2006 Donruss Threads Retail Green

*VETERANS 1-150: 3X TO 8X BASIC CARDS
*ROOKIES 151-225: .8X TO 2X BASIC CARDS
STATED PRINT RUN 100 SER.#'d SETS

2006 Donruss Threads Retail Red

*VETERANS 1-150: 2.5X TO 6X BASIC CARDS
*ROOKIES 151-225: 1X TO 2.5X BASIC CARDS
1-150 PRINT RUN 150 SER.#'d SETS
151-225 PRINT RUN 50 SER.#'d SETS

2006 Donruss Threads Retail Pewter

*VETERANS 1-150: 2X TO 5X BASIC CARDS
*ROOKIES: 151-225: .5X TO 1.2X
STATED PRINT RUN 250 SER.#'d SETS

2006 Donruss Threads Silver Holofoil

*VETERANS 1-150: 3X TO 8X BASIC CARDS
*ROOKIES 151-225: .8X TO 2X BASIC CARDS
STATED PRINT RUN 100 SER.#'d SETS

2006 Donruss Threads Century Collection Materials

*PRIME/25: .8X TO 2X BASIC INSERTS
1 Jim Brown 4.00 10.00
2 Forrest Gregg 2.00 5.00
3 Yale Lary 2.00 5.00
4 Charley Taylor 2.50 6.00
5 Lance Alworth 2.50 6.00
6 Cliff Branch 2.00 5.00
7 Bob Griese 3.00 8.00
8 Daryle Lamonica 2.00 5.00
9 Fred Biletnikoff 3.00 8.00
10 Paul Warfield 2.50 6.00
11 Earl Campbell 3.00 8.00
12 Joe Montana 10.00 25.00
13 John Riggins 2.50 6.00
14 Mark Gastineau 2.00 5.00
15 Ozzie Newsome 2.50 6.00
16 Tom Brady 10.00 25.00
17 Peyton Manning 8.00 20.00
18 Jerry Rice 6.00 15.00
19 Brett Favre 6.00 15.00
20 Curtis Martin 2.50 6.00

2006 Donruss Threads Century Legends Gold

GOLD ODDS 1:18 HOB, 1:81 RET
*BLUE/100: .8X TO 2X BASIC INSERTS
BLUE PRINT RUN 100 SER.#'d SETS
1 Lance Alworth 1.25 3.00
2 Fred Biletnikoff 1.50 4.00
3 Earl Campbell 1.50 4.00
4 Joe Montana 3.00 8.00
5 John Elway 2.50 6.00
6 Jim Kelly 1.50 4.00
7 Jim Brown 2.00 5.00
8 Tom Brady 2.00 5.00
9 Jerry Rice 2.50 6.00
10 Peyton Manning 2.00 5.00
11 Brett Favre 2.50 6.00
12 Jim Plunkett 1.25 3.00
13 Phil Simms 1.25 3.00
14 Thurman Thomas 1.25 3.00

2006 Donruss Threads Century Legends Materials

*PRIME/25: .8X TO 2X BASIC JSY/250
1 Lance Alworth 2.50 6.00
2 Fred Biletnikoff 3.00 8.00
3 Earl Campbell 3.00 8.00
4 Joe Montana 10.00 25.00
5 John Elway 5.00 12.00
6 Jim Kelly 3.00 8.00
7 Jim Brown/100 5.00 12.00
8 Tom Brady 10.00 25.00
9 Jerry Rice 6.00 15.00
10 Peyton Manning 8.00 20.00
11 Brett Favre 6.00 15.00
12 Jim Plunkett 2.50 6.00
13 Phil Simms 2.50 6.00
14 Thurman Thomas 2.50 6.00

2006 Donruss Threads Century Stars Gold

GOLD ODDS 1:18 HOB, 1:81 RET
*BLUE/100: .8X TO 2X BASIC INSERTS
BLUE PRINT RUN 100 SER.#'d SETS
1 Carson Palmer 1.00 2.50
2 Ben Roethlisberger 2.50 6.00
3 Brett Favre 2.50 6.00
4 Isaac Bruce .60 1.50
5 Jerome Bettis 1.00 2.50
6 Jerry Rice 2.50 6.00
7 LaDainian Tomlinson 1.00 2.50
8 Steve Smith 1.00 2.50
9 Marvin Harrison 1.00 2.50
10 Matt Hasselbeck .60 1.50
11 Michael Vick 1.00 2.50
12 Peyton Manning 2.00 5.00
13 Randy Moss 1.00 2.50
14 Shaun Alexander 1.25 3.00
15 Tom Brady 2.00 5.00

2006 Donruss Threads Century Stars Materials

*PRIME/25: .8X TO 2X BASIC INSERTS
1 Carson Palmer 2.50 6.00
2 Ben Roethlisberger 4.00 10.00
3 Brett Favre 6.00 15.00
4 Isaac Bruce 3.00 8.00
5 Jerome Bettis 3.00 8.00
6 Jerry Rice 6.00 15.00
7 LaDainian Tomlinson 3.00 8.00
8 Steve Smith 3.00 8.00
9 Marvin Harrison 2.50 6.00
10 Matt Hasselbeck 2.00 5.00
11 Michael Vick 2.50 6.00
12 Peyton Manning 8.00 20.00
13 Randy Moss 2.50 6.00
14 Shaun Alexander 2.00 5.00
15 Tom Brady 10.00 25.00

2006 Donruss Threads College Greats

STATED ODDS 1:989 RET
1 Peyton Manning 2.50 6.00
2 Carson Palmer .75 2.00
3 Ronnie Brown .75 2.00
4 Cadillac Williams .75 2.00
5 LaDainian Tomlinson 1.00 2.50
6 Cedric Benson .60 1.50
7 Hines Ward .75 2.00
8 Larry Johnson .60 1.50
9 Michael Vick .75 2.00
10 Willis McGahee .60 1.50
11 Reggie Bush 1.00 2.50
12 Matt Leinart .60 1.50
13 Vince Young .60 1.50
14 Jim Brown 1.25 3.00
15 Anquan Boldin .60 1.50
16 Chad Johnson .60 1.50
17 Ben Roethlisberger 1.25 3.00
18 Ken Kavanaugh .60 1.50
19 Jack Cloud
20 Doc Blanchard

2006 Donruss Threads College Greats Autographs

UNPRICED DUAL AUs SER.#'d TO 5
1 Peyton Manning SP 60.00 120.00
2 Carson Palmer SP 15.00 40.00
4 Cadillac Williams SP 15.00 40.00
6 Cedric Benson SP 15.00 40.00
7 Hines Ward SP 20.00 50.00
8 Larry Johnson SP 15.00 40.00
9 Michael Vick SP 30.00 60.00
10 Willis McGahee SP 15.00 40.00
11 Reggie Bush SP 12.00 30.00
12 Matt Leinart SP 12.00 30.00
13 Vince Young SP 10.00 25.00
14 Jim Brown SP 60.00 120.00
15 Anquan Boldin SP 15.00 40.00
16 Chad Johnson SP 15.00 40.00
17 Ben Roethlisberger SP 50.00 100.00
18 Ken Kavanaugh 10.00 25.00

2006 Donruss Threads College Greats Autographs Dual

STATED PRINT RUN 5 SER.#'d SETS
3 J.Elway/J.Montana EXCH
4 H Walker/S Alexander EXCH

2006 Donruss Threads College Gridiron Kings Gold

GOLD ODDS 1:19 HOB, 1:24 RET
UNPRICED FRAMED BLACK SER.#'d TO 10
*FRAMED BLUE/50: 1.2X TO 3X
FRAMED BLUE PRINT RUN 50 SER.#'d SETS
*FRAMED GREEN/25: 1.5X TO 4X
FRAMED GREEN PRINT RUN 25 SER.#'d SETS
*FRAMED RED/100: 1X TO 2.5X
FRAMED RED PRINT RUN 100 SER.#'d SETS
*GOLD HOLOFOIL/100: 1X TO 2.5X
GOLD HOLO.PRINT RUN 100 SER.#'d SETS
*PLATINUM/25: 1.5X TO 4X BASIC INSERTS
PLATINUM PRINT RUN 25 SER.#'d SETS
*SILVER HOLOFOIL/250: .6X TO 1.5X
SILVER HOLO.PRINT RUN 250 SER.#'d SETS
1 Marcus Allen 1.25 3.00
2 Terry Baker .75 2.00
3 Joe Bellino .75 2.00
4 Billy Cannon .75 2.00
5 John Cappelletti .75 2.00
6 Howard Cassady 1.25 3.00
7 Eric Crouch 1.25 3.00
8 John David Crow .75 2.00
9 Tony Dorsett 1.50 4.00
10 Doug Flutie 1.25 3.00
11 Paul Hornung 1.25 3.00
12 John Huarte .75 2.00
13 Dick Kazmaier .75 2.00
14 John Lattner .75 2.00
15 John Lujack 1.25 3.00
16 Steve Owens 1.25 3.00
17 Johnny Rodgers 1.25 3.00
18 Billy Sims 1.25 3.00
19 Roger Staubach 2.50 6.00
20 Matt Leinart .75 2.00
21 Reggie Bush 1.25 3.00
22 Eddie George 1.25 3.00
23 Jason White 1.25 3.00
24 Doak Walker 1.25 3.00
25 Jim Plunkett .75 2.00
26 Bo Jackson 1.50 4.00
27 Carson Palmer 1.25 3.00
28 Gary Beban .75 2.00
29 Glenn Davis .75 2.00
30 Pete Dawkins 1.25 3.00
31 Archie Griffin 1.25 3.00
32 Jay Berwanger .75 2.00
33 Nile Kinnick 1.25 3.00
34 Tom Harmon .75 2.00
35 Angelo Bertelli .75 2.00
36 Les Horvath .75 2.00
37 Leon Hart .75 2.00
38 Vic Janowicz .75 2.00
39 Doc Blanchard 1.25 3.00
40 Larry Kelley .75 2.00

2006 Donruss Threads College Gridiron Kings Autographs

1 Marcus Allen 15.00 40.00
2 Terry Baker 8.00 20.00
3 Joe Bellino 10.00 25.00
4 Billy Cannon 8.00 20.00
5 John Cappelletti 6.00 15.00
6 Howard Cassady 15.00 30.00
7 Eric Crouch 8.00 20.00
8 John David Crow 12.00 30.00
9 Tony Dorsett 15.00 40.00
10 Doug Flutie SP 25.00 40.00
11 Paul Hornung 15.00 40.00
12 John Huarte 15.00 40.00
13 Dick Kazmaier 15.00 40.00
14 John Lattner 10.00 25.00
15 John Lujack 15.00 40.00
16 Steve Owens 10.00 25.00
17 Johnny Rodgers 8.00 20.00
18 Billy Sims 10.00 25.00
19 Roger Staubach SP 75.00 135.00
20 Matt Leinart SP 25.00 60.00
21 Reggie Bush SP 15.00 40.00
22 Eddie George 25.00 50.00
23 Jason White 10.00 25.00
25 Jim Plunkett SP 10.00 25.00
26 Bo Jackson SP 50.00 80.00
27 Carson Palmer SP 40.00 80.00
28 Gary Beban SP 25.00 40.00
29 Glenn Davis SP 25.00 50.00
30 Pete Dawkins SP 25.00 40.00
31 Archie Griffin SP 25.00 40.00
39 Doc Blanchard SP No AU 3.00 8.00

2006 Donruss Threads Dynasty Gold

GOLD ODDS 1:24 HOB, 1:212 RET
*BLUE/100: .8X TO 2X BASIC INSERTS
BLUE PRINT RUN 100 SER.#'d SETS
1 Plunkett/Branch/Biletnikoff 1.25 3.00
2 Montana/Rice/Young 3.00 8.00
3 Roethlisberger/Bettis/Ward 3.00 8.00
4 Manning/James/Harrison 2.50 6.00
5 Brees/Tomlinson/Gates 1.50 4.00
6 Hasselbeck/Alexander/Jackson 1.50 4.00
7 Delhomme/Davis/Smith 1.25 3.00
8 Elway/Davis/Smith 2.50 6.00
9 Favre/Green/Walker 3.00 8.00
10 Kelly/Thomas/Reed 1.50 4.00

2006 Donruss Threads Dynasty Materials

STATED PRINT RUN 250 SER.#'d SETS
*PRIME/25: .8X TO 2X BASIC INSERTS
PRIME PRINT RUN 25 SER.#'d SETS
1 Plunkett/Branch/Biletnikoff 5.00 12.00
2 Montana/Rice/Young 25.00 50.00
3 Roethlisberger/Bettis/Ward 10.00 25.00
4 Manning/James/Harrison 12.00 30.00
5 Brees/Tomlinson/Gates 5.00 12.00
6 Hasselbeck/Alexander/Jackson 4.00 10.00
7 Delhomme/Davis/Smith 5.00 12.00
8 Elway/Davis/Smith 8.00 20.00
9 Favre/Green/Walker 10.00 25.00
10 Kelly/Thomas/Reed 5.00 12.00

2006 Donruss Threads Footballs

PRINT RUN 250 UNLESS NOTED
19 Anquan Boldin 3.00 8.00
20 Kurt Warner 4.00 10.00
21 Larry Fitzgerald 3.00 8.00
22 Alge Crumpler 3.00 8.00
23 Michael Vick 4.00 10.00
24 Warrick Dunn 3.00 8.00
25 Jamal Lewis/240 4.00 10.00
26 Ray Lewis/170 4.00 10.00
27 Eric Moulds/200 3.00 8.00
28 Josh Reed 2.50 6.00
30 Steve Smith 4.00 10.00
31 Brian Urlacher 4.00 10.00
32 Thomas Jones 3.00 8.00
33 Chad Johnson 3.00 8.00
34 Rudi Johnson 3.00 8.00
35 T.J. Houshmandzadeh 3.00 8.00
36 Reuben Droughns 2.50 6.00
37 Drew Bledsoe 4.00 10.00
38 Keyshawn Johnson 3.00 8.00
39 Jake Plummer 3.00 8.00
40 Rod Smith 3.00 8.00
41 Mike Anderson 3.00 8.00
42 Joey Harrington 3.00 8.00
43 Brett Favre 10.00 25.00
44 Donald Driver/60 4.00 10.00
46 Andre Johnson/140 5.00 12.00
47 David Carr/75 5.00 12.00
48 Domanick Davis/100 5.00 12.00
49 Edgerrin James/200 4.00 10.00
50 Marvin Harrison 4.00 10.00
51 Peyton Manning 8.00 20.00
52 Reggie Wayne/176 4.00 10.00
53 Jimmy Smith 3.00 8.00
54 Tony Gonzalez 3.00 8.00
55 Trent Green 3.00 8.00
56 Eddie Kennison 2.50 6.00
57 Chris Chambers 3.00 8.00
58 Zach Thomas 3.00 8.00
59 Daunte Culpepper/248 4.00 10.00
60 Corey Dillon/115 4.00 10.00
61 Deion Branch 3.00 8.00
62 Tedy Bruschi/88 6.00 15.00
63 Tom Brady 6.00 15.00
64 Deuce McAllister 3.00 8.00
65 Donte Stallworth 3.00 8.00
66 Jeremy Shockey 4.00 10.00
67 Tiki Barber 4.00 10.00
68 Chad Pennington 3.00 8.00
69 Curtis Martin 4.00 10.00
70 Donovan McNabb 4.00 10.00
71 Antwaan Randle El 3.00 8.00
72 Hines Ward 4.00 10.00
75 Keenan McCardell 2.50 6.00
76 LaDainian Tomlinson 4.00 10.00
81 Darrell Jackson 3.00 8.00
82 Joe Jurevicius 2.50 6.00
83 Matt Hasselbeck 4.00 10.00
84 Shaun Alexander 5.00 12.00
86 Marc Bulger 3.00 8.00
87 Steven Jackson 4.00 10.00
88 Torry Holt 3.00 8.00
91 Joey Galloway 3.00 8.00
95 Steve McNair 4.00 10.00

2006 Donruss Threads Generations Gold

GOLD ODDS 1:17 HOB, 1:40 RET
*BLUE/100: .8X TO 2X BASIC INSERTS
BLUE PRINT RUN 100 SER.#'d SETS
1 E.Campbell/C.Brown 1.00 2.50
2 P.Simms/C.Simms 1.00 2.50
3 B.Favre/A.Rodgers 2.50 6.00
4 O.Newsome/B.Edwards 1.00 2.50
5 B.Esiason/C.Palmer 1.25 3.00
6 R.Lott/R.Williams S 1.00 2.50
7 J.Rice/M.Harrison 1.50 4.00
8 C.Martin/E.James 1.00 2.50
9 S.Alexander/J.Jones 1.25 3.00
10 P.Warfield/R.Brown 1.00 2.50
11 T.Thomas/T.Bell 1.00 2.50
12 S.Young/A.Smith QB 1.25 3.00
13 J.Bettis/W.Parker 1.50 4.00
14 R.Moss/C.Johnson 1.00 2.50
15 J.Plunkett/C.Pennington 1.00 2.50
16 P.Manning/E.Manning 2.00 5.00
17 M.Singletary/J.Seau 1.00 2.50
18 P.Warfield/C.Chambers 1.00 2.50
19 J.Elway/B.Roethlisberger 3.00 8.00
20 W.Moon/D.McNabb 1.00 2.50

2006 Donruss Threads Generations Materials

STATED PRINT RUN 250 SER.#'d SETS
*PRIME/25: 1X TO 2.5X BASIC INSERTS
PRIME PRINT RUN 25 SER.#'d SETS
1 E.Campbell/C.Brown 4.00 10.00
2 P.Simms/C.Simms 3.00 8.00
3 B.Favre/A.Rodgers 10.00 25.00
4 O.Newsome/B.Edwards 3.00 8.00
5 B.Esiason/C.Palmer 3.00 8.00
6 R.Lott/R.Williams S 3.00 8.00
7 J.Rice/M.Harrison 8.00 20.00
8 C.Martin/E.James 3.00 8.00
9 S.Alexander/J.Jones 2.50 6.00
10 P.Warfield/R.Brown 3.00 8.00
11 T.Thomas/T.Bell 3.00 8.00
12 S.Young/A.Smith QB 5.00 12.00
13 J.Bettis/W.Parker 4.00 10.00
14 R.Moss/C.Johnson 3.00 8.00
15 J.Plunkett/C.Pennington 3.00 8.00
16 P.Manning/E.Manning 10.00 25.00
17 M.Singletary/J.Seau 4.00 10.00
18 P.Warfield/C.Chambers 3.00 8.00
19 J.Elway/B.Roethlisberger 6.00 15.00
20 W.Moon/D.McNabb 4.00 10.00

2006 Donruss Threads Jerseys

STATED PRINT RUN 19-250
1 Braylon Edwards/100 5.00 12.00
3 Julius Jones/80 5.00 12.00
4 Roy Williams S/250 4.00 10.00
5 Terry Glenn/200 3.00 8.00
6 Ashley Lelie/75 3.00 8.00
7 Kevin Jones/54 6.00 15.00
9 Roy Williams WR/244 4.00 10.00
10 Aaron Rodgers/50 20.00 50.00
11 Tatum Bell/200 3.00 8.00
12 Samkon Gado/25 8.00 20.00
15 Matt Jones/100 4.00 10.00
16 Larry Johnson/200 4.00 10.00
17 Byron Leftwich/250 3.00 8.00
18 Fred Taylor/250 2.50 6.00
19 Anquan Boldin/250 3.00 8.00
20 Kurt Warner/28 6.00 15.00
21 Larry Fitzgerald/250 4.00 10.00
22 Alge Crumpler/55 5.00 12.00
23 Michael Vick/250 4.00 10.00
24 Warrick Dunn/250 3.00 8.00
25 Jamal Lewis/250 3.00 8.00
26 Ray Lewis/75 5.00 12.00
28 Josh Reed/250 3.00 8.00
29 Lee Evans/50 4.00 10.00
30 Steve Smith/225 4.00 10.00
31 Brian Urlacher/250 4.00 10.00
32 Thomas Jones/250 3.00 8.00
33 Chad Johnson/150 4.00 10.00
34 Rudi Johnson/200 3.00 8.00
35 T.J. Houshmandzadeh/50 4.00 10.00
37 Drew Bledsoe/50 6.00 15.00
39 Jake Plummer/250 3.00 8.00
43 Brett Favre/155 10.00 25.00
46 Andre Johnson/182 3.00 8.00
47 David Carr/250 4.00 10.00
48 Domanick Davis/150 4.00 10.00
50 Marvin Harrison/200 4.00 10.00
51 Peyton Manning/92 10.00 25.00
52 Reggie Wayne/125 4.00 10.00
53 Jimmy Smith/115 4.00 10.00
55 Trent Green/50 5.00 12.00
57 Chris Chambers/35 5.00 12.00
58 Zach Thomas/19 6.00 15.00
60 Corey Dillon/43 5.00 12.00
61 Deion Branch/40 5.00 12.00
63 Tom Brady/45 10.00 25.00
64 Deuce McAllister/250 3.00 8.00
65 Donte Stallworth/55 4.00 10.00
66 Jeremy Shockey/250 4.00 10.00
67 Tiki Barber/45 6.00 15.00
68 Chad Pennington/250 3.00 8.00
69 Curtis Martin/190 4.00 10.00
70 Donovan McNabb/250 4.00 10.00
72 Hines Ward/215 4.00 10.00
73 Antonio Gates/200 4.00 10.00
75 Keenan McCardell/250 3.00 8.00
76 LaDainian Tomlinson/50 6.00 15.00
77 Alex Smith QB/55 6.00 15.00
81 Darrell Jackson/200 3.00 8.00
83 Matt Hasselbeck/43 6.00 15.00
84 Shaun Alexander/200 4.00 10.00
86 Marc Bulger/215 3.00 8.00
87 Steven Jackson/200 4.00 10.00
88 Torry Holt/45 5.00 12.00
89 Cadillac Williams/45 5.00 12.00
92 Michael Clayton/250 3.00 8.00
93 Chris Brown/45 4.00 10.00
94 Drew Bennett/250 3.00 8.00
95 Steve McNair/250 4.00 10.00
97 Clinton Portis/150 5.00 12.00
102 Ronnie Brown/150 4.00 10.00
105 Troy Williamson/107 4.00 10.00
111 LaMont Jordan/45 5.00 12.00
112 Randy Moss/55 6.00 15.00
113 Jerry Porter/163 3.00 8.00
114 Brian Westbrook/215 3.00 8.00
116 Joe Horn/250 3.00 8.00
117 Eli Manning/137 8.00 20.00
120 Ben Roethlisberger/40 15.00 40.00
121 Willie Parker/35 6.00 15.00
127 Dante Hall/68 4.00 10.00
135 Kyle Boller/29 4.00 10.00
137 Willis McGahee/107 5.00 12.00
139 Jake Delhomme/45 6.00 15.00
141 Keary Colbert/244 2.50 6.00
142 Stephen Davis/45 5.00 12.00
143 Todd Heap/250 3.00 8.00
144 J.P. Losman/37 4.00 10.00
145 Muhsin Muhammad/250 3.00 8.00
146 Carson Palmer/189 4.00 10.00
147 Cedric Benson/55 6.00 15.00
148 Rex Grossman/215 3.00 8.00

2006 Donruss Threads Jerseys Prime

COMMON CARD 5.00 12.00
SEMISTARS 6.00 15.00
UNLISTED STARS 8.00 20.00
PRIME PRINT RUN 5-25
SERIAL #'d UNDER 25 NOT PRICED
16 Larry Johnson 8.00 20.00
43 Brett Favre 20.00 50.00
51 Peyton Manning 15.00 40.00
63 Tom Brady 12.00 30.00
76 LaDainian Tomlinson 8.00 20.00
120 Ben Roethlisberger/24 30.00 80.00

2006 Donruss Threads Pro Gridiron Kings Gold

GOLD ODDS 1:12 HOB, 1:17 RET
UNPRICED FRAMED BLACK SER.#'d TO 10
*FRAMED BLUE/50: 1.2X TO 3X
FRAMED BLUE PRINT RUN 50 SER.#'d SETS
*FRAMED GREEN/25: 1.5X TO 4X
FRAMED GREEN PRINT RUN 25 SER.#'d SETS
*FRAMED RED/100: 1X TO 2.5X
FRAMED RED PRINT RUN 100 SER.#'d SETS
*GOLD HOLOFOIL/100: 1X TO 2.5X
GOLD HOLO.PRINT RUN 100 SER.#'d SETS
*PLATINUM/25: 1.5X TO 4X
PLATINUM PRINT RUN 25 SER.#'d SETS
*SILVER HOLOFOIL/250 .6X TO 1.5X
SILVER HOLO.PRINT RUN 250 SER.#'d SETS
1 Alex Smith QB .75 2.00
2 Andre Johnson .75 2.00
3 Ben Roethlisberger 1.25 3.00
4 Brett Favre 2.00 5.00
5 Cadillac Williams .75 2.00
6 Carson Palmer .75 2.00
7 Cedric Benson .60 1.50
8 Chad Johnson .60 1.50
9 Clinton Portis .60 1.50
10 Corey Dillon .60 1.50
11 Curtis Martin .75 2.00
12 Darrell Jackson .75 2.00
13 Domanick Davis .60 1.50
14 Donovan McNabb .75 2.00
15 Drew Bledsoe .75 2.00
16 Edgerrin James .75 2.00
17 Eli Manning .75 2.00
18 Hines Ward .75 2.00
19 Isaac Bruce 1.00 2.50
20 J.P. Losman .75 2.00
21 Jake Delhomme .60 1.50
22 Javon Walker .75 2.00
23 Jeremy Shockey .60 1.50
24 Jerome Bettis 1.00 2.50
25 Jimmy Smith .75 2.00
26 Julius Jones .60 1.50
27 Kevin Jones .60 1.50
28 Keyshawn Johnson .75 2.00
29 LaDainian Tomlinson 1.00 2.50
30 Larry Fitzgerald .75 2.00
31 Larry Johnson .60 1.50
32 Lee Evans .75 2.00
33 Marshall Faulk .75 2.00
34 Marvin Harrison .75 2.00
35 Matt Hasselbeck .60 1.50
36 Matt Jones .60 1.50
37 Michael Vick .75 2.00
38 Peyton Manning 2.50 6.00
39 Randy Moss .75 2.00
40 Reggie Brown .60 1.50
41 Reggie Wayne .75 2.00
42 Antonio Gates 1.00 2.50
43 Rod Smith .75 2.00
44 Ronnie Brown .75 2.00
45 Roy Williams WR .60 1.50
46 Rudi Johnson .60 1.50
47 Samkon Gado .60 1.50
48 Shaun Alexander .60 1.50
49 Stephen Davis .60 1.50
50 Steve Smith 1.00 2.50
51 Steven Jackson .60 1.50
52 T.J. Houshmandzadeh .60 1.50
53 Tatum Bell .60 1.50
54 Tiki Barber .75 2.00
55 Tom Brady 3.00 8.00
56 Tony Gonzalez .75 2.00
57 Torry Holt .75 2.00
58 Trent Green .60 1.50
59 Willie Parker .75 2.00
60 Willis McGahee .60 1.50

2006 Donruss Threads Pro Gridiron Kings Autographs

STATED PRINT RUN 5-25
UNPRICED MATERIAL AU PRINT RUN 5-20
UNPRICED MAT.PRIME AU PRINT RUN 2-10
13 Domanick Davis/25 10.00 25.00
40 Reggie Brown/25 10.00 25.00
46 Rudi Johnson/25 10.00 25.00
52 T.J. Houshmandzadeh/25 10.00 25.00
59 Willie Parker/25 20.00 50.00

2006 Donruss Threads Pro Gridiron Kings Materials

STATED PRINT RUN 90-250
*PRIME/15-25: 1X TO 2.5X JSY/150-250
*PRIME/15-25: .8X TO 2X JSY/90-147
PRIME SER.#'d UNDER 25 NOT PRICED
1 Alex Smith QB/125 4.00 10.00
2 Andre Johnson/137 4.00 10.00
3 Ben Roethlisberger/125 12.00 30.00
4 Brett Favre/250 8.00 20.00
5 Cadillac Williams/125 4.00 10.00
6 Carson Palmer/137 4.00 10.00
7 Cedric Benson/137 3.00 8.00
8 Chad Johnson/147 3.00 8.00
9 Clinton Portis/115 3.00 8.00
10 Corey Dillon/175 2.50 6.00
11 Curtis Martin/137 4.00 10.00
12 Darrell Jackson/175 3.00 8.00
13 Domanick Davis/137 3.00 8.00
14 Donovan McNabb/137 4.00 10.00
15 Drew Bledsoe/125 4.00 10.00
16 Edgerrin James/250 3.00 8.00
17 Eli Manning/155 3.00 8.00
18 Hines Ward/137 4.00 10.00
19 Isaac Bruce/250 4.00 10.00
20 J.P. Losman/90 4.00 10.00
21 Jake Delhomme/125 3.00 8.00
22 Javon Walker/230 3.00 8.00
23 Jeremy Shockey/250 2.50 6.00
24 Jerome Bettis/200 4.00 10.00
25 Jimmy Smith/137 4.00 10.00
26 Julius Jones/125 3.00 8.00
27 Kevin Jones/137 3.00 8.00
28 Keyshawn Johnson/230 3.00 8.00
29 LaDainian Tomlinson/137 5.00 12.00
30 Larry Fitzgerald/250 3.00 8.00
31 Larry Johnson/125 3.00 8.00
32 Lee Evans/125 4.00 10.00
33 Marshall Faulk/250 3.00 8.00
34 Marvin Harrison/250 3.00 8.00
35 Matt Hasselbeck/137 3.00 8.00
36 Matt Jones/125 3.00 8.00
37 Michael Vick/250 3.00 8.00
38 Peyton Manning/250 10.00 25.00
39 Randy Moss/125 4.00 10.00
40 Reggie Brown/125 3.00 8.00
41 Reggie Wayne/137 4.00 10.00
42 Antonio Gates/250 4.00 10.00
43 Rod Smith/250 3.00 8.00
44 Ronnie Brown/125 4.00 10.00
45 Roy Williams WR/225 2.50 6.00
46 Rudi Johnson/125 3.00 8.00
47 Samkon Gado/125 3.00 8.00
48 Shaun Alexander/125 3.00 8.00
49 Stephen Davis/137 3.00 8.00
50 Steve Smith/125 5.00 12.00
51 Steven Jackson/125 3.00 8.00
52 T.J. Houshmandzadeh/125 3.00 8.00
53 Tatum Bell/125 3.00 8.00
54 Tiki Barber/125 4.00 10.00
55 Tom Brady/250 12.00 30.00
56 Tony Gonzalez/137 4.00 10.00
57 Torry Holt/137 4.00 10.00
58 Trent Green/150 2.50 6.00
59 Willie Parker/125 4.00 10.00
60 Willis McGahee/137 3.00 8.00

2006 Donruss Threads Rookie Autographs

STATED PRINT RUN 100 UNLESS NOTED
151 Mathias Kiwanuka/50 10.00 25.00
152 Ingle Martin 8.00 20.00
153 Reggie McNeal Â• 6.00 15.00
154 Bruce Gradkowski 8.00 20.00
155 D.J. Shockley 8.00 20.00
156 Paul Pinegar 6.00 15.00
157 Brandon Kirsch 8.00 20.00
158 P.J. Daniels 6.00 15.00
159 Marques Hagans 6.00 15.00
160 Jerome Harrison 6.00 15.00
161 Wali Lundy 6.00 15.00
162 Cedric Humes 6.00 15.00
163 Quinton Ganther 6.00 15.00
164 Mike Bell 6.00 15.00
166 Anthony Fasano 6.00 15.00
167 Tony Scheffler 10.00 25.00
168 Leonard Pope 10.00 25.00
169 David Thomas 6.00 15.00
170 Dominique Byrd 6.00 15.00
171 Devin Hester 12.00 30.00
172 Willie Reid 8.00 20.00
173 Brad Smith 8.00 20.00
174 Cory Rodgers 6.00 15.00
175 Domenik Hixon 10.00 25.00
176 Jeremy Bloom 6.00 15.00
177 Jonathan Orr 8.00 20.00
178 Jeff Webb 8.00 20.00
179 Ethan Kilmer 8.00 20.00
180 Bennie Brazell 8.00 20.00
181 David Anderson 8.00 20.00
182 Kevin McMahan 8.00 20.00
183 Anthony Mix 8.00 20.00
184 D'Brickashaw Ferguson 6.00 15.00
185 Kamerion Wimbley 8.00 20.00
186 Tamba Hali 10.00 25.00
187 Haloti Ngata 8.00 20.00
188 Brodrick Bunkley 8.00 20.00
189 John McCargo 6.00 15.00
190 Claude Wroten 6.00 15.00
191 Gabe Watson 6.00 15.00
192 D'Qwell Jackson 6.00 15.00
193 Abdul Hodge 6.00 15.00
194 Ernie Sims 6.00 15.00
195 Chad Greenway 10.00 25.00
196 Bobby Carpenter 6.00 15.00
197 Manny Lawson 8.00 20.00
198 DeMeco Ryans 8.00 20.00
199 Rocky McIntosh 6.00 15.00
200 Thomas Howard 6.00 15.00
201 Jon Alston 6.00 15.00
202 A.J. Nicholson 6.00 15.00
203 Tye Hill 6.00 15.00
205 Johnathan Joseph 8.00 20.00
206 Kelly Jennings 8.00 20.00
207 Ashton Youboty 6.00 15.00
208 Alan Zemaitis 6.00 15.00
209 Jason Allen 8.00 20.00
210 Cedric Griffin 8.00 20.00
211 Ko Simpson 8.00 20.00
212 Pat Watkins 8.00 20.00
213 Donte Whitner 8.00 20.00
214 Bernard Pollard 8.00 20.00
215 Darnell Bing 8.00 20.00

2006 Donruss Threads Rookie Collection Materials

STATED PRINT RUN 500 SER.#'d SETS
*PRIME/25: 1X TO 2.5X BASIC INSERTS
PRIME PRINT RUN 25 SER.#'d SETS
1 Chad Jackson 2.00 5.00
2 Laurence Maroney 2.00 5.00
3 Tarvaris Jackson 2.00 5.00
4 Michael Huff 2.50 6.00
5 Mario Williams 3.00 8.00
6 Marcedes Lewis 2.00 5.00
7 Maurice Drew 3.00 8.00
8 Vince Young 2.00 5.00
9 LenDale White 2.00 5.00
10 Reggie Bush 3.00 8.00
11 Matt Leinart 2.00 5.00
12 Michael Robinson 2.00 5.00
13 Vernon Davis 2.50 6.00
14 Brandon Williams 2.00 5.00
15 Derek Hagan 2.50 6.00
16 Jason Avant 2.00 5.00
17 Brandon Marshall 4.00 10.00
18 Omar Jacobs 2.00 5.00
19 Santonio Holmes 2.50 6.00
20 Jerious Norwood 2.00 5.00
21 Demetrius Williams 2.00 5.00
22 Sinorice Moss 2.00 5.00
23 Leon Washington 2.00 5.00
24 Kellen Clemens 2.00 5.00
25 A.J. Hawk 2.50 6.00
26 Maurice Stovall 2.00 5.00
27 DeAngelo Williams 2.50 6.00
28 Charlie Whitehurst 2.00 5.00
29 Travis Wilson 2.00 5.00
30 Joe Klopfenstein 2.00 5.00
31 Brian Calhoun 2.00 5.00

2006 Donruss Threads Rookie Collection Material Autographs

STATED PRINT RUN 5-25
UNPRICED PRIME AU PRINT RUN 3-5
SERIAL #'d UNDER 25 NOT PRICED
3 Tarvaris Jackson/25 25.00 60.00

6 Marcedes Lewis/25	12.00	30.00
12 Michael Robinson/25	15.00	40.00

2006 Donruss Threads Rookie Collection Materials Combo

STATED PRINT RUN 500 SER.#'d SETS
*PRIME/25: 1X TO 2.5X BASIC INSERTS
PRIME PRINT RUN 25 SER.#'d SETS

1 V.Young/L.White	2.50	6.00
2 M.Lewis/M.Drew	4.00	10.00
3 C.Jackson/L.Maroney	2.50	6.00
4 O.Jacobs/S.Holmes	3.00	8.00
5 Moss/Dem.Williams	2.50	6.00
6 M.Robinson/B.Williams	2.50	6.00
7 R.Bush/M.Leinart	4.00	10.00
8 V.Davis/J.Klopfenstein	3.00	8.00
9 M.Williams/A.Hawk	4.00	10.00
10 B.Marshall/M.Stovall	5.00	12.00
11 T.Jackson/C.Whitehurst	2.50	6.00
12 D.Hagan/J.Avant	3.00	8.00
13 M.Huff/T.Wilson	3.00	8.00
14 K.Clemens/L.Washington	2.50	6.00
15 DeA.Williams/Calhoun	3.00	8.00

2006 Donruss Threads Rookie Collection Materials Triple

STATED PRINT RUN 500 SER.#'d SETS
*PRIME/25: .8X TO 2X BASIC INSERTS
PRIME PRINT RUN 25 SER.#'d SETS

1 Bush/Leinart/White	6.00	15.00
2 Robinson/Davis/Williams	5.00	12.00
3 Young/Huff/Wilson	5.00	12.00
4 Moss/Washington/Clemens	4.00	10.00
5 Lewis/Stovall/Klopfenstein	4.00	10.00
6 Holmes/Marshall/Williams	8.00	20.00
7 Jackson/Whitehurst/Jacobs	4.00	10.00
8 Drew/Williams/Norwood	6.00	15.00
9 Jackson/Avant/Maroney	4.00	10.00
10 Williams/Hawk/Hagan	6.00	15.00

2006 Donruss Threads Rookie Collection Materials Quad

STATED PRINT RUN 100 SER.#'d SETS
*PRIME: .8X TO 2X BASIC INSERTS
PRIME PRINT RUN 25 SER.#'d SETS

1 Young/White/Bush/Leinart	10.00	25.00
2 Davis/Holmes/Jackson/Moss	10.00	25.00
3 Drew/DeA.Will/Maron/Calhn	15.00	40.00
4 Jcksn/Jcbs/Clem/Whthrst	12.00	30.00

2007 Donruss Threads

This 294-card set was released in August, 2007. The set was issued into the hobby in five-card packs, with a $4 SRP, which came 24 packs to a box. Cards numbered 1-150 feature veterans while cards numbered 151-294 feature 2007 NFL rookies. The Rookie Cards numbered 151-225 were all issued to a stated print run of 999 serial numbered sets and cards 226-294 were signed by the player and were issued to stated print runs between 100 and 999 serial numbered copies. A few players did not return their signatures in time for pack out and we have notated those cards with an EXCH in our checklist.

COMP.SET w/o RC's (150) 10.00 25.00
226-250 AU ROOKIE PRINT RUN 198-999
251-294 AU ROOKIE PRINT RUN 100-210

1 Anquan Boldin	.25	.60
2 Larry Fitzgerald	.30	.75
3 Alge Crumpler	.30	.75
4 Michael Vick	.30	.75
5 Steve McNair	.30	.75
6 Ray Lewis	.40	1.00
7 Keyshawn Johnson	.30	.75
8 Steve Smith	.30	.75
9 Brian Urlacher	.40	1.00
10 Muhsin Muhammad	.25	.60
11 Chad Johnson	.25	.60
12 Rudi Johnson	.25	.60
13 T.J. Houshmandzadeh	.25	.60
14 Terry Glenn	.30	.75
15 Terrell Owens	.30	.75
16 Jon Kitna	.25	.60
17 Brett Favre	.75	2.00
18 Peyton Manning	1.00	2.50
19 Fred Taylor	.25	.60
20 Eddie Kennison	.25	.60
21 Larry Johnson	.25	.60
22 Tony Gonzalez	.30	.75
23 Trent Green	.25	.60
24 Chris Chambers	.25	.60
25 Marty Booker	.25	.60
26 Tom Brady	1.25	3.00
27 Donte Stallworth	.30	.75
28 Deuce McAllister	.30	.75
29 Drew Brees	.40	1.00
30 Reuben Droughns	.30	.75
31 Jeremy Shockey	.25	.60
32 Plaxico Burress	.25	.60
33 Chad Pennington	.25	.60
34 Jerricho Cotchery	.25	.60
35 Laveranues Coles	.25	.60
36 LaMont Jordan	.30	.75
37 Brian Westbrook UER	.25	.60
38 Donovan McNabb	.30	.75
39 Hines Ward	.30	.75
40 Antonio Gates	.40	1.00
41 LaDainian Tomlinson	.40	1.00
42 Arnaz Battle	.25	.60
43 Darrell Jackson	.25	.60
44 Deion Branch	.25	.60
45 Matt Hasselbeck	.25	.60
46 Jerramy Stevens	.25	.60
47 Shaun Alexander	.25	.60
48 Isaac Bruce	.40	1.00
49 Marc Bulger	.25	.60
50 Drew Bennett	.25	.60
51 Torry Holt	.30	.75
52 Joey Galloway	.30	.75
53 Mike Alstott	.25	.60
54 Travis Henry	.30	.75
55 Clinton Portis	.25	.60
56 Santana Moss	.30	.75
57 Edgerrin James	.30	.75
58 Matt Leinart	.25	.60
59 Jerious Norwood	.25	.60
60 Warrick Dunn	.25	.60
61 Mark Clayton	.25	.60
62 J.P. Losman	.25	.60
63 Josh Reed	.25	.60
64 Lee Evans	.30	.75
65 DeAngelo Williams	.25	.60
66 DeShaun Foster	.30	.75
67 Jake Delhomme	.25	.60
68 Bernard Berrian	.25	.60
69 Cedric Benson	.25	.60
70 Rex Grossman	.25	.60
71 Carson Palmer	.30	.75
72 Braylon Edwards	.25	.60
73 Kellen Winslow	.25	.60
74 Charlie Frye	.30	.75
75 Julius Jones	.25	.60
76 Marion Barber	.30	.75
77 Javon Walker	.30	.75
78 Jay Cutler	.25	.60
79 Mike Bell	.30	.75
80 Donald Driver	.30	.75
81 Greg Jennings	.25	.60
82 Andre Johnson	.30	.75
83 Matt Schaub	.25	.60
84 Wali Lundy	.25	.60
85 Joseph Addai	.25	.60
86 Marvin Harrison	.30	.75
87 Kevin Jones	.25	.60
88 Roy Williams WR	.25	.60
89 Mike Furrey	.30	.75
90 A.J. Hawk	.25	.60
91 Reggie Wayne	.30	.75
92 Dallas Clark	.30	.75
93 Byron Leftwich	.25	.60
94 Maurice Jones-Drew	.25	.60
95 Reggie Williams	.30	.75
96 Tony Romo	.50	1.25
97 Daunte Culpepper	.30	.75
98 Ronnie Brown	.25	.60
99 Chester Taylor	.25	.60
100 Travis Taylor	.25	.60
101 Ben Watson	.25	.60
102 Laurence Maroney	.30	.75
103 Bo Scaife	.25	.60
104 Peerless Price	.25	.60
105 Marques Colston	.25	.60
106 Reggie Bush	.25	.60
107 Brandon Jacobs	.25	.60
108 Eli Manning	.30	.75
109 Leon Washington	.25	.60
110 Kevan Barlow	.30	.75
111 Randy Moss	.30	.75
112 Troy Polamalu	.40	1.00
113 Willie Parker	.30	.75
114 Santonio Holmes	.25	.60
115 Philip Rivers	.40	1.00
116 Shawne Merriman	.25	.60
117 Alex Smith QB	.30	.75
118 Frank Gore	.30	.75
119 Vernon Davis	.25	.60
120 Reggie Brown	.25	.60
121 Ben Roethlisberger	.40	1.00
122 Steven Jackson	.25	.60
123 Bruce Gradkowski	.25	.60
124 Cadillac Williams	.30	.75
125 Chris Cooley	.25	.60
126 Michael Jenkins	.25	.60
127 Demetrius Williams	.25	.60
128 Roy Williams S	.25	.60
129 Owen Daniels	.25	.60
130 Hank Baskett	.30	.75
131 Marcedes Lewis	.25	.60
132 Brandon Marshall	.30	.75
133 John Madsen	.25	.60
134 Michael Huff	.30	.75
135 Joe Klopfenstein	.25	.60
136 Vincent Jackson	.25	.60
137 Todd Heap	.25	.60
138 Tarvaris Jackson	.25	.60
139 Troy Williamson	.25	.60
140 Ronald Curry	.25	.60
141 Ahman Green	.30	.75
142 LenDale White	.30	.75
143 Vince Young	.25	.60
144 Thomas Jones	.25	.60
145 Jamal Lewis	.30	.75
146 Joe Horn	.25	.60
147 Tatum Bell	.25	.60
148 Willis McGahee	.25	.60
149 Jason Campbell	.25	.60
150 Ladell Betts	.25	.60
151 John Broussard RC	2.00	5.00
152 Michael Allan RC	1.50	4.00
153 Tyler Thigpen RC	2.50	6.00
154 Chandler Williams RC	2.00	5.00
155 Eric Weddle RC	2.00	5.00
156 Derek Stanley RC	2.00	5.00
157 Justise Hairston RC	2.00	5.00
158 Johnathan Holland RC	2.00	5.00
159 Legedu Naanee RC	2.00	5.00
160 Courtney Taylor RC	1.50	4.00
161 David Irons RC	1.50	4.00
162 Joel Filani RC	1.50	4.00
163 H.B. Blades RC	1.50	4.00
164 Rufus Alexander RC	1.50	4.00
165 Roy Hall RC	2.50	6.00
166 Eric Frampton RC	2.00	5.00
167 Tim Shaw RC	2.00	5.00
168 Tymere Zimmerman RC	1.50	4.00
169 Jeff Rowe RC	1.50	4.00
170 Josh Gattis RC	1.50	4.00
171 Brandon Myles RC	2.00	5.00
172 Earl Everett RC	1.50	4.00
173 Steve Breaston RC	1.50	4.00
174 Ryan McBean RC	2.50	6.00
175 Scott Chandler RC	2.50	6.00
176 Chris Davis RC	1.50	4.00
177 Fred Bennett RC	1.50	4.00
178 Ryne Robinson RC	2.00	5.00
179 Zak DeOssie RC	2.00	5.00
180 Dwayne Wright RC	1.50	4.00
181 A.J. Davis RC	1.50	4.00
182 Ray McDonald RC	2.00	5.00
183 Daymeion Hughes RC	1.50	4.00
184 Michael Okwo RC	2.00	5.00
185 Aaron Rouse RC	1.50	4.00
186 Stewart Bradley RC	1.50	4.00
187 Jonathan Wade RC	1.50	4.00
188 Charles Johnson RC	1.50	4.00
189 Demarcus Tank Tyler RC	1.50	4.00
190 Mike Walker RC	2.50	6.00
191 James Jones RC	1.50	4.00
192 Matt Spaeth RC	2.50	6.00
193 Laurent Robinson RC	2.50	6.00
194 Jacoby Jones RC	1.50	4.00
195 Marcus McCauley RC	1.50	4.00
196 Buster Davis RC	2.00	5.00
197 Quentin Moses RC	1.50	4.00
198 Sabby Piscitelli RC	1.50	4.00
199 Dan Bazuin RC	2.00	5.00
200 Ikaika Alama-Francis RC	2.50	6.00
201 Victor Abiamiri RC	1.50	4.00
202 Tim Crowder RC	2.00	5.00
203 Josh Wilson RC	2.00	5.00
204 Eric Wright RC	1.50	4.00
205 David Harris RC	1.50	4.00
206 LaMarr Woodley RC	3.00	8.00
207 Chris Houston RC	1.50	4.00
208 Zach Miller RC	1.50	4.00
209 Aaron Fairooz RC	2.00	5.00
210 Alan Branch RC	1.50	4.00
211 Anthony Spencer RC	2.00	5.00
212 Jon Beason RC	1.50	4.00
213 Brandon Meriweather RC	2.00	5.00
214 Reggie Nelson RC	1.50	4.00
215 Aaron Ross RC	1.50	4.00
216 Michael Griffin RC	1.50	4.00
217 Ronnie McGill RC	2.00	5.00
218 Jarvis Moss RC	1.50	4.00
219 Darrelle Revis RC	2.00	5.00
220 Lawrence Timmons RC	2.50	6.00
221 Adam Carriker RC	1.50	4.00
222 Amobi Okoye RC	2.00	5.00
223 Jamaal Anderson RC	2.00	5.00
224 Syvelle Newton RC	2.00	5.00
225 Levi Brown RC	1.50	4.00
226 Chansi Stuckey AU/499 RC	5.00	12.00
227 Nate Ilaoa AU/999 RC	4.00	10.00
228 Brandon Siler AU/198 RC	4.00	10.00
229 Jason Snelling AU/999 RC	6.00	15.00
230 Kenneth Darby AU/999 RC	3.00	8.00
231 A.Bradshaw AU/999 RC	5.00	12.00
232 Thomas Clayton AU/763 RC	4.00	10.00
233 D.Baker AU/499 RC UER	4.00	10.00
234 Ben Patrick AU/849 RC	4.00	10.00
235 Jordan Kent AU/999 RC	4.00	10.00
236 Jordan Palmer AU/299 RC	5.00	12.00
237 Chris Leak AU/299 RC	4.00	10.00
238 Jon Cornish AU/876 RC	4.00	10.00
239 J.Zabransky AU/299 RC	4.00	10.00
240 R.McKnight AU/999 RC	3.00	8.00
241 Selvin Young AU/999 RC	8.00	20.00
242 Gary Russell AU/981 RC	4.00	10.00
243 Jerard Rabb AU/999 RC	4.00	10.00
244 J.Cornelius AU/581 RC	5.00	12.00
245 A.Coleman AU/781 RC	4.00	10.00
246 Danny Ware AU/999 RC	5.00	12.00
247 David Ball AU/999 RC	3.00	8.00
248 D'Juan Woods AU/450 RC	4.00	10.00
249 S.Steptoe AU/676 RC	4.00	10.00
250 Jarrett Hicks AU/999 RC	4.00	10.00
251 T.Edwards/140 AU RC	12.00	30.00
252 M.Lynch/100 AU RC	30.00	80.00
253 Chris Henry/105 AU RC	12.00	30.00
254 Paul Williams/200 AU RC	12.00	30.00
255 Sidney Rice/100 AU RC	15.00	40.00
256 A.Peterson/120 AU RC	150.00	300.00
257 Drew Stanton/140 AU RC	12.00	30.00
258 C.Johnson/105 AU RC	40.00	80.00
259 Yamon Figurs/150 AU RC	12.00	30.00
260 Troy Smith/100 AU RC	12.00	30.00
261 Brian Leonard/210 AU RC	12.00	30.00
262 Greg Olsen/125 AU RC	20.00	50.00
263 Kenny Irons/100 AU RC	12.00	30.00
264 Joe Thomas/120 AU RC	20.00	50.00
265 Brady Quinn/125 AU RC	12.00	30.00
266 B.Jackson/140 AU RC	12.00	30.00
267 Steve Smith/150 AU RC	25.00	60.00
268 Dwayne Jarrett/140 AU RC	15.00	40.00
269 Ted Ginn/100 AU RC	15.00	40.00
270 John Beck/120 AU RC	12.00	30.00
271 Lorenzo Booker/150 AU RC	15.00	40.00
272 Antonio Pittman/105 AU RC	12.00	30.00
273 R.Meachem/140 AU RC	15.00	40.00
274 Dwayne Bowe/100 AU RC	12.00	30.00
275 A.Gonzalez/160 AU RC	12.00	30.00
276 J.Russell/140 AU RC	25.00	60.00
277 Michael Bush/120 AU RC	12.00	30.00
278 J.Lee Higgins/175 AU RC	12.00	30.00
279 Kevin Kolb/100 AU RC	15.00	40.00
280 Gaines Adams/150 AU RC	15.00	40.00
281 Patrick Willis/150 AU RC	20.00	50.00
282 Jason Hill/120 AU RC	12.00	30.00
283 I.Stanback/200 AU RC	12.00	30.00
284 Kolby Smith/125 AU RC	12.00	30.00
285 Leon Hall/120 AU RC	12.00	30.00
286 Darius Walker/180 AU RC	12.00	30.00
287 D.Clowney/175 AU RC	12.00	30.00
288 LaRon Landry/150 AU RC	20.00	50.00
289 Paul Posluszny/180 AU RC	12.00	30.00
290 Garrett Wolfe/125 AU RC	12.00	30.00
291 Tony Hunt/120 AU RC		
293 D.Wynn/120 AU RC	12.00	30.00
294 Aundrae Allison/175 AU RC	12.00	30.00

2007 Donruss Threads Bronze Holofoil

*VETS 1-150: 2X TO 5X BASIC CARDS
*ROOKIES 151-225: .5X TO 1.2X BASIC CARDS
STATED PRINT RUN 250 SER.#'d SETS

2007 Donruss Threads Gold Holofoil

*VETS 1-150: 4X TO 10X BASIC CARDS
*ROOKIES 151-225: 1X TO 2.5X BASIC CARDS
STATED PRINT RUN 50 SER.#'d SETS

2007 Donruss Threads Platinum Holofoil

*VETS 1-150: 6X TO 15X BASIC CARDS
*ROOKIES 151-225: 1.5X TO 4X BASIC CARDS
STATED PRINT RUN 25 SER.#'d SETS

2007 Donruss Threads Retail Blue

*VETS 1-150: 2X TO 5X BASIC CARDS
*ROOKIES 151-225: .5X TO 1.2X BASIC CARDS
STATED PRINT RUN 350 SER.#'d SETS

2007 Donruss Threads Retail Rookies

*ROOKIES 151-225: .4X TO 1X BASIC CARDS
STATED PRINT RUN 999 SER.#'d SETS
PRODUCED ON WHITE CARD STOCK

2007 Donruss Threads Retail Green

*VETS 1-150: 2.5X TO 6X BASIC CARDS
*ROOKIES 151-225: .6X TO 1.5X BASIC CARDS
STATED PRINT RUN 200 SER.#'d SETS

2007 Donruss Threads Retail Red

*VETS 1-150: 1.5X TO 4X BASIC CARDS
*ROOKIES 151-225: .4X TO 1X BASIC CARDS

2007 Donruss Threads Silver Holofoil

*VETS 1-150: 3X TO 8X BASIC CARDS
*ROOKIES 151-225: .8X TO 2X BASIC CARDS
STATED PRINT RUN 100 SER.#'d SETS

2007 Donruss Threads Century Collection Materials

STATED PRINT RUN 16-250 SER.#'d SETS
*PRIME/25: .8X TO 2X JSY/190-250
*PRIME/25: .6X TO 1.5X JSY/16-77
*PRIME/10: .8X TO 2X JSY/100
PRIME PRINT RUN 10-25

1 Jerry Rice/250	6.00	15.00
2 Roger Craig Shoe/77	10.00	25.00
3 Dan Hampton/250	8.00	20.00
4 Jim McMahon/16	8.00	20.00
5 Walter Payton/200	12.50	30.00
6 John Elway/250	8.00	20.00
7 Dan Fouts/100	5.00	12.00
8 Jan Stenerud/250	6.00	15.00
9 Roger Staubach/250	8.00	20.00
10 Mark Duper/190	4.00	10.00
11 Lawrence Taylor/200	5.00	12.00
12 John Hannah/100	6.00	15.00
13 Tim Brown/250	4.00	10.00
14 Jack Youngblood/250	4.00	10.00
15 John Riggins/250	5.00	12.00

2007 Donruss Threads Century Legends Gold

GOLD STATED ODDS 1:18
*BLUE: .6X TO 1.5X GOLD
BLUE PRINT RUN 100 SER.#'d SETS

1 Brett Favre	2.50	6.00
2 Tom Brady	4.00	10.00
3 Peyton Manning	3.00	8.00
4 LaDainian Tomlinson	1.25	3.00
5 Gale Sayers	2.00	5.00
6 Jim Kelly	2.00	5.00
7 Jim Brown	2.50	6.00
8 Lance Alworth	1.50	4.00
9 Troy Aikman	2.50	6.00
10 Sam Huff	1.50	4.00
11 Warren Moon	2.00	5.00
12 Bo Jackson	2.50	6.00
13 Marcus Allen	2.00	5.00
14 Eric Dickerson	1.50	4.00
15 Fran Tarkenton	2.00	5.00

2007 Donruss Threads Century Legends Materials

STATED PRINT RUN 250 SER.#'d SETS
*PRIME/25: 1X TO 2.5X BASIC INSERTS
*PRIME/10-15: 1.2X TO 3X BASIC INSERTS
PRIME PRINT RUN 6-25

1 Brett Favre	8.00	20.00
2 Tom Brady	12.00	30.00
3 Peyton Manning	10.00	25.00
4 LaDainian Tomlinson	4.00	10.00
5 Gale Sayers	5.00	12.00
6 Jim Kelly	5.00	12.00
7 Jim Brown	6.00	15.00
8 Lance Alworth/175	6.00	15.00
9 Troy Aikman	6.00	15.00
10 Sam Huff	4.00	10.00
11 Warren Moon	5.00	12.00
12 Bo Jackson	6.00	15.00
13 Marcus Allen	5.00	12.00
14 Eric Dickerson	4.00	10.00
15 Fran Tarkenton	5.00	12.00

2007 Donruss Threads Century Stars Gold

GOLD STATED ODDS 1:13
*BLUE: .8X TO 2X BASIC INSERTS
BLUE PRINT RUN 100 SER.#'d SETS

1 Chad Johnson	.50	1.25
2 Brian Westbrook	.50	1.25
3 Tom Brady	2.50	6.00
4 Ben Roethlisberger	.75	2.00
5 Reggie Wayne	.60	1.50
6 Torry Holt	.60	1.50
7 Steven Jackson	.50	1.25
8 Eli Manning	.60	1.50
9 Willie Parker	.60	1.50
10 Matt Hasselbeck	.50	1.25
11 Michael Vick	.60	1.50
12 Terrell Owens	.60	1.50
13 Steve Smith	.60	1.50
14 Steve McNair	.60	1.50
15 Shaun Alexander	.50	1.25
16 Peyton Manning	2.00	5.00
17 Marvin Harrison	.60	1.50
18 Warrick Dunn	.50	1.25
19 Hines Ward	.60	1.50
20 Donovan McNabb	.60	1.50

2007 Donruss Threads Century Stars Materials

STATED PRINT RUN 250 SER.#'d SETS
*PRIME/25: .8X TO 2X BASIC JSY/170-250
*PRIME/25: .4X TO 1X BASIC JSY/32
*PRIME/25: .3X TO .8X BASIC JSY/12
PRIME PRINT RUN 25 SER.#'d SETS

1 Chad Johnson	1.50	4.00
2 Brian Westbrook/170	1.50	4.00
3 Tom Brady	8.00	20.00
4 Ben Roethlisberger	2.50	6.00
5 Reggie Wayne	2.00	5.00
6 Torry Holt	2.00	5.00
7 Steven Jackson/12	5.00	12.00
8 Eli Manning	2.00	5.00
9 Willie Parker/32	5.00	12.00
10 Matt Hasselbeck	1.50	4.00
11 Michael Vick	2.00	5.00
12 Terrell Owens	2.00	5.00
13 Steve Smith	2.00	5.00
14 Steve McNair	2.00	5.00
15 Shaun Alexander	1.50	4.00
16 Peyton Manning	6.00	15.00
17 Marvin Harrison	2.00	5.00
18 Warrick Dunn	1.50	4.00
19 Hines Ward	2.00	5.00
20 Donovan McNabb	2.00	5.00

2007 Donruss Threads College Greats

STATED ODDS 1:151

1 Barry Sanders	8.00	20.00
2 Tony Dorsett	5.00	12.00
3 Marcus Allen	5.00	12.00
4 Adrian Peterson	4.00	10.00
5 JaMarcus Russell	1.25	3.00
6 Brady Quinn	1.25	3.00
7 Tim Brown	5.00	12.00
8 Bo Jackson	6.00	15.00
9 Dan Marino	10.00	25.00
10 Mike Singletary	5.00	12.00
11 Roger Staubach	6.00	15.00
12 Lydell Mitchell	3.00	8.00
13 Raymond Berry	4.00	10.00
14 Lance Alworth	4.00	10.00
15 Lenny Moore	3.00	8.00
16 Ronnie Lott	4.00	10.00
17 Jim McMahon	6.00	15.00
18 Fran Tarkenton	5.00	12.00
19 Jack Youngblood	4.00	10.00
20 Kellen Winslow	4.00	10.00

2007 Donruss Threads College Greats Autographs

STATED ODDS 1:958
STATED PRINT RUN 2-500
SERIAL #'d UNDER 15 NOT PRICED
UNPRICED COMBO AUTO PRINT RUN 10

1 Barry Sanders/21	125.00	200.00
2 Tony Dorsett/33	25.00	50.00
3 Marcus Allen/33	30.00	60.00
4 Adrian Peterson/28	100.00	200.00
7 Tim Brown/20	30.00	60.00
8 Bo Jackson/20	75.00	150.00
10 Mike Singletary/20	15.00	40.00
12 Lydell Mitchell/500	5.00	12.00
14 Lance Alworth/15	60.00	120.00
16 Ronnie Lott/20	50.00	100.00
19 Jack Youngblood/20	15.00	40.00
20 Kellen Winslow/20	15.00	40.00

2007 Donruss Threads College Greats Autographs Combos

STATED ODDS 1:958
UNPRICED COMBO PRINT RUN 10

2007 Donruss Threads College Gridiron Kings Gold

GOLD STATED ODDS 1:17
*SLVR HOLO/250: .5X TO 1.2X BASIC INSERTS
SILVER HOLOFOIL PRINT RUN 250 SER.#'d SETS
*FRAMED RED/100: .8X TO 2X BASIC INSERTS
FRAMED RED PRINT RUN 100 SER.#'d SETS
*GOLD HOLO/100: .8X TO 2X BASIC INSERTS
GOLD HOLOFOIL PRINT RUN 100 SER.#'d SETS
*FRAMED BLUE/50: 1X TO 2.5X BASIC INSERTS
FRAMED BLUE PRINT RUN 50 SER.#'d SETS
*FRAMED GREEN/25: 1.2X TO 3X
FRAMED GREEN PRINT RUN 25 SER.#'d SETS
*PLATINUM/25: 1.2X TO 3X BASIC INSERTS
PLATINUM PRINT RUN 25 SER.#'d SETS
*FRAMED BLACK/10: 2X TO 5X BASIC INSERTS
FRAMED BLACK PRINT RUN 10 SER.#'d SETS

1 Vince Young	.60	1.50
2 Dan Marino	3.00	8.00
3 Tony Dorsett	1.50	4.00
4 Frank Gore	.75	2.00
5 Kenny Irons	.50	1.25
6 Robert Meachem	.60	1.50
7 Courtney Taylor	.50	1.25
8 Jayson Swain	.60	1.50
9 Dwayne Jarrett	.60	1.50
10 Steve Smith USC	.50	1.25
11 Adrian Peterson	1.50	4.00
12 Brandon Meriweather	.60	1.50
13 Greg Olsen	.75	2.00
14 Brady Quinn	.50	1.25
15 Jon Beason	.50	1.25
16 JaMarcus Russell	.50	1.25
17 Dwayne Bowe	.50	1.25
18 Craig Buster Davis	.50	1.25
19 LaRon Landry	.75	2.00
20 Devery Henderson	.60	1.50
21 Zach Miller	.50	1.25
22 Jordan Palmer	.60	1.50
23 Johnnie Lee Higgins	.50	1.25
24 Cadillac Williams	.75	2.00
25 Ronnie Brown	.60	1.50
26 Jay Cutler	.60	1.50
27 LenDale White	.75	2.00
28 Joseph Addai	.60	1.50
29 Mario Williams	.75	2.00
30 Mike Hass	.60	1.50
31 A.J. Hawk	.60	1.50
32 Demetrius Williams	.60	1.50
33 Marcedes Lewis	.60	1.50
34 Laurence Maroney	.75	2.00
35 Maurice Jones-Drew	.60	1.50
36 Maurice Stovall	.60	1.50
37 Travis Wilson	.60	1.50
38 Peyton Manning	2.50	6.00
39 Larry Fitzgerald	.75	2.00
40 Sinorice Moss	.75	2.00

2007 Donruss Threads College Gridiron Kings Autographs

STATED PRINT RUN 3-25

22 Jordan Palmer/25	15.00	30.00
23 Johnnie Lee Higgins/21	12.50	25.00
32 Demetrius Williams/25	10.00	25.00

2007 Donruss Threads College Gridiron Kings Materials

STATED PRINT RUN 25-250
*PRIME/25: .8X TO 2X BASIC JSY/175-250
*PRIME/25: .5X TO 1.2X BASIC JSY/25
*PRIME/10: 1X TO 2.5X BASIC JSY/175-250
PRIME PRINT RUN 5-25

1 Vince Young/100	3.00	8.00
2 Dan Marino	6.00	15.00
3 Tony Dorsett/25	6.00	15.00
4 Frank Gore	2.50	6.00
5 Kenny Irons	2.00	5.00
6 Robert Meachem	2.50	6.00
7 Courtney Taylor	2.00	5.00
8 Jayson Swain	2.50	6.00
9 Dwayne Jarrett/100	3.00	8.00
10 Steve Smith USC/100	2.50	6.00
11 Adrian Peterson	6.00	15.00
12 Brandon Meriweather	2.50	6.00
13 Greg Olsen	3.00	8.00
14 Brady Quinn	2.00	5.00
15 Jon Beason	2.00	5.00
16 JaMarcus Russell/100	2.50	6.00
17 Dwayne Bowe/100	2.50	6.00
18 Craig Buster Davis/100	2.50	6.00
19 LaRon Landry/100	4.00	10.00
20 Devery Henderson	2.00	5.00
21 Zach Miller	2.00	5.00
22 Jordan Palmer	2.50	6.00
23 Johnnie Lee Higgins	2.00	5.00
24 Cadillac Williams/175	2.50	6.00
25 Ronnie Brown	2.00	5.00
26 Jay Cutler	2.00	5.00
27 LenDale White/100	3.00	8.00
28 Joseph Addai/75	2.50	6.00
29 Mario Williams	2.50	6.00
30 Mike Hass	2.00	5.00
31 A.J. Hawk	2.00	5.00
32 Demetrius Williams/75	2.50	6.00
33 Marcedes Lewis	2.00	5.00
34 Laurence Maroney/200	2.50	6.00
35 Maurice Jones-Drew	2.00	5.00
36 Maurice Stovall	2.00	5.00
37 Travis Wilson	2.00	5.00
38 Peyton Manning	10.00	25.00
39 Larry Fitzgerald	2.50	6.00
40 Sinorice Moss	2.50	6.00

2007 Donruss Threads College Gridiron Kings Material Autographs

STATED PRINT RUN 12-25
UNPRICED PRIME PRINT RUN 5-10
SERIAL #'d UNDER 25 NOT PRICED

1 Vince Young	10.00	25.00
2 Dan Marino	150.00	250.00
3 Tony Dorsett	30.00	60.00
4 Frank Gore	12.00	30.00
6 Robert Meachem	12.00	30.00
7 Courtney Taylor	10.00	25.00
9 Dwayne Jarrett	12.00	30.00
10 Steve Smith USC	10.00	25.00
11 Adrian Peterson	150.00	300.00
12 Brandon Meriweather	12.00	30.00
13 Greg Olsen	15.00	40.00
14 Brady Quinn	10.00	25.00
15 Jon Beason	10.00	25.00
16 JaMarcus Russell	10.00	25.00
17 Dwayne Bowe	10.00	25.00
19 LaRon Landry	15.00	40.00
20 Devery Henderson	10.00	25.00
21 Zach Miller	10.00	25.00
22 Jordan Palmer	12.00	30.00
23 Johnnie Lee Higgins	10.00	25.00
24 Cadillac Williams	12.00	30.00
25 Ronnie Brown	10.00	25.00
26 Jay Cutler	10.00	25.00
31 A.J. Hawk	10.00	25.00
32 Demetrius Williams	10.00	25.00
35 Maurice Jones-Drew	10.00	25.00
38 Peyton Manning	125.00	250.00
39 Larry Fitzgerald	25.00	50.00

2007 Donruss Threads Dynasty Gold

GOLD STATED ODDS 1:31
*BLUE: .8X TO 2X BASIC INSERTS
BLUE PRINT RUN 100 SER.#'d SETS

1 Palmer/Johnson/Houshmandzadeh	1.50	4.00
2 Romo/Owens/Glenn	2.50	6.00
3 Manning/Harrison/Wayne	5.00	12.00
4 Leftwich/Taylor/Jones-Drew	1.25	3.00
5 Green/Johnson/Gonzalez	1.50	4.00
6 Brady/Maroney/Brown	6.00	15.00
7 Brees/McAllister/Bush	2.00	5.00
8 Manning/Shockey/Burress	1.50	4.00
9 Rivers/Tomlinson/Gates	2.00	5.00
10 Smith QB/Gore/Davis	1.50	4.00

2007 Donruss Threads Dynasty Materials

STATED PRINT RUN 250 SER.#'d SETS
*PRIME: .8X TO 2X BASIC INSERTS
PRIME PRINT RUN 25 SER.#'d SETS

1 Palmer/Johnson/Housh	6.00	15.00
2 Romo/Owens/Glenn	15.00	40.00
3 Manning/Harrison/Wayne	12.00	30.00
4 Leftwich/Taylor/Jones-Drew	6.00	15.00
5 Green/Johnson/Gonzalez	6.00	15.00
6 Brady/Maroney/Brown	8.00	20.00
7 Brees/McAllister/Bush	12.50	30.00
8 Manning/Shockey/Burress	8.00	20.00
9 Rivers/Tomlinson/Gates	8.00	20.00
10 Smith QB/Gore/Davis	8.00	20.00

2007 Donruss Threads Footballs

RANDOM INSERTS IN RETAIL PACKS
STATED PRINT RUN 10-250

1 Anquan Boldin	2.00	5.00
2 Larry Fitzgerald	2.50	6.00
3 Alge Crumpler	2.50	6.00
4 Michael Vick/40	4.00	10.00
5 Steve McNair	2.50	6.00
7 Keyshawn Johnson	2.50	6.00
8 Steve Smith	2.50	6.00
9 Brian Urlacher	3.00	8.00
10 Muhsin Muhammad	2.00	5.00
11 Chad Johnson	2.00	5.00
12 Rudi Johnson	2.00	5.00
13 T.J. Houshmandzadeh	2.00	5.00
14 Terry Glenn	2.50	6.00
15 Terrell Owens	2.50	6.00
16 Jon Kitna	2.00	5.00
18 Peyton Manning/55	12.00	30.00
19 Fred Taylor/125	2.50	6.00
20 Eddie Kennison	2.00	5.00
21 Larry Johnson/200	2.00	5.00
22 Tony Gonzalez	2.50	6.00
23 Trent Green	2.00	5.00
24 Chris Chambers	2.00	5.00
25 Marty Booker	2.00	5.00
26 Tom Brady	10.00	25.00
27 Donte Stallworth	2.50	6.00
28 Deuce McAllister	2.50	6.00
29 Drew Brees/65	5.00	12.00
30 Reuben Droughns	2.50	6.00
31 Jeremy Shockey	2.00	5.00
32 Plaxico Burress/75	3.00	8.00
33 Chad Pennington	2.00	5.00
34 Jerricho Cotchery	2.00	5.00
35 Laveranues Coles	2.00	5.00
36 LaMont Jordan	2.50	6.00
37 Brian Westbrook	2.00	5.00
38 Donovan McNabb	2.50	6.00
39 Hines Ward	2.50	6.00
40 Antonio Gates	3.00	8.00
41 LaDainian Tomlinson	3.00	8.00
42 Arnaz Battle	2.00	5.00
43 Darrell Jackson	2.00	5.00
44 Deion Branch	2.00	5.00
45 Matt Hasselbeck	2.00	5.00
46 Jerramy Stevens	2.00	5.00
47 Shaun Alexander	2.00	5.00
48 Isaac Bruce	3.00	8.00
49 Marc Bulger	2.00	5.00
50 Drew Bennett	2.00	5.00
51 Torry Holt	2.50	6.00
52 Joey Galloway	2.50	6.00
53 Mike Alstott	2.00	5.00
54 Travis Henry	2.50	6.00
55 Clinton Portis	2.00	5.00
56 Santana Moss	2.50	6.00

2007 Donruss Threads Generations Gold

GOLD STATED ODDS 1:18
*BLUE: .8X TO 2X BASIC INSERTS
BLUE PRINT RUN 100 SER.#'d SETS

1 D.Marino/D.Brees	3.00	8.00
2 D.Sanders/D.Hester	2.00	5.00
3 B.Sanders/L.Tomlinson	2.50	6.00
4 R.Cunningham/V.Young	1.25	3.00
5 M.Irvin/M.Harrison	1.50	4.00
6 T.Aikman/T.Romo	3.00	8.00
7 K.Winslow/J.Shockey	1.00	2.50
8 J.Montana/P.Manning	5.00	12.00
9 E.Dickerson/J.Addai	1.25	3.00
10 T.Dorsett/J.Jones	1.50	4.00
11 M.Singletary/S.Merriman	1.50	4.00
12 S.Alexander/M.Jones-Drew	1.00	2.50
13 S.Largent/D.Jackson	1.50	4.00
14 E.Manning/P.Rivers	1.50	4.00
15 R.Lott/T.Polamalu	1.50	4.00

2007 Donruss Threads Generations Materials

STATED PRINT RUN 250 SER.#'d SETS
*PRIME/25: .8X TO 2X BASIC INSERTS
PRIME PRINT RUN 25 SER.#'d SETS

1 D.Marino/D.Brees	10.00	25.00
2 D.Sanders/D.Hester	8.00	20.00
3 B.Sanders/L.Tomlinson	10.00	25.00
4 R.Cunningham/V.Young	8.00	20.00
5 M.Irvin/M.Harrison	6.00	15.00
6 T.Aikman/T.Romo	10.00	25.00
7 K.Winslow/J.Shockey	5.00	12.00
8 J.Montana/P.Manning	12.00	30.00
9 E.Dickerson/J.Addai	6.00	15.00
10 T.Dorsett/J.Jones	6.00	15.00
11 M.Singletary/S.Merriman	6.00	15.00
12 S.Alexander/M.Jones-Drew	6.00	15.00
13 S.Largent/D.Jackson	5.00	12.00
14 E.Manning/P.Rivers	6.00	15.00
15 R.Lott/T.Polamalu	6.00	15.00

2007 Donruss Threads Jerseys

STATED PRINT RUN 50-250
*PRIME/25: .8X TO 2X BASIC JSY/200-250
*PRIME/25: .6X TO 1.5X BASIC JSY/100-125
*PRIME/25: .5X TO 1.2X BASIC JSY/50
*PRIME/10: 1X TO 2.5X BASIC JSY/250
*PRIME/9: .8X TO 2X BASIC JSY/100
PRIME PRINT RUN 5-25

1 Anquan Boldin	2.00	5.00
2 Larry Fitzgerald	2.50	6.00
3 Alge Crumpler/100	3.00	8.00
4 Michael Vick	2.50	6.00
5 Steve McNair	2.50	6.00
6 Ray Lewis	3.00	8.00
7 Keyshawn Johnson	2.50	6.00
8 Steve Smith	2.50	6.00
9 Brian Urlacher	3.00	8.00
10 Muhsin Muhammad	2.00	5.00
11 Chad Johnson	2.00	5.00
12 Rudi Johnson	2.00	5.00
14 Terry Glenn	2.50	6.00
15 Terrell Owens	2.50	6.00
16 Jon Kitna	2.00	5.00
17 Brett Favre	6.00	15.00
18 Peyton Manning/100	10.00	25.00
20 Eddie Kennison	2.00	5.00
21 Larry Johnson	2.00	5.00
22 Tony Gonzalez	2.50	6.00
23 Trent Green	2.00	5.00
24 Chris Chambers	2.00	5.00
26 Tom Brady	10.00	25.00
27 Donte Stallworth/125	3.00	8.00
28 Deuce McAllister	2.50	6.00
29 Drew Brees/100	4.00	10.00
30 Reuben Droughns	2.50	6.00
31 Jeremy Shockey	2.00	5.00
32 Plaxico Burress/115	2.50	6.00
33 Chad Pennington	2.00	5.00
34 Jerricho Cotchery/100	2.50	6.00
35 Laveranues Coles	2.00	5.00
36 LaMont Jordan	2.50	6.00
38 Donovan McNabb	2.50	6.00
39 Hines Ward/200	2.50	6.00
40 Antonio Gates	3.00	8.00
41 LaDainian Tomlinson	3.00	8.00
43 Darrell Jackson	2.00	5.00
44 Deion Branch	2.00	5.00
45 Matt Hasselbeck	2.00	5.00
47 Shaun Alexander	2.00	5.00
48 Isaac Bruce	3.00	8.00
49 Marc Bulger	2.00	5.00
50 Drew Bennett/120	2.50	6.00
51 Torry Holt	2.50	6.00
52 Joey Galloway	2.50	6.00
53 Mike Alstott	2.00	5.00
54 Travis Henry	2.50	6.00
55 Clinton Portis	2.00	5.00
56 Santana Moss	2.50	6.00
57 Edgerrin James	2.50	6.00
58 Matt Leinart	2.00	5.00
59 Jerious Norwood	2.00	5.00
60 Warrick Dunn	2.00	5.00
61 Mark Clayton	2.00	5.00
62 J.P. Losman	2.00	5.00
63 Josh Reed	2.00	5.00
64 Lee Evans	2.50	6.00
65 DeAngelo Williams	2.00	5.00
66 DeShaun Foster	2.50	6.00
67 Jake Delhomme	2.00	5.00
68 Bernard Berrian	2.00	5.00
69 Cedric Benson	2.00	5.00
70 Rex Grossman	2.00	5.00
71 Carson Palmer	2.50	6.00
72 Braylon Edwards	2.00	5.00
74 Charlie Frye	2.50	6.00
75 Julius Jones	2.00	5.00
76 Marion Barber	2.50	6.00
77 Javon Walker	2.50	6.00
78 Jay Cutler	2.00	5.00
79 Mike Bell	2.50	6.00
80 Donald Driver	2.50	6.00
82 Andre Johnson	2.50	6.00
85 Joseph Addai	2.00	5.00
86 Marvin Harrison	2.50	6.00
87 Kevin Jones	2.00	5.00
88 Roy Williams WR	2.00	5.00
90 A.J. Hawk	2.00	5.00
91 Reggie Wayne/50	4.00	10.00
92 Dallas Clark	2.50	6.00
93 Byron Leftwich	2.00	5.00
95 Reggie Williams/245	2.50	6.00
96 Tony Romo	4.00	10.00
97 Daunte Culpepper	2.50	6.00
98 Ronnie Brown	2.00	5.00
99 Chester Taylor	2.00	5.00
101 Ben Watson/100	2.50	6.00
102 Laurence Maroney	2.50	6.00
104 Peerless Price	2.00	5.00
105 Marques Colston/100	2.50	6.00
107 Brandon Jacobs	2.00	5.00
108 Eli Manning	2.50	6.00
109 Leon Washington	2.00	5.00
110 Kevan Barlow	2.50	6.00
111 Randy Moss	2.50	6.00
112 Troy Polamalu	3.00	8.00
114 Santonio Holmes/125	2.50	6.00
115 Philip Rivers	3.00	8.00
116 Shawne Merriman	2.00	5.00
117 Alex Smith QB	2.50	6.00
118 Frank Gore	2.50	6.00
119 Vernon Davis	2.00	5.00
120 Reggie Brown	2.00	5.00
121 Ben Roethlisberger	3.00	8.00
123 Bruce Gradkowski	2.00	5.00
124 Cadillac Williams	2.50	6.00
126 Michael Jenkins	2.00	5.00
127 Demetrius Williams	2.00	5.00
128 Roy Williams S	2.00	5.00
130 Hank Baskett	2.50	6.00
132 Brandon Marshall	2.50	6.00
135 Joe Klopfenstein	2.00	5.00
137 Todd Heap	2.00	5.00
139 Troy Williamson	2.00	5.00
141 Ahman Green	2.50	6.00
142 LenDale White	2.50	6.00
143 Vince Young	2.00	5.00
145 Jamal Lewis	2.50	6.00
146 Joe Horn	2.00	5.00
147 Tatum Bell	2.00	5.00
148 Willis McGahee	2.00	5.00
149 Jason Campbell	2.00	5.00

2007 Donruss Threads Pro Gridiron Kings Gold

GOLD STATED ODDS 1:11
*SILVER HOLO/250: .5X TO 1.2X
SILVER HOLOFOIL PRINT RUN 250 SER.#'d SETS
*FRAMED RED: .8X TO 2X BASIC INSERTS
FRAMED RED PRINT RUN 100 SER.#'d SETS
*GOLD HOLO/100: .8X TO 2X BASIC INSERTS
GOLD HOLOFOIL PRINT RUN 100 SER.#'d SETS
*FRAMED BLUE/50: 1X TO 2.5X
FRAMED BLUE PRINT RUN 50 SER.#'d SETS
*FRAMED GREEN/25: 1.2X TO 3X
FRAMED GREEN PRINT RUN 25 SER.#'d SETS
*PLATINUM/25: 1.2X TO 3X BASIC INSERTS
PLATINUM PRINT RUN 25 SER.#'d SETS
*FRAMED BLACK: 2X TO 5X BASIC INSERTS
FRAMED BLACK PRINT RUN 10 SER.#'d SETS

1 Andre Johnson	.75	2.00
2 Bernard Berrian	.60	1.50
3 Brandon Jacobs	.60	1.50
4 Brandon Marshall	.75	2.00
5 Brian Urlacher	1.00	2.50
6 Cedric Benson	.60	1.50
7 Chester Taylor	.60	1.50
8 Chris Henry WR	.60	1.50
9 Corey Dillon	.60	1.50
10 Curtis Martin	.75	2.00
11 DeAngelo Williams	.60	1.50
12 DeMeco Ryans	.75	2.00
13 Demetrius Williams	.60	1.50
14 Devery Henderson	.60	1.50
15 Devin Hester	.75	2.00
16 Donald Driver	.75	2.00
17 Donovan McNabb	.75	2.00
18 Drew Brees	1.00	2.50
19 Eli Manning	.75	2.00
20 Fred Taylor	.60	1.50
21 Greg Jennings	.60	1.50
22 Hank Baskett	.75	2.00
23 Jerricho Cotchery	.60	1.50
24 LaMont Jordan	.75	2.00
25 Larry Johnson	.60	1.50
26 LenDale White	.75	2.00
27 Leon Washington	.60	1.50
28 Marion Barber	1.00	2.50
29 Matt Leinart	.60	1.50
30 Michael Turner	.60	1.50
31 Mike Furrey	.75	2.00
32 Mike Bell	.75	2.00
33 Patrick Crayton	.60	1.50
34 Reggie Bush	.60	1.50
35 Rex Grossman	.60	1.50
36 Ronnie Brown	.60	1.50
37 Santonio Holmes	.60	1.50
38 Shawne Merriman	.60	1.50
39 Steve Smith	.75	2.00
40 Thomas Jones	.60	1.50
41 T.J. Houshmandzadeh	.60	1.50
42 Tony Romo	1.25	3.00
43 Tony Scheffler	.75	2.00
44 Vernon Davis	.60	1.50
45 Vince Young	.60	1.50
46 Vincent Jackson	.60	1.50
47 Willie Parker	.75	2.00
48 Willis McGahee	.60	1.50
49 Cliff Harris	1.00	2.50
50 Larry Little	1.00	2.50
51 Rick Casares	1.00	2.50
52 Billy Howton	1.00	2.50
53 Boyd Dowler	1.00	2.50
54 Jim Brown	2.00	5.00
55 Don Perkins	1.00	2.50
56 Harlon Hill	1.00	2.50
57 Jethro Pugh	1.00	2.50
58 Jimmy Orr	1.00	2.50
59 Johnny Morris	1.00	2.50
60 Rosey Grier	1.00	2.50

2007 Donruss Threads Pro Gridiron Kings Autographs

STATED PRINT RUN 25-500 SER.#'d SETS

12 DeMeco Ryans/100	5.00	12.00
14 Devery Henderson/25	8.00	20.00
33 Patrick Crayton/25	10.00	25.00
46 Vincent Jackson/25	8.00	20.00
49 Cliff Harris/25	15.00	40.00
51 Rick Casares/25	15.00	40.00
52 Billy Howton/500	6.00	15.00
53 Boyd Dowler/500	8.00	20.00
56 Harlon Hill/500	6.00	15.00
57 Jethro Pugh/25	10.00	25.00
60 Rosey Grier/25	10.00	25.00

2007 Donruss Threads Pro Gridiron Kings Materials

STATED PRINT RUN 250 SER.#'d SETS
*PRIME/10-25: .8X TO 2X BASIC JSY
PRIME PRINT RUN 10-25

1 Andre Johnson	3.00	8.00
2 Bernard Berrian	2.50	6.00
3 Brandon Jacobs	2.50	6.00
4 Brandon Marshall	3.00	8.00
5 Brian Urlacher	4.00	10.00
6 Cedric Benson	2.50	6.00
7 Chester Taylor	2.50	6.00
8 Chris Henry WR	2.50	6.00
9 Corey Dillon	2.50	6.00
10 Curtis Martin	3.00	8.00
11 DeAngelo Williams	2.50	6.00
13 Demetrius Williams	2.50	6.00
15 Devin Hester	3.00	8.00
16 Donald Driver	3.00	8.00

17 Donovan McNabb 3.00 8.00
18 Drew Brees/50 6.00 15.00
19 Eli Manning 3.00 8.00
20 Fred Taylor/165 2.50 6.00
22 Hank Baskett 3.00 8.00
23 Jerricho Cotchery 2.50 6.00
24 LaMont Jordan 3.00 8.00
25 Larry Johnson 2.50 6.00
26 LenDale White 3.00 8.00
27 Leon Washington 2.50 6.00
28 Marion Barber 3.00 8.00
29 Matt Leinart 2.50 6.00
32 Mike Bell 3.00 8.00
34 Reggie Bush/100 2.50 6.00
35 Rex Grossman 2.50 6.00
36 Ronnie Brown 2.50 6.00
37 Santonio Holmes/200 2.50 6.00
38 Shawne Merriman 2.50 6.00
39 Steve Smith 3.00 8.00
40 Thomas Jones 2.50 6.00
41 T.J. Houshmandzadeh/150 2.50 6.00
42 Tony Romo 5.00 12.00
44 Vernon Davis 2.50 6.00
45 Vince Young 2.50 6.00
47 Willie Parker 3.00 8.00
48 Willis McGahee 2.50 6.00
50 Larry Little 3.00 8.00
54 Jim Brown 6.00 15.00

2007 Donruss Threads Pro Gridiron Kings Material Autographs

STATED PRINT RUN 25 SER.#'d SETS
UNPRICED PRIME PRINT RUN 2-10
1 Andre Johnson 15.00 40.00
2 Bernard Berrian 12.00 30.00
3 Brandon Jacobs 12.00 30.00
4 Brandon Marshall 15.00 40.00
6 Cedric Benson 12.00 30.00
7 Chester Taylor 12.00 30.00
10 Curtis Martin 30.00 60.00
11 DeAngelo Williams 12.00 30.00
13 Demetrius Williams 12.00 30.00
15 Devin Hester 15.00 40.00
16 Donald Driver 30.00 60.00
18 Drew Brees 50.00 100.00
20 Fred Taylor 12.00 30.00
22 Hank Baskett 15.00 40.00
23 Jerricho Cotchery 12.00 30.00
25 Larry Johnson 12.00 30.00
28 Marion Barber 15.00 40.00
34 Reggie Bush 30.00 80.00
35 Rex Grossman 12.00 30.00
36 Ronnie Brown 12.00 30.00
37 Santonio Holmes 12.00 30.00
39 Steve Smith 15.00 40.00
42 Tony Romo 75.00 150.00
44 Vernon Davis 12.00 30.00
48 Willis McGahee 12.00 30.00
50 Larry Little 30.00 60.00

2007 Donruss Threads Rookie Autographs

STATED PRINT RUN 100-250
160 Courtney Taylor/200 5.00 12.00
161 David Irons/250 4.00 10.00
162 Joel Filani/200 6.00 15.00
163 H.B. Blades/250 5.00 12.00
164 Rufus Alexander/250 6.00 15.00
166 Eric Frampton/250 5.00 12.00
167 Tim Shaw/250 5.00 12.00
168 Tymere Zimmerman/250 5.00 12.00
169 Jeff Rowe/100 8.00 20.00
170 Josh Gattis/250 4.00 10.00
171 Brandon Myles/250 5.00 12.00
172 Earl Everett/200 5.00 12.00
173 Steve Breaston/200 5.00 12.00
174 Ryan McBean/250 6.00 15.00
175 Scott Chandler/200 6.00 15.00
176 Chris Davis/100 8.00 20.00
177 Fred Bennett/250 4.00 10.00
178 Ryne Robinson/250 5.00 12.00
179 Zak DeOssie/250 5.00 12.00
180 Dwayne Wright/250 4.00 10.00
181 A.J. Davis/250 4.00 10.00
182 Ray McDonald/200 5.00 12.00
183 Daymeion Hughes/250 4.00 10.00
184 Michael Okwo/250 5.00 12.00
185 Aaron Rouse/250 5.00 12.00
186 Stewart Bradley/250 6.00 15.00
187 Jonathan Wade/250 5.00 12.00
190 Mike Walker/250 5.00 12.00
191 James Jones/100 15.00 40.00
192 Matt Spaeth/100 10.00 25.00
193 Laurent Robinson/200 6.00 15.00
194 Jacoby Jones/100 25.00 50.00
195 Marcus McCauley/250 4.00 10.00
196 Buster Davis/250 5.00 12.00
197 Quentin Moses/250 5.00 12.00
198 Sabby Piscitelli/250 6.00 15.00
199 Dan Bazuin/250 6.00 15.00
200 Ikaika Alama-Francis/250 8.00 20.00
201 Victor Abiamiri/200 6.00 15.00
202 Tim Crowder/250 5.00 12.00
203 Josh Wilson/200 5.00 12.00
204 Eric Wright/250 4.00 10.00
205 David Harris/250 5.00 12.00
206 LaMarr Woodley/200 8.00 20.00
207 Chris Houston/200 4.00 10.00
208 Zach Miller/100 8.00 20.00
209 Aaron Fairooz/250 5.00 12.00
211 Anthony Spencer/200 10.00 25.00
212 Jon Beason/100 8.00 20.00
213 Brandon Meriweather/200 6.00 15.00
214 Reggie Nelson/100 10.00 25.00
215 Aaron Ross/200 6.00 15.00
216 Michael Griffin/200 6.00 15.00
217 Ronnie McGill/250 5.00 12.00
219 Darrelle Revis/100 8.00 20.00
220 Lawrence Timmons/100 12.00 30.00
221 Adam Carriker/100 12.00 30.00
222 Amobi Okoye/100 10.00 25.00
223 Jamaal Anderson/100 10.00 25.00
224 Syvelle Newton/250 6.00 15.00
225 Levi Brown/250 6.00 15.00

2007 Donruss Threads Rookie Collection Materials

STATED PRINT RUN 500 SER.#'d SETS
*PRIME: .8X TO 2X BASIC INSERTS
PRIME PRINT RUN 25 SER.#'d SETS
1 Trent Edwards 1.50 4.00
2 Marshawn Lynch 3.00 8.00
3 Chris Henry RB 4.00 10.00
4 Paul Williams 3.00 8.00
5 Sidney Rice 6.00 15.00
6 Adrian Peterson 10.00 25.00
7 Drew Stanton 1.50 4.00
8 Calvin Johnson 5.00 12.00
9 Yamon Figurs 3.00 8.00
10 Troy Smith 4.00 10.00
11 Brian Leonard 4.00 10.00
12 Greg Olsen 2.50 6.00
13 Garrett Wolfe 3.00 8.00
14 Kenny Irons 3.00 8.00
15 Joe Thomas 3.00 8.00
16 Brady Quinn 1.50 4.00
17 Brandon Jackson 4.00 10.00
18 Steve Smith USC 1.50 4.00
19 Dwayne Jarrett 4.00 10.00
20 Ted Ginn Jr. 2.00 5.00
21 John Beck 4.00 10.00
22 Lorenzo Booker 3.00 8.00
23 Antonio Pittman 3.00 8.00
24 Robert Meachem 4.00 10.00
25 Dwayne Bowe 1.50 4.00
26 Anthony Gonzalez 1.50 4.00
27 JaMarcus Russell 1.50 4.00
28 Michael Bush 4.00 10.00
29 Johnnie Lee Higgins 3.00 8.00
30 Kevin Kolb 2.00 5.00
31 Tony Hunt 4.00 10.00
32 Patrick Willis 2.50 6.00
33 Jason Hill 3.00 8.00
34 Gaines Adams 4.00 10.00

2007 Donruss Threads Rookie Collection Material Autographs

STATED PRINT RUN 25 SER.#'d SETS
UNPRICED PRIME PRINT RUN 10
1 Trent Edwards 12.00 30.00
2 Marshawn Lynch 40.00 80.00
3 Chris Henry RB 12.00 30.00
4 Paul Williams 12.00 30.00
5 Sidney Rice 15.00 40.00
6 Adrian Peterson 175.00 350.00
7 Drew Stanton 12.00 30.00
8 Calvin Johnson 100.00 200.00
9 Yamon Figurs 12.00 30.00
10 Troy Smith 12.00 30.00
11 Brian Leonard 12.00 30.00
12 Greg Olsen 20.00 50.00
13 Garrett Wolfe 12.00 30.00
14 Kenny Irons 12.00 30.00
15 Joe Thomas
16 Brady Quinn 12.00 30.00
17 Brandon Jackson 12.00 30.00
18 Steve Smith USC 12.00 30.00
19 Dwayne Jarrett 15.00 40.00
20 Ted Ginn Jr. 15.00 40.00
21 John Beck 12.00 30.00
22 Lorenzo Booker 15.00 40.00
23 Antonio Pittman 12.00 30.00
24 Robert Meachem 15.00 40.00
25 Dwayne Bowe 12.00 30.00
26 Anthony Gonzalez 12.00 30.00
27 JaMarcus Russell 20.00 50.00
28 Michael Bush 12.00 30.00
29 Johnnie Lee Higgins 12.00 30.00
30 Kevin Kolb 15.00 40.00
31 Tony Hunt 12.00 30.00
32 Patrick Willis 40.00 80.00
33 Jason Hill 12.00 30.00
34 Gaines Adams 15.00 40.00

2007 Donruss Threads Rookie Collection Materials Combo

STATED PRINT RUN 500 SER.#'d SETS
*PRIME/25: .8X TO 2X BASIC COMBO
PRIME PRINT RUN 25 SER.#'d SETS
1 T.Edwards/M.Lynch 4.00 10.00
2 C.Henry RB/P.Williams 4.00 10.00
3 S.Rice/A.Peterson 6.00 15.00
4 D.Stanton/C.Johnson 6.00 15.00
5 R.Meachem/A.Pittman 5.00 12.00
6 J.Russell/M.Bush 2.00 5.00
7 K.Kolb/T.Hunt 2.50 6.00
8 B.Quinn/J.Thomas 3.00 8.00
9 J.Beck/T.Ginn Jr. 2.50 6.00
10 T.Smith/Y.Figurs 2.00 5.00
11 G.Olsen/G.Wolfe 3.00 8.00
12 P.Willis/J.Hill 3.00 8.00
13 D.Bowe/A.Gonzalez 2.00 5.00
14 S.Smith USC/D.Jarrett 2.50 6.00
15 B.Jackson/K.Irons 5.00 12.00

2007 Donruss Threads Rookie Collection Materials Triple

STATED PRINT RUN 500 SER.#'d SETS
*PRIME/25: .8X TO 2X BASIC INSERTS
PRIME PRINT RUN 25 SER.#'d SETS
1 Peterson/Lynch/Bush 15.00 40.00
2 Quinn/Stanton/Russell 8.00 20.00
3 Johnson/Bowe/Gonzalez 10.00 25.00
4 Meachem/Smith USC/Jarrett 5.00 12.00

2007 Donruss Threads Rookie Collection Materials Quad

STATED PRINT RUN 100 SER.#'d SETS
*PRIME/25: .8X TO 2X BASIC QUAD
PRIME PRINT RUN 25 SER.#'d SETS
1 Rssll/Jhnsn/Gnzlz/Jrrtt 15.00 40.00
2 Ptrsn/Gnn./Wlls/Lych 25.00 60.00
3 Qnn/Bwe/Mchm/Olsn 10.00 25.00

2008 Donruss Threads

COMP.SET w/o RC's (150) 10.00 25.00
UNSIGNED ROOKIE PRINT RUN 999
251-300 AU ROOKIE PRINT RUN 100-999
1 Anquan Boldin .20 .50
2 Larry Fitzgerald .25 .60
3 Warrick Dunn .20 .50
4 Derrick Mason .20 .50
5 Steve Smith .25 .60
6 Brian Urlacher .30 .75
7 Chad Johnson .20 .50
8 Terrell Owens .25 .60
9 Tony Gonzalez .25 .60
10 Rex Grossman .20 .50
11 Torry Holt .25 .60
12 Isaac Bruce .30 .75
13 Jeff Garcia .20 .50
14 Santana Moss .20 .50
15 LaDainian Tomlinson .30 .75
16 Matt Hasselbeck .20 .50
17 Julius Jones .20 .50
18 Earnest Graham .20 .50
19 Joey Galloway .25 .60
20 Ike Hilliard .20 .50
21 Vince Young .20 .50
22 Jason Taylor .25 .60
23 Tom Brady 1.00 2.50
24 Randy Moss .25 .60
25 Donte Stallworth .20 .50
26 Deuce McAllister .25 .60
27 Eli Manning .25 .60
28 Michael Strahan .25 .60
29 Thomas Jones .20 .50
30 Laveranues Coles .20 .50
31 Jerry Porter .20 .50
32 Correll Buckhalter .20 .50
33 Donovan McNabb .25 .60
34 Hines Ward .25 .60
35 Tony Scheffler .20 .50
36 Jason Witten .25 .60
37 DeMarcus Ware .25 .60
38 Jay Cutler .20 .50
39 Brandon Marshall .25 .60
40 Brandon Stokley .20 .50
41 Selvin Young .20 .50
42 Jon Kitna .20 .50
43 Roy Williams WR .20 .50
44 Shaun McDonald .20 .50
45 Calvin Johnson .30 .75
46 Aaron Rodgers .60 1.50
47 Ryan Grant .25 .60
48 Donald Driver .25 .60
49 Greg Jennings .20 .50
50 James Jones .20 .50
51 Matt Schaub .20 .50
52 Owen Daniels .20 .50
53 Andre Johnson .25 .60
54 Kevin Walter .25 .60
55 Ahman Green .25 .60
56 Peyton Manning .75 2.00
57 Marvin Harrison .25 .60
58 Joseph Addai .20 .50
59 Reggie Wayne .25 .60
60 Dallas Clark .20 .50
61 David Garrard .20 .50
62 Fred Taylor .20 .50
63 Maurice Jones-Drew .20 .50
64 Reggie Williams .25 .60
65 Larry Johnson .20 .50
66 Kolby Smith .20 .50
67 Dwayne Bowe .25 .60
68 Ted Ginn Jr. .20 .50
69 Ronnie Brown .20 .50
70 John Beck .20 .50
71 Tarvaris Jackson .20 .50
72 Adrian Peterson .30 .75
73 Chester Taylor .20 .50
74 Sidney Rice .20 .50
75 Wes Welker .25 .60
76 Laurence Maroney .25 .60
77 Drew Brees .30 .75
78 Reggie Bush .20 .50
79 Marques Colston .20 .50
80 Brandon Jacobs .20 .50
81 Plaxico Burress .20 .50
82 Derrick Ward .20 .50
83 Kellen Clemens .20 .50
84 Leon Washington .20 .50
85 Jerricho Cotchery .20 .50
86 Matt Leinart .20 .50
87 Edgerrin James .25 .60
88 JaMarcus Russell .20 .50
89 Justin Fargas .20 .50
90 Alge Crumpler .20 .50
91 Jerious Norwood .20 .50
92 Roddy White .20 .50
93 Ronald Curry .20 .50
94 Willis McGahee .20 .50
95 Mark Clayton .20 .50
96 Brian Westbrook .20 .50
97 Kevin Curtis .20 .50
98 Ed Reed .25 .60
99 Ray Lewis .30 .75
100 Reggie Brown .20 .50
101 Trent Edwards .20 .50
102 Marshawn Lynch .25 .60
103 Ben Roethlisberger .30 .75
104 Willie Parker .25 .60
105 Lee Evans .25 .60
106 Josh Reed .20 .50
107 Santonio Holmes .20 .50
108 Jake Delhomme .20 .50
109 DeShaun Foster .20 .50
110 Heath Miller .20 .50
111 Philip Rivers .30 .75
112 DeAngelo Williams .20 .50
113 Drew Carter .20 .50
114 Adrian Peterson Bears .20 .50
115 Antonio Gates .25 .60
116 Shawne Merriman .20 .50
117 Bernard Berrian .20 .50
118 Cedric Benson .20 .50
119 Vincent Jackson .20 .50
120 Alex Smith QB .25 .60
121 Devin Hester .25 .60
122 Carson Palmer .25 .60
123 Frank Gore .25 .60
124 T.J. Houshmandzadeh .20 .50
125 Rudi Johnson .20 .50
126 Vernon Davis .20 .50
127 Patrick Willis .25 .60
128 Kenny Watson .20 .50
129 Derek Anderson .20 .50
130 Jamal Lewis .25 .60
131 Kellen Winslow .20 .50
132 Maurice Morris .20 .50
133 Nate Burleson .20 .50
134 Braylon Edwards .20 .50
135 Josh Cribbs .20 .50
136 Deion Branch .20 .50
137 Marc Bulger .20 .50
138 Tony Romo .25 .60
139 Marion Barber .20 .50
140 Steven Jackson .20 .50
141 Randy McMichael .20 .50
142 Cadillac Williams .25 .60
143 LenDale White .20 .50
144 Chris Brown .20 .50
145 Roydell Williams .20 .50
146 Justin Gage .20 .50
147 Jason Campbell .20 .50
148 Clinton Portis .20 .50
149 Chris Cooley .20 .50
150 Ladell Betts .20 .50
151 A.Arrington AU/299 RC 3.00 8.00
152 Alex Brink/999 RC 2.00 5.00
153 Ali Highsmith AU/999 RC 3.00 8.00
154 Anthony Alridge AU/999 RC 3.00 8.00
155 Antoine Cason/999 RC 2.00 5.00
156 Antwaun Molden/999 RC 1.50 4.00
157 Aqib Talib/999 RC 2.50 6.00
158 Arman Shields/999 RC 2.00 5.00
159 Brad Cottam AU/299 RC 3.00 8.00
160 Brandon Flowers/999 RC 2.00 5.00
161 Bruce Davis/999 RC 2.00 5.00
162 Calais Campbell AU/299 RC 4.00 10.00
163 Caleb Campbell AU/299 RC 5.00 12.00
164 Charles Godfrey/999 RC 1.50 4.00
165 Ch.Washington AU/299 RC 4.00 10.00
166 Chevis Jackson AU/299 RC 3.00 8.00
167 Cory Boyd AU/299 RC 3.00 8.00
168 Craig Steltz AU/299 RC 3.00 8.00
169 Craig Stevens/999 RC 1.50 4.00
170 Curtis Lofton AU/299 RC 4.00 10.00
171 DaJuan Morgan/999 RC 2.00 5.00
172 Dantrell Savage AU/999 RC 4.00 10.00
173 Darius Reynaud AU/999 RC 3.00 8.00
174 Darrell Strong AU/999 RC 4.00 10.00
175 Davone Bess AU/999 RC 4.00 10.00
176 Derek Fine/999 RC 1.50 4.00
177 Derrick Harvey/999 RC 1.50 4.00
178 DJ Hall AU/999 RC 3.00 8.00
179 D.Rodgers-Cromartie/999 RC 2.00 5.00
180 Erin Henderson AU/999 RC 4.00 10.00
181 E.Wheelwright AU/755 RC 4.00 10.00
182 Fred Davis/999 RC 1.50 4.00
183 Gary Barnidge/999 RC 2.50 6.00
184 Joe Jon Finley/999 RC 1.50 4.00
185 Jacob Hester AU/299 RC 3.00 8.00
186 Jacob Tamme/999 RC 2.00 5.00
187 Jalen Parmele/999 RC 2.00 5.00
188 Jamar Adams AU/775 RC 3.00 8.00
189 Jason Rivers AU/999 RC 3.00 8.00
190 Jaymar Johnson/999 RC 1.50 4.00
191 Jed Collins AU/999 RC 4.00 10.00
192 Jermichael Finley/999 RC 1.50 4.00
193 Jerod Mayo/999 RC 2.50 6.00
194 John Carlson/999 RC 1.50 4.00
195 Jonathan Hefney AU/928 RC 3.00 8.00
196 Jordon Dizon AU/299 RC 3.00 8.00
197 Josh Morgan AU/499 RC 3.00 8.00
198 Justin Forsett AU/299 RC 4.00 10.00
199 Justin Harper/999 RC 1.50 4.00
200 Kalvin McRae AU/999 RC 3.00 8.00
201 Keenan Burton/999 RC 1.50 4.00
202 Kellen Davis AU/299 RC 3.00 8.00
203 Kenneth Moore/999 RC 1.50 4.00
204 Kentwan Balmer/999 RC 1.50 4.00
205 Kevin Robinson AU/299 RC 3.00 8.00
206 Lawrence Jackson/999 RC 1.50 4.00
207 Leodis McKelvin/999 RC 2.00 5.00
208 Marcus Henry/999 RC 1.50 4.00
209 Marcus Monk AU/350 RC 4.00 10.00
210 Marcus Smith AU/299 RC 4.00 10.00
211 Marcus Thomas AU/299 RC 4.00 10.00
212 Mario Urrutia/999 RC 1.50 4.00
213 Mark Bradford AU/999 RC 3.00 8.00
214 Martellus Bennett/999 RC 2.00 5.00
215 Martin Rucker AU/299 RC 3.00 8.00
216 Matt Sherry/999 RC 2.00 5.00
217 Owen Schmitt AU/199 RC 3.00 8.00
218 Pat Sims/999 RC 2.00 5.00
219 Patrick Lee/999 RC 1.50 4.00
220 Paul Hubbard AU/699 RC 3.00 8.00
221 Paul Smith AU/999 RC 3.00 8.00
222 Peyton Hillis AU/299 RC 6.00 15.00
223 Phillip Merling/999 RC 1.50 4.00
224 Philip Wheeler/999 RC 2.00 5.00
225 Pierre Garcon/999 RC 3.00 8.00
226 Quentin Groves AU/299 RC 4.00 10.00
227 Reggie Smith/999 RC 1.50 4.00
228 R.Grice-Mullen AU/999 RC 3.00 8.00
229 Ryan Torain AU/199 RC 5.00 12.00
230 Sam Keller AU/999 RC 3.00 8.00
231 Sedrick Ellis/999 RC 1.50 4.00
232 Shawn Crable AU/299 RC 3.00 8.00
233 A.Bowman AU/999 RC 4.00 10.00
234 Simeon Castille AU/805 RC 3.00 8.00
235 Steve Johnson/999 RC 3.00 8.00
236 Tavares Gooden/999 RC 1.50 4.00
237 Terrell Thomas/999 RC 1.50 4.00
238 Terrence Wheatley/999 RC 1.50 4.00
239 Robert Killebrew AU/830 RC 4.00 10.00
240 Thomas Brown/999 RC 1.50 4.00
241 Tim Hightower AU/299 RC 5.00 12.00
242 Tom Zbikowski/999 RC 2.00 5.00
243 Tom Santi/999 RC 2.00 5.00
244 Bernard Morris AU/999 RC 4.00 10.00
245 Tracy Porter AU/299 RC 4.00 10.00
246 Vernon Gholston/999 RC 1.50 4.00
247 Will Franklin AU/199 RC 4.00 10.00
248 Xavier Adibi/999 RC 1.50 4.00
249 Xavier Omon/999 RC 1.50 4.00
250 Zackary Bowman/999 RC 2.00 5.00
251 Brian Brohm AU/100 RC 8.00 20.00
252 Chad Henne AU/100 RC 10.00 25.00
253 Chris Long AU/100 RC 10.00 25.00
254 Donnie Avery AU/100 RC 10.00 25.00
255 Eddie Royal AU/100 RC 8.00 20.00
256 Felix Jones AU/100 RC 8.00 20.00
257 James Hardy AU/100 RC 8.00 20.00
258 J.David Booty AU/100 RC 8.00 20.00
259 Kevin Smith AU/100 RC 8.00 20.00
260 Malcolm Kelly AU/100 RC 8.00 20.00
261 Matt Forte AU/100 RC 12.00 30.00
262 Matt Ryan AU/100 RC 60.00 120.00
263 Ray Rice AU/100 RC 8.00 20.00
264 DeS.Jackson AU/105 RC 15.00 40.00
265 Andre Caldwell AU/120 RC 8.00 20.00
266 D.McFadden AU/120 RC 8.00 20.00
267 Dustin Keller AU/120 RC 10.00 25.00
268 Early Doucet AU/120 RC 8.00 20.00
269 Glenn Dorsey AU/120 RC 8.00 20.00
270 Jake Long AU/120 RC 12.00 30.00
271 Joe Flacco AU/120 RC 15.00 40.00
272 Kevin O'Connell AU/120 RC 8.00 20.00
273 Steve Slaton AU/120 RC 8.00 20.00
274 Limas Sweed AU/125 RC 8.00 20.00
275 Earl Bennett AU/140 RC 12.00 30.00
276 Chris Johnson AU/140 RC 10.00 25.00
277 Dexter Jackson AU/140 RC 12.00 30.00
278 Harry Douglas AU/140 RC 10.00 25.00
279 Jamaal Charles AU/140 RC 12.00 30.00
280 Jerome Simpson AU/140 RC 10.00 25.00
281 J.Stewart AU/140 RC 12.00 30.00
282 Devin Thomas AU/150 RC 8.00 20.00
283 Jordy Nelson AU/150 RC 25.00 50.00
284 M.Manningham AU/150 RC 8.00 20.00
285 R.Mendenhall AU/150 RC 8.00 20.00
286 Dennis Dixon AU/100 RC 8.00 20.00
287 Erik Ainge AU/100 RC EXCH 8.00 20.00
288 Mike Hart AU/100 RC 8.00 20.00
289 M.Jenkins AU/105 RC EXCH 8.00 20.00
290 Dan Connor AU/120 RC 8.00 20.00
291 Dorien Bryant AU/120 RC 10.00 25.00
292 Keith Rivers AU/120 RC 8.00 20.00
293 Kenny Phillips AU/120 RC 8.00 20.00
294 Matt Flynn AU/125 RC 8.00 20.00
295 Lavelle Hawkins AU/140 RC 10.00 25.00
296 Allen Patrick AU/140 RC 8.00 20.00
297 Andre Woodson AU/140 RC 8.00 20.00
298 Colt Brennan AU/140 RC 10.00 25.00
299 Josh Johnson AU/140 RC 8.00 20.00
300 Tashard Choice AU/150 RC 8.00 20.00

2008 Donruss Threads Bronze Holofoil

*VETS 1-150: 2X TO 5X BASIC CARDS
*ROOKIES 151-250: .5X TO 1.2X RETAIL RED
STATED PRINT RUN 250 SER.#'d SETS

2008 Donruss Threads Gold Holofoil

*VETS 1-150: 4X TO 10X BASIC CARDS
*ROOKIES 151-250: 1X TO 2.5X RETAIL RED
STATED PRINT RUN 50 SER.#'d SETS

2008 Donruss Threads Platinum Holofoil

*VETS 1-150: 6X TO 15X BASIC CARDS
*ROOKIES 151-250: 1.2X TO 3X RETAIL RED
STATED PRINT RUN 25 SER.#'d SETS

2008 Donruss Threads Retail Blue

*VETS 1-150: 2X TO 5X BASIC CARDS
*ROOKIES 151-250: .5X TO 1.2X RETAIL RED
RETAIL BLUE PRINT RUN 350

2008 Donruss Threads Retail Green

*VETS 1-150: 2.5X TO 6X BASIC CARDS
*ROOKIES 151-250: .6X TO 1.5X RETAIL RED
STATED PRINT RUN 200 SER.#'d SETS

2008 Donruss Threads Retail Red

*VETS 1-150: 1.5X TO 4X BASIC CARDS
COMMON ROOKIE (151-250) 1.25 3.00
ROOKIE SEMISTARS 1.50 4.00
ROOKIE UNL.STARS 2.00 5.00
RANDOM INSERTS IN RETAIL PACKS
152 Alex Brink 1.50 4.00
161 Bruce Davis 1.50 4.00
185 Jacob Hester 1.25 3.00
193 Jerod Mayo 2.00 5.00
217 Owen Schmitt 1.25 3.00
222 Peyton Hillis 2.00 5.00
242 Tom Zbikowski 1.50 4.00
246 Vernon Gholston 1.25 3.00

2008 Donruss Threads Retail Rookies

*ROOKIES: .4X TO 1X HOBBY RC
STATED PRINT RUN 999 SER.#'d SETS
PRINTED ON WHITE CARD STOCK

2008 Donruss Threads Silver Holofoil

*VETS 1-150: 3X TO 8X BASIC CARDS
*ROOKIES 151-250: .8X TO 2X RETAIL RED
STATED PRINT RUN 100 SER.#'d SETS

2008 Donruss Threads Century Collection Materials

STATED PRINT RUN 250 SER.#'d SETS
*PRIME/25-50: .8X TO 2X BASIC JSY
PRIME PRINT RUN 25-50
1 Mark Gastineau 2.00 5.00
2 Joe Klecko 2.00 5.00
3 Thurman Thomas 2.50 6.00
4 John Matuszak 3.00 8.00
5 Steve Largent 3.00 8.00
6 Jay Novacek 2.50 6.00
7 Jim Kelly 3.00 8.00
8 Dan Marino 6.00 15.00
9 Andre Reed 2.50 6.00
10 John Elway 5.00 12.00
11 Troy Aikman 4.00 10.00
12 Mike Singletary 3.00 8.00
13 Garo Yepremian 2.00 5.00
14 Jim McMahon 3.00 8.00
15 Chuck Foreman 2.00 5.00

2008 Donruss Threads Century Legends

*CENT.PROOF/100: .6X TO 1.5X BASIC INSERTS
CENTURY PROOF PRINT RUN 100 SER.#'d SETS
1 Emmitt Smith 2.00 5.00
2 Peyton Manning 3.00 8.00
3 Brett Favre 2.50 6.00
4 Walter Payton 2.50 6.00
5 Reggie White 1.25 3.00
6 Dan Marino 2.50 6.00
7 Tom Brady 4.00 10.00
8 Joe Montana 4.00 10.00
9 Roger Craig 1.00 2.50
10 Jim Kelly 1.25 3.00
11 Randy White 1.00 2.50
12 Tony Dorsett 1.25 3.00
13 Barry Sanders 2.00 5.00
14 John Elway 2.00 5.00
15 Otto Graham 1.00 2.50

2008 Donruss Threads Century Legends Materials

STATED PRINT RUN 250 SER.#'d SETS
*PRIME/25-50: .8X TO 2X BASIC INSERTS
PRIME PRINT RUN 10-50
1 Emmitt Smith 6.00 15.00
2 Peyton Manning 5.00 12.00
3 Brett Favre 8.00 20.00
4 Walter Payton 12.00 30.00
5 Reggie White 5.00 12.00
6 Dan Marino 8.00 20.00
7 Tom Brady 12.00 30.00
8 Joe Montana 12.00 30.00
9 Roger Craig 3.00 8.00
10 Jim Kelly 4.00 10.00
11 Randy White 4.00 10.00
12 Tony Dorsett 4.00 10.00
13 Barry Sanders 6.00 15.00
14 John Elway 6.00 15.00
15 Otto Graham 6.00 15.00

2008 Donruss Threads Century Stars

*CENT.PROOF/100: .8X TO 2X BASIC INSERTS
CENTURY PROOF PRINT RUN 100 SER.#'d SETS
1 Randy Moss .60 1.50
2 LaDainian Tomlinson .75 2.00
3 Peyton Manning 2.00 5.00
4 Torry Holt .60 1.50
5 Ben Roethlisberger .75 2.00
6 Chad Johnson .50 1.25
7 Brett Favre 1.50 4.00
8 Larry Johnson .50 1.25
9 Brian Westbrook .50 1.25
10 Devin Hester .60 1.50
11 Eli Manning .60 1.50
12 Fred Taylor .50 1.25
13 Terrell Owens .60 1.50
14 Tony Gonzalez .60 1.50
15 Tony Romo .60 1.50
16 Shaun Alexander .50 1.25
17 Marvin Harrison .60 1.50
18 Michael Strahan .60 1.50
19 Donald Driver .60 1.50
20 Tom Brady 2.50 6.00

2008 Donruss Threads Century Stars Materials

STATED PRINT RUN 250 SER.#'d SETS
*PRIME/50: .8X TO 2X BASIC JSYs
PRIME PRINT RUN 50 SER.#'d SETS
1 Randy Moss 2.50 6.00
2 LaDainian Tomlinson 3.00 8.00
3 Peyton Manning 8.00 20.00
4 Torry Holt 2.50 6.00
5 Ben Roethlisberger 3.00 8.00
6 Chad Johnson 2.00 5.00
7 Brett Favre 6.00 15.00
8 Larry Johnson 2.00 5.00
9 Brian Westbrook 2.00 5.00
10 Devin Hester 4.00 10.00
11 Eli Manning 2.50 6.00
12 Fred Taylor 2.00 5.00
13 Terrell Owens/135 2.50 6.00
14 Tony Gonzalez 2.50 6.00
15 Tony Romo 2.50 6.00
16 Shaun Alexander 2.00 5.00
17 Marvin Harrison 2.50 6.00
18 Michael Strahan 2.50 6.00
19 Donald Driver 3.00 8.00
20 Tom Brady 10.00 25.00

2008 Donruss Threads College Greats

1 Dave Casper .40 1.00
2 Joe Greene .60 1.50
3 Gale Sayers .60 1.50
4 John Elway 1.00 2.50
5 Emmitt Smith 1.00 2.50
6 Troy Aikman .75 2.00
7 Charlie Joiner .40 1.00
8 Y.A. Tittle .60 1.50
9 Roger Craig .50 1.25
10 Darren McFadden .40 1.00
11 Matt Ryan 1.25 3.00
12 Steve Slaton .40 1.00
13 Brian Brohm .40 1.00
14 Jonathan Stewart .60 1.50
15 Malcolm Kelly .40 1.00

2008 Donruss Threads College Greats Autographs

STATED PRINT RUN 25-100 SER.#'d SETS
1 Dave Casper/75 8.00 20.00
2 Joe Greene/40 15.00 30.00
3 Gale Sayers/50 40.00 80.00
4 John Elway/25 60.00 120.00
5 Emmitt Smith/22 175.00 300.00
6 Troy Aikman/20 40.00 100.00
7 Charlie Joiner/100 8.00 20.00
8 Y.A. Tittle/100 15.00 40.00
9 Roger Craig/75 12.00 30.00
10 Darren McFadden/25 10.00 25.00
11 Matt Ryan/25 75.00 150.00
12 Steve Slaton/25 6.00 15.00
13 Brian Brohm/25 12.00 30.00
14 Jonathan Stewart/25 10.00 25.00
15 Malcolm Kelly/25 6.00 15.00

2008 Donruss Threads College Greats Autographs Combo

STATED PRINT RUN 25 SER.#'d SETS
1 C.Benson/J.Charles 15.00 40.00
2 M.Lynch/D.Jackson 25.00 50.00
3 D.Dixon/J.Stewart 25.00 50.00
4 A.Peterson/M.Kelly 90.00 150.00
5 D.McFadden/F.Jones 10.00 25.00

2008 Donruss Threads College Gridiron Kings

*SILVER/250: .8X TO 2X BASIC INSERTS
SILVER PRINT RUN 250 SER.#'d SETS
*GOLD/100: 1X TO 2.5X BASIC INSERTS
GOLD PRINT RUN 100 SER.#'d SETS
*FRAMED RED/100: 1X TO 2.5X
FRAMED RED PRINT RUN 100 SER.#'d SETS
*FRAMED BLUE/50: 1.2X TO 3X
FRAMED BLUE PRINT RUN 50 SER.#'d SETS
*PLATINUM/25: 2X TO 5X BASIC INSERTS
PLATINUM PRINT RUN 25 SER.#'d SETS
*FRAMED GREEN/25: 2X TO 5X
FRAMED GREEN PRINT RUN 25 SER.#'d SETS
*FRAMED BLACK/10: 3X TO 8X
FRAMED BLACK PRINT RUN 10 SER.#'d SETS
1 Ali Highsmith .30 .75
2 Allen Patrick .30 .75
3 Antoine Cason .40 1.00
4 Brian Brohm .30 .75
5 Chad Henne .40 1.00
6 Chevis Jackson .30 .75
7 Chris Long .40 1.00
8 Colt Brennan .40 1.00
9 DJ Hall .30 .75
10 Dan Connor .30 .75
11 Dennis Dixon .30 .75
12 Early Doucet .30 .75
13 Eddie Royal .30 .75
14 Erik Ainge .30 .75
15 Ernie Wheelwright .40 1.00
16 Fred Davis .30 .75
17 Glenn Dorsey .30 .75
18 Harry Douglas .40 1.00
19 Jamar Adams .30 .75
20 John David Booty .30 .75
21 Jonathan Hefney .30 .75
22 Keith Rivers .30 .75
23 Kenny Phillips .30 .75
24 Lawrence Jackson .30 .75
25 Limas Sweed .30 .75
26 Marcus Monk .50 1.25
27 Matt Ryan 1.00 2.50
28 Mike Hart .30 .75
29 Quentin Groves .40 1.00
30 Robert Killebrew .40 1.00
31 Sedrick Ellis .30 .75
32 Shawn Crable .30 .75
33 Simeon Castille .30 .75
34 Terrell Thomas .30 .75
35 Xavier Adibi .30 .75
36 Adrian Arrington .30 .75
37 Aqib Talib .50 1.25
38 Brandon Flowers .40 1.00
39 Steve Largent .50 1.25
40 Darren McFadden .30 .75
41 DeSean Jackson .60 1.50
42 Felix Jones .30 .75
43 Jamaal Charles .50 1.25
44 Jonathan Stewart .50 1.25
45 Malcolm Kelly .30 .75
46 Mario Manningham .30 .75
47 Matt Flynn .30 .75
48 Rashard Mendenhall .30 .75
49 Steve Slaton .30 .75
50 Vernon Gholston .30 .75

2008 Donruss Threads College Gridiron Kings Autographs

STATED PRINT RUN 25 SER.#'d SETS
1 Ali Highsmith 6.00 15.00
2 Allen Patrick 8.00 20.00
3 Antoine Cason 8.00 20.00
4 Brian Brohm 6.00 15.00
5 Chad Henne 8.00 20.00
6 Chevis Jackson 6.00 15.00
7 Chris Long 8.00 20.00
8 Colt Brennan 8.00 20.00
9 DJ Hall 6.00 15.00
10 Dan Connor 6.00 15.00
11 Dennis Dixon 12.00 30.00
12 Early Doucet 6.00 15.00
13 Eddie Royal 6.00 15.00
14 Erik Ainge 6.00 15.00
15 Ernie Wheelwright 8.00 20.00
16 Fred Davis 6.00 15.00
17 Glenn Dorsey 6.00 15.00
18 Harry Douglas EXCH 8.00 20.00
19 Jamar Adams 6.00 15.00
20 John David Booty 6.00 15.00
21 Jonathan Hefney 6.00 15.00
22 Keith Rivers 6.00 15.00
23 Kenny Phillips EXCH 6.00 15.00
24 Lawrence Jackson 6.00 15.00
25 Limas Sweed 6.00 15.00
26 Marcus Monk 8.00 20.00
27 Matt Ryan 60.00 120.00
28 Mike Hart 6.00 15.00
29 Quentin Groves 8.00 20.00
30 Robert Killebrew 8.00 20.00
31 Sedrick Ellis 6.00 15.00
32 Shawn Crable 6.00 15.00
33 Simeon Castille 6.00 15.00
34 Terrell Thomas 6.00 15.00
35 Xavier Adibi 6.00 15.00
36 Adrian Arrington 6.00 15.00
37 Aqib Talib 10.00 25.00
38 Brandon Flowers 8.00 20.00
39 Steve Largent 12.00 30.00
40 Darren McFadden 6.00 15.00
41 DeSean Jackson 12.00 30.00
42 Felix Jones 6.00 15.00
43 Jamaal Charles 10.00 25.00
44 Jonathan Stewart 10.00 25.00
45 Malcolm Kelly 6.00 15.00
46 Mario Manningham 6.00 15.00
47 Matt Flynn 6.00 15.00
48 Rashard Mendenhall 6.00 15.00
49 Steve Slaton 6.00 15.00
50 Vernon Gholston 6.00 15.00

2008 Donruss Threads College Gridiron Kings Material Autographs

STATED PRINT RUN 30 SER.#'d SETS
1 Ali Highsmith 6.00 15.00
2 Allen Patrick 6.00 15.00
4 Brian Brohm 6.00 15.00
5 Chad Henne 8.00 20.00
6 Chevis Jackson 6.00 15.00
7 Chris Long 8.00 20.00
8 Colt Brennan 8.00 20.00
9 DJ Hall 6.00 15.00
10 Dan Connor 6.00 15.00
12 Early Doucet 6.00 15.00
13 Eddie Royal 6.00 15.00
14 Erik Ainge 20.00 40.00
15 Ernie Wheelwright 8.00 20.00
16 Fred Davis 6.00 15.00
17 Glenn Dorsey 6.00 15.00
18 Harry Douglas 10.00 25.00
20 John David Booty 6.00 15.00
21 Jonathan Hefney 6.00 15.00
22 Keith Rivers 6.00 15.00
23 Kenny Phillips EXCH 6.00 15.00
24 Lawrence Jackson 6.00 15.00
25 Limas Sweed 6.00 15.00
26 Marcus Monk 8.00 20.00
27 Matt Ryan 60.00 120.00
28 Mike Hart 6.00 15.00
30 Robert Killebrew 8.00 20.00
31 Sedrick Ellis 6.00 15.00
32 Shawn Crable 6.00 15.00
33 Simeon Castille 6.00 15.00
34 Terrell Thomas 6.00 15.00
35 Xavier Adibi 6.00 15.00
37 Aqib Talib 10.00 25.00
38 Brandon Flowers 8.00 20.00
39 Steve Largent 15.00 40.00
40 Darren McFadden 6.00 15.00
41 DeSean Jackson 20.00 50.00
42 Felix Jones 6.00 15.00
43 Jamaal Charles 10.00 25.00
44 Jonathan Stewart 10.00 25.00
45 Malcolm Kelly 6.00 15.00
48 Rashard Mendenhall 6.00 15.00
49 Steve Slaton 6.00 15.00

2008 Donruss Threads College Gridiron Kings Material Autographs Prime

*PRIME/15: .6X TO 1.5X BASIC INSERTS
PRIME PRINT RUN 10-15
8 Colt Brennan 12.00 30.00
11 Dennis Dixon 25.00 60.00
19 Jamar Adams 20.00 40.00
27 Matt Ryan 100.00 200.00
29 Quentin Groves 12.00 30.00
36 Adrian Arrington 10.00 25.00
46 Mario Manningham 20.00 50.00
47 Matt Flynn 10.00 25.00
50 Vernon Gholston 10.00 25.00

2008 Donruss Threads College Gridiron Kings Materials

STATED PRINT RUN 110-250
*PRIME/15-25: .8X TO 2X BASIC INSERTS
PRIME PRINT RUN 9-25
1 Ali Highsmith 2.00 5.00
2 Allen Patrick 2.00 5.00
4 Brian Brohm 2.00 5.00
5 Chad Henne 2.50 6.00
6 Chevis Jackson 2.00 5.00
7 Chris Long 2.50 6.00
8 Colt Brennan 2.50 6.00
9 DJ Hall 2.00 5.00
10 Dan Connor 2.00 5.00
12 Early Doucet 2.00 5.00
13 Eddie Royal 2.00 5.00
14 Erik Ainge 2.00 5.00
15 Ernie Wheelwright 2.50 6.00
16 Fred Davis 2.00 5.00
17 Glenn Dorsey 2.00 5.00
18 Harry Douglas/110 2.50 6.00
20 John David Booty 2.00 5.00
21 Jonathan Hefney 2.00 5.00
22 Keith Rivers 2.00 5.00
23 Kenny Phillips 2.00 5.00
24 Lawrence Jackson 2.00 5.00
25 Limas Sweed 2.00 5.00
26 Marcus Monk 2.50 6.00
27 Matt Ryan 6.00 15.00
28 Mike Hart 2.00 5.00
30 Robert Killebrew 2.50 6.00
31 Sedrick Ellis 2.00 5.00
32 Shawn Crable 2.00 5.00
33 Simeon Castille 2.00 5.00
34 Terrell Thomas 2.00 5.00
35 Xavier Adibi 2.00 5.00
37 Aqib Talib 3.00 8.00
38 Brandon Flowers 2.50 6.00
39 Steve Largent 4.00 10.00
40 Darren McFadden 2.00 5.00
41 DeSean Jackson 4.00 10.00
42 Felix Jones 2.00 5.00
43 Jamaal Charles 3.00 8.00
44 Jonathan Stewart/220 3.00 8.00
45 Malcolm Kelly 2.00 5.00
48 Rashard Mendenhall 2.00 5.00
49 Steve Slaton/165 2.00 5.00
50 Vernon Gholston/190 2.00 5.00

2008 Donruss Threads Crown Autographs

RANDOM INSERTS IN 2009 LIMITED PACKS
1 Brian Brohm 6.00 15.00
3 Darren McFadden 6.00 15.00
4 Dexter Jackson 10.00 25.00
5 Donnie Avery 8.00 20.00
6 Earl Bennett 10.00 25.00
7 Eddie Royal 6.00 15.00
8 Harry Douglas 8.00 20.00
9 Jamaal Charles 10.00 25.00
10 Jerome Simpson 8.00 20.00
11 John David Booty 6.00 15.00
12 Jordy Nelson 20.00 40.00
13 Kevin Smith 6.00 15.00
15 Matt Forte 10.00 25.00
17 Steve Slaton 6.00 15.00
19 Ray Rice 6.00 15.00
20 Matt Ryan 20.00 50.00
21 Mario Manningham 6.00 15.00
23 Kevin O'Connell 6.00 15.00
24 Jonathan Stewart 10.00 25.00
25 Joe Flacco 12.00 30.00
26 James Hardy 6.00 15.00
27 Jake Long 10.00 25.00
28 Felix Jones 6.00 15.00
29 Early Doucet 6.00 15.00
30 Dustin Keller 8.00 20.00
32 DeSean Jackson 12.00 30.00
33 Chad Henne 8.00 20.00

2008 Donruss Threads Crown Retail

RANDOM INSERTS IN RETAIL PACKS
1 Brian Brohm .40 1.00
2 Chris Johnson .50 1.25
3 Darren McFadden .40 1.00
4 Devin Thomas .40 1.00
5 Donnie Avery .50 1.25
6 Earl Bennett .60 1.50
7 Eddie Royal .40 1.00
8 Harry Douglas .50 1.25
9 Jamaal Charles .60 1.50
10 Jerome Simpson .50 1.25
11 John David Booty .40 1.00
12 Jordy Nelson 1.25 3.00
13 Kevin Smith .40 1.00
14 Malcolm Kelly .40 1.00
15 Matt Forte .60 1.50
16 Rashard Mendenhall .40 1.00
17 Steve Slaton .40 1.00
18 Glenn Dorsey .40 1.00
19 Ray Rice .40 1.00
20 Matt Ryan 1.25 3.00
21 Mario Manningham .40 1.00
22 Limas Sweed .40 1.00
23 Kevin O'Connell .40 1.00
24 Jonathan Stewart .60 1.50
25 Joe Flacco .75 2.00
26 James Hardy .40 1.00
27 Jake Long .60 1.50
28 Felix Jones .40 1.00
29 Early Doucet .40 1.00
30 Dustin Keller .50 1.25
31 Dexter Jackson .60 1.50
32 DeSean Jackson .75 2.00
33 Chad Henne .50 1.25
34 Andre Caldwell .40 1.00

2008 Donruss Threads Crowns

ONE PER DICK'S SPORT.GOODS BOX
1 Darren McFadden .40 1.00
2 Rashard Mendenhall .40 1.00
3 Matt Ryan 1.25 3.00
4 Jonathan Stewart .60 1.50
5 Joe Flacco .75 2.00
6 Felix Jones .40 1.00

2008 Donruss Threads Dynasty

*CENT.PROOF/100: .8X TO 2X BASIC INSERTS
CENTURY PROOF PRINT RUN 100 SER.#'d SETS
1 Brady/Moss/Bruschi 3.00 8.00
2 Lambert/Stallworth/Greene 1.00 2.50
3 Starr/Hornung/Gregg 1.50 4.00
4 Griese/Warfield/Yepremian 1.00 2.50
5 Aikman/Smith/Irvin 1.50 4.00
6 Montana/Rice/Craig 3.00 8.00
7 McMahon/Payton/Singletary 2.00 5.00
8 Kelly/Thomas/Reed 1.00 2.50
9 Brown/Graham/Groza 1.25 3.00
10 Staubach/Dorsett/White 1.25 3.00

2008 Donruss Threads Dynasty Materials

STATED PRINT RUN 180-250
*PRIME/25-50: .6X TO 1.5X BASIC JSYs
*PRIME/15: .8X TO 2X BASIC JSYs
PRIME PRINT RUN 15-50
1 Brady/Moss/Bruschi 25.00 60.00
2 Lambert/Stallworth/Greene 12.00 30.00
3 Starr/Hornung/Gregg 15.00 40.00
4 Griese/Warfield/Yepremian/180 8.00 20.00

5 Aikman/Smith/Irvin 15.00 40.00
6 Montana/Rice/Craig 15.00 40.00
7 McMahon/Payton/Singletary 20.00 50.00
8 Kelly/Thomas/Reed 8.00 20.00
9 Brown/Graham/Groza/235 12.00 30.00
10 Staubach/Dorsett/White 12.00 30.00

2008 Donruss Threads Footballs

RANDOM INSERTS IN RETAIL PACKS
STATED PRINT RUN 9-250
1 Anquan Boldin 2.50 6.00
2 Larry Fitzgerald 3.00 8.00
3 Warrick Dunn 2.50 6.00
4 Derrick Mason 2.50 6.00
5 Steve Smith 3.00 8.00
6 Brian Urlacher 4.00 10.00
7 Chad Johnson/139 2.50 6.00
8 Terrell Owens/165 3.00 8.00
9 Tony Gonzalez 3.00 8.00
11 Torry Holt/165 3.00 8.00
12 Isaac Bruce 4.00 10.00
13 Jeff Garcia/190 2.50 6.00
14 Santana Moss 2.50 6.00
15 LaDainian Tomlinson 4.00 10.00
16 Matt Hasselbeck/50 3.00 8.00
18 Earnest Graham 2.50 6.00
19 Joey Galloway 3.00 8.00
20 Ike Hilliard 2.50 6.00
21 Vince Young 2.50 6.00
22 Jason Taylor 3.00 8.00
23 Tom Brady 12.00 30.00
24 Randy Moss 3.00 8.00
25 Donte Stallworth/23 4.00 10.00
26 Deuce McAllister 3.00 8.00
27 Eli Manning 3.00 8.00
28 Michael Strahan 3.00 8.00
29 Thomas Jones 2.50 6.00
30 Laveranues Coles 2.50 6.00
31 Jerry Porter 2.50 6.00
32 Correll Buckhalter 2.50 6.00
33 Donovan McNabb 3.00 8.00

2008 Donruss Threads Generations

*CENT.PROOF/100: .8X TO 2X BASIC INSERTS
CENTURY PROOF PRINT RUN 100 SER.#'d SETS
1 P.Manning/E.Manning 2.50 6.00
2 T.Thomas/M.Lynch .75 2.00
3 D.Marino/B.Favre 2.00 5.00
4 S.Largent/D.Branch 1.00 2.50
5 R.Craig/F.Gore .75 2.00
6 J.Stallworth/S.Holmes .75 2.00
7 C.Foreman/A.Peterson 1.00 2.50
8 S.Sharpe/G.Jennings .75 2.00
9 D.Fouts/P.Rivers 1.00 2.50
10 G.Sayers/D.Hester 1.50 4.00
11 J.Novacek/J.Witten 1.25 3.00
12 M.Harrison/A.Gonzalez .75 2.00
13 J.Rice/R.Moss 2.00 5.00
14 M.Irvin/T.Owens 1.25 3.00
15 R.White/M.Strahan 1.00 2.50

2008 Donruss Threads Generations Materials

STATED PRINT RUN 250 SER.#'d SETS
*PRIME/35-50: .8X TO 2X BASIC JSYs
PRIME PRINT RUN 35-50
1 P.Manning/E.Manning 12.00 30.00
2 T.Thomas/M.Lynch 4.00 10.00
3 D.Marino/B.Favre 15.00 40.00
4 S.Largent/D.Branch 5.00 12.00
5 R.Craig/F.Gore 5.00 12.00
6 J.Stallworth/S.Holmes 5.00 12.00
7 C.Foreman/A.Peterson 8.00 20.00
8 S.Sharpe/G.Jennings 5.00 12.00
9 D.Fouts/P.Rivers 5.00 12.00
10 G.Sayers/D.Hester 8.00 20.00
11 J.Novacek/J.Witten 6.00 15.00
12 M.Harrison/A.Gonzalez 4.00 10.00
13 J.Rice/R.Moss 10.00 25.00
14 M.Irvin/T.Owens 6.00 15.00
15 R.White/M.Strahan 5.00 12.00

2008 Donruss Threads Jerseys

STATED PRINT RUN 9-250
1 Anquan Boldin 2.00 5.00
2 Larry Fitzgerald 2.50 6.00
4 Derrick Mason/20 4.00 10.00
5 Steve Smith/200 2.50 6.00
6 Brian Urlacher 3.00 8.00
7 Chad Johnson 2.00 5.00
9 Tony Gonzalez 2.50 6.00
10 Rex Grossman 2.00 5.00
11 Torry Holt 2.50 6.00
13 Jeff Garcia 2.00 5.00
14 Santana Moss 2.00 5.00
15 LaDainian Tomlinson 3.00 8.00
16 Matt Hasselbeck 2.00 5.00
19 Joey Galloway/50 3.00 8.00
20 Ike Hilliard 2.00 5.00
21 Vince Young 2.00 5.00
22 Jason Taylor 3.00 8.00
23 Tom Brady 10.00 25.00
24 Randy Moss 2.50 6.00
26 Deuce McAllister 2.50 6.00
27 Eli Manning 2.50 6.00
28 Michael Strahan 2.50 6.00
30 Laveranues Coles 2.00 5.00
32 Correll Buckhalter 2.00 5.00
33 Donovan McNabb 2.50 6.00
34 Hines Ward 2.50 6.00
36 Jason Witten 3.00 8.00
38 Jay Cutler 2.00 5.00
39 Brandon Marshall 2.50 6.00
42 Jon Kitna 2.00 5.00
43 Roy Williams WR 2.00 5.00
45 Calvin Johnson 3.00 8.00
46 Aaron Rodgers 10.00 25.00
47 Ryan Grant 2.50 6.00
48 Donald Driver 2.50 6.00
49 Greg Jennings 2.00 5.00
50 James Jones 2.00 5.00
51 Matt Schaub 2.00 5.00
53 Andre Johnson 2.50 6.00
55 Ahman Green/110 2.50 6.00
56 Peyton Manning 8.00 20.00
57 Marvin Harrison 2.50 6.00
58 Joseph Addai 2.00 5.00
59 Reggie Wayne 2.50 6.00
60 Dallas Clark 2.00 5.00
61 David Garrard 2.00 5.00
62 Fred Taylor 2.00 5.00
63 Maurice Jones-Drew 2.00 5.00
64 Reggie Williams 2.50 6.00
65 Larry Johnson 2.00 5.00
67 Dwayne Bowe 2.50 6.00
68 Ted Ginn Jr./125 2.00 5.00
69 Ronnie Brown 2.00 5.00
71 Tarvaris Jackson 2.00 5.00
72 Adrian Peterson 3.00 8.00
73 Chester Taylor 2.00 5.00
74 Sidney Rice 2.00 5.00
75 Wes Welker 2.50 6.00
76 Laurence Maroney 2.50 6.00
77 Drew Brees 3.00 8.00
78 Reggie Bush 2.00 5.00
79 Marques Colston 2.00 5.00
80 Brandon Jacobs 2.00 5.00
81 Plaxico Burress 2.00 5.00
84 Leon Washington 2.00 5.00
85 Jerricho Cotchery 2.00 5.00
86 Matt Leinart 2.00 5.00
87 Edgerrin James/30 4.00 10.00
89 Justin Fargas/200 2.00 5.00
90 Alge Crumpler 2.00 5.00
91 Jerious Norwood 2.00 5.00
92 Roddy White/225 2.00 5.00
94 Willis McGahee 2.00 5.00
95 Mark Clayton 2.00 5.00
96 Brian Westbrook 3.00 8.00
97 Kevin Curtis 2.00 5.00
99 Ray Lewis 3.00 8.00
100 Reggie Brown/60 2.50 6.00
101 Trent Edwards/140 2.00 5.00
102 Marshawn Lynch 2.50 6.00
103 Ben Roethlisberger 3.00 8.00
104 Willie Parker 2.50 6.00
105 Lee Evans 2.50 6.00
106 Josh Reed 2.00 5.00
107 Santonio Holmes 2.00 5.00
108 Jake Delhomme/105 2.00 5.00
110 Heath Miller 2.00 5.00
111 Philip Rivers 3.00 8.00
112 DeAngelo Williams 2.00 5.00
115 Antonio Gates 2.50 6.00
116 Shawne Merriman/160 2.00 5.00
118 Cedric Benson 2.00 5.00
119 Vincent Jackson 2.00 5.00
120 Alex Smith QB/70 3.00 8.00
121 Devin Hester 2.50 6.00
122 Carson Palmer 2.50 6.00
123 Frank Gore 2.50 6.00
124 T.J. Houshmandzadeh 2.00 5.00
125 Rudi Johnson 2.00 5.00
126 Vernon Davis 2.00 5.00
127 Patrick Willis 2.50 6.00
129 Derek Anderson 2.00 5.00
131 Kellen Winslow 2.00 5.00
133 Nate Burleson 2.00 5.00
134 Braylon Edwards 2.00 5.00
136 Deion Branch 2.00 5.00
137 Marc Bulger 2.00 5.00
138 Tony Romo 2.50 6.00
139 Marion Barber 2.00 5.00
140 Steven Jackson 2.00 5.00
141 Randy McMichael/15 4.00 10.00
142 Cadillac Williams 2.50 6.00
143 LenDale White/150 2.00 5.00
144 Chris Brown 2.00 5.00
147 Jason Campbell 2.00 5.00
148 Clinton Portis 2.00 5.00
149 Chris Cooley/155 3.00 8.00
150 Ladell Betts 2.00 5.00

2008 Donruss Threads Jerseys Prime

*PRIME/25-50: .8X TO 2X JSY/105-250
*PRIME/25-50: .6X TO 1.5X JSY/50-70
*PRIME/25-50: .5X TO 1.2X JSY/15-30
PRIME PRINT RUN 4-50
3 Warrick Dunn/25 4.00 10.00
8 Terrell Owens 5.00 12.00
99 Ray Lewis 10.00 25.00

2008 Donruss Threads Pro Gridiron Kings

*SILVER/250: .5X TO 1.2X BASIC INSERTS
SILVER PRINT RUN 250 SER.#'d SETS
*GOLD/100: .6X TO 1.5X BASIC INSERTS
GOLD PRINT RUN 100 SER.#'d SETS
*FRAMED RED/100: .6X TO 1.5X
FRAMED RED PRINT RUN 100 SER.#'d SETS
*FRAMED BLUE/50: .8X TO 2X
FRAMED BLUE PRINT RUN 50 SER.#'d SETS
*PLATINUM/25: 1.2X TO 3X BASIC INSERTS
PLATINUM PRINT RUN 25 SER.#'d SETS
*FRAMED GREEN/25: 1.2X TO 3X
FRAMED GREEN PRINT RUN 25 SER.#'d SETS
*FRAMED BLACK/10: 2X TO 5X
FRAMED BLACK PRINT RUN 10 SER.#'d SETS
1 Chad Johnson .50 1.25
2 Brian Westbrook .50 1.25
3 Willie Parker .60 1.50
4 Clinton Portis .50 1.25
5 Edgerrin James .60 1.50
6 Willis McGahee .50 1.25
7 Joseph Addai .50 1.25
8 Steven Jackson .50 1.25
9 Emmitt Smith 1.25 3.00
10 Randy White .60 1.50
11 Mark Gastineau .50 1.25
12 Joe Klecko .50 1.25
13 Chuck Foreman .50 1.25
14 John Matuszak .75 2.00
15 Vince Young .50 1.25
16 Drew Brees .75 2.00
17 Jon Kitna .50 1.25
18 Carson Palmer .60 1.50
19 Eli Manning .60 1.50
20 Reggie Wayne .60 1.50
21 Larry Fitzgerald .60 1.50
22 Torry Holt .60 1.50
23 Tony Gonzalez .60 1.50
24 Jason Witten .60 1.50
25 Wes Welker .60 1.50
26 Plaxico Burress .50 1.25
27 Greg Jennings .50 1.25
28 Antonio Gates .60 1.50
29 Adrian Peterson .75 2.00
30 Dwayne Bowe .60 1.50
31 Marshawn Lynch .60 1.50
32 Laurence Maroney .60 1.50
33 Randy Moss .60 1.50
34 Terrell Owens .60 1.50
35 Chris Cooley .50 1.25
36 Fred Taylor .50 1.25
37 Derek Anderson .50 1.25
38 Braylon Edwards .50 1.25
39 Marques Colston .50 1.25
40 T.J. Houshmandzadeh .50 1.25
41 Steve Smith .60 1.50
42 Lee Evans .60 1.50
43 Reggie Bush .50 1.25
44 Marion Barber .50 1.25
45 Jay Cutler .50 1.25
46 Donovan McNabb .60 1.50
47 Kurt Warner .60 1.50
48 Brandon Jacobs .50 1.25
49 Shaun Alexander .50 1.25
50 Maurice Jones-Drew .50 1.25
51A Brett Favre dropping back 3.00 8.00
51B Brett Favre holding towel 3.00 8.00
DM Darren McFadden 1.50 4.00
NNO Brett Favre Promo 3.00 8.00

2008 Donruss Threads Pro Gridiron Kings Autographs

STATED PRINT RUN 10-25
SERIAL #'d UNDER 25 NOT PRICED
3 Willie Parker/25 EXCH 15.00 40.00
10 Randy White/25 15.00 40.00
11 Mark Gastineau/25 EXCH 12.00 30.00
39 Marques Colston/25

2008 Donruss Threads Pro Gridiron Kings Materials

STATED PRINT RUN 250 SER.#'d SETS
*PRIME/20-50: .8X TO 2X BASIC INSERTS
PRIME PRINT RUN 20-50
1 Chad Johnson 2.00 5.00
2 Brian Westbrook 2.00 5.00
3 Willie Parker 2.50 6.00
4 Clinton Portis 2.00 5.00
5 Edgerrin James 2.50 6.00
6 Willis McGahee 2.00 5.00
7 Joseph Addai 2.00 5.00
8 Steven Jackson 2.00 5.00
9 Emmitt Smith 5.00 12.00
10 Randy White 2.50 6.00
11 Mark Gastineau 2.00 5.00
12 Joe Klecko 2.00 5.00
13 Chuck Foreman 2.00 5.00
14 John Matuszak 3.00 8.00
15 Vince Young 2.00 5.00
16 Drew Brees 3.00 8.00
17 Jon Kitna 2.00 5.00
18 Carson Palmer 2.50 6.00
19 Eli Manning 2.50 6.00
20 Reggie Wayne 2.50 6.00
21 Larry Fitzgerald 2.50 6.00
22 Torry Holt 2.50 6.00
23 Tony Gonzalez 2.50 6.00
24 Jason Witten 2.50 6.00
25 Wes Welker 2.50 6.00
26 Plaxico Burress 2.00 5.00
27 Greg Jennings 2.00 5.00
28 Antonio Gates 2.50 6.00
29 Adrian Peterson 3.00 8.00
30 Dwayne Bowe 2.50 6.00
31 Marshawn Lynch 2.50 6.00
32 Laurence Maroney 2.50 6.00
33 Randy Moss 2.50 6.00
34 Terrell Owens 2.50 6.00
35 Chris Cooley 2.00 5.00
36 Fred Taylor 2.00 5.00
37 Derek Anderson 2.00 5.00
38 Braylon Edwards 2.00 5.00
39 Marques Colston 2.00 5.00
40 T.J. Houshmandzadeh 2.00 5.00
41 Steve Smith 2.50 6.00
42 Lee Evans 2.50 6.00
43 Reggie Bush 2.00 5.00
44 Marion Barber 2.00 5.00
45 Jay Cutler 2.00 5.00
46 Donovan McNabb 2.50 6.00
47 Kurt Warner 2.50 6.00
48 Brandon Jacobs 2.00 5.00
49 Shaun Alexander 2.00 5.00
50 Maurice Jones-Drew 2.00 5.00

2008 Donruss Threads Rookie Autographs Silver

STATED PRINT RUN 50 SER.#'d SETS
155 Antoine Cason 6.00 15.00
157 Aqib Talib 8.00 20.00
160 Brandon Flowers 6.00 15.00
177 Derrick Harvey 5.00 12.00
179 Dominique Rodgers-Cromartie 6.00 15.00
182 Fred Davis 5.00 12.00
186 Jacob Tamme 6.00 15.00
192 Jermichael Finley 5.00 12.00
193 Jerod Mayo 8.00 20.00
194 John Carlson 5.00 12.00
201 Keenan Burton 5.00 12.00
204 Kentwan Balmer 5.00 12.00
206 Lawrence Jackson 5.00 12.00
207 Leodis McKelvin 6.00 15.00
214 Martellus Bennett 6.00 15.00
218 Pat Sims 6.00 15.00
223 Phillip Merling 5.00 12.00
227 Reggie Smith 5.00 12.00
231 Sedrick Ellis 5.00 12.00
237 Terrell Thomas 5.00 12.00
240 Thomas Brown 5.00 12.00
246 Vernon Gholston 5.00 12.00
248 Xavier Adibi 5.00 12.00

2008 Donruss Threads Rookie Collection Materials

STATED PRINT RUN 500 SER.#'d SETS
*PRIME/25: .8X TO 2X BASIC JSYs
PRIME PRINT RUN 25 SER.#'d SETS
1 Rashard Mendenhall 1.50 4.00
2 Mario Manningham 1.50 4.00
3 Jordy Nelson 5.00 12.00
4 Devin Thomas 1.50 4.00
5 Jonathan Stewart 2.50 6.00
6 Jerome Simpson 2.00 5.00
7 Jamaal Charles 2.50 6.00
8 Harry Douglas 2.00 5.00
9 Dexter Jackson 2.50 6.00
10 Chris Johnson 2.00 5.00
11 Earl Bennett 2.50 6.00
12 Limas Sweed 1.50 4.00
13 Steve Slaton 1.50 4.00
14 Kevin O'Connell 1.50 4.00
15 Joe Flacco 3.00 8.00
16 Jake Long 2.50 6.00
17 Glenn Dorsey 1.50 4.00
18 Early Doucet 1.50 4.00
19 Dustin Keller 2.00 5.00
20 Darren McFadden 1.50 4.00
21 Andre Caldwell 1.50 4.00
22 DeSean Jackson 3.00 8.00
23 Ray Rice 1.50 4.00
24 Matt Ryan 5.00 12.00
25 Matt Forte 2.50 6.00
26 Malcolm Kelly 1.50 4.00
27 Kevin Smith 1.50 4.00
28 John David Booty 1.50 4.00
29 James Hardy 1.50 4.00
30 Felix Jones 1.50 4.00
31 Eddie Royal 1.50 4.00
32 Donnie Avery 2.00 5.00
33 Chad Henne 2.00 5.00
34 Brian Brohm 1.50 4.00

2008 Donruss Threads Rookie Collection Materials Autographs

STATED PRINT RUN 25 SER.#'d SETS
UNPRICED PRIME PRINT RUN 10
1 Rashard Mendenhall 8.00 20.00
2 Mario Manningham 8.00 20.00
3 Jordy Nelson 25.00 50.00
4 Devin Thomas 8.00 20.00
5 Jonathan Stewart 12.00 30.00
6 Jerome Simpson 10.00 25.00
7 Jamaal Charles 12.00 30.00
8 Harry Douglas 10.00 25.00
9 Dexter Jackson 12.00 30.00
10 Chris Johnson 10.00 25.00
11 Earl Bennett 12.00 30.00
12 Limas Sweed 8.00 20.00
13 Steve Slaton 8.00 20.00
14 Kevin O'Connell 8.00 20.00
15 Joe Flacco 15.00 40.00
16 Jake Long 12.00 30.00
17 Glenn Dorsey 8.00 20.00
18 Early Doucet EXCH 8.00 20.00
19 Dustin Keller 10.00 25.00
20 Darren McFadden 6.00 15.00
21 Andre Caldwell 8.00 20.00
22 DeSean Jackson 15.00 40.00
23 Ray Rice 8.00 20.00
24 Matt Ryan 75.00 150.00
25 Matt Forte 30.00 60.00
26 Malcolm Kelly 8.00 20.00
27 Kevin Smith 8.00 20.00
28 John David Booty 8.00 20.00
29 James Hardy 8.00 20.00
30 Felix Jones 6.00 15.00
31 Eddie Royal 8.00 20.00
32 Donnie Avery 10.00 25.00
33 Chad Henne 10.00 25.00
34 Brian Brohm 8.00 20.00

2008 Donruss Threads Rookie Collection Materials Combo

STATED PRINT RUN 500 SER.#'d SETS
*PRIME/25: .8X TO 2X BASIC DUAL
PRIME PRINT RUN 25 SER.#'d SETS
1 M.Ryan/H.Douglas 6.00 15.00
2 J.Flacco/R.Rice 4.00 10.00
3 E.Bennett/M.Forte 5.00 12.00
4 A.Caldwell/J.Simpson 3.00 8.00
5 B.Brohm/J.Nelson 6.00 15.00
6 J.Charles/G.Dorsey 4.00 10.00
7 C.Henne/J.Long 3.00 8.00
8 R.Mendenhall/L.Sweed 2.00 5.00
9 J.Stewart/D.Jackson 4.00 10.00
10 D.Thomas/M.Kelly 5.00 12.00
11 M.Ryan/D.McFadden 6.00 15.00
12 M.Manningham/C.Henne 2.50 6.00
13 B.Brohm/H.Douglas 2.00 5.00
14 D.McFadden/F.Jones 2.00 5.00
15 L.Sweed/J.Charles 5.00 12.00

2008 Donruss Threads Rookie Collection Materials Quad

STATED PRINT RUN 100 SER.#'d SETS
*PRIME/25: .8X TO 2X BASIC QUAD
PRIME PRINT RUN 25 SER.#'d SETS
1 Ryan/Flacc/McFad/Stwrt 8.00 20.00
2 Jhnsn/Frte/Kelly/Sweed 4.00 10.00
3 McFad/Stew/Jnes/Mend 4.00 10.00
4 Ryan/Flacc/Brohm/Hnne 8.00 20.00
5 Avery/Thms/Nlsn/Hardy 8.00 20.00

2008 Donruss Threads National Convention

COMPLETE SET (6) 12.00 30.00
72 Adrian Peterson .60 1.50
121 Devin Hester .50 1.25
256 Felix Jones .60 1.50
262 Matt Ryan 2.00 5.00
266 Darren McFadden .60 1.50
281 Jonathan Stewart 1.00 2.50

2009 Donruss Threads

COMP.SET w/o RC's (100) 8.00 20.00
ROOKIE STICKER AU PRINT RUN 99-499
ROOKIE PATCH AU PRINT RUN 99-396
1 Kurt Warner .25 .60
2 Larry Fitzgerald .25 .60
3 Tim Hightower .20 .50
4 Matt Ryan .25 .60
5 Michael Turner .20 .50
6 Roddy White .20 .50
7 Derrick Mason .20 .50
8 Joe Flacco .25 .60
9 Willis McGahee .20 .50
10 Lee Evans .25 .60
11 Marshawn Lynch .25 .60
12 Terrell Owens .25 .60
13 DeAngelo Williams .20 .50
14 Jake Delhomme .20 .50
15 Jonathan Stewart .20 .50
16 Steve Smith .25 .60
17 Greg Olsen .25 .60
18 Kyle Orton .20 .50
19 Matt Forte .20 .50
20 Carson Palmer .25 .60
21 Cedric Benson .20 .50
22 Chad Ochocinco .20 .50
23 Brady Quinn .20 .50
24 Braylon Edwards .20 .50
25 Jamal Lewis .25 .60
26 Marion Barber .25 .60
27 Roy Williams WR .20 .50
28 Tony Romo .25 .60
29 Brandon Marshall .25 .60
30 Jay Cutler .20 .50
31 Correll Buckhalter .20 .50
32 Calvin Johnson .30 .75
33 Daunte Culpepper .25 .60
34 Kevin Smith .20 .50
35 Aaron Rodgers .60 1.50
36 Greg Jennings .20 .50
37 Ryan Grant .25 .60
38 Andre Johnson .25 .60
39 Matt Schaub .20 .50
40 Steve Slaton .20 .50
41 Anthony Gonzalez .20 .50
42 Joseph Addai .20 .50
43 Peyton Manning .75 2.00
44 Reggie Wayne .25 .60
45 David Garrard .20 .50
46 Marcedes Lewis .20 .50
47 Maurice Jones-Drew .20 .50
48 Dwayne Bowe .25 .60
49 Larry Johnson .20 .50
50 Matt Cassel .20 .50
51 Tony Gonzalez .25 .60
52 Chad Pennington .20 .50
53 Ricky Williams .25 .60
54 Ronnie Brown .20 .50
55 Adrian Peterson .30 .75
56 Bernard Berrian .20 .50
57 Visanthe Shiancoe .25 .60
58 Laurence Maroney .25 .60
59 Tom Brady 1.00 2.50
60 Wes Welker .25 .60
61 Randy Moss .25 .60
62 Drew Brees .30 .75
63 Marques Colston .20 .50
64 Reggie Bush .20 .50
65 Brandon Jacobs .20 .50
66 Eli Manning .25 .60
67 Kevin Boss .20 .50
68 Thomas Jones .20 .50
69 Jerricho Cotchery .20 .50
70 Leon Washington .20 .50
71 Darren McFadden .30 .75
72 JaMarcus Russell .20 .50
73 Zach Miller .20 .50
74 Brian Westbrook .20 .50
75 DeSean Jackson .25 .60
76 Donovan McNabb .25 .60
77 Ben Roethlisberger .30 .75
78 Santonio Holmes .20 .50
79 Willie Parker .20 .50
80 LaDainian Tomlinson .30 .75
81 Philip Rivers .30 .75
82 Vincent Jackson .20 .50
83 Frank Gore .25 .60
84 Shaun Hill .20 .50
85 Vernon Davis .20 .50
86 Julius Jones .20 .50
87 Matt Hasselbeck .20 .50
88 T.J. Houshmandzadeh .20 .50
89 Marc Bulger .20 .50
90 Steven Jackson .20 .50
91 Torry Holt .25 .60
92 Antonio Bryant .20 .50
93 Derrick Ward .20 .50
94 Kellen Winslow Jr. .20 .50
95 Chris Johnson .20 .50
96 Kerry Collins .20 .50
97 LenDale White .20 .50
98 Chris Cooley .20 .50
99 Clinton Portis .20 .50
100 Jason Campbell .20 .50
101 Aaron Brown RC 2.00 5.00
102 Aaron Kelly AU/199 RC 3.00 8.00
103 Aaron Maybin RC 2.00 5.00
104 Alphonso Smith RC 1.50 4.00
105 Andre Smith RC 1.50 4.00
106 Anthony Hill RC 1.50 4.00
107 Arian Foster RC 4.00 10.00
108 Asher Allen RC 1.50 4.00
109 Austin Collie AU/149 RC 4.00 10.00
110 Bernard Scott RC 2.50 6.00
111 Bradley Fletcher RC 1.50 4.00
112 Brandon Gibson AU/199 RC 4.00 10.00
113 Brian Hartline RC 2.50 6.00
114 Brooks Foster AU/199 RC 3.00 8.00
115 Cameron Morrah AU/499 RC 3.00 8.00
116 Chase Daniel RC 1.50 4.00
117 Chip Vaughn RC 1.50 4.00
118 Chris Ogbonnaya RC 2.00 5.00
119 Chris Owens RC 1.50 4.00
120 Clay Matthews AU/199 RC 35.00 60.00
121 Clint Sintim AU/99 RC 4.00 10.00
122 Cody Brown RC 1.50 4.00
123 Connor Barwin RC 2.00 5.00
124 Cornelius Ingram AU/199 RC 3.00 8.00
125 Curtis Painter RC 1.50 4.00
126 Darcel McBath RC 1.50 4.00
127 Darius Butler RC 2.00 5.00
128 Darius Passmore AU/199 RC 3.00 8.00
129 David Bruton RC 1.50 4.00
130 David Johnson RC 2.00 5.00
131 DeAndre Levy RC 2.00 5.00
132 Demetrius Byrd AU/499 RC 4.00 10.00
133 Devin Moore AU/249 RC 3.00 8.00
134 Davon Drew RC 1.50 4.00
135 D.Edison AU/199 RC 3.00 8.00
136 Eddie Williams RC 2.00 5.00
137 Eugene Monroe RC 1.50 4.00
138 Evander Hood RC 2.50 6.00
139 Gartrell Johnson RC 1.50 4.00
140 Gerald McRath RC 2.00 5.00
141 Glover Quin RC 2.00 5.00
142 Graham Harrell RC 1.50 4.00
143 Hunter Cantwell RC 1.50 4.00
144 Ian Johnson RC 1.50 4.00
145 Jairus Byrd RC 2.50 6.00
146 James Casey AU/199 RC 4.00 10.00
147 James Davis RC 1.50 4.00
148 James Laurinaitis AU/199 RC 6.00 15.00
149 Jarett Dillard AU/499 RC 3.00 8.00
150 Jason Phillips RC 2.00 5.00
151 Jason Williams RC 2.00 5.00
152 Jasper Brinkley RC 2.00 5.00
153 Javarris Williams RC 2.00 5.00
154 Jeremy Childs RC 1.50 4.00
155 Jerraud Powers RC 1.50 4.00
156 John Phillips RC 2.50 6.00
157 Johnny Knox AU/199 RC 4.00 10.00
158 Kaluka Maiava RC 1.50 4.00
159 Keenan Lewis RC 2.50 6.00
160 Keith Null RC 2.00 5.00
161 Kenny McKinley AU/199 RC 3.00 8.00
162 Kevin Barnes RC 1.50 4.00
163 Kevin Huber RC 1.50 4.00
164 Kevin Ogletree AU/199 RC 4.00 10.00
165 Lardarius Webb RC 2.50 6.00
166 Larry English AU/199 RC 4.00 10.00
167 Louis Delmas RC 2.00 5.00
168 Louis Murphy AU/299 RC 3.00 8.00
169 Manuel Johnson RC 1.50 4.00
170 Marcus Freeman RC 1.50 4.00
171 Marko Mitchell RC 1.50 4.00
172 Bear Pascoe RC 2.00 5.00
173 Michael Mitchell RC 1.50 4.00
174 Mike Goodson AU/399 RC 4.00 10.00
175 Nathan Brown AU/149 RC 5.00 12.00
176 Nic Harris RC 2.00 5.00
177 P.J. Hill AU/199 RC 3.00 8.00
178 Patrick Chung RC 1.50 4.00
179 Peria Jerry RC 1.50 4.00
180 Quan Cosby AU/149 RC 4.00 10.00
181 Quinn Johnson AU/149 RC 4.00 10.00
182 Quinten Lawrence RC 1.50 4.00
183 Rashad Johnson RC 1.50 4.00
184 Richard Quinn RC 2.00 5.00
185 Robert Ayers RC 1.50 4.00
186 Ryan Mouton RC 1.50 4.00
187 Sammie Stroughter RC 1.50 4.00
188 Scott McKillop RC 1.50 4.00
189 Sean Smith RC 1.50 4.00
190 Sen'Derrick Marks RC 1.50 4.00
191 Shawn Nelson No AU/149 RC 1.50 4.00
192 Sherrod Martin RC 1.50 4.00
193 Stanley Arnoux RC 2.00 5.00
194 Tiquan Underwood RC 1.50 4.00
195 Tony Fiammetta AU/199 RC 3.00 8.00
196 Travis Beckum AU/249 RC 3.00 8.00
197 Tyrell Sutton AU/499 RC 3.00 8.00
198 Tyrone McKenzie RC 2.00 5.00
199 Victor Butler RC 2.00 5.00
200 William Moore RC 1.50 4.00
201 Aaron Curry AU/275 RC 8.00 20.00
202 Andre Brown AU/175 RC 8.00 20.00
203 B.J. Raji AU/392 RC 6.00 15.00
204 Brandon Pettigrew AU/180 RC 6.00 15.00
205 Brandon Tate AU/200 RC 8.00 20.00
206 Brian Cushing AU/280 RC 5.00 12.00
207 Brian Orakpo AU/258 RC 6.00 15.00
208 Brian Robiskie AU/200 RC 6.00 15.00
209 Cedric Peerman AU/385 RC 5.00 12.00
210 Chase Coffman AU/385 RC 5.00 12.00
211 Chris Wells AU/175 RC 6.00 15.00
212 D.Heyward-Bey AU/250 RC 8.00 20.00
213 Derrick Williams AU/200 RC 6.00 15.00
214 Donald Brown AU/175 RC 6.00 15.00
215 Everette Brown AU/275 RC 5.00 12.00
216 Glen Coffee AU/270 RC 5.00 12.00
217 Hakeem Nicks AU/175 RC 8.00 20.00
218 Tyson Jackson AU/350 RC 5.00 12.00
219 Deon Butler AU/300 RC 5.00 12.00
220 Jared Cook AU/396 RC 6.00 15.00
221 Javon Ringer AU/180 RC 6.00 15.00
222 Jeremiah Johnson AU/175 RC 6.00 15.00
223 Jeremy Maclin AU/180 RC 8.00 20.00
224 J.Parker Wilson AU/180 RC 6.00 15.00
225 Josh Freeman AU/175 RC 6.00 15.00
226 Juaquin Iglesias AU/200 RC 6.00 15.00
227 Kenny Britt AU/175 RC 10.00 25.00
228 K.Moreno AU/180 RC 6.00 15.00
229 Kory Sheets AU/390 RC 6.00 15.00
230 LeSean McCoy AU/175 RC 12.00 30.00
231 Malcolm Jenkins AU/280 RC 5.00 12.00
232 Mark Sanchez AU/175 RC 25.00 60.00
233 Matthew Stafford AU/160 RC 30.00 80.00
234 Michael Crabtree AU/160 RC 10.00 25.00
235 Jason Smith AU/250 RC 5.00 12.00
236 Mike Thomas AU/390 RC 5.00 12.00
237 Mike Wallace AU/350 RC 8.00 20.00
238 M.Massaquoi AU/180 RC 6.00 15.00
239 Nate Davis AU/125 RC 6.00 15.00
240 Pat White AU/125 RC 8.00 20.00
241 Patrick Turner AU/300 RC 5.00 12.00
242 Percy Harvin AU/180 RC 6.00 15.00
243 Ramses Barden AU/300 RC 5.00 12.00
244 R.Jennings AU/160 RC 8.00 20.00
245 Rey Maualuga AU/280 RC 8.00 20.00
246 Rhett Bomar AU/175 RC 6.00 15.00
247 Shonn Greene AU/180 RC 6.00 15.00
248 Stephen McGee AU/200 RC 6.00 15.00
249 T.Brandstater AU/385 RC 6.00 15.00
250 Vontae Davis AU/275 RC 5.00 12.00
251 Brett Favre 10.00 25.00

2009 Donruss Threads Gold Holofoil

*VETS 1-100: 4X TO 10X BASIC CARDS
*ROOKIE 101-200: 1X TO 2.5X RETAIL RED
STATED PRINT RUN 50 SER.#'d SETS

2009 Donruss Threads Platinum Holofoil

*VETS 1-100: 5X TO 12X BASIC INSERTS
*ROOKIE 101-200: 1.2X TO 3X RETAIL RED
STATED PRINT RUN 25 SER.#'d SETS

2009 Donruss Threads Retail Green

*VETS 1-100: 3X TO 8X BASIC CARDS
*ROOKIE 101-200: .8X TO 2X RETAIL RED
STATED PRINT RUN 100 SER.#'d SETS

2009 Donruss Threads Retail Red

*VETS 1-100: 1.5X TO 4X BASIC CARDS
COMMON ROOKIE (101-200) 1.25 3.00
ROOKIE SEMISTARS 1.50 4.00
ROOKIE UNL.STARS 2.00 5.00
RANDOM INSERTS IN RETAIL PACKS
103 Aaron Maybin 1.50 4.00
116 Chase Daniel 1.50 4.00
120 Clay Matthews 5.00 12.00
138 Evander Hood 2.00 5.00
142 Graham Harrell 1.25 3.00
148 James Laurinaitis 1.25 3.00
157 Johnny Knox 1.50 4.00
185 Robert Ayers 1.25 3.00

2009 Donruss Threads Retail Rookies

*ROOKIES: .4X TO 1X BASIC CARDS
STATED PRINT RUN 999 SER.#'d SETS

2009 Donruss Threads Silver Holofoil

*VETS 1-100: 2X TO 5X BASIC CARDS
*ROOKIE 101-200: .5X TO 1.2X RETAIL RED
STATED PRINT RUN 250 SER.#'d SETS

2009 Donruss Threads Autographs Silver

STATED PRINT RUN 1-50
SERIAL #'d UNDER 20 NOT PRICED
3 Tim Hightower/25 6.00 15.00
5 Michael Turner/20 6.00 15.00
21 Cedric Benson/25 6.00 15.00
34 Kevin Smith/50 5.00 12.00
36 Greg Jennings/25 6.00 15.00
40 Steve Slaton/50 5.00 12.00
42 Joseph Addai/25 6.00 15.00
49 Larry Johnson/25 6.00 15.00
63 Marques Colston/50 5.00 12.00
73 Zach Miller/50 5.00 12.00
75 DeSean Jackson/40 6.00 15.00
93 Derrick Ward/30 6.00 15.00
109 Austin Collie/25 5.00 12.00
112 Brandon Gibson/25 6.00 15.00
114 Brooks Foster/25 5.00 12.00
115 Cameron Morrah/50 4.00 10.00
128 Darius Passmore/42 4.00 10.00
132 Demetrius Byrd/50 5.00 12.00
133 Devin Moore/25 5.00 12.00
135 Dominique Edison/25 5.00 12.00
146 James Casey/25 6.00 15.00
149 Jarett Dillard/50 4.00 10.00
157 Johnny Knox/25 6.00 15.00
161 Kenny McKinley/25 5.00 12.00
164 Kevin Ogletree/25 6.00 15.00
168 Louis Murphy/25 5.00 12.00
174 Mike Goodson/25 6.00 15.00
175 Nathan Brown/25 6.00 15.00
177 P.J. Hill/25 5.00 12.00
181 Quinn Johnson/25 5.00 12.00
191 Shawn Nelson/25 No AU 2.00 5.00
196 Travis Beckum/25 5.00 12.00
197 Tyrell Sutton/50 4.00 10.00

2009 Donruss Threads Century Collection Materials Prime

STATED PRINT RUN 18-50
*BASE JSY/250: .25X TO .6X PRIME/35-50
*BASE JSY/250: .2X TO .5X PRIME/18
*BASE JSY/100: .3X TO .8X PRIME/35-50
1 Antonio Gates/50 5.00 12.00
2 Ben Roethlisberger/50 6.00 15.00
3 Brandon Jacobs/50 4.00 10.00
4 Brian Westbrook/50 4.00 10.00
5 Clinton Portis/50 4.00 10.00
6 Donald Driver/50 5.00 12.00
7 Donovan McNabb/50 5.00 12.00
8 Eli Manning/35 5.00 12.00
9 Joseph Addai/50 4.00 10.00
10 LaDainian Tomlinson/50 6.00 15.00
11 Peyton Manning/18 20.00 50.00
12 Randy Moss/50 5.00 12.00
13 Ricky Williams/50 5.00 12.00
14 Tom Brady/50 20.00 50.00
15 Tony Gonzalez/50 5.00 12.00

2009 Donruss Threads Century Legends

*CENT.PROOF/100: .6X TO 1.5X BASIC INSERT
1 Archie Manning 1.25 3.00
2 Chuck Bednarik 1.25 3.00
3 Danny White 1.25 3.00
4 Dick Butkus 2.00 5.00
5 Frank Gifford 1.50 4.00
6 Jerry Rice 3.00 8.00
7 Jim Brown 2.00 5.00
8 Joe Montana 5.00 12.00
9 Joe Namath 2.00 5.00
10 Ozzie Newsome 1.25 3.00
11 Paul Hornung 1.50 4.00
12 Randy White 1.50 4.00
13 Steve Young 2.00 5.00
14 Thurman Thomas 1.25 3.00
15 Tommy McDonald 1.00 2.50

2009 Donruss Threads Century Legends Materials

STATED PRINT RUN 50-250
*PRIME/50: .8X TO 2X BASIC JSY/200-250
*PRIME/50: .6X TO 1.5X BASIC JSY/125
*PRIME/25-30: 1X TO 2.5X BASIC JSY/200-250
*PRIME/15: 1.2X TO 3X BASIC JSY/200-250
*PRIME/15: .8X TO 2X BASIC JSY/50
PRIME PRINT RUN 4-50
1 Archie Manning/250 5.00 12.00
2 Chuck Bednarik/200 5.00 12.00
3 Danny White/200 5.00 12.00
4 Dick Butkus/250 8.00 20.00
5 Frank Gifford/95 8.00 20.00
6 Jerry Rice/125 15.00 40.00
7 Jim Brown/100 10.00 25.00
8 Joe Montana/250 20.00 50.00
9 Joe Namath/50 12.00 30.00
10 Ozzie Newsome/250 5.00 12.00
11 Paul Hornung/250 6.00 15.00
12 Randy White/250 6.00 15.00
13 Steve Young/250 8.00 20.00
14 Thurman Thomas/250 5.00 12.00
15 Tommy McDonald/250 4.00 10.00

2009 Donruss Threads Century Stars

*CENT.PROOF/100: .6X TO 1.5X BASIC INSERT
1 Adrian Peterson 1.25 3.00
2 Ben Roethlisberger 1.25 3.00
3 Braylon Edwards .75 2.00
4 Chad Ochocinco .75 2.00
5 Clinton Portis .75 2.00
6 Donovan McNabb 1.00 2.50
7 Eli Manning 1.00 2.50
8 Frank Gore 1.00 2.50
9 Hines Ward 1.00 2.50
10 Larry Fitzgerald 1.00 2.50
11 Lee Evans 1.00 2.50
12 Marion Barber 1.00 2.50
13 Maurice Jones-Drew .75 2.00
14 Philip Rivers 1.25 3.00
15 Randy Moss 1.00 2.50
16 Reggie Wayne 1.00 2.50
17 Tom Brady 4.00 10.00
18 Tony Gonzalez 1.00 2.50
19 Tony Romo 1.00 2.50
20 Torry Holt 1.00 2.50

2009 Donruss Threads Century Stars Materials

STATED PRINT RUN 20-250
*PRIME/50: .8X TO 2X BASE JSY/250
*PRIME/50: .6X TO 1.5X BASE JSY/100
*PRIME/50: .5X TO 1.2X BASE JSY/65
*PRIME/50: .3X TO .8X BASE JSY/20
*PRIME/25: .8X TO 2X BASE JSY/100
PRIME PRINT RUN 5-50
1 Adrian Peterson/100 4.00 10.00
2 Ben Roethlisberger/100 4.00 10.00
3 Braylon Edwards/250 2.00 5.00
4 Chad Ochocinco/20 5.00 12.00
5 Clinton Portis/100 2.50 6.00
6 Donovan McNabb/250 2.50 6.00
7 Eli Manning/100 3.00 8.00
8 Frank Gore/100 3.00 8.00
9 Hines Ward/65 4.00 10.00
10 Larry Fitzgerald/100 3.00 8.00
11 Lee Evans/100 3.00 8.00
12 Marion Barber/100 3.00 8.00
13 Maurice Jones-Drew/100 2.50 6.00
14 Philip Rivers/100 4.00 10.00
15 Randy Moss/100 3.00 8.00
16 Reggie Wayne/100 3.00 8.00
17 Tom Brady/250 10.00 25.00
19 Tony Romo/250 2.50 6.00
20 Torry Holt/250 2.50 6.00

2009 Donruss Threads College Greats

1 Bob Lilly 1.25 3.00
2 Brandon Pettigrew .40 1.00
3 Carl Eller 1.00 2.50
4 Chris Wells .40 1.00
5 Ace Parker 1.00 2.50
6 Donald Brown .40 1.00
7 Earl Campbell 1.50 4.00
8 Graham Harrell .40 1.00
9 Hugh McElhenny 1.00 2.50
10 James Casey .50 1.25
11 Javon Ringer .40 1.00
12 Jeremy Maclin .50 1.25
13 Knowshon Moreno .40 1.00
14 LeSean McCoy 1.00 2.50
15 Mark Sanchez .40 1.00
16 Matthew Stafford 2.00 5.00
17 Michael Crabtree .60 1.50
18 Nate Davis .40 1.00
19 Percy Harvin .40 1.00
20 Shonn Greene .40 1.00

2009 Donruss Threads College Greats Autographs

STATED PRINT RUN 25-100
1 Bob Lilly/20 12.00 30.00
2 Brandon Pettigrew/50 5.00 12.00
3 Carl Eller/50 8.00 20.00
4 Chris Wells/25 6.00 15.00
5 Ace Parker/75 15.00 30.00
6 Donald Brown/25 6.00 15.00
7 Earl Campbell/25 15.00 40.00
8 Graham Harrell/50 12.00 30.00
9 Hugh McElhenny/100 8.00 20.00
10 James Casey/50 6.00 15.00
11 Javon Ringer/50 5.00 12.00
12 Jeremy Maclin/25 8.00 20.00
13 Knowshon Moreno/25 6.00 15.00
14 LeSean McCoy/25 15.00 40.00
15 Mark Sanchez/25 30.00 80.00
16 Matthew Stafford/25 40.00 100.00
17 Michael Crabtree/25 10.00 25.00
18 Nate Davis/50 5.00 12.00
19 Percy Harvin/25 6.00 15.00
20 Shonn Greene/50 5.00 12.00

2009 Donruss Threads College Gridiron Kings

*FRAMED BLACK/10: 2X TO 5X
*FRAMED BLUE/50: 1X TO 2.5X
*FRAMED GREEN/25: 1.2X TO 3X
*FRAMED RED/100: .8X TO 2X
1 Aaron Curry .75 2.00
2 Aaron Maybin .60 1.50
3 Andre Brown .60 1.50
4 B.J. Raji .60 1.50
5 Brandon Gibson .60 1.50
6 Brandon Pettigrew .50 1.25
7 Brandon Tate .60 1.50
8 Brian Cushing .50 1.25
9 Brian Orakpo .60 1.50
10 Brian Robiskie .50 1.25
11 Chase Coffman .50 1.25
12 Chris Wells .50 1.25
13 Darrius Heyward-Bey .75 2.00
14 Deon Butler .50 1.25
15 Derrick Williams .50 1.25
16 Donald Brown .50 1.25
17 Glen Coffee .50 1.25
18 Graham Harrell .50 1.25
19 Hakeem Nicks .60 1.50
20 James Casey .60 1.50
21 James Laurinaitis .50 1.25
22 Jared Cook .60 1.50
23 Jason Smith .50 1.25
24 Javon Ringer .50 1.25
25 Jeremiah Johnson .50 1.25
26 Jeremy Maclin .60 1.50
27 John Parker Wilson .50 1.25
28 Josh Freeman .50 1.25
29 Juaquin Iglesias .50 1.25
30 Kenny Britt .75 2.00
31 Kenny McKinley .50 1.25
32 Knowshon Moreno .50 1.25
33 LeSean McCoy 1.25 3.00
34 Malcolm Jenkins .50 1.25
35 Mark Sanchez .50 1.25
36 Matthew Stafford 2.50 6.00
37 Michael Crabtree .75 2.00
38 Mike Thomas .50 1.25
39 Mike Wallace .75 2.00
40 Mohamed Massaquoi .50 1.25
41 Pat White .60 1.50
42 Patrick Turner .50 1.25
43 Percy Harvin .50 1.25
44 Quan Cosby .50 1.25
45 Ramses Barden .50 1.25
46 Rey Maualuga .75 2.00
47 Rhett Bomar .50 1.25
48 Shonn Greene .50 1.25
49 Tyson Jackson .50 1.25
50 Vontae Davis .50 1.25

2009 Donruss Threads College Gridiron Kings Autographs

STATED PRINT RUN 25-163
1 Aaron Curry/50 8.00 20.00
3 Andre Brown/50 6.00 15.00
5 Brandon Gibson/25 8.00 20.00
6 Brandon Pettigrew/50 5.00 12.00
7 Brandon Tate/25 8.00 20.00
8 Brian Cushing/25 6.00 15.00
9 Brian Orakpo/25 8.00 20.00
10 Brian Robiskie/50 5.00 12.00
11 Chase Coffman/25 6.00 15.00
12 Chris Wells/25 6.00 15.00
13 Darrius Heyward-Bey/25 10.00 25.00
14 Deon Butler/50 5.00 12.00
15 Derrick Williams/25 6.00 15.00
16 Donald Brown/25 6.00 15.00
17 Glen Coffee/50 5.00 12.00
18 Graham Harrell/163 10.00 25.00
19 Hakeem Nicks/25 8.00 20.00
20 James Casey/50 6.00 15.00
21 James Laurinaitis/25 6.00 15.00

23 Jason Smith/50 5.00 12.00
24 Javon Ringer/50 5.00 12.00
26 Jeremy Maclin/25 8.00 20.00
28 Josh Freeman/25 6.00 15.00
31 Kenny McKinley/25 6.00 15.00
32 Knowshon Moreno/25 6.00 15.00
33 LeSean McCoy/25 15.00 40.00
35 Mark Sanchez/25 6.00 15.00
36 Matthew Stafford/25 30.00 80.00
37 Michael Crabtree/25 10.00 25.00
38 Mike Thomas/25 6.00 15.00
39 Mike Wallace/50 8.00 20.00
40 Mohamed Massaquoi/25 6.00 15.00
42 Patrick Turner/50 5.00 12.00
43 Percy Harvin/25 6.00 15.00
44 Quan Cosby/25 6.00 15.00
45 Ramses Barden/25 6.00 15.00
46 Rey Maualuga/25 10.00 25.00
47 Rhett Bomar/25 6.00 15.00
48 Shonn Greene/50 5.00 12.00
49 Tyson Jackson/25 6.00 15.00

2009 Donruss Threads College Gridiron Kings Materials

STATED PRINT RUN 25-250
5 Brandon Gibson/250 2.50 6.00
8 Brian Cushing/175 2.00 5.00
9 Brian Orakpo/30 5.00 12.00
11 Chase Coffman/250 2.00 5.00
12 Chris Wells/100 2.50 6.00
15 Derrick Williams/45 3.00 8.00
18 Graham Harrell/25 4.00 10.00
21 James Laurinaitis/85 2.50 6.00
25 Jeremiah Johnson/250 2.00 5.00
26 Jeremy Maclin/250 2.50 6.00
28 Josh Freeman/250 2.00 5.00
29 Juaquin Iglesias/25 4.00 10.00
31 Kenny McKinley/250 2.00 5.00
33 LeSean McCoy/250 5.00 12.00
35 Mark Sanchez/75 2.50 6.00
40 Mohamed Massaquoi/250 2.00 5.00
44 Quan Cosby/80 2.50 6.00
45 Ramses Barden/250 2.00 5.00
46 Rey Maualuga/95 4.00 10.00
47 Rhett Bomar/250 2.00 5.00
49 Tyson Jackson/250 2.00 5.00

2009 Donruss Threads College Gridiron Kings Materials Prime

PRIME PRINT RUN 5-50
5 Brandon Gibson/50 5.00 12.00
7 Brandon Tate/50 5.00 12.00
8 Brian Cushing/15 6.00 15.00
9 Brian Orakpo/50 5.00 12.00
11 Chase Coffman/50 4.00 10.00
12 Chris Wells/50 4.00 10.00
16 Donald Brown/50 4.00 10.00
18 Graham Harrell/50 4.00 10.00
21 James Laurinaitis/50 4.00 10.00
25 Jeremiah Johnson/50 4.00 10.00
26 Jeremy Maclin/25 6.00 15.00
28 Josh Freeman/50 4.00 10.00
29 Juaquin Iglesias/30 5.00 12.00
31 Kenny McKinley/50 4.00 10.00
33 LeSean McCoy/50 10.00 25.00
35 Mark Sanchez/15 6.00 15.00
40 Mohamed Massaquoi/25 5.00 12.00
44 Quan Cosby/50 4.00 10.00
45 Ramses Barden/30 5.00 12.00
46 Rey Maualuga/50 6.00 15.00
47 Rhett Bomar/50 4.00 10.00
49 Tyson Jackson/50 4.00 10.00

2009 Donruss Threads College Gridiron Kings Material Autographs

JSY AUTO PRINT RUN 9-25
SERIAL #'d UNDER 25 NOT PRICED
5 Brandon Gibson/25 10.00 25.00
8 Brian Cushing/25 8.00 20.00
9 Brian Orakpo/25 10.00 25.00
11 Chase Coffman/25 8.00 20.00
12 Chris Wells/25 8.00 20.00
18 Graham Harrell/25 20.00 50.00
21 James Laurinaitis/25 8.00 20.00
26 Jeremy Maclin/25 10.00 25.00
28 Josh Freeman/25 8.00 20.00
31 Kenny McKinley/25 8.00 20.00
33 LeSean McCoy/25 20.00 50.00
35 Mark Sanchez/25 40.00 100.00
36 Matthew Stafford/25 40.00 100.00
40 Mohamed Massaquoi/25 8.00 20.00
44 Quan Cosby/25 8.00 20.00
45 Ramses Barden/25 8.00 20.00
46 Rey Maualuga/25 12.00 30.00
47 Rhett Bomar/25 8.00 20.00
49 Tyson Jackson/25 8.00 20.00

2009 Donruss Threads Generations

*CENT.PROOF/100: .6X TO 1.5X BASE INSERTS
1 Newsome/Edwards 1.00 2.50
2 McDonald/Jackson 1.00 2.50
3 Campbell/Johnson 1.25 3.00
4 Hornung/Grant 1.25 3.00
5 Manning/Brees 1.25 3.00
6 Rice/Johnson 2.50 6.00
7 Ward/Holmes .75 2.00
8 Tomlinson/Peterson 1.00 2.50
9 Ochocinco/Johnson .75 2.00
10 Gonzalez/Bowe .75 2.00
11 Moss/Welker .75 2.00
12 Butkus/Urlacher 1.50 4.00
13 Williams/Stewart .60 1.50
14 Johnson/Charles .75 2.00
15 Westbrook/Barber .75 2.00

2009 Donruss Threads Generations Materials Prime

PRIME PRINT RUN 50 SER.#'d SETS
*BASE JSY/250: .25X TO .6X PRIME/50
*BASE JSY/80-130: .3X TO .8X PRIME/50
*BASE JSY/20: .6X TO 1.5X PRIME/50
1 Newsome/Edwards 5.00 12.00
3 Campbell/Johnson 6.00 15.00
4 Hornung/Grant 6.00 15.00
5 Manning/Brees 6.00 15.00
6 Rice/Johnson 12.00 30.00
7 Ward/Holmes 4.00 10.00
8 Tomlinson/Peterson 5.00 12.00
9 Ochocinco/Johnson 4.00 10.00
10 Gonzalez/Bowe 4.00 10.00
11 Moss/Welker 8.00 20.00
12 Butkus/Urlacher 8.00 20.00
13 Williams/Stewart 3.00 8.00
15 Westbrook/Barber 4.00 10.00

2009 Donruss Threads Jerseys

STATED PRINT RUN 2-250
2 Larry Fitzgerald/100 3.00 8.00
4 Matt Ryan/100 3.00 8.00
5 Michael Turner/100 2.50 6.00
6 Roddy White/100 2.50 6.00
7 Derrick Mason/250 2.00 5.00
8 Joe Flacco/160 3.00 8.00
9 Willis McGahee/250 2.00 5.00
10 Lee Evans/100 3.00 8.00
12 Terrell Owens/250 2.50 6.00
13 DeAngelo Williams/250 2.00 5.00
14 Jake Delhomme/250 2.00 5.00
16 Steve Smith/100 3.00 8.00
17 Greg Olsen/100 3.00 8.00
20 Carson Palmer/250 2.50 6.00
23 Brady Quinn/100 2.50 6.00
24 Braylon Edwards/100 2.50 6.00
26 Marion Barber/100 3.00 8.00
27 Roy Williams WR/119 2.50 6.00
28 Tony Romo/250 2.50 6.00
29 Brandon Marshall/100 3.00 8.00
32 Calvin Johnson/100 4.00 10.00
33 Daunte Culpepper/120 3.00 8.00
35 Aaron Rodgers/250 6.00 15.00
36 Greg Jennings/100 2.50 6.00
38 Andre Johnson/250 2.50 6.00
40 Steve Slaton/100 2.50 6.00
41 Anthony Gonzalez/250 2.00 5.00
42 Joseph Addai/250 2.00 5.00
43 Peyton Manning/250 8.00 20.00
44 Reggie Wayne/100 3.00 8.00
45 David Garrard/250 2.00 5.00
47 Maurice Jones-Drew/100 2.50 6.00
48 Dwayne Bowe/250 2.50 6.00
49 Larry Johnson/60 3.00 8.00
53 Ricky Williams/250 2.50 6.00
55 Adrian Peterson/100 4.00 10.00
58 Laurence Maroney/160 3.00 8.00
59 Tom Brady/250 10.00 25.00
62 Drew Brees/250 3.00 8.00
63 Marques Colston/250 2.00 5.00
64 Reggie Bush/130 2.50 6.00
65 Brandon Jacobs/100 2.50 6.00
66 Eli Manning/100 3.00 8.00
69 Jerricho Cotchery/250 2.00 5.00
71 Darren McFadden/100 4.00 10.00
72 JaMarcus Russell/250 2.00 5.00
74 Brian Westbrook/100 2.50 6.00
76 Donovan McNabb/250 2.50 6.00
77 Ben Roethlisberger/100 4.00 10.00
78 Santonio Holmes/100 2.50 6.00
80 LaDainian Tomlinson/250 3.00 8.00
81 Philip Rivers/100 4.00 10.00
83 Frank Gore/100 3.00 8.00
87 Matt Hasselbeck/250 2.00 5.00
89 Marc Bulger/250 2.00 5.00
92 Antonio Bryant/230 2.00 5.00
95 Chris Johnson/250 2.00 5.00
97 LenDale White/55 3.00 8.00
98 Chris Cooley/100 2.50 6.00
99 Clinton Portis/100 2.50 6.00
100 Jason Campbell/110 2.50 6.00

2009 Donruss Threads Jerseys Prime

PRIME PRINT RUN 2-50
2 Larry Fitzgerald/25 8.00 20.00
4 Matt Ryan/25 8.00 20.00
5 Michael Turner/50 5.00 12.00
6 Roddy White/50 5.00 12.00
7 Derrick Mason/50 5.00 12.00
9 Willis McGahee/50 5.00 12.00
10 Lee Evans/50 6.00 15.00
11 Marshawn Lynch/50 6.00 15.00
13 DeAngelo Williams/50 5.00 12.00
14 Jake Delhomme/50 5.00 12.00
15 Jonathan Stewart/50 5.00 12.00
16 Steve Smith/50 6.00 15.00
17 Greg Olsen/25 8.00 20.00
20 Carson Palmer/50 6.00 15.00
22 Chad Ochocinco/50 5.00 12.00
23 Brady Quinn/25 6.00 15.00
24 Braylon Edwards/50 5.00 12.00
26 Marion Barber/50 6.00 15.00
28 Tony Romo/50 6.00 15.00
29 Brandon Marshall/44 6.00 15.00
32 Calvin Johnson/50 8.00 20.00
35 Aaron Rodgers/50 15.00 40.00
36 Greg Jennings/50 5.00 12.00
37 Ryan Grant/50 6.00 15.00
38 Andre Johnson/50 6.00 15.00
40 Steve Slaton/50 5.00 12.00
42 Joseph Addai/50 5.00 12.00
43 Peyton Manning/25 25.00 60.00
44 Reggie Wayne/25 8.00 20.00
45 David Garrard/50 5.00 12.00
47 Maurice Jones-Drew/50 5.00 12.00
48 Dwayne Bowe/50 6.00 15.00
49 Larry Johnson/50 5.00 12.00
53 Ricky Williams/50 6.00 15.00
54 Ronnie Brown/50 5.00 12.00
55 Adrian Peterson/50 8.00 20.00
56 Bernard Berrian/50 5.00 12.00
58 Laurence Maroney/50 6.00 15.00
59 Tom Brady/50 25.00 60.00
60 Wes Welker/50 6.00 15.00
62 Drew Brees/50 8.00 20.00
63 Marques Colston/50 5.00 12.00
64 Reggie Bush/50 5.00 12.00
65 Brandon Jacobs/50 5.00 12.00
66 Eli Manning/25 8.00 20.00
69 Jerricho Cotchery/50 5.00 12.00
70 Leon Washington/30 6.00 15.00
71 Darren McFadden/25 10.00 25.00
72 JaMarcus Russell/50 5.00 12.00
74 Brian Westbrook/50 5.00 12.00
76 Donovan McNabb/50 6.00 15.00
77 Ben Roethlisberger/50 8.00 20.00
78 Santonio Holmes/50 5.00 12.00
79 Willie Parker/50 5.00 12.00
80 LaDainian Tomlinson/50 8.00 20.00
81 Philip Rivers/50 8.00 20.00
82 Vincent Jackson/20 6.00 15.00
83 Frank Gore/50 6.00 15.00
85 Vernon Davis/50 5.00 12.00
87 Matt Hasselbeck/50 5.00 12.00
89 Marc Bulger/40 5.00 12.00
90 Steven Jackson/50 5.00 12.00
95 Chris Johnson/25 5.00 12.00
97 LenDale White/50 5.00 12.00
98 Chris Cooley/50 5.00 12.00
99 Clinton Portis/50 5.00 12.00
100 Jason Campbell/50 5.00 12.00

2009 Donruss Threads Pro Gridiron Kings

*FRAMED BLACK/10: 1.5X TO 4X
*FRAMED BLUE/50: .8X TO 2X
*FRAMED GREEN/25: 1X TO 2.5X
*FRAMED RED/100: .6X TO 1.5X
1-50 RANDOM INSERTS IN PACKS
51-56 INSERTED INTO RETAIL PACKS
1 Adrian Arrington .75 2.00
2 A.J. Hawk .75 2.00
3 Andre Caldwell .75 2.00
4 Antoine Cason .75 2.00
5 Aqib Talib .75 2.00
6 Archie Manning 1.25 3.00
7 Brandon Flowers .75 2.00
8 Brandon Meriweather .75 2.00
9 Brian Brohm .75 2.00
10 Chad Henne 1.00 2.50
11 Charles Godfrey .75 2.00
12 Chuck Bednarik 1.25 3.00
13 Danny White 1.25 3.00
14 Davone Bess .75 2.00
15 Dick Butkus 2.00 5.00
16 Dominique Rodgers-Cromartie .75 2.00
17 Donnie Avery .75 2.00
18 Dustin Keller .75 2.00
19 Eddie Royal .75 2.00
20 Frank Gifford 1.50 4.00
21 Jacob Hester .75 2.00
22 Jamaal Charles 1.00 2.50
23 James Hardy 1.00 2.50
24 Jerious Norwood .75 2.00
25 Jerry Rice 3.00 8.00
26 Jim Brown 2.00 5.00
27 Joe Namath 2.00 5.00
28 John David Booty 1.00 2.50
29 Josh Morgan .75 2.00
30 Justin Fargas .75 2.00
31 Keith Rivers .75 2.00
32 Kevin Curtis .75 2.00
33 Kevin Smith .75 2.00
34 Leodis McKelvin .75 2.00
35 Marques Colston .75 2.00
36 Matt Leinart .75 2.00
37 Michael Bush .75 2.00
38 Mike Hart 1.00 2.50
39 Ozzie Newsome 1.25 3.00
40 Patrick Crayton .75 2.00
41 Patrick Willis 1.00 2.50
42 Paul Hornung 1.50 4.00
43 Randy White 1.50 4.00
44 Rashard Mendenhall .75 2.00
45 Ray Rice .75 2.00
46 Shawne Merriman .75 2.00
47 Steve Young 2.00 5.00
48 Ted Ginn, Jr. .75 2.00
49 Thurman Thomas 1.25 3.00
50 Tommy McDonald 1.00 2.50
51 Matthew Stafford 2.00 5.00
52 Mark Sanchez .40 1.00
53 Michael Crabtree .60 1.50
54 Knowhson Moreno .40 1.00
55 Darrius Heyward-Bey .60 1.50
56 LeSean McCoy 1.00 2.50

2009 Donruss Threads Pro Gridiron Kings Autographs

AUTO PRINT RUN 5-400
SERIAL #'d UNDER 25 NOT PRICED
1 Adrian Arrington/100 3.00 8.00
2 A.J. Hawk/100 3.00 8.00
3 Andre Caldwell/67 3.00 8.00
4 Antoine Cason/250 2.50 6.00
5 Aqib Talib/125 3.00 8.00
7 Brandon Flowers/80 3.00 8.00
8 Brandon Meriweather/400 2.50 6.00
9 Brian Brohm/40 4.00 10.00
10 Chad Henne/50 5.00 12.00
11 Charles Godfrey/300 2.50 6.00
14 Davone Bess/200 6.00 15.00
16 Dominique Rodgers-Cromartie/300 2.50 6.00
17 Donnie Avery/90 3.00 8.00
18 Dustin Keller/70 3.00 8.00
20 Eddie Royal/90 3.00 8.00
20 Frank Gifford/30 15.00 40.00
21 Jacob Hester/300 2.50 6.00
22 Jamaal Charles/70 4.00 10.00
23 James Hardy/90 4.00 10.00
24 Jerious Norwood/100 3.00 8.00
28 John David Booty/250 3.00 8.00
29 Josh Morgan/175 2.50 6.00
31 Keith Rivers/68 3.00 8.00
33 Kevin Smith/100 3.00 8.00
34 Leodis McKelvin/100 3.00 8.00
37 Michael Bush/125 3.00 8.00
38 Mike Hart/250 5.00 12.00
40 Patrick Crayton/250 2.50 6.00
41 Patrick Willis/75 4.00 10.00
42 Paul Hornung/25 12.00 30.00
43 Randy White/50 12.00 30.00
44 Rashard Mendenhall/50 4.00 10.00
45 Ray Rice/250 6.00 15.00
50 Tommy McDonald/60 10.00 25.00

2009 Donruss Threads Pro Gridiron Kings Materials

BASE JSY PRINT RUN 25-250
*PRIME/50: .6X TO 1.5X JSY/250
*PRIME/50: .5X TO 1.2X JSY/80
*PRIME/25: .8X TO 2X JSY/250
*PRIME/15: 1X TO 2.5X JSY/250
PRIME PRINT RUN 5-50
2 A.J. Hawk/250 2.50 6.00
6 Archie Manning/250 5.00 12.00
12 Chuck Bednarik/200 5.00 12.00
13 Danny White/200 5.00 12.00
15 Dick Butkus/250 8.00 20.00
20 Frank Gifford/25 12.00 30.00
24 Jerious Norwood/80 3.00 8.00
25 Jerry Rice/165 12.00 30.00
26 Jim Brown/50 12.00 30.00
27 Joe Namath/50 12.00 30.00
30 Justin Fargas/250 2.50 6.00
32 Kevin Curtis/250 2.50 6.00
35 Marques Colston/250 2.50 6.00
36 Matt Leinart/250 2.50 6.00
39 Ozzie Newsome/250 5.00 12.00
41 Patrick Willis/250 3.00 8.00
42 Paul Hornung/100 8.00 20.00
43 Randy White/100 8.00 20.00
46 Shawne Merriman/165 2.50 6.00
47 Steve Young/250 8.00 20.00
49 Thurman Thomas/250 5.00 12.00
50 Tommy McDonald/50 6.00 15.00

2009 Donruss Threads Pro Gridiron Kings Materials Autographs

JSY AUTO PRINT RUN 5-25
2 A.J. Hawk/25 8.00 20.00
6 Archie Manning/25 15.00 40.00
12 Chuck Bednarik/25 15.00 40.00
13 Danny White/20 15.00 40.00
15 Dick Butkus/25 25.00 60.00
20 Frank Gifford/25 20.00 50.00
24 Jerious Norwood/25 8.00 20.00
30 Justin Fargas/25 8.00 20.00
32 Kevin Curtis/25 8.00 20.00
35 Marques Colston/25 8.00 20.00
36 Matt Leinart/25 8.00 20.00
39 Ozzie Newsome/25 10.00 25.00
41 Patrick Willis/25 10.00 25.00
42 Paul Hornung/25 20.00 50.00
43 Randy White/25 20.00 50.00
47 Steve Young/25 25.00 60.00
49 Thurman Thomas/25 15.00 40.00
50 Tommy McDonald/25 12.00 30.00

2009 Donruss Threads Rookie Collection Materials

BASE JSY PRINT RUN 500 SER.#'d SETS
*PRIME/25: .8X TO 2X BASIC JSY
1 Andre Brown 2.00 5.00
2 Tyson Jackson 1.50 4.00
3 Chris Wells 1.50 4.00
4 Derrick Williams 1.50 4.00
5 Glen Coffee 1.50 4.00
6 Javon Ringer 1.50 4.00
7 Josh Freeman 1.50 4.00
8 Kenny Britt 2.50 6.00
9 LeSean McCoy 4.00 10.00
10 Matthew Stafford 8.00 20.00
11 Deon Butler 1.50 4.00
12 Mike Thomas 1.50 4.00
13 Mohamed Massaquoi 1.50 4.00
14 Pat White 2.00 5.00
15 Percy Harvin 1.50 4.00
16 Rhett Bomar 1.50 4.00
17 Stephen McGee 1.50 4.00
18 Jason Smith 1.50 4.00
19 Aaron Curry 2.50 6.00
20 Brandon Pettigrew 1.50 4.00
21 Brian Robiskie 1.50 4.00
22 Darrius Heyward-Bey 2.50 6.00
23 Donald Brown 1.50 4.00
24 Hakeem Nicks 2.00 5.00
25 Jeremy Maclin 2.00 5.00
26 Juaquin Iglesias 1.50 4.00
27 Knowshon Moreno 1.50 4.00
28 Mark Sanchez 1.50 4.00
29 Michael Crabtree 2.50 6.00
30 Mike Wallace 2.50 6.00
31 Nate Davis 1.50 4.00
32 Patrick Turner 1.50 4.00
33 Ramses Barden 1.50 4.00
34 Shonn Greene 1.50 4.00

2009 Donruss Threads Rookie Collection Materials Autographs

JSY AUTO PRINT RUN 50 SER.#'d SETS
*AU PRIME/25: .5X TO 1.2X BASIC JSY AU
1 Andre Brown 8.00 20.00
2 Tyson Jackson 6.00 15.00
3 Chris Wells 6.00 15.00
4 Derrick Williams 6.00 15.00
5 Glen Coffee 6.00 15.00
6 Javon Ringer 6.00 15.00
7 Josh Freeman 6.00 15.00
9 LeSean McCoy 15.00 40.00
10 Matthew Stafford 30.00 80.00
11 Deon Butler 6.00 15.00
12 Mike Thomas 6.00 15.00
13 Mohamed Massaquoi 6.00 15.00
15 Percy Harvin 6.00 15.00
16 Rhett Bomar 6.00 15.00
17 Stephen McGee 6.00 15.00
18 Jason Smith 6.00 15.00
19 Aaron Curry 10.00 25.00
20 Brandon Pettigrew 6.00 15.00
21 Brian Robiskie 6.00 15.00
22 Darrius Heyward-Bey 10.00 25.00
23 Donald Brown 6.00 15.00
24 Hakeem Nicks 8.00 20.00
25 Jeremy Maclin 8.00 20.00
27 Knowshon Moreno 6.00 15.00
28 Mark Sanchez 6.00 15.00
29 Michael Crabtree 10.00 25.00
30 Mike Wallace 10.00 25.00
31 Nate Davis 6.00 15.00
32 Patrick Turner 6.00 15.00
33 Ramses Barden 6.00 15.00
34 Shonn Greene 6.00 15.00

2009 Donruss Threads Rookie Collection Materials Combo

COMBO JSY PRINT RUN 500
*COMBO PRIME/25: .8X TO 2X BASIC CMBO
1 Massaquoi/Robiskie 1.50 4.00
2 Stafford/Pettigrew 8.00 20.00
3 Moreno/D.Brown 1.50 4.00
4 Turner/P.White 2.00 5.00
5 Hywrd-Bey/Crabtree 2.50 6.00
6 Bomar/A.Brown 2.00 5.00
7 Crabtree/N.Davis 2.50 6.00
8 Wells/Robiskie 1.50 4.00
9 Britt/Ringer 2.50 6.00
10 Sanchez/Greene 1.50 4.00
11 Stafford/Moreno 8.00 20.00
12 Nicks/Barden 2.00 5.00
13 Stafford/Sanchez 12.00 30.00
14 Pettigrew/D.Williams 1.50 4.00
15 Bomar/Nicks 2.00 5.00

2009 Donruss Threads Rookie Collection Materials Quad

QUAD JSY PRINT RUN 100 SER.#'d SETS
*PRIME/25: .8X TO 2X BASIC QUAD
1 Stfrd/Smth/Jcksn/Crry 12.00 30.00
2 Hywrd/Crbtr/Mclin/Hrvin 3.00 8.00
3 Stfrd/Snchz/Mrno/Brwn 15.00 40.00
4 Stfrd/Snchz/Frmn/Whte 15.00 40.00
5 Stfrd/Mrno/Hywrd/Pttgrw 12.00 30.00

2009 Donruss Threads Triple Threat

*CENT.PROOF/100: .6X TO 1.5X BASE INSERTS
1 Delhomme/S.Smith/D.Williams 1.00 2.50
2 Roethlisberger/Holmes/Parker 1.25 3.00
3 Schaub/A.Johnson/Slaton 1.00 2.50
4 Brady/S.Moss/Maroney 1.00 2.50
5 McNabb/D.Jackson/Westbrook 1.00 2.50
6 Flacco/Mason/McGahee 1.00 2.50
7 Ryan/R.White/Turner 1.00 2.50
8 Campbell/Cooley/Portis .75 2.00
9 Brees/Colston/Bush 1.25 3.00
10 Rodgers/Jennings/Grant 2.50 6.00

2009 Donruss Threads Triple Threat Materials

BASE JSY PRINT RUN 100-250
*PRIME/50: .8X TO 2X TRIPLE/230-250
*PRIME/50: .6X TO 1.5X TRIPLE/100
1 Delh/S.Smth/D.Will/250 5.00 12.00
2 Roeth/Holmes/Parker/100 8.00 20.00
3 Schaub/Jhnsn/Slaton/100 6.00 15.00
4 Brady/Moss/Marny/230 5.00 12.00
6 Flacco/Masn/McG/250 5.00 12.00
7 Ryan/R.White/Trner/100 6.00 15.00
8 Cmpbll/Cooly/Portis/250 4.00 10.00
9 Brees/Clstn/Bush/250 6.00 15.00
10 Rdgrs/Jenn/Grant/250 8.00 20.00

2003 Donruss/Playoff Holiday Cards Doubles

COMPLETE SET (14) 30.00 60.00
HH1 C.Palmer/K.Washington 7.50 20.00
HH2 K.Boller/M.Smith 3.00 8.00
HH3 D.Ragone/A.Johnson 5.00 12.00
HH4 B.Leftwich/D.Clark 5.00 12.00
HH5 K.Kingsbury/B.Johnson 2.50 6.00
HH6 T.Newman/T.Suggs 4.00 10.00
HH7 B.St.Pierre/T.Jacobs 2.50 6.00
HH8 O.Smith/N.Burleson 3.00 8.00
HH9 S.Wallace/K.Curtis 3.00 8.00
HH10 M.Trufant/W.McGahee 4.00 10.00
HH11 C.Brown/T.Calico 3.00 8.00
HH12 B.Johnson/A.Boldin 5.00 12.00
HH13 A.Pinner/L.Johnson 5.00 12.00
HH14 T.Johnson/J.Fargas 4.00 10.00

2003 Donruss/Playoff Holiday Cards Triples

COMPLETE SET (6) 20.00 50.00
HH1 C.Palmer/Br.Johnson/Be.Johnson 6.00 15.00
HH2 Byron Leftwich 6.00 15.00
Anquan Boldin/Kelly Washington
HH3 Kyle Boller/Taylor Jacobs/Kevin Curtis 4.00 10.00
HH4 Willis McGahee 4.00 10.00
Onterrio Smith/Teyo Johnson
HH5 Larry Johnson 6.00 15.00
Justin Fargas/Nate Burleson
HH6 Andre Johnson 4.00 10.00
Tyrone Calico/Dallas Clark

2003 Donruss/Playoff Holiday Cards Quads

COMPLETE SET (5) 20.00 50.00
HH1 Palmer/Boller/Leftwich/Wallace 7.50 20.00
HH2 Bryant Johnson 4.00 10.00
Tyrone Calico/Dallas Clark/Teyo Johnson
HH3 Justin Fargas/Larry Johnson 6.00 15.00
Willis McGahee/Onterrio Smith
HH4 Andre Johnson 4.00 10.00
Anquan Boldin/Taylor Jacobs/Nate Burleson
HH5 Terence Newman/Terrell Suggs 4.00 10.00
DeWayne Robertson/Marcus Trufant

2007 Donruss/Playoff Hawaii Trade Conference

COMPLETE SET (6) 8.00 20.00
1 Vince Young .60 1.50
2 Brett Favre 2.00 5.00
3 Reggie Bush .60 1.50
4 Peyton Manning 2.50 6.00
5 JaMarcus Russell .40 1.00
6 Adrian Peterson 1.25 3.00

2000 Dorling Kindersley QB Club Stickers

The book publisher Dorling Kindersley issued these stickers along with a book in which to paste them into. The stickers were printed in groups on 4-different page sized sheets within the book. To exist in single sticker form they actually would have had to be cut out by hand. We've included prices below for single stickers and listed them alphabetically beginning with the player subjects.

COMPLETE SET (50) 4.00 8.00
1 Troy Aikman .25 .60
2 Troy Aikman .25 .60
3 Jeff Blake .07 .20
4 Drew Bledsoe .15 .40
5 Drew Bledsoe .15 .40
6 Terrell Davis .25 .60
7 John Elway .40 1.00
8 John Elway .40 1.00
9 John Elway .40 1.00
10 Boomer Esiason .07 .20
11 Boomer Esiason .07 .20
12 Jim Everett .07 .20
13 Brett Favre .40 1.00
14 Brett Favre .40 1.00
15 Doug Flutie .15 .40
16 Gus Frerotte .07 .20
17 Jeff George .07 .20
18 Elvis Grbac .07 .20
19 Michael Irvin .07 .20
20 Brad Johnson .10 .30
21 Keyshawn Johnson .10 .30
22 Jim Kelly .10 .30
23 Bernie Kosar .07 .20
24 Bernie Kosar .07 .20
25 Bernie Kosar .07 .20
26 Peyton Manning .40 1.00
27 Dan Marino .40 1.00
28 Dan Marino .40 1.00
29 Donovan McNabb .20 .50
30 Donovan McNabb .20 .50
31 Steve McNair .10 .30
32 Neil O'Donnell .07 .20
33 Jake Plummer .10 .30
34 Jerry Rice .25 .60
35 Jerry Rice .25 .60
Steve Young
36 Barry Sanders .30 .75
37 Barry Sanders .30 .75
38 Junior Seau .07 .20
39 Junior Seau .07 .20
40 Phil Simms .07 .20
41 Kordell Stewart .07 .20
42 Vinny Testaverde .07 .20
43 Ricky Williams .20 .50
44 Ricky Williams .20 .50
45 Steve Young .15 .40
46 Cowboys Helmet .05 .15
47 Super Bowl Football .05 .15
48 Super Bowl Trophy .05 .15
49 Super Bowl XXXIII Program .05 .15
50 Super Bowl XXI Patch .05 .15

1949 Eagles Team Issue

This set of black and white photos was issued in 1949 by the Eagles in celebration of their 1948 NFL Championship team. Each photo measures roughly 8 3/4" by 10 1/2" and includes a facsimile autograph, the player's position, weight, height, and college below the photo. The photos are blankbacked and unnumbered.

COMPLETE SET (20) 250.00 400.00
1 Neill Armstrong 12.00 20.00
2 Russ Craft 12.00 20.00
3 Jack Ferrante 12.00 20.00
4 Noble Doss 12.00 20.00
4 Bucko Kilroy 15.00 25.00
5 Mario Giannelli 12.00 20.00
5 Vic Lindskog 12.00 20.00
6 Pat McHugh 12.00 20.00
7 Joe Muha 12.00 20.00
8 Jack Myers 12.00 20.00
9 Pete Pihos 25.00 40.00
10 Bosh Pritchard 15.00 25.00
11 George Savitsky 12.00 20.00
12 Vic Sears 12.00 20.00
13 Ernie Steele 12.00 20.00
14 Tommy Thompson 18.00 30.00
15 Steve Van Buren 35.00 60.00
16 Al Wistert 15.00 25.00
17 Alex Wojciechowicz 18.00 30.00
18 Team Photo 18.00 30.00

1950 Eagles Bulletin Pin-ups

These black and white premium photos measure roughly 8" x 10" and were issued by The Bulletin newspaper in the Philadelphia area. The photos are blankbacked and feature the newspaper's logo in the upper left corner, the team name in the lower left corner and the player's facsimile autograph in the lower right corner.

1 Greasy Neale 10.00 20.00
2 Bosh Pritchard 10.00 20.00
3 Steve Van Buren 15.00 30.00

1950 Eagles Team Issue

This set of black and white photos was issued around 1950 by the Eagles. Each photo is very similar to the 1949 issue with the differences being found in the text included below the player image. Some players were featured with the same photo in both years with only the difference in text. Each photo measures roughly 8 3/4" by 11" and includes a printed player name on a top row, followed by the player's position, height, weight, and college on a bottom row of type below the photo. The photos are blankbacked and unnumbered.

COMPLETE SET (10)
1 Neill Armstrong 12.00 20.00
2 Russ Craft 12.00 20.00
3 Bucko Kilroy 15.00 25.00
4 Pat McHugh 12.00 20.00
5 Joe Muha 12.00 20.00
6 Pete Pihos 25.00 40.00
7 Bosh Pritchard 15.00 25.00
8 Vic Sears 12.00 20.00
9 Steve Van Buren 35.00 60.00
10 Whitey Wistert 15.00 25.00

1956 Eagles Team Issue

The Philadelphia Eagles issued and distributed this set of player photos. Each measures approximately 8" by 10" and features a black and white photo on the cardfront with a blank cardback. The player's name, position (abbreviated), height, weight, and college affiliation appear below the photo with the team name above the picture. The checklist is thought to be incomplete. Any additions to this list are greatly appreciated.

1 Bibbles Bawel 10.00 20.00
2 Eddie Bell 10.00 20.00
3 Ken Keller 10.00 20.00
4 Bob Kelley 10.00 20.00
5 Bob Pellegrini 10.00 20.00
6 Rocky Ryan 10.00 20.00
7 Bill Stribling 10.00 20.00
8 Neil Worden 10.00 20.00

1959 Eagles Jay Publishing

This set features (approximately) 5" by 7" black-and-white player photos with the players in traditional football poses. The photos were packaged 12-per set and originally sold for 25-cents. The fronts include the player's name and team name (Philadelphia Eagles) below the player image. The backs are blank, unnumbered, and checklisted below in alphabetical order.

COMPLETE SET (11) 50.00 100.00
1 Bill Barnes 4.00 8.00
2 Chuck Bednarik 10.00 20.00
3 Tom Brookshier 5.00 10.00
4 Marion Campbell 4.00 8.00
5 Tommy McDonald 6.00 12.00
6 Clarence Peaks 4.00 8.00
7 Pete Retzlaff 5.00 10.00
8 Jesse Richardson 4.00 8.00
9 Norm Van Brocklin 10.00 20.00
10 Bobby Walston 4.00 8.00
11 Chuck Weber 4.00 8.00

1959 Eagles San Giorgio Flipbooks

This set features members of the Philadelphia Eagles printed on velum type paper stock created in a multi-image action sequence. The set is commonly referenced as the San Giorgio Macaroni Football Flipbooks. Members of the Philadelphia Eagles, Pittsburgh Steelers, and Washington Redskins were produced regionally with 15-players, reportedly, issued per team. Some players were produced in more than one sequence of poses with different captions and/or slightly different photos used. When the flipbooks are still in uncut form (which is most desirable), they measure approximately 5 3/4" by 3 9/16". The sheets are blank backed, in black and white, and provide 14-small numbered pages when cut apart. Collectors were encouraged to cut out each photo and stack them in such a way as to create a moving image of the player when flipped with the fingers. Any additions to this list are appreciated.

1A Bill Barnes 90.00 150.00
1B Bill Barnes 90.00 150.00
2 Chuck Bednarik 250.00 400.00
3 Proverb Jacobs 90.00 150.00
4 Tommy McDonald 175.00 300.00
5A Ed Meadows 90.00 150.00
5B Ed Meadows 90.00 150.00
6A Clarence Peaks 90.00 150.00
6B Clarence Peaks 90.00 150.00
7 Bob Pellegrini 90.00 150.00
8A Pete Retzlaff 100.00 175.00
8B Pete Retzlaff 100.00 175.00
8C Pete Retzlaff 100.00 175.00
9 Bobby Walston 90.00 150.00
10 Chuck Weber 90.00 150.00

1960 Eagles Team Issue

This 11-card team issued set measures approximately 5" by 7" and is printed on thin, slick card stock. The fronts feature black-and-white posed action player photos with white borders. The player's name is printed in black below the picture along with the team name "Eagles." The backs are blank. The cards are unnumbered and checklisted below in alphabetical order. Any additions to this list are appreciated.

COMPLETE SET (11) 60.00 120.00
1 Maxie Baughan 6.00 12.00
2 Chuck Bednarik 12.50 25.00
3 Don Burroughs 5.00 10.00
4 Jimmy Carr 6.00 12.00
5 Howard Keys 5.00 10.00
6 Ed Khayat 5.00 10.00
7 Jim McCusker 5.00 10.00
8 John Nocera 5.00 10.00
9 Nick Skorich CO 5.00 10.00
10 J.D. Smith 6.00 12.00
11 John Wittenborn 5.00 10.00

1961 Eagles Jay Publishing

This 12-card set features (approximately) 5" by 7" black-and-white player photos. The photos show players in traditional poses with the quarterback preparing to throw, the runner heading downfield, and the defenseman ready for the tackle. These cards were packaged 12 to a packet and originally sold for 25 cents. The backs are blank. The cards are unnumbered and checklisted below in alphabetical order.

COMPLETE SET (12) 40.00 80.00
1 Maxie Baughan 4.00 8.00
2 Jim McCusker 4.00 8.00
3 Tommy McDonald 6.00 12.00
4 Bob Pellegrini 4.00 8.00
5 Pete Retzlaff 5.00 10.00
6 Jesse Richardson 4.00 8.00
7 Joe Robb 4.00 8.00
8 Theron Sapp 4.00 8.00
9 J.D. Smith T 4.00 8.00
10 Bobby Walston 4.00 8.00
11 Jerry Williams ACO 4.00 8.00
12 John Wittenborn 4.00 8.00

1960-62 Eagles Team Issue

The Eagles issued this set of black and white player photos. Each measures approximately 8" by 10" and features the team name above the player photo with his name, vital statistics and college below. The backs are blank and unnumbered. The checklist below includes the known photos at this time. It's likely there were more produced. Any additions to this list would be appreciated.

COMPLETE SET (25) 150.00 300.00
1 Timmy Brown 7.50 15.00
2 Don Burroughs 7.50 15.00
3 Jimmy Carr 7.50 15.00
4 Irv Cross 7.50 15.00
5 Gene Gossage 7.50 15.00
6 Riley Gunnels 7.50 15.00
7 Bob Harrison 7.50 15.00
8 King Hill 7.50 15.00
9 Sonny Jurgensen 15.00 30.00
10 Jim McCusker 7.50 15.00
11 Alan Miller 7.50 15.00
12 John Nocera 7.50 15.00
13 Don Oakes 7.50 15.00
14 Clarence Peaks 7.50 15.00
15 Will Renfro 7.50 15.00
16 Theron Sapp 7.50 15.00
17 Buck Shaw CO 7.50 15.00
18 Nick Skorich CO 7.50 15.00
19 J.D. Smith T 7.50 15.00
20 Leo Sugar 7.50 15.00
21 Carl Taseff 7.50 15.00
22 John Tracey 7.50 15.00
23 Bobby Walston 7.50 15.00
24 Chuck Weber 7.50 15.00
25 John Wittenborn 7.50 15.00

1961 Eagles Team Issue 5x7

This team issued set measures approximately 5" by 7" and is printed on thin, slick card stock. The fronts feature black-and-white posed action player photos with white borders. The player's name is printed in black below the picture along with the team name "Philadelphia Eagles." The backs are blank. The cards are unnumbered and checklisted below in alphabetical order. Any additions to this list are appreciated.

COMPLETE SET (12) 75.00 150.00
1 Bill Barnes 6.00 12.00
2 Chuck Bednarik 10.00 20.00
3 Tom Brookshier 7.50 15.00
4 Timmy Brown 7.50 15.00
5 Marion Campbell 7.50 15.00
6 Stan Campbell 6.00 12.00
7 Jimmy Carr 6.00 12.00
8 Irv Cross 7.50 15.00
9 Sonny Jurgensen 15.00 25.00
10 Clarence Peaks 6.00 12.00
11 Jesse Richardson 6.00 12.00
12 Nick Skorich CO 6.00 12.00

1963 Eagles Phillies' Cigars

This attractive color football photo was part of a premium promotion for Phillies Cigars. It measures 6 1/2" by 9" and features a facsimile autograph on the cardfront. The cardback is blank.

1 Tommy McDonald 15.00 25.00

1964-66 Eagles Program Inserts

These photos were actually bound into Philadelphia Eagles game programs from 1964-66. Each one when cleanly cut from the program measures roughly 8 3/8" by 11" and features a black and white photo of an Eagles player (except for the photo of Giants Y.A. Tittle) on one side and a bio on the back along with two small photos. A facsimile autograph is included on the photo and the first 43-pictures in the series are numbered within the left side border while the remaining were issued without numbers. Early photos include a white border around all sides of the photo while later issues are borderless on three sides.

COMPLETE SET (53) 150.00 300.00
1 Timmy Brown 4.00 8.00
2 Ron Goodwin 3.00 6.00
3 Pete Retzlaff 4.00 8.00
4 Maxie Baughan 4.00 8.00
5 Y.A. Tittle 10.00 20.00
6 Don Burroughs 3.00 6.00
7 Norm Snead 6.00 12.00
8 Jim Ringo 6.00 12.00
9 Riley Gunnels 3.00 6.00
10 George Tarasovic 3.00 6.00
11 Earl Gros 3.00 6.00
12 Bob Brown 4.00 8.00
13 Irv Cross 4.00 8.00
14 Sam Baker 3.00 6.00
15 Ed Blaine 3.00 6.00
16 Nate Ramsey 3.00 6.00
17 Dave Lloyd 3.00 6.00
18 Ollie Matson 7.50 15.00
19 Pete Case 3.00 6.00
20 Mike Morgan 3.00 6.00
21 Bob Richards 3.00 6.00
22 Ray Poage 3.00 6.00
23 Don Hultz 3.00 6.00
24 Dave Graham 3.00 6.00
25 Floyd Peters 3.00 6.00
26 King Hill 4.00 8.00
27 John Meyers 3.00 6.00
28 Lynn Hoyem 3.00 6.00
29 Joe Scarpati 3.00 6.00
30 Jack Concannon 4.00 8.00
31 Jim Skaggs 3.00 6.00
32 Glenn Glass 3.00 6.00
33 Ralph Heck 3.00 6.00
34 Claude Crabb 3.00 6.00
35 Israel Lang 3.00 6.00
36 Tom Woodeshick 4.00 8.00
37 Ed Khayat 3.00 6.00
38 Roger Gill 3.00 6.00
39 Harold Wells 3.00 6.00
40 Lane Howell 3.00 6.00
41 Dave Recher 3.00 6.00
42 Fred Hill 3.00 6.00
43 Al Nelson 3.00 6.00
NNO Randy Beisler 3.00 6.00
NNO Dave Cahill 3.00 6.00
NNO Ben Hawkins 3.00 6.00
NNO Ike Kelley 3.00 6.00
NNO Aaron Martin 3.00 6.00
NNO Ron Medved 3.00 6.00
NNO Jim Nettles 3.00 6.00
NNO Gary Pettigrew 3.00 6.00
NNO Arunas Vasys 3.00 6.00
NNO Fred Whittingham 3.00 6.00

1965-66 Eagles Team Issue

The Eagles issued these black and white glossy player photos likely over a period of years. Each measures approximately 8" by 10" and features the player's name, position (spelled out in full) and team name below the photo. The backs are blank and unnumbered. The checklist below includes the known photos at this time. Any additions to this list would be appreciated.

COMPLETE SET (16) 125.00 250.00
1 Sam Baker 5.00 10.00
2 Sam Baker 5.00 10.00
3 Ed Blaine 5.00 10.00
4 Bob Brown T 6.00 12.00
5 Bob Brown T 6.00 12.00
6 Timmy Brown 6.00 12.00
7 Jack Concannon 5.00 10.00
8 Dave Graham 5.00 10.00
9 Earl Gros 5.00 10.00
10 Fred Hill 5.00 10.00
11 Lynn Hoyem 5.00 10.00
12 Dwight Kelley 5.00 10.00
13 Ed Khayat 5.00 10.00
14 Israel Lang 5.00 10.00
15 Dave Lloyd 5.00 10.00
16 Aaron Martin 5.00 10.00
17 Mike Morgan LB 5.00 10.00
18 Al Nelson 5.00 10.00
19 Jim Nettles 5.00 10.00
20 Floyd Peters 5.00 10.00
21 Ray Poage 5.00 10.00
22 Pete Retzlaff 6.00 12.00
23 Jim Ringo 6.00 12.00
24 Jim Skaggs 5.00 10.00
25 Norm Snead 6.00 12.00
26 Norm Snead 6.00 12.00
27 Norm Snead 6.00 12.00

1967 Eagles Program Inserts

These photos were actually bound into Philadelphia Eagles game programs from 1967 and are entitled "Eagles Portraits." Each one when cleanly cut from the program measures roughly 8 3/8" by 11" and features a black and white photo of an Eagles player on one side and a bio on the back along with two small photos. A facsimile autograph is included on the photo and each photo is numbered within the left side border. Each photo is borderless on three sides.

COMPLETE SET (14) 40.00 80.00
1 Timmy Brown 4.00 8.00
2 Dave Lloyd 3.00 6.00
3 Joe Scarpati 3.00 6.00
4 Bob Brown 4.00 8.00
5 Jim Ringo 6.00 12.00
6 Nate Ramsey 3.00 6.00
7 Israel Lang 3.00 6.00
8 Jim Skaggs 3.00 6.00
9 Norm Snead 6.00 12.00
10 Sam Baker 3.00 6.00
11 Tom Woodeshick 3.00 6.00
12 Tom Woodeshick 4.00 8.00
13 Don Hultz 3.00 6.00
14 Harold Wells 3.00 6.00

1968 Eagles Postcards

These photos measure approximately 4 1/4" by 5 1/2" and feature posed action black-and-white player photos with white borders. Each photo was taken outside unless noted below. The player's name and team name (measuring either 1 9/16" or 1 3/8") are printed in the bottom border. The Eagles issued Postcards over a number of years and this set is differentiated by the lack of a facsimile autograph on the cardfronts. Since the set is nearly identical to the 1969 issue, we've noted differences of like players below. Unless noted below, the backs include a postcard style format. The cards are unnumbered and checklisted below in alphabetical order.

COMPLETE SET (40) 150.00 300.00
1 Sam Baker 4.00 8.00
2 Gary Ballman 4.00 8.00
3 Randy Beisler 4.00 8.00
4 Bob Brown 6.00 12.00
5 Fred Brown 4.00 8.00
6 Gene Ceppetelli 4.00 8.00
7 Wayne Colman 4.00 8.00
8 Mike Ditka 10.00 20.00
9 Rick Duncan 4.00 8.00
10 Ron Goodwin 4.00 8.00
11 Ben Hawkins 4.00 8.00
12 Alvin Haymond 4.00 8.00
13 King Hill 4.00 8.00
14 John Huarte 4.00 8.00
15 Don Hultz 4.00 8.00
16 Ike Kelley 4.00 8.00
17 Jim Kelly 4.00 8.00
18 Izzy Lang 4.00 8.00
19 Dave Lloyd 4.00 8.00
20 John Mallory 4.00 8.00
21 Ron Medved 4.00 8.00
22 Frank Molden 4.00 8.00
23 Al Nelson 4.00 8.00
24 Jim Nettles 4.00 8.00
25 Mark Nordquist 4.00 8.00
26 Floyd Peters 4.00 8.00
27 Gary Pettigrew 4.00 8.00
28 Cyril Pinder 4.00 8.00
29 Nate Ramsey 4.00 8.00
30 Dave Recher 4.00 8.00

31 Tim Rossovich 4.00 8.00
32 Joe Scarpati 4.00 8.00
33 Norm Snead 5.00 10.00
34 Mel Tom 4.00 8.00
35 Arunas Vasys 4.00 8.00
36 Harold Wells 4.00 8.00
37 Harry Wilson 4.00 8.00
38 Tom Woodeshick 4.00 8.00
39 Adrian Young 4.00 8.00
40 Coaching Staff 4.00 8.00

1969 Eagles Postcards

These photos measure approximately 4 1/4" by 5 1/2" and feature posed action black-and-white player photos with white borders. Each photo was taken outside unless noted below. The player's name and team name (measuring either 1 9/16" or 1 3/8") are printed in the bottom border. The Eagles issued Postcards over a number of years and this set is differentiated by the lack of a facsimile autograph on the cardfronts. Since the set is nearly identical to the 1968 issue, we've noted differences of like players below. Unless noted below, the backs include a postcard style format. The cards are unnumbered and checklisted below in alphabetical order.

COMPLETE SET (41) 150.00 300.00
1 Sam Baker 4.00 8.00
2 Gary Ballman 4.00 8.00
3 Ronnie Blye 4.00 8.00
4 Bill Bradley 5.00 10.00
5 Ernest Calloway 4.00 8.00
6 Joe Carollo 4.00 8.00
7 Irv Cross 4.00 8.00
8 Mike Dirks 4.00 8.00
9 Mike Evans 4.00 8.00
10 Dave Graham 4.00 8.00
11 Tony Guillory 4.00 8.00
12 Dick Hart 4.00 8.00
13 Fred Hill 4.00 8.00
14 William Hobbs 4.00 8.00
15 Lane Howell 4.00 8.00
16 Chuck Hughes 4.00 8.00
17 Don Hultz 4.00 8.00
18 Harold Jackson 6.00 12.00
19 Harry Jones 4.00 8.00
20 Ike Kelley 4.00 8.00
21 Wade Key 4.00 8.00
22 Leroy Keyes 4.00 8.00
23 Kent Lawrence 4.00 8.00
24 Dave Lloyd 4.00 8.00
25 Ron Medved 4.00 8.00
26 George Mira 4.00 8.00
27 Al Nelson 4.00 8.00
28 Mark Nordquist 4.00 8.00
29 Floyd Peters 4.00 8.00
30 Gary Pettigrew 4.00 8.00
31 Cyril Pinder 4.00 8.00
32 Ron Porter 4.00 8.00
33 Nate Ramsey 4.00 8.00
34 Jimmy Raye 4.00 8.00
35 Tim Rossovich 4.00 8.00
36 Joe Scarpati 4.00 8.00
37 Jim Skaggs 4.00 8.00
38 Norm Snead 5.00 10.00
39 Mel Tom 4.00 8.00
40 Tom Woodeshick 4.00 8.00
41 Adrian Young 4.00 8.00

1970-71 Eagles Postcards

These postcards measure approximately 4 1/4" by 5 1/2" and feature posed action black-and-white player photos with white borders. Each photo was taken outside unless noted below. The player's name and team name (measuring either 1 9/16" or 1 3/8") are printed in the bottom border. The Eagles issued Postcards over a number of years and this set is differentiated by the facsimile autograph on the cardfronts. It is likely that our listing combines postcards that were released in 1970 and 1971. Several have been found with a Boy Scouts "BSA" logo near the photo. Unless noted below, the backs include a postcard style format. The cards are unnumbered and checklisted below in alphabetical order.

COMPLETE SET (53) 125.00 250.00
1 Henry Allison 3.00 6.00
2 Rick Arrington 3.00 6.00
3 Tom Bailey 3.00 6.00
4 Gary Ballman 3.00 6.00
5 Lee Bouggess 3.00 6.00
6 Lee Bouggess BSA 3.00 6.00
7 Bill Bradley 4.00 8.00
8 Ernie Calloway 3.00 6.00
9 Harold Carmichael 8.00 12.00
10 Joe Carollo 3.00 6.00
11 Bob Creech 3.00 6.00
12 Norm Davis 3.00 6.00
13 Tom Dempsey 3.00 6.00
14 Tom Dempsey BSA 3.00 6.00
15 Mike Dirks 3.00 6.00
16 Mike Evans 3.00 6.00
17 Happy Feller 3.00 6.00
18 Carl Gersbach 3.00 6.00
19 Dave Graham 3.00 6.00
20 Richard Harris 3.00 6.00
21 Dick Hart 3.00 6.00
22 Ben Hawkins 3.00 6.00
23 Fred Hill 3.00 6.00
24 Bill Hobbs 3.00 6.00
25 Don Hultz 3.00 6.00
26 Harold Jackson 4.00 8.00
27 Jay Johnson 3.00 6.00
28 Harry Jones 3.00 6.00
29 Ray Jones 3.00 6.00
30 Ike Kelley 3.00 6.00
31 Wade Key 3.00 6.00
32 Leroy Keyes 3.00 6.00
33 Pete Liske 3.00 6.00
34 Pete Liske BSA 3.00 6.00
35 Dave Lloyd 3.00 6.00
36 Ron Medved 3.00 6.00
37 Tom McNeill BSA 3.00 6.00
38 Mark Moseley 4.00 8.00
39 Al Nelson 3.00 6.00
40 Mark Nordquist 3.00 6.00
41 Gary Pettigrew 3.00 6.00
42 Steve Preece 3.00 6.00
43 Ron Porter 3.00 6.00
44 Nate Ramsey 3.00 6.00
45 Tim Rossovich 3.00 6.00
46 Jim Skaggs 3.00 6.00
47 Steve Smith T 3.00 6.00
48 Richard Stevens 3.00 6.00
49 Bill Walik 3.00 6.00
50 Jim Ward 3.00 6.00
51 Larry Watkins 3.00 6.00
52 Adrian Young 3.00 6.00
53 Coaching Staff 8.00 12.00
Cross
Levy

1972 Eagles Postcards

These photos measure approximately 4 1/4" by 5 1/2" and feature posed action black-and-white player photos with white borders. Each photo was taken outside unless noted below. The player's name and team name (measuring about 1 9/16") are printed in the bottom border. The Eagles issued Postcards over a number of years and this set is differentiated from the 1970-71 list by the lack of a facsimile autograph on the cardfronts. Unless noted below, the backs include a postcard style format. The cards are unnumbered and checklisted below in alphabetical order.

COMPLETE SET (6) 20.00 35.00
1 Henry Allison 3.00 6.00
2 Houston Antwine 3.00 6.00
3 Tony Baker 3.00 6.00
4 Larry Crowe 3.00 6.00
5 Harold Jackson 4.00 8.00
6 Jim Thrower 3.00 6.00

1972-73 Eagles Team Issue

These Philadelphia Eagles team issued photos measure approximately 8" by 10" and feature a black and white player photo on a glossy blankbacked card stock. The photos were likely issued over a number of years with many players issued in both a portrait and posed action format. Just the player's name and team name appear below the photo. The checklist is likely incomplete; any additions to this list would be appreciated.

COMPLETE SET (29) 75.00 150.00
1 Tom Bailey 3.00 6.00
Portrait
2 Herman Ball 3.00 6.00
3 Bill Bradley 4.00 8.00
Posed Action
4 Ron Bull 3.00 6.00
5 John Bunting 3.00 6.00
6 John Bunting 3.00 6.00
7 Bill Cody 3.00 6.00
Portrait
8 Larry Crowe 3.00 6.00
9 Larry Crowe 3.00 6.00
10 Albert Davis 3.00 6.00
11 Albert Davis 3.00 6.00
12 Stanley Davis 3.00 6.00
13 Stanley Davis 3.00 6.00
14 Mike Dunstan 3.00 6.00
15 Mike Dunstan 3.00 6.00
16 Lawrence Estes 3.00 6.00
Portrait
17 Mike Evans 3.00 6.00
18 Pat Gibbs 3.00 6.00
Posed Action
19 Harold Jackson 4.00 8.00
Posed Action
20 Wade Key 3.00 6.00
Posed Action
21 Kent Kramer 3.00 6.00
Portrait
22 Randy Logan 3.00 6.00
Posed Action
23 Tom Luken 3.00 6.00
Posed Action
24 Tom McNeill 3.00 6.00
25 Tom McNeill 3.00 6.00
26 Gary Pettigrew 3.00 6.00
Posed Action
27 Bob Picard 3.00 6.00
Posed Action
28 Ron Porter 3.00 6.00
Posed Action
29 Jerry Wampfler CO 3.00 6.00
30 Vern Winfield 3.00 6.00
Posed Action
31 Steve Zabel 3.00 6.00
Posed Action

1974 Eagles Postcards

These photos measure approximately 4 1/4" by 5 1/2" and feature posed action or portrait style black-and-white player photos with white borders. The player's name and team name (measuring about 1 9/16") are printed in the bottom border. The Eagles issued Postcards over a number of years and this set is very similar to the 1972 issue. The backs include a postcard style format. The photos are unnumbered and checklisted below in alphabetical order.

COMPLETE SET (45) 125.00 250.00
1 Tom Bailey 3.00 6.00
2 Bill Bergey 4.00 8.00
3 Mike Boryla 3.00 6.00
4 Bill Bradley 3.00 6.00
5 Norm Bulaich 3.00 6.00
6 John Bunting 3.00 6.00
7 Jim Cagle 3.00 6.00
8 Harold Carmichael 6.00 12.00
9 Wes Chesson 3.00 6.00
10 Tom Dempsey 3.00 6.00
11 Bill Dunstan 3.00 6.00
12 Charlie Ford 3.00 6.00
13 Roman Gabriel 5.00 10.00
14 Dean Halverson 3.00 6.00
15 Randy Jackson 3.00 6.00
16 Po James 3.00 6.00
17 Joe Jones 3.00 6.00
18 Roy Kirksey 3.00 6.00
19 Merritt Kersey 3.00 6.00
20 Wade Key 3.00 6.00
21 Kent Kramer 3.00 6.00
22 Joe Lavender 3.00 6.00
23 Frank LeMaster 3.00 6.00
24 Tom Luken 3.00 6.00
25 Larry Marshall 3.00 6.00
26 Guy Morriss 3.00 6.00
27 Mark Nordquist 3.00 6.00
28 Greg Oliver 3.00 6.00
29 John Outlaw 3.00 6.00
30 Artimus Parker 3.00 6.00
31 Jerry Patton 3.00 6.00
32 Bob Picard 3.00 6.00
33 John Reaves 3.00 6.00
34 Marion Reeves 3.00 6.00
35 Kevin Reilly 3.00 6.00
36 Charles Smith 3.00 6.00
37 Steve Smith 3.00 6.00
38 Jerry Sisemore 3.00 6.00
39 Richard Stevens 3.00 6.00
40 Mitch Sutton 3.00 6.00
41 Tom Sullivan 3.00 6.00
42 Will Wynn 3.00 6.00
43 Charlie Young 3.00 6.00
44 Steve Zabel 3.00 6.00
45 Don Zimmerman 3.00 6.00

1975 Eagles Postcards

Cards from this set measure approximately 4 1/4" by 5 1/2" and feature game action black-and-white player photos with white borders. The player's name, position (initials), Eagles logo and team name are printed in the bottom white margin. The backs include a postcard style format. The cards are unnumbered and checklisted below in alphabetical order. Any additions to the list below are appreciated.

COMPLETE SET (26) 75.00 135.00
1 George Amundson 3.00 6.00
2 Mike Boryla 3.00 6.00
3 Bill Bradley 3.00 6.00
4 Cliff Brooks 3.00 6.00
5 John Bunting 3.00 6.00
6 Tom Ehler 3.00 6.00
7 Roman Gabriel 6.00 10.00
8 Spike Jones 3.00 6.00
9 Keith Krepfle 3.00 6.00
10 Joe Lavender 3.00 6.00
11 Ron Lou 3.00 6.00
12 Art Malone 3.00 6.00
13 Rosie Manning 3.00 6.00
14 James McAlister 3.00 6.00
15 Guy Morriss 3.00 6.00
16 Horst Muhlmann 3.00 6.00
17 John Niland 3.00 6.00
18 John Outlaw 3.00 6.00
19 Artimus Parker 3.00 6.00
20 Don Ratliff 3.00 6.00
21 Jerry Sisemore 3.00 6.00
22 Charles Smith 3.00 6.00
23 Tom Sullivan 3.00 6.00
24 Stan Walters 3.00 6.00
25 Will Wynn 3.00 6.00
26 Don Zimmerman 3.00 6.00

1976 Eagles Team Issue

The Eagles issued these black and white glossy player photos in 1976. Each measures approximately 5" by 7" and features the player's name and position (initials) below the photo. The team name and year appear above the photo. The backs are blank and unnumbered. The checklist below includes the known photos at this time. Any additions to this list would be appreciated.

COMPLETE SET (7) 20.00 40.00
1 John Bunting 3.00 6.00
2 Harold Carmichael 4.00 8.00
3 Pete Lazetich 3.00 6.00
4 Guy Morriss 3.00 6.00
5 Jerry Sisemore 3.00 6.00
6 Charles Smith 3.00 6.00
7 Dick Vermeil CO 6.00 12.00

1977 Eagles Frito Lay

Cards from this set measure approximately 4 1/4" by 5 1/2" and feature portrait player photos on the fronts. The photo type differentiates this set from the 1978 set which otherwise follows the same type style and printing. It's likely that some of these player photos were released during both years. The team name and logo appear in the top border while the player's name, position, and Frito Lay (FL) logo appear in the bottom border. Most feature postcard style cardbacks. This release can be identified by the shorter "FL" Frito Lay logo in the lower right corner and the 1/8" left and right borders. Because this set is unnumbered, the cards are listed alphabetically.

COMPLETE SET (34) 100.00 200.00
1 Bill Bergey 4.00 8.00
2 John Bunting 3.00 6.00
3 Lem Burnham 3.00 6.00
4 Harold Carmichael 5.00 10.00
5 Mike Cordova 3.00 6.00
6 Herman Edwards 4.00 8.00
7 Tom Ehler 3.00 6.00
8 Cleveland Franklin 3.00 6.00
9 Dennis Franks 3.00 6.00
10 Roman Gabriel 5.00 10.00
11 Carl Hairston 3.00 6.00
12 Mike Hogan 3.00 6.00
13 Charlie Johnson 3.00 6.00
14 Eric Johnson 3.00 6.00
15 Wade Key 3.00 6.00
16 Pete Lazetich 3.00 6.00
17 Randy Logan 3.00 6.00
18 Herb Lusk 3.00 6.00
19 Larry Marshall 3.00 6.00
20 Wilbert Montgomery 4.00 8.00
21 Rocco Moore 3.00 6.00
22 Guy Morriss 3.00 6.00
23 Horst Muhlmann 3.00 6.00
24 John Outlaw 3.00 6.00
25 Vince Papale 7.50 15.00
26 James Reed 3.00 6.00
27 Kevin Russell 3.00 6.00
28 Jerry Sisemore 3.00 6.00
29 Manny Sistrunk 3.00 6.00
30 Charles Smith 3.00 6.00
31 Terry Tautolo 3.00 6.00
32 Art Thoms 3.00 6.00
33 Stan Walters 4.00 8.00
34 John Walton 3.00 6.00

1978 Eagles Frito Lay

Cards from this set measure approximately 4 1/4" by 5 1/2" and feature an action player photo on the fronts. The photo type differentiates this set from the 1977 set which otherwise follows the same type style and printing. It's likely that some of these player photos were released during both years. The team name and logo appear in the top border while the player's name, position, and Frito Lay (FL) logo appear in the bottom border. Most feature postcard style cardbacks. This release can be identified by the shorter "FL" Frito Lay logo in the lower right corner and the 1/8" left and right borders. Because this set is unnumbered, the cards are listed alphabetically.

COMPLETE SET (11) 30.00 60.00
1 Bill Bergey 4.00 8.00
2 Ken Clarke 3.00 6.00
3 Bob Howard 3.00 6.00
4 Keith Krepfle 3.00 6.00
5 Frank LeMaster 3.00 6.00
6 Mike Michel 3.00 6.00
7 Oren Middlebrook 3.00 6.00
8 Wilbert Montgomery 4.00 8.00
9 Mike Osborn 3.00 6.00
10 Reggie Wilkes 3.00 6.00
11 Charles Williams 3.00 6.00

1978 Eagles Team Issue

The Eagles issued these black and white glossy player photos in 1976. Each measures approximately 5" by 7" and features the player's name and position (initials) below the photo. The team name and year appear above the photo. The backs are blank and unnumbered. The checklist below includes the known photos at this time. Any additions to this list would be appreciated.

COMPLETE SET (15) 40.00 80.00
1 Rick Engles 3.00 6.00
2 Cleveland Franklin 3.00 6.00
3 Dennis Franks 3.00 6.00
4 Ed George 3.00 6.00
5 Eric Johnson 3.00 6.00
6 Oren Middlebrook 3.00 6.00
7 Mike Osborn 3.00 6.00
8 Richard Osborne 3.00 6.00
9 John Outlaw 3.00 6.00
10 Ken Payne 3.00 6.00
11 John Sanders 3.00 6.00
12 Manny Sistrunk 3.00 6.00
13 Terry Tautolo 3.00 6.00
14 John Walton 3.00 6.00
15 Charles Williams 3.00 6.00

1979 Eagles Frito Lay

The 1979 Frito Lay Eagles cards measure approximately 4 1/4" by 5 1/2" and feature an action player shot enclosed within a white border. The team name and mascot appear in the top border while the player's name, position, and "Lay's Brand Potato Chips" logo appear in the bottom border. Most feature postcard style cardbacks. Frito Lay sponsored several Eagles sets throughout the 1970s and '80s and it is likely that photos from this set were released over a period of years. This release can be specifically identified by the unique "Lay's Potato Chips" logo in the lower right corner. Because this set is unnumbered, the cards are listed alphabetically.

COMPLETE SET (30) 90.00 150.00
1 Larry Barnes 3.00 6.00
2 John Bunting 3.00 6.00
3 Lem Burnham 3.00 6.00
4 Billy Campfield 3.00 6.00
5 Harold Carmichael 5.00 10.00
6 Ken Clarke 3.00 6.00
7 Scott Fritzkee 3.00 6.00
8 Louie Giammona 3.00 6.00
9 Leroy Harris 3.00 6.00
10 Wally Henry 3.00 6.00
11 Bobby Lee Howard 3.00 6.00
12 Claude Humphrey 4.00 8.00
13 Charlie Johnson 3.00 6.00
14 Wade Key 3.00 6.00
15 Keith Krepfle 4.00 8.00
16 Frank LeMaster 3.00 6.00
17 Randy Logan 3.00 6.00
18 Rufus Mayes 3.00 6.00
19 Jerrold McRae 3.00 6.00
20 Wilbert Montgomery 4.00 8.00
21 Woody Peoples 3.00 6.00
22 Petey Perot 3.00 6.00
23 John Sanders 3.00 6.00
24 John Sciarra 3.00 6.00
25 Manny Sistrunk 3.00 6.00
26 Mark Slater 3.00 6.00
27 John Spagnola 3.00 6.00
28 Stan Walters 3.00 6.00
29 Reggie Wilkes 3.00 6.00
30 Brenard Wilson 3.00 6.00

1979 Eagles Team Sheets

This set consists of six 8" by 10" sheets that display five or eight glossy black-and-white player/coaches photos each. Each individual photo on the sheets measures approximately 2 1/4" by 3 1/4". An Eagles logo, team name and year appear above the photos at the top of each sheet and the backs are blank. The sheets are unnumbered and checklisted below alphabetically according to the player featured in the upper left corner.

COMPLETE SET (6) 20.00 40.00
1 Sheet 1 3.00 6.00
2 Sheet 2 4.00 8.00
3 Sheet 3 4.00 8.00
4 Sheet 4 3.00 6.00
5 Sheet 5 3.00 6.00
6 Sheet 6 5.00 10.00

1980 Eagles Frito Lay

COMPLETE SET (48) 125.00 250.00
1 Bill Bergey 3.00 8.00
2 Richard Blackmore 2.50 6.00
3 Thomas Brown 2.50 6.00
4 John Bunting 2.50 6.00
5 Lem Burnham 2.50 6.00
6 Billy Campfield 2.50 6.00
7 Harold Carmichael 4.00 10.00
8 Al Chesley 2.50 6.00
9 Ken Clarke 2.50 6.00
10 Ken Dunek 2.50 6.00
11 Herman Edwards 2.50 6.00
12 Scott Fitzkee 2.50 6.00
13 Tony Franklin 3.00 8.00
14 Louie Giammona 2.50 6.00
15 Carl Hairston 3.00 8.00
16 Perry Harrington 2.50 6.00
17 Leroy Harris 2.50 6.00
18 Dennis Harrison 2.50 6.00
19 Zac Henderson 2.50 6.00
20 Wally Henry 2.50 6.00
21 Rob Hertel 2.50 6.00
22 Claude Humphrey 3.00 8.00
23 Ron Jaworski 5.00 12.00
24 Charlie Johnson 2.50 6.00
25 Steve Kenney 2.50 6.00
26 Keith Krepfle 3.00 8.00
27 Frank LeMaster 2.50 6.00
28 Randy Logan 2.50 6.00
29 Wilbert Montgomery 3.00 8.00
30 Guy Morriss 2.50 6.00
31 Rodney Parker 2.50 6.00
32 Woody Peoples 2.50 6.00
33 Pete Perot 2.50 6.00
34 Ray Phillips 2.50 6.00
35 Joe Pisarcik 3.00 8.00
36 Jerry Robinson 2.50 6.00
37 Max Runager 2.50 6.00
38 John Sciarra 2.50 6.00
39 Jerry Sisemore 2.50 6.00
40 Mark Slater 2.50 6.00
41 Charles Smith 2.50 6.00
42 John Spagnola 2.50 6.00
43 Dick Vermeil 6.00 15.00
44 Steve Wagner 2.50 6.00
45 Stan Walters 2.50 6.00
46 Reggie Wilkes 2.50 6.00
47 Brenard Wilson 2.50 6.00
48 Roynell Young 2.50 6.00

1980 Eagles McDonald's Glasses

These standard-sized glasses were distributed by McDonald's in the Philadelphia area in 1980. Each glass contains 2 player drawings, with each player represented by a crude action drawing and a head shot superimposed over a fooball, with their name in script underneath the football. The glasses are unnumbered, and are catalogued below in alphabetical order by the first player name.

COMPLETE SET (5) 12.50 25.00
1 Bill Bergey 2.50 6.00
John Bunting
2 Billy Campfield 2.50 6.00
Wilbert Montgomery
3 Harold Carmichael 2.00 5.00
Randy Logan
4 Tony Franklin 2.00 5.00
Stan Walters
5 Ron Jaworski 3.00 8.00
Keith Krepfle

1983 Eagles Frito Lay

This set measures approximately 4 1/4" by 5 1/2" and features an action player shot and facsimile autograph enclosed in a white border. The team name and mascot appear in the top border while the player's name, position, and "Frito Lay" logo appear in the bottom border. Unless noted below, all cardbacks are blank. Frito Lay sponsored several Eagles sets throughout the 1970s and '80s. This release can be differentiated by the full "Frito Lay" logo in the lower right corner and the 1/8" left and right borders. Because this set is unnumbered, the cards are listed alphabetically.

COMPLETE SET (40) 100.00 200.00
1 Harvey Armstrong 2.50 6.00
2 Ron Baker 2.50 6.00
3 Bill Bergey 3.00 8.00
4 Greg Brown 2.50 6.00
5 Marion Campbell CO 2.50 6.00
6 Harold Carmichael 4.00 10.00
7 Ken Clarke 2.50 6.00
8 Dennis DeVaughn 2.50 6.00
9 Herman Edwards 2.50 6.00
10 Ray Ellis 2.50 6.00
11 Major Everett 2.50 6.00
12 Elbert Foules 2.50 6.00
13 Anthony Griggs 2.50 6.00
14 Michael Haddix 2.50 6.00
15 Perry Harrington 2.50 6.00
16 Dennis Harrison 2.50 6.00
17 Melvin Hoover 2.50 6.00
18 Wes Hopkins 2.50 6.00
19 Ron Jaworski 4.00 10.00
20 Vyto Kab 2.50 6.00
21 Steve Kenney 2.50 6.00
22 Rich Kraynak 2.50 6.00
23 Dean Miraldi 2.50 6.00
24 Leonard Mitchell 2.50 6.00
25 Wilbert Montgomery 3.00 8.00
26 Hubie Oliver 2.50 6.00
27 Joe Pisarcik 3.00 8.00
28 Mike Quick 3.00 8.00
29 Jerry Robinson 2.50 6.00
30 Max Runager 2.50 6.00
31 Lawrence Sampleton 2.50 6.00
32 Jody Schulz 2.50 6.00
33 Jerry Sisemore 2.50 6.00
34 John Spagnola 2.50 6.00
35 Reggie Wilkes 2.50 6.00
36 Joel Williams 2.50 6.00
37 Mike Williams 2.50 6.00
38 Tony Woodruff 2.50 6.00
39 Glen Young 2.50 6.00
40 Roynell Young 2.50 6.00

1984 Eagles Police

This numbered eight-card set features the Philadelphia Eagles. Backs are printed in black ink with red accent. Cards measure approximately 2 5/8" by 4 1/8". The set was sponsored by Frito-Lay, the local police department, and the Philadelphia Eagles.

COMPLETE SET (8) 2.50 6.00
1 Mike Quick .50 1.25
2 Dennis Harrison .20 .50
3 Jerry Robinson .30 .75
4 Wilbert Montgomery .50 1.25
5 Herman Edwards .20 .50
6 Kenny Jackson .30 .75
7 Anthony Griggs .20 .50
8 Ron Jaworski .60 1.50

1985 Eagles Police

This 16-card set is numbered on the back. The card backs are printed in black and red ink on white card stock. Cards measure 2 5/8" by 4 1/8". The set was sponsored by Frito-Lay, local Police Departments, and the Eagles. Uniform numbers are printed on the card front before the player's name.

COMPLETE SET (16) 3.00 8.00
1 Ken Clarke .20 .50
2 Roynell Young .30 .75
3 Ray Ellis .20 .50
4 Ron Baker .20 .50
5 John Spagnola .25 .60
6 Reggie Wilkes .20 .50
7 Ron Jaworski .50 1.25
8 Steve Kenney .20 .50
9 Paul McFadden .20 .50
10 Mike Quick .40 1.00
11 Hubie Oliver .20 .50
12 Greg Brown .25 .60
13 Anthony Griggs .20 .50
14 Michael Haddix .25 .60
15 Kenny Jackson .30 .75
16 Vyto Kab .20 .50

1985 Eagles TastyKake

Cards from this set measure approximately 4 1/4" by 5 1/2" and feature a close-up player photo within a white border. The team name and team logo appear in the top border while the player's name, position, and TastyKake and Philadelphia Daily News sponsorship logos appear in the bottom border. All are blankbacked.

COMPLETE SET (16) 40.00 80.00
1 Ron Baker 2.50 6.00
2 Greg Brown DE 2.50 6.00
3 Randall Cunningham 5.00 12.00
4 Byron Darby 2.50 6.00
5 Michael Haddix 2.50 6.00
6 Wes Hopkins 2.50 6.00
7 Earnest Jackson ERR 2.50 6.00
8 Steve Kenney 2.50 6.00
9 Rich Kraynak 2.50 6.00
10 Dave Little 2.50 6.00
11 Paul McFadden 2.50 6.00
12 Leonard Mitchell 2.50 6.00
13 Mike Quick 3.00 8.00
14 Ken Reeves 2.50 6.00
15 Mike Reichenbach 2.50 6.00
16 John Spagnola 2.50 6.00

1985 Eagles Team Issue

This 53-card team-issued set measures approximately 2 15/16" by 3 7/8". The fronts feature glossy color player photos bordered in white. The wider bottom border contains the player's name, position, and jersey number. Player information again appears on the top of the backs in green print; the career summary is printed in a black box that fills the rest of the backs. The cards are unnumbered and checklisted below alphabetically, with the miscellaneous cards listed at the end.

COMPLETE SET (53) 100.00 200.00
1 Harvey Armstrong 2.00 5.00
2 Ron Baker 2.00 5.00
3 Norman Braman PRES 2.00 5.00
4 Greg Brown 2.00 5.00
5 Marion Campbell CO 2.50 6.00
6 Jeff Christensen 2.00 5.00
7 Ken Clarke 2.00 5.00
8 Evan Cooper 2.00 5.00
9 Byron Darby 2.00 5.00
10 Mark Dennard 2.00 5.00
11 Herman Edwards 2.00 5.00
12 Ray Ellis 2.00 5.00
13 Major Everett 2.00 5.00
14 Gerry Feehery 2.00 5.00
15 Elbert Foules 2.00 5.00
16 Gregg Garrity 2.00 5.00
17 Anthony Griggs 2.00 5.00
18 Michael Haddix 2.00 5.00
19 Andre Hardy 2.00 5.00
20 Dennis Harrison 2.00 5.00
21 Joe Hayes 2.00 5.00
22 Melvin Hoover 2.00 5.00
23 Wes Hopkins 2.50 6.00
24 Mike Horan 2.00 5.00
25 Kenny Jackson 2.00 5.00
26 Ron Jaworski 3.00 8.00
27 Vyto Kab 2.00 5.00
28 Steve Kenney 2.00 5.00
29 Rich Kraynak 2.00 5.00
30 Dean May 2.00 5.00
31 Paul McFadden 2.00 5.00
32 Dean Miraldi 2.00 5.00
33 Leonard Mitchell 2.00 5.00
34 Wilbert Montgomery 2.50 6.00
35 Hubie Oliver 2.00 5.00
36 Mike Quick 2.50 6.00
37 Mike Reichenbach 2.00 5.00
38 Jerry Robinson 2.00 5.00
39 Rusty Russell 2.00 5.00
40 Lawrence Sampleton 2.00 5.00
41 Jody Schulz 2.00 5.00
42 John Spagnola 2.00 5.00
43 Tom Strauthers 2.00 5.00
44 Andre Waters 2.50 6.00
45 Reggie Wilkes 2.00 5.00
46 Joel Williams 2.00 5.00
47 Michael Williams 2.00 5.00
48 Brenard Wilson 2.00 5.00
49 Tony Woodruff 2.00 5.00
50 Roynell Young 2.00 5.00
51 Logo Card 2.00 5.00
52 1985 Schedule Card 2.00 5.00
53 Title Card 1985-86 2.00 5.00

1986 Eagles Frito Lay

Cards from this set measure approximately 4 1/4" by 5 1/2" and feature an action player shot and facsimile autograph enclosed within a white border. The team name and mascot appear in the top border while the player's name, position, and "Frito Lay" logo appear in the bottom border. All are blankbacked. Frito Lay sponsored several Eagles sets throughout the 1970s and '80s. This release can be differentiated by the full Frito Lay logo in the lower right corner and the 3/8" left and right borders. Because this set is unnumbered, the cards are listed alphabetically. Any additions to this checklist would be greatly appreciated.

COMPLETE SET 40.00 80.00
1 Ray Ellis 2.50 6.00
2 Wes Hopkins 2.50 6.00
3 Mike Horan 2.50 6.00
4 Earnest Jackson 3.00 8.00
5 Ron Jaworski 4.00 10.00
6 Ron Johnson WR 2.50 6.00
7 Mike Quick 3.00 8.00
8 Buddy Ryan CO 5.00 12.00
9 Tom Strauthers 2.50 6.00
10 Andre Waters 3.00 8.00
11 Reggie White 8.00 20.00

1986 Eagles Police

This 16-card set is numbered on the card backs, which are printed in black and red ink on white card stock. Cards measure approximately 2 5/8" by 4 1/8". The set was sponsored by Frito-Lay, local Police Departments, and the Eagles. Uniform numbers are printed on the card front before the player's name. Randall Cunningham's card predates his 1987 Topps Rookie Card by one year.

COMPLETE SET (16) 5.00 12.00
1 Greg Brown .15 .40
2 Reggie White 2.00 5.00
3 John Spagnola .15 .40
4 Mike Quick .30 .75
5 Ken Clarke .15 .40
6 Ken Reeves .15 .40
7 Mike Reichenbach .15 .40
8 Wes Hopkins .20 .50
9 Roynell Young .15 .40
10 Randall Cunningham 2.00 5.00
11 Paul McFadden .15 .40
12 Matt Cavanaugh .15 .40
13 Ron Jaworski .30 .75
14 Byron Darby .15 .40
15 Andre Waters .20 .50
16 Buddy Ryan CO .30 .75

1987 Eagles Police

This set of 12 cards featuring Philadelphia Eagles was issued very late in the year and was not widely distributed. Reportedly 10,000 sets were distributed by officers of the New Jersey police force. The cards measure approximately 2 3/4" by 4 1/8" and feature a crime prevention tip on the back. The set was sponsored by the New Jersey State Police Crime Prevention Resource Center. The cards are unnumbered and are listed alphabetically below for reference.

COMPLETE SET (12) 40.00 100.00
1 Ron Baker 2.50 6.00
2 Keith Byars 3.00 8.00
3 Ken Clarke 2.50 6.00
4 Randall Cunningham 8.00 20.00
5 Paul McFadden 2.50 6.00
6 Mike Quick 3.00 8.00
7 Mike Reidenbach 2.50 6.00
8 Buddy Ryan CO 3.00 8.00
9 John Spagnola 2.50 6.00
10 Anthony Toney 2.50 6.00
11 Andre Waters 3.00 8.00
12 Reggie White 8.00 20.00

1988 Eagles Police

The 1988 Police Philadelphia Eagles set contains 12 unnumbered cards measuring approximately 2 3/4" by 4 1/8". There are 11 player cards and one coach card. The format is very similar to the 1990 set, however for 1988 the player's name and his jersey number is immediately below the image with his height, position, and weight below that. The backs have safety tips. The cards are listed below in alphabetical order by subject's name.

COMPLETE SET (12) 30.00 80.00
1 Jerome Brown 2.50 6.00
2 Keith Byars 2.50 6.00
3 Randall Cunningham 6.00 15.00
4 Matt Darwin 2.00 5.00
5 Keith Jackson 3.00 8.00
6 Seth Joyner 2.50 6.00
7 Mike Quick 2.50 6.00
8 Buddy Ryan CO 4.00 10.00
9 Clyde Simmons 2.50 6.00
10 John Teltschik 2.00 5.00
11 Anthony Toney 2.00 5.00
12 Reggie White 6.00 15.00

1989 Eagles Daily News

This 24-card set which measures approximately 5 9/16" by 4 1/4" features black and white portrait photos of the players. Above the player's photo is the Eagle logo and the Philadelphia Eagles team name while underneath are advertisments for McDonald's, radio station KYW, and the Philadelphia Daily News. The backs are blank. This was the third season that the Eagles had participated in this project. We have checklisted this set in alphabetical order.

COMPLETE SET (24) 75.00 150.00
1 Eric Allen 3.00 8.00
2 Jerome Brown 3.00 8.00
3 Keith Byars 3.00 8.00
4 Cris Carter UER 6.00 15.00
5 Randall Cunningham 4.00 10.00
6 Matt Darwin 2.50 6.00
7 Gerry Feehery 2.50 6.00
8 Ron Heller 2.50 6.00
9A Terry Hoage 2.50 6.00
9B Terry Hoage 2.50 6.00
10 Wes Hopkins 2.50 6.00
11 Keith Jackson 3.00 8.00
12 Seth Joyner 3.00 8.00
13 Mike Pitts 2.50 6.00
14 Mike Quick 3.00 8.00
15 Mike Reichenbach 2.50 6.00
16 Clyde Simmons 3.00 8.00
17 John Spagnola 2.50 6.00
18 Junior Tautalatasi 2.50 6.00
19 John Teltschik 2.50 6.00
20 Anthony Toney 2.50 6.00
21 Andre Waters 3.00 8.00
22 Reggie White 6.00 15.00
23 Luis Zendejas 2.50 6.00

1989 Eagles Police Jumbo

Cards from this set were distributed by the New Jersey State Police in Trenton, New Jersey over a period of years. These large unnumbered cards measure approximately 8 1/2" by 11" and feature action player photos of members of the Philadelphia Eagles inside white borders. Player bio information is centered beneath the picture between the New Jersey State Police Crime Prevention Resource Center emblem and Security Savings Bank logo. The 1989 issue is nearly identical to the 1990 issue, but can be differentiated by the bank logo missing the FDIC notation. The back carries the title "Alcohol and Other Drugs: Facts and Myths" and features five questions and answers on this topic. Sponsor and team logos at the bottom round out the back. The cards are unnumbered and checklisted below alphabetically.

COMPLETE SET (8) 60.00 120.00
1 Cris Carter 15.00 40.00
2 Mike Golic 6.00 15.00
3 Keith Jackson 6.00 15.00
4 Clyde Simmons 6.00 15.00
5 John Teltschik 5.00 12.00
6 Anthony Toney 5.00 12.00
7 Andre Waters 6.00 15.00
8 Luis Zendejas 5.00 12.00

1989 Eagles Smokey

This 50-card set features members of the Philadelphia Eagles. The cards measure approximately 3" by 5". The full-color photo on the front covers the complete card, although the player's name, number, and position are overprinted in the lower right corner. Each card back shows a different fire safety cartoon. Backs are printed in green ink in deference to the Eagles colors. Cards are unnumbered, except for uniform number which appears on the card front and back; cards are ordered below by uniform number. In a few cases, there were two cards produced of the same player; typically the two can be distinguished by home and away colors. The complete set price below includes all the variations listed.

COMPLETE SET (50) 100.00 200.00
6 Matt Cavanaugh 1.60 4.00
8 Luis Zendejas 1.50 4.00
9 Don McPherson 1.50 4.00
10 John Teltschik 1.50 4.00
12A Randall Cunningham 6.00 15.00
12B Randall Cunningham 6.00 15.00
20 Andre Waters 2.00 5.00
21 Eric Allen 2.00 5.00
25 Anthony Toney 1.50 4.00
26 Michael Haddix 2.00 5.00
33 William Frizzell 1.50 4.00
34 Terry Hoage 1.50 4.00
35 Mark Konecny 1.50 4.00
41 Keith Byars 2.00 5.00
42 Eric Everett 1.50 4.00
43 Roynell Young 1.50 4.00
46 Izel Jenkins 1.50 4.00
48 Wes Hopkins 1.50 4.00
50 Dave Rimington 1.50 4.00
52 Todd Bell 1.50 4.00
53 Dwayne Jiles 1.50 4.00
55 Mike Reichenbach 1.50 4.00
56 Byron Evans 1.50 4.00
58 Ty Allert 1.50 4.00
59 Seth Joyner 2.00 5.00
61 Ben Tamburello 1.50 4.00
63 Ron Baker 1.50 4.00
66 Ken Reeves 1.50 4.00
68 Reggie Singletary 1.50 4.00
72 David Alexander 1.50 4.00
73 Ron Heller 1.50 4.00
74 Mike Pitts 1.50 4.00
78 Matt Darwin 1.50 4.00
80 Cris Carter 10.00 25.00
81 Kenny Jackson 1.50 4.00
82A Mike Quick 2.00 5.00
82B Mike Quick 2.00 5.00
83 Jimmie Giles 2.00 5.00
85 Ron Johnson WR 1.50 4.00
86 Gregg Garrity 1.50 4.00
88 Keith Jackson 2.00 5.00
89 David Little 1.50 4.00
90 Mike Golic 1.50 4.00
91 Scott Curtis 1.50 4.00
92 Reggie White 6.00 15.00
96 Clyde Simmons 2.00 5.00
97 John Klingel 1.50 4.00
99 Jerome Brown 2.00 5.00
NNO Buddy Ryan CO 3.00 8.00
NNO Buddy Ryan CO 3.00 8.00

1990 Eagles Police

Sponsored by the N.J. Crime Prevention Officer's Association and the New Jersey State Police Crime Prevention Resource Center, this 12-card set measures approximately 2 5/8" by 4 1/8" and features action player photos on a white card face. The team name appears above the photo between two helmet icons so this year is often confused with the 1988 Eagles Police set. Except for 1990, just the player's name is immediately below the image, then his height and weight are listed below his name and oriented to the left and his position and college name are oriented to the right. The backs contains sponsor logos, safety tips, and the slogan "Take a bite out of crime" by McGruff the crime dog. The cards are unnumbered and checklisted below in alphabetical order.

COMPLETE SET (12) 24.00 60.00
1 David Alexander 1.60 4.00
2 Eric Allen 2.00 5.00
3 Randall Cunningham 4.80 12.00
4 Keith Byars 2.00 5.00
5 Jeff Feagles 1.60 4.00
6 Mike Golic 1.60 4.00
7 Keith Jackson 2.00 5.00
8 Rich Kotite CO 1.60 4.00
9 Roger Ruzek 1.60 4.00
10 Mickey Shuler 1.60 4.00
11 Clyde Simmons 2.00 5.00
12 Reggie White 4.80 12.00

1990 Eagles Police Jumbo

Cards from this set were distributed by the New Jersey State Police in Trenton, New Jersey over a period of years. These large unnumbered cards measure approximately 8 1/2" by 11" and feature action player photos of members of the Philadelphia Eagles inside white borders. Player bio information is centered beneath the picture between the New Jersey State Police Crime Prevention Resource Center emblem and Security Savings Bank logo. The 1990 issue is nearly identical to the 1989 Issue, but can be differentiated by the bank logo including the FDIC notation. The back carries the title "Alcohol and Other Drugs: Facts and Myths" and features five questions and answers on this topic. Sponsor and team logos at the bottom round out the back. The cards are unnumbered and checklisted below alphabetically.

COMPLETE SET (15) 75.00 150.00
1 David Alexander 6.00 12.00
2 Eric Allen 7.50 15.00
3 Fred Barnett 7.50 15.00
4 Keith Byars 7.50 15.00
5 Randall Cunningham 12.50 25.00
6 Gregg Garrity 6.00 12.00
7 Mike Golic 7.50 15.00
(playing versus Browns)
8 Britt Hager 6.00 12.00
9 Ron Heller 6.00 12.00
10 Seth Joyner 7.50 15.00
11 Mike Pitts 6.00 12.00
12 Mike Schad 6.00 12.00
13 Jessie Small 6.00 12.00
14 Reggie White 15.00 30.00
15 Calvin Williams 7.50 15.00

1990 Eagles Sealtest Bookmarks

This six-card set (of bookmarks) which measures approximately 2" by 8" was produced by Sealtest to promote reading among children in Philadelphia. Apparently they were given out at The Free Library of Philadelphia on a weekly basis. The basic design of these bookmarks is identical to the 1990 Knudsen Chargers and 49ers bookmark sets. The color action player cut-out overlays a football stadium design. A box at the bottom whose color varies per bookmark gives biographical information and player profile. The backs have sponsor logos and describe two books that are available at the public library. The bookmarks are unnumbered and checklisted below in alphabetical order.

COMPLETE SET (6) 12.50 25.00
1 David Alexander 1.50 4.00
2 Eric Allen 2.00 5.00
3 Keith Byars 2.00 5.00
4 Randall Cunningham 4.00 8.00
5 Mike Pitts 1.50 4.00
6 Mike Quick 2.00 5.00

1991 Eagles Police Jumbo

1 Fred Barnett 7.50 15.00
2 Wes Hopkins 7.50 15.00
3 Keith Jackson 7.50 15.00
4 Clyde Simmons 7.50 15.00
5 Jessie Small 6.00 12.00
6 Ben Smith 6.00 12.00
7 Andre Waters 7.50 15.00
8 Calvin Williams 7.50 15.00

1992 Eagles Team Issue

These team issued photos measure approximately 4 1/4" by 5 1/2" and were produced for distribution by the Philadelphia Eagles. Each photo is blankbacked and unnumbered. Several photos were likely issued over a period of years. Any additions to this list would be appreciated.

COMPLETE SET (34) 60.00 120.00
1 David Alexander 1.50 4.00
2 Eric Allen 2.00 5.00
3 Fred Barnett 2.00 5.00
4 Pat Beach 1.50 4.00
5 Keith Byars 2.00 5.00
6 Antone Davis 1.50 4.00

7 Jeff Feagles 1.50 4.00
8 Mike Golic 1.50 4.00
9 Roy Green 2.00 5.00
10 Britt Hager 1.50 4.00
11 Andy Harmon 1.50 4.00
12 Wes Hopkins 1.50 4.00
13 Izel Jenkins 1.50 4.00
14 Tommy Jeter 1.50 4.00
15 Maurice Johnson 1.50 4.00
16 James Joseph 1.50 4.00
17 Seth Joyner 2.00 5.00
18 Rich Kotite 1.50 4.00
19 Scott Kowalkowski 1.50 4.00
20 Jim McMahon 3.00 8.00
21 Mark McMillian 1.50 4.00
22 Ken Rose 1.50 4.00
23 Roger Ruzek 1.50 4.00
24 Mike Schad 1.50 4.00
25 Rob Selby 1.50 4.00
26 Heath Sherman 1.50 4.00
27 Vai Sikahema 1.50 4.00
28 Clyde Simmons 2.00 5.00
29 William Thomas 2.00 5.00
30 Herschel Walker 3.00 8.00
31 Andre Waters 2.00 5.00
32 Casey Weldon 1.50 4.00
33 Reggie White 5.00 12.00
34 Calvin Williams 2.00 5.00

1997 Eagles Score

This 15-card set of the Philadelphia Eagles was distributed in five-card packs with a suggested retail price of $1.99. The fronts feature color action player photos with white borders and the player's name and team logo printed in team color foil at the bottom. The backs carry player information and career statistics. Platinum Team parallel cards were randomly seeded in packs featuring all foil cardfronts.

COMPLETE SET (15) 2.00 5.00
*PLATINUM TEAMS: 1X TO 2X
1 Irving Fryar .15 .40
2 Rodney Peete .15 .40
3 Ricky Watters .30 .75
4 Ty Detmer .30 .75
5 Troy Vincent .08 .25
6 Charlie Garner .15 .40
7 Jason Dunn .08 .25
8 Chris T. Jones .15 .40
9 William Thomas .08 .25
10 Brian Dawkins .30 .75
11 Bobby Taylor .08 .25
12 William Fuller .08 .25
13 Mike Mamula .08 .25
14 Ray Farmer .08 .25
15 Mark Seay .15 .40

2005 Eagles Activa Medallions

COMPLETE SET (25) 30.00 60.00
1 Keith Adams 1.25 3.00
2 David Akers 1.25 3.00
3 Shawn Andrews 1.25 3.00
4 Reggie Brown 1.25 3.00
5 Sheldon Brown 1.25 3.00
6 Brian Dawkins 1.25 3.00
7 Hank Fraley 1.25 3.00
8 Artis Hicks 1.25 3.00
9 Dirk Johnson 1.25 3.00
10 Dhani Jones 1.25 3.00
11 Jevon Kearse 1.25 3.00
12 Greg Lewis 1.25 3.00
13 Michael Lewis 1.25 3.00
14 Jerome McDougle 1.25 3.00
15 Donovan McNabb 1.50 4.00
16 Mike Patterson 1.25 3.00
17 Todd Pinkston 1.25 3.00
18 Jon Runyan 1.25 3.00
19 Lito Shepard 1.25 3.00
20 L.J. Smith 1.25 3.00
21 Tra Thomas 1.25 3.00
22 Jeremiah Trotter 1.25 3.00
23 Darwin Walker 1.25 3.00
24 Brian Westbrook 1.25 3.00
25 Eagles Logo 1.00 2.50

2005 Eagles Topps XXL

COMPLETE SET (4) 2.00 4.00
1 Donovan McNabb .60 1.50
2 Terrell Owens .50 1.25
3 Brian Westbrook .40 1.00
4 Brian Dawkins .40 1.00

2006 Eagles Topps

COMPLETE SET (12) 3.00 6.00
PHI1 Ryan Moats .25 .60
PHI2 L.J. Smith .25 .60
PHI3 Brian Dawkins .40 1.00
PHI4 Greg Lewis .25 .60
PHI5 Brian Westbrook .25 .60
PHI6 Donovan McNabb .30 .75
PHI7 Reggie Brown .25 .60
PHI8 Todd Pinkston .25 .60
PHI9 Jeremiah Trotter .25 .60
PHI10 Jevon Kearse .25 .60
PHI11 Brodrick Bunkley .30 .75
PHI12 Jason Avant .25 .60

2007 Eagles Topps

COMPLETE SET (12) 2.50 5.00
1 Brian Westbrook .40 1.00
2 L.J. Smith .40 1.00
3 Brian Dawkins .60 1.50
4 Donovan McNabb .50 1.25
5 Reggie Brown .40 1.00
6 Tony Hunt .40 1.00
7 Lito Sheppard .40 1.00
8 Kevin Curtis .40 1.00
9 Takeo Spikes .40 1.00
10 Jeremiah Trotter .40 1.00
11 David Akers .40 1.00
12 Kevin Kolb .50 1.25

2008 Eagles Donruss Thanksgiving Classic

Many fans who attended the 2008 Thanksgiving game in Philadelphia were treated to this complete set. Donruss reported that more than 120,000 cards were given away to fans at both the Dallas and Philadelphia games. Each team set also included one card from the NFL Network broadcasters set. The first four cards are numbered in the set and the final three did not feature card numbers but have been assigned card numbres below.

COMPLETE SET (7) 4.00 10.00
1 Donovan McNabb .75 2.00
2 Brian Dawkins 1.00 2.50
3 Brian Westbrook .60 1.50
4 Randall Cunningham .75 2.00
5 Brian Dawkins Youth Partnership 1.00 2.50
6 Swoop - Mascot .50 1.25
7 Pop Warner team of the year .50 1.25

2008 Eagles Topps

COMPLETE SET (12) 2.50 5.00
1 Brian Westbrook .40 1.00
2 Donovan McNabb .50 1.25
3 Kevin Curtis .40 1.00
4 Correll Buckhalter .40 1.00
5 Asante Samuel .40 1.00
6 Reggie Brown .40 1.00
7 Trent Cole .40 1.00
8 A.J. Feeley .40 1.00
9 L.J. Smith .40 1.00
10 Brian Dawkins .60 1.50
11 DeSean Jackson .75 2.00
12 Lito Sheppard .40 1.00

2012 Elite

COMP.SET w/o RC's (100) 8.00 20.00
101-200 ROOKIE PRINT RUN 699-999
1 Larry Fitzgerald .25 .60
2 Beanie Wells .20 .50
3 Kevin Kolb .20 .50
4 Michael Turner .20 .50
5 Julio Jones .30 .75
6 Roddy White .20 .50
7 Matt Ryan .25 .60
8 Ray Lewis .30 .75
9 Ray Rice .20 .50
10 Anquan Boldin .20 .50
11 Joe Flacco .25 .60
12 Ryan Fitzpatrick .20 .50
13 Fred Jackson .25 .60
14 Steve Johnson .25 .60
15 Cam Newton .30 .75
16 DeAngelo Williams .20 .50
17 Steve Smith WR .25 .60
18 Brian Urlacher .30 .75
19 Jay Cutler .20 .50
20 Devin Hester .25 .60
21 Matt Forte .20 .50
22 Andy Dalton .25 .60
23 Greg Little .20 .50
24 A.J. Green .30 .75
25 Colt McCoy .25 .60
26 Peyton Hillis .20 .50
27 DeMarcus Ware .30 .75
28 Tony Romo .25 .60
29 DeMarco Murray .25 .60
30 Jason Witten .25 .60
31 Von Miller .25 .60
32 Tim Tebow .30 .75
33 Willis McGahee .20 .50
34 Ndamukong Suh .25 .60
35 Matthew Stafford .25 .60
36 Calvin Johnson .30 .75
37 Charles Woodson .30 .75
38 Clay Matthews .30 .75
39 Aaron Rodgers .50 1.25
40 Greg Jennings .20 .50
41 Andre Johnson .25 .60
42 Arian Foster .25 .60
43 Matt Schaub .20 .50
44 Reggie Wayne .25 .60
45 Peyton Manning 1.00 2.50
46 Maurice Jones-Drew .20 .50
47 Blaine Gabbert .20 .50
48 Jamaal Charles .25 .60
49 Eric Berry .25 .60
50 Dwayne Bowe .25 .60
51 Matt Cassel .20 .50
52 Reggie Bush .20 .50
53 Brandon Marshall .25 .60
54 Jared Allen .20 .50
55 Adrian Peterson .30 .75
56 Christian Ponder .20 .50
57 Tom Brady .75 2.00
58 BenJarvus Green-Ellis .25 .60
59 Rob Gronkowski .30 .75
60 Wes Welker .25 .60
61 Drew Brees .30 .75
62 Darren Sproles .25 .60
63 Jimmy Graham .30 .75
64 Marques Colston .20 .50
65 Eli Manning .25 .60
66 Brandon Jacobs .20 .50
67 Victor Cruz .25 .60
68 Darrelle Revis .20 .50
69 Mark Sanchez .20 .50
70 Plaxico Burress .20 .50
71 Darren McFadden .20 .50
72 Richard Seymour .20 .50
73 Carson Palmer .25 .60
74 Michael Vick .25 .60
75 LeSean McCoy .30 .75
76 DeSean Jackson .25 .60
77 Ben Roethlisberger .30 .75
78 Rashard Mendenhall .20 .50
79 Troy Polamalu .30 .75
80 Heath Miller .20 .50
81 Philip Rivers .30 .75
82 Ryan Mathews .25 .60
83 Antonio Gates .25 .60
84 Vincent Jackson .20 .50
85 Patrick Willis .25 .60
86 Alex Smith QB .25 .60
87 Frank Gore .25 .60
88 Vernon Davis .20 .50
89 Tarvaris Jackson .20 .50
90 Marshawn Lynch .25 .60
91 Steven Jackson .20 .50
92 James Laurinaitis .20 .50
93 Sam Bradford .20 .50
94 LeGarrette Blount .25 .60
95 Josh Freeman .25 .60
96 Matt Hasselbeck .20 .50
97 Chris Johnson .20 .50
98 Nate Washington .20 .50
99 Brian Orakpo .25 .60
100 Roy Helu Jr. .20 .50
101 Andrew Luck/699 RC 15.00 40.00
102 Robert Griffin III/699 RC 1.50 4.00
103 Matt Kalil/799 RC 1.25 3.00
104 Morris Claiborne/799 RC 1.25 3.00
105 Justin Blackmon/699 RC 1.25 3.00
106 Trent Richardson/699 RC 1.25 3.00
107 Riley Reiff/999 RC 1.25 3.00
108 Quinton Coples/999 RC 1.25 3.00
109 Melvin Ingram/999 RC 1.25 3.00
110 Michael Brockers/999 RC 1.25 3.00
111 Ryan Tannehill/699 RC 2.00 5.00
112 David DeCastro/999 RC 1.25 3.00
113 Michael Floyd/699 RC 1.25 3.00
114 Luke Kuechly/999 RC 3.00 8.00
115 Janoris Jenkins/999 RC 1.50 4.00
116 Jonathan Martin/999 RC 1.25 3.00
117 Devon Still/999 RC 1.50 4.00
118 Dre Kirkpatrick/999 RC 1.25 3.00
119 Kendall Wright/799 RC 1.25 3.00
120 Fletcher Cox/999 RC 2.00 5.00
121 Courtney Upshaw/999 RC 1.50 4.00
122 Dontari Poe/999 RC 1.25 3.00
123 Rueben Randle/799 RC 1.25 3.00
124 Nick Perry/999 RC 1.50 4.00
125 Whitney Mercilus/999 RC 1.25 3.00
126 Dont'a Hightower/999 RC 2.00 5.00
127 Mark Barron/999 RC 1.25 3.00
128 Stephen Hill/799 RC 1.25 3.00
129 Zach Brown/999 RC 1.25 3.00
130 Andre Branch/999 RC 1.25 3.00
131 Dwayne Allen/799 RC 1.25 3.00
132 David Wilson/799 RC 1.25 3.00
133 Lamar Miller/799 RC 2.00 5.00
134 Brock Osweiler/799 RC 1.25 3.00
135 Lavonte David/999 RC 2.00 5.00
136 Alshon Jeffery/799 RC 2.50 6.00
137 Bobby Wagner/999 RC 2.00 5.00
138 Doug Martin/799 RC 2.00 5.00
139 Chris Givens/799 RC 1.25 3.00
140 Coby Fleener/799 RC 1.25 3.00
141 Brandon Weeden/699 RC 1.25 3.00
142 Jared Crick/999 RC 1.25 3.00
143 Shea McClellin/999 RC 1.50 4.00
144 Ronnell Lewis/999 RC 1.25 3.00
145 Orson Charles/999 RC 1.25 3.00
146 Vinny Curry/999 RC 1.50 4.00
147 Chandler Jones/999 RC 1.25 3.00
148 Isaiah Pead/799 RC 1.25 3.00
149 George Iloka/999 RC 1.25 3.00
150 Mohamed Sanu/799 RC 2.00 5.00
151 Nick Toon/799 RC 1.25 3.00
152 LaMichael James/799 RC 1.25 3.00
153 Kirk Cousins/999 RC 5.00 12.00
154 T.J. Graham/799 RC 1.25 3.00
155 Mychal Kendricks/999 RC 2.00 5.00
156 Juron Criner/999 RC 1.25 3.00
157 Stephon Gilmore/999 RC 1.50 4.00
158 Bernard Pierce/799 RC 1.25 3.00
159 Ladarius Green/999 RC 1.25 3.00
160 Cyrus Gray/999 RC 1.25 3.00
161 Brian Quick/799 RC 1.25 3.00
162 Nick Foles/799 RC 3.00 8.00
163 Ronnie Hillman/799 RC 1.25 3.00
164 Michael Egnew/799 RC 1.25 3.00
165 Keshawn Martin/999 RC 1.50 4.00
166 Chris Rainey/999 RC 1.25 3.00
167 Joe Adams/799 RC 1.25 3.00
168 Marvin Jones/999 RC 1.25 3.00
169 Ryan Lindley/999 RC 1.25 3.00
170 Greg Childs/999 RC 1.25 3.00
171 Jarius Wright/799 RC 1.25 3.00
172 Michael Smith/999 RC 1.50 4.00
173 Tommy Streeter/999 RC 1.25 3.00
174 Robert Turbin/799 RC 1.25 3.00
175 A.J. Jenkins/799 RC 1.25 3.00
176 DeVier Posey/799 RC 1.25 3.00
177 Bryce Brown/999 RC 1.25 3.00
178 Dan Herron/999 RC 1.25 3.00
179 Vick Ballard/999 RC 1.50 4.00
180 T.Y. Hilton/999 RC 2.50 6.00
181 Bruce Irvin/999 RC 1.50 4.00
182 Marvin McNutt/999 RC 1.25 3.00
183 Terrance Ganaway/999 RC 1.50 4.00
184 B.J. Coleman/999 RC 1.25 3.00
185 Alfred Morris/999 RC 1.25 3.00
186 Jeff Fuller/999 RC 1.25 3.00
187 Rishard Matthews/999 RC 1.25 3.00
188 B.J. Cunningham/799 RC 1.25 3.00
189 Ryan Broyles/799 RC 1.25 3.00
190 Russell Wilson/799 RC 10.00 25.00
191 Devon Wylie/999 RC 1.25 3.00
192 LaVon Brazill/999 RC 2.00 5.00
193 Travis Benjamin/999 RC 1.25 3.00
194 Kevin Zeitler/999 RC 1.25 3.00
195 Chandler Harnish/999 RC 1.25 3.00
196 Marc Tyler/999 RC 1.25 3.00
197 Harrison Smith/999 RC 1.25 3.00
198 Danny Coale/999 RC 1.25 3.00
199 Kellen Moore/999 RC 1.50 4.00
200 Case Keenum/999 RC 2.50 6.00

2012 Elite Aspirations

*VETS/70-99: 5X TO 12X BASIC CARDS
*ROOKIES/70-99: .8X TO 2X BASIC CARDS
*VETS/42-69: 6X TO 15X BASIC CARDS
*ROOKIES/42-69: 1X TO 2.5X BASIC CARDS
*VETS/31: 8X TO 20X BASIC CARDS
*ROOKIES/30: 1.2X TO 3X BASIC CARDS
*VETS/20: 10X TO 25X BASIC CARDS
*ROOKIES/23-29: 1.5X TO 4X BASIC CARDS
*VETS/10-19: 12X TO 30X BASIC CARDS
*ROOKIES/10-19: 2X TO 5X BASIC CARDS
STATED PRINT RUN 1-99
101 Andrew Luck/88 50.00 100.00

2012 Elite Status

*VETS/70-99: 5X TO 12X BASIC CARDS
*ROOKIES/70-99: .8X TO 2X BASIC CARDS
*VETS/40-69: 6X TO 15X BASIC CARDS
*ROOKIES/40-56: 1X TO 2.5X BASIC CARDS
*VETS/32-39: 8X TO 20X BASIC CARDS
*ROOKIES/30-32: 1.2X TO 3X BASIC CARDS
*VETS/20-29: 10X TO 25X BASIC CARDS
*ROOKIES/20-28: 1.5X TO 4X BASIC CARDS
*VETS/10-19: 12X TO 30X BASIC CARDS
*ROOKIES/10-19: 2X TO 5X BASIC CARDS
STATED PRINT RUN 1-99
101 Andrew Luck/12 125.00 200.00

2012 Elite Aspirations Autographs

1-100 VETERAN PRINT RUN 1-20
101-200 ROOKIE PRINT RUN 49
EXCH EXPIRATION: 1/25/2014
4 Michael Turner/20 8.00 20.00
15 Cam Newton/15 50.00 100.00
17 Steve Smith WR/20 10.00 25.00
20 Devin Hester/15 10.00 25.00
23 Greg Little/20 10.00 25.00
47 Blaine Gabbert/20 12.00 30.00
52 Reggie Bush/20 30.00 60.00
63 Jimmy Graham/20 12.00 30.00
64 Marques Colston/15 8.00 20.00
79 Troy Polamalu/20 40.00 80.00
87 Frank Gore/20 10.00 25.00
100 Roy Helu Jr./20 8.00 20.00
101 Andrew Luck/49 175.00 300.00
102 Robert Griffin III/49 8.00 20.00
103 Matt Kalil/49 6.00 15.00
104 Morris Claiborne/49 6.00 15.00
105 Justin Blackmon/49 6.00 15.00
106 Trent Richardson/49 6.00 15.00
107 Riley Reiff/49 6.00 15.00
108 Quinton Coples/49 6.00 15.00
109 Melvin Ingram/49 6.00 15.00
110 Michael Brockers/49 6.00 15.00
111 Ryan Tannehill/49 10.00 25.00
112 David DeCastro/49 6.00 15.00
113 Michael Floyd/49 6.00 15.00
114 Luke Kuechly/49 15.00 40.00
115 Janoris Jenkins/49 8.00 20.00
116 Jonathan Martin/49 6.00 15.00
117 Devon Still/49 8.00 20.00
118 Dre Kirkpatrick/49 EXCH 6.00 15.00
119 Kendall Wright/49 6.00 15.00
120 Fletcher Cox/49 10.00 25.00
121 Courtney Upshaw/49 8.00 20.00
122 Dontari Poe/49 6.00 15.00
123 Rueben Randle/49 6.00 15.00
124 Nick Perry/49 8.00 20.00
125 Whitney Mercilus/49 6.00 15.00
126 Dont'a Hightower/49 10.00 25.00
127 Mark Barron/49 6.00 15.00
128 Stephen Hill/49 6.00 15.00
129 Zach Brown/49 6.00 15.00
130 Andre Branch/49 6.00 15.00
131 Dwayne Allen/49 6.00 15.00
132 David Wilson/49 6.00 15.00
133 Lamar Miller/49 10.00 25.00
134 Brock Osweiler/49 6.00 15.00
135 Lavonte David/49 10.00 25.00
136 Alshon Jeffery/49 15.00 40.00
137 Bobby Wagner/49 10.00 25.00
138 Doug Martin/49 10.00 25.00
139 Chris Givens/49 6.00 15.00
140 Coby Fleener/49 6.00 15.00
141 Brandon Weeden/49 6.00 15.00
142 Jared Crick/49 6.00 15.00
143 Shea McClellin/49 8.00 20.00
144 Ronnell Lewis/49 6.00 15.00
145 Orson Charles/49 6.00 15.00
146 Vinny Curry/49 8.00 20.00
147 Chandler Jones/49 6.00 15.00
148 Isaiah Pead/49 6.00 15.00
149 George Iloka/49 6.00 15.00
150 Mohamed Sanu/49 10.00 25.00
151 Nick Toon/49 6.00 15.00
152 LaMichael James/49 6.00 15.00
153 Kirk Cousins/49 20.00 40.00
154 T.J. Graham/49 6.00 15.00
155 Mychal Kendricks/49 10.00 25.00
156 Juron Criner/49 6.00 15.00
157 Stephon Gilmore/49 8.00 20.00
158 Bernard Pierce/49 6.00 15.00
159 Ladarius Green/49 6.00 15.00
160 Cyrus Gray/49 6.00 15.00
161 Brian Quick/49 6.00 15.00
162 Nick Foles/49 15.00 40.00
163 Ronnie Hillman/49 EXCH 6.00 15.00
164 Michael Egnew/49 6.00 15.00
165 Keshawn Martin/49 8.00 20.00
166 Chris Rainey/49 6.00 15.00
167 Joe Adams/49 6.00 15.00
168 Marvin Jones/49 6.00 15.00
169 Ryan Lindley/49 6.00 15.00
170 Greg Childs/49 6.00 15.00
171 Jarius Wright/49 6.00 15.00
172 Michael Smith/49 EXCH 8.00 20.00
173 Tommy Streeter/49 6.00 15.00
174 Robert Turbin/49 8.00 20.00
175 A.J. Jenkins/49 6.00 15.00
176 DeVier Posey/49 6.00 15.00
177 Bryce Brown/49 6.00 15.00
178 Dan Herron/49 6.00 15.00
179 Vick Ballard/49 8.00 20.00
180 T.Y. Hilton/49 12.00 30.00
181 Bruce Irvin/49 8.00 20.00
182 Marvin McNutt/49 6.00 15.00
183 Terrance Ganaway/49 8.00 20.00
184 B.J. Coleman/49 6.00 15.00
185 Alfred Morris/49 6.00 15.00
186 Jeff Fuller/49 6.00 15.00
187 Rishard Matthews/49 6.00 15.00
188 B.J. Cunningham/49 6.00 15.00
189 Ryan Broyles/49 6.00 15.00
190 Russell Wilson/49 75.00 150.00
191 Devon Wylie/49 6.00 15.00
192 LaVon Brazill/49 10.00 25.00
193 Travis Benjamin/49 6.00 15.00
194 Kevin Zeitler/49 6.00 15.00
195 Chandler Harnish/49 6.00 15.00
196 Marc Tyler/49 6.00 15.00
197 Harrison Smith/49 6.00 15.00
198 Danny Coale/49 6.00 15.00
199 Kellen Moore/49 8.00 20.00
200 Case Keenum/49 12.00 30.00

2012 Elite Back to the Future Jerseys

STATED PRINT RUN 180-199
*PRIME/60-99: .5X TO 1.2X BASIC JSY
*PRIME/31-49: .6X TO 1.5X BASIC JSY
*PRIME/13: 1X TO 2.5X BASIC JSY
1 Dan Fouts/199 4.00 10.00
2 Bob Hayes/180 8.00 20.00
3 Knute Rockne/199 15.00 30.00
4 Buck Buchanan/199 3.00 8.00
5 Bob Griese/199 5.00 12.00
6 Rocket Ismail/199 4.00 10.00
7 Todd Christensen/199 3.00 8.00
8 Doug Williams/199 4.00 10.00
9 Sterling Sharpe/199 4.00 10.00
10 Mark Carrier/195 4.00 10.00
11 Ted Hendricks/199 3.00 8.00
12 Doak Walker/199 5.00 12.00
13 John Fuqua/199 4.00 10.00
14 Steve Young/199 5.00 12.00
15 Don Meredith/199 6.00 15.00
16 John Hadl/199 4.00 10.00
17 Deion Sanders/199 4.00 10.00
18 George Blanda/199 4.00 10.00
19 Otto Graham/199 5.00 12.00
20 Junior Seau/199 4.00 10.00

2012 Elite Craftsmen

STATED PRINT RUN 999 SER.#'d SETS
*GOLD/149: .6X TO 1.5X BASIC INSERTS
*BLACK/49: 1X TO 2.5X BASIC INSERTS
1 Andre Johnson 1.00 2.50
2 Ben Roethlisberger 1.25 3.00
3 Wes Welker 1.00 2.50
4 Reggie Wayne 1.00 2.50
5 Julio Jones 1.25 3.00
6 Darren McFadden .75 2.00
7 Peyton Manning 2.50 6.00
8 Hakeem Nicks .75 2.00
9 Miles Austin .75 2.00
10 Jason Witten 1.00 2.50
11 Michael Turner .75 2.00
12 Tony Romo 1.00 2.50
13 A.J. Green 1.25 3.00
14 Frank Gore 1.00 2.50
15 Darren Sproles 1.00 2.50

2012 Elite Craftsmen Jerseys Prime

STATED PRINT RUN 5-49
3 Wes Welker/25 6.00 15.00
6 Darren McFadden/25 5.00 12.00
8 Hakeem Nicks/49 4.00 10.00
9 Miles Austin/49 4.00 10.00
11 Michael Turner/49 4.00 10.00
12 Tony Romo/49 5.00 12.00
13 A.J. Green/49 6.00 15.00

2012 Elite Down and Distance Jerseys

STATED PRINT RUN 8-299
1 Matt Schaub/299 2.00 5.00
2 Aaron Ross/283 2.00 5.00
3 Anquan Boldin/299 2.00 5.00
4 Anthony Fasano/299 2.00 5.00
9 Brent Celek/299 2.00 5.00
10 Brian Hartline/47 5.00 12.00
11 Brian Urlacher/299 3.00 8.00
13 Cedric Benson/65 3.00 8.00
14 Devin Hester/36 5.00 12.00
15 Dez Bryant/299 3.00 8.00
16 Ed Reed/299 2.50 6.00
17 Haloti Ngata/299 2.00 5.00
18 Jacoby Ford/264 2.00 5.00
19 Jon Beason/19 5.00 12.00
20 Josh Cribbs/157 2.50 6.00
21 Knowshon Moreno/299 2.00 5.00
22 Mario Manningham/299 2.00 5.00
23 Mark Sanchez/299 2.00 5.00
24 Marques Colston/299 2.00 5.00
25 Miles Austin/299 2.00 5.00
26 Philip Rivers/63 5.00 12.00
27 Pierre Thomas/299 2.00 5.00
28 Shonn Greene/299 2.00 5.00
29 Tony Gonzalez/299 2.50 6.00
31 Devery Henderson/299 2.00 5.00
32 Joe Flacco/299 2.50 6.00
35 Eli Manning/299 4.00 10.00
36 Tony Romo/299 2.50 6.00
37 Steven Jackson/299 2.00 5.00
38 Hakeem Nicks/299 2.00 5.00
39 Sam Bradford/299 2.00 5.00
40 Reggie Wayne/299 2.50 6.00
41 Plaxico Burress/299 2.00 5.00
42 Patrick Willis/91 4.00 10.00
43 Wes Welker/19 6.00 15.00

2012 Elite Down and Distance Jerseys Prime

STATED PRINT RUN 2-49
2 Aaron Ross/49 4.00 10.00
3 Anquan Boldin/25 5.00 12.00
4 Anthony Fasano/49 4.00 10.00
5 Antonio Gates/49 5.00 12.00
9 Brent Celek/38 4.00 10.00
10 Brian Hartline/49 5.00 12.00
13 Cedric Benson/49 4.00 10.00
14 Devin Hester/49 5.00 12.00
15 Dez Bryant/49 6.00 15.00
16 Ed Reed/49 5.00 12.00
17 Haloti Ngata/49 4.00 10.00
19 Jon Beason/49 4.00 10.00
20 Josh Cribbs/16 5.00 12.00
22 Mario Manningham/49 4.00 10.00
24 Marques Colston/49 4.00 10.00
25 Miles Austin/49 4.00 10.00
27 Pierre Thomas/49 4.00 10.00
30 Chad Greenway/40 5.00 12.00
31 Devery Henderson/49 4.00 10.00
33 Vincent Jackson/49 4.00 10.00
35 Eli Manning/35 8.00 20.00
36 Tony Romo/49 5.00 12.00
38 Hakeem Nicks/49 4.00 10.00
43 Wes Welker/49 5.00 12.00

2012 Elite Down and Distance Jerseys Autographs

STATED PRINT RUN 5-15
7 Beanie Wells/15
26 Philip Rivers/15 12.00 30.00
27 Pierre Thomas/25 6.00 15.00
38 Hakeem Nicks/25 10.00 25.00
40 Reggie Wayne/15 EXCH

2012 Elite Down and Distance Jerseys Autographs Prime

PRIME STATED PRINT RUN 5-15
6 Asante Samuel/15 12.00 30.00

2012 Elite Hit List

STATED PRINT RUN 999 SER.#'d SETS
*BLACK/49: 1X TO 2.5X BASIC INSERTS
*GOLD/149: .6X TO 1.5X BASIC INSERTS
1 London Fletcher 1.00 2.50
2 D'Qwell Jackson .75 2.00
3 Chad Greenway 1.00 2.50
4 James Laurinaitis .75 2.00
5 Clay Matthews 1.25 3.00
6 Sean Lee 1.25 3.00
7 Curtis Lofton .75 2.00
8 Jason Babin .75 2.00
9 Jared Allen .75 2.00
10 Pat Angerer .75 2.00
11 James Anderson .75 2.00
12 Chris Long .75 2.00
13 NaVorro Bowman 1.00 2.50
14 Aldon Smith .75 2.00
15 Charles Woodson 1.25 3.00
16 Daryl Washington .75 2.00
17 Derrick Johnson .75 2.00
18 Desmond Bishop .75 2.00
19 Karlos Dansby .75 2.00
20 Lance Briggs 1.00 2.50

2012 Elite New Breed Jerseys

STATED PRINT RUN 199-399
*PRIME/50: .6X TO 1.5X BASIC JSY
*PRIME/25: .8X TO 2X BASIC JSY
1 Andrew Luck/199 12.00 30.00
2 Robert Griffin III/199 2.50 6.00
3 Trent Richardson/199 2.00 5.00
4 Justin Blackmon/199 2.00 5.00
5 Ryan Tannehill/199 3.00 8.00
6 Michael Floyd/299 2.00 5.00
7 Kendall Wright/299 2.00 5.00
8 Brandon Weeden/299 2.00 5.00
9 A.J. Jenkins/342 2.00 5.00
10 Doug Martin/399 3.00 8.00
11 David Wilson/399 2.00 5.00
12 Brian Quick/399 2.00 5.00
13 Coby Fleener/399 2.00 5.00
14 Stephen Hill/399 2.00 5.00
15 Alshon Jeffery/399 4.00 10.00
16 Isaiah Pead/399 2.00 5.00
17 Ryan Broyles/399 2.00 5.00
18 Brock Osweiler/399 2.00 5.00
19 LaMichael James/399 2.00 5.00
20 Rueben Randle/399 2.00 5.00
21 Dwayne Allen/399 2.00 5.00
22 Ronnie Hillman/399 2.00 5.00
23 DeVier Posey/399 2.00 5.00
24 T.J. Graham/399 2.00 5.00
25 Russell Wilson/399 12.00 30.00
26 Michael Egnew/399 2.00 5.00
27 Mohamed Sanu/399 3.00 8.00
28 Bernard Pierce/399 2.00 5.00
29 Nick Foles/399 5.00 12.00
30 Jarius Wright/399 2.00 5.00
31 Lamar Miller/399 3.00 8.00
32 Joe Adams/399 2.00 5.00
33 Robert Turbin/399 2.00 5.00
34 Chris Givens/399 2.00 5.00
35 Nick Toon/399 2.00 5.00

2012 Elite New Breed Jerseys Autographs

1-11 STATED PRINT RUN 25
12-35 STATED PRINT RUN 50
*PRIME/25: .5X TO 1.2X JSY AU/25
*PRIME/25: .6X TO 1.5X JSY AU/50
EXCH EXPIRATION: 1/25/2014
1 Andrew Luck/25 200.00 400.00
2 Robert Griffin III/25 10.00 25.00
3 Trent Richardson/25 8.00 20.00
4 Justin Blackmon/25 8.00 20.00
5 Ryan Tannehill/25 12.00 30.00
6 Michael Floyd/25 8.00 20.00
7 Kendall Wright/25 8.00 20.00
8 Brandon Weeden/25 8.00 20.00
9 A.J. Jenkins/25 8.00 20.00
10 Doug Martin/25 12.00 30.00
11 David Wilson/25 8.00 20.00
12 Brian Quick/50 6.00 15.00
13 Coby Fleener/50 6.00 15.00
14 Stephen Hill/50 6.00 15.00
15 Alshon Jeffery/50 12.00 30.00
16 Isaiah Pead/50 6.00 15.00
17 Ryan Broyles/50 6.00 15.00
18 Brock Osweiler/50 6.00 15.00
19 LaMichael James/50 6.00 15.00
20 Rueben Randle/50 6.00 15.00
21 Dwayne Allen/50 6.00 15.00
22 Ronnie Hillman/50 EXCH 6.00 15.00
23 DeVier Posey/50 6.00 15.00
24 T.J. Graham/50 6.00 15.00
25 Russell Wilson/50 75.00 125.00
26 Michael Egnew/50 6.00 15.00
27 Mohamed Sanu/50 10.00 25.00
28 Bernard Pierce/50 6.00 15.00
29 Nick Foles/50 15.00 40.00
30 Jarius Wright/50 6.00 15.00
31 Lamar Miller/50 10.00 25.00
32 Joe Adams/50 6.00 15.00
33 Robert Turbin/50 6.00 15.00
34 Chris Givens/50 6.00 15.00
35 Nick Toon/50 6.00 15.00

2012 Elite Passing the Torch Autograph

STATED PRINT RUN 5-25
EXCH EXPIRATION: 1/25/2014
1 Marino/Brees/20 250.00 350.00
2 K.Winslow/Gronk/20 75.00 135.00
4 Williams/Griffin/25 15.00 40.00
8 Esiason/A.Dalton/20 60.00 120.00
9 F.Taylor/M.Drew/20 40.00 80.00
10 J.Lofton/D.Driver/20 40.00 80.00
11 P.Manning/A.Luck/20 900.00 1500.00
12 E.Smith/Murray/20 100.00 200.00
13 Romnwsk/Millr/20 50.00 100.00
15 Ochocinco/Green/20 40.00 80.00
16 Plunkett/Palmer/20 EXCH
19 Tarkenton/C.Ponder/20 40.00 100.00
20 J.Elway/P.Manning/20 350.00 500.00

2012 Elite Prime Numbers

STATED PRINT RUN 999 SER.#'d SETS
*BLACK/49: 1X TO 2.5X BASIC INSERTS
*GOLD/149: .6X TO 1.5X BASIC INSERTS
1 Aaron Rodgers 2.00 5.00
2 Mike Wallace .75 2.00
3 Steve Smith WR 1.00 2.50
4 LeSean McCoy 1.25 3.00
5 Adrian Peterson 1.25 3.00
6 BenJarvus Green-Ellis 1.00 2.50
7 Calvin Johnson 1.25 3.00
8 Jermichael Finley .75 2.00
9 Matthew Stafford 1.00 2.50
10 Jordy Nelson 1.00 2.50
11 Jimmy Graham 1.25 3.00
12 Roddy White .75 2.00
13 Eli Manning 1.00 2.50
14 Steven Jackson .75 2.00
15 Andy Dalton 1.00 2.50
16 Marshawn Lynch 1.00 2.50
17 Victor Cruz 1.00 2.50
18 Brandon Marshall 1.00 2.50
19 Maurice Jones-Drew .75 2.00
20 Ahmad Bradshaw .75 2.00

2012 Elite Prime Numbers Jerseys Prime

STATED PRINT RUN 1-49
4 LeSean McCoy/48 6.00 15.00
9 Matthew Stafford/24 6.00 15.00
12 Roddy White/47 4.00 10.00
13 Eli Manning/43 5.00 12.00
15 Andy Dalton/49 5.00 12.00
18 Brandon Marshall/17 6.00 15.00
19 Maurice Jones-Drew/49 4.00 10.00

2012 Elite Rookie Hard Hats

STATED PRINT RUN 399 SER.#'d SETS
1 Andrew Luck 20.00 50.00
2 Robert Griffin III 2.50 6.00
3 Trent Richardson 2.00 5.00
4 Justin Blackmon 2.00 5.00
5 Ryan Tannehill 3.00 8.00
6 Michael Floyd 2.00 5.00
7 Kendall Wright 2.00 5.00
8 Brandon Weeden 2.00 5.00
9 A.J. Jenkins 2.00 5.00
10 Doug Martin 3.00 8.00
11 David Wilson 2.00 5.00
12 Alshon Jeffery 4.00 10.00
13 Bernard Pierce 2.00 5.00
14 Brian Quick 2.00 5.00
15 Brock Osweiler 2.00 5.00
16 Coby Fleener 2.00 5.00
17 DeVier Posey 2.00 5.00
18 Dwayne Allen 2.00 5.00
19 Isaiah Pead 2.00 5.00
20 Jarius Wright 2.00 5.00
21 Joe Adams 2.00 5.00
22 Lamar Miller 3.00 8.00
23 LaMichael James 2.00 5.00
24 Michael Egnew 2.00 5.00
25 Mohamed Sanu 3.00 8.00
26 Nick Foles 5.00 12.00
27 Nick Toon 2.00 5.00
28 Robert Turbin 2.00 5.00
29 Ronnie Hillman 2.00 5.00
30 Rueben Randle 2.00 5.00
31 Russell Wilson 15.00 40.00
32 Ryan Broyles 2.00 5.00
33 Stephen Hill 2.00 5.00
34 T.J. Graham 2.00 5.00
35 T.Y. Hilton 4.00 10.00
36 B.J. Coleman 2.00 5.00
37 Chandler Harnish 2.00 5.00
38 Chris Givens 2.00 5.00
39 Chris Rainey 2.00 5.00
40 Cyrus Gray 2.00 5.00
41 Dan Herron 2.00 5.00
42 Danny Coale 2.00 5.00
43 Devon Wylie 2.00 5.00
44 Juron Criner 2.00 5.00
45 Keshawn Martin 2.50 6.00
46 Kirk Cousins 8.00 20.00
47 Ladarius Green 2.00 5.00
48 Marvin Jones 2.00 5.00
49 Marvin McNutt 2.00 5.00
50 Orson Charles 2.00 5.00
51 Rishard Matthews 2.00 5.00
52 Ryan Lindley 2.00 5.00
53 Terrance Ganaway 2.50 6.00
54 Tommy Streeter 2.00 5.00
55 Travis Benjamin 2.00 5.00
56 Vick Ballard 2.50 6.00
57 Alfred Morris 2.00 5.00
58 Mark Barron 2.00 5.00
59 Dre Kirkpatrick 2.00 5.00
60 Morris Claiborne 2.00 5.00
61 Luke Kuechly 5.00 12.00
62 Melvin Ingram 2.00 5.00
63 Case Keenum 4.00 10.00
64 Jeff Fuller 2.00 5.00
65 Kellen Moore 2.50 6.00

2012 Elite Rookie Hard Hats Autographs

STATED PRINT RUN 49-199
1 Andrew Luck/49 100.00 200.00
2 Robert Griffin III/49 8.00 20.00
3 Trent Richardson/49 6.00 15.00
4 Justin Blackmon/49 6.00 15.00
5 Ryan Tannehill/49 10.00 25.00
6 Michael Floyd/49 6.00 15.00
7 Kendall Wright/49 6.00 15.00
8 Brandon Weeden/49 6.00 15.00
9 A.J. Jenkins/49 6.00 15.00
10 Doug Martin/49 10.00 25.00
11 David Wilson/49 6.00 15.00
12 Alshon Jeffery/99 10.00 25.00
13 Bernard Pierce/99 5.00 12.00
14 Brian Quick/99 5.00 12.00
15 Brock Osweiler/99 5.00 12.00
16 Coby Fleener/99 5.00 12.00
17 DeVier Posey/99 5.00 12.00
18 Dwayne Allen/99 5.00 12.00
19 Isaiah Pead/99 5.00 12.00
20 Jarius Wright/99 5.00 12.00
21 Joe Adams/99 10.00 25.00
22 Lamar Miller/99 8.00 20.00
23 LaMichael James/99 5.00 12.00
24 Michael Egnew/99 5.00 12.00
25 Mohamed Sanu/99 8.00 20.00
26 Nick Foles/99 12.00 30.00
27 Nick Toon/99 8.00 20.00
28 Robert Turbin/99 5.00 12.00
29 Ronnie Hillman/99 EXCH 5.00 12.00
30 Rueben Randle/99 5.00 12.00
31 Russell Wilson/99 60.00 120.00
32 Ryan Broyles/99 12.00 30.00
33 Stephen Hill/99 5.00 12.00
34 T.J. Graham/99 5.00 12.00
35 T.Y. Hilton/99 10.00 25.00
36 B.J. Coleman/199 4.00 10.00
37 Chandler Harnish/199 4.00 10.00
38 Chris Givens/199 4.00 10.00
39 Chris Rainey/199 4.00 10.00
40 Cyrus Gray/199 4.00 10.00
41 Dan Herron/199 4.00 10.00
42 Danny Coale/199 5.00 12.00
43 Devon Wylie/199 4.00 10.00
44 Juron Criner/199 8.00 20.00
45 Keshawn Martin/199 6.00 15.00
46 Kirk Cousins/199 15.00 40.00
47 Ladarius Green/199 4.00 10.00
48 Marvin Jones/199 4.00 10.00
49 Marvin McNutt/199 4.00 10.00
50 Orson Charles/199 4.00 10.00
51 Rishard Matthews/199 4.00 10.00
52 Ryan Lindley/199 4.00 10.00
53 Terrance Ganaway/199 6.00 15.00
54 Tommy Streeter/199 5.00 12.00
55 Travis Benjamin/199 4.00 10.00
56 Vick Ballard/199 5.00 12.00
57 Alfred Morris/199 4.00 10.00
58 Mark Barron/199 4.00 10.00
59 Dre Kirkpatrick/199 EXCH 4.00 10.00
60 Morris Claiborne/49* 6.00 15.00
61 Luke Kuechly/199 15.00 40.00
62 Melvin Ingram/199 4.00 10.00
63 Case Keenum/199 8.00 20.00
64 Jeff Fuller/199 4.00 10.00
65 Kellen Moore/199 5.00 12.00

2012 Elite Rookie Inscriptions Black Ink

ANNOUNCED PRINT RUN 8-75
3 Trent Richardson/25* 10.00 25.00
5 Ryan Tannehill/40* 12.00 30.00
6 Michael Floyd/40* 12.00 30.00
7 Kendall Wright/45* 8.00 20.00
9 A.J. Jenkins/75* 6.00 15.00
10 Doug Martin/45* 12.00 30.00
11 David Wilson/45* 8.00 20.00
12 Alshon Jeffery/50* 12.00 30.00
13 Bernard Pierce/45* 8.00 20.00
14 Brian Quick/25* 10.00 25.00
15 Brock Osweiler/35* 8.00 20.00
16 Coby Fleener/35* 8.00 20.00
17 DeVier Posey/45* 8.00 20.00
18 Dwayne Allen/45* 8.00 20.00
19 Isaiah Pead/75* 6.00 15.00
20 Chris Givens/30* 8.00 20.00
21 Joe Adams/50* 6.00 15.00
22 Lamar Miller/40* 12.00 30.00
23 LaMichael James/40* 8.00 20.00
25 Mohamed Sanu/55* 10.00 25.00
26 Nick Foles/50* 15.00 40.00
27 Nick Toon/21* 10.00 25.00
28 Robert Turbin/62* 6.00 15.00
29 Ronnie Hillman/35* 8.00 20.00
30 Rueben Randle/50* 6.00 15.00
31 Russell Wilson/35* 90.00 150.00
33 Stephen Hill/45* 8.00 20.00
34 T.J. Graham/40* 8.00 20.00

2012 Elite Rookie Inscriptions Blue Ink

ANNOUNCED PRINT RUN 15-196
1 Andrew Luck/40* 150.00 300.00
2 Robert Griffin III/40* 10.00 25.00
3 Trent Richardson/30* 8.00 20.00
4 Justin Blackmon/35* 8.00 20.00
5 Ryan Tannehill/15* 15.00 40.00
6 Michael Floyd/15* 12.00 30.00
7 Kendall Wright/15* 10.00 25.00
8 Brandon Weeden/55* 6.00 15.00
9 A.J. Jenkins/20* 10.00 25.00
10 Doug Martin/40* 12.00 30.00
11 David Wilson/40* 8.00 20.00
12 Alshon Jeffery/75* 12.00 30.00
13 Bernard Pierce/70* 6.00 15.00
14 Brian Quick/50* 6.00 15.00
15 Brock Osweiler/75* 6.00 15.00
16 Coby Fleener/15* 10.00 25.00
17 DeVier Posey/25* 10.00 25.00
18 Dwayne Allen/20* 10.00 25.00
19 Isaiah Pead/30* 8.00 20.00
20 Chris Givens/54* 6.00 15.00
21 Joe Adams/64* 6.00 15.00
22 Lamar Miller/25* 15.00 40.00
23 LaMichael James/75* 6.00 15.00
24 Michael Egnew/196* 5.00 12.00
25 Mohamed Sanu/64* 10.00 25.00
26 Nick Foles/38* 20.00 50.00
27 Nick Toon/79* 6.00 15.00
28 Robert Turbin/58* 6.00 15.00
29 Ronnie Hillman/75* 6.00 15.00
30 Rueben Randle/40* 8.00 20.00
31 Russell Wilson/50* 75.00 150.00
32 Ryan Broyles/150* 5.00 12.00
33 Stephen Hill/75* 6.00 15.00
34 T.J. Graham/40* 8.00 20.00

2012 Elite Rookie Inscriptions Green Ink

ANNOUNCED PRINT RUN 2-75
3 Trent Richardson/20* 10.00 25.00
5 Ryan Tannehill/30* 12.00 30.00
6 Michael Floyd/30* 12.00 30.00
7 Kendall Wright/15* 10.00 25.00
9 A.J. Jenkins/40* 8.00 20.00
10 Doug Martin/40* 12.00 30.00
11 David Wilson/55* 6.00 15.00
12 Alshon Jeffery/15* 20.00 50.00
13 Bernard Pierce 8.00 20.00
14 Brian Quick/30* 8.00 20.00
16 Coby Fleener/45* 8.00 20.00
17 DeVier Posey/55* 6.00 15.00
18 Dwayne Allen/75* 6.00 15.00
19 Isaiah Pead/50* 6.00 15.00
20 Chris Givens/25* 10.00 25.00
21 Joe Adams/56* 6.00 15.00
22 Lamar Miller/50* 10.00 25.00
23 LaMichael James/25* 10.00 25.00
25 Mohamed Sanu/45* 12.00 30.00
27 Nick Toon/32* 8.00 20.00
28 Robert Turbin/29* 10.00 25.00
30 Rueben Randle/25* 10.00 25.00
31 Russell Wilson/15* 125.00 200.00
34 T.J. Graham/35* 8.00 20.00

2012 Elite Rookie Inscriptions Red Ink

ANNOUNCED PRINT RUN 10-75
1 Andrew Luck/30* 150.00 300.00
2 Robert Griffin III/30* 10.00 25.00
3 Trent Richardson/15* 10.00 25.00
4 Justin Blackmon/30* 8.00 20.00
5 Ryan Tannehill/15* 15.00 40.00
7 Kendall Wright/30* 8.00 20.00
8 Brandon Weeden/30* 8.00 20.00
9 A.J. Jenkins/15* 10.00 25.00
10 Doug Martin/20* 15.00 40.00
11 David Wilson/40* 8.00 20.00
12 Alshon Jeffery/25* 20.00 50.00
14 Brian Quick/40* 8.00 20.00
15 Brock Osweiler/15* 10.00 25.00
16 Coby Fleener/50* 6.00 15.00
17 DeVier Posey/35* 8.00 20.00
18 Dwayne Allen/35* 8.00 20.00
19 Isaiah Pead/20* 10.00 25.00
20 Chris Givens/45* 8.00 20.00
21 Joe Adams/23* 10.00 25.00
22 Lamar Miller/30* 12.00 30.00
23 LaMichael James/15* 10.00 25.00
25 Mohamed Sanu/15* 15.00 40.00
26 Nick Foles/75* 15.00 40.00
27 Nick Toon/60* 6.00 15.00
28 Robert Turbin/37* 8.00 20.00
29 Ronnie Hillman/20* 10.00 25.00
30 Rueben Randle/30* 8.00 20.00
31 Russell Wilson/40* 75.00 150.00
33 Stephen Hill/20* 10.00 25.00
34 T.J. Graham/15* 10.00 25.00

2012 Elite Series

STATED PRINT RUN 999 SER.#'d SETS
*BLACK/49: 1X TO 2.5X BASIC INSERTS
*GOLD/149: .6X TO 1.5X BASIC INSERTS
1 Calvin Johnson 1.25 3.00
2 Greg Jennings .75 2.00
3 Rob Gronkowski 1.25 3.00
4 Chris Johnson .75 2.00
5 Arian Foster 1.00 2.50
6 DeAngelo Williams .75 2.00
7 Drew Brees 1.25 3.00
8 Aaron Rodgers 2.00 5.00
9 Ray Rice .75 2.00
10 Antonio Gates 1.00 2.50
11 Matt Ryan 1.00 2.50
12 Wes Welker 1.00 2.50
13 Larry Fitzgerald 1.00 2.50
14 Eli Manning 1.00 2.50
15 DeSean Jackson 1.00 2.50
16 Tom Brady 3.00 8.00
17 Dwayne Bowe 1.00 2.50
18 Michael Vick 1.00 2.50
19 Cam Newton 1.25 3.00
20 Maurice Jones-Drew .75 2.00

2012 Elite Series Jerseys Prime

STATED PRINT RUN 1-49
4 Chris Johnson/49 4.00 10.00
12 Wes Welker/49 5.00 12.00
20 Maurice Jones-Drew/49 4.00 10.00

2012 Elite Series Rookies
STATED PRINT RUN 999 SER.#'d SETS
*BLACK/49: 1X TO 2.5X BASIC INSERTS
*GOLD/149: .6X TO 1.5X BASIC INSERTS
1 Andrew Luck 8.00 20.00
2 Robert Griffin III 1.00 2.50
3 Trent Richardson .75 2.00
4 Justin Blackmon .75 2.00
5 Ryan Tannehill 1.25 3.00
6 Michael Floyd .75 2.00
7 Kendall Wright .75 2.00
8 Brandon Weeden .75 2.00
9 A.J. Jenkins .75 2.00
10 Doug Martin 1.25 3.00
11 David Wilson .75 2.00
12 Brian Quick .75 2.00
13 Coby Fleener .75 2.00
14 Stephen Hill .75 2.00
15 Alshon Jeffery 1.50 4.00
16 Isaiah Pead .75 2.00
17 Ryan Broyles .75 2.00
18 Brock Osweiler .75 2.00
19 LaMichael James .75 2.00
20 Rueben Randle .75 2.00
21 Dwayne Allen .75 2.00
22 Ronnie Hillman .75 2.00
23 DeVier Posey .75 2.00
24 T.J. Graham .75 2.00
25 Russell Wilson 6.00 15.00

2012 Elite Series Rookies Autographs
STATED PRINT RUN 99 SER.#'d SETS
1 Andrew Luck 50.00 100.00
2 Robert Griffin III 5.00 12.00
3 Trent Richardson 4.00 10.00
4 Justin Blackmon 4.00 10.00
5 Ryan Tannehill 6.00 15.00
6 Michael Floyd 4.00 10.00
7 Kendall Wright 4.00 10.00
8 Brandon Weeden 4.00 10.00
9 A.J. Jenkins 4.00 10.00
10 Doug Martin 6.00 15.00
11 David Wilson 4.00 10.00
12 Brian Quick 4.00 10.00
13 Coby Fleener 4.00 10.00
14 Stephen Hill 4.00 10.00
15 Alshon Jeffery 8.00 20.00
16 Isaiah Pead 4.00 10.00
17 Ryan Broyles 4.00 10.00
18 Brock Osweiler 4.00 10.00
19 LaMichael James 4.00 10.00
20 Rueben Randle 4.00 10.00
21 Dwayne Allen 4.00 10.00
22 Ronnie Hillman EXCH 4.00 10.00
23 DeVier Posey 4.00 10.00
24 T.J. Graham 4.00 10.00
25 Russell Wilson 60.00 125.00

2012 Elite Status Autographs
*1-100 VETS/15: .4X TO 1X ASPIRATION AU
1-100 VETERAN PRINT RUN 1-15
*ROOKIES/24: .6X TO 1.5X ASPRTION/49
101-200 ROOKIE PRINT RUN 24
79 Troy Polamalu/15 40.00 80.00
101 Andrew Luck/24 150.00 300.00
102 Robert Griffin III/24 12.00 30.00
106 Trent Richardson/24 10.00 25.00
111 Ryan Tannehill/24 15.00 40.00
185 Alfred Morris/24 10.00 25.00
190 Russell Wilson/24 150.00 250.00

2012 Elite Throwback Threads
STATED PRINT RUN 15-199
1 Marshall Faulk/199 4.00 10.00
2 Steven Jackson/110 3.00 8.00
3 Ozzie Newsome/199 4.00 10.00
4 Tony Gonzalez/199 4.00 10.00
5 Sterling Sharpe/199 4.00 10.00
6 Jay Novacek/199 4.00 10.00
7 Rocket Ismail/199 4.00 10.00
8 Jerry Rice/199 6.00 15.00
9 Darrell Green/126 5.00 12.00
12 Julius Peppers/199 4.00 10.00
13 Doug Flutie/199 4.00 10.00
14 Eddie George/199 4.00 10.00
15 Chris Johnson/199 3.00 8.00
16 E.George/C.Johnson/199 4.00 10.00
17 D.Flutie/Fitzpatrick/15 6.00 15.00
18 J.Novacek/J.Witten/111 4.00 10.00
19 M.Faulk/S.Jackson/108 4.00 10.00
20 O.Newsome/Gonzalez/199 4.00 10.00

2012 Elite Throwback Threads Prime
*PRIME/30-49: .6X TO 1.5X BASIC JSY
*PRIME/25: .8X TO 2X BASIC JSY
PRIME STATED PRINT RUN 11-49
10 DeAngelo Hall/31 5.00 12.00

2012 Elite Throwback Threads Autographs
STATED PRINT RUN 15 SER.#'d SETS
5 Sterling Sharpe 30.00 60.00
8 Jerry Rice 60.00 120.00
11 Richard Dent 25.00 50.00
13 Doug Flutie 12.00 30.00

2012 Elite Turn of the Century Autographs
STATED PRINT RUN 99-699
EXCH EXPIRATION: 1/25/2014
101 Andrew Luck/99 100.00 200.00
102 Robert Griffin III/99 15.00 40.00
103 Matt Kalil/399 3.00 8.00
104 Morris Claiborne/199 4.00 10.00
105 Justin Blackmon/99 5.00 12.00
106 Trent Richardson/99 5.00 12.00
107 Riley Reiff/399 3.00 8.00
108 Quinton Coples/399 3.00 8.00
109 Melvin Ingram/242 6.00 15.00
110 Michael Brockers/399 3.00 8.00
111 Ryan Tannehill/99 8.00 20.00
112 David DeCastro/399 3.00 8.00
113 Michael Floyd/99 5.00 12.00
114 Luke Kuechly/299 8.00 20.00
115 Janoris Jenkins/399 4.00 10.00
116 Jonathan Martin/399 3.00 8.00
117 Devon Still/399 4.00 10.00
118 Dre Kirkpatrick/299 EXCH 3.00 8.00
119 Kendall Wright/99 5.00 12.00
120 Fletcher Cox/399 5.00 12.00
121 Courtney Upshaw/299 4.00 10.00
122 Dontari Poe/599 3.00 8.00
123 Rueben Randle/99 5.00 12.00
124 Nick Perry/399 4.00 10.00
125 Whitney Mercilus/599 3.00 8.00
126 Dont'a Hightower/299 5.00 12.00
127 Mark Barron/299 3.00 8.00
128 Stephen Hill/99 5.00 12.00
129 Zach Brown/299 3.00 8.00
130 Andre Branch/599 3.00 8.00
131 Dwayne Allen/99 5.00 12.00
132 David Wilson/99 5.00 12.00
133 Lamar Miller/99 8.00 20.00
134 Brock Osweiler/99 5.00 12.00
135 Lavonte David/299 5.00 12.00
136 Alshon Jeffery/99 10.00 25.00
137 Bobby Wagner/299 5.00 12.00
138 Doug Martin/99 8.00 20.00
139 Chris Givens/199 4.00 10.00
140 Coby Fleener/99 5.00 12.00
141 Brandon Weeden/99 5.00 12.00
142 Jared Crick/599 3.00 8.00
143 Shea McClellin/299 4.00 10.00
144 Ronnell Lewis/599 3.00 8.00
145 Orson Charles/399 3.00 8.00
146 Vinny Curry/399 4.00 10.00
147 Chandler Jones/399 3.00 8.00
148 Isaiah Pead/99 5.00 12.00
149 George Iloka/699 3.00 8.00
150 Mohamed Sanu/99 8.00 20.00
151 Nick Toon/99 5.00 12.00
152 LaMichael James/99 5.00 12.00
153 Kirk Cousins/199 15.00 40.00
154 T.J. Graham/99 5.00 12.00
155 Mychal Kendricks/599 5.00 12.00
156 Juron Criner/399 3.00 8.00
157 Stephon Gilmore/599 4.00 10.00
158 Bernard Pierce/99 5.00 12.00
159 Ladarius Green/399 3.00 8.00
160 Cyrus Gray/199 4.00 10.00
161 Brian Quick/99 5.00 12.00
162 Nick Foles/99 12.00 30.00
163 Ronnie Hillman/99 EXCH 5.00 12.00
164 Michael Egnew/99 5.00 12.00
165 Keshawn Martin/399 4.00 10.00
166 Chris Rainey/199 4.00 10.00
167 Joe Adams/99 5.00 12.00
168 Marvin Jones/599 3.00 8.00
169 Ryan Lindley/199 4.00 10.00
170 Greg Childs/399 3.00 8.00
171 Jarius Wright/99 5.00 12.00
172 Michael Smith/399 EXCH 4.00 10.00
173 Tommy Streeter/399 3.00 8.00
174 Robert Turbin/99 5.00 12.00
175 A.J. Jenkins/99 5.00 12.00
176 DeVier Posey/99 5.00 12.00
177 Bryce Brown/399 3.00 8.00
178 Dan Herron/399 3.00 8.00
179 Vick Ballard/399 4.00 10.00
180 T.Y. Hilton/99 10.00 25.00
181 Bruce Irvin/399 5.00 12.00
182 Marvin McNutt/399 3.00 8.00
183 Terrance Ganaway/599 4.00 10.00
184 B.J. Coleman/599 5.00 12.00
185 Alfred Morris/399 3.00 8.00
186 Jeff Fuller/699 3.00 8.00
187 Rishard Matthews/599 3.00 8.00
188 B.J. Cunningham/599 3.00 8.00
189 Ryan Broyles/99 5.00 12.00
190 Russell Wilson/99 100.00 175.00
191 Devon Wylie/399 3.00 8.00
192 LaVon Brazill/399 5.00 12.00
193 Travis Benjamin/399 3.00 8.00
194 Kevin Zeitler/399 3.00 8.00
195 Chandler Harnish/399 3.00 8.00
196 Marc Tyler/699 3.00 8.00
197 Harrison Smith/399 3.00 8.00
198 Danny Coale/599 3.00 8.00
199 Kellen Moore/699 4.00 10.00
200 Case Keenum/699 6.00 15.00

2013 Elite
COMP.SET w/o RC's (100) 8.00 20.00
101-200 ROOKIE PRINT RUN 699-999
1 Larry Fitzgerald .25 .60
2 Rashard Mendenhall .20 .50
3 Patrick Peterson .20 .50
4 Matt Ryan .25 .60
5 Julio Jones .30 .75
6 Roddy White .20 .50
7 Steven Jackson .20 .50
8 Joe Flacco .25 .60
9 Torrey Smith .20 .50
10 Jacoby Jones .20 .50
11 Ray Rice .20 .50
12 C.J. Spiller .20 .50
13 Fred Jackson .25 .60
14 Steve Johnson .25 .60
15 Cam Newton .30 .75
16 Steve Smith .25 .60
17 DeAngelo Williams .20 .50
18 Jay Cutler .20 .50
19 Brandon Marshall .25 .60
20 Matt Forte .20 .50
21 Andy Dalton .25 .60
22 A.J. Green .30 .75
23 BenJarvus Green-Ellis .25 .60
24 Brandon Weeden .20 .50
25 Josh Gordon .20 .50
26 Trent Richardson .20 .50
27 Tony Romo .25 .60
28 Dez Bryant .30 .75
29 Jason Witten .25 .60
30 DeMarco Murray .25 .60
31 Peyton Manning .60 1.50
32 Demaryius Thomas .25 .60
33 Willis McGahee .20 .50
34 Matthew Stafford .25 .60
35 Calvin Johnson .30 .75
36 Mikel Leshoure .20 .50
37 Aaron Rodgers .50 1.25
38 James Jones .20 .50
39 Randall Cobb .25 .60
40 Matt Schaub .20 .50
41 Andre Johnson .20 .50
42 Arian Foster .25 .60
43 Andrew Luck .50 1.25
44 Reggie Wayne .25 .60
45 Vick Ballard .20 .50
46 Maurice Jones-Drew .20 .50
47 Cecil Shorts .20 .50
48 Justin Blackmon .20 .50
49 Jamaal Charles .25 .60
50 Dwayne Bowe .25 .60
51 Tamba Hali .20 .50
52 Ryan Tannehill .25 .60
53 Brian Hartline .20 .50
54 Mike Wallace .20 .50
55 Christian Ponder .20 .50
56 Greg Jennings .20 .50
57 A.Peterson UER NNO .30 .75
58 Tom Brady .75 2.00
59 Rob Gronkowski .30 .75
60 Danny Amendola .25 .60
61 Drew Brees .30 .75
62 Jimmy Graham .30 .75
63 Mark Ingram .25 .60
64 Eli Manning .25 .60
65 Hakeem Nicks .20 .50
66 David Wilson .20 .50
67 Mark Sanchez .20 .50
68 Santonio Holmes .20 .50
69 Bilal Powell .20 .50
70 Matt Flynn .20 .50
71 Denarius Moore .20 .50
72 Darren McFadden .25 .60
73 Michael Vick .25 .60
74 Jeremy Maclin .20 .50
75 LeSean McCoy .30 .75
76 Ben Roethlisberger .30 .75
77 Antonio Brown .30 .75
78 Jonathan Dwyer .20 .50
79 Sam Bradford .20 .50
80 Chris Givens .20 .50
81 Daryl Richardson .20 .50
82 Philip Rivers .30 .75
83 Antonio Gates .25 .60
84 Ryan Mathews .25 .60
85 Colin Kaepernick .25 .60
86 Michael Crabtree .20 .50
87 Frank Gore .25 .60
88 Vernon Davis .20 .50
89 Russell Wilson .60 1.50
90 Sidney Rice .20 .50
91 Marshawn Lynch .25 .60
92 Josh Freeman .25 .60
93 Vincent Jackson .20 .50
94 Doug Martin .25 .60
95 Jake Locker .25 .60
96 Kenny Britt .20 .50
97 Chris Johnson .20 .50
98 Robert Griffin III .20 .50
99 Pierre Garcon .25 .60
100 Alfred Morris .20 .50
101 Aaron Dobson/799 RC 1.00 2.50
102 Aaron Mellette/999 RC 1.00 2.50
103 Ace Sanders/799 RC 1.00 2.50
104 Arthur Brown/999 RC 1.00 2.50
105 Alec Ogletree/999 RC 1.00 2.50
106 Alex Okafor/999 RC 1.00 2.50
107 Andre Ellington/799 RC 1.00 2.50
108 Barkevious Mingo/899 RC 1.00 2.50
109 Bjoern Werner/899 RC 1.00 2.50
110 Chance Warmack/999 RC 1.00 2.50
111 Darius Slay/999 RC 1.00 2.50
112 Chris Gragg/799 RC 1.00 2.50
113 Chris Harper/899 RC 1.00 2.50
114 Christine Michael/899 RC 1.00 2.50
115 D.J. Hayden/999 RC 1.00 2.50
116 Eric Fisher/999 RC 1.00 2.50
117 Cobi Hamilton/799 RC 1.00 2.50
118 Knile Davis/699 RC 1.00 2.50
119 Conner Vernon/899 RC 1.00 2.50
120 Cordarrelle Patterson/699 RC 1.00 2.50
121 Corey Fuller/899 RC 1.00 2.50
122 Damontre Moore/999 RC 1.00 2.50
123 Da'Rick Rogers/799 RC 1.00 2.50
124 Datone Jones/999 RC 1.00 2.50
125 DeAndre Hopkins/699 RC 2.50 6.00
126 Dee Milliner/999 RC 1.00 2.50
127 Denard Robinson/799 RC 1.00 2.50
128 Desmond Trufant/999 RC 1.00 2.50
129 Dion Jordan/899 RC 1.00 2.50
130 Dion Sims/799 RC 1.00 2.50
131 Eddie Lacy/699 RC 1.00 2.50
132 EJ Manuel/699 RC 1.00 2.50
133 Eric Reid/899 RC 1.25 3.00
134 Gavin Escobar/799 RC 1.00 2.50
135 Geno Smith/699 RC 1.00 2.50
136 Giovani Bernard/799 RC 1.00 2.50
137 Jamar Taylor/999 RC 1.00 2.50
138 Jarvis Jones/899 RC 1.00 2.50
139 Jawan Jamison/799 RC 1.00 2.50
140 Cornellius Carradine/999 RC 1.00 2.50
141 Johnathan Franklin/899 RC 1.00 2.50
142 Dennis Johnson/899 RC 1.00 2.50
143 Johnthan Banks/999 RC 1.00 2.50
144 Jordan Poyer/999 RC 1.00 2.50
145 Jordan Reed/799 RC 1.50 4.00
146 Joseph Randle/799 RC 1.00 2.50
147 Josh Boyce/799 RC 1.00 2.50
148 Justin Hunter/699 RC 1.00 2.50
149 Keenan Allen/799 RC 2.00 5.00
150 Kenjon Barner/799 RC 1.00 2.50
151 Kenny Stills/799 RC 1.00 2.50
152 Kenny Vaccaro/899 RC 1.00 2.50
153 Kerwynn Williams/999 RC 1.00 2.50
154 Kevin Minter/999 RC 1.00 2.50
155 Landry Jones/899 RC 1.00 2.50
156 Le'Veon Bell/799 RC 3.00 8.00
157 Ezekiel Ansah/999 RC 1.00 2.50
158 Luke Joeckel/999 RC 1.00 2.50
159 Manti Te'o/899 RC 1.25 3.00
160 Marcus Davis/899 RC 1.00 2.50
161 Marcus Lattimore/899 RC 1.00 2.50
162 Margus Hunt/999 RC 1.00 2.50
163 Jasper Collins/899 RC 1.00 2.50
164 Markus Wheaton/799 RC 1.00 2.50
165 Marquess Wilson/799 RC 1.50 4.00
166 Marquise Goodwin/899 RC 1.00 2.50
167 Matt Barkley/699 RC 1.00 2.50
168 Matt Elam/999 RC 1.00 2.50
169 Mall Scott/899 RC 1.00 2.50
170 Mike Gillislee/899 RC 1.00 2.50
171 Mike Glennon/899 RC 1.00 2.50
172 Montee Ball/799 RC 1.00 2.50
173 Nick Kasa/899 RC 1.00 2.50
174 Phillip Thomas/999 RC 1.00 2.50
175 Quinton Patton/799 RC 1.00 2.50
176 Ray Graham/899 RC 1.00 2.50
177 Rex Burkhead/799 RC 1.25 3.00
178 Tyrann Mathieu/799 RC 1.50 4.00
179 Robert Woods/699 RC 1.50 4.00
180 Rodney Smith/899 RC 1.00 2.50
181 Ryan Nassib/799 RC 1.00 2.50
182 Ryan Otten/899 RC 1.00 2.50
183 Ryan Swope/899 RC 1.00 2.50
184 Sam Montgomery/999 RC 1.00 2.50
185 Sheldon Richardson/999 RC 1.00 2.50
186 Star Lotulelei/999 RC 1.25 3.00
187 Stedman Bailey/899 EC 1.00 2.50
188 Stepfan Taylor/799 RC 1.00 2.50
189 Tavarres King/899 RC 1.00 2.50
190 Tavon Austin/699 RC 1.25 3.00
191 Terrance Williams/799 RC 1.00 2.50
192 Theo Riddick/899 RC 1.00 2.50
193 Travis Kelce/899 RC 2.50 6.00
194 Tyler Bray/899 RC 1.00 2.50
195 Tyler Eifert/699 RC 1.00 2.50
196 Tyler Wilson/799 RC 1.00 2.50
197 Vance McDonald/899 RC 1.25 3.00
198 Xavier Rhodes/999 RC 1.00 2.50
199 Zac Dysert/899 RC 1.00 2.50
200 Zach Ertz/799 RC 2.00 5.00

2013 Elite Aspirations
*VETS/71-99: 5X TO 12X BASIC CARDS
*ROOKIES/70-99: .8X TO 2X BASIC CARDS
*VETS/54-68: 6X TO 15X BASIC CARDS
*ROOKIES/41-68: 1X TO 2.5X BASIC CARDS
*ROOKIES/30: 1.2X TO 3X BASIC CARDS
*VETS/20: 10X TO 25X BASIC CARDS
*ROOKIES/20-28: 1.5X TO 4X BASIC CARDS
*VETS/11-19: 12X TO 30X BASIC CARDS
*ROOKIES/11-18: 2X TO 5X BASIC CARDS

2013 Elite Status
*VETS/80-91: 5X TO 12X BASIC CARDS
*ROOKIES/70-99: .8X TO 2X BASIC CARDS
*VETS/42-46: 6X TO 15X BASIC CARDS
*ROOKIES/41-59: 1X TO 2.5X BASIC CARDS
*VETS/32-39: 8X TO 20X BASIC CARDS
*ROOKIES/30-38: 1.2X TO 3X BASIC CARDS
*VETS/20-29: 10X TO 25X BASIC CARDS
*ROOKIES/21-29: 1.5X TO 4X BASIC CARDS
*VETS/10-18: 12X TO 30X BASIC CARDS
*ROOKIES/10-19: 2X TO 5X BASIC CARDS

2013 Elite Status Gold
*GOLD/49: 6X TO 15X BASIC CARDS

2013 Elite Status Red
*RED/25: 10X TO 25X BASIC CARDS

2013 Elite Turn of the Century
*1-100 VETS/199: 3X TO 8X BASIC CARDS
*101-200 ROOKIE/199: .5X TO 1.2X BASIC RC

2013 Elite First and Goal Jerseys
*SECOND/49: .4X TO 1X FIRST JSY/99
*SECOND/25: .6X TO 1.5X FIRST JSY/49-99
*SECOND/15: .4X TO 1X FIRST JSY/17
*THIRD/15-25: .6X TO 1.5X FIRST JSY/49-99
*THIRD/13: .4X TO 1X FIRST JSY/17
*FOURTH/10: 1X TO 2.5X FIRST JSY/49-99
*FOURTH/10: .6X TO 1.5X FIRST JSY/17
1 Drew Brees/99 5.00 12.00
2 Adrian Peterson/99 5.00 12.00
3 Matthew Stafford/49 4.00 10.00
4 Arian Foster/17 6.00 15.00
5 Eli Manning/99 4.00 10.00
6 Alfred Morris/99 3.00 8.00
7 Tony Romo/99 4.00 10.00
8 A.J. Green/49 5.00 12.00
9 Philip Rivers/99 5.00 12.00
10 Brandon Marshall/49 4.00 10.00
11 Josh Freeman/99 4.00 10.00
12 Michael Crabtree/49 3.00 8.00
13 Peyton Manning/99 10.00 25.00
14 Demaryius Thomas/99 4.00 10.00
15 Ray Rice/99 3.00 8.00

2013 Elite Gridiron Gear Jerseys
1 Trent Richardson/99 3.00 8.00
2 Fred Jackson/149 3.00 8.00
3 Brian Urlacher/299 4.00 10.00
4 A.J. Green/99 5.00 12.00
6 Mark Sanchez/49 3.00 8.00
7 Brian Hartline/199 2.50 6.00
8 Ray Rice/149 2.50 6.00
9 Jared Allen/49 3.00 8.00
11 Roddy White/99 3.00 8.00
12 Matthew Stafford/99 4.00 10.00
13 Matt Forte/199 2.50 6.00
14 Knowshon Moreno/299 2.50 6.00
15 Matt Ryan/99 4.00 10.00
16 Beanie Wells/199 2.50 6.00
17 Darren McFadden/199 3.00 8.00
18 Eric Decker/99 3.00 8.00
19 Dez Bryant/99 5.00 12.00
20 Adrian Peterson/99 5.00 12.00
21 Larry Fitzgerald/199 3.00 8.00
22 Julio Jones/99 5.00 12.00
23 Golden Tate/199 2.50 6.00
24 DeMarco Murray/199 3.00 8.00
25 Tony Moeaki/299 2.50 6.00
26 Joe Flacco/199 3.00 8.00
27 Andy Dalton/99 4.00 10.00
28 Marcedes Lewis/99 3.00 8.00
29 C.J. Spiller/99 3.00 8.00
30 DeAngelo Williams/199 2.50 6.00
31 Malcom Floyd/199 2.50 6.00
32 DeMarcus Ware/99 5.00 12.00
34 Cameron Wake/199 2.50 6.00
35 Vonta Leach/299 2.50 6.00
36 Jamaal Charles/99 4.00 10.00
37 Joe Haden/299 2.50 6.00
38 Vernon Davis/49 3.00 8.00
39 Maurice Jones-Drew/99 3.00 8.00
40 Jimmy Graham/49 5.00 12.00
41 Philip Rivers/299 4.00 10.00
42 Tom Brady/49 12.00 30.00
43 BenJarvus Green-Ellis/99 4.00 10.00
44 Demaryius Thomas/199 3.00 8.00
45 Kenny Britt/49 3.00 8.00
46 Michael Crabtree/49 3.00 8.00
47 Ryan Tannehill/199 3.00 8.00
48 Haloti Ngata/299 2.50 6.00
49 Torrey Smith/49 3.00 8.00
50 Steve Johnson/199 3.00 8.00

2013 Elite Gridiron Gear Jerseys Prime
*PRIME/49: .6X TO 1.5X JSY/199-299
*PRIME/49: .5X TO 1.2X JSY/99
*PRIME/25: .8X TO 2X JSY/149-299
*PRIME/25: .6X TO 1.5X JSY/49-99
10 Devin Hester/25 6.00 15.00

2013 Elite Instant Impact Jerseys
PRIME/99: .8X TO 2X BASIC JSY/399
1 Geno Smith 1.50 4.00
2 Cordarrelle Patterson 1.50 4.00
3 Eddie Lacy 1.50 4.00
4 Keenan Allen 3.00 8.00
5 DeAndre Hopkins 4.00 10.00
6 Tavon Austin 2.00 5.00
7 Robert Woods 2.50 6.00
8 Quinton Patton 1.50 4.00
9 Giovani Bernard 1.50 4.00
10 Justin Hunter 1.50 4.00
11 Terrance Williams 1.50 4.00
12 EJ Manuel 1.50 4.00
13 Denard Robinson 1.50 4.00
14 Johnathan Franklin 1.50 4.00
15 Joseph Randle 1.50 4.00
16 Tyler Eifert 1.50 4.00
17 Zach Ertz 3.00 8.00
18 Montee Ball 1.50 4.00
19 Le'Veon Bell 5.00 12.00
20 Manti Te'o 2.00 5.00

2013 Elite New Breed Jerseys
PRIME/99: .8X TO 2X BASIC JSY/399
1 Geno Smith 1.50 4.00
2 Matt Barkley 1.50 4.00
3 Cordarrelle Patterson 1.50 4.00
4 Eddie Lacy 1.50 4.00
5 Keenan Allen 3.00 8.00
6 Mike Glennon 1.50 4.00
7 DeAndre Hopkins 4.00 10.00
8 Tavon Austin 2.00 5.00
9 Tyler Wilson 1.50 4.00
10 Robert Woods 2.50 6.00
11 Quinton Patton 1.50 4.00
12 Ryan Nassib 1.50 4.00
13 Giovani Bernard 1.50 4.00
14 Justin Hunter 1.50 4.00
15 Terrance Williams 1.50 4.00
16 Markus Wheaton 1.50 4.00
17 EJ Manuel 1.50 4.00
18 Denard Robinson 1.50 4.00
19 Johnathan Franklin 1.50 4.00
20 Joseph Randle 1.50 4.00
21 Tyler Eifert 1.50 4.00
22 Zach Ertz 3.00 8.00
23 Aaron Dobson 1.50 4.00
24 Knile Davis 1.50 4.00
25 Landry Jones 1.50 4.00
26 Montee Ball 1.50 4.00
27 Andre Ellington 1.50 4.00
28 Le'Veon Bell 5.00 12.00
29 Christine Michael 1.50 4.00
30 Stedman Bailey 1.50 4.00
31 Vance McDonald 2.00 5.00
32 Mike Gillislee 1.50 4.00
33 Jordan Reed 2.50 6.00
34 Stepfan Taylor 1.50 4.00
35 Manti Te'o 2.00 5.00
36 Marquise Goodwin 1.50 4.00
37 Marcus Lattimore 1.50 4.00
38 Gavin Escobar 1.50 4.00
39 Kenny Stills 1.50 4.00
40 Dion Jordan 1.50 4.00

2013 Elite New Breed Jerseys Autographs
*PRIME/49: .5X TO 1.2X JSY AU/99
1 Geno Smith 5.00 12.00
2 Matt Barkley 5.00 12.00
3 Cordarrelle Patterson 5.00 12.00
4 Eddie Lacy 5.00 12.00
5 Keenan Allen 12.00 30.00
6 Mike Glennon 5.00 12.00
7 DeAndre Hopkins 10.00 25.00
8 Tavon Austin 6.00 15.00
9 Tyler Wilson 5.00 12.00
10 Robert Woods 8.00 20.00
11 Quinton Patton 5.00 12.00
12 Ryan Nassib 5.00 12.00
13 Giovani Bernard 5.00 12.00
14 Justin Hunter 5.00 12.00
15 Terrance Williams 5.00 12.00
16 Markus Wheaton 5.00 12.00
17 EJ Manuel 5.00 12.00
18 Denard Robinson
19 Johnathan Franklin 5.00 12.00
20 Joseph Randle 5.00 12.00
21 Tyler Eifert 5.00 12.00
22 Zach Ertz 10.00 25.00
23 Aaron Dobson 5.00 12.00
24 Knile Davis 8.00 20.00
25 Landry Jones 5.00 12.00
26 Montee Ball 5.00 12.00
27 Andre Ellington 5.00 12.00
28 Le'Veon Bell 15.00 40.00
29 Christine Michael 5.00 12.00
30 Stedman Bailey 10.00 25.00
31 Vance McDonald
32 Mike Gillislee 8.00 20.00
33 Jordan Reed
34 Stepfan Taylor 5.00 12.00
35 Manti Te'o 6.00 15.00
36 Marquise Goodwin 5.00 12.00
37 Marcus Lattimore 5.00 12.00
38 Gavin Escobar 10.00 25.00
39 Kenny Stills 5.00 12.00
40 Dion Jordan 10.00 25.00

2013 Elite Panini Portraits Silve
*GOLD/49: .8X TO 2X BASIC INSERTS
*RED/25: 1.2X TO 3X BASIC INSERTS
1 Aaron Rodgers 4.00 10.00
2 Tom Brady 4.00 10.00
3 Peyton Manning 3.00 8.00
4 Calvin Johnson 1.50 4.00
5 Jason Witten 1.25 3.00
6 Matthew Stafford 1.25 3.00
7 Reggie Wayne 1.25 3.00
8 Jamaal Charles 1.25 3.00
9 Andrew Luck 2.50 6.00
10 Adrian Peterson 1.50 4.00
11 Drew Brees 1.50 4.00
12 Eli Manning 1.25 3.00
13 Colin Kaepernick 1.25 3.00
14 DeSean Jackson 1.25 3.00
15 Troy Polamalu 1.50 4.00
16 Philip Rivers 1.50 4.00
17 Frank Gore 1.25 3.00
18 Marshawn Lynch 1.25 3.00
19 Chris Johnson 1.00 2.50
20 Robert Griffin III 1.00 2.50

2013 Elite Passing the Torch Autographs
2 J.Witten/M.Irvin/25 90.00 150.00
11 D.Sanders/Claiborne/25 25.00 60.00
12 J.Allen/J.Randle/25 50.00 100.00
13 A.Morris/J.Riggins/25 50.00 100.00
14 D.Martin/W.Dunn/25 30.00 80.00
18 Hester/P.Peterson/25 25.00 50.00

2013 Elite Passing the Torch Silver
*GOLD/49: .8X TO 2X BASIC INSERTS
*RED/25: 1.2X TO 3X BASIC INSERTS
1 Marino/P.Manning 3.00 8.00
2 J.Witten/M.Irvin 1.50 4.00
3 E.Manning/P.Simms 1.25 3.00
4 A.Luck/C.Newton 2.50 6.00
5 C.Carter/R.Wayne 1.50 4.00
6 C.Johnson/J.Rice 2.50 6.00
7 Roethlisberger/RG3 1.50 4.00
8 D.Bledsoe/M.Stafford 1.25 3.00
9 Peterson/E.Campbell 1.50 4.00
10 M.Lynch/S.Alexander 1.25 3.00
11 D.Sanders/Claiborne 1.25 3.00
12 J.Allen/J.Randle 1.00 2.50
13 A.Morris/J.Riggins 1.25 3.00
14 D.Martin/W.Dunn 1.25 3.00
15 D.Thomas/R.Smith 1.25 3.00
16 J.Charles/P.Holmes 1.25 3.00
17 P.Manning/R.Wilson 3.00 8.00
18 D.Hester/P.Peterson 1.25 3.00
19 Kaepernick/S.Young 2.00 5.00
20 L.Kuechly/V.Miller 1.25 3.00

2013 Elite Playmakers Jerseys
1 Eli Manning/49 5.00 12.00
2 Adrian Peterson/49 6.00 15.00
3 Hakeem Nicks/49 4.00 10.00
4 Jamaal Charles/49 5.00 12.00
5 Reggie Bush/49 4.00 10.00
6 Torrey Smith/25 5.00 12.00
8 Ryan Mathews/49 5.00 12.00
9 Dwayne Bowe/49 5.00 12.00
10 Fred Davis/49 4.00 10.00
12 Vernon Davis/25 5.00 12.00
13 Shaun Alexander/49 4.00 10.00
14 Matt Ryan/49 5.00 12.00
15 Percy Harvin/49 4.00 10.00
16 Michael Crabtree/25 5.00 12.00
18 DeMarco Murray/49 5.00 12.00
19 A.J. Green/25 8.00 20.00
20 Julio Jones/25 8.00 20.00
21 Steve Johnson/49 5.00 12.00
22 Steven Jackson/49 4.00 10.00
23 C.J. Spiller/49 4.00 10.00
24 Maurice Jones-Drew/25 5.00 12.00
25 Mike Wallace/49 4.00 10.00
26 BenJarvus Green-Ellis/49 5.00 12.00
27 Matt Forte/49 4.00 10.00
28 Larry Fitzgerald/49 5.00 12.00
29 Julius Peppers/49 5.00 12.00
31 Josh Freeman/25 6.00 15.00
32 Sidney Rice/25 5.00 12.00
33 Mike Singletary/49 8.00 20.00
35 Jonathan Stewart/49 4.00 10.00
36 Michael Turner/49 4.00 10.00
37 Zach Miller/49 4.00 10.00
38 Miles Austin/25 5.00 12.00
39 Kenny Britt/25 5.00 12.00
40 Jermaine Gresham/49 5.00 12.00
41 Jason Witten/25 6.00 15.00
42 Marvin Harrison/25 8.00 20.00
43 Eric Decker/49 4.00 10.00
44 Andy Dalton/49 5.00 12.00
45 Jay Cutler/49 4.00 10.00
46 DeSean Jackson/49 5.00 12.00
48 Tony Romo/49 5.00 12.00
49 Jimmy Graham/25 8.00 20.00
50 Philip Rivers/49 6.00 15.00
51 Demaryius Thomas/49 5.00 12.00
52 Drew Brees/25 8.00 20.00
53 Sam Bradford/49 4.00 10.00
54 Marques Colston/25 5.00 12.00
55 Santonio Holmes/25 5.00 12.00
56 Von Miller/25 6.00 15.00
57 LaDainian Tomlinson/49 6.00 15.00
58 Steve Young/49 10.00 25.00
59 Christian Ponder/49 4.00 10.00
60 Steve Largent/49 8.00 20.00
61 Willis McGahee/25 5.00 12.00
62 Jacob Tamme/49 4.00 10.00
63 Wes Welker/49 5.00 12.00
64 Dez Bryant/25 8.00 20.00
67 Chris Long/49 4.00 10.00
68 Ahmad Bradshaw/49 4.00 10.00
69 Barry Sanders/25 15.00 40.00
70 Dan Marino/49 15.00 40.00
71 Randall Cunningham/49 6.00 15.00
74 Darren McFadden/49 5.00 12.00
75 Lawrence Taylor/49 8.00 20.00
76 Shonn Greene/49 4.00 10.00
77 Trent Richardson/25 5.00 12.00
78 Santana Moss/25 6.00 15.00
79 Troy Polamalu/25 8.00 20.00
80 Antonio Gates/25 6.00 15.00

2013 Elite Primary Colors Silver
*GOLD/49: .8X TO 2X BASIC INSERTS
*RED/25: 1.2X TO 3X BASIC INSERTS
1 Ray Rice 1.00 2.50
2 Vincent Jackson 1.00 2.50
3 Justin Blackmon 1.00 2.50
4 Michael Crabtree 1.00 2.50
5 Jay Cutler 1.00 2.50
6 Wes Welker 1.25 3.00
7 C.J. Spiller 1.00 2.50
8 Hakeem Nicks 1.00 2.50
9 Cam Newton 1.50 4.00
10 Tony Romo 1.25 3.00
11 Calvin Johnson 1.50 4.00
12 Andre Johnson 1.00 2.50
13 Andrew Luck 2.50 6.00
14 Carson Palmer 1.25 3.00
15 LeSean McCoy 1.50 4.00
16 Mike Wallace 1.00 2.50
17 Ryan Mathews 1.25 3.00
18 Russell Wilson 3.00 8.00
19 Sam Bradford 1.00 2.50
20 Pierre Garcon 1.25 3.00

2013 Elite Prime Numbers Jerseys Prime
1 Jamaal Charles/90 5.00 12.00
2 Adrian Peterson/70 6.00 15.00
4 Demaryius Thomas/90 5.00 12.00
5 Drew Brees/40 8.00 20.00
6 Torrey Smith/90 4.00 10.00
8 Matt Ryan/90 5.00 12.00
10 Eli Manning/20

2013 Elite Pro Bowl Standouts Jerseys
*PRIME/49: .6X TO 1.5X JSY/299
*PRIME/15-25: .8X TO 2X JSY/294-299
1 A.J. Green/299 4.00 10.00
2 David Akers/299 2.50 6.00
3 DeMarcus Ware/299 4.00 10.00
4 Drew Brees/299 4.00 10.00
5 Eli Manning/199 3.00 8.00
7 Jerod Mayo/75 4.00 10.00
8 Larry Fitzgerald/149 3.00 8.00
9 London Fletcher/299 3.00 8.00
10 Patrick Peterson/294 2.50 6.00
11 Philip Rivers/299 4.00 10.00
12 Steve Smith/299 3.00 8.00
13 Tony Gonzalez/299 3.00 8.00
14 Von Miller/299 3.00 8.00
15 Vonta Leach/299 2.50 6.00

2013 Elite Rookie Hard Hats
1 Aaron Dobson 1.25 3.00
2 Josh Boyce 1.25 3.00
3 Ezekiel Ansah 1.25 3.00
4 Zach Ertz 2.50 6.00
5 Matt Barkley 1.25 3.00
6 Jordan Poyer 1.25 3.00
7 Landry Jones 1.25 3.00
8 Jarvis Jones 1.25 3.00
9 Markus Wheaton 1.25 3.00
10 Le'Veon Bell 4.00 10.00
11 Tavarres King 1.25 3.00
12 Montee Ball 1.25 3.00
13 Zac Dysert 1.25 3.00
14 Giovani Bernard 1.25 3.00
15 Tyler Eifert 1.25 3.00
16 Cobi Hamilton 1.25 3.00
17 Rex Burkhead 1.50 4.00
18 Vance McDonald 1.50 4.00
19 Margus Hunt 1.25 3.00
20 Sheldon Richardson 1.25 3.00
21 Dee Milliner 1.25 3.00
22 Geno Smith 1.25 3.00
23 Eddie Lacy 1.25 3.00
24 Johnathan Franklin 1.25 3.00
25 Datone Jones 3.00 8.00
26 Eric Fisher 1.25 3.00
27 Kenjon Barner 1.25 3.00
28 Star Lotulelei 1.50 4.00
29 Keenan Allen 2.50 6.00
30 Chance Warmack 1.25 3.00
31 Manti Te'o 1.50 4.00
32 Tavon Austin 1.50 4.00
33 Alec Ogletree 1.25 3.00
34 Stedman Bailey 1.25 3.00
35 Johnthan Banks 1.25 3.00
36 Mike Glennon 1.25 3.00
37 Tyler Wilson 1.25 3.00
38 Nick Kasa 1.25 3.00
39 Darius Slay 1.25 3.00
40 EJ Manuel 1.25 3.00
41 Robert Woods 2.00 5.00
42 Marquise Goodwin 1.25 3.00
43 Da'Rick Rogers 2.50 6.00
44 Chris Gragg 1.25 3.00
45 Marcus Davis 1.25 3.00
46 Dennis Johnson 1.25 3.00
47 Damontre Moore 1.25 3.00
48 Ryan Nassib 1.25 3.00
49 Matt Scott 1.25 3.00
50 Ryan Otten 1.25 3.00
51 Ace Sanders 1.25 3.00
52 Luke Joeckel 1.25 3.00
53 Denard Robinson 1.25 3.00
54 Alex Okafor 1.25 3.00
55 Kevin Minter 1.25 3.00
56 Ryan Swope 1.25 3.00
57 Andre Ellington 1.25 3.00
58 Stepfan Taylor 1.25 3.00
59 Tyrann Mathieu 2.00 5.00
60 Marcus Lattimore 1.25 3.00
61 Quinton Patton 1.25 3.00
62 Eric Reid 1.50 4.00
63 Arthur Brown 1.25 3.00
64 DeAndre Hopkins 3.00 8.00
65 Sam Montgomery 1.25 3.00
66 Ray Graham 1.25 3.00
67 Knile Davis 1.25 3.00
68 D.J. Hayden 1.25 3.00
69 Mike Gillislee 1.25 3.00
70 Dion Jordan 1.25 3.00
71 Dion Sims 1.25 3.00
72 Jamar Taylor 1.25 3.00
73 Gavin Escobar 2.50 6.00
74 Joseph Randle 1.25 3.00
75 Terrance Williams 1.25 3.00
76 Christine Michael 1.25 3.00
77 Chris Harper 1.25 3.00
78 Justin Hunter 1.25 3.00
79 Marquess Wilson 2.00 5.00
80 Jasper Collins 1.25 3.00
81 Kenny Vaccaro 2.50 6.00
82 Kenny Stills 1.25 3.00
83 Conner Vernon 1.25 3.00
84 Aaron Mellette 2.00 5.00
85 Cornellius Carradine 1.25 3.00
86 Matt Elam 1.25 3.00
87 Theo Riddick 1.25 3.00
88 Corey Fuller 1.25 3.00
89 Rodney Smith 2.50 6.00
90 Xavier Rhodes 1.25 3.00
91 Cordarrelle Patterson 1.25 3.00
92 Tyler Bray 1.25 3.00
93 Travis Kelce 3.00 8.00
94 Barkevious Mingo 1.25 3.00
95 Bjoern Werner 1.25 3.00
96 Kerwynn Williams 1.25 3.00
97 Desmond Trufant 1.25 3.00
98 Jawan Jamison 2.50 6.00
99 Jordan Reed 2.00 5.00
100 Phillip Thomas 2.50 6.00

2013 Elite Rookie Hard Hats Autographs
1 Aaron Dobson/99 4.00 10.00
2 Josh Boyce/199 4.00 10.00
3 Ezekiel Ansah/49 5.00 12.00
4 Zach Ertz/199 8.00 20.00
5 Matt Barkley/99 4.00 10.00
6 Jordan Poyer/199 4.00 10.00
7 Landry Jones/99 4.00 10.00
8 Jarvis Jones/199 4.00 10.00
9 Markus Wheaton/99 4.00 10.00
10 Le'Veon Bell/199 12.00 30.00
11 Tavarres King/49 5.00 12.00
12 Montee Ball/199 4.00 10.00
13 Zac Dysert/99 4.00 10.00
14 Giovani Bernard/99 4.00 10.00
15 Tyler Eifert/199 4.00 10.00
16 Cobi Hamilton/49
17 Rex Burkhead/199 15.00 30.00
18 Vance McDonald/99
19 Margus Hunt/199 4.00 10.00
20 Sheldon Richardson/49
21 Dee Milliner/199 4.00 10.00
22 Geno Smith/99 4.00 10.00
23 Eddie Lacy/99 4.00 10.00
24 Johnathan Franklin/199 4.00 10.00
25 Datone Jones/199 4.00 10.00
26 Eric Fisher/199 4.00 10.00
27 Kenjon Barner/199 4.00 10.00
28 Star Lotulelei/49
29 Keenan Allen/99 8.00 20.00
30 Chance Warmack/199 4.00 10.00
31 Manti Te'o/199 5.00 12.00
32 Tavon Austin/199 5.00 12.00
33 Alec Ogletree/199 6.00 15.00
34 Stedman Bailey/199 4.00 10.00
35 Johnthan Banks/49 5.00 12.00
36 Mike Glennon/99 4.00 10.00
37 Tyler Wilson/99 4.00 10.00
38 Nick Kasa/199 4.00 10.00
39 Darius Slay/199 4.00 10.00
40 EJ Manuel/99 4.00 10.00
41 Robert Woods/99 6.00 15.00
42 Marquise Goodwin/199 4.00 10.00
43 Da'Rick Rogers/199 4.00 10.00
44 Chris Gragg/199 4.00 10.00
45 Marcus Davis/199 4.00 10.00
46 Dennis Johnson/199 5.00 12.00
47 Damontre Moore/199 4.00 10.00
48 Ryan Nassib/99 4.00 10.00
49 Matt Scott/199 4.00 10.00
50 Ryan Otten/199 4.00 10.00
51 Ace Sanders/199 8.00 20.00
52 Luke Joeckel/99 4.00 10.00
53 Denard Robinson/99
54 Alex Okafor/199 4.00 10.00
55 Kevin Minter/199 4.00 10.00
56 Ryan Swope/199 4.00 10.00
57 Andre Ellington/199 4.00 10.00
58 Stepfan Taylor/199 4.00 10.00
59 Tyrann Mathieu/199 6.00 15.00
60 Marcus Lattimore/199 4.00 10.00
61 Quinton Patton/199 4.00 10.00
62 Eric Reid/199 8.00 20.00
63 Arthur Brown/199 4.00 10.00
64 DeAndre Hopkins/99 10.00 25.00
65 Sam Montgomery/199 4.00 10.00
66 Ray Graham/49
67 Knile Davis/199 4.00 10.00
68 D.J. Hayden/49
69 Mike Gillislee/99 4.00 10.00
70 Dion Jordan/199 10.00 25.00
71 Dion Sims/199 4.00 10.00
72 Jamar Taylor/49
73 Gavin Escobar/199 8.00 20.00
74 Joseph Randle/199 4.00 10.00
75 Terrance Williams/99 4.00 10.00
76 Christine Michael/149 4.00 10.00
77 Chris Harper/49 5.00 12.00
78 Justin Hunter/199 4.00 10.00
79 Marquess Wilson/49
80 Jasper Collins/199 4.00 10.00
81 Kenny Vaccaro/199 4.00 10.00
82 Kenny Stills/199 4.00 10.00
83 Conner Vernon/99 4.00 10.00
84 Aaron Mellette/199 4.00 10.00
85 Cornellius Carradine/49
86 Matt Elam/199 4.00 10.00
87 Theo Riddick/49
88 Corey Fuller/199 4.00 10.00
89 Rodney Smith/199 5.00 12.00
90 Xavier Rhodes/199 4.00 10.00
91 Cordarrelle Patterson/99 4.00 10.00
92 Tyler Bray/199 4.00 10.00
93 Travis Kelce/199 15.00 40.00
94 Barkevious Mingo/199 4.00 10.00
95 Bjoern Werner/199 4.00 10.00
96 Kerwynn Williams/49
97 Desmond Trufant/199 4.00 10.00
98 Jawan Jamison/49
99 Jordan Reed/99
100 Phillip Thomas/199 4.00 10.00

2013 Elite Rookie Inscriptions Black Ink
SP GROUP A TOO SCARCE TO PRICE
SP GRP B ANNC'd PRINT RUN UNDER 50
2 Matt Barkley 15.00 40.00
3 Cordarrelle Patterson
4 Eddie Lacy SP B 8.00 20.00
5 Keenan Allen SP A
6 Mike Glennon
7 DeAndre Hopkins
8 Tavon Austin 8.00 20.00
9 Tyler Wilson 6.00 15.00
10 Robert Woods 10.00 25.00
11 Quinton Patton SP A
12 Ryan Nassib SP B 8.00 20.00
13 Giovani Bernard 6.00 15.00
14 Justin Hunter
15 Terrance Williams
16 Markus Wheaton
17 EJ Manuel SP A
18 Denard Robinson SP B 8.00 20.00
19 Johnathan Franklin 6.00 15.00
20 Joseph Randle
21 Tyler Eifert 6.00 15.00
22 Zach Ertz SP B 15.00 40.00
23 Aaron Dobson
24 Knile Davis SP B 15.00 40.00
25 Landry Jones SP B 10.00 25.00
26 Montee Ball 6.00 15.00
27 Andre Ellington SP B 8.00 20.00
28 Le'Veon Bell 20.00 50.00
29 Christine Michael SP B 10.00 25.00
30 Stedman Bailey 12.00 30.00
31 Vance McDonald
32 Mike Gillislee
33 Jordan Reed 10.00 25.00
34 Stepfan Taylor
35 Manti Te'o SP A
36 Marquise Goodwin
37 Marcus Lattimore SP B 8.00 20.00
38 Gavin Escobar
39 Kenny Stills SP A

2013 Elite Rookie Inscriptions Blue Ink
SP GROUP A TOO SCARCE TO PRICE
SP GRP B ANNC'd PRINT RUN UNDER 50
1 Geno Smith 5.00 12.00
2 Matt Barkley 12.00 30.00
3 Cordarrelle Patterson 5.00 12.00
4 Eddie Lacy 5.00 12.00
5 Keenan Allen 8.00 20.00
6 Mike Glennon 5.00 12.00
7 DeAndre Hopkins 8.00 20.00
8 Tavon Austin SP B 8.00 20.00
9 Tyler Wilson 5.00 12.00
10 Robert Woods SP A 8.00 20.00
11 Quinton Patton 5.00 12.00
12 Ryan Nassib SP A
13 Giovani Bernard 5.00 12.00
14 Justin Hunter 5.00 12.00
15 Terrance Williams 5.00 12.00
16 Markus Wheaton 5.00 12.00
17 EJ Manuel 12.00 30.00
18 Denard Robinson 5.00 12.00
19 Johnathan Franklin 5.00 12.00
20 Joseph Randle 5.00 12.00
21 Tyler Eifert SP B 6.00 15.00
22 Zach Ertz 10.00 25.00
23 Aaron Dobson 5.00 12.00
24 Knile Davis 8.00 20.00
25 Landry Jones 5.00 12.00
26 Montee Ball 5.00 12.00
27 Andre Ellington 5.00 12.00
28 Le'Veon Bell

29 Christine Michael 8.00 20.00
30 Stedman Bailey SP B 12.00 30.00
31 Vance McDonald 6.00 15.00
32 Mike Gillislee 8.00 20.00
33 Jordan Reed 8.00 20.00
34 Stepfan Taylor 5.00 12.00
35 Manti Te'o 15.00 40.00
36 Marquise Goodwin 5.00 12.00
37 Marcus Lattimore 5.00 12.00
38 Gavin Escobar 5.00 12.00
39 Kenny Stills 5.00 12.00

2013 Elite Rookie Inscriptions Green Ink

SP GROUP A TOO SCARCE TO PRICE
SP GRP B ANNC'd PRINT RUN UNDER 50
2 Matt Barkley SP B 25.00 60.00
3 Cordarrelle Patterson SP B 8.00 20.00
4 Eddie Lacy SP B 8.00 20.00
5 Keenan Allen SP A
6 Mike Glennon SP A 8.00 20.00
7 DeAndre Hopkins SP B 15.00 40.00
8 Tavon Austin 8.00 20.00
9 Tyler Wilson SP A
10 Robert Woods 10.00 25.00
11 Quinton Patton SP A
12 Ryan Nassib 6.00 15.00
13 Giovani Bernard SP B 8.00 20.00
14 Justin Hunter SP B 12.00 30.00
15 Terrance Williams 6.00 15.00
16 Markus Wheaton SP B 8.00 20.00
17 EJ Manuel SP B 30.00 80.00
18 Denard Robinson SP B
19 Johnathan Franklin SP A
20 Joseph Randle SP B 8.00 20.00
21 Tyler Eifert SP A
22 Zach Ertz 12.00 30.00
23 Aaron Dobson
24 Knile Davis SP A
25 Landry Jones 6.00 15.00
26 Montee Ball 6.00 15.00
27 Andre Ellington 6.00 15.00
28 Le'Veon Bell SP B 30.00 60.00
29 Christine Michael SP B 8.00 20.00
30 Stedman Bailey 12.00 30.00
31 Vance McDonald SP A
32 Mike Gillislee SP A
33 Jordan Reed SP B 12.00 30.00
34 Stepfan Taylor SP B
35 Manti Te'o SP A 10.00 25.00
36 Marquise Goodwin SP B 8.00 20.00
37 Marcus Lattimore SP B 8.00 20.00
38 Gavin Escobar SP A
39 Kenny Stills 6.00 15.00

2013 Elite Rookie Inscriptions Red Ink

SP GROUP A TOO SCARCE TO PRICE
SP GRP B ANNC'd PRINT RUN UNDER 50
1 Geno Smith SP B 8.00 20.00
2 Matt Barkley SP B
3 Cordarrelle Patterson SP B 8.00 20.00
4 Eddie Lacy SP B 8.00 20.00
5 Keenan Allen SP B
6 Mike Glennon SP A
7 DeAndre Hopkins SP B 15.00 40.00
8 Tavon Austin SP A
9 Tyler Wilson SP A
10 Robert Woods SP B
11 Quinton Patton SP B 8.00 20.00
12 Ryan Nassib 6.00 15.00
13 Giovani Bernard 6.00 15.00
14 Justin Hunter SP B 8.00 20.00
15 Terrance Williams SP B
16 Markus Wheaton SP B 8.00 20.00
17 EJ Manuel SP B 20.00 80.00
18 Denard Robinson SP B 8.00 20.00
19 Johnathan Franklin SP A
20 Joseph Randle SP B 8.00 20.00
21 Tyler Eifert 6.00 15.00
22 Zach Ertz 12.00 30.00
23 Aaron Dobson
24 Knile Davis SP A
25 Landry Jones SP B 8.00 20.00
26 Montee Ball SP A 8.00 20.00
27 Andre Ellington SP B 8.00 20.00
28 Le'Veon Bell 30.00 60.00
29 Christine Michael SP A
30 Stedman Bailey 12.00 30.00
31 Vance McDonald SP B 10.00 25.00
32 Mike Gillislee SP B
33 Jordan Reed 10.00 25.00
34 Stepfan Taylor SP B
35 Manti Te'o SP A
36 Marquise Goodwin SP B
37 Marcus Lattimore SP A
38 Gavin Escobar SP A
39 Kenny Stills SP B 8.00 20.00

2013 Elite Starstruck Silver

*GOLD/49: .8X TO 2X BASIC INSERTS
*RED/25: 1.2X TO 3X BASIC INSERTS
1 A.J. Green 1.50 4.00
2 Torrey Smith 1.00 2.50
3 Mike Wallace 1.00 2.50
4 Arian Foster 1.25 3.00
5 Chris Johnson 1.00 2.50
6 C.J. Spiller 1.00 2.50
7 Tom Brady 4.00 10.00
8 Peyton Manning 3.00 8.00
9 Jamaal Charles 1.25 3.00
10 Brandon Marshall 1.25 3.00
11 Calvin Johnson 1.50 4.00
12 Aaron Rodgers 2.50 6.00
13 Adrian Peterson 1.50 4.00
14 Julio Jones 1.50 4.00
15 Cam Newton 1.50 4.00
16 Drew Brees 1.50 4.00
17 Dez Bryant 1.50 4.00
18 Colin Kaepernick 1.25 3.00
19 Robert Griffin III 1.00 2.50
20 Russell Wilson 3.00 8.00

2013 Elite Status Autographs Gold

*GOLD/49: .6X TO 1.5X TOTC/199-299
*GOLD/49: .5X TO 1.2X TOTC/99-149

2013 Elite Status Autographs Red

132 EJ Manuel/25 25.00 60.00
172 Montee Ball/25 6.00 15.00
190 Tavon Austin/25 8.00 20.00

2013 Elite Turn of the Century Autographs

101 Aaron Dobson/299 3.00 8.00
102 Aaron Mellette/299 3.00 8.00
103 Ace Sanders/199 3.00 8.00
104 Arthur Brown/199 3.00 8.00
105 Alec Ogletree/299 3.00 8.00
106 Alex Okafor/299 3.00 8.00
107 Andre Ellington/299 3.00 8.00
108 Barkevious Mingo/299 3.00 8.00
109 Bjoern Werner/299 3.00 8.00
110 Chance Warmack/199 3.00 8.00
111 Darius Slay/199 3.00 8.00
112 Chris Gragg/299 3.00 8.00
113 Chris Harper/49
114 Christine Michael/149 4.00 10.00
115 D.J. Hayden/49
116 Eric Fisher/199 3.00 8.00
117 Cobi Hamilton/49
118 Knile Davis/199 3.00 8.00
119 Conner Vernon/199 3.00 8.00
120 Cordarrelle Patterson/299 3.00 8.00
121 Corey Fuller/299 3.00 8.00
122 Damontre Moore/299 3.00 8.00
123 Da'Rick Rogers/299 3.00 8.00
124 Datone Jones/199 3.00 8.00
125 DeAndre Hopkins/299 8.00 20.00
126 Dee Milliner/299 3.00 8.00
127 Denard Robinson/99 4.00 10.00
128 Desmond Trufant/299 3.00 8.00
129 Dion Jordan/199 3.00 8.00
130 Dion Sims/299 3.00 8.00
131 Eddie Lacy/299 3.00 8.00
132 EJ Manuel/99 4.00 10.00
133 Eric Reid/299 4.00 10.00
134 Gavin Escobar/299 3.00 8.00
135 Geno Smith/99 4.00 10.00
136 Giovani Bernard/299 3.00 8.00
137 Jamar Taylor/49
138 Jarvis Jones/299 3.00 8.00
139 Jawan Jamison/49
140 Cornellius Carradine/49
141 Johnathan Franklin/299 3.00 8.00
142 Dennis Johnson/199 3.00 8.00
143 Johnthan Banks/49
144 Jordan Poyer/299 3.00 8.00
145 Jordan Reed/99 6.00 15.00
146 Joseph Randle/299 3.00 8.00
147 Josh Boyce/299 3.00 8.00
148 Justin Hunter/199 3.00 8.00
149 Keenan Allen/299 6.00 15.00
150 Kenjon Barner/299 3.00 8.00
151 Kenny Stills/299 3.00 8.00
152 Kenny Vaccaro/299 3.00 8.00
153 Kerwynn Williams/49
154 Kevin Minter/299 3.00 8.00
155 Landry Jones/299 3.00 8.00
156 Le'Veon Bell/299 15.00 40.00
157 Ezekiel Ansah/49 5.00 12.00
158 Luke Joeckel/99 4.00 10.00
159 Manti Te'o/299 4.00 10.00
160 Marcus Davis/299 3.00 8.00
161 Marcus Lattimore/299 3.00 8.00
162 Margus Hunt/299 3.00 8.00
163 Jasper Collins/199 3.00 8.00
164 Markus Wheaton/299 3.00 8.00
165 Marquess Wilson/49
166 Marquise Goodwin/299 3.00 8.00
167 Matt Barkley/299 3.00 8.00
168 Matt Elam/299 3.00 8.00
169 Matt Scott/199 3.00 8.00
170 Mike Gillislee/99 4.00 10.00
171 Mike Glennon/299 3.00 8.00
172 Montee Ball/299 3.00 8.00
173 Nick Kasa/299 3.00 8.00
174 Phillip Thomas/299 3.00 8.00
175 Quinton Patton/299 3.00 8.00
176 Ray Graham/49
177 Rex Burkhead/299 4.00 10.00
178 Tyrann Mathieu/199 12.50 25.00
179 Robert Woods/299 5.00 12.00
180 Rodney Smith/299 3.00 8.00
181 Ryan Nassib/99 4.00 10.00
182 Ryan Otten/299 3.00 8.00
183 Ryan Swope/299 3.00 8.00
184 Sam Montgomery/299 3.00 8.00
185 Sheldon Richardson/49
186 Star Lotulelei/49
187 Stedman Bailey/299 3.00 8.00
188 Stepfan Taylor/299 3.00 8.00
189 Tavarres King/49
190 Tavon Austin/299 4.00 10.00
191 Terrance Williams/299 3.00 8.00
192 Theo Riddick/49
193 Travis Kelce/299 12.00 30.00
194 Tyler Bray/299 3.00 8.00
195 Tyler Eifert/299 3.00 8.00
196 Tyler Wilson/299 3.00 8.00
197 Vance McDonald/99
198 Xavier Rhodes/299 3.00 8.00
199 Zac Dysert/299 3.00 8.00
200 Zach Ertz/299 6.00 15.00

2013 Elite Zoning Commission Silver

*GOLD/49: .8X TO 2X BASIC INSERTS
*RED/25: 1.2X TO 3X BASIC INSERTS
1 Arian Foster 1.25 3.00
2 Alfred Morris 1.00 2.50
3 Adrian Peterson 1.50 4.00
4 Stevan Ridley 1.00 2.50
5 Marshawn Lynch 1.25 3.00
6 Doug Martin 1.25 3.00
7 Trent Richardson 1.00 2.50
8 Michael Turner 1.00 2.50
9 Mikel Leshoure 1.00 2.50
10 Ray Rice 1.00 2.50
11 James Jones 1.00 2.50
12 Eric Decker 1.00 2.50
13 Dez Bryant 1.50 4.00
14 A.J. Green 1.50 4.00
15 Rob Gronkowski 1.50 4.00
16 Brandon Marshall 1.25 3.00
17 Marques Colston 1.00 2.50
18 Victor Cruz 1.25 3.00
19 Julio Jones 1.50 4.00
20 Demaryius Thomas 1.25 3.00

2014 Elite

COMP.SET w/o RC's (100) 10.00 20.00
ROOKIE PRINT RUN 499-999
1 Carson Palmer .25 .60
2 Larry Fitzgerald .25 .60
3 Patrick Peterson .20 .50
4 Matt Ryan .25 .60
5 Julio Jones .30 .75
6 Steven Jackson .20 .50
7 Joe Flacco .25 .60
8 Torrey Smith .20 .50
9 Ray Rice .20 .50
10 EJ Manuel .20 .50
11 Steve Johnson .25 .60
12 C.J. Spiller .20 .50
13 Cam Newton .30 .75
14 Jerricho Cotchery .20 .50
15 Luke Kuechly .25 .60
16 Jay Cutler .20 .50
17 Brandon Marshall .20 .50
18 Jared Allen .20 .50
19 Andy Dalton .25 .60
20 A.J. Green .30 .75
21 Giovani Bernard .20 .50
22 Josh Gordon .20 .50
23 Jordan Cameron .20 .50
24 Joe Haden .20 .50
25 Tony Romo .25 .60
26 Dez Bryant .30 .75
27 DeMarco Murray .25 .60
28 Peyton Manning .60 1.50
29 Demaryius Thomas .25 .60
30 Wes Welker .25 .60
31 Montee Ball .20 .50
32 Matthew Stafford .25 .60
33 Calvin Johnson .30 .75
34 Ndamukong Suh .25 .60
35 Reggie Bush .20 .50
36 Aaron Rodgers .60 1.50
37 Jordy Nelson .25 .60
38 Eddie Lacy .20 .50
39 Andre Johnson .25 .60
40 Arian Foster .25 .60
41 J.J. Watt .30 .75
42 Andrew Luck .40 1.00
43 Reggie Wayne .25 .60
44 Trent Richardson .20 .50
45 Justin Blackmon .20 .50
46 Toby Gerhart .20 .50
47 Alex Smith .25 .60
48 Dwayne Bowe .25 .60
49 Jamaal Charles .25 .60
50 Derrick Johnson .20 .50
51 Ryan Tannehill .25 .60
52 Mike Wallace .20 .50
53 Knowshon Moreno .20 .50
54 Greg Jennings .20 .50
55 Adrian Peterson .30 .75
56 Kyle Rudolph .20 .50
57 Tom Brady .75 2.00
58 Julian Edelman .30 .75
59 Stevan Ridley .20 .50
60 Rob Gronkowski .30 .75
61 Drew Brees .30 .75
62 Marques Colston .20 .50
63 Jimmy Graham .30 .75
64 Eli Manning .25 .60
65 Victor Cruz .25 .60
66 Rueben Randle .20 .50
67 Geno Smith .20 .50
68 Chris Ivory .25 .60
69 Matt Schaub .20 .50
70 Darren McFadden .20 .50
71 Nick Foles .25 .60
72 Jeremy Maclin .20 .50
73 LeSean McCoy .30 .75
74 Ben Roethlisberger .30 .75
75 Antonio Brown .30 .75
76 Le'Veon Bell .25 .60
77 Philip Rivers .30 .75
78 Keenan Allen .25 .60
79 Ryan Mathews .25 .60
80 Colin Kaepernick .25 .60
81 Anquan Boldin .20 .50
82 Michael Crabtree .20 .50
83 Aldon Smith .20 .50
84 Russell Wilson .50 1.25
85 Percy Harvin .20 .50
86 Marshawn Lynch .25 .60
87 Richard Sherman .30 .75
88 Doug Baldwin .25 .60
89 Sam Bradford .20 .50
90 Jared Cook .20 .50
91 Tavon Austin .20 .50
92 Zac Stacy .20 .50
93 Josh McCown .20 .50
94 Vincent Jackson .20 .50
95 Doug Martin .25 .60
96 Kendall Wright .20 .50
97 Jake Locker .25 .60
98 Robert Griffin III .20 .50
99 DeSean Jackson .25 .60
100 Alfred Morris .20 .50
101 Aaron Donald/499 RC 2.50 6.00
102 Aaron Murray/999 RC 1.00 2.50
103 A.J. McCarron/999 RC 1.00 2.50
104 Allen Robinson/799 RC 1.50 4.00
105 Andre Williams/799 RC 1.00 2.50
106 Anthony Barr/499 RC 1.00 2.50
107 Taylor Lewan/799 RC 1.00 2.50
108 Austin Seferian-Jenkins/799 RC 1.00 2.50
109 Bishop Sankey/999 RC 1.00 2.50
110 Blake Bortles/499 RC 1.25 3.00
111 Brandin Cooks/499 RC 1.50 4.00
112 Brandon Coleman/799 RC 1.00 2.50
113 Brett Smith/799 RC 1.00 2.50
114 Bruce Ellington/799 RC 1.00 2.50
115 C.J. Fiedorowicz/799 RC 1.00 2.50
116 C.J. Mosley/499 RC 1.25 3.00
117 Calvin Pryor/499 RC 1.00 2.50
118 Carlos Hyde/999 RC 1.25 3.00
119 Charles Sims/999 RC 1.00 2.50
120 Marcus Smith/799 RC 1.00 2.50
121 Chris Smith/799 RC 1.00 2.50
122 Cody Latimer/999 RC 1.25 3.00
123 Connor Shaw/799 RC 1.00 2.50
124 Darqueze Dennard/499 RC 1.25 3.00
125 Davante Adams/999 RC 1.50 4.00
126 David Fales/799 RC 1.00 2.50
127 Justin Gilbert/999 RC 1.00 2.50
128 De'Anthony Thomas/799 RC 1.00 2.50
129 Dee Ford/499 RC 1.00 2.50
130 Deone Bucannon/499 RC 1.00 2.50
131 Derek Carr/999 RC 6.00 15.00
132 Devonta Freeman/799 RC 1.50 4.00
133 Donte Moncrief/799 RC 1.00 2.50
134 Dri Archer/999 RC 1.00 2.50
135 Ed Reynolds/799 RC 1.00 2.50
136 Eric Ebron/499 RC 1.25 3.00
137 Greg Robinson/499 RC 1.00 2.50
138 Ha Ha Clinton-Dix/499 RC 1.25 3.00
139 Jace Amaro/799 RC 1.00 2.50
140 Jadeveon Clowney/499 RC 1.25 3.00
141 Jake Matthews/499 RC 1.00 2.50
142 James Wilder Jr./799 RC 1.25 3.00
143 Jared Abbrederis/799 RC 1.00 2.50
144 Jarvis Landry/799 RC 2.00 5.00
145 Jason Verrett/499 RC 1.00 2.50
146 Jeff Janis/999 RC 1.00 2.50
147 Jeremy Hill/999 RC 1.25 3.00
148 Jerick McKinnon/999 RC 1.25 3.00
149 Jimmie Ward/499 RC 1.25 3.00
150 Jimmy Garoppolo/999 RC 8.00 20.00
151 Johnny Manziel/499 RC 1.50 4.00
152 Jordan Matthews/999 RC 1.50 4.00
153 Josh Huff/999 RC 1.25 3.00
154 Ka'Deem Carey/999 RC 1.00 2.50
155 Kelvin Benjamin/499 RC 1.50 4.00
156 Kevin Norwood/999 RC 1.00 2.50
157 Khalil Mack/499 RC 4.00 10.00
158 Kony Ealy/799 RC 1.25 3.00
159 Kyle Fuller/499 RC 1.00 2.50
160 Kyle Van Noy/799 RC 1.25 3.00
161 L'Damian Washington/999 RC 1.25 3.00
162 Lache Seastrunk/799 RC 1.00 2.50
163 Lamarcus Joyner/799 RC 1.25 3.00
164 Devin Street/999 RC 1.00 2.50
165 Louis Nix III/799 RC 1.00 2.50
166 Logan Thomas/999 RC 1.00 2.50
167 Marion Grice/999 RC 1.00 2.50
168 Marqise Lee/999 RC 1.25 3.00
169 Martavis Bryant/999 RC 1.25 3.00
170 Matt Hazel/799 RC 1.00 2.50
171 Michael Campanaro/999 RC 1.00 2.50
172 Michael Sam/799 RC 1.00 2.50
173 Mike Davis/799 RC 1.00 2.50
174 Mike Evans/499 RC 2.50 6.00
175 Odell Beckham Jr./499 RC 2.50 6.00
176 Paul Richardson/999 RC 1.25 3.00
177 Rajion Neal/799 RC 1.00 2.50
178 Ra'Shede Hageman/799 RC 1.00 2.50
179 Robert Herron/999 RC 1.00 2.50
180 Ryan Shazier/499 RC 1.50 4.00
181 Sammy Watkins/499 RC 1.50 4.00
182 Scott Crichton/799 RC 1.00 2.50
183 Shaq Evans/799 RC 1.00 2.50
184 Shayne Skov/799 RC 1.00 2.50
185 Stephon Tuitt/999 RC 1.50 4.00
186 Tajh Boyd/999 RC 1.00 2.50
187 Teddy Bridgewater/499 RC 1.50 4.00
188 Telvin Smith/999 RC 1.00 2.50
189 Terrance West/999 RC 1.00 2.50
190 Timmy Jernigan/999 RC 1.00 2.50
191 Tom Savage/999 RC 1.00 2.50
192 Travis Swanson/999 RC 1.00 2.50
193 Tre Mason/999 RC 1.00 2.50
194 Trent Murphy/999 RC 1.00 2.50
195 Trevor Reilly/999 RC 1.00 2.50
196 Troy Niklas/999 RC 1.00 2.50
197 Tyler Gaffney/999 RC 1.00 2.50
198 Bradley Roby/999 RC 1.00 2.50
199 Zach Mettenberger/999 RC 1.00 2.50
200 Zack Martin/499 RC 1.25 3.00

2014 Elite Clear

*VETS/72-99: 5X TO 12X BASIC CARDS
*ROOKIES/73-08: .8X TO 2X BASIC CARDS
*ROOKIES/64-68: .8X TO 2X BASIC CARDS

2014 Elite Aspirations

*VETS/70-99: 5X TO 12X BASIC CARDS
*ROOKIES/70-99: .8X TO 2X BASIC CARDS
*VETS/54-68: 6X TO 15X BASIC CARDS
*ROOKIES/41-49: 1X TO 2.5X BASIC CARDS
*ROOKIES/30-48: 1.2X TO 3X BASIC CARDS
*VETS/20-44: 10X TO 25X BASIC CARDS
*ROOKIES/20-28: 1.5X TO 4X BASIC CARDS

2014 Elite Status

*VETS/69-91: 3X TO 8X BASIC CARDS
*ROOKIES/64-99: .5X TO 1.2X BASIC CARDS
*VETS/42-59: 4X TO 10X BASIC CARDS
*ROOKIES/41-59: .6X TO 1.5X BASIC CARDS
*VETS/30-39: 5X TO 12X BASIC CARDS
*ROOKIES/30-38: .8X TO 2X BASIC CARDS
*VETS/20-29: 6X TO 15X BASIC CARDS
*ROOKIES/20-29: 1X TO 2.5X BASIC CARDS
27 DeMarco Murray/29 6.00 15.00
127 Justin Gilbert/21 8.00 20.00
159 Kyle Fuller/23 2.50 6.00

2014 Elite Status Gold

*GOLD VETS/49: 15X TO 40X BASIC CARDS
101 Aaron Donald AU/199 8.00 20.00
102 Aaron Murray AU/199 3.00 8.00
103 A.J. McCarron AU/25 6.00 15.00
104 Allen Robinson AU/199 5.00 12.00
105 Andre Williams AU/199 3.00 8.00
106 Anthony Barr AU/199 3.00 8.00
107 Taylor Lewan AU/199 3.00 8.00
108 Austin Seferian-Jenkins AU/199 3.00 8.00
109 Bishop Sankey AU/199 10.00 25.00
110 Blake Bortles AU/25 8.00 20.00
111 Brandin Cooks AU/199 5.00 12.00
112 Brandon Coleman AU/199 3.00 8.00
113 Brett Smith AU/49 4.00 10.00
114 Bruce Ellington AU/199 3.00 8.00
115 C.J. Fiedorowicz AU/199 3.00 8.00
117 Calvin Pryor AU/199 3.00 8.00
118 Carlos Hyde AU/199 4.00 10.00
119 Charles Sims AU/199 3.00 8.00
120 Marcus Smith AU/199 3.00 8.00
121 Chris Smith AU/199 3.00 8.00
122 Cody Latimer AU/199 4.00 10.00
123 Connor Shaw AU/199 3.00 8.00
124 Darqueze Dennard AU/199 4.00 10.00
126 David Fales AU/25
128 De'Anthony Thomas AU/199 3.00 8.00
129 Dee Ford AU/199 3.00 8.00
130 Deone Bucannon AU/199 3.00 8.00
131 Derek Carr AU/25 40.00 100.00
132 Devonta Freeman AU/199 5.00 12.00
133 Donte Moncrief AU/199 3.00 8.00
134 Dri Archer AU/199 3.00 8.00
135 Ed Reynolds AU/199 3.00 8.00
136 Eric Ebron AU/25 8.00 20.00
138 Ha Ha Clinton-Dix AU/199 4.00 10.00
139 Jace Amaro AU/199 3.00 8.00
140 J.Clowney AU/49 EXCH 4.00 10.00
141 Jake Matthews AU/199 3.00 8.00
142 James Wilder Jr. AU/199 4.00 10.00
143 Jared Abbrederis AU/199 3.00 8.00
145 Jason Verrett AU/199 3.00 8.00
146 Jeff Janis AU/199 3.00 8.00
147 Jeremy Hill AU/199 4.00 10.00
148 Jerick McKinnon AU/199 4.00 10.00
149 Jimmie Ward AU/199 4.00 10.00
150 Jimmy Garoppolo AU/25 50.00 125.00
151 Johnny Manziel AU/25 10.00 25.00
152 Jordan Matthews AU/199 5.00 12.00
153 Josh Huff AU/199 4.00 10.00
154 Ka'Deem Carey AU/199 3.00 8.00
155 Kelvin Benjamin AU/25 10.00 25.00
156 Kevin Norwood AU/199 3.00 8.00
157 Khalil Mack AU/199 12.00 30.00
158 Kony Ealy AU/199 4.00 10.00
159 Kyle Fuller AU/199 3.00 8.00
160 Kyle Van Noy AU/199 4.00 10.00
161 L'Damian Washington AU/199 4.00 10.00
162 Lache Seastrunk AU/99 3.00 8.00
163 Lamarcus Joyner AU/199 4.00 10.00
164 Devin Street AU/199 3.00 8.00
165 Louis Nix III AU/199 3.00 8.00
166 Logan Thomas AU/25 6.00 15.00
167 Marion Grice AU/199 3.00 8.00
168 Marqise Lee AU/25 8.00 20.00
169 Martavis Bryant AU/199 4.00 10.00
170 Matt Hazel AU/199 3.00 8.00
171 Michael Campanaro AU/199 3.00 8.00
172 Michael Sam AU/199 3.00 8.00
173 Mike Davis AU/199 3.00 8.00
174 Mike Evans AU/25
175 Odell Beckham Jr. AU/199 30.00 60.00
176 Paul Richardson AU/199 4.00 10.00
177 Rajion Neal AU/199 3.00 8.00
178 Ra'Shede Hageman AU/199 3.00 8.00
179 Robert Herron AU/199 3.00 8.00
180 Ryan Shazier AU/199 5.00 12.00
181 Sammy Watkins AU/25 10.00 25.00
182 Scott Crichton AU/199 3.00 8.00
183 Shaq Evans AU/199 3.00 8.00
184 Shayne Skov AU/199 3.00 8.00
186 Tajh Boyd AU/199 3.00 8.00
187 Teddy Bridgewater AU/25 10.00 25.00
188 Telvin Smith AU/199 3.00 8.00
189 Terrance West AU/199 3.00 8.00
190 Timmy Jernigan AU/199 3.00 8.00
191 Tom Savage AU/199 3.00 8.00
192 Travis Swanson AU/199 3.00 8.00
194 Trent Murphy AU/199 3.00 8.00
195 Trevor Reilly AU/199 3.00 8.00
196 Troy Niklas AU/199 3.00 8.00
197 Tyler Gaffney AU/199 3.00 8.00
198 Bradley Roby AU/199 3.00 8.00
200 Zack Martin AU/199 6.00 15.00

2014 Elite Status Red

*RED VETS/25: 8X TO 20X BASIC CARDS
*RED RK AU/49: .5X TO 1.2X GOLD AU/99-199
*RED RK AU/25: .5X TO 1.2X GOLD AU/49
*RED RK AU/15: .4X TO 1X GOLD AU/25

2014 Elite Turn of the Century

*VETS/199: 2.5X TO 6X BASIC CARDS
*ROOK/199: .5X TO 1.2X BASIC CARDS

2014 Elite Clarity

COMMON CARD 2.50 6.00
SEMISTARS 3.00 8.00
UNLISTED STARS 4.00 10.00
1 Rob Gronkowski 4.00 10.00
2 Adrian Peterson 4.00 10.00
3 C.J. Spiller 2.50 6.00
4 Ryan Tannehill 3.00 8.00
5 Chris Ivory 3.00 8.00
6 Joe Flacco 3.00 8.00
7 Giovani Bernard 2.50 6.00
8 Josh Gordon 2.50 6.00
9 Le'Veon Bell 3.00 8.00
10 Ben Roethlisberger 4.00 10.00
11 Arian Foster 3.00 8.00
12 Andrew Luck 5.00 12.00
13 Ace Sanders 2.50 6.00
14 Chris Johnson 2.50 6.00
15 Montee Ball 2.50 6.00
16 Peyton Manning 8.00 20.00
17 Jamaal Charles 3.00 8.00
18 Ryan Mathews 3.00 8.00
19 DeMarco Murray 3.00 8.00
20 Dez Bryant 4.00 10.00
21 Victor Cruz 3.00 8.00
22 LeSean McCoy 4.00 10.00
23 Alfred Morris 2.50 6.00
24 Robert Griffin III 2.50 6.00
25 Matt Forte 2.50 6.00
26 Alshon Jeffery 3.00 8.00
27 Reggie Bush 2.50 6.00
28 Calvin Johnson 4.00 10.00
29 Eddie Lacy 2.50 6.00
30 Steven Jackson 2.50 6.00
31 Cam Newton 4.00 10.00
32 DeAngelo Williams 2.50 6.00
33 Mark Ingram 3.00 8.00
34 Drew Brees 4.00 10.00
35 Doug Martin 3.00 8.00
36 Larry Fitzgerald 3.00 8.00
37 Zac Stacy 2.50 6.00
38 Frank Gore 3.00 8.00
39 Russell Wilson 6.00 15.00
40 Marshawn Lynch 3.00 8.00
41 Stevan Ridley 2.50 6.00
42 Ray Rice 2.50 6.00
43 Trent Richardson 2.50 6.00
44 Dwayne Bowe 3.00 8.00
45 Jeremy Maclin 2.50 6.00
46 Jordy Nelson 3.00 8.00
47 Andre Ellington 2.50 6.00
48 A.J. Green 4.00 10.00
49 Lamar Miller 2.50 6.00

2014 Elite Down and Distance Second

*FIRST/99: .3X TO .8X SECOND/49
*FIRST/49: .3X TO .8X SECOND/25
*THIRD/25: .6X TO 1.5X SECOND/49
1 Eddie Lacy/25 3.00 8.00
2 Keenan Allen/49 4.00 10.00
4 Julius Thomas/49 3.00 8.00
5 Russell Wilson/25 8.00 20.00
6 Larry Fitzgerald/49 4.00 10.00
7 Le'Veon Bell/49 4.00 10.00
8 Marques Colston/25 3.00 8.00
10 Jordan Cameron/49 3.00 8.00
12 Cordarrelle Patterson/25 8.00 20.00
13 Cam Newton/25 10.00 25.00
14 DeMarco Murray/49 4.00 10.00
15 Geno Smith/49 3.00 8.00
16 Andre Johnson/49 4.00 10.00
20 Manti Te'o/25 4.00 10.00
21 Peyton Manning/25 10.00 25.00
22 Anquan Boldin/25 3.00 8.00
25 Jordan Reed/49 3.00 8.00

2014 Elite Face 2 Face Silver

*GOLD/49: 1X TO 2.5X SILVER
*RED/25: 1.5X TO 4X SILVER
1 M.Crabtree/R.Sherman 1.25 3.00
2 D.Thomas/Chancellor 1.25 3.00
3 C.Kaepernick/R.Wilson 2.00 5.00
4 T.Brady/P.Manning 3.00 8.00
5 S.Smith/A.Talib 1.00 2.50
6 Cromartie/M.Wallace .75 2.00
7 E.Manuel/G.Smith .75 2.00
8 A.Green/J.Haden 1.25 3.00
9 A.Brown/L.Webb 1.25 3.00
10 J.Watt/A.Luck 3.00 8.00
11 D.Thomas/B.Flowers 1.00 2.50
12 J.Thomas/E.Weddle .75 2.00
13 E.Manning/T.Romo 1.00 2.50
14 R.Griffin III/N.Foles 1.00 2.50
15 D.Hall/D.Bryant 1.25 3.00
16 Stafford/C.Matthews 1.25 3.00
17 C.Johnsn/P.Petersn 1.25 3.00
18 C.Newton/D.Brees 1.25 3.00
19 S.Jackson/L.Kuechly 1.00 2.50
20 M.Lynch/N.Bowman 1.00 2.50

2014 Elite Gridiron Jersey Kings

*PRIME/25: .5X TO 1.2X BASIC JSY/49-99
*PRIME/25: .6X TO 1.5X BASIC JSY/149-199
1 A.J. Green/99 4.00 10.00
2 Adrian Peterson/49 8.00 20.00
3 Alfred Morris/149 2.00 5.00
4 Andy Dalton/199 2.50 6.00
5 Antonio Gates/99 2.50 6.00
6 Arian Foster/99 3.00 8.00
7 Brian Hartline/199 2.00 5.00
8 Malcolm Smith/99 4.00 10.00
9 C.J. Spiller/199 2.00 5.00
11 DeMarco Murray/99 3.00 8.00
12 Demaryius Thomas/199 2.50 6.00
13 Derrick Johnson/199 2.00 5.00
14 Reggie Bush/25 3.00 8.00
15 Dez Bryant/75 4.00 10.00
16 Dwayne Bowe/199 2.50 6.00
17 Eli Manning/199 2.50 6.00
18 Eric Berry/199 2.50 6.00
19 Cam Newton/49 8.00 20.00
20 Greg Olsen/49 3.00 8.00
21 Haloti Ngata/199 2.00 5.00
22 Jamaal Charles/199 2.50 6.00
23 Jason Witten/49 3.00 8.00
24 Jay Cutler/99 2.50 6.00
25 Giovani Bernard/99 2.50 6.00
26 Joe Flacco/199 2.50 6.00
27 Joe Haden/199 2.00 5.00
28 Josh Gordon/199 2.00 5.00
29 Julio Jones/49 4.00 10.00
30 Chris Ivory/99 3.00 8.00
31 Justin Blackmon/199 2.00 5.00
34 Larry Fitzgerald/199 2.50 6.00
35 Leonard Hankerson/99 2.50 6.00
36 LeSean McCoy/25
37 Marques Colston/49 2.50 6.00
41 Von Miller/25 4.00 10.00
42 Anquan Boldin/25 3.00 8.00
45 Pierre Garcon/25
46 Robert Griffin III/25 3.00 8.00
48 Robert Woods/49 3.00 8.00
49 Ryan Tannehill/199 2.50 6.00
50 Sam Bradford/49 2.50 6.00
51 Stevan Ridley/25 3.00 8.00
52 Steve Johnson/199 2.50 6.00
53 Tamba Hali/99 2.50 6.00
55 Terrell Suggs/199 2.00 5.00
56 Tony Romo/49 10.00 25.00
57 Torrey Smith/25 3.00 8.00
58 Tyler Eifert/25
59 Vontaze Burfict/99 2.50 6.00
60 Wes Welker/25 4.00 10.00
61 Shonn Greene/199 2.00 5.00
62 Kamerion Wimbley/199 2.00 5.00
63 Dannell Ellerbe/199 2.00 5.00
64 Kirk Cousins/199 3.00 8.00
65 Keenan Allen/99 3.00 8.00
66 EJ Manuel/25 3.00 8.00
67 Danny Woodhead/99 3.00 8.00
68 Aldon Smith/99 2.50 6.00
69 Carson Palmer/99 3.00 8.00
70 Vincent Jackson/25
71 Alex Smith/199 2.50 6.00
72 Julius Thomas/99 2.50 6.00
73 Earl Thomas/49 3.00 8.00

2014 Elite Legends of the Fall Silver

*GOLD/49: 1X TO 2.5X SILVER
*RED/25: 1.5X TO 4X SILVER
1 Tom Brady 3.00 8.00
2 Michael Vick 1.00 2.50
3 Terrell Suggs .75 2.00
4 Geno Atkins .75 2.00
5 Ben Roethlisberger 1.25 3.00
6 Andre Johnson 1.00 2.50
7 Reggie Wayne 1.00 2.50
8 Maurice Jones-Drew .75 2.00
9 Chris Johnson .75 2.00
10 Peyton Manning 2.50 6.00
11 Derrick Johnson .75 2.00
12 Antonio Gates .75 2.00
13 Tony Romo 1.00 2.50
14 Eli Manning 1.00 2.50
15 DeSean Jackson 1.00 2.50
16 Brian Orakpo .75 2.00
17 Charles Tillman 1.00 2.50
18 Ndamukong Suh 1.00 2.50
19 Clay Matthews 1.25 3.00
20 Greg Jennings .75 2.00
21 Roddy White .75 2.00
22 Steve Smith 1.00 2.50
23 Drew Brees 1.25 3.00
24 Vincent Jackson .75 2.00
25 Larry Fitzgerald 1.00 2.50
26 James Laurinaitis 1.00 2.50
27 Vernon Davis .75 2.00
28 Marshawn Lynch 1.00 2.50
29 Mario Williams .75 2.00
30 Mike Wallace .75 2.00

2014 Elite Marks

EMCJ C.J. Spiller/99 6.00 15.00
EMDP Dennis Pitta/99 6.00 15.00
EMEL Eddie Lacy/99 6.00 15.00
EMFG Frank Gore/15 12.00 30.00
EMGB Giovani Bernard/49 8.00 20.00
EMJB Jarrett Boykin/299 8.00 20.00
EMKAL Kiko Alonso/49 8.00 20.00
EMMB Marlon Brown/49 8.00 20.00
EMMR Matt Ryan/25
EMRS Richard Sherman/25 15.00 40.00
EMRT Ryan Tannehill/99 8.00 20.00
EMTH T.Y. Hilton/199 6.00 15.00
EMTM Tyrann Mathieu/49 10.00 25.00
EMZS Zac Stacy/25 10.00 25.00

2014 Elite New Breed Jerseys

*PRIME/99: .8X TO 2X JSY/299
1 Aaron Murray 1.25 3.00
2 A.J. McCarron 1.25 3.00
3 Allen Robinson 2.00 5.00
4 Andre Williams 1.25 3.00
5 Austin Seferian-Jenkins 1.25 3.00
6 Bishop Sankey 1.25 3.00
7 Blake Bortles 1.50 4.00
8 Brandin Cooks 2.00 5.00
9 De'Anthony Thomas 1.25 3.00
10 Carlos Hyde 1.50 4.00
11 Charles Sims 1.25 3.00
12 Davante Adams 2.00 5.00
13 Logan Thomas 1.25 3.00
14 Connor Shaw 1.25 3.00
15 Devonta Freeman 2.00 5.00
16 Donte Moncrief 1.25 3.00
17 Eric Ebron 1.50 4.00
18 Asa Watson 2.00 5.00
19 Jadeveon Clowney 1.50 4.00
20 Jarvis Landry 2.50 6.00
21 Jeremy Hill 1.50 4.00
22 Derek Carr 8.00 20.00
23 Jimmy Garoppolo 10.00 25.00
24 Johnny Manziel 2.00 5.00
25 Jordan Matthews 2.00 5.00
26 Ka'Deem Carey 4.00 10.00
27 Kelvin Benjamin 2.00 5.00
28 Cody Latimer 1.50 4.00
29 Marqise Lee 2.00 5.00
30 Dri Archer 1.25 3.00
31 Mike Evans 3.00 8.00
32 Odell Beckham Jr. 3.00 8.00
33 Paul Richardson 1.50 4.00
34 Khalil Mack 5.00 12.00
35 Sammy Watkins 2.00 5.00
36 Teddy Bridgewater 2.00 5.00
37 Terrance West 1.25 3.00
38 Tre Mason 1.25 3.00
39 Tajh Boyd 1.25 3.00
40 Tom Savage 2.00 5.00

2014 Elite New Breed Jerseys Autographs

1 Aaron Murray/149 6.00 15.00
3 Allen Robinson/149 5.00 12.00
4 Andre Williams/49 5.00 12.00
5 Austin Seferian-Jenkins/149 3.00 8.00
6 Bishop Sankey/149 15.00 40.00
8 Brandin Cooks/149 5.00 12.00
9 De'Anthony Thomas/149 3.00 8.00
10 Carlos Hyde/149 4.00 10.00
11 Charles Sims/149 3.00 8.00
13 Logan Thomas/25 6.00 15.00
14 Connor Shaw/149 3.00 8.00
15 Devonta Freeman/149 12.00 30.00
16 Donte Moncrief/149 8.00 20.00
17 Eric Ebron/25 8.00 20.00
19 Jadeveon Clowney/49 6.00 15.00
21 Jeremy Hill/149 4.00 10.00
23 Jimmy Garoppolo/49 60.00 125.00
24 Johnny Manziel/25 10.00 25.00
25 Jordan Matthews/149 5.00 12.00
26 Ka'Deem Carey/149 8.00 20.00
28 Cody Latimer/149 10.00 25.00
29 Marqise Lee/25 8.00 20.00
30 Dri Archer/149 3.00 8.00
31 Mike Evans/49 12.00 30.00
32 Odell Beckham Jr./149 30.00 60.00
33 Paul Richardson/149 4.00 10.00
34 Khalil Mack/149 12.00 30.00
35 Sammy Watkins/49 8.00 20.00
36 Teddy Bridgewater/49 8.00 20.00
37 Terrance West/149 3.00 8.00
39 Tajh Boyd/149 3.00 8.00
40 Tom Savage/149 3.00 8.00

2014 Elite New Breed Jerseys Autographs Prime

*PRIME/49: .6X TO 1.5X JSY AU/149
*PRIME/25: .5X TO 1.2X JSY AU/49
*PRIME/15: .6X TO 1.5X JSY AU/49
*PRIME/15 .5X TO 1.2X JSY AU/25

2014 Elite Passing the Torch Autographs

STATED PRINT RUN 2-25
UNPRICED PRINT RUN 2-20
3 A.Morris/E.Lacy/25 12.00 30.00
6 J.Bettis/L.Bell/25 100.00 200.00
8 J.Seau/M.Te'o/25 50.00 100.00
11 P.Burress/O.Beckham/25 60.00 125.00
13 D.Carr/J.Plunkett/25 50.00 100.00

2014 Elite Passing the Torch Silver

*GOLD/49: 1X TO 2.5X SILVER
*RED/25: 1.5X TO 4X SILVER
1 L.Kuechly/S.Richardson 1.00 2.50
2 R.Griffin III/E.Lacy .75 2.00
3 P.Manning/T.Brady 3.00 8.00
4 D.Brees/P.Manning 2.50 6.00
5 R.Wilson/W.Moon 2.00 5.00
6 C.Kaepernick/J.Montana 4.00 10.00
7 A.Luck/P.Manning 2.50 6.00
8 R.Sherman/M.Trufant 1.25 3.00
9 T.Austin/T.Holt .75 2.00
10 A.Johnson/D.Hopkins 1.00 2.50
11 M.Faulk/Z.Stacy 1.00 2.50
12 C.Patterson/R.Moss .75 2.00
13 A.Rodgers/B.Favre 4.00 10.00
14 G.Bernard/C.Dillon .75 2.00
15 E.Lacy/A.Green 1.00 2.50

2014 Elite Profiles Silver

*GOLD/49: 1X TO 2.5X SILVER
*RED/25: 1.5X TO 4X SILVER
1 Russell Wilson 2.00 5.00
2 Peyton Manning 2.50 6.00
3 Cam Newton 1.25 3.00
4 Colin Kaepernick 1.00 2.50
5 Richard Sherman 1.25 3.00

2014 Elite Rookie Autographs

*RED INK: .5X TO 1.2X BASIC AU
1 Aaron Murray 4.00 10.00
2 A.J. McCarron 4.00 10.00
3 Allen Robinson 6.00 15.00
4 Andre Williams 6.00 15.00
5 Austin Seferian-Jenkins 5.00 12.00
6 Bishop Sankey 6.00 15.00
7 Blake Bortles 5.00 12.00
8 Brandin Cooks 6.00 15.00
9 De'Anthony Thomas 6.00 15.00
10 Carlos Hyde 5.00 12.00
11 Charles Sims 5.00 12.00
12 Davante Adams 6.00 15.00
13 Logan Thomas 4.00 10.00
14 Derek Carr 15.00 40.00
15 Devonta Freeman 6.00 15.00
16 Donte Moncrief 5.00 12.00
17 Eric Ebron 5.00 12.00
18 Jace Amaro 4.00 10.00
19 Jadeveon Clowney 5.00 12.00
20 Jarvis Landry 6.00 15.00
21 Jeremy Hill 5.00 12.00
23 Jimmy Garoppolo 50.00 100.00
24 Johnny Manziel 6.00 15.00
25 Jordan Matthews 6.00 15.00
26 Ka'Deem Carey 4.00 10.00
27 Kelvin Benjamin 6.00 15.00
28 Cody Latimer 5.00 12.00
29 Marqise Lee 6.00 15.00
30 Dri Archer 4.00 10.00
31 Mike Evans 10.00 25.00
33 Paul Richardson 5.00 12.00
35 Sammy Watkins 6.00 15.00
36 Teddy Bridgewater 6.00 15.00
37 Terrance West 5.00 12.00
38 Tre Mason 8.00 20.00
39 Tajh Boyd 5.00 12.00
40 Tom Savage 6.00 15.00

2014 Elite Rookie Clear Signatures

1 Jadeveon Clowney 5.00 12.00
2 Blake Bortles 5.00 12.00
3 Sammy Watkins 6.00 15.00
4 Mike Evans 10.00 25.00
5 Eric Ebron 5.00 12.00
6 Johnny Manziel 6.00 15.00
7 Teddy Bridgewater 6.00 15.00
8 Derek Carr 25.00 60.00
9 Marqise Lee 12.00 30.00
10 Jeremy Hill 5.00 12.00
11 Cody Latimer 5.00 12.00
12 Tre Mason 4.00 10.00
13 Donte Moncrief 4.00 10.00
14 Dri Archer 4.00 10.00
15 Ka'Deem Carey 4.00 10.00
16 Logan Thomas 4.00 10.00
17 Tom Savage 4.00 10.00
18 A.J. McCarron 4.00 10.00
19 Bishop Sankey 4.00 10.00
20 Jordan Matthews 6.00 15.00

2014 Elite Rookie Debut Numbers

RN1 Anthony Barr 1.25 3.00
RN2 C.J. Mosley 1.50 4.00
RN3 Ha Ha Clinton-Dix 1.50 4.00
RN4 Marion Grice 1.25 3.00
RN5 DeMarcus Lawrence 1.50 4.00
RN6 Tyler Gaffney 1.25 3.00
RN7 C.J. Fiedorowicz 1.25 3.00
RN8 Josh Huff 1.50 4.00
RN9 John Brown 2.00 5.00
RN10 Jerick McKinnon 1.50 4.00
RN11 Bruce Ellington 1.25 3.00
RN12 Shaq Evans 1.25 3.00
RN13 Martavis Bryant 1.50 4.00
RN14 Kevin Norwood 1.25 3.00
RN15 James White 2.50 6.00
RN16 Devin Street 1.25 3.00
RN17 Jared Abbrederis 1.25 3.00
RN18 Zach Mettenberger 1.25 3.00
RN19 David Fales 1.25 3.00
RN20 Lache Seastrunk 1.25 3.00

2014 Elite Rookie Debut Numbers Autographs

AB Anthony Barr/199 6.00 15.00
BE Bruce Ellington/199 6.00 15.00
CJ C.J. Fiedorowicz/199 6.00 15.00
DF David Fales/25 6.00 15.00
DS Devin Street/199 6.00 15.00
HC Ha Ha Clinton-Dix/199 8.00 20.00
JA Jared Abbrederis/199 6.00 15.00
JB John Brown/199 12.00 30.00
JH Josh Huff/199 6.00 15.00
JM Jerick McKinnon/199 8.00 20.00
JW James White/199
KN Kevin Norwood/199 6.00 15.00
LS Lache Seastrunk/99 8.00 20.00
MB Martavis Bryant/199 8.00 20.00
MG Marion Grice/199 6.00 15.00
SE Shaq Evans/199 6.00 15.00
TG Tyler Gaffney/199 6.00 15.00

2014 Elite Rookie Inscriptions

1 Aaron Murray
2 A.J. McCarron 6.00 15.00
3 Allen Robinson 10.00 25.00
4 Andre Williams 6.00 15.00
5 Austin Seferian-Jenkins 6.00 15.00
6 Bishop Sankey 6.00 15.00
7 Blake Bortles 8.00 20.00
8 Brandin Cooks 10.00 25.00
9 De'Anthony Thomas 6.00 15.00
10 Carlos Hyde 12.00 30.00
11 Charles Sims 6.00 15.00
12 Davante Adams 10.00 25.00
13 Logan Thomas 6.00 15.00
14 Derek Carr 40.00 100.00
15 Devonta Freeman 10.00 25.00
16 Donte Moncrief 6.00 15.00
17 Eric Ebron 8.00 20.00
18 Jace Amaro 6.00 15.00
19 Jadeveon Clowney
20 Jarvis Landry 12.00 30.00
21 Jeremy Hill 8.00 20.00
23 Jimmy Garoppolo 50.00 100.00
24 Johnny Manziel 10.00 25.00
25 Jordan Matthews 10.00 25.00
26 Ka'Deem Carey 6.00 15.00
27 Kelvin Benjamin 10.00 25.00
28 Cody Latimer 8.00 20.00
29 Marqise Lee 8.00 20.00
30 Dri Archer
31 Mike Evans 15.00 40.00
32 Odell Beckham Jr. 30.00 60.00
33 Paul Richardson 8.00 20.00
35 Sammy Watkins 10.00 25.00
36 Teddy Bridgewater 10.00 25.00
37 Terrance West 6.00 15.00
38 Tre Mason
39 Tajh Boyd 6.00 15.00
40 Tom Savage 6.00 15.00

2014 Elite Rookie Premiere Signatures

1 Jadeveon Clowney 8.00 20.00
2 Blake Bortles 8.00 20.00
3 Sammy Watkins 10.00 25.00
4 Mike Evans 15.00 40.00
5 Eric Ebron 8.00 20.00
6 Johnny Manziel 10.00 25.00
7 Teddy Bridgewater 10.00 25.00
8 Derek Carr 25.00 60.00
9 Marqise Lee 8.00 20.00
10 Jeremy Hill 8.00 20.00
11 Cody Latimer 8.00 20.00
12 Tre Mason 6.00 15.00
13 Donte Moncrief 6.00 15.00
14 Dri Archer 6.00 15.00
15 Ka'Deem Carey 6.00 15.00
16 Logan Thomas 6.00 15.00
17 Tom Savage 6.00 15.00
18 A.J. McCarron 6.00 15.00
19 Bishop Sankey 6.00 15.00
20 Jordan Matthews 10.00 25.00

2014 Elite Series Silver

*GOLD/49: .8X TO 2X SILVER
*RED/25: 1.2X TO 3X SILVER
1 C.J. Spiller 1.00 2.50

2 Rob Gronkowski 1.50 4.00
3 Muhammad Wilkerson 1.00 2.50
4 Torrey Smith 1.00 2.50
5 A.J. Green 1.50 4.00
6 Josh Gordon 1.00 2.50
7 Antonio Brown 1.50 4.00
8 Arian Foster 1.25 3.00
9 Andrew Luck 2.00 5.00
10 Demaryius Thomas 1.25 3.00
11 Jamaal Charles 1.25 3.00
12 Philip Rivers 1.50 4.00
13 Dez Bryant 1.50 4.00
14 Victor Cruz 1.25 3.00
15 LeSean McCoy 1.50 4.00
16 Robert Griffin III 1.00 2.50
17 Brandon Marshall 1.00 2.50
18 Calvin Johnson 2.00 5.00
19 Aaron Rodgers 3.00 8.00
20 Adrian Peterson 1.50 4.00
21 Julio Jones 1.50 4.00
22 Cam Newton 1.50 4.00
23 Jimmy Graham 1.50 4.00
24 Doug Martin 1.25 3.00
25 Patrick Peterson 1.00 2.50
26 Zac Stacy 1.00 2.50
27 Colin Kaepernick 1.25 3.00
28 Russell Wilson 2.50 6.00
29 Richard Sherman 1.50 4.00
30 Wes Welker 1.25 3.00

2014 Elite Sophomore Swatches

1 Justin Hunter/99 2.00 5.00
2 Zac Stacy/49 2.00 5.00
3 Tyler Eifert/49 2.50 6.00
4 Giovani Bernard/99 2.00 5.00
5 Montee Ball/99 2.00 5.00
6 Mike Gillislee/99 2.00 5.00
7 Kenny Vaccaro/99 2.00 5.00
8 DeAndre Hopkins/99 2.50 6.00
9 Kiko Alonso/49 2.00 5.00
10 EJ Manuel/49 2.00 5.00
11 Eddie Lacy/49 2.00 5.00
12 Robert Woods/99 2.50 6.00
13 Manti Te'o/99 2.50 6.00
14 Keenan Allen/99 2.50 6.00
15 Tavon Austin/99 2.00 5.00
16 Barkevious Mingo/99 2.00 5.00
17 Knile Davis/99 2.00 5.00
18 Jordan Reed/99 2.00 5.00
19 Sheldon Richardson/99 2.00 5.00
20 Le'Veon Bell/99 5.00 12.00

2014 Elite Throwback Threads

1 Jake Plummer/60 3.00 8.00
2 Michael Vick/199 2.50 6.00
3 Ed Reed/199 2.50 6.00
4 Anquan Boldin/99 3.00 8.00
6 Willis McGahee/99 3.00 8.00
7 Thurman Thomas/99 4.00 10.00
8 Ryan Fitzpatrick/199 2.50 6.00
9 Jim Kelly/199 3.00 8.00
10 Darrelle Revis/199 2.00 5.00
11 Anthony Fasano/199 2.00 5.00
12 Walter Payton/25 20.00 50.00
13 Percy Harvin/199 2.00 5.00
14 Mike Singletary/49 5.00 12.00
15 Kyle Orton/199 2.00 5.00
16 Eric Decker/199 2.00 5.00
17 Greg Olsen/35 4.00 10.00
18 Elvis Dumervil/199 3.00 8.00
19 Boomer Esiason/199 2.50 6.00
20 Cris Collinsworth/25
21 Mike Wallace/199 2.00 5.00
23 Ozzie Newsome/199 2.50 6.00
24 Jim Brown/49 6.00 15.00
26 Colt McCoy/199 2.00 5.00
27 Ben Watson/199 2.00 5.00
28 Craig Morton/199 2.00 5.00
29 Emmitt Smith/99 8.00 20.00
30 Darren Sproles/99 4.00 10.00
31 Mario Manningham/199 2.00 5.00
32 Miles Austin/199 2.00 5.00
33 Roger Staubach/99 6.00 15.00
36 Terence Newman/199 2.00 5.00
37 Emmanuel Sanders/199 2.50 6.00
38 John Elway/199 5.00 12.00
39 Jay Cutler/199 2.00 5.00
40 Jake Plummer/199 2.00 5.00
41 Kenny Britt/199 2.00 5.00
42 Dustin Keller/199 2.00 5.00
43 Brandon Marshall/120 2.00 5.00
44 Barry Sanders/199 5.00 12.00
45 Knowshon Moreno/199 2.00 5.00
46 Jermichael Finley/199 2.00 5.00
47 Brett Favre/49 10.00 25.00
48 Matt Schaub/199 2.00 5.00
50 Fred Taylor/199 2.00 5.00
51 Joe Montana/199 12.00 30.00
53 Darrelle Revis/199 2.00 5.00
54 Karlos Dansby/199 2.00 5.00
55 Irving Fryar/65 3.00 8.00
56 Brandon Marshall/199 2.00 5.00
57 Reggie Bush/199 2.00 5.00
58 Sidney Rice/199 2.00 5.00
59 Wes Welker/99 8.00 20.00
61 Curtis Martin/199 2.50 6.00
62 Julius Peppers/199 2.50 6.00
63 Reggie Bush/199 2.00 5.00
64 Trent Richardson/199 2.00 5.00
65 Shonn Greene/199 2.00 5.00
66 Santana Moss/199 2.50 6.00
67 Maurice Jones-Drew/199 2.00 5.00
68 LaDainian Tomlinson/199 2.50 6.00
69 Jerry Rice/99 8.00 20.00
70 Darrius Heyward-Bey/92 3.00 8.00
71 Carson Palmer/199 2.50 6.00
72 Michael Vick/199 2.50 6.00
73 Jared Cook/199 2.00 5.00
74 Ahmad Bradshaw/199 2.00 5.00
75 Jerry Rice/199 5.00 12.00
76 Vincent Jackson/99 3.00 8.00
77 Shaun Alexander/25
78 Steven Jackson/199 2.00 5.00
79 Kurt Warner/49 4.00 10.00
80 Dallas Clark/199 2.00 5.00

2014 Elite Throwback Threads Prime

*PRIME/20-49: .5X TO 1.2X BASIC INSERTS
44 Barry Sanders/49 15.00 40.00
51 Joe Montana/49 50.00 120.00
56 Brandon Marshall/25 8.00 20.00
61 Curtis Martin/49 15.00 40.00
68 LaDainian Tomlinson/49 5.00 12.00

2014 Elite Turn of the Century Autographs

101 Aaron Donald 8.00 20.00
102 Aaron Murray 3.00 8.00
103 A.J. McCarron 5.00 12.00
104 Allen Robinson 5.00 12.00
105 Andre Williams 6.00 15.00
106 Anthony Barr 3.00 8.00
107 Taylor Lewan 3.00 8.00
108 Austin Seferian-Jenkins 3.00 8.00
109 Bishop Sankey 10.00 25.00
110 Blake Bortles 6.00 15.00
111 Brandin Cooks 5.00 12.00
112 Brandon Coleman 3.00 8.00
113 Brett Smith 3.00 8.00
114 Bruce Ellington 3.00 8.00
115 C.J. Fiedorowicz 3.00 8.00
117 Calvin Pryor 3.00 8.00
118 Carlos Hyde 4.00 10.00
119 Charles Sims 3.00 8.00
120 Marcus Smith 3.00 8.00
121 Chris Smith 3.00 8.00
122 Cody Latimer 4.00 10.00
123 Connor Shaw 3.00 8.00
124 Darqueze Dennard 4.00 10.00
126 David Fales 5.00 12.00
128 De'Anthony Thomas 3.00 8.00
129 Dee Ford 3.00 8.00
130 Deone Bucannon 3.00 8.00
131 Derek Carr 25.00 60.00
132 Devonta Freeman 5.00 12.00
133 Donte Moncrief 3.00 8.00
134 Dri Archer 3.00 8.00
135 Ed Reynolds 3.00 8.00
136 Eric Ebron 6.00 15.00
137 Greg Robinson 3.00 8.00
138 Ha Ha Clinton-Dix 4.00 10.00
139 Jace Amaro 3.00 8.00
140 Jadeveon Clowney 6.00 15.00
141 Jake Matthews 3.00 8.00
142 James Wilder Jr. 4.00 10.00
143 Jared Abbrederis 3.00 8.00
145 Jason Verrett 3.00 8.00
146 Jeff Janis 8.00 20.00
147 Jeremy Hill 4.00 10.00
148 Jerick McKinnon 5.00 12.00
149 Jimmie Ward 5.00 12.00
150 Jimmy Garoppolo 60.00 125.00
151 Johnny Manziel 8.00 20.00
152 Jordan Matthews 5.00 12.00
153 Josh Huff 4.00 10.00
154 Ka'Deem Carey 3.00 8.00
155 Kelvin Benjamin 8.00 20.00
156 Kevin Norwood 3.00 8.00
157 Khalil Mack 12.00 30.00
158 Kony Ealy 4.00 10.00
159 Kyle Fuller 3.00 8.00
160 Kyle Van Noy 4.00 10.00
161 L'Damian Washington 4.00 10.00
162 Lache Seastrunk 3.00 8.00
163 Lamarcus Joyner 4.00 10.00
164 Devin Street 3.00 8.00
165 Louis Nix III 3.00 8.00
166 Logan Thomas 5.00 12.00
167 Marion Grice 3.00 8.00
168 Marqise Lee 6.00 15.00
169 Martavis Bryant 4.00 10.00
170 Matt Hazel 3.00 8.00
171 Michael Campanaro 3.00 8.00
172 Michael Sam 8.00 20.00
173 Mike Davis 3.00 8.00
174 Mike Evans 12.00 30.00
175 Odell Beckham Jr. 30.00 60.00
176 Paul Richardson 4.00 10.00
177 Rajion Neal 5.00 12.00
178 Ra'Shede Hageman 3.00 8.00
179 Robert Herron 3.00 8.00
180 Ryan Shazier 5.00 12.00
181 Sammy Watkins 8.00 20.00
182 Scott Crichton 3.00 8.00
183 Shaq Evans 3.00 8.00
184 Shayne Skov 3.00 8.00
186 Tajh Boyd 3.00 8.00
187 Teddy Bridgewater 8.00 20.00
188 Telvin Smith 3.00 8.00
189 Terrance West 3.00 8.00
190 Timmy Jernigan 3.00 8.00
191 Tom Savage 6.00 15.00
192 Travis Swanson 3.00 8.00
194 Trent Murphy 3.00 8.00
195 Trevor Reilly 3.00 8.00
196 Troy Niklas 3.00 8.00
197 Tyler Gaffney 3.00 8.00
198 Bradley Roby 3.00 8.00
200 Zack Martin 6.00 15.00

2016 Elite

1 Matthew Stafford .25 .60
2 Jeremy Hill .20 .50
3 Marcus Mariota .30 .75
4 Jameis Winston .30 .75
5 Tom Brady .75 2.00
6 Carson Palmer .25 .60
7 DeMarco Murray .25 .60
8 Barry Sanders .50 1.25
9 Antonio Brown .30 .75
10 Franco Harris .30 .75
11 Calvin Johnson .30 .75
12 Golden Tate .20 .50
13 Delanie Walker .20 .50
14 Doug Martin .25 .60
15 Rob Gronkowski .30 .75
16 Larry Fitzgerald .25 .60
17 Jordan Matthews .25 .60
18 John Elway .50 1.25
19 Joe Flacco .25 .60
20 Marcus Allen .25 .60
21 Jay Cutler .20 .50
22 Jonathan Stewart .20 .50
23 Cam Newton .30 .75
24 Peyton Manning .60 1.50
25 Brandon Marshall .20 .50
26 Russell Wilson .40 1.00
27 Eli Manning .25 .60
28 Jerry Rice .50 1.25
29 Justin Forsett .25 .60
30 Warren Sapp .25 .60
31 Matt Forte .20 .50
32 Marcus Peters .20 .50
33 Greg Olsen .25 .60
34 Demaryius Thomas .25 .60
35 Darrelle Revis .20 .50
36 Marshawn Lynch .25 .60
37 Odell Beckham Jr. .30 .75
38 Joe Montana .75 2.00
39 Gary Barnidge .20 .50
40 Bo Jackson .40 1.00
41 Lamar Miller .20 .50
42 Julian Edelman .30 .75
43 Ted Ginn Jr. .20 .50
44 Jamaal Charles .25 .60
45 LeSean McCoy .30 .75
46 Todd Gurley .30 .75
47 Tony Romo .25 .60
48 Joe Namath .40 1.00
49 Isaiah Crowell .20 .50
50 Thurman Thomas .25 .60
51 DeAndre Hopkins .25 .60
52 Khalil Mack .30 .75
53 Matt Ryan .25 .60
54 Jeremy Maclin .20 .50
55 Sammy Watkins .30 .75
56 Nick Foles .25 .60
57 Dez Bryant .30 .75
58 Mike Ditka .30 .75
59 Teddy Bridgewater .25 .60
60 J.J. Watt .30 .75
61 Andrew Luck .40 1.00
62 Mike Evans .25 .60
63 Devonta Freeman .25 .60
64 Derek Carr .30 .75
65 Ryan Tannehill .25 .60
66 Colin Kaepernick .25 .60
67 A.J. Green .30 .75
68 Jim Kelly .30 .75
69 Adrian Peterson .30 .75
70 Latavius Murray .20 .50
71 T.Y. Hilton .25 .60
72 Emmanuel Sanders .30 .75
73 Julio Jones .30 .75
74 Amari Cooper .30 .75
75 Jarvis Landry .25 .60
76 Carlos Hyde .20 .50
77 Andy Dalton .25 .60
78 Tony Dorsett .30 .75
79 Aaron Rodgers .60 1.50
80 Frank Gore .25 .60
81 Blake Bortles .20 .50
82 Doug Baldwin .25 .60
83 Drew Brees .30 .75
84 Philip Rivers .30 .75
85 Kirk Cousins .30 .75
86 Emmitt Smith .50 1.25
87 Ben Roethlisberger .30 .75
88 Michael Strahan .25 .60
89 Jordy Nelson .25 .60
90 Darren McFadden .20 .50
91 Allen Robinson .25 .60
92 Eric Decker .20 .50
93 Brandin Cooks .25 .60
94 Antonio Gates .20 .50
95 DeSean Jackson .25 .60
96 Troy Aikman .40 1.00
97 Le'Veon Bell .25 .60
98 Larry Csonka .25 .60
99 Randall Cobb .25 .60
100 Chris Ivory .25 .60
101 Jalen Ramsey RC 1.50 4.00
102 Ronnie Stanley RC .75 2.00
103 DeForest Buckner RC .60 1.50
104 Jack Conklin RC 1.00 2.50
105 Leonard Floyd RC .75 2.00
106 Eli Apple RC .75 2.00
107 Vernon Hargreaves III RC 1.00 2.50
108 Sheldon Rankins RC .75 2.00
109 Laremy Tunsil RC .60 1.50
110 Karl Joseph RC .60 1.50
111 Taylor Decker RC .75 2.00
112 Keanu Neal RC .60 1.50
113 Shaq Lawson RC .60 1.50
114 Darron Lee RC .60 1.50
115 William Jackson III RC .75 2.00
116 Artie Burns RC .75 2.00
117 Kenny Clark RC .60 1.50
118 Robert Nkemdiche RC .75 2.00
119 Vernon Butler RC .60 1.50
120 Germain Ifedi RC .75 2.00
121 Emmanuel Ogbah RC .75 2.00
122 Kevin Dodd RC .60 1.50
123 Jaylon Smith RC .60 1.50
124 Myles Jack RC .75 2.00
125 Reggie Ragland RC .60 1.50
126 Austin Johnson RC .60 1.50
127 A'Shawn Robinson RC .60 1.50
128 Jarran Reed RC .60 1.50
129 Su'a Cravens RC .60 1.50
130 Mackensie Alexander RC .60 1.50
131 Vonn Bell RC .75 2.00
132 Maliek Collins RC .60 1.50
133 Will Redmond RC 1.00 2.50
134 Jonathan Bullard RC .60 1.50
135 Shilique Calhoun RC .60 1.50
136 Adolphus Washington RC .60 1.50
137 Austin Hooper RC .60 1.50
138 Kendall Fuller RC .75 2.00
139 Nick Vannett RC .60 1.50
140 Andrew Billings RC .75 2.00
141 Tajae Sharpe RC .75 2.00
142 DeAndre Washington RC .60 1.50
143 Jordan Payton RC .60 1.50
144 Tyreek Hill RC 2.50 6.00
145 Rashard Higgins RC .60 1.50
146 Moritz Bohringer RC .60 1.50
147 Jerell Adams RC .60 1.50
148 Jakeem Grant RC .60 1.50
149 Nate Sudfeld RC .60 1.50
150 Kolby Listenbee RC .60 1.50
151 Brandon Allen RC .60 1.50
152 Jeff Driskel RC .60 1.50
153 Kelvin Taylor RC .60 1.50
154 Aaron Burbridge RC .60 1.50
155 Brandon Doughty RC .60 1.50
156 Demarcus Ayers RC .60 1.50
157 Daniel Braverman RC .60 1.50
158 Thomas Duarte RC .60 1.50
159 Kenny Lawler RC 1.00 2.50
160 Scooby Wright III RC .60 1.50
161 Jared Goff RC 4.00 10.00
162 Carson Wentz RC 6.00 15.00
163 Joey Bosa RC 1.25 3.00
164 Ezekiel Elliott RC 3.00 8.00
165 Corey Coleman RC 1.00 2.50
166 Will Fuller RC 1.00 2.50
167 Josh Doctson RC .75 2.00
168 Laquon Treadwell RC .75 2.00
169 Paxton Lynch RC .60 1.50
170 Hunter Henry RC .75 2.00
171 Sterling Shepard RC .75 2.00
172 Derrick Henry RC 1.50 4.00
173 Michael Thomas RC 1.25 3.00
174 Christian Hackenberg RC .60 1.50
175 Tyler Boyd RC .75 2.00
176 Kenyan Drake RC 1.00 2.50
177 Braxton Miller RC .60 1.50
178 Leonte Carroo RC .60 1.50
179 C.J. Prosise RC .60 1.50
180 Jacoby Brissett RC .75 2.00
181 Cody Kessler RC .60 1.50
182 Connor Cook RC .75 2.00
183 Chris Moore RC .75 2.00
184 Malcolm Mitchell RC .60 1.50
185 Ricardo Louis RC .60 1.50
186 Pharoh Cooper RC .60 1.50
187 Tyler Ervin RC .60 1.50
188 Demarcus Robinson RC .60 1.50
189 Kenneth Dixon RC .60 1.50
190 Dak Prescott RC 3.00 8.00
191 Devontae Booker RC .75 2.00
192 Cardale Jones RC .60 1.50
193 Paul Perkins RC .60 1.50
194 Jordan Howard RC 1.50 4.00
195 Wendell Smallwood RC .60 1.50
196 Jonathan Williams RC .75 2.00
197 Kevin Hogan RC .75 2.00
198 Trevor Davis RC .60 1.50
199 Alex Collins RC .75 2.00
200 Keenan Reynolds RC .75 2.00

2016 Elite Black

*VETS/199: 1.2X TO 3X BASIC CARDS
*ROOKIES/199: .5X TO 1.2X BASIC CARDS

2016 Elite Purple

*VETS/25: 2.5X TO 6X BASIC CARDS
*ROOKIES/25: 1X TO 2.5X BASIC CARDS

2016 Elite Red

*VETS/49: 2X TO 5X BASIC CARDS
*ROOKIES/49: .8X TO 2X BASIC CARDS

2016 Elite Teal

*VETS/75: 1.5X TO 4X BASIC CARDS
*ROOKIES/75: .6X TO 1.5X BASIC CARDS

2016 Elite Back to the Future Materials

BFMAD Andy Dalton/299 2.50 6.00
BFMAG A.J. Green/299 3.00 8.00
BFMCK Colin Kaepernick/299 2.50 6.00
BFMDC Derek Carr/299 3.00 8.00
BFMDT Demaryius Thomas/249 2.50 6.00
BFMDW DeMarcus Ware/299 2.50 6.00
BFMJH Jeremy Hill/299 2.00 5.00
BFMKB Kelvin Benjamin/299 2.50 6.00
BFMLF Larry Fitzgerald/299 2.50 6.00
BFMLM Lamar Miller/299 2.00 5.00

2016 Elite Coverage Materials

*PRIME/99: .6X TO 1.5X BASIC JSY
*PRIME/49: .8X TO 2X BASIC JSY
1 Phillip Dorsett 1.50 4.00
2 Devonta Freeman 2.00 5.00
3 Teddy Bridgewater 2.00 5.00
4 Jadeveon Clowney 1.50 4.00
5 Jeremy Hill 1.50 4.00
6 Allen Robinson 2.00 5.00
7 Kelvin Benjamin 2.00 5.00
8 Brandin Cooks 2.00 5.00
9 Marcus Mariota 2.50 6.00
10 Davante Adams 1.50 4.00
11 Sammy Watkins 2.50 6.00
12 Donte Moncrief 2.00 5.00
13 Todd Gurley 2.50 6.00
14 Jameis Winston 2.50 6.00
15 Jeremy Langford 2.00 5.00
16 Amari Cooper 2.50 6.00
17 Kevin White 1.50 4.00
18 Buck Allen 1.50 4.00
19 Melvin Gordon 2.00 5.00
20 David Johnson 2.50 6.00
21 Stefon Diggs 2.00 5.00
22 Duke Johnson 1.50 4.00
23 Tyler Lockett 2.00 5.00
24 Jarvis Landry 2.00 5.00
25 Jordan Matthews 2.00 5.00
26 Blake Bortles 1.50 4.00
27 Khalil Mack 2.50 6.00
28 Carlos Hyde 1.50 4.00
29 Odell Beckham Jr. 2.50 6.00
30 Derek Carr 2.50 6.00

2016 Elite Craftsmen

*RED/75: .8X TO 2X BASIC INSERTS
*PURPLE/49: 1X TO 2.5X BASIC INSERTS
*ORANGE/25: 1.2X TO 3X BASIC INSERTS
CMAB Antonio Brown .75 2.00
CMAJ A.J. Green .75 2.00
CMAL Andrew Luck 1.00 2.50
CMAP Adrian Peterson .75 2.00
CMAR Aaron Rodgers 1.50 4.00
CMBR Ben Roethlisberger .75 2.00
CMDB Drew Brees .75 2.00
CMDF Devonta Freeman .60 1.50
CMDM Doug Martin .60 1.50
CMJJ Julio Jones .75 2.00
CMJW J.J. Watt .75 2.00
CMOB Odell Beckham Jr. .75 2.00
CMRS Richard Sherman .75 2.00
CMRW Russell Wilson 1.00 2.50
CMTB Tom Brady 2.00 5.00

2016 Elite Elitist

ELAB Antonio Brown 1.00 2.50
ELAL Andrew Luck 1.25 3.00
ELAP Adrian Peterson 1.00 2.50
ELAR Aaron Rodgers 2.00 5.00
ELBM Brandon Marshall .60 1.50
ELCN Cam Newton 1.00 2.50
ELDB Dez Bryant 1.00 2.50
ELDH DeAndre Hopkins .75 2.00
ELDJ DeSean Jackson .75 2.00
ELDM DeMarco Murray .75 2.00
ELDT Demaryius Thomas .75 2.00
ELJC Jamaal Charles .75 2.00
ELJF Joe Flacco .75 2.00
ELJG Jimmy Graham 1.00 2.50
ELJJ Julio Jones 1.00 2.50
ELJW J.J. Watt 1.00 2.50
ELLB Le'Veon Bell .75 2.00
ELLF Larry Fitzgerald .75 2.00
ELLM LeSean McCoy 1.00 2.50
ELOB Odell Beckham Jr. 1.00 2.50
ELPM Peyton Manning 2.00 5.00
ELRG Rob Gronkowski 1.00 2.50
ELRW Russell Wilson 1.25 3.00
ELTB Tom Brady 2.50 6.00
ELTR Tony Romo .75 2.00

2016 Elite Epic Materials

*PRIME/25: .6X TO 1.5X BASIC JSY/99
*PRIME/49: .5X TO 1.2X BASIC JSY/49
EMAL Andrew Luck/99 4.00 10.00
EMBR Ben Roethlisberger/49 10.00 25.00
EMCJ Calvin Johnson/49 4.00 10.00
EMEM Eli Manning/49 3.00 8.00
EMJC Jay Cutler/99 2.00 5.00
EMJF Joe Flacco/99 2.50 6.00
EMJW Jameis Winston/99 3.00 8.00
EMMM Marcus Mariota/99 3.00 8.00
EMMR Matt Ryan/49 3.00 8.00
EMTR Tony Romo/49 3.00 8.00

2016 Elite Etched In Time

*RED/75: .8X TO 2X BASIC INSERTS
*PURPLE/49: 1X TO 2.5X BASIC INSERTS
*ORANGE/25: 1.2X TO 3X BASIC INSERTS
ETAR Andre Reed .60 1.50
ETBF Brett Favre 1.50 4.00
ETBJ Bo Jackson 1.00 2.50
ETBL Bob Lilly .60 1.50
ETBS Barry Sanders 1.25 3.00
ETBS Bruce Smith .60 1.50
ETCM Curtis Martin .60 1.50
ETDM Dan Marino 1.50 4.00
ETDO Tony Dorsett .75 2.00
ETFH Franco Harris .75 2.00
ETFT Fran Tarkenton .75 2.00
ETFT Fred Taylor .50 1.25
ETGS Gale Sayers .75 2.00
ETJB Jerome Bettis .75 2.00
ETJK Jim Kelly .75 2.00
ETJM Joe Montana 2.00 5.00
ETJN Joe Namath 1.00 2.50
ETJR Jerry Rice 1.25 3.00
ETJR John Riggins .60 1.50
ETJT Joe Theismann .75 2.00
ETKW Kurt Warner .60 1.50
ETLC Larry Csonka .60 1.50
ETLT Lawrence Taylor .75 2.00
ETLT LaDainian Tomlinson .60 1.50
ETMA Marcus Allen .60 1.50
ETMF Marshall Faulk .60 1.50
ETMI Michael Irvin .75 2.00
ETMS Michael Strahan .60 1.50
ETRA Randy White .60 1.50
ETRB Raymond Berry .60 1.50
ETRI Ricky Williams .60 1.50
ETRO Rod Woodson .60 1.50
ETRS Roger Staubach 1.00 2.50
ETRT Ronnie Lott .60 1.50
ETSY Steve Young 1.00 2.50
ETTA Troy Aikman 1.00 2.50
ETTD Terrell Davis .60 1.50
ETTE Terry Bradshaw 1.00 2.50
ETTI Tim Brown .75 2.00
ETTT Thurman Thomas .60 1.50

2016 Elite Field Vision

*RED/49: .8X TO 2X BASIC INSERTS
*PURPLE/25: 1X TO 2.5X BASIC INSERTS
FVAL Andrew Luck 1.50 4.00
FVAR Aaron Rodgers 2.50 6.00
FVFJ Fred Jackson 1.00 2.50
FVJA Jared Allen .75 2.00
FVJC Jay Cutler .75 2.00
FVKM Khalil Mack 1.25 3.00
FVPM Peyton Manning 2.50 6.00
FVPR Philip Rivers 1.25 3.00
FVTB Tom Brady 3.00 8.00
FVVM Von Miller 1.00 2.50

2016 Elite Game Face

*RED/75: .75X TO 2X BASIC INSERTS
*PURPLE/49: 1X TO 2.5X BASIC INSERTS
*ORANGE/25: 1.2X TO 3X BASIC INSERTS
GFAL Andrew Luck 1.00 2.50
GFAP Adrian Peterson .75 2.00
GFAR Aaron Rodgers 1.50 4.00
GFBU Brian Urlacher .75 2.00
GFCN Cam Newton .75 2.00
GFDB Dez Bryant .75 2.00
GFES Emmitt Smith 1.25 3.00
GFJB Jerome Bettis .75 2.00
GFJC Jay Cutler .50 1.25
GFJW J.J. Watt .75 2.00
GFLC Larry Csonka .60 1.50
GFLT Lawrence Taylor .75 2.00
GFMS Mike Singletary .75 2.00
GFOB Odell Beckham Jr. .75 2.00
GFPM Peyton Manning 1.50 4.00
GFPR Philip Rivers .75 2.00
GFRS Richard Sherman .75 2.00
GFRW Russell Wilson 1.00 2.50
GFTB Tom Brady 2.00 5.00
GFWS Warren Sapp .60 1.50

2016 Elite Greatest Hits

GHAD Aaron Donald 1.00 2.50
GHBU Brian Urlacher 1.00 2.50
GHBW Bobby Wagner .60 1.50
GHCJ Chandler Jones .60 1.50
GHCM Clay Matthews 1.00 2.50
GHCW Cameron Wake .60 1.50
GHDW Donte Whitner .60 1.50
GHHS Harrison Smith .60 1.50
GHJH Justin Houston .60 1.50
GHJJ J.J. Watt 1.00 2.50
GHKC Kam Chancellor 1.00 2.50
GHKM Khalil Mack 1.00 2.50
GHLK Luke Kuechly .75 2.00
GHLT Lawrence Taylor 1.00 2.50
GHNB Navorro Bowman .75 2.00
GHNS Ndamukong Suh .75 2.00
GHPE Patrick Peterson .60 1.50
GHPP Paul Posluszny .60 1.50
GHRL Ronnie Lott .75 2.00
GHRQ Robert Quinn .75 2.00
GHSL Sean Lee .75 2.00
GHSR Sheldon Richardson .60 1.50
GHTM Tyrann Mathieu .75 2.00
GHTS Terrell Suggs .60 1.50
GHVM Von Miller .75 2.00

2016 Elite Home Field Advantage

HFAG Darrell Green .75 2.00
HFAJ A.J. Green 1.00 2.50
HFAP Adrian Peterson 1.00 2.50
HFAR Aaron Rodgers 2.00 5.00
HFBF Brett Favre 2.00 5.00
HFBR Ben Roethlisberger 1.00 2.50
HFBS Barry Sanders 1.50 4.00
HFDB Drew Brees 1.00 2.50
HFDE Derrick Brooks .60 1.50
HFDM Dan Marino 2.00 5.00
HFEM Eli Manning .75 2.00
HFJB Jerome Bettis 1.00 2.50
HFJC Jamaal Charles .75 2.00
HFJE John Elway 1.50 4.00
HFJJ J.J. Watt 1.00 2.50
HFJK Jim Kelly 1.00 2.50
HFJN Joe Namath 1.25 3.00
HFJW Jason Witten .75 2.00
HFLF Larry Fitzgerald .75 2.00
HFLT LaDainian Tomlinson .75 2.00
HFMS Matthew Stafford .75 2.00
HFPR Philip Rivers 1.00 2.50
HFTB Tom Brady 2.50 6.00
HFTI Tim Brown 1.00 2.50
HFTR Tony Romo .75 2.00

2016 Elite Lineage

*RED/49: 1X TO 2.5X BASIC INSERTS
*PUPRLE/25: 1.2X TO 3X BASIC INSERTS
LNBC T.Brown/A.Cooper 1.25 3.00
LNBR B.Roethlisberger/T.Bradshaw 1.50 4.00
LNFG M.Faulk/T.Gurley 1.25 3.00
LNFR A.Rodgers/B.Favre 2.50 6.00
LNHB F.Harris/L.Bell 1.25 3.00
LNIB M.Irvin/D.Bryant 1.25 3.00
LNSL G.Sayers/J.Langford 1.25 3.00
LNSR R.Staubach/T.Romo 1.50 4.00
LNTM L.McCoy/T.Thomas 1.25 3.00
LNWP C.Palmer/K.Warner 1.00 2.50

2016 Elite Master Craftsmen

*RED/49: .8X TO 2X BASIC INSERTS
*PURPLE/25: 1X TO 2.5 BASIC INSERTS
MCBS Barry Sanders 2.00 5.00
MCES Emmitt Smith 2.00 5.00
MCJE John Elway 2.00 5.00
MCJR Jerry Rice 2.00 5.00
MCPM Peyton Manning 2.50 6.00

2016 Elite Monument Marks

MMAG Ahman Green/15
MMBS Bruce Smith/25 15.00 30.00
MMCM Curtis Martin/25
MMDD Donald Driver/25 25.00 50.00
MMGS Gale Sayers/25
MMHW Hines Ward/25
MMJK Jim Kelly/15
MMJL Jamal Lewis/25 6.00 15.00
MMMA Marcus Allen/25 40.00 80.00
MMON Ozzie Newsome/25
MMRL Ronnie Lott/25 EXCH 15.00 40.00
MMSL Steve Largent/25
MMTB Tim Brown/25
MMTT Thurman Thomas/25

2016 Elite Passing the Torch Signatures

PTDW W.Dunn/D.Martin/25 30.00 80.00
PTHA A.Brown/H.Ward/25 125.00 200.00
PTJJ J.Cutler/J.McMahon/25 30.00 80.00
PTSA A.Reed/S.Watkins/25
PTSM S.Bartkowski/M.Ryan/25 30.00 80.00
PTTE E.Dickerson/T.Gurley II/25

2016 Elite Pen Pals

PPAC Alex Collins 5.00 12.00
PPBM Braxton Miller 4.00 10.00
PPCC Corey Coleman 6.00 15.00
PPCO Connor Cook 5.00 12.00
PPCH Christian Hackenberg 4.00 10.00
PPCJ Cardale Jones 4.00 10.00
PPCK Cody Kessler 4.00 10.00
PPCM Chris Moore 5.00 12.00
PPCP C.J. Prosise 4.00 10.00
PPCW Carson Wentz 40.00 80.00
PPDB Devontae Booker 5.00 12.00
PPDH Derrick Henry 10.00 25.00
PPDP Dak Prescott 50.00 100.00
PPDR Demarcus Robinson 4.00 10.00
PPEE Ezekiel Elliott 100.00 200.00
PPHH Hunter Henry 5.00 12.00
PPBR Jacoby Brissett 5.00 12.00
PPJB Joey Bosa 15.00 40.00
PPJD Josh Doctson 5.00 12.00
PPJG Jared Goff 50.00 100.00
PPJH Jordan Howard 10.00 25.00
PPJW Jonathan Williams 5.00 12.00
PPDX Kenneth Dixon 4.00 10.00
PPKD Kenyan Drake 6.00 15.00
PPKH Kevin Hogan 5.00 12.00
PPKR Keenan Reynolds 5.00 12.00
PPLC Leonte Carroo 4.00 10.00
PPLT Laquon Treadwell 20.00 40.00
PPMM Malcolm Mitchell 4.00 10.00
PPMT Michael Thomas 8.00 20.00
PPPC Pharoh Cooper 4.00 10.00
PPPL Paxton Lynch 4.00 10.00
PPPP Paul Perkins 4.00 10.00
PPRL Ricardo Louis 4.00 10.00
PPSS Sterling Shepard 5.00 12.00
PPTB Tyler Boyd 8.00 20.00
PPTD Trevor Davis 4.00 10.00
PPTE Tyler Ervin 4.00 10.00
PPWJ Will Fuller 6.00 15.00
PPWS Wendell Smallwood 4.00 10.00

2016 Elite Pen Pals Triples

PPTBCM Byd/Mre/Crroo 10.00 25.00
PPTBMJ Mllr/Jns/Bsa 15.00 40.00
PPTBWR Bker/Wllms/Rynlds
PPTCPH Prsctt/Cook/Hgn 50.00 100.00
PPTDFC Dctsn/Fllr/Clmn 12.00 30.00
PPTEHD Hnry/Ellt/Drke 125.00 250.00
PPTGWL Wntz/Lnch/Gff 250.00 400.00
PPTHWC Wllms/Cllns/Hnry
PPTKHB Ksslr/Hcknbrg/Brsstt 10.00 25.00
PPTLCD Dvs/Cpr/Louis 8.00 20.00
PPTMLR Mtchll/Louis/Rbnsn 8.00 20.00
PPTPED Prsse/Ervn/Dxn 8.00 20.00
PPTPHS Hwrd/Smllwd/Prkns 20.00 50.00
PPTTST Trdwll/Shprd/Thms 50.00 100.00

2016 Elite Prime Numbers 1st

*2ND/60-80: .4X TO 1X BASIC JSY/100
*2ND/60-80: .5X TO 1.2X BASIC JSY/600
*2ND/40-50: .6X TO 1.5X BASIC JSY/400-800
*2ND/20-30: .8X TO 2X BASIC JSY/400
*2ND/20-30: .6X TO 1.5X BASIC JSY/200
1 Dan Marino/100 15.00 30.00
2 Andy Dalton/600 2.00 5.00
3 Jameis Winston/400 2.50 6.00
4 Marcus Mariota/900 2.50 6.00
5 Joe Namath/100 10.00 25.00
6 Peyton Manning/100 10.00 25.00
7 Blake Bortles/400 1.50 4.00
8 Steve Young/200 4.00 10.00
9 Todd Gurley/800 2.50 6.00
10 Amari Cooper/600 2.50 6.00

2016 Elite Rookie Aspirations

RAAC Alex Collins .75 2.00
RACC Connor Cook .75 2.00
RACR Corey Coleman 1.00 2.50
RACH Christian Hackenberg .60 1.50
RACP C.J. Prosise .60 1.50
RACW Carson Wentz 6.00 15.00
RADB Devontae Booker .75 2.00
RADF DeForest Buckner .60 1.50
RADH Derrick Henry 1.50 4.00
RAEE Ezekiel Elliott 3.00 8.00
RAHH Hunter Henry .75 2.00
RAJB Joey Bosa 1.25 3.00
RAJD Josh Doctson .75 2.00
RAJG Jared Goff 4.00 10.00
RAJR Jalen Ramsey 1.00 2.50
RAJS Jaylon Smith .60 1.50
RAKD Kenneth Dixon .60 1.50
RALT Laquon Treadwell .75 2.00
RAMJ Myles Jack .75 2.00
RAMT Michael Thomas 1.25 3.00
RAPC Pharoh Cooper .60 1.50
RAPL Paxton Lynch .60 1.50
RASL Shaq Lawson .60 1.50
RATB Tyler Boyd .75 2.00
RAWF Will Fuller 1.00 2.50

2016 Elite Rookie Autographs

ERAAB Andrew Billings/99 4.00 10.00
ERAAG Aaron Green/99 3.00 8.00
ERAAH Austin Hooper/49 4.00 10.00
ERAAJ Austin Johnson/99 3.00 8.00
ERAAR A'Shawn Robinson/99 3.00 8.00
ERAAW Adolphus Washington/99 3.00 8.00
ERABA Bralon Addison/99 3.00 8.00
ERABU Jonathan Bullard/99 3.00 8.00
ERACA Cayleb Jones/99 3.00 8.00
ERACJ Chris Jones/49 4.00 10.00
ERACM Chris Moore/49 5.00 12.00
ERACN Carl Nassib/49 4.00 10.00
ERACP Charone Peake/99 3.00 8.00
ERACT Charles Tapper/99 4.00 10.00
ERADA Dominique Alexander/49 4.00 10.00
ERADB DeForest Buckner/99 3.00 8.00
ERADJ Deion Jones/99 3.00 8.00
ERADH Demarcus Robinson/49 4.00 10.00
ERADW DeAndre Washington/49 4.00 10.00
ERAEA Eli Apple/99 4.00 10.00
ERAEO Emmanuel Ogbah/99 4.00 10.00
ERAGG Glenn Gronkowski/99 3.00 8.00
ERAJB Joey Bosa/49
ERAJC Jeremy Cash/99 4.00 10.00
ERAJM Jalen Mills/99 4.00 10.00
ERAJP Joshua Perry/99 3.00 8.00
ERAJS Jaylon Smith/49 4.00 10.00
ERAKC Kamalei Correa/99 3.00 8.00
ERAKD Kevin Dodd/49 4.00 10.00
ERAKG Keyarris Garrett/99 3.00 8.00
ERAKL Kolby Listenbee/99 3.00 8.00
ERALT Laremy Tunsil/49 4.00 10.00
ERAMA Mackensie Alexander/99 3.00 8.00
ERAMC Maurice Canady/99 3.00 8.00
ERAMI Jaydon Mickens/49 4.00 10.00
ERAMJ Myles Jack/49
ERARR Reggie Ragland/99 3.00 8.00
ERASC Shilique Calhoun/99 3.00 8.00
ERASU Su'a Cravens/99 3.00 8.00
ERASW Scooby Wright III/99 3.00 8.00
ERATD Thomas Duarte/99 3.00 8.00
ERATH Tyler Higbee/49 4.00 10.00
ERATM Tre Madden/99 3.00 8.00
ERATS Tajae Sharpe/99 4.00 10.00

2016 Elite Signatures

ESAB Anquan Boldin/25
ESBF Bubba Franks/49 3.00 8.00
ESCC Chris Conley/99 2.50 6.00
ESCG Crockett Gillmore/99 2.50 6.00
ESCK Case Keenum/99 3.00 8.00
ESCP Clinton Portis/49
ESDB Deion Branch/49 3.00 8.00
ESDC David Cobb/99 2.50 6.00
ESDC2 Dallas Clark/49 10.00 25.00
ESDD Donald Driver/49 8.00 20.00
ESDD2 Dermontti Dawson/99 10.00 25.00
ESDH Devin Hester/25
ESDS Devin Smith/99 2.50 6.00
ESEE Eric Ebron/49 3.00 8.00
ESFB Fred Biletnikoff/25
ESFC Frank Clark/99 2.50 6.00
ESFT Fred Taylor/49 6.00 15.00
ESJA Joe Andruzzi/99 2.50 6.00
ESJF John Fuqua/49 8.00 20.00
ESJG Jimmy Garoppolo/49
ESJJ Jeff Janis/99 2.50 6.00
ESJL Jamal Lewis/99 3.00 8.00
ESJL2 Jeremy Langford/99 3.00 8.00
ESJS Jackie Smith/49 3.00 8.00
ESKA Colin Kaepernick/25 10.00 25.00
ESKE Kony Ealy/99 2.50 6.00
ESKS Kenny Stills/49 3.00 8.00
ESKW Kevin White/49 6.00 15.00
ESKW2 Karlos Williams/99 2.50 6.00
ESLB Lance Briggs/49 4.00 10.00
ESLC Landon Collins/99 2.50 6.00
ESLM Latavius Murray/99 2.50 6.00
ESLT Lawrence Taylor/25
ESMC Mark Chmura/49 3.00 8.00
ESMF Michael Floyd/49 8.00 20.00
ESNA Nelson Agholor/49 3.00 8.00
ESRB Robert Brooks/49 12.00 30.00
ESRM Ron Mix/99 2.50 6.00
ESSR Shane Ray/49 6.00 15.00
ESTB Tim Brown/25 8.00 20.00
ESTD Trent Dilfer/99 8.00 20.00
ESVJ Vincent Jackson/49 3.00 8.00
ESWD Warrick Dunn/25
ESZE Zach Ertz/99 3.00 8.00

2016 Elite Throwback Threads

*PRIME/49: .6X TO 1.5X BASIC JSY/299
*PRIME/49: .5X TO 1.2X BASIC JSY/99
*PRIME/25: .8X TO 2X BASIC JSY/299
*PRIME/25: .6X TO 1.5X BASIC JSY/99
TTBF Brett Favre/99 6.00 15.00
TTCC Cris Carter/299 2.50 6.00
TTCH Charles Haley/99 3.00 8.00
TTDB Derrick Brooks/299 1.50 4.00
TTDC Dallas Clark/299 1.50 4.00
TTDF Doug Flutie/299 2.00 5.00
TTDM Dan Marino/99 6.00 15.00
TTEC Earl Campbell/99 3.00 8.00
TTJE John Elway/99 5.00 12.00
TTJM Joe Montana/99 8.00 20.00
TTJR Jerry Rice/99 5.00 12.00
TTLT LaDainian Tomlinson/99 2.50 6.00
TTMC Jim McMahon/299 2.00 5.00
TTMS Mike Singletary/99 3.00 8.00
TTON Ozzie Newsome/299 2.00 5.00
TTRC Roger Craig/299 2.00 5.00
TTRL Ronnie Lott/299 2.00 5.00
TTSY Steve Young/99 4.00 10.00
TTWD Warrick Dunn/299 1.50 4.00
TTWM Warren Moon/99 3.00 8.00

2016 Elite Turn of the Century Autographs

TCAAC Alex Collins/99 6.00 15.00
TCABM Braxton Miller/99 5.00 12.00
TCACCO Connor Cook/25 10.00 25.00
TCACC Corey Coleman/49 10.00 25.00
TCACH Christian Hackenberg/49 6.00 15.00
TCACJ Cardale Jones/49 6.00 15.00
TCACK Cody Kessler/49 6.00 15.00
TCACM Chris Moore/49 8.00 20.00
TCACP C.J. Prosise/99 5.00 12.00
TCACW Carson Wentz/25 100.00 200.00
TCADB Devontae Booker/49 8.00 20.00
TCADH Derrick Henry/25 20.00 50.00
TCADP Dak Prescott/49 40.00 80.00
TCADR Demarcus Robinson/99 10.00 25.00
TCADW DeAndre Washington/49 6.00 15.00
TCAEE Ezekiel Elliott/25 200.00 400.00
TCAHH Hunter Henry/49 8.00 20.00
TCAJB Joey Bosa/49 12.00 30.00
TCAJD Josh Doctson/49 8.00 20.00
TCAJG Jared Goff/25 60.00 125.00
TCAJH Jordan Howard/99 12.00 30.00
TCAJW Jonathan Williams/99 6.00 15.00
TCADX Kenneth Dixon/49 EXCH 6.00 15.00
TCAKD Kenyan Drake/99 8.00 20.00
TCAKH Kevin Hogan/49 8.00 20.00
TCAKR Keenan Reynolds/99 6.00 15.00
TCALC Leonte Carroo/49 6.00 15.00
TCALT Laquon Treadwell/49 8.00 20.00
TCAMB Moritz Bohringer/49 6.00 15.00
TCAMT Michael Thomas/49 12.00 30.00
TCAPC Pharoh Cooper/99 5.00 12.00
TCAPL Paxton Lynch/25 8.00 20.00
TCAPP Paul Perkins/99 5.00 12.00
TCARL Ricardo Louis/99 5.00 12.00
TCASS Sterling Shepard/99 6.00 15.00
TCATB Tyler Boyd/49 25.00 50.00
TCATD Trevor Davis/49 6.00 15.00
TCATE Tyler Ervin/99 5.00 12.00
TCAWF Will Fuller/49 10.00 25.00
TCAWS Wendell Smallwood/99 5.00 12.00

2017 Elite

1 Carson Palmer .25 .60
2 David Johnson .30 .75
3 Larry Fitzgerald .25 .60
4 Matt Ryan .25 .60
5 Devonta Freeman .25 .60
6 Tevin Coleman .25 .60
7 Julio Jones .30 .75
8 Joe Flacco .25 .60
9 Kenneth Dixon .20 .50
10 Tyrod Taylor .25 .60
11 LeSean McCoy .30 .75
12 Sammy Watkins .30 .75
13 Cam Newton .30 .75
14 Jonathan Stewart .20 .50
15 Kelvin Benjamin .25 .60
16 Jordan Howard .30 .75
17 Alshon Jeffery .25 .60
18 Andy Dalton .25 .60
19 Jeremy Hill .20 .50
20 A.J. Green .30 .75
21 Isaiah Crowell .20 .50
22 Terrelle Pryor Sr. .20 .50
23 Corey Coleman .20 .50
24 Dak Prescott .30 .75
25 Ezekiel Elliott .40 1.00
26 Dez Bryant .30 .75
27 Cole Beasley .30 .75
28 Trevor Siemian .20 .50
29 C.J. Anderson .25 .60
30 Demaryius Thomas .25 .60
31 Paxton Lynch .20 .50
32 Matthew Stafford .25 .60
33 Golden Tate III .20 .50
34 Marvin Jones Jr. .20 .50
35 Aaron Rodgers .60 1.50
36 Jordy Nelson .25 .60
37 Davante Adams .25 .60
38 Ty Montgomery .20 .50
39 Jadeveon Clowney .20 .50
40 Lamar Miller .20 .50
41 DeAndre Hopkins .25 .60
42 J.J. Watt .30 .75
43 Andrew Luck .40 1.00
44 Frank Gore .25 .60
45 T.Y. Hilton .25 .60
46 Blake Bortles .20 .50
47 Allen Robinson .25 .60
48 Jalen Ramsey .20 .50
49 Alex Smith .25 .60
50 Tyreek Hill .30 .75
51 Travis Kelce .30 .75
52 Philip Rivers .30 .75
53 Melvin Gordon .25 .60
54 Joey Bosa .30 .75
55 Jared Goff .30 .75
56 Todd Gurley II .30 .75
57 Aaron Donald .30 .75
58 Ryan Tannehill .25 .60
59 Jay Ajayi .25 .60
60 Jarvis Landry .25 .60
61 Sam Bradford .20 .50
62 Adrian Peterson .30 .75
63 Stefon Diggs .25 .60
64 Tom Brady .75 2.00
65 Dion Lewis .20 .50
66 Rob Gronkowski .30 .75
67 Julian Edelman .30 .75
68 Drew Brees .30 .75
69 Brandin Cooks .25 .60
70 Michael Thomas .30 .75
71 Eli Manning .25 .60
72 Paul Perkins .20 .50
73 Odell Beckham Jr. .30 .75
74 Sterling Shepard .25 .60
75 Matt Forte .20 .50
76 Brandon Marshall .20 .50
77 Eric Decker .20 .50
78 Derek Carr .30 .75
79 Amari Cooper .30 .75
80 Khalil Mack .30 .75
81 Carson Wentz .40 1.00
82 Jordan Matthews .20 .50
83 Zach Ertz .25 .60
84 Ben Roethlisberger .30 .75
85 Le'Veon Bell .25 .60
86 Antonio Brown .30 .75
87 Eli Rogers .20 .50
88 Carlos Hyde .20 .50
89 Jeremy Kerley .20 .50
90 Russell Wilson .40 1.00
91 Thomas Rawls .20 .50
92 Doug Baldwin .25 .60
93 Jameis Winston .25 .60
94 Mike Evans .25 .60
95 Marcus Mariota .30 .75
96 DeMarco Murray .25 .60
97 Derrick Henry .25 .60
98 Kirk Cousins .30 .75
99 Robert Kelley .20 .50
100 Jordan Reed .20 .50

101 Chad Kelly RC .60 1.50
102 Brad Kaaya RC .60 1.50
103 Kevin King RC .75 2.00
104 Sefo Liufau RC .75 2.00
105 Tarik Cohen RC 1.25 3.00
106 Elijah McGuire RC .60 1.50
107 T.J. Logan RC 1.00 2.50
108 Aaron Jones RC 1.50 4.00
109 George Kittle RC .60 1.50
110 Jake Butt RC .75 2.00
111 Jonnu Smith RC .60 1.50
112 Gerald Everett RC .60 1.50
113 Adam Shaheen RC .60 1.50
114 Chad Williams RC .60 1.50
115 Jehu Chesson RC .75 2.00
116 Rodney Adams RC .60 1.50
117 Robert Davis RC .60 1.50
118 Isaiah McKenzie RC .60 1.50
119 Trent Taylor RC .75 2.00
120 DeAngelo Yancey RC .60 1.50
121 Travin Dural RC .75 2.00
122 Marshon Lattimore RC .75 2.00
123 Teez Tabor RC .75 2.00
124 Marlon Humphrey RC .60 1.50
125 Sidney Jones RC .60 1.50
126 Desmond King RC .75 2.00
127 Tre'Davious White RC .60 1.50
128 Jourdan Lewis RC .60 1.50
129 Cordrea Tankersley RC .75 2.00
130 Quincy Wilson RC .60 1.50
131 Myles Garrett RC 2.00 5.00
132 Solomon Thomas RC .60 1.50
133 Derek Barnett RC .75 2.00
134 Taco Charlton RC .60 1.50
135 Charles Harris RC .60 1.50
136 Carl Lawson RC .60 1.50
137 DeMarcus Walker RC .60 1.50
138 Malik McDowell RC .60 1.50
139 Caleb Brantley RC .60 1.50
140 Carlos Watkins RC .60 1.50
141 Reuben Foster RC .60 1.50
142 Raekwon McMillan RC .60 1.50
143 Jarrad Davis RC .75 2.00
144 Zach Cunningham RC .75 2.00
145 Tim Williams RC .75 2.00
146 Takkarist McKinley RC .60 1.50
147 T.J. Watt RC 2.00 5.00
148 Jabrill Peppers RC 1.00 2.50
149 Jamal Adams RC .60 1.50
150 Malik Hooker RC .60 1.50
151 Deshaun Watson RC 4.00 10.00
152 Mitchell Trubisky RC 3.00 8.00
153 DeShone Kizer RC .60 1.50
154 Nathan Peterman RC .75 2.00
155 Patrick Mahomes II RC 25.00 50.00
156 R. Joshua Dobbs RC .75 2.00
157 Davis Webb RC .60 1.50
158 C.J. Beathard RC .60 1.50
159 Leonard Fournette RC 2.00 5.00
160 Dalvin Cook RC 1.50 4.00
161 Christian McCaffrey RC 1.50 4.00
162 D'Onta Foreman RC .75 2.00
163 Samaje Perine RC .60 1.50
164 Alvin Kamara RC 2.50 6.00
165 Joe Mixon RC 1.25 3.00
166 Joe Williams RC .60 1.50
167 Wayne Gallman RC .75 2.00
168 Brian Hill RC .60 1.50
169 Jamaal Williams RC .60 1.50
170 Elijah Hood RC .60 1.50
171 Marlon Mack RC 1.00 2.50
172 Kareem Hunt RC 1.25 3.00
173 Jeremy McNichols RC .60 1.50
174 Donnel Pumphrey RC .75 2.00
175 James Conner RC 1.25 3.00
176 O.J. Howard RC .75 2.00
177 David Njoku RC .75 2.00
178 Mike Williams RC 1.00 2.50
179 John Ross RC .75 2.00
180 Corey Davis RC 1.00 2.50
181 JuJu Smith-Schuster RC 1.50 4.00
182 Dede Westbrook RC .60 1.50
183 Curtis Samuel RC .75 2.00
184 Amara Darboh RC .60 1.50
185 Isaiah Ford RC .60 1.50
186 Carlos Henderson RC .60 1.50
187 Malachi Dupre RC .60 1.50
188 Zay Jones RC .75 2.00
189 Cooper Kupp RC 1.00 2.50
190 Evan Engram RC .75 2.00
191 Ryan Switzer RC .75 2.00
192 Josh Reynolds RC .60 1.50
193 Kenny Golladay RC 1.00 2.50
194 Josh Malone RC .60 1.50
195 ArDarius Stewart RC .60 1.50
196 Chad Hansen RC .60 1.50
197 Mack Hollins RC .60 1.50
198 Chris Godwin RC .75 2.00
199 Taywan Taylor RC .60 1.50
200 Jonathan Allen RC .75 2.00

2017 Elite Aspirations Die Cut

*VETS/24: 3X TO 8X BASIC CARDS
*ROOKIES/24: 1.2X TO 3X BASIC CARDS

2017 Elite Blue

*VETS/25: 3X TO 8X BASIC CARDS
*ROOKIES/25: 1.2X TO 3X BASIC CARDS

2017 Elite Purple

*VETS/99: 1.5X TO 4X BASIC CARDS
*ROOKIES/99: .6X TO 1.5X BASIC CARDS

2017 Elite Red

*VETS/149: 1.2X TO 3X BASIC CARDS
*ROOKIES/149: .5X TO 1.2X BASIC CARDS

2017 Elite Status Die Cut

*VETS/24: 3X TO 8X BASIC CARDS
*ROOKIES/24: 1.2X TO 3X BASIC CARDS

2017 Elite Back to the Future Signatures

1 Michael Thomas/49 8.00 20.00
2 Dak Prescott/15 60.00 125.00
3 Sterling Shepard/99 5.00 12.00
4 Trevor Siemian/49 5.00 12.00
5 Eric Kendricks/99 4.00 10.00
6 Shaq Lawson/99 4.00 10.00
7 Carlos Hyde/99 4.00 10.00
8 Artie Burns/99 4.00 10.00
9 Thomas Rawls/49 5.00 12.00
10 Hunter Henry/99 4.00 10.00
11 Sean Davis/99 4.00 10.00
13 Reggie Ragland/99 4.00 10.00
14 Robert Nkemdiche/99 4.00 10.00
15 Cyrus Jones/99 4.00 10.00
16 Darron Lee/99 4.00 10.00
17 Myles Jack/99 4.00 10.00
18 Joey Bosa/49 8.00 20.00
19 Vernon Hargreaves III/99 4.00 10.00
20 Leonte Carroo/99 4.00 10.00

2017 Elite College Ties

1 D.Watson/M.Williams 3.00 8.00
2 J.Peppers/M.Trubisky 2.00 5.00
3 J.Hill/L.Fournette 1.25 3.00
4 D.Hopkins/M.Williams .60 1.50
5 D.Cook/D.Freeman 1.00 2.50
6 C.Woodson/J.Peppers .60 1.50
7 T.Watt/D.Watt 1.25 3.00
8 J.Allen/M.Dareus .50 1.25
9 A.Luck/C.McCaffrey 1.00 2.50
10 D.Barnett/A.Kamara 1.50 4.00
11 J.Butt/T.Charlton .50 1.25
12 A.Stewart/J.Jones .60 1.50
13 J.Mixon/A.Peterson .75 2.00
14 D.Foreman/R.Williams .50 1.25
15 E.Elliott/E.George .75 2.00
16 J.Adams/T.Mathieu .50 1.25
17 M.Garrett/M.Bennett 1.25 3.00
18 J.Graham/D.Njoku .60 1.50
19 T.Tabor/Q.Wilson .50 1.25
20 J.Kelly/B.Kaaya .60 1.50

2017 Elite Epic Materials

1 Antonio Brown/49 4.00 10.00
2 Tom Brady/25 12.00 30.00
3 Russell Wilson/49 5.00 12.00
4 Dak Prescott/49 4.00 10.00
5 Julio Jones/49 4.00 10.00
6 DeAndre Hopkins/49 3.00 8.00
7 Cam Newton/25 5.00 12.00
8 Khalil Mack/49 4.00 10.00
9 Le'Veon Bell/49 3.00 8.00
10 Ezekiel Elliott/49 5.00 12.00

2017 Elite Face to Face

*RED/99: .6X TO 1.5X BASIC INSERTS
*PURPLE/49: .8X TO 2X BASIC INSERTS
*ORANGE/25: 1X TO 2.5X BASIC INSERTS
1 R.Sherman/M.Crabtree 1.25 3.00
2 B.Favre/T.Aikman 2.50 6.00
3 B.Sanders/E.Smith 2.00 5.00
4 C.Newton/V.Miller 1.25 3.00
5 E.Reed/P.Manning 2.50 6.00
6 J.Watt/A.Luck 1.50 4.00
7 D.Sanders/J.Rice 2.00 5.00
8 J.Norman/D.Bryant 1.25 3.00
9 B.Rthlsbrgr/T.Brady 3.00 8.00
10 V.Burfict/A.Brown 1.25 3.00
11 A.Talib/S.Smith 1.00 2.50
12 T.Brady/M.Ryan 3.00 8.00
13 D.Revis/R.Moss 1.00 2.50
14 A.Peterson/B.Urlacher 1.25 3.00
15 E.George/R.Lewis 1.25 3.00

2017 Elite Family Ties

*RED/99: .6X TO 1.5X BASIC INSERTS
*PURPLE/49: .8X TO 2X BASIC INSERTS
*ORANGE/25: 1X TO 2.5X BASIC INSERTS
1 C.Long/H.Long 1.25 3.00
2 G.Grnkwski/R.Grnkwski 1.25 3.00
3 P.Manning/E.Manning 2.50 6.00
4 C.Matthews/J.Matthews 1.00 2.50
5 C.McCaffrey/E.McCaffrey 2.00 5.00
6 J.Kelce/T.Kelce 1.25 3.00
7 S.Sharpe/S.Sharpe 1.00 2.50
8 M.Pouncey/M.Pouncey .75 2.00
9 J.Watt/T.Watt 2.50 6.00
10 M.Bennett/M.Bennett .75 2.00

2017 Elite Field Vision

*RED/99: .6X TO 1.5X BASIC INSERTS
*PURPLE/49: .8X TO 2X BASIC INSERTS
*ORANGE/25: 1X TO 2.5X BASIC INSERTS
1 Dak Prescott 1.25 3.00
2 Carson Wentz 1.50 4.00
3 Luke Kuechly 1.00 2.50
4 Ben Roethlisberger 1.25 3.00
5 Earl Thomas III 1.00 2.50
6 Harrison Smith .75 2.00
7 Tom Brady 3.00 8.00
8 Cam Newton 1.25 3.00
9 Derek Carr 1.25 3.00
10 Adam Vinatieri .75 2.00

2017 Elite Fired Up

*RED/99: .6X TO 1.5X BASIC INSERTS
*PURPLE/49: .8X TO 2X BASIC INSERTS
*ORANGE/25: 1X TO 2.5X BASIC INSERTS
1 Aaron Rodgers 2.50 6.00
2 Andy Dalton 1.00 2.50
3 Steve Smith Sr. 1.00 2.50
4 Brian Urlacher 1.25 3.00
5 Cam Newton 1.25 3.00
6 Clay Matthews 1.00 2.50
7 Derek Carr 1.25 3.00
8 Dez Bryant 1.25 3.00
9 Drew Brees 1.25 3.00
10 Dak Prescott 1.25 3.00
11 Ezekiel Elliott 1.50 4.00
12 Russell Wilson 1.50 4.00
13 J.J. Watt 1.25 3.00
14 Khalil Mack 1.25 3.00
15 Travis Kelce 1.25 3.00
16 Antonio Brown 1.25 3.00
17 Marcus Mariota 1.25 3.00
18 Matt Ryan 1.00 2.50
19 Jarvis Landry 1.00 2.50
20 Philip Rivers 1.25 3.00
21 Larry Fitzgerald 1.00 2.50
22 Ray Lewis 1.25 3.00
23 Tom Brady 3.00 8.00
24 Von Miller 1.00 2.50
25 Warren Sapp 1.00 2.50

2017 Elite Home Field Advantage

1 Randy Moss .50 1.25
2 Brett Favre 1.25 3.00
3 Tom Brady 1.50 4.00
4 Dak Prescott .60 1.50
5 Odell Beckham Jr. .60 1.50
6 Cam Newton .60 1.50
7 Antonio Brown .60 1.50
8 Von Miller .50 1.25
9 Russell Wilson .75 2.00
10 Derek Carr .60 1.50
11 J.J. Watt .60 1.50
12 Matt Ryan .50 1.25
13 Kirk Cousins .60 1.50
14 Ezekiel Elliott .75 2.00
15 Landon Collins .40 1.00
16 Peyton Manning 1.25 3.00
17 Jerry Rice 1.00 2.50
18 Terry Bradshaw 1.00 2.50
19 Marcus Mariota .60 1.50
20 Aaron Rodgers 1.25 3.00

2017 Elite Man Coverage

1 Kevin Greene .50 1.25
2 Warren Sapp .50 1.25
3 Ed Reed .50 1.25
4 James Harrison .50 1.25
5 Steve Atwater .50 1.25
6 Bruce Smith .50 1.25
7 Mike Singletary .60 1.50
8 Ray Lewis .60 1.50
9 Lawrence Taylor .60 1.50
10 Joe Greene .60 1.50
11 Ronnie Lott .50 1.25
12 Darren Woodson .50 1.25
13 Navorro Bowman .50 1.25
14 Jamie Collins .40 1.00
15 Landon Collins .40 1.00
16 Kam Chancellor .60 1.50
17 Luke Kuechly .50 1.25
18 Clay Matthews .50 1.25
19 Harrison Smith .40 1.00
20 Sean Lee .50 1.25

2017 Elite Rookie Autographs

1 Marlon Humphrey/299 4.00 10.00
2 Marshon Lattimore/299 5.00 12.00
3 Zay Jones/299 5.00 12.00
4 Quincy Wilson/299 4.00 10.00
5 Adoree' Jackson/299 5.00 12.00
6 Sidney Jones/299 4.00 10.00
7 Desmond King/299 5.00 12.00
8 Cordrea Tankersley/299 5.00 12.00
9 Tre'Davious White/299 4.00 10.00
10 Gareon Conley/299 4.00 10.00
11 Dorok Barnott/299 5.00 12.00
12 Carl Lawson/299 4.00 10.00
13 Charles Harris/299 4.00 10.00
14 Taco Charlton/299 4.00 10.00
15 Jordan Willis/299 4.00 10.00
16 DeMarcus Walker/299 4.00 10.00
17 Solomon Thomas/299 4.00 10.00
18 Malik McDowell/299 4.00 10.00
19 Elijah Qualls/299 4.00 10.00
20 Caleb Brantley/299 4.00 10.00
21 Ryan Switzer/299 5.00 12.00
22 Raekwon McMillan/299 4.00 10.00
23 Zach Cunningham/299 5.00 12.00
24 Jarrad Davis/299 5.00 12.00
26 Tim Williams/299 5.00 12.00
28 T.J. Watt/299 12.00 30.00
29 Jamal Adams/149 10.00 25.00
30 Malik Hooker/299 4.00 10.00
32 Chad Kelly/299 4.00 10.00
33 R. Joshua Dobbs/299 5.00 12.00
34 Jamaal Williams/299 4.00 10.00
35 Jake Butt/299 5.00 12.00
36 Bucky Hodges/299 4.00 10.00
37 Jordan Leggett/299 4.00 10.00
38 Evan Engram/299 5.00 12.00
39 Travis Rudolph/299 4.00 10.00
40 Artavis Scott/299 4.00 10.00
41 Stacy Coley/299 4.00 10.00
42 De'Veon Smith/299 10.00 25.00
43 Corey Smith/299 6.00 15.00
44 Joseph Yearby/299 4.00 10.00
45 Devine Redding/299 4.00 10.00
46 Mitchell Trubisky/25 60.00 125.00
47 Leonard Fournette/25 60.00 125.00
48 Dalvin Cook/25 20.00 50.00
49 Mike Williams/25 12.00 30.00
50 John Ross/25 10.00 25.00

2017 Elite Rookie Elitist

1 Mitchell Trubisky 2.00 5.00
2 Deshaun Watson 2.50 6.00
3 Dalvin Cook 1.00 2.50
4 Leonard Fournette 1.25 3.00
5 Christian McCaffrey 1.00 2.50
6 Alvin Kamara 1.50 4.00
7 Joe Mixon .75 2.00
8 Mike Williams .60 1.50
9 Corey Davis .60 1.50
10 John Ross .50 1.25
11 JuJu Smith-Schuster 1.00 2.50
12 Jake Butt .50 1.25
13 O.J. Howard .50 1.25
14 David Njoku .50 1.25
15 Myles Garrett 1.25 3.00
16 Jonathan Allen .50 1.25
17 Solomon Thomas .40 1.00
18 Malik Hooker .40 1.00
19 Jamal Adams .40 1.00
20 Jabrill Peppers .60 1.50

2017 Elite Spellbound

*RED/99: .6X TO 1.5X BASIC INSERTS
*PURPLE/49: .8X TO 2X BASIC INSERTS
*ORANGE/25: 1X TO 2.5X BASIC INSERTS
1 Ezekiel Elliott E 1.50 4.00
2 Ezekiel Elliott L 1.50 4.00
3 Ezekiel Elliott L 1.50 4.00
4 Ezekiel Elliott I 1.50 4.00
5 Ezekiel Elliott O 1.50 4.00
6 Ezekiel Elliott T 1.50 4.00
7 Ezekiel Elliott T 1.50 4.00
8 Le'Veon Bell B 1.00 2.50
9 Le'Veon Bell E 1.00 2.50
10 Le'Veon Bell L 1.00 2.50
11 Le'Veon Bell L 1.00 2.50
12 Tom Brady B 3.00 8.00
13 Tom Brady R 3.00 8.00
14 Tom Brady A 3.00 8.00
15 Tom Brady D 3.00 8.00
16 Tom Brady Y 3.00 8.00
17 Aaron Rodgers R 2.50 6.00
18 Aaron Rodgers O 2.50 6.00
19 Aaron Rodgers D 2.50 6.00
20 Aaron Rodgers G 2.50 6.00
21 Aaron Rodgers E 2.50 6.00
22 Aaron Rodgers R 2.50 6.00
23 Aaron Rodgers S 2.50 6.00
24 Antonio Brown B 1.25 3.00
25 Antonio Brown R 1.25 3.00
26 Antonio Brown O 1.25 3.00
27 Antonio Brown W 1.25 3.00
28 Antonio Brown N 1.25 3.00
29 Julio Jones J 1.25 3.00
30 Julio Jones O 1.25 3.00
31 Julio Jones N 1.25 3.00
32 Julio Jones E 1.25 3.00
33 Julio Jones S 1.25 3.00
34 Odell Beckham Jr. B 1.25 3.00
35 Odell Beckham Jr. E 1.25 3.00
36 Odell Beckham Jr. C 1.25 3.00
37 Odell Beckham Jr. K 1.25 3.00
38 Odell Beckham Jr. H 1.25 3.00
39 Odell Beckham Jr. A 1.25 3.00
40 Odell Beckham Jr. M 1.25 3.00

2017 Elite Throwback Threads

1 Tony Dorsett/50 4.00 10.00
2 Emmitt Smith/50 6.00 15.00
3 Bobby Layne/50 3.00 8.00
4 Terry Bradshaw/99 5.00 12.00
5 Jerome Bettis/50 4.00 10.00
6 Marshall Faulk/50 3.00 8.00
7 Brett Favre/50 8.00 20.00
8 Sterling Sharpe/50 3.00 8.00
9 John Riggins/99 2.50 6.00
10 Clinton Portis/50 2.50 6.00

2017 Elite Throwback Threads Doubles

1 E.Smith/T.Dorsett/25
2 B.Layne/T.Bradshaw/25 15.00 40.00
3 J.Bettis/M.Faulk/15 6.00 15.00
5 C.Portis/J.Riggins/25 4.00 10.00

2017 Elite Title Waves

1 Dak Prescott .60 1.50
2 Matt Ryan .50 1.25
3 Tom Brady 1.50 4.00
4 Aaron Rodgers 1.25 3.00
5 Ezekiel Elliott .75 2.00
6 Drew Brees .60 1.50
7 Russell Wilson .75 2.00
8 Ben Roethlisberger .60 1.50
9 Alex Smith .50 1.25
10 DeAndre Hopkins .50 1.25
11 Peyton Manning 1.25 3.00
12 Jerry Rice 1.00 2.50
13 Eli Manning .50 1.25
14 Adrian Peterson .60 1.50
15 LaDainian Tomlinson .50 1.25
16 Terrell Davis .50 1.25
17 Jerome Bettis .60 1.50
18 Marshawn Lynch .50 1.25
19 Peyton Manning 1.25 3.00
20 Ray Lewis .60 1.50

2017 Elite Turn of the Century Autographs

1 Deshaun Watson/99 60.00 125.00
2 Mitchell Trubisky/99 25.00 60.00
3 DeShone Kizer/99 5.00 12.00
4 Brad Kaaya/99 5.00 12.00
5 Patrick Mahomes II/99 200.00 400.00
6 Jerod Evans/99 6.00 15.00
7 Davis Webb/99 5.00 12.00
8 R. Joshua Dobbs/99 6.00 15.00
9 Leonard Fournette/99 40.00 80.00
10 Dalvin Cook/99 12.00 30.00
11 Christian McCaffrey/99 40.00 80.00
12 D'Onta Foreman/99 6.00 15.00
13 Samaje Perine/99 5.00 12.00
14 Alvin Kamara/99 20.00 50.00
15 Joe Mixon/99 10.00 25.00
16 Matthew Dayes/99 5.00 12.00
17 Wayne Gallman/99 6.00 15.00
18 Brian Hill/99 5.00 12.00
19 Corey Clement/99 6.00 15.00
20 Elijah Hood/149 5.00 12.00
21 Marlon Mack/149 8.00 20.00
22 Kareem Hunt/149 10.00 25.00
23 Jeremy McNichols/149 5.00 12.00
24 Donnel Pumphrey/149 6.00 15.00
25 James Conner/149 10.00 25.00
26 O.J. Howard/99 6.00 15.00
27 Evan Engram/99 6.00 15.00
28 Mike Williams/99 8.00 20.00
29 John Ross/99 6.00 15.00
30 Corey Davis/99 8.00 20.00
31 JuJu Smith-Schuster/99 12.00 30.00
32 Dede Westbrook/99 5.00 12.00
33 Curtis Samuel/99 6.00 15.00
34 Amara Darboh/99 5.00 12.00
35 Isaiah Ford/99 5.00 12.00
36 Carlos Henderson/99 5.00 12.00
37 Malachi Dupre/99 5.00 12.00
38 Zay Jones/99 6.00 15.00
39 Cooper Kupp/99 8.00 20.00
40 Noah Brown/99 6.00 15.00
41 Ryan Switzer/99 6.00 15.00
42 Josh Reynolds/99 5.00 12.00
43 KD Cannon/149 5.00 12.00
44 Josh Malone/99 5.00 12.00
45 ArDarius Stewart/99 5.00 12.00
46 Chad Hansen/149 5.00 12.00
47 Shelton Gibson/149 5.00 12.00
48 Chris Godwin/149 6.00 15.00
49 Taywan Taylor/149 5.00 12.00
50 Jonathan Allen/99 6.00 15.00

2018 Elite

1 Dak Prescott .30 .75
2 Ezekiel Elliott .40 1.00
3 Dez Bryant .30 .75
4 DeMarcus Lawrence .20 .50
5 Eli Manning .25 .60
6 Odell Beckham Jr. .30 .75
7 Landon Collins .20 .50
8 Carson Wentz .40 1.00
9 Zach Ertz .25 .60
10 Alshon Jeffery .25 .60
11 Patrick Mahomes II .75 2.00
12 Josh Norman .20 .50
13 Samaje Perine .20 .50
14 Sam Bradford .20 .50
15 Larry Fitzgerald .25 .60
16 Chandler Jones .20 .50
17 Jared Goff .30 .75
18 Todd Gurley II .30 .75
19 Aaron Donald .30 .75
20 Robert Woods .25 .60
21 Jimmy Garoppolo .40 1.00
22 Tyrod Taylor .25 .60
23 Marquise Goodwin .20 .50
24 Russell Wilson .40 1.00
25 Doug Baldwin .25 .60
26 Richard Sherman .30 .75
27 Mitchell Trubisky .30 .75
28 Jordan Howard .30 .75
29 Allen Robinson .25 .60
30 Matthew Stafford .25 .60
31 Marvin Jones Jr. .20 .50
32 Darius Slay .20 .50
33 Aaron Rodgers .60 1.50
34 Jimmy Graham .30 .75
35 Clay Matthews .25 .60
36 Davante Adams .25 .60
37 Case Keenum .25 .60
38 Adam Thielen .30 .75
39 Harrison Smith .30 .75
40 Matt Ryan .25 .60
41 Julio Jones .30 .75
42 Devonta Freeman .25 .60
43 Cam Newton .30 .75
44 Luke Kuechly .25 .60
45 Christian McCaffrey .30 .75
46 Drew Brees .30 .75
47 Alvin Kamara .25 .60
48 Michael Thomas .30 .75
49 Jameis Winston .25 .60
50 Mike Evans .25 .60
51 Gerald McCoy .20 .50
52 Marcus Mariota .30 .75
53 Derrick Henry .30 .75
54 Delanie Walker .20 .50
55 Blake Bortles .20 .50
56 Leonard Fournette .30 .75
57 Jalen Ramsey .25 .60
58 Andrew Luck .40 1.00
59 Frank Gore .25 .60
60 T.Y. Hilton .25 .60
61 J.J. Watt .30 .75
62 Deshaun Watson .40 1.00
63 DeAndre Hopkins .25 .60
64 Ben Roethlisberger .30 .75
65 Antonio Brown .30 .75
66 T.J. Watt .25 .60
67 Le'Veon Bell .25 .60
68 A.J. McCarron .20 .50
69 Myles Garrett .30 .75
70 Josh Gordon .20 .50
71 Andy Dalton .25 .60
72 A.J. Green .30 .75
73 Joe Mixon .25 .60
74 Joe Flacco .25 .60
75 Alex Collins .20 .50
76 Terrell Suggs .20 .50
77 Derek Carr .30 .75
78 Amari Cooper .30 .75
79 Khalil Mack .30 .75
80 Joey Bosa .30 .75
81 Philip Rivers .30 .75
82 Melvin Gordon .25 .60
83 Keenan Allen .25 .60
84 Alex Smith .25 .60
85 Tyreek Hill .30 .75
86 Kareem Hunt .25 .60
87 Von Miller .25 .60
88 Demaryius Thomas .25 .60
89 Kirk Cousins .30 .75
90 Teddy Bridgewater .25 .60
91 Robby Anderson .20 .50
92 Tom Brady .75 2.00
93 Rob Gronkowski .30 .75
94 Brandin Cooks .25 .60
95 Danny Amendola .25 .60
96 Ryan Tannehill .25 .60
97 Jarvis Landry .25 .60
98 LeSean McCoy .30 .75
99 Kelvin Benjamin .25 .60
100 Kenyan Drake .20 .50
101 Dylan Cantrell/699 RC .50 1.25
102 Denzel Ward/699 RC 1.25 3.00
103 Minkah Fitzpatrick/699 RC 1.00 2.50
104 Tremaine Edmunds/699 RC 1.00 2.50
105 Roquan Smith/699 RC 1.50 4.00
106 Daron Payne/699 RC .75 2.00
107 Marcus Davenport/699 RC 1.00 2.50
108 Derwin James/699 RC 1.00 2.50
109 Joshua Jackson/699 RC 1.00 2.50
110 Maurice Hurst/699 RC .60 1.50
111 Vita Vea/699 RC .75 2.00
112 Rashaan Evans/699 RC .75 2.00
113 Isaiah Oliver/699 RC .50 1.25
114 Sam Hubbard/699 RC .60 1.50
115 Harold Landry/699 RC .50 1.25
116 Malik Jefferson/699 RC .60 1.50
117 Carlton Davis/699 RC .60 1.50
118 Harrison Phillips/699 RC .50 1.25
119 Leighton Vander Esch/699 RC 1.50 4.00
120 Arden Key/699 RC .50 1.25
121 Ronnie Harrison/699 RC .60 1.50
122 Justin Reid/699 RC .50 1.25
123 Derrick Nnadi/699 RC .50 1.25
124 Dorance Armstrong Jr./699 RC .50 1.25
125 Jaire Alexander/699 RC .75 2.00
126 M.J. Stewart/699 RC .50 1.25
127 Jerome Baker/699 RC .60 1.50
128 Ito Smith/699 RC .60 1.50
129 Jaylen Samuels/699 RC .60 1.50
130 Josey Jewell/699 RC .60 1.50
131 Mike Hughes/699 RC .75 2.00
132 Quenton Nelson/699 RC .75 2.00
133 Marquis Haynes/699 RC .50 1.25
134 Chad Thomas/699 RC .50 1.25
135 Donte Jackson/699 RC .75 2.00
136 Marcus Allen/699 RC .75 2.00
137 Tyquan Lewis/699 RC .60 1.50
138 Jordan Whitehead/699 RC .50 1.25
139 Anthony Averett/699 RC .60 1.50
140 Ogbonnia Okoronkwo/699 RC .75 2.00
141 Jalyn Holmes/699 RC .75 2.00
142 Daurice Fountain/699 RC .60 1.50
143 Duke Dawson/699 RC .50 1.25
144 Lorenzo Carter/699 RC .50 1.25
145 Shaquem Griffin/699 RC .75 2.00
146 Hayden Hurst/699 RC .60 1.50
147 Marquez Valdes-Scantling/699 RC .60 1.50
148 Auden Tate/699 RC .50 1.25
149 Ian Thomas/699 RC .50 1.25
150 J'Mon Moore/699 RC .50 1.25
151 Sam Darnold/399 RC 8.00 20.00
152 Josh Rosen/399 RC 2.00 5.00
153 Baker Mayfield/399 RC 8.00 20.00
154 Josh Allen/399 RC 4.00 10.00
155 Mason Rudolph/699 RC 1.25 3.00
156 Saquon Barkley/399 RC 8.00 20.00
157 Derrius Guice/399 RC 1.25 3.00
158 Nick Chubb/699 RC 1.50 4.00
159 Sony Michel/699 RC 1.50 4.00
160 Ronald Jones II/699 RC .50 1.25
161 Calvin Ridley/399 RC 1.50 4.00
162 Courtland Sutton/399 RC 1.00 2.50
163 Christian Kirk/699 RC .75 2.00
164 Anthony Miller/699 RC .75 2.00
165 D.J. Chark/699 RC .60 1.50
166 D.J. Moore/699 RC 1.00 2.50
167 Lamar Jackson/699 RC 6.00 15.00
168 Luke Falk/699 RC .60 1.50
169 Kyle Lauletta/699 RC .75 2.00
170 Mike White/699 RC .60 1.50
171 Josh Adams/699 RC 1.00 2.50
172 Royce Freeman/699 RC .60 1.50
173 Kerryon Johnson/699 RC .75 2.00
174 Rashaad Penny/699 RC .75 2.00
175 Kalen Ballage/699 RC .60 1.50
176 Nyheim Hines/699 RC .60 1.50
177 Bo Scarbrough/699 RC .60 1.50
178 James Washington/699 RC 1.00 2.50
179 Keke Coutee/699 RC .60 1.50
180 Marcell Ateman/699 RC .60 1.50
181 Michael Gallup/699 RC 1.00 2.50
182 Dante Pettis/699 RC .75 2.00
183 Deon Cain/699 RC .60 1.50
184 DaeSean Hamilton/699 RC .60 1.50
185 Tre'Quan Smith/699 RC .75 2.00
186 Jaleel Scott/699 RC .50 1.25
187 Terrell Edmunds/699 RC 1.50 4.00
188 Jordan Lasley/699 RC .50 1.25
189 Dallas Goedert/699 RC .60 1.50
190 Bradley Chubb/699 RC .75 2.00
191 Mike McGlinchey/699 RC 1.00 2.50
192 Riley Ferguson/699 RC .75 2.00
193 John Kelly/699 RC .60 1.50
194 Antonio Callaway/699 RC .60 1.50
195 Mark Walton/699 RC .60 1.50
196 Braxton Berrios/699 RC .50 1.25
197 Trey Quinn/699 RC .50 1.25
198 J.T. Barrett/699 RC .75 2.00
199 Mike Gesicki/699 RC .60 1.50
200 Mark Andrews/699 RC .75 2.00

2018 Elite Aspirations

*VETS/66-99: 2X TO 5X BASIC CARDS
*VETS/41-62: 2.5X TO 6X BASIC CARDS
*VETS/27-34: 3X TO 8X BASIC CARDS
*VETS/16-20: 4X TO 10X BASIC CARDS
*ROOK/66-99: .8X TO 2X BASIC CARDS/699
*ROOK/41-62: 1X TO 2.5X BASIC CARDS/699
*ROOK/27-34: 1.2X TO 3X BASIC CARDS/699
*ROOK/16-20: 1.5X TO 4X BASIC CARDS/699
*ROOK/66-99: .6X TO 1.5X BASIC CARDS/399
*ROOK/41-62: .8X TO 2X BASIC CARDS/399
*ROOK/27-34: 1X TO 2.5X BASIC CARDS/399
*ROOK/16-20: 1.2X TO 3X BASIC CARDS/399
153 Baker Mayfield/94 20.00 50.00
156 Saquon Barkley/74 12.00 30.00
167 Lamar Jackson/92 12.00 30.00

2018 Elite Aspirations Die Cut

*VETS/24: 4X TO 10X BASIC CARDS
*ROOK/24: 1.5X TO 4X BASIC CARDS/699
*ROOK/24: 1.2X TO 3X BASIC CARDS/399

2018 Elite Orange

*VETS/49: 2.5X TO 6X BASIC CARDS
*ROOKIES/25: 1.2X TO 3X BASIC CARDS/699
*ROOKIES/25: 1X TO 2.5X BASIC CARDS/399

2018 Elite Pink

*VETS: 1.5X TO 4X BASIC CARDS
*ROOKIES: .6X TO 1.5X BASIC CARDS/699

2018 Elite Purple

*VETS/99: 2X TO 5X BASIC CARDS
*ROOK/99: .8X TO 2X BASIC CARDS/699
*ROOK/99: .6X TO 1.5X BASIC CARDS/388

2018 Elite Red

*VETS/299: 1.2X TO 3X BASIC CARDS
*ROOKIES/199: .6X TO 1.5X BASIC CARDS/699
*ROOKIES/199: .5X TO 1.2X BASIC CARDS/399

2018 Elite Status

*VETS/66-99: 2X TO 5X BASIC CARDS
*VETS/38-59: 2.5X TO 6X BASIC CARDS
*VETS/25-34: 3X TO 8X BASIC CARDS
*VETS/15-24: 4X TO 10X BASIC CARDS
*ROOK/66-99: .8X TO 2X BASIC CARDS/699
*ROOK/38-59: 1X TO 2.5X BASIC CARDS/699
*ROOK/25-34: 1.2X TO 3X BASIC CARDS/699
*ROOK/15-24: 1.5X TO 4X BASIC CARDS/699
*ROOK/66-99: .6X TO 1.5X BASIC CARDS/399
*ROOK/38-59: .8X TO 2X BASIC CARDS/399
*ROOK/25-34: 1X TO 2.5X BASIC CARDS/399
*ROOK/15-24: 1.2X TO 3X BASIC CARDS/399
156 Saquon Barkley/26 20.00 50.00

2018 Elite Status Die Cut

*VETS/24: 4X TO 10X BASIC CARDS
*ROOK/24: 1.5X TO 4X BASIC CARDS/699
*ROOK/24: 1.2X TO 3X BASIC CARDS/399

2018 Elite Back to the Future Signatures

1 Jamison Crowder/75 4.00 10.00
2 Kenny Golladay/99 4.00 10.00
3 Marshon Lattimore/25 6.00 15.00
4 Joe Mixon/99 5.00 12.00
5 T.J. Watt/99 5.00 12.00
7 Alvin Kamara/49 12.00 30.00
8 Nelson Agholor/75 4.00 10.00
9 Jared Goff/25 15.00 40.00
10 Mitchell Trubisky/25 30.00 60.00
11 O.J. Howard/99 4.00 10.00
12 Patrick Mahomes II/25 40.00 80.00
13 Ezekiel Elliott/25
14 Alex Collins/75 4.00 10.00
15 Corey Davis/75 5.00 12.00
16 Vic Beasley Jr./75 4.00 10.00
17 Solomon Thomas/25 6.00 15.00
18 Jordan Howard/25
19 Adam Shaheen/49 8.00 20.00
20 D'Onta Foreman/75 4.00 10.00

2018 Elite Captain Clutch

1 Eli Manning .75 2.00
2 Joe Thomas .60 1.50
3 Drew Brees 1.00 2.50
4 Russell Wilson 1.25 3.00
5 Adam Vinatieri .60 1.50
6 Cam Newton 1.00 2.50
7 Larry Fitzgerald .75 2.00
8 Dan Bailey .60 1.50
9 Von Miller .75 2.00
10 Carson Wentz 1.25 3.00
11 Todd Gurley II 1.00 2.50
12 Travis Kelce 1.00 2.50
13 Jameis Winston .75 2.00
14 Dak Prescott 1.00 2.50
15 Andrew Luck 1.25 3.00
16 Derek Carr 1.00 2.50
17 Jason Witten .75 2.00
18 Marcus Mariota 1.00 2.50
19 Matt Ryan .75 2.00
20 Aaron Rodgers 2.00 5.00

2018 Elite Coverage Materials

*PRIME/49: .6X TO 1.5X BASIC JSY
1 Mitchell Trubisky 2.50 6.00
2 Deshaun Watson 5.00 12.00
3 Leonard Fournette 2.50 6.00
4 Alvin Kamara 2.00 5.00
5 Jared Goff 2.50 6.00
6 Joe Mixon 2.00 5.00
7 Corey Davis 2.00 5.00
8 Cooper Kupp 2.00 5.00
9 Ameer Abdullah 1.50 4.00
10 C.J. Anderson 2.00 5.00
11 Christian McCaffrey 2.50 6.00
12 Dalvin Cook 2.00 5.00
13 Evan Engram 1.50 4.00
14 Hunter Henry 1.50 4.00
15 Jabrill Peppers 1.50 4.00
16 Jamison Crowder 1.50 4.00
17 Joey Bosa 2.50 6.00
18 JuJu Smith-Schuster 2.50 6.00
19 Kareem Hunt 2.00 5.00
20 Kenyan Drake 1.50 4.00
21 Marlon Mack 1.50 4.00
22 Michael Thomas 2.50 6.00
23 Mike Williams 1.50 4.00
24 O.J. Howard 1.50 4.00
25 Ryan Switzer 1.50 4.00
26 Samaje Perine 1.50 4.00
27 Tyler Eifert 2.00 5.00
28 Tyreek Hill 2.50 6.00
29 Wayne Gallman 1.50 4.00
30 Will Fuller V 1.50 4.00

2018 Elite Craftsman Jerseys

*PRIME/49: .6X TO 1.5X BASIC JSY
*PRIME/25: .8X TO 2X BASIC JSY
*PRIME/20: 1X TO 2.5X BASIC JSY
1 Aaron Rodgers 6.00 15.00
2 Mike Evans 2.00 5.00
3 Carson Wentz 3.00 8.00
4 Dak Prescott 2.50 6.00
5 David Johnson 2.50 6.00
6 Jordan Howard 2.50 6.00
7 Devonta Freeman 2.00 5.00
8 Ezekiel Elliott 3.00 8.00
9 Jameis Winston 2.00 5.00
10 Khalil Mack 2.50 6.00
11 Patrick Mahomes II 6.00 15.00
12 Matt Ryan 2.00 5.00
13 Matthew Stafford 2.00 5.00
14 Mike Singletary 2.50 6.00
15 Terrell Suggs 1.50 4.00
16 Robert Kelley 1.50 4.00
17 Russell Wilson 3.00 8.00
18 T.Y. Hilton 2.00 5.00
19 T.J. Watt 2.00 5.00
20 Tony Romo 2.00 5.00

2018 Elite Deck

1 Tom Brady 2.50 6.00
2 Ezekiel Elliott 1.25 3.00
3 Dak Prescott 1.00 2.50
4 Aaron Rodgers 2.00 5.00
5 Julio Jones 1.00 2.50
6 Antonio Brown 1.00 2.50
7 Russell Wilson 1.25 3.00
8 Jordan Howard 1.00 2.50
9 Kareem Hunt .75 2.00
10 Deshaun Watson 1.25 3.00
11 Carson Wentz 1.25 3.00
12 J.J. Watt 1.00 2.50
13 Cam Newton 1.00 2.50
14 Ben Roethlisberger 1.00 2.50
15 Todd Gurley II 1.00 2.50
16 DeAndre Hopkins .75 2.00
17 Larry Fitzgerald .75 2.00
18 Drew Brees 1.00 2.50
19 Leonard Fournette 1.00 2.50
20 Adam Thielen 1.00 2.50

2018 Elite Dual Threats

*RED/99: .6X TO 1.5X BASIC INSERTS/299
*PURPLE/75: .6X TO 1.5X BASIC INSERTS/299
*ORANGE/25: 1X TO 2.5X BASIC INSERTS/299
1 Odell Beckham Jr. 1.25 3.00
2 Johnny Hekker .75 2.00
3 J.J. Watt 1.25 3.00
4 Tom Brady 3.00 8.00
5 Justin Tucker .75 2.00
6 Dez Bryant 1.25 3.00
7 Marcus Mariota 1.25 3.00
8 LaDainian Tomlinson 1.00 2.50
9 Nick Foles 1.00 2.50
10 Marquette King .75 2.00

2018 Elite Epic Materials

1 Blake Bortles 2.00 5.00
2 Clay Matthews 2.50 6.00
3 Derek Carr 3.00 8.00
4 Derrick Henry 3.00 8.00
5 Leonard Fournette 3.00 8.00
6 Earl Thomas III 2.50 6.00
7 Jadeveon Clowney 2.00 5.00
8 Luke Kuechly 2.50 6.00
9 Marcus Mariota 3.00 8.00
10 Melvin Gordon 2.50 6.00
11 O.J. Howard 2.00 5.00
12 Sterling Shepard 2.50 6.00
13 T.J. Watt 2.50 6.00
14 Todd Gurley II 3.00 8.00
15 Zach Ertz 2.50 6.00

2018 Elite Face to Face

*RED/99: .6X TO 1.5X BASIC INSERTS/299
*PURPLE/75: .6X TO 1.5X BASIC INSERTS/299
*ORANGE/25: 1X TO 2.5X BASIC INSERTS/299
1 A.Rodgers/B.Favre 2.50 6.00
2 V.Burfict/A.Brown 1.25 3.00
3 T.Suggs/T.Brady 3.00 8.00
4 C.Wentz/J.Goff 1.50 4.00
5 M.Ryan/D.Brees 1.25 3.00
6 A.Rodgers/M.Stafford 2.50 6.00
7 M.Gordon/T.Gurley II 1.25 3.00
8 A.Green/J.Jones 1.25 3.00
9 J.Winston/M.Mariota 1.25 3.00
10 T.Kelce/V.Miller 1.25 3.00
11 B.Roethlisberger/J.Flacco 1.25 3.00
12 E.Manning/P.Manning 2.50 6.00
13 A.Green/J.Ramsey 1.25 3.00
14 C.Long/K.Long .75 2.00
15 C.Wentz/D.Prescott 1.50 4.00

2018 Elite Field Vision

1 Jared Goff 1.25 3.00
2 Tom Brady 3.00 8.00
3 Dan Bailey .75 2.00
4 Von Miller 1.00 2.50
5 Melvin Gordon 1.00 2.50
6 Le'Veon Bell 1.00 2.50
7 Matthew Stafford 1.00 2.50
8 Russell Wilson 1.50 4.00
9 Blake Bortles .75 2.00
10 Derek Carr 1.25 3.00

2018 Elite Hard Hats

1 J.J. Watt 1.00 2.50
2 DeMarcus Lawrence .60 1.50
3 Chandler Jones .60 1.50
4 Joey Bosa 1.00 2.50
5 Calais Campbell .60 1.50
6 Everson Griffen .60 1.50
7 A.J. Bouye .60 1.50
8 Micah Hyde .60 1.50
9 Jalen Ramsey .75 2.00
10 Bobby Wagner .60 1.50
11 Landon Collins .60 1.50
12 Von Miller .75 2.00
13 Julius Peppers .75 2.00
14 Harrison Smith 1.00 2.50
15 Luke Kuechly .75 2.00
16 Myles Garrett 1.00 2.50
17 T.J. Watt .75 2.00
18 Marshon Lattimore .60 1.50
19 Tre'Davious White .60 1.50
20 Jamal Adams .75 2.00

2018 Elite Passing the Torch Dual Signatures

3 M.Gordon/L.Tomlinson/25 30.00 60.00
4 J.Charles/K.Hunt/25 10.00 25.00
5 E.Engram/J.Shockey/25 8.00 20.00
6 A.Kamara/R.Bush/25 15.00 40.00

2018 Elite Passing the Torch Signatures

1 Fred Taylor/25 6.00 15.00
2 Leonard Fournette/25
3 Jay Cutler/25 6.00 15.00
4 Mitchell Trubisky/25 30.00 60.00
5 LaDainian Tomlinson/25 EXCH 25.00 50.00
6 Melvin Gordon/49 6.00 15.00
7 Jamaal Charles/49 5.00 12.00
8 Kareem Hunt/49 12.00 30.00
9 Jeremy Shockey/49 EXCH 5.00 12.00
10 Evan Engram/49 EXCH 5.00 12.00
11 Reggie Bush/25 25.00 50.00
12 Alvin Kamara/49 12.00 30.00
14 Dalvin Cook/49 EXCH 25.00 50.00
15 Antonio Brown/15
16 JuJu Smith-Schuster/49 15.00 40.00
17 Eli Manning/15 20.00 50.00
18 Davis Webb/49 5.00 12.00
19 Kurt Warner/15 25.00 50.00
20 Jared Goff/15 20.00 50.00

2018 Elite Pen Pals

1 Josh Rosen 40.00 80.00
2 Sam Darnold 60.00 125.00
3 Josh Allen 50.00 100.00
4 Baker Mayfield 50.00 100.00
5 Mason Rudolph 10.00 25.00
6 Lamar Jackson 60.00 125.00
7 Keke Coutee 5.00 12.00
8 Mark Walton 5.00 12.00
9 Saquon Barkley 100.00 200.00
10 Derrius Guice 8.00 20.00
11 Ronald Jones II 4.00 10.00
12 Nick Chubb 12.00 30.00
13 Kerryon Johnson 6.00 15.00
14 Rashaad Penny 6.00 15.00
15 Royce Freeman 5.00 12.00
16 Sony Michel 15.00 40.00
17 J'Mon Moore 4.00 10.00
18 Kyle Lauletta 6.00 15.00
19 Mike White 5.00 12.00
20 Calvin Ridley 15.00 40.00
21 Courtland Sutton 6.00 15.00
22 Anthony Miller 6.00 15.00
23 Christian Kirk 6.00 15.00
24 Michael Gallup 8.00 20.00
25 James Washington 8.00 20.00
26 Daurice Fountain 5.00 12.00
27 Dante Pettis 6.00 15.00
28 Jaylen Samuels 5.00 12.00
29 Marquez Valdes-Scantling 5.00 12.00
30 DaeSean Hamilton 5.00 12.00
31 Tre'Quan Smith 6.00 15.00
32 D.J. Chark 5.00 12.00
33 Nyheim Hines 5.00 12.00
34 Mike Gesicki 5.00 12.00
35 Jaleel Scott 4.00 10.00
36 Hayden Hurst 5.00 12.00
37 Kalen Ballage 5.00 12.00
38 D.J. Moore 10.00 25.00
39 Bradley Chubb 6.00 15.00
40 Ito Smith 5.00 12.00

2018 Elite Pen Pals Duals

1 N.Chubb/B.Mayfield 100.00 200.00
2 J.Rosen/C.Kirk 20.00 50.00
3 C.Sutton/R.Freeman 10.00 25.00
4 J.Washington/M.Rudolph 15.00 40.00
5 S.Barkley/K.Lauletta 75.00 150.00
6 M.Gallup/M.White 12.00 30.00
7 H.Hurst/L.Jackson 50.00 100.00
8 J.Allen/S.Darnold 75.00 150.00
9 C.Ridley/D.Moore 15.00 40.00
10 R.Penny/S.Michel 20.00 50.00

2018 Elite Pen Pals Gold Ink

2 Sam Darnold 100.00 200.00
6 Lamar Jackson 125.00 250.00
9 Saquon Barkley 225.00 350.00

2018 Elite Primary Colors

*RED/99: .6X TO 1.5X BASIC INSERTS/299
*PURPLE/75: .6X TO 1.5X BASIC INSERTS/299
*ORANGE/25: 1X TO 2.5X BASIC INSERTS/299
1 Mitchell Trubisky 1.25 3.00
2 Matt Ryan 1.00 2.50
3 Joe Flacco 1.00 2.50
4 Cam Newton 1.25 3.00
5 A.J. Green 1.25 3.00
6 Dak Prescott 1.25 3.00
7 Von Miller 1.00 2.50
8 Matthew Stafford 1.00 2.50
9 Aaron Rodgers 2.50 6.00
10 J.J. Watt 1.25 3.00
11 Leonard Fournette 1.25 3.00
12 Todd Gurley II 1.25 3.00
13 Joey Bosa 1.25 3.00
14 Tom Brady 3.00 8.00
15 Drew Brees 1.25 3.00
16 Odell Beckham Jr. 1.25 3.00
17 Derek Carr 1.25 3.00
18 Carson Wentz 1.50 4.00
19 Antonio Brown 1.25 3.00
20 Russell Wilson 1.50 4.00
21 Jameis Winston 1.00 2.50
22 Marcus Mariota 1.25 3.00
23 Tyreek Hill 1.25 3.00
24 Adam Thielen 1.25 3.00
25 Jarvis Landry 1.00 2.50

2018 Elite Prime Targets Materials

1 Amari Cooper 4.00 10.00
2 Antonio Brown 4.00 10.00
3 Corey Davis 3.00 8.00
4 Davante Adams 3.00 8.00
5 DeAndre Hopkins 3.00 8.00
6 Doug Baldwin 3.00 8.00
7 Golden Tate III 2.50 6.00
8 Hunter Henry 2.50 6.00
9 A.J. Green 4.00 10.00

10 Jason Witten 3.00 8.00
11 Demaryius Thomas 3.00 8.00
12 Keenan Allen 3.00 8.00
13 Marqise Lee 2.50 6.00
14 Nelson Agholor 2.50 6.00
15 Stefon Diggs 3.00 8.00

2018 Elite Rookie Autographs

*RED/99: .5X TO 1.2X BASIC AU/199-299
*RED/15: .5X TO 1.2X BASIC AU/25
*PURPLE/49: .6X TO 1.5X BASIC AU/199-299
*PURPLE/49: .5X TO 1.2X BASIC AU/99
*ORANGE/25: .8X TO 2X BASIC AU/199-299
*ORANGE/25: .6X TO 1.5X BASIC AU/99
1 Dylan Cantrell/299 4.00 10.00
2 Denzel Ward/299 10.00 25.00
3 Minkah Fitzpatrick/299 8.00 20.00
4 Tremaine Edmunds/299 8.00 20.00
5 Roquan Smith/299 12.00 30.00
6 Daron Payne/299 6.00 15.00
7 Marcus Davenport/299 8.00 20.00
8 Derwin James/299 8.00 20.00
9 Joshua Jackson/299 8.00 20.00
10 Maurice Hurst/299 5.00 12.00
11 Vita Vea/299 6.00 15.00
12 Rashaan Evans/299 6.00 15.00
13 Isaiah Oliver/299 4.00 10.00
14 Sam Hubbard/299 5.00 12.00
15 Harold Landry/299 4.00 10.00
16 Malik Jefferson/299 5.00 12.00
17 Carlton Davis/299 5.00 12.00
18 Harrison Phillips/199 4.00 10.00
19 Leighton Vander Esch/199 12.00 30.00
20 Arden Key/299 4.00 10.00
21 Ronnie Harrison/299 5.00 12.00
22 Justin Reid/199 4.00 10.00
23 Derrick Nnadi/199 4.00 10.00
25 Jaire Alexander/199 6.00 15.00
27 Jerome Baker/199 5.00 12.00
28 Deontay Burnett/299 5.00 12.00
29 Riley Ferguson/299 6.00 15.00
30 Josey Jewell/99 6.00 15.00
31 Mike Hughes/299 6.00 15.00
32 Kurt Benkert/299 5.00 12.00
36 Marcus Allen/99 8.00 20.00
37 Tyquan Lewis/199 5.00 12.00
39 Anthony Averett/299 5.00 12.00
41 Jalyn Holmes/199 6.00 15.00
42 Simmie Cobbs Jr./299 6.00 15.00
44 Lorenzo Carter/299 4.00 10.00
45 Shaquem Griffin/199 6.00 15.00
46 Sam Darnold/25 40.00 80.00
47 Saquon Barkley/25 75.00 150.00
48 Josh Rosen/25
49 Josh Allen/25 30.00 80.00
50 Baker Mayfield/25 100.00 200.00

2018 Elite Rookie Elitist

1 Saquon Barkley 4.00 10.00
2 Josh Allen 2.00 5.00
3 Josh Rosen 1.50 4.00
4 Baker Mayfield 5.00 12.00
5 Lamar Jackson 3.00 8.00
6 Sam Darnold 3.00 8.00
7 Derwin James 1.00 2.50
8 Calvin Ridley 1.25 3.00
9 Sony Michel 1.50 4.00
10 Minkah Fitzpatrick 1.00 2.50
11 Christian Kirk .75 2.00
12 Derrius Guice 1.00 2.50
13 Courtland Sutton .75 2.00
14 Kerryon Johnson .75 2.00
15 Nick Chubb 1.50 4.00
16 Mason Rudolph 1.25 3.00
17 Riley Ferguson .75 2.00
18 Roquan Smith 1.50 4.00
19 Luke Falk .60 1.50
20 Mark Andrews .75 2.00

2018 Elite Signatures

2 Rich Gannon/49 6.00 15.00
4 Ottis Anderson/49 5.00 12.00
5 Vinny Testaverde/49 5.00 12.00
6 Mike Alstott/49 5.00 12.00
7 Lenny Moore/49
8 Y.A. Tittle/49 8.00 20.00
9 Daryle Lamonica/49 10.00 25.00
10 Fran Tarkenton/25 15.00 40.00
11 Mark Brunell/49 5.00 12.00
12 Paul Hornung/49 15.00 40.00
15 Roman Gabriel/49 12.00 30.00
16 Paul Warfield/49 6.00 15.00
17 Earl Campbell/25 12.00 30.00
18 Shaun Alexander/25 15.00 40.00
19 Ronnie Lott/25 25.00 50.00

2018 Elite Throwback Threads

*PRIME/15: .8X TO 2X BASIC JSY/99
1 Barry Sanders 5.00 12.00
2 Darren Woodson 2.50 6.00
3 Earl Campbell 3.00 8.00
4 Heath Miller 2.00 5.00
5 Howie Long 3.00 8.00
6 Jeremy Shockey 2.00 5.00
7 Jim Kelly 3.00 8.00
8 Joe Namath 4.00 10.00
9 Lawrence Taylor 3.00 8.00
10 Michael Vick 2.50 6.00

2018 Elite Throwback Threads Doubles

1 J.Cutler/M.Trubisky 5.00 12.00
2 E.Manning/P.Simms 4.00 10.00
3 E.Elliott/E.Smith 8.00 20.00
4 J.Charles/K.Hunt 4.00 10.00
5 T.Brdshw/B.Rthlsbrgr 12.00 30.00
6 M.Ryan/M.Vick 4.00 10.00
7 T.Romo/D.Prescott 5.00 12.00
8 T.Gonzalez/T.Kelce 5.00 12.00
9 E.Engram/J.Shockey 3.00 8.00
10 J.Goff/K.Warner 5.00 12.00

2018 Elite Title Waves

1 Aaron Rodgers 2.00 5.00
2 Ben Roethlisberger 1.00 2.50
3 Joe Montana 2.50 6.00
4 Drew Brees 1.00 2.50
5 Eli Manning .75 2.00
6 John Elway 1.50 4.00
7 Hines Ward .75 2.00
8 Jerry Rice 1.50 4.00
9 Kurt Warner .75 2.00
10 Steve Young 1.25 3.00
11 Peyton Manning 2.00 5.00
12 Ray Lewis 1.00 2.50
13 Nick Foles .75 2.00
14 Russell Wilson 1.25 3.00
15 Terry Bradshaw 1.50 4.00
16 Roger Staubach 1.25 3.00
17 Tom Brady 2.50 6.00
18 Von Miller .75 2.00
19 Phil Simms .75 2.00
20 Troy Aikman 1.25 3.00

2019 Elite

1 Tom Brady 2.00 5.00
2 Josh Allen .30 .75
3 Sam Darnold .30 .75
4 Lamar Jackson .30 .75
5 Ben Roethlisberger .25 .60
6 JuJu Smith-Schuster .30 .75
7 Baker Mayfield 2.00 5.00
8 A.J. Green .30 .75
9 Deshaun Watson .40 1.00
10 Andrew Luck .40 1.00
11 Kenyan Drake .20 .50
12 Derrick Henry .30 .75
13 Jalen Ramsey .25 .60
14 Patrick Mahomes II 2.00 5.00
15 Sammy Watkins .30 .75
16 Philip Rivers .30 .75
17 Von Miller .25 .60
18 Derek Carr .30 .75
19 Dak Prescott .30 .75
20 Ezekiel Elliott .40 1.00
21 Leighton Vander Esch .25 .60
22 Carson Wentz .40 1.00
23 Saquon Barkley 2.00 5.00
24 Odell Beckham Jr. .30 .75
25 Khalil Mack .30 .75
26 Mitchell Trubisky .30 .75
27 Adam Thielen .30 .75
28 Harrison Smith .20 .50
29 Aaron Rodgers .60 1.50
30 Davante Adams .25 .60
31 Matthew Stafford .25 .60
32 Drew Brees .30 .75
33 Michael Thomas .30 .75
34 Alvin Kamara .25 .60
35 Matt Ryan .30 .75
36 Julio Jones .30 .75
37 Cam Newton .30 .75
38 Mike Evans .25 .60
39 Todd Gurley II .30 .75
40 Jared Goff .30 .75
41 Aaron Donald .30 .75
42 Russell Wilson .40 1.00
43 Chris Carson .25 .60
44 Jimmy Garoppolo .30 .75
45 David Johnson .30 .75
46 J.J. Watt .30 .75
47 Terrell Suggs .20 .50
48 Myles Garrett .20 .50
49 Joe Mixon .25 .60
50 Marcus Mariota .30 .75
51 Josh Rosen .30 .75
52 Larry Fitzgerald .25 .60
53 Calvin Ridley .25 .60
54 Mark Ingram II .25 .60
55 Christian McCaffrey .30 .75
56 Luke Kuechly .25 .60
57 Roquan Smith .30 .75
58 Andy Dalton .25 .60
59 Jarvis Landry .25 .60
60 Joe Flacco .25 .60
61 Phillip Lindsay .30 .75
62 Kerryon Johnson .25 .60
63 Darius Slay .20 .50
64 Aaron Jones .25 .60
65 DeAndre Hopkins .25 .60
66 T.Y. Hilton .25 .60
67 Darius Leonard .25 .60
68 Leonard Fournette .30 .75
69 A.J. Bouye .20 .50
70 Travis Kelce .30 .75
71 Melvin Gordon III .25 .60
72 Joey Bosa .25 .60
73 Xavien Howard .20 .50
74 Kiko Alonso .20 .50
75 Kirk Cousins .30 .75
76 Sony Michel .30 .75
77 Julian Edelman .30 .75
78 Eli Manning .25 .60
79 Jamal Adams .25 .60
80 Le'Veon Bell .25 .60
81 Jared Cook .20 .50
82 Antonio Brown .30 .75
83 Alshon Jeffery .25 .60
84 Fletcher Cox .20 .50
85 James Conner .30 .75
86 Richard Sherman .25 .60
87 George Kittle .20 .50
88 Doug Baldwin .25 .60
89 Jameis Winston .25 .60
90 Tevin Coleman .20 .50
91 Harold Landry .20 .50
92 LeSean McCoy .30 .75
93 Tremaine Edmunds .25 .60
94 Amari Cooper .30 .75
95 Adrian Peterson .30 .75
96 Josh Norman .25 .60
97 Nick Chubb .30 .75
98 Robert Woods .25 .60
99 Bobby Wagner .20 .50
100 Chris Jones .20 .50
101 Nick Bosa RC 1.50 4.00
102 Dwayne Haskins RC 2.50 6.00
103 T.J. Hockenson RC 1.25 3.00
104 D.K. Metcalf RC 1.50 4.00
105 Marquise Brown RC 1.50 4.00
106 Kyler Murray RC 8.00 20.00
107 Drew Lock RC 2.50 6.00
108 Josh Jacobs RC 2.50 6.00
109 A.J. Brown RC 1.25 3.00
110 Daniel Jones RC 2.50 6.00
111 Will Grier RC 1.50 4.00
112 David Montgomery RC 2.00 5.00
113 Damien Harris RC 1.25 3.00
114 Deebo Samuel RC 1.25 3.00
115 Parris Campbell RC 1.25 3.00
116 Irv Smith Jr. RC 1.00 2.50
117 N'Keal Harry RC 1.50 4.00
118 Quinnen Williams RC .50 1.25
119 Terry McLaurin RC .60 1.50
120 Ryan Finley RC 1.00 2.50
121 Josh Allen RC 2.00 5.00
122 Darrell Henderson RC 1.25 3.00
123 Devin Singletary RC .60 1.50
124 Riley Ridley RC .75 2.00
125 Noah Fant RC 1.00 2.50
126 Rashan Gary RC 1.00 2.50
127 Greedy Williams RC 1.50 4.00
128 Deandre Baker RC 1.25 3.00
129 Devin White RC 1.50 4.00
130 Jarrett Stidham RC 1.50 4.00
131 Alexander Mattison RC 1.00 2.50
132 Hakeem Butler RC 1.00 2.50
133 Ed Oliver RC .75 2.00
134 Mecole Hardman Jr. RC 1.25 3.00
135 Clayton Thorson RC .75 2.00
136 Gardner Minshew II RC .75 2.00
137 Benny Snell Jr. RC 1.50 4.00
138 Tony Pollard RC 1.25 3.00
139 Bryce Love RC .75 2.00
140 Drew Sample RC .50 1.25
141 Gary Jennings Jr. RC .75 2.00
142 Diontae Johnson RC .60 1.50
143 Jalen Hurd RC .60 1.50
144 J.J. Arcega-Whiteside RC .75 2.00
145 Devin Bush II RC 2.00 5.00
146 Miles Boykin RC .60 1.50
147 Miles Sanders RC 1.25 3.00
148 Clelin Ferrell RC .75 2.00
149 Justice Hill RC .75 2.00
150 Andy Isabella RC .75 2.00
151 Josh Oliver RC .50 1.25
152 Jace Sternberger RC .60 1.50
153 Kahale Warring RC .60 1.50
154 Dawson Knox RC .60 1.50
155 Trevon Wesco RC .75 2.00
156 Foster Moreau RC .50 1.25
157 Ryquell Armstead RC .50 1.25
158 Zach Gentry RC .50 1.25
159 Hunter Renfrow RC 1.00 2.50
160 Qadree Ollison RC .60 1.50
161 Jordan Scarlett RC .50 1.25
162 Easton Stick RC .75 2.00
163 Darius Slayton RC .75 2.00
164 KeeSean Johnson RC .50 1.25
165 Kaden Smith RC .50 1.25
166 Trayveon Williams RC .60 1.50
167 Travis Fulgham RC .50 1.25
168 Ty Johnson RC 2.00 5.00
169 Juwann Winfree RC .50 1.25
170 Dexter Williams RC .60 1.50
171 Trace McSorley RC 1.25 3.00
172 Marcus Green RC .50 1.25
173 Travis Homer RC .50 1.25
174 Rodney Anderson RC .60 1.50
175 Darwin Thompson RC .75 2.00
176 Mike Weber RC .75 2.00
177 Myles Gaskin RC 1.00 2.50
178 Brett Rypien RC .60 1.50
179 Christian Wilkins RC 2.00 5.00
180 Brian Burns RC .60 1.50
181 Dexter Lawrence RC .75 2.00
182 Jeffery Simmons RC .50 1.25
183 Darnell Savage Jr. RC .75 2.00
184 Montez Sweat RC 1.50 4.00
185 Johnathan Abram RC .50 1.25
186 Jerry Tillery RC .60 1.50
187 L.J. Collier RC .50 1.25
188 Byron Murphy RC .50 1.25
189 Joejuan Williams RC .60 1.50
190 Marquise Blair RC .60 1.50
191 Juan Thornhill RC .50 1.25
192 Rock Ya-Sin RC .60 1.50
193 Jonah Williams RC 1.25 3.00
194 Chris Lindstrom RC .75 2.00
195 Garrett Bradbury RC .50 1.25
196 Lil'Jordan Humphrey RC .60 1.50
197 Kelvin Harmon RC .75 2.00
198 Tyree Jackson RC 1.25 3.00
199 Sean Murphy-Bunting RC .60 1.50
200 Trayvon Mullen Jr. RC .75 2.00

2019 Elite Aspirations

*VETS/65-99: 2X TO 5X BASIC CARDS
*VETS/37-64: 2.5X TO 6X BASIC CARDS
*VETS/15-20: 4X TO 10X BASIC CARDS
*ROOK/65-99: .8X TO 2X BASIC CARDS/699
*ROOK/37-64: 1X TO 2.5X BASIC CARDS/699
*ROOK/27: 1.2X TO 3X BASIC CARDS/699
*ROOK/15-20: 1.5X TO 4X BASIC CARDS/699

2019 Elite Green

*VETS: 1.5X TO 4X BASIC CARDS
*ROOKIES: .6X TO 1.5X BASIC CARDS

2019 Elite Orange

*VETS/49: 2.5X TO 6X BASIC CARDS
*ROOKIES/25: 1.2X TO 3X BASIC CARDS/699

2019 Elite Pink

*VETS: 1.5X TO 4X BASIC CARDS
*ROOKIES: .6X TO 1.5X BASIC CARDS/699

2019 Elite Purple

*VETS/99: 2X TO 5X BASIC CARDS
*ROOK/99: .8X TO 2X BASIC CARDS/699

2019 Elite Red

*VETS/299: 1.2X TO 3X BASIC CARDS
*ROOKIES/299: .5X TO 1.2X BASIC CARDS/699

2019 Elite Status

*VETS/73-99: 2X TO 5X BASIC CARDS
*VETS/35-63: 2.5X TO 6X BASIC CARDS
*VETS/25-34: 3X TO 8X BASIC CARDS
*VETS/15-24: 4X TO 10X BASIC CARDS
*ROOK/73-99: .8X TO 2X BASIC CARDS/699
*ROOK/35-63: 1X TO 2.5X BASIC CARDS/699
*ROOK/25-34: 1.2X TO 3X BASIC CARDS/699
*ROOK/15-24: 1.5X TO 4X BASIC CARDS/699

2019 Elite Status Die Cut

*VETS/24: 4X TO 10X BASIC CARDS
*ROOK/24: 1.5X TO 4X BASIC CARDS/699

2019 Elite Coverage Materials

*PRIME/49: .6X TO 1.5X BASIC JSY
1 Sony Michel 2.50 6.00
2 Dante Pettis 2.00 5.00
3 Mitchell Trubisky 2.50 6.00
4 Tyler Boyd 1.50 4.00
5 Josh Allen 2.50 6.00
6 Courtland Sutton 2.00 5.00
7 Nick Chubb 2.50 6.00
8 Ronald Jones II 1.50 4.00
9 Josh Rosen 2.50 6.00
10 Mike Williams 1.50 4.00
11 Marlon Mack 1.50 4.00
12 Michael Gallup 2.50 6.00
13 Kenyan Drake 1.50 4.00
14 Nelson Agholor 1.50 4.00
15 Calvin Ridley 2.00 5.00
16 Saquon Barkley 3.00 8.00
17 Leonard Fournette 2.50 6.00
18 Sam Darnold 2.50 6.00
19 Kerryon Johnson 2.00 5.00
20 Marquez Valdes-Scantling 2.00 5.00
21 Christian McCaffrey 2.50 6.00
22 Todd Gurley II 2.50 6.00
23 Lamar Jackson 2.50 6.00
24 Derrius Guice 2.00 5.00
25 Alvin Kamara 2.00 5.00
26 Rashaad Penny 1.50 4.00
27 James Conner 2.50 6.00
28 Deshaun Watson 3.00 8.00
29 Corey Davis 2.00 5.00
30 Stefon Diggs 2.00 5.00

2019 Elite Craftsman Jerseys

*PRIME/49: .6X TO 1.5X BASIC JSY
1 Derek Carr 2.50 6.00
2 Jameis Winston 2.00 5.00
3 Kirk Cousins 2.50 6.00
4 Marcus Mariota 2.50 6.00
5 Matthew Stafford 2.00 5.00
6 Carson Wentz 3.00 8.00
7 Jared Goff 2.50 6.00
8 Matt Ryan 2.50 6.00
9 Russell Wilson 3.00 8.00
10 Will Fuller V 1.50 4.00
11 Joe Mixon 2.00 5.00
12 Derrick Henry 2.50 6.00
13 Melvin Gordon III 2.00 5.00
14 Sterling Shepard 2.00 5.00
15 Tarik Cohen 2.00 5.00
16 Dalvin Cook 2.00 5.00
17 Devonta Freeman 2.00 5.00
18 Aaron Jones 2.00 5.00
19 Michael Thomas 2.50 6.00
20 Dak Prescott 2.50 6.00

2019 Elite Deck

1 Patrick Mahomes II 2.50 6.00
2 James Conner 1.00 2.50
3 Jarvis Landry .75 2.00
4 George Kittle .60 1.50
5 Andrew Luck 1.25 3.00
6 Phillip Lindsay 1.00 2.50
7 Stephon Gilmore .60 1.50
8 Baker Mayfield 1.50 4.00
9 Michael Thomas 1.00 2.50
10 Davante Adams .75 2.00
11 Zach Ertz .75 2.00
12 Saquon Barkley 1.25 3.00
13 Alvin Kamara .75 2.00
14 Aaron Donald 1.00 2.50
15 Khalil Mack 1.00 2.50
16 Patrick Peterson .60 1.50
17 Aaron Rodgers 2.00 5.00
18 Tom Brady 2.50 6.00
19 Ezekiel Elliott 1.25 3.00
20 Darius Leonard .75 2.00

2019 Elite Dual Threats

*GREEN: .3X TO .8X BASIC INSERTS
*PINK: .3X TO .8X BASIC INSERTS
*RED/99: .6X TO 1.5X BASIC INSERTS
*PURPLE/75: .6X TO 1.5X BASIC INSERTS
*ORANGE/25: 1X TO 2.5X BASIC INSERTS
1 Alejandro Villanueva 1.00 2.50
2 Larry Fitzgerald 1.00 2.50
3 Johnny Hekker .75 2.00
4 Ben Roethlisberger 1.00 2.50
5 Taysom Hill .75 2.00
6 Baker Mayfield 2.00 5.00
7 Julian Edelman 1.25 3.00
8 Jeff Heath .75 2.00
9 Derrick Henry 1.25 3.00
10 Pat McAfee 1.00 2.50

2019 Elite Field Vision

*GREEN: .3X TO .8X BASIC INSERTS
*PINK: .3X TO .8X BASIC INSERTS
*RED/99: .6X TO 1.5X BASIC INSERTS
*PURPLE/75: .6X TO 1.5X BASIC INSERTS
*ORANGE/25: 1X TO 2.5X BASIC INSERTS
1 Patrick Mahomes II 3.00 8.00
2 Tom Brady 3.00 8.00
3 Andrew Luck 1.50 4.00
4 Aaron Rodgers 2.50 6.00
5 Aaron Donald 1.25 3.00
6 Dak Prescott 1.25 3.00
7 Harrison Smith .75 2.00
8 Baker Mayfield 2.00 5.00
9 Saquon Barkley 1.50 4.00
10 Khalil Mack 1.25 3.00

2019 Elite Passing the Torch Signatures

2 Patrick Mahomes II/25 150.00 300.00
3 Joe Namath/15 60.00 125.00
4 Sam Darnold/15 EXCH
5 Jack Lambert/15 50.00 100.00
6 T.J. Watt/99 6.00 15.00
7 Terrell Davis/15 25.00 50.00
8 Phillip Lindsay/99 15.00 40.00
9 Brian Urlacher/15
10 Roquan Smith/49 10.00 25.00
11 Jim Kelly/15 25.00 50.00
12 Josh Allen/15 40.00 100.00
13 Hines Ward/25
14 JuJu Smith-Schuster/49 15.00 40.00
15 Jack Youngblood/49 6.00 15.00
16 Aaron Donald/49 10.00 25.00
17 Sean Lee/35 8.00 20.00
18 Leighton Vander Esch/49 30.00 60.00
19 Devin Hester/25 10.00 25.00
20 Tarik Cohen/49 8.00 20.00

2019 Elite Pen Pals

*BLUE: .5X TO 1.2X BASIC AU
1 Kyler Murray 60.00 125.00
2 Nick Bosa 12.00 30.00
3 Daniel Jones 30.00 60.00
4 T.J. Hockenson 10.00 25.00
5 Dwayne Haskins 40.00 80.00
6 Noah Fant 8.00 20.00
7 Josh Jacobs 20.00 50.00
8 Marquise Brown 12.00 30.00
9 N'Keal Harry 12.00 30.00
10 Drew Lock 20.00 50.00
11 Will Grier 12.00 30.00
12 Damien Harris 10.00 25.00
13 Darrell Henderson 10.00 25.00
14 David Montgomery 15.00 40.00
15 D.K. Metcalf 12.00 30.00
16 A.J. Brown 10.00 25.00
17 Parris Campbell 10.00 25.00
18 Deebo Samuel 10.00 25.00
19 Miles Sanders 10.00 25.00
20 J.J. Arcega-Whiteside 6.00 15.00
21 Irv Smith Jr. 8.00 20.00
22 Mecole Hardman Jr. 10.00 25.00
23 Andy Isabella 6.00 15.00
24 Diontae Johnson 5.00 12.00
25 Hunter Renfrow 8.00 20.00
26 Terry McLaurin 5.00 12.00
27 Miles Boykin 5.00 12.00
28 Alexander Mattison 8.00 20.00
29 Devin Singletary 5.00 12.00
30 Ryan Finley 8.00 20.00
31 Jarrett Stidham 12.00 30.00
32 Hakeem Butler 8.00 20.00
33 Bryce Love 6.00 15.00
34 Justice Hill 6.00 15.00
35 Gary Jennings Jr. 6.00 15.00
36 Benny Snell Jr. 12.00 30.00
37 Riley Ridley 6.00 15.00
38 Tony Pollard 10.00 25.00
39 Easton Stick 6.00 15.00
40 Darius Slayton 6.00 15.00

2019 Elite Playmakers

1 Tom Brady 2.50 6.00
2 Ezekiel Elliott 1.25 3.00
3 Saquon Barkley 1.25 3.00
4 Odell Beckham Jr. 1.00 2.50
5 Julio Jones 1.00 2.50
6 DeAndre Hopkins .75 2.00
7 Michael Irvin 1.25 3.00
8 Patrick Mahomes II 2.50 6.00
9 Barry Sanders 1.50 4.00
10 Marshall Faulk .75 2.00
11 Michael Vick .75 2.00
12 Devin Hester .75 2.00
13 Ed Reed .75 2.00
14 Bo Jackson 1.25 3.00
15 Deion Sanders .75 2.00
16 Todd Gurley II 1.00 2.50
17 Rob Gronkowski 1.00 2.50
18 Randy Moss .75 2.00
19 LaDainian Tomlinson .75 2.00
20 Jerry Rice 1.50 4.00

2019 Elite Primary Colors

*GREEN: .3X TO .8X BASIC INSERTS
*PINK: .3X TO .8X BASIC INSERTS
*RED/99: .6X TO 1.5X BASIC INSERTS
*PURPLE/75: .6X TO 1.5X BASIC INSERTS
*ORANGE/25: 1X TO 2.5X BASIC INSERTS
1 Matt Ryan 1.25 3.00
2 Carson Wentz 1.50 4.00
3 Lamar Jackson 1.25 3.00
4 A.J. Green 1.25 3.00
5 Sam Darnold 1.25 3.00
6 Baker Mayfield 2.00 5.00
7 Derrick Henry 1.25 3.00
8 Todd Gurley II 1.25 3.00
9 Andrew Luck 1.50 4.00
10 Tom Brady 3.00 8.00
11 Saquon Barkley 1.50 4.00
12 Von Miller 1.00 2.50
13 David Johnson 1.25 3.00
14 Kenyan Drake .75 2.00
15 Deshaun Watson 1.50 4.00
16 Derek Carr 1.25 3.00
17 Christian McCaffrey 1.25 3.00
18 JuJu Smith-Schuster 1.25 3.00
19 Aaron Rodgers 2.50 6.00
20 Russell Wilson 1.50 4.00
21 Matthew Stafford 1.00 2.50
22 Cam Newton 1.25 3.00
23 Dak Prescott 1.25 3.00
24 Drew Brees 1.25 3.00
25 Patrick Mahomes II 3.00 8.00

2019 Elite Rookie Elitist

1 Nick Bosa 1.50 4.00
2 Josh Allen 2.00 5.00
3 Dwayne Haskins 2.50 6.00
4 T.J. Hockenson 1.25 3.00
5 D.K. Metcalf 1.50 4.00
6 Marquise Brown 1.50 4.00
7 Kyler Murray 5.00 12.00
8 Drew Lock 2.50 6.00
9 Josh Jacobs 2.50 6.00
10 A.J. Brown 1.25 3.00
11 Daniel Jones 2.50 6.00
12 Will Grier 1.60 4.00
13 Darrell Henderson 1.25 3.00
14 Devin Singletary .60 1.50
15 Riley Ridley .75 2.00

2019 Elite Signatures

3 Ezekiel Elliott/25 60.00 125.00
4 Adam Thielen/25 60.00 125.00
5 DeAndre Hopkins/25 8.00 20.00
6 Clay Matthews/25 8.00 20.00
7 Patrick Mahomes II/25 150.00 250.00
8 Phillip Lindsay/99 12.00 30.00
9 Christian McCaffrey/25 25.00 60.00
10 Leighton Vander Esch/25 25.00 60.00
11 Curtis Martin/25 8.00 20.00
12 Joe Thomas/99 12.00 30.00
13 Jack Ham/75 8.00 20.00
14 Jason Taylor/25
15 Pat McAfee/75 15.00 40.00
17 Warren Moon/25 15.00 40.00
18 Doug Williams/25 8.00 20.00
19 Isaac Bruce/75 6.00 15.00
20 Philip Rivers/25 15.00 40.00

2019 Elite Spellbound

*GREEN: .3X TO .8X BASIC INSERTS
*PINK: .3X TO .8X BASIC INSERTS
*RED/99: .6X TO 1.5X BASIC INSERTS
*PURPLE/75: .6X TO 1.5X BASIC INSERTS
*ORANGE/25: 1X TO 2.5X BASIC INSERTS
1 Patrick Mahomes II 3.00 8.00
2 Patrick Mahomes II 3.00 8.00
3 Patrick Mahomes II 3.00 8.00
4 Patrick Mahomes II 3.00 8.00
5 Patrick Mahomes II 3.00 8.00
6 Patrick Mahomes II 3.00 8.00
7 Patrick Mahomes II 3.00 8.00
8 Khalil Mack 1.25 3.00
9 Khalil Mack 1.25 3.00
10 Khalil Mack 1.25 3.00
11 Khalil Mack 1.25 3.00
12 Baker Mayfield 2.00 5.00
13 Baker Mayfield 2.00 5.00
14 Baker Mayfield 2.00 5.00
15 Baker Mayfield 2.00 5.00
16 Baker Mayfield 2.00 5.00
17 Baker Mayfield 2.00 5.00
18 Baker Mayfield 2.00 5.00
19 Baker Mayfield 2.00 5.00
20 Jerry Rice 2.00 5.00
21 Jerry Rice 2.00 5.00
22 Jerry Rice 2.00 5.00
23 Jerry Rice 2.00 5.00
24 Brett Favre 2.50 6.00
25 Brett Favre 2.50 6.00
26 Brett Favre 2.50 6.00
27 Brett Favre 2.50 6.00
28 Brett Favre 2.50 6.00
29 Emmitt Smith 2.00 5.00
30 Emmitt Smith 2.00 5.00
31 Emmitt Smith 2.00 5.00
32 Emmitt Smith 2.00 5.00
33 Emmitt Smith 2.00 5.00
34 Saquon Barkley 1.50 4.00
35 Saquon Barkley 1.50 4.00
36 Saquon Barkley 1.50 4.00
37 Saquon Barkley 1.50 4.00
38 Saquon Barkley 1.50 4.00
39 Saquon Barkley 1.50 4.00
40 Saquon Barkley 1.50 4.00

2019 Elite Star Status

*GREEN: .3X TO .8X BASIC INSERTS
*PINK: .3X TO .8X BASIC INSERTS
*RED/99: .6X TO 1.5X BASIC INSERTS
*PURPLE/75: .6X TO 1.5X BASIC INSERTS
*ORANGE/25: 1X TO 2.5X BASIC INSERTS
1 Ben Roethlisberger 1.00 2.50
2 Patrick Mahomes II 3.00 8.00
3 Tom Brady 3.00 8.00
4 Aaron Rodgers 2.50 6.00
5 Andrew Luck 1.50 4.00
6 Ezekiel Elliott 1.50 4.00
7 Saquon Barkley 1.50 4.00
8 Joe Mixon 1.00 2.50
9 Nick Chubb 1.25 3.00
10 Julio Jones 1.25 3.00
11 DeAndre Hopkins 1.00 2.50
12 Michael Thomas 1.25 3.00
13 George Kittle .75 2.00
14 Aaron Donald 1.25 3.00
15 J.J. Watt 1.25 3.00

2019 Elite Throwback Threads

*PRIME/15: 1X TO 2.5X BASIC JSY/299
1 Howie Long 2.00 5.00
2 Peyton Manning 5.00 12.00
3 Brett Favre 5.00 12.00
4 Calvin Johnson 2.00 5.00
5 Bo Jackson 3.00 8.00
6 Zach Thomas 1.50 4.00
7 Archie Manning 2.00 5.00
8 Jerome Bettis 2.50 6.00
9 Drew Bledsoe 2.00 5.00
10 Fran Tarkenton 2.50 6.00

2019 Elite Title Waves

1 Tom Brady 2.50 6.00
2 Jared Goff 1.00 2.50
3 Patrick Mahomes II 2.50 6.00
4 Ben Roethlisberger .75 2.00
5 Ezekiel Elliott 1.25 3.00
6 Lamar Jackson 1.00 2.50
7 DeAndre Hopkins .75 2.00
8 Mitchell Trubisky 1.00 2.50
9 Drew Brees 1.00 2.50
10 Todd Gurley II 1.00 2.50
11 Sony Michel 1.00 2.50
12 Mike Alstott .60 1.50
13 Michael Strahan 1.00 2.50
14 Justin Tucker .60 1.50
15 Julian Edelman 1.00 2.50

2019 Elite Turn of the Century Autographs

1 Kyler Murray/99 100.00 200.00
2 Nick Bosa/99 15.00 40.00
3 Daniel Jones/99 50.00 100.00
4 T.J. Hockenson/99 12.00 30.00
5 Dwayne Haskins/99 60.00 125.00
6 Noah Fant/149 8.00 20.00
7 Josh Jacobs/99 25.00 60.00
8 Marquise Brown/99 15.00 40.00
9 N'Keal Harry/99 15.00 40.00
10 Drew Lock/99 25.00 60.00
11 Will Grier/99 15.00 40.00
12 Damien Harris/99 12.00 30.00
13 Darrell Henderson/149 10.00 25.00
14 David Montgomery/149 15.00 40.00
15 D.K. Metcalf/99 15.00 40.00
16 A.J. Brown/99 12.00 30.00
17 Parris Campbell/99 12.00 30.00
18 Deebo Samuel/99 12.00 30.00
19 Miles Sanders/99 12.00 30.00
20 J.J. Arcega-Whiteside/99 8.00 20.00
21 Irv Smith Jr./199 8.00 20.00
22 Mecole Hardman Jr./99 12.00 30.00
23 Andy Isabella/99 8.00 20.00
24 Diontae Johnson/149 5.00 12.00
25 Hunter Renfrow/199 8.00 20.00
26 Terry McLaurin/149 5.00 12.00
27 Miles Boykin/149 5.00 12.00
28 Alexander Mattison/199 8.00 20.00
29 Devin Singletary/199 5.00 12.00
30 Ryan Finley/99 10.00 25.00
31 Jarrett Stidham/149 12.00 30.00
32 Hakeem Butler/149 8.00 20.00
33 Bryce Love/99 8.00 20.00
34 Justice Hill/149 6.00 15.00
35 Gary Jennings Jr./199 6.00 15.00
36 Benny Snell Jr./199 12.00 30.00
37 Riley Ridley/199 6.00 15.00
38 Tony Pollard/149 10.00 25.00
39 Easton Stick/149 6.00 15.00
40 Darius Slayton/199 6.00 15.00
41 Kyler Murray/30 200.00 400.00
42 Nick Bosa/30 25.00 60.00
43 D.K. Metcalf/30 25.00 60.00
44 Will Grier/30 25.00 60.00
45 Mecole Hardman Jr./30 20.00 50.00
46 Alexander Mattison/30 15.00 40.00
47 A.J. Brown/30 20.00 50.00
48 Drew Lock/30 40.00 100.00
49 Josh Jacobs/30 40.00 100.00
50 Hunter Renfrow/30 15.00 40.00

2017 Elite Draft Picks

1 A.J. Green .30 .75
2 Aaron Rodgers .60 1.50
3 Adrian Peterson .30 .75
4 Allen Robinson .25 .60
5 Alshon Jeffery .25 .60
6 Amari Cooper .30 .75
7 Andrew Luck .40 1.00
8 Andy Dalton .25 .60
9 Antonio Brown .30 .75
10 Barry Sanders .50 1.25
11 Ben Roethlisberger .30 .75
12 Billy Sims .25 .60
13 Bo Jackson .40 1.00
14 Braxton Miller .20 .50
15 Brett Favre .60 1.50
16 Brian Bosworth .25 .60
17 Cam Newton .30 .75
18 Carlos Hyde .20 .50
19 Carson Wentz .40 1.00
20 Clay Matthews .20 .50
21 Corey Coleman .20 .50
22 Dak Prescott .30 .75
23 Dan Marino .60 1.50
24 David Johnson .30 .75
25 DeAndre Hopkins .25 .60
26 DeMarco Murray .25 .60
27 Derek Carr .30 .75
28 Derrick Henry .25 .60
29 Devonta Freeman .25 .60
30 Dez Bryant .30 .75
31 Drew Brees .30 .75
32 Earl Campbell .30 .75
33 Eddie Lacy .20 .50
34 Eli Manning .25 .60
35 Emmitt Smith .50 1.25
36 Eric Dickerson .30 .75
37 Ezekiel Elliott .40 1.00
38 Fran Tarkenton .30 .75
39 Frank Gore .25 .60
40 Gale Sayers .30 .75
41 Greg Olsen .25 .60
42 Hunter Henry .20 .50
43 Isaiah Crowell .20 .50
44 J.J. Watt .30 .75
45 Jameis Winston .25 .60
46 Jared Goff .30 .75
47 Jarvis Landry .25 .60
48 Jason Witten .25 .60
49 Jerry Rice .50 1.25
50 Jim Brown .40 1.00
51 Joe Flacco .25 .60
52 Joe Namath .40 1.00
53 John Elway .50 1.25
54 Jordan Howard .30 .75
55 Josh Doctson .20 .50
56 Julio Jones .30 .75
57 Keenan Allen .25 .60
58 Khalil Mack .30 .75
59 Kirk Cousins .30 .75
60 LaDainian Tomlinson .25 .60
61 Lamar Miller .20 .50
62 Laquon Treadwell .20 .50
63 Larry Fitzgerald .25 .60
64 Lawrence Taylor .30 .75
65 LeGarrette Blount .25 .60
66 LeSean McCoy .30 .75
67 Le'Veon Bell .25 .60
68 Luke Kuechly .25 .60
69 Marcus Allen .25 .60
70 Marcus Mariota .30 .75
71 Marshall Faulk .25 .60
72 Marvin Jones Jr. .20 .50
73 Matt Forte .20 .50
74 Matt Ryan .25 .60
75 Matthew Stafford .25 .60
76 Melvin Gordon .25 .60
77 Michael Thomas .30 .75
78 Mike Evans .25 .60
79 Odell Beckham Jr. .30 .75
80 Paxton Lynch .20 .50
81 Peyton Manning .60 1.50
82 Philip Rivers .30 .75
83 Red Grange .40 1.00
84 Rob Gronkowski .30 .75
85 Roger Staubach .40 1.00
86 Russell Wilson .40 1.00
87 Sammie Coates .20 .50
88 Sterling Shepard .25 .60
89 Steve Young .40 1.00
90 T.Y. Hilton .25 .60
91 Terry Bradshaw .50 1.25
92 Thomas Rawls .20 .50
93 Tim Tebow .30 .75
94 Todd Gurley II .30 .75
95 Tom Brady .75 2.00
96 Tony Dorsett .30 .75
97 Tony Romo .25 .60
98 Trevor Siemian .20 .50
99 Troy Aikman .40 1.00
100 Von Miller .25 .60
102 Jabrill Peppers RC 1.00 2.50
103 Malik McDowell RC .60 1.50
104 Deshaun Watson RC 4.00 10.00
105 Leonard Fournette RC 2.00 5.00
106 Teez Tabor RC .75 2.00
107 Jonathan Allen RC .75 2.00
108 Jamal Adams RC .60 1.50
109 Cam Robinson RC .60 1.50
110 Dalvin Cook RC 1.50 4.00
111 Marlon Humphrey RC .60 1.50
112 Mitchell Trubisky RC 3.00 8.00
113 JuJu Smith-Schuster RC 1.50 4.00
114 Tim Williams RC .75 2.00
115 Derek Barnett RC .75 2.00
116 Reuben Foster RC .60 1.50
117 Brad Kaaya RC .60 1.50
118 Christian McCaffrey RC 1.50 4.00
119 O.J. Howard RC .75 2.00
120 Mike Williams RC 1.00 2.50
121 Desmond King RC .75 2.00
122 Davis Webb RC .60 1.50
123 Carl Lawson RC .60 1.50
124 Dan Feeney RC 1.00 2.50
125 Josh Reynolds RC .60 1.50
126 Solomon Thomas RC .60 1.50
127 Dawuane Smoot RC .60 1.50
128 Zach Cunningham RC .75 2.00
129 Budda Baker RC .60 1.50
130 Matthew Dayes RC .60 1.50
131 Bucky Hodges RC .60 1.50
132 KD Cannon RC .60 1.50
133 Charles Harris RC .60 1.50
134 Malik Hooker RC .60 1.50
135 Sidney Jones RC .60 1.50
136 Jake Butt RC .75 2.00
137 Haason Reddick RC .60 1.50
138 Eddie Jackson RC .75 2.00
139 Marcus Williams RC .60 1.50
140 Chad Kelly RC .60 1.50
141 Jarrad Davis RC .75 2.00
142 Cordrea Tankersley RC .75 2.00
143 Isaiah Ford RC .60 1.50
144 Jerod Evans RC .75 2.00
145 Patrick Mahomes II RC 8.00 20.00
146 Adoree' Jackson RC .75 2.00
147 Charles Walker RC .60 1.50
148 John Ross RC .75 2.00
149 Cameron Sutton RC .60 1.50
150 Evan Engram RC .75 2.00
151 Tre'Davious White RC .60 1.50
152 Mitch Leidner RC 1.00 2.50
153 Samaje Perine RC .60 1.50
154 Corey Davis RC 1.00 2.50
155 Jourdan Lewis RC .60 1.50
156 Alvin Kamara RC 2.50 6.00
157 Travis Rudolph RC .60 1.50
158 Wayne Gallman RC .75 2.00
159 Jordan Leggett RC .60 1.50
160 Cooper Kupp RC 1.00 2.50
161 Joe Mixon RC 1.25 3.00
162 Artavis Scott RC .60 1.50
163 Jeremy McNichols RC .60 1.50
164 Dede Westbrook RC .60 1.50
165 Malachi Dupre RC .60 1.50
166 Curtis Samuel RC .75 2.00
167 Amara Darboh RC .60 1.50
168 Cooper Rush RC .75 2.00
169 Stacy Coley RC .60 1.50
170 Jeremy Sprinkle RC .60 1.50
171 James Quick RC .75 2.00
172 Ryan Switzer RC .75 2.00
173 ArDarius Stewart RC .60 1.50
174 Elijah Hood RC .60 1.50
175 Jehu Chesson RC .75 2.00
176 C.J. Beathard RC .60 1.50
177 Corey Clement RC .75 2.00
178 Zay Jones RC .75 2.00
179 Chris Godwin RC .75 2.00
180 Blake Jarwin RC .60 1.50
181 Seth Russell RC .75 2.00
182 Taywan Taylor RC .60 1.50
183 Donnel Pumphrey RC .75 2.00
184 Kareem Hunt RC 1.25 3.00
185 Shelton Gibson RC .60 1.50
186 Elijah McGuire RC .60 1.50
187 Travin Dural RC .75 2.00
188 Kenny Golladay RC 1.00 2.50
189 Damore'ea Stringfellow RC .75 2.00
190 Amba Etta-Tawo RC .60 1.50
191 Marlon Mack RC 1.00 2.50
192 Chad Hansen RC .60 1.50
193 James Conner RC 1.25 3.00
194 Brian Hill RC .60 1.50
195 Speedy Noil RC .60 1.50
196 R. Joshua Dobbs RC .75 2.00
197 Justin Davis RC 1.00 2.50
198 Fred Ross RC .60 1.50
199 Josiah Price RC .75 2.00
200 Noah Brown RC .75 2.00

2017 Elite Draft Picks Aspirations Blue

*VETS/25: 2.5X TO 6X BASIC CARDS
*ROOKIES/25: 1X TO 2.5X BASIC CARDS

2017 Elite Draft Picks Alma Mater

*HOLO: .5X TO 1.5X BASIC INSERTS
1 Cam Newton .75 2.00
2 Tom Brady 2.00 5.00
3 J.J. Watt .75 2.00
4 Antonio Brown .75 2.00
5 Adrian Peterson .75 2.00
6 Carson Wentz 1.00 2.50
7 Ezekiel Elliott 1.00 2.50
8 Dak Prescott .75 2.00
9 Aaron Rodgers 1.50 4.00
10 Rob Gronkowski .75 2.00

2017 Elite Draft Picks College Ties

*HOLO: .5X TO 1.2X BASIC INSERTS
1 L.Treadwell/C.Kelly .50 1.25
2 J.Witten/P.Manning 1.50 4.00
3 D.Henry/M.Ingram .60 1.50
4 M.Garrett/V.Miller .60 1.50
5 D.Watson/M.Williams 3.00 8.00
6 J.Winston/D.Cook 1.25 3.00
7 E.George/E.Elliott 1.00 2.50
8 C.McCaffrey/A.Luck 1.25 3.00
9 B.Sims/S.Perine .60 1.50
10 D.Westbrook/S.Perine .50 1.25
11 R.Williams/D.Foreman .60 1.50
12 M.Trubisky/R.Switzer 2.50 6.00
13 O.Beckham/L.Fournette 1.50 4.00
14 R.Wilson/J.Watt 1.00 2.50
15 B.Jackson/C.Newton 1.00 2.50
16 C.Woodson/T.Brady 2.00 5.00
17 D.Murray/A.Peterson .75 2.00
18 A.Dalton/L.Tomlinson .60 1.50
19 E.Smith/T.Tebow 1.25 3.00
20 J.Elway/C.McCaffrey 1.25 3.00

2017 Elite Draft Picks Draft Picks Autographs

102 Jabrill Peppers SP2 6.00 15.00
103 Malik McDowell SP1 3.00 8.00
104 Deshaun Watson SP2 30.00 60.00
105 Leonard Fournette SP2 30.00 60.00
107 Jonathan Allen SP2 5.00 12.00
108 Jamal Adams 2.50 6.00
110 Dalvin Cook SP2 10.00 25.00
112 Mitchell Trubisky SP2 40.00 80.00
113 JuJu Smith-Schuster SP1 8.00 20.00
114 Tim Williams SP1 4.00 10.00
115 Derek Barnett SP1 4.00 10.00
117 Brad Kaaya SP2 4.00 10.00
118 Christian McCaffrey SP2 30.00 60.00
119 O.J. Howard 3.00 8.00
120 Mike Williams SP2 6.00 15.00
121 Desmond King 3.00 8.00
122 Davis Webb SP2 4.00 10.00
123 Carl Lawson SP1 3.00 8.00
124 Dan Feeney 4.00 10.00
125 Josh Reynolds 2.50 6.00
126 Solomon Thomas 2.50 6.00
127 Dawuane Smoot 2.50 6.00
128 Zach Cunningham 3.00 8.00
129 Budda Baker 2.50 6.00
130 Matthew Dayes 2.50 6.00
132 KD Cannon SP2 4.00 10.00
133 Charles Harris SP1 3.00 8.00
134 Malik Hooker 2.50 6.00
135 Sidney Jones 2.50 6.00
136 Jake Butt 3.00 8.00
137 Haason Reddick 2.50 6.00
138 Eddie Jackson 3.00 8.00
139 Marcus Williams 2.50 6.00
140 Chad Kelly SP2 4.00 10.00
142 Cordrea Tankersley 3.00 8.00
143 Isaiah Ford SP1 3.00 8.00
144 Jerod Evans SP2 5.00 12.00
145 Patrick Mahomes II SP2 125.00 250.00
146 Adoree' Jackson 3.00 8.00
147 Charles Walker 2.50 6.00
148 John Ross SP2 5.00 12.00
149 Cameron Sutton 2.50 6.00
150 Evan Engram 3.00 8.00
151 Tre'Davious White 2.50 6.00
152 Mitch Leidner 4.00 10.00
153 Samaje Perine SP1 10.00 25.00
154 Corey Davis SP2 6.00 15.00
156 Alvin Kamara SP2 15.00 40.00
157 Travis Rudolph 2.50 6.00
159 Jordan Leggett 2.50 6.00
160 Cooper Kupp SP2 6.00 15.00
161 Joe Mixon SP1 6.00 15.00
162 Artavis Scott 2.50 6.00

163 Jeremy McNichols SP1 3.00 8.00
164 Dede Westbrook SP1 3.00 8.00
165 Malachi Dupre SP1 3.00 8.00
166 Curtis Samuel SP2 5.00 12.00
167 Amara Darboh SP1 3.00 8.00
168 Cooper Rush 3.00 8.00
169 Stacy Coley SP1 3.00 8.00
170 Jeremy Sprinkle 2.50 6.00
171 James Quick 3.00 8.00
172 Ryan Switzer 3.00 8.00
173 ArDarius Stewart 2.50 6.00
175 Jehu Chesson 3.00 8.00
176 C.J. Beathard SP2 4.00 10.00
177 Corey Clement SP1 4.00 10.00
178 Zay Jones SP2 5.00 12.00
179 Chris Godwin 8.00 20.00
180 Blake Jarwin 2.50 6.00
181 Seth Russell 3.00 8.00
182 DeShone Kizer SP2 4.00 10.00
183 Donnel Pumphrey SP1 4.00 10.00
184 Kareem Hunt SP1 8.00 20.00
185 Shelton Gibson 2.50 6.00
186 Elijah McGuire 2.50 6.00
187 Travin Dural 3.00 8.00
188 Pharaoh Brown 4.00 10.00
189 Damore'ea Stringfellow 3.00 8.00
190 Amba Etta-Tawo 2.50 6.00
191 Marlon Mack SP1 5.00 12.00
192 Chad Hansen 2.50 6.00
193 James Conner 5.00 12.00
194 Brian Hill SP2 4.00 10.00
195 Speedy Noil 2.50 6.00
197 Justin Davis 4.00 10.00
198 Fred Ross 2.50 6.00
199 Josiah Price 3.00 8.00
200 Noah Brown 3.00 8.00
201 Cole Hikutini 2.50 6.00
202 De'Veon Smith 6.00 15.00
204 Darrell Daniels 4.00 10.00
205 Ricky Seals-Jones 2.50 6.00
206 Gerald Everett 2.50 6.00
207 Jahad Thomas 2.50 6.00
208 Quincy Adeboyejo 2.50 6.00
209 Zach Pascal 2.50 6.00
210 Kenny Golladay 4.00 10.00
211 Michael Rector 2.50 6.00
214 Taco Charlton SP1 3.00 8.00
215 Anthony Walker Jr. 2.50 6.00
217 DeMarcus Walker 2.50 6.00
218 Carlos Watkins 2.50 6.00
219 Gareon Conley 2.50 6.00
221 Ryan Glasgow 2.50 6.00
222 Ryan Anderson 2.50 6.00
223 Chris Wormley 2.50 6.00
225 Daeshon Hall 2.50 6.00
226 Quincy Wilson 2.50 6.00
227 Marcus Maye 2.50 6.00
228 Steven Taylor 3.00 8.00
229 Jamaal Williams SP1 3.00 8.00
230 Bryan Cox 5.00 12.00
231 Marquez White 2.50 6.00
233 T.J. Watt 8.00 20.00
234 Marshon Lattimore SP1 4.00 10.00
235 Jaleel Johnson 5.00 12.00
236 Rushel Shell III 2.50 6.00
237 D'Onta Foreman SP2 5.00 12.00
238 Devine Redding 2.50 6.00
239 Jalen Reeves-Maybin 5.00 12.00
240 Davon Godchaux 2.50 6.00
241 Eddie Vanderdoes 2.50 6.00
242 Kendell Beckwith 2.50 6.00
243 Vince Biegel 5.00 12.00
244 Montravius Adams 3.00 8.00
245 Montae Nicholson 3.00 8.00
246 Matt Milano 3.00 8.00
247 Joseph Yearby SP2 4.00 10.00
248 Takkarist McKinley SP1 3.00 8.00
249 Josh Carraway 2.50 6.00
250 Ben Boulware 6.00 15.00
251 Damontae Kazee 3.00 8.00
252 Josh Malone 2.50 6.00
253 Keith Kelsey 2.50 6.00
254 Freddie Stevenson 3.00 8.00
255 Billy Brown 2.50 6.00
256 Kevin King 3.00 8.00
257 Chidobe Awuzie 3.00 8.00
258 Deatrich Wise Jr. 4.00 10.00
259 DeAngelo Yancey 2.50 6.00
260 Hardy Nickerson 2.50 6.00
261 Carlos Henderson SP1 3.00 8.00
262 Raekwon McMillan 2.50 6.00
263 Ejuan Price 2.50 6.00
264 Tony Conner 2.50 6.00
265 Justin Evans 2.50 6.00
266 Channing Stribling 3.00 8.00
267 Jordan Willis 2.50 6.00
268 Riley Bullough 2.50 6.00
269 Randall Goforth SP2 6.00 15.00
270 Calvin Munson 2.50 6.00
271 Fabian Moreau 2.50 6.00
272 Tyus Bowser 2.50 6.00
273 Ryan Ramczyk 2.50 6.00
275 Tanner Vallejo 4.00 10.00
276 Joe Mathis 2.50 6.00
277 Jalen Myrick 2.50 6.00
278 Des Lawrence 3.00 8.00
279 Sam Rogers 2.50 6.00
280 Ashton Lampkin 2.50 6.00
281 Marcus Cox 3.00 8.00
282 Obi Melifonwu 2.50 6.00
284 Trevor Knight 3.00 8.00
285 Phazahn Odom 2.50 6.00
286 Corey Smith 4.00 10.00
287 De'Angelo Henderson 2.50 6.00
289 Chris Carson 4.00 10.00
290 Gunner Kiel 4.00 10.00
291 Dare Ogunbowale 4.00 10.00
292 Brady Gustafson 2.50 6.00
293 Gabe Marks 2.50 6.00
295 Mack Hollins 2.50 6.00
296 Shock Linwood 3.00 8.00

2017 Elite Draft Picks Draft Picks Autographs Aspirations Blue

*BLUE/25: 1X TO 2.5X BASIC AU
*BLUE/25: .75X TO 2X BASIC AU SP1
*BLUE/25: .6X TO 1.5X BASIC AU SP2
104 Deshaun Watson 40.00 100.00
105 Leonard Fournette 40.00 100.00
145 Patrick Mahomes II 200.00 400.00

2017 Elite Draft Picks Draft Picks Autographs Aspirations Red

*RED/35-49: .8X TO 2X BASIC AU
*RED/35-49: .6X TO 1.5X BASIC AU SP1
*RED/35-49: .5X TO 1.2X BASIC AU SP2
104 Deshaun Watson/35 40.00 80.00
105 Leonard Fournette/35 30.00 80.00
145 Patrick Mahomes II/35 150.00 300.00

2017 Elite Draft Picks Draft Picks Autographs Status Die Cut Blue

*BLUE/25: 1X TO 2.5X BASIC AU
*BLUE/25: .75X TO 2X BASIC AU SP1
*BLUE/25: .6X TO 1.5X BASIC AU SP2
145 Patrick Mahomes II 200.00 400.00

2017 Elite Draft Picks Draft Picks Autographs Status Die Cut Purple

*PURPLE/99: .6X TO 1.5X BASIC AU
*PURPLE/99: .5X TO 1.2X BASIC AU SP1
*PURPLE/50: .6X TO 1.5X BASIC AU SP1
*PURPLE/50: .5X TO 1.2X BASIC AU SP2
145 Patrick Mahomes II/50 150.00 300.00

2017 Elite Draft Picks Draft Picks Autographs Status Die Cut Red

*RED/35-49: .8X TO 2X BASIC AU
*RED/35-49: .6X TO 1.5X BASIC AU SP1
*RED/35-49: .5X TO 1.2X BASIC AU SP2
104 Deshaun Watson/35 40.00 80.00
105 Leonard Fournette/35 40.00 80.00
145 Patrick Mahomes II/35 150.00 300.00

2017 Elite Draft Picks Passing the Torch

*HOLO: .5X TO 1.2X BASIC INSERTS
1 D.Henry/M.Mariota .75 2.00
2 J.Winston/M.Mariota .75 2.00
3 S.Bradford/T.Tebow .75 2.00
4 G.Rogers/M.Allen .60 1.50
5 E.Campbell/T.Dorsett .75 2.00
6 E.Campbell/R.Williams .75 2.00
7 B.Sanders/T.Thomas 1.25 3.00
8 E.George/E.Elliott 1.00 2.50
9 D.Pumphrey/M.Faulk .60 1.50
10 M.Gordon/L.Tomlinson .60 1.50
11 M.Gordon/S.Perine .60 1.50
12 S.Perine/B.Sims .60 1.50
13 A.Rodgers/J.Goff 1.50 4.00
14 E.Manning/A.Manning .60 1.50
15 D.Webb/J.Goff .75 2.00
16 A.Manning/P.Manning 1.50 4.00
17 E.Manning/P.Manning 1.50 4.00
18 A.Luck/J.Elway 1.25 3.00
19 D.Marino/T.Dorsett 1.50 4.00
20 C.Woodson/T.Brady 2.00 5.00

2018 Elite Draft Picks

1 A.J. Green .30 .75
2 Aaron Rodgers .60 1.50
3 Adam Thielen .30 .75
4 Adrian Peterson .30 .75
5 Amari Cooper .30 .75
6 Andrew Luck .40 1.00
7 Antonio Brown .30 .75
8 Barry Sanders .50 1.25
9 Barry Switzer .25 .60
10 Billy Cannon .20 .50
11 Billy Sims .25 .60
12 Bo Jackson .40 1.00
13 Brett Favre .60 1.50
14 Brian Bosworth .25 .60
15 Cam Newton .30 .75
16 Carson Wentz .40 1.00
17 Charles White .20 .50
18 Charles Woodson .30 .75
19 Christian McCaffrey .30 .75
20 Clay Helton .20 .50
21 Clay Matthews .25 .60
22 Colt McCoy .20 .50
23 Corey Davis .25 .60
24 Dak Prescott .30 .75
25 Dalvin Cook .25 .60
26 Dan Marino .60 1.50
27 David Johnson .30 .75
28 DeAndre Hopkins .25 .60
29 Dede Westbrook .20 .50
30 Deion Sanders .25 .60
31 Derek Carr .30 .75
32 Derrick Henry .30 .75
33 Deshaun Watson .40 1.00
34 Dez Bryant .30 .75
35 Dick Butkus .40 1.00
36 D'Onta Foreman .20 .50
37 Drew Brees .30 .75
38 Earl Campbell .30 .75
39 Ed Reed .25 .60
40 Emmitt Smith .50 1.25
41 Eric Dickerson .30 .75
42 Ezekiel Elliott .40 1.00
43 George Rogers .25 .60
44 J.J. Watt .30 .75
45 Jabrill Peppers .20 .50
46 Jameis Winston .25 .60
47 Jason Witten .25 .60
48 Jeremy Shockey .20 .50
49 Jerry Rice .50 1.25
50 Herschel Walker .30 .75
51 Alvin Kamara .25 .60
52 Joe Namath .40 1.00
53 John Elway .50 1.25
54 John Hannah .20 .50
55 Johnny Rodgers .25 .60
56 Jordan Howard .30 .75
57 Julio Jones .30 .75
58 Kareem Hunt .25 .60
59 Khalil Mack .30 .75
60 LaDainian Tomlinson .25 .60
61 Larry Fitzgerald .25 .60
62 Leonard Fournette .30 .75
63 Le'Veon Bell .25 .60
64 Mack Brown .20 .50
65 Major Applewhite .30 .75
66 Marcus Allen .30 .75
67 Marcus Dupree .25 .60
68 Marcus Mariota .30 .75
69 Matt Ryan .25 .60
70 Matthew Stafford .25 .60
71 Michael Irvin .30 .75
72 Michael Thomas .30 .75
73 Mike Rozier .25 .60
74 Mitchell Trubisky .30 .75
75 Ndamukong Suh .25 .60
76 Nick Saban .30 .75
77 Odell Beckham Jr. .30 .75
78 Ozzie Newsome .25 .60
79 Patrick Mahomes II .75 2.00
80 Peyton Manning .60 1.50
81 Randy Moss .25 .60
82 Ray Lewis .30 .75
83 Red Grange .40 1.00
84 Ricky Williams .25 .60
85 Roger Staubach .40 1.00
86 Ron Dayne .20 .50
87 Russell Wilson .40 1.00
88 Shaun Alexander .20 .50
89 Steve Spurrier .25 .60
90 Ted Hendricks .20 .50
91 Terry Bradshaw .50 1.25
92 Tim Tebow .30 .75
93 Todd Gurley II .30 .75
94 Tom Brady .75 2.00
95 Tony Dorsett .30 .75
96 Trevor Siemian .20 .50
97 Troy Aikman .40 1.00
98 Tyreek Hill .30 .75
99 Vince Young .20 .50
100 Von Miller .25 .60
101A Sam Darnold SP RC 6.00 15.00
(white jsy)
101B Sam Darnold SP 6.00 15.00
(red jsy)
102A Josh Rosen RC 1.50 4.00
(blue jsy)
102B Josh Rosen 1.50 4.00
(white jsy)
103A Josh Allen RC 2.00 5.00
(black jsy)
103B Josh Allen 2.00 5.00
(white jsy)
104A Lamar Jackson SP RC 6.00 15.00
(laces at side)
104B Lamar Jackson SP 6.00 15.00
(ball laces down)
105A Saquon Barkley RC 4.00 10.00
(white jsy)
105B Saquon Barkley 4.00 10.00
(dark jsy)
106A Derrius Guice SP RC 1.00 2.50
(ball in left arm)
106B Derrius Guice SP 1.00 2.50
(ball in right arm)
107A Courtland Sutton RC .75 2.00
(blue jsy)
107B Courtland Sutton .75 2.00
(white jsy)
108A James Washington RC 1.00 2.50
(white jsy)
108B James Washington 1.00 2.50
(black jsy)
109A Christian Kirk RC .75 2.00
(white jsy)
109B Christian Kirk .75 2.00
(maroon jsy)
110A Calvin Ridley SP RC 2.50 6.00
(white jsy)
110B Calvin Ridley SP 2.50 6.00
(red jsy)
111A Mason Rudolph RC 1.25 3.00
(ball in two hands)
111B Mason Rudolph 1.25 3.00
(ball in one hand)
112A Nick Chubb SP RC 3.00 8.00
(white jsy)
112B Nick Chubb 3.00 8.00
(red jsy)
113A Ronald Jones II RC .50 1.25
(ball low)
113B Ronald Jones II .50 1.25
(ball high)
114A Deon Cain RC .60 1.50
(catching)
114B Deon Cain .60 1.50
(running)
115A Mark Andrews RC .75 2.00
(ball in left hand)
115B Mark Andrews .75 2.00
(no ball)
116A Nyheim Hines RC .60 1.50
(red jsy)
116B Nyheim Hines .60 1.50
(black jsy)
117A Dante Pettis RC .75 2.00
(running)
117B Dante Pettis .75 2.00
(catching)
118A Hayden Hurst RC .60 1.50
(white jsy)
118B Hayden Hurst .60 1.50
(red jsy)
119A Bradley Chubb RC .75 2.00
(white jsy)
119B Bradley Chubb .75 2.00
(red jsy)
120A Luke Falk RC .60 1.50
(white jsy)
120B Luke Falk .60 1.50
(black jsy)
121A Bo Scarbrough SP RC 1.25 3.00
(white jsy)
121B Bo Scarbrough SP 1.25 3.00
(red jsy)
122A Minkah Fitzpatrick SP RC 2.00 5.00
(red jsy)
122B Minkah Fitzpatrick 2.00 5.00
(white jsy)
123A Simmie Cobbs Jr. RC .75 2.00
(red jsy)
123B Simmie Cobbs Jr. .75 2.00
(white jsy)
124A Deontay Burnett RC .60 1.50
(red jsy)
124B Deontay Burnett .60 1.50
(white jsy)
125A Dallas Goedert RC .60 1.50
(ball in right arm)
125B Dallas Goedert .60 1.50
(no ball)
126A Royce Freeman RC .60 1.50
(green jsy)
126B Royce Freeman .60 1.50
(white jsy)
127A Daron Payne RC .75 2.00
(white jsy)
127B Daron Payne .75 2.00
(red jsy)
128A Kamryn Pettway RC .75 2.00
(blue jsy)
128B Kamryn Pettway .75 2.00
(white jsy)
129A Derwin James RC 1.00 2.50
(white jsy)
129B Derwin James 1.00 2.50
(red jsy)
130A Allen Lazard RC .50 1.25
(two hands on ball)
130B Allen Lazard .50 1.25
(no ball)
131A D.J. Chark SP RC 1.25 3.00
(two hands on balll)
131B D.J. Chark SP 1.25 3.00
(no ball)
132A Mike Gesicki RC .60 1.50
(blue jsy)
132B Mike Gesicki .60 1.50
(white jsy)
133A DeAndre Goolsby RC .50 1.25
(standing straigh up)
133B DeAndre Goolsby .50 1.25
(bent over)
134A Dalton Schultz RC .60 1.50
(white jsy)
134B Dalton Schultz .60 1.50
(red jsy)
135A Anthony Miller RC .75 2.00
(white jsy)
135B Anthony Miller .75 2.00
(blue jsy)
136A Kalen Ballage RC .60 1.50
(maroon jsy)
136B Kalen Ballage .60 1.50
(black jsy)
137A John Kelly RC .60 1.50
(white jsy)
137B John Kelly .60 1.50
(gray jsy)
138A Troy Fumagalli RC .60 1.50
(white jsy)
138B Troy Fumagalli .60 1.50
(red jsy)
139A Baker Mayfield RC 5.00 12.00
(passing)
139B Baker Mayfield 5.00 12.00
(running)
140A Justin Jackson RC .60 1.50
(purple jsy)
140B Justin Jackson .60 1.50
(white jsy)
141A Connor Williams RC 1.00 2.50
(white jsy)
141B Connor Williams 1.00 2.50
(orange jsy)
142A Michael Gallup RC 1.00 2.50
(white jsy)
142B Michael Gallup 1.00 2.50
(green jsy)
143A Robert Foster RC .50 1.25
(running to the side)
143B Robert Foster .50 1.25
(running forward)
144A Jester Weah RC .50 1.25
(blue jsy)
144B Jester Weah .50 1.25
(white jsy)
145A Quadree Henderson RC .60 1.50
(navy jsy)
145B Quadree Henderson .60 1.50
(white jsy)
146A Rashaad Penny RC .75 2.00
(white jsy)
146B Rashaad Penny .75 2.00
(black jsy)
147A Akrum Wadley RC .50 1.25
(white jsy)
147B Akrum Wadley .50 1.25
(black jsy)
148A Kevin Toliver II SP RC 1.25 3.00
(looking straight)
148B Kevin Toliver II SP 1.25 3.00
(looking right)
149A Ronnie Harrison RC .60 1.50
(red jsy)
149B Ronnie Harrison .60 1.50
(white jsy)
150A Sam Hubbard RC .60 1.50
(running)
150B Sam Hubbard .60 1.50
(crouched)
152A Maurice Hurst RC .60 1.50
(yellow jsy)
152B Maurice Hurst .60 1.50
(blue jsy)
153A Harold Landry RC .50 1.25
(white jsy)
153B Harold Landry .50 1.25
(red jsy)
154A Arden Key RC .50 1.25
(looking straight)
154B Arden Key .50 1.25
(looking left)
158A Tarvarus McFadden SP RC 1.25 3.00
(bent over)
158B Tarvarus McFadden SP 1.25 3.00
(standing straight)
159 Minkah Fitzpatrick SP 10.00 25.00
160 Derwin James SP 10.00 25.00
161 Andrew Brown 2.50 6.00
162 Connor Williams 5.00 12.00
163 Dorian O'Daniel 2.50 6.00
164 Marcell Ateman 3.00 8.00
167 Ronnie Harrison 3.00 8.00
168 Bryce Bobo SP 5.00 12.00
169 Hayden Hurst 3.00 8.00
170 Devonte Boyd 2.50 6.00
171 Jake Wieneke SP 6.00 15.00
172 Matt Linehan SP 5.00 12.00
173 Kurt Benkert SP 6.00 15.00
174 J'Mon Moore 2.50 6.00
175 Dalyn Dawkins 2.50 6.00
176 Javon Wims SP 5.00 12.00
177 Christopher Herndon IV 2.50 6.00
178 Ian Thomas SP 5.00 12.00
179 Dimitri Flowers 2.50 6.00
180 Mark Walton SP 6.00 15.00
181 Lavon Coleman 3.00 8.00
182 Chase Edmonds 2.50 6.00
183 Riley Ferguson SP 8.00 20.00
184 Chase Litton 3.00 8.00
185 Marcus Baugh 2.50 6.00
186 Khalid Hill 3.00 8.00
187 Darren Carrington II SP 6.00 15.00
188 Cedrick Wilson Jr. SP 5.00 12.00
189 Austin Proehl 2.50 6.00
190 Max Browne SP 6.00 15.00
191 David Wells 2.50 6.00
192 Adam Breneman 3.00 8.00
194 Jaylen Samuels 3.00 8.00
195 Da'Shawn Hand 2.50 6.00
196 Vita Vea 4.00 10.00
197 Denzel Ward SP 12.00 30.00
198 Tyquan Lewis 3.00 8.00
199 Josh Sweat 3.00 8.00
200 Orlando Brown 4.00 10.00
201 Malik Jefferson 3.00 8.00
202 Derrick Nnadi 2.50 6.00
203 Brandon Facyson 2.50 6.00
204 Quin Blanding 2.50 6.00
205 Janarion Grant 2.50 6.00
207 Tremaine Edmunds SP 10.00 25.00
208 Jaire Alexander 4.00 10.00
209 Anthony Averett 3.00 8.00
210 Armani Watts 2.50 6.00
211 Marquis Haynes 2.50 6.00
213 Christian LaCouture 2.50 6.00
214 Keishawn Bierria 2.50 6.00
215 Chukwuma Okorafor 2.50 6.00
217 M.J. Stewart 2.50 6.00
219 Dorance Armstrong Jr. 2.50 6.00
220 Trenton Thompson 2.50 6.00
221 Jordan Thomas 3.00 8.00
222 Jalyn Holmes 4.00 10.00
223 Azeem Victor 3.00 8.00
224 Rashaan Evans SP 8.00 20.00
225 Mike McCray 3.00 8.00
226 Fred Warner 2.50 6.00
227 Duke Dawson 2.50 6.00
228 Roquan Smith 8.00 20.00
229 Kyzir White 4.00 10.00
230 Damon Webb 3.00 8.00
231 Harrison Phillips 2.50 6.00
232 Isaiah Oliver SP 5.00 12.00
233 Joshua Jackson SP 10.00 25.00
234 Jordan Lasley SP 5.00 12.00
235 Terrell Edmunds 8.00 20.00
237 Trey Marshall 3.00 8.00
238 Folorunso Fatukasi 2.50 6.00
239 Matthew Thomas 3.00 8.00
240 Duke Ejiofor 2.50 6.00
241 Jordan Whitehead 2.50 6.00
243 Josey Jewell 3.00 8.00
244 Deatrick Nichols 3.00 8.00
246 Rasheem Green 2.50 6.00
247 Marcus Allen 4.00 10.00
248 Micah Kiser 2.50 6.00
249 Tre Flowers 2.50 6.00
250 D.J. Reed 2.50 6.00
253 Auden Tate SP 5.00 12.00
254 DaeSean Hamilton 3.00 8.00
255 D.J. Moore SP 10.00 25.00
256 Kerryon Johnson SP 8.00 20.00
257 Billy Price 3.00 8.00
258 Ray-Ray McCloud 2.50 6.00
260 Sony Michel SP 15.00 40.00
261 Josh Adams SP 10.00 25.00
264 Trey Quinn 2.50 6.00
265 Kenny Hill 3.00 8.00
266 Martinas Rankin 2.50 6.00
268 Logan Woodside 4.00 10.00
270 J.T. Barrett SP 8.00 20.00
271 Lowell Lotulelei 2.50 6.00
272 Mike White 3.00 8.00
275 Jaleel Scott 2.50 6.00
276 Steve Ishmael 2.50 6.00
277 Kyle Allen SP 6.00 15.00
278 Tegray Scales 2.50 6.00
279 Austin Allen 3.00 8.00

2018 Elite Draft Picks Aspirations Blue

*VETS/25: 2.5X TO 6X BASIC CARDS
*ROOKIES/25: 1.5X TO 4X BASIC CARDS
*SP ROOK/25: .8X TO 2X BASIC CARDS

2018 Elite Draft Picks Aspirations Orange

*VETS: .8X TO 2X BASIC CARDS
*ROOKIES: .8X TO 2X BASIC CARDS
*SP ROOKIES: .4X TO 1X BASIC CARDS

2018 Elite Draft Picks Aspirations Purple

*VETS/99: 1.2X TO 3X BASIC CARDS
*ROOKIES/99: 1X TO 2.5X BASIC CARDS
*SP ROOK/99: .5X TO 1.2X BASIC CARDS

2018 Elite Draft Picks Aspirations Red

*VETS/49: 2X TO 5X BASIC CARDS
*ROOKIES/49: 1.2X TO 2X BASIC CARDS
*SP ROOK/49: .6X TO 1.5X BASIC CARDS

2018 Elite Draft Picks Status Die Cut Blue

*VETS/25: 2.5X TO 6X BASIC CARDS
*ROOKIES/25: 1.5X TO 4X BASIC CARDS
*SP ROOK/25: .8X TO 2X BASIC CARDS

2018 Elite Draft Picks Status Die Cut Purple

*VETS/99: 1.2X TO 3X BASIC CARDS
*ROOKIES/99: 1X TO 2.5X BASIC CARDS
*SP ROOK/99: .5X TO 1.2X BASIC CARDS

2018 Elite Draft Picks Status Die Cut Red

*VETS/49: 2X TO 5X BASIC CARDS
*ROOKIES/49: 1.2X TO 2X BASIC CARDS
*SP ROOK/49: .6X TO 1.5X BASIC CARDS

2018 Elite Draft Picks Chain Reaction

*HOLO/40: .8X TO 2X BASIC INSERTS
1 Saquon Barkley 4.00 10.00
2 Josh Allen 2.00 5.00
3 Calvin Ridley 1.25 3.00
4 Christian Kirk .75 2.00
5 Bo Scarbrough .60 1.50
6 Courtland Sutton .75 2.00
7 James Washington 1.00 2.50
8 Deon Cain .60 1.50
9 Josh Rosen 1.50 4.00
10 Deontay Burnett .60 1.50

2018 Elite Draft Picks College Ties

*HOLO/40: .8X TO 2X BASIC INSERTS
1 C.Helton/S.Darnold 3.00 8.00
2 J.Mora Jr./J.Rosen 1.50 4.00
3 B.Switzer/B.Sims .60 1.50
4 M.Brown/R.Williams .60 1.50
5 D.Henry/N.Saban .75 2.00
6 R.Jones II/S.Darnold 3.00 8.00
7 J.Washington/M.Rudolph 1.25 3.00
8 D.Guice/L.Fournette 1.00 2.50
9 B.Mayfield/D.Westbrook 5.00 12.00
10 B.Scarbrough/C.Ridley 1.25 3.00

2018 Elite Draft Picks Draft Picks Autographs

SP ANNC'D PRINT RUN 50 OR LESS
101 Sam Darnold SP 60.00 125.00
102 Josh Rosen SP 50.00 100.00
103 Josh Allen SP 50.00 100.00
105 Saquon Barkley SP 100.00 200.00
106 Derrius Guice SP 10.00 25.00
107 Courtland Sutton SP 8.00 20.00
108 James Washington SP 10.00 25.00
109 Christian Kirk SP 8.00 20.00
110 Calvin Ridley SP 12.00 30.00
111 Mason Rudolph SP 12.00 30.00
112 Nick Chubb SP 15.00 40.00
113 Ronald Jones II SP 5.00 12.00
114 Deon Cain SP 6.00 15.00
116 Nyheim Hines SP 6.00 15.00
117 Dante Pettis SP 8.00 20.00
119 Cam Serigne 2.50 6.00
120 Luke Falk SP 6.00 15.00
121 Bo Scarbrough SP 6.00 15.00
123 Simmie Cobbs Jr. SP 8.00 20.00
124 Deontay Burnett SP 6.00 15.00
125 Dallas Goedert SP 6.00 15.00
126 Royce Freeman SP 6.00 15.00
128 Kamryn Pettway SP 8.00 20.00
129 Richie James SP 5.00 12.00
130 Allen Lazard SP 5.00 12.00
131 D.J. Chark SP 6.00 15.00
132 Mike Gesicki SP 6.00 15.00
133 DeAndre Goolsby 2.50 6.00
134 Dalton Schultz 3.00 8.00
135 Anthony Miller SP 8.00 20.00
136 Kalen Ballage SP 6.00 15.00
137 John Kelly SP 6.00 15.00
138 Troy Fumagalli 3.00 8.00
139 Baker Mayfield SP 60.00 125.00
140 Justin Jackson SP 6.00 15.00
141 Phillip Lindsay 25.00 50.00
142 Michael Gallup SP 10.00 25.00
143 Robert Foster SP 5.00 12.00
144 Jester Weah SP 5.00 12.00
145 Quadree Henderson SP 6.00 15.00
146 Rashaad Penny SP 8.00 20.00
147 Akrum Wadley SP EXCH 5.00 12.00
150 Trevon Young 3.00 8.00
151 Bradley Chubb SP 8.00 20.00
152 Maurice Hurst SP 6.00 15.00
153 Harold Landry SP 5.00 12.00
154 Arden Key SP 5.00 12.00
155 Sam Hubbard 3.00 8.00
156 Ogbonnia Okoronkwo SP 8.00 20.00
157 Daron Payne SP 8.00 20.00

2018 Elite Draft Picks Draft Picks Autographs Aspirations Blue

*BLUE/30: 1X TO 2.5X BASIC AU
*BLUE/15: .6X TO 1.5X SP AU
101 Sam Darnold/15 100.00 200.00
102 Josh Rosen/15 75.00 150.00
103 Josh Allen/15 90.00 150.00
105 Saquon Barkley/15 200.00 300.00
139 Baker Mayfield/15 100.00 200.00

2018 Elite Draft Picks Draft Picks Autographs Aspirations Purple

*PURPLE/99: .6X TO 1.5X BASIC AU
*PURPLE/25: .5X TO 1.2X SP AU
101 Sam Darnold/25 75.00 150.00
102 Josh Rosen/25 60.00 125.00
103 Josh Allen/25 60.00 125.00
105 Saquon Barkley/25 150.00 250.00
139 Baker Mayfield/25 90.00 150.00

2018 Elite Draft Picks Draft Picks Autographs Aspirations Red

*RED/75: .6X TO 1.5X BASIC AU
*RED/20: .6X TO 1.5X SP AU
101 Sam Darnold/20 100.00 200.00
102 Josh Rosen/20 75.00 150.00
103 Josh Allen/20 90.00 150.00
105 Saquon Barkley/20 200.00 300.00
139 Baker Mayfield/20 100.00 200.00

2018 Elite Draft Picks Draft Picks Autographs Status Die Cut Blue

*BLUE/25: 1X TO 2.5X BASIC AU
*BLUE/25: .5X TO 1.2X SP AU
101 Sam Darnold 75.00 150.00
102 Josh Rosen 60.00 125.00
103 Josh Allen 60.00 125.00
105 Saquon Barkley 150.00 250.00
139 Baker Mayfield 90.00 150.00

2018 Elite Draft Picks Draft Picks Autographs Status Die Cut Purple

*PURPLE/99: .6X TO 1.5X BASIC AU
*PURPLE/49: .4X TO 1X SP AU
101 Sam Darnold/49 60.00 125.00
102 Josh Rosen/49 50.00 100.00
103 Josh Allen/49 50.00 100.00
105 Saquon Barkley/40 100.00 200.00
139 Baker Mayfield/49 75.00 125.00

2018 Elite Draft Picks Draft Picks Autographs Status Die Cut Red

*RED/49: .8X TO 2X BASIC AU
*RED/30: .5X TO 1.2X SP AU
101 Sam Darnold/30 75.00 150.00
102 Josh Rosen/30 60.00 125.00
103 Josh Allen/30 60.00 125.00
105 Saquon Barkley/30 150.00 250.00
139 Baker Mayfield/30 90.00 150.00

2018 Elite Draft Picks Elite Series

*HOLO/40: .8X TO 2X BASIC INSERTS
1 Sam Darnold 3.00 8.00
2 Saquon Barkley 4.00 10.00
3 Josh Rosen 1.50 4.00
4 Josh Allen 2.00 5.00
5 Derrius Guice 1.00 2.50
6 Calvin Ridley 1.25 3.00
7 Christian Kirk .75 2.00
8 Baker Mayfield 5.00 12.00
9 Courtland Sutton .75 2.00
10 Luke Falk .60 1.50

2018 Elite Draft Picks Passing the Torch

*HOLO/40: .8X TO 2X BASIC INSERTS
1 D.Henry/L.Jackson 3.00 8.00
2 M.Ingram/S.Bradford .60 1.50
3 R.Williams/R.Dayne .60 1.50
4 C.Woodson/R.Williams .75 2.00
5 C.Woodson/D.Wuerffel .75 2.00
6 C.White/G.Rogers .60 1.50
7 B.Sims/C.White .60 1.50
8 B.Sims/E.Campbell .75 2.00
9 B.Cannon/J.Bellino .50 1.25
10 G.Beban/S.Spurrier .60 1.50

2018 Elite Draft Picks Primary Colors

*HOLO/40: .8X TO 2X BASIC INSERTS
1 Sam Darnold 3.00 8.00
2 Saquon Barkley 4.00 10.00
3 Josh Rosen 1.50 4.00
4 Josh Allen 2.00 5.00
5 Derrius Guice 1.00 2.50
6 Calvin Ridley 1.25 3.00
7 Christian Kirk .75 2.00
8 Mason Rudolph 1.25 3.00
9 Courtland Sutton .75 2.00
10 Luke Falk .60 1.50

1991 ENOR Pro Football HOF Promos

This six-card standard-size promo set was issued to preview the 160-card 1991 ENOR Pro Football Hall of Fame set. Apart from a slightly different shade of colors and card numbering differences, these promo cards differ from their counterparts in that the Team NFL logo on their card backs is black and white, while on the regular series cards, it is red, white, and blue.

COMPLETE SET (6) 2.80 7.00
1 Pro Football Hall .40 1.00
2 Earl Campbell 1.20 3.00
3 John Hannah .40 1.00
4 Stan Jones .40 1.00
5 Jan Stenerud .40 1.00
6 Tex Schramm ADM .40 1.00

1991 ENOR Pro Football HOF

The 1991 Pro Football Hall of Fame set contains 160 standard-size cards. The set, which includes this year's inductees, was issued in factory sets and wax packs. The fronts feature a mix of color or black and white player photos, with black and gold borders (the photos were obtained from the NFL's extensive archives). The player's position and name are given in a black stripe below the picture. A purple box with the words "Pro Football Hall of Fame" in white appears at the lower right corner of the card face. The backs have biography, career summary, and the year the individual was inducted. The backs are predominantly orange in color and have a picture of the Hall of Fame building at the bottom. The numbering is essentially in alphabetical order by subject. Randomly inserted throughout the packs were coupon cards that entitled the collector to receive a free Hall of Fame Album and free admission to the Pro Football Hall of Fame (offer expired December 31, 1993). The front design of the Free Admission card shows four different scenes of the Hall of Fame.

COMPLETE SET (160) 7.50 20.00
1 Pro Football Hall of .08 .25
Fame (Canton, OH)
1A Free Admission .08 .25
Pro Football Hall of
Fame (Canton, OH)
2 Herb Adderley .08 .25
3 Lance Alworth .15 .40
4 Doug Atkins .08 .25
5 Red Badgro .07 .20
6 Cliff Battles .07 .20
7 Sammy Baugh .25 .60
8 Chuck Bednarik .15 .40
9A Bert Bell FOUND/OWN .10 .30
(Factory set version
in coat and tie on phone)
9B Bert Bell FOUND/OWN .10 .30
(Wax pack version in
Steelers tee shirt)
10 Bobby Bell .08 .25
11 Raymond Berry .15 .40
12 Charles W. Bidwill OWN .07 .20
13 Fred Biletnikoff .15 .40
14 George Blanda .15 .40
15 Mel Blount .15 .40
16 Terry Bradshaw .40 1.00
17 Jim Brown .40 1.00
18 Paul Brown CO OWN FND .10 .30
19 Roosevelt Brown .08 .25
20 Willie Brown .08 .25
21 Buck Buchanan .08 .25
22 Dick Butkus .30 .75
23 Earl Campbell .30 .75
24 Tony Canadeo .08 .25
25 Joe Carr PRES .07 .20
26 Guy Chamberlin .07 .20
27 Jack Christiansen .07 .20
28 Dutch Clark .08 .25
29 George Connor .08 .25
30 Jimmy Conzelman .07 .20
31 Larry Csonka .15 .40
32 Willie Davis .08 .25
33 Len Dawson .15 .40
34 Mike Ditka .30 .75
35 Art Donovan .10 .30
36 Paddy Driscoll .07 .20
37 Bill Dudley .08 .25
38 Turk Edwards .07 .20
39 Weeb Ewbank CO .07 .20
40 Tom Fears .08 .25
41 Ray Flaherty CO .07 .20
42 Len Ford .08 .25
43 Dan Fortmann .07 .20
44 Frank Gatski .07 .20
45 Bill George .08 .25
46 Frank Gifford .25 .60
47 Sid Gillman CO .07 .20
48 Otto Graham .30 .75
49 Red Grange .30 .75
50 Joe Greene .15 .40
51 Forrest Gregg .08 .25
52 Bob Griese .20 .50
53 Lou Groza .10 .30
54 Joe Guyon .07 .20
55 George Halas CO OWN FND .30 .75
56 Jack Ham .15 .40
57 John Hannah .08 .25
58 Franco Harris .25 .60
59 Ed Healey .07 .20
60 Mel Hein .07 .20
61 Ted Hendricks .08 .25
62 Fats Henry .07 .20
63 Arnie Herber .08 .25
64 Bill Hewitt .07 .20
65 Clarke Hinkle .07 .20
66 Elroy Hirsch .10 .30
67 Ken Houston .08 .25
68 Cal Hubbard .07 .20
69 Sam Huff .10 .30
70 Lamar Hunt OWN/FOUND .08 .25
71 Don Hutson .15 .40
72 John Henry Johnson .08 .25
73 Deacon Jones .10 .30
74 Stan Jones .07 .20
75 Sonny Jurgensen .10 .30
76 Walt Kiesling .07 .20
77 Frank (Bruiser) Kinard .07 .20
78 Earl (Curly) Lambeau .20 .50
CO/FOUND/OWN
79 Jack Lambert .25 .60
80 Tom Landry CO .30 .75
81 Dick Lane .08 .25
82 Jim Langer .08 .25
83 Willie Lanier .08 .25
84 Yale Lary .08 .25
85 Dante Lavelli .08 .25
86 Bobby Layne .25 .60
87 Tuffy Leemans .07 .20
88 Bob Lilly .15 .40
89 Sid Luckman .15 .40
90 Link Lyman .07 .20
91 Tim Mara FOUND/OWN .07 .20
92 Gino Marchetti .08 .25
93 Geo.Preston Marshall .07 .20
FOUND/OWN
94 Don Maynard .10 .30
95 George McAfee .07 .20
96 Mike McCormack .08 .25
97 Johnny Blood McNally .07 .20
98 Mike Michalske .07 .20
99 Wayne Millner .07 .20
100 Bobby Mitchell .10 .30
101 Ron Mix .08 .25
102 Lenny Moore .10 .30
103 Marion Motley .10 .30
(See also 130)
104 George Musso .08 .25
105 Bronko Nagurski .30 .75
106 Greasy Neale CO .07 .20
107 Ernie Nevers .08 .25
108 Ray Nitschke .20 .50
109 Leo Nomellini .08 .25
110 Merlin Olsen .10 .30
111 Jim Otto .10 .30
112 Steve Owen CO .07 .20
113 Alan Page .08 .25
114 Clarence(Ace) Parker .07 .20
115 Jim Parker .08 .25
116 1958 NFL Championship .07 .20
117 Pete Pihos .08 .25
118 Hugh(Shorty) Ray OFF .07 .20
119 Dan Reeves OWN .07 .20
120 Jim Ringo .08 .25
121 Andy Robustelli .08 .25
122 Art Rooney FOUND/ADMIN .10 .30
123 Pete Rozelle COMM .08 .25
124 Bob St.Clair .08 .25
125 Gale Sayers .30 .75
126 Joe Schmidt .08 .25
127 Tex Schramm ADM .07 .20
128 Art Shell .10 .30
129 Roger Staubach .40 1.00
130 Ernie Stautner UER .10 .30
(Numbered as 103)
131 Jan Stenerud .08 .25
132 Ken Strong .08 .25
133 Joe Stydahar .07 .20
134 Fran Tarkenton .25 .60
135 Charley Taylor .08 .25
136 Jim Taylor .10 .30
137 Jim Thorpe .30 .75
138 Y.A. Tittle .25 .60
139 George Trafton .07 .20
140 Charley Trippi .08 .25
141 Emlen Tunnell .08 .25
142 Bulldog Turner .10 .30
143 Johnny Unitas .60 1.50
144 Gene Upshaw .08 .25
145 Norm Van Brocklin .10 .30
146 Steve Van Buren .10 .30
147 Doak Walker .20 .50
148 Paul Warfield .10 .30
149 Bob Waterfield .10 .30
150 Arnie Weinmeister .07 .20
151 Bill Willis .08 .25
152 Larry Wilson .07 .20
153 Alex Wojciechowicz .07 .20
154 Willie Wood .08 .25
155 Enshrinement Day .07 .20
Hall of Fame
Induction Ceremony
156 Mementoes Exhibit .07 .20
Enshrinee Mementoes Room
157 Checklist 1 .07 .20
The Beginning
158 Checklist 2 .07 .20
The Early Years
159 Checklist 3 .07 .20
The Modern Era
160A Checklist 4 .07 .20
Evolution of Uniform
includes #133-160

1992 ENOR Pro Football HOF

1 Lem Barney .75 2.00
2 Al Davis .75 2.00
3 John Mackey B&W .75 2.00
4 John Riggins 1.00 2.50

1993 ENOR Pro Football HOF

1 Dan Fouts 2.00 5.00
2 Larry Little 2.00 5.00
3 Chuck Noll 2.00 5.00
4 Walter Payton 4.00 10.00
5 Bill Walsh 2.00 5.00

1994 ENOR Pro Football HOF

Packaged with 25 ProGard protective sheets, this six-card standard-size set was issued to commemorate five players and one coach who were inducted into the Football Hall of Fame in 1994. The cards have the same design as those in the 1991 ENOR set, except that they are unnumbered. The cards are listed below in alphabetical order.

COMPLETE SET (6) 20.00 40.00
1 Tony Dorsett 5.00 10.00
2 Bud Grant CO 3.00 6.00
3 Jim Johnson 3.00 6.00
4 Leroy Kelly 3.00 6.00
5 Jackie Smith 3.00 6.00
6 Randy White 4.00 8.00

1995 ENOR Pro Football HOF 5

This 5-card standard-size set was issued to commemorate the new inductees into the Pro Football Hall of Fame in 1995. The cards have the same design as those in the 1991 and 1995 ENOR sets, except that they are unnumbered. The cards are listed below in alphabetical order.

COMPLETE SET (5) 20.00 40.00

1 Jim Finks 4.00 8.00
2 Hank Jordan 5.00 10.00
3 Steve Largent 6.00 12.00
4 Lee Roy Selmon 4.00 8.00
5 Kellen Winslow 4.00 8.00

1995 ENOR Pro Football HOF 180

ENOR re-issued its 1991 Pro Football Hall of Fame set in factory set form in 1995. The 1995 release contains the first 159-cards from the 1991 set in original form plus 21 new cards including a re-worked checklist 4. The new cards carry a 1995 copyright date, while the first 159-cards are dated 1991. We've included single card prices for just the 21 new cards. The original 159-cards are priced previously under 1991 ENOR.

160B Checklist 4 includes 133-180 1.25 3.00
161 Lem Barney 1.25 3.00
162 Al Davis 2.00 5.00
163 John Mackey 1.25 3.00
164 John Riggins 2.00 5.00
165 Dan Fouts 2.00 5.00
166 Larry Little 1.25 3.00
167 Chuck Noll 1.50 4.00
168 Bill Walsh 2.00 5.00
169 Tony Dorsett 4.00 8.00
170 Bud Grant 1.50 4.00
171 Jim Johnson 1.25 3.00
172 Leroy Kelly 1.50 4.00
173 Jackie Smith 1.25 3.00
174 Randy White 2.00 5.00
175 O.J. Simpson 2.00 5.00
176 Jim Finks 1.25 3.00
177 Hank Jordan 1.50 4.00
178 Steve Largent 3.00 6.00
179 Lee Roy Selmon 1.25 3.00
180 Kellen Winslow 1.50 4.00

1996 ENOR Pro Football HOF

This five-card standard-size set was issued to commemorate the new inductees into the Pro Football Hall of Fame in 1996. The cards have the same design as those in the 1991 and 1995 ENOR sets, except that they are unnumbered. The cards are listed below in alphabetical order.

COMPLETE SET (5) 20.00 40.00
1 Lou Creekmur 4.00 8.00
2 Dan Dierdorf 4.00 8.00
3 Joe Gibbs 5.00 10.00
4 Charlie Joiner 4.00 8.00
5 Mel Renfro 4.00 8.00

2010 Epix

COMP.SET w/o RC's (100) 6.00 15.00
201-235 ROOKIE AU PRINT RUN 209-300
1 Chris Wells .12 .30
2 Larry Fitzgerald .15 .40
3 Matt Leinart .12 .30
4 Matt Ryan .15 .40
5 Michael Turner .12 .30
6 Roddy White .12 .30
7 Anquan Boldin .12 .30
8 Joe Flacco .15 .40
9 Ray Rice .12 .30
10 Lee Evans .15 .40
11 Marshawn Lynch .15 .40
12 Ryan Fitzpatrick .12 .30
13 DeAngelo Williams .12 .30
14 Matt Moore .12 .30
15 Steve Smith .15 .40
16 Devin Hester .15 .40
17 Jay Cutler .12 .30
18 Matt Forte .12 .30
19 Carson Palmer .15 .40
20 Cedric Benson .12 .30
21 Chad Ochocinco .12 .30
22 Jake Delhomme .12 .30
23 Josh Cribbs .12 .30
24 Mohamed Massaquoi .15 .40
25 Felix Jones .12 .30
26 Jason Witten .15 .40
27 Miles Austin .12 .30
28 Tony Romo .15 .40
29 Eddie Royal .12 .30
30 Knowshon Moreno .12 .30
31 Kyle Orton .12 .30
32 Calvin Johnson .20 .50
33 Matthew Stafford .15 .40
34 Nate Burleson .12 .30
35 Aaron Rodgers .40 1.00
36 Donald Driver .15 .40
37 Ryan Grant .15 .40
38 Andre Johnson .15 .40
39 Matt Schaub .12 .30
40 Steve Slaton .12 .30
41 Dallas Clark .12 .30
42 Joseph Addai .12 .30
43 Peyton Manning .50 1.25
44 Reggie Wayne .15 .40
45 David Garrard .12 .30
46 Maurice Jones-Drew .12 .30
47 Mike Sims-Walker .12 .30
48 Dwayne Bowe .15 .40
49 Jamaal Charles .15 .40
50 Matt Cassel .12 .30
51 Brandon Marshall .15 .40
52 Chad Henne .15 .40
53 Ronnie Brown .12 .30
54 Adrian Peterson .20 .50
55 Brett Favre .75 2.00
56 Sidney Rice .12 .30
57 Randy Moss .15 .40
58 Tom Brady .50 1.25
59 Wes Welker .15 .40
60 Drew Brees .20 .50
61 Marques Colston .12 .30
62 Pierre Thomas .12 .30
63 Brandon Jacobs .12 .30
64 Eli Manning .15 .40
65 Steve Smith USC .12 .30
66 Braylon Edwards .12 .30
67 LaDainian Tomlinson .20 .50
68 Mark Sanchez .12 .30
69 Shonn Greene .12 .30
70 Darren McFadden .12 .30
71 Jason Campbell .12 .30
72 Louis Murphy .12 .30
73 DeSean Jackson .15 .40
74 Kevin Kolb .12 .30
75 LeSean McCoy .20 .50
76 Ben Roethlisberger .20 .50
77 Hines Ward .15 .40
78 Rashard Mendenhall .12 .30
79 Antonio Gates .15 .40
80 Darren Sproles .15 .40
81 Philip Rivers .20 .50
82 Vincent Jackson .12 .30
83 Frank Gore .15 .40
84 Michael Crabtree .12 .30
85 Vernon Davis .12 .30
86 Julius Jones .12 .30
87 Matt Hasselbeck .12 .30
88 T.J. Houshmandzadeh .12 .30
89 Donnie Avery .12 .30
90 James Laurinaitis .15 .40
91 Steven Jackson .12 .30
92 Cadillac Williams .12 .30
93 Josh Freeman .15 .40
94 Kellen Winslow Jr. .12 .30
95 Chris Johnson .12 .30
96 Kenny Britt .12 .30
97 Vince Young .12 .30
98 Chris Cooley .12 .30
99 Clinton Portis .12 .30
100 Donovan McNabb .15 .40
101 Aaron Hernandez RC .60 1.50
102 Amari Spievey RC .60 1.50
103 Andre Anderson RC .60 1.50
104 Anthony Davis RC .75 2.00
105 Anthony Dixon RC .60 1.50
106 Anthony McCoy RC .60 1.50
107 Antonio Brown RC 5.00 12.00
108 Blair White RC .60 1.50
109 Brandon Graham RC .75 2.00
110 Brandon Spikes RC .60 1.50
111 Brian Price RC .60 1.50
112 Bryan Bulaga RC .60 1.50
113 Carlos Dunlap RC .60 1.50
114 Carlton Mitchell RC .60 1.50
115 Chad Jones RC .60 1.50
116 Charles Scott RC .60 1.50
117 Chris Cook RC .60 1.50
118 Chris McGaha RC .60 1.50
119 Corey Wootton RC .60 1.50
120 Dan LeFevour RC .60 1.50
121 Dan Williams RC .60 1.50
122 Daryl Washington RC .60 1.50
123 David Gettis RC .60 1.50
124 David Reed RC .60 1.50
125 Deji Karim RC .75 2.00
126 Dennis Pitta RC .60 1.50
127 Derrick Morgan RC .60 1.50
128 Devin McCourty RC .75 2.00
129 Dezmon Briscoe RC .60 1.50
130 Dominique Franks RC .60 1.50
131 Donald Butler RC .60 1.50
132 Earl Thomas RC 1.50 4.00
133 Ed Dickson RC .60 1.50
134 Everson Griffen RC .60 1.50
135 Freddie Barnes RC .60 1.50
136 Garrett Graham RC .60 1.50
137 Jacoby Ford RC .60 1.50
138 James Starks RC .75 2.00
139 Jared Odrick RC .75 2.00
140 Jarrett Brown RC .60 1.50
141 Jason Pierre-Paul RC 1.00 2.50
142 Jason Worilds RC .60 1.50
143 Javier Arenas RC .60 1.50
144 Jeremy Williams RC .60 1.50
145 Jermaine Cunningham RC .60 1.50
146 Jerome Murphy RC .75 2.00
147 Jerry Hughes RC .60 1.50
148 Jevan Snead RC .60 1.50
149 Jimmy Graham RC 1.50 4.00
150 Joe Haden RC 1.00 2.50
151 Joe Webb RC .60 1.50
152 John Conner RC .60 1.50
153 John Skelton RC .75 2.00
154 Joique Bell RC .60 1.50
155 Jonathan Crompton RC .60 1.50
156 Kareem Jackson RC .60 1.50
157 Kerry Meier RC .75 2.00
158 Koa Misi RC .75 2.00
159 Kyle Williams RC 1.00 2.50
160 Kyle Wilson RC .60 1.50
161 Lamarr Houston RC .75 2.00
162 LeGarrette Blount RC 1.25 3.00
163 Levi Brown RC .60 1.50
164 Linval Joseph RC .60 1.50
165 Lonyae Miller RC .75 2.00
166 Major Wright RC .60 1.50
167 Marc Mariani RC 1.00 2.50
168 Maurkice Pouncey RC .75 2.00
169 Mike Iupati RC 1.00 2.50
170 Mike Neal RC 1.00 2.50
171 Morgan Burnett RC .75 2.00
172 Myron Rolle RC .60 1.50
173 Nate Allen RC 1.00 2.50
174 NaVorro Bowman RC 1.25 3.00
175 Pat Angerer RC .60 1.50
176 Pat Paschall RC .60 1.50
177 Patrick Robinson RC .75 2.00
178 Perrish Cox RC .75 2.00
179 Ricky Sapp RC .60 1.50
180 Riley Cooper RC .60 1.50
181 Russell Okung RC .60 1.50
182 Rusty Smith RC 1.00 2.50
183 Sean Canfield RC .60 1.50
184 Sean Lee RC 1.25 3.00
185 Sean Weatherspoon RC .60 1.50
186 Sergio Kindle RC .60 1.50
187 Seyi Ajirotutu RC .60 1.50
188 Shay Hodge RC .60 1.50
189 T.J. Ward RC 1.00 2.50
190 Taylor Mays RC .60 1.50
191 Terrence Austin RC .75 2.00
192 Terrence Cody RC .60 1.50
193 Timothy Toone RC .75 2.00
194 Tony Moeaki RC .75 2.00
195 Tony Pike RC .60 1.50
196 Torell Troup RC .60 1.50
197 Trent Williams RC .75 2.00
198 Trindon Holliday RC 2.00 5.00
199 Tyson Alualu RC .60 1.50
200 Zac Robinson RC .75 2.00
201 C.J. Spiller AU/210 RC 5.00 12.00
202 Marcus Easley AU/210 RC 5.00 12.00
203 D.Thomas AU/210 RC 12.00 30.00
204 Eric Decker AU/300 RC 6.00 15.00
205 Tim Tebow AU/270 RC 25.00 60.00
206 J.Gresham AU/270 RC 5.00 12.00
207 Jordan Shipley AU/210 RC 5.00 12.00
208 Mike Kafka AU/210 RC 6.00 15.00
209 Eric Berry AU/210 RC 8.00 20.00
210 D.McCluster AU/300 RC 6.00 15.00
211 Armanti Edwards AU/210 RC 6.00 15.00
212 Brandon LaFell AU/210 RC 8.00 20.00
213 Jimmy Clausen AU/210 RC 5.00 12.00
214 Toby Gerhart AU/210 RC 5.00 12.00
215 Joe McKnight AU/210 RC 5.00 12.00
216 R.McClain AU/210 RC 5.00 12.00
217 E.Sanders AU/210 RC 8.00 20.00
218 Jonathan Dwyer AU/300 RC 5.00 12.00
219 Gerald McCoy AU/210 RC 5.00 12.00
220 Arrelious Benn AU/270 RC 5.00 12.00
221 Mike Williams AU/209 RC 5.00 12.00
222 Golden Tate AU/300 RC 6.00 15.00
223 Colt McCoy AU/270 RC 6.00 15.00
224 M.Hardesty AU/300 RC 5.00 12.00
225 Ben Tate AU/210 RC 5.00 12.00
226 Damian Williams AU/210 RC 5.00 12.00
227 Mardy Gilyard AU/210 RC 5.00 12.00
228 Sam Bradford AU/270 RC 6.00 15.00
229 Jahvid Best AU/270 RC 5.00 12.00
230 Ndamukong Suh AU/210 RC 10.00 25.00
231 Dez Bryant AU/300 RC 30.00 60.00
232 Rob Gronkowski AU/300 RC 30.00 60.00
233 Taylor Price AU/300 RC 5.00 12.00
234 Andre Roberts AU/210 RC 6.00 15.00
235 Ryan Mathews AU/210 RC 5.00 12.00

2010 Epix Gold

*VETS 1-100: 5X TO 12X BASIC CARDS
*ROOKIES 101-200: 1.2X TO 3X BASIC CARDS
STATED PRINT RUN 100 SER.#'d SETS

2010 Epix Platinum

*VETS 1-100: 6X TO 15X BASIC CARDS
*ROOKIES 101-200: 1.5X TO 4X BASIC CARDS
STATED PRINT RUN 50 SER.#'d SETS

2010 Epix Silver

*VETS 1-100: 3X TO 8X BASIC CARDS
*ROOKIES 101-200: .8X TO 2X BASIC CARDS
STATED PRINT RUN 250 SER.#'d SETS

2010 Epix Ball Hawks

1 DeMarcus Ware 1.00 2.50
2 Troy Polamalu 1.25 3.00
3 Darrelle Revis .75 2.00
4 Ray Lewis 1.25 3.00
5 Charles Woodson 1.25 3.00
6 Patrick Willis 1.00 2.50
7 Will Smith .75 2.00
8 Brian Urlacher 1.25 3.00
9 Jared Allen .75 2.00
10 Dwight Freeney .75 2.00

2010 Epix Ball Hawks Materials

STATED PRINT RUN 140-299
*PRIME/40-50: .8X TO 2X BASIC JSY
1 DeMarcus Ware/200 3.00 8.00
2 Troy Polamalu/299 3.00 8.00
3 Darrelle Revis/299 2.00 5.00
4 Ray Lewis/299 4.00 10.00
5 Charles Woodson/299 5.00 12.00
6 Patrick Willis/299 2.50 6.00
7 Will Smith/299 2.00 5.00
8 Brian Urlacher/299 3.00 8.00
9 Jared Allen/299 4.00 10.00
10 Dwight Freeney/140 2.00 5.00

2010 Epix Canton Lettermen Autographs

STATED PRINT RUN 30-50
1 Emmitt Smith/50 100.00 175.00
2 Jerry Rice/50 75.00 150.00
3 Russ Grimm/50 20.00 40.00
4 Rickey Jackson/50 30.00 60.00
5 Floyd Little/50 20.00 40.00
6 John Randle/50 15.00 40.00
8 Bart Starr/50 75.00 150.00
9 Dan Marino/50 100.00 175.00
10 Don Maynard/50 20.00 40.00
11 Jim Taylor/50 30.00 60.00
12 Joe Montana/50 75.00 150.00
13 Joe Namath/50 40.00 100.00
14 John Elway/30 90.00 150.00
16 Troy Aikman/50 40.00 80.00
17 Roger Staubach/50 50.00 100.00
18 Steve Largent/50 25.00 50.00
19 Rod Woodson/50 25.00 50.00

2010 Epix Dallas Cowboys Lettermen Autographs

STATED PRINT RUN 35-70
1 Bob Lilly/70 25.00 50.00
2 Chuck Howley/70 25.00 50.00
3 Cliff Harris/70 20.00 40.00
4 Darren Woodson/70 25.00 50.00
5 Deion Sanders/35 50.00 100.00
6 Ed Too Tall Jones/70 25.00 50.00
7 Emmitt Smith/35 100.00 175.00
8 Erik Williams/70 20.00 40.00
9 Everson Walls/70 20.00 40.00
11 John Niland/70 20.00 40.00
12 Mark Stepnoski/70 20.00 40.00
14 Mel Renfro/70 20.00 40.00
15 Michael Irvin/35 40.00 80.00
18 Roger Staubach/35 60.00 100.00
19 Tony Dorsett/35 30.00 60.00
20 Troy Aikman/70 40.00 80.00
21 Jason Witten/35 40.00 80.00
23 D.D. Lewis/35 25.00 50.00
25 Randy White/35 40.00 80.00

2010 Epix Epix Game Orange

*GAME EMERALD: .5X TO 1.2X GAME ORG
*GAME PURPLE: .6X TO 1.5X GAME ORG
*MOMENT EMERALD: .4X TO 1X GAME ORG
*MOMENT ORANGE: .5X TO 1.2X GAME ORG
*MOMENT PURPLE: .8X TO 2X GAME ORG
*SEASON EMERALD: .6X TO 1.5X GAME ORG
*SEASON ORANGE: .4X TO 1X GAME ORG
*SEASON PURPLE: .5X TO 1.2X GAME ORG
1 Sidney Rice .75 2.00
2 Santana Moss 1.00 2.50
3 Ronnie Brown .75 2.00
4 Reggie Wayne 1.00 2.50
5 Ray Rice .75 2.00
6 Randy Moss 1.00 2.50
7 Pierre Garcon 1.00 2.50
8 Peyton Manning 3.00 8.00
9 Patrick Willis 1.00 2.50
10 Michael Turner .75 2.00
11 Matthew Stafford 1.00 2.50
12 Matt Ryan 1.00 2.50
13 Matt Forte .75 2.00
14 Mark Sanchez .75 2.00
15 LeSean McCoy 1.25 3.00
16 Larry Fitzgerald 1.00 2.50
17 Kyle Orton .75 2.00
18 Kevin Boss .75 2.00
19 Joseph Addai .75 2.00
20 Joe Flacco 1.00 2.50
21 Jason Witten 1.00 2.50
22 Hines Ward 1.00 2.50
23 Greg Jennings .75 2.00
24 Felix Jones .75 2.00
25 Eddie Royal .75 2.00
26 Dwayne Bowe 1.00 2.50
27 Drew Brees 1.25 3.00
28 Donald Driver 1.00 2.50
29 Devery Henderson .75 2.00
30 Aaron Rodgers 2.50 6.00
31 Antonio Gates 1.00 2.50
32 Bernard Berrian .75 2.00
33 Brett Favre 2.50 6.00
34 Derrick Mason .75 2.00
35 David Garrard .75 2.00
36 Darrelle Revis .75 2.00
37 Wes Welker 1.00 2.50
38 Vincent Jackson .75 2.00
39 Vernon Davis .75 2.00
40 Tony Romo 1.00 2.50
41 Tom Brady 3.00 8.00
42 Terrell Suggs .75 2.00
43 Steve Smith 1.00 2.50
44 Shonn Greene .75 2.00
45 Andre Johnson 1.00 2.50
46 Austin Collie .75 2.00
47 Brandon Jacobs .75 2.00
48 Brian Urlacher 1.25 3.00
49 Cadillac Williams .75 2.00
50 Chris Cooley .75 2.00
51 Ray Lewis 1.25 3.00
52 Percy Harvin .75 2.00
53 Maurice Jones-Drew .75 2.00
54 Matt Hasselbeck .75 2.00
55 Marion Barber 1.00 2.50
56 Ladell Betts .75 2.00
57 Adrian Peterson 1.25 3.00
58 DeSean Jackson 1.00 2.50
59 Dustin Keller .75 2.00
60 Eli Manning 1.00 2.50
61 Heath Miller .75 2.00
62 Jay Cutler .75 2.00
63 Darren Sproles 1.00 2.50
64 Calvin Johnson 1.25 3.00
65 Clinton Portis .75 2.00
66 Chad Ochocinco .75 2.00
67 Carson Palmer 1.00 2.50
68 Braylon Edwards .75 2.00
69 Chris Wells .75 2.00
70 Visanthe Shiancoe 1.00 2.50
71 Troy Polamalu 1.25 3.00
72 T.J. Houshmandzadeh .75 2.00
73 Ryan Grant 1.00 2.50
74 Devin Hester 1.00 2.50
75 Ed Reed 1.00 2.50
76 Jamaal Charles 1.00 2.50
77 Josh Cribbs .75 2.00
78 Lee Evans 1.00 2.50
79 Matt Schaub .75 2.00
80 Philip Rivers 1.25 3.00
81 Reggie Bush .75 2.00
82 Tony Gonzalez 1.00 2.50
83 Roddy White .75 2.00
84 Miles Austin .75 2.00
85 Knowshon Moreno .75 2.00
86 Frank Gore 1.00 2.50
87 Donovan McNabb 1.00 2.50
88 DeAngelo Williams .75 2.00
89 Dallas Clark .75 2.00
90 Cedric Benson .75 2.00
91 Darren McFadden .75 2.00
92 Brent Celek .75 2.00
93 Jonathan Stewart .75 2.00
94 Marques Colston .75 2.00
95 Vince Young .75 2.00
96 Anthony Gonzalez .75 2.00
97 Pierre Thomas .75 2.00
98 Steven Jackson .75 2.00
99 Chris Johnson .75 2.00
100 Ben Roethlisberger 1.25 3.00

2010 Epix Epix Jerseys Blue

*PRIME/35-50: .8X TO 2X BASIC JSY
*PRIME/19-25: 1X TO 2.5X BASIC JSY
1 Sidney Rice 2.00 5.00
2 Santana Moss 2.50 6.00
3 Ronnie Brown 2.00 5.00
4 Reggie Wayne 2.50 6.00
6 Randy Moss 2.50 6.00
8 Peyton Manning 8.00 20.00
9 Patrick Willis 2.50 6.00
11 Matthew Stafford 2.50 6.00
12 Matt Ryan 2.50 6.00
13 Matt Forte 2.00 5.00
14 Mark Sanchez 2.00 5.00
15 LeSean McCoy 3.00 8.00
16 Larry Fitzgerald 2.50 6.00
17 Kyle Orton 2.00 5.00
18 Kevin Boss 2.00 5.00
19 Joseph Addai 2.00 5.00
20 Joe Flacco 2.50 6.00
21 Jason Witten 2.50 6.00
22 Hines Ward 2.50 6.00
23 Greg Jennings 2.00 5.00
24 Felix Jones 2.00 5.00
25 Eddie Royal 2.00 5.00
26 Dwayne Bowe 2.50 6.00
28 Donald Driver 2.50 6.00
29 Devery Henderson 2.00 5.00
31 Antonio Gates 2.50 6.00
32 Bernard Berrian 2.00 5.00
33 Brett Favre 12.00 30.00
34 Derrick Mason 2.00 5.00
35 David Garrard 2.00 5.00
36 Darrelle Revis 2.00 5.00
37 Wes Welker 2.50 6.00
38 Vincent Jackson 2.00 5.00
39 Vernon Davis 2.00 5.00
40 Tony Romo 2.50 6.00
41 Tom Brady 8.00 20.00
42 Terrell Suggs 2.00 5.00
43 Steve Smith 2.50 6.00
44 Shonn Greene 2.00 5.00
45 Andre Johnson 2.50 6.00
47 Brandon Jacobs 2.00 5.00
48 Brian Urlacher 3.00 8.00
49 Cadillac Williams 2.00 5.00
50 Chris Cooley 2.00 5.00
51 Ray Lewis 4.00 10.00
52 Percy Harvin 2.00 5.00
53 Maurice Jones-Drew 2.00 5.00
54 Matt Hasselbeck 2.00 5.00
55 Marion Barber 2.50 6.00
56 Ladell Betts 2.00 5.00
57 Adrian Peterson 3.00 8.00
59 Dustin Keller 2.00 5.00
60 Eli Manning 2.50 6.00
61 Heath Miller 2.00 5.00
62 Jay Cutler 2.00 5.00
63 Darren Sproles 2.50 6.00
64 Calvin Johnson 3.00 8.00
65 Clinton Portis 2.00 5.00
66 Chad Ochocinco 2.00 5.00
67 Carson Palmer 2.50 6.00
68 Braylon Edwards 2.00 5.00
69 Chris Wells 2.00 5.00
70 Visanthe Shiancoe 2.50 6.00
71 Troy Polamalu 3.00 8.00
74 Devin Hester 2.50 6.00
75 Ed Reed 2.50 6.00
76 Jamaal Charles 2.50 6.00
77 Josh Cribbs 2.00 5.00
78 Lee Evans 2.50 6.00
79 Matt Schaub 2.00 5.00
80 Philip Rivers 3.00 8.00
81 Reggie Bush 2.00 5.00
82 Tony Gonzalez 2.50 6.00
83 Roddy White 2.00 5.00
84 Miles Austin 2.00 5.00
85 Knowshon Moreno 2.00 5.00
86 Frank Gore 2.50 6.00
87 Donovan McNabb 2.50 6.00
88 DeAngelo Williams 2.00 5.00
89 Dallas Clark 2.00 5.00
90 Cedric Benson 2.00 5.00
91 Darren McFadden 2.00 5.00
93 Jonathan Stewart 2.00 5.00
94 Marques Colston 2.00 5.00
95 Vince Young 2.00 5.00
96 Anthony Gonzalez 2.00 5.00
98 Steven Jackson 2.00 5.00
99 Chris Johnson 2.00 5.00
100 Ben Roethlisberger 3.00 8.00

2010 Epix Epix Signatures Red

STATED PRINT RUN 1-25
14 Mark Sanchez/25 25.00 50.00
18 Kevin Boss/25 6.00 15.00
26 Dwayne Bowe/25 8.00 20.00
32 Bernard Berrian/25 6.00 15.00
38 Vincent Jackson/25 6.00 15.00
46 Austin Collie/25 6.00 15.00
61 Heath Miller/20 6.00 15.00
78 Lee Evans/25 8.00 20.00

2010 Epix Highlight Zone

1 Miles Austin .75 2.00
2 Chris Johnson .75 2.00
3 Drew Brees 1.25 3.00
4 Josh Cribbs .75 2.00
5 Randy Moss 1.00 2.50
6 Adrian Peterson 1.25 3.00
7 Aaron Rodgers 2.50 6.00
8 Philip Rivers 1.25 3.00
9 Sidney Rice .75 2.00
10 Vince Young .75 2.00
11 DeAngelo Williams .75 2.00
12 Peyton Manning 3.00 8.00
13 Maurice Jones-Drew .75 2.00
14 Felix Jones .75 2.00
15 Brett Favre 2.50 6.00

2010 Epix Highlight Zone Materials

STATED PRINT RUN 125-200
*PRIME/50: .6X TO 1.5X BASIC JSY
*PRIME/25: .8X TO 2X BASIC JSY
2 Chris Johnson/200 2.50 6.00
4 Josh Cribbs/200 2.50 6.00
5 Randy Moss/200 3.00 8.00
6 Adrian Peterson/200 4.00 10.00
8 Philip Rivers/125 4.00 10.00
9 Sidney Rice/200 2.50 6.00
10 Vince Young/200 2.50 6.00
11 DeAngelo Williams/200 2.50 6.00
12 Peyton Manning/200 10.00 25.00
13 Maurice Jones-Drew/200 2.50 6.00
14 Felix Jones/200 2.50 6.00
15 Brett Favre/200 8.00 20.00

2010 Epix Materials

STATED PRINT RUN 75-299
1 Chris Wells/299 2.00 5.00
2 Larry Fitzgerald/299 2.50 6.00
3 Matt Leinart/299 2.00 5.00
4 Matt Ryan/250 2.50 6.00
6 Roddy White/299 2.00 5.00
8 Joe Flacco/299 2.50 6.00
10 Lee Evans/299 2.50 6.00
13 DeAngelo Williams/200 2.50 6.00
15 Steve Smith/75 4.00 10.00
16 Devin Hester/299 2.50 6.00
18 Matt Forte/299 2.00 5.00
19 Carson Palmer/299 2.50 6.00
20 Cedric Benson/299 2.00 5.00
21 Chad Ochocinco/200 2.50 6.00
23 Josh Cribbs/299 2.00 5.00
24 Mohamed Massaquoi/299 2.50 6.00
25 Felix Jones/100 2.50 6.00
26 Jason Witten/100 3.00 8.00
28 Tony Romo/200 3.00 8.00
29 Eddie Royal/299 2.00 5.00
30 Knowshon Moreno/299 2.00 5.00
31 Kyle Orton/299 2.00 5.00
32 Calvin Johnson/299 3.00 8.00
33 Matthew Stafford/299 2.50 6.00
36 Donald Driver/299 2.50 6.00
38 Andre Johnson/299 2.50 6.00
39 Matt Schaub/299 2.00 5.00
40 Steve Slaton/299 2.00 5.00
41 Dallas Clark/299 2.00 5.00
42 Joseph Addai/75 3.00 8.00
43 Peyton Manning/185 10.00 25.00
44 Reggie Wayne/160 3.00 8.00
45 David Garrard/299 2.00 5.00
46 Maurice Jones-Drew/299 2.00 5.00
48 Dwayne Bowe/299 2.50 6.00
49 Jamaal Charles/299 2.50 6.00
53 Ronnie Brown/100 2.50 6.00
54 Adrian Peterson/200 4.00 10.00
55 Brett Favre/299 8.00 20.00
56 Sidney Rice/250 2.00 5.00
57 Randy Moss/299 2.50 6.00
58 Tom Brady/299 8.00 20.00
59 Wes Welker/150 3.00 8.00
61 Marques Colston/299 2.00 5.00
63 Brandon Jacobs/299 2.00 5.00
64 Eli Manning/200 3.00 8.00
66 Braylon Edwards/75 3.00 8.00
68 Mark Sanchez/200 2.50 6.00
70 Darren McFadden/299 2.00 5.00
71 Jason Campbell/299 2.00 5.00
72 Louis Murphy/299 2.00 5.00
74 Kevin Kolb/299 2.00 5.00
76 Ben Roethlisberger/125 4.00 10.00
77 Hines Ward/110 3.00 8.00
78 Rashard Mendenhall/170 2.50 6.00
79 Antonio Gates/299 2.50 6.00
80 Darren Sproles/299 2.50 6.00
81 Philip Rivers/125 4.00 10.00
82 Vincent Jackson/299 2.00 5.00
83 Frank Gore/299 2.50 6.00
84 Michael Crabtree/130 2.50 6.00
85 Vernon Davis/299 2.00 5.00
87 Matt Hasselbeck/299 2.00 5.00
91 Steven Jackson/299 2.00 5.00
92 Cadillac Williams/299 2.00 5.00
93 Josh Freeman/299 2.50 6.00
95 Chris Johnson/299 2.00 5.00
96 Kenny Britt/299 2.00 5.00
97 Vince Young/299 2.00 5.00
98 Chris Cooley/299 2.00 5.00
99 Clinton Portis/250 2.00 5.00
100 Donovan McNabb/299 2.50 6.00

2010 Epix Materials Prime

COMMON CARD/30-50 4.00 10.00
SEMISTARS/30-50 5.00 12.00
UNL.STARS/30-50 6.00 15.00
COMMON CARD/20-25 6.00 15.00
UNL.STARS/20-25 8.00 20.00
PRIME PRINT RUN 4-50
28 Tony Romo/50 5.00 12.00
43 Peyton Manning/40 15.00 40.00
54 Adrian Peterson/50 6.00 15.00
58 Tom Brady/50 15.00 40.00
68 Mark Sanchez/50 4.00 10.00

2010 Epix Odyssey Combo Materials

STATED PRINT RUN 10-200
1 Cedric Benson/200 2.50 6.00
2 Donovan McNabb/100 3.00 8.00
4 Jason Campbell/200 2.50 6.00
6 Michael Turner/10
10 Santana Moss/200 3.00 8.00
11 T.J. Houshmandzadeh/90 3.00 8.00
12 Brett Favre/200 20.00 50.00
18 Tony Gonzalez/15 6.00 15.00
19 Jay Cutler/45 4.00 10.00
20 Laveranues Coles/200 2.50 6.00

2010 Epix Odyssey Combo Materials Prime

COMMON CARD/50 5.00 12.00
UNL.STARS/50 6.00 15.00
COMMON CARD/25 6.00 15.00
PRIME PRINT RUN 5-50

2010 Epix Odyssey Materials

STATED PRINT RUN 40-299
1 Cedric Benson/299 2.00 5.00
2 Donovan McNabb/299 2.50 6.00
4 Jason Campbell/299 2.00 5.00
5 Anquan Boldin/40 4.00 10.00
7 Jake Delhomme/299 2.00 5.00
10 Santana Moss/299 2.50 6.00
12 Brett Favre/299 8.00 20.00
14 Santonio Holmes/190 2.50 6.00
15 Ted Ginn/299 2.00 5.00
16 Chad Pennington/299 2.00 5.00
17 Chester Taylor/299 2.00 5.00
19 Jay Cutler/299 2.00 5.00
20 Laveranues Coles/299 2.00 5.00

2010 Epix Odyssey Materials Prime

COMMON CARD/75 3.00 8.00
SEMISTARS/75 4.00 10.00
UNL.STARS/75 5.00 12.00
COMMON CARD/35-50 5.00 12.00
UNL.STARS/35-50 6.00 15.00
COMMON CARD/15 6.00 15.00
PRIME PRINT RUN 15-75

2010 Epix Rookie Campaign Materials

STATED PRINT RUN 499 SER.#'d SETS
*PRIME/50: .6X TO 1.5X BASIC JSY/499
1 Ryan Mathews 1.50 4.00
2 Taylor Price 1.50 4.00
3 Dez Bryant 6.00 15.00
4 Jahvid Best 1.50 4.00
5 Mardy Gilyard 1.50 4.00
6 Ben Tate 1.50 4.00
7 Colt McCoy 2.00 5.00
8 Mike Williams 1.50 4.00
9 Gerald McCoy 1.50 4.00
10 Emmanuel Sanders 2.50 6.00
11 Joe McKnight 1.50 4.00
12 Jimmy Clausen 1.50 4.00
13 Armanti Edwards 2.00 5.00
14 Eric Berry 2.50 6.00
15 Jordan Shipley 1.50 4.00
16 Tim Tebow 5.00 12.00
17 Demaryius Thomas 4.00 10.00
18 C.J. Spiller 1.50 4.00
19 Jonathan Dwyer 1.50 4.00
20 Arrelious Benn 1.50 4.00
21 Golden Tate 2.00 5.00
22 Montario Hardesty 1.50 4.00
23 Damian Williams 1.50 4.00
24 Sam Bradford 2.00 5.00
25 Ndamukong Suh 3.00 8.00
26 Rob Gronkowski 5.00 12.00
27 Andre Roberts 2.00 5.00
28 Rolando McClain 1.50 4.00
29 Toby Gerhart 1.50 4.00
30 Brandon LaFell 2.50 6.00
31 Dexter McCluster 2.00 5.00
32 Mike Kafka 2.00 5.00
33 Jermaine Gresham 1.50 4.00
34 Eric Decker 2.00 5.00
35 Marcus Easley 1.50 4.00

2010 Epix Rookie Campaign Materials Signatures

STATED PRINT RUN 100 SER.#'d SETS
1 Ryan Mathews 4.00 10.00
2 Taylor Price 4.00 10.00
3 Dez Bryant 30.00 60.00
4 Jahvid Best 4.00 10.00
5 Mardy Gilyard 4.00 10.00
6 Ben Tate 4.00 10.00
7 Colt McCoy 5.00 12.00
8 Mike Williams 4.00 10.00
10 Emmanuel Sanders 6.00 15.00
12 Jimmy Clausen 4.00 10.00
13 Armanti Edwards 5.00 12.00
14 Eric Berry 6.00 15.00
15 Jordan Shipley 4.00 10.00
16 Tim Tebow 30.00 60.00
18 C.J. Spiller 4.00 10.00
19 Jonathan Dwyer 4.00 10.00
20 Arrelious Benn 4.00 10.00
21 Golden Tate 5.00 12.00
22 Montario Hardesty 4.00 10.00
23 Damian Williams 4.00 10.00
24 Sam Bradford 5.00 12.00
25 Ndamukong Suh 8.00 20.00
26 Rob Gronkowski 25.00 50.00
27 Andre Roberts 5.00 12.00
28 Rolando McClain 4.00 10.00
29 Toby Gerhart 4.00 10.00
30 Brandon LaFell 6.00 15.00
31 Dexter McCluster 5.00 12.00
32 Mike Kafka 5.00 12.00
34 Eric Decker 5.00 12.00
35 Marcus Easley 4.00 10.00

2010 Epix Rookie Campaign Materials Prime Signatures

*PRIME/25: .6X TO 1.5X BASIC JSY AU/100
PRIME PRINT RUN 25 SER.#'d SETS
16 Tim Tebow 30.00 80.00

2010 Epix Rush Hour

1 Ryan Grant 1.00 2.50
2 Clinton Portis .75 2.00
3 Cadillac Williams .75 2.00
4 Cedric Benson .75 2.00
5 Chris Wells .75 2.00
6 LeSean McCoy 1.25 3.00
7 Ray Rice .75 2.00
8 Jonathan Stewart .75 2.00
9 Shonn Greene .75 2.00
10 Steven Jackson .75 2.00
11 Joseph Addai .75 2.00
12 Matt Forte .75 2.00
13 Darren Sproles 1.00 2.50
14 Reggie Bush .75 2.00
15 Rashard Mendenhall .75 2.00
16 Ronnie Brown .75 2.00
17 Knowshon Moreno .75 2.00
18 Marion Barber 1.00 2.50
19 Brandon Jacobs .75 2.00
20 Jamaal Charles 1.00 2.50

2010 Epix Rush Hour Materials

STATED PRINT RUN 95-150
*PRIME/50: .6X TO 1.5X BASIC JSY
*PRIME/15: .8X TO 2X BASIC JSY
2 Clinton Portis/150 2.50 6.00
3 Cadillac Williams/150 2.50 6.00
4 Cedric Benson/150 2.50 6.00
5 Chris Wells/150 2.50 6.00
6 LeSean McCoy/150 4.00 10.00
8 Jonathan Stewart/150 2.50 6.00
10 Steven Jackson/150 2.50 6.00
11 Joseph Addai/150 2.50 6.00
12 Matt Forte/150 2.50 6.00
13 Darren Sproles/150 3.00 8.00
14 Reggie Bush/95 2.50 6.00
15 Rashard Mendenhall/150 2.50 6.00
16 Ronnie Brown/150 2.50 6.00
17 Knowshon Moreno/150 2.50 6.00
18 Marion Barber/150 3.00 8.00
19 Brandon Jacobs/150 2.50 6.00
20 Jamaal Charles/150 3.00 8.00

2010 Epix Saints Who Dat Lettermen Autographs

STATED PRINT RUN 240 SER.#'d SETS
1 Tracy Porter 15.00 40.00
2 Garrett Hartley 15.00 40.00
3 Pierre Thomas 15.00 40.00
4 Marques Colston 15.00 40.00
5 Drew Brees 40.00 100.00

2010 Epix Signatures

VETERAN PRINT RUN 1-30
ROOKIE PRINT RUN 299-499
10 Lee Evans/25 8.00 20.00
29 Eddie Royal/30 5.00 12.00
64 Eli Manning/15 40.00 80.00
68 Mark Sanchez/25 25.00 50.00
72 Louis Murphy/50 5.00 12.00
74 Kevin Kolb/25 6.00 15.00
84 Michael Crabtree/25 12.00 30.00
96 Kenny Britt/25 6.00 15.00
101 Aaron Hernandez/499 3.00 8.00
103 Andre Anderson/499 3.00 8.00
105 Anthony Dixon/399 3.00 8.00
106 Anthony McCoy/499 3.00 8.00
107 Antonio Brown/499 30.00 60.00
108 Blair White/499 3.00 8.00
109 Brandon Graham/499 4.00 10.00
110 Brandon Spikes/499 3.00 8.00
112 Bryan Bulaga/499 3.00 8.00
113 Carlos Dunlap/499 3.00 8.00
114 Carlton Mitchell/499 3.00 8.00
115 Chad Jones/499 3.00 8.00
116 Charles Scott/499 3.00 8.00
118 Chris McGaha/499 3.00 8.00
119 Corey Wootton/499 3.00 8.00
120 Dan LeFevour/499 3.00 8.00
123 David Gettis/499 3.00 8.00
127 Derrick Morgan/499 3.00 8.00
128 Devin McCourty/499 4.00 10.00
129 Dezmon Briscoe/499 3.00 8.00
130 Dominique Franks/499 3.00 8.00
132 Earl Thomas/499 10.00 25.00
133 Ed Dickson/499 3.00 8.00
134 Everson Griffen/499 3.00 8.00
135 Freddie Barnes/499 3.00 8.00
136 Garrett Graham/499 3.00 8.00
137 Jacoby Ford/499 3.00 8.00
138 James Starks/499 4.00 10.00
140 Jarrett Brown/499 3.00 8.00
141 Jason Pierre-Paul/499 5.00 12.00
142 Jason Worilds/499 3.00 8.00
144 Jeremy Williams/499 3.00 8.00
147 Jerry Hughes/499 3.00 8.00
148 Jevan Snead/499 3.00 8.00
149 Jimmy Graham/499 12.50 25.00
150 Joe Haden/499 5.00 12.00
153 John Skelton/499 4.00 10.00
154 Joique Bell/499 3.00 8.00
155 Jonathan Crompton/499 3.00 8.00
156 Kareem Jackson/299 3.00 8.00
162 LeGarrette Blount/499 6.00 15.00
165 Lonyae Miller/499 4.00 10.00
171 Morgan Burnett/499 4.00 10.00
177 Patrick Robinson/499 4.00 10.00
178 Perrish Cox/499 4.00 10.00
179 Ricky Sapp/499 3.00 8.00
180 Riley Cooper/499 3.00 8.00
183 Sean Canfield/499 3.00 8.00
184 Sean Lee/499 6.00 15.00
185 Sean Weatherspoon/499 3.00 8.00
187 Seyi Ajirotutu/499 3.00 8.00
188 Shay Hodge/499 3.00 8.00
190 Taylor Mays/499 3.00 8.00
195 Tony Pike/499 3.00 8.00
200 Zac Robinson/499 4.00 10.00

2010 Epix Spellbound

1 Aaron Rodgers 4.00 10.00
2 Adrian Peterson 2.00 5.00
3 Andre Johnson 1.50 4.00
4 Brett Favre 4.00 10.00
5 Brian Urlacher 2.00 5.00
6 Calvin Johnson 2.00 5.00
7 Carson Palmer 1.50 4.00
8 Chad Ochocinco 1.25 3.00
9 Chris Johnson 1.25 3.00
10 Darrelle Revis 1.25 3.00
11 Darren Sproles 1.50 4.00
12 DeAngelo Williams 1.25 3.00
13 DeSean Jackson 1.50 4.00
14 Donovan McNabb 1.50 4.00
15 Drew Brees 2.00 5.00
16 Eli Manning 1.50 4.00
17 Frank Gore 1.50 4.00
18 Jamaal Charles 1.50 4.00
19 Jason Witten 1.50 4.00
20 Knowshon Moreno 1.25 3.00
21 Larry Fitzgerald 1.50 4.00
22 Mark Sanchez 1.25 3.00
23 Matt Ryan 1.50 4.00
24 Matthew Stafford 1.50 4.00
25 Maurice Jones-Drew 1.25 3.00
26 Michael Crabtree 1.25 3.00
27 Michael Turner 1.25 3.00
28 Ray Lewis 2.00 5.00
29 Ray Rice 1.25 3.00
30 Reggie Wayne 1.50 4.00
31 Steve Smith 1.50 4.00
32 Steven Jackson 1.25 3.00
33 Tom Brady 5.00 12.00
34 Tony Romo 1.50 4.00
35 Troy Polamalu 2.00 5.00
36 Vernon Davis 1.25 3.00

2010 Epix Sunday Showdown Materials

STATED PRINT RUN 5-200
*PRIME/50: .6X TO 1.5X BASIC DUAL JSY
1 D.Brees/D.Ware/5
2 T.Romo/E.Manning/200 4.00 10.00
3 P.Manning/T.Brady/200 12.00 30.00
4 Ochocinco/Polamalu/200 6.00 15.00
7 A.Peterson/R.Grant/14
8 P.Rivers/V.Young/200 4.00 10.00
9 C.Johnson/R.Lewis/200 6.00 15.00
10 L.Fitzgerald/F.Gore/200 4.00 10.00
11 C.Palmer/J.Flacco/200 4.00 10.00
12 S.Greene/R.Brown/110 3.00 8.00
13 McFadden/Moreno/200 4.00 10.00
14 C.Portis/L.McCoy/200 5.00 12.00
15 C.Johnson/M.Forte/200 5.00 12.00

1967-73 Equitable Sports Hall of Fame

This set consists of copies of art work found over a number of years in many national magazines, especially "Sports Illustrated," honoring sports heroes that Equitable Life Assurance Society selected to be in its very own Sports Hall of Fame. The cards consists of charcoal-type drawings on white backgrounds by artists, George Loh and Robert Riger, and measure approximately 11" by 7 3/4". The unnumbered cards have been assigned numbers below using a sport prefix (BB- baseball, BK- basketball, FB- football, HK- hockey, OT-other).

COMPLETE SET (95) 250.00 500.00
FB1 Jim Brown 4.00 8.00
FB2 Charley Conerly 2.00 4.00
FB3 Bill Dudley 1.25 2.50
FB4 Roman Gabriel 1.25 2.50
FB5 Red Grange 4.00 8.00
FB6 Elroy Hirsch 2.00 4.00
FB7 Jerry Kramer 2.00 4.00
FB8 Vince Lombardi 4.00 8.00
FB9 Earl Morrall 1.25 2.50
FB10 Bronko Nagurski 3.00 6.00
FB11 Gale Sayers 4.00 8.00
FB12 Jim Thorpe 4.00 8.00
FB13 Johnny Unitas 4.00 8.00
FB14 Alex Webster 2.00 4.00

1969 Eskimo Pie

The 1969 Eskimo Pie football card set contains 15 panel pairs of American Football League players. Each pair of individual player cards is most commonly collected together and, thus, cataloged as pairs below. Each could be cut off of Eskimo Pie Ice Cream boxes at the time and most, if not all, can also be found in a thinner sticker version originally attached to a green colored backing paper - two cards per panel for a total of four players. We've cataloged the card/box version below with a "C" suffix after the card number and an "S" suffix for the known sticker versions. This thin sticker version appears to be more difficult to find than the card/box version. The panels measure approximately 2 1/2" by 3" when neatly cut. The unnumbered pairs are checklisted below alphabetically according to the last name of the player on the left. The names are mistakenly reversed on the card containing Jim Otto and Len Dawson (card number 14). Finally, a 16th sticker was uncovered in 2012 which included an offer for four different NFL team logo jewelry premiums: tie clasp, tie tac, pendant, and charm bracelet with the Jets team logo featured. This premium offer sticker was issued along with the Lamonica/Frazier sticker pair and it measures the same size as a standard sticker pair. The catalog designation for this set is F73.

1C L.Alworth/J.Charles 100.00 200.00
1S L.Alworth/J.Charles 175.00 300.00
2C Al Atkinson/G.Goeddeke 100.00 200.00
2S Al Atkinson/G.Goeddeke 175.00 300.00
3S M.Briscoe/B.Shaw SP 350.00 600.00
4C G.Cappelletti/D.Livingston SP 250.00 400.00
4S G.Cappelletti/D.Livingston SP 350.00 600.00
5C E.Crabtree/J.Dunaway 100.00 200.00
5S E.Crabtree/J.Dunaway 175.00 300.00
6C B.Davidson/B.Griese 250.00 400.00
6S B.Davidson/B.Griese 400.00 600.00
7C H.Dixon/P.Beathard 100.00 175.00
7S H.Dixon/P.Beathard 150.00 250.00
8S M.Garrett/B.Hunt SP 250.00 400.00
9C D.Lamonica/W.Frazier 150.00 300.00
10C J.Lynch.J.Hadl 100.00 200.00
11C K.McCloughan/T.Regner 100.00 200.00
12C J.Nance/B.Neighbors SP 250.00 400.00
12S J.Nance/B.Neighbors SP 350.00 600.00
13C R.Norton/P.Costa 100.00 200.00
13S R.Norton/P.Costa 175.00 300.00
14C J.Otto/L.Dawson 250.00 400.00

15C M.Snell/D.Post 100.00 175.00
15S M.Snell/D.Post 150.00 250.00
16S Premium Offer Sticker 500.00 750.00

1995 ESPN Magazine

This set of 6-cards was released in ESPN magazine. It features ESPN broadcasters on cards styled after the 1956 Topps set. The cards were printed on thin glossy stock and issued as a perforated sheet. They were skip numbered.

COMPLETE SET (6) 7.50 15.00
7 Joe Theismann 2.00 5.00
12 Chris Berman 1.25 3.00
32 Chris Mortensen 1.25 3.00
57 Tom Jackson 1.25 3.00
70 Art Donovan 1.50 4.00
84 Sterling Sharpe 1.25 3.00

2000 eTopps

Available only through a limited offering on the Topps website, these cards were initially meant to be sold in a stock market like atmosphere on eBay. Each card was issued with an IPO price that ranged from $3.50-$9.50 per card. Announced print runs are included below.

ANNOUNCED RPINT RUNS BELOW
1 Ricky Williams/1423* 6.00 12.00
4 Daunte Culpepper/1000* 7.50 15.00
5 Peter Warrick/1000* 6.00 12.00
6 Emmitt Smith/938* 20.00 40.00
9 Peyton Manning/1000* 20.00 40.00
11 Ron Dayne/1000* 6.00 12.00
12 Randy Moss/982* 12.50 25.00
13 Eddie George/496* 15.00 30.00
18 Kurt Warner/1070* 7.50 15.00
21 Marshall Faulk/850* 6.00 12.00
23 Jamal Lewis/500* 30.00 60.00
24 Edgerrin James/758* 10.00 20.00

2001 eTopps

The 2001 eTopps cards were issued via Topps' website and initially sold exclusively on eBay's eTopps Trade Floor. Owners of the cards could hold the cards on account with Topps and freely trade those cards similar to shares of stock. They also could pay a fee to take actual delivery of their cards, but most are still held on account with Topps. Since most do not trade hands as physical cards, we've simply listed the checklist here without pricing.

1 Ray Lewis/649 4.00 8.00
2 Peter Warrick/281 7.50 15.00
3 James Stewart/465 2.50 5.00
4 Junior Seau/389 35.00 60.00
6 Amani Toomer/538 3.00 6.00
7 Elvis Grbac/230 35.00 60.00
8 David Boston/560 3.00 6.00
9 Jimmy Smith/354 10.00 20.00
10 Warrick Dunn/571 3.00 6.00
11 James Thrash/431 7.50 15.00
12 Joe Horn/606 2.50 5.00
13 Stephen Davis/236 7.50 15.00
14 Tyrone Wheatley/237 7.50 15.00
15 Brian Urlacher/1146 4.00 8.00
16 Fred Taylor/283 10.00 20.00
17 Jerry Rice/933 8.00 20.00
18 Keyshawn Johnson/254 20.00 35.00
19 Jay Fiedler/478 2.50 5.00
20 Jamal Anderson/274 10.00 20.00
21 Emmitt Smith/1975 6.00 12.00
22 Tiki Barber/861 3.00 6.00
23 Daunte Culpepper/457 3.00 6.00
24 Torry Holt/553 4.00 8.00
25 Peyton Manning/1104 12.50 25.00
26 Eddie George/292 7.50 15.00
27 Jamal Lewis/237 12.50 25.00
28 Ricky Williams/683 3.00 6.00
29 Ahman Green/1105 2.00 4.00
30 Ed McCaffrey/330 4.00 8.00
31 Curtis Martin/404 7.50 15.00
32 Isaac Bruce/772 2.50 6.00
33 Doug Flutie/684 3.00 6.00
34 Steve McNair/341 7.50 15.00
35 Donovan McNabb/987 4.00 8.00
36 Keenan McCardell/243 10.00 20.00
37 Charlie Batch/322 4.00 8.00
38 Cade McNown/333 7.50 15.00
39 Terrell Owens/528 6.00 12.00
40 Brad Johnson/231 50.00 100.00
41 Tim Dwight/586 5.00 10.00
42 Muhsin Muhammad/270 7.50 15.00
43 Kurt Warner/785 4.00 8.00
44 Lamar Smith/371 3.00 6.00
45 Brian Griese/505 2.50 5.00
46 Matthew Hatchette/317 3.00 6.00
47 Jeff Garcia/585 2.50 5.00
48 Derrick Mason/207 15.00 30.00
49 Drew Bledsoe/372 25.00 50.00
50 Marshall Faulk/2742 2.50 5.00
51 Corey Dillon/726 2.00 4.00
52 Tony Gonzalez/950 2.50 5.00
53 Chad Lewis/313 7.50 15.00
54 Shaun Alexander/1442 2.50 5.00
55 Edgerrin James/473 4.00 8.00
56 Eric Moulds/217 15.00 30.00
57 Aaron Brooks/434 2.50 5.00
58 Zach Thomas/380 7.50 15.00
59 Jerome Bettis/826 4.00 8.00
60 Shannon Sharpe/302 7.50 15.00
61 Kerry Collins/355 7.50 15.00
62 Ricky Watters/384 4.00 8.00
63 Tim Couch/677 2.00 4.00
64 Marvin Harrison/391 10.00 20.00
65 Tim Brown/377 12.50 25.00
66 Mark Brunell/299 7.50 15.00
67 Wayne Chrebet/380 4.00 8.00
68 Terry Glenn/260 12.50 25.00
69 Mike Anderson/352 2.50 5.00
70 Randy Moss/881 5.00 10.00
71 Freddie Jones/339 3.00 6.00
72 Ike Hilliard/280 5.00 10.00
73 Derrick Alexander/349 4.00 8.00
74 Travis Prentice/443 2.50 6.00
75 Brett Favre/1066 10.00 25.00
76 Rod Smith/521 2.00 4.00
77 Todd Pinkston/1005 2.00 4.00
78 Cris Carter/540 4.00 8.00
79 Rich Gannon/327 5.00 10.00
80 Charlie Garner/518 4.00 8.00
81 Michael Pittman/338 4.00 8.00
82 Jeff Graham/425 3.00 6.00
83 Albert Connell/275 5.00 10.00
84 Bill Schroeder/673 2.00 4.00
85 Jeff Blake/361 3.00 6.00
86 Jon Kitna/537 3.00 6.00
87 Qadry Ismail/431 12.50 25.00
88 Joey Galloway/413 4.00 8.00
89 Duce Staley/688 2.00 4.00
90 Troy Brown/559 2.00 4.00
91 Johnnie Morton/231 7.50 15.00
92 Chris Chandler/307 4.00 8.00
93 Donald Hayes/291 4.00 8.00
94 Mike Alstott/999 2.00 4.00
95 Vinny Testaverde/459 7.50 15.00
96 James Allen/467 3.00 6.00
97 Jake Plummer/600 2.50 5.00
98 Antonio Freeman/348 7.50 15.00
99 Darrell Jackson/502 3.00 6.00
100 Ron Dayne/257 4.00 8.00
101 Rob Johnson/389 2.50 5.00
102 Kordell Stewart/346 3.00 6.00
103 Akili Smith/202 15.00 30.00
104 Shawn Jefferson/226 7.50 15.00
105 Germane Crowell/281 3.00 6.00
106 Kevin Johnson/478 10.00 20.00
108 Marcus Robinson/662 2.00 4.00
109 Priest Holmes/418 5.00 10.00
111 Kevin Lockett/319 3.00 6.00
112 Tony Banks/186 60.00 100.00
113 Terrell Davis/269 15.00 30.00
114 Trent Green/313 4.00 8.00
115 Sylvester Morris/299 4.00 8.00
116 J.R. Redmond/272 20.00 40.00
117 Willie Jackson/282 5.00 10.00
118 Chad Pennington/507 4.00 8.00
119 Tai Streets/462 2.00 4.00
120 Matt Hasselbeck/237 25.00 50.00
121 LaMont Jordan/678 2.50 5.00
122 Quincy Morgan/811 2.00 4.00
123 Chad Johnson/331 40.00 80.00
124 Anthony Thomas/2186 2.00 4.00
125 Drew Brees/1290 20.00 50.00
126 Kevan Barlow/1724 2.00 4.00
127 Chris Chambers/1715 2.00 4.00
128 Mike McMahon/1697 2.00 4.00
129 Todd Heap/755 3.00 6.00
130 Robert Ferguson/315 10.00 20.00
131 Dan Morgan/645 2.00 4.00
132 Jesse Palmer/521 2.00 4.00
133 Travis Minor/637 3.00 6.00
134 Rudi Johnson/532 5.00 10.00
135 Rod Gardner/510 2.50 5.00
136 Snoop Minnis/837 2.00 4.00
137 Koren Robinson/482 2.50 5.00
138 Chris Weinke/875 3.00 6.00
139 James Jackson/1053 2.00 4.00
140 Michael Vick/5721 10.00 25.00
141 Marques Tuiasosopo/616 2.50 5.00
142 Michael Bennett/658 2.00 4.00
143 LaDainian Tomlinson/1536 12.00 30.00
144 Freddie Mitchell/634 2.00 4.00
145 Deuce McAllister/597 3.00 8.00
146 Quincy Carter/923 2.00 4.00
147 Santana Moss/620 4.00 8.00
148 David Terrell/638 2.00 4.00
149 Reggie Wayne/595 10.00 20.00
150 Travis Henry/1117 2.00 4.00

2001 eTopps Super Bowl XXXV Promos

Topps issued these 7-cards to promote the upcoming eTopps card releases for 2001. Each card features a 2000 NFL season award winner or starting quarterback in Super Bowl XXXV. The cards were distributed free to attendees of the 2001 NFL Experience Super Bowl Card Show in Tampa, Florida at the Topps booth one card at a time. The Super Bowl XXXV logo can be found on the cardfronts and the cardbacks feature an advertisement for eTopps cards. A Refractor parallel set was also produced with each being serial numbered of 2000-cards made.

COMPLETE SET (7) 35.00 50.00
*REFRACTORS: 1X TO 2X BASIC CARDS
1 Marshall Faulk NFL MVP 5.00 8.00
2 Marshall Faulk Off.POY 5.00 8.00
3 Brian Urlacher 6.00 12.00
4 Mike Anderson 10.00 20.00
5 Trent Dilfer 3.00 5.00
6 Kerry Collins 3.00 5.00
7 Ray Lewis 3.00 5.00

2002 eTopps

The 2002 eTopps cards were issued via Topps' website and initially sold exclusively on eBay's eTopps Trade Floor. Owner's of the cards could hold the cards on account with Topps and freely trade those cards similar to shares of stock. They also could pay a fee to take actual delivery of their cards, but most are still held on account with Topps. Since most of these cards do not trade hands as physical cards, we've simply listed the checklist here without pricing. We've also included the announced print runs when known. Card #76 was not issued. Collectors were given a chance in 2004 to have their Tom Brady and Brian Westbrook cards held in account signed by the athletes and certified by Topps. Each signed card was certified with a Topps hologram and accompanied by a matching card certificate of authenticity. We've listed those two variations below.

ANNOUNCED PRINT RUNS BELOW
1 Tom Brady/5000 10.00 20.00
2 Jeff Garcia/1724 1.25 3.00
3 Rod Smith/4000 1.00 2.50
4 Anthony Thomas/6000 1.25 3.00
5 Chris Chambers/4000 1.50 4.00
6 Kendrell Bell/5000 1.25 3.00
7 Curtis Martin/1311 1.50 4.00
8 Eddie George/3169 1.25 3.00
9 Stephen Davis/3961 1.25 3.00
10 Edgerrin James/3773 1.50 4.00
11 Michael Vick/6000 1.25 3.00
12 Peter Warrick/1533 1.25 3.00
13 Priest Holmes/5000 1.50 4.00
14 Jake Plummer/2000 1.25 3.00
15 Jimmy Smith/1692 1.25 3.00
16 Jerry Rice/2000 2.00 5.00
17 LaDainian Tomlinson/5000 1.50 4.00
18 Keyshawn Johnson/1492 1.25 3.00
19 Shaun Alexander/2986 1.50 4.00
20 Terrell Owens/5000 1.50 4.00
21 Rod Gardner/1757 1.50 4.00
22 Donovan McNabb/5000 1.50 4.00
23 Randy Moss/3000 1.50 4.00
24 Brian Griese/2909 1.25 3.00
25 Marcus Robinson/2000 1.25 3.00
26 Jamal Lewis/3528 1.50 4.00
27 Peyton Manning/2336 6.00 15.00
28 Mike McMahon/2790 1.25 3.00
29 Rich Gannon/3166 1.25 3.00
30 Jerome Bettis/2017 3.00 8.00
31 Matt Hasselbeck/3000 1.25 3.00
32 Marshall Faulk/3554 1.50 4.00
33 Plaxico Burress/3000 1.50 4.00
34 Ricky Williams/4000 1.25 3.00
35 Jay Fiedler/4000 1.00 2.50
36 Ahman Green/3730 1.50 4.00
37 Chris Weinke/2168 1.25 3.00
38 David Boston/2000 1.00 2.50
39 Troy Brown/3410 1.25 3.00
40 Tim Brown/1739 1.50 4.00
41 Darrell Jackson/4000 1.25 3.00
42 Steve McNair/2000 1.50 4.00
43 Torry Holt/4000 1.25 3.00
44 Tiki Barber/2000 1.50 4.00
45 Brett Favre/3466 4.00 10.00
46 Corey Dillon/4000 1.50 4.00
47 Emmitt Smith/2000 3.00 8.00
48 Marvin Harrison/4000 1.50 4.00
49 Daunte Culpepper/1508 1.50 4.00
50 Kurt Warner/1114 1.50 4.00
51 Tim Couch/5735 1.25 3.00
52 Eric Moulds/2000 1.25 3.00
53 Vinny Testaverde/3000 1.25 3.00
54 Trent Green/2000 1.25 3.00
55 Kordell Stewart/1538 1.25 3.00
56 Drew Brees/5000 1.50 4.00
57 Aaron Brooks/5000 1.25 3.00
58 Mark Brunell/4000 1.00 2.50
59 Tony Gonzalez/3274 1.25 3.00
60 Doug Flutie/1000 1.50 4.00
61 David Carr/6000 1.25 3.00
62 Travis Stephens/4000 1.00 2.50
63 Patrick Ramsey/5000 1.25 3.00
64 T.J. Duckett/6000 1.25 3.00
65 Javon Walker/5000 1.25 3.00
66 DeShaun Foster/3000 1.50 4.00
67 William Green/3000 1.25 3.00
68 Ashley Lelie/5000 1.25 3.00
69 Jabar Gaffney/5000 1.25 3.00
70 Ron Johnson/3000 1.00 2.50
71 Reche Caldwell/5000 1.00 2.50
72 Daniel Graham/4000 1.25 3.00
73 Josh Reed/3765 1.25 3.00
74 Andre Davis/2000 1.25 3.00
75 Joey Harrington/8000 1.25 3.00
77 Donte Stallworth/5000 1.25 3.00
78 Rohan Davey/3000 1.25 3.00
79 Maurice Morris/4000 1.25 3.00
80 Antwaan Randle El/4000 1.50 4.00
81 Cliff Russell/3000 1.00 2.50
82 Jeremy Shockey/7000 1.25 3.00
83 Julius Peppers/6000 1.50 4.00
84 Antonio Bryant/5000 1.25 3.00
85 Clinton Portis/6000 1.50 4.00
86 Ladell Betts/2302 1.25 3.00
87 Josh McCown/2127 1.50 4.00
88 Roy Williams/5000 1.50 4.00
89 Tim Carter/3000 1.25 3.00
90 Marquise Walker/2000 1.25 3.00
91 Chad Hutchinson/5000 1.00 2.50
92 Deion Branch/5000 1.50 4.00
93 Brian Westbrook/5000 3.00 6.00
94 Jonathan Wells/5000 1.00 2.50
95 Tommy Maddox/3397 1.25 3.00
96 Deuce McAllister/2822 1.50 4.00
97 Drew Bledsoe/2000 1.50 4.00
98 Brian Urlacher/2000 1.50 4.00
99 Donald Driver/2788 1.50 4.00
100 Peerless Price/2298 1.25 3.00
101 Chad Pennington/3000 1.50 4.00
102 Randy McMichael/2220 1.25 3.00
103 Marty Booker/1309 1.25 3.00
104 Hines Ward/2112 1.50 4.00
105 Warren Sapp/1621 1.25 3.00
106 Marc Bulger/3000 1.50 4.00
107 Lavernues Coles/2285 1.25 3.00

2002 eTopps Classic

1 Barry Sanders/3000 4.00 8.00
2 Ray Nitschke/983 10.00 20.00
3 Dan Marino/3000 6.00 12.00
4 Chuck Bednarik/1291 4.00 8.00
5 Sammy Baugh/1259 5.00 10.00
6 Frank Gifford/1270 4.00 8.00
7 Terry Bradshaw/3000 4.00 8.00
7 Kellen Winslow/777 6.00 12.00
8 Jim Brown/3000 4.00 8.00
9 Jim Kelly/985 7.50 15.00
10 Y.A. Tittle/1064 5.00 10.00
11 DeaconA Jones/865 6.00 12.00
11 Fran Tarkenton/1106 6.00 12.00
12 Joe Montana/3000 10.00 20.00
13 Joe Namath/3000 4.00 8.00
14 John Elway/2422 5.00 10.00
14 Elroy Hirsch/906 5.00 10.00
15 Norm Van Brocklin/975 6.00 12.00
19 Bubba Smith/805 5.00 10.00
20 Dan Fouts/843 7.50 15.00

2002 eTopps Event Series

ES8 Marvin Harrison/952* 3.00 8.00
ES6A Emmitt Smith/7184* 3.00 8.00
ES6B Jerry Rice/3579* 2.50 6.00

2003 eTopps

The 2003 eTopps cards were issued via Topps' website and initially sold exclusively on eBay's eTopps Trade Floor. Owner's of the cards could hold the cards on account with Topps and freely trade those cards similar to shares of stock. They also could pay a fee to take actual delivery of their cards, but most are still held on account with Topps. Since most of these cards do not trade hands as physical cards, we've simply listed the checklist here without pricing. We've also included the announced print runs when known. Collectors were given a chance in 2004 to have their Tom Brady card held in account signed and certified by Topps. Each signed card was certified with a Topps hologram and accompanied by a matching card certificate of authenticity.

ANNOUNCED PRINT RUNS BELOW
1 AaronA Brooks/638 2.50 5.00
2 Ahman Green/917 2.50 5.00
3 Amani Toomer/706 2.50 5.00
4 Brett Favre/1197 6.00 15.00
5 Brian Urlacher/1000 4.00 8.00
6 Brian Finneran/577 4.00 8.00
7 Chad Pennington/910 3.00 6.00
8 Clinton Portis/1495 2.50 5.00
9 Corey Dillon/1193 2.50 5.00
10 Curtis Martin/806 2.50 5.00
11 Darrell Jackson/1000 1.50 4.00
12 Jake Delhomme/1158 2.50 5.00
13 David Carr/1490 2.50 5.00
14 Derrick Mason/488 5.00 10.00
15 Deuce McAllister/772 3.00 6.00
16 Donald Driver/899 2.50 5.00
17 Donovan McNabb/812 4.00 8.00
18 Drew Bledsoe/918 2.50 5.00
19 Drew Brees/647 4.00 8.00
20 Kelly Holcomb/2565 1.25 3.00
21 Edgerrin James/920 2.50 5.00
22 Jamel White/1063 1.25 3.00
23 Hugh Douglas/578 4.00 8.00
24 Hines Ward/778 3.00 6.00
25 Jason Taylor/1012 1.50 4.00
26 Jeff Garcia/773 2.50 5.00
27 Jeremy Shockey/1763 4.00 8.00
28 Jerry Rice/1416 2.50 5.00
29 Jimmy Smith/785 1.50 4.00
30 Joe Horn/815 1.50 4.00
31 Joey Harrington/881 2.50 5.00
32 Kerry Collins/740 3.00 6.00
33 Keyshawn Johnson/1500 1.50 4.00
34 Kurt Warner/840 2.50 5.00
35 LaDainian Tomlinson/842 3.00 6.00
36 Marshall Faulk/634 5.00 10.00
37 Marty Booker/693 1.25 3.00
38 Marvin Harrison/1939 2.50 5.00
39 Michael Vick/1512 4.00 8.00
40 Peerless Price/724 1.50 4.00
41 Trent Green/1111 1.50 4.00
42 Troy Brown/1000 1.50 4.00
43 Priest Holmes/1033 2.50 5.00
44 Randy Moss/1050 3.00 6.00
45 Ray Lewis/1074 2.50 5.00
46 Rich Gannon/818 1.50 4.00
47 Ricky Williams/1052 2.50 5.00
48 Laveranues Coles/819 1.50 4.00
49 Rod Smith/951 1.25 3.00
50 Shaun Alexander/840 3.00 6.00
51 Steve McNair/1712 1.50 4.00
52 Terrell Owens/1003 2.50 5.00
53 Tiki Barber/1338 2.50 6.00
54 Champ Bailey/1072 2.50 5.00
55 Tom Brady/665 15.00 40.00
56 Tommy Maddox/772 1.50 4.00
57 Torry Holt/1069 2.50 5.00
58 Travis Henry/600 1.00 [illegible]
59 DeWayne Robertson/1197 1.25 3.00
60 Jerome McDougle/838 1.25 3.00
61 Andre Johnson/2551 1.50 4.00
62 Anquan Boldin/3500 1.50 4.00
63 Artose Pinner/1166 1.50 4.00
64 Bethel Johnson/1949 1.50 4.00
65 Brian St.Pierre/1511 1.25 3.00
66 Bryant Johnson/822 2.50 5.00
67 Byron Leftwich/5000 2.50 5.00
68 Carson Palmer/6000 5.00 12.00
69 Charles Rogers/2500 1.50 4.00
70 Chris Brown/1568 1.50 4.00
71 Chris Simms/1852 2.50 5.00
72 Dallas Clark/2829 4.00 10.00
73 Dave Ragone/842 1.50 4.00
74 Justin Fargas/2000 1.25 3.00
75 Kelley Washington/704 4.00 8.00
76 Kevin Curtis/785 4.00 8.00
77 Kliff Kingsbury/1000 1.50 4.00
78 Kyle Boller/3189 1.50 4.00
79 Larry Johnson/1858 3.00 8.00
80 Musa Smith/757 2.50 5.00
81 Nate Burleson/1491 1.25 3.00
82 Onterrio Smith/2000 1.50 4.00
83 Rex Grossman/3287 3.00 6.00
84 Seneca Wallace/1159 1.50 4.00
85 Taylor Jacobs/845 1.50 4.00
86 Terence Newman/1369 1.50 4.00
87 Terrell Suggs/1855 1.50 4.00
88 Teyo Johnson/1076 1.25 3.00
89 Tyrone Calico/1690 1.25 3.00
90 Willis McGahee/2000 2.50 5.00
91 Jerry Porter/1148 1.50 4.00
92 Dante Hall/2000 1.50 4.00
93 Trung Canidate/614 2.50 5.00
94 Curtis Conway/586 5.00 10.00
95 Kevin Faulk/689 4.00 8.00
96 Troy Hambrick/992 1.25 3.00
97 Domanick Davis/2000 1.50 4.00
98 Nick Barnett/955 1.50 4.00
99 Tim Rattay/880 2.50 5.00
100 Moe Williams/924 1.25 3.00
101 Correll Buckhalter/953 1.50 4.00
102 Steve Smith/765 3.00 6.00

2003 eTopps Classic

21 Lawrence Taylor/702 7.50 15.00
22 Gale Sayers/947 7.50 15.00
23 Johnny Unitas/661 12.50 25.00
24 Bo Jackson/1000 7.50 15.00
25 Walter Payton/1500 10.00 20.00
26 Phil Simms/781 10.00 20.00
27 Tony Dorsett/788 10.00 25.00
28 Steve Largent/639 7.50 15.00
29 Steve Young/592 75.00 125.00
30 Marcus Allen/722 10.00 20.00
31 Mike Singletary/953 6.00 12.00
32 Eric Dickerson/774 7.50 15.00
33 Otto Graham/547 10.00 20.00
34 Troy Aikman/587 12.50 25.00
35 Fred Biletnikoff/450 25.00 50.00
36 Jim Thorpe/785 6.00 15.00
37 Ronnie Lott/711 10.00 20.00
38 Jack Lambert/754 6.00 12.00
39 Raymond Berry/477 12.50 25.00
40 Earl Campbell/523 10.00 20.00

2003 eTopps Event Series

ES12 Jamal Lewis/938* 2.00 5.00

2004 eTopps

ANNOUNCED PRINT RUNS BELOW
1 Green Bay Packers/2500 2.50 6.00
2 Chicago Bears/1495 2.00 5.00
3 New England Patriots/2500 2.50 6.00
4 Cleveland Browns/1239 1.50 4.00
5 Carolina Panthers/1668 1.50 4.00
6 New York Jets/1510 1.50 4.00
7 Baltimore Ravens/1404 1.50 4.00
8 Detroit Lions/1192 1.50 4.00
9 Buffalo Bills/952 2.00 5.00
10 Washington Redskins/1283 2.00 5.00
11 Philadelphia Eagles/1750 1.50 4.00
12 Pittsburgh Steelers/1320 5.00 12.00
13 Seattle Seahawks/1632 1.50 4.00
14 New York Giants/981 2.50 6.00
15 Houston Texans/839 2.00 5.00
16 Minnesota Vikings/1123 2.50 6.00
17 Denver Broncos/777 2.50 6.00
18 Cincinnati Bengals/751 2.00 5.00
19 Jacksonville Jaguars/908 1.50 4.00
20 Tennessee Titans/685 2.00 5.00
21 Atlanta Falcons/1750 2.50 6.00
22 Tampa Bay Buccaneers/595 2.50 6.00
23 St. Louis Rams/758 2.50 6.00
24 Arizona Cardinals/584 2.50 6.00
25 Kansas City Chiefs/826 2.00 5.00
26 Indianapolis Colts/1750 2.00 5.00
27 Oakland Raiders/663 3.00 8.00
28 Dallas Cowboys/812 3.00 8.00
29 Miami Dolphins/672 2.50 6.00
30 New Orleans Saints/591 2.50 6.00
31 San Francisco 49ers/750 3.00 8.00
32 San Diego Chargers/900 2.50 6.00
33 Rashaun Woods/1250 1.50 4.00
34 Kellen Winslow/3750 2.50 6.00
35 Ben Roethlisberger/2500 6.00 15.00
36 Marvin Harrison/1250 2.00 5.00
37 Terrell Owens/1562 2.00 5.00
38 Stephen Davis/1250 1.50 4.00
39 Daunte Culpepper/1250 2.00 5.00
40 Roy Williams WR/2500 2.50 6.00
41 Brian Westbrook/1250 1.50 4.00
42 Julius Jones/1750 2.00 5.00
43 J.P. Losman/2500 2.00 5.00
44 Eli Manning/3750 8.00 20.00
45 Reggie Williams/2276 1.50 4.00
46 Tatum Bell/1750 2.00 5.00
47 Philip Rivers/2500 6.00 12.00
48 Matt Schaub/1750 5.00 10.00
49 LaDainian Tomlinson/1250 2.50 6.00
50 Rudi Johnson/1250 1.50 4.00
51 Robert Gallery/1750 2.50 6.00
52 Keary Colbert/1669 2.00 5.00
53 Greg Jones/1481 1.50 4.00
54 Priest Holmes/1738 2.00 5.00
55 Peyton Manning/1750 5.00 10.00
56 Deuce McAllister/1211 1.50 4.00
57 Larry Fitzgerald/2500 5.00 10.00
58 Steven Jackson/1750 3.00 8.00
59 Lee Evans/1540 2.50 6.00
60 Chad Pennington/1091 2.00 5.00
61 Chad Johnson/1573 2.00 5.00
62 Randy Moss/1250 2.00 5.00
63 Michael Clayton/1446 2.50 6.00
64 Kevin Jones/1750 2.50 6.00
65 Ben Watson/1113 1.50 4.00
66 Clinton Portis/1028 2.00 5.00
67 Hines Ward/871 2.50 6.00
68 Quentin Griffin/1750 1.50 4.00
69 Boo Williams/703 2.00 5.00
70 Tom Brady/1750 7.50 15.00
71 Adam Vinatieri/1250 2.00 5.00
72 Lee Suggs/1250 1.50 4.00
73 Chris Brown/1046 1.50 4.00
74 Drew Henson/1559 1.50 4.00
75 Michael Jenkins/995 2.50 6.00
76 Darius Watts/1042 1.50 4.00
77 Chris Perry/1133 2.50 6.00
78 Donovan McNabb/1418 2.50 6.00
79 Mike Vanderjagt/688 1.50 4.00
80 Tiki Barber/830 2.50 6.00
81 Takeo Spikes/710 2.50 6.00
82 Deion Sanders/1099 2.50 6.00
83 Mewelde Moore/1250 1.50 4.00
84 Brett Favre/900 7.50 15.00
85 LaVar Arrington/900 2.00 5.00
86 Jason Elam/900 1.50 4.00
87A Reuben Droughns/1282 1.50 4.00
87B Matt Hasselbeck/900 2.00 5.00
88 Antonio Gates/1000 2.50 6.00
89 Craig Krenzel/1000 2.00 5.00

2004 eTopps Autographs

3 C.Pennington 01eTop/19
4 C.Pennington 02eTop/54
5 C.Pennington 03eTop/27

2004 eTopps ECON Cleveland

These cards were given away to VIP attendees to the 2004 edition of The National Sports Collectors Convention in Cleveland. Each card features a famous Cleveland area athlete with The National logo at the top of the card and the eTopps and player names at the bottom.

3 Bernie Kosar/984* 2.00 5.00

2004 eTopps Event Series

ES14 Peyton Manning/2844* 2.00 5.00

2004 eTopps Event Series Playoffs

ES1 Marc Bulger/727 2.00 5.00
ES2 Chad Pennington/843 2.00 5.00
ES3 P.Manning/R.Wayne/1500 2.50 6.00
ES4 Daunte Culpepper/830 2.00 5.00
ES5 J.Bettis/D.Staley/1029 2.00 5.00
ES6 Michael Vick/990 2.00 5.00
ES7 Donovan McNabb/892 2.00 5.00
ES8 T.Brady/T.Bruschi/1207 2.50 6.00
ES9 B.Westbrook/B.Dawkins/923 2.00 5.00
ES10 Corey Dillon/1083 2.00 5.00
ES11 Rodney Harrison/987 2.00 5.00
ES12 Deion Branch/963 2.00 5.00

2005 eTopps

1 Michael Vick/1200 3.00 8.00
3 Alge Crumpler/690 2.50 6.00
4 Willis McGahee/885 2.50 6.00
5 Ben Roethlisberger/1200 5.00 10.00
7 T.J. Houshmandzadeh/881 2.50 6.00
8 Antonio Gates/852 3.00 8.00
9 J.P. Losman/1045 2.50 6.00
10 Shaun Alexander/893 3.00 8.00
13 Peyton Manning/1200 3.00 8.00
14 Julius Peppers/661 2.50 6.00
15 Clinton Portis/650 2.50 6.00
16 Randy Moss/1200 2.50 6.00
17 LaDainian Tomlinson/1200 2.50 6.00
18 Brett Favre/1200 6.00 12.00
19 Dunta Robinson/572 2.50 6.00
20 LaMont Jordan/660 2.50 6.00
21 Corey Dillon/591 2.00 5.00
22 Donovan McNabb/1169 2.00 5.00
23 Jason Witten/1012 2.50 6.00
24 Eli Manning/1200 2.50 6.00
25 Tony Gonzalez/638 2.50 6.00
26 Brandon Stokley/842 2.50 6.00
27 Larry Fitzgerald/684 2.50 6.00
28 Julius Jones/1200 2.00 5.00
29 Carson Palmer/1200 2.00 5.00
30 Tom Brady/1200 7.50 15.00
31 Byron Leftwich/667 2.00 5.00
32 Plaxico Burress/762 2.50 6.00
33 Brian Westbrook/786 2.50 6.00
34 Dwight Freeney/1026 2.00 5.00
35 Drew Brees/951 2.00 5.00
36 J.J. Arrington/2000 2.00 5.00
37 Cedric Benson/2000 2.00 5.00
38 Mark Bradley/1200 2.00 5.00
39 Reggie Brown/1200 2.00 5.00
40 Ronnie Brown/2000 3.00 8.00
41 Jason Campbell/1200 2.50 6.00
42 Maurice Clarett/1200 2.00 5.00
43 Mark Clayton/1200 2.00 5.00
44 Braylon Edwards/2000 3.00 8.00
45 Charlie Frye/1200 1.50 4.00
46 Frank Gore/1200 5.00 10.00
47 Vincent Jackson/1018 3.00 8.00
48 Matt Jones/1200 1.50 4.00
49 Stefan LeFors/1200 1.50 4.00
50 Heath Miller/1200 2.00 5.00
51 Ryan Moats/1158 2.00 5.00
52 Vernand Morency/1121 1.50 4.00
53 Terrence Murphy/1139 1.50 4.00
54 Kyle Orton/1200 1.50 4.00
55 Roscoe Parrish/1200 1.50 4.00
56 Courtney Roby/1200 1.50 4.00
57 Aaron Rodgers/1200 40.00 80.00
58 Mike Williams/2000 1.50 4.00
59 Eric Shelton/1200 1.50 4.00
60 Alex Smith/2400 6.00 12.00
62 Roddy White/1200 2.00 5.00
63 Cadillac Williams/2000 2.50 6.00
64 Troy Williamson/2000 1.50 4.00
67 Demarcus Ware/1127 2.50 6.00
68 Willie Parker/1200 2.00 5.00
69 Brandon Jones/599 2.50 6.00
70 Zach Thomas/600 2.00 5.00
71 Michael Strahan/741 2.00 5.00
72 Samie Parker/637 2.00 5.00
85 Mike Nugent/1200 1.50 4.00
86 Chris Henry/1067 1.50 4.00
87 David Greene/863 2.00 5.00
88 Brandon Jacobs/1200 2.50 6.00
89 Adrian McPherson/1200 1.50 4.00
TC1 Seattle Seahawks/1000 3.00 8.00
TC2 Indianapolis Colts/1000 2.50 6.00
TC3 Cincinnati Bengals/935 2.00 5.00
TC4 Chicago Bears/1000 2.00 5.00
TC5 New England Patriots/1000 2.50 6.00
TC6 Denver Broncos/947 2.00 5.00
TC7 New York Giants/881 2.00 5.00
TC8 Jacksonville Jaguars/476 3.00 8.00
TC9 Washington Redskins/604 2.50 6.00
TC10 Tampa Bay Buccaneers/647 2.50 6.00
TC11 Carolina Panthers/571 2.00 5.00
TC12 Pittsburgh Steelers/1000 3.00 8.00

2005 eTopps Autographs

BR1 Ben Roethlisberger 2004 eTopps/150
BW1 Brian Westbrook 2002 eTopps/143
CW1 Cadillac Williams 2005 eTopps/103
PM1 Peyton Manning 2000 eTopps/24
PM2 Peyton Manning 2001 eTopps/25
PM3 Peyton Manning 2002 eTopps/25
PM4 Peyton Manning 2005 eTopps/25
TB1 Tom Brady 2002 eTopps/155
TB2 Tom Brady 2003 eTopps/50

2005 eTopps Event Series

1 Brett Favre/1000 6.00 12.00
2 Peyton Manning 4.00 8.00
Eli Manning/1000

2005 eTopps Classic

41 Merlin Olsen/1000 4.00 8.00
42 Joe Greene/1000 4.00 8.00
43 Roger Staubach/2000 4.00 8.00
44 Reggie White/2000 4.00 8.00
45 Alan Page/1000 4.00 8.00
46 Ed Jones/1000 4.00 8.00
47 George Blanda/1000 4.00 8.00
48 Bob Lilly/1000 4.00 8.00
49 Brian Piccolo/1000 7.50 15.00
50 Herschel Walker/1000 4.00 8.00

2006 eTopps

1 Peyton Manning/849 4.00 10.00
2 Ben Roethlisberger/999 3.00 8.00
3 Steve Smith/999 1.50 4.00
4 Carson Palmer/849 3.00 8.00
5 Larry Johnson/899 2.50 6.00
6 Michael Huff/539 40.00 80.00
7 Chad Johnson/849 2.00 5.00
8 LaDainian Tomlinson/999 3.00 8.00
9 Michael Vick/999 1.50 4.00
10 Edgerrin James/547 2.00 5.00
11 Mario Williams/717 3.00 8.00
12 Tom Brady/749 12.50 25.00
13 Eli Manning/999 3.00 8.00
14 Marcedes Lewis/749 1.50 4.00
15 Terrell Owens/749 3.00 8.00
16 Donovan McNabb/460 3.00 8.00
17 Shaun Alexander/749 1.50 4.00
18 Brett Favre/749 7.50 15.00
20 Owen Daniels/599 2.00 5.00
21 Troy Polamalu/999 2.50 6.00
22 Anthony Fasano/499 2.50 6.00
23 Brian Urlacher/715 2.00 5.00
24 A.J. Hawk/183 100.00 175.00
25 Marques Colston/999 3.00 8.00
26 Kellen Clemens/499 7.50 15.00
27 Brodie Croyle/499 7.50 15.00
28 Jay Cutler/254 40.00 80.00
29 Bruce Gradkowski/999 2.00 5.00
30 Tarvaris Jackson/599 6.00 12.00
31 Demetrius Williams/499 2.50 6.00
32 Matt Leinart/2499 6.00 12.00
33 Vernon Davis/1454 3.00 8.00
34 D.J. Shockley/499 2.50 6.00
35 Dominique Byrd/499 1.50 4.00
36 Vince Young/2499 6.00 12.00
37 Joseph Addai/1499 7.50 15.00
38 Reggie Bush/2525 7.50 15.00
39 Brian Calhoun/762 1.50 4.00
40 Bernard Berrian/700 2.00 5.00
41 Maurice Jones-Drew/1499 4.00 10.00
42 Chester Taylor/749 2.00 5.00
43 Laurence Maroney/1499 4.00 10.00
44 Jerious Norwood/1113 3.00 8.00
45 Leon Washington/313 15.00 30.00
46 LenDale White/1499 2.50 6.00
47 DeAngelo Williams/1999 2.50 6.00
48 Tony Romo/999 10.00 20.00
50 Jerricho Cotchery/699 2.00 5.00
51 Mike Bell/249 12.50 25.00
52 Maurice Stovall/499 3.00 8.00
53 Derek Hagan/749 2.00 5.00
54 D'Brickashaw Ferguson/785 2.00 5.00
55 Devin Hester/599 6.00 15.00
56 Santonio Holmes/999 3.00 8.00
57 Chad Jackson/999 2.00 5.00
58 Greg Jennings/1759 2.50 6.00
60 Sinorice Moss/999 2.00 5.00
61 Drew Brees/700 3.00 8.00
62 Shawne Merriman/749 2.50 6.00
63 Michael Robinson/499 3.00 8.00
64 Wali Lundy/799 1.50 4.00

2006 eTopps Classic

51 Vince Papale/749 5.00 10.00
52 Bronko Nagurski/999 4.00 8.00
53 Paul Hornung/849 7.50 15.00
54 Jim Plunkett/749 5.00 10.00
55 Joe Theismann/749 5.00 10.00

2006 eTopps Event Series

3 Hines Ward 4.00 8.00
Jerome Bettis/1000

2006 eTopps Event Series Playoffs

1 Chicago Bears/1000 2.00 5.00
2 San Deigo Chargers/1000 2.00 5.00
3 Indianapolis Colts/799 2.00 5.00
4 Baltimore Ravens/799 2.00 5.00
5 Dallas Cowboys/999 3.00 8.00
6 New Orleans Saints/999 2.00 5.00
7 New England Patriots/899 2.50 6.00
8 Philadelphia Eagles/670 2.00 5.00
9 Seattle Seahawks/579 2.50 6.00
10 New York Jets/639 2.00 5.00
11 New York Giants/649 2.00 5.00
12 Kansas City Chiefs/599 2.50 6.00

2006 eTopps Event Series National VIP Promos

LB M.Leinart/R.Bush 2.00 5.00

2007 eTopps

1 Ben Roethlisberger/849 3.00 8.00
2 Peyton Manning/849 6.00 12.00
3 Randy Moss/749 6.00 12.00
4 Adrian Peterson/1999 25.00 40.00
5 Brandon Jackson/749 3.00 8.00
6 Tom Brady/749 15.00 30.00
7 Willis McGahee/749 2.00 5.00
8 Calvin Johnson/1999 3.00 8.00
9 Marshawn Lynch/999 10.00 20.00
10 Eli Manning/849 3.00 8.00
11 Thomas Jones/749 2.00 5.00
12 Anthony Gonzalez/749 3.00 8.00
13 James Jones/749 3.00 8.00
14 Brett Favre/499 30.00 50.00
15 Trent Edwards/749 7.50 15.00
16 Brian Leonard/749 2.00 5.00
17 Dwayne Bowe/2257 2.00 5.00
18 Vince Young/999 2.00 5.00
19 Greg Olsen/749 2.50 6.00
20 LaDainian Tomlinson/999 3.00 8.00
21 Reggie Bush/999 2.50 6.00
22 Sidney Rice/749 3.00 8.00
23 John Beck/749 5.00 10.00
24 Chad Johnson/749 2.00 5.00
25 Frank Gore/749 2.00 5.00
26 Selvin Young/749 5.00 10.00
27 Chris Henry/749 2.00 5.00
28 Braylon Edwards/749 2.50 6.00
29 Ted Ginn/1499 2.50 6.00
30 Wes Welker/749 2.50 6.00
31 DeShawn Wynn/749 2.00 5.00
32 Terrell Owens/499 25.00 50.00
33 Derek Anderson/749 3.00 8.00
34 Lorenzo Booker/749 2.00 5.00
35 Troy Smith/749 7.50 15.00
36 Tony Romo/999 5.00 10.00
37 Kevin Kolb/749 6.00 12.00
38 Brady Quinn/1499 6.00 12.00
39 T.J. Houshmandzadeh/749 2.00 5.00
40 Kolby Smith/749 2.50 6.00
41 Andre Hall/749 2.00 5.00
42 Brian Westbrook/749 2.50 6.00
43 JaMarcus Russell/1499 6.00 12.00
44 Zach Miller/499 7.50 15.00
45 Marion Barber/499 20.00 35.00
46 Ryan Grant/749 4.00 10.00
47 Drew Stanton/749 3.00 8.00

2007 eTopps Autographs

AF1 Anthony Fasano/2006 eTopps/49
AG1 Antonio Gates 2005 eTopps/75
AP1 Adrian Peterson/2007 eTopps/195 125.00 200.00
CP4 Chad Pennington 2004 eTopps Event Series/44
DA1 DeAngelo Williams 2006 eTopps/100
ES1 Emmitt Smith 2002 eTopps/25
ES2 Emmitt Smith 2002 eTopps Event Series/25
FG1 Frank Gore 2005 eTopps/99
GJ1 Greg Jennings 2006 eTopps/100
GS1 Gale Sayers 2003 eTopps Classic/50
JA1 Joseph Addai/2006 eTopps/100
JN1 Jerious Norwood/2006 eTopps/100
JP1 Jim Plunkett/2006 eTopps Classic/146
JT1 Joe Theismann/2006 eTopps Classic/150
LJ1 Larry Johnson 2003 eTopps/50
LT1 LaDainian Tomlinson 2001 eTopps/25 125.00 200.00
LT2 LaDainian Tomlinson 2006 eTopps/25
MC1 Marques Colston 2006 eTopps/100
MD1 Maurice Drew 2006 eTopps/100
ML1 Matt Leinart/2006 eTopps/100
MM1 Muhsin Muhammad 2006 eTopps/47
MS1 Maurice Stovall/2006 eTopps/49
PH1 Paul Hornung/2006 eTopps Classic/199
PM5 Peyton Manning/2006 eTopps/50
RB1 Reggie Bush/2006 eTopps/100 75.00 150.00
TD1 Terrell Davis 2001 eTopps/31
TD1 Tony Dorsett 2003 eTopps Classic/48
VP1 Vince Papale/2006 eTopps Classic/199
VY1 Vince Young/2006 eTopps/100
WP1 Willie Parker/2005 eTopps/50

2007 eTopps Event Series Playoffs

1 Green Bay Packers/999 3.00 6.00
2 Indianapolis Colts/999 3.00 6.00
3 New England Patriots/999 3.00 8.00
4 Dallas Cowboys/999 3.00 8.00
5 Tampa Bay Buccaneers/477 3.00 6.00
6 San Diego Chargers/586 3.00 6.00
7 Jacksonville Jaguars/590 3.00 6.00
8 Seattle Seahawks/497 3.00 6.00
9 New York Giants/641 3.00 6.00
10 Tennessee Titans/499 3.00 6.00
11 Washington Redskins/649 3.00 6.00
12 Pittsburgh Steelers/499 4.00 8.00

2008 eTopps

1 James Hardy/749
2 Matt Forte/999
3 Joe Flacco/999
4 Peyton Manning/849
5 Michael Turner/799
6 Eddie Royal/799
7 Jonathan Stewart/999
8 J.T. O'Sullivan/749
9 Felix Jones/999
10 Tim Hightower/799
11 Brett Favre/799
12 Steve Slaton/749
13 Chris Johnson/999
14 Matt Ryan/999
15 Matt Cassel/749
16 Rashard Mendenhall/1319
17 Drew Brees/699
18 DeSean Jackson/749
19 Kevin Smith/749
20 Adrian Peterson/799
21 Donnie Avery/699
22 Steve Breaston/699
23 Chad Pennington/499
24 Benjarvus Green-Ellis/749 7.50 15.00
25 Jamaal Charles/699
26 Clinton Portis/649
27 Dustin Keller/699
28 Brian Brohm/499
30 Ray Rice/699
31 Tony Romo/999
32 Andre Johnson/686
33 Darren McFadden/999
34 Kevin O'Connell/499
35 Peyton Hillis/499
36 Kurt Warner/599
37 Chad Henne/649
38 John Carlson/599
39 Davone Bess/699
40 Tashard Choice/499
41 New York Giants/999
42 Tennessee Titans/749
43 Pittsburgh Steelers/999
44 Arizona Cardinals/699
45 Indianapolis Colts/964
46 Carolina Panthers/749
47 Atlanta Falcons/699
48 San Diego Chargers/599
49 Philadelphia Eagles/694
50 Miami Dolphins/681
51 Minnesota Vikings/599
52 Baltimore Ravens/699
53 Colt Brennan/699
54 John David Booty/699

2008 eTopps Allen and Ginter Super Bowl Champions

1 Terry Bradshaw/749
2 John Elway/999
3 Joe Montana/999
4 Tom Brady/999
5 Troy Aikman/999
6 Joe Namath/999

2008 eTopps Allen and Ginter Yankee Tribute

5 Johnny Unitas/1499 * 4.00 10.00

2009 eTopps

1 Drew Brees/999
2 Chris Wells/749
3 Matthew Stafford/999
4 Brett Favre/999
5 Percy Harvin/999
6 Johnny Knox/749
7 Randy Moss/749
8 Peyton Manning/849
9 Ben Roethlisberger/849
10 Knowshon Moreno/749
11 Glen Coffee/749
12 Tom Brady/749
13 Steve Smith/749
14 Austin Collie/749
15 Kenny Britt/749
16 Josh Johnson/749
17 Adrian Peterson/999
18 Hakeem Nicks/749
19 Mike Wallace/749
20 Shonn Greene/749
21 Miles Austin/749
22 Kyle Orton/749
23 Mark Sanchez/999
24 Chris Johnson/749
26 LeSean McCoy/749
27 Cedric Benson/749
28 Mohamed Massaquoi/749
29 Josh Freeman/799
30 Reggie Wayne/749
31 Maurice Jones-Drew/749
32 Jason Snelling/669
33 Bernard Scott/729
34 Chris Jennings/609
35 Aaron Rodgers/649 6.00 12.00
36 Terrell Owens/599
37 Michael Crabtree/749
38 Donald Brown/699
39 Louis Murphy/699
40 Chad Ochocinco/599
41 Indianapolis Colts/749
42 New Orleans Saints/749
43 Minnesota Vikings/749
44 Tony Romo/749
45 San Diego Chargers/749
46 Arizona Cardinals/599
47 Philadelphia Eagles/659
48 Jared Allen/649
49 Cincinnati Bengals/539
50 New England Patriots/749
51 Dallas Cowboys/749
52 Green Bay Packers/749
53 New York Jets/499
54 Baltimore Ravens/509
55 Julian Edelman/649

2009 eTopps Allen and Ginter Super Bowl Champions

7 Brett Favre/999
8 Tom Landry/749
9 Emmitt Smith/999
10 Walter Payton/999
11 Jerry Rice/999
12 Peyton Manning/999
13 Roger Staubach/999
14 Tony Dorsett/999
15 Lawrence Taylor/999

1997 E-X2000

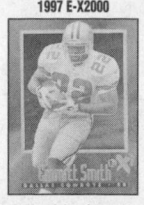

This 60-card, hobby-exclusive set features color action player images with a die-cut holofoil border and wet-look laminate. The player is silhouetted in front of a transparent window displaying a variety of sky patterns. The backs carry a modified mirror image of the front with 1996 season and career statistics.

COMPLETE SET (60) 12.50 30.00
1 Jake Plummer RC 4.00 10.00
2 Jamal Anderson .60 1.50
3 Rae Carruth RC .25 .60
4 Kerry Collins .60 1.50
5 Darnell Autry RC .60 1.50
6 Rashaan Salaam .25 .60
7 Troy Aikman 1.25 3.00
8 Deion Sanders .60 1.50
9 Emmitt Smith 2.00 5.00
10 Herman Moore .40 1.00
11 Barry Sanders 2.00 5.00
12 Mark Chmura .40 1.00
13 Brett Favre 2.50 6.00
14 Antonio Freeman .60 1.50
15 Reggie White .60 1.50
16 Cris Carter .60 1.50
17 Brad Johnson .60 1.50
18 Troy Davis RC .40 1.00
19 Danny Wuerffel RC .60 1.50
20 Dave Brown .25 .60
21 Ike Hilliard RC 1.25 3.00
22 Ty Detmer .40 1.00
23 Ricky Watters .40 1.00
24 Tony Banks .40 1.00
25 Eddie Kennison .40 1.00
26 Jim Druckenmiller RC .40 1.00
27 Jerry Rice 1.25 3.00
28 Steve Young .75 2.00
29 Trent Dilfer .60 1.50
30 Warrick Dunn RC 3.00 8.00
31 Terry Allen .60 1.50
32 Gus Frerotte .25 .60
33 Vinny Testaverde .40 1.00
34 Antowain Smith RC 2.50 6.00
35 Thurman Thomas .60 1.50
36 Jeff Blake .40 1.00
37 Carl Pickens .40 1.00
38 Terrell Davis .75 2.00
39 John Elway 2.00 5.00
40 Eddie George .60 1.50
41 Steve McNair .75 2.00
42 Marshall Faulk .75 2.00
43 Marvin Harrison .60 1.50
44 Mark Brunell .75 2.00
45 Marcus Allen .60 1.50
46 Elvis Grbac .40 1.00
47 Karim Abdul-Jabbar .40 1.00
48 Dan Marino 2.50 6.00
49 Drew Bledsoe .75 2.00
50 Terry Glenn .60 1.50
51 Curtis Martin .75 2.00
52 Keyshawn Johnson .60 1.50
53 Tim Brown .60 1.50
54 Jeff George .40 1.00
55 Jerome Bettis .60 1.50
56 Kordell Stewart .60 1.50
57 Stan Humphries .40 1.00
58 Junior Seau .60 1.50
59 Joey Galloway .40 1.00
60 Chris Warren .40 1.00

1997 E-X2000 Essential Credentials

*STARS: 8X TO 20X HI COLUMN
*RCs: 2.5X TO 6X BASIC CARDS
STATED PRINT RUN 100 SERIAL #'d SETS

1997 E-X2000 A Cut Above

Randomly inserted in packs at the rate of one in 288, this 10-card set features color images of some of the NFL's best players on sawblade die-cut cards with holographic foil backgrounds.

STATED ODDS 1:288
1 Barry Sanders 20.00 50.00
2 Brett Favre 25.00 60.00
3 Dan Marino 25.00 60.00
4 Eddie George 6.00 15.00
5 Emmitt Smith 20.00 50.00
6 Jerry Rice 15.00 40.00
7 Joey Galloway 5.00 12.00
8 John Elway 20.00 50.00
9 Mark Brunell 6.00 15.00
10 Terrell Davis 10.00 25.00

1997 E-X2000 Fleet of Foot

Randomly inserted in packs at the rate of one in 20, this 20-card set features color images of players known for their fast running. Each card is die cut in the shape of football cleats.

COMPLETE SET (20) 40.00 100.00
STATED ODDS 1:20
1 Antonio Freeman 2.50 6.00
2 Barry Sanders 8.00 20.00
3 Carl Pickens 1.50 4.00
4 Chris Warren 1.50 4.00
5 Curtis Martin 3.00 8.00
6 Deion Sanders 2.50 6.00
7 Emmitt Smith 8.00 20.00
8 Jerry Rice 5.00 12.00
9 Joey Galloway 1.50 4.00
10 Karim Abdul-Jabbar 1.50 4.00
11 Kordell Stewart 2.50 6.00
12 Lawrence Phillips 1.00 2.50
13 Mark Brunell 3.00 8.00
14 Marvin Harrison 2.50 6.00
15 Rae Carruth 1.00 2.50
16 Ricky Watters 1.50 4.00
17 Steve Young 3.00 8.00
18 Terrell Davis 3.00 8.00
19 Terry Glenn 2.50 6.00
20 Shawn Springs 1.50 4.00

1997 E-X2000 Star Date 2000

Randomly inserted in packs at the rate of one in nine, this 15-card set features color action images of young NFL players who appear to be on the road to stardom by the year 2000. Each card is printed on 100% holographic foil stock.

COMPLETE SET (15) 15.00 40.00
STATED ODDS 1:9
1 Curtis Martin 1.25 3.00
2 Darnell Autry .75 2.00
3 Darrell Russell .50 1.25
4 Eddie Kennison .75 2.00
5 Jim Druckenmiller .75 2.00
6 Karim Abdul-Jabbar 1.25 3.00
7 Kerry Collins .75 2.00
8 Keyshawn Johnson 1.25 3.00
9 Marvin Harrison 1.25 3.00
10 Orlando Pace 1.25 3.00
11 Pat Barnes 1.25 3.00
12 Reidel Anthony .75 2.00
13 Tim Biakabutuka .75 2.00
14 Warrick Dunn 2.00 5.00
15 Yatil Green .75 2.00

1998 E-X2001

The 1998 SkyBox E-X2001 hobby only set was issued in one series totalling 60 cards and was distributed in two-card packs with a suggested retail price of $3.99. The set features color action player images printed with holographic and gold-foil stamping and player-specific die-cuts mounted on durable, see-thru plastic stock. Two parallel versions of this set were also produced: Essential Credentials Now with a holofoil gold background and each card sequentially numbered according to the player's card number in the basic set; Essential Credentials Future with a holofoil rose colored background and each card sequentially numbered to the opposite of the player's card number in the basic set.

COMPLETE SET (60) 20.00 50.00
1 Kordell Stewart .20 .50
2 Steve Young .60 1.50
3 Mark Brunell .30 .75
4 Brett Favre 2.00 5.00
5 Barry Sanders 1.50 4.00
6 Warrick Dunn .30 .75
7 Jerry Rice 1.00 2.50
8 Dan Marino 2.00 5.00
9 Emmitt Smith 1.50 4.00
10 John Elway 2.00 5.00
11 Eddie George .30 .75
12 Jake Plummer .30 .75
13 Terrell Davis .30 .75
14 Curtis Martin .30 .75
15 Troy Aikman 1.00 2.50
16 Terry Glenn .20 .50
17 Mike Alstott .30 .75
18 Drew Bledsoe .30 .75
19 Keyshawn Johnson .30 .75
20 Dorsey Levens .20 .50
21 Elvis Grbac .20 .50
22 Ricky Watters .20 .50
23 Robert Smith .20 .50
24 Trent Dilfer .30 .75
25 Joey Galloway .20 .50
26 Rob Moore .20 .50
27 Steve McNair .30 .75
28 Jim Harbaugh .20 .50
29 Troy Davis .10 .30
30 Rob Johnson .20 .50
31 Shannon Sharpe .30 .75
32 Jerome Bettis .30 .75
33 Tim Brown .30 .75
34 Kerry Collins .20 .50
35 Garrison Hearst .20 .50
36 Antonio Freeman .30 .75
37 Charlie Garner .20 .50
38 Glenn Foley .10 .30
39 Yatil Green .10 .30
40 Tiki Barber .30 .75
41 Bobby Hoying .20 .50
42 Corey Dillon .20 .50
43 Antowain Smith .20 .50
44 Robert Edwards RC 1.00 2.50
45 Jammi German RC .60 1.50
46 Ahman Green RC 2.50 6.00
47 Hines Ward RC 5.00 10.00
48 Skip Hicks RC 1.00 2.50
49 Brian Griese RC 2.50 6.00
50 Charlie Batch RC 1.25 3.00
51 Jacquez Green RC 1.00 2.50
52 John Avery RC 1.00 2.50
53 Kevin Dyson RC 1.25 3.00
54 Peyton Manning RC 10.00 25.00
55 Randy Moss RC 6.00 15.00
56 Ryan Leaf RC 1.25 3.00
57 Curtis Enis RC .60 1.50
58 Charles Woodson RC 2.50 6.00
59 Robert Holcombe RC 1.00 2.50
60 Fred Taylor RC 2.00 5.00
NNO Jake Plummer PROMO .40 1.00
NNO Checklist Card 1 .10 .30
NNO Checklist Card 2 .10 .30

1998 E-X2001 Essential Credentials Future

*FUTURE/50-60: 25X TO 60X BASIC CARDS
*FUTURE/40-49: 40X TO 100X BASIC CARDS
*FUTURE/30-39: 50X TO 120X BASIC CARDS
*FUTURE/20-29: 60X TO 150X BASIC CARDS
*VETS FUT/10-19: 80X TO 200X BASIC CARDS
*ROOKIES FUT/10-19: 15X TO 40X BASIC RC
STATED PRINT RUN 1-60

1998 E-X2001 Essential Credentials Now

*ROOKIES NOW/50 60: 4X TO 10X BASIC RC
*ROOKIES NOW/44-49: 5X TO 12X BASIC RC
*VETS NOW/40-43: 40X TO 100X BASIC CARDS
*NOW/30-39: 50X TO 120X BASIC CARDS
*NOW/20-29: 60X TO 150X BASIC CARDS
*NOW/11-19: 80X TO 200X BASIC CARDS
STATED PRINT RUN 1-60
15 Troy Aikman/15 150.00 300.00
54 Peyton Manning/54 200.00 400.00

1998 E-X2001 Destination Honolulu

Randomly inserted in packs at the rate of one in 720, this 10-card set features color action player images printed on die-cut wooden card stock with one of five different statuesque backgrounds.

STATED ODDS 1:720 HOBBY
1 Peyton Manning 40.00 100.00
2 Terrell Davis 8.00 20.00
3 Corey Dillon 6.00 15.00
4 Eddie George 8.00 20.00
5 Emmitt Smith 30.00 80.00
6 Warrick Dunn 8.00 20.00
7 Brett Favre 40.00 100.00
8 Antowain Smith 6.00 15.00
9 Barry Sanders 30.00 80.00
10 Ryan Leaf 6.00 15.00

1998 E-X2001 Helmet Heroes

Randomly inserted in packs at the rate of one in 24, this 20-card set features color action player photos printed on team color-coded cards die-cut around the helmet at the card top.

COMPLETE SET (20) 60.00 120.00
STATED ODDS 1:24 HOBBY
1 Barry Sanders 5.00 12.00
2 Emmitt Smith 5.00 12.00
3 Brett Favre 6.00 15.00
4 Mark Brunell 1.00 2.50
5 Jerry Rice 3.00 8.00
6 Steve Young 2.00 5.00
7 Warrick Dunn 1.00 2.50
8 Kordell Stewart 1.00 2.50
9 John Elway 6.00 15.00
10 Troy Aikman 3.00 8.00
11 Dan Marino 6.00 15.00
12 Curtis Martin 1.00 2.50
13 Dorsey Levens 1.00 2.50
14 Jake Plummer 1.00 2.50
15 Corey Dillon 1.00 2.50
16 Yancey Thigpen .60 1.50
17 Randy Moss 5.00 12.00
18 Curtis Enis .50 1.25
19 Charles Woodson 2.00 5.00
20 Fred Taylor 1.50 4.00

1998 E-X2001 Star Date 2001

Randomly inserted in packs at the rate of one in 12, this 15-card set features color action player photos printed on thick, plastic card stock with flecks of foil running through it and highlighted with etched silver foil stamping.

COMPLETE SET (15) 15.00 40.00
STATED ODDS 1:12 HOBBY
1 Randy Moss 5.00 12.00
2 Fred Taylor 1.50 4.00
3 Corey Dillon .60 1.50
4 Jake Plummer .60 1.50
5 Antowain Smith .60 1.50
0 Wilmont Perry .25 .60
7 Donald Hayes .25 .60
8 Tavian Banks 2.50 6.00
9 John Dutton .25 .60
10 Kevin Dyson 1.00 2.50
11 Germane Crowell .40 1.00
12 Bobby Hoying .40 1.00
13 Jerome Pathon 1.00 2.50
14 Ryan Leaf 1.00 2.50
15 Peyton Manning 8.00 20.00

1999 E-X Century

This 90 card set is done on a thick transparent card stock with a color action shot of each player. Key rookies include Tim Couch, Edgerrin James, and Ricky Williams. Also randomly inserted in packs at a rate of 1 in 68 packs is the cross brand autographics insert set which features hand signed autographed cards of stars and rookies.

COMPLETE SET (90) 50.00 120.00
COMP.SET w/o SP's (60) 20.00 40.00
1 Keyshawn Johnson .30 .75
2 Natrone Means .30 .75
3 Antonio Freeman .30 .75
4 Muhsin Muhammad .25 .60
5 Curtis Martin .30 .75
6 Chris Chandler .30 .75
7 Priest Holmes .25 .60
8 Vinny Testaverde .25 .60
9 Tim Brown .40 1.00
10 Eddie George .30 .75
11 Brad Johnson .30 .75
12 Mike Alstott .25 .60
13 Dorsey Levens .30 .75
14 Jamal Anderson .30 .75
15 Herman Moore .30 .75
16 Brett Favre .75 2.00
17 John Elway .60 1.50
18 Steve Young .50 1.25
19 Warrick Dunn .25 .60
20 Fred Taylor .25 .60
21 Charlie Batch .25 .60
22 Jimmy Smith .30 .75
23 Steve McNair .30 .75
24 Jerry Rice 1.00 2.50
25 Dan Marino .75 2.00
26 Jake Plummer .25 .60
27 Marshall Faulk .30 .75
28 Garrison Hearst .25 .60
29 Terrell Davis .30 .75
30 Barry Sanders .60 1.50
31 Carl Pickens .30 .75
32 Jerome Bettis .40 1.00
33 Scott Mitchell .25 .60
34 Duce Staley .25 .60
35 Robert Smith .25 .60
36 Wayne Chrebet .25 .60
37 Steve Beuerlein .30 .75
38 Elvis Grbac .25 .60
39 Troy Aikman .50 1.25
40 Emmitt Smith .60 1.50
41 Joey Galloway .30 .75
42 Ryan Leaf .30 .75
43 Skip Hicks .25 .60
44 Cris Carter .40 1.00
45 Shannon Sharpe .30 .75
46 Mark Brunell .30 .75
47 Kerry Collins .25 .60
48 Corey Dillon .25 .60
49 Kordell Stewart .25 .60
50 Randy Moss .30 .75
51 Jon Kitna .25 .60
52 Deion Sanders .30 .75
53 Rod Smith .30 .75
54 Drew Bledsoe .30 .75
55 Torrell Owens .30 .75
56 Napoleon Kaufman .25 .60
57 Trent Green .25 .60
58 Ricky Watters .30 .75
59 Randall Cunningham .30 .75
60 Peyton Manning 1.25 3.00
61 Tim Couch RC 1.25 3.00
62 Amos Zereoue RC 1.00 2.50
63 Cade McNown RC 1.00 2.50
64 Donovan McNabb RC 3.00 8.00
65 Ricky Williams RC 1.50 4.00
66 Daunte Culpepper RC 1.50 4.00
67 Troy Edwards RC 1.00 2.50
68 Peerless Price RC 1.00 2.50
69 Edgerrin James RC 1.50 4.00
70 Champ Bailey RC 2.00 5.00
71 Akili Smith RC 1.00 2.50
72 Kevin Johnson RC 1.25 3.00
73 Cecil Collins RC 1.00 2.50
74 David Boston RC 1.00 2.50
75 Torry Holt RC 2.00 5.00
76 James Johnson RC 1.00 2.50
77 Na Brown RC 1.00 2.50
78 Rob Konrad RC 1.00 2.50
79 Mike Cloud RC 1.00 2.50
80 Craig Yeast RC 1.00 2.50
81 Brock Huard RC 1.00 2.50
82 Chris McAlister RC 1.00 2.50
83 Shaun King RC 1.00 2.50
84 Wane McGarity RC 1.00 2.50
85 Joe Germaine RC 1.25 3.00
86 D'Wayne Bates RC 1.00 2.50
87 Kevin Faulk RC 1.00 2.50
88 Antoine Winfield RC 1.00 2.50
89 Reginald Kelly RC 1.00 2.50
90 Antuan Edwards RC 1.00 2.50
P1 Jake Plummer Promo .40 1.00

1999 E-X Century Essential Credentials Future

*VETS/70-90: 8X TO 20X BASIC CARDS
*VETS/45-69: 12X TO 30X
*VETS/31-44: 20X TO 50X
*ROOKIES/20-30: 5X TO 10X
*ROOKIES/10-19: 6X TO 12X
STATED PRINT RUN 1-90

1999 E-X Century Essential Credentials Now

*ROOKIES/70-90: 2X TO 5X BASIC CARDS
*VETS/45-69: 12X TO 30X BASIC CARDS
*ROOKIES/45-69: 2.5X TO 6X
*VETS/30-44: 20X TO 50X
*VETS/20-29: 25X TO 60X
*VETS/10-19: 30X TO 80X
STATED PRINT RUN 1-90
CARDS #'d UNDER 10 NOT PRICED

1999 E-X Century Authen-Kicks

Randomly inserted in packs, This 12 card set features an actual piece of game used shoe worn in an NFL game by each respective player. All cards are hand numbered on the front showing how many were made of each.

1AK Travis McGriff/235 6.00 15.00
2AK Trent Green/190 12.50 30.00
3AK Brock Huard/280 6.00 15.00
4AK Randall Cunningham/290 15.00 40.00
5AK Donovan McNabb/210 30.00 60.00
6AK Torry Holt/285 10.00 25.00
7AK Joe Germaine/280 6.00 15.00
8AK Cade McNown/260 6.00 15.00
9AK Doug Flutie/215 12.50 30.00
10AK O.J. McDuffie/285 6.00 15.00
11AK Ricky Williams/215 12.50 30.00
12AK Dan Marino/285 40.00 80.00

1999 E-X Century Bright Lights

Randomy inserted at a rate of 1 in 24 packs, this insert set contains 24 cards and is done with a flourescent background of either purple or a lime green. An unexpected Orange version surfaced in packs due to a printing problem and seem to be harder to find than the original two colors intented for the insert.

COMPLETE SET (20) 50.00 120.00
STATED ODDS 1:24
*ORANGE: 1X TO 2.5X GREEN
1BL Randy Moss 1.50 4.00
2BL Tim Couch 1.50 4.00
3BL Eddie George 1.50 4.00
4BL Brett Favre 4.00 10.00
5BL Steve Young 2.50 6.00
6BL Barry Sanders 3.00 8.00
7BL Troy Aikman 2.50 6.00
8BL Jake Plummer 1.25 3.00
9BL Edgerrin James 2.00 5.00
10BL Terrell Davis 1.50 4.00
11BL Warrick Dunn 1.25 3.00
12BL Jerry Rice 5.00 12.00
13BL Fred Taylor 1.25 3.00
14BL Mark Brunell 1.50 4.00
15BL Emmitt Smith 3.00 8.00
16BL Ricky Williams 2.00 5.00
17BL Charlie Batch 1.25 3.00
18BL Jamal Anderson 1.50 4.00
19BL Peyton Manning 6.00 15.00
20BL Dan Marino 4.00 10.00

1999 E-X Century E-Xtraordinary

Randomly inserted in packs at a rate of 1 in 9 this 15 card insert set contains a 3-d type look with a small head shot of each player also on the card front. Set contains both rookies and star verteran players such as Dan Marino and Ricky Williams.

COMPLETE SET (15) 40.00 80.00
STATED ODDS 1:9
1XT Ricky Williams 1.00 2.50
2XT Corey Dillon .60 1.50
3XT Charlie Batch .60 1.50
4XT Terrell Davis .75 2.00
5XT Edgerrin James 1.00 2.50
6XT Jake Plummer .60 1.50
7XT Tim Couch .75 2.00
8XT Warrick Dunn .60 1.50
9XT Akili Smith .60 1.50
10XT Randy Moss .75 2.00
11XT Cade McNown .60 1.50
12XT Fred Taylor .60 1.50
13XT Donovan McNabb 2.00 5.00
14XT Torry Holt 1.25 3.00
15XT Peyton Manning 3.00 8.00

2000 E-X

Released in early October 2000, E-X features a 150-card base set comprised of 100 veteran cards and 50 short-printed rookie cards, each sequentially numbered to 1500. Base cards are holographic foil board and showcase full-color action photography. E-X was packaged in 24-pack boxes with each pack containing five cards and carried a suggested retail price of $4.99.

COMPLETE SET (150) 100.00 200.00
COMP.SET w/o RC's (100) 6.00 15.00
1 Tim Couch .20 .50
2 Daunte Culpepper .20 .50
3 Jake Reed .20 .50
4 Donovan McNabb .20 .50
5 Terry Glenn .20 .50
6 Vinny Testaverde .15 .40
7 Michael Westbrook .15 .40
8 Errict Rhett .20 .50
9 Joey Galloway .20 .50
10 O.J. McDuffie .20 .50
11 Rob Johnson .20 .50
12 Warren Sapp .20 .50
13 Brian Griese .15 .40
14 Derrick Mayes .15 .40
15 Ike Hilliard .15 .40
16 Kevin Dyson .20 .50
17 Shannon Sharpe .20 .50
18 Cade McNown .15 .40
19 Damon Huard .15 .40
20 James Stewart .15 .40
21 Kevin Johnson .15 .40
22 Muhsin Muhammad .15 .40
23 Shaun King .15 .40
24 Corey Dillon .15 .40
25 Fred Taylor .15 .40
26 Peyton Manning .60 1.50
27 Steve McNair .20 .50
28 Tim Brown .25 .60
29 Brad Johnson .20 .50
30 Edgerrin James .20 .50
31 Germane Crowell .15 .40
32 Kordell Stewart .15 .40
33 Randy Moss .20 .50
34 Tony Banks .15 .40
35 Akili Smith .15 .40
36 Charlie Batch .15 .40
37 Duce Staley .15 .40
38 Jerome Bettis .25 .60
39 Rich Gannon .20 .50
40 Steve Young .30 .75
41 Tony Gonzalez .20 .50
42 Curtis Martin .20 .50
43 Eddie George .20 .50
44 Marshall Faulk .20 .50
45 Troy Edwards .15 .40
46 Curtis Enis .15 .40
47 Jake Plummer .15 .40
48 Jon Kitna .15 .40
49 Qadry Ismail .15 .40
50 Terrell Davis .20 .50
51 Troy Aikman .30 .75
52 Elvis Grbac .15 .40
53 Jeff Blake .20 .50
54 Kurt Warner .40 1.00
55 Ricky Watters .20 .50
56 Torry Holt .20 .50
57 Brett Favre .50 1.25
58 Chris Chandler .20 .50
59 Eric Moulds .15 .40
60 Jimmy Smith .20 .50
61 Ricky Williams .20 .50
62 Antonio Freeman .20 .50
63 Curtis Conway .20 .50
64 Emmitt Smith .40 1.00
65 Kerry Collins .15 .40
66 Marvin Harrison .20 .50
67 Tyrone Wheatley .15 .40
68 Charlie Garner .20 .50
69 Derrick Alexander .15 .40
70 Jamal Anderson .20 .50
71 Mike Alstott .15 .40
72 Ryan Leaf .20 .50
73 Tim Biakabutuka .20 .50
74 Amani Toomer .15 .40
75 Dorsey Levens .20 .50
76 Frank Sanders .15 .40
77 Junior Seau .20 .50
78 Steve Beuerlein .20 .50
79 Wayne Chrebet .15 .40
80 Carl Pickens .20 .50
81 Drew Bledsoe .20 .50
82 Isaac Bruce .25 .60
83 Marcus Robinson .20 .50
84 Stephen Davis .15 .40
85 Cris Carter .25 .60
86 Ed McCaffrey .20 .50
87 Jerry Rice .60 1.50
88 Mark Brunell .20 .50
89 Peerless Price .20 .50
90 Terance Mathis .15 .40
91 Tony Martin .20 .50
92 Jevon Kearse .15 .40
93 Robert Smith .15 .40
94 Rob Moore .15 .40
95 Charles Johnson .15 .40
96 Doug Flutie .20 .50
97 Sean Dawkins .15 .40
98 Keenan McCardell .20 .50
99 Bill Schroeder .20 .50
100 Rod Smith .20 .50
101 Peter Warrick RC 1.50 4.00
102 Corey Simon RC 2.00 5.00
103 Danny Farmer RC 1.50 4.00
104 Jamal Lewis RC 2.50 6.00
105 Jerry Porter RC 2.50 6.00
106 Joe Hamilton RC 1.50 4.00
107 Marc Bulger RC 2.00 5.00
108 R.Jay Soward RC 1.50 4.00
109 Ron Dugans RC 1.50 4.00
110 Shaun Alexander RC 2.50 6.00
111 Travis Prentice RC 1.50 4.00
112 Anthony Becht RC 1.50 4.00
113 Bubba Franks RC 1.50 4.00
114 Chris Redman RC 1.50 4.00
115 Dennis Northcutt RC 1.50 4.00
116 Dez White RC 1.50 4.00
117 Gari Scott RC 1.50 4.00
118 Mareno Philyaw RC 1.50 4.00
119 Ron Dayne RC 2.50 6.00
120 Shyrone Stith RC 1.50 4.00
121 Tee Martin RC 1.50 4.00
122 Tom Brady RC 300.00 500.00
123 Trung Canidate RC 1.50 4.00
124 Chad Pennington RC 2.00 5.00
125 Chris Cole RC 2.00 5.00
126 Courtney Brown RC 2.00 5.00
127 Doug Chapman RC 1.50 4.00
128 Giovanni Carmazzi RC 1.50 4.00
129 J.R. Redmond RC 1.50 4.00
130 Michael Wiley RC 1.50 4.00
131 Reuben Droughns RC 1.50 4.00
132 Terrelle Smith RC 1.50 4.00
133 Thomas Jones RC 2.00 5.00
134 Travis Taylor RC 1.50 4.00
135 Anthony Lucas RC 1.50 4.00
136 Curtis Keaton RC 1.50 4.00
137 Frank Moreau RC 1.50 4.00
138 Darrell Jackson RC 1.50 4.00
139 Laveranues Coles RC 2.00 5.00
140 Brian Urlacher RC 8.00 20.00
141 Plaxico Burress RC 2.00 5.00
142 Sammy Morris RC 1.50 4.00
143 Sylvester Morris RC 1.50 4.00
144 Tim Rattay RC 2.00 5.00
145 Todd Pinkston RC 1.50 4.00
146 Troy Walters RC 1.50 4.00
147 Sebastian Janikowski RC 2.50 6.00
148 JaJuan Dawson RC 1.50 4.00
149 Trevor Gaylor RC 1.50 4.00
150 Rondell Mealey RC 1.50 4.00

2000 E-X Essential Credentials

*VETS 1-100: 12X TO 30X BASIC CARDS
1-100 VETERAN PRINT RUN 50
*ROOKIES 101-150: 1.5X TO 4X
101-150 ROOKIE PRINT RUN 25
122 Tom Brady 900.00 1500.00

2000 E-X E-Xceptional Red

Randomly inserted in packs at the rate of one in 12, this 15-card set features color player action photography set against a red 3-D background with silver foil highlights. A Green version (1:288 packs) and Blue (100-serial numbered sets) version were also produced.

COMPLETE SET (15) 10.00 25.00
STATED ODDS 1:12
*GREEN: 2.5X TO 6X BASIC INSERTS
GREEN STATED ODDS 1:288
*BLUE/100: 4X TO 10X BASIC INSERTS
BLUE PRINT RUN 100 SER.#'d SETS
1 Kurt Warner .60 1.50
2 Peyton Manning 1.00 2.50
3 Brett Favre .75 2.00
4 Tim Couch .30 .75
5 Keyshawn Johnson .30 .75
6 Mark Brunell .30 .75
7 Eddie George .30 .75
8 Edgerrin James .30 .75
9 Ricky Williams .30 .75
10 Randy Moss .30 .75
11 Jamal Lewis .40 1.00
12 Emmitt Smith .60 1.50
13 Thomas Jones .30 .75
14 Fred Taylor .25 .60
15 Chad Pennington .30 .75

2000 E-X E-Xciting

Randomly inserted in packs at the rate of one in 24, this 10-card set features a die-cut jersey card stock with player action photography and holofoil background.

COMPLETE SET (10) 12.00 30.00
STATED ODDS 1:24
1 Fred Taylor .60 1.50
2 Troy Aikman 1.25 3.00
3 Edgerrin James .75 2.00
4 Brett Favre 2.00 5.00
5 Peyton Manning 2.50 6.00
6 Emmitt Smith 1.50 4.00
7 Randy Moss .75 2.00
8 Kurt Warner 1.50 4.00
9 Marshall Faulk .75 2.00
10 Peter Warrick .60 1.50

2000 E-X E-Xplosive

Randomly inserted in packs at the rate of one in eight, this 20-card set features top NFL stars on a white background with an orange and red foil "explosion" on the left side of the card.

COMPLETE SET (20) 12.00 30.00
STATED ODDS 1:8
1 Kurt Warner 1.00 2.50
2 Marvin Harrison .50 1.25
3 Ricky Williams .50 1.25
4 Eddie George .50 1.25
5 Emmitt Smith 1.00 2.50
6 Troy Aikman .75 2.00
7 Randy Moss .50 1.25
8 Edgerrin James .50 1.25
9 Keyshawn Johnson .50 1.25
10 Tim Couch .50 1.25
11 Fred Taylor .40 1.00
12 Brett Favre 1.25 3.00
13 Peyton Manning 1.50 4.00
14 Donovan McNabb .50 1.25
15 Ron Dayne .60 1.50
16 Jake Plummer .40 1.00
17 Marshall Faulk .50 1.25
18 Travis Taylor .40 1.00
19 Terrell Davis .50 1.25
20 Shaun Alexander .60 1.50

2000 E-X Generation E-X

Randomly inserted in packs at the rate of one in four, this 15-card set features top draft picks on a black holographic foil background.

COMPLETE SET (15) 5.00 12.00
STATED ODDS 1:4
1 Peter Warrick .20 .50
2 Plaxico Burress .25 .60
3 R.Jay Soward .20 .50
4 Shaun Alexander .30 .75
5 Chad Pennington .25 .60
6 Giovanni Carmazzi .20 .50
7 Thomas Jones .25 .60
8 Todd Pinkston .20 .50
9 Chris Redman .20 .50
10 Jamal Lewis .30 .75
11 Ron Dayne .30 .75
12 Dez White .20 .50
13 J.R. Redmond .20 .50
14 Sylvester Morris .20 .50
15 Travis Taylor .20 .50

2000 E-X NFL Debut Postmarks

Randomly inserted in packs at the rate of one in 288, this 15-card set features "postcard" card-stock with a postal stamp and a shipping stamp.

COMPLETE SET (15) 40.00 100.00
STATED ODDS 1:288
1 Peter Warrick 1.50 4.00
2 Travis Taylor 1.50 4.00
3 Thomas Jones 2.00 5.00
4 Ron Dayne 2.50 6.00
5 Plaxico Burress 2.00 5.00
6 Sylvester Morris 1.50 4.00
7 Todd Pinkston 1.50 4.00
8 Jamal Lewis 2.50 6.00
9 Shaun Alexander 2.50 6.00
10 J.R. Redmond 1.50 4.00
11 Dennis Northcutt 1.50 4.00
12 Bubba Franks 1.50 4.00
13 R.Jay Soward 1.50 4.00
14 Jerry Porter 2.50 6.00
15 Chad Pennington 2.00 5.00

2001 E-X

This 140 card set was issued in four card packs which were packed 24 to a box. Cards numbered 91 through 140 featured rookies and were randomly inserted in packs. These cards were printed in quantities between 1000 and 1500 copies and most of the rookies featured signed some of the Rookie Cards.

COMP.SET w/o RC's (90) 10.00 25.00
91-140 ROOKIE PRINT RUN 1000-1500
1 Jamal Anderson .25 .60
2 Tim Couch .20 .50
3 Jeff Garcia .20 .50
4 Brett Favre .60 1.50
5 Donovan McNabb .25 .60
6 Kerry Collins .20 .50
7 Doug Flutie .25 .60
8 Steve McNair .25 .60
9 Kordell Stewart .20 .50
10 Daunte Culpepper .25 .60
11 Rich Gannon .25 .60
12 Kurt Warner .50 1.25
13 Brian Griese .20 .50
14 Brad Johnson .25 .60
15 Jake Plummer .20 .50
16 Mark Brunell .25 .60
17 Peyton Manning .75 2.00
18 Keyshawn Johnson .25 .60
19 Derrick Alexander .20 .50
20 Emmitt Smith .50 1.25
21 Rob Johnson .25 .60
22 Aaron Brooks .20 .50
23 Charlie Garner .25 .60
24 Lamar Smith .25 .60
25 Eddie George .30 .75
26 Marshall Faulk .25 .60
27 Tiki Barber .25 .60
28 Terrell Davis .25 .60
29 Jamal Lewis .30 .75
30 Edgerrin James .25 .60
31 Duce Staley .20 .50
32 Ricky Williams .25 .60
33 Dorsey Levens .25 .60
34 Jerome Bettis .30 .75
35 Ron Dayne .25 .60
36 Mike Anderson .20 .50
37 Peter Warrick .20 .50
38 Mike Alstott .20 .50
39 Fred Taylor .20 .50
40 Curtis Martin .25 .60
41 Warrick Dunn .20 .50
42 Vinny Testaverde .20 .50
43 Stephen Davis .20 .50
44 Ahman Green .25 .60
45 James Stewart .20 .50
46 Ricky Watters .25 .60
47 Ray Lewis .30 .75
48 Thomas Jones .20 .50
49 Zach Thomas .25 .60
50 Junior Seau .25 .60
51 Brian Urlacher .40 1.00
52 Isaac Bruce .30 .75
53 Corey Dillon .20 .50
54 Cris Carter .30 .75
55 Terrell Owens .25 .60
56 Drew Bledsoe .25 .60
57 Torry Holt .25 .60
58 Charlie Batch .20 .50
59 Germane Crowell .20 .50
60 Jimmy Smith .25 .60
61 Tim Biakabutuka .20 .50
62 Jay Fiedler .25 .60
63 Joey Galloway .25 .60
64 Michael Westbrook .20 .50
65 Shaun Alexander .20 .50
66 Matt Hasselbeck .20 .50
67 Elvis Grbac .25 .60
68 Derrick Mason .20 .50
69 Trent Green .20 .50
70 Wayne Chrebet .20 .50
71 Rod Smith .25 .60
72 Jerry Rice .60 1.50
73 Tim Brown .30 .75
74 Shannon Sharpe .25 .60
75 Joe Horn .20 .50
76 Randy Moss .25 .60
77 Amani Toomer .20 .50
78 Antonio Freeman .30 .75
79 Ed McCaffrey .25 .60
80 Marvin Harrison .25 .60
81 Muhsin Muhammad .20 .50
82 Chad Pennington .20 .50
83 Kevin Johnson .20 .50
84 Tony Gonzalez .25 .60
85 Terry Glenn .25 .60
86 David Boston .20 .50
87 Jevon Kearse .20 .50
88 Marcus Robinson .25 .60
89 Warren Sapp .25 .60
90 Eric Moulds .20 .50
91 Andre Carter/1250 RC 2.50 6.00
92 Kevan Barlow/1250 RC 2.50 6.00
93 Michael Bennett/1000 RC 2.50 6.00
94 Josh Booty/1500 RC 2.50 6.00
95 Drew Brees/1000 RC 100.00 200.00
96 Correll Buckhalter/1500 RC 2.00 5.00
97 Quincy Carter/1250 RC 2.50 6.00
98 Chris Chambers/1000 RC 2.00 5.00
99 Nick Goings/1500 RC 3.00 8.00
100 Kevin Kasper/1500 RC 2.00 5.00
101 Dave Dickenson/1500 RC 2.50 6.00
102 Robert Ferguson/1250 RC 3.00 8.00
103 Jamar Fletcher/1500 RC 2.00 5.00
104 Rod Gardner/1250 RC 2.50 6.00
105 Justin McCareins/1250 RC 2.50 6.00
106 Jason Brookins/1500 RC 3.00 8.00
107 Todd Heap/1500 RC 2.50 6.00
108 Travis Henry/1000 RC 2.50 6.00
109 Gerard Warren/1500 RC 2.50 6.00
110 James Jackson/1250 RC 2.00 5.00
111 Chad Johnson/1250 RC 3.00 8.00
112 Rudi Johnson/1500 RC 3.00 8.00
113 LaMont Jordan/1250 RC 3.00 8.00
114 Deuce McAllister/1250 RC 3.00 8.00
115 Mike McMahon/1250 RC 2.50 6.00
116 Snoop Minnis/1000 RC 2.00 5.00
117 Travis Minor/1500 RC 2.50 6.00
118 Freddie Mitchell/1000 RC 2.00 5.00
119 Quincy Morgan/1250 RC 2.50 6.00
120 Santana Moss/1250 RC 3.00 8.00
121 Cedrick Wilson/1500 RC 2.50 6.00
122 Jesse Palmer/1500 RC 2.50 6.00
123 Ken-Yon Rambo/1500 RC 2.00 5.00
124 Jamal Reynolds/1500 RC 2.00 5.00
125 Koren Robinson/1250 RC 2.50 6.00
126 Sage Rosenfels/1500 RC 2.50 6.00
127 Dan Morgan/1250 RC 2.50 6.00
128 Justin Smith/1500 RC 4.00 10.00
129 Fred Smoot/1500 RC 2.50 6.00
130 Vinny Sutherland/1500 RC 2.00 5.00
131 David Terrell/1000 RC 2.50 6.00
132 Anthony Thomas/1250 RC 3.00 8.00
133 L.Tomlinson/1000 RC 12.00 30.00
134 Dan Alexander/1500 RC 2.50 6.00
135 M.Tuiasosopo/1250 RC 2.50 6.00
136 Michael Vick/1000 RC 5.00 12.00
137 Steve Smith/1250 RC 6.00 15.00
138 Reggie Wayne/1250 RC 6.00 15.00
139 Chris Weinke/1000 RC 2.50 6.00
140 Alex Bannister/1250 RC 2.00 5.00

2001 E-X Essential Credentials

*VETS 1-90: 4X TO 10X BASIC CARDS
1-90 VETERAN PRINT RUN 299
*ROOKIES 91-140: 1.5X TO 4X
91-140 ROOKIE PRINT RUN 29
95 Drew Brees 400.00 800.00

2001 E-X Rookie Autographs

Randomly inserted in packs, these 39 cards feature the rookies who signed some of their cards for this product. Most of these signed cards were not ready in time for inclusion in the product and those cards could be redeemed until November 30, 2002. Each played signed a different number of cards and we have notated that amount in our checklist.

OVERALL AUTO/MEMORABILIA ODDS 1:10
ANNOUNCED PRINT RUNS BELOW
92 Kevan Barlow/275* 5.00 12.00
93 Michael Bennett/125* 6.00 15.00
95 Drew Brees/125* 800.00 1200.00
96 Correll Buckhalter/375* 4.00 10.00
98 Chris Chambers/125* 12.00 30.00
101 Dave Dickenson/375* 5.00 12.00
105 Justin McCareins/375* 5.00 12.00
107 Todd Heap/125* 6.00 15.00
110 James Jackson/375* 4.00 10.00
111 Chad Johnson/125* 30.00 80.00
112 Rudi Johnson/275* 6.00 15.00
114 Deuce McAllister/125* 12.00 30.00
115 Mike McMahon/375 5.00 12.00
117 Travis Minor/375* 5.00 12.00
119 Quincy Morgan/125* 6.00 15.00
120 Santana Moss/125* 8.00 20.00
122 Jesse Palmer/275* 5.00 12.00
124 Jamal Reynolds/125* 5.00 12.00
125 Koren Robinson/125* 6.00 15.00
126 Sage Rosenfels/275* 5.00 12.00
127 Dan Morgan/375* 5.00 12.00
128 Justin Smith/275* 8.00 20.00
130 Vinny Sutherland/375* 4.00 10.00
131 David Terrell/125* 6.00 15.00
132 Anthony Thomas/275* 6.00 15.00
134 Dan Alexander/125* 6.00 15.00
135 Marques Tuiasosopo/125* 6.00 15.00
136 Michael Vick/125* 100.00 200.00
137 Steve Smith/375* 50.00 100.00
139 Chris Weinke/125* 6.00 15.00
140 Alex Bannister/375* 4.00 10.00

2001 E-X Behind the Numbers Jerseys

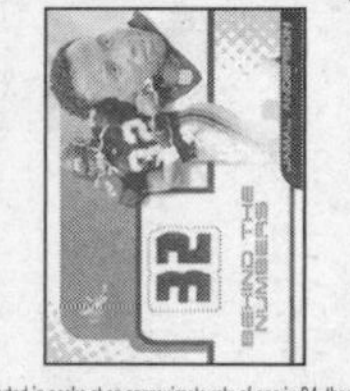

Inserted in packs at an approximate rate of one in 24, those cards have authentic game-worn swatched cut in the shape of the featured players uniform numbered. The print run for these cards are anywhere between 700 and 800 copies; for exact print runs, please see our checklist for specific information.

JERSEY/712-796 ODDS 1:24
OVERALL AUTO/MEMORABILIA ODDS 1:10
1 Mike Alstott/760 2.00 5.00
2 Jamal Anderson/768 2.50 6.00
3 Tim Brown/719 3.00 8.00
4 Isaac Bruce/720 3.00 8.00
5 Mark Brunell/792 2.50 6.00
6 Daunte Culpepper/789 2.50 6.00
7 Stephen Davis/752 2.00 5.00
8 Terrell Davis/770 2.50 6.00
9 Ron Dayne/773 2.50 6.00
10 Corey Dillon/772 2.00 5.00
11 Marshall Faulk/772 2.50 6.00
12 Brett Favre/796 6.00 15.00
13 Antonio Freeman/714 3.00 8.00
14 Jeff Garcia/795 2.00 5.00
15 Eddie George/773 3.00 8.00
16 Brian Griese/786 2.00 5.00
17 Marvin Harrison/712 2.50 6.00
18 Edgerrin James/768 2.50 6.00
19 Curtis Martin/772 2.50 6.00
20 Donovan McNabb/795 2.50 6.00
21 Randy Moss/716 2.50 6.00
22 Emmitt Smith/778 5.00 12.00
23 Fred Taylor/772 2.00 5.00
24 Ricky Williams/766 2.50 6.00

2001 E-X Behind the Numbers Jerseys Autographs

Randomly inserted in packs, a few of the players in this set autographed cards for this product. These cards are serial numbered to the player's uniform number. Due to market scarcity of some of these cards, not all of them are priced.

OVERALL AUTO/MEMORABILIA ODDS 1:10
1 Tim Brown/81 35.00 60.00
2 Isaac Bruce/80 15.00 40.00
3 Ron Dayne/27 15.00 40.00
4 Corey Dillon/28 12.00 30.00
5 Eddie George/27 30.00 60.00
6 Randy Moss/84 40.00 100.00
7 Emmitt Smith/22 175.00 300.00
8 Mike Alstott/40 12.00 30.00
9 Marvin Harrison/88 12.00 30.00
11 Stephen Davis/48 12.00 30.00
13 Marshall Faulk/28 40.00 100.00
18 Edgerrin James/32 15.00 40.00

2001 E-X Constant Threads

Inserted at stated odds of one in 40, these 20 cards have swatches of game-worn pieces from leading NFL players. Several players are represented by both jerseys and pants. A few players were inserted in lesser quantities and we have notated those in our checklist as SP's. Jerry Rice was issued in larger quantities and we have notated that as an DP.

STATED ODDS 1:40
OVERALL AUTO/MEMORABILIA ODDS 1:10
1 Tim Brown 3.00 8.00
2 Mark Brunell JSY 2.50 6.00
3 Mark Brunell Pants 2.50 6.00
4 Germane Crowell JSY 2.00 5.00
5 Germane Crowell Pants 2.00 5.00
6 Tim Dwight SP 3.00 8.00
7 Brett Favre 6.00 15.00
8 Doug Flutie 6.00 15.00
9 Eddie George SP 4.00 10.00
10 Torry Holt 2.50 6.00
11 Edgerrin James 2.50 6.00
12 Brad Johnson 2.50 6.00
13 Kevin Johnson SP 2.50 6.00
14 Dan Marino 10.00 25.00
15 Steve McNair 2.50 6.00
16 Herman Moore JSY 2.00 5.00
17 Herman Moore Pants 2.00 5.00
18 Jake Plummer Pants UER 2.00 5.00
19 Jerry Rice SP 8.00 20.00
20 Fred Taylor SP 2.50 6.00

2001 E-X E-Xtra Yards

Inserted in cards at stated odds of one in 20 retail, these 10 cards feature some of the leading offensive stars of the NFL featured in a television screen card design.
COMPLETE SET (10) 10.00 25.00
STATED ODDS 1:20 RETAIL
1 Randy Moss .60 1.50
2 Donovan McNabb .60 1.50
3 Eddie George .75 2.00
4 Kurt Warner 1.25 3.00
5 Marshall Faulk .60 1.50
6 Peyton Manning 2.00 5.00
7 Ricky Williams .60 1.50
8 Emmitt Smith 1.25 3.00
9 Jamal Lewis .75 2.00
10 Edgerrin James .60 1.50

2001 E-X Turf Team

Inserted at a stated rate of one in 240, these 20 cards have a piece of authentic artificial turf taken from Veterans Stadium in Philadelphia.
STATED ODDS 1:240
OVERALL AUTO/MEMORABILIA ODDS 1:10
1 Troy Aikman 4.00 10.00
2 Jamal Anderson 2.50 6.00
3 Drew Bledsoe 2.50 8.00
4 Stephen Davis 2.00 5.00
5 Ron Dayne 2.50 6.00
6 Corey Dillon 2.00 5.00
7 Marshall Faulk 2.50 6.00
8 Eddie George 3.00 8.00
9 Marvin Harrison 2.50 6.00
10 Torry Holt 2.50 6.00
11 Edgerrin James 2.50 6.00
12 Keyshawn Johnson 2.50 6.00
13 Peyton Manning 8.00 20.00
14 Donovan McNabb 2.50 6.00
15 Steve McNair 2.50 6.00
16 Jake Plummer 2.00 5.00
17 Emmitt Smith 5.00 12.00
18 Duce Staley 2.00 5.00
19 Kurt Warner 5.00 12.00
20 Peter Warrick 2.00 5.00

2004 E-X

E-X initially released in mid-February 2005. The base set consists of 65-cards including 16-rookies serial numberd to 500 and 9-rookie jersey serial numbered autographs. Hobby boxes contained 1-pack of 7-cards and carried an S.R.P. of $150 per pack. Two parallel sets and a variety of inserts can be found seeded in hobby and retail packs highlighted by the multi-tiered Clearly Authentics and Signings of the Times inserts. Some signed cards were issued via mail-in exchange or redemption cards with a number of those EXCH cards not yet appearing live on the secondary market as of the printing of this book.
UNSIGNED RC PRINT RUN 500 SER.#'d SETS
1 Travis Henry 1.00 2.50
2 Deion Sanders 1.25 3.00
3 Donovan McNabb 1.25 3.00
4 LaDainian Tomlinson 1.50 4.00
5 Shaun Alexander 1.00 2.50
6 Daunte Culpepper 1.25 3.00
7 Peyton Manning 4.00 10.00
8 Deuce McAllister 1.25 3.00
9 Marshall Faulk 1.25 3.00
10 Jamal Lewis 1.25 3.00
11 Chad Pennington 1.00 2.50
12 Clinton Portis 1.00 2.50
13 Brett Favre 3.00 8.00
14 Anquan Boldin 1.00 2.50
15 Priest Holmes 1.00 2.50
16 Brian Urlacher 1.50 4.00
17 David Carr 1.00 2.50
18 Joey Harrington 1.00 2.50
19 Tom Brady 6.00 15.00
20 Michael Vick 1.25 3.00
21 Jerry Rice 3.00 8.00
22 Mike Alstott 1.00 2.50
23 Keyshawn Johnson 1.25 3.00
24 Jeremy Shockey 1.00 2.50
25 Stephen Davis 1.00 2.50
26 Kevan Barlow 1.00 2.50
27 Carson Palmer 1.25 3.00
28 Steve McNair 1.25 3.00
29 Jake Plummer 1.00 2.50
30 Jeff Garcia 1.00 2.50
31 Byron Leftwich 1.00 2.50
32 Hines Ward 1.25 3.00
33 Randy Moss 1.25 3.00
34 Marvin Harrison 1.25 3.00
35 Terrell Owens 1.25 3.00
36 Ahman Green 1.25 3.00
37 Edgerrin James 1.25 3.00
38 Emmitt Smith 2.50 6.00
39 Torry Holt 1.25 3.00
40 Drew Bledsoe 1.25 3.00
42 P.Rivers JSY AU/90 RC 40.00 80.00
43 Larry Fitzgerald RC 8.00 20.00
44 Ro.Williams JSY AU/100 RC 20.00 50.00
45 D.Henson JSY AU/95 RC 12.50 30.00
46 Roethl. JSY AU/100 RC 100.00 200.00
48 Kellen Winslow RC 2.00 5.00
49 Chris Perry RC 2.00 5.00
50 Re.Williams JSY AU/100 RC 12.50 30.00
51 Steven Jackson RC 3.00 8.00
52 Rashaun Woods RC 2.00 5.00
53 Tatum Bell RC 2.00 5.00
54 J.P. Losman RC 2.00 5.00
55 Sean Taylor RC 12.00 30.00
56 M.Clayton JSY AU/80 RC 15.00 40.00
57 Lee Evans RC 3.00 8.00
58 Julius Jones RC 2.00 5.00
59 Jonathan Vilma RC 2.50 6.00
60 M.Jenkins JSY AU/96 RC 12.50 30.00
61 Greg Jones RC 2.00 5.00
62 Will Smith RC 2.50 6.00
63 Ernest Wilford RC 2.50 6.00
64 Quincy Wilson RC 2.00 5.00
65 Cody Pickett RC 2.00 5.00

2004 E-X Essential Credentials Future

*VET/40-65: 2X TO 5X BASIC CARDS
*VETS/26-39: 2.5X TO 6X BASIC CARDS
COMMON ROOKIE/20-25 5.00 12.00
COMMON ROOKIE/10-19 6.00 15.00
ROOK.SEMISTARS/10-19 8.00 20.00
ROOK.UNL.STARS/10-19 10.00 25.00
STATED PRINT RUN 1-65
41 Eli Manning/25 40.00 100.00
42 Philip Rivers/24 15.00 40.00
43 Larry Fitzgerald/23 20.00 50.00
44 Roy Williams WR/22 5.00 12.00
46 Ben Roethlisberger/20 40.00 100.00
51 Steven Jackson/15 10.00 25.00

2004 E-X Essential Credentials Now

*VETS/20-40: 2.5X TO 6X BASIC CARDS
*VETS/10-19: 3X TO 8X BASIC CARDS
COMMON ROOKIE/45-65 3.00 8.00
ROOK.SEMISTARS/45-65 4.00 10.00
ROOK.UNL.STARS/45-65 5.00 12.00
STATED PRINT RUN 1-65
41 Eli Manning/41 30.00 80.00
42 Philip Rivers/42 12.00 30.00
43 Larry Fitzgerald/43 15.00 40.00
44 Roy Williams WR/44 4.00 10.00
46 Ben Roethlisberger/46 25.00 60.00
51 Steven Jackson/51 5.00 12.00

2004 E-X Rookie Die Cuts

*DIE CUT/500: .4X TO 1X BASIC RCs
DIE CUT PRINT RUN 500 SER.#'d SETS
CARDS #41, 46 RELEASED IN LATE 2005
41 Eli Manning No Ser.# 12.00 30.00
46 Ben Roethlisberger No Ser.# 15.00 40.00

2004 E-X Rookie Jersey Autographs Gold

UNPRICED BURGUNDY PRINT RUN 5
UNPRICED EMERALD PRINT RUN 1
42 Philip Rivers/27 60.00 100.00
44 Roy Williams WR/54 15.00 40.00
45 Drew Henson/32 15.00 40.00
46 Ben Roethlisberger/77 100.00 200.00
50 Reggie Williams/73 10.00 25.00
56 Michael Clayton/24 15.00 40.00
60 Michael Jenkins/81 10.00 25.00

2004 E-X Rookie Dual Jersey Autographs Pewter

STATED PRINT RUN 9-63
41 Eli Manning/47 125.00 200.00
42 Philip Rivers/60 60.00 100.00
44 Roy Williams WR/26 25.00 60.00
45 Drew Henson/63 20.00 50.00
46 Ben Roethlisberger/55 100.00 200.00
49 Chris Perry/55 12.00 30.00
50 Reggie Williams/63 15.00 40.00
60 Michael Jenkins/54 15.00 40.00

2004 E-X Rookie Patch Autographs Tan

56 Michael Clayton/80 12.00 30.00

2004 E-X Check Mates Dual Autographs

STATED PRINT RUN 25 SER.#'d SETS
6 J.Elway/D.Marino 250.00 450.00
8 J.Kelly/S.Largent 60.00 120.00
11 E.Manning/P.Manning 175.00 300.00
13 J.Montana/S.Young 200.00 350.00

2004 E-X Classic ConnEXions Dual Jerseys

STATED PRINT RUN 22 SER.#'d SETS
DMJE D.Marino/J.Elway 30.00 60.00
DSMI D.Sanders/M.Irvin 15.00 40.00
FHTD F.Harris/T.Dorsett
FTDC F.Tarkenton/D.Culpepper
JKTA J.Kelly/T.Aikman
JLMS J.Lambert/M.Singletary 15.00 40.00
JMJN J.Montana/J.Namath 40.00 80.00
JMSY J.Montana/S.Young 20.00 50.00
JNMI J.Novacek/M.Irvin
JPRG J.Plunkett/R.Gannon 10.00 25.00
MSWP M.Singletary/W.Payton 40.00 80.00
PHBS P.Hornung/B.Starr 20.00 50.00
SLSA S.Largent/S.Alexander
SSJE S.Sharpe/J.Elway
SSSS St.Sharpe/Sh.Sharpe
TAES T.Aikman/E.Smith 20.00 50.00
TASY T.Aikman/S.Young
TTBS T.Thomas/B.Sanders
TTJK T.Thomas/J.Kelly 20.00 50.00
WPBS W.Payton/B.Sanders

2004 E-X Classic ConnEXions Triple Jerseys

UNPRICED PRINT RUN 13 SETS
UNPRICED EMERALD PRINT RUN 1 SET

2004 E-X Clearly Authentics Patch Silver

UNPRICED BLUE PRINT RUN 8 SETS
UNPRICED BRONZE PRINT RUN 11 SETS
UNPRICED BURGUNDY PRINT RUN 13 SETS
UNPRICED EMERALD PRINT RUN 1 SET
*GOLD/50: .5X TO 1.2X PATCH SILVER
GOLD PRINT RUN 50 SER.#'d SETS
*PEWTER/44: .6X TO 1.5X SILVER
PEWTER PRINT RUN 44 SER.#'d SETS
*DUAL TAN/22: .8X TO 2X SILVER
UNPRICED TURQUOISE SER.#'d 4-14
CAAB Anquan Boldin/81 7.50 20.00
CAAG Ahman Green/75 10.00 25.00
CABF Brett Favre/90 20.00 50.00
CABL Byron Leftwich/90 10.00 25.00
CABR Ben Roethlisberger/90 25.00 60.00
CABU Brian Urlacher/90 12.50 30.00
CACJ Chad Johnson/85 10.00 25.00
CACP Carson Palmer/90 10.00 25.00
CACP2 Clinton Portis/75 10.00 25.00
CACP3 Chad Pennington/90 10.00 25.00
CADC David Carr/65 10.00 25.00
CADC2 Daunte Culpepper/90 10.00 25.00
CADH Drew Henson/90 10.00 25.00
CADM Deuce McAllister/80 7.50 20.00
CADM2 Donovan McNabb/90 12.50 30.00
CADS Deion Sanders/65 15.00 40.00
CAEJ Edgerrin James/75 10.00 25.00
CAEM Eli Manning/90 20.00 50.00
CAES Emmitt Smith/90 12.50 30.00
CAJD Jake Delhomme/90 7.50 20.00
CAJH Joey Harrington/90 7.50 20.00
CAJL Jamal Lewis/90 7.50 20.00
CAJR Jerry Rice/80 15.00 40.00
CAJS Jeremy Shockey/80 10.00 25.00
CALF Larry Fitzgerald/90 12.50 30.00
CALT LaDainian Tomlinson/90 10.00 25.00
CAMF Marshall Faulk/90 7.50 20.00
CAMH Marvin Harrison/88 7.50 20.00
CAMV Michael Vick/90 15.00 40.00
CAPH Priest Holmes/90 12.50 30.00
CAPM Peyton Manning/90 15.00 40.00
CAPR Philip Rivers/50 15.00 40.00
CARL Ray Lewis/90 10.00 25.00
CARM Randy Moss/84 12.50 30.00
CASA Shaun Alexander/90 10.00 25.00
CASM Steve McNair/50
CATB Tom Brady/90 20.00 50.00
CATH Torry Holt/81 7.50 20.00
CATO Terrell Owens/81 10.00 25.00

2004 E-X Clearly Authentics Dual Emerald

UNPRICED EMERALD PRINT RUN 1 SET

2004 E-X Clearly Authentics Jersey Autographs

STATED PRINT RUN 2-100
SER.#'d UNDER 25 NOT PRICED
AB1 Anquan Boldin/100 12.00 30.00
AB2 Anquan Boldin/23 15.00 40.00
AG Ahman Green/85 20.00 40.00
BF1 Brett Favre/90 75.00 150.00
BL1 Byron Leftwich/100 15.00 40.00
BL2 Byron Leftwich/77 20.00 50.00
CJ1 Chad Johnson/65 12.00 30.00
CP2A Chad Pennington/80 15.00 40.00
DM1 Deuce McAllister/100 12.00 30.00
DM2 Deuce McAllister/88 15.00 40.00
EJ1 Edgerrin James/100 12.00 30.00
EJ2 Edgerrin James/52 20.00 50.00
JH1 Joey Harrington/36 20.00 50.00
JH2 Joey Harrington/95 15.00 40.00
KW Kellen Winslow Jr./90 20.00 50.00
MV1 Michael Vick/50 20.00 50.00
SJ1 Steven Jackson/100 6.00 15.00
SJ2 Steven Jackson/45 8.00 20.00
SM1 Santana Moss/90 12.00 30.00
SM2 Santana Moss/21
MV2 Michael Vick/22

2004 E-X Clearly Authentics Dual Jersey Autographs Pewter

UNPRICED BURGUNDY PRINT RUN 5 SETS
UNPRICED EMERALD PRINT RUN 1 SET
CAAR Anquan Boldin/41 15.00 40.00
CAAG Ahman Green/60 15.00 40.00
CAAJ Andre Johnson/39 20.00 50.00
CABL Byron Leftwich/68 15.00 40.00
CACJ Chad Johnson/39 15.00 40.00
CAEJ Edgerrin James/59 15.00 40.00
CAJD Jake Delhomme/46 15.00 40.00
CAJH Joey Harrington/74 12.00 30.00
CAJL Jamal Lewis/26 20.00 50.00
CAKW Kellen Winslow Jr./65 20.00 50.00
CAMV Michael Vick/104 30.00 60.00
CASA Shaun Alexander/30 15.00 40.00
CASJ Steven Jackson/56 10.00 25.00
CASM Santana Moss/54 15.00 40.00

2004 E-X Clearly Authentics Patch Autographs Tan

CARDS SER.#'d UNDER 25 NOT PRICED
CAAB Anquan Boldin/81 15.00 40.00
CAAG Ahman Green/30 20.00 50.00
CACJ Chad Johnson/85 15.00 40.00
CADM Deuce McAllister/26 20.00 50.00
CAEJ Edgerrin James/32 25.00 60.00
CAKW Kellen Winslow Jr./80 20.00 50.00
CASA Shaun Alexander/37 15.00 40.00
CASJ Steven Jackson/39 8.00 20.00
CASM Santana Moss/83 12.00 30.00

2004 E-X ConnEXions Dual Autographs

BBCB B.Bailey/C.Bailey/50 20.00 50.00
CJRJ C.Johnson/R.John/50 20.00 50.00
DFGP D.Flutie/G.Phelan/150 20.00 50.00
FFFH F.Fuqua/F.Harris/50 40.00 80.00
JMLM J.McCown/L.McC/50 20.00 50.00
RBTB R.Barber/T.Barber/150 20.00 50.00

2004 E-X Signings of the Times Jersey Bronze

BRONZE PRINT RUN 50 UNLESS NOTED
UNPRICED EMERALD PRINT RUN 1 SET
*GOLD: .6X TO 1.5X BRONZE
GOLD PRINT RUN 25 SER.#'d SETS
JK Jim Kelly 50.00 100.00
JM Joe Montana 75.00 150.00
RS Roger Staubach 50.00 100.00
SL Steve Largent/48 20.00 50.00
SY Steve Young 50.00 100.00
TA Troy Aikman 50.00 100.00
EC Earl Campbell No Auto 4.00 10.00

2004 E-X Signings of the Times Red

STATED PRINT RUN 50-350
AO Adewale Ogunleye/56 10.00 25.00
BB Boss Bailey/300 6.00 15.00
BS Billy Sims/255 12.00 30.00
BW Brian Westbrook/50 12.00 30.00
CB Champ Bailey/300 15.00 40.00
CC Chris Chambers/52 10.00 25.00
JB Jim Brown/100 40.00 80.00
JD Jake Delhomme/250 12.00 30.00
JM Josh McCown/250 12.00 30.00
LM Luke McCown/250 6.00 15.00
RG Rex Grossman/52 12.00 30.00
TA Troy Aikman/100 40.00 80.00
TB1 Tiki Barber/200 15.00 40.00
TB2 Troy Brown/350 10.00 25.00

1994 Excalibur Elway Promos

These three standard-size cards were issued to promote the 1994 Excalibur design and feature borderless color action shots of John Elway. The "X of 3" numbering on the back is preceded by an "SL" prefix.
COMPLETE SET (3) 4.80 12.00
COMMON CARD (SL1-SL3) 1.60 4.00

1994 Excalibur

The 1994 Collector's Edge Excalibur set consists of 75 standard-size cards based on the medieval theme of "Excalibur", the silver sword pulled from the stone in the legend of King Arthur. The cards are checklisted alphabetically according to teams. There are no key Rookie Cards in this set.
COMPLETE SET (75) 7.50 20.00
1 Bobby Hebert .08 .25
2 Deion Sanders .40 1.00
3 Andre Rison .20 .50
4 Cornelius Bennett .20 .50
5 Jim Kelly .30 .75
6 Andre Reed .20 .50
7 Bruce Smith .30 .75
8 Thurman Thomas .30 .75
9 Curtis Conway .30 .75
10 Richard Dent .20 .50
11 Jim Harbaugh .30 .75
12 Troy Aikman .75 2.00
13 Michael Irvin .30 .75
14 Russell Maryland .08 .25
15 Emmitt Smith 1.25 3.00
16 Steve Atwater .08 .25
17 Rod Bernstine .08 .25
18 John Elway 1.50 4.00
19 Glyn Milburn .20 .50
20 Shannon Sharpe .20 .50
21 Barry Sanders 1.25 3.00
22 Edgar Bennett .30 .75
23 Brett Favre 1.50 4.00
24 Sterling Sharpe .20 .50
25 Reggie White .30 .75
26 Warren Moon .30 .75
27 Wilber Marshall .08 .25
28 Haywood Jeffires .20 .50
29 Lorenzo White .08 .25
30 Quentin Coryatt .08 .25
31 Roosevelt Potts .08 .25
32 Jeff George .30 .75
33 Joe Montana 1.50 4.00
34 Neil Smith .20 .50
35 Marcus Allen .30 .75
36 Derrick Thomas .30 .75
37 Jeff Hostetler .20 .50
38 Tim Brown .30 .75
39 Rocket Ismail .20 .50
40 Randall Cunningham .30 .75
41 Jerome Bettis .40 1.00
42 Dan Marino 1.50 4.00
43 Keith Jackson .08 .25
44 O.J.McDuffie .30 .75
45 Drew Bledsoe .60 1.50
46 Leonard Russell .08 .25
47 Wade Wilson .08 .25
48 Eric Martin .08 .25
49 Phil Simms .20 .50
50 Gary Brown RB .30 .75
51 Rodney Hampton .20 .50
52 Boomer Esiason .20 .50
53 Johnny Johnson .08 .25
54 Ronnie Lott .20 .50
55 Fred Barnett .20 .50
56 Leroy Thompson .08 .25
57 Barry Foster .08 .25
58 Neil O'Donnell .30 .75
59 Stan Humphries .20 .50
60 Marion Butts .08 .25
61 Anthony Miller .20 .50
62 Natrone Means .30 .75
63 Dana Stubblefield .20 .50
64 John Taylor .20 .50
65 Ricky Watters .20 .50
66 Steve Young .60 1.50
67 Jerry Rice .75 2.00
68 Tom Rathman .08 .25
69 Rick Mirer .30 .75
70 Chris Warren .20 .50
71 Cortez Kennedy .20 .50
72 Mark Rypien .08 .25
73 Desmond Howard .20 .50
74 Art Monk .20 .50
75 Reggie Brooks .20 .50

1994 Excalibur FX

This seven-card standard-size set was randomly inserted in foil packs. On an acetate design, the player emerges from a cutout of a shield. The player's name, position and card number appear in a team colored label at the bottom right of the shield. A team helmet appears at the bottom of the card. Cards with a gold F/X shield impressed on the background were also produced.
COMPLETE SET (7) 7.50 20.00
STATED ODDS 1:7
*FX GOLD SHIELDS: 1.2X to 3X BASIC INSERTS
*EQ GOLD SHIELDS: SAME VALUE
ONE SET PER EDGEQUEST REDEMPTION
STATED ODDS 1:170
*EQ SILVER SHIELDS: SAME VALUE
ONE SET PER EDGEQUEST REDEMPTION
1 Emmitt Smith 4.00 8.00
2 Rodney Hampton .60 1.25
3 Jerome Bettis 1.25 2.50
4 Steve Young 2.00 4.00
5 Rick Mirer 1.00 2.00
6 John Elway 5.00 10.00
7 Troy Aikman UER 2.50 5.00

1994 Excalibur 22K

Randomly inserted in packs, this 25-card standard-size insert set showcases some of the NFL's top stars. All 25 card backs can be placed together to form a knight.
COMPLETE SET (25) 12.50 30.00
STATED ODDS 1:2
1 Troy Aikman 1.50 3.00
2 Michael Irvin .60 1.25
3 Emmitt Smith 2.50 5.00
4 Edgar Bennett .60 1.25
5 Brett Favre 3.00 6.00
6 Sterling Sharpe .30 .75
7 Rodney Hampton .30 .75
8 Jerome Bettis .75 1.50
9 Jerry Rice 1.50 3.00
10 Steve Young 1.25 2.50
11 Ricky Watters .30 .75
12 Thurman Thomas .60 1.25
13 John Elway 3.00 6.00
14 Shannon Sharpe .30 .75
15 Joe Montana 3.00 6.00
16 Marcus Allen .60 1.25
17 Tim Brown .60 1.25
18 Rocket Ismail .30 .75
19 Barry Foster .15 .40
20 Natrone Means .60 1.25
21 Rick Mirer .60 1.25
22 Dan Marino 3.00 6.00
23 AFC Card .15 .40
24 NFC Card .15 .40
25 Excalibur Card .15 .40
NNO Uncut Sheet 10.00 25.00

1995 Excalibur

For the second consecutive year, Collector's Edge issued an Excalibur brand. This 150-card medieval-themed card set was released in two series: the Sword (1-75) and the Stone (76-150). Fifteen-hundred, 12-box cases of each series were produced. The suggested retail price for each seven-card pack was $3.49. The cards are grouped alphabetically within teams. Jeff Blake is the only Rookie Card of note in this set. Collector's Edge issued a large number of Sword and Stone parallel cards for the base set as well as nearly every insert set. These Sword and Stone cards with printed with a bronze, silver, gold, or diamond "S/S" logo on the fronts and printed in quantities too low to establish secondary market values for.
COMPLETE SET (150) 15.00 30.00
COMP.SERIES 1 (75) 7.50 15.00
COMP.SERIES 2 (75) 7.50 15.00
1 Gary Clark .05 .15
2 Randal Hill .05 .15
3 Anthony Edwards .05 .15
4 Terance Mathis .10 .30
5 Erric Pegram .10 .30
6 Jeff George .10 .30
7 Pete Metzelaars .05 .15
8 Jim Kelly .20 .50
9 Andre Reed .10 .30
10 Lewis Tillman .05 .15
11 Curtis Conway .20 .50
12 Steve Walsh .05 .15
13 Derrick Fenner .05 .15
14 Harold Green .05 .15
15 Michael Jackson .10 .30
16 Eric Metcalf .10 .30
17 Antonio Langham .05 .15
18 Troy Aikman .75 2.00
19 Alvin Harper .05 .15
20 Jay Novacek .10 .30
21 John Elway 1.50 4.00
22 Glyn Milburn .05 .15
23 Steve Atwater .05 .15
24 Mel Gray .05 .15
25 Herman Moore .20 .50
26 Scott Mitchell .10 .30
27 Guy McIntyre .05 .15
28 Edgar Bennett .10 .30
29 Sterling Sharpe .10 .30
30 Gary Brown .05 .15
31 Haywood Jeffires .05 .15
32 Marshall Faulk 1.00 2.50
33 Roosevelt Potts .05 .15
34 Marcus Allen .20 .50
35 Willie Davis .10 .30
36 Lake Dawson .10 .30
37 Jeff Hostetler .10 .30
38 Rocket Ismail .10 .30
39 Troy Drayton .05 .15
40 Jerome Bettis .20 .50
41 Dan Marino 1.50 4.00
42 Mark Ingram .05 .15
43 O.J. McDuffie .20 .50
44 Warren Moon .10 .30
45 Qadry Ismail .10 .30
46 Jake Reed .10 .30
47 Ben Coates .10 .30
48 Vincent Brisby .05 .15
49 Michael Timpson .05 .15
50 Brad Daluiso .05 .15
51 Rodney Hampton .10 .30
52 Chris Calloway .05 .15
53 Rob Moore .10 .30
54 Boomer Esiason .10 .30
55 Michael Haynes .10 .30
56 Vaughn Dunbar .05 .15
57 Calvin Williams .10 .30
58 Herschel Walker .10 .30
59 Charlie Garner .20 .50
60 Neil O'Donnell .10 .30
61 Deon Figures .05 .15
62 Byron Bam Morris .05 .15
63 Junior Seau .20 .50
64 Leslie O'Neal .10 .30
65 Natrone Means .10 .30
66 Jerry Rice .75 2.00
67 Deion Sanders .50 1.25
68 William Floyd .10 .30
69 Chris Warren .10 .30
70 Cortez Kennedy .10 .30
71 Hardy Nickerson .05 .15
72 Craig Erickson .05 .15
73 Heath Shuler .10 .30
74 Reggie Brooks .10 .30
75 Henry Ellard .10 .30
76 Garrison Hearst .20 .50
77 Steve Beuerlein .10 .30
78 Seth Joyner .05 .15
79 Andre Rison .10 .30
80 Norm Johnson .05 .15
81 Craig Heyward .10 .30
82 Darryl Talley .05 .15
83 Kenneth Davis .05 .15
84 Bruce Smith .20 .50
85 Tom Waddle .05 .15
86 Erik Kramer .05 .15
87 Carl Pickens .10 .30
88 Dan Wilkinson .10 .30
89 Jeff Blake RC .30 .75
90 Vinny Testaverde .10 .30
91 Tommy Vardell .05 .15
92 Leroy Hoard .05 .15
93 Emmitt Smith 1.25 3.00
94 Michael Irvin .20 .50
95 Daryl Johnston .10 .30
96 Shannon Sharpe .10 .30
97 Anthony Miller .10 .30
98 Leonard Russell .05 .15
99 Barry Sanders 1.25 3.00
100 Brett Perriman .10 .30
101 Johnnie Morton .10 .30
102 Brett Favre 1.50 4.00
103 Bryce Paup .10 .30
104 Ernest Givins .05 .15
105 Webster Slaughter .05 .15
106 Jim Harbaugh .10 .30
107 Joe Montana 1.50 4.00
108 J.J. Birden .05 .15
109 Steve Bono .10 .30
110 James Jett .10 .30
111 Tim Brown .20 .50
112 Rob Fredrickson .05 .15
113 Chris Miller .05 .15
114 Bernie Parmalee .10 .30
115 Terry Kirby .10 .30
116 Bryan Cox .05 .15
117 Irving Fryar .10 .30
118 Terry Allen .10 .30
119 Cris Carter .20 .50
120 Fuad Reveiz .05 .15
121 Drew Bledsoe .50 1.25
122 Greg McMurtry .05 .15
123 Dave Brown .10 .30
124 Dave Meggett .05 .15
125 Johnny Johnson .05 .15
126 Ronnie Lott .10 .30
127 Johnny Mitchell .05 .15
128 Eric Martin .05 .15
129 Jim Everett .05 .15
130 Randall Cunningham .20 .50
131 Eric Allen .05 .15
132 Fred Barnett .10 .30
133 Barry Foster .10 .30
134 Kevin Greene .10 .30
135 Eric Green .05 .15
136 Stan Humphries .10 .30
137 Mark Seay .10 .30
138 Alfred Pupunu RC .05 .15
139 Steve Young .60 1.50
140 John Taylor .05 .15
141 Ricky Watters .10 .30
142 Brian Blades .10 .30
143 Rick Mirer .10 .30
144 Cortez Kennedy .10 .30
145 Jackie Harris .05 .15
146 Errict Rhett .10 .30
147 Trent Dilfer .20 .50
148 Brian Mitchell .05 .15
149 Ricky Ervins .05 .15
150 Darrell Green .05 .15

1995 Excalibur Die Cuts

*DIE CUTS: 2.5X TO 6X BASIC CARDS
STATED ODDS 1:9

1995 Excalibur Gold

*GOLDS: .4X to 1X BASIC CARDS

1995 Excalibur Challengers Draft Day Rookie Redemption Prizes

Cards from this 31-card standard-size set were available through a redemption program. Each exchange card found in packs was redeemed for the top rookie signed by the NFL team whose logo appeared on the cardfront. A gold parallel of each car din the set was also available by redeeming the Edgequest stone complete set.
COMPLETE SET (31) 12.00 30.00
ONE SILV.CARD PER TEAM LOGO REDEMP.
*GOLD CARDS: SAME VALUE
DD1 Derrick Alexander DE .40 1.00
DD2 Tony Boselli .75 2.00
DD3 Kyle Brady .60 1.50
DD4 Mark Bruener .60 1.50
DD5 Jamie Brown .40 1.00
DD6 Ruben Brown .75 2.00
DD7 Devin Bush .40 1.00
DD8 Kevin Carter .75 2.00
DD9 Ki-Jana Carter .75 2.00
DD10 Kerry Collins 1.25 3.00
DD11 Kordell Stewart 1.25 3.00
DD12 Mark Fields .75 2.00
DD13 Joey Galloway 1.25 3.00
DD14 Trezelle Jenkins .40 1.00
DD15 Ellis Johnson .40 1.00
DD16 Napoleon Kaufman 1.00 2.50
DD17 Ty Law 1.00 2.50
DD18 Mike Mamula .40 1.00
DD19 Steve McNair 2.50 6.00
DD20 Billy Milner .40 1.00
DD21 Craig Newsome .60 1.50
DD22 Craig Powell .40 1.00
DD23 Rashaan Salaam .75 2.00
DD24 Frank Sanders .75 2.00
DD25 Warren Sapp .60 1.50
DD26 Terrance Shaw .40 1.00
DD27 J.J.Stokes .75 2.00
DD28 Michael Westbrook .75 2.00
DD29 Tyrone Wheatley 1.00 2.50
DD30 Sherman Williams .60 1.50
DD31 Cover .40 1.00
Checklist Card

1995 Excalibur Dragon Slayers

This fourteen-card standard-size set was randomly inserted into "Stone" or series two packs. Several hobby publications designed two cards each for this set featuring leading NFL players. The cards are unnumbered and, thus, listed alphabetically.
COMPLETE SET (14) 15.00 30.00
STATED ODDS 1:12 STONE
1 Troy Aikman 2.00 4.00
2 Jerome Bettis .40 1.00
3 Drew Bledsoe 1.25 2.50
4 Marshall Faulk 2.50 5.00
5 Natrone Means .25 .60
6 Joe Montana 4.00 8.00
7 Byron Bam Morris .10 .30
8 Errict Rhett .25 .60
9 Jerry Rice 2.00 4.00
10 Barry Sanders 3.00 6.00
11 Deion Sanders 1.25 2.50
12 Junior Seau .40 1.00
13 Emmitt Smith 3.00 6.00
14 Ricky Watters .25 .60

1995 Excalibur EdgeTech

This 12-card standard-size set was randomly inserted in first series "Sword" packs. The cards are unnumbered and thus are listed alphabetically.
COMPLETE SET (12) 20.00 50.00
STATED ODDS 1:75 SWORD
1 Emmitt Smith 8.00 20.00
2 Errict Rhett .75 2.00
3 Steve Young 4.00 10.00
4 Jerry Rice 5.00 12.00
5 Ben Coates .75 2.00
6 Marcus Allen 1.25 3.00
7 John Elway 10.00 25.00
8 Keith Jackson .40 1.00
9 Garrison Hearst 1.25 3.00
10 Natrone Means .75 2.00
11 Michael Haynes .75 2.00
12 Byron Bam Morris .40 1.00

1995 Excalibur Rookie Roundtable

Randomly inserted into packs, this 25-card standard-size set subdivides into Sword Rookie Roundtable (1-13) and Stone Rookie Roundtable (14-25). The sword grouping features defensive players while the stone focuses on offensive players.
COMPLETE SET (25) 6.00 15.00
COMP.SERIES 1 (13) 2.00 5.00
COMP.SERIES 2 (12) 4.00 10.00
1-13 STATED ODDS 1:9 SWORD
14-25 STATED ODDS 1:9 STONE
1 Sam Adams .20 .50
2 Joe Johnson .20 .50
3 Tim Bowens .20 .50
4 Bryant Young .20 .50
5 Aubrey Beavers .20 .50
6 Willie McGinest .20 .50
7 Rob Fredrickson .20 .50
8 Lee Woodall .20 .50
9 Antonio Langham .20 .50
10 Dewayne Washington .20 .50
11 Darryl Morrison .20 .50
12 Keith Lyle .20 .50
13 Antonio Langham .20 .50
14 Darnay Scott .20 .50
15 Derrick Alexander WR .40 1.00
16 Todd Steussie .20 .50
17 Larry Allen .20 .50
18 Anthony Redmon .20 .50
19 Joe Panos .20 .50
20 Kevin Mawae .20 .50
21 Andrew Jordan .40 1.00
22 Heath Shuler .40 1.00
23 Marshall Faulk 3.00 8.00
24 Errict Rhett .40 1.00
25 Marshall Faulk POY 3.00 8.00

1995 Excalibur TekTech

This 12-card standard-size set was randomly inserted in second series "Stone" packs. The cards are unnumbered and thus are listed in alphabetical order.
COMPLETE SET (12) 20.00 50.00
SER.2 STATED ODDS 1:75 STONE
1 Troy Aikman 4.00 10.00
2 Jerome Bettis 1.00 2.50
3 Drew Bledsoe 2.50 6.00
4 Tim Brown 1.00 2.50
5 Marshall Faulk 5.00 12.00
6 Haywood Jeffires .30 .75
7 Dan Marino 8.00 20.00
8 Barry Sanders 6.00 15.00
9 Deion Sanders 2.50 6.00
10 Junior Seau 1.00 2.50
11 Darryl Talley .30 .75
12 Ricky Watters .60 1.50

1995 Excalibur 22K

This 50-card standard-size set was randomly inserted into packs. The fronts feature the word "Excalibur" in gold foil across over the player's photo. There was also a prism parallel version of the cards inserted which were limited to 200 of each player. These feature a raindrop look silver prismatic foil on plastic stock and do not contain the Excalibur name at the top of the card. A second and third parallel prism type was produced and released at a later date. Each of these does include the Excalibur name as well as a gold shield surrounding the 22K notation. The second version was printed on a silver prismatic paper stock and the third on a gold prismatic paper stock, each with a prismatic background featuring a circle within a square pattern. The silvers are numbered of 750 sets made and the golds of 250. Finally, four different Sword and Stone versions were released within those complete sets and some additional cards have been found with a gold foil crown and an actual jewel embedded into the card.
COMPLETE SET (50) 75.00 200.00
COMP.SWORD SER.1 (25) 40.00 100.00
COMP.STONE SER.2 (25) 40.00 100.00
1SW-25SW STATED ODDS 1:36 SWORD
1ST-25ST STATED ODDS 1:36 STONE
*PRISM: .6X TO 1.5X BASIC INSERTS
RAINDROP PRISM ANNC'D PRINT RUN 200
*GOLD SHIELD SILVER PRISM/750: .2X to .5X
GOLD SHIELD SILVER PRINT RUN 750
*GOLD SHIELD GOLD PRISM/250: .4X to 1X
GOLD SHIELD GOLD PRINT RUN 250
SWORD/STONE VERSIONS NOT PRICED
1SW Steve Young 2.50 6.00
2SW Barry Sanders 4.00 10.00
3SW John Elway 6.00 15.00
4SW Warren Moon 1.50 4.00
5SW Chris Warren 1.00 2.50
6SW William Floyd 1.00 2.50
7SW Jim Kelly 1.50 4.00
8SW Troy Aikman 3.00 8.00
9SW Jerome Bettis 1.50 4.00
10SW Terance Mathis 1.00 2.50
11SW Marcus Allen 1.50 4.00
12SW Antonio Langham .60 1.50
13SW Sterling Sharpe 1.50 4.00
14SW Leonard Russell .60 1.50
15SW Drew Bledsoe 1.50 4.00
16SW Rodney Hampton 1.00 2.50
17SW Herschel Walker 1.00 2.50
18SW Jim Everett 1.00 2.50
19SW Terry Allen 1.00 2.50
20SW Junior Seau 1.50 4.00
21SW Natrone Means 1.00 2.50
22SW Deion Sanders 2.00 5.00
23SW Charlie Garner 1.00 2.50
24SW Marshall Faulk 1.50 4.00
25SW Ben Coates 1.00 2.50
1ST Emmitt Smith 5.00 12.00
2ST Jerry Rice 4.00 10.00
3ST Stan Humphries .60 1.50
4ST Joe Montana 8.00 20.00
5ST Steve Atwater .60 1.50
6ST Eric Metcalf .60 1.50
7ST Andre Rison 1.00 2.50
8ST Brett Favre 10.00 25.00
9ST Dan Marino 8.00 20.00
10ST Byron Bam Morris .60 1.50
11ST Heath Shuler 1.00 2.50
12ST Trent Dilfer 1.50 4.00
13ST Errict Rhett 1.00 2.50
14ST Herman Moore 1.00 2.50
15ST Eric Allen .60 1.50
16ST Cris Carter 1.50 4.00
17ST Ronnie Lott 1.50 4.00
18ST Randall Cunningham 1.50 4.00
19ST Barry Foster .60 1.50
20ST John Taylor 1.00 2.50
21ST Rick Mirer 1.00 2.50
22ST Tim Brown 1.50 4.00
23ST Michael Irvin 1.50 4.00
24ST Ricky Watters 1.00 2.50
25ST Jay Novacek 1.00 2.50

1997 Excalibur

The 1997 Excalibur set was issued in one series totaling 150 cards and was distributed in six-card packs with a suggested retail price of $2.49. The cardfronts feature a foil stamped textured dragon detailed with black ink. The backs carry another player photo and player information and statistics. A second non-foil version of the set was released later. These cards were originally intended to be part of a retail parallel version set, but the idea was scrapped.
COMPLETE SET (150) 30.00 60.00
1 Larry Centers .30 .75
2 Leeland McElroy .20 .50
3 Simeon Rice .30 .75
4 Eric Swann .20 .50
5 Jamal Anderson .50 1.25
6 Bert Emanuel .30 .75
7 Eric Metcalf .30 .75
8 Ray Lewis .75 2.00
9 Derrick Alexander WR .30 .75
10 Michael Jackson .30 .75
11 Vinny Testaverde .30 .75
12 Todd Collins .20 .50
13 Jim Kelly .50 1.25
14 Eric Moulds .50 1.25
15 Andre Reed .30 .75
16 Bruce Smith .30 .75
17 Thurman Thomas .50 1.25
18 Tim Biakabutuka .30 .75
19 Kerry Collins .50 1.25
20 Kevin Greene .30 .75
21 Anthony Johnson .20 .50
22 Lamar Lathon .20 .50
23 Muhsin Muhammad .30 .75
24 Curtis Conway .30 .75
25 Bryan Cox .20 .50
26 Walt Harris .20 .50
27 Erik Kramer .20 .50
28 Rick Mirer .20 .50
29 Rashaan Salaam .20 .50
30 Jeff Blake .30 .75
31 Ki-Jana Carter .20 .50
32 Carl Pickens .30 .75
33 Troy Aikman 1.50 3.00
34 Michael Irvin .50 1.25
35 Daryl Johnston .30 .75
36 Emmitt Smith 2.50 5.00
37 Broderick Thomas .20 .50
38 Terrell Davis .60 1.50
39 John Elway 2.50 6.00
40 Anthony Miller .20 .50
41 John Mobley .20 .50
42 Shannon Sharpe .30 .75
43 Neil Smith .30 .75
44 Scott Mitchell .30 .75
45 Herman Moore .30 .75
46 Brett Perriman .20 .50
47 Barry Sanders 2.00 5.00
48 Edgar Bennett .30 .75
49 Robert Brooks .30 .75
50 Brett Favre 3.00 6.00
51 Antonio Freeman .50 1.25
52 Dorsey Levens .50 1.25
53 Reggie White .50 1.25
54 Eddie George .50 1.25
55 Darryll Lewis .20 .50
56 Steve McNair .60 1.50
57 Chris Sanders .20 .50
58 Marshall Faulk .60 1.50
59 Jim Harbaugh .30 .75
60 Marvin Harrison .50 1.25
61 Jimmy Smith .30 .75
62 Tony Brackens .20 .50
63 Mark Brunell .60 1.50
64 Kevin Hardy .20 .50
65 Keenan McCardell .30 .75
66 Natrone Means .30 .75
67 Marcus Allen .50 1.25
68 Elvis Grbac .30 .75
69 Derrick Thomas .50 1.25
70 Tamarick Vanover .30 .75
71 Karim Abdul-Jabbar .30 .75
72 Terrell Buckley .20 .50
73 Irving Fryar .30 .75
74 Dan Marino 2.50 6.00
75 O.J. McDuffie .30 .75
76 Zach Thomas .50 1.25
77 Terry Kirby .30 .75
78 Cris Carter .50 1.25
79 Brad Johnson .50 1.25
80 John Randle .30 .75
81 Jake Reed .30 .75
82 Robert Smith .30 .75
83 Drew Bledsoe .60 1.50
84 Ben Coates .30 .75
85 Terry Glenn .50 1.25
86 Ty Law .30 .75
87 Curtis Martin .60 1.50
88 Willie McGinest .20 .50
89 Mario Bates .20 .50
90 Jim Everett .20 .50
91 Wayne Martin .20 .50
92 Heath Shuler .20 .50
93 Torrance Small .20 .50
94 Ray Zellars .20 .50
95 Dave Brown .20 .50
96 Jason Sehorn .30 .75
97 Amani Toomer .30 .75
98 Tyrone Wheatley .30 .75
99 Hugh Douglas .20 .50
100 Aaron Glenn .20 .50
101 Jeff Graham .20 .50
102 Keyshawn Johnson .50 1.25
103 Adrian Murrell .30 .75
104 Neil O'Donnell .30 .75
105 Tim Brown .50 1.25
106 Jeff George .30 .75
107 Jeff Hostetler .20 .50
108 Napoleon Kaufman .50 1.25
109 Chester McGlockton .20 .50
110 Fred Barnett .20 .50
111 Ty Detmer .30 .75
112 Chris T. Jones .20 .50
113 Ricky Watters .30 .75
114 Bobby Engram .30 .75
115 Jerome Bettis .50 1.25
116 Charles Johnson .30 .75
117 Greg Lloyd .20 .50
118 Kordell Stewart .50 1.25
119 Yancey Thigpen .30 .75
120 Rod Woodson .30 .75
121 Stan Humphries .30 .75
122 Tony Martin .30 .75
123 Leonard Russell .20 .50
124 Junior Seau .50 1.25
125 Chad Brown .20 .50
126 John Friesz .20 .50
127 Joey Galloway .30 .75
128 Cortez Kennedy .20 .50
129 Warren Moon .50 1.25
130 Chris Warren .30 .75
131 Garrison Hearst .30 .75
132 Terrell Owens .60 1.50
133 Jerry Rice 1.50 3.00
134 Dana Stubblefield .20 .50
135 Bryant Young .20 .50
136 Steve Young .75 2.00
137 Tony Banks .30 .75
138 Isaac Bruce .50 1.25
139 Eddie Kennison .30 .75
140 Keith Lyle .20 .50
141 Lawrence Phillips .20 .50
142 Mike Alstott .50 1.25
143 Hardy Nickerson .20 .50
144 Errict Rhett .20 .50
145 Warren Sapp .30 .75
146 Gus Frerotte .20 .50
147 Sean Gilbert .20 .50
148 Ken Harvey .20 .50
149 Terry Allen .50 1.25
150 Michael Westbrook .30 .75

1997 Excalibur Non-Foil Parallel

COMP.NO-FOIL SET (150) 7.50 15.00
*NO-FOIL CARDS: .1X TO .25X FOILS

1997 Excalibur Castles
COMPLETE SET (25) 125.00 250.00
CASTLES: SAME PRICE AS OVERLORDS

1997 Excalibur Crusaders
Randomly inserted in retail premium packs only at a rate of one in 30, this 25-card set features action color player photos on acetate cards die cut in the shape of a knight chess piece. Each card is serial numbered of 750 sets produced.

COMPLETE SET (25) 75.00 150.00
STATED ODDS 1:30
STATED PRINT RUN 750 SERIAL #'d SETS
1 Brett Favre 15.00 40.00
2 Mark Brunell 4.00 10.00
3 Jim Kelly 3.00 8.00
4 Michael Westbrook 2.00 5.00
5 Emmitt Smith 12.50 30.00
6 Marshall Faulk 4.00 10.00
7 Kerry Collins 3.00 8.00
8 Jeff Hostetler 1.25 3.00
9 Rashaan Salaam 1.25 3.00
10 Garrison Hearst 2.00 5.00
11 Tamarick Vanover 2.00 5.00
12 Rodney Hampton 3.00 8.00
13 Leeland McElroy 1.25 3.00
14 Tony Banks 2.00 5.00
15 Deion Sanders 3.00 8.00
16 Errict Rhett 1.25 3.00
17 Thurman Thomas 3.00 8.00
18 Chris Warren 2.00 5.00
19 Andre Reed 2.00 5.00
20 Napoleon Kaufman 3.00 8.00
21 Terry Allen 3.00 8.00
22 Carl Pickens 2.00 5.00
23 Marvin Harrison 3.00 8.00
24 Lawrence Phillips 1.25 3.00
25 Troy Aikman 8.00 20.00

1997 Excalibur Dragon Slayers Redemption
This 12-card set was distributed via an instant win game card inserted into 1997 Excalibur packs. The cards were printed on silver foil board and individually numbered of 1000 sets produced.

COMPLETE SET (12) 15.00 40.00
STATED PRINT RUN 1000 SERIAL #'d SETS
1 Mark Brunell 2.00 5.00
2 Terrell Davis 2.50 6.00
3 Jim Druckenmiller 1.00 2.50
4 Warrick Dunn 2.00 5.00
5 Brett Favre 6.00 15.00
6 Terry Glenn 1.50 4.00
7 Keyshawn Johnson 1.50 4.00
8 Dan Marino 6.00 15.00
9 Curtis Martin 1.50 4.00
10 Emmitt Smith 4.00 10.00
11 Shawn Springs .60 1.50
12 Eddie George 2.00 5.00

1997 Excalibur Game Helmets
Randomly inserted in packs at a rate of one in 60, this set features color player photos that are enhanced with 22K gold foil and printed on extra thick plastic card stock. Each contains an authentic piece of a game-used helmet sandwiched between two layers of plastic stock. Six different autographed cards were also produced and each is clearly labled "Authentic Signature" within a box where the player signed. The Jerome Bettis AUTO was released as a dealer premium only and never issued in packs and the unsigned Jamal Anderson appeared on the market after Edge ceased card operations. The other five autographs were seeded at the rate of 1:350 packs. Of the player's who signed cards, there were unsigned copies also inserted of Brunell, Davis and Bettis. The unsigned copies do not contain the player's name on the cardfront like the other cards in the set. Reportedly, just 5-Brunell, 1-Terrell Davis, and 40-Bettis unsigned cards were released in packs but it appears that a larger quantity of these players hit the market at a later date. All other unsigned cards were produced in quantities of 249 each according to an anouncement from Edge.

COMP.UNSIGNED SET (25) 300.00 600.00
STATED PRINT RUN 249 UNSIGNED SETS
SIGNED CARDS STATED ODDS 1:350
1 Brett Favre 30.00 80.00
2 Mark Brunell SP 12.50 30.00
2AU Mark Brunell AU/700 10.00 25.00
3 Barry Sanders 25.00 60.00
4 John Elway 30.00 80.00
5 Emmitt Smith 25.00 60.00
6 Drew Bledsoe 12.50 30.00
7 Troy Aikman 20.00 50.00
8 Dan Marino 25.00 60.00
9 Eddie George 12.50 30.00
10 Terry Glenn 7.50 20.00
11 Keyshawn Johnson 12.50 30.00
12AU Terrell Davis AU/500 20.00 50.00
13 Curtis Martin 12.50 30.00
14 Steve McNair 12.50 30.00
15 Muhsin Muhammad 7.50 20.00
16 Antonio Freeman 8.00 20.00
17 Ricky Watters 7.50 20.00
18 Jerome Bettis SP 40.00 80.00
18AU Jerome Bettis AU/100 75.00 125.00
19 Herman Moore 6.00 15.00
20 Isaac Bruce 12.50 30.00
21 Deion Sanders 15.00 40.00
22 Cris Carter 15.00 40.00
23 Tim Biakabutuka 6.00 15.00
24 Karim Abdul-Jabbar 6.00 15.00
25 Mike Alstott 12.50 30.00
26 Jamal Anderson SP 12.50 30.00
26AU Jamal Anderson AU/100 20.00 50.00
27AU Kevin Greene AU/100 12.00 30.00
28 Tim Brown SP 30.00 60.00
28AU Tim Brown AU/100 20.00 50.00

1997 Excalibur Gridiron Wizards Draft
Randomly inserted in premium packs only at a rate of one in 20, this 25-card set features color photos of top players from the 1997 NFL draft. Each includes gold foil on the front and serial numbering on the back of 1000 cards produced. The unnumbered cards are listed alphabetically below.

COMPLETE SET (25) 60.00 120.00
STATED ODDS 1:20
STATED PRINT RUN 1000 SER.#'d SETS
1 Reidel Anthony 2.00 5.00
2 Darnell Autry 2.00 5.00
3 Tiki Barber 7.50 20.00
4 Pat Barnes 2.00 5.00
5 Peter Boulware 2.00 5.00
6 Chris Canty 1.25 3.00
7 Rae Carruth 1.25 3.00
8 Troy Davis 2.00 5.00
9 Corey Dillon 5.00 12.00
10 Jim Druckenmiller 2.00 5.00
11 Warrick Dunn 4.00 10.00
12 James Farrior 2.00 5.00
13 Tony Gonzalez 5.00 10.00
14 Yatil Green 2.00 5.00
15 Marcus Harris 1.25 3.00
16 Ike Hilliard 2.00 5.00
17 David LaFleur 1.25 3.00
18 Orlando Pace 2.00 5.00
19 Jake Plummer 5.00 12.00
20 Dwayne Rudd 1.25 3.00
21 Darrell Russell 1.25 3.00
22 Antowain Smith 3.00 8.00
23 Shawn Springs 2.00 5.00
24 Bryant Westbrook 1.25 3.00
25 Danny Wuerffel 2.00 5.00

1997 Excalibur Marauders
Randomly inserted in super premium packs only at a rate of one in 20, this 25-card set features color photos of 48 NFL stars back-to-back printed on extra thick card stock and a motion background creating a 3-D illusion. A "Supreme Edge" parallel version with each card numbered of 50 was randomly inserted in 1998 Collector's Edge Supreme Season Review packs.

COMPLETE SET (25) 75.00 200.00
STATED ODDS 1:20
*SUPREME EDGE: 2X TO 5X BASIC INS.
SUPREME EDGE PRINT RUN 50 SETS
1 T.Banks 2.50 6.00
A.Freeman
2 T.Biakabutuka 1.00 2.50
H.Shuler
3 E.Kennison 15.00 30.00
B.Favre
4 T.Collins 2.50 6.00
M.Allen
5 S.Sharpe 12.50 30.00
D.Marino
6 N.Kaufman 2.50 6.00
D.Howard
7 M.Muhammad 1.50 4.00
D.Levens
8 M.Alstott 3.00 8.00
D.Bledsoe
9 M.Westbrook 12.50 25.00
E.Smith
10 M.Harrison 2.50 6.00
H.Shuler
11 M.Faulk 3.00 8.00
J.Blake
12 L.Phillips 1.00 2.50
J.George
13 E.Bennett 1.00 2.50
T.Martin
14 K.Abdul-Jabbar 5.00 12.00
J.Rice
15 T.Owens 4.00 10.00
J.Harbaugh
16 I.Bruce 12.50 30.00
J.Elway
17 E.Metcalf 1.00 2.50
D.Brown
18 E.Kennison 2.50 6.00
J.Seau
19 E.George 2.50 6.00
M.Brunell
20 D.Sanders 4.00 8.00
C.Carter
21 E.Moulds 5.00 12.00
S.Young
22 C.Warren 1.50 4.00
B.Coates
23 C.Pickens 1.50 4.00
R.Brooks
24 B.Engram 2.50 6.00
T.Brown
25 B.Coates 7.50 15.00
T.Aikman

1997 Excalibur Overlords
Randomly inserted in super premium hobby packs only at the rate of one in 30, this 25-card set features action color player photos printed on cards die cut in the shape of the Excalibur dragon. The cards are essentially parallels of the Castles retail insert. The difference being on the front card design. The cardbacks of both sets are identical.

COMPLETE SET (25) 75.00 200.00
STATED ODDS 1:30
STATED PRINT RUN 750 SERIAL #'d SETS
CASTLE PRINT RUN 750 SERIAL #'d SETS
1 Jeff Blake 2.50 6.00
2 Mark Brunell 5.00 12.00
3 Bobby Engram 2.50 6.00
4 Joey Galloway 2.50 6.00
5 Eddie Kennison 2.50 6.00
6 Terrell Davis 5.00 12.00
7 Chris Calloway 2.50 6.00
8 Hardy Nickerson 1.50 4.00
9 Errict Rhett 1.50 4.00
10 Emmitt Smith 15.00 40.00
11 Kordell Stewart 4.00 10.00
12 Steve Young 6.00 15.00
13 Marcus Allen 4.00 10.00
14 Edgar Bennett 2.50 6.00
15 Robert Brooks 2.50 6.00
16 Kerry Collins 4.00 10.00
17 Todd Collins 1.50 4.00
18 Brett Favre 15.00 40.00
19 Gus Frerotte 1.50 4.00
20 Elvis Grbac 2.50 6.00
21 Jeff Hostetler 1.50 4.00
22 Tony Martin 2.50 6.00
23 Terrell Owens 5.00 12.00
24 Dorsey Levens 4.00 10.00
25 Thurman Thomas 4.00 10.00

1997 Excalibur Quest Redemption
Collectors who were able to spell the word "EDGE," by assembling the correct combination of letter cards found in 1997 Excalibur packs, received this set as a prize. Each card was printed on silver foil card stock and individually numbered of 1000 sets produced.

COMPLETE SET (12) 25.00 50.00
1 Jim Druckenmiller .75 2.00
2 Brett Favre 6.00 15.00
3 Joey Galloway 1.25 3.00
4 Eddie George 2.50 6.00
5 Terry Glenn .75 2.00
6 Marvin Harrison 1.25 3.00
7 Karim Abdul-Jabbar .75 2.00
8 Keyshawn Johnson 1.25 3.00
9 Eddie Kennison .75 2.00
10 Dan Marino 6.00 15.00
11 Curtis Martin 2.00 5.00
12 Emmitt Smith 4.00 10.00

1997 Excalibur 22K Knights
Randomly inserted in packs at a rate of one in 20, this 25-card set features player photos printed with a 22K Gold shield logo on backgrounds that come together to reveal a surprise Excalibur image. Each base insert card was serial numbered of 2000-sets made. A Black Magnum parallel was produced as well and distributed at the rate of 1:75 Super Premium packs. A "Supreme Edge" parallel version with each card numbered of 50 was randomly inserted in 1998 Collector's Edge Supreme Season Review packs.

COMPLETE SET (25) 100.00 200.00
STATED ODDS 1:20
STATED PRINT RUN 2000 SERIAL #'d SETS
*BLACK MAGNUMS: 1X TO 2.5X BASIC INSERTS
BL STATED ODDS 1:75 SUPER PREM.HOBBY
BL STATED PRINT RUN 250 SERIAL #'d SETS
*SUPREME EDGE: 1.2X TO 3X BASIC INSERTS
SUPREME EDGE STATED PRINT RUN 50 SETS
1 Troy Aikman 5.00 12.00
2 John Elway 10.00 25.00
3 Brett Favre 10.00 25.00
4 Dan Marino 10.00 25.00
5 Barry Sanders 8.00 20.00
6 Emmitt Smith 8.00 20.00
7 Mark Brunell 2.50 6.00
8 Jerry Rice 5.00 12.00
9 Terrell Davis 2.50 6.00
10 Natrone Means 1.25 3.00
11 Joey Galloway 1.25 3.00
12 Keyshawn Johnson 2.00 5.00
13 Curtis Martin 2.50 6.00
14 Herman Moore 1.25 3.00
15 Eddie George 2.00 5.00
16 Terry Glenn 2.00 5.00
17 Steve McNair 2.50 6.00
18 Marshall Faulk 2.50 6.00
19 Ricky Watters 1.25 3.00
20 Karim Abdul-Jabbar 1.25 3.00
21 Gus Frerotte .75 2.00
22 Terry Allen 2.00 5.00
23 Andre Reed 1.25 3.00
24 Jerome Bettis 2.00 5.00
25 Tim Brown 2.00 6.00

1997 Excalibur National
The 1997 Excalibur National set was released in single card form over the course of The National Sports Collector's Convention in Cleveland. Each card was printed on gold foil textured stock with a player photo and Excalibur logo on the cardfront. The cardbacks are essentially parallel to the base Excalibur release including the card number. A second card number was added, with each numbered "XX of 24."

COMPLETE SET (25) 50.00 125.00
1 Leeland McElroy .40 1.00
2 Mark Brunell 2.00 5.00
3 Emmitt Smith 4.00 10.00
4 Troy Aikman 2.40 6.00
5 Carl Pickens .80 2.00
6 Terrell Davis 3.00 8.00
7 John Elway 4.80 12.00
8 Eddie George 2.40 6.00
9 Brett Favre 4.80 12.00
10 Barry Sanders 4.00 10.00
11 Steve McNair 2.00 5.00
12 Eddie Kennison .80 2.00
13 Dan Marino 4.80 12.00
14 Cris Carter 1.20 3.00
15 Curtis Martin 2.00 5.00
16 Terry Glenn 1.20 3.00
17 Drew Bledsoe 2.00 5.00
18 Jerome Bettis 1.20 3.00
19 Kordell Stewart 1.50 4.00
20 Napoleon Kaufman 1.60 4.00
21 Joey Galloway 1.50 4.00
22 Kerry Collins .80 2.00
23 Jerry Rice 2.40 6.00
24 Isaac Bruce 1.20 3.00
NNO Checklist Card .40 1.00

1948-52 Exhibit W468 Black and White
Produced by the Exhibit Supply Company of Chicago, the 1948-52 Football Exhibit cards are unnumbered, blank-backed, and produced on thick card stock. Although we list the more common black and white cards below, some of the cards were issued in other colors as well including sepia, tan, green, red, pink, blue, and yellow. The primary method of distribution for the cards was through mechanical vending machines. Advertising panels on the front of these machines displayed from one to nine cards as well as the price for a card which was originally one-cent but later raised to two-cents. Each card measures approximately 3 1/4" by 5 3/8" and features a pro or college player. Several cards in the checklist below (Sammy Baugh, Glenn Dobbs, Otto Graham, Pat Harder, Jack Jacobs, Sid Luckman, Johnny Lujack, Marion Motley, Emil Sitko, Steve Van Buren, Bob Waterfield, and Tank Younger) have the same photo as in the Exhibit Sports Champions set of 1948; however, cards in this series do not have the single agate line of type describing the player at the bottom of the card. The cards were issued in three groups of 32 primarily during 1948, 1950, and 1951. We've included what is thought to be the year/years of issue for each card. The 16-cards in the 1951/1952 group are the most plentiful as they were reissued intact in sepia tone in 1952 (and perhaps 1953 as well). Some veteran collectors believe the second group may have been issued in 1949 rather than 1950. Cards issued during and after 1951 are marked as DP's as they are quite common compared to the other cards in the set. Several players, such as Creekmur, Houck, and Martin, are rumored to exist, but they have not been verified and are assumed not to exist in the checklist below. The American Card Catalog designation is W468. A football exhibit checklist card has also been found but was apparently produced in very limited quantity in 1950 only. This checklist card is known to exist in green and black-and-white and is identical to the Bednarik card but has the 32 players from the 1950 set listed on its front. The Bednarik checklist is usually found on the 9-card advertising display piece

COMPLETE SET (59) 2500.00 5000.00
1 Frankie Albert DP 3.00 8.00
2 Dick Barwegan DP 2.50 6.00
3 Sammy Baugh DP 12.50 25.00
4 Chuck Bednarik SP50 90.00 150.00
5 Tony Canadeo DP 6.00 15.00
6 Paul Christman 25.00 40.00
7 Bob Cifers SP48 175.00 300.00
8 Irv Comp SP48 175.00 300.00
9A Charley Conerly DP 6.00 15.00
9B Charley Conerly DP 6.00 15.00
10 George Connor DP 4.00 10.00
11 Tex Coulter SP48 175.00 300.00
12 Glenn Davis SP50 175.00 300.00
13 Glenn Dobbs 25.00 40.00
14 John Dottley DP 2.50 6.00
15 Bill Dudley 35.00 60.00
16 Tom Fears DP 5.00 12.00
17 Joe Geri DP 2.50 6.00
18 Otto Graham DP 15.00 30.00
19 Pat Harder 25.00 40.00
20 Elroy Hirsch DP 6.00 15.00
21 Dick Hoerner SP50 60.00 100.00
22 Bob Hoernschemeyer DP 2.50 6.00
23 Les Horvath SP48 175.00 300.00
24 Jack Jacobs SP48 175.00 300.00
25 Nate Johnson SP48 175.00 300.00
26 Charlie Justice SP50 90.00 150.00
27 Bobby Layne DP 10.00 25.00
28 Clyde LeForce SP48 175.00 300.00
29 Sid Luckman 45.00 80.00
30 Johnny Lujack 35.00 60.00
31 John Mastrangelo SP48 175.00 300.00
32 Ollie Matson DP 6.00 15.00
33 Bill McColl DP 2.50 6.00
34 Fred Morrison DP 2.50 6.00
35 Marion Motley DP 10.00 20.00
36 Chuck Ortmann DP 2.50 6.00
37 Joe Perry SP50 75.00 135.00
38 Pete Pihos 30.00 50.00
39 Steve Pritko SP48 175.00 300.00
40 George Ratterman DP 2.50 6.00
41 Jay Rhodemyre DP 2.50 6.00
42 Martin Ruby SP50 75.00 125.00
43 Julie Rykovich DP 2.50 6.00
44 Walt Schlinkman SP48 175.00 300.00
45 Emil Sitko DP 2.50 6.00
46 Vitamin Smith DP 2.50 6.00
47 Norm Standlee 25.00 40.00
48 George Taliaferro DP 2.50 6.00
49 Y.A. Tittle HOR 60.00 100.00
50 Charley Trippi DP 4.00 10.00
51 Frank Tripucka DP 3.00 8.00
52 Emlen Tunnell DP 5.00 12.00
53 Bulldog Turner DP 5.00 12.00
54 Steve Van Buren 35.00 60.00
55 Bob Waterfield DP 7.50 20.00
56 Herm Wedemeyer SP48 500.00 800.00
57 Bob Williams DP 2.50 6.00
58 Buddy Young DP 3.00 8.00
59 Tank Younger DP 3.00 8.00
NNO Checklist Card SP50 500.00 800.00

1948-52 Exhibit W468 Variations
1A Frankie Albert B&W PC 12.50 25.00
1B Frankie Albert Sepia 7.50 15.00
2B Dick Barwegan Sepia 6.00 12.00
3A Sammy Baugh B&W PC 25.00 50.00
3B Sammy Baugh Yellow 75.00 125.00
5B Tony Canadeo Sepia 15.00 30.00
6A Paul Christman Lt.Blue 60.00 100.00
7A Bob Cifers Dark Green 200.00 350.00
7B Bob Cifers Yellow 200.00 350.00
8A Irv Comp Yellow 200.00 350.00
9A Charley Conerly B&W PC 20.00 40.00
10B George Connor Sepia 10.00 20.00
11A Tex Coulter Green 200.00 350.00
11B Tex Coulter Pink 200.00 350.00
14B John Dottley Sepia 6.00 12.00
15A Bill Dudley Red 60.00 100.00
16A Tom Fears B&W PC 12.50 25.00
16B Tom Fears Sepia 12.50 25.00
17A Joe Geri Sepia 6.00 12.00
18A Otto Graham B&W PC 30.00 60.00
18B Otto Graham Sepia 30.00 60.00
19A Pat Harder Blue 50.00 80.00
20A Elroy Hirsch B&W PC 20.00 40.00
20B Elroy Hirsch Sepia 15.00 30.00
22B Bob Hoernschemeyer Sepia 6.00 12.00
23A Les Horvath Dark Red 200.00 350.00
23B Les Horvath Yellow 200.00 350.00
24A Jack Jacobs Dark Green 200.00 350.00
25A Nate Johnson Green 200.00 350.00
25B Nate Johnson Dark Red 200.00 350.00
27A Bobby Layne B&W PC 25.00 50.00
27B Bobby Layne Sepia 25.00 50.00
28A Clyde LeForce Green 200.00 350.00
29A Sid Luckman Lt.Green 90.00 150.00
30A Johnny Lujack Yellow 75.00 125.00
30B Johnny Lujack Pink 75.00 125.00
31A John Mastrangelo Lt.Blue 175.00 300.00
32A Ollie Matson B&W PC 20.00 40.00
32B Ollie Matson Sepia 15.00 30.00
33B Bill McColl Sepia 6.00 15.00
34A Fred Morrison B&W PC 25.00 50.00
34B Fred Morrison Sepia 6.00 12.00
34C Fred Morrison Tan 7.50 15.00
35A Marion Motley B&W PC 25.00 50.00
35B Marion Motley Sepia 20.00 40.00
36B Chuck Ortmann Sepia 6.00 12.00
38A Pete Pihos Yellow 60.00 100.00
39A Steve Pritko Yellow 200.00 350.00
40A George Ratterman B&W PC 12.50 25.00
40B George Ratterman Sepia 6.00 12.00
41B Jay Rhodemyre Sepia 6.00 12.00
41C Jay Rhodemyre Tan 7.50 15.00
43A Julie Rykovich B&W PC 12.50 25.00
43B Julie Rykovich Sepia 6.00 12.00
44A Walt Schlinkman Pink 200.00 350.00
45B Emil Sitko Sepia 6.00 12.00
48B George Taliaferro Sepia 6.00 12.00
48C George Taliaferro Tan 7.50 15.00
49A Y.A. Tittle Green 90.00 150.00
49B Y.A. Tittle Yellow 90.00 150.00
50A Charley Trippi B&W PC 15.00 30.00
50B Charley Trippi Sepia 10.00 20.00
51B Frank Tripucka Sepia 7.50 15.00
52B Emlen Tunnell Sepia 12.50 25.00
53A Bulldog Turner B&W PC 25.00 50.00
53B Bulldog Turner Green 60.00 100.00
53C Bulldog Turner Sepia 12.50 25.00
54A Steve Van Buren Lt.Blue 75.00 125.00
55A Bob Waterfield B&W PC 25.00 50.00
55B Bob Waterfield Sepia 15.00 40.00
56A Herm Wedemeyer Lt.Green 600.00 1000.00
57A Bob Williams B&W PC 25.00 50.00
57B Bob Williams Sepia 6.00 12.00
58A Buddy Young B&W PC 12.50 25.00
58B Buddy Young Sepia 7.50 15.00
58C Buddy Young Yellow 60.00 100.00
59B Tank Younger Sepia 6.00 12.00
NNO Chuck Bednarik CL Green 500.00 800.00

1926 Exhibit Red Grange One Minute to Play
These Exhibit cards were issued for the movie "One Minute to play' starring Red Grange. Each was produced in the standard oversized Exhibit style with a single color cardfront picturing Grange in a scene from the movie. The backs are blank.

1 Red Grange Green
2 Red Grange In sweater

2005 Exquisite Collection
This 127-card set was released in January, 2006. The set was Issued In a six-card pack with a $500 SRP. Cards numbered 1-42 feature veterans in team alphabetical order while cards numbered 43-127 were all signed by the rookie. Within the rookie subset, cards numbered 85-118 also have a player-worn jersey swatch. With the exception of the game-worn autographed cards, which had a stated print run of 199 serial numbered sets, all the cards in this set were issued to a stated print run of 150 serial numbered sets.

1-42 VETERAN PRINT RUN 150
ROOKIE AU PRINT RUN 150
ROOKIE JSY AU PRINT RUN 99-199
1 Larry Fitzgerald 12.00 30.00
2 Michael Vick 10.00 25.00
3 Jamal Lewis 10.00 25.00
4 Ray Lewis 12.00 30.00
5 Willis McGahee 8.00 20.00
6 Jake Delhomme 8.00 20.00
7 Brian Urlacher 12.00 30.00
8 Carson Palmer 10.00 25.00
9 Julius Jones 8.00 20.00
10 Drew Bledsoe 10.00 25.00
11 Jake Plummer 8.00 20.00
12 Kevin Jones 8.00 20.00
13 Roy Williams WR 8.00 20.00
14 Ahman Green 10.00 25.00
15 Brett Favre 20.00 50.00
16 David Carr 8.00 20.00
17 Edgerrin James 10.00 25.00
18 Marvin Harrison 10.00 25.00
19 Peyton Manning 20.00 50.00
20 Byron Leftwich 8.00 20.00
21 Priest Holmes 8.00 20.00
22 Daunte Culpepper 10.00 25.00
23 Tom Brady 25.00 60.00
24 Deuce McAllister 10.00 25.00
25 Eli Manning 20.00 50.00
26 Jeremy Shockey 8.00 20.00
27 Chad Pennington 8.00 20.00
28 Curtis Martin 10.00 25.00
29 Randy Moss 10.00 25.00
30 Donovan McNabb 10.00 25.00
31 Terrell Owens 10.00 25.00
32 Jerome Bettis 12.00 30.00
33 Ben Roethlisberger 15.00 40.00
34 Drew Brees 12.00 30.00
35 LaDainian Tomlinson 12.00 30.00
36 Antonio Gates 12.00 30.00
37 Shaun Alexander 8.00 20.00
38 Marc Bulger 8.00 20.00
39 Torry Holt 10.00 25.00
40 Steven Jackson 8.00 20.00
41 Steve McNair 10.00 25.00
42 Clinton Portis 8.00 20.00
43 Dan Orlovsky AU RC 10.00 25.00
44 Darren Sproles AU RC 20.00 50.00
45 Marion Barber AU RC 10.00 25.00
46 Chris Henry AU RC 12.00 30.00
47 Derek Anderson AU RC 12.00 30.00
48 Erasmus James AU RC 10.00 25.00
49 Thomas Davis AU RC 10.00 25.00
50 David Pollack AU RC 10.00 25.00
51 Fred Gibson AU RC 10.00 25.00
52 Craphonso Thorpe AU RC 10.00 25.00
53 Derrick Johnson AU RC 12.00 30.00
54 Brandon Jacobs AU RC 15.00 40.00
55 Adrian McPherson AU RC 10.00 25.00
56 Matt Cassel AU RC 10.00 25.00
57 Anthony Davis AU RC 10.00 25.00
58 Alvin Pearman AU RC 10.00 25.00
59 Brandon Jones AU RC 12.00 30.00
60 Jerome Mathis AU RC 15.00 40.00
61 Chase Lyman AU RC 10.00 25.00
62 Roydell Williams AU RC 12.00 30.00
63 DeMarcus Ware AU RC 125.00 250.00
64 Mike Patterson AU RC 10.00 25.00
65 Mike Nugent AU RC 12.00 30.00
66 Ryan Fitzpatrick AU RC 15.00 40.00
67 Barrett Ruud AU RC 12.00 30.00
68 Kevin Burnett AU RC 12.00 30.00
69 J.R. Russell AU RC 10.00 25.00
71 Marlin Jackson AU RC 10.00 25.00
72 Shawne Merriman AU RC 15.00 40.00
73 Alex Smith TE AU RC 10.00 25.00
74 Fabian Washington AU RC 10.00 25.00
75 Corey Webster AU RC 12.00 30.00
76 Larry Brackins AU RC 10.00 25.00
77 Kay-Jay Harris AU RC 10.00 25.00
78 Airese Currie AU RC 10.00 25.00
79 Taylor Stubblefield AU RC 10.00 25.00
80 James Kilian AU RC 10.00 25.00
81 Travis Johnson AU RC 10.00 25.00
82 Walter Reyes AU RC 10.00 25.00
83 Anttaj Hawthorne AU RC 10.00 25.00
84 Chad Owens AU RC 10.00 25.00
85 J.J. Arrington JSY AU RC 12.00 30.00
86 Mark Bradley JSY AU RC 10.00 25.00
87 Reggie Brown JSY AU RC 10.00 25.00
88 Jason Campbell JSY AU RC 10.00 25.00
89 Maurice Clarett JSY AU 10.00 25.00
90 Mark Clayton JSY AU RC 10.00 25.00
91 Ciatrick Fason JSY AU RC 10.00 25.00
92 Charlie Frye JSY AU RC 10.00 25.00
93 Frank Gore JSY AU RC 75.00 150.00
94 David Greene JSY AU RC 10.00 25.00
95 Vincent Jackson JSY AU RC 15.00 40.00
96 Adam Jones JSY AU RC 10.00 25.00
97 Matt Jones JSY AU RC 10.00 25.00
98 Stefan LeFors JSY AU RC 10.00 25.00
99 Heath Miller JSY AU RC 30.00 80.00
100 Ryan Moats JSY AU RC 10.00 25.00
101 Vernand Morency JSY AU RC 10.00 25.00
102 Terrence Murphy JSY AU RC 10.00 25.00
103 Kyle Orton JSY AU RC 15.00 40.00
104 Roscoe Parrish JSY AU RC 10.00 25.00
105 Courtney Roby JSY AU RC 10.00 25.00
106 Aaron Rodgers JSY AU RC 800.00 1500.00
107 Carlos Rogers JSY AU RC 15.00 40.00
108 Antrel Rolle JSY AU RC 30.00 60.00
109 Eric Shelton JSY AU RC 10.00 25.00
110 Andrew Walter JSY AU RC 10.00 25.00
111 Roddy White JSY AU RC 15.00 40.00
112 T.Williamson JSY AU/99 RC 20.00 50.00
113 Mike Williams JSY AU 15.00 40.00
114 Ro.Brown JSY AU/99 RC 20.00 50.00
115 B.Edwards JSY AU/99 RC 12.00 30.00
116 C.Benson JSY AU/99 RC 20.00 50.00
117 C.Williams JSY AU/99 RC 20.00 50.00
118 A.Smith QB JSY AU/99 RC 300.00 600.00
120 Tyson Thompson AU RC 10.00 25.00
121 Chris Carr AU RC 10.00 25.00
122 Fred Amey AU RC 10.00 25.00
123 Brodney Pool AU RC 10.00 25.00
124 Stanford Routt AU RC 10.00 25.00
125 Justin Tuck AU RC 50.00 100.00
126 Luis Castillo AU RC 10.00 25.00
127 Kirk Morrison AU RC 15.00 40.00
128 DeAndra Cobb AU RC 10.00 25.00

2005 Exquisite Collection Debut Signatures
STATED PRINT RUN 25 SER.#'d SETS
EDAJ Adam Jones 12.00 30.00
EDAN Antrel Rolle 20.00 50.00
EDAR Aaron Rodgers 350.00 600.00
EDAS Alex Smith QB 150.00 300.00
EDAW Andrew Walter 12.00 30.00
EDBE Braylon Edwards 12.00 30.00
EDCB Cedric Benson 12.00 30.00
EDCF Charlie Frye 12.00 30.00
EDCR Courtney Roby 12.00 30.00
EDCW Cadillac Williams 12.00 30.00
EDJC Jason Campbell 12.00 30.00
EDKO Kyle Orton 25.00 60.00
EDMA Mark Clayton 12.00 30.00
EDMC Maurice Clarett 12.00 30.00
EDMJ Matt Jones 12.00 30.00
EDMW Mike Williams 15.00 40.00
EDRB Reggie Brown 12.00 30.00
EDRM Ryan Moats 12.00 30.00
EDRO Ronnie Brown 40.00 100.00
EDRP Roscoe Parrish 12.00 30.00
EDRW Roddy White 20.00 50.00
EDTM Terrence Murphy 12.00 30.00
EDTW Troy Williamson 12.00 30.00
EDVJ Vincent Jackson 20.00 50.00
EDVM Vernand Morency 12.00 30.00

2005 Exquisite Collection Endorsement Autographs
STATED PRINT RUN 15 SER.#'d SETS
EEAB Anquan Boldin 12.00 30.00
EECB Chris Brown 12.00 30.00
EECJ Chad Johnson 12.00 30.00
EEDD Domanick Davis 12.00 30.00
EEJH Joe Horn 12.00 30.00
EEJI Jim Plunkett 20.00 50.00
EEJL James Lofton 20.00 50.00
EEJP J.P. Losman 12.00 30.00
EEJT Joe Theismann 40.00 80.00
EEKC Keary Colbert 12.00 30.00
EELJ Larry Johnson 12.00 30.00
EEMC Michael Clayton 12.00 30.00
EENB Nate Burleson 12.00 30.00
EERW Reggie Wayne 30.00 60.00
EETB Tiki Barber 30.00 60.00

2005 Exquisite Collection Patch Gold
GOLD PRINT RUN 35 SER.#'d SETS
*SILVER HOLO/15: .6X TO 1.5X GOLD/35
SILVER HOLO SER.#'d TO 15
EPAA Aaron Brooks 6.00 15.00
EPAB Anquan Boldin 6.00 15.00
EPAG Ahman Green 8.00 20.00
EPAJ Adam Jones 5.00 12.00
EPAL Marcus Allen 12.00 30.00
EPAN Antonio Gates 10.00 25.00
EPAR Aaron Rodgers 75.00 135.00
EPAS Alex Smith QB 20.00 50.00
EPAW Andrew Walter 6.00 15.00
EPBE Braylon Edwards 5.00 12.00
EPBF Brett Favre 20.00 50.00
EPBJ Bo Jackson 15.00 40.00
EPBK Bernie Kosar 8.00 20.00
EPBL Byron Leftwich 6.00 15.00
EPBN Reggie Brown 5.00 12.00
EPBR Ben Roethlisberger 15.00 40.00
EPBS Barry Sanders 20.00 50.00
EPCA Carlos Rogers 8.00 20.00
EPCB Cedric Benson 5.00 12.00
EPCF Charlie Frye 5.00 12.00
EPCJ Chad Johnson 6.00 15.00
EPCP Carson Palmer 8.00 20.00
EPCR Courtney Roby 5.00 12.00
EPCW Cadillac Williams 5.00 12.00
EPDB Drew Bledsoe 8.00 20.00
EPDD Domanick Davis 6.00 15.00
EPDE Deuce McAllister 8.00 20.00
EPDM1 Dan Marino Home 25.00 60.00
EPDM2 Dan Marino Away 25.00 60.00
EPDO Donovan McNabb 8.00 20.00
EPDR Drew Bennett 8.00 20.00
EPDS Deion Sanders 10.00 25.00
EPEC Earl Campbell 12.00 30.00
EPEJ Edgerrin James 8.00 20.00
EPEM Eli Manning 15.00 40.00
EPES Eric Shelton 5.00 12.00
EPFG Frank Gore 10.00 25.00
EPFR Fred Taylor 6.00 15.00
EPGO Tony Gonzalez 8.00 20.00
EPJA J.J. Arrington 6.00 15.00
EPJC Jason Campbell 5.00 12.00
EPJE John Elway 20.00 50.00
EPJH Joe Horn 6.00 15.00
EPJJ Julius Jones 6.00 15.00
EPJK Jim Kelly 12.00 30.00
EPJM Joe Montana 40.00 100.00
EPJP J.P. Losman 6.00 15.00
EPJT Joe Theismann 12.00 30.00
EPKC Keary Colbert 6.00 15.00
EPKO Kyle Orton 5.00 12.00
EPLE Lee Evans 8.00 20.00
EPLJ LaMont Jordan 8.00 20.00
EPLT LaDainian Tomlinson 10.00 25.00
EPMA Maurice Clarett 5.00 12.00
EPMB Marc Bulger 6.00 15.00
EPMC Mark Clayton 5.00 12.00
EPMI Michael Clayton 6.00 15.00
EPMJ Matt Jones 5.00 12.00
EPMK Mark Bradley 5.00 12.00
EPMM Muhsin Muhammad 6.00 15.00
EPMO Randy Moss 8.00 20.00
EPMV Michael Vick 8.00 20.00
EPMW Mike Williams 6.00 15.00
EPNB Nate Burleson 6.00 15.00
EPPM Peyton Manning 15.00 40.00
EPRB Ronnie Brown 6.00 15.00
EPRE Reggie Wayne 8.00 20.00
EPRM Ryan Moats 5.00 12.00
EPRO Roddy White 8.00 20.00
EPRP Roscoe Parrish 5.00 12.00
EPRW Roy Williams WR 6.00 15.00
EPSF Stefan LeFors 5.00 12.00
EPSJ Steven Jackson 6.00 15.00
EPTA Troy Aikman 15.00 40.00
EPTB Tiki Barber 8.00 20.00
EPTG Trent Green 6.00 15.00
EPTM Terrence Murphy 5.00 12.00
EPTW Troy Williamson 5.00 12.00
EPVJ Vincent Jackson 8.00 20.00

2005 Exquisite Collection Patch Duals
STATED PRINT RUN 25 SER.#'d SETS
AD A.Brooks/D.McAllister 12.00 30.00
AJ M.Allen/B.Jackson 25.00 60.00
BD T.Brady/C.Dillon 30.00 80.00
BJ M.Bulger/S.Jackson 10.00 25.00
BK B.Sanders/K.Jones 25.00 60.00
BL J.Bettis/J.Lewis 20.00 50.00
BM T.Brady/D.McNabb 30.00 80.00
CB C.Martin/J.Bettis 20.00 50.00
DJ T.Dorsett/J.Jones 15.00 40.00
EB J.Elway/T.Brady 40.00 100.00
EK J.Elway/B.Kosar 30.00 80.00
FM B.Favre/D.Marino 50.00 120.00
HG P.Holmes/T.Green 10.00 25.00
JC B.Jackson/E.Campbell 20.00 50.00
JD J.Montana/D.Marino 50.00 120.00
JJ J.Theismann/J.Montana 30.00 80.00
JM J.Jones/W.McGahee 10.00 25.00
JS B.Jackson/D.Sanders 25.00 60.00
JT E.James/L.Tomlinson 15.00 40.00
JW J.Losman/W.McGahee 10.00 25.00
KK J.Kelly/B.Kosar 20.00 50.00
KL J.Kelly/J.Losman 20.00 50.00
KW K.Jones/R.Williams 10.00 25.00
LM B.Leftwich/S.McNair 12.00 30.00
LS R.Lewis/D.Sanders 30.00 80.00
MB E.Manning/T.Barber 25.00 60.00
MF J.Montana/B.Favre 50.00 120.00
MH P.Manning/M.Harrison 30.00 80.00
MJ P.Manning/E.James 30.00 80.00
MM D.Marino/P.Manning 40.00 100.00
MO D.McNabb/T.Owens 12.00 30.00
MW P.Manning/R.Wayne 30.00 80.00
OM T.Owens/R.Moss 12.00 30.00
PJ C.Palmer/C.Johnson 12.00 30.00
RC R.Moss/C.Johnson 12.00 30.00
RP B.Roethlisberger/C.Palmer 20.00 50.00
SJ B.Sanders/J.Jones 25.00 60.00
SR Staubach/Roethlisberge 25.00 60.00
TM Tomlinson/McAllister 15.00 40.00
UL B.Urlchaer/R.Lewis 15.00 40.00
VB M.Vick/M.Bulger 12.00 30.00
VC M.Vick/D.Culpepper 12.00 30.00

2005 Exquisite Collection Patch Triples
STATED PRINT RUN 15 SER.#'d SETS
BAS Bldso/Aikmn/Stbch 25.00 60.00
DHP Dillon/Holmes/Portis 12.00 30.00
FAM Favre/Aikman/Mntna 60.00 150.00
JJJ Jones/Jones/Jackson 12.00 30.00
MEM Montna/Elwy/Marino 60.00 150.00
MFB Mann/Favre/Brady 80.00 200.00
MJH Mann/James/Harrisn 50.00 120.00
MMM P.Mann/Mntn/Mrino 60.00 150.00
MMT McGah/McAllis/LT 20.00 50.00
MOH Moss/Owens/Hrrisn 15.00 40.00
PAS Payton/Allen/Sanders 50.00 120.00
RCL Roeth/Culppr/Lftwch 30.00 80.00
VBF Vick/Brady/Favre 80.00 200.00

2005 Exquisite Collection Signatures
STATED PRINT RUN 10-35
ESAB Anquan Boldin 15.00 40.00
ESAG Ahman Green 12.00 30.00
ESAL Marcus Allen 30.00 80.00
ESAN Antonio Gates 25.00 60.00
ESAR Aaron Rodgers 350.00 600.00
ESAS Alex Smith QB 75.00 150.00
ESBF Brett Favre 150.00 300.00
ESBJ Bo Jackson 75.00 150.00
ESBK Bernie Kosar 20.00 50.00
ESBL Byron Leftwich 15.00 40.00
ESBR Ben Roethlisberger 60.00 120.00
ESBS Barry Sanders 100.00 200.00
ESCB Cedric Benson 12.00 30.00
ESCF Charlie Frye 12.00 30.00
ESCJ Chad Johnson 15.00 40.00
ESCP Carson Palmer 20.00 50.00
ESCW Cadillac Williams 12.00 30.00
ESDB Drew Bledsoe 20.00 50.00
ESDE Deuce McAllister 20.00 50.00
ESDM1 Dan Marino Home 75.00 150.00
ESDM2 Dan Marino Away 75.00 150.00
ESDS Deion Sanders 40.00 80.00
ESEC Earl Campbell 40.00 80.00
ESEJ Edgerrin James 12.00 30.00
ESEM Eli Manning 75.00 150.00
ESFT Fran Tarkenton 25.00 60.00
ESGS Gale Sayers 30.00 80.00
ESJA J.J. Arrington 15.00 40.00
ESJC Jason Campbell 12.00 30.00
ESJE John Elway 60.00 120.00
ESJJ Julius Jones 15.00 40.00
ESJK Jim Kelly 30.00 80.00
ESJL James Lofton 15.00 40.00
ESJM Joe Montana 100.00 200.00
ESJP J.P. Losman 15.00 40.00
ESJT Joe Theismann 25.00 60.00
ESKO Kyle Orton 12.00 30.00
ESLE Lee Evans 20.00 50.00
ESLJ LaMont Jordan 20.00 50.00
ESLT LaDainian Tomlinson 30.00 80.00
ESMA Maurice Clarett 12.00 30.00
ESMB Marc Bulger 15.00 40.00
ESMC Mark Clayton 12.00 30.00
ESMI Michael Clayton 15.00 40.00
ESMS Mike Singletary 30.00 80.00
ESMV Michael Vick 40.00 80.00
ESMW Mike Williams 15.00 40.00
ESNB Nate Burleson 15.00 40.00
ESPM Peyton Manning 100.00 200.00
ESRB Ronnie Brown 15.00 40.00
ESRE Reggie Wayne 20.00 50.00
ESRO Roddy White 20.00 50.00
ESRP Roscoe Parrish 12.00 30.00
ESRW Roy Williams WR/20 15.00 40.00
ESSJ Steven Jackson 15.00 40.00
ESTA Troy Aikman 50.00 120.00
ESTB Tiki Barber 20.00 50.00
ESTG Trent Green 15.00 40.00
ESTW Troy Williamson 12.00 30.00

2005 Exquisite Collection Signature Numbers
#'d UNDER 20 NOT PRICED DUE TO SCARCITY
SNBJ Bo Jackson/34 75.00 150.00
SNBS Barry Sanders/20 125.00 250.00
SNDS Deion Sanders/21 50.00 100.00
SNJJ Julius Jones/21
SNMA Marcus Allen/32 40.00 80.00
SNTD Tony Dorsett/33 60.00 100.00

2005 Exquisite Collection Signature Duals
STATED PRINT RUN 25 SER.#'d SETS
AC J.Arrington/M.Clarett 20.00 50.00
AH H.Adderley/P.Hornung 60.00 120.00
BJ M.Bulger/S.Jackson 25.00 60.00
BW R.Brown/C.Williams 40.00 100.00
DJ T.Dorsett/J.Jones 60.00 120.00
EA J.Elway/T.Aikman 125.00 250.00
EK J.Elway/B.Kosar 75.00 150.00
FM B.Favre/P.Manning 300.00 450.00
JS B.Jackson/D.Sanders 125.00 200.00
MM J.Montana/D.Marino 200.00 400.00
MS J.Montana/A.Smith QB 150.00 300.00
PJ C.Palmer/C.Johnson 25.00 60.00
RL Roethlis./Losman 75.00 150.00
SB G.Sayers/C.Benson 50.00 100.00
SR B.Sanders/R.Brown 100.00 200.00
TC J.Theismann/J.Campbell 20.00 50.00
TJ L.Tomlinson/E.James 40.00 100.00
WC R.White/M.Clayton 25.00 60.00
WE T.Williamson/B.Edwards 25.00 60.00
WW M.Williams/R.Williams WR 25.00 60.00

2005 Exquisite Collection Super Jersey Silver
STATED PRINT RUN 50 SER.#'d SETS
*GOLD/25: .5X TO 1.2X SILVER/50
SJAB Anquan Boldin 8.00 20.00
SJAG Ahman Green 10.00 25.00
SJAJ Adam Jones 6.00 15.00
SJAL Marcus Allen 12.00 30.00
SJAN Antonio Gates 12.00 30.00
SJAR Aaron Rodgers 50.00 100.00
SJAS Alex Smith QB 15.00 40.00
SJAW Andrew Walter 6.00 15.00
SJBD Brian Dawkins 12.00 30.00
SJBE Braylon Edwards 6.00 15.00
SJBF Brett Favre 20.00 50.00
SJBJ Bo Jackson 20.00 50.00
SJBK Bernie Kosar 10.00 25.00
SJBL Byron Leftwich 8.00 20.00
SJBN Reggie Brown 8.00 20.00
SJBR Ben Roethlisberger 15.00 40.00
SJBS Barry Sanders 20.00 50.00
SJCA Carlos Rogers 10.00 25.00
SJCB Cedric Benson 6.00 15.00
SJCF Charlie Frye 6.00 15.00
SJCJ Chad Johnson 8.00 20.00
SJCP Carson Palmer 10.00 25.00
SJCR Courtney Roby 6.00 15.00
SJCW Cadillac Williams 6.00 15.00
SJDB Drew Bledsoe 10.00 25.00
SJDD Domanick Davis 8.00 20.00
SJDE Deuce McAllister 10.00 25.00
SJDM1 Dan Marino Home 25.00 60.00
SJDM2 Dan Marino Away 15.00 40.00
SJDO Donovan McNabb 10.00 25.00
SJDR Drew Bennett 10.00 25.00
SJDS Deion Sanders 10.00 25.00
SJEC Earl Campbell 12.00 30.00
SJEJ Edgerrin James 10.00 25.00
SJEM Eli Manning 20.00 50.00
SJES Eric Shelton 6.00 15.00
SJFG Frank Gore 12.00 30.00
SJFT Fran Tarkenton 12.00 30.00
SJJA J.J. Arrington 8.00 20.00
SJJC Jason Campbell 6.00 15.00
SJJE John Elway 20.00 50.00
SJJH Joe Horn 8.00 20.00
SJJJ Julius Jones 8.00 20.00
SJJK Jim Kelly 12.00 30.00
SJJM Joe Montana 40.00 100.00
SJJP J.P. Losman 8.00 20.00
SJJT Joe Theismann 12.00 30.00
SJKC Keary Colbert 8.00 20.00
SJKO Kyle Orton 6.00 15.00
SJLE Lee Evans 10.00 25.00
SJLJ LaMont Jordan 10.00 25.00
SJLT LaDainian Tomlinson 12.00 30.00
SJMA Maurice Clarett 6.00 15.00
SJMB Marc Bulger 8.00 20.00
SJMC Mark Clayton 6.00 15.00
SJMJ Matt Jones 6.00 15.00
SJMK Mark Bradley 8.00 20.00
SJMM Muhsin Muhammad 8.00 20.00
SJMV Michael Vick 10.00 25.00
SJMW Mike Williams 8.00 20.00
SJNB Nate Burleson 8.00 20.00
SJPM Peyton Manning 30.00 80.00
SJRB Ronnie Brown 8.00 20.00
SJRE Reggie Wayne 10.00 25.00
SJRM Ryan Moats 6.00 15.00
SJRO Roddy White 10.00 25.00
SJRP Roscoe Parrish 6.00 15.00
SJRW Roy Williams WR 8.00 20.00
SJSA Shaun Alexander 8.00 20.00
SJSF Stefan LeFors 8.00 20.00
SJSJ Steven Jackson 8.00 20.00
SJTA Troy Aikman 15.00 40.00
SJTB Tiki Barber 10.00 25.00
SJTG Trent Green 8.00 20.00
SJTM Terrence Murphy 8.00 20.00
SJTW Troy Williamson 6.00 15.00
SJVJ Vincent Jackson 10.00 25.00
SJWM Willis McGahee 8.00 20.00

2005 Exquisite Collection Super Patch
STATED PRINT RUN 15 SER.#'d SETS
SUAB Anquan Boldin 20.00 50.00
SUAG Antonio Gates 30.00 80.00
SUBF Brett Favre 60.00 150.00
SUBK Bernie Kosar 25.00 60.00
SUBL Byron Leftwich 20.00 50.00
SUBO Bo Jackson 40.00 100.00
SUBR Ben Roethlisberger 50.00 125.00
SUBS Barry Sanders 50.00 120.00
SUCJ Chad Johnson 20.00 50.00
SUCP Carson Palmer 25.00 60.00
SUDB Drew Bledsoe 25.00 60.00
SUDD Domanick Davis 20.00 50.00
SUDE Deuce McAllister 25.00 60.00
SUDM Dan Marino 60.00 150.00
SUDO Donovan McNabb 25.00 60.00
SUDS Deion Sanders 25.00 60.00
SUEJ Edgerrin James 25.00 60.00
SUEM Eli Manning 50.00 125.00
SUJE John Elway 50.00 125.00
SUJJ Julius Jones 20.00 50.00
SUJM Joe Montana 100.00 250.00
SUJT Joe Theismann 30.00 80.00
SULE Lee Evans 25.00 60.00
SULT LaDainian Tomlinson 30.00 80.00
SUMA Marcus Allen 30.00 80.00
SUMB Marc Bulger 20.00 50.00
SUMC Michael Clayton 20.00 50.00
SUMS Mike Singletary 30.00 80.00
SUMV Michael Vick 25.00 60.00
SUNB Nate Burleson 20.00 50.00
SUPM Peyton Manning 80.00 200.00
SURO Roy Williams WR 20.00 50.00
SURS Roger Staubach 40.00 100.00
SURW Reggie Wayne 25.00 60.00
SUSJ Steven Jackson 20.00 50.00
SUTA Troy Aikman 40.00 100.00
SUTB Tiki Barber 20.00 50.00
SUTD Tony Dorsett 30.00 80.00
SUTG Trent Green 20.00 50.00
SUWP Walter Payton 80.00 200.00

2006 Exquisite Collection

This 135-card set was released in January, 2007. The set was issued into the hobby in six-card packs (actually a box) which had a $600 SRP. Cards numbered 1-60 are veterans in team alphabetical order while cards numbered 61-135 are 2006 rookies. The veteran players were all issued to a stated print run of 150 serial numbered sets while the rookies are all signed by the featured players and cards numbered 103-135 also feature player-worn swatches. Cards numbered 61-102 were also issued to a stated print run of 150 serial numbered sets while cards numbered 103-108 and 135 were issued to a stated print run of 99 serial numbered sets. Cards numbered 109-133 were issued to a stated print run of 225 serial numbered sets. Cards number 134, Jay Cutler, was issued to a stated print run of 20 serial numbered sets and is the key card to completing this set. A few players did not return their signatures in time for pack out and those signatures could be redeemed until January 9, 2010.

1-102 PRINT RUN 150
103-108/135 JSY AU PRINT RUN 99
109-133 JSY AU PRINT RUN 225
1 Larry Fitzgerald 8.00 20.00
2 Edgerrin James 8.00 20.00
3 Michael Vick 8.00 20.00
4 Warrick Dunn 6.00 15.00
5 Steve McNair 8.00 20.00
6 Jamal Lewis 8.00 20.00
7 J.P. Losman 8.00 20.00
8 Willis McGahee 6.00 15.00
9 Jake Delhomme 6.00 15.00
10 Steve Smith 10.00 25.00
11 Rex Grossman 6.00 15.00
12 Thomas Jones 6.00 15.00
13 Carson Palmer 8.00 20.00
14 Chad Johnson 8.00 20.00
15 Charlie Frye 6.00 15.00
16 Julius Jones 6.00 15.00
17 Terrell Owens 8.00 20.00
18 Jake Plummer 6.00 15.00
19 Tatum Bell 6.00 15.00
20 Kevin Jones 6.00 15.00
21 Roy Williams WR 6.00 15.00
22 Brett Favre 20.00 50.00
23 Ahman Green 8.00 20.00
24 David Carr 6.00 15.00
25 Andre Johnson 8.00 20.00
26 Peyton Manning 25.00 50.00
27 Marvin Harrison 8.00 20.00
28 Byron Leftwich 6.00 15.00
29 Fred Taylor 6.00 15.00
30 Trent Green 6.00 15.00
31 Larry Johnson 8.00 20.00
32 Daunte Culpepper 8.00 20.00
33 Ronnie Brown 8.00 20.00
34 Chester Taylor 6.00 15.00
35 Tom Brady 15.00 40.00
36 Corey Dillon 6.00 15.00
37 Drew Brees 12.00 30.00
38 Deuce McAllister 8.00 20.00
39 Eli Manning 8.00 20.00
40 Tiki Barber 8.00 20.00
41 Chad Pennington 6.00 15.00
42 Laveranues Coles 6.00 15.00
43 Randy Moss 8.00 20.00
44 LaMont Jordan 8.00 20.00
45 Donovan McNabb 8.00 20.00
46 Brian Westbrook 6.00 15.00
47 Ben Roethlisberger 12.00 30.00
48 Willie Parker 8.00 20.00
49 Philip Rivers 10.00 25.00
50 LaDainian Tomlinson 10.00 25.00
51 Alex Smith QB 6.00 15.00
52 Frank Gore 8.00 20.00
53 Matt Hasselbeck 6.00 15.00
54 Shaun Alexander 6.00 15.00
55 Marc Bulger 6.00 15.00
56 Steven Jackson 8.00 20.00
57 Cadillac Williams 8.00 20.00
58 Drew Bennett 6.00 15.00
59 Clinton Portis 8.00 20.00
60 Santana Moss 8.00 20.00
61 Andre Hall AU RC 6.00 15.00
62 Anthony Fasano AU RC 8.00 20.00
63 Antonio Cromartie AU RC 8.00 20.00
64 Derek Hagan AU RC 6.00 15.00
65 Brad Smith AU RC 8.00 20.00
66 Brodrick Bunkley AU RC 8.00 20.00
67 Bruce Gradkowski AU RC 8.00 20.00
68 Chad Greenway AU RC 10.00 25.00
69 Cory Rodgers AU RC 6.00 15.00
70 D.J. Shockley AU RC 8.00 20.00
71 Darrell Bing AU RC 8.00 20.00
72 Darrell Hackney AU RC 6.00 15.00
73 D.Ferguson AU RC 8.00 20.00
74 Dominique Byrd AU RC 6.00 15.00
75 Drew Olson AU RC 6.00 15.00
76 Ernie Sims AU RC 6.00 15.00
77 Garrett Mills AU RC 8.00 20.00
78 Gerald Riggs AU RC 6.00 15.00
79 Greg Jennings AU RC 10.00 25.00
80 Greg Lee AU RC 6.00 15.00
81 Ingle Martin AU RC 6.00 15.00
82 Jason Allen AU RC 6.00 15.00
83 Jerome Harrison AU RC 6.00 15.00
84 Jimmy Williams AU RC 6.00 15.00
85 Joseph Addai AU RC 6.00 15.00
86 Josh Betts AU RC 8.00 20.00
87 Kelly Jennings AU RC 8.00 20.00
88 Leonard Pope AU RC 10.00 25.00
89 Marcus McNeill AU RC 6.00 15.00
90 Martin Nance AU RC 6.00 15.00
91 Mathias Kiwanuka AU RC 10.00 25.00
92 Mike Bell AU RC 6.00 15.00
93 Mike Hass AU RC 6.00 15.00
94 Owen Daniels AU RC 10.00 25.00
95 P.J. Daniels AU RC 6.00 15.00
96 Reggie McNeal AU RC 6.00 15.00
97 Skyler Green AU RC 6.00 15.00
98 Terrence Whitehead AU RC 8.00 20.00
99 Thomas Howard AU RC 6.00 15.00
100 Tye Hill AU RC 6.00 15.00
101 Will Blackmon AU RC 6.00 15.00
102 Winston Justice AU RC 8.00 20.00
103 D.Williams JSY AU/99 RC 50.00 100.00
104 Matt Leinart JSY AU/99 RC 15.00 40.00
105 R.Bush JSY AU/99 RC 60.00 125.00
106 S.Holmes JSY AU/99 RC 30.00 80.00
107 Sin.Moss JSY AU/99 RC 25.00 60.00
108 V.Young JSY AU/99 RC 25.00 60.00
109 A.J. Hawk JSY AU RC 12.00 30.00
110 B.Marshall JSY AU RC 20.00 50.00
111 Brandon Williams JSY AU RC 8.00 20.00
112 Brian Calhoun JSY AU RC 8.00 20.00
113 Chad Jackson JSY AU RC 8.00 20.00
114 C.Whitehurst JSY AU RC 12.00 30.00
115 Dem.Williams JSY AU RC 8.00 20.00
116 Derek Hagan JSY AU RC 8.00 20.00
117 Jason Avant JSY AU RC 8.00 20.00
118 J.Norwood JSY AU RC 8.00 20.00
119 Joe Klopfenstein JSY AU RC 8.00 20.00
120 Kellen Clemens JSY AU RC 8.00 20.00
121 L.Maroney JSY AU RC 8.00 20.00
122 LenDale White JSY AU RC 8.00 20.00
123 L.Washington JSY AU RC 8.00 20.00
124 Marcedes Lewis JSY AU RC 8.00 20.00
125 Mario Williams JSY AU RC 15.00 40.00
126 Maurice Drew JSY AU RC 25.00 60.00
127 Maurice Stovall JSY AU RC 8.00 20.00
128 Michael Huff JSY AU RC 10.00 25.00
129 M.Robinson JSY AU RC 8.00 20.00
130 Omar Jacobs JSY AU RC 8.00 20.00
131 Tarv.Jackson JSY AU RC 8.00 20.00
132 Travis Wilson JSY AU RC 8.00 20.00
133 Vernon Davis JSY AU RC 10.00 25.00
134 Jay Cutler JSY AU/20 RC 250.00 500.00
135 M.Colston JSY AU/99 RC 75.00 150.00

2006 Exquisite Collection Gold

UNPRICED VETERAN 1-60 PRINT RUN 1
*ROOKIE AU 61-102: .5X TO 1.2X BASIC CARDS
*ROOK JSY AU/99 109-133: .5X TO 1.2X
ROOKIE PRINT RUN 60 SER.#'d SETS
105 Reggie Bush JSY AU/25 100.00 200.00
126 Maurice Drew JSY AU/99 40.00 100.00
133 Vernon Davis JSY AU/99 20.00 50.00

2006 Exquisite Collection Debut Signatures

STATED PRINT RUN 35 SER.#'d SETS
EDSAH A.J. Hawk 10.00 25.00
EDSCJ Chad Jackson 8.00 20.00
EDSDH Derek Hagan 10.00 25.00
EDSDW DeAngelo Williams 10.00 25.00
EDSJC Jay Cutler 10.00 25.00
EDSKC Kellen Clemens 8.00 20.00
EDSLE Marcedes Lewis 8.00 20.00
EDSLM Laurence Maroney 8.00 20.00
EDSLW LenDale White 8.00 20.00
EDSMD Maurice Drew 12.00 30.00
EDSMH Michael Huff 10.00 25.00
EDSML Matt Leinart 8.00 20.00
EDSMS Maurice Stovall 8.00 20.00
EDMW Mario Williams 12.00 30.00
EDSRB Reggie Bush 10.00 25.00
EDSSH Santonio Holmes 10.00 25.00
EDSSM Sinorice Moss 8.00 20.00
EDSTJ Tarvaris Jackson 8.00 20.00
EDSVD Vernon Davis 10.00 25.00
EDSVY Vince Young 8.00 20.00

2006 Exquisite Collection Endorsements

STATED PRINT RUN 35 SER.#'d SETS
UNPRICED HOLOFOIL PRINT RUN 1
EEAC Alge Crumpler
EEAD Joseph Addai 10.00 25.00
EEAG Antonio Gates 15.00 40.00
EEAH A.J. Hawk 12.00 30.00
EEBA Ronde Barber 10.00 25.00
EEBC Brian Calhoun 10.00 25.00
EEBE Braylon Edwards 10.00 25.00
EEBF Brett Favre 125.00 250.00
EEBG Bob Griese 25.00 60.00
EEBM Brandon Marshall 20.00 50.00
EEBR Ben Roethlisberger 75.00 135.00
EECB Cedric Benson 10.00 25.00
EECF Charlie Frye 12.00 30.00
EECJ Chad Jackson 10.00 25.00
EECS Chris Simms 10.00 25.00
EEDB Drew Bledsoe 12.00 30.00
EEDC Dwight Clark 12.00 30.00
EEDF D'Brickashaw Ferguson 10.00 25.00
EEDH Derek Hagan 12.00 30.00
EEDM Dan Marino 100.00 200.00
EEDW DeAngelo Williams
EEEM Eli Manning 60.00 100.00
EEFO DeShaun Foster 12.00 30.00
EEFT Fran Tarkenton 25.00 60.00
EEGS Gale Sayers 50.00 100.00
EEJA Jason Avant 10.00 25.00
EEJC Jay Cutler 75.00 150.00
EEJK Jim Kelly/30 40.00 100.00
EEJO LaMont Jordan 12.00 30.00
EEJT Joe Theismann 30.00 60.00
EEJW Jason Witten 25.00 60.00
EEKC Kellen Clemens 10.00 25.00
EEKJ Keyshawn Johnson 12.00 30.00
EELD Len Dawson 15.00 40.00
EELE Matt Leinart 30.00 60.00
EELG L.C. Greenwood 25.00 50.00
EELJ Larry Johnson 10.00 25.00
EELM Laurence Maroney 10.00 25.00
EELT Lofa Tatupu 10.00 25.00
EELW LenDale White 10.00 25.00
EEMB Marc Bulger 10.00 25.00
EEMC Michael Clayton 10.00 25.00
EEMD Maurice Drew 50.00 100.00
EEMH Michael Huff 12.00 30.00
EEML Marcedes Lewis 10.00 25.00
EEMM Muhsin Muhammad 10.00 25.00
EEMR Michael Robinson 10.00 25.00
EEMS Maurice Stovall 10.00 25.00
EEMW Mario Williams 15.00 40.00
EEOJ Omar Jacobs 10.00 25.00
EEPH Paul Hornung 30.00 60.00
EEPM Peyton Manning 100.00 200.00
EEPR Philip Rivers 30.00 60.00
EERB Reggie Bush 20.00 50.00
EERO Ronnie Brown 12.00 30.00
EERW Reggie Wayne 12.00 30.00
EETA Troy Aikman 60.00 120.00
EETB Tiki Barber 20.00 50.00
EETG Trent Green 10.00 25.00
EETH T.J. Houshmandzadeh 10.00 25.00
EETJ Tarvaris Jackson 10.00 25.00
EETW Travis Wilson 10.00 25.00
EEVD Vernon Davis 12.00 30.00
EEVY Vince Young 60.00 120.00
EEWH Charlie Whitehurst 25.00 40.00
EEWP Willie Parker 12.00 30.00

2006 Exquisite Collection Inscriptions

STATED PRINT RUN 25 SER.#'d SETS
UNPRICED HOLOFOIL PRINT RUN 1
EIBF Brett Favre 125.00 250.00
EIBR Ben Roethlisberger 60.00 120.00
EIBS Barry Sanders 100.00 200.00
EICW Cadillac Williams 20.00 50.00
EIDC Dwight Clark 25.00 60.00
EIJK Jim Kelly 50.00 100.00
EIKS Ken Stabler 50.00 100.00
EILC L.C. Greenwood 20.00 50.00
EIPM Peyton Manning 125.00 250.00
EISS Steve Smith 25.00 60.00
EITA Troy Aikman 40.00 100.00
EITD Tony Dorsett 30.00 80.00
EIWP Willie Parker 25.00 60.00

2006 Exquisite Collection Legendary Signatures

STATED PRINT RUN 10-25
UNPRICED HOLOFOIL PRINT RUN 1
SERIAL #'d UNDER 25 NOT PRICED
ELSBG Bob Griese 30.00 80.00
ELSDC Dwight Clark 25.00 60.00
ELSDF Dan Fouts 25.00 60.00
ELSDM Dan Marino 175.00 300.00
ELSFH Franco Harris 50.00 120.00
ELSGS Gale Sayers 30.00 80.00
ELSJE John Elway 75.00 150.00
ELSJK Jim Kelly 40.00 100.00
ELSJT Joe Theismann 25.00 60.00
ELSKS Ken Stabler 50.00 120.00
ELSLC L.C. Greenwood 25.00 60.00
ELSLD Len Dawson 25.00 60.00
ELSPH Paul Hornung 30.00 80.00
ELSTA Troy Aikman 75.00 150.00

2006 Exquisite Collection Maximum Jersey Silver

SILVER PRINT RUN 75 SER.#'d SETS
*GOLD/35: .6X TO 1.5X SILVER/75
GOLD PRINT RUN 35 SER.#'d SETS
UNPRICED SPECTRUM PRINT RUN 1
UNPRICED SIGNATURE PRINT RUN 5
XXLAG Antonio Gates 8.00 20.00
XXLAH A.J. Hawk 5.00 12.00
XXLBA Ronde Barber 5.00 12.00
XXLBC Brian Calhoun 4.00 10.00
XXLBE Braylon Edwards 5.00 12.00
XXLBF Brett Favre 15.00 40.00
XXLBM Brandon Marshall 8.00 20.00
XXLBR Ben Roethlisberger 10.00 25.00
XXLBU Reggie Bush 6.00 15.00
XXLBW Brandon Williams 4.00 10.00
XXLCB Cedric Benson 4.00 10.00
XXLCF Charlie Frye 6.00 15.00
XXLCJ Chad Jackson 4.00 10.00
XXLCL Mark Clayton 5.00 12.00
XXLCP Carson Palmer 6.00 15.00
XXLCS Chris Simms 5.00 12.00
XXLCU Kevin Curtis 6.00 15.00
XXLCW Cadillac Williams 6.00 15.00
XXLDB Drew Bledsoe 6.00 15.00
XXLDE Demetrius Williams 4.00 10.00
XXLDF DeShaun Foster 6.00 15.00
XXLDG David Givens 6.00 15.00
XXLDH Derek Hagan 5.00 12.00
XXLDM Derrick Mason 5.00 12.00
XXLDO Donovan McNabb 6.00 15.00
XXLDW DeAngelo Williams 6.00 15.00
XXLEM Eli Manning 6.00 15.00
XXLGJ Greg Jones 5.00 12.00
XXLHA Matt Hasselbeck 5.00 12.00
XXLHO T.J. Houshmandzadeh 5.00 12.00
XXLJA Jason Avant 4.00 10.00
XXLJC Jay Cutler 5.00 12.00
XXLJJ Julius Jones 5.00 12.00
XXLJK Joe Klopfenstein 4.00 10.00
XXLJN Jerious Norwood 4.00 10.00
XXLJO LaMont Jordan 6.00 15.00
XXLJW Jason Witten 6.00 15.00
XXLKC Kellen Clemens 4.00 10.00
XXLKJ Keyshawn Johnson 6.00 15.00
XXLKO Kyle Orton 6.00 15.00
XXLLE Byron Leftwich 6.00 15.00
XXLLJ Larry Johnson 5.00 12.00
XXLLM Laurence Maroney 4.00 10.00
XXLLT LaDainian Tomlinson 8.00 20.00
XXLLW LenDale White 8.00 20.00
XXLMA Matt Leinart 4.00 10.00
XXLMB Marc Bulger 6.00 15.00
XXLMC Deuce McAllister 6.00 15.00
XXLMD Maurice Drew 6.00 15.00
XXLMH Michael Huff 5.00 12.00
XXLMI Michael Clayton 5.00 12.00
XXLML Marcedes Lewis 4.00 10.00
XXLMM Muhsin Muhammad 6.00 15.00
XXLMR Michael Robinson 4.00 10.00
XXLMS Maurice Stovall 4.00 10.00
XXLMV Michael Vick 6.00 15.00
XXLMW Mario Williams 6.00 15.00
XXLNB Nate Burleson 5.00 12.00
XXLOJ Omar Jacobs 4.00 10.00
XXLPM Peyton Manning 20.00 50.00
XXLPR Philip Rivers 6.00 15.00
XXLRB Reggie Brown 5.00 12.00
XXLRJ Rudi Johnson 5.00 12.00
XXLRM Randy Moss 6.00 15.00
XXLRO Ronnie Brown 6.00 15.00
XXLRW Reggie Wayne 6.00 15.00
XXLSA Shaun Alexander 6.00 15.00
XXLSH Santonio Holmes 6.00 15.00
XXLSM Sinorice Moss 4.00 10.00
XXLSS Steve Smith 6.00 15.00
XXLTB Tedy Bruschi 6.00 15.00
XXLTG Trent Green 5.00 12.00
XXLTH Thomas Jones 5.00 12.00
XXLTI Tiki Barber 6.00 15.00
XXLTJ Tarvaris Jackson 4.00 10.00
XXLTO Tom Brady 25.00 60.00
XXLTW Travis Wilson 4.00 10.00
XXLVD Vernon Davis 5.00 12.00
XXLVY Vince Young 4.00 10.00
XXLWA Leon Washington 6.00 15.00
XXLWH Charlie Whitehurst 4.00 10.00
XXLWI Mike Williams 5.00 12.00
XXLWP Willie Parker 6.00 15.00

2006 Exquisite Collection Maximum Patch

STATED PRINT RUN 30 SER.#'d SETS
EMPBA Tiki Barber 12.00 30.00
EMPBF Brett Favre 30.00 80.00
EMPBL Byron Leftwich 10.00 25.00
EMPBR Ben Roethlisberger 20.00 50.00
EMPCJ Chad Jackson 10.00 25.00
EMPCP Carson Palmer 12.00 30.00
EMPCW Cadillac Williams 12.00 30.00
EMPDB Drew Bledsoe 12.00 30.00
EMPDC Daunte Culpepper 12.00 30.00
EMPDM Deuce McAllister 12.00 30.00
EMPDR Drew Brees 15.00 40.00
EMPDW DeAngelo Williams 12.00 30.00
EMPEJ Edgerrin James 12.00 30.00
EMPEM Eli Manning 15.00 40.00
EMPHW Hines Ward 12.00 30.00
EMPJJ Julius Jones 10.00 25.00
EMPJO Chad Johnson 12.00 30.00
EMPJP Jake Plummer 10.00 25.00
EMPLJ Larry Johnson 10.00 25.00
EMPLM Laurence Maroney 8.00 20.00
EMPLT LaDainian Tomlinson 15.00 40.00
EMPLW LenDale White 8.00 20.00
EMPMB Marc Bulger 10.00 25.00
EMPMC Donovan McNabb 12.00 30.00
EMPMH Marvin Harrison 12.00 30.00
EMPML Matt Leinart 8.00 20.00
EMPMV Michael Vick 12.00 30.00
EMPMW Mario Williams 12.00 30.00
EMPPM Peyton Manning 40.00 100.00
EMPPO Clinton Portis 10.00 25.00
EMPPR Philip Rivers 15.00 40.00
EMPRB Reggie Bush 12.00 30.00
EMPRJ Rudi Johnson 10.00 25.00
EMPRM Randy Moss 12.00 30.00
EMPRO Ronnie Brown 12.00 30.00
EMPSA Shaun Alexander 12.00 30.00
EMPSH Santonio Holmes 12.00 30.00
EMPTB Tom Brady 50.00 125.00
EMPTG Trent Green 10.00 25.00
EMPTO Terrell Owens 12.00 30.00
EMPVD Vernon Davis 10.00 25.00
EMPVY Vince Young 12.00 30.00

2006 Exquisite Collection Patch Silver

SILVER PRINT RUN 50 SER.#'d SETS
*GOLD/30: .5X TO 1.2X SILVER/50
GOLD PRINT RUN 30 SER.#'d SETS
UNPRICED SPECTRUM PRINT RUN 1
UNPRICED PATCH TRIO PRINT RUN 20
UNPRICED PATCH QUAD PRINT RUN 15
EPAB Anquan Boldin 6.00 15.00
EPAC Alge Crumpler 6.00 15.00
EPAG Ahman Green 6.00 15.00
EPAH A.J. Hawk 6.00 15.00
EPAR Antwaan Randle El 6.00 15.00
EPAS Alex Smith QB 6.00 15.00
EPBD Brian Dawkins 10.00 25.00
EPBE Braylon Edwards 6.00 15.00
EPBF Brett Favre 20.00 50.00
EPBL Byron Leftwich 6.00 15.00
EPBR Ben Roethlisberger 15.00 40.00
EPBS Barry Sanders 10.00 25.00
EPBU Brian Urlacher 10.00 25.00
EPBW Brian Westbrook 6.00 15.00
EPCC Chris Chambers 6.00 15.00
EPCF Charlie Frye 6.00 15.00
EPCJ Chad Johnson 6.00 15.00
EPCM Curtis Martin 8.00 20.00
EPCP Clinton Portis 6.00 15.00
EPCW Cadillac Williams 6.00 15.00
EPDB Drew Bledsoe 6.00 15.00
EPDC Daunte Culpepper 6.00 15.00
EPDF DeShaun Foster 6.00 15.00
EPDM Deuce McAllister 6.00 15.00
EPDR Drew Brees 10.00 25.00
EPDW DeAngelo Williams 6.00 15.00
EPEJ Edgerrin James 6.00 15.00
EPEM Eli Manning 8.00 20.00
EPER Ed Reed 8.00 20.00
EPFL Doug Flutie 12.00 30.00
EPFT Fred Taylor 6.00 15.00
EPGA Antonio Gates 10.00 25.00
EPGO Tony Gonzalez 8.00 20.00
EPHA Matt Hasselbeck 6.00 15.00
EPHO Torry Holt 8.00 20.00
EPIB Isaac Bruce 10.00 25.00
EPJA Chad Jackson 6.00 15.00
EPJE John Elway 20.00 50.00
EPJI Jim Plunkett 12.00 30.00
EPJJ Julius Jones 6.00 15.00
EPJK Jim Kelly 15.00 40.00
EPJL Jamal Lewis 8.00 20.00
EPJM Joe Montana 50.00 120.00
EPJO LaMont Jordan 8.00 20.00
EPJP Julius Peppers 8.00 20.00
EPJS Jeremy Shockey 6.00 15.00
EPJW Javon Walker 8.00 20.00
EPKJ Kevin Jones 6.00 15.00
EPKW Kurt Warner 8.00 20.00
EPLA LaVar Arrington 6.00 15.00
EPLJ Larry Johnson 6.00 15.00
EPLM Laurence Maroney 6.00 15.00
EPLT LaDainian Tomlinson 10.00 25.00
EPLW LenDale White 5.00 12.00
EPMA Dan Marino 30.00 80.00
EPMB Marc Bulger 6.00 15.00
EPMC Donovan McNabb 8.00 20.00
EPMF Marshall Faulk 8.00 20.00
EPMH Marvin Harrison 8.00 20.00
EPML Matt Leinart 5.00 12.00
EPMM Muhsin Muhammad 6.00 15.00
EPMO Sinorice Moss 6.00 15.00
EPMS Michael Strahan 8.00 20.00
EPMV Michael Vick 8.00 20.00
EPMW Mario Williams 8.00 20.00
EPOW Terrell Owens 8.00 20.00
EPPA Carson Palmer 8.00 20.00
EPPB Plaxico Burress 6.00 15.00
EPPL Jake Plummer 6.00 15.00
EPPM Peyton Manning 25.00 60.00
EPPR Philip Rivers 10.00 25.00
EPRB Reggie Bush 8.00 20.00
EPRJ Rudi Johnson 6.00 15.00
EPRL Ray Lewis 10.00 25.00
EPRM Randy Moss 8.00 20.00
EPRO Ronnie Brown 8.00 20.00
EPRW Roy Williams WR 6.00 15.00
EPSA Shaun Alexander 6.00 15.00
EPSH Santonio Holmes 6.00 15.00
EPSJ Steven Jackson 6.00 15.00
EPSM Steve McNair 6.00 15.00
EPSS Steve Smith 10.00 25.00
EPTA Tatum Bell 6.00 15.00
EPTB Tiki Barber 8.00 20.00
EPTD Tony Dorsett 15.00 40.00
EPTG Trent Green 6.00 15.00
EPTH T.J. Houshmandzadeh 6.00 15.00
EPTJ Thomas Jones 6.00 15.00
EPTO Tom Brady 30.00 80.00
EPTP Troy Polamalu 10.00 25.00
EPVD Vernon Davis 8.00 20.00
EPVY Vince Young 5.00 12.00
EPWA Reggie Wayne 8.00 20.00
EPWM Willis McGahee 6.00 15.00
EPWP Willie Parker 8.00 20.00

2006 Exquisite Collection Patch Combos

STATED PRINT RUN 25 SER.#'d SETS
AW J.Avant/B.Westbrook 10.00 25.00
BM R.Bush/D.McAllister 10.00 25.00
CS M.Clayton/M.Stovall 6.00 15.00
CW B.Calhoun/M.Williams 10.00 25.00
DH B.Dawkins/M.Huff 15.00 40.00
DW V.Davis/B.Williams 8.00 20.00
FJ M.Faulk/S.Jackson 12.00 30.00
HC D.Hagan/C.Chambers 12.00 30.00
JH O.Jacobs/S.Holmes 8.00 20.00
JL E.James/M.Leinart 8.00 20.00
JM C.Jackson/L.Maroney 8.00 20.00
JT L.Johnson/L.Tomlinson 15.00 40.00
JW T.Jackson/Whitehurst 6.00 15.00
LD M.Lewis/M.Drew 10.00 25.00
MB E.Manning/T.Barber 12.00 30.00
MF P.Manning/B.Favre 60.00 120.00
MW McNabb/Westbrook 12.00 30.00
NW Norwood/Washington 6.00 15.00
PJ C.Palmer/C.Johnson 12.00 30.00
PM C.Pennington/C.Martin 12.00 30.00
PW J.Peppers/M.Williams 10.00 25.00
RH Roethlisberger/Holmes 20.00 50.00
RW P.Rivers/C.Whitehurst 15.00 40.00
SR A.Smith/M.Robinson 12.00 30.00
TB T.Bell/B.Marshall 20.00 50.00
VY M.Vick/V.Young 8.00 20.00
WH M.Williams/A.Hawk 10.00 25.00
WW T.Wilson/D.Williams 6.00 15.00

2006 Exquisite Collection Patch Quads

ATJW Alexander/Tomlinson 15.00 40.00
Johnson/Williams
BDMJ Brdy/Dill/Mrny/Jckson 40.00 80.00
FVYL Fvre/Vick/Yng/Leinart 30.00 80.00
FWSP Fostr/Wllms/Smth/Pprs 15.00 40.00
GCDK Gats/Crmplr/Davis/Klopf 15.00 40.00
JHCK Jackson/Holt/Curtis/Klopfenstein 12.00 30.00
LJDL Lftwch/Jnes/Drw/Luis 10.00 25.00
MBMS Eli/Brbr/Moss/Shckey 12.00 30.00
MBPR P.Mnn/Brdy/Plmr/Roeth 50.00 120.00
MLLR McNr/Lwis/R.Lwis/Reed 15.00 40.00
MWBA McNabb/Westbrook/Brown/Avant 12.00 30.00
RPHJ Roeth/Prkr/Hlmes/Jacbs 20.00 50.00
WNCW White/Norwood/Calhoun/Washington 10.00 25.00
YLCJ Young/Leinart/Clemens/Jackson 10.00 25.00
YWGB Young/White/Givens/Bennett 12.00 30.00

2006 Exquisite Collection Patch Trios

STATED PRINT RUN 20 SER.#'d SETS
BLW Bush/Leinart/White 10.00 25.00
BMJ Brady/Maroney/Jackson 30.00 80.00
DWR Davis/Williams/Robinson 8.00 20.00
FBM Favre/Brady/Manning 40.00 100.00
FEW Frye/Edwards/Williams 8.00 20.00
FPW Foster/Peppers/Williams 8.00 20.00
GJG Green/Johnson/Gonzalez 12.00 30.00
JHK Jackson/Holt/Klopfenstein 12.00 30.00
MKS Marino/Kelly/Staubach 40.00 100.00
MLW McNair/Lewis/Williams 12.00 30.00
MMS Manning/Moss/Shockey 12.00 30.00
MWB McNabb/Westbrk/Brown 12.00 30.00
RHW Roeth/Holmes/Ward 20.00 50.00
STB Sanders/Tomlinson/Bush 15.00 40.00
WHH Williams/Hawk/Huff 10.00 25.00

2006 Exquisite Collection Signature Duals

DUAL SIGNATURE PRINT RUN 20
BB T.Barber/R.Barber 12.00 30.00
BJ D.Bledsoe/J.Jones
BW R.Bush/L.White 15.00 40.00
CC M.Clayton/M.Clayton 10.00 25.00
CD D.Clark/V.Davis 12.00 30.00
CW Clemens/Washington 10.00 25.00
EC J.Elway/J.Cutler 60.00 125.00
FE C.Frye/B.Edwards 12.00 30.00
HW D.Hagan/D.Williams 12.00 30.00
JR O.Jacobs/W.Reid 10.00 25.00
LD M.Lewis/M.Drew 25.00 60.00
MJ L.Maroney/J.Addai 10.00 25.00
RW P.Rivers/M.Williams
SB G.Sayers/C.Benson 25.00 50.00
SL K.Stabler/M.Leinart 40.00 80.00
TH L.Tatupu/A.Hawk 15.00 40.00
TW L.Tomlinson/D.Williams 40.00 80.00
WM R.Wayne/S.Moss 12.00 30.00
WR B.Williams/M.Robinson 10.00 25.00
YH V.Young/M.Huff 12.00 30.00

2006 Exquisite Collection Signature Numbers

STATED PRINT RUN 10-90 SER.#'d SETS
UNPRICED DUAL SIG PRINT RUN 20
UNPRICED QUAD SIG PRINT RUN 10
UNPRICED QUAD SIG LOGO PRINT RUN 10
UNPRICED TRIO SIG PRINT RUN 15
SERIAL #'d UNDER 25 NOT PRICED
ESNAG Antonio Gates/85 15.00 40.00
ESNAH A.J. Hawk/50 25.00 60.00
ESNBA Tiki Barber/21 20.00 50.00
ESNBC Brian Calhoun/29 15.00 40.00
ESNBR Ronnie Brown/23 20.00 50.00
ESNBS Barry Sanders/20 125.00 250.00
ESNCW Cadillac Williams/24 15.00 40.00
ESNDH Derek Hagan/82 12.00 30.00
ESNDW DeAngelo Williams/34 30.00 80.00
ESNGS Gale Sayers/40 60.00 100.00
ESNJA Jason Avant/81 10.00 25.00
ESNJJ Julius Jones/21 15.00 40.00
ESNJN Jerious Norwood/32 15.00 40.00
ESNJO LaMont Jordan/34 15.00 40.00
ESNKJ Keyshawn Johnson/19 12.00 30.00
ESNLJ Larry Johnson/27 15.00 40.00
ESNLM Laurence Maroney/39 10.00 25.00
ESNLW LenDale White/25 12.00 30.00
ESNMD Maurice Drew/32 30.00 80.00
ESNMH Michael Huff/24 15.00 40.00
ESNML Marcedes Lewis/89 10.00 25.00
ESNMR Michael Robinson/35 15.00 40.00
ESNMS Maurice Stovall/85 10.00 25.00
ESNMW Mario Williams/90 15.00 40.00
ESNRB Reggie Bush/25 20.00 50.00
ESNSM Sinorice Moss/83 10.00 25.00
ESNTW Travis Wilson/81 10.00 25.00
ESNVD Vernon Davis/85 12.00 30.00
ESNWA Leon Washington/29 15.00 40.00
ESNWI Demetrius Williams/87 10.00 25.00
ESNWP Willie Parker/39 15.00 40.00

2006 Exquisite Collection Signature Swatches

STATED PRINT RUN 25 SER.#'d SETS
UNPRICED SIG PATCH PRINT RUN 10
ESSAG Antonio Gates 20.00 50.00
ESSAH A.J. Hawk 15.00 40.00
ESSBA Tiki Barber 15.00 40.00
ESSBC Brian Calhoun 12.00 30.00
ESSBE Braylon Edwards 12.00 30.00
ESSBF Brett Favre 125.00 250.00
ESSBL Byron Leftwich 12.00 30.00
ESSBR Ben Roethlisberger 50.00 120.00
ESSBU Reggie Bush 20.00 50.00
ESSCB Cedric Benson 12.00 30.00
ESSCF Charlie Frye 15.00 40.00
ESSCJ Chad Jackson 12.00 30.00
ESSCS Chris Simms 12.00 30.00
ESSCW Cadillac Williams 15.00 40.00
ESSDB Drew Bledsoe 15.00 40.00
ESSDF DeShaun Foster 12.00 30.00
ESSDG David Givens 12.00 30.00
ESSDH Derek Hagan 12.00 30.00
ESSDM Deuce McAllister 15.00 40.00
ESSDW DeAngelo Williams 30.00 80.00
ESSEM Eli Manning 60.00 120.00
ESSHO T.J. Houshmandzadeh 12.00 30.00
ESSJJ Julius Jones 12.00 30.00
ESSJM Joe Montana 100.00 200.00
ESSJO LaMont Jordan 15.00 40.00
ESSKC Kellen Clemens 12.00 30.00
ESSKJ Keyshawn Johnson 15.00 40.00
ESSKO Kyle Orton 15.00 40.00
ESSLE Matt Leinart 12.00 30.00
ESSLJ Larry Johnson 12.00 30.00
ESSLM Laurence Maroney 12.00 30.00
ESSLT LaDainian Tomlinson 40.00 100.00
ESSLW LenDale White 15.00 40.00
ESSMB Marc Bulger 12.00 30.00
ESSMC Michael Clayton 12.00 30.00
ESSMD Maurice Drew 25.00 60.00
ESSMH Michael Huff 12.00 30.00
ESSML Marcedes Lewis 12.00 30.00
ESSMM Muhsin Muhammad 12.00 30.00
ESSMS Maurice Stovall 12.00 30.00
ESSMV Michael Vick 30.00 80.00
ESSMW Mario Williams 20.00 50.00
ESSPM Peyton Manning 100.00 200.00
ESSPR Philip Rivers 30.00 80.00
ESSRB Reggie Brown 12.00 30.00
ESSRJ Rudi Johnson 12.00 30.00
ESSRO Ronnie Brown 15.00 40.00
ESSRW Reggie Wayne 15.00 40.00
ESSSH Santonio Holmes 15.00 40.00
ESSSM Sinorice Moss 12.00 30.00
ESSSS Steve Smith 20.00 50.00
ESSTA Lofa Tatupu 15.00 40.00
ESSTD Tony Dorsett 30.00 80.00
ESSTG Trent Green 12.00 30.00
ESSTH Thomas Jones 12.00 30.00
ESSTJ Tarvaris Jackson 12.00 30.00
ESSVD Vernon Davis 15.00 40.00
ESSVY Vince Young 12.00 30.00
ESSWH Charlie Whitehurst 12.00 30.00
ESSWP Willie Parker

2006 Exquisite Collection Ticket Matchup Signatures

STATED PRINT RUN 25 SER.#'d SETS
BJ D.Bledsoe/K.Johnson 15.00 40.00
BM D.Bledsoe/E.Manning 50.00 100.00
BW R.Bush/D.Williams 20.00 50.00
CJ K.Clemens/T.Jackson 12.00 30.00
DK V.Davis/J.Klopfenstein 15.00 40.00
HG A.Hawk/C.Greenway 20.00 50.00
HJ D.Hagan/T.Jackson 15.00 40.00
JB L.Johnson/R.Brown 15.00 40.00
JH K.Johnson/S.Holmes 15.00 40.00
JJ C.Jackson/G.Jennings 20.00 50.00
LH M.Leinart/M.Huff 15.00 40.00
MA L.Maroney/J.Addai 12.00 30.00
MS S.Moss/M.Stovall 12.00 30.00
MY P.Manning/V.Young 75.00 150.00
RL B.Roethlisberger/B.Leftwich 60.00 120.00
TJ L.Tomlinson/L.Jordan 20.00 50.00
WB C.Williams/R.Bush 20.00 50.00
WD L.White/M.Drew 25.00 60.00

2007 Exquisite Collection

1-60 STATED PRINT RUN 150
61-102 AU ROOKIE PRINT RUN 150
104-125 JSY AU RC PRINT RUN 225
126-135 JSY AU RC PRINT RUN 99
1 Matt Leinart 5.00 12.00
2 Larry Fitzgerald 6.00 15.00
3 Julius Jones 5.00 12.00
4 Warrick Dunn 5.00 12.00
5 Steve McNair 5.00 12.00
6 Willis McGahee 5.00 12.00
7 J.P. Losman 5.00 12.00
8 Lee Evans 6.00 15.00
9 Jake Delhomme 5.00 12.00
10 Steve Smith 6.00 15.00
11 Rex Grossman 5.00 12.00
12 Cedric Benson 5.00 12.00
13 Carson Palmer 6.00 15.00
14 Chad Johnson 6.00 15.00
15 Jamal Lewis 5.00 12.00
16 Braylon Edwards 6.00 15.00
17 Tony Romo 20.00 50.00
18 Terrell Owens 6.00 15.00
19 Jay Cutler 6.00 15.00
20 Travis Henry 5.00 12.00
21 Jon Kitna 5.00 12.00
22 Roy Williams WR 5.00 12.00
23 Brett Favre 20.00 50.00
24 Donald Driver 6.00 15.00
25 Matt Schaub 6.00 15.00
26 Andre Johnson 5.00 12.00
27 Peyton Manning 20.00 50.00
28 Joseph Addai 5.00 12.00
29 David Garrard 5.00 12.00
30 Maurice Jones-Drew 5.00 12.00
31 Larry Johnson 5.00 12.00
32 Tony Gonzalez 6.00 15.00
33 Trent Green 5.00 12.00
34 Ronnie Brown 5.00 12.00
35 Tarvaris Jackson 5.00 12.00
36 Chester Taylor 5.00 12.00
37 Tom Brady 25.00 60.00
38 Randy Moss 6.00 15.00
39 Drew Brees 10.00 25.00
40 Reggie Bush 6.00 15.00
41 Eli Manning 6.00 15.00
42 Brandon Jacobs 5.00 12.00
43 Chad Pennington 5.00 12.00
44 Thomas Jones 5.00 12.00
45 Ronald Curry 5.00 12.00
46 Donovan McNabb 6.00 15.00
47 Brian Westbrook 6.00 15.00
48 Ben Roethlisberger 6.00 15.00
49 Willie Parker 5.00 12.00
50 Philip Rivers 8.00 20.00
51 LaDainian Tomlinson 6.00 15.00
52 Alex Smith QB 6.00 15.00
53 Frank Gore 6.00 15.00
54 Matt Hasselbeck 5.00 12.00
55 Shaun Alexander 5.00 12.00
56 Marc Bulger 5.00 12.00
57 Steven Jackson 6.00 15.00
58 Cadillac Williams 6.00 15.00
59 Vince Young 5.00 12.00
60 Jason Campbell 5.00 12.00
61 Aaron Ross AU RC 8.00 20.00
62 Adam Carriker AU RC 8.00 20.00
63 Ahmad Bradshaw AU RC 12.00 30.00
64 Amobi Okoye AU RC 8.00 20.00
65 Anthony Spencer AU RC 15.00 40.00
66 Aundrae Allison AU RC 8.00 20.00
67 Chris Davis AU RC 8.00 20.00
68 Chris Leak AU RC 8.00 20.00
69 Courtney Taylor AU RC 8.00 20.00
70 Korey Hall AU RC 10.00 25.00
71 Darrelle Revis AU RC 30.00 60.00
72 David Clowney AU RC 8.00 20.00
73 DeShawn Wynn AU RC 8.00 20.00
74 Dwayne Wright AU RC 8.00 20.00
75 Isaiah Stanback AU RC 8.00 20.00
76 Jacoby Jones AU RC 20.00 40.00
77 Jamaal Anderson AU RC 10.00 25.00
78 James Jones AU RC 8.00 20.00
79 Danny Ware AU RC 12.00 30.00
80 Jeff Rowe AU RC 8.00 20.00
81 Joel Filani AU RC 8.00 20.00
82 John Broussard AU RC 10.00 25.00
83 Jon Beason AU RC 8.00 20.00
84 Jordan Kent AU RC 10.00 25.00
85 Jordan Palmer AU RC 10.00 25.00
86 Justise Hairston AU RC 8.00 20.00
87 Kenneth Darby AU RC 8.00 20.00
88 Kolby Smith AU RC 8.00 20.00
89 LaRon Landry AU RC 12.00 30.00
90 Laurent Robinson AU RC 15.00 40.00
91 Lawrence Timmons AU RC 12.00 30.00
92 Legedu Naanee AU RC 10.00 25.00
93 Leon Hall AU RC 15.00 40.00
94 Michael Griffin AU RC 8.00 20.00
95 Mike Walker AU RC 12.00 30.00
96 Paul Posluszny AU RC 12.00 30.00
97 Reggie Nelson AU RC 8.00 20.00
98 Roy Hall AU RC 12.00 30.00
99 Ryne Robinson AU RC 8.00 20.00
100 Steve Breaston AU RC 15.00 40.00
101 Tyler Thigpen AU RC 12.00 30.00
102 Zach Miller AU RC 8.00 20.00
103 C.Davis JSY AU/30 RC 60.00 150.00
104 John Beck JSY AU RC 8.00 20.00
105 L.Booker JSY AU RC 15.00 40.00
106 Michael Bush JSY AU RC 12.00 30.00
107 T.Edwards JSY AU RC 12.00 30.00
108 Yamon Figurs JSY AU RC 12.00 30.00
109 Chris Henry JSY AU RC 12.00 30.00
110 J.Lee Higgins JSY AU RC 12.00 30.00
111 Jason Hill JSY AU RC 12.00 30.00
112 Tony Hunt JSY AU RC 12.00 30.00
113 Kenny Irons JSY AU RC 12.00 30.00
114 B.Jackson JSY AU RC 12.00 30.00
115 Kevin Kolb JSY AU RC 25.00 60.00
116 Brian Leonard JSY AU RC 12.00 30.00
117 Greg Olsen JSY AU RC 20.00 40.00
118 A.Pittman JSY AU RC 12.00 30.00
119 Sidney Rice JSY AU RC 25.00 60.00
120 Joe Thomas JSY AU RC 12.00 30.00
121 Steve Smith JSY AU RC 20.00 50.00
122 D.Stanton JSY AU RC 12.00 30.00
123 Paul Williams JSY AU RC 12.00 30.00
124 Patrick Willis JSY AU RC 20.00 50.00
125 Garrett Wolfe JSY AU RC 12.00 30.00
126 D.Bowe JSY AU RC 15.00 40.00
128 A.Gonzalez JSY AU RC 15.00 40.00
129 D.Jarrett JSY AU RC 20.00 50.00
130 C.Johnson JSY AU RC 200.00 400.00
131 M.Lynch JSY AU RC 60.00 125.00
132 R.Meachem JSY AU RC 15.00 40.00
133 A.Peterson JSY AU RC 500.00 1000.00
134 Brady Quinn JSY AU RC 15.00 40.00
135 J.Russell JSY AU RC 15.00 40.00

2007 Exquisite Collection Gold

1-60 VET UNPRICED PRINT RUN 1
*61-102 ROOKIE/60: .5X TO 1.2X BASE AU
*104-125 ROOKIE/99: .5X TO 1.2X BASE JSY AU
*126-135 ROOKIE/25: .5X TO 1.2X BASE JSY AU
61-102 ROOKIE AU PRINT RUN 60
104-125 ROOKIE JSY AU PRINT RUN 99
126-135 ROOKIE JSY AU PRINT RUN 25
130 Calvin Johnson JSY AU 600.00 1000.00
131 Marshawn Lynch JSY AU 175.00 300.00
133 Adrian Peterson JSY AU 1000.00 1800.00

2007 Exquisite Collection Debut Signatures

STATED PRINT RUN 20 SER.#'d SETS
UNPRICED GOLD SPECTRUM PRINT RUN 1
AG Anthony Gonzalez 10.00 25.00
AP Adrian Peterson 200.00 400.00
AP2 Adrian Peterson 200.00 400.00
BJ Brandon Jackson 10.00 25.00
BQ Brady Quinn 10.00 25.00
BQ2 Brady Quinn 10.00 25.00
CD Craig Buster Davis 10.00 25.00
CH Chris Henry RB 10.00 25.00
CJ Calvin Johnson 90.00 150.00
DB Dwayne Bowe 10.00 25.00
DB2 Dwayne Bowe 10.00 25.00
DJ Dwayne Jarrett 12.00 30.00
DS Drew Stanton 10.00 25.00
GO Greg Olsen 15.00 40.00
JB John Beck 10.00 25.00
JR JaMarcus Russell 10.00 25.00
JR2 JaMarcus Russell 10.00 25.00
KI Kenny Irons 10.00 25.00
KK Kevin Kolb 25.00 60.00
ML Marshawn Lynch 25.00 50.00
ML2 Marshawn Lynch 25.00 50.00
PI Antonio Pittman 10.00 25.00
PW Patrick Willis 15.00 40.00
RM Robert Meachem 20.00 50.00
RM2 Robert Meachem 12.00 30.00
SS Steve Smith USC 10.00 25.00
TE Trent Edwards 10.00 25.00
TG Ted Ginn Jr. 12.00 30.00
TG2 Ted Ginn Jr. 12.00 30.00
TH Tony Hunt 10.00 25.00

2007 Exquisite Collection Endorsements

STATED PRINT RUN 20 SER.#'d SETS
UNPRICED GOLD SPECTRUM PRINT RUN 1
AB Anquan Boldin 15.00 40.00
AS Alex Smith QB 20.00 50.00
BF Brett Favre 125.00 250.00
BJ Brandon Jacobs 15.00 40.00
BO Bo Jackson 30.00 80.00
BQ Brady Quinn 10.00 25.00
BU Reggie Bush 15.00 40.00
BU2 Reggie Bush 15.00 40.00
CJ Chad Johnson 15.00 40.00
CT Chester Taylor 15.00 40.00
DB Drew Brees 50.00 100.00
EM Eli Manning 60.00 120.00
FG Frank Gore 20.00 50.00
GS Gale Sayers 25.00 60.00
JA Joseph Addai 15.00 40.00
JC Jason Campbell 15.00 40.00
JO Calvin Johnson 30.00 80.00
JT Joe Theismann 25.00 60.00
LE Lee Evans 10.00 25.00
LF Larry Fitzgerald 20.00 50.00
LJ Larry Johnson 15.00 40.00
LT LaDainian Tomlinson 40.00 80.00
LY Marshawn Lynch 25.00 60.00
MA Marc Bulger 15.00 40.00
MB Marion Barber 20.00 50.00
ML Matt Leinart 15.00 40.00
PH Paul Hornung 25.00 50.00
PR Philip Rivers 25.00 60.00
RB Ronnie Brown 15.00 40.00
RW Reggie Wayne 20.00 50.00
SI Mike Singletary 25.00 60.00
SY Steve Young 50.00 120.00
TG Ted Ginn Jr. 12.00 30.00
TJ T.J. Houshmandzadeh 15.00 40.00
VY Vince Young 15.00 40.00
WP Willie Parker 15.00 40.00

2007 Exquisite Collection Inscriptions

STATED PRINT RUN 25 SER.#'d SETS
UNPRICED GOLD SPECTRUM PRINT RUN 1
AB Anquan Boldin 15.00 40.00
AS Alex Smith QB 20.00 50.00
BO Bo Jackson 60.00 120.00
CJ Chad Johnson 15.00 40.00
CW Cadillac Williams 12.00 30.00
DM Dan Marino 100.00 200.00
GS Gale Sayers 25.00 60.00
JA Joseph Addai 15.00 40.00
JN Joe Namath 50.00 100.00
JR JaMarcus Russell 10.00 25.00
LC L.C. Greenwood 15.00 40.00
LJ Larry Johnson 15.00 40.00
LT LaDainian Tomlinson 40.00 100.00
ML Matt Leinart 15.00 40.00
MS Mike Singletary 25.00 60.00
PH Paul Hornung 25.00 60.00
RB Reggie Bush 40.00 100.00
RW Reggie Wayne 20.00 50.00
VY Vince Young 15.00 40.00
WP Willie Parker 15.00 40.00

2007 Exquisite Collection Legendary Signatures

STATED PRINT RUN 20 SER.#'d SETS
UNPRICED GOLD SPECTRUM PRINT RUN 1
BO Bo Jackson 60.00 120.00
BS Barry Sanders
DM Dan Marino 100.00 200.00
DP Drew Pearson 20.00 50.00
ES Emmitt Smith 125.00 250.00
GS Gale Sayers 30.00 60.00
JM Joe Montana 100.00 200.00
JN Joe Namath 50.00 100.00
JT Joe Theismann 25.00 50.00
LC L.C. Greenwood 20.00 50.00
MS Mike Singletary 25.00 50.00
PH Paul Hornung 20.00 50.00
RC Roger Craig 20.00 50.00
SY Steve Young 60.00 120.00

2007 Exquisite Collection Maximum Jersey Silver

SILVER PRINT RUN 75 SER.#'d SETS
*SILVER SPECTRUM/15: .8X TO 2X BASIC JSY/75
SILVER SPECTRUM PRINT RUN 15 SER.#'d SETS
UNPRICED GOLD SPECTRUM PRINT RUN 1
AD Joseph Addai 5.00 12.00
AG Anthony Gonzalez 2.50 6.00
AJ Andre Johnson 6.00 15.00
AP Adrian Peterson 8.00 20.00
AP2 Adrian Peterson 8.00 20.00
AS Alex Smith QB 6.00 15.00
AV Adam Vinatieri 15.00 30.00
BA Champ Bailey 8.00 20.00
BF Brett Favre 20.00 50.00
BF2 Brett Favre 20.00 50.00
BJ Brandon Jackson 2.50 6.00
BL Byron Leftwich 5.00 12.00
BM Marion Barber 10.00 25.00
BO Dwayne Bowe 2.50 6.00
BO2 Dwayne Bowe 2.50 6.00
BQ Brady Quinn 2.50 6.00
BQ2 Brady Quinn 2.50 6.00
BR Ben Roethlisberger 12.00 30.00
BU Brian Urlacher 10.00 25.00
CB Cedric Benson 5.00 12.00
CH Chris Henry RB 2.50 6.00
CJ Calvin Johnson 8.00 20.00
CJ2 Calvin Johnson 8.00 20.00
CO Marques Colston 5.00 12.00
CP Carson Palmer 6.00 15.00
CT Chester Taylor 5.00 12.00
CU Jay Cutler 5.00 12.00
DB Drew Brees 6.00 15.00
DJ Dwayne Jarrett 3.00 8.00
DJ2 Dwayne Jarrett 3.00 8.00
DM Dan Marino 20.00 50.00
DM2 Dan Marino 20.00 50.00
DS Drew Stanton 2.50 6.00
DW DeAngelo Williams 5.00 12.00
EM Eli Manning 10.00 25.00
ER Ed Reed 8.00 20.00
FG Frank Gore 6.00 15.00
GA Gaines Adams 3.00 8.00
GL Terry Glenn 6.00 15.00
GS Gale Sayers 10.00 25.00
GW Garrett Wolfe 2.50 6.00
HI Johnnie Lee Higgins 2.50 6.00
HO Torry Holt 6.00 15.00
HU Tony Hunt 2.50 6.00
JA Jason Taylor 6.00 15.00
JB John Beck 2.50 6.00
JC Jason Campbell 5.00 12.00

JH Jason Hill 2.50 6.00
JJ Julius Jones 5.00 12.00
JM Joe Montana 30.00 80.00
JM2 Joe Montana 30.00 80.00
JN Joe Namath 12.00 30.00
JO Chad Johnson 5.00 12.00
JR JaMarcus Russell 2.50 6.00
JR2 JaMarcus Russell 2.50 6.00
JS Jeremy Shockey 5.00 12.00
JT Joe Thomas 4.00 10.00
JW Javon Walker 6.00 15.00
KI Kenny Irons 2.50 6.00
KK Kevin Kolb 3.00 8.00
KW Kellen Winslow 5.00 12.00
LB Lorenzo Booker 3.00 8.00
LJ Larry Johnson 5.00 12.00
LM Laurence Maroney 6.00 15.00
LT LaDainian Tomlinson 8.00 20.00
MB Marc Bulger 5.00 12.00
MC Donovan McNabb 6.00 15.00
ME Shawne Merriman 5.00 12.00
MH Matt Hasselbeck 5.00 12.00
MI Michael Bush 2.50 6.00
ML Marshawn Lynch 5.00 12.00
ML2 Marshawn Lynch 5.00 12.00
PI Antonio Pittman 2.50 6.00
PM Peyton Manning 12.00 30.00
PM2 Peyton Manning 12.00 30.00
PO Clinton Portis 5.00 12.00
PW Patrick Willis 4.00 10.00
RM Robert Meachem 3.00 8.00
RM2 Robert Meachem 3.00 8.00
RW Roy Williams WR 5.00 12.00
SA Shaun Alexander 5.00 12.00
SJ Steven Jackson 5.00 12.00
SM Steve Smith 6.00 15.00
SR Sidney Rice 3.00 8.00
SS Steve Smith USC 2.50 6.00
TB Tom Brady 25.00 60.00
TB2 Tom Brady 25.00 60.00
TE Trent Edwards 2.50 6.00
TG Ted Ginn Jr. 3.00 8.00
TG2 Ted Ginn Jr. 3.00 8.00
TH Joe Theismann 10.00 25.00
TH2 Joe Theismann 10.00 25.00
TS Troy Smith 2.50 6.00
VY Vince Young 5.00 12.00
VY2 Vince Young 5.00 12.00
WI Paul Williams 2.50 6.00
WM Willis McGahee 5.00 12.00
WM2 Willis McGahee 5.00 12.00
WP Walter Payton 20.00 50.00
WP2 Walter Payton 20.00 50.00

2007 Exquisite Collection Maximum Patch

PATCH PRINT RUN 25 SER.#'d SETS
UNPRICED PATCH GOLD SPECTRUM PRINT RUN 1
AG Antonio Gates 15.00 40.00
AP Adrian Peterson 15.00 40.00
BE Braylon Edwards 10.00 25.00
BQ Brady Quinn 5.00 12.00
BR Ben Roethlisberger 25.00 60.00
BU Brian Urlacher 20.00 50.00
CB Cedric Benson 10.00 25.00
CJ Chad Johnson 10.00 25.00
CP Clinton Portis 10.00 25.00
CW Cadillac Williams 12.00 30.00
DB Dwayne Bowe 5.00 12.00
DM Dan Marino 50.00 120.00
EJ Edgerrin James 12.00 30.00
ES Emmitt Smith 30.00 80.00
FG Frank Gore 12.00 30.00
FT Fred Taylor 10.00 25.00
GL Terry Glenn 12.00 30.00
JJ Julius Jones 10.00 25.00
JP Julius Peppers 12.00 30.00
JR JaMarcus Russell 5.00 12.00
JW Javon Walker 12.00 30.00
LE Lee Evans 12.00 30.00
LF Larry Fitzgerald 12.00 30.00
LJ Larry Johnson 10.00 25.00
LT LaDainian Tomlinson 15.00 40.00
MB Marion Barber 20.00 50.00
MC Donovan McNabb 12.00 30.00
MH Matt Hasselbeck 10.00 25.00
MJ Maurice Jones-Drew 10.00 25.00
ML Marshawn Lynch 10.00 25.00
PM Peyton Manning 30.00 80.00
PR Philip Rivers 15.00 40.00
RB Ronnie Brown 10.00 25.00
RM Randy Moss 12.00 30.00
RW Roy Williams WR 10.00 25.00
SA Shaun Alexander 10.00 25.00
TB Tom Brady 50.00 125.00
TG Ted Ginn Jr. 6.00 15.00
TH Torry Holt 12.00 30.00
TO Terrell Owens 12.00 30.00
TS Troy Smith 5.00 12.00
VY Vince Young 10.00 25.00

2007 Exquisite Collection Patch Combos

STATED PRINT RUN 25 SER.#'d SETS
UNPRICED PATCH QUAD PRINT RUN 10
UNPRICED PATCH TRIO PRINT RUN 15
AJ S.Alexander/S.Jackson 12.00 30.00
BF L.Fitzgerald/A.Boldin 12.00 30.00
BG D.Bowe/T.Ginn Jr. 15.00 40.00
BM E.Manning/P.Burress 15.00 40.00
CM T.Smith/M.Clayton 12.00 30.00
FM D.Marino/B.Favre 60.00 120.00
GG T.Gonzalez/A.Gates 12.00 30.00
GS A.Smith QB/F.Gore 12.00 30.00
HB M.Bulger/T.Holt 10.00 25.00
HW M.Harrison/R.Wayne 12.00 30.00
JB J.Jones/M.Barber 12.00 30.00
JH C.Johnson/T.Houshmandzadeh 12.00 30.00
JL L.Johnson/M.Lynch 15.00 40.00
LB R.Lewis/C.Bailey 15.00 40.00
MB P.Manning/T.Brady 40.00 100.00
MP D.McAllister/A.Pittman 10.00 25.00
MY D.McNabb/V.Young 15.00 40.00
PC J.Campbell/C.Portis 12.00 30.00
PR C.Palmer/B.Roethlisberger 20.00 50.00
QR J.Russell/B.Quinn 6.00 15.00
SJ S.Smith/D.Jarrett 12.00 30.00
SP W.Payton/E.Smith 60.00 120.00
ST J.Taylor/M.Strahan 12.00 30.00
TJ F.Taylor/M.Jones-Drew 15.00 40.00
TP A.Peterson/C.Taylor 30.00 80.00
TR L.Tomlinson/P.Rivers 20.00 50.00
WH H.Ward/S.Holmes 15.00 40.00
WJ R.Williams WR/C.Johnson 15.00 40.00

2007 Exquisite Collection Patch Gold

GOLD PRINT RUN 50 SER.#'d SETS
*SPECTRUM/15: .6X TO 1.5X GOLD/50
SPECTRUM PRINT RUN 15
AC Alge Crumpler 8.00 20.00
AD Joseph Addai 6.00 15.00
AG Anthony Gonzalez 3.00 8.00
AJ Andre Johnson 8.00 20.00
AN Antonio Gates 10.00 25.00
AP Adrian Peterson 10.00 25.00
AV Adam Vinatieri 15.00 40.00
BA Ronde Barber 6.00 15.00
BE Braylon Edwards 6.00 15.00
BF Brett Favre 25.00 60.00
BL Byron Leftwich 6.00 15.00
BO Dwayne Bowe 3.00 8.00
BQ Brady Quinn 3.00 8.00
BR Isaac Bruce 10.00 25.00
BS Barry Sanders 20.00 50.00
BU Brian Urlacher 10.00 25.00
BW Brian Westbrook 6.00 16.00
CB Champ Bailey 10.00 25.00
CJ Calvin Johnson 10.00 25.00
CL Mark Clayton 6.00 15.00
CO Marques Colston 6.00 15.00
CP Carson Palmer 8.00 20.00
CW Cadillac Williams 8.00 20.00
DB Drew Brees 10.00 25.00
DC Marion Barber 12.00 30.00
DE Deuce McAllister 8.00 20.00
DJ Dwayne Jarrett 8.00 20.00
DM Dan Marino 25.00 60.00
DO Donovan McNabb 8.00 20.00
ED Trent Edwards 3.00 8.00
EJ Edgerrin James 8.00 20.00
EM Eli Manning 12.00 30.00
ER Ed Reed 10.00 25.00
ES Emmitt Smith 20.00 50.00
FA Brett Favre 20.00 50.00
FG Frank Gore 8.00 20.00
FT Fred Taylor 6.00 15.00
GA Antonio Gates 10.00 25.00
GO Greg Olsen 10.00 25.00
GT Tony Gonzalez 8.00 20.00
GZ Tony Gonzalez 8.00 20.00
HM Heath Miller 6.00 15.00
HU Tony Hunt 6.00 15.00
HW Hines Ward 8.00 20.00
IB Isaac Bruce 10.00 25.00
JA Steven Jackson 6.00 15.00
JC Jay Cutler 6.00 15.00
JH Jason Witten 8.00 20.00
JJ Julius Jones 6.00 15.00
JK Jevon Kearse 6.00 15.00
JM Joe Montana 40.00 100.00
JO Chad Johnson 6.00 15.00
JP Julius Peppers 8.00 20.00
JR JaMarcus Russell 3.00 8.00
JS Jeremy Shockey 6.00 15.00
JT Jason Taylor 8.00 20.00
JU Julius Jones 6.00 15.00
JW Javon Walker 8.00 20.00
KJ Kevin Jones 6.00 15.00
LD Brian Leonard 6.00 15.00
LE Lee Evans 8.00 20.00
LF Larry Fitzgerald 8.00 20.00
LJ Larry Johnson 6.00 15.00
LT LaDainian Tomlinson 10.00 25.00
MA Matt Leinart 6.00 15.00
MB Marc Bulger 6.00 15.00
MC Deuce McAllister 8.00 20.00
ME Robert Meachem 6.00 15.00
MH Marvin Harrison 8.00 20.00
ML Marshawn Lynch 6.00 15.00
MS Michael Strahan 8.00 20.00
PB Plaxico Burress 6.00 15.00
PE Peyton Manning 20.00 50.00
PM Peyton Manning 20.00 50.00
PO Clinton Portis 6.00 15.00
PR Philip Rivers 10.00 25.00
RB Reggie Brown 6.00 15.00
RE Reggie Bush 6.00 15.00
RG Rex Grossman 6.00 15.00
RL Ray Lewis 10.00 25.00
RM Randy Moss 8.00 20.00
RO Ronnie Brown 6.00 15.00
RW Reggie Wayne 8.00 20.00
SA Shaun Alexander 6.00 15.00
SJ Steven Jackson 6.00 15.00
SM Shawne Merriman 6.00 15.00
SS Steve Smith 8.00 20.00
TA Fred Taylor 6.00 15.00
TE Tedy Bruschi 8.00 20.00
TG Ted Ginn Jr. 4.00 10.00
TH Torry Holt 8.00 20.00
TO Tom Brady 30.00 80.00
TR Tony Romo 12.00 30.00
TS Terrell Suggs 6.00 15.00
VY Vince Young 6.00 15.00
WD Warrick Dunn 6.00 15.00
WI Cadillac Williams 8.00 20.00
WP Willie Parker 8.00 20.00
WR Roy Williams S 6.00 15.00
ZT Zach Thomas 8.00 20.00

2007 Exquisite Collection Signature Combos

STATED PRINT RUN 25 SER.#'d SETS
UNPRICED SIG DUAL PATCH #'d TO 10
BL C.Bailey/J.Lynch 30.00 80.00
BS M.Bulger/M.Schaub 20.00 50.00
CT C.Johnson/T.Housh 25.00 60.00
EB E.Smith/B.Sanders 300.00 500.00
EL L.Evans/M.Lynch 30.00 80.00
FJ Fitzgerald/C.Johnson 75.00 150.00
GC F.Gore/R.Craig 30.00 80.00
GS Greenwood/Singletary 30.00 80.00
HG S.Holmes/T.Ginn Jr. 25.00 60.00
HJ Holmes/Jennings 25.00 60.00
HQ P.Hornung/B.Quinn 25.00 50.00
JB L.Johnson/D.Bowe 12.00 30.00
JT Bo Jcksn/Tmlinsn 75.00 150.00
LF M.Leinart/L.Fitzgerald 25.00 60.00
MJ E.Manning/B.Jacobs 40.00 80.00
MY J.Montana/S.Young 175.00 300.00
NM J.Namath/D.Marino 150.00 300.00
PB D.Pearson/M.Barber 25.00 60.00
PL W.Parker/M.Lynch 30.00 80.00
RD P.Rivers/C.Davis 25.00 60.00
SB Smith QB/Bush 30.00 80.00
SG A.Smith QB/F.Gore 30.00 80.00
SJ A.Smith QB/D.Jackson 20.00 50.00
SS G.Sayers/Singletary 60.00 120.00
ST B.Sanders/Tomlinson 175.00 350.00
WA R.Wayne/J.Addai
WB C.Williams/R.Brown 20.00 50.00
WJ D.Williams/D.Jarrett 25.00 60.00
WN D.Williams/J.Norwood 20.00 50.00

2007 Exquisite Collection Signature Jersey Numbers

STATED PRINT RUN 4-89
SERIAL #'d UNDER 18 NOT PRICED
AP Adrian Peterson/28 300.00 600.00
BJ Brandon Jacobs/27 15.00 40.00
BO Bo Jackson/34 60.00 120.00
BU Michael Bush/43 12.00 30.00
CB Champ Bailey/24 25.00 60.00
CD Craig Buster Davis/84 12.00 30.00
CH Chris Henry RB/29 15.00 40.00
CO Jerricho Cotchery/89 12.00 30.00
CT Chester Taylor/29 15.00 40.00
DB Dwayne Bowe/82 12.00 30.00
DJ Darrell Jackson/82 12.00 30.00
DW Dwayne Jarrett/80 15.00 40.00
GJ Greg Jennings/85 15.00 40.00
GS Gale Sayers/40 50.00 100.00
JA Brandon Jackson/32 15.00 40.00
LJ Larry Johnson/27 15.00 40.00
LT LaDainian Tomlinson/21 90.00 150.00
ML Marshawn Lynch/23 40.00 100.00
PM Peyton Manning/18 90.00 150.00
PW Patrick Willis/52 30.00 80.00
RC Roger Craig/33 20.00 50.00
SI Mike Singletary/50 30.00 60.00
TG Ted Ginn/19 25.00 60.00
VJ Vincent Jackson/83 12.00 30.00
WI DeAngelo Williams/34 20.00 50.00

2007 Exquisite Collection Signature Swatches Patch

STATED PRINT RUN 25 SER.#'d SETS
UNPRICED SIG SWATCH PRINT RUN 10
UNPRICED SIG SWATCH DUAL #'d TO 15
UNPRICED SIG SWATCH QUAD #'d TO 10
UNPRICED SIG QUAD PATCH #'d TO 5
AB Anquan Boldin 12.00 30.00
AD Joseph Addai 12.00 30.00
AG Anthony Gonzalez 10.00 25.00
AP Adrian Peterson 200.00 400.00
AS Alex Smith QB 30.00 60.00
BJ Brandon Jacobs 12.00 30.00
BQ Brady Quinn 10.00 25.00
BR Drew Brees 75.00 150.00
CB Champ Bailey 25.00 60.00
CJ Chad Johnson 12.00 30.00
CO Jerricho Cotchery 12.00 30.00
CT Chester Taylor 12.00 30.00
CW Cadillac Williams 15.00 40.00
DB Dwayne Bowe 10.00 25.00
DD Donald Driver 15.00 40.00
DJ Dwayne Jarrett 12.00 30.00
DJ2 Dwayne Jarrett 12.00 30.00
DW DeAngelo Williams 12.00 30.00
JA Darrell Jackson 12.00 30.00
JC Jason Campbell 12.00 30.00
JL John Lynch 15.00 40.00
JO Calvin Johnson 100.00 200.00
JR JaMarcus Russell 10.00 25.00
JR2 JaMarcus Russell 10.00 25.00
LE Lee Evans 15.00 40.00
LF Larry Fitzgerald 15.00 40.00
MA Marques Colston 12.00 30.00
MB Marc Bulger 12.00 30.00
MC Mark Clayton 12.00 30.00
ML Marshawn Lynch 40.00 100.00
ML2 Marshawn Lynch 40.00 100.00
PM Peyton Manning 100.00 200.00
PR Philip Rivers 20.00 50.00
RB Ronnie Brown 12.00 30.00
RM Robert Meachem 12.00 30.00
RW Reggie Wayne 15.00 40.00
SH Santonio Holmes 12.00 30.00
SR Sidney Rice 40.00 80.00
SS Steve Smith USC 10.00 25.00
TG Ted Ginn Jr. 12.00 30.00
TG2 Ted Ginn Jr. 12.00 30.00
VY Vince Young 12.00 30.00

2007 Exquisite Collection Signature Trios

STATED PRINT RUN 20 SER.#'d SETS
ABD Addai/Bowe/Davis 40.00 100.00
AWN Addai/Williams/Norwood 40.00 100.00
BBB Boldin/Brown/Berrian 25.00 60.00
BBC Brees/Bush/Colston 125.00 250.00
CCE Cotchery/Clayton/Evans 25.00 60.00
GGP Ginn Jr./Gonzalz/Pittman
GPH Greenwd/Parkr/Holmes 50.00 100.00
JGW Johnson/Gore/Williams 40.00 100.00
JHI Johnson/Housh/Irons 25.00 60.00
JTJ Jackson/Tomln/Johnsn 75.00 150.00
LBD Landry/Bowe/Davis 25.00 60.00
LFB Leinart/Fitzgerald/Boldin 40.00 100.00
LHJ Lynch/Henry/Jackson 40.00 80.00
MAW Manning/Addai/Wayne 125.00 250.00
MBG Marino/Brown/Ginn 100.00 175.00
MDG Meach/Davis/Gonzalz 30.00 80.00
MJS Eli/Jacobs/Smith USC 75.00 150.00
MRC Eli/Rivers/Campbell 60.00 120.00
MTQ Mont/Theis/Quinn 150.00 300.00
NFR Namath/Favre/Russell 200.00 400.00
PTR Ptrson/Taylor/Rice 150.00 300.00
RJP Russell/C.Jhnsn/Petrsn 150.00 300.00
SGJ Smith QB/Gore/Jackson 40.00 100.00
SSB Sayers/Singltry/Berrian 60.00 120.00
SST Smith/Sanders/Tomlin 250.00 500.00
TCL Theis/Cmpbll/Lndry 30.00 80.00
WEH Wayne/Evans/Housh 25.00 60.00
YLY Young/Leinart/Young 60.00 120.00

2007 Exquisite Collection Ticket Matchup Signatures

STATED PRINT RUN 30 SER.#'d SETS
AW J.Addai/D.Williams 20.00 50.00
CA C.Johnson/A.Boldin 75.00 150.00
FB B.Favre/M.Bulger 100.00 200.00
GJ F.Gore/B.Jacobs 25.00 60.00
GW F.Gore/D.Williams 25.00 60.00
JA L.Johnson/J.Addai 20.00 50.00
JB C.Johnson/D.Bowe 15.00 40.00
JE C.Johnson/L.Evans 15.00 40.00
LB M.Lynch/M.Barber 40.00 80.00
LJ M.Lynch/B.Jacobs 40.00 80.00
LQ M.Leinart/B.Quinn 25.00 60.00
MB P.Manning/D.Brees 125.00 250.00
MM Montana/Marino 200.00 400.00
PB W.Parker/R.Brown 25.00 60.00
PN A.Peterson/J.Norwood 125.00 250.00
SB A.Smith QB/M.Bulger 25.00 60.00
TJ L.Tomlinson/L.Johnson 25.00 60.00
WW C.Williams/D.Williams 25.00 60.00
YB V.Young/Bush 25.00 60.00
YR V.Young/P.Rivers 30.00 80.00

2007 Exquisite Collection Trophy Signature Patch

SIGNATURE PATCH PRINT RUN 25
UNPRICED SIG SWATCH PRINT RUN 10
ES Emmitt Smith 125.00 250.00
JA Joseph Addai 15.00 40.00
JL John Lynch 20.00 50.00
JN Joe Namath 60.00 120.00
JT Joe Theismann 25.00 60.00
PM Peyton Manning 100.00 200.00
RW Reggie Wayne 20.00 50.00
WP Willie Parker 20.00 50.00

2008 Exquisite Collection

This set was released on March 4, 2009. The base set consists of 177 cards. Cards 1-100 feature veterans serial numbered of 75. Cards 101-142 are autographed rookies serial numbered of 150, and cards 143-166 are autographed jersey rookies serial numbered of 199. Cards 167-176 are autographed jersey rookies serial numbered of 99. Card 177 is an autographed jersey card of Tiger Woods serial numbered of 10. This product was released with 7 cards per pack and 1 pack per hobby box.

1-100 VETERAN PRINT RUN 75
101-142 AU ROOKIE PRINT RUN 150
143-166 JSY AU RC PRINT RUN 191-199
167-176 JSY AU RC PRINT RUN 99
UNPRICED #177 PRINT RUN 10
1 Kurt Warner 8.00 20.00
2 Larry Fitzgerald 8.00 20.00
3 Anquan Boldin 6.00 15.00
4 Edgerrin James 8.00 20.00
5 Michael Turner 6.00 15.00
6 Roddy White 6.00 15.00
7 Willis McGahee 6.00 15.00
8 Ed Reed 8.00 20.00
9 Ray Lewis 10.00 25.00
10 Todd Heap 6.00 15.00
11 Trent Edwards 6.00 15.00
12 Marshawn Lynch 8.00 20.00
13 Lee Evans 8.00 20.00
14 Jake Delhomme 6.00 15.00
15 DeAngelo Williams 6.00 15.00
16 Steve Smith 8.00 20.00
17 Brian Urlacher 10.00 25.00
18 Kyle Orton 6.00 15.00
19 Devin Hester 8.00 20.00
20 Carson Palmer 8.00 20.00
21 Chad Johnson 6.00 15.00
22 T.J. Houshmandzadeh 6.00 15.00
23 Derek Anderson 6.00 15.00
24 Jamal Lewis 8.00 20.00
25 Kellen Winslow 6.00 15.00
26 Braylon Edwards 6.00 15.00
27 Tony Romo 8.00 20.00
28 Terrell Owens 8.00 20.00
29 Marion Barber 6.00 15.00
30 DeMarcus Ware 8.00 20.00
31 Jay Cutler 6.00 15.00
32 Brandon Marshall 8.00 20.00
33 Champ Bailey 8.00 20.00
34 Jon Kitna 6.00 15.00
35 Calvin Johnson 10.00 25.00
36 Roy Williams WR 6.00 15.00
37 Aaron Rodgers 40.00 80.00
38 Ryan Grant 8.00 20.00
39 Greg Jennings 6.00 15.00
40 Andre Johnson 8.00 20.00
41 Peyton Manning 25.00 50.00
42 Dallas Clark 6.00 15.00
43 Joseph Addai 6.00 15.00
44 Reggie Wayne 8.00 20.00
45 Fred Taylor 6.00 15.00
46 David Garrard 6.00 15.00
47 Maurice Jones-Drew 6.00 15.00
48 Selvin Young 6.00 15.00
49 Larry Johnson 6.00 15.00
50 Dwayne Bowe 8.00 20.00
51 Ronnie Brown 6.00 15.00
52 Joey Porter 6.00 15.00
53 Chad Pennington 6.00 15.00
54 Adrian Peterson 60.00 120.00
55 Jared Allen 6.00 15.00
56 Matt Jones 8.00 20.00
57 Tom Brady 15.00 40.00
58 Randy Moss 8.00 20.00
59 Rodney Harrison 6.00 15.00
60 Wes Welker 8.00 20.00
61 Drew Brees 12.00 30.00
62 Reggie Bush 6.00 15.00
63 Marques Colston 6.00 15.00
64 Eli Manning 12.00 30.00
65 Brandon Jacobs 6.00 15.00
66 Plaxico Burress 6.00 15.00
67 Brett Favre 25.00 60.00
68 Jerricho Cotchery 6.00 15.00
69 Laveranues Coles 6.00 15.00
70 JaMarcus Russell 6.00 15.00
71 Donovan McNabb 8.00 20.00
72 Brian Westbrook 6.00 15.00
73 Brian Dawkins 10.00 25.00
74 Willie Parker 8.00 20.00
75 Ben Roethlisberger 10.00 25.00
76 Troy Polamalu 10.00 25.00
77 Hines Ward 8.00 20.00
78 James Harrison 25.00 50.00
79 Philip Rivers 10.00 25.00
80 LaDainian Tomlinson 10.00 25.00
81 Antonio Gates 8.00 20.00
82 Antonio Cromartie 6.00 15.00
83 J.T. O'Sullivan 6.00 15.00
84 Patrick Willis 8.00 20.00
85 Frank Gore 8.00 20.00
86 Matt Hasselbeck 6.00 15.00
87 Jonathan Vilma 6.00 15.00
88 Lofa Tatupu 6.00 15.00
89 Marc Bulger 6.00 15.00
90 Torry Holt 8.00 20.00
91 Steven Jackson 6.00 15.00
92 Jeff Garcia 6.00 15.00
93 Earnest Graham 6.00 15.00
94 Joey Galloway 8.00 20.00
95 Vince Young 6.00 15.00
96 LenDale White 6.00 15.00
97 Santana Moss 6.00 15.00
98 Jason Campbell 6.00 15.00
99 Clinton Portis 6.00 15.00
100 Chris Cooley 6.00 15.00
101 Bruce Davis AU RC 8.00 20.00
102 Calais Campbell AU RC 8.00 20.00
103 Josh Johnson AU RC 6.00 15.00
104 Alex Brink AU RC 8.00 20.00
105 Andre Woodson AU RC 6.00 15.00
106 Antoine Cason AU RC 8.00 20.00
107 Aqib Talib AU RC 10.00 25.00
108 Chevis Jackson AU RC 6.00 15.00
109 Colt Brennan AU RC 8.00 20.00
110 DJ Hall AU RC 6.00 15.00
111 Dan Connor AU RC 6.00 15.00
112 Owen Schmitt AU RC 6.00 15.00
113 DeMario Pressley AU RC 8.00 20.00
114 Dennis Dixon AU RC 12.00 30.00
115 Dennis Keyes AU RC 6.00 15.00
116 Derrick Harvey AU RC 6.00 15.00
117 D.Rodgers-Cromartie AU RC 10.00 25.00
118 Mike Jenkins AU RC 6.00 15.00
119 Dwight Lowery AU RC 8.00 20.00
120 Erik Ainge AU RC 6.00 15.00
121 Erin Henderson AU RC 8.00 20.00
122 Chris Long AU RC 8.00 20.00
123 Frank Okam AU RC 6.00 15.00
124 Fred Davis AU RC 12.00 30.00
125 Tashard Choice AU RC 6.00 15.00
126 Jack Ikegwuonu AU RC 6.00 15.00
127 Jacob Hester AU RC 6.00 15.00
128 Jacob Tamme AU RC 12.00 30.00
129 Matt Flynn AU RC 25.00 50.00
130 Jermichael Finley AU RC 6.00 15.00
131 John Carlson AU RC 6.00 15.00
132 Justin Forsett AU RC 20.00 40.00
133 Justin King AU RC 8.00 20.00
134 Keenan Burton AU RC 6.00 15.00
135 Keith Rivers AU RC 6.00 15.00
136 Kenny Phillips AU RC 6.00 15.00
137 Lavelle Hawkins AU RC 8.00 20.00
138 Leodis McKelvin AU RC 8.00 20.00
139 Mike Hart AU RC 6.00 15.00
140 Ryan Clady AU RC 8.00 20.00
141 Sedrick Ellis AU RC 6.00 15.00
142 Vernon Gholston AU RC 6.00 15.00
143 Donnie Avery JSY AU RC 12.00 30.00
144 Earl Bennett JSY AU RC 15.00 40.00
145 J.David Booty JSY AU RC 10.00 25.00
146 Brian Brohm JSY AU RC 25.00 50.00
147 Andre Caldwell JSY AU RC 10.00 25.00
148 J.Charles JSY AU RC 40.00 80.00
150 Early Doucet JSY AU RC 10.00 25.00
151 Harry Douglas JSY AU RC 12.00 30.00
152 Matt Forte JSY AU RC 30.00 80.00
153 James Hardy JSY AU RC 10.00 25.00
154 DeS.Jackson JSY AU RC 20.00 50.00
155 Dexter Jackson JSY AU RC 15.00 40.00
156 Chris Johnson JSY AU RC 25.00 60.00
157 D.Keller JSY AU/191 RC 12.00 30.00
158 Malcolm Kelly JSY AU RC 10.00 25.00
159 M.Manningham JSY AU RC 30.00 60.00
160 Jordy Nelson JSY AU RC 30.00 60.00
161 K.O'Connell JSY AU RC 10.00 25.00
162 Ray Rice JSY AU RC 10.00 25.00
163 Eddie Royal JSY AU RC 10.00 25.00
164 J.Simpson JSY AU RC 12.00 30.00
165 Steve Slaton JSY AU RC 10.00 25.00
166 Jake Long JSY AU RC 20.00 50.00
167 D.McFadden JSY AU RC 15.00 40.00
168 Matt Ryan JSY AU RC 300.00 600.00
169 Felix Jones JSY AU RC 15.00 40.00
170 Joe Flacco JSY AU RC 60.00 125.00
171 R.Mendenhall JSY AU RC 15.00 40.00
172 Kevin Smith JSY AU RC 15.00 40.00
173 J.Stewart JSY AU RC 20.00 50.00
174 Limas Sweed JSY AU RC
175 Chad Henne JSY AU RC 20.00 50.00
176 Devin Thomas JSY AU RC 15.00 40.00

2008 Exquisite Collection Silver Holofoil

UNPRICED VET 1-100 PRINT RUN 1
*ROOKIE AU 101-142: .5X TO 1.2X BASE AU RC
ROOKIE AU 101-142 PRINT RUN 30
*JSY AU 143-166: .4X TO 1X JSY AU/191-199
ROOKIE JSY AU 143-166 PRINT RUN 75
*JSY AU 167-176: .5X TO 1.2X JSY AU/99
ROOKIE JSY AU 167-176 PRINT RUN 25
UNPRICED #177 PRINT RUN 3
148 Jamaal Charles JSY AU 40.00 80.00
152 Matt Forte JSY AU 40.00 100.00
154 DeSean Jackson JSY AU 30.00 80.00
156 Chris Johnson JSY AU 20.00 50.00
160 Jordy Nelson JSY AU 60.00 125.00
162 Ray Rice JSY AU 15.00 40.00
167 D.McFadden JSY AU/25 200.00 400.00
168 Matt Ryan JSY AU/25 2000.00 3000.00
169 Felix Jones JSY AU/25 25.00 60.00
170 Joe Flacco JSY AU/25 350.00 700.00
171 R.Mendenhall JSY AU/25 25.00 60.00
173 J.Stewart JSY AU/25 80.00 175.00
175 Chad Henne JSY AU/25 30.00 80.00

2008 Exquisite Collection Black and Gold Steelers Champion Redemptions

ANNOUNCED PRINT RUN 25-150
BGBR Ben Roethlisberger/25* 125.00 250.00
BGDS Donnie Shell/150* 20.00 40.00
BGFH Franco Harris/100* 30.00 60.00
BGJH Jack Ham/150* 25.00 50.00
BGLG L.C. Greenwood/150* 20.00 40.00
BGRB Rocky Bleier/150* 25.00 50.00

2008 Exquisite Collection Champions Signatures

AUTO STATED PRINT RUN 15
ECSBF Brett Favre EXCH 100.00 200.00
ECSEM Eli Manning 50.00 100.00
ECSFH Franco Harris 50.00 100.00
ECSJE John Elway 75.00 150.00
ECSPM Peyton Manning 75.00 150.00
ECSRC Roger Craig 20.00 50.00
ECSTB Terry Bradshaw 75.00 150.00

2008 Exquisite Collection Debut Signatures

GOLD PRINT RUN 15-60
EGDSCH Chad Henne/50 12.00 30.00
EGDSCL Chris Long/25 15.00 40.00
EGDSDM Darren McFadden/15 12.00 30.00
EGDSDT Devin Thomas/60 10.00 25.00
EGDSFJ Felix Jones/60 10.00 25.00
EGDSHD Harry Douglas/60 12.00 30.00
EGDSJF Joe Flacco/35 20.00 50.00
EGDSJH James Hardy/60 10.00 25.00
EGDSJS Jonathan Stewart/60 15.00 40.00
EGDSKS Kevin Smith/60 10.00 25.00
EGDSMF Matt Forte/60 15.00 40.00
EGDSMR Matt Ryan/15 150.00 300.00
EGDSRM Rashard Mendenhall/35 10.00 25.00
EGDSSS Steve Slaton/40 10.00 25.00

2008 Exquisite Collection Endorsements

STATED PRINT RUN 15-30
EEAP Adrian Peterson/15 100.00 200.00
EEAR Aaron Rodgers/30 200.00 400.00
EEBB Brian Bosworth/30 40.00 80.00
EEBF Brett Favre/30 100.00 200.00
EEBR Ben Roethlisberger/30 60.00 120.00
EEBS Barry Sanders/30 100.00 200.00
EECH Chad Henne/30 10.00 25.00
EECL Chris Long/30 10.00 25.00
EECP Clinton Portis/30 8.00 20.00
EEDA Donnie Avery/30 10.00 25.00
EEDG David Garrard/30 8.00 20.00
EEDJ Daryl Johnston/30 15.00 40.00
EEDT Devin Thomas/30 8.00 20.00
EEEM Eli Manning/30 30.00 60.00
EEES Emmitt Smith/30 75.00 150.00
EEFT Fran Tarkenton/30 25.00 60.00
EEJC Jason Campbell/30 8.00 20.00
EEJF Joe Flacco/30 15.00 40.00
EEJS Jonathan Stewart/30 12.00 30.00
EEJT Joe Theismann/30 20.00 50.00
EEKS Kevin Smith/30 8.00 20.00
EEKW Kurt Warner/30 40.00 80.00
EELE Jamal Lewis/30 10.00 25.00
EELT LaDainian Tomlinson/30 30.00 60.00
EEMA Peyton Manning/30 60.00 120.00
EEMF Matt Forte/30 12.00 30.00
EEML Marshawn Lynch/30 15.00 40.00
EEMR Matt Ryan/30 125.00 250.00
EEPH Paul Hornung/30 15.00 40.00
EEPM Peyton Manning/30 60.00 120.00
EERG Roman Gabriel/30 25.00 50.00
EERM Rashard Mendenhall/30 8.00 20.00
EEWI Kellen Winslow Sr./30 12.00 30.00
EEYT Y.A. Tittle/30 15.00 40.00

2008 Exquisite Collection Ensemble 3 Signatures

ENSEMBLE 3 PRINT RUN 10-20
UNPRICED ENSEMBLE 4 PRINT RUN 10
UNPRICED ENSEMBLE 6 PRINT RUN 6
UNPRICED ENSEMBLE 8 PRINT RUN 5
BJC Barbr/Jnes/Choice 25.00 50.00
BRO Ryan/O'Conn/Booty 75.00 150.00
CGR Gore/Rthmn/Craig 50.00 100.00
CMB Bowe/Mrshll/Ctch 15.00 40.00
FMR Fav/P.Man/Rmo 150.00 300.00
GGC Garrard/Cmpbll/Grcia 15.00 40.00
JTL Tmlnsn/LJ/Lewis 50.00 100.00
LPA Portis/Addai/Lewis 25.00 50.00
MFS McFad/Frte/K.Smth 40.00 100.00
RBF Rodgrs/Brohm/Flynn 150.00 300.00
SCW Watsn/Clark/Shcky 15.00 40.00
SWH Hawk/Ware/Schbl 25.00 50.00
TMT Eli/Tittle/Tarkntn 60.00 120.00
WGB Warnr/Grc/Blgr 30.00 60.00
WMR P.Man/Wrnr/Romo 125.00 200.00
WWH Willis/Ware/Hawk 25.00 50.00

2008 Exquisite Collection Generations Signatures

STATED PRINT RUN 15-35
UNPRICED PLATINUM PRINT RUN 1
AHM Harris/Andrsn/Mndn/35 40.00 80.00
CGR Craig/Rathman/Gore/35 40.00 80.00
FRB Fav/Rodgrs/Brhm/15 300.00 500.00
HHB Ham/Bosworth/Hawk/35 30.00 60.00
HSL Sayers/Harris/Lynch/25 50.00 100.00
MMM A.Mnn/P.Mann/Eli/15 300.00 450.00
SBJ Smith/Barber/Jones/15 125.00 250.00
TCJ Brenn/Theis/Cmpbll/25 25.00 60.00
TMT Tittle/Tarkenton/Eli/15 60.00 120.00
WBG Gbrl/Wrnr/Blgr/25 30.00 80.00

2008 Exquisite Collection Immortals Signatures

STATED PRINT RUN 10-55
SERIAL #'d UNDER 15 NOT PRICED
UNPRICED PLATINUM PRINT RUN 1
EGIIBS Barry Sanders/15 75.00 150.00
EGIIDB Dick Butkus/25 30.00 80.00
EGIIFT Fran Tarkenton/45 25.00 50.00
EGIIGS Gale Sayers/25 40.00 80.00
EGIIJH Jack Ham/35 30.00 60.00
EGIIKW Kellen Winslow Sr./25 12.00 30.00
EGIIPH Paul Hornung/55 15.00 40.00
EGIITB Terry Bradshaw/15 75.00 150.00
EGIIYT Y.A. Tittle/55 15.00 40.00

2008 Exquisite Collection Inscriptions

STATED PRINT RUN 30 SER.#'d SETS
UNPRICED PLATINUM PRINT RUN 1
UNPRICED QUAD AUTO PRINT RUN 4
EIBR Ben Roethlisberger 60.00 120.00
EICJ Chad Johnson 15.00 40.00
EIDJ Daryl Johnston 30.00 60.00
EIFH Franco Harris 40.00 80.00
EIJG Joe Greene 25.00 60.00
EIJK Jerry Kramer 20.00 40.00
EIML Marshawn Lynch 15.00 40.00
EIPH Paul Hornung 15.00 40.00

2008 Exquisite Collection Legendary Signatures

STATED PRINT RUN 35 SER.#'d SETS
UNPRICED PLATINUM PRINT RUN 1
ELBG Bob Griese 20.00 50.00
ELBS Barry Sanders 60.00 120.00
ELFH Franco Harris 30.00 80.00
ELFT Fran Tarkenton 25.00 60.00
ELJK Jerry Kramer 15.00 40.00
ELJR Jerry Rice 100.00 200.00
ELJT Joe Theismann 20.00 50.00
ELKA Ken Anderson 12.00 30.00
ELKW Kellen Winslow Sr. 12.00 30.00
ELPH Paul Hornung 15.00 40.00
ELTA Troy Aikman 50.00 100.00
ELTB Terry Bradshaw 60.00 120.00
ELYT Y.A. Tittle 15.00 40.00

2008 Exquisite Collection Legendary Signatures Gold Ink

BASIC GOLD INK PRINT RUN 10-60
*GOLD HOLO/15-30: .5X TO 1.2X GOLD INK
GOLD HOLOFOIL PRINT RUN 5-30
UNPRICED PLATINUM PRINT RUN 1
SERIAL #'d UNDER 15 NOT PRICED
EGSAM Archie Manning/40 15.00 40.00
EGSAR Aaron Rodgers/30 125.00 200.00
EGSBB Brian Brohm/40 10.00 25.00
EGSBG Bob Griese/40 15.00 40.00
EGSBG2 Bob Griese/40 15.00 40.00
EGSBJ Bo Jackson/35 60.00 120.00
EGSBR Ben Roethlisberger/15 60.00 120.00
EGSCH Chad Henne/60 10.00 25.00
EGSCL Chris Long/50 12.00 30.00
EGSCL2 Chris Long/50 12.00 30.00
EGSCP Clinton Portis/40 15.00 40.00
EGSDA Derek Anderson/40 15.00 40.00
EGSDB Dick Butkus/20 30.00 80.00
EGSDB2 Dick Butkus/20 30.00 80.00
EGSDM Darren McFadden/30 25.00 60.00
EGSDM2 Darren McFadden/30 25.00 60.00
EGSDT Devin Thomas/60 12.00 30.00
EGSDT2 Devin Thomas/60 12.00 30.00
EGSEB Earl Bennett/50 12.00 30.00
EGSEM Eli Manning/50 40.00 100.00
EGSEM2 Eli Manning/50 40.00 100.00
EGSFH Franco Harris/20 40.00 80.00
EGSFJ Felix Jones/60 8.00 20.00
EGSGS Gale Sayers/25 40.00 80.00
EGSHA James Hardy/50 12.00 30.00
EGSHD Harry Douglas/50 12.00 30.00
EGSJA Joseph Addai/15 15.00 40.00
EGSJC Jamaal Charles/50 15.00 40.00
EGSJF Joe Flacco/50 30.00 60.00
EGSJH Jack Ham/30 30.00 60.00
EGSJK Jerry Kramer/50 20.00 50.00
EGSJL Jake Long/50 12.00 30.00
EGSJN Jordy Nelson/50 30.00 60.00
EGSJS Jonathan Stewart/20 25.00 60.00
EGSJS2 Jonathan Stewart/20 25.00 60.00
EGSJT Joe Theismann/50 15.00 40.00
EGSJT2 Joe Theismann/50 15.00 40.00
EGSKS Kevin Smith/60 10.00 25.00
EGSKW Kellen Winslow Sr./45 12.00 30.00
EGSLE Jamal Lewis/40 10.00 25.00
EGSLT LaDainian Tomlinson/15 40.00 80.00
EGSMB Marion Barber/40 15.00 40.00
EGSPH Paul Hornung/50 15.00 40.00
EGSPH2 Paul Hornung/50 15.00 40.00
EGSPM Peyton Manning/25 60.00 120.00
EGSPM2 Peyton Manning/25 60.00 120.00
EGSRM Rashard Mendenhall/60 8.00 20.00
EGSRM2 Rashard Mendenhall/60 8.00 20.00
EGSSS Steve Slaton/40 15.00 40.00
EGSSS2 Steve Slaton/40 15.00 40.00
EGSTR Tony Romo/60 40.00 80.00
EGSYT Y.A. Tittle/50 15.00 40.00
EGSYT2 Y.A. Tittle/50 15.00 40.00

2008 Exquisite Collection Legendary Signatures Dual

STATED PRINT RUN 15
UNPRICED PLATINUM PRINT RUN 1
ELCAS O.Andrsn/B.Sims 20.00 50.00
ELCBH Bradshaw/F.Harris 100.00 175.00
ELCGG R.Gabriel/B.Griese 30.00 60.00
ELCHK Hornung/J.Kramer 30.00 60.00
ELCHT Y.Tittle/P.Hornung 30.00 60.00
ELCJP Theismnn/Hornung 30.00 60.00
ELCJR Johnston/Rathman 40.00 80.00
ELCTT F.Tarkenton/Y.Tittle 30.00 60.00

2008 Exquisite Collection Legendary Signatures Dual Gold Ink

STATED PRINT RUN 15-35
UNPRICED PLATINUM PRINT RUN 1
BJ Barber/Johnston/15 40.00 80.00
BR Roeth/Bradshaw/15 175.00 300.00
CS Simpson/Caldwell/35 15.00 40.00
DS J.Stewart/D.Dixon/15 40.00 80.00
DT Douglas/D.Thomas/35 15.00 40.00
FN J.Nelson/M.Flynn/35 40.00 100.00
FS M.Forte/K.Smith/35 15.00 40.00
JM McFadd/Bo Jcksn/15 75.00 150.00
LL C.Long/J.Long/35 15.00 40.00
RB A.Rodgers/B.Brohm/15 150.00 250.00
TB F.Tarkenton/J.Booty/35 30.00 60.00
WG Warner/Gabriel/15 EXCH 50.00 100.00
WH A.Hawk/P.Willis/25 25.00 50.00

2008 Exquisite Collection Legendary Signatures Trios

TRIOS PRINT RUN 10-15
UNPRICED PLATINUM PRINT RUN 1
ELTSASJ Jackson/Sims/Anderson/15 50.00 100.00

2008 Exquisite Collection Legendary Signatures Trios Gold Ink

STATED PRINT RUN 10-99
UNPRICED PLATINUM PRINT RUN 1
SERIAL #'d UNDER 20 NOT PRICED
ARJ Aikman/Jones/Romo/25 100.00 200.00
FJS Forte/Smith/Johnson/99 15.00 40.00
HAS Andrn/Sims/Hrng/99 25.00 50.00
HFB Henn/Flco/Bty/99 15.00 40.00
MCA Manning/Clark/Addai/20 100.00 200.00
SSS Sims/Sanders/Smith/25 75.00 150.00
TGT Tittle/Griese/Theis/75 40.00 80.00
WGC Garcia/Warner/Croyle/75 30.00 60.00

2008 Exquisite Collection Legendary Signatures Jersey Gold Ink

STATED PRINT RUN 35 SER.#'d SETS
*GOLD HOLO/20: .5X TO 1.2X JSY SIG/35
GOLD HOLOFOIL PRINT RUN 20
EGSJBB Brian Brohm 15.00 40.00
EGSJBF Brett Favre 125.00 200.00
EGSJBR Ben Roethlisberger 75.00 150.00
EGSJCH Chad Henne 12.00 30.00
EGSJCJ Chris Johnson 12.00 30.00
EGSJDM Darren McFadden 10.00 25.00
EGSJDT Devin Thomas 15.00 40.00
EGSJEM Eli Manning 50.00 100.00
EGSJFH Franco Harris 40.00 80.00
EGSJFJ Felix Jones 10.00 25.00
EGSJFT Fran Tarkenton 30.00 60.00
EGSJGS Gale Sayers 40.00 80.00
EGSJJF Joe Flacco 25.00 60.00
EGSJJS Jonathan Stewart 25.00 60.00
EGSJJT Joe Theismann 30.00 60.00
EGSJLT LaDainian Tomlinson 30.00 80.00
EGSJMK Malcolm Kelly 15.00 40.00
EGSJML Marshawn Lynch 20.00 50.00
EGSJMR Matt Ryan 75.00 150.00
EGSJPM Peyton Manning 75.00 150.00
EGSJPW Patrick Willis 15.00 40.00
EGSJRM Rashard Mendenhall 10.00 25.00

2008 Exquisite Collection Patch Combos

STATED PRINT RUN 35 SER.#'d SETS
*GOLD HOLO/15: .5X TO 1.2X COMBO/35
ECP1 D.McFadden/J.Stewart 6.00 16.00
ECP2 M.Ryan/J.Flacco 12.00 30.00
ECP3 R.Mendenhall/F.Jones 4.00 10.00
ECP4 D.Thomas/L.Sweed 4.00 10.00
ECP5 T.Brady/P.Manning 25.00 60.00
ECP6 E.Manning/P.Manning 25.00 60.00
ECP7 L.Tomlinson/A.Peterson 10.00 25.00
ECP8 W.Payton/M.Forte 30.00 80.00
ECP10 M.Ryan/C.Henne 12.00 30.00
ECP11 M.Kelly/D.Jackson 8.00 20.00
ECP12 B.Brohm/J.Booty 4.00 10.00
ECP13 R.Moss/T.Owens 8.00 20.00
ECP14 T.Romo/D.McNabb 8.00 20.00
ECP15 B.Urlacher/P.Willis 10.00 25.00
ECP17 K.Smith/B.Sanders 15.00 40.00
ECP19 M.Forte/E.Bennett 6.00 15.00
ECP20 M.Barber/J.Lewis 8.00 20.00
ECP21 C.Portis/C.Johnson 8.00 20.00
ECP22 J.Theismann/K.Stabler 10.00 25.00
ECP23 A.Rodgers/B.Brohm 20.00 50.00
ECP24 R.Mendenhall/L.Sweed 4.00 10.00
ECP25 B.Favre/J.Elway 25.00 60.00

2008 Exquisite Collection Patch Trios

STATED PRINT RUN 25 SER.#'d SETS
UNPRICED GOLD HOLOFOIL PRINT RUN 10
UNPRICED PLATINUM PRINT RUN 1
ETP1 McFadden/Stewart/Johnson 8.00 20.00
ETP2 Ryan/Brohm/Flacco 15.00 40.00
ETP3 Thomas/Nelson/Avery 15.00 40.00
ETP4 Brady/Manning/Romo 40.00 100.00
ETP5 Payton/Smith/Harris 40.00 100.00
ETP6 Peterson/Tomlinson/Lynch 12.00 30.00
ETP7 Harris/Bradshaw/Swann 30.00 80.00
ETP8 McFadden/Forte/Smith 8.00 20.00
ETP9 Jones/Mendenhall/Rice 5.00 12.00
ETP10 Moss/Owens/Johnson 10.00 25.00
ETP11 Willis/Ware/Schobel 10.00 25.00
ETP12 Anderson/Edwards/Lewis 10.00 25.00
ETP13 Favre/Rodgers/Brohm 25.00 60.00

2008 Exquisite Collection Patch Quads

QUAD PATCH PRINT RUN 15
UNPRICED GOLD HOLOFOIL PRINT RUN 4
UNPRICED PLATINUM PRINT RUN 1
EQP1 McFd/Mndhll/Jnes/Stew 10.00 25.00
EQP2 Ryan/Brhm/Henne/Flcco 20.00 50.00
EQP3 Kelly/Thoms/Swd/Mndhll 6.00 15.00
EQP4 Jcksn/Jcksn/Bntt/Avery 12.00 30.00
EQP5 Brady/Romo/P.Mann/Eli 40.00 100.00
EQP7 Ptrsn/Portis/Tomlin/LJ 15.00 40.00
EQP8 Moss/Owns/Jhnsn/Wyn 12.00 30.00
EQP9 Mntn/Rce/Brdshw/Swan 50.00 120.00
EQP10 Ptrsn/Paytn/Hrris/Sandrs 75.00 150.00

2008 Exquisite Collection Patch Duals

STATED PRINT RUN 50 SER.#'d SETS
*GOLD HOLO/15: .5X TO 1.2X PATCH/50
GOLD HOLOFOIL PRINT RUN 15
UNPRICED PLATINUM PRINT RUN 1
EP1 Darren McFadden 4.00 10.00
EP2 Matt Ryan 20.00 50.00
EP3 Rashard Mendenhall 4.00 10.00
EP4 Joe Flacco 8.00 20.00
EP5 Felix Jones 4.00 10.00
EP6 Jonathan Stewart 12.00 30.00
EP7 Brian Brohm 4.00 10.00
EP8 Steve Slaton 4.00 10.00
EP9 Limas Sweed 4.00 10.00
EP10 Peyton Manning 25.00 60.00
EP11 Tom Brady 30.00 80.00
EP16 Walter Payton 25.00 60.00
EP17 Tony Romo 8.00 20.00
EP18 Fran Tarkenton 12.00 30.00
EP19 Joe Theismann 12.00 30.00
EP20 Barry Sanders 20.00 50.00
EP21 Emmitt Smith 20.00 50.00
EP22 Jack Lambert 12.00 30.00
EP23 James Hardy 4.00 10.00
EP24 Chad Henne 5.00 12.00
EP25 Randy Moss 8.00 20.00
EP26 LaDainian Tomlinson 10.00 25.00
EP27 Donovan McNabb 8.00 20.00
EP28 Terrell Owens 8.00 20.00
EP29 Bo Jackson 15.00 40.00
EP30 Brett Favre 20.00 50.00
EP31 Marshawn Lynch 8.00 20.00
EP32 Chad Johnson 6.00 15.00
EP33 Kurt Warner 8.00 20.00
EP34 Chris Johnson 5.00 12.00
EP35 Darren McFadden 4.00 10.00
EP36 Matt Ryan 15.00 40.00
EP37 Jonathan Stewart 12.00 30.00
EP38 Felix Jones 4.00 10.00
EP39 Devin Thomas 4.00 10.00
EP40 Eli Manning 8.00 20.00
EP41 Joseph Addai 6.00 15.00
EP42 Kellen Winslow Sr. 10.00 25.00
EP43 Adrian Peterson 10.00 25.00
EP44 Rashard Mendenhall 4.00 10.00
EP45 Matt Forte 12.00 30.00
EP47 Malcolm Kelly 4.00 10.00
EP48 Jerry Rice 15.00 40.00
EP49 Mel Blount 10.00 25.00
EP50 Aaron Rodgers 20.00 50.00

2008 Exquisite Collection Rare Materials

STATED PRINT RUN 35 SER.#'d SETS
UNPRICED PLATINUM PRINT RUN 10
ERMAC Andre Caldwell 5.00 12.00
ERMBB Brian Brohm 5.00 12.00
ERMBE Braylon Edwards 8.00 20.00
ERMBJ Brandon Jacobs 8.00 20.00
ERMBS Barry Sanders 40.00 100.00
ERMCH Chad Henne 6.00 15.00
ERMCJ Chris Johnson 6.00 15.00
ERMDA Donnie Avery 6.00 15.00
ERMDJ DeSean Jackson 10.00 25.00
ERMDK Dustin Keller 6.00 15.00
ERMDM Darren McFadden 5.00 12.00
ERMDT Devin Thomas 5.00 12.00
ERMDW DeMarcus Ware 10.00 25.00
ERMEM Eli Manning 10.00 25.00
ERMER Eddie Royal 5.00 12.00
ERMFH Franco Harris 15.00 40.00
ERMFJ Felix Jones 5.00 12.00
ERMJB John David Booty 5.00 12.00
ERMJC Jamaal Charles 8.00 20.00
ERMJE John Elway 20.00 50.00
ERMJF Joe Flacco 10.00 25.00
ERMJO Chad Johnson 8.00 20.00
ERMJS Jonathan Stewart 8.00 20.00
ERMKO Kevin O'Connell 5.00 12.00
ERMKS Kevin Smith 5.00 12.00
ERMLS Limas Sweed 5.00 12.00
ERMLT LaDainian Tomlinson 12.00 30.00
ERMMF Matt Forte 8.00 20.00
ERMMK Malcolm Kelly 5.00 12.00
ERMMR Matt Ryan 15.00 40.00
ERMNE Jordy Nelson 25.00 50.00
ERMPM Peyton Manning 20.00 80.00

ERMRM Rashard Mendenhall 5.00 12.00
ERMRR Ray Rice 5.00 12.00
ERMSS Steve Slaton 5.00 12.00
ERMST Ken Stabler 15.00 40.00
ERMTB Tom Brady 40.00 100.00

2008 Exquisite Collection Signature Combos

STATED PRINT RUN 35 SER.#'d SETS
ECSAJ K.Anderson/B.Jones 15.00 40.00
ECSBR M.Ryan/B.Brohm 30.00 80.00
ECSHF J.Flacco/C.Henne 20.00 40.00
ECSHK P.Hornung/J.Kramer 30.00 60.00
ECSHT P.Hornung/Y.Tittle 30.00 60.00
ECSJB B.Bosworth/B.Jackson 50.00 100.00
ECSJR T.Rathman/D.Johnston 40.00 80.00
ECSJS F.Jones/K.Smith 10.00 25.00
ECSJT D.Thomas/D.Jackson 20.00 50.00
ECSLL C.Long/J.Long 15.00 40.00
ECSMA J.Addai/P.Manning 60.00 120.00
ECSMC P.Manning/D.Clark 60.00 120.00
ECSMM P.Manning/E.Manning 125.00 250.00
ECSSM J.Stewart/R.Mendenhall 15.00 40.00
ECSWH A.Hawk/D.Ware 20.00 50.00

2008 Exquisite Collection Signature Jersey

STATED PRINT RUN 25 SER.#'d SETS
UNPRICED PATCH AU PRINT RUN 10
ESSAP Adrian Peterson 100.00 200.00
ESSAR Aaron Rodgers 200.00 400.00
ESSBB Brian Brohm 8.00 20.00
ESSBR Ben Roethlisberger 75.00 150.00
ESSCH Chad Henne 10.00 25.00
ESSCJ Chris Johnson 12.00 30.00
ESSCP Clinton Portis 10.00 25.00
ESSDA Derek Anderson 10.00 25.00
ESSDB Dwayne Bowe 12.00 30.00
ESSDJ DeSean Jackson 40.00 80.00
ESSDM Darren McFadden 15.00 40.00
ESSDT Devin Thomas 10.00 25.00
ESSEM Eli Manning 50.00 100.00
ESSFH Franco Harris 40.00 80.00
ESSFJ Felix Jones 10.00 25.00
ESSJA Joseph Addai 10.00 25.00
ESSJB John David Booty 8.00 20.00
ESSJC Jamaal Charles 12.00 30.00
ESSJF Joe Flacco 20.00 50.00
ESSJL Jamal Lewis 12.00 30.00
ESSJN Jordy Nelson 30.00 60.00
ESSJR Jerry Rice 100.00 200.00
ESSJS Jonathan Stewart 30.00 60.00
ESSKO Kevin O'Connell 8.00 20.00
ESSKS Kevin Smith 8.00 20.00
ESSMF Matt Forte 30.00 80.00
ESSPM Peyton Manning 75.00 150.00
ESSPW Patrick Willis 20.00 50.00
ESSRC Roger Craig 12.00 30.00
ESSRM Rashard Mendenhall 10.00 25.00
ESSRR Ray Rice 10.00 25.00
ESSSS Steve Slaton 8.00 20.00
ESSTA Troy Aikman 50.00 100.00
ESSTB Terry Bradshaw 75.00 150.00
ESSTE Trent Edwards 10.00 25.00
ESSTR Tony Romo 50.00 100.00

2008 Exquisite Collection Signature Jersey Dual

DUAL JSY AU PRINT RUN 25
UNPRICED DUAL PATCH AU PRINT RUN 5
AR T.Aikman/T.Romo 75.00 150.00
BL Roethlisberger/L.Sweed 40.00 80.00
BN B.Brohm/J.Nelson 30.00 60.00
BR M.Ryan/B.Brohm 40.00 80.00
CG R.Craig/F.Gore 30.00 60.00
CW B.Watson/M.Lynch 20.00 50.00
EL T.Edwards/M.Lynch 20.00 50.00
EM J.Elway/B.Marshall 75.00 150.00
FO K.O'Connell/J.Flacco 20.00 50.00
FR J.Flacco/R.Rice 25.00 60.00
JE C.Johnson/B.Edwards
JS K.Smith/C.Johnson 15.00 40.00
LP C.Portis/J.Lewis 20.00 50.00
MJ D.McFadden/F.Jones 12.00 30.00
RM J.Rice/D.Maynard 100.00 200.00
SB E.Smith/M.Barber 100.00 200.00
SM Mendenhall/J.Stewart 20.00 50.00
TM Tomlinson/McFadden 15.00 40.00
WW D.Ware/A.Hawk

2008 Exquisite Collection Signature Jersey Numbers

STATED PRINT RUN 2-80
SERIAL #'d UNDER 21 NOT PRICED
UNPRICED PATCH PRINT RUN 10
ESNCP Clinton Portis/26 20.00 50.00
ESNES Emmitt Smith/22 125.00 250.00
ESNFJ Felix Jones/25 10.00 25.00
ESNJA Joseph Addai/29 20.00 50.00
ESNJR Jerry Rice/80 100.00 175.00
ESNJS Jonathan Stewart/28 25.00 60.00
ESNLT LaDainian Tomlinson/21 40.00 80.00
ESNPM Peyton Manning/18 75.00 150.00

2008 Exquisite Collection Signature Jersey Numbers Dual

STATED PRINT RUN RUN 15
UNPRICED DUAL PATCH AU PRINT RUN 5
FB B.Favre/B.Brohm 125.00 200.00
FR M.Ryan/J.Flacco 40.00 100.00
JF C.Johnson/M.Forte 20.00 50.00
JM B.Jackson/D.McFadden 60.00 120.00
JS J.Simpson/C.Johnson 15.00 40.00
MC P.Manning/D.Clark 75.00 150.00
PB J.Booty/A.Peterson 75.00 150.00
SJ E.Smith/F.Jones 125.00 200.00
WH D.Ware/A.Hawk 30.00 60.00

2008 Exquisite Collection Super Swatch

STATED PRINT RUN 50 SER.#'d SETS
*BLUE/20: .5X TO 1.2X SUPER SWATCH/50
BLUE PRINT RUN 20 SER.#'d SETS
UNPRICED BLUE PATCH PRINT RUN 5
UNPRICED GOLD HOLOFOIL PRINT RUN 5
UNPRICED PLATINUM PRINT RUN 1
UNPRICED SIGNATURE PRINT RUN 4
SSAN Derek Anderson 5.00 12.00
SSAP Adrian Peterson 8.00 20.00
SSAR Aaron Rodgers 15.00 40.00
SSAV Donnie Avery 4.00 10.00
SSBA Marion Barber 5.00 12.00
SSBB Brian Brohm 3.00 8.00
SSBC Brodie Croyle 6.00 15.00
SSBE Braylon Edwards 5.00 12.00
SSBF Brett Favre 15.00 40.00
SSBJ Bo Jackson 12.00 30.00
SSBO Brian Bosworth 10.00 25.00
SSBR Brian Brohm 3.00 8.00
SSBS Barry Sanders 15.00 40.00
SSBU Marc Bulger 5.00 12.00
SSCA Carson Palmer 6.00 15.00
SSCH Chad Henne 4.00 10.00
SSCJ Chad Johnson 5.00 12.00
SSCO Chris Johnson 4.00 10.00
SSCP Clinton Portis 5.00 12.00
SSCR Chris Johnson 4.00 10.00
SSDB Dwayne Bowe 6.00 15.00
SSDC Dallas Clark 5.00 12.00
SSDE Dexter Jackson 5.00 12.00
SSDG David Garrard 5.00 12.00
SSDJ DeSean Jackson 8.00 20.00
SSDM Darren McFadden 3.00 8.00
SSDO Donovan McNabb 6.00 15.00
SSDT Devin Thomas 3.00 8.00
SSEB Earl Bennett 5.00 12.00
SSEM Eli Manning 6.00 15.00
SSES Emmitt Smith 15.00 40.00
SSFA Brett Favre 15.00 40.00
SSFH Franco Harris 10.00 25.00
SSFJ Felix Jones 3.00 8.00
SSFL Joe Flacco 6.00 15.00
SSFT Fran Tarkenton 10.00 25.00
SSGS Gale Sayers 10.00 25.00
SSHE Chad Henne 4.00 10.00
SSJA Joseph Addai 5.00 12.00
SSJD Daryl Johnston 12.00 30.00
SSJDB John David Booty 3.00 8.00
SSJE John Elway 15.00 40.00
SSJF Joe Flacco 6.00 15.00
SSJH James Hardy 3.00 8.00
SSJL Jack Lambert 10.00 25.00
SSJO Felix Jones 3.00 8.00
SSJR Jerry Rice 20.00 50.00
SSJS Jonathan Stewart 10.00 25.00
SSJT Joe Theismann 10.00 25.00
SSKA Ken Anderson 8.00 20.00
SSKO Kevin O'Connell 3.00 8.00
SSKS Kevin Smith 3.00 8.00
SSKW Kurt Warner 6.00 15.00
SSLE Jamal Lewis 6.00 15.00
SSLJ Larry Johnson 5.00 12.00
SSLO Jake Long 5.00 12.00
SSLS Lynn Swann 15.00 40.00
SSLT LaDainian Tomlinson 8.00 20.00
SSMB Mel Blount 10.00 25.00
SSMC Darren McFadden 5.00 12.00
SSME Rashard Mendenhall 3.00 8.00
SSMF Matt Forte 10.00 25.00
SSMJ Joe Montana 30.00 80.00
SSMK Malcolm Kelly 3.00 8.00
SSML Marshawn Lynch 6.00 15.00
SSMO Randy Moss 6.00 15.00
SSMR Matt Ryan 15.00 40.00
SSNE Jordy Nelson 8.00 20.00
SSOA Ottis Anderson 6.00 15.00
SSPA Walter Payton 25.00 60.00
SSPE Peyton Manning 20.00 50.00
SSPH Paul Hornung 10.00 25.00
SSPM Peyton Manning 20.00 50.00
SSPW Patrick Willis 6.00 15.00
SSRC Roger Craig 8.00 20.00
SSRM Rashard Mendenhall 3.00 8.00
SSRO Ben Roethlisberger 8.00 20.00
SSRY Matt Ryan 15.00 40.00
SSSA Barry Sanders 15.00 40.00
SSSI Billy Sims 8.00 20.00
SSSM Kevin Smith 3.00 8.00
SSSS Steve Slaton 3.00 8.00
SSST Jonathan Stewart 10.00 25.00
SSSW Limas Sweed 3.00 8.00
SSTA Troy Aikman 12.00 30.00
SSTB Terry Bradshaw 12.00 30.00
SSTO Tom Brady 25.00 60.00
SSTR Tony Romo 6.00 15.00
SSVY Vince Young 5.00 12.00
SSWI Kellen Winslow Sr. 8.00 20.00
SSWP Walter Payton 25.00 60.00
SSWW Wes Welker 6.00 15.00

2009 Exquisite Collection

101-160 ROOKIE AU PRINT RUN 99
161-182 ROOK.JSY AU PRINT RUN 225
183-188 ROOKIE JSY AU PRINT RUN 99
1 Peyton Manning 25.00 50.00
2 Eli Manning 15.00 40.00
3 Adrian Peterson 40.00 80.00
4 Tony Romo 15.00 40.00
5 Drew Brees 10.00 25.00
6 LaDainian Tomlinson 8.00 20.00
7 Donovan McNabb 6.00 15.00
8 Tom Brady 20.00 50.00
9 Randy Moss 6.00 15.00
10 Steve Smith 6.00 15.00
11 Ben Roethlisberger 12.00 30.00
12 Matt Ryan 10.00 25.00
13 Joe Flacco 6.00 15.00
14 Matt Forte 5.00 12.00
15 Brian Westbrook 5.00 12.00
16 Philip Rivers 8.00 20.00
17 Jay Cutler 5.00 12.00
18 Kurt Warner 6.00 15.00
19 Larry Fitzgerald 6.00 15.00
20 Anquan Boldin 5.00 12.00
21 Chad Henne 6.00 15.00
22 Ray Lewis 8.00 20.00
23 Brady Quinn 5.00 12.00
24 Steven Jackson 5.00 12.00
25 Matt Cassel 5.00 12.00
26 Andre Johnson 6.00 15.00
27 Jake Delhomme 5.00 12.00
28 Matt Schaub 5.00 12.00
29 Frank Gore 6.00 15.00
30 Brian Urlacher 8.00 20.00
31 Matt Hasselbeck 5.00 12.00
32 Reggie Wayne 6.00 15.00
33 Steve Smith USC 6.00 15.00
34 Steve Slaton 5.00 12.00
35 Calvin Johnson 8.00 20.00
36 Kevin Smith 5.00 12.00
37 Devin Hester 6.00 15.00
38 Hines Ward 6.00 15.00
39 James Harrison 8.00 20.00
40 Trent Edwards 5.00 12.00
41 Marshawn Lynch 6.00 15.00
42 JaMarcus Russell 5.00 12.00
43 Chris Cooley 5.00 12.00
44 Carson Palmer 6.00 15.00
45 Chad Johnson 5.00 12.00
46 T.J. Houshmandzadeh 5.00 12.00
47 Aaron Rodgers 30.00 80.00
48 Greg Jennings 5.00 12.00
49 Ryan Grant 6.00 15.00
50 Bernard Berrian 5.00 12.00
51 Jason Campbell 5.00 12.00
52 David Garrard 5.00 12.00
53 Maurice Jones-Drew 5.00 12.00
54 Ed Reed 6.00 15.00
55 Jerricho Cotchery 5.00 12.00
56 Marques Colston 5.00 12.00
57 Reggie Bush 5.00 12.00
58 Mario Williams 6.00 15.00
59 DeMarcus Ware 6.00 15.00
60 Ronnie Brown 5.00 12.00
61 Ted Ginn 5.00 12.00
62 Asante Samuel 5.00 12.00
63 Troy Polamalu 8.00 20.00
64 Rashard Mendenhall 5.00 12.00
65 Marion Barber 6.00 15.00
66 Brandon Jacobs 5.00 12.00
67 Marc Bulger 5.00 12.00
68 Torry Holt 6.00 15.00
69 Jason Witten 6.00 15.00
70 Tony Gonzalez 6.00 15.00
71 DeSean Jackson 6.00 15.00
72 Kyle Orton 5.00 12.00
73 Shawne Merriman 5.00 12.00
74 Dwayne Bowe 6.00 15.00
75 Dwight Freeney 5.00 12.00
76 DeAngelo Williams 5.00 12.00
77 Roddy White 5.00 12.00
78 Braylon Edwards 5.00 12.00
79 Santonio Holmes 5.00 12.00
80 Champ Bailey 6.00 15.00
81 Cedric Benson 5.00 12.00
82 Nnamdi Asomugha 5.00 12.00
83 Lance Briggs 6.00 15.00
84 Adrian Wilson 6.00 12.00
85 Thomas Jones 5.00 12.00
86 Vince Young 5.00 12.00
87 Patrick Willis 6.00 15.00
88 Justin Tuck 5.00 12.00
89 Jared Allen 5.00 12.00
90 Julius Peppers 6.00 15.00
91 Antonio Bryant 5.00 12.00
92 Vernon Davis 5.00 12.00
93 Vincent Jackson 5.00 12.00
94 Darren McFadden 8.00 20.00
95 Roy Williams WR 5.00 12.00
96 Felix Jones 5.00 12.00
97 Michael Turner 5.00 12.00
98 Donald Driver 6.00 15.00
99 Dallas Clark 5.00 12.00
100 Brett Favre 30.00 80.00
101 Curtis Painter AU RC 8.00 20.00
102 Bernard Scott AU RC 12.00 30.00
103 James Laurinaitis AU RC 25.00 60.00
104 Malcolm Jenkins AU RC 8.00 20.00
105 Brian Orakpo AU RC 10.00 25.00
106 Graham Harrell AU RC 15.00 40.00
107 Brian Cushing AU RC 8.00 20.00
108 Rey Maualuga AU RC 12.00 30.00
109 Clay Matthews AU RC 100.00 200.00
110 Phil Loadholt AU RC 10.00 25.00
111 Duke Robinson AU RC 8.00 20.00
112 Terrance Taylor AU RC 10.00 25.00
113 Tyson Jackson AU RC 8.00 20.00
114 Brandon Tate AU RC 10.00 25.00
115 Darius Butler AU RC 10.00 25.00
116 Larry English AU RC 10.00 25.00
117 B.J. Raji AU RC 10.00 25.00
118 Eugene Monroe AU RC 8.00 20.00
119 Vontae Davis AU RC 8.00 20.00
120 Mike Thomas AU RC 8.00 20.00
121 Deon Butler AU RC 8.00 20.00
122 Chase Coffman AU RC 8.00 20.00
123 Richard Quinn AU RC 10.00 25.00
124 Travis Beckum AU RC 8.00 20.00
125 Brian Hartline AU RC 12.00 30.00
126 Mike Goodson AU RC 10.00 25.00
127 Austin Collie AU RC 8.00 20.00
128 Gartrell Johnson AU RC 8.00 20.00
129 Brooks Foster AU RC 8.00 20.00
130 Johnny Knox AU RC 10.00 25.00
131 Tom Brandstater AU RC 10.00 25.00
132 Mike Teel AU RC 10.00 25.00
133 Cedric Peerman AU RC 8.00 20.00
134 Andre Smith AU RC 8.00 20.00
135 Alex Mack AU RC 8.00 20.00
137 Michael Oher AU RC 12.00 30.00
138 Evander Hood AU RC 12.00 30.00
139 Patrick Chung AU RC 8.00 20.00
140 Mike Mitchell AU RC 8.00 20.00
141 Louis Delmas AU RC 10.00 25.00
142 Alphonso Smith AU RC 8.00 20.00
143 Clint Sintim AU RC 8.00 20.00
144 Sen'Derrick Marks AU RC 8.00 20.00
145 Cody Brown AU RC 8.00 20.00
146 Michael Johnson AU RC 8.00 20.00
148 Dominique Edison AU RC 8.00 20.00
149 Kenny McKinley AU RC 8.00 20.00
150 Cornelius Ingram AU RC 8.00 20.00
151 Aaron Brown AU RC 10.00 25.00
152 Bear Pascoe AU RC 10.00 25.00
153 Keith Null AU RC 10.00 25.00
154 Rashad Jennings AU RC 10.00 25.00
155 Quinten Lawrence AU RC 8.00 20.00
156 Javarris Williams AU RC 10.00 25.00
157 Mike Mickens AU RC 8.00 20.00
158 Julian Edelman AU RC 150.00 300.00
159 Chris Ogbonnaya AU RC 10.00 25.00
160 Quinn Johnson AU RC 8.00 20.00
161 J.Maclin JSY AU RC 15.00 40.00
162 Percy Harvin JSY AU RC 8.00 20.00
163 B.Robiskie JSY AU RC 8.00 20.00
164 H.Nicks JSY AU RC 10.00 25.00
165 R.Barden JSY AU RC 8.00 20.00
166 Rhett Bomar JSY AU RC 8.00 20.00
167 Pat White JSY AU RC 10.00 25.00
168 B.Pettigrew JSY AU RC 8.00 20.00
169 D.Williams JSY AU RC 8.00 20.00
170 Aaron Curry JSY AU RC 12.00 30.00
171 Kenny Britt JSY AU RC 8.00 20.00
172 S.McGee JSY AU RC 8.00 20.00
173 J.Iglesias JSY AU RC 8.00 20.00
174 Nate Davis JSY AU RC 8.00 20.00
175 Glen Coffee JSY AU RC 8.00 20.00
176 Jason Smith JSY AU RC 8.00 20.00
177 M.Wallace JSY AU RC 12.00 30.00
178 Javon Ringer JSY AU RC 8.00 20.00
179 S.Greene JSY AU RC 8.00 20.00
180 Andre Brown JSY AU RC 10.00 25.00
181 L.McCoy JSY AU RC 40.00 80.00
182 P.Turner JSY AU RC 8.00 20.00
183 M.Stafford JSY AU RC 300.00 600.00
184 K.Moreno JSY AU RC 15.00 40.00
185 M.Crabtree JSY AU RC 20.00 50.00
186 D.Heyward-Bey JSY AU RC 20.00 50.00
187 M.Sanchez JSY AU RC 20.00 50.00
188 D.Brown JSY AU RC 12.00 30.00
189 Chris Wells JSY AU RC 12.00 30.00
190 J.Freeman JSY AU RC 75.00 150.00

2009 Exquisite Collection Rookie Silver Holofoil

*ROOKIE AU 101-160: .5X TO 1.2X BASIC CARD
101-160 ROOKIE AU PRINT RUN 25
*ROOK.JSY AU 161-182: .5X TO 1.2X
161-182 ROOKIE AU PRINT RUN 99
*ROOK.JSY AU 183-188: .6X TO 1.5X
183-188 ROOKIE AU PRINT RUN 25
109 Clay Matthews AU 200.00 400.00
158 Julian Edelman AU 250.00 500.00
181 LeSean McCoy JSY AU 50.00 120.00
183 Matthew Stafford JSY AU 800.00 1500.00
185 Michael Crabtree JSY AU 75.00 150.00
187 Mark Sanchez JSY AU 100.00 200.00
190 Josh Freeman JSY AU 75.00 150.00

2009 Exquisite Collection Autobiography Jersey Signatures

STATED PRINT RUN 25-99
*GOLD/35: .5X TO 1.2X BASIC JSY AU
GOLD PRINT RUN 10-35
EXCH EXPIRATION: 3/6/2012
AB Anquan Boldin/99 10.00 25.00
AP Adrian Peterson/25 100.00 200.00
BM Brandon Marshall/99 12.00 30.00
BR Lance Briggs/99 12.00 30.00
BS Billy Sims/99 15.00 40.00
BW Brian Westbrook/75 15.00 40.00
CJ Chris Johnson/50 EXCH 50.00 100.00
DB Drew Brees/75 60.00 120.00
DM Donovan McNabb/25 30.00 60.00
DW DeMarcus Ware/99 25.00 50.00
EC Earl Campbell/75 30.00 60.00
EM Eli Manning/25 60.00 120.00
ES Emmitt Smith/25 100.00 200.00
FB Fred Biletnikoff/99 20.00 50.00
KW Kurt Warner/75 40.00 80.00
LE Lee Evans/99 12.00 30.00
LT Lawrence Taylor/99 30.00 60.00
MF Matt Forte/99 20.00 50.00
MT Michael Turner/75 15.00 40.00
MW Mario Williams/99 15.00 40.00
PH Paul Hornung/75 15.00 40.00
PM Peyton Manning/75 100.00 175.00
PS Phil Simms/75 20.00 50.00
RC Randall Cunningham/75 25.00 60.00
RO Ben Roethlisberger/25 60.00 120.00
RS Roger Staubach/75 50.00 100.00
RW Reggie Wayne/99 15.00 40.00
SL Steve Largent/75 20.00 50.00
SS Steve Slaton/99 10.00 25.00
TR Tony Romo/75 40.00 80.00

2009 Exquisite Collection Eight Patch

STATED PRINT RUN 20 SER.#'d SETS
1 Current RBs 1 40.00 100.00
2 Current WRs 1 30.00 60.00
3 Current QBs 1 100.00 [illegible]
4 Various QBs 1 100.00 200.00
5 Current RBs 2 30.00 80.00
6 Various WRs 1 50.00 100.00
7 2009 Rookies 1 50.00 100.00
8 2009 Rookie WRs 1 20.00 50.00
9 2009 Rookie WRs 2 15.00 40.00
10 Current QBs 2 50.00 100.00
11 Current RBs 3 40.00 100.00
12 Current WRs 2 20.00 50.00
13 Various QBs 2 60.00 150.00
14 2009 Rookies 2 20.00 50.00
15 Current Defense 1 40.00 80.00
16 QBs and WRs 1 75.00 150.00
17 QBs and WRs 2 30.00 60.00
18 Giants and Colts 40.00 80.00
19 Cowboys and Eagles 40.00 80.00
20 Chicago Bears 75.00 150.00
21 Cowboys and Raiders 60.00 120.00
22 Various QBs 3 60.00 150.00
23 Current QBs 3 30.00 60.00
24 Current Defense 2 40.00 80.00
25 Various QBs 4 75.00 150.00
26 Current Defense 3 40.00 80.00
27 Current QBs 4 100.00 200.00
28 Various Defense 1 50.00 100.00
29 QBs and WRs 3 40.00 80.00
30 Steelers 90.00 150.00
31 2009 Rookies 3 25.00 60.00
32 Current WRs 3 30.00 60.00
33 Retired RBs 75.00 150.00
34 2009 Rookies 4 30.00 80.00
35 Current RBs 4 50.00 100.00
36 Current RBs 5 40.00 100.00
37 Various Defense 2 30.00 60.00
38 QBs and WRs 4 50.00 100.00
39 Cowboys and Bears 75.00 150.00
40 Various QBs 5 100.00 200.00

2009 Exquisite Collection Endorsements

STATED PRINT RUN 25-99
*GOLD/15: .6X TO 1.5X AU/50-99
*GOLD/15: .5X TO 1.2X AU/25-35
GOLD PRINT RUN 15
EAB Anquan Boldin/65 6.00 15.00
EAC Aaron Curry/99 8.00 20.00
EAH Albert Haynesworth/75 8.00 20.00
EAP Adrian Peterson/25 60.00 120.00
EBP Brandon Pettigrew/99 5.00 12.00
EBR Brian Robiskie/99 5.00 12.00
EBW Brian Westbrook/35 8.00 20.00
ECJ Chris Johnson/75 6.00 15.00
ECP Clinton Portis/65 6.00 15.00
ECR Michael Crabtree/35 15.00 40.00
EDB Drew Brees/30 50.00 100.00
EDH Darrius Heyward-Bey/50 8.00 20.00
EDM Donovan McNabb/25 40.00 80.00
EEM Eli Manning/25 40.00 80.00
EHN Hakeem Nicks/99 6.00 15.00
EJA Jared Allen/75 15.00 40.00
EJM Jeremy Maclin/75 10.00 25.00
EJP Joey Porter/75 8.00 20.00
EKB Kenny Britt/99 8.00 20.00
ELB Lance Briggs/75 12.00 30.00
ELM LeSean McCoy/99 25.00 50.00
EMC Matt Cassel/50 10.00 25.00
EMF Matt Forte/50 10.00 30.00
EMJ Maurice Jones-Drew/75 6.00 15.00
EMR Matt Ryan/25 25.00 60.00
EMS Matthew Stafford/25 60.00 150.00
EMT Michael Turner/50 10.00 25.00
EMW Mario Williams/75 8.00 20.00
EPM Peyton Manning/50 75.00 125.00
EPW Patrick Willis/99 12.00 30.00
ERL Ray Lewis/60 50.00 100.00
ERO Ben Roethlisberger/25 50.00 100.00
ESA Mark Sanchez/35 15.00 40.00
ESG Shonn Greene/99 5.00 12.00
EWH Pat White/75 6.00 15.00

2009 Exquisite Collection Ensemble 2 Signatures

DUAL AUTO PRINT RUN 25-50
EXCH EXPIRATION: 3/8/2012
BN H.Nicks/R.Barden/50 8.00 20.00
BW L.Briggs/P.Willis/35 20.00 50.00
CH Heyward-By/Crabtree/35 10.00 25.00
CM McNabb/Cunningham/25 50.00 100.00
HW Haynesworth/Williams/50 15.00 40.00
KT J.Kelly/T.Thomas/35 40.00 80.00
MC B.Cushing/C.Matthews/50 40.00 80.00
ML Maynard/Largent/35 25.00 60.00
MM J.Maclin/L.McCoy/50 25.00 60.00
MS P.Mann/Staubach/25 90.00 150.00
RB J.Ringer/K.Britt/50 15.00 40.00
RH Robiskie/Harvin/50 15.00 40.00
SF G.Sayers/M.Forte/35 40.00 80.00
SP A.Peterson/B.Sims/25 75.00 150.00
SS M.Sanchez/Stafford/25 60.00 150.00
TR M.Ryan/M.Turner/25 40.00 80.00
WB A.Boldin/R.Wayne/35 15.00 40.00
WJ Westbrook/D.Jackson/35 20.00 50.00
WM C.Wells/K.Moreno/35 20.00 50.00

2009 Exquisite Collection Ensemble 3 Signatures

STATED PRINT RUN 10-30
EXCH EXPIRATION: 3/8/2012
BRH Hywrd/Rice/Brwn/20 125.00 200.00
CHM Mclin/Crbtree/Hrvin/20 12.00 30.00
FSJ Jhnsn/Frte/Slatn/20
KLP Karras/Lilly/Perry/20 40.00 80.00
MCM Cshing/Mtthws/Mluga/30 50.00 100.00
MMB Brwn/Morno/McCoy/20 50.00 100.00
MWB Brwn/P.Mann/Wyne/20 100.00 175.00
PJF Prt/Frt/Jns-Drw/20 30.00 60.00
RMG Ringer/McCoy/Grne/20 20.00 50.00
RWN Rbisk/Willi/icks/30 10.00 25.00
SKM Kelly/Simms/Moon/20 50.00 100.00
WAH Hynswrth/Ware/Allen/20 40.00 80.00
WMB Wells/Brown/Moreno/20 20.00 50.00
WTC Curry/Ware/LT/30

2009 Exquisite Collection Ensemble 4 Signatures

BPWT Prtr/White/Trnr/Brwn 20.00 50.00
CBJR Jhnstn/Cmpbll/Blr/Rthm 60.00 120.00
ECLB Bwe/Evns/Lnch/Cssel 25.00 60.00
IBNW Ncks/Igls/Wllce/Brdn 12.00 30.00
JJDC Crry/Jnkns/Jcksn/Dvis 8.00 20.00
RMBG Brwn/Ringr/McCy/Grne 20.00 50.00
SEKM Mrno/Klly/Elwy/Simms 175.00 300.00
SHBJ Jhnstn/Emitt/Hrris/Blr 150.00 250.00
SMCP Pettgr/Mrno/Stffrd/Crbtr 12.00 30.00
STPS Ptrsn/Sndrs/Syrs/Tmlin 250.00 400.00
WBBC Bldin/Brees/Wrnr/Clstn 75.00 150.00
WBBP Brks/Prtr/Brgs/Willis 60.00 120.00
WMBM Brees/Eli/Wrnr/P.Mnn 300.00 450.00
WMMB Wlls/Brwn/Mrno/McCy 20.00 50.00

2009 Exquisite Collection Inscriptions

IAK Alex Karras 40.00 80.00
IAP Alan Page 50.00 100.00
IBJ Bo Jackson 75.00 150.00
ICP Clinton Portis 40.00 80.00
IDB Drew Brees 100.00 200.00
IDJ Deacon Jones 50.00 100.00
IEC Earl Campbell 40.00 80.00
IKW Kurt Warner 75.00 150.00
ILM LeSean McCoy 50.00 100.00
ILT Lawrence Taylor
IMA Matthew Stafford 75.00 150.00
IMS Mark Sanchez 50.00 100.00
IPH Percy Harvin 20.00 50.00
IPM Peyton Manning 100.00 200.00
IPS Phil Simms 40.00 80.00
IRB Rocky Bleier 50.00 100.00
ISL Steve Largent 10.00 [illegible]
ITR Tony Romo 50.00 100.00
ITT Thurman Thomas 40.00 80.00

2009 Exquisite Collection Legendary Signatures

STATED PRINT RUN 15-45
EXCH EXPIRATION: 3/8/2012
LAP Alan Page/45 15.00 40.00
LBL Bob Lilly/45 12.00 30.00
LDJ Deacon Jones/45 12.00 30.00
LEC Earl Campbell/25 25.00 50.00
LES Emmitt Smith/15 125.00 250.00
LJE John Elway/15 125.00 250.00
LJH Jack Ham/35 25.00 50.00
LJR Jerry Rice/15 125.00 200.00
LLB Lem Barney/45 10.00 25.00
LRC Randall Cunningham/35 30.00 60.00
LRS Roger Staubach/25 EXCH 75.00 125.00
LSL Steve Largent/45 15.00 40.00
LSY Steve Young/15 40.00 80.00
LWM Warren Moon/25 30.00 60.00

2009 Exquisite Collection Legendary Signatures Dual

STATED PRINT RUN 20 SER.#'d SETS
BH Bradshaw/Harris EXCH
CM E.Campbell/W.Moon 30.00 60.00
JO D.Jones/M.Olsen 30.00 60.00
KT J.Kelly/T.Thomas 50.00 100.00
LJ B.Lilly/E.Jones EXCH
LM H.Moore/S.Largent 30.00 60.00
MM A.Mann/Marino 100.00 200.00
PS A.Page/B.Smith 30.00 60.00
TC Carson/L.Taylor 30.00 60.00
WB L.Barney/R.Woodson 40.00 100.00

2009 Exquisite Collection Legendary Signatures Trios

AEM Marino/Elway/Aikmn 250.00 400.00
HCS Sims/Cmpbll/F.Hrris 60.00 120.00
HKS Krmer/Singltry/Hrng 40.00 80.00
JOK Karras/D.Jnes/Olsen 50.00 100.00
LMM Mynrd/Moore/Lrgnt
MRL Moore/Rice/Largent 125.00 200.00
PJS Page/B.Smth/D.Jnes 30.00 60.00
SKM Kelly/Simms/Moon 75.00 150.00
SST B.Sndrs/Emit/T.Thms 200.00 350.00

2009 Exquisite Collection Notable Nameplates

STATED PRINT RUN 15 SER.#'d SETS
NAB Andre Brown 8.00 20.00
NAC Aaron Curry 10.00 25.00
NAP Adrian Peterson 15.00 40.00
NBA Ramses Barden 6.00 15.00
NBP Brandon Pettigrew 6.00 15.00
NBR Brian Robiskie 6.00 15.00
NBS Barry Sanders 30.00 80.00
NBU Deon Butler 6.00 15.00
NCW Chris Wells 12.00 30.00
NDB Donald Brown 6.00 15.00
NDH Darrius Heyward-Bey 10.00 25.00
NDM Dan Marino 40.00 100.00
NDW Derrick Williams 6.00 15.00
NEM Eli Manning 20.00 50.00
NGC Glen Coffee 6.00 15.00
NHN Hakeem Nicks 8.00 20.00
NJF Josh Freeman 6.00 15.00
NJI Juaquin Iglesias 6.00 15.00
NJM Jeremy Maclin 12.00 30.00
NJR Javon Ringer 6.00 15.00
NKB Kenny Britt 10.00 25.00
NKM Knowshon Moreno 6.00 15.00
NLM LeSean McCoy 15.00 40.00
NLT LaDainian Tomlinson 15.00 40.00
NMC Michael Crabtree 10.00 25.00
NMM Mohamed Massaquoi 6.00 15.00
NMS Mark Sanchez 6.00 15.00
NMT Mike Thomas 6.00 15.00
NMW Mike Wallace 10.00 25.00
NND Nate Davis 6.00 15.00
NPH Percy Harvin 6.00 15.00
NPM Peyton Manning 40.00 80.00
NPT Patrick Turner 6.00 15.00
NPW Pat White 8.00 20.00
NRB Rhett Bomar 6.00 15.00
NSG Shonn Greene 6.00 15.00
NST Matthew Stafford 30.00 80.00
NTB Tom Brady 40.00 80.00
NTH Mike Thomas 6.00 15.00
NTO Terrell Owens 12.00 30.00

2009 Exquisite Collection Patch

STATED PRINT RUN 75 SER.#'d SETS
*GOLD/40: .4X TO 1X BASIC PATCH/75
GOLD PRINT RUN 40 SER.#'d SETS
PAB Anquan Boldin 5.00 12.00
PAH A.J. Hawk 5.00 12.00
PAP Adrian Peterson 8.00 20.00
PAR Aaron Rodgers 30.00 60.00
PAS Aaron Schobel 8.00 20.00
PBD Brian Dawkins 8.00 20.00
PBJ Bo Jackson 15.00 40.00
PBO Dwayne Bowe 6.00 15.00
PBS Barry Sanders 15.00 40.00
PBU Brian Urlacher 10.00 25.00
PBW Brian Westbrook 8.00 20.00
PCJ Calvin Johnson 8.00 20.00
PCO Chad Johnson 5.00 12.00
PCP Clinton Portis 5.00 12.00
PCW Cadillac Williams 6.00 15.00
PDC Dallas Clark 5.00 12.00
PDH Devin Hester 6.00 15.00
PDJ Daryl Johnston 8.00 20.00
PDM Dan Marino 20.00 50.00
PDW DeAngelo Williams 5.00 12.00
PEM Eli Manning 6.00 15.00
PES Emmitt Smith 15.00 40.00
PFG Frank Gore 6.00 15.00
PGJ Greg Jennings 5.00 12.00
PJC Jason Campbell 5.00 12.00
PJK Jim Kelly 10.00 25.00
PJP Julius Peppers 6.00 15.00
PJR Jerry Rice 10.00 25.00
PJT Joe Theismann 10.00 25.00
PJW Jason Witten 6.00 15.00
PKW Kellen Winslow Sr. 8.00 20.00
PLJ Larry Johnson 5.00 12.00
PLT LaDainian Tomlinson 8.00 20.00
PMB Marion Barber 6.00 15.00
PMC Donovan McNabb 6.00 15.00
PML Marshawn Lynch 6.00 15.00
POW Terrell Owens 6.00 15.00
PPL Philip Rivers 8.00 20.00
PPM Peyton Manning 15.00 40.00
PPW Patrick Willis 6.00 15.00
PRB Ronnie Brown 5.00 12.00
PRL Ray Lewis 12.00 30.00
PRW Reggie Wayne 6.00 15.00
PSA Bob Sanders 6.00 15.00
PSJ Steven Jackson 5.00 12.00
PSM Shawne Merriman 5.00 12.00
PTO Tom Brady 25.00 60.00
PWI Willie Parker 5.00 12.00
PWP Walter Payton 25.00 60.00
PWW Wes Welker 10.00 25.00

2009 Exquisite Collection Patch Combos

STATED PRINT RUN 50 SER.#'d SETS
*GOLD/20: .6X TO 1.5X DUAL/50
GOLD STATED PRINT RUN 20
DM P.Manning/T.Brady 20.00 40.00
CC C.Johnson/C.Johnson 8.00 20.00
EB B.Sanders/E.Smith 25.00 50.00
EW L.Evans/W.Welker 10.00 25.00
GJ A.Gates/V.Jackson 5.00 12.00
[illegible]
JB M.Bulger/S.Jackson 5.00 12.00
JJ A.Johnson/G.Jennings 6.00 15.00
JP C.Palmer/C.Johnson 6.00 15.00
JW C.Johnson/W.Welker 10.00 25.00
KM D.Marino/J.Kelly 30.00 60.00
LU B.Urlacher/R.Lewis 10.00 25.00
MB D.McNabb/T.Brady 25.00 60.00
MM D.Marino/P.Manning 20.00 50.00
MR E.Manning/P.Rivers 8.00 20.00
OJ C.Johnson/T.Owens 6.00 15.00
PC C.Palmer/J.Campbell 6.00 15.00
PJ B.Jacobs/C.Portis 5.00 12.00
PS A.Peterson/B.Sanders 15.00 40.00
PW D.Ware/J.Peppers 8.00 20.00
RR A.Rodgers/P.Rivers 15.00 40.00
TP A.Peterson/L.Tomlinson 8.00 20.00
WG B.Westbrook/F.Gore 8.00 20.00
WM Westbrook/D.McNabb 6.00 15.00
WP H.Ward/W.Parker 12.00 30.00

2009 Exquisite Collection Patch Quads

QUAD PATCH PRINT RUN 20
QB Plmr/McNb/P.Mnn/Brdy 25.00 50.00
RB Prts/Will/Gre/Jns-Drw 20.00 40.00
WR Jhns/Jhns/Wyne/Smth 20.00 40.00
49OR Hywrd/Rice/Rice/Crbtr 15.00 40.00
BEAR Hestr/Sayrs/Frte/Pytn 30.00 60.00
FKTM Fvre/Mrino/Trkntn/Klly 50.00 120.00
LUMW Urlchr/Wre/Lwis/Mrmn 25.00 50.00
MRMR Rdgrs/Eli/P.Mnn/Rivrs 40.00 80.00
OJJS Jhnsn/Jhnsn/Smth/TO 20.00 40.00
TPBL Ptrsn/Tmln/Lnch/Brwn 30.00 60.00

2009 Exquisite Collection Patch Trios

STATED PRINT RUN 25 SER.#'d SETS
BRL Bruce/Rice/Largent 20.00 50.00
BRM Rodgers/Eli/Brady 50.00 100.00
DRF Rodgers/Favre/Driver 40.00 80.00
DSS Samuel/Sandrs/Dwkins 10.00 25.00
FBM Favre/Marino/Brady 50.00 100.00
JBL L.Jhnsn/Lnch/Brwn 10.00 25.00
JES Edwrds/Jhnsn/S.Smth 10.00 25.00
JJJ Johnsn/Johnsn/Johnsn 10.00 25.00
JTP Petrsn/Tomlin/L.Jhnsn 20.00 50.00
LUW Urlachr/Ware/Lewis 15.00 40.00
MBM Eli/P.Mann/Brady 25.00 50.00
MMM Marino/Eli/P.Mann 30.00 60.00
SSP Sanders/Emmitt/Payton 40.00 80.00
TKM Marino/Tarkntn/Kelly 30.00 60.00
WWS Ward/S.Smth/Welker 15.00 40.00

2009 Exquisite Collection Rare Materials

STATED PRINT RUN 35 SER.#'d SETS
4AB Andre Brown 8.00 20.00
4AC Aaron Curry 10.00 25.00
4AJ Andre Johnson 10.00 25.00
4AP Adrian Peterson
4BA Ramses Barden 6.00 15.00
4BF Brett Favre 40.00 100.00
4BJ Bo Jackson 20.00 50.00
4BO Anquan Boldin 8.00 20.00
4BP Brandon Pettigrew 6.00 15.00
4BR Brian Robiskie 6.00 15.00
4BU Deon Butler 6.00 15.00
4CJ Calvin Johnson 20.00 50.00
4CO Chad Johnson 8.00 20.00
4CP Carson Palmer 10.00 25.00
4CW Chris Wells 6.00 15.00
4DB Donald Brown 6.00 15.00
4DE DeAngelo Williams 8.00 20.00
4DH Darrius Heyward-Bey 10.00 25.00
4DM Dan Marino 30.00 80.00
4DO Donovan McNabb 15.00 40.00
4DW Derrick Williams 6.00 15.00
4FG Frank Gore 12.00 30.00
4GC Glen Coffee 6.00 15.00
4GS Gale Sayers
4HN Hakeem Nicks 8.00 20.00
4HO Paul Hornung
4JF Josh Freeman 6.00 15.00
4JK Jim Kelly 15.00 40.00
4JM Jeremy Maclin 8.00 20.00
4JR Javon Ringer 6.00 15.00
4JS Jason Smith 6.00 15.00
4KB Kenny Britt 10.00 25.00
4KM Knowshon Moreno 6.00 15.00
4LJ Larry Johnson 8.00 20.00
4LM LeSean McCoy 15.00 40.00
4LT LaDainian Tomlinson 12.00 30.00
4MA Marques Colston 8.00 20.00
4MC Michael Crabtree 10.00 25.00
4ML Marshawn Lynch 10.00 25.00
4MM Mohamed Massaquoi 6.00 15.00
4MS Mark Sanchez 6.00 15.00
4MT Mike Thomas 6.00 15.00
4MW Mike Wallace 10.00 25.00
4ND Nate Davis 6.00 15.00
4PH Percy Harvin 6.00 15.00
4PM Peyton Manning 40.00 80.00
4PT Patrick Turner 6.00 15.00
4PW Pat White 8.00 20.00
4RB Ronnie Brown 10.00 25.00
4RH Rhett Bomar 6.00 15.00
4RI Jerry Rice 40.00 80.00
4SG Shonn Greene 6.00 15.00
4SM Stephen McGee 6.00 15.00
4SS Steve Smith 10.00 25.00
4ST Matthew Stafford 15.00 40.00
4TJ Tyson Jackson 6.00 15.00
4TR Tony Romo 10.00 25.00
4UR Brian Urlacher 25.00 50.00
4VJ Vincent Jackson 8.00 20.00
4WP Walter Payton

2009 Exquisite Collection Rookie Big Patch Match-Up

STATED PRINT RUN 50 SER.#'d SETS
BC A.Brown/G.Coffee 6.00 15.00
BM R.Bomar/S.McGee 5.00 12.00
BN H.Nicks/R.Barden 6.00 15.00
CH Heyward-Bey/Crabtree 8.00 20.00
CM J.Maclin/M.Crabtree 8.00 20.00
FD J.Freeman/N.Davis 5.00 12.00
HM J.Maclin/P.Harvin 6.00 15.00
IM J.Iglesias/Massaquoi 5.00 12.00
MG L.McCoy/S.Greene 12.00 30.00
MN H.Nicks/J.Maclin 6.00 15.00
RB J.Ringer/K.Britt 8.00 20.00
RW B.Robiskie/M.Wallace 8.00 20.00
SG M.Sanchez/S.Greene 30.00 80.00
SP Pettigrew/M.Stafford 20.00 50.00
SS M.Sanchez/M.Stafford 20.00 50.00
SW D.Williams/M.Stafford 20.00 50.00
WC A.Curry/C.Wells 8.00 20.00
WM C.Wells/K.Moreno 5.00 12.00
WP Pettigrew/D.Williams 5.00 12.00
WT P.White/P.Turner 6.00 15.00

2009 Exquisite Collection Rookie Bookmark Patch Autographs

STATED PRINT RUN 35-99
*PLATINUM/50: .5X TO 1.2X DUAL AU/99
PLATINUM PRINT RUN 10-50
EXCH EXPIRATION: 3/5/2012
BC A.Curry/D.Butler/99 10.00 25.00
BG D.Brown/S.Greene/99 12.00 30.00
BM D.Brown/K.Moreno/35 12.00 30.00
BN H.Nicks/R.Bomar/99 12.00 30.00
BS M.Sanchez/R.Bomar/35 30.00 80.00
CC G.Coffee/Crabtree/35 20.00 50.00
CD Crabtree/N.Davis/35 20.00 50.00
CH Heywrd-By/Crabtree/35 20.00 50.00
CM J.Maclin/Crabtree/35 20.00 50.00
FD J.Freemn/N.Davis/99 10.00 25.00
GB A.Brwn/S.Greene/99 12.00 30.00
HB Heywrd-By/D.Butlr/99 12.00 30.00
HT M.Thoms/P.Harvin/99 10.00 25.00
IH J.Iglesias/P.Harvin/99 12.00 30.00
IP Pettigrw/J.Iglesias/99 10.00 25.00
JS J.Smith/T.Jackson/99 10.00 25.00
MB D.Butler/Massaquoi/99 10.00 25.00
MF J.Freemn/McGee/99 12.00 30.00
MM K.Moreno/L.McCoy/99 25.00 60.00
NB H.Nicks/K.Britt/99 15.00 40.00
RB B.Robiskie/K.Britt/99 15.00 40.00
RM Robiskie/Massaquoi/99 10.00 25.00
RW Robiskie/M.Wallace/99 10.00 25.00
SG Sanchez/S.Greene/35 15.00 40.00
SM K.Moreno/Stafford/35 60.00 120.00
SS M.Sanchez/Stafford/35 100.00 200.00
SW M.Stafford/P.White/35 50.00 120.00
TS M.Sanchez/P.Turner/35 40.00 100.00
TT M.Thomas/P.Turner/99 10.00 25.00
WB D.Butler/D.Williams/99 10.00 25.00
WD N.Davis/P.White/99 12.00 30.00
WG C.Wells/S.Greene/99 15.00 40.00
WH C.Wells/Heywrd-By/35 20.00 50.00
WI D.Williams/Iglesias/99 10.00 25.00
WM C.Wells/L.McCoy/99 12.00 30.00
WR B.Robiskie/C.Wells/99 20.00 50.00

2009 Exquisite Collection Signature Jersey

STATED PRINT RUN 20-50
EXCH EXPIRATION: 3/5/2012
SJAB Anquan Boldin/30 10.00 25.00
SJAC Aaron Curry/35 12.00 30.00
SJBG Bob Griese/30 20.00 50.00
SJBP Brandon Pettigrew/35 8.00 20.00
SJBR Brian Robiskie/35 8.00 20.00
SJBS Barry Sanders/20 100.00 175.00
SJCW Chris Wells/35 8.00 20.00
SJDB Drew Brees/25 75.00 135.00
SJDM Dan Marino/20 100.00 200.00
SJDW DeMarcus Ware/30 12.00 30.00
SJEM Eli Manning/20 40.00 80.00
SJFH Franco Harris/25 30.00 80.00
SJGS Gale Sayers/30 40.00 80.00
SJHN Hakeem Nicks/50 10.00 25.00
SJJE John Elway/30 75.00 150.00
SJJH Jack Ham/30 30.00 60.00
SJJI Juaquin Iglesias/50 8.00 20.00
SJJM Jeremy Maclin/35 10.00 25.00
SJKB Kenny Britt/50 12.00 30.00
SJKM Knowshon Moreno/35 8.00 20.00
SJKW Kurt Warner/30 30.00 80.00
SJLB Lance Briggs/30 25.00 50.00
SJLM LeSean McCoy/35 25.00 60.00
SJMA Peyton Manning/30 75.00 150.00
SJMC Michael Crabtree/30 40.00 80.00
SJMR Matt Ryan/20 40.00 80.00
SJMS Matthew Stafford/20 60.00 120.00
SJMT Michael Turner/30 10.00 25.00
SJMW Mario Williams/30 12.00 30.00
SJNI Hakeem Nicks/50 10.00 25.00
SJPM Peyton Manning/30 100.00 175.00
SJPS Phil Simms/30 12.00 30.00
SJPW Pat White/35 10.00 25.00
SJRC Randall Cunningham/30 30.00 60.00
SJSA Mark Sanchez/30 25.00 60.00
SJSG Shonn Greene/50 8.00 20.00
SJSL Steve Largent/30 30.00 60.00
SJTR Tony Romo/20 40.00 80.00
SJWM Warren Moon/30 25.00 60.00

2009 Exquisite Collection Signature Jersey Dual

STATED PRINT RUN 10-35
BC Curry/Butler/15 8.00 20.00
BN H.Nicks/R.Barden/35 6.00 15.00
HJ Hyneswrth/Jacksn/25 15.00 40.00
LB L.Briggs/R.Lewis/15 60.00 120.00
TJ B.Jacobs/M.Turner/15 10.00 25.00
WP Pettigrew/D.Willms/35 15.00 40.00

2009 Exquisite Collection Single Player Triple Patch

STATED PRINT RUN 30 SER.#'d SETS
3PAG Antonio Gates 10.00 25.00
3PAJ Andre Johnson 8.00 20.00
3PAP Adrian Peterson 40.00 80.00
3PBE Braylon Edwards 6.00 15.00
3PBF Brett Favre 75.00 150.00
3PBJ Brandon Jacobs 6.00 15.00
3PBP Brandon Pettigrew 5.00 12.00
3PBR Tedy Bruschi 10.00 25.00
3PBS Barry Sanders 20.00 50.00
3PBU Brian Urlacher 12.00 30.00
3PCJ Chad Johnson 6.00 15.00
3PCP Clinton Portis 6.00 15.00
3PCR Michael Crabtree 8.00 20.00
3PCW Chris Wells 12.00 30.00
3PDA Darren McFadden 10.00 25.00
3PDE DeAngelo Williams 6.00 15.00
3PDG David Garrard 6.00 15.00
3PDH Darrius Heyward-Bey 8.00 20.00
3PDM Donovan McNabb 12.00 30.00
3PDO Donald Brown 5.00 12.00
3PDW DeMarcus Ware 8.00 20.00
3PES Emmitt Smith 25.00 60.00
3PFG Frank Gore 12.00 30.00
3PFR Josh Freeman 5.00 12.00
3PFT Fred Taylor 6.00 15.00
3PJC Jason Campbell 6.00 15.00
3PJF Joe Flacco 12.00 30.00
3PJK Jim Kelly 12.00 30.00
3PJM Jeremy Maclin 6.00 15.00
3PJO Chris Johnson 12.00 30.00
3PJP Julius Peppers 8.00 20.00
3PJR Jerry Rice 25.00 60.00
3PJW Jason Witten 8.00 20.00
3PKM Knowshon Moreno 5.00 12.00
3PKW Kurt Warner 8.00 20.00
3PLE Lee Evans 8.00 20.00
3PLM LeSean McCoy 12.00 30.00
3PLT LaDainian Tomlinson 10.00 25.00
3PMB Marion Barber 8.00 20.00
3PMC Marques Colston 6.00 15.00
3PMF Matt Forte 6.00 15.00
3PML Marshawn Lynch 8.00 20.00
3PMR Matt Ryan 12.00 30.00
3PMS Matthew Stafford 20.00 50.00
3PPA Carson Palmer 8.00 20.00
3PPH Percy Harvin 6.00 15.00
3PPM Peyton Manning 25.00 60.00
3PRB Ronnie Brown 6.00 15.00
3PRE Reggie Bush 12.00 30.00
3PRI Jerry Rice 20.00 50.00
3PRW Reggie Wayne 8.00 20.00
3PSA Mark Sanchez 25.00 60.00
3PSJ Steven Jackson 6.00 15.00
3PSM Shawne Merriman 6.00 15.00
3PSS Steve Smith 8.00 20.00
3PTO LaDainian Tomlinson 10.00 25.00
3PTR Tony Romo 8.00 20.00
3PVJ Vincent Jackson 6.00 15.00
3PVY Vince Young 6.00 15.00
3PWW Wes Welker 12.00 30.00

2009-10 Exquisite Collection Rookie Patch Flashback

STATED PRINT RUN 25 SER.#'d SETS
78J Peyton Manning/25 400.00 700.00
78K John Elway/25 300.00 600.00
78L Jerry Rice/25 350.00 650.00
78M Barry Sanders/25 400.00 800.00
700 Adrian Peterson/25 400.00 [illegible]

2010 Exquisite Collection

1-99 VETERAN PRINT RUN 35
100-132 JSY AU RC PRINT RUN 75-120
133-190 AU ROOKIE PRINT RUN 65
EXCH EXPIRATION: 3/17/2013
1 Aaron Rodgers 25.00 60.00

2 Adrian Peterson 30.00 60.00
3 Ahmad Bradshaw 6.00 15.00
4 Alex Smith QB 8.00 20.00
5 Andre Johnson 8.00 20.00
6 Anquan Boldin 6.00 15.00
7 Arian Foster 10.00 25.00
8 Austin Collie 6.00 15.00
9 Ben Roethlisberger 12.00 30.00
10 Brandon Marshall 8.00 20.00
11 Brett Favre 60.00 120.00
12 Calvin Johnson 10.00 25.00
13 Zach Miller 6.00 15.00
14 Carson Palmer 8.00 20.00
15 Cedric Benson 6.00 15.00
16 Chad Henne 8.00 20.00
17 Chad Johnson 6.00 15.00
18 Charles Woodson 20.00 40.00
19 Peyton Hillis 8.00 20.00
20 Chris Johnson 12.00 30.00
21 Brandon Jacobs 6.00 15.00
22 Clay Matthews 20.00 40.00
23 Ryan Fitzpatrick 6.00 15.00
24 Dallas Clark 6.00 15.00
25 Darren McFadden 6.00 15.00
26 David Garrard 6.00 15.00
27 DeAngelo Williams 6.00 15.00
28 DeSean Jackson 8.00 20.00
29 Donovan McNabb 20.00 40.00
30 Drew Brees 25.00 50.00
31 Eli Manning 25.00 50.00
32 Felix Jones 6.00 15.00
33 Frank Gore 8.00 20.00
34 Greg Jennings 6.00 15.00
35 Hakeem Nicks 6.00 15.00
36 Hines Ward 8.00 20.00
37 Jamaal Charles 8.00 20.00
38 Jason Campbell 6.00 15.00
39 Jason Witten 8.00 20.00
40 Jay Cutler 6.00 15.00
41 Brandon Lloyd 6.00 15.00
42 Jeremy Maclin 6.00 15.00
43 Joe Flacco 8.00 20.00
44 Jonathan Stewart 6.00 15.00
45 Joseph Addai 6.00 15.00
46 Josh Freeman 8.00 20.00
47 Josh Cribbs 6.00 15.00
48 Kevin Kolb 6.00 15.00
49 Knowshon Moreno 6.00 15.00
50 Kyle Orton 6.00 15.00
51 LaDainian Tomlinson 10.00 25.00
52 Larry Fitzgerald 8.00 20.00
53 LeSean McCoy 10.00 25.00
54 Braylon Edwards 6.00 15.00
55 Marion Barber 8.00 20.00
56 Mark Sanchez 6.00 15.00
57 Marques Colston 6.00 15.00
58 Matt Cassel 6.00 15.00
59 Matt Forte 6.00 15.00
60 Matt Hasselbeck 6.00 15.00
61 Matt Ryan 8.00 20.00
62 Matt Schaub 6.00 15.00
63 Matthew Stafford 8.00 20.00
64 Maurice Jones-Drew 6.00 15.00
65 Michael Turner 6.00 15.00
66 Michael Vick 15.00 40.00
67 Mike Wallace 6.00 15.00
68 Miles Austin 6.00 15.00
69 Patrick Willis 8.00 20.00
70 Percy Harvin 6.00 15.00
71 Peyton Manning 50.00 100.00
72 Philip Rivers 10.00 25.00
73 Kenny Britt 6.00 15.00
74 Randy Moss 8.00 20.00
75 Rashard Mendenhall 6.00 15.00
76 Ray Lewis 12.00 30.00
77 Ray Rice 6.00 15.00
78 Reggie Wayne 8.00 20.00
79 Ricky Williams 8.00 20.00
80 Roddy White 6.00 15.00
81 Ronnie Brown 6.00 15.00
82 Santana Moss 6.00 15.00
83 Santonio Holmes 6.00 15.00
84 Shonn Greene 6.00 15.00
85 Sidney Rice 10.00 25.00
86 Steve Breaston 6.00 15.00
87 Steve Smith USC 6.00 15.00
88 Steve Smith 8.00 20.00
89 Steven Jackson 6.00 15.00
90 Terrell Owens 8.00 20.00
91 Thomas Jones 6.00 15.00
92 Tim Hightower 6.00 15.00
93 Tom Brady 40.00 80.00
94 Tony Romo 8.00 20.00
95 Troy Polamalu 10.00 25.00
96 Vernon Davis 6.00 15.00
97 Vince Young 6.00 15.00
98 Vincent Jackson 6.00 15.00
99 Wes Welker 8.00 20.00
100 D.Bryant JSY AU/75 RC 150.00 250.00
101 A.Benn JSY AU/75 RC 15.00 40.00
102 C.Spiller JSY AU/75 RC 15.00 40.00
103 C.McCoy JSY AU/75 RC 25.00 60.00
104 D.Thomas JSY AU/75 RC 40.00 100.00
105 D.McCluster JSY AU/75 RC 12.00 30.00
106 J.Clausen JSY AU/75 RC 25.00 50.00
107 N.Suh JSY AU/75 RC 30.00 80.00
108 R.Mathews JSY AU/75 RC 40.00 100.00
109 S.Bradford JSY AU/75 RC 20.00 50.00
110 T.Tebow JSY AU/75 RC 150.00 300.00
111 T.Gerhart JSY AU/75 RC 15.00 40.00
112 A.Roberts JSY AU/120 RC 12.00 30.00
113 A.Edwards JSY AU/120 RC 15.00 40.00
114 B.Tate JSY AU/120 RC 35.00 60.00
115 D.Williams JSY AU/120 RC 12.00 30.00
116 E.Sanders JSY AU/75 RC 25.00 60.00
117 Eric Berry JSY AU/75 25.00 60.00
118 E.Decker JSY AU/120 RC 25.00 60.00
119 G.McCoy JSY AU/120 RC 12.00 30.00
120 G.Tate JSY AU/120 RC 30.00 60.00
121 J.Best JSY AU/120 RC 12.00 30.00
122 J.Gresham JSY AU/120 RC 15.00 40.00
123 J.McKnight JSY AU/120 RC 15.00 40.00
124 J.Dwyer JSY AU/120 RC 12.00 30.00
125 J.Shipley JSY AU/120 RC 12.00 30.00
126 M.Easley JSY AU/120 RC 12.00 30.00
127 M.Gilyard JSY AU/120 RC 12.00 30.00
128 M.Kafka JSY AU/75 RC 20.00 50.00
129 M.Williams JSY AU/120 RC 20.00 50.00
130 M.Hardesty JSY AU/120 RC 12.00 30.00
131 Gronkowski JSY AU/120 RC 125.00 250.00
132 R.McClain JSY AU/120 RC 12.00 30.00
133 Anthony Dixon AU RC 8.00 20.00
134 Antonio Brown AU RC 150.00 300.00
135 Daryl Washington AU RC 25.00 50.00
136 Koa Misi AU RC 10.00 25.00
137 Brandon Graham AU RC 10.00 25.00
138 David Nelson AU RC 12.00 30.00
139 Carlton Mitchell AU RC 8.00 20.00
140 Charles Scott AU RC 8.00 20.00
141 Trent Williams AU RC 10.00 25.00
142 Dan LeFevour AU RC 8.00 20.00
143 Dan Williams AU RC 8.00 20.00
144 NaVorro Bowman AU RC 90.00 150.00
145 David Reed AU RC 8.00 20.00
146 Michael Hoomanawanui AU RC 8.00 20.00
147 Tyson Alualu AU RC 8.00 20.00
148 Dezmon Briscoe AU RC 8.00 20.00
149 Earl Thomas AU RC 20.00 50.00
150 Ed Dickson AU RC 15.00 40.00
151 Jacoby Ford AU RC 12.00 30.00
152 James Starks AU RC 20.00 50.00
153 Corey Peters AU RC 10.00 25.00
154 Taylor Mays AU RC 8.00 20.00
155 Jason Pierre-Paul AU RC EXCH 12.00 30.00
156 Jerry Hughes AU RC EXCH 15.00 40.00
157 J.Cunningham AU RC 8.00 20.00
158 Jimmy Graham AU RC 50.00 100.00
159 John Conner AU RC 8.00 20.00
160 Joe Webb AU RC 15.00 40.00
161 John Skelton AU RC 15.00 40.00
162 Anthony McCoy AU RC 8.00 20.00
163 Kareem Jackson AU RC 8.00 20.00
164 Kerry Meier AU RC 10.00 25.00
165 Sean Lee AU RC 50.00 100.00
166 LeGarrette Blount AU RC 40.00 80.00
167 Levi Brown AU RC 8.00 20.00
168 Taylor Price AU RC 8.00 20.00
169 Zac Robinson AU RC 10.00 25.00
170 Bryan Bulaga AU RC 12.00 30.00
171 Javier Arenas AU RC 8.00 20.00
172 Patrick Robinson AU RC 10.00 25.00
173 Riley Cooper AU RC 20.00 40.00
175 Rusty Smith AU RC 12.00 30.00
176 Garrett Graham AU RC 8.00 20.00
177 Rennie Curran AU RC 8.00 20.00
178 S.Weatherspoon AU RC 8.00 20.00
179 Sergio Kindle AU RC 8.00 20.00
180 Stafon Johnson AU RC 10.00 25.00
181 Aaron Hernandez AU RC 20.00 50.00
182 Tony Pike AU RC 8.00 20.00
183 Deji Karim AU RC 8.00 20.00
184 Brian Price AU RC 8.00 20.00
185 Lamarr Houston AU RC 10.00 25.00
186 T.J. Ward AU RC 12.00 30.00
187 Dennis Pitta AU RC 25.00 50.00
188 Jarrett Brown AU RC 10.00 25.00
189 Jonathan Crompton AU RC 8.00 20.00
190 Sean Canfield AU RC 8.00 20.00

2010 Exquisite Collection Autobiography Jersey Signatures

STATED PRINT RUN 20-99
EABAP Adrian Peterson/20 100.00 200.00
EABBB Brian Bosworth/20 40.00 80.00
EABBJ Bo Jackson/20 75.00 150.00
EABBR Drew Brees/20 50.00 100.00
EABBS Barry Sanders/20 75.00 150.00
EABCM Colt McCoy/20 50.00 120.00
EABCS C.J. Spiller/20 25.00 60.00
EABDJ DeSean Jackson/20 25.00 50.00
EABDM Dexter McCluster/99 10.00 25.00
EABDT Demaryius Thomas/99 20.00 50.00
EABEC Earl Campbell/20 40.00 80.00
EABEM Eli Manning/20 50.00 100.00
EABGT Golden Tate/99 15.00 40.00
EABJB Jahvid Best/99 8.00 20.00
EABJR Jerry Rice/20 125.00 200.00
EABJT Joe Theismann/20 30.00 80.00
EABNS Ndamukong Suh/20 100.00 200.00
EABPH Paul Hornung/99 30.00 60.00
EABPM Peyton Manning/20 125.00 200.00
EABRB Ronnie Brown/99 10.00 25.00
EABRM Ryan Mathews/99 8.00 20.00
EABSB Sam Bradford/20 40.00 100.00
EABSH Jordan Shipley/99 8.00 20.00
EABSI Billy Sims/20 30.00 60.00
EABSY Steve Young/20 60.00 120.00
EABTA Troy Aikman/20 75.00 125.00
EABTG Toby Gerhart/99 8.00 20.00
EABTT Tim Tebow/20 75.00 200.00

2010 Exquisite Collection Bio Script Signatures

STATED PRINT RUN 5-20
BSAH A.J. Hawk/20 15.00 40.00
BSCS C.J. Spiller/20 8.00 20.00
BSFG Frank Gore/20 12.00 30.00
BSMC Rolando McClain/20 8.00 20.00
BSRM Ryan Mathews/20 8.00 20.00
BSTH Thurman Thomas/20 15.00 40.00

2010 Exquisite Collection Draft Picks

STATED PRINT RUN 99 SER.#'d SETS
ERAD Andy Dalton 20.00 50.00
ERAG A.J. Green 20.00 50.00
ERBG Blaine Gabbert 20.00 50.00
ERCK Colin Kaepernick 20.00 50.00
ERCN Cam Newton 50.00 100.00
ERCP Christian Ponder 12.00 30.00
ERDC Delone Carter 12.00 30.00
ERDM DeMarco Murray 25.00 60.00
ERDT Daniel Thomas 15.00 40.00
ERER Evan Royster 12.00 30.00
ERGL Greg Little 15.00 40.00
ERGS Greg Salas 10.00 25.00
ERJJ Jerrel Jernigan 10.00 25.00
ERJL Jake Locker 20.00 50.00
ERJO Julio Jones 20.00 50.00
ERKH Kendall Hunter 12.00 30.00
ERLH Leonard Hankerson 12.00 30.00
ERMI Mark Ingram 25.00 60.00
ERND Noel Devine 10.00 25.00
ERNP Niles Paul 8.00 20.00
ERPA Prince Amukamara 12.00 30.00
ERPD Pat Devlin 12.00 30.00
ERRJ Ronald Johnson 10.00 25.00
ERRM Ryan Mallett 12.00 30.00
ERSV Shane Vereen 12.00 30.00
ERTS Torrey Smith 15.00 40.00
ERTT Tyrod Taylor 25.00 50.00
ERTY Titus Young 12.00 30.00
ERVB Vincent Brown 10.00 25.00
ERVM Von Miller 12.00 30.00

2010 Exquisite Collection Draft Picks Bronze

*BRONZE/25: .6X TO 1.5X BASIC INSERT/99
ERCN Cam Newton 100.00 200.00

2010 Exquisite Collection Endorsements

STATED PRINT RUN 10-50
EAB Arrelious Benn/50 6.00 15.00
EBT Ben Tate/50 6.00 15.00
EDC Dallas Clark/20 20.00 50.00
EDM Dexter McCluster/50 8.00 20.00
EDT Demaryius Thomas/50 15.00 40.00
EGJ Greg Jennings/20 10.00 25.00
EGT Golden Tate/50 8.00 20.00
EJA Jamaal Charles/20 15.00 40.00
EJB Jahvid Best/20 8.00 20.00
EJM Joe McKnight/50 6.00 15.00
EPA Alan Page/20 15.00 40.00
EPW Patrick Willis/20 15.00 40.00
ERM Ryan Mathews/20 8.00 20.00
ERO Rolando McClain/50 6.00 15.00
ESH Jordan Shipley/50 6.00 15.00
ETG Toby Gerhart/50 6.00 15.00

2010 Exquisite Collection Ensemble 2 Signatures

ENSEMBLE TWO AU PRINT RUN 10-25
GH Gronkowski/Hernandez/25 125.00 200.00
HW P.Willis/A.Hawk/25 30.00 60.00
TB A.Benn/G.Tate/25 12.00 30.00
TI G.Tate/R.Ismail/25 25.00 60.00
TT G.Tate/D.Thomas/25 25.00 60.00
TW D.Thomas/M.Williams/25 25.00 60.00

2010 Exquisite Collection Inscriptions

STATED PRINT RUN 5-25
IBS Billy Sims/25 15.00 40.00
IJB Jahvid Best/25 8.00 20.00
IPH Paul Hornung/25 20.00 50.00
IPW Patrick Willis/25 15.00 40.00

2010 Exquisite Collection Legacy Signatures

STATED PRINT RUN 5-20
LBK Bernie Kosar/20 15.00 40.00
LGR George Rogers/20 15.00 40.00
LJT Joe Theismann/20 15.00 40.00
LPH Paul Hornung/20 20.00 50.00
LRI Rocket Ismail/20 15.00 40.00
LSI Billy Sims/20 10.00 25.00
LSL Steve Largent/20 20.00 50.00

2010 Exquisite Collection NCAA All-Time Defense Autographs

STATED PRINT RUN 10-20
ATDAH A.J. Hawk/20 20.00 50.00
ATDAP Alan Page/20 15.00 40.00
ATDEB Eric Berry/20 50.00 120.00
ATDHC Harry Carson/20 12.00 30.00
ATDJY Jack Youngblood/20 15.00 40.00
ATDMW Mario Williams/20 12.00 30.00
ATDNS Ndamukong Suh/20 30.00 80.00
ATDPW Patrick Willis/20 15.00 40.00
ATDSM Bubba Smith/20 15.00 40.00

2010 Exquisite Collection NCAA All-Time Offense Autographs

STATED PRINT RUN 5-20
EXCH EXPIRATION: 3/18/2013
ATOKW Kellen Winslow Sr./20 15.00 40.00
ATOPH Paul Hornung/20 20.00 50.00
ATORG Roman Gabriel/20 EXCH 20.00 50.00
ATORI Rocket Ismail/20 30.00 60.00
ATOSI Billy Sims/20 15.00 40.00

2010 Exquisite Collection Patch Combos

STATED PRINT RUN 50 SER.#'d SETS
AB B.Sims/A.Peterson 20.00 50.00
AM T.Aikman/D.Marino 30.00 60.00
BH C.Henne/T.Brady 15.00 40.00
FR D.Flutie/M.Ryan 12.00 30.00
MB P.Manning/D.Brees 20.00 50.00
MC C.McCoy/J.Clausen 15.00 40.00
MM E.Manning/P.Manning 20.00 50.00
PB A.Peterson/S.Bradford 8.00 20.00
PJ A.Peterson/C.Johnson 15.00 40.00
PS M.Sanchez/C.Palmer 12.00 30.00
RB T.Brown/J.Rice 15.00 40.00
SC E.Campbell/B.Sanders 15.00 40.00
SP A.Peterson/B.Sanders 20.00 50.00
ST B.Sanders/T.Thomas 15.00 40.00
TB S.Bradford/T.Tebow 15.00 40.00
WC R.Williams/E.Campbell 12.00 30.00

2010 Exquisite Collection Patch Quads

STATED PRINT RUN 15 SER.#'d SETS
AEYM Aikmn/Mrno/Elwy/Yng 60.00 120.00
BRSR Schb/Romo/Brdy/Rivrs 25.00 60.00
BTWS Brynt/Shply/Wlfl/Thmas 25.00 60.00
CPTB Clsen/Tate/Brwn/Page 25.00 60.00
ESRW Wnsl/B.Snd/Elwy/Rce 40.00 100.00
FPTB Tebw/Plmr/Brdfrd/Fltie 25.00 60.00
MBBM Brees/P.Mnn/Eli/Brdy 40.00 80.00
MBMR Eli/P.Mann/Brees/Romo 30.00 60.00
PGJB Jhnsn/Brwn/Ptrsn/Gre 25.00 60.00
SSFP Plmr/Fltie/B.Sndrs/Sims 30.00 80.00
SWCS Sms/B.Snd/R.Wil/Camp 40.00 80.00
TMBC Clsn/Tbow/Brdfrd/McC 25.00 60.00
YKKG Klly/Kosr/Griese/Yng 40.00 80.00

2010 Exquisite Collection Patch Trios

STATED PRINT RUN 25 SER.#'d SETS
BCM Clausn/McCoy/Brdfrd 8.00 20.00
BPR Rivers/Brady/Palmer 30.00 80.00
BRL Brown/Largent/Rice 20.00 50.00
EAY Young/Elway/Aikman 25.00 60.00
EMA Aikman/Elway/Marino 30.00 80.00
MBB Brady/P.Mann/Brees 25.00 60.00
MMB Brees/P.Mann/E.Mann 25.00 60.00
MWC Clark/P.Mann/Wayne 15.00 40.00
RRR Rivers/Romo/Rodgers 20.00 50.00
SPB Bradford/Peterson/Sims 12.00 30.00
SRF Flutie/B.Sanders/Rice 15.00 40.00
SRM Rice/Marino/B.Sanders 30.00 80.00
TBC Bradfrd/Tebow/Clausn 20.00 50.00
TMB McCoy/Brdfrd/Tebow 20.00 50.00

2010 Exquisite Collection Premium Patch

STATED PRINT RUN 35-75
EPPAP Adrian Peterson/75 10.00 25.00
EPPAR Aaron Rodgers/50 40.00 80.00
EPPBB Brian Bosworth/75 12.00 30.00
EPPBJ Bo Jackson/50 15.00 40.00
EPPBK Bernie Kosar/50 6.00 15.00
EPPBR Tom Brady/75 15.00 40.00
EPPBS Barry Sanders/75 12.00 30.00
EPPCJ Calvin Johnson/35 10.00 25.00
EPPCM Colt McCoy/50 6.00 15.00
EPPCP Carson Palmer/75 6.00 15.00
EPPDB Drew Brees/35 10.00 25.00
EPPDF Doug Flutie/75 8.00 20.00
EPPDJ DeSean Jackson/50 6.00 15.00
EPPEC Earl Campbell/35 10.00 25.00
EPPEM Eli Manning/75 6.00 15.00
EPPFG Frank Gore/75 6.00 15.00
EPPGJ Greg Jennings/75 5.00 12.00
EPPJK Jim Kelly/75 8.00 20.00
EPPJN Chris Johnson/50 5.00 12.00
EPPJR Jerry Rice/75 12.00 30.00
EPPMA Miles Austin/75 5.00 12.00
EPPMS Mark Sanchez/75 5.00 12.00
EPPPM Peyton Manning/75 40.00 80.00
EPPPR Philip Rivers/50 8.00 20.00
EPPRW Reggie Wayne/35 8.00 20.00
EPPSB Sam Bradford/50 6.00 15.00
EPPSL Steve Largent/75 8.00 20.00
EPPSY Steve Young/75 12.00 30.00
EPPTA Troy Aikman/75 10.00 25.00
EPPTB Tim Brown/75 12.00 30.00
EPPTH Thurman Thomas/75 6.00 15.00
EPPTR Tony Romo/35 10.00 25.00
EPPTT Tim Tebow/50 25.00 60.00

2010 Exquisite Collection Rare Materials

STATED PRINT RUN 30-60
ERMAB Arrelious Benn/60 10.00 25.00
ERMAE Armanti Edwards/60 6.00 15.00
ERMAP Adrian Peterson/60 15.00 40.00
ERMAR Andre Roberts/60 6.00 15.00
ERMBL Brandon LaFell/60 8.00 20.00
ERMBR Dez Bryant/60 15.00 40.00
ERMBS Barry Sanders/60 20.00 50.00
ERMBT Ben Tate/60 5.00 12.00
ERMBU Brian Urlacher/60 15.00 40.00
ERMCH Chad Henne/30 10.00 25.00
ERMCJ Calvin Johnson/30 12.00 30.00
ERMCM Colt McCoy/60 6.00 15.00
ERMCS C.J. Spiller/60 5.00 12.00
ERMDB Drew Brees/30 12.00 30.00
ERMDJ DeSean Jackson/30 10.00 25.00
ERMDM Dan Marino/30 50.00 100.00
ERMDT Demaryius Thomas/60 12.00 30.00
ERMDW Damian Williams/60 5.00 12.00
ERMDX Dexter McCluster/60 6.00 15.00
ERMEB Eric Berry/60 8.00 20.00
ERMEC Earl Campbell/30 15.00 40.00
ERMED Eric Decker/60 6.00 15.00
ERMES Emmanuel Sanders/60 8.00 20.00
ERMGJ Greg Jennings/30 8.00 20.00
ERMGM Gerald McCoy/60 5.00 12.00
ERMGT Golden Tate/60 6.00 15.00
ERMJB Jahvid Best/60 5.00 12.00
ERMJC Jimmy Clausen/60 5.00 12.00
ERMJD Jonathan Dwyer/60 5.00 12.00
ERMJE John Elway/30 25.00 60.00
ERMJG Jermaine Gresham/60 5.00 12.00
ERMJK Jim Kelly/60 12.00 30.00
ERMJM Joe McKnight/60 5.00 12.00
ERMJN Chris Johnson/30 8.00 20.00
ERMJO Chad Johnson/60 6.00 15.00
ERMJR Jerry Rice/60 12.00 30.00
ERMJS Jordan Shipley/60 5.00 12.00
ERMLF Larry Fitzgerald/30 10.00 25.00
ERMMA Ryan Mathews/60 5.00 12.00
ERMMB Marion Barber/60 8.00 20.00
ERMME Marcus Easley/60 5.00 12.00
ERMMG Mardy Gilyard/60 5.00 12.00
ERMMH Montario Hardesty/60 10.00 25.00
ERMMK Mike Kafka/60 6.00 15.00
ERMMS Mark Sanchez/60 6.00 15.00
ERMMW Mike Williams/60 5.00 12.00
ERMNS Ndamukong Suh/60 15.00 40.00
ERMPM Peyton Manning/60 20.00 50.00
ERMPW Patrick Willis/60 12.00 30.00
ERMRB Ronnie Brown/60 10.00 25.00
ERMRG Rob Gronkowski/60 12.00 30.00
ERMRM Rolando McClain/60 5.00 12.00
ERMRW Ricky Williams/60 10.00 25.00
ERMSB Sam Bradford/60 6.00 15.00
ERMSY Steve Young/60 15.00 40.00
ERMTA Troy Aikman/60 15.00 40.00
ERMTB Tom Brady/60 25.00 60.00
ERMTG Toby Gerhart/60 5.00 12.00
ERMTR Tony Romo/60 8.00 20.00
ERMTT Tim Tebow/60 15.00 40.00

2010 Exquisite Collection Rookie Bookmark Patch Autographs

STATED PRINT RUN 50-99
BC S.Bradford/Clausen/50 30.00 60.00
BG T.Gerhart/J.Best/50 12.00 30.00
BH E.Berry/M.Hardesty/99 20.00 50.00
BM2 E.Berry/D.McCluster/50 15.00 40.00
BM R.Mathews/J.Best/50 12.00 30.00
BW A.Benn/M.Williams/99 12.00 30.00
DA A.Benn/D.Thomas/99 25.00 60.00
DG D.Thomas/G.Tate/50 30.00 80.00
DJ D.McCluster/J.Best/50 15.00 40.00
DT J.Dwyer/D.Thomas/99 12.00 30.00
GG Gresham/Gronkowski/50 30.00 80.00
MB S.Bradford/C.McCoy/50 30.00 60.00
MC C.McCoy/J.Clausen/50 15.00 40.00
MS C.McCoy/J.Shipley/50 30.00 80.00
NJ N.Suh/J.Best/50 25.00 60.00
SB C.Spiller/J.Best/50 12.00 30.00
SG J.Gresham/J.Shipley/50 15.00 40.00
SM R.Mathews/C.Spiller/50 12.00 30.00
TB S.Bradford/T.Tebow/50 60.00 120.00
TD D.Thomas/E.Decker/99 25.00 60.00
TT T.Tebow/D.Thomas/50 50.00 120.00
WT D.Williams/G.Tate/50 15.00 40.00
WW D.Williams/M.Williams/99 15.00 40.00

2010 Exquisite Collection Signature Jersey

STATED PRINT RUN 10-99
ESJAB Arrelious Benn/99 8.00 20.00
ESJDM Dexter McCluster/99 10.00 25.00
ESJDT Demaryius Thomas/99 20.00 50.00
ESJGT Golden Tate/99 10.00 25.00
ESJJB Jahvid Best/99 8.00 20.00
ESJMK Mike Kafka/99 10.00 25.00
ESJRM Rolando McClain/99 8.00 20.00
ESJSH Jordan Shipley/99 8.00 20.00
ESJTG Toby Gerhart/99 8.00 20.00

2010 Exquisite Collection Signature Jersey Dual

STATED PRINT RUN 5-25
BT G.Tate/A.Benn/25 12.00 30.00
TT G.Tate/D.Thomas/25 25.00 60.00

2010 Exquisite Collection Single Player Dual Patch

STATED PRINT RUN 25 SER.#'d SETS
EDPBB Brian Bosworth 10.00 25.00
EDPBK Bernie Kosar 10.00 25.00
EDPBS Barry Sanders 20.00 50.00
EDPDF Doug Flutie 10.00 25.00
EDPEC Earl Campbell 12.00 30.00
EDPJE John Elway 20.00 50.00
EDPJK Jim Kelly 12.00 30.00
EDPJR Jerry Rice 15.00 40.00
EDPSY Steve Young 15.00 40.00
EDPTA Troy Aikman 15.00 40.00
EDPTB Tim Brown 12.00 30.00
EDPTT Thurman Thomas 10.00 25.00

2010 Exquisite Collection Single Player Triple Patch

STATED PRINT RUN 50-75
ETPAJ Andre Johnson/75 8.00 20.00
ETPAP Adrian Peterson/75 10.00 25.00
ETPBS Barry Sanders/75 15.00 40.00
ETPCJ Calvin Johnson/50 10.00 25.00
ETPCP Carson Palmer/50 8.00 20.00
ETPDB Drew Brees/75 12.00 30.00
ETPDJ DeSean Jackson/75 8.00 20.00
ETPFG Frank Gore/50 8.00 20.00
ETPJC Jamaal Charles/75 8.00 20.00
ETPJR Jerry Rice/75 12.00 30.00
ETPMS Mark Sanchez/75 6.00 15.00
ETPPM Peyton Manning/50 25.00 60.00
ETPPR Philip Rivers/50 10.00 25.00
ETPRW Reggie Wayne/75 8.00 20.00
ETPSI Billy Sims/75 10.00 25.00
ETPTA Troy Aikman/50 15.00 40.00
ETPTB Tom Brady/75 20.00 50.00
ETPTR Tony Romo/75 8.00 20.00
ETPWW Wes Welker/75 8.00 20.00

2011 Exquisite Collection

EXCH EXPIRATION: 7/31/2014
1 Eddie George 6.00 15.00
2 Barry Sanders 15.00 40.00
3 Rocky Bleier 6.00 15.00
4 Gale Sayers 8.00 20.00
5 Mike Alstott 5.00 12.00
6 William Perry 5.00 12.00
7 Eric Metcalf 5.00 12.00
8 Bernie Kosar 6.00 15.00
9 Brian Bosworth 6.00 15.00
10 Floyd Little 5.00 12.00
11 Keith Jackson 5.00 12.00
12 Paul Hornung 8.00 20.00
13 Roman Gabriel 5.00 12.00
14 Steve Young 8.00 20.00
15 Warren Moon 8.00 20.00
16 Drew Bledsoe 6.00 15.00
17 Bo Jackson 10.00 25.00
18 John Cappelletti 5.00 12.00
19 Rocket Ismail 6.00 15.00
20 Tony Dorsett 8.00 20.00
21 Alan Page 5.00 12.00
22 Charles White 5.00 12.00
23 Kellen Winslow Sr. 5.00 12.00
24 Billy Sims 5.00 12.00
25 Thurman Thomas 6.00 15.00
26 Tim Brown 8.00 20.00
27 Troy Aikman 8.00 20.00
28 Dan Marino 15.00 40.00
29 Earl Campbell 8.00 20.00
30 Herschel Walker 8.00 20.00
31 Cris Carter 6.00 15.00
32 George Rogers 6.00 15.00
33 Doug Flutie 6.00 15.00
34 Andre Rison 5.00 12.00
35 Ozzie Newsome 6.00 15.00
36 Greg Pruitt 5.00 12.00
37 John Elway 15.00 40.00
38 Archie Griffin 6.00 15.00
39 Antonio Freeman 5.00 12.00
40 Rod Woodson 8.00 20.00
41 Tommy McDonald 6.00 15.00
42 Ken Stabler 8.00 20.00
43 Mike Singletary 8.00 20.00
44 Gino Torretta 5.00 12.00
45 Jim Kelly 8.00 20.00
46 Danny Wuerffel 5.00 12.00
47 Jim Plunkett 6.00 15.00
48 Johnny Rodgers 5.00 12.00
49 Anthony Carter 5.00 12.00
50 Andre Ware 6.00 15.00
51 Ty Detmer 5.00 12.00
52 Daryle Lamonica 5.00 12.00
53 Ron Dayne 6.00 15.00
54 Steve Owens 5.00 12.00
55 Jim McMahon 6.00 15.00
56 Gary Beban 5.00 12.00
57 Adrian Peterson 15.00 40.00
58 Drew Brees 12.50 25.00
59 Aaron Rodgers 25.00 50.00
60 Steven Jackson 5.00 12.00
61 Ras-I Dowling AU 6.00 15.00
62 Virgil Green AU 6.00 15.00
63 Von Miller AU 30.00 60.00
64 Aaron Williams AU 6.00 15.00
65 Ryan Whalen AU 6.00 15.00
66 Marcell Dareus AU 6.00 15.00
67 Kelvin Sheppard AU 6.00 15.00
68 Ricky Stanzi AU 12.00 30.00
69 Jabaal Sheard AU 6.00 15.00
70 Rob Housler AU 6.00 15.00
71 Justin Houston AU 20.00 40.00
73 Akeem Ayers AU 6.00 15.00
74 Luke Stocker AU 6.00 15.00
77 Stevan Ridley AU 6.00 15.00
78 Kris Durham AU 6.00 15.00
79 D.J. Williams AU 6.00 15.00
80 J.J. Watt AU 400.00 600.00
81 Evan Royster AU 20.00 50.00
82 Nick Fairley AU 20.00 50.00
83 Rahim Moore AU 6.00 15.00
84 Edmond Gates AU 6.00 15.00
85 Mike Pouncey AU 15.00 40.00
86 Lance Kendricks AU 6.00 15.00
87 Tyrod Taylor AU 30.00 60.00
88 Ryan Kerrigan AU 20.00 40.00
89 Nate Solder AU 6.00 15.00
90 Cecil Shorts AU 30.00 50.00
91 Corey Liuget AU 12.00 30.00
92 Anthony Castonzo AU 6.00 15.00
93 Prince Amukamara AU 6.00 15.00
95 Casey Matthews AU 6.00 15.00
96 Adrian Clayborn AU 12.00 30.00
97 Drake Nevis AU 6.00 15.00
98 Mason Foster AU 12.00 30.00
99 Phil Taylor AU 6.00 15.00
100 Stephen Paea AU 6.00 15.00
101 T.J. Yates AU 8.00 20.00
102 Terrelle Pryor AU 12.00 30.00
103 Allen Bailey AU 6.00 15.00
104 Jeremy Kerley AU 10.00 25.00
106 Anthony Allen AU 6.00 15.00
107 Cameron Jordan AU 8.00 20.00
108 Jimmy Smith AU 6.00 15.00
109 Bilal Powell AU 20.00 40.00
110 Nathan Enderle AU 6.00 15.00
111 Cameron Heyward AU 8.00 20.00
112 Jamie Harper AU EXCH 6.00 15.00
113 Stephen Burton AU 6.00 15.00
114 Mark Herzlich AU EXCH
115 Pat Devlin AU 12.00 30.00
116 John Clay AU 10.00 25.00
117 Noel Devine AU 10.00 25.00
118 Terrence Toliver AU 8.00 20.00
120 Derrick Locke AU 8.00 20.00
121 Ryan Williams JSY AU 30.00 80.00
122 Randall Cobb JSY AU 20.00 50.00
123 Greg Salas JSY AU 12.00 30.00
124 Jerrel Jernigan JSY AU 12.00 30.00
125 Leonard Hankerson JSY AU 15.00 40.00
126 Kendall Hunter JSY AU 12.00 30.00
127 Niles Paul JSY AU 12.00 30.00
128 Dion Lewis JSY AU 25.00 60.00
129 DeMarco Murray JSY AU 25.00 60.00
130 Tandon Doss JSY AU 12.00 30.00
131 Ronald Johnson JSY AU 12.00 30.00
132 Greg Little JSY AU 15.00 40.00
133 Titus Young JSY AU 15.00 40.00
134 Vincent Brown JSY AU 15.00 40.00
135 Mikel Leshoure JSY AU 15.00 40.00
136 Jacquizz Rodgers JSY AU 15.00 40.00
137 Jonathan Baldwin JSY AU 12.00 30.00
138 Roy Helu JSY AU 12.00 30.00
139 Shane Vereen JSY AU 15.00 40.00
140 Torrey Smith JSY AU 12.00 30.00
141 Austin Pettis JSY AU 20.00 50.00
142 Ryan Mallett JSY AU 12.00 30.00
143 Kyle Rudolph JSY AU 40.00 80.00
144 Daniel Thomas JSY AU 12.00 30.00
145 Andy Dalton JSY AU 50.00 100.00
146 Colin Kaepernick JSY AU 20.00 50.00
147 Delone Carter JSY AU 12.00 30.00
148 Dwayne Harris JSY AU 12.00 30.00
149 Jordan Todman JSY AU 12.00 30.00
150 Mark Ingram JSY AU 30.00 80.00
151 A.J. Green JSY AU 75.00 150.00
152 Cam Newton JSY AU 200.00 400.00
153 Blaine Gabbert JSY AU 25.00 60.00
154 Julio Jones JSY AU 100.00 200.00
155 Christian Ponder JSY AU 25.00 60.00
156 Jake Locker JSY AU 25.00 60.00

2011 Exquisite Collection Choice Signatures

CSAD Andy Dalton 10.00 25.00
CSAG A.J. Green 30.00 60.00
CSAL Alan Page 10.00 25.00
CSAP Adrian Peterson 60.00 120.00
CSAR Aaron Rodgers
CSAU Austin Pettis 10.00 25.00
CSAW Andre Ware 10.00 25.00
CSBB Brian Bosworth 15.00 40.00
CSBG Blaine Gabbert 6.00 15.00
CSBJ Bo Jackson 40.00 80.00
CSBK Bernie Kosar 15.00 30.00
CSBS Barry Sanders
CSCK Colin Kaepernick 10.00 25.00
CSCN Cam Newton 40.00 80.00
CSCP Christian Ponder 12.00 30.00
CSCW Charles White 8.00 20.00
CSDB Drew Brees
CSDE Ty Detmer
CSDF Doug Flutie 20.00 40.00
CSDL Dion Lewis
CSDM Dan Marino
CSDT Daniel Thomas 6.00 15.00
CSDW Danny Wuerffel 8.00 20.00
CSEC Earl Campbell 15.00 30.00
CSEG Eddie George 30.00 60.00
CSEM Eric Metcalf 8.00 20.00
CSGE George Rogers 10.00 25.00
CSGL Greg Little 8.00 20.00
CSGR Archie Griffin 15.00 40.00
CSGS Gale Sayers 30.00 60.00
CSGT Gino Torretta 8.00 20.00
CSHW Herschel Walker
CSJB Jonathan Baldwin 8.00 20.00
CSJE John Elway 60.00 120.00
CSJJ Julio Jones
CSJL Jake Locker 5.00 12.00
CSJM Jim McMahon 12.00 30.00
CSJR Jerry Rice 30.00 60.00
CSMI Mark Ingram 8.00 20.00
CSMS Mike Singletary 15.00 40.00
CSNP Niles Paul 8.00 20.00
CSPH Paul Hornung 15.00 30.00
CSRB Rocky Bleier 12.00 30.00
CSRC Randall Cobb 10.00 25.00
CSRH Roy Helu 10.00 25.00
CSRO Roger Craig
CSRW Ryan Williams 6.00 15.00
CSSI Billy Sims 8.00 20.00
CSSR Stevan Ridley 6.00 15.00
CSSV Shane Vereen 8.00 20.00
CSSY Steve Young 30.00 60.00
CSTA Troy Aikman 40.00 80.00
CSTB Tim Brown 20.00 40.00
CSTD Tony Dorsett 15.00 30.00
CSTR Tom Rathman
CSTS Torrey Smith 6.00 15.00
CSTT Thurman Thomas 15.00 30.00
CSTY Titus Young 6.00 15.00
NNO Dual Holder 2.50 6.00
NNO Quad Holder 3.00 8.00

2011 Exquisite Collection Dimension Autographs

DAC Anthony Carter 15.00 40.00
DAD Andy Dalton 30.00 80.00
DAG A.J. Green 60.00 120.00
DAR Aaron Rodgers 150.00 300.00
DBG Blaine Gabbert 15.00 40.00
DBJ Bo Jackson 50.00 120.00
DBK Bernie Kosar 20.00 50.00
DBS Barry Sanders 75.00 150.00
DCC Cris Carter 25.00 60.00
DCK Colin Kaepernick 25.00 60.00
DCN Cam Newton 75.00 150.00
DCP Christian Ponder 15.00 40.00
DCW Charles White 15.00 40.00
DDB Drew Brees 40.00 100.00
DDF Doug Flutie 20.00 50.00
DDL Daryle Lamonica 15.00 40.00
DDM Dan Marino 75.00 150.00
DEG Eddie George 40.00 100.00
DFL Floyd Little 25.00 60.00
DGR Archie Griffin 25.00 60.00
DHW Herschel Walker 50.00 100.00
DJB Jonathan Baldwin 25.00 60.00
DJE John Elway 50.00 100.00
DJJ Julio Jones 60.00 120.00
DJK Jim Kelly 30.00 80.00
DJL Jake Locker 15.00 40.00
DJM Jim McMahon 20.00 50.00
DJO Johnny Rodgers 15.00 40.00
DJP Jim Plunkett 20.00 50.00
DJR Jerry Rice 50.00 100.00
DKS Ken Stabler 25.00 60.00
DMI Mark Ingram 25.00 60.00
DON Ozzie Newsome 20.00 50.00
DRM Ryan Mallett 15.00 40.00
DRO George Rogers 15.00 40.00
DSY Steve Young 40.00 100.00
DTA Troy Aikman 50.00 100.00
DTB Tim Brown 40.00 80.00
DTD Tony Dorsett 40.00 80.00
DTT Thurman Thomas 25.00 60.00
DWM Warren Moon 25.00 60.00

2011 Exquisite Collection Draft Picks Bronze

STATED PRINT RUN 99 SER.#'d SETS
ERAJ Alshon Jeffery 15.00 40.00
ERAL Andrew Luck 150.00 300.00
ERBO Brock Osweiler 10.00 25.00
ERBP Bernard Pierce 12.00 30.00
ERBW Brandon Weeden 12.00 30.00
ERCK Case Keenum 10.00 25.00
ERDJ Dwight Jones 8.00 20.00
ERDM Doug Martin 15.00 40.00
ERDP DeVier Posey 8.00 20.00
ERIP Isaiah Pead 8.00 20.00
ERJB Justin Blackmon 6.00 15.00
ERJC Juron Criner 8.00 20.00
ERJF Jeff Fuller 8.00 20.00
ERKC Kirk Cousins 15.00 40.00
ERKM Kellen Moore 10.00 25.00
ERKW Kendall Wright 8.00 20.00
ERLJ LaMichael James 10.00 25.00
ERMF Michael Floyd 15.00 40.00
ERMS Mohamed Sanu 10.00 25.00
ERNF Nick Foles 25.00 60.00
ERNT Nick Toon 8.00 20.00
ERRB Ryan Broyles 12.00 30.00
ERRG Robert Griffin III 25.00 60.00
ERRH Ronnie Hillman 10.00 25.00
ERRL Ryan Lindley 8.00 20.00
ERRR Rueben Randle 8.00 20.00
ERRT Ryan Tannehill 10.00 25.00
ERRW Russell Wilson 90.00 150.00
ERTP Tauren Poole 8.00 20.00
ERTR Trent Richardson 20.00 50.00

2011 Exquisite Collection Draft Picks Silver

*SILVER/35: .6X TO 1.5X BRONZE/99
SILVER STATED PRINT RUN 35
ERRG Robert Griffin III 40.00 100.00
ERRW Russell Wilson 125.00 250.00

2011 Exquisite Collection Endorsements

STATED PRINT RUN 45-75
EXCH EXPIRATION: 7/31/2014
EAD Andy Dalton/75 12.00 30.00
EAG Archie Griffin/75 15.00 40.00
EAJ A.J. Green/75 25.00 60.00
EBG Blaine Gabbert/45 6.00 15.00
EBS Barry Sanders/45 75.00 150.00
ECK Colin Kaepernick/75 10.00 25.00
ECN Cam Newton/45 75.00 150.00
ECP Christian Ponder/75 6.00 15.00
ECW Charles White/75 10.00 25.00
EDB Drew Brees/45 40.00 80.00
EDT Daniel Thomas/75 6.00 15.00
EFL Floyd Little/75 12.00 30.00
EGB Gary Beban/75 10.00 25.00
EGL Greg Little/75 8.00 20.00
EGR George Rogers/75 10.00 25.00
EJE John Elway/45 60.00 120.00
EJL Jake Locker/75 6.00 15.00
EJO Johnny Rodgers/75 12.00 30.00
EJP Jim Plunkett/75 15.00 40.00
EJR Jerry Rice/45 50.00 120.00
EKR Kyle Rudolph/75 6.00 15.00
EKS Ken Stabler/75 15.00 40.00
EMI Mark Ingram/75 10.00 25.00
EML Mikel Leshoure/75 6.00 15.00
EMS Mike Singletary/75 15.00 40.00
EON Ozzie Newsome/75 12.00 30.00
ERB Rocky Bleier/75 15.00 40.00
ERD Ron Dayne/75 12.00 30.00
ESJ Steven Jackson/45 12.00 30.00
ESY Steve Young/45 30.00 80.00
ETA Troy Aikman/45 40.00 80.00
ETD Tony Dorsett/45 30.00 60.00
ETM Tommy McDonald/75 12.00 30.00
ETS Torrey Smith/75 6.00 15.00
ETT Thurman Thomas/75 15.00 40.00
ETY Titus Young/75 6.00 15.00
EVM Von Miller/75 15.00 40.00
EWI Ryan Williams/75 6.00 15.00
EWM Warren Moon/75 20.00 50.00

2011 Exquisite Collection Ensemble 2 Signatures

STATED PRINT RUN 25 SER.#'d SETS
E2BC T.Casillas/B.Bosworth 25.00 50.00
E2BI D.Brees/M.Ingram 40.00 80.00
E2BM B.Bosworth/T.Mandarich 25.00 50.00
E2BR A.Rodgers/D.Brees 250.00 400.00
E2DM T.Dorsett/D.Marino 150.00 250.00
E2GG E.George/A.Griffin 60.00 120.00
E2GJ J.Jones/A.Green 75.00 135.00
E2GP B.Gabbert/C.Ponder 10.00 25.00
E2JB J.Jones/J.Baldwin EXCH 40.00 80.00
E2JN C.Newton/B.Jackson 200.00 400.00
E2KK B.Kosar/J.Kelly 40.00 100.00
E2KT J.Kelly/T.Thomas 40.00 80.00
E2LG J.Locker/B.Gabbert 12.00 30.00
E2LH D.Lamonica/P.Hornung 20.00 50.00
E2NI C.Newton/M.Ingram 75.00 150.00
E2SW B.Sims/C.White 20.00 40.00
E2WT R.Williams/D.Thomas 20.00 40.00
E2WW C.White/H.Walker 30.00 60.00
E2YM J.McMahon/S.Young 40.00 80.00
E2YR S.Young/J.Rice 125.00 250.00

2011 Exquisite Collection Ensemble 3 Signatures

STATED PRINT RUN 15 SER.#'d SETS
E3BHP Hornung/Brown/Page 40.00 80.00
E3CGW Griffin/Campbell/Walker
E3EMA Marino/Aikman/Elway 250.00 400.00
E3GJB Baldwin/Jones/Green 60.00 120.00
E3ING Green/Ingram/Newton 100.00 200.00
E3IWT Ingram/Will/Thmas 30.00 60.00
E3JID Ingram/Jones/Dareus
E3KKT Kosar/Kelly/Torretta 40.00 80.00
E3NLG Gabbert/Locker/Newton 50.00 100.00
E3PDK Kaepernick/Ponder/Dalton 40.00 80.00
E3RCR Rathman/Rodgers/Craig 30.00 60.00
E3YMD McMahon/Young/Detmer 75.00 150.00

2011 Exquisite Collection Legacy Signatures

STATED PRINT RUN 20-45
LAC Anthony Carter/45 12.00 30.00
LAG Archie Griffin/45 15.00 40.00
LBJ Bo Jackson/45 75.00 150.00
LBS Barry Sanders/20 100.00 200.00
LCW Charles White/45 10.00 25.00
LDF Doug Flutie/20 15.00 40.00
LDL Daryle Lamonica/20 12.00 30.00
LEC Earl Campbell/45 20.00 50.00
LEG Eddie George/20 15.00 40.00
LGB Gary Beban/45 10.00 25.00
LGR George Rogers/45 10.00 25.00
LGS Gale Sayers/45 20.00 50.00
LHW Herschel Walker/45 20.00 50.00
LJE John Elway/20 60.00 120.00
LJO Johnny Rodgers/45 12.00 30.00
LJR Jerry Rice/20 75.00 150.00
LPH Paul Hornung/45 15.00 40.00
LTA Troy Aikman/20 50.00 100.00
LTD Tony Dorsett/20 25.00 60.00
LTM Tommy McDonald/45 12.00 30.00

2011 Exquisite Collection Masterpieces Autographs

STATED PRINT RUN 10-25
MAG Archie Griffin/25 25.00 60.00
MBB Brian Bosworth/25 20.00 50.00
MBJ Bo Jackson/25 60.00 125.00
MBK Bernie Kosar/25 15.00 40.00
MCN Cam Newton/25 125.00 250.00
MCW Charles White/25 12.00 30.00
MDF Doug Flutie/25 15.00 40.00
MGR George Rogers/25 15.00 40.00
MHW Herschel Walker/25 30.00 60.00
MJM Jim McMahon/25 15.00 40.00
MJR Johnny Rodgers/25 15.00 40.00
MPH Paul Hornung/25 20.00 50.00
MRI Rocket Ismail/25 15.00 40.00
MTD Tony Dorsett/25 30.00 60.00

2011 Exquisite Collection Rookie Bookmark Jersey Autographs

STATED PRINT RUN 40 SER.#'d SETS
EXCH EXPIRATION: 7/31/2014
RBMBL J.Baldwin/D.Lewis 12.00 30.00
RBMBY T.Young/J.Baldwin 10.00 25.00
RBMGD A.Green/A.Dalton 50.00 120.00
RBMGJ A.Green/J.Jones 75.00 135.00
RBMGP C.Ponder/B.Gabbert 15.00 40.00
RBMHC D.Carter/K.Hunter 10.00 25.00
RBMHH R.Helu/L.Hankerson 10.00 25.00
RBMHJ R.Johnson/K.Hunter 10.00 25.00
RBMHP N.Paul/R.Helu 25.00 60.00
RBMIG A.Green/Ingram 25.00 60.00
RBMIJ M.Ingram/J.Jones 30.00 80.00
RBMJB J.Jones/Baldwin EXCH 40.00 100.00
RBMKD A.Dalton/C.Kaepernick 50.00 100.00
RBMKR K.Hunter/R.Helu
RBMLG B.Gabbert/J.Locker 10.00 25.00
RBMLP J.Locker/C.Ponder 10.00 25.00
RBMLY G.Little/T.Young 12.00 30.00
RBMMH D.Harris/D.Murray 20.00 50.00
RBMNG B.Gabbert/C.Newton 40.00 80.00
RBMNI C.Newton/M.Ingram 50.00 100.00
RBMNL C.Newton/J.Locker 50.00 120.00
RBMPD C.Ponder/A.Dalton 20.00 50.00
RBMPH N.Paul/L.Hankerson 10.00 25.00
RBMPK C.Ponder/C.Kaepernick 40.00 80.00
RBMPM C.Ponder/R.Mallett 15.00 40.00
RBMPR C.Ponder/K.Rudolph 10.00 25.00
RBMRJ J.Jones/J.Rodgers EXCH 30.00 80.00
RBMSD T.Smith/T.Doss 10.00 25.00
RBMSP A.Pettis/G.Salas 10.00 25.00
RBMTV D.Thomas/S.Vereen 12.00 30.00
RBMVM S.Vereen/R.Mallett 12.00 30.00
RBMWL M.Leshoure/R.Williams 12.00 30.00
RBMWT R.Williams/D.Thomas 10.00 25.00
RBMYL M.Leshoure/T.Young 10.00 25.00
RBMYP T.Young/Pettis EXCH 10.00 25.00

2011 Exquisite Collection Signing Day

STATED PRINT RUN 15 SER.#'d SETS
SDAG A.J. Green 75.00 150.00
SDBG Bob Griese 25.00 60.00
SDBJ Bo Jackson 60.00 120.00
SDBS Barry Sanders 100.00 200.00
SDCN Cam Newton 125.00 250.00
SDDM Dan Marino 150.00 225.00
SDEG Eddie George
SDGR Archie Griffin 25.00 60.00
SDGS Gale Sayers 40.00 80.00
SDHW Herschel Walker 40.00 80.00
SDJB Jonathan Baldwin 15.00 40.00
SDJE John Elway 60.00 120.00
SDJJ Julio Jones 75.00 150.00
SDJM Jim McMahon 20.00 50.00
SDJR Jerry Rice 100.00 175.00
SDKJ Keith Jackson 15.00 40.00
SDMA Mike Alstott 25.00 60.00
SDMI Mark Ingram 25.00 60.00
SDRW Ryan Williams 15.00 40.00
SDWM Warren Moon 25.00 50.00

2012 Exquisite Collection

1-60 VETERAN PRINT RUN 85
61-120 ROOKIE AU PRINT RUN 99
121-143 ROOK.JSY AU PRINT RUN 150
144-150 ROOK.JSY AU PRINT RUN 99
QB EXCH EXPIRATION: 6/1/2015
ROOKIE AU EXCH EXPIRATION: 6/6/2015
1 Keith Jackson 2.50 6.00
2 Ken MacAfee 2.50 6.00
3 Warren Moon 4.00 10.00
4 Garrison Hearst 2.50 6.00
5 Warren Sapp 3.00 8.00
6 Roger Craig 3.00 8.00
7 Billy Cannon 2.50 6.00
8 Nick Buoniconti 2.50 6.00
9 Tedy Bruschi 3.00 8.00

10 Ken Stabler 4.00 10.00
11 Barry Sanders 6.00 15.00
12 Don Maynard 3.00 8.00
13 Paul Hornung 4.00 10.00
14 Gary Beban 2.50 6.00
15 Tim Tebow 5.00 12.00
16 Tony Dorsett 4.00 10.00
17 Vinny Testaverde 2.50 6.00
18 Mike Rozier 3.00 8.00
19 Bruce Smith 3.00 8.00
20 Bo Jackson 6.00 15.00
21 Troy Aikman 4.00 10.00
22 Doug Flutie 3.00 8.00
23 Johnny Lattner 2.50 6.00
24 Chris Weinke 2.50 6.00
25 Dan Marino 8.00 20.00
26 Archie Griffin 2.50 6.00
27 Joe Namath 6.00 15.00
28 Jake Plummer 2.50 6.00
29 Ozzie Newsome 3.00 8.00
30 Rich Gannon 2.50 6.00
31 Al Toon 2.50 6.00
32 Dan Fouts 3.00 8.00
33 Anthony Carter 2.50 6.00
34 Joe Theismann 3.00 8.00
35 Steve Young 4.00 10.00
36 Drew Bledsoe 3.00 8.00
37 George Rogers 2.50 6.00
38 Jim Kelly 4.00 10.00
39 Charlie Ward 2.50 6.00
40 Tommie Frazier 2.50 6.00
41 Jason White 3.00 8.00
42 Jerry Rice 5.00 12.00
43 Jerome Bettis 4.00 10.00
44 Daryle Lamonica 2.50 6.00
45 John Hannah 3.00 8.00
46 Earl Campbell 4.00 10.00
47 Andy Katzenmoyer 3.00 8.00
48 Robert Smith 3.00 8.00
49 Ty Detmer 2.50 6.00
50 Joe Washington 2.50 6.00
51 Billy Sims 3.00 8.00
52 Herschel Walker 4.00 10.00
53 Charles White 2.50 6.00
54 John Elway 5.00 12.00
55 Rodney Peete 2.50 6.00
56 Bart Starr 6.00 15.00
57 Aaron Rodgers 8.00 20.00
58 Archie Manning 3.00 8.00
59 Andre Ware 3.00 8.00
60 Brian Bosworth 3.00 8.00
61 Dan Herron AU 5.00 12.00
62 B.J. Cunningham AU 5.00 12.00
63 Marc Tyler AU 5.00 12.00
64 Matt Kalil AU 6.00 15.00
65 Laron Byrd AU 6.00 15.00
66 Stephon Gilmore AU 6.00 15.00
67 Dre Kirkpatrick AU 5.00 12.00
68 Janoris Jenkins AU 6.00 15.00
69 Casey Hayward AU 5.00 12.00
70 Andre Branch AU 5.00 12.00
71 Shea McClellin AU 6.00 15.00
72 Whitney Mercilus AU 5.00 12.00
73 Josh Gordon AU 12.00 30.00
75 Michael Brockers AU 5.00 12.00
76 Kendall Reyes AU 5.00 12.00
77 Mike Martin AU 6.00 15.00
78 Alameda Ta'amu AU 6.00 15.00
80 Dont'a Hightower AU 10.00 25.00
81 Mychal Kendricks AU 8.00 20.00
82 Bobby Wagner AU 8.00 20.00
83 David DeCastro AU 5.00 12.00
84 Cordy Glenn AU 6.00 15.00
85 Lavonte David AU 15.00 40.00
86 Ryan Lindley AU 5.00 12.00
87 Chandler Harnish AU 10.00 25.00
88 Tyler Hansen AU 5.00 12.00
89 Jordan Jefferson AU 6.00 15.00
90 Stephen Garcia AU 8.00 20.00
91 Jarrett Lee AU 8.00 20.00
92 Ronnie Hillman AU 25.00 50.00
93 Alfred Morris AU 5.00 12.00
96 Dwayne Allen AU 8.00 20.00
97 Michael Egnew AU 5.00 12.00
98 Ladarius Green AU 10.00 25.00
100 Brandon Thompson AU 6.00 15.00
101 T.J. Graham AU 5.00 12.00
102 Devon Wylie AU 5.00 12.00
103 Keshawn Martin AU 6.00 15.00
104 Greg Childs AU 5.00 12.00
105 Marvin Jones AU 8.00 20.00
106 Marvin McNutt AU 5.00 12.00
107 Rishard Matthews AU 5.00 12.00
108 Jeremy Ebert AU 5.00 12.00
110 Jarius Wright AU 5.00 12.00
111 Dwight Jones AU 5.00 12.00
112 Jermaine Kearse AU 15.00 40.00
113 Marquis Maze AU 5.00 12.00
114 Nelson Rosario AU 5.00 12.00
115 Tyler Shoemaker AU 6.00 15.00
116 Lavasier Tuinei AU 8.00 20.00
117 Cyrus Gray AU 5.00 12.00
118 Melvin Ingram AU 5.00 12.00
119 Jeff Fuller AU 5.00 12.00
120 Tauren Poole AU 5.00 12.00
121 Kendall Wright JSY AU 10.00 25.00
122 Brock Osweiler JSY AU 10.00 25.00
123 Nick Foles JSY AU 100.00 200.00
124 A.J. Jenkins JSY AU 10.00 25.00
125 Case Keenum JSY AU 20.00 50.00
126 Kellen Moore JSY AU 12.00 30.00
127 Russell Wilson JSY AU 150.00 300.00
128 Kirk Cousins JSY AU 60.00 125.00
129 Isaiah Pead JSY AU 10.00 25.00
130 LaMichael James JSY AU 10.00 25.00
131 Bernard Pierce JSY AU EXCH 40.00 80.00
132 Coby Fleener JSY AU 10.00 25.00
133 Brian Quick JSY AU 10.00 25.00
134 Stephen Hill JSY AU 10.00 25.00
135 Alshon Jeffery JSY AU 25.00 50.00
136 Ryan Broyles JSY AU 10.00 25.00
137 Rueben Randle JSY AU 10.00 25.00
138 DeVier Posey JSY AU 10.00 25.00
139 Mohamed Sanu JSY AU 15.00 40.00
140 Travis Benjamin JSY AU 10.00 25.00
141 Jarius Wright JSY AU 12.00 30.00
142 Nick Toon JSY AU 10.00 25.00
143 Juron Criner JSY AU 10.00 25.00
144 Robert Griffin III JSY AU 30.00 80.00
145 Ryan Tannehill JSY AU 40.00 100.00
146 Brandon Weeden JSY AU 15.00 40.00
147 Trent Richardson JSY AU 30.00 80.00
148 Doug Martin JSY AU 40.00 100.00
149 Justin Blackmon JSY AU 25.00 60.00
150 Michael Floyd JSY AU 30.00 80.00
QB2 QB Draft Trade Gold AU 800.00 1200.00
QB1 QB Draft Trade Silver 250.00 400.00
0 Andrew Luck Gold AU/99 300.00 600.00

2012 Exquisite Collection Art Autographs

EABB Brian Bosworth 25.00 50.00
EABL Justin Blackmon 12.00 30.00
EABO Brock Osweiler 40.00 80.00
EABQ Brian Quick 12.00 30.00
EABS Bart Starr 50.00 100.00
EABW Brandon Weeden 20.00 50.00
EACW Charlie Ward 12.00 30.00
EADF Doug Flutie 12.00 30.00
EADM Dan Marino 100.00 200.00
EADP DeVier Posey 12.00 30.00
EAJB Jerome Bettis 50.00 100.00
EAJE John Elway 60.00 120.00
EAJN Joe Namath 50.00 100.00
EAJP Jake Plummer 12.00 30.00
EAJR Jerry Rice 60.00 120.00
EAKC Kirk Cousins 75.00 150.00
EAKW Kendall Wright 12.00 30.00
EAMA Doug Martin 20.00 50.00
EAMF Michael Floyd 15.00 40.00
EAMS Mohamed Sanu 20.00 50.00
EANF Nick Foles 30.00 80.00
EAPL Jim Plunkett 12.00 30.00
EARB Ryan Broyles 12.00 30.00
EARG Robert Griffin III 15.00 40.00
EARR Rueben Randle 12.00 30.00
EART Ryan Tannehill 20.00 50.00
EASA Barry Sanders
EASH Stephen Hill 15.00 40.00
EASY Steve Young 30.00 60.00
EATA Troy Aikman 30.00 60.00
EATB Tedy Bruschi 15.00 40.00
EATR Trent Richardson 12.00 30.00
EATT Tim Tebow 40.00 100.00
EAVT Vinny Testaverde

2012 Exquisite Collection Choice Signatures

ESSAC Anthony Carter 6.00 15.00
ESSAG Archie Griffin 6.00 15.00
ESSAJ Alshon Jeffery 10.00 25.00
ESSAW Andre Ware 8.00 20.00
ESSBE Travis Benjamin 5.00 12.00
ESSBJ Bo Jackson 40.00 80.00
ESSBQ Brian Quick 5.00 12.00
ESSBS Barry Sanders 50.00 100.00
ESSBT Tedy Bruschi 12.00 30.00
ESSBW Brandon Weeden 5.00 12.00
ESSCK Case Keenum 10.00 25.00
ESSCW Charlie Ward 6.00 15.00
ESSDB Drew Bledsoe 8.00 20.00
ESSDF Doug Flutie 8.00 20.00
ESSDL Daryle Lamonica 6.00 15.00
ESSDM Doug Martin 10.00 25.00
ESSDP DeVier Posey 5.00 12.00
ESSEC Earl Campbell 20.00 40.00
ESSGB Gary Beban 6.00 15.00
ESSGR George Rogers 6.00 15.00
ESSHW Herschel Walker 12.00 30.00
ESSIP Isaiah Pead 5.00 12.00
ESSJA A.J. Jenkins 5.00 12.00
ESSJB Justin Blackmon 5.00 12.00
ESSJC Juron Criner 5.00 12.00
ESSJE John Elway 50.00 100.00
ESSJL Johnny Lattner 6.00 15.00
ESSJM Jim Kelly 20.00 40.00
ESSJN Joe Namath 30.00 60.00
ESSJP Jake Plummer 6.00 15.00
ESSJR Johnny Rodgers 8.00 20.00
ESSJW Joe Washington 6.00 15.00
ESSKC Kirk Cousins 20.00 50.00
ESSKJ Keith Jackson 6.00 15.00
ESSKM Ken MacAfee 6.00 15.00
ESSKW Kendall Wright 5.00 12.00
ESSLJ LaMichael James 5.00 12.00
ESSMA Dan Marino 60.00 120.00
ESSMF Michael Floyd 5.00 12.00
ESSMO Kellen Moore 6.00 15.00
ESSMR Mike Rozier 6.00 15.00
ESSMS Mohamed Sanu 8.00 20.00
ESSNF Nick Foles 12.00 30.00
ESSPH Paul Hornung 15.00 40.00
ESSRB Ryan Broyles 5.00 12.00
ESSRG Robert Griffin III 6.00 15.00
ESSRR Rueben Randle 5.00 12.00
ESSRT Ryan Tannehill 8.00 20.00
ESSSH Stephen Hill 5.00 12.00
ESSST Bart Starr 30.00 60.00
ESSSY Steve Young 25.00 50.00
ESSTF Tommie Frazier 6.00 15.00
ESSTR Trent Richardson 5.00 12.00
ESSTT Tim Tebow 30.00 80.00
ESSVT Vinny Testaverde 10.00 25.00
ESSWH Jason White 8.00 20.00
ESSWM Warren Moon 12.00 30.00
ESSWR Jarius Wright 5.00 12.00
NNO Dual Holder 2.50 6.00
NNO Quad Holder 3.00 8.00

2012 Exquisite Collection Dimension Autographs

EBAC Anthony Carter 20.00 40.00
EBAG Archie Griffin 20.00 40.00
EBAJ A.J. Jenkins 8.00 20.00
EBAL Alshon Jeffery 20.00 50.00
EBAR Aaron Rodgers 100.00 200.00
EBAW Andre Ware 8.00 20.00
EBBB Brian Bosworth 20.00 40.00
EBBJ Bo Jackson 40.00 100.00
EBBS Bart Starr 50.00 100.00
EBBT Travis Benjamin 8.00 20.00
EBBW Brandon Weeden 8.00 20.00
EBCK Case Keenum 15.00 40.00
EBDM Doug Martin 12.00 30.00
EBDP DeVier Posey 12.00 30.00
EBEC Earl Campbell 25.00 50.00
EBGB Gary Beban 8.00 20.00
EBGR George Rogers 8.00 20.00
EBHW Herschel Walker 20.00 50.00
EBJB Justin Blackmon 8.00 20.00
EBJE John Elway 50.00 100.00
EBJK Jim Kelly 25.00 50.00
EBJL Johnny Lattner 12.00 30.00
EBJN Joe Namath 50.00 100.00
EBJP Jake Plummer 10.00 25.00
EBJR Johnny Rodgers 10.00 25.00
EBJW Joe Washington 12.00 30.00
EBKC Kirk Cousins 30.00 80.00
EBKM Kellen Moore 10.00 25.00
EBKW Kendall Wright 8.00 20.00
EBMA Ken MacAfee 10.00 25.00
EBMF Michael Floyd 8.00 20.00
EBMR Mike Rozier 10.00 25.00
EBRG Robert Griffin III 10.00 25.00
EBRJ Jerry Rice 60.00 120.00
EBRT Ryan Tannehill 12.00 30.00
EBRW Russell Wilson 75.00 150.00
EBSA Barry Sanders 60.00 120.00
EBSY Steve Young 40.00 80.00
EBTF Tommie Frazier 12.00 30.00
EBTR Trent Richardson 8.00 20.00
EBWJ Jason White 10.00 25.00

2012 Exquisite Collection Draft Picks

ERAD Aaron Dobson 5.00 12.00
ERBA Montee Ball 3.00 8.00
ERCH Cobi Hamilton 4.00 10.00
ERCK Collin Klein 5.00 12.00
ERCP Cordarrelle Patterson 5.00 12.00
ERDH DeAndre Hopkins 8.00 20.00
ERDR Da'Rick Rogers 5.00 12.00
EREL Eddie Lacy 12.00 30.00
EREM EJ Manuel 6.00 15.00
ERGB Giovani Bernard 10.00 25.00
ERGS Geno Smith 6.00 15.00
ERJF Johnathan Franklin 5.00 12.00
ERJH Justin Hunter 6.00 15.00
ERJJ Jawan Jamison 3.00 8.00
ERJR Joseph Randle 4.00 10.00
ERKA Keenan Allen 10.00 25.00
ERKS Kenny Stills 6.00 15.00
ERLB Le'Veon Bell 8.00 20.00
ERLJ Landry Jones 5.00 12.00
ERMB Matt Barkley 6.00 15.00
ERMG Mike Glennon 8.00 20.00
ERMT Manti Te'o 10.00 25.00
ERMW Markus Wheaton 6.00 15.00
ERRN Ryan Nassib 6.00 15.00
ERRO Denard Robinson 6.00 15.00
ERRW Robert Woods 5.00 12.00
ERTA Tavon Austin 8.00 20.00
ERTB Tyler Bray 5.00 12.00
ERTW Tyler Wilson 5.00 12.00
ERZD Zac Dysert 5.00 12.00

2012 Exquisite Collection Endorsements

EEAJ Alshon Jeffery 15.00 40.00
EEAT Al Toon 8.00 20.00
EEAW Andre Ware 6.00 15.00
EEBB Brian Bosworth 10.00 25.00
EEBC Billy Cannon 12.00 30.00
EEBS Barry Sanders 60.00 120.00
EEBW Brandon Weeden 8.00 20.00
EECW Charlie Ward 8.00 20.00
EEDB Drew Bledsoe 20.00 40.00
EEDH Dan Herron 8.00 20.00
EEDK Dre Kirkpatrick 8.00 20.00
EEDL Daryle Lamonica 8.00 20.00
EEDM Dan Marino 75.00 135.00
EEDP DeVier Posey 8.00 20.00
EEJB Justin Blackmon 8.00 20.00
EEJC Juron Criner 6.00 15.00
EEJK Jim Kelly 25.00 50.00
EEJL Johnny Lattner 8.00 20.00
EEJN Joe Namath 40.00 80.00
EEJR Jerry Rice 40.00 100.00
EEKM Ken MacAfee 6.00 15.00
EEKW Kendall Wright 8.00 20.00
EELJ LaMichael James 8.00 20.00
EEMA Doug Martin 12.00 30.00
EEMB Michael Brockers 10.00 25.00
EEMF Michael Floyd 10.00 25.00
EEMK Kellen Moore 6.00 15.00
EENF Nick Foles 20.00 50.00
EEPH Paul Hornung 12.00 30.00
EERB Ryan Broyles 10.00 25.00
EERG Robert Griffin III 10.00 25.00
EERR Rueben Randle 8.00 20.00
EERT Ryan Tannehill 12.00 30.00
EESB Bart Starr 50.00 100.00
EESY Steve Young 30.00 60.00
EETR Trent Richardson 8.00 20.00
EETT Tim Tebow 30.00 80.00
EEVT Vinny Testaverde 15.00 30.00
EEWM Warren Moon 12.00 30.00

2012 Exquisite Collection Ensemble 2 Signatures

EE2BW B.Weeden/J.Blackmon 5.00 12.00
EE2CF N.Foles/K.Cousins 20.00 50.00
EE2CM Cunningham/K.Martin 8.00 20.00
EE2DR T.Dorsett/G.Rogers 15.00 40.00
EE2EM D.Marino/J.Elway 150.00 300.00
EE2FR T.Frazier/M.Rozier 15.00 40.00
EE2JC B.Jackson/E.Campbell 75.00 150.00
EE2LM J.Lattner/K.MacAfee 25.00 50.00
EE2NR A.Rodgers/J.Namath 150.00 250.00
EE2NS J.Namath/B.Starr 125.00 200.00
EE2PS M.Sanu/D.Posey 10.00 25.00
EE2RM D.Martin/T.Richardson 8.00 20.00
EE2RY A.Rodgers/S.Young 125.00 200.00
EE2TG R.Griffin III/R.Tannehill 8.00 20.00
EE2TH M.Tyler/C.Hayward 5.00 12.00
EE2TK V.Testaverde/J.Kelly 20.00 40.00
EE2WF D.Flutie/H.Walker 25.00 50.00
EE2WO R.Wilson/B.Osweiler 60.00 120.00
EE2YF D.Fouts/S.Young 60.00 120.00

2012 Exquisite Collection Ensemble 3 Signatures

EE3BJQ Bryls/Quick/Jeffery
EE3EYM Marino/Elway/Young
EE3HTL Lmnc/Thsmnn/Hrng
EE3JRM Rchrdsn/Jmes/Mrtn 10.00 25.00
EE3KMW Mre/Wilsn/Keenum 60.00 120.00
EE3NAR Namth/Aikman/Rice 125.00 200.00
EE3SGN Strr/Griffin/Namath
EE3SWB Bswrth/Sims/Whte 50.00 100.00
EE3TWG Weden/Tannhll/RGIII 10.00 25.00
EE3YFR Fouts/Rdgers/Young 175.00 300.00

2012 Exquisite Collection Inscriptions

EIAJ Alshon Jeffery 25.00 60.00
EIBS Barry Sanders
EIBT Brandon Thompson 15.00 40.00
EIBW Brandon Weeden 12.00 30.00
EIDB Drew Bledsoe 40.00 80.00
EIDF Doug Flutie 20.00 50.00
EIGB Gary Beban 12.00 30.00
EIJB Justin Blackmon 12.00 30.00
EIJL Johnny Lattner 15.00 40.00
EIMS Mohamed Sanu 20.00 50.00
EIRG Robert Griffin III 15.00 40.00
EIRR Rueben Randle 15.00 40.00
EIRT Ryan Tannehill 20.00 50.00
EISH Stephen Hill 15.00 40.00
EITA Troy Aikman 40.00 80.00

2012 Exquisite Collection Legacy Signatures

ELAC Anthony Carter 15.00 30.00
ELAG Archie Griffin 15.00 30.00
ELAK Andy Katzenmoyer 8.00 20.00
ELAW Andre Ware 6.00 15.00
ELBJ Bo Jackson 40.00 80.00
ELBS Bart Starr 50.00 100.00
ELCW Charlie Ward 8.00 20.00
ELDF Doug Flutie 15.00 30.00
ELEC Earl Campbell 20.00 40.00
ELGB Gary Beban 6.00 15.00
ELGR George Rogers 8.00 20.00
ELHW Herschel Walker 25.00 50.00
ELJE John Elway 50.00 100.00
ELJL Johnny Lattner 8.00 20.00
ELJN Joe Namath 40.00 80.00
ELJP Jake Plummer 8.00 20.00
ELJR Johnny Rodgers 8.00 20.00
ELJW Joe Washington 15.00 30.00
ELRJ Jerry Rice 50.00 100.00
ELSB Barry Sanders 60.00 120.00
ELTB Tedy Bruschi 12.00 30.00
ELTD Tony Dorsett 20.00 40.00
ELTF Tommie Frazier 8.00 20.00
ELVT Vinny Testaverde 15.00 30.00
ELWJ Jason White 6.00 15.00

2012 Exquisite Collection Rookie Bookmark Jersey Autographs

RBMAH S.Hill/D.Allen 10.00 25.00
RBMBJ Blackmon/Weeden 10.00 25.00
RBMBR Blackmon/Richardson 15.00 40.00
RBMBW K.Wright/Blackmon 10.00 25.00
RBMCC Cunningham/Cousins 40.00 100.00
RBMCW J.Wright/J.Criner 12.00 30.00
RBMHS D.Herron/M.Sanu 12.00 30.00
RBMJH A.Jeffery/S.Hill 15.00 40.00
RBMJR R.Randle/A.Jeffery 20.00 50.00
RBMJW A.Jeffery/K. Wright 25.00 60.00
RBMMM D.Martin/K.Moore 15.00 40.00
RBMPH D.Herron/D.Posey 10.00 25.00
RBMPJ D.Posey/A.Jeffery 15.00 40.00
RBMPR D.Posey/R.Randle 12.00 30.00
RBMPW D.Posey/J.Wright 10.00 25.00
RBMRB Benjamin/R.Randle 12.00 30.00
RBMRG Richardson/Griffin III 12.00 30.00
RBMRK K.Cousins/R.Wilson 80.00 200.00
RBMRN R.Wilson/N.Toon 75.00 150.00
RBMRW Richardson/Weeden 20.00 50.00
RBMSH S.Hill/M.Sanu 15.00 40.00
RBMTG Griffin III/Tannehill 15.00 40.00
RBMTL Richardson/L.James 20.00 50.00
RBMTW Tannehill/Weeden 15.00 40.00
RBMWG R.Griffin III/K.Wright 12.00 30.00
RBMWO R.Wilson/B.Osweiler 75.00 150.00

2012 Exquisite Collection Rookie Gold Holofoil

*121-143 AU/50: .8X TO 2X JSY AU/150
*144-150 AU/40: .5X TO 1.2X JSY AU/99
123 Nick Foles JSY AU 40.00 100.00
125 Case Keenum JSY AU 30.00 80.00
127 Russell Wilson JSY AU 500.00 1000.00
144 Robert Griffin III JSY AU 20.00 50.00
145 Ryan Tannehill JSY AU 25.00 60.00

2013 Exquisite Collection

1-60 STATED PRINT RUN 70
62-120 AU PRINT RUN 70
121-143 JSY AU PRINT RUN 125
144-150 JSY AU PRINT RUN 99
1 Andrew Luck 20.00 40.00
2 Barry Sanders 8.00 20.00
3 Jerry Rice 8.00 20.00
4 Eric Dickerson 4.00 10.00
5 Bo Jackson 10.00 25.00
6 John Elway 8.00 20.00
7 Kordell Stewart 4.00 10.00
8 Billy Sims 4.00 10.00
9 Doug Flutie 4.00 10.00
10 Ozzie Newsome 4.00 10.00
11 Dan Marino 10.00 25.00
12 Roger Craig 4.00 10.00
13 Natrone Means 3.00 8.00
14 Jerome Bettis 5.00 12.00
15 Bernie Kosar 4.00 10.00
16 Peyton Manning 30.00 80.00
17 Terrell Davis 4.00 10.00
18 Drew Bledsoe 4.00 10.00
19 Charley Taylor 3.00 8.00
20 Charlie Ward 3.00 8.00
21 LaDainian Tomlinson 4.00 10.00
22 Paul Hornung 5.00 12.00
23 Tedy Bruschi 4.00 10.00
24 Roman Gabriel 3.00 8.00
25 Ben Roethlisberger 5.00 12.00
26 Johnny Rodgers 3.00 8.00
27 Thurman Thomas 4.00 10.00
28 Warren Moon 5.00 12.00
29 Archie Griffin 5.00 12.00
30 Brian Bosworth 4.00 10.00
31 Steve Young 6.00 15.00
32 Jason White 3.00 8.00
33 Eddie George 4.00 10.00
34 Ickey Woods 3.00 8.00
35 Joe Namath 12.00 30.00
36 Ron Dayne 4.00 10.00
37 Dan Fouts 4.00 10.00
38 Joe Montana 15.00 40.00
39 Lawrence Taylor 5.00 12.00
40 Garrison Hearst 3.00 8.00
41 Ty Detmer 3.00 8.00
42 Jerry Rice 8.00 20.00
43 Drew Brees 5.00 12.00
44 Anthony Carter 3.00 8.00
45 Earl Campbell 5.00 12.00
46 Mike Alstott 3.00 8.00
47 Bart Starr 8.00 20.00
48 Rick Mirer 3.00 8.00
49 Tim Brown 5.00 12.00
50 Mike Vrabel 3.00 8.00
51 Irving Fryar 3.00 8.00
52 Randall Cunningham 4.00 10.00
53 Daryle Lamonica 3.00 8.00
54 Chris Weinke 3.00 8.00
55 Jim Kelly 5.00 12.00
56 Jim Plunkett 4.00 10.00
57 George Rogers 3.00 8.00
58 Craig Krenzel 3.00 8.00
59 Joe Theismann 5.00 12.00
60 John Elway 8.00 20.00
62 Collin Klein AU 8.00 20.00
63 B.J. Daniels AU 10.00 25.00
65 Damontre Moore AU 6.00 15.00
68 Tavarres King AU 6.00 15.00
70 Jawan Jamison AU 6.00 15.00
72 Stepfan Taylor AU 6.00 15.00
73 Aaron Mellette AU 15.00 40.00
75 Marquess Wilson AU 10.00 25.00
76 Matt Scott AU 6.00 15.00
77 Knile Davis AU 6.00 15.00
78 Da'Rick Rogers AU 6.00 15.00
80 Brad Sorensen AU 6.00 15.00
81 Xavier Rhodes AU 6.00 15.00
82 Dayne Crist AU 8.00 20.00
84 Spencer Ware AU 6.00 15.00
85 Rex Burkhead AU 8.00 20.00
86 Cierre Wood AU 6.00 15.00
87 Ray Graham AU 6.00 15.00
93 Marcus Davis AU 6.00 15.00
94 Theo Riddick AU 6.00 15.00
95 Conner Vernon AU 6.00 15.00
96 Will Davis AU 6.00 15.00
97 Corey Fuller AU 6.00 15.00
99 T.J. Moe AU 8.00 20.00
100 Eric Reid AU 25.00 50.00
101 Gavin Escobar AU 6.00 15.00
104 Vance McDonald AU 8.00 20.00
105 Justin Pugh AU 6.00 15.00
106 Luke Joeckel AU 6.00 15.00
107 Eric Fisher AU 6.00 15.00
108 Lane Johnson AU 8.00 20.00
109 D.J. Fluker AU 6.00 15.00
110 Sharrif Floyd AU 6.00 15.00
115 Datone Jones AU 6.00 15.00
116 Bjoern Werner AU 6.00 15.00
117 Alec Ogletree AU 6.00 15.00
118 Kevin Minter AU 6.00 15.00
119 Desmond Trufant AU 6.00 15.00
120 Dion Jordan AU 6.00 15.00
121 R.Nassib JSY AU 10.00 25.00
122 M.Gillislee JSY AU 10.00 25.00
123 M.Glennon JSY AU 10.00 25.00
124 Z.Dysert JSY AU 10.00 25.00
125 L.Jones JSY AU EX 10.00 25.00
126 Montee Ball JSY AU 10.00 25.00
127 Le'Veon Bell JSY AU 60.00 125.00
128 J.Randle JSY AU 10.00 25.00
129 Eddie Lacy JSY AU 10.00 25.00
130 D.Robinson JSY AU 10.00 25.00
131 M.Lattimore JSY AU 10.00 25.00
132 J.Franklin JSY AU 10.00 25.00
133 Tyler Eifert JSY AU 10.00 25.00
134 M.Wheaton JSY AU 10.00 25.00
135 J.Hunter JSY AU 10.00 25.00
136 C.Patterson JSY AU EX 10.00 25.00
137 T.Williams JSY AU 10.00 25.00
138 A.Dobson JSY AU 10.00 25.00
139 R.Woods JSY AU EX 15.00 40.00
140 K.Allen JSY AU EX 20.00 50.00
141 S.Bailey JSY AU 10.00 25.00
142 Kenny Stills JSY AU 10.00 25.00
143 Zach Ertz JSY AU 20.00 50.00
144 Geno Smith JSY AU 12.00 30.00
145 Matt Barkley JSY AU 12.00 30.00
146 EJ Manuel JSY AU 12.00 30.00
147 G.Bernard JSY AU 12.00 30.00
148 T.Austin JSY AU 15.00 40.00
149 D.Hopkins JSY AU 40.00 80.00
150 Manti Te'o JSY AU 15.00 40.00

2013 Exquisite Collection Silver Spectrum

*SILVER/20: .5X TO 1.2X JSY AU RC/125
*SILVER/20: .4X TO 1X JSY AU RC/99
129 Eddie Lacy
130 Denard Robinson 12.00 30.00
136 Cordarrelle Patterson EXCH 12.00 30.00
138 Aaron Dobson 30.00 80.00
144 Geno Smith 12.00 30.00
146 EJ Manuel
147 Giovani Bernard
148 Tavon Austin 15.00 40.00

2013 Exquisite Collection Dimension Autographs

DAD Aaron Dobson [illegible]
DAL Andrew Luck 40.00 80.00
DBA Montee Ball 15.00 40.00
DBD Drew Bledsoe 25.00 60.00
DBR Ben Roethlisberger 50.00 100.00
DBS Barry Sanders 50.00 100.00
DBT Tedy Bruschi 12.00 30.00
DCP Cordarrelle Patterson EXCH 8.00 20.00
DDB Drew Brees 40.00 100.00
DDF Doug Flutie 15.00 40.00
DDH DeAndre Hopkins 20.00 50.00
DDM Dan Marino 90.00 150.00
DED Eric Dickerson 25.00 50.00
DEG Eddie George 50.00 100.00
DEL Eddie Lacy 8.00 20.00
DEM EJ Manuel 25.00 60.00
DGB Giovani Bernard 8.00 20.00
DGS Geno Smith 8.00 20.00
DJB Jerome Bettis 40.00 80.00
DJE John Elway 50.00 100.00
DJH Justin Hunter 20.00 50.00
DJN Joe Namath 50.00 100.00
DJR Jerry Rice 75.00 150.00
DLB Le'Veon Bell 30.00 80.00
DLT LaDainian Tomlinson 20.00 50.00
DMB Matt Barkley 8.00 20.00
DMG Mike Glennon 8.00 20.00
DMT Manti Te'o 10.00 25.00
DON Ozzie Newsome 12.00 30.00
DPH Paul Hornung 15.00 40.00
DPM Peyton Manning 100.00 200.00
DRW Robert Woods 12.00 30.00
DSY Steve Young 30.00 60.00
DTA Tavon Austin 10.00 25.00
DTB Tim Brown EXCH
DTD Terrell Davis 25.00 50.00
DTE Tyler Eifert 8.00 20.00
DTT Thurman Thomas 12.00 30.00
DWM Warren Moon EXCH 15.00 40.00
DZE Zach Ertz 15.00 40.00

2013 Exquisite Collection Draft Picks Autographs

EXCH EXPIRATION: 5/20/2016
ERAR Allen Robinson/99 30.00 60.00
ERBB Blake Bortles/49 125.00 250.00
ERBC Brandon Coleman/99 10.00 25.00
ERBO Tajh Boyd/99 EXCH 15.00 40.00
ERBS Bishop Sankey/99 10.00 25.00
ERCB Brandin Cooks/99 EXCH 10.00 25.00
ERCH Carlos Hyde/99 15.00 40.00
ERCS Charles Sims/99 EXCH 10.00 25.00
ERDA Davante Adams/99 15.00 40.00
ERDC Derek Carr/75 100.00 200.00
ERDF David Fales/99 EXCH 10.00 25.00
ERDM Donte Moncrief/99 10.00 25.00
ERDS Devin Street/99 8.00 20.00
ERDT D.Thomas/99 EXCH 25.00 50.00
ERFM Devonta Freeman/99 40.00 80.00
ERGR Ryan Grant/99 EXCH 8.00 20.00
ERHJ Jeremy Hill/99 15.00 40.00
ERJA Jared Abbrederis/99 6.00 15.00
ERJG Jimmy Garoppolo/75 30.00 60.00
ERJH Josh Huff/99 8.00 20.00
ERJL Jarvis Landry/99 EXCH 25.00 50.00
ERJM Johnny Manziel/49 EXCH 40.00 80.00
ERJW James Wilder Jr./99 EXCH 10.00 25.00
ERKB Kelvin Benjamin/99 20.00 50.00
ERKC Ka'Deem Carey/99 10.00 25.00
ERLJ LeBron James/49 EXCH 250.00 500.00
ERLS Lache Seastrunk/99 8.00 20.00
ERLT Logan Thomas/99 EXCH 10.00 25.00
ERMB Martavis Bryant/99 EXCH 25.00 50.00
ERMD Mike Davis/99 8.00 20.00
ERME Mike Evans/75 12.00 30.00
ERMG Marion Grice/99 10.00 25.00
ERML Marqise Lee/75 EXCH 10.00 25.00
ERMU Aaron Murray/99 EXCH 15.00 40.00
EROB Odell Beckham Jr./99 EXCH 150.00 300.00
ERPR Paul Richardson/99 EXCH 8.00 20.00
ERRH Robert Herron/99 EXCH 6.00 15.00
ERSA Jalen Saunders/99 6.00 15.00
ERSB Brett Smith/99 EXCH 6.00 15.00
ERSM Stephen Morris/99 10.00 25.00
ERSW Sammy Watkins/75 25.00 50.00
ERTB Teddy Bridgewater/49 40.00 80.00
ERWH James White/99 EXCH 8.00 20.00
ERZM Zach Mettenberger/99 20.00 50.00

2013 Exquisite Collection Ensemble 2 Signatures

EE2BB Bettis/T.Brown EXCH 75.00 125.00
EE2BD J.Bettis/E.Dickerson 90.00 150.00
EE2BL G.Bernard/E.Lacy 40.00 80.00
EE2BM D.Brees/D.Marino
EE2BR Brees/Roethlisberger
EE2BW Barkley/Woods EXCH
EE2CG E.Campbell/E.George 100.00 175.00
EE2DB K.Davis/L.Bell
EE2ET T.Eifert/M.Te'o 8.00 20.00
EE2FF D.Fouts/D.Flutie
EE2HL Hornung/D.Lamonica
EE2JB Jackson/Brown EXCH
EE2ML P.Manning/A.Luck 500.00 700.00
EE2PH Patterson/Hunter EXCH
EE2RM J.Rice/J.Montana 150.00 250.00
EE2SA G.Smith/T.Austin 8.00 20.00
EE2SC B.Sims/R.Craig
EE2SM G.Smith/E.Manuel 6.00 15.00
EE2ST Sanders/Tomlnsn EXCH

2013 Exquisite Collection Exquisite Endorsements

EEAD Aaron Dobson/125 5.00 12.00
EEBA Montee Ball/125
EEBT Tedy Bruschi/125 8.00 20.00
EECP Cordarrelle Patterson/125 EXCH 5.00 12.00
EECW Charlie Ward/125 10.00 25.00
EEDF Doug Flutie/125 8.00 20.00
EEDH DeAndre Hopkins/125 12.00 30.00
EEEL Eddie Lacy/125 5.00 12.00
EEEM EJ Manuel/125 5.00 12.00
EEGB Giovani Bernard/125 5.00 12.00
EEIW Ickey Woods/125 6.00 15.00
EEJF Johnathan Franklin/125 5.00 12.00
EEJH Justin Hunter/125 10.00 25.00
EEJW Jason White/125
EELB Le'Veon Bell/125 25.00 50.00
EEMB Matt Barkley/125 10.00 25.00
EEMG Mike Glennon/125 5.00 12.00
EEMT Manti Te'o/125 6.00 15.00
EENM Natrone Means/125 6.00 15.00
EEON Ozzie Newsome/125 8.00 20.00
EERD Ron Dayne/125 8.00 20.00
EERG Roman Gabriel/125 6.00 15.00
EERN Ryan Nassib/125 5.00 12.00
EERW Robert Woods/125 EXCH 8.00 20.00
EETA Tavon Austin/125 6.00 15.00
EETD Terrell Davis/125 8.00 20.00
EETE Tyler Eifert/125 5.00 12.00

2013 Exquisite Collection Legendary

COMMON CARD/30-60 10.00 25.00
SEMISTARS/30-60 12.00 30.00
UNLISTED STARS/30-60 15.00 40.00
STATED PRINT RUN 10-60
ELAC Anthony Carter/60 10.00 25.00
ELAG Archie Griffin/60 10.00 25.00
ELAL Andrew Luck/40 75.00 150.00
ELDB Drew Brees/40 30.00 80.00
ELDF Doug Flutie/60 12.00 30.00
ELDL Daryle Lamonica/60 10.00 25.00
ELEC Earl Campbell/60 15.00 40.00
ELED Eric Dickerson/60 12.00 30.00
ELEG Eddie George/60 25.00 60.00
ELJE John Elway/30 50.00 100.00
ELJR Jerry Rice/30 50.00 100.00
ELPH Paul Hornung/60 15.00 40.00
ELPM Peyton Manning/30 125.00 250.00
ELRC Roger Craig/60 12.00 30.00
ELRD Ron Dayne/60 12.00 30.00
ELTS Terrell Davis/60 12.00 30.00
ELWM Warren Moon/60 EXCH 15.00 40.00

2013 Exquisite Collection Rookie Legacy Bookmark Jersey Autographs

STATED PRINT RUN 60 SER.#'d SETS
*PATCH/15: .6X TO 1.5X BASIC DUAL AU
RMBAH T.Austin/D.Hopkins 15.00 40.00
RMBAT M.Te'o/K.Allen EXCH 12.00 30.00
RMBBA T.Austin/S.Bailey 8.00 20.00
RMBBL M.Lattimore/M.Ball 6.00 15.00
RMBBW Barkley/Woods EXCH 10.00 25.00
RMBDW T.Williams/A.Dobson 6.00 15.00
RMBEB M.Ball/E.Lacy 6.00 15.00
RMBEE T.Eifert/Z.Ertz EXCH
RMBEH Ellington/Hopkins EXCH 40.00 80.00
RMBGL G.Bernard/L.Bell 40.00 100.00
RMBGN M.Glennon/R.Nassib 6.00 15.00
RMBJS L.Jones/K.Stills EXCH 6.00 15.00
RMBLB E.Lacy/G.Bernard 6.00 15.00
RMBLF E.Lacy/J.Franklin 6.00 15.00
RMBMS E.Manuel/G.Smith 6.00 15.00
RMBMW Manuel/Woods EXCH
RMBPD A.Dobson/C.Patterson 6.00 15.00
RMBPH Patterson/Hunter EXCH
RMBRG J.Randle/M.Gillislee 6.00 15.00
RMBRK D.Robinson/T.King 6.00 15.00
RMBSA G.Smith/T.Austin 8.00 20.00
RMBSB M.Barkley/G.Smith 6.00 15.00
RMBTE M.Te'o/T.Eifert 20.00 50.00
RMBWH M.Wheaton/J.Hunter 6.00 15.00

2014 Exquisite Collection

EXCH EXPIRATION: 3/21/2017
1 Matthew Stafford 4.00 10.00
2 Jerry Rice 8.00 20.00
3 Tiki Barber 4.00 10.00
4 Nick Saban 5.00 12.00
5 Steve Young 6.00 15.00
6 Marcus Allen 5.00 12.00
7 Barry Sanders 8.00 20.00
8 Donovan McNabb 4.00 10.00
9 Kellen Winslow Sr. 4.00 10.00
10 Peyton Manning 25.00 50.00
11 Brian Westbrook 3.00 8.00
12 Jerome Bettis 5.00 12.00
13 Peter Warrick 3.00 8.00
14 Jeff Garcia 3.00 8.00
15 John Elway 8.00 20.00
16 Mike Ditka 5.00 12.00
17 Eddie George 4.00 10.00
18 Chris Cooley 3.00 8.00
19 Bart Starr 8.00 20.00
20 Rod Woodson 4.00 10.00
21 Eric Dickerson 4.00 10.00
22 Terrell Davis 2.00 5.00
23 Ken Anderson 4.00 10.00
24 Vinny Testaverde 3.00 8.00
25 Trent Green 3.00 8.00
26 Troy Aikman 6.00 15.00
27 Earl Campbell 5.00 12.00
28 Bernie Kosar 4.00 10.00
29 James Lofton 3.00 8.00
30 Hines Ward 4.00 10.00
31 Kurt Warner 4.00 10.00
32 Ronde Barber 3.00 8.00
33 Donnie Shell 3.00 8.00
34 Deuce McAllister 4.00 10.00
35 Joe Namath 6.00 15.00
36 Brandon Jacobs 3.00 8.00
37 Steve Slaton 3.00 8.00
38 Tim Brown 5.00 12.00
39 Chuck Foreman 3.00 8.00
40 Ben Roethlisberger 10.00 25.00
41 Thurman Thomas 4.00 10.00
42 Joe Theismann 5.00 12.00
43 Joey Harrington 3.00 8.00
44 LaDainian Tomlinson 4.00 10.00
45 Emmitt Smith 8.00 20.00
46 Anthony Carter 3.00 8.00
47 Jim Kelly 5.00 12.00
48 Lawrence Taylor 5.00 12.00
49 Ahman Green 4.00 10.00
50 Bert Jones 3.00 8.00
51 Brett Smith AU 6.00 15.00
52 Bruce Ellington AU 6.00 15.00
53 David Fales AU EXCH 6.00 15.00
54 A.Seferian-Jenkins AU 6.00 15.00
55 Devin Street AU 6.00 15.00
56 Khalil Mack AU
57 Darqueze Dennard AU 8.00 20.00
58 Dri Archer AU 6.00 15.00
59 Calvin Pryor AU 6.00 15.00
60 Devonta Freeman AU 10.00 25.00
61 Robert Herron AU 6.00 15.00
62 Martavis Bryant AU 8.00 20.00
63 Troy Niklas AU 6.00 15.00
64 Ha Ha Clinton-Dix AU 8.00 20.00
65 Brandon Coleman AU 6.00 15.00
66 Jake Matthews AU 6.00 15.00
67 Jason Verrett AU 6.00 15.00
68 Michael Sam AU 6.00 15.00
69 Jeff Janis AU 6.00 15.00
70 Keith Wenning AU 8.00 20.00
71 Jared Abbrederis AU 6.00 15.00
72 Andre Williams AU
73 Mike Flacco AU 6.00 15.00
74 Taylor Lewan AU 6.00 15.00
75 Jalen Saunders AU 6.00 15.00
76 Shaquelle Evans AU 6.00 15.00
77 Lorenzo Taliaferro AU 6.00 15.00
78 Cody Hoffman AU 6.00 15.00
79 Jace Amaro AU 6.00 15.00
80 Stephen Morris AU 6.00 15.00
81 Marcus Smith AU 6.00 15.00
82 Tyler Gaffney AU 6.00 15.00
83 Jeremy Gallon AU 10.00 25.00
84 Kapri Bibbs AU 8.00 20.00
85 Cody Latimer AU 8.00 20.00
86 Anthony Barr AU 6.00 15.00
87 Rajion Neal AU 6.00 15.00
88 Trey Burton AU 6.00 15.00
89 Dee Ford AU 6.00 15.00
90 Keith Price AU 10.00 25.00
91 Mike Davis AU 6.00 15.00
92 Jerick McKinnon AU 8.00 20.00
93 C.J. Mosley AU 15.00 40.00
94 Lache Seastrunk AU 6.00 15.00
95 Kevin Norwood AU 6.00 15.00
96 James Wilder Jr. AU 8.00 20.00
97 Lamarcus Joyner AU 8.00 20.00
98 Tevin Reese AU 6.00 15.00
99 Arthur Lynch AU 6.00 15.00
100 Jordan Lynch AU 8.00 20.00
101 Ryan Grant AU 6.00 15.00
102 James White AU 12.00 30.00
103 Kyle Fuller AU 6.00 15.00
104 Marion Grice AU 6.00 15.00
105 Quincy Enunwa AU 10.00 25.00
106 Storm Johnson AU 6.00 15.00
107 Dominique Easley AU 6.00 15.00
108 Silas Redd AU 8.00 20.00
109 TJ Jones AU 10.00 25.00
110 Jeff Mathews AU 8.00 20.00
111 Jimmy Garoppolo JSY AU
112 Marqise Lee JSY AU 12.00 30.00
113 Carlos Hyde JSY AU 12.00 30.00
114 Paul Richardson JSY AU 12.00 30.00
115 Eric Ebron JSY AU 12.00 30.00
116 Z.Mettenberger JSY AU 10.00 25.00
117 Bruce Ellington JSY AU 10.00 25.00
118 Ka'Deem Carey JSY AU 10.00 25.00
120 Tom Savage JSY AU 12.00 30.00
121 Aaron Murray JSY AU 10.00 25.00
122 Kelvin Benjamin JSY AU 15.00 40.00
123 Bishop Sankey JSY AU 10.00 25.00
124 Jarvis Landry JSY AU EXCH 50.00 100.00
125 Terrance West JSY AU 10.00 25.00
126 Logan Thomas JSY AU 10.00 25.00
127 Allen Robinson JSY AU 40.00 80.00
128 Charles Sims JSY AU 10.00 25.00
129 Josh Huff JSY AU EXCH 12.00 30.00
130 Jeremy Hill JSY AU 12.00 30.00
131 Tajh Boyd JSY AU 10.00 25.00
132 Davante Adams JSY AU 15.00 40.00
133 D.Thomas JSY AU 10.00 25.00
134 Johnny Manziel JSY AU/75 20.00 50.00
135 Sammy Watkins JSY AU/75 20.00 50.00
136 T.Bridgewater JSY AU/75 20.00 50.00
137 Mike Evans JSY AU/75 25.00 60.00
138 Blake Bortles JSY AU/75 15.00 40.00
139 Brandin Cooks JSY AU/75 20.00 50.00
140 Derek Carr JSY AU/75 200.00 400.00
NNO Rookie Set EXCH

2014 Exquisite Collection Rookie Autographed Patches

*SILVER/20: .5X TO 1.2X JSY AU RC/110
*SILVER/20: .4X TO 1X JSY AU RC/75
116 Zach Mettenberger EXCH 12.00 30.00
130 Jeremy Hill 15.00 40.00
132 Davante Adams 20.00 50.00
134 Johnny Manziel EXCH 20.00 50.00
135 Sammy Watkins 20.00 50.00
138 Blake Bortles 15.00 40.00
140 Derek Carr 250.00 500.00

2014 Exquisite Collection Draft Picks

ERAA Ameer Abdullah 10.00 25.00
ERAC Amari Cooper 15.00 40.00
ERBB Brandon Bridge 5.00 12.00
ERBH Brett Hundley 10.00 25.00
ERBK Ben Koyack 3.00 8.00
ERBP Bryce Petty 5.00 12.00
ERBW Bo Wallace 10.00 25.00
ERCF Cody Fajardo 5.00 12.00
ERCS Sammie Coates 6.00 15.00
ERDE Devante Parker 12.00 30.00
ERDF Devin Funchess 6.00 15.00
ERDJ Duke Johnson 5.00 12.00
ERGG Garrett Grayson 8.00 20.00
ERHJ Justin Hardy 5.00 12.00
ERJH Josh Harper 4.00 10.00
ERJS Jaelen Strong 6.00 15.00
ERJW Jameis Winston 25.00 60.00
ERKW Kevin White 12.00 30.00
ERMD Mike Davis 5.00 12.00
ERMG Melvin Gordon III 20.00 50.00
ERMM Marcus Mariota 30.00 80.00
ERNO Nick O'Leary 6.00 15.00
ERRG Rashad Greene 5.00 12.00
ERSC Shane Carden 5.00 12.00
ERSM Sean Mannion 6.00 15.00
ERTC Tevin Coleman 5.00 12.00
ERTG Todd Gurley 25.00 50.00
ERTY T.J. Yeldon 12.00 30.00

2014 Exquisite Collection Exquisite Endorsements

EEAC Anthony Carter/40 10.00 25.00
EEAM Aaron Murray/40 10.00 25.00
EEAR Allen Robinson/40 15.00 40.00
EEBC Brandin Cooks/40 15.00 40.00
EEBK Bernie Kosar/25
EECA Derek Carr/25 40.00 100.00
EECH Carlos Hyde/40 12.00 30.00
EEDA Davante Adams/40 15.00 40.00
EEEC Earl Campbell/25 20.00 50.00
EEEE Eric Ebron/40 12.00 30.00
EEEG Eddie George/25 25.00 60.00
EEHW Hines Ward/25 25.00 60.00
EEJG Jimmy Garoppolo/40 50.00 100.00
EEJT Joe Theismann/25 15.00 40.00
EEKB Kelvin Benjamin/40 15.00 40.00
EEKC Ka'Deem Carey/40 10.00 25.00
EEME Mike Evans/25 30.00 80.00
EEML Marqise Lee/40 12.00 30.00
EEOB Odell Beckham Jr./40 EXCH 50.00 100.00
EESB Bishop Sankey/40 10.00 25.00
EESW Sammy Watkins/25 20.00 50.00
EETD Terrell Davis/25 8.00 20.00
EETT Thurman Thomas/25 15.00 40.00
EETW Terrance West/40 10.00 25.00
EEZM Zach Mettenberger/40 EXCH 10.00 25.00

2014 Exquisite Collection Signatures

ESAC Anthony Carter/99 8.00 20.00
ESAM Aaron Murray/99 8.00 20.00
ESBC Brandin Cooks/99 12.00 30.00
ESBW Brian Westbrook/99 8.00 20.00
ESCF Chuck Foreman/99 8.00 20.00
ESCH Carlos Hyde/99 10.00 25.00
ESDM Donovan McNabb/60 12.00 30.00
ESHW Hines Ward/60 25.00 50.00
ESJG Jimmy Garoppolo/99 50.00 100.00
ESJH Joey Harrington/99 8.00 20.00
ESJL James Lofton/99 8.00 20.00
ESJT Joe Theismann/60 15.00 40.00
ESKS Kellen Winslow Sr./60 12.00 30.00
ESME Mike Evans/60 15.00 40.00
ESRW Rod Woodson/60 15.00 40.00
ESSB Bishop Sankey/99 8.00 20.00
ESSW Sammy Watkins/60 15.00 40.00
ESTB Tiki Barber/99 10.00 25.00
ESTG Trent Green/99 8.00 20.00
ESTL Logan Thomas/99 8.00 20.00
ESTT Thurman Thomas/60 12.00 30.00
ESVT Vinny Testaverde/99 8.00 20.00

1971 Facsimile Photos

1 Danny Abramowicz 6.00 15.00
2 Lem Barney 8.00 20.00
3 Emerson Boozer 6.00 15.00
4 Terry Bradshaw 15.00 40.00
5 Larry Brown 6.00 15.00
6 Nick Buoniconti 8.00 20.00
7 Paul Costa 5.00 12.00
8 Bobby Douglass 6.00 15.00
9 Carl Eller 6.00 15.00
10 Jim Hart 6.00 15.00
11 Charley Johnson 6.00 15.00
12 Daryle Lamonica 6.00 15.00
13 Floyd Little 6.00 15.00
14 Spider Lockhart 5.00 12.00
15 Bill Nelsen 6.00 15.00
16 Ray Nitschke 10.00 25.00
17 Tommy Nobis 6.00 15.00
18 Johnny Robinson 6.00 15.00
19 Paul Robinson 5.00 12.00
20 Ron Sellers 5.00 12.00
21 Bubba Smith 8.00 20.00
22 Gene Washington 6.00 15.00
23 Tom Woodeshick 6.00 15.00

1990 FACT Pro Set Cincinnati

The 1990 Pro Set FACT (Football and Academics: A Cincinnati Team) set was aimed at fourth graders in 29 schools in the Cincinnati school system. The special cards were used as motivational learning tools to promote public health and education. Twenty-five cards per week were issued in 25-card cello packs for fifteen consecutive weeks beginning October 1990. Moreover, a Teacher Instructional Game Plan, measuring approximately 8 1/2" by 11" and containing answers to all of the questions, was also issued. The standard-size cards are identical to first series cards, with the exception that the backs have interactive educational (Math, grammar, and science) questions instead of player information. Each 1990 Pro Set first series card was reprinted. The cards are numbered on the back. Each cello-wrapped pack led off with a header card which indicated the "week" number at the bottom. Initially, the missing numbers from the first series were 338, 376, and 377 but the Eric Dickerson PB card surfaced in limited quantities nearly twenty years later.

COMPLETE SET (375) 720.00 1800.00
1 Barry Sanders W1 30.00 80.00
2 Joe Montana W1 50.00 120.00
3 Lindy Infante W1 UER 1.25 3.00
4 Warren Moon W1 UER 1.50 4.00
5 Keith Millard W1 1.25 3.00
6 Derrick Thomas W1 UER 1.50 4.00
7 Ottis Anderson W1 1.25 3.00
8 Joe Montana W2 50.00 120.00
9 Christian Okoye W2 1.25 3.00
10 Thurman Thomas W2 2.50 6.00
11 Mike Cofer W2 1.25 3.00
12 Dalton Hilliard W2 UER 1.25 3.00
13 Sterling Sharpe W2 2.50 6.00
14 Rich Camarillo W3 1.25 3.00
15 Walter Stanley W3 1.25 3.00
16 Rod Woodson W3 1.50 4.00
17 Felix Wright W3 1.25 3.00
18 Chris Doleman W3 1.25 3.00
19 Andre Ware W3 1.50 4.00
20 Mo Elewonibi W4 1.25 3.00
21 Percy Snow W4 1.25 3.00
22 Anthony Thompson W4 1.25 3.00
23 Buck Buchanan W4 1.25 3.00
24 Bob Griese W4 1.50 4.00
25 Franco Harris W5 1.50 4.00
26 Ted Hendricks W4 1.50 4.00
27 Jack Lambert W5 1.50 4.00
28 Tom Landry W5 1.50 4.00
29 Bob St.Clair W5 1.25 3.00
30 Aundray Bruce W5 UER 1.25 3.00
31 Tony Casillas W5 UER 1.25 3.00
32 Shawn Collins W5 1.25 3.00
33 Marcus Cotton W6 1.25 3.00
34 Bill Fralic W6 1.25 3.00
35 Chris Miller W6 1.50 4.00
36 Deion Sanders W6 UER 15.00 40.00
37 John Settle W6 1.25 3.00
38 Jerry Glanville CO W6 1.25 3.00
39 Cornelius Bennett W7 1.50 4.00
40 Jim Kelly W7 6.00 15.00
41 Mark Kelso W7 UER 1.25 3.00
42 Scott Norwood W7 1.25 3.00
43 Nate Odomes W7 1.25 3.00
44 Scott Radecic W7 1.25 3.00
45 Jim Ritcher W8 1.25 3.00
46 Leonard Smith W8 1.25 3.00
47 Darryl Talley W8 1.25 3.00
48 Marv Levy CO W8 1.25 3.00
49 Neal Anderson W8 1.50 4.00
50 Kevin Butler W8 1.25 3.00
51 Jim Covert W9 1.25 3.00
52 Richard Dent W9 1.50 4.00
53 Jay Hilgenberg W9 1.25 3.00
54 Steve McMichael W9 1.25 3.00
55 Ron Morris W9 1.25 3.00
56 John Roper W9 1.25 3.00
57 Mike Singletary W9 1.50 4.00
58 Keith Van Horne W10 1.25 3.00
59 Mike Ditka CO W10 1.50 4.00
60 Lewis Billups W10 1.25 3.00
61 Eddie Brown W10 1.25 3.00
62 Jason Buck W10 1.25 3.00
63 Rickey Dixon W10 1.25 3.00
64 Tim McGee W11 1.25 3.00
65 Eric Thomas W11 1.25 3.00
66 Ickey Woods W11 1.25 3.00
67 Carl Zander W11 1.25 3.00
68 Sam Wyche CO W11 1.25 3.00
69 Paul Farren W11 1.25 3.00
70 Thane Gash W12 1.25 3.00
71 David Grayson W12 1.25 3.00
72 Bernie Kosar W12 1.50 4.00
73 Reggie Langhorne W12 1.25 3.00
74 Eric Metcalf W12 1.50 4.00
75 Ozzie Newsome W12 1.50 4.00
76 Felix Wright W13 1.25 3.00
77 Bud Carson CO W13 1.25 3.00
78 Troy Aikman W13 30.00 80.00
79 Michael Irvin W13 5.00 12.00
80 Jim Jeffcoat W13 1.25 3.00
81 Crawford Ker W13 1.25 3.00
82 Eugene Lockhart W13 1.25 3.00
83 Kelvin Martin W14 1.25 3.00
84 Ken Norton Jr. W14 1.50 4.00
85 Jimmy Johnson CO W14 1.50 4.00
86 Steve Atwater W14 1.25 3.00
87 Tyrone Braxton W14 1.25 3.00
88 John Elway W14 40.00 100.00
89 Simon Fletcher W15 1.25 3.00
90 Ron Holmes W15 1.25 3.00
91 Bobby Humphrey W15 1.25 3.00
92 Vance Johnson W15 1.25 3.00
93 Ricky Nattiel W15 1.25 3.00
94 Dan Reeves CO W15 1.50 4.00
95 Jim Arnold W1 1.25 3.00
96 Jerry Ball W1 1.25 3.00
97 Bennie Blades W1 1.25 3.00
98 Lomas Brown W1 1.25 3.00
99 Michael Cofer W1 1.25 3.00
100 Richard Johnson W4 1.25 3.00
101 Eddie Murray W4 1.25 3.00
102 Barry Sanders W2 40.00 100.00
103 Chris Spielman W2 1.25 3.00
104 William White W2 1.25 3.00
105 Eric Williams W2 1.25 3.00
106 Wayne Fontes CO W3 UER 1.25 3.00
107 Brent Fullwood W3 1.25 3.00
108 Ron Hallstrom W3 1.25 3.00
109 Tim Harris W8 1.25 3.00
110 Johnny Holland W8 1.25 3.00
111 Perry Kemp W8 1.25 3.00
112 Don Majkowski W9 1.25 3.00
113 Mark Murphy W9 1.25 3.00
114 Sterling Sharpe W9 2.50 6.00
115 Ed West W9 1.25 3.00
116 Lindy Infante CO W9 1.25 3.00
117 Steve Brown W9 1.25 3.00
118 Ray Childress W10 1.25 3.00
119 Ernest Givins W10 1.25 3.00
120 John Grimsley W10 1.25 3.00
121 Alonzo Highsmith W10 1.25 3.00
122 Drew Hill W10 1.50 4.00
123 Bubba McDowell W10 1.25 3.00
124 Dean Steinkuhler W10 1.25 3.00
125 Lorenzo White W11 1.25 3.00
126 Tony Zendejas W11 1.25 3.00
127 Jack Pardee CO W11 1.25 3.00
128 Albert Bentley W11 1.25 3.00
129 Dean Biasucci W11 1.25 3.00
130 Duane Bickett W11 1.25 3.00
131 Bill Brooks W12 1.25 3.00
132 Jon Hand W12 1.25 3.00
133 Mike Prior W12 1.25 3.00
134 Andre Rison W12 1.60 4.00
135 Rohn Stark W12 1.25 3.00
136 Donnell Thompson W12 1.25 3.00
137 Clarence Verdin W13 1.25 3.00
138 Fredd Young W13 1.25 3.00
139 Ron Meyer CO W14 1.25 3.00
140 John Alt W14 1.25 3.00
141 Steve DeBerg W14 1.25 3.00
142 Irv Eatman W1 1.25 3.00
143 Dino Hackett W2 1.25 3.00
144 Nick Lowery W2 1.25 3.00
145 Bill Maas W2 1.25 3.00
146 Stephone Paige W5 1.25 3.00
147 Neil Smith W3 1.50 4.00
148 Marty Schottenheimer 1.25 3.00
149 Steve Beuerlein W3 1.50 4.00
150 Tim Brown W4 8.00 15.00
151 Mike Dyal W4 1.25 3.00
152 Mervyn Fernandez W4 1.25 3.00
153 Willie Gault W4 1.25 3.00
154 Bob Golic W5 1.25 3.00
155 Bo Jackson W5 2.50 6.00
156 Don Mosebar W5 1.25 3.00
157 Steve Smith W5 1.25 3.00
158 Greg Townsend W5 1.25 3.00
159 Bruce Wilkerson W6 1.25 3.00
160 Steve Wisniewski W6 1.25 3.00
161 Art Shell CO W6 1.50 4.00
162 Flipper Anderson W6 1.25 3.00
163 Greg Bell W6 UER 1.25 3.00
164 Henry Ellard W6 1.50 4.00
165 Jim Everett W6 1.25 3.00
166 Jerry Gray W7 1.25 3.00
167 Kevin Greene W7 1.50 4.00
168 Pete Holohan W13 1.25 3.00
169 Larry Kelm W13 1.25 3.00
170 Tom Newberry W13 1.25 3.00
171 Vince Newsome W13 1.25 3.00
172 Irv Pankey W14 1.25 3.00
173 Jackie Slater W14 1.25 3.00
174 Fred Strickland W14 1.25 3.00
175 Mike Wilcher W14 UER 1.25 3.00
176 John Robinson CO W7 1.25 3.00
177 Mark Clayton W7 1.50 4.00
178 Roy Foster W7 1.25 3.00
179 Harry Galbreath W7 1.25 3.00
180 Jim C. Jensen W8 1.25 3.00
181 Dan Marino W15 60.00 150.00
182 Louis Oliver W15 1.25 3.00
183 Sammie Smith W15 1.25 3.00
184 Brian Sochia W15 1.25 3.00
185 Don Shula CO W15 2.50 6.00
186 Joey Browner W8 1.25 3.00
187 Anthony Carter W15 1.50 4.00
188 Chris Doleman W8 1.25 3.00
189 Steve Jordan W4 1.25 3.00
190 Carl Lee W4 1.25 3.00
191 Randall McDaniel W5 1.50 4.00
192 Mike Merriweather W5 1.25 3.00
193 Keith Millard W14 1.25 3.00
194 Al Noga W12 1.25 3.00
195 Scott Studwell W5 1.25 3.00
196 Henry Thomas W12 1.25 3.00
197 Herschel Walker W5 1.50 4.00
198 Wade Wilson W5 1.50 4.00
199 Gary Zimmerman W5 1.25 3.00
200 Jerry Burns CO W6 1.25 3.00
201 Vincent Brown W6 1.25 3.00
202 Hart Lee Dykes W14 1.25 3.00
203 Sean Farrell W6 1.25 3.00
204 Fred Marion W6 1.25 3.00
205 Stanley Morgan W15 UER 1.50 4.00
(Text says he reached 10,000 yards fastest; 3 players did it in 10 seasons)
206 Eric Sievers W6 1.25 3.00
207 John Stephens W15 1.25 3.00
208 Andre Tippett W15 1.25 3.00
209 Rod Rust CO W15 1.25 3.00
210 Morten Andersen W6 1.25 3.00
211 Brad Edelman W12 1.25 3.00
212 John Fourcade W12 1.25 3.00
213 Dalton Hilliard W13 1.25 3.00
214 Rickey Jackson W13 1.25 3.00
215 Vaughan Johnson W13 1.25 3.00
216 Eric Martin W13 1.25 3.00
217 Sam Mills W7 1.25 3.00
218 Pal Swilling W7 UER 1.50 4.00
219 Frank Warren W7 1.25 3.00
220 Jim Wilks W7 1.25 3.00
221 Jim Mora CO W7 1.25 3.00
222 Raul Allegre W2 1.25 3.00
223 Carl Banks W1 1.25 3.00
224 Jumbo Elliott W1 1.25 3.00
225 Erik Howard W7 1.25 3.00
226 Pepper Johnson W2 1.25 3.00
227 Leonard Marshall W7 1.25 3.00
228 Dave Meggett W2 1.50 4.00
229 Bart Oates W3 1.25 3.00
230 Phil Simms W8 1.50 4.00
231 Lawrence Taylor W8 1.50 4.00
232 Bill Parcells CO W8 1.50 4.00
233 Troy Benson W8 1.25 3.00
234 Kyle Clifton W8 UER 1.25 3.00
235 Johnny Hector W8 1.25 3.00
236 Jeff Lageman W9 1.25 3.00
237 Pat Leahy W9 1.25 3.00
238 Freeman McNeil W9 1.50 4.00
239 Ken O'Brien W9 1.25 3.00
240 Al Toon W9 1.50 4.00
241 Jo Jo Townsell W9 1.25 3.00
242 Bruce Coslet CO W10 1.25 3.00
243 Eric Allen W10 1.25 3.00
244 Jerome Brown W10 1.50 4.00
245 Keith Byars W10 1.50 4.00
246 Cris Carter W13 15.00 40.00
247 Randall Cunningham W13 2.50 6.00
248 Keith Jackson W14 1.50 4.00
249 Mike Quick W14 1.50 4.00
250 Clyde Simmons W14 1.50 4.00
251 Andre Waters W14 1.25 3.00
252 Reggie White W15 2.50 6.00
253 Buddy Ryan CO W15 1.25 3.00
254 Rich Camarillo W15 1.25 3.00
255 Earl Ferrell W10 1.25 3.00
256 Roy Green W10 1.50 4.00
257 Ken Harvey W3 1.25 3.00
258 Ernie Jones W1 1.25 3.00
259 Tim McDonald W11 1.25 3.00
260 Timm Rosenbach W11 UER 1.25 3.00
261 Luis Sharpe W3 1.25 3.00
262 Vai Sikahema W3 1.25 3.00
263 J.T. Smith W1 1.25 3.00
264 Ron Wolfley W1 UER 1.25 3.00
265 Joe Bugel CO W11 1.25 3.00
266 Gary Anderson W11 1.25 3.00
267 Bubby Brister W1 1.50 4.00
268 Merril Hoge W11 1.25 3.00
269 Carnell Lake W2 1.25 3.00
270 Louis Lipps W11 1.25 3.00
271 David Little W3 1.25 3.00
272 Greg Lloyd W3 1.50 4.00
273 Keith Willis W11 1.25 3.00
274 Tim Worley W3 1.25 3.00
275 Chuck Noll CO W4 1.50 4.00
276 Marion Butts W4 1.25 3.00
277 Gill Byrd W2 1.25 3.00
278 Vencie Glenn W2 UER 1.25 3.00
279 Burt Grossman W4 1.25 3.00
280 Gary Plummer W4 1.25 3.00
281 Billy Ray Smith W12 1.25 3.00
282 Billy Joe Tolliver W12 1.25 3.00
283 Dan Henning CO W1 1.25 3.00
284 Harris Barton W1 1.25 3.00
285 Michael Carter W1 1.25 3.00
286 Mike Cofer W1 1.25 3.00
287 Roger Craig W1 1.50 4.00
288 Don Griffin W1 1.25 3.00
289 Charles Haley W2 1.25 3.00
290 Pierce Holt W2 1.25 3.00
291 Ronnie Lott W2 2.50 6.00
292 Guy McIntyre W2 1.25 3.00
293 Joe Montana W2 75.00 200.00
294 Tom Rathman W2 1.25 3.00
295 Jerry Rice W3 30.00 75.00
296 Jesse Sapolu W3 1.25 3.00
297 John Taylor W3 1.50 4.00
298 Michael Walter W3 1.25 3.00
299 George Seifert CO W3 1.50 4.00
300 Jeff Bryant W3 1.25 3.00
301 Jacob Green W4 1.25 3.00
302 Norm Johnson W4 UER 1.25 3.00
303 Bryan Millard W4 1.25 3.00
304 Joe Nash W4 1.25 3.00
305 Eugene Robinson W4 1.25 3.00
306 John L. Williams W14 1.25 3.00
307 David Wyman W14 1.25 3.00
308 Chuck Knox CO W14 1.25 3.00
309 Mark Carrier W14 1.50 4.00
310 Paul Gruber W14 1.25 3.00
311 Harry Hamilton W15 1.25 3.00
312 Bruce Hill W15 1.25 3.00
313 Donald Igwebuike W15 1.25 3.00
314 Kevin Murphy W15 1.25 3.00
315 Ervin Randle W12 1.25 3.00
316 Mark Robinson W12 1.25 3.00
317 Lars Tate W12 1.25 3.00
318 Vinny Testaverde W12 1.50 4.00
319 Ray Perkins CO W12 1.25 3.00
320 Earnest Byner W12 1.25 3.00
321 Gary Clark W12 1.50 4.00
322 Darryl Grant W13 1.25 3.00
323 Darrell Green W13 1.25 3.00
324 Jim Lachey W13 1.25 3.00
325 Charles Mann W13 1.25 3.00
326 Wilber Marshall W13 1.25 3.00
327 Ralf Mojsiejenko W13 1.25 3.00
328 Art Monk W15 2.50 6.00
329 Gerald Riggs W15 1.25 3.00
330 Mark Rypien W14 1.50 4.00
331 Ricky Sanders W4 1.25 3.00
332 Alvin Walton W4 1.25 3.00
333 Joe Gibbs CO W5 1.50 4.00
334 Aloha Stadium W5 1.25 3.00
335 Brian Blades PB W5 1.50 4.00
336 James Brooks PB W5 1.25 3.00
337 Shane Conlan PB W5 1.25 3.00
338 Eric Dickerson PB UER SP
339 Ray Donaldson PB W5 1.25 3.00
340 Ferrell Edmunds PB W6 1.25 3.00
341 Boomer Esiason PB W6 1.50 4.00
342 David Fulcher PB W6 1.25 3.00
343 Chris Hinton PB W6 1.25 3.00
344 Rodney Holman PB W6 1.25 3.00
345 Kent Hull PB W6 1.25 3.00
346 Tunch Ilkin PB W7 1.25 3.00
347 Mike Johnson PB W7 1.25 3.00
348 Greg Kragen PB W7 1.25 3.00
349 Dave Krieg PB W7 1.25 3.00
350 Albert Lewis PB W7 1.25 3.00
351 Howie Long PB W7 1.50 4.00
352 Bruce Matthews PB W8 1.50 4.00
353 Clay Matthews PB W8 1.25 3.00
354 Erik McMillan PB W8 1.25 3.00
355 Karl Mecklenburg PB W8 1.25 3.00
356 Anthony Miller PB W8 1.50 4.00
357 Frank Minnifield PB W8 1.25 3.00
358 Max Montoya PB W8 1.25 3.00
359 Warren Moon PB W10 2.50 6.00
360 Mike Munchak PB W9 1.50 4.00
361 Anthony Munoz PB W9 1.50 4.00
362 John Offerdahl PB W9 1.25 3.00
363 Christian Okoye PB W9 1.25 3.00
364 Leslie O'Neal PB W9 1.50 4.00
365 Rufus Porter PB W9 UER 1.25 3.00
366 Andre Reed PB W10 1.50 4.00
367 Johnny Rembert PB W10 1.25 3.00
368 Reggie Roby PB W10 1.25 3.00
369 Kevin Ross PB W10 1.25 3.00
370 Webster Slaughter PB 1.25 3.00
371 Bruce Smith PB W11 1.50 4.00
372 Dennis Smith PB W11 1.25 3.00
373 Derrick Thomas PB W11 1.50 4.00
374 Thurman Thomas PB W11 1.50 4.00
375 David Treadwell PB W11 1.25 3.00
376 Lee Williams PB W11 1.25 3.00

1991 FACT Pro Set Mobil

Sponsored by Pro Set and Mobil Oil, the 1991 Pro Set FACT (Football and Academics: A Championship Team) set marks the second year that Pro Set produced cards to serve as motivational learning tools to promote public health and education. This year's program was expanded to include all 26 NFL cities and to target 200,000 fourth grade students in low socio-economic areas. Six monthly lessons were featured in the set, and each lesson had an educational theme. Teachers utilized in-classroom educational materials and distributed a set of 17 Pro Set cards (along with one title/header card) each month, with the reverse sides carrying specific educational lessons corresponding to the educational theme. The standard-size cards are identical to first series cards, with the exception that the backs have interactive educational questions instead of player information. The particular set in which the card was issued is indicated below by S for set number.

COMPLETE SET (108) 100.00 250.00
3 Joe Montana S1 30.00 50.00
5 Mike Singletary S2 .80 2.00
12 Jay Novacek S3 .80 2.00
20 Ottis Anderson S2 .80 2.00
40 Tim Brown S1 3.20 8.00
44 Herschel Walker S1 .80 2.00
59 Eric Dorsey S3 .60 1.50
60 Jumbo Elliott S1 .60 1.50
63 Jeff Hostetler S2 .80 2.00
69 Eric Moore S4 .60 1.50
70 Bart Oates S3 .60 1.50
71 Gary Reasons S4 .60 1.50
75 Shane Conlan S3 .60 1.50
78 Jim Kelly S4 1.60 4.00
84 Darryl Talley S6 .60 1.50
90 Marv Levy CO S1 .60 1.50
94 Tim Green S2 .60 1.50
99 Jerry Glanville CO S3 .60 1.50
101 Mark Carrier S3 .60 1.50
104 Jim Harbaugh S6 .80 2.00
105 Brad Muster S4 .60 1.50
107 Keith Van Horne S6 .60 1.50
111 Boomer Esiason S1 .80 2.00
114 Rodney Holman S5 .60 1.50
116 Anthony Munoz S2 .80 2.00
117 Sam Wyche CO S4 .60 1.50
118 Paul Farren S6 .60 1.50
119 Thane Gash S3 .60 1.50
122 Clay Matthews S2 .60 1.50
123 Eric Metcalf S6 .80 2.00
127 Tommie Agee S4 .60 1.50
128 Troy Aikman S6 10.00 25.00
132 Michael Irvin S6 1.60 4.00
134 Daniel Stubbs S6 .60 1.50
136 Steve Atwater S1 .60 1.50
138 John Elway S2 16.00 40.00
141 Mark Jackson S6 .60 1.50
142 Karl Mecklenburg S3 .60 1.50
143 Doug Widell S2 .60 1.50
153 Wayne Fontes CO S2 .60 1.50
156 Don Majkowski S1 .60 1.50
157 Tony Mandarich S6 .60 1.50
158 Mark Murphy S6 .60 1.50
161 Sterling Sharpe S4 1.60 4.00
162 Lindy Infante CO S3 .60 1.50
163 Ray Childress S6 .60 1.50
166 Bruce Matthews S3 .80 2.00
167 Warren Moon S6 1.60 4.00
168 Mike Munchak S4 .80 2.00
169 Al Smith S6 .60 1.50
174 Bill Brooks S1 .80 2.00
179 Clarence Verdin S3 .60 1.50
182 Steve DeBerg S1 .60 1.50
185 Christian Okoye S3 .60 1.50
189 M.Schottenheimer CO S1 .60 1.50
191 Howie Long S2 .80 2.00
194 Steve Smith S4 .60 1.50
196 Lionel Washington S6 .60 1.50
198 Art Shell CO S3 .80 2.00
203 Buford McGee S2 .60 1.50
204 Tom Newberry S6 .60 1.50
205 Frank Stams S1 .60 1.50
210 Dan Marino S4 16.00 40.00
212 John Offerdahl S1 .60 1.50
216 Don Shula CO S4 .80 2.00
217 Darrell Fullington S6 .60 1.50
218 Tim Irwin S2 .60 1.50
219 Mike Merriweather S3 .60 1.50
231 Ed Reynolds S3 .60 1.50
238 Robert Massey S4 .60 1.50
246 James Hasty S1 .60 1.50
247 Erik McMillan S2 .60 1.50
249 Ken O'Brien S4 .60 1.50
260 Andre Waters S2 .60 1.50
270 Joe Bugel CO S2 .60 1.50
271 Gary Anderson S1 .60 1.50
272 Dermontti Dawson S4 .60 1.50
275 Tunch Ilkin S2 .60 1.50
282 Gill Byrd S4 .60 1.50
290 Michael Carter S2 .60 1.50
292 Pierce Holt S3 .60 1.50
297 George Seifert CO S1 .80 2.00
306 Chuck Knox CO S3 .60 1.50
310 Harry Hamilton S4 .60 1.50
321 Martin Mayhew S4 .60 1.50
322 Mark Rypien S1 .80 2.00
NNO S1 Title Card .60 1.50
NNO S2 Title Card .60 1.50
NNO S3 Title Card .60 1.50
NNO S4 Title Card .60 1.50
NNO S5 Title Card .60 1.50
NNO S6 Title Card .60 1.50

1992 FACT NFL Properties

Sponsored by NFL Properties, Inc., this 18-card FACT (Football and Academics: A Championship Team) set measures the standard size and features NFL star players. The color photos on the fronts are full-bleed on the sides but bordered by black above and below. In white block lettering, the top of each card reads "It's A Fact," while the bottom slogan varies from card to card. On a white background with "It's A Fact" printed in pale blue, the horizontal backs have an extended player quote on the theme of the card.

COMPLETE SET (18) 16.00 40.00
1 Warren Moon/Crack Kills 1.00 2.50
2 Boomer Esiason/Think Before You Drink 1.00 2.50
3 Troy Aikman/Play It Straight 2.00 5.00
4 Anthony Munoz/Quedate en la Escuela 1.00 2.50
5 Charles Mann/Steroids Destroy .60 1.50
6 Earnest Byner/Never Give Up .60 1.50
7 Joe Jacoby/Don't Pollute .60 1.50
8 Howie Long/Aids Kills 1.00 2.50
9 Dan Marino/School's The Ticket 6.00 15.00
10 Mike Singletary/Be The Best 1.00 2.50
11 Cornelius Bennett/Chill 1.00 2.50
12 Chris Doleman/Turn It Off 1.00 2.50
13 Jim Harbaugh/Eat To Win 1.00 2.50
14 Chris Hinton/Say It Don't Spray It .60 1.50
15 Nick Lowery/Heal The Planet .60 1.50
16 Rodney Peete/Respect The Law 1.00 2.50
17 Pat Swilling/Vote 1.00 2.50
18 Jim Everett/Study 1.00 2.50

1992 FACT Pro Set Mobil

Sponsored by Pro Set and Mobil Oil, the 1992 Pro Set FACT (Football and Academics: A Championship Team) set marks the third year that Pro Set produced cards to serve as motivational learning tools to promote public health and education. Six monthly lessons were featured in the set, and each lesson had an educational theme. Teachers utilized in-classroom educational materials and distributed a set of 18-Pro Set cards (including one title/header card) each month, with the reverse sides carrying specific educational lessons corresponding to the educational theme. The standard-size cards are identical to first series '92 Pro Set cards, with the exception of the backs featuring interactive educational questions instead of player information.

COMPLETE SET (108) 40.00 100.00
10 Michael Irvin SL .50 1.25
20 Pat Leahy M .40 1.00
76 Andro Collins .40 1.00
79 Jim Lachey .40 1.00
82 Martin Mayhew .40 1.00
83 Matt Millen .40 1.00
87 Mark Rypien .40 1.00
90 Joe Gibbs CO .50 1.25
98 James Lofton .50 1.25
104 Darryl Talley .40 1.00
108 Marv Levy CO .50 1.25
111 Moe Gardner .40 1.00
117 Jerry Glanville CO .40 1.00
118 Neal Anderson .40 1.00
119 Trace Armstrong .40 1.00
125 Tom Waddle .40 1.00
132 Anthony Munoz .50 1.25
135 David Shula CO .40 1.00
136 Mike Babb .40 1.00
137 Brian Brennan .40 1.00
141 Clay Matthews .40 1.00
142 Eric Metcalf .50 1.25
144 Bill Belichick CO .80 2.00
145 Steve Beuerlein .50 1.25
147 Ray Horton .40 1.00
152 Alexander Wright .40 1.00
153 Jimmy Johnson CO .50 1.25
155 John Elway 4.80 12.00
158 Karl Mecklenburg .40 1.00
161 Doug Widell .40 1.00
170 Chris Spielman .40 1.00
171 Wayne Fontes .40 1.00
173 Tony Mandarich .40 1.00
175 Bryce Paup .50 1.25
176 Sterling Sharpe .50 1.25
177 Darrell Thompson .40 1.00
180 Mike Holmgren CO .80 2.00
181 Ray Childress .40 1.00
183 Curtis Duncan .40 1.00
186 Warren Moon .80 2.00
189 Jack Pardee CO .40 1.00
192 Bill Brooks .40 1.00
195 Mike Prior .40 1.00
197 Clarence Verdin .40 1.00
199 John Alt .40 1.00
200 Deron Cherry .40 1.00
202 Nick Lowery .40 1.00
205 Joe Valerio .40 1.00
207 Marty Schottenheimer .40 1.00
210 Tim Brown .80 2.00
211 Howie Long .80 2.00
212 Ronnie Lott .80 2.00
216 Art Shell .50 1.25
222 Tom Newberry .40 1.00
225 Chuck Knox CO .40 1.00
230 Jim Jensen .40 1.00
231 Louis Oliver .40 1.00
234 Don Shula CO .80 2.00
238 Steve Jordan .40 1.00
241 Herschel Walker .50 1.25
242 Felix Wright .40 1.00
243 Dennis Green CO .40 1.00
248 Hugh Millen .40 1.00
250 Andre Tippett .40 1.00
252 Dick MacPherson CO .40 1.00
254 Bobby Hebert .40 1.00
259 Floyd Turner .40 1.00
261 Jim Mora CO .40 1.00
265 Jeff Hostetler .50 1.25
268 Gary Reasons .40 1.00
269 Everson Walls .40 1.00
270 Ray Handley CO .40 1.00
275 Jeff Lageman .40 1.00
277 Rob Moore .50 1.25
278 Lonnie Young .40 1.00
279 Bruce Coslet CO .40 1.00
283 Keith Jackson .50 1.25
286 Andre Waters .40 1.00
288 Rich Kotite CO .40 1.00
290 Garth Jax .40 1.00
291 Ernie Jones .40 1.00
297 Joe Bugel CO .40 1.00
298 Gary Anderson K .40 1.00
300 Eric Green .40 1.00
301 Bryan Hinkle .40 1.00
302 Tunch Ilkin .40 1.00
303 Louis Lipps .40 1.00
304 Neil O'Donnell .50 1.25
306 Bill Cowher CO .50 1.25
312 Henry Rolling .40 1.00
315 Bobby Ross CO .40 1.00
317 Michael Carter .40 1.00
320 Brent Jones .50 1.25
324 George Seifert CO .50 1.25
328 Tommy Kane .40 1.00
330 Dave Krieg .40 1.00
333 Tom Flores CO .40 1.00
336 Reuben Davis .40 1.00
342 Sam Wyche CO .40 1.00
375 Steve Atwater .40 1.00
386 Haywood Jeffires PROB .40 1.00
398 Richmond Webb PROB .40 1.00
NNO S1 Title Card .40 1.00
NNO S2 Title Card .40 1.00
NNO S3 Title Card .40 1.00
NNO S4 Title Card .40 1.00
NNO S5 Title Card .40 1.00
NNO S6 Title Card .40 1.00

1993 FACT Fleer Shell

This 108-card set was issued by Fleer and co-sponsored by Shell and Russell Athletic. The FACT (Football and Academics: A Championship Team) sets were originally produced by Pro Set to serve as motivational learning tools to promote public health and education. Teachers utilized in-classroom educational materials and distributed a set of 18 Fleer cards each month, with the reverse sides carrying specific educational lessons corresponding to the educational theme. The standard-size cards are identical to the regular 1993 Fleer set, with the exception that the backs include interactive educational questions along with player information. The cards are numbered on the back with 1-18 being in set 1, 19-36 in set 2, 37-54 in set 3, etc.

COMPLETE SET (108) 15.00 40.00
1 Stay in School .10 .30
2 Andre Rison .20 .50
3 Jim Kelly .30 .75
4 Mark Carrier DB .10 .30
5 David Fulcher .10 .30
6 Eric Metcalf .20 .50
7 Emmitt Smith 2.00 5.00
8 John Elway 2.40 6.00
9 Rodney Peete .20 .50
10 Brett Favre 2.40 6.00
11 Warren Moon .30 .75
12 Reggie Langhorne .10 .30
13 Christian Okoye .20 .50
14 Nick Bell .10 .30
15 Jim Everett .20 .50
16 Dan Marino 2.40 6.00
17 Chris Doleman .20 .50
18 Lennard Russell .20 .50
19 Stay Fit .10 .30
20 Sam Mills .10 .30
21 Rodney Hampton .20 .50
22 Rob Moore .20 .50
23 Seth Joyner .20 .50
24 Chris Chandler .20 .50
25 Barry Foster .20 .50
26 Stan Humphries .20 .50
27 Steve Young 1.00 2.50
28 Cortez Kennedy .20 .50
29 Reggie Cobb .10 .30
30 Mark Rypien .10 .30
31 Michael Haynes .20 .50
32 Thurman Thomas .30 .75
33 Tom Waddle .10 .30
34 Harold Green .10 .30
35 Tommy Vardell .10 .30
36 Michael Irvin .30 .75
37 Eat Smart .10 .30
38 Mike Croel .10 .30
39 Barry Sanders 2.00 5.00
40 Sterling Sharpe .30 .75
41 Haywood Jeffires .20 .50
42 Duane Bickett .10 .30
43 Nick Lowery .10 .30
44 Greg Townsend .10 .30
45 Todd Lyght .10 .30
46 Richmond Webb .10 .30
47 Cris Carter .60 1.50
48 Marv Cook .10 .30
49 Vaughan Johnson .10 .30
50 Pepper Johnson .10 .30
51 Kyle Clifton .10 .30
52 Fred Barnett .20 .50
53 Ken Harvey .10 .30
54 Rod Woodson .20 .50
55 Stay in Tune .10 .30
56 Marion Butts .10 .30
57 Ricky Watters .20 .50
58 Brian Blades .20 .50
59 Broderick Thomas .10 .30
60 Charles Mann .10 .30
61 Chris Hinton .10 .30
62 Cornelius Bennett .20 .50
63 Jim Harbaugh .20 .50
64 Tim Krumrie .10 .30
65 Bernie Kosar .20 .50
66 Troy Aikman 1.20 3.00
67 Shannon Sharpe .30 .75
68 Chris Spielman .20 .50
69 Brian Noble .10 .30
70 Curtis Duncan .10 .30
71 Quentin Coryatt .10 .30
72 Derrick Thomas .30 .75
73 Stay off Drugs .10 .30
74 Tim Brown .30 .75
75 Jackie Slater .10 .30
76 Keith Jackson .20 .50
77 Terry Allen .30 .75
78 Andre Tippett .10 .30
79 Morten Andersen .10 .30
80 Phil Simms .20 .50
81 Jeff Lageman .10 .30
82 Randall Cunningham .30 .75
83 Randal Hill .10 .30
84 Neil O'Donnell .20 .50
85 Gill Byrd .10 .30
86 John Taylor .20 .50
87 Eugene Robinson .10 .30
88 Paul Gruber .10 .30
89 Andre Collins .10 .30
90 Chris Miller .20 .50
91 Stay True to Yourself .10 .30
92 Andre Reed .20 .50
93 Richard Dent .20 .50
94 David Klingler .10 .30
95 Jay Novacek .20 .50
96 Steve Atwater .10 .30
97 Bennie Blades .10 .30
98 Terrell Buckley .10 .30
99 Ray Childress .10 .30
100 Harvey Williams .20 .50
101 Howie Long .30 .75
102 Lawrence Taylor .20 .50
103 Johnny Mitchell .10 .30
104 Carnell Lake .10 .30
105 Junior Seau .30 .75
106 Kevin Fagan .10 .30
107 Lawrence Dawsey .10 .30
108 Art Monk .20 .50

1993 FACT NFL Properties

COMPLETE SET (18) 10.00 25.00
1 Troy Aikman/Play It Straight 1.50 4.00
2 Cornelius Bennett/Chill .50 1.25
3 Chris Doleman/Turn It Off .50 1.25
4 Jim Harbaugh/Eat To Win .50 1.25
5 Chris Hinton/Say It Don't Spray It .30 .75
6 Howie Long/Aids Kills .50 1.25
7 Nick Lowery/Heal The Planet .30 .75
8 Charles Mann/Steroids Destroy .40 1.00
9 Dan Marino/School's The Ticket 3.00 8.00
10 Warren Moon/Crack Kills .50 1.25
11 Rod Bernstine/Jim Kelly .30 .75
We're The Same Inside
12 Rohn Stark/Smoking Is Stupid .30 .75
13 Michael Irvin/Respect the Law .50 1.25
14 Steve Young/Education Works 1.25 3.00
15 Bart Oates/Kids Deserve Love .30 .75
16 John Offerdahl .30 .75
Be buff!
17 Emmitt Smith/Don't Quit 2.50 6.00
18 Steve Beuerlein/Think before you drink .30 .75

1994 FACT Fleer Shell

For the second consecutive year, Fleer and Shell Oil teamed up to produce a 108-card FACT (Football and Academics: A Championship Team) set. Consisting of six 18-card subsets, each subset features one title card, 17 player cards, and a different theme. The fronts feature white-bordered color action photos with a gold-foil stamped player signature, name and position, and team logo. The horizontal backs carry a ghosted action shot, and a close-up color photo. The set is arranged according to themes as follows: Stay in School (1-18), Stay Fit (19-36), Eat Smart (37-54), Stay in Tune (55-72), Stay off Drugs (73-90), and Stay True to Yourself (91-108).

COMPLETE SET (108) 15.00 40.00
1 Cover Card .08 .25
2 Steve Beuerlein .15 .40
3 Erric Pegram .08 .25
4 Darryl Talley .08 .25
5 Tom Waddle .08 .25
6 Darryl Williams .08 .25
7 Tony Jones T .08 .25
8 Jay Novacek .08 .25
9 Simon Fletcher .08 .25
10 Jason Hanson .08 .25
11 Reggie White .25 .60
12 Ernest Givins .08 .25
13 Kerry Cash .08 .25
14 Joe Montana 2.40 6.00
15 Anthony Smith .08 .25
16 Jackie Slater .08 .25
17 Terry Kirby .15 .40
18 John Randle .15 .40
19 Cover Card .08 .25
20 Drew Bledsoe .80 2.00
21 Vaughan Johnson .08 .25
22 Greg Jackson .08 .25
23 Rob Moore .15 .40
24 Byron Evans .08 .25
25 Rod Woodson .15 .40
26 Junior Seau .25 .60
27 Steve Young .80 2.00
28 Cortez Kennedy .15 .40
29 Paul Gruber .08 .25
30 Darrell Green .08 .25
31 Tyronne Stowe .08 .25
32 Pierce Holt .08 .25
33 Steve Tasker .15 .40
34 Chris Zorich .15 .40
35 Ricardo McDonald .08 .25
36 Mark Carrier WR .15 .40
37 Cover Card .08 .25
38 Emmitt Smith 2.00 5.00
39 Shannon Sharpe .25 .60
40 Chris Spielman .15 .40
41 Ken Ruettgers .08 .25
42 Bubba McDowell .08 .25
43 Rohn Stark .08 .25
44 Derrick Thomas .15 .40
45 Tim Brown .25 .60
46 Shane Conlan .08 .25
47 Marco Coleman .08 .25
48 Steve Jordan .08 .25
49 Ben Coates .15 .40
50 Willie Roaf .08 .25
51 Carlton Bailey .08 .25
52 Ronnie Lott .15 .40
53 Eric Allen .08 .25
54 Dermontti Dawson .20 .50
55 Cover Card .08 .25
56 Ronnie Harmon .08 .25
57 Dana Stubblefield .15 .40
58 Rick Mirer .15 .40
59 Santana Dotson .08 .25
60 Jim Lachey .08 .25
61 Ricky Proehl .08 .25
62 Jessie Tuggle .08 .25
63 Jim Kelly .25 .60
64 Mark Carrier DB .08 .25
65 David Klingler .08 .25
66 Eric Turner .08 .25
67 Darrin Smith .08 .25
68 Glyn Milburn .15 .40
69 Herman Moore .25 .60
70 Sterling Sharpe .15 .40
71 Ray Childress .08 .25
72 Quentin Coryatt .08 .25
73 Cover Card .08 .25
74 Marcus Allen .25 .60
75 Jeff Hostetler .15 .40
76 Jerome Bettis .50 1.25
77 Richmond Webb .08 .25
78 Randall McDaniel .08 .25
79 Maurice Hurst .08 .25
80 Morten Andersen .08 .25
81 Dave Meggett .15 .40
82 Brian Washington .08 .25
83 Randall Cunningham .25 .60
84 Kevin Greene .15 .40
85 Leslie O'Neal .08 .25
86 Tim McDonald .08 .25
87 Eugene Robinson .08 .25
88 Hardy Nickerson .08 .25
89 Chip Lohmiller .08 .25
90 Jeff George .15 .40
91 Cover Card .08 .25
92 Cornelius Bennett .15 .40
93 Erik Kramer .08 .25
94 Tommy Vardell .08 .25
95 Troy Aikman 1.20 3.00
96 John Elway 2.00 5.00
97 Barry Sanders 1.60 4.00
98 Dan Saleaumua .08 .25
99 Dan Marino 2.00 5.00
100 Jack Del Rio .08 .25
101 Bruce Armstrong .08 .25
102 Renaldo Turnbull .08 .25
103 Phil Simms .15 .40
104 Boomer Esiason .15 .40
105 Fred Barnett .15 .40
106 Greg Lloyd .08 .25
107 John Carney .08 .25
108 Jerry Rice 1.20 3.00

1994 FACT NFL Properties

Sponsored by NFL Properties, Inc., this 18-card FACT (Football and Academics: A Championship Team) measures the standard-size and features NFL star players as well as Lesley Visser, a sports journalist. Inside a black picture frame, the fronts feature color posed photos. The words "It's A Fact" appears in white block lettering across the top, while the specific slogan, which varies from card to card, is printed across the bottom. On a white panel edged above and below in black, the backs present an extended player quote on the theme of the card.

COMPLETE SET (18) 10.00 25.00
1 Troy Aikman/Play It Straight 1.50 4.00
2 Cornelius Bennett/Chill .50 1.25
3 Lesley Visser ANN/Aim High .30 .75
4 Junior Seau/Eat Smart .50 1.25
5 Chris Hinton/Clean Up Your Act .30 .75
6 Howie Long/Plan Ahead .50 1.25
7 Nick Lowery/Heal The Planet .30 .75
8 Tony Casillas/Guns Are For Fools .30 .75
9 Dan Marino/School's The Ticket 3.00 8.00
10 Warren Moon/Make A Difference .50 1.25
11 Rod Bernstine/Jim Kelly/We're The Same Inside .30
.75
12 Rohn Stark/Smoking Is Stupid .30 .75
13 Michael Irvin/Respect the Law .50 1.25
14 Steve Young/Education Works 1.25 3.00
15 Bart Oates/Kids Deserve Love .30 .75
16 Erik Kramer/Be Fit! .30 .75
17 Emmitt Smith/Don't Quit 2.50 6.00
18 Steve Beuerlein/Think before you drink .30 .75

1994 FACT NFL Properties Artex

Issued in a cello pack, these three standard-size FACT cards are identical to their counterparts in the 18-card FACT set except for the numbering of cards 2-3 (Marino is #9 and Smith is #17 in the 18-card set) and the Artex Sportswear logo on their back. These sets were also distributed through various K-Mart outlets.

COMPLETE SET (3) 4.00 10.00
1 Troy Aikman/Play It Straight .80 2.00
2 Dan Marino/School's The Ticket 1.60 4.00
3 Emmitt Smith/Don't Quit 1.60 4.00

1995 FACT Fleer Shell

This FACT (Football and Academics: A Championship Team) set was produced by Fleer and Shell Oil and consists of six subsets of 18 cards each. The set features color action player photos with questions relating to the subset theme. The set is arranged according to themes as follows: Stay in School (1-18), Stay Fit (19-36), Eat Smart (37-54), Stay in Tune (55-72), Stay off Drugs (73-90), and Stay True to Yourself (91-108).

COMPLETE SET (108) 15.00 40.00
1 Cover Card .07 .20
2 Seth Joyner .07 .20
3 J.J. Birden .10 .30
4 Jim Kelly .25 .60
5 Pete Metzelaars .07 .20
6 Joe Cain .07 .20
7 Carl Pickens .10 .30
8 Leroy Hoard .10 .30
9 Troy Aikman 1.00 2.50
10 Steve Atwater .07 .20
11 Bennie Blades .07 .20
12 Brett Favre 2.00 5.00
13 Mel Gray .07 .20
14 Tony Bennett .07 .20
15 Steve Beuerlein .10 .30
16 Marcus Allen .25 .60
17 Tim Brown .25 .60
18 Tim Bowens .07 .20
19 Cover Card .07 .20
20 Jack Del Rio .07 .20
21 Drew Bledsoe 1.00 2.50
22 Jim Everett .07 .20
23 Michael Brooks .07 .20
24 Tony Casillas .07 .20
25 Fred Barnett .10 .30
26 Kevin Greene .10 .30
27 Jerome Bettis .25 .60
28 John Carney .07 .20
29 Ken Norton .10 .30
30 Cortez Kennedy .10 .30
31 Alvin Harper .07 .20
32 Henry Ellard .10 .30
33 Aeneas Williams .07 .20
34 Jeff George .10 .30
35 Bryce Paup .07 .20
36 Sam Mills .10 .30
37 Cover Card .07 .20
38 Mark Carrier .07 .20
39 Darnay Scott .10 .30
40 Pepper Johnson .07 .20
41 Michael Irvin .25 .60
42 John Elway 2.00 5.00
43 Herman Moore .25 .60
44 John Jurkovic .07 .20
45 Al Smith .07 .20
46 Steve Emtman .07 .20
47 Darren Carrington .07 .20
48 Kimble Anders .07 .20
49 Jeff Hostetler .10 .30
50 Eric Green .10 .30
51 Cris Carter .25 .60
52 Ben Coates .10 .30
53 Michael Haynes .07 .20
54 Dave Brown QB .10 .30
55 Cover Card .07 .20
56 Boomer Esiason .10 .30
57 Randall Cunningham .25 .60
58 Byron Bam Morris .07 .20
59 Sean Gilbert .10 .30
60 Stan Humphries .10 .30
61 Jerry Rice 1.00 2.50
62 Rick Mirer .10 .30
63 Hardy Nickerson .10 .30
64 Ricky Ervins .07 .20
65 Eric Swann .10 .30
66 Craig Heyward .10 .30
67 Andre Reed .10 .30
68 Frank Reich .10 .30
69 Steve Walsh .07 .20
70 Dan Wilkinson .07 .20
71 Vinny Testaverde .10 .30
72 Russell Maryland .07 .20
73 Cover Card .07 .20
74 Shannon Sharpe .10 .30
75 Brett Perriman .10 .30
76 Reggie White .25 .60
77 Mark Stepnoski .07 .20
78 Marshall Faulk 1.00 2.50
79 Reggie Cobb .07 .20
80 Lake Dawson .07 .20
81 Rocket Ismail .10 .30
82 Dan Marino 2.00 5.00
83 Warren Moon .25 .60
84 Willie McGinest .10 .30
85 William Roaf .07 .20
86 Rodney Hampton .10 .30
87 Marvin Washington .07 .20
88 Charlie Garner .25 .60
89 Neil O'Donnell .10 .30
90 Todd Lyght .07 .20
91 Cover Card .07 .20

92 Natrone Means .10 .30
93 Deion Sanders .40 1.00
94 Chris Warren .10 .30
95 Errict Rhett .10 .30
96 Ken Harvey .07 .20
97 Bruce Smith .25 .60
98 Chris Zorich .10 .30
99 Eric Turner .10 .30
100 Emmitt Smith 1.60 4.00
101 Barry Sanders 1.60 4.00
102 Neil Smith .10 .30
103 Chester McGlockton .07 .20
104 Fuad Reveiz .07 .20
105 Thomas Lewis .07 .20
106 Rod Woodson .10 .30
107 Junior Seau .10 .30
108 Steve Young .60 1.50

1995 FACT NFL Properties

This 18-card set was produced by the NFL to promote it's FACT (Football and Academics: a Championship Team) program. The cards feature black-bordered color player photos with the NFL logo and words, "IT'S A FACT," at the top. The subject and a related message are printed at the bottom. The backs carry a paragraph of the player's thoughts on the card subject.

COMPLETE SET (18) 12.00 30.00
1 Troy Aikman 1.50 4.00
2 Rocket Ismail .40 1.00
Qadry Ismail
3 Robin Roberts .30 .75
4 Junior Seau .50 1.25
5 Chris Hinton .30 .75
6 Sean Jones .30 .75
7 Thurman Thomas .60 1.50
8 Neil Smith .40 1.00
9 Dan Marino 3.00 8.00
10 Reggie Williams .30 .75
11 Rod Bernstine .30 .75
Jim Kelly
12 Drew Bledsoe 1.25 3.00
13 Michael Irvin .50 1.25
14 Steve Young 1.25 3.00
15 Jerry Rice 2.00 5.00
16 Herschel Walker .40 1.00
17 Emmitt Smith 2.50 6.00
18 Barry Sanders 2.50 6.00

1996 FACT Fleer Shell

This FACT set was produced by Fleer and sponsored by Shell Oil and consists of six subsets of 18-cards each. The set features color action player photos with questions relating to the subset theme. The set is essentially a parallel to the base 1996 Fleer set on the cardfronts with a community service message on the cardbacks.

COMPLETE SET (108) 15.00 25.00
1 Cover Card .05 .15
Stay in School
2 Garrison Hearst .08 .25
3 Jeff George .08 .25
4 Michael Jackson .05 .15
5 Jim Kelly .20 .50
6 Kerry Collins .20 .50
7 Curtis Conway .08 .25
8 Jeff Blake .20 .50
9 Troy Aikman .40 1.00
10 Steve Atwater .05 .15
11 Scott Mitchell .08 .25
12 Edgar Bennett .05 .15
13 Mel Gray .05 .15
14 Quentin Coryatt .05 .15
15 Tony Boselli .05 .15
16 Marcus Allen .20 .50
17 Dan Marino .60 1.50
18 Cris Carter .20 .50
19 Cover Card .05 .15
Stay Fit
20 Drew Bledsoe .30 .75
21 Mario Bates .05 .15
22 Dave Brown .05 .15
23 Kyle Brady .08 .25
24 Tim Brown .20 .50
25 William Fuller .05 .15
26 Greg Lloyd .05 .15
27 Isaac Bruce .20 .50
28 Marco Coleman .05 .15
29 Brent Jones .05 .15
30 Joey Galloway .20 .50
31 Trent Dilfer .08 .25
32 Terry Allen .08 .25
33 Rob Moore .08 .25
34 Craig Heyward .05 .15
35 Vinny Testaverde .08 .25
36 Bryce Paup .05 .15
37 Cover Card .05 .15
Eat Smart
38 Lamar Lathon .05 .15
39 Erik Kramer .05 .15
40 Ki-Jana Carter .08 .25
41 Daryl Johnston .05 .15
42 Terrell Davis .60 1.50
43 Herman Moore .08 .25
44 Mark Chmura .08 .25
45 Steve McNair .25 .60
46 Ken Dilger .05 .15
47 Mark Brunell .30 .75
48 Neil Smith .08 .25
49 O.J. McDuffie .08 .25
50 Qadry Ismail .08 .25
51 Ben Coates .08 .25
52 Jim Everett .05 .15
53 Rodney Hampton .05 .15
54 Hugh Douglas .08 .25
55 Cover Card .05 .15
Stay in Tune
56 Chester McGlockton .05 .15
57 Ricky Watters .08 .25
58 Kordell Stewart .20 .50
59 Troy Drayton .05 .15
60 Aaron Hayden .05 .15
61 Ken Norton .05 .15
62 Rick Mirer .08 .25
63 Hardy Nickerson .05 .15
64 Henry Ellard .05 .15
65 Aeneas Williams .05 .15
66 Terance Mathis .08 .25
67 Eric Turner .05 .15
68 Bruce Smith .08 .25
69 Tyrone Poole .05 .15
70 Rashaan Salaam .08 .25
71 Carl Pickens .08 .25
72 Deion Sanders .25 .60
73 Cover Card .05 .15
Stay off Drugs
74 John Elway .60 1.50
75 Barry Sanders .60 1.50
76 Robert Brooks .08 .25
77 Chris Sanders .05 .15
78 Marshall Faulk .20 .50
79 James O. Stewart .08 .25
80 Derrick Thomas .08 .25
81 Bernie Parmalee .05 .15
82 Robert Smith .20 .50
83 Curtis Martin .20 .50
84 Renaldo Turnbull .05 .15
85 Thomas Lewis .05 .15
86 Aaron Glenn .05 .15
87 Harvey Williams .05 .15
88 Calvin Williams .05 .15
89 Yancey Thigpen .05 .15
90 Leslie O'Neal .05 .15
91 Cover Card .05 .15
Stay True to Yourself
92 Stan Humphries .05 .15
93 Jerry Rice .40 1.00
94 Chris Warren .05 .15
95 Errict Rhett .08 .25
96 Heath Shuler .08 .25
97 Eric Metcalf .05 .15
98 Thurman Thomas .08 .25
99 Emmitt Smith .50 1.25
100 Shannon Sharpe .08 .25
101 Reggie White .20 .50
102 Rodney Thomas .05 .15
103 Jim Harbaugh .05 .15
104 Tamarick Vanover .08 .25
105 Neil O'Donnell .05 .15
106 Rod Woodson .08 .25
107 Junior Seau .08 .25
108 Steve Young .25 .60

1996 FACT NFL Properties

COMPLETE SET (18) 12.00 30.00
1 Troy Aikman/Play It Straight 1.50 4.00
2 Rocket Ismail .40 1.00
Qadry Ismail
Break free
3 Robin Roberts .30 .75
Dream big
4 Junior Seau/Eat Smart .50 1.25
5 Chris Hinton/Clean Up Your Act .30 .75
6 Sean Jones .30 .75
Career goals
7 Thurman Thomas .60 1.50
Heal The Planet
8 Neil Smith .40 1.00
Chill!
9 Dan Marino/School's The Ticket 3.00 8.00
10 Reggie Williams .30 .75
Plan ahead
11 Rod Bernstine/Jim Kelly/We're The Same Inside .30
.75
12 Drew Bledsoe 1.25 3.00
Smoking Is Stupid
13 Derrick Thomas .75 2.00
Read to succeed
14 Steve Young 1.25 3.00
Make a difference
15 Jerry Rice 2.00 5.00
Family matters
16 Herschel Walker .40 1.00
Be Fit!
17 Emmitt Smith/Don't Quit 2.50 6.00
18 Barry Sanders 2.50 6.00
Think, don't drink

1968-69 Falcons Team Issue

Printed on glossy thick paper stock, each of these black-and-white photos measure approximately 7 1/2" by 9 1/2" and have white borders. With the exception of the Berry photo (a portrait), all the photos are posed action shots. The cardbacks are blank. The photos are unnumbered and checklisted below in alphabetical order. Each includes the player's name and team name below the photo in the card border. This series can be differentiated from the 1970 and 1971 issues by the much larger type used in printing the player name and team name below the photo.

COMPLETE SET (23) 100.00 200.00
1 Bob Berry 5.00 10.00
2 Greg Brezina 5.00 10.00
3 Junior Coffey 5.00 10.00
4 Carlton Dabney 5.00 10.00
5 Bob Etter 5.00 10.00
6 Paul Gipson 5.00 10.00
7 Don Hansen 5.00 10.00
8 Bill Harris 5.00 10.00
9 Ralph Heck 5.00 10.00
10 Claude Humphrey 6.00 12.00
11 Randy Johnson 5.00 10.00
12 George Kunz 5.00 10.00
13 Errol Linden 5.00 10.00
14 Billy Lothridge 5.00 10.00
15 Tommy McDonald 7.50 15.00
16 Jim Mitchell 5.00 10.00
17 Tommy Nobis 7.50 15.00
18 Ken Reaves 5.00 10.00
19 Jerry Shay 5.00 10.00
20 John Small 5.00 10.00
21 Norm Van Brocklin CO 7.50 15.00
22 Harmon Wages 5.00 10.00
23 John Zook 5.00 10.00

1970 Falcons Stadium Issue

This 10-card set of the Atlanta Falcons features black and white player portraits in a white border and measures approximately 5 1/2" by 7 1/2". The backs are blank. The cards are unnumbered and checklisted below in alphabetical order.

COMPLETE SET (10) 40.00 80.00
1 Mike Brunson 5.00 10.00
2 Charlie Bryant 5.00 10.00
3 Sonny Campbell 5.00 10.00
4 Dean Halverson 5.00 10.00
5 Greg Lens 5.00 10.00
6 Randy Marshall 5.00 10.00
7 John Matlock 5.00 10.00
8 Gary Roberts 5.00 10.00
9 Jim Sullivan 5.00 10.00
10 Kenny Vinyard 5.00 10.00

1970 Falcons Team Issue

This set of the Atlanta Falcons features 8" by 10" black-and-white player photos with white borders. The photos are very similar to the 1971 set except that most players are wearing their black Falcons jersey and the pictures were taken inside the stadium. Unless noted below, all players also include their position (initials) below the photo along with their name and team name. The backs are blank. The cards are unnumbered and checklisted below in alphabetical order.

COMPLETE SET (41) 150.00 300.00
1 Ron Acks 5.00 10.00
2 Grady Allen 5.00 10.00
3A Bob Berry ERR 5.00 10.00
3B Bob Berry COR 5.00 10.00
4 Bob Breitenstein 5.00 10.00
5 Greg Brezina 5.00 10.00
6 Jim Butler 5.00 10.00
7 Gail Cogdill 5.00 10.00
8 Glen Condren 5.00 10.00
9 Ted Cottrell 5.00 10.00
10 Carlton Dabney 5.00 10.00
11 Mike Donohoe 5.00 10.00
12 Dick Enderle 5.00 10.00
13 Paul Flatley 5.00 10.00
14 Mike Freeman 5.00 10.00
15 Paul Gipson 5.00 10.00
16 Don Hansen 5.00 10.00
17 Tom Hayes 5.00 10.00
18 Dave Hettema 5.00 10.00
19 Claude Humphrey 6.00 12.00
20 Randy Johnson 6.00 12.00
21 George Kunz 5.00 10.00
22 Al Lavan 5.00 10.00
23 Bruce Lemmerman 5.00 10.00
24 Billy Lothridge 5.00 10.00
25 John Mallory 5.00 10.00
26 Art Malone 5.00 10.00
27 Andy Maurer 5.00 10.00
28 Tom McCauley 5.00 10.00
29 Jim Mitchell 5.00 10.00
30A Tommy Nobis 6.00 12.00
30B Tommy Nobis 6.00 12.00
31 Rudy Redmond 5.00 10.00
32 Bill Sandeman 5.00 10.00
33 Dick Shiner 5.00 10.00
34 John Small 5.00 10.00
35 Malcolm Snider 5.00 10.00
36 Todd Snyder 5.00 10.00
37 Norm Van Brocklin CO 6.00 12.00
38 Jeff Van Note 5.00 10.00
39 Harmon Wages 5.00 10.00
40 John Zook 5.00 10.00
41 Team Photo 5.00 10.00

1971 Falcons Team Issue

The 1971 Falcons Team Issue set consists of black-and-white photos measuring 8" by 10" with a white border on all four sides. The photos are similar to the 1970 set, but each player is wearing his red Falcons jersey and the pictures were taken outdoors. Only the player's name and team name appear below the photo. They are unnumbered and checklisted in alphabetical order.

COMPLETE SET (15) 75.00 150.00
1 Bob Berry 5.00 10.00
2 Mike Brunson 5.00 10.00
3 Ken Burrow 5.00 10.00
4 Sonny Campbell 5.00 10.00
5 Don Hansen 5.00 10.00
6 Leo Hart 5.00 10.00
7 Claude Humphrey 5.00 10.00
8 Ray Jarvis 5.00 10.00
9 Greg Lens 5.00 10.00
10 John Matlock 5.00 10.00
11 Tommy Nobis 6.00 12.00
12 Malcolm Snider 5.00 10.00
13 Pat Sullivan 6.00 12.00
14 Norm Van Brocklin CO 6.00 12.00
15 Harmon Wages 5.00 10.00

1973 Falcons Team Issue

The 1973 Falcons Team Issue features black-and-white photos measuring 8" by 10" with a white border. The photos are similar to the 1970 and 1972 sets, but the player's name and position initials (on the left) and the team name (on the right) are oriented very close to the outside borders. They are blankbacked, unnumbered and checklisted below in alphabetical order.

COMPLETE SET (11) 40.00 80.00
1 Greg Brezina 4.00 8.00
2 Ray Brown 4.00 8.00
3 Ken Burrow 4.00 8.00
4 Dave Hampton 4.00 8.00
5 Don Hansen 4.00 8.00
6A Claude Humphrey 5.00 10.00
(vertical)
6B Claude Humphrey 5.00 10.00
(horizontal)
7 Art Malone 4.00 8.00
8 Tommy Nobis 5.00 10.00
9 Ken Reaves 4.00 8.00
10 Bill Sandeman 4.00 8.00
11 Pat Sullivan 5.00 10.00

1975 Falcons Team Sheets

This three-card set was printed on sheets each measuring approximately 8 1/2" by 11" and features black-and-white player portraits. They were produced to be used by media and as public relations photos. Sheet 3 contains 15-players and the set title, while sheets 1 and 2 contain 16 players. The backs are blank.

COMPLETE SET (3) 10.00 20.00
1 Greg Brezina 2.50 5.00
Ray Brown
Ken Burrow
Rick Byas
La
2 Marion Campbell/ 5.00 10.00
3 Title Card/ 2.50 5.00

1978 Falcons Kinnett Dairies

These six blank-backed white panels measure approximately 4 1/4" by 6" and feature four black-and-white player headshots per panel, all framed by a thin red line. A narrow strip running across the center of the panel contains the sponsor name, the words "Atlanta Player Cards," and the NFLPA logo. The cards are unnumbered and checklisted below in the alphabetical order of the players shown in the upper left corners.

COMPLETE SET (6) 20.00 40.00
1 William Andrews 3.75 7.50
2 Warren Bryant 5.00 10.00
3 Wallace Francis 3.75 7.50
Mitchell TE
Van Note
East.
4 Dewey McClain 2.50 5.00
5 Robert Pennywell 2.50 5.00
6 Haskel Stanback 3.75 7.50

1980 Falcons Police

The 1980 Atlanta Falcons set contains 30 unnumbered cards each measuring approximately 2 5/8" by 4 1/8". Although uniform numbers can be found on the front of the cards, the cards have been listed alphabetically on the checklist below for convenience. Logos of the three sponsors, the Atlanta Police Athletic League, the Northside Atlanta Jaycees, and Coca-Cola, can be found on the back of the cards with short "Tips from the Falcons". Card backs have black printing with red accent. The Falcon helmet and stylized logo appear on the front of the cards with the player's name, uniform number, position, height, weight and college.

COMPLETE SET (30) 25.00 50.00
1 William Andrews 2.00 5.00
2 Steve Bartkowski 3.00 8.00
3 Bubba Bean .75 2.00
4 Warren Bryant .60 1.50
5 Rick Byas .60 1.50
6 Lynn Cain 1.25 3.00
7 Buddy Curry .60 1.50
8 Edgar Fields .60 1.50
9 Wallace Francis 1.50 4.00
10 Alfred Jackson 1.25 3.00
11 John James .60 1.50
12 Alfred Jenkins 1.50 4.00
13 Kenny Johnson .60 1.50
14 Mike Kenn 1.25 3.00
15 Fulton Kuykendall .75 2.00
16 Rolland Lawrence .75 2.00
17 Tim Mazzetti .60 1.50
18 Dewey McLean .60 1.50
19 Jeff Merrow .75 2.00
20 Junior Miller .75 2.00
21 Tom Pridemore .60 1.50
22 Frank Reed .60 1.50
23 Al Richardson .60 1.50
24 Dave Scott .60 1.50
25 Don Smith .60 1.50
26 Reggie Smith .60 1.50
27 R.C. Thielemann .75 2.00
28 Jeff Van Note 1.25 3.00
29 Joel Williams .60 1.50
30 Jeff Yeates .60 1.50

1981 Falcons Police

The 1981 Atlanta Falcons 30-card police set is unnumbered but has been listed in the checklist below by player uniform number. The cards measure approximately 2 5/8" by 4 1/8". The set is sponsored by the Atlanta Police Athletic League, whose logo appears on the front, and Coca-Cola and Chevron, whose logos appear on the back. The player's name and brief biographical data, in addition to "Tips from the Falcons," are contained on the backs of the cards. Card backs have black printing with red and blue accent on thin white card stock. The fronts inform the public that the Atlanta Falcons were the NFC Western Division Champions of 1980.

COMPLETE SET (30) 7.50 15.00
6 John James .15 .40
10 Steve Bartkowski 1.25 3.00
16 Reggie Smith .15 .40
18 Mick Luckhurst .15 .40
21 Lynn Cain .25 .60
23 Bobby Butler .15 .40
27 Tom Pridemore .15 .40
30 Scott Woerner .15 .40
31 William Andrews .60 1.50
36 Bob Glazebrook .15 .40
37 Kenny Johnson .15 .40
50 Buddy Curry .15 .40
51 Jim Laughlin .15 .40
54 Fulton Kuykendall .15 .40
56 Al Richardson .15 .40
57 Jeff Van Note .25 .60
58 Joel Williams .15 .40
65 Don Smith .15 .40
66 Warren Bryant .15 .40
68 R.C. Thielemann .15 .40
70 Dave Scott .15 .40
74 Wilson Faumuina .15 .40
75 Jeff Merrow .15 .40
78 Mike Kenn .25 .60
79 Jeff Yeates .15 .40
80 Junior Miller .25 .60
84 Alfred Jenkins .40 1.00
85 Alfred Jackson .30 .75
89 Wallace Francis .40 1.00
NNO Leeman Bennett CO .15 .40

1981 Falcons Team Issue

The 1981 Falcons Team Issue set was issued with a total of 22-cards. The black-and-white photos measure 8" by 10" and have a white border. The player's name and team name appear below the photo with some pictures also including the player's position (initials) between his name and team name. The cards are unnumbered and checklisted below in alphabetical order.

COMPLETE SET (22) 14.00 35.00
1 William Andrews 1.25 3.00
2 Lynn Cain 1.00 2.50
3 Buddy Curry .75 2.00
4 Tony Daykin .75 2.00
5 Wilson Faumuina .75 2.00
6 Wallace Francis .75 2.00
7 Bob Glazebrook .75 2.00
8 John James .75 2.00
9 Kenny Johnson .75 2.00
10 Mike Kenn .75 2.00
11 Jim Laughlin .75 2.00
12 Rolland Lawrence 1.00 2.50
13 James Mayberry .75 2.00
14 Tim Mazzetti .75 2.00
15 Junior Miller .75 2.00
16 Al Richardson .75 2.00
17 Eric Sanders .75 2.00
18 John Scully .75 2.00
19 Don Smith .75 2.00
20 Reggie Smith .75 2.00
21 Jeff Van Note 1.00 2.50
22 Joel Williams .75 2.00

1982 Falcons Frito Lay

This set was sponsored by Frito Lay and contains 28-photo cards. The cards measure approximately 4 1/4" by 5 1/2" and are printed on thin paper stock. The white-bordered fronts display black-and-white player photos with a facsimile autograph over the player image. The "Compliments of..." note and Frito Lay logo in the lower right corner rounds out the front. The backs are blank. The cards are unnumbered and checklisted below alphabetically.

COMPLETE SET (28) 48.00 120.00
1 William Andrews 3.00 8.00
2 Steve Bartkowski 3.00 8.00
3 Warren Bryant 1.50 4.00
4 Bobby Butler 1.50 4.00
5 Lynn Cain 1.50 4.00
6 Buddy Curry 1.50 4.00
7 Pat Howell 1.50 4.00
8 Alfred Jackson 2.00 5.00
9 Alfred Jenkins 2.00 5.00
10 Kenny Johnson 1.50 4.00
11 Earl Jones 1.50 4.00
12 Mike Kenn 1.50 4.00
13 Fulton Kuykendall 1.50 4.00
14 Jim Laughlin 1.50 4.00
15 Mick Luckhurst 1.50 4.00
16 Jeff Merrow 1.50 4.00
17 Russ Mikeska 1.50 4.00
18 Junior Miller 2.00 5.00
19 Tom Pridemore 1.50 4.00
20 Al Richardson 1.50 4.00
21 Gerald Riggs 2.00 5.00
22 Eric Sanders 1.50 4.00
23 Dave Scott 1.50 4.00
24 John Scully 1.50 4.00
25 Don Smith 1.50 4.00
26 Ray Strong 1.50 4.00
27 Lyman White 1.50 4.00
28 Joel Williams 1.50 4.00

1995 Falcons A and P Food Market

These 8 X 10 glossy black and white action photos were issued by A and P Food Stores for promotional autograph signings within their stores. These unnumbered photos are checklisted alphabetically below. The checklist below may be incomplete, any additional submissions would be welcomed.

COMPLETE SET (9) 10.00 25.00
1 Terance Mathis 2.40 6.00
2 Eric Metcalf 1.60 4.00
3 Ross Schulte 1.20 3.00
4 Ken Tippins 1.20 3.00
5 Jessie Tuggle 1.60 4.00
6 Scott Tyner 1.20 3.00
7 Darnell Walker 1.20 3.00
8 Thomas Williams 1.20 3.00
9 Mike Zandofsky 1.20 3.00

2006 Falcons Topps

COMPLETE SET (12) 3.00 6.00
ATL1 Keith Brooking .20 .50
ATL2 Roddy White .25 .60
ATL3 Michael Vick .30 .75
ATL4 Alge Crumpler .30 .75
ATL5 DeAngelo Hall .25 .60
ATL6 Patrick Kerney .25 .60
ATL7 Warrick Dunn .25 .60
ATL8 Matt Schaub .25 .60
ATL9 Brian Finneran .25 .60
ATL10 Michael Jenkins .25 .60
ATL11 T.J. Duckett .25 .60
ATL12 John Abraham .25 .60

2007 Falcons Donruss Thanksgiving Classic

COMPLETE SET (4) 2.00 5.00
1 Alge Crumpler .50 1.25
2 Jerious Norwood .40 1.00
3 Warrick Dunn .40 1.00
4 Joe Horn .40 1.00

2007 Falcons Topps

COMPLETE SET (12) 2.50 5.00
1 Alge Crumpler .50 1.25
2 Warrick Dunn .40 1.00
3 Michael Vick .50 1.25
4 Michael Jenkins .40 1.00
5 Roddy White .40 1.00
6 Jerious Norwood .40 1.00
7 Joe Horn .40 1.00
8 DeAngelo Hall .40 1.00
9 Keith Brooking .40 1.00
10 Rod Coleman .40 1.00
11 John Abraham .40 1.00
12 Jamaal Anderson .50 1.25

2008 Falcons Topps

COMPLETE SET (10) [illegible]
1 Joey Harrington .40 1.00
2 Roddy White .40 1.00
3 Jerious Norwood .40 1.00
4 Laurent Robinson .40 1.00
5 Chris Redman .40 1.00
6 Michael Turner .40 1.00
7 John Abraham .40 1.00
8 Michael Jenkins .40 1.00
9 Keith Brooking .40 1.00
10 Michael Boley .40 1.00
11 Matt Ryan 1.25 3.00
12 Harry Douglas .50 1.25

2008 Fathead Tradeables Game Time

Fatheads are 5x7 vinyls sticker featuring NFL players and team helmets. Each pack included one Team Helmet, 2-3 Game Time stickers and 1-2 Authentic insert stickers.

G1 Eli Manning .75 2.00
G2 Adrian Peterson 1.00 2.50
G3 Terrell Owens .75 2.00
G4 Tom Brady 3.00 8.00
G5 Peyton Manning 2.50 6.00
G6 LaDainian Tomlinson 1.00 2.50
G7 Larry Fitzgerald .75 2.00
G8 David Garrard .60 1.50
G9 Hines Ward .75 2.00
G10 Andre Johnson .75 2.00
G11 Willis McGahee .60 1.50
G12 Antonio Cromartie .60 1.50
G13 Reggie Wayne .75 2.00
G14 DeMarcus Ware .75 2.00
G15 Frank Gore .75 2.00
G16 LenDale White .60 1.50
G17 Chad Johnson .60 1.50
G18 Dwayne Bowe .75 2.00
G19 Michael Huff .60 1.50
G20 Keith Brooking .60 1.50
G21 Kellen Winslow .60 1.50
G22 Donovan McNabb .75 2.00
G23 Vince Young .60 1.50
G24 John Lynch .75 2.00
G25 Marvin Harrison .75 2.00
G26 Kyle Vanden Bosch .60 1.50
G27 TJ Houshmandzadeh .60 1.50
G28 Reggie Bush .60 1.50
G29 Steve Smith .75 2.00
G30 Joseph Addai .60 1.50
G31 Tedy Bruschi .75 2.00
G32 Matt Hasselbeck .60 1.50
G33 Brian Westbrook .60 1.50
G34 A.J. Hawk .60 1.50
G35 Brandon Marshall .75 2.00
G36 Jason Campbell .60 1.50
G37 JaMarcus Russell .60 1.50
G38 Michael Strahan .75 2.00
G39 Shawne Merriman .60 1.50
G40 Aaron Kampman .75 2.00
G41 Terence Newman .60 1.50
G42 Dallas Clark .60 1.50
G43 Jason Witten .75 2.00
G44 Anquan Boldin .60 1.50
G45 Brady Quinn .60 1.50
G46 Charles Woodson 1.00 2.50
G47 Marshawn Lynch .75 2.00
G48 James Harrison 1.00 2.50
G49 Steven Jackson .60 1.50
G50 Roddy White .60 1.50
G51 Derek Anderson .60 1.50
G52 Fred Taylor .60 1.50
G53 Marion Barber .60 1.50
G54 Larry Johnson .60 1.50
G55 Ed Reed .75 2.00
G56 Julian Peterson .60 1.50
G57 Ray Lewis 1.00 2.50
G58 Randy Moss .75 2.00
G59 Ronnie Brown .60 1.50
G60 Tony Romo .75 2.00
G61 Todd Heap .60 1.50
G62 Ronde Barber .60 1.50
G63 Calvin Johnson 1.00 2.50
G64 Derrick Mason .60 1.50
G65 Marc Bulger .60 1.50
G66 Ben Roethlisberger 1.00 2.50
G67 Brian Urlacher 1.00 2.50
G68 Wes Welker .75 2.00
G69 Willie Parker .75 2.00
G70 Jay Cutler .60 1.50
G71 Carson Palmer .75 2.00
G72 Darren Sharper .60 1.50
G73 Devin Hester .75 2.00
G74 Deuce McAllister .75 2.00
G75 Donald Driver .75 2.00
G76 Rudi Johnson .60 1.50
G77 Jason Taylor .75 2.00
G78 Richard Seymour .60 1.50
G79 Derrick Brooks .60 1.50
G80 Braylon Edwards .60 1.50
G81 Plaxico Burress .60 1.50
G82 Drew Brees 1.00 2.50
G83 Laveranues Coles .60 1.50
G84 Edgerrin James .75 2.00
G85 Santonio Holmes .60 1.50
G86 Antonio Gates .75 2.00
G87 Lance Briggs .75 2.00
G88 Greg Jennings .60 1.50
G89 Patrick Willis .75 2.00
G90 Tommie Harris .60 1.50
G91 Clinton Portis .60 1.50
G92 Jamal Lewis .75 2.00
G93 Jeff Garcia .60 1.50
G94 Marques Colston .60 1.50
G95 Mario Williams .75 2.00
G96 Brandon Jacobs .60 1.50
G97 Ernie Sims .60 1.50
G98 Lee Evans .75 2.00
G99 DeMeco Ryans .75 2.00
G100 Kellen Clemens .60 1.50
G101 Osi Umenyiora .60 1.50
G102 Brian Dawkins 1.00 2.50
G103 Chris Chambers .60 1.50
G104 Bob Sanders .75 2.00
G105 Julius Peppers .75 2.00
G106 Philip Rivers 1.00 2.50
G107 Trent Edwards .60 1.50
G108 Santana Moss .60 1.50
G109 Roy Williams WR .60 1.50
G110 Torry Holt .75 2.00
G111 Marcus Trufant .60 1.50
G112 Ryan Grant .75 2.00
G113 Troy Polamalu 1.00 2.50
G114 Lofa Tatupu .60 1.50
G115 Maurice Jones-Drew .60 1.50
G116 Joey Galloway .75 2.00
G117 Matt Schaub .60 1.50
G118 Jeremy Shockey .60 1.50
G119 Kamerion Wimbley .60 1.50
G120 Champ Bailey .75 2.00
G121 Chris Cooley .60 1.50
G122 Dwight Freeney .60 1.50
G123 Laurence Maroney .75 2.00
G124 Jerricho Cotchery .60 1.50
G125 Tony Gonzalez .75 2.00

2008 Fathead Tradeables Authentic

A1 Tom Brady 3.00 8.00
A2 LaDainian Tomlinson 1.00 2.50
A3 Peyton Manning 2.50 6.00
A4 Tony Romo .75 2.00
A5 Eli Manning .75 2.00
A6 Drew Brees 1.00 2.50
A7 Terrell Owens .75 2.00
A8 Adrian Peterson 1.00 2.50
A9 Brian Urlacher 1.00 2.50
A10 Champ Bailey .75 2.00
A11 Ben Roethlisberger 1.00 2.50
A12 Vince Young .60 1.50
[illegible]
A14 Clinton Portis .60 1.50
A15 Brian Westbrook .60 1.50
A16 Carson Palmer .75 2.00
A17 Shawne Merriman .60 1.50
A18 Steve Smith .75 2.00
A19 Larry Johnson .60 1.50
A20 Devin Hester .75 2.00
A21 Marvin Harrison .75 2.00
A22 Reggie Bush .60 1.50
A23 Troy Polamalu 1.00 2.50
A24 Ray Lewis 1.00 2.50
A25 Andre Johnson .75 2.00

2008 Fathead Tradeables Helmets

H1 Arizona Cardinals .60 1.50
H2 Atlanta Falcons .60 1.50
H3 Baltimore Ravens .60 1.50
H4 Buffalo Bills .60 1.50
H5 Carolina Panthers .60 1.50
H6 Chicago Bears .60 1.50
H7 Cincinnati Bengals .60 1.50
H8 Cleveland Browns .60 1.50
H9 Dallas Cowboys .60 1.50
H10 Denver Broncos .60 1.50
H11 Detroit Lions .60 1.50
H12 Green Bay Packers .60 1.50
H13 Houston Texans .60 1.50
H14 Indianapolis Colts .60 1.50
H15 Jacksonville Jaguars .60 1.50
H16 Kansas City Chiefs .60 1.50
H17 Miami Dolphins .60 1.50
H18 Minnesota Vikings .60 1.50
H19 New England Patriots .60 1.50
H20 New Orleans Saints .60 1.50
H21 New York Giants .60 1.50
H22 New York Jets .60 1.50
H23 Oakland Raiders .60 1.50
H24 Philadelphia Eagles .60 1.50
H25 Pittsburgh Steelers .60 1.50
H26 San Diego Chargers .60 1.50
H27 San Francisco 49ers .60 1.50
H28 Seattle Seahawks .60 1.50
H29 St. Louis Rams .60 1.50
H30 Tampa Bay Buccaneers .60 1.50
H31 Tennessee Titans .60 1.50
H32 Washington Redskins .60 1.50

2009 Fathead Tradeables Gameday

G1 Peyton Manning 2.50 6.00
G2 James Harrison 1.00 2.50
G3 Matt Ryan .75 2.00
G4 Tony Romo .75 2.00
G5 Lance Briggs .75 2.00
G6 Marion Barber .75 2.00
G7 Drew Brees 1.00 2.50
G8 Jared Allen .60 1.50
G9 Kyle Vanden Bosch .60 1.50
G10 Lee Evans .75 2.00
G11 Thomas Jones .60 1.50
G12 Reggie Bush .60 1.50
G13 DeSean Jackson .75 2.00
G14 Joe Flacco .75 2.00
G15 Chris Cooley .60 1.50
G16 Maurice Jones-Drew .60 1.50
G17 David Garrard .60 1.50
G18 Darrelle Revis .60 1.50
G19 Larry Johnson .60 1.50
G20 Ray Lewis 1.00 2.50
G21 Bernard Berrian .60 1.50
G22 Felix Jones .60 1.50
G23 Jamal Lewis .75 2.00
G24 Anquan Boldin .60 1.50
G25 Steven Jackson .60 1.50
G26 Antonio Bryant .60 1.50
G27 Julius Jones .60 1.50
G28 Dwayne Bowe .75 2.00
G29 Steve Smith .75 2.00
G30 Jason Campbell .60 1.50
G31 Ryan Grant .75 2.00
G32 Lamarr Woodley .60 1.50
G33 Philip Rivers 1.00 2.50
G34 Chad Pennington .60 1.50
G35 Jerod Mayo .75 2.00
G36 Greg Jennings .60 1.50
G37 Cortland Finnegan .60 1.50
G38 Matt Schaub .60 1.50
G39 Vincent Jackson .60 1.50
G40 Clinton Portis .60 1.50
G41 Derrick Mason .60 1.50
G42 Demeco Ryans .75 2.00
G43 Darren McFadden 1.00 2.50
G44 Antonio Gates .75 2.00
G45 Roy Williams WR .60 1.50
G46 Joe Thomas .75 2.00
G47 Trent Edwards .60 1.50
G48 Patrick Willis .75 2.00
G49 Nnamdi Asomugha .60 1.50
G50 Brady Quinn .60 1.50
G51 Heath Miller .60 1.50
G52 Ronnie Brown .60 1.50
G53 Champ Bailey .75 2.00
G54 Joey Porter .75 2.00
G55 Troy Polamalu 1.00 2.50
G56 Matt Hasselbeck .60 1.50
G57 Ed Reed .75 2.00
G58 Kerry Collins .60 1.50
G59 Reggie Wayne .75 2.00
G60 Adrian Peterson 1.00 2.50
G61 Adrian Wilson .60 1.50
G62 Jake Delhomme .60 1.50
G63 Jason Witten .75 2.00
G64 Kurt Warner .75 2.00
G65 Ben Roethlisberger 1.00 2.50
G66 Calvin Johnson 1.00 2.50
G67 Marshawn Lynch .75 2.00
G68 A.J. Hawk .60 1.50
G69 Aaron Rodgers 2.00 5.00
G70 Carson Palmer .75 2.00
G71 Jerricho Cotchery .60 1.50
G72 Jonathan Stewart .60 1.50
G73 Derrick Johnson .60 1.50
G74 Marques Colston .60 1.50
G75 Bob Sanders .75 2.00
G76 JaMarcus Russell .60 1.50
G77 Barrett Ruud .60 1.50
G78 Tom Brady 3.00 8.00
G79 Roddy White .60 1.50
G80 Eli Manning .75 2.00
G81 Chad Ochocinco .60 1.50
G82 LenDale White .60 1.50
G83 Donovan McNabb .75 2.00
G84 Aaron Kampman .75 2.00
G85 Larry Fitzgerald .75 2.00
G86 Donnie Avery .60 1.50
G87 Steve Slaton .60 1.50
G88 Dwight Freeney .60 1.50
G89 Randy Moss .75 2.00
G90 Antonio Pierce .60 1.50
G91 Julius Peppers .75 2.00
G92 LaDainian Tomlinson 1.00 2.50
G93 D'Qwell Jackson .60 1.50
G94 Willie Parker .60 1.50
G95 Charles Woodson 1.00 2.50
G96 Brian Urlacher 1.00 2.50
G97 Michael Turner .60 1.50
G98 Chris Johnson .60 1.50
G99 Shawne Merriman .60 1.50
G100 Matt Forte .60 1.50
G101 Brandon Marshall .75 2.00
G102 Jon Beason .60 1.50
G103 Asante Samuel .60 1.50
G104 Santana Moss .75 2.00
G105 Justin Tuck .60 1.50
G106 Terrell Suggs .60 1.50
G107 Jeremy Shockey .60 1.50
G108 Laron Landry .60 1.50
[illegible] .75 2.00
G110 Andre Johnson .75 2.00
G111 Braylon Edwards .60 1.50
G112 James Farrior .60 1.50
G113 Robert Mathis .60 1.50
G114 DeAngelo Williams .60 1.50
G115 Santonio Holmes .60 1.50
G116 Devin Hester .75 2.00
G117 Frank Gore .75 2.00
G118 Mario Williams .75 2.00
G119 Kevin Smith .60 1.50
G120 Brian Westbrook .60 1.50
G121 Brandon Jacobs .60 1.50
G122 Dallas Clark .60 1.50
G123 Eddie Royal .60 1.50
G124 Wes Welker .75 2.00
G125 Ronde Barber .60 1.50
G126 DeMarcus Ware .75 2.00
G127 Joseph Addai .60 1.50
G128 John Abraham .60 1.50

2009 Fathead Tradeables Authentic

A1 Troy Polamalu 1.00 2.50
A2 Larry Fitzgerald .75 2.00
A3 Donovan McNabb .75 2.00
A4 Randy Moss .75 2.00
A5 Peyton Manning 2.50 6.00
A6 Brian Urlacher 1.00 2.50
A7 Clinton Portis .60 1.50
A8 Marion Barber .75 2.00
A9 Aaron Rodgers 2.00 5.00
A10 Chris Johnson .60 1.50
A11 Marshawn Lynch .75 2.00
A12 Matt Ryan .75 2.00
A13 Eli Manning .75 2.00
A14 Steven Jackson .60 1.50
A15 Braylon Edwards .60 1.50

2009 Fathead Tradeables Helmets

COMPLETE SET (32) 12.00 30.00
H1 Arizona Cardinals .60 1.50
H2 Atlanta Falcons .60 1.50
H3 Baltimore Ravens .60 1.50
H4 Buffalo Bills .60 1.50
H5 Carolina Panthers .60 1.50
H6 Chicago Bears .60 1.50
H7 Cincinnati Bengals .60 1.50
H8 Cleveland Browns .60 1.50
H9 Dallas Cowboys .60 1.50
H10 Denver Broncos .60 1.50
H11 Detroit Lions .60 1.50
H12 Green Bay Packers .60 1.50
H13 Houston Texans .60 1.50
H14 Indianapolis Colts .60 1.50
H15 Jacksonville Jaguars .60 1.50
H16 Kansas City Chiefs .60 1.50
H17 Miami Dolphins .60 1.50
H18 Minnesota Vikings .60 1.50
H19 New England Patriots .60 1.50
H20 New Orleans Saints .60 1.50
H21 New York Giants .60 1.50
H22 New York Jets .60 1.50
H23 Oakland Raiders .60 1.50
H24 Philadelphia Eagles .60 1.50
H25 Pittsburgh Steelers .60 1.50
H26 San Diego Chargers .60 1.50
H27 San Francisco 49ers .60 1.50
H28 Seattle Seahawks .60 1.50
H29 St. Louis Rams .60 1.50
H30 Tampa Bay Buccaneers .60 1.50
H31 Tennessee Titans .60 1.50
H32 Washington Redskins .60 1.50

2010 Fathead Tradeables

1 Drew Brees 1.00 2.50
2 Peyton Manning 2.50 6.00
3 Chris Johnson .60 1.50
4 Charles Woodson 1.00 2.50
5 Larry Fitzgerald .75 2.00
6 Brett Favre 2.00 5.00
7 Darrelle Revis .60 1.50
8 Tom Brady 2.50 6.00
9 DeSean Jackson .75 2.00
10 Philip Rivers 1.00 2.50
11 Maurice Jones-Drew .60 1.50
12 Hines Ward .75 2.00
13 Patrick Willis .75 2.00
14 Roddy White .60 1.50
15 Ray Rice .60 1.50
16 Cedric Benson .60 1.50
17 Tony Romo .75 2.00
18 Matthew Stafford .75 2.00
19 Ricky Williams .75 2.00
20 Josh Cribbs .60 1.50
21 Knowshon Moreno .60 1.50
22 Eli Manning .75 2.00
23 James Harrison 1.00 2.50
24 Shawne Merriman .60 1.50
25 Kellen Winslow .60 1.50
26 Matt Schaub .60 1.50
27 Clinton Portis .60 1.50
28 Shonn Greene .60 1.50
29 Dwight Freeney .60 1.50
30 Percy Harvin .60 1.50
31 Donnie Avery .60 1.50
32 LeSean McCoy 1.00 2.50
33 Ryan Grant .75 2.00
34 Joe Flacco .75 2.00
35 Paul Posluszny .60 1.50
36 Jonathan Stewart .60 1.50
37 Carson Palmer .75 2.00
38 DeMarcus Ware .75 2.00
39 Marques Colston .60 1.50
40 Vincent Jackson .60 1.50
41 Vince Young .60 1.50
42 Nnamdi Asomugha .60 1.50
43 Matt Cassel .60 1.50
44 Andre Johnson .75 2.00
45 Matt Hasselbeck .60 1.50
46 Cadillac Williams .60 1.50
47 Steve Smith USC .60 1.50
48 Reggie Bush .60 1.50
49 Marion Barber .75 2.00
50 Donald Driver .75 2.00
51 Dallas Clark .60 1.50
52 Wes Welker .75 2.00
53 Heath Miller .60 1.50
54 Frank Gore .75 2.00
55 Darren McFadden .60 1.50
56 Vernon Davis .60 1.50
57 T.J. Houshmandzadeh .60 1.50
58 Steven Jackson .60 1.50
59 Jerod Mayo .75 2.00
60 Chad Henne .75 2.00
61 Adrian Peterson 1.00 2.50
62 Mark Sanchez .60 1.50
63 Rashard Mendenhall .60 1.50
64 DeAngelo Williams .60 1.50
65 Matt Forte .60 1.50
66 Ed Reed .75 2.00
67 Miles Austin .60 1.50
68 Champ Bailey .75 2.00
69 Kevin Kolb .60 1.50
70 Aaron Rodgers 2.00 5.00
71 Chad Ochocinco .60 1.50
72 Laurence Maroney .60 1.50
73 Darren Sharper .60 1.50
74 Brandon Meriweather .60 1.50
75 Darren Sproles .75 2.00
76 LaMarr Woodley .60 1.50
77 Chris Cooley .60 1.50
78 Matt Ryan .75 2.00
79 Beanie Wells .60 1.50
80 Jay Cutler .60 1.50
81 Felix Jones .60 1.50
82 Calvin Johnson 1.00 2.50
83 Joseph Addai .60 1.50
84 David Garrard [illegible]

85 Sidney Rice .60 1.50
86 Antonio Gates .75 2.00
87 Troy Polamalu 1.00 2.50
88 Jared Allen .60 1.50
89 Ronnie Brown .60 1.50
90 Brian Urlacher 1.00 2.50
91 Michael Turner .60 1.50
92 Lee Evans .75 2.00
93 Jason Witten .75 2.00
94 Steve Smith .75 2.00
95 Joe Thomas .60 1.50
96 Pierre Garcon .75 2.00
97 Dwayne Bowe .75 2.00
98 Randy Moss .75 2.00
99 Ray Lewis 1.00 2.50
100 Reggie Wayne .75 2.00

1993 Fax Pax World of Sport

The 1993 Fax Pax World of Sport set was issued in Great Britain and contains 40 standard size cards. This multisport set spotlights notable sports figures from around the world, who are the best in their respective sports. An Olympic subset of seven cards (28-34) is included. The full-bleed fronts feature color action and posed photos with a red-edged white stripe intersecting the photo across the bottom. Within the white stripe is displayed the athlete's name and his country's flag. The horizontal, white backs carry the athlete's name and sport at the top followed by biographical information. Career summary and statistics are printed within a gray box, edged in red.

COMPLETE SET (40) 6.00 15.00
15 Dan Marino 1.50 4.00
16 Joe Montana 1.50 4.00
17 Emmitt Smith 1.25 3.00

1993 FCA 50

This 50-card standard-size set was sponsored by Fellowship of Christian Athletes. The color player photos on the fronts are accented on three sides by a thin pink stripe; the card face itself shades from blue to white as one moves toward the bottom. The FCA logo, featuring a cross with two olive branches, is superimposed in the upper left corner, while the player's name is printed beneath the picture and his sport in the pink stripe on the left. On a blue background, the backs carry a close-up photo, biography, and the player's testimony.

COMPLETE SET (50) 10.00 20.00
2 Zenon Andrusyshyn FB .20 .50
3 Bobby Bowden CO FB .20 .50
5 John Brandes FB .20 .50
7 Brian Cabral FB .20 .50
9 Paul Coffman FB .20 .50
12 Doug Dawson FB .20 .50
13 Donnie Dee FB .20 .50
15 Mitch Donahue FB .20 .50
16 Curtis Duncan FB .20 .50
21 Bobby Hebert FB .30 .75
23 David Dean FB .20 .50
25 Brian Kinchen FB .20 .50
26 Todd Kinchen FB .20 .50
30 Neil Lomax FB .30 .75
32 Dan Meers FB Mascot .20 .50
33 Mike Merriweather FB .20 .50
34 Ken Norton Jr. FB .30 .75
38 Steve Pelluer FB .30 .75
44 R.C. Slocum CO FB .20 .50
45 Grant Teaff CO FB .20 .50
46 Pat Tilley FB .20 .50

1993 FCA Super Bowl

This six-card standard-size set features color player photos on a gradated blue background. The pictures are bordered on three sides by a thin hot pink line. The left side is bordered by a gradated blue border that also runs across the the bottom creating a double hot pink and blue bottom border. At the upper left of the picture is the FCA (Fellowship of Christian Athletes) emblem. The player's name appears in the bottom border, while his position is printed in the bottom margin. A hot pink stripe on the left edge contains the words "Professional Football." The backs are blue and display a color close-up photo, biographical information (including favorite scripture), and the player's testimony in yellow print.

COMPLETE SET (6) 6.00 15.00
1 Alfred Anderson .75 2.00
2 Bob Lilly 1.25 3.00
3 Tom Landry CO 1.50 4.00
4 Brent Jones .75 2.00
5 Bruce Matthews 1.00 2.50
6 Title Card .75 2.00

1992 Finest

Manufactured with Topps Poly-tech process, this 44-card standard-size set features 33 established NFL stars and 11 top rookies. Three thousand cases were produced, with 20 sets per case. The cards are checklisted alphabetically according to veterans (1-33) and rookies (34-44).

COMPLETE SET (45) 7.50 20.00
1 Neal Anderson .20 .50
2 Cornelius Bennett .20 .50
3 Marion Butts .10 .30
4 Anthony Carter .20 .50
5 Mike Croel .10 .30
6 John Elway 2.00 5.00
7 Jim Everett .20 .50
8 Ernest Givins .10 .30
9 Rodney Hampton .20 .50
10 Alvin Harper .10 .30
11 Michael Irvin .40 1.00
12 Rickey Jackson .10 .30
13 Seth Joyner .10 .30
14 James Lofton .20 .50
15 Ronnie Lott .20 .50
16 Eric Metcalf .20 .50
17 Chris Miller .20 .50
18 Art Monk .20 .50
19 Warren Moon .40 1.00
20 Rob Moore .20 .50
21 Anthony Munoz .20 .50
22 Christian Okoye .10 .30
23 Andre Rison .20 .50
24 Leonard Russell .10 .30
25 Mark Rypien .20 .50
26 Barry Sanders 2.00 5.00
27 Emmitt Smith 2.50 6.00
28 Pat Swilling .10 .30
29 John Taylor .20 .50
30 Derrick Thomas .40 1.00
31 Thurman Thomas .40 1.00
32 Reggie White .40 1.00
33 Rod Woodson .40 1.00
34 Edgar Bennett .20 .50
35 Terrell Buckley .10 .30
36 Keith Hamilton .20 .50
37 Amp Lee .10 .30
38 Ricardo McDonald .10 .30
39 Chris Mims .10 .30
40 Robert Porcher .40 1.00
41 Leon Searcy .10 .30
42 Siran Stacy .10 .30
43 Tommy Vardell .10 .30
44 Bob Whitfield .10 .30
NNO Checklist .10 .30

1994 Finest

The 1994 Finest football set consists of 220 standard-size cards. Specially designed refracting foil cards were produced for each of the 220 cards. One of these foil cards was inserted in approximately every nine packs. Thirty-seven cards displayed a special rookie design, and one of these rookie cards was included in each five-card pack. Moreover, oversized 4" by 6" versions of these 37 rookie cards were produced and inserted at a rate of one in each 24-count box. There are no key Rookie Cards in this set.

COMPLETE SET (220) 15.00 40.00
1 Emmitt Smith 2.50 6.00
2 Calvin Williams .30 .75
3 Mark Collins .20 .50
4 Steve McMichael .30 .75
5 Jim Kelly .60 1.50
6 Michael Dean Perry .30 .75
7 Wayne Simmons .20 .50
8 Rocket Ismail .30 .75
9 Mark Rypien .20 .50
10 Brian Blades .20 .50
11 Barry Word .20 .50
12 Jerry Rice 1.50 4.00
13 Derrick Fenner .20 .50
14 Karl Mecklenburg .20 .50
15 Reggie Cobb .20 .50
16 Eric Swann .20 .50
17 Neil Smith .30 .75
18 Barry Foster .20 .50
19 Willie Roaf .20 .50
20 Troy Drayton .20 .50
21 Warren Moon .50 1.25
22 Richmond Webb .20 .50
23 Anthony Miller .30 .75
24 Chris Slade .20 .50
25 Mel Gray .20 .50
26 Ronnie Lott .50 1.25
27 Andre Rison .30 .75
28 Jeff George .30 .75
29 John Copeland .20 .50
30 Derrick Thomas .50 1.25
31 Sterling Sharpe .30 .75
32 Chris Doleman .20 .50
33 Monte Coleman .20 .50
34 Mark Bavaro 3.00 .75
35 Kevin Williams WR .20 .50
36 Eric Metcalf .30 .75
37 Brent Jones .30 .75
38 Steve Tasker .30 .75
39 Dave Meggett .20 .50
40 Howie Long .50 1.25
41 Rick Mirer .30 .75
42 Jerome Bettis 1.50 4.00
43 Marion Butts .20 .50
44 Barry Sanders 2.50 6.00
45 Jason Elam .30 .75
46 Broderick Thomas .20 .50
47 Derek Brown RBK .20 .50
48 Lorenzo White .20 .50
49 Neil O'Donnell .30 .75
50 Chris Burkett .20 .50
51 John Offerdahl .20 .50
52 Rohn Stark .20 .50
53 Neal Anderson .30 .75
54 Steve Beuerlein .30 .75
55 Bruce Armstrong .20 .50
56 Lincoln Kennedy .20 .50
57 Darrell Green .30 .75
58 Ricardo McDonald .20 .50
59 Chris Warren .30 .75
60 Mark Jackson .20 .50
61 Pepper Johnson .20 .50
62 Chris Spielman .30 .75
63 Marcus Allen .50 1.25
64 Jim Everett .30 .75
65 Greg Townsend .20 .50
66 Cris Carter .50 1.25
67 Don Beebe .30 .75
68 Reggie Langhorne .20 .50
69 Randall Cunningham .50 1.25
70 Johnny Holland .20 .50
71 Morten Andersen .20 .50
72 Leonard Marshall .20 .50
73 Keith Jackson .30 .75
74 Leslie O'Neal .20 .50
75 Hardy Nickerson .30 .75
76 Dan Williams .20 .50
77 Steve Young 1.25 3.00
78 Deon Figures .20 .50
79 Michael Irvin .60 1.50
80 Luis Sharpe .20 .50
81 Andre Tippett .30 .75
82 Ricky Sanders .20 .50
83 Erric Pegram .20 .50
84 Albert Lewis .20 .50
85 Anthony Blaylock .20 .50
86 Pat Swilling .20 .50
87 Duane Bickett .20 .50
88 Myron Guyton .20 .50
89 Clay Matthews .20 .50
90 Jim McMahon .30 .75
91 Bruce Smith .50 1.25
92 Reggie White .50 1.25
93 Shannon Sharpe .50 1.25
94 Rickey Jackson .20 .50
95 Ronnie Harmon .20 .50
96 Terry McDaniel .20 .50
97 Bryan Cox .20 .50
98 Webster Slaughter .20 .50
99 Boomer Esiason .30 .75
100 Tim Krumrie .20 .50
101 Cortez Kennedy .30 .75
102 Henry Ellard .30 .75
103 Clyde Simmons .20 .50
104 Craig Erickson .20 .50
105 Eric Green .20 .50
106 Gary Clark .30 .75
107 Jay Novacek .30 .75
108 Dana Stubblefield .30 .75
109 Mike Johnson .20 .50
110 Ray Crockett .20 .50
111 Leonard Russell .20 .50
112 Robert Smith .50 1.25
113 Art Monk .30 .75
114 Ray Childress .20 .50
115 O.J.McDuffie .30 .75
116 Tim Brown .50 1.25
117 Kevin Ross .20 .50
118 Richard Dent .30 .75
119 John Elway 2.50 6.00
120 James Hasty .20 .50
121 Gary Plummer .20 .50
122 Pierce Holt .20 .50
123 Eric Martin .20 .50
124 Brett Favre 3.00 8.00
125 Cornelius Bennett .30 .75
126 Jessie Hester .20 .50
127 Lewis Tillman .20 .50
128 Qadry Ismail .30 .75
129 Jay Schroeder .20 .50
130 Curtis Conway .50 1.25
131 Santana Dotson .30 .75
132 Nick Lowery .20 .50
133 Lomas Brown .20 .50
134 Reggie Roby .20 .50
135 John L. Williams .20 .50
136 Vinny Testaverde .30 .75
137 Seth Joyner .20 .50
138 Ethan Horton .20 .50
139 Jackie Slater .20 .50
140 Rod Bernstine .20 .50
141 Rob Moore .30 .75
142 Dan Marino 2.50 6.00
143 Ken Harvey .20 .50
144 Ernest Givins .30 .75
145 Russell Maryland .20 .50
146 Drew Bledsoe 1.00 2.50
147 Kevin Greene .30 .75
148 Bobby Hebert .20 .50
149 Junior Seau .50 1.25
150 Tim McDonald .20 .50
151 Thurman Thomas .50 1.25
152 Phil Simms .30 .75
153 Terrell Buckley .20 .50
154 Sam Mills .20 .50
155 Anthony Carter .30 .75
156 Kelvin Martin .20 .50
157 Shane Conlan .20 .50
158 Irving Fryar .30 .75
159 Demetrius DuBose .20 .50
160 David Klingler .20 .50
161 Herman Moore .30 .75
162 Jeff Hostetler .30 .75
163 Tommy Vardell .20 .50
164 Craig Heyward .30 .75
165 Wilber Marshall .20 .50
166 Quentin Coryatt .20 .50
167 Glyn Milburn .20 .50
168 Fred Barnett .30 .75
169 Charles Haley .30 .75
170 Carl Banks .30 .75
171 Ricky Proehl .20 .50
172 Joe Montana 2.50 6.00
173 Johnny Mitchell .20 .50
174 Andre Reed .30 .75
175 Marco Coleman .20 .50
176 Vaughan Johnson .20 .50
177 Carl Pickens .30 .75
178 Dwight Stone .20 .50
179 Ricky Watters .30 .75
180 Michael Haynes .30 .75
181 Roger Craig .30 .75
182 Cleveland Gary .20 .50
183 Steve Emtman .20 .50
184 Patrick Bates .20 .50
185 Mark Carrier WR .30 .75
186 Brad Hopkins .20 .50
187 Dennis Smith .20 .50
188 Natrone Means .50 1.25
189 Michael Jackson .30 .75
190 Ken Norton Jr. .20 .50
191 Carlton Gray .20 .50
192 Edgar Bennett .50 1.25
193 Lawrence Taylor .50 1.25
194 Marv Cook .20 .50
195 Eric Curry .20 .50
196 Victor Bailey .20 .50
197 Ryan McNeil .20 .50
198 Rod Woodson .30 .75
199 Earnest Byner .20 .50
200 Marvin Jones .20 .50
201 Thomas Smith .20 .50
202 Troy Aikman 1.50 4.00
203 Audray McMillian .20 .50
204 Wade Wilson .20 .50
205 George Teague .20 .50
206 Deion Sanders .75 2.00
207 Will Shields .30 .75
208 John Taylor .30 .75
209 Jim Harbaugh .50 1.25
210 Micheal Barrow .20 .50
211 Harold Green .20 .50
212 Steve Everitt .20 .50
213 Flipper Anderson .20 .50
214 Rodney Hampton .30 .75
215 Steve Atwater .20 .50
216 James Trapp .20 .50
217 Terry Kirby .30 .75
218 Garrison Hearst .50 1.25
219 Jeff Bryant .20 .50
220 Roosevelt Potts .20 .50

1994 Finest Refractors

COMPLETE SET (220) 250.00 500.00
*REFRACTORS: 2.5X TO 6X BASIC CARDS

1994 Finest Rookie Jumbos

These oversized (4 1/4" by 6") versions of the 37 rookies from the 1994 Finest set were inserted at a rate of one in each 24-count box. Aside from their larger size, the cards are identical to the corresponding basic Finest cards.

COMPLETE SET (37) 40.00 100.00
ONE JUMBO CARD PER SEALED BOX
7 Wayne Simmons .50 1.25
19 Willie Roaf .50 1.25
20 Troy Drayton .50 1.25
24 Chris Slade .50 1.25
29 John Copeland .50 1.25
35 Kevin Williams WR 1.00 2.50
41 Rick Mirer 2.00 5.00
42 Jerome Bettis 6.00 15.00
45 Jason Elam 1.00 2.50
47 Derek Brown RBK .50 1.25
56 Lincoln Kennedy .50 1.25
78 Deon Figures .50 1.25
108 Dana Stubblefield 1.00 2.50
112 Robert Smith 2.00 5.00
115 O.J.McDuffie 2.00 5.00
128 Qadry Ismail 2.00 5.00
130 Curtis Conway 2.00 5.00
146 Drew Bledsoe 5.00 12.00
159 Demetrius DuBose .50 1.25
167 Glyn Milburn 1.00 2.50
184 Patrick Bates .50 1.25
186 Brad Hopkins .50 1.25
188 Natrone Means 2.00 5.00
191 Carlton Gray .50 1.25
195 Eric Curry .50 1.25
196 Victor Bailey .50 1.25
197 Ryan McNeil .50 1.25
200 Marvin Jones .50 1.25
201 Thomas Smith .50 1.25
205 George Teague .50 1.25
207 Will Shields 1.00 2.50
210 Micheal Barrow .50 1.25
212 Steve Everitt .50 1.25
216 James Trapp .50 1.25
217 Terry Kirby 2.00 5.00
218 Garrison Hearst 2.00 5.00
220 Roosevelt Potts .50 1.25

1995 Finest

This 275 standard-size set was issued in seven card packs. These packs were in 24 count boxes and had a suggested retail price of $5.00 per pack. These high-tech cards each came with a protective peel-off laminate that prevented the cards from being scratched. Rookie Cards in this set include Jeff Blake, Ki-Jana Carter, Kerry Collins, Joey Galloway, Curtis Martin, Rashaan Salaam and Michael Westbrook.

COMPLETE SET (275) 30.00 80.00
COMP.SERIES 1 (165) 10.00 20.00
COMP.SERIES 2 (110) 25.00 60.00
1 Natrone Means .25 .60
2 Dave Meggett .08 .25
3 Tim Bowens .08 .25
4 Jay Novacek .25 .60
5 Michael Jackson .25 .60
6 Calvin Williams .25 .60
7 Neil Smith .25 .60
8 Chris Gardocki .08 .25
9 Jeff Burris .08 .25
10 Warren Moon .25 .60
11 Gary Anderson K .08 .25
12 Bert Emanuel .50 1.25
13 Rick Tuten .08 .25
14 Steve Wallace .08 .25
15 Marion Butts .08 .25
16 Johnnie Morton .25 .60
17 Rob Moore .25 .60
18 Wayne Gandy .08 .25
19 Quentin Coryatt .25 .60
20 Richmond Webb .08 .25
21 Erric Rhett .25 .60
22 Joe Johnson .08 .25
23 Gary Brown .08 .25
24 Jeff Hostetler .25 .60
25 Larry Centers .25 .60
26 Tom Carter .08 .25
27 Steve Atwater .08 .25
28 Doug Pelfrey .08 .25
29 Bryce Paup .25 .60
30 Erik Williams .08 .25
31 Henry Jones .08 .25
32 Stanley Richard .08 .25
33 Marcus Allen .50 1.25
34 Antonio Langham .08 .25
35 Lewis Tillman .08 .25
36 Thomas Randolph .08 .25
37 Byron Bam Morris .08 .25
38 David Palmer .25 .60
39 Ricky Watters .25 .60
40 Brett Perriman .25 .60
41 Will Wolford .08 .25
42 Burt Grossman .08 .25
43 Vincent Brisby .08 .25
44 Ronnie Lott .25 .60
45 Brian Blades .25 .60
46 Brent Jones .08 .25
47 Anthony Newman .08 .25
48 Willie Roaf .08 .25
49 Paul Gruber .08 .25
50 Jeff George .25 .60
51 Jamir Miller .08 .25
52 Anthony Miller .25 .60
53 Darrell Green .08 .25
54 Steve Wisniewski .08 .25
55 Dan Wilkinson .25 .60
56 Brett Favre 2.00 5.00
57 Leslie O'Neal .25 .60
58 Keith Byars .08 .25
59 James Washington .08 .25
60 Andre Reed .25 .60
61 Ken Norton Jr. .25 .60
62 John Randle .25 .60
63 Lake Dawson .25 .60
64 Greg Montgomery .08 .25
65 Erric Pegram .25 .60
66 Steve Everitt .08 .25
67 Chris Brantley .08 .25
68 Rod Woodson .25 .60
69 Eugene Robinson .08 .25
70 Dave Brown .25 .60
71 Ricky Reynolds .08 .25
72 Rohn Stark .08 .25
73 Randal Hill .08 .25
74 Brian Washington .08 .25
75 Heath Shuler .25 .60
76 Darion Conner .08 .25
77 Terry McDaniel .08 .25
78 Al Del Greco .08 .25
79 Allen Aldridge .08 .25
80 Trace Armstrong .08 .25
81 Darnay Scott .25 .60
82 Charlie Garner .50 1.25
83 Harold Bishop .08 .25
84 Reggie White .50 1.25
85 Shawn Jefferson .08 .25
86 Irving Spikes .25 .60
87 Mel Gray .08 .25
88 D.J. Johnson .08 .25
89 Daryl Johnston .25 .60
90 Joe Montana 2.00 5.00
91 Michael Strahan .50 1.25
92 Robert Blackmon .08 .25
93 Ryan Yarborough .25 .60
94 Terry Allen .25 .60
95 Michael Haynes .25 .60
96 Jim Harbaugh .25 .60
97 Micheal Barrow .08 .25
98 John Thierry .08 .25
99 Seth Joyner .08 .25
100 Deion Sanders .75 2.00
101 Eric Turner .08 .25
102 LeShon Johnson .25 .60
103 John Copeland .08 .25
104 Cornelius Bennett .25 .60
105 Sean Gilbert .25 .60
106 Herschel Walker .25 .60
107 Henry Ellard .25 .60
108 Neil O'Donnell .25 .60
109 Charles Wilson .08 .25
110 Willie McGinest .25 .60
111 Tim Brown .50 1.25
112 Simon Fletcher .08 .25
113 Broderick Thomas .08 .25
114 Tom Waddle .08 .25
115 Jessie Tuggle .08 .25
116 Maurice Hurst .08 .25
117 Aubrey Beavers .08 .25
118 Donnell Bennett .25 .60
119 Shante Carver .08 .25
120 Eric Metcalf .25 .60
121 John Carney .08 .25
122 Thomas Lewis .25 .60
123 Johnny Mitchell .08 .25
124 Trent Dilfer .50 1.25
125 Marshall Faulk 1.25 3.00
126 Ernest Givins .08 .25
127 Aeneas Williams .08 .25
128 Bucky Brooks .08 .25
129 Todd Steussie .08 .25
130 Randall Cunningham .50 1.25
131 Reggie Brooks .25 .60
132 Morten Andersen .08 .25
133 James Jett .25 .60
134 George Teague .08 .25
135 John Taylor .08 .25
136 Charles Johnson .25 .60
137 Isaac Bruce 1.00 2.50
138 Jason Elam .25 .60
139 Carl Pickens .25 .60
140 Chris Warren .25 .60
141 Bruce Armstrong .08 .25
142 Mark Carrier DB .08 .25
143 Irving Fryar .25 .60
144 Van Malone .08 .25
145 Charles Haley .25 .60
146 Chris Calloway .08 .25
147 J.J. Birden .08 .25
148 Tony Bennett .08 .25
149 Lincoln Kennedy .08 .25
150 Stan Humphries .25 .60
151 Hardy Nickerson .08 .25
152 Randall McDaniel .08 .25
153 Marcus Robertson .08 .25
154 Ronald Moore .08 .25
155 Thurman Thomas .50 1.25
156 Tommy Vardell .08 .25
157 Ken Ruettgers .08 .25
158 Rob Fredrickson .08 .25
159 Johnny Bailey .08 .25
160 Greg Lloyd .25 .60
161 David Alexander .08 .25
162 Kevin Mawae .08 .25
163 Derek Brown RBK .08 .25
164 William Floyd .25 .60
165 Aaron Glenn .08 .25
166 Joey Galloway RC 2.00 5.00
167 Troy Drayton .08 .25
168 Dermontti Dawson .50 1.25
169 Ronald Moore .08 .25
170 Dan Marino 2.00 5.00
171 Dennis Gibson .08 .25
172 Raymont Harris .08 .25
173 Shannon Sharpe .25 .60
174 Kevin Williams .25 .60
175 Jim Everett .08 .25
176 Rocket Ismail .25 .60
177 Mark Fields RC .50 1.25
178 George Koonce .08 .25
179 Chris Hudson .08 .25
180 Jerry Rice 1.00 2.50
181 Dewayne Washington .25 .60
182 Dale Carter .25 .60
183 Pete Stoyanovich .08 .25
184 Blake Brockermeyer .08 .25
185 Troy Aikman 1.00 2.50
186 Jeff Blake RC 1.00 2.50
187 Troy Vincent .08 .25
188 Lamar Lathon .08 .25
189 Tony Boselli .50 1.25
190 Emmitt Smith 1.50 4.00
191 Bobby Houston .08 .25
192 Edgar Bennett .25 .60
193 Derrick Brooks RC 3.00 8.00
194 Ricky Proehl .08 .25
195 Rodney Hampton .25 .60
196 Dave Krieg .08 .25
197 Vinny Testaverde .25 .60
198 Erik Kramer .08 .25
199 Ben Coates .25 .60
200 Steve Young .75 2.00
201 Glyn Milburn .08 .25
202 Bryan Cox .08 .25
203 Luther Elliss .08 .25
204 Mark McMillian .08 .25
205 Jerome Bettis .50 1.25
206 Craig Heyward .25 .60
207 Ray Buchanan .08 .25
208 Kimble Anders .25 .60
209 Kevin Greene .25 .60
210 Eric Allen .08 .25
211 Ricardo McDonald .08 .25
212 Ruben Brown RC .60 1.50
213 Harvey Williams .08 .25
214 Broderick Thomas .08 .25
215 Frank Reich .08 .25
216 Frank Sanders RC .60 1.50
217 Craig Newsome .08 .25
218 Merton Hanks .08 .25
219 Chris Miller .08 .25
220 John Elway 2.00 5.00
221 Ernest Givins .08 .25
222 Boomer Esiason .25 .60
223 Reggie Roby .08 .25
224 Qadry Ismail .25 .60
225 Ki-Jana Carter RC .60 1.50
226 Leon Lett .08 .25
227 Eric Hill .08 .25
228 Scott Mitchell .25 .60
229 Craig Erickson .08 .25
230 Drew Bledsoe .75 2.00
231 Sean Landeta .08 .25
232 Barrett Brooks .08 .25
233 Brian Mitchell .08 .25
234 Tyrone Poole .50 1.25
235 Desmond Howard .25 .60
236 Wayne Simmons .08 .25
237 Michael Westbrook RC .60 1.50
238 Quinn Early .25 .60
239 Willie Davis .25 .60
240 Rashaan Salaam RC .30 .75
241 Devin Bush .08 .25
242 Dana Stubblefield .25 .60
243 Dexter Carter .08 .25
244 Shane Conlan .08 .25
245 Keith Elias RC .08 .25
246 Robert Brooks .50 1.25
247 Garrison Hearst .50 1.25
248 Eric Zeier RC .60 1.50
249 Nate Newton .25 .60
250 Barry Sanders 1.50 4.00
251 Dave Meggett .08 .25
252 Courtney Hawkins .08 .25
253 Cortez Kennedy .25 .60
254 Mario Bates .25 .60
255 Junior Seau .50 1.25
256 Brian Washington .08 .25
257 Darius Holland .08 .25
258 Jeff Graham .08 .25
259 Rob Moore .25 .60
260 Andre Rison .25 .60
261 Kerry Collins RC 2.50 6.00
262 Roosevelt Potts .08 .25
263 Cris Carter .50 1.25
264 Curtis Martin RC 6.00 12.00
265 Rick Mirer .25 .60
266 Mo Lewis .08 .25
267 Mike Sherrard .08 .25
268 Herman Moore .50 1.25
269 Eric Metcalf .25 .60
270 Ray Childress .08 .25
271 Chris Slade .08 .25
272 Michael Irvin .50 1.25
273 Jim Kelly .50 1.25
274 Terance Mathis .25 .60
275 LeRoy Butler .08 .25

1995 Finest Refractors

COMPLETE SET (275) 300.00 600.00
COMP.SERIES 1 (165) 100.00 200.00
COMP.SERIES 2 (110) 200.00 400.00
*REFRACT.STARS: 2.5X to 6 BASIC CARDS
*REFRACTOR RCs: 1.5X to 4X BASIC CARDS
STATED ODDS 1:12

1995 Finest Fan Favorites

Randomly inserted one in every 12 packs, this 25-card set spotlights some of the NFL's top playmakers. With a front design that is similar to the basic Finest cards, Fan Favorites are transparent with photos surrounded by purple. A Fan Favorite banner is at the top. At the bottom of the back is a brief biography.

COMPLETE SET (25) 25.00 60.00
STATED ODDS 1:12 SER.1
FF1 Drew Bledsoe 1.50 4.00
FF2 Jerome Bettis 1.00 2.50
FF3 Rick Mirer .50 1.25
FF4 Andre Rison .50 1.25
FF5 Troy Aikman 2.00 5.00
FF6 Cortez Kennedy .50 1.25
FF7 Emmitt Smith 3.00 8.00
FF8 Sterling Sharpe .50 1.25
FF9 Junior Seau 1.00 2.50
FF10 Michael Irvin 1.00 2.50
FF11 Jim Kelly 1.00 2.50
FF12 Steve Young 1.50 4.00
FF13 John Elway 4.00 10.00
FF14 Jerry Rice 2.00 5.00
FF15 Barry Sanders 3.00 8.00
FF16 Dan Marino 4.00 10.00
FF17 Dan Wilkinson .50 1.25
FF18 Reggie White 1.00 2.50
FF19 Deion Sanders 1.50 4.00
FF20 Willie McGinest .50 1.25
FF21 Stan Humphries .50 1.25
FF22 Heath Shuler .50 1.25
FF23 Natrone Means .50 1.25
FF24 Warren Moon .50 1.25
FF25 Marshall Faulk 2.50 6.00

1995 Finest Landmark

These standard-size "cards" are actually metal cards that were overlaid on a 4-ounce ingot of solid bronze. Using Topps' finest technology, the cards also feature the players personal achievements on the back. The first four cards were originally available only as a set through Topps direct mailers at a cost of $99 plus shipping. Two additional series were released later seperately and re-released together as "series two." These 12-card series two sets were available directly from Topps. We've assigned numbers to the cards alphabetically by series.

COMPLETE SET (16) 150.00 400.00
1 Troy Aikman 12.00 30.00
2 Jerry Rice 12.00 30.00
3 Emmitt Smith 16.00 40.00
4 Steve Young 8.00 20.00
5 Drew Bledsoe 10.00 25.00
6 Randall Cunningham 8.00 20.00
7 John Elway 20.00 50.00
8 Brett Favre 20.00 50.00
9 Michael Irvin 8.00 20.00
10 Jim Kelly 8.00 20.00
11 Dan Marino 20.00 50.00
12 Rick Mirer 4.80 12.00
13 Warren Moon 8.00 20.00
14 Barry Sanders 20.00 50.00
15 Junior Seau 8.00 20.00
16 Heath Shuler 4.00 12.00

1995-96 Finest Pro Bowl Jumbos

This 22-card set measures approximately 4" by 5 5/8". The fronts feature a color player cut-out on a metallic, lightning-effect background with the player's name printed in silver foil on a violet and black marblized band at the bottom. The cards are essentially enlarged versions of regular issue 1995 Finest cards and were distributed at the 1996 NFL Experience Pro Bowl show in Hawaii. The original card number is included on the backs as well as the new numbering of 22-cards. Refractor parallel versions of each card were produced in much shorter quantities. A poster sized Steve Young Finest promo card was produced as well and distributed at the Pro Bowl Card Show. It is priced separately below.

COMPLETE SET (22) 15.00 40.00
*REFRACTOR STARS: 5X TO 12X
1 Troy Aikman 2.00 5.00
2 Tim Brown .75 2.00
3 Cris Carter .75 2.00
4 Marshall Faulk 1.25 3.00
5 Brett Favre 5.00 10.00
6 Merton Hanks .40 1.00
7 Michael Irvin .75 2.00
8 Greg Lloyd .40 1.00
9 Dan Marino 5.00 10.00
10 Curtis Martin 2.00 5.00
11 Herman Moore .75 2.00
12 Terry McDaniel .40 1.00
13 Ken Norton .40 1.00
14 Bryce Paup .40 1.00
15 John Randle .75 2.00
16 Jerry Rice 2.00 5.00
17 Barry Sanders 4.00 8.00
18 Junior Seau .75 2.00
19 Steve Young 1.50 4.00
20 Reggie White .75 2.00
21 Chris Warren .40 1.00
22 Emmitt Smith 4.00 8.00
P1 Steve Young Promo 7.50 15.00

1996 Finest

This 359 card standard-size set was issued in two series by Topps. The set was issued in six-card packs and had a suggested retail price of $5 per pack. The set is broken down into a total of 220 bronze cards, 91 silver cards (1:4 packs), and 48 gold cards (1:24 packs). All of the cards feature chromium technology and the "Topps Finest" protector. Cards are numbered on the back both by set order and by card theme.

COMPLETE SET (359) 150.00 300.00
COMP.SERIES 1 (191) 100.00 200.00
COMP.SERIES 2 (168) 50.00 100.00
COMP.BRONZE SER.1 (110) 15.00 40.00
COMP.BRONZE SER.2 (110) 15.00 40.00
1 Kordell Stewart G 1.50 4.00
2 Jay Novacek B .25 .60
3 Ray Buchanan B .10 .30
4 Brett Favre S 5.00 12.00
5 Phil Hansen B .10 .30
6 Mike Mamula B .10 .30
7 Kimble Anders G .75 2.00
8 Merton Hanks G .75 2.00
9 Bernie Parmalee B .10 .30
10 Herman Moore B .25 .60
11 Shawn Jefferson B .10 .30
12 Chris Doleman B .10 .30
13 Erik Kramer B .25 .60
14 Chester McGlockton S .30 .75
15 Orlando Thomas B .10 .30
16 Terrell Davis B 1.50 4.00
17 Rick Mirer G 1.25 3.00
18 Roman Phifer B .10 .30
19 Trent Dilfer B .25 .60
20 Tyrone Hughes S .30 .75
21 Darnay Scott B .25 .60
22 Steve McNair B 1.50 4.00
23 Lamar Lathon B .10 .30
24 Ty Law S 1.25 3.00
25 Brian Mitchell S .30 .75
26 Thomas Randolph B .10 .30
27 Michael Jackson B .25 .60
28A Seth Joyner B .10 .30
28B Dan Saleaumua B UER .10 .30
29 Jeff Lageman B .10 .30
30 Darryl Williams B .10 .30
31 Darren Woodson S .60 1.50
32 Eric Pegram B .25 .60
33 Craig Newsome G .75 2.00
34 Sean Dawkins B .25 .60
35 Brian Mitchell S .30 .75
36 Bryce Paup G 1.25 3.00
37 Dana Stubblefield S .60 1.50
39 Henry Thomas B .10 .30
40 Dan Marino G 8.00 20.00
41 Kerry Collins S 1.25 3.00
42 Andre Coleman G .75 2.00
43 Pat Swilling B .10 .30
44 Marty Carter B .10 .30
45 Anthony Miller B .25 .60
46 Orlando Thomas S .30 .75
47 Kevin Carter G .75 2.00
48 Chris Warren B .25 .60
49 Derek Brown RBK B .10 .30
50 Jerry Rice S 3.00 8.00
51 Blaine Bishop B .10 .30
52 Jake Reed B .25 .60
53 Willie McGinest S .30 .75
54 Blake Brockermeyer S .30 .75
55 Vencie Glenn B .10 .30
56 Michael Westbrook S 1.25 3.00
57 Garrison Hearst S 1.25 3.00
58 Derrick Alexander WR B .25 .60
59 Kyle Brady S .60 1.50
60 Mark Brunell G 1.50 4.00
61 David Palmer G 1.25 3.00
62 Tim Brown S .60 1.50
63 Jeff Graham S .30 .75
64 Jessie Tuggle B .10 .30
65 Terrance Shaw B .10 .30
66 David Sloan B .25 .60
67 Dan Marino S 5.00 12.00
68 Brent Jones B .10 .30
69 Tamarick Vanover S 1.25 3.00
70 William Thomas B .10 .30
71 Robert Smith B .25 .60
72 Wayne Simmons B .10 .30
73 Jim Harbaugh B .25 .60
74 Daryl Johnston S .60 1.50
75 Carnell Lake G .75 2.00
76 Wayne Chrebet B .40 1.00
77 Chris Hudson B .10 .30
78 Frank Sanders S .60 1.50
79 Stevon Moore B .10 .30
80 Chris Calloway B .10 .30
81 Tom Carter B .10 .30
82 Dave Meggett B .10 .30
83 Sam Mills B .25 .60
84 Darryll Lewis S .30 .75
85 Carl Pickens S .60 1.50
86 Renaldo Turnbull B .10 .30
87 Derrick Brooks B .40 1.00
88 Jerome Bettis S 1.25 3.00
89 Eugene Robinson B .10 .30
90 Terrell Davis S 2.50 6.00
91 Rodney Thomas B .10 .30
92 Dan Wilkinson B .10 .30
93 Mark Fields B .10 .30
94 Warren Sapp B .10 .30
95 Curtis Martin B 1.50 4.00
96 Joey Galloway G 1.50 4.00
97 Ray Crockett B .10 .30
98 Ed McDaniel B .10 .30
99 Napoleon Kaufman S 1.25 3.00
100 Rashaan Salaam S .60 1.50
101 Craig Heyward B .10 .30
102 Ellis Johnson B .10 .30
103 Barry Sanders S 4.00 10.00
104 O.J. McDuffie B .25 .60
105 J.J. Stokes B .40 1.00
106 Mo Lewis B .10 .30
107 Tony Boselli S .60 1.50
108 Rob Moore B .25 .60
109 Eric Zeier S .60 1.50
110 Tyrone Wheatley B .25 .60
111 Ken Harvey B .10 .30
112 Melvin Tuten G .75 2.00
113 Willie Green B .10 .30
114 Willie Davis B .25 .60
115 Andy Harmon B .10 .30
116 Bruce Smith S 1.25 3.00
117 Bryan Cox B .10 .30
118 Zack Crockett S .30 .75
119 Bert Emanuel B .25 .60
120 Greg Lloyd B .25 .60
121 Aaron Glenn G .75 2.00
122 Willie Jackson B .25 .60
123 Lorenzo Lynch B .10 .30
124 Pepper Johnson B .10 .30
125 Joey Galloway S 1.25 3.00
126 Heath Shuler S .60 1.50
127 Curtis Martin S 2.50 6.00
128 Tyrone Poole B .10 .30
129 Neil Smith B .25 .60
130 Eddie Robinson B .10 .30
131 Bryce Paup B .25 .60
132 Brett Favre G 8.00 20.00
133 Ken Dilger G 1.25 3.00
134 Troy Aikman B 2.00 5.00
135 Greg Lloyd S .60 1.50
136 Chris Sanders B .25 .60
137 Marshall Faulk S 1.50 4.00
138 Jim Everett B .10 .30
139 Frank Sanders B .25 .60
140 Barry Sanders G 6.00 15.00
141 Cortez Kennedy B .25 .60
142 Glyn Milburn G .75 2.00
143 Derrick Alexander DE B .10 .30
144 Rob Fredrickson B .10 .30
145 Chris Zorich B .10 .30
146 Devin Bush B .10 .30
147 Tyrone Poole S .30 .75
148 Brett Perriman G 1.25 3.00
149 Troy Vincent B .10 .30
150 J.J. Stokes S 1.25 3.00
151 Deion Sanders B 1.00 2.50
152 James O. Stewart B .25 .60
153 Drew Bledsoe S 1.25 3.00
154 Terry McDaniel S .30 .75
155 Terrell Fletcher S .30 .75
156 Lawrence Dawsey B .10 .30
157 Robert Brooks B .40 1.00
158 Rashaan Salaam B .25 .60
159 Dave Brown S .30 .75
160 Kerry Collins G 1.50 4.00
161 Tim Brown B .25 .60
162 Brendan Stai B .10 .30
163 Sean Gilbert B .10 .30
164 Lee Woodall G .75 2.00
165 Jim Harbaugh S .60 1.50
166 Larry Brown S .30 .75
167 Neil Smith S .60 1.50
168 Herman Moore S .60 1.50
169 Calvin Williams B .25 .60
170 Deion Sanders S 2.00 5.00
171 Ruben Brown B .10 .30
172 Eric Green B .10 .30
173 Marshall Faulk G 2.00 5.00
174 Mark Chmura S .60 1.50
175 Jerry Rice B 2.00 5.00
176 Bruce Smith B .40 1.00
177 Mark Bruener B .10 .30
178 Troy Aikman G 3.00 8.00
179 Lamont Warren B .10 .30
180 Tamarick Vanover B .40 1.00
181 Chris Warren S .60 1.50
182 Scott Mitchell B .25 .60
183 Robert Brooks S 1.25 3.00
184 Steve McNair S 2.50 6.00
185 Kordell Stewart S 1.25 3.00
186 Terry Wooden B .10 .30
187 Ken Norton B .25 .60
188 Jeff Herrod B .10 .30
189 Charlie Garner S .60 1.50
190 Drew Bledsoe G 1.50 4.00
191 Checklist G .75 2.00
192 Gus Frerotte B .25 .60
193 Michael Irvin G 1.50 4.00
194 Brett Maxie B .10 .30
195 Harvey Williams S .30 .75
196 Warren Moon G 1.25 3.00
197 Jeff George S .60 1.50
198 Eddie Kennison B RC .40 1.00
199 Ricky Watters S .60 1.50
200 Steve Young G 3.00 8.00
201 Marcus Jones B RC .10 .30
202 Terry Allen B .25 .60
203 Leroy Hoard B .10 .30
204 Steve Bono S .60 1.50
205 Reggie White B .40 1.00
206 Larry Centers B .25 .60
207 Alex Van Dyke G RC 1.25 3.00
208 Vincent Brisby B .10 .30
209 Michael Timpson B .10 .30
210 Jeff Blake S 1.25 3.00
211 John Mobley B RC .10 .30
212 Clay Matthews B .25 .60
213 Shannon Sharpe B .25 .60
214 Tony Bennett B .10 .30
215 Phillippi Sparks S .30 .75
216 Mickey Washington B .10 .30
217 Fred Barnett B .25 .60
218 Michael Haynes B .25 .60
219 Stan Humphries B .25 .60
220 Cris Carter G 1.50 4.00
221 Winston Moss B .10 .30
222 Tim Biakabutuka B RC .40 1.00
223 Leeland McElroy B RC .25 .60
224 Vinnie Clark B .10 .30
225 Keyshawn Johnson B RC 2.00 5.00
226 William Floyd S .60 1.50
227 Troy Drayton S .30 .75
228 Tony Woods B .10 .30
229 Rodney Hampton S .60 1.50
230 John Elway G 8.00 20.00
231 Anthony Pleasant B .10 .30
232 Jeff George B .25 .60
233 Curtis Conway B .40 1.00
234 Charles Haley G 1.25 3.00
235 Jeff Lewis B RC .25 .60
236 Edgar Bennett B .25 .60
237 Regan Upshaw B RC .10 .30
238 William Fuller B .10 .30
239 Duane Clemons S RC .30 .75
240 Jim Kelly G 1.50 4.00
241 Willie Anderson B RC .10 .30
242 Derrick Thomas B .40 1.00
243 Marvin Harrison B RC 6.00 15.00
244 Darion Conner B .10 .30
245 Antonio Langham B .10 .30
246 Rodney Peete B .10 .30
247 Tim McDonald B .10 .30
248 Robert Jones B .10 .30
249 Curtis Conway S 1.25 3.00
250 Rodney Hampton G 1.25 3.00
251 Mark Carrier DB B .10 .30
252 Stephen Grant B .10 .30
253 John Mobley S .30 .75
254 Jeff Hostetler B .25 .60
255 Darrell Green B .10 .30
256 Errict Rhett G 1.25 3.00
257 Alex Molden G .75 2.00
258 Chris Slade S .30 .75

259 Derrick Thomas S 1.25 3.00
260 Kevin Hardy G 1.25 3.00
261 Eric Swann B .25 .60
262 Eric Metcalf S .60 1.50
263 Irv Smith B .10 .30
264 Tim McKyer B .10 .30
265 Emmitt Smith S 4.00 10.00
266 Sean Jones B .10 .30
267 Bryant Young G 1.25 3.00
268 Jeff Blake G 1.50 4.00
269 Jeff Hostetler S .60 1.50
270 Keyshawn Johnson G 1.50 4.00
271 Yancey Thigpen B .25 .60
272 Thurman Thomas S 1.25 3.00
273 Quentin Coryatt B .10 .30
274 Hardy Nickerson B .10 .30
275 Ricardo McDonald B .10 .30
276 Steve Atwater S .30 .75
277 Robert Blackmon B .10 .30
278 Junior Seau G 1.50 4.00
279 Alonzo Spellman B .10 .30
280 Isaac Bruce S 1.25 3.00
281 Rickey Dudley B RC .40 1.00
282 Joe Cain B .10 .30
283 Neil O'Donnell S .60 1.50
284 John Randle B .25 .60
285 Terry Kirby G 1.25 3.00
286 Vinny Testaverde B .25 .60
287 Jim Kelly S 1.25 3.00
288 Lawrence Phillips S 1.25 3.00
289 Henry Jones B .10 .30
290 Simeon Rice B RC 1.00 2.50
291 Terance Mathis S .30 .75
292 Errict Rhett S .60 1.50
293 Hugh Douglas G 1.25 3.00
294 Santo Stephens S .30 .75
295 Leslie O'Neal B .10 .30
296 Reggie White G 1.50 4.00
297 Greg Hill B .25 .60
298 Elvis Grbac G 1.50 4.00
299 Walt Harris S RC .30 .75
300 Emmitt Smith G 6.00 15.00
301 Eric Metcalf B .25 .60
302 Jamir Miller S .30 .75
303 Jerome Woods B RC .10 .30
304 Ben Coates S .60 1.50
305 Marcus Allen S 1.25 3.00
306 Anthony Smith B .10 .30
307 Darren Perry B .10 .30
308 Jonathan Ogden S RC 4.00 10.00
309 Ricky Watters G 1.25 3.00
310 John Elway S 5.00 12.00
311 James Hasty B .10 .30
312 Cris Carter B .40 1.00
313 Irving Fryar S .60 1.50
314 Lawrence Phillips B RC .25 .60
315 Junior Seau S 1.25 3.00
316 Alex Molden S RC .30 .75
317 Aeneas Williams B .10 .30
318 Eric Hill B .10 .30
319 Kevin Hardy B RC .40 1.00
320 Steve Young S 2.50 6.00
321 Chris Chandler B .25 .60
322 Rocket Ismail B .25 .60
323 Anthony Parker B .10 .30
324 John Thierry B .10 .30
325 Micheal Barrow B .10 .30
326 Henry Ford B .10 .30
327 Aaron Hayden B RC .10 .30
328 Terance Mathis B .10 .30
329 Kirk Pointer B RC .10 .30
330 Ray Mickens B RC .10 .30
331 Jermane Mayberry B RC .10 .30
332 Mario Bates B .25 .60
333 Carlton Gray B .10 .30
334 Derek Loville B .10 .30
335 Mike Alstott B RC 2.00 5.00
336 Eric Guliford B .10 .30
337 Marvcus Patton B .10 .30
338 Terrell Owens B RC 5.00 12.00
339 Lance Johnstone B RC .25 .60
340 Lake Dawson B .25 .60
341 Winslow Oliver B RC .10 .30
342 Adrian Murrell B .25 .60
343 Jason Belser B .10 .30
344 Brian Dawkins B RC 3.00 8.00
345 Reggie Brown B RC .10 .30
346 Shaun Gayle B .10 .30
347 Tony Brackens B RC .40 1.00
348 Thomas Lewis B .10 .30
349 Kelvin Pritchett B .10 .30
350 Bobby Engram B RC .40 1.00
351 Moe Williams B RC 1.00 2.50
352 Thomas Smith B .10 .30
353 Dexter Carter B .10 .30
354 Qadry Ismail B .25 .60
355 Marco Battaglia B RC .10 .30
356 Levon Kirkland B .10 .30
357 Eric Allen B .10 .30
358 Bobby Hoying B RC .40 1.00
359 Checklist B .10 .30

1996 Finest Refractors

COMP.BRONZE SET (220) 500.00 1000.00
COMP.BRONZE SER.1 (110) 250.00 500.00
COMP.BRONZE SER.2 (110) 250.00 500.00
*BRONZE VETS: 3X TO 8X BASIC CARDS
*BRONZE ROOKIE STARS: 1.5X TO 4X
*BRNZ ROOK.COMM/SEMI: 3X TO 8X
BRONZE REFRACTOR ODDS 1:12
*GOLD VETS: 2X TO 5X BASIC CARDS
GOLD REFRACTOR ODDS 1:288
*SILVER VETS: 2.5X TO 6X BASIC CARDS
SILVER REFRACTOR ODDS 1:48

1996-97 Finest Pro Bowl Jumbos

This 22-card set measures approximately 4" by 5-5/8". The fronts feature a color player photo on a metallic background. The cards are essentially enlarged versions of regular issue 1996 Finest gold cards but were distributed at the 1997 NFL Experience Pro Bowl show in Hawaii. Each is numbered "XX of 22" cards. Refractor parallel versions of each card were produced in much shorter quantities.

COMPLETE SET (22) 24.00 60.00
*REFRACTOR STARS: 6X TO 15X
1 Brett Favre 3.20 8.00
2 Herman Moore .60 1.50
3 Terrell Davis 2.00 5.00
4 Jerry Rice 2.00 5.00
5 Tim Brown .60 1.50
6 Dan Marino 3.20 8.00
7 Curtis Martin 1.60 4.00
8 Barry Sanders 3.20 8.00
9 Bruce Smith .80 2.00
10 Troy Aikman 2.00 5.00
11 Deion Sanders 1.20 3.00
12 Drew Bledsoe 1.60 4.00
13 Steve Young 1.60 4.00
14 Terry Allen .60 1.50
15 Reggie White .80 2.00
16 Shannon Sharpe .60 1.50
17 John Elway 3.20 8.00
18 Emmitt Smith 2.40 6.00
19 Keyshawn Johnson 1.20 3.00
20 Ben Coates .40 1.00
21 Ricky Watters .40 1.00
22 Junior Seau .80 2.00

1996-97 Finest Pro Bowl Promos 5X7

In addition to the 22-card Finest Pro Bowl set, six promo cards were released at the 1997 NFL Experience Pro Bowl Card Show in Hawaii. Each is simply an enlarged (5" by 7") copy of a 1996 Finest card. The backs carry a 1996 copyright date along with a player bio and card number. A Refractor parallel was also produced for each card.

COMPLETE SET (6) 14.00 35.00
*REFRACTORS: 4X TO 10X BASIC CARDS
1 Curtis Martin 2.00 5.00
2 Brett Favre 4.00 10.00
3 Barry Sanders 4.00 10.00
4 Jerry Rice 2.40 6.00
5 Troy Aikman 2.40 6.00
6 John Elway 4.00 10.00

1997 Finest

The 1997 Finest set was issued in two series totalling 350 cards and was distributed in six-card packs with a suggested retail price of $5. The set features borderless metallic design with the first 100 cards labeled as Common and highlighted in bronze. Cards #101-150 are labeled as Uncommon and are highlighted in silver with an insertion rate of one in four packs. The last 25 cards of Series 1 (#151-175) are labeled as Rare, are highlighted in gold, and carry an insertion rate of one in 24 packs. The set is also divided into five theme categories: Dynamos, Bulldozers, Masters, Hitmen, and Field Generals. The cards are numbered twice according to where they fall in the whole set and according to where they fall within each of the five themes. Series 2 features color action player photos printed on chromium cards. Cards #176-275 are the Common or Bronze cards; cards #276-325 are the Uncommon or Silver cards with an insertion rate of one in four; cards #326-350 are the Rare or Gold cards with an insertion rate of one in 24. Series 2 contains the following themes: Champions, Dominators, Impact, Stalwarts, and Masters. Series 2 cards are also numbered twice according to where they fall in the whole set and according to where they fall within each of the five themes.

COMPLETE SET (350) 250.00 500.00
COMP.SERIES 1 SET (175) 125.00 250.00
COMP.SERIES 2 SET (175) 125.00 250.00
COMP.BRONZE SET (200) 25.00 60.00
COMP.BRONZE SER.1 (100) 10.00 25.00
COMP.BRONZE SER.2 (100) 15.00 40.00
1 Mark Brunell B .60 1.50
2 Chris Slade B .25 .60
3 Chris Doleman B .25 .60
4 Chris Hudson B .25 .60
5 Karim Abdul-Jabbar B .40 1.00
6 Darren Perry B .25 .60
7 Daryl Johnston B .40 1.00
8 Rob Moore B UER .40 1.00
9 Robert Smith B .40 1.00
10 Terry Allen B .40 1.00
11 Jason Dunn B .25 .60
12 Henry Thomas B .25 .60
13 Rod Stephens B .25 .60
14 Ray Mickens B .25 .60
15 Ty Detmer B .40 1.00
16 Fred Barnett B .25 .60
17 Derrick Alexander WR B .40 1.00
18 Marcus Robertson B .25 .60
19 Robert Blackmon B .25 .60
20 Isaac Bruce B .60 1.50
21 Chester McGlockton B .25 .60
22 Stan Humphries B .40 1.00
23 Lonnie Marts B .25 .60
24 Jason Sehorn B .40 1.00
25 Bobby Engram B UER .40 1.00
26 Brett Perriman B UER .25 .60
27 Stevon Moore B .25 .60
28 Jamal Anderson B .40 1.00
29 Wayne Martin B .25 .60
30 Michael Irvin B UER .60 1.50
31 Thomas Smith B .25 .60
32 Tony Brackens B .25 .60
33 Eric Davis B .25 .60
34 James O.Stewart B .40 1.00
35 Ki-Jana Carter B .25 .60
36 Ken Norton B .25 .60
37 William Thomas B .25 .60
38 Tim Brown B .60 1.50
39 Lawrence Phillips B .25 .60
40 Ricky Watters B .40 1.00
41 Tony Bennett B .25 .60
42 Jessie Armstead B .25 .60
43 Trent Dilfer B .60 1.50
44 Rodney Hampton B .40 1.00
45 Sam Mills B .25 .60
46 Rodney Harrison B RC 1.25 3.00
47 Rob Fredrickson B .25 .60
48 Eric Hill B .25 .60
49 Bennie Blades B .25 .60
50 Eddie George B .60 1.50
51 Dave Brown B .25 .60
52 Raymont Harris B .25 .60
53 Steve Tovar B .25 .60
54 Thurman Thomas B .60 1.50
55 Leeland McElroy B .25 .60
56 Brian Mitchell B UER .25 .60
57 Eric Allen B .25 .60
58 Vinny Testaverde B .40 1.00
59 Marvin Washington B .25 .60
60 Junior Seau B .60 1.50
61 Bert Emanuel B .40 1.00
62 Kevin Carter B .25 .60
63 Mark Carrier DB B .25 .60
64 Andre Coleman B .25 .60
65 Chris Warren B .40 1.00
66 Aeneas Williams B .25 .60
67 Eugene Robinson B .25 .60
68 Darren Woodson B .25 .60
69 Anthony Johnson B .25 .60
70 Terry Glenn B .40 1.00
71 Troy Vincent B .25 .60
72 John Copeland B .25 .60
73 Warren Sapp B .40 1.00
74 Bobby Hebert B .25 .60
75 Jeff Hostetler B .25 .60
76 Willie Davis B .25 .60
77 Mickey Washington B .25 .60
78 Cortez Kennedy B .25 .60
79 Michael Strahan B .40 1.00
80 Jerome Bettis B .60 1.50
81 Andre Hastings B UER .25 .60
82 Simeon Rice B .40 1.00
83 Cornelius Bennett B .25 .60
84 Napoleon Kaufman B .40 1.00
85 Jim Harbaugh B .40 1.00
86 Aaron Hayden B .25 .60
87 Gus Frerotte B .25 .60
88 Jeff Blake B .40 1.00
89 Anthony Miller B UER .25 .60
90 Deion Sanders B .60 1.50
91 Curtis Conway B .40 1.00
92 William Floyd B .40 1.00
93 Eric Moulds B UER .40 1.00
94 Mel Gray B .25 .60
95 Andre Rison B UER .40 1.00
96 Eugene Daniel B .25 .60
97 Jason Belser B .25 .60
98 Mike Mamula B .25 .60
99 Jim Everett B .25 .60
100 Checklist B .25 .60
101 Drew Bledsoe S 1.25 3.00
102 Shannon Sharpe S .75 2.00
103 Ken Harvey S .50 1.25
104 Isaac Bruce S 1.25 3.00
105 Terry Allen S .75 2.00
106 Lawyer Milloy S .75 2.00
107 Ashley Ambrose S .50 1.25
108 Alfred Williams S .50 1.25
109 Hugh Douglas S .50 1.25
110 Junior Seau S 1.25 3.00
111 Kordell Stewart S .75 2.00
112 Adrian Murrell S .75 2.00
113 Byron Bam Morris S .50 1.25
114 Terrell Buckley S .50 1.25
115 Dan Marino S 5.00 12.00
116 Willie Clay S .50 1.25
117 Neil Smith S .75 2.00
118 Blaine Bishop S .50 1.25
119 John Mobley S .50 1.25
120 Herman Moore S .75 2.00
121 Keyshawn Johnson S 1.25 3.00
122 Boomer Esiason S .75 2.00
123 Marshall Faulk S 1.25 3.00
124 Keith Jackson S .50 1.25
125 Ricky Watters S .75 2.00
126 Carl Pickens S .75 2.00
127 Cris Carter S 1.25 3.00
128 Mike Alstott S 1.25 3.00
129 Simeon Rice S .75 2.00
130 Troy Aikman S 2.50 6.00
131 Tamarick Vanover S .75 2.00
132 Marquez Pope S .50 1.25
133 Winslow Oliver S .50 1.25
134 Edgar Bennett S .75 2.00
135 Dave Meggett S .50 1.25
136 Marcus Allen S 1.25 3.00
137 Jerry Rice S 2.50 6.00
138 Steve Atwater S .50 1.25
139 Tim McDonald S .50 1.25
140 Barry Sanders S 4.00 10.00
141 Eddie George S 1.25 3.00
142 Wesley Walls S .50 1.25
143 Jerome Bettis S 1.25 3.00
144 Kevin Greene S .75 2.00
145 Terrell Davis S 1.25 3.00
146 Gus Frerotte S .75 2.00
147 Joey Galloway S .75 2.00
148 Vinny Testaverde S .75 2.00
149 Hardy Nickerson S .50 1.25
150 Brett Favre S 5.00 12.00
151 Desmond Howard G 1.25 3.00
152 Keyshawn Johnson G 2.00 5.00
153 Tony Banks G 2.00 5.00
154 Chris Spielman G .60 1.50
155 Reggie White G 2.00 5.00
156 Zach Thomas G 2.00 5.00
157 Carl Pickens G 1.25 3.00
158 Karim Abdul-Jabbar G 2.00 5.00
159 Chad Brown G .60 1.50
160 Kerry Collins G 2.00 5.00
161 Marvin Harrison G 2.00 5.00
162 Steve Young G 3.00 8.00
163 Deion Sanders G 2.00 5.00
164 Trent Dilfer G 2.00 5.00
165 Barry Sanders G 6.00 15.00
166 Cris Carter G 2.00 5.00
167 Keenan McCardell G 1.25 3.00
168 Terry Glenn G 2.00 5.00
169 Emmitt Smith G 6.00 15.00
170 John Elway G 7.50 20.00
171 Jerry Rice G 4.00 10.00
172 Troy Aikman G 4.00 10.00
173 Curtis Martin G 2.00 5.00
174 Darrell Green G 1.25 3.00
175 Mark Brunell G 2.00 5.00
176 Corey Dillon B RC 3.00 8.00
177 Tyrone Poole B .25 .60
178 Anthony Pleasant B .25 .60
179 Frank Sanders B .40 1.00
180 Troy Aikman B 1.50 3.00
181 Bill Romanowski B .25 .60
182 Ty Law B .40 1.00
183 Orlando Thomas B .25 .60
184 Quentin Coryatt B .25 .60
185 Kenny Holmes B RC .40 1.00
186 Bryant Young B .25 .60
187 Michael Sinclair B .25 .60
188 Mike Tomczak B .25 .60
189 Bobby Taylor B .25 .60
190 Brett Favre B 3.00 6.00
191 Kent Graham B .25 .60
192 Jessie Tuggle B .25 .60
193 Jimmy Smith B .40 1.00
194 Greg Hill B .25 .60
195 Yatil Green B RC .25 .60
196 Mark Fields B .25 .60
197 Phillippi Sparks B .25 .60
198 Aaron Glenn B .25 .60
199 Pat Swilling B .25 .60
200 Barry Sanders B 2.00 5.00
201 Mark Chmura B .40 1.00
202 Marco Coleman B .25 .60
203 Merton Hanks B .25 .60
204 Brian Blades B .25 .60
205 Errict Rhett B .25 .60
206 Henry Ellard B .25 .60
207 Andre Reed B .40 1.00
208 Bryan Cox B .25 .60
209 Darnay Scott B .40 1.00
210 John Elway B 3.00 6.00
211 Glyn Milburn B .25 .60
212 Don Beebe B .25 .60
213 Kevin Lockett B RC .25 .60
214 Dorsey Levens B .60 1.50
215 Kordell Stewart B .60 1.50
216 Larry Centers B .40 1.00
217 Cris Carter B .60 1.50
218 Willie McGinest B .25 .60
219 Renaldo Wynn B RC .25 .60
220 Jerry Rice B 1.50 3.00
221 Reidel Anthony B RC .25 .60
222 Mark Carrier WR B .25 .60
223 Quinn Early B .25 .60
224 Chris Sanders B .25 .60
225 Shawn Springs B RC .25 .60
226 Kevin Smith B .25 .60
227 Ben Coates B .40 1.00
228 Tyrone Wheatley B .40 1.00
229 Antonio Freeman B .60 1.50
230 Dan Marino B 3.00 6.00
231 Dwayne Rudd B RC .40 1.00
232 Leslie O'Neal B .25 .60
233 Brent Jones B .25 .60
234 Jake Plummer B RC 3.00 8.00
235 Kerry Collins B .60 1.50
236 Rashaan Salaam B .25 .60
237 Tyrone Braxton B .25 .60
238 Herman Moore B .40 1.00
239 Keyshawn Johnson B .60 1.50
240 Drew Bledsoe B .60 1.50
241 Rickey Dudley B .40 1.00
242 Antowain Smith B RC 2.00 5.00
243 Jeff Lageman B .25 .60
244 Chris T. Jones B .25 .60
245 Steve Young B 1.00 2.50
246 Eddie Robinson B .25 .60
247 Chad Cota B .25 .60
248 Michael Jackson B .40 1.00
249 Robert Porcher B .25 .60
250 Reggie White B .60 1.50
251 Carnell Lake B .25 .60
252 Chris Calloway B .25 .60
253 Terance Mathis B .40 1.00
254 Carl Pickens B .40 1.00
255 Curtis Martin B .60 1.50
256 Jeff Graham B .25 .60
257 Regan Upshaw RC B .25 .60
258 Sean Gilbert B .25 .60
259 Will Blackwell B RC .25 .60
260 Emmitt Smith B 2.50 5.00
261 Reinard Wilson B RC .25 .60
262 Darrell Russell B RC .25 .60
263 Wayne Chrebet B .40 1.00
264 Kevin Hardy B .25 .60
265 Shannon Sharpe B .60 1.50
266 Harvey Williams B .25 .60
267 John Randle B .40 1.00
268 Tim Bowens B .25 .60
269 Tony Gonzalez B RC 3.00 8.00
270 Warrick Dunn B RC 2.50 6.00
271 Sean Dawkins B .25 .60
272 Darryll Lewis B .25 .60
273 Alonzo Spellman B .25 .60
274 Mark Collins B .25 .60
275 Checklist Card B .25 .60
276 Pat Barnes S RC .50 1.25
277 Dana Stubblefield S .75 2.00
278 Dan Wilkinson S .50 1.25
279 Bryce Paup S .50 1.25
280 Kerry Collins S 1.25 3.00
281 Derrick Brooks S 1.25 3.00
282 Walter Jones S RC 2.00 5.00
283 Terry McDaniel S .50 1.25
284 James Farrior S RC 1.25 3.00
285 Curtis Martin S 1.25 3.00
286 O.J. McDuffie S .75 2.00
287 Natrone Means S .75 2.00
288 Bryant Westbrook S RC .75 2.00
289 Peter Boulware S RC 1.25 3.00
290 Emmitt Smith S 4.00 10.00
291 Joey Kent S RC .75 2.00
292 Eddie Kennison S .75 2.00
293 LeRoy Butler S .50 1.25
294 Dale Carter S .50 1.25
295 Jim Druckenmiller S RC .75 2.00
296 Byron Hanspard S RC .75 2.00
297 Jeff Blake S .75 2.00
298 Levon Kirkland S .50 1.25
299 Michael Westbrook S .50 1.25
300 John Elway S 5.00 12.00
301 Lamar Lathon S .50 1.25
302 Ray Lewis S 2.00 5.00
303 Steve McNair S 1.25 3.00
304 Shawn Springs S .50 1.25
305 Karim Abdul-Jabbar S .75 2.00
306 Orlando Pace S RC 1.25 3.00
307 Scott Mitchell S .50 1.25
308 Walt Harris S .50 1.25
309 Bruce Smith S .75 2.00
310 Reggie White S 1.25 3.00
311 Eric Swann S .50 1.25
312 Derrick Thomas S 1.25 3.00
313 Tony Martin S .75 2.00
314 Darrell Russell S RC .75 2.00
315 Mark Brunell S 1.25 3.00
316 Trent Dilfer S 1.25 3.00
317 Irving Fryar S .50 1.25
318 Amani Toomer S .75 2.00
319 Jake Reed S .75 2.00
320 Steve Young S 2.00 5.00
321 Troy Davis S RC .75 2.00
322 Jim Harbaugh S .75 2.00
323 Neil O'Donnell S .50 1.25
324 Terry Glenn S .75 2.00
325 Deion Sanders S 1.25 3.00
326 Gus Frerotte G 1.25 3.00
327 Tom Knight G RC 1.25 3.00
328 Peter Boulware G 1.25 3.00
329 Jerome Bettis G 2.00 5.00
330 Orlando Pace G 2.00 5.00
331 Darnell Autry G RC 1.25 3.00
332 Ike Hilliard G RC 2.00 5.00
333 David LaFleur G RC .60 1.50
334 Jim Harbaugh G 1.25 3.00
335 Eddie George G 2.00 5.00
336 Vinny Testaverde G 1.25 3.00
337 Terry Allen G 1.25 3.00
338 Jim Druckenmiller G 1.25 3.00
339 Ricky Watters G 1.25 3.00
340 Brett Favre G 7.50 20.00
341 Simeon Rice G 1.25 3.00
342 Shannon Sharpe G 2.00 5.00
343 Kordell Stewart G 2.00 5.00
344 Isaac Bruce G 2.00 5.00
345 Drew Bledsoe G 2.00 5.00
346 Jeff Blake G 1.25 3.00
347 Herman Moore G 1.25 3.00
348 Junior Seau G 2.00 5.00
349 Rae Carruth G RC .60 1.50
350 Dan Marino G 7.50 20.00
P5 K.Abdul-Jabbar Promo .60 1.50
P20 Isaac Bruce Promo .75 2.00
P32 Tony Brackens Promo .60 1.50
P45 Sam Mills Promo .60 1.50
P70 Terry Glenn Promo .60 1.50
P87 Gus Frerotte Promo .60 1.50

1997 Finest Atomic Refractors

*GOLD: 2.5X TO 6X BASIC CARDS

1997 Finest Embossed

*SILVER: .8X TO 2X BASIC CARDS
SILVER STATED ODDS 1:16
*GOLD: 1X TO 2.5X BASIC CARDS
GOLD STATED ODDS 1:96

1997 Finest Embossed Refractors

*SILVER: 2X TO 5X BASIC CARDS
SILVER STATED ODDS 1:192
*GOLD: 3X TO 8X BASIC CARDS
GOLD STATED ODDS 1:1152

1997 Finest Refractors

*BRONZE VETS: 1.2X TO 3X BASIC CARDS
*BRONZE ROOKIES: 1X TO 2.5X
BRONZE REFRACTOR ODDS 1:12
*SILVER: 1X TO 2.5X BASIC CARDS
SILVER REFRACTOR ODDS 1:48
*GOLD: 1.2X TO 3X BASIC CARDS
GOLD REFRACTOR ODDS 1:288

1998 Finest Promos

This set of cards was distributed to hobbyists to promote the upcoming 1998 Finest football card release. Each card is nearly identical to the matching base issue card except for the card number on back.

COMPLETE SET (6) 4.00 10.00
PP1 Jerome Bettis .60 1.50
PP2 Cris Carter .60 1.50
PP3 Tony Gonzalez .80 2.00
PP4 Tim Brown .60 1.50
PP5 Mark Brunell 1.20 3.00
PP6 Antonio Freeman .60 1.50

1998 Finest

The 1998 Finest set was issued in two series totalling 270 cards and was distributed in six-card packs with a suggested price of $5. The fronts feature color action player photos printed on 29 pt. card stock, while the backs display player information. Series 1 contains the subset Rookies (121-150). The 120 cards in Series 2 are organized by player position, each of which is identified by a different graphic.

COMPLETE SET (270) 30.00 80.00
COMP.SERIES 1 (150) 20.00 50.00
COMP.SERIES 2 (120) 12.50 30.00
1 John Elway 1.50 4.00
2 Terance Mathis .25 .60
3 Jermaine Lewis .25 .60
4 Fred Lane .15 .40
5 Simeon Rice .25 .60
6 David Dunn .15 .40
7 Dexter Coakley .15 .40
8 Carl Pickens .25 .60
9 Antonio Freeman .40 1.00
10 Herman Moore .25 .60
11 Kevin Hardy .15 .40
12 Tony Gonzalez .40 1.00
13 O.J. McDuffie .25 .60
14 David Palmer .15 .40
15 Lawyer Milloy .25 .60
16 Danny Kanell .25 .60
17 Randal Hill .15 .40
18 Chris Slade .15 .40
19 Charlie Garner .25 .60
20 Mark Brunell .40 1.00
21 Donnell Woolford .15 .40
22 Freddie Jones .15 .40
23 Ken Norton .15 .40
24 Tony Banks .25 .60
25 Isaac Bruce .40 1.00
26 Willie Davis .15 .40
27 Cris Dishman .15 .40
28 Aeneas Williams .15 .40
29 Michael Booker .15 .40
30 Cris Carter .40 1.00
31 Michael McCrary .15 .40
32 Eric Moulds .40 1.00
33 Rae Carruth .15 .40
34 Bobby Engram .25 .60
35 Jeff Blake .25 .60
36 Deion Sanders .40 1.00
37 Rod Smith .25 .60
38 Bryant Westbrook .15 .40
39 Mark Chmura .25 .60
40 Tim Brown .40 1.00
41 Bobby Taylor .15 .40
42 James Stewart .25 .60
43 Kimble Anders .25 .60
44 Karim Abdul-Jabbar .40 1.00
45 Willie McGinest .15 .40
46 Jessie Armstead .15 .40
47 Brad Johnson .40 1.00
48 Greg Lloyd .15 .40
49 Stephen Davis .15 .40
50 Jerome Bettis .40 1.00
51 Warren Sapp .25 .60
52 Horace Copeland .15 .40
53 Chad Brown .15 .40
54 Chris Canty .15 .40
55 Robert Smith .40 1.00
56 Pete Mitchell .15 .40
57 Aaron Bailey .15 .40
58 Robert Porcher .15 .40
59 John Mobley .15 .40
60 Tony Martin .25 .60
61 Michael Irvin .40 1.00
62 Charles Way .15 .40
63 Raymont Harris .15 .40
64 Chuck Smith .15 .40
65 Larry Centers .15 .40
66 Greg Hill .15 .40
67 Kenny Holmes .15 .40
68 John Lynch .25 .60
69 Michael Sinclair .15 .40
70 Steve Young .50 1.25
71 Michael Strahan .25 .60
72 Levon Kirkland .15 .40
73 Rickey Dudley .15 .40
74 Marcus Allen .40 1.00
75 John Randle .25 .60
76 Erik Kramer .15 .40
77 Neil Smith .25 .60
78 Byron Hanspard .15 .40
79 Quinn Early .15 .40
80 Warren Moon .40 1.00
81 William Thomas .15 .40
82 Ben Coates .25 .60
83 Lake Dawson .15 .40
84 Steve McNair .40 1.00
85 Gus Frerotte .15 .40
86 Rodney Harrison .25 .60
87 Reggie White .40 1.00
88 Derrick Thomas .40 1.00
89 Dale Carter .15 .40
90 Warrick Dunn .40 1.00
91 Will Blackwell .15 .40
92 Troy Vincent .15 .40
93 Johnnie Morton .25 .60
94 David LaFleur .15 .40
95 Tony McGee .15 .40
96 Lonnie Johnson .15 .40
97 Thurman Thomas .40 1.00
98 Chris Chandler .25 .60
99 Jamal Anderson .40 1.00
100 Checklist .15 .40
101 Marshall Faulk .60 1.50
102 Chris Calloway .15 .40
103 Chris Spielman .15 .40
104 Zach Thomas .40 1.00
105 Jeff George .25 .60
106 Darrell Russell .15 .40
107 Darryll Lewis .15 .40
108 Reidel Anthony .25 .60
109 Terrell Owens .40 1.00
110 Rob Moore .25 .60
111 Darrell Green .25 .60
112 Merton Hanks .15 .40
113 Shawn Jefferson .15 .40
114 Chris Sanders .15 .40
115 Scott Mitchell .25 .60
116 Vaughn Hebron .15 .40
117 Ed McCaffrey .25 .60
118 Bruce Smith .25 .60
119 Peter Boulware .15 .40
120 Brett Favre 1.50 4.00
121 Peyton Manning RC 12.00 30.00
122 Brian Griese RC 1.00 2.50
123 Tavian Banks RC .60 1.50
124 Duane Starks RC .40 1.00
125 Robert Holcombe RC .60 1.50
126 Brian Simmons RC .60 1.50
127 Skip Hicks RC .60 1.50
128 Keith Brooking RC .75 2.00
129 Ahman Green RC 2.00 5.00
130 Jerome Pathon RC .75 2.00
131 Curtis Enis RC .40 1.00
132 Grant Wistrom RC .60 1.50
133 Germane Crowell RC .60 1.50
134 Jacquez Green RC .60 1.50
135 Randy Moss RC 6.00 15.00
136 Jason Peter RC .40 1.00
137 John Avery RC .60 1.50
138 Takeo Spikes RC .75 2.00
139 Pat Johnson RC .60 1.50
140 Andre Wadsworth RC .60 1.50
141 Fred Taylor RC 1.25 3.00
142 Charles Woodson RC 2.00 5.00
143 Marcus Nash RC .40 1.00
144 Robert Edwards RC .60 1.50
145 Kevin Dyson RC .75 2.00
146 Joe Jurevicius RC .75 2.00
147 Anthony Simmons RC .60 1.50
148 Hines Ward RC 5.00 10.00
149 Greg Ellis RC .40 1.00
150 Ryan Leaf RC .75 2.00
151 Jerry Rice .75 2.00
152 Tony Martin .25 .60
153 Checklist .15 .40
154 Rob Johnson .25 .60
155 Shannon Sharpe .25 .60
156 Bert Emanuel .25 .60
157 Eric Metcalf .15 .40
158 Natrone Means .25 .60
159 Derrick Alexander .25 .60
160 Emmitt Smith 1.25 3.00
161 Jeff Burris .15 .40
162 Chris Warren .25 .60
163 Corey Fuller .15 .40
164 Courtney Hawkins .15 .40
165 James McKnight .40 1.00
166 Shawn Springs .15 .40
167 Wayne Martin .15 .40
168 Michael Westbrook .25 .60
169 Michael Jackson .15 .40
170 Dan Marino 1.50 4.00
171 Amp Lee .15 .40
172 James Jett .25 .60
173 Ty Law .25 .60
174 Kerry Collins .25 .60
175 Robert Brooks .25 .60
176 Blaine Bishop .15 .40
177 Stephen Boyd .15 .40
178 Keyshawn Johnson .40 1.00
179 Deon Figures .15 .40
180 Allen Aldridge .15 .40
181 Corey Miller .15 .40
182 Chad Lewis .25 .60
183 Derrick Rodgers .15 .40
184 Troy Drayton .15 .40
185 Darren Woodson .15 .40
186 Ken Dilger .15 .40
187 Elvis Grbac .25 .60
188 Terrell Fletcher .15 .40
189 Frank Sanders .25 .60
190 Curtis Martin .40 1.00
191 Derrick Brooks .40 1.00
192 Darrien Gordon .15 .40
193 Andre Reed .25 .60
194 Darnay Scott .25 .60
195 Curtis Conway .25 .60
196 Tim McDonald .15 .40
197 Sean Dawkins .15 .40
198 Napoleon Kaufman .40 1.00
199 Willie Clay .15 .40
200 Terrell Davis .40 1.00
201 Wesley Walls .25 .60
202 Santana Dotson .15 .40
203 Frank Wycheck .15 .40
204 Wayne Chrebet .40 1.00
205 Andre Rison .25 .60
206 Jason Sehorn .25 .60
207 Jessie Tuggle .15 .40
208 Kevin Turner .15 .40
209 Jason Taylor .25 .60
210 Yancey Thigpen .15 .40
211 Jake Reed .25 .60
212 Carnell Lake .15 .40
213 Joey Galloway .25 .60
214 Andre Hastings .15 .40
215 Terry Allen .40 1.00
216 Jim Harbaugh .25 .60
217 Tony Banks .25 .60
218 Greg Clark .15 .40
219 Corey Dillon .40 1.00
220 Troy Aikman .75 2.00
221 Antowain Smith .40 1.00
222 Steve Atwater .15 .40
223 Trent Dilfer .40 1.00
224 Junior Seau .40 1.00
225 Garrison Hearst .40 1.00
226 Eric Allen .15 .40
227 Chad Cota .15 .40
228 Vinny Testaverde .25 .60
229 Duce Staley .50 1.25
230 Drew Bledsoe .60 1.50
231 Charles Johnson .15 .40
232 Jake Plummer .40 1.00
233 Errict Rhett .25 .60
234 Doug Evans .15 .40
235 Phillippi Sparks .15 .40
236 Ashley Ambrose .15 .40
237 Bryan Cox .15 .40
238 Kevin Smith .15 .40
239 Hardy Nickerson .15 .40
240 Terry Glenn .40 1.00
241 Lee Woodall .15 .40
242 Andre Coleman .15 .40
243 Michael Bates .15 .40
244 Mark Fields .15 .40
245 Eddie Kennison .25 .60
246 Dana Stubblefield .15 .40
247 Bobby Hoying .25 .60
248 Mo Lewis .15 .40
249 Derrick Mayes .25 .60
250 Eddie George .40 1.00
251 Mike Alstott .40 1.00
252 J.J. Stokes .25 .60
253 Adrian Murrell .25 .60
254 Kevin Greene .25 .60
255 LeRoy Butler .15 .40
256 Glenn Foley .25 .60
257 Jimmy Smith .25 .60
258 Tiki Barber .40 1.00
259 Irving Fryar .25 .60
260 Ricky Watters .25 .60
261 Jeff Graham .15 .40
262 Kordell Stewart .40 1.00
263 Rod Woodson .25 .60
264 Leslie Shepherd .15 .40
265 Ryan McNeil .15 .40
266 Ike Hilliard .25 .60
267 Keenan McCardell .25 .60
268 Marvin Harrison .40 1.00
269 Dorsey Levens .40 1.00
270 Barry Sanders 1.25 3.00

1998 Finest No-Protectors

COMPLETE SET (270) 150.00 300.00
*NO-PROT VETS: 1.25X TO 3X BASIC CARDS
*NO-PROT ROOKIES: .5X TO 1.2X BASIC RC
STATED ODDS 1:2 HOB/RET, 1 PER JUMBO

1998 Finest No-Protectors Refractors

*NP REF STARS: 6X TO 15X BASIC CARDS
*NP REF ROOKIES: 1.5X TO 4X BASIC RC
NP.REFRACT.ODDS 1:24 H/R, 1:10 JUM

1998 Finest Refractors

COMP.REFRACT.SET (270) 500.00 1000.00
*REF.VETS: 3X TO 8X BASIC CARDS
*REF.ROOKIES: 1X TO 2.5X BASIC RC
REFRACTOR ODDS 1:12H/R, 1:5J
1-120 REFRACTORS IN SERIES 1 PACKS
121-270 REFRACTORS SERIES 2 PACKS

1998 Finest Centurions

Randomly inserted in Series 1 packs at a rate of one in 125, this 20-card set features color action player photos and is sequentially numbered to 500.

COMPLETE SET (20) 125.00 250.00
CENTURIAN/500 ODDS 1:125H/R, 1:58J
*REFRACT/75: .75X TO 2X BASIC INSERT
REFRACTOR/75 ODDS 1:831H/R, 1:383J
C1 Brett Favre 25.00 60.00
C2 Eddie George 6.00 15.00
C3 Antonio Freeman 6.00 15.00
C4 Napoleon Kaufman 6.00 15.00
C5 Terrell Davis 6.00 15.00
C6 Keyshawn Johnson 6.00 15.00
C7 Peter Boulware 2.50 6.00
C8 Mike Alstott 6.00 15.00
C9 Jake Plummer 6.00 15.00
C10 Mark Brunell 6.00 15.00
C11 Marvin Harrison 6.00 15.00
C12 Antowain Smith 6.00 15.00
C13 Dorsey Levens 4.00 10.00
C14 Terry Glenn 4.00 10.00
C15 Warrick Dunn 6.00 15.00
C16 Joey Galloway 4.00 10.00
C17 Steve McNair 6.00 15.00
C18 Corey Dillon 6.00 15.00
C19 Drew Bledsoe 10.00 25.00
C20 Kordell Stewart 6.00 15.00

1998 Finest Future's Finest

Randomly inserted in Series 2 packs at the rate of one in 83, this 20-card set features color action photos of top young players who will be taking the game into the next century. The cards are sequentially numberd to 500. A refractive parallel version of this set was also produced with an insertion rate of 1:557 packs. These cards are sequentially numbered to 75.

COMPLETE SET (20) 125.00 250.00
STATED PRINT RUN 500 SERIAL #'d SETS
*REFRACTOR/75: 1.2X TO 3X BASIC INSERTS
REFRACTOR/75 ODDS 1:557
F1 Peyton Manning 25.00 60.00
F2 Napoleon Kaufman 5.00 12.00
F3 Jake Plummer 5.00 12.00
F4 Terry Glenn 5.00 12.00
F5 Ryan Leaf 5.00 12.00
F6 Drew Bledsoe 7.50 20.00
F7 Dorsey Levens 4.00 10.00
F8 Andre Wadsworth 4.00 10.00
F9 Joey Galloway 4.00 10.00
F10 Curtis Enis 4.00 10.00
F11 Warrick Dunn 5.00 12.00
F12 Kordell Stewart 4.00 10.00
F13 Randy Moss 15.00 40.00
F14 Robert Edwards 4.00 10.00
F15 Eddie George 5.00 12.00
F16 Fred Taylor 5.00 12.00
F17 Corey Dillon 5.00 12.00
F18 Brett Favre 20.00 50.00
F19 Kevin Dyson 5.00 12.00
F20 Terrell Davis 5.00 12.00

1998 Finest Jumbos 1

Randomly inserted in Series one boxes at the rate of one in three, this eight-card set features color player photos printed on large 3 1/2" by 5" cards. A refractive parallel version of this set was also produced with an insertion rate of one in 12 boxes.

COMPLETE SET (8) 50.00 100.00
STATED ODDS 1:3 BOXES
*REFRACTORS: .8X TO 2X BASIC INSERTS
REFRACTOR ODDS 1:12 BOXES
1 John Elway 8.00 20.00
2 Peyton Manning 15.00 40.00
3 Mark Brunell 2.00 5.00
4 Curtis Enis .60 1.50
5 Jerome Bettis 2.00 5.00
6 Ryan Leaf .60 1.50
7 Warrick Dunn 2.00 5.00
8 Brett Favre 8.00 20.00

1998 Finest Jumbos 2

Randomly inserted in Series two boxes at the rate of one in three, this seven-card set features color player photos printed on large 3 1/2" by 5" cards. A refractive parallel version of this set was also produced with an insertion rate of one in 12 boxes.

COMPLETE SET (7) 40.00 80.00
STATED ODDS 1:3 BOXES
*REFRACTORS: .8X TO 2X BASIC INSERTS
REFRACTOR STATED ODDS 1:12 BOXES
151 Jerry Rice 4.00 10.00
160 Emmitt Smith 6.00 15.00
170 Dan Marino 8.00 20.00
213 Joey Galloway 1.25 3.00
230 Drew Bledsoe 3.00 8.00
250 Eddie George 2.00 5.00
270 Barry Sanders 6.00 15.00

1998 Finest Mystery Finest 1

Randomly inserted in Series one packs at a rate of one in 36, this 50-card insert set features color action photos of two top players printed on double-sided cards. A refractive parallel set was also produced and seeded in packs at the rate of 1:144.

COMPLETE SET (50) 300.00 600.00
STATED ODDS 1:36H/R, 1:15J
*REFRACTORS: .6X TO 1.5X HI COL.
REFRACT.STATED ODDS 1:144H/R, 1:64J
M1 B.Favre / M.Brunell 10.00 25.00
M2 B.Favre / J.Plummer 10.00 25.00
M3 B.Favre / S.Young 10.00 25.00
M4 B.Favre / B.Favre 10.00 25.00
M5 M.Brunell / S.Young 4.00 10.00
M6 M.Brunell / M.Brunell 2.50 6.00
M7 J.Plummer / M.Brunell 3.00 8.00
M8 J.Plummer / J.Plummer 3.00 8.00
M9 S.Young / J.Plummer 4.00 10.00
M10 S.Young / S.Young 4.00 10.00
M11 J.Elway / D.Bledsoe 7.50 20.00
M12 J.Elway / T.Aikman 7.50 20.00
M13 J.Elway / D.Marino 10.00 25.00
M14 J.Elway / J.Elway 7.50 20.00
M15 D.Bledsoe / T.Aikman 5.00 12.00
M16 D.Bledsoe / D.Bledsoe 3.00 8.00
M17 T.Aikman / D.Marino 10.00 25.00
M18 T.Aikman / T.Aikman 5.00 12.00
M19 D.Marino / D.Bledsoe 10.00 25.00
M20 D.Marino / D.Marino 10.00 25.00
M21 K.Stewart / C.Dillon 2.50 6.00
M22 K.Stewart / T.Brown 2.50 6.00
M23 K.Stewart / B.Sanders 7.50 20.00
M24 K.Stewart / K.Stewart 2.50 6.00
M25 C.Dillon / T.Brown 3.00 8.00
M26 C.Dillon / C.Dillon 3.00 8.00
M27 T.Brown / B.Sanders 7.50 20.00
M28 T.Brown / T.Brown 3.00 8.00
M29 B.Sanders / C.Dillon 7.50 20.00
M30 B.Sanders / B.Sanders 7.50 20.00
M31 T.Davis / E.Smith 7.50 20.00
M32 T.Davis / J.Bettis 3.00 8.00
M33 T.Davis / E.George 3.00 8.00
M34 T.Davis / T.Davis 3.00 8.00
M35 E.Smith / E.George 7.50 20.00
M36 E.Smith / E.Smith 7.50 20.00

M37 J.Bettis 7.50 20.00
E.Smith
M38 J.Bettis 3.00 8.00
J.Bettis
M39 E.George 3.00 8.00
J.Bettis
M40 E.George 2.50 6.00
E.George
M41 H.Moore 6.00 15.00
J.Rice
M42 H.Moore 2.00 5.00
H.Moore
M43 W.Dunn 2.50 6.00
H.Moore
M44 W.Dunn 6.00 15.00
J.Rice
M45 W.Dunn 2.50 6.00
D.Levens
M46 W.Dunn 2.50 6.00
W.Dunn
M47 J.Rice 6.00 15.00
D.Levens
M48 J.Rice 7.50 20.00
J.Rice
M49 D.Levens 2.00 5.00
H.Moore
M50 D.Levens 2.00 5.00
D.Levens

1998 Finest Mystery Finest 2

Randomly inserted in Series two packs at the rate of one in 36, this 40-card set features color action photos of two players printed on double-sided cards. A refractive parallel version of this set was also produced and seeded in packs at the rate of 1:144.

STATED ODDS 1:36
*REFRACTORS: .6X TO 1.5X HI COL.
REFRACTOR STATED ODDS 1:144
M1 B.Favre 10.00 25.00
D.Marino
M2 B.Favre 12.00 30.00
P.Manning
M3 B.Favre 8.00 20.00
R.Leaf
M4 D.Marino 12.00 30.00
P.Manning
M5 D.Marino 8.00 20.00
R.Leaf
M6 P.Manning 10.00 25.00
R.Leaf
M7 B.Sanders 10.00 25.00
E.Smith
M8 B.Sanders 6.00 15.00
C.Enis
M9 B.Sanders 5.00 12.00
F.Taylor
M10 E.Smith 5.00 12.00
C.Enis
M11 E.Smith 5.00 12.00
F.Taylor
M12 C.Enis 2.50 6.00
F.Taylor
M13 J.Elway 8.00 20.00
J.Rice
M14 J.Elway 10.00 25.00
R.Moss
M15 J.Elway 8.00 20.00
C.Woodson
M16 J.Rice 8.00 20.00
R.Moss
M17 J.Rice 5.00 12.00
C.Woodson
M18 R.Moss 6.00 15.00
C.Woodson
M19 T.Davis 3.00 8.00
K.Stewart
M20 T.Davis 3.00 8.00
R.Watters
M21 T.Davis 3.00 8.00
K.Dyson
M22 K.Stewart 2.50 6.00
R.Watters
M23 K.Stewart 2.50 6.00
K.Dyson
M24 R.Watters 2.00 5.00
K.Dyson
M25 W.Dunn 3.00 8.00
E.George
M26 W.Dunn 2.00 5.00
C.Martin
M27 W.Dunn 2.50 6.00
R.Edwards
M28 E.George 3.00 8.00
C.Martin
M29 E.George 3.00 8.00
R.Edwards
M30 C.Martin 3.00 8.00
R.Edwards
M31 P.Manning 12.00 30.00
P.Manning
M32 R.Leaf 2.00 5.00
R.Leaf
M33 C.Enis 2.00 5.00
C.Enis
M34 F.Taylor 2.50 6.00
F.Taylor
M35 R.Moss 6.00 15.00
R.Moss
M36 C.Woodson 4.00 10.00
C.Woodson
M37 R.Watters 2.00 5.00
R.Watters
M38 K.Dyson 2.00 5.00
K.Dyson
M39 C.Martin 2.50 6.00
C.Martin
M40 R.Edwards 2.00 5.00
R.Edwards

1998 Finest Mystery Finest Jumbos 2

Randomly inserted in Series two boxes at the rate of one in four, this three-card set features color player photos printed on large 3 1/2" by 5" cards. A refractive parallel version of this set was also produced with an insertion rate of one in 17 boxes.

COMPLETE SET (3) 12.50 30.00
STATED ODDS 1:4 BOXES
*REFRACTORS: .75X TO 2X HI COL.
REFRACTOR STATED ODDS 1:17 BOXES
M3 B.Favre 6.00 15.00
R.Leaf
M8 B.Sanders 6.00 15.00
C.Enis
M16 J.Rice 12.50 25.00
R.Moss

1998 Finest Stadium Stars

Randomly inserted in Series 2 packs at the rate of one in 45, this 20-card set features action color player photos of current top NFL stars. A jumbo parallel version of this set was also produced with an insertion rate of 1:12 boxes.

COMPLETE SET (20) 40.00 100.00
STATED ODDS 1:45
S1 Barry Sanders 4.00 10.00
S2 Steve Young 1.50 4.00
S3 Emmitt Smith 4.00 10.00
S4 Mark Brunell 1.25 3.00
S5 Curtis Martin 1.25 3.00
S6 Kordell Stewart 1.25 3.00
S7 Jerry Rice 2.50 6.00
S8 Warrick Dunn 1.25 3.00
S9 Peyton Manning 10.00 20.00
S10 Brett Favre 5.00 12.00
S11 Terrell Davis 1.25 3.00
S12 Cris Carter 1.25 3.00
S13 Herman Moore .75 2.00
S14 Troy Aikman 2.50 6.00
S15 Tim Brown 1.25 3.00
S16 Dan Marino 5.00 12.00
S17 Drew Bledsoe 2.00 5.00
S18 Jerome Bettis 1.25 3.00
S19 Ryan Leaf .60 1.50
S20 John Elway 5.00 12.00

1998 Finest Undergrads

Randomly inserted in packs at a rate of one in 72, this 20-card set features color action photos of top young players in the NFL. A refractive parallel version of this set was also produced and seeded in packs at the rate of 1:216.

COMPLETE SET (20) 50.00 120.00
STATED ODDS 1:72H/R, 1:32J
*REFRACTORS: .6X TO 1.5X BASIC INSERTS
REFRACT.STATED ODDS 1:216H/R, 1:96J
U1 Warrick Dunn 1.00 2.50
U2 Tony Gonzalez 1.00 2.50
U3 Antowain Smith .60 1.50
U4 Jake Plummer 1.00 2.50
U5 Peter Boulware .30 .75
U6 Derrick Rodgers .30 .75
U7 Freddie Jones .30 .75
U8 Reidel Anthony .30 .75
U9 Bryant Westbrook .30 .75
U10 Corey Dillon 1.00 2.50
U11 Curtis Enis .30 .75
U12 Andre Wadsworth .60 1.50
U13 Fred Taylor 1.50 4.00
U14 Greg Ellis .30 .75
U15 Ryan Leaf .60 1.50
U16 Robert Edwards .60 1.50
U17 Germane Crowell .30 .75
U18 Brian Griese 2.00 5.00
U19 Kevin Dyson 1.00 2.50
U20 Peyton Manning 12.00 30.00

1998-99 Finest Pro Bowl Jumbos

This set of cards was distributed by Topps for the 1999 Pro Bowl Card Show in Hawaii. Each card measures roughly 4" by 5 5/8" and is essentially an enlarged version of the base Finest card with a Pro Bowl logo on the cardfronts. A Refractor version of each card was also issued.

COMPLETE SET (12) 20.00 50.00
*REFRACTORS: 3X TO 8X
1 John Elway 3.00 8.00
2 Steve Young 1.50 4.00
3 Brett Favre 3.00 8.00
4 Fred Taylor 2.00 5.00
5 Robert Edwards 1.25 3.00
6 Peyton Manning 4.00 10.00
7 Randy Moss 2.00 5.00
8 Jerry Rice 1.50 4.00
9 Dan Marino 3.00 8.00
10 Terrell Davis 1.50 4.00
11 Drew Bledsoe 1.25 3.00
12 Barry Sanders 2.50 6.00

1998-99 Finest Pro Bowl Promos 5X7

1 John Elway 3.00 8.00
2 Brett Favre 3.00 8.00
3 Terrell Davis 1.50 4.00
4 Randy Moss 2.00 5.00
5 Barry Sanders 2.50 6.00
6 Steve Young 1.25 3.00

1998-99 Finest Super Bowl Jumbos

This set of cards was distributed by Topps for the Super Bowl XXXIII Card Show in Miami. Each card measures roughly 4" by 5 5/8" and is essentially an enlarged version of the base Finest card. Each card was distributed in exchange for 5-Topps wrappers at the show.

COMPLETE SET (12) 24.00 60.00
1 John Elway 3.20 8.00
2 Steve Young 1.20 3.00
3 Brett Favre 3.20 8.00
4 Fred Taylor 2.40 6.00
5 Robert Edwards 1.20 3.00
6 Peyton Manning 4.00 10.00
7 Randy Moss 5.00 10.00
8 Jerry Rice 1.60 4.00
9 Dan Marino 3.20 8.00
10 Terrell Davis 2.40 6.00
11 Drew Bledsoe 1.20 3.00
12 Barry Sanders 3.20 8.00

1998-99 Finest Super Bowl Promos

This six card set and accompaning Refractors set was released at the 1999 Super Bowl Card Show in Miami and the Hawaii Trade Conference in February 1999. Each is numbered "X of 6" and features the Super Bowl XXXIII logo on the cardfront.

COMPLETE SET (6) 10.00 25.00
*REFRACTORS: 2X TO 4X BASE CARD
1 Terrell Davis 2.00 5.00
2 Steve Young 1.20 3.00
3 Brett Favre 2.40 6.00
4 Fred Taylor 1.60 4.00
5 Robert Edwards 1.20 3.00
6 Randy Moss 5.00 10.00

1999 Finest Promos

This set of cards was distributed to hobbyists to promote the upcoming 1999 Finest football card release. Each card is nearly identical to the matching base issue card except for the card number on the back.

COMPLETE SET (6) 3.00 8.00
PP1 Charlie Batch .40 1.00
PP2 Jimmy Smith .50 1.25
PP3 Jake Plummer .60 1.50
PP4 O.J. McDuffie .40 1.00
PP5 Curtis Martin .75 2.00
PP6 Corey Dillon .60 1.50

1999 Finest

The 1999 Finest set was released in mid September 1999 as a 175-card single series set consisting of 124 veterans and 51 bonus base cards, divided into three subsets, Rookies, Gems, and Sensations. The short printed Rookies subset contains the games best young players such as Edgerrin James and Ricky Williams each being designated with the Finest Rookie Card logo stamp. Gems showcases 11 of todays biggest stars with each cards background featuring an etched "gem" pattern. Sensations features 11 emerging talents such as Peyton Manning and Randy Moss. Each cards background is highlighted with a multi-etched design. Each base card is printed on a 27 pt. thickness stock. The S.R.P. is $5.00 per pack with five cards in a pack. Thirteen card collector packs, available exclusively through Home Team Advantage stores, contain eleven base cards plus two bonus cards with an S.R.P. of $10.00 per pack.

COMPLETE SET (175) 30.00 80.00
COMP.SET w/o SPs (124) 15.00 30.00
1 Peyton Manning 1.25 3.00
2 Priest Holmes .25 .60
3 Kordell Stewart .25 .60
4 Shannon Sharpe .30 .75
5 Andre Rison .30 .75
6 Rickey Dudley .25 .60
7 Duce Staley .25 .60
8 Randall Cunningham .30 .75
9 Warrick Dunn .25 .60
10 Dan Marino .75 2.00
11 Kevin Greene .40 1.00
12 Garrison Hearst .25 .60
13 Eric Moulds .25 .60
14 Marvin Harrison .30 .75
15 Eddie George .30 .75
16 Vinny Testaverde .25 .60
17 Brad Johnson .30 .75
18 Derrick Thomas .60 1.50
19 Chris Chandler .30 .75
20 Troy Aikman .50 1.25
21 Terance Mathis .25 .60
22 Terrell Owens .30 .75
23 Junior Seau .30 .75
24 Cris Carter .40 1.00
25 Fred Taylor .25 .60
26 Adrian Murrell .25 .60
27 Terry Glenn .30 .75
28 Rod Smith .30 .75
29 Darnay Scott .25 .60
30 Brett Favre .75 2.00
31 Cam Cleeland .25 .60
32 Ricky Watters .30 .75
33 Derrick Alexander .25 .60
34 Bruce Smith .30 .75
35 Steve McNair .30 .75
36 Wayne Chrebet .25 .60
37 Herman Moore .30 .75
38 Bert Emanuel .30 .75
39 Michael Irvin .40 1.00
40 Steve Young .50 1.25
41 Napoleon Kaufman .25 .60
42 Tim Biakabutuka .30 .75
43 Isaac Bruce .40 1.00
44 J.J. Stokes .25 .60
45 Antonio Freeman .30 .75
46 John Randle .40 1.00
47 Frank Sanders .25 .60
48 O.J. McDuffie .30 .75
49 Keenan McCardell .30 .75
50 Randy Moss .30 .75
51 Ed McCaffrey .30 .75
52 Yancey Thigpen .25 .60
53 Curtis Conway .30 .75
54 Mike Alstott .25 .60
55 Deion Sanders .30 .75
56 Dorsey Levens .30 .75
57 Joey Galloway .30 .75
58 Natrone Means .30 .75
59 Tim Brown .40 1.00
60 Jerry Rice 1.00 2.50
61 Robert Smith .25 .60
62 Carl Pickens .30 .75
63 Ben Coates .30 .75
64 Jerome Bettis .40 1.00
65 Corey Dillon .25 .60
66 Curtis Martin .30 .75
67 Jimmy Smith .30 .75
68 Keyshawn Johnson .30 .75
69 Charlie Batch .25 .60
70 Jamal Anderson .30 .75
71 Mark Brunell .30 .75
72 Antowain Smith .25 .60
73 Aeneas Williams .25 .60
74 Wesley Walls .30 .75
75 Jake Plummer .25 .60
76 Oronde Gadsden .25 .60
77 Gary Brown .25 .60
78 Peter Boulware .25 .60
79 Stephen Alexander .25 .60
80 Barry Sanders .60 1.50
81 Warren Sapp .30 .75
82 Michael Sinclair .25 .60
83 Freddie Jones .25 .60
84 Ike Hilliard .25 .60
85 Jake Reed .30 .75
86 Tim Dwight .30 .75
87 Johnnie Morton .30 .75
88 Robert Brooks .30 .75
89 Rocket Ismail .30 .75
90 Emmitt Smith .60 1.50
91 Ricky Proehl .25 .60
92 James Jett .25 .60
93 Karim Abdul-Jabbar .25 .60
94 Mark Chmura .25 .60
95 Andre Reed .40 1.00
96 Michael Westbrook .25 .60
97 Michael Strahan .30 .75
98 Chad Brown .25 .60
99 Trent Dilfer .25 .60
100 Terrell Davis .30 .75
101 Aaron Glenn .25 .60
102 Skip Hicks .25 .60
103 Tony Gonzalez .30 .75
104 Ty Law .40 1.00
105 Jermaine Lewis .25 .60
106 Ray Lewis .40 1.00
107 Zach Thomas .30 .75
108 Reidel Anthony .25 .60
109 Levon Kirkland .25 .60
110 Drew Bledsoe .30 .75
111 Bobby Engram .25 .60
112 Jerome Pathon .25 .60
113 Muhsin Muhammad .25 .60
114 Vonnie Holliday .25 .60
115 Bill Romanowski .30 .75
116 Marshall Faulk .30 .75
117 Ty Detmer .25 .60
118 Mo Lewis .25 .60
119 Charles Woodson .40 1.00
120 Doug Flutie .40 1.00
121 Jon Kitna .25 .60
122 Courtney Hawkins .25 .60
123 Trent Green .25 .60
124 John Elway .60 1.50
125 Barry Sanders GM 1.25 3.00
126 Brett Favre GM 1.50 4.00
127 Curtis Martin GM .60 1.50
128 Dan Marino GM 1.50 4.00
129 Eddie George GM .60 1.50
130 Emmitt Smith GM 1.25 3.00
131 Jamal Anderson GM .60 1.50
132 Jerry Rice GM 2.00 5.00
133 John Elway GM 1.25 3.00
134 Terrell Davis GM .60 1.50
135 Troy Aikman GM 1.00 2.50
136 Skip Hicks SN .50 1.25
137 Charles Woodson SN .75 2.00
138 Charlie Batch SN .50 1.25
139 Curtis Enis SN .50 1.25
140 Fred Taylor SN .50 1.25
141 Jake Plummer SN .50 1.25
142 Peyton Manning SN 2.50 6.00
143 Randy Moss SN .60 1.50
144 Corey Dillon SN .50 1.25
145 Priest Holmes SN .50 1.25
146 Warrick Dunn SN .50 1.25
147 Jevon Kearse RC .75 2.00
148 Chris Claiborne RC .60 1.50
149 Akili Smith RC .60 1.50
150 Brock Huard RC .60 1.50
151 Daunte Culpepper RC 1.00 2.50
152 Edgerrin James RC 1.00 2.50
153 Cecil Collins RC .60 1.50
154 Kevin Faulk RC .60 1.50
155 Amos Zereoue RC .60 1.50
156 James Johnson RC .60 1.50
157 Sedrick Irvin RC .60 1.50
158 Ricky Williams RC 1.00 2.50
159 Mike Cloud RC .60 1.50
160 Chris McAlister RC .60 1.50
161 Rob Konrad RC .60 1.50
162 Champ Bailey RC 1.25 3.00
163 Ebenezer Ekuban RC .60 1.50
164 Tim Couch RC .75 2.00
165 Cade McNown RC .60 1.50
166 Donovan McNabb RC 2.00 5.00
167 Joe Germaine RC .75 2.00
168 Shaun King RC .60 1.50
169 Peerless Price RC .60 1.50
170 Kevin Johnson RC .75 2.00
171 Troy Edwards RC .60 1.50
172 Karsten Bailey RC .60 1.50
173 David Boston RC .60 1.50
174 D'Wayne Bates RC .60 1.50
175 Torry Holt RC 1.25 3.00

1999 Finest Gold Refractors

*1-124 VETS: 12X TO 30X BASIC CARDS
*125-135 GEMS: 6X TO 15X BASIC CARDS
*136-146 SENSATION: 6X TO 15X BASIC SN
*147-175 ROOKIES: 5X TO 12X BASIC RC
STATED ODDS 1:72 H/R, 1:33 HTA
STATED PRINT RUN 100 SERIAL #'d SETS

1999 Finest Refractors

*1-124 VETS: 3X TO 8X BASIC CARDS
*125-135 GEMS: 1.5X TO 4X BASIC GEM
*136-146 SENSATION: 1.5X TO 4X BASIC SN
*147-175 ROOKIES: 1.5X TO 3X BASIC RC
STATED ODDS 1:12 H/R, 1:5 HTA

1999 Finest Double Team Left Side Refractors

Randomly inserted in packs at the rate of 1:50, this split screen card combines refractor and non-refractor technology on the same card. There are 14 paired players on seven different cards with the following cardfrontvariations; right side refractor/left side non-refractor, left side refractor/right side non-refractor, and dual refractor.

COMPLETE SET (7) 8.00 20.00
*RIGHT/LEFT REF.VARIATIONS EQUAL VALUE
STATED ODDS 1:50 H/R, 1:24 HTA
*DUAL REFRACTORS: .8X TO 2X
DUAL REFRACTOR ODDS 1:150H/R, 1:72HTA
DT1 Ak.Smith 1.25 3.00
C.Pickens
DT2 C.McNown 1.00 2.50
C.Enis
DT3 D.Flutie 1.50 4.00
E.Moulds
DT4 M.Brunell 1.25 3.00
F.Taylor
DT5 K.Stewart 1.50 4.00
J.Bettis
DT6 J.Kitna 1.25 3.00
J.Galloway
DT7 W.Dunn 1.00 2.50
M.Alstott

1999 Finest Future's Finest

Randomly inserted in packs at (1:253), this set contains the top rookies and is sequentially numbered to 500 with refractors sequentially numbered to 100. These cards have an "F" prefix.

COMPLETE SET (10) 25.00 60.00
FUTURE/500 ODDS 1:253 H/R, 1:117 HTA
*REFRACT/100: 1X TO 2.5X INSERT/500
REFRACT/100 ODDS 1:1262 H/R, 1:583 HTA
F1 Akili Smith 1.50 4.00
F2 Cade McNown 1.50 4.00
F3 Champ Bailey 3.00 8.00
F4 Daunte Culpepper 2.50 6.00
F5 David Boston 1.50 4.00
F6 Donovan McNabb 5.00 12.00
F7 Edgerrin James 2.50 6.00
F8 Ricky Williams 2.50 6.00
F9 Tim Couch 2.00 5.00
F10 Torry Holt 3.00 8.00

1999 Finest Leading Indicators

Randomly inserted in packs (1:30), this 10 card set of various stars features a unique, heat sensative, thermal ink technology used on the top third of the card and when touched on various spots reveals the players statistics. These cards have an "L" prefix and a peel back protective film covering the front of the card.

COMPLETE SET (10) 12.00 30.00
STATED ODDS 1:30 H/R, 1:14 HTA
L1 Jamal Anderson 1.50 4.00
L2 Doug Flutie 1.50 4.00
L3 Drew Bledsoe 2.00 5.00
L4 Eddie George 1.50 4.00
L5 Emmitt Smith 3.00 8.00
L6 John Elway 5.00 12.00
L7 Keyshawn Johnson 1.50 4.00
L8 Steve Young 2.00 5.00
L9 Terrell Owens 1.50 4.00
L10 Vinny Testaverde 1.00 2.50

1999 Finest Main Attractions Left Side Refractors

Randomly inserted in packs (1:50), this 7 card set, which pairs 14 players, combines refractor and non-refractor technology. There are three versions, non-refractor/refractor, refractor/non-refractor and refractor/refractor. These cards have an "MA" prefix.

COMPLETE SET (7) 15.00 40.00
*RIGHT/LEFT REF.VARIATIONS: SAME VALUE
STATED ODDS 1:50 H/R, 1:24 HTA
*DUAL REFRACTOR: .8X TO 2X BASIC INSERT
DUAL REFRACTOR ODDS 1:150H/R, 1:72HTA
MA1 C.Bailey 3.00 8.00
D.Sanders
MA2 D.Culpepper 2.50 6.00
S.McNair
MA3 D.McNabb 5.00 12.00
K.Stewart
MA4 E.James 4.00 10.00
M.Faulk
MA5 K.Faulk 2.50 6.00
W.Dunn
MA6 J.Germaine 4.00 10.00
T.Aikman
MA7 R Konrad 2.50 6.00
M.Alstott

1999 Finest Prominent Figures

Randomly inserted in packs, this set consisits of 6 separate statistical category cards, passing yards (1:25) and serial numbered to 5084, touchdown passes (1:2,634) and serial numbered to 48, rushing yards (1:60) and serial numbered to 2105, rushing touchdowns (1:5099) and serial numbered to 25, receiving yards (1:68) and serial numbered to 1848, and touchdown receptions (1:5,779) and serial numbered to 22. These cards are in refractor form with a "PF" prefix.

QB-YARDAGE PRINT RUN 5084 SER.#'d SETS
QB-YARDAGE ODDS 1:25H/R,1:11HTA
QB-TDs PRINT RUN 48 SER.#'d SETS
QB-TDs STATED ODDS 1:2634H/R,1:1220HTA
RB-TDs PRINT RUN 25 SER.#'d SETS
RB-TDs STATED ODDS 1:5099H/R,1:2333HTA
RB-YARDAGE PRINT RUN 2105 SER.#'d SETS
RB-YARD.STATED ODDS 1:60H/R,1:28HTA
WR-TDs PRINT RUN 22 SER.#'d SETS
WR-TDs STATED ODDS 1:5779H/R,1:2660HTA
WR-YARDAGE PRINT RUN 1848 SER.#'d SETS
WR-YARDAGE ODDS 1:68H/R, 1:32HTA
PF1 Brett Favre 4.00 10.00
PF2 Dan Marino 4.00 10.00
PF3 Drew Bledsoe 1.50 4.00
PF4 Jake Plummer .60 1.50
PF5 Mark Brunell .60 1.50
PF6 Peyton Manning 3.00 8.00
PF7 Randall Cunningham 1.00 2.50
PF8 Steve Young 1.50 4.00
PF9 Tim Couch 1.00 2.50
PF10 Vinny Testaverde .60 1.50
PF11 Brett Favre 60.00 150.00
PF12 Dan Marino 60.00 150.00
PF13 Drew Bledsoe 25.00 60.00
PF14 Jake Plummer 10.00 25.00
PF15 Mark Brunell 10.00 25.00
PF16 Peyton Manning 50.00 120.00
PF17 Randall Cunningham 15.00 40.00
PF18 Steve Young 25.00 60.00
PF19 Tim Couch 15.00 40.00
PF20 Vinny Testaverde .60 1.50
PF21 Barry Sanders 100.00 250.00
PF22 Curtis Martin 35.00 80.00
PF23 Eddie George 35.00 80.00
PF24 Emmitt Smith 60.00 150.00
PF25 Fred Taylor 35.00 80.00
PF26 Garrison Hearst 25.00 60.00
PF27 Jamal Anderson 25.00 60.00
PF28 Marshall Faulk 40.00 100.00
PF29 Ricky Williams 40.00 100.00
PF30 Terrell Davis 35.00 80.00
PF31 Barry Sanders 7.50 20.00
PF32 Curtis Martin 2.50 6.00
PF33 Eddie George 2.50 6.00
PF34 Emmitt Smith 5.00 12.00
PF35 Fred Taylor 2.50 6.00
PF36 Garrison Hearst 2.00 5.00
PF37 Jamal Anderson 2.00 5.00
PF38 Marshall Faulk 4.00 10.00
PF39 Ricky Williams 4.00 10.00
PF40 Terrell Davis 2.50 6.00
PF41 Antonio Freeman 25.00 60.00
PF42 David Boston 15.00 40.00
PF43 Cris Carter 25.00 60.00
PF44 Jerry Rice 60.00 150.00
PF45 Joey Galloway 15.00 40.00
PF46 Keyshawn Johnson 25.00 60.00
PF47 Randy Moss 75.00 150.00
PF48 Terrell Owens 25.00 60.00
PF49 Tim Brown 25.00 60.00
PF50 Torry Holt 30.00 80.00
PF51 Antonio Freeman 2.00 5.00
PF52 David Boston 2.00 5.00
PF53 Eric Moulds 2.00 5.00
PF54 Jerry Rice 5.00 12.00
PF55 Joey Galloway 1.25 3.00
PF56 Keyshawn Johnson 2.00 5.00
PF57 Randy Moss 5.00 12.00
PF58 Terrell Owens 2.00 5.00
PF59 Jimmy Smith 1.25 3.00
PF60 Torry Holt 4.00 10.00

1999 Finest Salute

These randomly inserted cards honor three 1998 season award winners all on one card: Randy Moss, Terrell Davis, and John Elway. The base card was inserted at the rate of 1:53. It is also available in a Refractor version (1:1900) and as a sequentially numbered to 100 die-cut Gold Refractor (1:12,384).

STATED ODDS 1:53 HOB, 1:25 HTA
REFRACTOR ODDS 1:1900 HOB,1:790 HTA
GOLD REF.ODDS 1:12,384 HOB,1:5782 HTA
GOLD REFRACTOR PRINT RUN 100 CARDS
FS T.Davis/Elway/Moss 4.00 10.00
FSR T.Davis/Elway/Moss REF 15.00 40.00
FSGR T.Davis/Elway/Moss GR/100 75.00 150.00

1999 Finest Team Finest

Randomly inserted in packs this set consists of three different versions: The base set Blue-sequentially numbered to 1500 with a blue refractor version numbered to 150, Red-sequentially numbered to 500 with a red refractor version numbered to 50, and Gold-sequentially numbered to 250 with a gold refractor version numbered to 25.

COMPLETE SET (10) 30.00 80.00
BLUE/1500 ODDS 1:84 HOB, 1:39 HTA
*BLUE REFRACTOR/150: 1.2X TO 3X BLUE
BLUE REF/150 ODDS 1:843 HOB,1:389 HTA
*GOLD/250: 1X TO 2.5X BLUE
GOLD/250 STATED ODDS 1:57 HTA
*GOLD REFRACTOR/25: 4X TO 10X BLUE
GOLD REFRACTOR/25 ODDS 1:573 HTA
*RED/500: .8X TO 2X BLUE
RED/500 STATED ODDS 1:29 HTA
*RED REFRACTOR/50: 2.5X TO 6X BLUE
RED REFRACTOR/50 ODDS 1:285 HTA
T1 Barry Sanders 3.00 8.00
T2 Brett Favre 4.00 10.00
T3 Dan Marino 4.00 10.00
T4 Drew Bledsoe 1.50 4.00
T5 Jamal Anderson 1.50 4.00
T6 John Elway 3.00 8.00
T7 Peyton Manning 6.00 15.00
T8 Randy Moss 1.50 4.00
T9 Terrell Davis 1.50 4.00
T10 Troy Aikman 2.50 6.00

1999-00 Finest Pro Bowl Jumbos

This set of cards was distributed by Topps directly to dealers at the 2000 Pro Bowl Card Show in Hawaii. Each card measures roughly 3 1/2" by 4 7/8" and is essentially an enlarged version of the Finest Pro Bowl and Super Bowl promos printed in the bi-fold format. A Refractor version was produced as well.

COMPLETE SET (12) 24.00 60.00
*REFRACTORS: 4X TO 10X BASIC CARDS
1 Brett Favre 3.20 8.00
2 Marvin Harrison .80 2.00
3 Marshall Faulk
4 Randy Moss 3.20 8.00
5 Kurt Warner 6.00 15.00
6 Stephen Davis .80 2.00
7 Peyton Manning 3.20 8.00
8 Edgerrin James 4.80 12.00
9 Drew Bledsoe 1.00 2.50
10 Emmitt Smith 2.00 5.00
11 Terrell Davis 2.00 5.00
12 Brad Johnson .80 2.00

1999-00 Finest Pro Bowl Promos

This 12-card standard sized set was released at the 2000 Pro Bowl Card Show in Hawaii. Each player's card is essentially a parallel to the Finest Super Bowl set released a week earlier in Atlanta except that the Super Bowl logo has been replaced by the Pro Bowl logo.

COMPLETE SET (12) 24.00 60.00
*REFRACTORS: 4X TO 10X BASIC CARDS
1 Brett Favre 3.20 8.00
2 Marvin Harrison .60 1.50
3 Marshall Faulk .60 1.50
4 Randy Moss 3.20 8.00
5 Kurt Warner 6.00 15.00
6 Stephen Davis .60 1.50
7 Peyton Manning 3.20 8.00
8 Edgerrin James 4.80 12.00
9 Drew Bledsoe 1.00 2.50
10 Emmitt Smith .60 1.50
11 Terrell Davis 2.00 5.00
12 Brad Johnson .60 1.50

1999-00 Finest Super Bowl Promos

This 12-card set and accompaning Refractors parallel set was released at the 2000 Super Bowl Card Show in Atlanta as a wrapper redemption. Eight player's cards were similar to their base 1999 Finest card with 4-additional player's added to the set. Each features the Super Bowl XXXIV logo on the cardfront and was produced in a bi-fold format.

COMPLETE SET (12) 24.00 60.00
*REFRACTORS: 4X TO 10X BASIC CARDS
1 Brett Favre 3.20 8.00
2 Marvin Harrison .60 1.50
3 Marshall Faulk .60 1.50
4 Randy Moss 3.20 8.00
5 Kurt Warner 6.00 15.00
6 Stephen Davis .60 1.50
7 Peyton Manning 3.20 8.00
8 Edgerrin James 4.80 12.00
9 Drew Bledsoe 1.00 2.50
10 Emmitt Smith 2.00 5.00
11 Terrell Davis 2.00 5.00
12 Brad Johnson .60 1.60

2000 Finest

Released as a 190-card base set, Finest football features 125 veteran cards, 40 rookie cards inserted in packs at one in 11 and one in five HTA sequentially numbered to 2400, 30 dual player Inherent Fire cards (card numbers 166-195) inserted at one in eight packs and one in three HTA, and 10 Gems cards (card numbers 195-205) inserted at one in 24 and one in nine HTA. Finest was packaged in 24-pack boxes with each pack containing five cards and carried a suggested retail price of $3.25; and Finest HTA was packaged in 12-pack boxes with packs containing 11 cards and carried a suggested retail price of $9.99. A special PSA redemption card limited to 10 total was inserted in packs at the rate of one in 12278 HTA which is redeemable for a complete set of the graded rookie subset.

COMPLETE SET (205) 150.00 300.00
COMP.SET w/o SP's (125) 12.50 30.00
126-165 ROOKIE/2400 ODDS 1:11, 1:5 HTA
1 Tim Dwight .25 .60
2 Cade McNown .20 .50
3 Drew Bledsoe .25 .60
4 Torry Holt .25 .60
5 Derrick Mayes .20 .50
6 Vinny Testaverde .20 .50
7 Patrick Jeffers .20 .50
8 Dorsey Levens .25 .60
9 James Johnson .20 .50
10 Champ Bailey .25 .60
11 Jeff George .25 .60
12 Shawn Jefferson .20 .50
13 Terrence Wilkins .20 .50
14 J.J. Stokes .25 .60
15 Doug Flutie .25 .60
16 Corey Dillon .20 .50
17 Rod Smith .25 .60
18 Jimmy Smith .25 .60
19 Amani Toomer .20 .50
20 Curtis Conway .25 .60
21 Brad Johnson .25 .60
22 Edgerrin James .25 .60
23 Derrick Alexander .20 .50
24 Terrell Owens .25 .60
25 Kurt Warner .50 1.25
26 Frank Sanders .20 .50
27 Tony Banks .20 .50
28 Troy Aikman .40 1.00
29 Curtis Enis .20 .50
30 Eddie George .25 .60
31 Bill Schroeder .25 .60
32 Kent Graham .20 .50
33 Mike Alstott .20 .50
34 Steve Young .40 1.00
35 Jacquez Green .20 .50
36 Frank Wycheck .25 .60
37 Kerry Collins .20 .50
38 Stephen Davis .20 .50
39 Tony Gonzalez .25 .60
40 Tyrone Wheatley .20 .50
41 Brett Favre .60 1.50
42 Joey Galloway .25 .60
43 Terrell Davis .25 .60
44 Marvin Harrison .25 .60
45 Zach Thomas .25 .60
46 Jerry Rice .75 2.00
47 Keyshawn Johnson .25 .60
48 Rob Johnson .25 .60
49 Rocket Ismail .25 .60
50 Elvis Grbac .20 .50
51 Warrick Dunn .20 .50
52 Jevon Kearse .20 .50
53 Albert Connell .20 .50
54 Muhsin Muhammad .20 .50
55 Carl Pickens .25 .60
56 Peyton Manning .75 2.00
57 Daunte Culpepper .25 .60
58 Ike Hilliard .20 .50
59 Steve McNair .25 .60
60 Sean Dawkins .20 .50
61 Steve Beuerlein .25 .60
62 Priest Holmes .20 .50
63 Jim Harbaugh .25 .60
64 Germane Crowell .20 .50
65 Cris Carter .30 .75
66 Jamal Anderson .25 .60
67 Kevin Johnson .20 .50
68 Herman Moore .20 .50
69 Ricky Williams .25 .60
70 Rich Gannon .25 .60
71 Isaac Bruce .30 .75
72 Peerless Price .25 .60
73 Az-Zahir Hakim .20 .50
74 Mark Brunell .25 .60
75 Rob Moore .20 .50
76 Antowain Smith .25 .60
77 Tim Biakabutuka .25 .60
78 Ed McCaffrey .25 .60
79 Tony Martin .25 .60
80 Marcus Robinson .25 .60
81 Kevin Dyson .25 .60
82 Wesley Walls .20 .50
83 Chris Chandler .25 .60
84 Keenan McCardell .25 .60
85 Napoleon Kaufman .25 .60
86 Emmitt Smith .50 1.25
87 James Stewart .20 .50
88 Tim Brown .30 .75
89 Ricky Watters .25 .60
90 Johnnie Morton .25 .60
91 Jake Plummer .20 .50
92 Olandis Gary .25 .60
93 Jerome Bettis .30 .75
94 Terry Glenn .25 .60
95 Kordell Stewart .20 .50
96 Charlie Garner .25 .60
97 Yancey Thigpen .20 .50
98 Michael Westbrook .20 .50
99 Bobby Engram .20 .50
100 Eric Moulds .20 .50
101 Darnay Scott .25 .60
102 Antonio Freeman .25 .60
103 Wayne Chrebet .20 .50
104 Akili Smith .20 .50
105 Jeff Blake .25 .60
106 Curtis Martin .25 .60
107 Errict Rhett .25 .60
108 Damon Huard .20 .50
109 Jeff Graham .20 .50
110 Terance Mathis .20 .50
111 Jon Kitna .20 .50
112 Tim Couch .25 .60
113 Fred Taylor .20 .50
114 Qadry Ismail .20 .50
115 Donovan McNabb .25 .60
116 Charles Johnson .20 .50
117 Troy Edwards .20 .50
118 Shaun King .20 .50
119 Charlie Batch .20 .50
120 Robert Smith .20 .50
121 Marshall Faulk .25 .60
122 Brian Griese .20 .50
123 O.J. McDuffie .25 .60
124 Randy Moss .25 .60
125 Duce Staley .20 .50
126 Peter Warrick RC 1.50 4.00
127 Dez White RC 1.50 4.00
128 Ron Dayne RC 2.50 6.00
129 J.R. Redmond RC 1.50 4.00
130 Thomas Jones RC 2.00 5.00
131 Plaxico Burress RC 2.00 5.00
132 Reuben Droughns RC 1.50 4.00
133 Shaun Alexander RC 2.50 6.00
134 Ron Dugans RC 1.50 4.00
135 Travis Prentice RC 1.50 4.00
136 Joe Hamilton RC 1.50 4.00
137 Curtis Keaton RC 1.50 4.00
138 Chris Redman RC 1.50 4.00
139 Chad Pennington RC 2.00 5.00
140 Travis Taylor RC 1.50 4.00
141 Bubba Franks RC 1.50 4.00
142 Dennis Northcutt RC 1.50 4.00
143 Jerry Porter RC 2.50 6.00
144 Sylvester Morris RC 1.50 4.00
145 Anthony Becht RC 1.50 4.00
146 Trung Canidate RC 1.50 4.00
147 Jamal Lewis RC 2.50 6.00
148 R.Jay Soward RC 1.50 4.00
149 Tee Martin RC 1.50 4.00
150 Courtney Brown RC 2.00 5.00
151 Brian Urlacher RC 8.00 20.00
152 Danny Farmer RC 1.50 4.00
153 Laveranues Coles RC 2.00 5.00
154 Todd Pinkston RC 1.50 4.00
155 Corey Simon RC 2.00 5.00
156 Spergon Wynn RC 1.50 4.00
157 Tim Rattay RC 2.00 5.00
158 Todd Husak RC 1.50 4.00
159 Aaron Shea RC 2.00 5.00
160 Giovanni Carmazzi RC 1.50 4.00
161 Trevor Gaylor RC 1.50 4.00
162 JaJuan Dawson RC 1.50 4.00
163 Jarious Jackson RC 2.00 5.00
164 Chris Samuels RC 2.50 6.00
165 Rob Morris RC 2.00 5.00
166 P.Warrick .60 1.50
R.Moss IF
167 R.Moss .60 1.50
P.Warrick IF
168 T.Prentice .50 1.25
S.Davis IF
169 S.Davis .50 1.25
T.Prentice IF
170 C.Redman 1.25 3.00
K.Warner IF
171 K.Warner 1.25 3.00
C.Redman IF
172 Syl.Morris .60 1.50
J.Smith IF
173 J.Smith .60 1.50
Syl.Morris IF
174 C.Pennington 2.00 5.00
P.Manning IF
175 P.Manning 2.00 5.00
C.Pennington IF
176 R.Soward .60 1.50
M.Harrison IF
177 M.Harrison .60 1.50
R.Soward IF
178 R.Dayne .75 2.00
J.Anderson IF
179 J.Anderson .75 2.00
R.Dayne IF
180 S.Alexander .50 1.25
E.George IF
181 E.George .50 1.25
S.Alexander IF
182 C.Brown .60 1.50
B.Smith IF
183 B.Smith .60 1.50
C.Brown IF
184 J.Lewis .50 1.25
E.James IF
185 E.James .50 1.25
J.Lewis IF
186 T.Canidate 1.25 3.00
E.Smith IF
187 E.Smith 1.25 3.00
T.Canidate IF
188 T.Taylor .75 2.00
C.Carter IF
189 C.Carter .75 2.00
T.Taylor IF
190 C.Keaton .60 1.50
M.Faulk IF
191 M.Faulk .60 1.50
C.Keaton IF
192 P.Burress 2.00 5.00
J.Rice IF
193 J.Rice 2.00 5.00
P.Burress IF
194 T.Jones .40 1.00
T.Davis IF
195 T.Davis .40 1.00
T.Jones IF
196 Peyton Manning GM 1.50 4.00
197 Randy Moss GM .50 1.25
198 Terrell Davis GM .50 1.25
199 Marshall Faulk GM .50 1.25
200 Edgerrin James GM .50 1.25
201 Emmitt Smith GM 1.00 2.50
202 Ricky Williams GM .50 1.25
203 Kurt Warner GM 1.00 2.50
204 Eddie George GM .50 1.25
205 Brett Favre GM 1.25 3.00

2000 Finest Gold/Refractors

*VETS 1-125: 5X TO 12X BASIC CARDS
1-125 VET/300 ODDS 1:26, 1:14 HTA
1-125 VETERAN PRINT RUN 300
*ROOKIES 126-165: 1X TO 2.5X
126-165 ROOKIE/200 ODDS 1:132, 1:54 HTA
126-165 ROOKIE PRINT RUN 200
*IF 166-195: 3X TO 8X BASIC CARDS
166-195 IF/100 ODDS 1:365, 1:134 HTA
166-195 IF PRINT RUN 100
*GM 196-205: 5X TO 12X BASIC CARDS
196-205 GM/50 ODDS 1:2372, 1:703 HTA
196-205 GM PRINT RUN 50

2000 Finest Moments

Randomly inserted in packs at the rate of one in 8, and one in four HTA, this 25-card set identifies and pictures 25 of the NFL's finest moments.

COMPLETE SET (25) 10.00 25.00
STATED ODDS 1:8, 1:4 HTA
*REFRACTOR: .8X TO 2X BASIC INSERTS
REFRACTOR ODDS 1:18, 1:8 HTA
FM1 Bart Starr 1.50 4.00
FM2 Phil Simms .60 1.50
FM3 John Elway 1.00 2.50
FM4 Dan Marino 1.25 3.00
FM5 Kellen Winslow .50 1.25
FM6 Franco Harris .75 2.00
FM7 Stephen Davis .40 1.00
FM8 Isaac Bruce .60 1.50
FM9 Edgerrin James .50 1.25
FM10 Marshall Faulk .50 1.25
FM11 Patrick Jeffers .40 1.00
FM12 Kurt Warner 1.00 2.50
FM13 Joe Montana 2.00 5.00
FM14 Kevin Carter .40 1.00
FM15 Andre Reed .60 1.50
FM16 Torry Holt .50 1.25
FM17 F.Wycheck .50 1.25
K.Dyson
FM18 Jason Elam .40 1.00
FM19 Mike Jones LB .40 1.00
FM20 Cade McNown .40 1.00
FM21 Germane Crowell .40 1.00
FM22 Bruce Matthews .40 1.00
FM23 Champ Bailey .50 1.25
FM24 Qadry Ismail .40 1.00
FM25 Tony Brackens .40 1.00

2000 Finest Moments Refractors Autographs

Randomly inserted in packs at the rate of one in 48, and 1:22 HTA this 25-card set parallels the Finest Moments Refractors set enhanced with authentic player autographs. Card #17 was issued with either a Frank Wycheck or a Kevin Dyson autograph on the front. Each card has a Topps "Genuine Issue" authenticity sticker on the back.

OVERALL STATED ODDS 1:48, 1:22 HTA
FM1 Bart Starr 90.00 150.00

FM2 Phil Simms 15.00 40.00
FM3 John Elway 75.00 150.00
FM4 Dan Marino 100.00 200.00
FM5 Kellen Winslow 20.00 50.00
FM6 Franco Harris 50.00 100.00
FM7 Stephen Davis 6.00 15.00
FM8 Isaac Bruce 25.00 60.00
FM9 Edgerrin James 8.00 20.00
FM10 Marshall Faulk 30.00 60.00
FM11 Patrick Jeffers 6.00 15.00
FM12 Kurt Warner 60.00 120.00
FM13 Joe Montana 75.00 150.00
FM14 Kevin Carter 6.00 15.00
FM15 Andre Reed 10.00 25.00
FM16 Torry Holt 8.00 20.00
FM17A F.Wycheck AU 8.00 20.00
K.Dyson
FM17B F.Wycheck 8.00 20.00
K.Dyson AU
FM18 Jason Elam 12.00 30.00
FM19 Mike Jones LB 6.00 15.00
FM20 Cade McNown 6.00 15.00
FM21 Germane Crowell 6.00 15.00
FM22 Bruce Matthews 6.00 15.00
FM23 Champ Bailey 10.00 25.00
FM24 Qadry Ismail 6.00 15.00
FM25 Tony Brackens 6.00 15.00

2000 Finest Moments Jumbos

Inserted at one per box, this set utilizes the card stock from the base Finest Moments insert set in jumbo card format.
COMPLETE SET (7) 12.50 30.00
ONE PER BOX
1 Bart Starr 2.50 6.00
2 Phil Simms 1.00 2.50
3 John Elway 1.50 4.00
4 Dan Marino 2.00 5.00
5 Edgerrin James .75 2.00
6 Marshall Faulk .75 2.00
7 Joe Montana 3.00 8.00

2000 Finest NFL Europe's Finest

Randomly inserted in packs at the rate of one in 24, and one in 12 HTA, this 10-card set spotlights 10 NFL players who have played European Football.
COMPLETE SET (10) 4.00 10.00
STATED ODDS 1:24, 1:12 HTA
E1 Kurt Warner 1.25 3.00
E2 Bill Schroeder .60 1.50
E3 Andy McCullough .50 1.25
E4 Dameyune Craig .50 1.25
E5 Marcus Robinson .60 1.50
E6 La'Roi Glover .50 1.25
E7 Damon Huard .50 1.25
E8 Brad Johnson .60 1.50
E9 Jake Delhomme .60 1.50
E10 Jon Kitna .50 1.25

2000 Finest Out of the Blue

Randomly inserted in packs at the rate of one in 24, and one in 12 HTA, this 15-card set features players who stepped their play up last season. Player action shots are set against a blue foil background.
COMPLETE SET (15) 7.50 20.00
STATED ODDS 1:24, 1:12 HTA
B1 Kurt Warner 1.00 2.50
B2 Patrick Jeffers .40 1.00
B3 Stephen Davis .40 1.00
B4 Amani Toomer .40 1.00
B5 Marcus Robinson .50 1.25
B6 Tyrone Wheatley .40 1.00
B7 Kevin Johnson .40 1.00
B8 Tony Gonzalez .50 1.25
B9 Olandis Gary .50 1.25
B10 Brad Johnson .50 1.25
B11 Germane Crowell .40 1.00
B12 Ricky Williams .50 1.25
B13 Edgerrin James .50 1.25
B14 Tim Couch .50 1.25
B15 Steve Beuerlein .50 1.25

2000 Finest Moments Pro Bowl Jerseys

Randomly inserted in packs at the rate of one in 77, and one in 35 HTA, this 33-card set features players that made their first appearance at the Pro Bowl in 2000. Each card features a swatch of the featured player's Pro Bowl jersey.
COMPLETE SET (33) 250.00 500.00
STATED ODDS 1:77, 1:35 HTA
KMC Kevin Mawae 4.00 10.00
MBP Mitch Berger 5.00 12.00
TTP Tom Tupa 4.00 10.00
BDFS Brian Dawkins 12.00 25.00
BJQB Brad Johnson 5.00 12.00
CDRB Corey Dillon 4.00 10.00
DCOLB Dexter Coakley 4.00 10.00
DSST Detron Smith 4.00 10.00
DSTE David Sloan 4.00 10.00
EJRB Edgerrin James 5.00 12.00
JKDE Jevon Kearse 4.00 10.00
KCDE Kevin Carter 4.00 10.00
KHOLB Kevin Hardy 4.00 10.00
KWQB Kurt Warner 10.00 25.00
LEILM Luther Elliss 4.00 10.00
LSFS Lance Schulters 4.00 10.00
LSOT Leon Searcy 4.00 10.00
MHWR Marvin Harrison 5.00 12.00
MMWR Muhsin Muhammad 4.00 10.00
OMPK Olindo Mare 4.00 10.00
OPOT Orlando Pace 4.00 10.00
RGQB Rich Gannon 5.00 12.00
SBILB Stephen Boyd 4.00 10.00
SBQB Steve Beuerlein 5.00 12.00
SDRB Stephen Davis 4.00 10.00
SMCB Sam Madison 4.00 10.00
TBDE Tony Brackens 4.00 10.00
TGTE Tony Gonzalez 5.00 12.00
TJOG Tre Johnson 4.00 10.00
TLCB Todd Lyght 4.00 10.00
TMKR Tremain Mack 4.00 10.00
TPILM Trevor Pryce 4.00 10.00
ZTILB Zach Thomas 5.00 12.00

2000 Finest Superstars

Randomly inserted in packs at the rate of one in 16, and one in eight HTA, this 15-card set features top NFL Star action photography on an all foil dufex card.
COMPLETE SET (15) 7.50 20.00
STATED ODDS 1:16, 1:8 HTA
S1 Dan Marino 1.00 2.50
S2 Eddie George .40 1.00
S3 Marshall Faulk .40 1.00
S4 Stephen Davis .30 .75
S5 Jerry Rice 1.25 3.00
S6 Emmitt Smith .75 2.00
S7 Terrell Davis .40 1.00
S8 Jimmy Smith .40 1.00
S9 Cris Carter .50 1.25
S10 Troy Aikman .60 1.50
S11 Curtis Martin .40 1.00
S12 Brett Favre 1.00 2.50
S13 Kurt Warner .75 2.00
S14 Marvin Harrison .40 1.00
S15 Steve Young .60 1.50

2000-01 Finest Pro Bowl Jumbos

This set was distributed to attendees (one card at a time) of the NFL Experience Pro Bowl Show in Hawaii in February 2001. The cards are essentially a Jumbo (roughly 4" by 5 5/8") version of the player's base 2000 Finest card with each featuring the Pro Bowl 2001 logo. A Jumbo Refractor parallel set was also produced.
COMPLETE SET (12) 15.00 30.00
*REFRACTORS: 3X TO 8X BASIC CARDS
1 Jeff Garcia 1.00 2.50
2 Randy Moss 2.50 6.00
3 Warren Sapp .60 1.50
4 Peyton Manning 2.50 6.00
5 Eddie George 1.25 3.00
6 Edgerrin James 2.50 6.00
7 Stephen Davis 1.00 2.50
8 Jamal Lewis 3.00 8.00
9 Marvin Harrison 1.00 2.50
10 Marshall Faulk 1.25 3.00
11 Rich Gannon 1.00 2.50
12 Daunte Culpepper 2.00 5.00

2000-01 Finest Pro Bowl Promos

These 6-cards were distributed to attendees (one card at a time) of the NFL Experience Pro Bowl Show in Hawaii in February 2001. The cards are essentially a parallel version of the player's base 2000 Finest card with each featuring the Pro Bowl 2001 logo.
COMPLETE SET (6) 12.50 25.00
1 Daunte Culpepper 2.00 5.00
2 Jamal Lewis 3.00 8.00
3 Peyton Manning 2.50 6.00
4 Edgerrin James 2.50 6.00
5 Randy Moss 2.50 6.00
6 Jeff Garcia 1.25 3.00

2000-01 Finest Super Bowl Jumbos

This set was distributed to hobby dealers primarily at the NFL Experience Super Bowl Card Show in Tampa, Florida. The cards are essentially a Jumbo (roughly 4" by 5 5/8") version of the player's base Issue card with each featuring the Super Bowl XXXV logo. A Jumbo Refractor parallel set was also produced.
COMPLETE SET (12) 18.00 30.00
*REFRACTORS: 2.5X TO 5X BASIC CARDS
1 Jeff Garcia .75 2.00
2 Randy Moss 2.00 5.00
3 Warren Sapp .50 1.25
4 Peyton Manning 2.50 6.00
5 Eddie George 1.25 3.00
6 Edgerrin James 2.50 6.00
7 Stephen Davis .75 2.00
8 Jamal Lewis 2.50 6.00
9 Marvin Harrison .75 2.00
10 Marshall Faulk 1.25 3.00
11 Rich Gannon 1.25 3.00
12 Daunte Culpepper 1.50 4.00

2001 Finest

This 140 card set was released in October, 2001. The set is broken down into two parts: The first 100 cards are veterans while the final 40 cards are 2001 NFL rookies serial numbered to 1000. The first 500 of those rookies were graded by PSA. Both the ungraded and graded rookies were inserted at a one per box level. Each box contained 10 packs and each box was supposed to contain the following elements: Graded Rookie Card, Sequentially numbered Rookie Card, three Relic Cards and 2 Autographed cards.
COMP.SET w/o SP's (100) 20.00 40.00
1 Eddie George .40 1.00
2 Jay Fiedler .30 .75
3 Peter Warrick .25 .60
4 Vinny Testaverde .25 .60
5 Charles Johnson .25 .60
6 Ahman Green .30 .75
7 Isaac Bruce .40 1.00
8 Junior Seau .30 .75
9 Daunte Culpepper .30 .75
10 Ike Hilliard .25 .60
11 Tony Banks .25 .60
12 Steve Beuerlein .30 .75
13 Jamal Anderson .30 .75
14 Tyrone Wheatley .30 .75
15 Sylvester Morris .25 .60
16 Edgerrin James .30 .75
17 Shaun King .25 .60
18 Terrell Owens .30 .75
19 Donovan Mcnabb .30 .75
20 Cade Mcnown .30 .75
21 Elvis Grbac .30 .75
22 James Stewart .25 .60
23 Joe Horn .25 .60
24 Randy Moss .30 .75
25 Matt Hasselbeck .25 .60
26 Jerome Bettis .40 1.00
27 Bill Schroeder .30 .75
28 Jake Plummer .25 .60
29 Rod Smith .30 .75
30 Akili Smith .25 .60
31 Jimmy Smith .30 .75
32 Oronde Gadsden .25 .60
33 Kerry Collins .25 .60
34 Warrick Dunn .25 .60
35 Jeff Graham .25 .60
36 Ray Lewis .40 1.00
37 Joey Galloway .30 .75
38 Tim Brown .40 1.00
39 Derrick Alexander .25 .60
40 Jerry Rice .75 2.00
41 Muhsin Muhammad .25 .60
42 Shawn Jefferson .25 .60
43 Curtis Martin .30 .75
44 Terry Glenn .30 .75
45 Marvin Harrison .30 .75
46 Mike Anderson .25 .60
47 Stephen Davis .25 .60
48 Chad Lewis .25 .60
49 Fred Taylor .25 .60
50 Corey Dillon .25 .60
51 Charlie Batch .25 .60
52 Kevin Johnson .25 .60
53 Brett Favre .75 2.00
54 Marshall Faulk .30 .75
55 Kordell Stewart .25 .60
56 Steve McNair .30 .75
57 Jeff Blake .30 .75
58 Eric Moulds .25 .60
59 Emmitt Smith .60 1.50
60 David Boston .25 .60
61 Cris Carter .40 1.00
62 Peyton Manning 1.00 2.50
63 Keyshawn Johnson .30 .75
64 Doug Flutie .30 .75
65 Drew Bledsoe .30 .75
66 Ricky Williams .30 .75
67 Keenan Mccardell .30 .75
68 Brian Urlacher .50 1.25
69 Jamal Lewis .40 1.00
70 Ed McCaffrey .30 .75
71 Antonio Freeman .40 1.00
72 Darrell Jackson .30 .75
73 Jeff George .30 .75
74 Chris Chandler .30 .75
75 Germane Crowell .25 .60
76 Tim Biakabutuka .25 .60
77 Jon Kitna .25 .60
78 Troy Brown .25 .60
79 Lamar Smith .30 .75
80 Derrick Mason .25 .60
81 Hines Ward .30 .75
82 Mark Brunell .30 .75
83 Trent Dilfer .25 .60
84 Tim Couch .25 .60
85 Donald Hayes .25 .60
86 Amani Toomer .25 .60
87 Tony Gonzalez .30 .75
88 Rich Gannon .30 .75
89 Rob Johnson .30 .75
90 Torry Holt .30 .75
91 Jeff Garcia .25 .60
92 Kurt Warner .60 1.50
93 Aaron Brooks .25 .60
94 Brian Griese .25 .60
95 James Allen .25 .60
96 Wayne Chrebet .25 .60
97 Tiki Barber .30 .75
98 Brad Johnson .30 .75
99 Ricky Watters .30 .75
100 Charlie Garner .30 .75
101 Andre Carter RC 1.50 4.00
102 Dan Morgan RC 1.50 4.00
103 Gerard Warren RC 1.50 4.00
104 Jesse Palmer RC 1.50 4.00
105 Josh Heupel RC 2.00 5.00
106 Justin Smith RC 2.50 6.00
107 LaMont Jordan RC 2.00 5.00
108 Leonard Davis RC 2.00 5.00
109 Marques Tuiasosopo RC 1.50 4.00
110 Snoop Minnis RC 1.25 3.00
111 Quincy Carter RC 1.50 4.00
112 Quincy Morgan RC 1.50 4.00
113 Richard Seymour RC 2.00 5.00
114 Rudi Johnson RC 2.00 5.00
115 Sage Rosenfels RC 1.50 4.00
116 Todd Heap RC 1.50 4.00
117 Travis Minor RC 1.50 4.00
118 Will Allen RC 2.00 5.00
119 Jamal Reynolds RC 1.25 3.00
120 Scotty Anderson RC 1.25 3.00
121 Anthony Thomas RC 2.00 5.00
122 Chad Johnson RC 2.00 5.00
123 Chris Chambers RC 1.25 3.00
124 Chris Weinke RC 1.50 4.00
125 David Terrell RC 1.50 4.00
126 Deuce McAllister RC 2.00 5.00
127 Drew Brees RC 150.00 300.00
128 Freddie Mitchell RC 1.25 3.00
129 James Jackson RC 1.25 3.00
130 Kevan Barlow RC 1.50 4.00
131 Koren Robinson RC 1.50 4.00
132 LaDainian Tomlinson RC 12.00 30.00
133 Michael Bennett RC 1.50 4.00
134 Michael Vick RC 12.00 30.00
135 Mike McMahon RC 1.50 4.00
136 Reggie Wayne RC 2.50 6.00
137 Robert Ferguson RC 3.00 8.00
138 Rod Gardner RC 2.50 6.00
139 Santana Moss RC 3.00 8.00
140 Travis Henry RC 2.50 6.00

2001 Finest Autographs

Inserted at an overall rate of one every five packs, these 25 cards are all autographed. The individual cards were inserted at rates anywhere between one in 10 packs and one in 1174 packs. Those cards which were available in far shorter quantities are notated in our checklist as SP's.
GROUP A STATED ODDS 1:1174
GROUP B, D, E STATED ODDS 1:220
GROUP C STATED ODDS 1:587
GROUP F STATED ODDS 1:176
GROUP G STATED ODDS 1:135
GROUP H STATED ODDS 1:98
GROUP I STATED ODDS 1:10
GROUP J STATED ODDS 1:84
GROUP K STATED ODDS 1:80
GROUP L STATED ODDS 1:59
GROUP M STATED ODDS 1:44
OVERALL STATED ODDS 1:5
FAAB Aaron Brooks K 5.00 12.00
FABN Bobby Newcombe M 6.00 15.00
FABS Bill Schroeder I 6.00 15.00
FACW Chris Weinke C SP 6.00 15.00
FADA Dan Alexander J 6.00 15.00
FADC Daunte Culpepper B SP 10.00 25.00
FADH Donald Hayes I 5.00 12.00
FAEG Eddie George B SP 8.00 20.00
FAEJ Edgerrin James A SP 25.00 50.00
FAEM Eric Moulds H 5.00 12.00
FAES Emmitt Smith D SP 60.00 120.00
FAJG Jeff Garcia E 10.00 25.00
FAJH Joe Horn I 5.00 12.00
FAJJ James Jackson I 5.00 12.00
FAJL Jamal Lewis G 8.00 20.00
FAJS Jimmy Smith I 6.00 15.00
FALS Lamar Smith I 6.00 15.00
FAMB Michael Bennett B SP 6.00 15.00
FAMR Marcus Robinson L 6.00 15.00
FARG Reggie Germany F 5.00 12.00
FASCM Sammy Morris D SP 5.00 12.00
FASM Sylvester Morris I 5.00 12.00
FASMO Santana Moss B SP 20.00 40.00
FATH Travis Henry I 6.00 15.00
FATM Travis Minor I 6.00 15.00

2001 Finest Moments Autographs

Inserted at an overall rate of one in 160, this set features some of the NFL leading stars. A few of the cards were available at a rate of one in 1760 packs while most of the cards were available at a rate of one in 176. Jeff Garcia and Michael Vick did not return their cards in time for the product pack out and those were issued as exchange cards with a redemption date of September 30, 2003.
STATED ODDS 1:160
FMACW Chris Weinke 6.00 15.00
FMADC Daunte Culpepper 10.00 25.00
FMAEJ Edgerrin James 12.00 30.00
FMAEM Eric Moulds 6.00 15.00
FMAJG Jeff Garcia 10.00 25.00
FMAMV Michael Vick 40.00 100.00

2001 Finest Moments Relics

Randomly inserted in packs at a rate of one in 176, these 10 cards feature leading NFL players along with a game-worn piece of uniform or football.
STATED ODDS 1:176
FMRCJ Chad Johnson 4.00 10.00
FMRDA Dan Alexander 3.00 8.00
FMRDC Daunte Culpepper 3.00 8.00
FMREJ Edgerrin James 3.00 8.00
FMRKB Kevan Barlow 3.00 8.00
FMRLJ LaMont Jordan 4.00 10.00
FMRLT LaDainian Tomlinson FB 12.00 30.00
FMRRG Rich Gannon 3.00 8.00
FMRRG Rod Gardner JSY 3.00 8.00
FMRRW Reggie Wayne 5.00 12.00

2001 Finest Rookie Premiere Jerseys

Inserted at an overall rate of one in five, these 22 cards feature some of the leading 2001 rookies along with a game-used jersey piece. The odds of a specific card ranged anywhere from one in 11 packs to one in 88 packs.
GROUP A STATED ODDS 1:88
GROUP B STATED ODDS 1:35
GROUP C STATED ODDS 1:11
GROUP D STATED ODDS 1:70
GROUP E STATED ODDS 1:15
OVERALL STATED ODDS 1:5
RPJAC Andre Carter A 3.00 8.00
RPJAT Anthony Thomas C 4.00 10.00
RPJCJ Chad Johnson B 4.00 10.00
RPJCW Chris Weinke E 3.00 8.00
RPJGW Gerard Warren A 3.00 8.00
RPJJH Josh Heupel B 4.00 10.00
RPJJP Jesse Palmer B 3.00 8.00
RPJJS Justin Smith A 5.00 12.00
RPJKB Kevan Barlow B 3.00 8.00
RPJKR Koren Robinson E 3.00 8.00
RPJLD Leonard Davis A 4.00 10.00
RPJMM Mike McMahon B 3.00 8.00
RPJMT Marques Tuiasosopo C 3.00 8.00
RPJMMI Snoop Minnis C 2.50 6.00
RPJRF Robert Ferguson 4.00 10.00
RPJRG Rod Gardner E 3.00 8.00
RPJRJ Rudi Johnson C 4.00 10.00
RPJRW Reggie Wayne E 5.00 12.00
RPJSM Santana Moss D 4.00 10.00
RPJSR Sage Rosenfels C 3.00 8.00
RPJTH Todd Heap C 3.00 8.00
RPJTM Travis Minor C 3.00 8.00

2001 Finest Stadium Throwback Relics

Randomly inserted in packs at a rate of one in 10, these 20 cards feature seat relics from old stadiums which are no longer used for NFL games. Each relic piece is cut in the shape of the teams logo at the time the vintage uniform and stadium were in use.
STATED ODDS 1:10
FSBF Brett Favre 5.00 12.00
FSCC Cris Carter 2.50 6.00
FSCD Corey Dillon 1.50 4.00
FSDB Drew Brees 10.00 25.00
FSDC Daunte Culpepper 2.00 5.00
FSDM Donovan McNabb 2.00 5.00
FSEJ Edgerrin James 2.00 5.00
FSEM Eric Moulds 1.50 4.00
FSJB Jerome Bettis 2.50 6.00
FSKR Koren Robinson 2.00 5.00
FSKW Kurt Warner 4.00 10.00
FSLT LaDainian Tomlinson 8.00 20.00
FSMF Marshall Faulk 2.00 5.00
FSMH Marvin Harrison 2.00 5.00
FSMM Snoop Minnis 1.50 4.00
FSPM Peyton Manning 6.00 15.00
FSRG Rod Gardner 2.00 5.00
FSRM Randy Moss 2.00 5.00
FSTC Tim Couch 1.50 4.00
FSTG Tony Gonzalez 2.00 5.00

2002 Finest

Released in late September, 2002, this set contains 62 veteran base cards, 14 veteran jersey cards, 40 rookies and 22 autographed rookies. The jersey cards #'d/999 were inserted 1:30, and the jersey cards #'d/499 were inserted 1:102 packs. The rookie autographs were inserted 1:18 packs. Please note some autographed rookies were issued via exchange card. The EXCH expiration date was September 30, 2004. The Hobby S.R.P. is $40.00/per mini-box. Each pack contains 5 cards. There are 6 packs per mini-box. Three mini-boxes per full box. Twelve boxes per case.
COMP.SET w/o SP's (62) 15.00 40.00
1 Peyton Manning 1.25 3.00
2 Troy Brown .30 .75
3 Curtis Martin .40 1.00
4 Kordell Stewart .30 .75
5 Michael Pittman .40 1.00
6 Rod Gardner .30 .75
7 Germane Crowell .30 .75
8 Terrell Davis .40 1.00
9 Eric Moulds .30 .75
10 Jake Plummer .30 .75
11 Tony Gonzalez .40 1.00
12 Ricky Williams .40 1.00
13 Deuce McAllister .40 1.00
14 Jerry Rice 1.00 2.50
15 Torry Holt .40 1.00
16 Michael Vick .40 1.00
17 David Terrell .30 .75
18 Terry Glenn .40 1.00
19 Mark Brunell .40 1.00
20 Vinny Testaverde .30 .75
21 Jerome Bettis .50 1.25
22 Randy Moss .40 1.00
23 Marvin Harrison .40 1.00
24 Chris Weinke .30 .75
25 Tiki Barber .40 1.00
26 Corey Bradford .30 .75
27 David Boston .30 .75
28 Emmitt Smith .75 2.00
29 Santana Moss .40 1.00
30 Brian Griese .30 .75
31 Priest Holmes .30 .75
32 Rich Gannon .40 1.00
33 Antowain Smith .40 1.00
34 Marcus Robinson .40 1.00
35 Warrick Dunn .30 .75
36 Daunte Culpepper .40 1.00
37 Shaun Alexander .30 .75
38 Kurt Warner .40 1.00
39 Quincy Carter .30 .75
40 Ray Lewis .50 1.25
41 Aaron Brooks .30 .75
42 Plaxico Burress .30 .75
43 Jamal Lewis .40 1.00
44 Ahman Green .40 1.00
45 Rod Smith .40 1.00
46 Tim Couch .30 .75
47 Muhsin Muhammad .30 .75
48 Drew Bledsoe .40 1.00
49 Anthony Thomas .40 1.00
50 Tom Brady 2.50 6.00
51 Trent Green .30 .75
52 Charlie Garner .40 1.00
53 Darrell Jackson .40 1.00
54 Mike McMahon .30 .75
55 Donovan McNabb .40 1.00
56 Fred Taylor .30 .75
57 Corey Dillon .30 .75
58 Keyshawn Johnson .40 1.00
59 Drew Brees 1.00 2.50
60 Steve McNair .40 1.00
61 Jimmy Smith .40 1.00
62 Terrell Owens .40 1.00
63 Eddie George JSY/499 6.00 15.00
64 Jeff Garcia JSY/999 4.00 10.00
65 LaDain Tomlinson JSY/999 6.00 15.00
66 Cris Carter JSY/499 8.00 20.00
67 Chris Chambers JSY/499 5.00 12.00
68 Brian Urlacher JSY/999 6.00 15.00
69 Tim Brown JSY/999 6.00 15.00
70 Marshall Faulk JSY/999 5.00 12.00
71 Stephen Davis JSY/999 4.00 10.00
72 Jevon Kearse JSY/999 4.00 10.00
73 Edgerrin James JSY/999 5.00 12.00
74 Mike Anderson JSY/999 4.00 10.00
75 Warren Sapp JSY/499 6.00 15.00
76 Brett Favre JSY/499 15.00 40.00
77 Julius Peppers RC 2.00 5.00
78 Tim Carter RC 1.00 2.50
79 Travis Stephens RC .75 2.00
80 Jabar Gaffney RC .75 2.00
81 Cliff Russell RC .75 2.00
82 Reche Caldwell RC 1.00 2.50
83 Maurice Morris RC 1.00 2.50
84 Antwaan Randle El RC 1.00 2.50
85 Ladell Betts RC 1.25 3.00
86 Daniel Graham RC 1.00 2.50
87 Jeremy Shockey RC 1.25 3.00
88 Mike Williams RC .75 2.00
89 Josh McCown RC 1.25 3.00
90 Rohan Davey RC 1.25 3.00
91 David Garrard RC 1.00 2.50
92 Dwight Freeney RC 1.50 4.00
93 Leonard Henry RC .75 2.00
94 Albert Haynesworth RC 1.25 3.00
95 Herb Haygood RC .75 2.00
96 Kurt Kittner RC .75 2.00
97 Jason McAddley RC 1.00 2.50
98 Bryan Thomas RC .75 2.00
99 Wendell Bryant RC .75 2.00
100 Mike Rumph RC .75 2.00
101 Chad Hutchinson RC .75 2.00
102 Brian Westbrook RC 1.50 4.00
103 Deion Branch RC 1.25 3.00
104 John Henderson RC 1.00 2.50
105 Jerramy Stevens RC 1.25 3.00
106 Tracey Wistrom RC 1.00 2.50
107 Phillip Buchanon RC 1.25 3.00
108 Matt Schobel RC 1.00 2.50
109 Ed Reed RC 5.00 12.00
110 Randy Fasani RC .75 2.00
111 Josh Scobey RC 1.00 2.50
112 Luke Staley RC .75 2.00
113 Anthony Weaver RC .75 2.00
114 Kyle Johnson RC .75 2.00
115 David Carr AU RC 5.00 12.00
116 Joey Harrington AU RC 5.00 12.00
117 Donte Stallworth AU RC 8.00 20.00
118 Ashley Lelie AU RC 5.00 12.00
119 Patrick Ramsey AU RC 6.00 15.00
120 William Green AU RC 6.00 15.00
121 Josh Reed AU RC 6.00 15.00
122 Clinton Portis AU RC 8.00 20.00
123 Antonio Bryant AU RC 8.00 20.00
124 Javon Walker AU RC 8.00 20.00
125 Roy Williams AU RC 5.00 12.00
126 Marquise Walker AU RC 5.00 12.00
127 Quentin Jammer AU RC 8.00 20.00
128 DeShaun Foster AU RC 8.00 20.00
129 Andre Davis AU RC 5.00 12.00
130 Ron Johnson AU RC 6.00 15.00
131 Lamar Gordon AU RC 6.00 15.00
132 T.J. Duckett AU/300 RC 5.00 12.00
133 Freddie Milons AU RC 5.00 12.00
134 Eric Crouch AU RC 8.00 20.00
135 Adrian Peterson AU RC 6.00 15.00
136 Damien Anderson AU RC 5.00 12.00

2002 Finest Refractors

*VETS 1-62: 3X TO 8X BASIC CARDS
1-62 VETERAN ODDS 1:12 PACKS
*JSY/250: .5X TO 1.2X BASE JSY/999
*JSY/250: .4X TO 1X BASE JSY/499
63-76 JERSEY ODDS 1:72 PACKS
*ROOKIES 77-114: 1.2X TO 3X
77-114 ROOKIE PRINT RUN 250
*ROOKIE AU 115-136: .6X TO 1.5X
115-136 ROOKIE AU/175 ODDS 1:66
115-136 PRINT RUN 175 SER.#'d SETS

2002 Finest Gold Refractors

*VETS 1-62: 12X TO 30X BASIC CARDS
*JSY/25: 1X TO 2.5X BASIC JSY/999
JSY/999 ODDS 1:1746 PACKS
*JSY/25: .8X TO 2X BASIC JSY/499
JSY/499 ODDS 1:1470 PACKS
*ROOKIES 77-114: 5X TO 12X
*ROOKIE AU 115-136: 1.2X TO 3X
GOLD REF/25 OVERALL ODDS 1:102
STATED PRINT RUN 25 SER.#'d SETS

2002 Finest Xfractors

*JSY/20: 1X TO 2.5X BASE JSY/999
*JSY/20: .8X TO 2X BASE JSY/499
*ROOKIES 77-114: 5X TO 12X
*ROOKIE AU 115-136: 1.2X TO 3X
XFRACTOR/20 ODDS 1:3810
STATED PRINT RUN 20 SER.#'d SETS

2003 Finest

Released in October of 2003, this set consists of 149 cards including 60 veterans, 40 rookies, 18 jerseys, and 31 rookie autographs. The boxes contained three mini-boxes of 6 packs, with each pack featuring five cards. The SRP for the mini-boxes was $40. Card #149 was initially issued in packs as an exchange card, but the card was never fulfilled.
COMP.SET w/o SP's (100) 20.00 50.00
101-118 GROUP A ODDS 1:171 MINI-BOXES
101-118 GROUP B ODDS 1:38 MINI-BOXES
101-118 GROUP C ODDS 1:4 MINI-BOXES
ROOKIE AU/999 ODDS 1:3 MINI-BOXES
ROOKIE AU/399 ODDS 1:30 MINI-BOXES
1 Chad Pennington .25 .60
2 Tommy Maddox .25 .60
3 Brett Favre .75 2.00
4 Eric Moulds .25 .60
5 Randy Moss .30 .75
6 Duce Staley .25 .60
7 Derrick Mason .25 .60
8 Shaun Alexander .25 .60
9 Peyton Manning 1.00 2.50
10 Kerry Collins .25 .60
11 Joe Horn .25 .60
12 Laveranues Coles .25 .60
13 Marty Booker .25 .60
14 Emmitt Smith .60 1.50
15 Edgerrin James .30 .75
16 Aaron Brooks .25 .60
17 Curtis Martin .30 .75
18 Hines Ward .30 .75
19 Rod Smith .30 .75
20 Priest Holmes .25 .60
21 Jerry Rice .75 2.00
22 Peerless Price .25 .60
23 Mark Brunell .30 .75
24 Trent Green .25 .60
25 David Boston .25 .60
26 Chris Chambers .25 .60
27 Marshall Faulk .30 .75
28 Fred Taylor .25 .60
29 Tim Couch .25 .60
30 Amani Toomer .25 .60
31 Travis Henry .25 .60
32 Jeff Blake .30 .75
33 Troy Brown .25 .60
34 Charlie Garner .30 .75
35 Tom Brady 1.25 3.00
36 Warrick Dunn .25 .60
37 Plaxico Burress .25 .60
38 Marvin Harrison .30 .75
39 Clinton Portis .25 .60
40 Deuce McAllister .30 .75
41 Matt Hasselbeck .25 .60
42 Jeff Garcia .25 .60
43 David Carr .25 .60
44 Ahman Green .30 .75
45 Eddie George .30 .75
46 Drew Brees .40 1.00
47 Tiki Barber .30 .75
48 Jay Fiedler .25 .60
49 Curtis Conway .25 .60
50 Steve McNair .30 .75
51 Donald Driver .30 .75
52 Jake Plummer .25 .60
53 Jamal Lewis .30 .75
54 Corey Dillon .25 .60
55 Stephen Davis .25 .60
56 Terrell Owens .30 .75
57 Torry Holt .30 .75
58 Chad Johnson .25 .60
59 Chad Hutchinson .25 .60
60 Kurt Warner .30 .75
61 Troy Polamalu RC 12.00 30.00
62 Eugene Wilson RC 1.25 3.00
63 Juston Wood RC .75 2.00
64 Anquan Boldin RC 1.25 3.00
65 Doug Gabriel RC 1.00 2.50
66 Domanick Davis RC 1.00 2.50
67 J.R. Tolver RC 1.00 2.50
68 Jerome McDougle RC .75 2.00
69 Keenan Howry RC .75 2.00
70 Teyo Johnson RC 1.00 2.50
71 Bethel Johnson RC .75 2.00
72 Ken Hamlin RC 1.25 3.00
73 L.J. Smith RC 1.25 3.00
74 Rashean Mathis RC .75 2.00
75 Arnaz Battle RC 1.25 3.00
76 B.J. Askew RC 1.00 2.50
77 Mike Doss RC 1.25 3.00
78 Kevin Curtis RC .75 2.00
79 Terence Newman RC 1.25 3.00
80 Shaun McDonald RC 1.00 2.50
81 Kevin Williams RC 1.25 3.00
82 Nate Burleson RC 1.00 2.50
83 Tyrone Calico RC .75 2.00
84 DeWayne White RC .75 2.00
85 Marcus Trufant RC 1.00 2.50
86 Nick Barnett RC 1.25 3.00
87 Bennie Joppru RC .75 2.00
88 Andre Woolfolk RC .75 2.00
89 Billy McMullen RC .75 2.00
90 Boss Bailey RC 1.00 2.50
91 William Joseph RC .75 2.00
92 Michael Haynes RC .75 2.00
93 DeWayne Robertson RC 1.00 2.50
94 LaTarence Dunbar RC .75 2.00
95 David Tyree RC 1.00 2.50
96 Walter Young RC .75 2.00
97 E.J. Henderson RC 1.00 2.50
98 Ty Warren RC 1.00 2.50
99 Zuriel Smith RC .75 2.00
100 Brock Forsey RC 1.00 2.50
101 Ricky Williams JSY C 4.00 10.00
102 Drew Bledsoe JSY C 4.00 10.00
103 Joey Harrington JSY C 3.00 8.00
104 Tim Brown JSY C 5.00 12.00
105 Brian Urlacher JSY C 5.00 12.00
106 Zach Thomas JSY C 4.00 10.00
107 Jeremy Shockey JSY C 3.00 8.00
108 Michael Strahan JSY A 5.00 12.00
109 Jason Taylor JSY C 4.00 10.00
110 Donovan McNabb JSY C 4.00 10.00
111 LaDainian Tomlinson JSY B 6.00 15.00
112 Rich Gannon JSY C 4.00 10.00
113 Brad Johnson JSY C 4.00 10.00
114 Daunte Culpepper JSY C 4.00 10.00
115 Michael Vick JSY C 4.00 10.00
116 Jimmy Smith JSY B 5.00 12.00
117 Keyshawn Johnson JSY C 5.00 12.00
118 Keith Brooking JSY C 4.00 10.00
119 Carson Palmer AU/399 RC 15.00 40.00
120 Byron Leftwich AU/399 RC 8.00 20.00
121 Chris Simms AU/399 RC 6.00 15.00
122 Kyle Boller AU/399 RC 6.00 15.00
123 Justin Fargas AU RC 6.00 15.00
124 Seneca Wallace AU RC 5.00 12.00
125 Larry Johnson AU RC 5.00 12.00
126 Kareem Kelly AU RC 4.00 10.00
127 Willis McGahee AU/399 RC 10.00 25.00
128 Kelley Washington AU RC 4.00 10.00
129 Brian St.Pierre AU RC 4.00 10.00
130 Kliff Kingsbury AU RC 6.00 15.00
131 Ken Dorsey AU RC 5.00 12.00
132 Bryant Johnson AU RC 6.00 15.00
133 Dallas Clark AU RC 10.00 25.00
134 Chris Brown AU RC 4.00 10.00
135 Taylor Jacobs AU RC 4.00 10.00
136 Artose Pinner AU RC 4.00 10.00
137 Lee Suggs AU RC 4.00 10.00
138 LaBrandon Toefield AU RC 4.00 10.00
139 Jason Witten AU RC 30.00 60.00
140 Brad Banks AU RC 5.00 12.00
141 Earnest Graham AU RC 8.00 20.00
142 Bobby Wade AU RC 5.00 12.00
143 Talman Gardner AU RC 4.00 10.00
144 Justin Gage AU RC 5.00 12.00
145 Sam Aiken AU RC 5.00 12.00
146 Musa Smith AU RC 4.00 10.00
147 Terrell Suggs AU RC 12.00 30.00
148 Brandon Lloyd AU RC 5.00 12.00
150 Rex Grossman AU RC 5.00 12.00

2003 Finest Refractors

*STARS 1-60: 2.5X TO 6X HI COL.
*ROOKIES 61-100: 1.5X TO 4X
1-100 ODDS 1:3 MINI-BOX
*VET JSY 101-118: .4X TO 1X GRP A-B
*VET JSY 101-118: .5X TO 1.2X GRP C
101-118 VET JSY ODDS 1:17 MINI-BOX
*ROOK.AU: .5X TO 1.2X BASE AU/399
*ROOK.AU: .8X TO 2X BASE AU/999
ROOKIE AU ODDS 1:10 MINI-BOXES
PRINT RUN 199 SERIAL #'d SETS
119 Carson Palmer AU 30.00 80.00
139 Jason Witten AU 50.00 100.00

2003 Finest Gold Refractors

*VETS 1-60: 6X TO 15X BASIC CARDS
*ROOKIES 61-100: 3X TO 8X
1-100 ODDS 1:12 MINI-BOX
*VET JSY 101-118: .5X TO 1.2X GRP A-B
*VET JSY 101-118: .6X TO 1.5X GRP C
101-118 VET JSY ODDS 1:68 MINI-BOX
*ROOK.AU/50: .8X TO 2X BASE AU/399
*ROOK.AU/50: 1.2X TO 3X BASE AU/999
119-150 ROOKIE AU ODDS 1:38 MINI-BOX
PRINT RUN 50 SERIAL #'d SETS
119 Carson Palmer AU 40.00 100.00
139 Jason Witten AU 125.00 200.00
150 Rex Grossman AU 15.00 40.00

2003 Finest Xfractors

*VETS 1-60: 3X TO 8X BASIC CARDS
*ROOKIES 61-100: 2X TO 5X
1-100 PRINT RUN 175
*VET JSY 101-118: .5X TO 1.2X GRP A-B
*VET JSY 101-118: .6X TO 1.5X GRP C
*ROOK.AU/50: .8X TO 2X BASE AU/399
*ROOK.AU/50: 1.2X TO 3X BASE AU/999
101-150 PRINT RUN 50
119 Carson Palmer AU 30.00 80.00
139 Jason Witten AU 125.00 200.00

2004 Finest

Finest initially released in early November 2004. The base set consists of 134-cards including 40-rookies (#61-100), 7-veteran jersey cards, and 27-signed and serial numbered rookies. Hobby boxes contained 18-packs of 5-cards and carried an S.R.P. of $6 per pack. Four basic parallel sets can be found seeded in hobby packs with four additional 1/1 Printing Plate parallels produced as well.
COMP.SET w/o SP's (100) 15.00 40.00
COMP.SET w/o RC's (60) 5.00 12.00
108-134 AU/399 RC STATED ODDS 1:120
108-134 AU/999 RC STATED ODDS 1:12
1 Steve McNair .25 .60
2 Corey Dillon .20 .50
3 Joey Harrington .20 .50
4 Travis Henry .20 .50
5 Donovan McNabb .25 .60
6 Jamal Lewis .25 .60
7 Jeff Garcia .20 .50
8 Fred Taylor .20 .50
9 Aaron Brooks .20 .50
10 Marc Bulger .20 .50
11 Keenan McCardell .20 .50
12 David Carr .20 .50
13 Charles Rogers .20 .50
14 Ray Lewis .30 .75
15 Priest Holmes .20 .50
16 Curtis Martin .25 .60
17 Plaxico Burress .20 .50
18 Shaun Alexander .20 .50
19 Brad Johnson .25 .60
20 Marvin Harrison .25 .60
21 Rod Smith .25 .60
22 Jake Delhomme .20 .50
23 Santana Moss .25 .60
24 Trent Green .20 .50
25 Michael Vick .25 .60
26 Tim Rattay .20 .50
27 Chris Chambers .20 .50
28 Robert Ferguson .20 .50
29 Tiki Barber .25 .60
30 Terrell Owens .25 .60
31 Marshall Faulk .25 .60
32 Quincy Carter .20 .50
33 Stephen Davis .20 .50
34 Josh McCown .25 .60
35 Jeremy Shockey .20 .50
36 Tommy Maddox .20 .50
37 Derrick Mason .20 .50
38 Kerry Collins .20 .50
39 Jimmy Smith .25 .60
40 Chad Pennington .20 .50
41 Domanick Davis .20 .50
42 Darrell Jackson .25 .60
43 Steve Smith .30 .75
44 Drew Bledsoe .25 .60
45 Deuce McAllister .25 .60
46 Jerry Porter .20 .50
47 Peerless Price .20 .50
48 Eric Moulds .20 .50
49 Garrison Hearst .20 .50
50 Brett Favre .60 1.50
51 Amani Toomer .20 .50
52 Andre Johnson .25 .60
53 Edgerrin James .25 .60
54 Rex Grossman .20 .50
55 Daunte Culpepper .25 .60
56 Tony Gonzalez .25 .60
57 Byron Leftwich .20 .50
58 Mark Brunell .25 .60
59 Laveranues Coles .20 .50
60 Matt Hasselbeck .20 .50
61 Chris Gamble RC .50 1.25
62 Michael Turner RC .50 1.25
63 Julius Jones RC .50 1.25
64 Dunta Robinson RC .50 1.25
65 Sean Taylor RC 3.00 8.00
66 Ahmad Carroll RC .50 1.25
67 Derrick Strait RC .50 1.25
68 Dontarrious Thomas RC .60 1.50
69 Jason Babin RC .75 2.00
70 Reggie Williams RC .50 1.25
71 Dwan Edwards RC .50 1.25
72 Rashaun Woods RC .50 1.25
73 Ricardo Colclough RC .50 1.25
74 Will Smith RC .60 1.50
75 Kellen Winslow RC .50 1.25
76 Roy Williams RC .50 1.25
77 B.J. Symons RC .50 1.25
78 Carlos Francis RC .50 1.25
79 Triandos Luke RC .50 1.25
80 Drew Henson RC .50 1.25
81 Keiwan Ratliff RC .50 1.25
82 Will Poole RC .75 2.00
83 Tommie Harris RC .60 1.50
84 Steven Jackson RC .75 2.00
85 Greg Jones RC .50 1.25
86 Vince Wilfork RC .75 2.00
87 DeAngelo Hall RC .75 2.00
88 Daryl Smith RC .50 1.25
89 Teddy Lehman RC .50 1.25
90 Casey Bramlet RC .50 1.25
91 Marcus Tubbs RC .50 1.25
92 Andy Hall RC .50 1.25
93 Jim Sorgi RC .60 1.50
94 Kenechi Udeze RC .60 1.50
95 Darius Watts RC .50 1.25
96 Tank Johnson RC .50 1.25
97 Matt Mauck RC .50 1.25
98 Bradlee Van Pelt RC .60 1.50
99 D.J. Williams RC .75 2.00
100 Larry Fitzgerald RC 2.00 5.00
101 Peyton Manning JSY 8.00 20.00
102 Clinton Portis JSY 2.00 5.00
103 Chad Johnson JSY 2.00 5.00
104 Randy Moss JSY 2.50 6.00
105 Tom Brady JSY 12.00 30.00
106 LaDainian Tomlinson JSY 3.00 8.00
107 Ahman Green JSY 2.50 6.00
108 Roethlisberger AU/399 RC 150.00 300.00
109 Philip Rivers AU/399 RC 100.00 200.00
110 Eli Manning AU/399 RC 75.00 150.00
111 Kevin Jones AU/399 RC 6.00 15.00
112 Bernard Berrian AU RC 4.00 10.00
113 Jeff Smoker AU RC 5.00 12.00
114 Mewelde Moore AU RC 5.00 12.00
115 Michael Clayton AU RC 5.00 12.00
116 Jonathan Vilma AU RC 5.00 12.00
117 Johnnie Morant AU RC 4.00 10.00
118 Devard Darling AU RC 4.00 10.00
119 Cedric Cobbs AU RC 4.00 10.00
120 Chris Perry AU/399 RC 5.00 12.00
121 Ernest Wilford AU RC 5.00 12.00
122 Michael Jenkins AU RC 4.00 10.00
123 Jerricho Cotchery AU RC 5.00 12.00
124 P.K. Sam AU RC 4.00 10.00
125 Tatum Bell AU RC 4.00 10.00
126 Derrick Hamilton AU RC 4.00 10.00
127 Luke McCown AU RC 4.00 10.00
128 Devery Henderson AU RC 4.00 10.00
129 Craig Krenzel AU RC 4.00 10.00
130 J.P. Losman AU RC 4.00 10.00
131 Lee Evans AU RC 6.00 15.00
132 Matt Schaub AU RC 6.00 15.00
133 Robert Gallery AU RC 5.00 12.00
134 Keary Colbert AU RC 4.00 10.00

2004 Finest Refractors

*STARS: 2.5X TO 6X BASE CARD HI
*ROOKIES 61-100: 1.5X TO 4X
1-100 SER.#'d TO 199, STATED ODDS 1:12
*VETERAN JSY: .5X TO 1.2X BASE JSYs
VETERAN JERSEY STATED ODDS 1:168
*ROOKIE AUs: .6X TO 1.5X BASE AU/999
ROOKIE AUTO SER.#'d TO 199, ODDS 1:48
108 Ben Roethlisberger AU 175.00 300.00
109 Philip Rivers AU 125.00 250.00
110 Eli Manning AU 75.00 150.00

2004 Finest Gold Refractors

*STARS: 6X TO 15X BASE CARD HI
*ROOKIES 61-100: 3X TO 8X BASE CARD HI
1-100 SER.#'d TO 50, STATED ODDS 1:48
*VETERAN JSY: 1.2X TO 3X BASE CARD HI
VETERAN JERSEY STATED ODDS 1:684
*ROOKIE AUs: 1.2X TO 3X BASE AU/999
ROOKIE AUTO SER.#'d TO 50, ODDS 1:180
108 Ben Roethlisberger AU 250.00 500.00
109 Philip Rivers AU 150.00 300.00
110 Eli Manning AU 200.00 400.00

2004 Finest Refractors Xfractors

1-100 STATED ODDS 1:468
VETERAN JERSEY STATED ODDS 1:8856
ROOKIE AUTO STATED ODDS 1:2166
UNPRICED XFRACTORS SER.#'d TO 5

2004 Finest Uncirculated Gold Xfractors

*STARS: 5X TO 12X BASE CARD HI
*ROOKIES: 2.5X TO 6X BASE CARD HI
STATED PRINT RUN 150 SER.#'d SETS

2005 Finest

This 183-card set was released in October, 2005. The set was issued through the hobby in five-card packs with an $8 SRP which came 18 packs to a box. Cards numbered 1-120 feature veterans while cards 121-183 were NFL rookies. In the rookie grouping, cards numbered 151-183 were all signed. Cards numbered 151-160 were signed to a stated print run of 299 serial numbered cards while there was no serial numbering for cards 151-183.
COMP.SET w/o AUs (150) 25.00 60.00
1 Muhsin Muhammad .20 .50
2 Kevin Jones .20 .50
3 Eli Manning .50 1.25
4 Kevan Barlow .20 .50
5 Randy Moss .25 .60
6 Brian Griese .20 .50
7 Dante Hall .20 .50
8 Chris Brown .20 .50
9 Antonio Gates .30 .75
10 Champ Bailey .25 .60
11 Eric Moulds .20 .50
12 Ray Lewis .30 .75
13 Larry Fitzgerald .30 .75
14 Byron Leftwich .20 .50
15 Marvin Harrison .25 .60
16 Stephen Davis .20 .50
17 Laveranues Coles .20 .50
18 Shaun Alexander .20 .50

19 Drew Bledsoe .25 .60
20 Sean Taylor .30 .75
21 Deuce McAllister .25 .60
22 Nate Burleson .20 .50
23 A.J. Feeley .20 .50
24 Jerome Bettis .30 .75
25 Torry Holt .25 .60
26 LaDainian Tomlinson .30 .75
27 Travis Henry .20 .50
28 T.J. Houshmandzadeh .20 .50
29 Fred Taylor .20 .50
30 Michael Jenkins .20 .50
31 Edgerrin James .25 .60
32 Terrell Owens .25 .60
33 Jason Witten .25 .60
34 Clinton Portis .20 .50
35 Deion Branch .20 .50
36 Priest Holmes .20 .50
37 Javon Walker .20 .50
38 Rex Grossman .20 .50
39 Domanick Davis .20 .50
40 Allen Rossum .20 .50
41 Dwight Freeney .20 .50
42 Jimmy Smith .25 .60
43 Tiki Barber .25 .60
44 Steve McNair .25 .60
45 Steven Jackson .20 .50
46 Joe Horn .20 .50
47 Randy McMichael .20 .50
48 J.P. Losman .20 .50
49 Warrick Dunn .20 .50
50 Tatum Bell .20 .50
51 Roy Williams WR .20 .50
52 Curtis Martin .25 .60
53 Donovan McNabb .25 .60
54 LaMont Jordan .25 .60
55 Marc Bulger .20 .50
56 Drew Bennett .25 .60
57 Julius Jones .20 .50
58 Santana Moss .25 .60
59 Michael Bennett .20 .50
60 Tony Gonzalez .25 .60
61 Jamal Lewis .25 .60
62 Keary Colbert .20 .50
63 Carson Palmer .25 .60
64 Dunta Robinson .20 .50
65 Brandon Stokley .20 .50
66 Brett Favre .60 1.50
67 Jonathan Vilma .20 .50
68 Darrell Jackson .20 .50
69 Michael Pittman .20 .50
70 Drew Brees .30 .75
71 Amani Toomer .20 .50
72 Corey Dillon .20 .50
73 Willis McGahee .20 .50
74 Michael Vick .25 .60
75 Chad Johnson .20 .50
76 Anquan Boldin .20 .50
77 Kerry Collins .20 .50
78 Marshall Faulk .25 .60
79 Roy Williams S .20 .50
80 Trent Green .20 .50
81 Chris Gamble .20 .50
82 Ahman Green .25 .60
83 Todd Heap .20 .50
84 Brandon Lloyd .20 .50
85 Andre Johnson .25 .60
86 Lee Suggs .20 .50
87 Plaxico Burress .20 .50
88 Hines Ward .25 .60
89 Rod Smith .25 .60
90 Joey Harrington .20 .50
91 Derrick Mason .20 .50
92 Rudi Johnson .20 .50
93 Isaac Bruce .30 .75
94 Chris Chambers .20 .50
95 Matt Hasselbeck .20 .50
96 Donte Stallworth .20 .50
97 Philip Rivers .30 .75
98 Michael Clayton .20 .50
99 Alge Crumpler .25 .60
100 Chad Pennington .20 .50
101 Brian Westbrook .20 .50
102 Daunte Culpepper .25 .60
103 Jeremy Shockey .20 .50
104 Jerry Porter .20 .50
105 Tom Brady 1.25 3.00
106 Lee Evans .25 .60
107 Jake Delhomme .20 .50
108 Ben Roethlisberger .50 1.25
109 Jake Plummer .20 .50
110 Charles Rogers .20 .50
111 Patrick Ramsey .25 .60
112 Reggie Wayne .25 .60
113 Reuben Droughns .20 .50
114 Aaron Brooks .20 .50
115 David Carr .20 .50
116 Thomas Jones .20 .50
117 Ashley Lelie .20 .50
118 Donald Driver .25 .60
119 Billy Volek .20 .50
120 Peyton Manning .75 2.00
121 Frank Gore RC 1.25 3.00
122 Adam Jones RC .60 1.50
123 Antrel Rolle RC 1.00 2.50
124 Roddy White RC 1.00 2.50
125 Derrick Johnson RC .75 2.00
126 Troy Williamson RC .60 1.50
127 Maurice Clarett .60 1.50
128 Dan Orlovsky RC .60 1.50
129 Andrew Walter RC .60 1.50
130 Reggie Brown RC .60 1.50
131 Matt Jones RC .60 1.50
132 David Greene RC .60 1.50
133 Jerome Mathis RC 1.00 2.50
134 Thomas Davis RC .60 1.50
135 Roscoe Parrish RC .60 1.50
136 Ciatrick Fason RC .60 1.50
137 David Pollack RC .60 1.50
138 Kyle Orton RC .60 1.50
139 Heath Miller RC 1.25 3.00
140 Courtney Roby RC .60 1.50
141 Terrence Murphy RC .60 1.50
142 DeMarcus Ware RC 2.00 5.00
143 Fabian Washington RC .60 1.50
144 J.J. Arrington RC .75 2.00
145 Fred Gibson RC .60 1.50
146 Carlos Rogers RC 1.00 2.50
147 Eric Shelton RC .60 1.50
148 Craphonso Thorpe RC .60 1.50
149 Anthony Davis RC .60 1.50
150 Marion Barber RC .60 1.50
151 Aaron Rodgers AU/299 RC 300.00 500.00
152 Alex Smith QB AU/299 RC 50.00 100.00
153 Braylon Edwards AU/299 RC 6.00 15.00
154 Cadillac Williams AU/299 RC 6.00 15.00
155 Cedric Benson AU/299 RC 15.00 20.00
156 Charlie Frye AU/299 RC 6.00 15.00
157 Jason Campbell AU/299 RC 4.00 10.00
158 Mark Clayton AU/299 RC 4.00 10.00
159 Mike Williams AU/299 5.00 12.00
160 Ronnie Brown AU/299 RC 5.00 12.00
161 Alex Smith TE AU RC 3.00 8.00
162 Alvin Pearman AU RC 3.00 8.00
163 Brandon Jacobs AU RC 6.00 15.00
164 Channing Crowder AU RC 4.00 10.00
165 Chris Henry AU RC 4.00 10.00
166 Courtney Roby AU RC 3.00 8.00
167 Derek Anderson AU RC 4.00 10.00
168 Mark Bradley AU RC 3.00 8.00
169 Ryan Fitzpatrick AU RC 5.00 12.00
170 Ryan Moats AU RC 3.00 8.00
171 Stefan LeFors AU RC 3.00 8.00
172 Steve Savoy AU RC 3.00 8.00
173 Tab Perry AU RC 3.00 8.00
174 Timmy Chang AU RC 3.00 8.00
175 Vincent Jackson AU RC 5.00 12.00
176 Charles Frederick AU RC 3.00 8.00
177 Kay-Jay Harris AU RC 3.00 8.00
178 Darren Sproles AU RC 8.00 20.00
179 Adrian McPherson AU RC 3.00 8.00
180 Craig Bragg AU RC 3.00 8.00
181 J.R. Russell AU RC 3.00 8.00
182 Gino Guidugli AU RC 3.00 8.00
183 Vernand Morency AU RC 3.00 8.00

2005 Finest Refractors

*VETERANS: 2X TO 5X BASIC CARDS
*ROOKIE 121-150: .6X TO 1.5X BASIC CARD
*ROOKIE AU 161-183: .4X TO 1X BASIC AU
STATED PRINT RUN 399 SER.#'d SETS

2005 Finest Xfractors

*VETERANS 1-120: 2.5X TO 6X BASIC CARDS
*ROOKIES 121-150: .8X TO 2X BASIC CARDS
*ROOKIE AU 161-183: .5X TO 1.2X
STATED PRINT RUN 250 SER.#'d SETS

2005 Finest Black Refractors

*VETERANS: 5X TO 12X BASIC CARDS
*ROOKIES 121-150: 1.5X TO 4X BASIC CARDS
*ROOKIE AU 161-183: 1X TO 2.5X
STATED PRINT RUN 99 SER.#'d SETS

2005 Finest Black Xfractors

*VETERANS: 10X TO 25X BASIC CARDS
*ROOKIES 121-150: 4X TO 10X BASIC CARDS
*ROOKIE AU 161-183: 2X TO 5X BASIC AUTOS
STATED PRINT RUN 25 SER.#'d SETS

2005 Finest Gold Refractors

*VETERANS: 6X TO 15X BASIC CARDS
*ROOKIES 121-150: 2.5X TO 6X BASIC CARDS
*ROOKIE AU 161-183: 1.2X TO 3X
STATED PRINT RUN 49 SER.#'d SETS

2005 Finest Green Refractors

*VETERANS: 3X TO 8X BASIC CARDS
*ROOKIES 121-150: 1X TO 2.5X BASIC CARDS
*ROOKIE AU 161-183: .6X TO 1.5X
STATED PRINT RUN 199 SER.#'d SETS

2005 Finest Green Xfractors

*VETERANS: 6X TO 15X BASIC CARDS
*ROOKIES 121-150: 2.5X TO 6X BASIC CARDS
*ROOKIE AU 161-183: 1.2X TO 3X
STATED PRINT RUN 50 SER.#'d SETS

2005 Finest Blue Refractors

*VETERANS: 2.5X TO 6X BASIC CARDS
*ROOKIES 121-150: .8X TO 2X BASIC CARDS
*ROOKIE AU 161-183: .5X TO 1.2X
STATED PRINT RUN 299 SER.#'d SETS

2005 Finest Blue Xfractors

*VETERANS: 4X TO 10X BASIC CARDS
*ROOKIES 121-150: 1.2X TO 3X BASIC CARDS
*ROOKIE AU 161-183: .8X TO 2X
STATED PRINT RUN 150 SER.#'d SETS

2005 Finest Autographs Refractor

UNPRICED SUPERFRACTORS #'d TO 1
*XFRACTOR/199: .6X TO 1.5X BASIC AU
FAAM Adrian McPherson 4.00 10.00
FAAR Antrel Rolle 6.00 15.00
FABJ Brandon Jones 5.00 12.00
FACF Ciatrick Fason 4.00 10.00
FACT Craphonso Thorpe 4.00 10.00
FADJ Derrick Johnson 5.00 12.00
FADO Dan Orlovsky 4.00 10.00
FADS Darren Sproles 6.00 15.00
FAFW Fabian Washington 4.00 10.00
FAKC Kevin Curtis 5.00 12.00
FAMB Marion Barber 4.00 10.00
FANB Nate Burleson 4.00 10.00
FAOS Onterrio Smith 4.00 10.00
FARP Roscoe Parrish 4.00 10.00
FARW Roddy White 6.00 15.00
FASM Shawne Merriman 6.00 15.00
FATB Tatum Bell 4.00 10.00
FATW Troy Williamson 4.00 10.00

2005 Finest Peyton Manning Finest Moments

COMMON CARD (FM1-FM49) 2.50 6.00
STATED PRINT RUN 599 SER.#'d SETS
UNPRICED AUTOS PRINT RUN 1 SET

2006 Finest

This 186-card set was released in October, 2006. The set was issued in five-card packs, with an $0.50 SRP, which came six packs to a mini-box and three mini-boxes to a full box. Cards numbered 1-105 feature veterans while cards numbered 106-186 feature rookies. Within the rookie subset, cards numbered 151-186 were signed by the featured players. A few of those players who signed cards autographed fewer cards then the other players and those signed cards were serial numbered. The serial numbering of those signed cards are notated in our checklist.

COMP.SET w/o AU's (150) 12.50 30.00
1 Muhsin Muhammad .20 .50
2 Kevin Jones .20 .50
3 Eli Manning .25 .60
4 Marion Barber .25 .60
5 Randy Moss .25 .60
6 Odell Thurman .20 .50
7 Dante Hall .20 .50
8 Chris Brown .20 .50
9 Antonio Gates .30 .75
10 Champ Bailey .25 .60
11 Eric Moulds .20 .50
12 Ray Lewis .30 .75
13 Larry Fitzgerald .25 .60
14 Byron Leftwich .20 .50
15 Marvin Harrison .25 .60
16 Larry Johnson .20 .50
17 Steve Smith .30 .75
18 Shaun Alexander .20 .50
19 Drew Bledsoe .25 .60
20 Joey Galloway .25 .60
21 Deuce McAllister .25 .60
22 Ben Obomanu RC 1.25 3.00
23 Chester Taylor .25 .60
24 Delanie Walker RC 2.00 5.00
25 Torry Holt .25 .60
26 LaDainian Tomlinson .30 .75
27 Derrick Mason .20 .50
28 T.J. Houshmandzadeh .20 .50
29 Fred Taylor .20 .50
30 Michael Jenkins .20 .50
31 Edgerrin James .25 .60
32 Terrell Owens .25 .60
33 Jason Witten .25 .60
34 Clinton Portis .20 .50
35 Deion Branch .20 .50
36 Priest Holmes .20 .50
37 Quinton Ganther RC 1.00 2.50
38 Kurt Warner .25 .60
39 Domanick Davis .20 .50
40 Chris Simms .20 .50
41 Dwight Freeney .20 .50
42 Daniel Bullocks RC 1.00 2.50
43 Tiki Barber .25 .60
44 Steve McNair .25 .60
45 Steven Jackson .20 .50
46 Joe Horn .20 .50
47 Randy McMichael .20 .50
48 Cedric Humes RC 1.00 2.50
49 Warrick Dunn .20 .50
50 Tatum Bell .20 .50
51 P.J. Pope RC 1.50 4.00
52 Curtis Martin .25 .60
53 Donovan McNabb .25 .60
54 LaMont Jordan .25 .60
55 Marc Bulger .20 .50
56 Drew Bennett .25 .60
57 Julius Jones .20 .50
58 Santana Moss .25 .60
59 Ronnie Brown .25 .60
60 Tony Gonzalez .25 .60
61 Jamal Lewis .25 .60
62 D.J. Shockley RC 1.25 3.00
63 Carson Palmer .25 .60
64 Jonathan Orr RC 1.25 3.00
65 Brandon Stokley .20 .50
66 Brett Favre .60 1.50
67 Jonathan Vilma .20 .50
68 Darrell Jackson .25 .60
69 Brian Urlacher .30 .75
70 Drew Brees .30 .75
71 Mike Williams .20 .50
72 Corey Dillon .20 .50
73 Willis McGahee .20 .50
74 Michael Vick .25 .60
75 Chad Johnson .20 .50
76 Anquan Boldin .20 .50
77 Shawne Merriman .25 .60
78 Willie Parker .25 .60
79 Roy Williams S .20 .50
80 Trent Green .20 .50
81 Chris Gamble .20 .50
82 Ahman Green .25 .60
83 Todd Heap .20 .50
84 Brett Basanez RC 1.50 4.00
85 Andre Johnson .25 .60
86 Abdul Hodge RC 1.00 2.50
87 Plaxico Burress .20 .50
88 Hines Ward .25 .60
89 Rod Smith .25 .60
90 Cadillac Williams .25 .60
91 Braylon Edwards .20 .50
92 Rudi Johnson .20 .50
93 Isaac Bruce .30 .75
94 Chris Chambers .20 .50
95 Matt Hasselbeck .20 .50
96 Donte Stallworth .20 .50
97 Philip Rivers .30 .75
98 Will Blackmon RC 1.00 2.50
99 Alge Crumpler .25 .60
100 Chad Pennington .20 .50
101 Darnell Bing RC 1.25 3.00
102 Daunte Culpepper .25 .60
103 Jeremy Shockey .20 .50
104 Jerry Porter .20 .50
105 Tom Brady 1.00 2.50
106 Jeff Webb RC 1.25 3.00
107 Jake Delhomme .20 .50
108 Ben Roethlisberger .40 1.00
109 Jake Plummer .20 .50
110 Paul Pinegar RC 1.00 2.50
111 Kevin McMahan RC 1.25 3.00
112 Reggie Wayne .25 .60
113 Bennie Brazell RC 1.25 3.00
114 Todd Watkins RC 1.00 2.50
115 David Carr .20 .50
116 Cory Rodgers RC 1.00 2.50
117 Leon Washington RC 1.00 2.50
118 Michael Strahan .25 .60
119 P.J. Daniels RC 1.00 2.50
120 Peyton Manning .75 2.00
121 Brandon Marshall RC 2.00 5.00
122 Jerome Harrison RC 1.00 2.50
123 Mario Williams RC 1.50 4.00
124 Ernie Sims RC 1.00 2.50
125 Devin Hester RC 2.00 5.00
126 Jimmy Williams RC 1.00 2.50
127 Charlie Whitehurst RC 1.00 2.50
128 Jason Avant RC 1.00 2.50
129 Marcus Vick RC 1.00 2.50
130 Mathias Kiwanuka RC 1.50 4.00
131 Brodrick Bunkley RC 1.25 3.00
132 Reggie McNeal RC 1.00 2.50
133 Dominique Byrd RC 1.00 2.50
134 Jason Allen RC 1.25 3.00
135 D'Qwell Jackson RC 1.00 2.50
136 Donte Whitner RC 1.25 3.00
137 Willie Reid RC 1.25 3.00
138 Kamerion Wimbley RC 1.25 3.00
139 Martin Nance RC 1.00 2.50
140 Haloti Ngata RC 1.25 3.00
141 Devin Aromashodu RC 1.00 2.50
142 Jeremy Bloom RC 1.00 2.50
143 Manny Lawson RC 1.25 3.00
144 Johnathan Joseph RC 1.25 3.00
145 Brad Smith RC 1.25 3.00
146 Thomas Howard RC 1.00 2.50
147 Demetrius Williams RC 1.00 2.50
148 Antonio Cromartie RC 1.25 3.00
149 Bobby Carpenter RC 1.00 2.50
150 Tamba Hali RC 1.50 4.00
151 Reggie Bush AU/199 RC 10.00 25.00
152 Matt Leinart AU/199 RC 8.00 20.00
153 Vince Young AU/199 RC 6.00 15.00
154 Jay Cutler AU/199 RC 8.00 20.00
155 S.Holmes AU/199 RC 8.00 20.00
156 LenDale White AU/199 RC 6.00 15.00
157 DeA.Williams AU/199 RC 8.00 20.00
158 Sinorice Moss AU/199 RC 6.00 15.00
159 Vernon Davis AU/199 RC 8.00 20.00
160 Joseph Addai AU/199 RC 6.00 15.00
161 Omar Jacobs AU/199 RC 6.00 15.00
162 Chad Jackson AU/199 RC 6.00 15.00
163 Chad Greenway AU RC 5.00 12.00
164 Maurice Drew AU RC 5.00 12.00
165 D.Ferguson AU RC 3.00 8.00
166 Anthony Fasano AU RC 3.00 8.00
167 Derek Hagan AU/199 RC 8.00 20.00
168 A.J. Hawk AU/199 RC 8.00 20.00
169 David Thomas AU RC 3.00 8.00
170 Brian Calhoun AU RC 3.00 8.00
171 Kellen Clemens AU RC 3.00 8.00
172 Tarvaris Jackson AU RC 3.00 8.00
173 Maurice Stovall AU RC 3.00 8.00
174 Michael Huff AU/199 RC 8.00 20.00
175 Greg Jennings AU RC 5.00 12.00
176 Joe Klopfenstein AU RC 3.00 8.00
177 Leonard Pope AU RC 5.00 12.00
178 Michael Robinson AU RC 3.00 8.00
179 Ingle Martin AU RC 4.00 10.00
180 Wali Lundy AU RC 3.00 8.00
181 Drew Olson AU RC 3.00 8.00
182 Jerious Norwood AU RC 3.00 8.00
183 Travis Wilson AU RC 3.00 8.00
184 Tye Hill AU RC 3.00 8.00
185 Brandon Williams AU RC 3.00 8.00
186 Marques Hagans AU RC 3.00 8.00

2006 Finest Black Refractors

*VETS: 5X TO 12X BASIC CARDS
*ROOKIES: 1.2X TO 3X BASIC CARDS
*ROOKIE AU: .8X TO 2X BASIC AU
STATED PRINT RUN 99 SER.#'d SETS

2006 Finest Black Xfractors

*VETERANS: 10X TO 25X BASIC CARDS
*ROOKIES: 2.5X TO 6X BASIC CARDS
*ROOKIE AU: 1.2X TO 3X BASIC CARDS
STATED PRINT RUN 25 SER.#'d SETS

2006 Finest Blue Refractors

*VETERANS: 2.5X TO 6X BASIC CARDS
*ROOKIES: .6X TO 1.5X BASIC CARDS
*ROOKIE AU: .5X TO 1.2X BASIC CARDS
STATED PRINT RUN 299 SER.#'d SETS

2006 Finest Blue Xfractors

*VETERANS: 4X TO 10X BASIC CARDS
*ROOKIES: 1X TO 2.5X BASIC CARDS
*ROOKIE AU: .6X TO 1.5X BASIC CARDS
STATED PRINT RUN 150 SER.#'d SETS

2006 Finest Gold Refractors

*VETERANS: 6X TO 15X BASIC CARDS
*ROOKIES: 1.5X TO 4X BASIC CARDS
*ROOKIE AU: 1X TO 2.5X BASIC CARDS
STATED PRINT RUN 49 SER.#'d SETS

2006 Finest Gold Xfractors

UNPRICED GOLD XFRACT #'d TO 10

2006 Finest Green Refractors

*VETERANS: 3X TO 8X BASIC CARDS
*ROOKIES: .8X TO 2X BASIC CARDS
*ROOKIE AU: .5X TO 1.2X BASIC CARDS
STATED PRINT RUN 199 SER.#'d SETS

2006 Finest Green Xfractors

*VETERANS: 6X TO 15X BASIC CARDS
*ROOKIES: 1.5X TO 4X BASIC CARDS
*ROOKIE AU: 1X TO 2.5X BASIC CARDS
STATED PRINT RUN 50 SER.#'d SETS

2006 Finest Refractors

*VETERANS: 2X TO 5X BASIC CARDS
*ROOKIES: .5X TO 1.2X BASIC CARDS
*ROOKIE AU: .4X TO 1X BASIC CARDS
*ROOKIE AU/50: .6X TO 1.5X BASIC CARDS
STATED PRINT RUN 50-399

2006 Finest SuperFractors

UNPRICED SUPERFRACTOR #'d TO 1

2006 Finest White Framed Refractors

UNPRICED WHITE REF #'d TO 1

2006 Finest White Framed Xfractors

UNPRICED WHT XFRACT #'d TO 1

2006 Finest Xfractors

*VETERANS: 2.5X TO 6X BASIC CARDS
*ROOKIES: .6X TO 1.5X BASIC CARDS
*ROOKIE AU: .4X TO 1X BASIC CARDS
*ROOKIE AU/25: 1X TO 2.5X AUTO/199
STATED PRINT RUN 25-250

2006 Finest Autographs Refractor

GROUP A ODDS 1:1896 HOB
GROUP B ODDS 1:126 HOB
GROUP C ODDS 1:36 HOB
*XFRCT/25: .6X TO 1.5X BASE GRP A
*XFRCT/25: .8X TO 2X BASE GRP B-C
XFRACTOR PRINT RUN 25
UNPRICED PRINT PLATES #'d TO 1
UNPRICED SUPERFRACTOR #'d TO 1
FABM Brandon Marshall C 8.00 20.00
FACH Cedric Humes C 3.00 8.00
FACR Cory Rodgers C 3.00 8.00
FADA Devin Aromashodu C 3.00 8.00
FAEM Eli Manning A 60.00 100.00
FAES Emmitt Smith A 150.00 250.00
FAJA Jason Avant B 3.00 8.00
FAJC Jay Cutler A 4.00 10.00
FAJH Jerome Harrison B 3.00 8.00
FALT LaDainian Tomlinson A 25.00 60.00
FAMK Mathias Kiwanuka C 5.00 12.00
FAML Matt Leinart A 10.00 25.00
FAPM Peyton Manning A 60.00 120.00
FAQG Quinton Ganther C 3.00 8.00
FARB Reggie Bush A 5.00 12.00
FASM Shawne Merriman A 8.00 20.00
FASS Steve Smith A 15.00 30.00
FAVY Vince Young A 12.00 30.00
FAWB Will Blackmon B 3.00 8.00
FAWJ Winston Justice C 4.00 10.00

2006 Finest Brett Favre Finest Moments

COMMON CARD (1-20) 2.50 6.00
*BLACK REFRACTOR/99: 1.2X TO 3X
*BLACK XFRACTOR/25: 3X TO 8X
*BLUE REFRACTOR/299: .6X TO 1.5X
*BLUE XFRACTOR/150: 1X TO 2.5X
*GOLD REFRACTOR/49: 2X TO 5X
*GOLD XFRACTOR/10: 6X TO 12X
*GREEN REFRACTOR/199: .8X TO 2X
*GREEN XFRACTOR/50: 2X TO 5X
UNPRICED PRINT PLATES #'d TO 1
*REFRACTOR/399: .5X TO 1.2X
UNPRICED SUPERFRACTOR #'d TO 1
UNPRICED WHT REFRACT #'d TO 1
UNPRICED WHT XFRACT #'d TO 1
*XFRACTOR/250: .8X TO 2X
UNPRICED AUTOS #'d TO 4
UNPRICED AU PRINT PLATES #'d TO 1

2006 Finest Johnny Unitas Finest Moments

COMMON CARD (1-10) 2.50 6.00
*BLACK REFRACTOR/99: 1X TO 2.5X
*BLUE REFRACTOR/299: .6X TO 1.5X
UNPRICED CUT AUTOS #'d TO 5
*GREEN REFRACTOR/199: .8X TO 2X
UNPRICED PRINT PLATES #'d TO 1
*REFRACTOR/399: .5X TO 1.2X
ONE UNITAS MOMENT PER HOBBY BOX

2007 Finest

This 150-card set was relased in October, 2007. The set was issued into the hobby in five-card packs, with a $10 SRP, which came 18 packs to a box. The set is divided between veterans which are cards 1-100 and 2007 NFL rookies which are cards 101-150.

COMPLETE SET (150) 25.00 60.00
UNPRICED PRINT.PLATE PRINT RUN 1
UNPRICED SUPERFRACTOR PRINT RUN 1
UNPRICED WHT XFRACTOR PRINT RUN 1
1 Peyton Manning .75 2.00
2 Drew Brees .30 .75
3 Donovan McNabb .25 .60
4 Tony Romo .40 1.00
5 Carson Palmer .25 .60
6 Marc Bulger .20 .50
7 Philip Rivers .30 .75
8 Tom Brady 1.00 2.50
9 J.P. Losman .20 .50
10 Steve McNair .25 .60
11 Eli Manning .25 .60
12 Matt Hasselbeck .20 .50
13 Alex Smith QB .25 .60
14 Ben Roethlisberger .30 .75
15 Matt Leinart .20 .50
16 Rex Grossman .20 .50
17 Brett Favre .60 1.50
18 Vince Young .20 .50
19 Jay Cutler .20 .50
20 Chad Pennington .20 .50
21 LaDainian Tomlinson .30 .75
22 Larry Johnson .20 .50
23 Frank Gore .25 .60
24 Steven Jackson .20 .50
25 Willie Parker .25 .60
26 Rudi Johnson .20 .50
27 Brian Westbrook .20 .50
28 Chester Taylor .20 .50
29 Travis Henry .25 .60
30 Thomas Jones .20 .50
31 Edgerrin James .25 .60
32 Fred Taylor .20 .50
33 Warrick Dunn .20 .50
34 Jamal Lewis .25 .60
35 Julius Jones .20 .50
36 Joseph Addai .20 .50
37 Ahman Green .25 .60
38 Deuce McAllister .25 .60
39 Ronnie Brown .20 .50
40 Maurice Jones-Drew .20 .50
41 DeShaun Foster .25 .60
42 Shaun Alexander .20 .50
43 Cadillac Williams .25 .60
44 Laurence Maroney .25 .60
45 Cedric Benson .20 .50
46 Dominic Rhodes .20 .50
47 Jerious Norwood .20 .50
48 Brandon Jacobs .20 .50
49 DeAngelo Williams .20 .50
50 Willis McGahee .20 .50
51 Clinton Portis .20 .50
52 Chad Johnson .20 .50
53 Marvin Harrison .25 .60
54 Roy Williams WR .20 .50
55 Reggie Wayne .25 .60
56 Donald Driver .25 .60
57 Lee Evans .25 .60
58 Anquan Boldin .20 .50
59 Torry Holt .25 .60
60 Terrell Owens .25 .60
61 Steve Smith .25 .60
62 Andre Johnson .25 .60
63 Laveranues Coles .20 .50
64 Javon Walker .25 .60
65 T.J. Houshmandzadeh .20 .50
66 Marques Colston .20 .50
67 Terry Glenn .25 .60
68 Plaxico Burress .20 .50
69 Hines Ward .25 .60
70 Jerricho Cotchery .20 .50
71 Larry Fitzgerald .25 .60
72 Braylon Edwards .20 .50
73 Santana Moss .25 .60
74 Santonio Holmes .20 .50
75 Mike Furrey .25 .60
76 Isaac Bruce .30 .75
77 Derrick Mason .20 .50
78 Randy Moss .25 .60
79 Greg Jennings .20 .50
80 Devin Hester .25 .60
81 Muhsin Muhammad .20 .50
82 Kellen Winslow .20 .50
83 Todd Heap .20 .50
84 Tony Gonzalez .25 .60
85 Antonio Gates .30 .75
86 Jeremy Shockey .20 .50
87 Jason Witten .25 .60
88 Randy McMichael .20 .50
89 Alge Crumpler .25 .60
90 L.J. Smith .20 .50
91 Champ Bailey .25 .60
92 DeAngelo Hall .20 .50
93 Asante Samuel .20 .50
94 Julius Peppers .25 .60
95 Jason Taylor .25 .60
96 Michael Strahan .25 .60
97 Shawne Merriman .20 .50
98 Brian Urlacher .30 .75
99 Troy Polamalu .30 .75
100 Ed Reed .25 .60
101 JaMarcus Russell RC 1.00 2.50
102 Brady Quinn RC 1.00 2.50
103 John Beck RC 1.00 2.50
104 Kevin Kolb RC 1.25 3.00
105 Trent Edwards RC 1.00 2.50
106 Troy Smith RC 1.00 2.50
107 Drew Stanton RC 1.00 2.50
108 Chris Leak RC 1.00 2.50
109 Jordan Palmer RC 1.25 3.00
110 Drew Tate RC 1.25 3.00
111 Isaiah Stanback RC 1.00 2.50
112 Adrian Peterson RC 15.00 40.00
113 Marshawn Lynch RC 2.00 5.00
114 Brandon Jackson RC 1.00 2.50
115 Kenny Irons RC 1.00 2.50
116 Michael Bush RC .75 2.00
117 Lorenzo Booker RC 1.25 3.00
118 Brian Leonard RC 1.00 2.50
119 Garrett Wolfe RC 1.00 2.50
120 Antonio Pittman RC 1.00 2.50
121 Selvin Young RC 1.00 2.50
122 Chris Henry RB RC 1.00 2.50
123 Tony Hunt RC 1.00 2.50
124 Kenneth Darby RC 1.00 2.50
125 Kolby Smith RC 1.00 2.50
126 Darius Walker RC 1.00 2.50
127 Greg Olsen RC 1.50 4.00
128 Dwayne Bowe RC 1.00 2.50
129 Craig Buster Davis RC 1.00 2.50
130 Ted Ginn Jr. RC 1.25 3.00
131 Anthony Gonzalez RC 1.00 2.50
132 Yamon Figurs RC 1.00 2.50
133 Jason Hill RC 1.00 2.50
134 Dwayne Jarrett RC 1.25 3.00
135 Calvin Johnson RC 10.00 25.00
136 Robert Meachem RC 1.25 3.00
137 Sidney Rice RC 1.25 3.00
138 Steve Smith USC RC 1.00 2.50
139 Paul Williams RC 1.00 2.50
140 Steve Breaston RC 1.00 2.50
141 David Clowney RC 1.00 2.50
142 Aundrae Allison RC 1.00 2.50
143 Ryne Robinson RC 1.25 3.00
144 Joe Thomas RC 1.50 4.00
145 Leon Hall RC 1.00 2.50
146 Gaines Adams RC 1.25 3.00
147 LaRon Landry RC 1.50 4.00
148 Amobi Okoye RC 1.25 3.00
149 Patrick Willis RC 1.50 4.00
150 Lawrence Timmons RC 1.50 4.00

2007 Finest Black Refractors

*VETS 1-100: 5X TO 12X BASIC CARDS
*ROOKIES 101-150: 1X TO 2.5X BASIC CARDS
BLK REF/99 ODDS 1:4 6-PACK MINI BOX

2007 Finest Blue Refractors

*VETS 1-100: 2.5X TO 6X BASIC CARDS
*ROOKIES 101-150: .5X TO 1.2X BASIC CARDS
BLUE REF/299 ODDS 1:2 6-PACK MINI BOX

2007 Finest Gold Refractors

*VETS 1-100: 6X TO 15X BASIC CARDS
*ROOKIES 101-150: 1.5X TO 4X BASIC CARDS
GOLD REF/50 ODDS 1:7 6-PACK MINI BOX
112 Adrian Peterson 60.00 120.00
135 Calvin Johnson 40.00 100.00

2007 Finest Green Refractors

*VETS 1-100: 3X TO 8X BASIC CARDS
*ROOKIES 101-150: .6X TO 1.5X BASIC CARDS
GRN REF/199 ODDS 1:2 6-PACK MINI BOX

2007 Finest Refractors

*VETS 1-100: 2.5X TO 6X BASIC CARDS
*ROOKIES 101-150: .5X TO 1.2X BASIC CARDS
ODDS 1:1 6-PACK MINI BOX
112 Adrian Peterson 20.00 50.00

2007 Finest Xfractors

*VETS 1-100: 8X TO 20X BASIC CARDS
*ROOKIES 101-150: 2X TO 5X BASIC CARDS
XFRACTOR/25 ODDS 1:14 6-PACK MINI BOX
102 Brady Quinn 5.00 12.00
112 Adrian Peterson 100.00 200.00
135 Calvin Johnson 40.00 80.00

2007 Finest Moments

STATED ODDS 1:1 6-PACK MINI BOX
*REFRACTORS: .5X TO 1.2X
REFRACT.ODDS 1:1 6-PACK MINI BOX
*BLUE REFRACTORS/299: .6X TO 1.5X
BLUE REF/299 ODDS 1:4 6-PACK MINI BOX
*GREEN REFRACTORS/199: .8X TO 2X
GREEN REF/199 ODDS 1:5 6-PACK MINI BOX
*BLACK REFRACTORS/99: 1X TO 2.5X
BLK REF/99 ODDS 1:10 6-PACK MINI BOX
*GOLD REFRACTORS/50: 1.2X TO 3X
GOLD REF/50 ODDS 1:20 6-PACK MINI BOX
*XFRACTORS/25: 2X TO 5X
XFRACT/25 ODDS 1:40 6-PACK MINI BOX
UNPRICED PRINT.PLATES PRINT RUN 1
UNPRICED SUPERFRACT.PRINT RUN 1
UNPRICED WHT XFRACT.PRINT RUN 1
AG Anthony Gonzalez .75 2.00
AP Adrian Peterson 2.50 6.00
BJ Brandon Jackson .75 2.00
BL Brian Leonard .75 2.00
BQ Brady Quinn .75 2.00
CJ Chad Johnson .75 2.00
CJA Chad Jackson .75 2.00
CJO Calvin Johnson 2.50 6.00
CW Cadillac Williams 1.00 2.50
DB Dwayne Bowe .75 2.00
DBR Drew Brees 1.25 3.00
DH Devin Hester 1.00 2.50
DJ Dwayne Jarrett 1.00 2.50
DS Drew Stanton .75 2.00
DW DeAngelo Williams .75 2.00
EM Eli Manning 1.00 2.50
FG Frank Gore 1.00 2.50
GJ Greg Jennings .75 2.00
GO Greg Olsen 1.25 3.00
JA Joseph Addai .75 2.00
JB John Beck .75 2.00
JC Jay Cutler .75 2.00
JN Jerious Norwood .75 2.00
JR JaMarcus Russell .75 2.00
KK Kevin Kolb 1.00 2.50
LB Lorenzo Booker 1.00 2.50
LJ Larry Johnson .75 2.00
LM Laurence Maroney 1.00 2.50
LT LaDainian Tomlinson 1.25 3.00
MB Michael Bush .75 2.00
MC Marques Colston .75 2.00
MD Maurice Jones-Drew .75 2.00
ML Matt Leinart .75 2.00
MLY Marshawn Lynch 1.50 4.00
MW Mario Williams 1.00 2.50
PM Peyton Manning 3.00 8.00
RB Reggie Bush .75 2.00
RM Robert Meachem 1.00 2.50
RW Roy Williams WR .75 2.00
SA Shaun Alexander .75 2.00
SH Santonio Holmes .75 2.00
SJ Steven Jackson .75 2.00
SR Sidney Rice 1.00 2.50
SS Steve Smith USC .75 2.00
SSM Steve Smith 1.00 2.50
TB Tom Brady 4.00 10.00
TG Ted Ginn Jr. 1.00 2.50
TJ Thomas Jones .75 2.00
VY Vince Young .75 2.00
WM Willis McGahee .75 2.00

2007 Finest Moments Autographs

GROUP A ODDS 1:328 6-PACK BOX
GROUP B ODDS 1:143 6-PACK BOX
GROUP C ODDS 1:125 6-PACK BOX
GROUP D ODDS 1:34 6-PACK BOX
*REFRACT/25: .4X TO 1X GROUP A-B AUs
*REFRACT/25: .6X TO 1.5X GROUP C-D AUs
REFRACT/25 ODDS 1:83 6-PACK BOX
UNPRICED SUPERFR.PRINT RUN 1
UNPRICED PRINT.PLATE PRINT RUN 1
AP Adrian Peterson A 125.00 250.00
BJ Brandon Jackson D 8.00 20.00
BL Brian Leonard D 8.00 20.00
BQ Brady Quinn A 15.00 40.00
CJ Chad Johnson B 8.00 20.00
DB Dwayne Bowe B 8.00 20.00
DW DeAngelo Williams B 8.00 20.00
FG Frank Gore B 10.00 25.00
GJ Greg Jennings C 8.00 20.00
JB John Beck D 8.00 20.00
JR JaMarcus Russell A 10.00 25.00
KK Kevin Kolb C 10.00 25.00
LJ Larry Johnson B 8.00 20.00
LT LaDainian Tomlinson A 30.00 80.00
MC Marques Colston B 8.00 20.00
ML Matt Leinart B 8.00 20.00
RB Reggie Bush A 20.00 50.00
RM Robert Meachem B 10.00 25.00
SA Shaun Alexander A 10.00 25.00
SJ Steven Jackson B 8.00 20.00
SS Steve Smith B 10.00 25.00
TB Tom Brady A 150.00 250.00
TG Ted Ginn Jr. B 10.00 25.00
TJ Thomas Jones B 8.00 20.00
VY Vince Young A 10.00 25.00

2007 Finest Moments Autographs Dual

STATED PRINT RUN 20 SER.#'d SETS
BG J.Beck/T.Ginn 25.00 60.00
BM D.Brees/R.Meachem 40.00 80.00
BQ T.Brady/B.Quinn 250.00 400.00
JL S.Jackson/B.Leonard 20.00 50.00
JS D.Jarrett/S.Smith 15.00 40.00
JT L.Johnson/L.Tomlinson 30.00 80.00
PL A.Peterson/M.Lynch 125.00 250.00
RJ J.Russell/C.Johnson 60.00 120.00
RP J.Russell/A.Peterson 100.00 200.00
RQ J.Russell/B.Quinn 30.00 80.00

2007 Finest Reggie Bush Finest Moments

COMMON CARD 2.00 5.00
REG.BUSH MOMENT/899 ODDS 1:36 HOB
*REFRACTORS/149: .6X TO 1.5X
REFRACTOR/149 ODDS 1:144 HOB
*XFRACTORS/50: 1X TO 2.5X
XFRACTOR/50 ODDS 1:414 HOB
UNPRICED GOLD REF. PRINT RUN 1

2007 Finest Rookie Autographs

GROUP A ODDS 1:415 6-PACK BOX
GROUP B ODDS 1:51 6-PACK BOX
GROUP C/D ODDS 1:33 6-PACK BOX
GROUP E ODDS 1:14 6-PACK BOX
GROUP F/G ODDS 1:17 6-PACK BOX
GROUP H ODDS 1:2 6-PACK BOX
*BLUE XFRACT/50: .4X TO 1X GRP A AU
*BLUE XFRACT/50: .6X TO 1.5X GRP B-H AU
BLUE XFRACT/50 1:21 6-PACK MINI BOX
UNPRICED BLK XFRACT/10 1:104 MINI BOX
UNPRICED GOLD XFRACT.PRINT RUN 1
UNPRICED PRINT.PLATE PRINT RUN 1
101 JaMarcus Russell A 8.00 20.00
102 Brady Quinn A 8.00 20.00
103 John Beck D 4.00 10.00
104 Kevin Kolb B 5.00 12.00
105 Trent Edwards D 4.00 10.00
106 Troy Smith B 4.00 10.00
107 Drew Stanton B 4.00 10.00
109 Jordan Palmer F 5.00 12.00
110 Drew Tate H 5.00 12.00
111 Isaiah Stanback H 4.00 10.00
112 Adrian Peterson A 150.00 300.00
113 Marshawn Lynch A 40.00 80.00
114 Brandon Jackson D 4.00 10.00
116 Michael Bush C 4.00 10.00
117 Lorenzo Booker E 5.00 12.00
118 Brian Leonard E 4.00 10.00
119 Garrett Wolfe E 4.00 10.00
120 Antonio Pittman E 4.00 10.00
121 Selvin Young H 4.00 10.00
122 Chris Henry RB H 4.00 10.00
123 Tony Hunt G 4.00 10.00
124 Kenneth Darby H 4.00 10.00
125 Kolby Smith H 4.00 10.00
126 Darius Walker H 4.00 10.00
127 Greg Olsen C 6.00 15.00
128 Dwayne Bowe B 4.00 10.00
129 Craig Buster Davis H 4.00 10.00
130 Ted Ginn Jr. B 5.00 12.00
131 Anthony Gonzalez C 4.00 10.00
132 Yamon Figurs H 4.00 10.00
133 Jason Hill F 4.00 10.00
134 Dwayne Jarrett B 5.00 12.00
135 Calvin Johnson A 60.00 120.00
136 Robert Meachem B 5.00 12.00
137 Sidney Rice B 5.00 12.00
138 Steve Smith USC F 4.00 10.00
139 Paul Williams H 4.00 10.00
140 Steve Breaston H 4.00 10.00
141 David Clowney H 4.00 10.00
142 Aundrae Allison G 4.00 10.00
143 Ryne Robinson H 5.00 12.00
144 Joe Thomas C 6.00 15.00
145 Leon Hall C 4.00 10.00
146 Gaines Adams B 5.00 12.00
147 LaRon Landry E 6.00 15.00
148 Amobi Okoye B 5.00 12.00
149 Patrick Willis C 6.00 15.00
150 Lawrence Timmons H 6.00 15.00

2007 Finest Rookie Autographs Green Xfractors

*GREEN XFRACT/25: .6X TO 1.5X GRP A AUs
*GREEN XFRACT/25: .8X TO 2X GRP B-H AUs
GREEN XFRACTORS PRINT RUN 25 SER.#'d SETS
104 Kevin Kolb 10.00 25.00
112 Adrian Peterson 250.00 400.00
135 Calvin Johnson 120.00 250.00

2007 Finest Vince Young Finest Moments

COMMON CARD 2.00 5.00
VIN.YOUNG MOMENT/899 ODDS 1:36 HOB
*REFRACTORS/149: .6X TO 1.5X
REFRACTOR/149 ODDS 1:144 HOB
*XFRACTORS/50: 1X TO 2.5X
XFRACTOR/50 ODDS 1:414 HOB
UNPRICED GOLD REF. PRINT RUN 1

2008 Finest

This set was released on September 17, 2008. The base set consists of 151 cards. Cards 1-100 and 151 feature veterans, and cards 101-150 are rookies serial numbered of 699.

COMP.SET w/o RC's (100) 10.00 25.00
ROOKIE REFRACTOR/699 ODDS 1:12
UNPRICED PRINT PLATE/1 ODDS 1:396
1 Drew Brees .30 .75
2 Tom Brady 1.00 2.50
3 Peyton Manning .75 2.00
4 Carson Palmer .25 .60
5 Ben Roethlisberger .40 1.00
6 Tony Romo .25 .60
7 Vince Young .20 .50
8 David Garrard .20 .50
9 Jeff Garcia .20 .50
10 Derek Anderson .20 .50
11 Matt Hasselbeck .20 .50
12 Donovan McNabb .25 .60
13 Philip Rivers .30 .75
14 Jay Cutler .20 .50
15 Matt Leinart .20 .50
16 Jason Campbell .20 .50
17 Matt Schaub .20 .50
18 Jon Kitna .20 .50
19 Marc Bulger .20 .50
20 Eli Manning .25 .60
21 Willie Parker .25 .60
22 Clinton Portis .20 .50
23 Adrian Peterson .30 .75
24 LaDainian Tomlinson .30 .75
25 Marion Barber .20 .50
26 Brian Westbrook .20 .50
27 Fred Taylor .20 .50
28 Marshawn Lynch .25 .60
29 Joseph Addai .20 .50
30 Willis McGahee .20 .50
31 Frank Gore .25 .60
32 Larry Johnson .20 .50
33 Jamal Lewis .25 .60
34 Edgerrin James .25 .60
35 Thomas Jones .20 .50
36 Brandon Jacobs .20 .50
37 LenDale White .20 .50
38 Justin Fargas .20 .50
39 Ryan Grant .25 .60
40 Earnest Graham .20 .50
41 Laurence Maroney .25 .60
42 Steven Jackson .20 .50
43 DeAngelo Williams .20 .50
44 Shaun Alexander .20 .50
45 Maurice Jones-Drew .20 .50
46 Reggie Bush .20 .50
47 Chester Taylor .20 .50
48 Rudi Johnson .20 .50
49 Ronnie Brown .20 .50
50 Travis Henry .20 .50
51 Cedric Benson .20 .50
52 Chad Johnson .20 .50
53 Reggie Wayne .25 .60
54 Anquan Boldin .20 .50
55 Randy Moss .25 .60
56 Plaxico Burress .20 .50
57 Terrell Owens .25 .60
58 Andre Johnson .25 .60
59 Larry Fitzgerald .25 .60
60 Braylon Edwards .20 .50
61 Steve Smith .25 .60
62 Wes Welker .25 .60
63 T.J. Houshmandzadeh .20 .50
64 Derrick Mason .20 .50
65 Brandon Marshall .25 .60
66 Marques Colston .20 .50
67 Bobby Engram .20 .50
68 Torry Holt .25 .60
69 Roddy White .20 .50
70 Jerricho Cotchery .20 .50
71 Donald Driver .25 .60
72 Roy Williams WR .20 .50
73 Hines Ward .25 .60
74 Santonio Holmes .20 .50
75 Joey Galloway .25 .60
76 Greg Jennings .20 .50
77 Dwayne Bowe .25 .60
78 Calvin Johnson .30 .75
79 Santana Moss .20 .50
80 Kevin Curtis .20 .50
81 Chris Chambers .20 .50
82 Kellen Winslow .20 .50
83 Tony Gonzalez .25 .60
84 Antonio Gates .25 .60
85 Jeremy Shockey .20 .50
86 Jason Witten .25 .60
87 Chris Cooley .20 .50
88 Owen Daniels .20 .50
89 Dallas Clark .20 .50
90 Vernon Davis .20 .50
91 Antonio Cromartie .20 .50
92 Marcus Trufant .20 .50
93 Terence Newman .20 .50
94 Osi Umenyiora .20 .50
95 Mario Williams .25 .60
96 Patrick Willis .25 .60
97 Shawne Merriman .20 .50
98 DeMarcus Ware .25 .60
99 Ed Reed .25 .60
100 Bob Sanders .25 .60
101 Erik Ainge RC 1.25 3.00
102 John David Booty RC 1.25 3.00
103 Colt Brennan RC 1.50 4.00
104 Brian Brohm RC 1.25 3.00
105 Joe Flacco RC 2.50 6.00
106 Chad Henne RC 1.50 4.00
107 Josh Johnson RC 1.25 3.00
108 Anthony Morelli RC 1.25 3.00
109 Matt Ryan RC 4.00 10.00
110 Andre Woodson RC 1.25 3.00
111 Kyle Wright RC 1.25 3.00
112 Jamaal Charles RC 2.00 5.00
113 Tashard Choice RC 1.25 3.00
114 Matt Forte RC 2.00 5.00
115 Mike Hart RC 1.25 3.00
116 Chris Johnson RC 1.50 4.00
117 Felix Jones RC 1.25 3.00
118 Darren McFadden RC 1.25 3.00
119 Rashard Mendenhall RC 1.25 3.00
120 Allen Patrick RC 1.25 3.00

121 Ray Rice RC 1.25 3.00
122 Dustin Keller RC 1.50 4.00
123 Steve Slaton RC 1.25 3.00
124 Kevin Smith RC 1.25 3.00
125 Jonathan Stewart RC 2.00 5.00
126 Kevin O'Connell RC 1.25 3.00
127 Adrian Arrington RC 1.25 3.00
128 Donnie Avery RC 1.50 4.00
129 Earl Bennett RC 2.00 5.00
130 Dexter Jackson RC 2.00 5.00
131 Jerome Simpson RC 1.50 4.00
132 Keenan Burton RC 1.25 3.00
133 Andre Caldwell RC 1.25 3.00
134 Early Doucet RC 1.25 3.00
135 Harry Douglas RC 1.50 4.00
136 James Hardy RC 1.25 3.00
137 Jordy Nelson RC 4.00 10.00
138 DeSean Jackson RC 2.50 6.00
139 Malcolm Kelly RC 1.25 3.00
140 Mario Manningham RC 1.25 3.00
141 Limas Sweed RC 1.25 3.00
142 Eddie Royal RC 1.25 3.00
143 Devin Thomas RC 1.25 3.00
144 John Carlson RC 1.25 3.00
145 Chris Long RC 1.50 4.00
146 Vernon Gholston RC 1.25 3.00
147 D.Rodgers-Cromartie RC 1.50 4.00
148 Keith Rivers RC 1.25 3.00
149 Jake Long RC 2.00 5.00
150 Glenn Dorsey RC 1.25 3.00
151 Brett Favre SP 20.00 40.00

2008 Finest Black Refractors/Xfractors

*VETS 1-100: 4X TO 10X BASIC CARDS
*ROOKIES 101-150: 1.5X TO 4X BASIC CARDS
1-100 REFRACTOR/99 ODDS 1:24
101-150 XFRACTOR/10 ODDS 1:474

2008 Finest Blue Refractors/Xfractors

*VETS 1-100: 2.5X TO 6X BASIC CARDS
*ROOKIES 101-150: .8X TO 2X BASIC CARDS
101-150 ROOKIE XFRACTOR/50 ODDS 1:96

2008 Finest Gold Refractors/Xfractors

*VETS 1-100: 5X TO 12X BASIC CARDS
1-100 VET REFRACTOR/50 ODDS 1:48
UNPRICED 101-150 XFRACT/1 ODDS 1:4812

2008 Finest Green Refractors/Xfractors

*VETS 1-100: 2.5X TO 6X BASIC CARDS
*ROOKIES 101-150: 1X TO 2.5X BASIC CARDS
1-100 VET REFRACTOR/299 ODDS 1:12
101-150 XFRACTOR/25 ODDS 1:192

2008 Finest Red Refractors

*VETS 1-100: 8X TO 20X BASIC CARDS
RED REFRACTOR/25 ODDS 1:96

2008 Finest Adrian Peterson Finest Moments

COMMON CARD (AP1-AP16) 3.00 8.00
*REFRACTOR/149: .5X TO 1.2X BASIC INSERTS
REFRACTORS PRINT RUN 149 SER.#'d SETS
*XFRACTOR/50: .6X TO 1.5X BASIC INSERTS
XFRACTORS PRINT RUN 50 SER.#'d SETS
UNPRICED GOLD REF. PRINT RUN 1
ONE PETERSON PER MINI-BOX

2008 Finest Autograph Patches

AUTO PATCH/15 ODDS 1:498
102 John David Booty 10.00 25.00
104 Brian Brohm 10.00 25.00
105 Joe Flacco 20.00 50.00
106 Chad Henne 12.00 30.00
109 Matt Ryan 100.00 200.00
112 Jamaal Charles 15.00 40.00
114 Matt Forte 15.00 40.00
116 Chris Johnson 12.00 30.00
117 Felix Jones 10.00 25.00
118 Darren McFadden 10.00 25.00
119 Rashard Mendenhall 10.00 25.00
121 Ray Rice 10.00 25.00
122 Dustin Keller 12.00 30.00
123 Steve Slaton 10.00 25.00
124 Kevin Smith 10.00 25.00
125 Jonathan Stewart 15.00 40.00
126 Kevin O'Connell 10.00 25.00
128 Donnie Avery 12.00 30.00
129 Earl Bennett 15.00 40.00
130 Dexter Jackson 15.00 40.00
131 Jerome Simpson 12.00 30.00
133 Andre Caldwell 10.00 25.00
134 Early Doucet 10.00 25.00
135 Harry Douglas 12.00 30.00
136 James Hardy 10.00 25.00
137 Jordy Nelson 40.00 80.00
138 DeSean Jackson 20.00 50.00
139 Malcolm Kelly 10.00 25.00
140 Mario Manningham 10.00 25.00
141 Limas Sweed 10.00 25.00
142 Eddie Royal 10.00 25.00
143 Devin Thomas 10.00 25.00
149 Jake Long 15.00 40.00
150 Glenn Dorsey 10.00 25.00

2008 Finest Autographs

GROUP A/40* ODDS 1:606
GROUP B/150* ODDS 1:126
GROUP C/400* ODDS 1:66
GROUP D/750* ODDS 1:84
GROUP E/1200* ODDS 1:102
GROUP F/1499* ODDS 1:54
GROUP G/1999* ODDS 1:18
ANNOUNCED PRINT RUNS BELOW
CARDS COULD BE SER.#'d VIA MAIL OFFER
UNPRICED BLACK XFRACT/5 ODDS 1:948
UNPRICED GOLD XFRACT/1 ODDS 1:4812
UNPRICED PRINT.PLATE/1 ODDS 1:1584
101 Erik Ainge/400* 3.00 8.00
102 John David Booty/40* 6.00 15.00
103 Colt Brennan/40* 8.00 20.00
104 Brian Brohm/40* 6.00 15.00
105 Joe Flacco/40* 12.00 30.00
106 Chad Henne/150* 5.00 12.00
107 Josh Johnson/1999* 2.50 6.00
108 Anthony Morelli/1499* 2.50 6.00
109 Matt Ryan/40* 60.00 120.00
110 Andre Woodson/40* 6.00 15.00
111 Kyle Wright/1200* 2.50 6.00
112 Jamaal Charles/400* 10.00 25.00
113 Tashard Choice/400* 3.00 8.00
114 Matt Forte/1999* 10.00 25.00
115 Mike Hart/1499* 2.50 6.00
116 Chris Johnson/1200* 3.00 8.00
117 Felix Jones/40* 6.00 15.00
118 Darren McFadden/40* 6.00 15.00
119 Rashard Mendenhall/40* 6.00 15.00
120 Allen Patrick/1999* 2.50 6.00
121 Ray Rice/150* 4.00 10.00
122 Dustin Keller/400* 4.00 10.00
123 Steve Slaton/150* 4.00 10.00
124 Kevin Smith/1999* 2.50 6.00
125 Jonathan Stewart/40* 10.00 25.00
126 Kevin O'Connell/150* 4.00 10.00
127 Adrian Arrington/1999* 2.50 6.00
128 Donnie Avery/1499* 3.00 8.00
129 Earl Bennett/750* 4.00 10.00
130 Dexter Jackson/150* 6.00 15.00
131 Jerome Simpson/150* 5.00 12.00
132 Keenan Burton/1999* 2.50 6.00
133 Andre Caldwell/1999* 2.50 6.00
134 Early Doucet/400* 3.00 8.00
135 Harry Douglas/1999* 3.00 8.00
136 James Hardy/150* 4.00 10.00
137 Jordy Nelson/150* 15.00 30.00
138 DeSean Jackson/400* 6.00 15.00
139 Malcolm Kelly/400* 3.00 8.00
140 Mario Manningham/750* 6.00 15.00
141 Limas Sweed/150* 4.00 10.00
142 Eddie Royal/1999* 2.50 6.00
143 Devin Thomas/150* 4.00 10.00
144 John Carlson/750* 2.50 6.00
145 Chris Long/150* 5.00 12.00
146 Vernon Gholston/150* 4.00 10.00
147 Dominique Rodgers-Cromartie/750* 3.00 8.00
148 Keith Rivers/400* 3.00 8.00
149 Jake Long/400* 5.00 12.00
150 Glenn Dorsey/150* EXCH 4.00 10.00
151 Brett Favre/25 175.00 300.00

2008 Finest Autographs Blue Xfractors

*BLUE XFRACT/30: .4X TO 1X BASIC AU/40
*BLUE XFRACT/30: .6X TO 1.5X BASIC AU/150
*BLUE XFRACT/30: .8X TO 2X BASIC AU/400
*BLUE XFRACT/30: 1X TO 2.5X BASIC AU/750-1999
BLUE XFRACTOR/30 ODDS 1:168
105 Joe Flacco 12.00 30.00
109 Matt Ryan 75.00 150.00
116 Chris Johnson 8.00 20.00
121 Ray Rice 6.00 15.00

2008 Finest Autographs Green Xfractors

*GRN XFRACT/30: .5X TO 1.2X BASIC AU/40
*GRN XFRACT/30: .8X TO 2X BASIC AU/150
*GRN XFRACT/30: 1X TO 2.5X BASIC AU/400
*GRN XFRACT/30: 1.2X TO 3X AUTO/750-1999
GREEN XFRACTOR/20 ODDS 1:252
105 Joe Flacco 15.00 40.00
109 Matt Ryan 125.00 250.00
116 Chris Johnson 10.00 25.00
121 Ray Rice 8.00 20.00

2008 Finest Moments

OVERALL MOMENTS ODDS 1:2
*REFRACTORS: .5X TO 1.2X BASIC INSERTS
*BLUE REF/299: .5X TO 1.2X BASIC INSERT
BLUE REFRACTOR/299 ODDS 1:18
*GREEN REF/199: .6X TO 1.5X BASIC INSERT
GREEN REFRACTOR/199 ODDS 1:24
*BLACK REFRACT/99: .8X TO 2X BASIC INSERTS
BLACK REFRACTOR/99 ODDS 1:48
*GOLD REFRACT/50: 1X TO 2.5X BASIC INSERTS
GOLD REFRACTOR/50 ODDS 1:96
*XFRACTOR/25: 1.5X TO 4X BASIC INSERTS
XFRACTOR/25 ODDS 1:192
UNPRICED WHITE XFRACT/1 ODDS 1:4812
UNPRICED SUPERFRACT/1 ODDS 1:4812
UNPRICED PRINT PLATE/1 ODDS 1:1203
FMAP Adrian Peterson 1.25 3.00
FMAW Andre Woodson .50 1.25
FMBB Bernard Berrian .75 2.00
FMBB Brian Brohm .50 1.25
FMBE Braylon Edwards .75 2.00
FMBS Barry Sanders 4.00 10.00
FMCB Colt Brennan .60 1.50
FMCH Chad Henne .60 1.50
FMCJ Chris Johnson .60 1.50
FMCL Chris Long .60 1.50
FMDB Drew Brees 1.25 3.00
FMDE Derek Anderson .75 2.00
FMDJ DeSean Jackson 1.00 2.50
FMDM Darren McFadden .50 1.25
FMDT Devin Thomas .50 1.25
FMED Early Doucet .50 1.25
FMEM Eli Manning 1.00 2.50
FMFJ Felix Jones .50 1.25
FMGD Glenn Dorsey .50 1.25
FMJB John David Booty .50 1.25
FMJC Jamaal Charles .75 2.00
FMJE John Elway 2.50 6.00
FMJF Joe Flacco 1.00 2.50
FMJH James Hardy .50 1.25
FMJL Jake Long .75 2.00
FMJM Joe Montana 5.00 12.00
FMJS Jonathan Stewart .75 2.00
FMLS Limas Sweed .50 1.25
FMLT LaDainian Tomlinson 1.25 3.00
FMLTA Lawrence Taylor 1.50 4.00
FMMF Matt Forte .75 2.00
FMMH Mike Hart .50 1.25
FMMK Malcolm Kelly .50 1.25
FMML Marshawn Lynch 1.00 2.50
FMMM Mario Manningham .50 1.25
FMMR Matt Ryan 1.50 4.00
FMPM Peyton Manning 3.00 8.00
FMRC Randall Cunningham 1.25 3.00
FMRG Ryan Grant 1.00 2.50
FMRM Randy Moss 1.00 2.50
FMRME Rashard Mendenhall .50 1.25
FMRR Ray Rice .50 1.25
FMRW Reggie Wayne 1.00 2.50
FMSJ Steven Jackson .75 2.00
FMSS Steve Slaton .50 1.25
FMTB Tom Brady 4.00 10.00
FMTO Terrell Owens 1.00 2.50
FMTR Tony Romo 1.00 2.50
FMVY Vince Young .75 2.00
FMWW Wes Welker 1.00 2.50

2008 Finest Moments Autographs

GROUP A ODDS 1:804
GROUP B ODDS 1:948
GROUP C ODDS 1:198
UNPRICED REFRACTOR/10 ODDS 1:948
UNPRICED SUPERFRACT/1 ODDS 1:10,152
UNPRICED PRINT PLATE/1 ODDS 1:3174
UNPRICED CUT AUTO/1 ODDS 1:23,712
FMAAP Adrian Peterson 100.00 175.00
FMAAW Andre Woodson 6.00 15.00
FMABB Brian Brohm 6.00 15.00
FMABE Braylon Edwards 6.00 15.00
FMABS Barry Sanders 60.00 120.00
FMACH Chad Henne 10.00 25.00
FMADM Darren McFadden 20.00 50.00
FMADT Devin Thomas 5.00 12.00
FMAEM Eli Manning 40.00 100.00
FMAFJ Felix Jones 6.00 15.00
FMAJE John Elway 75.00 150.00
FMAJF Joe Flacco 12.00 30.00
FMAJM Joe Montana 75.00 150.00
FMAJS Jonathan Stewart 20.00 50.00
FMALS Limas Sweed 5.00 12.00
FMALT LaDainian Tomlinson 40.00 80.00
FMALTA Lawrence Taylor 40.00 80.00
FMAMK Malcolm Kelly 5.00 12.00
FMAMR Matt Ryan 40.00 100.00
FMAPM Peyton Manning 75.00 150.00
FMARC Randall Cunningham 15.00 40.00
FMARM Randy Moss 60.00 120.00
FMARME Rashard Mendenhall 6.00 15.00
FMASJ Steven Jackson 6.00 15.00
FMATB Tom Brady 150.00 250.00

2008 Finest Moments Autographs Dual

DUAL AU/15 ODDS 1:1692
BH T.Brady/C.Henne 150.00 250.00
BM T.Brady/R.Moss 150.00 300.00
EK B.Edwards/M.Kelly 25.00 60.00
ML R.Mendenhall/M.Lynch 30.00 60.00
MM E.Manning/P.Manning 125.00 200.00
RM M.Ryan/D.McFadden 125.00 200.00
SM B.Sanders/D.McFadden 125.00 200.00
TC L.Taylor/R.Cunningham 50.00 100.00
TP L.Tomlinson/A.Peterson 75.00 150.00
WF A.Woodson/J.Flacco

2008 Finest Tom Brady Finest Moments

COMMON CARD (TB1-TB16) 2.50 6.00
STATED PRINT RUN 629 SER.#'d SETS
*REFRACTOR/149: .5X TO 1.2X BASIC INSERTS
REFRACTORS PRINT RUN 149 SER.#'d SETS
*XFRACTOR/50: .6X TO 1.5X BASIC INSERTS
XFRACTORS PRINT RUN 50 SER.#'d SETS
UNPRICED GOLD REF.PRINT RUN 1
ONE BRADY PER MINI BOX

2009 Finest

COMP.SET w/o AU's (100) 30.00 80.00
101-130 AUTO OVERALL ODDS 1:3 HOB
101-130 AU ANNOUNCED PRINT RUN 187-495
101-130 AU PER LETTER SER.#'s 17-102
1 Larry Fitzgerald .25 .60
2 Willis McGahee .20 .50
3 Darren McFadden .30 .75
4 Brett Favre 3.00 8.00
5 Brian Westbrook .20 .50
6 Anquan Boldin .20 .50
7 Hines Ward .25 .60
8 Drew Brees .30 .75
9 Terrell Owens .25 .60
10 Matt Ryan .25 .60
11 Steve Slaton .20 .50
12 Matt Cassel .20 .50
13 Clinton Portis .20 .50
14 Kurt Warner .25 .60
15 Santana Moss .25 .60
16 Steven Jackson .20 .50
17 Brandon Jacobs .20 .50
18 LaDainian Tomlinson .30 .75
19 DeAngelo Williams .20 .50
20 Marion Barber .25 .60
21 Randy Moss .25 .60
22 Aaron Rodgers .60 1.50
23 Jay Cutler .20 .50
24 Chad Ochocinco .20 .50
25 Adrian Peterson .30 .75
26 Joe Flacco .25 .60
27 Chris Johnson .20 .50
28 Reggie Wayne .25 .60
29 Tom Brady 1.00 2.50
30 Steve Smith .25 .60
31 Braylon Edwards .20 .50
32 Donovan McNabb .25 .60
33 Michael Turner .20 .50
34 Michael Vick .25 .60
35 Eli Manning .25 .60
36 Brandon Marshall .25 .60
37 Roy Williams WR .20 .50
38 Reggie Bush .20 .50
39 Philip Rivers .30 .75
40 Marshawn Lynch .25 .60
41 Tony Romo .25 .60
42 Jonathan Stewart .20 .50
43 Matt Forte .20 .50
44 Ryan Grant .25 .60
45 Ben Roethlisberger .30 .75
46 Dwayne Bowe .25 .60
47 Antonio Gates .25 .60
48 Maurice Jones-Drew .20 .50
49 DeSean Jackson .25 .60
50 Calvin Johnson .30 .75
51 Joseph Addai .20 .50
52 Eddie Royal .20 .50
53 Andre Johnson .25 .60
54 Jason Witten .25 .60
55 Ronnie Brown .20 .50
56 T.J. Houshmandzadeh .20 .50
57 Frank Gore .25 .60
58 LenDale White .20 .50
59 Greg Jennings .20 .50
60 Peyton Manning .75 2.00
61 Josh Freeman RC .60 1.50
62 Shonn Greene RC .60 1.50
63 Mike Wallace RC 1.00 2.50
64 Javon Ringer RC .60 1.50
65 Hakeem Nicks RC .75 2.00
66 Brandon Pettigrew RC .60 1.50
67 Brian Robiskie RC .60 1.50
68 Chris Wells RC .60 1.50
69 Pat White RC .75 2.00
70 Michael Crabtree RC 1.00 2.50
71 Mike Thomas RC .60 1.50
72 Nate Davis RC .60 1.50
73 Percy Harvin RC .60 1.50
74 Tyson Jackson RC .60 1.50
75 Darrius Heyward-Bey RC 1.00 2.50
76 Aaron Curry RC 1.00 2.50
77 Juaquin Iglesias RC .60 1.50
78 Mohamed Massaquoi RC .60 1.50
79 Andre Brown RC .75 2.00
80 Mark Sanchez RC .60 1.50
81 Jason Smith RC .60 1.50
82 Patrick Turner RC .60 1.50
83 Donald Brown RC .60 1.50
84 Derrick Williams RC .60 1.50
85 Jeremy Maclin RC .75 2.00
86 Rhett Bomar RC .60 1.50
87 Glen Coffee RC .60 1.50
88 James Davis RC .60 1.50
89 Jarett Dillard RC .60 1.50
90 Knowshon Moreno RC .60 1.50
91 Kenny Britt RC 1.00 2.50
92 Stephen McGee RC .60 1.50
93 Austin Collie RC .60 1.50
94 Gartrell Johnson RC .60 1.50
95 LeSean McCoy RC 1.50 4.00
96 Deon Butler RC .60 1.50
97 Brandon Tate RC .75 2.00
98 Tom Brandstater RC .75 2.00
99 Ramses Barden RC .60 1.50
100 Matthew Stafford RC 6.00 15.00
101 James Laurinaitis AU/330* 5.00 12.00
102 James Casey AU/495* 6.00 15.00
103 Brian Cushing AU/476* 5.00 12.00
105 Austin Collie AU/486* 5.00 12.00
106 Johnny Knox AU/408* 6.00 15.00
107 Chris Wells AU/245* 6.00 15.00
108 Quan Cosby AU/495* 5.00 12.00
109 Cedric Peerman AU/476* 5.00 12.00
110 Chase Coffman AU/378* 5.00 12.00
112 Glen Coffee AU/384* 5.00 12.00
113 Gartrell Johnson AU/476* 5.00 12.00
114 Rashad Jennings AU/464* 6.00 15.00
115 James Davis AU/495* 5.00 12.00
116 Jarett Dillard AU/476* 5.00 12.00
117 Jeremy Maclin AU/234* 6.00 15.00
119 Rey Maualuga AU/368* 8.00 20.00
120 Kenny Britt AU/245* 8.00 20.00
121 LeSean McCoy AU/245* 20.00 40.00
122 Nate Davis AU/495* 5.00 12.00
123 Percy Harvin AU/288* 5.00 12.00
124 Patrick Turner AU/384* 5.00 12.00
128 Shonn Greene AU/486* 5.00 12.00
129 Stephen McGee AU/395* 5.00 12.00
130 Tom Brandstater AU/187* 6.00 15.00

2009 Finest Blue Refractors 429

*VETS 1-60: 2.5X TO 6X BASIC CARDS
*ROOKIES 61-100: .6X TO 1.5X BASIC CARDS
1-100 BLUE REF PRINT RUN 429
4 Brett Favre 10.00 25.00
34 Michael Vick 1.50 4.00

2009 Finest Gold Refractors 75

*VETS 1-60: 4X TO 10X BASIC CARDS
*ROOKIES 61-100: 1X TO 2.5X BASIC CARDS
1-100 GOLD REF PRINT RUN 75
4 Brett Favre 20.00 40.00
34 Michael Vick 2.50 6.00

2009 Finest Green Refractors 199

*VETS 1-60: 3X TO 8X BASIC CARDS
*ROOKIES 61-100: .8X TO 2X BASIC CARDS
1-100 GREEN REF PRINT RUN 199
4 Brett Favre 12.50 30.00
34 Michael Vick 2.00 5.00

2009 Finest Pigskin Gold Refractors

*VETS 1-60: 6X TO 15X BASIC CARDS
*ROOKIES 61-100: 1.5X TO 4X BASIC CARDS
1-100 PIGSKIN GOLD REF PRINT RUN 25
4 Brett Favre 30.00 60.00
34 Michael Vick 4.00 10.00
100 Matthew Stafford 30.00 60.00

2009 Finest Pigskin Refractors

*VETS 1-60: 3X TO 8X BASIC CARDS
*ROOKIES 61-100: .8X TO 2X BASIC CARDS
1-100 PIGSKIN REF ODDS 1:9 HOB
4 Brett Favre 12.50 30.00
34 Michael Vick 2.00 5.00

2009 Finest Red Refractors 25

*VETS 1-60: 6X TO 15X BASIC CARDS
*ROOKIES 61-100: 1.5X TO 4X BASIC CARDS
1-100 RED REF PRINT RUN 25
4 Brett Favre 30.00 60.00
34 Michael Vick 6.00 15.00
100 Matthew Stafford 40.00 80.00

2009 Finest Refractors

*VETS 1-60: 2.5X TO 6X BASIC CARDS
*ROOKIES 61-100: .6X TO 1.5X BASIC CARDS
1-100 REFRACTOR ODDS 1:3 HOB
AUTO/40-80*: .6X TO 1.5X BASIC AU
AUTO/110: .5X TO 1.2X BASIC AU
101-130 AU ANNOUNCED PRINT RUN 40-110
101-130 AU PER LETTER SER.#'d TO 10
4 Brett Favre 6.00 15.00
34 Michael Vick 2.50 6.00

2009 Finest Moments Autographs

GROUP A/15 ODDS 1:138 HOB
GROUP B/25 ODDS 1:74 HOB
FMAAP Adrian Peterson/15 75.00 150.00
FMABE Braylon Edwards/25 12.00 30.00
FMACW Chris Wells/25 30.00 60.00
FMADB Drew Brees/15 50.00 100.00
FMADM Darren McFadden/15 15.00 40.00
FMAEM Eli Manning/15 50.00 100.00
FMAFG Frank Gore/25 12.00 30.00
FMAHN Hakeem Nicks/25 12.00 30.00
FMAJC Jay Cutler/15 15.00 40.00
FMAJF Joe Flacco/15 30.00 60.00
FMAJM Jeremy Maclin/25 20.00 50.00
FMAKM Knowshon Moreno/25 8.00 20.00
FMALT LaDainian Tomlinson/15 25.00 50.00
FMAMC Michael Crabtree/25 40.00 80.00
FMAMS Matthew Stafford/25 50.00 120.00
FMAPM Peyton Manning/15 90.00 150.00
FMARM Randy Moss/15 60.00 120.00
FMARW Reggie Wayne/15 15.00 40.00
FMATB Tom Brady/15 100.00 200.00
FMADEB Donald Brown/25 12.00 30.00
FMADHB Darrius Heyward-Bey/25 12.00 30.00
FMAJFR Josh Freeman/25 8.00 20.00
FMAMJS Mark Sanchez/25 40.00 100.00

2009 Finest Rookie Jersey Autographs

GROUP A/109 ODDS 1:17 HOB
GROUP B/209 ODDS 1:13 HOB
GROUP C/309 ODDS 1:8 HOB
GROUP D/409 ODDS 1:11 HOB
*REFRACT/50: .5X TO 1.2X BASIC AU/209-409
*REFRACT/50: .4X TO 1X BASIC AU/109
61 Josh Freeman/109 6.00 15.00
62 Shonn Greene/309 5.00 12.00
63 Mike Wallace/309 8.00 20.00
64 Javon Ringer/309 5.00 12.00
65 Hakeem Nicks/209 6.00 15.00
66 Brandon Pettigrew/209 5.00 12.00
67 Brian Robiskie/209 5.00 12.00
68 Chris Wells/109 6.00 15.00
69 Pat White/109 8.00 20.00
70 Michael Crabtree/109 10.00 25.00
71 Mike Thomas/409 5.00 12.00
72 Nate Davis/409 5.00 12.00
73 Percy Harvin/209 5.00 12.00
74 Tyson Jackson/209 5.00 12.00
75 Darrius Heyward-Bey/109 10.00 25.00
76 Aaron Curry/209 8.00 20.00
77 Juaquin Iglesias/309 5.00 12.00
78 Mohamed Massaquoi/309 5.00 12.00
79 Andre Brown/409 6.00 15.00
80 Mark Sanchez/109 15.00 40.00
81 Jason Smith/209 5.00 12.00
82 Patrick Turner/309 5.00 12.00
83 Donald Brown/109 6.00 15.00
84 Derrick Williams/309 5.00 12.00
85 Jeremy Maclin/109 8.00 20.00
86 Rhett Bomar/309 5.00 12.00
87 Glen Coffee/309 5.00 12.00
90 Knowshon Moreno/109 6.00 15.00
91 Kenny Britt/109 10.00 25.00
92 Stephen McGee/209 5.00 12.00
95 LeSean McCoy/109 20.00 50.00
96 Deon Butler/409 5.00 12.00
99 Ramses Barden/409 5.00 12.00
100 Matthew Stafford/109 25.00 60.00

2009 Finest Rookie Jersey Autographs Gold Refractors

*GOLD REF/25: .8X TO 2X BASIC AU/209-409
*GOLD REF/25: .6X TO 1.5X BASIC AU/109
GOLD REFRACTOR PRINT RUN 25
61 Josh Freeman 10.00 25.00
80 Mark Sanchez 60.00 120.00
100 Matthew Stafford 150.00 300.00

2009 Finest Rookie Jersey Autographs Red Refractors

*RED REF/15: .8X TO 2X BASIC AU/209-409
*RED REF/15: .6X TO 1.5X BASIC AU/109
RED REFRACTOR PRINT RUN 15
80 Mark Sanchez 50.00 120.00
100 Matthew Stafford 150.00 300.00

2010 Finest

COMPLETE SET (125) 30.00 60.00
1 Adrian Peterson .30 .75
2 Marcus Easley RC .50 1.25
3 Miles Austin .20 .50
4 Calvin Johnson .30 .75
5 Hines Ward .25 .60
6 Brandon Jacobs .20 .50
7 C.J. Spiller RC .50 1.25
8 Mark Sanchez .20 .50
9 Brent Celek .20 .50
10 Peyton Manning .75 2.00
11 Charles Woodson .30 .75
12 Steven Jackson .20 .50
13 Greg Jennings .20 .50
14 Matt Forte .20 .50
15 Jay Cutler .20 .50
16 Jason Witten .25 .60
17 Toby Gerhart RC .50 1.25
18 Reggie Bush .20 .50
19 Ray Rice .20 .50
20 Chris Johnson .20 .50
21 Matt Schaub .20 .50
22 Steve Smith .25 .60
23 Eric Decker RC .60 1.50
24 Emmanuel Sanders RC .75 2.00
25 Jerome Harrison .20 .50
26 DeMarcus Ware .25 .60
27 Jermaine Gresham RC .50 1.25
28 Hakeem Nicks .20 .50
29 Sidney Rice .20 .50
30 Andre Johnson .25 .60
31 Demaryius Thomas RC 1.25 3.00
32 Mardy Gilyard RC .50 1.25
33 Adrian Wilson .20 .50
34 Joseph Addai .20 .50
35 Darren McFadden .20 .50
36 Donovan McNabb .25 .60
37 Jonathan Dwyer RC .50 1.25
38 Mike Kafka RC .60 1.50
39 Fred Jackson .25 .60
40 Tom Brady .75 2.00
41 Damian Williams RC .50 1.25
42 Rob Gronkowski RC 1.50 4.00
43 Jimmy Clausen RC .50 1.25
44 Michael Crabtree .20 .50
45 Ray Lewis .30 .75
46 Jared Allen .20 .50
47 Lee Evans .25 .60
48 Ryan Grant .25 .60
49 Santonio Holmes .20 .50
50 Drew Brees .30 .75
51 Knowshon Moreno .20 .50
52 Ndamukong Suh RC 1.00 2.50
53 Ryan Mathews RC .50 1.25
54 Brandon Marshall .25 .60
55 DeAngelo Williams .20 .50
56 Aaron Rodgers .60 1.50
57 Steve Smith USC .20 .50
58 Mike Sims-Walker .20 .50
59 Jahvid Best RC .50 1.25
60 Maurice Jones-Drew .20 .50
61 Dwight Freeney .20 .50
62 Brett Favre .60 1.50
63 Ricky Williams .25 .60
64 LaDainian Tomlinson .30 .75
65 Golden Tate RC .60 1.50
66 Armanti Edwards RC .60 1.50
67 Reggie Wayne .25 .60
68 Rashard Mendenhall .20 .50
69 Tony Gonzalez .25 .60
70 Troy Polamalu .30 .75
71 Kellen Winslow .20 .50
72 Vincent Jackson .20 .50
73 Frank Gore .25 .60
74 Thomas Jones .20 .50
75 Matt Ryan .25 .60
76 Percy Harvin .20 .50
77 Colt McCoy RC .60 1.50
78 Michael Turner .20 .50
79 Wes Welker .25 .60
80 Chad Ochocinco .20 .50
81 Dexter McCluster RC .60 1.50
82 Mike Williams RC .50 1.25
83 Montario Hardesty RC .50 1.25
84 Kevin Kolb .20 .50
85 Darrelle Revis .20 .50
86 Jonathan Stewart .20 .50
87 Marques Colston .20 .50
88 Anquan Boldin .20 .50
89 Vince Young .20 .50
90 Larry Fitzgerald .25 .60
91 Taylor Price RC .50 1.25
92 Matthew Stafford .25 .60
93 Andre Roberts RC .60 1.50
94 Patrick Willis .25 .60
95 Elvis Dumervil .20 .50
96 Randy Moss .25 .60
97 Cedric Benson .20 .50
98 Eli Manning .25 .60
99 Shonn Greene .20 .50
100 Tim Tebow RC 1.50 4.00
101 Ben Tate RC .50 1.25
102 Eric Berry RC .75 2.00
103 Jamaal Charles .25 .60
104 Brandon LaFell RC .75 2.00
105 Joe Flacco .25 .60
106 T.J. Houshmandzadeh .20 .50
107 Ronnie Brown .20 .50
108 Antonio Gates .25 .60
109 DeSean Jackson .25 .60
110 Dez Bryant RC 1.25 3.00
111 Joe McKnight RC .50 1.25
112 Philip Rivers .30 .75
113 Chris Wells .20 .50
114 Roddy White .20 .50
115 LeSean McCoy .30 .75
116 Arrelious Benn RC .50 1.25
117 Pierre Thomas .20 .50
118 Gerald McCoy RC .50 1.25
119 Rolando McClain RC .50 1.25
120 Tony Romo .25 .60
121 Dallas Clark .20 .50
122 Jordan Shipley RC .50 1.25
123 Clinton Portis .20 .50
124 Marion Barber .25 .60
125 Sam Bradford RC .60 1.50

2010 Finest Black Refractors

*VETS: 5X TO 12X BASIC CARDS
*ROOKIES: 2X TO 5X BASIC CARDS
BLACK REFRACTOR PRINT RUN 99

2010 Finest Gold Refractors

*VETS: 6X TO 15X BASIC CARDS
*ROOKIES: 2.5X TO 6X BASIC CARDS
GOLD REFRACTOR PRINT RUN 50

2010 Finest Mosaic Refractors

*VETS: 12X TO 30X BASIC CARDS
*ROOKIES: 5X TO 12X BASIC CARDS
MOSAIC REFRACTOR PRINT RUN 10
100 Tim Tebow 100.00 250.00
125 Sam Bradford 40.00 80.00

2010 Finest Red Refractors

*VETS: 8X TO 20X BASIC CARDS
*ROOKIES: 3X TO 8X BASIC CARDS
RED REFRACTOR PRINT RUN 25

2010 Finest Refractors

*VETS: 2X TO 5X BASIC CARDS
*ROOKIES: .8X TO 2X BASIC CARDS
STATED ODDS 1:3 HOBBY

2010 Finest Xfractors

*VETS: 2.5X TO 6X BASIC CARDS
*ROOKIES: 1X TO 2.5X BASIC CARDS
XFRACTOR/399 ODDS 1:4 HOBBY

2010 Finest Atomic Refractor Rookies

COMPLETE SET (25) 40.00 80.00
ONE PER 6-PACK MINI HOBBY BOX
*GOLD/50: 1.2X TO 3X BASIC INSERTS
FAR1 Sam Bradford 1.00 2.50
FAR2 Eric Berry 1.25 3.00
FAR3 Ben Tate .75 2.00
FAR4 Dexter McCluster 1.00 2.50
FAR5 Ryan Mathews .75 2.00
FAR6 Jahvid Best .75 2.00
FAR7 Montario Hardesty .75 2.00
FAR8 Jermaine Gresham .75 2.00
FAR9 Mike Williams .75 2.00
FAR10 Dez Bryant 2.00 5.00
FAR11 Joe McKnight .75 2.00
FAR12 Colt McCoy 1.00 2.50
FAR13 Brandon LaFell 1.25 3.00
FAR14 Ndamukong Suh 1.50 4.00
FAR15 Jimmy Clausen .75 2.00
FAR16 Demaryius Thomas 2.00 5.00
FAR17 Jonathan Dwyer .75 2.00
FAR18 Golden Tate 1.00 2.50
FAR19 Rolando McClain .75 2.00
FAR20 C.J. Spiller .75 2.00
FAR21 Arrelious Benn .75 2.00
FAR22 Toby Gerhart .75 2.00
FAR23 Jordan Shipley .75 2.00
FAR24 Emmanuel Sanders 1.25 3.00
FAR25 Tim Tebow 2.50 6.00

2010 Finest Dual Jersey Autographs

STATED PRINT RUN 100-350
*REF/75: .6X TO 1.5X JSY AU/300-350
*REF/75: .5X TO 1.2X JSY AU/200-250
*REF/75: .4X TO 1X JSY AU/100-160
EXCH EXPIRATION: 9/30/2013
AB Arrelious Benn/250 4.00 10.00
AD Anthony Dixon/350 3.00 8.00
AE Armanti Edwards/350 4.00 10.00
AG Anthony Gonzalez/110 6.00 15.00
AH Aaron Hernandez/350 10.00 25.00
AR Andre Roberts/350 4.00 10.00
BL Brandon LaFell/250 6.00 15.00
BT Ben Tate/110 6.00 15.00
CH Chad Henne/110 12.00 30.00
CM Colt McCoy/100 8.00 20.00
CS C.J. Spiller/110 6.00 15.00
DB Dez Bryant/100 30.00 60.00
DK Dustin Keller/110 6.00 15.00
DM Dexter McCluster/160 6.00 15.00
DT Demaryius Thomas/100 15.00 40.00
DTH Devin Thomas/300 3.00 8.00
DW Damian Williams/250 4.00 10.00
EB Eric Berry/160 8.00 20.00
ED Eric Decker/350 4.00 10.00
EDO Early Doucet/300 3.00 8.00
ES Emmanuel Sanders/250 6.00 15.00
GM Gerald McCoy/110 6.00 15.00
GT Golden Tate/100 8.00 20.00
JA Joseph Addai/110 6.00 15.00
JB Jahvid Best/100 6.00 15.00
JC Jimmy Clausen/100 6.00 15.00
JD Jonathan Dwyer/350 3.00 8.00
JF Jacoby Ford/350 3.00 8.00
JFL Joe Flacco/110 20.00 50.00
JG Jermaine Gresham/200 4.00 10.00
JGR Jimmy Graham/300 12.00 30.00
JH James Hardy/300 3.00 8.00
JM Joe McKnight/200 4.00 10.00
JMA Jerod Mayo/110 8.00 20.00
JS Jordan Shipley/350 3.00 8.00
ME Marcus Easley/350 3.00 8.00
MG Mardy Gilyard/350 3.00 8.00
MH Montario Hardesty/200 4.00 10.00
MK Mike Kafka/250 5.00 12.00
MW Mike Williams 3.00 8.00
NS Ndamukong Suh/110 12.00 30.00
PM Peyton Manning/100 60.00 120.00
RG Rob Gronkowski/200 25.00 50.00
RM Rolando McClain/100 6.00 15.00
RMA Ryan Mathews/100 6.00 15.00
SB Sam Bradford/100 8.00 20.00
SS Steve Slaton/110 6.00 15.00
TG Toby Gerhart/200 4.00 10.00
TP Taylor Price/350 3.00 8.00
TT Tim Tebow/100 30.00 80.00

2010 Finest Dual Jersey Autographs Black Refractors

*BLACK REF: .8X TO 2X DUAL/300-350
*BLACK REF: .6X TO 1.5X DUAL/200-250
*BLACK REF: .5X TO 1.2X DUAL/160
*BLACK REF: .4X TO 1X DUAL/100-110
STATED PRINT RUN 50 SER.#'d SETS
EXCH EXPIRATION: 9/30/2013

2010 Finest Dual Jersey Autographs Gold Refractors

*GOLD REF: 1.2X TO 3X DUAL/300-350
*GOLD REF: 1X TO 2.5X DUAL/200-250
*GOLD REF: .8X TO 2X DUAL/160
*GOLD REF: .6X TO 1.5X DUAL/100-110
GOLD REFRACTOR PRINT RUN 25
EXCH EXPIRATION: 9/30/2013
PM Peyton Manning 75.00 150.00
SB Sam Bradford 12.00 30.00
TT Tim Tebow 50.00 120.00

2010 Finest Moments

COMPLETE SET (25) 25.00 50.00
ONE PER 6-PACK MINI HOBBY BOX
FM1 Dez Bryant 1.25 3.00
FM2 Jonathan Dwyer .50 1.25
FM3 Jermaine Gresham .50 1.25
FM4 Toby Gerhart .50 1.25
FM5 Montario Hardesty .50 1.25
FM6 LeSean McCoy 1.25 3.00
FM7 Rob Gronkowski 1.50 4.00
FM8 Ben Tate .50 1.25
FM9 Ryan Mathews .50 1.25
FM10 Adrian Peterson 1.25 3.00
FM11 Darren McFadden .75 2.00
FM12 Arrelious Benn .50 1.25
FM13 Brandon LaFell .75 2.00
FM14 Jimmy Clausen .50 1.25
FM15 Ray Rice .75 2.00
FM16 Earl Thomas 1.25 3.00
FM17 Marques Colston .75 2.00
FM18 Joe Flacco 1.00 2.50
FM19 DeSean Jackson 1.00 2.50
FM20 Sam Bradford .60 1.50
FM21 Mike Sims-Walker .75 2.00
FM22 Jonathan Stewart .75 2.00
FM23 Jamaal Charles 1.00 2.50
FM24 Brandon Marshall 1.00 2.50
FM25 Tim Tebow 1.50 4.00

2010 Finest Moments Autographs

GROUP A ODDS 1:402 HOB
GROUP B ODDS 1:186 HOB
GROUP C ODDS 1:42 HOB
AB Arrelious Benn C 3.00 8.00
AP Adrian Peterson B 40.00 100.00
BL Brandon LaFell C 5.00 12.00
BM Brandon Marshall B 8.00 20.00
BT Ben Tate C 3.00 8.00
DB Dez Bryant A 30.00 60.00
DJ DeSean Jackson C 10.00 25.00
DM Darren McFadden C 8.00 20.00
ET Earl Thomas C 12.00 30.00
JC Jimmy Clausen A 5.00 12.00
JCH Jamaal Charles B 6.00 15.00
JD Jonathan Dwyer C 3.00 8.00
JF Joe Flacco C 20.00 40.00
JG Jermaine Gresham C 3.00 8.00
JS Jonathan Stewart C 5.00 12.00
LM LeSean McCoy C 10.00 25.00
MC Marques Colston B 5.00 12.00
MH Montario Hardesty C 3.00 8.00
MSW Mike Sims-Walker C 5.00 12.00
RG Rob Gronkowski C 25.00 50.00
RMA Ryan Mathews B 3.00 8.00
RR Ray Rice A 10.00 25.00
SB Sam Bradford A 15.00 40.00
TG Toby Gerhart C 3.00 8.00
TT Tim Tebow A 40.00 80.00

2010 Finest Rookie Patch Autographs

STATED PRINT RUN 100-450
EXCH EXPIRATION: 9/30/2013
2 Marcus Easley/450 4.00 10.00
7 C.J. Spiller/150 6.00 15.00
17 Toby Gerhart/300 4.00 10.00
23 Eric Decker/400 5.00 12.00
24 Emmanuel Sanders/350 6.00 15.00
27 Jermaine Gresham/300 4.00 10.00
31 Demaryius Thomas/100 20.00 50.00
32 Mardy Gilyard/400 4.00 10.00
37 Jonathan Dwyer/400 4.00 10.00
38 Mike Kafka/250 6.00 15.00
41 Damian Williams/350 4.00 10.00
42 Rob Gronkowski/350 30.00 80.00
43 Jimmy Clausen/100 8.00 20.00
52 Ndamukong Suh/210 10.00 25.00
53 Ryan Mathews/150 6.00 15.00
59 Jahvid Best/150 6.00 15.00
65 Golden Tate/100 10.00 25.00
66 Armanti Edwards/400 5.00 12.00
77 Colt McCoy/100 10.00 25.00
81 Dexter McCluster/150 8.00 20.00
82 Mike Williams 4.00 10.00
83 Montario Hardesty/400 4.00 10.00
91 Taylor Price/400 4.00 10.00
93 Andre Roberts/450 5.00 12.00
100 Tim Tebow/100 25.00 60.00
101 Ben Tate/150 6.00 15.00
102 Eric Berry/150 10.00 25.00
104 Brandon LaFell/350 6.00 15.00
110 Dez Bryant/100 40.00 80.00
111 Joe McKnight 4.00 10.00
116 Arrelious Benn/300 4.00 10.00
118 Gerald McCoy/150 10.00 25.00
119 Rolando McClain/250 5.00 12.00
122 Jordan Shipley/350 4.00 10.00
125 Sam Bradford/100 8.00 20.00

2010 Finest Rookie Patch Autographs Black Refractors

*BLK REF: .6X TO 1.5X BASE JSY AU/300-450
*BLK REF: .5X TO 1.2X BASE JSY AU/210-250
*BLACK REF: .4X TO 1X BASE JSY AU/150
BLACK REFRACTOR PRINT RUN 75
EXCH EXPIRATION: 9/30/2013

2010 Finest Rookie Patch Autographs Gold Refractors

*GOLD REF: 1X TO 2.5X BASIC JSY AU/300-450
*GOLD REF: .8X TO 2X BASIC JSY AU/210-250
*GOLD REF: .6X TO 1.5X BASIC JSY AU/150
*GOLD REF: .6X TO 1.5X BASIC JSY AU/100
GOLD REFRACTOR PRINT RUN 25
EXCH EXPIRATION: 9/30/2013
100 Tim Tebow 75.00 150.00
110 Dez Bryant 75.00 150.00

2010 Finest Rookie Patch Autographs Red Refractors

*RED REF: .8X TO 2X BASIC JSY AU/300-450
*RED REF: .6X TO 1.5X BASIC JSY AU/210-250
*RED REF: .5X TO 1.2X BASIC JSY AU/150
*RED REF: .4X TO 1X BASIC JSY AU/100
RED REFRACTOR PRINT RUN 50
EXCH EXPIRATION: 9/30/2013
100 Tim Tebow 40.00 100.00
110 Dez Bryant 50.00 100.00

2010 Finest Rookie Patch Autographs Refractors

*REFRACT: .6X TO 1.5X BASIC JSY AU/300-450
*REFRACT: .5X TO 1.2X BASIC JSY AU/210-250
*REFRACT: .4X TO 1X BASIC JSY AU/150
REFRACTOR STATED PRINT RUN 99
EXCH EXPIRATION: 9/30/2013

2011 Finest

COMPLETE SET (125) 15.00 40.00
1 Michael Vick .25 .60
2 Pierre Garcon .25 .60
3 Jeremy Maclin .20 .50
4 Mike Wallace .20 .50
5 Jahvid Best .20 .50
6 Vernon Davis .20 .50
7 Greg Little RC .60 1.50
8 Greg Jennings .20 .50
9 Santana Moss .25 .60
10 Adrian Peterson .30 .75
11 Matt Schaub .20 .50
12 Julio Jones RC 1.50 4.00
13 Matt Ryan .25 .60
14 Ray Rice .20 .50
15 Ryan Torain .20 .50
16 Dallas Clark .20 .50
17 Ahmad Bradshaw .20 .50
18 Randall Cobb RC .75 2.00
19 Frank Gore .25 .60
20 Chris Johnson .20 .50
21 A.J. Green RC 1.25 3.00
22 Shane Vereen RC .60 1.50
23 Jon Baldwin RC .50 1.25
24 Edmond Gates RC .50 1.25
25 Tim Tebow .30 .75
26 Miles Austin .20 .50
27 Sidney Rice .20 .50
28 Von Miller RC .75 2.00
29 Jason Witten .25 .60
30 Arian Foster .20 .50
31 Cedric Benson .20 .50
32 Mike Williams .25 .60
33 Bilal Powell RC .60 1.50
34 Reggie Wayne .25 .60
35 Jamie Harper RC .50 1.25
36 Andre Johnson .25 .60
37 Brandon Marshall .25 .60
38 Jermichael Finley .20 .50
39 Austin Pettis RC .50 1.25
40 Roddy White .20 .50
41 Steven Jackson .20 .50
42 Vincent Jackson .20 .50
43 Jonathan Stewart .20 .50
44 Vincent Brown RC .50 1.25
45 Daniel Thomas RC .50 1.25
46 Michael Turner .20 .50
47 Christian Ponder RC .50 1.25
48 Ben Roethlisberger .30 .75
49 Jay Cutler .20 .50
50 Aaron Rodgers .50 1.25
51 Jerrel Jernigan RC .50 1.25
52 Colin Kaepernick RC .75 2.00
53 Thomas Jones .20 .50
54 Alex Green RC .50 1.25

55 Dwayne Bowe .25 .60
56 Kenny Britt .20 .50
57 Austin Collie .20 .50
58 Dez Bryant .30 .75
59 Santonio Holmes .20 .50
60 Drew Brees .30 .75
61 Maurice Jones-Drew .20 .50
62 Mike Tolbert .20 .50
63 Marcell Dareus RC .50 1.25
64 Brandon Lloyd .20 .50
65 Philip Rivers .30 .75
66 Eli Manning .25 .60
67 LeSean McCoy .30 .75
68 Johnny Knox .20 .50
69 Taiwan Jones RC .50 1.25
70 Tom Brady .75 2.00
71 Terrell Owens .25 .60
72 Anquan Boldin .20 .50
73 Ryan Mathews .25 .60
74 DeAngelo Williams .20 .50
75 Peyton Hillis .20 .50
76 Derrick Mason .20 .50
77 Jordan Todman RC .50 1.25
78 Darren McFadden .20 .50
79 BenJarvus Green-Ellis .20 .50
80 Peyton Manning .60 1.50
81 Torrey Smith RC .50 1.25
82 Delone Carter RC .50 1.25
83 Antonio Gates .20 .50
84 Shonn Greene .20 .50
85 Marshawn Lynch .25 .60
86 Mikel Leshoure RC .50 1.25
87 DeSean Jackson .25 .60
88 Josh Freeman .25 .60
89 Matthew Stafford .25 .60
90 Larry Fitzgerald .25 .60
91 Michael Crabtree .20 .50
92 Kyle Rudolph RC .50 1.25
93 Ryan Williams RC .50 1.25
94 Owen Daniels .20 .50
95 Stevan Ridley RC .50 1.25
96 Fred Jackson .20 .50
97 Beanie Wells .20 .50
98 Percy Harvin .20 .50
99 Jamaal Charles .25 .60
100 Blaine Gabbert RC .50 1.25
101 DeMarco Murray RC 1.00 2.50
102 Titus Young RC .50 1.25
103 Ryan Mallett RC .50 1.25
104 LaDainian Tomlinson .30 .75
105 Joseph Addai .20 .50
106 Mario Manningham .20 .50
107 Hakeem Nicks .20 .50
108 Steve Johnson .20 .50
109 Braylon Edwards .20 .50
110 Felix Jones .20 .50
111 Jake Locker RC .50 1.25
112 Matt Forte .20 .50
113 Knowshon Moreno .20 .50
114 Joe Flacco .25 .60
115 Marques Colston .20 .50
116 Andy Dalton RC 1.00 2.50
117 Calvin Johnson .30 .75
118 Tony Romo .25 .60
119 Wes Welker .25 .60
120 Mark Ingram RC .75 2.00
121 Leonard Hankerson RC .50 1.25
122 Kendall Hunter RC .50 1.25
123 LeGarrette Blount .25 .60
124 Rashard Mendenhall .20 .50
125 Cam Newton RC 2.50 6.00

2011 Finest Blue Refractors

*1-99 VETS/99: 6X TO 15X BASIC CARDS
*100-125 ROOKIE/99: 2.5X TO 6X BASIC RC
BLUE REFRACTOR/99 ODDS 1:24 HOB

2011 Finest Gold Refractors

*1-99 VETS/50: 8X TO 20X BASIC CARDS
*100-125 ROOKIE/50: 3X TO 8X BASIC RC
GOLD REFRACTOR/50 ODDS 1:42 HOB

2011 Finest Mosaic Refractors

*VETS/10: 20X TO 50X BASIC CARDS
*ROOKIES/10: 8X TO 20X BASIC CARDS
MOSAIC REFRACTOR/10 ODDS 1:210 HOB
125 Cam Newton 200.00 400.00

2011 Finest Red Refractors

*1-99 VETS/25: 10X TO 25X BASIC CARDS
*100-125 ROOKIE/99: 4X TO 10X BASIC RC
RED REFRACTOR/25 ODDS 1:84 HOB
125 Cam Newton 75.00 150.00

2011 Finest Refractors

*1-99 VETS: 2.5X TO 6X BASIC CARDS
*100-125 ROOKIES: 1X TO 2.5X BASIC RC

2011 Finest Xfractors

*1-99 VETS/399: 3X TO 8X BASIC CARDS
*100-125 ROOKIE/399: 1.2X TO 3X BASIC RC
STATED PRINT RUN 399 SER.#'d SETS

2011 Finest Atomic Refractor Rookies

*GOLD REF/50: 1.5X TO 4X BASIC INSERTS
*MOSAIC REF/10: 4X TO 10X BASIC INSERTS
*RED REF/25: 2.5X TO 6X BASIC INSERTS
FARAD Andy Dalton 2.00 5.00
FARAG A.J. Green 2.50 6.00
FARBG Blaine Gabbert 1.00 2.50
FARCK Colin Kaepernick 1.50 4.00
FARCN Cam Newton 8.00 20.00
FARCP Christian Ponder 1.00 2.50
FARDB Da'Quan Bowers 1.00 2.50
FARDM DeMarco Murray 2.00 5.00
FARGL Greg Little 1.25 3.00
FARJB Jon Baldwin 1.00 2.50
FARJH Jamie Harper 1.00 2.50
FARJJ Julio Jones 4.00 10.00
FARJJE Jerrel Jernigan 1.00 2.50
FARJL Jake Locker 1.00 2.50
FARKR Kyle Rudolph 1.00 2.50
FARLH Leonard Hankerson 1.00 2.50
FARMI Mark Ingram 1.50 4.00
FARML Mikel Leshoure 1.00 2.50
FARNF Nick Fairley 1.00 2.50
FARPA Prince Amukamara 1.00 2.50
FARRC Randall Cobb 1.50 4.00
FARRM Ryan Mallett 1.00 2.50
FARRW Ryan Williams 1.00 2.50
FARTS Torrey Smith 1.00 2.50
FARVM Von Miller 1.50 4.00

2011 Finest Jumbo Jersey Autographs

*BASE JSY AU/589: .25X TO .6X REF/75
*BASE JSY AU/339: .3X TO .8X REF/75
*BASE JSY AU/89-189: .4X TO 1X REF/75
EXCH EXPIRATION: 8/31/2014
AJRRM Ryan Mallett/189 5.00 12.00

2011 Finest Jumbo Jersey Autographs Gold Refractors

*GOLD REF/25: .6X TO 1.5X BASIC REF/75
AJRCN Cam Newton 175.00 350.00
AJRDB2 Drew Brees 75.00 135.00
AJRMV Michael Vick 40.00 100.00

2011 Finest Jumbo Jersey Autographs Red Refractors

*RED REF/10: .8X TO 2X BASIC REF/75
AJRAD Andy Dalton 20.00 50.00
AJRAJG A.J. Green 75.00 150.00
AJRCK Colin Kaepernick 15.00 40.00
AJRCN Cam Newton 250.00 500.00
AJRCP Christian Ponder 10.00 25.00
AJRJL Jake Locker 10.00 25.00
AJRMI Mark Ingram 75.00 150.00
AJRJJ2 Julio Jones 100.00 200.00

2011 Finest Jumbo Jersey Autographs Refractors

REFRACTOR STATED PRINT RUN 75
EXCH EXPIRATION: 8/31/2014
AJRAB Ahmad Bradshaw 6.00 15.00
AJRAG Alex Green 12.00 30.00
AJRAP Austin Pettis 5.00 12.00
AJRBP Bilal Powell 6.00 15.00
AJRCC Chris Cooley 10.00 25.00
AJRCS Cecil Shorts 5.00 12.00
AJRDB Dwayne Bowe 8.00 20.00
AJRDC Delone Carter 5.00 12.00
AJRDH David Harris 6.00 15.00
AJRDHA DeAngelo Hall 8.00 20.00
AJRDK Dustin Keller 6.00 15.00
AJRDM DeMarco Murray 10.00 25.00
AJRDMA Derrick Mason 6.00 15.00
AJRDT Daniel Thomas 5.00 12.00
AJREG Edmond Gates 5.00 12.00
AJRGL Greg Little 8.00 20.00
AJRJB Jon Baldwin 5.00 12.00
AJRJH Jamie Harper 5.00 12.00
AJRJJ Jerrel Jernigan 5.00 12.00
AJRJT Jordan Todman 5.00 12.00
AJRKH Kendall Hunter 10.00 25.00
AJRKM Knowshon Moreno 6.00 15.00
AJRKR Kyle Rudolph 5.00 12.00
AJRLH Leonard Hankerson 5.00 12.00
AJRLM LeSean McCoy 10.00 25.00
AJRMD Marcell Dareus 5.00 12.00
AJRML Mikel Leshoure 5.00 12.00
AJRNP Niles Paul 5.00 12.00
AJRPA Prince Amukamara 5.00 12.00
AJRPP Paul Posluszny 8.00 20.00
AJRPW Patrick Willis 10.00 25.00
AJRRC Randall Cobb 8.00 20.00
AJRRW Ryan Williams 5.00 12.00
AJRSH Santonio Holmes 10.00 25.00
AJRSR Sidney Rice 6.00 15.00
AJRSR2 Stevan Ridley 5.00 12.00
AJRSV Shane Vereen 6.00 15.00
AJRTD Tandon Doss 5.00 12.00
AJRTJ Taiwan Jones 5.00 12.00
AJRTS Torrey Smith 5.00 12.00
AJRTY Titus Young 5.00 12.00
AJRVB Vincent Brown 5.00 12.00
AJRVM Von Miller 12.00 30.00

2011 Finest Moments

*REFRACTORS: .6X TO 1.5X BASIC INSERTS
FMAB Antonio Brown 1.25 3.00
FMAJG A.J. Green 1.25 3.00
FMAP Adrian Peterson 1.25 3.00
FMAR Antrel Rolle .75 2.00
FMBG Blaine Gabbert .50 1.25
FMCN Cam Newton 2.50 6.00
FMDK Dustin Keller 1.00 2.50
FMDM DeMarco Murray 1.00 2.50
FMJB Jon Baldwin .50 1.25
FMJG Jabar Gaffney .75 2.00
FMJM Jerod Mayo .75 2.00
FMKR Kyle Rudolph .50 1.25
FMLH Leonard Hankerson .50 1.25
FMMI Mark Ingram .75 2.00
FMML Mikel Leshoure .50 1.25
FMMS Mark Sanchez .75 2.00
FMMT Mike Thomas 1.00 2.50
FMPH Peyton Hillis .75 2.00
FMRC Randall Cobb .75 2.00
FMRM Ryan Mallett .50 1.25
FMRW Ryan Williams .50 1.25
FMSV Shane Vereen .60 1.50
FMTJ Thomas Jones .75 2.00
FMTS Torrey Smith .50 1.25
FMTY Titus Young .50 1.25

2011 Finest Moments Autographs

STATED PRINT RUN 25 SER.#'d SETS
FMAAB Antonio Brown 10.00 25.00
FMAAJG A.J. Green 30.00 60.00
FMAAP Adrian Peterson 50.00 100.00
FMAAR Antrel Rolle 10.00 25.00
FMABG Blaine Gabbert 5.00 12.00
FMACN Cam Newton 75.00 150.00
FMADK Dustin Keller 6.00 15.00
FMADM DeMarco Murray 10.00 25.00
FMAJB Jon Baldwin 5.00 12.00
FMAJG Jabar Gaffney 6.00 15.00
FMAJM Jerod Mayo 6.00 15.00
FMAKR Kyle Rudolph 5.00 12.00
FMALH Leonard Hankerson 5.00 12.00
FMAMI Mark Ingram 8.00 20.00
FMAML Mikel Leshoure 5.00 12.00
FMAMS Mark Sanchez 25.00 60.00
FMAMT Mike Thomas 6.00 15.00
FMAPH Peyton Hillis 12.00 30.00
FMARC Randall Cobb 8.00 20.00
FMARM Ryan Mallett 5.00 12.00
FMARW Ryan Williams 5.00 12.00
FMASV Shane Vereen 6.00 15.00
FMATJ Thomas Jones 10.00 25.00
FMATS Torrey Smith 5.00 12.00
FMATY Titus Young 5.00 12.00

2011 Finest Rookie Autograph Refractors

REFRACTOR AU/30-150 ODDS 1:26 HOB
EXCH EXPIRATION: 8/31/2014
7 Greg Little/30 10.00 25.00
18 Randall Cobb/30 12.00 30.00
22 Shane Vereen/30 10.00 25.00
23 Jon Baldwin/30 8.00 20.00
24 Edmond Gates/150 6.00 15.00
28 Von Miller/30 20.00 50.00
33 Bilal Powell/30 10.00 25.00
35 Jamie Harper/90 15.00 40.00
39 Austin Pettis/150 6.00 15.00
44 Vincent Brown/150 6.00 15.00
45 Daniel Thomas/30 8.00 20.00
51 Jerrel Jernigan/30 8.00 20.00
54 Alex Green/150 6.00 15.00
63 Marcell Dareus/30 8.00 20.00
69 Taiwan Jones/90 6.00 15.00
77 Jordan Todman/90 6.00 15.00
81 Torrey Smith/30 8.00 20.00
82 Delone Carter/90 6.00 15.00
86 Mikel Leshoure/30 8.00 20.00
92 Kyle Rudolph/90 12.00 30.00
95 Stevan Ridley/90 6.00 15.00
101 DeMarco Murray/30 15.00 40.00
102 Titus Young/30 8.00 20.00
121 Leonard Hankerson/30 8.00 20.00
122 Kendall Hunter/150 6.00 15.00

2011 Finest Rookie Autograph Red Refractors

*RED REF/25: .5X TO 1.2X REF/90-150
*RED REF/25: .4X TO 1X REF/30
12 Julio Jones 75.00 150.00
93 Ryan Williams 8.00 20.00
101 DeMarco Murray 15.00 40.00

2011 Finest Rookie Patch Autographs

STATED PRINT RUN 100-599
EXCH EXPIRATION: 8/13/2014
*BLUE REF/75: .6X TO 1.5X PATCH AU/599
*BLUE REF/75: .5X TO 1.2X PATCH AU/310
*BLUE REF/75: .4X TO 1X PATCH AU/100
*RED REF/50: .8X TO 2X PATCH AU/599
*RED REF/50: .6X TO 1.5X PATCH AU/310
*RED REF/50: .5X TO 1.2X PATCH AU/100
RAPAD Andy Dalton/100 12.00 30.00
RAPAG Alex Green/599 4.00 10.00
RAPAJG A.J. Green/100 30.00 80.00
RAPAP Austin Pettis/599 4.00 10.00
RAPBP Bilal Powell/599 5.00 12.00
RAPCK Colin Kaepernick/100 10.00 25.00
RAPCN Cam Newton/100 60.00 120.00
RAPCP Christian Ponder/100 6.00 15.00
RAPCS Cecil Shorts/599 4.00 10.00
RAPDC Delone Carter/599 4.00 10.00
RAPDM DeMarco Murray/310 10.00 25.00
RAPDT Daniel Thomas/310 5.00 12.00
RAPEG Edmond Gates/599 4.00 10.00
RAPGL Greg Little/310 10.00 25.00
RAPJB Jon Baldwin/100 6.00 15.00
RAPJH Jamie Harper/599 4.00 10.00
RAPJJ Julio Jones/100 50.00 100.00
RAPJJE Jerrel Jernigan/310 6.00 15.00
RAPJR Jacquizz Rodgers/599 4.00 10.00
RAPJT Jordan Todman/599 4.00 10.00
RAPKH Kendall Hunter/599 8.00 20.00
RAPKR Kyle Rudolph/310 5.00 12.00
RAPLH Leonard Hankerson/310 5.00 12.00
RAPMD Marcell Dareus/100 6.00 15.00
RAPML Mikel Leshoure/100 6.00 15.00
RAPNP Niles Paul/599 4.00 10.00
RAPRC Randall Cobb/310 8.00 20.00
RAPRM Ryan Mallett/100 6.00 15.00
RAPRW Ryan Williams/100 6.00 15.00
RAPSR Stevan Ridley/599 4.00 10.00
RAPSV Shane Vereen/310 6.00 15.00
RAPTD Tandon Doss/599 5.00 12.00
RAPTJ Taiwan Jones/599 4.00 10.00
RAPTS Torrey Smith/310 5.00 12.00
RAPTY Titus Young/100 6.00 15.00
RAPVB Vincent Brown/599 4.00 10.00
RAPVM Von Miller/100 15.00 40.00

2011 Finest Rookie Patch Autographs Gold Refractors

*GOLD REF/25: 1X TO 2.5X PATCH AU/599
*GOLD REF/25: .8X TO 2X PATCH AU/310
*GOLD REF/25: .6X TO 1.5X PATCH AU/100
RAPAD Andy Dalton 20.00 50.00
RAPCN Cam Newton 100.00 200.00
RAPJL Jake Locker 10.00 25.00
RAPMI Mark Ingram 15.00 40.00

201/ inest Rookie Patch Autographs Refractors

*REFRACT/99: .6X TO 1.5X PATCH AU/599
*REFRACT/99: .5X TO 1.2X PATCH AU/310
*REFRACT/99: .4X TO 1X PATCH AU/100
RAPBG Blaine Gabbert 6.00 15.00
RAPCN Cam Newton 75.00 150.00

2012 Finest

COMPLETE SET (150) 30.00 80.00
COMP.SET w/o RC's (100) 8.00 20.00
TWO ROOKIES PER HOBBY PACK
1 Aaron Rodgers .50 1.25
2 Troy Polamalu .30 .75
3 Josh Freeman .25 .60
4 Kenny Britt .20 .50
5 Dez Bryant .30 .75
6 Victor Cruz .25 .60
7 Jahvid Best .20 .50
8 Jimmy Graham .30 .75
9 Demaryius Thomas .30 .75
10 Cam Newton .30 .75
11 Jason Pierre-Paul .20 .50
12 Vernon Davis .20 .50
13 Rashard Mendenhall .20 .50
14 Marshawn Lynch .25 .60
15 Andy Dalton .25 .60
16 Beanie Wells .20 .50
17 Patrick Willis .25 .60
18 Maurice Jones-Drew .20 .50
19 Julio Jones .30 .75
20 Calvin Johnson .30 .75
21 LaDainian Tomlinson .30 .75
22 Anquan Boldin .20 .50
23 Andre Johnson .25 .60
24 Brandon Marshall .25 .60
25 Michael Bush .20 .50
26 Wes Welker .25 .60
27 Ben Roethlisberger .30 .75
28 Percy Harvin .20 .50
29 DeMarco Murray .25 .60
30 Drew Brees .30 .75
31 Torrey Smith .20 .50
32 Jermichael Finley .20 .50
33 Doug Baldwin .30 .75
34 Reggie Wayne .25 .60
35 Mike Wallace .20 .50
36 Matt Forte .20 .50
37 Ryan Mathews .25 .60
38 Marques Colston .20 .50
39 Ed Reed .25 .60
40 Michael Vick .25 .60
41 Chris Johnson .20 .50
42 Ryan Fitzpatrick .20 .50
43 Larry Fitzgerald .25 .60
44 James Starks .20 .50
45 Mark Sanchez .20 .50
46 Shonn Greene .20 .50
47 Tim Tebow .30 .75
48 Fred Jackson .25 .60
49 LeGarrette Blount .25 .60
50 Tom Brady .75 2.00
51 Jason Witten .25 .60
52 Steven Jackson .20 .50
53 Carson Palmer .25 .60
54 Miles Austin .20 .50
55 Jay Cutler .20 .50
56 Brandon Pettigrew .20 .50
57 Jared Allen .20 .50
58 Mario Williams .20 .50
59 Jamaal Charles .25 .60
60 Peyton Manning .60 1.50
61 Jordy Nelson .25 .60
62 Reggie Bush .20 .50
63 Joe Flacco .25 .60
64 Sam Bradford .20 .50
65 Philip Rivers .30 .75
66 Daniel Thomas .20 .50
67 Steve Smith .25 .60
68 Ahmad Bradshaw .20 .50
69 Roddy White .20 .50
70 Adrian Peterson .30 .75
71 Cedric Benson .20 .50
72 A.J. Green .30 .75
73 Rob Gronkowski .30 .75
74 Dwayne Bowe .25 .60
75 Christian Ponder .20 .50
76 Darren McFadden .20 .50
77 Jake Locker .30 .75
78 Darren Sproles .25 .60
79 Matt Ryan .25 .60
80 Arian Foster .25 .60
81 Kevin Kolb .20 .50
82 Ndamukong Suh .25 .60
83 Matt Schaub .20 .50
84 Antonio Gates .25 .60
85 Greg Jennings .20 .50
86 Matt Flynn .20 .50
87 Michael Turner .20 .50
88 LeSean McCoy .30 .75
89 Hakeem Nicks .20 .50
90 Matthew Stafford .25 .60
91 Ray Rice .20 .50
92 Aaron Hernandez .25 .60
93 Tony Gonzalez .25 .60
94 Frank Gore .25 .60
95 Tony Romo .25 .60
96 Willis McGahee .20 .50
97 Roy Helu .20 .50
98 Vincent Jackson .20 .50
99 Alex Smith .25 .60
100 Eli Manning .25 .60
101 Brock Osweiler RC .50 1.25
102 Brandon Weeden RC .50 1.25
103 Nick Foles RC 1.25 3.00
104 Kirk Cousins RC 2.00 5.00
105 Ryan Lindley RC .50 1.25
106 David Wilson RC .50 1.25
107 Lamar Miller RC .75 2.00
108 Doug Martin RC .75 2.00
109 Isaiah Pead RC .50 1.25
110 Andrew Luck RC 6.00 15.00
111 A.J. Jenkins RC .50 1.25
112 LaMichael James RC .50 1.25
113 Bernard Pierce RC .50 1.25
114 Chris Rainey RC .50 1.25
115 Ronnie Hillman RC .50 1.25
116 Cyrus Gray RC .50 1.25
117 Michael Floyd RC .50 1.25
118 Kendall Wright RC .50 1.25
119 Alshon Jeffery RC 1.00 2.50
120 Robert Griffin III RC .60 1.50
121 Mohamed Sanu RC .75 2.00
122 Rueben Randle RC .50 1.25
123 Nick Toon RC .50 1.25
124 Stephen Hill RC .50 1.25
125 Trent Richardson RC .50 1.25
126 Brian Quick RC .50 1.25
127 Joe Adams RC .50 1.25
128 Chris Givens RC .50 1.25
129 Juron Criner RC .50 1.25
130 Justin Blackmon RC .50 1.25
131 Dwayne Allen RC .50 1.25
132 Coby Fleener RC .50 1.25
133 Morris Claiborne RC .50 1.25
134 T.J. Graham RC .50 1.25
135 Ryan Tannehill RC .75 2.00
136 Quinton Coples RC .50 1.25
137 Michael Brockers RC .50 1.25
138 Jarius Wright RC .50 1.25
139 Luke Kuechly RC 1.25 3.00
140 Russell Wilson RC 5.00 12.00
141 DeVier Posey RC .50 1.25
142 Marvin Jones RC .50 1.25
143 Vick Ballard RC .60 1.50
144 Ryan Broyles RC .50 1.25
145 Robert Turbin RC .50 1.25
146 Michael Egnew RC .50 1.25
147 Greg Childs RC .50 1.25
148 T.Y. Hilton RC 1.00 2.50
149 Matt Kalil RC .50 1.25
150 Tommy Streeter RC .50 1.25

2012 Finest Blue Refractors

*1-100 VETS/99: 5X TO 12X BASIC CARDS
*101-150 ROOKIE/99: 2X TO 5X BASIC RC
BLUE REFRACTOR/99 ODDS 1:24 HOB

2012 Finest Gold Refractors

*1-100 VETS/50: 8X TO 20X BASIC CARDS
*101-150 ROOKIE/50: 3X TO 8X BASIC RC
GOLD REF/50 ODDS 1:48 HOB
110 Andrew Luck 75.00 135.00
140 Russell Wilson 30.00 80.00

2012 Finest Prism Refractors

*1-100 VETS: 3X TO 8X BASIC CARDS
*101-150 ROOKIE: 1.2X TO 3X BASIC RC

2012 Finest Pulsar Refractors

*1-100 VETS/10: 15X TO 40X BASIC CARDS
*101-150 ROOKIE/10: 6X TO 15X BASIC RC
110 Andrew Luck 250.00 400.00
120 Robert Griffin III 10.00 25.00
135 Ryan Tannehill 12.00 30.00
140 Russell Wilson 125.00 250.00

2012 Finest Red Refractors

*1-100 VETS/25: 10X TO 25X BASIC CARDS
*101-150 ROOKIE/25: 4X TO 10X BASIC RC
RED REF/25 ODDS 1:96 HOB
110 Andrew Luck 150.00 300.00
120 Robert Griffin III 6.00 15.00
135 Ryan Tannehill 8.00 20.00
140 Russell Wilson 60.00 120.00

2012 Finest Refractors

*1-100 VETS: 2.5X TO 6X BASIC CARDS
*101-150 ROOKIE: 1X TO 2.5X BASIC RC
ONE REFRACTOR PER PACK OVERALL

2012 Finest Atomic Refractor Rookies

STATED ODDS 1:6
FARAL Andrew Luck 10.00 25.00
FARBO Brock Osweiler 1.00 2.50
FARBP Bernard Pierce 1.00 2.50
FARBQ Brian Quick 1.00 2.50
FARBW Brandon Weeden 1.00 2.50
FARCF Coby Fleener 1.00 2.50
FARCGI Chris Givens 1.00 2.50
FARDA Dwayne Allen 1.00 2.50
FARDM Doug Martin 1.50 4.00
FARDW David Wilson 1.00 2.50
FARIP Isaiah Pead 1.00 2.50
FARJB Justin Blackmon 1.00 2.50
FARKW Kendall Wright 1.00 2.50
FARLJ LaMichael James 1.00 2.50
FARLM Lamar Miller 1.50 4.00
FARMF Michael Floyd 1.00 2.50
FARMS Mohamed Sanu 1.50 4.00
FARNF Nick Foles 2.50 6.00
FARNT Nick Toon 1.00 2.50
FARRG Robert Griffin III 1.25 3.00
FARRH Ronnie Hillman 1.00 2.50
FARRR Rueben Randle 1.00 2.50
FARRT Ryan Tannehill 1.50 4.00
FARSH Stephen Hill 1.00 2.50
FARTR Trent Richardson 1.00 2.50

2012 Finest Atomic Refractor Rookies Autographs Gold Refractors

GOLD REF/25 AU ODDS 1:94
EXCH EXPIRATION: 8/31/2015
FARAAL Andrew Luck 500.00 800.00
FARABO Brock Osweiler 12.00 30.00
FARABP Bernard Pierce 12.00 30.00
FARABQ Brian Quick 15.00 40.00
FARABW Brandon Weeden 12.00 30.00
FARACF Coby Fleener 12.00 30.00
FARACGI Chris Givens 12.00 30.00
FARADA Dwayne Allen 12.00 30.00
FARADM Doug Martin 20.00 50.00
FARADW David Wilson 12.00 30.00
FARAIP Isaiah Pead 12.00 30.00
FARAJB Justin Blackmon 12.00 30.00
FARAKW Kendall Wright 12.00 30.00
FARALJ LaMichael James 12.00 30.00
FARALM Lamar Miller 20.00 50.00
FARAMF Michael Floyd 12.00 30.00
FARAMS Mohamed Sanu 20.00 50.00
FARANF Nick Foles 30.00 80.00
FARANT Nick Toon 15.00 40.00
FARARG Robert Griffin III 15.00 40.00
FARARH Ronnie Hillman 12.00 30.00
FARARR Rueben Randle 15.00 40.00
FARART Ryan Tannehill 20.00 50.00
FARASH Stephen Hill EXCH 12.00 30.00
FARATR Trent Richardson 12.00 30.00

2012 Finest Jumbo Jersey Autographs Blue Refractors

*BLUE REF/99: .4X TO 1X GOLD REF/75
AJRBW Brandon Weeden 4.00 10.00

2012 Finest Jumbo Jersey Autographs Gold Refractors

STATED PRINT RUN 75 SER.#'d SETS
*BASE REF/1368-1500: .25X TO .6X GLD REF/75
*BASE REF/299: .3X TO .8X GLD REF/75
*BASE REF/100: .4X TO 1X GOLD REF/75
AJRAG A.J. Green 12.00 30.00
AJRAJ Alshon Jeffery 12.00 30.00
AJRAJJ A.J. Jenkins 4.00 10.00
AJRBG Blaine Gabbert 12.00 30.00
AJRBO Brock Osweiler 4.00 10.00
AJRBP Bernard Pierce EXCH 4.00 10.00
AJRBQ Brian Quick 4.00 10.00
AJRCF Coby Fleener 4.00 10.00
AJRCGI Chris Givens 4.00 10.00
AJRCM Colt McCoy 10.00 25.00
AJRCP Christian Ponder 8.00 20.00
AJRDA Dwayne Allen 4.00 10.00
AJRDM Doug Martin 6.00 15.00
AJRDP DeVier Posey 4.00 10.00
AJRDW David Wilson 4.00 10.00
AJRIP Isaiah Pead 4.00 10.00
AJRJA Joe Adams 4.00 10.00
AJRJB Justin Blackmon 4.00 10.00
AJRJW Jarius Wright 4.00 10.00
AJRKW Kendall Wright 4.00 10.00
AJRLJ LaMichael James 4.00 10.00
AJRLM Lamar Miller 6.00 15.00
AJRME Michael Egnew 4.00 10.00
AJRMF Michael Floyd 4.00 10.00
AJRMI Mark Ingram 10.00 25.00
AJRMS Mohamed Sanu 6.00 15.00
AJRMSC Matt Schaub 8.00 20.00
AJRNF Nick Foles 25.00 60.00
AJRNT Nick Toon 4.00 10.00
AJRRB Ryan Broyles 8.00 20.00
AJRRH Ronnie Hillman 10.00 25.00
AJRRHE Roy Helu EXCH 8.00 20.00
AJRRR Rueben Randle 4.00 10.00
AJRRT Ryan Tannehill 6.00 15.00
AJRRTU Robert Turbin 4.00 10.00
AJRRW Russell Wilson 90.00 150.00
AJRSB Sam Bradford 12.00 30.00
AJRSH Stephen Hill 4.00 10.00
AJRTG T.J. Graham 4.00 10.00
AJRTS Torrey Smith 8.00 20.00
AJRTYH T.Y. Hilton 8.00 20.00

2012 Finest Jumbo Jersey Autographs Red Refractors

*RED/25: .6X TO 1.5X VET GOLD/75
*RED/25: .8X TO 2X ROOKIE GOLD/75
STATED PRINT RUN 25 SER.#'d SETS
AJRAB Ahmad Bradshaw 12.00 30.00
AJRAL Andrew Luck 300.00 500.00
AJRBW Brandon Weeden 8.00 20.00
AJRDB Dez Bryant 15.00 40.00
AJRDMC Darren McFadden 15.00 40.00
AJRJB Justin Blackmon 8.00 20.00
AJRMSA Mark Sanchez 12.00 30.00
AJRRG Robert Griffin III 10.00 25.00
AJRRT Ryan Tannehill 12.00 30.00
AJRRW Russell Wilson 250.00 400.00
AJRTR Trent Richardson 8.00 20.00

2012 Finest Lucky Cuts

LCAL STATED ODDS 1:59
LCAAL AUTO/10 ODDS 1:5866
LCPAL PATCH/25 ODDS 1:2345
LCAL Andrew Luck 20.00 50.00
LCPAL Andrew Luck Patch/25 75.00 135.00

2012 Finest Moments

STATED ODDS 1:5
*REFRACTORS: .6X TO 1.5X BASIC INSERTS
FMAJ Alshon Jeffery 1.00 2.50
FMAL Andrew Luck 5.00 12.00
FMBG Blaine Gabbert .75 2.00
FMBO Brock Osweiler .50 1.25
FMBW Brandon Weeden .50 1.25
FMCB Cedric Benson .75 2.00
FMCM Colt McCoy 1.00 2.50
FMDB Drew Brees 1.25 3.00
FMDM Doug Martin .75 2.00
FMDW David Wilson .50 1.25
FMJB Justin Blackmon .50 1.25
FMJM Jeremy Maclin .75 2.00
FMKW Kendall Wright .50 1.25
FMLM Lamar Miller .75 2.00
FMMF Michael Floyd .50 1.25
FMMI Mark Ingram 1.00 2.50
FMMS Mohamed Sanu .75 2.00
FMPB Plaxico Burress .75 2.00
FMRG Robert Griffin III .60 1.50
FMRR Rueben Randle .50 1.25
FMRT Ryan Tannehill .75 2.00
FMSB Sam Bradford .75 2.00
FMSS Steve Smith 1.00 2.50
FMTR Trent Richardson .50 1.25
FMVJ Vincent Jackson .75 2.00

2012 Finest Moments Autographs Refractors

STATED ODDS 1:94
FMAAJ Alshon Jeffery 10.00 25.00
FMAAL Andrew Luck 250.00 400.00
FMABG Blaine Gabbert 6.00 15.00
FMABO Brock Osweiler 5.00 12.00
FMABW Brandon Weeden 5.00 12.00
FMACB Cedric Benson 6.00 15.00
FMACM Colt McCoy 8.00 20.00
FMADB Drew Brees 40.00 80.00
FMADM Doug Martin 8.00 20.00
FMADW David Wilson 5.00 12.00
FMAJB Justin Blackmon 5.00 12.00
FMAJM Jeremy Maclin 6.00 15.00
FMAKW Kendall Wright 5.00 12.00
FMALM Lamar Miller 8.00 20.00
FMAMF Michael Floyd 5.00 12.00
FMAMI Mark Ingram 10.00 20.00
FMAMS Mohamed Sanu 8.00 20.00
FMAPB Plaxico Burress 6.00 15.00
FMARG Robert Griffin III 6.00 15.00
FMARR Rueben Randle 5.00 12.00
FMART Ryan Tannehill 8.00 20.00
FMASB Sam Bradford 15.00 30.00
FMASS Steve Smith 8.00 20.00
FMATR Trent Richardson 5.00 12.00
FMAVJ Vincent Jackson 6.00 15.00

2012 Finest Rookie Autograph Refractors

STATED PRINT RUN 20-112
EXCH EXPIRATION: 8/31/2015
101 Brock Osweiler/20 10.00 25.00
102 Brandon Weeden/20 10.00 25.00
103 Nick Foles/25 25.00 60.00
106 David Wilson/20 10.00 25.00
107 Lamar Miller/25 15.00 40.00
108 Doug Martin/25 15.00 40.00
109 Isaiah Pead/25 10.00 25.00
111 A.J. Jenkins/20 10.00 25.00
112 LaMichael James/25 10.00 25.00
113 Bernard Pierce/101 12.00 30.00
115 Ronnie Hillman/101 6.00 15.00
117 Michael Floyd/20 10.00 25.00
118 Kendall Wright/20 EXCH 10.00 25.00
119 Alshon Jeffery/25 20.00 50.00
121 Mohamed Sanu/25 15.00 40.00
122 Rueben Randle/25 10.00 25.00
123 Nick Toon/101 8.00 20.00
124 Stephen Hill/20 10.00 25.00
126 Brian Quick/25 10.00 25.00
127 Joe Adams/101 EXCH 6.00 15.00
128 Chris Givens/101 6.00 15.00
130 Justin Blackmon/20 10.00 25.00
131 Dwayne Allen/101 6.00 15.00
132 Coby Fleener/101 6.00 15.00
134 T.J. Graham/101 6.00 15.00
138 Jarius Wright/101 8.00 20.00
140 Russell Wilson/20 150.00 250.00
141 DeVier Posey/101 8.00 20.00
144 Ryan Broyles/101 6.00 15.00
145 Robert Turbin/101 6.00 15.00
146 Michael Egnew/101 6.00 15.00
148 T.Y. Hilton/101 12.00 30.00

2012 Finest Rookie Autograph Red Refractors

*RED REF/15: 1X TO 2.5X REF AU/101-112
*RED REF/15: .6X TO 1.5X REF AU/20-25
STATED PRINT RUN 15 SER.#'d SETS
110 Andrew Luck 700.00 1200.00
120 Robert Griffin III 20.00 50.00
125 Trent Richardson 15.00 40.00
135 Ryan Tannehill 25.00 60.00
140 Russell Wilson 300.00 500.00

2012 Finest Rookie Patch Autographs Blue Refractors

*GOLD REF/75: .4X TO 1X BLUE REF/99
*RED REF/50: .5X TO 1.2X BLUE REF/99
*REF/1353-1500: .25X TO .6X BLUE REF/99
*REF/250: .3X TO .8X BLUE REF/99
RAPAJ Alshon Jeffery 10.00 25.00
RAPAJJ A.J. Jenkins 5.00 12.00
RAPBO Brock Osweiler 5.00 12.00
RAPBP Bernard Pierce 10.00 25.00
RAPBQ Brian Quick 5.00 12.00
RAPBW Brandon Weeden 5.00 12.00
RAPCF Coby Fleener 5.00 12.00
RAPCGI Chris Givens 5.00 12.00
RAPDA Dwayne Allen 5.00 12.00
RAPDM Doug Martin 8.00 20.00
RAPDP DeVier Posey 5.00 12.00
RAPDW David Wilson 5.00 12.00
RAPIP Isaiah Pead 5.00 12.00
RAPJA Joe Adams 5.00 12.00
RAPJW Jarius Wright 5.00 12.00
RAPKW Kendall Wright 5.00 12.00
RAPLJ LaMichael James 5.00 12.00
RAPLM Lamar Miller 8.00 20.00
RAPME Michael Egnew 5.00 12.00
RAPMF Michael Floyd 5.00 12.00
RAPMS Mohamed Sanu 8.00 20.00
RAPNF Nick Foles 30.00 80.00
RAPNT Nick Toon 5.00 12.00
RAPRB Ryan Broyles 10.00 25.00
RAPRH Ronnie Hillman 5.00 12.00
RAPRR Rueben Randle 6.00 15.00
RAPRTU Robert Turbin 5.00 12.00
RAPRW Russell Wilson 75.00 150.00
RAPSH Stephen Hill 5.00 12.00
RAPTG T.J. Graham 5.00 12.00
RAPTYH T.Y. Hilton 12.00 30.00

2012 Finest Rookie Patch Autographs Pulsar Refractors

*PULSAR/25: .8X TO 2X BLUE REF/99
RAPAL Andrew Luck 500.00 800.00
RAPDM Doug Martin 15.00 40.00
RAPJB Justin Blackmon 10.00 25.00
RAPRG Robert Griffin III 12.00 30.00
RAPRT Ryan Tannehill 15.00 40.00
RAPRW Russell Wilson 200.00 400.00
RAPTR Trent Richardson 10.00 25.00

2013 Finest

COMPLETE SET (150) 20.00 50.00
1 Joe Flacco .25 .60
2 Jay Cutler .20 .50
3 Matthew Stafford .25 .60
4 DeMarco Murray .25 .60
5 Larry Fitzgerald .25 .60
6 Wes Welker .25 .60
7 David Wilson .20 .50
8 Stevan Ridley .20 .50
9 Clay Matthews .30 .75
10 Eli Manning .25 .60
11 Matt Schaub .20 .50
12 Brandon Weeden .20 .50
13 Steve Johnson .25 .60
14 Jake Locker .25 .60
15 Christian Ponder .20 .50
16 Earl Thomas .25 .60
17 Reggie Wayne .25 .60
18 Percy Harvin .20 .50
19 Roddy White .20 .50
20 Peyton Manning 1.50 4.00
21 Torrey Smith .20 .50
22 Matt Ryan .25 .60
23 Troy Polamalu .30 .75
24 Carson Palmer .25 .60
25 Cam Newton .30 .75
26 Jason Witten .25 .60
27 J.J. Watt .25 .60
28 Jamaal Charles .25 .60
29 Ed Reed .25 .60
30 Colin Kaepernick .25 .60
31 Dez Bryant .30 .75
32 Marshawn Lynch .25 .60
33 A.J. Green .30 .75
34 Andre Johnson .20 .50
35 Darren Sproles .25 .60
36 Von Miller .25 .60
37 Heath Miller .20 .50
38 Justin Blackmon .20 .50
39 Jared Allen .20 .50
40 Tom Brady .75 2.00
41 Maurice Jones-Drew .20 .50
42 Ryan Tannehill .25 .60
43 Jimmy Graham .30 .75
44 Vincent Jackson .20 .50
45 Marques Colston .20 .50
46 James Jones .20 .50
47 Matt Forte .20 .50
48 Andy Dalton .25 .60
49 Brandon Marshall .25 .60
50 Adrian Peterson .30 .75
51 Eric Decker .20 .50
52 Alfred Morris .20 .50
53 Mike Wallace .20 .50
54 Patrick Willis .25 .60
55 Philip Rivers .30 .75
56 Michael Crabtree .20 .50
57 Chris Johnson .20 .50
58 BenJarvus Green-Ellis .25 .60
59 Anquan Boldin .20 .50
60 Andrew Luck .50 1.25
61 Antonio Gates .25 .60
62 Greg Olsen .25 .60
63 Frank Gore .25 .60
64 Julio Jones .30 .75
65 Steven Jackson .20 .50
66 Kyle Rudolph .20 .50
67 Jeremy Maclin .20 .50
68 Arian Foster .25 .60
69 Santonio Holmes .20 .50
70 Drew Brees .30 .75
71 Jonathan Stewart .20 .50
72 Ben Roethlisberger .30 .75
73 Tim Tebow .25 .60
74 Danny Amendola .25 .60
75 Russell Wilson .60 1.50
76 Sam Bradford .20 .50
77 Victor Cruz .25 .60
78 Hakeem Nicks .20 .50
79 Darren McFadden .25 .60
80 Calvin Johnson .30 .75
81 Jermichael Finley .20 .50
82 Josh Freeman .25 .60
83 Dwayne Bowe .25 .60
84 Vernon Davis .20 .50
85 Kendall Wright .20 .50
86 Jason Pierre-Paul .20 .50
87 Doug Martin .25 .60
88 Willis McGahee .20 .50
89 Michael Vick .25 .60
90 Robert Griffin III .20 .50
91 Reggie Bush .20 .50
92 LeSean McCoy .30 .75
93 Demaryius Thomas .25 .60
94 C.J. Spiller .20 .50
06 Rob Cronkowski .30 .75
96 Tony Romo .25 .60
97 Randall Cobb .25 .60
98 Trent Richardson .20 .50
99 Ray Rice .20 .50
100 Aaron Rodgers .50 1.25
101 Mike Glennon RC .50 1.25
102 Zach Ertz RC 1.00 2.50
103 DeAndre Hopkins RC 1.25 3.00
104 Tyler Eifert RC .50 1.25
105 Tavon Austin RC .60 1.50
106 Tyler Wilson RC .50 1.25
107 Robert Woods RC .75 2.00
108 Quinton Patton RC .50 1.25
109 Ryan Nassib RC .50 1.25
110 Matt Barkley RC .50 1.25
111 Terrance Williams RC .50 1.25
112 Markus Wheaton RC .50 1.25
113 Aaron Dobson RC .50 1.25
114 Giovani Bernard RC .50 1.25
115 EJ Manuel RC .50 1.25
116 Justin Hunter RC .50 1.25
117 Joseph Randle RC .50 1.25
118 Chris Harper RC .50 1.25
119 Ezekiel Ansah RC .50 1.25
120 Montee Ball RC .50 1.25
121 Andre Ellington RC .50 1.25
122 Stepfan Taylor RC .50 1.25
123 Jordan Reed RC .75 2.00
124 Landry Jones RC .50 1.25
125 Cordarrelle Patterson RC .50 1.25
126 Luke Joeckel RC .50 1.25
127 Bjoern Werner RC .50 1.25
128 Dee Milliner RC .50 1.25
129 Jarvis Jones RC .50 1.25
130 Eddie Lacy RC .50 1.25
131 Manti Te'o RC .60 1.50
132 Cobi Hamilton RC .50 1.25
133 Gavin Escobar RC .50 1.25
134 Johnathan Franklin RC .50 1.25
135 Stedman Bailey RC .50 1.25
136 Tavarres King RC .50 1.25
137 Christine Michael RC .50 1.25
138 Marcus Lattimore RC .50 1.25
139 Ryan Swope RC .50 1.25
140 Keenan Allen RC 1.00 2.50
141 Le'Veon Bell RC 1.50 4.00
142 Mike Gillislee RC .50 1.25
143 Kenny Stills RC .50 1.25
144 Kenjon Barner RC .50 1.25
145 Denard Robinson RC .50 1.25
146 Geno Smith RC .50 1.25
147 Marquise Goodwin RC .50 1.25
148 Vance McDonald RC .60 1.50
149 Knile Davis RC .50 1.25
150 Dion Jordan RC .50 1.25
MA Mystery AUTO EXCH 40.00 100.00
US Uncut Sheet EXCH 60.00 150.00

2013 Finest Blue Refractors

*1-100 VETS/99: 4X TO 10X BASIC CARDS
*101-150 ROOKIE/99: 1.5X TO 4X BASIC RC
BLUE REF/99 ODDS 1:24 HOB

2013 Finest Camo Refractors

*1-100 VETS/10: 12X TO 30X BASIC CARDS
*101-200 ROOKIE/10: 5X TO 12X BASIC RC
CAMO/10 STATED ODDS 1:204 HOB

2013 Finest Gold Refractors

*1-100 VETS/75: 5X TO 12X BASIC CARDS
*101-150 ROOKIE/75: 2X TO 5X BASIC RC
GOLD REF/75 ODDS 1.30 HOB

2013 Finest Pink Refractors

*1-100 VETS/10: 12X TO 30X BASIC CARDS
*101-200 ROOKIE/10. 5X TO 12X BASIC RC
PINK/10 STATED ODDS 1:204 HOB

2013 Finest Prism Refractors

*1-100 VETS/25: 8X TO 20X BASIC CARDS
*101-150 ROOKIE/25: 3X TO 8X BASIC RC
PRISM REF/25 ODDS 1:84 HOB

2013 Finest Red Refractors

*1-100 VETS/50: 6X TO 15X BASIC CARDS
*101-150 ROOKIE/50: 2.5X TO 6X BASIC RC
RED REF/50 ODDS 1:42 HOB

2013 Finest Refractors

*1-100 VETS: 1.5X TO 4X BASIC CARDS
*101-150 ROOKIES: .6X TO 1.5X BASIC RC
REF STATED ODDS 1:3 HOB

2013 Finest Xfractors

*1-100 VETS. 3X TO 8X BASIC CARDS
*101-150 ROOKIES: 1.2X TO 3X BASIC RC
STATED ODDS 1:36 HOB

2013 Finest Atomic Refractor Rookies

STATED ODDS 1:36 HOBBY
FARAD Aaron Dobson 1.00 2.50
FARCM Christine Michael 1.00 2.50
FARCP Cordarrelle Patterson 1.00 2.50
FARDH DeAndre Hopkins 2.50 6.00
FARDRO Denard Robinson 1.00 2.50
FAREJM EJ Manuel 6.00 15.00
FAREL Eddie Lacy 1.00 2.50
FARGB Giovani Bernard 1.50 4.00
FARGS Geno Smith 1.00 2.50
FARJH Justin Hunter 1.00 2.50
FARJRE Jordan Reed 1.50 4.00
FARKA Keenan Allen 2.00 5.00
FARKS Kenny Stills 1.00 2.50
FARLB Le'Veon Bell 3.00 8.00
FARMB Matt Barkley 1.00 2.50
FARMBA Montee Ball 1.00 2.50
FARMGO Marquise Goodwin 1.00 2.50
FARML Marcus Lattimore 1.00 2.50
FARMT Manti Te'o 1.25 3.00
FARRW Robert Woods 1.50 4.00
FARSB Stedman Bailey 1.00 2.50
FARTA Tavon Austin 1.25 3.00
FARTE Tyler Eifert 1.00 2.50
FARTWI Terrance Williams 1.00 2.50
FARZE Zach Ertz 2.00 5.00

2013 Finest Atomic Refractor Rookies Autographs Red Refractors

ATOMIC ROOKIE AU/25 ODDS 1:492 HOB
FARAAD Aaron Dobson 25.00 60.00
FARACM Christine Michael 25.00 100.00
FARACP Cordarrelle Patterson 12.00 30.00
FARADH DeAndre Hopkins 30.00 80.00
FARADRO Denard Robinson 12.00 30.00
FARAEJM EJ Manuel 60.00 120.00
FARAEL Eddie Lacy 12.00 30.00
FARAGB Giovani Bernard 15.00 40.00
FARAGS Geno Smith 12.00 30.00
FARAJH Justin Hunter 12.00 30.00
FARAJRE Jordan Reed 25.00 50.00
FARAKA Keenan Allen 25.00 60.00
FARAKS Kenny Stills 12.00 30.00
FARALB Le'Veon Bell 75.00 125.00
FARAMB Matt Barkley 12.00 30.00
FARAMBA Montee Ball 12.00 30.00
FARAMGO Marquise Goodwin 15.00 40.00
FARAML Marcus Lattimore 12.00 30.00
FARAMT Manti Te'o 15.00 40.00
FARARW Robert Woods 20.00 50.00
FARASB Stedman Bailey 12.00 30.00
FARATA Tavon Austin 15.00 40.00
FARATE Tyler Eifert 12.00 30.00
FARATWI Terrance Williams 12.00 30.00
FARAZE Zach Ertz 25.00 60.00

2013 Finest Jumbo Jersey Autographs Gold Refractors

*BASE REF: .25X TO .6X GOLD REF/50
*BLUE REF/99: .3X TO .8X GOLD REF/50
*RED REF/75: .3X TO .8X GOLD REF/50
AJRAD Aaron Dobson 5.00 12.00

AJRAE Andre Ellington 5.00 12.00
AJRAL Andrew Luck 90.00 150.00
AJRAM Alfred Morris 6.00 15.00
AJRBC Brent Celek 6.00 15.00
AJRCM Christine Michael 12.00 30.00
AJRCP Cordarrelle Patterson 5.00 12.00
AJRDH DeAndre Hopkins 12.00 30.00
AJRDRO Denard Robinson 5.00 12.00
AJRDT Demaryius Thomas 12.00 30.00
AJREJM EJ Manuel 30.00 80.00
AJREL Eddie Lacy 5.00 12.00
AJRGB Giovani Bernard 5.00 12.00
AJRGE Gavin Escobar 5.00 12.00
AJRGS Geno Smith 5.00 12.00
AJRJF Johnathan Franklin 5.00 12.00
AJRJG Jimmy Graham 15.00 40.00
AJRJH Justin Hunter 5.00 12.00
AJRJJ Jarvis Jones 5.00 12.00
AJRJL James Laurinaitis 8.00 20.00
AJRJR Joseph Randle 5.00 12.00
AJRJRE Jordan Reed 8.00 20.00
AJRKA Keenan Allen 10.00 25.00
AJRKD Knile Davis 5.00 12.00
AJRKS Kenny Stills 5.00 12.00
AJRLB Le'Veon Bell 15.00 40.00
AJRLJ Landry Jones 5.00 12.00
AJRLM Lamar Miller 6.00 15.00
AJRMB Matt Barkley 5.00 12.00
AJRMBA Montee Ball 5.00 12.00
AJRMG Mike Glennon 5.00 12.00
AJRMGI Mike Gillislee 5.00 12.00
AJRMGO Marquise Goodwin 5.00 12.00
AJRML Marcus Lattimore 5.00 12.00
AJRMT Manti Te'o 6.00 15.00
AJRMW Markus Wheaton 5.00 12.00
AJRQP Quinton Patton 5.00 12.00
AJRRG3 Robert Griffin III 6.00 15.00
AJRRN Ryan Nassib 5.00 12.00
AJRRR Rueben Randle 6.00 15.00
AJRRW Robert Woods 8.00 20.00
AJRSB Stedman Bailey 5.00 12.00
AJRST Stepfan Taylor 6.00 15.00
AJRTE Tyler Eifert 5.00 12.00
AJRTW Tyler Wilson 5.00 12.00
AJRTWI Terrance Williams 10.00 25.00
AJRVB Vick Ballard 6.00 15.00
AJRVM Vance McDonald 6.00 15.00
AJRZE Zach Ertz 10.00 25.00

2013 Finest Jumbo Jersey Autographs Prism Refractors

*PRISM REF/25: .6X TO 1.5X GOLD REF/50
AJRAL Andrew Luck 75.00 150.00
AJREJM EJ Manuel 50.00 120.00
AJRMBA Montee Ball 8.00 20.00
AJRMG Mike Glennon 8.00 20.00

2013 Finest Jumbo Jersey Autographs Xfractors

*XFRACTOR/15: .8X TO 2X GOLD REF/50
AJRAL Andrew Luck 100.00 200.00
AJREJM EJ Manuel 100.00 200.00
AJRGS Geno Smith 10.00 25.00
AJRMBA Montee Ball 10.00 25.00

2013 Finest Moments

STATED ODDS 1:36 HOBBY
*PRISM REF/99: 1X TO 2.5X BASIC INSERTS
*REFRACTOR: 1X TO 2.5X BASIC INSERTS
FMAE Andre Ellington .50 1.25
FMAF Arian Foster 1.00 2.50
FMAL Andrew Luck 2.00 5.00
FMBH Brian Hartline .75 2.00
FMCP Cordarrelle Patterson .50 1.25
FMDH DeAndre Hopkins 1.25 3.00
FMDM DeMarco Murray 1.00 2.50
FMED Eric Decker .75 2.00
FMEL Eddie Lacy .50 1.25
FMGB Giovani Bernard .50 1.25
FMGS Geno Smith .50 1.25
FMGT Golden Tate .75 2.00
FMJF Jermichael Finley .75 2.00
FMMB Matt Barkley .50 1.25
FMMBA Montee Ball .50 1.25
FMMBU Michael Bush .75 2.00
FMMG Mike Glennon .50 1.25
FMMJD Maurice Jones-Drew .75 2.00
FMNB NaVorro Bowman 1.00 2.50
FMPG Pierre Garcon 1.00 2.50
FMRG Robert Griffin III .75 2.00
FMRR Ray Rice .75 2.00
FMSS Steve Smith 1.00 2.50
FMTW Tyler Wilson .50 1.25
FMVC Victor Cruz 1.00 2.50

2013 Finest Moments Autographs Refractors

STATED ODDS 1:816 HOBBY
EXCH EXPIRATION: 8/31/2016
FMAAE Andre Ellington 5.00 12.00
FMAAF Arian Foster 25.00 50.00
FMAAL Andrew Luck 90.00 150.00
FMABH Brian Hartline
FMACP Cordarrelle Patterson 5.00 12.00
FMADH DeAndre Hopkins 12.00 30.00
FMADM DeMarco Murray 10.00 25.00
FMAED Eric Decker 8.00 20.00
FMAEL Eddie Lacy 5.00 12.00
FMAGB Giovani Bernard 5.00 12.00
FMAGS Geno Smith 5.00 12.00
FMAGT Golden Tate EXCH 12.00 30.00
FMAJF Jermichael Finley 8.00 20.00
FMAKT Kenbrell Thompkins/200 Mystery 8.00 20.00
FMAMB Matt Barkley 5.00 12.00
FMAMBA Montee Ball 5.00 12.00
FMAMBU Michael Bush 6.00 15.00
FMAMG Mike Glennon EXCH 5.00 12.00
FMAMJD Maurice Jones-Drew 8.00 20.00
FMANB NaVorro Bowman 10.00 25.00
FMAPG Pierre Garcon 10.00 25.00
FMARR Ray Rice
FMASS Steve Smith EXCH 10.00 25.00
FMAST Stepfan Taylor 5.00 12.00
FMATW Tyler Wilson 10.00 25.00
FMAVC Victor Cruz 10.00 25.00

2013 Finest Rookie Autograph Blue Refractors

*BLUE REF/25: .5X TO 1.2X BASIC AU/50
115 EJ Manuel 40.00 100.00
141 Le'Veon Bell 60.00 120.00

2013 Finest Rookie Autograph Red Refractors

*RED REF/15: .6X TO 1.5X BASIC AU/50
RED REF/15 ODDS 1:510 HOB
115 EJ Manuel 40.00 100.00

2013 Finest Rookie Autograph Refractors

REFRACTOR AUTO/50 ODDS 1:156 HOB
101 Mike Glennon 8.00 20.00
102 Zach Ertz 15.00 40.00
103 DeAndre Hopkins 12.00 30.00
104 Tyler Eifert 8.00 20.00
105 Tavon Austin 10.00 25.00
106 Tyler Wilson 8.00 20.00
107 Robert Woods 10.00 25.00
108 Quinton Patton 8.00 20.00
109 Ryan Nassib 8.00 20.00
110 Matt Barkley 8.00 20.00
111 Terrance Williams 8.00 20.00
112 Markus Wheaton 8.00 20.00
113 Aaron Dobson 8.00 20.00
114 Giovani Bernard 8.00 20.00
115 EJ Manuel 20.00 50.00
116 Justin Hunter 8.00 20.00
117 Joseph Randle 8.00 20.00
119 Tyler Bray 8.00 20.00
120 Montee Ball 8.00 20.00
121 Andre Ellington 8.00 20.00
122 Stepfan Taylor 8.00 20.00
123 Jordan Reed 15.00 40.00
124 Landry Jones 10.00 25.00
125 Cordarrelle Patterson 8.00 20.00
130 Eddie Lacy 8.00 20.00
131 Manti Te'o 10.00 25.00
133 Gavin Escobar 8.00 20.00
134 Johnathan Franklin 8.00 20.00
135 Stedman Bailey 8.00 20.00
137 Christine Michael 8.00 20.00
138 Marcus Lattimore 8.00 20.00
140 Keenan Allen 10.00 25.00
141 Le'Veon Bell 30.00 80.00
142 Mike Gillislee 8.00 20.00
144 Kenny Stills 8.00 20.00
149 Denard Robinson 8.00 20.00
150 Geno Smith 8.00 20.00
151 Marquise Goodwin 8.00 20.00
153 Vance McDonald 10.00 25.00
154 Knile Davis 8.00 20.00

2013 Finest Rookie Patch Autographs Prism Refractors

*PRISM REF/25: .8X TO 2X RED REF/75
RAPGS Geno Smith 10.00 25.00
RAPTE Tyler Eilert 12.00 30.00

2013 Finest Rookie Patch Autographs Red Refractors

RED REF/75 ODDS 1:102 HOB
*BLUE REF/99: .4X TO 1X RED REF/75
*GOLD REF/50: .5X TO 1.2X RED REF/75
*BASE REF: .3X TO .8X RED REF/75
RAPAD Aaron Dobson 5.00 12.00
RAPAE Andre Ellington 5.00 12.00
RAPCM Christine Michael 12.00 30.00
RAPCP Cordarrelle Patterson 5.00 12.00
RAPDH DeAndre Hopkins 10.00 25.00
RAPDRO Denard Robinson 5.00 12.00
RAPGB Giovani Bernard 6.00 15.00
RAPGE Gavin Escobar 5.00 12.00
RAPGS Geno Smith 5.00 12.00
RAPJF Johnathan Franklin 5.00 12.00
RAPJH Justin Hunter 5.00 12.00
RAPJJ Jarvis Jones 5.00 12.00
RAPJR Joseph Randle 5.00 12.00
RAPJRE Jordan Reed 10.00 25.00
RAPKA Keenan Allen 10.00 25.00
RAPKD Knile Davis 5.00 12.00
RAPKS Kenny Stills 5.00 12.00
RAPLB Le'Veon Bell 30.00 80.00
RAPLJ Landry Jones 5.00 12.00
RAPMB Matt Barkley 5.00 12.00
RAPMBA Montee Ball 5.00 12.00
RAPMG Mike Glennon 5.00 12.00
RAPMGI Mike Gillislee 8.00 20.00
RAPMGO Marquise Goodwin 5.00 12.00
RAPML Marcus Lattimore 5.00 12.00
RAPMT Manti Te'o 6.00 15.00
RAPMW Markus Wheaton 5.00 12.00
RAPQP Quinton Patton 5.00 12.00
RAPRN Ryan Nassib 5.00 12.00
RAPRW Robert Woods 8.00 20.00
RAPSB Stedman Bailey 5.00 12.00
RAPST Stepfan Taylor 5.00 12.00
RAPTA Tavon Austin 6.00 15.00
RAPTE Tyler Eifert 5.00 12.00
RAPTW Tyler Wilson 5.00 12.00
RAPTWI Terrance Williams 5.00 12.00
RAPVM Vance McDonald 6.00 15.00
RAPZE Zach Ertz 10.00 25.00

2013 Finest Rookie Patch Autographs Xfractors

*XFRACTOR/15: 1X TO 2.5X RED REF/75
XFRACTOR/15 ODDS 1:510 HOB
RAPEJM EJ Manuel 75.00 150.00
RAPGS Geno Smith 12.00 30.00
RAPMG Mike Glennon 12.00 30.00

2014 Finest

COMPLETE SET (150)
1 Adrian Peterson .30 .75
2 Demaryius Thomas .25 .60
3 Alex Smith .25 .60
4 Josh Gordon .20 .50
5 Jimmy Graham .30 .75
6 Mike Wallace .20 .50
7 Antonio Brown .30 .75
8 Robert Quinn .25 .60
9 C.J. Spiller .20 .50
10 Jay Cutler .20 .50
11 Earl Thomas .25 .60
12 Andy Dalton .25 .60
13 Reggie Wayne .25 .60
14 Reggie Bush .20 .50
15 Cam Newton .30 .75
16 Mike Glennon .25 .60
17 Sean Lee .25 .60
18 Marshawn Lynch .25 .60
19 Larry Fitzgerald .25 .60
20 Julius Thomas .20 .50
21 Troy Polamalu .30 .75
22 Denarius Moore .20 .50
23 Richard Sherman .30 .75
24 Drew Brees .30 .75
25 Russell Wilson .50 1.25
26 Ace Sanders .20 .50
27 NaVorro Bowman .25 .60
28 Victor Cruz .25 .60
29 Montee Ball .20 .50
30 Jordy Nelson .25 .60
31 Jordan Cameron .20 .50
32 DeSean Jackson .25 .60
33 T.Y. Hilton .25 .60
34 Eddie Lacy .20 .50
35 Terrell Suggs .20 .50
36 Patrick Willis .25 .60
37 Cordarrelle Patterson .20 .50
38 Giovani Bernard .20 .50
39 Randall Cobb .25 .60
40 Patrick Peterson .20 .50
41 Kendall Wright .20 .50
42 Roddy White .20 .50
43 J.J. Watt .30 .75
44 Cecil Shorts .20 .50
45 DeAndre Hopkins .25 .60
46 Percy Harvin .20 .50
47 Ndamukong Suh .25 .60
48 Tavon Austin .20 .50
49 Pierre Garcon .25 .60
50 Peyton Manning .60 1.50
51 Luke Kuechly .25 .60
52 Robert Griffin III .20 .50
53 Rob Gronkowski .30 .75
54 Julio Jones .30 .75
55 Keenan Allen .25 .60
56 Dez Bryant .30 .75
57 Tony Romo .25 .60
58 EJ Manuel .20 .50
59 Ryan Tannehill .25 .60
60 Matt Ryan .25 .60
61 Von Miller .25 .60
62 Matt Forte .20 .50
63 Sheldon Richardson .20 .50
64 Geno Smith .20 .50
65 Julian Edelman .30 .75
66 Alfred Morris .25 .60
67 LeSean McCoy .30 .75
68 Eli Manning .25 .60
69 Colin Kaepernick .25 .60
70 Ray Rice .20 .50
71 Eric Berry .25 .60
72 Matthew Stafford .25 .60
73 Le'Veon Bell .25 .60
74 Zach Ertz .25 .60
75 Andrew Luck .40 1.00
76 Arian Foster .25 .60
77 Frank Gore .25 .60
78 Andre Johnson .25 .60
79 Pierre Thomas .20 .50
80 Clay Matthews .30 .75
81 Ryan Mathews .25 .60
82 Robert Mathis .20 .50
83 Vincent Jackson .20 .50
84 Darrelle Revis .20 .50
85 DeMarco Murray .25 .60
86 Brian Hartline .20 .50
87 Philip Rivers .30 .75
88 Kiko Alonso .20 .50
89 Aaron Rodgers .60 1.50
90 A.J. Green .30 .75
91 Brandon Marshall .20 .50
92 Joe Flacco .25 .60
93 Jamaal Charles .25 .60
94 Alshon Jeffery .25 .60
95 Wes Welker .25 .60
96 Michael Crabtree .20 .50
97 Tom Brady .75 2.00
98 Nick Foles .25 .60
99 Torrey Smith .20 .50
100 Calvin Johnson .30 .75
101 Blake Bortles RC .50 1.25
102 Jarvis Landry RC .75 2.00
103 Carlos Hyde RC .50 1.25
104 Austin Seferian-Jenkins RC .40 1.00
105 Jared Abbrederis RC .40 1.00
106 Taylor Lewan RC .40 1.00
107 Greg Robinson RC .40 1.00
108 Odell Beckham Jr. RC 1.00 2.50
109 Robert Herron RC .40 1.00
110 Jordan Matthews RC .60 1.50
111 Zach Mettenberger RC .40 1.00
112 Zack Martin RC .50 1.25
113 Brandin Cooks RC .60 1.50
114 Marqise Lee RC .50 1.25
115 Tre Mason RC .40 1.00
116 Jimmy Garoppolo RC 3.00 8.00
117 Martavis Bryant RC .50 1.25
118 Kelvin Benjamin RC .60 1.50
119 Khalil Mack RC 1.50 4.00
120 David Fales RC .40 1.00
121 Jeremy Hill RC .50 1.25
122 Derek Carr RC 2.50 6.00
123 Eric Ebron RC .50 1.25
124 Logan Thomas RC .40 1.00
125 Johnny Manziel RC .60 1.50
126 De'Anthony Thomas RC .40 1.00
127 Tajh Boyd RC .40 1.00
128 Jace Amaro RC .40 1.00
129 Ka'Deem Carey RC .40 1.00
130 Davante Adams RC .60 1.50
131 Jordan Lynch RC .50 1.25
132 Charles Sims RC .40 1.00
133 Michael Sam RC .40 1.00
134 Aaron Donald RC 1.00 2.50
135 Aaron Murray RC .40 1.00
136 Jake Matthews RC .40 1.00
137 Darqueze Dennard RC .50 1.25
138 Troy Niklas RC .40 1.00
139 Connor Shaw RC .40 1.00
140 C.J. Fiedorowicz RC .40 1.00
141 Sammy Watkins RC .60 1.50
142 Teddy Bridgewater RC .60 1.50
143 Bishop Sankey RC .40 1.00
144 Stephen Morris RC .40 1.00
145 Anthony Barr RC .40 1.00
146 Mike Evans RC 1.00 2.50
147 A.J. McCarron RC .40 1.00
148 Allen Robinson RC .60 1.50
149 Paul Richardson RC .50 1.25
150 Jadeveon Clowney RC .50 1.25
US Uncut Sheet EXCH 50.00 100.00

2014 Finest Blue Refractors

*VETS/99: 3X TO 8X BASIC CARDS
*ROOKIES/99: 1.5X TO 4X BASIC CARDS
STATED ODDS 1:5 HOBBY
108 Odell Beckham Jr. 15.00 40.00

2014 Finest Gold Refractors

*VETS/75: 3X TO 8X BASIC CARDS
*ROOKIES/75: 1.5X TO 4X BASIC CARDS

2014 Finest Red Refractors

*VETS/50: 5X TO 12X BASIC CARDS
*ROOKIES/50: 2.5X TO 6X BASIC CARDS
50 Peyton Manning 15.00 40.00

2014 Finest Refractors

*VETS: 1.5X TO 4X BASIC CARDS
*ROOKIES: .6X TO 1.5X BASIC CARDS

2014 Finest Xfractors

*1-100 VETS: 2X TO 5X BASIC CARDS
*101-150 ROOKIES: .8X TO 2X BASIC RC

2014 Finest Atomic Refractor Rookies

FARAM A.J. McCarron .60 1.50
FARAR Allen Robinson 1.00 2.50
FARBB Blake Bortles .75 2.00
FARBC Brandin Cooks 1.00 2.50
FARBS Bishop Sankey .60 1.50
FARCF C.J. Fiedorowicz .60 1.50
FARCH Carlos Hyde .75 2.00
FARCS Charles Sims .60 1.50
FARDA Davante Adams 1.00 2.50
FARDC Derek Carr 4.00 10.00
FARDD Darqueze Dennard .75 2.00
FARDF David Fales .60 1.50
FAREE Eric Ebron .75 2.00
FARJA Jace Amaro .60 1.50
FARJC Jadeveon Clowney .75 2.00
FARJG Jimmy Garoppolo 5.00 12.00
FARJH Jeremy Hill .75 2.00
FARJL Jarvis Landry 1.25 3.00
FARJM Johnny Manziel 1.00 2.50
FARKB Kelvin Benjamin 1.00 2.50
FARKC Ka'Deem Carey .60 1.50
FARKM Khalil Mack 2.50 6.00
FARLT Logan Thomas .60 1.50
FARMB Martavis Bryant .75 2.00
FARME Mike Evans 1.50 4.00
FARML Marqise Lee .75 2.00
FARMS Michael Sam .60 1.50
FAROB Odell Beckham Jr. 1.50 4.00
FARPR Paul Richardson .75 2.00
FARRH Robert Herron .60 1.50
FARSW Sammy Watkins 1.00 2.50
FARTB Tajh Boyd .60 1.50
FARTM Tre Mason .60 1.50
FARTS Tom Savage .60 1.50
FARZM Zach Mettenberger .60 1.50
FARAMU Aaron Murray .60 1.50
FARASJ Austin Seferian-Jenkins .60 1.50
FARCSH Connor Shaw .60 1.50
FARJMA Jordan Matthews 1.00 2.50
FARTBR Teddy Bridgewater 1.00 2.50

2014 Finest Atomic Refractor Rookies Autographs Red Refractors

FARAAM A.J. McCarron 10.00 25.00
FARABB Blake Bortles 12.00 30.00
FARABC Brandin Cooks 15.00 40.00
FARABS Bishop Sankey 10.00 25.00
FARACH Carlos Hyde 12.00 30.00
FARACC Charles Sims 10.00 25.00
FARADA Davante Adams 15.00 40.00
FARADD Darqueze Dennard 12.00 30.00
FARADF David Fales 10.00 25.00
FARAEE Eric Ebron 12.00 30.00
FARAJC Jadeveon Clowney 12.00 30.00
FARAJH Jeremy Hill 10.00 20.00
FARAJL Jarvis Landry 20.00 50.00
FARAJM Johnny Manziel 15.00 40.00
FARALT Logan Thomas 10.00 25.00
FARAMB Martavis Bryant 12.00 30.00
FARAME Mike Evans 25.00 60.00
FARAMS Michael Sam 10.00 25.00
FARAPR Paul Richardson 12.00 30.00
FARARH Robert Herron 10.00 25.00
FARATB Tajh Boyd 10.00 25.00
FARAZM Zach Mettenberger 10.00 25.00
FARAAMU Aaron Murray 10.00 25.00
FARACSH Connor Shaw 15.00 40.00
FARAJMA Jordan Matthews 15.00 40.00

2014 Finest Fantasy's Finest

*REFRACTOR: .6X TO 1.5X BASIC INSERTS
*PULSAR REF/99: .8X TO 2X BASIC INSERTS
FFAJ Alshon Jeffery 1.00 2.50
FFAP Adrian Peterson 1.25 3.00
FFBH Brian Hartline .75 2.00
FFDA Danny Amendola 1.00 2.50
FFDB Drew Brees 1.25 3.00
FFDJ DeSean Jackson 1.00 2.50
FFDW Danny Woodhead 1.00 2.50
FFEL Eddie Lacy .75 2.00
FFGB Giovani Bernard .75 2.00
FFGO Greg Olsen 1.00 2.50
FFJC Jordan Cameron .75 2.00
FFJE Julian Edelman 1.25 3.00
FFJN Jordy Nelson 1.00 2.50
FFJR Jordan Reed .75 2.00
FFJT Julius Thomas .75 2.00
FFLB Le'Veon Bell 1.00 2.50
FFLF Larry Fitzgerald 1.00 2.50
FFMF Matt Forte .75 2.00
FFML Marshawn Lynch 1.00 2.50
FFRB Reggie Bush .75 2.00
FFRM Ryan Mathews 1.00 2.50
FFRW Roddy White .75 2.00
FFSV Shane Vereen 1.00 2.50
FFVC Victor Cruz 1.00 2.50
FFZS Zac Stacy .75 2.00

2014 Finest Fantasy's Finest Autographs

STATED ODDS 1:198 HOBBY
FFAAF Arian Foster 8.00 20.00
FFAAJ Alshon Jeffery 8.00 20.00
FFAAP Adrian Peterson 40.00 80.00
FFABH Brian Hartline 6.00 15.00
FFACS C.J. Spiller
FFADB Drew Brees 50.00 100.00
FFADW Danny Woodhead EXCH 25.00 50.00
FFAEL Eddie Lacy 6.00 15.00
FFAGB Giovani Bernard 6.00 15.00
FFAGO Greg Olsen 8.00 20.00
FFAJC Jordan Cameron 6.00 15.00
FFAJE Julian Edelman EXCH 10.00 25.00
FFAJN Jordy Nelson 20.00 40.00
FFAJR Jordan Reed 6.00 15.00
FFAJT Julius Thomas 6.00 15.00
FFALB Le'Veon Bell 8.00 20.00
FFALF Larry Fitzgerald 25.00 50.00
FFAMF Matt Forte EXCH 6.00 15.00
FFAML Marshawn Lynch 8.00 20.00
FFARB Reggie Bush EXCH 30.00 60.00
FFARM Ryan Mathews 6.00 15.00
FFARW Roddy White 6.00 15.00
FFASV Shane Vereen 6.00 15.00
FFAVC Victor Cruz EXCH 8.00 20.00
FFAZS Zac Stacy EXCH 6.00 15.00

2014 Finest Fantasy's Finest Jumbo Jersey Autographs

STATED ODDS 1:595 MINI BOX
FFAJAF Arian Foster EXCH 15.00 40.00
FFAJAG A.J. Green UER 15.00 40.00
FFAJAJ Alshon Jeffery 12.00 30.00
FFAJAP Adrian Peterson 50.00 100.00
FFAJBH Brian Hartline 10.00 25.00
FFAJCP Cordarrelle Patterson 10.00 25.00
FFAJCS C.J. Spiller
FFAJDB Drew Brees 75.00 125.00
FFAJDJ DeSean Jackson
FFAJEL Eddie Lacy
FFAJGB Giovani Bernard
FFAJGO Greg Olsen 10.00 25.00
FFAJJJ Julio Jones
FFAJJR Jordan Reed
FFAJKM Knowshon Moreno
FFAJKW Kendall Wright EXCH
FFAJLB Le'Veon Bell 12.00 30.00
FFAJLF Larry Fitzgerald EXCH 20.00 50.00
FFAJMF Matt Forte
FFAJML Marshawn Lynch
FFAJRB Reggie Bush
FFAJRM Ryan Mathews 12.00 30.00
FFAJRW Roddy White 15.00 40.00
FFAJSV Shane Vereen
FFAJVC Victor Cruz EXCH

2014 Finest Jumbo Jersey Autographs Gold Refractors

*BASE REF: .25 TO .6X GOLD/50
*BLUE/99: .3X TO .8X GOLD/50
*RED/75: .3X TO .8X GOLD/50
AJRAG A.J. Green 12.00 30.00
AJRAJ Alshon Jeffery 12.00 30.00
AJRAM A.J. McCarron 5.00 12.00
AJRAMU Aaron Murray 5.00 12.00
AJRAR Allen Robinson 8.00 20.00
AJRASJ Austin Seferian-Jenkins 5.00 12.00
AJRBB Blake Bortles 6.00 15.00
AJRBC Brandin Cooks 8.00 20.00
AJRBSA Bishop Sankey 5.00 12.00
AJRCLA Cody Latimer 6.00 15.00
AJRCP Cordarrelle Patterson 6.00 15.00
AJRCS Charles Sims 5.00 12.00
AJRDA Davante Adams 8.00 20.00
AJRDC Derek Carr 30.00 80.00
AJRDFE Devonta Freeman 8.00 20.00
AJREE Eric Ebron 6.00 15.00
AJREL Eddie Lacy 6.00 15.00
AJRGB Giovani Bernard
AJRGS Geno Smith 6.00 15.00
AJRJAM Jace Amaro 5.00 12.00
AJRJC Jadeveon Clowney 6.00 15.00
AJRJG Jimmy Garoppolo 100.00 200.00
AJRJH Jeremy Hill 6.00 15.00
AJRJLA Jarvis Landry 10.00 25.00
AJRJM Jordan Matthews 8.00 20.00
AJRJMA Johnny Manziel 8.00 20.00
AJRKB Kelvin Benjamin 8.00 20.00
AJRKC Ka'Deem Carey 5.00 12.00
AJRKS Kenny Stills 6.00 15.00
AJRKW Kendall Wright 6.00 15.00
AJRLB Le'Veon Bell 12.00 30.00
AJRLT Logan Thomas 5.00 12.00
AJRME Mike Evans 12.00 30.00
AJRMG Marquise Goodwin 6.00 15.00
AJRML Marqise Lee 6.00 15.00
AJRMS Michael Sam 5.00 12.00
AJRPG Paul Richardson 6.00 15.00
AJRRM Keenan Allen 8.00 20.00
AJRRMA Ryan Mathews
AJRRW Robert Woods 8.00 20.00
AJRSW Sammy Watkins 15.00 40.00
AJRTB Tajh Boyd 5.00 12.00
AJRTBR Teddy Bridgewater 8.00 20.00
AJRTM Tre Mason 5.00 12.00
AJRTS Tom Savage 5.00 12.00
AJRTW Terrance West 5.00 12.00
AJRZE Zach Ertz 8.00 20.00
AJRZM Zach Mettenberger 5.00 12.00

2014 Finest Jumbo Jersey Autographs Pulsar Refractors

*PULSAR/25: .5X TO 1.2X GOLD/50
AJRJG Jimmy Garoppolo 200.00 300.00

2014 Finest Quarterback Cuts

FQCAM Aaron Murray 1.00 2.50
FQCBB Blake Bortles 1.25 3.00
FQCDC Derek Carr 6.00 15.00
FQCJG Jimmy Garoppolo 8.00 20.00
FQCJM Johnny Manziel 1.50 4.00
FQCLT Logan Thomas 1.00 2.50
FQCTB Teddy Bridgewater 1.50 4.00
FQCTS Tom Savage 1.00 2.50
FGCAMC A.J. McCarron 1.00 2.50
FQCTBY Tajh Boyd 1.00 2.50

2014 Finest Rookie Autograph Refractors

101 Blake Bortles 8.00 20.00
102 Jarvis Landry 15.00 40.00
103 Carlos Hyde 8.00 20.00
105 Jared Abbrederis 6.00 15.00
106 Taylor Lewan 6.00 15.00
107 Greg Robinson 6.00 15.00
108 Odell Beckham Jr. 60.00 120.00
109 Robert Herron 6.00 15.00
110 Jordan Matthews 10.00 25.00
111 Zach Mettenberger 6.00 15.00
112 Zack Martin 12.00 30.00
113 Brandin Cooks 10.00 25.00
114 Marqise Lee 8.00 20.00
115 Tre Mason 6.00 15.00
116 Jimmy Garoppolo 75.00 150.00
117 Martavis Bryant 8.00 20.00
118 Kelvin Benjamin 10.00 25.00
121 Jeremy Hill 8.00 20.00
122 Derek Carr 30.00 80.00
123 Eric Ebron 8.00 20.00
125 Johnny Manziel 10.00 25.00
128 Jace Amaro 6.00 15.00
130 Davante Adams 10.00 25.00
131 Jordan Lynch 8.00 20.00
132 Charles Sims 6.00 15.00
133 Michael Sam 6.00 15.00
134 Aaron Donald 15.00 40.00
135 Aaron Murray 6.00 15.00
136 Jake Matthews 6.00 15.00
137 Darqueze Dennard 8.00 20.00
138 Troy Niklas 6.00 15.00
140 C.J. Fiedorowicz 6.00 15.00
141 Sammy Watkins 10.00 25.00
142 Teddy Bridgewater 10.00 25.00
143 Bishop Sankey 8.00 20.00
145 Anthony Barr 6.00 15.00
146 Mike Evans 15.00 40.00
147 A.J. McCarron 6.00 15.00
148 Allen Robinson 10.00 25.00
150 Jadeveon Clowney 8.00 20.00
NNO Mystery EXCH/A.Hurns 15.00 40.00

2014 Finest Rookie Autograph Blue Refractors

*BLUE/25: .5X TO 1.2X BASIC AU/35
116 Jimmy Garoppolo 100.00 200.00

2014 Finest Rookie Autograph Red Refractors

*RED/15: .6X TO 1.5X BASIC AU/35
116 Jimmy Garoppolo 150.00 250.00

2014 Finest Rookie Patch Autographs Gold Refractors

*BASE REF: .25X TO .6X GOLD/50
*BLUE/99: .3X TO .8X GOLD/50
*RED/75: .3X TO .8X GOLD/50
RAPAM Aaron Murray 10.00 25.00
RAPAMC A.J. McCarron 5.00 12.00
RAPAR Allen Robinson 8.00 20.00
RAPASJ Austin Seferian-Jenkins 5.00 12.00
RAPBB Blake Bortles 6.00 15.00
RAPBC Brandin Cooks 8.00 20.00
RAPBS Bishop Sankey 5.00 12.00
RAPCLA Cody Latimer 6.00 15.00
RAPCS Charles Sims 5.00 12.00
RAPDA Davante Adams 8.00 20.00
RAPDC Derek Carr 60.00 120.00
RAPDM Donte Moncrief 5.00 12.00
RAPEE Eric Ebron 6.00 15.00
RAPJA Jace Amaro 5.00 12.00
RAPJC Jadeveon Clowney 6.00 15.00
RAPJG Jimmy Garoppolo 100.00 200.00
RAPJH Jeremy Hill 6.00 15.00
RAPJL Jarvis Landry 10.00 25.00
RAPJM Johnny Manziel 8.00 20.00
RAPJMA Jordan Matthews 8.00 20.00
RAPKB Kelvin Benjamin 8.00 20.00
RAPKC Ka'Deem Carey 5.00 12.00
RAPLT Logan Thomas 5.00 12.00
RAPME Mike Evans 12.00 30.00
RAPML Marqise Lee 6.00 15.00
RAPMS Michael Sam 5.00 12.00
RAPPR Paul Richardson 10.00 25.00
RAPSW Sammy Watkins 8.00 20.00
RAPTB Tajh Boyd 5.00 12.00
RAPTBR Teddy Bridgewater 8.00 20.00
RAPTM Tre Mason 10.00 25.00
RAPTS Tom Savage 5.00 12.00
RAPTW Terrance West 5.00 12.00

2014 Finest Rookie Patch Autographs Pulsar Refractors

*PULSAR/25: .5X TO 1.2X GOLD/50
RAPBB Blake Bortles 8.00 20.00
RAPJG Jimmy Garoppolo 200.00 300.00
RAPTBR Teddy Bridgewater 10.00 25.00

2015 Finest

1 Aaron Rodgers .60 1.50
2 Arian Foster .25 .60
3 Jeremy Langford RC .30 .75
4 Eric Ebron .20 .50
5 Antonio Brown .30 .75
6 Marshawn Lynch .25 .60
7 Tyler Lockett RC .50 1.25
8 Karlos Williams RC .30 .75
9 Ty Montgomery RC .30 .75
10 Mike Evans .25 .60
11 Eli Manning .25 .60
12 Cameron Artis-Payne RC .30 .75
13 T.J. Yeldon RC .30 .75
14 Cam Newton .30 .75
15 Demaryius Thomas .25 .60
16 Austin Hill RC .30 .75
17 Jay Cutler .20 .50
18 Phillip Dorsett RC .30 .75
19 Devin Smith RC .30 .75
20 Marcus Mariota RC 1.25 3.00
21 Vince Mayle RC .40 1.00
22 Eric Decker .20 .50
23 Travis Kelce .30 .75
24 Bryce Petty RC .30 .75
25 Andrew Luck .40 1.00
26 Justin Houston .20 .50
27 Justin Hardy RC .30 .75
28 Von Miller .25 .60
29 Tony Lippett RC .30 .75
30 Matt Ryan .25 .60
31 David Cobb RC .30 .75
32 Alfred Morris .20 .50
33 Kenny Bell RC .50 1.25
34 Golden Tate .20 .50
35 Jordy Nelson .25 .60
36 Sammie Coates RC .40 1.00
37 Devin Funchess RC .50 1.25
38 Brandon Marshall .20 .50
39 Sean Mannion RC .30 .75
40 Jeremy Hill .20 .50
41 Jason Witten .25 .60
42 Andy Dalton .25 .60
43 Drew Brees .30 .75
44 Donte Moncrief .25 .60
45 Amari Cooper RC 1.00 2.50
46 Robert Griffin III .20 .50
47 Danny Shelton RC .30 .75
48 Terrell Suggs .20 .50
49 Breshad Perriman RC .30 .75
50 Russell Wilson .40 1.00
51 Joe Flacco .25 .60
52 Mark Ingram .25 .60
53 Eddie Lacy .20 .50
54 Richard Sherman .30 .75
55 Ndamukong Suh .25 .60
56 Derek Carr .30 .75
57 Davante Adams .25 .60
58 Stefon Diggs RC .75 2.00
59 Josh Harper RC .30 .75
60 DeMarco Murray .25 .60
61 Alshon Jeffery .25 .60
62 Larry Donnell .20 .50
63 Tony Romo .25 .60
64 DeAndre Hopkins .25 .60
65 Darrelle Revis .20 .50
66 Peyton Manning .60 1.50
67 Javorius Allen RC .40 1.00
68 Jason Pierre-Paul .20 .50
69 Emmanuel Sanders .25 .60
70 Jameis Winston RC .75 2.00
71 Philip Rivers .30 .75
72 Patrick Peterson .20 .50
73 Rob Gronkowski .30 .75
74 Clive Walford RC .30 .75
75 Kelvin Benjamin .25 .60
76 Dorial Green-Beckham RC .30 .75
77 Jimmy Graham .30 .75
78 Larry Fitzgerald .25 .60
79 Landon Collins RC .40 1.00
80 Melvin Gordon RC .75 2.00
81 Sam Bradford .20 .50
82 Brandon Scherff RC .50 1.25
83 Duke Johnson RC .50 1.25
84 Matt Forte .20 .50
85 Todd Gurley RC 1.25 3.00
86 Garrett Grayson RC .30 .75
87 Clay Matthews .30 .75
88 Titus Davis RC .40 1.00
89 Jeremy Maclin .20 .50
90 Randall Cobb .25 .60
91 Julian Edelman .30 .75
92 Jaelen Strong RC .40 1.00
93 A.J. Green .30 .75
94 Andrus Peat RC .30 .75
95 Teddy Bridgewater .25 .60
96 Lamar Miller .20 .50
97 Rashad Greene RC .30 .75
98 Matt Jones RC .30 .75
99 Calvin Johnson .30 .75
100 Odell Beckham Jr. .30 .75
101 Colin Kaepernick .25 .60
102 Tre Mason .25 .60
103 Mike Davis RC .30 .75
104 Joique Bell .20 .50
105 DeVante Parker RC .50 1.25
106 Sammy Watkins .25 .60
107 Jay Ajayi RC .50 1.25
108 David Johnson RC .75 2.00
109 Shaq Thompson RC .40 1.00
110 Kevin White RC .40 1.00
111 Julio Jones .30 .75
112 Antonio Gates .20 .50
113 Nick Foles .25 .60
114 Nelson Agholor RC .40 1.00
115 J.J. Watt .30 .75
116 T.Y. Hilton .25 .60
117 Vic Beasley RC .40 1.00
118 Tre McBride RC .30 .75
119 Tevin Coleman RC .40 1.00
120 Brett Hundley RC .30 .75
121 Adrian Peterson .30 .75
122 Chris Conley RC .30 .75
123 Greg Olsen .25 .60
124 Alvin Dupree RC .40 1.00
125 Dez Bryant .30 .75
126 Randy Gregory RC .30 .75
127 LeSean McCoy .30 .75
128 Dante Fowler Jr. RC .50 1.25
129 Alex Smith .25 .60
130 Blake Bortles .20 .50
131 Jamison Crowder RC .40 1.00
132 Jeff Heuerman RC .40 1.00
133 Shane Ray RC .30 .75
134 Victor Cruz .25 .60
135 Jordan Matthews .25 .60
136 Andre Johnson .25 .60
137 Le'Veon Bell .25 .60
138 Julius Thomas .20 .50
139 Ameer Abdullah RC .50 1.25
140 Tom Brady .75 2.00
141 Johnny Manziel .25 .60
142 Luke Kuechly .25 .60
143 Jamaal Charles .25 .60
144 Maxx Williams RC .30 .75
145 C.J. Anderson .25 .60
146 Ben Roethlisberger .30 .75
147 Carlos Hyde .20 .50
148 Leonard Williams RC .30 .75
149 Ryan Tannehill .25 .60
150 Matthew Stafford .25 .60

2015 Finest Black Refractors

*VETS: 1.2X TO 3X BASIC CARDS
*ROOKIES: .8X TO 2X BASIC RC

2015 Finest Blue Refractors

*VETS/250: 1.5X TO 4X BASIC CARDS
*ROOKIES/250: 1X TO 2.5X BASIC CARDS

2015 Finest Camo Refractors

*VETS/10: 12X TO 30X BASIC CARDS
*ROOKIES/25: X TO X BASIC RC*ROOKIES/10: 5X TO 12X BASIC RC

2015 Finest Diamond Refractors

*VETS/60: 4X TO 10X BASIC CARDS
*ROOKIES/60: 2.5X TO 6X BASIC RC

2015 Finest Gold Refractors

*VETS/150: 2.5X TO 6X BASIC CARDS
*ROOKIES/150: 1.5X TO 4X BASIC RC

2015 Finest Pink Refractors

*VETS/25: 8X TO 20X BASIC CARDS
*ROOKIES/25: 4X TO 10X BASIC RC

2015 Finest Red Refractors

*VETS/99: 3X TO 8X BASIC CARDS
*ROOKIES/99: 2X TO 5X BASIC RC

2015 Finest Refractors

*VETS: 1.2X TO 3X BASIC CARDS
*ROOKIES: .8X TO 2X BASIC RC

2015 Finest Xfractors

*VETS: 1.5X TO 4X BASIC CARDS
*ROOKIES: 1X TO 2.5X BASIC RC

2015 Finest '95 Finest Autographs Refractors

95FRAAC Amari Cooper 40.00 80.00
95FRAAJ Alshon Jeffery 15.00 40.00
95FRARP Breshad Perriman 10.00 25.00
95FRADG Dorial Green-Beckham 10.00 25.00
95FRADJ Duke Johnson 15.00 40.00
95FRADP DeVante Parker 15.00 40.00
95FRAEL Eddie Lacy 12.00 30.00
95FRAJH Jeremy Hill 12.00 30.00
95FRAJM Jordan Matthews 15.00 40.00
95FRAJS Jaelen Strong 12.00 30.00
95FRAJW Jameis Winston 25.00 60.00
95FRAKB Kelvin Benjamin 15.00 40.00
95FRAKW Kevin White 12.00 30.00
95FRAME Mike Evans 15.00 40.00
95FRAMF Matt Forte 12.00 30.00
95FRAMG Melvin Gordon 25.00 60.00
95FRAMM Marcus Mariota 60.00 125.00
95FRATG Todd Gurley 100.00 200.00

2015 Finest '95 Finest Refractors

*GOLD REF/199: .6X TO 1.5X BASIC INSERTS
*GREEN REF/299: .5X TO 1.2X BASIC INSERTS
*PULSAR REF/50: 1.5X TO 4X BASIC INSERTS
*RED REF/99: .8X TO 2X BASIC INSERTS
*METAL/49: 1.5X TO 4X BASIC INSERTS
95FRRAC Amari Cooper 2.00 5.00
95FRRAJ Alshon Jeffery 1.25 3.00
95FRRAR Aaron Rodgers 3.00 8.00
95FRRBP Breshad Perriman .60 1.50
95FRRDG Dorial Green-Beckham .60 1.50
95FRRDJ Duke Johnson 1.00 2.50
95FRRDP DeVante Parker 1.00 2.50
95FRREL Eddie Lacy 1.00 2.50
95FRREM Eli Manning 1.25 3.00
95FRRJH Jeremy Hill 1.00 2.50
95FRRJM Jordan Matthews 1.25 3.00
95FRRJS Jaelen Strong .75 2.00
95FRRJW Jameis Winston 1.50 4.00
95FRRKB Kelvin Benjamin 1.25 3.00
95FRRKW Kevin White .75 2.00
95FRRME Mike Evans 1.25 3.00
95FRRMF Matt Forte 1.00 2.50
95FRRMG Melvin Gordon 1.50 4.00
95FRRMM Marcus Mariota 2.50 6.00
95FRROB Odell Beckham Jr. 1.50 4.00
95FRRPD Phillip Dorsett .60 1.50
95FRRPM Peyton Manning 3.00 8.00
95FRRRW Russell Wilson 2.00 5.00
95FRRTB Tom Brady 4.00 10.00
95FRRTG Todd Gurley 2.50 6.00

2015 Finest Atomic Refractor Rookies

*BLUE REF/299: .6X TO 1.5X BASIC INSERTS
*GOLD REF/199: .8X TO 2X BASIC INSERTS
*PULSAR REF/50: 2X TO 5X BASIC INSERTS
*RED REF/99: 1.X TO 3X BASIC INSERTS
ARDCAA Ameer Abdullah .50 1.25
ARDCAC Amari Cooper 1.00 2.50
ARDCBH Brett Hundley .30 .75
ARDCBP Breshad Perriman .30 .75
ARDCBPE Bryce Petty .30 .75
ARDCCA Cameron Artis-Payne .30 .75
ARDCCC Chris Conley .30 .75
ARDCDC David Cobb .30 .75
ARDCDF Devin Funchess .50 1.25
ARDCDG Dorial Green-Beckham .30 .75
ARDCDJ Duke Johnson .50 1.25
ARDCDJJ David Johnson .75 2.00
ARDCDP DeVante Parker .50 1.25
ARDCDS Devin Smith .30 .75
ARDCGG Garrett Grayson .30 .75
ARDCJA Jay Ajayi .50 1.25
ARDCJAL Javorius Allen .40 1.00
ARDCJL Jeremy Langford .30 .75
ARDCJS Jaelen Strong .40 1.00
ARDCJW Jameis Winston .75 2.00
ARDCKB Kenny Bell .50 1.25
ARDCKW Kevin White .40 1.00
ARDCKWI Karlos Williams .30 .75
ARDCMD Mike Davis .30 .75
ARDCMG Melvin Gordon .75 2.00
ARDCMM Marcus Mariota 1.25 3.00
ARDCMW Maxx Williams .30 .75
ARDCNA Nelson Agholor .40 1.00
ARDCPD Phillip Dorsett .30 .75
ARDCRG Rashad Greene .30 .75
ARDCSC Sammie Coates .40 1.00
ARDCSD Stefon Diggs .75 2.00
ARDCSM Sean Mannion .30 .75
ARDCTC Tevin Coleman .40 1.00
ARDCTG Todd Gurley 1.25 3.00
ARDCTL Tyler Lockett .50 1.25
ARDCTLI Tony Lippett .30 .75
ARDCTM Ty Montgomery .30 .75
ARDCTY T.J. Yeldon .30 .75
ARDCVM Vince Mayle .40 1.00

2015 Finest Atomic Refractor Rookies Autographs Refractors

*BLUE/25: .4X TO 1X BASIC AU
RADC2 Devin Funchess 12.00 30.00
RADC4 Todd Gurley 75.00 150.00
RADC5 Melvin Gordon 20.00 50.00
RADC6 DeVante Parker 12.00 30.00
RADC7 Brett Hundley 8.00 20.00
RADC8 Amari Cooper 40.00 100.00
RADC9 Kevin White 10.00 25.00
RADC10 Marcus Mariota 40.00 80.00
RADC11 Jameis Winston 20.00 50.00
RADC13 Ameer Abdullah 12.00 30.00
RADC14 Breshad Perriman 8.00 20.00
RADC16 Devin Smith 8.00 20.00
RADC19 Tyler Lockett 12.00 30.00
RADC20 Tevin Coleman 10.00 25.00
RADC22 Jay Ajayi 12.00 30.00
RADC23 Bryce Petty 8.00 20.00
RADC25 Jeremy Langford 8.00 20.00
RADC26 David Johnson 20.00 50.00
RADC27 Ty Montgomery 8.00 20.00
RADC28 T.J. Yeldon 8.00 20.00
RADC29 Mike Davis 8.00 20.00
RADC30 Rashad Greene 8.00 20.00

2015 Finest Jumbo Jersey Autographs Refractors

*BASE REF: .3X TO .8X BLUE/150
AJRRBH Brett Hundley 2.00 5.00

2015 Finest Jumbo Jersey Autographs Blue Refractors

AJRRAA Ameer Abdullah 4.00 10.00
AJRRBPE Bryce Petty 2.50 6.00
AJRRCA Cameron Artis-Payne 2.50 6.00
AJRRCC Chris Conley 2.50 6.00
AJRRCW Clive Walford 2.50 6.00
AJRRDA Davante Adams 4.00 10.00
AJRRDCO David Cobb 2.50 6.00
AJRRDG Dorial Green-Beckham 2.50 6.00
AJRRDJ Duke Johnson 4.00 10.00
AJRRDJO David Johnson 10.00 25.00
AJRRDM Donte Moncrief 4.00 10.00
AJRRDS Devin Smith 2.50 6.00
AJRRJA Jay Ajayi 4.00 10.00
AJRRJAL Javorius Allen 3.00 8.00
AJRRJC Jamison Crowder 3.00 8.00
AJRRJHA Justin Hardy 2.50 6.00
AJRRJL Jeremy Langford 10.00 25.00
AJRRKBE Kenny Bell 4.00 10.00
AJRRKWI Karlos Williams 2.50 6.00
AJRRMD Mike Davis 2.50 6.00
AJRRMJ Matt Jones 2.50 6.00
AJRRMW Maxx Williams 2.50 6.00
AJRRRG Rashad Greene 2.50 6.00
AJRRSC Sammie Coates 3.00 8.00
AJRRSM Sean Mannion 2.50 6.00
AJRRTL Tyler Lockett 4.00 10.00
AJRRTM Ty Montgomery 2.50 6.00
AJRRTY T.J. Yeldon 2.50 6.00
AJRRVM Vince Mayle 3.00 8.00

2015 Finest Jumbo Jersey Autographs Camo Refractors

*CAMO REF/15: 1.5X TO 4X BLUE/150
AJRRAC Amari Cooper 100.00 200.00
AJRRJW Jameis Winston 25.00 60.00
AJRRKW Kevin White 12.00 30.00
AJRRMM Marcus Mariota 40.00 80.00
AJRRNA Nelson Agholor 12.00 30.00

AJRRPD Phillip Dorsett 10.00 25.00
AJRRSW Sammy Watkins 15.00 40.00
AJRRTG Todd Gurley 50.00 125.00

2015 Finest Jumbo Jersey Autographs Diamond Refractors

*DIAMOND/60: .6X TO 1.5X BLUE/150
AJRRAC Amari Cooper 40.00 80.00
AJRRBP Breshad Perriman 4.00 10.00
AJRRDF Devin Funchess 6.00 15.00
AJRRDP DeVante Parker 6.00 15.00
AJRRJS Jaelen Strong 5.00 12.00
AJRRKB Kelvin Benjamin 6.00 15.00
AJRRKW Kevin White 5.00 12.00
AJRRME Mike Evans 6.00 15.00
AJRRMG Melvin Gordon 15.00 40.00
AJRRNA Nelson Agholor 5.00 12.00
AJRRPD Phillip Dorsett 4.00 10.00
AJRRSW Sammy Watkins 6.00 15.00
AJRRTG Todd Gurley 25.00 50.00

2015 Finest Jumbo Jersey Autographs Gold Refractors

*GOLD REF/99: .5X TO 1.2X BLUE/150
AJRRBP Breshad Perriman 3.00 8.00
AJRRDF Devin Funchess 5.00 12.00
AJRRNA Nelson Agholor 4.00 10.00
AJRRPD Phillip Dorsett 3.00 8.00

2015 Finest Jumbo Jersey Autographs Pink Refractors

*PINK REF/10: 1.5X TO 4X BLUE/150
AJRRAC Amari Cooper 150.00 250.00
AJRRJW Jameis Winston 25.00 60.00
AJRRKW Kevin White 12.00 30.00
AJRRMM Marcus Mariota 50.00 100.00
AJRRNA Nelson Agholor 12.00 30.00
AJRRPD Phillip Dorsett 10.00 25.00
AJRRSW Sammy Watkins 15.00 40.00
AJRRTG Todd Gurley 50.00 125.00

2015 Finest Jumbo Jersey Autographs Pulsar Refractors

*PULSAR REF/35: 1X TO 2.5X BLUE/150
AJRRAC Amari Cooper 60.00 120.00
AJRRDP DeVante Parker 10.00 25.00
AJRRJS Jaelen Strong 8.00 20.00
AJRRJW Jameis Winston 15.00 40.00
AJRRKB Kelvin Benjamin 8.00 20.00
AJRRKW Kevin White 8.00 20.00
AJRRME Mike Evans 10.00 25.00
AJRRMM Marcus Mariota 25.00 50.00
AJRRNA Nelson Agholor 8.00 20.00
AJRRPD Phillip Dorsett 6.00 15.00
AJRRSW Sammy Watkins 10.00 25.00
AJRRTG Todd Gurley 30.00 80.00

2015 Finest Jumbo Jersey Autographs Xfractors

*XFRACTOR/20: 1.2X TO 3X BLUE/150
AJRRAC Amari Cooper 75.00 150.00
AJRRJW Jameis Winston 20.00 50.00
AJRRKW Kevin White 10.00 25.00
AJRRMM Marcus Mariota 40.00 80.00
AJRRNA Nelson Agholor 10.00 25.00
AJRRPD Phillip Dorsett 8.00 20.00
AJRRSW Sammy Watkins 12.00 30.00
AJRRTG Todd Gurley 40.00 100.00

2015 Finest Quarterback Cuts

*GOLD REF/75: 2X TO 5X BASIC INSERTS
*PULSAR REF/25: 3X TO 8X BASIC INSERTS
*RED REF/50: 2.5X TO 6X BASIC INSERTS
QBCAL Andrew Luck 1.00 2.50
QBCAR Aaron Rodgers 1.50 4.00
QBCBB Blake Bortles .50 1.25
QBCBH Brett Hundley .30 .75
QBCBP Bryce Petty .30 .75
QBCBR Ben Roethlisberger .75 2.00
QBCCN Cam Newton .75 2.00
QBCEM Eli Manning .60 1.50
QBCGG Garrett Grayson .30 .75
QBCJW Jameis Winston .75 2.00
QBCMM Marcus Mariota 1.25 3.00
QBCMR Matt Ryan .60 1.50
QBCMS Matthew Stafford .60 1.50
QBCPM Peyton Manning 1.50 4.00
QBCPR Philip Rivers .75 2.00
QBCRT Ryan Tannehill .60 1.50
QBCRW Russell Wilson 1.00 2.50
QBCTB Tom Brady 2.00 6.00
QBCTR Tony Romo .60 1.50
QBCTBR Teddy Bridgewater .60 1.50

2015 Finest Rookie Autograph Refractors

*BLUE REF/25: .4X TO 1X BASIC AU/30
*RED REF/15: .5X TO 1.2X BASIC AU/30
13 T.J. Yeldon 6.00 15.00
19 Devin Smith 6.00 15.00
20 Marcus Mariota 40.00 80.00
37 Devin Funchess 10.00 25.00
45 Amari Cooper 50.00 100.00
47 Danny Shelton 6.00 15.00
49 Breshad Perriman 6.00 15.00
70 Jameis Winston 40.00 80.00
79 Landon Collins 8.00 20.00
80 Melvin Gordon 12.00 30.00
82 Brandon Scherff 10.00 25.00
85 Todd Gurley 50.00 100.00
94 Andrus Peat 6.00 15.00
105 DeVante Parker 10.00 25.00
107 Jay Ajayi 10.00 25.00
109 Shaq Thompson 8.00 20.00
110 Kevin White 8.00 20.00
117 Vic Beasley 8.00 20.00
120 Brett Hundley 6.00 15.00
124 Alvin Dupree 8.00 20.00
128 Dante Fowler Jr. 10.00 25.00
133 Shane Ray 6.00 15.00
139 Ameer Abdullah 10.00 25.00

2015 Finest Rookie Patch Autographs Blue Refractors

*BASE REF: .3X TO .8X BLUE/150
RRAPAA Ameer Abdullah 4.00 10.00
RRAPBPE Bryce Petty 2.50 6.00
RRAPCA Cameron Artis-Payne 2.50 6.00
RRAPCC Chris Conley 2.50 6.00
RRAPCW Clive Walford 2.50 6.00
RRAPDC David Cobb 2.50 6.00
RRAPDG Dorial Green-Beckham 2.50 6.00
RRAPDJ Duke Johnson 4.00 10.00
RRAPDJO David Johnson 10.00 25.00
RRAPDS Devin Smith 2.50 6.00
RRAPJA Jay Ajayi 4.00 10.00
RRAPJAL Javorius Allen 3.00 8.00
RRAPJC Jamison Crowder 3.00 8.00
RRAPJHA Justin Hardy 2.50 6.00
RRAPJL Jeremy Langford 10.00 25.00
RRAPKWI Karlos Williams 2.50 6.00
RRAPMD Mike Davis 2.50 6.00
RRAPMJ Matt Jones 2.50 6.00
RRAPMW Maxx Williams 2.50 6.00
RRAPRG Rashad Greene 2.50 6.00
RRAPSC Sammie Coates 3.00 8.00
RRAPSD Stefon Diggs 6.00 15.00
RRAPSM Sean Mannion 2.50 6.00
RRAPTL Tyler Lockett 4.00 10.00
RRAPTM Ty Montgomery 2.50 6.00
RRAPTY T.J. Yeldon 2.50 6.00
RRAPVM Vince Mayle 3.00 8.00

2015 Finest Rookie Patch Autographs Camo Refractors

*CAMO REF/15: 1.5X TO 4X BLUE/150
RRAPAC Amari Cooper 150.00 250.00
RRAPBH Brett Hundley 10.00 25.00
RRAPBP Breshad Perriman 10.00 25.00
RRAPDF Devin Funchess 15.00 40.00
RRAPDP DeVante Parker 15.00 40.00
RRAPJS Jaelen Strong 12.00 30.00
RRAPJW Jameis Winston 25.00 60.00
RRAPKW Kevin White 12.00 30.00
RRAPMM Marcus Mariota 50.00 100.00
RRAPNA Nelson Agholor 12.00 30.00
RRAPPD Phillip Dorsett 10.00 25.00
RRAPTG Todd Gurley 100.00 200.00

2015 Finest Rookie Patch Autographs Diamond Refractors

*DIAMOND/60: .6X TO 1.5X BLUE/150
RRAPBP Breshad Perriman 4.00 10.00
RRAPDF Devin Funchess 6.00 15.00
RRAPPD Phillip Dorsett 4.00 10.00

2015 Finest Rookie Patch Autographs Gold Refractors

*GOLD REF/99: .5X TO 1.2X BLUE/150
RRAPBP Breshad Perriman 3.00 8.00
RRAPDF Devin Funchess 5.00 12.00
RRAPMG Melvin Gordon 8.00 20.00
RRAPPD Phillip Dorsett 3.00 8.00

2015 Finest Rookie Patch Autographs Pink Refractors

*PINK REF/10: 1.5X TO 4X BLUE/150
RRAPAC Amari Cooper 150.00 250.00
RRAPBH Brett Hundley 10.00 25.00
RRAPBP Breshad Perriman 10.00 25.00
RRAPDF Devin Funchess 15.00 40.00
RRAPDP DeVante Parker 15.00 40.00
RRAPJS Jaelen Strong 12.00 30.00
RRAPJW Jameis Winston 25.00 60.00
RRAPKW Kevin White 12.00 30.00
RRAPMM Marcus Mariota 60.00 125.00
RRAPNA Nelson Agholor 12.00 30.00
RRAPPD Phillip Dorsett 10.00 25.00
RRAPTG Todd Gurley 125.00 250.00

2015 Finest Rookie Patch Autographs Pulsar Refractors

*PULSAR REF/35: 1X TO 2.5X BLUE/150
RRAPAC Amari Cooper 75.00 150.00
RRAPBH Brett Hundley 6.00 15.00
RRAPBP Breshad Perriman 6.00 15.00
RRAPDF Devin Funchess 10.00 25.00
RRAPJS Jaelen Strong 8.00 20.00
RRAPJW Jameis Winston 15.00 40.00
RRAPKW Kevin White 8.00 20.00
RRAPMM Marcus Mariota 40.00 80.00
RRAPNA Nelson Agholor 8.00 20.00
RRAPPD Phillip Dorsett 6.00 15.00
RRAPTG Todd Gurley 60.00 125.00

2015 Finest Rookie Patch Autographs Xfractors

*XFRACTOR/20: 1.2X TO 3X BLUE/150
RRAPAC Amari Cooper 100.00 200.00
RRAPBH Brett Hundley 8.00 20.00
RRAPBP Breshad Perriman 8.00 20.00
RRAPDF Devin Funchess 12.00 30.00
RRAPDP DeVante Parker 12.00 30.00
RRAPJS Jaelen Strong 10.00 25.00
RRAPJW Jameis Winston 20.00 50.00
RRAPKW Kevin White 10.00 25.00
RRAPMM Marcus Mariota 50.00 100.00
RRAPNA Nelson Agholor 10.00 25.00
RRAPPD Phillip Dorsett 8.00 20.00
RRAPTG Todd Gurley 75.00 150.00

1995 Flair

The debut issue for Flair contains 220 standard size cards. Rookie Cards include Ki-Jana Carter, Kerry Collins, Curtis Martin, Steve McNair, Rashaan Salaam, J.J. Stokes, Kordell Stewart and Michael Westbrook.
COMPLETE SET (220) 12.50 30.00
1 Larry Centers .15 .40
2 Garrison Hearst .30 .75
3 Seth Joyner .07 .20
4 Dave Krieg .07 .20
5 Rob Moore .15 .40
6 Frank Sanders RC .30 .75
7 Eric Swann .15 .40
8 Devin Bush .07 .20
9 Chris Doleman .07 .20
10 Bert Emanuel .30 .75
11 Jeff George .15 .40
12 Craig Heyward .15 .40
13 Terance Mathis .15 .40
14 Eric Metcalf .15 .40
15 Cornelius Bennett .15 .40
16 Jeff Burris .07 .20
17 Todd Collins RC 1.00 2.50
18 Russell Copeland .07 .20
19 Jim Kelly .30 .75
20 Andre Reed .15 .40
21 Bruce Smith .30 .75
22 Don Beebe .07 .20
23 Mark Carrier WR .15 .40
24 Kerry Collins RC 1.00 2.50
25 Barry Foster .15 .40
26 Pete Metzelaars .07 .20
27 Tyrone Poole .30 .75
28 Frank Reich .07 .20
29 Curtis Conway .30 .75
30 Chris Gedney .07 .20
31 Jeff Graham .07 .20
32 Raymont Harris .07 .20
33 Erik Kramer .07 .20
34 Rashaan Salaam RC .15 .40
35 Lewis Tillman .07 .20
36 Michael Timpson .07 .20
37 Jeff Blake RC .40 1.00
38 Ki-Jana Carter RC .30 .75
39 Tony McGee .07 .20
40 Carl Pickens .15 .40
41 Corey Sawyer .07 .20
42 Darnay Scott .15 .40
43 Dan Wilkinson .15 .40
44 Derrick Alexander WR .30 .75
45 Leroy Hoard .07 .20
46 Michael Jackson .15 .40
47 Antonio Langham .07 .20
48 Andre Rison .15 .40
49 Vinny Testaverde .15 .40
50 Eric Turner .07 .20
51 Troy Aikman .75 2.00
52 Charles Haley .15 .40
53 Michael Irvin .30 .75
54 Daryl Johnston .15 .40
55 Leon Lett .07 .20
56 Jay Novacek .15 .40
57 Emmitt Smith 1.25 3.00
58 Kevin Williams WR .15 .40
59 Steve Atwater .07 .20
60 Rod Bernstine .07 .20
61 John Elway 1.50 4.00
62 Glyn Milburn .07 .20
63 Anthony Miller .15 .40
64 Mike Pritchard .07 .20
65 Shannon Sharpe .15 .40
66 Scott Mitchell .15 .40
67 Herman Moore .30 .75
68 Johnnie Morton .15 .40
69 Brett Perriman .15 .40
70 Barry Sanders 1.25 3.00
71 Chris Spielman .15 .40
72 Edgar Bennett .15 .40
73 Robert Brooks .30 .75
74 Brett Favre 1.50 4.00
75 LeShon Johnson .15 .40
76 Sean Jones .07 .20
77 George Teague .07 .20
78 Reggie White .30 .75
79 Micheal Barrow .07 .20
80 Gary Brown .07 .20
81 Mel Gray .07 .20
82 Haywood Jeffires .07 .20
83 Steve McNair RC 1.50 4.00
84 Rodney Thomas RC .15 .40
85 Trev Alberts .07 .20
86 Flipper Anderson .07 .20
87 Tony Bennett .07 .20
88 Quentin Coryatt .15 .40
89 Sean Dawkins .15 .40
90 Craig Erickson .07 .20
91 Marshall Faulk 1.00 2.50
92 Steve Beuerlein .15 .40
93 Tony Boselli RC .30 .75
94 Reggie Cobb .07 .20
95 Ernest Givins .07 .20
96 Desmond Howard .15 .40
97 Jeff Lageman .07 .20
98 James O. Stewart RC .60 1.50
99 Marcus Allen .30 .75
100 Steve Bono .15 .40
101 Dale Carter .15 .40
102 Willie Davis .15 .40
103 Lake Dawson .15 .40
104 Greg Hill .15 .40
105 Neil Smith .15 .40
106 Tim Bowens .07 .20
107 Bryan Cox .07 .20
108 Irving Fryar .15 .40
109 Eric Green .07 .20
110 Terry Kirby .15 .40
111 Dan Marino 1.50 4.00
112 O.J. McDuffie .30 .75
113 Bernie Parmalee .15 .40
114 Derrick Alexander DE RC .07 .20
115 Cris Carter .30 .75
116 Qadry Ismail .15 .40
117 Warren Moon .15 .40
118 Jake Reed .15 .40
119 Robert Smith .30 .75
120 Dewayne Washington .15 .40
121 Drew Bledsoe .50 1.25
122 Vincent Brisby .07 .20
123 Ben Coates .15 .40
124 Curtis Martin RC 1.50 4.00
125 Willie McGinest .15 .40
126 Dave Meggett .07 .20
127 Chris Slade UER 126 .07 .20
128 Eric Allen .07 .20
129 Mario Bates .15 .40
130 Jim Everett .07 .20
131 Michael Haynes .15 .40
132 Tyrone Hughes .15 .40
133 Renaldo Turnbull .07 .20
134 Ray Zellars RC .15 .40
135 Michael Brooks .07 .20
136 Dave Brown .15 .40
137 Rodney Hampton .15 .40
138 Thomas Lewis .15 .40
139 Mike Sherrard .07 .20
140 Herschel Walker .15 .40
141 Tyrone Wheatley RC .60 1.50
142 Kyle Brady RC .30 .75
143 Boomer Esiason .15 .40
144 Aaron Glenn .07 .20
145 Mo Lewis .07 .20
146 Johnny Mitchell .07 .20
147 Ronald Moore .07 .20
148 Joe Aska .15 .40
149 Tim Brown .30 .75
150 Jeff Hostetler .15 .40
151 Rocket Ismail .15 .40
152 Napoleon Kaufman RC .60 1.50
153 Chester McGlockton .15 .40
154 Harvey Williams .07 .20
155 Fred Barnett .15 .40
156 Randall Cunningham .30 .75
157 Charlie Garner .30 .75
158 Mike Mamula RC .07 .20
159 Kevin Turner .07 .20
160 Ricky Watters .15 .40
161 Calvin Williams .15 .40
162 Mark Bruener RC .15 .40
163 Kevin Greene .15 .40
164 Charles Johnson .15 .40
165 Greg Lloyd .15 .40
166 Byron Bam Morris .07 .20
167 Neil O'Donnell .15 .40
168 Kordell Stewart RC .75 2.00
169 John L. Williams .07 .20
170 Rod Woodson .15 .40
171 Jerome Bettis .30 .75
172 Isaac Bruce .50 1.25
173 Kevin Carter RC .30 .75
174 Troy Drayton .07 .20
175 Sean Gilbert .15 .40
176 Carlos Jenkins .07 .20
177 Todd Lyght .07 .20
178 Chris Miller .07 .20
179 Andre Coleman .07 .20
180 Stan Humphries .15 .40
181 Shawn Jefferson .07 .20
182 Natrone Means .15 .40
183 Leslie O'Neal .15 .40
184 Junior Seau .30 .75
185 Mark Seay .15 .40
186 William Floyd .15 .40
187 Merton Hanks .07 .20
188 Brent Jones .07 .20
189 Ken Norton .15 .40
190 Jerry Rice .75 2.00
191 Deion Sanders .40 1.00
192 J.J. Stokes RC .30 .75
193 Dana Stubblefield .15 .40
194 Steve Young .60 1.50
195 Sam Adams .07 .20
196 Brian Blades .15 .40
197 Joey Galloway RC .75 2.00
198 Cortez Kennedy .15 .40
199 Rick Mirer .15 .40
200 Chris Warren .15 .40
201 Derrick Brooks RC .75 2.00
202 Lawrence Dawsey .07 .20
203 Trent Dilfer .30 .75
204 Alvin Harper .07 .20
205 Jackie Harris .07 .20
206 Courtney Hawkins .07 .20
207 Hardy Nickerson .07 .20
208 Errict Rhett .15 .40
209 Warren Sapp RC .75 2.00
210 Terry Allen .15 .40
211 Tom Carter .07 .20
212 Henry Ellard .15 .40
213 Darrell Green .07 .20
214 Brian Mitchell .07 .20
215 Heath Shuler .15 .40
216 Michael Westbrook RC .30 .75
217 Tydus Winans .07 .20
218 Checklist .07 .20
219 Checklist .07 .20
220 Checklist .15 .40
S1 Michael Irvin Sample .50 1.25

1995 Flair Hot Numbers

This 10 card set was randomly inserted into packs at a rate of one in six packs. Card fronts have different color backgrounds similar to the team's colors with different statistical numbers shadowed in the background. At the bottom is the set name followed by the team name and finally, the player's name. Card backs are horizontal with a player shot and a statistical summary of that particular player's prior year.
COMPLETE SET (10) 12.50 30.00
STATED ODDS 1:6
1 Jeff Blake .50 1.25
2 Tim Brown .50 1.25
3 Drew Bledsoe 1.50 4.00
4 Ben Coates .50 1.25
5 Trent Dilfer .50 1.25
6 Brett Favre 5.00 12.00
7 Dan Marino 4.00 10.00
8 Byron Bam Morris .50 1.25
9 Ricky Watters .50 1.25
10 Steve Young 2.00 5.00

1995 Flair TD Power

Randomly inserted in packs at a rate of one in twelve, this 10 card set features players who frequent the endzone. Card fronts have silver on one side and purple on the other in the background with a "TD Power" logo beside the player. The player's name and team are located at the bottom of the card. Card backs are similar to the fronts with a statistical summary beside the player.
COMPLETE SET (10) 7.50 20.00
STATED ODDS 1:12
1 Marshall Faulk 2.00 5.00
2 Natrone Means .30 .75
3 William Floyd .30 .75
4 Byron Bam Morris .15 .40
5 Errict Rhett .30 .75
6 Andre Rison .30 .75
7 Jerry Rice 1.50 4.00
8 Barry Sanders 2.50 6.00
9 Emmitt Smith 2.50 6.00
10 Chris Warren .30 .75

1995 Flair Wave of the Future

This die cut 10 card set was randomly inserted into packs at a rate of one in 37 and focus on rookie players from 1995. Card fronts contain a die cut head shot of the player with the Wave of the Future logo and the player's name written in script at the bottom. Card backs contain commentary on the player
COMPLETE SET (9) 20.00 50.00
STATED ODDS 1:37
1 Kyle Brady 1.00 2.50
2 Ki-Jana Carter 2.50 6.00
3 Kerry Collins 4.00 10.00
4 Joey Galloway 4.00 10.00
5 Steve McNair 7.50 20.00
6 Rashaan Salaam 2.50 6.00
7 James O. Stewart 3.00 8.00
8 Michael Westbrook 2.50 6.00
9 Tyrone Wheatley 3.00 8.00

2002 Flair

Released in September, 2002, this set contains 100 veterans and 35 rookies. The rookies are serial #'d to 1250. Each box contained 10 packs of 5 cards. Cases were available in either 12, 6 or 4 box configurations.
COMP.SET w/o SP's (90) 10.00 25.00
1 Jeff Garcia .30 .75
2 Jevon Kearse .30 .75
3 Chris Weinke .30 .75
4 Ray Lewis .50 1.25
5 Donovan McNabb .40 1.00
6 Tiki Barber .40 1.00
7 Rich Gannon .40 1.00
8 Jamal Anderson .40 1.00
9 Curtis Martin .40 1.00
10 Darrell Jackson .40 1.00
11 Ricky Williams .40 1.00
12 Drew Brees 1.00 2.50
13 Mark Brunell .40 1.00
14 Johnnie Morton .40 1.00
15 Quincy Carter .30 .75
16 Brian Urlacher .50 1.25
17 Peerless Price .30 .75
18 Drew Bledsoe .40 1.00
19 Aaron Brooks .30 .75
20 Derrick Mason .30 .75
21 Charlie Garner .40 1.00
22 Mike Alstott .30 .75
23 Freddie Mitchell .30 .75
24 Isaac Bruce .50 1.25
25 Hines Ward .40 1.00
26 Doug Flutie .40 1.00
27 Terrell Owens .40 1.00
28 Peyton Manning 1.25 3.00
29 Ron Dayne .40 1.00
30 Peter Warrick .30 .75
31 Randy Moss .40 1.00
32 Priest Holmes .30 .75
33 Joey Galloway .40 1.00
34 Jimmy Smith .40 1.00
35 Marvin Harrison .40 1.00
36 Junior Seau .40 1.00
37 Zach Thomas .40 1.00
38 Antowain Smith .40 1.00
39 Marty Booker .30 .75
40 Deuce McAllister .40 1.00
41 Rod Smith .40 1.00
42 Michael Westbrook .30 .75
43 Antonio Freeman .50 1.25
44 Kerry Collins .30 .75
45 Koren Robinson .30 .75
46 Jamal Lewis .40 1.00
47 Duce Staley .30 .75
48 Jerome Bettis .50 1.25
49 David Terrell .30 .75
50 Daunte Culpepper .40 1.00
51 Tim Couch .30 .75
52 Brian Griese .30 .75
53 Marshall Faulk .40 1.00
54 Brad Johnson .40 1.00
55 Eddie George .40 1.00
56 Kurt Warner .40 1.00
57 Steve McNair .40 1.00
58 Stephen Davis .30 .75
59 Corey Dillon .30 .75
60 Troy Brown .30 .75
61 Warrick Dunn .30 .75
62 Ed McCaffrey .40 1.00
63 Amani Toomer .30 .75
64 Rod Gardner .30 .75
65 Mike McMahon .30 .75
66 Wayne Chrebet .30 .75
67 Jake Plummer .30 .75
68 Edgerrin James .40 1.00
69 Eric Moulds .30 .75
70 Tony Gonzalez .40 1.00
71 Marcus Robinson .40 1.00
72 Muhsin Muhammad .30 .75
73 Trent Dilfer .30 .75
74 Kevin Johnson .30 .75
75 Fred Taylor .30 .75
76 Terrell Davis .40 1.00
77 Emmitt Smith .75 2.00
78 Az-Zahir Hakim .30 .75
79 Tim Brown .50 1.25
80 Jerry Rice 1.00 2.50
81 Warren Sapp .40 1.00
82 Michael Strahan .40 1.00
83 Garrison Hearst .30 .75
84 David Boston .30 .75
85 Michael Vick .40 1.00
86 Anthony Thomas .40 1.00
87 Ahman Green .40 1.00
88 Chris Chambers .30 .75
89 Tom Brady 2.50 6.00
90 Plaxico Burress .30 .75
91 LaDainian Tomlinson .50 1.25
92 Shaun Alexander .30 .75
93 Torry Holt .40 1.00
94 Kordell Stewart .30 .75
95 Chad Pennington .30 .75
96 Chris Redman .30 .75
97 Kendrell Bell .30 .75
98 Michael Bennett .30 .75
99 Joe Horn .30 .75
100 Brett Favre 1.00 2.50
101 David Carr RC 1.25 3.00
102 Joey Harrington RC 1.25 3.00
103 Ashley Lelie RC 1.25 3.00
104 Javon Walker RC 2.00 5.00
105 Reche Caldwell RC 1.50 4.00
106 Andre Davis RC 1.25 3.00
107 William Green RC 1.50 4.00
108 Antonio Bryant RC 2.00 5.00
109 Clinton Portis RC 2.00 5.00
110 Luke Staley RC 1.25 3.00
111 Josh Reed RC 1.50 4.00
112 Ron Johnson RC 1.50 4.00
113 Lamar Gordon RC 1.25 3.00
114 Cliff Russell RC 1.25 3.00
115 Eric Crouch RC 2.00 5.00
116 Ladell Betts RC 2.00 5.00
117 Patrick Ramsey RC 1.50 4.00
118 Adrian Peterson RC 1.50 4.00
119 DeShaun Foster RC 2.00 5.00
120 Tim Carter RC 1.50 4.00
121 Jabar Gaffney RC 1.25 3.00
122 T.J. Duckett RC 1.25 3.00
123 Julius Peppers RC 3.00 8.00
124 Rohan Davey RC 2.00 5.00
125 Antwaan Randle El RC 1.50 4.00
126 Jeremy Shockey RC 2.00 5.00
127 Donte Stallworth RC 2.00 5.00
128 Marquise Walker RC 1.25 3.00
129 Brian Westbrook RC 2.50 6.00
130 Randy Fasani RC 1.25 3.00
131 Jonathan Wells RC 1.50 4.00
132 Travis Stephens RC 1.25 3.00
133 Daniel Graham RC 1.50 4.00
134 Maurice Morris RC 1.50 4.00
135 David Garrard RC 1.50 4.00

2002 Flair Collection

*VETS/200: 2.5X TO 6X BASIC CARDS
1-100 VETERAN PRINT RUN 200
*ROOKIES/50: 1.2X TO 3X
101-135 ROOKIE PRINT RUN 50

2002 Flair Franchise Favorites

Inserted into packs at a rate of 1:4, this set features players who are favorites of their beloved franchises.
COMPLETE SET (18) 15.00 40.00
STATED ODDS 1:4
1 Donovan McNabb .60 1.50
2 Tim Brown .75 2.00
3 Michael Vick .60 1.50
4 Peerless Price .50 1.25
5 Anthony Thomas .60 1.50
6 Corey Dillon .50 1.25
7 Emmitt Smith 1.25 3.00
8 Brett Favre 1.50 4.00
9 Edgerrin James .60 1.50
10 Fred Taylor .50 1.25
11 Tony Gonzalez .60 1.50
12 Daunte Culpepper .60 1.50
13 Tom Brady 4.00 10.00
14 Deuce McAllister .60 1.50
15 Jerome Bettis .75 2.00
16 LaDainian Tomlinson .75 2.00
17 Kurt Warner .60 1.50
18 Eddie George .60 1.50

2002 Flair Franchise Favorites Jerseys

Inserted at a rate of 1:10, cards in this set feature a swatch of game used memorabilia.
STATED ODDS 1:10
1 Jerome Bettis 5.00 12.00
2 Daunte Culpepper 4.00 10.00
3 Corey Dillon 3.00 8.00
4 Brett Favre 10.00 25.00
5 Eddie George 4.00 10.00
6 Edgerrin James 4.00 10.00
7 Donovan McNabb 4.00 10.00
8 Fred Taylor SP/300* 3.00 8.00
9 Anthony Thomas 4.00 10.00
10 LaDainian Tomlinson 5.00 12.00
11 Michael Vick 4.00 10.00
12 Kurt Warner 4.00 10.00

2002 Flair Franchise Tools Memorabilia

Inserted at a rate of 1:40, this set features players who exhibit the tools necessary to become superstars with a swatch of a jersey and a football on each card. A gold parallel is also available, which features cards serial #'d to 50.
STATED ODDS 1:40
*GOLD/50: .8X TO 2X BASIC JSY-FB
GOLD/50: .6X TO 1.5X JSY-FB/50-100
GOLD PRINT RUN 50 SER.#'d SETS
1 Ladell Betts 5.00 12.00
2 Tim Carter 4.00 10.00
3 Rohan Davey 5.00 12.00
4 Andre Davis 3.00 8.00
5 T.J. Duckett SP/100* 4.00 10.00
6 DeShaun Foster SP/250* 5.00 12.00
7 Jabar Gaffney 3.00 8.00
8 David Garrard 4.00 10.00
9 Joey Harrington SP/200* 3.00 8.00
10 Ron Johnson 4.00 10.00
11 Ashley Lelie SP/75* 4.00 10.00
12 Maurice Morris 4.00 10.00
13 Clinton Portis SP/50* 6.00 15.00
14 Patrick Ramsey SP/200* 4.00 10.00
15 Antwaan Randle El SP/200* 4.00 10.00
16 Cliff Russell 3.00 8.00
17 Jeremy Shockey 6.00 15.00
18 Donte Stallworth SP/100* 6.00 15.00
19 Travis Stephens 3.00 8.00
20 Javon Walker 5.00 12.00

2002 Flair Jersey Heights

Inserted at a rate of 1:10, this set features players who have soared high above all others to become superstars.
STATED ODDS 1:10
1 Ricky Williams 1.25 3.00
2 Marvin Harrison 1.25 3.00
3 Brian Urlacher 1.50 4.00
4 Terrell Davis 1.25 3.00
5 Randy Moss 1.25 3.00
6 Fred Taylor 1.00 2.50
7 Aaron Brooks 1.00 2.50
8 Jerry Rice 3.00 8.00
9 Curtis Martin 1.25 3.00
10 Kordell Stewart 1.00 2.50
11 Doug Flutie 1.25 3.00
12 Steve McNair 1.25 3.00
13 Marshall Faulk 1.25 3.00
14 Jeff Garcia 1.00 2.50
15 Brian Griese 1.00 2.50
16 Isaac Bruce 1.50 4.00
17 Drew Bledsoe 1.25 3.00
18 Rich Gannon 1.25 3.00

2002 Flair Jersey Heights Jerseys

Inserted at a rate of 1:18, this set features swatches of game used memorabilia. There is also a Hot Numbers parallel, that is serial #'d to 100.
STATED ODDS 1:18
*HOT NUMBER/100: .8X TO 2X BASIC JSY
HOT NUMBER JSY PRINT RUN 100
1 Drew Bledsoe 3.00 8.00
2 Aaron Brooks 2.50 6.00
3 Isaac Bruce 4.00 10.00
4 Doug Flutie 3.00 8.00
5 Rich Gannon 3.00 8.00
6 Jeff Garcia 2.50 6.00
7 Brian Griese 2.50 6.00
8 Steve McNair 3.00 8.00
9 Randy Moss 3.00 8.00
10 Kordell Stewart 2.50 6.00
11 Brian Urlacher 4.00 10.00

2002 Flair Sweet Swatch Memorabilia

Inserted one per box as a boxtopper, this set features oversized cards containing a swatch of game worn memorabilia. Also available are patch versions, that are serial #'d to 150.
STATED ODDS ONE PER BOX
ANNC'D PRINT RUN 375-750
*PATCH/150-300: .8X TO 2X BASIC JSY
PATCH PRINT RUN 150-300
AGSS Ahman Green/750* 5.00 12.00
BFSS Brett Favre/400* 12.00 30.00
CMSS Curtis Martin/400* 5.00 12.00
DCSS Daunte Culpepper/400* 5.00 12.00
EGSS Eddie George/400* 5.00 12.00
EJSS Edgerrin James/400* 5.00 12.00
JPSS Jake Plummer/400* 4.00 10.00
KWSS Kurt Warner/400* 5.00 12.00
MHSS Marvin Harrison/450* 5.00 12.00
MVSS Michael Vick/400* 5.00 12.00
TCSS Tim Couch/400* 4.00 10.00
THSS Torry Holt/375* 5.00 12.00
TOSS Terrell Owens/400* 5.00 12.00

2002 Flair Sweet Swatch Memorabilia Autographs

Randomly inserted as a boxtopper, these oversized cards feature autographs from some of the NFL's best current players, along with Joe Montana. A gold version is also available, and they are serial #'d to 50.
RANDOM INSERTS IN BOXES
ANNC'D PRINT RUN 50-800
*GOLD/50: .6X TO 1.5X BASIC AUTO
GOLD PRINT RUN 50 SER.#'d SETS
1 Kurt Warner/500* 12.00 30.00
2 Jeff Garcia/500* 10.00 25.00
3 Donovan McNabb/500* 12.00 30.00
4 Joe Montana SP/50* 75.00 150.00
5 Chad Pennington/800* 10.00 25.00

2003 Flair

Released in June of 2003, this set consists of 90 veterans and 40 rookies which were serial numbered to 500. Boxes contained 20 packs of five cards. Each hobby box also contained one oversized pack containing a Sweet Swatch Jumbo autograph or memorabilia card. The pack SRP was $5.99.
COMP.SET w/o SP's (90) 10.00 25.00
91-130 ROOKIE PRINT RUN 500
1 Jamal Lewis .30 .75
2 Aaron Brooks .25 .60
3 Joey Harrington .25 .60
4 Brett Favre .75 2.00
5 Donovan McNabb .30 .75
6 Marcel Shipp .25 .60
7 Michael Vick .30 .75
8 David Carr .25 .60
9 Tommy Maddox .25 .60
10 Drew Brees .40 1.00
11 Chad Pennington .25 .60
12 Drew Bledsoe .30 .75
13 Rich Gannon .30 .75
14 Kurt Warner .30 .75
15 Brian Griese .25 .60
16 William Green .25 .60
17 Jake Plummer .25 .60
18 Eric Moulds .25 .60
19 Peyton Manning 1.00 2.50
20 Keyshawn Johnson .40 1.00
21 Travis Henry .25 .60
22 Tiki Barber .30 .75
23 Emmitt Smith .60 1.50
24 Michael Bennett .25 .60
25 Curtis Martin .30 .75
26 Donald Driver .30 .75
27 Clinton Portis .25 .60
28 Eddie George .30 .75
29 Marshall Faulk .30 .75
30 Jeremy Shockey .25 .60
31 Ahman Green .30 .75
32 Priest Holmes .25 .60
33 Edgerrin James .30 .75
34 Plaxico Burress .25 .60
35 Ricky Williams .30 .75
36 Anthony Thomas .30 .75
37 Jerome Bettis .40 1.00
38 Shaun Alexander .25 .60
39 Fred Taylor .25 .60
40 Isaac Bruce .40 1.00
41 Mike Alstott .25 .60
42 Peerless Price .25 .60
43 Corey Dillon .25 .60
44 Amani Toomer .25 .60
45 Warrick Dunn .25 .60
46 Tim Brown .40 1.00
47 Deuce McAllister .30 .75
48 Terrell Owens .30 .75
49 Stephen Davis .25 .60
50 Torry Holt .30 .75
51 Duce Staley .25 .60
52 Jimmy Smith .30 .75
53 Ray Lewis .40 1.00
54 Brian Urlacher .40 1.00
55 Zach Thomas .30 .75
56 Joey Galloway .30 .75
57 LaDainian Tomlinson .40 1.00
58 Chris Chambers .25 .60
59 Ronde Barber .25 .60
60 Randy Moss .30 .75
61 Tom Brady 1.50 4.00
62 Jerry Porter .25 .60
63 Patrick Ramsey .30 .75
64 Derrick Mason .25 .60
65 Daunte Culpepper .30 .75
66 Marty Booker .25 .60
67 Steve McNair .30 .75
68 Hines Ward .30 .75
69 Matt Hasselbeck .25 .60
70 Joe Horn .25 .60
71 Mark Brunell .30 .75
72 Laveranues Coles .25 .60
73 Chad Hutchinson .25 .60
74 Tony Gonzalez .30 .75
75 Jeff Garcia .25 .60
76 Kendrell Bell .25 .60
77 Kerry Collins .25 .60
78 Warren Sapp .30 .75
79 Tim Couch .25 .60
80 Jerry Rice .75 2.00
81 Koren Robinson .30 .75
82 Antwaan Randle El .25 .60
83 Donte Stallworth .25 .60
84 Shannon Sharpe .30 .75
85 Chad Johnson .25 .60
86 Todd Heap .25 .60
87 Rod Gardner .25 .60
88 Marvin Harrison .30 .75
89 David Boston .25 .60
90 Julius Peppers .40 1.00
91 Byron Leftwich RC 3.00 8.00
92 Terrell Suggs RC 3.00 8.00
93 Kelley Washington RC 2.50 6.00
94 Brandon Lloyd RC 4.00 10.00
95 Kliff Kingsbury RC 4.00 10.00
96 Willis McGahee RC 3.00 8.00
97 Terence Newman RC 4.00 10.00
98 Bryant Johnson RC 4.00 10.00
99 Musa Smith RC 2.50 6.00
100 Ken Dorsey RC 3.00 8.00
101 Larry Johnson RC 3.00 8.00
102 DeWayne Robertson RC 3.00 8.00
103 Onterrio Smith RC 2.50 6.00
104 Tyrone Calico RC 2.50 6.00
105 Kareem Kelly RC 2.50 6.00
106 Chris Brown RC 2.50 6.00
107 Andrew Pinnock RC 3.00 8.00
108 Taylor Jacobs RC 2.50 6.00
109 Dallas Clark RC 4.00 10.00
110 Marcus Trufant RC 3.00 8.00
111 Charles Rogers RC 3.00 8.00
112 Lee Suggs RC 2.50 6.00
113 Rex Grossman RC 3.00 8.00
114 Doug Gabriel RC 3.00 8.00
115 Arnaz Battle RC 4.00 10.00
116 William Joseph RC 2.50 6.00
117 Justin Fargas RC 4.00 10.00
118 Anquan Boldin RC 4.00 10.00
119 Teyo Johnson RC 3.00 8.00
120 Bobby Wade RC 3.00 8.00
121 Brian St.Pierre RC 2.50 6.00
122 Carson Palmer RC 5.00 12.00
123 Kyle Boller RC 2.50 6.00
124 Andre Johnson RC 6.00 15.00
125 Dave Ragone RC 2.50 6.00
126 Chris Simms RC 2.50 6.00
127 Seneca Wallace RC 3.00 8.00
128 Justin Gage RC 3.00 8.00
129 LaBrandon Toefield RC 2.50 6.00
130 Talman Gardner RC 2.50 6.00

2003 Flair Collection

*VETS 1-90: 4X TO 10X BASIC CARDS
*91-130 ROOKIES: .5X TO 1.2X
STATED PRINT RUN 125 SER.#'d SETS

2003 Flair A Cut Above

Randomly inserted into packs, this set features game used jersey swatches. Each card is serial numbered to 500. In addition, there is a Final Cut parallel set that is serial numbered to 50 and features patch swatches.
STATED PRINT RUN 500 SER.#'d SETS
*FINAL CUT/50: .8X TO 2X BASE JSY/500
FINAL CUT PRINT RUN 50 SER.#'d SETS
ACADB Drew Bledsoe 4.00 10.00
ACADC Daunte Culpepper 4.00 10.00
ACAEJ Edgerrin James 4.00 10.00
ACAIB Isaac Bruce 5.00 12.00
ACAJH Joe Horn 3.00 8.00
ACAKJ Keyshawn Johnson 5.00 12.00
ACAMA Mike Alstott 3.00 8.00
ACAMF Marshall Faulk 4.00 10.00
ACAPP Peerless Price 3.00 8.00
ACATB Tim Brown 5.00 12.00

2003 Flair Canton Calling

Inserted into packs at a rate of 1:20, this set features game used jersey swatches from future Hall of Famers. There is also a patch version of each card serial numbered to 150.
STATED ODDS 1:20
*PATCH/150: .6X TO 1.5X BASIC JSY
PATCHES PRINT RUN 150 SER.#'d SETS
CCBF Brett Favre 10.00 25.00
CCCC Cris Carter 5.00 12.00
CCCD Corey Dillon 3.00 8.00
CCCM Curtis Martin 4.00 10.00
CCEM Ed McCaffrey 4.00 10.00
CCES Emmitt Smith 8.00 20.00
CCJR Jerry Rice 10.00 25.00
CCJS Junior Seau 4.00 10.00
CCKW Kurt Warner 4.00 10.00
CCMF Marshall Faulk 4.00 10.00
CCRM Randy Moss 4.00 10.00
CCRW Ray Lewis 5.00 12.00
CCTG Tony Gonzalez 4.00 10.00
CCTO Terrell Owens 4.00 10.00

2003 Flair Sunday Showdown Jerseys

Randomly inserted into packs, this set features game used jersey swatches, with each card being serial numbered to 500. Please note that Marvin Harrison cards feature pant swatches. A patch version of this set also exists, with each card serial numbered to 100.
STATED PRINT RUN 500 SER.#'d SETS
*PATCH/100: .5X TO 1.2X BASE JSY/500
PATCHES PRINT RUN 100 SER.#'d SETS
SSAG A.Green JSY / B.Urlacher 3.00 8.00
SSBU A.Green / B.Urlacher JSY 3.00 8.00
SSCC M.Harrison / C.Chambers JSY 2.50 6.00
SSCP C.Portis JSY / L.Tomlinson 3.00 8.00
SSDB Drew Bledsoe 2.50 6.00
SSDM D.McNabb JSY / J.Shockey 2.50 6.00
SSDM Deuce McAllister 2.50 6.00
SSEG F.Taylor / E.George JSY 2.50 6.00
SSFT F.Taylor JSY / E.George 2.50 6.00
SSJL J.Lewis JSY / W.Green 2.50 6.00
SSJP J.Peppers JSY / D.Carr 3.00 8.00
SSJS D.McNabb / J.Shockey JSY 2.50 6.00
SSMH M.Harrison PANTS / C.Chambers 2.50 6.00
SSRG R.Gannon JSY / D.Brees 3.00 8.00
SSSM S.McNair JSY / P.Manning 8.00 20.00
SSWG J.Lewis / W.Green JSY 2.50 6.00

2003 Flair Sunday Showdown Dual Patches

Randomly inserted into packs, this set features two swatches of game used jersey. Each card is serial numbered to 50.
STATED PRINT RUN 50 SER.#'d SETS
AGBU A.Green/B.Urlacher 6.00 15.00
DMJS D.McNabb/J.Shockey 5.00 12.00
FTEG F.Taylor/E.George 5.00 12.00
JHDC J.Harrington/D.Culpepper 5.00 12.00
JLWG J.Lewis/W.Green 5.00 12.00
MADM M.Alstott/D.McAllister 5.00 12.00
MHCC M.Harrison/C.Chambers 5.00 12.00
SMPM S.McNair/P.Manning 15.00 40.00

2003 Flair Sweet Swatch Autographs

This set features authentic player autographs, with each card serial numbered to 175. A Gold version serial numbered to 25, and a Masterpiece version serial numbered to 1 also exist.
STATED PRINT RUN 175 SER.#'d SETS
*GOLD/25: .8X TO 2X BASIC AU/175
GOLD PRINT RUN 25 SER.#'d SETS
UNPRICED MASTERPIECE PRINT RUN 1
LT LaDainian Tomlinson 40.00 80.00
TB Tom Brady 100.00 200.00
WM Willis McGahee 15.00 40.00

2003 Flair Sweet Swatch Jerseys

Randomly inserted into packs, this set features game used jersey swatches, with each card serial numbered to 200. A patch version, serial numbered to 25 was also issued.
STATED PRINT RUN 200 SER.#'d SETS
*PATCH/25: .8X TO 2X BASE JSY/200
*JUMBO/180-520: .4X TO 1X BASE JSY/200
*JUMBO PATCH/61-165: .6X TO 1.5X BASE JSY/200
UNPRICED MASTERPIECE JUMBO #'d TO 1

AB Aaron Brooks 2.00 5.00
CM Curtis Martin 2.50 6.00
CP Chad Pennington 2.00 5.00
DB Drew Brees 3.00 8.00
DC David Carr 2.00 5.00
DM Deuce McAllister 2.50 6.00
ES Emmitt Smith 5.00 12.00
HW Hines Ward 2.50 6.00
JH Joey Harrington 2.00 5.00
KB Kendrell Bell 2.00 5.00
LT LaDainian Tomlinson 3.00 8.00
MB Michael Bennett 2.00 5.00
MH Marvin Harrison 2.50 6.00
MV Michael Vick 2.50 6.00
PH Priest Holmes 2.00 5.00
PM Peyton Manning 8.00 20.00
PP Peerless Price 2.00 5.00
RM Randy Moss 2.50 6.00
RW Ricky Williams 2.50 6.00
TG Tony Gonzalez 2.50 6.00

2003 Flair Sweet Swatch Jerseys Patches Jumbo

Randomly inserted into box topper packs, this set features swatches of game used jersey patches. Each card is serial numbered to various quantities as listed below.
STATED PRINT RUN 61-165

2003 Flair Sweet Swatch Jerseys Duals Jumbo

Randomly inserted into box topper packs, cards in this set feature two swatches of game used jersey on dual-player cards. Each was serial numbered to 25.
STATED PRINT RUN 25 SER.#'d SETS

CPCM C.Pennington/C.Martin 6.00 15.00
DBLT D.Brees/L.Tomlinson 10.00 25.00
DCJH D.Carr/J.Harrington
DMAB D.McAllister/A.Brooks
ESRW E.Smith/R.Williams 10.00 25.00
MVPP M.Vick/P.Price 8.00 20.00
PHTG P.Holmes/T.Gonzalez 6.00 15.00
PMMH P.Manning/M.Harrison 12.00 30.00
RMMB R.Moss/M.Bennett

2004 Flair

Flair initially released in mid-July 2004. The base set consists of -cards including 5-Power Pick short prints at the end of the set. Hobby boxes contained 1-pack of 12-cards and retail contained 24-packs of 4-cards with an S.R.P. of $2.99 per pack. Two parallel sets and a variety of inserts can be found seeded in hobby and retail packs highlighted by the multi-tiered Autograph Collection and Significant Cuts inserts. Some signed cards were issued via mail-in exchange or redemption cards with a number of those EXCH cards not yet appearing live on the secondary market as of the printing of this book.
COMP.SET w/o SP's (60) 20.00 40.00
ROOKIE STATED ODDS 1:100 RETAIL
ROOKIE PRINT RUN 799 SER.#'d SETS

1 Clinton Portis .40 1.00
2 Deuce McAllister .50 1.25
3 Marshall Faulk .50 1.25
4 Tom Brady 2.50 6.00
5 Ahman Green .50 1.25
6 LaDainian Tomlinson .60 1.50
7 Lee Suggs .50 1.25
8 Amani Toomer .40 1.00
9 Priest Holmes .40 1.00
10 Peerless Price .40 1.00
11 Warren Sapp .50 1.25
12 Andre Davis .40 1.00
13 Chad Pennington .40 1.00
14 Quincy Carter .40 1.00
15 Santana Moss .50 1.25
16 Antonio Bryant .50 1.25
17 Jerry Porter .40 1.00
18 Laveranues Coles .40 1.00
19 Daunte Culpepper .50 1.25
20 Stephen Davis .40 1.00
21 Rich Gannon .50 1.25
22 Chad Johnson .40 1.00
23 Ashley Lelie .40 1.00
24 Ray Lewis .60 1.50
25 Joey Harrington .40 1.00
26 Brian Westbrook .40 1.00
27 Marvin Harrison .50 1.25
28 Torry Holt .50 1.25
29 Kevan Barlow .40 1.00
30 Peyton Manning 1.50 4.00
31 Andre Johnson .50 1.25
32 Steve Smith .60 1.50
33 Troy Brown .40 1.00
34 Brian Urlacher .60 1.50
35 Anquan Boldin .40 1.00
36 Matt Hasselbeck .40 1.00
37 Edgerrin James .50 1.25
38 Dante Hall .40 1.00
39 Brad Johnson .50 1.25
40 Jamal Lewis .50 1.25
41 Rudi Johnson .40 1.00
42 Michael Strahan .50 1.25
43 Donovan McNabb .50 1.25
44 Steve McNair .50 1.25
45 Ricky Williams .50 1.25
46 Jake Delhomme .40 1.00
47 Patrick Ramsey .50 1.25
48 Randy Moss .50 1.25
49 David Carr .40 1.00
50 Jeff Garcia .40 1.00
51 Shaun Alexander .40 1.00
52 Byron Leftwich .40 1.00
53 Michael Vick .50 1.25
54 Brett Favre 1.25 3.00
55 Hines Ward .50 1.25
56 Chris Chambers .40 1.00
57 Eddie George .50 1.25
58 Eric Moulds .40 1.00
59 Plaxico Burress .40 1.00
60 Charles Rogers .40 1.00
61 Eli Manning RC 12.00 30.00
62 Larry Fitzgerald RC 4.00 10.00
63 Chris Perry RC 1.00 2.50
64 Ben Roethlisberger RC 12.00 30.00
65 Roy Williams RC 1.00 2.50
66 Kellen Winslow RC 1.00 2.50
67 Steven Jackson RC 1.50 4.00
68 Kevin Jones RC 1.25 3.00
69 Reggie Williams RC 1.00 2.50
70 Michael Clayton RC 1.25 3.00
71 Rashaun Woods RC 1.00 2.50
72 Ben Troupe RC 1.00 2.50
73 Greg Jones RC 1.00 2.50
74 J.P. Losman RC 1.00 2.50
75 Philip Rivers RC 3.00 8.00
76 Michael Jenkins RC 1.00 2.50
77 Darius Watts RC 1.00 2.50
78 Michael Turner RC 1.00 2.50
79 Lee Evans RC 1.50 4.00
80 Drew Henson RC 1.00 2.50
81 Luke McCown RC 1.00 2.50
82 Julius Jones RC 1.00 2.50
83 Bernard Berrian RC 1.00 2.50
84 Keary Colbert RC 1.00 2.50
85 Tatum Bell RC 1.00 2.50

2004 Flair Collection Row 1

*STARS: 2X TO 5X BASE CARD HI
*ROOKIES: .8X TO 2X BASIC CARDS
ROW 1/2 OVERALL ODDS 1:7H, 1:55R
ROW 1 PRINT RUN 100 SER.#'d SETS
UNPRICED ROW 2 PRINT RUN 1 SET

2004 Flair Autograph Collection Bronze

OVERALL AUTO ODDS 1:1 HOB
UNPRICED MASTERPIECE #'d OF 1

ACAL Ashley Lelie/150 5.00 12.00
ACBR Ben Roethlisberger/250 50.00 100.00
ACDC David Carr/100 5.00 12.00
ACDHA Dante Hall/150 5.00 12.00
ACEM Eli Manning/200 40.00 100.00
ACJD Jake Delhomme/150 5.00 12.00
ACJJ Julius Jones/150 5.00 12.00
ACJL J.P. Losman/150 5.00 12.00
ACKJ Kevin Jones/150 6.00 15.00
ACLE Lee Evans/220 6.00 15.00
ACLF Larry Fitzgerald/82 30.00 80.00
ACMC Michael Clayton/150 6.00 15.00
ACMJ Michael Jenkins/150 5.00 12.00
ACPRA Patrick Ramsey/158 6.00 15.00
ACPRI Philip Rivers/350 20.00 50.00
ACRAW Rashaun Woods/350 4.00 10.00
ACREW Reggie Williams/350 4.00 10.00
ACRG Rex Grossman/150 5.00 12.00
ACROW Roy Williams WR/150 5.00 12.00
ACSJ Steven Jackson/150 8.00 20.00
ACTB Tatum Bell/150 5.00 12.00
ACWM Willis McGahee/175 5.00 12.00

2004 Flair Autograph Collection Silver

SILVER PRINT RUN 100 SER.#'d SETS

ACKW Kellen Winslow 20.00 50.00
ACLF Larry Fitzgerald 30.00 80.00

2004 Flair Autograph Collection Gold Parchment

*GOLD/25: .8X TO 2X BRNZ/82-175
*GOLD/25: 1X TO 2.5X BRNZ/200-350
GOLD PRINT RUN 25 SER.#'d SETS

ACBR Ben Roethlisberger 100.00 200.00
ACEM Eli Manning 125.00 200.00
ACLF Larry Fitzgerald 40.00 100.00
ACPRI Philip Rivers 40.00 100.00

2004 Flair Cuts and Glory Bronze

BRONZE PRINT RUN 100 SER.#'d SETS
*SILVER/50: .6X TO 1.5X BRONZE AU/100
SILVER PRINT RUN 50 SER.#'d SETS
GOLD STATED PRINT RUN 10-15
UNPRICED MASTERPIECE PRINT RUN 1 SET

CAGAB Anquan Boldin 8.00 20.00
CAGAG Ahman Green 10.00 25.00
CAGBL Byron Leftwich 8.00 20.00
CAGBW Brian Westbrook 8.00 20.00
CAGDC David Carr 8.00 20.00
CAGDF DeShaun Foster 10.00 25.00
CAGDM Donovan McNabb 15.00 40.00
CAGJD Jake Delhomme 8.00 20.00
CAGKB Kyle Boller 8.00 20.00
CAGMF Marshall Faulk 10.00 25.00
CAGMH Matt Hasselbeck 8.00 20.00
CAGSM Santana Moss 10.00 25.00
CHAD Chad Pennington 8.00 20.00

2004 Flair Gridiron Cuts Green

GREEN STATED ODDS 1:48 RETAIL
*BLUE/200: .5X TO 1.2X GREEN JSY
BLUE PRINT RUN 200 SER.#'d SETS
*DIE CUT PATCH/25: 1.5X TO 4X GREEN JSY
DIE CUT PATCH PRINT RUN 25 SER.#'d SETS
UNPRICED PURPLE PRINT RUN 1 SET
*RED/150: .5X TO 1.2X GREEN JSY
RED PRINT RUN 150 SER.#'d SETS
*SILVER/75: .8X TO 2X GREEN JSY
SILVER PRINT RUN 75 SER.#'d SETS
UNPRICED GOLD PRINT RUN 10 SETS

GCAG Ahman Green 2.50 6.00
GCAJ Andre Johnson 2.50 6.00
GCBF Brett Favre 6.00 15.00
GCCR Charles Rogers 2.00 5.00
GCDC Daunte Culpepper 2.50 6.00
GCDC2 David Carr 2.00 5.00
GCDM Deuce McAllister 2.50 6.00
GCDM2 Donovan McNabb 2.50 6.00
GCES Emmitt Smith 5.00 12.00
GCJH Joey Harrington 2.00 5.00
GCJL Jamal Lewis 2.50 6.00
GCLT LaDainian Tomlinson 3.00 8.00
GCMF Marshall Faulk 2.50 6.00
GCMH Matt Hasselbeck 2.00 5.00
GCPM Peyton Manning 8.00 20.00
GCRM Randy Moss 2.50 6.00
GCSA Shaun Alexander 2.00 5.00
GCSM Steve McNair 2.50 6.00
GCTB Tom Brady 12.00 30.00
GCTH Torry Holt 2.50 6.00

2004 Flair Hot Numbers

STATED PRINT RUN 500 SER.#'d SETS
*GOLD/52-99: 1.2X TO 3X BASIC INSERTS
*GOLD/21-37: 1.5X TO 4X BASIC INSERTS
*GOLD/10-19: 2X TO 5X BASIC INSERTS
GOLDS/3-8 NOT PRICED DUE TO SCARCITY
GOLD STATED PRINT RUN 3-99

1HN Peyton Manning 6.00 15.00
2HN Brett Favre 5.00 12.00
3HN Shaun Alexander 1.50 4.00
4HN Charles Rogers 1.50 4.00
5HN Jamal Lewis 2.00 5.00
6HN Clinton Portis 1.50 4.00
7HN Jeremy Shockey 1.50 4.00
8HN Daunte Culpepper 2.00 5.00
9HN Jake Delhomme 1.50 4.00
10HN Tom Brady 10.00 25.00
11HN Quincy Carter 1.50 4.00
12HN Donovan McNabb 2.00 5.00
13HN Byron Leftwich 1.50 4.00
14HN Santana Moss 2.00 5.00
15HN Marvin Harrison 2.00 5.00
16HN Randy Moss 2.00 5.00
17HN Laveranues Coles 1.50 4.00
18HN Andre Johnson 2.00 5.00
19HN Marshall Faulk 2.00 5.00
20HN Edgerrin James 2.00 5.00
21HN Ray Lewis 2.50 6.00
22HN Joey Harrington 1.50 4.00
23HN David Carr 1.50 4.00
24HN Ahman Green 2.00 5.00
25HN Torry Holt 2.00 5.00
26HN Chad Pennington 1.50 4.00
27HN LaDainian Tomlinson 2.50 6.00
28HN Chad Johnson 1.50 4.00
29HN Priest Holmes 1.50 4.00
30HN Marc Bulger 1.50 4.00
31HN Roy Williams S 1.50 4.00
32HN Plaxico Burress 1.50 4.00
33HN Jerry Porter 1.50 4.00
34HN Warren Sapp 2.00 5.00
35HN Brian Urlacher 2.50 6.00

2004 Flair Hot Numbers Game Used Green

STATED ODDS 1:48 RETAIL
*BLUE/200: .5X TO 1.2X GREEN JSY
BLUE PRINT RUN 200 SER.#'d SETS
*DIE CUT PATCH/25: 1.5X TO 4X GREEN JSY
DC PATCH PRINT RUN 25 SER.#'d SETS
GOLD/21-54: 1.5X TO 4X GREEN JSY
*GOLD/80-99: .8X TO 2X GREEN JSY
GOLDS/3-18 NOT PRICED DUE TO SCARCITY
GOLDS #'d TO PLAYER'S JERSEY NUMBER
UNPRICED PURPLE PRINT RUN 1 SET
*RED/150: .5X TO 1.2X GREEN JSY
RED PRINT RUN 150 SER.#'d SETS
*SILVER/75: .8X TO 2X GREEN JSY
SILVER PRINT RUN 75 SER.#'d SETS

HNAG Ahman Green 2.50 6.00
HNAJ Andre Johnson 2.50 6.00
HNBF Brett Favre 6.00 15.00
HNBL Byron Leftwich 2.00 5.00
HNBU Brian Urlacher 3.00 8.00
HNCJ Chad Johnson 2.00 5.00
HNCP Chad Pennington 2.00 5.00
HNCR Charles Rogers 2.00 5.00
HNDC David Carr 2.00 5.00
HNDC Daunte Culpepper 2.50 6.00
HNDM Donovan McNabb 2.50 6.00
HNEJ Edgerrin James 2.50 6.00
HNJD Jake Delhomme 2.00 5.00
HNJH Joey Harrington 2.00 5.00
HNJL Jamal Lewis 2.50 6.00
HNJP Jerry Porter 2.00 5.00
HNJS Jeremy Shockey 2.00 5.00
HNLT LaDainian Tomlinson 3.00 8.00
HNMF Marshall Faulk 2.50 6.00
HNMH Marvin Harrison 2.50 6.00
HNPB Plaxico Burress 2.00 5.00
HNPH Priest Holmes 2.00 5.00
HNPM Peyton Manning 8.00 20.00
HNQC Quincy Carter 2.00 5.00
HNRL Ray Lewis 3.00 8.00
HNRW Roy Williams S 2.00 5.00
HNSA Shaun Alexander 2.00 5.00
HNTB Tom Brady 12.00 30.00
HNTH Torry Holt 2.50 6.00
HNWS Warren Sapp 2.50 6.00

2004 Flair Lettermen

STATED PRINT RUN 4-10 SETS
NOT PRICED DUE TO SCARCITY

2004 Flair Power Swatch Blue

BLUE PRINT RUN 200 SER.#'d SETS
*DIE CUT PATCH/25: 1.2X TO 3X BLUE JSY
DIE CUT PATCH PRINT RUN 25 SER.#'d SETS
*GOLDS/28-48: 1X TO 2.5X BLUE JSY
*GOLDS/80-88: .6X TO 1.5X BLUE JSY
GOLDS/5-8 NOT PRICED DUE TO SCARCITY
GOLDS #'d TO PLAYER'S JERSEY NUMBER
UNPRICED PURPLE PRINT RUN 1 SET
*RED/150: .4X TO 1X BLUE JSY
RED PRINT RUN 150 SER.#'d SETS
*SILVER/75: .6X TO 1.5X BLUE JSY
SILVER PRINT RUN 75 SER.#'d SETS

PSAB Anquan Boldin 2.50 6.00
PSAJ Andre Johnson 3.00 8.00
PSBL Byron Leftwich 2.50 6.00
PSCJ Chad Johnson 2.50 6.00
PSDM Donovan McNabb 3.00 8.00
PSEJ Edgerrin James 3.00 8.00
PSJS Jeremy Shockey 2.50 6.00
PSMF Marshall Faulk 3.00 8.00
PSMH Marvin Harrison 3.00 8.00
PSMV Michael Vick 3.00 8.00
PSPH Priest Holmes 2.50 6.00
PSRG Rex Grossman 2.50 6.00
PSRM Randy Moss 3.00 8.00
PSRW Ricky Williams 3.00 8.00
PSST Stephen Davis 2.50 6.00

2004 Flair SIGnificant Cuts

STATED PRINT RUN 25-100

AV Adam Vinatieri/58 50.00 100.00
BL Byron Leftwich/25 20.00 40.00
BS Barry Sanders/50 75.00 150.00
BW Brian Westbrook/25 20.00 40.00
DM2 Donovan McNabb/100 15.00 40.00
DM3 Deuce McAllister/100 10.00 25.00
JH Joey Harrington/50 10.00 25.00
PM Peyton Manning/75 50.00 100.00
SA Shaun Alexander/100 12.00 30.00
CP2 Chad Pennington/25 20.00 40.00

1997 Flair Showcase Row 2

The 1997 Flair Showcase set was issued in one series totalling 360 cards and was distributed in five-card packs with a suggested retail price of $4.99. This hobby exclusive set is divided into three 120-card sets (Row 2/Style, Row1/Grace, and Row0/Showcase) and features holographic, foil fronts with an action photo of the player silhouetted over a larger black-and-white head-shot image in the background. The backs carry a third photo, bio information and year-by-year and career statistics. The 24 pt. card stock is laminated with a shiny glossy coating for a super-premium style.
COMPLETE SET (120) 15.00 40.00

1 Jerry Rice .75 2.00
2 Mark Brunell .50 1.25
3 Eddie Kennison .25 .60
4 Brett Favre 1.50 4.00
5 Karim Abdul-Jabbar .25 .60
6 David LaFleur RC .15 .40
7 John Elway 1.50 4.00
8 Troy Aikman .75 2.00
9 Steve McNair .50 1.25
10 Kordell Stewart .40 1.00
11 Drew Bledsoe .50 1.25
12 Kerry Collins .40 1.00
13 Dan Marino 1.50 4.00
14 Steve Young .50 1.25
15 Marvin Harrison .40 1.00
16 Lawrence Phillips .15 .40
17 Jeff Blake .25 .60
18 Yatil Green RC .25 .60
19 Jake Plummer RC 1.50 4.00
20 Barry Sanders 1.25 3.00
21 Deion Sanders .40 1.00
22 Emmitt Smith 1.25 3.00
23 Rae Carruth RC .15 .40
24 Chris Warren .25 .60
25 Terry Glenn .40 1.00
26 Jim Druckenmiller RC .25 .60
27 Eddie George .40 1.00
28 Curtis Martin .50 1.25
29 Warrick Dunn RC 1.50 4.00
30 Terrell Davis .50 1.25
31 Rashaan Salaam .15 .40
32 Marcus Allen .40 1.00
33 Jeff George .25 .60
34 Thurman Thomas .40 1.00
35 Keyshawn Johnson .40 1.00
36 Jerome Bettis .40 1.00
37 Larry Centers .25 .60
38 Tony Banks .25 .60
39 Marshall Faulk .50 1.25
40 Mike Alstott .40 1.00
41 Elvis Grbac .25 .60
42 Errict Rhett .15 .40
43 Edgar Bennett .25 .60
44 Jim Harbaugh .25 .60
45 Antonio Freeman .50 1.25
46 Tiki Barber RC 3.00 8.00
47 Tim Biakabutuka .25 .60
48 Joey Galloway .30 .75
49 Tony Gonzalez RC 3.00 8.00
50 Keenan McCardell .25 .60
51 Darnay Scott .25 .60
52 Brad Johnson .50 1.25
53 Herman Moore .25 .60
54 Reidel Anthony RC .50 1.25
55 Junior Seau .40 1.00
56 Ricky Watters .25 .60
57 Amani Toomer .25 .60
58 Andre Reed .25 .60
59 Antowain Smith RC 1.00 2.50
60 Ike Hilliard RC .60 1.50
61 Byron Hanspard RC .30 .75
62 Robert Smith .25 .60
63 Gus Frerotte .15 .40
64 Charles Way .15 .40
65 Trent Dilfer .40 1.00
66 Adrian Murrell .25 .60
67 Stan Humphries .25 .60
68 Robert Brooks .25 .60
69 Jamal Anderson .40 1.00
70 Natrone Means .25 .60
71 John Friesz .15 .40
72 Ki-Jana Carter .15 .40
73 Marc Edwards RC .15 .40
74 Michael Westbrook .25 .60
75 Neil O'Donnell .25 .60
76 Scott Mitchell .25 .60
77 Wesley Walls .25 .60
78 Bruce Smith .25 .60
79 Corey Dillon RC 1.50 4.00
80 Wayne Chrebet .40 1.00
81 Tony Martin .25 .60
82 Jimmy Smith .25 .60
83 Terry Allen .40 1.00
84 Shannon Sharpe .25 .60
85 Derrick Alexander WR .25 .60
86 Garrison Hearst .25 .60
87 Tamarick Vanover .25 .60
88 Michael Irvin .40 1.00
89 Mark Chmura .25 .60
90 Bert Emanuel .25 .60
91 Eric Metcalf .25 .60
92 Reggie White .40 1.00
93 Carl Pickens .25 .60
94 Chris Sanders .15 .40
95 Frank Sanders .25 .60
96 Desmond Howard .25 .60
97 Michael Jackson .25 .60
98 Tim Brown .40 1.00
99 O.J. McDuffie .25 .60
100 Mario Bates .15 .40
101 Warren Moon .40 1.00
102 Curtis Conway .25 .60
103 Irving Fryar .25 .60
104 Isaac Bruce .40 1.00
105 Cris Carter .40 1.00
106 Chris Chandler .25 .60
107 Charles Johnson .25 .60
108 Kevin Lockett RC .25 .60
109 Rob Moore .25 .60
110 Napoleon Kaufman .40 1.00
111 Henry Ellard .15 .40
112 Vinny Testaverde .25 .60
113 Rick Mirer .15 .40
114 Ty Detmer .25 .60
115 Todd Collins .15 .40
116 Jake Reed .25 .60
117 Dave Brown .15 .40
118 Dedric Ward RC .25 .60
119 Heath Shuler .15 .40
120 Ben Coates .25 .60
S1 Rae Carruth Sample .08 .25

1997 Flair Showcase Row 1

COMPLETE SET (120) 50.00 120.00
*STARS 1-40: 1X TO 2X ROW 2
*RCs 1-40: .5X TO 1.2X ROW 2
ROW 1 1-40 ODDS 1:2.5
*STARS 41-80: .5X TO 1.2X ROW 2
*RCs 41-80: .5X TO 1.2X ROW 2
ROW 1 41-80 ODDS 1:2
*STARS 81-120: 1.2X TO 3X ROW 2
*RCs 81-120: .8X TO 2X ROW 2
ROW 1 81-120 ODDS 1:3

1997 Flair Showcase Row 0

COMPLETE SET (120) 400.00 800.00
*STARS 1-40: 5X TO 12X ROW 2
*RCs 1-40: 3X TO 8X ROW 2
ROW 0 1-40 ODDS 1:24
*STARS 41-80: 3X TO 8X ROW 2
*RCs 41-80: 2X TO 5X ROW 2
ROW 0 41-80 ODDS 1:12
*STARS 81-120: 2X TO 5X ROW 2
*RCs 81-120: 1.2X TO 3X ROW 2
ROW 0 81-120 ODDS 1:5

1997 Flair Showcase Legacy Collection

*VETS 1-40: 10X TO 25X ROW 2
*ROOKIE STARS 1-40: 6X TO 15X ROW 2
*VETS 41-80: 6X TO 15X ROW 2
*ROOKIE STARS 41-80: 4X TO 10X ROW 2
*LEGACY 81-120: 8X TO 20X ROW 2
STATED PRINT RUN 100 SER.#'d SETS
THREE CARDS PER PLAYER: SAME PRICE

1997 Flair Showcase Hot Hands

Randomly inserted in packs at the rate of one in 90, this 12-card set features color photos of the best of the best players in the NFL. The backs carry player information.
COMPLETE SET (12) 40.00 100.00
STATED ODDS 1:90

HH1 Kerry Collins 3.00 8.00
HH2 Emmitt Smith 10.00 25.00
HH3 Terrell Davis 4.00 10.00
HH4 Brett Favre 12.50 30.00
HH5 Eddie George 3.00 8.00
HH6 Marvin Harrison 3.00 8.00
HH7 Mark Brunell 4.00 10.00
HH8 Dan Marino 12.50 30.00
HH9 Curtis Martin 4.00 10.00
HH10 Terry Glenn 3.00 8.00
HH11 Keyshawn Johnson 3.00 8.00
HH12 Jerry Rice 6.00 15.00

1997 Flair Showcase Midas Touch

Randomly inserted in packs at the rate of one in 20, this 12-card set features color photos of superstars who turn footballs to gold with touched by one of them. The backs carry player information.
COMPLETE SET (12) 30.00 80.00
STATED ODDS 1:20

MT1 Troy Aikman 5.00 12.00
MT2 John Elway 10.00 25.00
MT3 Barry Sanders 8.00 20.00
MT4 Marshall Faulk 3.00 8.00
MT5 Karim Abdul-Jabbar 1.50 4.00
MT6 Drew Bledsoe 3.00 8.00
MT7 Ricky Watters 1.50 4.00
MT8 Kordell Stewart 2.50 6.00
MT9 Tony Martin 1.50 4.00
MT10 Steve Young 3.00 8.00
MT11 Joey Galloway 2.00 5.00
MT12 Isaac Bruce 2.50 6.00

1997 Flair Showcase Now and Then

Randomly inserted in packs at the rate of one in 400, this four-card set features color photos of 12 superstars as they debuted as rookies and now guide the NFL toward the 21st Century. Each card displays photos of three different players.

COMPLETE SET (4) 60.00 120.00
STATED ODDS 1:400

NT1 Marino 20.00 50.00
Elway
Green
NT2 Aikman 20.00 50.00
BSanders
Deion
NT3 E.Smith 10.00 25.00
Warren
Seau
NT4 Favre 12.50 30.00
HMoore
Watters

1997 Flair Showcase Wave of the Future

Randomly inserted in packs at the rate of one in four, this 25-card set features color photos of top rookies. The backs carry player information.
COMPLETE SET (25) 15.00 30.00
STATED ODDS 1:4

WF1 Mike Adams .30 .75
WF2 John Allred .30 .75
WF3 Pat Barnes .75 2.00
WF4 Kenny Bynum .30 .75
WF5 Will Blackwell .50 1.25
WF6 Peter Boulware .75 2.00
WF7 Greg Clark .30 .75
WF8 Troy Davis .50 1.25
WF9 Albert Connell .75 2.00
WF10 Jay Graham .50 1.25
WF11 Leon Johnson .50 1.25
WF12 Damon Jones .30 .75
WF13 Freddie Jones .50 1.25
WF14 George Jones .50 1.25
WF15 Chad Levitt .30 .75
WF16 Joey Kent .75 2.00
WF17 Danny Wuerffel .75 2.00
WF18 Orlando Pace .75 2.00
WF19 Darnell Autry .50 1.25
WF20 Sedrick Shaw .50 1.25
WF21 Shawn Springs .50 1.25
WF22 Duce Staley 2.50 6.00
WF23 Darrell Russell .30 .75
WF24 Bryant Westbrook .30 .75
WF25 Antwuan Wyatt .30 .75

1998 Flair Showcase Row 3

The 1998 Flair Showcase set was issued in one series totalling 80 cards and was distributed in five-card packs with a suggested retail price of $4.99. This hobby exclusive set is divided into four 80-card versions (Row 3/Flair/Showtime, Row 2/Style/Showstopper, Row 1/Grace/Showdown, and Row 0/Showcase/Showpiece) and features holographic foil fronts with an action photo of the player silhouetted over a larger black-and-white head-shot image in the background coated with a protective laminate finish. The backs display another player photo with player information and career statistics
COMPLETE SET (80) 40.00 80.00
ROW 3 FLAIR 1-20 STATED ODDS 1:0.9
ROW 3 FLAIR 21-40 STATED ODDS 1:1.1
ROW 3 FLAIR 41-60 STATED ODDS 1:1.4
ROW 3 FLAIR 61-80 STATED ODDS 1:1.8

1 Brett Favre 1.25 3.00
2 Emmitt Smith 1.00 2.50
3 Peyton Manning RC 8.00 20.00
4 Mark Brunell .40 1.00
5 Randy Moss RC 4.00 10.00
6 Jerry Rice .60 1.50
7 John Elway 1.25 3.00
8 Troy Aikman .60 1.50
9 Warrick Dunn .40 1.00
10 Kordell Stewart .40 1.00
11 Drew Bledsoe .50 1.25
12 Eddie George .40 1.00
13 Dan Marino 1.25 3.00
14 Antowain Smith .40 1.00
15 Curtis Enis RC .30 .75
16 Jake Plummer .40 1.00
17 Steve Young .40 1.00
18 Ryan Leaf RC .60 1.50
19 Terrell Davis .40 1.00
20 Barry Sanders 1.00 2.50
21 Corey Dillon .40 1.00
22 Fred Taylor RC 1.00 2.50
23 Herman Moore .25 .60
24 Marshall Faulk .50 1.25
25 John Avery RC .25 .60
26 Terry Glenn .40 1.00
27 Keyshawn Johnson .40 1.00
28 Charles Woodson RC 1.25 3.00
29 Garrison Hearst .40 1.00
30 Steve McNair .40 1.00
31 Deion Sanders .40 1.00
32 Robert Holcombe RC .25 .60
33 Jerome Bettis .40 1.00
34 Robert Edwards RC .50 1.25
35 Skip Hicks RC .50 1.25
36 Marcus Nash RC .30 .75
37 Fred Lane .15 .40
38 Kevin Dyson RC .60 1.50
39 Dorsey Levens .40 1.00
40 Jacquez Green RC .50 1.25
41 Shannon Sharpe .30 .75
42 Michael Irvin .50 1.25
43 Jim Harbaugh .30 .75
44 Curtis Martin .50 1.25
45 Bobby Hoying .30 .75
46 Trent Dilfer .50 1.25
47 Yancey Thigpen .20 .50
48 Warren Moon .50 1.25
49 Danny Kanell .30 .75
50 Rob Johnson .30 .75
51 Carl Pickens .30 .75
52 Scott Mitchell .30 .75
53 Tim Brown .50 1.25
54 Tony Banks .50 1.25
55 Jamal Anderson .50 1.25
56 Kerry Collins .30 .75
57 Elvis Grbac .30 .75
58 Mike Alstott .50 1.25
59 Glenn Foley .30 .75
60 Brad Johnson .50 1.25
61 Robert Brooks .50 1.25
62 Irving Fryar .50 1.25
63 Natrone Means .50 1.25
64 Rae Carruth .30 .75
65 Isaac Bruce .75 2.00
66 Andre Rison .50 1.25
67 Jeff George .50 1.25
68 Charles Way .30 .75
69 Derrick Alexander .50 1.25
70 Michael Jackson .30 .75
71 Rob Moore .50 1.25
72 Ricky Watters .50 1.25
73 Curtis Conway .50 1.25
74 Antonio Freeman .75 2.00
75 Jimmy Smith .50 1.25
76 Troy Davis .30 .75
77 Robert Smith .75 2.00
78 Terry Allen .75 2.00
79 Joey Galloway .50 1.25
80 Charles Johnson .30 .75
P16 Jake Plummer promo .50 1.25
NNO Checklist Card .15 .40

1998 Flair Showcase Row 2

COMPLETE SET (80) 60.00 120.00
*STARS 1-20: 1X TO 2.5X ROW 3
*ROOKIES 1-20: .5X TO 1.2X ROW 3
ROW 2 STYLE 1-20 STATED ODDS 1:3
*STARS 21-40: .75X TO 2X ROW 3
*ROOKIES 21-40: .6X TO 1.5X ROW 3
ROW 2 STYLE 21-40 STATED ODDS 1:2.5
*STARS 41-60: 1X TO 2.5X ROW 3
ROW 2 STYLE 41-60 STATED ODDS 1:4
*STARS 61-80: .6X TO 1.5X ROW 3
ROW 2 STYLE 61-80 STATED ODDS 1:3.4
P16 Jake Plummer promo .50 1.25

1998 Flair Showcase Row 1

*STARS 1-20: 3X TO 8X ROW 3
*ROOKIES 1-20: 1.5X TO 4X ROW 3
ROW 1 GRACE 1-20 STATED ODDS 1:16
*STARS 21-40: 4X TO 10X ROW 3
*ROOKIES 21-40: 2X TO 5X ROW 3
ROW 1 GRACE 21-40 STATED ODDS 1:24
*STARS 41-60: 1.2X TO 3X ROW 3
ROW 1 GRACE 41-60 STATED ODDS 1:6
*STARS 61-80: 1.2X TO 3X ROW 3
ROW 1 GRACE 61-80 STATED ODDS 1:9.6
P16 Jake Plummer promo .50 1.25

1998 Flair Showcase Row 0

*STARS 1-20: 10X TO 25X ROW 3
*ROOKIES 1-20: 3X TO 8X ROW 3
ROW 0 SHOWCASE 1-20 PRINT RUN 250
*STARS 21-40: 6X TO 15X ROW 3
*ROOKIES 21-40: 2.5X TO 6X ROW 3
ROW 0 SHOWCASE 21-40 PRINT RUN 500
*STARS 41-60: 5X TO 12X ROW 3
ROW 0 SHOWCASE 41-60 PRINT RUN 1000
*STARS 61-80: 2.5X TO 6X ROW 3
ROW 0 SHOWCASE 61-80 PRINT RUN 2000
P16 Jake Plummer promo .50 1.25

1998 Flair Showcase Legacy Collection Row 3

*VETS 1-40: 8X TO 20X BASIC ROW 3
*ROOKIES 1-40: 4X TO 10X BASIC ROW 3
*VETS 41-60: 6X TO 15X BASIC ROW 3
*VETS 61-80: 6X TO 15X BASIC ROW 3
STATED PRINT RUN 100 SER.#'d SETS
*ROW 0/1/2 CARDS: .4X TO 1X ROW 3
UNPRICED MASTERPIECES #'d TO 1

3 Peyton Manning 100.00 200.00
28 Charles Woodson 50.00 100.00

1998 Flair Showcase Feature Film

Randomly inserted in packs at the rate of one in 60, this 10-card set features actual slides from the Showcase set mounted on black-and-white player photos with the photographer's name printed on the card. A very rare Feature Film Master parallel version of this set was also produced with the original slide and signature of photographer printed on each card. Each card is numbered 1-of-1 and includes the word "original" on the cardback.
COMPLETE SET (10) 75.00 150.00
STATED ODDS 1:60
UNPRICED MASTERS SERIAL #'d TO 1

1 Terrell Davis 4.00 10.00
2 Brett Favre 12.50 30.00
3 Antowain Smith 4.00 10.00
4 Emmitt Smith 10.00 25.00
5 Dan Marino 12.50 30.00
6 Kordell Stewart 4.00 10.00
7 Warrick Dunn 4.00 10.00
8 Barry Sanders 10.00 25.00
9 Peyton Manning 12.00 30.00
10 Ryan Leaf 1.25 3.00

1999 Flair Showcase

Released as a 192-card set, the 1999 Flair Showcase set is divided into three subsets. The power version contains 32 cards featuring a full color action photo set against a silver silhouette background, the passion version is comprised of 64 cards that feature two full color action photos set against the player's jersey number, and the Showcase version features 96 players and rookies on a split-front card with two silhouette photos segmented by an action shot. The last 32 cards in this set are numbered out of 1999. 1999 Flair Showcase was packaged in 24-pack boxes with packs of five cards each and carried a suggested retail price of $4.99.
COMPLETE SET (192) 300.00 600.00
COMP.SET w/o SPs (160) 20.00 50.00

1 Troy Aikman PW .40 1.00
2 Jamal Anderson PW .25 .60
3 Charlie Batch PW .20 .50
4 Jerome Bettis PW .30 .75
5 Drew Bledsoe PW .25 .60
6 Mark Brunell PW .25 .60
7 Randall Cunningham PW .25 .60
8 Terrell Davis PW .25 .60
9 Corey Dillon PW .20 .50
10 Warrick Dunn PW .20 .50
11 Curtis Enis PW .20 .50
12 Marshall Faulk PW .25 .60
13 Brett Favre PW .60 1.50
14 Doug Flutie PW .30 .75
15 Eddie George PW .25 .60
16 Brian Griese PW .20 .50
17 Keyshawn Johnson PW .25 .60
18 Peyton Manning PW 1.00 2.50
19 Dan Marino PW .60 1.50
20 Curtis Martin PW .25 .60
21 Steve McNair PW .25 .60
22 Randy Moss PW .25 .60
23 Terrell Owens PW .25 .60
24 Jake Plummer PW .20 .50
25 Jerry Rice PW .75 2.00
26 Barry Sanders PW .50 1.25
27 Antowain Smith PW .20 .50
28 Emmitt Smith PW .50 1.25
29 Kordell Stewart PW .20 .50
30 J.J. Stokes PW .20 .50
31 Fred Taylor PW .20 .50
32 Steve Young PW .40 1.00
33 Troy Aikman PN .40 1.00
34 Mike Alstott PN .20 .50
35 Jamal Anderson PN .25 .60
36 Charlie Batch PN .20 .50
37 Jerome Bettis PN .30 .75
38 Drew Bledsoe PN .25 .60
39 Mark Brunell PN .25 .60
40 Cris Carter PN .30 .75
41 Mark Chmura PN .20 .50
42 Wayne Chrebet PN .20 .50
43 Kerry Collins PN .20 .50
44 Randall Cunningham PN .25 .60
45 Terrell Davis PN .25 .60
46 Trent Dilfer PN .20 .50
47 Corey Dillon PN .20 .50
48 Warrick Dunn PN .20 .50
49 Kevin Dyson PN .20 .50
50 Curtis Enis PN .20 .50
51 Marshall Faulk PN .25 .60
52 Brett Favre PN .60 1.50
53 Doug Flutie PN .30 .75
54 Antonio Freeman PN .25 .60
55 Eddie George PN .25 .60
56 Terry Glenn PN .25 .60
57 Tony Gonzalez PN .25 .60
58 Elvis Grbac PN .20 .50
59 Jacquez Green PN .20 .50
60 Brian Griese PN .20 .50
61 Marvin Harrison PN .25 .60
62 Garrison Hearst PN .20 .50
63 Skip Hicks PN .20 .50
64 Priest Holmes PN .20 .50
65 Michael Irvin PN .30 .75
66 Brad Johnson PN .25 .60
67 Keyshawn Johnson PN .25 .60
68 Napoleon Kaufman PN .20 .50
69 Dorsey Levens PN .25 .60
70 Peyton Manning PN 1.00 2.50
71 Dan Marino PN .60 1.50
72 Curtis Martin PN .25 .60
73 Ed McCaffrey PN .25 .60
74 Keenan McCardell PN .25 .60
75 O.J. McDuffie PN .25 .60
76 Steve McNair PN .25 .60
77 Scott Mitchell PN .20 .50
78 Randy Moss PN .25 .60
79 Eric Moulds PN .20 .50
80 Terrell Owens PN .25 .60
81 Lawrence Phillips PN .25 .60
82 Jake Plummer PN .20 .50
83 Jerry Rice PN .75 2.00
84 Andre Rison PN .25 .60
85 Barry Sanders PN .50 1.25
86 Shannon Sharpe PN .25 .60
87 Antowain Smith PN .20 .50
88 Emmitt Smith PN .50 1.25
89 Rod Smith PN .25 .60
90 Duce Staley PN .20 .50
91 Kordell Stewart PN .20 .50
92 J.J. Stokes PN .20 .50
93 Fred Taylor PN .20 .50
94 Vinny Testaverde PN .20 .50
95 Ricky Watters PN .25 .60
96 Steve Young PN .40 1.00
97 Mike Alstott .20 .50
98 Jamal Anderson .25 .60
99 Charlie Batch .20 .50
100 Jerome Bettis .30 .75
101 Tim Biakabutuka .25 .60
102 Drew Bledsoe .25 .60
103 Tim Brown .30 .75
104 Mark Brunell .25 .60
105 Cris Carter .30 .75
106 Chris Chandler .25 .60
107 Mark Chmura .20 .50
108 Wayne Chrebet .20 .50
109 Ben Coates .25 .60
110 Kerry Collins .20 .50
111 Randall Cunningham .25 .60
112 Trent Dilfer .20 .50
113 Corey Dillon .20 .50
114 Warrick Dunn .20 .50
115 Kevin Dyson .20 .50
116 Curtis Enis .20 .50
117 Marshall Faulk .25 .60
118 Doug Flutie .30 .75
119 Antonio Freeman .25 .60
120 Joey Galloway .25 .60
121 Rich Gannon .25 .60
122 Eddie George .25 .60
123 Terry Glenn .25 .60
124 Tony Gonzalez .25 .60
125 Elvis Grbac .20 .50
126 Jacquez Green .20 .50
127 Brian Griese .20 .50
128 Marvin Harrison .25 .60
129 Garrison Hearst .20 .50
130 Skip Hicks .20 .50
131 Priest Holmes .20 .50
132 Michael Irvin .30 .75
133 Brad Johnson .25 .60
134 Napoleon Kaufman .20 .50
135 Terry Kirby .20 .50
136 Dorsey Levens .25 .60
137 Curtis Martin .25 .60
138 Ed McCaffrey .25 .60
139 Keenan McCardell .25 .60
140 O.J. McDuffie .25 .60
141 Steve McNair .25 .60
142 Natrone Means .25 .60
143 Scott Mitchell .20 .50
144 Herman Moore .25 .60
145 Eric Moulds .20 .50
146 Terrell Owens .25 .60
147 Lawrence Phillips .25 .60
148 Jerry Rice .75 2.00
149 Andre Rison .25 .60
150 Deion Sanders .25 .60
151 Shannon Sharpe .25 .60
152 Antowain Smith .20 .50
153 Rod Smith .25 .60
154 Duce Staley .20 .50
155 Kordell Stewart .20 .50
156 J.J. Stokes .20 .50
157 Vinny Testaverde .20 .50
158 Yancey Thigpen .20 .50
159 Ricky Watters .25 .60
160 Steve Young .40 1.00
161 Troy Aikman/1999 3.00 8.00
162 Champ Bailey RC 4.00 10.00
163 Karsten Bailey RC 2.00 5.00
164 D'Wayne Bates RC 2.00 5.00
165 David Boston RC 2.00 5.00
166 Mike Cloud RC 2.00 5.00
167 Cecil Collins RC 2.00 5.00
168 Tim Couch RC 2.50 6.00
169 Daunte Culpepper RC 3.00 8.00
170 Terrell Davis/1999 3.00 8.00
171 Troy Edwards RC 2.00 5.00
172 Kevin Faulk RC 2.00 5.00
173 Brett Favre/1999 5.00 12.00
174 Torry Holt RC 4.00 10.00
175 Sedrick Irvin RC 2.00 5.00
176 Edgerrin James RC 6.00 15.00
177 James Johnson RC 2.00 5.00
178 Kevin Johnson RC 2.50 6.00
179 Keyshawn Johnson/1999 2.00 5.00
180 Peyton Manning/1999 8.00 20.00
181 Dan Marino/1999 5.00 12.00
182 Donovan McNabb RC 6.00 15.00
183 Cade McNown RC 2.00 5.00
184 Joe Montgomery RC 2.00 5.00
185 Randy Moss/1999 5.00 12.00
186 Jake Plummer/1999 1.50 4.00
187 Peerless Price RC 2.50 6.00
188 Barry Sanders/1999 4.00 10.00
189 Akili Smith RC 2.00 5.00
190 Emmitt Smith/1999 4.00 10.00
191 Fred Taylor/1999 1.50 4.00
192 Ricky Williams RC 3.00 8.00
P24 Jake Plummer PW Promo .40 1.00
P82 Jake Plummer PN Promo .40 1.00
P147 Jake Plummer Promo .40 1.00

1999 Flair Showcase Legacy Collection

*VETS/99: 8X TO 20X BASIC CARDS
*VET/99: 1X TO 2.5X VET/1999
*ROOKIES/99: .8X TO 2X RC/1999
STATED PRINT RUN 99 SERIAL #'d SETS
UNPRICED MASTERPIECES SER.#'d TO 1

1999 Flair Showcase Class of '99

Randomly inserted in packs, this 15-card set showcases 1999 rookies on a split-front card featuring a silhouette shot and an action shot. Each card is sequentially numbered out of 500.
COMPLETE SET (15)
STATED PRINT RUN 500 SER.#'d SETS

1 Tim Couch 2.50 6.00
2 Donovan McNabb 6.00 15.00
3 Akili Smith 2.00 5.00
4 Cade McNown 2.00 5.00
5 Daunte Culpepper 3.00 8.00
6 Ricky Williams 3.00 8.00
7 Edgerrin James 5.00 12.00
8 Kevin Faulk 2.00 5.00
9 Torry Holt 4.00 10.00
10 David Boston 2.00 5.00
11 Sedrick Irvin 2.00 5.00
12 Peerless Price 2.00 5.00
13 Joe Germaine 2.50 6.00
14 Brock Huard 2.00 5.00
15 Shaun King 2.00 5.00

1999 Flair Showcase Feel The Game

Randomly seeded in packs at the rate of one in 168, this 10 card set features swatches of game-used memorabilia such as jerseys, gloves, and shoes.

STATED ODDS 1:168
1FG Edgerrin James Glove 40.00 100.00
2FG Antowain Smith Shorts 6.00 15.00
3FG Peyton Manning JSY 20.00 50.00
4FG Cecil Collins Shoes 6.00 15.00
5FG Brett Favre JSY 20.00 50.00
6FG Jake Plummer Shoes 7.50 20.00
7FG Dan Marino JSY 25.00 60.00
8FG Sean Dawkins Shoes 6.00 15.00
9FG Torry Holt Shoes 10.00 25.00
10FG Marshall Faulk JSY 12.50 30.00

1999 Flair Showcase First Rounders

Randomly seeded in packs at the rate of one in 10, this 10-card set features top draft picks on an all foil card showing players in action. Background colors match each player's team colors.

COMPLETE SET (10) 15.00 40.00
STATED ODDS 1:10
1FR Tim Couch .75 2.00
2FR Donovan McNabb 2.00 5.00
3FR Akili Smith .60 1.50
4FR Cade McNown .60 1.50
5FR Daunte Culpepper 1.00 2.50
6FR David Boston .60 1.50
7FR Torry Holt 1.25 3.00
8FR Ricky Williams 1.00 2.50
9FR Edgerrin James 1.00 2.50
10FR Troy Edwards .60 1.50

1999 Flair Showcase Shrine Time

Randomly inserted in packs, this 15-card set picks players most likely to make the football hall of fame. Each card sets the featured player on a trophy-like gold pedistal and is highlighted with gold foil and gold foil stamping. Each card is sequentially numbered out of 1500.

COMPLETE SET (15) 50.00 100.00
STATED PRINT RUN 1500 SER.#'d SETS
1 Peyton Manning 6.00 15.00
2 Fred Taylor 1.25 3.00
3 Terrell Owens 1.50 4.00
4 Charlie Batch 1.25 3.00
5 Jerry Rice 5.00 12.00
6 Randy Moss 1.50 4.00
7 Warrick Dunn 1.25 3.00
8 Mark Brunell 1.50 4.00
9 Emmitt Smith 3.00 8.00
10 Eddie George 1.50 4.00
11 Barry Sanders 3.00 8.00
12 Terrell Davis 1.50 4.00
13 Dan Marino 4.00 10.00
14 Troy Aikman 2.50 6.00
15 Brett Favre 4.00 10.00

2006 Flair Showcase

This 268-card set was released in November, 2006. The set was issued in five-card packs, with a $4.99 SRP, which came 18 packs to a box. The set is broken down into veterans (1-100, 237-268) both groupings of which are in team alphabetical order and rookies (101-236) also broken down several times into team alphabetical order. The following groups of cards have these stated print runs: Cards numbered 101-142 were issued to a stated print run of 699 serial numbered copies, Cards numbered 143-184 were issued to a stated print run of 499 serial numbered sets, cards numbered 185-226 were issued to a stated print run of 299 serial numbered sets and the veterans from 237-268 were issued to a stated print run of 999 serial numbered sets.

COMP.SET w/o SP's (100) 8.00 20.00
101-142 PRINT RUN 699 SER.#'d SETS
143-184 PRINT RUN 499 SER.#'d SETS
185-226 PRINT RUN 299 SER.#'d SETS
227-236 PRINT RUN 199 SER.#'d SETS
237-268 PRINT RUN 999 SER.#'d SETS
1 Edgerrin James .25 .60
2 Larry Fitzgerald .25 .60
3 Anquan Boldin .20 .50
4 Michael Vick .25 .60
5 Warrick Dunn .20 .50
6 Roddy White .20 .50
7 Steve McNair .25 .60
8 Jamal Lewis .25 .60
9 Derrick Mason .20 .50
10 Willis McGahee .20 .50
11 Lee Evans .25 .60
12 J.P. Losman .25 .60
13 Jake Delhomme .20 .50
14 DeShaun Foster .25 .60
15 Steve Smith .30 .75
16 Rex Grossman .20 .50
17 Thomas Jones .20 .50
18 Muhsin Muhammad .20 .50
19 Brian Urlacher .30 .75
20 Carson Palmer .25 .60
21 Rudi Johnson .20 .50
22 Chad Johnson .20 .50
23 Charlie Frye .25 .60
24 Reuben Droughns .25 .60
25 Braylon Edwards .20 .50
26 Drew Bledsoe .25 .60
27 Julius Jones .20 .50
28 Terrell Owens .25 .60
29 Jake Plummer .20 .50
30 Tatum Bell .20 .50
31 Javon Walker .25 .60
32 Kevin Jones .20 .50
33 Roy Williams WR .20 .50
34 Mike Williams .20 .50
35 Brett Favre .60 1.50
36 Ahman Green .25 .60
37 Donald Driver .25 .60
38 David Carr .20 .50
39 Eric Moulds .20 .50
40 Andre Johnson .25 .60
41 Peyton Manning .75 2.00
42 Marvin Harrison .25 .60
43 Reggie Wayne .25 .60
44 Byron Leftwich .20 .50
45 Fred Taylor .20 .50
46 Ernest Wilford .20 .50
47 Trent Green .20 .50
48 Larry Johnson .20 .50
49 Tony Gonzalez .25 .60
50 Eddie Kennison .20 .50
51 Daunte Culpepper .25 .60
52 Ronnie Brown .25 .60
53 Chris Chambers .20 .50
54 Brad Johnson .25 .60
55 Chester Taylor .25 .60
56 Troy Williamson .20 .50
57 Tom Brady 1.00 2.50
58 Corey Dillon .20 .50
59 Troy Brown .20 .50
60 Drew Brees .30 .75
61 Deuce McAllister .25 .60
62 Joe Horn .20 .50
63 Eli Manning .25 .60
64 Tiki Barber .25 .60
65 Plaxico Burress .20 .50
66 Jeremy Shockey .20 .50
67 Chad Pennington .20 .50
68 Curtis Martin .25 .60
69 Laveranues Coles .20 .50
70 Aaron Brooks .20 .50
71 LaMont Jordan .25 .60
72 Randy Moss .25 .60
73 Jerry Porter .20 .50
74 Donovan McNabb .25 .60
75 Brian Westbrook .20 .50
76 Reggie Brown .20 .50
77 Ben Roethlisberger .40 1.00
78 Willie Parker .25 .60
79 Hines Ward .25 .60
80 Philip Rivers .30 .75
81 LaDainian Tomlinson .30 .75
82 Antonio Gates .30 .75
83 Alex Smith QB .25 .60
84 Frank Gore .25 .60
85 Antonio Bryant .20 .50
86 Matt Hasselbeck .20 .50
87 Shaun Alexander .20 .50
88 Nate Burleson .20 .50
89 Marc Bulger .20 .50
90 Steven Jackson .20 .50
91 Torry Holt .25 .60
92 Chris Simms .20 .50
93 Cadillac Williams .25 .60
94 Joey Galloway .25 .60
95 Kerry Collins .20 .50
96 David Givens .25 .60
97 Drew Bennett .25 .60
98 Mark Brunell .25 .60
99 Clinton Portis .20 .50
100 Santana Moss .25 .60
101 Todd Watkins RC 1.50 4.00
102 Adam Jennings RC 2.00 5.00
103 David Pittman RC 2.00 5.00
104 Dawan Landry RC 2.50 6.00
105 Ko Simpson RC 2.00 5.00
106 James Anderson RC 1.50 4.00
107 Dusty Dvoracek RC 2.50 6.00
108 Jamar Williams RC 2.00 5.00
109 Bennie Brazell RC 2.00 5.00
110 Leon Williams RC 2.00 5.00
111 Lawrence Vickers RC 2.00 5.00
112 Elvis Dumervil RC 2.50 6.00
113 Domenik Hixon RC 2.50 6.00
114 Antoine Bethea RC 2.50 6.00
115 David Anderson RC 2.00 5.00
116 Freddie Keiaho RC 2.00 5.00
117 Clint Ingram RC 2.50 6.00
118 Jeff Webb RC 2.00 5.00
119 Devin Aromashodu RC 1.50 4.00
120 Mike Hass RC 1.50 4.00
121 Josh Lay RC 1.50 4.00
122 Marques Colston RC 2.50 6.00
123 Gerris Wilkinson RC 1.50 4.00
124 Barry Cofield RC 2.50 6.00
125 Guy Whimper RC 1.50 4.00
126 Nick Mangold RC 1.25 3.00
127 Anthony Schlegel RC 2.00 5.00
128 Eric Smith RC 2.00 5.00
129 Darnell Bing RC 2.00 5.00
130 Anthony Smith RC 2.50 6.00
131 Charlie Whitehurst RC 1.50 4.00
132 Delanie Walker RC 3.00 8.00
133 Marcus Hudson RC 2.00 5.00
134 David Kirtman RC 2.00 5.00
135 Victor Adeyanju RC 2.00 5.00
136 Davin Joseph RC 2.00 5.00
137 Marcus McNeill RC 1.50 4.00
138 Calvin Lowry RC 2.50 6.00
139 Stephen Tulloch RC 2.00 5.00
140 Terna Nande RC 2.00 5.00
141 Jonathan Orr RC 2.00 5.00
142 Jon Alston RC 1.50 4.00
143 Jimmy Williams RC 2.00 5.00
144 D.J. Shockley RC 2.50 6.00
145 Demetrius Williams RC 2.00 5.00
146 P.J. Daniels RC 2.00 5.00
147 Quinn Sypniewski RC 2.50 6.00
148 Ashton Youboty RC 2.00 5.00
149 Richard Marshall RC 2.50 6.00
150 Jeff King RC 2.50 6.00
151 Danieal Manning RC 3.00 8.00
152 Reggie McNeal RC 2.00 5.00
153 D'Qwell Jackson RC 2.00 5.00
154 Jerome Harrison RC 2.00 5.00
155 Skyler Green RC 2.00 5.00
156 Brandon Marshall RC 4.00 10.00
157 Daniel Bullocks RC 2.00 5.00
158 Abdul Hodge RC 2.00 5.00
159 Cory Rodgers RC 2.00 5.00
160 Ingle Martin RC 2.50 6.00
161 Stephen Gostkowski RC 10.00 25.00
162 Wali Lundy RC 2.00 5.00
163 Bernard Pollard RC 2.50 6.00
164 Marcus Vick RC 2.00 5.00
165 Cedric Griffin RC 2.50 6.00
166 Garrett Mills RC 2.50 6.00
167 Roman Harper RC 2.50 6.00
168 Brad Smith RC 2.50 6.00
169 Leon Washington RC 2.00 5.00
170 Ahmad Brooks RC 3.00 8.00
171 Thomas Howard RC 2.00 5.00
172 Jason Avant RC 2.00 5.00
173 Jeremy Bloom RC 2.00 5.00
174 Omar Jacobs RC 2.00 5.00
175 Mike Bell RC 2.00 5.00
176 Cedric Humes RC 2.00 5.00
177 Michael Robinson RC 2.00 5.00
178 Ben Obomanu RC 2.50 6.00
179 Darryl Tapp RC 2.50 6.00
180 Claude Wroten RC 2.00 5.00
181 Dominique Byrd RC 2.00 5.00
182 Marques Hagans RC 2.00 5.00
183 Bruce Gradkowski RC 2.50 6.00
184 Rocky McIntosh RC 2.00 5.00
185 Leonard Pope RC 3.00 8.00
186 Jerious Norwood RC 2.00 5.00
187 Haloti Ngata RC 2.50 6.00
188 Donte Whitner RC 2.50 6.00
189 John McCargo RC 2.00 5.00
190 Devin Hester RC 4.00 10.00
191 Johnathan Joseph RC 2.50 6.00
192 Kamerion Wimbley RC 2.50 6.00
193 Travis Wilson RC 2.00 5.00
194 Bobby Carpenter RC 2.00 5.00
195 Anthony Fasano RC 2.00 5.00
196 Tony Scheffler RC 3.00 8.00
197 Ernie Sims RC 2.00 5.00
198 Brian Calhoun RC 2.00 5.00
199 A.J. Hawk RC 2.50 6.00
200 Greg Jennings RC 3.00 8.00
201 Mario Williams RC 3.00 8.00
202 DeMeco Ryans RC 2.50 6.00
203 Marcedes Lewis RC 2.00 5.00
204 Maurice Drew RC 3.00 8.00
205 Tamba Hali RC 3.00 8.00
206 Brodie Croyle RC 2.00 5.00
207 Jason Allen RC 2.50 6.00
208 Derek Hagan RC 2.50 6.00
209 Chad Greenway RC 3.00 8.00
210 Tarvaris Jackson RC 2.00 5.00
211 Chad Jackson RC 2.00 5.00
212 David Thomas RC 2.00 5.00
213 Mathias Kiwanuka RC 3.00 8.00
214 Sinorice Moss RC 2.00 5.00
215 D'Brickashaw Ferguson RC 2.00 5.00
216 Kellen Clemens RC 2.00 5.00
217 Michael Huff RC 2.50 6.00
218 Brodrick Bunkley RC 2.50 6.00
219 Willie Reid RC 2.50 6.00
220 Antonio Cromartie RC 2.50 6.00
221 Manny Lawson RC 2.50 6.00
222 Brandon Williams RC 2.00 5.00
223 Kelly Jennings RC 2.50 6.00
224 Tye Hill RC 2.00 5.00
225 Joe Klopfenstein RC 2.00 5.00
226 Maurice Stovall RC 2.00 5.00
227 Matt Leinart RC 2.50 6.00
228 DeAngelo Williams RC 3.00 8.00
229 Jay Cutler RC 3.00 8.00
230 Joseph Addai RC 2.50 6.00
231 Laurence Maroney RC 2.50 6.00
232 Reggie Bush RC 4.00 10.00
233 Santonio Holmes RC 3.00 8.00
234 Vernon Davis RC 3.00 8.00
235 Vince Young RC 2.50 6.00
236 LenDale White RC 2.50 6.00
237 Edgerrin James 1.25 3.00
238 Michael Vick 1.25 3.00
239 Jamal Lewis 1.25 3.00
240 Willis McGahee 1.00 2.50
241 Steve Smith 1.50 4.00
242 Brian Urlacher 1.50 4.00
243 Carson Palmer 1.25 3.00
244 Charlie Frye 1.25 3.00
245 Terrell Owens 1.25 3.00
246 Jake Plummer 1.00 2.50
247 Kevin Jones 1.00 2.50
248 Brett Favre 3.00 8.00
249 David Carr 1.00 2.50
250 Peyton Manning 4.00 10.00
251 Byron Leftwich 1.00 2.50
252 Larry Johnson 1.00 2.50
253 Daunte Culpepper 1.25 3.00
254 Brad Johnson 1.25 3.00
255 Tom Brady 5.00 12.00
256 Drew Brees 1.50 4.00
257 Eli Manning 1.25 3.00
258 Curtis Martin 1.25 3.00
259 Randy Moss 1.25 3.00
260 Donovan McNabb 1.25 3.00
261 Ben Roethlisberger 2.00 5.00
262 LaDainian Tomlinson 1.50 4.00
263 Alex Smith QB 1.25 3.00
264 Shaun Alexander 1.00 2.50
265 Marc Bulger 1.00 2.50
266 Cadillac Williams 1.25 3.00
267 Drew Bennett 1.25 3.00
268 Clinton Portis 1.00 2.50

2006 Flair Showcase Emerald

*VETS 1-100: 5X TO 12X BASIC CARDS
1-100 PRINT RUN 50 SER.#'d SETS
*ROOKIES 101-142: 1X TO 2.5X
*ROOKIES 143-184: .8X TO 2X
*ROOKIES 185-226: .8X TO 2X
*ROOKIES 227-236: .6X TO 1.5X
*VETS 237-268: 1.5X TO 4X BASIC CARDS
101-236 PRINT RUN 25 SER.#'d SETS

2006 Flair Showcase Gold

*VETS 1-100: 3X TO 8X BASIC CARDS
*ROOKIES 101-142: .6X TO 1.5X
*ROOKIES 143-184: .5X TO 1.2X
*ROOKIES 185-226: .5X TO 1.2X
1-226 PRINT RUN 99 SER.#'d SETS
*ROOKIES 227-236: .5X TO 1.2X
*VETS 237-268: .8X TO 2X BASIC CARDS
227-268 PRINT RUN 75 SER.#'d SETS

2006 Flair Showcase Autographics

AUAF Anthony Fasano 6.00 15.00
AUAH Andre Hall 5.00 12.00
AUBA Ronde Barber SP 10.00 25.00
AUBB Brodrick Bunkley 4.00 10.00
AUBC Brian Calhoun 8.00 20.00
AUBD Brian Dawkins 10.00 25.00
AUBG Bruce Gradkowski 6.00 15.00
AUBM Brandon Marshall 10.00 25.00
AUBR Reggie Brown SP 6.00 15.00
AUCJ Chad Jackson 8.00 20.00
AUCS Chris Simms SP 6.00 15.00
AUCU Kevin Curtis 4.00 10.00
AUCW Charlie Whitehurst 8.00 20.00
AUDF D'Brickashaw Ferguson 6.00 15.00
AUDM DonTrell Moore 4.00 10.00
AUDW DeAngelo Williams SP 15.00 40.00
AUES Ernie Sims 6.00 15.00
AUJA Joseph Addai 10.00 25.00
AUJC Jay Cutler SP 12.00 30.00
AUJJ Julius Jones SP 15.00 30.00
AUJK Joe Klopfenstein 4.00 10.00
AUJW Jimmy Williams 4.00 10.00
AUKC Kellen Clemens 6.00 15.00
AUKJ Kelly Jennings 4.00 10.00
AULJ Larry Johnson 8.00 20.00
AULP Leonard Pope SP 6.00 15.00
AULT Lofa Tatupu 10.00 25.00
AULW LenDale White SP 10.00 25.00
AUMB Mike Bell 8.00 20.00
AUMC Deuce McAllister SP 8.00 20.00
AUMI Mike Williams 4.00 10.00
AUMM Marcus McNeill 4.00 10.00
AUMN Martin Nance 4.00 10.00
AUMS Maurice Stovall 6.00 15.00
AUMU Muhsin Muhammad SP 8.00 20.00
AUMW Mario Williams 8.00 20.00
AUPR Philip Rivers 15.00 40.00
AURB Reggie Bush SP 15.00 40.00
AURM Reggie McNeal 6.00 15.00
AUSM Sinorice Moss 8.00 20.00
AUSS Steve Smith SP 15.00 30.00
AUTB Tedy Bruschi 20.00 40.00
AUTH Tye Hill 6.00 15.00
AUTJ Thomas Jones 8.00 20.00
AUTR Travis Wilson 4.00 10.00
AUTW Terrence Whitehead 4.00 10.00
AUVD Vernon Davis SP 10.00 25.00

2006 Flair Showcase Clear Path to Greatness

CPTG1 A.J. Hawk 4.00 10.00
CPTG2 Anthony Fasano 3.00 8.00
CPTG3 Brandon Marshall 6.00 15.00
CPTG4 Brandon Williams 3.00 8.00
CPTG5 Brian Calhoun 3.00 8.00
CPTG6 Brodie Croyle 3.00 8.00
CPTG7 Chad Jackson 3.00 8.00
CPTG8 Charlie Whitehurst 3.00 8.00
CPTG9 D'Brickashaw Ferguson 3.00 8.00
CPTG10 DeAngelo Williams 4.00 10.00
CPTG11 Demetrius Williams 3.00 8.00
CPTG12 Derek Hagan 4.00 10.00
CPTG13 Donte Whitner 4.00 10.00
CPTG14 Ernie Sims 3.00 8.00
CPTG15 Greg Jennings 5.00 12.00
CPTG16 Jason Allen 4.00 10.00
CPTG17 Jason Avant 3.00 8.00
CPTG18 Jay Cutler 4.00 10.00
CPTG19 Jerious Norwood 3.00 8.00
CPTG20 Joe Klopfenstein 3.00 8.00
CPTG21 Joseph Addai 3.00 8.00
CPTG22 Kamerion Wimbley 4.00 10.00
CPTG23 Kellen Clemens 3.00 8.00
CPTG24 Laurence Maroney 3.00 8.00
CPTG25 LenDale White 3.00 8.00
CPTG26 Leon Washington 3.00 8.00
CPTG27 Marcedes Lewis 3.00 8.00
CPTG28 Mario Williams 5.00 12.00
CPTG29 Matt Leinart 3.00 8.00
CPTG30 Maurice Drew 5.00 12.00
CPTG31 Maurice Stovall 3.00 8.00
CPTG32 Michael Huff 4.00 10.00
CPTG33 Michael Robinson 3.00 8.00
CPTG34 Omar Jacobs 3.00 8.00
CPTG35 Reggie Bush 5.00 12.00
CPTG36 Santonio Holmes 4.00 10.00
CPTG37 Sinorice Moss 3.00 8.00
CPTG38 Tarvaris Jackson 3.00 8.00
CPTG39 Travis Wilson 3.00 8.00
CPTG40 Tye Hill 3.00 8.00
CPTG41 Vernon Davis 4.00 10.00
CPTG42 Vince Young 3.00 8.00

2006 Flair Showcase Fresh Ink

FIAG Antonio Gates 8.00 20.00
FIAH A.J. Hawk 15.00 40.00
FIAY Ashton Youboty SP 5.00 12.00
FIBE Braylon Edwards SP 5.00 12.00
FIBI Darnell Bing 6.00 15.00
FIBW Brandon Williams 5.00 12.00
FIBY Dominique Byrd 5.00 12.00
FICG Chad Greenway 8.00 20.00
FICI Clint Ingram 8.00 20.00
FICR Cory Rodgers 5.00 12.00
FIDD Drew Bennett 6.00 15.00
FIDF DeShaun Foster 6.00 15.00
FIDG David Givens 6.00 15.00
FIDH Darrell Hackney 6.00 15.00
FIDM Derrick Mason 5.00 12.00
FIDO Drew Olson 5.00 12.00
FIDR DeMeco Ryans 6.00 15.00
FIEM Eli Manning SP 25.00 60.00
FIGJ Greg Jennings 8.00 20.00
FIGL Greg Lee 5.00 12.00
FIGR Gerald Riggs 6.00 15.00
FIHA Derek Hagan 6.00 15.00
FIHB Hank Baskett 5.00 12.00
FIHO T.J. Houshmandzadeh 5.00 12.00
FIHU Michael Huff 6.00 15.00
FIJB Josh Betts 6.00 15.00
FIJH Jerome Harrison 5.00 12.00
FIJN Jerious Norwood 5.00 12.00
FIJW Jason Witten SP 20.00 40.00
FIKO Kyle Orton SP 5.00 12.00
FILE Matt Leinart SP 20.00 50.00
FILJ LaMont Jordan SP 6.00 15.00
FILM Laurence Maroney 8.00 20.00
FILW Leon Washington 5.00 12.00
FIMD Maurice Drew 12.00 30.00
FIMH Mike Hass 5.00 12.00
FIMK Mathias Kiwanuka 8.00 20.00
FIMR Michael Robinson 5.00 12.00
FINB Nate Burleson 5.00 12.00
FIOD Owen Daniels 8.00 20.00
FIOJ Omar Jacobs 5.00 12.00
FIPM Peyton Manning 50.00 100.00
FIRJ Rudi Johnson SP 5.00 12.00
FIRW Reggie Wayne 6.00 15.00
FISH Santonio Holmes SP 10.00 25.00
FITH Thomas Howard 5.00 12.00
FITJ Tarvaris Jackson 5.00 12.00
FIVY Vince Young SP 12.00 30.00
FIWJ Winston Justice SP 6.00 15.00
FIWP Willie Parker SP 10.00 25.00

2006 Flair Showcase Hot Hands

HH1 Anquan Boldin .75 2.00
HH2 Bob Sanders 1.00 2.50
HH3 Brian Dawkins 1.25 3.00
HH4 Chad Johnson .75 2.00
HH5 Champ Bailey 1.00 2.50
HH6 Chris Chambers .75 2.00
HH7 Darren Sharper .75 2.00
HH8 DeAngelo Hall .75 2.00
HH9 Donald Driver 1.00 2.50
HH10 Ed Reed 1.00 2.50
HH11 Hines Ward 1.00 2.50
HH12 Javon Walker 1.00 2.50
HH13 Joey Galloway 1.00 2.50
HH14 Ken Lucas .75 2.00
HH15 Larry Fitzgerald 1.00 2.50
HH16 Marvin Harrison 1.00 2.50
HH17 Nathan Vasher .75 2.00
HH18 Plaxico Burress .75 2.00
HH19 Randy Moss 1.00 2.50
HH20 Ronde Barber .75 2.00
HH21 Santana Moss 1.00 2.50
HH22 Steve Smith 1.25 3.00
HH23 Terrell Owens 1.00 2.50
HH24 Torry Holt 1.00 2.50
HH25 Troy Polamalu 1.25 3.00

2006 Flair Showcase Hot Numbers

HN1 Anquan Boldin .75 2.00
HN2 Antonio Gates 1.25 3.00
HN3 Ben Roethlisberger 1.50 4.00
HN4 Brett Favre 2.50 6.00
HN5 Brian Urlacher 1.25 3.00
HN6 Carson Palmer 1.00 2.50
HN7 Chad Johnson .75 2.00
HN8 Champ Bailey 1.00 2.50
HN9 Donovan McNabb 1.00 2.50
HN10 Dwight Freeney .75 2.00
HN11 Edgerrin James 1.00 2.50
HN12 Eli Manning 1.00 2.50
HN13 Julius Peppers 1.00 2.50
HN14 LaDainian Tomlinson 1.25 3.00
HN15 Larry Johnson .75 2.00
HN16 Michael Vick 1.00 2.50
HN17 Peyton Manning 3.00 8.00
HN18 Randy Moss 1.00 2.50
HN19 Santana Moss 1.00 2.50
HN20 Shaun Alexander .75 2.00
HN21 Steve Smith 1.25 3.00
HN22 Terrell Owens 1.00 2.50
HN23 Tiki Barber 1.00 2.50
HN24 Tom Brady 4.00 10.00
HN25 Tony Gonzalez 1.00 2.50

2006 Flair Showcase Lettermen

UNPRICED LETTERMEN PRINT RUN 4-10

2006 Flair Showcase Showcase Stars

SS1 Antonio Gates 1.25 3.00
SS2 Brett Favre 2.50 6.00
SS3 Brian Urlacher 1.25 3.00
SS4 Carson Palmer 1.00 2.50
SS5 Chad Johnson .75 2.00
SS6 Clinton Portis .75 2.00
SS7 Dwight Freeney .75 2.00
SS8 Edgerrin James 1.00 2.50
SS9 LaDainian Tomlinson 1.25 3.00
SS10 Larry Johnson .75 2.00
SS11 Michael Vick 1.00 2.50
SS12 Peyton Manning 3.00 8.00
SS13 Randy Moss 1.00 2.50
SS14 Santana Moss 1.00 2.50
SS15 Shaun Alexander .75 2.00
SS16 Steve Smith 1.25 3.00
SS17 Terrell Owens 1.00 2.50
SS18 Tiki Barber 1.00 2.50
SS19 Tom Brady 4.00 10.00
SS20 Troy Polamalu 1.25 3.00

2006 Flair Showcase Showcase Stitches Jersey

*PATCHES: .8X TO 2X BASIC INSERTS
PATCH PRINT RUN 50 SER.#'d SETS
SHSAC Alge Crumpler 3.00 8.00
SHSAH A.J. Hawk 2.00 5.00
SHSAS Alex Smith QB 3.00 8.00
SHSBC Brian Calhoun 2.50 6.00
SHSBL Byron Leftwich 2.50 6.00
SHSBU Reggie Bush 2.50 6.00
SHSBW Brandon Williams 1.50 4.00
SHSCJ Chad Jackson 2.50 6.00
SHSCW Cadillac Williams 3.00 8.00
SHSDB Drew Bledsoe 3.00 8.00
SHSDH Derek Hagan 2.00 5.00
SHSDM Deuce McAllister 3.00 8.00
SHSDW DeAngelo Williams 2.00 5.00
SHSEJ Edgerrin James 3.00 8.00
SHSJC Jay Cutler 2.00 5.00
SHSJP Jake Plummer 2.50 6.00
SHSJS Jeremy Shockey 2.50 6.00
SHSKJ Kevin Jones 2.50 6.00
SHSKO Kyle Orton 2.50 6.00
SHSLJ Larry Johnson 2.50 6.00
SHSLM Laurence Maroney 1.50 4.00
SHSLW LenDale White 1.50 4.00
SHSMD Maurice Drew 2.50 6.00
SHSMH Michael Huff 2.00 5.00
SHSML Matt Leinart 1.50 4.00
SHSMS Maurice Stovall 1.50 4.00
SHSMW Mario Williams 2.50 6.00
SHSOJ Omar Jacobs 2.50 6.00
SHSPB Plaxico Burress 2.50 6.00
SHSPH Priest Holmes 2.50 6.00
SHSRB Ronnie Brown 3.00 8.00
SHSRM Randy Moss 3.00 8.00
SHSRW Reggie Wayne 3.00 8.00
SHSSH Santonio Holmes 2.00 5.00
SHSSJ Steven Jackson 2.50 6.00
SHSSM Sinorice Moss 1.50 4.00
SHSTB Tatum Bell 2.50 6.00
SHSTJ Tarvaris Jackson 1.50 4.00
SHSTO Terrell Owens 3.00 8.00
SHSTW Troy Williamson 2.50 6.00
SHSVD Vernon Davis 2.00 5.00
SHSVY Vince Young 1.50 4.00

2006 Flair Showcase Wave of the Future

WOTF1 Alex Smith QB 1.25 3.00
WOTF2 Antonio Gates 1.50 4.00
WOTF3 Ben Roethlisberger 2.00 5.00
WOTF4 Braylon Edwards 1.00 2.50
WOTF5 Cadillac Williams 1.25 3.00
WOTF6 Chad Jackson 1.00 2.50
WOTF7 Chris Simms 1.00 2.50
WOTF8 Eli Manning 1.25 3.00
WOTF9 Jay Cutler .60 1.50
WOTF10 Joseph Addai .50 1.25
WOTF11 Julius Jones 1.00 2.50
WOTF12 Kellen Clemens 1.00 2.00
WOTF13 Kevin Jones 1.00 2.50
WOTF14 Larry Fitzgerald 1.25 3.00
WOTF15 Larry Johnson 1.00 2.50
WOTF16 Laurence Maroney .50 1.25
WOTF17 LenDale White .50 1.25
WOTF18 Lofa Tatupu 1.00 2.50
WOTF19 Mario Williams .75 2.00
WOTF20 Matt Leinart .50 1.25
WOTF21 Philip Rivers 1.50 4.00
WOTF22 Reggie Bush .75 2.00
WOTF23 Ronnie Brown 1.25 3.00
WOTF24 Santonio Holmes .60 1.50
WOTF25 Shawne Merriman 1.25 3.00
WOTF26 Steven Jackson 1.00 2.50
WOTF27 Tatum Bell 1.00 2.50
WOTF28 Vernon Davis .60 1.50
WOTF29 Vince Young .50 1.25
WOTF30 Willie Parker 1.25 3.00

2014 Flair Showcase

COMP.SET w/o SP's (150) 20.00 40.00
ROW 0 SP STATED ODDS 1:3 PACKS
1 Marqise Lee R2 .40 1.00
2 Johnny Manziel R2 .50 1.25
3 Ka'Deem Carey R2 .30 .75
4 Darqueze Dennard R2 .40 1.00
5 Sammy Watkins R2 .50 1.25
6 Ha Ha Clinton-Dix R2 .40 1.00
7 Brandon Coleman R2 .30 .75
8 James White R2 .60 1.50
9 Yawin Smallwood R2 .30 .75
10 Teddy Bridgewater R2 .50 1.25
11 Martavis Bryant R2 .40 1.00
12 Carlos Hyde R2 .40 1.00
13 Jalen Saunders R2 .30 .75
14 Khalil Mack R2 1.25 3.00
15 Mike Evans R2 .75 2.00
16 Jake Matthews R2 .30 .75
17 Cody Latimer R2 .40 1.00
18 James Wilder Jr. R2 .40 1.00
19 Mike Flacco R2 .30 .75
20 Blake Bortles R2 .40 1.00
21 Jared Abbrederis R2 .30 .75
22 Jeremy Hill R2 .40 1.00
23 Jeff Janis R2 .30 .75
24 Stephon Tuitt R2 .50 1.25
25 Eric Ebron R2 .40 1.00
26 Chris Borland R2 .30 .75
27 Kevin Norwood R2 .30 .75
28 Marion Grice R2 .30 .75
29 Jace Amaro R2 .30 .75
30 Aaron Murray R2 .30 .75
31 Robert Herron R2 .30 .75
32 Devonta Freeman R2 .50 1.25
33 Antonio Richardson R2 .50 1.25
34 Ross Cockrell R2 .30 .75
35 Kelvin Benjamin R2 .50 1.25
36 Logan Thomas R2 .30 .75
37 Cody Hoffman R2 .30 .75
38 Antonio Andrews R2 .30 .75
39 Dominique Easley R2 .30 .75
40 Tom Savage R2 .30 .75
41 Donte Moncrief R2 .30 .75
42 Lache Seastrunk R2 .30 .75
43 Josh Stewart R2 .50 1.25
44 Anthony Barr R2 .30 .75
45 Odell Beckham Jr. R2 .75 2.00
46 Dee Ford R2 .30 .75
47 Tevin Reese R2 .30 .75
48 George Atkinson III R2 .30 .75
49 Stanley Jean-Baptiste R2 .60 1.50
50 Brett Smith R2 .30 .75
51 Josh Huff R2 .40 1.00
52 Stephen Morris R2 .30 .75
53 Shaquelle Evans R2 .30 .75
54 Shayne Skov R2 .30 .75
55 Allen Robinson R2 .50 1.25
56 Dion Bailey R2 .30 .75
57 Matt Hazel R2 .30 .75
58 De'Anthony Thomas R2 .30 .75
59 Austin Seferian-Jenkins R2 .30 .75
60 Derek Carr R2 2.00 5.00
61 Bruce Ellington R2 .30 .75
62 Bishop Sankey R2 .30 .75
63 Dri Archer R2 .30 .75
64 Ryan Shazier R2 .50 1.25
65 Brandin Cooks R2 .50 1.25
66 Zack Martin R2 .40 1.00
67 Quincy Enunwa R2 .50 1.25
68 Tyler Gaffney R2 .30 .75
69 Ryan Hewitt R2 .30 .75
70 Jimmy Garoppolo R2 2.50 6.00
71 Mike Davis R2 .30 .75
72 Rajion Neal R2 .30 .75
73 Isaiah Burse R2 .30 .75
74 Bashaud Breeland R2 .30 .75
75 Paul Richardson R2 .40 1.00
76 Ego Ferguson R2 .30 .75
77 Austin Franklin R2 .40 1.00
78 Silas Redd R2 .40 1.00
79 Marcel Jensen R2 .30 .75
80 Zach Mettenberger R2 .30 .75
81 Ryan Grant R2 .30 .75
82 Terrance West R2 .30 .75
83 Trey Burton R2 .30 .75
84 Victor Hampton R2 .40 1.00
85 Davante Adams R2 .50 1.25
86 Kyle Van Noy R2 .40 1.00
87 Derel Walker R2 .40 1.00
88 Kapri Bibbs R2 .40 1.00
89 Arthur Lynch R2 .30 .75
90 David Fales R2 .30 .75
91 TJ Jones R2 .50 1.25
92 Charles Sims R2 .30 .75
93 Noel Grigsby R2 .30 .75
94 Terrence Brooks R2 .30 .75
95 Jarvis Landry R2 .60 1.50
96 Weston Richburg R2 .30 .75
97 Ryan Lankford R2 .30 .75
98 Andre Williams R2 .30 .75
99 Devin Street R2 .30 .75
100 Tajh Boyd R2 .30 .75
101 Teddy Bridgewater R1 .50 1.25
102 Blake Bortles R1 .40 1.00
103 Johnny Manziel R1 .50 1.25
104 Jimmy Garoppolo R1 2.50 6.00
105 Zach Mettenberger R1 .30 .75
106 Derek Carr R1 2.00 5.00
107 Aaron Murray R1 .30 .75
108 David Fales R1 .30 .75
109 Brett Smith R1 .30 .75
110 Tajh Boyd R1 .30 .75
111 Tom Savage R1 .30 .75
112 Logan Thomas R1 .30 .75
113 Stephen Morris R1 .30 .75
114 Sammy Watkins R1 .50 1.25
115 Marqise Lee R1 .40 1.00
116 Mike Evans R1 .75 2.00
117 Kelvin Benjamin R1 .50 1.25
118 Allen Robinson R1 .50 1.25
119 Odell Beckham Jr. R1 .75 2.00
120 Brandin Cooks R1 .50 1.25
121 Cody Latimer R1 .40 1.00
122 Martavis Bryant R1 .40 1.00
123 Paul Richardson R1 .40 1.00
124 Davante Adams R1 .50 1.25
125 Jarvis Landry R1 .60 1.50
126 Josh Huff R1 .40 1.00
127 Jared Abbrederis R1 .30 .75
128 Bruce Ellington R1 .30 .75
129 Donte Moncrief R1 .30 .75
130 Kevin Norwood R1 .30 .75
131 Devin Street R1 .30 .75
132 TJ Jones R1 .50 1.25
133 Dri Archer R1 .30 .75
134 Carlos Hyde R1 .40 1.00
135 Ka'Deem Carey R1 .30 .75
136 Lache Seastrunk R1 .30 .75
137 Terrance West R1 .30 .75
138 Andre Williams R1 .30 .75
139 Charles Sims R1 .30 .75
140 Devonta Freeman R1 .50 1.25
141 Jeremy Hill R1 .40 1.00
142 Bishop Sankey R1 .30 .75
143 James White R1 .60 1.50
144 De'Anthony Thomas R1 .30 .75
145 Jerick Mckinnon R1 .40 1.00
146 James Wilder Jr. R1 .40 1.00
147 Marion Grice R1 .30 .75
148 Eric Ebron R1 .40 1.00
149 Jace Amaro R1 .30 .75
150 Austin Seferian-Jenkins R1 .30 .75
151 Blake Bortles R0 .60 1.50
152 Mike Evans R0 1.25 3.00
153 Logan Thomas R0 .50 1.25
154 Eric Ebron R0 .60 1.50
155 Teddy Bridgewater R0 .75 2.00
156 Ka'Deem Carey R0 .50 1.25
157 Tom Savage R0 .50 1.25
158 Odell Beckham Jr. R0 1.25 3.00
159 Carlos Hyde R0 .60 1.50
160 Johnny Manziel R0 .75 2.00
161 Sammy Watkins R0 .75 2.00
162 De'Anthony Thomas R0 .50 1.25
163 Allen Robinson R0 .75 2.00
164 Jeremy Hill R0 .60 1.50
165 Aaron Murray R0 .50 1.25
166 Marqise Lee R0 .60 1.50
167 Charles Sims R0 .50 1.25
168 Davante Adams R0 .75 2.00
169 Bishop Sankey R0 .50 1.25
170 Derek Carr R0 3.00 8.00
171 Kelvin Benjamin R0 .75 2.00
172 Jace Amaro R0 .50 1.25
173 Cody Latimer R0 .60 1.50
174 Brandin Cooks R0 .75 2.00
175 Jimmy Garoppolo R0 4.00 10.00
176 John Elway R0 1.25 3.00
177 Barry Sanders R0 1.25 3.00
178 Joe Montana R0 2.00 5.00
179 LaDainian Tomlinson R0 .60 1.50
180 Peyton Manning R0 1.50 4.00
181 Bo Jackson R0 1.00 2.50
182 Ben Roethlisberger R0 .75 2.00
183 Jerome Bettis R0 .75 2.00
184 Steve Young R0 1.00 2.50
185 Archie Griffin R0 .50 1.25
186 Matthew Stafford R0 .60 1.50
187 Eric Dickerson R0 .60 1.50
188 Joe Namath R0 1.00 2.50
189 Thurman Thomas R0 .60 1.50
190 Bart Starr R0 1.25 3.00
191 Earl Campbell R0 .75 2.00
192 Dan Fouts R0 .60 1.50
193 Jerry Rice R0 1.25 3.00
194 Warren Moon R0 .75 2.00
195 Tim Brown R0 .75 2.00
196 Drew Brees R0 .75 2.00
197 Roger Craig R0 .60 1.50
198 Terrell Davis R0 .30 .75
199 Joe Theismann R0 .75 2.00
200 Tedy Bruschi R0 .60 1.50

2014 Flair Showcase Legacy

*LEGACY/150: 1.5X TO 4X BASIC ROW 2
*LEGACY/100: 2X TO 5X BASIC ROW 1
*LEGACY/50: 1.5X TO 4X BASIC ROW 0 SP
OVERALL STATED ODDS 1:6 PACKS
119 Odell Beckham Jr. R1 15.00 40.00
177 Barry Sanders R0 12.00 30.00
178 Joe Montana R0 12.00 30.00
180 Peyton Manning R0 30.00 60.00
181 Bo Jackson R0 8.00 20.00
188 Joe Namath R0 10.00 25.00
193 Jerry Rice R0 10.00 25.00

2014 Flair Showcase Autographs

1-100 STATED ODDS 1:10
101-150 STATED ODDS 1:48
151-175 STATED ODDS 1:144
176-200 STATED ODDS 1:288
OVERALL STATED ODDS 1:12
1 Marqise Lee R2 3.00 8.00
2 Johnny Manziel R2 4.00 10.00
3 Ka'Deem Carey R2 6.00 15.00
4 Darqueze Dennard R2 3.00 8.00
5 Sammy Watkins R2 4.00 10.00
6 Ha Ha Clinton-Dix R2
7 Brandon Coleman R2
8 James White R2
9 Yawin Smallwood R2 2.50 6.00
10 Teddy Bridgewater R2 4.00 10.00
11 Martavis Bryant R2 3.00 8.00
12 Carlos Hyde R2 3.00 8.00
13 Jalen Saunders R2 5.00 12.00
14 Khalil Mack R2 10.00 25.00
15 Mike Evans R2 6.00 15.00
16 Jake Matthews R2
17 Cody Latimer R2 6.00 15.00
18 James Wilder Jr. R2
19 Mike Flacco R2 2.50 6.00
20 Blake Bortles R2 3.00 8.00
21 Jared Abbrederis R2 2.50 6.00
22 Jeremy Hill R2
23 Jeff Janis R2 6.00 15.00
24 Stephon Tuitt R2
25 Eric Ebron R2 3.00 8.00
26 Chris Borland R2 2.50 6.00
27 Kevin Norwood R2 2.50 6.00
28 Marion Grice R2 2.50 6.00
29 Jace Amaro R2
30 Aaron Murray R2 2.50 6.00
31 Robert Herron R2
32 Devonta Freeman R2 8.00 20.00
33 Antonio Richardson R2 4.00 10.00
34 Ross Cockrell R2 2.50 6.00
35 Kelvin Benjamin R2 4.00 10.00
36 Logan Thomas R2
37 Cody Hoffman R2 2.50 6.00
38 Antonio Andrews R2 2.50 6.00
39 Dominique Easley R2 2.50 6.00
40 Tom Savage R2
41 Donte Moncrief R2 2.50 6.00
42 Lache Seastrunk R2 2.50 6.00
43 Josh Stewart R2 4.00 10.00
44 Anthony Barr R2 2.50 6.00
45 Odell Beckham Jr. R2
46 Dee Ford R2 2.50 6.00
47 Tevin Reese R2 2.50 6.00
48 George Atkinson III R2
49 Stanley Jean-Baptiste R2 5.00 12.00
50 Brett Smith R2 2.50 6.00
51 Josh Huff R2
52 Stephen Morris R2 2.50 6.00
53 Shaquelle Evans R2 2.50 6.00
54 Shayne Skov R2 2.50 6.00
55 Allen Robinson R2 4.00 10.00
56 Dion Bailey R2 2.50 6.00
57 Matt Hazel R2 2.50 6.00
58 De'Anthony Thomas R2 2.50 6.00
59 Austin Seferian-Jenkins R2
60 Derek Carr R2 30.00 80.00
61 Bruce Ellington R2
62 Bishop Sankey R2 10.00 25.00
63 Dri Archer R2 2.50 6.00
64 Ryan Shazier R2 4.00 10.00
65 Brandin Cooks R2 15.00 40.00
66 Zack Martin R2
67 Quincy Enunwa R2
68 Tyler Gaffney R2
69 Ryan Hewitt R2 2.50 6.00
70 Jimmy Garoppolo R2 40.00 80.00
71 Mike Davis R2
72 Rajion Neal R2 2.50 6.00
73 Isaiah Burse R2
74 Bashaud Breeland R2 5.00 12.00
75 Paul Richardson R2
76 Ego Ferguson R2
77 Austin Franklin R2
78 Silas Redd R2 5.00 12.00
79 Marcel Jensen R2 2.50 6.00
80 Zach Mettenberger R2 2.50 6.00
81 Ryan Grant R2 5.00 12.00
82 Terrance West R2 8.00 20.00
83 Trey Burton R2 2.50 6.00
84 Victor Hampton R2
85 Davante Adams R2
86 Kyle Van Noy R2
87 Derel Walker R2 3.00 8.00
88 Kapri Bibbs R2
89 Arthur Lynch R2
90 David Fales R2 2.50 6.00
91 TJ Jones R2
92 Charles Sims R2
93 Noel Grigsby R2 2.50 6.00
94 Terrence Brooks R2
95 Jarvis Landry R2
96 Weston Richburg R2 2.50 6.00
97 Ryan Lankford R2 2.50 6.00
98 Andre Williams R2
99 Devin Street R2 6.00 15.00
100 Tajh Boyd R2
101 Teddy Bridgewater R1
102 Blake Bortles R1 4.00 10.00
103 Johnny Manziel R1 5.00 12.00
104 Jimmy Garoppolo R1 40.00 80.00
105 Zach Mettenberger R1 3.00 8.00
106 Derek Carr R1 30.00 80.00
107 Aaron Murray R1 3.00 8.00
108 David Fales R1 3.00 8.00
109 Brett Smith R1 4.00 10.00
110 Tajh Boyd R1 3.00 8.00
111 Tom Savage R1
112 Logan Thomas R1 3.00 8.00
113 Stephen Morris R1 3.00 8.00
114 Sammy Watkins R1 5.00 12.00
115 Marqise Lee R1
116 Mike Evans R1 8.00 20.00
117 Kelvin Benjamin R1 5.00 12.00
118 Allen Robinson R1 5.00 12.00
119 Odell Beckham Jr. R1
120 Brandin Cooks R1
121 Cody Latimer R1 4.00 10.00
122 Martavis Bryant R1 4.00 10.00
123 Paul Richardson R1 6.00 15.00
124 Davante Adams R1
125 Jarvis Landry R1 6.00 15.00
126 Josh Huff R1 4.00 10.00
127 Jared Abbrederis R1 3.00 8.00
128 Bruce Ellington R1
129 Donte Moncrief R1 3.00 8.00
130 Kevin Norwood R1 3.00 8.00
131 Devin Street R1 3.00 8.00
132 TJ Jones R1
133 Dri Archer R1 3.00 8.00
134 Carlos Hyde R1 4.00 10.00
135 Ka'Deem Carey R1 3.00 8.00
136 Lache Seastrunk R1 3.00 8.00
137 Terrance West R1 8.00 20.00
138 Andre Williams R1
139 Charles Sims R1
140 Devonta Freeman R1 10.00 25.00
141 Jeremy Hill R1 4.00 10.00
142 Bishop Sankey R1 10.00 25.00
143 James White R1 6.00 15.00
144 De'Anthony Thomas R1 3.00 8.00
145 Jerick Mckinnon R1 4.00 10.00
146 James Wilder Jr. R1 4.00 10.00
147 Marion Grice R1 3.00 8.00
148 Eric Ebron R1
149 Jace Amaro R1 3.00 8.00
150 Austin Seferian-Jenkins R1 3.00 8.00
151 Blake Bortles R0 5.00 12.00
152 Mike Evans R0 10.00 25.00
153 Logan Thomas R0 6.00 15.00
154 Eric Ebron R0 6.00 15.00
155 Teddy Bridgewater R0 6.00 15.00
156 Ka'Deem Carey R0 5.00 12.00
157 Tom Savage R0
158 Odell Beckham Jr. R0 40.00 80.00
159 Carlos Hyde R0 5.00 12.00
160 Johnny Manziel R0 6.00 15.00
161 Sammy Watkins R0 6.00 15.00
162 De'Anthony Thomas R0 4.00 10.00
163 Allen Robinson R0 6.00 15.00
164 Jeremy Hill R0 5.00 12.00
165 Aaron Murray R0 4.00 10.00
166 Marqise Lee R0
167 Charles Sims R0
168 Davante Adams R0 6.00 15.00
169 Bishop Sankey R0 10.00 25.00
170 Derek Carr R0 20.00 40.00
171 Kelvin Benjamin R0 6.00 15.00
172 Jace Amaro R0 4.00 10.00
173 Cody Latimer R0
174 Brandin Cooks R0 8.00 20.00
175 Jimmy Garoppolo R0 40.00 80.00
176 John Elway R0 50.00 100.00
177 Barry Sanders R0
178 Joe Montana R0
179 LaDainian Tomlinson R0 20.00 40.00
180 Peyton Manning R0
181 Bo Jackson R0 50.00 100.00
182 Ben Roethlisberger R0
183 Jerome Bettis R0 40.00 80.00
184 Steve Young R0 12.00 30.00
185 Archie Griffin R0
186 Matthew Stafford R0 20.00 40.00
187 Eric Dickerson R0 20.00 40.00
188 Joe Namath R0 40.00 80.00
189 Thurman Thomas R0 8.00 20.00
190 Bart Starr R0
191 Earl Campbell R0 10.00 25.00
192 Dan Fouts R0 20.00 40.00
193 Jerry Rice R0 50.00 100.00
194 Warren Moon R0 10.00 25.00
195 Tim Brown R0
196 Drew Brees R0
197 Roger Craig R0 8.00 20.00
198 Terrell Davis R0 4.00 10.00
199 Joe Theismann R0 10.00 25.00
200 Tedy Bruschi R0 8.00 20.00

2014 Flair Showcase Jambalaya

STATED ODDS 1:144
1 Johnny Manziel 15.00 40.00
2 Sammy Watkins 40.00 80.00
3 Joe Montana 40.00 100.00
4 Derek Carr 30.00 60.00

5 Blake Bortles 12.00 30.00
6 Jerry Rice 25.00 60.00
7 John Elway 40.00 80.00
8 Ben Roethlisberger 20.00 50.00
9 Marqise Lee 12.00 30.00
10 Joe Namath 30.00 60.00
11 Eric Ebron 12.00 30.00
12 Jimmy Garoppolo 80.00 200.00
13 Dan Marino 30.00 80.00
14 Matthew Stafford 12.00 30.00
15 Drew Brees 25.00 50.00
16 Peyton Manning 75.00 150.00
17 Barry Sanders 25.00 60.00
18 Bishop Sankey 10.00 25.00
19 Bo Jackson 50.00 100.00
20 Mike Evans 25.00 60.00
21 Teddy Bridgewater 15.00 40.00

2014 Flair Showcase Jerseys

101-150 STATED ODDS 1:18
151-175 STATED ODDS 1:48
176-200 STATED ODDS 1:96
OVERALL STATED ODDS 1:12
101 Teddy Bridgewater R1 2.00 5.00
102 Blake Bortles R1 1.50 4.00
103 Johnny Manziel R1 2.00 5.00
104 Jimmy Garoppolo R1 10.00 25.00
105 Zach Mettenberger R1 1.25 3.00
106 Derek Carr R1 4.00 10.00
107 Aaron Murray R1 1.25 3.00
110 Tajh Boyd R1 1.25 3.00
111 Tom Savage R1 1.25 3.00
112 Logan Thomas R1 1.25 3.00
113 Stephen Morris R1 2.00 5.00
114 Sammy Watkins R1 4.00 10.00
115 Marqise Lee R1 1.50 4.00
116 Mike Evans R1 3.00 8.00
117 Kelvin Benjamin R1 2.00 5.00
118 Allen Robinson R1 2.00 5.00
119 Odell Beckham Jr. R1 3.00 8.00
120 Brandin Cooks R1 2.00 5.00
122 Martavis Bryant R1 1.50 4.00
123 Paul Richardson R1 1.50 4.00
124 Davante Adams R1 2.00 5.00
125 Jarvis Landry R1 2.50 6.00
126 Josh Huff R1 1.50 4.00
127 Jared Abbrederis R1 1.25 3.00
128 Bruce Ellington R1 1.25 3.00
129 Donte Moncrief R1 1.25 3.00
134 Carlos Hyde R1 1.50 4.00
135 Ka'Deem Carey R1 1.25 3.00
136 Lache Seastrunk R1 1.25 3.00
137 Terrance West R1 1.25 3.00
138 Andre Williams R1 1.25 3.00
139 Charles Sims R1 1.25 3.00
140 Devonta Freeman R1 2.00 5.00
141 Jeremy Hill R1 1.50 4.00
142 Bishop Sankey R1 1.25 3.00
143 James White R1 2.50 6.00
144 De'Anthony Thomas R1 1.25 3.00
146 James Wilder Jr. R1 1.50 4.00
147 Marion Grice R1 1.25 3.00
148 Eric Ebron R1 1.50 4.00
149 Jace Amaro R1 1.25 3.00
150 Austin Seferian-Jenkins R1 1.25 3.00
151 Blake Bortles R0 2.00 5.00
152 Mike Evans R0 4.00 10.00
153 Logan Thomas R0 1.50 4.00
154 Eric Ebron R0 2.00 5.00
155 Teddy Bridgewater R0 2.50 6.00
156 Ka'Deem Carey R0 1.50 4.00
157 Tom Savage R0 1.50 4.00
158 Odell Beckham Jr. R0 4.00 10.00
159 Carlos Hyde R0 2.00 5.00
160 Johnny Manziel R0 2.50 6.00
161 Sammy Watkins R0 5.00 12.00
162 De'Anthony Thomas R0 1.50 4.00
163 Allen Robinson R0 2.50 6.00
164 Jeremy Hill R0 2.00 5.00
165 Aaron Murray R0 1.50 4.00
166 Marqise Lee R0 2.00 5.00
167 Charles Sims R0 1.50 4.00
168 Davante Adams R0 2.50 6.00
169 Bishop Sankey R0 1.50 4.00
170 Derek Carr R0 5.00 12.00
171 Kelvin Benjamin R0 2.50 6.00
172 Jace Amaro R0 1.50 4.00
174 Brandin Cooks R0 2.50 6.00
175 Jimmy Garoppolo R0 12.00 30.00
176 John Elway R0 8.00 20.00
177 Barry Sanders R0 12.00 30.00
178 Joe Montana R0 12.00 30.00
180 Peyton Manning R0 10.00 25.00
181 Bo Jackson R0 12.00 30.00
183 Jerome Bettis R0 5.00 12.00
184 Steve Young R0 6.00 15.00
185 Archie Griffin R0 3.00 8.00
186 Matthew Stafford R0 4.00 10.00
187 Eric Dickerson R0 4.00 10.00
188 Joe Namath R0 6.00 15.00
189 Thurman Thomas R0 5.00 12.00
190 Bart Starr R0 8.00 20.00
191 Earl Campbell R0 5.00 12.00
192 Dan Fouts R0 4.00 10.00
193 Jerry Rice R0 12.00 30.00
194 Warren Moon R0 10.00 25.00
195 Tim Brown R0 5.00 12.00
196 Drew Brees R0 5.00 12.00
197 Roger Craig R0 4.00 10.00
198 Terrell Davis R0 3.00 8.00
199 Joe Theismann R0 5.00 12.00
200 Tedy Bruschi R0 4.00 10.00

2014 Flair Showcase Metal Universe

STATED ODDS 1:4
M1 Johnny Manziel .60 1.50
M2 Sammy Watkins .60 1.50
M3 Blake Bortles .50 1.25
M4 Odell Beckham Jr. 1.00 2.50
M5 Peyton Manning 1.25 3.00
M6 Mike Evans 1.00 2.50
M7 Logan Thomas .40 1.00
M8 Davante Adams .60 1.50
M9 Bishop Sankey .40 1.00
M10 Joe Montana 1.50 4.00
M11 Brandin Cooks .60 1.50
M12 Tom Savage .40 1.00
M13 Cody Latimer .50 1.25
M14 Teddy Bridgewater .60 1.50
M15 Barry Sanders 1.00 2.50
M16 Aaron Murray .40 1.00
M17 Kelvin Benjamin .60 1.50
M18 Jimmy Garoppolo 3.00 8.00
M19 Charles Sims .40 1.00
M20 Dan Marino 1.25 3.00
M21 Allen Robinson .60 1.50
M22 Zach Mettenberger .40 1.00
M23 Carlos Hyde .50 1.25
M24 Eric Ebron .50 1.25
M25 Matthew Stafford .50 1.25
M26 Marqise Lee .50 1.25
M27 Jeremy Hill .50 1.25
M28 Tajh Boyd .40 1.00
M29 Paul Richardson .50 1.25
M30 Derek Carr 2.50 6.00

2014 Flair Showcase Metal Universe Precious Metal Gems Magenta

*SINGLES: 5X TO 12X BASIC INSERTS
M5 Peyton Manning 50.00 100.00
M10 Joe Montana 40.00 80.00
M20 Dan Marino 40.00 80.00

2014 Flair Showcase Metal Universe Precious Metal Gems Teal

*TEAL/100: 2.5X TO 6X BASIC INSERTS
M5 Peyton Manning 20.00 50.00

2014 Flair Showcase Patch Autographs

STATED PRINT RUN 5-125
UNPRICED PRINT RUN 5-15
101 Teddy Bridgewater/25 12.00 30.00
102 Blake Bortles/25 10.00 25.00
103 Johnny Manziel/25 12.00 30.00
104 Jimmy Garoppolo/125 12.00 30.00
105 Zach Mettenberger/125 5.00 12.00
106 Derek Carr/125 20.00 50.00
107 Aaron Murray/125 5.00 12.00
110 Tajh Boyd/125
111 Tom Savage/125 5.00 12.00
112 Logan Thomas/125 5.00 12.00
114 Sammy Watkins/25 12.00 30.00
115 Marqise Lee/125 6.00 15.00
116 Mike Evans/25 20.00 50.00
117 Kelvin Benjamin/125 8.00 20.00
118 Allen Robinson/125 8.00 20.00
119 Odell Beckham Jr./125 40.00 80.00
120 Brandin Cooks/125
122 Martavis Bryant/125 6.00 15.00
123 Paul Richardson/125 10.00 25.00
124 Davante Adams/125 8.00 20.00
125 Jarvis Landry/125 10.00 25.00
126 Josh Huff/125 6.00 15.00
127 Jared Abbrederis/125 5.00 12.00
128 Bruce Ellington/125
129 Donte Moncrief/125 5.00 12.00
134 Carlos Hyde/125 6.00 15.00
135 Ka'Deem Carey/125 6.00 15.00
136 Lache Seastrunk/125 6.00 15.00
137 Terrance West/125 5.00 12.00
139 Charles Sims/125
140 Devonta Freeman/125 15.00 40.00
141 Jeremy Hill/125 6.00 15.00
142 Bishop Sankey/125 5.00 12.00
148 Eric Ebron/125 6.00 15.00
151 Blake Bortles/15 15.00 40.00
152 Mike Evans/15 25.00 60.00
153 Logan Thomas/49 6.00 15.00
154 Eric Ebron/49 8.00 20.00
155 Teddy Bridgewater/15 15.00 40.00
156 Ka'Deem Carey/49 8.00 20.00
157 Tom Savage/49 6.00 15.00
158 Odell Beckham Jr./49 40.00 100.00
159 Carlos Hyde/49 8.00 20.00
161 Sammy Watkins/15
162 De'Anthony Thomas/49 6.00 15.00
163 Allen Robinson/49 10.00 25.00
164 Jeremy Hill/49 8.00 20.00
165 Aaron Murray/49 6.00 15.00
166 Marqise Lee/49 8.00 20.00
167 Charles Sims/49
168 Davante Adams/49 10.00 25.00
169 Bishop Sankey/49 6.00 15.00
170 Derek Carr/49 40.00 100.00
171 Kelvin Benjamin/49 10.00 25.00
172 Jace Amaro/49
174 Brandin Cooks/49
175 Jimmy Garoppolo/49 50.00 125.00

1960 Fleer

The 1960 Fleer set of 132 standard-size cards was Fleer's first venture into football card production. This set features players of the American Football League's debut season. Several well-known coaches are featured in the set; the set is the last regular issue set to feature coaches (on their own specific card) until the 1989 Pro Set release. The card backs are printed in red and black. The key card in the set is Jack Kemp's Rookie Card. Other Rookie Cards include Sid Gillman, Ron Mix and Hank Stram. The cards are frequently found off-centered as Fleer's first effort into the football card market left much to be desired in the area of quality control. A large quantity of color separations and "proofs" are widely available.

COMPLETE SET (132) 500.00 750.00
WRAPPER (5-CENT) 20.00 25.00
1 Harvey White RC 12.00 20.00
2 Tom Corky Tharp RC 2.00 4.00
3 Dan McGrew RC 2.00 4.00
4 Bob White RC 2.00 4.00
5 Dick Jamieson RC 2.00 4.00
6 Sam Salerno RC 2.00 4.00
7 Sid Gillman CO RC 12.00 20.00
8 Ben Preston RC 2.00 4.00
9 George Blanch RC 2.00 4.00
10 Bob Stransky RC 2.00 4.00
11 Fran Curci RC 2.00 4.00
12 George Shirkey RC 2.00 4.00
13 Paul Larson 2.00 4.00
14 John Stolte RC 2.00 4.00
15 Serafino Fazio RC 2.50 5.00
16 Tom Dimitroff RC 2.00 4.00
17 Elbert Dubenion RC 6.00 12.00
18 Hogan Wharton RC 2.00 4.00
19 Tom O'Connell 2.00 4.00
20 Sammy Baugh CO 25.00 40.00
21 Tony Sardisco RC 2.00 4.00
22 Alan Cann RC 2.00 4.00
23 Mike Hudock RC 2.00 4.00
24 Bill Atkins RC 2.00 4.00
25 Charlie Jackson RC 2.00 4.00
26 Frank Tripucka 3.00 6.00
27 Tony Teresa RC 2.00 4.00
28 Joe Amstutz RC 2.00 4.00
29 Bob Fee RC 2.00 4.00
30 Jim Baldwin RC 2.00 4.00
31 Jim Yates RC 2.00 4.00
32 Don Flynn RC 2.00 4.00
33 Ken Adamson RC 2.00 4.00
34 Ron Drzewiecki 2.00 4.00
35 J.W. Slack RC 2.00 4.00
36 Bob Yates RC 2.00 4.00
37 Gary Cobb RC 2.00 4.00
38 Jacky Lee RC 2.50 5.00
39 Jack Spikes RC 2.50 5.00
40 Jim Padgett RC 2.00 4.00
41 Jack Larscheid UER RC 2.00 4.00
42 Bob Reifsnyder RC 2.00 4.00
43 Fran Rogel 2.00 4.00
44 Ray Moss RC 2.00 4.00
45 Tony Banfield RC 2.50 5.00
46 George Herring RC 2.00 4.00
47 Willie Smith RC 2.00 4.00
48 Buddy Allen RC 2.00 4.00
49 Bill Brown LB RC 2.00 4.00
50 Ken Ford RC 2.00 4.00
51 Billy Kinard RC 2.00 4.00
52 Buddy Mayfield RC 2.00 4.00
53 Bill Krisher RC 2.00 4.00
54 Frank Bernardi RC 2.00 4.00
55 Lou Saban CO RC 2.50 5.00
56 Gene Cockrell RC 2.00 4.00
57 Sam Sanders RC 2.00 4.00
58 George Blanda 30.00 50.00
59 Sherrill Headrick RC 2.50 5.00
60 Carl Larpenter RC 2.00 4.00
61 Gene Prebola RC 2.00 4.00
62 Dick Chorovich RC 2.00 4.00
63 Bob McNamara RC 2.00 4.00
64 Tom Saidock RC 2.00 4.00
65 Willie Evans RC 2.00 4.00
66 Billy Cannon RC UER 10.00 20.00
67 Sam McCord RC 2.00 4.00
68 Mike Simmons RC 2.00 4.00
69 Jim Swink RC 2.50 5.00
70 Don Hitt RC 2.00 4.00
71 Gerhard Schwedes RC 2.00 4.00
72 Thurlow Cooper RC 2.00 4.00
73 Abner Haynes RC 10.00 20.00
74 Billy Shoemake RC 2.00 4.00
75 Marv Lasater RC 2.00 4.00
76 Paul Lowe RC 7.50 15.00
77 Bruce Hartman RC 2.00 4.00
78 Blanche Martin RC 2.00 4.00
79 Gene Grabosky RC 2.00 4.00
80 Lou Rymkus CO 2.50 5.00
81 Chris Burford RC 4.00 8.00
82 Don Allen RC 2.00 4.00
83 Bob Nelson C RC 2.00 4.00
84 Jim Woodard RC 2.00 4.00
85 Tom Rychlec RC 2.00 4.00
86 Bob Cox RC 2.00 4.00
87 Jerry Cornelison RC 2.00 4.00
88 Jack Work 2.00 4.00
89 Sam DeLuca RC 2.00 4.00
90 Rommie Loudd RC 2.00 4.00
91 Teddy Edmondson RC 2.00 4.00
92 Buster Ramsey CO 2.00 4.00
93 Doug Asad RC 2.00 4.00
94 Jimmy Harris 2.00 4.00
95 Larry Cundiff RC 2.00 4.00
96 Richie Lucas RC 3.00 6.00
97 Don Norwood RC 2.00 4.00
98 Larry Grantham RC 2.50 5.00
99 Bill Mathis RC 3.00 6.00
100 Mel Branch RC 2.50 5.00
101 Marvin Terrell RC 2.00 4.00
102 Charlie Flowers RC 2.00 4.00
103 John McMullan RC 2.00 4.00
104 Charlie Kaaihue RC 2.00 4.00
105 Joe Schaffer RC 2.00 4.00
106 Al Day RC 2.00 4.00
107 Johnny Carson 2.00 4.00
108 Alan Goldstein RC 2.00 4.00
109 Doug Cline RC 2.00 4.00
110 Al Carmichael 2.00 4.00
111 Bob Dee RC 2.00 4.00
112 John Bredice RC 2.00 4.00
113 Don Floyd RC 2.00 4.00
114 Ronnie Cain RC 2.00 4.00
115 Stan Flowers RC 2.00 4.00
116 Hank Stram CO RC 25.00 40.00
117 Bob Dougherty RC 2.00 4.00
118 Ron Mix RC 25.00 40.00
119 Roger Ellis RC 2.00 4.00
120 Elvin Caldwell RC 2.00 4.00
121 Bill Kimber RC 2.00 4.00
122 Jim Matheny RC 2.00 4.00
123 Curley Johnson RC 2.00 4.00
124 Jack Kemp RC 60.00 120.00
125 Ed Denk RC 2.00 4.00
126 Jerry McFarland RC 2.00 4.00
127 Dan Lanphear RC 2.00 4.00
128 Paul Maguire RC 10.00 18.00
129 Ray Collins 2.00 4.00
130 Ron Burton RC 3.00 6.00
131 Eddie Erdelatz CO RC 2.00 4.00
132 Ron Beagle RC ! 7.50 15.00

1960 Fleer AFL Team Decals

This set of nine logo decals was inserted with the 1960 Fleer regular issue inaugural AFL football set. These inserts measure approximately 2 1/4" by 3" and one decal was to be inserted in each wax pack. The decals are unnumbered and are ordered below alphabetically by team name for convenience. There is one decal for each of the eight AFL teams as well as a decal with the league logo. The backs of the decal backing contained instructions on the proper application of the decal.

COMPLETE SET (9) 100.00 200.00
1 AFL Logo 12.50 25.00
2 Boston Patriots 10.00 20.00
3 Buffalo Bills 12.50 25.00
4 Dallas Texans 15.00 30.00
5 Denver Broncos 12.50 25.00
6 Houston Oilers 12.50 25.00
7 Los Angeles Chargers 12.50 25.00
8 New York Titans 10.00 20.00
9 Oakland Raiders 15.00 30.00

1960 Fleer College Pennant Decals

This set of 19 pennant decal pairs was distributed as an insert with the 1960 Fleer regular issue inaugural AFL football set along with and at the same time as the AFL Team Decals described immediately above. Some dealers feel that these college decals are tougher to find than the AFL team decals. These inserts were approximately 2 1/4" by 3" and one decal was to be inserted in each wax pack. The decals are unnumbered and are ordered below alphabetically according to the lower alphabetically of each college pair. The backs of the decal backing contained instructions on the proper application of the decal printed in very light blue.

COMPLETE SET (19) 87.50 175.00
1 Alabama 6.00 12.00
Yale
2 Army 3.75 7.50
Mississippi
3 California 3.75 7.50
Indiana
4 Duke 10.00 20.00
Notre Dame
5 Florida St. 6.00 12.00
Kentucky
6 Georgia 6.00 12.00
Oklahoma
7 Houston 3.75 7.50
Iowa
8 Idaho St. 3.75 7.50
Penn.
9 Iowa St. 6.00 12.00
Penn State
10 Kansas 5.00 10.00
UCLA
11 Marquette 3.75 7.50
New Mexico
12 Maryland 3.75 7.50
Missouri
13 Miss.South. 3.75 7.50
N.Carolina
14 Navy 5.00 10.00
Stanford
15 Nebraska 6.00 12.00
Purdue
16 Pittsburgh 3.75 7.50
Utah
17 SMU 3.75 7.50
West Virginia
18 So.Carolina 5.00 10.00
USC
19 Wake Forest 3.75 7.50
Wisconsin

1961 Fleer

The 1961 Fleer football set contains 220 standard-size cards. The set contains NFL (1-132) and AFL (133-220) players. The cards are grouped alphabetically by team nicknames within league. The backs are printed in black and lime green on a white card stock. The AFL cards are often found in uncut sheet form. The key Rookie Cards in this set are John Brodie, Tom Flores, Don Maynard, Don Meredith, and Jim Otto.

COMPLETE SET (220) 1000.00 1600.00
WRAPPER (5-CENT, SER.1) 20.00 25.00
WRAPPER (5-CENT, SER.2) 25.00 30.00
1 Ed Brown 7.50 15.00
2 Rick Casares 3.00 6.00
3 Willie Galimore 3.00 6.00
4 Jim Dooley 2.50 4.00
5 Harlon Hill 2.50 4.00
6 Stan Jones 4.00 8.00
7 J.C. Caroline 2.50 4.00
8 Joe Fortunato 2.50 4.00
9 Doug Atkins 4.00 8.00
10 Milt Plum 3.00 6.00
11 Jim Brown 90.00 150.00
12 Bobby Mitchell 5.00 10.00
13 Ray Renfro 3.00 6.00
14 Gern Nagler 2.50 4.00
15 Jim Shofner 2.50 4.00
16 Vince Costello 2.50 4.00
17 Galen Fiss RC 2.50 4.00
18 Walt Michaels 3.00 6.00
19 Bob Gain 2.50 4.00
20 Mal Hammack 2.50 4.00
21 Frank Mestnik RC 2.50 4.00
22 Bobby Joe Conrad 3.00 6.00
23 John David Crow 3.00 6.00
24 Sonny Randle RC 3.00 6.00
25 Don Gillis 2.50 4.00
26 Jerry Norton 2.50 4.00
27 Bill Stacy RC 2.50 4.00
28 Leo Sugar 2.50 4.00
29 Frank Fuller 2.50 4.00
30 Johnny Unitas 35.00 60.00
31 Alan Ameche 4.00 8.00
32 Lenny Moore 7.50 15.00
33 Raymond Berry 7.50 15.00
34 Jim Mutscheller 2.50 4.00
35 Jim Parker 4.00 8.00
36 Bill Pellington 2.50 4.00
37 Gino Marchetti 5.00 10.00
38 Gene Lipscomb 4.00 8.00
39 Art Donovan 7.50 15.00
40 Eddie LeBaron 3.00 6.00
41 Don Meredith RC 90.00 150.00
42 Don McIlhenny 2.50 4.00
43 L.G. Dupre 2.50 4.00
44 Fred Dugan RC 2.50 4.00
45 Billy Howton 3.00 6.00
46 Duane Putnam 2.50 4.00
47 Gene Cronin 2.50 4.00
48 Jerry Tubbs 2.50 4.00
49 Clarence Peaks 2.50 4.00
50 Ted Dean RC 2.50 4.00
51 Tommy McDonald 4.00 8.00
52 Bill Barnes 2.50 4.00
53 Pete Retzlaff 3.00 6.00
54 Bobby Walston 2.50 4.00
55 Chuck Bednarik 6.00 12.00
56 Maxie Baughan RC 3.00 6.00
57 Bob Pellegrini 2.50 4.00
58 Jesse Richardson 2.50 4.00
59 John Brodie RC 30.00 50.00
60 J.D. Smith RB 3.00 6.00
61 Ray Norton RC 2.50 4.00
62 Monty Stickles RC 2.50 4.00
63 Bob St.Clair 4.00 8.00
64 Dave Baker RC 2.50 4.00
65 Abe Woodson 2.50 4.00
66 Matt Hazeltine 2.50 4.00
67 Leo Nomellini 5.00 10.00
68 Charley Conerly 5.00 10.00
69 Kyle Rote 4.00 8.00
70 Jack Stroud RC 2.50 4.00
71 Roosevelt Brown 4.00 8.00
72 Jim Patton 2.50 4.00
73 Erich Barnes 2.50 4.00
74 Sam Huff 7.50 15.00
75 Andy Robustelli 5.00 10.00
76 Dick Modzelewski RC 2.50 4.00
77 Roosevelt Grier 4.00 8.00
78 Earl Morrall 4.00 8.00
79 Jim Ninowski 2.50 4.00
80 Nick Pietrosante RC 3.00 6.00
81 Howard Cassady 3.00 6.00
82 Jim Gibbons 2.50 4.00
83 Gail Cogdill RC 3.00 6.00
84 Dick Lane 4.00 8.00
85 Yale Lary 4.00 8.00
86 Joe Schmidt 4.00 8.00
87 Darris McCord 2.50 4.00
88 Bart Starr 35.00 60.00
89 Jim Taylor 30.00 50.00
90 Paul Hornung 30.00 55.00
91 Tom Moore RC 4.00 8.00
92 Boyd Dowler RC 7.50 15.00
93 Max McGee 4.00 8.00
94 Forrest Gregg 5.00 10.00
95 Jerry Kramer 5.00 10.00
96 Jim Ringo 4.00 8.00
97 Bill Forester 3.00 6.00
98 Frank Ryan 3.00 6.00
99 Ollie Matson 6.00 12.00
100 Jon Arnett 3.00 6.00
101 Dick Bass RC 3.00 6.00
102 Jim Phillips 2.50 4.00
103 Del Shofner 3.00 6.00
104 Art Hunter 2.50 4.00
105 Lindon Crow 2.50 4.00
106 Les Richter 3.00 6.00
107 Lou Michaels 2.50 4.00
108 Ralph Guglielmi 2.50 4.00
109 Don Bosseler 2.50 4.00
110 John Olszewski 2.50 4.00
111 Bill Anderson 2.50 4.00
112 Joe Walton 2.50 4.00
113 Jim Schrader 2.50 4.00
114 Gary Glick 2.50 4.00
115 Ralph Felton 2.50 4.00
116 Bob Toneff 2.50 4.00
117 Bobby Layne 25.00 40.00
118 John Henry Johnson 4.00 8.00
119 Tom Tracy 3.00 6.00
120 Jimmy Orr RC 4.00 8.00
121 John Nisby 2.50 4.00
122 Dean Derby 2.50 4.00
123 John Reger 2.50 4.00
124 George Tarasovic 2.50 4.00
125 Ernie Stautner 5.00 10.00
126 George Shaw 2.50 4.00
127 Hugh McElhenny 6.00 12.00
128 Dick Haley RC 2.50 4.00
129 Dave Middleton 2.50 4.00
130 Perry Richards RC 2.50 4.00
131 Gene Johnson DB RC 2.50 4.00
132 Don Joyce RC 2.50 4.00
133 Johnny Green RC 4.00 8.00
134 Wray Carlton RC 4.00 8.00
135 Richie Lucas 4.00 8.00
136 Elbert Dubenion 4.00 8.00
137 Tom Rychlec 3.50 6.00
138 Mack Yoho RC 3.50 6.00
139 Phil Blazer RC 3.50 6.00
140 Dan McGrew 3.50 6.00
141 Bill Atkins 3.50 6.00
142 Archie Matsos RC 3.50 6.00
143 Gene Grabosky 3.50 6.00
144 Frank Tripucka 5.00 10.00
145 Al Carmichael 3.50 6.00
146 Bob McNamara 3.50 6.00
147 Lionel Taylor RC 7.50 15.00
148 Eldon Danenhauer RC 3.50 6.00
149 Willie Smith 3.50 6.00
150 Carl Larpenter 3.50 6.00
151 Ken Adamson 3.50 6.00
152 Goose Gonsoulin UER RC 5.00 10.00
153 Joe Young RC 3.50 6.00
154 Gordy Holz RC 3.50 6.00
155 Jack Kemp 35.00 60.00
156 Charlie Flowers 3.50 6.00
157 Paul Lowe 5.00 10.00
158 Don Norton RC 3.50 6.00
159 Howard Clark RC 3.50 6.00
160 Paul Maguire 7.50 15.00
161 Ernie Wright RC 4.00 8.00
162 Ron Mix 7.50 15.00
163 Fred Cole RC 3.50 6.00
164 Jim Sears RC 3.50 6.00
165 Volney Peters 3.50 6.00
166 George Blanda 25.00 40.00
167 Jacky Lee 4.00 8.00
168 Bob White 3.50 6.00
169 Doug Cline 3.50 6.00
170 Dave Smith RB RC 3.50 6.00
171 Billy Cannon 7.50 15.00
172 Bill Groman RC 3.50 6.00
173 Al Jamison RC 3.50 6.00
174 Jim Norton RC 3.50 6.00
175 Dennit Morris RC 3.50 6.00
176 Don Floyd 3.50 6.00
177 Butch Songin 3.50 6.00
178 Billy Lott RC 3.50 6.00
179 Ron Burton 5.00 10.00
180 Jim Colclough RC 3.50 6.00
181 Charley Leo RC 3.50 6.00
182 Walt Cudzik RC 3.50 6.00
183 Fred Bruney 3.50 6.00
184 Ross O'Hanley RC 3.50 6.00
185 Tony Sardisco 3.50 6.00
186 Harry Jacobs RC 3.50 6.00
187 Bob Dee 3.50 6.00
188 Tom Flores RC 15.00 30.00
189 Jack Larscheid 3.50 6.00
190 Dick Christy RC 3.50 6.00
191 Alan Miller RC 3.50 6.00
192 James Smith 3.50 6.00
193 Gerald Burch RC 3.50 6.00
194 Gene Prebola 3.50 6.00
195 Alan Goldstein 3.50 6.00
196 Don Manoukian RC 3.50 6.00
197 Jim Otto RC 40.00 75.00
198 Wayne Crow 3.50 6.00
199 Cotton Davidson RC 4.00 8.00
200 Randy Duncan RC 4.00 8.00
201 Jack Spikes 4.00 8.00
202 Johnny Robinson RC 7.50 15.00
203 Abner Haynes 7.50 15.00
204 Chris Burford 4.00 8.00
205 Bill Krisher 3.50 6.00
206 Marvin Terrell 3.50 6.00
207 Jimmy Harris 3.50 6.00
208 Mel Branch 4.00 8.00
209 Paul Miller 3.50 6.00
210 Al Dorow 3.50 6.00
211 Dick Jamieson 3.50 6.00
212 Pete Hart RC 3.50 6.00
213 Bill Shockley RC 3.50 6.00
214 Dewey Bohling RC 3.50 6.00
215 Don Maynard RC 40.00 80.00
216 Bob Mischak RC 3.50 6.00
217 Mike Hudock 3.50 6.00
218 Bob Reifsnyder 3.50 6.00
219 Tom Saidock 3.50 6.00
220 Sid Youngelman 12.00 20.00

1961 Fleer Magic Message Blue Inserts

This unattractive set contains 40 cards that were inserted in 1961 Fleer football wax packs. The cards are light blue in color and measure approximately 3" by 2 1/8". The fronts feature a question and a crude line drawing. For the answer, the collector is instructed to "Turn card and wet; when dry, wet again." A tag line at the bottom of the front indicates that the cards were printed by Business Service of Long Island, New York. The backs are blank, and the cards are numbered on the front in the lower right corner.

COMPLETE SET (40) 75.00 150.00
1 When was the first 2.00 4.00
2 Which school was 2.00 4.00
3 What famous coach was 2.00 4.00
4 Which college coach 2.00 4.00
5 What is meant by two 2.00 4.00
6 When was the only 2.00 4.00
7 What is a Sudden 2.00 4.00
8 What is the longest 2.00 4.00
9 What famous Colorado 2.00 4.00
10 What Michigan All- 3.00 6.00
11 The North-South game 2.00 4.00
12 The Army-Navy game has 2.00 4.00
13 What slugging major 2.00 4.00
14 What All-Americans were 2.00 4.00
15 Which team was called 2.00 4.00
16 When was the first 2.00 4.00
17 What is the record 2.00 4.00
18 What is the longest 2.00 4.00
19 Who was the first 2.00 4.00
20 Which team was the 2.00 4.00
21 Who was the first 2.00 4.00
22 When was the first 2.00 4.00
23 What is the longest 2.00 4.00
24 What is the origin of 2.00 4.00
25 What player was 3.00 6.00
26 What is the record 2.00 4.00
27 What player ran the 2.00 4.00
28 When was the first 2.00 4.00
29 When and by whom was 2.00 4.00
30 When was the forward 2.00 4.00
31 What was the first 2.00 4.00
32 When was the first 2.00 4.00
33 Where is the Football 2.00 4.00
34 Who were the Four 2.00 4.00
35 When was the first 2.00 4.00
36 Who holds the record 2.00 4.00
37 Who was known as the 3.00 6.00
38 Has the Rose Bowl 2.00 4.00
39 Which team featured 2.00 4.00
40 Where and when was the 3.00 6.00

1961 Fleer Wallet Pictures

These "cards" were issued as part of the 1961-62 issue of Complete Sports Pro-Football Illustrated magazine. The magazine section was entitled "Wallet Picture Album, photos courtesy of Frank H. Fleer Corp." The AFL and NFL sections were issued seperately and each photo inside the magazine was printed in black and white on newsprint stock. The pictures were to be cut from the pages and, once neatly cut, the photos measure roughly 2 1/2" by 3 3/8" with the backs including only the player's name and team name. The interior pages included 52-NFL players and 90-AFL players. Twelve additional photos were included as the back cover to the magazine and they measure roughly 2 3/8" by 2 3/8" when neatly cut out. Those twleve were printed on white stock with a light single color tone. Most of the photos were the same as used for the 1961 Fleer card set. We've arranged the unnumbered photos below alphabetically by team and then by player starting with the AFL (1-90) then the NFL (91-145).

COMPLETE SET (145) 125.00 300.00
1 Tommy Addison .75 2.00
2 Jim Colclough .75 2.00
3 Walt Cudzik .75 2.00
4 Bob Dee .75 2.00
5 Harry Jacobs .75 2.00
6 Charley Leo .75 2.00
7 Billy Lott .75 2.00
8 Ross O'Hanley .75 2.00
9 Tony Sardisco UER .75 2.00
10 Butch Songin .75 2.00
11 Bill Atkins .75 2.00
12 Phil Blazer .75 2.00
13 Wray Carlton .75 2.00
14 Monte Crockett .75 2.00
15 Elbert Dubenion 1.00 2.50
16 Wilmer Fowler .75 2.00
17 Gene Grabosky .75 2.00
18 Richie Lucas 1.00 2.50
19 Archie Matsos .75 2.00
20 Richard McCabe .75 2.00
21 Dan McGrew UER .75 2.00
22 Tom Rychlec .75 2.00
23 Laverne Torczon .75 2.00
24 Mack Yoho .75 2.00
25 Mel Branch .75 2.00
26 Chris Burford .75 2.00
27 Cotton Davidson .75 2.00
28 Randy Duncan .75 2.00
29 Jimmy Harris .75 2.00
30 E.J. Holub .75 2.00
31 Bill Krisher .75 2.00
32 Paul Miller .75 2.00
33 Johnny Robinson 1.00 2.50
34 Jack Spikes .75 2.00
35 Marvin Terrell .75 2.00
36 Ken Adamson .75 2.00
37 Al Carmichael .75 2.00
38 Eldon Danenhauer .75 2.00
39 Goose Gonsoulin .75 2.00
40 Gordy Holz .75 2.00
41 Carl Larpenter .75 2.00
42 Bud McFadin .75 2.00
43 Bob McNamara .75 2.00
44 Dave Rolle .75 2.00
45 Willie Smith .75 2.00
46 Lionel Taylor 1.50 4.00
47 Frank Tripucka UER 1.50 4.00
48 Joe Young .75 2.00
49 George Blanda 4.00 10.00
50 Doug Cline .75 2.00
51 Don Floyd .75 2.00
52 Bobby Gordon .75 2.00
53 Bill Groman .75 2.00
54 Al Jamison .75 2.00
55 Jacky Lee .75 2.00
56 Richard Michael .75 2.00
57 Dennit Morris .75 2.00
58 Jim Norton .75 2.00
59 Dave Smith .75 2.00
60 Bob White .75 2.00
61 Dewey Bohling .75 2.00
62 Pete Hart .75 2.00
63 Mike Hudock .75 2.00
64 Bob Mischak .75 2.00
65 Sid Youngelman .75 2.00
66 Gerald Burch .75 2.00
67 Dick Christy .75 2.00
68 Bob Coolbaugh .75 2.00
69 Wayne Crow .75 2.00
70 Don Deskins .75 2.00
71 Tom Flores 1.50 4.00
72 Alan Goldstein .75 2.00
73 Jack Larscheid .75 2.00
74 Dan Manoukian .75 2.00
75 Alan Miller UER .75 2.00
76 Jim Otto 3.00 8.00
77 Charley Powell .75 2.00
78 Gene Prebola .75 2.00
79 Jim Smith RB .75 2.00
80 Howard Clark .75 2.00
81 Fred Cole .75 2.00
82 Charlie Flowers .75 2.00
83 Dick Harris .75 2.00
84 Jack Kemp 6.00 15.00
85 Paul Lowe 1.00 2.50
86 Ron Mix 1.50 4.00
87 Don Norton .75 2.00
88 Volney Peters .75 2.00
89 Jim Sears .75 2.00
90 Ernie Wright 1.00 2.50
91 Alan Ameche 1.00 2.50
92 Raymond Berry 3.00 8.00
93 Lenny Moore 2.50 6.00
94 Jim Mutscheller .75 2.00
95 Ed Brown 1.00 2.50
96 Rick Casares 1.00 2.50
97 J.C. Caroline .75 2.00
98 Willie Galimore .75 2.00
99 Harlon Hill UER .75 2.00
100 Bobby Mitchell 2.00 5.00
101 Gern Nagler .75 2.00
102 Milt Plum 1.00 2.50
103 Ray Renfro 1.00 2.50
104 Billy Howton UER 1.00 2.50
105 Don Meredith 6.00 15.00
106 Howard Cassady 1.00 2.50
107 Gail Cogdill .75 2.00
108 Dick Lane 1.50 4.00
109 Nick Pietrosante .75 2.00
110 Paul Hornung 6.00 15.00
111 Tom Moore 1.00 2.50
112 Bart Starr 10.00 25.00
113 Jim Taylor 5.00 12.00
114 Les Richter .75 2.00
115 Frank Ryan 1.00 2.50
116 Del Shofner .75 2.00
117 Dick Haley UER .75 2.00
118 Perry Richards .75 2.00
119 Charley Conerly UER 2.00 5.00
120 Kyle Rote 1.00 2.50
121 Bill Barnes .75 2.00
122 Chuck Bednarik 2.00 5.00
123 Clarence Peaks .75 2.00
124 Pete Retzlaff 1.00 2.50
125 Bobby Walston .75 2.00
126 Dean Derby .75 2.00
127 John Henry Johnson 1.50 4.00
128 Bobby Layne 4.00 10.00
129 Jimmy Orr 1.00 2.50
130 Tom Tracy 1.00 2.50
131 Bobby Joe Conrad .75 2.00
132 John David Crow 1.00 2.50
133 Mal Hammack .75 2.00
134 Sonny Randle .75 2.00
135 Bill Stacy UER .75 2.00
136 Dave Baker .75 2.00
137 John Brodie 3.00 8.00
138 Matt Hazeltine .75 2.00
139 Ray Norton .75 2.00
140 J.D.Smith RB .75 2.00
141 Bill Anderson .75 2.00
142 Don Bosseler .75 2.00
143 Ralph Guglielmi .75 2.00
144 John Olszewski .75 2.00
145 Joe Walton .75 2.00

1962 Fleer

The 1962 Fleer football set contains 88 standard-size cards featuring AFL players only. The set was issued in six-card nickel packs which came 24 packs to a box with a slab of bubble gum. Card numbering is alphabetical by team city. The card backs are printed in black and blue on a white card stock. Key Rookie Cards in this set are Gino Cappelletti, Charlie Hennigan, Ernie Ladd and Fred Williamson.

COMPLETE SET (88) 500.00 900.00
WRAPPER (5-CENT) 100.00 200.00
1 Billy Lott 8.00 16.00
2 Ron Burton 5.00 10.00
3 Gino Cappelletti RC 10.00 20.00
4 Babe Parilli 5.00 10.00
5 Jim Colclough 3.50 7.00
6 Tony Sardisco 3.50 7.00
7 Walt Cudzik 3.50 7.00
8 Bob Dee 3.50 7.00
9 Tommy Addison RC 4.00 8.00
10 Harry Jacobs 3.50 7.00
11 Ross O'Hanley 3.50 7.00
12 Art Baker 3.50 7.00
13 Johnny Green 3.50 7.00
14 Elbert Dubenion 5.00 10.00
15 Tom Rychlec 3.50 7.00
16 Billy Shaw RC 20.00 40.00
17 Ken Rice 3.50 7.00
18 Bill Atkins 3.50 7.00
19 Richie Lucas 4.00 8.00
20 Archie Matsos 3.50 7.00
21 Laverne Torczon 3.50 7.00
22 Warren Rabb RC UER 3.50 7.00
23 Jack Spikes 4.00 8.00
24 Cotton Davidson 4.00 8.00
25 Abner Haynes 7.50 15.00
26 Jimmy Saxton RC 3.50 7.00
27 Chris Burford 4.00 8.00
28 Bill Miller RC 3.50 7.00
29 Sherrill Headrick 4.00 8.00
30 E.J.Holub RC 4.00 8.00
31 Jerry Mays RC 5.00 10.00
32 Mel Branch 4.00 8.00
33 Paul Rochester RC 3.50 7.00
34 Frank Tripucka 5.00 10.00
35 Gene Mingo 3.50 7.00
36 Lionel Taylor 6.00 12.00
37 Ken Adamson 3.50 7.00
38 Eldon Danenhauer 3.50 7.00
39 Goose Gonsoulin 5.00 10.00
40 Gordy Holz 3.50 7.00
41 Bud McFadin 4.00 8.00
42 Jim Stinnette RC 3.50 7.00
43 Bob Hudson RC 3.50 7.00
44 George Herring 3.50 7.00
45 Charley Tolar RC 3.50 7.00
46 George Blanda 30.00 50.00
47 Billy Cannon 7.50 15.00
48 Charlie Hennigan RC 7.50 15.00
49 Bill Groman 3.50 7.00
50 Al Jamison 3.50 7.00
51 Tony Banfield 3.50 7.00
52 Jim Norton 3.50 7.00
53 Dennit Morris 3.50 7.00
54 Don Floyd 3.50 7.00
55 Ed Husmann UER RC 3.50 7.00
56 Robert Brooks RC 3.50 7.00
57 Al Dorow 3.50 7.00
58 Dick Christy 3.50 7.00
59 Don Maynard 30.00 50.00
60 Art Powell 5.00 10.00
61 Mike Hudock 3.50 7.00
62 Bill Mathis 4.00 8.00
63 Butch Songin 3.50 7.00
64 Larry Grantham 3.50 7.00
65 Nick Mumley RC 3.50 7.00
66 Tom Saidock 3.50 7.00
67 Alan Miller 3.50 7.00
68 Tom Flores 7.50 15.00
69 Bob Coolbaugh 3.50 7.00
70 George Fleming RC 3.50 7.00
71 Wayne Hawkins RC 4.00 8.00
72 Jim Otto 25.00 40.00
73 Wayne Crow 3.50 7.00
74 Fred Williamson RC 18.00 30.00
75 Tom Louderback RC 3.50 7.00
76 Volney Peters 3.50 7.00
77 Charley Powell RC 3.50 7.00
78 Don Norton 3.50 7.00
79 Jack Kemp 50.00 100.00
80 Paul Lowe 5.00 10.00
81 Dave Kocourek 3.50 7.00
82 Ron Mix 7.50 15.00
83 Ernie Wright 5.00 10.00
84 Dick Harris RC 3.50 7.00
85 Bill Hudson RC 3.50 7.00
86 Ernie Ladd RC 15.00 25.00
87 Earl Faison RC 4.00 8.00
88 Ron Nery 9.00 18.00

1963 Fleer

The 1963 Fleer football set of 88 standard-size cards features AFL players only. Card numbers is in team order. Card numbers 6 and 64 are more difficult to obtain than the other cards in the set; their shortage is believed to be attributable to their possible replacement on the printing sheet by the unnumbered checklist. The card backs are printed in red and black on a white card stock. The set price below does not include the checklist card. Cards with numbers divisible by four can be found with or without a red stripe on the bottom of the card back; it is thought that those without the red stripe are in lesser supply. Currently, there is no difference in value. The key Rookie Cards in this set are Lance Alworth, Nick Buoniconti, and Len Dawson.

COMPLETE SET (88) 1200.00 1800.00
WRAPPER (5-CENT) 60.00 120.00
1 Larry Garron RC 10.00 20.00
2 Babe Parilli 5.00 10.00
3 Ron Burton 6.00 12.00
4 Jim Colclough 4.00 8.00
4B Jim Colclough NS 4.00 8.00
5 Gino Cappelletti 6.00 12.00
6 Charles Long SP RC 45.00 80.00
7 Billy Neighbors RC 4.00 8.00
8 Dick Felt RC 4.00 8.00
8B Dick Felt NS RC 4.00 8.00
9 Tommy Addison 4.00 8.00
10 Nick Buoniconti RC 45.00 80.00
11 Larry Eisenhauer RC 4.00 8.00
12 Bill Mathis 4.00 8.00
12B Bill Mathis NS 4.00 8.00
13 Lee Grosscup RC 5.00 10.00
14 Dick Christy 4.00 8.00
15 Don Maynard 30.00 50.00
16 Alex Kroll RC 4.00 8.00
16B Alex Kroll NS RC 4.00 8.00
17 Bob Mischak 4.00 8.00
18 Dainard Paulson RC 4.00 8.00
19 Lee Riley 4.00 8.00
20 Larry Grantham 5.00 10.00
20B Larry Grantham NS 5.00 10.00
21 Hubert Bobo RC 4.00 8.00
22 Nick Mumley 4.00 8.00
23 Cookie Gilchrist RC 30.00 50.00
24 Jack Kemp 75.00 150.00
24B Jack Kemp NS 75.00 150.00
25 Wray Carlton 4.00 8.00
26 Elbert Dubenion 5.00 10.00
27 Ernie Warlick RC 5.00 10.00
28 Billy Shaw 7.50 15.00
28B Billy Shaw NS 7.50 15.00
29 Ken Rice 4.00 8.00
30 Booker Edgerson RC 4.00 8.00
31 Ray Abruzzese RC UER 4.00 8.00
(name misspelled Abbruzzese)
32 Mike Stratton RC 7.50 15.00
32B Mike Stratton NS RC 7.50 15.00
33 Tom Sestak RC 6.00 12.00
34 Charley Tolar 4.00 8.00
35 Dave Smith RB 4.00 8.00
36 George Blanda 30.00 50.00
36B George Blanda NS 30.00 50.00
37 Billy Cannon 7.50 15.00
38 Charlie Hennigan 5.00 10.00
39 Bob Talamini RC 4.00 8.00
40 Jim Norton 4.00 8.00
40B Jim Norton NC 4.00 8.00
41 Tony Banfield 4.00 8.00
42 Doug Cline 4.00 8.00
43 Don Floyd 4.00 8.00
44 Ed Husmann 4.00 8.00
44B Ed Husmann NS 4.00 8.00
45 Curtis McClinton RC 7.50 15.00

46 Jack Spikes 5.00 10.00
47 Len Dawson RC 150.00 250.00
48 Abner Haynes 7.50 15.00
48B Abner Haynes NS 7.50 15.00
49 Chris Burford 5.00 10.00
50 Fred Arbanas RC 6.00 12.00
51 Johnny Robinson 5.00 10.00
52 E.J. Holub 5.00 10.00
52B E.J. Holub NS 5.00 10.00
53 Sherrill Headrick 5.00 10.00
54 Mel Branch 5.00 10.00
55 Jerry Mays 5.00 10.00
56 Cotton Davidson 5.00 10.00
56B Cotton Davidson NS 5.00 10.00
57 Clem Daniels RC 10.00 20.00
58 Bo Roberson RC 5.00 10.00
59 Art Powell 6.00 12.00
60 Bob Coolbaugh 4.00 8.00
60B Bob Coolbaugh NS 4.00 8.00
61 Wayne Hawkins 4.00 8.00
62 Jim Otto 18.00 30.00
63 Fred Williamson 10.00 20.00
64 Bob Dougherty SP 60.00 120.00
64B Bob Dougherty SP NS 60.00 120.00
65 Dalva Allen RC 4.00 8.00
66 Chuck McMurtry RC 4.00 8.00
67 Gerry McDougall RC 4.00 8.00
68 Tobin Rote 5.00 10.00
68B Tobin Rote NS 5.00 10.00
69 Paul Lowe 6.00 12.00
70 Keith Lincoln RC 25.00 40.00
71 Dave Kocourek 4.00 8.00
72 Lance Alworth RC 125.00 250.00
72B Lance Alworth NS RC 125.00 250.00
73 Ron Mix 15.00 25.00
74 Charlie McNeil RC 4.00 8.00
75 Emil Karas RC 4.00 8.00
76 Ernie Ladd 10.00 20.00
76B Ernie Ladd NS 10.00 20.00
77 Earl Faison 4.00 8.00
78 Jim Stinnette 4.00 8.00
79 Frank Tripucka 6.00 12.00
80 Don Stone RC 4.00 8.00
80B Don Stone NS RC 4.00 8.00
81 Bob Scarpitto RC 4.00 8.00
82 Lionel Taylor 6.00 12.00
83 Jerry Tarr RC 4.00 8.00
84 Eldon Danenhauer 4.00 8.00
84B Eldon Danenhauer NS 4.00 8.00
85 Goose Gonsoulin 5.00 10.00
86 Jim Fraser RC 4.00 8.00
87 Chuck Gavin RC 4.00 8.00
88 Bud McFadin ! 10.00 20.00
88B Bud McFadin NS 10.00 20.00
NNO Checklist SP ! 250.00 350.00

1968 Fleer Big Signs

This set of 26 "Big Signs" was produced by Fleer. They are blank backed and measure approximately 7 3/4" by 11 1/2" with rounded corners. They are unnumbered so they are listed below alphabetically by team city name. They are credited at the bottom as 1968 in roman numerals, but in fact were probably issued several years later, perhaps as late as 1974. As another point of reference in dating the set, the New England Patriots changed their name from Boston in 1970. There were two distinct versions of this set, with each version including all 26 teams. The 1970 version was issued in a green box, while the 1974 version was issued in a brown box. Both boxes carry a 1968 copyright date; however, 1974 is generally considered to be the issue date of the second series. Though they are considerably different in design, the size of the collectibles is similar. The generic drawings (of a faceless player from each team) are in color with a white border. The set was licensed by NFL Properties so there are no players shown.

COMPLETE SET (26) 150.00 250.00
1 Atlanta Falcons 5.00 10.00
2 Baltimore Colts 5.00 10.00
3 Buffalo Bills 5.00 10.00
4 Chicago Bears 6.00 12.00
5 Cincinnati Bengals 5.00 10.00
6 Cleveland Browns 5.00 10.00
7 Dallas Cowboys 10.00 20.00
8 Denver Broncos 5.00 10.00
9 Detroit Lions 5.00 10.00
10 Green Bay Packers 10.00 20.00
11 Houston Oilers 5.00 10.00
12 Kansas City Chiefs 5.00 10.00
13 Los Angeles Rams 5.00 10.00
14 Miami Dolphins 7.50 15.00
15 Minnesota Vikings 5.00 10.00
16 New England Patriots 5.00 10.00
17 New Orleans Saints 5.00 10.00
18 New York Giants 5.00 10.00
19 New York Jets 5.00 10.00
20 Oakland Raiders 10.00 20.00
21 Philadelphia Eagles 5.00 10.00
22 Pittsburgh Steelers 7.50 15.00
23 St. Louis Cardinals 5.00 10.00
24 San Diego Chargers 5.00 10.00
25 San Francisco 49ers 7.50 15.00
26 Washington Redskins 7.50 15.00

1972 Fleer Quiz

The 28 cards in this set measure approximately 2 1/2" by 4" and feature three questions and (upside down) answers about football players and events. The cards were issued one per pack with Fleer cloth team patches. The words "Official Football Quiz" are printed at the top and are accented by the NFL logo. The backs are blank. The cards are numbered in the lower right hand corner.

COMPLETE SET (28) 25.00 50.00
COMMON CARD (1-28) 1.00 2.00

1972-73 Fleer Cloth Patches

These cloth stickers were issued 3-per pack as a stand alone product, inserted one per pack in 1972 Fleer Quiz, and two per pack in 1973 Fleer Pro Scouting Report. Each blankbacked sticker includes one small team name sticker at the top and a larger team helmet or team logo at the bottom. We've catalogued and priced the stickers as pairs according to the smaller team name sticker first and the larger sticker second. Many of the stickers were identical for both years (and all contain a 1972 copyright date) except for the conference champions stickers as noted below. Variations on some sticker combinations do exist and we have cataloged all known versions below. The 1972-73 helmet stickers can be differentiated from the 1974-75 listings (those also feature a 1972 copyright year) by a single-bar face mask design instead of dual-bar. The glue used for these stickers tends to break down over time and will cause spots to bleed through to the fronts and separation of the sticker from the backing is quite common, therefore they are extremely condition sensitive.

1972-73 Fleer Cloth Patches

COMPLETE SET (64) 125.00 250.00
1 Bears Name 4.00 8.00
Cowboys Small Helmet
2 Bears Name 3.00 6.00
Jets helmet
3 Bengals Name 2.50 5.00
Cardinals Helmet
4 Bengals Name 3.00 6.00
Giants Logo Blue
5A Bills Name 4.00 10.00
Chiefs Logo ERR
5B Bills Name 2.50 5.00
Chiefs Logo Gold
6 Bills Name 4.00 8.00
Cowboys Large Helmet
7 Broncos Name 2.50 5.00
Colts Helmet
8 Broncos Name 2.50 5.00
Patriots Logo
9 Broncos Name 4.00 8.00
Redskins Helmet
10 Browns Name 2.50 5.00
Chargers Helmet
11 Browns Name 2.50 5.00
Saints Helmet
12 Cardinals Name Gold 2.50 5.00
Bengals Logo
13 Cardinals Name 4.00 8.00
Raiders Helmet
14A Chargers Name Lt Blue 3.00 6.00
Bears Helmet White C
14B Chargers Name Lt Blue 3.00 6.00
Bears Helmet Orange C
15 Chiefs Name 2.50 5.00
Browns Helmet
16 Chiefs Name 2.50 5.00
NFL Logo
17 Chiefs Name 2.50 5.00
Rams Helmet
18 Colts Name 2.50 5.00
Saints Logo
19 Colts Name 4.00 8.00
Steelers Logo
20 Cowboys Name 4.00 8.00
Broncos Helmet
21A Cowboys Name 4.00 8.00
Dolphins Helmet Print
21B Cowboys Name 4.00 8.00
Dolphins Helmet Script
22 Dolphins Name 3.00 6.00
Vikings Helmet
23 Eagles Name 2.50 5.00
Chiefs Helmet
24 Eagles Name 4.00 8.00
Steelers Helmet
25 Falcons Name 3.00 6.00
Browns Logo
26 Falcons Name 3.00 6.00
Giants Logo Red
27 Falcons Name 2.50 5.00
Oilers Helmet
28 49ers Name 3.00 6.00
Colts Logo
29 49ers Name 4.00 8.00
Packers Logo
30 Giants Name Red 3.00 6.00
Bills Logo
31 Giants Name Blue 2.50 5.00
Lions Logo
32 Jets Name 4.00 8.00
Broncos Logo
33 Jets Name 2.50 5.00
Falcons Logo
34 Lions Name 2.50 5.00
Oilers Logo
35 Lions Name 2.50 5.00
Rams Logo Y
36 Lions Name 2.50 5.00
Rams Logo W
37 Oilers Name 2.50 5.00
Cardinals Logo
38 Oilers Name 2.50 5.00
Eagles Helmet
39 Packers Name 3.00 6.00
Chargers Logo Lt Blue
40 Packers Name 3.00 6.00
Eagles Logo
41 Patriots Name 2.50 5.00
Falcons Helmet
42 Patriots Name 3.00 6.00
Jets Logo
43 Raiders Name 4.00 8.00
Redskins Logo Gold
44 Raiders Name 3.00 6.00
Giants Helmet
45A Rams Name 4.00 8.00
Dolphins Logo Print
45B Rams Name 4.00 8.00
Dolphins Logo Script
46 Rams Name/49ers Logo 4.00 8.00
47 Redskins Name 2.50 5.00
Bengals Helmet
48 Redskins Name/49ers Helmet 4.00 8.00
49 Saints Name 2.50 5.00
Lions Helmet
50 Saints Name 4.00 8.00
Raiders Logo
51 Steelers Name 4.00 8.00
Packers Helmet
52 Steelers Name 3.00 6.00
Rams Helmet
53 Steelers Name 3.00 6.00
Vikings Logo
54 Vikings Name 3.00 6.00
Bears Logo
55 Vikings Name 3.00 6.00
Bills Helmet
56 Vikings Name 2.50 5.00
Patriots Helmet
57 AFC Champ Dolphins 4.00 8.00
NFL Logo
58 AFC Conference 4.00 8.00
NFL Logo
59 NFC Champ Redskins 4.00 8.00
NFL Logo
60 NFC Conference 4.00 8.00
NFL Logo

1973 Fleer Pro Bowl Scouting Report

The 14 cards in this set measure approximately 2 1/2" by 4" and feature an explanation of the ideal size, responsibilities, and assignments of each player on the team. Each card shows a different position. Color artwork illustrates examples of how a player might appear. A diagram shows the position on the field. The words "AFC-NFC Pro Bowl Scouting Cards" are printed at the top and are accented by the NFL logo and underscored by a blue stripe. The backs are blank. The cards are unnumbered and checklisted below in alphabetical order. The cards came one per pack with two cloth football logo patches that are dated 1972. It appears that the same cloth patches were sold each year from 1972 to 1975. In the first year, they were sold alone in packs, while in the following years, they were sold again through packs with the Scouting Report and Hall of Fame issues, respectively.

COMPLETE SET (14) 20.00 40.00
1 Center 1.50 3.00
2 Cornerback 1.50 3.00
3 Defensive End 1.50 3.00
4 Defensive Tackle 1.50 3.00
5 Guard 1.50 3.00
6 Kicker 1.50 3.00
7 Linebacker 1.50 3.00
8 Offensive Tackle 1.50 3.00
9 Punter 1.50 3.00
10 Quarterback 1.50 3.00
11 Running Back 1.50 3.00
12 Safety 1.50 3.00
13 Tight End 1.50 3.00
14 Wide Receiver 1.50 3.00

1974 Fleer Big Signs

This set of 26 "Big Signs" was produced by Fleer in 1974. They are blank backed and measure approximately 7 3/4" by 11 1/2" with rounded corners. They are unnumbered so they are listed below alphabetically by team city name. They are credited at the bottom as 1968 in roman numerals, but in fact were probably issued several years later, perhaps as late as 1974. As another point of reference in dating the set, the New England Patriots changed their name from Boston in 1970. There were two distinct versions of this set, with each version including all 26 teams. The 1968 version was issued in a green box, while the 1974 version was issued in a brown box. Both boxes carry a 1968 copyright date; however, 1974 is generally considered to be the issue date of this second series. Though they are considerably different in design, the size of the collectibles is similar. The generic drawings (of a faceless player from each team) are in color with a white border. The set was licensed by NFL Properties so there are no players identifiably shown.

COMPLETE SET (26) 60.00 100.00
1 Atlanta Falcons 2.00 4.00
2 Baltimore Colts 2.00 4.00
3 Buffalo Bills 2.00 4.00
4 Chicago Bears 2.00 4.00
5 Cincinnati Bengals 2.00 4.00
6 Cleveland Browns 2.00 4.00
7 Dallas Cowboys 4.00 8.00
8 Denver Broncos 2.00 4.00
9 Detroit Lions 2.00 4.00
10 Green Bay Packers 4.00 8.00
11 Houston Oilers 2.00 4.00
12 Kansas City Chiefs 2.00 4.00
13 Los Angeles Rams 2.00 4.00
14 Miami Dolphins 3.00 6.00
15 Minnesota Vikings 2.00 4.00
16 New England Patriots 2.00 4.00
17 New Orleans Saints 2.00 4.00
18 New York Giants 2.00 4.00
19 New York Jets 2.00 4.00
20 Oakland Raiders 4.00 8.00
21 Philadelphia Eagles 2.00 4.00
22 Pittsburgh Steelers 3.00 6.00
23 St. Louis Cardinals 2.00 4.00
24 San Diego Chargers 2.00 4.00
25 San Francisco 49ers 3.00 6.00
26 Washington Redskins 3.00 6.00

1974 Fleer Hall of Fame

The 1974 Fleer Hall of Fame football card set contains 50 players inducted into the Pro Football Hall of Fame in Canton, Ohio. The cards measure approximately 2 1/2" by 4". The fronts feature black and white photos, white borders, and a cartoon head of a football player flanked by the words "The Immortal Roll." The backs contain biographical data and a stylized Pro Football Hall of Fame logo. The cards are unnumbered and can be distinguished from cards of the 1975 Fleer Hall of Fame set by this lack of numbering as well as the white border on the fronts. The cards are arranged and numbered below alphabetically by player's name for convenience. The cards were originally issued in wax packs with one Hall of Fame card and two cloth team logo stickers.

COMPLETE SET (50) 35.00 70.00
1 Cliff Battles .50 1.25
2 Sammy Baugh 1.50 3.00
3 Chuck Bednarik .75 1.50
4 Bert Bell COMM .40 1.00
OWN
5 Paul Brown CO 1.00 2.00
OWN
FOUND
6 Joe Carr PRES .40 1.00
7 Guy Chamberlin .40 1.00
8 Dutch Clark .50 1.25
9 Jimmy Conzelman .40 1.00
10 Art Donovan .75 1.50
11 Paddy Driscoll .40 1.00
12 Bill Dudley .50 1.25
13 Dan Fortmann .40 1.00
14 Otto Graham 1.50 3.00
15 Red Grange 2.00 4.00
16 George Halas CO 1.00 2.00
OWN
17 Mel Hein .40 1.00
18 Fats Henry .40 1.00
19 Bill Hewitt .40 1.00
20 Clarke Hinkle .40 1.00
21 Elroy Hirsch .75 1.50
22 Robert(Cal) Hubbard .40 1.00
23 Lamar Hunt OWN .40 1.00
FOUNDER
24 Don Hutson .50 1.25
25 Earl Lambeau CO .40 1.00
26 Bobby Layne 1.25 2.50
27 Vince Lombardi CO 2.00 4.00
28 Sid Luckman 1.00 2.00
29 Gino Marchetti .50 1.25
30 Ollie Matson .75 1.50
31 George McAfee .50 1.25
32 Hugh McElhenny .75 1.50
33 Johnny Blood McNally .40 1.00
34 Marion Motley .75 1.50
35 Bronko Nagurski 1.25 2.50
36 Ernie Nevers .50 1.25
37 Leo Nomellini .50 1.25
38 Steve Owen CO .40 1.00
39 Joe Perry .75 1.50
40 Pete Pihos .50 1.25
41 Andy Robustelli .75 1.50
42 Ken Strong .50 1.25
43 Jim Thorpe 2.00 4.00
44 Y.A. Tittle 1.25 2.50
45 Charley Trippi .50 1.25
46 Emlen Tunnell .50 1.25
47 Bulldog Turner .75 1.50
48 Norm Van Brocklin 1.00 2.00
49 Steve Van Buren .75 1.50
50 Bob Waterfield 1.00 2.00

1974-75 Fleer Cloth Patches

These cloth stickers were inserted one per pack in 1974 and 1975 Fleer Hall of Fame packs although each includes a 1972 copyright year on the fronts. The blankbacked stickers include one small team name sticker at the top and a larger team helmet or team logo at the bottom. We've catalogued and priced the stickers as pairs according to the smaller team name sticker first and the larger sticker second. Most of the stickers were nearly identical for both years except that the 1974 issue features no trademark (TM) notation on the fronts while the 1975 stickers include two trademark (TM) symbols. They are also very similar to the 1972-73 stickers and are often confused with them due to the 1972 copyright year printed on the fronts. However, the helmet stickers can be differentiated from the 1972-73 listings by the double-bar face mask design instead of single-bar. Most of the 1974 team logo stickers cannot be differentiated from the 1972-73 logo stickers and therefore are not listed below. However, the 1975 team logo stickers are priced below (marked with an *) since they do feature the trademark (TM) symbol distinction on the logo sticker portion. The glue used for these stickers tends to break down over time and will cause spots to bleed through to the fronts and separation of the sticker from the backing is quite common, therefore they are extremely condition sensitive.

COMPLETE SET (62) 125.00 250.00
1 Bears Name 4.00 8.00
Cowboys Small Helmet
2 Bears Name 3.00 6.00
Jets helmet
3 Bengals Name 2.50 5.00
Cardinals Helmet
4 Bengals Name 3.00 6.00
Giants Logo TM *
5A Bills Name 2.50 5.00
Chiefs Logo Yellow No TM
5B Bills Name 2.50 5.00
Chiefs Logo Yellow TM
6 Bills Name 4.00 8.00
Cowboys Large Helmet
7 Broncos Name 2.50 5.00
Colts Helmet
8 Broncos Name 2.50 5.00
Patriots Logo *
9 Broncos Name 4.00 8.00
Redskins Helmet
10 Browns Name 2.50 5.00
Chargers Helmet
11 Browns Name 2.50 5.00
Saints Helmet
12A Cardinals Name Yell No TM 2.50 5.00
Bengals Logo
12B Cardinals Name Yellow TM 2.50 5.00
Bengals Logo
13 Cardinals Name 4.00 8.00
Raiders Helmet
14 Chargers Name Dark Blue 3.00 6.00
Bears Helmet Orange C
15 Chiefs Name 2.50 5.00
Browns Helmet
16 Chiefs Name 2.50 5.00
NFL Logo *
17 Colts Name 2.50 5.00
Saints Logo *
18 Colts Name 4.00 8.00
Steelers Logo *
19 Cowboys Name 4.00 8.00
Broncos Helmet
20 Cowboys Name 4.00 8.00
Dolphins Helmet
21 Dolphins Name 3.00 6.00
Vikings Helmet
22 Eagles Name 2.50 5.00
Chiefs Helmet
23 Eagles Name 4.00 8.00
Steelers Helmet
24 Falcons Name 3.00 6.00
Browns Logo *
25 Falcons Name 3.00 6.00
Giants Logo *
26 Falcons Name 2.50 5.00
Oilers Helmet
27 49ers Name 3.00 6.00
Colts Logo *
28 49ers Name 4.00 8.00
Packers Logo *
29 Giants Name 3.00 6.00
Bills Logo *
30 Giants Name 2.50 5.00
Lions Logo *
31 Jets Name 4.00 8.00
Broncos Logo *
32 Jets Name 2.50 5.00
Falcons Logo *
33 Lions Name 2.50 5.00
Oilers Logo *
34 Lions Name 2.50 5.00
Rams Logo Y
35 Oilers Name 2.50 5.00
Cardinals Logo *
36 Oilers Name 2.50 5.00
Eagles Helmet
37A Packers Name 3.00 6.00
Chargers Logo dark blue No TM
37B Packers Name/Chargers Logo * 3.00 6.00
38 Packers Name 3.00 6.00
Eagles Logo *
39 Patriots Name 2.50 5.00
Falcons Helmet
40 Patriots Name 3.00 6.00
Jets Logo *
41A Raiders Name 4.00 8.00
Redskins Logo Yellow TM
41B Raiders Name/Redskins Logo * 4.00 8.00
42 Raiders Name 3.00 6.00
Giants Helmet
43 Rams Name 4.00 8.00
Dolphins Logo *
44 Rams Name/49ers Logo * 4.00 8.00
45 Redskins Name 2.50 5.00
Bengals Helmet
46 Redskins Name/49ers Helmet 4.00 8.00
47 Saints Name 2.50 5.00
Lions Helmet
48 Saints Name 4.00 8.00
Raiders Logo *
49 Steelers Name 4.00 8.00
Packers Helmet
50 Steelers Name 3.00 6.00
Rams Helmet
51 Steelers Name 3.00 6.00
Vikings Logo *
52 Vikings Name 3.00 6.00
Bears Logo *
53 Vikings Name 3.00 6.00
Bills Helmet
54 Vikings Name 2.50 5.00
Patriots Helmet
55 AFC Conference 4.00 8.00
AFC Logo
56 AFC Conference 4.00 8.00
AFC Logo
57 NFC Conference/NFC Logo 4.00 8.00
58 NFC Conference 4.00 8.00
NFC Logo

1975 Fleer Hall of Fame

The 1975 Fleer Hall of Fame football card set contains 84 cards. The cards measure 2 1/2" by 4". Except for the change in border color from white to brown and the different set numbering contained on the backs of the cards, fifty of the cards in this set are very similar to the cards in the 1974 Fleer set. Thirty-four additional cards have been added to this set in comparison to the 1974 set. These cards are numbered and were issued in wax packs with cloth team logo stickers.

COMPLETE SET (84) 40.00 80.00
1 Jim Thorpe 1.50 3.00
2 Cliff Battles .40 1.00
3 Bronko Nagurski 1.00 2.00
4 Red Grange 1.50 3.00
5 Guy Chamberlin .30 .75
6 Joe Carr PRES .30 .75
7 George Halas .75 1.50
CO/OWN//FOUNDER
8 Jimmy Conzelman .30 .75
9 George McAfee .40 1.00
10 Clarke Hinkle .30 .75
11 Paddy Driscoll .30 .75
12 Mel Hein .30 .75
13 Johnny Blood McNally .30 .75
14 Dutch Clark .40 1.00
15 Steve Owen CO .30 .75
16 Bill Hewitt .30 .75
17 Cal Hubbard .30 .75
18 Don Hutson .63 1.25
19 Ernie Nevers .40 1.00
20 Dan Fortmann .30 .75
21 Ken Strong .40 1.00
22 Chuck Bednarik .63 1.25
23 Bert Bell COMM/OWN .30 .75
24 Paul Brown CO/OWN/FOUND .75 1.50
25 Art Donovan .63 1.25
26 Bill Dudley .40 1.00
27 Otto Graham 1.00 2.00
28 Fats Henry .40 1.00
29 Elroy Hirsch .63 1.25
30 Lamar Hunt OWN/FOUND .30 .75
31 Curly Lambeau .30 .75
CO/OWN/FOUNDER
32 Vince Lombardi CO 1.50 3.00
33 Sid Luckman .75 1.50
34 Gino Marchetti .40 1.00
35 Ollie Matson .63 1.25
36 Hugh McElhenny .63 1.25
37 Marion Motley .40 1.00
38 Leo Nomellini .40 1.00
39 Joe Perry .63 1.25
40 Andy Robustelli .40 1.00
41 Pete Pihos .40 1.00
42 Y.A. Tittle 1.00 2.00
43 Charley Trippi .40 1.00
44 Emlen Tunnell .40 1.00
45 Bulldog Turner .63 1.25
46 Norm Van Brocklin .75 1.50
47 Steve Van Buren .63 1.25
48 Bob Waterfield .75 1.50
49 Bobby Layne 1.00 2.00
50 Sammy Baugh 1.25 2.50
51 Joe Guyon .30 .75
52 Roy(Link) Lyman .30 .75
53 George Trafton .30 .75
54 Turk Edwards .30 .75
55 Ed Healey .30 .75
56 Mike Michalske .30 .75
57 Alex Wojciechowicz .30 .75
58 Dante Lavelli .63 1.25
59 George Connor .40 1.00
60 Wayne Millner .30 .75
61 Jack Christiansen .30 .75
62 Roosevelt Brown .30 .75
63 Joe Stydahar .30 .75
64 Ernie Stautner .40 1.00
65 Jim Parker .40 1.00
66 Raymond Berry .63 1.25
67 George Preston Marshall .30 .75
OWN/FOUND
68 Clarence(Ace) Parker .30 .75
69 Greasy Neale CO .30 .75
70 Tim Mara OWN/FOUND .30 .75
71 Hugh (Shorty) Ray OFF .30 .75
72 Tom Fears .40 1.00
73 Arnie Herber .30 .75
74 Walt Kiesling .30 .75
75 Frank (Bruiser) Kinard .30 .75
76 Tony Canadeo .30 .75
77 Bill George .30 .75
78 Art Rooney .30 .75
FOUND/OWN/ADMIN
79 Joe Schmidt .40 1.00
80 Dan Reeves OWN .30 .75
81 Lou Groza .63 1.25
82 Charles W. Bidwill OWN .30 .75
83 Lenny Moore .63 1.25
84 Dick (Night Train) Lane .40 1.00

1976 Fleer Cloth Patches

These cloth stickers were sold as a stand alone product and do not feature any copyright year on them. The blankbacked stickers include one small team name sticker at the top and a larger team helmet or team logo at the bottom. We've catalogued and priced the stickers as pairs according to the smaller team name sticker first and the larger sticker second. Many of the stickers can be confused with the 1972-73 and 1974-75 sets, but this year has no date designation. The glue used for these stickers tends to break down over time and will cause spots to bleed through to the fronts and separation of the sticker from the backing is quite common, therefore they are extremely condition sensitive.

1 Bears Name 3.00 6.00
Cowboys Small Helmet
2 Bears Name 2.50 5.00
Jets helmet
3 Bengals Name 2.00 4.00
Cardinals Helmet
4 Bengals Name 2.50 5.00
Giants Logo
5 Bills Name 2.00 4.00
Chiefs Logo
6 Bills Name 3.00 6.00
Cowboys Large Helmet
7 Broncos Name 2.00 4.00
Colts Helmet
8 Broncos Name 2.00 4.00
Patriots Logo
9 Broncos Name 3.00 6.00
Redskins Helmet
10 Browns Name 2.00 4.00
Chargers Helmet
11 Browns Name 2.00 4.00
Saints Helmet
12 Buccaneers Name 2.00 4.00
Seahawks Helmet
13 Buccaneers Name 2.00 4.00
Seahawks Logo
14 Cardinals Name 2.00 4.00
Bengals Logo
15 Cardinals Name 3.00 6.00
Raiders Helmet
16 Chargers Name 2.50 5.00
Bears Helmet
17 Chiefs Name 2.50 5.00
Browns Helmet
18 Colts Name 2.00 4.00
Saints Logo
19 Colts Name 3.00 6.00
Steelers Logo
20 Cowboys Name 3.00 6.00
Broncos Helmet
21 Cowboys Name 3.00 6.00
Dolphins Helmet
22 Dolphins Name 2.50 5.00
Vikings Logo
23 Eagles Name 2.00 4.00
Chiefs Helmet
24 Eagles Name 3.00 6.00
Steelers Helmet
25 Falcons Name 2.50 5.00
Browns Logo
26 Falcons Name 2.00 4.00
Oilers Helmet
27 49ers Name 2.50 5.00
Colts Logo
28 49ers Name 3.00 6.00
Packers Logo
29 Giants Name 2.50 5.00
Bills Logo
30 Giants Name 2.00 4.00
Lions Logo
31 Jets Name 3.00 6.00
Broncos Logo
32 Jets Name 2.00 4.00
Falcons Logo
33 Lions Name 2.00 4.00
Oilers Helmet
34 Lions Name 2.00 4.00
Rams Logo
35 Oilers Name 2.00 4.00
Cardinals Logo
36 Oilers Name 2.00 4.00
Eagles Helmet
37 Packers Name 2.50 5.00
Chargers Logo
38 Packers Name 2.50 5.00
Eagles Logo
39 Patriots Name 2.00 4.00
Falcons Helmet
40 Patriots Name 2.50 5.00
Jets Logo
41 Raiders Name 3.00 6.00
Redskins Logo
42 Raiders Name 2.50 5.00
Giants Helmet
43 Rams Name 3.00 6.00
Dolphins Logo
44 Rams Name/49ers Logo 3.00 6.00
45 Redskins Name 2.00 4.00
Bengals Helmet
46 Redskins Name/49ers Helmet 3.00 6.00
47 Saints Name 2.00 4.00
Lions Helmet
48 Seahawks Name 2.00 4.00
Buccaneers Helmet
49 Saints Name 3.00 6.00
Raiders Logo
50 Seahawks Name 2.00 4.00
Buccaneers Logo
51 Steelers Name 3.00 6.00
Packers Helmet
52 Steelers Name 2.50 5.00
Rams Helmet
53 Steelers Name 2.50 5.00
Vikings Logo
54 Vikings Name 2.50 5.00
Bears Logo
55 Vikings Name 2.50 5.00
Bills Helmet
56 Vikings Name 2.00 4.00
Patriots Helmet

1976 Fleer Hi Gloss Patches

Fleer issued these helmet and logo stickers in 1976 as a separate product packaged in its own wrapper with two Hi Gloss paper stickers and one Cloth Patch in each pack. Each card is blankbacked and features a small team name sticker at the top and a larger logo or helmet sticker at the bottom. We've cataloged the set in order by the team name on top. Note that no year of issue was printed on the stickers.

COMPLETE SET (56) 125.00 225.00
*CLOTH VERSION: .5X TO 1.2X
1 Bears Name 3.00 6.00
Cowboys Small Helmet
2 Bears Name 2.50 5.00
Jets helmet
3 Bengals Name 2.00 4.00
Cardinals Helmet
4 Bengals Name 2.50 5.00
Giants Logo
5 Bills Name 2.00 4.00
Chiefs Logo
6 Bills Name 3.00 6.00
Cowboys Large Helmet
7 Broncos Name 2.00 4.00
Colts Helmet
8 Broncos Name 2.00 4.00
Patriots Logo
9 Broncos Name 3.00 6.00
Redskins Helmet
10 Browns Name 2.00 4.00
Chargers Helmet
11 Browns Name 2.00 4.00
Saints Helmet
12 Buccaneers Name 2.00 4.00
Seahawks Helmet
13 Buccaneers Name 2.00 4.00
Seahawks Logo
14 Cardinals Name 2.00 4.00
Bengals Logo
15 Cardinals Name 3.00 6.00
Raiders Helmet
16 Chargers Name 2.50 5.00
Bears Helmet
17 Chiefs Name 2.50 5.00
Browns Helmet
18 Colts Name 2.00 4.00
Saints Logo
19 Colts Name 3.00 6.00
Steelers Logo
20 Cowboys Name 3.00 6.00
Broncos Helmet
21 Cowboys Name 3.00 6.00
Dolphins Helmet
22 Dolphins Name 2.50 5.00
Vikings Logo
23 Eagles Name 2.00 4.00
Chiefs Helmet
24 Eagles Name 3.00 6.00
Steelers Helmet
25 Falcons Name 2.50 5.00
Browns Logo
26 Falcons Name 2.00 4.00
Oilers Helmet
27 49ers Name 2.50 5.00
Colts Logo
28 49ers Name 3.00 6.00
Packers Logo
29 Giants Name 2.50 5.00
Bills Logo
30 Giants Name 2.00 4.00
Lions Logo
31 Jets Name 3.00 6.00
Broncos Logo
32 Jets Name 2.00 4.00
Falcons Logo
33 Lions Name 2.00 4.00
Oilers Helmet
34 Lions Name 2.00 4.00
Rams Logo
35 Oilers Name 2.00 4.00
Cardinals Logo
36 Oilers Name 2.00 4.00
Eagles Helmet
37 Packers Name 2.50 5.00
Chargers Logo
38 Packers Name 2.50 5.00
Eagles Logo
39 Patriots Name 2.00 4.00
Falcons Helmet
40 Patriots Name 2.50 5.00
Jets Logo
41 Raiders Name 2.50 5.00
Giants Helmet
42 Raiders Name 3.00 6.00
Redskins Logo
43 Rams Name 3.00 6.00
Dolphins Logo
44 Rams Name/49ers Logo 3.00 6.00
45 Redskins Name 2.00 4.00
Bengals Helmet
46 Redskins Name/49ers Helmet 3.00 6.00
47 Saints Name 2.00 4.00
Lions Helmet
48 Saints Name 3.00 6.00
Raiders Logo
49 Seahawks Name 2.00 4.00
Buccaneers Helmet
50 Seahawks Name 2.00 4.00
Buccaneers Logo
51 Steelers Name 3.00 6.00
Packers Helmet
52 Steelers Name 2.50 5.00
Rams Helmet
53 Steelers Name 2.50 5.00
Vikings Logo
54 Vikings Name 2.50 5.00
Bears Logo
55 Vikings Name 2.50 5.00
Bills Helmet
56 Vikings Name 2.00 4.00
Patriots Helmet

1976 Fleer Team Action

This 66-card standard-size set contains cards picturing action scenes with two cards for every NFL team and then a card for each previous Super Bowl. The first card in each team pair, i.e., the odd-numbered card, is an offensive card; the even-numbered cards are defensive scenes. Cards have a white border with a red outline on the front; the backs are printed with black ink on white cardboard stock with a light blue NFL emblem superimposed in the middle of the write-up on the back of the card. These cards are actually stickers as they may be peeled and stuck. The instructions on the back of the sticker say, "For use as sticker, bend corner and peel." The cards were issued in four-card packs with no inserts, unlike earlier Fleer football issues.

COMPLETE SET (66) 300.00 600.00
1 Baltimore Colts 4.50 9.00
2 Baltimore Colts 4.00 8.00
3 Buffalo Bills 4.00 8.00
4 Buffalo Bills 4.00 8.00
5 Cincinnati Bengals 4.00 8.00
6 Cincinnati Bengals 6.00 12.00
7 Cleveland Browns 4.00 8.00
8 Cleveland Browns 4.00 8.00
9 Denver Broncos 4.00 8.00
10 Denver Broncos 4.00 8.00
11 Houston Oilers 5.00 10.00
12 Houston Oilers 6.00 12.00
13 Kansas City Chiefs 4.00 8.00
14 Kansas City Chiefs 4.00 8.00
15 Miami Dolphins 6.00 12.00
16 Miami Dolphins 5.00 10.00
17 New England Patriots 4.00 8.00
18 New England Patriots 4.00 8.00
19 New York Jets 7.50 15.00
20 New York Jets 6.00 12.00
21 Oakland Raiders 5.00 10.00
22 Oakland Raiders 5.00 10.00
23 Pittsburgh Steelers 7.50 15.00
24 Pittsburgh Steelers 6.00 12.00
25 San Diego Chargers 4.00 8.00
26 San Diego Chargers 4.00 8.00
27 Tampa Bay Buccaneers 4.00 8.00
28 Tampa Bay Buccaneers 4.00 8.00
29 Atlanta Falcons 4.00 8.00
30 Atlanta Falcons 4.00 8.00
31 Chicago Bears 4.00 8.00
32 Chicago Bears 4.00 8.00
33 Dallas Cowboys 5.00 10.00
34 Dallas Cowboys 5.00 10.00
35 Detroit Lions 4.00 8.00
36 Detroit Lions 4.00 8.00
37 Green Bay Packers 4.00 8.00
38 Green Bay Packers 4.00 8.00
39 Los Angeles Rams 4.00 8.00
40 Los Angeles Rams 4.00 8.00
41 Minnesota Vikings 6.00 12.00
42 Minnesota Vikings 4.00 8.00
43 New York Giants 4.00 8.00
44 New York Giants 4.00 8.00
45 New Orleans Saints 5.00 10.00
46 New Orleans Saints 4.00 8.00
47 Philadelphia Eagles 4.00 8.00
48 Philadelphia Eagles 4.00 8.00
49 San Francisco 49ers 4.00 8.00
50 San Francisco 49ers 4.00 8.00
51 St. Louis Cardinals 5.00 10.00
52 St. Louis Cardinals 4.00 8.00
53 Seattle Seahawks 4.00 8.00
54 Seattle Seahawks 4.00 8.00
55 Washington Redskins 5.00 10.00
56 Washington Redskins 4.00 8.00
57 Super Bowl I 6.00 12.00
58 Super Bowl II 6.00 12.00
59 Super Bowl III 6.00 12.00
60 Super Bowl IV 6.00 12.00
61 Super Bowl V 6.00 12.00
62 Super Bowl VI 10.00 20.00
63 Super Bowl VII 7.50 15.00
64 Super Bowl VIII 7.50 15.00
65 Super Bowl IX 6.00 12.00
66 Super Bowl X 25.00 40.00

1977 Fleer Team Action

The 1977 Fleer Teams in Action football set contains 67 standard-size cards depicting action scenes. There are two cards for each NFL team and one card for each Super Bowl. The first card in each team pair, i.e., the odd-numbered card, is an offensive card; the even-numbered cards are defensive scenes. The cards have white borders and the backs are printed in dark blue ink on gray stock. The cards are numbered and contain a 1977 copyright date. The cards were issued in four-card wax packs along with four team logo stickers.

COMPLETE SET (67) 40.00 80.00
1 Baltimore Colts 1.25 2.50
2 Baltimore Colts .63 1.25
3 Buffalo Bills .63 1.25
4 Buffalo Bills .63 1.25
5 Cincinnati Bengals 1.00 2.00
6 Cincinnati Bengals .63 1.25
7 Cleveland Browns .75 1.50
8 Cleveland Browns .63 1.25
9 Denver Broncos .63 1.25
10 Denver Broncos .63 1.25
11 Houston Oilers .63 1.25
12 Houston Oilers .63 1.25
13 Kansas City Chiefs .63 1.25
14 Kansas City Chiefs .63 1.25
15 Miami Dolphins .75 1.50
16 Miami Dolphins .75 1.50
17 New England Patriots .63 1.25
18 New England Patriots .63 1.25
19 New York Jets 4.00 8.00
20 New York Jets .63 1.25
21 Oakland Raiders .75 1.50
22 Oakland Raiders .75 1.50
23 Pittsburgh Steelers 1.00 2.00
24 Pittsburgh Steelers .75 1.50
25 San Diego Chargers 2.00 4.00
26 San Diego Chargers .63 1.25
27 Seattle Seahawks 1.00 2.00
28 Seattle Seahawks .75 1.50
29 Atlanta Falcons .63 1.25
30 Atlanta Falcons .63 1.25
31 Chicago Bears 3.00 6.00
32 Chicago Bears .63 1.25
33 Dallas Cowboys .75 1.50
34 Dallas Cowboys 1.25 2.50
35 Detroit Lions .63 1.25
36 Detroit Lions .63 1.25
37 Green Bay Packers .63 1.25
38 Green Bay Packers 3.00 6.00
39 Los Angeles Rams .63 1.25
40 Los Angeles Rams .63 1.25
41 Minnesota Vikings .63 1.25
42 Minnesota Vikings .63 1.25
43 New Orleans Saints .63 1.25
44 New Orleans Saints .63 1.25
45 New York Giants .63 1.25
46 New York Giants .63 1.25
47 Philadelphia Eagles .63 1.25
48 Philadelphia Eagles .63 1.25
49 St. Louis Cardinals .75 1.50
50 St. Louis Cardinals .63 1.25
51 San Francisco 49ers .75 1.50
52 San Francisco 49ers .75 1.50
53 Tampa Bay Buccaneers .63 1.25
54 Tampa Bay Buccaneers .63 1.25
55 Washington Redskins 1.25 2.50
56 Washington Redskins .75 1.50
57 Super Bowl I .75 1.50
58 Super Bowl II .75 1.50
59 Super Bowl III .75 1.50
60 Super Bowl IV .75 1.50
61 Super Bowl V .75 1.50
62 Super Bowl VI 2.00 4.00
63 Super Bowl VII 1.25 2.50
64 Super Bowl VIII 1.25 2.50
65 Super Bowl IX .75 1.50
66 Super Bowl X 2.00 4.00
67 Super Bowl XI 2.00 4.00

1977 Fleer Team Action Stickers

This set of stickers was issued one per pack in the 1977 Fleer Team Action card release. Each NFL team is represented with two stickers, with all but the Cowboys and Seahawks having both a helmet sticker and logo/insignia sticker. Several were produced with slight color variations in the border as noted below. Although these and other similar stickers were released over a number of years, the exact year of issue can be identified by the unique sticker back -- an artist's drawing of fingers peeling away a Jets helmet sticker. Two separate posters were also released to house the stickers; one for each conference. Each sticker measures roughly 2 3/8" by 2 3/4."

COMPLETE SET (65) 100.00 200.00
1A Atlanta Falcons Helmet 1.25 3.00
1B Atlanta Falcons Helmet 1.25 3.00
2 Atlanta Falcons 1.25 3.00
Logo
3A Baltimore Colts Helmet 1.25 3.00
3B Baltimore Colts Helmet 1.25 3.00
4 Baltimore Colts 1.25 3.00
Logo
5 Buffalo Bills 1.50 4.00
Helmet
6 Buffalo Bills 1.50 4.00
Logo

7A Chicago Bears Helmet 1.50 4.00
7B Chicago Bears Helmet (red border) 1.50 4.00
8 Chicago Bears Logo 1.50 4.00
9 Cincinnati Bengals Helmet 1.25 3.00
10 Cincinnati Bengals Logo 1.25 3.00
11 Cleveland Browns Helmet 1.50 4.00
12 Cleveland Browns Logo 1.50 4.00
13 Dallas Cowboys Helmet 2.00 5.00
14 Dallas Cowboys Helmet 2.00 5.00
15 Denver Broncos Helmet 2.00 5.00
16 Denver Broncos Logo 2.00 5.00
17 Detroit Lions Helmet 1.25 3.00
18 Detroit Lions Logo 1.25 3.00
19 Green Bay Packers Helmet 2.00 5.00
20 Green Bay Packers Logo 2.00 5.00
21 Houston Oilers Helmet 1.25 3.00
22 Houston Oilers Logo 1.25 3.00
23 Kansas City Chiefs Helmet 1.25 3.00
24 Kansas City Chiefs Logo 1.25 3.00
25 Los Angeles Rams Helmet 1.25 3.00
26A Los Angeles Rams Logo 1.25 3.00
26B Los Angeles Rams Logo 1.25 3.00
27 Miami Dolphins Helmet 2.00 5.00
28 Miami Dolphins Logo 2.00 5.00
29 Minnesota Vikings Helmet 1.50 4.00
30 Minnesota Vikings Logo 1.50 4.00
31A New England Patriots Helmet 1.25 3.00
31B New England Patriots Helmet 1.25 3.00
32 New England Patriots Logo 1.25 3.00
33 New Orleans Saints Helmet 1.25 3.00
34 New Orleans Saints Logo 1.25 3.00
35 New York Giants Helmet 1.50 4.00
36 New York Giants Logo 1.50 4.00
37 New York Jets Helmet 1.50 4.00
38A New York Jets Logo 1.50 4.00
38B New York Jets Logo (green border) 1.50 4.00
39 Oakland Raiders Helmet 2.00 5.00
40A Oakland Raiders Logo 2.00 5.00
40B Oakland Raiders Logo 2.00 5.00
41A Philadelphia Eagles Helmet 1.25 3.00
41B Philadelphia Eagles Helmet (green border) 1.25 3.00
42 Philadelphia Eagles Logo 1.25 3.00
43 Pittsburgh Steelers Helmet 2.00 5.00
44A Pittsburgh Steelers Logo 2.00 5.00
44B Pittsburgh Steelers Logo (yellow border) 2.00 5.00
45 St. Louis Cardinals Helmet 1.25 3.00
46 St. Louis Cardinals Logo 1.25 3.00
47 San Diego Chargers Helmet 1.25 3.00
48 San Diego Chargers Logo 1.25 3.00
49 San Francisco 49ers Helmet 2.00 5.00
50 San Francisco 49ers Logo 2.00 5.00
51 Seattle Seahawks Helmet 1.25 3.00
52 Seattle Seahawks Helmet 1.25 3.00
53 Tampa Bay Bucs Helmet 1.25 3.00
54 Tampa Bay Bucs Logo 1.25 3.00
55 Washington Redskins Helmet 2.00 5.00
56 Washington Redskins Logo 2.00 5.00
NNO AFC Poster 5.00 10.00
NNO NFC Poster 5.00 10.00

1978 Fleer Team Action

The 1978 Fleer Teams in Action football set contains 68 action scenes. The cards measure the standard size. As in the previous year, each team is depicted on two cards and each Super Bowl is depicted on one card. The additional card in comparison to last year's set comes from the additional Super Bowl which was played during the year. The fronts have yellow borders. The card backs are printed with black ink on gray stock. The cards are numbered and feature a 1978 copyright date. Cards were issued in wax packs of seven team cards plus four team logo stickers.

COMPLETE SET (68) 20.00 40.00
1 Atlanta Falcons .63 1.25
2 Atlanta Falcons .25 .50
3 Baltimore Colts .25 .50
4 Baltimore Colts .25 .50
5 Buffalo Bills .25 .50
6 Buffalo Bills .25 .50
7 Chicago Bears 3.00 6.00
8 Chicago Bears .25 .50
9 Cincinnati Bengals .75 1.50
10 Cincinnati Bengals .25 .50
11 Cleveland Browns .38 .75
12 Cleveland Browns .50 1.00
13 Dallas Cowboys 3.00 6.00
14 Dallas Cowboys .50 1.00
15 Denver Broncos .25 .50
16 Denver Broncos 2.00 4.00
17 Detroit Lions .25 .50
18 Detroit Lions .25 .50
19 Green Bay Packers .25 .50
20 Green Bay Packers .25 .50
21 Houston Oilers .25 .50
22 Houston Oilers .25 .50
23 Kansas City Chiefs .25 .50
24 Kansas City Chiefs .25 .50
25 Los Angeles Rams .25 .50
26 Los Angeles Rams .25 .50
27 Miami Dolphins 1.50 3.00
28 Miami Dolphins .38 .75
29 Minnesota Vikings .50 1.00
30 Minnesota Vikings .25 .50
31 New England Patriots .25 .50
32 New England Patriots .25 .50
33 New Orleans Saints .25 .50
34 New Orleans Saints .25 .50
35 New York Giants .25 .50
36 New York Giants .25 .50
37 New York Jets .25 .50
38 New York Jets .25 .50
39 Oakland Raiders .50 1.00
40 Oakland Raiders .50 1.00
41 Philadelphia Eagles .40 1.00
42 Philadelphia Eagles .25 .50
43 Pittsburgh Steelers .38 .75
44 Pittsburgh Steelers .75 1.50
45 St. Louis Cardinals .25 .50
46 St. Louis Cardinals .25 .50
47 San Diego Chargers .25 .50
48 San Diego Chargers .25 .50
49 San Francisco 49ers .50 1.00
50 San Francisco 49ers .50 1.00
51 Seattle Seahawks .25 .50
52 Seattle Seahawks .25 .50
53 Tampa Bay Buccaneers .25 .50
54 Tampa Bay Buccaneers .25 .50
55 Washington Redskins .38 .75
56 Washington Redskins .38 .75
57 Super Bowl I 1.00 2.00
58 Super Bowl II .38 .75
59 Super Bowl III .38 .75
60 Super Bowl IV .38 .75
61 Super Bowl V .38 .75
62 Super Bowl VI .38 .75
63 Super Bowl VII .38 .75
64 Super Bowl VIII 1.00 2.00
65 Super Bowl IX 1.50 3.00
66 Super Bowl X .38 .75
67 Super Bowl XI .75 1.50
68 Super Bowl XII 2.00 4.00

1978 Fleer Team Action Stickers

This set of stickers was issued one per pack in the 1978 Fleer Team Action card release and is virtually identical to the 1979 set. Each NFL team is represented with two stickers, with all but the Cowboys and Seahawks having both a helmet sticker and logo/insignia sticker. Several were produced with slight color variations in the border as noted below. Although these and other similar stickers were released over a number of years, the exact year of issue can be identified by the unique sticker back -- a puzzle piece that forms a photo from Super Bowl XII when fully assembled. Note that there are a number of puzzle back variations for each team. Very few collectors attempt to assemble a full set with all back variations. Reportedly, there are 170-total different sticker combinations of fronts and backs. We've noted the number of known back variations for each sticker below. Each sticker measures roughly 2 3/8" by 2 3/4."

COMPLETE SET (65) 70.00 120.00
1A Atlanta Falcons Helmet 1 .75 1.50
1B Atlanta Falcons Helmet 3 .75 1.50
2 Atlanta Falcons Logo 3 .75 1.50
3A Baltimore Colts Helmet 1 1.25 2.50
3B Baltimore Colts Helmet 2 (yellow border) 1.25 2.50
4 Baltimore Colts Logo 3 1.25 2.50
5 Buffalo Bills Helmet 3 1.25 2.50
6 Buffalo Bills Logo 3 1.25 2.50
7A Chicago Bears Helmet 1 1.25 2.50
7B Chicago Bears Helmet 2 (red border) .75 1.50
8 Chicago Bears Logo 3 1.25 2.50
9 Cincinnati Bengals Helmet 3 .75 1.50
10 Cincinnati Bengals Logo 3 .75 1.50
11 Cleveland Browns Helmet 3 1.25 2.50
12 Cleveland Browns Logo 3 1.25 2.50
13 Dallas Cowboys Helmet 3 2.00 4.00
14 Dallas Cowboys Helmet 3 2.00 4.00
15 Denver Broncos Helmet 2 2.00 4.00
16 Denver Broncos Logo 3 .75 1.50
17 Detroit Lions Helmet 2 .75 1.50
18 Detroit Lions Logo 3 .75 1.50
19 Green Bay Packers Helmet 3 2.00 4.00
20 Green Bay Packers Logo 3 2.00 4.00
21 Houston Oilers Helmet 4 .75 1.50
22 Houston Oilers Logo 3 .75 1.50
23 Kansas City Chiefs Helmet 3 .75 1.50
24 Kansas City Chiefs Logo 3 .75 1.50
25 Los Angeles Rams Helmet 3 .75 1.50
26A Los Angeles Rams blue .75 1.50
26B Los Angeles Rams Red .75 1.50
27 Miami Dolphins Helmet 3 2.00 4.00
28 Miami Dolphins Logo 3 1.50 3.00
29 Minnesota Vikings Helmet 3 1.25 2.50
30 Minnesota Vikings Logo 3 1.25 2.50
31A New England Pats Helmet 1 (blue border) .75 1.50
31B New England Pats Helmet 2 .75 1.50
32 New England Pats Logo 3 .75 1.50
33 New Orleans Saints Helmet 3 .75 1.50
34 New Orleans Saints Logo 3 .75 1.50
35 New York Giants Helmet 3 1.25 2.50
36 New York Giants Logo 3 1.25 2.50
37 New York Jets Helmet 3 1.25 2.50
38A New York Jets Logo 1 (blue border) .75 1.50
38B New York Jets Logo 3 1.25 2.50
39 Oakland Raiders Helmet 3 2.00 4.00
40A Oakland Raiders Logo 1 (blue border) .75 1.50
40B Oakland Raiders Logo 3 2.00 4.00
41A Philadelphia Eagles Helmet 1 .75 1.50
41B Philadelphia Eagles Helmet 2 .75 1.50
42 Philadelphia Eagles Logo 3 .75 1.50
43 Pittsburgh Steelers Helmet 3 2.00 4.00
44A Pittsburgh Steelers Logo 1 .75 1.50
44B Pittsburgh Steelers Logo 3 2.00 4.00
45 St. Louis Cardinals Helmet 3 .75 1.50
46 St. Louis Cardinals Logo 3 .75 1.50
47 San Diego Chargers Helmet 2 .75 1.50
48 San Diego Chargers Logo 3 .75 1.50
49 San Francisco 49ers Helmet 3 2.00 4.00
50 San Francisco 49ers Logo 3 2.00 4.00
51 Seattle Seahawks Helmet 3 .75 1.50
52 Seattle Seahawks Helmet 3 .75 1.50
53 Tampa Bay Bucs Helmet 3 .75 1.50
54 Tampa Bay Bucs Logo 3 .75 1.50
55 Washington Redskins Helmet 3 2.00 4.00
56 Washington Redskins Logo 3 2.00 4.00

1979 Fleer Team Action

The 1979 Fleer Teams in Action football set mirrors the previous two sets in design (colorful action scenes with specific players not identified) and contains an additional card for the most recent Super Bowl making a total of 69 standard-size cards in the set. The fronts have white borders, and the backs are printed in black ink on gray stock. The backs have a 1979 copyright date. The card numbering follows team name alphabetical order followed by Super Bowl cards in chronological order. Cards were issued in wax packs of seven team cards plus three team logo stickers.

COMPLETE SET (69) 15.00 30.00
1 Atlanta Falcons .50 1.00
2 Atlanta Falcons .20 .40
3 Baltimore Colts .20 .40
4 Baltimore Colts .20 .40
5 Buffalo Bills .20 .40
6 Buffalo Bills .20 .40
7 Chicago Bears .20 .40
8 Chicago Bears .20 .40
9 Cincinnati Bengals .20 .40
10 Cincinnati Bengals .20 .40
11 Cleveland Browns .20 .40
12 Cleveland Browns .20 .40
13 Dallas Cowboys 1.50 3.00
14 Dallas Cowboys .30 .60
15 Denver Broncos .20 .40
16 Denver Broncos .20 .40
17 Detroit Lions .20 .40
18 Detroit Lions .20 .40
19 Green Bay Packers .20 .40
20 Green Bay Packers .20 .40
21 Houston Oilers 3.00 6.00
22 Houston Oilers .20 .40
23 Kansas City Chiefs .20 .40
24 Kansas City Chiefs .20 .40
25 Los Angeles Rams .20 .40
26 Los Angeles Rams .20 .40
27 Miami Dolphins .30 .60
28 Miami Dolphins .30 .60
29 Minnesota Vikings .20 .40
30 Minnesota Vikings .20 .40
31 New England Patriots .20 .40
32 New England Patriots .20 .40
33 New Orleans Saints .50 1.00
34 New Orleans Saints .20 .40
35 New York Giants .20 .40
36 New York Giants .20 .40
37 New York Jets .20 .40
38 New York Jets .20 .40
39 Oakland Raiders 1.00 2.00
40 Oakland Raiders .30 .60
41 Philadelphia Eagles .20 .40
42 Philadelphia Eagles .20 .40
43 Pittsburgh Steelers .30 .60
44 Pittsburgh Steelers .50 1.00
45 St. Louis Cardinals .30 .60
46 St. Louis Cardinals .20 .40
47 San Diego Chargers .20 .40
48 San Diego Chargers .20 .40
49 San Francisco 49ers .30 .60
50 San Francisco 49ers .30 .60
51 Seattle Seahawks .20 .40
52 Seattle Seahawks .20 .40
53 Tampa Bay Buccaneers .20 .40
54 Tampa Bay Buccaneers .20 .40
55 Washington Redskins .30 .60
56 Washington Redskins .30 .60
57 Super Bowl I .50 1.00
58 Super Bowl II .75 1.50
59 Super Bowl III .30 .60
60 Super Bowl IV .30 .60
61 Super Bowl V .30 .60
62 Super Bowl VI 1.00 2.00
63 Super Bowl VII .30 .60
64 Super Bowl VIII 1.00 2.00
65 Super Bowl IX 1.50 3.00
66 Super Bowl X .30 .60
67 Super Bowl XI .30 .60
68 Super Bowl XII .30 .60
69 Super Bowl XIII .75 1.50

1979 Fleer Team Action Stickers

This set of stickers was issued one per pack in the 1979 Fleer Team Action card release and is virtually identical to the 1978 set. Each NFL team is represented with two stickers, with all but the Cowboys and Seahawks having both a helmet sticker and logo/insignia sticker. Several were produced with slight color variations in the border as noted below. Although these and other similar stickers were released over a number of years, the exact year of issue can be identified by the unique sticker back -- a puzzle piece that forms a photo from Super Bowl XIII when fully assembled. Note that there are a number of puzzle back variations for each team. Very few collectors attempt to assemble a full set with all back variations. Reportedly, there are 170-total different sticker combinations of fronts and backs. We've noted the number of known back variations for each sticker below. Each sticker measures roughly 2 3/8" by 2 3/4."

COMPLETE SET (65) 30.00 60.00
1A Atlanta Falcons Helmet 1 .50 1.00
1B Atlanta Falcons Helmet 3 .50 1.00
2 Atlanta Falcons Logo 3 .50 1.00
3A Baltimore Colts Helmet 1 .75 1.50
3B Baltimore Colts Helmet 2 (yellow border) .75 1.50
4 Baltimore Colts Logo 3 .75 1.50
5 Buffalo Bills Helmet 3 .75 1.50
6 Buffalo Bills Logo 3 .75 1.50
7A Chicago Bears Helmet 1 .75 1.50
7B Chicago Bears Helmet 2 (red border) .75 1.50
8 Chicago Bears Logo 3 .75 1.50
9 Cincinnati Bengals Helmet 3 .50 1.00
10 Cincinnati Bengals Logo 3 .50 1.00
11 Cleveland Browns Helmet 3 .75 1.50
12 Cleveland Browns Logo 3 .75 1.50
13 Dallas Cowboys Helmet 3 1.25 2.50
14 Dallas Cowboys Helmet 3 1.25 2.50
15 Denver Broncos Helmet 2 .75 1.50
16 Denver Broncos Logo 3 .75 1.50
17 Detroit Lions Helmet 2 .50 1.00
18 Detroit Lions Logo 3 .50 1.00
19 Green Bay Packers Helmet 3 1.25 2.50
20 Green Bay Packers Logo 3 1.25 2.50
21 Houston Oilers Helmet 4 .50 1.00
22 Houston Oilers Logo 3 .50 1.00
23 Kansas City Chiefs Helmet 3 .50 1.00
24 Kansas City Chiefs Logo 3 .50 1.00
25 Los Angeles Rams Helmet 3 .50 1.00
26A Los Angeles Rams Logo 1#(blue border) .50 1.00
26B Los Angeles Rams Logo 3 .50 1.00
27 Miami Dolphins Helmet 3 1.25 2.50
28 Miami Dolphins Logo 3 1.25 2.50
29 Minnesota Vikings Helmet 3 .75 1.50
30 Minnesota Vikings Logo 3 .75 1.50
31A New England Pats Helmet 1 (blue border) .50 1.00
31B New England Pats Helmet 2 .50 1.00
32 New England Pats Logo 3 .50 1.00
33 New Orleans Saints Helmet 3 .50 1.00
34 New Orleans Saints Logo 3 .50 1.00
35 New York Giants Helmet 3 .75 1.50
36 New York Giants Logo 3 .75 1.50
37 New York Jets Helmet 3 .75 1.50
38A New York Jets Logo 1 (blue border) .75 1.50
38B New York Jets Logo 3 .75 1.50
39 Oakland Raiders Helmet 3 1.25 2.50
40A Oakland Raiders Logo 1 (blue border) 1.25 2.50
40B Oakland Raiders Logo 3 1.25 2.50
41A Philadelphia Eagles Helmet 1 .50 1.00
41B Philadelphia Eagles Helmet 2 .50 1.00
42 Philadelphia Eagles Logo 3 .50 1.00
43 Pittsburgh Steelers Helmet 3 1.25 2.50
44A Pittsburgh Steelers Logo 1 1.25 2.50
44B Pittsburgh Steelers Logo 3 1.25 2.50
45 St. Louis Cardinals Helmet 3 .50 1.00
46 St. Louis Cardinals Logo 3 .50 1.00
47 San Diego Chargers Helmet 2 .50 1.00
48 San Diego Chargers Logo 3 .50 1.00
49 San Francisco 49ers Helmet 3 1.25 2.50
50 San Francisco 49ers Logo 3 1.25 2.50
51 Seattle Seahawks Helmet 3 .50 1.00
52 Seattle Seahawks Helmet 3 .50 1.00
53 Tampa Bay Bucs Helmet 3 .50 1.00
54 Tampa Bay Bucs Logo 3 .50 1.00
55 Washington Redskins Helmet 3 .75 1.50
56 Washington Redskins Logo 3 .75 1.50

1980 Fleer Team Action

The 1980 Fleer Teams in Action football set continues the tradition of earlier sets but has one additional card for the most recent Super Bowl, i.e., now 70 full color standard-size cards in the set. The fronts have white borders and the backs are printed in black on gray stock. The cards are numbered on back and feature a 1980 copyright date. The card numbering follows team name alphabetical order followed by Super Bowl cards in chronological order. Cards were issued in seven-card wax packs along with three team logo stickers.

COMPLETE SET (70) 10.00 20.00
1 Atlanta Falcons .30 .75
2 Atlanta Falcons .12 .30
3 Baltimore Colts .12 .30
4 Baltimore Colts .12 .30
5 Buffalo Bills .12 .30
6 Buffalo Bills .12 .30
7 Chicago Bears 1.50 4.00
8 Chicago Bears .12 .30
9 Cincinnati Bengals .12 .30
10 Cincinnati Bengals .12 .30
11 Cleveland Browns .40 1.00
12 Cleveland Browns .12 .30
13 Dallas Cowboys .75 2.00
14 Dallas Cowboys .25 .60
15 Denver Broncos .12 .30
16 Denver Broncos .12 .30
17 Detroit Lions .12 .30
18 Detroit Lions .12 .30
19 Green Bay Packers .12 .30
20 Green Bay Packers .12 .30
21 Houston Oilers .12 .30
22 Houston Oilers .12 .30
23 Kansas City Chiefs .12 .30
24 Kansas City Chiefs .12 .30
25 Los Angeles Rams .12 .30
26 Los Angeles Rams .12 .30
27 Miami Dolphins .12 .30
28 Miami Dolphins .12 .30
29 Minnesota Vikings .12 .30
30 Minnesota Vikings .12 .30
31 New England Patriots .12 .30
32 New England Patriots .12 .30
33 New Orleans Saints .12 .30
34 New Orleans Saints .40 1.00
35 New York Giants 1.00 2.50
36 New York Giants .12 .30
37 New York Jets .12 .30
38 New York Jets .12 .30
39 Oakland Raiders .12 .30
40 Oakland Raiders .12 .30
41 Philadelphia Eagles .12 .30
42 Philadelphia Eagles .12 .30
43 Pittsburgh Steelers .75 2.00
44 Pittsburgh Steelers .12 .30
45 St. Louis Cardinals .40 1.00
46 St. Louis Cardinals .12 .30
47 San Diego Chargers .12 .30
48 San Diego Chargers .12 .30
49 San Francisco 49ers .12 .30
50 San Francisco 49ers .12 .30
51 Seattle Seahawks .12 .30
52 Seattle Seahawks .12 .30
53 Tampa Bay Buccaneers .12 .30
54 Tampa Bay Buccaneers 1.25 3.00
55 Washington Redskins .12 .30
56 Washington Redskins .12 .30
57 Super Bowl I .20 .50
58 Super Bowl II .40 1.00
59 Super Bowl III 1.00 2.50
60 Super Bowl IV .20 .50
61 Super Bowl V .20 .50
62 Super Bowl VI 1.00 2.50
63 Super Bowl VII .20 .50
64 Super Bowl VIII .20 .50
65 Super Bowl IX .60 1.50
66 Super Bowl X .40 1.00
67 Super Bowl XI .20 .50
68 Super Bowl XII .20 .50
69 Super Bowl XIII .75 2.00
70 Super Bowl XIV .60 1.50

1980 Fleer Team Action Stickers

This set of stickers was issued one per pack in the 1980 Fleer Team Action card release and is virtually identical to the 1977 set. Each NFL team is represented with two stickers, with all but the Cowboys and Seahawks having both a helmet sticker and logo/insignia sticker. Several were produced with slight color variations in the border as noted below. Although these and other similar stickers were released over a number of years, the exact year of issue can be identified by the unique blank white sticker back. Each sticker measures roughly 2 3/8" by 2 3/4."

COMPLETE SET (65) 25.00 50.00
1A Atlanta Falcons Helmet .30 .75
1B Atlanta Falcons Helmet .30 .75
2 Atlanta Falcons Logo .30 .75
3A Baltimore Colts Helmet .50 1.25
3B Baltimore Colts Helmet .50 1.25
4 Baltimore Colts Logo .50 1.25
5 Buffalo Bills Helmet .50 1.25
6 Buffalo Bills Logo .50 1.25
7A Chicago Bears Helmet .50 1.25
7B Chicago Bears Helmet (red border) .50 1.25
8 Chicago Bears Logo .50 1.25
9 Cincinnati Bengals Helmet .30 .75
10 Cincinnati Bengals Logo .30 .75
11 Cleveland Browns Helmet .50 1.25
12 Cleveland Browns Logo .50 1.25
13 Dallas Cowboys Helmet .75 2.00
14 Dallas Cowboys Helmet .75 2.00
15 Denver Broncos Helmet .50 1.25
16 Denver Broncos Logo .50 1.25
17 Detroit Lions Helmet .30 .75
18 Detroit Lions Logo .30 .75
19 Green Bay Packers Helmet .75 2.00
20 Green Bay Packers Logo .75 2.00
21 Houston Oilers Helmet .30 .75
22 Houston Oilers Logo .30 .75
23 Kansas City Chiefs Helmet .30 .75
24 Kansas City Chiefs Logo .30 .75
25 Los Angeles Rams Helmet .30 .75
26A Los Angeles Rams Logo .30 .75
26B Los Angeles Rams Logo .30 .75
27 Miami Dolphins Helmet .75 2.00
28 Miami Dolphins Logo .75 2.00
29 Minnesota Vikings Helmet .50 1.25
30 Minnesota Vikings Logo .50 1.25
31A New England Patriots Helmet .30 .75
31B New England Patriots Helmet .30 .75
32 New England Patriots Logo .30 .75
33 New Orleans Saints Helmet .30 .75
34 New Orleans Saints Logo .30 .75
35 New York Giants Helmet .50 1.25
36 New York Giants Logo .50 1.25
37 New York Jets Helmet .50 1.25
38A New York Jets Logo .50 1.25
38B New York Jets Logo (green border) .50 1.25
39 Oakland Raiders Helmet .75 2.00
40A Oakland Raiders Logo .75 2.00
40B Oakland Raiders Logo .75 2.00
41A Philadelphia Eagles Helmet .30 .75
41B Philadelphia Eagles Helmet (green border) .30 .75
42 Philadelphia Eagles Logo .30 .75
43 Pittsburgh Steelers Helmet .75 2.00
44A Pittsburgh Steelers Logo .75 2.00
44B Pittsburgh Steelers Logo (yellow border) .75 2.00
45 St. Louis Cardinals Helmet .30 .75
46 St. Louis Cardinals Logo .30 .75
47 San Diego Chargers Helmet .30 .75
48 San Diego Chargers Logo .30 .75
49 San Francisco 49ers Helmet .75 2.00
50 San Francisco 49ers Logo .75 2.00
51 Seattle Seahawks Helmet .30 .75
52 Seattle Seahawks Helmet .30 .75
53 Tampa Bay Bucs Helmet .30 .75
54 Tampa Bay Bucs Logo .30 .75
55 Washington Redskins Helmet .50 1.25
56 Washington Redskins Logo .50 1.25

1981 Fleer Team Action

The 1981 Fleer Teams in Action football set deviates from previous years in that, while each team is depicted on two cards and each Super Bowl is depicted on one card, an additional group of cards (72-88) have been added to make the set number 88 standard-size cards, no doubt to accomodate the press sheet size. The card numbering follows team name alphabetical order followed by Super Bowl cards in chronological order and the last group of miscellaneous cards. The card fronts are in full color with white borders, and the card backs are printed in blue and red on white stock. The backs feature a 1981 copyright. Cards were issued in eight-card wax packs along with three team logo stickers.

COMPLETE SET (88) 8.00 20.00
1 Atlanta Falcons .20 .50
2 Atlanta Falcons .10 .25
3 Baltimore Colts .10 .25
4 Baltimore Colts .10 .25
5 Buffalo Bills .10 .25
6 Buffalo Bills .10 .25
7 Chicago Bears 1.00 2.50
8 Chicago Bears .10 .25
9 Cincinnati Bengals .10 .25
10 Cincinnati Bengals .10 .25
11 Cleveland Browns .15 .40
12 Cleveland Browns .20 .50
13 Dallas Cowboys .20 .50
14 Dallas Cowboys .20 .50
15 Denver Broncos .10 .25
16 Denver Broncos .10 .25
17 Detroit Lions .20 .50
18 Detroit Lions .10 .25
19 Green Bay Packers .10 .25
20 Green Bay Packers .10 .25
21 Houston Oilers .10 .25
22 Houston Oilers .10 .25
23 Kansas City Chiefs .10 .25
24 Kansas City Chiefs .10 .25
25 Los Angeles Rams .10 .25
26 Los Angeles Rams .10 .25
27 Miami Dolphins .15 .40
28 Miami Dolphins .15 .40
29 Minnesota Vikings .10 .25
30 Minnesota Vikings .10 .25
31 New England Patriots .10 .25
32 New England Patriots .40 1.00
33 New Orleans Saints .20 .50
34 New Orleans Saints .10 .25
35 New York Giants .10 .25
36 New York Giants .10 .25
37 New York Jets .15 .40
38 New York Jets .10 .25
39 Oakland Raiders .15 .40
40 Oakland Raiders .15 .40
41 Philadelphia Eagles .10 .25
42 Philadelphia Eagles .10 .25
43 Pittsburgh Steelers .40 1.00
44 Pittsburgh Steelers .15 .40
45 St. Louis Cardinals .10 .25
46 St. Louis Cardinals .10 .25
47 San Diego Chargers .10 .25
48 San Diego Chargers .10 .25
49 San Francisco 49ers .15 .40
50 San Francisco 49ers .15 .40
51 Seattle Seahawks .10 .25
52 Seattle Seahawks .10 .25
53 Tampa Bay Buccaneers .10 .25
54 Tampa Bay Buccaneers .10 .25
55 Washington Redskins .15 .40
56 Washington Redskins .15 .40
57 Super Bowl I .20 .50
58 Super Bowl II .10 .25
59 Super Bowl III .10 .25
60 Super Bowl IV .10 .25
61 Super Bowl V .10 .25
62 Super Bowl VI .15 .40
63 Super Bowl VII .10 .25
64 Super Bowl VIII .40 1.00
65 Super Bowl IX .40 1.00
66 Super Bowl X .15 .40
67 Super Bowl XI .40 1.00
68 Super Bowl XII .75 2.00
69 Super Bowl XIII 1.00 2.50
70 Super Bowl XIV .40 1.00
71 Super Bowl XV .15 .40
72 Training Camp .20 .50
73 Practice Makes .10 .25
74 Airborn Carrier .10 .25
75 The National Anthem .10 .25
76 Filling Up .10 .25
77 Away In Time .75 2.00
78 Flat Out .10 .25
79 Halftime .10 .25
80 Warm Ups Patriots .10 .25
81 Getting To The .10 .25
82 Souvenir (Crowd) .10 .25
83 A Game Of Inches .10 .25
84 The Overview .10 .25
85 The Dropback .10 .25
86 Pregame Huddle .10 .25
87 Every Way But Loose UER .10 .25
88 Mudders UER .15 .40

1981 Fleer Team Action Stickers

Fleer re-designed the Team Action Sticker sets in 1981 to feature the team's helmet or logo against a green football field pattern. This set was issued one sticker per pack and features each NFL team in two different stickers. The cardbacks contain the team's 1981 NFL schedule and each sticker measures roughly 2 1/4" by 2 3/4." Over the years a large number of variations have been discovered, but we've listed only the more significant variations below. Minor variations in colors and tones exist on virtually every sticker and some collectors attempt to assemble complete sets of all minor variations.

COMPLETE SET (56) 20.00 50.00
1 Atlanta Falcons Helmet .30 .75
2 Atlanta Falcons Logo .30 .75
3A Baltimore Colts Helmet COR .50 1.25
3B Baltimore Colts Helmet ERR .50 1.25
3C Baltimore Colts Helmet ERR .50 1.25
4A Baltimore Colts Logo COR .50 1.25
4B Baltimore Colts Logo ERR .50 1.25
5A Buffalo Bills Helmet .50 1.25
5B Buffalo Bills Helmet .50 1.25
6 Buffalo Bills Logo .50 1.25
7A Chicago Bears Helmet .50 1.25
7B Chicago Bears Helmet .50 1.25
8 Chicago Bears Logo .50 1.25
9A Cincinnati Bengals Large Helmet .30 .75
9B Cincinnati Bengals Large Helmet .30 .75
10A Cincinnati Bengals Small Helmet .30 .75
10B Cincinnati Bengals Small Helmet .30 .75
11 Cleveland Browns Large Helmet .50 1.25
12 Cleveland Browns Small Helmet .50 1.25
13 Dallas Cowboys Helmet .75 2.00
14 Dallas Cowboys Helmet .75 2.00
15 Denver Broncos Helmet .50 1.25
16 Denver Broncos Logo .50 1.25
17A Detroit Lions Helmet .30 .75
17B Detroit Lions Helmet .30 .75
18A Detroit Lions Logo .30 .75
18B Detroit Lions Logo .30 .75
19A Green Bay Packers Helmet .75 2.00
19B Green Bay Packers Helmet .75 2.00
20A Green Bay Packers Logo .75 2.00
20B Green Bay Packers Logo .75 2.00
21A Houston Oilers Helmet .30 .75
21B Houston Oilers Helmet .30 .75
22 Houston Oilers Logo .30 .75
23 Kansas City Chiefs Helmet .30 .75
24 Kansas City Chiefs Logo .30 .75
25A Los Angeles Rams Helmet .30 .75
25B Los Angeles Rams Helmet .30 .75
26A L.A. Rams Logo White .30 .75
26B L.A. Rams Logo Orange .30 .75
27A Miami Dolphins Helmet .75 2.00
27B Miami Dolphins Helmet .75 2.00
28 Miami Dolphins Logo .75 2.00
29 Minnesota Vikings Helmet .50 1.25
30 Minnesota Vikings Logo .50 1.25
31 New England Patriots Helmet .30 .75
32 New England Patriots Logo .30 .75
33A New Orleans Saints Helmet .30 .75
33B New Orleans Saints Holmot .30 .75
34 New Orleans Saints Logo .30 .75
35 New York Giants Large Helmet .50 1.25
36 New York Giants Small Helmet .50 1.25
37 New York Jets Large Helmet .50 1.25
38 New York Jets Logo .50 1.25
39A Oakland Raiders Helmet .75 2.00
39B Oakland Raiders Helmet .75 2.00
40 Oakland Raiders Logo .75 2.00
41 Philadelphia Eagles Helmet .30 .75
42 Philadelphia Eagles Logo .30 .75
43A Pittsburgh Steelers Helmet .75 2.00
43b Pittsburgh Steelers Helmet .75 2.00
44 Pittsburgh Steelers Logo .75 2.00
45A St. Louis Cardinals Helmet .30 .75
45B St. Louis Cardinals Helmet .30 .75
46 St. Louis Cardinals Logo .30 .75
47 San Diego Chargers Helmet .30 .75
48 San Diego Chargers Logo .30 .75
49A San Francisco 49ers Helmet .75 2.00
49B San Francisco 49ers Helmet .75 2.00
50 San Francisco 49ers Logo .75 2.00
51A Seattle Seahawks Helmet .30 .75
51B Seattle Seahawks Large Helmet .30 .75
52 Seattle Seahawks Helmet .30 .75
53A Tampa Bay Bucs Helmet .30 .75
53B Tampa Bay Bucs Helmet .30 .75
54 Tampa Bay Bucs Logo .30 .75
55A Washington Redskins Helmet .50 1.25
55B Washington Redskins Helmet .50 1.25
56 Washington Redskins Logo .50 1.25

1982 Fleer Team Action

The 1982 Fleer Teams in Action football set is very similar to the 1981 set (with again 88 standard-size cards) and other Fleer Teams in Action sets of previous years. The backs are printed in yellow and gray on a white stock. These cards feature a 1982 copyright date. The card numbering follows team name alphabetical order followed by Super Bowl cards in chronological order and NFL Team Highlights cards. Cards were issued in wax packs of seven team cards along with three team logo stickers.

COMPLETE SET (88) 14.00 35.00
1 Atlanta Falcons .25 .60
2 Atlanta Falcons .10 .25
3 Baltimore Colts .15 .40
4 Baltimore Colts .10 .25
5 Buffalo Bills .15 .40
6 Buffalo Bills .10 .25
7 Chicago Bears 1.00 2.50
8 Chicago Bears .10 .25
9 Cincinnati Bengals .10 .25
10 Cincinnati Bengals .10 .25
11 Cleveland Browns .15 .40
12 Cleveland Browns .10 .25
13 Dallas Cowboys .40 1.00
14 Dallas Cowboys .15 .40
15 Denver Broncos .15 .40
16 Denver Broncos .10 .25
17 Detroit Lions .10 .25
18 Detroit Lions .15 .40
19 Green Bay Packers .10 .25
20 Green Bay Packers .10 .25
21 Houston Oilers 1.50 4.00
22 Houston Oilers .10 .25
23 Kansas City Chiefs .10 .25
24 Kansas City Chiefs .10 .25
25 Los Angeles Rams .10 .25
26 Los Angeles Rams .30 .75
27 Miami Dolphins .15 .40
28 Miami Dolphins .15 .40
29 Minnesota Vikings .10 .25
30 Minnesota Vikings .10 .25
31 New England Patriots .10 .25
32 New England Patriots .10 .25
33 New Orleans Saints .15 .40
34 New Orleans Saints .10 .25
35 New York Giants .10 .25
36 New York Giants .50 1.25
37 New York Jets .15 .40
38 New York Jets .10 .25
39 Oakland Raiders .15 .40
40 Oakland Raiders .15 .40
41 Philadelphia Eagles .15 .40
42 Philadelphia Eagles .30 .75
43 Pittsburgh Steelers .15 .40
44 Pittsburgh Steelers .15 .40
45 St. Louis Cardinals .15 .40
46 St. Louis Cardinals .10 .25
47 San Diego Chargers .10 .25
48 San Diego Chargers .10 .25
49 San Francisco 49ers 6.00 15.00
50 San Francisco 49ers .20 .50
51 Seattle Seahawks .30 .75
52 Seattle Seahawks .15 .40
53 Tampa Bay Buccaneers .15 .40
54 Tampa Bay Buccaneers .10 .25
55 Washington Redskins .30 .75
56 Washington Redskins .15 .40
57 Super Bowl I .20 .50
58 Super Bowl II .10 .25
59 Super Bowl III .10 .25
60 Super Bowl IV .10 .25
61 Super Bowl V .10 .25
62 Super Bowl VI .40 1.00
63 Super Bowl VII .30 .75
64 Super Bowl VIII .40 1.00

65 Super Bowl IX .10 .25
66 Super Bowl X .60 1.50
67 Super Bowl XI .15 .40
68 Super Bowl XII .60 1.50
69 Super Bowl XIII .50 1.25
70 Super Bowl XIV .10 .25
71 Super Bowl XV .15 .40
72 Super Bowl XVI .40 1.00
73 NFL Team Highlights 5.00 12.00
74 NFL Team Highlights .40 1.00
75 NFL Team Highlights .10 .25
76 NFL Team Highlights .10 .25
77 NFL Team Highlights .25 .60
78 NFL Team Highlights .10 .25
79 NFL Team Highlights .10 .25
80 NFL Team Highlights .10 .25
81 NFL Team Highlights .10 .25
82 NFL Team Highlights .10 .25
83 NFL Team Highlights LT .10 .25
84 NFL Team Highlights .10 .25
85 NFL Team Highlights .10 .25
86 NFL Team Highlights .40 1.00
87 NFL Team Highlights .10 .25
88 NFL Team Highlights .15 .40

1982 Fleer Team Action Stickers

Fleer again re-designed the Team Action Sticker sets in 1982 to feature the team's helmet or logo against a gold colored background along with a team name sticker. This set was issued one sticker per pack and features all NFL teams with most in two different stickers. Cardbacks contain the team's 1982 NFL schedule printed in red ink. Each sticker measures roughly 2" by 3."

COMPLETE SET (50) 20.00 50.00
1 Atlanta Falcons Helmet .30 .75
2 Atlanta Falcons Logo .30 .75
3 Baltimore Colts Helmet .50 1.25
4 Baltimore Colts Helmet .50 1.25
5 Buffalo Bills Helmet .50 1.25
6 Buffalo Bills Logo .50 1.25
7 Chicago Bears Helmet .50 1.25
8 Chicago Bears Logo .50 1.25
9 Cincinnati Bengals Helmet .50 1.25
10 Cleveland Browns Helmet .50 1.25
11 Dallas Cowboys Helmet .75 2.00
12 Dallas Cowboys Helmet .75 2.00
13 Denver Broncos Helmet .50 1.25
14 Denver Broncos Logo .50 1.25
15 Detroit Lions Helmet .30 .75
16 Detroit Lions Logo .30 .75
17 Green Bay Packers Helmet .75 2.00
18 Green Bay Packers Helmet .75 2.00
19 Houston Oilers Helmet .30 .75
20 Houston Oilers Logo .30 .75
21 Kansas City Chiefs Helmet .30 .75
22 Kansas City Chiefs Logo .30 .75
23 Los Angeles Rams Helmet .30 .75
24 Los Angeles Rams Logo .30 .75
25 Miami Dolphins Helmet .75 2.00
26 Miami Dolphins Logo .75 2.00
27 Minnesota Vikings Helmet .50 1.25
28 Minnesota Vikings Logo .50 1.25
29 New England Patriots Helmet .30 .75
30 New England Patriots Logo .30 .75
31 New Orleans Saints Helmet .30 .75
32 New Orleans Saints Logo .30 .75
33 New York Giants Helmet .50 1.25
34 New York Giants Helmet .50 1.25
35 New York Jets Logo .50 1.25
36 Oakland Raiders Helmet .75 2.00
37 Oakland Raiders Logo .75 2.00
38 Philadelphia Eagles Helmet .30 .75
39 Philadelphia Eagles Logo .30 .75
40 Pittsburgh Steelers Helmet .75 2.00
41 Pittsburgh Steelers Logo .75 2.00
42 St. Louis Cardinals Helmet .30 .75
43 St. Louis Cardinals Logo .30 .75
44 San Diego Chargers Helmet .30 .75
45 San Francisco 49ers Helmet .75 2.00
46 San Francisco 49ers Logo .75 2.00
47 Seattle Seahawks Helmet .30 .75
48 Tampa Bay Bucs Helmet .30 .75
49 Tampa Bay Bucs Logo .30 .75
50 Washington Redskins Helmet .50 1.25
51 Washington Redskins Logo .50 1.25

1983 Fleer Team Action

The 1983 Fleer Teams in Action football set contains 88 standard-size cards. There are two cards numbered 67, one of which was obviously intended to be card number 66. The backs are printed in blue on white card stock. These cards feature a 1983 copyright date. The card numbering follows team name alphabetical order followed by Super Bowl cards in chronological order and NFL Team Highlights cards. Cards were issued in seven-card packs along with three team logo stickers.

COMPLETE SET (88) 8.00 20.00
1 Atlanta Falcons .40 1.00
2 Atlanta Falcons .10 .25
3 Baltimore Colts .10 .25
4 Baltimore Colts .10 .25
5 Buffalo Bills .10 .25
6 Buffalo Bills .10 .25
7 Chicago Bears 1.00 2.50
8 Chicago Bears .10 .25
9 Cincinnati Bengals .10 .25
10 Cincinnati Bengals .10 .25
11 Cleveland Browns .10 .25
12 Cleveland Browns .10 .25
13 Dallas Cowboys .50 1.25
14 Dallas Cowboys .15 .40
15 Denver Broncos .10 .25
16 Denver Broncos .10 .25
17 Detroit Lions .10 .25
18 Detroit Lions .10 .25
19 Green Bay Packers .30 .75
20 Green Bay Packers .10 .25
21 Houston Oilers .10 .25
22 Houston Oilers .10 .25
23 Kansas City Chiefs .10 .25
24 Kansas City Chiefs .15 .40
25 Los Angeles Raiders .20 .50
26 Los Angeles Raiders .15 .40
27 Los Angeles Rams .10 .25
28 Los Angeles Rams .10 .25
29 Miami Dolphins .15 .40
30 Miami Dolphins .15 .40
31 Minnesota Vikings .15 .40
32 Minnesota Vikings .10 .25
33 New England Patriots .10 .25
34 New England Patriots 1.00 2.50
35 New Orleans Saints .10 .25
36 New Orleans Saints .50 1.25
37 New York Giants .10 .25
38 New York Giants .10 .25
39 New York Jets .10 .25
40 New York Jets .10 .25
41 Philadelphia Eagles .15 .40
42 Philadelphia Eagles .15 .40
43 Pittsburgh Steelers .40 1.00
44 Pittsburgh Steelers .30 .75
45 St. Louis Cardinals .10 .25
46 St. Louis Cardinals .10 .25
47 San Diego Chargers .10 .25
48 San Diego Chargers .10 .25
49 San Francisco 49ers .15 .40
50 San Francisco 49ers .15 .40
51 Seattle Seahawks .15 .40
52 Seattle Seahawks .10 .25
53 Tampa Bay Buccaneers .10 .25
54 Tampa Bay Buccaneers .10 .25
55 Washington Redskins .15 .40
56 Washington Redskins .15 .40
57 Super Bowl I .30 .75
58 Super Bowl II .10 .25
59 Super Bowl III .10 .25
60 Super Bowl IV .10 .25
61 Super Bowl V .60 1.50
62 Super Bowl VI .40 1.00
63 Super Bowl VII .15 .40
64 Super Bowl VIII .30 .75
65 Super Bowl IX .40 1.00
66 Super Bowl X UER .60 1.50
67 Super Bowl XI .15 .40
68 Super Bowl XII .10 .25
69 Super Bowl XIII .60 1.50
70 Super Bowl XIV .10 .25
71 Super Bowl XV .10 .25
72 Super Bowl XVI .10 .25
73 Super Bowl XVII .30 .75
74 NFL Team Highlights .40 1.00
75 NFL Team Highlights .10 .25
76 NFL Team Highlights .10 .25
77 NFL Team Highlights .10 .25
78 NFL Team Highlights .15 .40
79 NFL Team Highlights .10 .25
80 NFL Team Highlights .10 .25
81 NFL Team Highlights .10 .25
82 NFL Team Highlights .10 .25
83 NFL Team Highlights .10 .25
84 NFL Team Highlights .10 .25
85 NFL Team Highlights .10 .25
86 NFL Team Highlights .10 .25
87 NFL Team Highlights .10 .25
88 NFL Team Highlights .15 .40

1983 Fleer Team Action Stickers

The 1983 Fleer Team Action Sticker set is virtually identical to the 1982 release. Each features the team's helmet or logo against a gold colored background along with a team name sticker. This set was issued one sticker per pack and features all NFL teams with most in two different stickers. The cardbacks contain the team's 1983 NFL schedule printed in red ink. Each sticker measures roughly 2" by 3."

COMPLETE SET (51) 14.00 35.00
1 Atlanta Falcons Helmet .25 .60
2 Atlanta Falcons Logo .25 .60
3 Baltimore Colts Helmet SL .40 1.00
4 Baltimore Colts Helmet LL .40 1.00
5 Buffalo Bills Helmet .40 1.00
6 Buffalo Bills Logo .40 1.00
7 Chicago Bears Helmet .40 1.00
8 Chicago Bears Logo .40 1.00
9 Cincinnati Bengals Helmet .40 1.00
10 Cleveland Browns Helmet .40 1.00
11 Dallas Cowboys Large Helmet .60 1.50
12 Dallas Cowboys Small Helmet Logo .60 1.50
13 Denver Broncos Helmet .40 1.00
14 Denver Broncos Logo .40 1.00
15 Detroit Lions Helmet .25 .60
16 Detroit Lions Logo .25 .60
17 Green Bay Packers Helmet .60 1.50
18 Green Bay Packers Helmet .60 1.50
19 Houston Oilers Helmet .25 .60
20 Houston Oilers Logo .25 .60
21 Kansas City Chiefs Helmet .25 .60
22 Kansas City Chiefs Logo .25 .60
23 Los Angeles Raiders Helmet .60 1.50
24 Los Angeles Raiders Logo .60 1.50
25 Los Angeles Rams Helmet .25 .60
26 Los Angeles Rams Logo .25 .60
27 Miami Dolphins Helmet .60 1.50
28 Miami Dolphins Logo .60 1.50
29 Minnesota Vikings Helmet .40 1.00
30 Minnesota Vikings Logo .40 1.00
31 New England Patriots Helmet .25 .60
32 New England Patriots Logo .25 .60
33 New Orleans Saints Logo .25 .60
34 New Orleans Saints Helmet .25 .60
35 New York Giants Helmet .40 1.00
36 New York Giants Helmet .40 1.00
37 New York Jets Helmet .40 1.00
38 Philadelphia Eagles Helmet .25 .60
39 Philadelphia Eagles Logo .25 .60
40 Pittsburgh Steelers Helmet .60 1.50
41 Pittsburgh Steelers Logo .60 1.50
42 St. Louis Cardinals Helmet .25 .60
43 St. Louis Cardinals Logo .25 .60
44 San Diego Chargers Helmet .25 .60
45 San Francisco 49ers Helmet .60 1.50
46 San Francisco 49ers Logo .60 1.50
47 Seattle Seahawks Helmet .25 .60
48 Tampa Bay Bucs Helmet .25 .60
49 Tampa Bay Bucs Logo .25 .60
50 Washington Redskins Helmet .40 1.00
51 Washington Redskins Logo .40 1.00

1984 Fleer Team Action

The 1984 Fleer Teams in Action football card set contains 88 standard-size cards. The cards feature a 1984 copyright date. The cards show action scenes with specific players not identified. There is a green border on the fronts of the cards with the title of the card inside a yellow strip; the backs are red and white. The card fronts are in full color. The card numbering follows team name alphabetical order (with the exception of the Indianapolis Colts whose last-minute move from Baltimore aparently put them out of order) followed by Super Bowl cards in chronological order and NFL Team Highlights cards. Cards were issued in seven-card wax packs along with three team logo stickers.

COMPLETE SET (88) 8.00 20.00
1 Atlanta Falcons .15 .40
2 Atlanta Falcons .10 .25
3 Indianapolis Colts .10 .25
4 Indianapolis Colts .10 .25
5 Buffalo Bills .10 .25
6 Buffalo Bills .10 .25
7 Chicago Bears 1.00 2.50
8 Chicago Bears .10 .25
9 Cincinnati Bengals .10 .25
10 Cincinnati Bengals .10 .25
11 Cleveland Browns .10 .25
12 Cleveland Browns .10 .25
13 Dallas Cowboys .20 .50
14 Dallas Cowboys .25 .60
15 Denver Broncos .10 .25
16 Denver Broncos .10 .25
17 Detroit Lions .15 .40
18 Detroit Lions .25 .60
19 Green Bay Packers .10 .25
20 Green Bay Packers .10 .25
21 Houston Oilers 1.50 4.00
22 Houston Oilers .10 .25
23 Kansas City Chiefs .10 .25
24 Kansas City Chiefs .10 .25
25 Los Angeles Raiders .75 2.00
26 Los Angeles Raiders .40 1.00
27 Los Angeles Rams .10 .25
28 Los Angeles Rams .10 .25
29 Miami Dolphins .15 .40
30 Miami Dolphins .15 .40
31 Minnesota Vikings .10 .25
32 Minnesota Vikings .10 .25
33 New England Patriots .15 .40
34 New England Patriots 1.25 3.00
35 New Orleans Saints .10 .25
36 New Orleans Saints .10 .25
37 New York Giants .10 .25
38 New York Giants .10 .25
39 New York Jets .10 .25
40 New York Jets .10 .25
41 Philadelphia Eagles .10 .25
42 Philadelphia Eagles .10 .25
43 Pittsburgh Steelers .15 .40
44 Pittsburgh Steelers .15 .40
45 St. Louis Cardinals .10 .25
46 St. Louis Cardinals .10 .25
47 San Diego Chargers .10 .25
48 San Diego Chargers .10 .25
49 San Francisco 49ers .15 .40
50 San Francisco 49ers .25 .60
51 Seattle Seahawks .10 .25
52 Seattle Seahawks .10 .25
53 Tampa Bay Buccaneers .10 .25
54 Tampa Bay Buccaneers .10 .25
55 Washington Redskins .25 .60
56 Washington Redskins .15 .40
57 Super Bowl I .20 .50
58 Super Bowl II .30 .75
59 Super Bowl III .10 .25
60 Super Bowl IV .10 .25
61 Super Bowl V .20 .50
62 Super Bowl VI .50 1.25
63 Super Bowl VII .25 .60
64 Super Bowl VIII .30 .75
65 Super Bowl IX .50 1.25
66 Super Bowl X .30 .75
67 Super Bowl XI .10 .25
68 Super Bowl XII .40 1.00
69 Super Bowl XIII .30 .75
70 Super Bowl XIV .30 .75
71 Super Bowl XV .10 .25
72 Super Bowl XVI .10 .25
73 Super Bowl XVII .10 .25
74 Super Bowl XVIII .30 .75
75 NFL Team Highlights .10 .25
76 NFL Team Highlights .10 .25
77 NFL Team Highlights .10 .25
78 NFL Team Highlights .10 .25
79 NFL Team Highlights .15 .40
80 NFL Team Highlights .10 .25
81 NFL Team Highlights .10 .25
82 NFL Team Highlights .10 .25
83 NFL Team Highlights .10 .25
84 NFL Team Highlights .10 .25
85 NFL Team Highlights .10 .25
86 NFL Team Highlights .10 .25
87 NFL Team Highlights .10 .25
88 NFL Team Highlights .25 .60

1984 Fleer Team Action Stickers

The 1984 Fleer Team Action Sticker set is virtually identical to the 1983 release with only a small change in the border color. Each features the team's helmet or logo against a yellow colored background along with a team name sticker. This set was issued one sticker per pack and features all NFL teams with most in two different stickers. The cardbacks contain the team's 1984 NFL schedule printed in blue ink. Each sticker measures roughly 2" by 3."

COMPLETE SET (51) 14.00 35.00
1 Atlanta Falcons Helmet .25 .60
2 Atlanta Falcons Logo .25 .60
3 Buffalo Bills Helmet .40 1.00
4 Buffalo Bills Logo .40 1.00
5 Chicago Bears Helmet .40 1.00
6 Chicago Bears Logo .40 1.00
7 Cincinnati Bengals Helmet .25 .60
8 Cleveland Browns Helmet .40 1.00
9 Dallas Cowboys Helmet .60 1.50
10 Dallas Cowboys Helmet .60 1.50
11 Denver Broncos Helmet .40 1.00
12 Denver Broncos Logo .40 1.00
13 Detroit Lions Helmet .25 .60
14 Detroit Lions Logo .25 .60
15 Green Bay Packers Helmet .60 1.50
16 Green Bay Packers Helmet .60 1.50
17 Houston Oilers Helmet .25 .60
18 Houston Oilers Logo .25 .60
19 Indianapolis Colts Helmet SL .40 1.00
20 Indianapolis Colts Helmet LL .40 1.00
21 Kansas City Chiefs Helmet .25 .60
22 Kansas City Chiefs Logo .25 .60
23 Los Angeles Raiders Helmet .60 1.50
24 Los Angeles Raiders Logo .60 1.50
25 Los Angeles Rams Helmet .25 .60
26 Los Angeles Rams Logo .25 .60
27 Miami Dolphins Helmet .60 1.50
28 Miami Dolphins Logo .60 1.50
29 Minnesota Vikings Helmet .40 1.00
30 Minnesota Vikings Logo .40 1.00
31 New England Patriots Helmet .25 .60
32 New England Patriots Logo .25 .60
33 New Orleans Saints Helmet .25 .60
34 New Orleans Saints Logo .25 .60
35 New York Giants Helmet .40 1.00
36 New York Giants Helmet .40 1.00
37 New York Jets Logo .40 1.00
38 Philadelphia Eagles Helmet .25 .60
39 Philadelphia Eagles Logo .25 .60
40 Pittsburgh Steelers Helmet .60 1.50
41 Pittsburgh Steelers Logo .60 1.50
42 St. Louis Cardinals Helmet .25 .60
43 St. Louis Cardinals Logo .25 .60
44 San Diego Chargers Helmet .25 .60
45 San Francisco 49ers Helmet .60 1.50
46 San Francisco 49ers Logo .60 1.50
47 Seattle Seahawks Helmet .25 .60
48 Tampa Bay Bucs Helmet .25 .60
49 Tampa Bay Bucs Logo .25 .60
50 Washington Redskins Helmet .40 1.00
51 Washington Redskins Logo .40 1.00

1985 Fleer Team Action

This 88-card standard-size set, entitled Fleer Teams in Action, is essentially organized alphabetically by the name of the team. There are three cards for each team, the first subtitled "On Offense" with offensive team statistics on the back, the second "On Defense" with defensive team statistics on the back, and the third "In Action" with a team schedule for the upcoming 1985 season. The last four cards feature highlights of the previous three Super Bowls and Pro Bowl. The cards are typically oriented horizontally. The cards feature a 1985 copyright date. The cards show full-color action scenes with specific players not identified. The card backs are printed in orange and black on white card stock. Cards were issued in wax packs of 15 cards and one sticker.

COMPLETE SET (88) 10.00 25.00
1 Atlanta Falcons .15 .40
2 Atlanta Falcons .10 .25
3 Atlanta Falcons .25 .60
4 Buffalo Bills .10 .25
5 Buffalo Bills .10 .25
6 Buffalo Bills .10 .25
7 Chicago Bears .75 2.00
8 Chicago Bears .10 .25
9 Chicago Bears .30 .75
10 Cincinnati Bengals .10 .25
11 Cincinnati Bengals .10 .25
12 Cincinnati Bengals .10 .25
13 Cleveland Browns .10 .25
14 Cleveland Browns .10 .25
15 Cleveland Browns .10 .25
16 Dallas Cowboys .40 1.00
17 Dallas Cowboys .50 1.25
18 Dallas Cowboys .25 .60
19 Denver Broncos .10 .25
20 Denver Broncos .10 .25
21 Denver Broncos .10 .25
22 Detroit Lions .10 .25
23 Detroit Lions .10 .25
24 Detroit Lions .10 .25
25 Green Bay Packers .15 .40
26 Green Bay Packers .40 1.00
27 Green Bay Packers .10 .25
28 Houston Oilers 1.50 4.00
29 Houston Oilers .10 .25
30 Houston Oilers .10 .25
31 Indianapolis Colts .10 .25
32 Indianapolis Colts .10 .25
33 Indianapolis Colts .10 .25
34 Kansas City Chiefs .10 .25
35 Kansas City Chiefs .10 .25
36 Kansas City Chiefs .10 .25
37 Los Angeles Raiders .15 .40
38 Los Angeles Raiders .15 .40
39 Los Angeles Raiders .15 .40
40 Los Angeles Rams .40 1.00
41 Los Angeles Rams .10 .25
42 Los Angeles Rams .10 .25
43 Miami Dolphins .15 .40
44 Miami Dolphins .15 .40
45 Miami Dolphins 4.00 10.00
46 Minnesota Vikings .10 .25
47 Minnesota Vikings .10 .25
48 Minnesota Vikings .10 .25
49 New England Patriots .10 .25
50 New England Patriots .10 .25
51 New England Patriots .10 .25
52 New Orleans Saints .10 .25
53 New Orleans Saints .10 .25
54 New Orleans Saints .10 .25
55 New York Giants .10 .25
56 New York Giants .10 .25
57 New York Giants .20 .50
58 New York Jets .10 .25
59 New York Jets .10 .25
60 New York Jets .10 .25
61 Philadelphia Eagles .10 .25
62 Philadelphia Eagles .10 .25
63 Philadelphia Eagles .10 .25
64 Pittsburgh Steelers .15 .40
65 Pittsburgh Steelers .15 .40
66 Pittsburgh Steelers .15 .40
67 St.Louis Cardinals .10 .25
68 St.Louis Cardinals .10 .25
69 St.Louis Cardinals .20 .50
70 San Diego Chargers .10 .25
71 San Diego Chargers .10 .25
72 San Diego Chargers .10 .25
73 San Francisco 49ers .15 .40
74 San Francisco 49ers .15 .40
75 San Francisco 49ers 3.00 8.00
76 Seattle Seahawks .15 .40
77 Seattle Seahawks .15 .40
78 Seattle Seahawks .10 .25
79 Tampa Bay Buccaneers .10 .25
80 Tampa Bay Buccaneers .10 .25
81 Tampa Bay Buccaneers .25 .60
82 Washington Redskins .25 .60
83 Washington Redskins .15 .40
84 Washington Redskins .15 .40
85 Super Bowl XIX .25 .60
86 Super Bowl XIX 2.00 5.00
87 Super Bowl XIX .15 .40
88 1985 Pro Bowl .15 .40

1985 Fleer Team Action Stickers

The 1985 Fleer Team Action Sticker set is very similar to previous releases. Each features the team's helmet or logo against a blue colored background along with a team name sticker. This set was issued one sticker per pack and features all NFL teams with most in two different stickers. The cardbacks contain an offer to participate in a Fleer Cheer Contest. Each sticker measures roughly 2" by 3."

COMPLETE SET (50) 15.00 30.00
1 Atlanta Falcons Helmet .30 .75
2 Atlanta Falcons Logo .30 .75
3 Buffalo Bills Helmet .40 1.00
4 Buffalo Bills Logo .40 1.00
5 Chicago Bears Helmet .40 1.00
6 Chicago Bears Logo .40 1.00
7 Cincinnati Bengals Helmet .30 .75
8 Cleveland Browns Helmet .40 1.00
9 Dallas Cowboys Helmet .60 1.50
10 Dallas Cowboys Helmet .60 1.50
11 Denver Broncos Helmet .40 1.00
12 Denver Broncos Logo .40 1.00
13 Detroit Lions Helmet .30 .75
14 Detroit Lions Logo .30 .75
15 Green Bay Packers Helmet .60 1.50
16 Green Bay Packers Helmet .60 1.50
17 Houston Oilers Helmet .30 .75
18 Houston Oilers Logo .30 .75
19 Indianapolis Colts Small Helmet .40 1.00
20 Indianapolis Colts Large Helmet .40 1.00
21 Kansas City Chiefs Helmet .30 .75
22 Kansas City Chiefs Logo .30 .75
23 Los Angeles Raiders Helmet .60 1.50
24 Los Angeles Raiders Logo .60 1.50
25 Los Angeles Rams Helmet .30 .75
26 Los Angeles Rams Logo .30 .75
27 Miami Dolphins Helmet .60 1.50
28 Miami Dolphins Logo .60 1.50
29 Minnesota Vikings Helmet .40 1.00
30 Minnesota Vikings Logo .40 1.00
31 New England Patriots Helmet .30 .75
32 New England Patriots Logo .30 .75
33 New Orleans Saints Helmet .30 .75
34 New Orleans Saints Logo .30 .75
35 New York Giants Helmet .40 1.00
36 New York Jets Logo .40 1.00
37 Philadelphia Eagles Helmet .30 .75
38 Philadelphia Eagles Logo .30 .75
39 Pittsburgh Steelers Helmet .60 1.50
40 Pittsburgh Steelers Logo .60 1.50
41 St. Louis Cardinals Helmet .30 .75
42 St. Louis Cardinals Logo .30 .75
43 San Diego Chargers Helmet .30 .75
44 San Francisco 49ers Helmet .60 1.50
45 San Francisco 49ers Logo .60 1.50
46 Seattle Seahawks Helmet .30 .75
47 Tampa Bay Bucs Helmet .30 .75
48 Tampa Bay Bucs Logo .30 .75
49 Washington Redskins Helmet .40 1.00
50 Washington Redskins Logo .40 1.00

1986 Fleer Team Action

This 88-card standard-size set, entitled "Live Action Football," is essentially organized alphabetically by the name of the team. There are three cards for each team; the first subtitled "On Offense" with offensive team statistics on the back, the second "On Defense" with defensive team statistics on the back, and the third "In Action" with a team schedule for the upcoming 1986 season. The last four cards feature highlights of the previous three Super Bowls and Pro Bowl. The cards are typically oriented horizontally. The cards feature a 1986 copyright date. The cards show full-color action scenes (with a light blue border around the photo) with specific players not identified. The card backs are printed in blue and black on white card stock. Cards were issued in wax packs of seven team action cards and three team logo stickers.

COMPLETE SET (88) 10.00 25.00
1 Atlanta Falcons .15 .40
2 Atlanta Falcons .10 .25
3 Atlanta Falcons .10 .25
4 Buffalo Bills .10 .25
5 Buffalo Bills .10 .25
6 Buffalo Bills .10 .25
7 Chicago Bears .60 1.50
8 Chicago Bears .30 .75
9 Chicago Bears .30 .75
10 Cincinnati Bengals .15 .40
11 Cincinnati Bengals .10 .25
12 Cincinnati Bengals .30 .75
13 Cleveland Browns .40 1.00
14 Cleveland Browns .10 .25
15 Cleveland Browns .10 .25
16 Dallas Cowboys .40 1.00
17 Dallas Cowboys .20 .50
18 Dallas Cowboys .20 .50
19 Denver Broncos 3.00 8.00
20 Denver Broncos .10 .25
21 Denver Broncos .10 .25
22 Detroit Lions .10 .25
23 Detroit Lions .10 .25
24 Detroit Lions .10 .25
25 Green Bay Packers .10 .25
26 Green Bay Packers .10 .25
27 Green Bay Packers .10 .25
28 Houston Oilers .10 .25
29 Houston Oilers .10 .25
30 Houston Oilers .10 .25
31 Indianapolis Colts .10 .25
32 Indianapolis Colts .10 .25
33 Indianapolis Colts .10 .25
34 Kansas City Chiefs .10 .25
35 Kansas City Chiefs .10 .25
36 Kansas City Chiefs .10 .25
37 Los Angeles Raiders .10 .25
38 Los Angeles Raiders .10 .25
39 Los Angeles Raiders .10 .25
40 Los Angeles Rams .25 .60
41 Los Angeles Rams .10 .25
42 Los Angeles Rams .10 .25
43 Miami Dolphins .10 .25
44 Miami Dolphins .10 .25
45 Miami Dolphins .10 .25
46 Minnesota Vikings .10 .25
47 Minnesota Vikings .60 1.50
48 Minnesota Vikings .10 .25
49 New England Patriots .10 .25
50 New England Patriots .10 .25
51 New England Patriots .10 .25
52 New Orleans Saints .10 .25
53 New Orleans Saints .10 .25
54 New Orleans Saints .10 .25
55 New York Giants .20 .50
56 New York Giants .10 .25
57 New York Giants .10 .25
58 New York Jets .10 .25
59 New York Jets .10 .25
60 New York Jets .10 .25
61 Philadelphia Eagles .20 .50
62 Philadelphia Eagles .10 .25
63 Philadelphia Eagles .10 .25
64 Pittsburgh Steelers .10 .25
65 Pittsburgh Steelers .15 .40
66 Pittsburgh Steelers .15 .40
67 St.Louis Cardinals .10 .25
68 St.Louis Cardinals .10 .25
69 St.Louis Cardinals .10 .25
70 San Diego Chargers UER .10 .25
71 San Diego Chargers .15 .40
72 San Diego Chargers .10 .25
73 San Francisco 49ers 2.50 6.00
74 San Francisco 49ers .15 .40
75 San Francisco 49ers .20 .50
76 Seattle Seahawks .10 .25
77 Seattle Seahawks .10 .25
78 Seattle Seahawks .25 .60
79 Tampa Bay Buccaneers .10 .25
80 Tampa Bay Buccaneers .10 .25
81 Tampa Bay Buccaneers .10 .25
82 Washington Redskins .15 .40
83 Washington Redskins .20 .50
84 Washington Redskins .15 .40
85 Super Bowl XX .60 1.50
86 Super Bowl XX .20 .50
87 Super Bowl XX .10 .25
88 Pro Bowl 1986 .30 .75

1986 Fleer Team Action Stickers

The 1986 Fleer Team Action Sticker set is very similar to previous releases. Each features the team's helmet or logo against a blue colored background along with a team name sticker. The helmets were re-designed with a new facemask. This set was issued one sticker per pack and features all NFL teams with most in two different stickers. There are no known variations and cardbacks contain advertisements for various Fleer Candy products printed with red ink. Each sticker measures roughly 2" by 3."

COMPLETE SET (49) 10.00 25.00
1 Atlanta Falcons Helmet .20 .50
2 Atlanta Falcons Logo .20 .50
3 Buffalo Bills Helmet .30 .75
4 Buffalo Bills Logo .30 .75
5 Chicago Bears Helmet .30 .75
6 Chicago Bears Logo .30 .75
7 Cincinnati Bengals Helmet .20 .50
8 Cleveland Browns Helmet .30 .75
9 Dallas Cowboys Helmet .50 1.25
10 Dallas Cowboys Helmet .50 1.25
11 Denver Broncos Helmet .30 .75
12 Denver Broncos Logo .30 .75
13 Detroit Lions Helmet .20 .50
14 Detroit Lions Logo .20 .50
15 Green Bay Packers Helmet .50 1.25
16 Houston Oilers Helmet .20 .50
17 Houston Oilers Logo .20 .50
18 Indianapolis Colts Helmet SL .30 .75
19 Indianapolis Colts Helmet LL .30 .75
20 Kansas City Chiefs Helmet .20 .50
21 Kansas City Chiefs Logo .20 .50
22 Los Angeles Raiders Helmet .50 1.25
23 Los Angeles Raiders Logo .50 1.25
24 Los Angeles Rams Helmet .20 .50
25 Los Angeles Rams Logo .20 .50
26 Miami Dolphins Helmet .50 1.25
27 Miami Dolphins Logo .50 1.25
28 Minnesota Vikings Helmet .30 .75
29 Minnesota Vikings Logo .30 .75
30 New England Patriots Helmet .20 .50
31 New England Patriots Logo .20 .50
32 New Orleans Saints Helmet .20 .50
33 New Orleans Saints Logo .20 .50
34 New York Giants Helmet .30 .75
35 New York Jets Logo .30 .75
36 Philadelphia Eagles Helmet .20 .50
37 Philadelphia Eagles Logo .20 .50
38 Pittsburgh Steelers Helmet .50 1.25
39 Pittsburgh Steelers Logo .50 1.25
40 St. Louis Cardinals Helmet .20 .50
41 St. Louis Cardinals Logo .20 .50
42 San Diego Chargers Helmet .20 .50
43 San Francisco 49ers Helmet .50 1.25
44 San Francisco 49ers Logo .50 1.25
45 Seattle Seahawks Helmet .20 .50
46 Tampa Bay Bucs Helmet .20 .50
47 Tampa Bay Bucs Logo .20 .50
48 Washington Redskins Helmet .30 .75
49 Washington Redskins Logo .30 .75

1987 Fleer Team Action

This 88-card standard-size set, entitled "Live Action Football," is essentially organized alphabetically by the name of the team. There are two cards for each team; basically odd-numbered cards feature the team's offense and even-numbered cards feature the team's defense. The cards are typically oriented horizontally. The cards feature a 1987 copyright date. The cards show full-color action scenes (with a yellow and black border around the photo) with specific players not identified. The card backs are printed in gold and black on white card stock. Cards were issued in wax packs of seven team action cards and three team logo stickers.

COMPLETE SET (88) 20.00 35.00
1 Atlanta Falcons .12 .30
2 Atlanta Falcons .08 .20
3 Buffalo Bills .08 .20
4 Buffalo Bills UER .08 .20
5 Chicago Bears .50 1.25
6 Chicago Bears .12 .30
7 Cincinnati Bengals .08 .20
8 Cincinnati Bengals UER .08 .20
9 Cleveland Browns .08 .20
10 Cleveland Browns .08 .20
11 Dallas Cowboys .12 .30
12 Dallas Cowboys .12 .30
13 Denver Broncos 1.50 4.00
14 Denver Broncos .08 .20
15 Detroit Lions .08 .20
16 Detroit Lions .08 .20
17 Green Bay Packers .08 .20
18 Green Bay Packers .08 .20
19 Houston Oilers .08 .20
20 Houston Oilers .08 .20
21 Indianapolis Colts .08 .20
22 Indianapolis Colts .08 .20
23 Kansas City Chiefs .08 .20
24 Kansas City Chiefs .30 .75
25 Los Angeles Raiders .40 1.00
26 Los Angeles Raiders .12 .30
27 Los Angeles Rams .12 .30
28 Los Angeles Rams .08 .20
29 Miami Dolphins .12 .30
30 Miami Dolphins .12 .30
31 Minnesota Vikings .08 .20
32 Minnesota Vikings .08 .20
33 New England Patriots .12 .30
34 New England Patriots .08 .20
35 New Orleans Saints .08 .20
36 New Orleans Saints .08 .20
37 New York Giants .08 .20
38 New York Giants .30 .75
39 New York Jets .08 .20
40 New York Jets .08 .20
41 Philadelphia Eagles .08 .20
42 Philadelphia Eagles .50 1.25
43 Pittsburgh Steelers .12 .30
44 Pittsburgh Steelers .12 .30
45 St. Louis Cardinals .08 .20
46 St. Louis Cardinals .08 .20
47 San Diego Chargers .08 .20
48 San Diego Chargers .08 .20
49 San Francisco 49ers UER .12 .30
50 San Francisco 49ers .12 .30
51 Seattle Seahawks .08 .20
52 Seattle Seahawks .08 .20
53 Tampa Bay Buccaneers 1.25 3.00
54 Tampa Bay Buccaneers .08 .20
55 Washington Redskins .12 .30
56 Washington Redskins .12 .30
57 AFC Championship Game .08 .20
58 AFC Divisional Playoff .08 .20
59 AFC Divisional Playoff .08 .20
60 AFC Wild Card Game .08 .20
61 NFC Championship .20 .50
62 NFC Divisional Playoff .12 .30
63 NFC Divisional Playoff .12 .30
64 NFC Wild Card Game .20 .50
65 Super Bowl I .08 .20
66 Super Bowl II .20 .50
67 Super Bowl III .08 .20
68 Super Bowl IV .08 .20
69 Super Bowl V .12 .30
70 Super Bowl VI .50 1.25
71 Super Bowl VII .20 .50
72 Super Bowl VIII .20 .50
73 Super Bowl IX .20 .50
74 Super Bowl X .20 .50
75 Super Bowl XI .08 .20
76 Super Bowl XII .30 .75
77 Super Bowl XIII .40 1.00
78 Super Bowl XIV .12 .30
79 Super Bowl XV .12 .30
80 Super Bowl XVI .12 .30
81 Super Bowl XVII .08 .20
82 Super Bowl XVIII .08 .20
83 Super Bowl XIX 2.00 5.00
84 Super Bowl XX .12 .30
85 Super Bowl XXI .20 .50
86 Super Bowl XXI .08 .20
87 Super Bowl XXI .20 .50
88 Super Bowl XXI .12 .30

1987 Fleer Team Action Stickers

The 1987 Fleer Team Action Sticker set is very similar to previous releases. Each features the team's helmet or logo against a blue colored background along with a team name sticker. This set was issued one sticker per pack and features all NFL teams with most in two different stickers. There are no known variations and cardbacks contain advertisements for various Fleer Candy products printed with blue ink. Each sticker measures roughly 2" by 3."

COMPLETE SET (49) 8.00 20.00
1 Atlanta Falcons Helmet .15 .40
2 Atlanta Falcons Logo .15 .40
3 Buffalo Bills Helmet .25 .60
4 Buffalo Bills Logo .25 .60
5 Chicago Bears Helmet .25 .60
6 Chicago Bears Logo .25 .60
7 Cincinnati Bengals Helmet .15 .40
8 Cleveland Browns Helmet .25 .60
9 Dallas Cowboys Helmet .40 1.00
10 Dallas Cowboys Helmet .40 1.00
11 Denver Broncos Helmet .25 .60
12 Denver Broncos Logo .25 .60
13 Detroit Lions Helmet .15 .40
14 Detroit Lions Logo .15 .40
15 Green Bay Packers Helmet .40 1.00
16 Houston Oilers Helmet .15 .40
17 Houston Oilers Logo .15 .40
18 Indianapolis Colts Helmet SL .25 .60
19 Indianapolis Colts Helmet LL .25 .60

Card		
20 Kansas City Chiefs Helmet	.15	.40
21 Kansas City Chiefs Logo	.15	.40
22 Los Angeles Raiders Helmet	.40	1.00
23 Los Angeles Raiders Logo	.40	1.00
24 Los Angeles Rams Helmet	.15	.40
25 Los Angeles Rams Logo	.15	.40
26 Miami Dolphins Helmet	.40	1.00
27 Miami Dolphins Logo	.40	1.00
28 Minnesota Vikings Helmet	.25	.60
29 Minnesota Vikings Logo	.25	.60
30 New England Patriots Helmet	.15	.40
31 New England Patriots Logo	.15	.40
32 New Orleans Saints Helmet	.15	.40
33 New Orleans Saints Logo	.15	.40
34 New York Giants Helmet	.25	.60
35 New York Jets Logo	.25	.60
36 Philadelphia Eagles Helmet	.15	.40
37 Philadelphia Eagles Logo	.15	.40
38 Pittsburgh Steelers Helmet	.40	1.00
39 Pittsburgh Steelers Logo	.40	1.00
40 St. Louis Cardinals Helmet	.15	.40
41 St. Louis Cardinals Logo	.15	.40
42 San Diego Chargers Helmet	.15	.40
43 San Francisco 49ers Helmet	.40	1.00
44 San Francisco 49ers Logo	.40	1.00
45 Seattle Seahawks Helmet	.15	.40
46 Tampa Bay Bucs Helmet	.15	.40
47 Tampa Bay Bucs Logo	.15	.40
48 Washington Redskins Helmet	.25	.60
49 Washington Redskins Logo	.25	.60

1988 Fleer Team Action

This 88-card standard-size set, entitled "Live Action Football," is essentially organized alphabetically by the nickname of the team within each conference. There are two cards for each team. Basically odd-numbered cards feature the team's offense and even-numbered cards feature the team's defense. The Super Bowl cards included in this set are subtitled "Super Bowls of the Decade." The cards are typically oriented horizontally. The cards feature a 1988 copyright date. The cards show full-color action scenes with specific players not identified. The card backs are printed in blue and green on white card stock. Cards were issued in wax packs of seven team action cards and three team logo stickers.

Card		
COMPLETE SET (88)	20.00	35.00
1 Cincinnati Bengals Offense	.20	.50
2 Cincinnati Bengals Defense	.08	.20
3 Buffalo Bills Offense	.40	1.00
4 Buffalo Bills Defense	.08	.20
5 Denver Broncos Offense	1.25	3.00
6 Denver Broncos Defense	.08	.20
7 Cleveland Browns Offense	.12	.30
8 Cleveland Browns Defense	.12	.30
9 San Diego Chargers Offense	.08	.20
10 San Diego Chargers Defense	.08	.20
11 Kansas City Chiefs Offense	.08	.20
12 Kansas City Chiefs Defense	.08	.20
13 Indianapolis Colts Offense	.08	.20
14 Indianapolis Colts Defense	.08	.20
15 Miami Dolphins Offense	2.00	5.00
16 Miami Dolphins Defense	.12	.30
17 New York Jets Offense	.08	.20
18 New York Jets Defense	.08	.20
19 Houston Oilers Offense	.30	.75
20 Houston Oilers Defense	.08	.20
21 New England Patriots Offense	.12	.30
22 New England Patriots Defense	.12	.30
23 Los Angeles Raiders Offense	.20	.50
24 Los Angeles Raiders Defense	.12	.30
25 Seattle Seahawks Offense	.08	.20
26 Seattle Seahawks Defense	.08	.20
27 Pittsburgh Steelers Offense	.12	.30
28 Pittsburgh Steelers Defense	.12	.30
29 Chicago Bears Offense	.08	.20
30 Chicago Bears Defense	.08	.20
31 Tampa Bay Buccaneers Offense	.20	.50
32 Tampa Bay Buccaneers Defense	.08	.20
33 Phoenix Cardinals Offense	.08	.20
34 Phoenix Cardinals Defense	.12	.30
35 Dallas Cowboys Offense	.12	.30
36 Dallas Cowboys Defense	.12	.30
37 Philadelphia Eagles Offense	.20	.50
38 Philadelphia Eagles Defense	.30	.75
39 Atlanta Falcons Offense	.08	.20
40 Atlanta Falcons Defense	.08	.20
41 San Francisco 49ers Offense	.12	.30
42 San Francisco 49ers Defense	.20	.50
43 New York Giants Offense	.12	.30
44 New York Giants Defense	.08	.20
45 Detroit Lions Offense	.08	.20
46 Detroit Lions Defense	.08	.20
47 Green Bay Packers Offense	.08	.20
48 Green Bay Packers Defense	.08	.20
49 Los Angeles Rams Offense	.08	.20
50 Los Angeles Rams Defense	.08	.20
51 Washington Redskins Offense	.12	.30
52 Washington Redskins Defense	.12	.30
53 New Orleans Saints Offense	.08	.20
54 New Orleans Saints Defense	.08	.20
55 Minnesota Vikings Offense	.08	.20
56 Minnesota Vikings Defense	.08	.20
57 Super Bowl XXII	.08	.20
58 Super Bowl Checklist	.08	.20
59 Super Bowl Checklist	.40	1.00
60 Super Bowl XXI	.20	.50
61 Super Bowl XX	.40	1.00
62 Super Bowl XIX	.12	.30
63 Super Bowl XVIII	.20	.50
64 Super Bowl XVII	.08	.20
65 Super Bowl XVI	1.00	2.50
66 Super Bowl XV	.12	.30
67 Super Bowl XIV	.08	.20
68 NFC Championship	.08	.20
69 AFC Championship	.40	1.00
70 NFC Playoff Game	1.00	2.50
71 NFC Playoff Game	.08	.20
72 AFC Playoff Game	.12	.30
73 AFC Playoff Game	.08	.20
74 NFC Wild Card Game	.08	.20
75 AFC Wild Card Game	.08	.20
76 League Leading Team	.12	.30
77 League Leading Team	1.50	4.00
78 League Leading Team	.08	.20
79 League Leading Team	.08	.20
80 League Leading Team	.12	.30
81 League Leading Team	.08	.20
82 League Leading Team	.08	.20
83 League Leading Team	.08	.20
84 League Leading Team	.08	.20
85 League Leading Team	.08	.20
86 League Leading Team	.12	.30
87 League Leading Team	.08	.20
88 League Leading Team	.20	.50

1988 Fleer Team Action Stickers

The 1988 Fleer Team Action Sticker set is very similar to previous releases. Each features the team's helmet or logo against a red colored background along with a team name sticker. This set was issued one sticker per pack and features all NFL teams with most in two different stickers. There are no known variations and cardbacks contain the team's 1988 NFL Schedule printed in blue ink. Each sticker measures roughly 2" by 3."

Card		
COMPLETE SET (49)	8.00	20.00
1 Atlanta Falcons Helmet	.15	.40
2 Atlanta Falcons Logo	.15	.40
3 Buffalo Bills Helmet	.25	.60
4 Buffalo Bills Logo	.25	.60
5 Chicago Bears Helmet	.25	.60
6 Chicago Bears Logo	.25	.60
7 Cincinnati Bengals Helmet	.15	.40
8 Cleveland Browns Helmet	.25	.60
9 Dallas Cowboys Large Helmet	.40	1.00
10 Dallas Cowboys Small Helmet	.40	1.00
11 Denver Broncos Helmet	.25	.60
12 Denver Broncos Logo	.25	.60
13 Detroit Lions Helmet	.15	.40
14 Detroit Lions Logo	.15	.40
15 Green Bay Packers Helmet	.40	1.00
16 Houston Oilers Helmet	.15	.40
17 Houston Oilers Logo	.15	.40
18 Indianapolis Colts Helmet (COLTS printed in smaller letters on front)	.25	.60
19 Indianapolis Colts Helmet (COLTS printed in larger letters on front)	.25	.60
20 Kansas City Chiefs Helmet	.15	.40
21 Kansas City Chiefs Logo	.15	.40
22 Los Angeles Raiders Helmet	.40	1.00
23 Los Angeles Raiders Logo	.40	1.00
24 Los Angeles Rams Helmet	.15	.40
25 Los Angeles Rams Logo	.15	.40
26 Miami Dolphins Helmet	.40	1.00
27 Miami Dolphins Logo	.40	1.00
28 Minnesota Vikings Helmet	.25	.60
29 Minnesota Vikings Logo	.25	.60
30 New England Patriots Helmet	.15	.40
31 New England Patriots Logo	.15	.40
32 New Orleans Saints Helmet	.15	.40
33 New Orleans Saints Logo	.15	.40
34 New York Giants Helmet	.25	.60
35 New York Jets Logo	.25	.60
36 Philadelphia Eagles Helmet	.15	.40
37 Philadelphia Eagles Logo	.15	.40
38 Phoenix Cardinals Helmet	.15	.40
39 Phoenix Cardinals Logo	.15	.40
40 Pittsburgh Steelers Helmet	.40	1.00
41 Pittsburgh Steelers Logo	.40	1.00
42 San Diego Chargers Helmet	.15	.40
43 San Francisco 49ers Helmet	.40	1.00
44 San Francisco 49ers Logo	.40	1.00
45 Seattle Seahawks Helmet	.15	.40
46 Tampa Bay Bucs Helmet	.15	.40
47 Tampa Bay Bucs Logo	.15	.40
48 Washington Redskins Helmet	.25	.60
49 Washington Redskins Logo	.25	.60

1990 Fleer

The 1990 Fleer set contains 400 standard-size cards. This set was issued in fifteen-card baggy packs as well as 43 card pre-priced ($1.49) jumbo packs. The card numbering is alphabetical within team which are are essentially ordered by their respective order of finish during the 1989 season. The following cards have AFC logo location variations: 18, 20-22, 24, 27-30, 32, 49-56, 58, 60, 110-111, 113-117, 119, 122, 124, 198, 200-211, 213-217, and 221-223. Jim Covert (290) and Mark May (162) can be found with or without a thin line just above the text on the back. Rookie Cards include Jeff George and Jeff Hostetler.

Card		
COMPLETE SET (400)	5.00	12.00
1 Harris Barton	.02	.05
2 Chet Brooks	.02	.05
3 Michael Carter	.02	.05
4 Mike Cofer UER	.02	.05
5 Roger Craig	.04	.10
6 Kevin Fagan RC	.02	.05
7 Charles Haley UER	.04	.10
8 Pierce Holt RC	.02	.05
9 Ronnie Lott	.04	.10
10A Joe Montana ERR	.50	1.25
10B Joe Montana COR	.50	1.25
11 Bubba Paris	.02	.05
12 Tom Rathman	.02	.05
13 Jerry Rice	.30	.75
14 John Taylor	.08	.25
15 Keena Turner	.02	.05
16 Michael Walter	.02	.05
17 Steve Young	.20	.50
18 Steve Atwater	.02	.05
19 Tyrone Braxton	.02	.05
20 Michael Brooks RC	.02	.05
21 John Elway	.50	1.25
22 Simon Fletcher	.02	.05
23 Bobby Humphrey	.02	.05
24 Mark Jackson	.02	.05
25 Vance Johnson	.02	.05
26 Greg Kragen	.02	.05
27 Ken Lanier RC	.02	.05
28 Karl Mecklenburg	.02	.05
29 Orson Mobley RC	.02	.05
30 Steve Sewell	.02	.05
31 Dennis Smith	.02	.05
32 David Treadwell	.02	.05
33 Flipper Anderson	.02	.05
34 Greg Bell	.02	.05
35 Henry Ellard	.04	.10
36 Jim Everett	.04	.10
37 Jerry Gray	.02	.05
38 Kevin Greene	.04	.10
39 Pete Holohan	.02	.05
40 LeRoy Irvin	.02	.05
41 Mike Lansford	.02	.05
42 Buford McGee RC	.02	.05
43 Tom Newberry	.02	.05
44 Vince Newsome RC	.02	.05
45 Jackie Slater	.02	.05
46 Mike Wilcher	.02	.05
47 Matt Bahr	.02	.05
48 Brian Brennan	.02	.05
49 Thane Gash RC	.02	.05
50 Mike Johnson	.02	.05
51 Bernie Kosar	.04	.10
52 Reggie Langhorne	.02	.05
53 Tim Manoa	.02	.05
54 Clay Matthews	.04	.10
55 Eric Metcalf	.08	.25
56 Frank Minnifield	.02	.05
57 Gregg Rakoczy UER RC	.02	.05
58 Webster Slaughter	.04	.10
59 Bryan Wagner	.02	.05
60 Felix Wright	.02	.05
61 Raul Allegre	.02	.05
62 Ottis Anderson UER	.04	.10
63 Carl Banks	.02	.05
64 Mark Bavaro	.02	.05
65 Maurice Carthon	.02	.05
66 Mark Collins UER	.02	.05
67 Jeff Hostetler RC	.08	.25
68 Erik Howard	.02	.05
69 Pepper Johnson	.02	.05
70 Sean Landeta	.02	.05
71 Lionel Manuel	.02	.05
72 Leonard Marshall	.02	.05
73 Dave Meggett	.04	.10
74 Bart Oates	.02	.05
75 Doug Riesenberg RC	.02	.05
76 Phil Simms	.04	.10
77 Lawrence Taylor	.08	.25
78 Eric Allen	.02	.05
79 Jerome Brown	.02	.05
80 Keith Byars	.02	.05
81 Cris Carter	.20	.50
82A Byron Evans ERR RC	.05	.15
82B Randall Cunningham	.05	.15
83A Ron Heller ERR RC	.05	.15
83B Byron Evans COR RC	.05	.15
84 Ron Heller COR RC	.02	.05
85 Terry Hoage RC	.02	.05
86 Keith Jackson	.04	.10
87 Seth Joyner	.04	.10
88 Mike Quick	.02	.05
89 Mike Schad	.02	.05
90 Clyde Simmons	.02	.05
91 John Teltschik	.02	.05
92 Anthony Toney	.02	.05
93 Reggie White	.08	.25
94 Ray Berry	.02	.05
95 Joey Browner	.02	.05
96 Anthony Carter	.04	.10
97 Chris Doleman	.02	.05
98 Rick Fenney	.02	.05
99 Rich Gannon RC	.60	1.50
100 Hassan Jones	.02	.05
101 Steve Jordan	.02	.05
102 Rich Karlis	.02	.05
103 Andre Ware RC	.08	.25
104 Kirk Lowdermilk	.02	.05
105 Keith Millard	.02	.05
106 Scott Studwell	.02	.05
107 Herschel Walker	.04	.10
108 Wade Wilson	.04	.10
109 Gary Zimmerman	.04	.10
110 Don Beebe	.04	.10
111 Cornelius Bennett	.04	.10
112 Shane Conlan	.02	.05
113 Jim Kelly	.08	.25
114 Scott Norwood UER	.02	.05
115 Mark Kelso UER	.02	.05
116 Larry Kinnebrew	.02	.05
117 Pete Metzelaars	.02	.05
118 Scott Radecic	.02	.05
119 Andre Reed	.08	.25
120 Jim Ritcher RC	.02	.05
121 Bruce Smith	.08	.25
122 Leonard Smith	.02	.05
123 Art Still	.02	.05
124 Thurman Thomas	.08	.25
125 Steve Brown	.02	.05
126 Ray Childress	.02	.05
127 Ernest Givins	.04	.10
128 John Grimsley	.02	.05
129 Alonzo Highsmith	.02	.05
130 Drew Hill	.02	.05
131 Bruce Matthews	.04	.10
132 Johnny Meads	.02	.05
133 Warren Moon UER	.08	.25
134 Mike Munchak	.04	.10
135 Mike Rozier	.02	.05
136 Dean Steinkuhler	.02	.05
137 Lorenzo White	.02	.05
138 Tony Zendejas	.02	.05
139 Gary Anderson K	.02	.05
140 Bubby Brister	.02	.05
141 Thomas Everett	.02	.05
142 Derek Hill RC	.02	.05
143 Merril Hoge	.02	.05
144 Tim Johnson	.02	.05
145 Louis Lipps	.04	.10
146 David Little	.02	.05
147 Greg Lloyd	.08	.25
148 Mike Mularkey	.02	.05
149 John Rienstra RC	.02	.05
150 Gerald Williams UER RC	.02	.05
151 Keith Willis UER	.02	.05
152 Rod Woodson	.08	.25
153 Tim Worley	.02	.05
154 Gary Clark	.08	.25
155 Darryl Grant	.02	.05
156 Darrell Green	.04	.10
157 Joe Jacoby	.02	.05
158 Jim Lachey	.02	.05
159 Chip Lohmiller	.02	.05
160 Charles Mann	.02	.05
161 Wilber Marshall	.02	.05
162 Mark May	.02	.05
163 Ralf Mojsiejenko	.02	.05
164 Art Monk UER	.04	.10
165 Gerald Riggs	.04	.10
166 Mark Rypien	.04	.10
167 Ricky Sanders	.02	.05
168 Don Warren	.02	.05
169 Robert Brown RC	.02	.05
170 Blair Bush	.02	.05
171 Brent Fullwood	.02	.05
172 Tim Harris	.02	.05
173 Chris Jacke	.02	.05
174 Perry Kemp	.02	.05
175 Don Majkowski	.02	.05
176 Tony Mandarich	.02	.05
177 Mark Murphy	.02	.05
178 Brian Noble	.02	.05
179 Ken Ruettgers	.02	.05
180 Sterling Sharpe	.08	.25
181 Ed West RC	.02	.05
182 Keith Woodside	.02	.05
183 Morten Andersen	.02	.05
184 Stan Brock	.02	.05
185 Jim Dombrowski RC	.02	.05
186 John Fourcade	.02	.05
187 Bobby Hebert	.02	.05
188 Craig Heyward	.04	.10
189 Dalton Hilliard	.02	.05
190 Rickey Jackson	.04	.10
191 Buford Jordan	.02	.05
192 Eric Martin	.02	.05
193 Robert Massey	.02	.05
194 Sam Mills	.04	.10
195 Pat Swilling	.04	.10
196 Jim Wilks	.02	.05
197 John Alt RC	.02	.05
198 Walker Lee Ashley RC	.02	.05
199 Steve DeBerg	.02	.05
200 Leonard Griffin RC	.02	.05
201 Albert Lewis	.02	.05
202 Nick Lowery	.02	.05
203 Bill Maas	.02	.05
204 Pete Mandley	.02	.05
205 Chris Martin RC	.02	.05
206 Christian Okoye	.02	.05
207 Stephone Paige	.02	.05
208 Kevin Porter RC	.02	.05
209 Derrick Thomas	.08	.25
210 Lewis Billups	.02	.05
211 James Brooks	.04	.10
212 Jason Buck	.02	.05
213 Rickey Dixon RC	.02	.05
214 Boomer Esiason	.04	.10
215 David Fulcher	.02	.05
216 Rodney Holman	.02	.05
217 Lee Johnson	.02	.05
218 Tim Krumrie	.02	.05
219 Tim McGee	.02	.05
220 Anthony Munoz	.04	.10
221 Bruce Reimers RC	.02	.05
222 Leon White	.02	.05
223 Ickey Woods	.02	.05
224 Harvey Armstrong RC	.02	.05
225 Michael Ball RC	.02	.05
226 Chip Banks	.02	.05
227 Pat Beach	.02	.05
228 Duane Bickett	.02	.05
229 Bill Brooks	.02	.05
230 Jon Hand	.02	.05
231 Andre Rison	.08	.25
232 Rohn Stark	.02	.05
233 Donnell Thompson	.02	.05
234 Jack Trudeau	.02	.05
235 Clarence Verdin	.02	.05
236 Mark Clayton	.04	.10
237 Jeff Cross	.02	.05
238 Jeff Dellenbach RC	.02	.05
239 Mark Duper	.04	.10
240 Ferrell Edmunds	.02	.05
241 Hugh Green UER	.02	.05
242 E.J. Junior	.02	.05
243 Marc Logan	.02	.05
244 Dan Marino	.50	1.25
245 John Offerdahl	.02	.05
246 Reggie Roby	.02	.05
247 Sammie Smith	.02	.05
248 Pete Stoyanovich	.02	.05
249 Marcus Allen	.08	.25
250 Eddie Anderson RC	.02	.05
251 Steve Beuerlein	.04	.10
252 Mike Dyal RC	.02	.05
253 Mervyn Fernandez	.02	.05
254 Bob Golic	.02	.05
255 Mike Harden	.02	.05
256 Bo Jackson	.10	.30
257 Howie Long UER	.08	.25
258 Don Mosebar	.02	.05
259 Jay Schroeder	.02	.05
260 Steve Smith	.02	.05
261 Greg Townsend	.02	.05
262 Lionel Washington	.02	.05
263 Brian Blades	.04	.10
264 Jeff Bryant	.02	.05
265 Grant Feasel RC	.02	.05
266 Jacob Green	.02	.05
267 James Jefferson	.02	.05
268 Norm Johnson	.02	.05
269 Dave Krieg UER	.04	.10
270 Travis McNeal	.02	.05
271 Joe Nash	.02	.05
272 Rufus Porter	.02	.05
273 Kelly Stouffer	.02	.05
274 John L. Williams	.02	.05
275 Jim Arnold	.02	.05
276 Jerry Ball	.02	.05
277 Bennie Blades	.02	.05
278 Lomas Brown	.02	.05
279 Michael Cofer	.02	.05
280 Bob Gagliano	.02	.05
281 Richard Johnson	.02	.05
282 Eddie Murray	.02	.05
283 Rodney Peete	.04	.10
284 Barry Sanders	.50	1.25
285 Eric Sanders RC	.02	.05
286 Chris Spielman	.08	.25
287 Eric Williams RC	.02	.05
288 Neal Anderson	.04	.10
289A Kevin Butler P/P	.08	.25
289B Kevin Butler K/P	.08	.25
289C Kevin Butler P/K	.08	.25
289D Kevin Butler K/K	.02	.05
290 Jim Covert	.02	.05
291 Richard Dent	.04	.10
292 Dennis Gentry	.02	.05
293 Jim Harbaugh	.08	.25
294 Jay Hilgenberg	.02	.05
295 Vestee Jackson	.02	.05
296 Steve McMichael	.04	.10
297 Ron Morris	.02	.05
298 Brad Muster	.02	.05
299 Mike Singletary	.04	.10
300 James Thornton UER	.02	.05
301 Mike Tomczak	.04	.10
302 Keith Van Horne	.02	.05
303 Chris Bahr UER	.02	.05
304 Martin Bayless RC	.02	.05
305 Marion Butts	.04	.10
306 Gill Byrd	.02	.05
307 Arthur Cox	.02	.05
308 Burt Grossman	.02	.05
309 Jamie Holland	.02	.05
310 Jim McMahon	.04	.10
311 Anthony Miller	.08	.25
312 Leslie O'Neal	.04	.10
313 Billy Ray Smith	.02	.05
314 Tim Spencer	.02	.05
315 Broderick Thompson RC	.02	.05
316 Lee Williams	.02	.05
317 Bruce Armstrong	.02	.05
318 Tim Goad RC	.02	.05
319 Steve Grogan	.04	.10
320 Roland James	.02	.05
321 Cedric Jones RC	.02	.05
322 Fred Marion	.02	.05
323 Stanley Morgan	.02	.05
324 Robert Perryman	.02	.05
325 Johnny Rembert	.02	.05
326 Ed Reynolds	.02	.05
327 Kenneth Sims	.02	.05
328 John Stephens	.02	.05
329 Danny Villa RC	.02	.05
330 Robert Awalt	.02	.05
331 Anthony Bell	.02	.05
332 Rich Camarillo	.02	.05
333 Earl Ferrell	.02	.05
334 Roy Green	.04	.10
335 Gary Hogeboom	.02	.05
336 Cedric Mack	.02	.05
337 Freddie Joe Nunn	.02	.05
338 Luis Sharpe	.02	.05
339 Vai Sikahema	.02	.05
340 J.T. Smith	.02	.05
341 Tom Tupa RC	.02	.05
342 Percy Snow RC	.02	.05
343 Mark Carrier WR	.08	.25
344 Randy Grimes	.02	.05
345 Paul Gruber	.02	.05
346 Ron Hall	.02	.05
347 Jeff George RC	.20	.50
348 Bruce Hill UER	.02	.05
349 William Howard UER	.02	.05
350 Donald Igwebuike	.02	.05
351 Chris Mohr RC	.02	.05
352 Winston Moss RC	.02	.05
353 Ricky Reynolds	.02	.05
354 Mark Robinson	.02	.05
355 Lars Tate	.02	.05
356 Vinny Testaverde	.04	.10
357 Broderick Thomas	.02	.05
358 Troy Benson	.02	.05
359 Jeff Criswell RC	.02	.05
360 Tony Eason	.02	.05
361 James Hasty	.02	.05
362 Johnny Hector	.02	.05
363 Bobby Humphery UER	.02	.05
364 Pat Leahy	.02	.05
365 Erik McMillan	.02	.05
366 Freeman McNeil	.02	.05
367 Ken O'Brien	.02	.05
368 Ron Stallworth	.02	.05
369 Al Toon	.04	.10
370 Blair Thomas RC	.02	.05
371 Aundray Bruce	.02	.05
372 Tony Casillas	.02	.05
373 Shawn Collins	.02	.05
374 Evan Cooper	.02	.05
375 Bill Fralic	.02	.05
376 Scott Fulhage	.02	.05
377 Mike Gann	.02	.05
378 Ron Heller TE	.02	.05
379 Keith Jones	.02	.05
380 Mike Kenn	.02	.05
381 Chris Miller	.08	.25
382 Deion Sanders UER	.20	.50
383 John Settle	.02	.05
384 Troy Aikman	.30	.75
385 Bill Bates	.04	.10
386 Willie Broughton	.02	.05
387 Steve Folsom	.02	.05
388 Ray Horton UER	.02	.05
389 Michael Irvin	.08	.25
390 Jim Jeffcoat	.02	.05
391 Eugene Lockhart	.02	.05
392 Kelvin Martin RC	.02	.05
393 Nate Newton	.04	.10
394 Mike Saxon UER	.02	.05
395 Derrick Shepard RC	.02	.05
396 Steve Walsh	.04	.10
397 Joe Montana Rice MVP's	.30	.75
398 Checklist Card UER	.02	.05
399 Checklist Card UER	.02	.05
400 Checklist Card	.02	.05

1990 Fleer All-Pros

The 1990 Fleer All-Pro set contains 25 standard-size cards. These cards were randomly distributed in Fleer poly packs, approximately five per box.

Card		
COMPLETE SET (25)	2.50	6.00
1 Joe Montana	.60	1.50
2 Jerry Rice	.40	1.00
3 Keith Jackson	.04	.10
4 Barry Sanders	.60	1.50
5 Christian Okoye	.02	.05
6 Tom Newberry	.02	.05
7 Jim Covert	.02	.05
8 Anthony Munoz	.04	.10
9 Mike Munchak	.04	.10
10 Jay Hilgenberg	.02	.05
11 Chris Doleman	.02	.05
12 Keith Millard	.02	.05
13 Derrick Thomas	.10	.30
14 Lawrence Taylor	.10	.30
15 Karl Mecklenburg	.02	.05
16 Reggie White	.10	.30
17 Tim Harris	.02	.05
18 David Fulcher	.02	.05
19 Ronnie Lott	.04	.10
20 Eric Allen	.02	.05
21 Steve Atwater	.02	.05
22 Rich Camarillo	.02	.05
23 Morten Andersen	.02	.05
24 Andre Reed	.10	.30
25 Rod Woodson	.10	.30

1990 Fleer Stars and Stripes

This 90-card standard size set was issued by Fleer in conjunction with their subsidiary, the Asher Candy Company, in a packaging which included two red, white, and blue striped candy sticks as well as eight cards. This set features members of the 1990 Pro Bowl teams as well as ten of the leading rookies in the 1990 season. Cards were arranged as follows, AFC Pro Bowlers (1-39), NFC Pro Bowlers (40-80), and leading draftees (81-90). Some of the same mistakes made in the regular Fleer set were carried over into the Stars'n'Stripes set including the misspelling of Dave Krieg's name as Kreig. Since this set did not sell that well at the retail level, much of the production was remaindered. However some of these leftover sealed cases are susceptible to damaged cards from the candy "leaking" into or onto the cards.

Card		
COMPLETE SET (90)	4.80	12.00
1 Warren Moon	.20	.50
2 Reggie Roby	.05	.15
3 David Treadwell	.05	.15
4 Dave Krieg UER	.10	.30
5 James Brooks	.05	.15
6 Erik McMillan	.05	.15
7 Rod Woodson	.10	.30
8 Albert Lewis	.05	.15
9 Kevin Ross	.05	.15
10 Frank Minnifield	.05	.15
11 David Fulcher	.05	.15
12 Thurman Thomas	.20	.50
13 Christian Okoye	.05	.15
14 Dennis Smith	.05	.15
15 Johnny Rembert	.05	.15
16 Ray Donaldson	.05	.15
17 John Offerdahl	.05	.15
18 Clay Matthews	.05	.15
19 Shane Conlan	.05	.15
20 Derrick Thomas	.10	.30
21 Tunch Ilkin	.05	.15
22 Mike Munchak	.10	.30
23 Max Montoya	.05	.15
24 Kent Hull	.05	.15
25 Greg Kragen	.05	.15
26 Bruce Matthews	.10	.30
27 Howie Long	.20	.50
28 Chris Hinton	.05	.15
29 Anthony Munoz	.05	.15
30 Bruce Smith	.10	.30
31 Ferrell Edmunds	.05	.15
32 Rodney Holman	.05	.15
33 Andre Reed	.10	.30
34 Webster Slaughter	.05	.15
35 Anthony Miller	.10	.30
36 Brian Blades	.05	.15
37 Leslie O'Neal	.05	.15
38 Rufus Porter	.05	.15
39 Lee Williams	.05	.15
40 Eddie Murray	.05	.15
41 Mark Rypien	.05	.15
42 Randall Cunningham	.20	.50
43 Rich Camarillo	.05	.15
44 Barry Sanders	1.60	4.00
45 Dalton Hilliard	.05	.15
46 Eric Allen	.05	.15
47 Brent Fullwood	.05	.15
48 Ron Wolfley	.05	.15
49 Jerry Gray	.05	.15
50 Dave Meggett	.05	.15
51 Roger Craig	.10	.30
52 Carl Lee	.05	.15
53 Ronnie Lott	.20	.50
54 Tim McDonald	.05	.15
55 Joey Browner	.05	.15
56 Mike Singletary	.10	.30
57 Vaughan Johnson	.05	.15
58 Chris Spielman	.05	.15
59 Doug Smith	.05	.15
60 Lawrence Taylor	.20	.50
61 Chris Doleman	.05	.15
62 Guy McIntyre	.05	.15
63 Jay Hilgenberg	.05	.15
64 Randall McDaniel	.10	.30
65 Gary Zimmerman	.05	.15
66 Luis Sharpe	.05	.15
67 Charles Mann	.05	.15
68 Keith Millard	.05	.15
69 Jackie Slater	.05	.15
70 Bill Fralic	.05	.15
71 Henry Ellard	.10	.30
72 Jerry Rice	.80	2.00
73 Steve Jordan	.05	.15
74 Sterling Sharpe	.10	.30
75 Keith Jackson	.05	.15
76 Mark Carrier WR	.10	.30
77 Kevin Greene	.10	.30
78 Reggie White	.20	.50
79 Jerry Ball	.05	.15
80 Tim Harris	.05	.15
81 Jeff George	.20	.50
82 Blair Thomas	.05	.15
83 Cortez Kennedy	.25	.60
84 Junior Seau	.20	.50
85 Mark Carrier DB	.05	.15
86 Andre Ware	.10	.30
87 Chris Singleton	.05	.15
88 Percy Snow	.05	.15
89 Steve Broussard	.05	.15
90 Rodney Hampton	.10	.30

1990 Fleer Update

This 120-card standard size set features some of the leading rookies and traded players in their new uniforms. The set is the same design as the regular issue with color photos bordered by a team color. The set is arranged in team order. The cards are numbered on the back with a "U" prefix. Rookie Cards include Brad Baxter, Mark Carrier (DB), Reggie Cobb, Andre Collins, Barry Foster, Eric Green, Harold Green, Rodney Hampton, Leroy Hoard, Stan Humphries, Haywood Jeffires, Johnny Johnson, Brent Jones, Cortez Kennedy, Rob Moore, Ken Norton Jr., Junior Seau, Emmitt Smith and Calvin Williams.

Card		
COMP.FACT.SET (120)	12.50	25.00
U1 Albert Bentley	.02	.05
U2 Dean Biasucci	.02	.05
U3 Ray Donaldson	.02	.05
U4 Jeff George	.50	1.25
U5 Ray Agnew RC	.02	.05
U6 Greg McMurtry RC	.02	.05
U7 Chris Singleton RC	.02	.05
U8 James Francis RC	.02	.05
U9 Harold Green RC	.04	.10
U10 John Elliott	.02	.05
U11 Rodney Hampton RC	.08	.25
U12 Gary Reasons	.02	.05
U13 Lewis Tillman	.02	.05
U14 Everson Walls	.02	.05
U15 David Alexander RC	.02	.05
U16 Jim McMahon	.04	.10
U17 Ben Smith RC	.02	.05
U18 Andre Waters	.04	.10
U19 Calvin Williams RC	.04	.10
U20 Earnest Byner	.04	.10
U21 Andre Collins RC	.02	.05
U22 Russ Grimm	.04	.10
U23 Stan Humphries RC	.08	.25
U24 Martin Mayhew RC	.02	.05
U25 Barry Foster RC	.08	.25
U26 Eric Green RC	.04	.10
U27 Tunch Ilkin	.02	.05
U28 Hardy Nickerson	.04	.10
U29 Jerrol Williams	.02	.05
U30 Mike Baab	.02	.05
U31 Leroy Hoard RC	.20	.50
U32 Eddie Johnson RC	.02	.05
U33 William Fuller	.04	.10
U34 Haywood Jeffires RC	.08	.25
U35 Don Maggs RC	.02	.05
U36 Allen Pinkett	.02	.05
U37 Robert Awalt	.02	.05
U38 Dennis McKinnon	.02	.05
U39 Ken Norton Jr. RC	.08	.25
U40 Emmitt Smith RC	6.00	15.00
U41 Alexander Wright RC	.02	.05
U42 Eric Hill	.02	.05
U43 Johnny Johnson RC	.04	.10
U44 Timm Rosenbach	.02	.05
U45 Anthony Thompson RC	.02	.05
U46 Dexter Carter RC	.02	.05
U47 Eric Davis UER RC	.04	.10
U48 Keith DeLong	.02	.05
U49 Brent Jones RC	.08	.25
U50 Darryl Pollard RC	.02	.05
U51 Steve Wallace RC	.08	.25
U52 Bern Brostek RC	.02	.05
U53 Aaron Cox	.02	.05
U54 Cleveland Gary	.02	.05
U55 Fred Strickland RC	.02	.05
U56 Pat Terrell RC	.02	.05
U57 Steve Broussard RC	.02	.05
U58 Scott Case	.02	.05
U59 Brian Jordan RC	.04	.10
U60 Andre Rison	.08	.25
U61 Kevin Haverdink RC	.02	.05
U62 Rueben Mayes	.02	.05
U63 Steve Walsh	.04	.10
U64 Greg Bell	.02	.05
U65 Tim Brown	.08	.25
U66 Willie Gault	.04	.10
U67 Vance Mueller RC	.02	.05
U68 Bill Pickel	.02	.05
U69 Aaron Wallace RC	.04	.10
U70 Glenn Parker RC	.02	.05
U71 Frank Reich	.08	.25
U72 Leon Seals RC	.02	.05
U73 Darryl Talley	.02	.05
U74 Brad Baxter RC	.02	.05
U75 Jeff Criswell	.02	.05
U76 Jeff Lageman	.02	.05
U77 Rob Moore RC	.60	1.50
U78 Blair Thomas	.04	.10
U79 Louis Oliver	.02	.05
U80 Tony Paige	.02	.05
U81 Richmond Webb RC	.02	.05
U82 Robert Blackmon RC	.02	.05
U83 Derrick Fenner RC	.02	.05
U84 Andy Heck	.02	.05
U85 Cortez Kennedy RC	.20	.50
U86 Terry Wooden RC	.02	.05
U87 Jeff Donaldson	.02	.05
U88 Tim Grunhard RC	.02	.05
U89 Emile Harry RC	.02	.05
U90 Dan Saleaumua	.02	.05
U91 Percy Snow	.02	.05
U92 Andre Ware	.08	.25
U93 Darrell Fullington RC	.02	.05
U94 Mike Merriweather	.02	.05
U95 Henry Thomas	.02	.05
U96 Robert Brown	.02	.05
U97 LeRoy Butler RC	.08	.25
U98 Anthony Dilweg	.02	.05
U99 Darrell Thompson RC	.02	.05
U100 Keith Woodside	.02	.05
U101 Gary Plummer	.02	.05
U102 Junior Seau RC	2.00	5.00
U103 Billy Joe Tolliver	.02	.05
U104 Mark Vlasic	.02	.05
U105 Gary Anderson RB	.02	.05
U106 Ian Beckles RC	.02	.05
U107 Reggie Cobb RC	.02	.05
U108 Keith McCants RC	.02	.05
U109 Mark Bortz RC	.02	.05
U110 Maury Buford	.02	.05
U111 Mark Carrier RC DB	.08	.25
U112 Dan Hampton	.04	.10
U113 William Perry	.04	.10
U114 Ron Rivera	.02	.05
U115 Lemuel Stinson	.02	.05
U116 Melvin Bratton RC	.02	.05
U117 Gary Kubiak RC	.08	.25
U118 Alton Montgomery RC	.02	.05
U119 Ricky Nattiel	.02	.05
U120 Checklist 1-132	.02	.05

1991 Fleer

This 432-card standard-size set features color action photos with the player removed from the action. The card numbering is alphabetical by player within team by conference. Subsets include Hot Hitters (396-407), League Leaders (408-419) and Rookie Prospects (420-428). Rookie Cards in this set include Russell Maryland.

Card		
COMPLETE SET (432)	4.00	10.00
1 Shane Conlan	.01	.05
2 John Davis RC	.01	.05
3 Kent Hull	.01	.05
4 James Lofton	.02	.10
5 Keith McKeller	.01	.05
6 Scott Norwood	.01	.05
7 Nate Odomes	.01	.05
8 Andre Reed	.02	.10
9 Jim Ritcher	.01	.05
10 Leon Seals	.01	.05
11 Bruce Smith	.08	.25
12 Leonard Smith	.01	.05
13 Steve Tasker	.02	.10
14 Thurman Thomas	.08	.25
15 Lewis Billups	.01	.05
16 James Brooks	.02	.10
17 Eddie Brown	.01	.05
18 Carl Carter	.01	.05
19 Boomer Esiason	.02	.10
20 James Francis	.01	.05
21 David Fulcher	.01	.05
22 Harold Green	.02	.10
23 Rodney Holman	.01	.05
24 Bruce Kozerski	.01	.05
25 Tim McGee	.01	.05
26 Anthony Munoz	.02	.10
27 Bruce Reimers	.01	.05
28 Ickey Woods	.01	.05
29 Carl Zander	.01	.05
30 Mike Baab	.01	.05
31 Brian Brennan	.01	.05
32 Rob Burnett RC	.02	.10
33 Paul Farren	.01	.05
34 Thane Gash	.01	.05
35 David Grayson	.01	.05
36 Mike Johnson	.01	.05
37 Reggie Langhorne	.01	.05
38 Kevin Mack	.01	.05
39 Eric Metcalf	.02	.10
40 Frank Minnifield	.01	.05
41 Gregg Rakoczy	.01	.05
42 Felix Wright	.01	.05
43 Steve Atwater	.01	.05
44 Michael Brooks	.01	.05
45 John Elway	.50	1.25
46 Simon Fletcher	.01	.05
47 Bobby Humphrey	.01	.05
48 Mark Jackson	.01	.05
49 Keith Kartz	.01	.05
50 Clarence Kay	.01	.05
51 Greg Kragen	.01	.05
52 Karl Mecklenburg	.01	.05
53 Warren Powers	.01	.05
54 Dennis Smith	.01	.05
55 Jim Szymanski	.01	.05
56 David Treadwell	.01	.05
57 Michael Young	.01	.05
58 Ray Childress	.01	.05
59 Curtis Duncan	.01	.05
60 William Fuller	.02	.10
61 Ernest Givins	.02	.10
62 Drew Hill	.01	.05
63 Haywood Jeffires	.02	.10
64 Richard Johnson DB	.01	.05
65 Sean Jones	.02	.10
66 Don Maggs	.01	.05
67 Bruce Matthews	.02	.10
68 Johnny Meads	.01	.05
69 Greg Montgomery	.01	.05
70 Warren Moon	.08	.25
71 Mike Munchak	.02	.10
72 Allen Pinkett	.01	.05
73 Lorenzo White	.01	.05
74 Pat Beach	.01	.05
75 Albert Bentley	.01	.05
76 Dean Biasucci	.01	.05
77 Duane Bickett	.01	.05
78 Bill Brooks	.01	.05
79 Sam Clancy	.01	.05
80 Ray Donaldson	.01	.05
81 Jeff George	.08	.25
82 Alan Grant	.01	.05
83 Jessie Hester	.01	.05
84 Jeff Herrod	.01	.05
85 Rohn Stark	.01	.05
86 Jack Trudeau	.01	.05
87 Clarence Verdin	.01	.05
88 John Alt	.01	.05
89 Steve DeBerg	.01	.05
90 Tim Grunhard	.01	.05
91 Dino Hackett	.01	.05
92 Jonathan Hayes	.01	.05
93 Albert Lewis	.01	.05
94 Nick Lowery	.01	.05
95 Bill Maas UER	.01	.05
96 Christian Okoye	.01	.05
97 Stephone Paige	.01	.05
98 Kevin Porter	.01	.05
99 David Szott RC	.01	.05
100 Derrick Thomas	.08	.25
101 Barry Word FFC	.01	.05
102 Marcus Allen	.08	.25
103 Thomas Benson	.01	.05
104 Tim Brown	.08	.25
105 Riki Ellison	.01	.05
106 Mervyn Fernandez	.01	.05
107 Willie Gault	.02	.10
108 Bob Golic	.01	.05
109 Ethan Horton FFC	.01	.05
110 Bo Jackson	.10	.30
111 Howie Long	.08	.25
112 Don Mosebar	.01	.05
113 Jerry Robinson	.01	.05
114 Jay Schroeder	.01	.05
115 Steve Smith	.01	.05
116 Greg Townsend	.01	.05
117 Steve Wisniewski	.01	.05
118 Mark Clayton	.02	.10
119 Mark Duper	.02	.10
120 Ferrell Edmunds	.01	.05
121 Hugh Green	.01	.05
122 David Griggs	.01	.05
123 Jim C. Jensen	.01	.05
124 Dan Marino	.50	1.25
125 Tim McKyer	.01	.05
126 John Offerdahl	.01	.05
127 Louis Oliver	.01	.05
128 Tony Paige	.01	.05
129 Reggie Roby	.01	.05
130 Keith Sims	.01	.05
131 Sammie Smith	.01	.05
132 Pete Stoyanovich	.01	.05

133 Richmond Webb .01 .05
134 Bruce Armstrong .01 .05
135 Vincent Brown .01 .05
136 Hart Lee Dykes .01 .05
137 Irving Fryar .02 .10
138 Tim Goad .01 .05
139 Tommy Hodson .01 .05
140 Maurice Hurst .01 .05
141 Ronnie Lippett .01 .05
142 Greg McMurtry .01 .05
143 Ed Reynolds .01 .05
144 John Stephens .01 .05
145 Andre Tippett .01 .05
146 Danny Villa .01 .05
147 Brad Baxter .01 .05
148 Kyle Clifton .01 .05
149 Jeff Criswell .01 .05
150 James Hasty .01 .05
151 Jeff Lageman .01 .05
152 Pat Leahy .01 .05
153 Rob Moore .08 .25
154 Al Toon .02 .10
155 Gary Anderson K .01 .05
156 Bubby Brister .01 .05
157 Chris Calloway .01 .05
158 Donald Evans .01 .05
159 Eric Green .01 .05
160 Bryan Hinkle .01 .05
161 Merril Hoge .01 .05
162 Tunch Ilkin .01 .05
163 Louis Lipps .01 .05
164 David Little .01 .05
165 Mike Mularkey .01 .05
166 Gerald Williams .01 .05
167 Warren Williams .01 .05
168 Rod Woodson .08 .25
169 Tim Worley .01 .05
170 Martin Bayless .01 .05
171 Marion Butts .02 .10
172 Gill Byrd .01 .05
173 Frank Cornish .01 .05
174 Arthur Cox .01 .05
175 Burt Grossman .01 .05
176 Anthony Miller .02 .10
177 Leslie O'Neal .02 .10
178 Gary Plummer .01 .05
179 Junior Seau .08 .25
180 Billy Joe Tolliver .01 .05
181 Derrick Walker RC .01 .05
182 Lee Williams .01 .05
183 Robert Blackmon .01 .05
184 Brian Blades .02 .10
185 Grant Feasel .01 .05
186 Derrick Fenner .01 .05
187 Andy Heck .01 .05
188 Norm Johnson .01 .05
189 Tommy Kane .01 .05
190 Cortez Kennedy .08 .25
191 Dave Krieg .02 .10
192 Travis McNeal .01 .05
193 Eugene Robinson .01 .05
194 Chris Warren FFC .08 .25
195 John L. Williams .01 .05
196 Steve Broussard .01 .05
197 Scott Case .01 .05
198 Shawn Collins .01 .05
199 Darion Conner UER .01 .05
200 Tory Epps .01 .05
201 Bill Fralic .01 .05
202 Michael Haynes FFC .08 .25
203 Chris Hinton .01 .05
204 Keith Jones .01 .05
205 Brian Jordan .02 .10
206 Mike Kenn .01 .05
207 Chris Miller .02 .10
208 Andre Rison .02 .10
209 Mike Rozier .01 .05
210 Deion Sanders .15 .40
211 Gary Wilkins .01 .05
212 Neal Anderson .02 .10
213 Trace Armstrong .01 .05
214 Mark Bortz .01 .05
215 Kevin Butler .01 .05
216 Mark Carrier DB .02 .10
217 Wendell Davis FFC .01 .05
218 Richard Dent .02 .10
219 Dennis Gentry .01 .05
220 Jim Harbaugh .08 .25
221 Jay Hilgenberg .01 .05
222 Steve McMichael .02 .10
223 Ron Morris .01 .05
224 Brad Muster .01 .05
225 Mike Singletary .02 .10
226 James Thornton .01 .05
227 Tommie Agee .01 .05
228 Troy Aikman .30 .75
229 Jack Del Rio .02 .10
230 Issiac Holt .01 .05
231 Ray Horton .01 .05
232 Jim Jeffcoat .01 .05
233 Eugene Lockhart .01 .05
234 Kelvin Martin .01 .05
235 Nate Newton .02 .10
236 Mike Saxon .01 .05
237 Emmitt Smith 1.00 2.50
238A Daniel Stubbs .02 .10
238B Daniel Stubbs .02 .10
239 Jim Arnold .01 .05
240 Jerry Ball .01 .05
241 Bennie Blades .01 .05
242 Lomas Brown .01 .05
243 Robert Clark .01 .05
244 Mike Cofer .01 .05
245 Mel Gray .02 .10
246 Rodney Peete .02 .10
247 Barry Sanders .50 1.25
248 Andre Ware .02 .10
249 Matt Brock RC .01 .05
250 Robert Brown .01 .05
251 Anthony Dilweg .01 .05
252 Johnny Holland .01 .05
253 Tim Harris .01 .05
254 Chris Jacke .01 .05
255 Perry Kemp .01 .05
256 Don Majkowski UER .01 .05
257 Tony Mandarich .01 .05
258 Mark Murphy .01 .05
259 Brian Noble .01 .05
260 Jeff Query .01 .05
261 Sterling Sharpe .08 .25
262 Ed West .01 .05
263 Keith Woodside .01 .05
264 Flipper Anderson .01 .05
265 Aaron Cox .01 .05
266 Henry Ellard .02 .10
267 Jim Everett .02 .10
268 Cleveland Gary .01 .05
269 Kevin Greene .02 .10
270 Pete Holohan .01 .05
271 Mike Lansford .01 .05
272 Duval Love RC .01 .05
273 Buford McGee .01 .05
274 Tom Newberry .01 .05
275 Jackie Slater .01 .05
276 Frank Stams .01 .05
277 Alfred Anderson .01 .05
278 Joey Browner .01 .05
279 Anthony Carter .02 .10
280 Chris Doleman .01 .05
281 Rick Fenney .01 .05
282 Rich Gannon .08 .25
283 Hassan Jones .01 .05
284 Steve Jordan .01 .05
285 Carl Lee .01 .05
286 Randall McDaniel .02 .10
287 Keith Millard .01 .05
288 Herschel Walker .02 .10
289 Wade Wilson .02 .10
290 Gary Zimmerman .02 .10
291 Morten Andersen .01 .05
292 Jim Dombrowski .01 .05
293 Gill Fenerty .01 .05
294 Craig Heyward .02 .10
295 Dalton Hilliard .01 .05
296 Rickey Jackson .01 .05
297 Vaughan Johnson .01 .05
298 Eric Martin .01 .05
299 Robert Massey .01 .05
300 Rueben Mayes .01 .05
301 Sam Mills .01 .05
302 Brett Perriman .08 .25
303 Pat Swilling .02 .10
304 Steve Walsh .01 .05
305 Ottis Anderson .02 .10
306 Matt Bahr .01 .05
307 Mark Bavaro .01 .05
308 Maurice Carthon .01 .05
309 Mark Collins .01 .05
310 John Elliott .01 .05
311 Rodney Hampton .08 .25
312 Jeff Hostetler .02 .10
313 Erik Howard .01 .05
314 Pepper Johnson .01 .05
315 Sean Landeta .01 .05
316 Dave Meggett .02 .10
317 Bart Oates .01 .05
318 Phil Simms .02 .10
319 Lawrence Taylor .08 .25
320 Reyna Thompson .01 .05
321 Everson Walls .01 .05
322 Eric Allen .01 .05
323 Fred Barnett FFC .08 .25
324 Jerome Brown .01 .05
325 Keith Byars .01 .05
326 Randall Cunningham .08 .25
327 Byron Evans .01 .05
328 Ron Heller .01 .05
329 Keith Jackson .02 .10
330 Seth Joyner .02 .10
331 Heath Sherman .01 .05
332 Clyde Simmons .01 .05
333 Ben Smith .01 .05
334 Anthony Toney .01 .05
335 Andre Waters .01 .05
336 Reggie White .08 .25
337 Calvin Williams .02 .10
338 Anthony Bell .01 .05
339 Rich Camarillo .01 .05
340 Roy Green .01 .05
341 Tim Jorden RC .01 .05
342 Cedric Mack .01 .05
343 Dexter Manley .01 .05
344 Freddie Joe Nunn .01 .05
345 Ricky Proehl .01 .05
346 Tootie Robbins .01 .05
347 Timm Rosenbach .01 .05
348 Luis Sharpe .01 .05
349 Vai Sikahema .01 .05
350 Anthony Thompson .01 .05
351 Lonnie Young .01 .05
352 Dexter Carter .01 .05
353 Mike Cofer .01 .05
354 Kevin Fagan .01 .05
355 Don Griffin .01 .05
356 Charles Haley UER .02 .10
357 Pierce Holt .01 .05
358 Brent Jones .08 .25
359 Guy McIntyre .01 .05
360 Joe Montana .50 1.25
361 Darryl Pollard .01 .05
362 Tom Rathman .01 .05
363 Jerry Rice .30 .75
364 Bill Romanowski .01 .05
365 John Taylor .02 .10
366 Steve Wallace .02 .10
367 Steve Young .30 .75
368 Gary Anderson RB .01 .05
369 Ian Beckles .01 .05
370 Mark Carrier WR .08 .25
371 Reggie Cobb .01 .05
372 Reuben Davis .01 .05
373 Randy Grimes .01 .05
374 Wayne Haddix .01 .05
375 Ron Hall .01 .05
376 Harry Hamilton .01 .05
377 Bruce Hill .01 .05
378 Keith McCants .01 .05
379 Bruce Perkins .01 .05
380 Vinny Testaverde UER .02 .10
381 Broderick Thomas .01 .05
382 Jeff Bostic .01 .05
383 Earnest Byner .01 .05
384 Gary Clark .08 .25
385 Darryl Grant .01 .05
386 Darrell Green .01 .05
387 Stan Humphries .08 .25
388 Jim Lachey .01 .05
389 Charles Mann .01 .05
390 Wilber Marshall .01 .05
391 Art Monk .02 .10
392 Gerald Riggs .01 .05
393 Mark Rypien .02 .10
394 Ricky Sanders .01 .05
395 Don Warren .01 .05
396 Bruce Smith HIT .02 .10
397 Reggie White HIT .02 .10
398 Lawrence Taylor HIT .02 .10
399 David Fulcher HIT .01 .05
400 Derrick Thomas HIT .02 .10
401 Mark Carrier DB HIT .01 .05
402 Mike Singletary HIT .02 .10
403 Charles Haley HIT .01 .05
404 Jeff Cross HIT .01 .05
405 Leslie O'Neal HIT .02 .10
406 Tim Harris HIT .01 .05
407 Steve Atwater HIT .01 .05
408 Joe Montana LL UER .20 .50
409 Randall Cunningham LL .02 .10
410 Warren Moon LL .02 .10
411 Andre Rison LL UER 412 .02 .10
412 Haywood Jeffires LL .02 .10
413 Stephone Paige LL .01 .05
414 Phil Simms LL .02 .10
415 Barry Sanders LL .20 .50
416 Bo Jackson LL .02 .10
417 Thurman Thomas LL .02 .10
418 Emmitt Smith LL .50 1.25
419 John L. Williams LL .01 .05
420 Nick Bell RC .01 .05
421 Eric Bieniemy RC .01 .05
422 Mike Dumas UER RC .01 .05
423 Russell Maryland RC .08 .25
424 Derek Russell RC .01 .05
425 Chris Smith RC .01 .05
426 Mike Stonebreaker RP RC .01 .05
427 Pat Tyrance RP .01 .05
428 Kenny Walker RC .01 .05
429 Checklist 1-108 UER .01 .05
430 Checklist 109-216 .01 .05
431 Checklist 217-324 .01 .05
432 Checklist 325-432 .01 .05

1991 Fleer All-Pros

This 26-card standard size set was issued as a random insert in packs.The set features attractive full-color photography. A small player photo is superimposed over a larger up-close player photo on front. A "Fleer All-Pro '91" banner is accompanied by player and team name and position. The card backs contain a large body of text.

COMPLETE SET (26) 2.00 5.00
1 Andre Reed UER .02 .10
2 Bobby Humphrey .01 .05
3 Kent Hull .01 .05
4 Mark Bortz .01 .05
5 Bruce Smith .08 .25
6 Greg Townsend .01 .05
7 Ray Childress .01 .05
8 Andre Rison .02 .10
9 Barry Sanders .50 1.25
10 Bo Jackson .10 .30
11 Neal Anderson .02 .10
12 Keith Jackson .02 .10
13 Derrick Thomas .08 .25
14 John Offerdahl .01 .05
15 Lawrence Taylor .08 .25
16 Darrell Green .01 .05
17 Mark Carrier DB UER .02 .10
18 David Fulcher UER .01 .05
19 Joe Montana .50 1.25
20 Jerry Rice .30 .75
21 Charles Haley .02 .10
22 Mike Singletary .02 .10
23 Nick Lowery .01 .05
24 Jim Lachey UER .01 .05
25 Anthony Munoz .02 .10
26 Thurman Thomas .08 .25

1991 Fleer Pro-Vision

This ten-card standard size set was randomly inserted in packs. The fronts feature artworks with the player's name at the bottom. The backs contain a large write-up describing the player's career highlights.

COMPLETE SET (10) 2.00 5.00
1 Joe Montana .60 1.50
2 Barry Sanders .60 1.50
3 Lawrence Taylor .10 .30
4 Mike Singletary .02 .10
5 Dan Marino .60 1.50
6 Bo Jackson .15 .40
7 Randall Cunningham .10 .30
8 Bruce Smith .10 .30
9 Derrick Thomas .10 .30
10 Howie Long .10 .30

1991 Fleer Stars and Stripes

This 140-card standard-size set marked the second year that Fleer, in conjunction with Asher Candy, marketed a set sold with candy sticks. The set features full-color game action shots on the front and a large color portrait, as well as complete statistical information on the back. The cards are arranged by alphabetical team order within each conference.

COMPLETE SET (140) 4.80 12.00
1 Shane Conlan .02 .10
2 Kent Hull .02 .10
3 Andre Reed .07 .20
4 Bruce Smith .07 .20
5 Thurman Thomas .10 .30
6 James Brooks .02 .10
7 Boomer Esiason .07 .20
8 David Fulcher .02 .10
9 Rodney Holman .02 .10
10 Anthony Munoz .07 .20
11 Reggie Langhorne .02 .10
12 Clay Matthews .02 .10
13 Eric Metcalf .07 .20
14 Gregg Rakoczy .02 .10
15 Steve Atwater .02 .10
16 John Elway 1.00 2.50
17 Bobby Humphrey .02 .10
18 Karl Mecklenburg .02 .10
19 Dennis Smith .02 .10
20 Ray Childress .02 .10
21 Ernest Givins .02 .10
22 Haywood Jeffires .07 .20
23 Warren Moon .10 .30
24 Mike Munchak .07 .20
25 Albert Bentley .02 .10
26 Jeff George .07 .20
27 Rohn Stark .02 .10
28 Clarence Verdin .02 .10
29 Albert Lewis .02 .10
30 Nick Lowery .02 .10
31 Christian Okoye .02 .10
32 Stephone Paige .02 .10
33 Derrick Thomas .07 .20
34 Barry Word .02 .10
35 Bo Jackson .10 .30
36 Howie Long .10 .30
37 Greg Townsend .02 .10
38 Steve Wisniewski UER .02 .10
39 Mark Clayton .02 .10
40 Dan Marino 1.00 2.50
41 John Offerdahl .02 .10
42 Richmond Webb .02 .10
43 Irving Fryar .07 .20
44 Ed Reynolds .02 .10
45 John Stephens .02 .10
46 Rob Moore .10 .30
47 Ken O'Brien .02 .10
48 Al Toon .02 .10
49 Bubby Brister .02 .10
50 Eric Green .02 .10
51 Merril Hoge .02 .10
52 David Little .02 .10
53 Rod Woodson .07 .20
54 Marion Butts .02 .10
55 Leslie O'Neal .02 .10
56 Junior Seau .10 .30
57 Billy Joe Tolliver .02 .10
58 Cortez Kennedy .07 .20
59 Dave Krieg .02 .10
60 John L. Williams .02 .10
61 Steve Broussard .02 .10
62 Bill Fralic .02 .10
63 Andre Rison .07 .20
64 Neal Anderson .02 .10
65 Mark Carrier DB .02 .10
66 Richard Dent .02 .10
67 Jim Harbaugh .07 .20
68 Mike Singletary .07 .20
69 Troy Aikman .50 1.25
70 Emmitt Smith 1.25 3.00
71 Mel Gray .02 .10
72 Rodney Peete .02 .10
73 Barry Sanders 1.00 2.50
74 Tim Harris .02 .10
75 Perry Kemp .02 .10
76 Sterling Sharpe .07 .20
77 Henry Ellard .07 .20
78 Jim Everett .02 .10
79 Kevin Greene .07 .20
80 Jackie Slater .02 .10
81 Joey Browner .02 .10
82 Chris Doleman .02 .10
83 Steve Jordan .02 .10
84 Carl Lee .02 .10
85 Herschel Walker .07 .20
86 Morten Andersen .02 .10
87 Dalton Hilliard .02 .10
88 Vaughan Johnson .02 .10
89 Steve Walsh .02 .10
90 Ottis Anderson .02 .10
91 John Elliott .02 .10
92 Rodney Hampton .07 .20
93 Sean Landeta .02 .10
94 Dave Meggett .02 .10
95 Phil Simms .07 .20
96 Lawrence Taylor .07 .20
97 Randall Cunningham .10 .30
98 Keith Jackson .02 .10
99 Seth Joyner .02 .10
100 Reggie White .10 .30
101 Roy Green .02 .10
102 Johnny Johnson .02 .10
103 Ricky Proehl .02 .10
104 Tootie Robbins .02 .10
105 Kevin Fagan UER .02 .10
106 Charles Haley .07 .20
107 Guy McIntyre .02 .10
108 Joe Montana 1.00 2.50
109 Tom Rathman .02 .10
110 Jerry Rice .50 1.25
111 John Taylor .07 .20
112 Wayne Haddix .02 .10
113 Vinny Testaverde .02 .10
114 Earnest Byner .02 .10
115 Gary Clark .07 .20
116 Darrell Green .02 .10
117 Jim Lachey .02 .10
118 Art Monk .07 .20
119 Mark Rypien .02 .10
120 Nick Bell .02 .10
121 Eric Bieniemy .02 .10
122 Jarrod Bunch .02 .10
123 Aaron Craver .02 .10
124 Lawrence Dawsey .02 .10
125 Mike Dumas .02 .10
126 Jeff Graham .10 .30
127 Paul Justin .02 .10
128 Darryll Lewis UER .02 .10
129 Todd Marinovich .02 .10
130 Russell Maryland .07 .20
131 Kanavis McGhee .02 .10
132 Ernie Mills .02 .10
133 Herman Moore .30 .75
134 Godfrey Myles .02 .10
135 Browning Nagle .02 .10
136 Esera Tuaolo .02 .10
137 Mark Vander Poel .02 .10
138 Harvey Williams .07 .20
139 Chris Zorich .02 .10
140 Checklist Card UER .02 .10

1992 Fleer Prototypes

The 1992 Fleer Prototype football set contains six standard-size cards. The cards were distributed as two-card and three-card panels or strips in an attempt to show off the new design features of the 1992 Fleer football cards. The cards prominently pronounce "1992 Pre-Production Sample" in the middle of the reverse.

93 Mike Croel .30 .75
191 Tim Brown .50 1.25
428 Mark Rypien .30 .75
435 Terrell Buckley .30 .75
457 Barry Sanders LL 2.00 5.00
475 Emmitt Smith PV 2.00 5.00

1992 Fleer

The 1992 Fleer football set contains 480 standard-size cards. The cards were available in 17-card wax packs, 42-card rack packs, and 32-card cello packs. The cards are checklisted alphabetically according to teams. Subsets included are Prospects (432-451), League Leaders (452-470), Pro-Visions (471-476), and Checklists (477-480). Rookie Cards include Edgar Bennett, Steve Bono, Amp Lee and Tommy Vardell.

COMPLETE SET (480) 5.00 10.00
1 Steve Broussard .01 .05
2 Rick Bryan .01 .05
3 Scott Case .01 .05
4 Tory Epps .01 .05
5 Bill Fralic .01 .05
6 Moe Gardner .01 .05
7 Michael Haynes .02 .10
8 Chris Hinton .01 .05
9 Brian Jordan .02 .10
10 Mike Kenn .01 .05
11 Tim McKyer .01 .05
12 Chris Miller .02 .10
13 Erric Pegram .02 .10
14 Mike Pritchard .02 .10
15 Andre Rison .02 .10
16 Jessie Tuggle .01 .05
17 Carlton Bailey RC .02 .10
18 Howard Ballard .01 .05
19 Don Beebe .01 .05
20 Cornelius Bennett .02 .10
21 Shane Conlan .01 .05
22 Kent Hull .01 .05
23 Mark Kelso .01 .05
24 James Lofton .02 .10
25 Keith McKeller .01 .05
26 Scott Norwood .01 .05
27 Nate Odomes .01 .05
28 Frank Reich .02 .10
29 Jim Ritcher .01 .05
30 Leon Seals .01 .05
31 Darryl Talley .01 .05
32 Steve Tasker .02 .10
33 Thurman Thomas .08 .25
34 Will Wolford .01 .05
35 Neal Anderson .01 .05
36 Trace Armstrong .01 .05
37 Mark Carrier DB .01 .05
38 Richard Dent .02 .10
39 Shaun Gayle .01 .05
40 Jim Harbaugh .08 .25
41 Jay Hilgenberg .01 .05
42 Darren Lewis .01 .05
43 Steve McMichael .02 .10
44 Brad Muster .01 .05
45 William Perry .02 .10
46 John Roper .01 .05
47 Lemuel Stinson .01 .05
48 Stan Thomas .01 .05
49 Keith Van Horne .01 .05
50 Tom Waddle .01 .05
51 Donnell Woolford .01 .05
52 Chris Zorich .02 .10
53 Eddie Brown .01 .05
54 James Francis .01 .05
55 David Fulcher .01 .05
56 David Grant .01 .05
57 Harold Green .01 .05
58 Rodney Holman .01 .05
59 Lee Johnson .01 .05
60 Tim Krumrie .01 .05
61 Anthony Munoz .02 .10
62 Joe Walter RC .01 .05
63 Mike Baab .01 .05
64 Stephen Braggs .01 .05
65 Richard Brown RC .01 .05
66 Dan Fike .01 .05
67 Scott Galbraith RC .01 .05
68 Randy Hilliard RC .01 .05
69 Michael Jackson .02 .10
70 Tony Jones T .01 .05
71 Ed King .01 .05
72 Kevin Mack .01 .05
73 Clay Matthews .02 .10
74 Eric Metcalf .02 .10
75 Vince Newsome .01 .05
76 John Rienstra .01 .05
77 Steve Beuerlein .02 .10
78 Larry Brown DB .01 .05
79 Tony Casillas .01 .05
80 Alvin Harper .02 .10
81 Issiac Holt .01 .05
82 Ray Horton .01 .05
83 Michael Irvin .08 .25
84 Daryl Johnston .08 .25
85 Kelvin Martin .01 .05
86 Nate Newton .02 .10
87 Ken Norton .02 .10
88 Jay Novacek .02 .10
89 Emmitt Smith .60 1.50
90 Vinson Smith RC .01 .05
91 Mark Stepnoski .02 .10
92 Steve Atwater .01 .05
93 Mike Croel .01 .05
94 John Elway .50 1.25
95 Simon Fletcher .01 .05
96 Gaston Green .01 .05
97 Mark Jackson .01 .05
98 Keith Kartz .01 .05
99 Greg Kragen .01 .05
100 Greg Lewis .01 .05
101 Karl Mecklenburg .01 .05
102 Derek Russell .01 .05
103 Steve Sewell .01 .05
104 Dennis Smith .01 .05
105 David Treadwell .01 .05
106 Kenny Walker .01 .05
107 Doug Widell .01 .05
108 Michael Young .01 .05
109 Jerry Ball .01 .05
110 Bennie Blades .01 .05
111 Lomas Brown .01 .05
112 Scott Conover RC .01 .05
113 Ray Crockett .01 .05
114 Mike Farr .01 .05
115 Mel Gray .02 .10
116 Willie Green .01 .05
117 Tracy Hayworth RC .01 .05
118 Erik Kramer .02 .10
119 Herman Moore .08 .25
120 Dan Owens .01 .05
121 Rodney Peete .02 .10
122 Brett Perriman .08 .25
123 Barry Sanders .50 1.25
124 Chris Spielman .02 .10
125 Marc Spindler .01 .05
126 Tony Bennett .01 .05
127 Matt Brock .01 .05
128 LeRoy Butler .01 .05
129 Johnny Holland .01 .05
130 Perry Kemp .01 .05
131 Don Majkowski .01 .05
132 Mark Murphy .01 .05
133 Brian Noble .01 .05
134 Bryce Paup .08 .25
135 Sterling Sharpe .08 .25
136 Scott Stephen .01 .05
137 Darrell Thompson .01 .05
138 Mike Tomczak .01 .05
139 Esera Tuaolo .01 .05
140 Keith Woodside .01 .05
141 Ray Childress .01 .05
142 Cris Dishman .01 .05
143 Curtis Duncan .01 .05
144 John Flannery .01 .05
145 William Fuller .02 .10
146 Ernest Givins .02 .10
147 Haywood Jeffires .02 .10
148 Sean Jones .02 .10
149 Lamar Lathon .01 .05
150 Bruce Matthews .01 .05
151 Bubba McDowell .01 .05
152 Johnny Meads .01 .05
153 Warren Moon .08 .25
154 Mike Munchak .02 .10
155 Al Smith .01 .05
156 Doug Smith .01 .05
157 Lorenzo White .01 .05
158 Michael Ball .01 .05
159 Chip Banks .01 .05
160 Duane Bickett .01 .05
161 Bill Brooks .01 .05
162 Ken Clark .01 .05
163 Jon Hand .01 .05
164 Jeff Herrod .01 .05
165 Jessie Hester .01 .05
166 Scott Radecic .01 .05
167 Rohn Stark .01 .05
168 Clarence Verdin .01 .05
169 John Alt .01 .05
170 Tim Barnett .01 .05
171 Tim Grunhard .01 .05
172 Dino Hackett .01 .05
173 Jonathan Hayes .01 .05
174 Bill Maas .01 .05
175 Chris Martin .01 .05
176 Christian Okoye .01 .05
177 Stephone Paige .01 .05
178 Jayice Pearson RC .01 .05
179 Kevin Porter .01 .05
180 Kevin Ross .01 .05
181 Dan Saleaumua .01 .05
182 Tracy Simien RC .01 .05
183 Neil Smith .08 .25
184 Derrick Thomas .08 .25
185 Robb Thomas .01 .05
186 Mark Vlasic .01 .05
187 Barry Word .01 .05
188 Marcus Allen .08 .25
189 Eddie Anderson .01 .05
190 Nick Bell .01 .05
191 Tim Brown .08 .25
192 Scott Davis .01 .05
193 Riki Ellison .01 .05
194 Mervyn Fernandez .01 .05
195 Willie Gault .02 .10
196 Jeff Gossett .01 .05
197 Ethan Horton .01 .05
198 Jeff Jaeger .01 .05
199 Howie Long .08 .25
200 Ronnie Lott .02 .10
201 Todd Marinovich .01 .05
202 Don Mosebar .01 .05
203 Jay Schroeder .01 .05
204 Greg Townsend .01 .05
205 Lionel Washington .01 .05
206 Steve Wisniewski .01 .05
207 Flipper Anderson .01 .05
208 Bern Brostek .01 .05
209 Robert Delpino .01 .05
210 Henry Ellard .02 .10
211 Jim Everett .02 .10
212 Cleveland Gary .01 .05
213 Kevin Greene .02 .10
214 Darryl Henley .01 .05
215 Damone Johnson .01 .05
216 Larry Kelm .01 .05
217 Todd Lyght .01 .05
218 Jackie Slater .01 .05
219 Michael Stewart .01 .05
220 Pat Terrell UER .01 .05
221 Robert Young .01 .05
222 Mark Clayton .02 .10
223 Bryan Cox .02 .10
224 Aaron Craver .01 .05
225 Jeff Cross .01 .05
226 Mark Duper .01 .05
227 Harry Galbreath .01 .05
228 David Griggs .01 .05
229 Mark Higgs .01 .05
230 Vestee Jackson .01 .05
231 John Offerdahl .01 .05
232 Louis Oliver .01 .05
233 Tony Paige .01 .05
234 Reggie Roby .01 .05
235 Sammie Smith .01 .05
236 Pete Stoyanovich .01 .05
237 Richmond Webb .01 .05
238 Terry Allen .08 .25
239 Ray Berry .01 .05
240 Joey Browner .01 .05
241 Anthony Carter .02 .10
242 Cris Carter .20 .50
243 Chris Doleman .01 .05
244 Rich Gannon .08 .25
245 Tim Irwin .01 .05
246 Steve Jordan .01 .05
247 Carl Lee .01 .05
248 Randall McDaniel .02 .10
249 Mike Merriweather .01 .05
250 Harry Newsome .01 .05
251 John Randle .02 .10
252 Henry Thomas .01 .05
253 Herschel Walker .02 .10
254 Ray Agnew .01 .05
255 Bruce Armstrong .01 .05
256 Vincent Brown .01 .05
257 Marv Cook .01 .05
258 Irving Fryar .02 .10
259 Pat Harlow .01 .05
260 Tommy Hodson .01 .05
261 Maurice Hurst .01 .05
262 Ronnie Lippett .01 .05
263 Eugene Lockhart .01 .05
264 Greg McMurtry .01 .05
265 Hugh Millen .01 .05
266 Leonard Russell .02 .10
267 Andre Tippett .01 .05
268 Brent Williams .01 .05
269 Morten Andersen .01 .05
270 Gene Atkins .01 .05
271 Wesley Carroll .01 .05
272 Jim Dombrowski .01 .05
273 Quinn Early .02 .10
274 Gill Fenerty .01 .05
275 Bobby Hebert .01 .05
276 Joel Hilgenberg .01 .05
277 Rickey Jackson .01 .05
278 Vaughan Johnson .01 .05
279 Eric Martin .01 .05
280 Brett Maxie .01 .05
281 Fred McAfee RC .01 .05
282 Sam Mills .01 .05
283 Pat Swilling .02 .10
284 Floyd Turner .01 .05
285 Steve Walsh .01 .05
286 Frank Warren .01 .05
287 Stephen Baker .01 .05
288 Maurice Carthon .01 .05
289 Mark Collins .01 .05
290 John Elliott .01 .05
291 Myron Guyton .01 .05
292 Rodney Hampton .02 .10
293 Jeff Hostetler .02 .10
294 Mark Ingram .01 .05
295 Pepper Johnson .01 .05
296 Sean Landeta .01 .05
297 Leonard Marshall .01 .05
298 Dave Meggett .02 .10
299 Bart Oates .01 .05
300 Phil Simms .02 .10
301 Reyna Thompson .01 .05
302 Lewis Tillman .01 .05
303 Brad Baxter .01 .05
304 Kyle Clifton .01 .05
305 James Hasty .01 .05
306 Joe Kelly .01 .05
307 Jeff Lageman .01 .05
308 Mo Lewis .01 .05
309 Erik McMillan .01 .05
310 Rob Moore .02 .10
311 Tony Stargell .01 .05
312 Jim Sweeney .01 .05
313 Marvin Washington .01 .05
314 Lonnie Young .01 .05
315 Eric Allen .01 .05
316 Fred Barnett .08 .25
317 Jerome Brown .01 .05
318 Keith Byars .01 .05
319 Wes Hopkins .01 .05
320 Keith Jackson .02 .10
321 James Joseph .01 .05
322 Seth Joyner .02 .10
323 Jeff Kemp .01 .05
324 Roger Ruzek .01 .05
325 Clyde Simmons .01 .05
326 William Thomas .01 .05
327 Reggie White .08 .25
328 Calvin Williams .02 .10
329 Rich Camarillo .01 .05
330 Ken Harvey .01 .05
331 Eric Hill .01 .05
332 Johnny Johnson .01 .05
333 Ernie Jones .01 .05
334 Tim Jorden .01 .05
335 Tim McDonald .01 .05
336 Freddie Joe Nunn .01 .05
337 Luis Sharpe .01 .05
338 Eric Swann .02 .10
339 Aeneas Williams .02 .10
340 Gary Anderson K .01 .05
341 Bubby Brister .01 .05
342 Adrian Cooper .01 .05
343 Barry Foster .02 .10
344 Eric Green .01 .05
345 Bryan Hinkle .01 .05
346 Tunch Ilkin .01 .05
347 Carnell Lake .01 .05
348 Louis Lipps .01 .05
349 David Little .01 .05
350 Greg Lloyd .02 .10
351 Neil O'Donnell .08 .25
352 Dwight Stone .01 .05
353 Rod Woodson .08 .25
354 Rod Bernstine .01 .05
355 Eric Bieniemy .01 .05
356 Marion Butts .01 .05
357 Gill Byrd .01 .05
358 John Friesz .02 .10
359 Burt Grossman .01 .05
360 Courtney Hall .01 .05
361 Ronnie Harmon .01 .05
362 Shawn Jefferson .01 .05
363 Nate Lewis .01 .05
364 Craig McEwen RC .01 .05
365 Eric Moten .01 .05
366 Joe Phillips .01 .05
367 Gary Plummer .01 .05
368 Henry Rolling .01 .05
369 Broderick Thompson .01 .05
370 Harris Barton .01 .05
371 Steve Bono RC .08 .25
372 Todd Bowles .08 .25
373 Dexter Carter .01 .05
374 Michael Carter .01 .05
375 Mike Cofer .01 .05
376 Keith DeLong .01 .05
377 Charles Haley .02 .10
378 Merton Hanks .02 .10
379 Tim Harris .01 .05
380 Brent Jones .02 .10
381 Guy McIntyre .01 .05
382 Tom Rathman .01 .05
383 Bill Romanowski .01 .05
384 Jesse Sapolu .01 .05
385 John Taylor .02 .10
386 Steve Young .25 .60
387 Robert Blackmon .01 .05
388 Brian Blades .02 .10
389 Jacob Green .01 .05
390 Dwayne Harper .01 .05
391 Andy Heck .01 .05
392 Tommy Kane .01 .05
393 John Kasay .01 .05
394 Cortez Kennedy .02 .10
395 Bryan Millard .01 .05
396 Rufus Porter .01 .05
397 Eugene Robinson .01 .05
398 John L. Williams .01 .05
399 Terry Wooden .01 .05
400 Gary Anderson RB .01 .05
401 Ian Beckles .01 .05
402 Mark Carrier WR .02 .10
403 Reggie Cobb .01 .05
404 Lawrence Dawsey .02 .10
405 Ron Hall .01 .05
406 Keith McCants .01 .05
407 Charles McRae .01 .05
408 Tim Newton .01 .05
409 Jesse Solomon .01 .05
410 Vinny Testaverde .02 .10
411 Broderick Thomas .01 .05
412 Robert Wilson .01 .05
413 Jeff Bostic .01 .05
414 Earnest Byner .01 .05
415 Gary Clark .08 .25
416 Andre Collins .01 .05
417 Brad Edwards .01 .05
418 Kurt Gouveia .01 .05
419 Darrell Green .01 .05
420 Joe Jacoby .01 .05
421 Jim Lachey .01 .05
422 Chip Lohmiller .01 .05
423 Charles Mann .01 .05
424 Wilber Marshall .01 .05
425 Ron Middleton RC .01 .05
426 Brian Mitchell .02 .10
427 Art Monk .02 .10
428 Mark Rypien .01 .05
429 Ricky Sanders .01 .05
430 Mark Schlereth RC .01 .05
431 Fred Stokes .01 .05
432 Edgar Bennett RC .08 .25
433 Brian Bollinger RC .01 .05
434 Joe Bowden RC .01 .05
435 Terrell Buckley RC .01 .05
436 Willie Clay RC .01 .05
437 Steve Gordon RC .01 .05
438 Keith Hamilton RC .02 .10
439 Carlos Huerta .01 .05
440 Matt LaBounty RC .01 .05
441 Amp Lee RC .01 .05
442 Ricardo McDonald RC .01 .05
443 Chris Mims RC .02 .10
444 Michael Moody RC .01 .05
445 Patrick Rowe RC .01 .05
446 Leon Searcy RC .02 .10
447 Siran Stacy RC .01 .05
448 Kevin Turner RC .01 .05
449 Tommy Vardell RC .02 .10
450 Bob Whitfield RC .01 .05
451 Darryl Williams RC .01 .05
452 Thurman Thomas LL .02 .10
453 Emmitt Smith LL .30 .75
454 Haywood Jeffires LL .01 .05
455 Michael Irvin LL .02 .10
456 Mark Clayton LL .01 .05
457 Barry Sanders LL .25 .60
458 Pete Stoyanovich LL .01 .05
459 Chip Lohmiller LL .01 .05
460 William Fuller LL .01 .05
461 Pat Swilling LL .01 .05
462 Ronnie Lott LL .01 .05
463 Ray Crockett LL .01 .05
464 Tim McKyer LL .01 .05
465 Aeneas Williams LL .01 .05
466 Rod Woodson LL .02 .10
467 Mel Gray LL .01 .05
468 Nate Lewis LL .01 .05
469 Steve Young LL .10 .30
470 Reggie Roby LL .01 .05
471 John Elway PV .25 .60
472 Ronnie Lott PV .01 .05
473 Art Monk PV UER .01 .05
474 Warren Moon PV .02 .10
475 Emmitt Smith PV .30 .75
476 Thurman Thomas PV .02 .10
477 Checklist 1-120 .01 .05
478 Checklist 121-240 .01 .05
479 Checklist 241-360 .01 .05
480 Checklist 361-480 .01 .05

1992 Fleer All-Pros

This 24-card standard-size set was randomly inserted in packs. On a dark blue card face, the fronts feature color player cut outs superimposed on a red, white, and blue NFL logo emblem. The player's name and position appear in gold foil lettering at the lower left corner. The backs carry a color head shot and player profile on a pink background.

COMPLETE SET (24) 2.00 5.00
1 Marv Cook .02 .10
2 Mike Kenn .02 .10
3 Steve Wisniewski .02 .10
4 Jim Ritcher .02 .10
5 Jim Lachey .02 .10
6 Michael Irvin .30 .75
7 Andre Rison .10 .30
8 Thurman Thomas .30 .75
9 Barry Sanders 2.00 4.00
10 Bruce Matthews .02 .10
11 Mark Rypien .02 .10
12 Jeff Jaeger .02 .10
13 Reggie White .30 .75
14 Clyde Simmons .02 .10
15 Pat Swilling .10 .30
16 Sam Mills .02 .10
17 Ray Childress .02 .10
18 Jerry Ball .02 .10
19 Derrick Thomas .30 .75
20 Darrell Green .02 .10
21 Ronnie Lott .10 .30
22 Steve Atwater .02 .10
23 Mark Carrier DB .02 .10
24 Jeff Gossett .02 .10

1992 Fleer Rookie Sensations

This 20-card standard size set was inserted in 1992 Fleer cello packs. The color action player photos on the fronts are slightly tilted to the left and have shadow borders on the left and bottom. The card face is designed like a football field, with a green background sectioned off by white yard line markers. At the card top, the words "Rookie Sensations" are accented by gold foil stripes representing the flight of a football, while the player's name appears in gold foil lettering below the picture. The backs have a similar design to the fronts and present a career summary.

COMPLETE SET (20) 4.00 10.00
RANDOM INSERTS IN JUMBO PACKS
1 Moe Gardner .15 .40
2 Mike Pritchard .40 1.00
3 Stan Thomas .15 .40
4 Larry Brown DB .15 .40
5 Todd Lyght .15 .40
6 James Joseph .15 .40
7 Aeneas Williams .40 1.00
8 Michael Jackson .40 1.00
9 Ed King .15 .40
10 Mike Croel .15 .40
11 Kenny Walker .15 .40
12 Tim Barnett .15 .40
13 Nick Bell .15 .40
14 Todd Marinovich .15 .40
15 Leonard Russell .40 1.00
16 Pat Harlow .15 .40
17 Mo Lewis .15 .40
18 John Kasay .15 .40
19 Lawrence Dawsey .40 1.00
20 Charles McRae .15 .40

1992 Fleer Mark Rypien

This 15-card standard-size set chronicles the career of Mark Rypien, Super Bowl XXVI's Most Valuable Player. The first 12 cards were randomly inserted in packs. Collectors could also obtain three additional cards (13-15) of him by mailing in ten Fleer pack proofs of purchase. Rypien autographed over 2,000 of his cards. On a dark blue card face, the fronts feature color action photos outlined in the team's colors. The words "Mark Rypien Performance Highlights" appear in gold-foil lettering above the picture. The backs carry capsule summaries of different phases of Rypien's career.

COMPLETE SET (12) 1.50 3.00
COMMON RYPIEN (1-12) .10 .30
COMMON SEND-OFF (13-15) .20 .50
AU Mark Rypien AUTO 12.50 30.00

1992 Fleer Team Leaders

This 24-card standard-size set was inserted in 1992 Fleer rack packs. Each rack contained either a Team Leader card or a Mark Rypien insert. The cards are arranged alphabetically according to team in the NFC (1-13) and AFC

(14-24).
COMPLETE SET (24) 15.00 40.00
ONE TL OR RYPIEN PER RACK PACK
1 Chris Miller .25 .60
2 Neal Anderson .08 .25
3 Emmitt Smith 4.00 10.00
4 Chris Spielman .25 .60
5 Brian Noble .08 .25
6 Jim Everett .25 .60
7 Joey Browner .08 .25
8 Sam Mills .08 .25
9 Rodney Hampton .25 .60
10 Reggie White .60 1.50
11 Tim McDonald .08 .25
12 Charles Haley .25 .60
13 Mark Rypien .08 .25
14 Cornelius Bennett .25 .60
15 Clay Matthews .25 .60
16 John Elway 3.00 8.00
17 Warren Moon .60 1.50
18 Derrick Thomas .60 1.50
19 Greg Townsend .08 .25
20 Bruce Armstrong .08 .25
21 Brad Baxter .08 .25
22 Rod Woodson .60 1.50
23 Marion Butts .08 .25
24 Rufus Porter .08 .25

1993 Fleer

The 1993 Fleer football set consists of 500 standard-size cards. Cards were available in 15 and 29-card packs as well as 27-card rack packs. Topical subsets featured are Award Winners (236-240, 253-257), League Leaders (241-243, 258-262), and Pro Visions (246-248, 263-264). Rookie Cards include Dave Brown. A Promo Panel with eight cards was produced and is priced as uncut at the end of our checklist.
COMPLETE SET (500) 10.00 20.00
1 Dan Saleaumua .01 .05
2 Bryan Cox .01 .05
3 Dermontti Dawson .02 .10
4 Michael Jackson .02 .10
5 Calvin Williams .02 .10
6 Terry McDaniel .01 .05
7 Jack Del Rio .01 .05
8 Steve Atwater .01 .05
9 Ernie Jones .01 .05
10 Brad Muster .01 .05
11 Harold Green .01 .05
12 Eric Bieniemy .01 .05
13 Eric Dorsey .01 .05
14 Fred Barnett .02 .10
15 Cleveland Gary .01 .05
16 Darion Conner .01 .05
17 Jerry Ball .01 .05
18 Tony Casillas .01 .05
19 Brian Blades .02 .10
20 Tony Bennett .01 .05
21 Reggie Cobb .01 .05
22 Kurt Gouveia .01 .05
23 Greg McMurtry .01 .05
24 Kyle Clifton .01 .05
25 Trace Armstrong .01 .05
26 Terry Allen .08 .25
27 Steve Bono .02 .10
28 Barry Word .01 .05
29 Mark Duper .01 .05
30 Nate Newton .02 .10
31 Will Wolford .01 .05
32 Curtis Duncan .01 .05
33 Nick Bell .01 .05
34 Don Beebe .01 .05
35 Mike Croel .01 .05
36 Rich Camarillo .01 .05
37 Wade Wilson .01 .05
38 John Taylor .02 .10
39 Marion Butts .01 .05
40 Rodney Hampton .02 .10
41 Seth Joyner .01 .05
42 Wilber Marshall .01 .05
43 Bobby Hebert .01 .05
44 Bennie Blades .01 .05
45 Thomas Everett .01 .05
46 Ricky Sanders .01 .05
47 Matt Brock .01 .05
48 Lawrence Dawsey .01 .05
49 Brad Edwards .01 .05
50 Vincent Brown .01 .05
51 Jeff Lageman .01 .05
52 Mark Carrier DB .01 .05
53 Cris Carter .08 .25
54 Brent Jones .02 .10
55 Barry Foster .02 .10
56 Derrick Thomas .08 .25
57 Scott Zolak .01 .05
58 Mark Stepnoski .01 .05
59 Eric Metcalf .02 .10
60 Al Smith .01 .05
61 Ronnie Harmon .01 .05
62 Cornelius Bennett .02 .10
63 Karl Mecklenburg .01 .05
64 Chris Chandler .02 .10
65 Toi Cook .01 .05
66 Tim Krumrie .01 .05
67 Gill Byrd .01 .05
68 Mark Jackson .01 .05
69 Tim Harris .01 .05
70 Shane Conlan .01 .05
71 Moe Gardner .01 .05
72 Lomas Brown .01 .05
73 Charles Haley .02 .10
74 Mark Rypien .01 .05
75 LeRoy Butler .01 .05
76 Steve DeBerg .01 .05
77 Darrell Green .01 .05
78 Marv Cook .01 .05
79 Chris Burkett .01 .05
80 Richard Dent .02 .10
81 Roger Craig .02 .10
82 Amp Lee .01 .05
83 Eric Green .01 .05
84 Willie Davis .08 .25
85 Mark Higgs .01 .05
86 Carlton Haselrig .01 .05
87 Tommy Vardell .01 .05
88 Haywood Jeffires .02 .10
89 Tim Brown .08 .25
90 Randall McDaniel .02 .10
91 John Elway .60 1.50
92 Ken Harvey .01 .05
93 Joel Hilgenberg .01 .05
94 Steve Wallace .01 .05
95 Stan Humphries .02 .10
96 Greg Jackson .01 .05
97 Clyde Simmons .01 .05
98 Jim Everett .02 .10
99 Michael Haynes .02 .10
100 Mel Gray .02 .10
101 Alvin Harper .02 .10
102 Art Monk .02 .10
103 Brett Favre .75 2.00
104 Keith McCants .01 .05
105 Charles Mann .01 .05
106 Leonard Russell .02 .10
107 Mo Lewis .01 .05
108 Shaun Gayle .01 .05
109 Chris Doleman .01 .05
110 Tim McDonald .01 .05
111 Louis Oliver .01 .05
112 Greg Lloyd .02 .10
113 Chip Banks .01 .05
114 Sean Jones .01 .05
115 Ethan Horton .01 .05
116 Kenneth Davis .01 .05
117 Simon Fletcher .01 .05
118 Johnny Johnson .01 .05
119 Vaughan Johnson .01 .05
120 Derrick Fenner .01 .05
121 Nate Lewis .01 .05
122 Pepper Johnson .01 .05
123 Heath Sherman .01 .05
124 Darryl Henley .01 .05
125 Pierce Holt .01 .05
126 Herman Moore .08 .25
127 Michael Irvin .08 .25
128 Tommy Kane .01 .05
129 Jackie Harris .01 .05
130 Hardy Nickerson .02 .10
131 Chip Lohmiller .01 .05
132 Andre Tippett .01 .05
133 Leonard Marshall .01 .05
134 Craig Heyward .02 .10
135 Anthony Carter .02 .10
136 Tom Rathman .01 .05
137 Lorenzo White .01 .05
138 Nick Lowery .01 .05
139 John Offerdahl .01 .05
140 Neil O'Donnell .08 .25
141 Clarence Verdin .01 .05
142 Ernest Givins .02 .10
143 Todd Marinovich .01 .05
144 Jeff Wright .01 .05
145 Michael Brooks .01 .05
146 Freddie Joe Nunn .01 .05
147 William Perry .02 .10
148 Daniel Stubbs .01 .05
149 Morten Andersen .01 .05
150 Dave Meggett .01 .05
151 Andre Waters .01 .05
152 Todd Lyght .01 .05
153 Chris Miller .02 .10
154 Rodney Peete .01 .05
155 Jim Jeffcoat .01 .05
156 Cortez Kennedy .02 .10
157 Johnny Holland .01 .05
158 Ricky Reynolds .04 .05
159 Kevin Greene .02 .10
160 Jeff Herrod .01 .05
161 Bruce Matthews .01 .05
162 Anthony Smith .01 .05
163 Henry Jones .01 .05
164 Rob Burnett .01 .05
165 Eric Swann .02 .10
166 Tom Waddle .01 .05
167 Alfred Williams .01 .05
168 Darren Carrington RC .01 .05
169 Mike Sherrard .01 .05
170 Frank Reich .02 .10
171 Anthony Newman RC .01 .05
172 Mike Pritchard .02 .10
173 Andre Ware .01 .05
174 Daryl Johnston .08 .25
175 Rufus Porter .01 .05
176 Reggie White .08 .25
177 Charles Mincy RC .01 .05
178 Pete Stoyanovich .01 .05
179 Rod Woodson .08 .25
180 Anthony Johnson .02 .10
181 Cody Carlson .01 .05
182 Gaston Green .01 .05
183 Audray McMillian .01 .05
184 Mike Johnson .01 .05
185 Aeneas Williams .01 .05
186 Jarrod Bunch .01 .05
187 Dennis Smith .01 .05
188 Quinn Early .02 .10
189 James Hasty .01 .05
190 Darryl Talley .01 .05
191 Jon Vaughn .01 .05
192 Andre Rison .02 .10
193 Kelvin Pritchett .01 .05
194 Ken Norton Jr. .02 .10
195 Chris Warren .02 .10
196 Sterling Sharpe .08 .25
197 Christian Okoye .01 .05
198 Richmond Webb .01 .05
199 James Francis .01 .05
200 Reggie Langhorne .01 .05
201 J.J. Birden .01 .05
202 Aaron Wallace .01 .05
203 Henry Thomas .01 .05
204 Clay Matthews .02 .10
205 Robert Massey .01 .05
206 Donnell Woolford .01 .05
207 Ricky Watters .08 .25
208 Wayne Martin .01 .05
209 Rob Moore .02 .10
210 Steve Tasker .02 .10
211 Jackie Slater .01 .05
212 Steve Young .30 .75
213 Barry Sanders .50 1.25
214 Jay Novacek .02 .10
215 Eugene Robinson .01 .05
216 Duane Bickett .01 .05
217 Broderick Thomas .01 .05
218 David Fulcher .01 .05
219 Rohn Stark .01 .05
220 Warren Moon .08 .25
221 Steve Wisniewski .01 .05
222 Nate Odomes .01 .05
223 Shannon Sharpe .08 .25
224 Byron Evans .01 .05
225 Mark Collins .01 .05
226 Rod Bernstine .01 .05
227 Sam Mills .01 .05
228 Marvin Washington .01 .05
229 Thurman Thomas .08 .25
230 Brent Williams .01 .05
231 Jessie Tuggle .01 .05
232 Chris Spielman .02 .10
233 Emmitt Smith .60 1.50
234 John L. Williams .01 .05
235 Jeff Cross .01 .05
236 Chris Doleman AW .01 .05
237 John Elway AW .30 .75
238 Barry Foster AW .01 .05
239 Cortez Kennedy AW .01 .05
240 Steve Young AW .15 .40
241 Barry Foster LL .01 .05
242 Warren Moon LL .01 .05
243 Sterling Sharpe LL .01 .05
244 Emmitt Smith LL .30 .75
245 Thurman Thomas LL .02 .10
246 Michael Irvin PV .02 .10
247 Steve Young PV .15 .40
248 Barry Foster PV .01 .05
249 Checklist .01 .05
250 Checklist .01 .05
251 Checklist .01 .05
252 Checklist .01 .05
253 Troy Aikman AW .15 .40
254 Jason Hanson AW .01 .05
255 Carl Pickens AW .02 .10
256 Santana Dotson AW .01 .05
257 Dale Carter AW .01 .05
258 Clyde Simmons LL .01 .05
259 Audray McMillian LL .01 .05
260 Henry Jones LL .01 .05
261 Deion Sanders LL .08 .25
262 Haywood Jeffires LL .01 .05
263 Deion Sanders PV .08 .25
264 Andre Reed PV .02 .10
265 Vince Workman .01 .05
266 Robert Brown .01 .05
267 Ray Agnew .01 .05
268 Ronnie Lott .02 .10
269 Wesley Carroll .01 .05
270 John Randle .02 .10
271 Rodney Culver .01 .05
272 David Alexander .01 .05
273 Troy Aikman .30 .75
274 Bernie Kosar .02 .10
275 Scott Case .01 .05
276 Dan McGwire .01 .05
277 John Alt .01 .05
278 Dan Marino .60 1.50
279 Santana Dotson .02 .10
280 Johnny Mitchell .01 .05
281 Alonzo Spellman .01 .05
282 Adrian Cooper .01 .05
283 Gary Clark .02 .10
284 Vance Johnson .01 .05
285 Eric Martin .01 .05
286 Jesse Solomon .01 .05
287 Carl Banks .01 .05
288 Harris Barton .01 .05
289 Jim Harbaugh .08 .25
290 Bubba McDowell .01 .05
291 Anthony McDowell RC .01 .05
292 Terrell Buckley .01 .05
293 Bruce Armstrong .01 .05
294 Kurt Barber .01 .05
295 Reginald Jones .01 .05
296 Steve Jordan .01 .05
297 Kerry Cash .01 .05
298 Ray Crockett .01 .05
299 Keith Byars .01 .05
300 Russell Maryland .01 .05
301 Johnny Bailey .01 .05
302 Vinnie Clark .01 .05
303 Terry Wooden .01 .05
304 Harvey Williams .02 .10
305 Marco Coleman .01 .05
306 Mark Wheeler .01 .05
307 Greg Townsend .01 .05
308 Tim McGee .01 .05
309 Donald Evans .01 .05
310 Randal Hill .01 .05
311 Kenny Walker .01 .05
312 Dalton Hilliard .01 .05
313 Howard Ballard .01 .05
314 Phil Simms .02 .10
315 Jerry Rice .40 1.00
316 Courtney Hall .01 .05
317 Darren Lewis .01 .05
318 Greg Montgomery .01 .05
319 Paul Gruber .01 .05
320 George Koonce RC .01 .05
321 Eugene Chung .01 .05
322 Mike Brim .01 .05
323 Patrick Hunter .01 .05
324 Todd Scott .01 .05
325 Steve Emtman .01 .05
326 Andy Harmon RC .02 .10
327 Larry Brown DB .01 .05
328 Chuck Cecil .01 .05
329 Tim McKyer .01 .05
330 Jeff Bryant .01 .05
331 Tim Barnett .01 .05
332 Irving Fryar .02 .10
333 Tyji Armstrong .01 .05
334 Brad Baxter .01 .05
335 Shane Collins .01 .05
336 Jeff Graham .02 .10
337 Ricky Proehl .01 .05
338 Tommy Maddox .08 .25
339 Jim Dombrowski .01 .05
340 Bill Brooks .01 .05
341 Dave Brown RC .08 .25
342 Eric Davis .01 .05
343 Leslie O'Neal .02 .10
344 Jim Morrissey .01 .05
345 Mike Munchak .02 .10
346 Ron Hall .01 .05
347 Brian Noble .01 .05
348 Chris Singleton .01 .05
349 Boomer Esiason .02 .10
350 Ray Roberts .01 .05
351 Gary Zimmerman .01 .05
352 Quentin Coryatt .02 .10
353 Willie Green .01 .05
354 Randall Cunningham .08 .25
355 Kevin Smith .02 .10
356 Michael Dean Perry .02 .10
357 Tim Green .01 .05
358 Dwayne Harper .01 .05
359 Dale Carter .01 .05
360 Keith Jackson .02 .10
361 Martin Mayhew .01 .05
362 Brian Washington .01 .05
363 Earnest Byner .01 .05
364 D.J. Johnson .01 .05
365 Timm Rosenbach .01 .05
366 Doug Widell .01 .05
367 Vaughn Dunbar .01 .05
368 Phil Hansen .01 .05
369 Mike Fox .01 .05
370 Dana Hall .01 .05
371 Junior Seau .08 .25
372 Steve McMichael .02 .10
373 Eddie Robinson .01 .05
374 Milton Mack RC .01 .05
375 Mike Prior .01 .05
376 Jerome Henderson .01 .05
377 Scott Mersereau .01 .05
378 Neal Anderson .01 .05
379 Harry Newsome .01 .05
380 John Baylor .01 .05
381 Bill Fralic .01 .05
382 Mark Bavaro .01 .05
383 Robert Jones .01 .05
384 Tyronne Stowe .01 .05
385 Deion Sanders .20 .50
386 Robert Blackmon .01 .05
387 Neil Smith .08 .25
388 Mark Ingram .01 .05
389 Mark Carrier WR .02 .10
390 Browning Nagle .01 .05
391 Ricky Ervins .01 .05
392 Carnell Lake .01 .05
393 Luis Sharpe .01 .05
394 Greg Kragen .01 .05
395 Tommy Barnhardt .01 .05
396 Mark Kelso .01 .05
397 Kent Graham RC .08 .25
398 Bill Romanowski .01 .05
399 Anthony Miller .02 .10
400 John Roper .01 .05
401 Lamar Rogers .01 .05
402 Troy Auzenne .01 .05
403 Webster Slaughter .01 .05
404 David Brandon .01 .05
405 Chris Hinton .01 .05
406 Andy Heck .01 .05
407 Tracy Simien .01 .05
408 Troy Vincent .01 .05
409 Jason Hanson .01 .05
410 Rod Jones CB RC .01 .05
411 Al Noga .01 .05
412 Ernie Mills .01 .05
413 Willie Gault .01 .05
414 Henry Ellard .02 .10
415 Rickey Jackson .01 .05
416 Bruce Smith .08 .25
417 Derek Brown TE .01 .05
418 Kevin Fagan .01 .05
419 Gary Plummer .01 .05
420 Wendell Davis .01 .05
421 Craig Thompson .01 .05
422 Wes Hopkins .01 .05
423 Ray Childress .01 .05
424 Pat Harlow .01 .05
425 Howie Long .08 .25
426 Shane Dronett .01 .05
427 Sean Salisbury .01 .05
428 Dwight Hollier RC .01 .05
429 Brett Perriman .08 .25
430 Donald Hollas RC .01 .05
431 Jim Lachey .01 .05
432 Darren Perry .01 .05
433 Lionel Washington .01 .05
434 Sean Gilbert .02 .10
435 Gene Atkins .01 .05
436 Jim Kelly .08 .25
437 Ed McCaffrey .08 .25
438 Don Griffin .01 .05
439 Jerrol Williams .01 .05
440 Bryce Paup .02 .10
441 Darryl Williams .01 .05
442 Vai Sikahema .01 .05
443 Cris Dishman .01 .05
444 Kevin Mack .01 .05
445 Winston Moss .01 .05
446 Tyrone Braxton .01 .05
447 Mike Merriweather .01 .05
448 Tony Paige .01 .05
449 Robert Porcher .01 .05
450 Ricardo McDonald .01 .05
451 Danny Copeland .01 .05
452 Tony Tolbert .01 .05
453 Eric Dickerson .02 .10
454 Flipper Anderson .01 .05
455 Dave Krieg .02 .10
456 Brad Lamb RC .01 .05
457 Bart Oates .01 .05
458 Guy McIntyre .01 .05
459 Stanley Richard .01 .05
460 Edgar Bennett .08 .25
461 Pat Carter .01 .05
462 Eric Allen .01 .05
463 William Fuller .01 .05
464 James Jones DT .01 .05
465 Chester McGlockton .02 .10
466 Charles Dimry .01 .05
467 Tim Grunhard .01 .05
468 Jarvis Williams .01 .05
469 Tracy Scroggins .01 .05
470 David Klingler .01 .05
471 Andre Collins .01 .05
472 Erik Williams .01 .05
473 Eddie Anderson .01 .05
474 Marc Boutte .01 .05
475 Joe Montana .60 1.50
476 Andre Reed .02 .10
477 Lawrence Taylor .08 .25
478 Jeff George .08 .25
479 Chris Mims .01 .05
480 Ken Ruettgers .01 .05
481 Roman Phifer .01 .05
482 William Thomas .01 .05
483 Lamar Lathon .01 .05
484 Vinny Testaverde .02 .10
485 Mike Kenn .01 .05
486 Greg Lewis .01 .05
487 Chris Martin .01 .05
488 Maurice Hurst .01 .05
489 Pat Swilling .01 .05
490 Carl Pickens .02 .10
491 Tony Smith RB .01 .05
492 James Washington .01 .05
493 Jeff Hostetler .02 .10
494 Jeff Chadwick .01 .05
495 Kevin Ross .01 .05
496 Jim Ritcher .01 .05
497 Jessie Hester .01 .05
498 Burt Grossman .01 .05
499 Keith Van Horne .01 .05
500 Gerald Robinson .01 .05
P1 Promo Panel 2.00 5.00

1993 Fleer All-Pros

Randomly inserted into foil packs, this 25-card standard-size set features the best of the NFL at each offensive and defensive position. The set is checklisted in alphabetical order.
COMPLETE SET (25) 10.00 25.00
1 Steve Atwater .15 .40
2 Rich Camarillo .15 .40
3 Ray Childress .15 .40
4 Chris Doleman .15 .40
5 Barry Foster .30 .75
6 Henry Jones .15 .40
7 Cortez Kennedy .30 .75
8 Nick Lowery .15 .40
9 Wilber Marshall .15 .40
10 Bruce Matthews .15 .40
11 Randall McDaniel .15 .40
12 Audray McMillian .15 .40
13 Sam Mills .15 .40
14 Jay Novacek .30 .75
15 Jerry Rice 3.00 8.00
16 Junior Seau .75 2.00
17 Sterling Sharpe .75 2.00
18 Clyde Simmons .15 .40
19 Emmitt Smith 5.00 12.00
20 Derrick Thomas .75 2.00
21 Steve Wallace .15 .40
22 Richmond Webb .15 .40
23 Steve Wisniewski .15 .40
24 Rod Woodson .75 2.00
25 Steve Young 2.50 6.00

1993 Fleer Prospects

Randomly inserted into foil packs, this 30-card standard-size set features the top 1993 NFL draft picks. This set started Fleer's tradition of issuing cards of current year rookies as an insert.
COMPLETE SET (30) 15.00 40.00
1 Drew Bledsoe ! 5.00 12.00
2 Garrison Hearst 1.50 4.00
3 John Copeland .30 .75
4 Eric Curry .30 .75
5 Curtis Conway 1.25 3.00
6 Lincoln Kennedy .30 .75
7 Jerome Bettis 6.00 15.00
8 Patrick Bates .30 .75
9 Brad Hopkins .30 .75
10 Tom Carter .30 .75
11 Irv Smith .30 .75
12 Robert Smith 2.50 6.00
13 Deon Figures .30 .75
14 Leonard Renfro .30 .75
15 O.J.McDuffie 1.25 3.00
16 Dana Stubblefield .60 1.50
17 Todd Kelly .30 .75
18 George Teague .30 .75
19 Demetrius DuBose .30 .75
20 Coleman Rudolph .30 .75
21 Carlton Gray .30 .75
22 Troy Drayton .30 .75
23 Natrone Means UER 1.25 3.00
24 Qadry Ismail 1.25 3.00
25 Gino Torretta .60 1.50
26 Carl Simpson .30 .75
27 Glyn Milburn .30 .75
28 Chad Brown LB .30 .75
29 Reggie Brooks .30 .75
30 Billy Joe Hobert .60 1.50

1993 Fleer Rookie Sensations

This 20-card standard-size set was randomly inserted in jumbo packs.The set is checklisted in alphabetical order.
COMPLETE SET (20) 30.00 80.00
RANDOM INSERTS IN JUMBO PACKS
1 Dale Carter 2.50 6.00
2 Eugene Chung 2.00 5.00
3 Marco Coleman 2.50 6.00
4 Quentin Coryatt 2.00 5.00
5 Santana Dotson 2.00 5.00
6 Vaughn Dunbar 2.00 5.00
7 Steve Emtman 2.50 6.00
8 Sean Gilbert 2.50 6.00
9 Dana Hall 2.00 5.00
10 Jason Hanson 2.00 5.00
11 Robert Jones 2.00 5.00
12 David Klingler 2.50 6.00
13 Amp Lee 2.00 5.00
14 Troy Auzenne 2.00 5.00
15 Ricardo McDonald 2.00 5.00
16 Chris Mims 2.00 5.00
17 Johnny Mitchell 2.50 6.00
18 Carl Pickens 2.50 6.00
19 Darren Perry 2.00 5.00
20 Troy Vincent 2.50 6.00

1993 Fleer Team Leaders

Randomly inserted into foil packs, this five-card standard-size set showcases 1992's brightest stars. On a sky blue background laced with lightning streaks, the fronts feature full-bleed color action player cut outs. The words "Team Leader" and the player's name are gold foil stamped at the bottom. Inside a gold border on a sky blue panel, the backs present a player profile and a second color player cut out.
COMPLETE SET (5) 15.00 30.00
1 Brett Favre 8.00 15.00
2 Derrick Thomas 1.00 2.00
3 Steve Young 3.00 6.00
4 John Elway 6.00 12.00
5 Cortez Kennedy .30 .75

1993 Fleer Steve Young

Randomly inserted in packs, this ten-card standard-size set spotlights Steve Young, the NFL's MVP for the 1992 season. Young autographed more than 2,000 of his cards. It is thought that he signed all 10-cards. Through a mail-in offer, for ten 1993 Fleer Football wrappers plus $1, the collector could receive three additional Steve Young "Performance Highlights" cards (#11-13). The fronts feature color action player photos bordered in white. The player's name and "Performance Highlights" are gold-foil stamped at the upper left corner.
COMPLETE SET (10) 3.00 8.00
COMMON YOUNG (1-10) .40 1.00
COMMON SEND-OFF (11-13) .75 2.00

1993 Fleer Steve Young Autographs

COMMON AUTO (1-10) 20.00 50.00

1993 Fleer Fruit of the Loom

This 50-card standard-size set issued by Fleer was sponsored by Fruit of the Loom. Each specially marked underwear package contained six cards. The color action player photos on the fronts are framed with silver metallic borders. At the bottom of the photo, the player's last name is printed in transparent lettering that has an embossed look. The team affiliation and position appear at the lower right corner. Fruit of the Loom's logo is in the upper left corner. On a team color-coded panel, the horizontal backs carry a close-up color shot, biography, player profile, team logo, and statistics.
COMPLETE SET (50) 70.00 175.00
1 Andre Rison 1.20 3.00
2 Deion Sanders 4.00 8.00
3 Neal Anderson .50 1.25
4 Jim Harbaugh 1.20 3.00
5 Bernie Kosar .80 2.00
6 Eric Metcalf .80 2.00
7 John Elway 10.00 20.00
8 Karl Mecklenburg .50 1.25
9 Sterling Sharpe .80 2.00
10 Reggie White 1.20 3.00
11 Steve Emtman .50 1.25
12 Jeff George 1.20 3.00
13 Willie Gault .50 1.25
14 Jim Kelly 1.20 3.00
15 Thurman Thomas 1.20 3.00
16 Harold Green .50 1.25
17 Carl Pickens .80 2.00
18 Troy Aikman 6.00 12.00
19 Emmitt Smith 6.00 15.00
20 Barry Sanders 6.00 15.00
21 Pat Swilling .50 1.25
22 Haywood Jeffires .50 1.25
23 Warren Moon 1.20 3.00
24 Derrick Thomas 1.20 3.00
25 Christian Okoye .50 1.25
26 Flipper Anderson .50 1.25
27 Jim Everett .50 1.25
28 Keith Jackson .50 1.25
29 Dan Marino 10.00 20.00
30 Andre Tippett .50 1.25
31 Lawrence Taylor 1.20 3.00
32 Randall Cunningham 1.20 3.00
33 Barry Foster .50 1.25
34 Rod Woodson .80 2.00
35 Jerry Rice 6.00 12.00
36 Steve Young 5.00 10.00
37 Reggie Cobb .50 1.25
38 Roger Craig .80 2.00
39 Chris Doleman .50 1.25
40 Morten Andersen .50 1.25
41 Dalton Hilliard .50 1.25
42 Ronnie Lott .80 2.00
43 Chris Chandler .80 2.00
44 Stan Humphries .80 2.00
45 Junior Seau 1.20 3.00
46 Brian Blades .50 1.25
47 Cortez Kennedy .80 2.00
48 Wilber Marshall .50 1.25
49 Art Monk .80 2.00
50 Checklist Card .50 1.25

1994 Fleer

The 1994 Fleer set consists of 480 standard-size cards. The cards are grouped alphabetically within teams and checklisted alphabetically according to teams. A "Fleer Hot Pack" was inserted in about every other box. It looks like a regular pack but it is filled with 15 insert cards. Otherwise, one insert card was included per pack. Cards were available in 15 and 21-card packs.There are no key Rookie Cards in this set. A Jerome Bettis prototype/promo card was produced and priced below.
COMPLETE SET (480) 10.00 20.00
1 Michael Bankston .01 .05
2 Steve Beuerlein .02 .10
3 John Booty .01 .05
4 Rich Camarillo .01 .05
5 Chuck Cecil .01 .05
6 Larry Centers .08 .25
7 Gary Clark .02 .10
8 Garrison Hearst .08 .25
9 Eric Hill .01 .05
10 Randal Hill .01 .05
11 Ronald Moore .01 .05
12 Ricky Proehl .01 .05
13 Luis Sharpe .01 .05
14 Clyde Simmons .01 .05
15 Tyronne Stowe .01 .05
16 Eric Swann .02 .10
17 Aeneas Williams .01 .05
18 Darion Conner .01 .05
19 Moe Gardner .01 .05
20 Jumpy Geathers .01 .05
21 Jeff George .08 .25
22 Roger Harper .01 .05
23 Bobby Hebert .01 .05
24 Pierce Holt .01 .05
25 D.J. Johnson .01 .05
26 Mike Kenn .01 .05
27 Lincoln Kennedy .01 .05
28 Erric Pegram .01 .05
29 Mike Pritchard .01 .05
30 Andre Rison .02 .10
31 Deion Sanders .20 .50
32 Tony Smith RB .01 .05
33 Jesse Solomon .01 .05
34 Jessie Tuggle .01 .05
35 Don Beebe .01 .05
36 Cornelius Bennett .02 .10
37 Bill Brooks .01 .05
38 Kenneth Davis .01 .05
39 John Fina .01 .05
40 Phil Hansen .01 .05
41 Kent Hull .01 .05
42 Henry Jones .01 .05
43 Jim Kelly .08 .25
44 Pete Metzelaars .01 .05
45 Marvcus Patton .01 .05
46 Andre Reed .02 .10
47 Frank Reich .02 .10
48 Bruce Smith .08 .25
49 Thomas Smith .01 .05
50 Darryl Talley .01 .05
51 Steve Tasker .02 .10
52 Thurman Thomas .08 .25
53 Jeff Wright .01 .05
54 Neal Anderson .01 .05
55 Trace Armstrong .01 .05
56 Troy Auzenne .01 .05
57 Joe Cain RC .01 .05
58 Mark Carrier DB .01 .05
59 Curtis Conway .08 .25
60 Richard Dent .02 .10
61 Shaun Gayle .01 .05
62 Andy Heck .01 .05
63 Dante Jones .01 .05
64 Erik Kramer .02 .10
65 Steve McMichael .02 .10
66 Terry Obee .01 .05
67 Vinson Smith .01 .05
68 Alonzo Spellman .01 .05
69 Tom Waddle .01 .05
70 Donnell Woolford .01 .05
71 Tim Worley .01 .05
72 Chris Zorich .01 .05
73 Mike Brim .01 .05
74 John Copeland .01 .05
75 Derrick Fenner .01 .05
76 James Francis .01 .05
77 Harold Green .01 .05
78 Rod Jones CB .01 .05
79 David Klingler .01 .05
80 Bruce Kozerski .01 .05
81 Tim Krumrie .01 .05
82 Ricardo McDonald .01 .05
83 Tim McGee .01 .05
84 Tony McGee .01 .05
85 Louis Oliver .01 .05
86 Carl Pickens .02 .10
87 Jeff Query .01 .05
88 Daniel Stubbs .01 .05
89 Steve Tovar .01 .05
90 Alfred Williams .01 .05
91 Darryl Williams .01 .05
92 Rob Burnett .01 .05
93 Mark Carrier WR .02 .10
94 Leroy Hoard .01 .05
95 Michael Jackson .02 .10
96 Mike Johnson .01 .05
97 Pepper Johnson .01 .05
98 Tony Jones T .01 .05
99 Clay Matthews .01 .05
100 Eric Metcalf .02 .10
101 Stevon Moore .01 .05
102 Michael Dean Perry .02 .10
103 Anthony Pleasant .01 .05
104 Vinny Testaverde .02 .10
105 Eric Turner .01 .05
106 Tommy Vardell .01 .05
107 Troy Aikman .40 1.00
108 Larry Brown DB .01 .05
109 Dixon Edwards .01 .05
110 Charles Haley .02 .10
111 Alvin Harper .02 .10
112 Michael Irvin .08 .25
113 Jim Jeffcoat .01 .05
114 Daryl Johnston .02 .10
115 Leon Lett .01 .05
116 Russell Maryland .01 .05
117 Nate Newton .01 .05
118 Ken Norton Jr. .02 .10
119 Jay Novacek .02 .10
120 Darrin Smith .01 .05
121 Emmitt Smith .60 1.50
122 Kevin Smith .01 .05
123 Mark Stepnoski .01 .05
124 Tony Tolbert .01 .05
125 Erik Williams .01 .05
126 Kevin Williams WR .02 .10
127 Darren Woodson .02 .10
128 Steve Atwater .01 .05
129 Rod Bernstine .01 .05
130 Ray Crockett .01 .05
131 Mike Croel .01 .05
132 Robert Delpino .01 .05
133 Shane Dronett .01 .05
134 Jason Elam .02 .10
135 John Elway .75 2.00
136 Simon Fletcher .01 .05
137 Greg Kragen .01 .05
138 Karl Mecklenburg .01 .05
139 Glyn Milburn .02 .10
140 Anthony Miller .02 .10
141 Derek Russell .01 .05
142 Shannon Sharpe .02 .10
143 Dennis Smith .01 .05
144 Dan Williams .01 .05
145 Gary Zimmerman .01 .05
146 Bennie Blades .01 .05
147 Lomas Brown .01 .05
148 Bill Fralic .01 .05
149 Mel Gray .01 .05
150 Willie Green .01 .05
151 Jason Hanson .01 .05
152 Robert Massey .01 .05
153 Ryan McNeil .01 .05
154 Scott Mitchell .02 .10
155 Derrick Moore .01 .05
156 Herman Moore .08 .25
157 Brett Perriman .02 .10
158 Robert Porcher .01 .05
159 Kelvin Pritchett .01 .05
160 Barry Sanders .60 1.50
161 Tracy Scroggins .01 .05
162 Chris Spielman .02 .10
163 Pat Swilling .01 .05
164 Edgar Bennett .08 .25
165 Robert Brooks .08 .25
166 Terrell Buckley .01 .05
167 LeRoy Butler .01 .05
168 Brett Favre .75 2.00
169 Harry Galbreath .01 .05
170 Jackie Harris .01 .05
171 Johnny Holland .01 .05
172 Chris Jacke .01 .05
173 George Koonce .01 .05
174 Bryce Paup .02 .10
175 Ken Ruettgers .01 .05
176 Sterling Sharpe .02 .10
177 Wayne Simmons .01 .05
178 George Teague .01 .05
179 Darrell Thompson .01 .05
180 Reggie White .08 .25
181 Gary Brown .01 .05
182 Cody Carlson .01 .05
183 Ray Childress .01 .05
184 Cris Dishman .01 .05
185 Ernest Givins .02 .10
186 Haywood Jeffires .02 .10
187 Sean Jones .01 .05
188 Lamar Lathon .01 .05
189 Bruce Matthews .01 .05
190 Bubba McDowell .01 .05
191 Glenn Montgomery .01 .05
192 Greg Montgomery .01 .05
193 Warren Moon .08 .25
194 Bo Orlando .01 .05
195 Marcus Robertson .01 .05
196 Eddie Robinson .01 .05
197 Webster Slaughter .01 .05
198 Lorenzo White .01 .05
199 John Baylor .01 .05
200 Jason Belser .01 .05
201 Tony Bennett .01 .05
202 Dean Biasucci .01 .05
203 Ray Buchanan .01 .05
204 Kerry Cash .01 .05
205 Quentin Coryatt .01 .05
206 Eugene Daniel .01 .05
207 Steve Emtman .01 .05
208 Jon Hand .01 .05
209 Jim Harbaugh .08 .25
210 Jeff Herrod .01 .05
211 Anthony Johnson .02 .10
212 Roosevelt Potts .01 .05
213 Rohn Stark .01 .05
214 Will Wolford .01 .05
215 Marcus Allen .08 .25
216 John Alt .01 .05
217 Kimble Anders .02 .10
218 J.J. Birden .01 .05
219 Dale Carter .01 .05
220 Keith Cash .01 .05
221 Tony Casillas .01 .05
222 Willie Davis .02 .10
223 Tim Grunhard .01 .05
224 Nick Lowery .01 .05
225 Charles Mincy .01 .05
226 Joe Montana .75 2.00
227 Dan Saleaumua .01 .05
228 Tracy Simien .01 .05
229 Neil Smith .02 .10
230 Derrick Thomas .08 .25
231 Eddie Anderson .01 .05
232 Tim Brown .08 .25
233 Nolan Harrison .01 .05
234 Jeff Hostetler .02 .10
235 Rocket Ismail .02 .10
236 Jeff Jaeger .01 .05
237 James Jett .01 .05
238 Joe Kelly .01 .05
239 Albert Lewis .01 .05
240 Terry McDaniel .01 .05
241 Chester McGlockton .01 .05
242 Winston Moss .01 .05
243 Gerald Perry .01 .05
244 Greg Robinson .01 .05
245 Anthony Smith .01 .05
246 Steve Smith .01 .05
247 Greg Townsend .01 .05
248 Lionel Washington .01 .05
249 Steve Wisniewski .01 .05
250 Alexander Wright .01 .05
251 Flipper Anderson .01 .05
252 Jerome Bettis .20 .50
253 Marc Boutte .01 .05
254 Shane Conlan .01 .05
255 Troy Drayton .01 .05
256 Henry Ellard .02 .10
257 Sean Gilbert .01 .05
258 Nate Lewis .01 .05
259 Todd Lyght .01 .05
260 Chris Miller .01 .05
261 Anthony Newman .01 .05
262 Roman Phifer .01 .05
263 Henry Rolling .01 .05
264 T.J.Rubley RC .01 .05
265 Jackie Slater .01 .05
266 Fred Stokes .01 .05
267 Robert Young .01 .05
268 Gene Atkins .01 .05
269 J.B. Brown .01 .05
270 Keith Byars .01 .05
271 Marco Coleman .01 .05
272 Bryan Cox .01 .05
273 Jeff Cross .01 .05
274 Irving Fryar .02 .10
275 Mark Higgs .01 .05
276 Dwight Hollier .01 .05
277 Mark Ingram .01 .05
278 Keith Jackson .01 .05
279 Terry Kirby .08 .25
280 Bernie Kosar .02 .10
281 Dan Marino .75 2.00
282 O.J.McDuffie .08 .25
283 Keith Sims .01 .05
284 Pete Stoyanovich .01 .05
285 Troy Vincent .01 .05
286 Richmond Webb .01 .05
287 Terry Allen .02 .10
288 Anthony Carter .02 .10
289 Cris Carter .20 .50
290 Jack Del Rio .01 .05
291 Chris Doleman .01 .05
292 Vencie Glenn .01 .05
293 Scottie Graham RC .02 .10
294 Chris Hinton .01 .05
295 Qadry Ismail .08 .25
296 Carlos Jenkins .01 .05
297 Steve Jordan .01 .05
298 Carl Lee .01 .05
299 Randall McDaniel .02 .10
300 John Randle .02 .10
301 Todd Scott .01 .05
302 Robert Smith .08 .25
303 Fred Strickland .01 .05
304 Henry Thomas .01 .05
305 Bruce Armstrong .01 .05
306 Harlon Barnett .01 .05
307 Drew Bledsoe .30 .75
308 Vincent Brown .01 .05
309 Ben Coates .02 .10
310 Todd Collins .01 .05
311 Myron Guyton .01 .05
312 Pat Harlow .01 .05
313 Maurice Hurst .01 .05
314 Leonard Russell .01 .05
315 Chris Slade .01 .05
316 Michael Timpson .01 .05
317 Andre Tippett .01 .05
318 Morten Andersen .01 .05
319 Derek Brown RBK .01 .05
320 Vince Buck .01 .05
321 Toi Cook .01 .05
322 Quinn Early .02 .10
323 Jim Everett .02 .10
324 Michael Haynes .02 .10
325 Tyrone Hughes .02 .10
326 Rickey Jackson .01 .05
327 Vaughan Johnson .01 .05
328 Eric Martin .01 .05
329 Wayne Martin .01 .05
330 Sam Mills .01 .05
331 Willie Roaf .01 .05
332 Irv Smith .01 .05
333 Keith Taylor .01 .05
334 Renaldo Turnbull .01 .05
335 Carlton Bailey .01 .05
336 Michael Brooks .01 .05

337 Jarrod Bunch .01 .05
338 Chris Calloway .01 .05
339 Mark Collins .01 .05
340 Howard Cross .01 .05
341 Stacey Dillard RC .01 .05
342 John Elliott .01 .05
343 Rodney Hampton .02 .10
344 Greg Jackson .01 .05
345 Mark Jackson .01 .05
346 Dave Meggett .01 .05
347 Corey Miller .01 .05
348 Mike Sherrard .01 .05
349 Phil Simms .02 .10
350 Lewis Tillman .01 .05
351 Brad Baxter .01 .05
352 Kyle Clifton .01 .05
353 Boomer Esiason .02 .10
354 James Hasty .01 .05
355 Bobby Houston .01 .05
356 Johnny Johnson .01 .05
357 Jeff Lageman .01 .05
358 Mo Lewis .01 .05
359 Ronnie Lott .02 .10
360 Leonard Marshall .01 .05
361 Johnny Mitchell .01 .05
362 Rob Moore .02 .10
363 Eric Thomas .01 .05
364 Brian Washington .01 .05
365 Marvin Washington .01 .05
366 Eric Allen .01 .05
367 Fred Barnett .02 .10
368 Bubby Brister .01 .05
369 Randall Cunningham .08 .25
370 Byron Evans .01 .05
371 William Fuller .01 .05
372 Andy Harmon .01 .05
373 Seth Joyner .01 .05
374 William Perry .02 .10
375 Leonard Renfro .01 .05
376 Heath Sherman .01 .05
377 Ben Smith .01 .05
378 William Thomas .01 .05
379 Herschel Walker .02 .10
380 Calvin Williams .02 .10
381 Chad Brown .01 .05
382 Dermontti Dawson .02 .10
383 Deon Figures .01 .05
384 Barry Foster .01 .05
385 Jeff Graham .01 .05
386 Eric Green .01 .05
387 Kevin Greene .02 .10
388 Carlton Haselrig .01 .05
389 Levon Kirkland .01 .05
390 Carnell Lake .01 .05
391 Greg Lloyd .02 .10
392 Neil O'Donnell .08 .25
393 Darren Perry .01 .05
394 Dwight Stone .01 .05
395 Leroy Thompson .01 .05
396 Rod Woodson .02 .10
397 Marion Butts .01 .05
398 John Carney .01 .05
399 Darren Carrington .01 .05
400 Burt Grossman .01 .05
401 Courtney Hall .01 .05
402 Ronnie Harmon .01 .05
403 Stan Humphries .02 .10
404 Shawn Jefferson .01 .05
405 Vance Johnson .01 .05
406 Chris Mims .01 .05
407 Leslie O'Neal .01 .05
408 Stanley Richard .01 .05
409 Junior Seau .08 .25
410 Harris Barton .01 .05
411 Dennis Brown .01 .05
412 Eric Davis .01 .05
413 Merton Hanks .02 .10
414 John Johnson .01 .05
415 Brent Jones .02 .10
416 Marc Logan .01 .05
417 Tim McDonald .01 .05
418 Gary Plummer .01 .05
419 Tom Rathman .01 .05
420 Jerry Rice .40 1.00
421 Bill Romanowski .01 .05
422 Jesse Sapolu .01 .05
423 Dana Stubblefield .02 .10
424 John Taylor .02 .10
425 Steve Wallace .01 .05
426 Ted Washington .01 .05
427 Ricky Watters .02 .10
428 Troy Wilson RC .01 .05
429 Steve Young .30 .75
430 Howard Ballard .01 .05
431 Michael Bates .01 .05
432 Robert Blackmon .01 .05
433 Brian Blades .02 .10
434 Ferrell Edmunds .01 .05
435 Carlton Gray .01 .05
436 Patrick Hunter .01 .05
437 Cortez Kennedy .02 .10
438 Kelvin Martin .01 .05
439 Rick Mirer .08 .25
440 Nate Odomes .01 .05
441 Ray Roberts .01 .05
442 Eugene Robinson .01 .05
443 Rod Stephens .01 .05
444 Chris Warren .02 .10
445 John L. Williams .01 .05
446 Terry Wooden .01 .05
447 Marty Carter .01 .05
448 Reggie Cobb .01 .05
449 Lawrence Dawsey .01 .05
450 Santana Dotson .02 .10
451 Craig Erickson .01 .05
452 Thomas Everett .01 .05
453 Paul Gruber .01 .05
454 Courtney Hawkins .01 .05
455 Martin Mayhew .01 .05
456 Hardy Nickerson .02 .10
457 Ricky Reynolds .01 .05
458 Vince Workman .01 .05
459 Reggie Brooks .02 .10
460 Earnest Byner .01 .05
461 Andre Collins .01 .05
462 Brad Edwards .01 .05
463 Kurt Gouveia .01 .05
464 Darrell Green .01 .05
465 Ken Harvey .01 .05
466 Ethan Horton .01 .05
467 A.J. Johnson .01 .05
468 Tim Johnson .01 .05
469 Jim Lachey .01 .05
470 Chip Lohmiller .01 .05
471 Art Monk .02 .10
472 Sterling Palmer RC .01 .05
473 Mark Rypien .01 .05
474 Ricky Sanders .01 .05
475 Checklist 1-106 .01 .05
476 Checklist 107-214 .01 .05
477 Checklist 215-317 .01 .05
478 Checklist 318-409 .01 .05
479 Checklist 410-480 .01 .05
Inserts
480 Inserts Checklist .01 .05
P244 Jerome Bettis Promo .40 1.00

1994 Fleer All-Pros

Randomly inserted in packs, these 24 standard-size cards present Fleer's choices for leading offensive and defensive players from both conferences. The cards are numbered on the back as "X of 24."

COMPLETE SET (24) 7.50 20.00
1 Troy Aikman 1.25 3.00
2 Eric Allen .07 .20
3 Jerome Bettis .60 1.50
4 Barry Foster .07 .20
5 Michael Irvin .30 .75
6 Cortez Kennedy .10 .30
7 Joe Montana 2.50 6.00
8 Hardy Nickerson .07 .20
9 Jerry Rice 1.25 3.00
10 Andre Rison .10 .30
11 Barry Sanders 2.00 5.00
12 Deion Sanders .60 1.50
13 Junior Seau .30 .75
14 Shannon Sharpe .10 .30
15 Sterling Sharpe .10 .30
16 Bruce Smith .30 .75
17 Emmitt Smith 2.00 5.00
18 Neil Smith .10 .30
19 Derrick Thomas .30 .75
20 Thurman Thomas .30 .75
21A R.Turnbull ERR R.White .40 1.00
21B Renaldo Turnbull COR .07 .20
22 Reggie White .30 .75
23 Rod Woodson .10 .30
24 Steve Young 1.00 2.50

1994 Fleer Award Winners

Randomly inserted in packs, this five-card standard-size set focuses on the Super Bowl MVP, the AFC and NFC Offensive Rookies of the Year, the NFL Defensive Player of the Year and the NFL Rookie of the Year. The set is numbered on the back as "X of 5." The set is checklisted in alphabetical order.

COMPLETE SET (5) 1.50 4.00
1 Jerome Bettis .30 .75
2 Rick Mirer .10 .30
3 Deion Sanders .40 1.00
4 Emmitt Smith 1.25 2.50
5 Dana Stubblefield .10 .30

1994 Fleer Jerome Bettis

Randomly inserted in packs, this 12-card standard-size set details Jerome Bettis' achievements at Notre Dame and as a 1993 rookie star with the Los Angeles Rams. Three mail-in cards (13-15) could be obtained for 10 1994 Fleer Football wrappers plus 1.50.

COMPLETE SET (15) 3.00 8.00
COMPLETE SET (12) 2.50 6.00
COMMON BETTIS (1-12) .25 .60
COMMON SEND-OFF (13-15) .40 1.00

1994 Fleer League Leaders

The 1994 Fleer League Leaders 10-card, standard-size set highlights top-ranked players in passing, rushing and receiving from the 1993 campaign. The cards were randomly inserted in packs. The set is checklisted in alphabetical order.

COMPLETE SET (10) 4.00 10.00
1 Marcus Allen .20 .50
2 Tim Brown .20 .50
3 John Elway 1.50 4.00
4 Tyrone Hughes .07 .20
5 Jerry Rice .75 2.00
6 Sterling Sharpe .07 .20
7 Emmitt Smith 1.25 3.00
8 Neil Smith .07 .20
9 Thurman Thomas .20 .50
10 Steve Young .60 1.50

1994 Fleer Living Legends

These horizontally designed metallized cards were inserted at a rate of approximately one in 60 wax packs. The six-card standard size set features NFL stars with long records of achievement in the league. The set is checklisted in alphabetical order.

COMPLETE SET (6) 12.50 30.00
STATED ODDS 1:60 HOB/JUM
1 Marcus Allen .60 1.50
2 John Elway 5.00 12.00
3 Joe Montana 5.00 12.00
4 Jerry Rice 2.50 6.00
5 Emmitt Smith 4.00 10.00
6 Reggie White .60 1.50

1994 Fleer Prospects

Randomly inserted in packs, this 25-card standard size set features leading 1994 rookie prospects. Pictured in his collegiate uniform, the player is superimposed over a the fiery background of a steel mill. The set is checklisted in alphabetical order.

COMPLETE SET (25) 6.00 15.00
1 Sam Adams .25 .60
2 Trev Alberts .25 .60
3 Derrick Alexander WR .40 1.00
4 Mario Bates .40 1.00
5 Jeff Burris .25 .60
6 Shante Carver .15 .40
7 Marshall Faulk 2.50 6.00
8 William Floyd .40 1.00
9 Rob Fredrickson .25 .60
10 Wayne Gandy .15 .40
11 Charlie Garner 1.00 2.50
12 Aaron Glenn .40 1.00
13 Charles Johnson .40 1.00
14 Joe Johnson .15 .40
15 Tre Johnson .15 .40
16 Antonio Langham .25 .60
17 Chuck Levy .15 .40
18 Willie McGinest .40 1.00
19 David Palmer .40 1.00
20 Errict Rhett UER .40 1.00
21 Jason Sehorn .40 1.00
22 Heath Shuler .40 1.00
23 Charlie Ward .40 1.00
24 Dewayne Washington .25 .60
25 Bryant Young .40 1.00

1994 Fleer Pro-Vision

This nine-card standard-size set was randomly inserted in packs. When placed together, they form a colorful puzzle. The nine-card jumbo parallel set was distributed one set per hobby case.

COMPLETE SET (9) 2.50 6.00
*JUMBO CARDS: 1.2X TO 3X BASIC CARDS
ONE JUMBO SET PER HOBBY CASE
1 Rodney Hampton .05 .15
2 Ricky Watters .05 .15
3 Rick Mirer .15 .40
4 Brett Favre 1.50 3.00
5 Troy Aikman .75 1.50
6 Jerome Bettis .30 .75
7 Joe Montana 1.50 3.00
8 Cornelius Bennett .05 .15
9 Rod Woodson .05 .15

1994 Fleer Rookie Exchange

Identical in design to the basic set, these 12 standard-size cards could be obtained by sending in a Rookie Exchange card that was randomly inserted in packs. The set features rookies that appeared in their respective NFL uniforms subsequent to the printing of the basic Fleer set.

COMPLETE SET (12) 12.50 30.00
ONE SET PER TRADE CARD BY MAIL
1 Derrick Alexander WR 1.25 3.00
2 Trent Dilfer 2.50 6.00
3 Marshall Faulk 7.50 20.00
4 Charlie Garner 3.00 8.00
5 Greg Hill 1.25 3.00
6 Charles Johnson 1.25 3.00
7 Antonio Langham .40 1.00
8 Willie McGinest 1.25 3.00
9 Heath Shuler 1.25 3.00
10 Dewayne Washington .60 1.50
11 Dan Wilkinson .60 1.50
12 Bryant Young 1.25 3.00
NNO Rookie Exch.Expired .20 .50

1994 Fleer Rookie Sensations

Randomly inserted in 21-card jumbo packs, the Rookie Sensations set contains 20 standard size cards of players that were rookies in 1993. The set is checklisted in alphabetical order.

COMPLETE SET (20) 50.00 100.00
RANDOM INSERTS IN JUMBO PACKS
1 Jerome Bettis 5.00 12.00
2 Drew Bledsoe 7.50 20.00
3 Reggie Brooks 2.50 6.00
4 Tom Carter 1.50 4.00
5 John Copeland 1.50 4.00
6 Jason Elam 1.50 4.00
7 Garrison Hearst 3.00 8.00
8 Tyrone Hughes 1.50 4.00
9 James Jett 3.00 8.00
10 Lincoln Kennedy 1.50 4.00
11 Terry Kirby 3.00 8.00
12 Glyn Milburn 2.50 6.00
13 Rick Mirer 3.00 8.00
14 Ronald Moore 1.50 4.00
15 Willie Roaf 1.50 4.00
16 Wayne Simmons 1.50 4.00
17 Chris Slade 1.50 4.00
18 Darrin Smith 1.50 4.00
19 Dana Stubblefield 2.50 6.00
20 George Teague 1.50 4.00

1994 Fleer Scoring Machines

Inserted in 15-card packs, this 20-card standard size set highlights top scorers in the NFL in recent seasons. The set is checklisted in alphabetical order.

COMPLETE SET (20) 15.00 40.00
1 Marcus Allen .50 1.25
2 Natrone Means 1.00 2.50
3 Jerome Bettis 1.00 2.50
4 Tim Brown .50 1.25
5 Barry Foster .08 .25
6 Rodney Hampton .20 .50
7 Michael Irvin .50 1.25
8 Nick Lowery .08 .25
9 Dan Marino 4.00 10.00
10 Joe Montana 4.00 10.00
11 Warren Moon .50 1.25
12 Andre Reed .20 .50
13 Jerry Rice 2.00 5.00
14 Andre Rison .20 .50
15 Barry Sanders 3.00 8.00
16 Shannon Sharpe .20 .50
17 Sterling Sharpe .20 .50
18 Emmitt Smith 3.00 8.00
19 Thurman Thomas .50 1.25
20 Ricky Watters .20 .50

1994 Fleer Patriots Tickets

COMPLETE SET (10) 40.00 80.00
1 Bruce Armstrong 3.00 8.00
2 Drew Bledsoe 5.00 12.00
3 Tim Brown 5.00 12.00
4 Vincent Brown 3.00 8.00
5 Gino Cappelletti '63 Fleer 4.00 10.00
6 Ben Coates 4.00 10.00
7 Pat Harlow 3.00 8.00
8 Dan Marino 8.00 20.00
9 Junior Seau 5.00 12.00
10 Bruce Smith 5.00 12.00

1995 Fleer

The 1995 Fleer set consists of 400 standard-size cards issued as one series. The cards were issued in 11-card packs with a suggested retail price of $1.49. These packs included nine basic cards, one insert and one Flair preview card. Hot packs containing only insert cards were included one out of 72 packs. Seventeen-card jumbo ($2.29) included 15 basic cards, one insert as well as one Flair preview. The cards are grouped alphabetically within teams, and checklisted alphabetically according to teams. Jeff Blake is the key Rookie Card in this set. A Promo Panel of three cards was produced and is priced at the end of our checklist as an uncut panel.

COMPLETE SET (400) 12.00 30.00
1 Michael Bankston .02 .10
2 Larry Centers .07 .20
3 Gary Clark .02 .10
4 Eric Hill .02 .10
5 Seth Joyner .02 .10
6 Dave Krieg .02 .10
7 Lorenzo Lynch .02 .10
8 Jamir Miller .02 .10
9 Ronald Moore .02 .10
10 Ricky Proehl .02 .10
11 Clyde Simmons .02 .10
12 Eric Swann .07 .20
13 Aeneas Williams .02 .10
14 J.J. Birden .02 .10
15 Chris Doleman .02 .10
16 Bert Emanuel .10 .30
17 Jumpy Geathers .02 .10
18 Jeff George .07 .20
19 Roger Harper .02 .10
20 Craig Heyward .07 .20
21 Pierce Holt .02 .10
22 D.J. Johnson .02 .10
23 Terance Mathis .07 .20
24 Clay Matthews .07 .20
25 Andre Rison .07 .20
26 Chuck Smith .02 .10
27 Jessie Tuggle .02 .10
28 Cornelius Bennett .07 .20
29 Bucky Brooks .02 .10
30 Jeff Burris .02 .10
31 Russell Copeland .02 .10
32 Matt Darby .02 .10
33 Phil Hansen .02 .10
34 Henry Jones .02 .10
35 Jim Kelly .10 .30
36 Mark Maddox RC .02 .10
37 Bryce Paup .07 .20
38 Andre Reed .07 .20
39 Bruce Smith .10 .30
40 Darryl Talley .02 .10
41 Dewell Brewer RC .02 .10
42 Mike Fox .02 .10
43 Eric Guliford .02 .10
44 Lamar Lathon .02 .10
45 Pete Metzelaars .02 .10
46 Sam Mills .07 .20
47 Frank Reich .02 .10
48 Rod Smith DB .07 .20
49 Jack Trudeau .02 .10
50 Trace Armstrong .02 .10
51 Joe Cain .02 .10
52 Mark Carrier DB .02 .10
53 Curtis Conway .10 .30
54 Shaun Gayle .02 .10
55 Jeff Graham .02 .10
56 Raymont Harris .02 .10
57 Erik Kramer .02 .10
58 Lewis Tillman .02 .10
59 Tom Waddle .02 .10
60 Steve Walsh .02 .10
61 Donnell Woolford .02 .10
62 Chris Zorich .02 .10
63 Jeff Blake RC .25 .60
64 Mike Brim .02 .10
65 Steve Broussard .02 .10
66 James Francis .02 .10
67 Ricardo McDonald .02 .10
68 Tony McGee .02 .10
70 Darnay Scott .07 .20
71 Steve Tovar .02 .10
72 Dan Wilkinson .07 .20
73 Alfred Williams .02 .10
74 Darryl Williams .02 .10
75 Derrick Alexander WR .10 .30
76 Randy Baldwin .02 .10
77 Carl Banks .02 .10
78 Rob Burnett .02 .10
79 Steve Everitt .02 .10
80 Leroy Hoard .02 .10
81 Michael Jackson .07 .20
82 Pepper Johnson .02 .10
83 Tony Jones T .02 .10
84 Antonio Langham .02 .10
85 Eric Metcalf .07 .20
86 Stevon Moore .02 .10
87 Anthony Pleasant .02 .10
88 Vinny Testaverde .07 .20
89 Eric Turner .02 .10
90 Troy Aikman .40 1.00
91 Charles Haley .07 .20
92 Michael Irvin .10 .30
93 Daryl Johnston .07 .20
94 Robert Jones .02 .10
95 Leon Lett .02 .10
96 Russell Maryland .02 .10
97 Nate Newton .07 .20
98 Jay Novacek .07 .20
99 Darrin Smith .02 .10
100 Emmitt Smith .60 1.50
101 Kevin Smith .02 .10
102 Erik Williams .02 .10
103 Kevin Williams WR .07 .20
104 Darren Woodson .07 .20
105 Elijah Alexander .02 .10
106 Steve Atwater .02 .10
107 Ray Crockett .02 .10
108 Shane Dronett .02 .10
109 Jason Elam .07 .20
110 John Elway .75 2.00
111 Simon Fletcher .02 .10
112 Glyn Milburn .02 .10
113 Anthony Miller .07 .20
114 Michael Dean Perry .02 .10
115 Mike Pritchard .02 .10
116 Derek Russell .02 .10
117 Leonard Russell .02 .10
118 Shannon Sharpe .07 .20
119 Gary Zimmerman .02 .10
120 Bennie Blades .02 .10
121 Lomas Brown .02 .10
122 Willie Clay .02 .10
123 Mike Johnson .02 .10
124 Robert Massey .02 .10
125 Scott Mitchell .07 .20
126 Herman Moore .10 .30
127 Brett Perriman .07 .20
128 Robert Porcher .02 .10
129 Barry Sanders .60 1.50
130 Chris Spielman .07 .20
131 Henry Thomas .02 .10
132 Edgar Bennett .07 .20
134 LeRoy Butler .02 .10
135 Brett Favre .75 2.00
136 Sean Jones .02 .10
137 John Jurkovic .02 .10
138 George Koonce .02 .10
139 Wayne Simmons .02 .10
140 George Teague .02 .10
141 Reggie White .10 .30
142 Micheal Barrow .02 .10
143 Gary Brown .02 .10
144 Cody Carlson .02 .10
145 Ray Childress .02 .10
146 Cris Dishman .02 .10
147 Ernest Givins .02 .10
148 Mel Gray .02 .10
149 Darryll Lewis .02 .10
150 Bruce Matthews .02 .10
151 Marcus Robertson .02 .10
152 Webster Slaughter .02 .10
153 Al Smith .02 .10
154 Mark Stepnoski .02 .10
155 Trev Alberts .02 .10
156 Flipper Anderson .02 .10
157 Jason Belser .02 .10
158 Tony Bennett .02 .10
159 Ray Buchanan .02 .10
160 Quentin Coryatt .07 .20
161 Sean Dawkins .07 .20
162 Steve Emtman .02 .10
163 Marshall Faulk .50 1.25
164 Stephen Grant RC .02 .10
165 Jim Harbaugh .07 .20
166 Jeff Herrod .02 .10
167 Tony Siragusa .02 .10
168 Steve Beuerlein .07 .20
169 Darren Carrington .02 .10
170 Reggie Cobb .02 .10
171 Kelvin Martin .02 .10
172 Kelvin Pritchett .02 .10
173 Joel Smeenge .02 .10
174 James Williams LB .02 .10
175 Marcus Allen .10 .30
176 Kimble Anders .07 .20
177 Dale Carter .07 .20
178 Mark Collins .02 .10
179 Willie Davis .07 .20
180 Lake Dawson .07 .20
181 Greg Hill .07 .20
182 Darren Mickell RC .02 .10
183 Joe Montana .75 2.00
184 Tracy Simien .02 .10
185 Neil Smith .07 .20
186 William White .02 .10
187 Greg Biekert .02 .10
188 Tim Brown .10 .30
189 Rob Fredrickson .02 .10
190 Andrew Glover RC .02 .10
191 Nolan Harrison .02 .10
192 Jeff Hostetler .07 .20
193 Rocket Ismail .07 .20
194 Terry McDaniel .02 .10
195 Chester McGlockton .07 .20
196 Winston Moss .02 .10
197 Anthony Smith .02 .10
198 Harvey Williams .02 .10
199 Steve Wisniewski .02 .10
200 Johnny Bailey .02 .10
201 Jerome Bettis .10 .30
202 Isaac Bruce .20 .50
203 Shane Conlan .02 .10
204 Troy Drayton .02 .10
205 Sean Gilbert .07 .20
206 Jessie Hester .02 .10
207 Jimmie Jones .02 .10
208 Todd Lyght .02 .10
209 Chris Miller .02 .10
210 Roman Phifer .02 .10
211 Marquez Pope .02 .10
212 Robert Young .02 .10
213 Gene Atkins .02 .10
214 Aubrey Beavers .02 .10
215 Tim Bowens .02 .10
216 Bryan Cox .02 .10
217 Jeff Cross .02 .10
218 Irving Fryar .07 .20
219 Eric Green .02 .10
220 Mark Ingram .02 .10
221 Terry Kirby .07 .20
222 Dan Marino .75 2.00
223 O.J. McDuffie .10 .30
224 Bernie Parmalee .07 .20
225 Keith Sims .02 .10
226 Irving Spikes .07 .20
227 Michael Stewart .02 .10
228 Troy Vincent .02 .10
229 Richmond Webb .02 .10
230 Terry Allen .07 .20
231 Cris Carter .10 .30
232 Jack Del Rio .02 .10
233 Vencie Glenn .02 .10
234 Qadry Ismail .07 .20
235 Carlos Jenkins .02 .10
236 Ed McDaniel .02 .10
237 Randall McDaniel .05 .15
238 Warren Moon .07 .20
239 Anthony Parker .02 .10
240 John Randle .07 .20
241 Jake Reed .07 .20
242 Fuad Reveiz .02 .10
243 Broderick Thomas .02 .10
244 Dewayne Washington .07 .20
245 Bruce Armstrong .02 .10
246 Drew Bledsoe .25 .60
247 Vincent Brisby .02 .10
248 Vincent Brown .02 .10
249 Marion Butts .02 .10
250 Ben Coates .07 .20
251 Tim Goad .02 .10
252 Myron Guyton .02 .10
253 Maurice Hurst .02 .10
254 Mike Jones .02 .10
255 Willie McGinest .07 .20
256 Dave Meggett .02 .10
257 Ricky Reynolds .02 .10
258 Chris Slade .07 .20
259 Michael Timpson .02 .10
260 Mario Bates .07 .20
261 Derek Brown RBK .02 .10
262 Darion Conner .02 .10
263 Quinn Early .07 .20
264 Jim Everett .02 .10
265 Michael Haynes .07 .20
266 Tyrone Hughes .07 .20
267 Joe Johnson .02 .10
268 Wayne Martin .02 .10
269 Willie Roaf .02 .10
270 Irv Smith .02 .10
271 Jimmy Spencer .02 .10
272 Winfred Tubbs .02 .10
273 Renaldo Turnbull .02 .10
274 Michael Brooks .02 .10
275 Dave Brown .07 .20
276 Chris Calloway .02 .10
277 Jesse Campbell .02 .10
278 Howard Cross .02 .10
279 John Elliott .02 .10
280 Keith Hamilton .02 .10
281 Rodney Hampton .07 .20
282 Thomas Lewis .07 .20
283 Thomas Randolph .02 .10
284 Mike Sherrard .02 .10
285 Michael Strahan .10 .30
286 Brad Baxter .02 .10
287 Tony Casillas .02 .10
288 Kyle Clifton .02 .10
289 Boomer Esiason .07 .20
290 Aaron Glenn .02 .10
291 Bobby Houston .02 .10
292 Johnny Johnson .02 .10
293 Jeff Lageman .02 .10
294 Mo Lewis .02 .10
295 Johnny Mitchell .02 .10
296 Rob Moore .07 .20
297 Marcus Turner .02 .10
298 Marvin Washington .02 .10
299 Eric Allen .02 .10
300 Fred Barnett .07 .20
301 Randall Cunningham .10 .30
302 Byron Evans .02 .10
303 William Fuller .02 .10
304 Charlie Garner .10 .30
305 Andy Harmon .02 .10
306 Greg Jackson .02 .10
307 Bill Romanowski .02 .10
308 William Thomas .02 .10
309 Herschel Walker .07 .20
310 Calvin Williams .07 .20
311 Michael Zordich .02 .10
312 Chad Brown .07 .20
313 Dermontti Dawson .15 .40
314 Barry Foster .07 .20
315 Kevin Greene .07 .20
316 Charles Johnson .07 .20
317 Levon Kirkland .02 .10
318 Carnell Lake .02 .10
319 Greg Lloyd .07 .20
320 Byron Bam Morris .02 .10
321 Neil O'Donnell .07 .20
322 Darren Perry .02 .10
323 Ray Seals .02 .10
324 John L. Williams .02 .10
325 Rod Woodson .07 .20
326 John Carney .02 .10
327 Andre Coleman .02 .10
328 Courtney Hall .02 .10
329 Ronnie Harmon .02 .10
330 Dwayne Harper .02 .10
331 Stan Humphries .07 .20
332 Shawn Jefferson .02 .10
333 Tony Martin .07 .20
334 Natrone Means .07 .20
335 Chris Mims .02 .10
336 Leslie O'Neal .07 .20
337 Alfred Pupunu RC .02 .10
338 Junior Seau .10 .30
339 Mark Seay .07 .20
340 Eric Davis .02 .10
341 William Floyd .07 .20
342 Merton Hanks .02 .10
343 Rickey Jackson .02 .10
344 Brent Jones .02 .10
345 Tim McDonald .02 .10
346 Ken Norton Jr. .07 .20
347 Gary Plummer .02 .10
348 Jerry Rice .40 1.00
349 Deion Sanders .15 .40
350 Jesse Sapolu .02 .10
351 Dana Stubblefield .07 .20
352 John Taylor .02 .10
353 Steve Wallace .02 .10
354 Ricky Watters .07 .20
355 Lee Woodall .02 .10
356 Bryant Young .07 .20
357 Steve Young .30 .75
358 Sam Adams .02 .10
359 Howard Ballard .02 .10
360 Robert Blackmon .02 .10
361 Brian Blades .07 .20
362 Carlton Gray .02 .10
363 Cortez Kennedy .07 .20
364 Rick Mirer .07 .20
365 Eugene Robinson .02 .10
366 Chris Warren .07 .20
367 Terry Wooden .02 .10
368 Brad Culpepper RC .02 .10
369 Lawrence Dawsey .02 .10
370 Trent Dilfer .10 .30
371 Santana Dotson .02 .10
372 Craig Erickson .02 .10
373 Thomas Everett .02 .10
374 Paul Gruber .02 .10
375 Alvin Harper .02 .10
376 Jackie Harris .02 .10
377 Courtney Hawkins .02 .10
378 Martin Mayhew .02 .10
379 Hardy Nickerson .02 .10
380 Errict Rhett .07 .20
381 Charles Wilson .02 .10
382 Reggie Brooks .07 .20
383 Tom Carter .02 .10
384 Andre Collins .02 .10
385 Henry Ellard .07 .20
386 Ricky Ervins .02 .10
387 Darrell Green .02 .10
388 Ken Harvey .02 .10
389 Brian Mitchell .02 .10
390 Stanley Richard .02 .10
391 Heath Shuler .07 .20
392 Rod Stephens .02 .10
393 Tyronne Stowe .02 .10
394 Tydus Winans .02 .10
395 Tony Woods .02 .10
396 Checklist .02 .10
397 Checklist .02 .10
398 Checklist .02 .10
399 Checklist .02 .10
400 Checklist .02 .10
P1 Promo Panel 1.00 2.50
Bettis
Mirer
R.Brooks

1995 Fleer Aerial Attack

This six-card standard-size set was randomly inserted into packs at a rate of one in 37. Featured in this set are leading passers and receivers. These cards contain a player photo against a metallic, etched foil design. The words "Aerial Attack" are in the lower left corner in gold foil. The player's name is identified in gold foil across the bottom. The back is divided between player information as well as another photo.

COMPLETE SET (6) 15.00 30.00
STATED ODDS 1:37
1 Tim Brown 1.25 2.50
2 Dan Marino 8.00 15.00
3 Joe Montana 8.00 15.00
4 Jerry Rice 4.00 8.00
5 Andre Rison .75 1.50
6 Sterling Sharpe .75 1.50

1995 Fleer Flair Preview

As a preview to the 1995 Flair issue, these 30 standard-size cards were inserted one per Fleer regular and jumbo pack. The fronts feature two photos on an etched foil surface with glossy polylaminate coating. The player's name and team name are on the bottom of the card. The backs mention that the card is a 1995 Flair Preview and gives some player highlights.

COMPLETE SET (30) 7.50 20.00
ONE PER PACK
1 Aeneas Williams .07 .20
2 Jeff George .15 .40
3 Andre Reed .15 .40
4 Kerry Collins .40 1.00
5 Mark Carrier DB .07 .20
6 Jeff Blake .50 1.25
7 Leroy Hoard .07 .20
8 Emmitt Smith 1.25 3.00
9 Shannon Sharpe .15 .40
10 Barry Sanders 1.25 3.00
11 Reggie White .25 .60
12 Bruce Matthews .07 .20
13 Marshall Faulk 1.00 2.50
14 Tony Boselli .07 .20
15 Joe Montana 1.50 4.00
16 Tim Brown .25 .60
17 Jerome Bettis .25 .60
18 Dan Marino 1.50 4.00
19 Cris Carter .25 .60
20 Drew Bledsoe .50 1.25
21 Willie Roaf .07 .20
22 Rodney Hampton .15 .40
23 Rob Moore .15 .40
24 Fred Barnett .15 .40
25 Rod Woodson .15 .40
26 Natrone Means .15 .40
27 Jerry Rice .75 2.00
28 Chris Warren .15 .40
29 Errict Rhett .15 .40
30 Henry Ellard .15 .40

1995 Fleer Gridiron Leaders

This 10-card standard-size set was inserted at a ratio of one in every four packs. The fronts feature the player's photo set against a geometric background. The words "Gridiron Leader" run vertically across the left border, while the player is identified in the bottom right corner. The back has a player close-up along with career highlights.

COMPLETE SET (10) 2.50 6.00
STATED ODDS 1:4
1 Cris Carter .15 .40
2 Ben Coates .08 .25
3 Marshall Faulk .75 1.50
4 Jerry Rice .60 1.25
5 Barry Sanders 1.00 2.00
6 Deion Sanders .20 .50
7 Emmitt Smith 1.00 2.00
8 Eric Turner .02 .10
9 Chris Warren .08 .25
10 Steve Young .40 1.00

1995 Fleer Prospects

This 20-card standard-size set was inserted one in every six packs. Players featured were expected by Fleer to go high in the 1995 draft. The fronts have a player photo against a multi-colored background. "NFL Prospects" is in the lower left corner with the player name at the bottom. The back contains another shot as well as some pertinent information.

COMPLETE SET (20) 10.00 20.00
STATED ODDS 1:6
1 Tony Boselli .60 1.50
2 Kyle Brady .30 .75
3 Ruben Brown .60 1.50
4 Kevin Carter .60 1.50
5 Ki-Jana Carter .60 1.50
6 Kerry Collins 1.25 3.00
7 Luther Elliss .20 .50
8 Jimmy Hitchcock .20 .50
9 Jack Jackson .20 .50
10 Ellis Johnson .20 .50
11 Rob Johnson .60 1.50
12 Steve McNair 2.00 5.00
13 Rashaan Salaam .60 1.50
14 Warren Sapp .20 .50
15 J.J.Stokes .60 1.50
16 Bobby Taylor .60 1.50
17 John Walsh .20 .50
18 Michael Westbrook .60 1.50
19 Tyrone Wheatley .75 2.00
20 Sherman Williams .30 .75

1995 Fleer Pro-Vision

This six-card standard-size set features some of the NFL's leading players. They were inserted at a rate of one per six packs. The card illustrations on front were done by sports artist Wayne Anthony Still. The artwork is consistent with the team nickname. The player's name and team is identified in gold-foil in the lower right corner. The back contains player profile information.

COMPLETE SET (6) 1.00 2.50
STATED ODDS 1:6
1 Natrone Means .07 .20
2 Sterling Sharpe .07 .20
3 Ken Norton .07 .20
4 Drew Bledsoe .25 .60
5 Marshall Faulk .50 1.25
6 Tim Brown .10 .30

1995 Fleer Rookie Sensations

This 20-card standard-size set was issued in jumbo packs only. They were released at a rate of one every three packs. Players featured in this set were among the best 1994 rookies. Fronts feature an embossed player photo with player name and the words "Rookie Sensation" on the left side. The back contains a player profile and player photo.

COMPLETE SET (20) 20.00 40.00
STATED ODDS 1:3 JUMBO
1 Derrick Alexander WR 2.00 4.00
2 Mario Bates .50 1.25
3 Tim Bowens .50 1.25
4 Lake Dawson 1.00 2.50
5 Bert Emanuel 2.00 4.00
6 Marshall Faulk 4.00 10.00
7 William Floyd 1.00 2.50
8 Rob Fredrickson .50 1.25
9 Greg Hill 1.00 2.50
10 Charles Johnson 1.00 2.50
11 Antonio Langham .50 1.25
12 Willie McGinest 1.00 2.50
13 Byron Bam Morris .50 1.25
14 Errict Rhett 1.00 2.50
15 Darnay Scott 3.00 6.00
16 Heath Shuler 1.00 2.50
17 Dewayne Washington .50 1.25
18 Dan Wilkinson .50 1.25
19 Lee Woodall .50 1.25
20 Bryant Young 1.00 2.50

1995 Fleer TD Sensations

This 10-card standard-size set was issued in 11-card packs at a rate of one in every three packs. Players featured in this set excelled in getting the ball into the end zone. The borderless fronts feature action shots of the player. The backs are split between another action shot as well as some highlights.

COMPLETE SET (10) 4.00 8.00
STATED ODDS 1:3 FOIL
1 Marshall Faulk .75 1.50
2 Dan Marino 1.25 2.50
3 Natrone Means .08 .25
4 Herman Moore .15 .40
5 Jerry Rice .60 1.25
6 Sterling Sharpe .08 .25
7 Emmitt Smith 1.00 2.00
8 Chris Warren .08 .25
9 Ricky Watters .08 .25
10 Steve Young .40 1.00

1995 Fleer Bettis/Mirer Sheet

At the Super Bowl card show in Miami, commemorative sheets of Bettis and Mirer insert cards could be purchased for five wrappers and 1.00. Just 2,500 were produced; 400 of these were signed by one of the two players and sold for 25.00. The sheets measure 8 1/2" by 11". One side features ten insert cards of Jerome Bettis, while the other side shows ten Rick Mirer insert cards. Sheets containing autograph's of Bettis and Mirer were embossed with the Fleer mark of Authenticity stamp.

1 Jerome Bettis .80 2.00
2 Jerome Bettis 12.50 25.00
AU

1995 Fleer Shell

Produced by Fleer, this 10-card set was issued by Shell in the "Drive to the Super Bowl XXX" sweepstakes. The standard-size cards are perforated at one end and were originally attached to a tab card of equal size. The tab features three rub-offs on its front and abbreviated rules on its back. The three rub-offs were titled "your score," "their score," and "prize." If the first rub-off had a higher score than the second one, then the holder could scratch the prize box to determine the prize. The contest expired 9/17/95. The cards themselves feature horizontal fronts with either color or black and white action photos that fade along the edges into white borders. The card title and final game score are presented in a yellow rectangle at the bottom. The circumstances surrounding the particular game are summarized on the back. Reportedly, 65 million game pieces (cards) were created.

COMPLETE SET (10) 3.20 8.00
1 Super Bowl XXIII .80 2.00
2 1967 NFL Championship Game .50 1.25
3 1986 AFC Championship Game .30 .75
4 Super Bowl XIII .50 1.25
5 1975 NFC Divisional Playoffs .30 .75
6 1968 AFL Championship Game .30 .75
7 1981 NFC Championship Game .40 1.00
8 1983 NFC Championship Game .40 1.00
9 1969 AFL Divisional Playoffs .40 1.00
10 Super Bowl V .40 1.00

1996 Fleer

The 1996 Fleer set was issued in one series totalling 200 cards. The 11-card packs retail for $1.49 each. The cards are grouped alphabetically within teams and checklisted below alphabetically according to teams. The set contains the topical subsets: Rookies (141-180) and PFW Weekly Previews (181-197). A three-card promo sheet (cards numbered S1-S3) was produced and is priced below in complete sheet form.

COMPLETE SET (200) 7.50 20.00
1 Garrison Hearst .07 .20
2 Rob Moore .07 .20
3 Frank Sanders .07 .20
4 Eric Swann .02 .10
5 Aeneas Williams .02 .10
6 Jeff George .07 .20
7 Craig Heyward .02 .10
8 Terance Mathis .02 .10
9 Eric Metcalf .02 .10
10 Michael Jackson .07 .20
11 Andre Rison .07 .20
12 Vinny Testaverde .07 .20
13 Eric Turner .02 .10
14 Darick Holmes .02 .10
15 Jim Kelly .10 .30
16 Bryce Paup .02 .10
17 Bruce Smith .07 .20
18 Thurman Thomas .10 .30
19 Kerry Collins .10 .30
20 Lamar Lathon .02 .10
21 Derrick Moore .02 .10
22 Tyrone Poole .02 .10
23 Curtis Conway .10 .30
24 Bryan Cox .02 .10
25 Erik Kramer .02 .10
26 Rashaan Salaam .07 .20
27 Jeff Blake .10 .30
28 Ki-Jana Carter .07 .20
29 Carl Pickens .07 .20
30 Darnay Scott .07 .20
31 Troy Aikman .30 .75
32 Charles Haley .07 .20
33 Michael Irvin .10 .30
34 Daryl Johnston .07 .20
35 Jay Novacek .02 .10
36 Deion Sanders .15 .40
37 Emmitt Smith .50 1.25
38 Steve Atwater .02 .10
39 Terrell Davis .25 .60
40 John Elway .60 1.50
41 Anthony Miller .07 .20
42 Shannon Sharpe .07 .20
43 Scott Mitchell .07 .20
44 Herman Moore .07 .20
45 Johnnie Morton .07 .20
46 Brett Perriman .02 .10
47 Barry Sanders .50 1.25
48 Edgar Bennett .07 .20
49 Robert Brooks .10 .30
50 Mark Chmura .07 .20
51 Brett Favre .60 1.50
52 Reggie White .10 .30
53 Mel Gray .02 .10
54 Steve McNair .25 .60
55 Chris Sanders .07 .20

56 Rodney Thomas .02 .10
57 Quentin Coryatt .02 .10
58 Sean Dawkins .02 .10
59 Ken Dilger .07 .20
60 Marshall Faulk .15 .40
61 Jim Harbaugh .07 .20
62 Tony Boselli .02 .10
63 Mark Brunell .20 .50
64 Natrone Means .07 .20
65 James O.Stewart .07 .20
66 Marcus Allen .10 .30
67 Steve Bono .02 .10
68 Neil Smith .07 .20
69 Derrick Thomas .10 .30
70 Tamarick Vanover .07 .20
71 Fred Barnett .02 .10
72 Eric Green .02 .10
73 Dan Marino .60 1.50
74 O.J. McDuffie .07 .20
75 Bernie Parmalee .02 .10
76 Cris Carter .10 .30
77 Qadry Ismail .07 .20
78 Warren Moon .07 .20
79 Jake Reed .07 .20
80 Robert Smith .07 .20
81 Drew Bledsoe .20 .50
82 Vincent Brisby .02 .10
83 Ben Coates .07 .20
84 Curtis Martin .25 .60
85 Dave Meggett .02 .10
86 Mario Bates .07 .20
87 Jim Everett .02 .10
88 Michael Haynes .02 .10
89 Renaldo Turnbull .02 .10
90 Dave Brown .02 .10
91 Rodney Hampton .07 .20
92 Thomas Lewis .02 .10
93 Tyrone Wheatley .07 .20
94 Kyle Brady .02 .10
95 Hugh Douglas .07 .20
96 Aaron Glenn .02 .10
97 Jeff Graham .02 .10
98 Adrian Murrell .07 .20
99 Neil O'Donnell .07 .20
100 Tim Brown .10 .30
101 Jeff Hostetler .02 .10
102 Napoleon Kaufman .10 .30
103 Chester McGlockton .02 .10
104 Harvey Williams .02 .10
105 William Fuller .02 .10
106 Charlie Garner .07 .20
107 Ricky Watters .07 .20
108 Calvin Williams .02 .10
109 Jerome Bettis .10 .30
110 Greg Lloyd .07 .20
111 Byron Bam Morris .02 .10
112 Kordell Stewart .10 .30
113 Yancey Thigpen .07 .20
114 Rod Woodson .07 .20
115 Isaac Bruce .10 .30
116 Troy Drayton .02 .10
117 Leslie O'Neal .02 .10
118 Steve Walsh .02 .10
119 Marco Coleman .02 .10
120 Aaron Hayden .02 .10
121 Stan Humphries .07 .20
122 Junior Seau .10 .30
123 William Floyd .07 .20
124 Brent Jones .02 .10
125 Ken Norton .02 .10
126 Jerry Rice .30 .75
127 J.J. Stokes .10 .30
128 Steve Young .25 .60
129 Brian Blades .02 .10
130 Joey Galloway .10 .30
131 Rick Mirer .07 .20
132 Chris Warren .07 .20
133 Trent Dilfer .10 .30
134 Alvin Harper .02 .10
135 Hardy Nickerson .02 .10
136 Errict Rhett .07 .20
137 Terry Allen .07 .20
138 Henry Ellard .02 .10
139 Heath Shuler .07 .20
140 Michael Westbrook .10 .30
141 Karim Abdul-Jabbar RC .10 .30
142 Mike Alstott RC .40 1.00
143 Marco Battaglia RC .02 .10
144 Tim Biakabutuka RC .10 .30
145 Tony Brackens RC .10 .30
146 Duane Clemons RC .02 .10
147 Ernie Conwell RC .02 .10
148 Chris Darkins RC .02 .10
149 Stephen Davis RC .60 1.50
150 Brian Dawkins RC .50 1.25
151 Rickey Dudley RC .10 .30
152 Jason Dunn RC .07 .20
153 Bobby Engram RC .10 .30
154 Daryl Gardener RC .02 .10
155 Eddie George RC .50 1.25
156 Terry Glenn RC .40 1.00
157 Kevin Hardy RC .10 .30
158 Walt Harris RC .02 .10
159 Marvin Harrison RC 1.00 2.50
160 Bobby Hoying RC .10 .30
161 Keyshawn Johnson RC .40 1.00
162 Cedric Jones RC .02 .10
163 Marcus Jones RC .02 .10
164 Eddie Kennison RC .10 .30
165 Ray Lewis RC 3.00 8.00
166 Derrick Mayes RC .10 .30
167 Leeland McElroy RC .07 .20
168 Johnny McWilliams RC .07 .20
169 John Mobley RC .02 .10
170 Alex Molden RC .02 .10
171 Eric Moulds RC .50 1.25
172 Muhsin Muhammad RC UER .40 1.00
173 Jonathan Ogden RC .40 1.00
174 Lawrence Phillips RC .10 .30
175 Stanley Pritchett RC .07 .20
176 Simeon Rice RC .30 .75
177 Bryan Still RC .07 .20
178 Amani Toomer RC .40 1.00
179 Regan Upshaw RC .02 .10
180 Alex Van Dyke RC .07 .20
181 Barry Sanders PFW .25 .60
182 Marcus Allen PFW .10 .30
183 Bryce Paup PFW .02 .10
184 Jerry Rice PFW .15 .40
185 D.Howard .07 .20
B.Christian PFW
186 Leon Lett PFW .02 .10
187 Brett Favre PFW .30 .75
188 G.Lloyd .02 .10
D.Thomas PFW
189 Jeff Blake PFW .07 .20
190 Emmitt Smith PFW .25 .60
191 J.Elway .15 .40
J.Hostetler PFW
192 Chiefs PFW .02 .10
193 Marshall Faulk PFW .10 .30
194 T.Aikman .15 .40
S.Young PFW
195 Dan Marino PFW .30 .75
196 Donta Jones PFW .02 .10
197 Jim Kelly PFW .10 .30
198 Checklist .02 .10
199 Checklist .02 .10
200 Checklist .02 .10
P1 Promo Sheet 1.50 4.00
WFloyd
TDil
Favre

1996 Fleer Breakthroughs

Randomly inserted in packs at the rate of one in three, this 24-card set features photos of players chosen by Pro Football Weekly to have had career seasons, including some '96 rookies highlighted in 100% etched foil design.

COMPLETE SET (24) 6.00 15.00
STATED ODDS 1:3
1 Tim Bowens .15 .40
2 Kyle Brady .15 .40
3 Devin Bush .15 .40
4 Kevin Carter .15 .40
5 Ki-Jana Carter .30 .75
6 Kerry Collins .50 1.25
7 Trent Dilfer .50 1.25
8 Ken Dilger .30 .75
9 Joey Galloway .50 1.25
10 Aaron Hayden .15 .40
11 Napoleon Kaufman .50 1.25
12 Craig Newsome .15 .40
13 Tyrone Poole .15 .40
14 Jake Reed .30 .75
15 Rashaan Salaam .30 .75
16 Chris Sanders .30 .75
17 Frank Sanders .30 .75
18 Kordell Stewart .50 1.25
19 J.J. Stokes .50 1.25
20 Bobby Taylor .15 .40
21 Orlando Thomas .15 .40
22 Michael Timpson .15 .40
23 Tamarick Vanover .30 .75
24 Michael Westbrook .50 1.25

1996 Fleer RAC Pack

Randomly inserted in packs at the rate of one in 18, this 10-card set features photos of receivers who excel at racking up Run After Catch yardage in 100% etched foil and color foil stamped design.

COMPLETE SET (10) 6.00 15.00
STATED ODDS 1:18
1 Robert Brooks 1.50 4.00
2 Tim Brown 1.50 4.00
3 Isaac Bruce 1.50 4.00
4 Cris Carter 1.50 4.00
5 Curtis Conway 1.50 4.00
6 Michael Irvin 1.50 4.00
7 Eric Metcalf .50 1.25
8 Herman Moore 1.00 2.50
9 Carl Pickens 1.00 2.50
10 Jerry Rice 4.00 10.00

1996 Fleer Rookie Autographs

Randomly inserted in hobby packs only at a rate of one in 288, this three-card autographed set features players that Fleer felt would make an impact in their Rookie season.

COMPLETE SET (3) 30.00 60.00
STATED ODDS 1:288 HOBBY
*BLUE SIGS: .6X TO 1.5X BASIC AUTOS
A1 Tim Biakabutuka 5.00 12.00
A2 Eddie George 6.00 15.00
A3 Leeland McElroy 5.00 12.00

1996 Fleer Rookie Sensations

Randomly inserted at the rate of one in 72 packs, this 11-card set features color photos of some of the NFL's best 1996 rookies printed on colorful plastic cards. Seeded 1:960 packs was a special Rookie Sensations Hot Packs containing specially marked versions of all 11 Rookie Sensations insert cards with a special Hot Packs logo.

COMPLETE SET (11) 25.00 60.00
STATED ODDS 1:72
*HOT PACK: .3X TO .8X BASIC INSERTS
HOT PACK SET STATED ODDS 1:960
1 Karim Abdul-Jabbar 2.00 5.00
2 Tim Biakabutuka UER 2.00 5.00
3 Rickey Dudley 1.25 3.00
4 Eddie George 4.00 10.00
5 Terry Glenn 3.00 8.00
6 Kevin Hardy 1.25 3.00
7 Marvin Harrison 7.50 20.00
8 Keyshawn Johnson 3.00 8.00
9 Jonathan Ogden 4.00 10.00
10 Lawrence Phillips 2.00 5.00
11 Simeon Rice 5.00 12.00

1996 Fleer Rookie Write-Ups

Randomly inserted in hobby packs only at the rate of one in 12, this 10-card set features color player images of rookies entering the NFL in '96 whose scouting reports are similar to those of previous rookies. The backs carry a player head photo with a paragraph stating the name of the previous rookie and why he and the pictured rookie are similar.

COMPLETE SET (10) 6.00 15.00
STATED ODDS 1:12 HOBBY
1 Tim Biakabutuka .30 .75
2 Rickey Dudley .30 .75
3 Eddie George 1.25 3.00
4 Terry Glenn 1.00 2.50
5 Kevin Hardy .30 .75
6 Marvin Harrison 2.50 6.00
7 Keyshawn Johnson 1.00 2.50
8 Leeland McElroy .20 .50
9 Lawrence Phillips .30 .75
10 Simeon Rice .75 2.00

1996 Fleer Statistically Speaking

Randomly inserted in packs at the rate of one in 37, this 20-card set features player images of the NFL's statistical standouts printed on plastic cards in hot colors with statistics as the background.

COMPLETE SET (20) 25.00 60.00
STATED ODDS 1:37
1 Troy Aikman 2.50 6.00
2 Larry Centers .60 1.50
3 Ben Coates .60 1.50
4 Brett Favre 5.00 12.00
5 Joey Galloway 1.00 2.50
6 Rodney Hampton .60 1.50
7 Dan Marino 5.00 12.00
8 Curtis Martin 2.00 5.00
9 Anthony Miller .40 1.00
10 Brian Mitchell .60 1.50
11 Herman Moore .60 1.50
12 Errict Rhett .60 1.50
13 Rashaan Salaam .40 1.00
14 Barry Sanders 4.00 10.00
15 Deion Sanders 1.25 3.00
16 Emmitt Smith 4.00 10.00
17 Kordell Stewart .60 1.50
18 Chris Warren .40 1.00
19 Ricky Watters .60 1.50
20 Steve Young 2.00 5.00

1997 Fleer

The 1997 Fleer set was issued in one series totaling 450 cards and features full-bleed action player photos with the Textured Legend matte finish making the cards especially suitable for autographs. The player's name is printed in gold foil block type with his team and position in gold foil script below. The set was distributed in 10-card foil packs with a suggested retail price of $1.49. A special Emerald Reggie White signed card numbered of 80 was randomly inserted in special retail packs.

COMPLETE SET (450) 15.00 40.00
1 Mark Brunell .40 1.00
2 Andre Reed .20 .50
3 Darrell Green .20 .50
4 Mario Bates .10 .30
5 Eddie George .30 .75
6 Cris Carter .30 .75
7 Terrell Owens .40 1.00
8 Bill Romanowski .10 .30
9 Isaac Bruce .30 .75
10 Eric Curry .10 .30
11 Danny Kanell .10 .30
12 Ki-Jana Carter .10 .30
13 Antonio Freeman .30 .75
14 Ricky Watters .20 .50
15 Ty Law .20 .50
16 Alonzo Spellman .10 .30
17 Kordell Stewart .30 .75
18 Jerry Rice .60 1.50
19 Derrick Alexander WR .20 .50
20 Barry Sanders 1.00 2.50
21 Keyshawn Johnson .30 .75
22 Emmitt Smith 1.00 2.50
23 Ricky Proehl .10 .30
24 Daryl Gardener .10 .30
25 Dan Saleaumua .10 .30
26 Kevin Greene .20 .50
27 Junior Seau .30 .75
28 Randall McDaniel .10 .30
29 Marshall Faulk .40 1.00
30 Lorenzo Lynch .10 .30
31 Terance Mathis .20 .50
32 Warren Sapp .20 .50
33 Chris Sanders .10 .30
34 Tom Carter .10 .30
35 Aeneas Williams .10 .30
36 Lawrence Phillips .10 .30
37 John Elway 1.25 3.00
38 Stanley Richard .10 .30
39 Darryl Williams .10 .30
40 Phillippi Sparks .10 .30
41 Tedy Bruschi .60 1.50
42 Merton Hanks .10 .30
43 Ray Lewis .50 1.25
44 Erik Williams .10 .30
45 Jason Gildon .10 .30
46 George Koonce .10 .30
47 Louis Oliver .10 .30
48 Muhsin Muhammad .20 .50
49 Daryl Hobbs .10 .30
50 Terry Glenn .30 .75
51 Marvin Harrison .30 .75
52 Brian Dawkins .30 .75
53 Dale Carter .10 .30
54 Alex Molden .10 .30
55 Raymont Harris .10 .30
56 Jeff Burris .10 .30
57 Don Beebe .10 .30
58 Jamir Miller .10 .30
59 Carl Pickens .20 .50
60 Antonio London .10 .30
61 Courtney Hall .10 .30
62 Derrick Brooks .30 .75
63 Chris Boniol .10 .30
64 Jeff Lageman .10 .30
65 Roy Barker .10 .30
66 Devin Bush .10 .30
67 Aaron Glenn .10 .30
68 Wayne Simmons .10 .30
69 Steve Atwater .10 .30
70 Jimmie Jones .10 .30
71 Mark Carrier WR .10 .30
72 Chris Chandler .20 .50
73 Andy Harmon .10 .30
74 John Friesz .10 .30
75 Karim Abdul-Jabbar .20 .50
76 Levon Kirkland .10 .30
77 Torrance Small .10 .30
78 Harvey Williams .10 .30
79 Chris Calloway .10 .30
80 Vinny Testaverde .20 .50
81 Bryant Young .10 .30
82 Ray Buchanan .10 .30
83 Robert Smith .20 .50
84 Robert Brooks .20 .50
85 Ray Crockett .10 .30
86 Bennie Blades .10 .30
87 Mark Carrier DB .10 .30
88 Mike Tomczak .10 .30
89 Darick Holmes .10 .30
90 Drew Bledsoe .40 1.00
91 Darren Woodson .10 .30
92 Dan Wilkinson .10 .30
93 Charles Way .10 .30
94 Ray Farmer .10 .30
95 Marcus Allen .30 .75
96 Marco Coleman .10 .30
97 Zach Thomas .30 .75
98 Wesley Walls .20 .50
99 Frank Wycheck .10 .30
100 Troy Aikman .60 1.50
101 Clyde Simmons .10 .30
102 Courtney Hawkins .10 .30
103 Chuck Smith .10 .30
104 Neil O'Donnell .20 .50
105 Kevin Carter .10 .30
106 Chris Slade .10 .30
107 Jessie Armstead .10 .30
108 Sean Dawkins .10 .30
109 Robert Blackmon .10 .30
110 Kevin Smith .10 .30
111 Lonnie Johnson .10 .30
112 Craig Newsome .10 .30
113 Jonathan Ogden .10 .30
114 Chris Zorich .10 .30
115 Tim Brown .30 .75
116 Fred Barnett .10 .30
117 Michael Haynes .10 .30
118 Eric Hill .10 .30
119 Ronnie Harmon .10 .30
120 Sean Gilbert .10 .30
121 Derrick Alexander DE .10 .30
122 Derrick Thomas .30 .75
123 Tyrone Wheatley .20 .50
124 Cortez Kennedy .10 .30
125 Jeff George .20 .50
126 Chad Cota .10 .30
127 Gary Zimmerman .10 .30
128 Johnnie Morton .20 .50
129 Chad Brown .10 .30
130 Marvcus Patton .10 .30
131 James O.Stewart .20 .50
132 Terry Kirby .20 .50
133 Chris Mims .10 .30
134 William Thomas .10 .30
135 Steve Tasker .10 .30
136 Jason Belser .10 .30
137 Bryan Cox .10 .30
138 Jessie Tuggle .10 .30
139 Ashley Ambrose .10 .30
140 Mark Chmura .20 .50
141 Jeff Hostetler .10 .30
142 Rich Owens .10 .30
143 Willie Davis .10 .30
144 Hardy Nickerson .10 .30
145 Curtis Martin .40 1.00
146 Ken Norton .10 .30
147 Victor Green .10 .30
148 Anthony Miller .10 .30
149 John Kasay .10 .30
150 O.J. McDuffie .20 .50
151 Darren Perry .10 .30
152 Luther Elliss .10 .30
153 Greg Hill .10 .30
154 John Randle .20 .50
155 Stephen Grant .10 .30
156 Leon Lett .10 .30
157 Darrien Gordon .10 .30
158 Ray Zellars .10 .30
159 Michael Jackson .20 .50
160 Leslie O'Neal .10 .30
161 Bruce Smith .20 .50
162 Santana Dotson .10 .30
163 Bobby Hebert .10 .30
164 Keith Hamilton .10 .30
165 Tony Boselli .10 .30
166 Alfred Williams .10 .30
167 Ty Detmer .20 .50
168 Chester McGlockton .10 .30
169 William Floyd .20 .50
170 Bruce Matthews .10 .30
171 Simeon Rice .20 .50
172 Scott Mitchell .20 .50
173 Ricardo McDonald .10 .30
174 Tyrone Poole .10 .30
175 Greg Lloyd .10 .30
176 Bruce Armstrong .10 .30
177 Erik Kramer .10 .30
178 Kimble Anders .20 .50
179 Lamar Smith .30 .75
180 Tony Tolbert .10 .30
181 Joe Aska .10 .30
182 Eric Allen .10 .30
183 Eric Turner .10 .30
184 Brad Johnson .30 .75
185 Tony Martin .20 .50
186 Mike Mamula .10 .30
187 Irving Spikes .10 .30
188 Keith Jackson .10 .30
189 Carlton Bailey .10 .30
190 Tyrone Braxton .10 .30
191 Chad Bratzke .10 .30
192 Adrian Murrell .20 .50
193 Roman Phifer .10 .30
194 Todd Collins .10 .30
195 Chris Warren .20 .50
196 Kevin Hardy .10 .30
197 Rick Mirer .10 .30
198 Cornelius Bennett .10 .30
199 Jimmy Hitchcock .10 .30
200 Michael Irvin .30 .75
201 Quentin Coryatt .10 .30
202 Reggie White .30 .75
203 Larry Centers .20 .50
204 Rodney Thomas .10 .30
205 Dana Stubblefield .10 .30
206 Rod Woodson .20 .50
207 Rhett Hall .10 .30
208 Steve Tovar .10 .30
209 Michael Westbrook .20 .50
210 Steve Wisniewski .10 .30
211 Carlester Crumpler .10 .30
212 Elvis Grbac .20 .50
213 Tim Bowens .10 .30
214 Robert Porcher .10 .30
215 John Carney .10 .30
216 Anthony Newman .10 .30
217 Earnest Byner .10 .30
218 Dewayne Washington .10 .30
219 Willie Green .10 .30
220 Terry Allen .30 .75
221 William Fuller .10 .30
222 Al Del Greco .10 .30
223 Trent Dilfer .30 .75
224 Michael Dean Perry .10 .30
225 Larry Allen .10 .30
226 Mark Bruener .10 .30
227 Clay Matthews .10 .30
228 Reuben Brown UER .10 .30
229 Edgar Bennett .20 .50
230 Neil Smith .20 .50
231 Ken Harvey .10 .30
232 Kyle Brady .10 .30
233 Corey Miller .10 .30
234 Tony Siragusa .10 .30
235 Todd Sauerbrun .10 .30
236 Daniel Stubbs .10 .30
237 Robb Thomas .10 .30
238 Jimmy Smith .20 .50
239 Marquez Pope .10 .30
240 Tim Biakabutuka .20 .50
241 Jamie Asher .10 .30
242 Steve McNair .40 1.00
243 Harold Green .10 .30
244 Frank Sanders .20 .50
245 Joe Johnson .10 .30
246 Eric Bieniemy .10 .30
247 Kevin Turner .10 .30
248 Rickey Dudley .20 .50
249 Orlando Thomas .10 .30
250 Dan Marino 1.25 3.00
251 Deion Sanders .30 .75
252 Dan Williams .10 .30
253 Sam Cash .10 .30
254 Lonnie Marts .10 .30
255 Mo Lewis .10 .30
256 Charles Johnson .20 .50
257 Chris Jacke .10 .30
258 Keenan McCardell .20 .50
259 Donnell Woolford .10 .30
260 Terrance Shaw .10 .30
261 Jason Dunn .10 .30
262 Willie McGinest .10 .30
263 Ken Dilger .10 .30
264 Keith Lyle .10 .30
265 Antonio Langham .10 .30
266 Carlton Gray .10 .30
267 LeShon Johnson .10 .30
268 Thurman Thomas .30 .75
269 Jesse Campbell .10 .30
270 Carnell Lake .10 .30
271 Cris Dishman .10 .30
272 Kevin Williams .10 .30
273 Troy Brown .20 .50
274 William Roaf .10 .30
275 Terrell Davis .40 1.00
276 Herman Moore .20 .50
277 Walt Harris .10 .30
278 Mark Collins .10 .30
279 Bert Emanuel .20 .50
280 Qadry Ismail .20 .50
281 Phil Hansen .10 .30
282 Steve Young .40 1.00
283 Michael Sinclair .10 .30
284 Jeff Graham .10 .30
285 Sam Mills .10 .30
286 Terry McDaniel .10 .30
287 Eugene Robinson .10 .30
288 Tony Bennett .10 .30
289 Daryl Johnston .20 .50
290 Eric Swann .10 .30
291 Byron Bam Morris .10 .30
292 Thomas Lewis .10 .30
293 Terrell Fletcher .10 .30
294 Gus Frerotte .10 .30
295 Stanley Pritchett .10 .30
296 Mike Alstott .30 .75
297 Will Shields .10 .30
298 Errict Rhett .10 .30
299 Garrison Hearst .20 .50
300 Kerry Collins .30 .75
301 Darryll Lewis .10 .30
302 Chris T. Jones .10 .30
303 Yancey Thigpen .20 .50
304 Jackie Harris .10 .30
305 Steve Christie .10 .30
306 Gilbert Brown .20 .50
307 Terry Wooden .10 .30
308 Pete Mitchell .10 .30
309 Tim McDonald .10 .30
310 Jake Reed .20 .50
311 Ed McCaffrey .20 .50
312 Chris Doleman .10 .30
313 Eric Metcalf .20 .50
314 Ricky Reynolds .10 .30
315 David Sloan .10 .30
316 Marvin Washington .10 .30
317 Herschel Walker .20 .50
318 Michael Timpson .10 .30
319 Blaine Bishop .10 .30
320 Irv Smith .10 .30
321 Seth Joyner .10 .30
322 Terrell Buckley .10 .30
323 Michael Strahan .20 .50
324 Sam Adams .10 .30
325 Leslie Shepherd .10 .30
326 James Jett .20 .50
327 Anthony Pleasant .10 .30
328 Lee Woodall .10 .30
329 Shannon Sharpe .20 .50
330 Jamal Anderson .30 .75
331 Andre Hastings .10 .30
332 Troy Vincent .10 .30
333 Sean LaChapelle .10 .30
334 Winslow Oliver .10 .30
335 Sean Jones .10 .30
336 Darnay Scott .20 .50
337 Todd Lyght .10 .30
338 Leonard Russell .10 .30
339 Nate Newton .10 .30
340 Zack Crockett .10 .30
341 Amp Lee .10 .30
342 Bobby Engram .20 .50
343 Mike Hollis .10 .30
344 Rodney Hampton .20 .50
345 Mel Gray .10 .30
346 Van Malone .10 .30
347 Aaron Craver .10 .30
348 Jim Everett .10 .30
349 Trace Armstrong .10 .30
350 Pat Swilling .10 .30
351 Brent Jones .10 .30
352 Chris Spielman .10 .30
353 Brett Perriman .10 .30
354 Brian Kinchen .10 .30
355 Joey Galloway .20 .50
356 Henry Ellard .10 .30
357 Ben Coates .20 .50
358 Dorsey Levens .30 .75
359 Charlie Garner .20 .50
360 Eric Pegram .10 .30
361 Anthony Johnson .10 .30
362 Rashaan Salaam .10 .30
363 Jeff Blake .20 .50
364 Kent Graham .10 .30
365 Broderick Thomas .10 .30
366 Richmond Webb .10 .30
367 Alfred Pupunu .10 .30
368 Mark Stepnoski .10 .30
369 David Dunn .10 .30
370 Bobby Houston .10 .30
371 Anthony Parker .10 .30
372 Quinn Early .10 .30
373 LeRoy Butler .10 .30
374 Kurt Gouveia .10 .30
375 Greg Biekert .10 .30
376 Jim Harbaugh .20 .50
377 Eric Bjornson .10 .30
378 Craig Heyward .10 .30
379 Steve Bono .20 .50
380 Tony Banks .20 .50
381 John Mobley .10 .30
382 Irving Fryar .20 .50
383 Dermontti Dawson .25 .60
384 Eric Davis .10 .30
385 Natrone Means .20 .50
386 Jason Sehorn .20 .50
387 Michael McCrary .10 .30
388 Corwin Brown .10 .30
389 Kevin Glover .10 .30
390 Jerris McPhail .10 .30
391 Bobby Taylor .10 .30
392 Tony McGee .10 .30
393 Curtis Conway .20 .50
394 Napoleon Kaufman .30 .75
395 Brian Blades .10 .30
396 Richard Dent .10 .30
397 Dave Brown .10 .30
398 Stan Humphries .20 .50
399 Stevon Moore .10 .30
400 Brett Favre 1.50 3.00
401 Jerome Bettis .30 .75
402 Darrin Smith .10 .30
403 Chris Penn .10 .30
404 Rob Moore .20 .50
405 Micheal Barrow .10 .30
406 Tony Brackens .10 .30
407 Wayne Martin .10 .30
408 Warren Moon .30 .75
409 Jason Elam .20 .50
410 J.J. Birden .10 .30
411 Hugh Douglas .10 .30
412 Lamar Lathon .10 .30
413 John Kidd .10 .30
414 Bryce Paup .10 .30
415 Shawn Jefferson .10 .30
416 Leeland McElroy SS .10 .30
417 Elbert Shelley SS .10 .30
418 Jermaine Lewis SS .20 .50
419 Eric Moulds SS .30 .75
420 Michael Bates SS .10 .30
421 John Mangum SS .10 .30
422 Corey Sawyer SS .10 .30
423 Jim Schwantz SS RC .10 .30
424 Rod Smith WR SS .30 .75
425 Glyn Milburn SS .10 .30
426 Desmond Howard SS .20 .50
427 John Henry Mills SS RC .10 .30
428 Cary Blanchard SS RC .10 .30
429 Chris Hudson SS .10 .30
430 Tamarick Vanover SS .20 .50
431 Kirby Dar Dar SS RC .20 .50
432 David Palmer SS .10 .30
433 Dave Meggett SS .10 .30
434 Tyrone Hughes SS .10 .30
435 Amani Toomer SS .20 .50
436 Wayne Chrebet SS .20 .50
437 Carl Kidd RC SS .10 .30
438 Derrick Witherspoon SS .10 .30
439 Jahine Arnold SS .10 .30
440 Andre Coleman SS .10 .30
441 Jeff Wilkins SS .10 .30
442 Jay Bellamy SS RC .10 .30
443 Eddie Kennison SS .20 .50
444 Nilo Silvan SS .10 .30
445 Brian Mitchell SS .10 .30
446 Garrison Hearst CL .20 .50
447 Napoleon Kaufman CL .30 .75
448 Brian Mitchell CL .10 .30
449 Rodney Hampton CL .10 .30
450 Edgar Bennett CL .10 .30
S1 Mark Chmura Sample .40 1.00
AU1 Reggie White AUTO 75.00 125.00

1997 Fleer Crystal Silver

COMPLETE SET (445) 60.00 120.00
*1-445 SILVER: 1.5X TO 3X BASIC CARDS
STATED ODDS 1:2

1997 Fleer Tiffany Blue

COMPLETE SET (445) 500.00 1000.00
*1-445 BLUE: 10X TO 25X BASIC CARDS
STATED ODDS 1:20 HOBBY

1997 Fleer All-Pros

Randomly inserted in retail packs only at a rate of one in 30, this 24-card set features color player photos of first-time and regular All-Pro players.

COMPLETE SET (24) 60.00 120.00
STATED ODDS 1:36 RETAIL
1 Troy Aikman 5.00 12.00
2 Larry Allen 1.00 2.50
3 Drew Bledsoe 3.00 8.00
4 Terrell Davis 3.00 8.00
5 Dermontti Dawson 2.00 5.00
6 John Elway 10.00 25.00
7 Brett Favre 8.00 20.00
8 Herman Moore 1.50 4.00
9 Jerry Rice 5.00 12.00
10 Barry Sanders 8.00 20.00
11 Shannon Sharpe 1.50 4.00
12 Erik Williams 1.00 2.50
13 Ashley Ambrose 1.00 2.50
14 Chad Brown 1.00 2.50
15 LeRoy Butler 1.00 2.50
16 Kevin Greene 1.50 4.00
17 Sam Mills 1.00 2.50
18 John Randle 1.50 4.00
19 Deion Sanders 2.50 6.00
20 Junior Seau 2.50 6.00
21 Bruce Smith 1.50 4.00
22 Alfred Williams 1.00 2.50
23 Darren Woodson 1.00 2.50
24 Bryant Young 1.00 2.50

1997 Fleer Decade of Excellence

Randomly inserted in hobby packs only at a rate of one in 36, this 12-card set pays tribute to players whose careers began in 1987 or earlier and features 1987 photography and design details. A silver foil Rare Traditions parallel set was also issued and randomly seeded in packs.

COMPLETE SET (12) 20.00 50.00
STATED ODDS 1:36 HOBBY
*RARE TRAD.: 1X TO 2.5X BASIC INSERTS
1 Marcus Allen 1.50 4.00
2 Cris Carter 1.50 4.00
3 John Elway 6.00 15.00
4 Irving Fryar 1.00 2.50
5 Darrell Green 1.00 2.50
6 Dan Marino 6.00 15.00
7 Jerry Rice 3.00 8.00
8 Bruce Smith 1.00 2.50
9 Herschel Walker 1.00 2.50
10 Reggie White 1.50 4.00
11 Rod Woodson 1.00 2.50
12 Steve Young 2.00 5.00

1997 Fleer Game Breakers

Randomly inserted in retail packs only at a rate of one in two, this 20-card set features color photos of players who can break a game wide open. The tougher Supreme parallels combines a matte-finish background with a fully sculptured embossed player image covered in glossy UV coating. They were inserted at the rate of 1:18 hobby and retail packs.

COMPLETE SET (20) 7.50 15.00
STATED ODDS 1:2 RETAIL
*SUPREMES: 2X TO 5X BASIC INSERTS
SUPREME ODDS 1:18 HOB/RET
1 Troy Aikman .75 2.00
2 Jerome Bettis .40 1.00
3 Drew Bledsoe .50 1.25
4 Isaac Bruce .40 1.00
5 Mark Brunell .50 1.25
6 Kerry Collins .40 1.00
7 Terrell Davis .50 1.25
8 Marshall Faulk .50 1.25
9 Antonio Freeman .40 1.00
10 Joey Galloway .25 .60
11 Terry Glenn .40 1.00
12 Desmond Howard .25 .60
13 Keyshawn Johnson .40 1.00
14 Eddie Kennison .25 .60
15 Curtis Martin .50 1.25
16 Herman Moore .25 .60
17 Lawrence Phillips .15 .40
18 Barry Sanders 1.25 3.00
19 Shannon Sharpe .25 .60
20 Emmitt Smith 1.25 3.00

1997 Fleer Million Dollar Moments

Each 1997 Fleer and Ultra pack included one Million Dollar Moments game piece as part of a Sweepstakes promotion with a $1 million top prize. Ten free game pieces could be received via mail as well. The contest ended April 30, 1998. The cards include a notable NFL event on the fronts (along with the player's photo) with the game rules on the card backs. Cards #46-50 pulled from packs were the contest winner cards and could be exchanged (along with the other 45-cards) for a chance to win various prizes including $1000 hobby shopping sprees. Card #50 could be redeemed (with the other 49-cards) for the $1 million dollar prize. Finally, the first 45-cards could be redeemed along with $5.95 for a prize set version including the final five-cards. The prize set is identical to the pack inserts except for the line of text on the cardbacks that mentions the cards not being eligible for the contest.

COMPLETE SET (45) 2.00 4.00
COMP.PRIZE SET (50) 6.00 10.00
*PRIZE CARDS: SAME PRICE AS INSERTS
46A-50A: PRICED ONLY AS PRIZE VERSIONS
ONE PER PACK IN FLEER PRODUCTS
1 Checklist Card .01 .05
2 Troy Aikman .20 .50
3 Sid Luckman .05 .15
4 Barry Sanders .20 .50
5 Tom Fears .05 .15
6 Reggie White .08 .25
7 Lou Groza .05 .15
8 John Elway .20 .50
9 Raymond Berry .05 .15
10 Marcus Allen .08 .25
11 Paul Hornung .08 .25
12 Herschel Walker .05 .15
13 Norm Van Brocklin .05 .15
14 Bruce Smith .05 .15
15 Bill Wade .01 .05
16 Andre Reed .05 .15
17 Gale Sayers .08 .25
18 Terrell Davis .15 .40
19 Jim Bakken .01 .05
20 Marshall Faulk .10 .30
21 Tom Dempsey .01 .05
22 Dan Marino .40 1.00
23 Garo Yepremian .01 .05
24 Jerry Rice .20 .50
25 Herman Edwards .01 .05
26 Derrick Thomas .05 .15
27 Kellen Winslow .01 .05
28 Steve Young .08 .25
29 Tony Dorsett .08 .25
30 Desmond Howard .05 .15
31 Roger Craig .01 .05
32 Drew Bledsoe .10 .30
33 Doug Williams .01 .05
34 Jerome Bettis .08 .25
35 Bobby Layne .05 .15
36 Junior Seau .08 .25
37 Roman Gabriel .01 .05
38 Cris Carter .08 .25
39 Drew Pearson .05 .15
40 Warren Moon .08 .25
41 Wesley Walker .01 .05
42 Ricky Watters .05 .15
43 Carl Eller .01 .05
44 Kordell Stewart .15 .40
45 John Mackey .01 .05
46A Thurman Thomas Prize .08 .25
47A Ken Stabler Prize .20 .50
48A Emmitt Smith Prize .75 2.00
49A Jim Brown Prize .20 .50
50A Eddie George Prize .30 .75

1997 Fleer Prospects

Randomly inserted in packs at a rate of one in six, this 10-card set features color photos of the top prospects from the 1997 NFL draft with college statistics and commentary on their anticipated impact as pros.

COMPLETE SET (10) 6.00 12.00
STATED ODDS 1:6
1 Peter Boulware .75 2.00
2 Rae Carruth .40 1.00
3 Jim Druckenmiller .60 1.50
4 Warrick Dunn 1.25 3.00
5 Tony Gonzalez 1.50 4.00
6 Yatil Green .40 1.00
7 Ike Hilliard .75 2.00
8 Orlando Pace .75 2.00
9 Darrell Russell .40 1.00
10 Shawn Springs .60 1.50

1997 Fleer Rookie Sensations

Randomly inserted in packs at a rate of one in four, this 20-card set features color photos of high-impact rookies from the 1996 season. The card design includes textured border and single-level embossed player image.

COMPLETE SET (20) 10.00 25.00
STATED ODDS 1:4
1 Karim Abdul-Jabbar .75 2.00
2 Mike Alstott 1.25 3.00
3 Tony Banks .75 2.00
4 Tony Brackens .50 1.25
5 Rickey Dudley .75 2.00
6 Bobby Engram .75 2.00
7 Eddie George 1.25 3.00
8 Terry Glenn 1.25 3.00
9 Kevin Hardy .50 1.25
10 Marvin Harrison 1.25 3.00
11 Keyshawn Johnson 1.25 3.00
12 Eddie Kennison .75 2.00
13 Jermaine Lewis .75 2.00
14 Ray Lewis 2.00 5.00
15 John Mobley .50 1.25
16 Eric Moulds 1.25 3.00
17 Jonathan Ogden .50 1.25
18 Lawrence Phillips .50 1.25
19 Simeon Rice .75 2.00
20 Zach Thomas 1.25 3.00

1997 Fleer Thrill Seekers

Randomly inserted in packs at a rate of one in 288, this 12-card set features color photos of players who are known for making the big play. Both player image and background have a shimmery metallic look.

COMPLETE SET (12) 100.00 200.00
STATED ODDS 1:288
1 Karim Abdul-Jabbar 2.50 6.00
2 Jerome Bettis 4.00 10.00
3 Terrell Davis 5.00 12.00
4 John Elway 15.00 40.00
5 Brett Favre 15.00 40.00
6 Eddie George 4.00 10.00
7 Terry Glenn 4.00 10.00
8 Keyshawn Johnson 4.00 10.00
9 Dan Marino 15.00 40.00
10 Curtis Martin 5.00 12.00
11 Deion Sanders 4.00 10.00
12 Emmitt Smith 12.50 30.00

1997 Fleer SkyBox Brett Favre Promo

1 Brett Favre/2500 2.00 5.00

2006 Fleer

This 200-card set was released in June, 2006. The set was issued into the hobby in 10-card packs, with a $1.59 SRP, which came 36 packs to a box. Cards 1-100 feature veterans sequenced in alphabetical team order while cards 101-200 feature 2006 rookies sequenced in first name alphabetical order. Those rookie cards were inserted into packs at a stated rate of two per.

COMPLETE SET (200) 20.00 50.00
COMP.SET w/o RC's (100) 6.00 15.00
TWO ROOKIES PER PACK
ONE INSERT CARD PER PACK
1 Anquan Boldin .12 .30
2 Larry Fitzgerald .15 .40
3 J.J. Arrington .12 .30
4 Michael Vick .15 .40
5 Warrick Dunn .12 .30
6 Roddy White .12 .30
7 Jamal Lewis .15 .40
8 Kyle Boller .12 .30
9 Derrick Mason .12 .30
10 Willis McGahee .12 .30
11 J.P. Losman .15 .40
12 Lee Evans .15 .40
13 Steve Smith .20 .50
14 Jake Delhomme .12 .30
15 DeShaun Foster .15 .40
16 Rex Grossman .12 .30
17 Brian Urlacher .20 .50
18 Thomas Jones .12 .30
19 Carson Palmer .15 .40
20 Chad Johnson .12 .30
21 Rudi Johnson .12 .30
22 Charlie Frye .15 .40
23 Braylon Edwards .12 .30
24 Reuben Droughns .15 .40
25 Julius Jones .12 .30
26 Drew Bledsoe .15 .40
27 Terry Glenn .15 .40
28 Jake Plummer .12 .30
29 Tatum Bell .12 .30
30 Champ Bailey .15 .40
31 Rod Smith .15 .40
32 Roy Williams WR .12 .30
33 Kevin Jones .12 .30
34 Mike Williams .12 .30
35 Brett Favre .40 1.00
36 Ahman Green .15 .40
37 Javon Walker .15 .40
38 David Carr .12 .30
39 Andre Johnson .15 .40
40 Domanick Davis .12 .30
41 Peyton Manning .50 1.25
42 Edgerrin James .15 .40
43 Marvin Harrison .15 .40
44 Reggie Wayne .15 .40
45 Byron Leftwich .12 .30
46 Fred Taylor .12 .30
47 Ernest Wilford .12 .30
48 Larry Johnson .12 .30
49 Trent Green .12 .30
50 Tony Gonzalez .15 .40
51 Ronnie Brown .15 .40
52 Ricky Williams .12 .30
53 Chris Chambers .12 .30
54 Daunte Culpepper .15 .40
55 Troy Williamson .12 .30
56 Brad Johnson .15 .40
57 Tom Brady .60 1.50
58 Deion Branch .12 .30
59 Corey Dillon .12 .30
60 Deuce McAllister .15 .40
61 Donte Stallworth .12 .30

62 Joe Horn .12 .30
63 Eli Manning .15 .40
64 Tiki Barber .15 .40
65 Plaxico Burress .12 .30
66 Jeremy Shockey .12 .30
67 Chad Pennington .12 .30
68 Curtis Martin .15 .40
69 Laveranues Coles .12 .30
70 Randy Moss .15 .40
71 Aaron Brooks .12 .30
72 LaMont Jordan .15 .40
73 Donovan McNabb .15 .40
74 Brian Westbrook .12 .30
75 Terrell Owens .15 .40
76 Ben Roethlisberger .25 .60
77 Hines Ward .15 .40
78 Willie Parker .15 .40
79 Heath Miller .12 .30
80 LaDainian Tomlinson .20 .50
81 Drew Brees .20 .50
82 Antonio Gates .20 .50
83 Alex Smith QB .15 .40
84 Antonio Bryant .12 .30
85 Frank Gore .15 .40
86 Shaun Alexander .12 .30
87 Matt Hasselbeck .12 .30
88 Darrell Jackson .15 .40
89 Marc Bulger .12 .30
90 Steven Jackson .12 .30
91 Torry Holt .15 .40
92 Cadillac Williams .15 .40
93 Chris Simms .12 .30
94 Joey Galloway .15 .40
95 Steve McNair .15 .40
96 Chris Brown .12 .30
97 Drew Bennett .15 .40
98 Clinton Portis .12 .30
99 Santana Moss .15 .40
100 Mark Brunell .15 .40
101 A.J. Hawk RC .60 1.50
102 A.J. Nicholson RC .50 1.25
103 Abdul Hodge RC .50 1.25
104 Andre Hall RC .60 1.50
105 Anthony Fasano RC .50 1.25
106 Antonio Cromartie RC .60 1.50
107 Ashton Youboty RC .50 1.25
108 Bobby Carpenter RC .50 1.25
109 Brad Smith RC .60 1.50
110 Greg Jennings RC .75 2.00
111 Brandon Williams RC .50 1.25
112 Brian Calhoun RC .50 1.25
113 Brodie Croyle RC .50 1.25
114 Brodrick Bunkley RC .60 1.50
115 Bruce Gradkowski RC .60 1.50
116 Chad Greenway RC .75 2.00
117 Chad Jackson RC .50 1.25
118 Charles Davis RC .60 1.50
119 Charles Gordon RC .50 1.25
120 Charlie Whitehurst RC .50 1.25
121 Claude Wroten RC .50 1.25
122 Cory Rodgers RC .50 1.25
123 D.J. Shockley RC .60 1.50
124 Darnell Bing RC .60 1.50
125 Darrell Hackney RC .60 1.50
126 David Thomas RC .50 1.25
127 D'Brickashaw Ferguson RC .50 1.25
128 DeAngelo Williams RC .60 1.50
129 DeMeco Ryans RC .60 1.50
130 Demetrius Williams RC .50 1.25
131 Derek Hagan RC .60 1.50
132 Devin Hester RC 1.00 2.50
133 Dominique Byrd RC .50 1.25
134 DonTrell Moore RC .60 1.50
135 D'Qwell Jackson RC .50 1.25
136 Drew Olson RC .50 1.25
137 Elvis Dumervil RC .75 2.00
138 Ernie Sims RC .50 1.25
139 Garrett Mills RC .60 1.50
140 Gerald Riggs RC .60 1.50
141 Greg Lee RC .50 1.25
142 Haloti Ngata RC .60 1.50
143 Hank Baskett RC .50 1.25
144 Jason Allen RC .60 1.50
145 Jason Avant RC .50 1.25
146 Jay Cutler RC .60 1.50
147 Jeff Webb RC .60 1.50
148 Jeremy Bloom RC .50 1.25
149 Jerome Harrison RC .50 1.25
150 Jimmy Williams RC .50 1.25
151 Joe Klopfenstein RC .50 1.25
152 Johnathan Joseph RC .60 1.50
153 Joseph Addai RC .50 1.25
154 Jovon Bouknight RC .60 1.50
155 Kai Parham RC .75 2.00
156 Kamerion Wimbley RC .60 1.50
157 Kellen Clemens RC .50 1.25
158 Kelly Jennings RC .60 1.50
159 Ko Simpson RC .60 1.50
160 Laurence Maroney RC .50 1.25
161 Lawrence Vickers RC .60 1.50
162 LenDale White RC .50 1.25
163 Leon Washington RC .50 1.25
164 Leonard Pope RC .75 2.00
165 Manny Lawson RC .60 1.50
166 Marcedes Lewis RC .50 1.25
167 Marcus McNeill RC .50 1.25
168 Donte Whitner RC .60 1.50
169 Mario Williams RC .75 2.00
170 Martin Nance RC .50 1.25
171 Mathias Kiwanuka RC .75 2.00
172 Matt Bernstein RC .50 1.25
173 Matt Leinart RC .50 1.25
174 Maurice Drew RC .75 2.00
175 Maurice Stovall RC .50 1.25
176 Michael Huff RC .60 1.50
177 Michael Robinson RC .50 1.25
178 Mike Hass RC .50 1.25
179 Omar Jacobs RC .50 1.25
180 Orien Harris RC .60 1.50
181 Owen Daniels RC .75 2.00
182 Miles Austin RC .60 1.50
183 Reggie Bush RC .75 2.00
184 Reggie McNeal RC .50 1.25
185 Santonio Holmes RC .60 1.50
186 Sinorice Moss RC .50 1.25
187 Skyler Green RC .50 1.25
188 Tony Scheffler RC .75 2.00
189 Tamba Hali RC .75 2.00
190 Tarvaris Jackson RC .50 1.25
191 Thomas Howard RC .50 1.25
192 Tim Day RC .60 1.50
193 Todd Watkins RC .50 1.25
194 Travis Wilson RC .50 1.25
195 Tye Hill RC .50 1.25
196 Vernon Davis RC .60 1.50
197 Vince Young RC .50 1.25
198 Wali Lundy RC .50 1.25
199 Will Blackmon RC .50 1.25
200 Winston Justice RC .60 1.50

2006 Fleer Gold

*VETERANS 1-100: 5X TO 12X BASIC CARDS
*ROOKIES 101-200: 1X TO 2.5X BASIC CARDS

2006 Fleer Silver

*VETERANS 1-100: 3X TO 8X BASIC CARDS
*ROOKIES 101-200: .6X TO 1.5X BASIC CARDS

2006 Fleer Autographics

AUAG Antonio Gates
AUAV Jason Avant 5.00 12.00
AUBA Ronde Barber 5.00 12.00
AUBE Braylon Edwards
AUBL Byron Leftwich
AUBY Dominique Byrd 5.00 12.00
AUCG Chad Greenway 8.00 20.00
AUCJ Chad Jackson 5.00 12.00
AUCW Cadillac Williams
AUDB Drew Bledsoe
AUDF D'Brickashaw Ferguson 5.00 12.00
AUDO Drew Olson
AUDR DeMeco Ryans 10.00 25.00
AUDW DeAngelo Williams SP 25.00 60.00
AUGR Gerald Riggs 6.00 15.00
AUHB Hank Baskett
AUJC Jay Cutler SP
AUJH Jerome Harrison 5.00 12.00
AUKJ Keyshawn Johnson
AUKO Kyle Orton 5.00 12.00
AULE Matt Leinart SP
AULJ Larry Johnson SP 12.00 30.00
AULM Laurence Maroney
AULP Leonard Pope 8.00 20.00
AULT LaDainian Tomlinson SP
AULW Leon Washington 15.00 30.00
AUMD Maurice Drew 30.00 60.00
AUMK Mathias Kiwanuka 8.00 20.00
AUML Marcedes Lewis 5.00 12.00
AUMO Sinorice Moss SP 5.00 12.00
AURB Reggie Bush SP 8.00 20.00
AURJ Rudi Johnson 5.00 12.00
AURM Reggie McNeal 5.00 12.00
AURY Ryan Moats 5.00 12.00
AUTH T.J. Houshmandzadeh
AUTJ Thomas Jones 5.00 12.00
AUTW Travis Wilson 5.00 12.00
AUWH LenDale White SP
AUWI Jason Witten 20.00 40.00

2006 Fleer Fabrics

FFAB Aaron Brooks 2.00 5.00
FFAC Alge Crumpler 2.50 6.00
FFAG Ahman Green 2.50 6.00
FFAL Ashley Lelie 2.00 5.00
FFAR Antwaan Randle El 2.00 5.00
FFBL Byron Leftwich 2.00 5.00
FFBR Troy Brown 2.00 5.00
FFBU Marc Bulger 2.00 5.00
FFBW Brian Westbrook 2.00 5.00
FFCF Charlie Frye 2.50 6.00
FFCM Curtis Martin 2.50 6.00
FFCP Chad Pennington 2.00 5.00
FFCW Cadillac Williams 2.50 6.00
FFDB Drew Brees 3.00 8.00
FFDC David Carr 2.00 5.00
FFDD Domanick Davis SP 2.50 6.00
FFDM Deuce McAllister 2.50 6.00
FFEJ Edgerrin James 2.50 6.00
FFGR Trent Green 2.00 5.00
FFHO Torry Holt SP 2.50 6.00
FFIB Isaac Bruce 3.00 8.00
FFJD Jake Delhomme SP 2.50 6.00
FFJG Jeff Garcia 2.00 5.00
FFJJ Julius Jones 2.00 5.00
FFJL Jamal Lewis 2.50 6.00
FFJM Josh McCown 2.00 5.00
FFJO Larry Johnson 2.00 5.00
FFJP Jake Plummer 2.00 5.00
FFJS Jeremy Shockey 2.00 5.00
FFJW Javon Walker 2.50 6.00
FFKJ Kevin Jones 2.00 5.00
FFKM Keenan McCardell 2.50 6.00
FFKO Kyle Orton 2.00 5.00
FFLA LaVar Arrington 2.00 5.00
FFMB Mark Brunell 2.50 6.00
FFMF Marshall Faulk 2.50 6.00
FFMH Matt Hasselbeck 2.00 5.00
FFPB Plaxico Burress 2.00 5.00
FFPM Peyton Manning SP 10.00 25.00
FFPO Jerry Porter 2.00 5.00
FFPR Philip Rivers 3.00 8.00
FFRB Ronnie Brown 2.50 6.00
FFRG Rex Grossman 2.00 5.00
FFRM Randy Moss 2.50 6.00
FFRW Ricky Williams 2.00 5.00
FFSD Stephen Davis 2.00 5.00
FFSJ Steven Jackson 2.00 5.00
FFSM Steve McNair 2.50 6.00
FFTA Tatum Bell 2.00 5.00
FFTB Tom Brady SP 12.00 30.00
FFTG Tony Gonzalez SP 3.00 8.00
FFTH Todd Heap 2.00 5.00
FFTO Terrell Owens 2.50 6.00
FFTW Troy Williamson 2.00 5.00
FFWA Reggie Wayne 2.50 6.00
FFWO Charles Woodson 3.00 8.00
FFZT Zach Thomas 2.50 6.00
FFEJ2 Edgerrin James 2.50 6.00

2006 Fleer Faces of the Game

COMPLETE SET (10) 8.00 20.00
FGBA Tiki Barber .60 1.50
FGBF Brett Favre 1.50 4.00
FGCJ Chad Johnson .50 1.25
FGDM Donovan McNabb .60 1.50
FGHW Hines Ward .60 1.50
FGLT LaDainian Tomlinson .75 2.00
FGMV Michael Vick .60 1.50
FGPM Peyton Manning 2.00 5.00
FGSA Shaun Alexander .50 1.25
FGTB Tom Brady 2.50 6.00

2006 Fleer Fantastic 40

RANDOM INSERTS IN WAL-MART PACKS
F40AB Anquan Boldin .40 1.00
F40AG Antonio Gates .60 1.50
F40BA Tiki Barber .50 1.25
F40BF Brett Favre 1.25 3.00
F40BR Ben Roethlisberger .75 2.00
F40CC Chris Chambers .40 1.00
F40CD Corey Dillon .40 1.00
F40CJ Chad Johnson .40 1.00
F40CM Curtis Martin .50 1.25
F40CP Carson Palmer .50 1.25
F40CW Cadillac Williams .50 1.25
F40DC Daunte Culpepper .50 1.25
F40DM Donovan McNabb .50 1.25
F40EJ Edgerrin James .50 1.25
F40EM Eli Manning .50 1.25
F40HA Matt Hasselbeck .40 1.00
F40HW Hines Ward .50 1.25
F40JG Joey Galloway .50 1.25
F40JJ Julius Jones .40 1.00
F40JL Jamal Lewis .50 1.25
F40JP Jake Plummer .40 1.00
F40LF Larry Fitzgerald .50 1.25
F40LJ Larry Johnson .40 1.00
F40LT LaDainian Tomlinson .60 1.50
F40MH Marvin Harrison .50 1.25
F40MV Michael Vick .50 1.25
F40PM Peyton Manning 1.50 4.00
F40PO Clinton Portis .40 1.00
F40RB Ronnie Brown .50 1.25
F40RJ Rudi Johnson .40 1.00
F40RM Randy Moss .50 1.25
F40RW Reggie Wayne .50 1.25
F40SA Shaun Alexander .40 1.00
F40SM Santana Moss .50 1.25
F40SS Steve Smith .60 1.50
F40TB Tom Brady 2.00 5.00
F40TG Tony Gonzalez .50 1.25
F40TH Torry Holt .50 1.25
F40TO Terrell Owens .50 1.25
F40WD Warrick Dunn .40 1.00

2006 Fleer Fantasy Standouts

COMPLETE SET (20) 10.00 25.00
FSBR Tom Brady 2.50 6.00
FSCJ Chad Johnson .50 1.25
FSCP Clinton Portis .50 1.25
FSDM Donovan McNabb .60 1.50
FSEJ Edgerrin James .60 1.50
FSEM Eli Manning .60 1.50
FSHA Marvin Harrison .60 1.50
FSJO LaMont Jordan .60 1.50
FSLF Larry Fitzgerald .60 1.50
FSLJ Larry Johnson .50 1.25
FSLT LaDainian Tomlinson .75 2.00
FSMH Matt Hasselbeck .50 1.25
FSPA Carson Palmer .60 1.50
FSPM Peyton Manning 2.00 5.00
FSRJ Rudi Johnson .50 1.25
FSRM Randy Moss .60 1.50
FSSA Shaun Alexander .50 1.25
FSSS Steve Smith .75 2.00
FSTB Tiki Barber .60 1.50
FSTH Torry Holt .60 1.50

2006 Fleer Fresh Faces

COMPLETE SET (18) 15.00 40.00
FRAH A.J. Hawk .60 1.50
FRCJ Chad Jackson .50 1.25
FRCR Brodie Croyle .50 1.25
FRDF D'Brickashaw Ferguson .50 1.25
FRDW DeAngelo Williams .60 1.50
FRJA Joseph Addai .50 1.25
FRJC Jay Cutler .60 1.50
FRLM Laurence Maroney .50 1.25
FRLW LenDale White .50 1.25
FRMH Michael Huff .60 1.50
FRML Matt Leinart .50 1.25
FRMS Maurice Stovall .50 1.25
FRMW Mario Williams .75 2.00
FRRB Reggie Bush .75 2.00
FRSH Santonio Holmes .60 1.50
FRSM Sinorice Moss .50 1.25
FRVD Vernon Davis .60 1.50
FRVY Vince Young .50 1.25

2006 Fleer Seek and Destroy

COMPLETE SET (10) 6.00 15.00
SDBU Brian Urlacher 1.25 3.00
SDCB Champ Bailey 1.00 2.50
SDDF Dwight Freeney .75 2.00
SDJP Julius Peppers 1.00 2.50
SDJV Jonathan Vilma .75 2.00
SDMS Michael Strahan 1.00 2.50
SDRL Ray Lewis 1.25 3.00
SDSM Shawne Merriman 1.00 2.50
SDTB Tedy Bruschi 1.00 2.50
SDTP Troy Polamalu 1.25 3.00

2006 Fleer Stretching the Field

COMPLETE SET (10) 6.00 15.00
SFAB Anquan Boldin .60 1.50
SFCJ Chad Johnson .60 1.50
SFJG Joey Galloway .75 2.00
SFLF Larry Fitzgerald .75 2.00
SFMH Marvin Harrison .75 2.00
SFPB Plaxico Burress .60 1.50
SFRM Randy Moss .75 2.00
SFSM Santana Moss .75 2.00
SFSS Steve Smith 1.00 2.50
SFTH Torry Holt .75 2.00

2006 Fleer The Franchise

COMPLETE SET (32) 12.00 30.00
TFAS Alex Smith QB .75 2.00
TFBF Brett Favre 2.00 5.00
TFBJ Brad Johnson .75 2.00
TFBL Byron Leftwich .60 1.50
TFBR Ben Roethlisberger 1.25 3.00
TFBU Brian Urlacher 1.00 2.50
TFCF Charlie Frye .75 2.00
TFCP Carson Palmer .75 2.00
TFCW Cadillac Williams .75 2.00
TFDC David Carr .60 1.50
TFDM Deuce McAllister .75 2.00
TFEM Eli Manning .75 2.00
TFJJ Julius Jones .60 1.50
TFJP Jake Plummer .60 1.50
TFKJ Kevin Jones .60 1.50
TFLF Larry Fitzgerald .75 2.00
TFLJ Larry Johnson .60 1.50
TFLT LaDainian Tomlinson 1.00 2.50
TFMB Marc Bulger .60 1.50
TFMC Donovan McNabb .75 2.00
TFMV Michael Vick .75 2.00
TFPE Chad Pennington .60 1.50
TFPM Peyton Manning 2.50 6.00
TFPO Clinton Portis .60 1.50
TFRB Ronnie Brown .75 2.00
TFRL Ray Lewis 1.00 2.50
TFRM Randy Moss .75 2.00
TFSA Shaun Alexander .60 1.50
TFSM Steve McNair .75 2.00
TFSS Steve Smith 1.00 2.50
TFTB Tom Brady 3.00 8.00
TFWM Willis McGahee .60 1.50

2002 Fleer Collectibles

This set of cards was issued one card at a time packaged with a 1:55 scale Howler die-cast car. Each card and die-cast combo was issued together in a blister style package. The cards feature foil highlights and a "Fleer Collectibles" logo on the front. The cardbacks include a brief player bio and a large card number at the top. One card and die-cast was produced for each NFL team.

COMPLETE SET (32) 25.00 60.00
1 Michael Vick .75 2.00
2 Brian Urlacher 1.00 2.50
3 Emmitt Smith 1.50 4.00
4 Mike McMahon .60 1.50
5 Brett Favre 2.00 5.00
6 Kurt Warner .75 2.00
7 Daunte Culpepper .75 2.00
8 Aaron Brooks .60 1.50
9 Tiki Barber .75 2.00
10 Donovan McNabb .75 2.00
11 Jake Plummer .60 1.50
12 Jeff Garcia .60 1.50
13 Keyshawn Johnson .75 2.00
14 Stephen Davis .60 1.50
15 Eric Moulds 1.00 2.50
16 Corey Dillon .60 1.50
17 Ray Lewis 1.00 2.50
18 Brian Griese .60 1.50
19 Peyton Manning 2.50 6.00
20 Eddie George .75 2.00
21 Tony Gonzalez .75 2.00
22 Tim Brown 1.00 2.50
23 Chris Chambers .60 1.50
24 Tom Brady 5.00 12.00
25 Curtis Martin .75 2.00
26 Jerome Bettis 1.00 2.50
27 LaDainian Tomlinson 1.00 2.50
28 Trent Dilfer .60 1.50
29 Mark Brunell .75 2.00
30 Muhsin Muhammad .60 1.50
31 Tim Couch .60 1.50
32 Tony Boselli .75 2.00

2004 Fleer Authentic Player Autographs

Cards from this set were issued as replacements for a variety of older autograph exchange cards from different Fleer football products. Each card includes a cut signature of the featured player with his name above the player image and the notation "Player Autograph Card." The Fleer logo appears at the top of the card but no specific Fleer brand is mentioned. Some players have more than one serial numbered version as noted below while others feature a swatch of jersey as well as the signature. However, on some cards, little or no difference can be found between the serial numbered versions except for the serial numbering while others were printed with a variation in the foil color used.

BL1 Byron Leftwich JSY/50 10.00 25.00
BL2 Byron Leftwich JSY/75 10.00 25.00
DC1 David Carr/25 12.00 30.00
DC2 David Carr/75 10.00 25.00
DC3 David Carr/100 10.00 25.00
DC4 David Carr/250 8.00 20.00
JL1 Jamal Lewis/25 8.00 20.00
JL2 Jamal Lewis/100 8.00 20.00
MH1 Matt Hasselbeck/50 10.00 25.00
MH2 Matt Hasselbeck/75 10.00 25.00
MH3 Matt Hasselbeck/100 10.00 25.00
MV1 Michael Vick JSY/25 25.00 50.00
MV2 Michael Vick JSY/50 25.00 50.00
MV3 Michael Vick JSY/100 25.00 50.00

2005 Fleer Authentic Player Autographs

Cards from this set first hit the secondary market in Spring 2005. They were issued as replacements for a variety of older autograph exchange cards from different Fleer football products. Each card includes a cut signature of the featured player with his first inital and last name above the player image and the simple set name "Authentic Player Autograph." The Fleer logo appears at the bottom of the card but no specific Fleer brand is mentioned. Most players have more than serial numbered version as noted below. However little or no difference can be found between the versions except for the serial numbering.

AM2 Archie Manning/150 7.50 20.00
BR1 Ben Roethlisberger/50 90.00 150.00
CC1 Chris Chambers/50 5.00 12.00
CC2 Chris Chambers/150 5.00 12.00
CC4 Chris Chambers/300 5.00 12.00
DH1 Drew Henson/50 7.50 20.00
DH2 Drew Henson/150 7.50 20.00
DS2 Donte Stallworth/150 5.00 12.00
JM1 Josh McCown/50 6.00 15.00
JM2 Josh McCown/150 6.00 15.00
JM3 Josh McCown/300 6.00 15.00
KW1 Kellen Winslow Jr./50 7.50 20.00
KW2 Kellen Winslow Jr./150 7.50 20.00
WM1 Willis McGahee/50 7.50 20.00
AM1 Archie Manning/50 7.50 20.00
CC3 Chris Chambers JSY/100 6.00 15.00
DS1 Donte Stallworth/50 6.00 15.00
SJ1 Steven Jackson/50 10.00 25.00
JMJ2 Josh McCown JSY/100 7.50 20.00
JMJ1 Josh McCown JSY/25 7.50 20.00

2002 Fleer Authentix

Released in June 2002, this 140-card base set includes 100 veterans and 40 rookies. The rookies are numbered to 1,250. Some Hot Boxes exist which contain a bonus pack with a memorabilia card of the team noted on the box. The card fronts feature a color action shot surrounded by a white border. The background resembles that of a game ticket. Special "Home Team Edition" foil boxes were produced for these teams: Dallas Cowboys, Green Bay Packers, San Francisco 49ers, Pittsburgh Steelers, Miami Dolphins, and Philadelphia Eagles. Each of the Home Team boxes included additional cards from the second series (cards #141-230) of players from the team featured in that box as well as randomly seeded parallel inserts for that team. Due to market scarcity, the basic issue Hometown Heroes subset cards (#141-230) are not priced below.

COMP.SET w/o SP's (100) 7.50 20.00
1 Jake Plummer .20 .50
2 Chad Pennington .20 .50
3 Corey Bradford .20 .50
4 Mike Anderson .20 .50
5 Donovan McNabb .25 .60
6 Brian Griese .20 .50
7 Keyshawn Johnson .25 .60
8 Michael Strahan .25 .60
9 Rod Smith .25 .60
10 Warren Sapp .25 .60
11 Joe Horn .20 .50
12 Anthony Thomas .25 .60
13 Jeff Garcia .20 .50
14 Michael Bennett .20 .50
15 Richard Huntley .20 .50
16 Doug Flutie .25 .60
17 Tony Gonzalez .25 .60
18 David Boston .20 .50
19 Freddie Mitchell .20 .50
20 Terrell Davis .25 .60
21 Torry Holt .25 .60
22 Drew Bledsoe .25 .60
23 Peter Warrick .20 .50
24 Darrell Jackson .25 .60
25 Chris Chambers .20 .50
26 Marvin Harrison .25 .60
27 Warrick Dunn .20 .50
28 Tim Brown .30 .75
29 Terry Glenn .25 .60
30 Rod Gardner .20 .50
31 Aaron Brooks .20 .50
32 Johnnie Morton .25 .60
33 Steve McNair .25 .60
34 Deuce McAllister .25 .60
35 Emmitt Smith .50 1.25
36 Isaac Bruce .30 .75
37 Cris Carter .30 .75
38 Marty Booker .20 .50
39 Garrison Hearst .20 .50
40 Jay Fiedler .25 .60
41 Eric Moulds .20 .50
42 Hines Ward .25 .60
43 Peyton Manning .75 2.00
44 Trent Dilfer .20 .50
45 Ricky Williams .25 .60
46 Quincy Carter .20 .50
47 Kurt Warner .25 .60
48 Tom Brady 1.50 4.00
49 Chris Weinke .20 .50
50 LaDainian Tomlinson .30 .75
51 Antowain Smith .25 .60
52 Corey Dillon .20 .50
53 Shaun Alexander .20 .50
54 Daunte Culpepper .25 .60
55 Ray Lewis .30 .75
56 Kordell Stewart .20 .50
57 Trent Green .20 .50
58 Chris Redman .20 .50
59 Plaxico Burress .20 .50
60 Fred Taylor .20 .50
61 Snoop Minnis .20 .50
62 Jerry Rice .60 1.50
63 James Allen .20 .50
64 Peerless Price .20 .50
65 Curtis Martin .25 .60
66 Mike McMahon .20 .50
67 Brad Johnson .25 .60
68 Troy Brown .20 .50
69 Jamal Lewis .25 .60
70 Jerome Bettis .30 .75
71 Dominic Rhodes .20 .50
72 Az-Zahir Hakim .20 .50
73 Rich Gannon .25 .60
74 Ahman Green .25 .60
75 Eddie George .25 .60
76 Tim Couch .20 .50
77 Ricky Watters .25 .60
78 Randy Moss .25 .60
79 Brian Urlacher .30 .75
80 Terrell Owens .25 .60
81 Jimmy Smith .25 .60
82 Travis Henry .20 .50
83 Drew Brees .60 1.50
84 Priest Holmes .20 .50
85 Michael Vick .25 .60
86 James Thrash .25 .60
87 Jamie Sharper .25 .60
88 Marcus Robinson .25 .60
89 Laveranues Coles .25 .60
90 Brett Favre .60 1.50
91 Stephen Davis .20 .50
92 Tiki Barber .25 .60
93 Kevin Johnson .20 .50
94 Marshall Faulk .25 .60
95 Mark Brunell .25 .60
96 Jamal Anderson .25 .60
97 Duce Staley .20 .50
98 Edgerrin James .25 .60
99 Kevan Barlow .20 .50
100 Kerry Collins .20 .50
101 David Carr RC 1.50 4.00
102 Joey Harrington RC 1.50 4.00
103 William Green RC 2.00 5.00
104 Donte Stallworth RC 2.50 6.00
105 Ashley Lelie RC 1.50 4.00
106 Jabar Gaffney RC 1.50 4.00
107 Antonio Bryant RC 2.50 6.00
108 Josh Reed RC 2.00 5.00
109 Daniel Graham RC 2.00 5.00
110 Reche Caldwell RC 2.00 5.00
111 Jeremy Shockey RC 2.50 6.00
112 T.J. Duckett RC 1.50 4.00
113 Marquise Walker RC 1.50 4.00
114 Lamar Gordon RC 2.00 5.00
115 DeShaun Foster RC 2.50 6.00
116 Patrick Ramsey RC 2.00 5.00
117 Andre Davis RC 1.50 4.00
118 Ron Johnson RC 2.00 5.00
119 Luke Staley RC 1.50 4.00
120 Clinton Portis RC 2.50 6.00
121 Freddie Milons RC 1.50 4.00
122 Javon Walker RC 2.50 6.00
123 David Garrard RC 2.00 5.00
124 Kurt Kittner RC 1.50 4.00
125 Adrian Peterson RC 2.00 5.00
126 Roy Williams RC 1.50 4.00
127 Maurice Morris RC 2.00 5.00
128 Cliff Russell RC 1.50 4.00
129 Antwaan Randle El RC 2.00 5.00
130 Verron Haynes RC 1.50 4.00
131 Eric Crouch RC 2.50 6.00
132 Kahlil Hill RC 1.50 4.00
133 Brian Westbrook RC 3.00 8.00
134 Travis Stephens RC 1.50 4.00
135 Julius Peppers RC 4.00 10.00
136 Quentin Jammer RC 2.50 6.00
137 Rohan Davey RC 2.50 6.00
138 Ladell Betts RC 2.50 6.00
139 Tim Carter RC 2.00 5.00
140 Josh McCown RC 2.50 6.00
141 Emmitt Smith HH 1.50 4.00
142 Quincy Carter HH .60 1.50
143 Joey Galloway HH .75 2.00
144 Anthony Wright HH .60 1.50
145 La'Roi Glover HH .60 1.50
146 Greg Ellis HH .60 1.50
147 Dexter Coakley HH .60 1.50
148 Dat Nguyen HH .60 1.50
149 Darren Woodson HH .75 2.00
150 Troy Hambrick HH .60 1.50
151 Larry Allen HH 1.00 2.50
152 Ebenezer Ekuban HH .60 1.50
153 Reggie Swinton HH .60 1.50
154 Michael Wiley HH .60 1.50
155 Duane Hawthorne HH .60 1.50
156 Brett Favre HH 2.00 5.00
157 Ahman Green HH .75 2.00
158 Terry Glenn HH .75 2.00
159 Donald Driver HH .75 2.00
160 Ryan Longwell HH .60 1.50
161 Nate Wayne HH .60 1.50
162 Darren Sharper HH .60 1.50
163 Kabeer Gbaja-Biamila HH .60 1.50
164 Vonnie Holliday HH .60 1.50
165 Bubba Franks HH .60 1.50
166 LeRoy Butler HH .75 2.00
167 Dorsey Levens HH .75 2.00
168 William Henderson HH .60 1.50
169 Tyrone Williams HH .60 1.50
170 Robert Ferguson HH .75 2.00
171 Jeff Garcia HH .60 1.50
172 Garrison Hearst HH .60 1.50
173 Terrell Owens HH .75 2.00
174 Kevan Barlow HH .60 1.50
175 J.J. Stokes HH .60 1.50
176 Tai Streets HH .60 1.50
177 Eric Johnson HH .60 1.50
178 Fred Beasley HH .60 1.50
179 Tim Rattay HH .75 2.00
180 Derek Smith HH RC 1.00 2.50
181 Zack Bronson HH .60 1.50
182 Ahmed Plummer HH .60 1.50
183 Bryant Young HH .60 1.50
184 Vinny Sutherland HH .60 1.50
185 Andre Carter HH .60 1.50
186 Kordell Stewart HH .60 1.50
187 Jerome Bettis HH 1.00 2.50
188 Hines Ward HH .75 2.00
189 Plaxico Burress HH .60 1.50
190 Kendrell Bell HH .60 1.50
191 Amos Zereoue HH .60 1.50
192 Jason Gildon HH .75 2.00
193 Chad Scott HH .60 1.50
194 Joey Porter HH .75 2.00
195 Hank Poteat HH .60 1.50
196 Troy Edwards HH .60 1.50
197 Lee Flowers HH .60 1.50
198 Aaron Smith HH RC 6.00 15.00
199 Dan Kreider HH RC 6.00 15.00
200 Tommy Maddox HH .60 1.50
201 Jay Fiedler HH .75 2.00
202 Ricky Williams HH .75 2.00
203 Chris Chambers HH .60 1.50
204 Oronde Gadsden HH .60 1.50
205 Travis Minor HH .60 1.50
206 Zach Thomas HH .75 2.00
207 Jason Taylor HH .75 2.00
208 Olindo Mare HH .60 1.50
209 Sam Madison HH .60 1.50
210 Patrick Surtain HH .60 1.50
211 Tim Bowens HH .60 1.50
212 Daryl Gardener HH .60 1.50
213 Dedric Ward HH .60 1.50
214 James McKnight HH .60 1.50
215 Deon Dyer HH .60 1.50
216 Donovan McNabb HH .75 2.00
217 Duce Staley HH .60 1.50
218 James Thrash HH .75 2.00
219 Correll Buckhalter HH .60 1.50
220 Freddie Mitchell HH .60 1.50
221 Chad Lewis HH .60 1.50
222 Hugh Douglas HH .60 1.50
223 Brian Dawkins HH 1.00 2.50
224 David Akers HH .60 1.50
225 Troy Vincent HH .75 2.00
226 Bobby Taylor HH .75 2.00
227 Rod Smart HH RC 1.00 2.50
228 Todd Pinkston HH .60 1.50
229 Corey Simon HH .60 1.50
230 A.J. Feeley HH .60 1.50

2002 Fleer Authentix Front Row

*VETS 1-100: 4X TO 10X BASIC CARDS
*ROOKIES 101-140: .8X TO 2X
STATED PRINT RUN 150 SER.#'d SETS

2002 Fleer Authentix Second Row

*VETS 1-100: 3X TO 8X BASIC CARDS
*ROOKIES 101-140: .6X TO 1.5X
STATED PRINT RUN 250 SER.#'d SETS

2002 Fleer Authentix Buy Backs

Randomly inserted into Home Team packs, these cards feature authentic autographs, a special Authentic Fleer Buy Back logo, along with various serial numbering.

1 K.Barlow 01Leg/42
4 Q.Carter 01Leg/41
6 C.Chambers 01Leg/40
8 R.Ferguson 01Leg/58
9 B.Franks 01E-X/20
10 F.Mitchell 01Leg/42
12 T.Pinkston 01E-X/20

2002 Fleer Authentix Hometown Heroes

Randomly inserted in packs at a rate of 1:6, this 15-card insert set shows a skyline view of the city for which the player plays. Cards were inserted at a rate of 1:6.

COMPLETE SET (15) 10.00 25.00
STATED ODDS 1:6
1 Michael Vick .60 1.50
2 William Green .60 1.50
3 Donte Stallworth .75 2.00
4 Ashley Lelie .50 1.25
5 Anthony Thomas .60 1.50
6 Eddie George .60 1.50
7 Peyton Manning 2.00 5.00
8 Ricky Williams .60 1.50
9 Tom Brady 4.00 10.00
10 Kurt Warner .60 1.50
11 Daunte Culpepper .60 1.50
12 David Carr .50 1.25
13 Joey Harrington .50 1.25
14 Edgerrin James .60 1.50
15 Randy Moss .60 1.50

2002 Fleer Authentix Hometown Heroes Memorabilia

Inserted one per Home Team Edition Box, this 30-card insert set parallels the basic Hometown Heroes set with each card featuring a swatch of game used memorabilia. All were jersey swatches unless noted below. Several players not found in the Hometown Heroes base set were added to this set.

ONE PER HOME TEAM EDITION BOX
*CHINATOWN/50: .8X TO 2X BASIC JSY
49ERS CHINATOWN PRINT RUN 50
UNPRICED 49ERS FISHER.WHARF #'d TO 5
UNPRICED 49ERS LOMBARD ST. #'d TO 1
*LOWER.GRNVL/25: 1X TO 2.5X BASIC JSY
COWBOY LOWER GRNVILLE #'d TO 25
UNPRICED COWBOY HIGH.PARK #'d TO 5
UNPRICED COWBOY WEST END #'d TO 1
*FT.LAUDER/50: .8X TO 2X BASIC JSY
DOLPHIN FT.LAUDERDALE #'d TO 50
UNPRICED DOLPHIN S.BEACH #'d TO 5
UNPRICED DOLPHIN OCEAN DR.#'d TO 1
*SOUTH ST/25: 1X TO 2.5X BASIC JSY
EAGLE SOUTH ST.PRINT RUN 25
UNPRICED EAGLE MANAYUNK #'d TO 5
UNPRICED EAGLE PENN'S LAND. #'d TO 1
*KEWAUNEE/25: 1X TO 2.5X BASIC JSY
PACKERS KEWAUNEE #'d TO 25
UNPRICED PACKER IOLA #'d TO 5
UNPRICED PACKER BAY BEACH #'d TO 1
*OHIO RIVER/25: 1X TO 2.5X BASIC JSY
STEELER OHIO RIVER #'d TO 25
UNPRICED STEELER ALLEGHENY #'d TO 5
UNPRICED STEELER MONGHLA #'d TO 1
HHM49 J.Garcia/T.Owens 8.00 20.00
HHMBD Brian Dawkins 8.00 20.00
HHMBF Brett Favre 15.00 40.00
HHMBS Bart Starr Pants 20.00 50.00
HHMCO T.Aikman/E.Smith 15.00 40.00
HHMDL Dorsey Levens SP 6.00 15.00
HHMDM2 Donovan McNabb 6.00 15.00
HHMDM1 Dan Marino 15.00 40.00
HHMDO J.Taylor/S.Madison 8.00 20.00
HHMDS Duce Staley 5.00 12.00
HHMEA B.Dawkins/T.Vincent 10.00 25.00
HHMES Emmitt Smith 12.00 30.00
HHMJB Jerome Bettis 8.00 20.00
HHMJG Jeff Garcia 5.00 12.00
HHMJR Jerry Rice 15.00 40.00
HHMJT Jason Taylor 6.00 15.00
HHMKS Kordell Stewart 5.00 12.00
HHMPA B.Favre/D.Levens 20.00 50.00
HHMPB Plaxico Burress 5.00 12.00
HHMPH Paul Hornung Pants 12.00 30.00
HHMRN Ray Nitschke Pants 15.00 40.00
HHMRS Roger Staubach 12.00 30.00
HHMSM Sam Madison
HHMST K.Stewart/J.Bettis 10.00 25.00
HHMTA Troy Aikman 10.00 25.00
HHMTD Tony Dorsett Pants 10.00 25.00
HHMTO Terrell Owens 6.00 15.00
HHMTP Todd Pinkston SP 5.00 12.00
HHMTV Troy Vincent 6.00 15.00
HHMZT Zach Thomas 6.00 15.00

2002 Fleer Authentix Jersey Authentix Ripped

Inserted in packs at a rate of 1:11, this 30-card features the design of a ripped ticket stub, along with a piece of game used memorabilia.

STATED ODDS 1:11
*UNRIPPED/50: .8X TO 2X BASIC JSY
UNRIPPED PRINT RUN 50 SER.#'d SETS
*RIPPED PRO BOWL: .6X TO 1.5X BASIC JSY
RIPPED PB RANDOM INSERTS IN PACKS
UNPRICED UNRIPPED PRO BOWL #'d TO 1
JAAF Antonio Freeman 5.00 12.00
JABF Brett Favre 10.00 25.00
JABU Brian Urlacher 5.00 12.00
JACD Corey Dillon 3.00 8.00
JACP Chad Pennington 3.00 8.00
JACW Charles Woodson 5.00 12.00
JADB1 David Boston 3.00 8.00
JADB2 Drew Bledsoe 4.00 10.00
JADM Donovan McNabb 4.00 10.00
JADW Dez White 3.00 8.00
JAEJ Edgerrin James 4.00 10.00
JAEM1 Ed McCaffrey 4.00 10.00
JAEM2 Eric Moulds 3.00 8.00
JAGC Germane Crowell 3.00 8.00
JAIB Isaac Bruce 5.00 12.00
JAJA Jamal Anderson 4.00 10.00
JAJG Jeff Garcia 3.00 8.00
JAJS Jimmy Smith 4.00 10.00
JAKJ Kevin Johnson 3.00 8.00
JAKM Keenan McCardell 4.00 10.00
JAKW Kurt Warner 4.00 10.00
JAMF Marshall Faulk 4.00 10.00
JAPW Peter Warrick 3.00 8.00
JARD Ron Dayne 4.00 10.00
JASD Stephen Davis 3.00 8.00
JATB Tim Brown 5.00 12.00
JATH Torry Holt 4.00 10.00
JATP Todd Pinkston 3.00 8.00
JATS Thomas Jones 3.00 8.00
JAWS Warren Sapp 4.00 10.00

2002 Fleer Authentix Stadium Classics

This 15-card set is randomly inserted in packs at a rate of 1:12.

COMPLETE SET (15) 20.00 50.00
STATED ODDS 1:12
1 Donovan McNabb 1.00 2.50
2 Marshall Faulk 1.00 2.50
3 Mark Brunell 1.00 2.50
4 Brett Favre 2.50 6.00
5 Emmitt Smith 2.00 5.00
6 Kurt Warner 1.00 2.50
7 Daunte Culpepper 1.00 2.50
8 Jerry Rice 2.50 6.00
9 Tim Couch .75 2.00
10 Edgerrin James 1.00 2.50
11 Randy Moss 1.00 2.50
12 Fred Taylor .75 2.00
13 Brian Urlacher 1.25 3.00
14 Jeff Garcia .75 2.00
15 Shaun Alexander .75 2.00

2002 Fleer Authentix Stadium Classics Memorabilia

Inserted into packs at a rate of 1:58, this 14-card set offers cards with both a swatch from a game-worn jersey as well as a piece of a stadium seat. Each card featured silver foil highlights on the front. A gold foil parallel version was also produced with each card being serial numbered to 100.

STATED ODDS 1:58
*GOLD/100: .6X TO 1.5X BASIC JSY
GOLD STATED PRINT RUN 100
SCBA Brian Urlacher 5.00 12.00
SCBF Brett Favre 10.00 25.00
SCDC Daunte Culpepper 4.00 10.00
SCDM Donovan McNabb 4.00 10.00
SCEJ Edgerrin James 4.00 10.00
SCES Emmitt Smith 8.00 20.00
SCFT Fred Taylor 3.00 8.00
SCJG Jeff Garcia 3.00 8.00
SCJR Jerry Rice 10.00 25.00
SCKW Kurt Warner 4.00 10.00
SCMB Mark Brunell 4.00 10.00
SCMF Marshall Faulk 4.00 10.00
SCRM Randy Moss 4.00 10.00
SCTC Tim Couch 3.00 8.00

2002 Fleer Authentix Ticket for Four

This 5-card insert set was serial numbered to 200. Each card features four of the NFL's top players along with swatches of jersey from all four.

STATED PRINT 200 SER.#'d SETS
1 Favre/Culp/McNab/Couch 15.00 40.00
2 Bo/R.Will/Faulk/S.Davis 10.00 25.00
3 Owns/Bstn/R.Smith/Ti.Brwn 8.00 20.00
4 Seau/B.Smith/Urlchr/Sapp 8.00 20.00
5 Warner/Faulk/Holt/Bruce 8.00 20.00

2002 Fleer Authentix Ticket Stubs

Available as box toppers in Home Team boxes, this set includes a ticket stub from an actual NFL game. The cards also measure slightly smaller than standard size.

2003 Fleer Authentix

Released in July of 2003, this set consists of 165 cards, including 100 veterans, 30 rookies, and 35 Hometown Heroes subset cards. The rookies are serial numbered to 1250. The Hometown Heroes cards are only available in Home Team Edition boxes. Boxes featured 24 packs of 5 cards, with an SRP of $3.99. In addition to hobby boxes, Fleer also produced Home Team Edition boxes for the Dallas Cowboys, Green Bay Packers, New York Giants, Oakland Raiders, and Pittsburgh Steelers. Each Home Team Editon box contained one special pack with a Hometown Heroes memorabilia card, along with three Hometown Heroes subset cards.

COMP.SET w/o SP's (100) 7.50 20.00
1 Donovan McNabb .25 .60
2 Tim Brown .30 .75
3 Donald Driver .25 .60
4 Eddie George .25 .60
5 Curtis Martin .25 .60
6 Chad Hutchinson .20 .50
7 Shaun Alexander .20 .50
8 Kerry Collins .20 .50
9 Trent Green .20 .50
10 Marc Bulger .20 .50
11 Donte Stallworth .20 .50
12 Julius Peppers .30 .75
13 Ronde Barber .20 .50
14 Jason Taylor .25 .60
15 Eric Moulds .20 .50
16 Amos Zereoue .20 .50
17 Fred Taylor .20 .50
18 Jake Plummer .20 .50
19 Jerry Rice .60 1.50
20 Quincy Morgan .20 .50
21 Koren Robinson .25 .60
22 Tom Brady 1.25 3.00
23 Brian Urlacher .30 .75
24 Terrell Owens .25 .60
25 Priest Holmes .20 .50
26 Brett Favre .60 1.50
27 Derrick Mason .20 .50
28 Charlie Garner .25 .60
29 Clinton Portis .20 .50
30 Warren Sapp .25 .60
31 Joe Horn .20 .50
32 Michael Lewis .20 .50
33 Torry Holt .25 .60
34 Aaron Brooks .20 .50
35 William Green .20 .50
36 Matt Hasselbeck .20 .50
37 Ricky Williams .25 .60
38 Travis Henry .20 .50
39 Junior Seau .25 .60
40 Duce Staley .20 .50
41 Todd Heap .20 .50
42 Hines Ward .25 .60
43 David Carr .20 .50
44 Rod Gardner .20 .50
45 Deuce McAllister .25 .60
46 Chad Johnson .20 .50
47 Garrison Hearst .20 .50
48 Daunte Culpepper .25 .60
49 Ray Lewis .30 .75
50 Plaxico Burress .20 .50
51 Randy Moss .25 .60
52 Drew Bledsoe .25 .60
53 LaDainian Tomlinson .30 .75
54 Chris Chambers .20 .50
55 Chris Redman .20 .50
56 Jerome Bettis .30 .75
57 Tony Gonzalez .25 .60
58 Michael Vick .25 .60
59 Tommy Maddox .20 .50
60 Marvin Harrison .25 .60
61 Stephen Davis .20 .50
62 Chad Pennington .20 .50
63 James Stewart .20 .50
64 Simeon Rice .20 .50
65 Jeremy Shockey .20 .50
66 Emmitt Smith .50 1.25
67 Marshall Faulk .25 .60
68 Troy Brown .20 .50
69 Warrick Dunn .20 .50
70 David Boston .20 .50
71 Edgerrin James .25 .60
72 Patrick Ramsey .25 .60
73 Rich Gannon .25 .60
74 Ed McCaffrey .25 .60
75 Kurt Warner .25 .60
76 Marty Booker .20 .50
77 Tai Streets .20 .50
78 Michael Bennett .20 .50
79 Peerless Price .20 .50
80 Drew Brees .30 .75
81 Mark Brunell .25 .60
82 Jamal Lewis .25 .60
83 Brad Johnson .25 .60
84 Jimmy Smith .25 .60
85 T.J. Duckett .20 .50
86 Todd Pinkston .20 .50
87 Joey Harrington .20 .50
88 Derrick Brooks .20 .50
89 Laveranues Coles .20 .50
90 Shannon Sharpe .25 .60
91 Keyshawn Johnson .30 .75
92 Tiki Barber .25 .60
93 Corey Dillon .20 .50
94 Jeff Garcia .20 .50
95 Peyton Manning .75 2.00
96 Marcel Shipp .20 .50
97 Brian Dawkins .30 .75
98 Ahman Green .25 .60
99 Steve McNair .25 .60

100 Amani Toomer .20 .50
101 Carson Palmer RC 2.50 6.00
102 Taylor Jacobs RC 1.25 3.00
103 Kyle Boller RC 1.25 3.00
104 Anquan Boldin RC 2.00 5.00
105 Willis McGahee RC 1.50 4.00
106 Kevin Curtis RC 1.25 3.00
107 Musa Smith RC 1.25 3.00
108 Dallas Clark RC 2.00 5.00
109 Larry Johnson RC 1.50 4.00
110 Billy McMullen RC 1.25 3.00
111 B.J. Askew RC 1.50 4.00
112 Bennie Joppru RC 1.25 3.00
113 Bryant Johnson RC 2.00 5.00
114 Byron Leftwich RC 1.50 4.00
115 Onterrio Smith RC 1.25 3.00
116 Justin Fargas RC 2.00 5.00
117 Terence Newman RC 2.00 5.00
118 Andre Johnson RC 3.00 8.00
119 Rex Grossman RC 1.50 4.00
120 Tyrone Calico RC 1.25 3.00
121 Chris Simms RC 1.25 3.00
122 Kelley Washington RC 1.25 3.00
123 Dave Ragone RC 1.25 3.00
124 Teyo Johnson RC 1.50 4.00
125 Seneca Wallace RC 1.50 4.00
126 Lee Suggs RC 1.25 3.00
127 Chris Brown RC 1.25 3.00
128 L.J. Smith RC 2.00 5.00
129 Charles Rogers RC 1.50 4.00
130 Terrell Suggs RC 1.50 4.00
131 Antonio Bryant HH 1.25 3.00
132 Roy Williams HH 1.25 3.00
133 Joey Galloway HH 1.50 4.00
134 Dexter Coakley HH 1.50 4.00
135 Greg Ellis HH 2.00 5.00
136 Troy Hambrick HH 1.25 3.00
137 La'Roi Glover HH 1.25 3.00
138 Tony Fisher HH 1.25 3.00
139 Javon Walker HH 1.50 4.00
140 Robert Ferguson HH 1.25 3.00
141 Bubba Franks HH 1.50 4.00
142 Kabeer Gbaja-Biamila HH 1.25 3.00
143 Na'il Diggs HH 1.25 3.00
144 Darren Sharper HH 1.25 3.00
145 Jerry Porter HH 1.25 3.00
146 Doug Jolley HH 1.25 3.00
147 Sebastian Janikowski HH 1.25 3.00
148 Rod Woodson HH 1.50 4.00
149 Phillip Buchanon HH 1.25 3.00
150 Charles Woodson HH 2.00 5.00
151 Zack Crockett HH 1.50 4.00
152 Michael Strahan HH 1.50 4.00
153 Dhani Jones HH RC 2.00 5.00
154 Will Allen HH 1.50 4.00
155 Will Peterson HH 1.50 4.00
156 Ron Dixon HH 1.25 3.00
157 Mike Barrow HH 1.25 3.00
158 Ike Hilliard HH 1.25 3.00
159 Antwaan Randle El HH 1.25 3.00
160 Joey Porter HH 2.00 5.00
161 Jason Gildon HH 1.50 4.00
162 Chris Fuamatu-Ma'afala HH 1.50 4.00
163 Kendrell Bell HH 1.25 3.00
164 Chad Scott HH 1.25 3.00
165 Dan Kreider HH 2.00 5.00

2003 Fleer Authentix Balcony

*VETS 1-100: 2X TO 5X BASE CARDS
*ROOKIES 101-130: .5X TO 1.2X
STATED PRINT RUN 250 SER.#'d SETS

2003 Fleer Authentix Booster Tickets Lower Level

*LUXURY BOX: 1.2X TO 3X LOWER LEVEL
*UPPER LEVEL: .8X TO 2X LOWER LEVEL
OVERALL ANNC'D BOOSTER PRINT RUN 250
101 Carson Palmer 2.50 6.00
102 Taylor Jacobs 1.25 3.00
103 Kyle Boller 1.25 3.00
104 Anquan Boldin 2.00 5.00
105 Willis McGahee 1.50 4.00
106 Kevin Curtis 1.25 3.00
107 Musa Smith 1.25 3.00
108 Dallas Clark 2.00 5.00
109 Larry Johnson 1.50 4.00
110 Billy McMullen 1.25 3.00
111 B.J. Askew 1.50 4.00
112 Bennie Joppru 1.25 3.00
113 Bryant Johnson 2.00 5.00
114 Byron Leftwich 1.50 4.00
115 Onterrio Smith 1.25 3.00
116 Justin Fargas 2.00 5.00
117 Terence Newman 2.00 5.00
118 Andre Johnson 3.00 8.00
119 Rex Grossman 1.50 4.00
120 Tyrone Calico 1.25 3.00
121 Chris Simms 1.25 3.00
122 Kelley Washington 1.25 3.00
123 Dave Ragone 1.25 3.00
124 Teyo Johnson 1.50 4.00
125 Seneca Wallace 1.50 4.00
126 Lee Suggs 1.25 3.00
127 Chris Brown 1.25 3.00
128 L.J. Smith 2.00 5.00
129 Charles Rogers 1.50 4.00
130 Terrell Suggs 1.50 4.00

2003 Fleer Authentix Club Box

*VETS 1-100: 3X TO 8X BASIC CARDS
*ROOKIES 101-130: .8X TO 2X
STATED PRINT RUN 100 SER.#'d SETS

2003 Fleer Authentix Standing Room Only

*VETS 1-100: 10X TO 25X BASIC CARDS
*ROOKIES 101-30: 1.5X TO 4X
PRINT RUN 25 SER.#'d SETS

2003 Fleer Authentix Autographs

Randomly inserted into packs, this set features cards with an authentic player autograph. Please note that all cards found in packs from this set were exchange cards. There is no expiration date listed on the cards. Each card features an image of the player who will sign the card.
AABU Brian Urlacher EXCH 3.00 8.00
AACP Chad Pennington 8.00 20.00
AACPX Chad Pennington EXCH 1.50 4.00
AADM Donovan McNabb 15.00 40.00
AADMX Donovan McNabb EXCH 3.00 8.00
AAJH Joey Harrington 6.00 15.00
AAJHX Joey Harrington EXCH 1.00 2.50
AAMB Michael Bennett 5.00 12.00
AAMBX Michael Bennett EXCH .75 2.00
AAMV Michael Vick 15.00 40.00
AAMVX Michael Vick EXCH 2.50 6.00
AAPB Plaxico Burress 6.00 15.00
AAPBX Plaxico Burress EXCH 1.00 2.50

2003 Fleer Authentix Hometown Heroes Memorabilia

Inserted one per Home Team Edition pack, this set features game worn jersey swatches.
ONE PER HOME TEAM BOX
AB Antonio Bryant 4.00 10.00
AG Ahman Green 5.00 12.00
BF Brett Favre 12.00 30.00
DD Donald Driver 5.00 12.00
HW Hines Ward 5.00 12.00
JB Jerome Bettis 6.00 15.00
JG Joey Galloway 5.00 12.00
JR Jerry Rice 12.00 30.00
JS Jeremy Shockey 4.00 10.00
MS Michael Strahan 5.00 12.00
PB Plaxico Burress 4.00 10.00
RG Rich Gannon 5.00 12.00
RW Roy Williams 4.00 10.00
TB1 Tiki Barber 5.00 12.00
TB2 Tim Brown 6.00 15.00
WPB H.Ward/P.Burress 6.00 15.00
BFAG B.Favre/A.Green 15.00 40.00
JGAB J.Galloway/A.Bryant 6.00 15.00
JRRG J.Rice/R.Gannon 15.00 40.00
JSTB J.Shockey/T.Barber 6.00 15.00

2003 Fleer Authentix Jersey Authentix Ripped

Inserted at a rate of 1:18, this set features game worn jersey swatches. Card design is meant to resemble a torn ticket. An Unripped parallel set also exists, with each card serial numbered to 50, and having the appearance of an unripped ticket.
STATED ODDS 1:18
*UNRIPPED/50: .8X TO 2X RIPPED JSY
UNRIPPED PRINT RUN 50 SER.#'d SETS
JAAB Antonio Bryant 2.50 6.00
JACP Clinton Portis 2.50 6.00
JACP2 Chad Pennington 2.50 6.00
JADM1 Deuce McAllister 3.00 8.00
JADM2 Donovan McNabb 3.00 8.00
JAJG Jeff Garcia 2.50 6.00
JAJH Joey Harrington 2.50 6.00
JABU Brian Urlacher 4.00 10.00
JALT LaDainian Tomlinson 4.00 10.00
JAMB Michael Bennett 2.50 6.00
JAMF Marshall Faulk 3.00 8.00
JAPB Plaxico Burress 2.50 6.00
JARM Randy Moss 3.00 8.00
JARW Ricky Williams 3.00 8.00
JATH Travis Henry 2.50 6.00

2003 Fleer Authentix Jersey Authentix Ripped Pro Bowl

Randomly inserted into packs, this set features game worn jersey swatches, along with a Pro Bowl logo ticket, built into the card design. Each card is serial numbered to various quantities. An Unripped parallel version exists, with each card being a 1/1.
STATED PRINT RUN 19-103
UNPRICED UNRIPPED PRINT RUN 1
JADM1 Deuce McAllister/91 4.00 10.00
JADM2 Donovan McNabb/39 5.00 12.00
JAJG Jeff Garcia/87 3.00 8.00
JABU Brian Urlacher/50 5.00 12.00
JALT LaDainian Tomlinson/103 5.00 12.00
JAMB Michael Bennett/19 4.00 10.00
JAMF Marshall Faulk/80 4.00 10.00
JARM Randy Moss/66 4.00 10.00
JARW Ricky Williams/74 4.00 10.00
JATH Travis Henry/42 4.00 10.00

2003 Fleer Authentix Jersey Authentix Autographs Pro Bowl

Randomly inserted into packs, this set is a parallel of the Jersey Authentix Autographs set. Each card is serial numbered to 75. Please note that Michael Vick was issued in packs as an exchange card. No expiration date was listed on the card. A Super Bowl parallel also exists, with each card serial numbered to 25.
PRO BOWL PRINT RUN 75 SER.#'d SETS
*REG.SEASON/270: .3X TO .8X PRO BOWL/75
*REG.SEASON/100-135: .4X TO 1X PB/75
*REG.SEASON/25: .6X TO 1.5X PRO BOWL/75
AJACP Chad Pennington 15.00 40.00
AJAMV Michael Vick 25.00 60.00
AJAWM Willis McGahee 15.00 40.00

2003 Fleer Authentix Jersey Authentix Game of the Week Ripped

Inserted into packs at a rate of 1:240, this set features game worn jersey swatches from two players who will match up against one another during the 2003 season. An Unripped version also exists, with each card serial numbered to 50.
RIPPED STATED ODDS 1:240
*UNRIPPED/50: .6X TO 1.5X BASE DUAL JSY
UNRIPPED PRINT RUN 50 SER.#'d SETS
ABDM A.Bryant/D.McAllister 3.00 8.00
CPDM C.Pennington/D.McNabb 3.00 8.00
CPLT C.Portis/L.Tomlinson 4.00 10.00
CPTH C.Pennington/T.Henry 2.50 6.00
DMRW D.McNabb/R.Williams 3.00 8.00
JHMB J.Harrington/M.Bennett 2.50 6.00
MFJG M.Faulk/J.Garcia 3.00 8.00
MFPB M.Faulk/P.Burress 3.00 8.00
RMBU R.Moss/B.Urlacher 4.00 10.00
THAB T.Henry/A.Bryant 2.50 6.00

2003 Fleer Authentix Stadium Classics

COMPLETE SET (10) 12.50 30.00
STATED ODDS 1:12
1SC Brian Urlacher 1.25 3.00
2SC Donovan McNabb 1.00 2.50
3SC Peyton Manning 3.00 8.00
4SC Deuce McAllister 1.00 2.50
5SC Brett Favre 2.50 6.00
6SC Chad Pennington .75 2.00
7SC Randy Moss 1.00 2.50
8SC Michael Vick 1.00 2.50
9SC Ricky Williams 1.00 2.50
10SC LaDainian Tomlinson 1.25 3.00

2003 Fleer Authentix Ticket Studs

Inserted at a rate of 1:26, this set resembles an admission ticket, and features top NFL superstars.
STATED ODDS 1:26
1TS Michael Vick 1.25 3.00
2TS Tom Brady 6.00 15.00
3TS Brett Favre 3.00 8.00
4TS Emmitt Smith 2.50 6.00
5TS Randy Moss 1.25 3.00
6TS Jerry Rice 3.00 8.00
7TS Peyton Manning 4.00 10.00
8TS Chad Pennington 1.00 2.50
9TS Donovan McNabb 1.25 3.00
10TS LaDainian Tomlinson 1.50 4.00
11TS Jeremy Shockey 1.00 2.50
12TS Drew Brees 1.50 4.00
13TS Brian Urlacher 1.50 4.00
14TS Clinton Portis 1.00 2.50
15TS David Carr 1.00 2.50

2003 Fleer Authentix Ticket Studs Jerseys

Inserted at a rate of 1:24, this set resembles an admission ticket, and features top NFL superstars, along with a swatch of game worn jersey.
STATED ODDS 1:24
TSBF Brett Favre 8.00 20.00
TSBU Brian Urlacher 4.00 10.00
TSCP1 Chad Pennington 2.50 6.00
TSCP2 Clinton Portis 2.50 6.00
TSDB Drew Brees 4.00 10.00
TSDC David Carr 2.50 6.00
TSDM Donovan McNabb 3.00 8.00
TSES Emmitt Smith 6.00 15.00
TSJR Jerry Rice 8.00 20.00
TSJS Jeremy Shockey 2.50 6.00
TSLT LaDainian Tomlinson 4.00 10.00
TSMV Michael Vick 3.00 8.00
TSPM Peyton Manning 10.00 25.00
TSRM Randy Moss 3.00 8.00
TSTB Tom Brady 15.00 40.00

2004 Fleer Authentix

Fleer Authentix initially released in late July 2004. The base set consists of 150-cards including 30-rookies, 10-rookies issued with an autograph of that playerâ€™s teamâ€™s coach, and 10-additional veteran Home Team cards. Hobby boxes contained 24 packs of 5 cards and carried an S.R.P. of $4.99 per pack. Five parallel sets and a variety of inserts can be found seeded in hobby and retail packs highlighted by the multi-tiered Autograph inserts. Some signed cards were issued via mail-in exchange or redemption cards with a number of those EXCH cards not yet appearing live on the secondary market as of the printing of this book.
COMP.SET w/o SP's (100) 10.00 25.00
OVERALL ROOKIE 101-140 ODDS 1:12H, 1:60R
131-140 PRINT RUN 250 SER.#'d SETS
1 Tom Brady 1.25 3.00
2 Amani Toomer .20 .50
3 Terry Glenn .25 .60
4 Eddie George .25 .60
5 Bryant Johnson .20 .50
6 Carson Palmer .25 .60
7 Matt Hasselbeck .20 .50
8 Randy Moss .25 .60
9 Chad Johnson .20 .50
10 Darrell Jackson .25 .60
11 Chris Chambers .20 .50
12 Jake Delhomme .20 .50
13 Plaxico Burress .20 .50
14 Marvin Harrison .25 .60
15 Drew Bledsoe .25 .60
16 Terrell Owens .25 .60
17 Andre Johnson .25 .60
18 Anquan Boldin .20 .50
19 Jeremy Shockey .20 .50
20 Champ Bailey .25 .60
21 Shaun Alexander .20 .50
22 DantÃ© Hall .20 .50
23 Julius Peppers .25 .60
24 Duce Staley .20 .50
25 Domanick Davis .20 .50
26 Quentin Griffin .20 .50
27 Clinton Portis .20 .50
28 Aaron Brooks .20 .50
29 Justin McCareins .20 .50
30 Joey Galloway .25 .60
31 David Boston .20 .50
32 Lee Suggs .25 .60
33 Torry Holt .25 .60
34 Daunte Culpepper .25 .60
35 Brian Urlacher .30 .75
36 Kevan Barlow .20 .50
37 Fred Taylor .20 .50
38 Eric Moulds .20 .50
39 Donovan McNabb .25 .60
40 Edgerrin James .25 .60
41 Ray Lewis .30 .75
42 Rich Gannon .25 .60
43 Joey Harrington .20 .50
44 Laveranues Coles .20 .50
45 Ricky Williams .25 .60
46 Rex Grossman .20 .50
47 Drew Brees .30 .75
48 Priest Holmes .20 .50
49 Travis Henry .20 .50
50 Tim Rattay .20 .50
51 Tony Gonzalez .25 .60
52 Stephen Davis .20 .50
53 Hines Ward .25 .60
54 Peyton Manning .75 2.00
55 Peerless Price .20 .50
56 Jerry Rice .60 1.50
57 David Carr .20 .50
58 Jamal Lewis .25 .60
59 Tim Brown .30 .75
60 Warren Sapp .25 .60
61 Tommy Maddox .20 .50
62 Joe Horn .20 .50
63 Roy Williams S .20 .50
64 Charlie Garner .25 .60
65 Deion Branch .20 .50
66 Corey Dillon .20 .50
67 Marc Bulger .20 .50
68 Trent Green .20 .50
69 Michael Vick .25 .60
70 Chad Pennington .20 .50
71 Charles Rogers .20 .50
72 Mark Brunell .25 .60
73 Tiki Barber .25 .60
74 Jeff Garcia .20 .50
75 Marshall Faulk .25 .60
76 DeShaun Foster .25 .60
77 LaVar Arrington .20 .50
78 Byron Leftwich .20 .50
79 Willis McGahee .20 .50
80 Brian Westbrook .20 .50
81 Ahman Green .25 .60
82 Kyle Boller .20 .50
83 Jevon Kearse .20 .50
84 Donald Driver .25 .60
85 Warrick Dunn .20 .50
86 Santana Moss .25 .60
87 Keyshawn Johnson .25 .60
88 Steve McNair .25 .60
89 Deuce McAllister .25 .60
90 A.J. Feeley .20 .50
91 Keenan McCardell .20 .50
92 Michael Bennett .20 .50
93 Terrell Suggs .20 .50
94 LaDainian Tomlinson .30 .75
95 Brett Favre .60 1.50
96 Emmitt Smith .50 1.25
97 Curtis Martin .25 .60
98 Jake Plummer .20 .50
99 Derrick Mason .20 .50
100 Ty Law .30 .75
101 Ben Troupe RC 1.25 3.00
102 DeAngelo Hall RC 2.00 5.00
103 Eli Manning RC 10.00 25.00
104 Cody Pickett RC 1.25 3.00
105 Matt Schaub RC 1.25 3.00
106 J.P. Losman RC 1.25 3.00
107 Chris Perry RC 1.25 3.00
108 Steven Jackson RC 2.00 5.00
109 Kevin Jones RC 1.50 4.00
110 Michael Turner RC 1.25 3.00
111 Philip Rivers RC 4.00 10.00
112 Quincy Wilson RC 1.25 3.00
113 Luke McCown RC 1.25 3.00
114 Greg Jones RC 1.25 3.00
115 Julius Jones RC 1.25 3.00
116 Sean Taylor RC 8.00 20.00
117 Kellen Winslow RC 1.25 3.00
118 Rashaun Woods RC 1.25 3.00
119 Ben Watson RC 1.50 4.00
120 Devery Henderson RC 1.25 3.00
121 Ernest Wilford RC 1.50 4.00
122 Michael Jenkins RC 1.25 3.00
123 Roy Williams RC 1.25 3.00
124 Lee Evans RC 2.00 5.00
125 Bernard Berrian RC 1.25 3.00
126 Mewelde Moore RC 1.50 4.00
127 Jammal Lord RC 1.25 3.00
128 Darius Watts RC 1.25 3.00
129 Derrick Hamilton RC 1.25 3.00
130 Devard Darling RC 1.25 3.00
131 A.Hall RC/Reid AU RC 6.00 15.00
132 T.Bell RC/Shanahan AU 12.50 30.00
133 D.Henson RC/Parcells AU 15.00 40.00
134 Roethlisber RC/Cowh.AU 30.00 80.00
135 Gallery RC/N.Turner AU RC 10.00 25.00
136 Cobbs RC/Belichick AU 50.00 100.00
137 Re.Williams RC/Del Rio AU 5.00 12.00
138 L.Fitzgerald RC/Green AU 12.50 30.00
139 Clayton RC/Gruden AU RC 10.00 25.00
140 K.Colbert RC/Fox AU RC 10.00 25.00
141 Najeh Davenport HT .50 1.25
142 Javon Walker HT .50 1.25
143 Robert Ferguson HT .50 1.25
144 Nick Barnett HT .50 1.25
145 Kabeer Gbaja-Biamila HT .50 1.25
146 Terence Newman HT .60 1.50
147 Dexter Coakley HT .50 1.25
148 Darren Woodson HT .60 1.50
149 Jason Witten HT .60 1.50
150 Antonio Bryant HT .60 1.50

2004 Fleer Authentix Balcony Blue

*VETS 1-100: 5X TO 12X BASIC CARDS
*ROOKIES 101-130: .8X TO 2X
*ROOKIES 131-140: .5X TO 1.2X
*VETS 141-150: 2X TO 5X
STATED PRINT RUN 75 SER.#'d SETS

2004 Fleer Authentix Club Box Gold

*VETS 1-100: 10X TO 25X
*ROOKIES 101-130: 1.5X TO 4X
*ROOKIES 131-140: 1.2X TO 3X
*VETS 141-150: 4X TO 10X
STATED PRINT RUN 25 SER.#'d SETS
134 Roethlisberger/Cowher AU 60.00 150.00

2004 Fleer Authentix General Admission Green

*VETS 1-100: 4X TO 10X BASIC CARDS
*ROOKIES 101-130: .6X TO 1.5X
*ROOKIES 131-140: .5X TO 1.2X
*VETS 141-150: 1.5X TO 4X
OVERALL PARALLEL ODDS 1:8 HOB, 1:48 RET
STATED PRINT RUN 100 SER.#'d SETS

2004 Fleer Authentix Mezzanine Bronze

*VETS 1-100: 6X TO 15X
*ROOKIES 101-130: 1X TO 2.5X
*ROOKIES 131-140: .6X TO 1.5X
*VETS 141-150: 2.5X TO 6X
STATED PRINT RUN 50 SER.#'d SETS

2004 Fleer Authentix Standing Room Only Purple

*VETS 1-100: 15X TO 40X BASIC CARDS
*ROOKIES 101-130: 2.5X TO 6X
*ROOKIES 131-140: 2X TO 5X
*VETS 141-150: 6X TO 15X
STATED PRINT RUN 10 SER.#'d SETS
134 Roethlisberger/Cowher AU 125.00 250.00

2004 Fleer Authentix Autographs General Admission

GENERAL ADMISSION PRINT RUN 100
*BALCONY/75: .4X TO 1X GEN.ADM/100
BALCONY PRINT RUN 75 SER.#'d SETS
*CLUB BOX/25: .8X TO 2X GEN.ADM/100
CLUB BOX PRINT RUN 25 SER.#'d SETS
*MEZZANINE/50: .5X TO 1.2X GEN.ADM/100
MEZZANINE PRINT RUN 50 SER.#'d SETS
UNPRICED STANDING ROOM #'d TO 5
AABW Brian Westbrook 6.00 15.00
AADH Dante Hall 6.00 15.00
AAJW2 Jason Witten 12.00 30.00
AAMJ Michael Jenkins 6.00 15.00
AATC Tyrone Calico 8.00 20.00
AAWM Willis McGahee 6.00 15.00

2004 Fleer Authentix Autographed Jersey Balcony

*BALCONY: .5X TO 1.2X GEN.ADMISS.
BALCONY PRINT RUN 50 SER.#'d SETS

2004 Fleer Authentix Autographed Jersey General Admission

GENERAL ADMISSION PRINT RUN 75
UNPRICED STANDING ROOM #'d TO 1
AJABW Brian Westbrook 8.00 20.00
AJADH Dante Hall 8.00 20.00
AJAJD Jake Delhomme 8.00 20.00
AJAJW2 Jason Witten 15.00 40.00
AJAMH Matt Hasselbeck 8.00 20.00
AJATC Tyrone Calico 10.00 25.00
AJAWM Willis McGahee 8.00 20.00

2004 Fleer Authentix Autographed Jersey Mezzanine

*MEZZANINE/25: .8X TO 2X GEN.ADMISS.
MEZZANINE PRINT RUN 25 SER.#'d SETS

2004 Fleer Authentix Draft Day Tickets

STATED ODDS 1:240 H, 1:480 R
DDTBR Ben Roethlisberger 20.00 50.00
DDTEM Eli Manning 20.00 50.00
DDTKW Kellen Winslow Jr. 2.50 6.00
DDTLE Lee Evans 4.00 10.00
DDTLF Larry Fitzgerald 10.00 25.00
DDTPR Philip Rivers 12.00 30.00
DDTRW Roy Williams WR 2.50 6.00
DDTRW2 Reggie Williams 2.50 6.00
DDTRW3 Rashaun Woods 2.50 6.00
DDTSJ Steven Jackson 4.00 10.00

2004 Fleer Authentix Hot Ticket

STATED ODDS 1:12 H, 1:18 R
1HT Donovan McNabb 1.00 2.50
2HT Tom Brady 5.00 12.00
3HT Brett Favre 2.50 6.00
4HT Clinton Portis .75 2.00
5HT Michael Vick 1.00 2.50
6HT Jeremy Shockey .75 2.00
7HT Peyton Manning 3.00 8.00
8HT Emmitt Smith 2.00 5.00
9HT Chad Pennington .75 2.00
10HT Randy Moss 1.00 2.50
11HT Ricky Williams 1.00 2.50
12HT Byron Leftwich .75 2.00
13HT Brian Urlacher 1.25 3.00
14HT Terrell Owens 1.00 2.50
15HT Jerry Rice 2.50 6.00

2004 Fleer Authentix Hot Ticket Jersey

STATED PRINT RUN 200-500
*PATCH/54-81: .8X TO 2X JSY/410-500
*PATCH/84: .5X TO 1.2X JSY/200
*PATCH/34: 1X TO 2.5X JSY/500
*PATCH/18-26: 1.2X TO 3X JSY/410-500
PATCH STATED PRINT RUN 4-84
UNPRICED NFL SHIELD SER.#'d TO 1
HTBF Brett Favre/500 6.00 15.00
HTBL Byron Leftwich/500 2.00 5.00
HTBU Brian Urlacher/450 3.00 8.00
HTCP Chad Pennington/500 2.00 5.00
HTCP2 Clinton Portis/500 2.00 5.00
HTDM Donovan McNabb/500 2.50 6.00
HTES Emmitt Smith/485 5.00 12.00
HTJR Jerry Rice/410 6.00 15.00
HTJS Jeremy Shockey/500 2.00 5.00
HTMV Michael Vick/200 4.00 10.00
HTPM Peyton Manning/500 8.00 20.00
HTRM Randy Moss/500 2.50 6.00
HTRW Ricky Williams/500 2.50 6.00
HTTB Tom Brady/500 8.00 20.00
HTTO Terrell Owens/460 2.50 6.00

2004 Fleer Authentix Jersey Authentix Balcony

BALCONY PRINT RUN 150 SER.#'d SETS
*GEN.ADM/205-350: .3X TO .8X BALCONY
*GEN.ADM/145-170: .4X TO 1X BALCONY
*CLUB BOX/25: 1X TO 2.5X BALCONY
CLUB BOX PRINT RUN 25 SER.#'d SETS
*MEZZANINE/75: .6X TO 1.5X BALCONY
MEZZANINE PRINT RUN 75 SER.#'d SETS
*STAND.ROOM/10: 1.5X TO 4X BALCONY
STANDING ROOM ONLY PRINT RUN 10
JAAB Anquan Boldin 2.50 6.00
JAAG Ahman Green HT 3.00 8.00
JAAJ Andre Johnson 3.00 8.00
JABF Brett Favre HT 8.00 20.00
JABL Byron Leftwich 2.50 6.00
JABW Brian Westbrook 2.50 6.00
JACJ Chad Johnson 2.50 6.00
JACP Clinton Portis 2.50 6.00
JACP2 Chad Pennington 2.50 6.00
JADC Daunte Culpepper 3.00 8.00
JADM Donovan McNabb 3.00 8.00
JADM2 Deuce McAllister 3.00 8.00
JAEJ Edgerrin James 3.00 8.00
JAES Emmitt Smith 6.00 15.00
JAJH Joey Harrington 2.50 6.00
JAJL Jamal Lewis 3.00 8.00
JAJR Jerry Rice 8.00 20.00
JAJS Jeremy Shockey 2.50 6.00
JAKG Donald Driver HT 3.00 8.00
JALA LaVar Arrington 8.00 20.00
JALT LaDainian Tomlinson 4.00 10.00
JAMF Marshall Faulk 3.00 8.00
JAMH Marvin Harrison 3.00 8.00
JAMV Michael Vick 3.00 8.00
JAPM Peyton Manning 10.00 25.00
JAQC Quincy Carter HT 2.50 6.00
JARM Randy Moss 3.00 8.00
JARW Ricky Williams 3.00 8.00
JARW2 Roy Williams S HT 2.50 6.00
JASA Shaun Alexander 2.50 6.00
JASM Santana Moss 3.00 8.00
JASM2 Steve McNair 3.00 8.00
JATB Tom Brady 15.00 40.00
JATN Terence Newman HT 3.00 8.00
JATO Terrell Owens 3.00 8.00

2004 Fleer Authentix Monday Night Matchup Jersey

STATED PRINT RUN 10-160
*PATCH/10: 1X TO 2.5X JSY/80-160
*PATCH/10: .8X TO 2X JSY/40-70
*PATCH/10: .6X TO 1.5X JSY/30
*PATCH/10: .5X TO 1.2X JSY/20
*PATCH/10: .4X TO 1X JSY/10
PATCH STATED PRINT RUN 10
AGEG A.Green/E.George/50 5.00 12.00
BFMF B.Favre/M.Faulk/120 10.00 25.00
CPJP C.Palmer/J.Plummer/70 5.00 12.00
CPRW C.Portis/Ro.Will.S/30 5.00 12.00
CPRW Pennington/Ri.Will./80 4.00 10.00
DBMF D.Brooks/M.Faulk/60 5.00 12.00
DCPM Manning/Culpepper/90 12.00 30.00
DMKJ Key.John./McNabb/100 4.00 10.00
JDBF J.Delhomme/B.Favre/10 30.00 80.00
RLPH J.Lewis/P.Holmes/40 5.00 12.00
RWTB Ri.Williams/T.Brady/150 20.00 50.00
SARW Alexander/Ro.Will.S/130 3.00 8.00
SMTG McNair/T.Gonzalez/140 4.00 10.00
TGTB T.Green/T.Brady/110 20.00 50.00
THTO T.Holt/T.Owens/160 4.00 10.00
TORM T.Owens/R.Moss/20 8.00 20.00

2004 Fleer Authentix Stadium Standouts

COMPLETE SET (10) 10.00 25.00
STATED ODDS 1:8 HOB, 1:12 RET
1SS Ricky Williams .75 2.00
2SS Anquan Boldin .60 1.50
3SS Tom Brady 4.00 10.00
4SS Brett Favre 2.00 5.00
5SS Peyton Manning 2.50 6.00
6SS Marshall Faulk .75 2.00
7SS Michael Vick .75 2.00
8SS David Carr .60 1.50
9SS Carson Palmer .75 2.00
10SS Randy Moss .75 2.00

2004 Fleer Authentix Tailgate Trios Jerseys

STATED PRINT RUN 75 SER.#'d SETS
*HOMETOWN/25: .6X TO 1.5X BASIC INSERTS
HOMETOWN 25 PRINT RUN 25 SETS
UNPRICED HOMETOWN 5 PRINT RUN 5
BHM Brooks/Horn/McAllister 8.00 20.00
BJG Bryant/Keyshawn/Glenn 8.00 20.00
BMH Bledsoe/Moulds/Henry 8.00 20.00
BWM Burress/Ward/Maddox 8.00 20.00
DGF Driver/Green/Favre 20.00 50.00
GRB Gannon/Rice/Brown 20.00 50.00
HBF Holt/Bruce/Faulk 10.00 25.00
HJA Hassel./Jackson/Alexander 8.00 20.00
HJM Harrison/James/P.Manning 25.00 60.00
MCB R.Moss/Culpep./Bennett 8.00 20.00
MMG McNair/Mason/George 8.00 20.00
OMW McNabb/Owens/Westbr. 8.00 20.00
PCB Portis/Coles/Brunell 8.00 20.00
PMM Penning/S.Moss/Martin 8.00 20.00
TSB Toomer/Shockey/Barber 8.00 20.00

2001 Fleer Authority

This 155 card set was issued by Fleer in November, 2001. The first 100 cards in the set are veterans while cards 101-155 are rookie cards which are serial numbered to 1350.
COMP.SET w/o SP's (100) 10.00 25.00
1 Brian Urlacher .40 1.00
2 James Stewart .20 .50
3 Lamar Smith .25 .60
4 Curtis Martin .25 .60
5 Shannon Sharpe .25 .60
6 Germane Crowell .20 .50
7 Daunte Culpepper .25 .60
8 Charlie Garner .25 .60
9 Jake Plummer .20 .50
10 Eric Moulds .20 .50
11 Brett Favre .60 1.50
12 Robert Smith .20 .50
13 Tim Brown .30 .75
14 David Boston .20 .50
15 Cade McNown .25 .60
16 Ahman Green .25 .60
17 Terry Glenn .25 .60
18 Wayne Chrebet .20 .50
19 Jamal Lewis .30 .75
20 Peter Warrick .20 .50
21 Peyton Manning .75 2.00
22 Ricky Williams .25 .60
23 Donovan McNabb .25 .60
24 Isaac Bruce .30 .75
25 Tim Couch .20 .50
26 Marvin Harrison .25 .60
27 Kerry Collins .20 .50
28 Kordell Stewart .20 .50
29 Keyshawn Johnson .25 .60
30 Kevin Johnson .20 .50
31 Mark Brunell .25 .60
32 Ron Dayne .25 .60
33 Doug Flutie .25 .60
34 Warrick Dunn .20 .50
35 Emmitt Smith .50 1.25
36 Jimmy Smith .25 .60
37 Amani Toomer .20 .50
38 Chad Pennington .20 .50
39 Steve McNair .25 .60
40 Brian Griese .20 .50
41 Derrick Alexander .20 .50
42 Vinny Testaverde .20 .50
43 Torrell Owens .25 .60
44 Derrick Mason .20 .50
45 Mike Anderson .20 .50
46 Michael Westbrook .20 .50
47 Rich Gannon .25 .60
48 Shaun Alexander .20 .50
49 Jevon Kearse .20 .50
50 Ed McCaffrey .25 .60
51 Tony Gonzalez .25 .60
52 Tyrone Wheatley .25 .60
53 Kurt Warner .50 1.25
54 Stephen Davis .20 .50
55 Rod Smith .25 .60
56 Deion Sanders .25 .60
57 Brad Johnson .25 .60
58 Ike Hilliard .20 .50
59 Trent Green .20 .50
60 Terrell Davis .25 .60
61 Warren Sapp .25 .60
62 Marshall Faulk .25 .60
63 Tiki Barber .25 .60
64 Keenan McCardell .25 .60
65 Joey Galloway .25 .60
66 Frank Wycheck .20 .50
67 Ricky Watters .25 .60
68 Joe Horn .20 .50
69 Fred Taylor .20 .50
70 Troy Aikman .40 1.00
71 Mike Alstott .20 .50
72 Matt Hasselbeck .20 .50
73 Aaron Brooks .20 .50
74 Terrence Wilkins .20 .50
75 Travis Prentice .20 .50
76 Eddie George .30 .75
77 Jeff Garcia .20 .50
78 Randy Moss .25 .60
79 Edgerrin James .25 .60
80 Corey Dillon .20 .50
81 Torry Holt .25 .60
82 Todd Pinkston .20 .50
83 Drew Bledsoe .25 .60
84 Antonio Freeman .30 .75
85 Marcus Robinson .25 .60
86 Muhsin Muhammad .20 .50
87 Junior Seau .25 .60
88 Zach Thomas .25 .60
89 Dorsey Levens .25 .60
90 Tim Biakabutuka .20 .50
91 Elvis Grbac .25 .60
92 Jerome Bettis .30 .75
93 Cris Carter .30 .75
94 Jerry Rice .60 1.50
95 Rob Johnson .25 .60
96 Thomas Jones .20 .50
97 Duce Staley .20 .50
98 Ray Lucas .20 .50
99 Charlie Batch .20 .50
100 Jamal Anderson .25 .60
101 Michael Vick RC 2.50 6.00
102 Drew Brees RC 12.00 30.00
103 Andre Carter RC 1.25 3.00
104 David Terrell RC 1.25 3.00
105 Koren Robinson RC 1.25 3.00
106 Rod Gardner RC 1.25 3.00
107 Santana Moss RC 1.50 4.00
108 Deuce McAllister RC 1.50 4.00
109 Freddie Mitchell RC 1.00 2.50
110 Michael Bennett RC 1.25 3.00
111 Reggie Wayne RC 2.00 5.00
112 Todd Heap RC 1.25 3.00
113 LaDainian Tomlinson RC 5.00 12.00
114 Chad Johnson RC 1.50 4.00
115 Anthony Thomas RC 1.50 4.00
116 Robert Ferguson RC 1.50 4.00
117 LaMont Jordan RC 1.50 4.00
118 Chris Chambers RC 1.00 2.50
119 Travis Henry RC 1.25 3.00
120 Marques Tuiasosopo RC 1.25 3.00
121 James Jackson RC 1.00 2.50
122 Heath Evans RC 1.25 3.00
123 Travis Minor RC 1.25 3.00
124 Rudi Johnson RC 1.50 4.00
125 Chris Weinke RC 1.25 3.00
126 Sage Rosenfels RC 1.25 3.00
127 Fred Smoot RC 1.25 3.00
128 Correll Buckhalter RC 1.00 2.50
129 Justin McCareins RC 1.25 3.00
130 Jesse Palmer RC 1.25 3.00
131 Scotty Anderson RC 1.00 2.50
132 Kevan Barlow RC 1.25 3.00
133 John Capel RC 1.00 2.50
134 Mike McMahon RC 1.25 3.00
135 Snoop Minnis RC 1.00 2.50
136 Quincy Morgan RC 1.25 3.00
137 Vinny Sutherland RC 1.00 2.50
138 Dan Alexander RC 1.25 3.00
139 Cedrick Wilson RC 1.25 3.00
140 Josh Booty RC 1.25 3.00
141 Bobby Newcombe RC 1.25 3.00
142 Josh Heupel RC 1.50 4.00
143 Ken-Yon Rambo RC 1.00 2.50
144 Eddie Berlin RC 1.00 2.50
145 Reggie Germany RC 1.00 2.50
146 Quincy Carter RC 1.25 3.00
147 Steve Smith RC 3.00 8.00
148 Dan Morgan RC 1.25 3.00
149 Chris Barnes RC 1.00 2.50
150 Alex Bannister RC 1.00 2.50
151 A.J. Feeley RC 1.25 3.00
152 Jason Brookins RC 1.50 4.00
153 Kevin Kasper RC 1.00 2.50
154 Nick Goings RC 1.50 4.00
155 Gerard Warren RC 1.25 3.00

2001 Fleer Authority Prominence 25

*ROOKIES 101-155: 2X TO 5X BASIC CARD
STATED PRINT RUN 25 SER.#'d SETS

2001 Fleer Authority Prominence 75

*VETS 1-100: 6X TO 15X BASIC CARDS
*ROOKIES 101-155: 1X TO 2.5X
STATED PRINT RUN 75 SER.#'d SETS

2001 Fleer Authority Prominence 125

*VETS 1-100: 5X TO 12X BASIC CARDS
STATED PRINT RUN 125 SER.#'d SETS

2001 Fleer Authority Autographs

Randomly inserted into packs, these 30 cards feature a mix of rookies and veterans who signed cards for the Fleer Authority product. Each player signed a different quantity of cards. The card are not serial numbered but the print runs below were provided by Fleer. The overall odds of finding an autographed card is one in 59 packs. Please note that some cards were available in packs of 2002 Fleer Platinum. Randy Moss was only available in Fleer Platinum packs.
STATED ODDS 1:59 HOB, 1:206 RET
ANNOUNCED PRIINT RUNS 25-500
1 Shaun Alexander/500* 6.00 15.00
2 Drew Brees/150* 300.00 600.00
3 Isaac Bruce/95* 8.00 20.00
4 Chris Chambers/450* 3.00 8.00
5 Wayne Chrebet/500* 3.00 8.00
6 Daunte Culpepper/25* 12.00 30.00
7 Stephen Davis/500* 3.00 8.00
8 Corey Dillon/500* 3.00 8.00
9 Marshall Faulk/25* 12.00 30.00
10 Travis Henry/400* 4.00 10.00
11 Josh Heupel/500* 5.00 12.00
12 Torry Holt/500* 5.00 12.00
13 Edgerrin James/25* 12.00 30.00
14 Jamal Lewis/450* 5.00 12.00
15 Deuce McAllister 8.00 20.00
16 Donovan McNabb/100* 15.00 40.00
17 Travis Minor/500* 4.00 10.00
18 Quincy Morgan/500* 4.00 10.00
19 Randy Moss 25.00 50.00
20 Santana Moss/250* 5.00 12.00
21 Kon Yon Rambo/500* 3.00 8.00
22 Sage Rosenfels/500* 4.00 10.00
23 Jimmy Smith/225* 4.00 10.00
24 Duce Staley/250* 3.00 8.00
25 David Terrell/225* 4.00 10.00
26 Anthony Thomas/500* 5.00 12.00
27 LaDainian Tomlinson/250* 40.00 100.00
28 Marques Tuiasosopo/500* 4.00 10.00
29 Chris Weinke/100* 6.00 15.00
2X Drew Brees EXCH 4.00 10.00

2001 Fleer Authority Figure

Randomly inserted, this 20 card set features a veteran and a rookie from the same team. These cards are serial numbered to 1750.
COMPLETE SET (20) 12.50 30.00
STATED PRINT RUN 1750 SER.#'d SETS
1 M.Vick/J.Anderson .60 1.50
2 D.Brees/D.Flutie 3.00 8.00
3 D.Terrell/M.Robinson .30 .75
4 K.Robinson/M.Hasselbeck .30 .75
5 R.Gardner/S.Davis .30 .75
6 S.Moss/W.Chrebet .40 1.00
7 D.McAllister/R.Williams .40 1.00
8 D.Morgan/B.Urlacher .50 1.25
9 R.Wayne/M.Harrison .50 1.25
10 M.Tuiasosopo/T.Brown .40 1.00
11 F.Mitchell/D.McNabb .30 .75
12 Q.Morgan/T.Couch .30 .75
13 C.Johnson/P.Warrick .40 1.00
14 R.Ferguson/B.Favre .75 2.00
15 J.Heupel/C.Weinke .40 1.00
16 A.Thomas/C.McNown .40 1.00
17 Q.Carter/E.Smith .60 1.50
18 K.Barlow/J.Garcia .30 .75
19 J.Jackson/E.James .30 .75
20 M.Bennett/R.Moss .30 .75

2001 Fleer Authority Goal Line Gear

Cards in this set feature different types of uniform swatches from a variety of players. Each was randomly inserted in packs at a rate of one in 14. Most cards included a printed serial number as noted below. Several of the card from this set were not inserted in packs but surfaced in early 2006 following the liquidation of the company's assets. Most of those did not feature a serial number.
STATED ODDS 1:14 HOB, 1:44 RET
1 David Boston Hat/100 4.00 10.00
2 David Boston JSY/450 2.50 6.00
3 Mark Brunell Hat/100 5.00 12.00
4 Mark Brunell JSY/650 3.00 8.00
5 Tim Couch Hat/200 3.00 8.00
6 Tim Couch Pants/800 2.50 6.00
7 Ron Dayne JSY/800 3.00 8.00
8 Warrick Dunn JSY/800 2.50 6.00
9 Marshall Faulk FB/200 4.00 10.00
10 Marshall Faulk Hat/200 4.00 10.00
11 Marshall Faulk JSY/500 3.00 8.00
12 Marshall Faulk Pants/175 4.00 10.00
13 Brett Favre JSY/200 10.00 25.00
14 Rich Gannon JSY/800 3.00 8.00
15 Eddie George Hat/200 5.00 12.00
16 Eddie George JSY/800 4.00 10.00
17 Marvin Harrison JSY/550 3.00 8.00
18 Marvin Harrison Pants/325 4.00 10.00
19 Torry Holt Hat/200 4.00 10.00
20 Torry Holt JSY/800 3.00 8.00
21 Torry Holt Pants/300 4.00 10.00
22 Torry Holt Shoes/400 3.00 8.00
23 Edgerrin James FB/200 4.00 10.00
24 Edgerrin James Pants/800 3.00 8.00
25 Kevin Johnson Hat/100 4.00 10.00
26 Kevin Johnson Pants/400 2.50 6.00
27 Thomas Jones Hat/100 4.00 10.00
28 Thomas Jones JSY/100 4.00 10.00
29 Jevon Kearse Hat/100 4.00 10.00
30 Jevon Kearse JSY/650 2.50 6.00
31 Jevon Kearse Pants/200 3.00 8.00
32 Donovan McNabb FB/200 4.00 10.00
33 Donovan McNabb Hat/300 4.00 10.00
34 Donovan McNabb JSY/625 3.00 8.00
35 Donovan McNabb Pants/800 3.00 8.00
36 Steve McNair Hat/100 5.00 12.00
37 Cade McNown Jsy 3.00 8.00
38 Cade McNown Hat 3.00 8.00
39 Chad Pennington JSY/800 2.50 6.00
40 Jake Plummer Hat/100 4.00 10.00
41 Jake Plummer JSY/250 3.00 8.00
42 Jake Plummer Pants/900 2.50 6.00
43 Warren Sapp JSY/800 3.00 8.00
44 Junior Seau JSY/800 3.00 8.00
45 Emmitt Smith FB/200 8.00 20.00
46 Emmitt Smith JSY/600 6.00 15.00
47 Duce Staley Hat/100 4.00 10.00
48 R.Jay Soward JSY 2.50 6.00
49 Duce Staley JSY/150 4.00 10.00
50 Fred Taylor FB/100 4.00 10.00
51 Fred Taylor Hat/750 2.50 6.00
52 Fred Taylor JSY/360 3.00 8.00
53 Brian Urlacher Hat/200 6.00 15.00
54 Brian Urlacher JSY/200 6.00 15.00
55 Kurt Warner FB/100 10.00 25.00
56 Kurt Warner Hat/100 10.00 25.00
57 Kurt Warner JSY/250 8.00 20.00
58 Kurt Warner Pants/150 10.00 25.00
59 Dez White Hat 3.00 8.00
60 Dez White JSY 3.00 8.00

2001 Fleer Authority Seal of Approval

This 15 card set features the stories of how 15 leading players made their journey from the draft to their current NFL team.
COMPLETE SET (15) 30.00 60.00
STATED ODDS 1:80 HOB, 1:120 RET
1 Donovan McNabb 1.25 3.00
2 Emmitt Smith 2.50 6.00
3 Edgerrin James 1.25 3.00
4 Brett Favre 3.00 8.00
5 Michael Vick 2.50 6.00
6 Daunte Culpepper 1.25 3.00
7 Eddie George 1.50 4.00
8 LaDainian Tomlinson 2.50 6.00
9 Jamal Lewis 1.50 4.00
10 Marshall Faulk 1.25 3.00
11 Peyton Manning 4.00 10.00
12 Randy Moss 1.25 3.00
13 Ricky Williams 1.25 3.00
14 Fred Taylor 1.00 2.50
15 Kurt Warner 2.50 6.00

2001 Fleer Authority We're Number One

This 10 card insert set features players who were selected as the first overall draft pick.
COMPLETE SET (10) 12.50 25.00
STATED ODDS 1:20 HOB, 1:40 RET
1 Tim Couch .60 1.50
2 Drew Bledsoe .75 2.00
3 Troy Aikman 1.50 4.00
4 Bo Jackson 1.50 4.00
5 George Rogers 1.00 2.50
6 Earl Campbell 1.25 3.00
7 Jim Plunkett 1.00 2.50
8 Terry Bradshaw 1.50 4.00
9 Paul Hornung 1.25 3.00
10 Michael Vick 1.00 2.50

2001 Fleer Authority We're Number One Autographs

This 10 card parallel insert set features players who were selected as the first overall draft pick. These cards were all authentically signed by the featured player.
STATED ODDS 1:100
1 Troy Aikman 30.00 80.00
2 Drew Bledsoe 15.00 30.00
3 Terry Bradshaw 50.00 100.00
4 Earl Campbell 15.00 30.00
5 Irving Fryar 15.00 30.00
6 Paul Hornung 15.00 30.00
7 Bo Jackson 50.00 120.00
8 Jim Plunkett 10.00 20.00
9 George Rogers 15.00 30.00
10 Michael Vick 20.00 50.00

2001 Fleer Authority We're Number One Jerseys

This six-card insert is a quasi parallel to the We're Number One insert set features players who were selected as the first overall draft pick. These six cards include swatches of authentic memorabilia from the featured player.

STATED ODDS 1:100
1 Drew Bledsoe 2.50 6.00
2 Terry Bradshaw 12.00 30.00
3 Tim Couch 2.00 5.00
4 John Elway 5.00 12.00
5 Bo Jackson 4.00 10.00
6 Jim Plunkett 2.50 6.00

2003 Fleer Avant

Released in November of 2003, this set consists of 90 cards, including 60 veterans and 30 rookies. Rookies 61-90 are serial numbered to 699. Boxes contained 18 packs of 4 cards. SRP was $7.99.

COMP.SET w/o SP's (60) 12.50 30.00
ROOKIE PRINT RUN 699 SER.#'d SETS
1 Priest Holmes .30 .75
2 Hines Ward .40 1.00
3 Patrick Ramsey .40 1.00
4 Deuce McAllister .40 1.00
5 Tony Gonzalez .40 1.00
6 Daunte Culpepper .40 1.00
7 Edgerrin James .40 1.00
8 Jeremy Shockey .30 .75
9 Donovan McNabb .40 1.00
10 Eddie George .40 1.00
11 Ray Lewis .50 1.25
12 LaDainian Tomlinson .50 1.25
13 Peyton Manning 1.25 3.00
14 Charlie Garner .40 1.00
15 Brad Johnson .40 1.00
16 David Carr .30 .75
17 Jerry Rice 1.00 2.50
18 Keyshawn Johnson .50 1.25
19 Ahman Green .40 1.00
20 Rich Gannon .40 1.00
21 William Green .30 .75
22 Torry Holt .40 1.00
23 Brett Favre 1.00 2.50
24 Curtis Martin .40 1.00
25 Derrick Brooks .30 .75
26 Joey Harrington .30 .75
27 Chad Pennington .30 .75
28 Koren Robinson .40 1.00
29 Clinton Portis .30 .75
30 Michael Strahan .40 1.00
31 Marvin Harrison .40 1.00
32 Travis Henry .30 .75
33 Aaron Brooks .30 .75
34 Antwaan Randle El .30 .75
35 Antonio Bryant .30 .75
36 Shaun Alexander .30 .75
37 Jake Plummer .30 .75
38 Emmitt Smith .75 2.00
39 Plaxico Burress .30 .75
40 Peerless Price .30 .75
41 Drew Bledsoe .40 1.00
42 Jeff Garcia .30 .75
43 Fred Taylor .30 .75
44 Correll Buckhalter .30 .75
45 Steve McNair .40 1.00
46 Stephen Davis .30 .75
47 Terrell Owens .40 1.00
48 Corey Dillon .30 .75
49 Marshall Faulk .40 1.00
50 Tom Brady 2.00 5.00
51 Tiki Barber .40 1.00
52 Michael Vick .40 1.00
53 Drew Brees .50 1.25
54 Chad Johnson .30 .75
55 Randy Moss .40 1.00
56 Eric Moulds .30 .75
57 Brian Urlacher .50 1.25
58 Kurt Warner .40 1.00
59 Ricky Williams .40 1.00
60 Laveranues Coles .30 .75
61 Carson Palmer RC 2.50 6.00
62 Charles Rogers RC 1.50 4.00
63 Andre Johnson RC 3.00 8.00
64 DeWayne Robertson RC 1.50 4.00
65 Terence Newman RC 2.00 5.00
66 Byron Leftwich RC 1.50 4.00
67 Terrell Suggs RC 1.50 4.00
68 Bryant Johnson RC 2.00 5.00
69 Kyle Boller RC 1.25 3.00
70 Rex Grossman RC 1.50 4.00
71 Willis McGahee RC 1.50 4.00
72 Dallas Clark RC 2.00 5.00
73 Larry Johnson RC 1.50 4.00
74 Bennie Joppru RC 1.25 3.00
75 Taylor Jacobs RC 1.25 3.00
76 Anquan Boldin RC 2.00 5.00
77 Tyrone Calico RC 1.25 3.00
78 L.J. Smith RC 2.00 5.00
79 Teyo Johnson RC 1.50 4.00
80 Kelley Washington RC 1.25 3.00
81 Jason Witten RC 5.00 12.00
82 Nate Burleson RC 1.50 4.00
83 Musa Smith RC 1.25 3.00
84 Tony Hollings RC 1.50 4.00
85 Chris Brown RC 1.25 3.00
86 Billy McMullen RC 1.25 3.00
87 Chris Simms RC 1.25 3.00
88 Artose Pinner RC 1.25 3.00
89 Quentin Griffin RC 1.50 4.00
90 Onterrio Smith RC 1.25 3.00

2003 Fleer Avant Black

*VETS 1-60: 2X TO 5X BASIC CARDS
*ROOKIES 61-90: .8X TO 2X
BLACK/199 STATED ODDS 1:3
STATED PRINT RUN 199 SER.#'d SETS

2003 Fleer Avant Candid Collection

OVERALL #'d INSERT ODDS 1:199
STATED PRINT RUN 99 SER.#'d SETS
1 Donovan McNabb 2.50 6.00
2 Brett Favre 6.00 15.00
3 Terrell Owens 2.50 6.00
4 Michael Vick 2.50 6.00
5 Kurt Warner 2.50 6.00
6 Emmitt Smith 5.00 12.00
7 Clinton Portis 2.00 5.00
8 Rich Gannon 2.50 6.00
9 Ricky Williams 2.50 6.00
10 Daunte Culpepper 2.50 6.00
11 Peyton Manning 8.00 20.00
12 Chad Pennington 2.00 5.00
13 Warren Sapp 2.50 6.00
14 Shaun Alexander 2.00 5.00
15 Priest Holmes 2.00 5.00
16 LaDainian Tomlinson 3.00 8.00
17 Jeremy Shockey 2.00 5.00
18 Randy Moss 2.50 6.00
19 Joey Harrington 2.00 5.00
20 David Carr 2.00 5.00

2003 Fleer Avant Candid Collection Jerseys

Randomly inserted in packs, this set features game worn jersey swatches. Each card is serial numbered to 100.

OVERALL MEMORABILIA ODDS 1:3
STATED PRINT RUN 100 SER.#'d SETS
1 Daunte Culpepper 2.50 6.00
2 Brett Favre 6.00 15.00
3 Joey Harrington 2.00 5.00
4 Priest Holmes 2.00 5.00
5 Peyton Manning 8.00 20.00
6 Donovan McNabb 2.50 6.00
7 Terrell Owens 2.50 6.00
8 Clinton Portis 2.00 5.00
9 Warren Sapp 2.50 6.00
10 Jeremy Shockey 2.00 5.00

2003 Fleer Avant Draw Play

COMPLETE SET (15) 15.00 40.00
OVERALL #'d INSERT ODDS 1:199
STATED PRINT RUN 535 SER.#'d SETS
1 Ricky Williams 1.00 2.50
2 Michael Vick 1.00 2.50
3 Travis Henry .75 2.00
4 Deuce McAllister 1.00 2.50
5 Clinton Portis .75 2.00
6 Ahman Green 1.00 2.50
7 Priest Holmes .75 2.00
8 Marshall Faulk 1.00 2.50
9 Emmitt Smith 2.00 5.00
10 LaDainian Tomlinson 1.25 3.00
11 Steve McNair 1.00 2.50
12 Daunte Culpepper 1.00 2.50
13 Tiki Barber 1.00 2.50
14 Donovan McNabb 1.00 2.50
15 Edgerrin James 1.00 2.50

2003 Fleer Avant Draw Play Jerseys

Randomly inserted in packs, this set features game worn jersey swatches of top NFL running backs.

OVERALL MEMORABILIA ODDS 1:3
SER.#'d UNDER 20 NOT PRICED
1 Marshall Faulk/28 5.00 12.00
2 Edgerrin James/32 5.00 12.00
3 Deuce McAllister/26 5.00 12.00
5 LaDainian Tomlinson/21 6.00 15.00

2003 Fleer Avant Materials Blue

Randomly inserted in packs, this set features game used jersey swatches. Each card is serial numbered to 250. Please note that there is both a Red and a Patch parallel of this set. The Red parallel is serial numbered to 75, and the Patch parallel is serial numbered to 25.

BLUE PRINT RUN 250 SER.#'d SETS
*PATCH/25: .8X TO 2X BLUE JSY
PATCHES PRINT RUN 25 SER.#'d SETS
*RED/75: .6X TO 1.5X BLUE JSY
RED PRINT RUN 75 SER.#'d SETS
OVERALL MEMORABILIA ODDS 1:3
1 Drew Bledsoe 2.50 6.00
2 Tom Brady 12.00 30.00
3 Drew Brees 3.00 8.00
4 David Carr 2.00 5.00
5 Daunte Culpepper 2.50 6.00
6 Corey Dillon 2.00 5.00
7 Marshall Faulk 2.50 6.00
8 Brett Favre 6.00 15.00
9 Rich Gannon 2.50 6.00
10 Eddie George 2.50 6.00
11 Ahman Green 2.50 6.00
12 Rex Grossman 2.50 6.00
13 Joey Harrington 2.00 5.00
14 Torry Holt 2.50 6.00
15 Taylor Jacobs 2.00 5.00
16 Edgerrin James 2.50 6.00
17 Andre Johnson 5.00 12.00
18 Larry Johnson 2.50 6.00
19 Byron Leftwich 2.50 6.00
20 Peyton Manning 8.00 20.00
21 Deuce McAllister 2.50 6.00
22 Donovan McNabb 2.50 6.00
23 Steve McNair 2.50 6.00
24 Peerless Price 2.00 5.00
25 Antwaan Randle El 2.00 5.00
26 Jeremy Shockey 2.00 5.00
27 Chris Simms 2.00 5.00
28 LaDainian Tomlinson 3.00 8.00
29 Brian Urlacher 3.00 8.00
30 Hines Ward 2.50 6.00

2003 Fleer Avant Work of Heart

COMPLETE SET (10) 15.00 40.00
PRINT RUN 300 SER.#'d SETS
OVERALL #'d INSERT ODDS 1:199
1 Brett Favre 3.00 8.00
2 Marshall Faulk 1.25 3.00
3 Jerry Rice 3.00 8.00
4 Michael Vick 1.25 3.00
5 Jeff Garcia 1.00 2.50
6 Joey Harrington 1.00 2.50
7 Edgerrin James 1.25 3.00
8 Donovan McNabb 1.25 3.00
9 Jeremy Shockey 1.00 2.50
10 Randy Moss 1.25 3.00

2003 Fleer Avant Work of Heart Jerseys

Randomly inserted in packs, this set features game worn jersey swatches. Each card is serial numbered to 300.

OVERALL MEMORABILIA ODDS 1:3
STATED PRINT RUN 300 SER.#'d SETS
1 Brett Favre 8.00 20.00
2 Marshall Faulk 3.00 8.00
3 Jerry Rice 8.00 20.00
4 Michael Vick 3.00 8.00
5 Jeff Garcia 2.50 6.00
6 Joey Harrington 2.50 6.00
7 Edgerrin James 3.00 8.00
8 Donovan McNabb 3.00 8.00
9 Jeremy Shockey 2.50 6.00
10 Randy Moss 3.00 8.00

2002 Fleer Box Score

Released in late November 2002, this set consists of 240-cards including 115-veterans, 35-rookies, 30-rising stars, 30-quarterbacks, and 30-all-pros. The rookies were serial numbered to 1500. Cards 151-180 were only available in rising stars mini boxes, cards 181-210 were only found in QBC mini boxes, and cards 211-240 were only found in All Pro mini boxes.

COMP.SET w/o SP's (115) 10.00 25.00
1 Brian Urlacher .40 1.00
2 Edgerrin James .30 .75
3 Ricky Williams .30 .75
4 Tim Brown .40 1.00
5 Tim Couch .25 .60
6 Kurt Warner .30 .75
7 Kendrell Bell .25 .60
8 Daunte Culpepper .30 .75
9 Anthony Thomas .30 .75
10 Marvin Harrison .30 .75
11 Jerry Rice .75 2.00
12 Eddie George .30 .75
13 Donovan McNabb .30 .75
14 Chris Chambers .25 .60
15 Emmitt Smith .60 1.50
16 David Boston .25 .60
17 Plaxico Burress .25 .60
18 Randy Moss .30 .75
19 Peyton Manning 1.00 2.50
20 Michael Vick .30 .75
21 Marshall Faulk .30 .75
22 Tom Brady 2.00 5.00
23 LaDainian Tomlinson .40 1.00
24 Shaun Alexander .25 .60
25 Curtis Martin .30 .75
26 Brett Favre .75 2.00
27 Drew Bledsoe .30 .75
28 Jeff Garcia .25 .60
29 Terrell Davis .30 .75
30 Corey Dillon .25 .60
31 Troy Brown .25 .60
32 Drew Brees .75 2.00
33 Jamal Lewis .30 .75
34 Derrick Alexander .25 .60
35 Az-Zahir Hakim .25 .60
36 Antowain Smith .30 .75
37 Muhsin Muhammad .25 .60
38 Warrick Dunn .25 .60
39 Curtis Conway .30 .75
40 Antonio Freeman .40 1.00
41 Bill Schroeder .25 .60
42 Joe Horn .25 .60
43 Peerless Price .25 .60
44 Ahman Green .30 .75
45 Marcus Robinson .30 .75
46 Aaron Brooks .25 .60
47 Cris Carter .40 1.00
48 Tiki Barber .30 .75
49 Terry Glenn .30 .75
50 Ed McCaffrey .30 .75
51 Darrell Jackson .30 .75
52 Garrison Hearst .25 .60
53 Hines Ward .30 .75
54 Deuce McAllister .30 .75
55 Rod Gardner .25 .60
56 Amani Toomer .25 .60
57 Thomas Jones .25 .60
58 Travis Henry .25 .60
59 Koren Robinson .25 .60
60 Travis Taylor .25 .60
61 Ron Dayne .30 .75
62 Robert Ferguson .30 .75
63 Chad Pennington .25 .60
64 James Allen .25 .60
65 Chris Weinke .25 .60
66 Torry Holt .30 .75
67 Chris Chandler .30 .75
68 Shane Matthews .25 .60
69 Ike Hilliard .25 .60
70 Charlie Garner .30 .75
71 Laveranues Coles .30 .75
72 Lamar Smith .25 .60
73 Rob Johnson .30 .75
74 Qadry Ismail .25 .60
75 James Jackson .25 .60
76 Wayne Chrebet .25 .60
77 Priest Holmes .25 .60
78 Michael Westbrook .25 .60
79 Michael Pittman .30 .75
80 Derrick Mason .25 .60
81 Dominic Rhodes .25 .60
82 Eric Moulds .25 .60
83 Fred Taylor .25 .60
84 Corey Bradford .25 .60
85 Steve McNair .30 .75
86 Tyrone Wheatley .30 .75
87 Peter Warrick .25 .60
88 Freddie Mitchell .25 .60
89 Peter Boulware .25 .60
90 Kevin Johnson .25 .60
91 Jermaine Lewis .25 .60
92 Joey Galloway .30 .75
93 Stephen Davis .25 .60
94 James Thrash .30 .75
95 James Stewart .25 .60
96 Quincy Morgan .25 .60
97 Dorsey Levens .30 .75
98 Johnnie Morton .30 .75
99 Rocket Ismail .30 .75
100 Rod Smith .30 .75
101 David Terrell .25 .60
102 Kordell Stewart .25 .60
103 Marty Booker .25 .60
104 Brian Griese .25 .60
105 Snoop Minnis .25 .60
106 Jake Plummer .25 .60
107 Keenan McCardell .30 .75
108 Duce Staley .25 .60
109 Isaac Bruce .40 1.00
110 Bubba Franks .25 .60
111 Keyshawn Johnson .30 .75
112 Kevan Barlow .25 .60
113 Reggie Wayne .30 .75
114 Michael Bennett .25 .60
115 Santana Moss .30 .75
116 David Carr RC .60 1.50
117 Joey Harrington RC .60 1.50
118 Antwaan Randle El RC .75 2.00
119 Eric Crouch RC 1.00 2.50
120 Javon Walker RC 1.00 2.50
121 William Green RC .75 2.00
122 Patrick Ramsey RC .75 2.00
123 Clinton Portis RC 1.00 2.50
124 Andre Davis RC .60 1.50
125 T.J. Duckett RC .60 1.50
126 Ladell Betts RC 1.00 2.50
127 Marquise Walker RC .60 1.50
128 Maurice Morris RC .75 2.00
129 Brian Westbrook RC 1.25 3.00
130 Phillip Buchanon RC 1.00 2.50
131 Tim Carter RC .75 2.00
132 Zak Kustok RC .60 1.50
133 Chester Taylor RC 1.00 2.50
134 Josh Reed RC .75 2.00
135 Kurt Kittner RC .60 1.50
136 Cliff Russell RC .60 1.50
137 Travis Fisher RC .75 2.00
138 Jerramy Stevens RC 1.00 2.50
139 Verron Haynes RC .60 1.50
140 Ricky Williams RC .75 2.00
141 Randy McMichael RC 1.00 2.50
142 Dwight Freeney RC 1.25 3.00
143 Lito Sheppard RC 1.00 2.50
144 Mike Williams RC .60 1.50
145 Jason McAddley RC .75 2.00
146 Deion Branch RC 1.00 2.50
147 Daniel Graham RC .75 2.00
148 J.T. O'Sullivan RC .75 2.00
149 Freddie Milons RC .60 1.50
150 Ron Johnson RC .75 2.00
151 Ashley Lelie RC .40 1.00
152 Roy Williams RC .40 1.00
153 Donte Stallworth RC .60 1.50
154 Randy Fasani RC .40 1.00
155 Antonio Bryant RC .60 1.50
156 Julius Peppers RC 1.00 2.50
157 Jabar Gaffney RC .40 1.00
158 Chad Hutchinson RC .40 1.00
159 DeShaun Foster RC .60 1.50
160 Micah Ross RC .40 1.00
161 Rocky Calmus RC .50 1.25
162 Travis Stephens RC .40 1.00
163 Quentin Jammer RC .60 1.50
164 Napoleon Harris RC .50 1.25
165 Jeremy Shockey RC .60 1.50
166 Rohan Davey RC .60 1.50
167 Najeh Davenport RC .40 1.00
168 Adrian Peterson RC .50 1.25
169 Ed Reed RC 2.50 6.00
170 Ben Leber RC .40 1.00
171 Robert Thomas RC .40 1.00
172 Lamar Gordon RC .50 1.25
173 Reche Caldwell RC .50 1.25
174 Michael Lewis RC .50 1.25
175 Ryan Sims RC .60 1.50
176 David Garrard RC .50 1.25
177 Jonathan Wells RC .50 1.25
178 Albert Haynesworth RC .60 1.50
179 Josh McCown RC .60 1.50
180 John Henderson RC .50 1.25
181 Jake Plummer QBC .30 .75
182 Michael Vick QBC .40 1.00
183 Chris Redman QBC .30 .75
184 Drew Bledsoe QBC .40 1.00
185 Jim Miller QBC .30 .75
186 Jon Kitna QBC .30 .75
187 Tim Couch QBC .30 .75
188 Quincy Carter QBC .30 .75
189 Brian Griese QBC .30 .75
190 Mike McMahon QBC .30 .75
191 Brett Favre QBC 1.00 2.50
192 David Carr QBC .30 .75
193 Peyton Manning QBC 1.25 3.00
194 Mark Brunell QBC .40 1.00
195 Trent Green QBC .30 .75
196 Jay Fiedler QBC .40 1.00
197 Daunte Culpepper QBC .40 1.00
198 Tom Brady QBC 2.50 6.00
199 Aaron Brooks QBC .30 .75
200 Kerry Collins QBC .30 .75
201 Vinny Testaverde QBC .30 .75
202 Rich Gannon QBC .40 1.00
203 Donovan McNabb QBC .40 1.00
204 Kordell Stewart QBC .30 .75
205 Doug Flutie QBC .40 1.00
206 Jeff Garcia QBC .30 .75
207 Trent Dilfer QBC .30 .75
208 Kurt Warner QBC .40 1.00
209 Brad Johnson QBC .40 1.00
210 Steve McNair QBC .40 1.00
211 Sam Madison AP .30 .75
212 Bruce Matthews AP .30 .75
213 Brett Favre AP 1.00 2.50
214 Cris Carter AP .50 1.25
215 Michael Strahan AP .40 1.00
216 Ray Lewis AP .50 1.25
217 Randy Moss AP .40 1.00
218 Jerome Bettis AP .50 1.25
219 Warren Sapp AP .40 1.00
220 Junior Seau AP .40 1.00
221 Emmitt Smith AP .75 2.00
222 Jimmy Smith AP .40 1.00
223 Mike Alstott AP .30 .75
224 Zach Thomas AP .40 1.00
225 Marshall Faulk AP .40 1.00
226 John Lynch AP .40 1.00
227 Larry Allen AP .50 1.25
228 Kurt Warner AP .40 1.00
229 Eddie George AP .40 1.00
230 Tony Gonzalez AP .40 1.00
231 Marvin Harrison AP .40 1.00
232 Terrell Davis AP .40 1.00
233 Peyton Manning AP 1.25 3.00
234 Terrell Owens AP .40 1.00
235 Jevon Kearse AP .30 .75
236 Jerry Rice AP 1.00 2.50
237 Shannon Sharpe AP .40 1.00
238 Rod Woodson AP .50 1.25
239 Mark Brunell AP .40 1.00
240 Tim Brown AP .50 1.25

2002 Fleer Box Score Classic Miniatures

COMPLETE SET (30) 12.50 30.00
*MINIS: .8X TO 2X BASIC CARDS
CLASSIC MINIATURE SET IN MINI BOXES

2002 Fleer Box Score Classic Miniatures First Edition

*MIN FIRST EDIT/100: 3X TO 8X BASIC CARDS
FIRST EDITION PRINT RUN 100

2002 Fleer Box Score First Edition

*VETS 1-115: 3X TO 8X BASIC CARDS
*ROOKIES 116-150: .8X TO 2X
*ROOKIES 151-180: 1.2X TO 3X
*QBC 181-210: 2.5X TO 6X
*AP 211-240: 2.5X TO 6X
STATED PRINT RUN 100 SER.#'d SETS

2002 Fleer Box Score All Pro Roster Jerseys

Inserted one per All Pro mini box, this set features authentic player jersey swatches from three or four NFL superstars.

ONE PER ALL PRO MINI BOX
1 Carter/Moss/Rice/Brown 12.00 30.00
2 Favre/E.Smith/Rice/Moss 12.00 30.00
3 Favre/Warner/Mann/Brunell 15.00 40.00
4 Gonzalez/Sharpe/Alstott 5.00 12.00
5 Madison/Lynch/Woodson 6.00 15.00
6 Seau/Lewis/Z.Thomas 5.00 12.00
7 E.Smith/Faulk/Grge/T.Dav 10.00 25.00
8 J.Smith/Harrison/Owens 5.00 12.00
9 Strahan/Kearse/Sapp 5.00 12.00
10 Warn/Faulk/Mann/Grge 15.00 40.00

2002 Fleer Box Score Classic Miniatures Jerseys

Inserted at a rate of one per classic miniatures box, this 10-card set features mini versions of the regular issue set along with a swatch of game used jersey.

ONE PER CLASSIC MINIATURES MINI BOX
1 Brian Urlacher 4.00 10.00
2 Ricky Williams 3.00 8.00
3 Tom Brady 20.00 50.00
4 Shaun Alexander 2.50 6.00
5 Anthony Thomas 3.00 8.00
6 Chris Chambers 2.50 6.00
7 David Boston 2.50 6.00
8 LaDainian Tomlinson 4.00 10.00
9 Plaxico Burress 2.50 6.00
10 Corey Dillon 2.50 6.00

2002 Fleer Box Score Debuts

Randomly inserted in packs, this 15-card set features top rookies with debut stats on the card fronts. The cards were serial numbered to 2002.

COMPLETE SET (15) 15.00 40.00
STATED PRINT RUN 2002 SER.#'d SETS
1 Antwaan Randle El .75 2.00
2 T.J. Duckett .60 1.50
3 Donte Stallworth 1.00 2.50
4 Deion Branch 1.00 2.50
5 William Green .75 2.00
6 Brian Westbrook 1.25 3.00
7 Jabar Gaffney .60 1.50
8 Clinton Portis 1.00 2.50
9 Joey Harrington .60 1.50
10 Andre Davis .60 1.50
11 Javon Walker 1.00 2.50
12 Antonio Bryant 1.00 2.50
13 Jeremy Shockey 1.00 2.50
14 Josh Reed .75 2.00
15 David Carr .60 1.50

2002 Fleer Box Score Jersey Rack Quads

Randomly inserted in packs, this 7-card set features four NFL stars on each card along with a swatch of game-used jersey per player. The cards were serial numbered to 100.

STATED PRINT RUN 100 SER.#'d SETS
1 Grg/McN/McNabb/Free 10.00 25.00
2 Garcia/TO/Faulk/Warner 8.00 20.00
3 Moss/Culp/Grn/Favre 20.00 50.00
4 Lewis/Mann/Emmitt/Tlr 25.00 60.00
5 Bost/Harr/Tomlnsn/Martin 10.00 25.00
6 R.Will/Chamb/Edge/Marvin 8.00 20.00
7 Brady/Smith/Faulk/Warner 50.00 120.00

2002 Fleer Box Score Jersey Rack Triples

Randomly inserted in packs, this 7-card set features three NFL stars on the card fronts along with a swatch of game-used jersey per player. The cards were serial numbered to 300.

STATED PRINT RUN 300 SER.#'d SETS
1 Brady/Favre/Warner 25.00 60.00
2 Moss/Rice/Holt 15.00 40.00
3 Stewart/Burress/Bettis 8.00 20.00
4 Thomas/Green/Alexander 6.00 15.00
5 Vick/Culpepper/McNabb 6.00 15.00

2002 Fleer Box Score Press Clippings

Inserted in packs at a rate of 1:18, this 15-card sets features both rookies and veterans who often make the newspaper headlines.

STATED ODDS 1:18
1 David Carr .75 2.00
2 Joey Harrington .75 2.00
3 Drew Bledsoe 1.00 2.50
4 Michael Vick 1.00 2.50
5 Kordell Stewart .75 2.00
6 Aaron Brooks .75 2.00
7 Donovan McNabb 1.00 2.50
8 Rich Gannon 1.00 2.50
9 Drew Brees 2.50 6.00
10 Peyton Manning 3.00 8.00
11 Tom Brady 6.00 15.00
12 Brett Favre 2.50 6.00
13 Jeff Garcia .75 2.00
14 Kurt Warner 1.00 2.50
15 Daunte Culpepper 1.00 2.50

2002 Fleer Box Score Press Clippings Jerseys

Inserted in packs at a rate of 1:14, this 15-card sets features both rookies and veterans cards with the addition of a swatch of game used jersey. A Patch version of each card was also produced and serial numbered of 50.

STATED ODDS 1:14
*PATCH/50: 1X TO 2.5X BASIC JSY
PATCHES PRINT RUN 50 SER.#'d SETS
1 Shaun Alexander 2.50 6.00
2 Jerome Bettis 4.00 10.00
3 David Boston 2.50 6.00
4 Tim Couch 2.50 6.00
5 Marvin Harrison 3.00 8.00
6 Torry Holt 3.00 8.00
7 Jamal Lewis 3.00 8.00
8 Curtis Martin 3.00 8.00
9 Jerry Rice 6.00 15.00
10 Emmitt Smith 6.00 15.00
11 Fred Taylor 2.50 6.00
12 Anthony Thomas 3.00 8.00
13 LaDainian Tomlinson 4.00 10.00
14 Brian Urlacher 4.00 10.00
15 Michael Vick 3.00 8.00

2002 Fleer Box Score QBXtra Jerseys

Inserted at a rate of one per QB Club mini box, this 10-card set features swatches of game worn jersey cut out in the shape of an "X" on the card front

ONE PER QBC MINI BOX
1 Tom Brady SP 20.00 50.00
2 Tim Couch 2.50 6.00
3 Daunte Culpepper 3.00 8.00
4 Brett Favre 8.00 20.00
5 Jeff Garcia 2.50 6.00
6 Brian Griese 2.50 6.00
7 Peyton Manning SP 10.00 25.00
8 Donovan McNabb 3.00 8.00
9 Michael Vick SP 3.00 8.00
10 Kurt Warner 3.00 8.00

2002 Fleer Box Score Red Shirt Freshman

Inserted at a rate of one per rising stars mini box, this 10-card set features rookie-player game-worn jersey cards with the player being outlined in a red border.

ONE PER RISING STARS MINI BOX
1 Deion Branch 3.00 8.00
2 Antonio Bryant 3.00 8.00
3 David Carr 2.00 5.00
4 DeShaun Foster 3.00 8.00
5 William Green 2.50 6.00
6 Joey Harrington 2.00 5.00
7 Clinton Portis SP 3.00 8.00
8 Josh Reed 2.50 6.00
9 Jeremy Shockey 3.00 8.00
10 Javon Walker 3.00 8.00

2002 Fleer Box Score Yard Markers

Inserted at a rate of 1:9, this 20-card set features top NFL veterans with a significant 2001 stat on the card front along with the title "Yard Markers."

COMPLETE SET (20) 15.00 40.00
STATED ODDS 1:9
1 Tom Brady 5.00 12.00
2 Antowain Smith .75 2.00
3 Randy Moss .75 2.00
4 Daunte Culpepper .75 2.00
5 Edgerrin James .75 2.00
6 Peyton Manning 2.50 6.00
7 Eddie George .75 2.00
8 Steve McNair .75 2.00
9 Ricky Williams .75 2.00
10 Chris Chambers .60 1.50
11 Jeff Garcia .60 1.50
12 Terrell Owens .75 2.00
13 Marshall Faulk .75 2.00
14 Kurt Warner .75 2.00
15 Donovan McNabb .75 2.00
16 Freddie Mitchell .60 1.50
17 Ahman Green .75 2.00
18 Brett Favre 2.00 5.00
19 Plaxico Burress .60 1.50
20 Kordell Stewart .60 1.50

2002 Fleer Box Score Yard Markers Jerseys

Inserted at a rate of 1:14, this 20-card set features top NFL veterans with a significant 2001 stat on the card front along with the words "Yard Markers." The cards also contain a swatch of game worn jersey within the letter "Y" on the front.

STATED ODDS 1:14
1 Tom Brady 25.00 60.00
2 Plaxico Burress 3.00 8.00
3 Chris Chambers 3.00 8.00
4 Daunte Culpepper 4.00 10.00
5 Marshall Faulk 4.00 10.00
6 Brett Favre 10.00 25.00
7 Antonio Freeman 5.00 12.00
8 Jeff Garcia 3.00 8.00
9 Eddie George 4.00 10.00
10 Ahman Green 4.00 10.00
11 Edgerrin James 4.00 10.00
12 Peyton Manning 12.00 30.00
13 Donovan McNabb 4.00 10.00
14 Steve McNair 4.00 10.00
15 Randy Moss 4.00 10.00
16 Terrell Owens 4.00 10.00
17 Antowain Smith 4.00 10.00
18 Kordell Stewart 3.00 8.00
19 Kurt Warner 4.00 10.00
20 Ricky Williams 4.00 10.00

2002 Fleer Box Score Yard Markers Duals

Inserted at a rate of 1:108,this 10 card set features two top NFL veterans with a significant 2001 stat on card front and back per player along with the words yard markers.

COMPLETE SET (10) 25.00 60.00
STATED ODDS 1:108
1 T.Brady/A.Smith 10.00 25.00
2 R.Moss/D.Culpepper 1.50 4.00
3 E.James/P.Manning 5.00 12.00
4 E.George/S.McNair 1.50 4.00
5 R.Williams/C.Chambers 1.50 4.00
6 J.Garcia/T.Owens 1.50 4.00
7 M.Faulk/W.Warner 1.50 4.00
8 D.McNabb/F.Mitchell 1.50 4.00
9 A.Green/B.Favre 4.00 10.00
10 P.Burress/K.Stewart 1.25 3.00

2002 Fleer Box Score Yard Markers Duals Jerseys

Randomly inserted in packs,this 10 card set features two top NFL veterans with a significant 2001 stat on card front and back per player along with the words yard markers. Cards also feature a swatch of game worn jersey on card front and back for each player cut out in the shape of a "Y"

STATED PRINT RUN 100 SER.#'d SETS
1 T.Brady/A.Smith 30.00 80.00
2 P.Burress/K.Stewart 4.00 10.00
3 M.Faulk/K.Warner 5.00 12.00
4 J.Garcia/T.Owens 5.00 12.00
5 E.George/S.McNair 5.00 12.00
6 A.Green/B.Favre 12.00 30.00
7 E.James/P.Manning 15.00 40.00
8 D.McNabb/A.Freeman 6.00 15.00
9 R.Moss/D.Culpepper 5.00 12.00
10 R.Williams/C.Chambers 5.00 12.00

1998 Fleer Brilliants

The 1998 Fleer Brilliants set was issued in one series totalling 150 cards and was distriubted in five-card packs with a suggested price of $4.99. The set featues color action player photos printed using super-bright mirror foil laminate on 24 pt. plastic styrene card stock with an etched radial pattern background. The set contains a 50-card Rookie subset seeded into packs at the rate of 1:2.

COMPLETE SET (150) 40.00 100.00
1 John Elway .75 2.00
2 Curtis Conway .40 1.00
3 Danny Wuerffel .40 1.00
4 Emmitt Smith .75 2.00
5 Marvin Harrison .40 1.00
6 Antowain Smith .40 1.00
7 James Stewart .30 .75
8 Junior Seau .40 1.00
9 Herman Moore .40 1.00
10 Drew Bledsoe .40 1.00
11 Rae Carruth .30 .75
12 Trent Dilfer .40 1.00
13 Derrick Alexander .40 1.00
14 Ike Hilliard .30 .75
15 Bruce Smith .40 1.00
16 Warren Moon .50 1.25
17 Jermaine Lewis .30 .75
18 Mike Alstott .30 .75
19 Robert Brooks .40 1.00
20 Jerome Bettis .50 1.25
21 Brett Favre 1.00 2.50
22 Garrison Hearst .30 .75
23 Neil O'Donnell .40 1.00
24 Joey Galloway .40 1.00
25 Barry Sanders .75 2.00
26 Donnell Bennett .30 .75
27 Jamal Anderson .40 1.00
28 Isaac Bruce .50 1.25
29 Chris Chandler .40 1.00
30 Kordell Stewart .30 .75
31 Corey Dillon .30 .75
32 Troy Aikman .60 1.50
33 Frank Sanders .30 .75
34 Cris Carter .50 1.25
35 Greg Hill .30 .75
36 Tony Martin .40 1.00
37 Shannon Sharpe .40 1.00
38 Wayne Chrebet .30 .75
39 Trent Green .30 .75
40 Warrick Dunn .30 .75
41 Michael Irvin .50 1.25
42 Eddie George .40 1.00
43 Carl Pickens .40 1.00
44 Wesley Walls .40 1.00
45 Steve McNair .40 1.00
46 Bert Emanuel .40 1.00
47 Terry Glenn .40 1.00
48 Elvis Grbac .40 1.00
49 Charles Way .30 .75
50 Steve Young .60 1.50
51 Deion Sanders .40 1.00
52 Keyshawn Johnson .40 1.00
53 Kerry Collins .30 .75
54 O.J. McDuffie .40 1.00
55 Ricky Watters .40 1.00
56 Derrick Thomas .50 1.25
57 Antonio Freeman .50 1.25
58 Jake Plummer .30 .75
59 Andre Reed .50 1.25
60 Jerry Rice 1.25 3.00
61 Dorsey Levens .40 1.00
62 Eddie Kennison .30 .75
63 Marshall Faulk .40 1.00
64 Michael Jackson .30 .75
65 Karim Abdul-Jabbar .30 .75
66 Andre Rison .40 1.00
67 Glenn Foley .30 .75
68 Jake Reed .40 1.00
69 Tony Banks .40 1.00
70 Dan Marino 1.00 2.50
71 Bryan Still .30 .75
72 Tim Brown .50 1.25
73 Charles Johnson .30 .75
74 Jeff George .40 1.00
75 Jimmy Smith .40 1.00
76 Ben Coates .40 1.00
77 Rob Moore .30 .75
78 Johnnie Morton .40 1.00
79 Peter Boulware .30 .75
80 Curtis Martin .40 1.00
81 James McKnight .30 .75
82 Danny Kanell .30 .75
83 Brad Johnson .40 1.00
84 Amani Toomer .30 .75
85 Terry Allen .40 1.00
86 Rod Smith .40 1.00
87 Keenan McCardell .40 1.00
88 Leslie Shepherd .30 .75
89 Irving Fryar .40 1.00
90 Terrell Davis .40 1.00
91 Robert Smith .30 .75
92 Duce Staley .30 .75
93 Rickey Dudley .30 .75
94 Bobby Hoying .40 1.00
95 Terrell Owens .40 1.00
96 Fred Lane .30 .75
97 Natrone Means .40 1.00
98 Yancey Thigpen .30 .75
99 Reggie White .50 1.25
100 Mark Brunell .40 1.00
101 Ahman Green RC 1.25 3.00
102 Skip Hicks RC .75 2.00
103 Hines Ward RC 4.00 10.00
104 Marcus Nash RC .60 1.50
105 Terry Hardy RC .60 1.50
106 Patrick Johnson RC .75 2.00
107 Tremayne Stephens RC .60 1.50
108 Joe Jurevicius RC 1.00 2.50
109 Moses Moreno RC .60 1.50
110 Charles Woodson RC 2.50 6.00
111 Kevin Dyson RC .75 2.00
112 Alvis Whitted RC .75 2.00
113 Michael Pittman RC 1.00 2.50
114 Stephen Alexander RC .75 2.00
115 Tavian Banks RC .75 2.00
116 John Avery RC .75 2.00
117 Keith Brooking RC 1.00 2.50
118 Jerome Pathon RC .75 2.00
119 Terry Fair RC .75 2.00
120 Peyton Manning RC 12.00 30.00
121 R.W. McQuarters RC 1.00 2.50
122 Charlie Batch RC 1.00 2.50
123 Jonathan Quinn RC .75 2.00
124 Chris Fuamatu-Ma'afala RC .75 2.00
125 Jacquez Green RC .75 2.00
126 Germane Crowell RC .60 1.50
127 Oronde Gadsden RC .75 2.00
128 Koy Detmer .75 2.00
129 Robert Holcombe RC .60 1.50
130 Curtis Enis RC .75 2.00
131 Brian Griese RC 1.25 3.00
132 Tony Simmons RC .75 2.00
133 Vonnie Holliday RC .75 2.00
134 Alonzo Mayes RC .60 1.50
135 Jon Ritchie RC .75 2.00
136 Robert Edwards RC .75 2.00
137 Mike Vanderjagt RC .75 2.00
138 Jonathan Linton RC .75 2.00
139 Fred Taylor RC 1.25 3.00
140 Randy Moss RC 5.00 12.00
141 Rod Rutledge RC .60 1.50
142 Andre Wadsworth RC 1.00 2.50
143 Rashaan Shehee RC .60 1.50
144 Shaun Williams RC .75 2.00
145 Mikhael Ricks RC .75 2.00
146 Wade Richey RC .60 1.50
147 Carlos King RC .60 1.50
148 Tim Dwight RC 1.00 2.50
149 Scott Frost RC .60 1.50
150 Ryan Leaf RC .75 2.00
P74 Jeff George Promo .40 1.00

1998 Fleer Brilliants 24-Karat Gold

*1-100 VETS/24: 10X TO 25X BASIC CARDS
*101-150 ROOKIES/24: 4X TO 10X
STATED PRINT RUN 24 SETS
25 Barry Sanders 300.00 500.00
60 Jerry Rice 300.00 500.00
120 Peyton Manning 500.00 1000.00
139 Fred Taylor 60.00 125.00

1998 Fleer Brilliants Blue

COMPLETE SET (150) 150.00 300.00
*1-100 VETS: 1.5X TO 4X BASIC CARDS
*101-150 ROOKIES: .6X TO 1.5X BASIC CARDS
1-100 VETERAN STATED ODDS 1:3
101-150 ROOKIE STATED ODDS 1:6

1998 Fleer Brilliants Gold

*1-100 VETS/99: 8X TO 20X BASIC CARDS
*101-150 ROOKIES/99: 2X TO 5X
STATED PRINT RUN 99 SER.#'d SETS

1998 Fleer Brilliants Illuminators

Randomly inserted into packs at the rate of one in 10, this 15-card set features color action player photos printed on team color coded super bright mirror foil cards.

COMPLETE SET (15) 30.00 60.00
STATED ODDS 1:10
1 Robert Edwards .75 2.00
2 Fred Taylor 1.50 4.00
3 Kordell Stewart 1.50 4.00
4 Troy Aikman 3.00 8.00
5 Curtis Enis .50 1.25
6 Drew Bledsoe 2.50 6.00
7 Curtis Martin 1.50 4.00
8 Joey Galloway 1.00 2.50
9 Jerome Bettis 1.50 4.00
10 Glenn Foley 1.00 2.50
11 Karim Abdul-Jabbar 1.50 4.00
12 Jake Plummer 1.50 4.00
13 Jerry Rice 3.00 8.00
14 Charlie Batch 1.00 2.50
15 Jacquez Green .75 2.00

1998 Fleer Brilliants Shining Stars

Randomly inserted into packs at the rate of one in 20, this 15-card set features color action photos of top players printed on two-sided super bright mirror foil cards. A Shining Stars Pulsars parallel set was also produced which features two-sided rainbow holographic foil cards with an embossed star pattern in the background.

COMPLETE SET (15) 30.00 80.00
STATED ODDS 1:20
*PULSAR STARS: 2X TO 5X BASIC INSERTS
*PULSAR ROOKIES: 1.2X TO 3X BAS.INS.
PULSARS STATED ODDS 1:400
1 Terrell Davis 1.50 4.00
2 Emmitt Smith 4.00 10.00
3 Barry Sanders 4.00 10.00
4 Mark Brunell 1.25 3.00
5 Brett Favre 5.00 12.00
6 Ryan Leaf 1.00 2.50
7 Randy Moss 3.00 8.00
8 Warrick Dunn 1.25 3.00
9 Peyton Manning 8.00 20.00
10 Corey Dillon 1.25 3.00
11 Dan Marino 5.00 12.00
12 Keyshawn Johnson 1.25 3.00
13 John Elway 4.00 10.00
14 Eddie George 1.25 3.00
15 Antowain Smith 1.00 2.50

1999 Fleer Focus

Released as a 175-card set, 1999 Fleer Focus football is comprised of 100 veteran cards and 75 rookie subset cards seeded at one in two packs. Base cards are white-bordered and highlighted with gold foil. Rookie cards are divided up into four tiers, Quarterbacks are serial numbered out of 2250, Running Backs are numbered out of 2500, Receivers are numbered out 3850, and Defense/others are not serial numbered. Fleer Focus was packaged in 24-pack boxes with five cards per pack and carried a suggested retail price of $2.99.

COMPLETE SET (175) 100.00 200.00
COMP.SET w/o SP's (100) 20.00 40.00
1 Randy Moss .25 .60
2 Andre Rison .25 .60
3 Ed McCaffrey .25 .60
4 Jerry Rice .75 2.00
5 Tim Biakabutuka .25 .60
6 Wayne Chrebet .20 .50
7 Deion Sanders .25 .60
8 Ricky Watters .25 .60
9 Skip Hicks .20 .50
10 Charlie Batch .20 .50
11 Joey Galloway .25 .60
12 Stephen Alexander .20 .50
13 Curtis Conway .25 .60
14 Garrison Hearst .20 .50
15 Kerry Collins .20 .50
16 Cris Carter .30 .75
17 Eddie George .25 .60
18 Eric Moulds .20 .50
19 Vinny Testaverde .20 .50
20 Curtis Enis .20 .50
21 Gary Brown .20 .50
22 Junior Seau .25 .60
23 Kevin Dyson .20 .50
24 Jeff Blake .25 .60
25 Herman Moore .25 .60
26 Natrone Means .25 .60
27 Terry Glenn .25 .60
28 Fred Taylor .20 .50
29 Ben Coates .25 .60
30 Corey Dillon .20 .50
31 Eddie Kennison .25 .60
32 Byron Bam Morris .20 .50
33 Doug Pederson .20 .50
34 Jamal Anderson .25 .60
35 Michael Westbrook .20 .50
36 Peyton Manning 1.00 2.50
37 Carl Pickens .25 .60
38 Drew Bledsoe .25 .60
39 Jim Harbaugh .25 .60
40 Kurt Warner RC 2.00 5.00
41 Mark Chmura .20 .50
42 Hines Ward .25 .60
43 Terry Kirby .20 .50
44 Brett Favre .60 1.50
45 Kordell Stewart .20 .50
46 Leslie Shepherd .20 .50
47 Marshall Faulk .25 .60
48 Troy Aikman .40 1.00
49 Isaac Bruce .30 .75
50 Michael Irvin .30 .75

51 Robert Smith .20 .50
52 Dorsey Levens .25 .60
53 Duce Staley .20 .50
54 Jake Plummer .20 .50
55 Adrian Murrell .20 .50
56 Antonio Freeman .25 .60
57 Jerome Bettis .30 .75
58 Elvis Grbac .20 .50
59 Keyshawn Johnson .25 .60
60 Steve Beuerlein .25 .60
61 Yancey Thigpen .20 .50
62 Doug Flutie .30 .75
63 Jacquez Green .20 .50
64 Jimmy Smith .25 .60
65 Tim Brown .30 .75
66 Jason Sehorn .25 .60
67 Muhsin Muhammad .20 .50
68 Shannon Sharpe .25 .60
69 Terrell Owens .25 .60
70 Keenan McCardell .25 .60
71 Rich Gannon .25 .60
72 Scott Mitchell .20 .50
73 Warrick Dunn .20 .50
74 Brad Johnson .25 .60
75 Charles Johnson .20 .50
76 Chris Chandler .25 .60
77 Marcus Pollard .20 .50
78 Mike Alstott .20 .50
79 Bubby Brister .20 .50
80 Jon Kitna .20 .50
81 Randall Cunningham .25 .60
82 Antowain Smith .20 .50
83 Curtis Martin .25 .60
84 Steve McNair .25 .60
85 Tony Gonzalez .25 .60
86 O.J. McDuffie .25 .60
87 Steve Young .40 1.00
88 Terrell Davis .25 .60
89 Mark Brunell .25 .60
90 Napoleon Kaufman .20 .50
91 Priest Holmes .20 .50
92 Trent Dilfer .20 .50
93 Brian Griese .20 .50
94 J.J. Stokes .20 .50
95 Karim Abdul-Jabbar .20 .50
96 Barry Sanders .50 1.25
97 Dan Marino .60 1.50
98 Emmitt Smith .50 1.25
99 Marvin Harrison .25 .60
100 Rod Smith .25 .60
101 Champ Bailey RC .75 2.00
102 Fernando Bryant RC .40 1.00
103 Chris Claiborne RC .40 1.00
104 Antuan Edwards RC .40 1.00
105 Martin Gramatica RC .40 1.00
106 Andy Katzenmoyer RC .50 1.25
107 Jevon Kearse RC .50 1.25
108 Chris McAlister RC .40 1.00
109 Al Wilson RC .60 1.50
110 Antoine Winfield RC .40 1.00
111 Karsten Bailey RC 1.00 2.50
112 D'Wayne Bates RC 1.00 2.50
113 Marty Booker RC 1.00 2.50
114 David Boston RC 1.00 2.50
115 Na Brown RC 1.00 2.50
116 Desmond Clark RC 1.25 3.00
117 Dameane Douglas RC 1.00 2.50
118 Donald Driver RC 10.00 25.00
119 Troy Edwards RC 1.00 2.50
120 Torry Holt RC 2.00 5.00
121 Kevin Johnson RC 1.25 3.00
122 Reginald Kelly RC 1.00 2.50
123 Jimmy Kleinsasser RC 1.50 4.00
124 Jeremy McDaniel RC 1.00 2.50
125 Darnell McDonald RC 1.00 2.50
126 Travis McGriff RC 1.00 2.50
127 Billy Miller RC 1.00 2.50
128 Dee Miller RC 1.00 2.50
129 Peerless Price RC 1.00 2.50
130 Troy Smith RC 1.25 3.00
131 Brandon Stokley RC 1.25 3.00
132 Wane McGarity RC 1.00 2.50
133 Mark Campbell RC 1.00 2.50
134 Jerame Tuman RC 1.00 2.50
135 Craig Yeast RC 1.00 2.50
136 Jerry Azumah RC 1.50 4.00
137 Marlon Barnes RC 1.50 4.00
138 Michael Basnight RC 1.50 4.00
139 Shawn Bryson RC 1.50 4.00
140 Mike Cloud RC 1.50 4.00
141 Cecil Collins RC 1.50 4.00
142 Autry Denson RC 1.50 4.00
143 Kevin Faulk RC 1.50 4.00
144 Jermaine Fazande RC 1.50 4.00
145 Jim Finn RC 1.50 4.00
146 Madre Hill RC 1.50 4.00
147 Sedrick Irvin RC 1.50 4.00
148 Terry Jackson RC 1.50 4.00
149 Edgerrin James RC 2.50 6.00
150 James Johnson RC 1.50 4.00
151 Rob Konrad RC 1.50 4.00
152 Joel Makovicka RC 1.50 4.00
153 Cecil Martin RC 1.50 4.00
154 Joe Montgomery RC 1.50 4.00
155 De'Mond Parker RC 1.50 4.00
156 Sirr Parker RC 1.50 4.00
157 Jeff Paulk RC 1.50 4.00
158 Nick Williams RC 1.50 4.00
159 Ricky Williams RC 2.50 6.00
160 Amos Zereoue RC 1.50 4.00
161 Michael Bishop RC 2.00 5.00
162 Aaron Brooks RC 2.00 5.00
163 Tim Couch RC 2.00 5.00
164 Scott Covington RC 1.50 4.00
165 Daunte Culpepper RC 2.50 6.00
166 Kevin Daft RC 1.50 4.00
167 Joe Germaine RC 2.00 5.00
168 Chris Greisen RC 1.50 4.00
169 Brock Huard RC 1.50 4.00
170 Shaun King RC 1.50 4.00
171 Cory Sauter RC 1.50 4.00
172 Donovan McNabb RC 5.00 12.00
173 Cade McNown RC 1.50 4.00
174 Chad Plummer RC 1.50 4.00
175 Akili Smith RC 1.50 4.00
P1 Promo Sheet 1.50 4.00
P54 Jake Plummer PROMO .40 1.00

1999 Fleer Focus Stealth

*STARS 1-100: 3X TO 8X HI COL.
*101-110 RCs: .8X TO 2X
*111-135 RCs: .6X TO 1.5X
*136-175 RCs: .5X TO 1.2X
STATED PRINT RUN 300 SER.#'d SETS

1999 Fleer Focus Feel the Game

Randomly inserted in packs at the rate of one in 192, this 10-card set features players paired with a swatch of an authentic game-used jersey.

COMPLETE SET (10) 125.00 300.00
STATED ODDS 1:192
1FG Vinny Testaverde 6.00 15.00
2FG Mark Brunell 12.50 30.00
3FG Brett Favre Shoe 30.00 80.00
4FG Fred Taylor 12.50 30.00
5FG Jeff Blake 6.00 15.00
6FG Emmitt Smith 15.00 40.00
7FG Joe Germaine 6.00 15.00
8FG Cecil Collins 6.00 15.00
9FG Charles Woodson 10.00 25.00
10FG Kurt Warner 15.00 40.00

1999 Fleer Focus Fresh Ink

Randomly inserted in packs at the rate of one in 48, this 37-card set features close-up player photos paired with an authentic autograph.

STATED ODDS 1:48
1 Reidel Anthony 5.00 12.00
2 Charlie Batch 5.00 12.00
3 Jeff Blake 8.00 20.00
4 Darrin Chiaverini 5.00 12.00
5 Wayne Chrebet 6.00 15.00
6 Daunte Culpepper 10.00 25.00
7 Terrell Davis 10.00 25.00
8 Koy Detmer 5.00 12.00
9 Corey Dillon 8.00 20.00
10 Troy Edwards 5.00 12.00
11 Doug Flutie 10.00 25.00
12 Eddie George 10.00 25.00
13 Trent Green 8.00 20.00
14 Marvin Harrison 12.50 30.00
15 Torry Holt 10.00 25.00
16 Sedrick Irvin 5.00 12.00
17 Edgerrin James 12.50 30.00
18 Brad Johnson 8.00 20.00
19 Charles Johnson 5.00 12.00
20 Jon Kitna 10.00 25.00
21 Jim Kleinsasser 8.00 20.00
22 Peyton Manning 60.00 100.00
23 O.J. McDuffie 5.00 12.00
24 Travis McGriff 5.00 12.00
25 Donovan McNabb 25.00 60.00
26 Cade McNown 5.00 12.00
27 Joe Montgomery 5.00 12.00
28 Randy Moss 30.00 60.00
29 Jake Plummer 8.00 20.00
30 Akili Smith 5.00 12.00
31 Antowain Smith 6.00 15.00
32 Duce Staley 10.00 25.00
33 Brandon Stokley 8.00 20.00
34 Fred Taylor 10.00 25.00
35 Vinny Testaverde 8.00 20.00
36 Ricky Williams 10.00 25.00
37 Steve Young 20.00 50.00

1999 Fleer Focus Glimmer Men

Randomly inserted in packs at the rate of one in 20, this 10-card set features an all-foil base card highlighted with silver and gold foil stamping.

COMPLETE SET (10) 20.00 40.00
STATED ODDS 1:20
1R Tim Couch 1.25 3.00
2R Barry Sanders 4.00 10.00
3R Terrell Davis 1.25 3.00
4R Dan Marino 4.00 10.00
5R Troy Aikman 2.50 6.00
6R Brett Favre 4.00 10.00
7R Randy Moss 3.00 8.00
8R Emmitt Smith 2.50 6.00
9R Edgerrin James 2.50 6.00
10R Fred Taylor 1.25 3.00

1999 Fleer Focus Reflexions

Randomly inserted in packs, this 10-card set features all-foil cards accentuated with gold and silver foil highlights. Each card is serial numbered out of 100.

COMPLETE SET (10) 150.00 300.00
STATED PRINT RUN 100 SER.#'d SETS
1R Tim Couch 7.50 20.00
2R Barry Sanders 15.00 40.00
3R Terrell Davis 5.00 12.00
4R Dan Marino 15.00 40.00
5R Troy Aikman 10.00 25.00
6R Brett Favre 15.00 40.00
7R Randy Moss 12.50 30.00
8R Emmitt Smith 10.00 25.00
9R Edgerrin James 20.00 40.00
10R Fred Taylor 5.00 12.00

1999 Fleer Focus Sparklers

Randomly seeded in packs at the rate of one in 10, this 15-card set showcases top rookies on an all silver-foil card highlighed with gold-foil stamping.

COMPLETE SET (15) 12.50 30.00
STATED ODDS 1:10
1S Tim Couch .60 1.50
2S Donovan McNabb 2.50 6.00
3S Akili Smith .60 1.50
4S Cade McNown .60 1.50
5S Daunte Culpepper 2.00 5.00
6S Ricky Williams 1.00 2.50
7S Edgerrin James 2.00 5.00
8S Kevin Faulk .60 1.50
9S Torry Holt 1.25 3.00
10S David Boston .60 1.50
11S Sedrick Irvin .60 1.50
12S Peerless Price .60 1.50
13S Troy Edwards .60 1.50
14S Brock Huard .60 1.50
15S Shaun King .60 1.50

1999 Fleer Focus Wondrous

These cards were randomly inserted in 2000 Fleer Focus packs at the rate of 1:20. The player selection includes a mix of veterans, young stars, and 1999 draft picks.

COMPLETE SET 30.00 60.00
STATED ODDS 1:20
1W Peyton Manning 4.00 10.00
2W Fred Taylor .75 2.00
3W Tim Couch 1.00 2.50
4W Charlie Batch .75 2.00
5W Jerry Rice 3.00 8.00
6W Randy Moss 1.00 2.50
7W Warrick Dunn .75 2.00
8W Mark Brunell 1.00 2.50
9W Emmitt Smith 2.00 5.00
10W Eddie George 1.00 2.50
11W Brian Griese .75 2.00
12W Terrell Davis 1.00 2.50
13W Dan Marino 2.50 6.00
14W Ricky Williams 1.25 3.00
15W Brett Favre 2.50 6.00
16W Jake Plummer .75 2.00
17W Troy Aikman 1.50 4.00
18W Drew Bledsoe 1.00 2.50
19W Edgerrin James 1.25 3.00
20W Cade McNown .75 2.00

2000 Fleer Focus

Released as a 260-card set, Fleer Focus features 200 base issue cards and 60 sequentially numbered rookie cards. Card numbers 201-211 are numbered to 3999, card numbers 212-233 are numbered to 1999, card numbers 234-250 are numbered to 2499, and card numbers 251-260 are numbered to 2999. Focus was packaged in 24-pack boxes with packs containing 10 cards and carried a suggested retail price of $2.99.

COMPLETE SET (260) 200.00 400.00
COMP.SET w/o SPs (200) 10.00 25.00
201-211 ROOKIE PRINT RUN 3999
212-233 ROOKIE PRINT RUN 1999
234-250 ROOKIE PRINT RUN 2499
251-260 ROOKIE PRINT RUN 2999
1 Tim Couch .20 .50
2 Germane Crowell .15 .40
3 Curtis Martin .20 .50
4 Samari Rolle .15 .40
5 Brian Griese .15 .40
6 Kerry Collins .15 .40
7 Jevon Kearse .15 .40
8 Rocket Ismail .20 .50
9 Cam Cleeland .15 .40
10 Warrick Dunn .15 .40
11 Carl Pickens .20 .50
12 Cris Carter .25 .60
13 Mike Pritchard .15 .40
14 Corey Dillon .15 .40
15 Randy Moss .20 .50
16 Derrick Mayes .15 .40
17 Marcus Robinson .20 .50
18 Thurman Thomas .20 .50
19 J.J. Stokes .20 .50
20 Muhsin Muhammad .15 .40
21 Derrick Alexander .15 .40
22 Curtis Conway .20 .50
23 Qadry Ismail .15 .40
24 Ken Dilger .15 .40
25 Troy Edwards .15 .40
26 Shawn Jefferson .15 .40
27 Terrence Wilkins .15 .40
28 Duce Staley .15 .40
29 Aeneas Williams .15 .40
30 Antonio Freeman .20 .50
31 Tim Brown .25 .60
32 Darrell Green .20 .50
33 Herman Moore .15 .40
34 Vinny Testaverde .15 .40
35 Yancey Thigpen .15 .40
36 Emmitt Smith .40 1.00
37 Ricky Williams .20 .50
38 Keyshawn Johnson .20 .50
39 Eddie Kennison .15 .40
40 Zach Thomas .20 .50
41 Shawn Springs .15 .40
42 Wesley Walls .15 .40
43 Andre Rison .20 .50
44 Jerry Rice .60 1.50
45 Rob Johnson .20 .50
46 Keenan McCardell .20 .50
47 Ryan Leaf .20 .50
48 Michael McCrary .15 .40
49 Marvin Harrison .20 .50
50 Donovan McNabb .20 .50
51 Curtis Enis .15 .40
52 Tony Martin .20 .50
53 Jeff Garcia .15 .40
54 Tim Biakabutuka .20 .50
55 Tony Gonzalez .20 .50
56 Jim Harbaugh .20 .50
57 Peerless Price .20 .50
58 Fred Taylor .15 .40
59 Kordell Stewart .15 .40
60 Chris Chandler .20 .50
61 Bill Schroeder .20 .50
62 Charles Woodson .25 .60
63 Terance Mathis .15 .40
64 Brett Favre .50 1.25
65 Rickey Dudley .15 .40
66 Rob Moore .15 .40
67 Charlie Batch .15 .40
68 Wayne Chrebet .15 .40
69 Jeff George .20 .50
70 Olandis Gary .20 .50
71 Amani Toomer .15 .40
72 Kevin Dyson .20 .50
73 Darrin Chiaverini .15 .40
74 Willie McGinest .20 .50
75 Ricky Proehl .15 .40
76 Craig Yeast .15 .40
77 Dwayne Rudd .15 .40
78 Marshall Faulk .20 .50
79 Bobby Engram .15 .40
80 Jay Fiedler .20 .50
81 Jon Kitna .15 .40
82 Patrick Jeffers .15 .40
83 James Johnson .15 .40
84 Charlie Garner .20 .50
85 Eric Moulds .15 .40
86 Mark Brunell .20 .50
87 Richard Huntley .15 .40
88 Frank Sanders .15 .40
89 Robert Porcher .15 .40
90 Aaron Glenn .15 .40
91 Stephen Davis .15 .40
92 Ed McCaffrey .20 .50
93 Pete Mitchell .15 .40
94 Frank Wycheck .20 .50
95 David LaFleur .15 .40
96 Jake Delhomme RC .20 .50
97 John Lynch .20 .50
98 Michael Pittman .15 .40
99 Andy Katzenmoyer .15 .40
100 Isaac Bruce .25 .60
101 Terry Kirby .15 .40
102 Kevin Faulk .15 .40
103 Kevin Carter .15 .40
104 Darnay Scott .20 .50
105 Robert Smith .15 .40
106 Brian Mitchell .15 .40
107 Shane Matthews .15 .40
108 O.J. McDuffie .20 .50
109 Bryant Young .15 .40
110 Jay Riemersma .15 .40
111 Elvis Grbac .15 .40
112 Jermaine Fazande .15 .40
113 Jonathan Linton .15 .40
114 Kyle Brady .15 .40
115 Junior Seau .20 .50
116 Shannon Sharpe .20 .50
117 Jerome Pathon .15 .40
118 Jerome Bettis .25 .60
119 O.J. Santiago .15 .40
120 Ahman Green .20 .50
121 Troy Vincent .15 .40
122 David Boston .15 .40
123 James Stewart .15 .40
124 Ray Lucas .15 .40
125 Brad Johnson .20 .50
126 Rod Smith .20 .50
127 Joe Jurevicius .15 .40
128 Eddie George .20 .50
129 Darren Woodson .20 .50
130 Jake Reed .20 .50
131 Mike Alstott .15 .40
132 Leslie Shepherd .15 .40
133 Terry Glenn .20 .50
134 Az-Zahir Hakim .15 .40
135 Alonzo Mayes .15 .40
136 Sam Madison .15 .40
137 Ricky Watters .20 .50
138 Antowain Smith .20 .50
139 Jimmy Smith .20 .50
140 Hines Ward .20 .50
141 Priest Holmes .15 .40
142 Edgerrin James .20 .50
143 Charles Johnson .15 .40
144 Jamal Anderson .20 .50
145 Dorsey Levens .20 .50
146 Rich Gannon .20 .50
147 Champ Bailey .20 .50
148 Bill Romanowski .15 .40
149 Jason Sehorn .15 .40
150 Steve McNair .20 .50
151 Jermaine Lewis .15 .40
152 Cornelius Bennett .15 .40
153 Torrance Small .15 .40
154 Tim Dwight .20 .50
155 Corey Bradford .15 .40
156 Napoleon Kaufman .20 .50
157 Jake Plummer .15 .40
158 David Sloan .15 .40
159 Dedric Ward .15 .40
160 Michael Westbrook .15 .40
161 Terrell Davis .20 .50
162 Ike Hilliard .15 .40
163 Derrick Brooks .15 .40
164 Greg Ellis .15 .40
165 Keith Poole .15 .40
166 Jacquez Green .15 .40
167 Joey Galloway .20 .50
168 Lawyer Milloy .15 .40
169 Warren Sapp .20 .50
170 Takeo Spikes .15 .40
171 John Randle .25 .60
172 Torry Holt .20 .60
173 Cade McNown .15 .40
174 Damon Huard .15 .40
175 Terrell Owens .20 .50
176 Steve Beuerlein .20 .50
177 Tony Richardson RC .15 .40
178 Jeff Graham .15 .40
179 Doug Flutie .20 .50
180 Kevin Hardy .15 .40
181 Mark Bruener .20 .50
182 Tony Banks .15 .40
183 Peyton Manning .60 1.50
184 Hugh Douglas .15 .40
185 Simeon Rice .20 .50
186 Terry Fair .15 .40
187 James Jett .20 .50
188 Albert Connell .15 .40
189 Troy Aikman .30 .75
190 Jeff Blake .20 .50
191 Shaun King .15 .40
192 Kevin Johnson .15 .40
193 Drew Bledsoe .20 .50
194 Kurt Warner .40 1.00
195 Akili Smith .15 .40
196 Daunte Culpepper .20 .50
197 Sean Dawkins .15 .40
198 Natrone Means .20 .50
199 Kimble Anders .15 .40
200 Steve Young .30 .75
201 Courtney Brown RC 1.00 2.50
202 Chris Samuels RC 1.25 3.00
203 Corey Simon RC 1.00 2.50
204 Deon Grant RC .75 2.00
205 Darren Howard RC .75 2.00
206 Rob Morris RC 1.00 2.50
207 Ahmed Plummer RC .75 2.00
208 Anthony Becht RC .75 2.00
209 Brian Urlacher RC 4.00 10.00
210 Shaun Ellis RC 1.00 2.50
211 Bubba Franks RC .75 2.00
212 Plaxico Burress RC 1.50 4.00
213 R.Jay Soward RC 1.25 3.00
214 Dez White RC 1.25 3.00
215 Peter Warrick RC 1.25 3.00
216 Jerry Porter RC 2.00 5.00
217 Ron Dugans RC 1.25 3.00
218 Laveranues Coles RC 1.50 4.00
219 Travis Taylor RC 1.25 3.00
220 Anthony Lucas RC 1.25 3.00
221 Sylvester Morris RC 1.25 3.00
222 Dennis Northcutt RC 1.25 3.00
223 Chafie Fields RC 1.25 3.00
224 Danny Farmer RC 1.25 3.00
225 Chris Cole RC 1.50 4.00
226 Sherrod Gideon RC 1.25 3.00
227 Todd Pinkston RC 1.25 3.00
228 Gari Scott RC 1.25 3.00
229 Darrell Jackson RC 1.25 3.00
230 JaJuan Dawson RC 1.25 3.00
231 Trevor Gaylor RC 1.25 3.00
232 Bashir Yamini RC 1.25 3.00
233 Quinton Spotwood RC 1.25 3.00
234 Michael Wiley RC 1.00 2.50
235 Ron Dayne RC 1.50 4.00
236 Thomas Jones RC 1.25 3.00
237 Jamal Lewis RC 1.50 4.00
238 Travis Prentice RC 1.00 2.50
239 J.R. Redmond RC 1.00 2.50
240 Trung Canidate RC 1.00 2.50
241 Shaun Alexander RC 1.50 4.00
242 Frank Murphy RC 1.00 2.50
243 Shyrone Stith RC 1.00 2.50
244 Rondell Mealey RC 1.00 2.50
245 Terrelle Smith RC 1.00 2.50
246 Reuben Droughns RC 1.00 2.50
247 Chad Morton RC 1.25 3.00
248 Mike Anderson RC 1.00 2.50
249 Paul Smith RC 1.00 2.50
250 Curtis Keaton RC 1.00 2.50
251 Jarious Jackson RC 1.25 3.00
252 Marc Bulger RC 1.25 3.00
253 Tee Martin RC 1.00 2.50
254 Todd Husak RC 1.00 2.50
255 Joe Hamilton RC 1.00 2.50
256 Doug Johnson RC 1.00 2.50
257 Giovanni Carmazzi RC 1.00 2.50
258 Chris Redman RC 1.00 2.50
259 Tim Rattay RC 1.25 3.00
260 Chad Pennington RC 1.25 3.00
P16 Tim Couch Promo .40 1.00

2000 Fleer Focus Draft Position

*VETS/823-1220: 2.5X TO 6X BASIC CARD
*VETS/401-735: 3X TO 8X BASIC CARD
*VETS/300-331: 4X TO 10X BASIC CARD
*VETS/201-230: 5X TO 12X BASIC CARD
*VETS/90-131: 6X TO 15X BASIC CARD
1-200 VETERAN PRINT RUN 90-1220
*201-211 ROOK/202-226: 1X TO 2.5X
*201-211 ROOK/101-128: 1.2X TO 3X
*212-233 ROOK/405-634: .4X TO 1X
*212-233 ROOK/304-318: .5X TO 1.2X
*212-233 ROOK/201-216 .6X TO 1.5X
*212-233 ROOK/100-129: .8X TO 2X
*234-250 ROOK/402-746: .5X TO 1.2X
*234-250 ROOK/301-319: .6X TO 1.5X
*234-250 ROOK/105-131: 1X TO 2.5X
*251-260 ROOK/403-728: .5X TO 1.2X
*251-260 ROOK/303-313: .6X TO 1.5X
*251-260 ROOK/100-118: 1X TO 2.5X
201-260 ROOKIE PRINT RUN 100-746

2000 Fleer Focus Good Hands

Randomly inserted in packs at the rate of one in 18, this 15-card set features all foil cards with player action photos set agains a background with a hand print.

COMPLETE SET (15) 12.50 30.00
STATED ODDS 1:18
*TD/12-17: 6X TO 15X BASIC INSERTS
TD EDITION PRINT RUN 1-17
1 Keyshawn Johnson .60 1.50
2 Joey Galloway .60 1.50
3 Jerry Rice 2.00 5.00
4 Cris Carter .75 2.00
5 Randy Moss .60 1.50
6 Marvin Harrison .60 1.50
7 Marcus Robinson .60 1.50
8 Edgerrin James .60 1.50
9 Tim Brown .75 2.00
10 Jimmy Smith .60 1.50
11 Isaac Bruce .75 2.00
12 Peter Warrick .50 1.25
13 Marshall Faulk .60 1.50
14 Germane Crowell .50 1.25
15 Plaxico Burress .60 1.50

2000 Fleer Focus Last Man Standing

Randomly inserted in packs at the rate of one in 12, this 25-card all-foil set features both portrait style photography and action shots.

COMPLETE SET (25) 25.00 60.00
STATED ODDS 1:12
*TD/42: 5X TO 12X BASIC INSERTS
*TD/20-28: 6X TO 15X BASIC INSERTS
*TD/11-18: 8X TO 20X BASIC INSERTS
TD EDITION PRINT RUN 2-42
1 Tim Couch .50 1.25
2 Randy Moss .50 1.25
3 Akili Smith .40 1.00
4 Peyton Manning 1.50 4.00
5 Kurt Warner 1.00 2.50
6 Ricky Williams .50 1.25
7 Edgerrin James .50 1.25
8 Eddie George .50 1.25
9 Emmitt Smith 1.00 2.50
10 Terrell Davis .50 1.25
11 Brett Favre 1.25 3.00
12 Brian Griese .40 1.00
13 Donovan McNabb .50 1.25
14 Charlie Batch .40 1.00
15 Shaun King .40 1.00
16 Marshall Faulk .50 1.25
17 Jake Plummer .40 1.00
18 Cade McNown .40 1.00
19 Jerry Rice 1.50 4.00
20 Troy Aikman .75 2.00
21 Keyshawn Johnson .50 1.25
22 Peter Warrick .40 1.00
23 Ron Dayne .60 1.50
24 Mark Brunell .50 1.25
25 Fred Taylor .40 1.00

2000 Fleer Focus Sparklers

Randomly inserted in packs at the rate of one in six, this 15-card set spotlights 2000 NFL top draft picks. Cards are all foil with backgrounds to match each respective player's team colors.

COMPLETE SET (15) 12.50 30.00
STATED ODDS 1:6
*TD/32-40: 8X TO 20X BASIC INSERTS
*TD/20-26: 10X TO 25X BASIC INSERTS
*TD/11-18: 12X TO 30X BASIC INSERTS
TD EDITION PRINT RUN 5-40
1 Chad Pennington .30 .75
2 Ron Dayne .40 1.00
3 Shaun Alexander .40 1.00
4 Plaxico Burress .30 .75
5 Peter Warrick .25 .60
6 Thomas Jones .30 .75
7 Chris Redman .25 .60
8 Sylvester Morris .25 .60
9 J.R. Redmond .25 .60
10 Dez White .25 .60
11 Jamal Lewis .40 1.00
12 Travis Taylor .25 .60
13 R.Jay Soward .25 .60
14 Todd Pinkston .25 .60
15 Dennis Northcutt .25 .60

2000 Fleer Focus Star Studded

Randomly inserted in packs at the rate of one in 24, this 25-card set features a plastic die cut card stock with enhanced rainbow holofoil stamping.

COMPLETE SET (25) 60.00 120.00
STATED ODDS 1:24
*TD/40-42: 3X TO 8X BASIC INSERTS
*TD/20-28: 4X TO 10X BASIC INSERTS
*TD/11-19: 5X TO 12X BASIC INSERTS
TD EDITION PRINT RUN 2-42
1 Peyton Manning 2.50 6.00
2 Fred Taylor .60 1.50
3 Tim Couch .75 2.00
4 Charlie Batch .60 1.50
5 Jerry Rice 2.50 6.00
6 Randy Moss .75 2.00
7 Ron Dayne 1.00 2.50
8 Mark Brunell .75 2.00
9 Emmitt Smith 1.50 4.00
10 Thomas Jones .75 2.00
11 Brian Griese .60 1.50
12 Terrell Davis .75 2.00
13 Brad Johnson .75 2.00
14 Ricky Williams .75 2.00
15 Brett Favre 2.00 5.00
16 Jake Plummer .60 1.50
17 Troy Aikman 1.25 3.00
18 Drew Bledsoe .75 2.00
19 Edgerrin James .75 2.00
20 Steve McNair .75 2.00
21 Doug Flutie .75 2.00
22 Chad Pennington .75 2.00
23 Jamal Lewis 1.00 2.50
24 Plaxico Burress .75 2.00
25 Kurt Warner 1.50 4.00

2001 Fleer Focus

This 230 card set was issued in fall, 2001. The set consists of 180 veterans and fifty 2001 NFL rookies. The Rookie Cards, numbered from 181 through 230 had a stated print run of 1850 sets.

COMP.SET w/o SP's (180) 10.00 25.00
181-230 ROOKIE PRINT RUN 1850
1 Marshall Faulk .20 .50
2 Randy Moss .20 .50
3 Cade McNown .20 .50
4 Jeff Graham .15 .40
5 Donovan McNabb .20 .50
6 Shannon Sharpe .20 .50
7 Todd Pinkston .15 .40
8 Terrence Wilkins .15 .40
9 Michael Strahan .20 .50
10 Rich Gannon .20 .50
11 Germane Crowell .15 .40
12 Warren Sapp .20 .50
13 La'Roi Glover .15 .40
14 Peter Warrick .15 .40
15 Shaun Alexander .15 .40
16 Ray Lucas .15 .40
17 Muhsin Muhammad .15 .40
18 Curtis Conway .20 .50
19 R.Jay Soward .15 .40
20 Jamal Lewis .25 .60
21 Tony Gonzalez .20 .50
22 Bill Schroeder .20 .50
23 Frank Sanders .15 .40
24 Charles Woodson .25 .60
25 Johnnie Morton .20 .50
26 Frank Wycheck .15 .40
27 Ron Dayne .20 .50
28 Travis Prentice .15 .40
29 Isaac Bruce .25 .60
30 Drew Bledsoe .20 .50
31 James Allen .15 .40
32 Matt Hasselbeck .15 .40
33 Zach Thomas .20 .50
34 Shawn Bryson .15 .40
35 Jerry Rice .50 1.25
36 Mike Cloud .15 .40
37 Sammy Morris .15 .40
38 Corey Simon .15 .40
39 Peyton Manning .60 1.50
40 Thomas Jones .15 .40
41 Tyrone Wheatley .20 .50
42 Herman Moore .15 .40
43 Jeff George .20 .50
44 Kerry Collins .15 .40
45 Rocket Ismail .20 .50
46 Andre Rison .20 .50
47 David Sloan .15 .40
48 Michael Westbrook .15 .40
49 Ron Dixon .15 .40
50 Randall Cunningham .20 .50
51 Keyshawn Johnson .20 .50
52 Aaron Brooks .15 .40
53 Corey Dillon .15 .40
54 John Randle .20 .50
55 Cris Carter .25 .60
56 Donald Hayes .15 .40
57 Hines Ward .20 .50
58 Edgerrin James .20 .50
59 Terance Mathis .15 .40
60 Doug Johnson .15 .40
61 Rod Smith .20 .50
62 Kevin Dyson .15 .40
63 Amani Toomer .15 .40
64 Courtney Brown .15 .40
65 Mike Alstott .15 .40
66 Kevin Faulk .15 .40
67 Shane Matthews .15 .40
68 Ricky Watters .20 .50
69 Peter Boulware .15 .40
70 Tim Biakabutuka .15 .40
71 Troy Aikman .30 .75
72 Keenan McCardell .20 .50
73 Priest Holmes .15 .40
74 Duce Staley .15 .40
75 Antonio Freeman .25 .60
76 David Boston .15 .40
77 Chad Pennington .15 .40
78 Brian Griese .15 .40
79 Stephen Davis .15 .40
80 Curtis Martin .20 .50
81 Tony Banks .15 .40
82 Warrick Dunn .15 .40
83 Willie McGinest .15 .40
84 Marty Booker .15 .40
85 James Williams .15 .40
86 Oronde Gadsden .15 .40
87 Patrick Jeffers .15 .40
88 Junior Seau .20 .50
89 Frank Moreau .15 .40
90 Ray Lewis .25 .60
91 Doug Flutie .20 .50
92 Jimmy Smith .20 .50
93 Qadry Ismail .15 .40
94 Jeremiah Trotter .15 .40
95 Dorsey Levens .20 .50
96 Michael Pittman .20 .50
97 Wayne Chrebet .15 .40
98 Mike Anderson .15 .40
99 Derrick Mason .15 .40
100 Jason Sehorn .20 .50
101 Kevin Johnson .15 .40
102 Terrell Owens .20 .50
103 Lamar Smith .20 .50
104 Eric Moulds .15 .40
105 Jerome Bettis .25 .60
106 Marvin Harrison .20 .50
107 Shawn Jefferson .15 .40
108 Rickey Dudley .15 .40
109 James Stewart .15 .40
110 Bruce Smith .20 .50
111 Matthew Hatchette .15 .40
112 Emmitt Smith .40 1.00
113 Steve McNair .20 .50
114 Ricky Williams .20 .50
115 Tim Couch .15 .40
116 Darrell Jackson .20 .50
117 Doug Chapman .15 .40
118 Jeff Lewis .15 .40
119 Freddie Jones .15 .40
120 Sylvester Morris .15 .40
121 Elvis Grbac .20 .50
122 Plaxico Burress .15 .40
123 Marcus Pollard .15 .40
124 Chris Chandler .20 .50
125 James Thrash .20 .50
126 Brett Favre .50 1.25
127 Jake Plummer .15 .40
128 Vinny Testaverde .15 .40
129 Terrell Davis .20 .50
130 Jevon Kearse .15 .40
131 Albert Connell .15 .40
132 Dennis Northcutt .15 .40
133 Az-Zahir Hakim .15 .40
134 J.R. Redmond .15 .40
135 Marcus Robinson .20 .50
136 Eddie George .25 .60
137 Ike Hilliard .15 .40
138 Hugh Douglas .15 .40
139 Kurt Warner .40 1.00
140 Terry Glenn .20 .50
141 Brian Urlacher .30 .75
142 Charlie Garner .20 .50
143 Jay Fiedler .20 .50
144 Rob Johnson .20 .50
145 Kordell Stewart .15 .40
146 Mark Brunell .20 .50
147 Travis Taylor .15 .40
148 Laveranues Coles .20 .50
149 Ed McCaffrey .20 .50
150 Jacquez Green .15 .40
151 Joe Horn .15 .40
152 Darnay Scott .20 .50
153 Torry Holt .20 .50
154 Daunte Culpepper .20 .50
155 Wesley Walls .15 .40
156 Jeff Garcia .15 .40
157 Derrick Alexander .15 .40
158 Peerless Price .15 .40
159 Bobby Shaw .15 .40
160 Fred Taylor .15 .40
161 Chris Redman .25 .60
162 Tim Brown .25 .60
163 Charlie Batch .15 .40
164 Champ Bailey .20 .50
165 Tiki Barber .20 .50
166 Joey Galloway .20 .50
167 Brad Johnson .20 .50
168 Jeff Blake .20 .50
169 Jon Kitna .15 .40
170 Trent Green .15 .40
171 Troy Brown .15 .40
172 Eddie Kennison .20 .50
173 J.J. Stokes .15 .40
174 James McKnight .15 .40
175 Jeremy McDaniel .15 .40
176 Richard Huntley .15 .40
177 Kyle Brady .15 .40
178 Jamal Anderson .20 .50
179 Chad Lewis .15 .40
180 Ahman Green .20 .50
181 Michael Vick RC 2.50 6.00
182 Deuce McAllister RC 1.50 4.00
183 David Terrell RC 1.25 3.00
184 Koren Robinson RC 1.25 3.00
185 LaDainian Tomlinson RC 5.00 12.00
186 Michael Bennett RC 1.25 3.00
187 Chris Chambers RC 1.00 2.50
188 Chad Johnson RC 1.50 4.00
189 Santana Moss RC 1.50 4.00
190 Todd Heap RC 1.25 3.00
191 Freddie Mitchell RC 1.00 2.50
192 Quincy Morgan RC 1.25 3.00
193 Rod Gardner RC 1.25 3.00
194 Kevan Barlow RC 1.25 3.00
195 Drew Brees RC 15.00 40.00
196 Robert Ferguson RC 1.50 4.00
197 Ken-Yon Rambo RC 1.00 2.50
198 Travis Henry RC 1.25 3.00
199 LaMont Jordan RC 1.50 4.00
200 Chris Weinke RC 1.25 3.00
201 Sage Rosenfels RC 1.25 3.00
202 Josh Heupel RC 1.50 4.00
203 Quincy Carter RC 1.25 3.00
204 Jesse Palmer RC 1.25 3.00
205 Mike McMahon RC 1.25 3.00
206 Rudi Johnson RC 1.50 4.00
207 Anthony Thomas RC 1.50 4.00
208 James Jackson RC 1.00 2.50
209 Snoop Minnis RC 1.00 2.50
210 Derek Combs RC 1.00 2.50
211 Ronney Daniels RC 1.00 2.50
212 Alex Bannister RC 1.00 2.50
213 Cedrick Wilson RC 1.25 3.00
214 Travis Minor RC 1.25 3.00
215 Marques Tuiasosopo RC 1.25 3.00
216 Reggie Wayne RC 2.00 5.00
217 Josh Booty RC 1.25 3.00
218 Jamal Reynolds RC 1.00 2.50
219 Gerard Warren RC 1.25 3.00
220 Justin Smith RC 2.00 5.00
221 Andre Carter RC 1.25 3.00
222 Milton Wynn RC 1.00 2.50
223 Fred Smoot RC 1.25 3.00
224 Jamar Fletcher RC 1.00 2.50
225 Dan Morgan RC 1.25 3.00
226 Jonathan Carter RC 1.00 2.50
227 Correll Buckhalter RC 1.00 2.50
228 Kevin Kasper RC 1.00 2.50
229 Derrick Blaylock RC 1.25 3.00
230 Justin McCareins RC 1.25 3.00

2001 Fleer Focus Numbers

*VETS/200-403: 3X TO 8X BASIC CARDS
*ROOKIES/200-403: .5X TO 1.2X
*VETS/100-199: 5X TO 12X BASIC CARDS
*ROOKIES/100-199: .8X TO 2X
*VETS/70-99: 6X TO 15X BASIC CARDS
*ROOKIES/70-99: 1X TO 2.5X
*VETS/45-69: 8X TO 20X BASIC CARDS
*ROOKIES/45-69: 1.2X TO 3X
*VETS/30-44: 12X TO 30X BASIC CARDS
*ROOKIES/30-44: 2X TO 5X
*VETS/20-29: 15X TO 40X BASIC CARDS
*VETS/10-19: 20X TO 50X BASIC CARDS
195 Drew Brees/309 50.00 100.00

2001 Fleer Focus Certified Cuts

Inserted at a rate of one in 72, these 18 cards feature players "cut" autographs pasted onto a card. A few cards were printed in lesser quantity and those are notated as a SP. In addition, a few players were not ready when this product was released and were available as exchange cards. Those exchange cards were redeemable until August 31, 2002.

STATED ODDS 1:72
CCCC Chris Chambers 5.00 12.00
CCCW Chris Weinke SP 6.00 15.00
CCDB Drew Brees SP 75.00 125.00
CCDM Deuce McAllister 8.00 20.00
CCDM2 Donovan McNabb SP 25.00 50.00
CCDT David Terrell 6.00 15.00
CCJH Josh Heupel 8.00 20.00
CCJJ James Jackson 5.00 12.00
CCJP Jesse Palmer 6.00 15.00
CCKB Kevan Barlow 6.00 15.00
CCKR Koren Robinson 6.00 15.00
CCLJ LaMont Jordan EXCH 1.25 3.00
CCLT LaDainian Tomlinson 30.00 80.00
CCMB Michael Bennett 6.00 15.00
CCMV Michael Vick SP 60.00 100.00
CCRJ Rudi Johnson 8.00 20.00
CCRW Reggie Wayne EXCH 1.50 4.00
CCSM Santana Moss 8.00 20.00

2001 Fleer Focus Property Of

Issued at a stated rate of one in 192, these 10 card feature a game-worn uniform swatch in addition to a photo of the featured player. In addition, a shirts/skins parallel was issued and these cards have a stated print run of 50 serial numbered copies.

STATED ODDS 1:192
*SHIRTS/SKINS/50: .6X TO 1.5X JSY
SHIRTS/SKINS PRINT RUN 50
POBF Brett Favre 6.00 15.00
POCD Corey Dillon 2.00 5.00
PODM Dan Marino 6.00 15.00
POJR Jerry Rice 6.00 15.00
POKS Kordell Stewart 2.00 5.00
POKW Kurt Warner 5.00 12.00
POMF Marshall Faulk 2.50 6.00
PORL Ray Lewis 3.00 8.00
PORS Rod Smith 2.50 6.00
POWC Wayne Chrebet 2.00 5.00

2001 Fleer Focus Rookie Premiere Jersey

Inserted at a rate of one in 65, these 36 cards feature rookies from the 2001 NFL season along with a game-worn uniform swatch.

STATED ODDS 1:65
*SHIRTS/SKINS/50: .6X TO 1.5X JSY
SHIRTS/SKINS PRINT RUN 50
RPAC Andre Carter 2.00 5.00
RPAT Anthony Thomas 2.50 6.00
RPCC Chris Chambers 1.50 4.00
RPCJ Chad Johnson 2.50 6.00
RPCW Chris Weinke 2.00 5.00
RPDB Drew Brees 30.00 60.00
RPDM1 Dan Morgan 2.00 5.00
RPDM2 Deuce McAllister 2.50 6.00
RPDT David Terrell 2.00 5.00
RPFM Freddie Mitchell 1.50 4.00
RPGW Gerard Warren 2.00 5.00
RPJH Josh Heupel 2.50 6.00
RPJJ James Jackson 1.50 4.00
RPJP Jesse Palmer 2.00 5.00
RPJS Justin Smith 3.00 8.00
RPKB Kevan Barlow 2.00 5.00
RPKR Koren Robinson 2.00 5.00
RPLD Leonard Davis 2.50 6.00
RPLT LaDainian Tomlinson 8.00 20.00
RPMB Michael Bennett 2.00 5.00
RPMM1 Mike McMahon 2.00 5.00
RPMM2 Snoop Minnis 1.50 4.00
RPMT Marques Tuiasosopo 2.00 5.00
RPMV Michael Vick 4.00 10.00
RPQC Quincy Carter 2.00 5.00
RPQM Quincy Morgan 2.00 5.00
RPRF Robert Ferguson 2.50 6.00
RPRG Rod Gardner 2.00 5.00
RPRJ Rudi Johnson 2.50 6.00
RPRS Richard Seymour 2.50 6.00
RPRW Reggie Wayne 3.00 8.00
RPSM Santana Moss 2.50 6.00
RPSR Sage Rosenfels 2.00 5.00
RPTH1 Todd Heap 2.00 5.00
RPTH2 Travis Henry 2.00 5.00
RPTM Travis Minor 2.00 5.00

2001 Fleer Focus Tag Team

Inserted at a rate of one in 140, these 29 cards feature the players photo along with a piece of memorabilia.

STATED ODDS 1:140
TTBF Brett Favre 10.00 25.00
TTBJ Bo Jackson 6.00 15.00
TTBU Brian Urlacher 6.00 15.00
TTDC Daunte Culpepper 4.00 10.00
TTDM1 Dan Marino 10.00 25.00
TTDM2 Deuce McAllister 5.00 12.00
TTDM3 Donovan McNabb 4.00 10.00
TTED Eric Dickerson 4.00 10.00
TTEG Eddie George 5.00 12.00
TTEJ Edgerrin James 4.00 10.00
TTES Emmitt Smith 8.00 20.00
TTJE John Elway 8.00 20.00
TTJM Joe Montana 15.00 40.00
TTJR Jerry Rice 10.00 25.00
TTJU Johnny Unitas 10.00 25.00
TTMA Marcus Allen 5.00 12.00
TTMF Marshall Faulk 4.00 10.00
TTPH Paul Hornung Pants 5.00 12.00
TTRC Randall Cunningham 4.00 10.00
TTRM Randy Moss 4.00 10.00
TTRS Roger Staubach 6.00 15.00
TTSM Steve McNair 4.00 10.00
TTSY Steve Young 6.00 15.00
TTTA Troy Aikman 6.00 15.00
TTTD1 Terrell Davis 4.00 10.00
TTTD2 Tony Dorsett 5.00 12.00
TTWM Warren Moon 5.00 12.00
TTWP1 Walter Payton 12.00 30.00
TTWP2 William Perry 3.00 8.00

2001 Fleer Focus Tag Team Tandems

Randomly inserted in packs, these 15 cards feature two players with a commonality as well as two pieces of memorabilia. These cards were serial numbered to 50

STATED PRINT RUN 50 SER.#'d SETS
BJMA B.Jackson/M.Allen 12.00 30.00
DCWM D.Culpepper/W.Moon 10.00 25.00

DMRC McNabb/Cunningham 8.00 20.00
DMRW D.McAllister/R.Williams 10.00 25.00
ESTD E.Smith/T.Dorsett 15.00 40.00
JETD J.Elway/T.Davis 8.00 20.00
JMSY J.Montana/S.Young 30.00 80.00
JRSY J.Rice/S.Young 20.00 50.00
JUEJ J.Unitas/E.James 8.00 20.00
MFED M.Faulk/E.Dickerson 8.00 20.00
PHBF P.Hornung/B.Favre 20.00 50.00
RMDC R.Moss/D.Culpepper 8.00 20.00
SMEG S.McNair/E.George 10.00 25.00
TARS T.Aikman/R.Staubach 12.00 30.00
WPBU W.Perry/B.Urlacher 12.00 30.00

2001 Fleer Focus Toast of the Town

Inserted at a rate of one in six, these 20 cards feature the player's photo set against a map of their home city.

COMPLETE SET (20) 15.00 40.00
STATED ODDS 1:6
1 Donovan McNabb .60 1.50
2 Brett Favre 1.50 4.00
3 Jerome Bettis .75 2.00
4 Stephen Davis .50 1.25
5 Emmitt Smith 1.25 3.00
6 Cris Carter .75 2.00
7 Peyton Manning 2.00 5.00
8 Eddie George .75 2.00
9 Edgerrin James .60 1.50
10 Daunte Culpepper .60 1.50
11 Kurt Warner 1.25 3.00
12 Mark Brunell .60 1.50
13 Randy Moss .60 1.50
14 Marvin Harrison .60 1.50
15 Jamal Lewis .75 2.00
16 Warren Sapp .60 1.50
17 Jerry Rice 1.50 4.00
18 Ricky Williams .60 1.50
19 Ron Dayne .60 1.50
20 Brian Griese .50 1.25

2001 Fleer Focus Tunnel Vision

Inserted at a rate of one in 12, these 15 cards give the effect of a player leaving a wind tunnel. The player's photo is on the right of the card while the words "Tunnel Vision" is on the left. The player's name and team affiliation is on the bottom.

COMPLETE SET (15) 15.00 40.00
STATED ODDS 1:12
1 Peyton Manning 2.00 5.00
2 Jamal Lewis .75 2.00
3 Emmitt Smith 1.25 3.00
4 Eddie George .75 2.00
5 Michael Vick .75 2.00
6 Brett Favre 1.50 4.00
7 Ricky Williams .60 1.50
8 Edgerrin James .60 1.50
9 Ron Dayne .60 1.50
10 Eric Moulds .50 1.25
11 Tim Brown .75 2.00
12 Terrell Davis .60 1.50
13 Jevon Kearse .50 1.25
14 Peter Warrick .50 1.25
15 Ray Lewis .75 2.00

2002 Fleer Focus JE

Released in October 2002, this 160 card-set was made up of 100 veterans and 60 rookies. Boxes contained 24 packs with 7 cards per pack. The rookies were serial numbered to 1850. Boxes contained 1 oversized materialistic jumbo card as a box topper.

COMP.SET w/o SP's (100) 7.50 20.00
ROOKIE PRINT RUN 1850 SER.#'d SETS
1 Tom Brady 1.50 4.00
2 Curtis Martin .25 .60
3 Brett Favre .60 1.50
4 Michael Pittman .25 .60
5 Donovan McNabb .25 .60
6 Quincy Carter .20 .50
7 Trent Dilfer .20 .50
8 Troy Brown .20 .50
9 Ed McCaffrey .25 .60
10 Shaun Alexander .20 .50
11 Daunte Culpepper .25 .60
12 Marty Booker .20 .50
13 Junior Seau .25 .60
14 Zach Thomas .25 .60
15 Muhsin Muhammad .20 .50
16 Kordell Stewart .20 .50
17 Jimmy Smith .25 .60
18 David Boston .20 .50
19 Laveranues Coles .25 .60
20 Emmitt Smith .50 1.25
21 Darrell Jackson .25 .60
22 Charlie Garner .25 .60
23 Marcus Robinson .25 .60
24 Drew Brees .60 1.50
25 Tony Gonzalez .25 .60
26 James Allen .20 .50
27 Steve McNair .25 .60
28 Kerry Collins .20 .50
29 Az-Zahir Hakim .20 .50
30 Marshall Faulk .25 .60
31 Derrick Mason .20 .50
32 Rod Smith .25 .60
33 Torry Holt .25 .60
34 Jake Plummer .20 .50
35 Kevin Johnson .20 .50
36 Kevan Barlow .20 .50
37 Priest Holmes .20 .50
38 Anthony Thomas .25 .60
39 Jerome Bettis .30 .75
40 Johnnie Morton .25 .60
41 Eric Moulds .20 .50
42 James Thrash .25 .60
43 Jamie Sharper .25 .60
44 Eddie George .25 .60
45 Randy Moss .25 .60
46 Tim Couch .20 .50
47 Terrell Owens .25 .60
48 Jay Fiedler .25 .60
49 Travis Henry .20 .50
50 Hines Ward .25 .60
51 Ricky Williams .25 .60
52 Brian Urlacher .30 .75
53 LaDainian Tomlinson .30 .75
54 Trent Green .20 .50
55 Chris Redman .20 .50
56 Deuce McAllister .25 .60
57 Mark Brunell .25 .60
58 Jamal Lewis .25 .60
59 Freddie Mitchell .20 .50
60 Peyton Manning .75 2.00
61 Stephen Davis .20 .50
62 Tiki Barber .25 .60
63 Terry Glenn .25 .60
64 Keyshawn Johnson .25 .60
65 Aaron Brooks .20 .50
66 Brian Griese .20 .50
67 Koren Robinson .20 .50
68 Michael Bennett .20 .50
69 Ray Lewis .30 .75
70 Rich Gannon .25 .60
71 Marvin Harrison .25 .60
72 Rod Gardner .20 .50
73 Chad Pennington .20 .50
74 Terrell Davis .25 .60
75 Isaac Bruce .30 .75
76 Peter Warrick .20 .50
77 Jeff Garcia .20 .50
78 Chris Chambers .20 .50
79 Chris Weinke .20 .50
80 Plaxico Burress .20 .50
81 Edgerrin James .25 .60
82 Drew Bledsoe .25 .60
83 Duce Staley .20 .50
84 Fred Taylor .20 .50
85 Warrick Dunn .20 .50
86 Jerry Rice .60 1.50
87 Ahman Green .25 .60
88 Warren Sapp .25 .60
89 Michael Strahan .25 .60
90 Bill Schroeder .20 .50
91 Kurt Warner .25 .60
92 Antowain Smith .25 .60
93 Corey Dillon .20 .50
94 Garrison Hearst .20 .50
95 Joey Galloway .25 .60
96 Michael Vick .25 .60
97 Tim Brown .30 .75
98 Corey Bradford .20 .50
99 Brad Johnson .25 .60
100 Joe Horn .20 .50
101 Quentin Jammer RC 1.25 3.00
102 Rohan Davey RC 1.25 3.00
103 David Garrard RC 1.00 2.50
104 Ron Johnson RC 1.00 2.50
105 Jeremy Shockey RC 1.25 3.00
106 Marquise Walker RC .75 2.00
107 Luke Staley RC .75 2.00
108 Josh Scobey RC 1.00 2.50
109 Adrian Peterson RC 1.00 2.50
110 Lito Sheppard RC 1.25 3.00
111 Daniel Graham RC 1.00 2.50
112 Ryan Sims RC 1.25 3.00
113 William Green RC 1.00 2.50
114 Ashley Lelie RC .75 2.00
115 Deion Branch RC 1.25 3.00
116 Omar Easy RC 1.00 2.50
117 Jake Schifino RC .75 2.00
118 Donte Stallworth RC 1.25 3.00
119 Craig Nall RC 1.00 2.50
120 Clinton Portis RC 1.25 3.00
121 Brandon Doman RC .75 2.00
122 Eric Crouch RC 1.25 3.00
123 Josh McCown RC 1.25 3.00
124 Cliff Russell RC .75 2.00
125 T.J. Duckett RC .75 2.00
126 Jason McAddley RC 1.00 2.50
127 Chad Hutchinson RC .75 2.00
128 Jonathan Wells RC 1.00 2.50
129 Antwaan Randle El RC 1.00 2.50
130 Terry Charles RC .75 2.00
131 Lamar Gordon RC 1.00 2.50
132 Antonio Bryant RC 1.25 3.00
133 Brian Westbrook RC 1.50 4.00
134 Javon Walker RC 1.25 3.00
135 J.T. O'Sullivan RC 1.00 2.50
136 Maurice Morris RC 1.00 2.50
137 Tim Carter RC 1.00 2.50
138 Antwoine Womack RC .75 2.00
139 Ladell Betts RC 1.25 3.00
140 Joey Harrington RC .75 2.00
141 Chester Taylor RC 1.25 3.00
142 David Carr RC .75 2.00
143 Roy Williams RC .75 2.00
144 Reche Caldwell RC 1.00 2.50
145 Lamont Brightful RC .75 2.00
146 Patrick Ramsey RC 1.00 2.50
147 Travis Stephens RC .75 2.00
148 Andre Davis RC .75 2.00
149 Herb Haygood RC .75 2.00
150 Randy Fasani RC .75 2.00
151 Jabar Gaffney RC .75 2.00
152 Kahlil Hill RC .75 2.00
153 Julius Peppers RC 2.00 5.00
154 Kurt Kittner RC .75 2.00
155 DeShaun Foster RC 1.25 3.00
156 Verron Haynes RC .75 2.00
157 Josh Reed RC 1.00 2.50
158 Freddie Milons RC .75 2.00
159 Robert Thomas RC .75 2.00
160 Sam Simmons RC .75 2.00

2002 Fleer Focus JE Jersey Numbers

*VETS/80-99: 4X TO 10X BASIC CARDS
*ROOKIES/80-99: .8X TO 2X
*VETS/45-55: 5X TO 12X BASIC CARDS
*ROOKIES/45-55: 1X TO 2.5X
*VETS/30-43: 8X TO 20X BASIC CARDS
*ROOKIES/30-43: 1.5X TO 4X
*VETS/20-29: 12X TO 30X BASIC CARDS
*ROOKIES/20-29: 2.5X TO 6X
*VETS/10-19: 20X TO 50X BASIC CARDS
*ROOKIES/10-19: 4X TO 10X
SERIAL #'d UNDER 10 NOT PRICED

2002 Fleer Focus JE Jersey Numbers Century

*VETS: 2.5X TO 6X BASIC CARDS
*ROOKIES: .6X TO 1.5X BASIC CARDS
STATED PRINT RUN 101-199

2002 Fleer Focus JE Franchise Focus

Inserted in packs at a rate of 1:12, this 32 card set features color action shots with each teams respective colors in background.

STATED ODDS 1:12
1 David Boston .75 2.00
2 Michael Vick 1.00 2.50
3 Ray Lewis 1.25 3.00
4 Drew Bledsoe 1.00 2.50
5 Julius Peppers 2.00 5.00
6 Brian Urlacher 1.25 3.00
7 Corey Dillon .75 2.00
8 Tim Couch .75 2.00
9 Emmitt Smith 2.00 5.00
10 Rod Smith 1.00 2.50
11 Joey Harrington .75 2.00
12 Brett Favre 2.50 6.00
13 David Carr .75 2.00
14 Peyton Manning 3.00 8.00
15 Jimmy Smith 1.00 2.50
16 Tony Gonzalez 1.00 2.50
17 Ricky Williams 1.00 2.50
18 Randy Moss 1.00 2.50
19 Tom Brady 6.00 15.00
20 Aaron Brooks .75 2.00
21 Michael Strahan 1.00 2.50
22 Curtis Martin 1.00 2.50
23 Jerry Rice 2.50 6.00
24 Donovan McNabb 1.00 2.50
25 Jerome Bettis 1.25 3.00
26 Junior Seau 1.00 2.50
27 Jeff Garcia .75 2.00
28 Shaun Alexander .75 2.00
29 Kurt Warner 1.00 2.50
30 Keyshawn Johnson 1.00 2.50
31 Eddie George 1.00 2.50
32 Stephen Davis .75 2.00

2002 Fleer Focus JE Franchise Focus Jerseys

Inserted in packs at a rate of 1:82, this 10 card set features color action shots with each teams respective color in the background along with a swatch of game used jersey.

STATED ODDS 1:82
1 Tim Couch 2.00 5.00
2 Stephen Davis 2.00 5.00
3 Keyshawn Johnson 2.50 6.00
4 Ray Lewis 3.00 8.00
5 Donovan McNabb 2.50 6.00
6 Randy Moss 2.50 6.00
7 Junior Seau 2.50 6.00
8 Brian Urlacher 3.00 8.00
9 Kurt Warner 2.50 6.00
10 Ricky Williams 2.50 6.00

2002 Fleer Focus JE Franchise Focus Rivals

Randomly inserted in packs, this 10 card set features NFL rivals with a swatch of game worn jersey for each player. The cards were serial numbered on back to 100.

STATED PRINT RUN 100 SER.#'d SETS
ABMV A.Brooks/M.Vick 3.00 8.00
CMRB C.Martin/T.Brady 20.00 50.00
DBSA D.Boston/S.Alexander 2.50 6.00
DMMS D.McNabb/M.Strahan 3.00 8.00
ESSD E.Smith/S.Davis 6.00 15.00
JGKW J.Garcia/K.Warner 3.00 8.00
JRJS J.Rice/J.Seau 8.00 20.00
JSEG J.Smith/E.George 3.00 8.00
RMBF R.Moss/B.Favre 8.00 20.00
TCJB T.Couch/J.Bettis 4.00 10.00

2002 Fleer Focus JE Freeze Frame

Inserted in packs at a rate of 1:24, this 15 card set features color action fronts along with a film cell.

STATED ODDS 1:24
1 Kurt Warner 1.25 3.00
2 Eddie George 1.25 3.00
3 Marshall Faulk 1.25 3.00
4 Emmitt Smith 2.50 6.00
5 Randy Moss 1.25 3.00
6 Brett Favre 3.00 8.00
7 Drew Bledsoe 1.25 3.00
8 LaDainian Tomlinson 1.50 4.00
9 Tom Brady 8.00 20.00
10 Donovan McNabb 1.25 3.00
11 Ricky Williams 1.25 3.00
12 Jerry Rice 3.00 8.00
13 Daunte Culpepper 1.25 3.00
14 Peyton Manning 4.00 10.00
15 Brian Urlacher 1.50 4.00

2002 Fleer Focus JE Freeze Frame Jerseys

Inserted in packs at a rate of 1:187, this 10 card set features color action fronts along with a film cell and a swatch of game worn jersey.

STATED ODDS 1:187
*PATCH/50: .6X TO 1.5X BASIC JSY
PATCHES PRINT RUN 50 SER.#'d SETS
1 Marshall Faulk 3.00 8.00
2 Brett Favre 8.00 20.00
3 Eddie George 3.00 8.00
4 Peyton Manning 10.00 25.00
5 Donovan McNabb 3.00 8.00
6 Randy Moss 3.00 8.00
7 Emmitt Smith 6.00 15.00
8 Brian Urlacher 4.00 10.00
9 Kurt Warner 3.00 8.00
10 Ricky Williams 3.00 8.00

2002 Fleer Focus JE Lettermen

Randomly inserted as hobby only box toppers, these 20-cards feature jumbo material swatches of an actual letter cut from the player's jersey nameplate. Each letter is considered a 1 of 1. Due to market scarcity, no pricing is provided.

UNPRICED LETTERMEN #'d TO 1

2002 Fleer Focus JE Materialistic Home

Inserted in packs at a rate of 1:24, this 15-card set features the player's action photo set against a fabric material background.

STATED ODDS 1:24
*AWAY/50: .8X TO 2X HOME JSY
AWAY PRINT RUN 50 SER.#'d SETS
1 Kurt Warner 2.50 6.00
2 Tom Brady 15.00 40.00
3 Daunte Culpepper 2.50 6.00
4 Drew Bledsoe 2.50 6.00
5 Emmitt Smith 5.00 12.00
6 Jerry Rice 6.00 15.00
7 Eddie George 2.50 6.00
8 Donovan McNabb 2.50 6.00
9 Brett Favre 6.00 15.00
10 Peyton Manning 8.00 20.00
11 Randy Moss 2.50 6.00
12 Marshall Faulk 2.50 6.00
13 Ricky Williams 2.50 6.00
14 Brian Urlacher 3.00 8.00
15 Edgerrin James 2.50 6.00

2002 Fleer Focus JE Materialistic Jumbos

Inserted at a rate of one per hobby box, this 15 card set was done as a sealed oversized pack box topper. The cards feature the player's action photo set against a material background.

STATED ODDS ONE PER BOX
*GOLD/50: 1X TO 2.5X BASIC INSERT
GOLD PRINT RUN 50 SER.#'d SETS
1 Joey Harrington 1.25 3.00
2 William Green 1.50 4.00
3 Donte Stallworth 2.00 5.00
4 Ashley Lelie 1.25 3.00
5 Jabar Gaffney 1.25 3.00
6 Antonio Bryant 2.00 5.00
7 Josh Reed 1.50 4.00
8 Antwaan Randle El 1.50 4.00
9 Reche Caldwell 1.50 4.00
10 Javon Walker 2.00 5.00
11 T.J. Duckett 1.25 3.00
12 Marquise Walker 1.25 3.00
13 Clinton Portis 2.00 5.00
14 DeShaun Foster 2.00 5.00
15 Patrick Ramsey 1.50 4.00

2002 Fleer Focus JE Materialistic Plus

Randomly inserted in packs, this 10 card set fetaures a color action photo set against a material background. Cards also contain a swatch of game used jersey and are serial numbered to 250.

STATED PRINT RUN 250 SER.#'d SETS
1 Brett Favre 10.00 25.00
2 Eddie George 4.00 10.00
3 Peyton Manning 12.00 30.00
4 Donovan McNabb 4.00 10.00
5 Randy Moss 4.00 10.00
6 Emmitt Smith 8.00 20.00
7 Brian Urlacher 5.00 12.00
8 Kurt Warner 4.00 10.00
9 Ricky Williams 4.00 10.00
10 Marshall Faulk 4.00 10.00

2002 Fleer Focus JE ROY Collection

Inserted in packs at a rate of 1:144, this 15 card set features past players who received rookie of the year honors.

STATED ODDS 1:144
1 Emmitt Smith 5.00 12.00
2 Curtis Martin 2.50 6.00
3 Anthony Thomas 2.50 6.00
4 Brian Urlacher 3.00 8.00
5 Jerome Bettis 3.00 8.00
6 Edgerrin James 2.50 6.00
7 Jevon Kearse 2.00 5.00
8 Marshall Faulk 2.50 6.00
9 Eric Dickerson 2.50 6.00
10 Randy Moss 2.50 6.00
11 Tony Dorsett 3.00 8.00
12 Kendrell Bell 2.00 5.00
13 Eddie George 2.50 6.00
14 Charles Woodson 3.00 8.00
15 Warrick Dunn 2.00 5.00

2002 Fleer Focus JE ROY Collection Jerseys

Inserted in packs at a rate of 1:187, this 15 card set features past players who received rookie of the year honors. The cards also contain a swatch of game worn jersey within the letter "O" on the card front.

STATED ODDS 1:187
*PATCH/97-101: .6X TO 1.5X BASIC JSY
PATCH PRINT RUN 97-101
1 Kendrell Bell SP 4.00 10.00
2 Tony Dorsett SP 10.00 25.00
3 Warrick Dunn 4.00 10.00
4 Marshall Faulk 5.00 12.00
5 Eddie George 5.00 12.00
6 Jevon Kearse 4.00 10.00
7 Randy Moss 5.00 12.00
8 Anthony Thomas SP 5.00 12.00
9 Brian Urlacher SP 6.00 15.00

2003 Fleer Focus

Released in November of 2003, this set features 160 cards consisting of 120 veterans and 40 rookies. Rookies 121-160 are serial numbered to 699. Boxes contained 24 packs of 5 cards. SRP was $2.99.

COMP.SET w/o SP's (120) 10.00 25.00
121-160 ROOKIE PRINT RUN 699
1 Tony Gonzalez .25 .60
2 Aaron Brooks .20 .50
3 Joey Harrington .20 .50
4 Brett Favre .60 1.50
5 Donovan McNabb .25 .60
6 Jerome Bettis .30 .75
7 Michael Vick .25 .60
8 Travis Taylor .20 .50
9 Jay Fiedler .20 .50
10 David Boston .20 .50
11 Peerless Price .20 .50
12 Kevan Barlow .20 .50
13 LaDainian Tomlinson .30 .75
14 Jevon Kearse .20 .50
15 Peyton Manning .75 2.00
16 T.J. Duckett .20 .50
17 Drew Brees .30 .75
18 Brian Dawkins .30 .75
19 Charles Woodson .30 .75
20 Emmitt Smith .50 1.25
21 Joe Jurevicius .25 .60
22 Duce Staley .20 .50
23 Rod Gardner .20 .50
24 Jamal Lewis .25 .60
25 Jeff Garcia .20 .50
26 Clinton Portis .20 .50
27 Priest Holmes .20 .50
28 Mike Alstott .20 .50
29 Shaun Alexander .20 .50
30 Randy Moss .25 .60
31 Eric Moulds .20 .50
32 Troy Brown .20 .50
33 Michael Bennett .20 .50
34 Ricky Williams .25 .60
35 Champ Bailey .25 .60
36 Hugh Douglas .20 .50
37 Travis Henry .20 .50
38 Daunte Culpepper .25 .60
39 Koren Robinson .25 .60
40 Todd Heap .20 .50
41 John Abraham .25 .60
42 Drew Bledsoe .25 .60
43 Tom Brady 1.25 3.00
44 Torry Holt .25 .60
45 Jake Delhomme .20 .50
46 Joe Horn .20 .50
47 Julius Peppers .30 .75
48 Ray Lewis .30 .75
49 Deuce McAllister .25 .60
50 Marshall Faulk .25 .60
51 Takeo Spikes .20 .50
52 Kordell Stewart .20 .50
53 Brian Urlacher .30 .75
54 Zach Thomas .25 .60
55 Kurt Warner .25 .60
56 Peter Warrick .20 .50
57 Marty Booker .20 .50
58 Warren Sapp .25 .60
59 Jon Kitna .20 .50
60 Chad Johnson .20 .50
61 Jeremy Shockey .20 .50
62 Keyshawn Johnson .30 .75
63 Kelly Holcomb .20 .50
64 Corey Dillon .20 .50
65 Tiki Barber .25 .60
66 Eddie George .25 .60
67 Joey Galloway .25 .60
68 Tim Couch .20 .50
69 Amani Toomer .20 .50
70 Steve McNair .25 .60
71 Troy Hambrick .20 .50
72 William Green .20 .50
73 Chad Pennington .20 .50
74 Laveranues Coles .20 .50
75 Quincy Carter .20 .50
76 Antonio Bryant .20 .50
77 Curtis Martin .25 .60
78 Terrell Owens .25 .60
79 Patrick Ramsey .25 .60
80 Ashley Lelie .20 .50
81 Donte Stallworth .20 .50
82 Roy Williams .20 .50
83 Charlie Garner .25 .60
84 Chris Chambers .20 .50
85 Warrick Dunn .20 .50
86 Shannon Sharpe .25 .60
87 Rod Smith .25 .60
88 Marvin Harrison .25 .60
89 Rich Gannon .25 .60
90 Stephen Davis .20 .50
91 James Stewart .20 .50
92 Tim Brown .30 .75
93 Anthony Thomas .25 .60
94 Stacey Mack .20 .50
95 Jake Plummer .20 .50
96 Jerry Rice .60 1.50
97 Quincy Morgan .20 .50
98 Dwight Freeney .20 .50
99 Jason Taylor .25 .60
100 Ahman Green .25 .60
101 Hines Ward .25 .60
102 Kerry Collins .20 .50
103 Plaxico Burress .20 .50
104 Santana Moss .25 .60
105 Michael Strahan .25 .60
106 Donald Driver .25 .60
107 Tommy Maddox .20 .50
108 Jerry Porter .20 .50
109 David Carr .20 .50
110 Garrison Hearst .20 .50
111 Edgerrin James .25 .60
112 Isaac Bruce .30 .75
113 Marc Bulger .20 .50
114 Brad Johnson .25 .60
115 Fred Taylor .20 .50
116 Derrick Brooks .20 .50
117 Jimmy Smith .25 .60
118 Derrick Mason .20 .50
119 Mark Brunell .25 .60
120 Trent Green .20 .50
121 Mike Doss RC 2.00 5.00
122 Carson Palmer RC 2.50 6.00
123 Charles Rogers RC 1.50 4.00
124 Andre Johnson RC 3.00 8.00
125 Tony Hollings RC 1.50 4.00
126 Terence Newman RC 2.00 5.00
127 Byron Leftwich RC 1.50 4.00
128 Terrell Suggs RC 1.50 4.00
129 Bryant Johnson RC 2.00 5.00
130 Kyle Boller RC 1.25 3.00
131 Rex Grossman RC 1.50 4.00
132 Willis McGahee RC 1.50 4.00
133 Dallas Clark RC 2.00 5.00
134 Bobby Wade RC 1.50 4.00
135 Tony Romo RC 30.00 60.00
136 Michael Haynes RC 1.25 3.00
137 Bethel Johnson RC 1.25 3.00
138 Anquan Boldin RC 2.00 5.00
139 Seneca Wallace RC 1.50 4.00
140 Nick Barnett RC 2.00 5.00
141 Teyo Johnson RC 1.50 4.00
142 Kelley Washington RC 1.25 3.00
143 Nate Burleson RC 1.50 4.00
144 Ken Dorsey RC 1.50 4.00
145 Dewayne White RC 1.25 3.00
146 Chris Kelsay RC 1.50 4.00
147 Dave Ragone RC 1.25 3.00
148 David Tyree RC 1.50 4.00
149 Billy McMullen RC 1.25 3.00
150 Chris Simms RC 1.25 3.00
151 Onterrio Smith RC 1.25 3.00
152 Marcus Trufant RC 1.50 4.00
153 Jason Witten RC 5.00 12.00
154 Johnathan Sullivan RC 1.25 3.00
155 Kevin Williams RC 2.00 5.00
156 Justin Fargas RC 2.00 5.00
157 Domanick Davis RC 1.50 4.00
158 LaBrandon Toefield RC 1.25 3.00
159 Shaun McDonald RC 1.50 4.00
160 Brandon Lloyd RC 2.00 5.00

2003 Fleer Focus Anniversary Gold

*VETS 1-120: 5X TO 12X BASIC CARDS
*ROOKIES 121-160: .8X TO 2X
STATED PRINT RUN 50 SER.#'d SETS
135 Tony Romo 75.00 125.00

2003 Fleer Focus Anniversary Silver

*VETS 1-120: 8X TO 20X BASIC CARDS
*ROOKIES 121-160: 1.2X TO 3X
STATED PRINT RUN 25 SER.#'d SETS
135 Tony Romo 125.00 200.00

2003 Fleer Focus Numbers Century

*VETS 1-120: 3X TO 8X BASIC CARDS
*ROOKIES 121-160: .5X TO 1.2X
STATED PRINT RUN 100 SER.#'d SETS
UNPRICED DECADE SER.#'d TO 10
135 Tony Romo 40.00 80.00

2003 Fleer Focus Numbers Decade

UNPRICED DECADE SER.#'d TO 10
NOT PRICED DUE TO SCARCITY

2003 Fleer Focus Diamond Focus

This set features die cut cards of some of the NFL's biggest superstars. Each card is serial numbered to 350.

STATED PRINT RUN 350 SER.#'d SETS
1 Ricky Williams 1.50 4.00
2 Chad Pennington 1.25 3.00
3 Michael Vick 1.50 4.00
4 Brett Favre 4.00 10.00
5 Peyton Manning 5.00 12.00
6 Marshall Faulk 1.50 4.00
7 Carson Palmer 1.50 4.00
8 Charles Rogers 1.50 4.00
9 Willis McGahee 1.00 2.50
10 Andre Johnson 2.00 5.00
11 Byron Leftwich 1.00 2.50
12 Kyle Boller 1.25 3.00
13 LaDainian Tomlinson 2.00 5.00
14 Drew Bledsoe 1.50 4.00
15 Jerry Rice 4.00 10.00

2003 Fleer Focus Diamond Focus Jerseys 200

Randomly inserted in packs, this set features game worn jersey swatches. Each card is die cut and serial numbered to 200.

STATED PRINT RUN 200 SER.#'d SETS
*JERSEYS/100: .5X TO 1.2X JSY/200
*JERSEYS/50: .8X TO 2X JSY/200
JERSEYS/5 TOO SCARCE TO PRICE
1 Drew Bledsoe 2.00 5.00
2 Marshall Faulk 2.00 5.00
3 Brett Favre 5.00 12.00
4 Peyton Manning 6.00 15.00
5 Chad Pennington 1.50 4.00
6 Jerry Rice 5.00 12.00
7 Charles Rogers 2.00 5.00
8 LaDainian Tomlinson 2.50 6.00
9 Michael Vick 2.00 5.00
10 Ricky Williams 2.00 5.00

2003 Fleer Focus Emerald Focus

This set features die cut cards of some of the NFL's brightest stars. Each card is serial numbered to 500.

COMPLETE SET (10) 20.00 50.00
STATED PRINT RUN 500 SER.#'d SETS
1 Donovan McNabb 1.25 3.00
2 Kurt Warner 1.25 3.00
3 David Carr 1.00 2.50
4 Tom Brady 6.00 15.00
5 Brian Urlacher 1.50 4.00
6 Randy Moss 1.25 3.00
7 Joey Harrington 1.00 2.50
8 Edgerrin James 1.25 3.00
9 Emmitt Smith 2.50 6.00
10 Jeremy Shockey 1.00 2.50

2003 Fleer Focus Emerald Focus Jerseys 250

Randomly inserted in packs, this set features game worn jersey swatches. Each card is die cut and serial numbered to 250.

STATED PRINT RUN 250 SER.#'d SETS
*JERSEYS/150: .5X TO 1.2X JSY/250
*JERSEYS/75: .6X TO 1.5X JSY/250
JERSEYS/10 TOO SCARCE TO PRICE
1 Tom Brady 15.00 40.00
2 David Carr 2.50 6.00
3 Joey Harrington 2.50 6.00
4 Edgerrin James 3.00 8.00
5 Jeremy Shockey 2.50 6.00
6 Donovan McNabb 3.00 8.00
7 Randy Moss 3.00 8.00
8 Emmitt Smith 6.00 15.00
9 Brian Urlacher 4.00 10.00
10 Kurt Warner 3.00 8.00

2003 Fleer Focus Extra Effort

COMPLETE SET (10) 15.00 40.00
STATED PRINT RUN 500 SER.#'d SETS
1 Emmitt Smith 2.50 6.00
2 Brett Favre 3.00 8.00
3 Hines Ward 1.25 3.00
4 Jerry Rice 3.00 8.00
5 Jeff Garcia 1.00 2.50
6 Chad Pennington 1.00 2.50
7 Eric Moulds 1.00 2.50
8 Daunte Culpepper 1.25 3.00
9 Fred Taylor 1.00 2.50
10 Drew Brees 1.50 4.00

2003 Fleer Focus Shirtified

COMPLETE SET (15) 12.00 30.00
STATED PRINT RUN 750 SER.#'d SETS
1 Torry Holt 1.00 2.50
2 Michael Vick 1.00 2.50
3 Jeremy Shockey .75 2.00
4 Terrell Owens 1.00 2.50
5 Plaxico Burress .75 2.00
6 Steve McNair 1.00 2.50
7 Ricky Williams 1.00 2.50
8 Tim Brown 1.25 3.00
9 Brian Urlacher 1.25 3.00
10 Priest Holmes .75 2.00
11 Tommy Maddox .75 2.00
12 Deuce McAllister 1.00 2.50
13 Marvin Harrison 1.00 2.50
14 Clinton Portis .75 2.00
15 Tiki Barber 1.00 2.50

2003 Fleer Focus Shirtified Jerseys 175

Randomly inserted in packs, this set features game worn jersey swatches. Each card is serial numbered to 175.

STATED PRINT RUN 175 SER.#'d SETS
*JERSEYS/75: .6X TO 1.5X JSY/175
*NAMEPLATE/25: 1.5X TO 3X JSY/175
UNPRICED NFL LOGO PRINT RUN 1
*NUMBERS/80-90: .6X TO 1.5X JSY/175
*NUMBERS/52-54: .8X TO 2X JSY/175
*NUMBERS/31-37: 1X TO 2.5X JSY/175
*NUMBERS/20-27: 1.2X TO 3X JSY/175
NUMBERS STATED PRINT RUN 4-90
1 Shaun Alexander 2.50 6.00
2 Tiki Barber 3.00 8.00
3 Tim Brown 4.00 10.00
4 Plaxico Burress 2.50 6.00
5 Daunte Culpepper 3.00 8.00
6 Brett Favre 8.00 20.00
7 Eddie George 4.00 10.00
8 William Green 2.50 6.00
9 Marvin Harrison 3.00 8.00
10 Travis Henry 2.50 6.00
11 Priest Holmes 2.50 6.00
12 Torry Holt 3.00 8.00
13 Andre Johnson 4.00 10.00
14 Ray Lewis 4.00 10.00
15 Tommy Maddox 2.50 6.00
16 Deuce McAllister 3.00 8.00
17 Steve McNair 3.00 8.00
18 Terrell Owens 3.00 8.00
19 Julius Peppers 4.00 10.00
20 Clinton Portis 2.50 6.00
21 Jeremy Shockey 2.50 6.00
22 Emmitt Smith 6.00 15.00
23 Brian Urlacher 4.00 10.00
24 Michael Vick 3.00 8.00
25 Ricky Williams 3.00 8.00

2003 Fleer Focus Shirtified Jerseys Numbers

Randomly inserted in packs, this set features game worn jersey swatches. Each card is serial numbered to the player's jersey number. Cards with print runs under 12 are not priced due to scarcity.

NUMBERS STATED PRINT RUN 4-90

2001 Fleer Game Time

Fleer Game Time released in July of 2001. The 150-card set featured 110 veterans and 40 rookies called Next Game. The cardfronts had 3 pictures of the featured player, a full color photo is the main focus, a two-color image of the the main photo is used in the background, and the headshot was taken from the main photo and placed on the left side of the card. The cardbacks were horizontal and contained statistics up through 2000. The rookie cards were serial numbered to 2001.

COMP.SET w/o SP's (110) 6.00 15.00
1 Donovan McNabb .15 .40
2 Travis Prentice .12 .30
3 Keenan McCardell .15 .40
4 Kurt Warner .30 .75
5 Ray Lewis .20 .50
6 Terrell Davis .15 .40
7 Kevin Faulk .12 .30
8 Terrell Owens .15 .40
9 Jeff George .15 .40
10 Dennis Northcutt .12 .30
11 Fred Taylor .12 .30
12 Cris Carter .20 .50
13 Aaron Brooks .12 .30
14 Marshall Faulk .15 .40
15 David Boston .12 .30
16 Rocket Ismail .15 .40
17 Jerome Bettis .20 .50
18 Warrick Dunn .12 .30
19 Corey Dillon .12 .30
20 Mark Brunell .15 .40
21 Torry Holt .15 .40
22 Michael McCrary .12 .30
23 Rod Smith .15 .40
24 Charlie Garner .15 .40
25 Bruce Smith .15 .40
26 Doug Johnson .12 .30
27 Brian Griese .12 .30
28 Jeff Garcia .12 .30
29 Eddie George .20 .50
30 Shawn Bryson .12 .30
31 Marvin Harrison .15 .40
32 Hugh Douglas .12 .30
33 Terance Mathis .12 .30
34 Emmitt Smith .30 .75
35 Lamar Smith .15 .40
36 Junior Seau .15 .40
37 Steve McNair .15 .40
38 Jake Plummer .12 .30
39 Tim Couch .12 .30
40 Jay Fiedler .15 .40
41 Plaxico Burress .12 .30
42 Keyshawn Johnson .15 .40
43 Jason Taylor .20 .50
44 Charlie Batch .12 .30
45 Terry Glenn .15 .40
46 Laveranues Coles .15 .40
47 Darrell Jackson .16 .40
48 Jamal Lewis .20 .50
49 Ed McCaffrey .15 .40
50 Vinny Testaverde .12 .30
51 Ricky Watters .15 .40
52 Champ Bailey .15 .40
53 Peter Warrick .12 .30
54 Eric Moulds .12 .30
55 Michael Strahan .15 .40
56 Warren Sapp .15 .40
57 Tony Gonzalez .15 .40
58 Kerry Collins .12 .30
59 Shaun King .12 .30
60 Jason Sehorn .15 .40
61 Marcus Robinson .15 .40
62 James Stewart .12 .30
63 Curtis Martin .15 .40
64 Brian Urlacher .25 .60
65 Germane Crowell .12 .30
66 Wesley Walls .12 .30
67 Antonio Freeman .20 .50
68 Ron Dayne .15 .40
69 Tyrone Wheatley .15 .40
70 Zach Thomas .15 .40
71 Shannon Sharpe .15 .40
72 Mike Anderson .12 .30
73 Wayne Chrebet .12 .30
74 Shaun Alexander .12 .30
75 Stephen Davis .12 .30
76 Derrick Mason .12 .30
77 Dorsey Levens .15 .40
78 Jessie Armstead .12 .30
79 Rich Gannon .15 .40
80 Muhsin Muhammad .12 .30
81 Brett Favre .40 1.00
82 Randy Moss .15 .40
83 Joe Horn .12 .30
84 Charles Woodson .20 .50
85 Brad Hoover .15 .40
86 Terrence Wilkins .12 .30
87 Sylvester Morris .12 .30
88 Tim Brown .20 .50
89 Jamal Anderson .15 .40
90 Joey Galloway .15 .40
91 Drew Bledsoe .15 .40
92 Rodney Harrison .12 .30
93 Jevon Kearse .12 .30
94 Rob Johnson .15 .40
95 Edgerrin James .15 .40
96 Thomas Jones .12 .30
97 Courtney Brown .12 .30
98 Jimmy Smith .15 .40
99 Ricky Williams .15 .40
100 Isaac Bruce .20 .50
101 Akili Smith .12 .30
102 Derrick Alexander .12 .30
103 Daunte Culpepper .15 .40
104 Amani Toomer .12 .30
105 Mike Alstott .12 .30
106 Sam Cowart .12 .30
107 Peyton Manning .50 1.25
108 Robert Smith .12 .30
109 Duce Staley .12 .30
110 Cade McNown .15 .40
111 Michael Vick RC 2.50 6.00
112 David Terrell RC 1.25 3.00
113 Deuce McAllister RC 1.50 4.00
114 Koren Robinson RC 1.25 3.00
115 Rod Gardner RC 1.25 3.00
116 Chris Chambers RC 1.00 2.50
117 Santana Moss RC 1.50 4.00
118 Reggie Wayne RC 2.00 5.00
119 Quincy Morgan RC 1.25 3.00
120 Rudi Johnson RC 1.50 4.00
121 Robert Ferguson RC 1.50 4.00
122 Ja'Mar Toombs RC 1.00 2.50
123 Michael Bennett RC 1.25 3.00
124 Ronney Daniels RC 1.00 2.50
125 Drew Brees RC 15.00 40.00
126 Josh Heupel RC 1.50 4.00
127 Chris Weinke RC 1.25 3.00
128 LaDainian Tomlinson RC 5.00 12.00
129 Chad Johnson RC 1.50 4.00
130 LaMont Jordan RC 1.50 4.00
131 Freddie Mitchell RC 1.00 2.50
132 Anthony Thomas RC 1.50 4.00
133 Ben Leard RC 1.00 2.50
134 Sage Rosenfels RC 1.25 3.00
135 Marques Tuiasosopo RC 1.25 3.00
136 Gerard Warren RC 1.25 3.00
137 Jamar Fletcher RC 1.00 2.50
138 Justin Smith RC 2.00 5.00
139 Dan Morgan RC 1.25 3.00
140 Jamal Reynolds RC 1.00 2.50
141 Shaun Rogers RC 1.50 4.00
142 Todd Heap RC 1.25 3.00
143 Travis Minor RC 1.25 3.00
144 Mike McMahon RC 1.25 3.00
145 Travis Henry RC 1.25 3.00
146 Kevan Barlow RC 1.25 3.00
147 Javon Green RC 1.00 2.50
148 Ken-Yon Rambo RC 1.00 2.50
149 Tim Hasselbeck RC 1.25 3.00
150 Snoop Minnis RC 1.00 2.50
CL1 Checklist .05 .15
CL2 Checklist .05 .15

2001 Fleer Game Time Extra

*VETS 1-110: 2.5X TO 6X BASIC CARDS
*ROOKIES 111-150: .8X TO 2X
OVERALL STATED ODDS 1:8
111-150 ROOKIE PRINT RUN 201

2001 Fleer Game Time Crunch Time

Randomly inserted in packs of 2001 Fleer Game Time at a rate of 1:4 hobby, and 1:5 retail, this 20-card set featured players who get the ball at crunch-time. The cardfronts featured a horizontal design with silver-foil lettering and highlights. The cardfronts also had raised the seams on the picture of the football. The cards numbering carried an 'of 20 CT' suffix.

COMPLETE SET (20) 7.50 20.00
STATED ODDS 1:4 HOB, 1:5 RET
1 Emmitt Smith 1.25 3.00
2 Isaac Bruce .75 2.00
3 James Stewart .50 1.25
4 Warrick Dunn .50 1.25
5 Jake Plummer .50 1.25
6 Shannon Sharpe .60 1.50
7 Robert Smith .50 1.25
8 Jamal Anderson .60 1.50
9 Terrell Owens .60 1.50
10 Marcus Robinson .60 1.50
11 Ed McCaffrey .60 1.50
12 Jamal Lewis .75 2.00
13 Amani Toomer .50 1.25
14 Jerome Bettis .75 2.00
15 Cris Carter .75 2.00
16 Stephen Davis .50 1.25
17 Marvin Harrison .60 1.50
18 Joe Horn .50 1.25
19 Tim Couch .50 1.25
20 Drew Bledsoe .60 1.50

2001 Fleer Game Time Double Trouble

The Double Trouble set was randomly inserted in packs of 2001 Fleer GameTime at a rate of 1:24 hobby, and 1:30 retail. These cards featured 2 teammates on the cardfronts. The card design consisted of 2 die-cut edges, silver-foil highlights, and 2 of the 4 photos in full color and the other 2 with rainbow-holofoil technology. The cardbacks carried an 'of 15 DT' suffix.

COMPLETE SET (15) 12.50 30.00
STATED ODDS 1:24 HOB. 1:30 RET.
1 D.Culpepper/R.Moss .75 2.00
2 K.Warner/M.Faulk 1.50 4.00
3 P.Manning/E.James 2.50 6.00
4 W.Dunn/Key.Johnson .60 1.50
5 B.Favre/A.Freeman 2.00 5.00
6 T.Barber/R.Dayne .75 2.00
7 C.Dillon/P.Warrick .60 1.50
8 D.McNabb/D.Staley .75 2.00
9 F.Taylor/J.Smith .75 2.00
10 R.Gannon/T.Brown 1.00 2.50
11 S.McNair/E.George 1.00 2.50
12 C.Martin/W.Chrebet .75 2.00
13 R.Williams/A.Brooks .75 2.00
14 D.Alexander/T.Gonzalez .75 2.00
15 B.Griese/T.Davis .75 2.00

2001 Fleer Game Time Eleven-Up

Randomly inserted in packs of 2001 Fleer GameTime at a rate of 1:12 hobby and 1: 15 retail, this 15-card set featured some of the top players from the NFL. The set design was cut into the shape of a clipboard. The detail even went as far as raising the card were the clip was located and using a metallic silver for its realistic look. The cardbacks had a small full color photo of the featured player and a brief description of a highlight from this past season. The cards carried an 'of 15 E' suffix for their numbering.

COMPLETE SET (15) 12.50 30.00
STATED ODDS 1:12 HOB. 1:15 RET.
1 Jamal Lewis 1.00 2.50
2 Randy Moss .75 2.00
3 Ricky Williams .75 2.00
4 Terrell Davis .75 2.00
5 Donovan McNabb .75 2.00
6 Curtis Martin .75 2.00
7 Brett Favre 2.00 5.00
8 Aaron Brooks .60 1.50
9 Kurt Warner 1.50 4.00
10 Eddie George 1.00 2.50
11 Daunte Culpepper .75 2.00
12 Jamal Anderson .75 2.00
13 Marshall Faulk .75 2.00
14 Ray Lewis 1.00 2.50
15 Ron Dayne .75 2.00

2001 Fleer Game Time Fame Time Jerseys

Randomly inserted in packs of 2001 Fleer GameTime, this 11-card set featured 11 Hall of Famers. These cards featured jersey swatches and were hand serially numbered to 100 on the fronts. The set name "Fame Time" was printed in gold foil against a red colored background near the top of the cards.

STATED PRINT RUN 100 SER.#'d SETS
*RED: .3X TO .8X BASIC JSY
1 Terry Bradshaw 8.00 20.00
2 Eric Dickerson 5.00 12.00
3 Tony Dorsett 6.00 15.00
4 Paul Hornung 6.00 15.00
5 Howie Long 6.00 15.00
6 Joe Montana 20.00 50.00
7 Walter Payton 15.00 40.00
8 Roger Staubach 8.00 20.00
9 Fran Tarkenton 6.00 15.00
10 Lawrence Taylor 6.00 15.00
11 Johnny Unitas 12.00 30.00

2001 Fleer Game Time Fame Time Jerseys Autographs

Randomly inserted in packs of 2001 Fleer GameTime, this set featured ten Hall of Famers. These cards featured jersey

swatches and autographs and were hand serially numbered to 25. Each also features red foil on the set name at the top of the cardfront. Please note that at the time of release these cards were issued as exchange cards that carried an expiration date of July 2002.
STATED PRINT RUN 25 SER.#'d SETS

1 Terry Bradshaw	100.00	200.00
2 Eric Dickerson	30.00	80.00
3 Tony Dorsett	60.00	120.00
4 Paul Hornung	30.00	80.00
5 Howie Long	60.00	120.00
6 Joe Montana	150.00	300.00
7 Roger Staubach	75.00	150.00
8 Fran Tarkenton	30.00	80.00
10 Johnny Unitas	175.00	300.00

2001 Fleer Game Time In the Zone

Randomly inserted in packs of 2001 Fleer GameTime at a rate of 1:73 hobby-only, this 14-card set featured game-used pylons from the endzone and Indy's RCA Dome. The set featured players who charged into Indy's endzone in 2000.
STATED ODDS 1:73

CM Curtis Martin	2.50	6.00
DB Drew Bledsoe	2.00	5.00
DC Daunte Culpepper	2.00	5.00
EJ Edgerrin James	2.00	5.00
JR J.R. Redmond	1.50	4.00
JS James Stewart	1.50	4.00
JS Jimmy Smith	2.00	5.00
MH Marvin Harrison	2.00	5.00
OG Oronde Gadsden	1.50	4.00
PM Peyton Manning	6.00	15.00
PP Peerless Price	1.50	4.00
RG Rich Gannon	2.00	5.00
RM Randy Moss	2.00	5.00
TW Tyrone Wheatley	2.00	5.00

2001 Fleer Game Time Uniformity

Randomly inserted in packs of 2001 Fleer GameTime at a rate of 1:19 hobby-only. This set featured swatches of game jerseys or pants from some of the top players in the NFL. The unnumbered cards are listed alphabetically below.
STATED ODDS 1:19 HOBBY

1 Jessie Armstead	2.00	5.00
2 Champ Bailey	2.50	6.00
3 David Boston	2.00	5.00
4 Kyle Brady Pants	2.00	5.00
5 Courtney Brown	2.00	5.00
6 Isaac Bruce	3.00	8.00
7 Mark Brunell	2.50	6.00
8 Plaxico Burress	2.00	5.00
9 Trung Canidate Pants	2.00	5.00
10 Wayne Chrebet	2.00	5.00
11 Tim Couch Pants	2.00	5.00
12 Marshall Faulk Pants	2.50	6.00
13 Marvin Harrison	2.50	6.00
14 Torry Holt	2.50	6.00
15 Kevin Johnson Pants	2.00	5.00
16 Jevon Kearse	2.00	5.00
17 Shaun King	2.00	5.00
18 Dorsey Levens	2.50	6.00
19 Dan Marino	6.00	15.00
20 Keenan McCardell	2.50	6.00
21 Donovan McNabb	2.50	6.00
22 Cade McNown	2.50	6.00
23 Jake Plummer	2.00	5.00
24 Travis Prentice	2.00	5.00
25 Peerless Price	2.00	5.00
26 Chris Redman	3.00	8.00
27 Jerry Rice	6.00	15.00
28 Marcus Robinson	2.50	6.00
29 Corey Simon	2.00	5.00
30 Jimmy Smith	2.50	6.00
31 Duce Staley	2.00	5.00
32 Kordell Stewart	2.00	5.00
33 Michael Strahan Pants	2.50	6.00
34 Fred Taylor	2.00	5.00
35 Kurt Warner	5.00	12.00

2000 Fleer Gamers

Released as a 145-card set, Fleer Gamers features 100 veteran cards and 45 rookie cards. Base card is half foil and features full color action player shots, and the Next Gamers rookie cards feature an all-foil card stock. Fleer Gamers was packaged in 24-pack boxes with packs containing five cards and carried a suggested retail price of $3.99.

COMPLETE SET (145)	50.00	100.00
COMP.SET w/o SPs (100)	7.50	20.00
1 Edgerrin James	.20	.50
2 Tim Couch	.20	.50
3 Cris Carter	.25	.60
4 Rich Gannon	.20	.50
5 Akili Smith	.15	.40
6 Muhsin Muhammad	.15	.40
7 Dorsey Levens	.20	.50
8 Dedric Ward	.15	.40
9 Jevon Kearse	.15	.40
10 Peerless Price	.20	.50
11 Mike Alstott	.15	.40
12 Michael Strahan	.20	.50
13 Stephen Davis	.15	.40
14 Rob Moore	.15	.40
15 James Stewart	.15	.40
16 Robert Smith	.15	.40
17 Napoleon Kaufman	.20	.50
18 Peyton Manning	.60	1.50
19 Keyshawn Johnson	.20	.50
20 Tony Martin	.20	.50
21 Jermaine Fazande	.15	.40
22 Jamal Anderson	.20	.50
23 Ed McCaffrey	.20	.50
24 Drew Bledsoe	.20	.50
25 Duce Staley	.15	.40
26 Warrick Dunn	.15	.40
27 Chris Chandler	.20	.50
28 Olandis Gary	.20	.50
29 Terry Glenn	.20	.50
30 Donovan McNabb	.20	.50
31 Torry Holt	.20	.50
32 Tim Dwight	.20	.50
33 Terrell Davis	.20	.50
34 Tony Simmons	.15	.40
35 Jerome Bettis	.25	.60
36 Az-Zahir Hakim	.15	.40
37 Darrin Chiaverini	.15	.40
38 Fred Taylor	.15	.40
39 Jon Kitna	.15	.40
40 Tony Banks	.15	.40
41 Brian Griese	.15	.40
42 Jeff Blake	.20	.50
43 Kordell Stewart	.15	.40
44 Isaac Bruce	.25	.60
45 Shannon Sharpe	.20	.50
46 Rocket Ismail	.20	.50
47 Ricky Williams	.20	.50
48 Marshall Faulk	.20	.50
49 Qadry Ismail	.15	.40
50 Joey Galloway	.20	.50
51 Jake Reed	.20	.50
52 Kurt Warner	.40	1.00
53 Cade McNown	.15	.40
54 Herman Moore	.15	.40
55 Curtis Martin	.20	.50
56 Steve McNair	.20	.50
57 Tim Biakabutuka	.20	.50
58 Brett Favre	.50	1.25
59 Wayne Chrebet	.15	.40
60 Eddie George	.20	.50
61 Troy Aikman	.30	.75
62 Jimmy Smith	.20	.50
63 Derrick Mayes	.15	.40
64 Emmitt Smith	.40	1.00
65 Mark Brunell	.20	.50
66 Ricky Watters	.20	.50
67 Marcus Robinson	.20	.50
68 Randy Moss	.20	.50
69 Troy Edwards	.15	.40
70 Carl Pickens	.20	.50
71 Damon Huard	.15	.40
72 Mikhael Ricks	.15	.40
73 David Boston	.15	.40
74 Charlie Batch	.15	.40
75 Randall Cunningham	.20	.50
76 Tim Brown	.25	.60
77 Shaun King	.15	.40
78 Darnay Scott	.20	.50
79 Derrick Alexander	.15	.40
80 Steve Young	.30	.75
81 Kevin Johnson	.15	.40
82 Elvis Grbac	.15	.40
83 Tai Streets	.15	.40
84 Steve Beuerlein	.20	.50
85 Antonio Freeman	.20	.50
86 Vinny Testaverde	.15	.40
87 Brad Johnson	.20	.50
88 Curtis Enis	.15	.40
89 Jay Fiedler	.20	.50
90 Junior Seau	.20	.50
91 Eric Moulds	.15	.40
92 Jake Plummer	.15	.40
93 Amani Toomer	.15	.40
94 Champ Bailey	.20	.50
95 Germane Crowell	.15	.40
96 Tony Gonzalez	.20	.50
97 Jerry Rice	.60	1.50
98 Rob Johnson	.20	.50
99 Marvin Harrison	.20	.50
100 Kerry Collins	.15	.40
101 Thomas Jones RC	.75	2.00
102 Jarious Jackson RC	.75	2.00
103 R.Jay Soward RC	.60	1.50
104 Trung Canidate RC	.60	1.50
105 Travis Taylor RC	.60	1.50
106 Giovanni Carmazzi RC	.60	1.50
107 Jerry Porter RC	1.00	2.50
108 Chris Redman RC	.60	1.50
109 Tee Martin RC	.60	1.50
110 Dez White RC	.60	1.50
111 Danny Farmer RC	.60	1.50
112 Brian Urlacher RC	3.00	8.00
113 Reuben Droughns RC	.60	1.50
114 Marc Bulger RC	.75	2.00
115 Peter Warrick RC	.60	1.50
116 Plaxico Burress RC	.75	2.00
117 Ron Dugans RC	.60	1.50
118 Gari Scott RC	.60	1.50
119 Curtis Keaton RC	.60	1.50
120 Corey Simon RC	.75	2.00
121 Rob Morris RC	.75	2.00
122 Chad Morton RC	.75	2.00
123 Hank Poteat RC	.60	1.50
124 Ahmed Plummer RC	.60	1.50
125 Bashir Yamini RC	.60	1.50
126 J.R. Redmond RC	.60	1.50
127 Travis Prentice RC	.60	1.50
128 Todd Pinkston RC	.60	1.50
129 Courtney Brown RC	.75	2.00
130 Laveranues Coles RC	.75	2.00
131 Jamal Lewis RC	1.00	2.50
132 Tim Rattay RC	.75	2.00
133 Anthony Becht RC	.60	1.50
134 Chris Cole RC	.75	2.00
135 Ron Dayne RC	1.00	2.50
136 Sylvester Morris RC	.60	1.50
137 Joe Hamilton RC	.60	1.50
138 Dennis Northcutt RC	.60	1.50
139 Doug Johnson RC	.60	1.50
140 Shyrone Stith RC	.60	1.50
141 Darrell Jackson RC	.60	1.50
142 Michael Wiley RC	.60	1.50
143 Chad Pennington RC	.75	2.00
144 Bubba Franks RC	.60	1.50
145 Shaun Alexander RC	1.00	2.50

2000 Fleer Gamers Extra

COMPLETE SET (145)	100.00	200.00

*VETS 1-100: 1.5X TO 4X BASIC CARDS
1-100 VETERAN ODDS 1:8
*ROOKIES 101-145: .6X TO 1.5X
101-145 ROOKIE ODDS 1:24

2000 Fleer Gamers Change the Game

Randomly inserted in packs at the rate of one in 24, this 15-card set features an all foil card stock with full color player action shots. Background foil is set to match each respective player's team.

COMPLETE SET (15)	25.00	60.00
STATED ODDS 1:24		
1 Kurt Warner	1.00	2.50
2 Brett Favre	1.25	3.00
3 Eddie George	.50	1.25
4 Keyshawn Johnson	.50	1.25
5 Randy Moss	.50	1.25
6 Tim Couch	.50	1.25
7 Ricky Williams	.50	1.25
8 Peyton Manning	1.50	4.00
9 Terrell Davis	.50	1.25
10 Troy Aikman	.75	2.00
11 Fred Taylor	.40	1.00
12 Cade McNown	.40	1.00
13 Edgerrin James	.50	1.25
14 Peter Warrick	.40	1.00
15 Jamal Lewis	.60	1.50

2000 Fleer Gamers Contact Sport

Randomly inserted in packs at the rate of one in four, this 20-card set features four action shots in silver foil and one color portrait of each featured player.

COMPLETE SET (20)	10.00	25.00
STATED ODDS 1:4		
1 Peter Warrick	.20	.50
2 Jamal Lewis	.30	.75
3 Thomas Jones	.25	.60
4 Plaxico Burress	.25	.60
5 Travis Taylor	.20	.50
6 Ron Dayne	.30	.75
7 Bubba Franks	.20	.50
8 Chad Pennington	.25	.60
9 Shaun Alexander	.30	.75
10 Sylvester Morris	.20	.50
11 R.Jay Soward	.20	.50
12 Trung Canidate	.20	.50
13 Dennis Northcutt	.20	.50
14 Todd Pinkston	.20	.50
15 Jerry Porter	.30	.75
16 Travis Prentice	.20	.50
17 Courtney Brown	.25	.60
18 Ron Dugans	.20	.50
19 Dez White	.20	.50
20 Chris Redman	.20	.50

2000 Fleer Gamers Uniformity

Randomly inserted in packs at the rate of one in 44, this 34-card set features swatches of authentic game-worn jerseys or pants. The Charlie Batch cards include either a jersey or pants swatch and are titled "uniform" cards. This set is not numbered, therefore, numbers have been assigned alphabetically.
STATED ODDS 1:44

1 Troy Aikman	5.00	12.00
2 Jamal Anderson Pants	2.50	6.00
3 Charlie Batch Uniform	2.00	5.00
4 David Boston Pants	2.00	5.00
5 Tim Brown	3.00	8.00
6 Isaac Bruce Pants	3.00	8.00
7 Mark Brunell	2.50	6.00
8 Chris Chandler Pants	2.50	6.00
9 Tim Couch Pants	2.50	6.00
10 Germane Crowell Pants	2.00	5.00
11 Randall Cunningham	2.50	6.00
12 Stephen Davis	2.00	5.00
13 Tim Dwight Pants	2.50	6.00
14 Curtis Enis	2.00	5.00
15 Marshall Faulk	2.50	6.00
16 Az-Zahir Hakim	2.00	5.00
17 Marvin Harrison Pants	2.50	6.00
18 Torry Holt Pants	2.50	6.00
19 Edgerrin James Pants	2.50	6.00
20 Kevin Johnson Pants	2.00	5.00
21 Terry Kirby Pants	2.00	5.00
22 John Lynch	2.50	6.00
23 Peyton Manning Pants	8.00	20.00
24 Ed McCaffrey	2.50	6.00
25 Herman Moore Pants	2.00	5.00
26 Rob Moore Pants	2.00	5.00
27 Johnnie Morton Pants	2.50	6.00
28 Jake Plummer Pants	2.00	5.00
29 Jerry Rice	8.00	20.00
30 Frank Sanders Pants	2.00	5.00
31 Bruce Smith	2.50	6.00
32 Emmitt Smith	5.00	12.00
33 Kurt Warner	5.00	12.00
34 Steve Young	4.00	10.00

2000 Fleer Gamers Yard Chargers

Released as a three tier insert set, card numbers 1-5 are inserted at the rate of one in nine, 6-10 are inserted at the rate of one in 24, and card numbers 11-15 are inserted at the rate of one in 144. Base cards feature full color action photography set on a holographic foil card stock.

COMPLETE SET (15)	25.00	60.00
1-5 STATED ODDS 1:9		
6-10 STATED ODDS 1:24		
11-15 STATED ODDS 1:144		
1 Marvin Harrison	.40	1.00
2 Randy Moss	.40	1.00
3 Keyshawn Johnson	.40	1.00
4 Tim Brown	.50	1.25
5 Jerry Rice	1.25	3.00
6 Terrell Davis	.60	1.50
7 Emmitt Smith	1.25	3.00
8 Eddie George	.60	1.50
9 Edgerrin James	.60	1.50
10 Marshall Faulk	.60	1.50
11 Tim Couch	2.00	5.00
12 Kurt Warner	4.00	10.00
13 Peyton Manning	6.00	15.00
14 Brett Favre	5.00	12.00
15 Troy Aikman	3.00	8.00

2001 Fleer Genuine

Fleer Genuine was released in July of 2001. The base set consisted of 155 cards, with the last 30 from the set being short-printed rookies. The rookies were serial numbered to 1000, and each had a swatch of a jersey. The cardfronts were highlighted by silver foil lettering and the border is split vertically with the left side white and the right side a team color.

COMP.SET w/o RC's (125)	10.00	25.00
1 Donovan McNabb	.25	.60
2 Daunte Culpepper	.25	.60
3 Derrick Alexander	.20	.50
4 Jessie Armstead	.20	.50
5 Hines Ward	.25	.60
6 Peter Warrick	.20	.50
7 Jay Fiedler	.25	.60
8 Cris Carter	.30	.75
9 Az-Zahir Hakim	.20	.50
10 Michael Westbrook	.20	.50
11 Akili Smith	.20	.50
12 Lamar Smith	.25	.60
13 Eric Moulds	.20	.50
14 Shaun Alexander	.20	.50
15 Jeff George	.25	.60
16 Brad Hoover	.25	.60
17 Brian Griese	.20	.50
18 Keenan McCardell	.25	.60
19 Freddie Jones	.20	.50
20 Brian Urlacher	.40	1.00
21 Thomas Jones	.20	.50
22 Charlie Batch	.20	.50
23 Aaron Brooks	.20	.50
24 Hugh Douglas	.20	.50
25 Mike Alstott	.20	.50
26 Darrell Russell	.20	.50
27 Muhsin Muhammad	.20	.50
28 Rocket Ismail	.25	.60
29 Fred Taylor	.20	.50
30 Tyrone Wheatley	.25	.60
31 Rodney Harrison	.20	.50
32 Curtis Martin	.25	.60
33 Jason Sehorn	.25	.60
34 James McKnight	.20	.50
35 Jimmy Smith	.25	.60
36 Laveranues Coles	.25	.60
37 Jeff Garcia	.20	.50
38 Sam Cowart	.20	.50
39 Joey Galloway	.25	.60
40 Mark Brunell	.25	.60
41 Vinny Testaverde	.20	.50
42 Terrell Owens	.25	.60
43 Ray Lewis	.30	.75
44 Ahman Green	.25	.60
45 Ron Dayne	.25	.60
46 Samari Rolle	.20	.50
47 Shawn Bryson	.20	.50
48 Emmitt Smith	.50	1.25
49 Terrence Wilkins	.20	.50
50 Charlie Garner	.25	.60
51 Rob Johnson	.25	.60
52 Courtney Brown	.20	.50
53 Edgerrin James	.25	.60
54 Kurt Warner	.50	1.25
55 Michael McCrary	.20	.50
56 Dennis Northcutt	.20	.50
57 Marvin Harrison	.25	.60
58 Rich Gannon	.25	.60
59 Marshall Faulk	.25	.60
60 Travis Prentice	.20	.50
61 Terrell Davis	.25	.60
62 Charles Woodson	.30	.75
63 Isaac Bruce	.30	.75
64 Tim Couch	.20	.50
65 Oronde Gadsden	.20	.50
66 Randy Moss	.25	.60
67 Torry Holt	.25	.60
68 Shannon Sharpe	.25	.60
69 Antonio Freeman	.30	.75
70 Michael Strahan	.25	.60
71 Jevon Kearse	.20	.50
72 Jamal Lewis	.30	.75
73 Peyton Manning	.75	2.00
74 Amani Toomer	.20	.50
75 Derrick Mason	.20	.50
76 Jake Plummer	.20	.50
77 Rod Smith	.25	.60
78 Terry Glenn	.25	.60
79 Plaxico Burress	.20	.50
80 Warren Sapp	.25	.60
81 Jamal Anderson	.25	.60
82 James Stewart	.20	.50
83 Ricky Williams	.25	.60
84 Chad Lewis	.20	.50
85 Shaun King	.20	.50
86 Wesley Walls	.20	.50
87 Mike Anderson	.20	.50
88 Corey Simon	.20	.50
89 Wayne Chrebet	.20	.50
90 Junior Seau	.25	.60
91 Terance Mathis	.20	.50
92 Germane Crowell	.20	.50
93 Joe Horn	.20	.50
94 Duce Staley	.20	.50
95 Keyshawn Johnson	.25	.60
96 Qadry Ismail	.20	.50
97 Dorsey Levens	.25	.60
98 Kerry Collins	.20	.50
99 Corey Dillon	.20	.50
100 Zach Thomas	.25	.60
101 Chad Pennington	.20	.50
102 Ricky Watters	.25	.60
103 Bruce Smith	.25	.60
104 David Boston	.20	.50
105 Ed McCaffrey	.25	.60
106 Kevin Faulk	.20	.50
107 Jerome Bettis	.30	.75
108 Warrick Dunn	.20	.50
109 Tim Brown	.30	.75
110 Marcus Robinson	.25	.60
111 Tony Gonzalez	.25	.60
112 Drew Bledsoe	.25	.60
113 Darrell Jackson	.25	.60
114 Stephen Davis	.20	.50
115 Doug Johnson	.20	.50
116 Brett Favre	.60	1.50
117 Darren Howard	.20	.50
118 Cade McNown	.25	.60
119 Steve McNair	.25	.60
120 James Allen	.20	.50
121 Sylvester Morris	.20	.50
122 J.R. Redmond	.20	.50
123 Jacquez Green	.20	.50
124 Champ Bailey	.25	.60
125 Eddie George	.30	.75
126 Michael Vick JSY RC	6.00	15.00
127 David Terrell JSY RC	3.00	8.00
128 Deuce McAllister JSY RC	4.00	10.00
129 Koren Robinson JSY RC	3.00	8.00
130 Rod Gardner JSY RC	3.00	8.00
131 Chris Chambers JSY RC	2.50	6.00
132 Santana Moss JSY RC	4.00	10.00
133 Reggie Wayne JSY RC	5.00	12.00
134 Quincy Morgan JSY RC	3.00	8.00
135 Rudi Johnson JSY RC	4.00	10.00
136 Robert Ferguson JSY RC	4.00	10.00
137 Todd Heap JSY RC	3.00	8.00
138 Michael Bennett JSY RC	3.00	8.00
139 Jesse Palmer JSY RC	3.00	8.00
140 Drew Brees JSY RC	30.00	60.00
141 James Jackson JSY RC	2.50	6.00
142 Chris Weinke JSY RC	3.00	8.00
143 LaDainian Tomlinson JSY RC	12.00	30.00
144 Chad Johnson JSY RC	4.00	10.00
145 Quincy Carter JSY RC	3.00	8.00
146 Freddie Mitchell JSY RC	2.50	6.00
147 Anthony Thomas JSY RC	4.00	10.00
148 Travis Henry JSY RC	3.00	8.00
149 Snoop Minnis JSY RC	2.50	6.00
150 Marques Tuiasosopo JSY RC	3.00	8.00
151 Travis Minor JSY RC	3.00	8.00
152 Mike McMahon JSY RC	3.00	8.00
153 Josh Heupel JSY RC	4.00	10.00
154 Sage Rosenfels JSY RC	3.00	8.00
155 Kevan Barlow JSY RC	3.00	8.00

2001 Fleer Genuine Coverage Plus Jerseys

Randomly inserted into 2001 Fleer Genuine packs at a rate of 1:24. The cards featured a swatch of an authentic game-worn uniform. The cardbacks featured a congratulations message from Fleer.
STATED ODDS 1:24

1 Courtney Brown	2.00	5.00
2 Isaac Bruce	3.00	8.00
3 Mark Brunell	2.50	6.00
4 Az-Zahir Hakim	2.00	5.00
5 Marvin Harrison	2.50	6.00
6 Torry Holt	2.50	6.00
7 Edgerrin James	2.50	6.00
8 Brad Johnson	2.50	6.00
9 Kevin Johnson	2.00	5.00
10 Rob Johnson	2.50	6.00
11 Thomas Jones	2.00	5.00
12 Ed McCaffrey	2.50	6.00
13 Keenan McCardell	2.50	6.00
14 Cade McNown	2.50	6.00
15 Eric Moulds	2.00	5.00
16 Jake Plummer	2.00	5.00
17 Travis Prentice	2.00	5.00
18 Marcus Robinson	2.50	6.00
19 Warren Sapp	2.50	6.00
20 Corey Simon	2.00	5.00
21 Jimmy Smith	2.50	6.00
22 Duce Staley	2.00	5.00
23 Fred Taylor	2.00	5.00
24 Brian Urlacher	4.00	10.00
25 Kurt Warner	5.00	12.00
26 Dez White	2.50	6.00

2001 Fleer Genuine Final Cut Jerseys

Randomly inserted into 2001 Fleer Genuine packs at a rate of 1:24. The cards featured a swatch of an authentic game-worn uniform. The cardfronts featured a photo of the player and a photo of a stadium in the background which was in black and white. The cardbacks featured a congratulations message from Fleer.
STATED ODDS 1:24

1 Troy Aikman	4.00	10.00
2 Jamal Anderson	2.50	6.00
3 Charlie Batch	2.00	5.00
4 David Boston	2.00	5.00
5 Isaac Bruce	3.00	8.00
6 Tim Couch	2.00	5.00
7 Terrell Davis	2.50	6.00
8 Kevin Dyson	2.00	5.00
9 L.C. Greenwood	2.00	5.00
10 Marvin Harrison	2.50	6.00
11 Edgerrin James	2.50	6.00
12 Rob Johnson	2.50	6.00
13 Jevon Kearse	2.00	5.00
14 Jim Kelly	3.00	8.00
15 James Lofton	2.00	5.00
16 Ed McCaffrey	2.50	6.00
17 Rob Moore	2.00	5.00
18 Johnnie Morton	2.50	6.00
19 Jake Plummer	2.00	5.00
20 Jerry Rice	6.00	15.00
21 Mike Singletary	3.00	8.00
22 Emmitt Smith	5.00	12.00
23 Charles Woodson	3.00	8.00
24 Steve Young	4.00	10.00

2001 Fleer Genuine Future Swatch Tandems

Randomly inserted into 2001 Fleer Genuine packs, this five-card set featured a swatch of an authentic game-worn uniform from both players on the card. The cardfronts featured a photo of each player. The cardbacks featured a congratulations message from Fleer. The cards were serial numbered to 50.
STATED PRINT RUN 50 SER.#'d SETS

1 M.Vick/D.Brees	20.00	50.00
2 D.Terrell/A.Thomas	5.00	12.00
3 S.Moss/R.Wayne	6.00	15.00
4 D.McAllister/L.Tomlinson	15.00	40.00
5 K.Robinson/R.Gardner	4.00	10.00

2001 Fleer Genuine Hawaii Live O

Randomly inserted into packs of 2001 Fleer Genuine at a rate of 1:23, this 15-card set featured players from the 2001 Pro Bowl in Hawaii. The cards were die-cut and featured some gold-foil lettering and a photo of Aloha Stadium in the background. The cards carried an 'of 15 HO' suffix for the card numbering.

COMPLETE SET (15)	10.00	25.00
STATED ODDS 1:23		
1 Daunte Culpepper	.75	2.00
2 Donovan McNabb	.75	2.00
3 Torry Holt	.75	2.00
4 Terrell Owens	.75	2.00
5 Jimmy Smith	.75	2.00
6 Jeff Garcia	.60	1.50
7 Rich Gannon	.75	2.00
8 Peyton Manning	2.50	6.00
9 Joe Horn	.60	1.50
10 Tony Gonzalez	.75	2.00
11 Edgerrin James	.75	2.00
12 Eddie George	1.00	2.50
13 Corey Dillon	.60	1.50
14 Warrick Dunn	.60	1.50
15 Marvin Harrison	.75	2.00

2001 Fleer Genuine Names of the Game Jerseys

Randomly inserted into 2001 Fleer Genuine packs, this 17-card set featured a swatch of an authentic game-worn uniform. The cardfronts featured a photo of the player and a photo of the shadow of the player in the background. The cardbacks featured a congratulations message from Fleer. The cards were serial numbered to 100.
STATED PRINT RUN 100 SER.#'d SETS

1 Daunte Culpepper	4.00	10.00
2 Terrell Davis	4.00	10.00
3 Ron Dayne	4.00	10.00
4 Eric Dickerson	4.00	10.00
5 Tony Dorsett	5.00	12.00
6 Edgerrin James	4.00	10.00
7 Jevon Kearse	3.00	8.00
8 Curtis Martin	4.00	10.00
9 Steve McNair	4.00	10.00
10 Joe Montana	15.00	40.00
11 Randy Moss	4.00	10.00
12 Walter Payton	12.00	30.00
13 William Perry	3.00	8.00
14 Deion Sanders	4.00	10.00
15 Roger Staubach	6.00	15.00
16 Lawrence Taylor	5.00	12.00
17 Johnny Unitas	10.00	25.00

2001 Fleer Genuine Names of the Game Jerseys Autographs

Randomly inserted into 2001 Fleer Genuine packs, this set featured a swatch of an authentic game-worn uniform and an autograph. The cardfronts featured a photo of the player and a photo of the shadow of the player in the background. The cardbacks featured a congratulations message from Fleer. The cards were serial numbered to 50. Please note at the time of its release the cards were all issued as exchange/redemptions.
STATED PRINT RUN 50 SER.#'d SETS

3 Ron Dayne	12.50	30.00
4 Eric Dickerson	30.00	60.00
5 Tony Dorsett	40.00	80.00
6 Edgerrin James	20.00	50.00
7 Joe Montana	100.00	200.00
8 Randy Moss	40.00	100.00
9 William Perry	30.00	60.00
10 Roger Staubach	75.00	150.00
11 Lawrence Taylor	40.00	80.00
12 Johnny Unitas	200.00	350.00

2001 Fleer Genuine Pennant Aggression

Randomly inserted in packs of 2001 Fleer Genuine at a rate of 1:23, this 10-card set had the design of a pennant. The cardfronts were highlighted with rainbow-holofoil lettering. The card numbering carried an 'of 10 PA' suffix.

COMPLETE SET (10)	7.50	20.00
STATED ODDS 1:23		
1 Kurt Warner	1.25	3.00
2 Brett Favre	1.50	4.00
3 Emmitt Smith	1.25	3.00
4 Daunte Culpepper	.60	1.50
5 Terrell Davis	.60	1.50
6 Peyton Manning	2.00	5.00
7 Eddie George	.75	2.00
8 Donovan McNabb	.60	1.50
9 Ricky Williams	.60	1.50
10 Tim Couch	.50	1.25

2001 Fleer Genuine Seek and Deploy

Randomly inserted in packs of 2001 Fleer Genuine at a rate of 1:23, this 15-card set featured a die-cut design in the shape of a bomb. The cardfronts were highlighted by rainbow holofoil lettering. The card number carried an 'of 15 SD' suffix.

COMPLETE SET (15)	12.50	30.00
STATED ODDS 1:23		
1 Jamal Lewis	1.00	2.50
2 Randy Moss	.75	2.00
3 Ricky Williams	.75	2.00
4 Terrell Davis	.75	2.00
5 Donovan McNabb	.75	2.00
6 Curtis Martin	.75	2.00
7 Brett Favre	2.00	5.00
8 Aaron Brooks	.60	1.50
9 Kurt Warner	1.50	4.00
10 Eddie George	1.00	2.50
11 Daunte Culpepper	.75	2.00
12 Jamal Anderson	.75	2.00
13 Marshall Faulk	.75	2.00
14 Ray Lewis	1.00	2.50
15 Ron Dayne	.75	2.00

2002 Fleer Genuine

Released in December, 2002, this set features 125 veterans and 50 rookies. The rookies were serial #'d to 599. Each box contained 24 packs of 5 cards.

COMP.SET w/o SP's (125)	7.50	20.00
126-175 ROOKIE PRINT RUN 599		
1 Brian Urlacher	.30	.75
2 Keyshawn Johnson	.25	.60
3 Donovan McNabb	.25	.60
4 Tim Couch	.20	.50
5 Junior Seau	.25	.60
6 Eric Moulds	.20	.50
7 Randy Moss	.25	.60
8 Rod Smith	.25	.60
9 Torry Holt	.25	.60
10 Plaxico Burress	.20	.50
11 Kordell Stewart	.20	.50
12 Brett Favre	.60	1.50
13 Stephen Davis	.20	.50
14 Santana Moss	.25	.60
15 Kurt Warner	.25	.60
16 Jake Plummer	.20	.50
17 Jimmy Smith	.25	.60
18 Quincy Carter	.20	.50
19 Marvin Harrison	.25	.60
20 Fred Taylor	.20	.50
21 Warren Sapp	.25	.60
22 Curtis Martin	.25	.60
23 Isaac Bruce	.30	.75
24 Drew Brees	.60	1.50
25 Ray Lewis	.30	.75
26 Hines Ward	.25	.60
27 Koren Robinson	.20	.50
28 Jevon Kearse	.20	.50
29 Jerry Rice	.60	1.50
30 Jeff Garcia	.20	.50
31 Edgerrin James	.25	.60
32 Warrick Dunn	.20	.50
33 Ricky Williams	.25	.60
34 Doug Flutie	.25	.60
35 Brian Griese	.20	.50
36 Chad Pennington	.20	.50
37 Duce Staley	.20	.50
38 Eddie George	.25	.60
39 Daunte Culpepper	.25	.60
40 Jerome Bettis	.30	.75
41 Michael Vick	.25	.60
42 Tim Brown	.30	.75
43 Tom Brady	1.50	4.00
44 Steve McNair	.25	.60
45 Terrell Owens	.25	.60
46 Corey Dillon	.20	.50
47 Peyton Manning	.75	2.00
48 Rich Gannon	.25	.60
49 Emmitt Smith	.50	1.25
50 David Boston	.20	.50
51 Mark Brunell	.25	.60
52 Ron Dayne	.25	.60
53 Wayne Chrebet	.20	.50
54 Terrell Davis	.25	.60
55 Zach Thomas	.25	.60
56 Kevin Johnson	.20	.50
57 Marshall Faulk	.25	.60
58 Anthony Thomas	.25	.60
59 Deuce McAllister	.25	.60
60 LaDainian Tomlinson	.30	.75
61 Thomas Jones	.20	.50
62 Ahman Green	.25	.60
63 Aaron Brooks	.20	.50
64 Courtney Brown	.20	.50
65 Chris Chambers	.20	.50
66 Jamal Lewis	.25	.60
67 David Terrell	.20	.50
68 Tony Gonzalez	.25	.60
69 Laveranues Coles	.25	.60
70 Shaun Alexander	.20	.50
71 Chris Weinke	.20	.50
72 Antowain Smith	.25	.60
73 Rod Gardner	.20	.50
74 Mike Anderson	.20	.50
75 Antonio Freeman	.30	.75
76 Kevan Barlow	.20	.50
77 Jim Miller	.20	.50
78 Bill Schroeder	.20	.50
79 Joe Horn	.20	.50
80 Travis Henry	.20	.50
81 Michael Bennett	.20	.50
82 Michael Pittman	.25	.60
83 Keenan McCardell	.25	.60
84 Amani Toomer	.20	.50
85 Peerless Price	.20	.50
86 Az-Zahir Hakim	.20	.50
87 James Thrash	.25	.60
88 Drew Bledsoe	.25	.60
89 Mike McMahon	.20	.50
90 Derrick Mason	.20	.50
91 Joey Galloway	.20	.50
92 Snoop Minnis	.20	.50
93 Ed McCaffrey	.25	.60
94 Johnnie Morton	.25	.60
95 Richard Huntley	.20	.50
96 Troy Brown	.20	.50
97 Shane Matthews	.20	.50
98 Muhsin Muhammad	.20	.50
99 David Patten	.20	.50
100 Jon Kitna	.20	.50
101 Terrence Wilkins	.20	.50
102 Kerry Collins	.20	.50
103 Tiki Barber	.25	.60
104 Fred Beasley	.20	.50
105 Trent Dilfer	.20	.50
106 Chris Redman	.20	.50
107 Jay Fiedler	.25	.60
108 Charlie Garner	.25	.60
109 Mike Alstott	.20	.50
110 Darnay Scott	.25	.60
111 Garrison Hearst	.20	.50
112 James Jackson	.20	.50
113 Darrell Jackson	.25	.60
114 Freddie Mitchell	.20	.50
115 Brad Johnson	.25	.60
116 Olandis Gary	.25	.60
117 Priest Holmes	.20	.50
118 Vinny Testaverde	.20	.50
119 Takeo Spikes	.20	.50
120 Marty Booker	.20	.50
121 Curtis Conway	.25	.60
122 Jacquez Green	.20	.50
123 Champ Bailey	.25	.60
124 Trent Green	.20	.50
125 Terry Glenn	.25	.60
126 Ladell Betts RC	2.00	5.00
127 DeShaun Foster RC	2.00	5.00
128 Maurice Morris RC	1.50	4.00
129 Chester Taylor RC	2.00	5.00
130 Randy McMichael RC	2.00	5.00
131 Verron Haynes RC	1.25	3.00
132 Cliff Russell RC	1.25	3.00
133 Brandon Doman RC	1.25	3.00
134 Ashley Lelie RC	1.25	3.00
135 Roy Williams RC	1.25	3.00
136 Antonio Bryant RC	2.00	5.00
137 William Green RC	1.50	4.00
138 Clinton Portis RC	2.00	5.00
139 J.T. O'Sullivan RC	1.50	4.00
140 Javon Walker RC	2.00	5.00
141 Randy Fasani RC	1.25	3.00
142 Chad Hutchinson RC	1.25	3.00
143 Ben Leber RC	1.25	3.00
144 Tim Carter RC	1.50	4.00
145 Jason McAddley RC	1.50	4.00
146 Donte Stallworth RC	2.00	5.00
147 Andre Davis RC	1.25	3.00
148 Julius Peppers RC	3.00	8.00
149 Patrick Ramsey RC	1.50	4.00
150 Deion Branch RC	2.00	5.00
151 Jonathan Wells RC	1.50	4.00
152 Jabar Gaffney RC	1.25	3.00
153 Josh McCown RC	2.00	5.00
154 Jeremy Shockey RC	2.00	5.00
155 Eric Crouch RC	2.00	5.00
156 Joey Harrington RC	1.25	3.00
157 Jerramy Stevens RC	2.00	5.00
158 T.J. Duckett RC	1.25	3.00
159 Ron Johnson RC	1.50	4.00
160 Josh Reed RC	1.50	4.00
161 Reche Caldwell RC	1.50	4.00
162 Lamar Gordon RC	1.50	4.00
163 David Garrard RC	1.50	4.00
164 Freddie Milons RC	1.25	3.00
165 Marquise Walker RC	1.25	3.00
166 Rohan Davey RC	2.00	5.00
167 Coy Wire RC	1.50	4.00
168 Quentin Jammer RC	2.00	5.00
169 Omar Easy RC	1.50	4.00
170 Kurt Kittner RC	1.25	3.00
171 Travis Stephens RC	1.25	3.00
172 David Carr RC	1.25	3.00
173 Daniel Graham RC	1.50	4.00
174 Antwaan Randle El RC	1.50	4.00
175 Brian Westbrook RC	2.50	6.00

2002 Fleer Genuine Reflection Ascending

*VETS/100-125: 3X TO 8X
*VETS/70-99: 4X TO 10X
*VETS/45-69: 5X TO 12X
*VETS/30-44: 6X TO 15X
*VETS/20-29: 10X TO 25X
*VETS/10-19: 15X TO 40X
STATED PRINT RUN 1-125
SER.#'d UNDER 10 NOT PRICED

2002 Fleer Genuine Reflection Descending

*VETS/100-125: 3X TO 8X
*VETS/70-99: 4X TO 10X
*VETS/45-69: 5X TO 12X
*VETS/30-44: 6X TO 15X
*VETS/20-29: 10X TO 25X
*VETS/10-19: 15X TO 40X
STATED PRINT RUN 1-125
SER.#'d UNDER 10 NOT PRICED

2002 Fleer Genuine Article

Inserted at a rate of 1:24, this set features authentic jersey swatches of many of the NFL's best players. In addition, there is also an Insider parallel which features a pull out section of the card. The Insider cards were serial #'d to 500. Finally, a Tags version was also produced with each being serial numbered between 5 and 19-copies.
STATED ODDS 1:24
*INSIDER/500: .5X TO 1.2X BASIC JSY
INSIDER PRINT RUN 500 SER.#'d SETS
UNPRICED TAG PRINT RUN 5-19

GABF Brett Favre	5.00	12.00
GABU Brian Urlacher	2.50	6.00
GADB Drew Brees	5.00	12.00
GADC Daunte Culpepper	2.00	5.00
GAES Emmitt Smith	4.00	10.00
GAIB Isaac Bruce	2.50	6.00
GAJB Jerome Bettis	2.50	6.00
GAJG Jeff Garcia	1.50	4.00
GAJR Jerry Rice	5.00	12.00
GAJS Junior Seau	2.00	5.00
GAKJ Keyshawn Johnson	2.00	5.00
GAKR Koren Robinson	1.50	4.00
GALT LaDainian Tomlinson	2.50	6.00
GAPM Peyton Manning	6.00	15.00
GAQC Quincy Carter	1.50	4.00
GARL Ray Lewis	2.50	6.00
GARM Randy Moss	2.00	5.00
GARS Rod Smith	2.00	5.00
GASD Stephen Davis	1.50	4.00
GASM Santana Moss	2.00	5.00
GATB Tom Brady	12.00	30.00
GATH Torry Holt	2.00	5.00
GAWS Warren Sapp	2.00	5.00
GAZT Zach Thomas	2.00	5.00

2002 Fleer Genuine Authen-Kicks

Inserted at a rate of 1:240, this set features swatches of game used shoes. A Combos parallel was also produced with each also including a swatch of game used jersey. Those are serial numbered of 25.
STATED ODDS 1:240
*COMBO/25: .8X TO 2X BASIC INSERTS
COMBO STATED PRINT RUN 25

ADM Donovan McNabb	3.00	8.00
AEJ Edgerrin James	3.00	8.00
AMH Marvin Harrison	3.00	8.00
APM Peyton Manning	10.00	25.00
ARGO Rich Gannon	3.00	8.00
ATH Torry Holt	3.00	8.00

2002 Fleer Genuine Names of the Game

Inserted at a rate of 1:20, this set features top NFL players in a horizontal card design that highlights the first letter of the players first name.

COMPLETE SET (20)	15.00	40.00
STATED ODDS 1:20		
1 Kurt Warner	.75	2.00
2 Brett Favre	2.00	5.00
3 Brian Urlacher	1.00	2.50
4 Jeff Garcia	.60	1.50
5 Donovan McNabb	.75	2.00
6 Tom Brady	5.00	12.00
7 Tim Couch	.60	1.50
8 Daunte Culpepper	.75	2.00
9 Michael Vick	.75	2.00
10 Edgerrin James	.75	2.00
11 Marshall Faulk	.75	2.00
12 Emmitt Smith	1.50	4.00
13 Eddie George	.75	2.00
14 Jerome Bettis	1.00	2.50
15 Drew Brees	2.00	5.00
16 Quincy Carter	.60	1.50
17 Randy Moss	.75	2.00
18 Isaac Bruce	1.00	2.50
19 Jerry Rice	2.00	5.00
20 Junior Seau	.75	2.00

2002 Fleer Genuine Names of the Game Jerseys

Randomly inserted into packs, this set features authentic jersey swatches, with each card serial numbered to 500.
STATED PRINT RUN 500 SER.#'d SETS

1 Jerome Bettis	2.50	6.00
2 Tom Brady	15.00	40.00
3 Drew Brees	5.00	12.00
4 Isaac Bruce	2.50	6.00
5 Quincy Carter	1.50	4.00
6 Tim Couch	1.50	4.00
7 Daunte Culpepper	2.00	5.00
8 Marshall Faulk	2.00	5.00
9 Brett Favre	5.00	12.00
10 Jeff Garcia	1.50	4.00
11 Eddie George	2.00	5.00
12 Edgerrin James	2.00	5.00
13 Donovan McNabb	2.00	5.00
14 Randy Moss	2.00	5.00
15 Jerry Rice	5.00	12.00
16 Junior Seau	2.00	5.00
17 Emmitt Smith	4.00	10.00
18 Brian Urlacher	2.50	6.00
19 Michael Vick	2.00	5.00
20 Kurt Warner	2.00	5.00

2002 Fleer Genuine Names of the Game Jerseys Duals

Randomly inserted into packs, this set features two swatches of game worn jerseys from two NFL superstars. Each card is serial numbered to 50.
STATED PRINT RUN 50 SER.#'d SETS

BFDC B.Favre/D.Culpepper	20.00	50.00
BUJS B.Urlacher/J.Seau	10.00	25.00
DBQC D.Brees/Q.Carter	20.00	50.00
EGJB E.George/J.Bettis	12.00	30.00
EJMF E.James/M.Faulk	8.00	20.00
ESJR E.Smith/J.Rice	20.00	50.00
KWDM K.Warner/D.McNabb	8.00	20.00
MVJG M.Vick/J.Garcia	8.00	20.00
RMIB R.Moss/I.Bruce	10.00	25.00
TBTC T.Brady/T.Couch	50.00	125.00

2002 Fleer Genuine TD Threats

Inserted at a rate of 1:8, this set features two players of the same position who are pure touchdown threats.
STATED ODDS 1:8

1 E.James/E.George	.60	1.50
2 T.Owens/T.Brown	.75	2.00
3 E.Smith/M.Faulk	1.25	3.00
4 D.Boston/J.Smith	.60	1.50
5 S.Moss/R.Moss	.60	1.50
6 D.Culpepper/T.Couch	.60	1.50
7 D.McNabb/P.Manning	2.00	5.00
8 J.Rice/C.Chambers	1.50	4.00
9 E.Moulds/R.Smith	.60	1.50
10 F.Taylor/L.Tomlinson	.75	2.00
11 D.Staley/J.Bettis	.75	2.00
12 M.Vick/B.Favre	1.50	4.00
13 T.Brady/D.Brees	4.00	10.00
14 A.Green/C.Martin	.60	1.50
15 K.Warner/J.Garcia	.60	1.50
16 Q.Carter/J.Plummer	.50	1.25

17 T.Davis/C.Dillon .60 1.50
18 M.Brunell/K.Stewart .60 1.50
19 H.Ward/P.Burress .60 1.50
20 J.Horn/T.Holt .60 1.50
21 B.Griese/D.Bledsoe .60 1.50
22 D.Stallworth/D.Jackson .75 2.00
23 R.Gardner/D.Terrell .50 1.25
24 D.McAllister/A.Thomas .60 1.50
25 A.Brooks/D.Carr .50 1.25

2002 Fleer Genuine TD Threats Jerseys

Inserted at a rate of 1:22, this set features authentic NFL jerseys from the top touchdown artists in the league.
STATED ODDS 1:22
*PATCH/56-73: .6X TO 1.5X BASIC DUAL
*PATCH/36-38: 1X TO 2.5X BASIC DUAL
*PATCH/21-26: 1.2X TO 3X BASIC DUAL
*PATCH/10-19: 1.5X TO 4X BASIC DUAL
PATCH STATED PRINT RUN 8-73
PATCH SER.#'d UNDER 10 NOT PRICED
1 E.James/E.George 2.50 6.00
2 T.Owens/T.Brown 3.00 8.00
3 E.Smith/M.Faulk 5.00 12.00
4 D.Boston/J.Smith 2.50 6.00
5 S.Moss/R.Moss 2.50 6.00
6 D.Culpepper/T.Couch 2.50 6.00
7 D.McNabb/P.Manning 8.00 20.00
8 J.Rice/C.Chambers 6.00 15.00
9 E.Moulds/R.Smith 2.50 6.00
10 F.Taylor/L.Tomlinson 3.00 8.00
11 M.Vick/B.Favre 6.00 15.00
12 T.Brady/D.Brees 15.00 40.00
13 A.Green/C.Martin 2.50 6.00
14 K.Warner/J.Garcia 2.50 6.00
15 Q.Carter/J.Plummer 2.00 5.00
16 T.Davis/C.Dillon 2.50 6.00
17 M.Brunell/K.Stewart 2.50 6.00
18 H.Ward/P.Burress 2.50 6.00
19 J.Horn/T.Holt 2.50 6.00

2003 Fleer Genuine Insider

Released in August of 2003, this set consists of 140 cards, including 100 veterans and 40 rookies. Rookies 101-110 are serial numbered to 499. Rookies 111-130 are serial numbered to 799. Rookies 131-140 are serial numbered to 350. Boxes contained 24 packs of 5 cards.
COMP.SET w/o SP's (100) 7.50 20.00
101-110 ROOKIE PRINT RUN 499
111-130 ROOKIE PRINT RUN 799
131-140 ROOKIE PRINT RUN 350
1 Donovan McNabb .30 .75
2 Rich Gannon .30 .75
3 Joey Harrington .25 .60
4 Eddie George .30 .75
5 Jeremy Shockey .25 .60
6 Tim Couch .25 .60
7 Shaun Alexander .25 .60
8 Tiki Barber .30 .75
9 Antonio Bryant .25 .60
10 Marc Bulger .25 .60
11 Tom Brady 1.50 4.00
12 Julius Peppers .40 1.00
13 Junior Seau .30 .75
14 Trent Green .25 .60
15 Eric Moulds .25 .60
16 Santana Moss .30 .75
17 Hugh Douglas .25 .60
18 Emmitt Smith .60 1.50
19 Tim Brown .40 1.00
20 William Green .25 .60
21 Koren Robinson .30 .75
22 Randy Moss .30 .75
23 Anthony Thomas .30 .75
24 Terrell Owens .30 .75
25 Fred Taylor .25 .60
26 Ahman Green .30 .75
27 Derrick Mason .25 .60
28 Chad Pennington .25 .60
29 Shannon Sharpe .30 .75
30 Warren Sapp .30 .75
31 Deuce McAllister .30 .75
32 Rod Smith .30 .75
33 Torry Holt .30 .75
34 Joe Horn .25 .60
35 Chad Johnson .25 .60
36 Matt Hasselbeck .25 .60
37 Chris Chambers .25 .60
38 Travis Henry .25 .60
39 David Boston .25 .60
40 Tony Gonzalez .30 .75
41 Todd Heap .25 .60
42 Hines Ward .30 .75
43 Brett Favre .75 2.00
44 Rod Gardner .25 .60
45 Donte Stallworth .25 .60
46 Corey Dillon .25 .60
47 Garrison Hearst .25 .60
48 Ricky Williams .30 .75
49 Ray Lewis .40 1.00
50 Plaxico Burress .25 .60
51 Michael Bennett .25 .60
52 Stephen Davis .25 .60
53 LaDainian Tomlinson .40 1.00
54 Priest Holmes .25 .60
55 Jonathan Wells .25 .60
56 Jerome Bettis .40 1.00
57 Jimmy Smith .30 .75
58 Michael Vick .30 .75
59 Tommy Maddox .25 .60
60 Edgerrin James .30 .75
61 Laveranues Coles .25 .60
62 Curtis Conway .25 .60
63 Clinton Portis .25 .60
64 Derrick Brooks .25 .60
65 Amani Toomer .25 .60
66 Roy Williams .25 .60
67 Marshall Faulk .30 .75
68 Daunte Culpepper .30 .75
69 Peerless Price .25 .60
70 Marcel Shipp .25 .60
71 David Carr .25 .60
72 Patrick Ramsey .30 .75
73 Charlie Garner .30 .75
74 Jake Plummer .25 .60
75 Kurt Warner .30 .75
76 Brian Urlacher .40 1.00
77 Tai Streets .25 .60
78 Jason Taylor .30 .75
79 Drew Bledsoe .30 .75
80 Drew Brees .40 1.00
81 Peyton Manning 1.00 2.50
82 Jamal Lewis .30 .75
83 Antwaan Randle El .25 .60
84 Mark Brunell .30 .75
85 Warrick Dunn .25 .60
86 Brian Dawkins .40 1.00
87 James Stewart .25 .60
88 Ronde Barber .25 .60
89 Curtis Martin .30 .75
90 Jon Kitna .25 .60
91 Keyshawn Johnson .40 1.00
92 Aaron Brooks .25 .60
93 Marty Booker .25 .60
94 Jeff Garcia .25 .60
95 Marvin Harrison .30 .75
96 T.J. Duckett .25 .60
97 Jerry Rice .75 2.00
98 Donald Driver .30 .75
99 Steve McNair .30 .75
100 Kerry Collins .25 .60
101 Carson Palmer RC 3.00 8.00
102 Kyle Boller RC 1.50 4.00
103 Willis McGahee RC 2.00 5.00
104 Larry Johnson RC 2.00 5.00
105 Bryant Johnson RC 2.50 6.00
106 Byron Leftwich RC 2.00 5.00
107 Andre Johnson RC 4.00 10.00
108 Rex Grossman RC 2.00 5.00
109 Kelley Washington RC 1.50 4.00
110 Charles Rogers RC 2.00 5.00
111 Taylor Jacobs RC 1.25 3.00
112 Sam Aiken RC 1.50 4.00
113 Dallas Clark RC 2.00 5.00
114 B.J. Askew RC 1.50 4.00
115 Quentin Griffin RC 1.50 4.00
116 Terence Newman RC 2.00 5.00
117 Chris Simms RC 1.25 3.00
118 Brandon Lloyd RC 2.00 5.00
119 Lee Suggs RC 1.25 3.00
120 L.J. Smith RC 2.00 5.00
121 Anquan Boldin RC 2.00 5.00
122 Musa Smith RC 1.25 3.00
123 Billy McMullen RC 1.25 3.00
124 Bennie Joppru RC 1.25 3.00
125 Justin Fargas RC 2.00 5.00
126 Tyrone Calico RC 1.25 3.00
127 Dave Ragone RC 1.25 3.00
128 Seneca Wallace RC 1.50 4.00
129 Chris Brown RC 1.25 3.00
130 Terrell Suggs RC 1.50 4.00
131 Bethel Johnson RC 2.00 5.00
132 Nate Burleson RC 2.50 6.00
133 Teyo Johnson RC 2.50 6.00
134 Kevin Curtis RC 2.00 5.00
135 Jason Witten RC 8.00 20.00
136 Artose Pinner RC 2.00 5.00
137 Boss Bailey RC 2.50 6.00
138 Jerome McDougle RC 2.00 5.00
139 LaBrandon Toefield RC 2.00 5.00
140 Domanick Davis RC 2.50 6.00

2003 Fleer Genuine Insider Mini 149

*SINGLES: .3X TO .8X BASIC CARDS
STATED PRINT RUN 149 SER.#'d SETS

2003 Fleer Genuine Insider Reflection

*VETS 1-100: 3X TO 8X BASIC CARDS
*ROOKIES 111-130: 1X TO 2.5X
STATED PRINT RUN 99 SER.#'d SETS

2003 Fleer Genuine Insider Genuine Article

Inserted at a rate of 1:24 packs, this set features authentic game worn jersey swatches. A patch parallel also exists, with each card serial numbered to 50.
STATED ODDS 1:24
*PATCHES: .8X TO 2X BASIC JSY
PATCH PRINT RUN 50 SER.#'d SETS
GAAB Aaron Brooks 2.00 5.00
GABF Brett Favre 6.00 15.00
GABU Brian Urlacher 3.00 8.00
GACP Clinton Portis 2.00 5.00
GACP2 Chad Pennington 2.00 5.00
GADB Drew Brees 3.00 8.00
GADC Daunte Culpepper 2.50 6.00
GADC2 David Carr 2.00 5.00
GADM Donovan McNabb 2.50 6.00
GADM2 Deuce McAllister 2.50 6.00
GAES Emmitt Smith 5.00 12.00
GAJH Joey Harrington 2.00 5.00
GAJR Jerry Rice 6.00 15.00
GAJS Jeremy Shockey 2.00 5.00
GAKW Kurt Warner 2.50 6.00
GALT LaDainian Tomlinson 3.00 8.00
GAMF Marshall Faulk 2.50 6.00
GAMH Marvin Harrison 2.50 6.00
GAMV Michael Vick 2.50 6.00
GAPM Peyton Manning 8.00 20.00
GARM Randy Moss 2.50 6.00
GARW Ricky Williams 2.50 6.00
GATB Tom Brady 12.00 30.00
GATO Terrell Owens 2.50 6.00

2003 Fleer Genuine Insider Autographs

Inserted at a rate of 1:24, this set features authentic player autographs. Please note that David Carr and Roy Williams were only available in packs as exchange cards.
STATED ODDS 1:24
AICS Chris Simms 8.00 20.00
AIDB Drew Brees 30.00 60.00
AIDC David Carr EXCH 1.00 2.50
AIKB Kyle Boller 6.00 15.00
AIKW Kelley Washington 6.00 15.00
AILJ Larry Johnson 10.00 25.00
AIMB Michael Bennett 6.00 15.00
AIRW Roy Williams EXCH 1.00 2.50
AITM Tommy Maddox 10.00 25.00

2003 Fleer Genuine Insider Tools of the Game

COMPLETE SET (15) 15.00 40.00
STATED ODDS 1:8
1 Brett Favre 2.00 5.00
2 Clinton Portis .60 1.50
3 Donovan McNabb .75 2.00
4 Daunte Culpepper .75 2.00
5 LaDainian Tomlinson 1.00 2.50
6 Tom Brady 4.00 10.00
7 Peyton Manning 2.50 6.00
8 Emmitt Smith 1.50 4.00
9 Brian Urlacher 1.00 2.50
10 Michael Vick .75 2.00
11 Randy Moss .75 2.00
12 Marshall Faulk .75 2.00
13 Kurt Warner .75 2.00
14 Marvin Harrison .75 2.00
15 Joey Harrington .60 1.50

2003 Fleer Genuine Insider Tools of the Game Memorabilia

Randomly inserted into packs, this set features authentic game worn jerseys. Each card is serial numbered to 199.
STATED PRINT RUN 199 SER.#'d SETS
TGBF Brett Favre 6.00 15.00
TGBU Brian Urlacher 3.00 8.00
TGCP Clinton Portis 2.00 5.00
TGDC Daunte Culpepper 2.50 6.00
TGDM Donovan McNabb 2.50 6.00
TGJH Joey Harrington 2.00 5.00
TGJR Jerry Rice 6.00 15.00
TGKW Kurt Warner 2.50 6.00
TGLT LaDainian Tomlinson 3.00 8.00
TGMF Marshall Faulk 2.50 6.00
TGMH Marvin Harrison 2.50 6.00
TGMV Michael Vick 2.50 6.00
TGPM Peyton Manning 8.00 20.00
TGRM Randy Moss 2.50 6.00
TGTB Tom Brady 12.00 30.00

2003 Fleer Genuine Insider Tools of the Game Memorabilia Duals

Randomly inserted into packs, this set features swatches of game used jersey and pants. Each card is serial numbered to 99.
STATED PRINT RUN 99 SER.#'d SETS
TGBF Brett Favre 10.00 25.00
TGBU Brian Urlacher 5.00 12.00
TGDC Daunte Culpepper 4.00 10.00
TGDM Donovan McNabb 4.00 10.00
TGKW Kurt Warner 4.00 10.00
TGMF Marshall Faulk 4.00 10.00
TGMH Marvin Harrison 4.00 10.00
TGMV Michael Vick 4.00 10.00
TGPM Peyton Manning 12.00 30.00
TGRM Randy Moss 4.00 10.00

2003 Fleer Genuine Insider Touchdown Threats

COMPLETE SET (10) 15.00 40.00
STATED ODDS 1:20
1 D.McNabb/M.Vick .75 2.00
2 B.Favre/P.Manning 2.50 6.00
3 J.Shockey/T.Heap .60 1.50
4 R.Moss/T.Owens .75 2.00
5 L.Tomlinson/C.Portis 1.00 2.50
6 E.Smith/J.Rice 2.00 5.00
7 D.McAllister/T.Henry .75 2.00
8 Ri.Williams/F.Taylor .75 2.00
9 M.Faulk/E.James .75 2.00
10 D.Carr/C.Pennington .60 1.50

2003 Fleer Genuine Insider Touchdown Threats Jerseys

Inserted at a rate of 1:48, this set features authentic game worn jersey swatches.
STATED ODDS 1:48
BFPM B.Favre JSY/P.Manning 8.00 20.00
BFPM1 B.Favre/P.Manning JSY 8.00 20.00
DCCP D.Carr JSY/C.Pennington 2.00 5.00
DCCP1 D.Carr/C.Pennington JSY 2.00 5.00
DMMV D.McNabb JSY/M.Vick 2.50 6.00
DMMV1 D.McNabb/M.Vick JSY 2.50 6.00
ESJR E.Smith JSY/J.Rice 6.00 15.00
JSTH J.Shockey JSY/T.Heap 2.00 5.00
LTCP L.Tomlinson JSY/C.Portis 3.00 8.00
LTCP1 L.Tomlinson/C.Portis JSY 3.00 8.00
MFEJ M.Faulk JSY/E.James 2.50 6.00
MFEJ1 M.Faulk/E.James JSY 2.50 6.00
RMTO R.Moss JSY/T.Owens 2.50 6.00
RMTO1 R.Moss/T.Owens JSY 2.50 6.00
RWFT Ri.Will.JSY/F.Taylor 2.50 6.00

2003 Fleer Genuine Insider Touchdown Threats Jersey Duals

Randomly inserted into packs, this set features two game worn jersey swatches from NFL superstars.
STATED PRINT RUN 200 SER.#'d SETS
BFPM B.Favre/P.Manning 12.00 30.00
DCCP D.Carr/C.Pennington 3.00 8.00
DMMV D.McNabb/M.Vick 4.00 10.00
ESJR E.Smith/J.Rice 10.00 25.00
LTCP L.Tomlinson/C.Portis 5.00 12.00
MFEJ M.Faulk/E.James 4.00 10.00
RMTO R.Moss/T.Owens 4.00 10.00

2004 Fleer Genuine

Fleer Genuine initially released in late October 2004. The base set consists of 100-cards including 25-rookies serial numbered to 500. Hobby boxes contained 12-packs of 5-cards. One parallel set and a variety of inserts can be found seeded in hobby and retail packs highlighted by the multi-tiered Big Time Autograph inserts. Some signed cards were issued via mail-in exchange or redemption cards with a number of those EXCH cards not yet appearing live on the secondary market as of the printing of this book.
76-100 ROOKIE PRINT RUN 500 SER.#'d SETS
1 Anquan Boldin .25 .60
2 Rod Smith .30 .75
3 Randy Moss .30 .75
4 Drew Brees .40 1.00
5 Jamal Lewis .30 .75
6 Ahman Green .30 .75
7 Aaron Brooks .25 .60
8 Torry Holt .30 .75
9 Steve Smith .40 1.00
10 Marvin Harrison .30 .75
11 Santana Moss .30 .75
12 Eddie George .30 .75
13 Lee Suggs .30 .75
14 Randy McMichael .25 .60
15 Hines Ward .30 .75
16 Drew Bledsoe .30 .75
17 Andre Johnson .30 .75
18 Jeremy Shockey .25 .60
19 Mike Alstott .25 .60
20 Chad Johnson .25 .60
21 Priest Holmes .25 .60
22 Brian Westbrook .25 .60
23 Rudi Johnson .25 .60
24 Keyshawn Johnson .30 .75
25 Chris Chambers .25 .60
26 LaDainian Tomlinson .40 1.00
27 Ray Lewis .40 1.00
28 Brett Favre .75 2.00
29 Deuce McAllister .30 .75
30 Marshall Faulk .30 .75
31 Brian Urlacher .40 1.00
32 Byron Leftwich .25 .60
33 Jerry Rice .75 2.00
34 Clinton Portis .25 .60
35 Derrick Mason .25 .60
36 Emmitt Smith .60 1.50
37 Plaxico Burress .25 .60
38 Peerless Price .25 .60
39 Joey Harrington .25 .60
40 Corey Dillon .25 .60
41 Matt Hasselbeck .25 .60
42 Stephen Davis .25 .60
43 Peyton Manning 1.00 2.50
44 Tiki Barber .30 .75
45 Derrick Brooks .25 .60
46 Jeff Garcia .25 .60
47 Trent Green .25 .60
48 Donovan McNabb .30 .75
49 Michael Vick .30 .75
50 Jake Plummer .25 .60
51 Tom Brady 1.50 4.00
52 Brandon Lloyd .30 .75
53 Eric Moulds .25 .60
54 David Carr .25 .60
55 Joe Horn .25 .60
56 Isaac Bruce .40 1.00
57 Rex Grossman .25 .60
58 Fred Taylor .25 .60
59 Rich Gannon .30 .75
60 Laveranues Coles .25 .60
61 T.J. Duckett .25 .60
62 Charles Rogers .25 .60
63 Deion Branch .25 .60
64 Shaun Alexander .25 .60
65 Jake Delhomme .25 .60
66 Edgerrin James .30 .75
67 Chad Pennington .25 .60
68 Steve McNair .30 .75
69 Carson Palmer .30 .75
70 Tony Gonzalez .30 .75
71 Terrell Owens .30 .75
72 Josh McCown .30 .75
73 Ashley Lelie .25 .60
74 Daunte Culpepper .30 .75
75 Kevan Barlow .25 .60
76 Eli Manning RC 8.00 20.00
77 Larry Fitzgerald RC 4.00 10.00
78 Philip Rivers RC 3.00 8.00
79 Kellen Winslow RC 1.00 2.50
80 Roy Williams RC 1.00 2.50
81 Reggie Williams RC 1.00 2.50
82 Ben Roethlisberger RC 8.00 20.00
83 Lee Evans RC 1.50 4.00
84 Michael Clayton RC 1.25 3.00
85 J.P. Losman RC 1.00 2.50
86 Steven Jackson RC 1.50 4.00
87 Chris Perry RC 1.00 2.50
88 Michael Jenkins RC 1.00 2.50
89 Kevin Jones RC 1.25 3.00
90 Rashaun Woods RC 1.00 2.50
91 Ben Watson RC 1.25 3.00
92 Ben Troupe RC 1.00 2.50
93 Tatum Bell RC 1.00 2.50
94 Julius Jones RC 1.00 2.50
95 Devery Henderson RC 1.00 2.50
96 Darius Watts RC 1.00 2.50
97 Greg Jones RC 1.00 2.50
98 Keary Colbert RC 1.00 2.50
99 Derrick Hamilton RC 1.00 2.50
100 Drew Henson RC 1.00 2.50

2004 Fleer Genuine Reflections

*STARS: 3X TO 8X BASE CARD HI
1-75 PRINT RUN 99 SER.#'d SETS
76-100 SER.#'d TO DRAFT PICK POSITION
ROOKIES SER.#'d UNDER 20 NOT PRICED
85 J.P. Losman/22 4.00 10.00
86 Steven Jackson/24 6.00 15.00
87 Chris Perry/26 4.00 10.00
88 Michael Jenkins/29 4.00 10.00
89 Kevin Jones/30 4.00 10.00
90 Rashaun Woods/31 3.00 8.00
91 Ben Watson/32 4.00 10.00
92 Ben Troupe/40 3.00 8.00
93 Tatum Bell/41 3.00 8.00
94 Julius Jones/43 3.00 8.00
95 Devery Henderson/50 2.00 5.00
96 Darius Watts/54 2.00 5.00
97 Greg Jones/55 2.00 5.00
98 Keary Colbert/62 2.00 5.00
99 Derrick Hamilton/77 2.00 5.00
100 Drew Henson/192 1.25 3.00

2004 Fleer Genuine At Large

STATED ODDS 1:45
1AL Anquan Boldin 1.00 2.50
2AL LaDainian Tomlinson 1.50 4.00
3AL Michael Vick 1.25 3.00
4AL Daunte Culpepper 1.25 3.00
5AL Brian Urlacher 1.50 4.00
6AL Ahman Green 1.25 3.00
7AL Peyton Manning 4.00 10.00
8AL Byron Leftwich 1.00 2.50
9AL Priest Holmes 1.00 2.50
10AL Chad Pennington 1.00 2.50
11AL Jeremy Shockey 1.00 2.50
12AL Joe Horn 1.00 2.50
13AL Santana Moss 1.25 3.00
14AL Donovan McNabb 1.25 3.00
15AL Randy Moss 1.25 3.00

2004 Fleer Genuine At Large Patch Autographs

STATED PRINT RUN 25-44
AB Anquan Boldin/25 15.00 40.00
BL Byron Leftwich/25 30.00 60.00
CP Chad Pennington/44 40.00 100.00

2004 Fleer Genuine At Large Patch White

WHITE PRINT RUN 75 SER.#'d SETS
*BLACK BORDER/35: .5X TO 1.2X WHT/75
BLACK PRINT RUN 35 SER.#'d SETS
*ORANGE/10: 1X TO 2.5X WHITE/75
ORANGE PRINT RUN 10 SETS
AB Anquan Boldin 2.50 6.00
AB2 Aaron Brooks 2.50 6.00
AG Ahman Green 3.00 8.00
BL Byron Leftwich 2.50 6.00
BU Brian Urlacher 4.00 10.00
CC Chris Chambers 2.50 6.00
CP Chad Pennington 2.50 6.00
DB Derrick Brooks 2.50 6.00
DC Daunte Culpepper 3.00 8.00
DM Donovan McNabb 3.00 8.00
HW Hines Ward 3.00 8.00
JD Jake Delhomme 2.50 6.00
JF Justin Fargas 3.00 8.00
JH Joey Harrington 2.50 6.00
JH2 Joe Horn 2.50 6.00
JL Jamal Lewis 3.00 8.00
JS Jeremy Shockey 2.50 6.00
LT LaDainian Tomlinson 4.00 10.00
MA Mike Alstott 2.50 6.00
MF Marshall Faulk 3.00 8.00
MH Matt Hasselbeck 2.50 6.00
MV Michael Vick 3.00 8.00
PH Priest Holmes 2.50 6.00
PM Peyton Manning 10.00 25.00
RG Rich Gannon 3.00 8.00
RG2 Rex Grossman 2.50 6.00
RM Randy Moss 3.00 8.00
RW Roy Williams S 2.50 6.00
SM Santana Moss 3.00 8.00
TH Travis Henry 2.50 6.00

2004 Fleer Genuine Big Time

STATED ODDS 1:500
1BT Clinton Portis 3.00 8.00
2BT Donovan McNabb 4.00 10.00
3BT Jeff Garcia 3.00 8.00
4BT Chad Johnson 3.00 8.00
5BT Michael Vick 4.00 10.00
6BT Tony Gonzalez 4.00 10.00
7BT Deuce McAllister 4.00 10.00
8BT Carson Palmer 4.00 10.00
9BT Peyton Manning 12.00 30.00
10BT LaDainian Tomlinson 5.00 12.00
11BT Brett Favre 10.00 25.00
12BT Marvin Harrison 4.00 10.00
13BT Terrell Owens 4.00 10.00
14BT Priest Holmes 3.00 8.00
15BT Jamal Lewis 4.00 10.00

2004 Fleer Genuine Big Time Autographs Blue

BLUE BORDER PRINT RUN 150
*ORANGE/25: .8X TO 2X BLUE/150
ORANGE BORDER PRINT RUN 25
*RED/50: .5X TO 1.2X BLUE/150
RED BORDER PRINT RUN 50
CJ Chad Johnson 5.00 12.00
CP2 Chris Perry 5.00 12.00
DM Deuce McAllister 6.00 15.00
DS Donte Stallworth 5.00 12.00
JJ Joe Jurevicius 5.00 12.00
JL Jamal Lewis 6.00 15.00
RW Reggie Williams 5.00 12.00

2004 Fleer Genuine Big Time Jersey Autographs White

WHITE BORDER PRINT RUN 75 SER.#'d SETS
*BLACK BORDER: .6X TO 1.5X WHITE
BLACK BORDER PRINT RUN 25 SER.#'d SETS
CJ Chad Johnson 10.00 25.00

2004 Fleer Genuine Big Time Patch Autographs

STATED PRINT RUN 25 SER.#'d SETS
DM Deuce McAllister 25.00 60.00

2004 Fleer Genuine Big Time Patch Black

BLACK BORDER PRINT RUN 25
UNPRICED ORANGE PRINT RUN 5 SETS
*WHITE BORDER/54-97: .25X TO .6X BLACK
*WHITE BORDER/31-44: .3X TO .8X BLACK
*WHITE BORDER/21-28: .4X TO 1X BLACK
WHITE BORDER SER.#'d TO JSY NUMBER
BB Boss Bailey 6.00 15.00
BF Brett Favre 20.00 50.00
BU Brian Urlacher 10.00 25.00
CJ Chad Johnson 6.00 15.00
CM Curtis Martin 8.00 20.00
CP Carson Palmer 8.00 20.00
CP2 Clinton Portis 6.00 15.00
DC David Carr 6.00 15.00
DM Deuce McAllister 8.00 20.00
DM2 Donovan McNabb 8.00 20.00
DS Donte Stallworth 6.00 15.00
FM Freddie Mitchell 6.00 15.00
FT Fred Taylor 6.00 15.00
IB Isaac Bruce 10.00 25.00
JG Jeff Garcia 6.00 15.00
JL Jamal Lewis 8.00 20.00
JP Julius Peppers 8.00 20.00
LS Lee Suggs 8.00 20.00
LT LaDainian Tomlinson 10.00 25.00
MH Marvin Harrison 8.00 20.00
MV Michael Vick 8.00 20.00
PB Plaxico Burress 6.00 15.00
PH Priest Holmes 6.00 15.00
PM Peyton Manning 25.00 60.00
PP Peerless Price 6.00 15.00
PW Peter Warrick 6.00 15.00
TB Tiki Barber 8.00 20.00
TG Tony Gonzalez 8.00 20.00
TO Terrell Owens 8.00 20.00
ZT Zach Thomas 8.00 20.00

2004 Fleer Genuine Genuine Article

COMPLETE SET (15) 12.50 30.00
STATED ODDS 1:7
1GA Brett Favre 2.00 5.00
2GA Marvin Harrison .75 2.00
3GA Clinton Portis .60 1.50
4GA Peyton Manning 2.50 6.00
5GA Randy Moss .75 2.00
6GA Donovan McNabb .75 2.00
7GA Tom Brady 4.00 10.00
8GA Terrell Owens .75 2.00
9GA Torry Holt .75 2.00
10GA Steve McNair .75 2.00
11GA Ray Lewis 1.00 2.50
12GA Michael Vick .75 2.00
13GA Deuce McAllister .75 2.00
14GA Shaun Alexander .60 1.50
15GA Priest Holmes .60 1.50

2004 Fleer Genuine Genuine Article Jerseys Red

*ORANGE BORDER/25: 1.2X TO 3X RED
ORANGE BORDER PRINT RUN 25
*WHITE BORDER/150: .6X TO 1.5X RED
WHITE BORDER PRINT RUN 150
BF Brett Favre 6.00 15.00
CP Clinton Portis 2.00 5.00
DM Deuce McAllister 2.50 6.00
DM2 Donovan McNabb 2.50 6.00
MH Marvin Harrison 2.50 6.00
MV Michael Vick 2.50 6.00
PH Priest Holmes 2.00 5.00
PM Peyton Manning 8.00 20.00
RL Ray Lewis 3.00 8.00
RM Randy Moss 2.50 6.00
SA Shaun Alexander 2.00 5.00
SM Steve McNair 2.50 6.00
TB Tom Brady 12.00 30.00
TH Torry Holt 2.50 6.00
TO Terrell Owens 2.50 6.00

2004 Fleer Genuine Genuine Article Jersey Autographs Silver

SILVER BORDER PRINT RUN 100
UNPRICED ORANGE PRINT RUN 1 SET
SA Shaun Alexander 15.00 40.00

1997 Fleer Goudey

The 1997 Fleer Goudey set was issued in two series, each totaling 150 cards.The small almost square shaped (2 3/8" x 2 7/8") cards measured the same as the 1930's Goudey sets. Inspired by the classic look of the 1930's cards these cards have the same "Art Deco-style" graphics and same matte finish. The cards in Series 1 were issued in 10 card packs in 36 count hobby boxes. An unnumbered base card of Brett Favre was released to promote the set.
COMPLETE SET (150) 6.00 15.00
1 Michael Jackson .10 .30
2 Ray Lewis .30 .75
3 Vinny Testaverde .10 .30
4 Eric Turner .07 .20
5 Jim Kelly .20 .50
6 Bryce Paup .07 .20
7 Andre Reed .10 .30
8 Bruce Smith .10 .30
9 Thurman Thomas .20 .50
10 Jeff Blake .10 .30
11 Ki-Jana Carter .07 .20
12 Carl Pickens .10 .30
13 Darnay Scott .10 .30
14 Terrell Davis .25 .60
15 John Elway .75 2.00
16 Anthony Miller .07 .20
17 John Mobley .07 .20
18 Shannon Sharpe .10 .30
19 Chris Chandler .10 .30
20 Eddie George .20 .50
21 Steve McNair .25 .60
22 Chris Sanders .07 .20
23 Quentin Coryatt .07 .20
24 Sean Dawkins .07 .20
25 Ken Dilger .07 .20
26 Marshall Faulk .25 .60
27 Jim Harbaugh .10 .30
28 Marvin Harrison .20 .50
29 Tony Brackens .07 .20
30 Mark Brunell .25 .60
31 Kevin Hardy .07 .20
32 Keenan McCardell .10 .30
33 James O.Stewart .10 .30
34 Marcus Allen .20 .50
35 Steve Bono .10 .30
36 Dale Carter .07 .20
37 Neil Smith .10 .30
38 Derrick Thomas .20 .50
39 Tamarick Vanover .10 .30
40 Karim Abdul-Jabbar .10 .30
41 Dan Marino .75 2.00
42 O.J. McDuffie .10 .30
43 Stanley Pritchett .07 .20
44 Zach Thomas .20 .50
45 Drew Bledsoe .25 .60
46 Ben Coates .10 .30
47 Terry Glenn .20 .50
48 Shawn Jefferson .07 .20
49 Curtis Martin .25 .60
50 Dave Meggett .07 .20
51 Hugh Douglas .07 .20
52 Keyshawn Johnson .20 .50
53 Adrian Murrell .10 .30
54 Tim Brown .20 .50
55 Rickey Dudley .10 .30
56 Jeff Hostetler .07 .20
57 Napoleon Kaufman .20 .50
58 Chester McGlockton .07 .20
59 Jerome Bettis .20 .50
60 Andre Hastings .07 .20
61 Greg Lloyd .07 .20
62 Kordell Stewart .20 .50
63 Yancey Thigpen .10 .30
64 Rod Woodson .10 .30
65 Andre Coleman .07 .20
66 Stan Humphries .10 .30
67 Tony Martin .10 .30
68 Leonard Russell .07 .20
69 Junior Seau .20 .50
70 Brian Blades .07 .20
71 Joey Galloway .10 .30
72 Chris Warren .10 .30
73 Larry Centers .10 .30
74 Leeland McElroy .07 .20
75 Simeon Rice .10 .30
76 Frank Sanders .10 .30
77 Eric Swann .07 .20
78 Jamal Anderson .20 .50
79 Bert Emanuel .10 .30
80 Terance Mathis .10 .30
81 Eric Metcalf .10 .30
82 Tim Biakabutuka .10 .30
83 Kerry Collins .20 .50
84 Kevin Greene .10 .30
85 Muhsin Muhammad .10 .30
86 Wesley Walls .10 .30
87 Curtis Conway .10 .30
88 Bryan Cox .07 .20
89 Walt Harris .07 .20
90 Erik Kramer .07 .20
91 Rashaan Salaam .07 .20
92 Troy Aikman .40 1.00
93 Michael Irvin .20 .50
94 Daryl Johnston .10 .30
95 Leon Lett .07 .20
96 Deion Sanders .20 .50
97 Emmitt Smith .60 1.50
98 Scott Mitchell .10 .30
99 Herman Moore .10 .30
100 Johnnie Morton .10 .30
101 Brett Perriman .07 .20
102 Barry Sanders .60 1.50
103 Edgar Bennett .10 .30
104 Robert Brooks .10 .30
105 Brett Favre .75 2.00
106 Antonio Freeman .20 .50
107 Keith Jackson .07 .20
108 Reggie White .20 .50
109 Cris Carter .20 .50
110 Warren Moon .20 .50
111 John Randle .10 .30
112 Jake Reed .10 .30
113 Robert Smith .10 .30
114 Jim Everett .07 .20
115 Michael Haynes .07 .20
116 Alex Molden .07 .20
117 Ray Zellars .07 .20
118 Chris Calloway .07 .20
119 Rodney Hampton .10 .30
120 Phillippi Sparks .07 .20
121 Amani Toomer .10 .30
122 Ty Detmer .10 .30
123 Jason Dunn .07 .20
124 Irving Fryar .10 .30
125 Chris T. Jones .07 .20
126 Ricky Watters .10 .30
127 Tony Banks .10 .30
128 Isaac Bruce .20 .50
129 Eddie Kennison .10 .30
130 Lawrence Phillips .07 .20
131 Merton Hanks .07 .20
132 Terry Kirby .10 .30
133 Ken Norton .07 .20
134 Jerry Rice .40 1.00
135 J.J. Stokes .10 .30
136 Steve Young .25 .60
137 Alvin Harper .07 .20
138 Jackie Harris .07 .20
139 Hardy Nickerson .07 .20
140 Errict Rhett .07 .20
141 Terry Allen .20 .50
142 Henry Ellard .07 .20
143 Gus Frerotte .07 .20
144 Brian Mitchell .07 .20
145 Michael Westbrook .10 .30
146 Chuck Bednarik .10 .30
146AU Chuck Bednarik AUTO 20.00 50.00
147 Y.A. Tittle .10 .30
147AU Y.A. Tittle AUTO 20.00 50.00
148 Checklist .07 .20
149 Checklist .07 .20
150 Checklist .07 .20
P1 Brett Favre Promo .75 2.00

1997 Fleer Goudey Gridiron Greats

COMPLETE SET (147) 40.00 80.00
*GRID.GREATS STARS: 2.5X TO 5X
STATED ODDS 1:3

1997 Fleer Goudey Bednarik Says

Inserted at the rate of one in 60 hobby and one in 72 retail packs, this 15 card insert highlights Bednarik's personally chosen Top 15 current day defenders. The cards measure 2 3/8" x 2 7/8".
COMPLETE SET (15) 40.00 80.00
STATED ODDS 1:60
1 Kevin Greene 2.00 4.00
2 Ray Lewis 3.00 8.00
3 Greg Lloyd 1.25 2.50
4 Chester McGlockton 1.25 2.50
5 Hardy Nickerson 1.25 2.50
6 Bryce Paup 1.25 2.50
7 Simeon Rice 2.00 4.00
8 Deion Sanders 3.00 6.00
9 Junior Seau 3.00 6.00
10 Bruce Smith 2.00 4.00
11 Derrick Thomas 3.00 6.00
12 Zach Thomas 3.00 6.00
13 Eric Turner 1.25 2.50
14 Reggie White 4.00 8.00
15 Rod Woodson 2.00 4.00

1997 Fleer Goudey Heads Up

This 20 card insert can be found in one in 30 hobby and one in 36 retail packs. Inspired by Goudey's 1938 "Heads Up" cards, the set's design has oversized head photos on black and white cartoon body drawings on a foil enhanced card stock. The cards measure 2 3/8" x 2 7/8".
COMPLETE SET (20) 50.00 100.00
STATED ODDS 1:30
1 Troy Aikman 4.00 10.00
2 Marcus Allen 2.00 5.00
3 Tim Biakabutuka 1.25 3.00
4 Robert Brooks 1.25 3.00
5 Isaac Bruce 2.00 5.00
6 Kerry Collins 2.00 5.00
7 Terrell Davis 2.50 6.00
8 Brett Favre 8.00 20.00
9 Terry Glenn 2.00 5.00
10 Rodney Hampton 1.25 3.00
11 Michael Irvin 2.00 5.00
12 Chris T. Jones .75 2.00
13 Carl Pickens 1.25 3.00
14 Barry Sanders 6.00 15.00
15 Kordell Stewart 2.00 5.00
16 Thurman Thomas 2.00 5.00
17 Tamarick Vanover 1.25 3.00
18 Chris Warren 1.25 3.00
19 Ricky Watters 1.25 3.00
20 Steve Young 2.50 6.00

1997 Fleer Goudey Pigskin 2000

Inserted at a rate of one 360 hobby packs, this 15 card set highlights up-and-coming players that could be the future of the NFL in the year 2000. The cards utilize a multi-colored foil style that Fleer says embodies the "card of the future" design. The cards measure 2 3/8" x 2 7/8".
COMPLETE SET (15) 100.00 200.00
STATED ODDS 1:360
1 Karim Abdul-Jabbar 4.00 10.00
2 Jeff Blake 4.00 10.00
3 Drew Bledsoe 8.00 20.00
4 Robert Brooks 4.00 10.00
5 Terrell Davis 8.00 20.00
6 Marshall Faulk 8.00 20.00
7 Joey Galloway 4.00 10.00
8 Eddie George 6.00 15.00
9 Terry Glenn 6.00 15.00
10 Keyshawn Johnson 6.00 15.00
11 Chris T. Jones 2.50 6.00
12 Curtis Martin 8.00 20.00
13 Steve McNair 8.00 20.00
14 Lawrence Phillips 2.50 6.00
15 Kordell Stewart 6.00 15.00

1997 Fleer Goudey Tittle Says

Coming out of packs at the rate of one in 72 hobby and one in 85 retail packs, this 20 card set highlights Tittle's personal Top 20 current day offensive players. The cards measuring 2 3/8" x 2 7/8", show a picture of the player on a white background that also includes a large "Y" and "A" on the card fronts. The player's name is written in gold foil stamping.
COMPLETE SET (20) 75.00 150.00
STATED ODDS 1:72
1 Karim Abdul-Jabbar 1.25 3.00
2 Jerome Bettis 2.00 5.00
3 Tim Brown 2.00 5.00
4 Isaac Bruce 2.00 5.00
5 Cris Carter 2.00 5.00
6 Curtis Conway 1.25 3.00
7 John Elway 8.00 20.00
8 Marshall Faulk 2.50 6.00
9 Brett Favre 8.00 20.00
10 Joey Galloway 1.25 3.00
11 Eddie George 2.00 5.00
12 Keyshawn Johnson 2.00 5.00
13 Dan Marino 8.00 20.00
14 Curtis Martin 2.50 6.00
15 Herman Moore 1.25 3.00
16 Jerry Rice 4.00 10.00
17 Barry Sanders 6.00 15.00
18 Emmitt Smith 6.00 15.00
19 Thurman Thomas 2.00 5.00
20 Ricky Watters 1.25 3.00

1997 Fleer Goudey II

The 1997 Fleer Goudey set was issued in two series, each totaling 150 cards. Series II cards were issued in eight-card packs with a suggested retail price of $1.49. These cards were designed to match the card stock, color (off-white), size and graphics of the 1934 Goudey set. The back of each card displayed what Gale Sayers reported on the pictured player. Series II contained three Gale Sayers commemorative cards that were seeded at 1:9 packs with one percent foil stamped as "Rare Traditions" versions. A Reggie White promo card was released to promote the set that is identical to the base #92 Reggie White card except that it was printed on white card stock instead of off-white. Additionally there was a Reggie White display card measuring standard size that was to be used in the retailer's box display.
COMPLETE SET (150) 7.50 20.00
1 Gale Sayers SP .20 .50
1AU Gale Sayers AUTO 25.00 60.00
1RT Gale Sayers Rare Trad. 2.50 6.00
2 Vinny Testaverde .10 .30
3 Jeff George .10 .30
4 Brett Favre .75 2.00
5 Eddie Kennison .10 .30
6 Ken Norton .07 .20
7 John Elway .75 2.00
8 Troy Aikman .40 1.00
9 Steve McNair .25 .60
10 Kordell Stewart .20 .50
11 Drew Bledsoe .25 .60
12 Kerry Collins .20 .50
13 Dan Marino .75 2.00
14 Brad Johnson .20 .50
15 Todd Collins .07 .20
16 Ki-Jana Carter .07 .20
17 Pat Barnes RC .20 .50
18 Aeneas Williams .07 .20
19 Keyshawn Johnson .20 .50
20 Barry Sanders .60 1.50
21 Tiki Barber RC 1.25 3.00
22 Emmitt Smith .60 1.50
23 Kevin Hardy .07 .20
24 Mario Bates .07 .20
25 Ricky Watters .10 .30
26 Chris Canty RC .07 .20
27 Eddie George .20 .50
28 Curtis Martin .25 .60
29 Adrian Murrell .10 .30
30 Terrell Davis .25 .60
31 Rashaan Salaam .07 .20
32 Marcus Allen .20 .50
33 Karim Abdul-Jabbar .20 .50
34 Thurman Thomas .20 .50
35 Marvin Harrison .20 .50
36 Jerome Bettis .20 .50
37 Larry Centers .10 .30
38 Stan Humphries .10 .30
39 Lawrence Phillips .07 .20
40 Gale Sayers SP .20 .50
40AU Gale Sayers AUTO 25.00 60.00
40RT Gale Sayers Rare Trad. 2.50 6.00
41 Henry Ellard .07 .20
42 Chris Warren .10 .30
43 Robert Brooks .10 .30
44 Sedrick Shaw RC .10 .30
45 Muhsin Muhammad .10 .30
46 Napoleon Kaufman .20 .50
47 Reidel Anthony RC .20 .50
48 Jamal Anderson .20 .50
49 Scott Mitchell .10 .30
50 Mark Brunell .25 .60
51 William Thomas .07 .20
52 Bryan Cox .07 .20
53 Carl Pickens .10 .30
54 Chris Spielman .07 .20
55 Junior Seau .20 .50
56 Hardy Nickerson .07 .20
57 Dwayne Rudd RC .20 .50
58 Peter Boulware RC .20 .50
59 Jim Druckenmiller RC .10 .30
60 Michael Westbrook .10 .30
61 Shawn Springs RC .10 .30
62 Zach Thomas .20 .50
63 David LaFleur RC .07 .20
64 Darrell Russell RC .07 .20
65 Jake Plummer RC .75 2.00
66 Tim Biakabutuka .10 .30
67 Tyrone Wheatley .10 .30
68 Elvis Grbac .10 .30
69 Antonio Freeman .20 .50
70 Wayne Chrebet .20 .50
71 Walter Jones RC .30 .75
72 Marshall Faulk .25 .60
73 Jason Dunn .07 .20
74 Darnay Scott .10 .30
75 Errict Rhett .07 .20
76 Orlando Pace RC .20 .50
77 Natrone Means .10 .30
78 Bruce Smith .10 .30
79 Jamie Sharper RC .10 .30
80 Jerry Rice .40 1.00
81 Tim Brown .20 .50
82 Brian Mitchell .07 .20
83 Andre Reed .10 .30
84 Herman Moore .10 .30
85 Rob Moore .10 .30
86 Rae Carruth RC .07 .20
87 Bert Emanuel .10 .30
88 Michael Irvin .20 .50
89 Mark Chmura .10 .30
90 Tony Brackens .07 .20

91 Kevin Greene .10 .30
92 Reggie White .20 .50
93 Derrick Thomas .20 .50
94 Troy Davis RC .10 .30
95 Greg Lloyd .07 .20
96 Cortez Kennedy .07 .20
97 Simeon Rice .10 .30
98 Terrell Owens .25 .60
99 Hugh Douglas .07 .20
100 Terry Glenn .20 .50
101 Jim Harbaugh .10 .30
102 Shannon Sharpe .10 .30
103 Joey Kent RC .20 .50
104 Jeff Blake .10 .30
105 Terry Allen .20 .50
106 Cris Carter .20 .50
107 Amani Toomer .10 .30
108 Derrick Alexander WR .10 .30
109 Darnell Autry RC .10 .30
110 Irving Fryar .10 .30
111 Bryant Westbrook RC .07 .20
112 Tony Banks .10 .30
113 Michael Booker RC .07 .20
114 Yatil Green RC .10 .30
115 James Farrior RC .20 .50
116 Warrick Dunn RC .60 1.50
117 Greg Hill .07 .20
118 Tony Martin .10 .30
119 Chris Sanders .07 .20
120 Charles Johnson .10 .30
121 John Mobley .07 .20
122 Keenan McCardell .10 .30
123 Willie McGinest .07 .20
124 O.J. McDuffie .10 .30
125 Deion Sanders .20 .50
126 Curtis Conway .10 .30
127 Desmond Howard .10 .30
128 Johnnie Morton .10 .30
129 Ike Hilliard RC .30 .75
130 Gus Frerotte .07 .20
131 Tom Knight .07 .20
132 Sean Dawkins .07 .20
133 Isaac Bruce .20 .50
134 Wesley Walls .10 .30
135 Danny Wuerffel RC .20 .50
136 Tony Gonzalez RC .75 2.00
137 Ben Coates .10 .30
138 Joey Galloway .10 .30
139 Michael Jackson .10 .30
140 Steve Young .25 .60
141 Corey Dillon RC .75 2.00
142 Jake Reed .10 .30
143 Edgar Bennett .10 .30
144 Ty Detmer .10 .30
145 Darrell Green .10 .30
146 Antowain Smith RC .50 1.25
147 Mike Alstott .20 .50
148 Checklist .07 .20
149 Checklist .07 .20
150 Gale Sayers SP .20 .50
150AU Gale Sayers AUTO 25.00 60.00
150RT Gale Sayers Rare Trad. 2.50 6.00
D92 Reggie White Display card .40 1.00
P92 Reggie White Promo .40 1.00

1997 Fleer Goudey II Greats

*GREATS STARS: 15X TO 40X HI COL.
*GREATS RCs: 15X TO 30X HI COL.
STATED PRINT RUN 150 SERIAL #'d SETS
40 Gale Sayers AUTO 15.00 30.00

1997 Fleer Goudey II Gridiron Greats

COMPLETE SET (148) 60.00 120.00
*STARS: 2.5X TO 5X BASIC CARDS
*RC'S: 1.25X TO 2.5X BASIC CARDS
STATED ODDS 1:3

1997 Fleer Goudey II Big Time Backs

Randomly inserted in Series 2 packs at the rate of one in 72, this 10-card set features color action photos of top quarterbacks and running backs who are known for their "Big Time" play and have the statistics to prove it. An unannounced parallel set entitled "Stealth" was also randomly inserted into packs. The parallels were printed on actual wood stock and individually numbered of 10-sets produced.

COMPLETE SET (10) 125.00 250.00
STATED ODDS 1:72
UNPRICED WOODEN CARDS #'d OF 10
1 Karim Abdul-Jabbar 4.00 10.00
2 Marcus Allen 4.00 10.00
3 Jerome Bettis 4.00 10.00
4 Terrell Davis 5.00 12.00
5 Brett Favre 15.00 40.00
6 Eddie George 4.00 10.00
7 Dan Marino 15.00 40.00
8 Curtis Martin 5.00 12.00
9 Barry Sanders 12.50 30.00
10 Emmitt Smith 12.50 30.00

1997 Fleer Goudey II Glory Days

Randomly inserted in Series 2 retail packs only at the rate of one in 18, this 15-card set features color action photos of top NFL players who could be considered the "gladiators" of their teams.

COMPLETE SET (15) 35.00 70.00
STATED ODDS 1:18 RETAIL
1 Troy Aikman 5.00 12.00
2 Isaac Bruce 2.50 6.00
3 Mark Brunell 3.00 8.00
4 Cris Carter 2.50 6.00
5 Joey Galloway 1.50 4.00
6 Terry Glenn 2.50 6.00
7 Marvin Harrison 2.50 6.00
8 Dan Marino 10.00 25.00
9 Deion Sanders 2.50 6.00
10 Shannon Sharpe 1.50 4.00
11 Bruce Smith 1.50 4.00
12 Emmitt Smith 8.00 20.00
13 Kordell Stewart 2.50 6.00
14 Ricky Watters 1.50 4.00
15 Reggie White 2.50 6.00

1997 Fleer Goudey II Rookie Classics

Randomly inserted in packs at the rate of one in three, this 20-card set features color action photos of the top high impact rookies from the NFL Draft Class of 1997.

COMPLETE SET (20) 7.50 15.00
STATED ODDS 1:3
1 Reidel Anthony .30 .75
2 Pat Barnes .30 .75
3 Peter Boulware .30 .75
4 Rae Carruth .10 .30
5 Troy Davis .20 .50
6 Corey Dillon 1.25 3.00
7 Jim Druckenmiller .20 .50
8 Warrick Dunn 1.00 2.50
9 Tony Gonzalez 1.25 3.00
10 Yatil Green .20 .50
11 Ike Hilliard .50 1.25
12 Walter Jones .50 1.25
13 David LaFleur .10 .30
14 Orlando Pace .30 .75
15 Jake Plummer 1.25 3.00
16 Darrell Russell .10 .30
17 Antowain Smith .75 2.00
18 Shawn Springs .20 .50
19 Bryant Westbrook .10 .30
20 Danny Wuerffel .30 .75

1997 Fleer Goudey II Vintage Goudey

Randomly inserted in hobby packs only at the rate of one in 36, this 15-card set features color action photos of players considered throwbacks to old-time football. Redemption cards for original 1933 Sport Kings football cards of legends Red Grange, Jim Thorpe and Knute Rockne could also be found in packs.

COMPLETE SET (15) 75.00 150.00
STATED ODDS 1:36 HOBBY
1 Karim Abdul-Jabbar 3.00 8.00
2 Kerry Collins 3.00 8.00
3 Terrell Davis 4.00 10.00
4 John Elway 12.50 30.00
5 Brett Favre 12.50 30.00
6 Eddie George 3.00 8.00
7 Terry Glenn 3.00 8.00
8 Keyshawn Johnson 3.00 8.00
9 Curtis Martin 4.00 10.00
10 Herman Moore 2.00 5.00
11 Jerry Rice 6.00 15.00
12 Barry Sanders 10.00 25.00
13 Deion Sanders 3.00 8.00
14 Zach Thomas 3.00 8.00
15 Steve Young 4.00 10.00

2004 Fleer Inscribed

Fleer Inscribed initially released in mid-October 2004. The base set consists of 100-cards including 25-rookies serial numbered to 750. The boxes contained 24-packs of 5-cards each. Two parallel sets and a variety of inserts can be found seeded in packs highlighted by the multi-tiered Autograph inserts. Most signed cards were issued via mail-in exchange or redemption cards with a number of those EXCH cards not yet appearing live on the secondary market as of the printing of this book.

COMP.SET w/o SP's (75) 10.00 25.00
76-100 RC ODDS: 1:12 HOB, 1:100 RET
76-100 RC PRINT RUN 750 SER.#'d SETS
UNPRICED RED PRINT RUN 5 SETS
1 Terrell Owens .30 .75
2 David Carr .25 .60
3 Jerry Porter .25 .60
4 Charles Rogers .25 .60
5 Torry Holt .30 .75
6 Byron Leftwich .25 .60
7 Laveranues Coles .25 .60
8 Edgerrin James .30 .75
9 Brian Urlacher .40 1.00
10 Hines Ward .30 .75
11 LaDainian Tomlinson .40 1.00
12 Ahman Green .30 .75
13 Kevan Barlow .25 .60
14 Trent Green .25 .60
15 Deuce McAllister .30 .75
16 Lee Suggs .30 .75
17 Drew Brees .40 1.00
18 Randy Moss .30 .75
19 Brandon Lloyd .30 .75
20 Jeff Garcia .25 .60
21 Roy Williams S .25 .60
22 Daunte Culpepper .30 .75
23 Matt Hasselbeck .25 .60
24 Keyshawn Johnson .30 .75
25 Michael Vick .30 .75
26 Shaun Alexander .25 .60
27 Chad Pennington .25 .60
28 Ashley Lelie .25 .60
29 Anquan Boldin .25 .60
30 Carson Palmer .30 .75
31 Jeremy Shockey .25 .60
32 Peerless Price .25 .60
33 Chad Johnson .25 .60
34 Tiki Barber .30 .75
35 Warrick Dunn .25 .60
36 Jamal Lewis .30 .75
37 Brian Westbrook .25 .60
38 Stephen Davis .25 .60
39 Steve McNair .30 .75
40 Donovan McNabb .30 .75
41 Fred Taylor .25 .60
42 Clinton Portis .25 .60
43 Santana Moss .30 .75
44 Rod Smith .30 .75
45 Josh McCown .30 .75
46 Ray Lewis .40 1.00
47 Marshall Faulk .30 .75
48 Eric Moulds .25 .60
49 Jerry Rice .75 2.00
50 Jake Delhomme .25 .60
51 Tony Gonzalez .30 .75
52 Aaron Brooks .25 .60
53 Randy McMichael .25 .60
54 David Boston .25 .60
55 Plaxico Burress .25 .60
56 Rich Gannon .30 .75
57 Brett Favre .75 2.00
58 Isaac Bruce .40 1.00
59 Tom Brady 1.50 4.00
60 Priest Holmes .25 .60
61 Joe Horn .25 .60
62 Troy Brown .25 .60
63 Jake Plummer .25 .60
64 Derrick Brooks .25 .60
65 Marvin Harrison .30 .75
66 LaVar Arrington .25 .60
67 Drew Bledsoe .30 .75
68 Steve Smith .40 1.00
69 Peyton Manning 1.00 2.50
70 Rex Grossman .25 .60
71 Corey Dillon .25 .60
72 Mike Alstott .25 .60
73 Andre Johnson .30 .75
74 Joey Harrington .25 .60
75 Tyrone Calico .30 .75
76 Eli Manning RC 10.00 25.00
77 Larry Fitzgerald RC 5.00 12.00
78 Philip Rivers RC 4.00 10.00
79 Kellen Winslow RC 1.25 3.00
80 Roy Williams RC 1.25 3.00
81 Reggie Williams RC 1.25 3.00
82 Ben Roethlisberger RC 10.00 25.00
83 Lee Evans RC 2.00 5.00
84 Michael Clayton RC 1.50 4.00
85 J.P. Losman RC 1.25 3.00
86 Steven Jackson RC 2.00 5.00
87 Chris Perry RC 1.25 3.00
88 Michael Jenkins RC 1.25 3.00
89 Kevin Jones RC 1.50 4.00
90 Rashaun Woods RC 1.25 3.00
91 Ben Watson RC 1.50 4.00
92 Ben Troupe RC 1.25 3.00
93 Tatum Bell RC 1.25 3.00
94 Julius Jones RC 1.25 3.00
95 Devery Henderson RC 1.25 3.00
96 Darius Watts RC 1.25 3.00
97 Greg Jones RC 1.25 3.00
98 Keary Colbert RC 1.25 3.00
99 Derrick Hamilton RC 1.25 3.00
100 Bernard Berrian RC 1.25 3.00

2004 Fleer Inscribed Black Border Gold

*1-75 VETS: 2X TO 5X BASIC CARDS
*76-100 ROOKIES: .6X TO 1.5X BASIC CARDS
STATED PRINT RUN 199 SER.#'d SETS

2004 Fleer Inscribed Autographs Bronze

*BRONZE: .4X TO 1X SILVER AUTO
BRONZE STATED PRINT RUN 50-350
LF Larry Fitzgerald/50 40.00 80.00

2004 Fleer Inscribed Autographs Purple

STATED PRINT RUN 21-88
AB Antonio Bryant/88 8.00 20.00
DH Dante Hall/82 10.00 25.00
DS Donte Stallworth/83 10.00 25.00
KW Kelley Washington/87 8.00 20.00
WM Willis McGahee/21 12.00 30.00
CJ Chad Johnson/85 10.00 25.00

2004 Fleer Inscribed Autographs Silver

SILVER STATED PRINT RUN 100-450
*RED/25: 1X TO 2.5X SILVER/300-450
RED STATED PRINT RUN 25
*GOLD/300-450: .4X TO 1X SLVR/300-450
AB Antonio Bryant/300 8.00 20.00
DH Dante Hall/350 6.00 15.00
DS Donte Stallworth/450 6.00 15.00
JL J.P. Losman/100 8.00 20.00
LM Luke McCown/300 6.00 15.00
WM Willis McGahee/350 6.00 15.00

2004 Fleer Inscribed Award Winners

STATED PRINT RUN 150 SER.#'d SETS
1AW Randy Moss 1.50 4.00
2AW Ray Lewis 2.00 5.00
3AW Warrick Dunn 1.25 3.00
4AW Edgerrin James 1.50 4.00
5AW Brian Urlacher 2.00 5.00
6AW Derrick Brooks 1.25 3.00
7AW Tommy Maddox 1.25 3.00
8AW Marshall Faulk 1.50 4.00
9AW Priest Holmes 1.25 3.00
10AW Jevon Kearse 1.25 3.00
11AW Warren Sapp 1.50 4.00
12AW Michael Strahan 1.50 4.00
13AW Eddie George 1.50 4.00
14AW Clinton Portis 1.25 3.00
15AW Anquan Boldin 1.25 3.00

2004 Fleer Inscribed Award Winners Autographs

STATED PRINT RUN 100 SER.#'d SETS
AWAAB Anquan Boldin/100 10.00 25.00

2004 Fleer Inscribed Award Winners Autographs Notated

NOTATED STATED PRINT RUN 3-97
AWAWD Warrick Dunn/97 10.00 25.00

2004 Fleer Inscribed Award Winners Jersey Silver

SILVER PRINT RUN 175 SER.#'d SETS
*COPPER/75: .6X TO 1.5X SILVER/175
COPPER PRINT RUN 75 SER.#'d SETS
*PURPLE PATCH/49: .8X TO 2X SILVER/175
PURPLE PRINT RUN 49 SER.#'d SETS
AWJAB Anquan Boldin 2.50 6.00
AWJBU Brian Urlacher 4.00 10.00
AWJCP Clinton Portis 2.50 6.00
AWJDB Derrick Brooks 2.50 6.00
AWJEG Eddie George 3.00 8.00
AWJEJ Edgerrin James 3.00 8.00
AWJJK Jevon Kearse 2.50 6.00
AWJMF Marshall Faulk 3.00 8.00
AWJMS Michael Strahan 3.00 8.00
AWJPH Priest Holmes 2.50 6.00
AWJRL Ray Lewis 6.00 15.00
AWJRM Randy Moss 3.00 8.00
AWJTM Tommy Maddox 2.50 6.00
AWJWD Warrick Dunn 2.50 6.00
AWJWS Warren Sapp 3.00 8.00

2004 Fleer Inscribed Names of the Game

STATED PRINT RUN 299 SER.#'d SETS
1NG Priest Holmes .60 1.50
2NG LaDainian Tomlinson 1.00 2.50
3NG Donovan McNabb .75 2.00
4NG Deuce McAllister .75 2.00
5NG Edgerrin James .75 2.00
6NG Plaxico Burress .60 1.50
7NG Jake Plummer .60 1.50
8NG Steve McNair .75 2.00
9NG Boo Williams .60 1.50
10NG Jevon Kearse .60 1.50
11NG Tiki Barber .75 2.00
12NG Peyton Manning 2.50 6.00
13NG Peerless Price .60 1.50
14NG Jerome Bettis 1.00 2.50
15NG Tom Brady 4.00 10.00
16NG Dante Hall .60 1.50
17NG Randy Moss .75 2.00
18NG Emmitt Smith 1.50 4.00
19NG Ahman Green .75 2.00
20NG Daunte Culpepper .75 2.00
21NG Kellen Winslow Jr. .50 1.25
22NG Terrell Owens .60 1.50
23NG Larry Fitzgerald 2.00 5.00
24NG Eli Manning 4.00 10.00
25NG Dick Butkus 2.00 5.00
26NG Ken Stabler 2.00 5.00
27NG Paul Hornung 1.25 3.00
28NG Earl Campbell 1.00 2.50
29NG John Elway 4.00 10.00
30NG Dan Marino 5.00 12.00

2004 Fleer Inscribed Names of the Game Autographs

STATED PRINT RUN 99 SER.#'d SETS
*NOTATED/25: .5X TO 1.2X BASIC AU/99
NOTATED STATED PRINT RUN 25
NGADH Dante Hall 6.00 15.00
NGADM2 Deuce McAllister 8.00 20.00
NGADM3 Dan Marino 100.00 175.00
NGAEM Eli Manning 75.00 150.00
NGAJE John Elway 50.00 100.00

2004 Fleer Inscribed Names of the Game Jersey Copper

COPPER PRINT RUN 225 SER.#'d SETS
*GOLD/150: .5X TO 1.2X COPPER JSY
GOLD PRINT RUN 150 SER.#'d SETS
*PURPLE PATCH/33: 1X TO 2.5X COPPER
PURPLE PRINT RUN 33 SER.#'d SETS
*RED/79: .6X TO 1.5X COPPER JSY
RED PRINT RUN 79 SER.#'d SETS
*SILVER: .3X TO .8X COPPER JSY
NGJAG Ahman Green 2.50 6.00
NGJBW Boo Williams 2.00 5.00
NGJDC Daunte Culpepper 2.50 6.00
NGJDH Dante Hall 2.00 5.00
NGJDM Dan Marino 6.00 15.00
NGJDM2 Deuce McAllister 2.50 6.00
NGJDM3 Donovan McNabb 2.50 6.00
NGJEC Earl Campbell 3.00 8.00
NGJEJ Edgerrin James 2.50 6.00
NGJEM Eli Manning 6.00 15.00
NGJES Emmitt Smith 5.00 12.00
NGJJB Jerome Bettis 3.00 8.00
NGJJE John Elway 5.00 12.00
NGJJK Jevon Kearse 2.00 5.00
NGJJP Jake Plummer 2.00 5.00
NGJKS Ken Stabler 4.00 10.00
NGJKW Kellen Winslow Jr. 2.00 5.00
NGJLF Larry Fitzgerald 3.00 8.00
NGJLT LaDainian Tomlinson 3.00 8.00
NGJPB Plaxico Burress 2.00 5.00
NGJPH Paul Hornung 3.00 8.00
NGJPM Peyton Manning 8.00 20.00
NGJPP Peerless Price 2.00 5.00
NGJPH2 Priest Holmes 2.00 5.00
NGJRM Randy Moss 2.50 6.00
NGJSM Steve McNair 2.50 6.00
NGJTB Tiki Barber 2.50 6.00
NGJTO Terrell Owens 2.50 6.00
NGJTB2 Tom Brady 6.00 15.00

2004 Fleer Inscribed Valuable Players

STATED PRINT RUN 74-104
1VP Dan Marino/84 7.50 20.00
2VP John Elway/87 6.00 15.00
3VP Earl Campbell/79 2.00 5.00
4VP Emmitt Smith/93 4.00 10.00
5VP Ken Stabler/74 3.00 8.00
6VP Brett Favre/95 5.00 12.00
7VP Marshall Faulk/100 2.00 5.00
8VP Rich Gannon/103 1.25 3.00
9VP Steve McNair/104 2.00 5.00
10VP Peyton Manning/104 2.50 6.00

2004 Fleer Inscribed Valuable Players Autographs

STATED PRINT RUN 199 SER.#'d SETS
UNPRICED NOTATED PRINT RUN 9 SETS
VPADM Dan Marino 75.00 150.00
VPAJE John Elway 50.00 100.00

2004 Fleer Inscribed Valuable Players Jersey Blue

STATED PRINT RUN 74-104
UNPRICED MASTERPIECE PRINT RUN 1 SET
BF Brett Favre/95 12.00 30.00
DM Dan Marino/84 15.00 40.00
EC Earl Campbell/79 8.00 20.00
ES Emmitt Smith/93 10.00 25.00
JE John Elway/87 12.00 30.00
KS Ken Stabler/74 10.00 25.00
MF Marshall Faulk/100 5.00 12.00
PM Peyton Manning/104 15.00 40.00
RG Rich Gannon/103 5.00 12.00
SM Steve McNair/104 5.00 12.00

2001 Fleer Legacy

This 120 card set was released in December, 2001. It was issued in five card packs with an SRP of $4.99 per pack which came 24 to a box. Cards numbered 91-120 featured rookies and were serial numbered to 999. The first 300 of those rookie cards featured a "postmark" on them as part of an insert set.

COMP.SET w/o SP's (90) 10.00 25.00
91-120 ROOKIE PRINT RUN 999
1 Donovan McNabb .25 .60
2 Doug Flutie .25 .60
3 Amani Toomer .20 .50
4 Jay Fiedler .25 .60
5 Antonio Freeman .30 .75
6 Jon Kitna .20 .50
7 Jake Plummer .20 .50
8 Ricky Watters .25 .60
9 Jerry Rice .60 1.50
10 Troy Brown .20 .50
11 Jimmy Smith .25 .60
12 Edgerrin James .25 .60
13 Todd Pinkston .20 .50
14 Eric Moulds .20 .50
15 Stephen Davis .20 .50
16 Matt Hasselbeck .20 .50
17 Vinny Testaverde .20 .50
18 Priest Holmes .20 .50
19 Mike Anderson .20 .50
20 Shane Matthews .20 .50
21 Qadry Ismail .20 .50
22 Torry Holt .25 .60
23 Duce Staley .20 .50
24 Ahman Green .25 .60
25 Corey Dillon .20 .50
26 Peerless Price .20 .50
27 Steve McNair .25 .60
28 Junior Seau .25 .60
29 Doug Chapman .20 .50
30 Mark Brunell .25 .60
31 Joey Galloway .25 .60
32 James Allen .20 .50
33 David Boston .20 .50
34 Marshall Faulk .25 .60
35 Shaun Alexander .20 .50
36 Wayne Chrebet .20 .50
37 Randy Moss .25 .60
38 Marvin Harrison .25 .60
39 Tim Couch .20 .50
40 Jamal Anderson .20 .50
41 Warren Sapp .25 .60
42 Brad Johnson .25 .60
43 Kerry Collins .20 .50
44 Derrick Alexander .20 .50
45 Terrell Davis .25 .60
46 Tiki Barber .25 .60
47 Trent Green .20 .50
48 James Stewart .20 .50
49 Kevin Johnson .20 .50
50 Ray Lewis .30 .75
51 Warrick Dunn .20 .50
52 Tim Brown .30 .75
53 Daunte Culpepper .25 .60
54 Fred Taylor .20 .50
55 Brian Griese .20 .50
56 Wesley Walls .20 .50
57 Rob Johnson .25 .60
58 Travis Taylor .20 .50
59 Jeff Garcia .20 .50
60 Rich Gannon .25 .60
61 Cris Carter .30 .75
62 Peyton Manning .75 2.00
63 Peter Warrick .20 .50
64 Terance Mathis .20 .50
65 Kurt Warner .50 1.25
66 Kordell Stewart .20 .50
67 Aaron Brooks .20 .50
68 JaJuan Dawson .20 .50
69 Elvis Grbac .25 .60
70 Keyshawn Johnson .25 .60
71 Terrell Owens .25 .60
72 Curtis Martin .25 .60
73 Lamar Smith .25 .60
74 Rod Smith .25 .60
75 Tim Biakabutuka .20 .50
76 Thomas Jones .20 .50
77 Isaac Bruce .30 .75
78 Joe Horn .20 .50
79 Drew Bledsoe .25 .60
80 Oronde Gadsden .20 .50
81 Brett Favre .60 1.50
82 Emmitt Smith .50 1.25
83 Muhsin Muhammad .20 .50
84 Eddie George .30 .75
85 Jerome Bettis .30 .75
86 Ricky Williams .25 .60
87 Tony Gonzalez .25 .60
88 Germane Crowell .20 .50
89 Brian Urlacher .40 1.00
90 Shawn Jefferson .20 .50
91 Michael Vick RC 4.00 10.00
92 David Terrell RC 2.00 5.00
93 Chris Chambers RC 1.50 4.00
94 Freddie Mitchell RC 1.50 4.00
95 Drew Brees RC 50.00 100.00
96 LaMont Jordan RC 2.50 6.00
97 Quincy Carter RC 2.00 5.00
98 Anthony Thomas RC 2.50 6.00
99 LaDainian Tomlinson RC 8.00 20.00
100 Santana Moss RC 2.50 6.00
101 Rod Gardner RC 2.00 5.00
102 Nick Goings RC 2.50 6.00
103 Sage Rosenfels RC 2.00 5.00
104 Mike McMahon RC 2.00 5.00
105 Snoop Minnis RC 1.50 4.00
106 Michael Bennett RC 2.00 5.00
107 Todd Heap RC 2.00 5.00
108 Kevan Barlow RC 2.00 5.00
109 Travis Henry RC 2.00 5.00
110 Jason Brookins RC 2.50 6.00
111 Rudi Johnson RC 2.50 6.00
112 Reggie Wayne RC 3.00 8.00
113 Koren Robinson RC 2.00 5.00
114 Chad Johnson RC 2.50 6.00
115 Quincy Morgan RC 2.00 5.00
116 Robert Ferguson RC 2.50 6.00
117 Chris Weinke RC 2.00 5.00
118 Jesse Palmer RC 2.00 5.00
119 James Jackson RC 1.50 4.00
120 Deuce McAllister RC 2.50 6.00

2001 Fleer Legacy Ultimate Legacy

*VETS 1-90: 3X TO 8X BASIC CARDS
*ROOKIES 91-120: .5X TO 1.2X
STATED PRINT RUN 250
95 Drew Brees 75.00 150.00

2001 Fleer Legacy Rookie Postmarks

Randomly inserted in packs, the first 300 of each rookie card featured a postmark dating their first game in the NFL.

FIRST 300 SER.#'d RCs POSTMARKED
FIRST 100 #'d POSTMARKS WERE SIGNED
91 Michael Vick 3.00 8.00
92 David Terrell 1.50 4.00
93 Chris Chambers 1.25 3.00
94 Freddie Mitchell 1.25 3.00
95 Drew Brees 60.00 125.00
96 LaMont Jordan 2.00 5.00
97 Quincy Carter 1.50 4.00
98 Anthony Thomas 2.00 5.00
99 LaDainian Tomlinson 6.00 15.00
100 Santana Moss 2.00 5.00
101 Rod Gardner 1.50 4.00
102 Nick Goings 2.00 5.00
103 Sage Rosenfels 1.50 4.00
104 Mike McMahon 1.50 4.00
105 Snoop Minnis 1.25 3.00
106 Michael Bennett 1.50 4.00
107 Todd Heap 1.50 4.00
108 Kevan Barlow 1.50 4.00
109 Travis Henry 1.50 4.00
110 Jason Brookins 2.00 5.00
111 Rudi Johnson 2.00 5.00
112 Reggie Wayne 2.50 6.00
113 Koren Robinson 1.50 4.00
114 Chad Johnson 2.00 5.00
115 Quincy Morgan 1.50 4.00
116 Robert Ferguson 2.00 5.00
117 Chris Weinke 1.50 4.00
118 Jesse Palmer 1.50 4.00
119 James Jackson 1.25 3.00
120 Deuce McAllister 2.00 5.00

2001 Fleer Legacy Rookie Postmarks Autographs

Randomly inserted in packs, the first 300-cards of the 999-serial numbered rookies featured a postmark dating their first game in the NFL. Eleven players signed the first 100 of those cards for inclusion in this insert set. Each was initially inserted in packs as a redemption card.

FIRST 100 #'d POSTMARKS SIGNED
91 Michael Vick 125.00 200.00
92 David Terrell 8.00 20.00
93 Chris Chambers 6.00 15.00
95 Drew Brees 300.00 600.00
100 Santana Moss 10.00 25.00
103 Sage Rosenfels 8.00 20.00
104 Mike McMahon 8.00 20.00
106 Michael Bennett 8.00 20.00
108 Kevan Barlow 8.00 20.00
114 Chad Johnson 30.00 80.00
118 Jesse Palmer 8.00 20.00

2001 Fleer Legacy 1000 Yard Club Jerseys

Inserted at stated odds of one in 115, these 22-cards feature jersey swatches of players who reached 1,000 yards rushing or receiving at least once in their career. The Barry Sanders card appeared on the secondary market only after Fleer ceased operations.

STATED ODDS 1:115
OVERALL MEMORABILIA ODDS 1:12
BS Barry Sanders 5.00 12.00
CD Corey Dillon 2.00 5.00
CM Curtis Martin 2.50 6.00
DS Duce Staley 2.00 5.00
EJ Edgerrin James 2.50 6.00
FS Frank Sanders 2.00 5.00
FT Fred Taylor 2.00 5.00
IB Isaac Bruce 3.00 8.00
JA Jamal Anderson 2.50 6.00
JB Jerome Bettis 3.00 8.00
JL Jamal Lewis 3.00 8.00
MH Marvin Harrison 2.50 6.00
MR Marcus Robinson 2.50 6.00
RM Randy Moss 10.00 25.00
RS Rod Smith 2.50 6.00
SD Stephen Davis 2.00 5.00
TB Tiki Barber 2.50 6.00
TH Torry Holt 2.50 6.00
TO Terrell Owens 2.50 6.00
WC Wayne Chrebet 2.00 5.00
WD Warrick Dunn 2.00 5.00
EMC Ed McCaffrey 2.50 6.00
EMO Eric Moulds 2.00 5.00

2001 Fleer Legacy 1000 Yard Club Dual Jerseys

Randomly inserted in packs, these cards feature two swatches of game-used jerseys from players who had reached the 1,000 yard mark plateau as least once in their career. The two Barry Sanders cards appeared on the market only after Fleer ceased operations.

STATED PRINT RUN 400 SER.#'d SETS
OVERALL MEMORABILIA ODDS 1:12
BSRM B.Sanders/R.Moss 6.00 15.00
CDTD C.Dillon/T.Davis 3.00 8.00
EGWD E.George/W.Dunn 4.00 10.00
EMJS E.McCaffrey/J.Smith 3.00 8.00
IBMR I.Bruce/M.Robinson 4.00 10.00
IBTO I.Bruce/T.Owens 4.00 10.00
JABS J.Anderson/B.Sanders 6.00 15.00
JBEJ J.Bettis/E.James 4.00 10.00
JBFT J.Bettis/F.Taylor 4.00 10.00
MHIB M.Harrison/I.Bruce 4.00 10.00
MHRS M.Harrison/Rod Smith 3.00 8.00
MRMH M.Robinson/M.Harrison 3.00 8.00
RSEM Rod Smith/E.McCaffrey 3.00 8.00
SDDS S.Davis/D.Staley 2.50 6.00
SDTD S.Davis/T.Davis 3.00 8.00
SDWD S.Davis/W.Dunn 2.50 6.00
TBEG T.Barber/E.George 4.00 10.00
TBWD T.Barber/W.Dunn 2.50 6.00
WCCM W.Chrebet/C.Martin 3.00 8.00
WCJM W.Chrebet/J.Smith 3.00 8.00

2001 Fleer Legacy Game Issue 2nd Quarter

Randomly inserted in packs, these cards feature game-worn jerseys of NFL stars. These cards say 2nd quarter on the front and are serial numbered to 100.

2ND QUARTER PRINT RUN 100
*1ST QUARTER: .4X TO 1X 2ND QUARTER
*3RD QUARTER/50: .5X TO 1.2X 2ND QRTR
3RD QUARTER PRINT RUN 50
*4TH QUARTER/25: 1X TO 2.5X 2ND QRTR
4TH QUARTER PRINT RUN 25
OVERALL MEMORABILIA ODDS 1:12
BF Brett Favre 6.00 15.00
BG Brian Griese 2.00 5.00
BJ Bo Jackson 4.00 10.00
CC Cris Carter 3.00 8.00
DB David Boston 2.00 5.00
DC Daunte Culpepper 2.50 6.00
DM Donovan McNabb 2.50 6.00
EJ Edgerrin James 2.50 6.00
GC Germane Crowell 2.00 5.00
JG Jeff Garcia 2.00 5.00
JP Jake Plummer 2.00 5.00
KJ Kevin Johnson 2.00 5.00
KS Kordell Stewart 2.00 5.00
KW Kurt Warner 5.00 12.00
MB Mark Brunell 2.50 6.00
RD Ron Dayne 2.50 6.00
RG Rich Gannon 2.50 6.00
RJ Rob Johnson 2.50 6.00
RL Ray Lewis 3.00 8.00
VT Vinny Testaverde 2.00 5.00

2001 Fleer Legacy Hall of Fame Material

Issued at stated odds of one in 288, these cards feature game-worn uniform swatches of players looking like they are on their way to induction in the Football Hall of Fame. These cards are designed in the way the busts at Canton are.

STATED ODDS 1:288
OVERALL MEMORABILIA ODDS 1:12
BF Brett Favre 8.00 20.00
BJ Bo Jackson 5.00 12.00
DM Dan Marino 8.00 20.00
ES Emmitt Smith 6.00 15.00
JE John Elway 6.00 15.00
JR Jerry Rice 8.00 20.00
JS Junior Seau 3.00 8.00
MA Marcus Allen 4.00 10.00
MF Marshall Faulk 3.00 8.00
TA Troy Aikman 5.00 12.00

2001 Fleer Legacy Triple Threads

Inserted at stated odds of one in 48, these 30 cards feature three jersey swatches from leading rookies of 2001.

STATED ODDS 1:48
OVERALL MEMORABILIA ODDS 1:12
BBJ Barlow/Bennett/R.Jhnsn 4.00 10.00
CGR Chambrs/Grdner/Rbnson 3.00 8.00
CMF Chmbers/Minnis/Frguson 4.00 10.00
FWM Ferguson/Wayne/Minnis 5.00 12.00
HCV Heupel/Carter/Vick 6.00 15.00
HMC Heap/Morgan/Chambers 3.00 8.00
HPT Heupel/Palmr/Tuiasosopo 4.00 10.00
HRH Heupel/Rosenfels/Heap 4.00 10.00
HTJ Henry/Thomas/J.Jacksn 4.00 10.00
JHM C.Johnson/Heap/S.Moss 4.00 10.00
JJM R.Johnsn/J.Jacksn/Minor 4.00 10.00
MFM Morgan/Ferguson/Minnis 4.00 10.00
MHB Minor/Henry/Bennett 3.00 8.00
MJJ McAllistr/R.Jhnsn/C.Jhnsn 4.00 10.00
MMJ S.Moss/Mitchell/C.Jhnsn 4.00 10.00
MMT McAllister/Minor/Thomas 4.00 10.00
MPW McMahon/Palmer/Weinke 3.00 8.00
MTR McMahn/Tuiassopo/Rosnfls 3.00 8.00
MWT McMhn/Weinke/Tuisospo 3.00 8.00
PBR Palmer/Brees/Rosenfels 15.00 40.00
RMM Rbinson/Mitchell/Mrgan 3.00 8.00
TBH Tomlinson/Barlow/Henry 12.00 30.00
TGW Terrell/Gardner/Wayne 5.00 12.00
TJB Thomas/Jackson/Barlow 4.00 10.00
TMB Tomlnsn/McAllstr/Benntt 12.00 30.00
TMG Terrell/Mitchell/Gardner 3.00 8.00
VBC Vick/Brees/Carter 15.00 40.00
VTT Vick/Tomlinson/Terrell 12.00 30.00
WBC Weinke/Brees/Carter 15.00 40.00
WMR Wayne/Moss/Robinson 5.00 12.00

2002 Fleer Maximum

This 290-card base set contains 250 veterans and 40 rookies. The rookies are divided into subsets: Maximum Rookie Home Whites sequentially numbered to 3500 and Maximum Rookie True Colors sequentially numbered to 3500.

COMP.SET w/o RC's (250) 10.00 25.00
251-290 ROOKIE PRINT RUN 3500
1 Tom Brady 1.50 4.00
2 Kurt Warner .25 .60
3 Mike McMahon .20 .50
4 Ronney Jenkins .20 .50
5 Tyrone Wheatley .25 .60
6 Germane Crowell .20 .50
7 James Jackson .20 .50
8 Eric Metcalf .20 .50
9 Muhsin Muhammad .20 .50
10 Tony Richardson .20 .50
11 Wayne Chrebet .20 .50
12 Daunte Culpepper .25 .60
13 Trent Dilfer .20 .50
14 Kevin Dyson .25 .60
15 Chris Fuamatu-Ma'afala .20 .50
16 Dominic Rhodes .20 .50
17 David Terrell .20 .50
18 Rod Woodson .30 .75
19 Anthony Wright .20 .50
20 Jerome Bettis .30 .75
21 Kendrell Bell .20 .50
22 Edgerrin James .25 .60
23 Jamal Lewis .25 .60
24 Jim Miller .20 .50
25 Warren Sapp .25 .60
26 Clint Stoerner .20 .50
27 Michael Strahan .25 .60
28 Vinny Sutherland .20 .50
29 Mike Alstott .20 .50
30 Jay Fiedler .25 .60
31 Willie Jackson .20 .50
32 Earl Little RC .25 .60
33 Robert Porcher .20 .50
34 Junior Seau .25 .60
35 Darrick Vaughn .20 .50
36 Wesley Walls .25 .60
37 Michael Westbrook .20 .50
38 Freddie Mitchell .20 .50
39 Drew Bledsoe .25 .60
40 Gus Frerotte .20 .50
41 Travis Henry .20 .50
42 MarTay Jenkins .20 .50
43 Curtis Keaton .20 .50
44 Keenan McCardell .25 .60
45 Neil O'Donnell .25 .60
46 Chad Pennington .20 .50
47 Charlie Rogers .20 .50
48 Hines Ward .25 .60
49 Jason Gildon .25 .60
50 Travis Taylor .20 .50
51 Dre Bly .20 .50
52 Oronde Gadsden .25 .60
53 Danny Wuerffel .20 .50
54 Jamir Miller .20 .50
55 Cory Schlesinger .20 .50
56 LaDainian Tomlinson .30 .75
57 Michael Vick .25 .60
58 Chris Weinke .20 .50
59 Brandon Stokley .20 .50
60 James Allen .20 .50
61 Correll Buckhalter .20 .50
62 Jameel Cook .20 .50
63 Deuce McAllister .25 .60
64 Travis Minor .20 .50
65 James Stewart .20 .50
66 Kwamie Lassiter .20 .50
67 Jamel White .20 .50
68 Ronde Barber .20 .50
69 Kevan Barlow .20 .50
70 Marty Booker .20 .50
71 Peter Boulware .20 .50
72 Quincy Carter .20 .50
73 Warrick Dunn .20 .50
74 Brett Favre .60 1.50
75 Chad Lewis .20 .50
76 Jeff Ogden .25 .60
77 Todd Sauerbrun .20 .50
78 Ricky Williams .25 .60
79 Charlie Batch .20 .50
80 Courtney Brown .20 .50
81 Stephen Davis .20 .50
82 Fred Smoot .25 .60
83 Marshall Faulk .25 .60
84 Doug Flutie .25 .60
85 Rich Gannon .25 .60
86 Dante Hall .20 .50
87 Frank Sanders .20 .50
88 Antowain Smith .25 .60
89 Tiki Barber .25 .60
90 Fred Beasley .20 .50
91 Jason Brookins .20 .50
92 Rocket Ismail .25 .60
93 Bubba Franks .20 .50
94 Joey Galloway .25 .60
95 Keyshawn Johnson .25 .60
96 Donovan McNabb .25 .60
97 Lamar Smith .20 .50
98 Corey Bradford .20 .50
99 Kerry Collins .20 .50
100 Autry Denson .20 .50
101 Antonio Freeman .30 .75
102 Fred Taylor .20 .50
103 Troy Hambrick .20 .50
104 Brad Johnson .25 .60
105 Brian Mitchell .25 .60
106 Zach Thomas .25 .60
107 Michael Bennett .20 .50
108 Ron Dayne .25 .60
109 Jeff Garcia .20 .50
110 Ahman Green .25 .60
111 Scotty Anderson .20 .50
112 Qadry Ismail .20 .50
113 Ed McCaffrey .25 .60
114 Shaun King .20 .50
115 Duce Staley .20 .50
116 Travis Brown .20 .50
117 Mark Brunell .25 .60
118 Chris Cole .20 .50
119 Aaron Glenn .20 .50
120 Darrell Jackson .25 .60
121 Jevon Kearse .20 .50
122 Randy Moss .25 .60
123 Hank Poteat .20 .50
124 Brian Urlacher .30 .75
125 Mike Anderson .20 .50
126 David Akers .20 .50
127 Laveranues Coles .25 .60
128 Eddie George .25 .60
129 J.J. Stokes .20 .50
130 Matt Hasselbeck .20 .50
131 Nate Jacquet .20 .50
132 Anthony Thomas .25 .60
133 Terrence Wilkins .20 .50
134 Tim Couch .20 .50
135 Ty Detmer .20 .50
136 Rod Gardner .20 .50
137 Charlie Garner .25 .60
138 Terry Glenn .25 .60
139 Az-Zahir Hakim .20 .50
140 Donald Hayes .20 .50
141 Priest Holmes .20 .50
142 Jermaine Wiggins .20 .50
143 Aaron Brooks .20 .50
144 Alge Crumpler .25 .60
145 Benjamin Gay .20 .50
146 Marcellus Wiley .20 .50
147 Torry Holt .25 .60
148 Desmond Howard .25 .60
149 Richard Huntley .20 .50
150 Bryan Johnson RC .25 .60
151 Terry Kirby .20 .50
152 Snoop Minnis .20 .50
153 David Boston .20 .50
154 Shawn Bryson .20 .50
155 Scott Covington .20 .50
156 Terrell Davis .25 .60
157 Damon Gibson .20 .50
158 Curtis Martin .25 .60
159 Derrick Mason .20 .50
160 Jacquez Green .20 .50
161 Chad Scott .20 .50
162 Tony Boselli .25 .60
163 Derrick Alexander .20 .50
164 Ian Gold .20 .50
165 Rob Johnson .25 .60
166 Thomas Jones .20 .50
167 Steve Smith .30 .75
168 Jonathan Quinn .20 .50
169 Mack Strong .20 .50
170 Vinny Testaverde .20 .50
171 Frank Wycheck .20 .50
172 Amos Zereoue .20 .50
173 Chris Chambers .20 .50
174 Joe Horn .20 .50
175 Kevin Johnson .20 .50
176 Ryan McNeil .20 .50
177 Marcus Pollard .20 .50
178 Jerry Rice .60 1.50
179 Jon Kitna .20 .50
180 Maurice Smith .20 .50
181 Jerome Pathon .20 .50
182 Darrien Gordon .20 .50
183 Champ Bailey .25 .60
184 Drew Brees .60 1.50
185 Troy Brown .20 .50
186 Brian Griese .20 .50
187 Jamal Anderson .25 .60
188 Eric Moulds .20 .50
189 Darnay Scott .25 .60
190 Jimmy Smith .25 .60
191 Ricky Watters .25 .60
192 Craig Yeast .20 .50
193 Michael Bates .20 .50
194 Trung Canidate .20 .50
195 David Dunn .20 .50
196 Tim Dwight .20 .50
197 Trent Green .20 .50
198 David Patten .20 .50
199 Jake Plummer .20 .50
200 Rod Smith .25 .60
201 Alex Van Pelt .20 .50
202 Peter Warrick .20 .50
203 Shaun Alexander .20 .50
204 Plaxico Burress .20 .50
205 Byron Chamberlain .20 .50
206 Peyton Manning .75 2.00
207 Marcus Robinson .25 .60
208 Desmond Clark .20 .50
209 Reggie Swinton .20 .50
210 Amani Toomer .20 .50
211 Karl Williams .20 .50
212 Larry Centers .20 .50
213 Corey Dillon .20 .50
214 Jason Elam .20 .50
215 Arnold Jackson .20 .50
216 Stacey Mack .20 .50
217 Steve McNair .25 .60
218 Santana Moss .25 .60
219 Koren Robinson .20 .50
220 Kordell Stewart .20 .50
221 Spergon Wynn .20 .50
222 Todd Bouman .20 .50
223 Marvin Harrison .25 .60
224 Joe Jurevicius .20 .50
225 Terry Allen .25 .60

226 Jermaine Lewis .20 .50
227 Terrell Owens .25 .60
228 Shane Matthews .20 .50
229 Emmitt Smith .50 1.25
230 Jeremiah Trotter .20 .50
231 Tony Banks .20 .50
232 Tim Brown .30 .75
233 Isaac Bruce .30 .75
234 Curtis Conway .25 .60
235 Marc Edwards .20 .50
236 Tony Gonzalez .25 .60
237 Deltha O'Neal .20 .50
238 Michael Pittman .25 .60
239 Peerless Price .20 .50
240 Takeo Spikes .20 .50
241 Charlie Clemons RC .20 .50
242 Garrison Hearst .20 .50
243 Ike Hilliard .20 .50
244 Leonard Johnson .20 .50
245 Chris Redman .20 .50
246 Ray Lewis .30 .75
247 John Lynch .25 .60
248 Bill Schroeder .20 .50
249 James Thrash .25 .60
250 Chad Johnson .20 .50
251 David Carr RC .60 1.50
252 Joey Harrington RC .60 1.50
253 DeShaun Foster RC 1.00 2.50
254 William Green RC .75 2.00
255 Julius Peppers RC 1.50 4.00
256 Javon Walker RC 1.00 2.50
257 Ashley Lelie RC .60 1.50
258 Adrian Peterson RC .75 2.00
259 Patrick Ramsey RC .75 2.00
260 Kurt Kittner RC .60 1.50
261 Josh Reed RC .75 2.00
262 David Garrard RC .75 2.00
263 Reche Caldwell RC .75 2.00
264 Quentin Jammer RC 1.00 2.50
265 Rohan Davey RC 1.00 2.50
266 Eric Crouch RC 1.00 2.50
267 Kahlil Hill RC .60 1.50
268 Antwaan Randle El RC .75 2.00
269 Josh McCown RC 1.00 2.50
270 Maurice Morris RC .75 2.00
271 Jeremy Shockey RC 1.00 2.50
272 Travis Stephens RC .60 1.50
273 Jonathan Wells RC .75 2.00
274 Roy Williams RC .60 1.50
275 Brian Westbrook RC 1.25 3.00
276 Daniel Graham RC .75 2.00
277 Marquise Walker RC .60 1.50
278 Lamar Gordon RC .75 2.00
279 Jason McAddley RC .75 2.00
280 Jabar Gaffney RC .60 1.50
281 Luke Staley RC .60 1.50
282 Clinton Portis RC 1.00 2.50
283 Cliff Russell RC .60 1.50
284 Andre Davis RC .60 1.50
285 Ron Johnson RC .75 2.00
286 Ladell Betts RC 1.00 2.50
287 T.J. Duckett RC .60 1.50
288 Donte Stallworth RC 1.00 2.50
289 Antonio Bryant RC 1.00 2.50
290 Chad Hutchinson RC .60 1.50

2002 Fleer Maximum To The Max

*VETS 1-250: 2.5X TO 6X BASIC CARDS
1-250 VETERAN PRINT RUN 250
*ROOKIES 251-290: 2X TO 5X
251-290 ROOKIE PRINT RUN 100

2002 Fleer Maximum Dressed to Thrill

Randomly inserted in packs at a rate of 1:16, this 23-card set contains game-worn jersey swatches from many of the NFL's most exciting players
STATED ODDS 1:16 HOB, 1:72 RET
1 Courtney Brown 1.50 4.00
2 Tim Brown 2.50 6.00
3 Mark Brunell 2.00 5.00
4 Plaxico Burress 1.50 4.00
5 Trung Canidate 1.50 4.00
6 Stephen Davis 1.50 4.00
7 Corey Dillon 1.50 4.00
8 Brett Favre 5.00 12.00
9 Rich Gannon 2.00 5.00
10 Tony Gonzalez 2.00 5.00
11 Marvin Harrison 2.00 5.00
12 Jevon Kearse 1.50 4.00
13 Donovan McNabb 2.00 5.00
14 Eric Moulds 1.50 4.00
15 Terrell Owens 2.00 5.00
16 Jerry Rice 5.00 12.00
17 Marcus Robinson 2.00 5.00
18 Warren Sapp 2.00 5.00
19 Ricky Williams 2.00 5.00
20 Vinny Testaverde 1.50 4.00
21 Zach Thomas 2.00 5.00
22 LaDainian Tomlinson 2.50 6.00
23 Peter Warrick 1.50 4.00

2002 Fleer Maximum Dressed to Thrill Nameplates

Sequentially numbered to 100, this 15-card insert offers game-worn jersey name plate swatches from many of the NFL's top performers.
STATED PRINT RUN 100 SER.#'d SETS
1 Courtney Brown 5.00 12.00
2 Tim Brown 8.00 20.00
3 Trung Canidate 5.00 12.00
4 Corey Dillon 5.00 12.00
5 Brett Favre 15.00 40.00
6 Rich Gannon 6.00 15.00
7 Tony Gonzalez 6.00 15.00
8 Donovan McNabb 6.00 15.00
9 Terrell Owens 6.00 15.00
10 Warren Sapp 6.00 15.00
11 Vinny Testaverde 5.00 12.00
12 Zach Thomas 6.00 15.00
13 LaDainian Tomlinson 8.00 20.00
14 Peter Warrick 5.00 12.00
15 Ricky Williams 6.00 15.00

2002 Fleer Maximum Dressed to Thrill Numbers

Sequentially numbered to 250, this 21-card insert offers game-worn jersey number swatches from many of the NFL's top performers.
STATED PRINT RUN 250 SER.#'d SETS
1 Jamal Anderson 5.00 12.00
2 Courtney Brown 4.00 10.00
3 Tim Brown 6.00 15.00
4 Mark Brunell 5.00 12.00
5 Trung Canidate 4.00 10.00
6 Corey Dillon 4.00 10.00
7 Brett Favre 12.00 30.00
8 Rich Gannon 5.00 12.00
9 Tony Gonzalez 5.00 12.00
10 Marvin Harrison 5.00 12.00
11 Jevon Kearse 4.00 10.00
12 Donovan McNabb 5.00 12.00
13 Terrell Owens 5.00 12.00
14 Jerry Rice 12.00 30.00
15 Marcus Robinson 5.00 12.00
16 Warren Sapp 5.00 12.00
17 Vinny Testaverde 4.00 10.00
18 Zach Thomas 5.00 12.00
19 LaDainian Tomlinson 6.00 15.00
20 Peter Warrick 4.00 10.00
21 Ricky Williams 5.00 12.00

2002 Fleer Maximum First and Ten

Randomly inserted into packs, this set features two cards, each of which features ten of the NFL's top players from each conference along with a jersey swatch. Each card is serial numbered to 25.
STATED PRINT RUN 25 SER.#'d SETS
1 AFC 125.00 250.00
2 NFC 150.00 300.00

2002 Fleer Maximum K Corps

This 58-card insert is sequentially numbered to the 2001 season yardage total of each featured player. Cards were randomly inserted into packs.
1-18 PRINT RUN 3040-4830
19-58 PRINT RUN 1003-1598
1 Kurt Warner/4830 .75 2.00
2 Peyton Manning/4131 2.50 6.00
3 Brett Favre/3921 2.00 5.00
4 Aaron Brooks/3832 .60 1.50
5 Rich Gannon/3828 .75 2.00
6 Trent Green/3783 .60 1.50
7 Kerry Collins/3764 .60 1.50
8 Jake Plummer/3653 .60 1.50
9 Jeff Garcia/3538 .60 1.50
10 Doug Flutie/3464 .75 2.00
11 Brad Johnson/3406 .75 2.00
12 Steve McNair/3350 .75 2.00
13 Mark Brunell/3309 .75 2.00
14 Jay Fiedler/3290 .75 2.00
15 Donovan McNabb/3233 .75 2.00
16 Jon Kitna/3216 .60 1.50
17 Kordell Stewart/3109 .60 1.50
18 Tim Couch/3040 .60 1.50
19 David Boston/1598 1.00 2.50
20 Priest Holmes/1555 1.00 2.50
21 Marvin Harrison/1524 1.25 3.00
22 Curtis Martin/1513 1.25 3.00
23 Stephen Davis/1432 1.00 2.50
24 Terrell Owens/1412 1.25 3.00
25 Ahman Green/1387 1.25 3.00
26 Marshall Faulk/1382 1.25 3.00
27 Jimmy Smith/1373 1.25 3.00
28 Torry Holt/1363 1.25 3.00
29 Rod Smith/1343 1.25 3.00
30 Shaun Alexander/1318 1.00 2.50
31 Corey Dillon/1315 1.00 2.50
32 Keyshawn Johnson/1266 1.25 3.00
33 Joe Horn/1265 1.00 2.50
34 Ricky Williams/1245 1.25 3.00
35 LaDainian Tomlinson/1236 1.50 4.00
36 Randy Moss/1233 1.25 3.00
37 Garrison Hearst/1206 1.00 2.50
38 Troy Brown/1199 1.00 2.50
39 Anthony Thomas/1183 1.25 3.00
40 Tim Brown/1199 1.50 4.00
41 Antowain Smith/1157 1.25 3.00
42 Johnnie Morton/1154 1.25 3.00
43 Jerry Rice/1139 3.00 8.00
44 Derrick Mason/1128 1.00 2.50
45 Curtis Conway/1125 1.25 3.00
46 Keenan McCardell/1110 1.25 3.00
47 Isaac Bruce/1106 1.50 4.00
48 Dominic Rhodes/1104 1.00 2.50
49 Kevin Johnson/1097 1.00 2.50
50 Darrell Jackson/1081 1.25 3.00
51 Jerome Bettis/1072 1.50 4.00
52 Marty Booker/1071 1.00 2.50
53 Qadry Ismail/1059 1.00 2.50
54 Amani Toomer/1054 1.00 2.50
55 Willie Jackson/1046 1.00 2.50
56 Emmitt Smith/1021 2.50 6.00
57 Plaxico Burress/1008 1.00 2.50
58 Hines Ward/1003 1.25 3.00

2002 Fleer Maximum Playbook X's and O's

Inserted in packs at a rate of 1:6, this 20-card insert features a playbook like design with action shots of many of the NFL's best.
COMPLETE SET (20) 12.00 30.00
STATED ODDS 1:6 HOB, 1:8 RET
1 Tom Brady 4.00 10.00
2 Tiki Barber .60 1.50
3 Brian Griese .50 1.25
4 Jake Plummer .50 1.25
5 Chris Chambers .50 1.25
6 Terrell Davis .60 1.50
7 Daunte Culpepper .60 1.50
8 Ron Dayne .60 1.50
9 Cris Carter .75 2.00
10 Jamal Lewis .60 1.50
11 Duce Staley .50 1.25
12 Brian Urlacher .75 2.00
13 Edgerrin James .60 1.50
14 Michael Vick .60 1.50
15 Drew Brees 1.50 4.00
16 Jerry Rice 1.50 4.00
17 Marshall Faulk .60 1.50
18 Brett Favre 1.50 4.00
19 Jerome Bettis .75 2.00
20 Kurt Warner .60 1.50

2002 Fleer Maximum Playbook Xs Jerseys

This set is similar in design to the Playbook X's and O's set, with the addition of a jersey swatch. There is an O's parallel that is serial #'d to 50.
X's JERSEY ODDS 1:24 HOB, 1:144 RET
*O's JSY/50: .8X TO 2X X's JSY
O's STATED PRINT RUN 50
1 Jerome Bettis 3.00 8.00
2 Drew Brees 6.00 15.00
3 Cris Carter 3.00 8.00
4 Daunte Culpepper 2.50 6.00
5 Ron Dayne 2.50 6.00
6 Marshall Faulk 2.50 6.00
7 Brett Favre 6.00 15.00
8 Brian Griese 2.00 5.00
9 Edgerrin James 2.50 6.00
10 Jamal Lewis 2.50 6.00
11 Jake Plummer 2.00 5.00
12 Jerry Rice 6.00 15.00
13 Duce Staley 2.00 5.00
14 Brian Urlacher 3.00 8.00
15 Kurt Warner 2.50 6.00

2002 Fleer Maximum Post Pattern

Inserted into packs at a rate of 1:40, this set features an authentic piece of NFL goal post from an NFL game.
STATED ODDS 1:40 HOB, 1:72 RET
1 Edgerrin James 2.50 6.00
2 Marvin Harrison 2.50 6.00
3 Curtis Martin 2.50 6.00
4 Mark Brunell 2.50 6.00
5 Fred Taylor 2.00 5.00
6 Tim Brown 3.00 8.00
7 Randy Moss 2.50 6.00
8 Daunte Culpepper 2.50 6.00
9 Emmitt Smith 5.00 12.00
10 Steve McNair 2.50 6.00

1999 Fleer Mystique

Released as a 160-card set, 1999 Fleer Mystique is comprised of 100 veterans, 50 rookies which are sequentially numbered to 2999, and 10 star player cards which are sequentially numbered to 2500. Each pack contained one "covered" card which had to be peeled to reveal either a numbered insert/basic card or one of the few non-numbered base cards. Mystique was packaged in 24-pack boxes with each pack containing four cards and carried a suggested retail price of $4.99.
COMPLETE SET (160) 100.00 200.00
COMP.SHORT SET (100) 25.00 50.00
1 Terrell Davis SP .50 1.25
2 Jerome Bettis SP .60 1.50
3 J.J. Stokes .25 .60
4 Frank Wycheck .30 .75
5 O.J. McDuffie .30 .75
6 Johnnie Morton .30 .75
7 Marshall Faulk SP .50 1.25
8 Ryan Leaf .30 .75
9 Sean Dawkins .25 .60
10 Brett Favre SP 1.25 3.00
11 Steve Young SP .75 2.00
12 Jimmy Smith .30 .75
13 Isaac Bruce .40 1.00
14 Trent Dilfer .25 .60
15 Brian Mitchell .30 .75
16 Kordell Stewart SP .40 1.00
17 Herman Moore .30 .75
18 Troy Aikman SP .75 2.00
19 Cris Carter .40 1.00
20 Barry Sanders SP 1.00 2.50
21 Tony Gonzalez .30 .75
22 Skip Hicks .25 .60
23 Steve McNair SP .50 1.25
24 Brad Johnson .30 .75
25 Mark Chmura .25 .60
26 Randall Cunningham SP .50 1.25
27 Jerry Rice SP 1.50 4.00
28 Jamie Asher .25 .60
29 Brian Griese SP .40 1.00
30 Peyton Manning SP 2.00 5.00
31 Keith Poole .25 .60
32 Wayne Chrebet .25 .60
33 Rich Gannon .30 .75
34 Michael Irvin .40 1.00
35 Yancey Thigpen .25 .60
36 Corey Dillon .25 .60
37 Steve Beuerlein .30 .75
38 Terry Kirby .25 .60
39 Jacquez Green .25 .60
40 Mark Brunell SP .50 1.25
41 Rickey Dudley .25 .60
42 Shannon Sharpe .30 .75
43 Andre Rison .30 .75
44 Chris Chandler .30 .75
45 Fred Taylor SP .40 1.00
46 Kerry Collins .25 .60
47 Antowain Smith SP .40 1.00
48 Wesley Walls .30 .75
49 Rob Moore .25 .60
50 Dan Marino SP 1.25 3.00
51 Robert Smith .25 .60
52 Keenan McCardell .30 .75
53 Joey Galloway .30 .75
54 Fred Lane .25 .60
55 Napoleon Kaufman .25 .60
56 Curtis Martin .30 .75
57 Rod Smith .30 .75
58 Curtis Conway .30 .75
59 Kevin Dyson .25 .60
60 Warrick Dunn SP .40 1.00
61 Ahman Green .30 .75
62 Duce Staley .25 .60
63 Emmitt Smith SP 1.00 2.50
64 Adrian Murrell .25 .60
65 Dorsey Levens .30 .75
66 Drew Bledsoe SP .50 1.25
67 Ed McCaffrey .30 .75
68 Natrone Means .30 .75
69 Deion Sanders .30 .75
70 Keyshawn Johnson SP .50 1.25
71 Antonio Freeman .30 .75
72 James Stewart .25 .60
73 Ben Coates .30 .75
74 Priest Holmes .25 .60
75 Jake Reed .30 .75
76 Mike Alstott .25 .60
77 Vinny Testaverde .25 .60
78 Ricky Watters .30 .75
79 Garrison Hearst .25 .60
80 Junior Seau .30 .75
81 Tim Brown .40 1.00
82 Jamal Anderson .30 .75
83 Robert Brooks .30 .75
84 Marc Edwards .30 .75
85 Curtis Enis .25 .60
86 Doug Flutie .40 1.00
87 Terry Glenn .30 .75
88 Charlie Batch SP .40 1.00
89 Marvin Harrison .30 .75
90 Jake Plummer SP .40 1.00
91 Terrell Owens .30 .75
92 Scott Mitchell .25 .60
93 Tim Dwight .30 .75
94 Eddie George SP .50 1.25
95 Ike Hilliard .25 .60
96 Robert Holcombe .25 .60
97 Charles Johnson .25 .60
98 Eric Moulds .25 .60
99 Michael Westbrook .25 .60
100 Randy Moss SP .50 1.25
101 Tim Couch RC 1.50 4.00
102 Donovan McNabb RC 8.00 20.00
103 Akili Smith RC 1.25 3.00
104 Cade McNown RC 1.25 3.00
105 Daunte Culpepper RC 2.00 5.00
106 Ricky Williams RC 2.00 5.00
107 Edgerrin James RC 2.00 5.00
108 Kevin Faulk RC 1.25 3.00
109 Torry Holt RC 2.50 6.00
110 David Boston RC 1.25 3.00
111 Chris Claiborne RC 1.25 3.00
112 Mike Cloud RC 1.25 3.00
113 Joe Germaine RC 1.50 4.00
114 Cecil Collins RC 1.25 3.00
115 Tim Alexander RC 1.25 3.00
116 Brandon Stokley RC 1.50 4.00
117 Lamarr Glenn RC 1.25 3.00
118 Shawn Bryson RC 1.25 3.00
119 Jeff Paulk RC 1.25 3.00
120 Kevin Johnson RC 1.50 4.00
121 Charlie Rogers RC 1.25 3.00
122 Joe Montgomery RC 1.25 3.00
123 Travis McGriff RC 1.25 3.00
124 Dee Miller RC 1.25 3.00
125 Rob Konrad RC 1.25 3.00
126 Peerless Price RC 1.25 3.00
127 D'Wayne Bates RC 1.25 3.00
128 Craig Yeast RC 1.25 3.00
129 Malcolm Johnson RC 1.25 3.00
130 Brock Huard RC 1.25 3.00
131 Sedrick Irvin RC 1.25 3.00
132 Troy Smith RC 1.50 4.00
133 Troy Edwards RC 1.25 3.00
134 Al Wilson RC 2.00 5.00
135 Terry Jackson RC 1.25 3.00
136 Dameane Douglas RC 1.25 3.00
137 Amos Zereoue RC 1.25 3.00
138 Shaun King RC 1.25 3.00
139 James Johnson RC 1.25 3.00
140 Jermaine Fazande RC 1.25 3.00
141 Autry Denson RC 1.25 3.00
142 Darran Hall RC 1.25 3.00
143 Na Brown RC 1.25 3.00
144 Mike Lucky RC 1.25 3.00
145 Karsten Bailey RC 1.25 3.00
146 Kevin Daft RC 1.25 3.00
147 Sean Bennett RC 1.25 3.00
148 Madre Hill RC 1.25 3.00
149 Michael Bishop RC 1.50 4.00
150 Scott Covington RC 1.25 3.00
151 Randy Moss STAR 1.25 3.00
152 Fred Taylor STAR 1.00 2.50
153 Brett Favre STAR 3.00 8.00
154 Dan Marino STAR 3.00 8.00
155 Terrell Davis STAR 1.25 3.00
156 Barry Sanders STAR 2.50 6.00
157 Emmitt Smith STAR 2.50 6.00
158 Jake Plummer STAR 1.00 2.50
159 Warrick Dunn STAR 1.00 2.50
160 Troy Aikman STAR 2.00 5.00
P80 Doug Flutie Promo .50 1.25

1999 Fleer Mystique Gold

COMPLETE SET (100) 150.00 300.00
*GOLD STARS: 2X TO 5X HI COL.
*GOLD SP STARS: 2.5X TO 6X HI COL.
GOLDS RANDOM INSERTS IN PACKS

1999 Fleer Mystique Feel the Game

Randomly inserted in packs, this 10-card set features player photos coupled with a swatch of a game-used jersey or sock. Each card was released in different hand numbered print runs.
COMPLETE SET (10) 150.00 300.00
1 Terrell Davis/545 10.00 25.00
2 Charles Johnson/325 8.00 20.00
3 Jon Kitna/640 6.00 15.00
4 Dorsey Levens/515 6.00 15.00
5 Dan Marino Sock/220 30.00 80.00
6 Curtis Martin/690 10.00 25.00
7 Johnnie Morton/580 6.00 15.00
8 Randy Moss/510 10.00 25.00
9 Brandon Stokley Glv/85 15.00 40.00
10 Steve Young/580 20.00 40.00

1999 Fleer Mystique Fresh Ink

Randomly inserted in packs, this 30-card set features player photos set behind an authentic autograph. The cards were released in different print run numbers and each was hand serial numbered on the cardfront.
STATED PRINT RUN 45-750
1 Charlie Batch/250 8.00 20.00
2 Mark Brunell/45 30.00 60.00
3 Shawn Bryson/650 5.00 12.00
4 Cecil Collins/725 5.00 12.00
5 Daunte Culpepper/300 12.00 30.00
6 Randall Cunningham/200 15.00 40.00
7 Terrell Davis/50 40.00 80.00
8 Sean Dawkins/700 5.00 12.00
9 Corey Dillon/250 8.00 20.00
10 Dameane Douglas/750 5.00 12.00
11 Tim Dwight/725 8.00 20.00
12 Troy Edwards/200 8.00 20.00
13 Doug Flutie/250 12.00 30.00
14 Eddie George/250 10.00 25.00
15 Joe Germaine/575 5.00 12.00
16 Trent Green/350 10.00 25.00
17 Torry Holt/350 10.00 25.00
18 Brock Huard/700 8.00 20.00
19 Edgerrin James/150 12.00 30.00
20 Brad Johnson/300 10.00 25.00
21 Jon Kitna/350 8.00 20.00
22 Peyton Manning/250 60.00 120.00
23 Randy Moss/150 30.00 80.00
24 Doug Pederson/750 5.00 12.00
25 Jake Plummer/300 8.00 20.00
26 Peerless Price/675 8.00 20.00
27 Akili Smith/100 5.00 12.00
28 Emmitt Smith/125 100.00 175.00
29 Antowain Smith/150 10.00 25.00
30 Ricky Williams/150 12.00 30.00

1999 Fleer Mystique NFL 2000

Randomly seeded in packs, this 10-card set showcases the NFL's young talent. Base cards are printed on all-holographic card stock, and each card is sequentially numbered to 999.
COMPLETE SET (10) 20.00 40.00
STATED PRINT RUN 999 SER.#'d SETS
1N Peyton Manning 6.00 15.00
2N Ryan Leaf .75 2.00
3N Charlie Batch 2.00 5.00
4N Fred Taylor 2.00 5.00
5N Keyshawn Johnson 1.25 3.00
6N J.J. Stokes 1.25 3.00
7N Jake Plummer 1.25 3.00
8N Brian Griese 2.00 5.00
9N Antowain Smith 1.25 3.00
10N Jamal Anderson 1.25 3.00

1999 Fleer Mystique Protential

Randomly inserted in packs, this 10-card set includes top draft picks on a base card where background color matches team color, and card is enhanced with silver foil highlights. Each card is sequentially numbered to 1999.
COMPLETE SET (10) 30.00 60.00
STATED PRINT RUN 1999 SER.#'d SETS
1PT Tim Couch 2.00 5.00
2PT Donovan McNabb 6.00 15.00
3PT Akili Smith 2.00 5.00
4PT Cade McNown 2.00 5.00
5PT Daunte Culpepper 5.00 12.00
6PT Ricky Williams 2.50 6.00
7PT Edgerrin James 5.00 12.00
8PT Kevin Faulk 2.00 5.00
9PT Torry Holt 3.00 8.00
10PT David Boston 2.00 5.00

1999 Fleer Mystique Star Power

Randomly inserted in packs, this 10-card set highlights top NFL stars on an all-foil card with a star background. Each card is sequentially numbered to 100.
COMPLETE SET (10) 150.00 300.00
STATED PRINT RUN 100 SER.#'d SETS
1SP Randy Moss 20.00 50.00
2SP Warrick Dunn 8.00 20.00
3SP Mark Brunell 6.00 15.00
4SP Emmitt Smith 15.00 40.00
5SP Eddie George 8.00 20.00
6SP Barry Sanders 25.00 60.00
7SP Terrell Davis 8.00 20.00
8SP Dan Marino 25.00 60.00
9SP Troy Aikman 15.00 40.00
10SP Brett Favre 25.00 60.00

2000 Fleer Mystique

Released as a 145-card set, Fleer Mystique is comprised of 100 veteran cards and 45 rookie cards sequentially numbered to 2000. Base cards are all foil and feature full color action photography with the word mystique appearing behind the player in silver foil. All inserts and rookie cards were produced with an opaque covering that needed to be peeled to reveal the card. Mystique was packaged in 20-pack boxes with packs containing five cards and carried a suggested retail price of $4.99.
COMPLETE SET (145) 125.00 250.00
COMP.SET w/o SP's (100) 6.00 15.00
1 Tim Couch .25 .60
2 Edgerrin James .25 .60
3 Terrell Davis .25 .60
4 Eddie George .25 .60
5 Jevon Kearse .20 .50
6 Mike Alstott .20 .50
7 Tony Martin .25 .60
8 Jermaine Fazande .20 .50
9 Akili Smith .20 .50
10 Damon Huard .20 .50
11 Kordell Stewart .20 .50
12 Peyton Manning .75 2.00
13 Michael Westbrook .20 .50
14 Tim Biakabutuka .25 .60
15 Curtis Martin .25 .60
16 Shaun King .20 .50
17 Jamal Anderson .25 .60
18 Terry Allen .25 .60
19 Sean Dawkins .20 .50
20 Muhsin Muhammad .20 .50
21 Vinny Testaverde .20 .50
22 Warren Sapp .25 .60
23 Wesley Walls .20 .50
24 Mark Brunell .25 .60
25 Tim Brown .30 .75
26 Kevin Dyson .25 .60
27 Curtis Enis .20 .50
28 Keenan McCardell .25 .60
29 Rich Gannon .25 .60
30 Jermaine Lewis .20 .50
31 Johnnie Morton .25 .60
32 Kerry Collins .20 .50
33 Az-Zahir Hakim .20 .50
34 Cade McNown .20 .50
35 Jimmy Smith .25 .60
36 Tyrone Wheatley .20 .50
37 Marcus Robinson .25 .60
38 Fred Taylor .20 .50
39 Donovan McNabb .25 .60
40 Steve McNair .25 .60
41 Corey Dillon .20 .50
42 Tony Gonzalez .25 .60
43 Duce Staley .20 .50
44 Albert Connell .20 .50
45 Isaac Bruce .30 .75
46 Troy Aikman .40 1.00
47 Charlie Garner .25 .60
48 Kevin Johnson .20 .50
49 Cris Carter .30 .75
50 Ryan Leaf .25 .60
51 Doug Flutie .25 .60
52 Brett Favre .60 1.50
53 Joe Montgomery .20 .50
54 Torry Holt .25 .60
55 Jonathan Linton .20 .50
56 Antonio Freeman .25 .60
57 Amani Toomer .20 .50
58 Kurt Warner .50 1.25
59 Jake Plummer .20 .50
60 Rob Johnson .25 .60
61 Randy Moss .25 .60
62 Jerry Rice .75 2.00
63 Chris Chandler .25 .60
64 Joey Galloway .25 .60
65 Olandis Gary .25 .60
66 Drew Bledsoe .25 .60
67 Steve Beuerlein .25 .60
68 Marvin Harrison .25 .60
69 Keyshawn Johnson .25 .60
70 Warrick Dunn .20 .50
71 Tim Dwight .25 .60
72 Brian Griese .20 .50
73 Terry Glenn .25 .60
74 Jon Kitna .20 .50
75 Qadry Ismail .20 .50
76 Germane Crowell .20 .50
77 Ricky Williams .25 .60
78 Marshall Faulk .25 .60
79 Karim Abdul-Jabbar .20 .50
80 James Johnson .20 .50
81 Hines Ward .25 .60
82 Frank Sanders .20 .50
83 Emmitt Smith .50 1.25
84 Robert Smith .20 .50
85 Steve Young .40 1.00
86 Darnay Scott .25 .60
87 Tamarick Vanover .20 .50
88 Troy Edwards .20 .50
89 Brad Johnson .25 .60
90 Tony Banks .20 .50
91 Charlie Batch .20 .50
92 Jeff Blake .25 .60
93 Ricky Watters .25 .60
94 Carl Pickens .25 .60
95 Elvis Grbac .20 .50
96 Jerome Bettis .30 .75
97 Eric Moulds .20 .50
98 Dorsey Levens .25 .60
99 Wayne Chrebet .20 .50
100 Stephen Davis .20 .50
101 Shaun Alexander RC 1.50 4.00
102 Sebastian Janikowski RC 1.50 4.00
103 Tom Brady RC 150.00 250.00
104 Courtney Brown RC 1.25 3.00
105 Marc Bulger RC 1.25 3.00
106 Plaxico Burress RC 1.25 3.00
107 Trung Canidate RC 1.00 2.50
108 Giovanni Carmazzi RC 1.00 2.50
109 Trevor Gaylor RC 1.00 2.50
110 Laveranues Coles RC 1.25 3.00
111 Ron Dayne RC 1.50 4.00
112 Reuben Droughns RC 1.00 2.50
113 Danny Farmer RC 1.00 2.50
114 Chafie Fields RC 1.00 2.50
115 Bubba Franks RC 1.00 2.50
116 Sherrod Gideon RC 1.00 2.50
117 Joe Hamilton RC 1.00 2.50
118 Chris Cole RC 1.25 3.00
119 Darrell Jackson RC 1.00 2.50
120 Thomas Jones RC 1.25 3.00
121 Jamal Lewis RC 1.50 4.00
122 Anthony Lucas RC 1.00 2.50
123 Tee Martin RC 1.00 2.50
124 Frank Murphy RC 1.00 2.50
125 Rondell Mealey RC 1.00 2.50
126 Sylvester Morris RC 1.00 2.50
127 Dennis Northcutt RC 1.00 2.50
128 Chad Pennington RC 1.25 3.00
129 Travis Prentice RC 1.00 2.50
130 Tim Rattay RC 1.25 3.00
131 Chris Redman RC 1.00 2.50
132 J.R. Redmond RC 1.00 2.50
133 R.Jay Soward RC 1.00 2.50
134 Quinton Spotwood RC 1.00 2.50
135 Shyrone Stith RC 1.00 2.50
136 Travis Taylor RC 1.00 2.50
137 Troy Walters RC 1.00 2.50
138 Peter Warrick RC 1.00 2.50
139 Dez White RC 1.00 2.50
140 Michael Wiley RC 1.00 2.50
141 Jerry Porter RC 1.50 4.00
142 Mareno Philyaw RC 1.00 2.50
143 Anthony Becht RC 1.00 2.50
144 JaJuan Dawson RC 1.00 2.50
145 Ron Dugans RC 1.00 2.50

2000 Fleer Mystique Gold

*VETS 1-100: 1.5X TO 4X BASIC CARDS
*ROOKIES 101-145: .4X TO 1X
GOLD STATED ODDS 1:20
103 Tom Brady 150.00 250.00

2000 Fleer Mystique Big Buzz

Randomly inserted in packs at the rate of one in 10, this 10-card set features top rated rookies from the 2000 draft in action with the words Big Buzz across the card front.
COMPLETE SET (10) 6.00 15.00
STATED ODDS 1:10
1 Peter Warrick .30 .75
2 Shaun Alexander .50 1.25
3 Ron Dayne .50 1.25
4 Joe Hamilton .30 .75
5 Thomas Jones .40 1.00
6 Jamal Lewis .50 1.25
7 Chad Pennington .40 1.00
8 Tim Rattay .40 1.00
9 Chris Redman .30 .75
10 Plaxico Burress .40 1.00

2000 Fleer Mystique Canton Calling

Randomly inserted in packs at the rate of one in 20, this 10-card set features an all silver foil card stock with players in action set against the famous dome roof of the Canton Hall of Fame.
COMPLETE SET (10) 10.00 25.00
STATED ODDS 1:20
1 Jerry Rice 2.00 5.00
2 Troy Aikman 1.00 2.50
3 Dan Marino 1.50 4.00
4 Brett Favre 1.50 4.00
5 Peyton Manning 2.00 5.00
6 Emmitt Smith 1.25 3.00
7 Randy Moss .60 1.50
8 Marvin Harrison .60 1.50
9 Marshall Faulk .60 1.50
10 Thurman Thomas .60 1.50

2000 Fleer Mystique Destination Tampa

Randomly inserted in packs at the rate of one in 10, this 10-card set features players in action set against palm trees and blue skies. The words Destination Tampa appear in red lettering along the bottom of the card.
COMPLETE SET (10) 6.00 15.00
STATED ODDS 1:10
1 Kurt Warner .75 2.00
2 Peyton Manning 1.25 3.00
3 Brett Favre 1.00 2.50
4 Tim Couch .40 1.00
5 Keyshawn Johnson .40 1.00
6 Mark Brunell .40 1.00
7 Eddie George .40 1.00
8 Edgerrin James .40 1.00
9 Ricky Williams .40 1.00
10 Randy Moss .40 1.00

2000 Fleer Mystique Numbers Game

Randomly inserted in packs at the rate of one in 40, this 10-card set features an all foil card stock with player action photos set against a colored background to match the respective team colors. Cards are enhanced with silver foil highlights.
COMPLETE SET (10) 15.00 40.00
STATED ODDS 1:40
*RED ZONE/100: 1.5X TO 4X BASIC INSERTS
RED ZONE PRINT RUN 100
1 Kurt Warner 2.00 5.00
2 Peyton Manning 3.00 8.00
3 Keyshawn Johnson 1.00 2.50
4 Terrell Davis 1.00 2.50
5 Brett Favre 2.50 6.00
6 Jevon Kearse .75 2.00
7 Troy Aikman 1.50 4.00
8 Edgerrin James 1.00 2.50
9 Eddie George 1.00 2.50
10 Marshall Faulk 1.00 2.50

2000 Fleer Mystique Running Men

Randomly inserted in packs at the rate of one in five, this 20-card set features full color player action photography set against a fade to black background. Cards are enhanced with silver foil.
COMPLETE SET (20) 5.00 12.00
STATED ODDS 1:5
1 Antowain Smith .40 1.00
2 Corey Dillon .30 .75
3 Terrell Davis .40 1.00
4 Edgerrin James .40 1.00
5 Fred Taylor .30 .75
6 Kevin Faulk .30 .75
7 Jerome Bettis .50 1.25
8 Ricky Watters .40 1.00
9 Eddie George .40 1.00
10 Jamal Anderson .40 1.00
11 Tim Biakabutuka .40 1.00
12 Curtis Enis .30 .75
13 Emmitt Smith .75 2.00
14 James Stewart .30 .75
15 Dorsey Levens .40 1.00
16 Robert Smith .30 .75
17 Duce Staley .30 .75
18 Marshall Faulk .40 1.00
19 Stephen Davis .30 .75
20 Mike Alstott .30 .75

2003 Fleer Mystique

Released in September of 2003, this set consists of 130 cards including 80 veterans and 50 rookies. The rookies were serial numbered to 699, and were inserted into packs at a rate of 1:15. Boxes contained 20 packs of 4 cards, with one pack containing a sealed mystery pack. Pack SRP was $5.99.
COMP. SET w/o SP's (80) 12.00 30.00
81-130 ROOKIE/699 ODDS 1:15
1 Emmitt Smith .60 1.50
2 Marcel Shipp .25 .60
3 Michael Vick .30 .75
4 Warrick Dunn .25 .60
5 T.J. Duckett .25 .60
6 Peerless Price .25 .60
7 Ray Lewis .40 1.00
8 Todd Heap .25 .60
9 Jamal Lewis .30 .75
10 Eric Moulds .25 .60
11 Drew Bledsoe .30 .75
12 Travis Henry .25 .60
13 Stephen Davis .25 .60
14 Julius Peppers .40 1.00
15 Marty Booker .25 .60
16 Brian Urlacher .40 1.00
17 Chad Johnson .25 .60
18 Corey Dillon .25 .60
19 William Green .25 .60
20 Tim Couch .25 .60
21 Joey Galloway .30 .75
22 Chad Hutchinson .25 .60
23 Jake Plummer .25 .60
24 Ed McCaffrey .30 .75
25 Clinton Portis .25 .60
26 Joey Harrington .25 .60
27 Ahman Green .30 .75
28 Brett Favre .75 2.00
29 Jabar Gaffney .25 .60
30 David Carr .25 .60
31 Peyton Manning 1.00 2.50
32 Marvin Harrison .30 .75
33 Edgerrin James .30 .75
34 Mark Brunell .30 .75
35 Fred Taylor .25 .60
36 Trent Green .25 .60
37 Priest Holmes .25 .60
38 Tony Gonzalez .30 .75
39 Chris Chambers .25 .60
40 Zach Thomas .30 .75
41 Ricky Williams .30 .75
42 Michael Bennett .25 .60
43 Daunte Culpepper .30 .75
44 Randy Moss .30 .75
45 Deion Branch .25 .60
46 Tom Brady 1.50 4.00
47 Aaron Brooks .25 .60
48 Deuce McAllister .30 .75
49 Joe Horn .25 .60
50 Jeremy Shockey .25 .60
51 Amani Toomer .25 .60
52 Tiki Barber .30 .75
53 Chad Pennington .25 .60
54 Curtis Martin .30 .75
55 Rich Gannon .30 .75
56 Tim Brown .40 1.00
57 Jerry Rice .75 2.00
58 Donovan McNabb .30 .75
59 Duce Staley .25 .60
60 Hines Ward .30 .75
61 Tommy Maddox .25 .60
62 Plaxico Burress .25 .60
63 Jerome Bettis .40 1.00
64 David Boston .25 .60
65 Drew Brees .40 1.00
66 LaDainian Tomlinson .40 1.00
67 Jeff Garcia .25 .60
68 Terrell Owens .30 .75
69 Koren Robinson .30 .75
70 Shaun Alexander .25 .60
71 Kurt Warner .30 .75
72 Torry Holt .30 .75
73 Marshall Faulk .30 .75
74 Keyshawn Johnson .40 1.00
75 Mike Alstott .25 .60
76 Warren Sapp .30 .75
77 Steve McNair .30 .75
78 Eddie George .30 .75
79 Patrick Ramsey .30 .75
80 Rod Gardner .25 .60
81 Bennie Joppru RC 1.25 3.00
82 Musa Smith RC 1.25 3.00
83 Ken Dorsey RC 1.50 4.00
84 Billy McMullen RC 1.25 3.00
85 Bethel Johnson RC 1.25 3.00
86 Terence Newman RC 2.00 5.00
87 Jason Witten RC 5.00 12.00
88 Jimmy Kennedy RC 1.50 4.00
89 Johnathan Sullivan RC 1.25 3.00
90 Chris Simms RC 1.25 3.00
91 Brian St.Pierre RC 1.25 3.00
92 Quentin Griffin RC 1.50 4.00
93 Tyrone Calico RC 1.25 3.00
94 DeWayne Robertson RC 1.50 4.00
95 Bryant Johnson RC 2.00 5.00
96 Charles Rogers RC 1.50 4.00
97 William Joseph RC 1.25 3.00
98 Dallas Clark RC 2.00 5.00
99 Michael Haynes RC 1.25 3.00
100 Larry Johnson RC 1.50 4.00
101 Terrell Suggs RC 1.50 4.00
102 Marcus Trufant RC 1.50 4.00
103 Dave Ragone RC 1.25 3.00
104 Seneca Wallace RC 1.50 4.00
105 Willis McGahee RC 1.50 4.00
106 Andre Woolfolk RC 1.25 3.00
107 LaBrandon Toefield RC 1.25 3.00
108 Andre Johnson RC 3.00 8.00
109 Lee Suggs RC 1.25 3.00
110 Brandon Lloyd RC 2.00 5.00
111 Kyle Boller RC 1.25 3.00
112 B.J. Askew RC 1.50 4.00
113 Anquan Boldin RC 2.00 5.00
114 Kelley Washington RC 1.25 3.00
115 Kevin Williams RC 2.00 5.00
116 Kliff Kingsbury RC 2.00 5.00
117 Jerome McDougle RC 1.25 3.00
118 L.J. Smith RC 2.00 5.00
119 J.R. Tolver RC 1.50 4.00
120 Carson Palmer RC 2.50 6.00
121 Kevin Curtis RC 1.25 3.00
122 Shaun McDonald RC 1.50 4.00
123 Byron Leftwich RC 1.50 4.00
124 Bobby Wade RC 1.50 4.00
125 Nate Burleson RC 1.50 4.00
126 Justin Fargas RC 2.00 5.00
127 DeWayne White RC 1.25 3.00
128 Taylor Jacobs RC 1.25 3.00
129 Rex Grossman RC 1.50 4.00
130 Boss Bailey RC 1.50 4.00
P28 Brett Favre PROMO 1.00 2.50
P41 Ricky Williams PROMO .50 1.25
P123 Byron Leftwich PROMO .75 2.00

2003 Fleer Mystique Gold

*1-80 VETS/150: 4X TO 10X BASIC CARDS
1-80 VET STATED PRINT RUN 150
*81-130 ROOKIES: .8X TO 2X
81-130 ROOKIE PRINT RUN 75
OVERALL STATED ODDS 1:15

2003 Fleer Mystique Rookie Blue

*ROOKIES: .5X TO 1.2X BASIC CARDS
STATED PRINT RUN 350 SER.#'d SETS

2003 Fleer Mystique Awe Pairs

COMPLETE SET (20) 25.00 60.00
STATED PRINT RUN 250 SER.#'d SETS
UNPRICED GOLD PRINT RUN 6-12
1 D.Bledsoe/T.Henry 1.25 3.00
2 P.Manning/M.Harrison 4.00 10.00
3 T.Maddox/P.Burress 1.00 2.50
4 M.Faulk/T.Holt 1.25 3.00
5 R.Williams/C.Chambers 1.25 3.00
6 T.Green/P.Holmes 1.00 2.50
7 S.McNair/E.George 1.25 3.00
8 D.McNabb/D.Staley 1.25 3.00
9 R.Gannon/T.Brown 1.50 4.00
10 C.Pennington/C.Martin 1.25 3.00
11 D.Brees/L.Tomlinson 1.50 4.00
12 K.Collins/J.Shockey 1.00 2.50
13 K.Johnson/M.Alstott 1.50 4.00
14 M.Bennett/R.Moss 1.25 3.00
15 J.Garcia/T.Owens 1.25 3.00
16 B.Favre/D.Driver 3.00 8.00
17 J.Lewis/T.Heap 1.25 3.00
18 K.Robinson/S.Alexander 1.25 3.00
19 A.Brooks/D.McAllister 1.25 3.00
20 M.Vick/W.Dunn 1.25 3.00

2003 Fleer Mystique Awe Pairs Jerseys

This set features two authentic game worn jersey swatches. Each card is serial numbered to 199.
STATED PRINT RUN 199 SER.#'d SETS
ABDM A.Brooks/D.McAllister 3.00 8.00
DBLT D.Brees/L.Tomlinson 4.00 10.00
DBTH D.Bledsoe/T.Henry 3.00 8.00
DMDS D.McNabb/D.Staley 3.00 8.00
JGTO J.Garcia/T.Owens 3.00 8.00
JLTH J.Lewis/T.Heap 3.00 8.00
KCJS K.Collins/J.Shockey 2.50 6.00
KJMA K.Johnson/M.Alstott 4.00 10.00
KRSA K.Robinson/S.Alexander 3.00 8.00
MBRM M.Bennett/R.Moss 3.00 8.00
MFTH M.Faulk/T.Holt 3.00 8.00
PMMH P.Manning/M.Harrison 10.00 25.00
RGTB R.Gannon/T.Brown 4.00 10.00
RWCC R.Williams/C.Chambers 3.00 8.00
SMEG S.McNair/E.George 3.00 8.00
TMPB T.Maddox/P.Burress 2.50 6.00

2003 Fleer Mystique End Zone Eminence

COMPLETE SET (10) 10.00 25.00
STATED PRINT RUN 100 SER.#'d SETS
*GOLD/77-88: .5X TO 1.2X BASIC INSERT
*GOLD/54-67: .6X TO 1.5X BASIC INSERT
*GOLD/26: .8X TO 2X BASIC INSERT
GOLD PRINT RUN 26-88
1 Priest Holmes 1.00 2.50
2 Shaun Alexander 1.00 2.50
3 Ricky Williams 1.25 3.00
4 Clinton Portis 1.00 2.50
5 Deuce McAllister 1.25 3.00
6 LaDainian Tomlinson 1.50 4.00
7 Travis Henry 1.00 2.50
8 Eddie George 1.25 3.00
9 Terrell Owens 1.25 3.00
10 Hines Ward 1.25 3.00

2003 Fleer Mystique End Zone Eminence Jerseys

Randomly inserted into packs, this set features authentic game worn jersey swatches. Each card is serial numbered to 100.
STATED PRINT RUN 100 SER.#'d SETS
CP Clinton Portis 2.50 6.00
DM Deuce McAllister 3.00 8.00
EG Eddie George 3.00 8.00
HW Hines Ward 3.00 8.00
LT LaDainian Tomlinson 4.00 10.00
PH Priest Holmes 2.50 6.00
RW Ricky Williams 3.00 8.00
SA Shaun Alexander 2.50 6.00
TH Travis Henry 2.50 6.00
TO Terrell Owens 3.00 8.00

2003 Fleer Mystique Ink Appeal

Randomly inserted into packs, this set features authentic player autographs. Each card is serial numbered to various quantities between 20-75.
INK APPEAL PRINT RUN 20-75
AJ Andre Johnson/75 30.00 60.00
DM Donovan McNabb/20 25.00 60.00
LT LaDainian Tomlinson/75 50.00 100.00
MB Michael Bennett/20 15.00 40.00
PB Plaxico Burress/20 12.00 30.00
TB Tom Brady/75 100.00 200.00
WM Willis McGahee/55 25.00 60.00

2003 Fleer Mystique Ink Appeal Gold

Randomly inserted into packs, this set features authentic player autographs. Each card is serial numbered to various quantities, and features gold foil accents.
GOLD PRINT RUN 3-80
SERIAL #'d UNDER 20 NOT PRICED
AJ Andre Johnson/80 40.00 80.00
LT LaDainian Tomlinson/21 60.00 120.00
MB Michael Bennett/23 15.00 40.00
PB Plaxico Burress/80 10.00 25.00
WM Willis McGahee/21 30.00 80.00

2003 Fleer Mystique Rare Finds

COMPLETE SET (10) 12.00 30.00
STATED PRINT RUN 350 SER.#'d SETS
1 Ri.Williams/Holmes/Tomlinson 1.25 3.00
2 Faulk/McAllister/Alexander 1.00 2.50
3 Gannon/Bledsoe/Manning 3.00 8.00
4 Favre/Brooks/Vick 2.50 6.00
5 Harrison/Ward/Moulds 1.00 2.50
6 Moss/Owens/Johnson 1.25 3.00
7 Peppers/Urlacher/Lewis 1.25 3.00
8 Carr/Harrington/Ramsey 1.00 2.50
9 Portis/Henry/Green .75 2.00
10 Rice/Brown/Porter 2.50 6.00

2003 Fleer Mystique Rare Finds Autographs

Randomly inserted into packs, this set features authentic player autographs. Each card is serial numbered to 100.
STATED PRINT RUN 100 SER.#'d SETS
CP Chad Pennington 8.00 20.00
DM Donovan McNabb 20.00 50.00
JH Joey Harrington 8.00 20.00
MB Michael Bennett 8.00 20.00
PB Plaxico Burress 8.00 20.00

2003 Fleer Mystique Rare Finds Jersey Autographs

Randomly inserted into packs, this set features game worn jersey swatches and authentic player autographs. Each card is serial numbered to 50.
STATED PRINT RUN 50 SER.#'d SETS
CP Chad Pennington 12.00 30.00
DM Donovan McNabb 30.00 80.00
JH Joey Harrington 12.00 30.00
MB Michael Bennett 12.00 30.00
PB Plaxico Burress 12.00 30.00

2003 Fleer Mystique Rare Finds Jersey Singles

Randomly inserted into packs, this set features game worn jersey swatches. Each card is serial numbered to 299.
STATED PRINT RUN 299 SER.#'d SETS
BF Favre JSY/Brooks/Vick 8.00 20.00
BU Urlacher JSY/Peppers/Lewis 4.00 10.00
CP Portis JSY/Henry/Green 2.50 6.00
DB Bledsoe JSY/Gannon/Manning 4.00 10.00
DC Carr JSY/Harrington/Ramsey 3.00 8.00
DM McAllister JSY/Faulk/Alex. 3.00 8.00
HW Ward JSY/Harrison/Moulds 3.00 8.00
JH Harrington JSY/Carr/Ramsey 3.00 8.00
JP Peppers JSY/Urlacher/Lewis 4.00 10.00
MF Faulk JSY/McAllist/Alexand 3.00 8.00
MH Harrison JSY/Ward/Moulds 3.00 8.00
RW Williams JSY/Holmes/Tomlin 4.00 10.00
TO Owens JSY/Moss/Johnson 4.00 10.00
WG Green JSY/Henry/Portis 4.00 10.00

2003 Fleer Mystique Rare Finds Jersey Doubles

Randomly inserted into packs, this set features two game worn jersey swatches. Each card is serial numbered to 250.
STATED PRINT RUN 250 SER.#'d SETS
CPTH Portis JSY/Henry JSY/Grn 4.00 10.00
DBPM Gann/Bleds JSY/Mann JSY 15.00 40.00
DCJH Carr JSY/Harr JSY/Ramsey 5.00 12.00
DMSA Faulk/McAll JSY/Alex JSY 5.00 12.00
JPBU Pepp JSY/Urlac JSY/Lewis 6.00 15.00
MFDM Faulk JSY/McAll JSY/Alex 5.00 12.00
MHHW Har JSY/WardJSY/Moulds 5.00 12.00
RWLT Wilms JSY/Hlms/Toml JSY 6.00 15.00
RWPH Wilms JSY/HlmsJSY/Toml 6.00 15.00
TOKJ Moss/Owens JSY/John JSY 6.00 15.00

2003 Fleer Mystique Rare Finds Jersey Triples

Randomly inserted into packs, this set features three game worn jersey swatches. Each card is serial numbered to 150.
STATED PRINT RUN 150 SER.#'d SETS
CPTHWG Portis/Henry/Green 5.00 12.00
DCJHPR Carr/Harrington/Ramsey 6.00 15.00
JPBURL Peppers/Urlacher/Lewis 8.00 20.00
MFDMSA Faulk/McAllister/Alexander 6.00 15.00
MHHWEM Harrison/Ward/Moulds 6.00 15.00
RGDBPM Gannon/Bledsoe/Manning 20.00 50.00
RWPHLT Williams/Holmes/Tomlinson 8.00 20.00

2003 Fleer Mystique Secret Weapons

COMPLETE SET (15) 15.00 40.00
STATED PRINT RUN 500 SER.#'d SETS
*GOLD/80-83: .8X TO 2X BASIC INSERT
*GOLD/55: 1X TO 2.5X BASIC INSERT
*GOLD/34-41: 1.2X TO 3X BASIC INSERT
*GOLD/21-22: 1.5X TO 4X BASIC INSERT
GOLD PRINT RUN 2-80
1 Willis McGahee .75 2.00
2 Carson Palmer 1.25 3.00
3 Charles Rogers .75 2.00
4 Byron Leftwich .75 2.00
5 Andre Johnson 1.50 4.00
6 Larry Johnson .75 2.00
7 Quentin Griffin .75 2.00
8 Dave Ragone .60 1.50
9 Kyle Boller .60 1.50
10 Chris Simms .60 1.50
11 Terrell Suggs .75 2.00
12 Rex Grossman .75 2.00
13 Bryant Johnson 1.00 2.50
14 Seneca Wallace .75 2.00
15 Terence Newman 1.00 2.50

2003 Fleer Mystique Shining Stars

COMPLETE SET (15) 15.00 40.00
STATED PRINT RUN 500 SER.#'d SETS
*GOLD/192-326: .6X TO 1.5X BASIC INSERTS
*GOLD/85-164: .8X TO 2X BASIC INSERTS
*GOLD/47-60: 1X TO 2.5X BASIC INSERTS
*GOLD/27: 1.5X TO 4X BASIC INSERTS
GOLD PRINT RUN 2-326
1 Emmitt Smith 1.50 4.00
2 Michael Vick .75 2.00
3 Brian Urlacher 1.00 2.50
4 Joey Harrington .60 1.50
5 Brett Favre 2.00 5.00
6 Peyton Manning 2.50 6.00
7 Tom Brady 4.00 10.00
8 Kurt Warner .75 2.00
9 Jeremy Shockey .60 1.50
10 Jerry Rice 2.00 5.00
11 Marshall Faulk .75 2.00
12 Randy Moss .75 2.00
13 Donovan McNabb .75 2.00
14 Corey Dillon .60 1.50
15 David Carr .00 1.50

2003 Fleer Mystique Shining Stars Jerseys

Randomly inserted into packs, this set features game worn jersey swatches. Each card is serial numbered to 250. A patch version, featuring cards serial numbered to 25 also exists, and are not priced due to scarcity.
STATED PRINT RUN 250 SER.#'d SETS
*PATCH/25: 1X TO 2.5X BASIC JSY
PATCH STATED PRINT RUN 25
BF Brett Favre 6.00 15.00
BU Brian Urlacher 3.00 8.00
CD Corey Dillon 2.00 5.00
DC David Carr 2.00 5.00
DM Donovan McNabb 2.50 6.00
ES Emmitt Smith 5.00 12.00
JH Joey Harrington 2.00 5.00
JR Jerry Rice 6.00 15.00
JS Jeremy Shockey 2.00 5.00
KW Kurt Warner 2.50 6.00
MF Marshall Faulk 2.50 6.00
PM Peyton Manning 8.00 20.00
TB Tom Brady 12.00 30.00

2002 Fleer Platinum

Released in late December 2002, this set features 320 cards including 230 veterans, and 90 rookies. Rookies 231-290 were found in all packs. Rookies 291-300 were only available in wax packs, and rookies 301-310 were only available in jumbo packs. Each box contained 10 wax packs of 10 cards, 4 jumbo packs of 25 cards, and one rack pack of 45 cards.
COMP.SET w/o RC's (230) 12.00 30.00
1 Donovan McNabb .25 .60
2 Tom Brady 1.50 4.00
3 Kurt Warner .25 .60
4 Jerry Porter .20 .50
5 LaDainian Tomlinson .30 .75
6 Rod Gardner .20 .50
7 Dorsey Levens .25 .60
8 Drew Bledsoe .25 .60
9 David Terrell .20 .50
10 Ahman Green .25 .60
11 D'Wayne Bates .20 .50
12 Wayne Chrebet .20 .50
13 Doug Flutie .25 .60
14 Steve McNair .25 .60
15 Nate Clements .20 .50
16 Gerard Warren .20 .50
17 James Allen .20 .50
18 David Patten .20 .50
19 Jerry Rice .60 1.50
20 Garrison Hearst .20 .50
21 Samari Rolle .20 .50
22 Jay Riemersma .20 .50
23 Quincy Carter .20 .50
24 Lamar Smith .20 .50
25 Jacquez Green .20 .50
26 John Abraham .25 .60
27 Kevin Dyson .25 .60
28 James Thrash .25 .60
29 Todd Heap .20 .50
30 Gus Frerotte .20 .50
31 Terry Glenn .25 .60
32 Mark Brunell .25 .60
33 Randy Moss .25 .60
34 John Lynch .25 .60
35 Curtis Conway .25 .60
36 Bill Romanowski .25 .60
37 Thomas Jones .20 .50
38 Dez White .20 .50
39 Greg Ellis .20 .50
40 Trent Green .20 .50
41 Deuce McAllister .25 .60
42 Hines Ward .25 .60
43 Isaac Bruce .30 .75
44 Edgerrin James .25 .60
45 Chad Lewis .20 .50
46 Ray Lewis .30 .75
47 Corey Dillon .20 .50
48 Brett Favre .60 1.50
49 Daunte Culpepper .25 .60
50 Vinny Testaverde .20 .50
51 Warren Sapp .25 .60
52 Corey Simon .20 .50
53 Chris McAlister .20 .50
54 Peter Warrick .20 .50
55 Luther Elliss .20 .50
56 Sam Madison .20 .50
57 Will Allen .20 .50
58 Michael Pittman .25 .60
59 Jamal Lewis .25 .60
60 Takeo Spikes .20 .50
61 Robert Porcher .20 .50
62 Peyton Manning .75 2.00
63 Robert Edwards .20 .50
64 Rob Johnson .25 .60
65 Willie Jackson .20 .50
66 Dan Morgan .20 .50
67 Ian Gold .20 .50
68 Donald Driver .25 .60
69 Fred Taylor .20 .50
70 Dante Hall .20 .50
71 Jerome Pathon .20 .50
72 Amos Zereoue .20 .50
73 Darrell Jackson .25 .60
74 Chris Redman .20 .50
75 Chad Johnson .20 .50
76 Az-Zahir Hakim .20 .50
77 Jermaine Lewis .20 .50
78 Zach Thomas .25 .60
79 Michael Strahan .25 .60
80 Junior Seau .25 .60
81 Brad Johnson .25 .60
82 Keith Brooking .20 .50
83 Shawn Springs .20 .50
84 Tim Couch .20 .50
85 Bill Schroeder .20 .50
86 Jamie Sharper .25 .60
87 Ricky Williams .25 .60
88 Ron Dayne .25 .60
89 Brian Finneran .20 .50
90 Kevin Johnson .20 .50
91 Scotty Anderson .20 .50
92 Chris Chambers .20 .50
93 Amani Toomer .20 .50
94 Jeff Garcia .20 .50
95 Chad Brown .20 .50
96 Rodney Peete .25 .60
97 Dennis Northcutt .20 .50
98 Jamel White .20 .50
99 Patrick Johnson .20 .50
100 Ty Law .30 .75
101 Charles Woodson .30 .75
102 Stephen Davis .20 .50
103 Charlie Garner .25 .60
104 Courtney Brown .20 .50
105 Aaron Glenn .20 .50
106 Antowain Smith .25 .60
107 Tim Brown .30 .75
108 Shane Matthews .20 .50
109 Warrick Dunn .20 .50
110 Wesley Walls .25 .60
111 Jason Elam .20 .50
112 Jay Fiedler .25 .60
113 Kerry Collins .20 .50
114 Jerome Bettis .30 .75
115 Koren Robinson .20 .50
116 Patrick Kerney .20 .50
117 Muhsin Muhammad .20 .50
118 Mike McMahon .20 .50
119 Qadry Ismail .20 .50
120 Oronde Gadsden .20 .50
121 Tiki Barber .25 .60
122 Kordell Stewart .20 .50
123 Shaun Alexander .20 .50
124 Jake Plummer .20 .50
125 Marty Booker .20 .50
126 La'Roi Glover .20 .50
127 Marvin Harrison .25 .60
128 Bobby Shaw .20 .50
129 Kevin Faulk .20 .50
130 Drew Brees .60 1.50
131 Marshall Faulk .25 .60
132 MarTay Jenkins .20 .50
133 Anthony Thomas .25 .60
134 Brian Griese .20 .50
135 Johnnie Morton .25 .60
136 Aaron Brooks .20 .50
137 Ernie Conwell .20 .50
138 Rod Smith .25 .60
139 Antonio Freeman .30 .75
140 Travis Taylor .20 .50
141 Jon Kitna .20 .50
142 Robert Ferguson .25 .60
143 Derrick Alexander .20 .50
144 Laveranues Coles .25 .60
145 Keyshawn Johnson .25 .60
146 Freddie Jones .20 .50
147 Jim Miller .20 .50
148 Mike Anderson .20 .50
149 Marcus Pollard .20 .50
150 Priest Holmes .20 .50
151 Joe Horn .20 .50
152 Plaxico Burress .20 .50
153 Shannon Sharpe .25 .60
154 Michael Vick .25 .60
155 Steve Smith .30 .75
156 Ed McCaffrey .25 .60
157 Eddie Kennison .25 .60
158 Darren Howard .20 .50
159 Trent Dilfer .20 .50
160 Peerless Price .20 .50
161 Quincy Morgan .20 .50
162 Corey Bradford .20 .50
163 Jimmy Smith .25 .60
164 Troy Brown .20 .50
165 Rich Gannon .25 .60
166 Kevan Barlow .20 .50
167 Jevon Kearse .20 .50
168 David Boston .20 .50
169 Marcel Shipp .20 .50
170 Joey Galloway .25 .60
171 Kyle Brady .20 .50
172 Donald Hayes .20 .50
173 Chad Scott .20 .50
174 Torry Holt .25 .60
175 Champ Bailey .25 .60
176 Travis Henry .20 .50
177 Troy Hambrick .20 .50
178 Hardy Nickerson .20 .50
179 Michael Bennett .20 .50
180 Chad Pennington .20 .50
181 Eric Johnson .20 .50
182 Derrick Mason .20 .50
183 Kwamie Lassiter .20 .50
184 Brian Urlacher .30 .75
185 Olandis Gary .25 .60
186 Tony Gonzalez .25 .60
187 David Sloan .20 .50
188 Kendrell Bell .20 .50
189 Jamie Martin .25 .60
190 Eric Moulds .20 .50
191 Emmitt Smith .50 1.25
192 Bubba Franks .20 .50
193 Byron Chamberlain .20 .50
194 Santana Moss .25 .60
195 Dana Stubblefield .20 .50
196 Eddie George .25 .60
197 Brian Dawkins .30 .75
198 Stephen Alexander .20 .50
199 Terrell Owens .25 .60
200 Curtis Martin .25 .60
201 Larry Izzo UH .20 .50
202 Brian Simmons UH .20 .50
203 Jason Fisk UH RC .20 .50
204 Carlos Emmons UH .20 .50
205 Justin McCareins UH .25 .60
206 Adam Vinatieri UH .20 .50
207 Cornelius Griffin UH .20 .50
208 Trevor Pryce UH .20 .50
209 Sam Shade UH .20 .50
210 Rod Smart UH RC .25 .60
211 Tony Richardson UH .20 .50
212 Kevin Kasper UH .20 .50
213 Rodney Harrison UH .20 .50
214 Patrick Surtain UH .20 .50
215 Fred Beasley UH .20 .50
216 James Farrior UH .20 .50
217 Rosevelt Colvin UH RC .40 1.00
218 Anthony McFarland UH .20 .50
219 Dat Nguyen UH .20 .50
220 Greg Comella UH .20 .50
221 Rob Konrad UH .20 .50
222 London Fletcher UH .25 .60
223 Omar Stoutmire UH .20 .50
224 Warrick Holdman UH .20 .50
225 Bob Christian UH .20 .50
226 David Akers UH .20 .50
227 Tony Brackens UH .20 .50
228 Deon Grant UH .20 .50
229 Olin Kreutz UH RC .40 1.00
230 Gary Walker UH .20 .50
231 Lito Sheppard RC 1.00 2.50
232 Kalimba Edwards RC .75 2.00
233 Hayden Epstein RC .60 1.50
234 Napoleon Harris RC .75 2.00
235 Josh McCown RC 1.00 2.50
236 J.T. O'Sullivan RC .75 2.00
237 Omar Easy RC .75 2.00
238 Adrian Peterson RC .75 2.00
239 Jarrod Baxter RC .60 1.50
240 John Henderson RC .75 2.00
241 Jon McGraw RC .60 1.50
242 Terry Jones RC .60 1.50
243 Ron Johnson RC .75 2.00
244 Josh Reed RC .75 2.00
245 Jason McAddley RC .75 2.00
246 Sheldon Brown RC 1.00 2.50
247 Rocky Bernard RC .75 2.00
248 Nick Davis RC .60 1.50
249 Robert Thomas RC .60 1.50
250 Rohan Davey RC 1.00 2.50
251 Seth Burford RC .60 1.50
252 Najeh Davenport RC .60 1.50
253 Verron Haynes RC .60 1.50
254 Tellis Redmon RC .60 1.50
255 Vernon Fox RC .60 1.50
256 Willie Offord RC .60 1.50
257 Marquise Walker RC .60 1.50
258 Antonio Bryant RC 1.00 2.50
259 Andre Davis RC .60 1.50
260 Eddie Drummond RC .60 1.50
261 Marques Anderson RC .75 2.00
262 Charles Stackhouse RC .60 1.50
263 Rocky Calmus RC .75 2.00
264 Mike Williams RC .60 1.50
265 Brandon Doman RC .60 1.50
266 Maurice Morris RC .75 2.00
267 Ladell Betts RC 1.00 2.50
268 Ricky Williams RC .75 2.00
269 Tony Fisher RC .60 1.50
270 Michael Lewis RC .75 2.00
271 Jerramy Stevens RC 1.00 2.50
272 Reche Caldwell RC .75 2.00
273 Antwaan Randle El RC .75 2.00
274 Charles Grant RC 1.00 2.50
275 Lee Mays RC .60 1.50
276 Phillip Buchanon RC 1.00 2.50
277 Carlos Hall RC .60 1.50
278 Billy Cundiff RC .75 2.00
279 Saleem Rasheed RC .60 1.50
280 David Garrard RC .75 2.00
281 Preston Parsons RC .60 1.50
282 Travis Stephens RC .60 1.50
283 Clinton Portis RC 1.00 2.50
284 James Mungro RC 1.00 2.50
285 Tank Williams RC .75 2.00
286 Ed Reed RC 4.00 10.00
287 Javon Walker RC 1.00 2.50
288 Cliff Russell RC .60 1.50
289 Daryl Jones RC .60 1.50
290 Freddie Milons RC .60 1.50
291 Dwight Freeney RC 2.50 6.00
292 Lamar Gordon RC 1.50 4.00
293 Donte Stallworth RC 2.00 5.00
294 Craig Nall RC 1.50 4.00
295 Coy Wire RC 1.50 4.00
296 T.J. Duckett RC 1.25 3.00
297 Jeremy Shockey RC 2.00 5.00
298 Patrick Ramsey RC 1.50 4.00
299 Chester Taylor RC 2.00 5.00
300 Tim Carter RC 1.50 4.00
301 Joey Harrington RC 1.50 4.00
302 Roy Williams RC 1.50 4.00
303 Julius Peppers RC 4.00 10.00
304 William Green RC 2.00 5.00
305 Ashley Lelie RC 1.50 4.00
306 Rock Cartwright RC 2.50 6.00
307 DeShaun Foster RC 2.50 6.00
308 Marc Boerigter RC 2.50 6.00
309 Chad Hutchinson RC 1.50 4.00
310 Daniel Graham RC 2.00 5.00
311 Ryan Sims RC 3.00 8.00
312 Kurt Kittner RC 2.00 5.00
313 Jabar Gaffney RC 2.00 5.00
314 David Carr RC 2.00 5.00
315 Brian Westbrook RC 4.00 10.00
316 Randy Fasani RC 2.00 5.00
317 Randy McMichael RC 3.00 8.00
318 Ben Leber RC 2.00 5.00
319 Jonathan Wells RC 2.50 6.00
320 Deion Branch RC 3.00 8.00

2002 Fleer Platinum Finish

*VETS 1-230: 4X TO 10X BASIC CARDS
*ROOKIES 231-290: 1.5X TO 4X
*ROOKIES 291-300: .8X TO 2X
*ROOKIES 301-310: .6X TO 1.5X
*ROOKIES 311-320: .5X TO 1.2X
STATED PRINT RUN 100 SER.#'d SETS

2002 Fleer Platinum Bad to the Bone

Inserted at a rate of 1:12 wax, 1:6 jumbo, and 1:3 rack packs, this set features 20 of the coolest, hippest 2002 NFL rookies.
COMPLETE SET (20) 20.00 50.00
STATED ODDS 1:12, 1:6 JUM, 1:3 RACK
BB1 Julius Peppers 1.50 4.00
BB2 Josh Reed .75 2.00
BB3 Antonio Bryant 1.00 2.50
BB4 DeShaun Foster 1.00 2.50
BB5 Joey Harrington .60 1.50
BB6 Patrick Ramsey .75 2.00
BB7 Jeremy Shockey 1.00 2.50
BB8 Marquise Walker .60 1.50
BB9 Reche Caldwell .75 2.00
BB10 Jabar Gaffney .60 1.50
BB11 Antwaan Randle El .75 2.00
BB12 Donte Stallworth 1.00 2.50
BB13 Roy Williams .60 1.50
BB14 Tim Carter .75 2.00
BB15 T.J. Duckett .60 1.50
BB16 William Green .75 2.00
BB17 Ashley Lelie .60 1.50
BB18 Clinton Portis 1.00 2.50
BB19 Javon Walker 1.00 2.50
BB20 Andre Davis .60 1.50

2002 Fleer Platinum Guts and Glory

Inserted at a rate of 1:4 wax, 1:2 jumbo, and 1:1 rack packs, this set features 20 of the NFL's most hard-nosed players.
COMPLETE SET (20) 12.00 30.00
STATED ODDS 1:4, 1:2 JUM, 1:1 RACK
1 Zach Thomas .75 2.00
2 Junior Seau .75 2.00
3 Michael Strahan .75 2.00
4 Mike Alstott .60 1.50
5 Darren Woodson .75 2.00
6 Garrison Hearst .60 1.50
7 Jake Plummer .60 1.50
8 Grant Wistrom .60 1.50
9 Wayne Chrebet .60 1.50
10 Rich Gannon .75 2.00
11 Brian Griese .60 1.50
12 Ed McCaffrey .75 2.00
13 Jerome Bettis 1.00 2.50
14 Tedy Bruschi .75 2.00
15 Keith Brooking .60 1.50
16 Peter Boulware .60 1.50
17 Brian Dawkins 1.00 2.50
18 Vinny Testaverde .60 1.50
19 Warren Sapp .75 2.00
20 Antowain Smith .75 2.00

2002 Fleer Platinum Inside the Playbook

Designed to look like a real NFL playbook, this set features an actual play, and each card was serial #'d to 400.
STATED PRINT RUN 400 SER.#'d SETS
1 Jake Plummer 1.25 3.00
2 Michael Vick 1.50 4.00
3 Ray Lewis 2.00 5.00
4 Drew Bledsoe 1.50 4.00
5 Julius Peppers 3.00 8.00
6 Brian Urlacher 2.00 5.00
7 Corey Dillon 1.25 3.00
8 Tim Couch 1.25 3.00
9 Emmitt Smith 3.00 8.00
10 Rod Smith 1.50 4.00
11 Joey Harrington 1.25 3.00
12 Brett Favre 4.00 10.00
13 David Carr 1.25 3.00
14 Peyton Manning 5.00 12.00
15 Jimmy Smith 1.50 4.00
16 Tony Gonzalez 1.50 4.00
17 Ricky Williams 1.50 4.00
18 Randy Moss 1.50 4.00
19 Tom Brady 10.00 25.00
20 Deuce McAllister 1.50 4.00
21 Jeremy Shockey 2.00 5.00
22 Curtis Martin 1.50 4.00
23 Jerry Rice 4.00 10.00
24 Donovan McNabb 1.50 4.00
25 Hines Ward 1.50 4.00
26 LaDainian Tomlinson 2.00 5.00
27 Terrell Owens 1.50 4.00
28 Shaun Alexander 1.25 3.00
29 Marshall Faulk 1.50 4.00
30 Keyshawn Johnson 1.50 4.00
31 Steve McNair 1.50 4.00
32 Stephen Davis 1.25 3.00

2002 Fleer Platinum Inside the Playbook Jerseys

Limited to only 250 copies, this set features authentic jersey swatches from many of the NFL's best.
STATED PRINT RUN 250 SER.#'d SETS
1 Tim Couch 2.00 5.00
2 Stephen Davis 2.00 5.00
3 Corey Dillon 2.00 5.00
4 Marshall Faulk 2.50 6.00
5 Brett Favre 6.00 15.00
6 Joey Harrington 2.00 5.00
7 Keyshawn Johnson 2.50 6.00
8 Ray Lewis 3.00 8.00
9 Peyton Manning 8.00 20.00
10 Curtis Martin 2.50 6.00
11 Donovan McNabb 2.50 6.00
12 Steve McNair 2.50 6.00
13 Randy Moss 2.50 6.00
14 Terrell Owens 2.50 6.00
15 Julius Peppers 5.00 12.00
16 Jake Plummer 2.00 5.00
17 Jerry Rice 6.00 15.00
18 Emmitt Smith 5.00 12.00
19 Jimmy Smith 2.50 6.00
20 Rod Smith 2.50 6.00
21 LaDainian Tomlinson 3.00 8.00
22 Brian Urlacher 3.00 8.00
23 Michael Vick 2.50 6.00
24 Hines Ward 2.50 6.00
25 Ricky Williams 2.50 6.00

2002 Fleer Platinum Nameplates

Inserted at a rate of 1:8 jumbo packs, this set features premium jersey swatches taken from the players actual nameplates. Each card was serial #'d to varying quantities.
NAMEPLATE/20-240 ODDS 1:8 JUMBO
STATED PRINT RUN 20-240
NAG Ahman Green/33 10.00 25.00
NAH Az-Zahir Hakim/45 4.00 10.00
NAS Antowain Smith/60 4.00 10.00
NBF Brett Favre/33 25.00 60.00
NBG Brian Griese/20 10.00 25.00
NBS Bruce Smith/40 5.00 12.00
NBU Brian Urlacher/65 5.00 12.00
NCC Chris Chambers/80 3.00 8.00
NCD Corey Dillon/90 3.00 8.00
NCP Clinton Portis/50 6.00 15.00
NDB1 David Boston/48 4.00 10.00
NDB2 Drew Brees/135 8.00 20.00
NDC Daunte Culpepper/200 2.50 6.00
NDF Doug Flutie/44 5.00 12.00
NEM1 Ed McCaffrey/240 2.50 6.00
NEM2 Eric Moulds/100 2.50 6.00
NES Emmitt Smith/150 6.00 15.00
NHW Hines Ward/52 5.00 12.00
NIB Isaac Bruce/95 5.00 12.00
NJB Jerome Bettis/52 6.00 15.00
NJG Jeff Garcia/70 3.00 8.00
NJK Jevon Kearse/45 4.00 10.00
NJM Johnnie Morton/90 4.00 10.00
NJP1 Jake Plummer/125 2.50 6.00
NJP2 Julius Peppers/54 10.00 25.00
NJR Jerry Rice/35 25.00 60.00
NJS Jimmy Smith/45 5.00 12.00
NKD Kevin Dyson/80 4.00 10.00
NKJ Kevin Johnson/75 3.00 8.00
NKR Koren Robinson/60 3.00 8.00
NKS Kordell Stewart/60 3.00 8.00
NKW Kurt Warner/75 4.00 10.00
NLT LaDainian Tomlinson/150 4.00 10.00
NMA Mike Alstott/65 3.00 8.00
NMB Mark Brunell/150 3.00 8.00
NMF Marshall Faulk/40 5.00 12.00
NMH Marvin Harrison/55 5.00 12.00
NPB Plaxico Burress/130 2.50 6.00
NPM Peyton Manning/55 15.00 40.00
NPW Peter Warrick/65 3.00 8.00
NQC Quincy Carter/95 3.00 8.00
NRL Ray Lewis/35 8.00 20.00
NRM Randy Moss/40 5.00 12.00
NRS Rod Smith/110 3.00 8.00
NSD Stephen Davis/75 3.00 8.00
NSM1 Steve McNair/50 5.00 12.00
NSM2 Santana Moss/20 12.00 30.00
NTB1 Tim Brown/105 4.00 10.00
NTB2 Tom Brady/61 25.00 60.00
NTC Tim Couch/35 5.00 12.00
NTD Terrell Davis/40 5.00 12.00
NTH Torry Holt/60 4.00 10.00
NTO Terrell Owens/45 5.00 12.00
NVT Vinny Testaverde/75 3.00 8.00
NWS Warren Sapp/110 3.00 8.00
NZT Zach Thomas/60 4.00 10.00

2002 Fleer Platinum Portraits

Inserted at a rate of 1:20 wax, 1:10 jumbo, and 1:5 rack packs, this set features 25 of the NFL's top players, in a card designed to look like a picture in a frame.
COMPLETE SET (20) 20.00 50.00
STATED ODDS 1:20, 1:10 JUM, 1:5 RACK
1 Brett Favre 2.00 5.00
2 Jerry Rice 2.00 5.00
3 Emmitt Smith 1.50 4.00
4 Michael Vick .75 2.00
5 Marshall Faulk .75 2.00
6 Peyton Manning 2.50 6.00
7 Kurt Warner .75 2.00
8 Donovan McNabb .75 2.00
9 Tom Brady 5.00 12.00
10 Ricky Williams .75 2.00
11 LaDainian Tomlinson 1.00 2.50
12 Drew Brees 2.00 5.00
13 Daunte Culpepper .75 2.00
14 Randy Moss .75 2.00
15 Brian Urlacher 1.00 2.50
16 Jeff Garcia .60 1.50
17 Jerome Bettis 1.00 2.50
18 Clinton Portis .50 1.25
19 Fred Taylor .60 1.50
20 Julius Peppers .75 2.00

2002 Fleer Platinum Portraits Memorabilia

Inserted at a rate of 1:66 wax packs, this set features authentic swatches of game worn memorabilia. In addition there was also a patch version serial numbered to 100 and inserted in wax packs only.
STATED ODDS 1:66 WAX PACK
SOME PRINT RUNS FLEER ANNOUNCED
*PATCH/100: .6X TO 1.5X BASIC JSY
*PATCH/100: .5X TO 1.2X JSY SP
PATCHES PRINT RUN 100 SER.#'d SETS
PATCH/100 ISSUED IN WAX PACKS
PPBU Brian Urlacher 2.50 6.00
PPCP Clinton Portis 2.50 6.00
PPDB Drew Brees 5.00 12.00
PPDC Daunte Culpepper 2.00 5.00
PPDM Donovan McNabb 2.00 5.00
PPES Emmitt Smith SP/326* 5.00 12.00
PPFT Fred Taylor 1.50 4.00
PPJG Jeff Garcia 1.50 4.00
PPJP Julius Peppers 4.00 10.00
PPJR Jerry Rice 5.00 12.00
PPKW Kurt Warner 2.00 5.00
PPLT LaDainian Tomlinson 2.50 6.00
PPMF Marshall Faulk Pants 2.00 5.00
PPMV Michael Vick 2.00 5.00
PPPM Peyton Manning SP/380* 8.00 20.00
PPRM Randy Moss SP/393* 2.50 6.00
PPRW Ricky Williams 2.00 5.00

2002 Fleer Platinum Run with History Jerseys

Randomly inserted into packs, this set was made to commemorate Emmitt Smith's 2002 Run with History. Each card is serial #'d to 222. Please note that Troy Aikman signed all 222 of his Aikman/Emmitt cards. The Aikman/Emmitt card was issued via redemption with an expiration date of 1/1/2004.
STATED PRINT RUN 222 SER.#'d SETS
ESBS E.Smith/D.Sanders 35.00 00.00
ESES Emmitt Smith 20.00 50.00
ESTA E.Smith/Aikman AU 50.00 120.00
ESTD E.Smith/T.Dorsett 35.00 60.00
ESWP E.Smith/W.Payton 40.00 100.00
NNO Smith/Snd/Aik/Dor/Pay/22 175.00 300.00

2002 Fleer Platinum Run with History Jersey Autographs

Randomly inserted into packs, this set was made to commemorate Emmitt Smith's 2002 Run with History. It is a signed parallel version of the first 20-serial numbered cards from the basic issue inserts. The Aikman/Emmitt card was issued via redemption with an expiration date of 1/1/2004.
FIRST 20 CARDS OF PRINT RUN SIGNED
ESBS E.Smith AU/B.Sanders 150.00 300.00
ESES Emmitt Smith AU 150.00 300.00
ESTA E.Smith AU/T.Aikman AU 200.00 400.00
ESTD E.Smith AU/T.Dorsett 150.00 300.00
ESWP E.Smith AU/W.Payton 150.00 300.00

2003 Fleer Platinum

Released in July of 2003, this set consists of 270 cards, including 210 veterans, and 60 rookies. Cards 211-240 were inserted at a rate of 1:2 jumbo packs, one per rack pack, and 1:14 wax packs. Cards 241-250 were serial numbered to 1500, and were only available in wax packs. Cards 251-260 were serial numbered to 750, and were only available in jumbo packs. Cards 261-270 were serial numbered to 500, and were only available in rack packs. Boxes contained 14 wax packs of 7 cards, 4 jumbo packs of 20 cards, and 1 rack pack with 30 cards.
COMP.SET w/o SP's (210) 12.00 30.00
1 Donovan McNabb .25 .60
2 Jonathan Wells .20 .50
3 Amos Zereoue .20 .50
4 Ray Lewis .30 .75
5 Trent Green .20 .50
6 Jeff Garcia .20 .50
7 Marty Booker .20 .50
8 Antowain Smith .25 .60
9 Brad Johnson .25 .60
10 Joey Galloway .25 .60
11 Chad Pennington .20 .50
12 Patrick Ramsey .25 .60
13 James Stewart .20 .50
14 Charles Woodson .30 .75
15 Warrick Dunn .20 .50
16 Marvin Harrison .25 .60
17 Jerome Bettis .30 .75
18 Muhsin Muhammad .20 .50
19 Zach Thomas .25 .60
20 Darrell Jackson .25 .60
21 Kelly Holcomb .20 .50
22 Deuce McAllister .25 .60
23 Mike Alstott .20 .50
24 Kabeer Gbaja-Biamila .20 .50
25 Todd Pinkston .20 .50
26 Chris Redman .20 .50
27 Jimmy Smith .25 .60
28 Tim Dwight .20 .50
29 Kordell Stewart .20 .50
30 Daunte Culpepper .25 .60
31 Isaac Bruce .30 .75
32 William Green .20 .50
33 Tiki Barber .25 .60
34 Jevon Kearse .20 .50
35 Ashley Lelie .20 .50
36 Charlie Garner .25 .60
37 Marcel Shipp .20 .50
38 Corey Bradford .20 .50
39 Hines Ward .25 .60
40 Josh Reed .20 .50
41 Jay Fiedler .20 .50
42 Matt Hasselbeck .20 .50
43 Corey Dillon .20 .50
44 David Patten .20 .50
45 Warren Sapp .25 .60
46 Chad Johnson .20 .50
47 Troy Brown .20 .50
48 Keyshawn Johnson .30 .75
49 Roy Williams .20 .50
50 Curtis Martin .25 .60
51 Rod Gardner .20 .50
52 David Carr .20 .50
53 Tommy Maddox .20 .50
54 Todd Heap .20 .50
55 Hugh Douglas .20 .50
56 Julian Peterson .20 .50
57 Julius Peppers .30 .75
58 Sam Madison .25 .60
59 Jerramy Stevens .25 .60
60 Andre Davis .20 .50
61 Joe Horn .20 .50
62 Ronde Barber .20 .50
63 Joey Harrington .20 .50
64 Jerry Porter .20 .50
65 T.J. Duckett .20 .50
66 Edgerrin James .25 .60
67 Joey Porter .30 .75
68 Brian Urlacher .30 .75
69 Randy Moss .25 .60
70 Torry Holt .25 .60
71 Quincy Morgan .20 .50
72 Amani Toomer .20 .50
73 Derrick Mason .20 .50
74 Donald Driver .25 .60
75 Duce Staley .20 .50
76 Peerless Price .20 .50
77 Mark Brunell .25 .60
78 David Boston .20 .50
79 Takeo Spikes .20 .50
80 Ricky Williams .25 .60
81 Shaun Alexander .20 .50
82 Jon Kitna .20 .50
83 Deion Branch .20 .50
84 Derrick Brooks .20 .50
85 Rod Smith .25 .60
86 Rich Gannon .25 .60
87 Jason McAddley .20 .50
88 Jabar Gaffney .20 .50
89 Plaxico Burress .20 .50
90 Troy Hambrick .20 .50
91 Santana Moss .25 .60
92 Champ Bailey .25 .60
93 Bubba Franks .25 .60
94 Brian Westbrook .20 .50
95 Ed Reed .25 .60
96 Priest Holmes .20 .50
97 Terrell Owens .25 .60
98 Anthony Thomas .25 .60
99 Michael Bennett .20 .50
100 Marshall Faulk .25 .60
101 Kevin Johnson .20 .50
102 Kerry Collins .20 .50
103 Eddie George .25 .60
104 Shannon Sharpe .25 .60
105 Tim Brown .30 .75
106 Brian Finneran .20 .50
107 Reggie Wayne .25 .60
108 Drew Brees .30 .75
109 Jake Delhomme .20 .50
110 Chris Chambers .20 .50
111 Maurice Morris .20 .50
112 Antonio Bryant .20 .50
113 Michael Strahan .25 .60
114 Laveranues Coles .20 .50
115 Ahman Green .25 .60
116 Jeff Blake .25 .60
117 Jamal Lewis .25 .60
118 Fred Taylor .20 .50
119 Marcellus Wiley .20 .50
120 Stephen Davis .20 .50
121 Randy McMichael .20 .50
122 Kurt Warner .25 .60
123 Tim Couch .20 .50
124 Aaron Brooks .20 .50
125 John Lynch .25 .00
126 Clinton Portis .20 .50
127 Wayne Chrebet .20 .50
128 Emmitt Smith .50 1.25
129 Aaron Glenn .20 .50
130 Antwaan Randle El .20 .50
131 Travis Henry .20 .50
132 Tony Gonzalez .25 .60
133 Garrison Hearst .20 .50
134 Drew Bledsoe .25 .60
135 Eddie Kennison .20 .50
136 Kevan Barlow .20 .50
137 David Terrell .20 .50
138 Tom Brady 1.25 3.00
139 Joe Jurevicius .25 .60
140 Terry Glenn .25 .60
141 Curtis Conway .20 .50
142 Trung Canidate .20 .50
143 Javon Walker .25 .60
144 Brian Dawkins .30 .75
145 Keith Brooking .25 .60
146 Dwight Freeney .20 .50
147 LaDainian Tomlinson .30 .75
148 Kevin Dyson .20 .50
149 Jason Taylor .25 .60
150 Koren Robinson .25 .60
151 Dennis Northcutt .20 .50
152 Donte Stallworth .20 .50
153 Steve McNair .25 .60
154 Ed McCaffrey .25 .60
155 Jerry Rice .60 1.50
156 Travis Taylor .20 .50
157 Kyle Brady .20 .50
158 Quentin Jammer .20 .50
159 DeShaun Foster .25 .60
160 Derrius Thompson .20 .50
161 Marc Bulger .20 .50
162 Chad Hutchinson .20 .50
163 Jeremy Shockey .20 .50
164 Frank Wycheck .20 .50
165 Brett Favre .60 1.50
166 Phillip Buchanon .20 .50
167 Michael Vick .25 .60
168 Peyton Manning .75 2.00
169 Kendrell Bell .20 .50
170 Eric Moulds .20 .50
171 Johnnie Morton .25 .60
172 Tai Streets .20 .50
173 Ron Dugans .20 .50
174 Ty Law .30 .75
175 Simeon Rice .20 .50
176 Jake Plummer .20 .50
177 John Abraham .25 .60
178 Fred Smoot .20 .50
179 Arizona TC .15 .40
Shipp
180 Atlanta TC/Vick .20 .50
181 Baltimore TC/Lewis .25 .60
182 Buffalo TC/Bledsoe .20 .50
183 Carolina TC/Weinke .20 .50
184 Chicago TC/Thomas .20 .50
185 Cincinnati TC/Dillon .15 .40
186 Cleveland TC/J.White .15 .40
187 Dallas TC/Hambrick .15 .40
188 Denver TC/Wilson .15 .40
189 Detroit TC/Schlesinger .15 .40
190 Green Bay TC/Fisher .15 .40
191 Houston TC/Carr .15 .40
192 Indianapolis TC/Manning .60 1.50
193 Jacksonville TC/Taylor .15 .40
194 Kansas City TC/Green .15 .40
195 Miami TC/Fiedler .15 .40
196 Minnesota TC/Williams .15 .40
197 New England TC/Johnson .15 .40
198 New Orleans TC/McAllister .20 .50
199 NY Giants TC/Barrow .15 .40
200 NY Jets TC/Jordan .20 .50
201 Oakland TC/Wheatley .20 .50
202 Philadelphia TC/Staley .15 .40
203 Pittsburgh TC/Maddox .15 .40
204 San Diego TC/Tomlinson .25 .60
205 San Francisco TC/Hearst .15 .40
206 Seattle TC/Hasselbeck .15 .40
207 St. Louis TC/Warner .20 .50
208 Tampa Bay TC/Stecker .15 .40
209 Tennessee TC/Smith .15 .40
210 Washington TC/Ramsey .20 .50
211 L.J. Smith RC 1.00 2.50
212 Taylor Jacobs RC .60 1.50
213 J.R. Tolver RC .75 2.00
214 Musa Smith RC .60 1.50
215 Bennie Joppru RC .60 1.50
216 Ken Dorsey RC .75 2.00
217 Kareem Kelly RC .60 1.50
218 Andre Woolfolk RC .60 1.50
219 Brian St.Pierre RC .60 1.50
220 Jerome McDougle RC .60 1.50
221 Avon Cobourne RC .60 1.50
222 William Joseph RC .60 1.50
223 Dallas Clark RC 1.00 2.50
224 Anquan Boldin RC 1.00 2.50
225 Mike Doss RC 1.00 2.50
226 Cecil Sapp RC .60 1.50
227 Domanick Davis RC .75 2.00
228 Brad Banks RC .75 2.00
229 Justin Gage RC .75 2.00
230 Nate Burleson RC .75 2.00
231 Earnest Graham RC 1.00 2.50
232 DeWayne White RC .60 1.50
233 Kevin Williams RC 1.00 2.50
234 Billy McMullen RC .60 1.50
235 Talman Gardner RC .60 1.50
236 Marcus Trufant RC .75 2.00
237 Quentin Griffin RC .75 2.00
238 LaBrandon Toefield RC .60 1.50
239 Kliff Kingsbury RC 1.00 2.50
240 Doug Gabriel RC .75 2.00
241 Kyle Boller RC 1.00 2.50
242 Dave Ragone RC 1.00 2.50
243 Larry Johnson RC 1.25 3.00
244 Lee Suggs RC 1.00 2.50
245 Charles Rogers RC 1.25 3.00
246 Jimmy Kennedy RC 1.25 3.00
247 Onterrio Smith RC 1.00 2.50
248 Artose Pinner RC 1.00 2.50
249 Tyrone Calico RC 1.00 2.50
250 Terence Newman RC 1.50 4.00
251 Byron Leftwich RC 1.50 4.00
252 Kelley Washington RC 1.25 3.00
253 Justin Fargas RC 2.00 5.00
254 DeWayne Robertson RC 1.50 4.00
255 Boss Bailey RC 1.50 4.00
256 Sam Aiken RC 1.50 4.00
257 Bryant Johnson RC 2.00 5.00
258 Rex Grossman RC 1.50 4.00
259 Teyo Johnson RC 1.50 4.00
260 Willis McGahee RC 1.50 4.00
261 Carson Palmer RC 3.00 8.00
262 Chris Simms RC 1.50 4.00
263 Andre Johnson RC 4.00 10.00
264 Seneca Wallace RC 2.00 5.00
265 Terrell Suggs RC 2.00 5.00
266 Chris Brown RC 1.50 4.00
267 Kevin Curtis RC 1.50 4.00
268 Brandon Lloyd RC 2.50 6.00
269 Jason Witten RC 6.00 15.00
270 Bobby Wade RC 2.00 5.00

2003 Fleer Platinum Finish

*VETS/1-210: 5X TO 12X BASIC CARDS
*ROOKIES 211-240: 1.5X TO 4X
*ROOKIES 241-250: 1X TO 2.5X
*ROOKIES 251-260: .8X TO 2X
*ROOKIES 261-270: .6X TO 1.5X
STATED PRINT RUN 100 SER.#'d SETS

2003 Fleer Platinum Alma Materials
Inserted one per rack pack, this set features game worn jersey swatches.
ONE PER RACK PACK
1 Ken Dorsey 2.50 6.00
2 Justin Fargas 3.00 8.00
3 Quentin Griffin 2.50 6.00
4 Edgerrin James 2.50 6.00
5 Peyton Manning 8.00 20.00
6 Carson Palmer 4.00 10.00
7 Julius Peppers 3.00 8.00
8 Michael Vick 2.50 6.00
9 Seneca Wallace 2.50 6.00

2003 Fleer Platinum Alma Materials Prep to Pro
Randomly inserted into packs, this set features cards with two jersey swatches; one from his current NFL team, and one from his college team. Each card is serial numbered to 200.
STATED PRINT RUN 200 SER.#'d SETS
1 Edgerrin James 3.00 8.00
2 Peyton Manning 10.00 25.00
3 Julius Peppers 4.00 10.00
4 Michael Vick 3.00 8.00

2003 Fleer Platinum Big Signs
COMPLETE SET (10) 6.00 15.00
ODDS 1:2 JUM, 1:RACK, 1:7 WAX
*PLATINUM/100: 1.5X TO 4X BASIC INSERTS
PLATINUM PRINT RUN 100 SER.#'d SETS
1 Donovan McNabb .60 1.50
2 Brett Favre 1.50 4.00
3 Ricky Williams .60 1.50
4 Brian Urlacher .75 2.00
5 Clinton Portis .50 1.25
6 Jeremy Shockey .50 1.25
7 Jerry Rice 1.50 4.00
8 Randy Moss .60 1.50
9 Chad Pennington .50 1.25
10 Michael Vick .60 1.50

2003 Fleer Platinum Big Signs Autographs
Randomly inserted into packs, this set features authentic player autographs, with each card serial numbered to 200. Please note that Chad Pennington was only available in packs as an exchange card.
STATED PRINT RUN 200 SER.#'d SETS
BSACP Clinton Portis 20.00 40.00
BSADM Donovan McNabb 20.00 40.00

2003 Fleer Platinum Patch of Honor
Inserted at a rate of 1:8 jumbo packs, this set features game worn patch swatches. Each card is serial numbered to varying quantities.
PATCH/142-220 ODDS 1:8 JUMBO
STATED PRINT RUN 142-220
PHBF Brett Favre/220 12.00 30.00
PHBU Brian Urlacher/220 6.00 15.00
PHCM Curtis Martin/220 5.00 12.00
PHCP Clinton Portis/220 4.00 10.00
PHCP2 Chad Pennington/219 4.00 10.00
PHDC Daunte Culpepper/220 5.00 12.00
PHDM Donovan McNabb/220 5.00 12.00
PHDM2 Deuce McAllister/220 5.00 12.00
PHEG Eddie George/220 5.00 12.00
PHES Emmitt Smith/220 10.00 25.00
PHFT Fred Taylor/220 4.00 10.00
PHHT Travis Henry/215 4.00 10.00
PHHW Hines Ward/219 5.00 12.00
PHJG Jeff Garcia/220 4.00 10.00
PHJR Jerry Rice/205 12.00 30.00
PHJS Jeremy Shockey/220 4.00 10.00
PHLT LaDainian Tomlinson/220 6.00 15.00
PHMF Marshall Faulk/220 5.00 12.00
PHMH Marvin Harrison/219 5.00 12.00
PHMV Michael Vick/219 5.00 12.00
PHPH Priest Holmes/220 4.00 10.00
PHPM0 Peyton Manning/220 15.00 40.00
PHRL Ray Lewis/220 6.00 15.00
PHRM Randy Moss/220 5.00 12.00
PHRW0 Ricky Williams/220 5.00 12.00
PHSA Shaun Alexander/220 4.00 10.00
PHTB Tom Brady/220 25.00 60.00
PHTB2 Tim Brown/142 6.00 15.00
PHTO Terrell Owens/220 5.00 12.00
PHWS Warren Sapp/220 5.00 12.00

2003 Fleer Platinum Portrayals
COMPLETE SET (15) 15.00 40.00
ODDS 1:4 JUM, 1:2 RACK, 1:14 WAX
*PLATINUM/100: 1X TO 2.5X BASIC INSERT
PLATINUM PRINT RUN 100 SER.#'d SETS
1 LaDainian Tomlinson 1.00 2.50
2 Shaun Alexander .60 1.50
3 Ray Lewis 1.00 2.50
4 Brett Favre 2.00 5.00
5 Jerry Rice 2.00 5.00
6 Joey Harrington .60 1.50
7 Donovan McNabb .75 2.00
8 Brian Urlacher 1.00 2.50
9 Jeremy Shockey .60 1.50
10 Emmitt Smith 1.50 4.00
11 Chad Pennington .60 1.50
12 Randy Moss .75 2.00
13 Michael Vick .75 2.00
14 Clinton Portis .60 1.50
15 Ricky Williams .75 2.00

2003 Fleer Platinum Portrayals Jerseys
Inserted into wax packs at a rate of 1:50, this set features authentic game worn jersey swatches. A patch version was also created, with each card serial numbered to 100.
STATED ODDS 1:50 WAX
*PATCH/100: 1X TO 2.5X BASIC JSY
PATCHES PRINT RUN 100 SER.#'d SETS
PPBF Brett Favre 6.00 15.00
PPBU Brian Urlacher 3.00 8.00
PPDM Donovan McNabb 2.50 6.00
PPJH Joey Harrington 2.00 5.00
PPJR0 Jerry Rice 6.00 15.00
PPJS Jeremy Shockey 2.00 5.00
PPMV Michael Vick 2.50 6.00
PPRL Ray Lewis 3.00 8.00
PPRM Randy Moss 2.50 6.00
PPSA Shaun Alexander 2.00 5.00

2003 Fleer Platinum Pro Bowl Scouting Report
COMPLETE SET (15) 20.00 50.00
STATED PRINT RUN 400 SER.#'d SETS
*PLATINUM/100: .6X TO 1.5X BASIC INSERTS
PLATINUM PRINT RUN 100 SER.#'d SETS
1 Ricky Williams 1.25 3.00
2 Rich Gannon 1.25 3.00
3 Drew Bledsoe 1.25 3.00
4 Brad Johnson 1.25 3.00
5 Jeff Garcia 1.00 2.50
6 Donovan McNabb 1.25 3.00
7 Peyton Manning 4.00 10.00
8 Todd Heap 1.00 2.50
9 Terrell Owens 1.25 3.00
10 Marshall Faulk 1.25 3.00
11 Marvin Harrison 1.25 3.00
12 Deuce McAllister 1.25 3.00
13 LaDainian Tomlinson 1.50 4.00
14 Eric Moulds 1.00 2.50
15 Jerry Rice 3.00 8.00

2003 Fleer Platinum Pro Bowl Scouting Report Jerseys
Randomly inserted into packs, this set is serial numbered to 250, and features swatches of game worn jerseys.
STATED PRINT RUN 250 SER.#'d SETS
PBSRDM Deuce McAllister 3.00 8.00
PBSRJG Jeff Garcia 2.50 6.00
PBSRJR Jerry Rice 8.00 20.00
PBSRLT LaDainian Tomlinson 4.00 10.00
PBSRMH Marvin Harrison 3.00 8.00
PBSRPM Peyton Manning 10.00 25.00
PBSRRG Rich Gannon 3.00 8.00
PBSRRW Ricky Williams 3.00 8.00
PBSRTH Todd Heap 2.50 6.00
PBSRTO Terrell Owens 3.00 8.00

2004 Fleer Platinum
Fleer Platinum initially released in early September 2004. The base set consists of 185-cards including 50-rookies featuring prints runs between 299 and 999. Hobby boxes contained sixteen 7-card packs and four 20-card jumbo packs and carried an S.R.P. of $6 per pack. One parallel set and a variety of inserts can be found seeded in hobby and retail packs highlighted by the Pro Material Jersey Autograph inserts. Some signed cards were issued via mail-in exchange or redemption cards with a number of those EXCH cards not yet appearing live on the secondary market as of the printing of this book.
COMP.SET w/o SP's (135) 7.50 20.00
136-145 RC PRINT RUN 299 SER.#'d SETS
146-155 RC PRINT RUN 499 SER.#'d SETS
156-165 RC PRINT RUN 799 SER.#'d SETS
166-185 RC PRINT RUN 999 SER.#'d SETS
1 Joey Harrington .20 .50
2 Kyle Boller .20 .50
3 Randy McMichael .20 .50
4 David Tyree .20 .50
5 Darrell Jackson .25 .60
6 Brian Urlacher .30 .75
7 Ahman Green .25 .60
8 Onterrio Smith .20 .50
9 Jevon Kearse .20 .50
10 Eddie George .25 .60
11 Julius Peppers .25 .60
12 Donald Driver .25 .60
13 Randy Moss .25 .60
14 Brian Westbrook .20 .50
15 Derrick Brooks .20 .50
16 Jamal Lewis .25 .60
17 Artose Pinner .20 .50
18 Ricky Williams .25 .60
19 Chad Pennington .20 .50
20 Matt Hasselbeck .20 .50
21 Josh McCown .25 .60
22 Carson Palmer .25 .60
23 Byron Leftwich .20 .50
24 Tedy Bruschi .25 .60
25 Duce Staley .20 .50
26 Laveranues Coles .20 .50
27 Drew Bledsoe .25 .60
28 Shannon Sharpe .25 .60
29 A.J. Feeley .20 .50
30 Santana Moss .25 .60
31 Adam Archuleta .20 .50
32 Travis Henry .20 .50
33 Ashley Lelie .20 .50
34 Dante Hall .20 .50
35 Curtis Martin .25 .60
36 Isaac Bruce .30 .75
37 Eric Moulds .20 .50
38 Jake Plummer .20 .50
39 Trent Green .20 .50
40 Shaun Ellis .20 .50
41 Torry Holt .25 .60
42 T.J. Duckett .20 .50
43 Quincy Morgan .20 .50
44 Jabar Gaffney .20 .50
45 Tiki Barber .25 .60
46 Tim Rattay .20 .50
47 Champ Bailey .25 .60
48 Tony Gonzalez .25 .60
49 Rich Gannon .25 .60
50 Marshall Faulk .25 .60
51 Jake Delhomme .20 .50
52 Antonio Bryant .25 .60
53 Priest Holmes .20 .50
54 Jerry Rice .60 1.50
55 Marc Bulger .20 .50
56 Stephen Davis .20 .50
57 Roy Williams S .20 .50
58 Willis McGahee .20 .50
59 Julian Peterson .25 .60
60 Thomas Jones .20 .50
61 Dre Bly .20 .50
62 Corey Dillon .20 .50
63 Tommy Maddox .20 .50
64 Derrick Mason .20 .50
65 Marty Booker .20 .50
66 Brett Favre .60 1.50
67 Tom Brady 1.25 3.00
68 Correll Buckhalter .20 .50
69 Steve McNair .25 .60
70 Alge Crumpler .25 .60
71 Quincy Carter .20 .50
72 Andre Johnson .25 .60
73 Jeremy Shockey .20 .50
74 Kevan Barlow .20 .50
75 Jerry Porter .20 .50
76 Ray Lewis .30 .75
77 Keyshawn Johnson .25 .60
78 Domanick Davis .20 .50
79 Michael Strahan .25 .60
80 Brandon Lloyd .25 .60
81 Anquan Boldin .20 .50
82 Chad Johnson .20 .50
83 Jimmy Smith .25 .60
84 Troy Brown .20 .50
85 Hines Ward .25 .60
86 Tyrone Calico .25 .60
87 Marcel Shipp .20 .50
88 Peter Warrick .20 .50
89 Reggie Wayne .25 .60
90 Aaron Brooks .20 .50
91 Antwaan Randle El .20 .50
92 Mark Brunell .25 .60
93 Todd Heap .20 .50
94 Charles Rogers .20 .50
95 Chris Chambers .20 .50
96 Amani Toomer .20 .50
97 Shaun Alexander .25 .60
98 Michael Vick .25 .60
99 Jeff Garcia .20 .50
100 Edgerrin James .25 .60
101 Deuce McAllister .25 .60
102 LaDainian Tomlinson .30 .75
103 Warrick Dunn .20 .50
104 Andre Davis .20 .50
105 Peyton Manning .75 2.00
106 Boo Williams .20 .50
107 Drew Brees .30 .75
108 Rex Grossman .20 .50
109 Javon Walker .20 .50
110 Michael Bennett .20 .50
111 Terrell Owens .25 .60
112 Michael Pittman .25 .60
113 Emmitt Smith .50 1.25
114 Rudi Johnson .20 .50
115 Fred Taylor .20 .50
116 Deion Branch .20 .50
117 Plaxico Burress .20 .50
118 Clinton Portis .20 .50
119 DeShaun Foster .25 .60
120 Najeh Davenport .20 .50
121 Daunte Culpepper .25 .60
122 Donovan McNabb .25 .60
123 Charles Lee .20 .50
124 Peerless Price .20 .50
125 Lee Suggs .25 .60
126 Marvin Harrison .25 .60
127 Joe Horn .20 .50
128 Antonio Gates .30 .75
129 Steve Smith .30 .75
130 David Carr .20 .50
131 Jason Taylor .25 .60
132 Phillip Buchanon .25 .60
133 Brad Johnson .25 .60
134 Takeo Spikes .20 .50
135 Koren Robinson .20 .50
136 Eli Manning RC 15.00 40.00
137 Ben Roethlisberger RC 15.00 40.00
138 Drew Henson RC 2.00 5.00
139 Kellen Winslow RC 2.00 5.00
140 Kevin Jones RC 2.50 6.00
141 Larry Fitzgerald RC 8.00 20.00
142 Roy Williams RC 2.00 5.00
143 Philip Rivers RC 6.00 15.00
144 Lee Evans RC 3.00 8.00
145 Julius Jones RC 2.00 5.00
146 Chris Perry RC 1.25 3.00
147 Michael Clayton RC 1.50 4.00
148 Sean Taylor RC 8.00 20.00
149 Reggie Williams RC 1.25 3.00
150 Steven Jackson RC 2.00 5.00
151 Tatum Bell RC 1.25 3.00
152 Keary Colbert RC 1.25 3.00
153 J.P. Losman RC 1.25 3.00
154 Devery Henderson RC 1.25 3.00
155 Ben Troupe RC 1.25 3.00
156 Luke McCown RC 1.00 2.50
157 Greg Jones RC 1.00 2.50
158 Ben Watson RC 1.25 3.00
159 Bernard Berrian RC 1.00 2.50
160 Devard Darling RC 1.00 2.50
161 Cedric Cobbs RC 1.00 2.50
162 Darius Watts RC 1.00 2.50
163 Derrick Hamilton RC 1.00 2.50
164 Matt Schaub RC 1.00 2.50
165 Mewelde Moore RC 1.25 3.00
166 Michael Jenkins RC .75 2.00
167 Rashaun Woods RC .75 2.00
168 Quincy Wilson RC .75 2.00
169 Jonathan Vilma RC 1.00 2.50
170 Jerricho Cotchery RC 1.00 2.50
171 John Navarre RC .75 2.00
172 Josh Harris RC .75 2.00
173 Teddy Lehman RC .75 2.00
174 Ernest Wilford RC 1.00 2.50
175 P.K. Sam RC .75 2.00
176 Jeff Smoker RC 1.00 2.50
177 Chris Gamble RC .75 2.00
178 Johnnie Morant RC .75 2.00
179 DeAngelo Hall RC 1.25 3.00
180 Vince Wilfork RC 1.25 3.00
181 Michael Turner RC .75 2.00
182 Robert Gallery RC 1.00 2.50
183 Ricardo Colclough RC .75 2.00
184 Kenechi Udeze RC 1.00 2.50
185 Dunta Robinson RC .75 2.00

2004 Fleer Platinum Finish
*VETS: 4X TO 10X BASIC CARDS
*ROOKIES 136-145: .5X TO 1.2X BASE RCs
*ROOKIES 146-155: .8X TO 2X BASE RCs
*ROOKIES 156-165: 1X TO 2.5X BASE RCs
*ROOKIES 166-185: 1.2X TO 3X BASE RCs
STATED PRINT RUN 100 SER.#'d SETS

2004 Fleer Platinum Autographs Blue
BLUE AU/15-99 ODDS 1:256 HOBBY
BLUE #'d UNDER 20 NOT PRICED
UNPRICED RED PRINT RUN 5 SETS
14 Brian Westbrook/43 12.50 30.00
16 Jamal Lewis/23 15.00 40.00
19 Chad Pennington/71 15.00 40.00
50 Marshall Faulk/15 30.00 60.00
51 Jake Delhomme/35 15.00 40.00
81 Anquan Boldin/19 15.00 40.00
101 Deuce McAllister/47 15.00 40.00
122 Donovan McNabb/19 30.00 60.00
138 Drew Henson/99 12.50 30.00

2004 Fleer Platinum Deep Six
STATED ODDS 1:108 HOB/JUM, 1:270 RET
1DS Harrington/Ro.Williams WR 1.25 3.00
2DS E.Manning/J.Shockey 8.00 20.00
3DS D.McNabb/T.Owens 2.50 6.00
4DS D.Culpepper/R.Moss 2.50 6.00
5DS D.Carr/A.Johnson 2.50 6.00
6DS C.Pennington/S.Moss 2.50 6.00
7DS M.Vick/M.Jenkins 2.50 6.00
8DS P.Manning/M.Harrison 8.00 20.00
9DS D.Bledsoe/E.Moulds 2.50 6.00
10DS R.Gannon/J.Rice 6.00 15.00

2004 Fleer Platinum Jerseys
OVERALL JERSEY ODDS 1:4 JUMBO
STATED PRINT RUN 40-765
*NAMEPLATE/105-120: .8X TO 2X JSY/765
*NAMEPLATE/40-60: 1.2X TO 3X JSY/765
*NAMEPLATE/25-35: 1.5X TO 4X JSY/765
NAMEPLATE/25-120 INSERTS IN JUMBO
UNPRICED PATCH PRINT RUN 5 SETS
1 Joey Harrington/765 2.00 5.00
6 Brian Urlacher/80 5.00 12.00
22 Carson Palmer/120 4.00 10.00
41 Torry Holt/765 2.50 6.00
66 Brett Favre/765 6.00 15.00
67 Tom Brady/765 12.00 30.00
69 Steve McNair/765 2.50 6.00
73 Jeremy Shockey/100 3.00 8.00
76 Ray Lewis/765 3.00 8.00
90 Aaron Brooks/765 2.00 5.00
98 Michael Vick/40 5.00 12.00
101 Deuce McAllister/765 2.50 6.00
102 LaDainian Tomlinson/765 3.00 8.00
105 Peyton Manning/765 8.00 20.00
121 Daunte Culpepper/220 4.00 10.00
126 Marvin Harrison/765 2.50 6.00
130 David Carr/765 2.00 5.00

2004 Fleer Platinum Platinum Memorabilia
STATED ODDS 1:24 HOB, 1:96 RET
*DUAL/50: .8X TO 2X SINGLE JSY
*DUAL/50: .6X TO 1.5X SINGLE JSY SP
DUAL PRINT RUN 50 SER.#'d SETS
PMAG Ahman Green SP 3.00 8.00
PMBF Brett Favre 6.00 15.00
PMBL Byron Leftwich 2.00 5.00
PMCJ Chad Johnson SP 2.50 6.00
PMCP Chad Pennington SP 2.50 6.00
PMCP2 Clinton Portis 2.00 5.00
PMDC David Carr 2.00 5.00
PMDM Donovan McNabb SP 3.00 8.00
PMDM2 Deuce McAllister 2.50 6.00
PMJH Joey Harrington 2.00 5.00
PMJL Jamal Lewis 2.50 6.00
PMJR Jerry Rice SP 8.00 20.00
PMJS Jeremy Shockey SP 2.50 6.00
PMLT LaDainian Tomlinson 3.00 8.00
PMMF Marshall Faulk 2.50 6.00
PMMH Marvin Harrison 2.50 6.00
PMMV Michael Vick SP 3.00 8.00
PMPH Priest Holmes 2.00 5.00
PMPM Peyton Manning 8.00 20.00
PMRI Ricky Williams SP 3.00 8.00
PMRM Randy Moss 2.50 6.00
PMRW Roy Williams S SP 2.50 6.00
PMSA Shaun Alexander SP 2.50 6.00
PMSM Steve McNair 2.50 6.00
PMTB Tom Brady 12.00 30.00

2004 Fleer Platinum Platinum Portraits
COMPLETE SET (10) 8.00 20.00
STATED ODDS 1:18 HOB,1:4 JUM, 1:24 RET
1PP Deuce McAllister .60 1.50
2PP Marshall Faulk .60 1.50
3PP Brian Westbrook .50 1.25
4PP Shaun Alexander .50 1.25
5PP Andre Johnson .60 1.50
6PP Charles Rogers .50 1.25
7PP Brett Favre 1.50 4.00
8PP Edgerrin James .60 1.50
9PP Byron Leftwich .50 1.25
10PP Hines Ward .60 1.50

2004 Fleer Platinum Platinum Portraits Jersey
STATED ODDS 1:48 HOB, 1:120 RET
*PATCH/80-100: .6X TO 1.5X BASIC JSY
PATCH PRINT RUN 80-100 SER.#'d SETS
PPAJ Andre Johnson SP 3.00 8.00
PPBF Brett Favre 8.00 20.00
PPBL Byron Leftwich 2.50 6.00
PPBW Brian Westbrook 2.50 6.00
PPCR Charles Rogers SP 2.50 6.00
PPDM Deuce McAllister 3.00 8.00
PPEJ Edgerrin James 3.00 8.00
PPHW Hines Ward 3.00 8.00
PPMF Marshall Faulk 3.00 8.00
PPSA Shaun Alexander SP 2.50 6.00

2004 Fleer Platinum Pro Material Jerseys
ONE PER RACK PACK
STATED PRINT RUN 250 SER.#'d SETS
*DIE CUT/99: .6X TO 1.5X BASIC JSY
DIE CUT PRINT RUN 99 SER.#'d SETS
UNPRICED DC PATCH PRINT RUN 5 SETS
PMBB Bernard Berrian 2.00 5.00
PMBR Ben Roethlisberger 12.00 30.00
PMBT Ben Troupe 2.00 5.00
PMBW Ben Watson 2.50 6.00
PMCC Cedric Cobbs 2.00 5.00
PMCP Chris Perry 2.00 5.00
PMDD Devard Darling 2.00 5.00
PMDH DeAngelo Hall 3.00 8.00
PMDH2 Derrick Hamilton 2.00 5.00
PMDH3 Devery Henderson 2.00 5.00
PMDW Darius Watts 2.00 5.00
PMEM Eli Manning 12.00 30.00
PMGJ Greg Jones 2.00 5.00
PMJJ Julius Jones 2.00 5.00
PMJL J.P. Losman 2.00 5.00
PMKC Keary Colbert 2.00 5.00
PMKJ Kevin Jones 3.00 8.00
PMKW Kellen Winslow Jr. 2.00 5.00
PMLE Lee Evans 3.00 8.00
PMLF Larry Fitzgerald 8.00 20.00
PMLM Luke McCown 2.00 5.00
PMMC Michael Clayton 2.50 6.00
PMMJ Michael Jenkins 2.00 5.00
PMMM Mewelde Moore 2.50 6.00
PMMS Matt Schaub 2.00 5.00
PMPR Philip Rivers 6.00 15.00
PMRW Reggie Williams 2.00 5.00
PMRW2 Roy Williams WR 2.00 5.00
PMRW3 Rashaun Woods 2.00 5.00
PMSJ Steven Jackson 3.00 8.00
PMTB Tatum Bell 2.00 5.00

2004 Fleer Platinum Pro Material Jerseys Autographs
JSY AU/10-394 ODDS 1:4 RACK PACK
UNPRICED DC PATCH PRINT RUN 5
PMCP Chris Perry/394 5.00 12.00
PMEM Eli Manning/224 60.00 120.00
PMKC Keary Colbert/78 6.00 15.00
PMMC Michael Clayton/166 8.00 20.00
PMPR Philip Rivers/294 30.00 60.00
PMRW Rashaun Woods/274 5.00 12.00
PMSJ Steven Jackson/22 25.00 60.00

2004 Fleer Platinum Pro Material Jerseys Autographs Die Cut
DIE CUT PRINT RUN 25 SER.#'d SETS
PMBR Ben Roethlisberger 125.00 250.00
PMCP Chris Perry 10.00 25.00
PMEM Eli Manning 100.00 200.00
PMKC Keary Colbert 10.00 25.00
PMLF Larry Fitzgerald 60.00 120.00
PMMC Michael Clayton 12.00 30.00
PMMS Matt Schaub 15.00 40.00
PMPR Philip Rivers 60.00 125.00
PMRW Rashaun Woods 10.00 25.00
PMSJ Steven Jackson 20.00 50.00

2004 Fleer Platinum Scouting Report
STATED ODDS 1:60 H,1:160 JUM,1:432 R
STATED PRINT RUN 250 SER.#'d SETS
1SR Tom Brady 8.00 20.00
2SR Peyton Manning 5.00 12.00
3SR Priest Holmes 1.25 3.00
4SR Donovan McNabb 1.50 4.00
5SR Torry Holt 1.50 4.00
6SR Clinton Portis 1.25 3.00
7SR LaDainian Tomlinson 2.00 5.00
8SR Jeremy Shockey 1.25 3.00
9SR Steve McNair 1.50 4.00
10SR Chad Pennington 1.25 3.00
11SR Michael Vick 1.50 4.00
12SR Brett Favre 4.00 10.00
13SR Randy Moss 1.50 4.00
14SR Byron Leftwich 1.25 3.00
15SR David Carr 1.25 3.00
16SR Ricky Williams 1.50 4.00
17SR Stephen Davis 1.25 3.00
18SR Terrell Owens 1.50 4.00
19SR Marvin Harrison 1.50 4.00
20SR Jerry Rice 4.00 10.00

2004 Fleer Platinum Scouting Report Jersey
STATED PRINT RUN 35-250
SRBF Brett Favre 8.00 20.00
SRBL Byron Leftwich 2.50 6.00
SRCP2 Clinton Portis 2.50 6.00
SRDC David Carr 2.50 6.00
SRDM Donovan McNabb/35 5.00 12.00
SRJR Jerry Rice 8.00 20.00
SRJS Jeremy Shockey 2.50 6.00
SRLT LaDainian Tomlinson 4.00 10.00
SRMH Marvin Harrison 3.00 8.00
SRMV Michael Vick 3.00 8.00
SRPH Priest Holmes 2.50 6.00
SRPM Peyton Manning 10.00 25.00
SRRM Randy Moss 3.00 8.00
SRSD Stephen Davis 2.50 6.00
SRSM Steve McNair 3.00 8.00
SRTB Tom Brady 15.00 40.00
SRTH Torry Holt 3.00 8.00
SRTO Terrell Owens 3.00 8.00

2004 Fleer Platinum Youth Movement
COMPLETE SET (15) 12.50 30.00
STATED ODDS 1:9 HOB, 1:2 JUM, 1:8 RET
1YM Eli Manning 2.50 6.00
2YM Kevin Jones .40 1.00
3YM Philip Rivers 1.00 2.50
4YM Kellen Winslow Jr. .30 .75
5YM Ben Roethlisberger 2.50 6.00
6YM Roy Williams WR .30 .75
7YM Drew Henson .30 .75
8YM Larry Fitzgerald 1.25 3.00
9YM J.P. Losman .30 .75
10YM Steven Jackson .50 1.25
11YM Chris Perry .30 .75
12YM Reggie Williams .30 .75
13YM Michael Clayton .40 1.00
14YM Lee Evans .50 1.25
15YM Tatum Bell .30 .75

2001 Fleer Premium
Fleer released Premium in August of 2001. This 250-card set featured 200 base cards and 50 rookies which were short printed. The rookies were serial numbered to 2001. The base set design used foilboard and gold-foil highlights fro the lettering and logo. The cards were issued in eight card packs with an SRP of $3.99 per pack and 24 packs in the box.
COMP.SET w/o SP's (200) 10.00 25.00
201-250 ROOKIE PRINT RUN 2001
1 Ricky Williams .20 .50
2 Dez White .20 .50
3 Jay Riemersma .15 .40
4 Derrick Mason .15 .40
5 Chad Lewis .15 .40
6 Shaun King .15 .40
7 Jevon Kearse .15 .40
8 Bobby Engram .15 .40
9 Warrick Dunn .15 .40
10 Randall Cunningham .20 .50
11 Stephen Alexander .15 .40
12 Jimmy Smith .20 .50
13 Az-Zahir Hakim .15 .40
14 Antonio Freeman .25 .60
15 Curtis Conway .20 .50
16 Tim Biakabutuka .15 .40
17 Peter Warrick .15 .40
18 Kurt Warner .40 1.00
19 Brian Urlacher .30 .75
20 Rod Smith .20 .50
21 Frank Sanders .15 .40
22 Trevor Pryce .15 .40
23 Sammy Morris .15 .40
24 Cade McNown .20 .50
25 Keyshawn Johnson .20 .50
26 Tim Couch .15 .40
27 Dedric Ward .15 .40
28 Bill Schroeder .20 .50
29 John Randle .20 .50
30 Donovan McNabb .20 .50
31 Marvin Harrison .20 .50
32 Trent Dilfer .15 .40
33 David Boston .15 .40
34 Donnell Bennett .15 .40
35 Trace Armstrong .15 .40
36 Sam Adams .15 .40
37 Jeremiah Trotter .15 .40
38 Zach Thomas .20 .50
39 Shawn Jefferson .15 .40
40 J.J. Stokes .15 .40
41 Akili Smith .15 .40
42 Tony Siragusa .20 .50
43 William Roaf .15 .40
44 Muhsin Muhammad .15 .40
45 Terance Mathis .15 .40
46 Tee Martin .20 .50
47 Ray Lewis .25 .60
48 Matt Hasselbeck .15 .40
49 Todd Pinkston .15 .40
50 Rob Johnson .20 .50
51 Edgerrin James .20 .50
52 Rocket Ismail .20 .50
53 Trent Green .15 .40
54 Tim Dwight .20 .50
55 Anthony Becht .15 .40
56 Jessie Armstead .15 .40
57 Mike Anderson .15 .40
58 Jamal Anderson .20 .50
59 Anthony Wright .15 .40
60 Regan Upshaw .15 .40
61 John Holecek .15 .40
62 Shaun Alexander .15 .40
63 Troy Aikman .30 .75
64 Peter Boulware .15 .40
65 Hines Ward .20 .50
66 Michael Strahan .20 .50
67 Herman Moore .15 .40
68 Rich Gannon .20 .50
69 Ken Dilger .15 .40
70 Terrell Davis .20 .50
71 Terrence Wilkins .15 .40
72 Fred Taylor .15 .40
73 Napoleon Kaufman .15 .40
74 Tony Horne .15 .40
75 Ahman Green .20 .50
76 Jay Fiedler .20 .50
77 Albert Connell .15 .40
78 Charlie Batch .15 .40
79 James Allen .15 .40
80 Sylvester Morris .15 .40
81 Isaac Bruce .25 .60
82 Charles Woodson .25 .60
83 Lamar Smith .20 .50
84 Peyton Manning .60 1.50
85 Sam Madison .15 .40
86 Olandis Gary .15 .40
87 Kevin Faulk .15 .40
88 Jeff Garcia .15 .40
89 JaJuan Dawson .15 .40
90 Sam Cowart .15 .40
91 David Sloan .15 .40
92 Bobby Shaw .15 .40
93 Travis Prentice .15 .40
94 Terrell Owens .20 .50
95 John Lynch .20 .50
96 Jim Harbaugh .20 .50
97 Brian Griese .15 .40
98 Jeff Graham .15 .40
99 La'Roi Glover .15 .40
100 Joey Galloway .20 .50
101 Wesley Walls .15 .40
102 Vinny Testaverde .15 .40
103 Jason Taylor .25 .60
104 Darnay Scott .20 .50
105 Samari Rolle .15 .40
106 Adrian Murrell .20 .50
107 Eric Moulds .15 .40
108 Keenan McCardell .20 .50
109 Donald Hayes .15 .40
110 Brett Favre .50 1.25
111 Troy Edwards .15 .40
112 Ron Dayne .20 .50
113 Daunte Culpepper .20 .50
114 Chris Chandler .20 .50
115 Mark Brunell .20 .50
116 Courtney Brown .15 .40
117 Aaron Brooks .15 .40
118 Fred Beasley .15 .40
119 Mike Alstott .15 .40
120 Tyrone Wheatley .20 .50
121 R.Jay Soward .15 .40
122 Deion Sanders .20 .50
123 Jake Reed .20 .50
124 Jamal Lewis .25 .60
125 Tony Gonzalez .20 .50
126 Terrell Fletcher .15 .40
127 Wayne Chrebet .15 .40
128 Cris Carter .25 .60
129 Drew Bledsoe .20 .50
130 Tiki Barber .20 .50
131 Derrick Alexander .15 .40
132 Frank Wycheck .15 .40
133 Jerome Pathon .15 .40
134 Warren Sapp .20 .50
135 Joe Horn .15 .40
136 Ricky Watters .20 .50
137 Amani Toomer .15 .40
138 Bruce Smith .20 .50
139 Andre Rison .20 .50
140 J.R. Redmond .15 .40
141 Steve McNair .20 .50
142 Michael McCrary .15 .40
143 Ike Hilliard .15 .40
144 Charlie Garner .20 .50
145 Mark Bruener .20 .50
146 Emmitt Smith .40 1.00
147 Darren Sharper .20 .50
148 Peerless Price .15 .40
149 Johnnie Morton .20 .50
150 Curtis Martin .20 .50
151 Joe Johnson .15 .40
152 MarTay Jenkins .15 .40
153 Priest Holmes .15 .40
154 Terry Glenn .20 .50
155 Oronde Gadsden .15 .40
156 Germane Crowell .15 .40
157 Steve Beuerlein .20 .50
158 Champ Bailey .20 .50
159 Troy Vincent .20 .50
160 James Stewart .15 .40
161 Jerry Rice .50 1.25
162 Randy Moss .20 .50
163 Dave Moore .15 .40
164 Ed McCaffrey .20 .50
165 Thomas Jones .15 .40
166 Rickey Dudley .15 .40
167 Hugh Douglas .15 .40
168 Stephen Davis .15 .40
169 Kerry Collins .15 .40
170 Cam Cleeland .15 .40
171 Stephen Boyd .15 .40
172 Jerome Bettis .25 .60
173 Aeneas Williams .15 .40
174 Chad Pennington .15 .40
175 Dorsey Levens .20 .50
176 Desmond Howard .20 .50
177 Torry Holt .20 .50
178 Plaxico Burress .15 .40
179 Kevin Johnson .15 .40
180 Kyle Brady .15 .40
181 Jake Plummer .15 .40
182 Brad Johnson .20 .50
183 Eddie George .25 .60
184 Corey Dillon .15 .40
185 Curtis Enis .15 .40
186 Tim Brown .25 .60
187 Tony Boselli .20 .50
188 Duce Staley .15 .40
189 Junior Seau .20 .50
190 Marshall Faulk .20 .50
191 Kordell Stewart .15 .40
192 Corey Simon .15 .40
193 Shannon Sharpe .20 .50
194 Marcus Robinson .20 .50
195 Carl Pickens .20 .50
196 Doug Flutie .20 .50
197 Freddie Jones .15 .40
198 Patrick Jeffers .15 .40
199 Shawn Bryson .15 .40
200 Kevin Dyson .15 .40
201 David Terrell RC 1.25 3.00
202 Dan Morgan RC 1.25 3.00
203 Chris Weinke RC 1.25 3.00
204 Correll Buckhalter RC 1.00 2.50
205 Chad Johnson RC 1.50 4.00
206 LaDainian Tomlinson RC 5.00 12.00
207 Reggie Wayne RC 2.00 5.00
208 Tim Hasselbeck RC 1.25 3.00
209 Michael Vick RC 2.50 6.00
210 Heath Evans RC 1.25 3.00
211 Damione Lewis RC 1.25 3.00
212 Richard Seymour RC 1.50 4.00
213 Quincy Morgan RC 1.25 3.00
214 Drew Brees RC 25.00 50.00
215 Freddie Mitchell RC 1.00 2.50
216 Justin McCareins RC 1.25 3.00
217 Mike McMahon RC 1.25 3.00
218 Derrick Gibson RC 1.00 2.50
219 Rudi Johnson RC 1.50 4.00
220 Todd Heap RC 1.25 3.00
221 Josh Booty RC 1.25 3.00
222 Justin Smith RC 2.00 5.00
223 Marcus Stroud RC 1.25 3.00
224 Rod Gardner RC 1.25 3.00
225 Vinny Sutherland RC 1.00 2.50
226 Marques Tuiasosopo RC 1.25 3.00
227 Anthony Thomas RC 1.50 4.00
228 Bobby Newcombe RC 1.25 3.00
229 Michael Bennett RC 1.25 3.00
230 Snoop Minnis RC 1.00 2.50
231 Travis Minor RC 1.25 3.00
232 Travis Henry RC 1.25 3.00
233 Kevan Barlow RC 1.25 3.00
234 Gerard Warren RC 1.25 3.00
235 Sage Rosenfels RC 1.25 3.00
236 Chris Chambers RC 1.00 2.50
237 James Jackson RC 1.00 2.50
238 Deuce McAllister RC 1.50 4.00
239 Koren Robinson RC 1.25 3.00
240 Andre Carter RC 1.25 3.00
241 Santana Moss RC 1.50 4.00
242 LaMont Jordan RC 1.50 4.00
243 Ken-Yon Rambo RC 1.00 2.50
244 Jamal Reynolds RC 1.00 2.50
245 Fred Smoot RC 1.25 3.00
246 Robert Ferguson RC 1.50 4.00
247 Alex Bannister RC 1.00 2.50
248 Dan Alexander RC 1.25 3.00
249 Nate Clements RC 1.25 3.00
250 Quincy Carter RC 1.25 3.00
CL1 Checklist .05 .15
CL2 Checklist .05 .15

2001 Fleer Premium Star Ruby
*VETS 1-200: 6X TO 15X BASIC CARDS
*ROOKIES 201-250: 1X TO 2.5X
STATED PRINT RUN 125 SER.#'d SETS

2001 Fleer Premium Clothes to the Game
Inserted in packs at a rate of one in 59, these 21 cards have pieces of game-used equipment on them and honor some of the NFL's stars.
STATED ODDS 1:59
1 Jessie Armstead 2.00 5.00
2 Champ Bailey 2.50 6.00
3 David Boston 2.00 5.00
4 Courtney Brown 2.00 5.00
5 Isaac Bruce 3.00 8.00
6 Ken Dilger 2.00 5.00
7 Curtis Enis 2.00 5.00
8 E.G. Green 2.00 5.00
9 Marvin Harrison 2.50 6.00
10 Torry Holt 2.50 6.00
11 Edgerrin James 2.50 6.00
12 Cade McNown 2.50 6.00
13 Johnnie Morton 2.50 6.00
14 Todd Pinkston 2.00 5.00
15 Michael Pittman 2.50 6.00
16 Jake Plummer 2.00 5.00
17 Travis Prentice 2.00 5.00
18 Jerry Rice 6.00 15.00
19 R.Jay Soward 2.00 5.00
20 Kordell Stewart 2.00 5.00
21 Kurt Warner 5.00 12.00

2001 Fleer Premium Commanding Respect
Issued at a rate of one in 20, this 15 card set features players who are among the most respected by their peers in the NFL.
COMPLETE SET (15) 7.50 20.00
STATED ODDS 1:20
1 Brian Griese .50 1.25
2 Jamal Lewis .75 2.00
3 Fred Taylor .50 1.25
4 Stephen Davis .50 1.25
5 Marcus Robinson .60 1.50
6 Marvin Harrison .60 1.50
7 Marshall Faulk .60 1.50
8 Doug Flutie .60 1.50
9 Jamal Anderson .60 1.50
10 Donovan McNabb .60 1.50
11 Steve McNair .60 1.50
12 Jeff Garcia .50 1.25
13 Daunte Culpepper .60 1.50
14 Isaac Bruce .75 2.00
15 Jimmy Smith .60 1.50

2001 Fleer Premium Greatest Plays
This set features some of the most memorable plays football history celebrated on cards. They were inserted at a rate of one per 10 packs. Although the set was scheduled to conatin 21-cards, cards numbered 1 and 7 were intended to have been pulled from production. However, some copies of both cards have surfaced on the secondary market.
COMP.SET w/o SP's (19) 12.50 30.00
STATED ODDS 1:10
1 Dave Casper SP 10.00 20.00
2 Emmitt Smith 1.00 2.50
3 Roger Staubach 1.00 2.50
4 Jerry Rice 1.25 3.00
5 Doug Flutie .60 1.50
6 Earl Campbell .75 2.00
7 Bart Starr SP 15.00 30.00
8 John Elway 1.25 3.00
9 Joe Montana 2.50 6.00
10 Dan Marino 1.50 4.00
11 Dwight Clark .60 1.50
12 Franco Harris .75 2.00
13 Gale Sayers .75 2.00
14 Ken Stabler 1.00 2.50
15 Steve Young 1.00 2.50
16 William Perry .50 1.25
17 Michael Westbrook .50 1.25
18 Kordell Stewart .40 1.00
19 Terry Bradshaw 1.00 2.50
20 Tony Dorsett .75 2.00
21 Eric Dickerson .60 1.50

2001 Fleer Premium Greatest Plays Jerseys
This quasi-parallel to the Greatest Plays set has game-used swatches from some of the players involved in those all-time plays. These cards were issued at a rate of one in 91.
STATED ODDS 1:91
1 Tony Dorsett 10.00 25.00
2 John Elway 15.00 40.00
3 Doug Flutie 10.00 25.00
4 Dan Marino 15.00 40.00
5 Joe Montana 12.00 30.00
6 Jerry Rice 12.00 30.00
7 Bart Starr 12.00 30.00
8 Steve Young 10.00 25.00

2001 Fleer Premium Home Field Advantage
Issued at a rate of one per 72 packs, these cards spotlight some of the game's top players and their accomplishments on their home turf.
COMPLETE SET (12) 20.00 50.00
STATED ODDS 1:72
1 Eddie George 1.50 4.00
2 Edgerrin James 1.25 3.00
3 Ricky Williams 1.25 3.00
4 Jeff Garcia 1.00 2.50
5 Brett Favre 3.00 8.00
6 Warrick Dunn 1.00 2.50
7 Donovan McNabb 1.25 3.00
8 Brian Urlacher 2.00 5.00
9 Kurt Warner 2.50 6.00
10 Emmitt Smith 2.50 6.00
11 Rich Gannon 1.25 3.00
12 Cris Carter 1.50 4.00

2001 Fleer Premium Home Field Advantage Turf
This parallel set of the Home Field Advantage insert set includes an actual piece of game-used turf which is embedded on the card. These cards, which were randomly inserted in packs, had a stated print run of 314.
STATED PRINT RUN 314 SER.#'d SETS
1 Cris Carter 6.00 15.00
2 Warrick Dunn 4.00 10.00
3 Brett Favre 12.00 30.00
4 Rich Gannon 5.00 12.00
5 Jeff Garcia 4.00 10.00
6 Eddie George 6.00 15.00
7 Edgerrin James 5.00 12.00
8 Donovan McNabb 5.00 12.00
9 Emmitt Smith 10.00 25.00
10 Brian Urlacher 8.00 20.00
11 Kurt Warner 10.00 25.00
12 Ricky Williams 5.00 12.00

2001 Fleer Premium Performers Jerseys
Randomly inserted in packs, these 20 cards feature game-used uniform swatches from some of the NFL's leading stars. These cards had a stated print run of 900.
STATED PRINT RUN 900 SER.#'d SETS
1 Jerome Bettis 2.50 6.00
2 David Boston 1.50 4.00
3 Az-Zahir Hakim 1.50 4.00
4 Torry Holt 2.00 5.00
5 Edgerrin James 2.00 5.00
6 Kevin Johnson 1.50 4.00
7 Rob Johnson 2.00 5.00
8 Thomas Jones 1.50 4.00
9 Jim Kelly 2.50 6.00
10 Jamal Lewis 2.50 6.00
11 Keenan McCardell 2.00 5.00
12 Donovan McNabb 2.00 5.00
13 Cade McNown 2.00 5.00
14 Jake Plummer 1.50 4.00
15 Travis Prentice 1.50 4.00
16 Jerry Rice 5.00 12.00
17 Marcus Robinson 2.00 5.00
18 Duce Staley 1.50 4.00
19 Kordell Stewart 1.50 4.00
20 Kurt Warner 4.00 10.00

2001 Fleer Premium Respect Patches
Randomly inserted in packs, these 15 cards feature game-used uniform patches from some of the NFL's leading stars. These cards had a stated print run of 80.
STATED PRINT RUN 80 SER.#'d SETS
1 Jamal Anderson 4.00 10.00
2 Isaac Bruce 5.00 12.00
3 Daunte Culpepper 4.00 10.00
4 Stephen Davis 3.00 8.00
5 Marshall Faulk 4.00 10.00
6 Doug Flutie 4.00 10.00
7 Jeff Garcia 3.00 8.00
8 Brian Griese 3.00 8.00
9 Marvin Harrison 4.00 10.00
10 Jamal Lewis 5.00 12.00
11 Donovan McNabb 4.00 10.00
12 Steve McNair 4.00 10.00
13 Marcus Robinson 4.00 10.00
14 Jimmy Smith 4.00 10.00
15 Fred Taylor 3.00 8.00

2001 Fleer Premium Rookie Game Ball

This semi-parallel to some of the final 50 cards in the premium set feature the 2001 Rookies with a piece of a NFL game football on them. Randomly inserted in packs, these cards are skip-numbered and have a stated print run of 250 cards.

STATED PRINT RUN 250 SER.#'d SETS
201 David Terrell 2.50 6.00
202 Dan Morgan 2.50 6.00
203 Chris Weinke 2.50 6.00
205 Chad Johnson 3.00 8.00
206 LaDainian Tomlinson 10.00 25.00
207 Reggie Wayne 4.00 10.00
209 Michael Vick 5.00 12.00
213 Quincy Morgan 2.50 6.00
214 Drew Brees 50.00 100.00
215 Freddie Mitchell 2.00 5.00
219 Rudi Johnson 3.00 8.00
224 Rod Gardner 2.50 6.00
226 Marques Tuiasosopo 2.50 6.00
227 Anthony Thomas 3.00 8.00
229 Michael Bennett 2.50 6.00
230 Snoop Minnis 2.00 5.00
231 Travis Minor 2.50 6.00
232 Travis Henry 2.50 6.00
233 Kevan Barlow 2.50 6.00
236 Chris Chambers 2.00 5.00
237 James Jackson 2.00 5.00
238 Deuce McAllister 3.00 8.00
239 Koren Robinson 2.50 6.00
241 Santana Moss 3.00 8.00
250 Quincy Carter 2.50 6.00

2001 Fleer Premium Rookie Revolution

Inserted in packs at a rate of one in 10, this 10 card set feature some of the leading 2001 NFL rookies.

COMPLETE SET (10) 10.00 25.00
STATED ODDS 1:10
1 Deuce McAllister .60 1.50
2 David Terrell .50 1.25
3 Drew Brees 6.00 15.00
4 Chad Johnson .60 1.50
5 LaDainian Tomlinson 2.00 5.00
6 Marques Tuiasosopo .50 1.25
7 Michael Vick 1.00 2.50
8 Michael Bennett .50 1.25
9 Anthony Thomas .60 1.50
10 Santana Moss .60 1.50

2001 Fleer Premium Rookie Revolution Autographs

Randomly Inserted in packs, this 10 card set feature autographs of the players in the Rookie Revolution set. Each player signed 50 serial numbered cards for the set. Deuce McAllister did not sign his cards in time for inclusion in packs and the collectors who pulled that card had until September 1, 2002 to redeem the card. When these finally surfaced, they were not serial numbered.

STATED PRINT RUN 50 SER.#'d SETS
1 Michael Bennett 8.00 20.00
2 Drew Brees 150.00 300.00
3 Chad Johnson 10.00 25.00
3X Chad Johnson EXCH 1.00 2.50
4 Deuce McAllister 10.00 25.00
5 Santana Moss 10.00 25.00
6 David Terrell 8.00 20.00
7 Anthony Thomas 10.00 25.00
8 LaDainian Tomlinson 75.00 150.00
9 Marques Tuiasosopo 8.00 20.00
10 Michael Vick 75.00 150.00

2001 Fleer Premium Solid Performers

Inserted at a rate of one in 20, this 20 card set commends players who play to their best each week during the season.

COMPLETE SET (20) 12.00 30.00
STATED ODDS 1:20
1 Jerome Bettis .75 2.00
2 David Boston .50 1.25
3 Cade McNown .60 1.50
4 Keenan McCardell .60 1.50
5 Thomas Jones .50 1.25
6 Edgerrin James .60 1.50
7 Torry Holt .60 1.50
8 Az-Zahir Hakim .50 1.25
9 Jake Plummer .50 1.25
10 Travis Prentice .50 1.25
11 Marcus Robinson .60 1.50
12 Duce Staley .50 1.25
13 Kurt Warner 1.25 3.00
14 Kordell Stewart .50 1.25
15 Rob Johnson .60 1.50
16 Jamal Lewis .75 2.00
17 Donovan McNabb .60 1.50
18 Kevin Johnson .50 1.25
19 Jim Kelly .75 2.00
20 Jerry Rice 1.50 4.00

2001 Fleer Premium Suiting Up Jerseys

Issued exclusively in retail packs at a rate of one in 109, this 19 card set features uniform pieces of some players who don't always get featured in these jersey sets.

STATED ODDS 1:109 RETAIL
1 Jessie Armstead 2.00 5.00
2 Champ Bailey 2.50 6.00
3 David Boston 2.00 5.00
4 Courtney Brown 2.00 5.00
5 Isaac Bruce 3.00 8.00
6 Ken Dilger 2.00 5.00
7 Curtis Enis 2.00 5.00
8 E.G. Green 2.00 5.00
9 Marvin Harrison 2.50 6.00
10 Torry Holt 2.50 6.00
11 Edgerrin James 2.50 6.00
12 Cade McNown 2.50 6.00
13 Johnnie Morton 2.50 6.00
14 Todd Pinkston 2.00 5.00
15 Michael Pittman 2.50 6.00
16 Jake Plummer 2.00 5.00
17 Travis Prentice 2.00 5.00
18 Jerry Rice 6.00 15.00
19 R.Jay Soward 2.00 5.00

2002 Fleer Premium

Released in September 2002, this 200-card set contains 130 veterans and 39 rookies. S.R.P. was $2.99 per pack. Both hobby and retail boxes contained 24 packs each with 5 cards per pack. Rookies were serial numbered to 1250.

COMP.SET w/o SP's (160) 15.00 40.00
131-170 ROOKIE PRINT RUN 1250
1 Kevin Dyson .30 .75
2 Kerry Collins .25 .60
3 Marty Booker .25 .60
4 Curtis Conway .30 .75
5 Drew Bledsoe .30 .75
6 Kurt Warner .30 .75
7 Hines Ward .30 .75
8 Terrell Owens .30 .75
9 Todd Pinkston .25 .60
10 Eric Moulds .25 .60
11 Quincy Morgan .25 .60
12 Fred Taylor .25 .60
13 Santana Moss .30 .75
14 Peyton Manning 1.00 2.50
15 Qadry Ismail .25 .60
16 Mike McMahon .25 .60
17 David Patten .25 .60
18 Wayne Chrebet .25 .60
19 David Terrell .25 .60
20 Corey Bradford .25 .60
21 Derrick Mason .25 .60
22 Anthony Thomas .30 .75
23 James Allen .25 .60
24 Vinny Testaverde .25 .60
25 Trent Green .25 .60
26 Thomas Jones .25 .60
27 Rocket Ismail .30 .75
28 Duce Staley .25 .60
29 Drew Brees .75 2.00
30 Chris Chandler .30 .75
31 Kordell Stewart .25 .60
32 Koren Robinson .25 .60
33 Jon Kitna .25 .60
34 Jamie Sharper .30 .75
35 Germane Crowell .25 .60
36 Lamar Smith .25 .60
37 LaDainian Tomlinson .40 1.00
38 Freddie Mitchell .25 .60
39 Corey Dillon .25 .60
40 Isaac Bruce .40 1.00
41 James Thrash .30 .75
42 Brian Griese .25 .60
43 Marvin Harrison .30 .75
44 Aaron Brooks .25 .60
45 Rich Gannon .30 .75
46 Mike Alstott .25 .60
47 Shannon Sharpe .30 .75
48 Travis Henry .25 .60
49 Keyshawn Johnson .30 .75
50 Daunte Culpepper .30 .75
51 James Jackson .25 .60
52 Justin McCareins .30 .75
53 Quincy Carter .25 .60
54 Stephen Davis .25 .60
55 Joey Galloway .30 .75
56 Joe Horn .25 .60
57 Plaxico Burress .25 .60
58 Brett Favre .75 2.00
59 Brian Urlacher .40 1.00
60 David Boston .25 .60
61 Darrell Jackson .30 .75
62 Trung Canidate .25 .60
63 Shaun Alexander .25 .60
64 Steve McNair .30 .75
65 Doug Flutie .30 .75
66 LaMont Jordan .30 .75
67 Rod Smith .30 .75
68 Marshall Faulk .30 .75
69 Tiki Barber .30 .75
70 James Stewart .25 .60
71 Frank Wycheck .25 .60
72 Peerless Price .25 .60
73 Derrick Alexander .25 .60
74 Charlie Garner .30 .75
75 Peter Warrick .25 .60
76 Warren Sapp .30 .75
77 Kevan Barlow .25 .60
78 Edgerrin James .30 .75
79 Willie Jackson .25 .60
80 Keenan McCardell .30 .75
81 Bill Schroeder .25 .60
82 Curtis Martin .30 .75
83 Torry Holt .30 .75
84 Tony Gonzalez .30 .75
85 Jeff Garcia .25 .60
86 Travis Taylor .25 .60
87 Johnnie Morton .30 .75
88 Tim Couch .25 .60
89 Troy Brown .25 .60
90 Emmitt Smith .60 1.50
91 Aeneas Williams .25 .60
92 Rod Gardner .25 .60
93 Brandon Stokley .25 .60
94 Warrick Dunn .25 .60
95 Jay Riemersma .25 .60
96 Kevin Johnson .25 .60
97 Antowain Smith .30 .75
98 James McKnight .25 .60
99 Amani Toomer .25 .60
100 Ricky Williams .30 .75
101 Priest Holmes .25 .60
102 Muhsin Muhammad .25 .60
103 Jake Plummer .25 .60
104 Marcus Robinson .30 .75
105 Donovan McNabb .30 .75
106 Tom Brady 2.00 5.00
107 Jimmy Smith .30 .75
108 Jamal Lewis .30 .75
109 Antonio Freeman .40 1.00
110 Ron Dayne .30 .75
111 Tim Brown .40 1.00
112 Chris Chambers .25 .60
113 Garrison Hearst .25 .60
114 Michael Vick .30 .75
115 Snoop Minnis .25 .60
116 Terrell Davis .30 .75
117 Ahman Green .30 .75
118 Donald Hayes .25 .60
119 Jermaine Lewis .25 .60
120 Chad Johnson .25 .60
121 Jay Fiedler .30 .75
122 Randy Moss .30 .75
123 Wesley Walls .30 .75
124 Eddie George .30 .75
125 Jerry Rice .75 2.00
126 Michael Bennett .25 .60
127 Jerome Bettis .40 1.00
128 Mark Brunell .30 .75
129 Adam Vinatieri .25 .60
130 Ed McCaffrey .30 .75
131 Maurice Morris RC 1.25 3.00
132 Ron Johnson RC 1.25 3.00
133 Antwaan Randle El RC 1.25 3.00
134 Brian Westbrook RC 2.00 5.00
135 Julius Peppers RC 2.50 6.00
136 Travis Stephens RC 1.00 2.50
137 David Carr RC 1.00 2.50
138 Clinton Portis RC 1.50 4.00
139 Reche Caldwell RC 1.25 3.00
140 Tim Carter RC 1.25 3.00
141 Daniel Graham RC 1.25 3.00
142 Rohan Davey RC 1.50 4.00
143 T.J. Duckett RC 1.00 2.50
144 Luke Staley RC 1.00 2.50
145 Ashley Lelie RC 1.00 2.50
146 Josh Reed RC 1.25 3.00
147 Randy Fasani RC 1.00 2.50
148 Andre Davis RC 1.00 2.50
149 Joey Harrington RC 1.00 2.50
150 David Garrard RC 1.25 3.00
151 Ladell Betts RC 1.50 4.00
152 Donte Stallworth RC 1.50 4.00
153 Adrian Peterson RC 1.25 3.00
154 Lamar Gordon RC 1.25 3.00
155 Jonathan Wells RC 1.25 3.00
156 Jabar Gaffney RC 1.00 2.50
157 Patrick Ramsey RC 1.25 3.00
158 Roy Williams RC 1.00 2.50
159 Jeremy Shockey RC 1.50 4.00
160 Javon Walker RC 1.50 4.00
161 Marquise Walker RC 1.00 2.50
162 Antonio Bryant RC 1.50 4.00
163 Josh McCown RC 1.50 4.00
164 Najeh Davenport RC 1.00 2.50
165 William Green RC 1.25 3.00
166 Jerramy Stevens RC 1.50 4.00
167 DeShaun Foster RC 1.50 4.00
168 Cliff Russell RC 1.00 2.50
169 Kurt Kittner RC 1.00 2.50
170 Eric Crouch RC 1.50 4.00
171 Michael Pittman PP .30 .75
172 Darnay Scott PP .30 .75
173 Charles Woodson PP .40 1.00
174 Ty Law PP .40 1.00
175 Tony Boselli PP .30 .75
176 Zach Thomas PP .30 .75
177 Trent Dilfer PP .25 .60
178 Bubba Franks PP .25 .60
179 Laveranues Coles PP .30 .75
180 John Lynch PP .30 .75
181 Kendrell Bell PP .25 .60
182 Mike Anderson PP .25 .60
183 Amos Zereoue PP .25 .60
184 Michael Strahan PP .30 .75
185 Chad Lewis PP .25 .60
186 Travis Minor PP .25 .60
187 Jevon Kearse PP .25 .60
188 Darren Sharper PP .25 .60
189 Az-Zahir Hakim PP .25 .60
190 Ray Lewis PP .40 1.00
191 Deuce McAllister PP .30 .75
192 Chris Weinke PP .25 .60
193 Desmond Howard PP .30 .75
194 Dominic Rhodes PP .25 .60
195 Joe Jurevicius PP .25 .60
196 Tim Dwight PP .25 .60
197 Jeff Zgonina PP .25 .60
198 Junior Seau PP .30 .75
199 Rosevelt Colvin PP RC .50 1.25
200 Chad Pennington PP .25 .60

2002 Fleer Premium Star Ruby

*VETS 1-130: 2.5X TO 6X BASIC CARDS
*ROOKIES 131-170: 1X TO 2.5X
STATED PRINT RUN 100 SER.#'d SETS

2002 Fleer Premium All-Pro Team

Randomly inserted in packs, this 25-card set features current all-pro players. The cards were serial numbered to 1000.

COMPLETE SET (25) 25.00 60.00
STATED PRINT RUN 1000 SER.#'d SETS
1 David Boston .75 2.00
2 Jerome Bettis 1.25 3.00
3 Brett Favre 2.50 6.00
4 Brian Urlacher 1.25 3.00
5 Marshall Faulk 1.00 2.50
6 Rich Gannon 1.00 2.50
7 Emmitt Smith 2.00 5.00
8 Corey Dillon .75 2.00
9 Jerry Rice 2.50 6.00
10 Donovan McNabb 1.00 2.50
11 Curtis Martin 1.00 2.50
12 Isaac Bruce 1.25 3.00
13 Junior Seau 1.00 2.50
14 Jeff Garcia .75 2.00
15 Mike Alstott .75 2.00
16 Ray Lewis 1.25 3.00
17 Daunte Culpepper 1.00 2.50
18 Tony Gonzalez 1.00 2.50
19 Terrell Owens 1.00 2.50
20 Peyton Manning 3.00 8.00
21 Randy Moss 1.00 2.50
22 Kurt Warner 1.00 2.50
23 Jimmy Smith 1.00 2.50
24 Edgerrin James 1.00 2.50
25 Tom Brady 6.00 15.00

2002 Fleer Premium All-Pro Team Jerseys

Inserted in packs at a rate of 1:36 hobby and 1:150 retail, this 16-card set features current all-pro players along with a swatch of game worn jersey on the card front.

STATED ODDS 1:36 HOB, 1:150 RET
1 David Boston 2.50 6.00
2 Tom Brady 20.00 50.00
3 Daunte Culpepper 3.00 8.00
4 Corey Dillon 2.50 6.00
5 Brett Favre 8.00 20.00
6 Jeff Garcia 2.50 6.00
7 Ray Lewis 4.00 10.00
8 Curtis Martin 3.00 8.00
9 Randy Moss 3.00 8.00
10 Terrell Owens 3.00 8.00
11 Jerry Rice 8.00 20.00
12 Junior Seau 3.00 8.00
13 Emmitt Smith 6.00 15.00
14 Jimmy Smith 3.00 8.00
15 Brian Urlacher 4.00 10.00
16 Kurt Warner 3.00 8.00

2002 Fleer Premium All-Pro Team Jersey Patches

Randomly inserted in packs, this 19-card set fetaures current all-pros along with a swatch of game used jersey patch on the card front. The cards were hand numbered on front to 100.

STATED PRINT RUN 100 SER.#'d SETS
1 Mike Alstott 5.00 12.00
2 Jerome Bettis 8.00 20.00
3 David Boston 5.00 12.00
4 Tom Brady 40.00 100.00
5 Isaac Bruce 8.00 20.00
6 Daunte Culpepper 6.00 15.00
7 Corey Dillon 5.00 12.00
8 Marshall Faulk 6.00 15.00
9 Brett Favre 15.00 40.00
10 Rich Gannon 6.00 15.00
11 Jeff Garcia 5.00 12.00
12 Edgerrin James 6.00 15.00
13 Ray Lewis 10.00 25.00
14 Donovan McNabb 6.00 15.00
15 Randy Moss 6.00 15.00
16 Terrell Owens 6.00 15.00
17 Jerry Rice 15.00 40.00
18 Brian Urlacher 8.00 20.00
19 Kurt Warner 6.00 15.00

2002 Fleer Premium All-Rookie Team

Inserted in packs at a rate of 1:6 hobby and retail,this 15 card set features the hottest first year players in the NFL.

STATED ODDS 1:6 HOB/RET
1 David Carr .30 .75
2 William Green .40 1.00
3 Ashley Lelie .30 .75
4 Clinton Portis .50 1.25
5 Reche Caldwell .40 1.00
6 Donte Stallworth .50 1.25
7 DeShaun Foster .50 1.25
8 T.J. Duckett .30 .75
9 Antwaan Randle El .40 1.00
10 Julius Peppers .75 2.00
11 Joey Harrington .30 .75
12 Jabar Gaffney .30 .75
13 Antonio Bryant .50 1.25
14 Ladell Betts .50 1.25
15 Ron Johnson .40 1.00

2002 Fleer Premium All-Rookie Team Memorabilia

Randomly inserted in packs,this 8 card set features the hottest first year players in the NFL along with a swatch of game used jersey. Cards were serial numbered to 50.

STATED PRINT RUN 50 SER.#'d SETS
1 T.J. Duckett 4.00 10.00
2 DeShaun Foster 6.00 15.00
3 Jabar Gaffney 4.00 10.00
4 William Green 5.00 12.00
5 Joey Harrington 4.00 10.00
6 Ashley Lelie 4.00 10.00
7 Julius Peppers 10.00 25.00
8 Donte Stallworth 6.00 15.00

2002 Fleer Premium Fantasy Team

Randomly inserted in packs,this 20 cards set features top notch fantasy football scorers and were serial numbered to 1200.

COMPLETE SET (20) 25.00 60.00
STATED PRINT RUN 1200 SER.#'d SETS
1 Kurt Warner .75 2.00
2 Peyton Manning 2.50 6.00
3 Brett Favre 2.00 5.00
4 Michael Vick .75 2.00
5 Tom Brady 5.00 12.00
6 Edgerrin James .75 2.00
7 Marshall Faulk .75 2.00
8 Ricky Williams .75 2.00
9 Emmitt Smith 1.50 4.00
10 Anthony Thomas .75 2.00
11 Randy Moss .75 2.00
12 Jerry Rice 2.00 5.00
13 Marvin Harrison .75 2.00
14 Chris Chambers .60 1.50
15 Torry Holt .75 2.00
16 David Carr .60 1.50
17 Joey Harrington .60 1.50
18 William Green .75 2.00
19 Donte Stallworth 1.00 2.50
20 Ashley Lelie .60 1.50

2002 Fleer Premium Fantasy Team Memorabilia

Inserted in packs at a rate of 1:60 hobby and 1:240 retail, this 20-card set features top-notch fantasy football scorers along with a swatch of game used jersey or pants.

STATED ODDS 1:60 HOB, 1:240 RET
1 Tom Brady 20.00 50.00
2 Brett Favre 8.00 20.00
3 William Green 3.00 8.00
4 Joey Harrington 2.50 6.00
5 Marvin Harrison Pants 3.00 8.00
6 Torry Holt 3.00 8.00
7 Edgerrin James 3.00 8.00
8 Randy Moss 3.00 8.00
9 Jerry Rice 8.00 20.00
10 Emmitt Smith 6.00 15.00
11 Anthony Thomas 3.00 8.00
12 Kurt Warner 3.00 8.00
13 Ricky Williams 3.00 8.00

2002 Fleer Premium Fantasy Team Memorabilia Duals

Randomly inserted in packs,this 5 card set features a swatch of game worn jersey patch and a swatch of sideline cap. Cards were hand numbered on back to 75.

STATED PRINT RUN 75 SER.#'d SETS
1 William Green 8.00 20.00
2 Joey Harrington 6.00 15.00
3 Donte Stallworth 10.00 25.00
4 Anthony Thomas 8.00 20.00
5 Michael Vick 8.00 20.00

2002 Fleer Premium Prem Team

Inserted in packs at a rate of 1:12 hobby and retail, this 27-card set features premium players at each position.

COMPLETE SET (27) 50.00 100.00
STATED ODDS 1:12 HOB/RET
*RUBY/500: .5X TO 1.2X BASIC INSERTS
RUBY PRINT RUN 500 SER.#'d SETS
1 Jeff Garcia 1.00 2.50
2 Garrison Hearst 1.00 2.50
3 Emmitt Smith 2.50 6.00
4 Brett Favre 3.00 8.00
5 Ahman Green 1.25 3.00
6 Plaxico Burress 1.00 2.50
7 Jerome Bettis 1.50 4.00
8 Kordell Stewart 1.00 2.50
9 Kendrell Bell 1.00 2.50
10 Randall Cunningham 1.25 3.00
11 Donovan McNabb 1.25 3.00
12 Duce Staley 1.00 2.50
13 Chad Lewis 1.00 2.50
14 Ricky Williams 1.25 3.00
15 Zach Thomas 1.25 3.00
16 Rich Gannon 1.25 3.00
17 Jerry Rice 3.00 8.00
18 Tim Brown 1.50 4.00
19 Brian Urlacher 1.50 4.00
20 Marcus Robinson 1.25 3.00
21 Anthony Thomas 1.25 3.00
22 Kurt Warner 1.25 3.00
23 Marshall Faulk 1.25 3.00
24 Isaac Bruce 1.50 4.00
25 Brian Griese 1.00 2.50
26 Terrell Davis 1.25 3.00
27 Ed McCaffrey 1.25 3.00

2002 Fleer Premium Prem Team Jerseys

Inserted in packs at a rate of 1:10 hobby and 1:65 retail,this 15 card set features premium players along with a swatch of game used jersey.

STATED ODDS 1:10 HOB, 1:65 RET
1 Jerome Bettis 6.00 15.00
2 Tim Brown 4.00 10.00
3 Terrell Davis 3.00 8.00
4 Brett Favre 8.00 20.00
5 Rich Gannon 3.00 8.00
6 Jeff Garcia 2.50 6.00
7 Brian Griese 2.50 6.00
8 Jerry Rice 8.00 20.00
9 Emmitt Smith 6.00 15.00
10 Duce Staley 2.50 6.00
11 Anthony Thomas 3.00 8.00
12 Brian Urlacher 4.00 10.00
13 Kurt Warner 3.00 8.00
14 Ricky Williams 3.00 8.00
15 Donovan McNabb 3.00 8.00

2002 Fleer Premium Prem Team Jersey Patches

Randomly inserted in packs,this 13 card set features premium players along with a swatch of game used jersey patch. Cards were serial numbered to 100.

STATED PRINT RUN 100 SER.#'d SETS
1 Jerome Bettis 15.00 40.00
2 Tim Brown 10.00 25.00
3 Brett Favre 20.00 50.00
4 Rich Gannon 8.00 20.00
5 Jeff Garcia 6.00 15.00
6 Brian Griese 6.00 15.00
7 Donovan McNabb 8.00 20.00
8 Jerry Rice 20.00 50.00
9 Emmitt Smith 15.00 40.00
10 Duce Staley 6.00 15.00
11 Kordell Stewart 6.00 15.00
12 Anthony Thomas 8.00 20.00
13 Brian Urlacher 10.00 25.00
14 Kurt Warner 8.00 20.00
15 Ricky Williams 8.00 20.00

2012 Fleer Retro Metal Universe

COMPLETE SET (100) 10.00 25.00
THREE METAL CARDS PER PACK
M1 Troy Aikman .40 1.00
M2 Joe Theismann .25 .60
M3 Jim Plunkett .25 .60
M4 Roger Staubach .40 1.00
M5 Johnny Rodgers .25 .60
M6 Tim Tebow .30 .75
M7 Tony Dorsett .30 .75
M8 Dan Marino .60 1.50
M9 Jim Kelly .30 .75
M10 Bart Starr .50 1.25
M11 Billy Sims .25 .60
M12 John Elway .60 1.50
M13 Jerry Rice .50 1.25
M14 Ken Stabler .30 .75
M15 Johnny Lattner .20 .50
M16 Jerome Bettis .30 .75
M17 Anthony Carter .20 .50
M18 Daryle Lamonica .20 .50
M19 Don Maynard .25 .60
M20 Drew Bledsoe .40 1.00
M21 George Rogers .20 .50
M22 Barry Sanders .60 1.50
M23 Garrison Hearst .20 .50
M24 Charlie Ward .20 .50
M25 Dan Fouts .25 .60
M26 Roger Craig .25 .60
M27 Mike Rozier .20 .50
M28 Bo Jackson .50 1.25
M29 Bruce Smith .25 .60
M30 Archie Manning .30 .75
M31 Rich Gannon .20 .50
M32 Vinny Testaverde .20 .50
M33 Steve Young .40 1.00
M34 Archie Griffin .20 .50
M35 Aaron Rodgers .60 1.50
M36 Joe Namath .60 1.50
M37 Brian Bosworth .25 .60
M38 Doug Flutie .25 .60
M39 Earl Campbell .30 .75
M40 Drew Brees .50 1.25
M41 Robert Griffin III .25 .60
M42 Trent Richardson .20 .50
M43 Justin Blackmon .20 .50
M44 Ryan Tannehill .30 .75
M45 Michael Floyd .20 .50
M46 Brandon Weeden .20 .50
M47 Doug Martin .30 .75
M48 A.J. Jenkins .20 .50
M49 Kendall Wright .20 .50
M50 Brock Osweiler .20 .50
M51 Nick Foles .50 1.25
M52 Brian Quick .20 .50
M53 Case Keenum .40 1.00
M54 Kellen Moore .25 .60
M55 Coby Fleener .20 .50
M56 Stephen Hill .20 .50
M57 Alshon Jeffery .40 1.00
M58 Isaiah Pead .20 .50
M59 Ryan Broyles .20 .50
M60 LaMichael James .20 .50
M61 Rueben Randle .20 .50
M62 DeVier Posey .20 .50
M63 Russell Wilson 1.50 4.00
M64 Mohamed Sanu .30 .75
M65 Bernard Pierce .20 .50
M66 Travis Benjamin .20 .50
M67 Kirk Cousins .75 2.00
M68 Jarius Wright .20 .50
M69 Nick Toon .20 .50
M70 Juron Criner .20 .50
M71 Melvin Ingram .20 .50
M72 Dwayne Allen .20 .50
M73 Cyrus Gray .20 .50
M74 B.J. Cunningham .20 .50
M75 Dan Herron .20 .50
M76 Matt Kalil .20 .50
M77 Mark Barron .20 .50
M78 Luke Kuechly .50 1.25
M79 Stephon Gilmore .25 .60
M80 Dontari Poe .20 .50
M81 Michael Brockers .20 .50
M82 Dre Kirkpatrick .20 .50
M83 Shea McClellin .25 .60
M84 David DeCastro .20 .50
M85 Dont'a Hightower .30 .75
M86 Whitney Mercilus .20 .50
M87 Andre Branch .20 .50
M88 Janoris Jenkins .25 .60
M89 Cordy Glenn .25 .60
M90 Mychal Kendricks .30 .75
M91 Bobby Wagner .30 .75
M92 Kendall Reyes .20 .50
M93 Lavonte David .30 .75
M94 Casey Hayward .20 .50
M95 Ronnie Hillman .20 .50
M96 T.J. Graham .20 .50
M97 Michael Egnew .20 .50
M98 Mike Martin .25 .60
M99 Devon Wylie .20 .50
M100 Alameda Ta'amu .25 .60

2012 Fleer Retro Metal Universe Precious Metal Gems Blue

*1-40 VETS/50: 15X TO 40X BASIC CARDS
*41-100 ROOKIE/50: 10X TO 25X BASIC CARD
M44 Ryan Tannehill 8.00 20.00
M46 Brandon Weeden 5.00 12.00
M63 Russell Wilson 40.00 100.00
M78 Luke Kuechly 20.00 40.00

2012 Fleer Retro Metal Universe Precious Metal Gems Red

*1-40 VETS/100: 10X TO 25X BASIC CARD
*41-100 ROOKIE/100: 6X TO 15X BASIC CARD
M44 Ryan Tannehill 5.00 12.00
M63 Russell Wilson 40.00 100.00

2012 Fleer Retro 1960 Fleer

60AG Archie Griffin 3.00 8.00
60AR Aaron Rodgers 8.00 20.00
60BJ Bo Jackson 6.00 15.00
60BS Barry Sanders 12.00 30.00
60DB Drew Bledsoe 6.00 15.00
60DM Dan Marino 12.00 30.00
60EC Earl Campbell 5.00 12.00
60JE John Elway 8.00 20.00
60JK Jim Kelly 5.00 12.00
60JN Joe Namath 12.00 30.00
60JR Jerry Rice 8.00 20.00
60RG Robert Griffin III 2.00 5.00
60RS Roger Staubach 6.00 15.00
60SM Bruce Smith 4.00 10.00
60ST Bart Starr 8.00 20.00
60SY Steve Young 6.00 15.00
60TA Troy Aikman 6.00 15.00
60TD Tony Dorsett 5.00 12.00
60TT Tim Tebow 5.00 12.00
60WM Warren Moon 5.00 12.00

2012 Fleer Retro 1960 Fleer Autographs

EXCH EXPIRATION: 2/13/2015
60AG Archie Griffin 15.00 40.00
60AR Aaron Rodgers SP EXCH 125.00 225.00
60BJ Bo Jackson SP 50.00 100.00
60BS Barry Sanders SP 125.00 200.00
60DB Drew Bledsoe 40.00 80.00
60DM Dan Marino SP EXCH 125.00 200.00
60EC Earl Campbell 12.00 30.00
60JE John Elway SP 75.00 150.00
60JK Jim Kelly 60.00 120.00
60JN Joe Namath SP EXCH 60.00 100.00
60JR Jerry Rice SP 75.00 150.00
60RG Robert Griffin III 5.00 12.00
60RS Roger Staubach SP EXCH 40.00 80.00
60SM Bruce Smith SP EXCH
60ST Bart Starr SP 75.00 125.00
60SY Steve Young SP EXCH
60TA Troy Aikman SP 100.00 175.00
60TD Tony Dorsett SP 25.00 50.00
60TT Tim Tebow 40.00 80.00
60WM Warren Moon 25.00 50.00

2012 Fleer Retro 1961 Fleer

61AC Anthony Carter 1.50 4.00
61AM Archie Manning 2.50 6.00
61AW Andre Ware 2.00 5.00
61BC Billy Cannon 2.50 6.00
61BS Billy Sims 2.00 5.00
61CW Charlie Ward 1.50 4.00
61DF Doug Flutie 2.00 5.00
61DL Daryle Lamonica 1.50 4.00
61DM Don Maynard 2.00 5.00
61GH Garrison Hearst 1.50 4.00
61GR George Rogers 1.50 4.00
61JB Jerome Bettis 2.50 6.00
61JL Johnny Lattner 1.50 4.00
61JP Jim Plunkett 2.00 5.00
61JR Johnny Rodgers 2.00 5.00
61JT Joe Theismann 2.50 6.00
61KS Ken Stabler 2.50 6.00
61MR Mike Rozier 1.50 4.00
61NB Nick Buoniconti 1.50 4.00
61PL Jake Plummer 1.50 4.00
61RC Roger Craig 2.00 5.00
61RG Rich Gannon 1.50 4.00
61RR Rudy Ruettiger 2.00 5.00
61TF Tommie Frazier 1.50 4.00
61VT Vinny Testaverde 1.50 4.00

2012 Fleer Retro 1961 Fleer Autographs

61AC Anthony Carter 15.00 40.00
61AM Archie Manning EXCH
61AW Andre Ware EXCH
61BC Billy Cannon EXCH
61BS Billy Sims 10.00 25.00
61CW Charlie Ward EXCH
61DF Doug Flutie EXCH
61DL Daryle Lamonica 10.00 25.00
61DM Don Maynard EXCH
61GH Garrison Hearst EXCH 10.00 25.00
61GR George Rogers EXCH
61JB Jerome Bettis 50.00 100.00
61JL Johnny Lattner
61JP Jim Plunkett EXCH 15.00 40.00
61JR Johnny Rodgers 12.00 30.00
61JT Joe Theismann 15.00 40.00
61MR Mike Rozier EXCH
61NB Nick Buoniconti 15.00 40.00
61PL Jake Plummer 12.00 30.00
61RC Roger Craig 10.00 25.00
61RG Rich Gannon EXCH
61RR Rudy Ruettiger 12.00 30.00
61TF Tommie Frazier EXCH 10.00 25.00
61VT Vinny Testaverde

2012 Fleer Retro 1962 Fleer

62AJ A.J. Jenkins .75 2.00
62AT Al Toon 1.50 4.00
62BO Brock Osweiler .75 2.00
62BP Bernard Pierce .75 2.00
62BQ Brian Quick 1.25 3.00
62BR Tim Brown 2.50 6.00
62BW Brandon Weeden .75 2.00
62CF Coby Fleener .75 2.00
62CK Case Keenum 1.50 4.00
62CW Chris Weinke 1.50 4.00
62DM Doug Martin 1.25 3.00
62DP DeVier Posey 1.25 3.00
62IP Isaiah Pead 1.25 3.00
62JA Jason White 2.00 5.00
62JB Justin Blackmon .75 2.00
62JE Alshon Jeffery 1.50 4.00
62JH John Hannah 2.50 6.00
62JW Joe Washington 1.50 4.00
62KJ Keith Jackson 1.50 4.00
62KM Ken MacAfee 1.50 4.00
62KW Kendall Wright .75 2.00
62LJ LaMichael James .75 2.00
62MF Michael Floyd .75 2.00
62MO Kellen Moore 1.00 2.50
62MS Mohamed Sanu 1.25 3.00
62NF Nick Foles 2.00 5.00
62RB Ryan Broyles .75 2.00
62RP Rodney Peete 1.50 4.00
62RR Rueben Randle .75 2.00
62RT Ryan Tannehill 1.25 3.00
62RW Russell Wilson 8.00 20.00
62SH Stephen Hill .75 2.00
62TB Travis Benjamin .75 2.00
62TR Trent Richardson .75 2.00
62WH Charles White 1.50 4.00

2012 Fleer Retro 1962 Fleer Autographs

62AJ A.J. Jenkins
62AT Al Toon
62BO Brock Osweiler 15.00 40.00
62BP Bernard Pierce EXCH
62BQ Brian Quick
62BR Tim Brown 20.00 40.00
62BW Brandon Weeden 12.00 30.00
62CF Coby Fleener
62CK Case Keenum SP
62CW Chris Weinke
62DM Doug Martin EXCH 12.00 30.00
62DP DeVier Posey 10.00 25.00
62IP Isaiah Pead 10.00 25.00
62JA Jason White 10.00 25.00
62JB Justin Blackmon 8.00 20.00
62JE Alshon Jeffery EXCH 15.00 40.00
62JH John Hannah EXCH
62JW Joe Washington
62KJ Keith Jackson 10.00 25.00
62KM Ken MacAfee 8.00 20.00
62KW Kendall Wright 8.00 20.00
62LJ LaMichael James 12.00 30.00
62MF Michael Floyd
62MO Kellen Moore EXCH
62MS Mohamed Sanu 10.00 25.00
62NF Nick Foles EXCH 10.00 25.00
62RB Ryan Broyles EXCH
62RP Rodney Peete EXCH
62RR Rueben Randle EXCH
62RT Ryan Tannehill
62RW Russell Wilson 75.00 150.00
62SH Stephen Hill
62TB Travis Benjamin EXCH
62TR Trent Richardson 15.00 40.00
62WH Charles White EXCH 10.00 25.00

2012 Fleer Retro 1963 Fleer

63AB Andre Branch 1.25 3.00
63AT Alameda Ta'amu 1.25 3.00
63BA Mark Barron .75 2.00
63BC B.J. Cunningham 1.25 3.00
63BW Bobby Wagner 1.25 3.00
63CG Cordy Glenn 1.25 3.00
63CH Casey Hayward .75 2.00
63DA Dwayne Allen .75 2.00
63DB Drew Brees 2.50 6.00
63DD David DeCastro .75 2.00
63DH Dont'a Hightower 1.25 3.00
63DK Dre Kirkpatrick .75 2.00
63DP Dontari Poe .75 2.00
63DW Devon Wylie 1.25 3.00
63GB Gary Beban 1.50 4.00
63GR Cyrus Gray .75 2.00
63HE Dan Herron 1.25 3.00
63JC Juron Criner 1.25 3.00
63JJ Janoris Jenkins 1.00 2.50
63JW Jarius Wright .75 2.00
63KC Kirk Cousins 3.00 8.00
63KE Mychal Kendricks 1.25 3.00
63KR Kendall Reyes 1.25 3.00
63LD Lavonte David 1.25 3.00
63LK Luke Kuechly 2.00 5.00
63MB Michael Brockers .75 2.00
63ME Michael Egnew 1.25 3.00
63MI Melvin Ingram .75 2.00
63MK Matt Kalil .75 2.00
63MM Mike Martin 1.00 2.50
63NT Nick Toon 1.25 3.00
63RG Roman Gabriel 1.50 4.00
63RH Ronnie Hillman .75 2.00
63RS Robert Smith 1.50 4.00
63SG Stephon Gilmore 1.00 2.50
63SM Shea McClellin 1.00 2.50
63SO Steve Owens 2.00 5.00
63TG T.J. Graham 1.25 3.00
63WM Whitney Mercilus .75 2.00
63WS Warren Sapp 2.00 5.00

2012 Fleer Retro 1963 Fleer Autographs

EXCH EXPIRATION: 2/13/2015
63AB Andre Branch
63AT Alameda Ta'amu
63BA Mark Barron 12.00 30.00
63BC B.J. Cunningham EXCH 12.00 30.00
63BW Bobby Wagner 10.00 25.00
63CG Cordy Glenn EXCH
63CH Casey Hayward EXCH 8.00 20.00
63DA Dwayne Allen
63DB Drew Brees EXCH
63DD David DeCastro
63DH Dont'a Hightower 10.00 25.00
63DK Dre Kirkpatrick 8.00 20.00
63DP Dontari Poe EXCH 8.00 20.00
63DW Devon Wylie
63GB Gary Beban
63GR Cyrus Gray EXCH
63HE Dan Herron 10.00 25.00
63JC Juron Criner 10.00 25.00
63JJ Janoris Jenkins 10.00 25.00
63JW Jarius Wright EXCH 8.00 20.00
63KC Kirk Cousins 12.00 30.00
63KE Mychal Kendricks EXCH
63KR Kendall Reyes EXCH 10.00 25.00
63LD Lavonte David EXCH
63LK Luke Kuechly EXCH
63MB Michael Brockers
63ME Michael Egnew EXCH
63MI Melvin Ingram 10.00 25.00
63MK Matt Kalil
63MM Mike Martin EXCH
63NT Nick Toon EXCH
63RG Roman Gabriel 10.00 25.00
63RH Ronnie Hillman 12.00 30.00
63RS Robert Smith EXCH 20.00 40.00
63SG Stephon Gilmore
63SM Shea McClellin EXCH
63SO Steve Owens 10.00 25.00
63TG T.J. Graham 8.00 20.00
63WM Whitney Mercilus 8.00 20.00
63WS Warren Sapp EXCH 20.00 40.00

2012 Fleer Retro Autographics 1997

97AB Andre Branch 5.00 12.00
97AC Anthony Carter 10.00 25.00
97AJ Alshon Jeffery 6.00 15.00
97AM Archie Manning 12.00 30.00
97BE Jerome Bettis 35.00 60.00
97BS Bart Starr 50.00 100.00
97BT Brandon Thompson SP
97CJ Cam Johnson SP
97CW Charlie Ward 4.00 10.00
97DA Dwayne Allen 3.00 8.00
97DK Dre Kirkpatrick SP
97DP DeVier Posey 5.00 12.00
97EP Eric Page 4.00 10.00
97GA Rich Gannon 4.00 10.00
97GC Greg Childs 3.00 8.00
97GR George Rogers 4.00 10.00
97GU Ray Guy 5.00 12.00
97HS Harrison Smith SP
97JB Justin Blackmon SP 6.00 15.00
97JC Josh Chapman 6.00 15.00
97JL Johnny Lattner 4.00 10.00
97KC Kirk Cousins 12.00 30.00
97KM Kellen Moore 4.00 10.00
97KO Kelechi Osemele 4.00 10.00
97MA Ken MacAfee 4.00 10.00
97MB Mark Barron 3.00 8.00
97MF Michael Floyd 3.00 8.00
97MI Melvin Ingram 3.00 8.00
97MR Mike Rozier 4.00 10.00
97MS Mohamed Sanu 5.00 12.00
97MT Marc Tyler 3.00 8.00
97NF Nick Foles 8.00 20.00
97NT Nick Toon 3.00 8.00
97RB Ryan Broyles 10.00 25.00
97RG Robert Griffin III SP 4.00 10.00
97RH Ronnie Hillman 8.00 20.00
97RL Ronnie Lott 15.00 35.00
97RP Rodney Peete 4.00 10.00
97RS Robert Smith 8.00 20.00
97RT Ryan Tannehill SP 5.00 12.00
97RW Russell Wilson 50.00 100.00
97SO Steve Owens 5.00 12.00
97TB Tedy Bruschi 10.00 20.00
97TF Tommie Frazier 5.00 12.00
97TP Tauren Poole SP 6.00 15.00
97TR Trent Richardson SP 15.00 40.00
97VT Vinny Testaverde 8.00 20.00
97WA Joe Washington 6.00 15.00
97WE Chris Weinke 4.00 10.00
97WH Charles White 4.00 10.00

2012 Fleer Retro Autographics 1998

98AJ Alshon Jeffery 6.00 15.00
98AK Andy Katzenmoyer 8.00 20.00
98AM Alfred Morris 3.00 8.00
98BC Billy Cannon 15.00 30.00
98BP Bernard Pierce 6.00 15.00
98BQ Brian Quick 3.00 8.00
98BS Bruce Smith 10.00 25.00
98BW Brandon Weeden 3.00 8.00
98CW Chris Weinke 4.00 10.00
98DA Dwayne Allen 3.00 8.00
98DB Drew Brees SP 40.00 80.00
98DF Dan Fouts 20.00 40.00
98DM Don Maynard 5.00 12.00
98FL Doug Flutie 12.50 25.00
98GB Gary Beban 4.00 10.00
98GH Garrison Hearst 4.00 10.00
98GR Robert Griffin III SP 4.00 10.00
98GU Ray Guy 5.00 12.00
98JB Justin Blackmon 3.00 8.00
98JC Jared Crick 3.00 8.00
98JF Jeff Fuller 3.00 8.00
98JH John Hannah 5.00 12.00
98JL Johnny Lattner 4.00 10.00
98KC Kirk Cousins 12.00 30.00
98KM Ken MacAfee 4.00 10.00
98KT Keith Tandy 4.00 10.00
98KW Kendall Wright 3.00 8.00
98LJ LaMichael James 3.00 8.00
98ME Davin Meggett SP
98MF Michael Floyd 3.00 8.00
98MI Melvin Ingram SP 8.00 20.00
98MO Kellen Moore 4.00 10.00
98MR Mike Rozier 4.00 10.00
98MS Mohamed Sanu 5.00 12.00
98NF Nick Foles 8.00 20.00
98NT Nick Toon 3.00 8.00
98QC Quinton Coples SP 8.00 20.00
98RG Rich Gannon 4.00 10.00
98RT Ryan Tannehill 5.00 12.00
98RW Russell Wilson 40.00 80.00
98SI Billy Sims 5.00 12.00
98SY Steve Young SP 60.00 120.00
98TB Tedy Bruschi 10.00 20.00
98TF Tommie Frazier 5.00 12.00
98TG T.J. Graham SP
98TR Trent Richardson SP 15.00 40.00
98TS Tyler Shoemaker 4.00 10.00
98WA Charlie Ward 5.00 12.00
98WM Whitney Mercilus 3.00 8.00
98WS Warren Sapp 8.00 20.00

2012 Fleer Retro Autographics 1999

99AJ Alshon Jeffery 6.00 15.00
99AK Andy Katzenmoyer 6.00 15.00
99AM Archie Manning 12.00 30.00
99BQ Brian Quick 3.00 8.00
99BW Brandon Weeden 3.00 8.00
99CU Courtney Upshaw 4.00 10.00
99CW Charlie Ward 5.00 12.00
99DD David DeCastro 3.00 8.00

99DJ Dwight Jones 3.00 8.00
99DM Doug Martin 5.00 12.00
99GA Rich Gannon 4.00 10.00
99GH Garrison Hearst 4.00 10.00
99GU Ray Guy 5.00 12.00
99IP Isaiah Pead 3.00 8.00
99JA Joe Adams 4.00 10.00
99JB Justin Blackmon 3.00 8.00
99JH John Hannah 5.00 12.00
99JJ Jordan Jefferson SP
99JL Johnny Lattner 4.00 10.00
99JP Jake Plummer 5.00 12.00
99KC Kirk Cousins 12.00 30.00
99KJ Keith Jackson 6.00 15.00
99KM Kellen Moore 4.00 10.00
99KO Kelechi Osemele 4.00 10.00
99MA Don Maynard 5.00 12.00
99MB Mark Barron 3.00 8.00
99MC Da'Jon McKnight SP
99ME Michael Egnew 3.00 8.00
99MF Michael Floyd 3.00 8.00
99MI Melvin Ingram EXCH 3.00 8.00
99MM Marquis Maze 4.00 10.00
99MN Marvin McNutt 6.00 15.00
99MS Mohamed Sanu 5.00 12.00
99MT Marc Tyler 3.00 8.00
99NF Nick Foles 8.00 20.00
99NT Nick Toon 3.00 8.00
99PH Paul Hornung 8.00 20.00
99RC Roger Craig 6.00 15.00
99RG Robert Griffin III SP 4.00 10.00
99RL Ryan Lindley 4.00 10.00
99RP Rodney Peete 4.00 10.00
99RR Rueben Randle 3.00 8.00
99RT Ryan Tannehill 5.00 12.00
99RW Russell Wilson 60.00 100.00
99TB Tedy Bruschi 10.00 20.00
99TD Ty Detmer 5.00 12.00
99TF Tommie Frazier 5.00 12.00
99TP Tauren Poole 6.00 15.00
99TR Trent Richardson SP 15.00 40.00
99WE Chris Weinke 4.00 10.00

2012 Fleer Retro Autographics 2000

00AJ A.J. Jenkins 3.00 8.00
00AK Andy Katzenmoyer 8.00 20.00
00AT Al Toon SP 8.00 20.00
00AW Andre Ware 5.00 12.00
00BQ Brian Quick 3.00 8.00
00BW Brandon Weeden 3.00 8.00
00CW Charles White 4.00 10.00
00DH Dan Herron 6.00 15.00
00DJ Dwight Jones 3.00 8.00
00DP Dan Persa SP
00GA Rich Gannon 5.00 12.00
00GH Garrison Hearst 4.00 10.00
00GU Ray Guy 5.00 12.00
00JB Justin Blackmon SP 6.00 15.00
00JH John Hannah 5.00 12.00
00JJ Janoris Jenkins 4.00 10.00
00JL Johnny Lattner 4.00 10.00
00JM Jonathan Martin SP
00JP Jake Plummer 5.00 12.00
00JW Jason White 5.00 12.00
00KC Kirk Cousins 12.00 30.00
00KM Kellen Moore 4.00 10.00
00KW Kendall Wright 3.00 8.00
00LJ LaMichael James 3.00 8.00
00LK Luke Kuechly 8.00 20.00
00MA Keshawn Martin 4.00 10.00
00MB Mark Barron 3.00 8.00
00MF Michael Floyd 3.00 8.00
00MI Melvin Ingram 3.00 8.00
00MM Marvin McNutt 6.00 15.00
00MR Mike Rozier 4.00 10.00
00MS Mohamed Sanu 5.00 12.00
00MT Marc Tyler 3.00 8.00
00NF Nick Foles 8.00 20.00
00NT Nick Toon 3.00 8.00
00PE Pat Edwards SP
00RG Robert Griffin III SP 4.00 10.00
00RL Ronnell Lewis 3.00 8.00
00RO Roman Gabriel SP 6.00 15.00
00RP Rodney Peete 4.00 10.00
00RT Ryan Tannehill SP 5.00 12.00
00RW Russell Wilson 50.00 100.00
00TB Tedy Bruschi 10.00 20.00
00TC Tank Carder 5.00 12.00
00TF Tommie Frazier 4.00 10.00
00TR Trent Richardson SP 15.00 40.00
00VT Vinny Testaverde 8.00 20.00
00WA Charlie Ward 5.00 12.00
00WS Warren Sapp 8.00 20.00

2012 Fleer Retro E-X A Cut Above

1 Drew Brees 6.00 15.00
2 Doug Flutie 4.00 10.00
3 Herschel Walker 5.00 12.00
4 Steve Young 6.00 15.00
5 Justin Blackmon 2.00 5.00
6 Barry Sanders 12.00 30.00
7 Joe Theismann 4.00 10.00
8 Tim Tebow 5.00 12.00
9 Bo Jackson 8.00 20.00
10 Dan Marino 12.00 30.00
11 Janoris Jenkins 4.00 10.00
12 Drew Bledsoe 6.00 15.00
13 Aaron Rodgers 12.00 30.00
14 Jim Kelly 5.00 12.00
15 Jerry Rice 8.00 20.00
16 Russell Wilson 20.00 50.00
17 Joe Namath 12.00 30.00
18 Trent Richardson 2.00 5.00
19 John Elway 10.00 25.00
20 Troy Aikman 6.00 15.00
21 Earl Campbell 5.00 12.00
22 Brandon Weeden 2.00 5.00
23 Robert Griffin III 2.50 6.00
24 Alfred Morris 2.00 5.00
25 Ryan Tannehill 3.00 8.00

2012 Fleer Retro Flair Showcase Hot Hands

HH1 Bo Jackson 8.00 20.00
HH2 Roger Staubach 6.00 15.00
HH3 Dan Marino 12.00 30.00
HH4 John Elway 10.00 25.00
HH5 Barry Sanders 12.00 30.00
HH6 Bruce Smith 4.00 10.00
HH7 Jerry Rice 8.00 20.00
HH8 Tim Tebow 5.00 12.00
HH9 Steve Young 6.00 15.00
HH10 Robert Griffin III 2.50 6.00
HH11 Alfred Morris 2.00 5.00
HH12 Michael Floyd 2.00 5.00
HH13 Brian Quick 3.00 8.00
HH14 Justin Blackmon 2.00 5.00
HH15 Joe Namath 12.00 30.00
HH16 A.J. Jenkins 2.00 5.00
HH17 Trent Richardson 2.00 5.00
HH18 Bart Starr 8.00 20.00
HH19 Drew Bledsoe 6.00 15.00
HH20 Brandon Weeden 2.00 5.00
HH21 Doug Martin 3.00 8.00
HH22 Brock Osweiler 2.00 5.00
HH23 Dan Fouts 4.00 10.00
HH24 Kendall Wright 2.00 5.00
HH25 Tony Dorsett 5.00 12.00
HH26 Ryan Tannehill 3.00 8.00
HH27 Aaron Rodgers 12.00 30.00
HH28 Russell Wilson 20.00 50.00
HH29 Jim Kelly 5.00 12.00
HH30 Nick Foles 5.00 12.00
HH31 Janoris Jenkins 4.00 10.00
HH32 Earl Campbell 5.00 12.00
HH33 Archie Griffin 5.00 12.00
HH34 Troy Aikman 6.00 15.00
HH35 Drew Brees 6.00 15.00

2012 Fleer Retro Flair Showcase Legacy Row 0

FL1 Robert Griffin III 2.50 6.00
FL2 Jerome Bettis 4.00 10.00
FL3 Paul Hornung 4.00 10.00
FL4 Earl Campbell 4.00 10.00
FL5 Joe Namath 6.00 15.00
FL6 Drew Bledsoe 6.00 15.00
FL7 Vinny Testaverde 2.50 6.00
FL8 Charles White 2.50 6.00
FL9 Warren Moon 4.00 10.00
FL10 Trent Richardson 2.00 5.00
FL11 Bart Starr 6.00 15.00
FL12 Drew Brees 6.00 15.00
FL13 Anthony Carter 2.50 6.00
FL14 Justin Blackmon 2.00 5.00
FL15 Herschel Walker 4.00 10.00
FL16 Ozzie Newsome 3.00 8.00
FL17 Roger Staubach 5.00 12.00
FL18 Tim Brown 4.00 10.00
FL19 Rich Gannon 2.50 6.00
FL20 Mark Barron 2.00 5.00
FL21 Ken Stabler 4.00 10.00
FL22 Roman Gabriel 2.50 6.00
FL23 Brock Osweiler 2.00 5.00
FL24 Roger Craig 3.00 8.00
FL25 Steve Young 5.00 12.00
FL26 Kellen Moore 2.50 6.00
FL27 Ronnie Lott 3.00 8.00
FL28 Tim Tebow 6.00 15.00
FL29 Nick Foles 5.00 12.00
FL30 Brandon Weeden 2.00 5.00
FL31 Robert Smith 2.50 6.00
FL32 Brian Bosworth 3.00 8.00
FL33 Billy Sims 3.00 8.00
FL34 A.J. Jenkins 2.00 5.00
FL35 Kendall Wright 2.00 5.00
FL36 Janoris Jenkins 2.50 6.00
FL37 Daryle Lamonica 2.50 6.00
FL38 Johnny Rodgers 3.00 8.00
FL39 Warren Sapp 3.00 8.00
FL40 Garrison Hearst 2.50 6.00
FL41 Jason White 3.00 8.00
FL42 Ryan Broyles 2.00 5.00
FL43 Russell Wilson 25.00 50.00
FL44 Ken MacAfee 2.50 6.00
FL45 Luke Kuechly 5.00 12.00
FL46 Joe Washington 3.00 8.00
FL47 Ricky Watters 3.00 8.00
FL48 Nick Buoniconti 2.50 6.00
FL49 Alfred Morris 2.00 5.00
FL50 Dont'a Hightower 3.00 8.00
FL51 Rodney Peete 2.50 6.00
FL52 Coby Fleener 2.00 5.00
FL53 Jim Plunkett 3.00 8.00
FL54 Keith Jackson 2.50 6.00
FL55 Archie Griffin 2.50 6.00
FL56 Al Toon 2.50 6.00
FL57 Ryan Tannehill 3.00 8.00
FL58 Jake Plummer 2.50 6.00
FL59 Gary Beban 2.50 6.00
FL60 Mike Rozier 2.50 6.00
FL61 Case Keenum 4.00 10.00
FL62 Billy Cannon 2.50 6.00
FL63 Stephen Hill 2.00 5.00
FL64 Johnny Lattner 2.50 6.00
FL65 Michael Floyd 2.00 5.00
FL66 Bruce Smith 3.00 8.00
FL67 Bo Jackson 8.00 20.00
FL68 George Rogers 2.50 6.00
FL69 Chris Weinke 2.50 6.00
FL70 LaMichael James 2.00 5.00
FL71 Alshon Jeffery 4.00 10.00
FL72 Charlie Ward 2.50 6.00
FL73 Rudy Ruettiger 3.00 8.00
FL74 Archie Manning 4.00 10.00
FL75 Isaiah Pead 2.00 5.00
FL76 Doug Flutie 3.00 8.00
FL77 Dan Fouts 3.00 8.00
FL78 Dan Marino 8.00 20.00
FL79 John Hannah 3.00 8.00
FL80 Jim Kelly 4.00 10.00
FL81 DeVier Posey 2.00 5.00
FL82 Tommie Frazier 2.50 6.00
FL83 Andy Katzenmoyer 2.50 6.00
FL84 Melvin Ingram 2.00 5.00
FL85 Ray Guy 2.50 6.00
FL86 Jerry Rice 6.00 15.00
FL87 John Elway 8.00 20.00
FL88 Rueben Randle 2.00 5.00
FL89 Aaron Rodgers 20.00 40.00
FL90 Barry Sanders 10.00 25.00
FL91 Tedy Bruschi 3.00 8.00
FL92 Ty Detmer 2.50 6.00
FL93 Brian Quick 2.50 6.00
FL94 Doug Martin 3.00 8.00
FL95 Don Maynard 3.00 8.00
FL96 Tony Dorsett 4.00 10.00
FL97 Joe Theismann 4.00 10.00
FL98 Steve Owens 3.00 8.00
FL99 Troy Aikman 6.00 15.00
FL100 Andre Ware 3.00 8.00

2012 Fleer Retro Golden Touch

1GT Steve Young 6.00 15.00
2GT Alfred Morris 2.00 5.00
3GT Russell Wilson 25.00 60.00
4GT Justin Blackmon 2.00 5.00
5GT Earl Campbell 5.00 12.00
6GT Brandon Weeden 2.00 5.00
7GT Drew Brees 6.00 15.00
8GT Herschel Walker 5.00 12.00
9GT John Elway 8.00 20.00
10GT Jerry Rice 8.00 20.00
11GT Joe Namath 8.00 20.00
12GT Ryan Tannehill 3.00 8.00
13GT Drew Bledsoe 4.00 10.00
14GT Robert Griffin III 2.50 6.00
15GT Tim Tebow 5.00 12.00
16GT Aaron Rodgers 8.00 20.00
17GT Troy Aikman 6.00 15.00
18GT Janoris Jenkins 2.50 6.00
19GT Trent Richardson 2.00 5.00
20GT Bo Jackson 6.00 15.00
21GT Dan Marino 10.00 25.00
22GT Doug Martin 3.00 8.00
23GT Barry Sanders 8.00 20.00
24GT Joe Theismann 4.00 10.00
25GT Michael Floyd 2.00 5.00

2012 Fleer Retro Jambalaya

STATED ODDS 1:360
1JB Robert Griffin III 15.00 40.00
2JB Trent Richardson 15.00 40.00
3JB Aaron Rodgers 60.00 120.00
4JB Jerry Rice 40.00 80.00
5JB John Elway 60.00 120.00
6JB Dan Marino 50.00 100.00
7JB Barry Sanders 40.00 100.00
8JB Troy Aikman 25.00 60.00
9JB Steve Young 30.00 60.00
10JB Joe Namath 60.00 120.00
11JB Drew Bledsoe 40.00 80.00
12JB Bo Jackson 50.00 100.00
13JB Roger Staubach 20.00 50.00
14JB Tony Dorsett 25.00 50.00
15JB Doug Flutie 20.00 40.00
16JB Jim Kelly 25.00 50.00
17JB Tim Tebow 40.00 100.00
18JB Archie Griffin 15.00 30.00
19JB Dan Fouts 25.00 50.00
20JB Earl Campbell 15.00 40.00
21JB Ryan Tannehill 20.00 50.00

2012 Fleer Retro Metal Universe Hardware

1H John Elway 8.00 20.00
2H Steve Young 6.00 15.00
3H Dan Fouts 4.00 10.00
4H Justin Blackmon 1.50 4.00
5H Roger Staubach 6.00 15.00
6H Jerome Bettis 5.00 12.00
7H Drew Bledsoe 4.00 10.00
8H Troy Aikman 6.00 15.00
9H Joe Theismann 4.00 10.00
10H Tim Tebow 6.00 15.00
11H Don Maynard 4.00 10.00
12H Drew Brees 5.00 12.00
13H Vinny Testaverde 3.00 8.00
14H Herschel Walker 5.00 12.00
15H Jerry Rice 10.00 25.00
16H Trent Richardson 1.50 4.00
17H Barry Sanders 8.00 20.00
18H Paul Hornung 5.00 12.00
19H Tony Dorsett 5.00 12.00
20H Bart Starr 12.00 30.00
21H Bo Jackson 8.00 20.00
22H Jake Plummer 3.00 8.00
23H Earl Campbell 5.00 12.00
24H Joe Namath 15.00 40.00
25H Jim Kelly 5.00 12.00
26H Alfred Morris 1.50 4.00
27H Aaron Rodgers 25.00 50.00
28H Doug Flutie 4.00 10.00
29H Dan Marino 12.00 30.00
30H Robert Griffin III 2.00 5.00

2012 Fleer Retro Playmakers Theatre

PM1 Janoris Jenkins 4.00 10.00
PM2 John Elway 12.00 30.00
PM3 Aaron Rodgers 20.00 50.00
PM4 Robert Griffin III 4.00 10.00
PM5 Jerome Bettis 8.00 20.00
PM6 Alfred Morris 3.00 8.00
PM7 Doug Flutie 6.00 15.00
PM8 Bo Jackson 10.00 25.00
PM9 Dan Marino 15.00 40.00
PM10 Joe Namath 25.00 50.00
PM11 Drew Bledsoe 8.00 20.00
PM12 Barry Sanders 12.00 30.00
PM13 Steve Young 10.00 25.00
PM14 Tim Tebow 8.00 20.00
PM15 Troy Aikman 10.00 25.00
PM16 Drew Brees 10.00 25.00
PM17 Jerry Rice 10.00 25.00
PM18 Russell Wilson 40.00 80.00
PM19 Earl Campbell 5.00 12.00
PM20 Vinny Testaverde 5.00 12.00

2012 Fleer Retro Premium Intimidation Nation

1IN Mark Barron 1.50 4.00
2IN Jerry Rice 8.00 20.00
3IN Janoris Jenkins 3.00 8.00
4IN Dont'a Hightower 2.50 6.00
5IN Joe Theismann 4.00 10.00
6IN Russell Wilson 20.00 40.00
7IN Bruce Smith 4.00 10.00
8IN Melvin Ingram 3.00 8.00
9IN Dan Fouts 4.00 10.00
10IN Trent Richardson 1.50 4.00
11IN Brandon Weeden 1.50 4.00
12IN Drew Brees 5.00 12.00
13IN Luke Kuechly 6.00 15.00
14IN Tim Tebow 5.00 12.00
15IN Roger Staubach 6.00 15.00
16IN Ryan Tannehill 2.50 6.00
17IN Drew Bledsoe 6.00 15.00
18IN Troy Aikman 6.00 15.00
19IN Robert Griffin III 2.00 5.00
20IN Bo Jackson 6.00 15.00
21IN Steve Young 6.00 15.00
22IN Alfred Morris 1.50 4.00
23IN Joe Namath 12.00 30.00
24IN Aaron Rodgers 12.00 30.00
25IN Bart Starr 8.00 20.00
26IN Dan Marino 10.00 25.00
27IN Herschel Walker 5.00 12.00
28IN Justin Blackmon 1.50 4.00
29IN John Elway 8.00 20.00
30IN Barry Sanders 10.00 25.00

2012 Fleer Retro Rookie Sensations

STATED ODDS 1:3
RS1 Robert Griffin III .50 1.25
RS2 Trent Richardson .40 1.00
RS3 Justin Blackmon .40 1.00
RS4 Ryan Tannehill .60 1.50
RS5 Michael Floyd .40 1.00
RS6 Brandon Weeden .40 1.00
RS7 Doug Martin 1.00 2.50
RS8 A.J. Jenkins .40 1.00
RS9 Kendall Wright .40 1.00
RS10 Brock Osweiler .40 1.00
RS11 Nick Foles 1.00 2.50
RS12 Brian Quick .40 1.00
RS13 Case Keenum .75 2.00
RS14 Kellen Moore .50 1.25
RS15 Coby Fleener .40 1.00
RS16 Stephen Hill .40 1.00
RS17 Alshon Jeffery .75 2.00
RS18 Isaiah Pead .40 1.00
RS19 Ryan Broyles .40 1.00
RS20 LaMichael James .40 1.00
RS21 Rueben Randle .40 1.00
RS22 DeVier Posey .40 1.00
RS23 Russell Wilson 5.00 12.00
RS24 Mohamed Sanu .60 1.50
RS25 Bernard Pierce .40 1.00
RS26 Travis Benjamin .40 1.00
RS27 Kirk Cousins 1.50 4.00
RS28 Jarius Wright .40 1.00
RS29 Nick Toon .40 1.00
RS30 Juron Criner .40 1.00
RS31 Melvin Ingram .40 1.00
RS32 Dwayne Allen .40 1.00
RS33 Cyrus Gray .40 1.00
RS34 B.J. Cunningham .40 1.00
RS35 Dan Herron .40 1.00
RS36 Matt Kalil .40 1.00
RS37 Mark Barron .40 1.00
RS38 Luke Kuechly 1.00 2.50
RS39 Stephon Gilmore .50 1.25
RS40 Dontari Poe .40 1.00
RS41 Michael Brockers .40 1.00
RS42 Dre Kirkpatrick .40 1.00
RS43 Shea McClellin .50 1.25
RS44 David DeCastro .40 1.00
RS45 Dont'a Hightower .60 1.50
RS46 Whitney Mercilus .40 1.00
RS47 Andre Branch .40 1.00
RS48 Janoris Jenkins .50 1.25
RS49 Cordy Glenn .50 1.25
RS50 Mychal Kendricks .60 1.50
RS51 Bobby Wagner .60 1.50
RS52 Kendall Reyes .40 1.00
RS53 Lavonte David .60 1.50
RS54 Casey Hayward .40 1.00
RS55 Ronnie Hillman .40 1.00
RS56 T.J. Graham .40 1.00
RS57 Michael Egnew .40 1.00
RS58 Mike Martin .50 1.25
RS59 Devon Wylie .40 1.00
RS60 Alameda Ta'amu .50 1.25
RS61 Ladarius Green .40 1.00
RS62 Kyle Wilber .60 1.50
RS63 Orson Charles .40 1.00
RS64 Keshawn Martin .50 1.25
RS65 Rhett Ellison .50 1.25
RS66 Greg Childs .40 1.00
RS67 Marvin Jones .40 1.00
RS68 Alfred Morris .40 1.00
RS69 Ryan Lindley .40 1.00
RS70 Marvin McNutt .40 1.00
RS71 Rishard Matthews .40 1.00
RS72 Jeremy Ebert .40 1.00
RS73 Cam Johnson .60 1.50
RS74 Eric Page .50 1.25
RS75 Brandon Bolden .60 1.50
RS76 Chandler Harnish .40 1.00
RS77 Dwight Jones .40 1.00
RS78 Jarrett Lee .60 1.50
RS79 Jeff Fuller .40 1.00
RS80 Jermaine Kearse .60 1.50
RS81 Jordan Jefferson .50 1.25
RS82 Laron Byrd .50 1.25
RS83 Lavasier Tuinei .60 1.50
RS84 Marc Tyler .40 1.00
RS85 Marquis Maze .40 1.00
RS86 Nelson Rosario .40 1.00
RS87 Stephen Garcia .60 1.50
RS88 Tauren Poole .40 1.00
RS89 Tyler Hansen .40 1.00
RS90 Tyler Shoemaker .50 1.25
RS91 Ronnell Lewis .50 1.25
RS92 Jared Crick .40 1.00
RS93 Harrison Smith .40 1.00
RS94 Pat Edwards .50 1.25
RS95 Courtney Upshaw .50 1.25
RS96 Kelechi Osemele .40 1.00
RS97 Joe Adams .40 1.00
RS98 Keith Tandy .50 1.25
RS99 Da'Jon McKnight .50 1.25
RS100 Dan Persa .50 1.25

2012 Fleer Retro Rookie Sensations Autographs

EXCH EXPIRATION: 2/13/2015
RS1 Robert Griffin III 3.00 8.00
RS2 Trent Richardson SP 10.00 25.00
RS3 Justin Blackmon 2.50 6.00
RS4 Ryan Tannehill 4.00 10.00
RS5 Michael Floyd 2.50 6.00
RS6 Brandon Weeden 2.50 6.00
RS7 Doug Martin 4.00 10.00
RS8 A.J. Jenkins 2.50 6.00
RS9 Kendall Wright 2.50 6.00
RS10 Brock Osweiler SP 8.00 20.00
RS11 Nick Foles 6.00 15.00
RS12 Brian Quick 2.50 6.00
RS13 Case Keenum 12.00 30.00
RS14 Kellen Moore 3.00 8.00
RS15 Coby Fleener 2.50 6.00
RS16 Stephen Hill 2.50 6.00
RS17 Alshon Jeffery 5.00 12.00
RS18 Isaiah Pead 4.00 10.00
RS19 Ryan Broyles 2.50 6.00
RS20 LaMichael James 2.50 6.00
RS21 Rueben Randle 2.50 6.00
RS22 DeVier Posey 6.00 15.00
RS23 Russell Wilson 40.00 80.00
RS24 Mohamed Sanu 4.00 10.00
RS25 Bernard Pierce 6.00 15.00
RS26 Travis Benjamin 2.50 6.00
RS27 Kirk Cousins 10.00 25.00
RS28 Jarius Wright 2.50 6.00
RS29 Nick Toon 2.50 6.00
RS30 Juron Criner 2.50 6.00
RS31 Melvin Ingram EXCH 2.50 6.00
RS32 Dwayne Allen 2.50 6.00
RS33 Cyrus Gray 5.00 12.00
RS34 B.J. Cunningham 5.00 12.00
RS35 Dan Herron SP 5.00 12.00
RS36 Matt Kalil 2.50 6.00
RS37 Mark Barron 2.50 6.00
RS38 Luke Kuechly 6.00 15.00
RS39 Stephon Gilmore SP 3.00 8.00
RS40 Dontari Poe SP
RS41 Michael Brockers SP
RS42 Dre Kirkpatrick SP EXCH 2.50 6.00
RS43 Shea McClellin SP EXCH
RS44 David DeCastro 2.50 6.00
RS45 Dont'a Hightower SP EXCH
RS46 Whitney Mercilus 2.50 6.00
RS47 Andre Branch 2.50 6.00
RS48 Janoris Jenkins 3.00 8.00
RS49 Cordy Glenn SP 3.00 8.00
RS50 Mychal Kendricks SP
RS51 Bobby Wagner SP
RS52 Kendall Reyes SP
RS53 Lavonte David SP
RS54 Casey Hayward SP 2.50 6.00
RS55 Ronnie Hillman 2.50 6.00
RS56 T.J. Graham 2.50 6.00
RS57 Michael Egnew 2.50 6.00
RS58 Mike Martin SP 25.00 50.00
RS59 Devon Wylie SP 2.50 6.00
RS60 Alameda Ta'amu SP
RS61 Ladarius Green SP
RS62 Kyle Wilber SP 4.00 10.00
RS63 Orson Charles 2.50 6.00
RS64 Keshawn Martin SP 3.00 8.00
RS65 Rhett Ellison SP 3.00 8.00
RS66 Greg Childs 2.50 6.00
RS67 Marvin Jones SP 2.50 6.00
RS68 Alfred Morris 2.50 6.00
RS69 Ryan Lindley 2.50 6.00
RS70 Marvin McNutt 2.50 6.00
RS71 Rishard Matthews SP
RS72 Jeremy Ebert SP 2.50 6.00
RS73 Cam Johnson 4.00 10.00
RS74 Eric Page 3.00 8.00
RS75 Brandon Bolden SP 15.00 30.00
RS76 Chandler Harnish 2.50 6.00
RS77 Dwight Jones 2.50 6.00
RS78 Jarrett Lee SP 5.00 12.00
RS79 Jeff Fuller 2.50 6.00
RS80 Jermaine Kearse SP
RS81 Jordan Jefferson 3.00 8.00
RS82 Laron Byrd SP
RS83 Lavasier Tuinei SP 4.00 10.00
RS84 Marc Tyler 2.50 6.00
RS85 Marquis Maze 3.00 8.00
RS86 Nelson Rosario SP
RS88 Tauren Poole 4.00 10.00
RS89 Tyler Hansen SP 2.50 6.00
RS90 Tyler Shoemaker 3.00 8.00
RS91 Ronnell Lewis 2.50 6.00
RS92 Jared Crick 2.50 6.00
RS93 Harrison Smith EXCH 6.00 15.00
RS94 Pat Edwards SP
RS95 Courtney Upshaw SP
RS96 Kelechi Osemele 2.50 6.00
RS97 Joe Adams SP 2.50 6.00
RS98 Keith Tandy 3.00 8.00
RS99 Da'Jon McKnight SP
RS100 Dan Persa SP

2012 Fleer Retro Thunder Noyz Boyz

1NB Jerry Rice 10.00 25.00
2NB Drew Brees 8.00 20.00
3NB Barry Sanders 12.00 30.00
4NB Aaron Rodgers 12.00 30.00
5NB Dan Marino 12.00 30.00
6NB Tim Tebow 6.00 15.00
7NB John Elway 10.00 25.00
8NB Drew Bledsoe 6.00 15.00
9NB Trent Richardson 2.50 6.00
10NB Russell Wilson 20.00 50.00
11NB Steve Young 8.00 20.00
12NB Joe Namath 12.00 30.00
13NB Robert Griffin III 3.00 8.00
14NB Troy Aikman 8.00 20.00
15NB Alfred Morris 2.50 6.00

2012 Fleer Retro Ultra

COMPLETE SET (50) 6.00 15.00
ONE PER PACK
1 Jim Kelly .40 1.00
2 Johnny Rodgers .30 .75
3 Charles White .25 .60
4 Nick Buoniconti .25 .60
5 Troy Aikman .50 1.25
6 Rodney Peete .25 .60
7 Andre Ware .30 .75
8 Ken Stabler .40 1.00
9 Jerry Rice .60 1.50
10 Drew Brees .40 1.00
11 Billy Cannon .25 .60
12 Archie Manning .30 .75
13 Aaron Rodgers .60 1.50
14 Archie Griffin .25 .60
15 Joe Theismann .30 .75
16 Mike Rozier .25 .60
17 Joe Washington .25 .60
18 Don Maynard .30 .75
19 Dan Marino .75 2.00
20 Earl Campbell .40 1.00
21 Barry Sanders .60 1.50
22 Jim Plunkett .30 .75
23 Roger Craig .30 .75
24 Jerome Bettis .40 1.00
25 Bart Starr .60 1.50
26 Charlie Ward .25 .60
27 Drew Bledsoe .30 .75
28 Garrison Hearst .25 .60
29 Vinny Testaverde .25 .60
30 Tim Brown .40 1.00
31 Rudy Ruettiger .30 .75
32 Bruce Smith .30 .75
33 Steve Young .50 1.25
34 George Rogers .25 .60
35 Johnny Lattner .25 .60
36 Roger Staubach .50 1.25
37 Tony Dorsett .40 1.00
38 Al Toon .25 .60
39 Bo Jackson .50 1.25
40 Tim Tebow .40 1.00
41 Anthony Carter .25 .60
42 Ken MacAfee .25 .60
43 Tommie Frazier .25 .60
44 Dan Fouts .30 .75
45 Joe Namath .60 1.50
46 Jake Plummer .25 .60
47 Daryle Lamonica .25 .60
48 John Elway .60 1.50
49 Rich Gannon .25 .60
50 Billy Sims .30 .75

2012 Fleer Retro Ultra Stars

1US John Elway 8.00 20.00
2US Barry Sanders 10.00 25.00
3US Jim Plunkett 3.00 8.00
4US Brian Bosworth 4.00 10.00
5US Aaron Rodgers 12.00 30.00
6US Doug Flutie 3.00 8.00
7US Daryle Lamonica 2.50 6.00
8US Bruce Smith 3.00 8.00
9US Vinny Testaverde 2.50 6.00
10US Tony Dorsett 4.00 10.00
11US Brandon Weeden 1.50 4.00
12US Bart Starr 6.00 15.00
13US Warren Sapp 3.00 8.00
14US Steve Young 5.00 12.00
15US Dan Marino 8.00 20.00
16US Tim Tebow 4.00 10.00
17US Joe Namath 10.00 25.00
18US Troy Aikman 5.00 12.00
19US Alfred Morris 1.50 4.00
20US Robert Griffin III 2.00 5.00
21US Ryan Tannehill 2.50 6.00
22US Bo Jackson 8.00 20.00
23US Paul Hornung 4.00 10.00
24US Russell Wilson 12.00 30.00
25US Ozzie Newsome 3.00 8.00
26US Janoris Jenkins 2.00 5.00
27US Jerry Rice 6.00 15.00
28US Justin Blackmon 1.50 4.00
29US Drew Bledsoe 5.00 12.00
30US Jake Plummer 2.50 6.00
31US Archie Griffin 4.00 10.00
32US Joe Theismann 3.00 8.00
33US Dan Fouts 3.00 8.00
34US Jim Kelly 4.00 10.00
35US Trent Richardson 1.50 4.00
36US Roger Staubach 5.00 12.00
37US George Rogers 2.50 6.00
38US Jerome Bettis 4.00 10.00
39US Earl Campbell 4.00 10.00
40US Drew Brees 6.00 15.00

2013 Fleer Retro Ultra

COMPLETE SET (100) 20.00 40.00
THREE ULTRA PER PACK
1 Andrew Luck .50 1.25
2 Dan Fouts .25 .60
3 Jerry Rice .50 1.25
4 Giovani Bernard .20 .50
5 Zac Dysert .20 .50
6 Dan Marino .60 1.50
7 Ben Roethlisberger .30 .75
8 Le'Veon Bell .60 1.50
9 Ozzie Newsome .25 .60
10 Kordell Stewart .20 .50
11 Warren Moon .30 .75
12 B.J. Daniels .30 .75
13 Joe Theismann .30 .75
14 Montee Ball .20 .50
15 Drew Brees .30 .75
16 Earl Campbell .30 .75
17 Ron Dayne .25 .60
18 Irving Fryar .20 .50
19 LaDainian Tomlinson .25 .60
20 Barry Sanders .50 1.25
21 Natrone Means .20 .50
22 Eddie Lacy .20 .50
23 Akeem Spence .20 .50
24 Ickey Woods .20 .50
25 Joe Montana 1.00 2.50
26 John Elway .50 1.25
27 Craig Krenzel .20 .50
28 Mike Glennon .20 .50
29 Steve Young .40 1.00
30 Landry Jones .20 .50
31 Knile Davis .20 .50
32 Matt Barkley .20 .50
33 Roger Craig .25 .60
34 Thurman Thomas .25 .60
35 Doug Flutie .25 .60
36 Jerome Bettis .30 .75
37 Johnny Rodgers .20 .50
38 Gerald Hodges .25 .60
39 Eric Dickerson .25 .60
40 Bo Jackson .40 1.00
41 Terrell Davis .25 .60
42 Eddie George .25 .60
43 Jim Plunkett .25 .60
44 Daryle Lamonica .20 .50
45 Archie Griffin .20 .50
46 Tedy Bruschi .25 .60
47 Tim Brown .30 .75
48 EJ Manuel .20 .50
49 Geno Smith .20 .50
50 Ryan Nassib .20 .50
51 Johnathan Franklin .20 .50
52 Tavon Austin .25 .60
53 Tyler Eifert .20 .50
54 Eric Fisher .20 .50
55 Marcus Lattimore .20 .50
56 DeAndre Hopkins .50 1.25
57 Daimion Stafford .25 .60
58 Zach Ertz .40 1.00
59 Luke Joeckel .20 .50
60 Stepfan Taylor .20 .50
61 Cordarrelle Patterson .20 .50
62 Dion Jordan .20 .50
63 Gavin Escobar .20 .50
65 Michael Buchanan .30 .75
66 Justin Hunter .20 .50
67 Rex Burkhead .25 .60
68 Robert Woods .30 .75
69 Tyler Bray .20 .50
70 Chris Thompson .20 .50
71 Aaron Dobson .20 .50
72 Lane Johnson .25 .60
73 Alec Ogletree .20 .50
74 Mike Gillislee .20 .50
75 Terrance Williams .20 .50
76 Theo Riddick .20 .50
77 Andre Ellington .20 .50
78 Keenan Allen .40 1.00
79 Ezekiel Ansah .20 .50
80 Kenjon Barner .20 .50
81 Marquise Goodwin .20 .50
82 Matt Elam .20 .50
83 Cobi Hamilton .20 .50
84 Markus Wheaton .20 .50
85 Ryan Swope .20 .50
86 Vance McDonald .25 .60
87 Stedman Bailey .20 .50
88 Corey Fuller .20 .50
89 Josh Boyce .20 .50
90 Manti Te'o .25 .60
91 Star Lotulelei .25 .60
92 Chris Harper .20 .50
93 Eric Reid .25 .60
94 D.J. Fluker .20 .50
95 Denard Robinson .20 .50
96 Justin Pugh .20 .50
97 Kenny Stills .20 .50
98 Sheldon Richardson .20 .50
99 Tavarres King .20 .50
100 Kenny Vaccaro .20 .50

2013 Fleer Retro '96-97 Flair Row 2

STATED ODDS 1:200
*LEGACY/100: 1.5X TO 4X BASIC INSERT
0 Andrew Luck 1.50 4.00

2013 Fleer Retro '98 Metal Universe

STATED ODDS 1:4
*M1-M25 TEAL/50: 5X TO 12X
*M26-M50 TEAL/50: 4X TO 10X
M1 Jerry Rice 1.00 2.50
M2 Barry Sanders 1.00 2.50
M3 Joe Montana 2.00 5.00
M4 Bo Jackson .75 2.00
M5 LaDainian Tomlinson .50 1.25
M6 Steve Young .75 2.00
M7 Ben Roethlisberger .60 1.50
M8 Joe Namath 1.00 2.50
M9 Eddie George .50 1.25
M10 Thurman Thomas .50 1.25
M11 Dan Fouts .50 1.25
M12 Andrew Luck 1.00 2.50
M13 Dan Marino 1.25 3.00
M14 Tedy Bruschi .50 1.25
M15 Drew Brees .60 1.50
M16 Peyton Manning 2.50 6.00
M17 Kordell Stewart .40 1.00
M18 Tim Brown .60 1.50
M19 Warren Moon .60 1.50
M20 Herschel Walker .60 1.50
M21 Eric Dickerson .50 1.25
M22 Jerome Bettis .60 1.50
M23 John Elway 1.00 2.50
M24 Jim Kelly .60 1.50
M25 Terrell Davis .50 1.25
M26 Geno Smith .25 .60
M27 Giovani Bernard .25 .60
M28 Tavon Austin .30 .75
M29 Le'Veon Bell .75 2.00
M30 EJ Manuel .25 .60
M31 DeAndre Hopkins .60 1.50
M32 Montee Ball .25 .60
M33 Robert Woods .40 1.00
M34 Tyler Eifert .25 .60
M35 Matt Barkley .25 .60
M36 Eddie Lacy .25 .60
M37 Keenan Allen .50 1.25
M38 Marcus Lattimore .25 .60
M39 Markus Wheaton .25 .60
M40 Mike Glennon .25 .60
M41 Cordarrelle Patterson .25 .60
M42 Aaron Dobson .25 .60
M43 Knile Davis .25 .60
M44 Tyler Wilson .25 .60
M45 Josh Boyce .25 .60
M46 Manti Te'o .30 .75
M47 Justin Hunter .25 .60
M48 Stedman Bailey .25 .60
M49 Zach Ertz .50 1.25
M50 Ryan Nassib .25 .60

2013 Fleer Retro Buyback Autographs

12 A.Manning '92ULT/18 40.00 80.00
M30 A.Manning '98METU/17 40.00 80.00

2013 Fleer Retro E-X Century

STATED ODDS 1:6
1 Andrew Luck 1.00 2.50
2 Thurman Thomas .50 1.25
3 Eddie George .50 1.25
4 Jerome Bettis .75 2.00
5 Dan Marino 1.25 3.00
6 Roger Craig .50 1.25
7 John Elway 1.00 2.50
8 Bo Jackson .75 2.00
9 Warren Moon .60 1.50
10 LaDainian Tomlinson .50 1.25
11 Steve Young .75 2.00
12 Lawrence Taylor .60 1.50
13 Drew Bledsoe .50 1.25
14 Jerry Rice 1.00 2.50
15 Eric Dickerson .50 1.25
16 Peyton Manning 2.50 6.00
17 Tedy Bruschi .50 1.25
18 Ben Roethlisberger .60 1.50
19 Billy Sims .50 1.25
20 Mike Alstott .40 1.00
21 Drew Brees .60 1.50
22 Paul Hornung .60 1.50
23 Joe Namath 2.00 5.00
24 Doug Flutie .50 1.25
25 Barry Sanders 1.00 2.50
26 Ron Dayne .50 1.25
27 Herschel Walker .60 1.50
28 Joe Montana 2.00 5.00
29 Ty Detmer .40 1.00
30 Alan Page .40 1.00
31 Daryle Lamonica .40 1.00
32 Dan Fouts .50 1.25
33 Matt Barkley .25 .60
34 Giovani Bernard .25 .60
35 Manti Te'o .30 .75
36 Tavon Austin .30 .75
37 EJ Manuel .25 .60
38 Montee Ball .25 .60
39 DeAndre Hopkins .60 1.50
40 Cordarrelle Patterson .25 .60
41 Le'Veon Bell .75 2.00
42 Geno Smith .25 .60

2013 Fleer Retro E-X Century Essential Credentials Future

1 Andrew Luck/42 50.00 100.00
5 Dan Marino/38 40.00 100.00
16 Peyton Manning/27 75.00 150.00
23 Joe Namath/20 30.00 80.00
25 Barry Sanders/18 50.00 100.00
28 Joe Montana/15 75.00 150.00

2013 Fleer Retro E-X Century Essential Credentials Now

*VETS/15-29: 6X TO 15X BASIC INSERT
*VETS/30-32: 5X TO 12X BASIC INSERT
*ROOKIE/33-42: 5X TO 12X BASIC INSERT
16 Peyton Manning/16 175.00 300.00
28 Joe Montana/28 50.00 100.00

2013 Fleer Retro Flair Showcase

STATED ODDS 1:2
*LEGACY VET/150: 2X TO 5X BASIC INSERTS
*LEGACY ROOK/150: 1.5X TO 4X BASIC INSERTS
1 Drew Brees .60 1.50
2 John Elway 1.00 2.50
3 Peyton Manning 2.50 6.00
4 LaDainian Tomlinson .50 1.25
5 Eddie George .50 1.25
6 Bo Jackson .75 2.00
7 Jerry Rice 1.00 2.50
8 Craig Krenzel .40 1.00
9 Drew Bledsoe .50 1.25
10 Charley Taylor .40 1.00
11 Geno Smith .25 .60
12 Andrew Luck 1.00 2.50
13 Thurman Thomas .50 1.25
14 Ben Roethlisberger .60 1.50
15 Markus Wheaton .25 .60
16 Ty Detmer .40 1.00
17 Eddie Lacy .25 .60
18 Tyler Eifert .25 .60
19 Roman Gabriel .40 1.00
20 Dan Marino 1.25 3.00
21 Matt Barkley .25 .60
22 Giovani Bernard .25 .60
23 Manti Te'o .30 .75
24 Jerome Bettis .60 1.50
25 Herschel Walker .60 1.50
26 Marquise Goodwin .25 .60
27 Le'Veon Bell .75 2.00
28 Dan Fouts .50 1.25
29 EJ Manuel .25 .60
30 Marcus Lattimore .25 .60
31 Ezekiel Ansah .25 .60
32 Alan Page .40 1.00
33 Roger Craig .50 1.25
34 Johnathan Franklin .25 .60
35 Stedman Bailey .25 .60
36 Zach Ertz .50 1.25
37 Barry Sanders 1.00 2.50
38 Kordell Stewart .40 1.00
39 Lawrence Taylor .60 1.50
40 Dee Milliner .25 .60
41 Warren Moon .60 1.50
42 Star Lotulelei .30 .75
43 Tedy Bruschi .50 1.25
44 Ickey Woods .40 1.00
45 Randall Cunningham .50 1.25
46 Kenny Stills .25 .60
47 Corey Fuller .25 .60
48 Steve Young .75 2.00
49 Mike Glennon .25 .60
50 Josh Boyce .25 .60
51 Kenjon Barner .25 .60
52 Keenan Allen .50 1.25
53 Matt Scott .25 .60
54 Lane Johnson .30 .75
55 Denard Robinson .25 .60
56 Theo Riddick .25 .60
57 Kenny Vaccaro .25 .60
58 Ryan Nassib .25 .60
59 Gavin Escobar .25 .60
60 Terrance Williams .25 .60
61 Xavier Rhodes .25 .60
62 Bjoern Werner .25 .60
63 Andre Ellington .25 .60
64 Aaron Dobson .25 .60
65 Rex Burkhead .30 .75
66 Spencer Ware .25 .60
67 Chris Harper .25 .60
68 Jordan Reed .40 1.00
69 T.J. McDonald .25 .60
70 Tim Brown .60 1.50
71 Tavon Austin .30 .75
72 Knile Davis .25 .60
73 Eric Fisher .25 .60
74 Eric Reid .30 .75
75 Tavarres King .25 .60
76 Vance McDonald .30 .75
77 Marquess Wilson .40 1.00
78 DeAndre Hopkins .60 1.50
79 Travis Kelce .60 1.50
80 Zac Dysert .25 .60
81 Aaron Mellette .25 .60
82 Joseph Randle .25 .60
83 Cordarrelle Patterson .25 .60
84 Tyler Bray .25 .60
85 Desmond Trufant .25 .60
86 Mike Gillislee .25 .60
87 Brad Sorensen .25 .60
88 Dion Jordan .25 .60
89 Landry Jones .25 .60
90 Sheldon Richardson .25 .60
91 Cobi Hamilton .25 .60
92 Justin Hunter .25 .60
93 Matt Elam .25 .60
94 Montee Ball .25 .60
95 Robert Woods .40 1.00
96 Alec Ogletree .25 .60
97 Tyler Wilson .25 .60
98 Stepfan Taylor .25 .60
99 Nick Kasa .25 .60

2013 Fleer Retro Flair Showcase Shrine Time

STATED PRINT RUN 25 SER.#'d SETS
ST1 Peyton Manning 50.00 120.00
ST2 Drew Brees 10.00 25.00
ST3 Barry Sanders 30.00 60.00
ST4 John Elway 20.00 50.00
ST5 Thurman Thomas 8.00 20.00
ST6 Joe Montana 30.00 60.00
ST7 Ben Roethlisberger 12.00 30.00
ST8 Jerome Bettis 12.00 30.00
ST9 Jerry Rice 15.00 40.00
ST10 Tim Brown 10.00 25.00
ST11 Dan Marino 30.00 60.00
ST12 Andrew Luck 25.00 50.00
ST13 Doug Flutie 8.00 20.00
ST14 Dan Fouts 8.00 20.00
ST15 Joe Namath
ST16 Terrell Davis 8.00 20.00
ST17 Steve Young 12.00 30.00
ST18 LaDainian Tomlinson 8.00 20.00
ST19 Drew Bledsoe 8.00 20.00
ST20 Eric Dickerson 8.00 20.00
ST21 Tedy Bruschi 8.00 20.00
ST22 Eddie George 8.00 20.00
ST23 Jim Kelly 10.00 25.00
ST24 Bo Jackson 12.00 30.00
ST25 Bart Starr

2013 Fleer Retro Fleer Focus Wondrous

STATED ODDS 1:90
W1 Andrew Luck 8.00 20.00
W2 Dan Marino 5.00 12.00
W3 Jerry Rice 4.00 10.00
W4 Peyton Manning 25.00 50.00
W5 Joe Namath 10.00 25.00
W6 Barry Sanders 4.00 10.00
W7 John Elway 4.00 10.00
W8 Billy Sims 2.00 5.00
W9 Ben Roethlisberger 2.50 6.00
W10 Steve Young 3.00 8.00
W11 Randall Cunningham 2.00 5.00
W12 Joe Montana 6.00 15.00
W13 Bo Jackson 3.00 8.00

W14 Joe Theismann 2.50 6.00
W15 EJ Manuel .75 2.00
W16 Montee Ball .75 2.00
W17 Drew Brees 2.50 6.00
W18 Matt Barkley .75 2.00
W19 Tavon Austin 1.00 2.50
W20 Dan Fouts 2.00 5.00
W21 Giovani Bernard .75 2.00
W22 LaDainian Tomlinson 2.00 5.00
W23 Geno Smith .75 2.00
W24 Charley Taylor 1.50 4.00
W25 Manti Te'o 1.00 2.50

2013 Fleer Retro Fleer Greats of the Game Autographs

GROUP A ODDS 1:485
GROUP B ODDS 1:71
OVERALL ODDS 1:62
EXCH EXPIRATION: 3/1/2016
AC58 Anthony Carter B 8.00 20.00
AD38 Aaron Dobson B 3.00 8.00
AL1 Andrew Luck A 50.00 100.00
BB45 Jim Plunkett A 8.00 20.00
BJ33 Bo Jackson A 100.00 200.00
BR8 Ben Roethlisberger A 40.00 80.00
BS4 Barry Sanders A 75.00 125.00
CP15 Cordarrelle Patterson B EXCH 3.00 8.00
DB28 Drew Brees A
DH10 DeAndre Hopkins B 8.00 20.00
DJ51 Dion Jordan B 3.00 8.00
DM2 Dan Marino A 90.00 150.00
DR55 Denard Robinson B 3.00 8.00
ED41 Eric Dickerson A
EG26 Eddie George A 50.00 100.00
EL23 Eddie Lacy B 3.00 8.00
EM3 EJ Manuel B 8.00 20.00
ER48 Eric Reid B 4.00 10.00
GB7 Giovani Bernard B 3.00 8.00
GE56 Gavin Escobar B 3.00 8.00
GS9 Geno Smith B EXCH 3.00 8.00
IW59 Ickey Woods B 5.00 12.00
JB24 Jerome Bettis A 40.00 80.00
JB53 Josh Boyce B 3.00 8.00
JE16 John Elway A
JF30 Johnathan Franklin B 3.00 8.00
JH57 Justin Hunter B 3.00 8.00
JM11 Joe Montana A
JN21 Joe Namath A 40.00 80.00
JR6 Jerry Rice A 60.00 120.00
KA36 Keenan Allen B 8.00 20.00
KD27 LaDainian Tomlinson A 20.00 40.00
KS50 Kenny Stills B 3.00 8.00
LB12 Le'Veon Bell B 10.00 25.00
MB14 Matt Barkley B 3.00 8.00
MB17 Montee Ball B 3.00 8.00
MG19 Mike Glennon B 3.00 8.00
MG40 Dan Fouts A 25.00 50.00
MT20 Manti Te'o B 4.00 10.00
NM35 Natrone Means B 5.00 12.00
RC47 Roger Craig B 6.00 15.00
RD18 Ron Dayne A 10.00 25.00
RN29 Ryan Nassib B 3.00 8.00
RW25 Robert Woods B 5.00 12.00
SB44 Stedman Bailey B 3.00 8.00
SY49 Steve Young A 30.00 60.00
TA5 Tavon Austin B 4.00 10.00
TB39 Tedy Bruschi B 6.00 15.00
TD52 Terrell Davis B 12.00 30.00
TT13 Thurman Thomas A
ZE54 Zach Ertz B 6.00 15.00

2013 Fleer Retro Fleer Rookie Sensations Autographs

GROUP A ODDS 1:629
GROUP B ODDS 1:315
GROUP C ODDS 1:227
GROUP D ODDS 1:124
GROUP E ODDS 1:55
GROUP F/G ODDS 1:53
OVERALL ODDS 1:18
UNPRICED LUCK '93 ODDS 10,015
RS1 Jelani Jenkins F 3.00 8.00
RS2 Tavon Austin A 4.00 10.00
RS4 Xavier Rhodes C 3.00 8.00
RS5 D.J. Swearinger E 2.50 6.00
RS7 Barrett Jones G 2.50 6.00
RS8 DeAndre Hopkins A 8.00 20.00
RS10 Travis Kelce C 8.00 20.00
RS12 Brandon McGee D 3.00 8.00
RS13 B.W. Webb E 3.00 8.00
RS14 Cameron Marshall F 2.50 6.00
RS15 Zaviar Gooden D 4.00 10.00
RS17 Conner Vernon B 3.00 8.00
RS18 Cordarrelle Patterson A 3.00 8.00
RS20 Tyler Wilson D 3.00 8.00
RS23 Aaron Mellette C 3.00 8.00
RS24 Da'Rick Rogers F 3.00 8.00
RS25 Dayne Crist F 3.00 8.00
RS27 Dion Sims F 2.50 6.00
RS28 Tyler Eifert C 3.00 8.00
RS30 Montee Ball A 3.00 8.00
RS31 Erik Highsmith E 3.00 8.00
RS32 Everett Dawkins C 3.00 8.00
RS33 Marquess Wilson F 4.00 10.00
RS34 Sylvester Williams B 3.00 8.00
RS35 Jawan Jamison E 2.50 6.00
RS36 Jeff Tuel D 5.00 12.00
RS37 Le'Veon Bell A
RS38 Jesse Williams E 4.00 10.00
RS39 John Boyett B 4.00 10.00
RS41 Jack Doyle D 3.00 8.00
RS42 Jordan Poyer E 3.00 8.00
RS43 Joseph Fauria F 2.50 6.00
RS45 Keith Pough D 3.00 8.00
RS46 Kevin Reddick E 2.50 6.00
RS48 Khaseem Greene C 3.00 8.00
RS49 Kwame Geathers F 2.50 6.00
RS51 Leon McFadden D 4.00 10.00
RS53 Malliciah Goodman E 2.50 6.00
RS54 Marc Anthony B 3.00 8.00
RS55 Marcus Davis F 3.00 8.00
RS56 Manti Te'o A 4.00 10.00
RS57 Matt Scott E 3.00 8.00
RS58 Michael Mauti F 5.00 12.00
RS59 Matt Barkley A 3.00 8.00
RS60 Michael Williams E 3.00 8.00
RS61 Mike Shanahan E 3.00 8.00
RS62 Mitchell Gale E 2.50 6.00
RS63 Nick Kasa B 3.00 8.00
RS65 Eddie Lacy A 3.00 8.00
RS66 Philip Lutzenkirchen C 5.00 12.00
RS67 Ray Graham C 3.00 8.00
RS68 Mike Glennon A
RS69 Roy Roundtree D 8.00 20.00
RS71 Ryan Otten E 2.50 6.00
RS73 Seth Doege B 5.00 12.00
RS75 Geno Smith A 3.00 8.00
RS76 Skye Dawson C 4.00 10.00
RS77 EJ Manuel A 3.00 8.00
RS78 Spencer Ware C 3.00 8.00
RS79 Ricky Wagner E 2.50 6.00
RS81 Rodney Smith F 2.50 6.00
RS82 Tommy Bohanon D 4.00 10.00
RS83 Tony Jefferson E 3.00 8.00
RS84 Travis Howard E 6.00 15.00
RS86 Uzoma Nwachukwu A 4.00 10.00
RS88 Zach Line F 2.50 6.00
RS89 Zach Maynard E 3.00 8.00
RS90 Ryan Nassib A
RS92 Josh Johnson F 2.50 6.00
RS93 Emory Blake F 2.50 6.00
RS94 Sheldon Price D 3.00 8.00
RS95 Blidi Wreh-Wilson B 4.00 10.00
RS97 Landry Jones C 3.00 8.00
RS98 Oday Aboushi E 2.50 6.00
RS99 Giovani Bernard A 3.00 8.00

2013 Fleer Retro Fleer Tradition Electrifying

STATED ODDS 1:72
1 Andrew Luck 6.00 15.00
2 Tavon Austin 1.00 2.50
3 EJ Manuel .75 2.00
4 Steve Young 3.00 8.00
5 Giovani Bernard .75 2.00
6 Jerome Bettis 4.00 10.00
7 John Elway 4.00 10.00
8 Joe Montana 6.00 15.00
9 Dan Fouts 2.00 5.00
10 Geno Smith .75 2.00
11 LaDainian Tomlinson 2.00 5.00
12 Jerry Rice 4.00 10.00
13 Dan Marino 5.00 12.00
14 Manti Te'o 1.00 2.50
15 Drew Brees 2.50 6.00
16 Montee Ball .75 2.00
17 Matt Barkley .75 2.00
18 Ben Roethlisberger 2.50 6.00
19 Eric Dickerson 2.00 5.00
20 Peyton Manning 12.00 30.00

2013 Fleer Retro Fleer Tradition Under Pressure

STATED ODDS 1:108
UP1 Andrew Luck 6.00 15.00
UP2 Joe Montana 8.00 20.00
UP3 Dan Marino 5.00 12.00
UP4 Ben Roethlisberger 2.50 6.00
UP5 Bo Jackson 3.00 8.00
UP6 Peyton Manning 12.00 30.00
UP7 Jerry Rice 4.00 10.00
UP8 Barry Sanders 4.00 10.00
UP9 John Elway 4.00 10.00
UP10 Dan Fouts 2.00 5.00
UP11 Drew Brees 2.50 6.00
UP12 LaDainian Tomlinson 2.00 5.00
UP13 Eddie George 2.00 5.00
UP14 Eric Dickerson 2.00 5.00
UP15 DeAndre Hopkins 2.00 5.00
UP16 Geno Smith .75 2.00
UP17 Giovani Bernard .75 2.00
UP18 Montee Ball .75 2.00
UP19 EJ Manuel .75 2.00
UP20 Tavon Austin 1.00 2.50

2013 Fleer Retro Metal Universe

STATED ODDS 1:2
M101 Andrew Luck 1.50 4.00
M102 Peyton Manning 1.00 2.50
M103 LaDainian Tomlinson .40 1.00
M104 Ben Roethlisberger .50 1.25
M105 Joe Montana 1.50 4.00
M106 EJ Manuel .20 .50
M107 Tavon Austin .25 .60
M108 Manti Te'o .25 .60
M109 Marquise Goodwin .20 .50
M110 Eddie Lacy .20 .50
M111 Ryan Nassib .20 .50
M112 Eric Fisher .20 .50
M113 Tyler Eifert .20 .50
M114 DeAndre Hopkins .50 1.25
M115 Johnathan Franklin .20 .50
M116 Dee Milliner .20 .50
M117 Geno Smith .20 .50
M118 Denard Robinson .20 .50
M119 Cordarrelle Patterson .20 .50
M120 Luke Joeckel .20 .50
M121 Le'Veon Bell .60 1.50
M122 Matt Barkley .20 .50
M123 Tavarres King .20 .50
M124 Justin Hunter .20 .50
M125 Marcus Lattimore .20 .50
M126 Zach Ertz .40 1.00
M127 Mike Glennon .20 .50
M128 Dion Jordan .20 .50
M129 Robert Woods .30 .75
M130 Josh Boyce .20 .50
M131 Eric Reid .25 .60
M132 Tyler Wilson .20 .50
M133 Desmond Trufant .20 .50
M134 Giovani Bernard .20 .50
M135 Kenny Vaccaro .20 .50
M136 Aaron Dobson .20 .50
M137 Sheldon Richardson .20 .50
M138 Knile Davis .20 .50
M139 Stedman Bailey .20 .50
M140 Joseph Randle .20 .50
M141 Terrance Williams .20 .50
M142 Barkevious Mingo .20 .50
M143 Keenan Allen .40 1.00
M144 Stepfan Taylor .20 .50
M145 Montee Ball .20 .50
M146 Alec Ogletree .20 .50
M147 Landry Jones .20 .50
M148 Kenny Stills .20 .50
M149 Gavin Escobar .20 .50
M150 Ezekiel Ansah .20 .50

2013 Fleer Retro Metal Universe Planet Metal

STATED ODDS 1:144
PM1 Drew Brees 3.00 8.00
PM2 Dan Marino 8.00 20.00
PM3 Barry Sanders 5.00 12.00
PM4 John Elway 5.00 12.00
PM5 Andrew Luck 10.00 25.00
PM6 Steve Young 4.00 10.00
PM7 Matt Barkley 1.00 2.50
PM8 Tim Brown 3.00 8.00
PM9 Tavon Austin 1.25 3.00
PM10 Peyton Manning 40.00 80.00
PM11 Joe Montana 10.00 25.00
PM12 Giovani Bernard 1.00 2.50
PM13 Bo Jackson 4.00 10.00
PM14 Manti Te'o 1.25 3.00
PM15 Jerry Rice 5.00 12.00
PM16 Ben Roethlisberger 3.00 8.00
PM17 EJ Manuel 1.00 2.50
PM18 Tedy Bruschi 2.50 6.00
PM19 Geno Smith 1.00 2.50
PM20 LaDainian Tomlinson 2.50 6.00

2013 Fleer Retro Metal Universe Precious Metal Gems Blue

*VETS/50: 6X TO 15X BASIC INSERT
*ROOKIE/50: 5X TO 12X BASIC INSERT
M101 Andrew Luck 50.00 120.00

2013 Fleer Retro Metal Universe Precious Metal Gems Red

*VETS/100: 5X TO 12X BASIC INSERT
*ROOKIE/100: 4X TO 10X BASIC INSERT
M101 Andrew Luck 50.00 100.00
M102 Peyton Manning 30.00 80.00

2013 Fleer Retro Metal Universe Quasars

STATED ODDS 1:54
Q1 Tavon Austin 1.00 2.50
Q2 Matt Barkley .75 2.00
Q3 Keenan Allen 1.50 4.00
Q4 Giovani Bernard .75 2.00
Q5 DeAndre Hopkins 2.00 5.00
Q6 Eddie Lacy .75 2.00
Q7 EJ Manuel .75 2.00
Q8 Manti Te'o 1.00 2.50
Q9 Cordarrelle Patterson .75 2.00
Q10 Le'Veon Bell 2.50 6.00
Q11 Tyler Eifert .75 2.00
Q12 Justin Hunter .75 2.00
Q13 Aaron Dobson .75 2.00
Q14 Geno Smith .75 2.00
Q15 Montee Ball .75 2.00
Q16 Zach Ertz 1.50 4.00
Q17 Robert Woods 1.25 3.00
Q18 Terrance Williams .75 2.00
Q19 Mike Glennon .75 2.00
Q20 Marquise Goodwin .75 2.00

2013 Fleer Retro Skybox Premium Players

STATED ODDS 1:120
PP1 Peyton Manning 20.00 50.00
PP2 Barry Sanders 5.00 12.00
PP3 Dan Marino 10.00 25.00
PP4 Terrell Davis 2.50 6.00
PP5 Drew Bledsoe 2.50 6.00
PP6 Jerome Bettis 3.00 8.00
PP7 John Elway 5.00 12.00
PP8 Bo Jackson 5.00 12.00
PP9 Joe Montana 8.00 20.00
PP10 Eddie George 2.50 6.00
PP11 Thurman Thomas 2.50 6.00
PP12 Andrew Luck 8.00 20.00
PP13 Joe Namath 5.00 12.00
PP14 Earl Campbell 3.00 8.00
PP15 Jim Kelly 3.00 8.00
PP16 Herschel Walker 3.00 8.00
PP17 Jerry Rice 5.00 12.00
PP18 Ben Roethlisberger 3.00 8.00
PP19 Steve Young 4.00 10.00
PP20 Joe Theismann 3.00 8.00
PP21 LaDainian Tomlinson 2.50 6.00
PP22 Drew Brees 3.00 8.00
PP23 Warren Moon 3.00 8.00
PP24 Eric Dickerson 2.50 6.00
PP25 Tedy Bruschi 2.50 6.00

2013 Fleer Retro Skybox Premium Prime Time Rookies Autographs

EXCH EXPIRATION: 3/1/2016
PTR1 Tavon Austin/25 5.00 12.00
PTR2 EJ Manuel/25 4.00 10.00
PTR3 Giovani Bernard/25 4.00 10.00
PTR4 Manti Te'o/25
PTR5 Geno Smith/25 EXCH 4.00 10.00
PTR6 Matt Barkley/25
PTR7 Justin Hunter/75 3.00 8.00
PTR8 Tyler Eifert/75 3.00 8.00
PTR9 C.Patterson/75 EXCH 3.00 8.00
PTR10 DeAndre Hopkins/75 8.00 20.00
PTR11 Ryan Nassib/75 8.00 20.00
PTR12 Le'Veon Bell/75 10.00 25.00
PTR13 Johnathan Franklin/75 3.00 8.00
PTR14 Knile Davis/75 3.00 8.00
PTR15 Robert Woods/75 5.00 12.00
PTR16 Montee Ball/75 EXCH 3.00 8.00
PTR17 Mike Glennon/75 3.00 8.00
PTR19 Eddie Lacy/75 3.00 8.00
PTR20 Aaron Dobson/75 3.00 8.00
PTR21 Zach Ertz/75 6.00 15.00

2013 Fleer Retro Ultra Autographs

UNPRICED GRP A ODDS 1:27,540
GROUP B ODDS 1:390
GROUP C ODDS 1:304
GROUP D ODDS 1:140
GROUP E ODDS 1:86
GROUP F ODDS 1:78
OVERALL ODDS 1:27
1 Andrew Luck B 50.00 100.00
2 Dan Fouts B 8.00 20.00
3 Jerry Rice B
4 Giovani Bernard B 6.00 15.00
5 Zac Dysert F 2.50 6.00
6 Dan Marino B 150.00 300.00
7 Ben Roethlisberger B 30.00 60.00
8 Le'Veon Bell C 10.00 25.00
9 Ozzie Newsome D 6.00 15.00
11 Warren Moon B 10.00 25.00
12 B.J. Daniels E 4.00 10.00
13 Joe Theismann C 10.00 25.00
14 Montee Ball D 2.50 6.00
15 Drew Brees A
16 Earl Campbell B 12.00 30.00
17 Ron Dayne B 8.00 20.00
18 Irving Fryar D 5.00 12.00
19 LaDainian Tomlinson B
20 Barry Sanders B 60.00 100.00
21 Natrone Means D 5.00 12.00
22 Eddie Lacy F 2.50 6.00
23 Akeem Spence F 2.50 6.00
24 Ickey Woods D 5.00 12.00
25 Joe Montana B 60.00 100.00
26 John Elway B 50.00 100.00
27 Craig Krenzel D 5.00 12.00
28 Mike Glennon F 2.50 6.00
29 Steve Young B 30.00 60.00
31 Knile Davis F 2.50 6.00
32 Matt Barkley D 2.50 6.00
33 Roger Craig D 6.00 15.00
34 Thurman Thomas B 8.00 20.00
35 Doug Flutie B 8.00 20.00
36 Jerome Bettis B
37 Johnny Rodgers C 6.00 15.00
38 Gerald Hodges F 3.00 8.00
39 Eric Dickerson B 25.00 50.00
40 Bo Jackson B 60.00 120.00
41 Terrell Davis C 8.00 20.00
42 Eddie George C 30.00 80.00
43 Jim Plunkett B
44 Daryle Lamonica B 6.00 15.00
45 Archie Griffin C
46 Tedy Bruschi C 8.00 20.00
47 Tim Brown B
48 EJ Manuel C 3.00 8.00
49 Geno Smith E 2.50 6.00
50 Ryan Nassib E 6.00 15.00
51 Johnathan Franklin D 2.50 6.00
52 Tavon Austin F 3.00 8.00
53 Tyler Eifert D 2.50 6.00
54 Eric Fisher C 3.00 8.00
55 Marcus Lattimore D 2.50 6.00
56 DeAndre Hopkins D 6.00 15.00
57 Daimion Stafford F 6.00 15.00
59 Luke Joeckel E 2.50 6.00
60 Stepfan Taylor C 3.00 8.00
61 Cordarrelle Patterson F 2.50 6.00
62 Dion Jordan E 2.50 6.00
63 Gavin Escobar E 2.50 6.00
66 Justin Hunter C 3.00 8.00
67 Rex Burkhead F 6.00 15.00
68 Robert Woods C 5.00 12.00
69 Tyler Bray B 3.00 8.00
70 Chris Thompson E 2.50 6.00
71 Aaron Dobson E 2.50 6.00
72 Lane Johnson E 3.00 8.00
74 Mike Gillislee F 2.50 6.00
75 Terrance Williams D 2.50 6.00
76 Theo Riddick F 2.50 6.00
77 Andre Ellington D 8.00 20.00
78 Keenan Allen C 6.00 15.00
80 Kenjon Barner D 2.50 6.00
81 Marquise Goodwin E 2.50 6.00
82 Matt Elam E 2.50 6.00
83 Cobi Hamilton F 2.50 6.00
84 Markus Wheaton E 2.50 6.00
85 Ryan Swope F 2.50 6.00
86 Vance McDonald E 3.00 8.00
87 Stedman Bailey D 5.00 12.00
88 Corey Fuller E 2.50 6.00
89 Josh Boyce E 2.50 6.00
90 Manti Te'o C 12.00 30.00
92 Chris Harper E 2.50 6.00
93 Eric Reid E 3.00 8.00
94 D.J. Fluker F 2.50 6.00
95 Denard Robinson D 2.50 6.00
96 Justin Pugh E 2.50 6.00
97 Kenny Stills E 2.50 6.00
99 Tavarres King D 2.50 6.00
100 Kenny Vaccaro E 2.50 6.00

2013 Fleer Retro Ultra Exclamation Points

STATED ODDS 1:360
EP1 Andrew Luck 40.00 80.00
EP2 Eddie George 4.00 10.00
EP3 Barry Sanders 8.00 20.00
EP4 Peyton Manning 75.00 135.00
EP5 Bo Jackson 8.00 20.00
EP6 Dan Marino 40.00 80.00
EP7 Dan Fouts 4.00 10.00
EP8 Ben Roethlisberger 5.00 12.00
EP9 Drew Brees 5.00 12.00
EP10 EJ Manuel 2.00 5.00
EP11 Geno Smith 2.00 5.00
EP12 Giovani Bernard 2.00 5.00
EP13 Jerome Bettis 5.00 12.00
EP14 Jerry Rice 8.00 20.00
EP15 Joe Montana 40.00 80.00
EP16 Drew Bledsoe 4.00 10.00
EP17 John Elway 8.00 20.00
EP18 LaDainian Tomlinson 4.00 10.00
EP19 Steve Young 6.00 15.00
EP20 Tavon Austin 2.50 6.00
EP21 Thurman Thomas 4.00 10.00

2013 Fleer Retro Ultra Touchdown Royalty

STATED ODDS 1:36
TK1 John Elway 3.00 8.00
TK2 Barry Sanders 5.00 12.00
TK3 Joe Montana 5.00 12.00
TK4 Bo Jackson 2.50 6.00
TK5 LaDainian Tomlinson 1.50 4.00
TK6 Jerome Bettis 3.00 8.00
TK7 Ben Roethlisberger 2.00 5.00
TK8 Steve Young 2.50 6.00
TK9 Terrell Davis 1.50 4.00
TK10 Joe Namath 5.00 12.00
TK11 Drew Bledsoe 1.50 4.00
TK12 Andrew Luck 5.00 12.00
TK13 Dan Marino 4.00 10.00
TK14 Jerry Rice 3.00 8.00
TK15 Drew Brees 2.00 5.00
TK16 Peyton Manning 10.00 25.00
TK17 Thurman Thomas 1.50 4.00
TK18 Eddie George 1.50 4.00
TK19 Eric Dickerson 1.50 4.00
TK20 Tim Brown 2.00 5.00

2013 Fleer Retro Z-Force Rave Review

STATED ODDS 1:180
RR1 Peyton Manning 40.00 80.00
RR2 John Elway 6.00 15.00
RR3 Jerome Bettis 5.00 12.00
RR4 Jerry Rice 6.00 15.00
RR5 Dan Marino 12.00 30.00
RR6 Joe Montana 25.00 50.00
RR7 Barry Sanders 6.00 15.00
RR8 Andrew Luck 10.00 25.00
RR9 Joe Namath 5.00 12.00
RR10 EJ Manuel 1.50 4.00
RR11 Randall Cunningham 3.00 8.00
RR12 Drew Brees 4.00 10.00
RR13 Warren Moon 4.00 10.00
RR14 Bart Starr 5.00 12.00
RR15 Giovani Bernard 1.50 4.00
RR16 Tim Brown 4.00 10.00
RR17 Geno Smith 1.50 4.00
RR18 Eric Dickerson 3.00 8.00
RR19 Paul Hornung 4.00 10.00
RR20 Tavon Austin 2.00 5.00
RR21 LaDainian Tomlinson 3.00 8.00
RR22 Steve Young 5.00 12.00
RR23 Tedy Bruschi 3.00 8.00
RR24 Jim Plunkett 3.00 8.00
RR25 Manti Te'o 2.00 5.00

2000 Fleer Showcase

Released in late November 2000, Showcase features a 160-card base set comprised of 100 Veteran cards, 20 Rookie cards, numbers 101-120, sequentially numbered to 1000, and 40 Rookie cards, numbers 121-160, sequentially numbered to 2000. Base cards are all holographic foil and are enhanced with gold foil highlights. Showcase was packaged in 24-pack boxes with packs containing five cards and carried a suggested retail price of $4.99.

COMP.SET w/o SP's (100) 10.00 25.00
1 Tim Couch .25 .60
2 Deion Sanders .25 .60
3 Darnay Scott .25 .60
4 Brett Favre .60 1.50
5 Mark Brunell .25 .60
6 Randy Moss .25 .60
7 Tyrone Wheatley .20 .50
8 Isaac Bruce .30 .75
9 Eddie George .25 .60
10 Troy Aikman .40 1.00
11 Charlie Batch .20 .50
12 Marvin Harrison .25 .60
13 Terry Glenn .25 .60
14 Charles Johnson .20 .50
15 Jerry Rice .75 2.00
16 Kurt Warner .50 1.25
17 Kevin Johnson .20 .50
18 Jay Fiedler .25 .60
19 Vinny Testaverde .20 .50
20 Curtis Enis .20 .50
21 Elvis Grbac .20 .50
22 Kordell Stewart .20 .50
23 Jamal Anderson .25 .60
24 Dorsey Levens .25 .60
25 Derrick Mayes .20 .50
26 Marcus Robinson .25 .60
27 Cam Cleeland .20 .50
28 Charlie Garner .25 .60
29 Germane Crowell .20 .50
30 Cade McNown .20 .50
31 Tony Gonzalez .25 .60
32 Shaun King .20 .50
33 Wayne Chrebet .20 .50
34 Muhsin Muhammad .20 .50
35 Olandis Gary .25 .60
36 Ray Lewis .30 .75
37 Terrell Davis .25 .60
38 Steve Beuerlein .25 .60
39 James Stewart .20 .50
40 Jon Kitna .20 .50
41 Tim Biakabutuka .25 .60
42 Ryan Leaf .25 .60
43 Mike Alstott .20 .50
44 Yancey Thigpen .20 .50
45 Champ Bailey .25 .60
46 Peerless Price .25 .60
47 Ken Dilger .20 .50
48 Dorrick Alexander .20 .50
49 Drew Bledsoe .25 .60
50 Jerome Bettis .30 .75
51 Jermaine Fazande .20 .50
52 Joey Galloway .25 .60
53 Jeff Blake .25 .60
54 Emmitt Smith .50 1.25
55 Ricky Williams .25 .60
56 Marshall Faulk .25 .60
57 Stephen Davis .20 .50
58 Rob Johnson .25 .60
59 Brian Griese .20 .50
60 Damon Huard .20 .50
61 Jevon Kearse .20 .50
62 Doug Flutie .25 .60
63 Curtis Martin .25 .60
64 Torry Holt .25 .60
65 David Boston .20 .50
66 Cris Carter .30 .75
67 Jason Sehorn .20 .50
68 Keyshawn Johnson .25 .60
69 Chris Chandler .25 .60
70 Antonio Freeman .25 .60
71 Kerry Collins .20 .50
72 Akili Smith .20 .50
73 Troy Edwards .20 .50
74 Tim Dwight .25 .60
75 Donovan McNabb .25 .60
76 Tony Banks .20 .50
77 Ed McCaffrey .25 .60
78 Errict Rhett .25 .60
79 Fred Taylor .20 .50
80 Terrell Owens .25 .60
81 Steve McNair .25 .60
82 Rob Moore .20 .50
83 Jimmy Smith .25 .60
84 Daunte Culpepper .25 .60
85 Carl Pickens .25 .60
86 Moses Moreno .20 .50
87 Brad Johnson .25 .60
88 Jake Plummer .20 .50
89 Edgerrin James .25 .60
90 Zach Thomas .25 .60
91 Rich Gannon .25 .60
92 Warrick Dunn .20 .50
93 Shannon Sharpe .25 .60
94 Peyton Manning .75 2.00
95 Keenan McCardell .25 .60
96 Tony Simmons .20 .50
97 Duce Staley .20 .50
98 Corey Dillon .20 .50
99 Tim Brown .30 .75
100 Ricky Watters .25 .60
101 Peter Warrick RC 2.00 5.00
102 Shaun Alexander RC 3.00 8.00
103 Anthony Becht RC 2.00 5.00
104 Courtney Brown RC 2.50 6.00
105 Plaxico Burress RC 2.50 6.00
106 Trung Canidate RC 2.00 5.00
107 Giovanni Carmazzi RC 2.00 5.00
108 Laveranues Coles RC 2.50 6.00
109 Ron Dayne RC 3.00 8.00
110 Reuben Droughns RC 2.00 5.00
111 Danny Farmer RC 2.00 5.00
112 Bubba Franks RC 2.00 5.00
113 Thomas Jones RC 2.50 6.00
114 Jamal Lewis RC 3.00 8.00
115 Sylvester Morris RC 2.00 5.00
116 Chad Pennington RC 2.50 6.00
117 Travis Prentice RC 2.00 5.00
118 J.R. Redmond RC 2.00 5.00
119 R.Jay Soward RC 2.00 5.00
120 Dez White RC 2.00 5.00
121 Sebastian Janikowski RC 2.00 5.00
122 Todd Pinkston RC 1.25 3.00
123 Marc Bulger RC 1.50 4.00
124 Ron Dugans RC 1.25 3.00
125 Joe Hamilton RC 1.25 3.00
126 Curtis Keaton RC 1.25 3.00
127 Tee Martin RC 1.25 3.00
128 Dennis Northcutt RC 1.25 3.00
129 Corey Simon RC 1.50 4.00
130 Chris Redman RC 1.25 3.00
131 Brian Urlacher RC 6.00 15.00
132 Travis Taylor RC 1.25 3.00
133 Michael Wiley RC 1.25 3.00
134 Tim Rattay RC 1.50 4.00
135 Jerry Porter RC 2.00 5.00
136 Tom Brady RC 600.00 1000.00
137 Deon Dyer RC 1.25 3.00
138 Mareno Philyaw RC 1.25 3.00
139 Spergon Wynn RC 1.25 3.00
140 John Abraham RC 2.00 5.00
141 Ahmed Plummer RC 1.25 3.00
142 Chris Hovan RC 1.50 4.00
143 Rob Morris RC 1.50 4.00
144 Keith Bulluck RC 1.50 4.00
145 JaJuan Dawson RC 1.25 3.00
146 Chris Cole RC 1.50 4.00
147 Chafie Fields RC 1.25 3.00
148 Darrell Jackson RC 1.25 3.00
149 Marcus Knight RC 1.25 3.00
150 Gari Scott RC 1.25 3.00
151 Kwame Cavil RC 1.25 3.00
152 Frank Moreau RC 1.25 3.00
153 Doug Chapman RC 1.25 3.00
154 Erron Kinney RC 1.25 3.00
155 Ron Dixon RC 1.25 3.00
156 Ben Kelly RC 1.25 3.00
157 Bashir Yamini RC 1.25 3.00
158 Anthony Lucas RC 1.25 3.00
159 Avion Black RC 1.25 3.00
160 Ian Gold RC 1.25 3.00

2000 Fleer Showcase Rookie Showcase Firsts

Randomly inserted in packs, this 60-card set parallels the base set Rookie subset cards with each featuring a horizontal card design instead of vertical. Each card was also sequentially numbered to 250.

*1-20: .5X TO 1.2X BASIC RC/1000
*21-60: .8X TO 2X BASIC RC/2000
SHOWCASE FIRST PRINT RUN 250
36 Tom Brady 1500.00 2500.00

2000 Fleer Showcase Legacy

*VETS 1-100: 15X TO 40X BASIC CARDS
*ROOKIES 101-120: 1.5X TO 4X
*ROOKIES 121-160: 2.5X TO 6X
LEGACY PRINT RUN 20 SER.#'d SETS
136 Tom Brady 6000.00 10000.00

2000 Fleer Showcase Air to the Throne

Randomly inserted in packs at the rate of one in 10, this 10-card set featrues to top up and coming quarterbacks in action set against a blue background with a gold portrait in the upper left hand corner.

COMPLETE SET (10) 5.00 12.00
STATED ODDS 1:10
1 Peyton Manning 1.50 4.00
2 Charlie Batch .40 1.00
3 Giovanni Carmazzi .40 1.00
4 Brian Griese .40 1.00
5 Daunte Culpepper .50 1.25
6 Steve McNair .50 1.25
7 Brad Johnson .50 1.25
8 Rob Johnson .50 1.25
9 Cade McNown .40 1.00
10 Chad Pennington .50 1.25

2000 Fleer Showcase License to Skill

Randomly seeded in packs at the rate of one in 20, this 10-card set features a die cut base card along the top edges in the form of a semi circle. Player action photography is set against a blue background with silver foil highlights.

COMPLETE SET (10) 10.00 25.00
STATED ODDS 1:20
1 Tim Couch .50 1.25
2 Keyshawn Johnson .50 1.25
3 Peyton Manning 1.50 4.00
4 Brett Favre 1.25 3.00
5 Terrell Davis .50 1.25
6 Cade McNown .40 1.00
7 Marvin Harrison .50 1.25
8 Eddie George .50 1.25
9 Randy Moss .50 1.25
10 Emmitt Smith 1.00 2.50

2000 Fleer Showcase Mission Possible

Randomly inserted in packs at the rate of one in 5, this 10-card set features top NFL stars on top and bottom black bordered card with both an action and portrait photos against a "fire" background.

COMPLETE SET (10) 3.00 8.00
STATED ODDS 1:5
1 Tim Couch .30 .75
2 Brett Favre .75 2.00
3 Ricky Williams .30 .75
4 Akili Smith .25 .60
5 Shaun King .25 .60
6 Marvin Harrison .30 .75
7 Vinny Testaverde .25 .60
8 Terrell Davis .30 .75
9 Edgerrin James .30 .75
10 Eddie George .30 .75

2000 Fleer Showcase Next

Randomly inserted in packs at the rate of one in 2.5, this 20-card set features top 2000 rookies in action on an all silver foil insert card.

COMPLETE SET (20) 7.50 20.00
STATED ODDS 1:2.5
1 Peter Warrick .20 .50
2 Bubba Franks .20 .50
3 Jamal Lewis .30 .75
4 Anthony Becht .20 .50
5 R.Jay Soward .20 .50
6 Courtney Brown .25 .60
7 Plaxico Burress .25 .60
8 Trung Canidate .20 .50
9 Chris Redman .20 .50
10 Laveranues Coles .25 .60
11 Ron Dayne .30 .75
12 Reuben Droughns .20 .50
13 Danny Farmer .20 .50
14 Travis Prentice .20 .50
15 Dez White .20 .50
16 Shaun Alexander .30 .75
17 Thomas Jones .25 .60
18 J.R. Redmond .20 .50
19 Sylvester Morris .20 .50
20 Chad Pennington .25 .60

2000 Fleer Showcase Super Natural

Randomly inserted in packs at the rate of one in 20, this 10-card set features an embossed "Super Natural" logo along the top edge of the card with player action shots set against an all foil background.

COMPLETE SET (10) 10.00 25.00
STATED ODDS 1:20
1 Randy Moss .50 1.25
2 Marshall Faulk .50 1.25
3 Edgerrin James .50 1.25
4 Terrell Davis .50 1.25
5 Kurt Warner 1.00 2.50
6 Fred Taylor .40 1.00
7 Peyton Manning 1.50 4.00
8 Brett Favre 1.25 3.00
9 Brad Johnson .50 1.25
10 Warrick Dunn .40 1.00

2000 Fleer Showcase Touch Football

These card were randomly inserted in packs at the rate of one in 150. Fleer painted the hands of top rookies with white paint and had them hold footballs. They then added a swatch of those footballs featuring part of the player's handprint to each card. The unnumbered cards are listed alphabetically.

STATED ODDS 1:150
1 Shaun Alexander 3.00 8.00
2 Anthony Becht 2.00 5.00
3 Courtney Brown 2.50 6.00
4 Plaxico Burress 2.50 6.00
5 Trung Canidate 2.00 5.00
6 Laveranues Coles 2.50 6.00
7 Ron Dayne 3.00 8.00
8 Reuben Droughns 2.00 5.00
9 Ron Dugans 2.00 5.00
10 Danny Farmer 2.00 5.00
11 Bubba Franks 2.00 5.00
12 Joe Hamilton 2.00 5.00
13 Thomas Jones 2.50 6.00
14 Curtis Keaton 2.00 5.00
15 Jamal Lewis 3.00 8.00
16 Tee Martin 2.00 5.00
17 Sylvester Morris 2.00 5.00
18 Dennis Northcutt 2.00 5.00
19 Chad Pennington 2.50 6.00
20 Todd Pinkston 2.00 5.00
21 Jerry Porter 3.00 8.00
22 Travis Prentice 2.00 5.00
23 Chris Redman 2.00 5.00
24 J.R. Redmond 2.00 5.00
25 Corey Simon 2.50 6.00
26 R.Jay Soward 2.00 5.00
27 Travis Taylor 2.00 5.00
28 Brian Urlacher 10.00 25.00
29 Peter Warrick 2.00 5.00
30 Dez White 2.00 5.00

2001 Fleer Showcase

This 160 card set was issued in September, 2001. The cards were issued in five card packs with a suggested retail price of $4.99 per pack. Twenty four packs were included in each box. The last 60 cards in the set were short printed as cards numbered 101 through 115 were inserted at a rate of two per box. The final 45 cards of the set featured Rookie Cards and they were all printed in different amounts. Cards numbered 116 to 125 had a print run of 500, cards numbered from 126 through 145 had a print run of 1500 and cards numbered 146 through 160 had a print run of 2500 cards. In addition, an signed Avant Card of Donovan McNabb (numbered to 300) was randomly inserted in packs.

COMP.SET w/o SP's (100) 10.00 25.00
146-160 ROOKIE PRINT RUN 2000
1 Cris Carter .30 .75
2 Sylvester Morris .20 .50
3 Vinny Testaverde .20 .50
4 Jevon Kearse .20 .50
5 Terance Mathis .20 .50
6 Mike Anderson .20 .50
7 Aaron Brooks .20 .50
8 Jerry Rice .60 1.50
9 Mike Alstott .20 .50
10 Jon Kitna .20 .50
11 Derrick Alexander .20 .50
12 Shaun Alexander .20 .50
13 Thomas Jones .20 .50
14 James Stewart .20 .50
15 Ron Dayne .25 .60
16 Az-Zahir Hakim .20 .50
17 Terrell Owens .25 .60
18 Travis Prentice .20 .50
19 Lamar Smith .25 .60
20 James Thrash .25 .60
21 Doug Flutie .25 .60
22 Derrick Mason .20 .50
23 Ray Lewis .30 .75
24 Ed McCaffrey .25 .60
25 Ricky Williams .25 .60
26 Tyrone Wheatley .25 .60
27 Chris Chandler .25 .60
28 Rod Smith .25 .60
29 Joe Horn .20 .50
30 Jerome Bettis .30 .75
31 Brian Urlacher .40 1.00
32 Dorsey Levens .25 .60
33 Kordell Stewart .20 .50
34 Michael Westbrook .20 .50
35 Jamal Anderson .25 .60
36 Charlie Batch .20 .50
37 Kerry Collins .20 .50
38 Jake Plummer .20 .50
39 Robert Porcher .20 .50
40 Jason Sehorn .25 .60
41 Junior Seau .25 .60
42 Warren Sapp .25 .60
43 Champ Bailey .25 .60
44 Jamal Lewis .30 .75
45 Tony Banks .20 .50
46 Doug Chapman .20 .50
47 Stephen Davis .20 .50
48 Elvis Grbac .25 .60
49 Joey Galloway .25 .60
50 Terry Glenn .25 .60
51 Todd Pinkston .20 .50
52 JaJuan Dawson .20 .50
53 Zach Thomas .25 .60
54 Tim Couch .20 .50
55 Cade McNown .25 .60
56 Charlie Garner .25 .60
57 Jeff George .25 .60
58 Peerless Price .20 .50
59 Tony Gonzalez .25 .60
60 Rob Johnson .25 .60
61 Keenan McCardell .25 .60
62 Eric Moulds .20 .50
63 Jimmy Smith .25 .60
64 Jeff Garcia .20 .50
65 Rod Woodson .30 .75
66 Brian Griese .20 .50
67 Kevin Faulk .20 .50
68 Plaxico Burress .20 .50
69 Isaac Bruce .30 .75
70 Keyshawn Johnson .25 .60
71 Tim Biakabutuka .20 .50
72 Mark Brunell .25 .60
73 Wesley Walls .20 .50
74 Jerome Pathon .20 .50
75 Wayne Chrebet .20 .50
76 Muhsin Muhammad .20 .50
77 Marvin Harrison .25 .60
78 David Boston .20 .50
79 Germane Crowell .20 .50
80 Tiki Barber .25 .60
81 Laveranues Coles .25 .60
82 Tim Brown .30 .75
83 Matt Hasselbeck .20 .50
84 Brad Johnson .25 .60
85 Marcus Robinson .25 .60
86 Ahman Green .25 .60
87 Curtis Martin .25 .60
88 Peter Warrick .20 .50
89 Ray Lucas .20 .50
90 Duce Staley .20 .50
91 Darrell Jackson .25 .60
92 Steve McNair .25 .60
93 Rickey Dudley .20 .50
94 Jason Taylor .30 .75
95 Rich Gannon .25 .60
96 Torry Holt .25 .60
97 James Allen .20 .50
98 Antonio Freeman .30 .75
99 Trent Green .20 .50
100 Ricky Watters .25 .60
101 Corey Dillon AC 1.00 2.50
102 Emmitt Smith AC 2.50 6.00
103 Terrell Davis AC 1.25 3.00
104 Brett Favre AC 3.00 8.00
105 Peyton Manning AC 4.00 10.00
106 Edgerrin James AC 1.25 3.00
107 Fred Taylor AC 1.00 2.50
108 Daunte Culpepper AC 1.25 3.00
109 Randy Moss AC 1.25 3.00
110 Drew Bledsoe AC 1.25 3.00
111 Donovan McNabb AC 1.25 3.00
112 Kurt Warner AC 2.50 6.00
113 Marshall Faulk AC 1.25 3.00
114 Warrick Dunn AC 1.00 2.50
115 Eddie George AC 1.50 4.00
116 Michael Vick AC RC 6.00 15.00
117 David Terrell AC RC 3.00 8.00
118 Deuce McAllister AC RC 4.00 10.00
119 Koren Robinson AC RC 3.00 8.00
120 Rod Gardner AC RC 3.00 8.00
121 Santana Moss AC RC 4.00 10.00
122 Drew Brees AC RC 60.00 125.00
123 Chris Weinke AC RC 3.00 8.00
124 LaDainian Tomlinson AC RC 12.00 30.00
125 Freddie Mitchell AC RC 2.50 6.00
126 Chris Chambers RC 1.25 3.00
127 Reggie Wayne RC 2.50 6.00
128 Quincy Morgan RC 1.50 4.00
129 Rudi Johnson RC 2.00 5.00
130 Robert Ferguson RC 2.00 5.00
131 Todd Heap RC 1.50 4.00
132 Michael Bennett RC 1.50 4.00
133 Jesse Palmer RC 1.50 4.00
134 James Jackson RC 1.25 3.00
135 Chad Johnson RC 2.00 5.00
136 LaMont Jordan RC 2.00 5.00
137 Anthony Thomas RC 2.00 5.00
138 Travis Henry RC 1.50 4.00
139 Snoop Minnis RC 1.25 3.00
140 Marques Tuiasosopo RC 1.50 4.00
141 Travis Minor RC 1.50 4.00
142 Mike McMahon RC 1.50 4.00
143 Josh Heupel RC 2.00 5.00
144 Sage Rosenfels RC 1.50 4.00
145 Quincy Carter RC 1.50 4.00
146 Alge Crumpler RC 2.00 5.00
147 Kevan Barlow RC 1.50 4.00
148 Heath Evans RC 1.50 4.00
149 Correll Buckhalter RC 1.25 3.00
150 Justin McCareins RC 1.50 4.00
151 Reggie Germany RC 1.25 3.00
152 Vinny Sutherland RC 1.25 3.00
153 Scotty Anderson RC 1.25 3.00
154 Tim Hasselbeck RC 1.50 4.00
155 Alex Bannister RC 1.25 3.00
156 Andre Carter RC 1.50 4.00
157 Adam Archuleta RC 1.50 4.00
158 Ken-Yon Rambo RC 1.25 3.00
159 Gerard Warren RC 1.50 4.00
160 Justin Smith RC 2.50 6.00
CL1 Checklist .05 .15
CL2 Checklist .05 .15
NNO D.McNabb AU/300 15.00 40.00

2001 Fleer Showcase Legacy

*VETS 1-100: 6X TO 15X BASIC CARDS
*VETS AC 101-115: 1.5X TO 4X
*ROOKIES 116-125: .8X TO 2X
*ROOKIES 126-145: 1.2X TO 3X
*ROOKIES 146-160: 1.2X TO 3X
STATED PRINT RUN 50 SER.#'d SETS

2001 Fleer Showcase Awards Showcase

Inserted at a rate of 1:20 retail packs, this set highlights NFL award winning performers.

STATED ODDS 1:20 RETAIL
1 Randy Moss 1.00 2.50
2 Marvin Harrison 1.00 2.50
3 Tony Gonzalez 1.00 2.50
4 Rich Gannon 1.00 2.50
5 Marshall Faulk 1.00 2.50
6 Edgerrin James 1.00 2.50
7 Warren Sapp 1.00 2.50
8 Ray Lewis 1.25 3.00
9 Brian Urlacher 1.50 4.00
10 Chris Weinke 1.00 2.50
11 Eric Moulds .75 2.00
12 Isaac Bruce 1.25 3.00
13 Daunte Culpepper 1.00 2.50
14 Curtis Martin 1.00 2.50
15 Kurt Warner 2.00 5.00
16 Mike Anderson .75 2.00

17 Robert Smith .75 2.00
18 Jamal Lewis 1.25 3.00
19 Rod Smith 1.00 2.50
20 Junior Seau 1.00 2.50

2001 Fleer Showcase Awards Showcase Memorabilia

This set, which was randomly inserted in packs featues a mix of current stars and all time greats. These cards feature a piece of game-used memorabilia on it.
STATED PRINT RUN 100 SER.#'d SETS
1 Marcus Allen 5.00 12.00
2 Terry Bradshaw 6.00 15.00
3 Terrell Davis 4.00 10.00
4 Eric Dickerson 4.00 10.00
5 Tony Dorsett 5.00 12.00
6 Marshall Faulk 4.00 10.00
7 Brett Favre 10.00 25.00
8 Eddie George 5.00 12.00
9 Edgerrin James 4.00 10.00
10 Joe Montana 15.00 40.00
11 Randy Moss 8.00 20.00
12 Walter Payton 12.00 30.00
13 Jerry Rice 10.00 25.00
14 Emmitt Smith 8.00 20.00
15 Fran Tarkenton 5.00 12.00
16 Lawrence Taylor 5.00 12.00
17 Johnny Unitas 10.00 25.00
18 Steve Young 6.00 15.00

2001 Fleer Showcase Awards Showcase Memorabilia Autographs

Randomly inserted in packs, these 14 card semi-parallel set has the players signature on their award showcase memorabilia card. These cards were serial numbered to 25 and since these cards were redemptions, the lucky collectors who pulled these cards from packs had until October 1, 2002 to redeem these cards.
STATED PRINT RUN 25 SER.#'d SETS
1 Marcus Allen 30.00 80.00
2 Terry Bradshaw 100.00 200.00
4 Eric Dickerson 30.00 80.00
5 Tony Dorsett 40.00 100.00
6 Marshall Faulk 30.00 80.00
7 Edgerrin James 30.00 80.00
8 Joe Montana 125.00 250.00
9 Randy Moss 60.00 120.00
11 Emmitt Smith 150.00 300.00
13 Lawrence Taylor 40.00 100.00
14 Johnny Unitas 250.00 400.00

2001 Fleer Showcase Patchwork

Inserted in packs at a rate on one in 20, this 33 card set features pieces of game-used jerseys of leading NFL stars. These horizontal cards feature a jersey piece is on the left side with the word "Patchwork" and the players name and team in the middle. The player's photo is on the bottom of the card.
STATED ODDS 1:20
1 Troy Aikman 4.00 10.00
2 Jamal Anderson 2.50 6.00
3 Charlie Batch 2.00 5.00
4 Drew Bledsoe 2.50 6.00
5 Mark Brunell 2.50 6.00
6 Chris Chandler 2.50 6.00
7 Terrell Davis 2.50 6.00
8 Marshall Faulk 2.50 6.00
9 Brian Griese 2.00 5.00
10 Marvin Harrison 2.50 6.00
11 Torry Holt 2.50 6.00
12 Edgerrin James 2.50 6.00
13 Dorsey Levens SP 3.00 8.00
14 Ronnie Lott 2.50 6.00
15 Dan Marino 6.00 15.00
16 Steve McNair 2.50 6.00
17 Johnnie Morton 2.50 6.00
18 Todd Pinkston 2.00 5.00
19 Travis Prentice 2.00 5.00
20 Peerless Price 2.00 5.00
21 Chris Redman 3.00 8.00
22 Jerry Rice 6.00 15.00
23 Warren Sapp 2.50 6.00
24 Deion Sanders 2.50 6.00
25 Junior Seau 2.50 6.00
26 Bruce Smith 2.50 6.00
27 Rod Smith 2.50 6.00
28 Fred Taylor 2.00 5.00
29 Lawrence Taylor 3.00 8.00
30 Brian Urlacher 4.00 10.00
31 Kurt Warner 5.00 12.00
32 Charles Woodson 3.00 8.00
33 Steve Young 4.00 10.00

2001 Fleer Showcase Stitches

This 17 card set, which was inserted at a rate of one in 20 packs features a game-used jersey piece of leading NFL stars. These horizontal cards feaure the player's photo on the right, along with a smaller shaded version of that version on the left side. The jersey piece is in the middle and on the bottom is the player's name and the insert set identification.
STATED ODDS 1:20
1 Cris Carter 3.00 8.00
2 Daunte Culpepper 2.50 6.00
3 Corey Dillon 2.00 5.00
4 John Elway 5.00 12.00
5 Marshall Faulk 2.50 6.00
6 Brett Favre 6.00 15.00
7 Marvin Harrison 2.50 6.00
8 Dan Marino 6.00 15.00
9 Steve McNair 2.50 6.00
10 Joe Montana 10.00 25.00
11 Todd Pinkston 2.00 5.00
12 Robert Smith 2.00 5.00
13 Fred Taylor 2.00 5.00
14 Kurt Warner 5.00 12.00
15 Peter Warrick 2.00 5.00
16 Ricky Williams 2.50 6.00
17 Steve Young 4.00 10.00

2002 Fleer Showcase

Released in May 2002, this 166 card set is composed of 125 basic cards, 10 Avant veteran cards and 6 rookie Avant cards serial numbered to 500 and 25 Rookie Showcase serial numbered to 1500. The veteran Avant cards were issued at a stated rate of one in 12. Boxes contained 24 packs per box with 5 cards per pack. SRP per pack was $4.99.
COMP.SET w/o SP's (125) 10.00 25.00
136-141 ROOKIE AC PRINT RUN 500
142-166 ROOKIE PRINT RUN 1500
1 Kevin Johnson .25 .60
2 Chris Walsh .25 .60
3 Vinny Testaverde .25 .60
4 Kordell Stewart .25 .60
5 Chris Redman .25 .60
6 Johnnie Morton .30 .75
7 Tony Gonzalez .30 .75
8 Torry Holt .30 .75
9 Champ Bailey .30 .75
10 Eric Moulds .25 .60
11 Az-Zahir Hakim .25 .60
12 Mark Brunell .30 .75
13 Laveranues Coles .30 .75
14 Kevan Barlow .25 .60
15 Stephen Davis .25 .60
16 Benjamin Gay .25 .60
17 Randy Moss .30 .75
18 Hines Ward .30 .75
19 Brian Urlacher .40 1.00
20 Dominic Rhodes .25 .60
21 David Patten .25 .60
22 Tim Brown .40 1.00
23 Trent Dilfer .25 .60
24 David Boston .25 .60
25 Quincy Carter .25 .60
26 Daunte Culpepper .30 .75
27 Plaxico Burress .25 .60
28 Michael Pittman .30 .75
29 Joey Galloway .30 .75
30 Jason Taylor .30 .75
31 Drew Brees .75 2.00
32 Jamal Anderson .30 .75
33 Dat Nguyen .25 .60
34 Chris Chambers .25 .60
35 Tiki Barber .30 .75
36 LaDainian Tomlinson .40 1.00
37 Peter Warrick .25 .60
38 Bubba Franks .25 .60
39 Joe Horn .25 .60
40 Correll Buckhalter .25 .60
41 Mike Alstott .25 .60
42 Brian Finneran .25 .60
43 Troy Hambrick .25 .60
44 Zach Thomas .30 .75
45 Kerry Collins .25 .60
46 Junior Seau .30 .75
47 Alvis Whitted .25 .60
48 Terrell Davis .30 .75
49 Ricky Williams .30 .75
50 Curtis Conway .30 .75
51 Travis Taylor .25 .60
52 Brian Griese .25 .60
53 Sylvester Morris .25 .60
54 Amani Toomer .25 .60
55 Jeff Garcia .25 .60
56 Michael McCrary .25 .60
57 Ahman Green .30 .75
58 Trent Green .25 .60
59 Trung Canidate .25 .60
60 Jamal Lewis .30 .75
61 Larry Foster .25 .60
62 Priest Holmes .25 .60
63 Isaac Bruce .40 1.00
64 Bruce Smith .30 .75
65 Darnay Scott .30 .75
66 Terry Glenn .30 .75
67 Darren Howard .25 .60
68 Hugh Douglas .25 .60
69 Milton Wynn .25 .60
70 Tim Couch .25 .60
71 Bill Schroeder .25 .60
72 Michael Strahan .30 .75
73 James Thrash .30 .75
74 Steve McNair .30 .75
75 Patrick Jeffers .30 .75
76 Marcus Pollard .25 .60
77 Willie McGinest .30 .75
78 Santana Moss .30 .75
79 Grant Wistrom .25 .60
80 Jim Miller .25 .60
81 Marvin Harrison .30 .75
82 Troy Brown .25 .60
83 Rich Gannon .30 .75
84 Shaun Alexander .25 .60
85 Jake Plummer .25 .60
86 Quincy Morgan .25 .60
87 Michael Bennett .25 .60
88 Jerome Bettis .40 1.00
89 Marty Booker .25 .60
90 Trevor Insley .25 .60
91 Adam Vinatieri .25 .60
92 Charles Woodson .40 1.00
93 Darrell Jackson .30 .75
94 Corey Dillon .25 .60
95 Corey Bradford .25 .60
96 Deuce McAllister .30 .75
97 Todd Pinkston .25 .60
98 Warren Sapp .30 .75
99 Alex Van Pelt .25 .60
100 Mike McMahon .25 .60
101 Fred Taylor .25 .60
102 Ron Dayne .30 .75
103 Ernie Conwell .25 .60
104 Rod Gardner .25 .60
105 Muhsin Muhammad .25 .60
106 Reggie Wayne .30 .75
107 Antowain Smith .30 .75
108 Chad Pennington .25 .60
109 Koren Robinson .25 .60
110 Travis Henry .25 .60
111 Ed McCaffrey .30 .75
112 Keenan McCardell .30 .75
113 Curtis Martin .30 .75
114 Bryant Young .25 .60
115 Derrick Mason .25 .60
116 Anthony Thomas .30 .75
117 Jermaine Lewis .25 .60
118 Aaron Brooks .25 .60
119 Charlie Garner .30 .75
120 Keyshawn Johnson .30 .75
121 Chris Weinke .25 .60
122 Rod Smith .30 .75
123 Jimmy Smith .30 .75
124 Terrell Owens .30 .75
125 Eddie George .30 .75
126 Tom Brady AC 6.00 15.00
127 Donovan McNabb AC 1.00 2.50
128 Kurt Warner AC 1.00 2.50
129 Peyton Manning AC 3.00 8.00
130 Marshall Faulk AC 1.00 2.50
131 Michael Vick AC 1.00 2.50
132 Emmitt Smith AC 2.00 5.00
133 Jerry Rice AC 2.50 6.00
134 Edgerrin James AC 1.00 2.50
135 Brett Favre AC 2.50 6.00
136 David Carr AC RC 2.00 5.00
137 Joey Harrington AC RC 2.00 5.00
138 Ashley Lelie AC RC 2.00 5.00
139 William Green AC RC 2.50 6.00
140 T.J. Duckett AC RC 2.00 5.00
141 Donte Stallworth AC RC 3.00 8.00
142 Ron Johnson RC 1.50 4.00
143 Jeremy Shockey RC 2.00 5.00
144 Daniel Graham RC 1.50 4.00
145 Reche Caldwell RC 1.50 4.00
146 Antonio Bryant RC 2.00 5.00
147 DeShaun Foster RC 2.00 5.00
148 Clinton Portis RC 2.00 5.00
149 Patrick Ramsey RC 1.50 4.00
150 Lamar Gordon RC 1.50 4.00
151 Josh Reed RC 1.50 4.00
152 Ladell Betts RC 2.00 5.00
153 Kurt Kittner RC 1.25 3.00
154 Jabar Gaffney RC 1.25 3.00
155 Josh McCown RC 2.00 5.00
156 Marquise Walker RC 1.25 3.00
157 Brian Westbrook RC 2.50 6.00
158 Andre Davis RC 1.25 3.00
159 David Garrard RC 1.50 4.00
160 Cliff Russell RC 1.25 3.00
161 Julius Peppers RC 3.00 8.00
162 Adrian Peterson RC 1.50 4.00
163 Antwaan Randle El RC 1.50 4.00
164 Javon Walker RC 2.00 5.00
165 Rohan Davey RC 2.00 5.00
166 Luke Staley RC 1.25 3.00

2002 Fleer Showcase Legacy

*VETS 1-125: 5X TO 12X BASIC CARDS
*AC VETS 126-135: 1.5X TO 4X
*ROOKIE AC 136-141: .6X TO 1.5X
*ROOKIES 142-166: 1X TO 2.5X
STATED PRINT RUN 100 SER.#'d SETS
UNPRICED MASTERPIECES #d TO 1

2002 Fleer Showcase Masterpiece

STATED PRINT RUN 1 SER.#'d SET
UNPRICED MASTERPIECE PRINT RUN 1

2002 Fleer Showcase Air to the Throne

Inserted in packs at a rate of 1 in 8, this 20 card set features some of the greatest past and present quarterbacks.
COMPLETE SET (17) 20.00 50.00
STATED ODDS 1:8
AT16, AT17, AT19 NOT RELEASED
AT1 Mark Brunell 1.00 2.50
AT2 Tim Couch .75 2.00
AT3 Daunte Culpepper 1.00 2.50
AT4 Brett Favre 2.50 6.00
AT5 Rich Gannon 1.00 2.50
AT6 Jeff Garcia .75 2.00
AT7 Brian Griese .75 2.00
AT8 Kurt Warner 1.00 2.50
AT9 Donovan McNabb 1.00 2.50
AT10 Steve McNair 1.00 2.50
AT11 Jake Plummer .75 2.00
AT12 Kordell Stewart .75 2.00
AT13 Troy Aikman 1.50 4.00
AT14 Jim Kelly 1.25 3.00
AT15 John Elway 2.00 5.00
AT18 Dan Marino 2.50 6.00
AT20 Roger Staubach 1.50 4.00

2002 Fleer Showcase Air to the Throne Jerseys

Inserted in packs at a rate of 1 in 24, this set features some of the greatest past and present quarterbacks to ever play in the NFL. Each unnumbered card features a swatch of game worn jersey.
STATED ODDS 1:24
*GOLD/50: .8X TO 2X BASIC JSY
GOLD STATED PRINT RUN 50 SER.#'d SETS
1 Troy Aikman 6.00 15.00
2 Mark Brunell 4.00 10.00
3 Tim Couch 3.00 8.00
4 Daunte Culpepper 4.00 10.00
5 John Elway 8.00 20.00
6 Brett Favre 10.00 25.00
7 Rich Gannon 4.00 10.00
8 Jeff Garcia 3.00 8.00
9 Brian Griese 3.00 8.00
10 Jim Kelly 5.00 12.00
11 Dan Marino 10.00 25.00
12 Donovan McNabb 4.00 10.00
13 Steve McNair 4.00 10.00
14 Joe Montana 15.00 40.00
15 Jake Plummer 3.00 8.00
16 Roger Staubach 6.00 15.00
17 Kordell Stewart 3.00 8.00
18 Kurt Warner 4.00 10.00

2002 Fleer Showcase Football's Best

Randomly inserted in packs, this 32 card set features full color horizontal action shots of top NFL stars. Cards are serial numbered to 799.
COMPLETE SET (32) 50.00 120.00
STATED PRINT RUN 799 SER.#'d SETS
FB1 Edgerrin James 1.50 4.00
FB2 Shaun Alexander 1.25 3.00
FB3 Mike Alstott 1.25 3.00
FB4 Tiki Barber 1.50 4.00
FB5 Jerome Bettis 2.00 5.00
FB6 David Boston 1.25 3.00
FB7 Tim Brown 2.00 5.00
FB8 Isaac Bruce 2.00 5.00
FB9 Plaxico Burress 1.25 3.00
FB10 Tim Couch 1.25 3.00
FB11 Wayne Chrebet 1.25 3.00
FB12 Daunte Culpepper 1.50 4.00
FB13 Stephen Davis 1.25 3.00
FB14 Terrell Davis 1.50 4.00
FB15 Ron Dayne 1.50 4.00
FB16 Corey Dillon 1.25 3.00
FB17 Marshall Faulk 1.50 4.00
FB18 Brett Favre 4.00 10.00
FB19 Rich Gannon 1.50 4.00
FB20 Eddie George 1.50 4.00
FB21 Randy Moss 1.50 4.00
FB22 Junior Seau 1.50 4.00
FB23 Jerry Rice 4.00 10.00
FB24 Torry Holt 1.50 4.00
FB25 Jamal Anderson 1.50 4.00
FB26 Ray Lewis 2.00 5.00
FB27 Antowain Smith 1.50 4.00
FB28 Peter Warrick 1.25 3.00
FB29 Ed McCaffrey 1.50 4.00
FB30 Marvin Harrison 1.50 4.00
FB31 Jimmy Smith 1.50 4.00
FB32 Fred Taylor 1.25 3.00

2002 Fleer Showcase Football's Best Memorabilia

Inserted in packs at a rate of 1 in 15, this 31 card set features full color horizontal action shots with a piece of game of game-used jersey on the card front.
STATED ODDS 1:15
*SILVER PATCH/100: .6X TO 1.5X BASIC JSY
SILVER PATCH PRINT RUN 100 SER.#'d SETS
*GOLD PATCH/25: 1.5X TO 4X BASIC JSY
GOLD PATCH PRINT RUN 25 SER.#'d SETS
FB1 Mike Alstott 3.00 8.00
FB2 Jamal Anderson 4.00 10.00
FB3 Tiki Barber 4.00 10.00
FB4 Jerome Bettis 12.00 30.00
FB5 David Boston 3.00 8.00
FB6 Tim Brown 5.00 12.00
FB7 Isaac Bruce 5.00 12.00
FB8 Plaxico Burress 3.00 8.00
FB9 Wayne Chrebet 3.00 8.00
FB10 Tim Couch 3.00 8.00
FB11 Daunte Culpepper 4.00 10.00
FB12 Stephen Davis 3.00 8.00
FB13 Terrell Davis 4.00 10.00
FB14 Ron Dayne 4.00 10.00
FB15 Corey Dillon 3.00 8.00
FB16 Marshall Faulk 4.00 10.00
FB17 Brett Favre 10.00 25.00
FB18 Rich Gannon 4.00 10.00
FB19 Eddie George 4.00 10.00
FB20 Marvin Harrison 4.00 10.00
FB21 Torry Holt 4.00 10.00
FB22 Edgerrin James 4.00 10.00
FB23 Ray Lewis 5.00 12.00
FB24 Ed McCaffrey 4.00 10.00
FB25 Randy Moss 4.00 10.00
FB26 Jerry Rice 10.00 25.00
FB27 Junior Seau 4.00 10.00
FB28 Antowain Smith 4.00 10.00
FB29 Jimmy Smith 4.00 10.00
FB30 Fred Taylor 3.00 8.00
FB31 Peter Warrick 3.00 8.00

2002 Fleer Showcase Top to Bottom

Randomly inserted in packs, this 8 card set features a full color action shots on card front along with a swatch of game used jersey with a swatch of game used pants directly beneath it. Cards are serial numbered to 250.
STATED PRINT RUN 250 SER.#'d SETS
1 David Boston 4.00 10.00
2 Eddie George 5.00 12.00
3 Marvin Harrison 5.00 12.00
4 Edgerrin James 5.00 12.00
5 Jake Plummer 4.00 10.00
6 Marcus Robinson 5.00 12.00
7 Duce Staley 4.00 10.00
8 Brian Urlacher 6.00 15.00

2003 Fleer Showcase

Released in June of 2003, this product features 100 veterans, and 40 rookies. The veterans were broken down as follows: 1-45 were only available in jersey packs, 46-90 in leather packs, 91-95 were found in jersey packs and were serial numbered to 650, while cards 96-100 were found in leather packs and were serial numbered to 350. Rookie Cards 101-110 are serial numbered to 350 or 650. Rookie Cards 111-140 are serial numbered to 750, with cards 111-125 available in jersey packs, and cards 126-140 available in leather packs. Each box contained two 12-pack mini-boxes, one Leather Edition and one Jersey Edition. Each pack featured five cards for an SRP of $4.99.
COMP.SET w/o SP's (90) 10.00 25.00
1 Edgerrin James .30 .75
2 Donald Driver .30 .75
3 Drew Brees .40 1.00
4 Corey Dillon .25 .60
5 Jerome Bettis .40 1.00
6 Charlie Garner .30 .75
7 Eddie George .30 .75
8 Mark Brunell .30 .75
9 David Boston .25 .60
10 Todd Heap .25 .60
11 Terrell Owens .30 .75
12 Tommy Maddox .25 .60
13 Keyshawn Johnson .40 1.00
14 Jamal Lewis .30 .75
15 Zach Thomas .30 .75
16 Isaac Bruce .40 1.00
17 Michael Bennett .25 .60
18 Rod Smith .30 .75
19 Eric Moulds .25 .60
20 T.J Duckett .25 .60
21 Hines Ward .30 .75
22 Tiki Barber .30 .75
23 Julius Peppers .40 1.00
24 Rich Gannon .30 .75
25 Rod Gardner .25 .60
26 Curtis Martin .30 .75
27 Donte Stallworth .25 .60
28 Anthony Thomas .30 .75
29 Warren Sapp .30 .75
30 Jake Plummer .25 .60
31 Patrick Ramsey .30 .75
32 Tai Streets .25 .60
33 Matt Hasselbeck .25 .60
34 James Stewart .25 .60
35 Chad Hutchinson .25 .60
36 Hugh Douglas .25 .60
37 Jimmy Smith .30 .75
38 Kerry Collins .25 .60
39 Junior Seau .30 .75
40 Ed McCaffrey .30 .75
41 Marshall Faulk .30 .75
42 Deuce McAllister .30 .75
43 Drew Bledsoe .30 .75
44 Brian Urlacher .40 1.00
45 William Green .25 .60
46 Chris Chambers .25 .60
47 Daunte Culpepper .30 .75
48 Warrick Dunn .25 .60
49 Antwaan Randle El .25 .60
50 Joey Harrington .25 .60
51 Tim Brown .40 1.00
52 Duce Staley .25 .60
53 Laveranues Coles .25 .60
54 Ray Lewis .40 1.00
55 Marvin Harrison .30 .75
56 Tony Gonzalez .30 .75
57 Torry Holt .30 .75
58 Jeff Garcia .25 .60
59 Peerless Price .25 .60
60 Marcel Shipp .25 .60
61 Brian Finneran .25 .60
62 Fred Taylor .25 .60
63 Koren Robinson .30 .75
64 Shaun Alexander .25 .60
65 Plaxico Burress .25 .60
66 Ahman Green .30 .75
67 Simeon Rice .25 .60
68 Joe Horn .25 .60
69 Steve McNair .30 .75
70 Amani Toomer .25 .60
71 Kendrell Bell .25 .60
72 Marty Booker .25 .60
73 Stephen Davis .25 .60
74 David Carr .25 .60
75 Garrison Hearst .25 .60
76 Joey Galloway .30 .75
77 Aaron Brooks .25 .60
78 Mike Alstott .25 .60
79 Shannon Sharpe .30 .75
80 Derrick Mason .25 .60
81 Tim Couch .25 .60
82 Chad Johnson .25 .60
83 Jason Taylor .30 .75
84 Travis Henry .25 .60
85 Curtis Conway .25 .60
86 Peyton Manning 1.00 2.50
87 Kurt Warner .30 .75
88 LaDainian Tomlinson .40 1.00
89 Emmitt Smith .60 1.50
90 Priest Holmes .25 .60
91 Ricky Williams AC 1.50 4.00
92 Brett Favre AC 4.00 10.00
93 Clinton Portis AC 1.25 3.00
94 Randy Moss AC 1.50 4.00
95 Tom Brady AC 8.00 20.00
96 Chad Pennington AC 1.50 4.00
97 Michael Vick AC 2.00 5.00
98 Jeremy Shockey AC 1.50 4.00
99 Donovan McNabb AC 2.00 5.00
100 Jerry Rice AC 5.00 12.00
101 Carson Palmer AC/350 RC 5.00 12.00
102 Lee Suggs AC/650 RC 2.00 5.00
103 Larry Johnson AC/350 RC 3.00 8.00
104 Taylor Jacobs AC/650 RC 2.00 5.00
105 Andre Johnson AC/350 RC 6.00 15.00
106 Justin Fargas AC/650 RC 3.00 8.00
107 Charles Rogers AC/350 RC 3.00 8.00
108 Willis McGahee AC/650 RC 2.50 6.00
109 Byron Leftwich AC/350 RC 3.00 8.00
110 Kyle Boller AC/650 RC 2.00 5.00
111 Bobby Wade RC 2.50 6.00
112 Brian St.Pierre RC 2.00 5.00
113 Doug Gabriel RC 2.50 6.00
114 Chris Brown RC 2.00 5.00
115 DeWayne Robertson RC 2.50 6.00
116 Anquan Boldin RC 3.00 8.00
117 Brandon Lloyd RC 3.00 8.00
118 Brad Banks RC 2.50 6.00
119 Dallas Clark RC 3.00 8.00
120 Artose Pinner RC 2.00 5.00
121 Dave Ragone RC 2.00 5.00
122 Arnaz Battle RC 3.00 8.00
123 Andrew Pinnock RC 2.50 6.00
124 Billy McMullen RC 2.00 5.00
125 Avon Cobourne RC 2.00 5.00
126 Terence Newman RC 3.00 8.00
127 Jimmy Kennedy RC 2.50 6.00
128 Terrell Suggs RC 2.50 6.00
129 Rex Grossman RC 2.50 6.00
130 Musa Smith RC 2.00 5.00
131 William Joseph RC 2.00 5.00
132 Tyrone Calico RC 2.00 5.00
133 Teyo Johnson RC 2.50 6.00
134 Onterrio Smith RC 2.00 5.00
135 Mike Doss RC 3.00 8.00
136 Kliff Kingsbury RC 3.00 8.00
137 Kelley Washington RC 2.00 5.00
138 Kareem Kelly RC 2.00 5.00
139 Jason Gesser RC 2.50 6.00
140 Chris Simms RC 2.00 5.00

2003 Fleer Showcase Legacy

*VETS 1-90: 3X TO 8X BASIC CARDS
*AC VETS 91-95: .8X TO 2X
*AC VETS 96-100: .6X TO 1.5X
*AC ROOKIES: .4X TO 1X AC RC/350
*AC ROOKIES: .5X TO 1.2X AC RC/650
*ROOKIES 111-140: .8X TO 2X
STATED PRINT RUN 125 SER.#'d SETS
UNPRICED MASTERPIECES #'d TO 1

2003 Fleer Showcase Avant Card Jerseys

This set is a game used jersey parallel of the Avant Card subset. Each card features game used jersey swatches, and is serial numbered to 999. Each card was available in either leather packs or jersey packs, which is noted after the players name as JE or LE.
STATED PRINT RUN 999 SER.#'d SETS
AVBF Brett Favre JE 6.00 15.00
AVCP Chad Pennington LE 2.00 5.00
AVCP2 Clinton Portis JE 2.00 5.00
AVDM Donovan McNabb LE 2.50 6.00
AVJR Jerry Rice LE 6.00 15.00
AVJS Jeremy Shockey LE 2.00 5.00
AVMV Michael Vick LE 2.50 6.00
AVRM Randy Moss JE 2.50 6.00
AVRW Ricky Williams JE 2.50 6.00
AVTB Tom Brady JE 12.00 30.00

2003 Fleer Showcase Football's Best

COMPLETE SET (8) 8.00 20.00
STATED ODDS 1:12 LEATHER
1 Michael Vick 1.00 2.50
2 Ricky Williams 1.00 2.50
3 Brian Urlacher 1.25 3.00
4 Jeff Garcia .75 2.00
5 Chad Pennington .75 2.00
6 William Green .75 2.00
7 Kurt Warner 1.00 2.50
8 Drew Bledsoe 1.00 2.50

2003 Fleer Showcase Football's Best Jerseys

Inserted at a rate of 1:28 leather packs, and 1:38 jersey packs, this set features swatches of game used jersey. A Gold version also exists, with each card being serial numbered to 150.
STATED ODDS 1:28 LEA, 1:38 JER
*GOLD/150: .6X TO 1.5X BASIC JSY
GOLD PRINT RUN 150 SER.#'d SETS
FBAG Ahman Green LE 2.50 6.00
FBBU Brian Urlacher JE 3.00 8.00
FBCP Chad Pennington JE 2.00 5.00
FBDC David Carr LE 2.00 5.00
FBEG Eddie George JE 2.50 6.00
FBEM Eric Moulds JE 2.00 5.00
FBES Emmitt Smith JE 5.00 12.00
FBJG Jeff Garcia LE 2.00 5.00
FBJK Jevon Kearse LE 2.00 5.00
FBJS Jeremy Shockey JE 2.00 5.00
FBKJ Keyshawn Johnson LE 3.00 8.00
FBKR Koren Robinson JE 2.50 6.00
FBKW Kurt Warner LE 2.50 6.00
FBMB Michael Bennett LE 2.00 5.00
FBMF Marshall Faulk JE 2.50 6.00
FBMV Michael Vick LE 2.50 6.00
FBPB Plaxico Burress JE 2.00 5.00
FBRW Ricky Williams LE 2.50 6.00
FBWG William Green LE 2.00 5.00
FBWS Warren Sapp JE 2.50 6.00

2003 Fleer Showcase Hot Hands

Inserted into leather packs at a rate of 1:144, this set features a die-cut design in the shape of a football.
STATED ODDS 1:144 LEATHER
1 Jerry Rice 6.00 15.00
2 Randy Moss 2.50 6.00
3 Terrell Owens 2.50 6.00
4 Marvin Harrison 2.50 6.00
5 Jeremy Shockey 2.00 5.00
6 Marshall Faulk 2.50 6.00
7 Priest Holmes 2.00 5.00
8 Deuce McAllister 2.50 6.00

2003 Fleer Showcase Hot Hands Jerseys

Randomly inserted into leather packs, this set features swatches of game used jerseys. Each card is serial numbered to 599.
STATED PRINT RUN 599 SER.#'d SETS
ISSUED IN LEATHER PACKS
HHAB Antonio Bryant 2.50 6.00
HHAR Antwaan Randle El 2.50 6.00
HHDB David Boston 2.50 6.00
HHDB2 Drew Brees 4.00 10.00
HHDC Daunte Culpepper 3.00 8.00
HHDM Deuce McAllister 3.00 8.00
HHEM Eric Moulds 2.50 6.00
HHJR Jerry Rice 8.00 20.00
HHJS Jeremy Shockey 2.50 6.00
HHKR Koren Robinson 3.00 8.00
HHKW Kurt Warner 3.00 8.00
HHLT LaDainian Tomlinson 4.00 10.00
HHMF Marshall Faulk 3.00 8.00
HHMH Marvin Harrison 3.00 8.00
HHPH Priest Holmes 2.50 6.00
HHPM Peyton Manning 10.00 25.00
HHPP Peerless Price 2.50 6.00
HHRM Randy Moss 3.00 8.00
HHTH Todd Heap 2.50 6.00
HHTO Terrell Owens 3.00 8.00

2003 Fleer Showcase Sweet Stitches

Inserted at a rate of 1:12 jersey packs, this set features an embossed design meant to resemble stitches from a football.
COMPLETE SET (8) 10.00 25.00
STATED ODDS 1:12 JERSEY
1 Brett Favre 2.50 6.00
2 Clinton Portis .75 2.00
3 Donovan McNabb 1.00 2.50
4 Daunte Culpepper 1.00 2.50
5 LaDainian Tomlinson 1.25 3.00
6 Tom Brady 5.00 12.00
7 Peyton Manning 3.00 8.00
8 Emmitt Smith 2.00 5.00

2003 Fleer Showcase Sweet Stitches Jerseys

Randomly inserted into jersey packs, this set features game used jersey swatches. Each card is serial numbered to 899. A patch version also exists, with each card serial numbered to 201.
STATED PRINT RUN 899 SER.#'d SETS
ISSUED IN JERSEY PACKS
*PATCH/201: .6X TO 1.5X BASIC JSY
PATCHES PRINT RUN 201 SER.#'d SETS
*PURPLE PATCH/46-56: 1X TO 2.5X BASIC JSY
*PURPLE PATCH/27: 1.2X TO 3X BASIC JSY
PURPLE PATCH PRINT RUN 27-56
1 Drew Brees 3.00 8.00
2 Antonio Bryant 2.00 5.00
3 David Carr 2.00 5.00
4 Daunte Culpepper 2.50 6.00
5 Brett Favre 6.00 15.00
6 Eddie George 2.50 6.00
7 Ahman Green 2.50 6.00
8 Edgerrin James 2.50 6.00
9 Peyton Manning 8.00 20.00
10 Donovan McNabb 2.50 6.00
11 Clinton Portis 2.00 5.00
12 Peerless Price 2.00 5.00
13 Antwaan Randle El 2.00 5.00
14 Emmitt Smith 5.00 12.00
15 LaDainian Tomlinson 3.00 8.00

2004 Fleer Showcase

Showcase released in early June of 2004 and was Fleer's second football product of the year. The base set consists of 149-cards including 100-veterans and 48-rookies each serial numbered to 599. Hobby box included 20-packs with 5-cards per pack at an SRP of $6.50 and retail boxes contained 24-packs of 4-cards with an SRP of $2.99. Card #150, Mike Williams, was initially pulled from the pack-out after he was declared ineligible for the NFL Draft. Copies of the card hit the secondary in late 2005, however, after the Fleer inventory liquidation sale took place. Due to the unique distribution of the card, it is not considered a Rookie Card. Two parallel sets and a large section of inserts with a variety of game-used versions can be found seeded in packs. Insert highlights include Sweet Sigs autographs produced in three foil colors and Feature Film with each card produced with an original photographic slide.
COMP.SET w/o SP's (100) 10.00 25.00
UNPRICED MASTERPIECE PRINT RUN 1
1 Jamal Lewis .30 .75
2 Kevan Barlow .25 .60
3 Travis Henry .25 .60
4 Jon Kitna .25 .60
5 David Boston .25 .60
6 Andre Davis .25 .60
7 Steve McNair .30 .75
8 Freddie Mitchell .25 .60
9 Plaxico Burress .25 .60
10 Jake Delhomme .25 .60
11 Andre Johnson .30 .75
12 T.J. Duckett .25 .60
13 Ray Lewis .40 1.00
14 Shaun Alexander .25 .60
15 Stephen Davis .25 .60
16 Priest Holmes .25 .60
17 Edgerrin James .30 .75
18 Josh McCown .30 .75
19 Jerry Rice .75 2.00
20 Fred Taylor .25 .60
21 Marty Booker .25 .60
22 Eddie George .30 .75
23 Jake Plummer .25 .60
24 LaDainian Tomlinson .40 1.00
25 David Carr .25 .60
26 Keenan McCardell .25 .60
27 Jerry Porter .25 .60
28 Drew Bledsoe .30 .75
29 Brian Dawkins .25 .60
30 Curtis Martin .30 .75
31 Troy Brown .25 .60
32 Peyton Manning 1.00 2.50
33 Clinton Portis .25 .60
34 Brett Favre .75 2.00
35 Joey Harrington .25 .60
36 Tiki Barber .30 .75
37 Hines Ward .30 .75
38 Laveranues Coles .25 .60
39 Deuce McAllister .30 .75
40 Kyle Boller .25 .60
41 Jeff Garcia .25 .60
42 Julius Peppers .30 .75
43 Chris Chambers .25 .60
44 Willis McGahee .25 .60
45 Michael Vick .30 .75
46 Carson Palmer .30 .75
47 Ricky Williams .30 .75
48 Matt Hasselbeck .25 .60
49 Anquan Boldin .25 .60
50 Tony Gonzalez .30 .75
51 Marvin Harrison .30 .75
52 Santana Moss .30 .75
53 Ahman Green .30 .75
54 Eric Moulds .25 .60
55 Byron Leftwich .25 .60
56 Daunte Culpepper .30 .75
57 Terrell Owens .30 .75
58 Kerry Collins .25 .60
59 Tommy Maddox .25 .60
60 Chad Johnson .25 .60
61 Rich Gannon .30 .75
62 Patrick Ramsey .30 .75
63 Quincy Morgan .25 .60
64 Koren Robinson .25 .60
65 Deion Branch .25 .60
66 Rex Grossman .25 .60
67 Damerien McCants .25 .60
68 Ashley Lelie .25 .60
69 Roy Williams S .25 .60
70 Michael Bennett .25 .60
71 Domanick Davis .25 .60
72 Warren Sapp .30 .75
73 Randy Moss .30 .75
74 Drew Brees .40 1.00
75 Brian Westbrook .25 .60
76 Kelly Holcomb .25 .60
77 Jason Taylor .30 .75
78 Charles Rogers .25 .60
79 Marc Bulger .25 .60
80 Donald Driver .30 .75
81 Trent Green .25 .60
82 Peerless Price .25 .60
83 Quincy Carter .25 .60
84 Torry Holt .30 .75
85 Derrick Mason .25 .60
86 Donte Stallworth .25 .60
87 Derrick Brooks .25 .60
88 Dre Bly .25 .60
89 Antonio Bryant .30 .75
90 DeShaun Foster .30 .75
91 Emmitt Smith .60 1.50
92 Chad Pennington .25 .60
93 Jeremy Shockey .25 .60
94 Aaron Brooks .25 .60
95 Marshall Faulk .30 .75
96 Dante Hall .25 .60
97 Brian Urlacher .40 1.00
98 Corey Dillon .25 .60
99 Donovan McNabb .30 .75
100 Tom Brady 1.50 4.00
101 Derrick Strait RC 1.25 3.00
102 Michael Clayton RC 1.50 4.00
103 Larry Fitzgerald RC 5.00 12.00
104 Chris Gamble RC 1.25 3.00
105 Devery Henderson RC 1.25 3.00
106 Steven Jackson RC 2.00 5.00
107 Michael Jenkins RC 1.25 3.00
108 Greg Jones RC 1.25 3.00
109 Kevin Jones RC 1.50 4.00
110 Eli Manning RC 10.00 25.00
111 Chris Perry RC 1.25 3.00
112 Philip Rivers RC 4.00 10.00
113 Ben Roethlisberger RC 10.00 25.00
114 Bernard Berrian RC 1.25 3.00
115 Sean Taylor RC 6.00 15.00
116 Reggie Williams RC 1.25 3.00
117 Roy Williams RC 1.25 3.00
118 Kellen Winslow RC 1.25 3.00
119 Rashaun Woods RC 1.25 3.00
120 J.P. Losman RC 1.25 3.00
121 Will Poole RC 2.00 5.00
122 Will Smith RC 1.50 4.00
123 Devard Darling RC 1.25 3.00
124 Jonathan Vilma RC 1.50 4.00
125 Drew Henson RC 1.25 3.00
126 Michael Turner RC 1.25 3.00
127 Lee Evans RC 2.00 5.00
128 Ernest Wilford RC 1.50 4.00
129 Cedric Cobbs RC 1.25 3.00
130 Ricardo Colclough RC 1.25 3.00
131 Ryan Dinwiddie RC 1.25 3.00
132 DeAngelo Hall RC 2.00 5.00
133 Cody Pickett RC 1.25 3.00
134 Quincy Wilson RC 1.25 3.00
135 Ahmad Carroll RC 1.25 3.00
136 Robert Gallery RC 1.50 4.00
137 John Navarre RC 1.25 3.00
138 P.K. Sam RC 1.25 3.00
139 Jeff Smoker RC 1.50 4.00
140 Ben Troupe RC 1.25 3.00
141 Marquise Hill RC 1.25 3.00
142 D.J. Williams RC 2.00 5.00
143 Tommie Harris RC 1.50 4.00
144 Ben Watson RC 1.50 4.00
145 Tatum Bell RC 1.25 3.00
146 B.J. Symons RC 1.25 3.00
147 Matt Schaub RC 1.25 3.00
148 Casey Clausen RC 1.50 4.00
149 Jason Fife RC 1.25 3.00
150 Mike Williams No Ser.# 3.00 8.00

2004 Fleer Showcase Legacy

*VETS 1-100: 3X TO 8X BASIC CARDS
*ROOKIES 101-149: .8X TO 2X BASIC CARD
STATED PRINT RUN 125 SER.#'d SETS

2004 Fleer Showcase Feature Film

STATED ODDS 1:480 HOB,1:2000 RET
STATED PRINT RUN 50 SER.#'d SETS
1FF Brian Urlacher 8.00 20.00
2FF Jerry Rice 15.00 40.00
3FF Michael Vick 6.00 15.00
4FF Jeremy Shockey 5.00 12.00
5FF Emmitt Smith 12.00 30.00
6FF Brett Favre 15.00 40.00
7FF David Carr 5.00 12.00
8FF Joey Harrington 5.00 12.00
9FF Randy Moss 6.00 15.00
10FF Peyton Manning 20.00 50.00

2004 Fleer Showcase Feature Film Game Used

OVERALL GAME USED ODDS 1:10H,1:24R
STATED PRINT RUN 25 SER.#'d SETS
FFBF Brett Favre 25.00 60.00
FFBU Brian Urlacher 12.00 30.00
FFDC David Carr 8.00 20.00
FFES Emmitt Smith 20.00 50.00
FFJH Joey Harrington 8.00 20.00
FFJR Jerry Rice 25.00 60.00
FFJS Jeremy Shockey 8.00 20.00
FFMV Michael Vick 10.00 25.00
FFPM Peyton Manning 30.00 80.00
FFRM Randy Moss 10.00 25.00

2004 Fleer Showcase Grace

COMPLETE SET (20) 15.00 40.00
STATED ODDS 1:8 HOB/RET
1SG Brian Urlacher 1.25 3.00
2SG Plaxico Burress .75 2.00
3SG Andre Johnson 1.00 2.50
4SG Shaun Alexander .75 2.00
5SG Stephen Davis .75 2.00
6SG Edgerrin James 1.00 2.50
7SG LaDainian Tomlinson 1.25 3.00
8SG Peyton Manning 3.00 8.00
9SG Clinton Portis .75 2.00
10SG Brett Favre 2.50 6.00
11SG Deuce McAllister 1.00 2.50
12SG Julius Peppers 1.00 2.50
13SG Jerry Rice 2.50 6.00
14SG Ricky Williams 1.00 2.50
15SG Daunte Culpepper 1.00 2.50
16SG Santana Moss 1.00 2.50
17SG Roy Williams S .75 2.00
18SG Chad Pennington .75 2.00
19SG Donovan McNabb 1.00 2.50
20SG Tom Brady 5.00 12.00

2004 Fleer Showcase Grace Game Used

Fleer issued these cards as parallels to the basic issue Grace insert. Each card includes a swatch of game used jersey from the featured player with six different cards issued for each player. The cards vary based upon serial numbering and foil color used on the fronts. We've added cards numbers below for each player to ease in cataloging and identifying the versions. Each player has two silver foil cards - one not serial numbered (listed as "1" below) and one serial numbered to 100 (listed as "3" below). Other colors include: blue (listed as "2" below, serial #'d of 300), gold (listed as "4" below), green (listed as "5" below, serial #'d to player's jersey number), and red (listed as "6" below, serial #'d to 2003 team wins).
OVERALL GAME USED ODDS 1:10H,1:24R
SERIAL #'d UNDER 16 NOT PRICED
UNPRICED MASTERPIECE PRINT RUN 1
AJ1 Andre Johnson 3.00 8.00
AJ2 Andre Johnson/300 3.00 8.00
AJ3 Andre Johnson/100 4.00 10.00
AJ5 Andre Johnson/80 4.00 10.00
BF1 Brett Favre 8.00 20.00
BF2 Brett Favre/300 8.00 20.00
BF3 Brett Favre/100 10.00 25.00
BF4 Brett Favre/358 8.00 20.00
BU1 Brian Urlacher 4.00 10.00
BU2 Brian Urlacher/300 4.00 10.00
BU3 Brian Urlacher/100 5.00 12.00
BU5 Brian Urlacher/54 12.00 30.00
CP1 Clinton Portis 2.50 6.00
CP2 Clinton Portis/300 2.50 6.00
CP3 Clinton Portis/100 3.00 8.00
CP4 Clinton Portis/31 6.00 15.00
CP5 Clinton Portis/26 8.00 20.00
DC1 Daunte Culpepper 3.00 8.00
DC2 Daunte Culpepper/300 3.00 8.00
DC3 Daunte Culpepper/100 4.00 10.00
DC4 Daunte Culpepper/116 4.00 10.00
EJ1 Edgerrin James 3.00 8.00
EJ2 Edgerrin James/300 3.00 8.00
EJ3 Edgerrin James/100 4.00 10.00
EJ4 Edgerrin James/52 6.00 15.00
EJ5 Edgerrin James/32 8.00 20.00
JP1 Julius Peppers 3.00 8.00
JP2 Julius Peppers/300 3.00 8.00
JP3 Julius Peppers/100 4.00 10.00
JP5 Julius Peppers/90 4.00 10.00
JR1 Jerry Rice 8.00 20.00
JR2 Jerry Rice/300 8.00 20.00
JR3 Jerry Rice/100 10.00 25.00
JR4 Jerry Rice/205 8.00 20.00
JR5 Jerry Rice/80 10.00 25.00
LT1 LaDainian Tomlinson 4.00 10.00
LT2 LaDainian Tomlinson/300 4.00 10.00
LT3 LaDainian Tomlinson/100 5.00 12.00
LT4 LaDainian Tomlinson/42 8.00 20.00
LT5 LaDainian Tomlinson/21 12.00 30.00
PB1 Plaxico Burress 2.50 6.00
PB2 Plaxico Burress/300 2.50 6.00
PB3 Plaxico Burress/100 3.00 8.00
PB4 Plaxico Burress/17 8.00 20.00
PB5 Plaxico Burress/80 3.00 8.00
PM1 Peyton Manning 10.00 25.00
PM2 Peyton Manning/300 10.00 25.00
PM3 Peyton Manning/100 12.00 30.00
PM4 Peyton Manning/176 10.00 25.00
PM5 Peyton Manning/18 30.00 80.00
RW1 Ricky Williams 3.00 8.00
RW2 Ricky Williams/300 3.00 8.00
RW3 Ricky Williams/100 4.00 10.00
RW4 Ricky Williams/45 6.00 15.00
RW5 Ricky Williams/34 8.00 20.00
SA1 Shaun Alexander 2.50 6.00
SA2 Shaun Alexander/300 2.50 6.00
SA3 Shaun Alexander/100 3.00 8.00
SA4 Shaun Alexander/52 5.00 12.00
SA5 Shaun Alexander/37 6.00 15.00
SD1 Stephen Davis 2.50 6.00
SD2 Stephen Davis/300 2.50 6.00
SD3 Stephen Davis/100 3.00 8.00
SD4 Stephen Davis/56 5.00 12.00
SD5 Stephen Davis/48 5.00 12.00
SM1 Santana Moss 3.00 8.00
SM2 Santana Moss/300 3.00 8.00
SM3 Santana Moss/100 4.00 10.00
SM4 Santana Moss/16 10.00 25.00
SM5 Santana Moss/83 4.00 10.00
TB1 Tom Brady 10.00 25.00
TB2 Tom Brady/300 10.00 25.00
TB3 Tom Brady/100 12.00 30.00
TB4 Tom Brady/71 12.00 30.00
DEM1 Deuce McAllister 3.00 8.00
DEM2 Deuce McAllister/300 3.00 8.00
DEM3 Deuce McAllister/100 4.00 10.00
DEM4 Deuce McAllister GLD/26 10.00 25.00
DEM5 Deuce McAllister GRN/26 10.00 25.00
DOM1 Donovan McNabb 3.00 8.00
DOM2 Donovan McNabb/300 3.00 8.00
DOM3 Donovan McNabb/100 4.00 10.00
DOM4 Donovan McNabb/104 4.00 10.00
ROY1 Roy Williams S 2.50 6.00
ROY2 Roy Williams S/300 2.50 6.00
ROY3 Roy Williams S/100 3.00 8.00
ROY5 Roy Williams S/31 6.00 15.00
CHAD1 Chad Pennington 2.50 6.00
CHAD2 Chad Pennington/300 2.50 6.00
CHAD3 Chad Pennington/100 3.00 8.00
CHAD4 Chad Pennington/41 5.00 12.00

2004 Fleer Showcase Hot Hands
STATED ODDS 1:240 HOB,1:480 RET
1HH Anquan Boldin 3.00 8.00
2HH Ahman Green 4.00 10.00
3HH Chad Johnson 3.00 8.00
4HH Jeremy Shockey 3.00 8.00
5HH Priest Holmes 3.00 8.00
6HH Torry Holt 4.00 10.00
7HH Marvin Harrison 4.00 10.00
8HH LaDainian Tomlinson 5.00 12.00
9HH Deuce McAllister 4.00 10.00
10HH Randy Moss 4.00 10.00

2004 Fleer Showcase Hot Hands Game Used
STATED PRINT RUN 50 SER.#'d SETS
HHAB Anquan Boldin 5.00 12.00
HHAG Ahman Green 6.00 15.00
HHCJ Chad Johnson 5.00 12.00
HHDM Deuce McAllister 6.00 15.00
HHJS Jeremy Shockey 5.00 12.00
HHLT LaDainian Tomlinson 8.00 20.00
HHMH Marvin Harrison 6.00 15.00
HHPH Priest Holmes 5.00 12.00
HHRM Randy Moss 6.00 15.00
HHTH Torry Holt 6.00 15.00

2004 Fleer Showcase Playmakers
COMPLETE SET (15) 15.00 40.00
STATED ODDS 1:24 HOB/RET
1PM Jamal Lewis 1.25 3.00
2PM Michael Vick 1.25 3.00
3PM Marvin Harrison 1.25 3.00
4PM Ahman Green 1.25 3.00
5PM Terrell Owens 1.25 3.00
6PM Chad Johnson 1.00 2.50
7PM Marshall Faulk 1.25 3.00
8PM Priest Holmes 1.00 2.50
9PM Hines Ward 1.25 3.00
10PM Ricky Williams 1.25 3.00
11PM Randy Moss 1.25 3.00
12PM Charles Rogers 1.00 2.50
13PM Donovan McNabb 1.25 3.00
14PM Anquan Boldin 1.00 2.50
15PM Chad Pennington 1.00 2.50

2004 Fleer Showcase Playmakers Game Used
Fleer issued these cards as parallels to the basic issue Playmakers insert. Each card includes a swatch of game used jersey from the featured player with six different cards issued for each player. The cards vary based on serial numbering and foil color used on the fronts. We've added card numbers below for each player to ease in cataloging and identifying the versions: silver foil (listed as "1" below and serial #'d of 300), gold (listed as "2" below and serial #'d of 100), a second gold foil (listed as "3" below and serial #'d to career touchdown total), blue (listed as "4" below and serial #'d to 2003 touchdown total), green (listed as "5" below serial #'d to the player's jersey number), and red (listed as "6" below serial numbered to the player's career starts).
JERSEYS SER.#'d UNDER 20 NOT PRICED
OVERALL GAME USED ODDS 1:10H,1:24R
UNPRICED MASTERPIECE PRINT RUN 1
AB1 Anquan Boldin/300 2.50 6.00
AB2 Anquan Boldin/100 3.00 8.00
AB5 Anquan Boldin/81 3.00 8.00
AB6 Anquan Boldin/16 8.00 20.00
AG1 Ahman Green/300 3.00 8.00
AG2 Ahman Green/100 4.00 10.00
AG3 Ahman Green/42 6.00 15.00
AG4 Ahman Green/15 10.00 25.00
AG5 Ahman Green/30 8.00 20.00
AG6 Ahman Green/57 6.00 15.00
CJ1 Chad Johnson/300 2.50 6.00
CJ2 Chad Johnson/100 3.00 8.00
CJ3 Chad Johnson/16 8.00 20.00
CJ5 Chad Johnson/85 3.00 8.00
CJ6 Chad Johnson/21 8.00 20.00
CP1 Chad Pennington/300 2.50 6.00
CP2 Chad Pennington/100 3.00 8.00
CP3 Chad Pennington/41 5.00 12.00
CP4 Chad Pennington/15 8.00 20.00
CP6 Chad Pennington/21 8.00 20.00
CR1 Charles Rogers/300 2.50 6.00
CR2 Charles Rogers/100 3.00 8.00
CR5 Charles Rogers/80 3.00 8.00
DM1 Donovan McNabb/300 3.00 8.00
DM2 Donovan McNabb/100 4.00 10.00
DM3 Donovan McNabb/104 4.00 10.00
DM4 Donovan McNabb/19 10.00 25.00
DM6 Donovan McNabb/64 6.00 15.00
HW1 Hines Ward/300 3.00 8.00
HW2 Hines Ward/100 4.00 10.00
HW3 Hines Ward/37 8.00 20.00
HW5 Hines Ward/86 4.00 10.00
HW6 Hines Ward/77 4.00 10.00
JL1 Jamal Lewis/300 3.00 8.00
JL2 Jamal Lewis/100 4.00 10.00
JL3 Jamal Lewis/27 10.00 25.00
JL5 Jamal Lewis/31 8.00 20.00
JL6 Jamal Lewis/44 6.00 15.00
MF1 Marshall Faulk/300 3.00 8.00
MF2 Marshall Faulk/100 4.00 10.00
MF3 Marshall Faulk/131 4.00 10.00
MF5 Marshall Faulk/28 10.00 25.00
MF6 Marshall Faulk/141 4.00 10.00
MH1 Marvin Harrison/300 3.00 8.00
MH2 Marvin Harrison/100 4.00 10.00
MH3 Marvin Harrison/83 4.00 10.00
MH5 Marvin Harrison/88 4.00 10.00
MH6 Marvin Harrison/121 4.00 10.00
MV1 Michael Vick/300 3.00 8.00
MV2 Michael Vick/100 4.00 10.00
MV3 Michael Vick/32 8.00 20.00
MV6 Michael Vick/21 10.00 25.00
PH1 Priest Holmes/300 2.50 6.00
PH2 Priest Holmes/100 3.00 8.00
PH3 Priest Holmes/72 3.00 8.00
PH4 Priest Holmes/27 8.00 20.00
PH5 Priest Holmes/31 6.00 15.00
PH6 Priest Holmes/65 5.00 12.00
RM1 Randy Moss/300 3.00 8.00
RM2 Randy Moss/100 4.00 10.00
RM3 Randy Moss/77 4.00 10.00
RM4 Randy Moss/17 10.00 25.00
RM5 Randy Moss/84 4.00 10.00
RM6 Randy Moss/91 4.00 10.00
RW1 Ricky Williams/300 3.00 8.00
RW2 Ricky Williams/100 4.00 10.00
RW3 Ricky Williams/45 6.00 15.00
RW5 Ricky Williams/34 8.00 20.00
RW6 Ricky Williams/70 4.00 10.00
TO1 Terrell Owens/300 3.00 8.00
TO2 Terrell Owens/100 4.00 10.00
TO3 Terrell Owens/83 4.00 10.00
TO5 Terrell Owens/81 4.00 10.00
TO6 Terrell Owens/107 4.00 10.00

2004 Fleer Showcase Sweet Sigs Gold
OVERALL AUTO STATED ODDS 1:20H, 1:24R
CARDS #'d UNDER 20 NOT PRICED
AL Ashley Lelie JSY/85 8.00 20.00
AM1 Archie Manning/50 10.00 25.00
CJ1 Chad Johnson/148 8.00 20.00
CJ2 Chad Johnson JSY/85 8.00 20.00
DF DeShaun Foster JSY/20 20.00 50.00
DS Donte Stallworth JSY/83 8.00 20.00
JD Jake Delhomme JSY/17 15.00 40.00
KJ Kevin Jones/34 15.00 40.00
LE Lee Evans/88 12.00 30.00
MC Michael Clayton/88 10.00 25.00
MW Mike Williams No AU 4.00 10.00
RG1 Rex Grossman/76 8.00 20.00
ROW Roy Williams WR/88 8.00 20.00
SA Shaun Alexander JSY/37 12.00 30.00
WP Will Poole/29 25.00 60.00

2004 Fleer Showcase Sweet Sigs Red
RED FOIL AU/12-68 ODDS 1:20H, 1:24R
CARDS #'d UNDER 20 NOT PRICED
AL Ashley Lelie/15 15.00 40.00
AM Archie Manning/42 30.00 60.00
AV Adam Vinatieri/46 50.00 100.00
BL Byron Leftwich/43 10.00 25.00
BR Ben Roethlisberger/68 60.00 120.00
CJ Chad Johnson/15 15.00 40.00
DC David Carr/67 10.00 25.00
DF DeShaun Foster/30 15.00 40.00
DH Drew Henson/26 15.00 40.00
DM Donovan McNabb/45 25.00 60.00
DS Donte Stallworth/67 10.00 25.00
EM Eli Manning/41 60.00 120.00
JD Jake Delhomme/33 12.00 30.00
KJ Kevin Jones/16 20.00 50.00
LE Lee Evans/12 25.00 60.00
MC Michael Clayton/12 20.00 50.00
RG Rex Grossman/38 12.00 30.00
ROW Roy Williams WR/12 15.00 40.00
SA Shaun Alexander/38 12.00 30.00
WP Will Poole/22 25.00 60.00

2004 Fleer Showcase Sweet Sigs Silver
The Sweet Sigs autograph inserts were issued in three foil colors with each player having up to two silver foil versions as noted below. Many cards were issued via mail redemption. Donovan McNabb was only produced in the Gold and Red foil varieties. Finally, some cards were released to the market unsigned after Fleer liquidated old inventory.
OVERALL AUTO ODDS 1:20H, 1:24R
STATED PRINT RUN 25-300
AL1 Ashley Lelie/300 6.00 15.00
AL2 Ashley Lelie/100 8.00 20.00
AV1 Adam Vinatieri/200 35.00 60.00
AV2 Adam Vinatieri/100 40.00 80.00
BL1 Byron Leftwich/250 6.00 15.00
BL2 Byron Leftwich/100 8.00 20.00
BR1 Ben Roethlisberger/270 40.00 100.00
BR2 Ben Roethlisberger/100 50.00 120.00
CJ1 Chad Johnson/148 8.00 20.00
CJ2 Chad Johnson/100 8.00 20.00
DC1 David Carr/25 15.00 40.00
DC2 David Carr/100 8.00 20.00
DF1 DeShaun Foster/300 8.00 20.00
DF2 DeShaun Foster/100 10.00 25.00
DH1 Drew Henson/50 10.00 25.00
DH2 Drew Henson/100 8.00 20.00
DS1 Donte Stallworth/60 10.00 25.00
DS2 Donte Stallworth/100 8.00 20.00
EM1 Eli Manning/200 25.00 60.00
EM2 Eli Manning/100 30.00 80.00
JD1 Jake Delhomme/275 10.00 25.00
JD2 Jake Delhomme/100 8.00 20.00
KJ1 Kevin Jones/300 8.00 20.00
KJ2 Kevin Jones/100 10.00 25.00
LE1 Lee Evans/300 10.00 25.00
LE2 Lee Evans/100 12.00 30.00
MC1 Michael Clayton/300 8.00 20.00
MC2 Michael Clayton/100 10.00 25.00
RG2 Rex Grossman/100 25.00 50.00
SA1 Shaun Alexander/125 8.00 20.00
SA2 Shaun Alexander/100 8.00 20.00
WP1 Will Poole/149 12.00 30.00
WP2 Will Poole/100 12.00 30.00
ROW1 Roy Williams WR/300 6.00 15.00
ROW2 Roy Williams WR/100 8.00 20.00
EC1 Earl Campbell No Auto 3.00 8.00
MW1 Mike Williams No Auto 3.00 8.00

2003 Fleer Snapshot
Released in January of 2004, this set consists of 135 cards including 90 veterans and 45 rookies. Rookies 91-135 are serial numbered to 500 and were inserted at a rate of 1:8 packs. Boxes contained 24 packs of 5 cards.
COMP.SET w/o SP's (90) 10.00 25.00
91-135 ROOKIE/500 ODDS 1:8
1 Trent Green .25 .60
2 Chad Johnson .25 .60
3 Randy Moss .30 .75
4 Brett Favre .75 2.00
5 Terrell Owens .30 .75
6 LaDainian Tomlinson .40 1.00
7 Michael Vick .30 .75
8 Jerry Rice .75 2.00
9 David Carr .25 .60
10 Chad Pennington .25 .60
11 Torry Holt .30 .75
12 Edgerrin James .30 .75
13 Travis Henry .25 .60
14 Warrick Dunn .25 .60
15 Laveranues Coles .25 .60
16 Fred Taylor .25 .60
17 Todd Heap .25 .60
18 Tim Brown .40 1.00
19 Donovan McNabb .30 .75
20 Marvin Harrison .30 .75
21 Patrick Ramsey .30 .75
22 Troy Brown .25 .60
23 Antonio Bryant .25 .60
24 Donte Stallworth .25 .60
25 Joe Horn .25 .60
26 Clinton Portis .25 .60
27 Kurt Warner .30 .75
28 Quincy Morgan .25 .60
29 James Stewart .25 .60
30 Ashley Lelie .25 .60
31 Kerry Collins .25 .60
32 Julius Peppers .40 1.00
33 Brad Johnson .30 .75
34 Ricky Williams .30 .75
35 Ahman Green .30 .75
36 Plaxico Burress .25 .60
37 Amani Toomer .25 .60
38 Brian Urlacher .40 1.00
39 Eddie George .30 .75
40 Tony Gonzalez .30 .75
41 Chris Chambers .25 .60
42 Tommy Maddox .25 .60
43 Drew Brees .40 1.00
44 Anthony Thomas .30 .75
45 Brian Griese .25 .60
46 Ray Lewis .40 1.00
47 Peerless Price .25 .60
48 Charlie Garner .30 .75
49 Stacey Mack .25 .60
50 Rod Gardner .25 .60
51 Jevon Kearse .25 .60
52 Tim Couch .25 .60
53 Koren Robinson .30 .75
54 Daunte Culpepper .30 .75
55 Tom Brady 1.50 4.00
56 Jeff Blake .30 .75
57 Jeff Garcia .25 .60
58 Mike Alstott .25 .60
59 Corey Dillon .25 .60
60 Antwaan Randle El .25 .60
61 Deuce McAllister .30 .75
62 William Green .25 .60
63 Shaun Alexander .25 .60
64 Eric Moulds .25 .60
65 Jamal Lewis .30 .75
66 Rich Gannon .30 .75
67 Tiki Barber .30 .75
68 Peyton Manning 1.00 2.50
69 Marshall Faulk .30 .75
70 Hines Ward .30 .75
71 Drew Bledsoe .30 .75
72 Stephen Davis .25 .60
73 Mark Brunell .30 .75
74 Priest Holmes .25 .60
75 Duce Staley .25 .60
76 Jerome Bettis .40 1.00
77 Rod Smith .30 .75
78 Marty Booker .25 .60
79 Aaron Brooks .25 .60
80 Jake Plummer .25 .60
81 Warren Sapp .30 .75
82 David Boston .25 .60
83 Joey Harrington .25 .60
84 Emmitt Smith .60 1.50
85 Jimmy Smith .30 .75
86 Curtis Martin .30 .75
87 Keyshawn Johnson .40 1.00
88 Steve McNair .30 .75
89 Donald Driver .30 .75
90 Jeremy Shockey .25 .60
91 Tyrone Calico RC 1.50 4.00
92 Sam Aiken RC 2.00 5.00
93 Jason Witten RC 6.00 15.00
94 Dave Ragone RC 1.50 4.00
95 Billy McMullen RC 1.50 4.00
96 Musa Smith RC 1.50 4.00
97 Kelley Washington RC 1.50 4.00
98 Larry Johnson RC 2.00 5.00
99 Dallas Clark RC 2.50 6.00
100 Andre Johnson RC 4.00 10.00
101 Artose Pinner RC 1.50 4.00
102 B.J. Askew RC 2.00 5.00
103 Rex Grossman RC 2.00 5.00
104 Kevin Williams RC 2.50 6.00
105 Terence Newman RC 2.50 6.00
106 Teyo Johnson RC 2.00 5.00
107 Kevin Curtis RC 1.50 4.00
108 Brandon Lloyd RC 2.50 6.00
109 Kyle Boller RC 1.50 4.00
110 Bethel Johnson RC 1.50 4.00
111 E.J. Henderson RC 2.00 5.00
112 Quentin Griffin RC 2.00 5.00
113 Jerome McDougle RC 1.50 4.00
114 Justin Fargas RC 2.50 6.00
115 Michael Haynes RC 1.50 4.00
116 Tony Hollings RC 2.00 5.00
117 Bryant Johnson RC 2.50 6.00
118 L.J. Smith RC 2.50 6.00
119 Nate Burleson RC 2.00 5.00
120 Taylor Jacobs RC 1.50 4.00
121 Byron Leftwich RC 2.00 5.00
122 Charles Rogers RC 2.00 5.00
123 Chris Brown RC 1.50 4.00
124 DeWayne Robertson RC 2.00 5.00
125 Terrell Suggs RC 2.00 5.00
126 Johnathan Sullivan RC 1.50 4.00
127 Willis McGahee RC 2.00 5.00
128 Anquan Boldin RC 2.50 6.00
129 Chris Simms RC 1.50 4.00
130 Carson Palmer RC 3.00 8.00
131 Marcus Trufant RC 2.00 5.00
132 Jimmy Kennedy RC 2.00 5.00
133 Onterrio Smith RC 1.50 4.00
134 Boss Bailey RC 2.00 5.00
135 William Joseph RC 1.50 4.00

2003 Fleer Snapshot Projections
COMPLETE SET (15) 30.00 80.00
PRINT RUN 199 SER.#'d SETS
1 Ricky Williams 2.00 5.00
2 Donovan McNabb 2.00 5.00
3 Brett Favre 5.00 12.00
4 Jerry Rice 5.00 12.00
5 Edgerrin James 2.00 5.00
6 Eddie George 2.00 5.00
7 Tom Brady 10.00 25.00
8 Marshall Faulk 2.00 5.00
9 Fred Taylor 1.50 4.00
10 Peyton Manning 6.00 15.00
11 Randy Moss 2.00 5.00
12 Chad Pennington 1.50 4.00
13 Kurt Warner 2.00 5.00
14 Tim Brown 2.50 6.00
15 Emmitt Smith 4.00 10.00

2003 Fleer Snapshot Projections Jerseys Silver
This set features game worn jersey swatches on cards with silver highlights. Each Silver card is serial numbered to 250. There is also a Gold version of this set, which features game worn jersey swatches on cards with gold highlights. Each Gold card is serial numbered to 50.
SILVER PRINT RUN 250 SER.#'d SETS
OVERALL MEM/AUTO ODDS 1:8
*GOLD/50: .8X TO 2X SILVER/250
GOLD PRINT RUN 50 SER.#'d SETS
NPBF Brett Favre 6.00 15.00
NPCP Chad Pennington 2.00 5.00
NPDM Donovan McNabb 2.50 6.00
NPEG Eddie George 2.50 6.00
NPEJ Edgerrin James 2.50 6.00
NPFT Fred Taylor 2.00 5.00
NPJR Jerry Rice 6.00 15.00
NPKW Kurt Warner 2.50 6.00
NPMF Marshall Faulk 2.50 6.00
NPPM Peyton Manning 8.00 20.00
NPRM Randy Moss 2.50 6.00
NPRWO Ricky Williams 2.50 6.00
NPTB Tom Brady 12.00 30.00
NPTB Tim Brown 3.00 8.00

2003 Fleer Snapshot Rookie Slides
This set features 35mm film slides of top NFL rookies imbedded in the cards. Each card is serial numbered to 50.
STATED PRINT RUN 50 SER.#'d SETS
1 Tyrone Calico 3.00 8.00
2 Sam Aiken 4.00 10.00
3 Jason Witten 12.00 30.00
4 Dave Ragone 3.00 8.00
5 Billy McMullen 3.00 8.00
6 Musa Smith 3.00 8.00
7 Kelley Washington 3.00 8.00
8 Larry Johnson 4.00 10.00
9 Dallas Clark 5.00 12.00
10 Andre Johnson 8.00 20.00
11 Artose Pinner 3.00 8.00
12 B.J. Askew 4.00 10.00
13 Rex Grossman 4.00 10.00
14 Kevin Williams 5.00 12.00
15 Terence Newman 5.00 12.00
16 Teyo Johnson 4.00 10.00
17 Kevin Curtis 3.00 8.00
18 Brandon Lloyd 5.00 12.00
19 Kyle Boller 3.00 8.00
20 Bethel Johnson 3.00 8.00
21 E.J. Henderson 4.00 10.00
22 Quentin Griffin 4.00 10.00
23 Jerome McDougle 3.00 8.00
24 Justin Fargas 5.00 12.00
25 Michael Haynes 3.00 8.00
26 Tony Hollings 4.00 10.00
27 Bryant Johnson 5.00 12.00
28 L.J. Smith 5.00 12.00
29 Nate Burleson 4.00 10.00
30 Taylor Jacobs 3.00 8.00
31 Byron Leftwich 4.00 10.00
32 Charles Rogers 4.00 10.00
33 Chris Brown 3.00 8.00
34 DeWayne Robertson 4.00 10.00
35 Terrell Suggs 4.00 10.00
36 Johnathan Sullivan 3.00 8.00
37 Willis McGahee 4.00 10.00
38 Anquan Boldin 5.00 12.00
39 Chris Simms 3.00 8.00
40 Carson Palmer 6.00 15.00
41 Marcus Trufant 4.00 10.00
42 Jimmy Kennedy 4.00 10.00
43 Onterrio Smith 3.00 8.00
44 Boss Bailey 4.00 10.00
45 William Joseph 3.00 8.00

2003 Fleer Snapshot Seal of Approval
STATED ODDS 1:12
*GOLD/99: .8X TO 2X BASIC INSERTS
GOLD PRINT RUN 99 SER.#'d SETS
1 Clinton Portis 1.00 2.50
2 David Carr 1.00 2.50
3 Joey Harrington 1.00 2.50
4 Antwaan Randle El 1.00 2.50
5 Jeremy Shockey 1.00 2.50
6 Michael Vick 1.25 3.00
7 Drew Brees 1.50 4.00
8 Tommy Maddox 1.00 2.50
9 LaDainian Tomlinson 1.50 4.00
10 Deuce McAllister 1.25 3.00
11 Brett Favre 3.00 8.00
12 Jerry Rice 3.00 8.00
13 Eric Moulds 1.00 2.50
14 Ricky Williams 1.25 3.00
15 Terrell Owens 1.25 3.00
16 Taylor Jacobs .60 1.50
17 Larry Johnson .75 2.00
18 Rex Grossman .75 2.00
19 Bryant Johnson 1.00 2.50
20 Kyle Boller .60 1.50
21 Andre Johnson 1.50 4.00
22 Charles Rogers .75 2.00
23 Byron Leftwich .75 2.00
24 Willis McGahee .75 2.00
25 Carson Palmer 1.25 3.00

2003 Fleer Snapshot Seal of Approval Jerseys Bronze
This set features jersey swatches on cards with bronze highlights. Each Bronze card is serial numbered to 375. There is also a Gold version of this set, which features jersey swatches on cards with gold highlights. Each Gold card is serial numbered to 99.
STATED PRINT RUN 375 SER.#'d SETS
OVERALL MEM/AUTO ODDS 1:8
*GOLD/99: .6X TO 1.5X BRONZE JSY
GOLD PRINT RUN 99 SER.#'d SETS
SAAJ Andre Johnson 4.00 10.00
SAAR Antwaan Randle El 1.50 4.00
SABF Brett Favre 5.00 12.00
SABL Byron Leftwich 2.00 5.00
SACP Clinton Portis 1.50 4.00
SACP Carson Palmer 3.00 8.00
SACR Charles Rogers 2.00 5.00
SADB Drew Brees 2.50 6.00
SADC David Carr 1.50 4.00
SADM Deuce McAllister 2.00 5.00
SAEM Eric Moulds 1.50 4.00
SAJH Joey Harrington 1.50 4.00
SAJR Jerry Rice 5.00 12.00
SAKB Kyle Boller 1.50 4.00
SALJ Larry Johnson 2.00 5.00
SALT LaDainian Tomlinson 2.50 6.00
SAMV Michael Vick 2.00 5.00
SARG Rex Grossman 2.00 5.00
SARW Ricky Williams 2.00 5.00
SATJ Taylor Jacobs 1.50 4.00
SATM Tommy Maddox 1.50 4.00
SATO Terrell Owens 2.00 5.00

2003 Fleer Snapshot Slides
Randomly inserted in packs, this set features 35mm film slides imbedded in the cards. Each card is serial numbered to 100.
PRINT RUN 100 SERIAL #'d SETS
1 Randy Moss 3.00 8.00
2 Brett Favre 8.00 20.00
3 LaDainian Tomlinson 4.00 10.00
4 Michael Vick 3.00 8.00
5 Jerry Rice 8.00 20.00
6 Chad Pennington 2.50 6.00
7 Donovan McNabb 3.00 8.00
8 Marvin Harrison 3.00 8.00
9 Clinton Portis 2.50 6.00
10 Ricky Williams 3.00 8.00
11 Daunte Culpepper 3.00 8.00
12 Tom Brady 15.00 40.00
13 Deuce McAllister 3.00 8.00
14 Shaun Alexander 2.50 6.00
15 Jamal Lewis 3.00 8.00
16 Peyton Manning 10.00 25.00
17 Marshall Faulk 3.00 8.00
18 Stephen Davis 2.50 6.00
19 Priest Holmes 2.50 6.00
20 Jeremy Shockey 2.50 6.00

2003 Fleer Snapshot Slides Autographs
This set features 35mm film slides imbedded in cards along with an authentic player autograph on the card. Each card is serial numbered to 50. There is also a Gold parallel of this set. The Gold autographs are serial numbered to 10 and are not priced due to scarcity.
PRINT RUN 50 SERIAL #'d SETS
OVERALL MEM/AUTO ODDS 1:8
UNPRICED GOLD PRINT RUN 10
1 T.J. Duckett 8.00 20.00
2 Joey Harrington 8.00 20.00
3 Josh Reed 8.00 20.00
4 Donte Stallworth 8.00 20.00
5 DeShaun Foster 10.00 25.00
6 Julius Peppers 50.00 100.00
7 Javon Walker 10.00 25.00
8 Daniel Graham 8.00 20.00
9 Ashley Lelie 8.00 20.00
10 Clinton Portis 8.00 20.00
11 Jabar Gaffney 8.00 20.00
12 Andre Davis 8.00 20.00
13 Antwaan Randle El 8.00 20.00
14 William Green 8.00 20.00
15 Patrick Ramsey 10.00 25.00
16 Roy Williams 8.00 20.00
17 Antonio Bryant 8.00 20.00
18 Ladell Betts 8.00 20.00
19 Tim Carter 8.00 20.00
20 Josh McCown 10.00 25.00

2003 Fleer Snapshot We're Number One
Randomly inserted in packs, each player in this set has two different cards: one is serial numbered to the year in which they were drafted, and the other is die cut and serial numbered to the last two digits of the year in which they were drafted.
STATED PRINT RUN 1-2003
1A Carson Palmer/2003 1.00 2.50
2A David Carr/2002 1.00 2.50
3A Michael Vick/2001 1.25 3.00
4A Tim Couch/1999 1.00 2.50
4B Tim Couch/99 2.00 5.00
5A Peyton Manning/1998 4.00 10.00
5B Peyton Manning/98 8.00 20.00
6A Keyshawn Johnson/1996 1.50 4.00
6B Keyshawn Johnson/96 3.00 8.00
7A Drew Bledsoe/1993 1.25 3.00
7B Drew Bledsoe/93 2.50 6.00

2003 Fleer Snapshot We're Number One Jerseys
Cards in this set are die cut and feature a jersey swatch. Each card is serial numbered to 111. Please note that there is a Gold version of this set. The Gold set features jersey swatches on die cut cards serial numbered to 25.
STATED PRINT RUN 111 SER.#'d SETS
*GOLD/25: .8X TO 2X BASIC JSY
GOLD STATED PRINT RUN 25
1 Carson Palmer 4.00 10.00
2 David Carr 2.00 5.00
3 Michael Vick 2.50 6.00
4 Tim Couch 2.00 5.00
5 Peyton Manning 8.00 20.00
6 Keyshawn Johnson 3.00 8.00
7 Drew Bledsoe 2.50 6.00

2004 Fleer Sweet Sigs
Fleer Sweet Sigs initially released in late November 2004. The base set consists of 100-cards including 25-rookies serial numbered to 999 at the end of the set. Hobby boxes contained 12-packs of 6-cards each. Two parallel sets and a variety of inserts can be found seeded in hobby and retail packs highlighted by the multi-tiered Autograph inserts. Some signed cards were issued via mail-in exchange or redemption cards with a number of those EXCH cards not yet appearing live on the secondary market as of the printing of this book.
COMP.SET w/o RC's (75) 6.00 15.00
1 Brett Favre .60 1.50
2 Daunte Culpepper .25 .60
3 Marshall Faulk .25 .60
4 Ashley Lelie .20 .50
5 Rex Grossman .20 .50
6 Jeff Garcia .20 .50
7 Jake Plummer .20 .50
8 Tony Gonzalez .25 .60
9 Terrell Owens .25 .60
10 Plaxico Burress .20 .50
11 Michael Vick .25 .60
12 Carson Palmer .25 .60
13 Charles Rogers .20 .50
14 Corey Dillon .20 .50
15 Aaron Brooks .20 .50
16 Torry Holt .25 .60
17 Joey Galloway .25 .60
18 Mark Brunell .25 .60
19 Anquan Boldin .20 .50
20 Domanick Davis .20 .50
21 Edgerrin James .25 .60
22 Hines Ward .25 .60
23 Kyle Boller .20 .50
24 Kurt Warner .25 .60
25 Matt Hasselbeck .20 .50
26 Chris Chambers .20 .50
27 Deuce McAllister .25 .60
28 Chad Pennington .20 .50
29 Eddie George .25 .60
30 Ray Lewis .30 .75
31 Ahman Green .25 .60
32 Marvin Harrison .25 .60
33 Tiki Barber .25 .60
34 Jerry Rice .60 1.50
35 Emmitt Smith .50 1.25
36 Chad Johnson .20 .50
37 Roy Williams S .20 .50
38 Peyton Manning .75 2.00
39 Stephen Davis .20 .50
40 Jamal Lewis .25 .60
41 David Carr .20 .50
42 A.J. Feeley .20 .50
43 Jerry Porter .20 .50
44 Willis McGahee .20 .50
45 Quincy Morgan .20 .50
46 Fred Taylor .20 .50
47 Trent Green .20 .50
48 Donovan McNabb .25 .60
49 Marc Bulger .20 .50
50 LaVar Arrington .20 .50
51 Joey Harrington .20 .50
52 Jake Delhomme .20 .50
53 Jeremy Shockey .20 .50
54 LaDainian Tomlinson .30 .75
55 Brian Urlacher .30 .75
56 Rudi Johnson .20 .50
57 Shaun Alexander .20 .50
58 Charlie Garner .25 .60
59 Eric Moulds .20 .50
60 Tom Brady 1.25 3.00
61 Curtis Martin .25 .60
62 Koren Robinson .20 .50
63 Steve McNair .25 .60
64 Travis Henry .20 .50
65 Julius Peppers .25 .60
66 Keyshawn Johnson .25 .60
67 Andre Johnson .25 .60
68 Priest Holmes .20 .50
69 Drew Brees .30 .75
70 Rich Gannon .25 .60
71 Randy Moss .25 .60
72 Peerless Price .20 .50
73 Drew Bledsoe .25 .60
74 Byron Leftwich .20 .50
75 Clinton Portis .20 .50
76 Roy Williams RC 1.00 2.50
77 Eli Manning RC 8.00 20.00
78 Kevin Jones RC 1.25 3.00
79 Tatum Bell RC 1.00 2.50
80 DeAngelo Hall RC 1.50 4.00
81 Michael Clayton RC 1.25 3.00
82 Rashaun Woods RC 1.00 2.50
83 Darius Watts RC 1.00 2.50
84 J.P. Losman RC 1.00 2.50
85 Drew Henson RC 1.00 2.50
86 Philip Rivers RC 3.00 8.00
87 Ben Roethlisberger RC 8.00 20.00
88 Larry Fitzgerald RC 4.00 10.00
89 Chris Perry RC 1.00 2.50
90 Devery Henderson RC 1.00 2.50
91 Sean Taylor RC 6.00 15.00
92 Reggie Williams RC 1.00 2.50
93 Lee Evans RC 1.50 4.00
94 Julius Jones RC 1.00 2.50
95 Dunta Robinson RC 1.00 2.50
96 Michael Jenkins RC 1.00 2.50
97 Greg Jones RC 1.00 2.50
98 Kellen Winslow RC 1.00 2.50
99 Steven Jackson RC 1.50 4.00
100 Matt Schaub RC 1.00 2.50

2004 Fleer Sweet Sigs Black
*VETS/80-90: 4X TO 10X BASIC CARDS
*ROOKIES/80-83: .8X TO 2X
*VETS/48-56: 5X TO 12X
*VETS/30-37: 6X TO 15X
*ROOKIES/33-39: 1.2X TO 3X
*VETS/20-28: 8X TO 20X
*ROOKIES/21-26: 1.5X TO 4X
*VETS/10-19: 12X TO 30X
*ROOKIES/10-19: 2.5X TO 6X
CARDS SER.#'d TO JERSEY NUMBER
CARDS #'d UNDER 25 NOT PRICED

2004 Fleer Sweet Sigs Gold
*VETS: 4X TO 10X BASIC CARDS
*ROOKIES: .9X TO 2X BASIC CARDS
STATED PRINT RUN 99 SER.#'d SETS

2004 Fleer Sweet Sigs Autographs Copper
UNPRICED MASTERPIECE PRINT RUN 1
BR Ben Roethlisberger/200 30.00 80.00
BW Brian Westbrook/150 5.00 12.00
CC Chris Chambers 5.00 12.00
CJ Chad Johnson/100 5.00 12.00
DC David Carr/40 8.00 20.00
EG Eddie George/27 12.00 30.00
GJ Greg Jones/175 4.00 10.00
JD Jake Delhomme/32 8.00 20.00
JE John Elway/16 40.00 80.00
JJ Joe Jurevicius/75 6.00 15.00
KB Kyle Boller/75 6.00 15.00
MC Michael Clayton/205 5.00 12.00
MV Michael Vick/45 30.00 60.00
PR Philip Rivers/175 12.00 30.00
RG Rex Grossman/125 5.00 12.00
RJ Rudi Johnson/143 5.00 12.00
RW5 Rashaun Woods/150 4.00 10.00
TC Tyrone Calico/175 5.00 12.00
CRP Chris Perry 4.00 10.00
DAH Dante Hall/15 8.00 20.00
DEH Devery Henderson/150 4.00 10.00
DRH Drew Henson/50 6.00 15.00

2004 Fleer Sweet Sigs Autographs Gold
GOLD PRINT RUN 3-29
BW Brian Westbrook/18 6.00 15.00
CB Chris Brown/29 6.00 15.00
GJ Greg Jones/29 6.00 15.00
JD Jake Delhomme/17 6.00 15.00
JJ Joe Jurevicius/30 6.00 15.00
JM Joe Montana/16 125.00 200.00
KC Keary Colbert/29 6.00 15.00
MC Michael Clayton/29 8.00 20.00
PR Philip Rivers/17 40.00 80.00
RW5 Rashaun Woods/15 6.00 15.00
DEH Devery Henderson/19 6.00 15.00

2004 Fleer Sweet Sigs Autographs Silver
SILVER PRINT RUN 11-153 CARDS
SILVERS SER.#'d UNDER 25 NOT PRICED
AB Anquan Boldin/54 5.00 12.00
AG Ahman Green/76 6.00 15.00
BF Brett Favre/33 150.00 250.00
BW Brian Westbrook/91 5.00 12.00
CB Chris Brown/86 5.00 12.00
DH Dante Hall/153 4.00 10.00
GJ Greg Jones/55 5.00 12.00
KB Kyle Boller/19 6.00 15.00
KC Keary Colbert/62 5.00 12.00
RG Rex Grossman/22 6.00 15.00
RJ Rudi Johnson/150 4.00 10.00
TC Tyrone Calico/60 6.00 15.00
CRP Chris Perry/26 6.00 15.00
DAM Dan Marino/27 150.00 300.00
DEH Devery Henderson/50 5.00 12.00
RW5 Rashaun Woods/31 6.00 15.00

2004 Fleer Sweet Sigs End Zone Kings
STATED ODDS 1:12 HOB/RET
1 Ahman Green .75 2.00
2 Priest Holmes .60 1.50
3 LaDainian Tomlinson 1.00 2.50
4 Jamal Lewis .75 2.00
5 Clinton Portis .60 1.50
6 Marshall Faulk .75 2.00
7 Marvin Harrison .75 2.00
8 Tony Gonzalez .75 2.00
9 Hines Ward .75 2.00
10 Peyton Manning 2.50 6.00
11 Steve McNair .75 2.00
12 Daunte Culpepper .75 2.00
13 Terrell Owens .75 2.00
14 Chad Pennington .60 1.50
15 Randy Moss .75 2.00

2004 Fleer Sweet Sigs End Zone Kings Jersey Silver
SILVER PRINT RUN 99-225
*GOLD/50: .8X TO 2X SILVER
GOLD PRINT RUN 50 SER.#'d SETS
*RED: .3X TO .8X SILVER
RED STATED ODDS 1:108 RETAIL
*BLACK DUAL: .8X TO 2X SILVER
AG Ahman Green/209 3.00 8.00
CP Chad Pennington/127 2.50 6.00
CP2 Clinton Portis/215 2.50 6.00
DC Daunte Culpepper/122 3.00 8.00
HW Hines Ward/223 3.00 8.00
JL Jamal Lewis/220 3.00 8.00
LT LaDainian Tomlinson/186 4.00 10.00
MF Marshall Faulk/208 3.00 8.00
MH Marvin Harrison/221 3.00 8.00
PH Priest Holmes/175 2.50 6.00
PM Peyton Manning/99 10.00 25.00
RM Randy Moss/212 3.00 8.00
SM Steve McNair/136 3.00 8.00
TG Tony Gonzalez/225 3.00 8.00
TO Terrell Owens/220 3.00 8.00

2004 Fleer Sweet Sigs End Zone Kings Jersey Quads
STATED PRINT RUN 12-35
GFMO Grn/Flk/R.Mss/Owns/33 25.00 60.00
PCMM Pnn/Clp/P.Mn/McNr/35 30.00 80.00
PTFH Prtis/Tmln/Flk/Hlms/26 20.00 50.00
WHMO Wrd/Hrsn/R.Mss/Own/27 20.00 50.00

2004 Fleer Sweet Sigs Gridiron Heroes
STATED ODDS 1:6 HOB/RET
1GH Brett Favre 2.00 5.00
2GH Michael Vick .75 2.00
3GH Jerry Rice 2.00 5.00
4GH Emmitt Smith 1.50 4.00
5GH Byron Leftwich .60 1.50
6GH Donovan McNabb .75 2.00
7GH Clinton Portis .60 1.50
8GH Shaun Alexander .60 1.50
9GH Tom Brady 4.00 10.00
10GH Eli Manning 2.50 6.00
11GH David Carr .60 1.50
12GH Chad Johnson .60 1.50
13GH Brian Urlacher 1.00 2.50
14GH Joey Harrington .60 1.50
15GH Andre Johnson .75 2.00
16GH Corey Dillon .60 1.50
17GH Drew Bledsoe .75 2.00
18GH Plaxico Burress .60 1.50
19GH Edgerrin James .75 2.00
20GH Larry Fitzgerald 1.25 3.00
21GH Carson Palmer .75 2.00
22GH Philip Rivers 1.00 2.50
23GH Kellen Winslow Jr. .60 1.50
24GH Charles Rogers .60 1.50
25GH Jeremy Shockey .60 1.50

2004 Fleer Sweet Sigs Gridiron Heroes Jersey Silver
SILVER PRINT RUN 35-230
*BLACK/80-85: .6X TO 1.5X SILVER
*BLACK/54: .8X TO 2X SILVER
*BLACK/26-32: 1X TO 2.5X SILVER
*BLACK/26-32: .6X TO 1.5X SILVER/35
BLACK SER.#'d TO JERSEY NUMBER
BLACK SER.#'d UNDER 25 NOT PRICED
*GOLD/50: .8X TO 2X SILVER/155-230
*GOLD/50: .5X TO 1.2X SILVER/35
*RED: .3X TO .8X SILVER/155-230
*RED: .2X TO .5X SILVER/35
RED STATED ODDS 1:108 RETAIL
UNPRICED NFL LOGO PRINT RUN 1
AJ Andre Johnson/198 3.00 8.00
BF Brett Favre/230 8.00 20.00
BL Byron Leftwich/199 2.50 6.00
BU Brian Urlacher/155 4.00 10.00
CD Corey Dillon/210 2.50 6.00
CJ Chad Johnson/229 2.50 6.00
CP2 Clinton Portis/189 2.50 6.00
CR Charles Rogers/228 2.50 6.00
DB Drew Bledsoe/203 3.00 8.00
DC David Carr/227 2.50 6.00
DM Donovan McNabb/215 3.00 8.00
EJ Edgerrin James/216 3.00 8.00
ES Emmitt Smith/35 10.00 25.00
JH Joey Harrington/230 2.50 6.00
JR Jerry Rice/200 8.00 20.00
JS Jeremy Shockey/224 2.50 6.00
MV Michael Vick/213 3.00 8.00
PB Plaxico Burress/209 2.50 6.00
TB Tom Brady/226 15.00 40.00
CAP Carson Palmer/223 3.00 8.00

2004 Fleer Sweet Sigs Gridiron Heroes Jersey Duals
STATED PRINT RUN 2-36
CARDS SER.#'d UNDER 20 NOT PRICED
BD T.Brady/C.Dillon/36 20.00 50.00
CJ D.Carr/A.Johnson/34 12.50 30.00
HR Harrington/C.Rogers/25 12.50 30.00
JP E.James/C.Portis/21 12.50 30.00
JP2 C.Johnson/C.Palmer/29 10.00 25.00
SF E.Smith/L.Fitzgerald/31 15.00 40.00
VL M.Vick/B.Leftwich/28 20.00 50.00

2004 Fleer Sweet Sigs Gridiron Heroes Jersey Quads
STATED PRINT RUN 29-42
BFSR Brdy/Fvr/Emm/Rce/32 40.00 100.00
BJJF Brr/C.Jhn/A.Jhn/Ftz/29 15.00 40.00
JPDA Jms/Prts/Dlln/Alx/37 15.00 40.00
VHLM Vck/Hrrin/Lft/McNb/42 25.00 60.00

2004 Fleer Sweet Sigs Sweet Stitches Jersey Silver
SILVER PRINT RUN 99-250
*BLACK/15-48: 1X TO 2.5X SILVER
BLACK PRINT RUN 15-48
*GOLD/50: .8X TO 2X SILVER
GOLD PRINT RUN 50 SER.#'d SETS
*RED: .3X TO .8X SILVER
RED STATED ODDS 1:108 RETAIL
AB Anquan Boldin/244 2.50 6.00
AB2 Aaron Brooks/250 2.50 6.00
AL Ashley Lelie/230 2.50 6.00
AT Amani Toomer/244 2.50 6.00
BU Brian Urlacher/189 4.00 10.00
CC Chris Chambers/236 2.50 6.00
CM Curtis Martin/248 3.00 8.00
DB Drew Bledsoe/239 3.00 8.00
DB2 Drew Brees/125 4.00 10.00
DD Domanick Davis/198 2.50 6.00
DH Dante Hall/239 2.50 6.00
DH2 Drew Henson/99 2.50 6.00
DS Donte Stallworth/223 2.50 6.00
EG0 Eddie George/236 3.00 8.00
HW Hines Ward/232 3.00 8.00
JD Jake Delhomme/247 2.50 6.00
JP Julius Peppers/221 3.00 8.00
JS Jeremy Shockey/230 2.50 6.00
KB Kyle Boller/226 2.50 6.00
LS Lee Suggs/231 3.00 8.00
MH Matt Hasselbeck/190 2.50 6.00
MP Marcus Pollard/210 2.50 6.00
PP Peerless Price/240 2.50 6.00
RG Rex Grossman/246 2.50 6.00
RJ Rudi Johnson/246 2.50 6.00
RL Ray Lewis/247 4.00 10.00
SD Stephen Davis/238 2.50 6.00
SM Santana Moss/239 3.00 8.00
TG Tony Gonzalez/201 3.00 8.00
ZT Zach Thomas/217 3.00 8.00

2004 Fleer Sweet Sigs Sweet Stitches Jersey Quads
STATED PRINT RUN 2-33
BBGS Bll/Bld/Grs/L.Sgs/26 15.00 40.00
BLSM Bld/Lel/Stll/S.Ms/33 15.00 40.00
CTMM Chm/Z.Th/Mrt/S.Ms/33 15.00 40.00
GSPF Gnz/Shk/Pll/Frnks/25 20.00 50.00
JSDG R.Jn/L.Sgs/D.Dv/Grf/27 12.00 30.00
MGDG Mrtn/Grg/S.Dv/Grn/28 20.00 50.00

2002 Fleer Throwbacks
Released in September 2002, this 125 card set features 54 retired legends, 46 active veterans and 25 rookies. The rookies were inserted at a rate of 1:4 packs. Pack SRP was $5.99. Boxes contained 24 packs of 5 cards.
COMP.SET w/o SP's (100) 12.50 30.00
1 Terry Bradshaw .75 2.00
2 Franco Harris .60 1.50
3 Y.A. Tittle .60 1.50
4 Tony Dorsett .60 1.50
5 Paul Hornung .60 1.50
6 Rocky Bleier .50 1.25
7 Archie Griffin .40 1.00
8 Dwight Clark .50 1.25
9 Bo Jackson .75 2.00
10 Fran Tarkenton .60 1.50
11 Howie Long .60 1.50
12 Bob Griese .60 1.50
13 George Rogers .40 1.00
14 Roger Craig .50 1.25
15 Jim Plunkett .50 1.25
16 Eric Dickerson .50 1.25
17 Marcus Allen .60 1.50
18 Roger Staubach .75 2.00
19 Lawrence Taylor .60 1.50
20 Joe Greene .60 1.50
21 Earl Campbell .60 1.50
22 Dave Casper .40 1.00
23 Charles White .40 1.00
24 Fred Biletnikoff .60 1.50
25 Dan Pastorini .40 1.00
26 John Cappelletti .40 1.00
27 Paul Warfield .50 1.25
28 Ozzie Newsome .50 1.25
29 Johnny Rodgers .50 1.25
30 William Perry .50 1.25
31 Charley Taylor .40 1.00
32 Deacon Jones .50 1.25
33 Bubba Smith .50 1.25
34 James Lofton .40 1.00
35 Mike Rozier .50 1.25
36 Ray Nitschke .60 1.50
37 Dan Fouts .50 1.25
38 Bob Lilly .50 1.25
39 Ronnie Lott .50 1.25
40 Barry Sanders 1.00 2.50
41 Troy Aikman .75 2.00
42 John Elway 1.00 2.50
43 Irving Fryar .40 1.00
44 Jim Kelly .60 1.50
45 Jim McMahon .60 1.50
46 Joe Montana 2.00 5.00
47 Warren Moon .60 1.50
48 Jay Novacek .50 1.25
49 Mel Renfro .40 1.00
50 Mike Singletary .60 1.50
51 Johnny Unitas 1.00 2.50
52 Steve Young .75 2.00
53 Walter Payton 2.50 6.00
54 Dan Marino 1.25 3.00
55 Torry Holt .30 .75
56 Rod Smith .30 .75
57 Priest Holmes .25 .60
58 Anthony Thomas .30 .75
59 Curtis Martin .30 .75
60 LaDainian Tomlinson .40 1.00
61 Antowain Smith .30 .75
62 Terrell Owens .30 .75
63 Tony Gonzalez .30 .75
64 Steve McNair .30 .75
65 Jerome Bettis .40 1.00
66 Rich Gannon .30 .75
67 Jake Plummer .25 .60
68 Jamal Lewis .30 .75
69 Drew Brees .75 2.00
70 Jovon Kearse .25 .60
71 Keyshawn Johnson .30 .75
72 Kordell Stewart .25 .60
73 Tim Brown .40 1.00
74 Vinny Testaverde .25 .60

75 Tom Brady 2.00 5.00
76 Drew Bledsoe .30 .75
77 Stephen Davis .25 .60
78 Marvin Harrison .30 .75
79 Brian Griese .25 .60
80 Michael Vick .30 .75
81 Emmitt Smith .60 1.50
82 Edgerrin James .30 .75
83 Mark Brunell .30 .75
84 Tim Couch .25 .60
85 Randy Moss .30 .75
86 Brian Urlacher .40 1.00
87 Marshall Faulk .30 .75
88 Corey Dillon .25 .60
89 Eddie George .30 .75
90 Terrell Davis .30 .75
91 Brett Favre .75 2.00
92 Peyton Manning 1.00 2.50
93 Fred Taylor .25 .60
94 Daunte Culpepper .30 .75
95 Ricky Williams .30 .75
96 Jerry Rice .75 2.00
97 Donovan McNabb .30 .75
98 Doug Flutie .30 .75
99 Jeff Garcia .25 .60
100 Kurt Warner .30 .75
101 Antonio Bryant RC .75 2.00
102 Reche Caldwell RC .60 1.50
103 David Carr RC .50 1.25
104 Tim Carter RC .60 1.50
105 Rohan Davey RC .75 2.00
106 Andre Davis RC .50 1.25
107 T.J. Duckett RC .50 1.25
108 DeShaun Foster RC .75 2.00
109 Jabar Gaffney RC .50 1.25
110 William Green RC .60 1.50
111 Joey Harrington RC .50 1.25
112 Ron Johnson RC .60 1.50
113 Ashley Lelie RC .50 1.25
114 Josh McCown RC .75 2.00
115 Julius Peppers RC 1.25 3.00
116 Clinton Portis RC .75 2.00
117 Patrick Ramsey RC .60 1.50
118 Antwaan Randle El RC .60 1.50
119 Josh Reed RC .60 1.50
120 Cliff Russell RC .50 1.25
121 Jeremy Shockey RC .75 2.00
122 Donte Stallworth RC .75 2.00
123 Travis Stephens RC .50 1.25
124 Javon Walker RC .75 2.00
125 Marquise Walker RC .50 1.25

2002 Fleer Throwbacks Classic Clippings

Inserted at a rate of 1:24 packs, this set features swatches of game used memorabilia from some of the NFL's greatest retired players.
STATED ODDS 1:24 HOB, 1:240 RET
1 Fred Biletnikoff 6.00 15.00
2 Earl Campbell 6.00 15.00
3 Dave Casper 4.00 10.00
4 John Elway 10.00 25.00
5 Irving Fryar 4.00 10.00
6 Bob Lilly 5.00 12.00
7 Ronnie Lott 5.00 12.00
8 Joe Montana DP 10.00 25.00
9 Dan Marino DP 10.00 25.00
10 Jay Novacek 5.00 12.00
11 Walter Payton 20.00 50.00
12 Barry Sanders 10.00 25.00
13 Steve Young 8.00 20.00

2002 Fleer Throwbacks Classic Numbers

This set is a partial parallel to the Classic Clippings set. Each card features premium swatches, and the cards are serial numbered to 100.
STATED PRINT RUN 100 SER.#'d SETS
1 Barry Sanders 20.00 50.00
2 Marcus Allen 12.00 30.00
3 Brett Favre 30.00 80.00
4 Irving Fryar 8.00 20.00
5 Steve Young 25.00 50.00
6 Jim Plunkett 10.00 25.00

2002 Fleer Throwbacks Greats of the Game Autographs

Inserted in packs at a rate of 1:48, these cards feature crisp, clean signatures from many of the NFL's best retired players, along with several current superstars. Please note that the year on the front and the copyright on the back of these cards is listed as 2001 since this was intended to be an insert in a 2001 product that was never released. Some cards were issued via redemption only. The EXCH expiration date for this set was September 1, 2003. Finally, some cards hit the market in unsigned form (although the congratulations message was still on the cardbacks) after Fleer ceased operations and old card inventory was sold at auction.
STATED ODDS 1:48 HOB, 1:240 RET
1 Marcus Allen 20.00 40.00
2 Fred Biletnikoff 15.00 40.00
3 Rocky Bleier SP 40.00 80.00
4 Terry Bradshaw SP 75.00 150.00
5 Earl Campbell 20.00 40.00
6 John Cappelletti 10.00 25.00
7 Dave Casper 10.00 25.00
8 Dwight Clark 10.00 25.00
9 Roger Craig 10.00 25.00
10 Daunte Culpepper 10.00 25.00
11 Eric Dickerson 15.00 30.00
12 Tony Dorsett 30.00 60.00
13 Joe Greene 25.00 60.00
14 Bob Griese 15.00 40.00
15 Archie Griffin 12.00 30.00
16 Franco Harris 35.00 60.00
17 Paul Hornung 25.00 50.00
18 Bo Jackson 50.00 80.00
19 Deacon Jones 10.00 25.00
20 Howie Long 25.00 50.00
21 Joe Montana 60.00 120.00
22 Randy Moss SP 50.00 100.00
23 Ozzie Newsome 10.00 25.00
24 Dan Pastorini 8.00 20.00
25 William Perry 10.00 25.00
26 Jim Plunkett 10.00 25.00
27 George Rogers 6.00 15.00
28 Johnny Rodgers 8.00 20.00
29 Mike Rozier 8.00 20.00
30 Bubba Smith 15.00 30.00
31 Emmitt Smith SP 175.00 300.00
32 Roger Staubach SP 50.00 80.00
33 Fran Tarkenton 15.00 40.00
34 Charley Taylor 8.00 20.00
35 Lawrence Taylor 25.00 50.00
36 Y.A. Tittle 15.00 40.00
37 Johnny Unitas SP 300.00 450.00
38 Paul Warfield 8.00 20.00
39 Charles White 8.00 20.00

2002 Fleer Throwbacks Lambeau Legends

Inserted at a rate of 1:48, this set showcases some of the best players ever to play at Lambeau field. Each card contains a swatch of game used memorabilia.
STATED ODDS 1:48 HOB, 1:240 RET
1 Paul Hornung 8.00 20.00
2 Brett Favre 10.00 25.00
3 Dorsey Levens 4.00 10.00
4 Ray Nitschke 8.00 20.00
5 Antonio Freeman 5.00 12.00
6 Ahman Green 4.00 10.00

2002 Fleer Throwbacks On 2 Canton

Inserted at a rate of 1:6 packs, this set features five Hall of Famers along with five future Hall of Famers.
STATED ODDS 1:12 HOB/RET
1 W.Payton/E.Smith 4.00 10.00
2 B.Griese/B.Griese 1.00 2.50
3 F.Tarkenton/D.Culpepper 1.00 2.50
4 R.Moss/J.Rice 2.00 5.00
5 E.Campbell/R.Williams 1.00 2.50

2002 Fleer Throwbacks On 2 Canton Memorabilia

This set parallels the base On 2 Canton set, with the addition of a piece of memorabilia for each player. The cards in this set were sequentially #'d to 50.
STATED PRINT RUN 50 SER.#'d SETS
1 E.Campbell/R.Williams 15.00 40.00
2 D.Marino/J.Montana 50.00 125.00
3 R.Moss/J.Rice 30.00 80.00
4 W.Payton/E.Smith 40.00 100.00
5 F.Tarkenton/D.Culpepper 15.00 40.00

2002 Fleer Throwbacks QB Collection

This set is serial #'d to 1500, and features some of the top QB's from yesterday and today.
COMPLETE SET (17) 20.00 50.00
STATED PRINT RUN 1500 SER.#'d SETS
1 Donovan McNabb .75 2.00
2 Warren Moon 1.25 3.00
3 Jim Plunkett 1.00 2.50
4 Kurt Warner .75 2.00
5 Steve Young 1.50 4.00
6 Daunte Culpepper .75 2.00
7 Brett Favre 2.00 5.00
8 Peyton Manning 2.50 6.00
9 Jeff Garcia .60 1.50
10 Dan Fouts 1.00 2.50
11 John Elway 2.00 5.00
12 Jim McMahon 1.25 3.00
13 Jim Kelly 1.25 3.00
14 Troy Aikman 1.50 4.00
15 Y.A. Tittle 1.25 3.00
16 Fran Tarkenton 1.25 3.00
17 Bob Griese 1.25 3.00

2002 Fleer Throwbacks QB Collection Memorabilia

This set parallels the QB Collection set, and features swatches of game used memorabilia. This set was inserted into packs at a rate of 1:48.
STATED ODDS 1:48 HOB, 1:240 RET
1 Troy Aikman 8.00 20.00
2 Daunte Culpepper 5.00 12.00
3 John Elway 10.00 25.00
4 Brett Favre 12.00 30.00
5 Dan Fouts 5.00 12.00
6 Jeff Garcia 4.00 10.00
8 Jim Kelly 6.00 15.00
10 Jim McMahon 6.00 15.00
11 Donovan McNabb 5.00 12.00
13 Jim Plunkett 5.00 12.00
16 Kurt Warner 5.00 12.00
17 Steve Young 8.00 20.00

2002 Fleer Throwbacks QB Collection Dream Backfield

This set was inserted at a rate of 1:24, and features a top QB and RB from 4 different teams, making up a Dream Backfield combination.
STATED ODDS 1:24 HOB/RET
1 B.Favre/P.Hornung 2.50 6.00
2 W.Moon/E.Campbell 1.25 3.00
3 K.Warner/E.Dickerson 1.00 2.50
4 D.Fouts/L.Tomlinson 1.25 3.00

2002 Fleer Throwbacks QB Collection Dream Backfield Memorabilia

This set is a parallel to QB Collection Dream Backfield, and features a swatch of game used memorabilia from one of the players.
STATED ODDS 1:30 HOB, 1:240 RET
1 P.Hornung JSY/B.Favre 7.50 20.00
2 E.Campbell JSY/W.Moon 6.00 15.00
3 E.Dickerson JSY/K.Warner 6.00 15.00
4 L.Tomlinson JSY/D.Fouts 6.00 15.00

2002 Fleer Throwbacks QB Collection Dream Backfield Memorabilia Duals

This set is a parallel to QB Collection Dream Backfield, and features a swatch of game used memorabilia from both players.
STATED ODDS 1:120 HOB, 1:480 RET
1 B.Favre/P.Hornung 30.00 60.00
2 W.Moon/E.Campbell 12.50 25.00
3 K.Warner/E.Dickerson 12.50 30.00
4 D.Fouts/L.Tomlinson 12.50 25.00

2002 Fleer Throwbacks Super Stars

Inserted at a rate of 1:6, this set highlights 7 of the NFL's all time greatest players.
COMPLETE SET (7) 7.50 20.00
STATED 1:6 HOB, 1:8 RET
1 Jerry Rice 2.00 5.00
2 Terrell Davis .75 2.00
3 Marcus Allen 1.00 2.50
4 Jim Plunkett .75 2.00
5 Fred Biletnikoff 1.00 2.50
7 Emmitt Smith 1.50 4.00
8 John Elway 1.50 4.00

2002 Fleer Throwbacks Super Stars Memorabilia

Inserted in packs at a rate of 1:48, cards in this set feature a swatch of game used memorabilia from some of the NFL's best players.
STATED ODDS 1:48 HOB, 1:240 RET
1 Marcus Allen 6.00 15.00
2 Fred Biletnikoff 6.00 15.00
3 Terrell Davis 5.00 12.00
4 John Elway 10.00 25.00
5 Jim Plunkett 5.00 12.00
6 Jerry Rice 12.00 30.00
7 Emmitt Smith 12.00 30.00

1998 Fleer Tradition

The 1998 Fleer Tradition set was issued in one series totalling 250 cards. The 10-card packs retail for $1.59 each. The fronts feature full-bleed color action photos with a clean background. The Fleer Tradition logo is found is the upper right corner. The backs offer complete stats on the featured player.
COMPLETE SET (250) 20.00 40.00
1 Brett Favre .75 2.00
2 Barry Sanders .60 1.50
3 John Elway .75 2.00
4 Emmitt Smith .60 1.50
5 Dan Marino .75 2.00
6 Eddie George .20 .50
7 Jerry Rice .40 1.00
8 Jake Plummer .20 .50
9 Joey Galloway .10 .30
10 Mike Alstott .20 .50
11 Brian Mitchell .07 .20
12 Keyshawn Johnson .20 .50
13 Jerald Moore .07 .20
14 Randal Hill .07 .20
15 Byron Hanspard .07 .20
16 Jeff George .10 .30
17 Terry Glenn .20 .50
18 Jerome Bettis .20 .50
19 Curtis Conway .10 .30
20 Fred Lane .07 .20
21 Isaac Bruce .20 .50
22 Tiki Barber .20 .50
23 Bobby Hoying .10 .30
24 Marcus Allen .20 .50
25 Dana Stubblefield .07 .20
26 Peter Boulware .07 .20
27 John Randle .10 .30
28 Jason Sehorn .10 .30
29 Rod Smith .10 .30
30 Michael Sinclair .07 .20
31 Marshall Faulk .25 .60
32 Karl Williams .07 .20
33 Kordell Stewart .20 .50
34 Corey Dillon .20 .50
35 Bryant Young .07 .20
36 Charlie Garner .10 .30
37 Andre Reed .10 .30
38 Ray Buchanan .07 .20
39 Brett Perriman .07 .20
40 Leon Lett .07 .20
41 Keenan McCardell .10 .30
42 Eric Swann .07 .20
43 Leslie Shepherd .07 .20
44 Curtis Martin .20 .50
45 Andre Rison .10 .30
46 Keith Lyle .07 .20
47 Rae Carruth .07 .20
48 William Henderson .10 .30
49 Sean Dawkins .07 .20
50 Terrell Davis .20 .50
51 Tim Brown .20 .50
52 Willie McGinest .07 .20
53 Jermaine Lewis .10 .30
54 Ricky Watters .10 .30
55 Freddie Jones .07 .20
56 Robert Smith .20 .50
57 Reidel Anthony .10 .30
58 James Stewart .10 .30
59 Earl Holmes RC .20 .50
60 Dale Carter .07 .20
61 Michael Irvin .20 .50
62 Jason Taylor .10 .30
63 Eric Metcalf .07 .20
64 LeRoy Butler .07 .20
65 Jamal Anderson .20 .50
66 Jamie Asher .07 .20
67 Chris Sanders .07 .20
68 Warren Sapp .10 .30
69 Ray Zellars .07 .20
70 Carl Pickens .10 .30
71 Garrison Hearst .20 .50
72 Eddie Kennison .10 .30
73 John Mobley .07 .20
74 Rob Johnson .10 .30
75 William Thomas .07 .20
76 Drew Bledsoe .30 .75
77 Micheal Barrow .07 .20
78 Jim Harbaugh .10 .30
79 Terry McDaniel .07 .20
80 Johnnie Morton .10 .30
81 Danny Kanell .10 .30
82 Larry Centers .07 .20
83 Courtney Hawkins .07 .20
84 Tony Brackens .07 .20
85 Tony Gonzalez .20 .50
86 Aaron Glenn .07 .20
87 Cris Carter .20 .50
88 Chuck Smith .07 .20
89 Tamarick Vanover .07 .20
90 Karim Abdul-Jabbar .20 .50
91 Bryant Westbrook .07 .20
92 Mike Pritchard .07 .20
93 Darren Woodson .07 .20
94 Wesley Walls .10 .30
95 Tony Banks .10 .30
96 Michael Westbrook .10 .30
97 Shannon Sharpe .10 .30
98 Jeff Blake .10 .30
99 Terrell Owens .20 .50
100 Warrick Dunn .20 .50
101 Levon Kirkland .07 .20
102 Frank Wycheck .07 .20
103 Gus Frerotte .07 .20
104 Simeon Rice .10 .30
105 Shawn Jefferson .07 .20
106 Irving Fryar .10 .30
107 Michael McCrary .07 .20
108 Robert Brooks .10 .30
109 Chris Chandler .10 .30
110 Junior Seau .20 .50
111 O.J. McDuffie .10 .30
112 Glenn Foley .10 .30
113 Darryl Williams .07 .20
114 Elvis Grbac .10 .30
115 Napoleon Kaufman .20 .50
116 Anthony Miller .07 .20
117 Troy Davis .07 .20
118 Charles Way .07 .20
119 Scott Mitchell .10 .30
120 Ken Harvey .07 .20
121 Tyrone Hughes .07 .20
122 Mark Brunell .20 .50
123 David Palmer .07 .20
124 Rob Moore .10 .30
125 Kerry Collins .10 .30
126 Will Blackwell .07 .20
127 Ray Crockett .07 .20
128 Leslie O'Neal .07 .20
129 Antowain Smith .20 .50
130 Carlester Crumpler .07 .20
131 Michael Jackson .07 .20
132 Trent Dilfer .20 .50
133 Dan Williams .07 .20
134 Dorsey Levens .20 .50
135 Ty Law .10 .30
136 Rickey Dudley .07 .20
137 Jessie Tuggle .07 .20
138 Darrien Gordon .07 .20
139 Kevin Turner .07 .20
140 Willie Davis .07 .20
141 Zach Thomas .20 .50
142 Tony McGee .07 .20
143 Dexter Coakley .07 .20
144 Troy Brown .10 .30
145 Leeland McElroy .07 .20
146 Michael Strahan .10 .30
147 Ken Dilger .07 .20
148 Bryce Paup .07 .20
149 Herman Moore .10 .30
150 Reggie White .20 .50
151 Dewayne Washington .07 .20
152 Natrone Means .10 .30
153 Ben Coates .10 .30
154 Bert Emanuel .10 .30
155 Steve Young .25 .60
156 Jimmy Smith .10 .30
157 Darrell Green .10 .30
158 Troy Aikman .40 1.00
159 Greg Hill .07 .20
160 Raymont Harris .07 .20
161 Troy Drayton .07 .20
162 Stevon Moore .07 .20
163 Warren Moon .20 .50
164 Wayne Martin .07 .20
165 Jason Gildon .07 .20
166 Chris Calloway .07 .20
167 Aeneas Williams .07 .20
168 Michael Bates .07 .20
169 Hugh Douglas .07 .20
170 Brad Johnson .20 .50
171 Bruce Smith .10 .30
172 Neil Smith .10 .30
173 James McKnight .20 .50
174 Robert Porcher .07 .20
175 Merton Hanks .07 .20
176 Ki-Jana Carter .07 .20
177 Mo Lewis .07 .20
178 Chester McGlockton .07 .20
179 Zack Crockett .07 .20
180 Derrick Thomas .20 .50
181 J.J. Stokes .10 .30
182 Derrick Rodgers .07 .20
183 Daryl Johnston .10 .30
184 Chris Penn .07 .20
185 Steve Atwater .07 .20
186 Amp Lee .07 .20
187 Frank Sanders .10 .30
188 Chris Slade .07 .20
189 Mark Chmura .10 .30
190 Kimble Anders .10 .30
191 Charles Johnson .07 .20
192 William Floyd .07 .20
193 Jay Graham .07 .20
194 Hardy Nickerson .07 .20
195 Terry Allen .20 .50
196 James Jett .10 .30
197 Jessie Armstead .07 .20
198 Yancey Thigpen .10 .30
199 Terance Mathis .10 .30
200 Steve McNair .20 .50
201 Wayne Chrebet .20 .50
202 Jamir Miller .07 .20
203 Duce Staley .25 .60
204 Deion Sanders .20 .50
205 Carnell Lake .07 .20
206 Ed McCaffrey .10 .30
207 Shawn Springs .07 .20
208 Tony Martin .10 .30
209 Jerris McPhail .07 .20
210 Darnay Scott .10 .30
211 Jake Reed .10 .30
212 Adrian Murrell .10 .30
213 Quinn Early .07 .20
214 Marvin Harrison .20 .50
215 Ryan McNeil .07 .20
216 Derrick Alexander .10 .30
217 Ray Lewis .20 .50
218 Antonio Freeman .20 .50
219 Dwayne Rudd .07 .20
220 Muhsin Muhammad .10 .30
221 Kevin Hardy .07 .20
222 Andre Hastings .07 .20
223 John Avery RC .30 .75
224 Keith Brooking RC .50 1.25
225 Kevin Dyson RC .50 1.25
226 Robert Edwards RC .30 .75
227 Greg Ellis RC .20 .50
228 Curtis Enis RC .20 .50
229 Terry Fair RC .30 .75
230 Ahman Green RC 1.50 4.00
231 Jacquez Green RC .30 .75
232 Brian Griese RC 1.25 3.00
233 Skip Hicks RC .30 .75
234 Ryan Leaf RC .50 1.25
235 Peyton Manning RC 7.50 15.00
236 R.W. McQuarters RC .30 .75
237 Randy Moss RC 4.00 10.00
238 Marcus Nash RC .20 .50
239 Anthony Simmons RC .30 .75
240 Brian Simmons RC .30 .75
241 Takeo Spikes RC .50 1.25
242 Duane Starks RC .20 .50
243 Fred Taylor RC .75 2.00
244 Andre Wadsworth RC .30 .75
245 Shaun Williams RC .30 .75
246 Grant Wistrom RC .30 .75
247 Charles Woodson RC 1.50 4.00
248 Checklist .07 .20
249 Checklist .07 .20
250 Checklist .07 .20
P16 Jeff George Promo .40 1.00

1998 Fleer Tradition Heritage

*1-250 VETS: 15X TO 40X BASIC CARDS
*221-247 ROOKIES: 5X TO 12X
HERITAGE PRINT RUN 125 SERIAL #'d SETS

1998 Fleer Tradition Big Numbers

Randomly inserted in packs at a rate of one in four, this 99-card set features nine different top skill-position players printed on 11-slightly different versions of interactive cards. Each unnumbered card was bi-fold with the front designed like a typical insert card, the back blank, and the inside sections featuring all of the rules of the contest along with the point value for that card (0-9 points or wild card). Cards of the same player could be combined to form that player's total 1998 passing yardage, rushing or receiving yardage for a chance to win various prizes including a trip to the 2000 Pro Bowl. The most common prize was a 9-card glossy stock prize set of the nine featured players. The prize set was also available for $3 plus any 4-Big Numbers redemption inserts. We've cataloged the inserts alphabetically by player with each in order from 0-9 points with the wild card version last. All cards for each payer are valued equally.
COMPLETE SET (99) 40.00 100.00
STATED ODDS 1:4
EACH HAS 11-CARDS OF EQUAL VALUE
BN1A Tim Brown 0 .30 .75
BN2A Cris Carter 0 .30 .75
BN3A Terrell Davis 0 .30 .75
BN4A John Elway 0 1.25 3.00
BN5A Brett Favre 0 1.25 3.00
BN6A Eddie George 0 .30 .75
BN7A Dorsey Levens 0 .30 .75
BN8A Herman Moore 0 .20 .50
BN9A Steve Young 0 .40 1.00

1998 Fleer Tradition Big Numbers Prizes

This 9-card set was issued via a mail redemption offer through the Big Numbers inserts in packs of 1998 Fleer. A collector could receive a set for $3 plus four Big Numbers insert bi-fold cards. Each card was printed on glossy stock and is a finished version of that player's bi-fold insert card complete with a traditional cardback.
COMPLETE SET (9) 6.00 15.00
SET ISSUED VIA MAIL REDEMPTION
1BN Tim Brown .50 1.25
2BN Cris Carter .50 1.25
3BN Terrell Davis .50 1.25
4BN John Elway 2.00 5.00
5BN Brett Favre 2.00 5.00
6BN Eddie George .50 1.25
7BN Dorsey Levens .50 1.25
8BN Herman Moore .30 .75
9BN Steve Young .60 1.50

1998 Fleer Tradition Playmakers Theatre

Randomly inserted in packs, this 15-card set features color action photos of the top NFL players and is sequentially numbered to 100.
STATED PRINT RUN 100 SER.#'d SETS
PT1 Terrell Davis 12.00 30.00
PT2 Corey Dillon 10.00 25.00
PT3 Warrick Dunn 10.00 25.00
PT4 John Elway 60.00 120.00
PT5 Brett Favre 100.00 200.00
PT6 Antonio Freeman 12.00 30.00
PT7 Joey Galloway 10.00 25.00
PT8 Eddie George 10.00 25.00
PT9 Terry Glenn 10.00 25.00
PT10 Dan Marino 60.00 120.00
PT11 Curtis Martin 12.00 30.00
PT12 Jake Plummer 10.00 25.00
PT13 Barry Sanders 60.00 120.00
PT14 Deion Sanders 15.00 40.00
PT15 Kordell Stewart 8.00 20.00

1998 Fleer Tradition Red Zone Rockers

Randomly inserted in packs at a rate of one in 32, this 10-card set features color action photos of players who consistantly stick the ball in the end zone.
COMPLETE SET (10) 30.00 60.00
STATED ODDS 1:32
RZ1 Jerome Bettis 2.00 5.00
RZ2 Drew Bledsoe 3.00 8.00
RZ3 Mark Brunell 2.00 5.00
RZ4 Corey Dillon 2.00 5.00
RZ5 Joey Galloway 1.25 3.00
RZ6 Keyshawn Johnson 2.00 5.00
RZ7 Dorsey Levens 2.00 5.00
RZ8 Dan Marino 8.00 20.00
RZ9 Barry Sanders 6.00 15.00
RZ10 Emmitt Smith 6.00 15.00

1998 Fleer Tradition Rookie Sensations

Randomly inserted in packs at a rate of one in 16, this 15-card set features color action photos of top new NFL Rookies.
COMPLETE SET (15) 30.00 60.00
STATED ODDS 1:16
1RS John Avery .50 1.25
2RS Keith Brooking .75 2.00
3RS Kevin Dyson .75 2.00
4RS Robert Edwards .50 1.25
5RS Greg Ellis .30 .75
6RS Curtis Enis .30 .75
7RS Terry Fair .50 1.25
8RS Ryan Leaf .75 2.00
9RS Peyton Manning 8.00 20.00
10RS Randy Moss 6.00 15.00
11RS Marcus Nash .30 .75
12RS Fred Taylor 1.25 3.00
13RS Andre Wadsworth .50 1.25
14RS Grant Wistrom .50 1.25
15RS Charles Woodson 2.00 5.00

1999 Fleer Tradition

This 300 card set was issued in August, 1999. The cards were in 10 card packs. Cards numbered from 251 through 300 feature the leading rookies entering the 1999 season. Notable Rookie Cards include Tim Couch, Edgerrin James and Ricky Williams. Four unnumbered checklist cards were issued at a rate of one every six packs.
COMPLETE SET (300) 20.00 40.00
1 Randy Moss .15 .40
2 Peyton Manning .60 1.50
3 Barry Sanders .30 .75
4 Terrell Davis .15 .40
5 Brett Favre .40 1.00
6 Fred Taylor .12 .30
7 Jake Plummer .12 .30
8 John Elway .30 .75
9 Emmitt Smith .30 .75
10 Kerry Collins .12 .30
11 Peter Boulware .12 .30
12 Jamal Anderson .15 .40
13 Doug Flutie .20 .50
14 Michael Bates .12 .30
15 Corey Dillon .12 .30
16 Curtis Conway .15 .40
17 Ty Detmer .12 .30
18 Robert Brooks .15 .40
19 Dale Carter .12 .30
20 Charlie Batch .12 .30
21 Ken Dilger .12 .30
22 Troy Aikman .25 .60
23 Tavian Banks .12 .30
24 Cris Carter .20 .50
25 Derrick Alexander WR .12 .30
26 Chris Bordano RC .12 .30
27 Karim Abdul-Jabbar .12 .30
28 Jessie Armstead .15 .40
29 Drew Bledsoe .15 .40
30 Brian Dawkins .20 .50
31 Wayne Chrebet .12 .30
32 Garrison Hearst .12 .30
33 Eric Allen .15 .40
34 Tony Banks .15 .40
35 Jerome Bettis .20 .50
36 Stephen Alexander .12 .30
37 Rodney Harrison .12 .30
38 Mike Alstott .12 .30
39 Chad Brown .12 .30
40 Johnny McWilliams .12 .30
41 Kevin Dyson .12 .30
42 Keith Brooking .15 .40
43 Jim Harbaugh .15 .40
44 Bobby Engram .12 .30
45 John Holecek .12 .30
46 Steve Beuerlein .15 .40
47 Tony McGee .12 .30
48 Greg Ellis .12 .30
49 Corey Fuller .12 .30
50 Stephen Boyd .12 .30
51 Marshall Faulk .15 .40
52 LeRoy Butler .15 .40
53 Reggie Barlow .12 .30
54 Randall Cunningham .15 .40
55 Aeneas Williams .12 .30
56 Kimble Anders .12 .30
57 Cam Cleeland .12 .30
58 John Avery .12 .30
59 Gary Brown .12 .30
60 Ben Coates .15 .40
61 Koy Detmer .12 .30
62 Bryan Cox .15 .40
63 Edgar Bennett .15 .40
64 Tim Brown .20 .50
65 Isaac Bruce .20 .50
66 Eddie George .15 .40
67 Reidel Anthony .12 .30
68 Charlie Jones .12 .30
69 Terry Allen .15 .40
70 Joey Galloway .15 .40
71 Jamir Miller .12 .30
72 Will Blackwell .12 .30
73 Ray Buchanan .12 .30
74 Priest Holmes .12 .30
75 Michael Irvin .20 .50
76 Jonathan Linton .12 .30
77 Curtis Enis .12 .30
78 Neil O'Donnell .15 .40
79 Tim Biakabutuka .15 .40
80 Terry Kirby .12 .30
81 Germane Crowell .12 .30
82 Jason Elam .12 .30
83 Mark Chmura .12 .30
84 Marvin Harrison .15 .40
85 Jimmy Hitchcock .12 .30
86 Tony Brackens .12 .30
87 Sean Dawkins .12 .30
88 Tony Gonzalez .15 .40
89 Kent Graham .12 .30
90 Oronde Gadsden .12 .30
91 Hugh Douglas .15 .40
92 Robert Edwards .12 .30
93 R.W. McQuarters .12 .30
94 Aaron Glenn .12 .30
95 Kevin Carter .12 .30
96 Rickey Dudley .12 .30
97 Derrick Brooks .20 .50
98 Mark Bruener .12 .30
99 Darrell Green .20 .50
100 Jessie Tuggle .12 .30
101 Freddie Jones .12 .30
102 Rob Moore .12 .30
103 Ahman Green .15 .40
104 Chris Chandler .15 .40
105 Steve McNair .15 .40
106 Kevin Greene .20 .50
107 Jermaine Lewis .12 .30
108 Erik Kramer .15 .40
109 Eric Moulds .12 .30
110 Terry Fair .12 .30
111 Carl Pickens .15 .40
112 La'Roi Glover RC .20 .50
113 Chris Spielman .15 .40
114 Leroy Hoard .12 .30
115 Mark Brunell .15 .40
116 Patrick Jeffers RC .20 .50
117 Elvis Grbac .12 .30
118 Ike Hilliard .12 .30
119 Sam Madison .12 .30
120 Terrell Owens .15 .40
121 Rich Gannon .15 .40
122 Skip Hicks .12 .30
123 Eric Green .12 .30
124 Trent Dilfer .12 .30
125 Terry Glenn .15 .40
126 Trent Green .12 .30
127 Charles Johnson .12 .30
128 Adrian Murrell .12 .30
129 Jason Gildon .15 .40
130 Tim Dwight .15 .40
131 Ryan Leaf .15 .40
132 Rocket Ismail .15 .40
133 Jon Kitna .12 .30
134 Alonzo Mayes .12 .30
135 Yancey Thigpen .12 .30
136 David LaFleur .12 .30
137 Ray Lewis .20 .50
138 Herman Moore .15 .40
139 Brian Griese .12 .30
140 Antonio Freeman .15 .40
141 Darnay Scott .12 .30
142 Ed McDaniel .12 .30
143 Andre Reed .20 .50
144 Andre Hastings .12 .30
145 Chris Warren .15 .40
146 Kevin Hardy .12 .30
147 Joe Jurevicius .12 .30
148 Jerome Pathon .12 .30
149 Duce Staley .12 .30
150 Dan Marino .40 1.00
151 Jerry Rice .50 1.25
152 Byron Bam Morris .12 .30
153 Az-Zahir Hakim .12 .30
154 Ty Law .20 .50
155 Warrick Dunn .12 .30
156 Keyshawn Johnson .15 .40
157 Brian Mitchell .15 .40
158 James Jett .12 .30
159 Fred Lane .12 .30
160 Courtney Hawkins .12 .30
161 Andre Wadsworth .12 .30
162 Natrone Means .15 .40
163 Andrew Glover .12 .30
164 Anthony Simmons .12 .30
165 Leon Lett .12 .30
166 Frank Wycheck .15 .40
167 Barry Minter .12 .30
168 Michael McCrary .12 .30
169 Johnnie Morton .15 .40
170 Jay Riemersma .12 .30
171 Vonnie Holliday .12 .30
172 Brian Simmons .12 .30
173 Joe Johnson .12 .30
174 Ed McCaffrey .15 .40
175 Jason Sehorn .15 .40
176 Keenan McCardell .15 .40
177 Bobby Taylor .15 .40
178 Andre Rison .15 .40
179 Greg Hill .12 .30
180 O.J. McDuffie .15 .40
181 Darren Woodson .15 .40
182 Willie McGinest .15 .40
183 J.J. Stokes .12 .30
184 Leon Johnson .12 .30
185 Bert Emanuel .15 .40
186 Napoleon Kaufman .12 .30
187 Leslie Shepherd .12 .30
188 Levon Kirkland .12 .30
189 Simeon Rice .12 .30
190 Mikhael Ricks .12 .30
191 Robert Smith .12 .30
192 Michael Sinclair .12 .30
193 Muhsin Muhammad .12 .30
194 Duane Starks .12 .30
195 Terance Mathis .12 .30
196 Antowain Smith .12 .30
197 Tony Parrish .12 .30
198 Takeo Spikes .12 .30
199 Ernie Mills .12 .30
200 John Mobley .12 .30
201 Robert Porcher .12 .30
202 Pete Mitchell .12 .30
203 Darick Holmes .12 .30
204 Derrick Thomas .20 .50
205 David Palmer .12 .30
206 Jason Taylor .15 .40
207 Sammy Knight .12 .30
208 Dwayne Rudd .12 .30
209 Lawyer Milloy .12 .30
210 Michael Strahan .15 .40
211 Mo Lewis .12 .30
212 William Thomas .12 .30
213 Darrell Russell .12 .30
214 Brad Johnson .15 .40
215 Kordell Stewart .12 .30
216 Robert Holcombe .12 .30
217 Junior Seau .15 .40
218 Jacquez Green .12 .30
219 Shawn Springs .12 .30
220 Michael Westbrook .12 .30
221 Rod Woodson .20 .50
222 Frank Sanders .12 .30
223 Bruce Smith .15 .40
224 Eugene Robinson .15 .40
225 Bill Romanowski .15 .40
226 Wesley Walls .15 .40
227 Jimmy Smith .15 .40
228 Deion Sanders .15 .40
229 Lamar Thomas .12 .30
230 Dorsey Levens .15 .40
231 Tony Simmons .12 .30
232 John Randle .20 .50
233 Curtis Martin .15 .40
234 Bryant Young .15 .40
235 Charles Woodson .20 .50
236 Charles Way .12 .30
237 Zach Thomas .15 .40
238 Ricky Proehl .12 .30
239 Ricky Watters .15 .40
240 Hardy Nickerson .12 .30
241 Shannon Sharpe .15 .40
242 O.J. Santiago .12 .30
243 Vinny Testaverde .12 .30
244 Roell Preston .12 .30
245 James Stewart .12 .30
246 Jake Reed .15 .40
247 Steve Young .25 .60
248 Shaun Williams .12 .30
249 Rod Smith .15 .40
250 Warren Sapp .15 .40
251 Champ Bailey RC .40 1.00
252 Karsten Bailey RC .20 .50
253 D'Wayne Bates RC .20 .50
254 Michael Bishop RC .25 .60
255 David Boston RC .20 .50
256 Na Brown RC .20 .50
257 Fernando Bryant RC .20 .50
258 Shawn Bryson RC .20 .50
259 Darrin Chiaverini RC .20 .50
260 Chris Claiborne RC .20 .50
261 Mike Cloud RC .20 .50
262 Cecil Collins RC .20 .50
263 Tim Couch RC .25 .60
264 Scott Covington RC .20 .50
265 Daunte Culpepper RC .30 .75
266 Antuan Edwards RC .20 .50
267 Troy Edwards RC .20 .50
268 Ebenezer Ekuban RC .20 .50
269 Kevin Faulk RC .20 .50
270 Jermaine Fazande RC .20 .50
271 Joe Germaine RC .25 .60
272 Martin Gramatica RC .20 .50
273 Torry Holt RC .40 1.00
274 Brock Huard RC .20 .50
275 Sedrick Irvin RC .20 .50
276 Sheldon Jackson RC .20 .50
277 Edgerrin James RC .30 .75
278 James Johnson RC .20 .50
279 Kevin Johnson RC .25 .60
280 Malcolm Johnson RC .20 .50
281 Andy Katzenmoyer RC .25 .60
282 Jevon Kearse RC .25 .60
283 Patrick Kerney RC .20 .50
284 Shaun King RC .20 .50
285 Jim Kleinsasser RC .30 .75
286 Rob Konrad RC .20 .50
287 Chris McAlister RC .20 .50
288 Donovan McNabb RC 2.00 5.00
289 Cade McNown RC .20 .50
290 Dee Miller RC .20 .50
291 Joe Montgomery RC .20 .50
292 De'Mond Parker RC .20 .50
293 Peerless Price RC .20 .50
294 Akili Smith RC .20 .50
295 Justin Swift RC .20 .50
296 Jerame Tuman RC .20 .50
297 Ricky Williams RC .30 .75
298 Antoine Winfield .20 .50
299 Craig Yeast RC .20 .50
300 Amos Zereoue RC .20 .50
P6 Fred Taylor Promo .40 1.00

1999 Fleer Tradition Blitz Collection

COMPLETE SET (300) 50.00 120.00
*BC STARS: 1.2X TO 3X BASIC CARDS
*BLITZ COLL.RCs: .5X TO 1.2X BASIC CARDS
ONE BLITZ COLLECTION PER RETAIL PACK

1999 Fleer Tradition Trophy Collection

*TC STARS: 50X TO 120X BASIC CARDS
*TC ROOKIES: 8X TO 20X
STATED PRINT RUN 20 SERIAL #'d SETS

1999 Fleer Tradition Aerial Assault

Issued one every 24 packs, these 15 cards showcase players who are known for either throwing or catching a football. The players photo is shot against a background of a target.
COMPLETE SET (15) 25.00 50.00
STATED ODDS 1:24
1 Troy Aikman 2.00 5.00
2 Jamal Anderson 1.00 2.50
3 Charlie Batch 1.00 2.50
4 Mark Brunell 1.00 2.50
5 Terrell Davis 1.00 2.50
6 John Elway 3.00 8.00
7 Brett Favre 3.00 8.00
8 Keyshawn Johnson 1.00 2.50
9 Jon Kitna 1.00 2.50
10 Peyton Manning 3.00 8.00
11 Dan Marino 3.00 8.00
12 Randy Moss 2.50 6.00
13 Eric Moulds 1.00 2.50
14 Jake Plummer .60 1.50
15 Jerry Rice 2.00 5.00

1999 Fleer Tradition Fresh Ink

The first 14 cards listed below were inserted randomly into Fleer Tradition packs. Each was signed by the player featured and included a congratulatory message on the card's back. The cards were hand serial numbered on the front to 200. The cards are unnumbered so we have sequenced them in alphabetical order. Additional non-serial numbered cards and players, such as Troy Edwards, surfaced much later after old Fleer inventory was released following their close.
ANNOUNCED PRINT RUN 200 SETS
1 Champ Bailey 15.00 30.00
2 David Boston 6.00 15.00
3 Chris Claiborne 6.00 15.00
4 Torry Holt 8.00 20.00
5 Edgerrin James 15.00 40.00
6 James Johnson 6.00 15.00
7 Kevin Johnson 7.50 20.00
8 Jevon Kearse 10.00 25.00
9 Shaun King 6.00 15.00
10 Rob Konrad 7.50 20.00
11 Donovan McNabb 30.00 80.00
12 Cade McNown 7.50 20.00
13 Akili Smith 7.50 20.00
14 Ricky Williams 12.00 30.00

1999 Fleer Tradition Rookie Sensations

Issued one every six packs, these cars feature 20 players drafted in 1999 who looked like they would make an impact in the NFL. The players are profiled against their team backgrounds which are in 100 percent silver foil.
COMPLETE SET (20) 15.00 40.00
STATED ODDS 1:6
1 Champ Bailey .75 2.00
2 Michael Bishop .60 1.50
3 David Boston .60 1.50
4 Chris Claiborne .20 .50
5 Tim Couch .60 1.50
6 Daunte Culpepper 2.50 6.00
7 Troy Edwards .40 1.00
8 Kevin Faulk .60 1.50
9 Torry Holt 1.50 4.00
10 Brock Huard .60 1.50
11 Edgerrin James 2.50 6.00
12 Kevin Johnson .60 1.50
13 Shaun King .40 1.00
14 Rob Konrad .60 1.50
15 Chris McAlister .40 1.00
16 Donovan McNabb 3.00 8.00
17 Cade McNown .40 1.00
18 Peerless Price .60 1.50
19 Akili Smith .40 1.00
20 Ricky Williams 1.25 3.00

1999 Fleer Tradition Under Pressure

Inserted one every 96 packs, these cards feature players who thrive in tough situations. Each card features a sculpture embossed player image against brilliant color backgrounds on patterned holofoil.
COMPLETE SET (15) 50.00 120.00
STATED ODDS 1:96
1 Charlie Batch 3.00 8.00
2 Terrell Davis 3.00 8.00
3 Warrick Dunn 3.00 8.00
4 John Elway 10.00 25.00
5 Brett Favre 10.00 25.00
6 Keyshawn Johnson 3.00 8.00
7 Peyton Manning 10.00 25.00
8 Dan Marino 10.00 25.00
9 Curtis Martin 3.00 8.00
10 Randy Moss 8.00 20.00
11 Jake Plummer 2.00 5.00
12 Barry Sanders 10.00 25.00
13 Emmitt Smith 6.00 15.00
14 Fred Taylor 3.00 8.00
15 Charles Woodson 3.00 8.00

1999 Fleer Tradition Unsung Heroes

This insert set, inserted at a rate of one in two, features 30 players who were voted as good representatives for their teams in the 1998 season. The cards were also issued at the NFL Players Awards Banquet with a different suffix on the card numbers.
COMPLETE SET (30) 5.00 10.00
STATED ODDS 1:3
1UH Tommy Bennett .25 .60
2UH Lester Archambeau .25 .60
3UH James Jones DT .25 .60
4UH Phil Hansen .25 .60
5UH Anthony Johnson .25 .60
6UH Bobby Engram .25 .60
7UH Eric Bieniemy .25 .60
8UH Daryl Johnston .25 .60
9UH Maa Tanuvasa .25 .60
10UH Stephen Boyd .25 .60
11UH Adam Timmerman .25 .60
12UH Ken Dilger .25 .60
13UH Bryan Barker .25 .60
14UH Rich Gannon .40 1.00
15UH O.J. Brigance .25 .60
16UH Jeff Christy .25 .60
17UH Shawn Jefferson .25 .60
18UH Aaron Craver .25 .60
19UH Chris Calloway .25 .60

20UH Pepper Johnson .25 .60
21UH Greg Biekert .25 .60
22UH Duce Staley .25 .60
23UH Courtney Hawkins .25 .60
24UH D'Marco Farr .25 .60
25UH Rodney Harrison .25 .60
26UH Ray Brown .25 .60
27UH Jon Kitna .40 1.00
28UH Brad Culpepper .25 .60
29UH Steve Jackson .25 .60
30UH Brian Mitchell .25 .60

1999 Fleer Tradition Unsung Heroes Banquet

This set was distributed to attendees of the NFL Player's Inc. Unsung Heroes Awards Banquet on April 16, 1999. Each card features a full color photo of the player on front with a player profile on back. The cards were also issued in Fleer packs as an insert with a different suffix on the card numbers.

COMPLETE SET (31) 16.00 40.00
1AB Tommy Bennett .50 1.25
2AB Lester Archambeau .50 1.25
3AB James Jones DT .50 1.25
4AB Phil Hansen .50 1.25
5AB Anthony Johnson .50 1.25
6AB Bobby Engram .80 2.00
7AB Eric Bieniemy .50 1.25
8AB Daryl Johnston .80 2.00
9AB Maa Tanuvasa .50 1.25
10AB Stephen Boyd .50 1.25
11AB Adam Timmerman .50 1.25
12AB Ken Dilger .80 2.00
13AB Bryan Barker .50 1.25
14AB Rich Gannon 1.20 3.00
15AB O.J. Brigance .50 1.25
16AB Jeff Christy .50 1.25
17AB Shawn Jefferson .50 1.25
18AB Aaron Craver .50 1.25
19AB Chris Calloway .80 2.00
20AB Pepper Johnson .50 1.25
21AB Greg Biekert .50 1.25
22AB Duce Staley 1.20 3.00
23AB Courtney Hawkins .50 1.25
24AB D'Marco Farr .50 1.25
25AB Rodney Harrison .50 1.25
26AB Ray Brown OL .50 1.25
27AB Jon Kitna 1.20 3.00
28AB Brad Culpepper .50 1.25
29AB Steve Jackson .50 1.25
30AB Brian Mitchell .50 1.25
NNO Checklist Card UER .50 1.25

2000 Fleer Tradition

Released in late September 2000, Fleer features a 400-card base set comprised of 303 Veterans, 31 Rpploe Singles, 31 Rookies to Watch, 31 Team Action cards, and 4 Checklists. Base cards are white bordered and feature both action and portrait photos coupled with a facsimile player autograph on a single color background resembling sets from the 1950's. Fleer was packaged in 36-pack boxes with packs containing 10 cards.

COMPLETE SET (400) 25.00 60.00
1 Kevin Johnson .12 .30
2 Chris Chandler .15 .40
3 Peerless Price .15 .40
4 Andre Rison .15 .40
5 Curtis Enis .12 .30
6 Tim Couch .15 .40
7 Brian Dawkins .20 .50
8 Akili Smith .12 .30
9 Kevin Faulk .12 .30
10 Joey Galloway .15 .40
11 Bill Romanowski .12 .30
12 Charlie Batch .12 .30
13 Terrence Wilkins .12 .30
14 Kevin Hardy .12 .30
15 Cade McNown .12 .30
16 Elvis Grbac .12 .30
17 Cris Carter .20 .50
18 Willie McGinest .15 .40
19 Michael Bishop .12 .30
20 Lee Woodall .12 .30
21 Jake Reed .15 .40
22 Bryan Cox .12 .30
23 Chris Sanders .12 .30
24 Tavian Banks .12 .30
25 Levon Kirkland .12 .30
26 James Hundon .12 .30
27 Junior Seau .15 .40
28 Darren Woodson .15 .40
29 Kevin Carter .12 .30
30 Joe Jurevicius .12 .30
31 John Lynch .15 .40
32 Steve McNair .15 .40
33 Jake Plummer .12 .30
34 Antonio Freeman .15 .40
35 Peter Boulware .12 .30
36 Brad Johnson .15 .40
37 Bobby Engram .12 .30
38 David Boston .12 .30
39 Jason Tucker .12 .30
40 Troy Brown .12 .30
41 Brian Griese .12 .30
42 Dorsey Levens .15 .40
43 Cornelius Bennett .12 .30
44 Donovan McNabb .15 .40
45 Rob Johnson .15 .40
46 Robert Smith .12 .30
47 Stanley Pritchett .12 .30
48 Tedy Bruschi .30 .75
49 Dan Marino .40 1.00
50 Amani Toomer .12 .30
51 Aaron Glenn .12 .30
52 Rickey Dudley .12 .30
53 Tim Brown .20 .50
54 Jim Harbaugh .15 .40
55 Terrell Owens .15 .40
56 Jason Sehorn .12 .30
57 Cortez Kennedy .15 .40
58 London Fletcher RC .40 1.00
59 Simeon Rice .15 .40
60 Shaun King .12 .30
61 Stephen Davis .12 .30
62 Andre Wadsworth .12 .30
63 Kyle Brady .12 .30
64 Priest Holmes .12 .30
65 Patrick Jeffers .12 .30
66 Barry Minter .12 .30
67 Curtis Martin .15 .40
68 Darrin Chiaverini .12 .30
69 Robert Thomas .12 .30
70 Samari Rolle .12 .30
71 Robert Porcher .12 .30
72 Jerry Rice .50 1.25
73 Bill Schroeder .15 .40
74 Chad Bratzke .12 .30
75 Tony Brackens .12 .30
76 O.J. McDuffie .15 .40
77 John Randle .20 .50
78 Michael Pittman .12 .30
79 Drew Bledsoe .15 .40
80 Ike Hilliard .12 .30
81 Victor Green .12 .30
82 Duce Staley .12 .30
83 Bruce Smith .15 .40
84 Amos Zereoue .12 .30
85 Charlie Garner .15 .40
86 Shawn Springs .12 .30
87 Kurt Warner .30 .75
88 Eddie George .15 .40
89 Michael Westbrook .12 .30
90 Dexter Coakley .12 .30
91 Rob Moore .12 .30
92 Duane Starks .12 .30
93 Steve Beuerlein .15 .40
94 Marty Booker .12 .30
95 Karim Abdul-Jabbar .12 .30
96 Troy Aikman .25 .60
97 Germane Crowell .12 .30
98 Matt Hasselbeck .12 .30
99 E.G. Green .12 .30
100 Mark Brunell .15 .40
101 Tony Martin .15 .40
102 Darrell Green .15 .40
103 Ricky Williams .15 .40
104 Michael Strahan .15 .40
105 Vinny Testaverde .12 .30
106 Charles Johnson .12 .30
107 Hines Ward .15 .40
108 Bryant Young .12 .30
109 Mo Lewis .12 .30
110 Greg Clark .12 .30
111 Jon Kitna .12 .30
112 Jacquez Green .12 .30
113 Kevin Dyson .15 .40
114 Stephen Alexander .12 .30
115 Cam Cleeland .12 .30
116 Keith Poole .12 .30
117 Az-Zahir Hakim .12 .30
118 Tim Dwight .15 .40
119 Corey Bradford .12 .30
120 Carlos Emmons .12 .30
121 Trent Dilfer .12 .30
122 Lance Schulters .12 .30
123 Byron Hanspard .12 .30
124 Tim Biakabutuka .15 .40
125 Eddie Kennison .12 .30
126 Terry Kirby .12 .30
127 Mike McKenzie .12 .30
128 Fred Beasley .12 .30
129 Chad Brown .12 .30
130 Terrell Davis .15 .40
131 Herman Moore .12 .30
132 Vonnie Holliday .12 .30
133 Jim Miller .12 .30
134 Peyton Manning .50 1.25
135 Derrick Alexander .12 .30
136 Oronde Gadsden .15 .40
137 Robert Griffith .12 .30
138 Troy Edwards .12 .30
139 Damon Huard .12 .30
140 Jessie Armstead .12 .30
141 Charles Woodson .20 .50
142 Troy Vincent .12 .30
143 Natrone Means .15 .40
144 Jeff Garcia .12 .30
145 Terry Glenn .15 .40
146 Marshall Faulk .15 .40
147 Pat Johnson .12 .30
148 Frank Wycheck .15 .40
149 Champ Bailey .15 .40
150 Jamal Anderson .15 .40
151 Doug Flutie .15 .40
152 Michael Bates .12 .30
153 Corey Dillon .12 .30
154 Keith McKenzie .12 .30
155 Orpheus Roye .12 .30
156 Olandis Gary .15 .40
157 Johnnie Morton .15 .40
158 Brett Favre .40 1.00
159 Adrian Murrell .12 .30
160 Fred Taylor .12 .30
161 Tony Gonzalez .15 .40
162 Zach Thomas .15 .40
163 Randy Moss .15 .40
164 Marcus Robinson .15 .40
165 Tiki Barber .15 .40
166 Rich Gannon .15 .40
167 Jeremiah Trotter RC .40 1.00
168 Jermaine Fazande .12 .30
169 Steve Young .25 .60
170 Isaac Bruce .20 .50
171 Warrick Dunn .12 .30
172 Yancey Thigpen .12 .30
173 Rod Smith .15 .40
174 Albert Connell .12 .30
175 Freddie Jones .12 .30
176 Terance Mathis .12 .30
177 Eric Moulds .12 .30
178 Brian Mitchell .12 .30
179 Wesley Walls .12 .30
180 Carl Pickens .15 .40
181 Errict Rhett .15 .40
182 Madre Hill .12 .30
183 Jason Elam .12 .30
184 Greg Ellis .12 .30
185 David Sloan .12 .30
186 Edgerrin James .15 .40
187 Jimmy Smith .15 .40
188 Tony Richardson RC .12 .30
189 James Hasty .12 .30
190 Sam Madison .12 .30
191 Tony Simmons .12 .30
192 Andre Hastings .12 .30
193 Keyshawn Johnson .15 .40
194 Na Brown .12 .30
195 Napoleon Kaufman .15 .40
196 Torrance Small .12 .30
197 Curtis Conway .15 .40
198 Jeff Graham .12 .30
199 Jason Hanson .12 .30
200 Derrick Mayes .12 .30
201 Torry Holt .15 .40
202 Warren Sapp .15 .40
203 Kimble Anders .12 .30
204 Blaine Bishop .12 .30
205 Leroy Hoard .12 .30
206 Larry Centers .12 .30
207 O.J. Santiago .12 .30
208 Antowain Smith .15 .40
209 Chuck Smith .12 .30
210 Takeo Spikes .12 .30
211 Rocket Ismail .15 .40
212 Ed McCaffrey .15 .40
213 Karsten Bailey .12 .30
214 Terry Fair .12 .30
215 Ken Dilger .12 .30
216 Jamie Martin .12 .30
217 Cris Dishman .12 .30
218 Jay Fiedler .15 .40
219 Lawyer Milloy .12 .30
220 Jake Delhomme RC .15 .40
221 Wayne Chrebet .15 .40
222 Darrell Russell .12 .30
223 Christian Fauria .12 .30
224 Jerome Bettis .20 .50
225 Ryan Leaf .15 .40
226 Ricky Watters .15 .40
227 Keenan McCardell .15 .40
228 Grant Wistrom .12 .30
229 Jevon Kearse .12 .30
230 Frank Sanders .12 .30
231 Shannon Sharpe .15 .40
232 Jonathan Linton .12 .30
233 Alonzo Mayes .12 .30
234 Jason Garrett .20 .50
235 Kordell Stewart .12 .30
236 David LaFleur .12 .30
237 Kenny Bynum .12 .30
238 Byron Chamberlain .12 .30
239 Tyrone Davis .12 .30
240 Jerome Pathon .12 .30
241 Alvis Whitted .12 .30
242 Kevin Lockett .12 .30
243 Matthew Hatchette .12 .30
244 Rod Woodson .20 .50
245 Joe Horn .15 .40
246 Ronnie Powell .12 .30
247 Dedric Ward .12 .30
248 James Johnson .12 .30
249 James Jett .15 .40
250 Bobby Shaw RC .12 .30
251 J.J. Stokes .15 .40
252 Paul Shields RC .12 .30
253 Sean Dawkins .12 .30
254 Hardy Nickerson .12 .30
255 Stephen Boyd .12 .30
256 Chris Warren .12 .30
257 Kerry Collins .12 .30
258 Isaac Byrd .12 .30
259 Bobby Hoying .12 .30
260 Daunte Culpepper .15 .40
261 Moe Williams .12 .30
262 Kamil Loud .12 .30
263 Derrick Brooks .12 .30
264 Jay Riemersma .12 .30
265 Ray Lucas .12 .30
266 Jason Gildon .12 .30
267 James Stewart .12 .30
268 Marcellus Wiley .12 .30
269 Craig Yeast .12 .30
270 Michael Basnight .12 .30
271 Tyrone Wheatley .12 .30
272 Martin Gramatica .12 .30
273 Phillip Daniels RC .12 .30
274 Richard Huntley .12 .30
275 Muhsin Muhammad .12 .30
276 Todd Lyght .12 .30
277 Carlester Crumpler .12 .30
278 Jeff Lewis .12 .30
279 Jeff George .15 .40
280 Jeff Blake .15 .40
281 Michael McCrary .12 .30
282 Shawn Jefferson .12 .30
283 Mark Bruener .15 .40
284 Donnie Abraham .12 .30
285 Yatil Green .12 .30
286 Jermaine Lewis .12 .30
287 Rob Fredrickson .12 .30
288 Thurman Thomas .15 .40
289 Kent Graham .12 .30
290 Darnay Scott .15 .40
291 Tony Graziani .15 .40
292 Qadry Ismail .12 .30
293 Aeneas Williams .12 .30
294 Marvin Harrison .15 .40
295 Jimmy Hitchcock .12 .30
296 Bob Christian .12 .30
297 Pete Mitchell .12 .30
298 Mike Alstott .12 .30
299 Emmitt Smith .30 .75
300 Trevor Pryce .12 .30
301 Tony Banks .12 .30
302 Mikhael Ricks .12 .30
303 Randall Cunningham .15 .40
304 Thomas Jones RC .25 .60
305 Mark Simoneau RC .20 .50
306 Jamal Lewis RC .30 .75
307 Kwame Cavil RC .20 .50
308 Rashard Anderson RC .20 .50
309 Brian Urlacher RC 1.00 2.50
310 Peter Warrick RC .20 .50
311 Courtney Brown RC .25 .60
312 Michael Wiley RC .20 .50
313 Chris Cole RC .25 .60
314 Reuben Droughns RC .20 .50
315 Bubba Franks RC .20 .50
316 Rob Morris RC .25 .60
317 R.Jay Soward RC .20 .50
318 Sylvester Morris RC .20 .50
319 Ben Kelly RC .20 .50
320 Doug Chapman RC .20 .50
321 J.R. Redmond RC .20 .50
322 Darren Howard RC .20 .50
323 Ron Dayne RC .30 .75
324 Chad Pennington RC .25 .60
325 Jerry Porter RC .30 .75
326 Corey Simon RC .25 .60
327 Plaxico Burress RC .25 .60
328 Trung Canidate RC .20 .50
329 Rogers Beckett RC .20 .50
330 Giovanni Carmazzi RC .20 .50
331 Shaun Alexander RC .30 .75
332 Joe Hamilton RC .20 .50
333 Keith Bulluck RC .25 .60
334 Todd Husak RC .20 .50
335 D.Walker RC/R.Thompson RC .20 .50
336 M.Philyaw RC/A.Midget RC .20 .50
337 C.Redman RC/T.Taylor RC .20 .50
338 Sam.Morris RC/A.Black RC .20 .50
339 D.Grant RC/A.McKinley RC .20 .50
340 D.White RC/F.Murphy RC .20 .50
341 C.Keaton RC/R.Dugans RC .20 .50
342 Prentice RC/Northcutt RC .20 .50
343 O.Grant RC/D.Goodrich RC .20 .50
344 D.O'Neal RC/I.Gold RC .20 .50
345 S.McDougle RC/B.Green RC .20 .50
346 A.Lucas RC/N.Diggs RC .20 .50
347 M.Washington RC/D.Kendra RC .25 .60
348 T.Slaughter RC/S.Stith RC .20 .50
349 W.Bartee RC/F.Moreau RC .20 .50
350 D.Dyer RC/T.Wade RC .20 .50
351 C.Hovan RC/T.Walters .25 .60
352 T.Brady RC/Stachelski RC 15.00 40.00
353 M.Bulger RC/T.Smith RC .25 .60
354 C.Griffin RC/R.Dixon RC .20 .50
355 L.Coles RC/A.Becht RC .25 .60
356 Janikowski RC/Lechler RC .30 .75
357 T.Pinkston RC/G.Scott RC .20 .50
358 D.Farmer RC/T.Martin RC .20 .50
359 B.Young RC/J.Shepherd RC .20 .50
360 J.Seider RC/T.Gaylor RC .20 .50
361 T.Rattay RC/C.Fields RC .25 .60
362 D.Jackson RC/J.Williams RC .20 .50
363 N.Webster RC/J.Whalen RC .20 .50
364 E.Kinney RC/C.Coleman RC .20 .50
365 C.Samuels RC/L.Murray RC .30 .75
366 Cardinals IA/Plummer .12 .30
367 Falcons IA/Chandlr/Andrson .12 .30
368 Ravens IA/Boulware .12 .30
369 Bills IA/Flutie .10 .25
370 Panthers IA/Beuerlein .12 .30
371 Bears IA/McNown .12 .30
372 Bengals IA/Dillon .12 .30
373 Browns IA/Couch .12 .30
374 Cowboys IA/Smith .20 .50
375 Broncos IA/Gary .12 .30
376 Lions IA/Batch .12 .30
377 Packers IA/Levens .12 .30
378 Colts IA/James .10 .25
379 Jaguars IA/Brackens .12 .30
380 Chiefs IA/Grbac .12 .30
381 Dolphins IA/Marino .25 .60
382 Vikings IA/Rob.Smith .12 .30
383 Patriots IA/Bledsoe .10 .25
384 Saints IA/Williams .10 .25
385 Giants IA/Armstead .12 .30
386 Jets IA/Martin .10 .25
387 Raiders IA/Kaufman .12 .30
388 Eagles IA/McNabb .10 .25
389 Steelers IA/Bettis .12 .30
390 Rams IA/Faulk .10 .25
391 Chargers IA/Fazande .12 .30
392 49ers IA/Garner .12 .30
393 Seahawks IA/Kennedy .12 .30
394 Buccaneers IA/Alstott .07 .20
395 Titans IA/McNair .10 .25
396 Redskins IA/S.Davis .12 .30
397 Tim Couch CL .12 .30
398 Peyton Manning CL .30 .75
399 Kurt Warner CL .20 .50
400 Randy Moss CL .10 .25

2000 Fleer Tradition Autographics

Fleer released these inserts in virtually every football product that was issued in 2000. Each card includes an authentic player autograph along with a color photo of the featured player. All cards included the Fleer Certificate of Authenticity on the cardback and were unnumbered.

DOMINION STATED ODDS 1:192
E-X STATED ODDS 1:24
FLEER STAT.ODDS 1:144 HOB, 1:192 RET
FLEER FOCUS ODDS 1:72 HOB, 1:144 RET
FLEER GAMERS STATED ODDS 1:287
FLEER MYSTIQUE STAT.ODDS 1:120
FLEER SHOWCASE STAT.ODDS 1:24
IMPACT STATED ODDS 1:216
METAL STATED ODDS 1:96
SKYBOX AND ULTRA STATED ODDS 1:72
1 Karim Abdul-Jabbar 4.00 10.00
2 Troy Aikman 60.00 120.00
3 Shaun Alexander 6.00 15.00
4 Terry Allen 5.00 12.00
5 Mike Alstott 8.00 20.00
6 Kimble Anders 4.00 10.00
7 Jamal Anderson 5.00 12.00
8 Mike Anderson 4.00 10.00
9 Champ Bailey 10.00 25.00
10 Charlie Batch 4.00 10.00
11 Donnell Bennett 4.00 10.00
12 Jerome Bettis 40.00 80.00
13 Tim Biakabutuka 5.00 12.00
14 Drew Bledsoe 12.00 30.00
15 David Boston 4.00 10.00
16 Peter Boulware 4.00 10.00
17 Tom Brady 300.00 600.00
18 Tim Brown 15.00 40.00
19 Isaac Bruce 6.00 15.00
20 Mark Brunell 5.00 12.00
21 Marc Bulger 5.00 12.00
22 Trung Canidate 4.00 10.00
23 Giovanni Carmazzi 4.00 10.00
24 Cris Carter 15.00 40.00
26 Darrin Chiaverini 4.00 10.00
27 Wayne Chrebet 4.00 10.00
28 Laveranues Coles 5.00 12.00
29 Kerry Collins 4.00 10.00
30 Tim Couch 5.00 12.00
31 Germane Crowell 4.00 10.00
32 Daunte Culpepper 5.00 12.00
33 Stephen Davis 4.00 10.00
34 Terrell Davis 12.00 30.00
35 Ron Dayne 6.00 15.00
36 Jake Delhomme 6.00 15.00
37 Corey Dillon 4.00 10.00
38 Reuben Droughns 4.00 10.00
39 Ron Dugans 4.00 10.00
40 Tim Dwight 5.00 12.00
41 Deon Dyer 4.00 10.00
42 Kevin Dyson 5.00 12.00
43 Troy Edwards 4.00 10.00
44 Danny Farmer 4.00 10.00
45 Kevin Faulk 4.00 10.00
46 Marshall Faulk 15.00 40.00
47 Christian Fauria 4.00 10.00
48 Jermaine Fazande 4.00 10.00
49 Jay Fiedler 5.00 12.00
50 Chafie Fields 4.00 10.00
51 Bubba Franks 4.00 10.00
52 Rich Gannon 6.00 15.00
53 Jeff Garcia 4.00 10.00
54 Charlie Garner 5.00 12.00
55 Olandis Gary 5.00 12.00
56 Jason Garrett 6.00 15.00
57 Trevor Gaylor 4.00 10.00
58 Eddie George 5.00 12.00
59 Sherrod Gideon 4.00 10.00
60 Tony Gonzalez 12.00 30.00
61 Jeff Graham 4.00 10.00
62 Tony Graziani 5.00 12.00
63 Damon Griffin 4.00 10.00
64 Az-Zahir Hakim 4.00 10.00
65 Joe Hamilton 4.00 10.00
66 Marvin Harrison 10.00 25.00
67 Tony Hartley 4.00 10.00
68 Priest Holmes 4.00 10.00
69 Torry Holt 8.00 20.00
70 Tony Horne 4.00 10.00
71 Damon Huard 4.00 10.00
73 Rocket Ismail 8.00 20.00
74 Darrell Jackson 4.00 10.00
75 Edgerrin James 5.00 12.00
76 Sebastian Janikowski 6.00 15.00
77 Patrick Jeffers 4.00 10.00
79 Brad Johnson 5.00 12.00
80 Kevin Johnson 4.00 10.00
81 Keyshawn Johnson 5.00 12.00
82 Rob Johnson 5.00 12.00
83 Thomas Jones 6.00 15.00
85 Curtis Keaton 4.00 10.00
86 Terry Kirby 4.00 10.00
87 Jon Kitna 4.00 10.00
88 Marcus Knight 4.00 10.00
89 Dorsey Levens 5.00 12.00
90 Jamal Lewis 6.00 15.00
92 Ray Lucas 4.00 10.00
93 Curtis Martin 20.00 50.00
94 Tee Martin 4.00 10.00
95 Shane Matthews 4.00 10.00
96 Derrick Mayes 4.00 10.00
97 Ed McCaffrey 5.00 12.00
98 Keenan McCardell 5.00 12.00
99 O.J.McDuffie 5.00 12.00
100 Cade McNown 4.00 10.00
101 Rondell Mealey 4.00 10.00
102 Joe Montgomery 4.00 10.00
103 Herman Moore 4.00 10.00
105 Sylvester Morris 4.00 10.00
106 Johnnie Morton 5.00 12.00
107 Randy Moss 30.00 60.00
108 Eric Moulds 4.00 10.00
109 Muhsin Muhammad 4.00 10.00
110 Dennis Northcutt 4.00 10.00
111 Terrell Owens 8.00 20.00
112 Chad Pennington 6.00 15.00
113 Mareno Philyaw 4.00 10.00
115 Jake Plummer 4.00 10.00
117 Travis Prentice 4.00 10.00
118 Peerless Price 5.00 12.00
119 John Randle 10.00 25.00
120 Tim Rattay 5.00 12.00
121 Chris Redman 4.00 10.00
122 J.R. Redmond 4.00 10.00
123 Jake Reed 5.00 12.00
124 Jerry Rice 75.00 135.00
125 Jay Riemersma 4.00 10.00
126 Jon Ritchie 4.00 10.00
127 Marcus Robinson 5.00 12.00
128 Warren Sapp 15.00 40.00
129 Bill Schroeder 5.00 12.00
130 Gari Scott 4.00 10.00
131 Jason Sehorn 4.00 10.00
132 Shannon Sharpe 10.00 25.00
133 David Sloan 4.00 10.00
134 Akili Smith 4.00 10.00
135 Antowain Smith 5.00 12.00
136 Emmitt Smith 100.00 200.00
137 Jimmy Smith 5.00 12.00
138 Rod Smith 5.00 12.00
139 R.Jay Soward 4.00 10.00
140 Quinton Spotwood 4.00 10.00
141 Shawn Springs 4.00 10.00
142 Duce Staley 4.00 10.00
143 Kordell Stewart 4.00 10.00
144 Shyrone Stith 4.00 10.00
145 Michael Strahan 15.00 40.00
147 Amani Toomer 4.00 10.00
148 Troy Walters 4.00 10.00
149 Dedric Ward 4.00 10.00
150 Kurt Warner 25.00 50.00
151 Peter Warrick 4.00 10.00
152 Chris Watson 4.00 10.00
154 Tyrone Wheatley 4.00 10.00
155 Dez White 4.00 10.00
156 Michael Wiley 4.00 10.00
157 Terrence Wilkins 4.00 10.00
159 Ricky Williams 12.00 30.00
160 Frank Wycheck 5.00 12.00

2000 Fleer Tradition Autographics Gold

*GOLD/50: .8X TO 2X BASIC AUTO
GOLD PRINT RUN 50 SER.#'d SETS
17 Tom Brady 500.00 1000.00
124 Jerry Rice 125.00 250.00
136 Emmitt Smith 150.00 300.00

2000 Fleer Tradition Autographics Silver

*SILVER/250: .5X TO 1.2X BASIC AUTO
SILVER PRINT RUN 250 SER.#'d SETS
17 Tom Brady 300.00 600.00
25 Kwame Cavil 5.00 12.00
124 Jerry Rice 75.00 150.00
136 Emmitt Smith 100.00 200.00
146 Travis Taylor 5.00 12.00

2000 Fleer Tradition Feel the Game

Fleer released these inserts in five different football products that were issued in 2000. Each card includes an authentic player worn jersey or uniform swatch along with a color photo of the featured player. All cards were unnumbered. Note that some cards were issued with variations in terms of type of swatch used or the color of the jersey the player is wearing in the photo on the card.

E-X STATED ODDS 1:72
FLEER FOCUS STAT.ODDS 1:144 H, 1:288 R
FLEER MYSTIQUE STAT.ODDS 1:120
FLEER SHOWCASE STAT.ODDS 1:72
ULTRA STATED ODDS 1:144
*GOLD/50: .8X TO 2X BASIC JSY
GOLD PRINT RUN 50 SER.#'d SETS
1 Karim Abdul-Jabbar 2.00 5.00
2 Troy Aikman Blue 4.00 10.00
3 Troy Aikman White 4.00 10.00
4 Jamal Anderson 2.50 6.00
5 Drew Bledsoe 2.50 6.00
6 David Boston 2.00 5.00
7 Tim Brown 3.00 8.00
8 Mark Brunell 2.50 6.00
9 Chris Chandler 2.50 6.00
10 Curtis Conway 2.50 6.00
11 Curtis Conway Pants 2.50 6.00
12 Tim Couch 2.50 6.00
13 Germane Crowell 2.00 5.00
14 Terrell Davis 2.50 6.00
15 Tim Dwight Pants 2.50 6.00
16 Kevin Dyson Blue 2.50 6.00
17 Kevin Dyson White 2.50 6.00
18 Kevin Dyson Pants 2.50 6.00
19 Curtis Enis 2.00 5.00
20 Curtis Enis Pants 2.00 5.00
21 Brett Favre 6.00 15.00
22 Doug Flutie 2.50 6.00
23 Antonio Freeman 2.50 6.00
24 Eddie George 2.50 6.00
25 Eddie George Pants 2.50 6.00
26 Terry Glenn 2.50 6.00
27 Trent Green Blue 2.00 5.00
29 Brian Griese 2.00 5.00
30 Az-Zahir Hakim Pants 2.00 5.00
31 Marvin Harrison 2.50 6.00
32 Torry Holt 2.50 6.00
33 Edgerrin James 2.50 6.00
34 Kevin Johnson 2.00 5.00
35 Rob Johnson 2.50 6.00
36 Jevon Kearse Blue 2.00 5.00
37 Jevon Kearse White 2.00 5.00
38 Terry Kirby 2.00 5.00
39 Dorsey Levens 2.50 6.00
40 Peyton Manning 8.00 20.00
41 Terrance Mathis 2.00 5.00
42 Shane Matthews Pants 2.00 5.00
43 Steve McNair Blue 2.50 6.00
44 Steve McNair White 2.50 6.00
45 Steve McNair Pants 2.50 6.00
46 Cade McNown Pants 2.00 5.00
47 Herman Moore 2.00 5.00
48 Rob Moore 2.00 5.00
49 Johnnie Morton Blue 2.50 6.00
50 Johnnie Morton White 2.50 6.00
51 Jake Plummer White 2.00 5.00
52 Jake Plummer Red 2.00 5.00
53 Jerry Rice 8.00 20.00
54 Marcus Robinson Pants 2.50 6.00
55 Deion Sanders Blue 2.50 6.00
56 Deion Sanders White 2.50 6.00
57 Frank Sanders 2.00 5.00
58 Junior Seau 2.50 6.00
59 Shannon Sharpe 2.50 6.00
60 Emmitt Smith Blue 5.00 12.00
61 Emmitt Smith White 5.00 12.00
62 Jimmy Smith 2.50 6.00
63 Rod Smith 2.50 6.00
64 J.J. Stokes 2.50 6.00
65 Kordell Stewart 2.00 5.00
66 Fred Taylor 2.00 5.00
67 Amani Toomer 2.00 5.00
68 Kurt Warner Pants 5.00 12.00
69 Charles Woodson 3.00 8.00

2000 Fleer Tradition Genuine Coverage

Fleer released these inserts in four football products that were issued in 2000. Each card includes a swatch from an authentic player worn jersey or uniform along with a color photo of the featured player. All cards were unnumbered and have been assigned card numbers below according to alphabetical order. Several cards (Jamal Anderson, Germane Crowell, Kevin Johnson, Jake Plummer) from the set surfaced in early 2006 following the liquidation of the company's assets.

DOMINION STATED ODDS 1:720
METAL GEN.COVER.OR AUTO.ODDS 1:96
SKYBOX H STATED ODDS 1:144
SKYBOX HR STATED ODDS 1:288
1 Troy Aikman 6.00 15.00
2 Shaun Alexander 5.00 12.00
3 Jamal Anderson 4.00 10.00
4 Charlie Batch 3.00 8.00
5 David Boston 3.00 8.00
6 Courtney Brown 4.00 10.00
7 Isaac Bruce 5.00 12.00
8 Mark Brunell 4.00 10.00
9 Chris Chandler 4.00 10.00
10 Darrin Chiaverini 3.00 8.00
11 Tim Couch 4.00 10.00
12 Germane Crowell 3.00 8.00
13 Sean Dawkins 3.00 8.00
14 Ron Dayne 5.00 12.00
15 Corey Dillon 3.00 8.00
16 Reuben Droughns 3.00 8.00
17 Tim Dwight 4.00 10.00
18 Bubba Franks 3.00 8.00
19 Marvin Harrison 4.00 10.00
20 Torry Holt 4.00 10.00
21 Kevin Johnson 3.00 8.00
22 Terry Kirby 3.00 8.00
23 Shane Matthews 3.00 8.00
24 Ed McCaffrey 4.00 10.00
25 Cade McNown 3.00 8.00
26 Herman Moore 3.00 8.00
27 Rob Moore 3.00 8.00
28 Sylvester Morris 3.00 8.00
29 Johnnie Morton 4.00 10.00
30 Chad Pennington 4.00 10.00
31 Jake Plummer 3.00 8.00
32 Jerry Porter 5.00 12.00
33 Travis Prentice 3.00 8.00
34 J.R. Redmond 3.00 8.00
35 Marcus Robinson 4.00 10.00
36 Frank Sanders 3.00 8.00
37 Peter Warrick 3.00 8.00

2000 Fleer Tradition Genuine Coverage Nostalgic

Randomly inserted in packs at the rate of one in 360 hobby or one in 720 retail, this nine card set features swatches of vintage game used jerseys worn by 2000 football rookies.

STATED ODDS 1:360 HOB, 1:720 RET
1 Chad Pennington 4.00 10.00
2 Ron Dayne 5.00 12.00
3 Plaxico Burress 4.00 10.00
4 Brian Urlacher 15.00 40.00
5 Bubba Franks 3.00 8.00
6 Jerry Porter 5.00 12.00
7 Trung Canidate 3.00 8.00
8 Dez White 3.00 8.00
9 Courtney Brown 4.00 10.00

2000 Fleer Tradition Patchworks

Fleer released these inserts in various 2000 SkyBox hobby products. Each card includes a patch swatch from an authentic player worn jersey along with a color photo of the featured player. We've cataloged the cards as a Fleer set instead of SkyBox since Fleer is prominantly noted on the cards as the manufacturer. The unnumbered cards have been listed alphabetically. Several cards in the checklist, such as Ron Dayne and Peter Warrick, appeared on the market only after Fleer ceased operations and old inventory was released to the secondary market.

RANDOM INSERTS IN SKYBOX HOBBY
1 Troy Aikman 4.00 10.00
2 Shaun Alexander 3.00 8.00
3 Jamal Anderson 2.50 6.00
4 Drew Bledsoe 2.50 6.00
5 Mark Brunell 2.50 6.00
6 Tim Couch 2.50 6.00
7 Ron Dayne 3.00 8.00
8 Brett Favre 6.00 15.00
9 Eddie George 2.50 6.00
10 Marvin Harrison 2.50 6.00
11 Peyton Manning 8.00 20.00
12 Edgerrin James 2.50 6.00
13 Cade McNown 2.00 5.00
14 Jake Plummer 2.00 5.00
15 Jerry Rice 8.00 20.00
16 Junior Seau 2.50 6.00
17 Emmitt Smith 5.00 12.00
18 Fred Taylor 2.00 5.00
19 Kurt Warner 5.00 12.00
20 Peter Warrick SP 2.50 6.00

2000 Fleer Tradition Rookie Retro

Randomly inserted in packs at the rate of one in 36, this 10-card set features this years most promising rookies on an embossed card stock with rainbow holofoil highlights.

COMPLETE SET (10) 10.00 25.00
STATED ODDS 1:36
1 Chad Pennington .60 1.50
2 Ron Dayne .75 2.00
3 Plaxico Burress .60 1.50
4 Brian Urlacher 2.50 6.00
5 Bubba Franks .50 1.25
6 Jerry Porter .75 2.00
7 Trung Canidate .50 1.25
8 Dez White .50 1.25
9 Courtney Brown .60 1.50
10 Shaun Alexander .75 2.00

2000 Fleer Tradition Throwbacks

Randomly inserted in packs at the rate of one in three, this 20-card set features some of the NFL's finest in action on an all foil insert card.

COMPLETE SET (20) 3.00 8.00
STATED ODDS 1:3
1 Troy Aikman .40 1.00
2 Junior Seau .25 .60
3 Ron Dayne .30 .75
4 Steve Young .40 1.00
5 Wesley Walls .20 .50
6 Duce Staley .20 .50
7 Brian Urlacher 1.00 2.50
8 Jerome Bettis .30 .75
9 Marshall Faulk .25 .60
10 Doug Flutie .25 .60
11 Brett Favre .60 1.50
12 Warren Sapp .25 .60
13 Charlie Batch .20 .50
14 Mike Alstott .20 .50
15 Cade McNown .20 .50
16 Jon Kitna .20 .50
17 Emmitt Smith .50 1.25
18 Tony Gonzalez .25 .60
19 Zach Thomas .25 .60
20 Cris Carter .30 .75

2000 Fleer Tradition Tradition of Excellence

Randomly inserted in packs at the rate of one in nine, this 20-card set features both rookies and veterans, in action and portrait photograpy, on a card with gold foil stamping highlights.

COMPLETE SET (20) 15.00 40.00
STATED ODDS 1:9
1 Brett Favre 1.00 2.50
2 Randy Moss .40 1.00
3 Tim Couch .40 1.00
4 Peter Warrick .30 .75
5 Ron Dayne .50 1.25
6 Kurt Warner .75 2.00
7 Jevon Kearse .30 .75
8 Ricky Williams .40 1.00
9 Keyshawn Johnson .40 1.00
10 Emmitt Smith .75 2.00
11 Donovan McNabb .40 1.00
12 Jamal Lewis .50 1.25
13 Jerry Rice 1.25 3.00
14 Eddie George .40 1.00
15 Peyton Manning 1.25 3.00
16 Stephen Davis .30 .75
17 Thomas Jones .40 1.00
18 Plaxico Burress .40 1.00
19 Troy Aikman .60 1.50
20 Edgerrin James .40 1.00

2000 Fleer Tradition Whole Ten Yards

Randomly inserted in packs at the rate of one in 18, this 10-card set features veteran players on an embossed card stock with rainbow holofoil highlights.

COMPLETE SET (15) 12.50 30.00
STATED ODDS 1:18
1 Edgerrin James .50 1.25
2 Stephen Davis .40 1.00
3 Kurt Warner 1.00 2.50
4 Keyshawn Johnson .50 1.25
5 Mark Brunell .50 1.25
6 Peyton Manning 1.50 4.00
7 Emmitt Smith 1.00 2.50
8 Peter Warrick .40 1.00
9 Brett Favre 1.25 3.00
10 Marshall Faulk .50 1.25
11 Fred Taylor .40 1.00
12 Shaun Alexander .60 1.50
13 Terrell Davis .50 1.25
14 Eddie George .50 1.25
15 Randy Moss .50 1.25

2000 Fleer Tradition Glossy

COMP.FACT.SET (406) 30.00 60.00
COMP.SET w/o SP's (400) 15.00 30.00
*1-400 VETS: .5X TO 1.2X BASIC CARD
*304-365 ROOKIES: .5X TO 1.2X
401-450 PRINT RUN 750 SETS
7500 FACTORY SETS PRODUCED
401 JaJuan Dawson RC .75 2.00
402 Mike Anderson RC .75 2.00
403 Windrell Hayes RC .75 2.00
404 Shockmain Davis RC .75 2.00
405 Dante Hall RC .75 2.00
406 Charles Lee RC .75 2.00
407 Maurice Smith RC .75 2.00
408 Obafemi Ayanbadejo RC 1.00 2.50
409 Travis Taylor .75 2.00
410 Dez White .75 2.00
411 Sammy Morris .75 2.00
412 Darrell Jackson .75 2.00
413 Todd Pinkston .75 2.00
414 Ron Dixon .75 2.00
415 Frank Moreau .75 2.00
416 James Williams .75 2.00
417 Lenzie Jackson RC .75 2.00
418 Chad Morton RC 1.00 2.50
419 Matt Lytle RC .75 2.00
420 Travis Prentice .75 2.00
421 Laveranues Coles 1.00 2.50
422 Clint Stoerner RC 1.25 3.00
423 Karon Coleman RC .75 2.00
424 Ron Dugans .75 2.00
425 Dennis Northcutt .75 2.00
426 Herbert Goodman RC .75 2.00
427 Dane Looker RC 1.25 3.00
428 Mike Brown RC .75 2.00
429 Derrius Thompson RC .75 2.00
430 Danny Farmer .75 2.00
431 Bashir Yamini RC .75 2.00
432 Trevor Gaylor .75 2.00
433 Erron Kinney RC .75 2.00
434 James Hodgins RC .75 2.00
435 Aaron Shea RC 1.00 2.50
436 Patrick Pass RC .75 2.00
437 Terrelle Smith .75 2.00
438 Avion Black .75 2.00
439 Deltha O'Neal .75 2.00
440 Chris Coleman .75 2.00
441 Reggie Jones RC .75 2.00
442 Shyrone Stith .75 2.00
443 Aaron Stecker RC .75 2.00
444 Chris Redman .75 2.00
445 Curtis Keaton .75 2.00
446 Jamel White RC .75 2.00
447 Troy Walters .75 2.00
448 Spergon Wynn .75 2.00
449 Ronney Jenkins RC .75 2.00
450 Doug Johnson RC .75 2.00

2000 Fleer Tradition Glossy Traditional Threads

Randomly inserted in factory sets at the rate of one in one, this 40-card set features players in action with a swatch of a game worn jersey. Each card is sequentially numbered. No card numbers are present, so the set is listed in alphabetical order.

ONE PER FACTORY SET
1 Troy Aikman/140 6.00 15.00
2 Jamal Anderson/225 3.00 8.00
3 Charlie Batch/55 5.00 12.00
4 Drew Bledsoe/325 3.00 8.00
5 David Boston/55 5.00 12.00
6 Tim Brown/81 6.00 15.00
7 Mark Brunell/700 2.50 6.00
8 Tim Couch/430 2.50 6.00
9 Germane Crowell/82 4.00 10.00
10 Stephen Davis/155 3.00 8.00
11 Terrell Davis/100 5.00 12.00
12 Curtis Enis/44 5.00 12.00
13 Marshall Faulk/275 3.00 8.00
14 Brett Favre/585 6.00 15.00
15 Antonio Freeman/86 5.00 12.00
16 Brian Griese/165 3.00 8.00
17 Marvin Harrison/250 3.00 8.00
18 Torry Holt/55 6.00 15.00
19 Edgerrin James/285 3.00 8.00
20 Dorsey Levens/25 8.00 20.00
21 Peyton Manning/345 10.00 25.00
22 Dan Marino/140 10.00 25.00
23 Steve McNair/200 3.00 8.00
25 Johnnie Morton/25 8.00 20.00
26 Jake Plummer/250 2.50 6.00
27 Junior Seau/55 6.00 15.00
28 Antowain Smith/26 8.00 20.00
29 Emmitt Smith/750 5.00 12.00
30 Rod Smith/25 8.00 20.00
31 Fred Taylor/325 2.50 6.00
32 Vinny Testaverde/225 2.50 6.00
33 Amani Toomer/25 6.00 15.00
34 Kurt Warner/700 5.00 12.00
35 Steve Young/125 8.00 20.00

2001 Fleer Tradition

In July of 2001 Fleer released its base set of what is also referred to as Fleer Tradition. The version was available at retail stores nationwide.The cards had a vintage look to them. The cardfronts had a color photo of the the player close up and a color photo of the player in action and a faded stadium scene photo in the background. The cards were set horizontally. The cardbacks had the old greyback stock and no UV coating. The cardbacks also featured a small comic reminiscent of older cards. The cardfronts did not have a glossy coating.

COMPLETE SET (450) 20.00 40.00
1 Thomas Jones .15 .40
2 Bruce Smith .20 .50
3 Marvin Harrison .20 .50
4 Darrell Jackson .20 .50
5 Trent Green .15 .40
6 Wesley Walls .15 .40
7 Jimmy Smith .20 .50
8 Isaac Bruce .25 .60
9 Jamal Anderson .20 .50
10 Marty Booker .15 .40
11 Elvis Grbac .20 .50
12 Joe Jurevicius .15 .40
13 Reidel Anthony .15 .40
14 Darnay Scott .20 .50
15 Oronde Gadsden .15 .40
16 Shawn Bryson .15 .40
17 Jonathan Ogden .20 .50
18 Aaron Shea .15 .40
19 Randy Moss .20 .50
20 Eddie George .25 .60
21 Stephen Davis .15 .40
22 Emmitt Smith .40 1.00
23 Willie McGinest .15 .40
24 Trent Dilfer .15 .40
25 Peter Boulware .15 .40
26 Rod Smith .20 .50
27 Ricky Williams .20 .50
28 Albert Connell .15 .40
29 Robert Porcher .15 .40
30 Jessie Armstead .15 .40
31 Shane Matthews .15 .40
32 Eric Moulds .15 .40
33 Kurt Schulz .15 .40
34 Richie Anderson .15 .40
35 Ron Dugans .15 .40
36 Steve Beuerlein .20 .50
37 Darren Sharper .20 .50
38 Andre Rison .20 .50
39 Courtney Brown .15 .40

Card	Low	High
40 Eddie Kennison	.20	.50
41 Ken Dilger	.15	.40
42 Charles Johnson	.15	.40
43 Dexter Coakley	.15	.40
44 Akili Smith	.15	.40
45 R.Jay Soward	.15	.40
46 Danny Farmer	.15	.40
47 Dez White	.20	.50
48 Olandis Gary	.15	.40
49 Wali Rainer	.15	.40
50 Derrick Alexander	.15	.40
51 Donnie Abraham	.15	.40
52 David Sloan	.15	.40
53 Larry Allen	.25	.60
54 Sam Madison	.15	.40
55 Troy Edwards	.15	.40
56 Ryan Longwell	.20	.50
57 Brian Griese	.15	.40
58 John Randle	.20	.50
59 Reggie Jones	.15	.40
60 Mike Peterson	.15	.40
61 Bill Romanowski	.20	.50
62 Kevin Faulk	.15	.40
63 Tai Streets	.15	.40
64 Tony Brackens	.15	.40
65 James Stewart	.15	.40
66 Joe Horn	.15	.40
67 Kurt Warner	.40	1.00
68 Eric Hicks RC	.25	.60
69 Bryan Westbrook	.15	.40
70 Tiki Barber	.20	.50
71 Frank Sanders	.15	.40
72 Olindo Mare	.15	.40
73 Bill Schroeder	.20	.50
74 Anthony Becht	.15	.40
75 Rob Johnson	.20	.50
76 Troy Brown	.15	.40
77 Chad Bratzke	.15	.40
78 Rickey Dudley	.15	.40
79 Doug Johnson	.15	.40
80 Joe Johnson	.15	.40
81 Keenan McCardell	.20	.50
82 Tim Brown	.25	.60
83 Blaine Bishop	.15	.40
84 Ron Dixon	.15	.40
85 Michael Cloud	.15	.40
86 Todd Pinkston	.15	.40
87 Shannon Sharpe	.20	.50
88 Marvin Jones	.15	.40
89 Zach Thomas	.20	.50
90 Kordell Stewart	.15	.40
91 Champ Bailey	.20	.50
92 Jacquez Green	.15	.40
93 Daunte Culpepper	.20	.50
94 Freddie Jones	.15	.40
95 Donald Hayes	.15	.40
96 Rich Gannon	.20	.50
97 Ty Law	.25	.60
98 Grant Wistrom	.15	.40
99 James Allen	.15	.40
100 Corey Simon	.15	.40
101 Jeff Blake	.20	.50
102 Bryant Young	.20	.50
103 Craig Yeast	.15	.40
104 Bobby Shaw	.15	.40
105 Kerry Collins	.15	.40
106 Brock Huard	.15	.40
107 JaJuan Dawson	.15	.40
108 Jeff Graham	.15	.40
109 Chad Pennington	.15	.40
110 Jake Plummer	.15	.40
111 James McKnight	.15	.40
112 Terrell Owens	.20	.50
113 Mo Lewis	.15	.40
114 Jeremy McDaniel	.15	.40
115 Ed McCaffrey	.20	.50
116 Ricky Watters	.20	.50
117 Jerry Porter	.15	.40
118 Shawn Jefferson	.15	.40
119 Charlie Batch	.15	.40
120 Justin Watson	.15	.40
121 Donovan McNabb	.20	.50
122 Shaun King	.15	.40
123 Brett Favre	.50	1.25
124 Ronald McKinnon	.15	.40
125 Richard Huntley	.15	.40
126 Ray Lewis	.25	.60
127 Jerome Pathon	.15	.40
128 Sam Cowart	.15	.40
129 Ryan Leaf	.15	.40
130 Greg Clark	.15	.40
131 Tony Boselli	.20	.50
132 Frank Wychock	.15	.40
133 Charlie Garner	.20	.50
134 Tony Siragusa	.20	.50
135 Sylvester Morris	.15	.40
136 Qadry Ismail	.15	.40
137 Jon Kitna	.15	.40
138 James Thrash	.20	.50
139 Lamar Smith	.20	.50
140 Brad Johnson	.20	.50
141 London Fletcher	.20	.50
142 Tim Biakabutuka	.15	.40
143 Ed McDaniel	.15	.40
144 Tony Parrish	.15	.40
145 David Boston	.15	.40
146 Brian Urlacher	.30	.75
147 Drew Bledsoe	.20	.50
148 David Patten	.15	.40
149 Marcellus Wiley	.15	.40
150 Peter Warrick	.15	.40
151 La'Roi Glover	.15	.40
152 Troy Aikman	.30	.75
153 Chris Chandler	.20	.50
154 Travis Prentice	.15	.40
155 Ike Hilliard	.15	.40
156 John Mobley	.15	.40
157 Warren Sapp	.20	.50
158 Joey Galloway	.20	.50
159 Laveranues Coles	.20	.50
160 Germane Crowell	.15	.40
161 Jamal Lewis	.25	.60
162 Mike Anderson	.15	.40
163 Charles Woodson	.25	.60
164 Antonio Freeman	.25	.60
165 Derrick Mason	.15	.40
166 Chris Claiborne	.15	.40
167 Brian Mitchell	.20	.50
168 Mike Vanderjagt	.15	.40
169 Rod Woodson	.25	.60
170 Doug Chapman	.15	.40
171 John Lynch	.20	.50
172 Kevin Hardy	.15	.40
173 Sam Shade	.15	.40
174 Edgerrin James	.20	.50
175 Brian Dawkins	.15	.40
176 Donnie Edwards	.15	.40
177 Patrick Jeffers	.15	.40
178 Mark Brunell	.20	.50
179 Junior Seau	.20	.50
180 Trace Armstrong	.15	.40
181 Marcus Robinson	.20	.50
182 Tony Gonzalez	.20	.50
183 J.J. Stokes	.15	.40
184 Jake Reed	.20	.50
185 Corey Dillon	.15	.40
186 Jay Fiedler	.20	.50
187 Christian Fauria	.15	.40
188 Sammy Knight	.15	.40
189 Kevin Johnson	.15	.40
190 Matthew Hatchette	.15	.40
191 Az-Zahir Hakim	.15	.40
192 Keith Hamilton	.15	.40
193 Darren Woodson	.20	.50
194 Terry Glenn	.20	.50
195 Simeon Rice	.20	.50
196 Keyshawn Johnson	.20	.50
197 Terrell Davis	.20	.50
198 William Roaf	.15	.40
199 Doug Flutie	.20	.50
200 Kevin Carter	.15	.40
201 Stephen Boyd	.15	.40
202 Michael Strahan	.20	.50
203 Ray Buchanan	.15	.40
204 Tyrone Wheatley	.20	.50
205 Jason Hanson	.15	.40
206 Wayne Chrebet	.15	.40
207 Samari Rolle	.15	.40
208 Duce Staley	.15	.40
209 Dorsey Levens	.20	.50
210 Sebastian Janikowski	.15	.40
211 Duane Starks	.15	.40
212 Jason Gildon	.15	.40
213 Terrence Wilkins	.15	.40
214 Eric Allen	.20	.50
215 Deion Sanders	.20	.50
216 Curtis Conway	.20	.50
217 Fred Taylor	.15	.40
218 Troy Vincent	.20	.50
219 Mike Minter RC	.20	.50
220 Jeff Garcia	.15	.40
221 Tony Richardson	.15	.40
222 Jerome Bettis	.25	.60
223 Chad Morton	.15	.40
224 Tony Horne	.15	.40
225 Dave Moore	.15	.40
226 Victor Green	.15	.40
227 Chris Sanders	.15	.40
228 Marshall Faulk	.20	.50
229 Cris Carter	.25	.60
230 Rodney Harrison	.15	.40
231 Tim Couch	.15	.40
232 Antowain Smith	.20	.50
233 Lawyer Milloy	.15	.40
234 Lance Schulters	.15	.40
235 Michael Wiley	.15	.40
236 Steve McNair	.20	.50
237 Aaron Brooks	.15	.40
238 Anthony Simmons	.15	.40
239 Dwayne Carswell	.15	.40
240 Priest Holmes	.15	.40
241 Amani Toomer	.15	.40
242 Aeneas Williams	.15	.40
243 MarTay Jenkins	.15	.40
244 Jeff George	.20	.50
245 Vinny Testaverde	.15	.40
246 Peerless Price	.15	.40
247 Bubba Franks	.15	.40
248 Randall Cunningham	.20	.50
249 Aaron Glenn	.20	.50
250 Terance Mathis	.15	.40
251 Peyton Manning	.60	1.50
252 Terrell Buckley	.20	.50
253 Greg Biekert	.15	.40
254 Martin Gramatica	.15	.40
255 Kyle Brady	.15	.40
256 Johnnie Morton	.20	.50
257 Jeremiah Trotter	.15	.40
258 Travis Taylor	.15	.40
259 Frank Moreau	.15	.40
260 LeRoy Butler	.20	.50
261 Plaxico Burress	.15	.40
262 Randall Godfrey	.15	.40
263 Jason Taylor	.25	.60
264 Jeff Burris	.15	.40
265 Jim Harbaugh	.20	.50
266 Marco Coleman	.15	.40
267 Robert Smith	.15	.40
268 Mike Hollis	.15	.40
269 Jerry Rice	.50	1.25
270 Muhsin Muhammad	.15	.40
271 J.R. Redmond	.15	.40
272 Brian Walker	.15	.40
273 Orlando Pace	.15	.40
274 Cade McNown	.20	.50
275 Darren Howard	.15	.40
276 Ron Dayne	.20	.50
277 Shaun Alexander	.15	.40
278 Brandon Bennett	.15	.40
279 Jason Sehorn	.20	.50
280 Matt Hasselbeck	.15	.40
281 Michael Pittman	.20	.50
282 Dennis Northcutt	.15	.40
283 Dedric Ward	.15	.40
284 Curtis Martin	.20	.50
285 Sammy Morris	.15	.40
286 Rocket Ismail	.20	.50
287 Jon Ritchie	.15	.40
288 Shaun Ellis	.15	.40
289 Tim Dwight	.20	.50
290 Trevor Pryce	.15	.40
291 Warrick Dunn	.15	.40
292 Napoleon Kaufman	.15	.40
293 Mike Alstott	.15	.40
294 Herman Moore	.15	.40
295 Chad Lewis	.15	.40
296 Hugh Douglas	.15	.40
297 Chris Redman	.25	.60
298 Ahman Green	.20	.50
299 Hines Ward	.20	.50
300 Mark Bruener	.20	.50
301 Jevon Kearse	.15	.40
302 Jermaine Fazande	.15	.40
303 Terrell Fletcher	.15	.40
304 Torry Holt	.20	.50
305 Chris McAlister	.15	.40
306 Jason Elam	.15	.40
307 Fred Beasley	.15	.40
308 Frank Wycheck UH	.15	.40
309 Michael McCrary UH	.15	.40
310 Mark Brunell UH	.20	.50
311 Tim Couch UH	.15	.40
312 Takeo Spikes UH	.15	.40
313 Jerome Bettis UH	.25	.60
314 Zach Thomas UH	.20	.50
315 Drew Bledsoe UH	.20	.50
316 Wayne Chrebet UH	.15	.40
317 Jay Riemersma UH	.15	.40
318 Marvin Harrison UH	.20	.50
319 Ed McCaffrey UH	.20	.50
320 Tony Gonzalez UH	.20	.50
321 Tim Brown UH	.25	.60
322 Junior Seau UH	.20	.50
323 Shawn Springs UH	.15	.40
324 Troy Aikman UH	.30	.75
325 Pat Tillman UH RC	8.00	20.00
326 David Akers UH RC	.15	.40
327 Michael Strahan UH	.20	.50
328 Darrell Green UH	.25	.60
329 Kurt Warner UH	.40	1.00
330 Jeff Garcia UH	.15	.40
331 Aaron Brooks UH	.15	.40
332 Jamal Anderson UH	.20	.50
333 Brad Hoover UH	.20	.50
334 Cris Carter UH	.25	.60
335 Derrick Brooks UH	.15	.40
336 Antonio Freeman UH	.25	.60
337 Luther Elliss UH	.15	.40
338 James Allen UH	.15	.40
339 Arizona Cardinals TC	.20	.50
340 Atlanta Falcons TC	.20	.50
341 Baltimore Ravens TC	.15	.40
342 Buffalo Bills TC	.15	.40
343 Carolina Panthers TC	.15	.40
344 Chicago Bears TC	.25	.60
345 Cincinnati Bengals TC	.20	.50
346 Cleveland Browns TC	.15	.40
347 Cowboys TC/E.Smith	.30	.75
348 Denver Broncos TC	.20	.50
349 Detroit Lions TC	.15	.40
350 Packers TC/Favre	.40	1.00
351 Indianapolis Colts TC Edgerrin James	.20	.50
352 Jacksonville Jaguars TC	.20	.50
353 Kansas City Chiefs TC	.15	.40
354 Miami Dolphins TC	.20	.50
355 Minnesota Vikings TC	.25	.60
356 New England Patriots TC	.25	.60
357 New Orleans Saints TC	.15	.40
358 New York Giants TC	.20	.50
359 New York Jets TC	.20	.50
360 Oakland Raiders TC	.20	.50
361 Philadelphia Eagles TC	.25	.60
362 Pittsburgh Steelers TC	.25	.60
363 San Diego Chargers TC	.15	.40
364 San Francisco 49ers TC	.15	.40
365 Seattle Seahawks TC	.15	.40
366 St. Louis Rams TC Kurt Warner	.25	.60
367 Tampa Bay Buccaneers TC	.20	.50
368 Tennessee Titans TC	.20	.50
369 Washington Redskins TC	.15	.60
370 Buffalo Bills TL	.15	.40
371 Indianapolis Colts TL	.25	.60
372 Miami Dolphins TL	.15	.40
373 New England Patriots TL	.20	.50
374 New York Jets TL	.20	.50
375 Baltimore Ravens TL	.20	.50
376 Cincinnati Bengals TL	.15	.40
377 Cleveland Browns TL	.15	.40
378 Jacksonville Jaguars TL	.20	.50
379 Pittsburgh Steelers TL	.25	.60
380 Tennessee Titans TL	.20	.50
381 Denver Broncos TL	.20	.50
382 Kansas City Chiefs TL	.20	.50
383 Oakland Raiders TL	.20	.50
384 San Diego Chargers TL	.20	.50
385 Seattle Seahawks TL	.15	.40
386 Arizona Cardinals TL	.15	.40
387 Dallas Cowboys TL	.25	.60
388 New York Giants TL	.20	.50
389 Philadelphia Eagles TL	.20	.50
390 Washington Redskins TL	.20	.50
391 Chicago Bears TL	.15	.40
392 Detroit Lions TL	.15	.40
393 Green Bay Packers TL	.25	.60
394 Minnesota Vikings TL	.25	.60
395 Tampa Bay Buccaneers TL	.20	.50
396 Atlanta Falcons TL	.15	.40
397 Carolina Panthers TL	.15	.40
398 New Orleans Saints TL	.20	.50
399 San Francisco 49ersTL	.20	.50
400 St. Louis Rams TL	.25	.60
401 Michael Vick RC	3.00	8.00
402 Drew Brees RC	10.00	25.00
403 Michael Bennett RC	.30	.75
404 David Terrell RC	.30	.75
405 Deuce McAllister RC	.40	1.00
406 Santana Moss RC	.40	1.00
407 Koren Robinson RC	.30	.75
408 Chris Weinke RC	.30	.75
409 Reggie Wayne RC	.50	1.25
410 Rod Gardner RC	.30	.75
411 James Jackson RC	.25	.60
412 Travis Henry RC	.30	.75
413 Josh Heupel RC	.40	1.00
414 LaDainian Tomlinson RC	3.00	8.00
415 Chad Johnson RC	.40	1.00
416 Sage Rosenfels RC	.30	.75
417 Quincy Morgan RC	.30	.75
418 Ken-Yon Rambo RC	.25	.60
419 LaMont Jordan RC	.40	1.00
420 Anthony Thomas RC	.40	1.00
421 Dave Dickenson RC	.30	.75
422 Travis Minor RC	.30	.75
423 Kevan Barlow RC	.30	.75
424 Chris Chambers RC	.25	.60
425 Richard Seymour RC	.40	1.00
426 Gerard Warren RC	.30	.75
427 Jamar Fletcher RC	.25	.60
428 Freddie Mitchell RC	.25	.60
429 Jamal Reynolds RC	.25	.60
430 Marques Tuiasosopo RC	.30	.75
431 Snoop Minnis RC	.25	.60
432 Mike McMahon RC	.30	.75
433 Robert Ferguson RC	.40	1.00
434 Ronney Daniels RC	.25	.60
435 Rudi Johnson RC	.40	1.00
436 Vinny Sutherland RC	.25	.60
437 Josh Booty RC	.30	.75
438 Reggie White RC	.25	.60
439 Todd Heap RC	.30	.75
440 Justin Smith RC	.50	1.25
441 Andre Carter RC	.30	.75
442 Bobby Newcombe RC	.30	.75
443 Alex Bannister RC	.25	.60
444 Correll Buckhalter RC	.25	.60
445 Quincy Carter RC	.30	.75
446 Jesse Palmer RC	.30	.75
447 Heath Evans RC	.30	.75
448 Dan Morgan RC	.30	.75
449 Justin McCareins RC	.30	.75
450 Alge Crumpler RC	.40	1.00

2001 Fleer Tradition Art of a Champion

Art of a Champion cards were inserted in packs of Fleer at the rate of 1:240 and Fleer Glossy at 1:120. The 10-card set featured artwork of some of biggest names in pro football. The cardfronts featured the artwork framed with a black and white border, and a gold foil stamp used for the Fleer Tradition logo. The cardbacks feature a 'Congratulations!' message on them. The cardbacks also carried an 'of 10 AC' suffix for the card numbering.

STATED ODDS 1:120 GLOSSY, 1:240 RETAIL

Card	Low	High
1 Drew Brees	8.00	20.00
2 Daunte Culpepper	1.50	4.00
3 Ron Dayne	1.50	4.00
4 Marshall Faulk	1.50	4.00
5 Eddie George	2.00	5.00
6 Edgerrin James	1.50	4.00
7 Jamal Lewis	2.00	5.00
8 Randy Moss	1.50	4.00
9 Fred Taylor	1.25	3.00
10 Michael Vick	3.00	8.00

2001 Fleer Tradition Art of a Champion Autographs

Art of a Champion cards were inserted in packs of Fleer retail and Fleer Glossy hobby. The set featured artwork of some of biggest names in pro football. The cardfronts featured the artwork framed with a black and white border, and a gold foil stamp used for the Fleer Tradition logo. The cardbacks feature a 'Congratulations!' message on them. The cardbacks also carried an 'of 10 AC' suffix for the card numbering. This was the autographed version of the insert.

RANDOM INSERTS IN GLOSSY AND RETAIL

Card	Low	High
1 Drew Brees	150.00	300.00
2 Daunte Culpepper	15.00	40.00
4 Marshall Faulk	25.00	50.00
5 Eddie George	15.00	40.00
6 Edgerrin James	15.00	40.00
7 Jamal Lewis	15.00	40.00
10 Michael Vick	60.00	120.00

2001 Fleer Tradition Autographics

The 2001 Fleer Autographics cards were randomly seeded in only 2001 Fleer Game Time (1:96) and Fleer Genuine packs. Many were issued via mail redemption cards which carried an expiration date of 7/31/2002. Deuce McAllister surfaced after Fleer ceased card operations.

STATED ODDS 1:96 RETAIL GAME TIME

Card	Low	High
1 Shaun Alexander	3.00	8.00
2 Mike Anderson	3.00	8.00
3 Drew Brees	150.00	300.00
4 Isaac Bruce SP	6.00	15.00
5 Mark Brunell SP	5.00	12.00
6 Chris Chambers	3.00	8.00
8 Daunte Culpepper SP	5.00	12.00
9 Stephen Davis	3.00	8.00
10 Ron Dayne	4.00	10.00
11 Corey Dillon	3.00	8.00
12 Marshall Faulk SP	5.00	12.00
14 Brian Griese	3.00	8.00
15 Travis Henry	4.00	10.00
16 Josh Heupel	5.00	12.00
17 Torry Holt	4.00	10.00
18 Edgerrin James SP	5.00	12.00
21 Donovan McNabb SP	15.00	40.00
22 Travis Minor	4.00	10.00
23 Randy Moss SP	30.00	60.00
24 Santana Moss	5.00	12.00
25 Ken-Yon Rambo	3.00	8.00
26 Koren Robinson SP	5.00	12.00
27 Marcus Robinson	4.00	10.00
28 Sage Rosenfels	4.00	10.00
29 Jimmy Smith	4.00	10.00
30 Duce Staley SP	4.00	10.00
31 David Terrell	4.00	10.00
32 Anthony Thomas	5.00	12.00
33 LaDainian Tomlinson	20.00	50.00
34 Marques Tuiasosopo	4.00	10.00
36 Kurt Warner SP	25.00	50.00
37 Reggie Wayne EXCH	1.00	2.50
38 Chris Weinke SP	5.00	12.00
20 Deuce McAllister	8.00	20.00

2001 Fleer Tradition Conference Clash

The Conference Clash set was inserted in packs of 2001 Fleer retail (1:40 packs) and Fleer Glossy hobby at a rate of 1:24. The set featured cards with two players on opposing teams who were involved in conference battles and during the past season. The teams selected for the cards have been long running rivals from the NFL. The cards carried an 'of 15 CC' suffix for the card numbering.

Card	Low	High
COMPLETE SET (15)	15.00	40.00
STATED ODDS 1:24 GLOSSY, 1:40 RETAIL		
1 P.Manning/D.Bledsoe	2.50	6.00
2 R.Moss/Key.Johnson	.75	2.00
3 S.Davis/E.Smith	1.50	4.00
4 J.Garcia/K.Warner	1.50	4.00
5 J.Lewis/E.George	1.00	2.50
6 T.Aikman/D.McNabb	1.25	3.00
7 E.James/C.Martin	.75	2.00
8 T.Owens/I.Bruce	1.00	2.50
9 B.Favre/D.Culpepper	2.00	5.00
10 C.Dillon/F.Taylor	.60	1.50
11 R.Williams/M.Faulk	.75	2.00
12 M.Brunell/T.Couch	.75	2.00
13 T.Holt/J.Rice	2.00	5.00
14 S.Alexander/T.Davis	.75	2.00
15 E.Moulds/M.Harrison	.75	2.00

2001 Fleer Tradition Grass Roots

Randomly inserted in packs of 2001 Fleer retail (1:40 packs) and Fleer Glossy hobby (1:24), this 10-card set featured some players who showed that they were big rushing threats. The cardfronts had a color photo of the featured player with green and white photo of a stadium as the backdrop along with some gold-foil highlights. The cards carried an 'of 10GR' suffix for the card numbering.

Card	Low	High
COMPLETE SET (10)	7.50	20.00
STATED ODDS 1:24 GLOSSY, 1:40 RETAIL		
1 Donovan McNabb	.75	2.00
2 Edgerrin James	.75	2.00
3 Ricky Williams	.75	2.00
4 Fred Taylor	.60	1.50
5 Terrell Davis	.75	2.00
6 Eddie George	1.00	2.50
7 Jamal Lewis	1.00	2.50
8 Marshall Faulk	.75	2.00
9 Daunte Culpepper	.75	2.00
10 Emmitt Smith	1.50	4.00

2001 Fleer Tradition Grass Roots Turf

Randomly inserted in packs of 2001 Fleer retail and Fleer Glossy hobby, this 10-card set featured some players who showed that they were big rushing threats. The cardfronts had a color photo of the featured player with green and white photo of a stadium as the backdrop along with some gold-foil highlights. Each card included a small piece of turf attached to the cardfront as a parallel to the base Grass Roots insert set. The cards carried an 'of 10GR' suffix for the card numbering.

RANDOM INSERTS IN GLOSSY AND RETAIL

Card	Low	High
1 Donovan McNabb	6.00	15.00
2 Edgerrin James	6.00	15.00
3 Ricky Williams	6.00	15.00
4 Fred Taylor	5.00	12.00
5 Terrell Davis	6.00	15.00
6 Eddie George	8.00	20.00
7 Jamal Lewis	8.00	20.00
8 Marshall Faulk	6.00	15.00
9 Daunte Culpepper	6.00	15.00
10 Emmitt Smith	12.00	30.00

2001 Fleer Tradition Keeping Pace

Randomly inserted in packs of 2001 Fleer retail (1:20 packs) and Fleer Glossy hobby (1:12). The 15-card set featured rookies from the 2001 NFL season pictured in their college uniforms and small logo from the NFL team that drafted them. The cardfronts were highlighted with silver-foil highlights. The cards carried an 'of 15 KP' suffix for the card numbering.

Card	Low	High
COMPLETE SET (15)	12.50	30.00
STATED ODDS 1:12 GLOSSY, 1:20 RETAIL		
1 Michael Vick	.75	2.00
2 Drew Brees	2.00	5.00
3 Michael Bennett	.40	1.00
4 David Terrell	.40	1.00
5 Deuce McAllister	.50	1.25
6 Santana Moss	.50	1.25
7 Koren Robinson	.40	1.00
8 Chris Weinke	.40	1.00
9 Reggie Wayne	.60	1.50
10 Rod Gardner	.40	1.00
11 James Jackson	.30	.75
12 Travis Henry	.40	1.00
13 Josh Heupel	.50	1.25
14 LaDainian Tomlinson	1.50	4.00
15 Chad Johnson	.50	1.25

2001 Fleer Tradition Rookie Retro Threads

Randomly inserted in packs of Fleer retail and Fleer Glossy hobby, this set featured swatches of old school jerseys, helmets and footballs from a rookie photo shoot. The stated odds for the Rookie Retro Threads was 1:24 Glossy, and 1:240 retail.

STATED ODDS 1:24 GLOSSY,1:240 RET

Card	Low	High
1 Kevan Barlow FB	2.50	6.00
2 Kevan Barlow JSY	2.50	6.00
3 Michael Bennett FB	2.50	6.00
4 Michael Bennett JSY	2.50	6.00
5 Drew Brees FB	10.00	25.00
6 Drew Brees JSY	10.00	25.00
7 Andre Carter JSY	2.50	6.00
8 Quincy Carter JSY	2.50	6.00
9 Chris Chambers FB	2.00	5.00
10 Chris Chambers JSY	2.00	5.00
11 Robert Ferguson FB	3.00	8.00
12 Robert Ferguson JSY	3.00	8.00
13 Rod Gardner FB	2.50	6.00
14 Rod Gardner JSY	2.50	6.00
15 Travis Henry FB	2.50	6.00
16 Travis Henry JSY	2.50	6.00
17 Josh Heupel FB	3.00	8.00
18 Josh Heupel JSY	3.00	8.00
19 James Jackson JSY	2.00	5.00
20 Deuce McAllister FB	3.00	8.00
21 Mike McMahon FB	2.50	6.00
22 Mike McMahon JSY	2.50	6.00
23 Travis Minor FB	2.50	6.00
24 Travis Minor JSY	2.50	6.00
25 Freddie Mitchell FB	2.00	5.00
26 Freddie Mitchell JSY	2.00	5.00
27 Quincy Morgan JSY	2.50	6.00
28 Santana Moss JSY	3.00	8.00
29 Jesse Palmer FB	2.50	6.00
30 Jesse Palmer JSY	2.50	6.00
31 Koren Robinson FB	2.50	6.00
32 Sage Rosenfels FB	2.50	6.00
33 Sage Rosenfels JSY	2.50	6.00
34 David Terrell JSY	2.50	6.00
35 Anthony Thomas FB	3.00	8.00
36 Anthony Thomas JSY	3.00	8.00
37 LaDainian Tomlinson FB	6.00	15.00
38 LaDainian Tomlinson JSY	6.00	15.00
39 Marques Tuiasosopo FB	2.50	6.00
40 Marques Tuiasosopo JSY	2.50	6.00
41 Michael Vick FB	4.00	10.00
42 Michael Vick JSY	4.00	10.00
43 Reggie Wayne JSY	4.00	10.00
44 Chris Weinke FB	2.50	6.00
45 Bennett/Tomlinson HEL	6.00	15.00
46 D.Brees/L.Tomlinson FB	10.00	25.00
47 D.Brees/M.Vick HEL	10.00	25.00
48 R.Gardner/F.Mitchell HEL	2.50	6.00
49 T.Heap/S.Minnis FB	2.50	6.00
50 J.Jackson/Q.Morgan FB	2.00	5.00
51 R.Johnson/C.Johnson FB	3.00	8.00
52 D.McAllister/M.Vick FB	4.00	10.00
53 D.Morgan/C.Weinke FB	2.50	6.00
54 S.Moss/R.Wayne FB	4.00	10.00
55 S.Moss/R.Wayne HEL	4.00	10.00
56 K.Robinson/D.Terrell HEL	2.50	6.00
57 K.Robinson/Q.Carter FB	2.50	6.00
58 S.Rosenfels/R.Gardner FB	2.50	6.00
59 D.Terrell/A.Thomas FB	3.00	8.00

2001 Fleer Tradition Throwbacks

Randomly inserted in packs of 2001 Fleer retail (1:20) and Fleer Glossy hobby (1:12). This 20-card set featured players that had an old school style of play. The cardfronts were very basic with silver-foil highlights. The cardbacks were horizontal and carried an 'of 20 TB' suffix for the card numbering.

Card	Low	High
COMPLETE SET (20)	20.00	50.00
STATED ODDS 1:12 GLOSSY, 1:20 RETAIL		
1 Jamal Lewis	.75	2.00
2 Eddie George	.75	2.00
3 Marvin Harrison	.60	1.50
4 Brett Favre	1.50	4.00
5 Donovan McNabb	.60	1.50
6 Troy Aikman	1.00	2.50
7 Edgerrin James	.60	1.50
8 Brian Urlacher	1.00	2.50
9 Stephen Davis	.50	1.25
10 Daunte Culpepper	.60	1.50
11 Jerry Rice	1.50	4.00
12 Emmitt Smith	1.25	3.00
13 Kurt Warner	1.25	3.00
14 Ricky Williams	.60	1.50
15 Cris Carter	.75	2.00
16 Mark Brunell	.60	1.50
17 Ron Dayne	.60	1.50
18 Peyton Manning	2.00	5.00
19 Randy Moss	.60	1.50
20 Brian Griese	.50	1.25

2001 Fleer Tradition Glossy

In July of 2001 Fleer released the glossy version of what is also referred to as Fleer Tradition. The Glossy set was only available at hobby shops.The cards had a vintage look to them. The cardfronts had a color photo of the the player close up and a color photo of the player in action and a faded stadium scene photo in the background. The cards were set horizontally. The cardbacks had the old greyback stock and no UV coating. The cardbacks also featured a small comic reminiscent of older cards.

Card	Low	High
COMP.SET w/o SP's (400)	20.00	40.00
*1-400 GLOSSY: .5X TO 1.2X BASIC CARDS		
401-500 ROOKIE PRINT RUN 2001		
325 Pat Tillman UH RC	8.00	20.00
402 Drew Brees RC	20.00	50.00

2001 Fleer Tradition Glossy Rookie Minis

*MINI/350: .5X TO 1.2X GLOSSY RC
STATED PRINT RUN 350 SER.#'d SETS

2001 Fleer Tradition Glossy Rookie Stickers

*STICKER/699: .4X TO 1X GLOSSY RC
STATED PRINT RUN 699 SER.#'d SETS

2001 Fleer Tradition Glossy Nameplates

Nameplates were inserted in cello and jumbo packs of 2001 Fleer and Fleer Glossy. The cards featured a swatch cut from the players' Nameplate patch. The cardfronts had a license plate design with the player's name representing the license plate numbers and letters. The cardbacks carried a Congratulations message.

RANDOM INSERTS IN CELLO/JUMBO PACKS

Card	Low	High
1 Ron Dayne	8.00	20.00
2 Kurt Warner	15.00	40.00
3 Curtis Martin	8.00	20.00
4 Jake Plummer	6.00	15.00
5 Mark Brunell	8.00	20.00
6 Drew Bledsoe	8.00	20.00
7 Kevin Johnson	6.00	15.00
8 Brian Griese	6.00	15.00
9 Terrell Owens	8.00	20.00
10 Brian Urlacher	12.00	30.00
11 Jamal Anderson	8.00	20.00
12 Isaac Bruce	10.00	25.00
13 Jerome Bettis	10.00	25.00
14 Fred Taylor	6.00	15.00
15 Tim Couch	6.00	15.00
16 Stephen Davis	6.00	15.00
17 Warrick Dunn	6.00	15.00
18 Rod Smith	8.00	20.00
19 Marshall Faulk	8.00	20.00
20 Thomas Jones	6.00	15.00
21 Emmitt Smith	15.00	40.00
22 Marcus Robinson	8.00	20.00
23 Daunte Culpepper	8.00	20.00
24 Antonio Freeman	10.00	25.00
25 Marvin Harrison	8.00	20.00
26 Dan Marino	20.00	50.00
27 Steve Young	15.00	40.00
28 Deion Sanders	8.00	20.00
29 Edgerrin James	8.00	20.00
30 Jerry Rice	15.00	40.00

2001 Fleer Tradition Glossy Traditional Threads

Randomly inserted one in every rack pack of Fleer Glossy, this 34-card set featured some of the top players from the NFL. The cards had a swatch from a game-used jersey on them. The Fleer logo had the word 'Glossy' under it, which was different than the other inserts from the glossy sets that were also included in the regular Fleer set.

ONE PER GLOSSY RACK PACK

Card	Low	High
1 Troy Aikman	4.00	10.00
2 Jamal Anderson	2.50	6.00
3 Jerome Bettis	3.00	8.00
4 Drew Bledsoe	2.50	6.00
5 Isaac Bruce	3.00	8.00
6 Mark Brunell	2.50	6.00
7 Tim Couch	2.00	5.00
8 Daunte Culpepper	2.50	6.00
9 Stephen Davis	2.00	5.00
10 Ron Dayne	2.50	6.00
11 Warrick Dunn	2.00	5.00
12 Marshall Faulk	2.50	6.00
13 Brett Favre	6.00	15.00
14 Antonio Freeman	3.00	8.00
15 Eddie George	3.00	8.00
16 Brian Griese	2.00	5.00
17 Marvin Harrison	2.50	6.00
18 Edgerrin James	2.50	6.00
19 Kevin Johnson	2.00	5.00
20 Thomas Jones	2.00	5.00
22 Ray Lewis	3.00	8.00
23 Dan Marino	6.00	15.00
24 Curtis Martin	2.50	6.00
25 Randy Moss	2.50	6.00
26 Terrell Owens	2.50	6.00
27 Jake Plummer	2.00	5.00
28 Jerry Rice	6.00	15.00
29 Rod Smith	2.50	6.00
30 Jimmy Smith	2.50	6.00
31 Kordell Stewart	2.00	5.00
32 Fred Taylor	2.00	5.00
33 Brian Urlacher	4.00	10.00
34 Kurt Warner	5.00	12.00
35 Steve Young	4.00	10.00

2002 Fleer Tradition

Released in August 2002, this 300-card set contains 260 veterans and 40 rookies. S.R.P. is $1.99 per pack. Both hobby and retail boxes contained 24 packs, each with 10 cards per pack.

Card	Low	High
COMPLETE SET (300)	30.00	80.00
1 Jeff Garcia	.15	.40
2 Brian Simmons	.15	.40
3 Kordell Stewart	.15	.40
4 Chris Weinke	.15	.40
5 Donovan McNabb	.20	.50
6 Antoine Winfield	.15	.40
7 Ray Lewis	.25	.60
8 Drew Brees	.50	1.25
9 Frank Sanders	.15	.40
10 Rich Gannon	.20	.50
11 Jamal Anderson	.20	.50
12 Curtis Martin	.20	.50
13 Darrell Jackson	.20	.50
14 Micheal Barrow	.15	.40
15 Jeff Wilkins	.15	.40
16 Ricky Williams	.20	.50
17 Brad Johnson	.20	.50
18 Tedy Bruschi	.20	.50
19 Frank Wycheck	.15	.40
20 Byron Chamberlain	.15	.40
21 Terry Glenn	.20	.50
22 James McKnight	.15	.40
23 Thomas Jones	.15	.40
24 Jamie Sharper	.20	.50
25 Trent Green	.15	.40
26 Mike Rucker RC	.25	.60
27 Mark Brunell	.20	.50
28 Takeo Spikes	.15	.40
29 Dominic Rhodes	.15	.40
30 Jim Miller	.15	.40
31 Corey Bradford	.15	.40
32 Jamir Miller	.15	.40
33 Johnnie Morton	.20	.50
34 Rocket Ismail	.20	.50
35 Mike Anderson	.15	.40
36 James Allen	.15	.40
37 Quincy Carter	.15	.40
38 Germane Crowell	.15	.40
39 Quincy Morgan	.15	.40
40 Kabeer Gbaja-Biamila	.15	.40
41 Reggie Wayne	.20	.50
42 Brian Urlacher	.25	.60
43 Stacey Mack	.15	.40
44 Justin Smith	.20	.50
45 Snoop Minnis	.15	.40
46 Donald Hayes	.15	.40
47 Jay Fiedler	.20	.50
48 Nate Clements	.15	.40
49 Drew Bledsoe	.20	.50
50 Peter Boulware	.15	.40
51 Lawyer Milloy	.15	.40
52 Michael Pittman	.20	.50
53 Aaron Brooks	.15	.40
54 Maurice Smith	.15	.40
55 Ike Hilliard	.15	.40
56 Derrick Mason	.15	.40
57 LaMont Jordan	.20	.50
58 Charlie Garner	.20	.50
59 Mike Alstott	.15	.40
60 Freddie Mitchell	.15	.40
61 Isaac Bruce	.25	.60
62 Hines Ward	.20	.50
63 John Randle	.20	.50
64 Doug Flutie	.20	.50
65 Terrell Owens	.20	.50
66 Garrison Hearst	.15	.40
67 Rodney Harrison	.15	.40
68 Koren Robinson	.15	.40
69 Amos Zereoue	.15	.40
70 Aeneas Williams	.15	.40
71 Hugh Douglas	.15	.40
72 Jacquez Green	.15	.40
73 Sebastian Janikowski	.15	.40
74 Kevin Dyson	.20	.50
75 Terance Mathis	.15	.40
76 Vinny Testaverde	.15	.40
77 Kwamie Lassiter	.15	.40
78 Ron Dayne	.20	.50
79 Jonathan Ogden	.20	.50
80 Charlie Clemons RC	.15	.40
81 Peter Warrick	.15	.40
82 Adam Vinatieri	.15	.40
83 Ted Washington	.15	.40
84 Randy Moss	.20	.50
85 Rosevelt Colvin RC	.30	.75
86 Oronde Gadsden	.15	.40
87 Anthony Henry	.15	.40
88 Priest Holmes	.15	.40
89 Joey Galloway	.20	.50
90 Jimmy Smith	.20	.50
91 Bill Romanowski	.20	.50
92 Chris Claiborne	.15	.40
93 Marvin Harrison	.20	.50
94 Vonnie Holliday	.15	.40
95 Darren Sharper	.15	.40
96 Chad Bratzke	.15	.40
97 James Stewart	.15	.40
98 Fred Taylor	.15	.40
99 Jason Elam	.15	.40
100 Keyshawn Johnson	.20	.50
101 Dexter Coakley	.15	.40
102 Zach Thomas	.20	.50
103 Jamel White	.15	.40
104 Antowain Smith	.20	.50
105 Marty Booker	.15	.40
106 Deuce McAllister	.20	.50
107 Adam Archuleta	.15	.40
108 Rod Smith	.20	.50
109 Tony Boselli	.20	.50
110 Joe Johnson	.15	.40
111 Simeon Rice	.15	.40
112 Cory Schlesinger	.15	.40
113 La'Roi Glover	.15	.40
114 Tiki Barber	.20	.50
115 Michael Westbrook	.15	.40
116 Antonio Freeman	.25	.60
117 Kerry Collins	.15	.40
118 Laveranues Coles	.20	.50
119 Jay Feely	.15	.40
120 Champ Bailey	.20	.50
121 Peyton Manning	.60	1.50
122 Chad Pennington	.15	.40
123 Anthony Dorsett	.15	.40
124 Jamal Lewis	.20	.50
125 Marcus Pollard	.15	.40
126 Charles Woodson	.25	.60
127 Duce Staley	.15	.40
128 Travis Henry	.15	.40
129 Tony Brackens	.15	.40
130 Jeremiah Trotter	.15	.40
131 Jerome Bettis	.25	.60
132 Chad Johnson	.15	.40
133 Lamar Smith	.15	.40
134 Joey Porter	.20	.50
135 Curtis Conway	.20	.50
136 David Terrell	.15	.40
137 Daunte Culpepper	.20	.50
138 Chris Fuamatu-Ma'afala	.15	.40
139 J.J. Stokes	.15	.40
140 Tim Couch	.15	.40
141 Ty Law	.25	.60
142 Vinny Sutherland	.15	.40
143 Trung Canidate	.15	.40
144 Larry Allen	.25	.60
145 Darren Howard	.15	.40
146 Ricky Watters	.20	.50
147 Grant Wistrom	.15	.40
148 Brian Griese	.15	.40
149 Jason Sehorn	.20	.50
150 Marshall Faulk	.20	.50
151 Martin Gramatica	.15	.40
152 Robert Porcher	.15	.40
153 Richie Anderson	.15	.40
154 Derrick Brooks	.15	.40
155 Jevon Kearse	.15	.40
156 Bill Schroeder	.15	.40
157 Marvin Jones	.15	.40
158 Eddie George	.20	.50
159 Keith Brooking	.15	.40
160 Ryan Longwell	.15	.40
161 Brian Dawkins	.25	.60
162 Chris Redman	.15	.40
163 Az-Zahir Hakim	.15	.40
164 James Thrash	.20	.50
165 Rob Johnson	.20	.50
166 Hardy Nickerson	.15	.40
167 Chad Scott	.15	.40
168 Jon Kitna	.15	.40
169 Donnie Edwards	.15	.40
170 Andre Carter	.15	.40
171 Warrick Holdman	.15	.40
172 Jason Taylor	.20	.50
173 Levon Kirkland	.15	.40
174 Mike Brown	.15	.40
175 David Patten	.15	.40
176 Kurt Warner	.20	.50
177 Fred Smoot	.20	.50
178 Dat Nguyen	.15	.40
179 Joe Horn	.15	.40
180 John Lynch	.20	.50
181 Troy Hambrick	.15	.40
182 John Carney	.15	.40
183 Wesley Walls	.20	.50
184 Deltha O'Neal	.15	.40
185 Joe Jurevicius	.15	.40
186 Steve McNair	.20	.50
187 Scotty Anderson	.15	.40
188 John Abraham	.20	.50
189 Stephen Davis	.15	.40
190 Nate Wayne	.15	.40
191 Corey Simon	.15	.40
192 Joel Makovicka	.15	.40
193 Rob Morris	.15	.40
194 Correll Buckhalter	.15	.40
195 Qadry Ismail	.15	.40
196 Keenan McCardell	.20	.50
197 Jason Gildon	.20	.50
198 Peerless Price	.15	.40
199 Tony Richardson	.15	.40
200 Kevan Barlow	.15	.40
201 Corey Dillon	.15	.40
202 Sam Madison	.15	.40
203 Chad Brown	.15	.40
204 Dez White	.15	.40
205 Troy Brown	.15	.40
206 Orlando Pace	.15	.40
207 Jermaine Lewis	.15	.40
208 Willie Jackson	.15	.40
209 Warrick Dunn	.15	.40
210 James Jackson	.15	.40
211 Sammy Knight	.15	.40
212 Ronde Barber	.15	.40
213 Ed McCaffrey	.20	.50
214 Amani Toomer	.15	.40
215 Rod Gardner	.15	.40
216 Mike McMahon	.15	.40
217 Wayne Chrebet	.15	.40
218 Jake Plummer	.15	.40
219 Bubba Franks	.15	.40
220 Shane Lechler	.15	.40
221 Travis Taylor	.15	.40
222 Edgerrin James	.20	.50
223 David Akers	.15	.40
224 Eric Moulds	.15	.40
225 Mike Vanderjagt	.15	.40
226 Kendrell Bell	.15	.40
227 Darnay Scott	.20	.50
228 Tony Gonzalez	.20	.50
229 Marcellus Wiley	.15	.40
230 Marcus Robinson	.20	.50
231 Muhsin Muhammad	.15	.40
232 Trent Dilfer	.15	.40
233 Kevin Johnson	.15	.40
234 Travis Minor	.15	.40
235 London Fletcher	.20	.50
236 Reggie Swinton	.15	.40
237 Michael Bennett	.15	.40
238 Brett Favre DD	.40	1.00
239 Terrell Davis DD	.15	.40
240 Emmitt Smith DD	.30	.75
241 Shannon Sharpe DD	.15	.40
242 Cris Carter DD	.20	.50
243 Tim Brown DD	.20	.50
244 Jerry Rice DD	.40	1.00
245 Bruce Smith DD	.15	.40
246 Warren Sapp DD	.15	.40
247 Michael Strahan DD	.15	.40
248 Junior Seau DD	.15	.40
249 Darrell Green DD	.20	.50
250 Rod Woodson DD	.20	.50
251 David Boston BB	.15	.40
252 Michael Vick BB	.15	.40
253 Anthony Thomas BB	.15	.40
254 Ahman Green BB	.15	.40
255 Chris Chambers BB	.12	.30
256 Tom Brady BB	1.00	2.50
257 Plaxico Burress BB	.12	.30
258 LaDainian Tomlinson BB	.20	.50
259 Shaun Alexander BB	.12	.30
260 Torry Holt BB	.15	.40
261 Julius Peppers RC	1.00	2.50
262 William Green RC	.50	1.25
263 Joey Harrington RC	.40	1.00
264 Jabar Gaffney RC	.40	1.00
265 T.J. Duckett RC	.40	1.00
266 Antwaan Randle El RC	.50	1.25
267 Javon Walker RC	.60	1.50
268 David Carr RC	.40	1.00
269 DeShaun Foster RC	.60	1.50
270 Donte Stallworth RC	.60	1.50
271 Antonio Bryant RC	.60	1.50
272 Clinton Portis RC	.60	1.50
273 Josh Reed RC	.50	1.25
274 Ashley Lelie RC	.40	1.00
275 Patrick Ramsey RC	.50	1.25

276 J.Wells RC/A.Peterson RC .50 1.25
277 Q.Jammer RC/R.Williams RC .60 1.50
278 J.Shockey RC/D.Graham RC .60 1.50
279 E.Crouch RC/Applewhite RC .60 1.50
280 Buchanon RC/Sheppard RC .60 1.50
281 K.Hill RC/D.Branch RC .60 1.50
282 R.Sims RC/W.Bryant RC .60 1.50
283 J.Scobey RC/Westbrook RC .75 2.00
284 L.Betts RC/O.Easy RC .60 1.50
285 A.Davis RC/D.Jones RC .40 1.00
286 C.Russell RC/C.Taylor RC .60 1.50
287 McAddley RC/J.McCown RC .60 1.50
288 D.Garrard RC/R.Davey RC .60 1.50
289 M.Walker RC/R.Johnson RC .50 1.25
290 L.Staley RC/L.Gordon RC .50 1.25
291 R.Caldwell RC/L.Mays RC .50 1.25
292 R.Thomas RC/N.Harris RC .50 1.25
293 M.Morris RC/J.Stevens RC .50 1.25
294 K.Kittner RC/R.Fasani RC .40 1.00
295 R.Calmus RC/J.Schifino RC .50 1.25
296 T.Carter RC/F.Milons RC .50 1.25
297 Wistrom RC/Stephens RC .50 1.25
298 M.Williams RC/D.Freeney RC .75 2.00
299 Hendersn RC/Hayneswrth RC .60 1.50
300 N.Davenport RC/C.Nall RC .50 1.25

2002 Fleer Tradition Minis

*VETS 1-260: 6X TO 15X BASIC CARDS
*ROOKIES 261-300: 2.5X TO 6X
STATED PRINT RUN 125 SER.#'d SETS

2002 Fleer Tradition Tiffany

*VETS 1-260: 4X TO 10X BASIC CARDS
*ROOKIES 261-300: 1.5X TO 4X
STATED PRINT 225 SER.#'d SETS

2002 Fleer Tradition Career Highlights

Inserted at a rate of 1:24, this set showcases the careers of ten of the NFL's best.

COMPLETE SET (10) 15.00 40.00
STATED ODDS 1:24
1 Peyton Manning 3.00 8.00
2 Brett Favre 2.50 6.00
3 Kurt Warner 1.00 2.50
4 Emmitt Smith 2.00 5.00
5 Marshall Faulk 1.00 2.50
6 Jerome Bettis 1.25 3.00
7 Jerry Rice 2.50 6.00
8 Cris Carter 1.25 3.00
9 Randy Moss 1.00 2.50
10 Michael Strahan 1.00 2.50

2002 Fleer Tradition Classic Combinations Hobby

This 35-card insert set is divided into four tiers. Cards 1-10 are #'d/2000, cards 11-20 are #'d/1000, cards 21-30 are #'d/500, and cards 31-35 are #'d/250. The Hobby version features the first player's name printed in blue foil while the Retail version has the player's name in red foil. The retail cards were seeded at the rate of 1:12 retail packs.

1-10 PRINT RUN 2000
11-20 PRINT RUN 1000
21-30 PRINT RUN 500
31-35 PRINT RUN 250
*RETAIL 1-10: .3X TO .8X HOBBY INSERTS
*RETAIL 11-20: .25X TO .6X HOBBY INSERTS
*RETAIL 21-30: .2X TO .5X HOBBY INSERTS
*RETAIL 31-35: .15X TO .4X HOBBY INSERTS
1 K.Bell/B.Urlacher 1.00 2.50
2 D.Culpepper/R.Moss .75 2.00
3 E.Campbell/E.George 1.00 2.50
4 P.Hornung/B.Favre 2.00 5.00
5 P.Manning/E.James 2.50 6.00
6 D.McNabb/D.Culpepper .75 2.00
7 B.Griese/T.Brady 5.00 12.00
8 J.Rice/T.Brown 2.00 5.00
9 A.Thomas/W.Payton 4.00 10.00
10 T.Holt/K.Robinson .75 2.00
11 J.Rice/C.Carter 2.50 6.00
12 C.Chambers/P.Burress .75 2.00
13 M.Vick/D.McNabb 1.00 2.50
14 K.Warner/M.Faulk 1.00 2.50
15 B.Favre/D.Culpepper 2.50 6.00
16 J.Garcia/K.Warner 1.00 2.50
17 P.Manning/J.Lewis 3.00 8.00
18 E.Campbell/R.Williams 1.25 3.00
19 D.Carr/P.Manning 3.00 8.00
20 J.Elway/B.Griese 2.00 5.00
21 J.Garcia/T.Owens 1.25 3.00
22 E.Dickerson/M.Faulk 1.25 3.00
23 E.Smith/M.Allen 2.50 6.00
24 R.Staubach/E.Smith 2.50 6.00
25 T.Davis/C.Martin 1.25 3.00
26 E.Smith/W.Payton 6.00 15.00
27 J.Montana/K.Warner 5.00 12.00
28 K.Stewart/J.Bettis 1.50 4.00
29 E.George/A.Griffin 1.25 3.00
30 J.Elway/T.Davis 2.50 6.00
31 B.Griese/B.Griese 2.00 5.00
32 J.Harrington/D.Carr 1.25 3.00
33 B.Griese/D.Brees 4.00 10.00
34 R.Moss/J.Rice 4.00 10.00
35 E.Smith/F.Taylor 3.00 8.00

2002 Fleer Tradition Classic Combinations Memorabilia

Inserted into packs at a rate of 1:24, this set feature single swatches of game used memorabilia.

STATED ODDS 1:24
1 M.Allen JSY/Smith 10.00 25.00
2 T.Brady JSY/Br.Griese 12.00 30.00
3 D.Brees JSY/Bo.Griese 8.00 20.00
4 E.Campbell JSY/George 6.00 15.00
5 E.Campbell JSY/Williams 6.00 15.00
6 C.Carter JSY/Rice 6.00 15.00
7 D.Culpepper JSY/McNabb 6.00 15.00
8 D.Culpepper JSY/Moss 6.00 15.00
9 E.Dickerson JSY/Faulk 6.00 15.00
10 J.Elway JSY/Davis 15.00 40.00
11 J.Elway JSY/Br.Griese 15.00 40.00
12 M.Faulk JSY/Dickerson 6.00 15.00
13 M.Faulk JSY/Warner 6.00 15.00
14 B.Favre JSY/Culpepper 12.00 30.00
15 B.Favre JSY/Hornung 12.00 30.00
16 J.Garcia JSY/Owens 6.00 15.00
17 J.Garcia JSY/Warner 6.00 15.00
18 E.George JSY/Campbell 5.00 12.00
19 T.Holt JSY/Robinson 6.00 15.00
20 J.Lewis JSY/Manning 5.00 12.00
21 D.McNabb JSY/Culpepper 6.00 15.00
22 D.McNabb JSY/Vick 8.00 20.00
23 J.Montana JSY/Warner 20.00 50.00
24 R.Moss JSY/Culpepper 8.00 20.00
25 R.Moss JSY/Rice 8.00 20.00
26 T.Owens JSY/Garcia 6.00 15.00
27 W.Payton JSY/Smith 20.00 50.00
28 W.Payton JSY/Thomas 25.00 60.00
29 J.Rice JSY/Carter 10.00 25.00
30 J.Rice JSY/Moss 10.00 25.00
31 E.Smith JSY/Allen 12.00 30.00
32 E.Smith JSY/Payton 12.00 30.00
33 E.Smith JSY/Taylor 12.00 30.00
34 R.Staubach JSY/Smith 15.00 40.00
35 A.Thomas JSY/Payton 6.00 15.00
36 B.Urlacher JSY/Bell 8.00 20.00
37 M.Vick JSY/McNabb 8.00 20.00
38 K.Warner JSY/Faulk 6.00 15.00
39 K.Warner JSY/Montana 6.00 15.00
40 R.Williams JSY/Campbell 6.00 15.00

2002 Fleer Tradition Classic Combinations Memorabilia Duals

Randomly inserted into packs, this set features dual swatches of game used memorabilia. Each card is serial #'d to 100.

STATED PRINT RUN 100 SER.#'d SETS
1 M.Allen/E.Smith 15.00 40.00
2 E.Campbell/E.George 10.00 25.00
3 E.Campbell/R.Williams 10.00 25.00
4 J.Rice/C.Carter 20.00 50.00
5 D.Culpepper/R.Moss 8.00 20.00
6 T.Davis/C.Martin 8.00 20.00
7 E.Dickerson/M.Faulk 8.00 20.00
8 J.Elway/T.Davis 15.00 40.00
9 J.Elway/B.Griese 15.00 40.00
10 B.Favre/D.Culpepper 20.00 50.00
11 J.Garcia/T.Owens 8.00 20.00
12 B.Griese/T.Brady 50.00 125.00
13 P.Hornung/B.Favre 40.00 100.00
14 D.McNabb/D.Culpepper 8.00 20.00
15 D.McNabb/M.Vick 8.00 20.00
16 J.Montana/K.Warner 30.00 80.00
17 W.Payton/E.Smith 40.00 100.00
18 R.Moss/J.Rice 20.00 50.00
19 R.Staubach/E.Smith 15.00 40.00
20 F.Taylor/E.Smith 15.00 40.00
21 A.Thomas/W.Payton 40.00 100.00
22 K.Warner/M.Faulk 8.00 20.00
23 K.Warner/J.Garcia 8.00 20.00

2002 Fleer Tradition Golden Memories

Inserted into packs at a rate of 1:8, this set highlights some of the NFL's brightest moments.

COMPLETE SET (15) 12.50 30.00
STATED ODDS 1:8
1 America Tribute .60 1.50
2 Kurt Warner .60 1.50
3 Tom Brady 4.00 10.00
4 David Carr .50 1.25
5 Shaun Alexander .50 1.25
6 Anthony Thomas .60 1.50
7 Kendrell Bell .50 1.25
8 Michael Vick .60 1.50
9 Donovan McNabb .60 1.50
10 LaDainian Tomlinson .75 2.00
11 Brian Urlacher .75 2.00
12 Marshall Faulk .60 1.50
13 Edgerrin James .60 1.50
14 Terrell Owens .60 1.50
15 Tim Brown .75 2.00

2002 Fleer Tradition Headliners

Inserted into packs at a rate of 1:24, this set features cartoon like drawings with actual photos of the players face.

COMPLETE SET (20) 30.00 80.00
STATED ODDS 1:24
1 Donovan McNabb 1.25 3.00
2 Marshall Faulk 1.25 3.00
3 Randy Moss 1.25 3.00
4 Emmitt Smith 2.50 6.00
5 Jeff Garcia 1.00 2.50
6 Tim Brown 1.50 4.00
7 Brian Urlacher 1.50 4.00
8 Jerome Bettis 1.50 4.00
9 Edgerrin James 1.25 3.00
10 Kurt Warner 1.25 3.00
11 Terrell Davis 1.25 3.00
12 Tim Couch 1.00 2.50
13 Ricky Williams 1.25 3.00
14 Daunte Culpepper 1.25 3.00
15 Jerry Rice 3.00 8.00
16 Curtis Martin 1.25 3.00
17 Peyton Manning 4.00 10.00
18 Eddie George 1.25 3.00
19 Tom Brady 8.00 20.00
20 Brett Favre 3.00 8.00

2002 Fleer Tradition Rookie Sensations

Randomly inserted into packs, this set of 2002 rookies is serial #'d to 1250.

COMPLETE SET (20) 30.00 80.00
STATED PRINT RUN 1250 SER.#'d SETS
1 David Carr .60 1.50
2 Joey Harrington .60 1.50
3 William Green .75 2.00
4 Ashley Lelie .60 1.50
5 Donte Stallworth 1.00 2.50
6 T.J. Duckett .60 1.50
7 DeShaun Foster 1.00 2.50
8 Josh Reed .75 2.00
9 Jabar Gaffney .60 1.50
10 Clinton Portis 1.00 2.50
11 Antonio Bryant 1.00 2.50
12 Reche Caldwell .75 2.00
13 Julius Peppers 1.50 4.00
14 Ron Johnson .75 2.00
15 Javon Walker 1.00 2.50
16 Josh McCown 1.00 2.50
17 Marquise Walker .60 1.50
18 Patrick Ramsey .75 2.00
19 Antwaan Randle El .75 2.00
20 Andre Davis .60 1.50

2002 Fleer Tradition School Colors

Randomly inserted into packs, this set is serial #'d to 750, and is designed to resemble a college pennant. Each pennant depicts the players alma mater.

COMPLETE SET (15) 20.00 50.00
STATED PRINT RUN 750 SER.#'d SETS
1 Santana Moss 1.25 3.00
2 Edgerrin James 1.25 3.00
3 David Terrell 1.00 2.50
4 Anthony Thomas 1.25 3.00
5 Dan Morgan 1.00 2.50
6 Rod Gardner 1.00 2.50
7 Archie Griffin 1.00 2.50
8 Drew Brees 3.00 8.00
9 Chad Johnson 1.00 2.50
10 Chris Weinke 1.00 2.50
11 Reggie Wayne 1.25 3.00
12 DeShaun Foster 1.50 4.00
13 Robert Ferguson 1.25 3.00
14 Tom Brady 8.00 20.00
15 David Carr 1.00 2.50

2002 Fleer Tradition School Colors Memorabilia

This 12-card set includes a single-swatch of game-worn jersey and is inserted into packs at a rate of 1:30.

STATED ODDS 1:30
1 Drew Brees 10.00 25.00
2 Robert Ferguson 4.00 10.00
3 DeShaun Foster 5.00 12.00
4 Rod Gardner 3.00 8.00
5 Archie Griffin 3.00 8.00
6 Edgerrin James 4.00 10.00
7 Chad Johnson 3.00 8.00
8 Dan Morgan 3.00 8.00
9 Santana Moss 4.00 10.00
10 David Terrell 3.00 8.00
11 Anthony Thomas 4.00 10.00
12 Chris Weinke 3.00 8.00

2002 Fleer Tradition School Colors Memorabilia Duals

This 5-card set includes a dual-swatch of game-worn jersey and is inserted into packs at a rate of 1:211.

STATED ODDS 1:211
1 Edgerrin James 8.00 20.00
2 Dan Morgan 6.00 15.00
3 Santana Moss 8.00 20.00
4 David Terrell 6.00 15.00
5 Anthony Thomas 8.00 20.00

2003 Fleer Tradition

Released in September of 2003, this set consists of 270 veterans, 10 single player rookie cards, and 20 triple player rookie cards.

COMPLETE SET (300) 15.00 40.00
1 Aaron Glenn .15 .40
2 Jerry Rice .50 1.25
3 Chad Hutchinson .15 .40
4 Kris Jenkins .15 .40
5 Ed Reed .20 .50
6 Ed McCaffrey .20 .50
7 Rod Gardner .15 .40
8 Aaron Brooks .15 .40
9 Chad Pennington .15 .40
10 Jevon Kearse .15 .40
11 Kurt Warner .20 .50
12 Eddie George .20 .50
13 Ron Dugans .15 .40
14 Adam Vinatieri .15 .40
15 Jimmy Smith .20 .50
16 Chad Johnson .15 .40
17 Kyle Brady .15 .40
18 Eddie Kennison .15 .40
19 Joe Jurevicius .20 .50
20 Ronde Barber .15 .40
21 Adam Archuleta .15 .40
22 Champ Bailey .20 .50
23 Joe Horn .15 .40
24 Ladell Betts .15 .40
25 Edgerrin James .20 .50
26 Rosevelt Colvin .20 .50
27 Ahman Green .20 .50
28 Joey Porter .25 .60
29 Charles Woodson .25 .60
30 Lance Schulters .15 .40
31 Edgerton Hartwell .15 .40
32 Joey Galloway .20 .50
33 Roy Williams .15 .40
34 Al Wilson .15 .40
35 Charlie Garner .20 .50
36 John Lynch .20 .50
37 La'Roi Glover .15 .40
38 Emmitt Smith .40 1.00
39 Ryan Longwell .20 .50
40 Alge Crumpler .20 .50
41 John Abraham .20 .50
42 Chris Hovan .20 .50
43 Laveranues Coles .15 .40
44 Eric Hicks .15 .40
45 Johnnie Morton .20 .50
46 Sam Madison .20 .50
47 Amani Toomer .15 .40
48 Chris Redman .15 .40
49 Jon Kitna .15 .40
50 Leonard Little .15 .40
51 Eric Moulds .15 .40
52 Santana Moss .20 .50
53 Amos Zereoue .15 .40
54 Jonathan Wells .15 .40
55 Chris Chambers .15 .40
56 London Fletcher .20 .50
57 Frank Wycheck .15 .40
58 Josh McCown .20 .50
59 Shannon Sharpe .20 .50
60 Andre Carter .15 .40
61 Corey Dillon .15 .40
62 Josh Reed .15 .40
63 Marc Boerigter .15 .40
64 Fred Smoot .15 .40
65 Shaun Alexander .15 .40
66 Andre Davis .15 .40
67 Julian Peterson .15 .40
68 Corey Bradford .15 .40
69 Marc Bulger .15 .40
70 Fred Taylor .15 .40
71 Junior Seau .20 .50
72 Simeon Rice .15 .40
73 Anthony Thomas .20 .50
74 Correll Buckhalter .15 .40
75 Justin Smith .20 .50
76 Marcel Shipp .15 .40
77 Garrison Hearst .15 .40
78 Stacey Mack .15 .40
79 Antowain Smith .20 .50
80 Kabeer Gbaja-Biamila .15 .40
81 Curtis Martin .20 .50
82 Marcellus Wiley .15 .40
83 Gary Walker .15 .40
84 Kalimba Edwards .15 .40
85 Stephen Davis .15 .40
86 Antwaan Randle El .15 .40
87 Curtis Conway .15 .40
88 Keith Brooking .20 .50
89 Mark Word RC .15 .40
90 Greg Ellis .25 .60
91 Steve McNair .20 .50
92 Ashley Lelie .15 .40
93 Kelly Holcomb .15 .40
94 Darrell Jackson .20 .50
95 Mark Brunell .20 .50
96 Hugh Douglas .15 .40
97 Kendrell Bell .15 .40
98 Steve Smith .25 .60
99 Bill Schroeder .15 .40
100 Darren Howard .20 .50
101 Kevan Barlow .15 .40
102 Marshall Faulk .20 .50
103 Ike Hilliard .15 .40
104 T.J. Duckett .15 .40
105 Bobby Taylor .20 .50
106 Kevin Carter .15 .40
107 Darren Sharper .15 .40
108 Marty Booker .15 .40
109 Isaac Bruce .25 .60
110 Kevin Hardy .15 .40
111 Tai Streets .15 .40
112 Brad Johnson .20 .50
113 Daunte Culpepper .20 .50
114 Kevin Johnson .15 .40
115 Matt Hasselbeck .15 .40
116 Jabar Gaffney .15 .40
117 Takeo Spikes .15 .40
118 Brett Favre .50 1.25
119 Keyshawn Johnson .25 .60
120 David Akers .20 .50
121 Maurice Morris .15 .40
122 Jake Delhomme .15 .40
123 Kordell Stewart .15 .40
124 Terrell Davis .20 .50
125 Brian Kelly .15 .40
126 David Terrell .15 .40
127 Koren Robinson .20 .50
128 Michael Strahan .20 .50
129 Jake Plummer .15 .40
130 Terrell Owens .20 .50
131 Brian Urlacher .25 .60
132 David Patten .15 .40
133 Michael Vick .20 .50
134 Jamal Lewis .20 .50
135 Terry Glenn .20 .50
136 Brian Simmons .15 .40
137 David Boston .15 .40
138 Michael Bennett .15 .40
139 James Stewart .15 .40
140 Tiki Barber .20 .50
141 Brian Griese .15 .40
142 Deion Branch .15 .40
143 Mike Peterson .15 .40
144 James Mungro .15 .40
145 Tim Couch .15 .40
146 Brian Dawkins .25 .60
147 Dennis Northcutt .15 .40
148 Mike Alstott .15 .40
149 James Thrash .15 .40
150 Tim Brown .25 .60
151 Brian Finneran .15 .40
152 Derrick Brooks .15 .40
153 Muhsin Muhammad .15 .40
154 Jason Elam .15 .40
155 Tim Dwight .15 .40
156 Bruce Smith .20 .50
157 Derrick Mason .15 .40
158 Napoleon Harris .15 .40
159 Jason Gildon .20 .50
160 Todd Heap .15 .40
161 Aaron Schobel .20 .50
162 Derrius Thompson .15 .40
163 Nate Clements .20 .50
164 Jason McAddley .15 .40
165 Todd Pinkston .15 .40
166 Bubba Franks .20 .50
167 Deuce McAllister .20 .50
168 Patrick Surtain .15 .40
169 Javon Walker .20 .50
170 Tom Brady 1.00 2.50
171 Dexter Coakley .20 .50
172 Patrick Kerney .15 .40
173 Jay Fiedler .15 .40
174 Tommy Maddox .15 .40
175 Donald Driver .20 .50
176 Patrick Ramsey .20 .50
177 Olandis Gary .15 .40
178 Tony Gonzalez .20 .50
179 Donnie Edwards .15 .40
180 Peter Boulware .20 .50
181 Jeff Blake .20 .50
182 Torry Holt .20 .50
183 Donovan McNabb .20 .50
184 Peter Warrick .15 .40
185 Jeff Garcia .15 .40
186 Travis Henry .15 .40
187 Doug Jolley .15 .40
188 Peyton Manning .60 1.50
189 Jerome Bettis .25 .60
190 Travis Taylor .15 .40
191 Drew Brees .25 .60
192 Phillip Buchanon .15 .40
193 Jerramy Stevens .20 .50
194 Trent Green .15 .40
195 Duce Staley .15 .40
196 Plaxico Burress .15 .40
197 Jerry Porter .15 .40
198 Trevor Pryce .20 .50
199 Dwight Freeney .15 .40
200 Quincy Morgan .15 .40
201 Troy Vincent .20 .50
202 Randy McMichael .15 .40
203 Troy Hambrick .15 .40
204 Randy Moss .20 .50
205 Troy Brown .15 .40
206 Ray Lewis .25 .60
207 Trung Canidate .15 .40
208 Raynoch Thompson .15 .40
209 Ty Law .25 .60
210 Reggie Wayne .20 .50
211 Warren Sapp .20 .50
212 Richard Seymour .20 .50
213 Warrick Dunn .15 .40
214 Robert Ferguson .15 .40
215 Wayne Chrebet .15 .40
216 Rod Coleman RC .15 .40
217 Will Allen .20 .50
218 Rod Woodson .20 .50
219 Zach Thomas .20 .50
220 Rod Smith .20 .50
221 Ricky Williams .20 .50
222 LaDainian Tomlinson .25 .60
223 Priest Holmes .15 .40
224 Rich Gannon .20 .50
225 Drew Bledsoe .20 .50
226 Kerry Collins .15 .40
227 Marvin Harrison .20 .50
228 Hines Ward .20 .50
229 Peerless Price .15 .40
230 Jason Taylor .20 .50
231 Jeremy Shockey .15 .40
232 Clinton Portis .15 .40
233 Antonio Bryant .15 .40
234 Donte Stallworth .15 .40
235 David Carr .15 .40
236 Joey Harrington .15 .40
237 William Green .15 .40
238 Julius Peppers .25 .60
239 Shipp/Thompson/Wilson .12 .30
240 Michael Vick .15 .40
Warrick Dunn
Brian Finneran
Keith Brooking
241 Lewis/Hartwell/Taylor/Reed .15 .40
242 Bled/Henry/Mould/Fletch .15 .40
243 Peppers/Smith/Muhammad .20 .50
244 Booker/Urlacher/Thomas .20 .50
245 Dillon/Smith/Johnson/Kitna .15 .40
246 Couch/Green/Morgan/Word .12 .30
247 Hutchinson/Galloway/Williams/Ellis .20 .50
248 Portis/Smith/Wilson .15 .40
249 Joey Harrington .12 .30
James Stewart
Bill Schroeder
Kalimba Edwards
250 Favre/Grn/Driver/KGB .40 1.00
251 Carr/Wells/Bradford/Glenn .12 .30
252 Mann/James/Harr/Freen .50 1.25
253 Brunell/Taylor/Smith/McCree .15 .40
254 Green/Holmes/Kenn/Hicks .12 .30
255 Willms/Chamb/Thom/Tayl .15 .40
256 Culp/Benn/Moss/Williams .15 .40
257 Brady/Smith/Brown/Vina .75 2.00
258 Brooks/McAllister/Horn/Howard .15 .40
259 Collins/Barber/Toomer/Strahan .15 .40
260 Pennington/Martin/Chrebet/Abraham .15 .40
261 Gann/Grnr/Rice/Wdsn .40 1.00
262 McNabb/Staley/Pinkston/Taylor .15 .40
263 Maddox/Zereoue/Ward/Gildon/Porter .15 .40
264 Brees/Tomlinson/Edwards .20 .50
265 Garcia/Hearst/Owens/Carter .15 .40
266 Hasselbeck/Alexander/Robin/Tongue .15 .40
267 Bulger/Faulk/Holt/Little .15 .40
268 B.John/Key.John/S.Rice/Kelly .40 1.00
269 McNair/George/Mason/Schulters .15 .40
270 Ramsey/Gardner/Smoot .15 .40
271 Carson Palmer RC .60 1.50
272 Kyle Boller RC .30 .75
273 Byron Leftwich RC .40 1.00
274 Willis McGahee RC .40 1.00
275 Larry Johnson RC .40 1.00
276 Charles Rogers RC .40 1.00
277 Andre Johnson RC .75 2.00
278 Bryant Johnson RC .50 1.25
279 Rex Grossman RC .40 1.00
280 Taylor Jacobs RC .30 .75
281 Rober RC/Sull RC/Will RC .50 1.25
282 Bennie Joppru RC .40 1.00
Domanick Davis RC
Dave Ragone RC
283 Witt RC/Clark RC/Smith RC 1.25 3.00
284 Edwds RC/Smith RC/Bail RC .40 1.00
285 Lee Suggs RC .30 .75
Chris Brown RC
Onterrio Smith RC
286 Griff RC/Pinn RC/Askew RC .40 1.00
287 Farg RC/Gabr RC/Johns RC .50 1.25
288 Kenn RC/Joseph RC/Warr RC .40 1.00
289 Sug RC/Hayn RC/McDo RC .40 1.00
290 Wash RC/Curt RC/Burles RC .40 1.00
291 Wall RC/Dors RC/Simms RC .40 1.00
292 Wade RC/Aiken RC/Gage RC .40 1.00
293 McCull RC/Sapp RC/Grah RC .50 1.25
294 Kelly RC/Gard RC/Tolv RC .40 1.00
295 Jhnsn RC/Bld RC/Calic RC .50 1.25
296 Lyd RC/McMl RC/McD RC .50 1.25
297 Kels RC/White RC/Doss RC .50 1.25
298 Newm RC/Truf RC/Wool RC .50 1.25
299 Romo RC/King.RC/St.P RC 5.00 12.00
300 Pinn RC/Toef RC/Cobou RC .40 1.00

2003 Fleer Tradition Minis

*VETS 1-270: 5X TO 12X BASIC CARDS
*ROOKIES 271-300: 2.5X TO 6X
STATED PRINT RUN 125 SER.#'d SETS
RANDOM INSERTS IN RETAIL PACKS
299 K.Kingsbury/T.Romo/B.St.Pierre 20.00 50.00

2003 Fleer Tradition Tiffany

*VETS 1-270: 3X TO 8X BASIC CARDS
*ROOKIES 271-300: 1.5X TO 4X
STATED PRINT RUN 200 SER.#'d SETS
299 K.Kingsbury/T.Romo/B.St.Pierre 12.00 30.00

2003 Fleer Tradition Classic Combinations

1-10 STATED PRINT RUN 1500 SER.#'d SETS
11-20 STATED PRINT RUN 750 SER.#'d SETS
21-30 STATED PRINT RUN 375 SER.#'d SETS
1 E.Campbell/P.Holmes 1.00 2.50
2 P.Burress/C.Rogers .75 2.00
3 E.Jones/T.Suggs .50 1.25
4 E.James/W.McGahee .50 1.25
5 M.Allen/C.Palmer .75 2.00
6 F.Tarkenton/C.Pennington 1.00 2.50
7 M.Vick/B.Leftwich .75 2.00
8 D.Flutie/D.Bledsoe .75 2.00
9 P.Manning/T.Henry 2.50 6.00
10 K.Stabler/R.Gannon 1.25 3.00
11 R.Moss/T.Owens 1.00 2.50
12 Bo.Griese/Ri.Williams 1.00 2.50
13 R.Lott/Ro.Williams 1.00 2.50
14 J.Ham/K.Bell 1.00 2.50
15 D.Carr/A.Johnson 1.25 3.00
16 B.Favre/K.Warner 2.50 6.00
17 F.Biletnikoff/J.Rice 2.50 6.00
18 J.Harrington/C.Rogers .60 1.50
19 C.Pennington/B.Leftwich .60 1.50
20 K.Stabler/M.Vick 1.50 4.00
21 F.Tarkenton/B.Favre 3.00 8.00
22 D.McNabb/M.Harrison 1.25 3.00
23 C.Portis/W.McGahee .75 2.00
24 E.Smith/R.Grossman 2.50 6.00
25 J.Ham/B.Urlacher 1.50 4.00
26 M.Allen/M.Faulk 1.50 4.00
27 J.Shockey/A.Johnson 1.50 4.00
28 F.Biletnikoff/T.Brown 1.50 4.00
29 C.Palmer/B.Leftwich 1.25 3.00
30 E.Jones/J.Peppers 1.50 4.00

2003 Fleer Tradition Classic Combinations Memorabilia

Inserted into packs at a rate of 1:72, this set features authentic game worn jersey swatches.

STATED ODDS 1:72
1 E.Campbell JSY/P.Holmes 5.00 12.00
2 M.Allen JSY/C.Palmer 5.00 12.00
3 Bo.Griese JSY/Ri.Williams 5.00 12.00
4 M.Vick JSY/K.Stabler 5.00 12.00
5 K.Warner JSY/B.Favre 6.00 15.00
6 F.Biletnikoff JSY/T.Brown 5.00 12.00
7 F.Biletnikoff JSY/J.Rice 5.00 12.00
8 M.Vick JSY/B.Leftwich 3.00 8.00
9 E.Jones JSY/T.Suggs 3.00 8.00
10 R.Lott JSY/Ro.Williams 5.00 12.00
11 D.Flutie JSY/D.Bledsoe 3.00 8.00
12 C.Pennington JSY/F.Tark. 4.00 10.00
13 C.Portis JSY/W.McGahee 1.50 4.00
14 M.Allen JSY/M.Faulk 5.00 12.00
15 J.Shockey JSY/A.Johnson 4.00 10.00
16 D.Bledsoe JSY/D.Flutie 3.00 8.00
17 B.Urlacher JSY/J.Ham 4.00 10.00
18 P.Holmes JSY/E.Campbell 4.00 10.00
19 P.Burress JSY/C.Rogers 3.00 8.00
20 P.Manning JSY/T.Henry 10.00 25.00
21 E.James JSY/W.McGahee 5.00 12.00
22 T.Brown JSY/F.Biletnikoff 4.00 10.00
23 M.Harrison JSY/D.McNabb 3.00 8.00
24 Ric.Williams JSY/Bo.Griese 4.00 10.00
25 T.Owens JSY/R.Moss 3.00 8.00

2003 Fleer Tradition Classic Combinations Memorabilia Duals

1 E.Campbell/P.Holmes 6.00 15.00
2 F.Biletnikoff/T.Brown 6.00 15.00
3 E.Jones/J.Peppers 6.00 15.00
4 D.Flutie/D.Bledsoe 5.00 12.00
5 M.Allen/M.Faulk 6.00 15.00
6 F.Biletnikoff/J.Rice 12.00 30.00
7 D.McNabb/M.Harrison 5.00 12.00
8 P.Manning/T.Henry 15.00 40.00
9 B.Favre/K.Warner 12.00 30.00
10 R.Moss/T.Owens 5.00 12.00
11 R.Lott/Ro.Williams 5.00 12.00
12 F.Tarkenton/B.Favre 12.00 30.00
13 B.Griese/R.Williams 6.00 15.00
14 K.Stabler/M.Vick 8.00 20.00
15 F.Tarkenton/C.Pennington 6.00 15.00

2003 Fleer Tradition Rookie Sensations

STATED PRINT RUN 1250 SER.#'d SETS
1 Kyle Boller .60 1.50
2 Taylor Jacobs .60 1.50
3 Terence Newman 1.00 2.50
4 Kelley Washington .60 1.50
5 Carson Palmer 1.25 3.00
6 Byron Leftwich .75 2.00
7 Willis McGahee .75 2.00
8 Bethel Johnson .60 1.50
9 Kevin Curtis .60 1.50
10 Charles Rogers .75 2.00
11 Rex Grossman .75 2.00
12 Larry Johnson .75 2.00
13 Anquan Boldin 1.00 2.50
14 Andre Johnson 1.50 4.00
15 Bryant Johnson 1.00 2.50
16 Terrell Suggs .75 2.00
17 Tyrone Calico .60 1.50
18 Chris Simms .60 1.50
19 DeWayne Robertson .75 2.00
20 Nate Burleson .75 2.00

2003 Fleer Tradition Standouts

COMPLETE SET (10) 10.00 25.00
STATED ODDS 1:36
1 Ricky Williams .75 2.00
2 Michael Vick .75 2.00
3 Brett Favre 2.00 5.00
4 Randy Moss .75 2.00
5 Chad Pennington .60 1.50
6 Jerry Rice 2.00 5.00
7 Clinton Portis .60 1.50
8 Brian Urlacher 1.00 2.50
9 Donovan McNabb .75 2.00
10 Tom Brady 4.00 10.00

2003 Fleer Tradition Throwbacks

COMPLETE SET (10) 15.00 40.00
STATED ODDS 1:72
1 Marcus Allen 2.00 5.00
2 Bob Griese 2.00 5.00
3 Jack Ham 1.50 4.00
4 Ken Stabler 2.50 6.00
5 Fran Tarkenton 2.00 5.00
6 Earl Campbell 2.00 5.00
7 Fred Biletnikoff 2.00 5.00
8 Ed Too Tall Jones 1.25 3.00
9 Ronnie Lott 1.50 4.00
10 Doug Flutie 1.50 4.00

2003 Fleer Tradition Throwbacks Memorabilia

Inserted into packs at a rate of 1:288, this set features authentic game worn jersey swatches. A patch version also exists, with each card serial numbered to 100.

STATED ODDS 1:288
*PATCH/100: .6X TO 1.5X BASIC JSY
PATCHES PRINT RUN 100 SER.#'d SETS
1 Marcus Allen 3.00 8.00
2 Earl Campbell 3.00 8.00
3 Bob Griese 3.00 8.00
4 Ronnie Lott 2.50 6.00
5 Fran Tarkenton 3.00 8.00

2004 Fleer Tradition

Fleer Tradition initially released in early July 2004. The base set consists of 360-cards including 20-rookies and 10-multi player rookie cards. Hobby boxes contained 36-packs of 10-cards each and carried and S.R.P. of $1.49. Four parallel sets and a variety of inserts can be found seeded in hobby and retail packs highlighted by the multi-tiered Rookie Throwback Threads inserts.

COMPLETE SET (360) 50.00 100.00
COMP.SET w/o SP's (330) 15.00 30.00
331-350 ROOKIE STATED ODDS 1:4 H/R
351-360 ROOKIE STATED ODDS 1:18H, 1:24R
1 Dolphins TL .15 .40
2 Bills TL .15 .40
3 Patriots TL .30 .75
4 Jets TL .15 .40
5 Colts TL .30 .75
6 Jaguars TL .15 .40
7 Titans TL .08 .25
8 Texans TL .15 .40
9 Raiders TL .25 .60
10 Broncos TL .15 .40
11 Chiefs TL .15 .40
12 Chargers TL .20 .50
13 Steelers TL .25 .60
14 Browns TL .08 .25
15 Bengals TL .15 .40
16 Ravens TL .15 .40
17 Eagles TL .15 .40
18 Giants TL .15 .40
19 Redskins TL .15 .40
20 Cowboys TL .15 .40
21 Vikings TL .25 .60
22 Packers TL .30 .75
23 Bears TL .25 .60
24 Lions TL .15 .40
25 49ers TL .15 .40
26 Rams TL .15 .40
27 Seahawks TL .15 .40
28 Cardinals TL .08 .25
29 Panthers TL .15 .40
30 BuccaneersTL .08 .25
31 Falcons TL .08 .25
32 Saints TL .15 .40
33 Anquan Boldin .12 .30
34 Michael Vick .15 .40
35 Kyle Boller .12 .30
36 Aeneas Williams .12 .30
37 Jake Delhomme .12 .30
38 Rex Grossman .12 .30
39 Carson Palmer .15 .40
40 Quincy Morgan .12 .30
41 Terry Glenn .15 .40
42 Jake Plummer .12 .30
43 Joey Harrington .12 .30
44 Brett Favre .40 1.00
45 Jeff Garcia .12 .30
46 Peyton Manning .50 1.25
47 Byron Leftwich .12 .30
48 Trent Green .12 .30
49 A.J. Feeley .12 .30
50 Daunte Culpepper .15 .40
51 Tom Brady .75 2.00
52 Aaron Brooks .12 .30
53 Kerry Collins .12 .30
54 Chad Pennington .12 .30
55 Rich Gannon .15 .40
56 Donovan McNabb .15 .40
57 Tommy Maddox .12 .30
58 Drew Brees .20 .50
59 Terrell Owens .15 .40
60 Matt Hasselbeck .12 .30
61 Kurt Warner .15 .40
62 Brad Johnson .15 .40
63 Jerome Bettis .20 .50
64 Keith Bulluck .12 .30
65 Rod Gardner .12 .30
66 Eddie George .15 .40
67 Warren Sapp .15 .40
68 Marc Bulger .12 .30
69 Shaun Alexander .12 .30
70 Tai Streets .12 .30
71 LaDainian Tomlinson .20 .50
72 Steve McNair .15 .40
73 Brian Westbrook .12 .30
74 Jerry Rice .40 1.00
75 Santana Moss .15 .40
76 Moe Williams .12 .30
77 Deuce McAllister .15 .40
78 Adam Vinatieri .12 .30
79 Randy Moss .15 .40
80 Ricky Williams .15 .40
81 Priest Holmes .12 .30
82 Jimmy Smith .15 .40
83 Edgerrin James .15 .40
84 Andre Johnson .15 .40
85 Ahman Green .12 .30
86 Charles Rogers .15 .40
87 Champ Bailey .12 .30
88 Roy Williams S .15 .40
89 Tim Couch .12 .30
90 Corey Dillon .12 .30
91 Thomas Jones .12 .30
92 Stephen Davis .12 .30
93 Travis Henry .15 .40
94 Jamal Lewis .12 .30
95 Warrick Dunn .30 .75
96 Emmitt Smith .15 .40
97 Mark Brunell .12 .30
98 Willis McGahee .12 .30
99 Duce Staley .15 .40
100 Lee Suggs .15 .40
101 Rod Smith .15 .40
102 Marvin Harrison .12 .30
103 Larry Johnson .12 .30
104 Michael Bennett .12 .30
105 Donte Stallworth .15 .40
106 DeShaun Foster .15 .40
107 Hines Ward .12 .30
108 T.J. Duckett .20 .50
109 Brian Urlacher .12 .30
110 Boss Bailey .20 .50
111 Tim Brown .12 .30
112 David Boston .15 .40
113 Marshall Faulk .15 .40
114 Jason Witten .12 .30
115 Richard Seymour
116 Domanick Davis .12 .30
117 Jon Kitna .12 .30
118 Ray Lewis .20 .50
119 Tedy Bruschi .15 .40
120 Chris Chambers .12 .30
121 Freddie Mitchell .12 .30
122 Amani Toomer .12 .30
123 Curtis Martin .15 .40
124 Eric Moulds .12 .30
125 Darrell Jackson .15 .40
126 Clinton Portis .12 .30
127 Jay Fiedler .12 .30
128 Todd Heap .12 .30
129 Dexter Jackson .12 .30
130 James Jackson .12 .30
131 Shannon Sharpe .15 .40
132 Donald Driver .15 .40
133 Billy Miller .12 .30
134 Dante Hall .12 .30
135 Onterrio Smith .12 .30
136 Joe Horn .12 .30
137 Shaun Ellis .12 .30
138 L.J. Smith .15 .40
139 Jerry Porter .12 .30
140 Reggie Wayne .15 .40
141 Derrick Brooks .12 .30
142 Terrell Suggs .12 .30
143 Randy McMichael .12 .30
144 Mike Alstott .12 .30
145 Nate Poole RC .20 .50
146 Chris Brown .12 .30
147 Torry Holt .15 .40
148 Adewale Ogunleye .15 .40
149 Peter Warrick .12 .30
150 Alge Crumpler .15 .40
151 Charlie Garner .15 .40
152 Jeremy Shockey .12 .30
153 Simeon Rice .12 .30
154 Julian Peterson .15 .40
155 Patrick Ramsey .15 .40
156 Shawn Springs .12 .30
157 Marcus Stroud .12 .30
158 Keyshawn Johnson .15 .40
159 Steve Smith .20 .50
160 Ty Law .20 .50
161 Derrick Mason .12 .30
162 Josh Reed .12 .30
163 Fred Smoot .12 .30
164 Muhsin Muhammad .12 .30
165 Justin Gage .15 .40
166 Chad Johnson .12 .30
167 Dennis Northcutt .12 .30
168 Joey Galloway .15 .40
169 Ashley Lelie .12 .30
170 Casey Fitzsimmons .12 .30
171 Dwight Freeney .12 .30
172 Nick Barnett .12 .30
173 LaBrandon Toefield .12 .30
174 Jabar Gaffney .12 .30
175 Tony Gonzalez .15 .40
176 Zach Thomas .15 .40
177 Nate Burleson .15 .40
178 Deion Branch .12 .30
179 Boo Williams .12 .30
180 Michael Strahan .15 .40
181 Anthony Becht .12 .30
182 Charles Woodson .20 .50
183 Sheldon Brown .12 .30
184 Kendrell Bell .12 .30
185 Kassim Osgood .12 .30
186 Tony Parrish .12 .30
187 Marcel Shipp .12 .30
188 Bobby Engram .12 .30
189 Keith Brooking .12 .30
190 Isaac Bruce .20 .50
191 Travis Taylor .12 .30
192 Charles Lee .12 .30
193 Takeo Spikes .12 .30
194 Justin McCareins .12 .30
195 Julius Peppers .15 .40
196 LaVar Arrington .12 .30
197 Dez White .15 .40
198 Rudi Johnson .12 .30
199 Andre Davis .12 .30
200 Quincy Carter .12 .30
201 Quentin Griffin .12 .30
202 Dallas Clark .12 .30
203 Artose Pinner .12 .30
204 Kevin Johnson .12 .30
205 Kabeer Gbaja-Biamila .12 .30
206 Marcus Coleman .12 .30
207 Johnnie Morton .15 .40
208 Jason Taylor .15 .40
209 Kevin Williams .12 .30
210 David Givens .12 .30
211 Charles Grant .12 .30
212 Ike Hilliard .12 .30
213 Wayne Chrebet .12 .30
214 Teyo Johnson .12 .30
215 Brian Dawkins .12 .30
216 Antwaan Randle El .12 .30
217 Eric Parker .15 .40
218 Josh McCown .15 .40
219 Tim Rattay .12 .30
220 Brian Finneran .12 .30
221 Chad Brown .12 .30
222 Ed Reed .15 .40
223 Dane Looker .12 .30
224 Aaron Schobel .12 .30
225 Joe Jurevicius .12 .30
226 Ricky Manning .12 .30
227 Jevon Kearse .12 .30
228 Laveranues Coles .12 .30
229 Kelley Washington .12 .30
230 William Green .12 .30
231 Terence Newman .15 .40
232 Bryant Johnson .12 .30
233 Peerless Price .12 .30
234 Peter Boulware .12 .30
235 Drew Bledsoe .15 .40
236 Kris Jenkins .15 .40
237 Marty Booker .12 .30
238 Matt Schobel .12 .30
239 Earl Little .12 .30
240 Antonio Bryant .15 .40
241 Al Wilson .12 .30
242 Dre Bly .12 .30
243 Javon Walker .12 .30
244 David Carr .12 .30
245 Mike Vanderjagt .12 .30
246 Fred Taylor .12 .30
247 Eddie Kennison .15 .40
248 Patrick Surtain .12 .30
249 Jim Kleinsasser .12 .30
250 Daniel Graham .12 .30
251 Jerome Pathon .12 .30
252 Tiki Barber .15 .40
253 John Abraham .12 .30
254 Justin Fargas .15 .40
255 Correll Buckhalter .12 .30
256 Plaxico Burress .12 .30
257 Quentin Jammer .12 .30
258 Kevan Barlow .12 .30
259 Koren Robinson .12 .30
260 Leonard Little .12 .30
261 John Lynch .15 .40
262 Tyrone Calico .15 .40
263 Taylor Jacobs .12 .30
264 Joey Porter .15 .40
265 Freddie Jones .12 .30
266 Marcus Pollard .12 .30
267 Mike Peterson .12 .30
268 Justin Griffith .12 .30
269 Shawn Bryson .12 .30
270 Will Allen .12 .30
271 Antonio Gates .20 .50

272 Chris McAlister .12 .30
273 Tony Hollings .12 .30
274 Cedrick Wilson .12 .30
275 Adam Archuleta .12 .30
276 London Fletcher .15 .40
277 Drew Bennett .15 .40
278 Rod Smart .15 .40
279 LaMont Jordan .15 .40
280 Jerry Azumah .12 .30
281 Bubba Franks .12 .30
282 Troy Edwards .12 .30
283 Willie McGinest .15 .40
284 Morten Andersen .12 .30
285 Dat Nguyen .12 .30
286 Samari Rolle .12 .30
287 Brian Simmons .12 .30
288 Chike Okeafor .15 .40
289 Rodney Harrison .12 .30
290 Jason Elam .12 .30
291 Tim Dwight .12 .30
292 Corey Bradford .12 .30
293 Charles Tillman .15 .40
294 Tim Carter .12 .30
295 Ahmed Plummer .12 .30
296 Troy Walters .12 .30
297 Michael Lewis .15 .40
298 Tory James .12 .30
299 Doug Flutie .15 .40
300 Az-Zahir Hakim .12 .30
301 Itula Mili .12 .30
302 Jamie Sharper .12 .30
303 Vonnie Holliday .12 .30
304 Brian Russell RC .20 .50
305 Bryan Gilmore .12 .30
306 Darren Sharper .12 .30
307 Kyle Brady .12 .30
308 David Tyree .12 .30
309 Andre Carter .12 .30
310 Lawyer Milloy .12 .30
311 David Terrell .12 .30
312 Richie Anderson .12 .30
313 Darren Howard .12 .30
314 Sebastian Janikowski .12 .30
315 Kimo von Oelhoffen .12 .30
316 Donnie Edwards .15 .40
317 Brandon Lloyd .15 .40
318 Robert Ferguson .12 .30
319 Derek Smith .12 .30
320 Anthony Thomas .15 .40
321 Ken Hamlin .12 .30
322 Ronde Barber .12 .30
323 Erron Kinney .12 .30
324 Tom Brady AW .60 1.50
325 Peyton Manning AW .40 1.00
326 Steve McNair AW .12 .30
327 Jamal Lewis AW .12 .30
328 Ray Lewis AW .15 .40
329 Anquan Boldin AW .10 .25
330 Terrell Suggs AW .10 .25
331 Eli Manning RC 4.00 10.00
332 Larry Fitzgerald RC 2.00 5.00
333 Ben Roethlisberger RC 4.00 10.00
334 Tatum Bell RC .50 1.25
335 Roy Williams RC .50 1.25
336 Drew Henson RC .50 1.25
337 Philip Rivers RC 4.00 10.00
338 Rashaun Woods RC .50 1.25
339 Kevin Jones RC .60 1.50
340 Sean Taylor RC 3.00 8.00
341 Steven Jackson RC .75 2.00
342 Kellen Winslow RC .50 1.25
343 Chris Perry RC .50 1.25
344 J.P. Losman RC .50 1.25
345 Greg Jones RC .50 1.25
346 Reggie Williams RC .50 1.25
347 Michael Clayton RC .60 1.50
348 Jonathan Vilma RC .60 1.50
349 Julius Jones RC .50 1.25
350 Michael Jenkins RC .50 1.25
351 E.Manning/Rivers/Roethlis. 15.00 30.00
352 Fitzgerald/Re.Will/Ro.Will. 3.00 8.00
353 Evans RC/Berr.RC/Ham.RC .50 1.25
354 Ude.RC/Poole RC/Colb.RC .75 2.00
355 Gamb.RC/Rob.RC/Hall RC .75 2.00
356 Trou.RC/Wats.RC/Harts.RC .60 1.50
357 Darl.RC/Morant RC/Wilf.RC .60 1.50
358 McCo.RC/Pick.RC/Sch.RC .50 1.25
359 Bell/Turn.RC/Cobbs RC .50 1.25
360 Moore RC/Wils.RC/Kni.RC .60 1.50

2004 Fleer Tradition Blue

*VETS: 1X TO 2.5X BASIC CARDS
*ROOKIES 331-350: .6X TO 1.5X
*ROOKIES 351-360: .6X TO 1.5X

2004 Fleer Tradition Crystal

*VETS: 5X TO 12X BASIC CARDS
*ROOKIES 331-350: 2.5X TO 6X
*ROOKIES 351-360: 2.5X TO 6X
1-330 PRINT RUN 150 SER.#'d SETS
331-350 PRINT RUN 75 SER.#'d SETS
351-360 PRINT RUN 25 SER.#'d SETS

2004 Fleer Tradition Draft Day

*ROOKIES 331-350: 1X TO 2.5X
*ROOKIES 351-360: 1X TO 2.5X
DRAFT DAY/375 ODDS ONE PER HOT PACK
STATED PRINT RUN 375 SER.#'d SETS

2004 Fleer Tradition Green

*VETS: 1.5X TO 4X BASIC CARDS
*ROOKIES 331-350: 1X TO 2.5X
*ROOKIES 351-360: 1X TO 2.5X

2004 Fleer Tradition Classic Combinations

COMBOS/250 ODDS 1:144 H, 1:360 R
STATED PRINT RUN 250 SER.#'d SETS
1CC J.Rice/L.Fitzgerald 5.00 12.00
2CC Rivers/E.Manning 10.00 25.00
3CC P.Manning/E.Manning 12.50 25.00
4CC C.Palmer/C.Perry 1.50 4.00
5CC Pennington/Roethlisberger 10.00 25.00
6CC C.Portis/T.Bell 1.25 3.00
7CC T.Brady/D.Henson 8.00 20.00
8CC J.Shockey/K.Winslow Jr. 1.25 3.00
9CC M.Vick/K.Jones 1.50 4.00
10CC Ro.Williams S/S.Taylor 8.00 20.00
11CC Ri.Williams/Ro.Will.WR 1.50 4.00
12CC A.Boldin/G.Jones 1.25 3.00
13CC Ch.Johnson/S.Jackson 2.00 5.00
14CC B.Leftwich/Reg.Williams 1.25 3.00
15CC C.Rogers/Ro.Williams WR 1.25 3.00
16CC B.Favre/P.Rivers 4.00 10.00
17CC R.Moss/R.Woods 1.50 4.00
18CC C.Chambers/L.Evans 2.00 5.00
19CC D.Henson/J.Jones 1.25 3.00
20CC P.Ramsey/J.Losman 1.50 4.00

2004 Fleer Tradition Gridiron Tributes

COMPLETE SET (20) 15.00 40.00
STATED ODDS 1:6 HOB/RET
1GT Steve McNair .60 1.50
2GT Tom Brady 3.00 8.00
3GT Peyton Manning 2.00 5.00
4GT Chad Pennington .50 1.25
5GT Donovan McNabb .60 1.50
6GT Brett Favre 1.50 4.00
7GT Jerry Rice 1.50 4.00
8GT Emmitt Smith 1.25 3.00
9GT Ricky Williams .60 1.50
10GT Priest Holmes .50 1.25
11GT LaDainian Tomlinson .75 2.00
12GT Jeremy Shockey .50 1.25
13GT Byron Leftwich .50 1.25
14GT Marvin Harrison .60 1.50
15GT Jamal Lewis .60 1.50
16GT Ahman Green .60 1.50
17GT Brian Urlacher .75 2.00
18GT Michael Vick .60 1.50
19GT Clinton Portis .50 1.25
20GT Randy Moss .60 1.50

2004 Fleer Tradition Gridiron Tributes Game Used

STATED ODDS 1:51 HOB, 1:192 RET
*PATCH/50: 1X TO 2.5X BASIC JSY
PATCH STATED PRINT RUN 50
GTAG Ahman Green 2.50 6.00
GTBF Brett Favre 6.00 15.00
GTBL Byron Leftwich 2.00 5.00
GTBU Brian Urlacher 3.00 8.00
GTCP Chad Pennington 2.00 5.00
GTCP2 Clinton Portis 2.00 5.00
GTDM Donovan McNabb 2.50 6.00
GTES Emmitt Smith 5.00 12.00
GTJL Jamal Lewis 2.50 6.00
GTJR Jerry Rice 6.00 15.00
GTJS Jeremy Shockey 2.00 5.00
GTLT LaDainian Tomlinson 3.00 8.00
GTMH Marvin Harrison 2.50 6.00
GTMV Michael Vick 2.50 6.00
GTPH Priest Holmes 2.00 5.00
GTPM Peyton Manning 8.00 20.00
GTRM Randy Moss 2.50 6.00
GTRW Ricky Williams 2.50 6.00
GTSM Steve McNair 2.50 6.00
GTTB Tom Brady 12.00 30.00

2004 Fleer Tradition Rookie Hat's Off

HAT'S OFF/100 ODDS 1:9 HOT PACKS
HOBR Ben Roethlisberger 20.00 50.00
HOCP Chris Perry 4.00 10.00
HOEM Eli Manning 20.00 50.00
HOGJ Greg Jones 4.00 10.00
HOJJ Julius Jones 4.00 10.00
HOJL J.P. Losman 4.00 10.00
HOKJ Kevin Jones 5.00 12.00
HOKW Kellen Winslow Jr. 4.00 10.00
HOLE Lee Evans 6.00 15.00
HOLF Larry Fitzgerald 15.00 40.00
HOMC Michael Clayton 5.00 12.00
HOMJ Michael Jenkins 4.00 10.00
HOPR Philip Rivers 15.00 40.00
HORW Roy Williams WR 4.00 10.00
HORW2 Rashaun Woods 4.00 10.00
HORW3 Reggie Williams 4.00 10.00
HOSJ Steven Jackson 6.00 15.00
HOTB Tatum Bell 4.00 10.00

2004 Fleer Tradition Rookie Throwback Threads Footballs

FOOTBALL ODDS 1:108 HOB, 1:480 RET
*HELMETS: .5X TO 1.2X FOOTBALLS
HELMET ODDS 1:360 HOB, 1:960 RET
*JERSEYS: .3X TO .8X FOOTBALLS
JERSEY ODDS 1:58 HOB, 1:240 RET
*JERSEY/BALL: 1X TO 2.5X FOOTBALLS
JSY/BALL PRINT RUN 50 SER.#'d SETS
*JERSEY/HELMET: 1.2X TO 3X FOOTBALLS
JSY/HELMET PRINT RUN 25 SER.#'d SETS
TTBR Ben Roethlisberger 20.00 50.00
TTCP Chris Perry 2.50 6.00
TTEM Eli Manning Blue 15.00 40.00
TTGJ Greg Jones 2.50 6.00
TTJJ Julius Jones 2.50 6.00
TTJL J.P. Losman 2.50 6.00
TTKJ Kevin Jones 3.00 8.00
TTKW Kellen Winslow Jr. Wht 2.50 6.00
TTLE Lee Evans 4.00 10.00
TTLF Larry Fitzgerald 10.00 25.00
TTLM Luke McCown 2.50 6.00
TTMC Michael Clayton 3.00 8.00
TTMJ Michael Jenkins 2.50 6.00
TTMS Matt Schaub 2.50 6.00
TTPR Philip Rivers 10.00 25.00
TTRW Roy Williams WR 2.50 6.00
TTSJ Steven Jackson 4.00 10.00
TTTB Tatum Bell 2.50 6.00
TTEM2 Eli Manning Wht 15.00 40.00
TTKW2 Kellen Winslow Jr. Blue 2.50 6.00
TTRW2 Rashaun Woods 2.50 6.00
TTRW3 Reggie Williams 2.50 6.00

2004 Fleer Tradition Rookie Throwback Threads Dual Jerseys

STATED PRINT RUN 100 SER.#'d SETS
*PATCH/75: .5X TO 1.2X BASIC DUAL
PATCH PRINT RUN 75 SER.#'d SETS
EMEM Eli Manning Dual 20.00 50.00
EMKW E.Manning/K.Winslow Jr. 20.00 50.00
EMPR E.Manning/P.Rivers 20.00 50.00
JLLM J.Losman/L.McCown 5.00 12.00
KJRW K.Jones/Ro.Williams WR 6.00 15.00
KWKW Kellen Winslow Dual 5.00 12.00
KWLM K.Winslow/L.McCown 5.00 12.00
LFMC Fitzgerald/Clayton no SN 12.00 30.00
MJCP M.Jenkins/C.Perry 5.00 12.00
PRBR P.Rivers/Roethlisberger 25.00 60.00
RWTB R.Woods/T.Bell 5.00 12.00
SJKJ S.Jackson/K.Jones 8.00 20.00
SJTB S.Jackson/T.Bell 8.00 20.00

2004 Fleer Tradition Signing Day

COMPLETE SET (15) 20.00 50.00
STATED ODDS 1:12 HOB, 1:24 RET
*CHROME/50: 2.5X TO 6X BASIC INSERT
CHROME PRINT RUN 50 SER.#'d SETS
1SD Eli Manning 4.00 10.00
2SD Larry Fitzgerald 2.00 5.00
3SD Ben Roethlisberger 4.00 10.00
4SD J.P. Losman .50 1.25
5SD Roy Williams WR .50 1.25
6SD Steven Jackson .75 2.00
7SD Rashaun Woods .50 1.25
8SD Reggie Williams .50 1.25
9SD Michael Jenkins .50 1.25
10SD Philip Rivers 1.50 4.00
11SD Drew Henson .50 1.25
12SD Kevin Jones .60 1.50
13SD Lee Evans .75 2.00
14SD Michael Clayton .60 1.50
15SD Chris Perry .50 1.25

1995 FlickBall NFL Helmets

FlickBall produced its first full set of "paper footballs" in 1995 as NFL Team Helmets. Each flickball features an NFL helmet or Super Bowl logo and were packaged 6 per pack. There were two special inaugural season expansion team flickballs (#61-62) randomly inserted at the rate of 1:48 packs. They are not considered part of the complete set price.

COMPLETE SET (60) 8.00 20.00
1 Dallas Cowboys .20 .50
2 New York Giants .10 .30
3 Arizona Cardinals .10 .30
4 Philadelphia Eagles .10 .30
5 Washington Redskins .20 .50
6 Minnesota Vikings .10 .30
7 Chicago Bears .10 .30
8 Green Bay Packers .20 .50
9 Detroit Lions .10 .30
10 Tampa Bay Buccaneers .10 .30
11 San Francisco 49ers .20 .50
12 New Orleans Saints .10 .30
13 Atlanta Falcons .10 .30
14 Carolina Panthers .20 .50
15 St.Louis Rams .10 .30
16 New England Patriots .10 .30
17 Miami Dolphins .20 .50
18 Buffalo Bills .10 .30
19 Indianapolis Colts .10 .30
20 New York Jets .10 .30
21 Pittsburgh Steelers .20 .50
22 Cleveland Browns .10 .30
23 Cincinnati Bengals .10 .30
24 Jacksonville Jaguars .20 .50
25 Houston Oilers .10 .30
26 San Diego Chargers .10 .30
27 Oakland Raiders .20 .50
28 Kansas City Chiets .10 .30
29 Denver Broncos .10 .30
30 Seattle Seahawks .10 .30
31 Super Bowl I .10 .30
32 Super Bowl II .10 .30
33 Super Bowl III .10 .30
34 Super Bowl IV .10 .30
35 Super Bowl V .10 .30
36 Super Bowl VI .10 .30
37 Super Bowl VII .10 .30
38 Super Bowl VIII .10 .30
39 Super Bowl IX .10 .30
40 Super Bowl X .10 .30
41 Super Bowl XI .10 .30
42 Super Bowl XII .10 .30
43 Super Bowl XIII .10 .30
44 Super Bowl XIV .10 .30
45 Super Bowl XV .10 .30
46 Super Bowl XVI .10 .30
47 Super Bowl XVII .10 .30
48 Super Bowl XVIII .10 .30
49 Super Bowl XIX .10 .30
50 Super Bowl XX .10 .30
51 Super Bowl XXI .10 .30
52 Super Bowl XXII .10 .30
53 Super Bowl XXIII .10 .30
54 Super Bowl XXIV .10 .30
55 Super Bowl XXV .10 .30
56 Super Bowl XXVI .10 .30
57 Super Bowl XXVII .10 .30
58 Super Bowl XXVIII .10 .30
59 Super Bowl XXIX .10 .30
60 Super Bowl XXX Logo .10 .30
61 Carolina Panthers 1.60 4.00
62 Jacksonville Jaguars 1.60 4.00

1995 FlickBall Prototypes

FlickBall produced this set as Prototypes for its 1996 premier FlickBall release. The 10-card, football-shaped set measures approximately 2 1/4" by 1 1/4" and features a finger-size cut-out space called the "flick zone" used to "flick" the card (ball) as part of a football game. The fronts feature color player photos while the backs include logos and the "Pre-Production" title. Card number seven is called a "Double Flick" and has a different player on each side. The cards are unnumbered and checklisted below in alphabetical order.

COMPLETE SET (10) 2.00 5.00
1 Bill Bates .07 .20
2 Jeff Blake .25 .60
3 Drew Bledsoe .30 .75
4 Brett Favre 1.00 2.50
5 Kevin Greene .07 .20
6 Daryl Johnston .07 .20
7 Steve McNair .50 1.25
Kerry Collins
8 Jerry Rice .40 1.00
9 Tamarick Vanover .15 .40
10 Chris Warren .07 .20

1996 FlickBall

FlickBall produced a complete 100-card set in 1996. The flickballs were packaged seven to a blister pack and included several random insert sets.

COMPLETE SET (100) 12.00 30.00
1 Troy Aikman .60 1.50
2 Emmitt Smith 1.00 2.50
3 Michael Irvin .15 .40
4 Deion Sanders .30 .75
5 Bill Bates .08 .25
6 Rodney Peete .05 .15
7 Ricky Watters .08 .25
8 Fred Barnett .05 .15
9 Dave Krieg .05 .15
10 Larry Centers .08 .25
11 Garrison Hearst .08 .25
12 Dave Brown .05 .15
13 Rodney Hampton .08 .25
14 Mike Sherrard .05 .15
15 Gus Frerotte .08 .25
16 Henry Ellard .05 .15
17 Darrell Green .05 .15
18 Scott Mitchell .08 .25
19 Barry Sanders 1.20 3.00
20 Herman Moore .08 .25
21 Erik Kramer .05 .15
22 Curtis Conway .08 .25
23 Jeff Graham .05 .15
24 Brett Favre 1.20 3.00
25 Edgar Bennett .08 .25
26 Robert Brooks .08 .25
27 Reggie White .15 .40
28 Warren Moon .08 .25
29 Robert Smith .15 .40
30 Cris Carter .15 .40
31 Trent Dilfer .15 .40
32 Errict Rhett .08 .25
33 Santana Dotson .05 .15
34 Steve Young .50 1.25
35 Jerry Rice .60 1.50
36 Merton Hanks .05 .15
37 Ken Norton .05 .15
38 Jesse Sapolu .05 .15
39 Jim Everett .05 .15
40 Willie Roaf .05 .15
41 Tyrone Hughes .05 .15
42 Chris Miller .05 .15
43 Isaac Bruce .15 .40
44 Shane Conlan .05 .15
45 Jeff George .08 .25
46 Eric Metcalf .05 .15
47 Craig Heyward .05 .15
48 Sam Mills .05 .15
49 Mark Carrier WR .05 .15
50 Brett Maxie .05 .15
51 Jim Kelly .15 .40
52 Andre Reed .08 .25
53 Bruce Smith .08 .25
54 Bryce Paup .05 .15
55 Jim Harbaugh .08 .25
56 Marshall Faulk .30 .75
57 Sean Dawkins .05 .15
58 Dan Marino 1.20 3.00
59 Terry Kirby .08 .25
60 O.J. McDuffie .08 .25
61 Bernie Parmalee .05 .15
62 Wayne Chrebet .08 .25
63 Adrian Murrell .08 .25
64 Ronald Moore .05 .15
65 Drew Bledsoe .50 1.25
66 Vincent Brisby .05 .15
67 Vincent Brown .05 .15
68 Neil O'Donnell UER .08 .25
69 Erric Pegram .05 .15
70 Rohn Stark .05 .15
71 Kevin Greene .08 .25
72 Greg Lloyd .08 .25
73 Todd McNair .05 .15
74 Mark Stepnoski .05 .15
75 Bruce Matthews .05 .15
76 Jeff Blake .08 .25
77 Carl Pickens .08 .25
78 John Copeland .05 .15
79 Vinny Testaverde .08 .25
80 Andre Rison .08 .25
81 Leroy Hoard .05 .15
82 Mark Brunell .50 1.25
83 Cedric Tillman .05 .15
84 Desmond Howard .08 .25
85 Stan Humphries .08 .25
86 Natrone Means .08 .25
87 Junior Seau .08 .25
88 Steve Bono .05 .15
89 Marcus Allen .15 .40
90 Derrick Thomas .08 .25
91 Neil Smith .05 .15
92 Rick Mirer .08 .25
93 Chris Warren .08 .25
94 Cortez Kennedy .05 .15
95 Jeff Hostetler .05 .15
96 Tim Brown .15 .40
97 Terry McDaniel .05 .15
98 John Elway 1.20 3.00
99 Shannon Sharpe .08 .25
100 Steve Atwater .05 .15

1996 FlickBall Commemoratives

These four inserts into 1996 FlickBall blister packs were hand numbered of 700. They feature four standout NFL players and were inserted at the rate of 1:357 packs.

COMPLETE SET (4) 28.00 70.00
C1 Emmitt Smith 8.00 20.00
C2 Dan Marino 8.00 20.00
C3 Brett Favre 8.00 20.00
C4 Curtis Martin 6.00 15.00

1996 FlickBall DoubleFlicks

These 12-card were randomly inserted into 1996 FlickBall packs at the average rate of 1:3. They feature one player from the same position on each side of the card.

COMPLETE SET (12) 8.00 20.00
DF1 Dan Marino 1.60 4.00
D.Bledsoe
DF2 Troy Aikman 1.00 2.50
S.Young
DF3 K.Collins .80 2.00
S.McNair
DF4 E.Zeier 1.20 3.00
K.Stewart
DF5 E.Smith 1.20 3.00
M.Faulk
DF6 B.Sanders 1.20 3.00
E.Rhett
DF7 C.Martin 2.00 5.00
T.Davis
DF8 R.Salaam .60 1.50
N.Kaufman
DF9 M.Irvin .80 2.00
J.Rice
DF10 T.Brown .50 1.25
C.Carter
DF11 J.Galloway .60 1.50
J.J. Stokes
DF12 F.Sanders .50 1.25
M.Westbrook

1996 FlickBall Hawaiian Flicks

These 4-cards were randomly inserted into 1996 FlickBall blister packs at the rate of 1:8. They feature NFL players native to Hawaii.

COMPLETE SET (4) 2.00 5.00
H1 Mark Tuinei .40 1.00
H2 Jesse Sapolu .40 1.00
H3 Jason Elam .40 1.00
H4 Junior Seau .80 2.00

1996 FlickBall PreviewFlick Cowboys

Random 1996 FlickBall packs contained these 8-cards. They feature Dallas Cowboys players and carry a "P" card number prefix. The insertion ratio was 1:4 packs.

COMPLETE SET (8) 2.40 6.00
P1 Daryl Johnston .40 1.00
P2 Jay Novacek .40 1.00
P3 Kevin Williams WR .30 .75
P4 Charles Haley .40 1.00
P5 Darren Woodson .30 .75
P6 Leon Lett .30 .75
P7 Chad Hennings .30 .75
P8 Mark Tuinei .30 .75

1996 FlickBall Rookies

Randomly inserted into 1996 FlickBall packs at the rate of 1:2, these 20-cards feature top 1995 NFL rookies.

COMPLETE SET (20) 6.00 15.00
R1 Sherman Williams .10 .30
R2 Mike Mamula .10 .30
R3 Frank Sanders .30 .75
R4 Steve Stenstrom .10 .30
R5 Michael Westbrook .40 1.00
R6 Warren Sapp .15 .40
R7 Rashaan Salaam .15 .40
R8 J.J. Stokes .25 .60
R9 Kevin Carter .10 .30
R10 Kerry Collins .60 1.50
R11 Curtis Martin .80 2.00
R12 Kordell Stewart .80 2.00
R13 Steve McNair 1.00 2.50
R14 Rodney Thomas .15 .40
R15 Eric Zeier .15 .40
R16 Tony Boselli .15 .40
R17 Tamarick Vanover .15 .40
R18 Joey Galloway .60 1.50
R19 Napoleon Kaufman .50 1.25
R20 Terrell Davis 2.00 5.00

1996 FlickBall Team Sets

MGwhiz, Inc., the makers or FlickBall products, developed this set as a test. The three teams were primarily distributed in their respective areas. Each team was individually packaged with five players and one team helmet mounted on a display backer board. We've added the team name initials to the card numbers below to assist with cataloging. There are no prefixes on the actual card numbers.

COMPLETE SET (18) 6.00 15.00
COMP.COWBOYS SET (6) 2.80 7.00
COMP.VIKINGS SET (6) 1.40 3.50
COMP.PACKERS SET (6) 2.00 5.00
DC1 Troy Aikman .80 2.00
DC2 Deion Sanders .50 1.25
DC3 Emmitt Smith 1.20 3.00
DC4 Daryl Johnston .30 .75
DC5 Cowboys Helmet .20 .50
DC6 Darren Woodson .20 .50
MV1 Warren Moon .30 .75
MV2 Cris Carter .30 .75
MV3 Robert Smith .30 .75
MV4 Qadry Ismail .20 .50
MV5 Vikings Helmet .20 .50
MV6 David Palmer .20 .50
GBP1 Brett Favre 1.60 4.00
GBP2 Edgar Bennett .30 .75
GBP3 Reggie White .40 1.00
GBP4 Robert Brooks .60 1.50
GBP5 Packers Helmet .20 .50
GBP6 George Teague .20 .50

1997 FlickBall ProFlick

The 1997 ProFlicks were similar to past Flickball releases except for the "card" like design. Each ProFlick was produced and inserted in a 2" by 3" holder that roughly resembles a card. Packs contained 4-ProFlicks with one of the four being from the foil parallel set. A six-piece Rookies insert set was also produced.

COMPLETE SET (44) 12.00 30.00
1 Troy Aikman .80 2.00
2 Terry Allen .30 .75
3 Jerome Bettis .30 .75
4 Drew Bledsoe .60 1.50
5 Tim Brown .30 .75
6 Isaac Bruce .30 .75
7 Mark Brunell .80 2.00
8 Larry Centers .08 .25
9 Mark Chmura .15 .40
10 Kerry Collins .30 .75
11 Terrell Davis 1.20 3.00
12 Ty Detmer .15 .40
13 John Elway 1.60 4.00
14 Marshall Faulk .30 .75
15 Brett Favre 1.60 4.00
16 Joey Galloway .40 1.00
17 Kevin Greene .08 .25
18 Jim Harbaugh .15 .40
19 Desmond Howard .15 .40
20 Brad Johnson .30 .75
21 Napoleon Kaufman .30 .75
22 Erik Kramer .08 .25
23 Dan Marino 1.60 4.00
24 Curtis Martin .50 1.25
25 Tony Martin .15 .40
26 Steve McNair .60 1.50
27 Natrone Means .15 .40
28 Herman Moore .15 .40
29 Adrian Murrell .15 .40
30 Carl Pickens .15 .40
31 Jerry Rice .80 2.00
32 Rashaan Salaam .15 .40
33 Barry Sanders 1.60 4.00
34 Deion Sanders .40 1.00
35 Junior Seau .15 .40
36 Emmitt Smith 1.20 3.00
37 Jimmy Smith .15 .40
38 Kordell Stewart .40 1.00
39 Vinny Testaverde .15 .40
40 Herschel Walker .15 .40
41 Ricky Watters .15 .40
42 Reggie White .30 .75
43 Steve Young .30 .75
44 Ray Zellars .08 .25

1997 FlickBall ProFlick Foils

ProFlick packs contained four-ProFlicks with one of the four being from this foil parallel set. Each foil "card" is a parallel to the base cards with a prismatic foil design on the cardfronts.

COMPLETE SET (44) 25.00 60.00
*FOILS: .8X TO 2X BASIC CARDS

1997 FlickBall ProFlick QB Greats

Six top NFL quarterbacks are featured in this ProFlick set. Each of the "cards" was printed in both standard card stock as well as prismatic silver foil stock and randomly inserted into special retail packs.

COMPLETE SET (6) 15.00 40.00
*FOIL: .6X TO 1.5X BASIC INSERTS
QB1 Troy Aikman 1.50 4.00
QB2 Drew Bledsoe 1.25 3.00
QB3 Mark Brunell 1.00 2.50
QB4 John Elway 3.00 8.00
QB5 Brett Favre 3.00 8.00
QB6 Dan Marino 3.00 8.00

1997 FlickBall ProFlick Rookies

This 6-card set was randomly inserted into 1997 ProFlicks packs. Each features a top 1996 NFL rookie. Reportedly, they were inserted at the rate of 1:48 packs.

COMPLETE SET (6) 30.00 50.00
*FOIL: .6X TO 1.5X BASIC INSERTS
R1 Karim Abdul-Jabbar 2.00 5.00
R2 Eddie George 4.00 10.00
R3 Terry Glenn 2.50 6.00
R4 Kevin Hardy 1.50 4.00
R5 Marvin Harrison 5.00 12.00
R6 Keyshawn Johnson 3.00 8.00

1997 FlickBall QB Club

MGwhiz, Inc., the makers or FlickBall products, developed this set featuring members of Quarterback Club. Two groups of six players each were packaged mounted on a display backer board, which was numbered of 2-different boards made. We've priced the flickballs separately, although they're most commonly sold in intact on sheets (display boards) of six.

COMPLETE SET (12) 4.00 10.00
1 Troy Aikman .40 1.00
2 Jerry Rice .40 1.00
3 Brett Favre .80 2.00
4 John Elway .80 2.00
5 Junior Seau .20 .50
6 Jim Harbaugh .20 .50
7 Dan Marino .80 2.00
8 Emmitt Smith .60 1.50
9 Steve Young .30 .75
10 Drew Bledsoe .30 .75
11 Barry Sanders .80 2.00
12 Mark Brunell .30 .75

2003 Flipp Sports Booklets

These booklets were issued to show, if fanned in quick order, two fast action photos of the featured player(s). Each player is mentioned on the outside covers and the inside covers feature biographical information as well as career statistics. Since these booklets are not numbered, we have sequenced them alphabetically.

1 Tiki Barber/Jeremy Shockey 1.25 3.00
2 Jerry Rice 2.00 5.00

1974 Florida Blazers WFL Team Issue

These photos were issued by the team for promotional purposes and fan mail requests. Each includes a black and white image printed above the subject's name and team logo. Each measures 5 1/2" by 7."

COMPLETE SET (10) 25.00 60.00
1 Chuck Beatty 3.00 8.00
2 Bob Davis 3.00 8.00
3 Billy Hobbs 3.00 8.00
4 Billie Hayes 3.00 8.00
5 Rommie Loudd Mgr. 3.00 8.00
6 Jack Pardee CO 4.00 10.00
7 Tommy Reamon 3.00 8.00
8 John Ricca 3.00 8.00
9 Lou Ross 3.00 8.00
10 Paul Vellano 3.00 8.00

1988 Football Heroes Sticker Book

This sticker book contains 20 pages and measures approximately 9 1/4" by 12 1/2". It serves as an introduction to American football, with a discussion of how the game is played and a glossary of terms. The bulk of the book discusses various positions (e.g., quarterbacks, running backs, tight ends, wide receivers, kickers, offensive linemen, and defensive linemen), and outstanding NFL players who fill these positions. The stickers are approximately 3" in height and issued on two sheets, with 15 stickers per sheet. They are to be pasted on a glossy "Football Heroes" poster, which has an imitation-wood picture frame and slots for only 15 player stickers. The cards are unnumbered and checklisted below in alphabetical order.

COMPLETE SET (30) 125.00 250.00
1 Marcus Allen 4.00 10.00
2 Gary Anderson K 1.50 4.00
3 Brian Bosworth 2.00 5.00
4 Anthony Carter 2.00 5.00
5 Deron Cherry 1.50 4.00
6 Eric Dickerson 2.00 5.00
7 John Elway 10.00 25.00
8 Bo Jackson 5.00 12.00
9 Rich Karlis 1.50 4.00
10 Bernie Kosar 2.00 5.00
11 Steve Largent 4.00 10.00
12 Mick Luckhurst 1.50 4.00
13 Dexter Manley 1.50 4.00
14 Dan Marino 12.00 30.00
15 Jim McMahon 2.00 5.00
16 Joe Montana 15.00 40.00
17 Joe Morris 1.50 4.00
18 Anthony Munoz 2.00 5.00
19 Ozzie Newsome 2.00 5.00
20 Walter Payton 15.00 40.00
21 William Perry 2.00 5.00
22 Jerry Rice 8.00 20.00
23 Ricky Sanders 1.50 4.00
24 Phil Simms 2.00 5.00
25 Mike Singletary 2.50 6.00
26 Dwight Stephenson 2.00 5.00
27 Lawrence Taylor 2.50 6.00
28 Herschel Walker 2.50 6.00
29 Doug Williams 2.00 5.00
30 Kellen Winslow 2.00 5.00

1985-88 Football Immortals

This set was produced and released in factory set form in 1985, 1987 and 1988. With a few exceptions, the majority of the cards in the factory sets are exactly the same therefore they are combined below. The 1985 set had 135 cards and the 1987 and 1988 sets had 142 cards. In the checklist below the variation cards are listed using the following convention, that the A (or first) variety is from 1985 and the B variety is the version that was released with the 1987 and 1988 sets. Cards 6-128 are essentially in alphabetical order by subject's name. The cards are standard size. The horizontal card backs are light green and black on white card stock. The card photos are in black and white inside two color borders. The outer, thicker border is gold metallic. The inner border is color coded according to the number of the card, red border (1-45), blue border (46-90), green border (91-135), and yellow border (136-144). The set is titled "Football Immortals" at the top of every cardfront. Since all members of the set are Football Hall of Famers, their year of induction is given on the front and back of each card.

COMPLETE SET (150) 100.00 200.00
COMP.FACT.SET 1985 (135) 15.00 30.00
COMP.FACT.SET 1987 (142) 50.00 100.00
1 Pete Rozelle .75 2.00
2 Joe Namath 1.50 4.00
3 Frank Gatski .75 2.00
4 O.J. Simpson 1.00 2.50
5 Roger Staubach 1.50 4.00
6 Herb Adderley 1.00 2.50
7 Lance Alworth 1.00 2.50
8 Doug Atkins 1.00 2.50
9 Red Badgro .75 2.00
10 Cliff Battles .75 2.00
11 Sammy Baugh 1.25 3.00
12 Raymond Berry 1.00 2.50
13 Charles W. Bidwill .75 2.00
14 Chuck Bednarik 1.00 2.50
15 Bert Bell .75 2.00
16 Bobby Bell 1.00 2.50
17 George Blanda 1.00 2.50
18 Jim Brown 1.50 4.00
19 Paul Brown 1.00 2.50
20 Roosevelt Brown .75 2.00
21 Ray Flaherty .75 2.00
22 Len Ford .75 2.00
23 Dan Fortmann .75 2.00
24 Bill George .75 2.00
25 Art Donovan 1.00 2.50
26 Paddy Driscoll .75 2.00
27 Jimmy Conzelman .75 2.00
28 Willie Davis 1.00 2.50
29 Dutch Clark 1.00 2.50
30 George Connor .75 2.00
31 Guy Chamberlin .75 2.00
32 Jack Christiansen .75 2.00
33 Tony Canadeo 1.00 2.50
34 Joe Carr .75 2.00
35 Willie Brown 1.00 2.50
36 Dick Butkus 1.25 3.00
37 Bill Dudley .75 2.00
38 Turk Edwards 1.00 2.50
39 Weeb Ewbank .75 2.00
40 Tom Fears .75 2.00
41 Otto Graham 1.25 3.00
42 Red Grange 1.25 3.00
43 Frank Gifford 1.00 2.50
44 Sid Gillman .75 2.00
45 Forrest Gregg 1.00 2.50
46 Lou Groza 1.00 2.50
47 Joe Guyon .75 2.00
48 George Halas 1.25 3.00
49 Ed Healey .75 2.00
50 Mel Hein .75 2.00
51 Fats Henry .75 2.00
52 Arnie Herber 1.00 2.50
53 Bill Hewitt .75 2.00
54 Clarke Hinkle 1.00 2.50
55 Elroy Hirsch 1.00 2.50
56 Robert(Cal) Hubbard .75 2.00
57 Sam Huff 1.00 2.50
58 Lamar Hunt .75 2.00
59 Don Hutson 1.00 2.50
60 Dave(Deacon) Jones 1.00 2.50
61 Sonny Jurgensen 1.00 2.50
62 Walt Kiesling .75 2.00
63 Frank(Bruiser) Kinard .75 2.00
64 Earl(Curly) Lambeau 1.00 2.50
65 Dick(Night Train)Lane 1.00 2.50
66 Yale Lary .75 2.00
67 Dante Lavelli 1.00 2.50
68 Bobby Layne 1.00 2.50
69 Tuffy Leemans .75 2.00
70 Bob Lilly 1.00 2.50
71 Vince Lombardi 2.50 6.00
72 Sid Luckman 1.00 2.50
73 Link Lyman .75 2.00
74 Tim Mara .75 2.00
75 Gino Marchetti 1.00 2.50
76 Geo.Preston Marshall .75 2.00
77 Ollie Matson 1.00 2.50
78 George McAfee .75 2.00
79 Mike McCormack .75 2.00
80 Hugh McElhenny 1.00 2.50
81 Johnny Blood McNally 1.00 2.50
82 Mike Michalske .75 2.00
83 Wayne Millner .75 2.00
84 Bobby Mitchell 1.00 2.50
85 Ron Mix .75 2.00
86 Lenny Moore 1.00 2.50
87 Marion Motley 1.00 2.50
88 George Musso .75 2.00
89 Bronko Nagurski 1.50 4.00
90 Greasy Neale .75 2.00
91 Ernie Nevers .75 2.00
92 Ray Nitschke 1.00 2.50
93 Leo Nomellini .75 2.00
94 Merlin Olsen 1.00 2.50
95 Jim Otto 1.00 2.50
96 Steve Owen .75 2.00
97 Clarence(Ace) Parker .75 2.00
98 Jim Parker .75 2.00
99 Joe Perry 1.00 2.50
100 Pete Pihos .75 2.00
101 Hugh(Shorty) Ray .75 2.00
102 Dan Reeves OWN .75 2.00
103 Jim Ringo 1.00 2.50
104 Andy Robustelli 1.00 2.50
105 Art Rooney .75 2.00
106 Gale Sayers 1.25 3.00
107 Joe Schmidt 1.00 2.50
108 Bart Starr 1.50 4.00
109 Ernie Stautner 1.00 2.50
110 Ken Strong .75 2.00
111 Joe Stydahar .75 2.00
112 Charley Taylor .75 2.00
113 Jim Taylor 1.00 2.50
114 Jim Thorpe 1.50 4.00
115 Y.A. Tittle 1.00 2.50
116 George Trafton .75 2.00
117 Charley Trippi .75 2.00
118 Emlen Tunnell .75 2.00
119 Bulldog Turner 1.00 2.50
120 Johnny Unitas 1.50 4.00
121 Norm Van Brocklin 1.00 2.50
122 Steve Van Buren 1.00 2.50
123 Paul Warfield 1.00 2.50
124 Bob Waterfield 1.00 2.50
125 Arnie Weinmeister .75 2.00
126 Bill Willis .75 2.00
127 Larry Wilson .75 2.00
128 Alex Wojciechowicz .75 2.00
129 Pro Football .75 2.00
130A Jim Thorpe Statue 1.25 3.00
130B Doak Walker 2.50 6.00
131A Enshrinement 1.00 2.50
131B Willie Lanier 1.50 4.00
132 Pro Football HOF .75 2.00
133A Eric Dickerson 1.25 3.00
133B Paul Hornung 3.00 8.00
134A Walter Payton 2.50 6.00
134B Ken Houston 1.50 4.00
135A Super Bowl Display 1.00 2.50
135B Fran Tarkenton 4.00 10.00
136 Don Maynard 2.00 5.00
137 Larry Csonka 3.00 8.00
138 Joe Greene 3.00 8.00
139 Len Dawson 2.50 6.00
140 Gene Upshaw 1.50 4.00
141A Jim Langer 1.50 4.00
141B Fred Biletnikoff 10.00 20.00
142A John Henry Johnson 1.50 4.00
142B Mike Ditka 12.50 25.00
143 Jack Ham 10.00 20.00
144 Alan Page 10.00 20.00

1988 Foot Locker Slam Fest

This nine-card set was produced by Foot Locker to commemorate the "Foot Locker Slam Fest" slam dunk contest, televised on ESPN on May 17, 1988. The cards were given out in May at participating Foot Locker stores to customers. Between May 18 and July 31, customers could turn in the winner's card (Mike Conley) and receive a free pair of Wilson athletic shoes and 50 percent off any purchase at Foot Locker. These standard size cards (2 1/2" by 3 1/2") feature color posed shots of the participants, who were professional athletes from sports other than basketball. The pictures have magenta and blue borders on a white card face. A colored banner with the words "Foot Locker" overlays the top of the picture. A line drawing of a referee overlays the lower left corner of the picture. The backs are printed in blue on white and promote the slam dunk contest and an in-store contest. The cards are unnumbered and checklisted below in alphabetical order.

COMPLETE SET (9) 12.00 30.00
1 Carl Banks FB .75 2.00
4 Bo Jackson BB/FB 2.50 6.00
5 Keith Jackson FB .75 2.00
7 Ricky Sanders FB .75 2.00

1989 Foot Locker Slam Fest

This ten-card standard-size set was produced by Foot Locker and Nike to commemorate the "Foot Locker Slam Fest" slam dunk contest, which was televised during halftimes of NBC college basketball games through March 12, 1989. The cards were wrapped in cellophane and issued with one stick of gum. They were given out at participating Foot Locker stores upon request with a purchase. The cards feature color posed shots of the participants, who were professional athletes from sports other than basketball. A banner with the words "Foot Locker" traverses the top of the card face. The cards are unnumbered and checklisted below in alphabetical order.

COMPLETE SET (10) 3.20 8.00
2 Keith Jackson FB .20 .50
4 Eric Dickerson FB .60 1.50
8 Mike Quick FB .20 .50

1991 Foot Locker Slam Fest

This 30-card standard-size set was issued by Foot Locker in three ten-card series to commemorate the "Foot Locker Slam Fest" dunk contest televised during halftimes of NBC college basketball games through March 10, 1991. Each set contained two Domino's Pizza coupons and a 5.00 discount coupon on any purchase of 50.00 or more at Foot Locker. The set was released in substantial quantity after the promotional coupons expired. The fronts feature both posed and action photos enclosed in an arch like double red borders. The card top carries a blue border with "Foot Locker" in blue print on a white background. Beneath the photo appears "Limited Edition" and the player's name. The backs present career highlights, card series, and numbers placed within an arch of double red borders. The player's name and team name appear in black lettering at the bottom. The cards are numbered on the back; the card numbering below adds the number 10 to each card number in the second series and 20 to each card number in the third series.

COMPLETE SET (30) 2.00 5.00
6 Deion Sanders BB .30 .75
FB
8 Tim Brown FB .10 .25
22 Bo Jackson BB .10 .25
FB
27 Eric Dickerson FB .06 .15

2005 Ford Promos

3 Brett Favre 2.00 5.00

1966 Fortune Shoes

Fortune Shoe Company sponsored this set of 9" by 12" black-and-white pencil sketches. The unnumbered cards are blankbacked and were printed on thick paper stock. Any additions to this list would be appreciated.

COMPLETE SET (9) 125.00 250.00
1 Roman Gabriel 12.50 25.00
2 Charley Johnson 10.00 20.00
3 John Henry Johnson 15.00 25.00
4 Don Meredith 15.00 30.00
5 Lenny Moore 15.00 25.00
6 Frank Ryan 10.00 20.00
7 Gale Sayers 25.00 50.00
8 Jim Taylor 15.00 30.00
9 John Unitas 25.00 50.00

2003 Fort Wayne Freedom UIF

1 Vernard Alsberry .20 .50
2 Jason Battershell .20 .50
3 Carlton Bragg .20 .50
4 Andrae Brooks .20 .50
5 Ron Brown .20 .50
6 Lewis Carter .20 .50
7 Pat Cavanaugh .20 .50
8 Vbrian Ceaser .20 .50
9 Jamar Cottee .20 .50
10 Rachman Crable .20 .50
11 Charles Dempsey .20 .50
12 John Diettrich .20 .50
13 Jeremy Dutcher .20 .50
14 Alf Fertil .20 .50
15 Rocky Harvey .20 .50
16 Rich Huff (HC) .20 .50
17 Robin Johnson .20 .50
18 Kevin Kemp .20 .50
19 Dietrich Lapsley .20 .50
20 Dayna Overton .20 .50
21 Patrick Paulsen .20 .50
22 Remele Penick .20 .50
23 Bobby Petras .20 .50
24 Adrian Reese .20 .50
25 Juliamn Reese .20 .50
26 Antoine Taylor .20 .50
27 Evan Triggs .20 .50
28 Lamont White .20 .50
29 Team Card .20 .50

2004 Fort Wayne Freedom UIF

1 Al Baysinger .20 .50
2 Chris Bell .20 .50
3 Andrae Brooks .20 .50
4 Nick Brownfield .20 .50
5 Lewis Carter .20 .50
6 Jamar Cottee .20 .50
7 Rachman Crable .20 .50
8 John Diettrich .20 .50
9 Alf Fertil .20 .50
10 Alen Ganaway .20 .50
11 Jamie Hanton .20 .50
12 Rocky Harvey .20 .50
13 Scott Heighland .20 .50
14 Lamar Martin .20 .50
15 Dayna Overton .20 .50
16 Remele Penick .20 .50
17 Bobby Petras .20 .50
18 Adrian Reese .20 .50
19 Ernie Smith .20 .50
20 Luther Stroder .20 .50
21 Jremy Swonger .20 .50
22 Antoine Taylor .20 .50
23 Adam Walter .20 .50

24 Adam Wheatley .20 .50
25 Bryan White .20 .50
26 Team Card .20 .50

2005 Fort Wayne Freedom UIF

1 Chris Bell OL .20 .50
2 Andrae Brooks .20 .50
3 Lewis Carter .20 .50
4 Rachman Crable .20 .50
5 Jeremy Dutcher .20 .50
6 Alf Fertil .20 .50
7 Alan Ganaway .20 .50
8 Jamarkus Gorman .20 .50
9 Mike Hanley .20 .50
10 Rocky Harvey .20 .50
11 Scott Heighland .20 .50
12 Lamar Martin .20 .50
13 Terrance Miles .20 .50
14 Dayna Overton .20 .50
15 Remele Oenick .20 .50
16 Bobby Petras .20 .50
17 Adrian Reese .20 .50
18 Scott Russell .20 .50
19 Bill Skelton .20 .50
20 Carlos Smith .20 .50
21 Luther Stroder .20 .50
22 Noah Swartz .20 .50
23 Evan Triggs .20 .50
24 Bryan White .20 .50
25 Team Card .20 .50

2006 Fort Wayne Freedom UIF

1 Andrae Brooks .20 .50
2 Lewis Carter .20 .50
3 Rachman Crable .20 .50
4 Doug Daniel .20 .50
5 Alf Fertil .20 .50
6 Alan Ganaway .20 .50
7 Jamarkus Gorman .20 .50
8 Randall Guzman .20 .50
9 Michael Hanley .20 .50
10 Rocky Harvey .20 .50
11 Scott Heighland .20 .50
12 Jamie Holman .20 .50
13 Mike Lane .20 .50
14 Lamar Martin .20 .50
15 Ronnie McCrae .20 .50
16 Dan Musielewicz .20 .50
17 Keith Recker .20 .50
18 Adrian Reese .20 .50
19 Scott Russell .20 .50
20 Bill Skelton .20 .50
21 Luther Stroder .20 .50
22 Noah Swartz .20 .50
23 Bryan White .20 .50
24 Johnell Wyatte .20 .50

2008 Fort Wayne Freedon CIFL

COMPLETE SET (24) 5.00 10.00
1 Shonn Bell .30 .75
2 Lewis Carter .20 .50
3 Brian Clawson .20 .50
4 Kota-Carone Colors .20 .50
5 Travis Colston .20 .50
6 Thad Conley .20 .50
7 Rachman Crable .20 .50
8 Alfred Fertil .20 .50
9 Rocky Harvey .20 .50
10 Scott Heighland .20 .50
11 Eric Hooks .20 .50
12 Justin Hoover .20 .50
13 Brandon Hurd .20 .50
14 Glenn Johnson .20 .50
15 Jeffrey Lewis .20 .50
16 Ronnie McCrae .20 .50
17 Remele Penick .20 .50
18 Craig Plaster .20 .50
19 Adrian Reese .20 .50
20 JaRell Smith .20 .50
21 Luther Stroder .20 .50
22 Antoine Taylor .20 .50
23 Bo Thompson .20 .50
24 Team Card .20 .50

1953-55 49ers Burgermeister Beer Team Photos

These oversized (roughly 6 1/4" by 9") color team photos were sponsored by Burgermeister Beer and distributed in the San Francisco area. Each were printed on thin card stock and featured a Burgermeister ad on the back along with the 49ers logo.

1953 San Francisco 49ers 25.00 50.00
1954 San Francisco 49ers 25.00 50.00
1955 San Francisco 49ers 25.00 50.00

1955 49ers Christopher Dairy

These cards were part of milk cartons released around 1955 by Christopher Dairy Farms. Two players were apparently included on each carton and printed in blue and white with the player's name and position next to the image. Three unfolded cartons were uncovered in 2001, but it is not yet known if these 6 constitute a full set. Any additions to this list are appreciated.

COMPLETE SET (6) 500.00 800.00
1 John Henry Johnson 125.00 200.00
2 Clay Matthews Sr. 75.00 125.00
3 Dick Moegle 75.00 125.00
4 Joe Perry 150.00 250.00
5 Bob St.Clair 90.00 150.00
6 Bob Toneff 75.00 125.00

1955 49ers Team Issue

This 38-card set measures approximately 4 1/4" by 6 1/4". The front features a black and white posed action photo enclosed by a white border, with the player's signature across the bottom portion of the picture. The back of the card lists the player's name, position, height, weight, and college, along with basic biographical information. Many of the cards in this and the other similar team issue sets are only distinguishable as to year by comparing text on the card back; the first few words of text are provided for many of the cards parenthetically below. The set was available direct from the team as part of a package for their fans. The cards are unnumbered and hence are listed alphabetically for convenience.

COMPLETE SET (38) 250.00 400.00
1 Frankie Albert CO 5.00 10.00
2 Joe Arenas 4.00 8.00
3 Harry Babcock 4.00 8.00
4 Ed Beatty 4.00 8.00
5 Phil Bengtson CO 4.00 8.00
6 Rex Berry 4.00 8.00
7 Hardy Brown 4.00 10.00
8 Marion Campbell 4.00 10.00
9 Al Carapella 4.00 8.00
10 Paul Carr 4.00 8.00
11 Maury Duncan 4.00 8.00
12 Bob Hantla 4.00 8.00
13 Carroll Hardy 4.00 8.00
14 Matt Hazeltine 4.00 8.00
15 Howard(Red) Hickey CO 4.00 8.00
16 Doug Hogland 4.00 8.00
17 Bill Johnson C 4.00 8.00
18 John Henry Johnson 15.00 30.00
19 Eldred Kraemer 4.00 8.00
20 Bud Laughlin 4.00 8.00
21 Bobby Luna 4.00 8.00
22 George Maderos 4.00 8.00
23 Clay Matthews Sr. 4.00 10.00
24 Hugh McElhenny 15.00 30.00
25 Dick Moegle 5.00 10.00
26 Leo Nomellini 12.50 25.00
27 Lou Palatella 4.00 8.00
28 Joe Perry 15.00 30.00
29 Charley Powell 4.00 8.00
30 Gordy Soltau 4.00 8.00
31 Bob St. Clair 12.50 25.00
32 Tom Stolhandske 4.00 8.00
33 R.Storey 4.00 8.00
B.Fouts
Strader
34 Red Strader CO 4.00 8.00
35 Y.A. Tittle 20.00 40.00
36 Bob Toneff 4.00 8.00
37 Billy Wilson 4.00 10.00
38 Sid Youngelman 4.00 8.00

1956 49ers Team Issue

This set measures approximately 4 1/8" by 6 1/4". The front features a black and white posed action photo enclosed by a white border, with the player's signature across the bottom portion of the picture. The back of the card lists the player's name, position, height, weight, and college, along with basic biographical information. Many of the cards in this and the other similar team issue sets are only distinguishable as to year by comparing text on the card back; the first few words of text are provided for many of the cards parenthetically below. The set was available direct from the team as part of a package for their fans. The cards are unnumbered and hence are listed alphabetically for convenience. It is likely that this set contains more than the number of cards listed below. Any additions to this list are appreciated.

COMPLETE SET (35) 200.00 350.00
1 Frankie Albert CO 5.00 10.00
2 Joe Arenas 4.00 8.00
3 Ed Beatty 4.00 8.00
4 Phil Bengtson CO 4.00 8.00
5 Rex Berry 4.00 8.00
6 Bruce Bosley 4.00 8.00
7 Fred Bruney 4.00 8.00
8 Paul Carr 4.00 8.00
9 Clyde Conner 4.00 8.00
10 Paul Goad 4.00 8.00
11 Matt Hazeltine 4.00 8.00
12 Ed Henke 4.00 8.00
13 Bill Herchman 4.00 8.00
14 Howard(Red) Hickey CO 4.00 8.00
15 Bill Jessup 4.00 8.00
16 Bill Johnson C 4.00 8.00
17 John Henry Johnson 18.00 30.00
18 George Maderos 4.00 8.00
19 Hugh McElhenny 15.00 30.00
20 Dick Moegle 5.00 10.00
21 Earl Morrall 12.00 20.00
22 George Morris 4.00 8.00
23 Leo Nomellini 12.50 25.00
24 Lou Palatella 4.00 8.00
25 Joe Perry 15.00 30.00
26 Charley Powell 4.00 8.00
27 Leo Rucka 4.00 8.00
28 Ed Sharkey 4.00 8.00
29 Charles Smith 4.00 8.00
30 Gordy Soltau 4.00 8.00
31 R.Storey 4.00 8.00
B.Fouts
32 Bob St. Clair 10.00 20.00
33 Y.A. Tittle 25.00 40.00
34 Bob Toneff 4.00 8.00
35 Billy Wilson 4.00 8.00

1956-61 49ers Falstaff Beer Team Photos

These oversized (roughly 6 1/4" by 9") color team photos were sponsored by Falstaff Beer and distributed in the San Francisco area. Each was printed on card stock and features advertising and/or photos of the coaching staff on the back. Note that blankbacked reprints of the photos have circulated for a number of years.

1956 San Francisco 49ers 20.00 40.00
1957 San Francisco 49ers 20.00 40.00
1958 San Francisco 49ers 20.00 40.00
1959 San Francisco 49ers 20.00 40.00
1960 San Francisco 49ers 20.00 40.00
1961 San Francisco 49ers 20.00 40.00

1957 49ers Team Issue

This 43-card set measures approximatey 4 1/8" by 6 1/4". The front features a black and white posed action photo enclosed by a white border, with the player's signature across the bottom portion of the picture. For those players who were included in the 1956 set, the same photos were used in the 1957 set, with the exception of Bill Johnson, who appears as a coach in the 1957 set. The back lists the player's name, position, height, weight, and college, along with basic biographical information. Many of the cards in this and the other similar team issue sets are only distinguishable as to year by comparing text on the card back; the first few words of text are provided for many of the cards parenthetically below. The set was available direct from the team as part of a package for their fans. The John Brodie card in this set predates his Topps and Fleer Rookie Cards by four years. The cards are unnumbered and hence are listed alphabetically for convenience.

COMPLETE SET (43) 250.00 400.00
1 Frankie Albert CO 5.00 10.00
2 Joe Arenas 4.00 8.00
3 Gene Babb 4.00 8.00
4 Larry Barnes 4.00 8.00
5 Phil Bengtson CO 4.00 8.00
6 Bruce Bosley 4.00 8.00
7 John Brodie 20.00 40.00
8 Paul Carr 4.00 8.00
9 Clyde Conner 4.00 8.00
10 Ted Connolly 4.00 8.00
11 Bobby Cross 4.00 8.00
12 Mark Duncan CO 4.00 8.00
13 B.Fouts 4.00 8.00
L.Simmons
Albert
14 John Gonzaga 4.00 8.00
15 Tom Harmon ANN 5.00 10.00
16 Matt Hazeltine 4.00 8.00
17 Ed Henke 4.00 8.00
18 Bill Herchman 4.00 8.00
19 Howard(Red) Hickey CO 4.00 8.00
20 Bob Holladay 4.00 8.00
21 Bill Jessup 4.00 8.00
22 Bill Johnson CO 4.00 8.00
23 Marv Matuszak 4.00 8.00
24 Hugh McElhenny 12.50 25.00
25 Dick Moegle 5.00 10.00
26 Frank Morze 4.00 8.00
27 Leo Nomellini 10.00 20.00
28 R.C. Owens 5.00 10.00
29 Lou Palatella 4.00 8.00
30 Joe Perry 12.50 25.00
31 Charley Powell 4.00 8.00
32 Jim Ridlon 4.00 8.00
33 Karl Rubke 4.00 8.00
34 J.D. Smith 5.00 10.00
35 Gordy Soltau 4.00 8.00
36 Bob St. Clair 7.50 15.00
37 Bill Stits 4.00 8.00
38 Y.A. Tittle 20.00 40.00
39 Bob Toneff 4.00 8.00
40A Lynn Waldorf Dir. 4.00 8.00
40B Lynn Waldorf Dir. 4.00 8.00
41 Val Joe Walker 4.00 8.00
42 Billy Wilson 4.00 8.00
43 49ers Coaches 5.00 10.00

1958 49ers Team Issue

This 44-card set measures approximately 4 1/8" by 6 1/4". The front features a black and white posed action photo enclosed by a white border, with the player's signature across the bottom portion of the picture. The back lists the player's name, position, height, weight, and college, along with basic biographical information. Many of the cards in this and the other similar team issue sets are only distinguishable as to year by comparing text on the card back; the first few words of text are provided for many of the cards parenthetically below. The set was available direct from the team as part of a package for their fans. The John Brodie card in this set holds particular interest to some collectors in that it precedes Brodie's Topps and Fleer Rookie Cards by three years. The cards are unnumbered and hence are listed alphabetically for convenience.

COMPLETE SET (44) 250.00 400.00
1 Frankie Albert CO 5.00 10.00
2 Bill Atkins 4.00 8.00
3 Gene Babb 4.00 8.00
4 Phil Bengtson CO 4.00 8.00
5 Bruce Bosley 4.00 8.00
6 John Brodie 15.00 30.00
7 Clyde Conner 4.00 8.00
8 Ted Connolly 4.00 8.00
9 Fred Dugan 4.00 8.00
10 Mark Duncan CO 4.00 8.00
11 Bob Fouts 4.00 8.00
Simmons
Albert
12 John Gonzaga 4.00 8.00
13 Tom Harmon ANN 5.00 10.00
14 Matt Hazeltine 4.00 8.00
15 Ed Henke 4.00 8.00
16 Bill Herchman 4.00 8.00
17 Howard(Red) Hickey CO 4.00 8.00
18 Bill Jessup 4.00 8.00
19 Bill Johnson CO 4.00 8.00
20 Marv Matuszak 4.00 8.00
21 Hugh McElhenny 12.50 25.00
22 Jerry Mertens 4.00 8.00
23 Dick Moegle 5.00 10.00
24 Dennit Morris 4.00 8.00
25 Frank Morze 4.00 8.00
26 Leo Nomellini 10.00 20.00
27 R.C. Owens 5.00 10.00
28 Jim Pace 4.00 8.00
29 Lou Palatella 4.00 8.00
30 Joe Perry 12.50 25.00
31 Jim Ridlon 4.00 8.00
32 Karl Rubke 4.00 8.00
33 J.D. Smith 5.00 10.00
34 Gordy Soltau 4.00 8.00
35 Bob St. Clair 7.50 15.00
36 Bill Stits 4.00 8.00
37 John Thomas 4.00 8.00
38 Y.A. Tittle 17.50 35.00
39 Bob Toneff 4.00 8.00
40 Lynn Waldorf Dir. 4.00 8.00
41 Billy Wilson 4.00 8.00
42 John Wittenborn 4.00 8.00
43 Abe Woodson 5.00 10.00
44 49ers Coaches 5.00 10.00

1959 49ers Team Issue

This 45-card set measures approximately 4 1/8" by 6 1/4". The front features a black and white posed action photo enclosed by a white border, with the player's signature across the bottom portion of the picture. The back lists the player's name, position, height, weight, and college, along with basic biographical information. Many of the cards in this and the other similar team issue sets are only distinguishable as to year by comparing text on the card back; the first few words of text are provided for many of the cards parenthetically below. The set was available direct from the team as part of a package for their fans. The cards are unnumbered and hence are listed alphabetically for convenience.

COMPLETE SET (45) 250.00 400.00
1 Bill Atkins 4.00 8.00
2 Dave Baker 4.00 8.00
3 Bruce Bosley 4.00 8.00
4 John Brodie 12.50 25.00
5 Jack Christiansen CO 7.50 15.00
6 Monte Clark 4.00 8.00
7 Clyde Conner 4.00 8.00
8 Ted Connolly 4.00 8.00
9 Tommy Davis 4.00 8.00
10 Eddie Dove 4.00 8.00
11 Fred Dugan 4.00 8.00
12 Mark Duncan CO 4.00 8.00
13 Bob Fouts ANN 4.00 8.00
14 John Gonzaga 4.00 8.00
15 Bob Harrison 4.00 8.00
16 Matt Hazeltine 4.00 8.00
17 Ed Henke 4.00 8.00
18 Bill Herchman 4.00 8.00
19 Howard(Red) Hickey CO 4.00 8.00
20 Russ Hodges ANN 4.00 8.00
21 Bill Johnson CO 4.00 8.00
22 Charlie Krueger 4.00 8.00
23 Lenny Lyles 4.00 8.00
24 Hugh McElhenny 12.50 25.00
25 Jerry Mertens 4.00 8.00
26 Dick Moegle 5.00 10.00
27 Frank Morze 4.00 8.00
28 Leo Nomellini 10.00 20.00
29 Clancy Osborne 4.00 8.00
30 R.C. Owens 5.00 10.00
31 Joe Perry 12.50 25.00
32 Jim Ridlon 4.00 8.00
33 Karl Rubke 4.00 8.00
34 Bob St.Clair 7.50 15.00
35 Henry Schmidt 4.00 8.00
36 Bob Shaw CO 4.00 8.00
37 Lon Simmons ANN 4.00 8.00
38 J.D. Smith 5.00 10.00
39 John Thomas 4.00 8.00
40 Y.A. Tittle 15.00 30.00
41 Jerry Tubbs 4.00 8.00
42 Lynn Waldorf Dir. 4.00 8.00
43 Billy Wilson 4.00 8.00
44 John Wittenborn 4.00 8.00
45 Abe Woodson 5.00 10.00

1960 49ers Team Issue

This 44-card set measures approximately 4 1/8" by 6 1/4". The front features a black-and-white posed action photo with white borders. The player's facsimile autograph is inscribed across the picture. The back lists the player's name, position, height, weight, age, college, along with career summary and biographical notes. The set was available direct from the team as part of a package for their fans. The photos are unnumbered and checklisted below in alphabetical order.

COMPLETE SET (44) 200.00 350.00
1 Dave Baker 4.00 8.00
2 Bruce Bosley 4.00 8.00
3 John Brodie 12.50 25.00
4 Jack Christiansen ACO 6.00 12.00
5 Monte Clark 4.00 8.00
6 Dan Colchico 4.00 8.00
7 Clyde Conner 4.00 8.00
8 Ted Connolly 4.00 8.00
9 Tommy Davis 4.00 8.00
10 Eddie Dove 4.00 8.00
11 Mark Duncan ACO 4.00 8.00
12 Bob Fouts ANN 4.00 8.00
13 Bob Harrison 4.00 8.00
14 Matt Hazeltine 4.00 8.00
15 Ed Henke 4.00 8.00
16 Howard(Red) Hickey CO 4.00 8.00
17 Russ Hodges ANN 4.00 8.00
18 Bill Johnson CO 4.00 8.00
19 Gordon Kelley 4.00 8.00
20 Charlie Krueger 4.00 8.00
21 Lenny Lyles 4.00 8.00
22 Hugh McElhenny 12.50 25.00
23 Mike Magac 4.00 8.00
24 Jerry Mertens 4.00 8.00
25 Frank Morze 4.00 8.00
26 Leo Nomellini 10.00 20.00
27 Clancy Osborne 4.00 8.00
28 R.C. Owens 5.00 10.00
29 Jim Ridlon 4.00 8.00
30 C.R. Roberts 4.00 8.00
31 Len Rohde 4.00 8.00
32 Karl Rubke 4.00 0.00
33 Bob St.Clair 6.00 12.00
34 Henry Schmidt 4.00 8.00
35 Lon Simmons ANN 4.00 8.00
36 J.D. Smith 4.00 8.00
37 Gordy Soltau ANN 4.00 8.00
38 Monty Stickles 4.00 8.00
39 John Thomas 4.00 8.00
40 Y.A. Tittle 15.00 30.00
41 Lynn Waldorf Dir. 4.00 8.00
42 Bobby Waters 4.00 8.00
43 Billy Wilson 4.00 8.00
44 Abe Woodson 5.00 10.00

1961 49ers Team Issue

The 49ers issued this set of large (approximately 8" by 10") black and white player photos in 1961. The team logo (old style) and basic player information is contained beneath the player image. The photos are unnumbered and listed below alphabetically. Note that these photos are similar to other 49ers photos, but can be identified by the size (8" by 10") and by the text (position is in lower and upper case letters) and format used to identify the player's weight (example of style: 6-1).

COMPLETE SET (31) 125.00 250.00
1 Bruce Bosley 4.00 8.00
2 John Brodie 10.00 20.00
3 Bernie Casey 4.00 8.00
4 Monte Clark 4.00 8.00
5 Clyde Conner 4.00 8.00
6 Bill Cooper 4.00 8.00
7 Lou Cordileone 4.00 8.00
8 Tommy Davis 5.00 10.00
9 Bob Harrison 4.00 8.00
10 Matt Hazeltine 4.00 8.00
11 Ed Henke 4.00 8.00
12 Howard Red Hickey CO 4.00 8.00
13 Jim Johnson 5.00 10.00
14 Carl Kammerer 4.00 8.00
15 Billy Kilmer 7.50 15.00
16 Roland Lakes 4.00 8.00
17 Bill Lopasky 4.00 8.00
18 Hugh McElhenny 7.50 15.00
19 Dale Messer 4.00 8.00
20 Leo Nomellini 6.00 12.00
21 Ray Norton 4.00 8.00
22 R.C. Owens 5.00 10.00
23 Jim Ridlon 4.00 8.00
24 Karl Rubke 4.00 8.00
25 Bob St. Clair 5.00 10.00
26 Monty Stickles 4.00 8.00
27 Aaron Thomas 4.00 8.00
28 John Thomas 4.00 8.00
29 Y.A. Tittle 12.50 25.00
30 Abe Woodson 5.00 10.00
31 Bill Johnson 7.50 15.00
Jack Christiansen
Billy Wilson

1963 49ers Team Issue

The 49ers issued this set of large (approximately 8" by 10 7/8") black and white player photos around 1963. The team logo (old style) and basic player information is contained beneath the player image. The photos are unnumbered and listed below alphabetically. Note that these photos are similar to other 49ers photos, but can be identified by the larger size (8" by 10 7/8") and by the larger text used on the player's name (4/32" high) as well as the format used to identify the player's weight (example of style: 6' 1"). Note that the player's position was also printed in upper and lower case letters which helps to differentiate this year from later years.

COMPLETE SET (7) 25.00 50.00
1 Eddie Dove 4.00 8.00
2 Mike Magac 4.00 8.00
3 Ed Pine 4.00 8.00
4 Len Rohde 4.00 8.00
5 Monty Stickles 4.00 8.00
6 John Thomas 4.00 8.00
7 Bob Waters 4.00 8.00

1964 49ers Team Issue

The 49ers issued this set of large (approximately 8" by 10 7/8") black and white player photos around 1964. The team logo (old style) and basic player information is contained beneath the player image. The photos are unnumbered and listed below alphabetically. Note that these photos are similar to other 49ers photos, but can be identified by the larger size (8" by 10 7/8") and by the smaller text used on the player's name (3/32" high) and the format used to identify the player's height (example of style: 6' 1"). Note that the player's position was also printed in upper and lower case letters which helps to differentiate this year from later years.

COMPLETE SET (16) 60.00 120.00
1 Kermit Alexander 4.00 8.00
2 John Brodie 7.50 15.00
3 Bernie Casey 5.00 10.00
4 Jack Christiansen CO 6.00 12.00
5 Dan Colchico 4.00 8.00
6 Tommy Davis 5.00 10.00
7 Leon Donohue 4.00 8.00
8 Charlie Krueger 4.00 8.00
9 Roland Lakes 4.00 8.00
10 Don Lisbon 4.00 8.00
11 Clark Miller 4.00 8.00
12 Walter Rock 4.00 8.00
13 Karl Rubke 4.00 8.00
14 Chuck Sieminski 4.00 8.00
15 J.D. Smith 5.00 10.00
16 Abe Woodson 4.00 8.00

1965 49ers Team Issue

The 49ers issued this set of large (approximately 8" by 10 7/8") black and white player photos around 1965. The team logo (old style) and basic player information is contained beneath the player image. The photos are unnumbered and listed below alphabetically. Note that these are virtually identical to the 1964 photos and likely were issued over a period of years. However, we've cataloged below photos which include distinct variations over the 1964 issue.

1 Kermit Alexander 4.00 8.00
2 John Brodie 7.50 15.00
3 Bernie Casey 4.00 8.00
4 Dave Wilcox 5.00 10.00

1966 49ers Team Issue

The 49ers issued this set of large (approximately 8" by 10 7/8") black and white player photos around 1966. The team logo (old style) and basic player information is contained beneath the player image. The photos are unnumbered and listed below alphabetically. Note that these photos are similar to other 49ers photos, but can be identified by the larger size (8" by 10 7/8") and by the text style used on the player's position which was printed in all capital letters.

COMPLETE SET (8) 40.00 80.00
1 Kermit Alexander 4.00 8.00
2 Tommy Davis 5.00 10.00
3 Billy Kilmer 7.50 15.00
4 Elbert Kimbrough 4.00 8.00
5 Dave Kopay 4.00 8.00
6 Charlie Krueger 4.00 8.00
7 Gary Lewis 4.00 8.00
8 George Mira 4.00 8.00
9 Ken Willard 5.00 10.00

1967 49ers Team Issue

This team issue set measures approximately 8" by 11" and features black and white posed action photos of the San Francisco 49ers on thin card stock. The backs are blank. The player's name, position, height, and weight are printed in the white lower border in all caps. The set is very similar to the 1968 and 1971-72 releases, but the size is slightly smaller. The team logo that appears in the white border below the player photo is also slightly different than the 1968 photos. Because this set is unnumbered, the photos are listed alphabetically.

COMPLETE SET 60.00 120.00
1 John David Crow 5.00 10.00
2 Tommy Davis 5.00 10.00
3 George Donnelly 4.00 8.00
4 Charlie Johnson DT 4.00 8.00
5 John Brodie 7.50 15.00
6 George Mira 4.00 8.00
7 Howard Mudd 4.00 8.00
8 Sonny Randle 4.00 8.00
9 Dave Wilcox 5.00 10.00
10 Dick Witcher 4.00 8.00
11 Ken Willard 5.00 10.00
12 Bob Windsor 4.00 8.00
13 Steve Spurrier 20.00 40.00

1968 49ers Team Issue

This team issue set measures approximately 8 1/2" by 11" and features black and white posed action photos of the San Francisco 49ers on thin card stock. The backs are blank. The player's name, position, height, and weight are printed in the white lower border in all caps. The set is very similar to the 1971-72 release, but the team logo is printed in black and silver. It also appears in the white border below the player information. Because this set is unnumbered, the players and coaches are listed alphabetically. Steve Spurrier's card predates his Rookie Card by four years.

COMPLETE SET (38) 125.00 250.00
1 Kermit Alexander 5.00 10.00
2 Cas Banaszek 4.00 8.00
3 Ed Beard 4.00 8.00
4 Forrest Blue 4.00 8.00
5 Bruce Bosley 4.00 8.00
6 John Brodie 7.50 15.00
7 Elmer Collett 4.00 8.00
8 Doug Cunningham 4.00 8.00
9 Tommy Davis 5.00 10.00
10 Earl Edwards 4.00 8.00
11 Kevin Hardy 4.00 8.00
12 Matt Hazeltine 4.00 8.00
13 Stan Hindman 4.00 8.00
14 Tom Holzer 4.00 8.00
15 Jim Johnson 6.00 12.00
16 Charlie Krueger 4.00 8.00
17 Roland Lakes 4.00 8.00
18 Gary Lewis 4.00 8.00
19 Kay McFarland 4.00 8.00
20 Clifton McNeil 4.00 8.00
21 George Mira 5.00 10.00
22 Eugene Moore 4.00 8.00
23 Howard Mudd 4.00 8.00
24 Dick Nolan CO 4.00 8.00
25 Frank Nunley 4.00 8.00
26 Don Parker 4.00 8.00
27 Mel Phillips 4.00 8.00
28 Al Randolph 4.00 8.00
29 Len Rohde 4.00 8.00
30 Steve Spurrier 20.00 40.00
31 John Thomas 4.00 8.00
32 Bill Tucker 4.00 8.00
33 Gene Washington 5.00 10.00
34 Dave Wilcox 5.00 10.00
35 Ken Willard 5.00 10.00
36 Bob Windsor 4.00 8.00
37 Dick Witcher 4.00 8.00
38 Team Photo 7.50 15.00

1968 49ers Volpe Tumblers

These 49ers artist's renderings were part of a plastic cup tumbler product produced in 1968. The noted sports artist Volpe created the artwork which includes an action scene and a player portrait. The "cards" are unnumbered, each measures approximately 5" by 8 1/2" and is curved in the shape required to fit inside a plastic cup. There are likely 12 cups included in this set. Any additions to this list are appreciated.

COMPLETE SET (3) 62.50 125.00
1 John Brodie 30.00 60.00
2 John David Crow 20.00 40.00
3 Charlie Krueger 15.00 30.00

1969 49ers Team Issue 4X5

These small (roughly 4" by 5") black and white photos look very similar to the 1971 release. Each includes a player photo along with his team name, player name, and position. The cardbacks are blank. We've noted text or photo differences below on players that were included in both sets.

COMPLETE SET (20) 40.00 80.00
1 Elmer Collett 2.50 5.00
2 Tommy Davis 3.00 6.00
3 Earl Edwards 2.50 5.00
4 Johnny Fuller 2.50 5.00
5 Harold Hays 2.50 5.00
6 Stan Hindman 2.50 5.00
7 Roland Lakes 2.50 5.00
8 Gary Lewis 2.50 5.00
9 Frank Nunley 2.50 5.00
10 Clifton McNeil 2.50 5.00
11 Mel Phillips 2.50 5.00
12 Al Randolph 2.50 5.00
13 Len Rohde 2.50 5.00
14 Jim Sniadecki 2.50 5.00
15 Sam Silas 2.50 5.00
16 Jimmy Thomas 2.50 5.00
17 Bill Tucker 2.50 5.00
18 Bob Windsor 2.50 5.00
19 Dick Witcher 3.00 6.00
20 John Woitt 2.50 5.00

1971 49ers Team Issue 4X5

These small (roughly 4" by 5") black and white photos look very similar to the 1969 release. Each includes a player photo along with his team name, player name, and position. The cardbacks are blank. We've noted text or photo differences below on players that were included in both sets.

COMPLETE SET (20) 40.00 80.00
1 Elmer Collett 2.50 4.00
2 Earl Edwards 2.50 4.00
3 Johnny Fuller 2.50 4.00
4 Tony Harris 2.50 4.00
5 Tommy Hart 3.00 6.00
6 Stan Hindman 2.50 4.00
7 Bob Hoskins 2.50 4.00
8 John Isenbarger 2.50 4.00
9 Jim McCann 2.50 4.00
10 Frank Nunley 2.50 4.00
11 Mel Phillips 2.50 4.00
12 Preston Riley 2.50 4.00
13 Len Rohde 2.50 5.00
14 Larry Schreiber 2.50 4.00
15 Mike Simpson 2.50 4.00
16 Jim Sniadecki 2.50 4.00
17 Jimmy Thomas 2.50 4.00
18 Vic Washington 2.50 5.00
19 Bob Windsor 2.50 5.00
20 Dick Witcher 2.50 5.00

1971 49ers Postcards

The San Francisco 49ers distributed this set of oversized postcards in 1971. Each measures approximately 5 3/4" by 8 7/8" and features a borderless black and white player photo on front with a postcard style back. The player's name, position, helmet logo, and some vital statistics are featured within a white border area below the photo. The unnumbered cardbacks also contain extensive player career information and stats.

COMPLETE SET (47) 200.00 400.00
1 Cas Banaszak 6.25 12.50
2 Ed Beard 5.00 10.00
3 Randy Beisler 5.00 10.00
4 Bill Belk 6.25 12.50
5 Forrest Blue 6.25 12.50
6 John Brodie 10.00 20.00
7 Elmer Collett 5.00 10.00
8 Doug Cunningham 5.00 10.00
9 Earl Edwards 5.00 10.00
10 Johnny Fuller 5.00 10.00
11 Bruce Gossett 6.25 12.50
12 Cedrick Hardman 6.25 12.50
13 Tony Harris 5.00 10.00
14 Tommy Hart 6.25 12.50
15 Stan Hindman 5.00 10.00
16 Bob Hoskins 5.00 10.00
17 Marty Huff 5.00 10.00
18 John Isenbarger 5.00 10.00
19 Ernie Janet 5.00 10.00
20 Jimmy Johnson 7.50 15.00
21 Charlie Krueger 6.25 12.50
22 Ted Kwalick 6.25 12.50
23 Jim McCann 5.00 10.00
24 Dick Nolan CO 6.25 12.50
25 Frank Nunley 5.00 10.00
26 Joe Orduna 5.00 10.00
27 Willie Parker 5.00 10.00
28 Woody Peoples 5.00 10.00
29 Mel Phillips 6.25 12.50
30 Joe Reed 6.25 12.50
31 Preston Riley 5.00 10.00
32 Len Rohde 6.25 12.50
33 Larry Schreiber 5.00 10.00
34 Sam Silas 5.00 10.00
35 Mike Simpson 5.00 10.00
36 Jim Sniadecki 5.00 10.00
37 Steve Spurrier 20.00 40.00
38 Bruce Taylor 6.25 12.50
39 Jimmy Thomas 5.00 10.00
40 Skip Vanderbundt 6.25 12.50
41 Gene Washington 6.25 12.50
42 Vic Washington 6.25 12.50
43 John Watson 5.00 10.00
44 Dave Wilcox 6.25 12.50
45 Ken Willard 6.25 12.50
46 Bob Windsor 5.00 10.00
47 Dick Witcher 5.00 10.00
48 Coaching Staff 6.25 12.50

1971-72 49ers Team Issue

This team issue set measures approximately 8 1/2" by 11" and features black and white posed action photos of the San Francisco 49ers on thin card stock. The backs are blank. The player's name, position, height, and weight are printed in the white lower border in all caps. The set is very similar to the 1967 and 1968 releases, but the team logo is printed in all black and appears in the white border below the player information. Because this set is unnumbered, the players are listed alphabetically.

COMPLETE SET (5) 15.00 30.00
1 Ed Beard 4.00 8.00
2 Bill Belk 4.00 8.00
3 John Brodie 7.50 15.00
4 Bruce Gossett 4.00 8.00
5 Ted Kwalick 4.00 8.00

1972 49ers Redwood City Tribune

This set of six (approximately) 3" by 5 1/2" facsimile autograph cards features black-and-white head shots with white borders. The player's name is printed beneath the picture and in a large space immediately beneath, the card carries the player's signature. The bottom of the front reads "49er autograph card courtesy of Redwood City Tribune." The cards are unnumbered and checklisted below in alphabetical order. The set's date is bracketed by the fact that Frank Edwards last year with the San Francisco 49ers was 1972 and Larry Schreiber's first year with the 49ers was 1971.

COMPLETE SET (6) 37.50 75.00
1 Earl Edwards 3.75 7.50
2 Frank Nunley 3.75 7.50
3 Len Rohde 3.75 7.50
4 Larry Schreiber 3.75 7.50
5 Steve Spurrier 20.00 40.00
6 Gene Washington 6.25 12.50

1972-75 49ers Team Issue

The 49ers released similar player photos over a period of years in the 1970s. For ease in cataloging, we've included them together below. There are likely many missing from the checklist, any additions to the list would be appreciated. Each photo measures approximately 7" by 11" and was printed on very thin glossy stock. The fronts feature black-and-white action player photos on a white background. The player's picture measures roughly 6 1/4" by 7 1/2" and the cardbacks are blanks. The player's name, biographical information, career highlights, and a personal profile are printed in the white margin at the bottom. Most also include a 49ers helmet logo below the image. The player's statistics and years pro notation help in identifying the year of issue. The cards are unnumbered and checklisted below in alphabetical order.

1 Cas Banaszek 4.00 8.00
2 Forrest Blue 4.00 8.00
3 Bruce Gossett 4.00 8.00
4 Windlan Hall 1974 4.00 8.00
5 Cedrick Hardman 4.00 8.00
6 Mike Holmes 4.00 8.00
7 Tom Hull 1974 4.00 8.00
8 Wilbur Jackson 1974 5.00 10.00
9 Jim Johnson 1974 6.00 12.00
10 Manfred Moore 1974 4.00 8.00
11 Mel Phillips 1972 4.00 8.00
12 Steve Spurrier 1974 12.50 25.00
13 Bruce Taylor 4.00 8.00
14 Skip Vanderbundt 4.00 8.00
15 Gene Washington 1973 5.00 10.00
16 Gene Washington 1975 5.00 10.00
17 John Watson 1974 4.00 8.00

1977 49ers Team Issue

These team issued photos of the San Francisco 49ers measure approximately 5" by 8" and feature black-and-white player photos within a white border. The player's name is pirnted in all caps below the picture with his jersey number, position, height, weight, and college printed below that. The backs are blank so the cards are unnumbered and checklisted below in alphabetical order. It is thought that these photos may have been issued over a period of years since they closely resemble the 1980-82 release.

1 Cleveland Elam 2.00 5.00
2 Jim Plunkett 3.00 8.00
3 Dave Washington 2.00 5.00

1980-82 49ers Team Issue

This team issue set of the San Francisco 49ers measures approximately 5" by 8" and features a black-and-white player photo in a white border. The players name, jersey number, height, weight, and college are printed in the wide bottom margin. The backs are blank. The cards are unnumbered and checklisted below in alphabetical order. It is thought that these photos may have been issued over a period of years since some feature the player's name in all caps while others use both upper and lower case letters. The set features an early Joe Montana card that is thought to have been issued in 1982.

COMPLETE SET (55) 125.00 250.00
1 Dan Audick 1.25 3.00
2 John Ayers 1.25 3.00
3 Jean Barrett 1.25 3.00
4 Guy Benjamin 1.25 3.00
5 Dwaine Board 1.25 3.00
6 Bob Bruer 1.25 3.00
7 Ken Bungarda 1.25 3.00
8 Dan Bunz 1.25 3.00
9 John Choma 1.25 3.00
10 Ricky Churchman 1.25 3.00
11 Dwight Clark 3.00 8.00
12 Earl Cooper 1.25 3.00
13 Randy Cross 1.50 4.00
14 Johnny Davis 1.25 3.00
15 Fred Dean 1.50 4.00
16 Walt Downing 1.25 3.00
17 Walt Easley 1.25 3.00
18 Lenvil Elliott 1.25 3.00
19 Keith Fahnhorst 1.25 3.00
20 Bob Ferrell 1.25 3.00
21 Phil Francis 1.25 3.00
22 Rick Gervais 1.25 3.00
23 Willie Harper 1.25 3.00
24 John Harty 1.25 3.00
25 Dwight Hicks 1.50 4.00
26 Scott Hilton 1.25 3.00
27 Paul Hofer 1.25 3.00
28 Pete Kugler 1.25 3.00
29 Amos Lawrence 1.25 3.00
30 Bobby Leopold 1.25 3.00
31 Ronnie Lott 6.00 15.00
32 Saladin Martin 1.25 3.00
33 Milt McColl 1.25 3.00
34 Jim Miller P 1.25 3.00
35 Joe Montana 90.00 150.00
36 Ricky Patton 1.25 3.00
37 Lawrence Pillers 1.25 3.00
38 Craig Puki 1.25 3.00
39 Fred Quillan 1.25 3.00
40 Eason Ramson 1.25 3.00
41 Archie Reese 1.25 3.00
42 Jack Reynolds 1.50 4.00
43 Bill Ring 1.25 3.00
44 Mike Shumann 1.25 3.00
45 Freddie Solomon 2.00 5.00
46 Scott Stauch 1.25 3.00
47 Jim Stuckey 1.25 3.00
48 Lynn Thomas 1.25 3.00
49 Keena Turner 1.25 3.00
50 Jimmy Webb 1.25 3.00
51 Ray Wersching 1.25 3.00
52 Carlton Williamson 1.25 3.00
53 Mike Wilson 1.25 3.00
54 Eric Wright 1.50 4.00
55 Charlie Young 1.50 4.00

1982 49ers Prints

These large (roughly 11 1/2" by 18") prints were sponsored by Taco Bell and Dr. Pepper and issued in 1982. Each features several 49ers players in a color artist's rendering format on thick paper stock. The backs feature the art's title and a write-up on the featured players along with the Taco Bell and Dr. Pepper logos.

COMPLETE SET (4) 30.00 75.00
1 Deanfence 6.00 15.00
2 Joe, Freddie, and Dwight 15.00 40.00
3 The Unsung Ones 4.00 10.00
4 Very Special Teams 4.00 10.00

1984 49ers Police

This set of 12 cards was issued in three panels of four cards each. Individual cards measure approximately 2 1/2" by 4 1/16" and feature the San Francisco 49ers. Since the cards are unnumbered, they are ordered and numbered below alphabetically by the subject's name. The set is sponsored by 7-Eleven, Dr. Pepper, and KCBS.

COMPLETE SET (12) 12.00 30.00
1 Dwaine Board .20 .50
2 Roger Craig 2.00 5.00
3 Riki Ellison .20 .50
4 Keith Fahnhorst .20 .50
5 Joe Montana 8.00 20.00
Clark
6 Jack Reynolds .30 .75
7 Freddie Solomon .30 .75
8 Keena Turner .30 .75
9 Wendell Tyler .30 .75
10 Bill Walsh CO 1.50 4.00
11 Ray Wersching .20 .50
12 Eric Wright .20 .50

1985 49ers Police

This set of 16 cards was issued in four panels of four cards each. Individual cards measure approximately 2 1/2" by 4" and feature the San Francisco 49ers. Since the cards are unnumbered, they are ordered and numbered below alphabetically by the subject's name. The set is differentiated from the similar 1984 Police 49ers set since this 1985 set is only sponsored by 7-Eleven and Dr. Pepper.

COMPLETE SET (16) 10.00 25.00
1 John Ayers .15 .40
2 Roger Craig .75 2.00
3 Fred Dean .30 .75
4 Riki Ellison .20 .50
5 Keith Fahnhorst .15 .40
6 Russ Francis .30 .75
7 Dwight Hicks .20 .50
8 Ronnie Lott 1.25 3.00
9 Dana McLemore .15 .40
10 Joe Montana 6.00 15.00
11 Todd Shell .20 .50
12 Freddie Solomon .30 .75
13 Keena Turner .20 .50
14 Bill Walsh CO .50 1.25
15 Ray Wersching .15 .40
16 Eric Wright .20 .50

1985 49ers Smokey

is set of seven large (approximately 2 15/16" by 4 3/8") cards was issued in the Summer of 1985 and features the San Francisco 49ers and Smokey Bear. The card backs are printed in black on a thin white card stock. Card backs have a cartoon fire safety message and a facsimile autograph of the player. Smokey Bear is pictured on each card along with the player (or players).

COMPLETE SET (7) 40.00 80.00
1 Group Picture 8.00 20.00
2 Joe Montana 30.00 60.00
3 Jack Reynolds 1.25 3.00
4 Eric Wright 1.25 3.00
5 Dwight Hicks 1.25 3.00
6 Dwight Clark 2.50 6.00
7 Keena Turner 1.25 3.00

1987 49ers Ace Fact Pack

This 33-card set measures approximately 2 1/4" by 3 5/8". This set was manufactured in West Germany (by Ace Fact Pack) for release in Great Britain and features rounded corners and a playing card type of design on the back. There are 22 player cards in this set and we have checklisted those cards in alphabetical order.

COMPLETE SET (33) 250.00 500.00
1 John Ayers 2.00 5.00
2 Dwaine Board 2.00 5.00
3 Michael Carter 2.50 6.00
4 Dwight Clark 4.00 10.00
5 Roger Craig 6.00 15.00
6 Joe Cribbs 2.50 6.00
7 Randy Cross 2.50 6.00
8 Riki Ellison 2.00 5.00
9 Jim Fahnhorst 2.00 5.00
10 Keith Fahnhorst 2.00 5.00
11 Russ Francis 2.50 6.00
12 Don Griffin 2.00 5.00

13 Ronnie Lott 10.00 25.00
14 Milt McColl 2.00 5.00
15 Tim McKyer 2.00 5.00
16 Joe Montana 125.00 300.00
17 Bubba Paris 2.00 5.00
18 Fred Quillan 2.00 5.00
19 Jerry Rice 75.00 150.00
20 Manu Tuiasosopo 2.00 5.00
21 Keena Turner 2.00 5.00
22 Carlton Williamson 2.00 5.00
23 49ers Helmet 2.00 5.00
24 49ers Information 2.00 5.00
25 49ers Uniform 2.00 5.00
26 Game Record Holders 2.00 5.00
27 Season Record Holders 2.00 5.00
28 Career Record Holders 2.00 5.00
29 Record 1967-86 2.00 5.00
30 1986 Team Statistics 2.00 5.00
31 All-Time Greats 2.00 5.00
32 Roll of Honour 2.00 5.00
33 Candlestick Park 2.00 5.00

1988 49ers Police

e 1988 Police San Francisco 49ers set contains 20 unnumbered cards measuring approximately 2 1/2" by 4". There are 19 player cards and one coach card. The fronts are basically "pure" with white borders. The backs have a football tip and a McGruff crime tip. The cards are listed below in alphabetical order by subject's name. The set is sponsored by 7-Eleven and Oscar Mayer, which differentiates this set from the similar-looking 1985 Police 49ers set.

COMPLETE SET (20) 25.00 60.00
1 Harris Barton .30 .75
2 Dwaine Board .20 .50
3 Michael Carter .20 .50
4 Roger Craig .40 1.00
5 Randy Cross .30 .75
6 Riki Ellison .20 .50
7 John Frank .20 .50
8 Jeff Fuller .20 .50
9 Pete Kugler .20 .50
10 Ronnie Lott 1.00 2.50
11 Joe Montana 8.00 20.00
12 Tom Rathman .30 .75
13 Jerry Rice 8.00 20.00
14 Jeff Stover .20 .50
15 Keena Turner .30 .75
16 Bill Walsh CO .60 1.50
17 Michael Walter .20 .50
18 Mike Wilson .20 .50
19 Eric Wright .30 .75
20 Steve Young 6.00 15.00

1988 49ers Smokey

is 35-card set features members of the San Francisco 49ers. The cards measure approximately 5" by 8". The printing on the card back is in black ink on white card stock. The cards are unnumbered except for uniform number; they are ordered below alphabetically for convenience. Each card back contains a fire safety cartoon (usually) featuring Smokey. Reportedly the Dwaine Board card is more difficult to find than the other cards in the set.

COMPLETE SET (35) 60.00 150.00
1 Harris Barton .60 1.50
2 Dwaine Board SP 3.00 8.00
3 Michael Carter .60 1.50
4 Bruce Collie .40 1.00
5 Roger Craig 1.50 4.00
6 Randy Cross .75 2.00
7 Eddie DeBartolo Jr. .75 2.00
8 Riki Ellison .40 1.00
9 Kevin Fagan .40 1.00
10 Jim Fahnhorst .40 1.00
11 John Frank .60 1.50
12 Jeff Fuller .40 1.00
13 Don Griffin .60 1.50
14 Charles Haley 1.25 3.00
15 Ron Heller TE .40 1.00
16 Tom Holmoe .40 1.00
17 Pete Kugler .40 1.00
18 Ronnie Lott 2.00 5.00
19 Tim McKyer .60 1.50
20 Joe Montana 20.00 50.00
21 Tory Nixon .40 1.00
22 Bubba Paris .60 1.50
23 John Paye .40 1.00
24 Tom Rathman .75 2.00
25 Jerry Rice 20.00 50.00
26 Jeff Stover .40 1.00
27 Harry Sydney .40 1.00
20 John Taylor 1.50 4.00
29 Keena Turner .60 1.50
30 Steve Wallace .60 1.50
31 Bill Walsh CO 1.25 3.00
32 Michael Walter .40 1.00
33 Mike Wilson .40 1.00
34 Eric Wright .60 1.50
35 Steve Young 10.00 25.00

1990 49ers Knudsen

is six-card set of bookmarks measures approximately 2" by 8" was produced by Knudsen's to help promote readership by people under 15 years old in the San Francisco area. They were given out in San Francisco libraries on a weekly basis. Between the Knudsen company name, the front features a color action photo of the player superimposed on a football stadium. The field is green, the bleachers are yellow with gray print, and the scoreboard above the player reads "The Reading Team". The box below the player gives brief biographical information and player highlights. The back has logos of the sponsors and describes two books that are available at the public library. We have checklisted this set in alphabetical order because they are otherwise unnumbered except for the player's uniform number displayed on the card front.

COMPLETE SET (6) 20.00 50.00
1 Roger Craig 1.60 4.00
2 Ronnie Lott 2.00 5.00
3 Joe Montana 8.00 20.00
4 Jerry Rice 8.00 20.00
5 George Seifert CO 1.60 4.00
6 Michael Walter 1.20 3.00

1990-91 49ers SF Examiner

This 16-card San Francisco Examiner 49ers set was issued on two unperforated sheets measuring approximately 14" by 11". Each sheet featured eight cards, with a newspaper headline at the top of the sheet reading "San Francisco Examiner Salutes the 49ers' Finest". If the cards were cut, they would measure approximately 3 1/4" by 4 1/8". The front design has color game shots, with a thin orange border on a red card face. A gold plaque at the card top reads "SF Examiner's Finest," while the gold plaque at the bottom has the player's position and name. The horizontally oriented backs have a black and white head shot, biographical information, statistics, and player profile. The cards are unnumbered and checklisted below in alphabetical order.

COMPLETE SET (16) 30.00 50.00
1 Harris Barton .50 1.25
2 Michael Carter .50 1.25
3 Mike Cofer .50 1.25
4 Roger Craig .75 2.00
5 Kevin Fagan .50 1.25
6 Don Griffin .50 1.25
7 Charles Haley .75 2.00
8 Pierce Holt .50 1.25
9 Brent Jones .75 2.00
10 Ronnie Lott 1.50 4.00
11 Guy McIntyre .50 1.25
12 Matt Millen .50 1.25
13 Joe Montana 10.00 20.00
14 Tom Rathman .75 2.00
15 Jerry Rice 7.50 15.00
16 John Taylor .75 2.00

1992 49ers FBI

is 40-card standard-size set was sponsored by the San Francisco 49ers and the FBI (Federal Bureau of Investigation). According to the title card, a different pack of cards was available free with the 49ers' edition of GameDay Magazine at regular season home games each week at Candlestick Park. The fronts display color action player photos with white borders. In red and white lettering, the player's first and last names are overprinted on the photo at the upper left and lower right corners respectively. The team helmet at the lower left corner rounds out the front. Inside white borders on brick-red background, the backs feature a color close-up photo (inside a football helmet design), biographical information, and a public service message in the form of a player quote.

COMPLETE SET (40) 16.00 40.00
1 Michael Carter .20 .50
2 Kevin Fagan .20 .50
3 Charles Haley .40 1.00
4 Guy McIntyre .20 .50
5 George Seifert CO .40 1.00
6 Harry Sydney .20 .50
7 John Taylor .50 1.25
8 Michael Walter .20 .50
9 Steve Young 4.00 10.00
10 Mike Cofer .20 .50
11 Keith DeLong .20 .50
12 Don Griffin .20 .50
13 Pierce Holt .30 .75
14 Mike Sherrard .40 1.00
15 Larry Roberts .20 .50
16 Bill Romanowski .20 .50
17 Tom Rathman .40 1.00
18 Jesse Sapolu .30 .75
19 Brent Jones .40 1.00
20 Brian Bollinger .20 .50
21 Eric Davis .20 .50
22 Antonio Goss .20 .50
23 Alan Grant .20 .50
24 Harris Barton .30 .75
25 Ricky Watters 1.60 4.00
26 Darin Jordan .20 .50
27 Odessa Turner .20 .50
28 David Wilkins LB .20 .50
29 Merton Hanks .40 1.00
30 David Whitmore .20 .50
31 Joe Montana 6.00 15.00
32 Klaus Wilmsmeyer .20 .50
33 Tim Harris .30 .75
34 Roy Foster .20 .50
35 Bill Musgrave .30 .75
36 Dana Hall .30 .75
37 Steve Wallace .30 .75
38 Steve Bono .80 2.00
39 Jerry Rice 4.80 12.00
NNO Title Card .30 .75

1994 49ers Pro Mags/Pro Tags

Issued in a black cardboard box and featuring the San Francisco 49ers, this set consists of six Pro Mags and six Pro Tags, both with rounded corners and measuring 2 1/8" by 3 3/8". Each box was individually numbered out of 750. On a team color-coded background, the magnet fronts display borderless color action player photos. The player's name in big gold-foil letters appears along the left side, with the team name below. A gold-foil Super Bowl XXIX logo is printed in the lower right corner. On a computerized team color-coded background, the tag fronts feature a color action player cutout superimposed on the Roman numerals XXIX printed vertically in block lettering. The player's name is gold foil-stamped across the bottom, with a gold-foil Super Bowl XXIX logo between the first and last name. The backs carry a color closeup photo, an autograph strip, and player profile. The magnets and tags are unnumbered and checklisted below in alphabetical order, first the magnets (1-6) and then the tags (7-12).

COMPLETE SET (12) 8.00 20.00
1 Ken Norton Jr. .50 1.25
2 Jerry Rice 1.20 3.00
3 Deion Sanders .80 2.00
4 John Taylor .50 1.25
5 Ricky Watters .60 1.50
6 Steve Young 1.00 2.50
7 Ken Norton Jr. .50 1.25
8 Jerry Rice 1.20 3.00
9 Deion Sanders .80 2.00
10 John Taylor .50 1.25
11 Ricky Watters .60 1.50
12 Steve Young 1.00 2.50

1994-95 49ers Then and Now Coins

Each coin in this set measures 1 1/4" in diameter and features a member of the 49ers from the past or present. The reverse side of the coins features the year "1994-95" and set name and 49ers logo. The unnumbered coins were minted in a silver colored heavy alloy metal. A colorful album to house the collection was also produced.

COMPLETE SET (20) 125.00 200.00
1 John Brodie 4.00 10.00
2 Dwight Clark 4.00 10.00
3 Dwight Clark The Catch 5.00 12.00
4 Roger Craig 5.00 12.00
5 Randy Cross 4.00 10.00
6 Ronnie Lott 6.00 15.00
7 Leo Nomellini 4.00 10.00
8 R.C. Owens 4.00 10.00
9 Joe Perry 5.00 12.00
10 Jerry Rice 7.50 20.00
11 Jerry Rice 127 TDs 7.50 20.00
12 George Seifert CO 4.00 10.00
13 John Taylor 4.00 10.00
14 Y.A. Tittle 5.00 12.00
15 Keena Turner 4.00 10.00
16 Bill Walsh CO 5.00 12.00
17 Gene Washington 4.00 10.00
18 Eric Wright 4.00 10.00
19 Steve Young 6.00 15.00
20 Team of the Decade Copper 5.00 12.00
NNO Album 5.00 12.00

1995 49ers CommCard Phone Cards

Five 49ers players were featured on prepaid phone cards by CommCard. The various denominations included: 10, 29, 49, and 75-minutes.

COMPLETE SET (5) 2.00 5.00
1 Richard Dent .60 1.50
2 Merton Hanks .40 1.00
3 Tim McDonald .40 1.00
4 Bart Oates .40 1.00
5 Jesse Sapolu .40 1.00

1996 49ers Save Mart Cards/Coins

The San Francisco 49ers, in conjunction with Save Mart Supermarkets, produced this nine card and coin set commemorating the team's Super Bowl teams past and present. The card fronts feature color action player photos with the player's name printed diagonally on one side of the cardfront. The backs display the complete nine-card checklist and individual card numbers. We've listed the cards below using a "CA" prefix. The coin fronts feature a player likeness with the player's name and jersey number. The backs display the 49ers team logo. The coins are unnumbered but have been listed below alphabetically using a "CO" prefix. A cardboard holder featuring Jerry Rice and Steve Young was produced to house the set.

COMP.CARD/COIN SET (18) 16.00 40.00
COMPLETE CARD SET (9) 10.00 25.00
COMPLETE COIN SET (9) 8.00 20.00
CA1 Steve Young 2.00 5.00
CA2 Roger Craig 1.00 2.50
CA3 Jerry Rice 2.40 6.00
CA4 Ronnie Lott 1.20 3.00
CA5 Ken Norton .75 2.00
CA6 Dwight Clark 1.00 2.50
CA7 Brent Jones .75 2.00
CA8 Joe Montana 3.20 8.00
CA9 S.Young 2.00 5.00
Rice
Super Bowl
CO1 Dwight Clark 1.00 2.50
CO2 Roger Craig 1.00 2.50
CO3 Brent Jones .75 2.00
CO4 Ronnie Lott 1.00 2.50
CO5 Joe Montana 2.40 6.00
CO6 Ken Norton .75 2.00
CO7 Jerry Rice 2.00 5.00
CO8 Steve Young 1.60 4.00
CO9 Super Bowl XXIX Trophy 1.20 3.00
NNO Set Display Holder 1.60 4.00

1997 49ers Collector's Choice

Upper Deck released several team sets in 1997 in a blister pack wrapper. Each of the 14-cards in this set are very similar to the base Collector's Choice cards except for the card numbering on the cardback. A cover/checklist card was added featuring the team helmet.

COMPLETE SET (14) 1.20 3.00
SF1 Dana Stubblefield .05 .15
SF2 Merton Hanks .02 .10
SF3 Terrell Owens .40 1.00
SF4 Brent Jones .02 .10
SF5 Ken Norton Jr. .02 .10
SF6 Jerry Rice .40 1.00
SF7 Terry Kirby .05 .15
SF8 Bryant Young .05 .15
SF9 Jim Druckenmiller .05 .15
SF10 William Floyd .05 .15
SF11 Steve Young .25 .60
SF12 Lee Woodall .02 .10
SF13 Garrison Hearst .05 .15
SF14 49ers Logo .25 .60
Checklist

1997 49ers Score

is 15-card set of the San Francisco 49ers was distributed in five-card packs with a suggested retail price of $1.99. The fronts feature color action player photos with white borders and the player's name and team logo printed in team color foil at the bottom. The backs carry player information and career statistics. A Platinum Team parallel set was randomly inserted in packs and featured red foil on the cardfronts.

COMPLETE SET (15) 3.20 8.00
*PLATINUM TEAMS: 1X TO 2X
1 Jerry Rice .80 2.00
2 Steve Young .60 1.50
3 Garrison Hearst .30 .75
4 Terry Kirby .15 .40
5 Brent Jones .08 .25
6 J.J. Stokes .30 .75
7 Terrell Owens .50 1.25
8 William Floyd .15 .40
9 Ken Norton Jr. .08 .25
10 Bryant Young .15 .40
11 Dana Stubblefield .15 .40
12 Ted Popson .08 .25
13 Roy Barker .08 .25
14 Tyronne Drakeford .08 .25
15 Merton Hanks .08 .25

1998 49ers UD Choice

COMPLETE SET (11) 3.00 8.00
SF1 Terrell Owens .40 1.00
SF2 Merton Hanks .20 .50
SF3 Chris Doleman .20 .50
SF4 Steve Young .60 1.50
SF5 Chuck Levy .20 .50
SF6 J.J. Stokes .20 .50
SF7 Ken Norton .20 .50
SF8 R.W. McQuarters .20 .50
SF9 Jerry Rice 1.00 2.50
SF10 Garrison Hearst .30 .75
SF11 Ty Detmer .30 .75

2002 49ers Topps Coke

is set was produced by Topps and sponsored by Coca-Cola. Each card features a red border with the Coke logo on the front and a standard cardback.

1 Jeff Garcia .50 1.25
2 Terrell Owens .75 2.00
3 Tai Streets .40 1.00
4 Garrison Hearst .50 1.25
5 Kevan Barlow .50 1.25
6 Eric Johnson .50 1.25
7 Bryant Young .40 1.00
8 Dana Stubblefield .40 1.00
9 Derek Smith LB .40 1.00
10 Jeff Ulbrich .40 1.00
11 Andre Carter .40 1.00
12 Ahmed Plummer .40 1.00

2006 49ers Topps

COMPLETE SET (12) 3.00 6.00
SF1 Alex Smith QB .30 .75
SF2 Kevan Barlow .25 .60
SF3 Arnaz Battle .25 .60
SF4 Frank Gore .30 .75
SF5 Derrick Johnson .25 .60
SF6 Shawntae Spencer .25 .60
SF7 Bryant Young .25 .60
SF8 Antonio Bryant .25 .60
SF9 Maurice Hicks .25 .60
SF10 Trent Dilfer .25 .60
SF11 Vernon Davis .30 .75
SF12 Manny Lawson .30 .75

2007 49ers Topps

COMPLETE SET (12) 2.50 6.00
1 Frank Gore .50 1.25
2 Vernon Davis .40 1.00
3 Alex Smith QB .50 1.25
4 Arnaz Battle .40 1.00
5 Ashley Lelie .50 1.25
6 Nate Clements .40 1.00
7 Manny Lawson .40 1.00
8 Bryant Young .40 1.00
9 Walt Harris .40 1.00
10 Jason Hill .40 1.00
11 Darrell Jackson .40 1.00
12 Patrick Willis .60 1.50

2008 49ers Topps

COMPLETE SET (12) 2.50 5.00
1 Vernon Davis .40 1.00
2 Patrick Willis .50 1.25
3 DeShaun Foster .40 1.00
4 Frank Gore .50 1.25
5 Trent Dilfer .40 1.00
6 Isaac Bruce .60 1.50
7 Alex Smith QB .50 1.25
8 Arnaz Battle .40 1.00
9 Nate Clements .40 1.00
10 Micheal Lewis .40 1.00
11 Josh Morgan .40 1.00
12 Kentwan Balmer .40 1.00

2009 49ers Breast Cancer Awareness

This three card set was issued at a home game in 2009. Each unnumbered card was created by one of the three NFL licensed manufacturers and features the pink ribbon breast cancer awareness logo on the fronts.

COMPLETE SET (3) 2.00 5.00
1 Vernon Davis Panini .60 1.50
2 Frank Gore Upper Deck .75 2.00
3 Patrick Willis Topps .75 2.00

2012 49ers Topps Super Bowl XLVII

COMPLETE SET (5) 3.00 6.00
AS Aldon Smith .40 1.00
CK Colin Kaepernick .50 1.25
FG Frank Gore .50 1.25
MC Michael Crabtree .40 1.00
PW Patrick Willis .50 1.25

1989 Franchise Game

The 1989 NFL Franchise Game was produced by Rohrwood Enterprises of Loveland, Colorado. The game is modeled after Monopoly, in that players begin with a sum of money (54.5 million dollars) and travel around the board, acquiring "property" (i.e., players) in exchange for money. The object of the game is to build a team of 23 players who fill all the different positions required by the team and who are under contract. The game cards measure approximately 3" by 3 1/2" and feature action player photos with rounded corners and white borders. Some collectors have observed a variation in photographic quality. The player's name and team appear above the picture, while the draft round, number of points player is worth to the franchise, and his salary are printed below the picture. The card backs display a teal panel printed with the home cities of NFL teams. A large numeral or acronym appears in the center of the panel. The player's position is printed across the top. The cards are unnumbered and checklisted below alphabetically according to and within teams. In addition to these player cards, the set includes 28 unnumbered team cards displaying the team helmet and 13 generic coaches' cards.

COMPLETE SET (332) 100.00 250.00
1 Neal Anderson .60 1.50
2 Kevin Butler .30 .75
3 Jim Covert .30 .75
4 Dave Duerson .30 .75
5 Dan Hampton .60 1.50
6 Jay Hilgenberg .30 .75
7 Mike Richardson .30 .75
8 Ron Rivera .30 .75
9 Mike Singletary .60 1.50
10 Mike Tomczak .30 .75
11 Keith Van Horne .30 .75
12 Lewis Billups .30 .75
13 Jim Breech .30 .75
14 James Brooks .30 .75
15 Eddie Brown .60 1.50
16 Ross Browner .30 .75
17 Jason Buck .30 .75
18 Cris Collinsworth .60 1.50
19 Eddie Edwards .30 .75
20 Boomer Esiason .60 1.50
21 David Fulcher .30 .75
22 Ray Horton .30 .75
23 Tim Krumrie .30 .75
24 Max Montoya .30 .75
25 Anthony Munoz .60 1.50
26 Jim Skow .30 .75
27 Reggie Williams .30 .75
28 Ickey Woods .30 .75
29 Cornelius Bennett 1.25 3.00
30 Shane Conlan .30 .75
31 Joe Devlin .30 .75
32 Nate Odomes .30 .75
33 Scott Norwood .30 .75
34 Andre Reed .60 1.50
35 Jim Ritcher .30 .75
36 Fred Smerlas .30 .75
37 Bruce Smith .60 1.50
38 Art Still .30 .75
39 Keith Bishop .30 .75
40 Bill Bryan .30 .75
41 Tony Dorsett 1.25 3.00
42 Simon Fletcher .30 .75
43 Mike Harden .30 .75
44 Mark Haynes .30 .75
45 Mike Horan .30 .75
46 Vance Johnson .30 .75
47 Rulon Jones .30 .75
48 Rich Karlis .30 .75
49 Karl Mecklenburg .30 .75
50 Dennis Smith .30 .75
51 Dave Studdard .30 .75
52 Andre Townsend .30 .75
53 Steve Watson .30 .75
54 Sammy Winder .30 .75
55 Matt Bahr .30 .75
56 Rickey Bolden .30 .75
57 Earnest Byner .30 .75
58 Sam Clancy .30 .75
59 Hanford Dixon .30 .75
60 Bob Golic .30 .75
61 Carl Hairston .30 .75
62 Eddie Johnson .30 .75
63 Kevin Mack .30 .75
64 Clay Matthews .30 .75
65 Frank Minnifield .30 .75
66 Ozzie Newsome .60 1.50
67 Cody Risien .30 .75
68 John Cannon .30 .75
69 Ron Holmes .30 .75
70 Winston Moss .30 .75
71 Rob Taylor T .30 .75
72 Joe Bostic .30 .75
73 Roy Green .30 .75
74 Ricky Hunley .30 .75
75 E.J. Junior .30 .75
76 Neil Lomax .30 .75
77 Tim McDonald .30 .75
78 Cedric Mack .30 .75
79 Freddie Joe Nunn .30 .75
80 Gary Anderson .60 1.50
81 Keith Baldwin .30 .75
82 Gill Byrd .30 .75
83 Elvis Patterson .30 .75
84 Gary Plummer .30 .75
85 Billy Ray Smith .30 .75
86 Lee Williams .30 .75
87 Mike Bell .30 .75
88 Lloyd Burruss .30 .75
89 Carlos Carson .30 .75
90 Deron Cherry .30 .75
91 Jack Del Rio 1.25 3.00
92 Irv Eatman .30 .75
93 Dino Hackett .30 .75
94 Bill Kenney .30 .75
95 Albert Lewis .30 .75
96 David Lutz .30 .75
97 Bill Maas .30 .75
98 Stephone Paige .60 1.50
99 Neil Smith 1.25 3.00
100 Dean Biasucci .30 .75
101 Duane Bickett .30 .75
102 Chris Chandler 1.25 3.00
103 Eugene Daniel .30 .75
104 Ray Donaldson .30 .75
105 Jon Hand .30 .75
106 Chris Hinton .30 .75
107 Joe Klecko .30 .75
108 Cliff Odom .30 .75
109 Rohn Stark .30 .75
110 Donnell Thompson .30 .75
111 Willie Tullis .30 .75
112 Freddie Young .30 .75
113 Michael Downs .30 .75
114 Michael Irvin 2.00 5.00
115 Jim Jeffcoat .30 .75
116 Ed(Too Tall) Jones .60 1.50
117 Tom Rafferty .30 .75
118 Herschel Walker .60 1.50
119 Everson Walls .30 .75
120 Danny White .60 1.50
121 Randy White .60 1.50
122 Bob Brudzinski .30 .75
123 Mark Clayton .60 1.50
124 Mark Duper .60 1.50
125 Ron Jaworski .60 1.50
126 Paul Lankford .30 .75
127 Dan Marino 8.00 20.00
128 John Offerdahl .30 .75
129 Reggie Roby .30 .75
130 Dwight Stephenson 1.25 3.00
131 Randall Cunningham 1.25 3.00
132 Ron Heller .30 .75
133 Mike Quick .60 1.50
134 Ken Reeves .30 .75
135 Dave Rimington .30 .75
136 Reggie Singletary .30 .75
137 Andre Waters .30 .75
138 Reggie White 1.25 3.00
139 Roynell Young .30 .75
140 Aundray Bruce .30 .75
141 Bobby Butler .30 .75
142 Bill Fralic .30 .75
143 Mike Kenn .30 .75
144 Chris Miller .60 1.50
145 John Settle .30 .75
146 George Yarno .30 .75
147 Michael Carter .30 .75
148 Wes Chandler .60 1.50
149 Roger Craig .60 1.50
150 Randy Cross .30 .75
151 Riki Ellison .30 .75
152 Jim Fahnhorst .30 .75
153 Charles Haley .60 1.50
154 Barry Helton .30 .75
155 Guy McIntyre .30 .75
156 Tim McKyer .30 .75
157 Joe Montana 10.00 25.00
158 Jerry Rice 5.00 12.00
159 Keena Turner .30 .75
160 Eric Wright .30 .75
161 Steve Young 3.00 8.00
162 Raul Allegre .30 .75
163 Ottis Anderson .30 .75
164 Billy Ard .30 .75
165 Carl Banks .30 .75
166 Mark Bavaro .30 .75
167 Jim Burt .30 .75
168 Harry Carson .30 .75
169 John Elliott .30 .75
170 Terry Kinard .30 .75
171 Sean Landeta .30 .75
172 Lionel Manuel .30 .75
173 Joe Morris .60 1.50
174 Bart Oates .30 .75
175 Phil Simms .60 1.50
176 Pat Leahy .30 .75
177 Marty Lyons .30 .75
178 Erik McMillan .30 .75
179 Freeman McNeil .60 1.50
180 Scott Mersereau .30 .75
181 Ken O'Brien .60 1.50
182 Jim Sweeney .30 .75
183 Al Toon .60 1.50
184 Wesley Walker .60 1.50
185 Jim Arnold .30 .75
186 Bennie Blades .30 .75
187 Mike Cofer .30 .75
188 Keith Ferguson .30 .75
189 Steve Mott .30 .75
190 Eddie Murray .30 .75
191 Harvey Salem .30 .75
192 Bobby Watkins .30 .75
193 Keith Bostic .30 .75
194 Richard Byrd .30 .75
195 Ray Childress .30 .75
196 Ernest Givins .30 .75
197 Kenny Johnson .30 .75
198 Sean Jones .30 .75
199 Robert Lyles .30 .75
200 Bruce Matthews .30 .75
201 Johnny Meads .30 .75
202 Warren Moon 1.25 3.00
203 Mike Munchak .60 1.50
204 Mike Rozier .30 .75
205 Dean Steinkuhler .30 .75
206 Tony Zendejas .30 .75
207 Mark Cannon .30 .75
208 Alphonso Carreker .30 .75
209 Phillip Epps .30 .75
210 Tim Harris .30 .75
211 Brian Noble .30 .75
212 Raymond Clayborn .30 .75
213 Steve Grogan .60 1.50
214 Roland James .30 .75
215 Fred Marion .30 .75
216 Stanley Morgan .60 1.50
217 Kenneth Sims .30 .75
218 Andre Tippett .60 1.50
219 Marcus Allen 1.25 3.00
220 Chris Bahr .30 .75
221 Steve Beuerlein 1.25 3.00
222 Tim Brown 2.50 6.00
223 Todd Christensen .30 .75
224 Ron Fellows .30 .75
225 Willie Gault .30 .75
226 Mike Haynes .60 1.50
227 Bo Jackson .60 1.50
228 James Lofton .60 1.50
229 Howie Long 1.25 3.00
230 Vann McElroy .30 .75
231 Rod Martin .30 .75
232 Matt Millen .30 .75
233 Bill Pickel .30 .75
234 Jay Schroeder .30 .75
235 Stacey Toran .30 .75
236 Greg Townsend .30 .75
237 Greg Bell .30 .75
238 Henry Ellard .60 1.50
239 Jerry Gray .30 .75
240 LeRoy Irvin .30 .75
241 Gary Jeter .30 .75
242 Johnnie Johnson .30 .75
243 Larry Kelm .30 .75
244 Mike Lansford .30 .75
245 Shawn Miller .30 .75
246 Mel Owens .30 .75
247 Jackie Slater .30 .75
248 Charles White .30 .75
249 Jeff Bostic .30 .75
250 Kelvin Bryant .30 .75
251 Dave Butz .30 .75
252 Gary Clark .60 1.50
253 Steve Cox .30 .75
254 Darryl Grant .30 .75
255 Darrell Green .60 1.50
256 Joe Jacoby .30 .75
257 Mel Kaufman .30 .75
258 Jim Lachey .30 .75
259 Dexter Manley .30 .75
260 Charles Mann .30 .75
261 Mark May .30 .75
262 Art Monk .60 1.50
263 Ricky Sanders .30 .75
264 Alvin Walton .30 .75
265 Doug Williams .60 1.50
266 Morten Andersen .60 1.50
267 Bruce Clark .30 .75
268 Jim Dombrowski .30 .75
269 Mel Gray .30 .75
270 Bobby Hebert .30 .75
271 Rickey Jackson .30 .75
272 Van Jakes .30 .75
273 Steve Korte .30 .75
274 Rueben Mayes .30 .75
275 Sam Mills .60 1.50
276 Dave Waymer .30 .75
277 Jeff Bryant .30 .75
278 Blair Bush .30 .75
279 Jacob Green .30 .75
280 Melvin Jenkins .30 .75
281 Norm Johnson .30 .75
282 Dave Krieg .60 1.50
283 Bryan Millard .30 .75
284 Ruben Rodriguez .30 .75
285 Terry Taylor .30 .75
286 Curt Warner .30 .75
287 Tony Woods .30 .75
288 Gary Anderson .30 .75
289 Tunch Ilkin .30 .75
290 Earnest Jackson .30 .75
291 Louis Lipps .30 .75
292 Mike Webster .60 1.50
293 Rod Woodson 1.25 3.00
294 Joey Browner .30 .75
295 Anthony Carter .60 1.50
296 Chris Doleman .60 1.50
297 Tim Irwin .30 .75
298 Tommy Kramer .60 1.50
299 Carl Lee .30 .75
300 Kirk Lowdermilk .30 .75
301 Keith Millard .30 .75
302 Scott Studwell .30 .75
303 Wade Wilson .60 1.50
304 Gary Zimmerman .50 1.25
T1 Atlanta Falcons .20 .50
T2 Buffalo Bills .20 .50
T3 Chicago Bears .20 .50
T4 Cincinnati Bengals .20 .50
T5 Cleveland Browns .20 .50
T6 Dallas Cowboys .30 .75
T7 Denver Broncos .30 .75
T8 Detroit Lions .20 .50
T9 Green Bay Packers .30 .75
T10 Houston Oilers .20 .50
T11 Indianapolis Colts .20 .50
T12 Kansas City Chiefs .20 .50
T13 Los Angeles Raiders .30 .75
T14 Los Angeles Rams .20 .50
T15 Miami Dolphins .30 .75
T16 Minnesota Vikings .20 .50
T17 New England Patriots .20 .50
T18 New Orleans Saints .20 .50
T19 New York Giants .20 .50
T20 New York Jets .20 .50
T21 Philadelphia Eagles .20 .50
T22 Phoenix Cardinals .20 .50
T23 Pittsburgh Steelers .30 .75
T24 San Diego Chargers .20 .50
T25 San Francisco 49ers .30 .75
T26 Seattle Seahawks .20 .50
T27 Tampa Bay Buccaneers .20 .50
T28 Washington Redskins .30 .75

1972-74 Franklin Mint HOF Coins Bronze

sued by the Pro Football Hall of Fame in Canton, Ohio and the Franklin Mint, this collection of 50-coins honors inducted players and coaches chosen by the Hall's Selection Committee. The larger coins were released by subsciption over the course of three years. The year of issue can be found on the serrated edge of the coin in very fine print. Reported mintage figures were 1,946 silver coins and 1,802 bronze coins with each coin containing 1-ounce of metal. The fronts feature a double image: a large portrait and an action scene. The unnumbered backs carry the Hall of Fame Logo, the player's name, position and a summary of his accomplishments. Each set came with a colorful album with a black-and-white action pencil drawing and a biography for each player. Another cardboard "mount" album was issued for use in housing the larger coin set. In 1976, the set was re-released in miniature form (roughly 1/2" diameter) as a complete set. These "minis" were issued sealed on a backer board and came with a jewelry style case to house the coins.

COMPLETE SET (50) 250.00 500.00
*SILVER MINI COINS: .3X TO .8X BRONZE
1 Cliff Battles 4.00 10.00
2 Sammy Baugh 10.00 25.00
3 Chuck Bednarik 6.00 15.00
4 Bert Bell 4.00 10.00
5 Paul Brown 74 6.00 15.00
6 Joe Carr 4.00 10.00
7 Guy Chamberlin 4.00 10.00
8 Dutch Clark 5.00 12.00
9 Jimmy Conzelman 4.00 10.00
10 Art Donovan 6.00 15.00
11 Paddy Driscoll 4.00 10.00
12 Bill Dudley 5.00 12.00
13 Dan Fortmann 4.00 10.00
14 Otto Graham 73 10.00 25.00
15 Red Grange 72 12.00 30.00
16 George Halas 74 8.00 20.00
17 Mel Hein 4.00 10.00
18 Fats Henry 5.00 12.00
19 Bill Hewitt 4.00 10.00
20 Clarke Hinkle 4.00 10.00
21 Elroy Hirsch 73 6.00 15.00
22 Cal Hubbard 4.00 10.00
23 Lamar Hunt 74 4.00 10.00
24 Don Hutson 6.00 15.00
25 Curly Lambeau 5.00 12.00
26 Bobby Layne 73 8.00 20.00
27 Vince Lombardi 74 15.00 40.00
28 Sid Luckman 8.00 20.00
29 Gino Marchetti 5.00 12.00
30 Ollie Matson 6.00 15.00
31 George McAfee 5.00 12.00
32 Hugh McElhenny 73 6.00 15.00
33 Johnny Blood McNally 4.00 10.00
34 Marion Motley 73 6.00 15.00
35 Bronko Nagurski 12.00 30.00
36 Ernie Nevers 72 5.00 12.00
37 Leo Nomellini 74 5.00 12.00
38 Steve Owen 4.00 10.00
39 Joe Perry 73 5.00 12.00
40 Pete Pihos 73 5.00 12.00
41 Andy Robustelli 5.00 12.00
42 Ken Strong 5.00 12.00
43 Jim Thorpe 12.00 30.00
44 Y.A. Tittle 74 8.00 20.00
45 Charley Trippi 73 5.00 12.00
46 Emlen Tunnell 74 5.00 12.00
47 Bulldog Turner 5.00 12.00
48 Norm Van Brocklin 74 6.00 15.00
49 Steve Van Buren 73 6.00 15.00
50 Bob Waterfield 73 6.00 15.00

1972-74 Franklin Mint HOF Coins Silver

1 Cliff Battles 30.00 40.00
2 Sammy Baugh 30.00 40.00
3 Chuck Bednarik 30.00 40.00
4 Bert Bell 30.00 40.00
5 Paul Brown 74 30.00 40.00
6 Joe Carr 30.00 40.00
7 Guy Chamberlin 30.00 40.00
8 Dutch Clark 30.00 40.00
9 Jimmy Conzelman 30.00 40.00
10 Art Donovan 30.00 40.00
11 Paddy Driscoll 30.00 40.00
12 Bill Dudley 30.00 40.00
13 Dan Fortmann 30.00 40.00
14 Otto Graham 73 30.00 40.00
15 Red Grange 72 30.00 50.00
16 George Halas 74 30.00 40.00
17 Mel Hein 30.00 40.00
18 Fats Henry 30.00 40.00
19 Bill Hewitt 30.00 40.00
20 Clarke Hinkle 30.00 40.00
21 Elroy Hirsch 73 30.00 40.00
22 Cal Hubbard 30.00 40.00
23 Lamar Hunt 74 30.00 40.00
24 Don Hutson 30.00 40.00
25 Curly Lambeau 30.00 40.00
26 Bobby Layne 73 30.00 40.00
27 Vince Lombardi 74 30.00 60.00
28 Sid Luckman 30.00 40.00
29 Gino Marchetti 30.00 40.00
30 Ollie Matson 30.00 40.00
31 George McAfee 30.00 40.00
32 Hugh McElhenny 73 30.00 40.00
33 Johnny Blood McNally 30.00 40.00
34 Marion Motley 73 30.00 40.00
35 Bronko Nagurski 30.00 50.00
36 Ernie Nevers 72 30.00 40.00
37 Leo Nomellini 74 30.00 40.00
38 Steve Owen 30.00 40.00
39 Joe Perry 73 30.00 40.00
40 Pete Pihos 73 30.00 40.00
41 Andy Robustelli 30.00 40.00
42 Ken Strong 30.00 40.00
43 Jim Thorpe 30.00 50.00
44 Y.A. Tittle 74 30.00 40.00
45 Charley Trippi 73 30.00 40.00
46 Emlen Tunnell 74 30.00 40.00
47 Bulldog Turner 30.00 40.00
48 Norm Van Brocklin 74 30.00 40.00
49 Steve Van Buren 73 30.00 40.00
50 Bob Waterfield 73 30.00 40.00

1990 Fresno Bandits Smokey

This 25-card standard-size set features the Fresno Bandits, a semi-professional football team. The fronts display black-and-white posed player photos inside white borders. Red and black designs edge the picture. The Smokey the Bear logo appears in the upper left corner, while the team logo is printed in the lower right. The backs carry biography, a black-and-white photo picturing the player with Smokey, and a safety slogan. The cards are unnumbered and checklisted below in alphabetical order.

COMPLETE SET (25) 10.00 25.00
1 Allan Blades .50 1.25
2 Corey Clark .50 1.25
3 Darryl Duke .50 1.25
4 Heikoti Fakava .50 1.25
5 Charles Frazier .50 1.25
6 Chris Geile .50 1.25
7 Mike Henson .50 1.25
8 James Hickey .50 1.25
9 Anthony Howard .50 1.25
10 Derrick Jinks .50 1.25
11 Anthony Jones .50 1.25
12 Marvin Jones .50 1.25
13 Mike Jones .50 1.25
14 Steve Loop .50 1.25
15 Thomas Ireland .50 1.25
16 Jay Lynch .50 1.25
17 Sheldon Martin .50 1.25
18 Chuckie McCutchen .50 1.25
19 Lance Oberparleiter .50 1.25
20 Darrell Rosette .50 1.25
21 Fred Sims .50 1.25
22 Bryan Turner .50 1.25
23 Jim Woods CO .50 1.25
24 Rick Zumwalt .50 1.25
25 Coaching Staff .50 1.25

1991 Fresno Bandits Smokey

This 27-card set of the Fresno Brandits was sponsored by Sierra National Forest and Fresno-Kings Ranger Unit. The fronts feature black-and-white player photos. The backs carry player information and a fire prevention cartoon starring Smokey the Bear. The cards are unnumbered and checklisted below in alphabetical order.

COMPLETE SET (27) 10.00 25.00
1 Kyle Cabott .40 1.00
2 Derrick Chachere .40 1.00
3 Eric Coleman WR .40 1.00
4 Steve Domingos .40 1.00
5 Carlos Hannon .40 1.00
6 Tim Hardin .40 1.00
7 Mike Henson .40 1.00
8 Keith Hill .40 1.00
9 Jeff Hulsey .40 1.00
10 Keith Jenkins .40 1.00
11 Derrick Jinks .60 1.50
12 Niko Liulamaga .40 1.00
13 Steve Loop .40 1.00
14 Stacy Marshall .40 1.00
15 Bob Martin CO .40 1.00
16 Sheldon Martin .40 1.00
17 Daren Miller .40 1.00
18 Kevin Newton .40 1.00
19 Shante' Rhodes .40 1.00
20 James Sanders .40 1.00
21 Sandy Sledge .40 1.00
22 Anthony Stiff .40 1.00
23 Bryan Tobey .40 1.00
24 JJ Velasco .40 1.00
25 Dave Walter .40 1.00
26 Derrick Williams .40 1.00
27 Smokey Bear CL .40 1.00

1989 Frito Lay Stickers

ese tiny (roughly 1-1/2" x 1-1/2") blankbacked color stickers feature one NFL player on the front along with his name, position, and team name. They were issued in bags of various Frito Lay chips and involve a redemption program around the winner of Super Bowl XXIV. The stickers were licensed through the NFLPA and MSA.

1 Bennie Blades 6.00 15.00
2 Bill Brooks 6.00 15.00
3 James Brooks 8.00 20.00
4 Joey Browner 6.00 15.00
5 Deron Cherry 6.00 15.00
6 Jim Everett 8.00 20.00
7 Willie Gault 8.00 20.00
8 Darrell Green 10.00 25.00
9 Roy Green 6.00 15.00
10 Dalton Hilliard 6.00 15.00
11 Vance Johnson 6.00 15.00
12 Louis Lipps 8.00 20.00
13 Dan Marino 50.00 100.00
14 Joe Montana 50.00 100.00
15 Warren Moon 10.00 25.00
16 Ozzie Newsome 8.00 20.00
17 Sterling Sharpe 8.00 20.00
18 Phil Simms 10.00 25.00
19 Mike Singletary 12.00 30.00
20 Tim Spencer 6.00 15.00
21 Andre Tippett 8.00 20.00
22 Al Toon 8.00 20.00
23 Everson Walls 6.00 15.00
24 James Wilder 6.00 15.00

1963 Gad Fun Cards

This set of 1963 Fun Cards were issued by a sports illustrator by the name of Gad from Minneapolis, Minnesota. The cards are printed on cardboard stock paper. The borderless fronts have black and white line drawings. A fun sport's fact or player career statistic is depicted in the drawing. The backs of the first six cards display numbers used to play the game explained on card number 6. The other backs carry a cartoon with a joke or riddle. Copyright information is listed on the lower portion of the card.

COMPLETE SET (84) 37.50 75.00
74 Minnesota Football Team/1949 .25 .50
81 Highest Football Game Score .25 .50

1992 GameDay Draft Day Promos

is 13-card promo set was produced by NFL Properties. In the May 1, 1992 edition of USA Today, an ad ran offering to the public 2,500 sets for 50.00 each with the proceeds going to NFL Charities. Other unnumbered sets (originally reported as 10,000 sets but later discovered to be only a small percentage of the original reported amount with many of these other sets missing one player) were also available through various media and dealer channels. The cards were patterned after 1965 Topps football and thus measure approximately 2 1/2" by 4 11/16". Several cards of the same player were issued to reflect different draft day scenarios; 13 different combos existed. Card fronts feature a full-color action picture in a small colored border enclosed by a white border. The team name beneath the photo is in gray lettering, while the player's name appears in block lettering. The title "NFL GameDay" is below the name. Horizontal backs feature the player's team helmet in a box, biography, and the NFL Draft logo in the white border on the far left. A full-color photo is also on the back along with a summary of the player's collegiate career. Although all the cards are numbered "1" on the back, they are checklisted below in alphabetical order according to the player's last name.

COMPLETE SET (13) 6.00 15.00
1A Quentin Coryatt .60 1.50
1B Vaughn Dunbar .60 1.50
1C Vaughn Dunbar .60 1.50
1D Vaughn Dunbar .60 1.50
1E Steve Emtman .60 1.50
1F Steve Emtman .60 1.50
1G Desmond Howard 1.20 3.00
1H Desmond Howard 1.20 3.00
1I David Klingler .60 1.50
1J David Klingler .60 1.50
1K Troy Vincent .60 1.50
1L Troy Vincent .60 1.50
1M Troy Vincent .60 1.50

1992 GameDay

is 500-card set measures 2 1/2" by 4 11/16" and was issued in 12 card packs. In terms of card size, it is the largest basic issue set since 1965 Topps. The set includes 14 multi-player special cards which feature 56 rookies chosen after the third round of the 1992 draft. Rookie Cards include Edgar Bennett, Steve Bono, Robert Brooks, Terrell Buckley, Mark Chmura, Marco Coleman, Quentin Coryatt, Steve Emtman, Chester McGlockton, Johnny Mitchell, Carl Pickens, and Tommy Vardell.

COMPLETE SET (500) 25.00 50.00
1 Jim Kelly .15 .40
2 Mark Ingram .02 .10
3 Travis McNeal .02 .10
4 Ricky Ervins .02 .10
5 Joe Montana .75 2.00
6 Broderick Thompson .02 .10
7 Darion Conner .02 .10
8 Jim Harbaugh .15 .40
9 Harvey Williams .07 .20
10 Chip Banks .02 .10
11 Henry Thomas .02 .10
12 Derek Brown TE RC .02 .10
13 James Joseph .02 .10
14 Kevin Fagan .02 .10
15 Chuck Klingbeil RC .02 .10
16 Harlon Barnett .02 .10
17 Jim Price .02 .10
18 Terrell Buckley RC .02 .10
19 Paul McJulien RC .02 .10
20 James Hasty .02 .10
21 James Francis .02 .10
22 Andre Tippett .02 .10
23 John Elway .60 1.50
24 Eric Dickerson .07 .20
25 James Jefferson .02 .10
26 Danny Noonan .02 .10
27 Warren Moon .15 .40
28 Gene Atkins .02 .10
29 Jessie Hester .02 .10
30 K.Smith RBK/Mooney/Hum RC .02 .10
31 Toby Caston RC .02 .10
32 Howard Dinkins RC .02 .10
33 James Patton RC .02 .10
34 Walter Reeves .02 .10
35 Johnny Mitchell RC .02 .10
36 Mike Brim RC .02 .10
37 Irving Fryar .07 .20
38 Lewis Billups .02 .10
39 Alonzo Spellman RC .07 .20
40 John Friesz .07 .20
41 Patrick Hunter .02 .10
42 Reuben Davis .02 .10
43 Mys/Harper/Thom/Frier RC .02 .10
44 Siran Stacy RC .02 .10
45 Stephone Paige .02 .10
46 Eddie Robinson RC .02 .10
47 Tracy Scroggins RC .02 .10
48 David Klingler RC .02 .10
49A Deion Sanders ERR .25 .60
49B Deion Sanders COR .25 .60
50 Tom Waddle .02 .10
51 Gary Anderson RB .02 .10
52 Kevin Butler .02 .10
53 Bruce Smith .15 .40
54 Steve Sewell .02 .10
55 Wesley Walls .02 .10
56 Lawrence Taylor .15 .40
57 Mike Merriweather .02 .10
58 Roman Phifer .02 .10
59 Shaun Gayle .02 .10
60 Marc Boutte RC .02 .10
61 Tony Mayberry RC .02 .10
62 Antone Davis UER .02 .10
63 Rod Bernstine .02 .10
64 Shane Collins RC .02 .10
65 Martin Bayless .02 .10
66 Corey Harris RC .02 .10
67 Jason Hanson RC .07 .20
68 John Fina RC .02 .10
69 Cornelius Bennett .07 .20
70 Mark Bortz .02 .10
71 Gary Anderson K .02 .10
72 Paul Siever RC .02 .10
73 Flipper Anderson .02 .10
74 Shane Dronett RC .02 .10
75 Brian Noble .02 .10
76 Tim Green .02 .10
77 Percy Snow .02 .10
78 Greg McMurtry .02 .10
79 Dana Hall RC .02 .10
80 Tyji Armstrong RC .02 .10
81 Gary Clark .07 .20
82 Steve Emtman RC .02 .10
83 Eric Moore .02 .10
84 Brent Jones .07 .20
85 Ray Seals RC .02 .10
86 James Jones DT .02 .10
87 Jeff Hostetler .07 .20
88 Keith Jackson .07 .20
89 Gary Plummer .02 .10
90 Robert Blackmon .02 .10
91 Larry Tharpe/Hamlet RC .02 .10
92 Greg Skrepenak RC .02 .10
93 Kevin Call .02 .10
94 Clarence Kay .02 .10
95 William Fuller .02 .10
96 Troy Auzenne RC .02 .10
97 Carl Pickens RC .15 .40
98 Lorenzo White .02 .10
99 Doug Smith .02 .10
100 Dale Carter RC .07 .20
101 Fred McAfee RC .02 .10
102 Jack Del Rio .02 .10
103 Vaughn Dunbar RC .02 .10
104 J.J. Birden .02 .10
105 Harris Barton .02 .10
106 Ray Ethridge RC .02 .10
107 John Gesek .02 .10
108 Mike Singletary .07 .20
109 Mark Rypien .02 .10
110 Robb Thomas .02 .10
111 Joe Kelly .02 .10
112 Ben Smith .02 .10
113 Neil O'Donnell .07 .20
114 John L. Williams .02 .10
115 Mike Sherrard .02 .10
116 Chad Hennings RC .07 .20
117 Henry Ellard .07 .20
118 Jay Hilgenberg .02 .10
119 Charles Dimry .02 .10
120 Chuck Smith RC .02 .10
121 Brian Mitchell .07 .20
122 Eric Allen .02 .10
123 Nate Lewis .02 .10
124 Kevin Ross .02 .10
125 Jimmy Smith RC 1.25 3.00
126 Kevin Smith RC .02 .10
127 Larry Webster RC .02 .10
128 Marv Cook .02 .10
129 Calvin Williams .07 .20
130 Harry Swayne RC .02 .10
131 Jimmie Jones .02 .10
132 Ethan Horton .02 .10
133 Chris Mims RC .02 .10
134 Derrick Thomas .15 .40
135 Gerald Dixon RC .02 .10
136 Gary Zimmerman .02 .10
137 Robert Jones RC .02 .10
138 Steve Broussard .02 .10
139 David Wyman .02 .10
140 Ian Beckles .02 .10
141 Steve Bono RC .15 .40
142 Cris Carter .20 .50
143 Anthony Carter .07 .20
144 Greg Townsend .02 .10
145 Al Smith .02 .10
146 Troy Vincent RC .02 .10
147 Jessie Tuggle .02 .10
148 David Fulcher .02 .10
149 Johnny Rembert .02 .10
150 Ernie Jones .02 .10
151 Mark Royals .02 .10
152 Jeff Bryant .02 .10
153 Vai Sikahema .02 .10
154 Tony Woods .02 .10
155 Bowden/Dowdell/Miles RC .02 .10
156 Mark Carrier WR .07 .20
157 Joe Nash .02 .10
158 Keith Van Horne .02 .10
159 Kelvin Martin .02 .10
160 Peter Tom Willis .02 .10
161 Richard Johnson CB .02 .10
162 Louis Oliver .02 .10
163 Nick Lowery .02 .10
164 Ricky Proehl .02 .10
165 Terance Mathis .07 .20
166 Keith Sims .02 .10
167 E.J. Junior .02 .10
168 Scott Mersereau .02 .10
169 Tom Rathman .02 .10
170 Robert Harris RC .02 .10
171 Ashley Ambrose RC .15 .40
172 David Treadwell .02 .10
173 Mark Green .02 .10
174 Clayton Holmes RC .02 .10
175 Tony Sacca RC .02 .10
176 Wes Hopkins .02 .10
177 Mark Wheeler RC .02 .10
178 Robert Clark .02 .10
179 Eugene Daniel .02 .10
180 Rob Burnett .02 .10
181 Al Edwards .02 .10
182 Clarence Verdin .02 .10
183 Tom Newberry .02 .10
184 Mike Jones .02 .10
185 Roy Foster .02 .10
186 Leslie O'Neal .07 .20
187 Izel Jenkins .02 .10
188 Detmer .15 .40
Clay
McDan
Ev.
189 Mike Tomczak .02 .10
190 Leonard Wheeler RC .02 .10
191 Gaston Green .02 .10
192 Maury Buford .02 .10
193 Jeremy Lincoln RC .02 .10
194 Todd Collins RC .02 .10
195 Billy Ray Smith .02 .10
196 Renaldo Turnbull .02 .10
197 Michael Carter .02 .10
198 R.E.White/Milst/Lambert RC .02 .10
199 Shawn Collins .02 .10
200 Issiac Holt .02 .10
201 Irv Eatman .02 .10
202 Anthony Thompson .02 .10
203 Chester McGlockton RC .07 .20
204 Curtis Whitley .02 .10
Crooms RC
205 James Brown RC .02 .10
206 Marvin Washington .02 .10
207 Richard Cooper RC .02 .10
208 Jim C. Jensen .02 .10
209 Sam Seale .02 .10
210 Andre Reed .07 .20
211 Thane Gash .02 .10
212 Randal Hill .02 .10
213 Brad Baxter .02 .10
214 Michael Cofer .02 .10
215 Ray Crockett .02 .10
216 Tony Mandarich .02 .10
217 Warren Williams .02 .10
218 Erik Kramer .07 .20
219 Bubby Brister .07 .20
220 Steve Young .30 .75
221 Jeff George .15 .40
222 James Washington .02 .10
223 Bruce Alexander RC .02 .10
224 Broderick Thomas .02 .10
225 Bern Brostek .02 .10
226 Brian Blades .07 .20
227 Troy Aikman .40 1.00
228 Aaron Wallace .02 .10
229 Tommy Jeter RC .02 .10
230 Russell Maryland .02 .10
231 Charles Haley .07 .20
232 James Lofton .07 .20
233 William White .02 .10
234 Tim McGee .02 .10
235 Haywood Jeffires .07 .20
236 Charles Mann .02 .10
237 Robert Lyles .02 .10
238 Rohn Stark .02 .10
239 Jim Morrissey .02 .10
240 Mel Gray .07 .20
241 Barry Word .02 .10
242 Dave Widell RC .02 .10
243 Sean Gilbert RC .07 .20
244 Tommy Maddox RC .75 2.00
245 Bernie Kosar .07 .20
246 John Roper .02 .10
247 Mark Higgs .02 .10
248 Rob Moore .07 .20
249 Dan Fike .02 .10
250 Dan Saleaumua .02 .10
251 Tim Krumrie .02 .10
252 Tony Casillas .02 .10
253 Jayice Pearson RC .02 .10
254 Dan Marino .60 1.50
255 Tony Martin .07 .20
256 Mike Fox .02 .10
257 Courtney Hawkins RC .07 .20
258 Leonard Marshall .02 .10
259 Willie Gault .07 .20
260 Al Toon .07 .20
261 Browning Nagle .02 .10
262 Ronnie Lott .07 .20
263 Sean Jones .02 .10
264 Ernest Givins .07 .20
265 Ray Donaldson .02 .10
266 Vaughan Johnson .02 .10
267 Tommy Hodson .02 .10
268 Chris Doleman .02 .10
269 Pat Swilling .02 .10
270 Merril Hoge .02 .10
271 Bill Maas .02 .10
272 Sterling Sharpe .15 .40
273 Mitchell Price .02 .10
274 Richard Brown RC .02 .10
275 Randall Cunningham .15 .40
276 Chris Martin .02 .10
277 Courtney Hall .02 .10
278 Michael Walter .02 .10
279 Ricardo McDonald/Lump. RC .02 .10
280 Bill Brooks .02 .10
281 Jay Schroeder .02 .10
282 John Stephens .02 .10
283 William Perry .07 .20
284 Floyd Turner .02 .10
285 Carnell Lake .02 .10
286 Joel Steed RC .02 .10
287 Vinnie Clark .02 .10
288 Ken Norton .07 .20
289 Eric Thomas .02 .10
290 Derrick Fenner .02 .10
291 Tony Smith RC .02 .10
292 Eric Metcalf .07 .20
293 Roger Craig .07 .20
294 Leon Searcy RC .02 .10
295 Tyrone Legette RC .02 .10
296 Rob Taylor .02 .10
297 Eric Williams .02 .10
298 David Little .02 .10
299 Wayne Martin .02 .10
300 Eric Martin .02 .10
301 Jim Everett .07 .20
302 Michael Dean Perry .07 .20
303 Dwayne White RC .02 .10
304 Greg Lloyd .07 .20
305 Ricky Reynolds .02 .10
306 Anthony Smith .02 .10
307 Robert Delpino .02 .10
308 Ken Clark .02 .10
309 Chris Jacke .02 .10
310 C.Thompson/K.Wilms RC .02 .10
311 Doug Widell .02 .10
312 Sammie Smith .02 .10
313 Ken O'Brien .02 .10
314 Timm Rosenbach .02 .10
315 Jesse Sapolu .02 .10
316 Ronnie Harmon .02 .10
317 Bill Pickel .02 .10
318 Lonnie Young .02 .10
319 Chris Burkett .02 .10
320 Ervin Randle .02 .10
321 Ed West .02 .10
322 Tom Thayer .02 .10
323 Keith McKeller .02 .10
324 Webster Slaughter .02 .10
325 Duane Bickett .02 .10
326 Howie Long .15 .40
327 Sam Mills .02 .10
328 Mike Golic .02 .10
329 Bruce Armstrong .02 .10
330 Pat Terrell .02 .10
331 Mike Pritchard .07 .20
332 Audray McMillian .02 .10
333 Marquez Pope RC .02 .10
334 Pierce Holt .02 .10
335 Erik Howard .02 .10
336 Jerry Rice .40 1.00
337 Vinny Testaverde .07 .20
338 Bart Oates .02 .10
339 Nolan Harrison RC .02 .10
340 Chris Goode .02 .10
341 Ken Ruettgers .02 .10
342 Brad Muster .02 .10
343 Paul Farren .02 .10
344 Corey Miller RC .02 .10
345 Brian Washington .02 .10
346 Jim Sweeney .02 .10
347 Keith McCants .02 .10
348 Louis Lipps .02 .10
349 Keith Byars .02 .10
350 Steve Walsh .02 .10
351 Jeff Jaeger .02 .10
352 Christian Okoye .02 .10
353 Cris Dishman .02 .10
354 Keith Kartz .02 .10
355 Harold Green .02 .10
356 Richard Shelton RC .02 .10
357 Jacob Green .02 .10
358 Al Noga .02 .10
359 Dean Biasucci .02 .10
360 Jeff Herrod .02 .10
361 Bennie Blades .02 .10
362 Mark Vlasic .02 .10
363 Chris Miller .07 .20
364 Bubba McDowell .02 .10
365 Tyronne Stowe RC .02 .10
366 Jon Vaughn .02 .10
367 Winston Moss .02 .10
368 Levon Kirkland RC .02 .10
369 Ted Washington .02 .10
370 Cortez Kennedy .07 .20
371 Jeff Feagles .02 .10
372 Aundray Bruce .02 .10
373 Michael Irvin .15 .40
374 Lemuel Stinson .02 .10
375 Billy Joe Tolliver .02 .10
376 Anthony Munoz .07 .20
377 Nate Newton .02 .10
378 Steve Smith .02 .10
379 Eugene Chung RC .02 .10
380 Bryan Hinkle .02 .10
381 Dan McGwire .02 .10
382 Jeff Cross .02 .10
383 Ferrell Edmunds .02 .10
384 Craig Heyward .07 .20
385 Shannon Sharpe .15 .40
386 Anthony Miller .07 .20
387 Eugene Lockhart .02 .10
388 Darryl Henley .02 .10
389 LeRoy Butler .02 .10
390 Scott Fulhage .02 .10
391 Andre Ware .02 .10
392 Lionel Washington .02 .10
393 Rick Fenney .02 .10
394 John Taylor .07 .20
395 Chris Singleton .02 .10
396 Monte Coleman .02 .10
397 Brett Perriman .07 .20
398 Hugh Millen .02 .10
399 Dennis Gentry .02 .10
400 Eddie Anderson .02 .10
401 Olberding .02 .10
Sabb
Widmer RC
402 Brent Williams .02 .10
403 Tony Zendejas .02 .10
404 Donnell Woolford .02 .10
405 Boomer Esiason .07 .20
406 Gill Fenerty .02 .10
407 Kurt Barber RC .02 .10
408 William Thomas .02 .10
409 Keith Henderson .02 .10
410 Paul Gruber .02 .10
411 Alfred Oglesby .02 .10
412 Wendell Davis .02 .10
413 Robert Brooks RC .30 .75
414 Ken Willis .02 .10
415 Aaron Cox .02 .10
416 Thurman Thomas .15 .40
417 Alton Montgomery .02 .10
418 Mike Prior .02 .10
419 Albert Bentley .02 .10
420 John Randle .07 .20
421 Dermontti Dawson .08 .20
422 Phillippi Sparks RC .02 .10
423 Michael Jackson .07 .20
424 Carl Banks .02 .10
425 Chris Zorich .07 .20
426 Dwight Stone .02 .10
427 Bryan Millard .02 .10
428 Neal Anderson .02 .10
429 Michael Haynes .07 .20
430 Michael Young .02 .10
431 Dennis Byrd .02 .10
432 Fred Barnett .07 .20
433 Junior Seau .15 .40
434 Mark Clayton .07 .20
435 Marco Coleman RC .02 .10
436 Lee Williams .02 .10
437 Stan Thomas .02 .10
438 Lawrence Dawsey .07 .20
439 Tommy Vardell RC .02 .10
440 Steve Israel RC .02 .10
441 Ray Childress .02 .10
442 Darren Woodson RC .15 .40
443 Lamar Lathon .02 .10
444 Reggie Roby .02 .10
445 Eric Green .02 .10
446 Mark Carrier DB .02 .10
447 Kevin Walker .02 .10
448 Vince Workman .02 .10
449 Leonard Griffin .02 .10
450 Robert Porcher RC .15 .40
451 Hart Lee Dykes .02 .10
452 Thomas McLemore RC .02 .10
453 Jamie Dukes RC .02 .10
454 Bill Romanowski .02 .10
455 Deron Cherry .02 .10
456 Burt Grossman .02 .10
457 Lance Smith .02 .10
458 Jay Novacek .07 .20
459 Erric Pegram .07 .20
460 Reggie Rutland .02 .10
461 Rickey Jackson .02 .10
462 Dennis Brown .02 .10
463 Neil Smith .15 .40
464 Rich Gannon .15 .40
465 Herman Moore .15 .40
466 Rodney Peete .07 .20
467 Alvin Harper .07 .20
468 Andre Rison .07 .20
469 Rufus Porter .02 .10
470 Robert Wilson .02 .10
471 Phil Simms .07 .20
472 Art Monk .07 .20
473 Mike Tice .02 .10
474 Quentin Coryatt RC .02 .10
475 Chris Hinton .02 .10
476 Vance Johnson .02 .10
477 Kyle Clifton .02 .10
478 Garth Jax .02 .10
479 Ray Agnew .02 .10
480 Patrick Rowe RC .02 .10
481 Joe Jacoby .02 .10
482 Bruce Pickens .02 .10
483 Keith DeLong .02 .10
484 Eric Swann .07 .20
485 Steve McMichael .07 .20
486 Leroy Hoard .07 .20
487 Rickey Dixon .02 .10
488 Robert Perryman .02 .10
489 Darryl Williams RC .02 .10
490 Emmitt Smith .75 2.00
491 Dino Hackett .02 .10
492 Earnest Byner .02 .10
493 B.Richardson .02 .10
Davis RC
494 Bill Johnson RC .02 .10
495 Ashm .02 .10
Campb RB
Harris
Lest RC
496 Nick Bell .02 .10
497 Jerry Ball .02 .10
498 E.Bennett/M.Chmura RC .15 .40
499 Steve Christie .02 .10
500 Kenneth Davis .02 .10
P1 Promo Sheet 2.00 5.00

1992 GameDay Promo Sheets

These 6-card perforated sheets were issued to preview the 1992 GameDay football card set. Each card appears to be exactly like the basic pack version single card but on close inspection differences on the cardbacks can be found as noted below.

5 Joe Montana 1.50 4.00
49 Deion Sanders .75 2.00
56 Lawrence Taylor .50 1.25
109 Mark Rypien .40 1.00
227 Troy Aikman 1.00 2.50
245 Bernie Kosar .40 1.00
268 Chris Doleman .30 .75
269 Pat Swilling .30 .75
275 Randall Cunningham .40 1.00
326 Howie Long .50 1.25
416 Thurman Thomas .60 1.50
492 Earnest Byner .30 .75
S1 Montana/LT/Rypien/Kosar 3.00 8.00
Doleman/Cunningham
S2 Deion/Aikman/T.Thomas 3.00 8.00
Long/Swilling/Byner

1992 GameDay National

e cards in this 46-card preview set were given away during the 13th National Sports Card Convention in Atlanta, Georgia. An attractive black vinyl notebook with a cardboard slip cover was available to hold the cards. Like the 1965 Topps football set, these cards measure approximately 2 1/2" by 4 11/16". The players featured on each card front are in color against a black and white background. The horizontally oriented backs have career statistics, biography, and a color head shot. The cards are numbered on the back. Reportedly the cards of Deron Cherry, Mark Rypien, and Deion Sanders were individually distributed in limited quantities at the National in Atlanta.

COMPLETE SET (46) 20.00 50.00
1 Deion Sanders 1.20 3.00
2 Jim Kelly .40 1.00
3 Jim Harbaugh .20 .50
4 Boomer Esiason .20 .50
5 Bernie Kosar .20 .50
6 Troy Aikman 1.60 4.00
7 John Elway 3.20 8.00
8 Rodney Peete .08 .25
9 Sterling Sharpe .20 .50
10 Warren Moon .40 1.00
11 Jeff George .20 .50
12 Derrick Thomas .20 .50
13 Howie Long .20 .50
14 Jim Everett .08 .25
15 Dan Marino 3.20 8.00
16 Chris Doleman .08 .25
17 Irving Fryar .08 .25
18 Pat Swilling .08 .25
19 Lawrence Taylor .40 1.00
20 Ken O'Brien .08 .25
21 Randall Cunningham .40 1.00
22 Timm Rosenbach .08 .25
23 Bubby Brister .40 1.00
24 John Friesz .08 .25
25 Joe Montana 3.20 8.00
26 Dan McGwire .08 .25
27 Vinny Testaverde .20 .50
28 Mark Rypien SP .08 .25
29 Ronnie Lott .40 1.00
30 Marco Coleman .08 .25
31 Rob Moore .20 .50
32 Bill Pickel .08 .25
33 Brad Baxter .08 .25
34 Steve Broussard .08 .25
35 Darion Conner .08 .25
36 Chris Hinton .08 .25
37 Erric Pegram .08 .25
38 Jessie Tuggle .08 .25
39 Billy Joe Tolliver .08 .25
40 David Klingler .20 .50
41 Michael Irvin .40 1.00
42 Emmitt Smith 3.20 8.00
43 Quentin Coryatt .20 .50
44 Steve Emtman .08 .25
45 Deron Cherry .40 1.00
46 Ricky Ervins .08 .25

1992-93 GameDay Gamebreakers

This 14-card set was first made available at the Super Bowl card show to preview the 1993 design. The cards, patterned after 1965 Topps football, measure approximately 2 1/2" by 4 11/16". The checklist card is printed with the individual number of the set and the total number produced (5,000).

COMPLETE SET (14) 3.20 8.00
1 Marco Coleman .07 .20
2 Bill Cowher CO .10 .30
3 John Elway 1.20 3.00
4 Barry Foster .07 .20
5 Cortez Kennedy .10 .30
6 James Lofton .10 .30
7 Art Monk .10 .30
8 Jerry Rice .60 1.50
9 Sterling Sharpe .10 .30
10 Emmitt Smith 1.20 3.00
11 Thurman Thomas .20 .50
12 Gino Torretta .07 .20
13 Steve Young .50 1.25
14 Checklist Card .07 .20

1992-93 GameDay Super Bowl Program Promos

This six-card promo set was inserted one card per 1993 Super Bowl program. Each card measures approximately 2 1/2" by 4 3/4". The cards are numbered on the back and identified as promo cards.

COMPLETE SET (6) 4.80 12.00
1 Troy Aikman 2.00 5.00
2 Terry Allen .80 2.00
3 Ray Childress .50 1.25
4 Marco Coleman .50 1.25
5 Barry Foster .50 1.25
6 Sterling Sharpe .80 2.00

1993 GameDay

sued by Fleer in 12-card packs, this set consists of 480 cards measuring approximately 2 1/2" by 4 3/4". Rookie Cards include Jerome Bettis, Drew Bledsoe, Reggie Brooks, Curtis Conway, Andre Hastings, Garrison Hearst, Qadry Ismail, Terry Kirby, O.J. McDuffie, Natrone Means, Glyn Milburn, Rick Mirer, Roosevelt Potts, Robert Smith, Dana Stubblefield and Kevin Williams. A six-card promo sheet was produced and priced below.

COMPLETE SET (480) 12.50 30.00
1 Troy Aikman .30 .75
2 Terry Allen .08 .25
3 Ray Childress .01 .05
4 Marco Coleman .01 .05
5 Barry Foster .02 .10
6 Sterling Sharpe .08 .25
7 Steve McMichael .02 .10
8 Steve Young .30 .75
9 Derrick Thomas .08 .25
10 John Elway .60 1.50
11 Drew Bledsoe RC 1.00 2.50
12 Jim Kelly .08 .25
13 Dan Marino .60 1.50
14 Mo Lewis .01 .05
15 David Klingler .01 .05
16 Darrell Green .01 .05
17 James Francis .01 .05
18 John Copeland RC .02 .10
19 Terry McDaniel .01 .05
20 Barry Sanders .50 1.25
21 Deion Sanders .20 .50
22 Emmitt Smith .60 1.50
23 Marion Butts .01 .05
24 Darryl Talley .01 .05
25 Randall Cunningham .08 .25
26 Rod Woodson .08 .25
27 Terrell Buckley .01 .05
28 Michael Haynes .02 .10
29 Tony Jones T .01 .05
30 Santana Dotson .02 .10
31 Lomas Brown .01 .05
32 Eric Metcalf .02 .10
33 Morten Andersen .01 .05
34 Reggie Cobb .01 .05
35 Ferrell Edmunds .01 .05
36 Joe Montana .60 1.50
37 Ken Harvey .01 .05
38 Rodney Hampton .02 .10
39 Kurt Gouveia .01 .05
40 Ken Norton Jr. .02 .10
41 Frank Reich .02 .10
42 Kevin Greene .02 .10
43 Cleveland Gary .01 .05
44 Maurice Hurst .01 .05
45 Troy Vincent .01 .05
46 Eric Curry RC .01 .05
47 Curtis Conway RC .15 .40
48 Christian Okoye .01 .05
49 Tunch Ilkin .01 .05
50 Michael Irvin .08 .25
51 Bart Oates .01 .05
52 Pepper Johnson .01 .05
53 Vaughan Johnson .01 .05
54 Lawrence Taylor .08 .25
55 Junior Seau .08 .25
56 Michael Brooks .01 .05
57 Neal Anderson .01 .05
58 D.J. Johnson .01 .05
59 Seth Joyner .01 .05
60 Marvin Washington .01 .05
61 Ernest Givins .02 .10
62 Jaime Fields RC .01 .05
63 Vincent Brown .01 .05
64 Randall McDaniel .02 .10
65 Tommy Maddox .08 .25
66 Steve Everitt RC .01 .05
67 Brian Noble .01 .05
68 Bryce Paup .02 .10
69 Brad Baxter .01 .05
70 Demetrius DuBose RC .01 .05
71 Duane Bickett .01 .05
72 Mark Rypien .01 .05
73 Harris Barton .01 .05
74 Bruce Matthews .01 .05
75 Irving Fryar .02 .10
76 Steve Wisniewski .01 .05
77 Will Shields RC .08 .25
78 Tom Carter RC .02 .10
79 Steve Emtman .01 .05
80 Jerry Rice .40 1.00
81 Art Monk .02 .10
82 Tony Tolbert .01 .05
83 Johnny Mitchell .01 .05
84 Deon Figures RC .01 .05
85 Marv Cook .01 .05
86 Darion Conner .01 .05
87 Ricky Proehl .01 .05
88 Tony Bennett .01 .05
89 Jay Schroeder .01 .05
90 Neil Smith .08 .25
91 Jarvis Williams .01 .05
92 James Hasty .01 .05
93 Anthony Miller .02 .10
94 Thomas Smith RC .02 .10
95 Richard Dent .02 .10
96 Henry Jones .01 .05
97 Renaldo Turnbull .01 .05
98 Jason Hanson .01 .05
99 Cortez Kennedy .02 .10
100 Brett Favre .75 2.00
101 Anthony Carter .02 .10
102 Cris Carter .08 .25
103 Dana Stubblefield RC .08 .25
104A Nick Bell .01 .05
104B Don Griffin UER .01 .05
105 Marcus Allen .08 .25
106 Neil O'Donnell .08 .25
107 Steve DeBerg .01 .05
108 Leonard Russell .02 .10
109 Ethan Horton .01 .05
110 William Perry .02 .10
112 Clarence Verdin .01 .05
113 Amp Lee .01 .05
114 Earnest Byner .01 .05
115 Ricky Reynolds .01 .05
116 Tom Waddle .01 .05
117 Robert Jones .01 .05
118 Willie Davis .02 .10
119 Chris Miller .02 .10
120 Drew Hill .01 .05
121 Warren Moon .08 .25
122 Flipper Anderson .01 .05
123 George Teague RC .02 .10
124 John L. Williams .01 .05
125 Ed McCaffrey .08 .25
126 Eric Green .01 .05
127 Scott Mersereau .01 .05
128 Charles Mann .01 .05
129 Todd Lyght .01 .05
130 Rodney Culver .01 .05
131 Richmond Webb .01 .05
132 John Parrella RC .01 .05
133 Reggie Brooks RC .02 .10
134 Lincoln Kennedy RC .01 .05
135 Tim Johnson .01 .05
136 Robert Massey .01 .05
137 Keith Jackson .02 .10
138 Alfred Williams .01 .05
139 Leroy Hoard .02 .10
140 Jessie Tuggle .01 .05
141 Chris Mims .01 .05
142 Herschel Walker .02 .10
143 Clyde Simmons .01 .05
144 Dana Hall .01 .05
145 Nate Newton .02 .10
146 Dennis Smith .01 .05
147 Rich Camarillo .01 .05
148 Chris Spielman .02 .10
149 Jim Dombrowski .01 .05
150 Steve Beuerlein .02 .10
151 Mark Clayton .01 .05
152 Lee Williams .01 .05
153 Robert Smith RC .50 1.25
154 Greg Jackson .01 .05
155 Jay Hilgenberg .01 .05
156 Howard Ballard .01 .05
157 Mike Compton RC .08 .25
158 Brent Williams .01 .05
159 Tommy Kane .01 .05
160 Barry Word .01 .05
161 Darren Lewis .01 .05
162 Steve Atwater .01 .05
163 Gary Clark .02 .10
164 Donnell Woolford .01 .05
165 Henry Thomas .01 .05
166 Tim Brown .08 .25
167 Andre Ware .01 .05
168 Jackie Harris .01 .05
169 Browning Nagle .01 .05
170 Chris Singleton .01 .05
171 Ronnie Lott .02 .10
172 Leonard Marshall .01 .05
173 Dale Carter .01 .05
174 Bruce Armstrong .01 .05
175 Tommy Vardell .01 .05
176 Bubba McDowell .01 .05
177 Patrick Bates RC .01 .05
178 Tyji Armstrong .01 .05
179 Keith Byars .01 .05
180 Boomer Esiason .02 .10
181 Ricky Watters .08 .25
182 Keith Sims .01 .05
183 Burt Grossman .01 .05
184 Richard Cooper .01 .05
185 Marc Boutte .01 .05
186 Shane Conlan .01 .05
187 Luis Sharpe .01 .05
188 O.J.McDuffie RC .08 .25
189 Harvey Williams .02 .10
190 Blair Thomas .01 .05
191 Charles Haley .02 .10
192 Chip Lohmiller .01 .05
193 Vinny Testaverde .02 .10
194 Desmond Howard .02 .10
195 Johnny Johnson .01 .05
196 Bennie Blades .01 .05
197 Jeff Wright .01 .05
198 Cody Carlson .01 .05
199 Micheal Barrow RC .08 .25
200 Pat Swilling .01 .05
201 Willie Roaf RC .10 .30
202 Michael Walter .01 .05
203 Kevin Fagan .01 .05
204 Nate Odomes .01 .05
205 Michael Dean Perry .02 .10
206 Bruce Pickens .01 .05
207 Mel Gray .02 .10
208 Jack Trudeau .01 .05
209 Ricky Sanders .01 .05
210 Bobby Hebert .01 .05
211 Craig Heyward .02 .10
212 Eric Bieniemy .01 .05
213 Andre Rison .02 .10
214 Bernie Kosar .02 .10
215 Lester Holmes .01 .05
216 Marcus Buckley RC .01 .05
217 Tony Casillas .01 .05
218 Cornelius Bennett .02 .10
219 Kyle Clifton .01 .05
220 Kirk Lowdermilk .01 .05
221 Leon Searcy .01 .05
222 Gary Anderson K .01 .05
223 Tim Barnett .01 .05
224 Gene Atkins .01 .05
225 Jeff Cross .01 .05
226 Darrin Smith RC .02 .10
227 Rohn Stark .01 .05
228 Chris Warren .02 .10
229 Eric Allen .01 .05
230 Wayne Simmons RC .01 .05
231 Al Smith .01 .05
232 Reggie Rivers RC .01 .05
233 Kevin Smith .02 .10
234 Vince Workman .01 .05
235 Thurman Thomas .08 .25
236 Kevin Williams RC WR .08 .25
237 Dan McGwire .01 .05
238 Greg Lloyd .02 .10
239 Ray Buchanan RC .08 .25
240 Shannon Sharpe .08 .25
241 Ricardo McDonald .01 .05
242 Aaron Wallace .01 .05
243 Chris Hinton .01 .05
244 Bill Romanowski .01 .05
245 Randal Hill .01 .05
246 Ray Agnew .01 .05
247 Todd Kelly RC .01 .05
248 John Stephens .01 .05
249 Sean Salisbury .01 .05
250 Roger Craig .02 .10
251 Dave Krieg .02 .10
252 Brian Blades .02 .10
253 Jarrod Bunch .01 .05
254 Phil Simms .02 .10
255 Keith Van Horne .01 .05
256 Jim Price .01 .05
257 Garrison Hearst RC .30 .75
258 Dorrick Walker .01 .05
259 Mike Pritchard .02 .10
260 Leonard Renfro RC .01 .05
261 Rodney Peete .01 .05
262 Jeff Bryant .01 .05
263 Dermontti Dawson .02 .10
264 Greg McMurtry .01 .05
265 Wendell Davis .01 .05
266 Kerry Cash .01 .05
267 Jackie Slater .01 .05
268 Sam Mills .01 .05
269 Carlton Bailey .01 .05
270 Mark Wheeler .01 .05
271 Darren Perry .01 .05
272 Todd Scott .01 .05
273 Johnny Holland .01 .05
274 Mike Croel .01 .05
275 Shane Dronett .01 .05
276 Andre Collins .01 .05
277 Eric Swann .02 .10
278 Jessie Hester .01 .05
279 Bryan Cox .01 .05
280 Mark Jackson .01 .05
281 Thomas Everett .01 .05
282 James Lofton .02 .10
283 Carl Pickens .02 .10
284 Mark Carrier WR .02 .10
285 Heath Sherman .01 .05
286 Chris Burkett .01 .05
287 Coleman Rudolph RC .01 .05
288 Todd Marinovich .01 .05
289 Nate Lewis .01 .05
290 Fred Barnett .02 .10
291 Jim Lachey .01 .05
292 Jerry Ball .01 .05
293 Jeff George .08 .25
294 William Fuller .01 .05
295 Courtney Hawkins .01 .05
296 Kelvin Martin .01 .05
297 Trace Armstrong .01 .05
298 Carl Banks .01 .05
299 Terry Kirby RC .08 .25
300 John Offerdahl .01 .05
301 Harry Swayne .01 .05
302 Wilber Marshall .01 .05
303 Guy McIntyre .01 .05
304 Steve Wallace .01 .05
305 Chris Slade RC .02 .10
306 Anthony Newman .01 .05
307 Chip Banks .01 .05
308 Carlton Gray RC .01 .05
309 Wayne Martin .01 .05
310 Tom Rathman .01 .05
311 Shaun Gayle .01 .05
312 Billy Joe Hobert RC .08 .25
313 Matt Brock .01 .05
314 Arthur Marshall RC .01 .05
315 Wade Wilson .01 .05
316 Michael Jackson .02 .10
317 Bruce Kozerski .01 .05
318 Reggie Langhorne .01 .05
319 Jerrol Williams .01 .05
320 Aeneas Williams .01 .05
321 Tony McGee RC .02 .10
322 Carl Simpson RC .01 .05
323 Russell Maryland .01 .05
324 Nick Lowery .01 .05
325 Steve Tasker .02 .10
326 Alvin Harper .02 .10
327 Haywood Jeffires .02 .10
328 Hardy Nickerson .02 .10
329 Alonzo Spellman .01 .05
330 Eric Dickerson .02 .10
331 Scott Zolak .01 .05
332 Darryl Henley .01 .05
333 Daniel Stubbs .01 .05
334 Andy Heck .01 .05
335 Mark May .01 .05
336 Roosevelt Potts RC .01 .05
337 Erik Howard .01 .05
338 Sean Gilbert .02 .10
339 Jerome Bettis RC 2.50 6.00
340 Darren Carrington RC .01 .05
341 Gill Byrd .01 .05
342 John Friesz .02 .10
343 Roger Harper RC .01 .05
344 Fred Stokes .01 .05
345 Stanley Richard .01 .05
346 Johnny Bailey .01 .05
347 David Wyman .01 .05
348 Merril Hoge .01 .05
349 Brett Perriman .08 .25
350 Kelvin Pritchett .01 .05
351 Rod Bernstine .01 .05
352 Jim Ritcher .01 .05
353 Mark Stepnoski .01 .05
354 Jeff Lageman .01 .05
355 Darrien Gordon RC .01 .05
356 Don Mosebar .01 .05
357 Simon Fletcher .01 .05
358 Charles Mincy RC .01 .05
359 Ron Hall .01 .05
360 Brent Jones .02 .10
361 Byron Evans .01 .05
362 Dan Footman RC .01 .05
363 Mark Higgs .01 .05
364 Brian Washington .01 .05
365 Brad Hopkins RC .01 .05
366 Tracy Simien .01 .05
367 Derrick Fenner .01 .05
368 Lorenzo White .01 .05
369 Marvin Jones RC .01 .05
370 Chris Doleman .01 .05
371 Jeff Herrod .01 .05
372 Jim Harbaugh .08 .25
373 Jim Jeffcoat .01 .05
374 Michael Strahan RC 1.00 2.50
375 Ricky Ervins .01 .05
376 Joel Hilgenberg .01 .05
377 Curtis Duncan .01 .05
378 Glyn Milburn RC .08 .25
379 Jack Del Rio .01 .05
380 Eric Martin .01 .05
381 Dave Meggett .01 .05
382 Jeff Hostetler .02 .10
383 Greg Townsend .01 .05
384 Brad Muster .01 .05
385 Irv Smith RC .01 .05
386 Chris Jacke .01 .05
387 Ernest Dye RC .01 .05
388 Henry Ellard .02 .10
389 John Taylor .02 .10
390 Chris Chandler .02 .10
391 Larry Centers RC .08 .25
392 Henry Rolling .01 .05
393 Dan Saleaumua .01 .05
394 Moe Gardner .01 .05
395 Darryl Williams .01 .05
396 Paul Gruber .01 .05
397 Dwayne Harper .01 .05
398 Pat Harlow .01 .05
399 Rickey Jackson .01 .05
400 Quentin Coryatt .02 .10
401 Steve Jordan .01 .05
402 Rick Mirer RC .08 .25
403 Howard Cross .01 .05
404 Mike Johnson .01 .05
405 Broderick Thomas .01 .05
406 Stan Humphries .02 .10
407 Ronnie Harmon .01 .05
408 Andy Harmon RC .02 .10
409 Troy Drayton RC .02 .10
410 Dan Williams RC .01 .05
411 Mark Bavaro .01 .05
412 Bruce Smith .08 .25
413 Elbert Shelley RC .01 .05
414 Tim McGee .01 .05
415 Tim Harris .01 .05
416 Rob Moore .02 .10
417 Rob Burnett .01 .05

418 Howie Long .08 .25
419 Chuck Cecil .01 .05
420 Carl Lee .01 .05
421 Anthony Smith .01 .05
422 Jeff Graham .02 .10
423 Clay Matthews .02 .10
424 Jay Novacek .02 .10
425 Phil Hansen .01 .05
426 Andre Hastings RC .02 .10
427 Toi Cook .01 .05
428 Rufus Porter .01 .05
429 Mike Pitts .01 .05
430 Eddie Robinson .01 .05
431 Herman Moore .08 .25
432 Erik Kramer .02 .10
433 Mark Carrier DB .01 .05
434 Natrone Means RC .08 .25
435 Carnell Lake .01 .05
436 Carlton Haselrig .01 .05
437 John Randle .02 .10
438 Louis Oliver .01 .05
439 Ray Roberts .01 .05
440 Leslie O'Neal .02 .10
441 Reggie White .08 .25
442 Dalton Hilliard .01 .05
443 Tim Krumrie .01 .05
444 LeRoy Butler .01 .05
445 Greg Kragen .01 .05
446 Anthony Johnson .02 .10
447 Audray McMillian .01 .05
448 Lawrence Dawsey .01 .05
449 Pierce Holt .01 .05
450 Brad Edwards .01 .05
451 J.J. Birden .01 .05
452 Mike Munchak .02 .10
453 Tracy Scroggins .01 .05
454 Mike Tomczak .01 .05
455 Harold Green .01 .05
456 Vaughn Dunbar .01 .05
457 Calvin Williams .02 .10
458 Pete Stoyanovich .01 .05
459 Willie Gault .01 .05
460 Ken Ruettgers .01 .05
461 Eugene Robinson .01 .05
462 Larry Brown DB .01 .05
463 Antonio London RC .01 .05
464 Andre Reed .02 .10
465 Daryl Johnston .08 .25
466 Karl Mecklenburg .01 .05
467 David Lang .01 .05
468 Bill Brooks .01 .05
469 Jim Everett .02 .10
470 Qadry Ismail RC .08 .25
471 Vai Sikahema .01 .05
472 Andre Tippett .01 .05
473 Eugene Chung .01 .05
474 Cris Dishman .01 .05
475 Tim McDonald .01 .05
476 Freddie Joe Nunn .01 .05
477 Checklist 1-134 .01 .05
478 Checklist 135-268 .01 .05
479 Checklist 269-402 .01 .05
480 CL 403-480 .01 .05
Inserts
P1 Promo Sheet 1.20 3.00

1993 GameDay Gamebreakers

The GameDay Gamebreakers set consists of 20 cards measuring approximately 2 1/2" by 4 3/4". Randomly inserted in packs at a rate of one in four, this set spotlights top stars who can break open a game. The cards are numbered as "X" of 20.

COMPLETE SET (20) 10.00 25.00
STATED ODDS 1:3
1 Troy Aikman .75 2.00
2 Brett Favre 2.00 5.00
3 Steve Young .75 2.00
4 Dan Marino 1.50 4.00
5 Joe Montana 1.50 4.00
6 Jim Kelly .25 .60
7 Emmitt Smith 1.50 4.00
8 Ricky Watters .25 .60
9 Barry Foster .08 .25
10 Barry Sanders 1.25 3.00
11 Michael Irvin .25 .60
12 Thurman Thomas .25 .60
13 Sterling Sharpe .25 .60
14 Jerry Rice 1.00 2.50
15 Andre Rison .08 .25
16 Deion Sanders .50 1.25
17 Harold Green .05 .15
18 Lorenzo White .05 .15
19 Terry Allen .25 .60
20 Haywood Jeffires .08 .25

1993 GameDay Rookie Standouts

The GameDay Rookie Standouts set consists of 16 cards measuring approximately 2 1/2" by 4 3/4". Randomly inserted in packs at a rate of one in four, the set spotlights top picks of the 1993 NFL Draft. The cards are numbered as "X" of 16.

COMPLETE SET (16) 10.00 25.00
STATED ODDS 1:4
1 Drew Bledsoe 5.00 12.00
2 Rick Mirer .50 1.25
3 Garrison Hearst 1.50 4.00
4 Jerome Bettis 12.50 30.00
5 Marvin Jones .08 .25
6 Reggie Brooks .20 .50
7 O.J.McDuffie .50 1.25
8 Qadry Ismail .50 1.25
9 Glyn Milburn .50 1.25
10 Andre Hastings .20 .50
11 Curtis Conway .75 2.00
12 Eric Curry .08 .25
13 John Copeland .20 .50
14 Kevin Williams WR .50 1.25
15 Patrick Bates .08 .25
16 Lincoln Kennedy .08 .25

1993 GameDay Second Year Stars

The GameDay Second Year Stars set consists of 16 cards measuring approximately 2 1/2" by 4 3/4". Randomly inserted in packs at a rate of one in four, the set spotlights 1992 rookies.

COMPLETE SET (16) 2.50 6.00
STATED ODDS 1:4
1 Carl Pickens .40 1.00
2 David Klingler .20 .50
3 Santana Dotson .40 1.00
4 Chris Mims .20 .50
5 Steve Emtman .20 .50
6 Marco Coleman .20 .50
7 Robert Jones .20 .50
8 Dale Carter .20 .50
9 Troy Vincent .20 .50
10 Tracy Scroggins .20 .50
11 Vaughn Dunbar .20 .50
12 Quentin Coryatt .40 1.00
13 Dana Hall .20 .50
14 Terrell Buckley .20 .50
15 Tommy Vardell .20 .50
16 Johnny Mitchell .20 .50

1994 GameDay

asuring 2 1/2" by 4 3/4", this 420-card set features full-bleed action photos on front with the player's name and team name at the bottom. The backs have a player photo with statistics and a write-up at the bottom. Biographical information runs along the right border. The players are grouped alphabetically within teams, and checklisted below alphabetically according to teams. Rookie Cards in this set include Mario Bates, Isaac Bruce, Bert Emanuel, Marshall Faulk, Errict Rhett, Darnay Scott and Heath Shuler. A Reggie Brooks promo card was produced and is priced below.

COMPLETE SET (420) 15.00 30.00
1 Michael Bankston .01 .05
2 Steve Beuerlein .02 .10
3 Gary Clark .02 .10
4 Garrison Hearst .08 .25
5 Eric Hill .01 .05
6 Randal Hill .01 .05
7 Seth Joyner .01 .05
8 Jim McMahon .02 .10
9 Jamir Miller RC .02 .10
10 Ronald Moore .01 .05
11 Ricky Proehl .01 .05
12 Luis Sharpe .01 .05
13 Clyde Simmons .01 .05
14 Eric Swann .02 .10
15 Aeneas Williams .01 .05
16 Chris Doleman .01 .05
17 Bert Emanuel RC .08 .25
18 Moe Gardner .01 .05
19 Jeff George .08 .25
20 Roger Harper .01 .05
21 Pierce Holt .01 .05
22 Lincoln Kennedy .01 .05
23 Erric Pegram .01 .05
24 Andre Rison .02 .10
25 Deion Sanders .20 .50
26 Tony Smith RB .01 .05
27 Jessie Tuggle .01 .05
28 Don Beebe .01 .05
29 Cornelius Bennett .02 .10
30 Bill Brooks .01 .05
31 Bucky Brooks RC .01 .05
32 Jeff Burris RC .02 .10
33 Kenneth Davis .01 .05
34 Phil Hansen .01 .05
35 Kent Hull .01 .05
36 Henry Jones .01 .05
37 Jim Kelly .08 .25
38 Pete Metzelaars .01 .05
39 Marvcus Patton .01 .05
40 Andre Reed .02 .10
41 Bruce Smith .08 .25
42 Thomas Smith .01 .05
43 Darryl Talley .01 .05
44 Steve Tasker .02 .10
45 Thurman Thomas .08 .25
46 Jeff Wright .01 .05
47 Trace Armstrong .01 .05
48 Joe Cain .01 .05
49 Mark Carrier DB .01 .05
50 Curtis Conway .08 .25
51 Shaun Gayle .01 .05
52 Dante Jones .01 .05
53 Erik Kramer .02 .10
54 Terry Obee .01 .05
55 Vinson Smith .01 .05
56 Alonzo Spellman .01 .05
57 John Thierry RC .01 .05
58 Tom Waddle .01 .05
59 Donnell Woolford .01 .05
60 Tim Worley .01 .05
61 Chris Zorich .01 .05
62 Mike Brim .01 .05
63 John Copeland .01 .05
64 Derrick Fenner .01 .05
65 James Francis .01 .05
66 Harold Green .01 .05
67 David Klingler .01 .05
68 Ricardo McDonald .01 .05
69 Tony McGee .01 .05
70 Carl Pickens .02 .10
71 Jeff Query .01 .05
72 Darnay Scott RC .20 .50
73 Steve Tovar .01 .05
74 Dan Wilkinson RC .02 .10
75 Alfred Williams .01 .05
76 Darryl Williams .01 .05
77 Derrick Alexander WR RC .08 .25
78 Rob Burnett .01 .05
79 Steve Everitt .01 .05
80 Michael Jackson .02 .10
81 Pepper Johnson .01 .05
82 Tony Jones T .01 .05
83 Antonio Langham RC .02 .10
84 Eric Metcalf .02 .10
85 Stevon Moore .01 .05
86 Michael Dean Perry .02 .10
87 Anthony Pleasant .01 .05
88 Vinny Testaverde .02 .10
89 Eric Turner .01 .05
90 Tommy Vardell .01 .05
91 Troy Aikman .40 1.00
92 Larry Brown DB .01 .05
93 Shante Carver RC .01 .05
94 Charles Haley .02 .10
95 Alvin Harper .02 .10
96 Michael Irvin .08 .25
97 Daryl Johnston .02 .10
98 Leon Lett .01 .05
99 Russell Maryland .01 .05
100 Nate Newton .01 .05
101 Jay Novacek .02 .10
102 Darrin Smith .01 .05
103 Emmitt Smith .60 1.50
104 Kevin Smith .01 .05
105 Mark Stepnoski .01 .05
106 Tony Tolbert .01 .05
107 Erik Williams .01 .05
108 Kevin Williams WR .02 .10
109 Darren Woodson .02 .10
110 Allen Aldridge RC .01 .05
111 Steve Atwater .01 .05
112 Rod Bernstine .01 .05
113 Ray Crockett .01 .05
114 Mike Croel .01 .05
115 Robert Delpino .01 .05
116 Shane Dronett .01 .05
117 Jason Elam .02 .10
118 John Elway .75 2.00
119 Simon Fletcher .01 .05
120 Glyn Milburn .02 .10
121 Anthony Miller .02 .10
122 Mike Pritchard .01 .05
123 Shannon Sharpe .02 .10
124 Dan Williams .01 .05
125 Bennie Blades .01 .05
126 Lomas Brown .01 .05
127 Anthony Carter .02 .10
128 Mel Gray .01 .05
129 Jason Hanson .01 .05
130 Robert Massey .01 .05
131 Ryan McNeil .01 .05
132 Scott Mitchell .02 .10
133 Herman Moore .08 .25
134 Johnnie Morton RC .20 .50
135 Brett Perriman .02 .10
136 Robert Porcher .01 .05
137 Barry Sanders .60 1.50
138 Tracy Scroggins .01 .05
139 Chris Spielman .02 .10
140 Pat Swilling .01 .05
141 Edgar Bennett .08 .25
142 Robert Brooks .08 .25
143 Terrell Buckley .01 .05
144 LeRoy Butler .01 .05
145 Reggie Cobb .01 .05
146 Curtis Duncan .01 .05
147 Brett Favre .75 2.00
148 Sean Jones .01 .05
149 George Koonce .01 .05
150 Ken Ruettgers .01 .05
151 Sterling Sharpe .02 .10
152 Wayne Simmons .01 .05
153 Aaron Taylor RC .01 .05
154 George Teague .01 .05
155 Reggie White .08 .25
156 Micheal Barrow .01 .05
157 Gary Brown .01 .05
158 Rich Camarillo .01 .05
159 Cody Carlson .01 .05
160 Ray Childress .01 .05
161 Cris Dishman .01 .05
162 Henry Ford RC .01 .05
163 Ernest Givins .02 .10
164 Steve Jackson .01 .05
165 Haywood Jeffires .02 .10
166 Bruce Matthews .01 .05
167 Bubba McDowell .01 .05
168 Marcus Robertson .01 .05
169 Eddie Robinson .01 .05
170 Webster Slaughter .01 .05
171 Trev Alberts RC .02 .10
172 Tony Bennett .01 .05
173 Ray Buchanan .01 .05
174 Kerry Cash .01 .05
175 Quentin Coryatt .01 .05
176 Eugene Daniel .01 .05
177 Sean Dawkins RC .08 .25
178 Steve Emtman .01 .05
179 Marshall Faulk RC 2.00 5.00
180 Jon Hand .01 .05
181 Jim Harbaugh .08 .25
182 Jeff Herrod .01 .05
183 Roosevelt Potts .01 .05
184 Rohn Stark .01 .05
185 Marcus Allen .08 .25
186 Donnell Bennett RC .08 .25
187 J.J. Birden .01 .05
188 Dale Carter .01 .05
189 Mark Collins .01 .05
190 Willie Davis .02 .10
191 Lake Dawson RC .02 .10
192 Tim Grunhard .01 .05
193 Greg Hill RC .08 .25
194 Joe Montana .75 2.00
195 Tracy Simien .01 .05
196 Neil Smith .02 .10
197 Derrick Thomas .08 .25
198 Tim Brown .08 .25
199 James Folston RC .01 .05
200 Rob Fredrickson RC .02 .10
201 Nolan Harrison .01 .05
202 Jeff Hostetler .02 .10
203 Rocket Ismail .02 .10
204 Jeff Jaeger .01 .05
205 James Jett .01 .05
206 Terry McDaniel .01 .05
207 Chester McGlockton .01 .05
208 Winston Moss .01 .05
209 Tom Rathman .01 .05
210 Anthony Smith .01 .05
211 Harvey Williams .02 .10
212 Steve Wisniewski .01 .05
213 Alexander Wright .01 .05
214 Flipper Anderson .01 .05
215 Jerome Bettis .20 .50
216 Isaac Bruce RC 2.00 4.00
217 Troy Drayton .01 .05
218 Wayne Gandy RC .01 .05
219 Sean Gilbert .01 .05
220 Nate Lewis .01 .05
221 Todd Lyght .01 .05
222 Chris Miller .01 .05
223 Anthony Newman .01 .05
224 Roman Phifer .01 .05
225 Henry Rolling .01 .05
226 Jackie Slater .01 .05
227 Fred Stokes .01 .05
228 Gene Atkins .01 .05
229 Aubrey Beavers RC .01 .05
230 Tim Bowens RC .02 .10
231 J.B. Brown .01 .05
232 Keith Byars .01 .05
233 Marco Coleman .01 .05
234 Bryan Cox .01 .05
235 Jeff Cross .01 .05
236 Irving Fryar .02 .10
237 Mark Ingram .01 .05
238 Keith Jackson .01 .05
239 Terry Kirby .08 .25
240 Dan Marino .75 2.00
241 Michael Stewart .01 .05
242 Troy Vincent .01 .05
243 Richmond Webb .01 .05
244 Terry Allen .02 .10
245 Cris Carter .20 .50
246 Jack Del Rio .01 .05
247 Vencie Glenn .01 .05
248 Chris Hinton .01 .05
249 Qadry Ismail .08 .25
250 Carlos Jenkins .01 .05
251 Randall McDaniel .02 .10
252 Warren Moon .08 .25
253 David Palmer RC .08 .25
254 John Randle .02 .10
255 Jake Reed .02 .10
256 Todd Scott .01 .05
257 Todd Steussie RC .02 .10
258 Henry Thomas .01 .05
259 Dewayne Washington RC .02 .10
260 Bruce Armstrong .01 .05
261 Drew Bledsoe .30 .75
262 Vincent Brisby .02 .10
263 Vincent Brown .01 .05
264 Marion Butts .01 .05
265 Ben Coates .02 .10
266 Pat Harlow .01 .05
267 Maurice Hurst .01 .05
268 Willie McGinest RC .08 .25
269 Chris Slade .01 .05
270 Michael Timpson .01 .05
271 Morten Andersen .01 .05
272 Mario Bates RC .08 .25
273 Derek Brown RBK .01 .05
274 Quinn Early .02 .10
275 Jim Everett .02 .10
276 Michael Haynes .02 .10
277 Tyrone Hughes .02 .10
278 Joe Johnson RC .01 .05
279 Eric Martin .01 .05
280 Wayne Martin .01 .05
281 Sam Mills .01 .05
282 Willie Roaf .01 .05
283 Irv Smith .01 .05
284 Renaldo Turnbull .01 .05
285 Carlton Bailey .01 .05
286 Michael Brooks .01 .05
287 Dave Brown .02 .10
288 Jarrod Bunch .01 .05
289 Howard Cross .01 .05
290 John Elliott .01 .05
291 Keith Hamilton .01 .05
292 Rodney Hampton .02 .10
293 Mark Jackson .01 .05
294 Thomas Lewis RC .02 .10
295 Dave Meggett .01 .05
296 Corey Miller .01 .05
297 Mike Sherrard .01 .05
298 Brad Baxter .01 .05
299 Kyle Clifton .01 .05
300 Boomer Esiason .02 .10
301 Aaron Glenn RC .08 .25
302 James Hasty .01 .05
303 Johnny Johnson .01 .05
304 Jeff Lageman .01 .05
305 Mo Lewis .01 .05
306 Ronnie Lott .02 .10
307 Johnny Mitchell .01 .05
308 Art Monk .02 .10
309 Rob Moore .02 .10
310 Brian Washington .01 .05
311 Marvin Washington .01 .05
312 Ryan Yarborough RC .01 .05
313 Eric Allen .01 .05
314 Victor Bailey .01 .05
315 Fred Barnett .02 .10
316 Mark Bavaro .01 .05
317 Randall Cunningham .08 .25
318 Byron Evans .01 .05
319 William Fuller .01 .05
320 Charlie Garner RC .50 1.25
321 Andy Harmon .01 .05
322 Vaughn Hebron .01 .05
323 Mark McMillian .01 .05
324 Bill Romanowski .01 .05
325 William Thomas .01 .05
326 Greg Townsend .01 .05
327 Herschel Walker .02 .10
328 Bernard Williams RC .01 .05
329 Calvin Williams .02 .10
330 Dermontti Dawson .02 .10
331 Deon Figures .01 .05
332 Barry Foster .01 .05
333 Eric Green .01 .05
334 Kevin Greene .02 .10
335 Carlton Haselrig .01 .05
336 Charles Johnson RC .08 .25
337 Levon Kirkland .01 .05
338 Carnell Lake .01 .05
339 Greg Lloyd .02 .10
340 Neil O'Donnell .08 .25
341 Darren Perry .01 .05
342 Dwight Stone .01 .05
343 John L. Williams .01 .05
344 Rod Woodson .02 .10
345 John Carney .01 .05
346 Darren Carrington .01 .05
347 Isaac Davis RC .01 .05
348 Courtney Hall .01 .05
349 Ronnie Harmon .01 .05
350 Dwayne Harper .01 .05
351 Stan Humphries .02 .10
352 Shawn Jefferson .01 .05
353 Vance Johnson .01 .05
354 Natrone Means .08 .25
355 Chris Mims .01 .05
356 Leslie O'Neal .01 .05
357 Stanley Richard .01 .05
358 Junior Seau .08 .25
359 Harris Barton .01 .05
360 Eric Davis .01 .05
361 Richard Dent .02 .10
362 William Floyd RC .08 .25
363 Merton Hanks .02 .10
364 Brent Jones .02 .10
365 Marc Logan .01 .05
366 Tim McDonald .01 .05
367 Ken Norton .02 .10
368 Jerry Rice .40 1.00
369 Jesse Sapolu .01 .05
370 Dana Stubblefield .02 .10
371 John Taylor .02 .10
372 Ricky Watters .02 .10
373 Bryant Young RC .15 .40
374 Steve Young .30 .75
375 Sam Adams RC .02 .10
376 Michael Bates .01 .05
377 Robert Blackmon .01 .05
378 Brian Blades .02 .10
379 Ferrell Edmunds .01 .05
380 John Kasay .01 .05
381 Cortez Kennedy .02 .10
382 Kelvin Martin .01 .05
383 Rick Mirer .08 .25
384 Rufus Porter .01 .05
385 Eugene Robinson .01 .05
386 Rod Stephens .01 .05
387 Chris Warren .02 .10
300 Marty Carter .01 .05
389 Horace Copeland .01 .05
390 Eric Curry .01 .05
391 Lawrence Dawsey .01 .05
392 Trent Dilfer RC .50 1.25
393 Santana Dotson .02 .10
394 Craig Erickson .01 .05
395 Thomas Everett .01 .05
396 Paul Gruber .01 .05
397 Jackie Harris .01 .05
398 Courtney Hawkins .01 .05
399 Martin Mayhew .01 .05
400 Hardy Nickerson .02 .10
401 Errict Rhett RC .08 .25
402 Vince Workman .01 .05
403 Reggie Brooks .02 .10
404 Tom Carter .01 .05
405 Andre Collins .01 .05
406 Henry Ellard .02 .10
407 Kurt Gouveia .01 .05
408 Darrell Green .01 .05
409 Ken Harvey .01 .05
410 Ethan Horton .01 .05
411 Desmond Howard .02 .10
412 Jim Lachey .01 .05
413 Sterling Palmer RC .01 .05
414 Heath Shuler RC .08 .25
415 Tyronne Stowe .01 .05
416 Tony Woods .01 .05
417 Checklist 1-124 .01 .05
418 Checklist 125-243 .01 .05
419 Checklist 244-358 .01 .05
420 CL 359-420 .01 .05
Inserts
P1 Reggie Brooks Promo .20 .50

1994 GameDay Flashing Stars

ndomly inserted in packs, this four-card set spotlights outstanding young players. The cards measure 2 1/2" by 4 3/4". Prismatic foil fronts contain a player photo and the Flashing Stars logo. The backs have a photo and a write-up. The set is numbered as "X" of 4 and is sequenced in alphabetical order.

COMPLETE SET (4) 7.50 20.00
1 Jerome Bettis 1.50 4.00
2 Rick Mirer .75 2.00
3 Jerry Rice 3.00 8.00
4 Emmitt Smith 5.00 12.00

1994 GameDay Gamebreakers

Randomly inserted in packs, this 16-card set spotlights clutch running backs, quarterbacks and receivers. The cards measure 2 1/2" by 4 3/4". Card fronts contain a large black and white photo with the same photo in color toward the bottom left. The word "Gamebreaker" runs across the card. The backs have a color player photo with a write-up. The set is numbered as "X" of 16 and is sequeneced in alphabetical order.

COMPLETE SET (16) 6.00 15.00
1 Troy Aikman .60 1.50
2 Marcus Allen .15 .40
3 Tim Brown .15 .40
4 John Elway 1.25 3.00
5 Michael Irvin .15 .40
6 Dan Marino 1.25 3.00
7 Joe Montana 1.25 3.00
8 Jerry Rice .60 1.50
9 Andre Rison .05 .15
10 Barry Sanders 1.00 2.50
11 Deion Sanders .30 .75
12 Sterling Sharpe .05 .15
13 Emmitt Smith 1.00 2.50
14 Thurman Thomas .15 .40
15 Rod Woodson .05 .15
16 Steve Young .50 1.25

1994 GameDay Rookie Standouts

ndomly inserted in packs, this 16-card set contains top 1994 rookies. The cards measure 2 1/2" by 4 3/4". These cards are distinguished by a "3-D embossed" design on front. The player photo occupies the entire front with the player's name in gold letters at the bottom. The backs have a close-up photo with highlights. The set is numbered as "X" of 16 and is sequenced in alphabetical order.

COMPLETE SET (16) 4.00 10.00
1 Sam Adams .05 .15
2 Trev Alberts .05 .15
3 Lake Dawson .05 .15
4 Trent Dilfer .75 2.00
5 Marshall Faulk 3.00 8.00
6 Aaron Glenn .15 .40
7 Charles Johnson .15 .40
8 Willie McGinest .15 .40
9 Jamir Miller .05 .15
10 Johnnie Morton .30 .75
11 David Palmer .15 .40
12 Errict Rhett .15 .40
13 Heath Shuler .15 .40
14 John Thierry .02 .10
15 Dan Wilkinson .05 .15
16 Bryant Young .15 .40

1994 GameDay Second Year Stars

Looking back on top rookies from 1993, this 16-card set was randomly inserted in packs. Action oriented fronts contain two photos and the player's name in gold foil. Background color is consistent with team colors. The backs are designed much like the front, except for one photo and highlights. The cards are numbered as "X" of 16 and are sequenced in alphabetical order.

COMPLETE SET (16) 2.50 6.00
1 Jerome Bettis .75 2.00
2 Drew Bledsoe 1.25 3.00
3 Reggie Brooks .15 .40
4 Tom Carter .07 .20
5 Eric Curry .07 .20
6 Steve Everitt .07 .20
7 Tyrone Hughes .15 .40
8 James Jett .07 .20
9 Terry Kirby .40 1.00
10 Natrone Means .40 1.00
11 Rick Mirer .40 1.00
12 Ronald Moore .07 .20
13 Willie Roaf .07 .20
14 Chris Slade .07 .20
15 Darrin Smith .07 .20
16 Dana Stubblefield .15 .40

1971 Gatorade Team Lids

These lids were actually the tops off bottles of Gatorade sold during the 1971 and 1972 NFL seasons. Each white colored lid had a dark outline of an NFL helmet with the team name printed underneath.

COMPLETE SET (26) 75.00 150.00
1 Atlanta Falcons 2.50 5.00
2 Baltimore Colts 3.00 6.00
3 Buffalo Bills 2.50 5.00
4 Chicago Bears 3.00 6.00
5 Cincinnati Bengals 2.50 5.00
6 Cleveland Browns 3.00 6.00
7 Dallas Cowboys 4.00 8.00
8 Denver Broncos 3.00 6.00
9 Detroit Lions 2.50 5.00
10 Green Bay Packers 4.00 8.00
11A Houston Oilers 4.00 10.00
11B Houston Oilers 2.50 5.00
12 Kansas City Chiefs 2.50 5.00
13A Los Angeles Rams 4.00 10.00
13B Los Angeles Rams 2.50 5.00
14 Miami Dolphins 4.00 8.00
15 Minnesota Vikings 3.00 6.00
16 New England Patriots 2.50 5.00
17 New Orleans Saints 2.50 5.00
18 New York Giants 2.50 5.00
19 Now York Jets 2.50 5.00
20 Oakland Raiders 4.00 8.00
21 Philadelphia Eagles 2.50 5.00
22 Pittsburgh Steelers 4.00 8.00
23 San Diego Chargers 2.50 5.00
24 San Francisco 49ers 4.00 8.00
25 St. Louis Cardinals 2.50 5.00
26A Washington Redskins 4.00 8.00
26B Washington Redskins 4.00 8.00

1997 George Teague Softball

This card set was issued for the Geaorge Teague vs. Michael Bolton Celebrity Softball Challenge event. The two single Teague cards are similar in design to the 1997 Ultra football card set on the fronts with a newly designed cardback. The set was sponsored by the Rebecca Fund and Michael Bolton Foundation.

COMPLETE SET (32) 12.50 25.00
1 Mike Bolen .40 1.00
2 Micheal Bolton .60 1.50
3 Micheal Bolton .60 1.50
4 Gilbert Brown .75 2.00
5 Mugs Cain .40 1.00
6 Johnny Dodd .40 1.00
7 Bucky Ford .40 1.00
8 Phil Higgins .40 1.00
9 Bill Jartz .40 1.00
10 Charles Jordan .60 1.50
11 John Jurkovic .75 2.00
12 Louis Levin .40 1.00
13 Tom Mulhern .40 1.00
14 Murphy in the morning .40 1.00
15 Tim Nass .40 1.00
16 Bobby Olah .40 1.00
17 Bernie Parmalee .75 2.00
18 Ron Peterson .40 1.00
19 Lee Ann Rimes .60 1.50
20 Jim Schwantz .60 1.50
21 Donnie Slye .40 1.00
22 Jimmy Slye .40 1.00
23 Rebecca Slye .40 1.00
24 George Teague .60 1.50
25 George Teague .60 1.50
26 J.T. Teague .40 1.00
27 Quinn Teague .40 1.00
28 Adam Timmerman .60 1.50
29 Richie Vaughn .40 1.00
30 Gary Whitefield .40 1.00
31 Shawn Wooden .60 1.50
32 Cover Card .40 1.00
Team Photo

1956 Giants Team Issue

The 1956 Giants Team Issue set contains 36 cards measuring approximately 4 7/8" by 6 7/8". The fronts have black and white posed player photos with white borders. A facsimile autograph appears below the picture. The backs have brief biographical information and career highlights. The cards are unnumbered and checklisted below in alphabetical order. Many of the cards in this set are similar to the 1957 release and are only distinguishable by the differences noted below in parenthesis. We've included the first line of text on the cardback of some to help differentiate the two sets.

COMPLETE SET (36) 125.00 250.00
1 Bill Austin 4.00 8.00
2 Ray Beck 4.00 8.00
3 Roosevelt Brown 6.00 12.00
4 Hank Burnine 4.00 8.00
5 Don Chandler 4.00 8.00
6 Bobby Clatterbuck 4.00 8.00
7 Charley Conerly 10.00 20.00
8 Frank Gifford 20.00 40.00
9 Roosevelt Grier 6.00 12.00
10 Don Heinrich 4.00 8.00
11 John Hermann 4.00 8.00
12 Jim Lee Howell CO 4.00 8.00
13 Sam Huff 10.00 20.00
14 Ed Hughes 4.00 8.00
15 Gerald Huth 4.00 8.00
16 Jim Katcavage 4.00 8.00
17 Gene Kirby ANN 4.00 8.00
18 Ken MacAfee E 4.00 8.00
19 Dick Modzelewski 4.00 8.00
20 Henry Moore 4.00 8.00
21 Dick Nolan 4.00 8.00
22 Jim Patton 4.00 8.00
23 Andy Robustelli 7.50 15.00
24 Kyle Rote 5.00 10.00
25 Chris Schenkel ANN 4.00 8.00
26 Bob Schnelker 4.00 8.00
27 Jack Stroud 4.00 8.00
28 Harland Svare 4.00 8.00
29 Bill Svoboda 4.00 8.00
30 Bob Topp 4.00 8.00
31 Mel Triplett 4.00 8.00
32 Emlen Tunnell 6.00 12.00
33 Alex Webster 5.00 10.00
34 Ray Wietecha 4.00 8.00
35 Dick Yelvington 4.00 8.00
36 Walt Yowarsky 4.00 8.00

1957 Giants Team Issue

is 36-card set measures approximately 4 7/8" by 6 7/8". The cardfronts have a black and white player photo printed on thin card stock with a white border. The cardbacks give biographical and statistical information. This set features one of the earliest Vince Lombardi cards. The cards are unnumbered and checklisted below in alphabetical order. Many of the cards in this set are similar to the 1956 release and are only distinguishable by the differences noted below in parenthesis. We've included the first line of text on the cardback of some to help differentiate the two sets.

COMPLETE SET (36) 150.00 300.00
1 Ben Agajanian 4.00 8.00
2 Bill Austin 4.00 8.00
3 Ray Beck 4.00 8.00
4 John Bookman 4.00 8.00
5 Roosevelt Brown 6.00 12.00
6 Don Chandler 4.00 8.00
7 Bobby Clatterbuck 4.00 8.00
8 Charley Conerly 10.00 20.00
9 Gene Filipski 4.00 8.00
10 Frank Gifford 15.00 30.00
11 Don Heinrich 4.00 8.00
12 Sam Huff 6.00 12.00
13 Ed Hughes 4.00 8.00
14 Gerald Huth 4.00 8.00
15 Jim Katcavage 4.00 8.00
16 Les Keiter ANN 4.00 8.00
17 Cliff Livingston 4.00 8.00
18 Ken MacAfee E 4.00 8.00
19 Dennis Mendyk 4.00 8.00
20 Dick Modzelewski 4.00 8.00
21 Dick Nolan 4.00 8.00
22 Jim Patton 4.00 8.00
23 Andy Robustelli 6.00 12.00
24 Kyle Rote 5.00 10.00
25 Chris Schenkel ANN 4.00 8.00
26 Jack Spinks 4.00 8.00
27 Jack Stroud 4.00 8.00
28 Harland Svare 4.00 8.00
29 Bill Svoboda 4.00 8.00
30 Mel Triplett 4.00 8.00
31 Emlen Tunnell 6.00 12.00
32 Alex Webster 5.00 10.00
33 Ray Wietecha 4.00 8.00
34 Dick Yelvington 4.00 8.00
35 Walt Yowarsky 4.00 8.00
36 Giants Coaches 30.00 60.00

1959 Giants Shell Glasses

ese four drinking glasses were issued by Shell Gasoline Stations around 1959. Each features the same artwork and captions found on the 1959 Giants Shell Posters with the image etched on the glass with a frosted background.

COMPLETE SET (4) 100.00 200.00
1 Frank Gifford 40.00 80.00
2 Sam Huff 30.00 60.00
3 Dick Modzelewski 20.00 40.00
4 Kyle Rote 25.00 50.00

1959 Giants Shell Posters

is set of ten posters was distributed by Shell Oil in 1959. The pictures are black and white drawings by Robert Riger, and measure approximately 11 3/4" by 13 3/4". The unnumbered posters are arranged alphabetically by the player's last name and feature members of the New York Giants.

COMPLETE SET (10) 75.00 150.00
1 Charley Conerly 7.50 15.00
2 Frank Gifford 18.00 30.00
3 Sam Huff 12.00 20.00
4 Dick Modzelewski 6.00 12.00
5 Jim Patton 6.00 12.00
6 Andy Robustelli 7.50 15.00
7 Kyle Rote 7.50 15.00
8 Bob Schnelker 6.00 12.00
9 Pat Summerall 7.50 15.00
10 Alex Webster 7.50 15.00
R.Brown

1960 Giants Jay Publishing

is 12-card set features (approximately) 5" by 7" black-and-white player photos. The photos show players in traditional poses with the quarterback preparing to throw, the runner heading downfield, and the defenseman ready for the tackle. These cards were packaged 12 to a packet and originally sold for 25 cents. The backs are blank. The cards are unnumbered and checklisted in alphabetical order.

COMPLETE SET (12) 75.00 135.00
1 Roosevelt Brown 6.00 12.00
2 Don Chandler 3.00 6.00
3 Charley Conerly 10.00 20.00
4 Frank Gifford 17.50 35.00
5 Roosevelt Grier 5.00 10.00
6 Sam Huff 10.00 20.00
7 Phil King 3.00 6.00
8 Andy Robustelli 7.50 15.00
9 Kyle Rote 4.00 8.00
10 Bob Schnelker 3.00 6.00
11 Pat Summerall 7.50 15.00
12 Alex Webster 4.00 8.00

1961 Giants Jay Publishing

This 12-card set features (approximately) 5" by 7" black-and-white player photos. The photos show players in traditional poses with the quarterback preparing to throw, the runner heading downfield, and the defenseman ready for the tackle. These cards were packaged 12 to a packet and originally sold for 25 cents. The backs are blank. The cards are unnumbered and checklisted below in alphabetical order.

COMPLETE SET (12) 50.00 100.00
1 Roosevelt Brown 4.00 8.00
2 Don Chandler 3.00 6.00
3 Charley Conerly 7.50 15.00
4 Roosevelt Grier 4.00 8.00
5 Sam Huff 6.00 12.00
6 Dick Modzelewski 3.00 6.00
7 Jimmy Patton 3.00 6.00
8 Jim Podoley 3.00 6.00
9 Andy Robustelli 5.00 10.00
10 Allie Sherman CO 3.00 6.00
11 Del Shofner 4.00 8.00
12 Y.A. Tittle 12.50 25.00

1962 Giants Team Issue

The New York Giants issued this set of player photos in 1962. The photos were distributed in set form complete with a paper checklist of the 10-players. Each measures approximately 8" by 10" and features a black and white photo with only the player's name directly below the picture within the border. The cards are blankbacked and unnumbered.

COMPLETE SET (10) 75.00 150.00
1 Roosevelt Brown 7.50 15.00
2 Don Chandler 6.00 12.00
3 Frank Gifford 17.50 35.00
4 Sam Huff 10.00 20.00
5 Dick Lynch 6.00 12.00
6 Jim Patton 6.00 12.00
7 Andy Robustelli 10.00 20.00
8 Del Shofner 7.50 15.00
9 Y.A. Tittle 12.50 25.00
10 Alex Webster 6.00 12.00

1965 Giants Team Issue Color

is set was originally released as a poster-sized sheet of color photos with facsimile player signatures. When cut, the photos measure roughly 5" by 7". The set is unnumbered and listed below alphabetically with prices for cut cards..

COMPLETE SET (15) 75.00 150.00
1 Roosevelt Brown 7.50 15.00
2 Tucker Frederickson 5.00 10.00
3 Jerry Hillebrand 5.00 10.00
4 Jim Katcavage 5.00 10.00
5 Spider Lockhart 6.00 12.00
6 Dick Lynch 5.00 10.00
7 Chuck Mercein 5.00 10.00
8 Earl Morrall 6.00 12.00
9 Joe Morrison 6.00 12.00
10 Del Shofner 6.00 12.00
11 Lou Slaby 5.00 10.00
12 Aaron Thomas 5.00 10.00
13 Steve Thurlow 5.00 10.00
14 Ernie Wheelwright 5.00 10.00
15 Giants Team Photo 6.00 12.00

1965-68 Giants Team Issue

e Giants issued a large number of roughly 8" x 10" black and white photos in the mid 1960s. Each photo includes only the player's name and position below the image in all capital letters and the backs are blank. Many player's were issued in various different poses as well as with variations in the text below the photo. We've included this detail below when known. Additions to this list are appreciated.

1A Erich Barnes 5.00 10.00
(Def. Halfback)
1B Erich Barnes 5.00 10.00
(Def. Halfback)
1C Erich Barnes 5.00 10.00
(Defensive Back)
2 Roosevelt Brown 7.50 15.00
3 Henry Carr 5.00 10.00
4A Clarence Childs 5.00 10.00
Defensive Back, name
and position 1 1/4-in apart)
4B Clarence Childs 5.00 10.00
Defensive Back, name
and position 1 1/4-in apart)
5 Darrell Dess 5.00 10.00
6 Scott Eaton 5.00 10.00
7 Tucker Frederickson 6.00 12.00
8A Jerry Hillebrand 5.00 10.00
(Linebacker, name and
position 1 3/8-in apart)
8B Jerry Hillebrand 5.00 10.00
(Linebacker, name and
position 3/4-in apart)
9A Jim Katcavage 5.00 10.00
(Defensive End)
9B Jim Katcavage 5.00 10.00
(Def. End, name and
position 2 3/8-in apart)
9C Jim Katcavage 5.00 10.00
(Def. End, name and
position 1 1/4-in apart)
10A Ernie Koy 6.00 12.00
(Offensive Back)
10B Ernie Koy 6.00 12.00
(Running Back)
11 Greg Larson 5.00 10.00
12 Dick Lynch 5.00 10.00
13 Earl Morrall 6.00 12.00
14 Joe Morrison 6.00 12.00
15 Allie Sherman CO 6.00 12.00
(At chalkboard)
16 Del Shofner 6.00 12.00
17 Andy Stynchula 5.00 10.00
18 Fran Tarkenton 12.50 25.00
19 Aaron Thomas 5.00 10.00

1966 Giants Team Issue Color

This set was originally released as a poster-sized sheet of color photos with facsimile player signatures. When cut, the photos measure roughly 5" by 7". The set is unnumbered and listed below alphabetically with prices for cut photos.

1 Henry Carr 5.00 10.00
2 Tucker Frederickson 5.00 10.00
3 Pete Gogolak 5.00 10.00
4 Jerry Hillebrand 5.00 10.00
5 Homer Jones 5.00 10.00
6 Jim Katcavage 5.00 10.00
7 Ernie Koy 5.00 10.00
8 Spider Lockhart 6.00 12.00
9 Chuck Mercein 5.00 10.00
10 Earl Morrall 7.50 15.00
11 Joe Morrison 6.00 12.00
12 Jim Prestel 5.00 10.00
13 Aaron Thomas 5.00 10.00
14 Go-Go Giants '66 Title 5.00 10.00
15 Earl Morrall Action 7x10 6.00 12.00

1972 Giants Team Issue

These photos were issued by the Giants in 1972. Each measures roughly 4" by 5" with a white border on all 4-sides of the player image. The player's name and position is included below the photo and the cardbacks are blank and unnumbered.

COMPLETE SET (18) 50.00 100.00
1 Pete Athas 4.00 8.00
2 Bobby Duhon 4.00 8.00
3 Charlie Evans 4.00 8.00
4 Jim Files 4.00 8.00
5 Pete Gogolak 4.00 8.00
6 Jack Gregory 4.00 8.00
7 Bob Grim 4.00 8.00
8 Don Herrmann 4.00 8.00
9 Rich Houston 4.00 8.00
10 Pat Hughes 4.00 8.00
11 Randy Johnson 5.00 10.00
12 Ron Johnson 4.00 8.00
13 Carl Lockhart 4.00 8.00
14 Eldridge Small 4.00 8.00
15 Joe Taffoni 4.00 8.00
16 Rocky Thompson 4.00 8.00
17 Dave Tipton 4.00 8.00
18 Willie Williams 4.00 8.00

1973 Giants Color Litho

ch of these color lithos measures approximately 8 1/2" by 11" and is blank backed. There is no card border and a facsimile autograph appears within a white triangle below the player photo.

COMPLETE SET (8) 25.00 50.00
1 Jim Files 3.00 6.00
2 Jack Gregory 3.00 6.00
3 Ron Johnson 4.00 8.00
4 Greg Larson 3.00 6.00
5 Spider Lockhart 4.00 8.00
6 Norm Snead 5.00 10.00
7 Bob Tucker 4.00 8.00
8 Brad Van Pelt 4.00 8.00

1974 Giants Color Litho

Each of these color photos measures approximately 8 1/2" by 11" and is blankbacked. The photos are borderless and the player's name appears in white in the lower left or right of the player image.

COMPLETE SET (8) 25.00 50.00

1 Pete Athas 3.00 6.00
2 Pete Gogolak 3.00 6.00
3 Bob Grim 4.00 8.00
4 Don Herrmann 3.00 6.00
5 Pat Hughes 3.00 6.00
6 Bob Hyland 3.00 6.00
7 Ron Johnson 4.00 8.00
8 John Mendenhall 3.00 6.00

1974 Giants Team Issue

This photo pack set was issued by the Giants in 1974. Each photo measures roughly 8 1/2" by 10" with a white border on all 4-sides of the player image. The player's name and position is included below the photo and the cardbacks are blank and unnumbered.

COMPLETE SET (8) 25.00 50.00
1 Chuck Crist 3.00 6.00
2 Pete Gogolak 3.00 6.00
3 Bob Grim 3.00 6.00
4 Brian Kelley 3.00 6.00
5 Spider Lockhart 4.00 8.00
6 Norm Snead 5.00 10.00
7 Doug Van Horn 3.00 6.00
8 Willie Young 3.00 6.00

1975 Giants Team Issue

This photos were issued by the Giants around 1975. Each measures roughly 8" by 10" with a white border on all 4-sides of the player image. Just the player's name and position are included below the photo and the backs are blank and unnumbered.

1 Bobby Brooks 5.00 10.00
2 Pete Gogolak 5.00 10.00
3 Ron Johnson 6.00 12.00
4 Norm Snead 6.00 12.00
5 Willie Young 5.00 10.00

1979 Giants Team Sheets

is set consists of eight 8" by 10" sheets that display 5-8 black-and-white player/coach photos on each. Each individual photo measures approximately 2 1/4" by 3 1/4" and includes the player's name, jersey number, position, and brief vital stats below the photo. "1979 New York Football Giants" appears across the top of each sheet and the backs are blank. The sheets are unnumbered and checklisted below alphabetically according to the player featured in the upper left corner.

COMPLETE SET (8) 25.00 50.00
1 Sheet 1 4.00 8.00
2 Sheet 2 3.00 6.00
3 Sheet 3 5.00 10.00
4 Sheet 4 3.00 6.00
5 Sheet 5 3.00 6.00
6 Sheet 6 5.00 10.00
7 Sheet 7 3.00 6.00
8 Sheet 8 3.00 6.00

1981 Giants Team Sheets

is set consists of eight 8" by 10" sheets that display four to eight black-and-white player/coach photos on each. Each individual photo measures approximately 2 1/4" by 3 1/4" and includes the player's name, jersey number, position, and brief vital stats below the photo. "1981 New York Football Giants" appears across the top of each sheet and the backs are blank. The sheets are unnumbered and checklisted below alphabetically according to the player featured in the upper left corner.

COMPLETE SET (9) 40.00 75.00
1 Sheet 1 2.50 6.00
2 Sheet 2 2.50 6.00
3 Sheet 3 4.00 10.00
4 Sheet 4 3.00 8.00
5 Sheet 5 4.00 10.00
6 Sheet 6 2.50 6.00
7 Sheet 7 2.50 6.00
8 Sheet 8 6.00 15.00
9 Sheet 9 6.00 15.00

1987 Giants Ace Fact Pack

This 33-card set, which measures approximately 2 1/4" by 3 5/8", was made in West Germany (by Ace Fact Pack) for distribution in England. This set features rounded corners and the back says "Ace" as if they were playing cards. We have checklisted the players in the set in alphabetical order.

COMPLETE SET (33) 50.00 120.00
1 Billy Ard 1.25 3.00
2 Carl Banks 2.50 6.00
3 Mark Bavaro 2.50 6.00
4 Brad Benson 1.25 3.00
5 Harry Carson 2.50 6.00
6 Maurice Carthon UER 2.00 5.00
7 Mark Collins 2.00 5.00
8 Chris Godfrey 1.25 3.00
9 Kenny Hill 1.25 3.00
10 Erik Howard 2.00 5.00
11 Bobby Johnson 1.25 3.00
12 Leonard Marshall 2.50 6.00
13 George Martin 2.00 5.00
14 Joe Morris 2.00 5.00
15 Karl Nelson 1.25 3.00
16 Bart Oates UER 2.00 5.00
17 Gary Reasons 1.25 3.00
18 Stacy Robinson 1.25 3.00
19 Phil Simms 6.00 15.00
20 Lawrence Taylor 10.00 25.00
21 Herb Welch 1.25 3.00
22 Perry Williams 1.25 3.00
23 Giants Helmet 1.25 3.00
24 Giants Information 1.25 3.00
25 Giants Uniforms 1.25 3.00
26 Game Record Holders 1.25 3.00
27 Season Record Holders 1.25 3.00
28 Career Record Holders 1.25 3.00
29 Record 1967-86 1.25 3.00
30 1986 Team Statistics 1.25 3.00
31 All-Time Greats 1.25 3.00
32 Roll of Honour 1.25 3.00
33 Giants Stadium 1.25 3.00

1987 Giants Police

This set of 12 cards featuring New York Giants was issued very late in the year and was not widely distributed. Reportedly 10,000 sets were distributed by officers of the New Jersey police force. Cards measure approximately 2 3/4" by 4 1/8" and feature a crime prevention tip on the back. The set was sponsored by the New Jersey State Police Crime Prevention Resource Center. The Giants helmet appears below the player photo which differentiates this set from the very similar 1988 Police Giants set. These unnumbered cards are listed alphabetically in the checklist below.

COMPLETE SET (12) 50.00 125.00
1 Carl Banks 4.00 10.00
2 Mark Bavaro 3.00 8.00
3 Brad Benson 2.50 6.00
4 Jim Burt 2.50 6.00
5 Harry Carson 3.00 8.00
6 Maurice Carthon 2.50 6.00
7 Sean Landeta 2.50 6.00
8 Leonard Marshall 3.00 8.00
9 George Martin 2.50 6.00
10 Joe Morris 4.00 10.00
11 Bill Parcells CO 10.00 25.00
12 Phil Simms 12.00 30.00

1988 Giants Police

e 1988 Police New York Giants set contains 12 unnumbered cards measuring approximately 2 3/4" by 4 1/8". There are 11 player cards and one coach card. The backs have safety tips. The cards are listed below in alphabetical order by subject's name. The Giants team name and helmets appear above the player photo which differentiates this set from the very similar 1987 Police Giants set.

COMPLETE SET (12) 50.00 125.00
1 Billy Ard 2.50 6.00
2 Jim Burt 2.50 6.00
3 Harry Carson 4.00 10.00
4 Maurice Carthon 2.50 6.00
5 Leonard Marshall 4.00 10.00
6 George Martin 2.50 6.00
7 Phil McConkey 2.50 6.00
8 Joe Morris 3.00 8.00
9 Karl Nelson 2.50 6.00
10 Bart Oates 2.50 6.00
11 Bill Parcells CO 10.00 25.00
12 Phil Simms 12.00 30.00

1992 Giants Police

is 12-card set was printed and distributed by the New Jersey State Police Crime Prevention Resource Center. The cards measure approxiamtely 2 3/4" by 4 1/8". The fronts display color action player photos bordered in white. The team name appears at the top between two representations of the team helmet, while player information is printed beneath the picture. In dark blue print on white, the backs carry logos, "Tips from the Giants" in the form of public service announcements, and the McGruff the Crime Dog "Take a Bite out of Crime" slogan. The cards are unnumbered and checklisted below in alphabetical order.

COMPLETE SET (12) 32.00 80.00
1 Ottis Anderson 3.20 8.00
2 Matt Bahr 2.00 5.00
3 Eric Dorsey 2.00 5.00
4 John Elliott 2.00 5.00
5 Ray Handley CO 2.00 5.00
6 Jeff Hostetler 3.20 8.00
7 Erik Howard 2.00 5.00
8 Pepper Johnson 2.40 6.00
9 Leonard Marshall 2.40 6.00
10 Bart Oates 2.00 5.00
11 Gary Reasons 2.00 5.00
12 Phil Simms 8.00 20.00

1997 Giants Score

This 15-card set of the New York Giants was distributed in five-card packs with a suggested retail price of $1.99. The fronts feature color action player photos with white borders and the player's name and team logo printed in team color foil at the bottom. The backs carry player information and career statistics. Platinum Team parallel cards were randomly seeded in packs featuring all foil cardfronts.

COMPLETE SET (15) 2.40 6.00
*PLATINUM TEAMS: 1X TO 2X
1 Thomas Lewis .08 .25
2 Dave Brown .15 .40
3 Rodney Hampton .30 .75
4 Tyrone Wheatley .30 .75
5 Cedric Jones DE .08 .25
6 Amani Toomer .30 .75
7 Michael Strahan .15 .40
8 Chris Calloway .15 .40
9 Jessie Armstead .08 .25
10 Corey Miller .08 .25
11 Jason Sehorn .15 .40
12 Phillippi Sparks .08 .25
13 Charles Way .30 .75
14 Corey Widmer .08 .25
15 Danny Kanell .40 1.00

2004 Giants NY Post Stickers

This set of stickers was issued over a series of weeks within the NY Post newspaper. Each sheet features stickers of a number of Giants players intended to be pasted into an album.

COMPLETE SET (6) 5.00 12.00
1 Sheet 1 1.50 4.00
2 Sheet 2 1.00 2.50
3 Sheet 3 1.00 2.50
4 Sheet 4 1.00 2.50
5 Sheet 5 1.00 2.50
NNO Album .60 1.50

2004 Giants Upper Deck Dunkin Donuts

COMPLETE SET (6) 5.00 12.00
1 Tiki Barber .50 1.25
2 Eli Manning 2.50 6.00
3 Jeremy Shockey .40 1.00
4 Michael Strahan .50 1.25
5 Amani Toomer .40 1.00
6 Kurt Warner .50 1.25

2005 Giants Topps XXL

COMPLETE SET (4) 2.00 5.00
1 Eli Manning 1.00 2.50
2 Jeremy Shockey .40 1.00
3 Plaxico Burress .30 .75
4 Tiki Barber .40 1.00

2006 Giants Topps

COMPLETE SET (12) 3.00 6.00
NYG1 Jeremy Shockey .25 .60
NYG2 Mathias Kiwanuka .40 1.00
NYG3 Eli Manning .30 .75
NYG4 Antonio Pierce .25 .60
NYG5 Tiki Barber .30 .75
NYG6 Amani Toomer .25 .60
NYG7 Osi Umenyiora .25 .60
NYG8 Plaxico Burress .25 .60
NYG9 Michael Strahan .30 .75
NYG10 LaVar Arrington .25 .60
NYG11 Sam Madison .25 .60
NYG12 Sinorice Moss .25 .60

2006 Giants Upper Deck Wachovia

rds from this set were issued at the October 8, 2006 New York Giants home game. The cards were produced by Upper Deck and sponsored by Wachovia Bank.

COMPLETE SET (20) 6.00 15.00
1 LaVar Arrington .40 1.00
2 Tiki Barber .50 1.25
3 Plaxico Burress .40 1.00
4 Will Demps .60 1.50
5 Jeff Feagles .30 .75
6 Jay Feely .30 .75
7 Mathias Kiwanuka .60 1.50
8 Eli Manning .50 1.25
9 Kareem McKenzie .30 .75
10 Sinorice Moss .40 1.00
11 Shaun O'Hara .60 1.50
12 Luke Petitgout .30 .75
13 Antonio Pierce .40 1.00
14 Jeremy Shockey .40 1.00
15 Chris Snee 3.00 8.00
16 Michael Strahan .50 1.25
17 Amani Toomer .40 1.00
18 David Tyree .40 1.00
19 Osi Umenyiora .40 1.00
20 Gibril Wilson .40 1.00

2007 Giants Merrick Mint Quarters

COMPLETE SET (11) 60.00 100.00
1 Plaxico Burress 5.00 10.00
2 Brandon Jacobs 5.00 10.00
3 Eli Manning 6.00 12.00
4 Eli Manning MVP 6.00 12.00
5 Antonio Pierce 5.00 10.00
6 Jeremy Shockey 5.00 10.00
7 Michael Strahan 5.00 10.00
8 Amani Toomer 5.00 10.00
9 Justin Tuck 5.00 10.00
10 David Tyree 5.00 10.00
11 Osi Umenyiora 5.00 10.00

2007 Giants Topps

COMPLETE SET (12) 3.00 6.00
1 Plaxico Burress .40 1.00
2 Eli Manning .50 1.25
3 Reuben Droughns .50 1.25
4 Brandon Jacobs .40 1.00
5 Sinorice Moss .50 1.25
6 Jeremy Shockey .40 1.00
7 Michael Strahan .50 1.25
8 Steve Smith .40 1.00
9 Antonio Pierce .40 1.00
10 Amani Toomer .40 1.00
11 Osi Umenyiora .40 1.00
12 Aaron Ross .40 1.00

2008 Giants Topps

COMPLETE SET (12) 2.50 5.00
1 Eli Manning .50 1.25
2 Brandon Jacobs .40 1.00
3 Jeremy Shockey .40 1.00
4 Osi Umenyiora .40 1.00
5 Michael Strahan .50 1.25
6 Plaxico Burress .40 1.00
7 Steve Smith USC .50 1.25
8 Justin Tuck .40 1.00
9 Ahmad Bradshaw .40 1.00
10 Antonio Pierce .40 1.00
11 Amani Toomer .40 1.00
12 Mario Manningham .40 1.00

2008 Giants Topps Super Bowl XLII

COMP.FACT.SET (27) 10.00 20.00
1 Eli Manning .50 1.25
2 Brandon Jacobs .40 1.00
3 Ahmad Bradshaw .40 1.00
4 Plaxico Burress .40 1.00
5 Amani Toomer .40 1.00
6 Steve Smith USC .50 1.25
7 David Tyree .40 1.00
8 Kevin Boss .40 1.00
9 Shaun O'Hara .40 1.00
10 Chris Snee .40 1.00
11 Kareem McKenzie .40 1.00
12 Michael Strahan .50 1.25
13 Osi Umenyiora .40 1.00
14 Jeremy Shockey .40 1.00
15 Fred Robbins .40 1.00
16 Antonio Pierce .40 1.00
17 Kawika Mitchell .40 1.00
18 Sam Madison .40 1.00
19 Corey Webster .40 1.00
20 Aaron Ross .40 1.00
21 Justin Tuck .40 1.00
22 Gibril Wilson .40 1.00
23 New York Giants Win .50 1.25
24 David Tyree TD Catch .40 1.00
25 David Tyree Catch .40 1.00
26 Plaxico Burress TD .40 1.00
27 Jay Alford Sack .40 1.00

2008 Giants Upper Deck Super Bowl XLII

COMP.FACT SET (51) 10.00 20.00
1 Eli Manning .40 1.00
2 R.W. McQuarters .30 .75
3 Antonio Pierce .30 .75
4 David Diehl .30 .75
5 Corey Webster .30 .75
6 Shaun O'Hara .30 .75
7 Barry Cofield .30 .75
8 Kevin Boss .30 .75
9 Reggie Torbor .30 .75
10 Sam Madison .30 .75
11 Jeff Feagles .30 .75
12 Madison Hedgecock .30 .75
13 David Tyree .30 .75
14 Grey Ruegamer .30 .75
15 Gerris Wilkinson .30 .75
16 Reuben Droughns .40 1.00
17 Domenik Hixon .40 1.00
18 Kawika Mitchell .30 .75
19 Ahmad Bradshaw .30 .75
20 Jeremy Shockey .30 .75
21 Justin Tuck .30 .75
22 Amani Toomer .30 .75
23 Fred Robbins .30 .75
24 James Butler .30 .75
25 Brandon Jacobs .30 .75
26 Osi Umenyiora .30 .75
27 Aaron Ross .30 .75
28 Derrick Ward .30 .75
29 Chris Snee .30 .75
30 Michael Strahan .40 1.00
31 Gibril Wilson .30 .75
32 Sinorice Moss .40 1.00
33 Lawrence Tynes .30 .75
34 Jay Alford .30 .75
35 Kareem McKenzie .30 .75
36 Zak DeOssie .30 .75
37 Kevin Dockery .30 .75
38 Rich Seubert .30 .75
39 Michael Johnson .30 .75
40 Plaxico Burress .30 .75
MM1 R.W. McQuarters MM .30 .75
MM2 Lawrence Tynes MM .30 .75
MM3 David Tyree MM .30 .75
MM4 Plaxico Burress MM .30 .75
SH1 Osi Umenyiora SH .30 .75
SH2 Michael Strahan SH .40 1.00
SH3 Derrick Ward SH .30 .75
SH4 Plaxico Burress SH .30 .75
SH5 Brandon Jacobs SH .30 .75
MVP1 Eli Manning MVP .40 1.00
NYG1 Giants Team Jumbo 1.25 3.00

2009 Giants BP Mini Posters

These mini posters measuring roughly 9 1/2" by 12" feature great moments in Giants history. They were created for and distributed by BP Stores in the New York area.

COMPLETE SET (10) 10.00 20.00
1 Joe Morris .75 2.00
2 Super Bowl Celebration .75 2.00
3 Tiki Barber 1.00 2.50
4 Kerry Collins 1.00 2.50
5 Osi Umenyiora .75 2.00
6 Joe Danelo .75 2.00
7 Lawrence Taylor 1.25 3.00
8 Phil Simms 1.25 3.00
9 Phil McConkey .75 2.00
10 Eli Manning 1.25 3.00

2009 Giants Breast Cancer Awareness

This three card set was issued at a home game in 2009. Each unnumbered card was created by one of the three NFL licensed manufacturers and features the pink ribbon breast cancer awareness logo on the fronts.

COMPLETE SET (3) 2.50 6.00
1 Eli Manning Panini .75 2.00
2 Justin Tuck Topps .60 1.50
3 Brandon Jacobs Upper Deck .60 1.50

2011 Giants Topps Super Bowl XLVI

This set was issued via a wrapper redemption program at the 2012 Super Bowl Card Show.

COMPLETE SET (5) 3.00 8.00
1 Eli Manning .60 1.50
2 Victor Cruz .60 1.50
3 Ahmad Bradshaw .50 1.25
4 Hakeem Nicks .50 1.25
5 Jason Pierre-Paul .50 1.25

2012 Giants Panini Super Bowl XLVI

COMPLETE SET (9) 4.00 10.00
1 Eli Manning .60 1.50
2 Ahmad Bradshaw .50 1.25
3 Brandon Jacobs .50 1.25
4 Hakeem Nicks .50 1.25
5 Victor Cruz .60 1.50
6 Jason Pierre-Paul .50 1.25
7 Justin Tuck .50 1.25
8 Osi Umenyiora .50 1.25
9 Antrel Rolle .50 1.25

2014 Giants Panini Super Bowl XLVIII

MPLETE SET (10) 2.50 6.00
ISSUED AS PART OF 40-CARD FACT.SET
1 Eli Manning .50 1.25
2 Andre Brown .40 1.00
3 David Wilson .40 1.00
4 Victor Cruz .50 1.25
5 Hakeem Nicks .40 1.00
6 Jason Pierre-Paul .40 1.00
7 Justin Tuck .40 1.00
8 Antrel Rolle .40 1.00
9 Prince Amukamara .40 1.00
10 Josh Brown .40 1.00

1969 Glendale Stamps

This set contains 312 stamps featuring NFL players each measuring approximately 1 13/16" by 2 15/16". The stamps were meant to be pasted in an accompanying album, which itself measures approximately 9" by 12". The stamps and the album positions are unnumbered so the stamps are ordered and numbered below according to the team order that they appear in the book. The team order is alphabetical as well, according to the city name. The stamp of O.J. Simpson predates his 1970 Topps Rookie Card by one year and the stamp of Gene Upshaw predates his Rookie Card by three years.

COMPLETE SET (312) 200.00 350.00
1 Bob Berry .30 .75
2 Clark Miller .30 .75
3 Jim Butler .30 .75
4 Junior Coffey .30 .75
5 Paul Flatley .30 .75
6 Randy Johnson .30 .75
7 Charlie Bryant .30 .75
8 Billy Lothridge .30 .75
9 Tommy Nobis .75 1.50
10 Claude Humphrey .30 .75
11 Ken Reaves .30 .75
12 Jerry Simmons .30 .75
13 Mike Curtis .40 1.00
14 Dennis Gaubatz .30 .75
15 Jerry Logan .30 .75
16 Lenny Lyles .30 .75
17 John Mackey 1.00 2.00
18 Tom Matte .30 .75
19 Lou Michaels .30 .75
20 Jimmy Orr .30 .75
21 Willie Richardson .30 .75
22 Don Shinnick .30 .75
23 Dan Sullivan .30 .75
24 Johnny Unitas 10.00 20.00
25 Houston Antwine .30 .75
26 John Bramlett .30 .75
27 Aaron Marsh .30 .75
28 R.C. Gamble .30 .75
29 Gino Cappelletti .40 1.00
30 John Charles .30 .75
31 Larry Eisenhauer .30 .75
32 Jon Morris .30 .75
33 Jim Nance .30 .75
34 Len St. Jean .30 .75
35 Mike Taliaferro .30 .75
36 Jim Whalen .30 .75
37 Stew Barber .30 .75
38 Al Bemiller .30 .75
39 George(Butch) Byrd .30 .75
40 Booker Edgerson .30 .75
41 Harry Jacobs .30 .75
42 Jack Kemp 10.00 20.00
43 Ron McDole .30 .75
44 Joe O'Donnell .30 .75
45 John Pitts .30 .75
46 George Saimes .30 .75
47 Mike Stratton .30 .75
48 O.J. Simpson 7.50 15.00
49 Ronnie Bull .30 .75
50 Dick Butkus 7.50 15.00
51 Jim Cadile .30 .75
52 Jack Concannon .30 .75
53 Dick Evey .30 .75
54 Bennie McRae .30 .75
55 Ed O'Bradovich .30 .75
56 Brian Piccolo 12.50 25.00
57 Mike Pyle .30 .75
58 Gale Sayers 7.50 15.00
59 Dick Gordon .30 .75
60 Roosevelt Taylor .30 .75
61 Al Beauchamp .30 .75
62 Dave Middendorf .30 .75
63 Harry Gunner .30 .75
64 Bobby Hunt .30 .75
65 Bob Johnson .30 .75
66 Charley King .30 .75
67 Andy Rice .30 .75
68 Paul Robinson .30 .75
69 Bill Staley .30 .75
70 Pat Matson .30 .75
71 Bob Trumpy .50 1.25
72 Sam Wyche 2.00 4.00
73 Erich Barnes .30 .75
74 Gary Collins .30 .75
75 Ben Davis .30 .75
76 John Demarie .30 .75
77 Gene Hickerson .40 1.00
78 Jim Houston .30 .75
79 Ernie Kellerman .30 .75
80 Leroy Kelly 1.25 2.50
81 Dale Lindsey .30 .75
82 Bill Nelsen .30 .75
83 Jim Kanicki .30 .75
84 Dick Schafrath .30 .75
85 George Andrie .30 .75
86 Mike Clark .30 .75
87 Cornell Green .30 .75
88 Bob Hayes 1.00 2.00
89 Chuck Howley .40 1.00
90 Lee Roy Jordan .75 1.50
91 Bob Lilly 2.50 5.00
92 Craig Morton .40 1.00
93 John Niland .30 .75
94 Dan Reeves 2.50 5.00
95 Mel Renfro 1.00 2.00
96 Lance Rentzel .30 .75
97 Tom Beer .30 .75
98 Billy Van Heusen .30 .75
99 Mike Current .30 .75
100 Al Denson .30 .75
101 Pete Duranko .30 .75
102 George Goeddeke .30 .75
103 John Huard .30 .75
104 Rich Jackson .30 .75
105 Pete Jacques .30 .75
106 Fran Lynch .30 .75
107 Floyd Little .75 1.50
108 Steve Tensi .30 .75
109 Lem Barney 1.25 2.50
110 Nick Eddy .30 .75
111 Mel Farr .30 .75
112 Ed Flanagan .30 .75
113 Larry Hand .30 .75
114 Alex Karras 1.25 2.50
115 Dick LeBeau .30 .75
116 Mike Lucci .30 .75
117 Earl McCullouch .30 .75
118 Bill Munson .30 .75
119 Jerry Rush .30 .75
120 Wayne Walker .30 .75
121 Herb Adderley 1.00 2.00
122 Donny Anderson .40 1.00
123 Lee Roy Caffey .30 .75
124 Carroll Dale .30 .75
125 Willie Davis 1.00 2.00
126 Boyd Dowler .30 .75
127 Marv Fleming .30 .75
128 Bob Jeter .30 .75
129 Hank Jordan 1.00 2.00
130 Dave Robinson .40 1.00
131 Bart Starr 10.00 20.00
132 Willie Wood 1.00 2.00
133 Pete Beathard .30 .75
134 Jim Beirne .30 .75
135 Garland Boyette .30 .75
136 Woody Campbell .30 .75
137 Miller Farr .30 .75
138 Hoyle Granger .30 .75
139 Mac Haik .30 .75
140 Ken Houston 1.25 2.50
141 Bobby Maples .30 .75
142 Alvin Reed .30 .75
143 Don Trull .30 .75
144 George Webster .30 .75
145 Bobby Bell 1.00 2.00
146 Aaron Brown .30 .75
147 Buck Buchanan 1.00 2.00
148 Len Dawson 4.00 8.00
149 Mike Garrett .40 1.00
150 Robert Holmes .30 .75
151 Willie Lanier 1.25 2.50
152 Frank Pitts .30 .75
153 Johnny Robinson .40 1.00
154 Jan Stenerud 1.25 2.50
155 Otis Taylor .40 1.00
156 Jim Tyrer .30 .75
157 Dick Bass .30 .75
158 Maxie Baughan .30 .75
159 Richie Petitbon .30 .75
160 Roger Brown .30 .75
161 Roman Gabriel .50 1.25
162 Bruce Gossett .30 .75
163 Deacon Jones 1.00 2.00
164 Tom Mack .50 1.25
165 Tommy Mason .30 .75
166 Ed Meador .30 .75
167 Merlin Olsen 1.25 2.50
168 Pat Studstill .30 .75
169 Jack Clancy .30 .75
170 Maxie Williams .30 .75
171 Larry Csonka 7.50 15.00
172 Jim Warren .30 .75
173 Norm Evans .30 .75
174 Rick Norton .30 .75
175 Bob Griese 6.00 12.00
176 Howard Twilley .30 .75
177 Billy Neighbors .30 .75
178 Nick Buoniconti .75 1.50
179 Tom Goode .30 .75
180 Dick Westmoreland .30 .75
181 Grady Alderman .30 .75
182 Bill Brown .30 .75
183 Fred Cox .30 .75
184 Clint Jones .30 .75
185 Joe Kapp .40 1.00
186 Paul Krause .40 1.00
187 Gary Larsen .30 .75
188 Jim Marshall 1.00 2.00
189 Dave Osborn .30 .75
190 Alan Page 2.50 5.00
191 Mick Tingelhoff .40 1.00
192 Roy Winston .30 .75
193 Dan Abramowicz .30 .75
194 Doug Atkins 1.00 2.00
195 Bo Burris .30 .75
196 John Douglas .30 .75
197 Don Shy .30 .75
198 Billy Kilmer .40 1.00
199 Tony Lorick .30 .75
200 Dave Parks .30 .75
201 Dave Rowe .30 .75
202 Monty Stickles .30 .75
203 Steve Stonebreaker .30 .75
204 Del Williams .30 .75
205 Pete Case .30 .75
206 Tommy Crutcher .30 .75
207 Scott Eaton .30 .75
208 Tucker Frederickson .30 .75
209 Pete Gogolak .30 .75
210 Homer Jones .30 .75
211 Ernie Koy .30 .75
212 Spider Lockhart .30 .75
213 Bruce Maher .30 .75
214 Aaron Thomas .30 .75
215 Fran Tarkenton 6.00 12.00
216 Jim Katcavage .30 .75
217 Al Atkinson .30 .75
218 Emerson Boozer .30 .75
219 John Elliott .30 .75
220 Dave Herman .30 .75
221 Winston Hill .30 .75
222 Jim Hudson .30 .75
223 Pete Lammons .30 .75
224 Gerry Philbin .30 .75
225 George Sauer Jr. .30 .75
226 Joe Namath 12.50 25.00
227 Matt Snell .40 1.00
228 Jim Turner .30 .75
229 Fred Biletnikoff 2.00 4.00
230 Willie Brown 1.00 2.00
231 Billy Cannon .40 1.00
232 Dan Conners .30 .75
233 Ben Davidson .40 1.00
234 Hewritt Dixon .30 .75
235 Daryle Lamonica .50 1.25
236 Ike Lassiter .30 .75
237 Kent McCloughan .30 .75
238 Jim Otto 1.00 2.00
239 Harry Schuh .30 .75
240 Gene Upshaw 1.25 2.50
241 Gary Ballman .30 .75
242 Joe Carollo .30 .75
243 Dave Lloyd .30 .75
244 Fred Hill .30 .75
245 Al Nelson .30 .75
246 Joe Scarpati .30 .75
247 Sam Baker .30 .75
248 Fred Brown .30 .75
249 Floyd Peters .30 .75
250 Nate Ramsey .30 .75
251 Norm Snead .40 1.00
252 Tom Woodeshick .30 .75
253 John Hilton .30 .75
254 Kent Nix .30 .75
255 Paul Martha .30 .75
256 Ben McGee .30 .75
257 Andy Russell .40 1.00
258 Dick Shiner .30 .75
259 J.R. Wilburn .30 .75
260 Marv Woodson .30 .75
261 Earl Gros .30 .75
262 Dick Hoak .30 .75
263 Roy Jefferson .30 .75
264 Larry Gagner .30 .75
265 Johnny Roland .30 .75
266 Jackie Smith 1.00 2.00
267 Jim Bakken .30 .75
268 Don Brumm .30 .75
269 Bob DeMarco .30 .75
270 Irv Goode .30 .75
271 Ken Gray .30 .75
272 Charley Johnson .40 1.00
273 Ernie McMillan .30 .75
274 Larry Stallings .30 .75
275 Jerry Stovall .30 .75
276 Larry Wilson .75 1.50
277 Chuck Allen .30 .75
278 Lance Alworth 2.50 5.00
279 Kenny Graham .30 .75
280 Steve DeLong .30 .75
281 Willie Frazier .30 .75
282 Gary Garrison .30 .75
283 Sam Gruneisen .30 .75
284 John Hadl .50 1.25
285 Brad Hubbert .30 .75
286 Ron Mix .75 1.50
287 Dick Post .30 .75
288 Walt Sweeney .30 .75
289 Kermit Alexander .30 .75
290 Ed Beard .30 .75
291 Bruce Bosley .30 .75
292 John Brodie 1.25 2.50
293 Stan Hindman .30 .75
294 Jim Johnson 1.00 2.00
295 Charlie Krueger .30 .75
296 Clifton McNeil .30 .75
297 Gary Lewis .30 .75
298 Howard Mudd .30 .75
299 Dave Wilcox .40 1.00
300 Ken Willard .30 .75
301 Charlie Gogolak .30 .75
302 Len Hauss .30 .75
303 Sonny Jurgensen 2.50 5.00
304 Carl Kammerer .30 .75
305 Walter Rock .30 .75
306 Ray Schoenke .30 .75
307 Chris Hanburger .40 1.00
308 Tom Brown .30 .75
309 Sam Huff 1.25 2.50
310 Bob Long .30 .75
311 Vince Promuto .30 .75
312 Pat Richter .30 .75
NNO Stamp Album 10.00 20.00

1989-97 Goal Line HOF

ese attractive cards were issued by subscription per series of 30. They were sent out one series at a time in a custom box. The cards are postcard-size drawings (a full-color action painting) measuring approximately 4" by 6". The card backs contain brief biographical information and are printed in black on white card stock. Each card contains the specific set serial number out of 5,000 at the bottom of the cardbacks. The back also feature the player's name, college, position, NFL years, pro team, and the date he was enshrined in the Hall of Fame. The players featured are all members of the Pro Football Hall of Fame in Canton, Ohio. The second series was produced in 1990, the third series in 1991, and so forth. Collectors who ordered series five before August 31, 1993, received a free commemorative ticket signed by Pete Elliott (Commissioner of the Pro Football Hall of Fame) and were entered into a drawing for one of three uncut sheets of series five. In total, 50 fifth-series uncut sheets were produced, and they were signed and numbered by the artist. Within each series the cards have been numbered alphabetically. They are considered ideal for autographing and are often found signed. The artist for the set was Gary Thomas. Collectors who have been purchasing this set over the years have the continuation right to receive the same serial numbered card whenever the next series is issued.

COMPLETE SET (189) 300.00 600.00
1 Lance Alworth 12.50 25.00
2 Red Badgro 2.00 5.00
3 Cliff Battles 1.50 4.00
4 Mel Blount 12.50 25.00
5 Terry Bradshaw 20.00 40.00
6 Jim Brown 15.00 30.00
7 George Connor 10.00 20.00
8 Turk Edwards 1.50 4.00
9 Tom Fears 10.00 20.00
10 Frank Gifford 12.50 25.00
11 Otto Graham 7.50 15.00
12 Red Grange 3.00 8.00
13 George Halas 2.50 6.00
14 Clarke Hinkle 1.50 4.00
15 Robert(Cal) Hubbard 1.50 4.00
16 Sam Huff 12.50 25.00
17 Frank(Bruiser) Kinard 1.50 4.00
18 Dick(Night Train) Lane 2.00 5.00
19 Sid Luckman 2.50 6.00
20 Bobby Mitchell 10.00 20.00
21 Merlin Olsen 10.00 20.00
22 Jim Parker 10.00 20.00
23 Joe Perry 12.50 25.00
24 Pete Rozelle 2.00 5.00
25 Art Shell 10.00 20.00
26 Fran Tarkenton 10.00 20.00
27 Jim Thorpe 3.00 8.00
28 Paul Warfield 12.50 25.00
29 Larry Wilson 10.00 20.00
30 Willie Wood 10.00 20.00
31 Doug Atkins 1.00 2.50
32 Bobby Bell 1.00 2.50
33 Raymond Berry 1.25 3.00
34 Paul Brown .60 1.50
35 Guy Chamberlin .60 1.50
36 Dutch Clark .60 1.50
37 Jimmy Conzelman .60 1.50
38 Len Dawson 1.25 3.00
39 Mike Ditka 2.50 6.00
40 Dan Fortmann .60 1.50
41 Frank Gatski 1.00 2.50
42 Bill George .60 1.50
43 Elroy Hirsch 1.25 3.00
44 Paul Hornung 1.50 4.00
45 John Henry Johnson 1.00 2.50
46 Walt Kiesling .60 1.50
47 Yale Lary 1.00 2.50
48 Bobby Layne 1.25 3.00
49 Tuffy Leemans .60 1.50
50 Geo.Preston Marshall .60 1.50
51 George McAfee 1.00 2.50
52 Wayne Millner .60 1.50
53 Bronko Nagurski 1.50 4.00
54 Joe Namath 4.00 10.00
55 Ray Nitschke 1.25 3.00
56 Jim Ringo 1.00 2.50
57 Art Rooney .60 1.50
58 Joe Stydahar .60 1.50
59 Charley Taylor 1.25 3.00
60 Charley Trippi 1.00 2.50
61 Fred Biletnikoff 1.25 3.00
62 Buck Buchanan .60 1.50
63 Dick Butkus 2.00 5.00
64 Earl Campbell 1.50 4.00
65 Tony Canadeo 1.00 2.50
66 Art Donovan 1.25 3.00
67 Ray Flaherty .60 1.50
68 Forrest Gregg 1.00 2.50
69 Lou Groza 1.25 3.00
70 John Hannah 1.00 2.50
71 Don Hutson 1.00 2.50
72 Deacon Jones 1.25 3.00
73 Stan Jones 1.00 2.50
74 Sonny Jurgensen 1.25 3.00
75 Vince Lombardi 1.25 3.00
76 Tim Mara .60 1.50
77 Ollie Matson 1.00 2.50
78 Mike McCormack 1.00 2.50
79 Johnny Blood McNally .60 1.50
80 Marion Motley 1.25 3.00
81 George Musso 1.00 2.50
82 Greasy Neale .60 1.50
83 Clarence(Ace) Parker 1.00 2.50
84 Pete Pihos 1.00 2.50
85 Tex Schramm 1.00 2.50
86 Roger Staubach 3.00 8.00
87 Jan Stenerud 1.00 2.50
88 Y.A. Tittle 1.50 4.00
89 Bulldog Turner 1.00 2.50
90 Steve Van Buren 1.00 2.50
91 Herb Adderley 1.00 2.50
92 Lem Barney 1.00 2.50
93 Sammy Baugh 2.00 5.00
94 Chuck Bednarik 1.25 3.00
95 Charles W. Bidwill .60 1.50
96 Willie Brown 1.25 3.00
97 Al Davis 1.50 4.00
98 Bill Dudley 1.00 2.50
99 Weeb Ewbank 1.00 2.50
100 Len Ford .60 1.50
101 Sid Gillman 1.00 2.50
102 Jack Ham 1.25 3.00
103 Mel Hein .60 1.50
104 Bill Hewitt .60 1.50
105 Dante Lavelli 1.00 2.50
106 Bob Lilly 1.25 3.00
107 John Mackey 1.00 2.50
108 Hugh McElhenny 1.25 3.00
109 Mike Michalske .60 1.50
110 Ron Mix 1.00 2.50
111 Leo Nomellini 1.00 2.50
112 Steve Owen .60 1.50
113 Alan Page 1.25 3.00
114 Dan Reeves OWN .60 1.50
115 John Riggins 1.25 3.00
116 Gale Sayers 2.00 5.00
117 Ken Strong .60 1.50
118 Gene Upshaw 1.00 2.50
119 Norm Van Brocklin 1.50 4.00
120 Alex Wojciechowicz .60 1.50
121 Bert Bell COMM .60 1.50
122 George Blanda 1.50 4.00
123 Joe Carr .60 1.50
124 Larry Csonka 1.50 4.00
125 Paddy Driscoll .60 1.50
126 Dan Fouts 1.25 3.00
127 Bob Griese 1.50 4.00
128 Ed Healey .60 1.50
129 Fats Henry .60 1.50
130 Ken Houston 1.00 2.50
131 Lamar Hunt OWN 1.00 2.50
132 Jack Lambert 1.25 3.00
133 Tom Landry 1.50 4.00
134 Willie Lanier 1.00 2.50
135 Larry Little 1.00 2.50
136 Don Maynard 1.00 2.50
137 Lenny Moore 1.25 3.00
138 Chuck Noll CO 1.25 3.00
139 Jim Otto 1.25 3.00
140 Walter Payton 4.00 10.00
141 Hugh(Shorty) Ray OFF .60 1.50
142 Andy Robustelli 1.00 2.50
143 Bob St. Clair 1.00 2.50
144 Joe Schmidt 1.25 3.00
145 Jim Taylor 1.25 3.00
146 Doak Walker 1.25 3.00
147 Bill Walsh CO 1.25 3.00
148 Bob Waterfield 1.25 3.00
149 Arnie Weinmeister 1.00 2.50
150 Bill Willis 1.00 2.50
151 Roosevelt Brown 1.00 2.50
152 Jack Christiansen .60 1.50
153 Willie Davis 1.00 2.50
154 Tony Dorsett 2.00 5.00
155 Bud Grant 1.00 2.50
156 Joe Greene 1.50 4.00
157 Joe Guyon .60 1.50
158 Franco Harris 1.50 4.00
159 Ted Hendricks 1.25 3.00
160 Arnie Herber .60 1.50
161 Jim Johnson 1.00 2.50
162 Leroy Kelly 1.25 3.00
163 Curly Lambeau .60 1.50
164 Jim Langer 1.00 2.50
165 Link Lyman .60 1.50
166 Gino Marchetti 1.00 2.50
167 Ernie Nevers 1.25 3.00
168 O.J. Simpson 1.50 4.00
169 Jackie Smith 1.00 2.50
170 Bart Starr 3.00 8.00
171 Ernie Stautner 1.25 3.00
172 George Trafton .60 1.50
173 Emlen Tunnell .60 1.50
174 Johnny Unitas 3.00 8.00
175 Randy White 1.25 3.00
176 Jim Finks 1.25 3.00
177 Hank Jordan 1.25 3.00
178 Steve Largent 2.00 5.00
179 Lee Roy Selmon 1.50 4.00
180 Kellen Winslow 2.00 5.00
181 Lou Creekmur 1.50 4.00
182 Dan Dierdorf 2.00 5.00
183 Joe Gibbs 1.50 4.00
184 Charlie Joiner 2.00 5.00
185 Mel Renfro 2.00 5.00
186 Mike Haynes 1.50 4.00
187 Wellington Mara 1.50 4.00
188 Don Shula 2.50 6.00
189 Mike Webster 1.50 4.00

1989-97 Goal Line HOF Autographs

COMPLETE SET (141) 3000.00 5000.00
1 Lance Alworth 30.00 60.00
2 Red Badgro 25.00 40.00
4 Mel Blount 20.00 40.00
5 Terry Bradshaw 40.00 75.00
6 Jim Brown 40.00 75.00
7 George Connor 15.00 30.00
9 Tom Fears 25.00 40.00
10 Frank Gifford 30.00 50.00
11 Otto Graham 20.00 40.00
12 Red Grange 200.00 350.00
16 Sam Huff 20.00 40.00
18 Dick(Night Train) Lane 15.00 30.00
19 Sid Luckman 125.00 200.00
20 Bobby Mitchell 15.00 30.00
21 Merlin Olsen 20.00 40.00
22 Jim Parker 15.00 30.00
23 Joe Perry 20.00 40.00
24 Pete Rozelle 175.00 300.00
25 Art Shell 15.00 30.00
26 Fran Tarkenton 25.00 50.00
28 Paul Warfield 20.00 40.00
29 Larry Wilson 12.50 25.00
30 Willie Wood 15.00 30.00
31 Doug Atkins 7.50 15.00
32 Bobby Bell 10.00 20.00
33 Raymond Berry 12.50 25.00
34 Paul Brown 125.00 200.00
38 Len Dawson 15.00 30.00
39 Mike Ditka 20.00 40.00
40 Dan Fortmann 125.00 200.00
41 Frank Gatski 12.50 25.00
43 Elroy Hirsch 15.00 30.00
44 Paul Hornung 15.00 30.00
45 John Henry Johnson 10.00 20.00
47 Yale Lary 10.00 20.00
51 George McAfee 7.50 15.00
54 Joe Namath 50.00 100.00
55 Ray Nitschke 35.00 60.00
56 Jim Ringo 15.00 30.00
59 Charley Taylor 12.50 25.00
60 Charley Trippi 10.00 20.00
61 Fred Biletnikoff 15.00 30.00
62 Buck Buchanan 75.00 125.00
63 Dick Butkus 25.00 40.00
64 Earl Campbell 20.00 40.00
65 Tony Canadeo 15.00 30.00
66 Art Donovan 12.50 25.00
67 Ray Flaherty 100.00 175.00
68 Forrest Gregg 12.50 25.00
69 Lou Groza 15.00 30.00
70 John Hannah 12.50 25.00
71 Don Hutson 125.00 200.00
72 Deacon Jones 12.50 25.00
73 Stan Jones 10.00 20.00
74 Sonny Jurgensen 30.00 45.00
77 Ollie Matson 15.00 30.00
78 Mike McCormack 10.00 20.00
80 Marion Motley 30.00 50.00
81 George Musso 15.00 30.00
83 Clarence Ace Parker 10.00 20.00
84 Pete Pihos 15.00 30.00

85 Tex Schramm 20.00 40.00
86 Roger Staubach 40.00 75.00
87 Jan Stenerud 10.00 20.00
88 Y.A. Tittle 15.00 30.00
89 Bulldog Turner 30.00 50.00
90 Steve Van Buren 10.00 20.00
91 Herb Adderley 10.00 20.00
92 Lem Barney 12.50 25.00
93 Sammy Baugh 40.00 80.00
94 Chuck Bednarik 10.00 20.00
96 Willie Brown 10.00 20.00
97 Al Davis OWN 400.00 600.00
98 Bill Dudley 12.50 25.00
99 Weeb Ewbank 25.00 40.00
101 Sid Gillman 12.50 25.00
102 Jack Ham 15.00 30.00
105 Dante Lavelli 12.50 25.00
106 Bob Lilly 12.50 25.00
107 John Mackey 10.00 20.00
108 Hugh McElhenny 10.00 20.00
110 Ron Mix 12.50 25.00
111 Leo Nomellini 15.00 30.00
113 Alan Page 15.00 30.00
115 John Riggins 90.00 150.00
116 Gale Sayers 30.00 50.00
118 Gene Upshaw 12.50 25.00
120 Alex Wojciechowicz 1500.00 2000.00
122 George Blanda 35.00 60.00
124 Larry Csonka 25.00 40.00
126 Dan Fouts 25.00 40.00
127 Bob Griese 20.00 40.00
130 Ken Houston 10.00 20.00
131 Lamar Hunt OWN 12.50 25.00
132 Jack Lambert 30.00 50.00
133 Tom Landry 50.00 80.00
134 Willie Lanier 10.00 20.00
135 Larry Little 10.00 20.00
136 Don Maynard 10.00 20.00
137 Lenny Moore 10.00 20.00
138 Chuck Noll CO 15.00 30.00
139 Jim Otto 10.00 20.00
140 Walter Payton 175.00 300.00
142 Andy Robustelli 10.00 20.00
143 Bob St. Clair 10.00 20.00
144 Joe Schmidt 10.00 20.00
145 Jim Taylor 15.00 30.00
146 Doak Walker 60.00 100.00
147 Bill Walsh CO 30.00 50.00
149 Arnie Weinmeister 25.00 40.00
150 Bill Willis 10.00 20.00
151 Roosevelt Brown 12.50 25.00
153 Willie Davis 10.00 20.00
154 Tony Dorsett 25.00 40.00
155 Bud Grant 30.00 50.00
156 Joe Greene 15.00 30.00
158 Franco Harris 30.00 50.00
159 Ted Hendricks 12.50 25.00
161 Jim Johnson 10.00 20.00
162 Leroy Kelly 12.50 25.00
164 Jim Langer 10.00 20.00
166 Gino Marchetti 12.50 25.00
168 O.J. Simpson 50.00 80.00
169 Jackie Smith 10.00 20.00
170 Bart Starr 75.00 125.00
171 Ernie Stautner 12.50 25.00
174 Johnny Unitas 90.00 150.00
175 Randy White 15.00 30.00
178 Steve Largent 15.00 30.00
179 Lee Roy Selmon 10.00 20.00
180 Kellen Winslow 25.00 40.00
181 Lou Creekmur 10.00 20.00
182 Dan Dierdorf 12.50 25.00
183 Joe Gibbs 30.00 45.00
184 Charlie Joiner 10.00 20.00
185 Mel Renfro 10.00 20.00
186 Mike Haynes 15.00 30.00
187 Wellington Mara 20.00 40.00
188 Don Shula CO 30.00 50.00
189 Mike Webster 75.00 125.00

1989-97 Goal Line HOF Proofs

MPLETE SET (189) 500.00 800.00
*PROOFS: .6X TO 1.5X BASIC CARDS

1998 Goal Line HOF

This update set was released by Goal Line Art primarily to collectors who held the rights to the original numbered sets. This set was issued in a blue and white factory set styled box. All five new inductees were included.

COMPLETE SET (5) 8.00 20.00
190 Paul Krause 1.60 4.00
191 Tommy McDonald 1.60 4.00
192 Anthony Munoz 1.60 4.00
193 Mike Singletary 2.40 6.00
194 Dwight Stephenson 2.40 6.00

1998 Goal Line HOF Autographs

This set was issued unsigned in 1998 to subscription holders. Although the cards were not released signed, the set is popular with autograph collectors and commonly traded signed.

190 Paul Krause 12.50 25.00
191 Tommy McDonald 7.50 15.00
192 Anthony Munoz 10.00 20.00
193 Mike Singletary 20.00 35.00
194 Dwight Stephenson 12.50 25.00

1999 Goal Line HOF

is update set was released by Goal Line Art primarily to collectors who held the rights to the original numbered sets. This set was issued in a red and white factory set styled box. All five new inductees were included. 5000 sets were produced.

COMPLETE SET (5) 10.00 20.00
195 Eric Dickerson 3.00 6.00
196 Tom Mack 2.00 4.00
197 Ozzie Newsome 3.00 6.00
198 Billy Shaw 2.00 4.00
199 Lawrence Taylor 3.00 6.00

1999 Goal Line HOF Autographs

This set was issued unsigned in 1998 to subscription holders. Although the cards were not released signed, the set is popular with autograph collectors and commonly traded signed.

195 Eric Dickerson 25.00 40.00
196 Tom Mack 12.50 25.00
197 Ozzie Newsome 20.00 35.00
198 Billy Shaw 12.50 25.00
199 Lawrence Taylor 20.00 40.00

2000 Goal Line HOF

This update set was released by Goal Line Art primarily to collectors who held the rights to the original numbered sets. This set was issued in a factory set box. Five new inductees were included. Reportedly, 5000 sets were produced.

COMPLETE SET (5) 15.00 25.00
200 Howie Long 3.00 6.00
201 Ronnie Lott 3.00 6.00
202 Joe Montana 5.00 10.00
203 Dan Rooney 2.00 4.00
204 Dave Wilcox 2.00 4.00

2000 Goal Line HOF Autographs

200 Howie Long 40.00 75.00
201 Ronnie Lott 25.00 40.00
202 Joe Montana 75.00 125.00
203 Dan Rooney 30.00 50.00
204 Dave Wilcox 12.50 25.00

2001 Goal Line HOF

This update set was released by Goal Line Art primarily to collectors who held the rights to the original numbered sets. This set was issued in a factory set box. Six new inductees were included. Reportedly, 5000 sets were produced.

COMPLETE SET (7) 15.00 30.00
205 Nick Buoniconti 4.00 8.00
206 Marv Levy 3.00 6.00
207 Mike Munchak 3.00 6.00
208 Jackie Slater 3.00 6.00
209 Lynn Swann 5.00 10.00
210 Ron Yary 3.00 6.00
211 Jack Youngblood 4.00 8.00

2001 Goal Line HOF Autographs

205 Nick Buoniconti 20.00 35.00
206 Marv Levy 30.00 50.00
207 Mike Munchak 25.00 40.00
208 Jackie Slater 20.00 35.00
209 Lynn Swann 50.00 100.00
210 Ron Yary 20.00 35.00
211 Jack Youngblood 20.00 35.00

2002 Goal Line HOF

This update set was released by Goal Line Art primarily to collectors who held the rights to the original numbered sets. This set was issued in a factory set box. Four new inductees were included. Reportedly, 5000 sets were produced.

COMPLETE SET (5) 12.50 25.00
212 George Allen 3.00 6.00
213 Dave Casper 4.00 8.00
214 Dan Hampton 3.00 6.00
215 Jim Kelly 5.00 10.00
216 John Stallworth 4.00 8.00

2002 Goal Line HOF Autographs

213 Dave Casper 15.00 30.00
214 Dan Hampton 15.00 30.00
215 Jim Kelly 30.00 50.00
216 John Stallworth 20.00 40.00

2003 Goal Line HOF

This update set was released by Goal Line Art primarily to collectors who held the rights to the original numbered sets. This set was issued in a factory set box. Five new inductees were included for 2003. Reportedly, 5000 sets were produced.

COMPLETE SET (5) 15.00 25.00
217 Marcus Allen 4.00 10.00
218 Elvin Bethea 2.50 6.00
219 Joe DeLamielleure 2.50 6.00
220 James Lofton 3.00 8.00
221 Hank Stram 2.50 6.00

2003 Goal Line HOF Autographs

217 Marcus Allen 25.00 40.00
218 Elvin Bethea 20.00 35.00
219 Joe DeLamielleure 20.00 35.00
220 James Lofton 20.00 35.00
221 Hank Stram 60.00 100.00

2004 Goal Line HOF

This update set was released by Goal Line Art primarily to collectors who held the rights to the original numbered sets. This set was issued in a factory set box. Four new inductees were included for 2004. Reportedly, 5000 sets were produced.

COMPLETE SET (4) 15.00 25.00
222 Bob Brown 3.00 6.00
223 Carl Eller 3.00 6.00
224 John Elway 5.00 10.00
225 Barry Sanders 5.00 10.00

2004 Goal Line HOF Autographs

222 Bob Brown 15.00 30.00
223 Carl Eller 15.00 30.00
224 John Elway 125.00 200.00
225 Barry Sanders 90.00 150.00

2005 Goal Line HOF

COMPLETE SET (4) 15.00 30.00
226 Benny Friedman 3.00 6.00
227 Dan Marino 5.00 10.00
228 Fritz Pollard 3.00 6.00
229 Steve Young 4.00 8.00

2005 Goal Line HOF Autographs

7 Dan Marino 125.00 200.00
229 Steve Young 40.00 80.00

2006 Goal Line HOF

COMPLETE SET (6) 15.00 30.00
230 Troy Aikman 4.00 8.00
231 Harry Carson 3.00 6.00
232 John Madden 3.00 6.00
233 Warren Moon 3.00 6.00
234 Reggie White 4.00 8.00
235 Rayfield Wright 3.00 6.00

2006 Goal Line HOF Autographs

230 Troy Aikman 90.00 150.00
231 Harry Carson 15.00 30.00
232 John Madden 40.00 75.00
233 Warren Moon 20.00 40.00
235 Rayfield Wright 15.00 30.00

2007 Goal Line HOF

COMPLETE SET (6) 15.00 30.00
236 Gene Hickerson 2.50 5.00
237 Michael Irvin 3.00 6.00
238 Bruce Matthews 2.50 5.00
239 Charlie Sanders 2.50 5.00
240 Thurman Thomas 3.00 6.00
241 Roger Wehrli 2.50 5.00

2007 Goal Line HOF Autographs

236 Gene Hickerson
237 Michael Irvin 25.00 50.00
238 Bruce Matthews 12.50 25.00
239 Charlie Sanders 12.50 25.00
240 Thurman Thomas 25.00 50.00
241 Roger Wehrli 12.50 25.00

2008 Goal Line HOF

COMPLETE SET (6) 15.00 30.00
242 Fred Dean 2.50 5.00
243 Darrell Green 3.00 6.00
244 Art Monk 3.00 6.00
245 Emmitt Thomas 2.50 5.00
246 Andre Tippett 2.50 5.00
247 Gary Zimmerman 2.50 5.00

2008 Goal Line HOF Autographs

242 Fred Dean 12.50 25.00
243 Darrell Green 15.00 30.00
244 Art Monk 25.00 50.00
245 Emmitt Thomas 12.50 25.00
246 Andre Tippett 12.50 25.00
247 Gary Zimmerman 12.50 25.00

2009 Goal Line HOF

COMPLETE SET (6) 15.00 30.00
248 Bob Hayes 2.50 5.00
249 Randall McDaniel 2.50 5.00
250 Bruce Smith 3.00 6.00
251 Derrick Thomas 2.50 5.00
252 Ralph Wilson Jr. 2.50 5.00
253 Rod Woodson 2.50 5.00

2009 Goal Line HOF Autographs

249 Randall McDaniel 12.50 25.00
250 Bruce Smith 15.00 30.00
252 Ralph Wilson Jr. 20.00 40.00
253 Rod Woodson 15.00 30.00

2010 Goal Line HOF

COMPLETE SET (7) 25.00 40.00
254 Russ Grimm 2.50 6.00
255 Rickey Jackson 2.50 6.00
256 Dick LeBeau 2.50 6.00
257 Floyd Little 2.50 6.00
258 John Randle 2.50 6.00
259 Jerry Rice 3.00 8.00
260 Emmitt Smith 3.00 8.00

2011 Goal Line HOF

COMPLETE SET (7) 25.00 35.00
1 Richard Dent 3.00 6.00
2 Marshall Faulk 4.00 8.00
3 Chris Hanburger 3.00 6.00
4 Les Richter 3.00 6.00
5 Ed Sabol 3.00 6.00
6 Deion Sanders 4.00 8.00
7 Shannon Sharpe 3.00 6.00

2012 Goal Line HOF

COMPLETE SET (6) 25.00 35.00
1 Jack Butler 3.00 6.00
2 Dermontti Dawson 3.00 6.00
3 Chris Doleman 3.00 6.00
4 Cortez Kennedy 3.00 6.00
5 Curtis Martin 4.00 8.00
6 Willie Roaf 3.00 6.00

2013 Goal Line HOF

COMPLETE SET (7) 25.00 35.00
1 Larry Allen 3.00 6.00
2 Cris Carter 4.00 8.00
3 Curley Culp 3.00 6.00
4 Jonathan Ogden 3.00 6.00
5 Bill Parcells 3.00 6.00
6 Dave Robinson 3.00 6.00
7 Warren Sapp 3.00 6.00

1888 Goodwin Champions N162

This 50-card set issued by Goodwin was one of the major competitors to the N28 and N29 sets marketed by Allen and Ginter. It contains individuals representing 18 sports, with eight baseball players pictured. Each color card is backlisted and bears advertising for "Old Judge" and "Gypsy Queen" cigarettes on the front. The set was released to the public in 1888 and an album (catalog: A36) is associated with it as a premium issue.

12 Harry Beecher (Football) 3000.00 4500.00

2003 Grand Rapids Rampage AFL

This set was sponsored by Choice Marketing, Inc. and features members of the Grand Papids Rampage of the Arena Football League. Each card includes the team name and player name below the color player photo on the front. The cardbacks are printed in black and white and feature another player photo and a player bio.

COMPLETE SET (10) 5.00 10.00
1 Chris Avery .40 1.00
2 Clint Dolezel .75 2.00
3 Cecil Doggette .40 1.00
4 Brian Gowins .40 1.00
5 Willis Marshall .40 1.00
6 Corey Mayfield .40 1.00
7 Ricky Ross .40 1.00
8 Chris Ryan .40 1.00
9 Terrill Shaw .75 2.00
10 Steve Smith .60 1.50

2003 Grand Rapids Rampage AFL Team Issue

COMPLETE SET (23) 75.00 150.00
1 Nick Browder 3.00 8.00
2 DeAuntae Brown 3.00 8.00
3 Charles Butler 3.00 8.00
4 Gary Compton 3.00 8.00
5 Clint Dolezel 4.00 10.00
6 Jason Gamble 3.00 8.00
7 Brian Gowins 3.00 8.00
8 Lamar Grant 3.00 8.00
9 Gary Isza 3.00 8.00
10 Madison Johnson 3.00 8.00
11 Rod Manuel 3.00 8.00
12 Willis Marshall 3.00 8.00
13 Corey Mayfield 3.00 8.00
14 Travis McDonald 3.00 8.00
15 Tristan Moss 3.00 8.00
16 Umar Muhammad 3.00 8.00
17 Demo Odems 3.00 8.00
18 Albert Reese 3.00 8.00
19 Mark Ricks 3.00 8.00
20 Steve Smith 3.00 8.00
21 Joe Wylie 3.00 8.00
22 Lucas Yarnell 3.00 8.00
23 Blitz Mascot 3.00 8.00

2000 Greats of the Game

leased in early January 2001, this 134-card set features base cards with maroon borders, a white out background and full color player action shots with silver foil highlights. Card numbers 131-134 were added late as redemptions and were limited in production to 500 of each card with #134, Mike Anderson, released as an autograph. Greats of the game was packaged in 24-pack boxes with each pack containing five cards and carried a suggested retail price of $4.99.

COMP.SET w/o SP's (100) 20.00 40.00
131-134 ROOKIE PRINT RUN 500
1 Terry Bradshaw .60 1.50
2 Paul Hornung .25 .60
3 Tony Dorsett .25 .60
4 L.C. Greenwood .15 .40
5 Ozzie Newsome .15 .40
6 Michael Irvin .25 .60
7 Art Donovan .15 .40
8 Don Maynard .20 .50
9 Bobby Mitchell .20 .50
10 Bob Lilly .20 .50
11 Earl Morrall .15 .40
12 Harvey Martin .15 .40
13 Dan Fouts .20 .50
14 Joe Theismann .25 .60
15 Roger Staubach .30 .75
16 Otto Graham .20 .50
17 Cliff Branch .15 .40
18 Sonny Jurgensen .25 .60
19 Eric Dickerson .20 .50
20 Lee Roy Selmon .15 .40
21 Roger Craig .20 .50
22 Raymond Berry .20 .50
23 Bob Hayes .20 .50
24 Steve Largent .25 .60
25 Lenny Moore .15 .40
26 Chuck Bednarik .20 .50
27 Ken Stabler .30 .75
28 William Perry .15 .40
29 Joe Greene .25 .60
30 Joe Namath .50 1.25
31 Jim Kelly .25 .60
32 Steve Young .30 .75
33 Randy White .20 .50
34 Lawrence Taylor .25 .60
35 Franco Harris .30 .75
36 Marcus Allen .25 .60
37 Mike Singletary .25 .60
38 Fran Tarkenton .25 .60
39 Mel Renfro .15 .40
40 Len Dawson .25 .60
41 Carl Eller .15 .40
42 Chuck Foreman .15 .40
43 Gino Marchetti .15 .40
44 Jim Marshall .15 .40
45 Jack Ham .25 .60
46 Mercury Morris .15 .40
47 Anthony Munoz .20 .50
48 Herschel Walker .25 .60
49 Drew Pearson .20 .50
50 John Elway .40 1.00
51 George Blanda .20 .50
52 Earl Campbell .25 .60
53 Bart Starr .60 1.50
54 Dan Marino .50 1.25
55 Johnny Unitas .60 1.50
56 Sammy Baugh .25 .60
57 Steve Van Buren .15 .40
58 Mel Blount .20 .50
59 Fred Biletnikoff .25 .60
60 John Brodie .20 .50
61 Daryle Lamonica .15 .40
62 James Lofton .15 .40
63 Ronnie Lott .25 .60
64 Gale Sayers .25 .60
65 Art Monk .25 .60
66 Jim Plunkett .20 .50
67 Charlie Joiner .15 .40
68 Deacon Jones .20 .50
69 Paul Warfield .25 .60
70 Jim Otto .15 .40
71 Billy Kilmer .20 .50
72 Archie Manning .20 .50
73 Alex Karras .20 .50
74 Tom Matte .15 .40
75 Jay Novacek .20 .50
76 Charley Taylor .15 .40
77 Sam Huff .20 .50
78 Jack Lambert .25 .60
79 Mike Ditka .25 .60
80 Frank Gifford .25 .60
81 Jim Thorpe .40 1.00
82 Walter Payton 1.00 2.50
83 Doak Walker .25 .60
84 Sid Luckman .20 .50
85 Bronko Nagurski .25 .60
86 Alan Ameche .15 .40
87 Merlin Olsen .15 .40
88 Dick Butkus .30 .75
89 Elroy Hirsch .20 .50
90 Max McGee .20 .50
91 Ray Nitschke .30 .75
92 Phil Simms .25 .60
93 Vince Lombardi CC .50 1.25
94 Tom Landry CC .30 .75
95 Bill Walsh CC .20 .50
96 Mike Ditka CC .25 .60
97 Jimmy Johnson CC .20 .50
98 Chuck Noll CC .20 .50
99 Dan Reeves CC .20 .50
100 Don Shula CC .25 .60
101 Peter Warrick RC 1.25 3.00
102 Thomas Jones RC 1.50 4.00
103 Jamal Lewis RC 2.00 5.00
104 Chad Pennington RC 1.50 4.00
105 Chris Redman RC 1.25 3.00
106 Ron Dayne RC 2.00 5.00
107 Trung Canidate RC 1.25 3.00
108 Shaun Alexander RC 2.00 5.00
109 Plaxico Burress RC 1.50 4.00
110 J.R. Redmond RC 1.25 3.00
111 Travis Taylor RC 1.25 3.00
112 Dez White RC 1.25 3.00
113 Todd Pinkston RC 1.25 3.00
114 Laveranues Coles RC 1.50 4.00
115 Dennis Northcutt RC 1.25 3.00
116 Jerry Porter RC 2.00 5.00
117 R.Jay Soward RC 1.25 3.00
118 Sylvester Morris RC 1.25 3.00
119 Ron Dugans RC 1.25 3.00
120 Travis Prentice RC 1.25 3.00
121 Tee Martin RC 1.25 3.00
122 James Williams RC 1.25 3.00
123 Trevor Gaylor RC 1.25 3.00
124 Shyrone Stith RC 1.25 3.00
125 Frank Moreau RC 1.25 3.00
126 Kwame Cavil RC 1.25 3.00
127 Ron Dixon RC 1.25 3.00
128 Darrell Jackson RC 1.25 3.00
129 Sammy Morris RC 1.25 3.00
130 JaJuan Dawson RC 1.25 3.00
131 Doug Johnson RC 2.50 6.00
132 Brian Urlacher RC 12.00 30.00
133 Brad Hoover RC 3.00 8.00
134 Mike Anderson AUTO RC 15.00 30.00

2000 Greats of the Game Gold Border Autographs

ndomly inserted in Hobby packs at the rate of one in 24 and Retail packs at the rate of one in 40, this 85-card set utilizes the base set card format enhanced with a gold border and an authentic player autograph. Some cards were issued via mail redemptions that carried an expiration date of 12/01/2001.

STATED ODDS 1:24 HOB, 1:40 RET
1 Marcus Allen 25.00 50.00
2 Sammy Baugh SP 60.00 125.00
3 Chuck Bednarik 10.00 25.00
4 Raymond Berry 12.00 30.00
5 Fred Biletnikoff 10.00 25.00
6 George Blanda 20.00 50.00
7 Mel Blount 25.00 60.00
8 Terry Bradshaw 60.00 120.00
9 Cliff Branch 12.00 30.00
11 Earl Campbell 25.00 50.00
12 Roger Craig 10.00 25.00
13 Len Dawson 12.00 30.00
14 Eric Dickerson 15.00 40.00
15 Mike Ditka 20.00 50.00
16 Mike Ditka CC 15.00 40.00
17 Art Donovan 12.00 30.00
18 Tony Dorsett 30.00 60.00
19 Carl Eller 15.00 40.00
20 John Elway SP 60.00 120.00
21 Chuck Foreman 12.00 30.00
22 Dan Fouts 15.00 40.00
23 Frank Gifford SP 40.00 80.00
24 Otto Graham 25.00 60.00
25 Joe Greene 30.00 60.00
26 L.C. Greenwood 15.00 40.00
27 Jack Ham 15.00 40.00
28 Franco Harris 20.00 50.00
29 Bob Hayes 75.00 150.00
30 Paul Hornung 10.00 25.00
31 Sam Huff 12.00 30.00
32 Michael Irvin 25.00 50.00
33 Jimmy Johnson SP 15.00 40.00
34 Charlie Joiner 10.00 25.00
35 Deacon Jones 12.00 30.00
36 Sonny Jurgensen 20.00 50.00
37 Alex Karras 15.00 40.00
38 Jim Kelly 25.00 50.00
39 Billy Kilmer 12.00 30.00
40 Jack Lambert 60.00 120.00
41 Daryle Lamonica 15.00 40.00
42 Steve Largent 15.00 40.00
43 Bob Lilly 12.00 30.00
44 James Lofton 15.00 40.00
45 Ronnie Lott 25.00 50.00
46 Archie Manning 15.00 40.00
47 Gino Marchetti 15.00 40.00
48 Dan Marino SP 75.00 150.00
49 Jim Marshall 12.00 30.00
50 Harvey Martin 12.00 30.00
51 Tom Matte 12.00 30.00
52 Don Maynard 12.00 30.00
53 Bobby Mitchell 10.00 25.00
54 Art Monk 25.00 50.00
55 Lenny Moore 15.00 40.00
56 Earl Morrall 10.00 25.00
57 Mercury Morris 12.00 25.00
58 Anthony Munoz 12.00 30.00
59 Joe Namath 40.00 100.00
60 Ozzie Newsome 12.00 30.00
61 Chuck Noll SP 40.00 80.00
62 Jay Novacek 12.00 30.00
63 Jim Otto 10.00 25.00
64 Drew Pearson 12.00 30.00
65 William Perry 12.00 30.00
66 Jim Plunkett 12.00 30.00
67 Dan Reeves SP 10.00 25.00
68 Mel Renfro 12.00 30.00
69 Gale Sayers 15.00 40.00
70 Lee Roy Selmon 12.00 30.00
71 Don Shula SP 25.00 60.00
72 Mike Singletary 15.00 40.00
73 Ken Stabler 20.00 50.00
74 Bart Starr SP 150.00 250.00
75 Roger Staubach SP 50.00 120.00
76 Fran Tarkenton 20.00 50.00
77 Charley Taylor 10.00 25.00
78 Lawrence Taylor SP 15.00 40.00
79 Joe Theismann 15.00 40.00
80 Johnny Unitas SP 200.00 350.00
81 Steve Van Buren SP 150.00 300.00
82 Herschel Walker 15.00 40.00
83 Bill Walsh 75.00 150.00
84 Paul Warfield 12.00 30.00
85 Randy White 12.00 30.00
86 Steve Young 40.00 80.00

2000 Greats of the Game Cowboy Clippings

ndomly inserted in Hobby packs at the rate of one in 72, this 9-card set features swatches of game used jersey from the Dallas Cowboys greats. Cards feature a full color action shot of the player and a jersey swatch in the shape of the Dallas Star. Card #3CCL was never issued.

STATED ODDS 1:72 HOB
1CCL Troy Aikman 20.00 50.00
2CCL Tony Dorsett 12.00 30.00
4CCL Michael Irvin 10.00 25.00
5CCL Tom Landry SP 250.00 400.00
6CCL Bob Lilly 10.00 25.00
7CCL Harvey Martin Shoes SP 75.00 135.00
8CCL Jay Novacek 12.00 30.00
9CCL Mel Renfro 12.00 30.00
10CCL Roger Staubach 20.00 50.00

2000 Greats of the Game Feel The Game Classics

ndomly seeded in Hobby packs at the rate of one in 36, this 20-card set features swatches of game used memorabilia such as jerseys and pants. An action shot of the showcased player is placed to the left of a football shaped memorabilia swatch. Three players were issued with two different material types creating a total of 23 unique cards.

STATED ODDS 1:36 HOB
1 Marcus Allen 6.00 15.00
2 Fred Biletnikoff 6.00 15.00
3 Terry Bradshaw 8.00 20.00
4 Eric Dickerson 5.00 12.00
5 John Elway 10.00 25.00
6 L.C. Greenwood Jersey 4.00 10.00
7 L.C. Greenwood Shoe 4.00 10.00
8 Paul Hornung Pants 6.00 15.00
9 Jim Kelly 6.00 15.00
10 James Lofton 4.00 10.00
11 Ronnie Lott 6.00 15.00
12 Dan Marino Wht 12.00 30.00
13 Dan Marino Teal 12.00 30.00
14 Joe Namath 10.00 25.00
15 Walter Payton 15.00 40.00
16 Jim Plunkett Blk 5.00 12.00
17 Jim Plunkett Wht 5.00 12.00
18 Mike Singletary 6.00 15.00
19 Bart Starr Pants 15.00 40.00
20 Fran Tarkenton 10.00 25.00
21 Lawrence Taylor 6.00 15.00
22 Johnny Unitas 15.00 40.00
23 Steve Young 8.00 20.00

2000 Greats of the Game Retrospection Collection

ndomly inserted in packs at the rate of one in six, this 10-card set features a throwback Fleer design from the early sixties sporting a white border, large player name box on the bottom, and silver foil highlights.

COMPLETE SET (10) 6.00 15.00
STATED ODDS 1:6
1RC Terry Bradshaw 1.00 2.50
2RC John Elway .60 1.50
3RC Roger Staubach .50 1.25
4RC Franco Harris .40 1.00
5RC Paul Hornung .40 1.00
6RC Dan Marino .75 2.00
7RC Fran Tarkenton .40 1.00
8RC Joe Namath .75 2.00
9RC Walter Payton 1.50 4.00
10RC Jim Thorpe .60 1.50

2004 Greats of the Game

eats of the Game was produced by Fleer and initially released in mid-December 2004. The base set consists of 86-cards including 20-rookies serial numbered to 999 at the end of the set. Note that cards #35, 39, and 41 reportedly were not produced but a few copies of each appeared on the market after Fleer ceased operations. Hobby boxes contained 15-packs of 5-cards each while retail boxes contained 20-packs of 4-cards each. One parallel set and a variety of inserts can be found seeded in hobby and retail packs highlighted by one of the most popular insert sets of the year -- Gold Border Autographs.

COMP.SET w/o RC's (67) 15.00 40.00
ROOKIE/999 ODDS: 1:15 HOB, 1:24 RET
1 Jim Brown 1.00 2.50
2 Jim Thorpe .75 2.00
3 Terry Bradshaw 1.00 2.50
4 Fran Tarkenton .75 2.00
5 Joe Namath 1.25 3.00
6 Joe Montana 2.50 6.00
7 George Rogers .50 1.25
8 Marcus Allen .75 2.00
9 Walter Payton 3.00 8.00
10 Dick Butkus 1.00 2.50
11 Dan Fouts .60 1.50
12 Kellen Winslow Sr. .75 2.00
13 Sammy Baugh .75 2.00
14 Bart Starr 2.00 5.00
15 Steve Young 1.00 2.50
16 Sid Luckman .75 2.00
17 Y.A. Tittle .75 2.00
18 Dan Marino 1.50 4.00
19 Paul Hornung .75 2.00
20 John Elway 1.25 3.00
21 Earl Campbell .75 2.00
22 Max McGee .60 1.50
23 Alan Ameche .50 1.25
24 Bronko Nagurski .75 2.00
25 Elroy Hirsch .60 1.50
26 Jack Lambert 1.00 2.50
27 Sam Huff .60 1.50
28 Jay Novacek .60 1.50
29 Roger Staubach 1.00 2.50
30 Bob Hayes .60 1.50
31 Ken Stabler 1.00 2.50
32 Chuck Bednarik .60 1.50
33 Ronnie Lott .75 2.00
34 Steve Van Buren .60 1.50
35 Art Monk SP 15.00 40.00
36 Gale Sayers .75 2.00
37 Jim Otto .50 1.25
38 Jim Plunkett .60 1.50
40 Don Maynard .60 1.50
41 John Riggins .60 1.50
42 Billy Sims .60 1.50
43 Franco Harris 1.00 2.50
44 Tony Dorsett .75 2.00
45 Wilbert Montgomery .50 1.25
46 Eric Dickerson SP 5.00 12.00
47 Jim Taylor .75 2.00
48 George Blanda .75 2.00
49 Cris Carter .75 2.00
50 Mike Quick .50 1.25
51 James Lofton .50 1.25
52 Lawrence Taylor .75 2.00
53 Roger Craig .75 2.00
54 Paul Warfield .60 1.50
55 Dan Pastorini .50 1.25
56 Ozzie Newsome .60 1.50
57 Charley Taylor .60 1.50
58 Deacon Jones .60 1.50
59 Bob Lilly .75 2.00
60 Mike Singletary .75 2.00
61 Warren Moon .75 2.00
62 Charles White .50 1.25
63 Bob Griese .75 2.00
64 Dwight Clark .60 1.50
65 Joe Greene .75 2.00
66 Dave Casper .50 1.25
67 Harold Carmichael .50 1.25
68 Drew Pearson .60 1.50
69 Tony Hill .50 1.25
70 Ray Nitschke .75 2.00
71 Eli Manning RC 8.00 20.00
72 Philip Rivers RC 3.00 8.00
73 Ben Roethlisberger RC 8.00 20.00
74 Julius Jones RC 1.00 2.50
75 Larry Fitzgerald RC 4.00 10.00
76 Steven Jackson RC 1.50 4.00
77 Kevin Jones RC 1.25 3.00
78 Tatum Bell RC 1.00 2.50
79 Rashaun Woods RC 1.00 2.50
80 Roy Williams RC 1.00 2.50
81 Lee Evans RC 1.50 4.00
82 Michael Clayton RC 1.25 3.00
83 J.P. Losman RC 1.00 2.50
84 Drew Henson RC 1.00 2.50
85 Kellen Winslow RC 1.00 2.50
86 Chris Perry RC 1.00 2.50
87 Reggie Williams RC 1.00 2.50
88 Michael Jenkins RC 1.00 2.50
89 Darius Watts RC 1.00 2.50
90 Keary Colbert RC 1.00 2.50

2004 Greats of the Game Green/Red

*VETS 1-70: 1.2X TO 3X BASE CARD HI
VETERAN GREEN PRINT RUN 500 SETS
*ROOKIES 71-90: 1X TO 2.5X
ROOKIE RED PRINT RUN 99 SETS
STATED ODDS 1:7.5 HOB, 1:24 RET

2004 Greats of the Game Classic Combos

C T.Aikman/M.Irvin/1995 2.50 6.00
2CC T.Bradshaw/L.Swann SP 30.00 80.00
3CC K.Stabler/Biletnikoff/1977 2.00 5.00
4CC Staubach/D.Pearson/1974 2.00 5.00
5CC J.Montana/D.Clark/1981 5.00 12.00
6CC D.Marino/M.Clayton/1984 4.00 10.00
7CC S.Young/J.Rice/1995 3.00 8.00
8CC J.Namath/D.Maynard/1965 2.50 6.00
9CC B.Griese/P.Warfield/1970 1.50 4.00
10CC D.Fouts/K.Winslow/1981 1.50 4.00

2004 Greats of the Game Classic Combos Autographs

PRICED SINGLE AU PRINT RUN 10
UNPRICED DUAL AU PRINT RUN 10
4CC2 Staubach No AU/D.Pearson No AU 15.00 40.00

2004 Greats of the Game Glory of Their Time

ATED PRINT RUN 1960-1997
GOT1 Joe Namath/1967 2.50 6.00
GOT2 Troy Aikman/1992 2.00 5.00
GOT3 Walter Payton/1977 6.00 15.00
GOT4 Joe Montana/1987 5.00 12.00
GOT5 Bart Starr/1966 4.00 10.00
GOT6 Paul Hornung/1960 1.50 4.00
GOT7 Dan Marino/1984 3.00 8.00
GOT8 Roger Staubach/1979 2.00 5.00
GOT9 Warren Moon/1990 1.50 4.00
GOT10 Jack Lambert/1976 2.00 5.00
GOT11 Franco Harris/1979 2.00 5.00
GOT12 Steve Young/1994 2.00 5.00
GOT13 Eric Dickerson/1984 1.50 4.00
GOT14 Lawrence Taylor/1986 1.50 4.00
GOT15 Tony Dorsett/1981 1.50 4.00
GOT16 Ronnie Lott/1986 1.50 4.00
GOT17 Earl Campbell/1980 1.50 4.00
GOT18 Gale Sayers/1965 1.50 4.00
GOT19 Jim Kelly/1991 1.50 4.00
GOT20 Bob Griese/1977 1.50 4.00
GOT21 John Elway/1993 2.50 6.00
GOT22 Barry Sanders/1997 2.50 6.00
GOT23 Jim Plunkett/1985 1.25 3.00
GOT24 Bob Lilly/1963 1.50 4.00
GOT25 Fran Tarkenton/1975 1.50 4.00
GOT26 Mel Renfro/1969 1.25 3.00
GOT27 Fred Biletnikoff/1969 1.50 4.00
GOT28 Shannon Sharpe/1996 1.25 3.00
GOT29 Thurman Thomas/1992 1.25 3.00
GOT30 Michael Irvin/1995 1.50 4.00

2004 Greats of the Game Glory of Their Time Game Used Red

D STATED ODDS 1:24 HOBBY
*GOLD: .4X TO 1X RED
GOLD STATED ODDS 1:24 RETAIL
*SILVER/300: .5X TO 1.2X RED
SILVER PRINT RUN 300 SER.#'d SETS
*PATCH/25: 1X TO 2.5X RED
PATCH PRINT RUN 25 SER.#'d SETS
ALL ARE JERSEY SWATCH UNLESS NOTED
BG Bob Griese 3.00 8.00
BS Barry Sanders 5.00 12.00
BS Bart Starr Pants 8.00 20.00
DM Dan Marino 6.00 15.00
EC Earl Campbell 3.00 8.00
FB Fred Biletnikoff 3.00 8.00
FH Franco Harris 4.00 10.00
FT Fran Tarkenton 3.00 8.00
GS Gale Sayers 3.00 8.00
JE John Elway 5.00 12.00
JK Jim Kelly 3.00 8.00
JL Jack Lambert 4.00 10.00
JM Joe Montana 10.00 25.00
JP Jim Plunkett 2.50 6.00
LT Lawrence Taylor 3.00 8.00
MF Mel Renfro 2.50 6.00
MI Michael Irvin 3.00 8.00
PH Paul Hornung Pants 3.00 8.00
RL Ronnie Lott 3.00 8.00
RS Roger Staubach 4.00 10.00
SS Shannon Sharpe SP 2.50 6.00
SY Steve Young 4.00 10.00
TA Troy Aikman 4.00 10.00
TD Tony Dorsett 3.00 8.00
TT Thurman Thomas 2.50 6.00
WM Warren Moon 3.00 8.00
WP Walter Payton 12.00 30.00

2004 Greats of the Game Gold Border Autographs

ATED ODDS 1:15 HOB, 1:288 RET
BG Bob Griese 15.00 40.00
BL Bob Lilly 10.00 25.00
BR Ben Roethlisberger 100.00 200.00
BS1 Bart Starr SP 60.00 120.00
BS2 Billy Sims 10.00 25.00
CB Chuck Bednarik 10.00 26.00
CC Cris Carter 15.00 40.00
CT Charley Taylor 7.50 20.00
CW Charles White 7.50 20.00
DF Dan Fouts 15.00 40.00
DJ Deacon Jones 10.00 25.00
ED Eric Dickerson 15.00 40.00
FH Franco Harris 25.00 50.00
FT Fran Tarkenton 15.00 40.00
GB George Blanda 12.00 30.00
GS Gale Sayers 30.00 60.00
HC Harold Carmichael 7.50 20.00
JB Jim Brown SP 100.00 200.00
JE John Elway 75.00 150.00
JG Joe Greene 30.00 50.00
JM Joe Montana 60.00 120.00
JN Jay Novacek SP 15.00 40.00
JO Jim Otto 12.00 30.00
JP Jim Plunkett 10.00 25.00
JT Jim Taylor 40.00 80.00
KC Keary Colbert 7.50 20.00
KS Ken Stabler 15.00 40.00
LT Lawrence Taylor SP 25.00 60.00
MC Michael Clayton 10.00 25.00
MD Mike Ditka 25.00 50.00
MJ Michael Jenkins SP 10.00 25.00
MQ Mike Quick 10.00 25.00
MS Mike Singletary 10.00 25.00
ON Ozzie Newsome 7.50 20.00
PH Paul Hornung 15.00 40.00
PW Paul Warfield SP 15.00 40.00
RC Roger Craig 15.00 40.00
RL Ronnie Lott 15.00 40.00
RS Roger Staubach SP 50.00 100.00
RW2 Roy Williams WR SP 15.00 40.00
SH Sam Huff 12.00 30.00
SV Steve Van Buren SP 125.00 250.00
SY Steve Young SP 50.00 100.00
TH Tony Hill 15.00 40.00
YT Y.A. Tittle 12.00 30.00
DCA Dave Casper 10.00 25.00
DCL Dwight Clark 10.00 25.00
DMY Don Maynard 7.50 20.00
DPA Dan Pastorini 7.50 20.00
DPE Drew Pearson 10.00 25.00
DPE2 Pearson ERR Hens.AU 15.00 40.00
JLA Jack Lambert 40.00 80.00
JNA Joe Namath SP 60.00 120.00
KWS Kellen Winslow Sr. 10.00 25.00
KWS2 Winslow Sr. ERR Jr.AU 15.00 40.00
WMN Warren Moon SP 20.00 50.00
WMY Wilbert Montgomery 7.50 20.00

2004 Greats of the Game Personality Cut Autographs

UNPRICED CUT AUTO PRINT RUN 1

1998 Green Bay Bombers PIFL

COMPLETE SET (30) 7.50 15.00
1 Coaches .30 .75
Dave Hochtritt#Dave Pisarik
Bob Canney
Bud Keyes
2 Mario Russo CO .30 .75
3 Joel Banda .30 .75
4 Dan Blohm .30 .75
5 Darrick Bolton .30 .75
6 Troy Bonk .30 .75
7 Bruce Breecher .30 .75
8 Tyrone Brown .30 .75
9 Derric Coakley .30 .75
10 Heath Garland .30 .75
11 Mark Grapentine .30 .75
12 Todd Hanley .30 .75
13 Willie High .30 .75
14 Jim Hobbins .30 .75
15 Shane Konop .30 .75
16 Dan Luedtke .30 .75
17 Bryan Mader .30 .75
18 Jay McDonagh .30 .75
19 Chris Perry .30 .75
20 Derf Reese .30 .75
21 Eric Rice .30 .75
22 Darrick Sanders .30 .75
23 Kelly Schmitt .30 .75
24 Sahl Shaheed .30 .75
25 Matt Teske .30 .75
26 Jeason Thomas .30 .75
27 Jeff Timmerman .30 .75
28 Mike Whitehouse .30 .75
29 Bomber Explosion .30 .75
30 Checklist .30 .75

1991 Greenleaf Puzzles

eenleaf Steel Rule Die Corp. produced these NFL player puzzles. Each measures roughly 4-1/2" by 6-3/8" and is sealed within a cardboard frame and thick plastic cover. The puzzle backs contain a postcard style format along with a short write-up on the featured player. The checklist below is presumed to be incomplete.

1001 Jim Kelly 1.25 3.00
1004 Warren Moon 1.00 2.50
1005 Dan Marino 3.00 8.00
1007 John Elway 2.50 6.00
1010 Lawrence Taylor 1.00 2.50
1011 Earnest Byner .75 2.00
1012 Tom Rathman .75 2.00
1013 Randall Cunningham 1.00 2.50
1014 Neal Anderson .75 2.00
1015 Troy Aikman 1.50 4.00
1016 Thurman Thomas 1.25 3.00
1018 Christian Okoye .75 2.00
1019 Pat Swilling .75 2.00

2012 Gridiron

MP.SET w/o RC's (200) 10.00 25.00
201-300 ROOKIES ONE PER HOBBY PACK
301-335 ROOKIE JSY AU PRINT RUN 199-299
1 Cam Newton .30 .75
2 Beanie Wells .20 .50
3 Early Doucet .20 .50
4 Kevin Kolb .20 .50
5 Larry Fitzgerald .25 .60
6 Patrick Peterson .20 .50
7 Ryan Williams .20 .50
8 Julio Jones .30 .75
9 Jacquizz Rodgers .25 .60
10 Michael Turner .20 .50
11 Matt Ryan .25 .60
12 Roddy White .20 .50
13 Tony Gonzalez .25 .60
14 Anquan Boldin .20 .50
15 Ed Reed .25 .60
16 Joe Flacco .25 .60
17 Ray Lewis .30 .75
18 Ray Rice .20 .50
19 Terrell Suggs .20 .50
20 Torrey Smith .20 .50
21 C.J. Spiller .20 .50
22 Fred Jackson .25 .60
23 Mario Williams .20 .50
24 Ryan Fitzpatrick .20 .50
25 Steve Johnson .25 .60
26 David Nelson .20 .50
27 DeAngelo Williams .20 .50
28 Jonathan Stewart .20 .50
29 Jon Beason .20 .50
30 Greg Olsen .25 .60
31 Steve Smith WR .25 .60
32 Brandon Marshall .25 .60
33 Lance Briggs .25 .60
34 Devin Hester .25 .60
35 Jay Cutler .20 .50
36 Julius Peppers .25 .60
37 Matt Forte .20 .50
38 A.J. Green .30 .75
39 Andy Dalton .25 .60
40 BenJarvus Green-Ellis .25 .60
41 Bernard Scott .20 .50

42 Jermaine Gresham .20 .50
43 Ben Watson .20 .50
44 Colt McCoy .25 .60
45 D'Qwell Jackson .20 .50
46 Greg Little .20 .50
47 Josh Cribbs .20 .50
48 Mohamed Massaquoi .20 .50
49 DeMarco Murray .25 .60
50 DeMarcus Ware .30 .75
51 Dez Bryant .30 .75
52 Jason Witten .25 .60
53 Miles Austin .20 .50
54 Tony Romo .25 .60
55 Brandon Carr .20 .50
56 Champ Bailey .25 .60
57 Demaryius Thomas .30 .75
58 Elvis Dumervil .20 .50
59 Eric Decker .20 .50
60 Peyton Manning .60 1.50
61 Von Miller .25 .60
62 Willis McGahee .20 .50
63 Brandon Pettigrew .20 .50
64 Calvin Johnson .30 .75
65 Jahvid Best .20 .50
66 Stephen Tulloch .20 .50
67 Matthew Stafford .25 .60
68 Ndamukong Suh .25 .60
69 Aaron Rodgers .50 1.25
70 Charles Woodson .30 .75
71 Clay Matthews .30 .75
72 Greg Jennings .20 .50
73 Jermichael Finley .20 .50
74 Jordy Nelson .25 .60
75 Andre Johnson .25 .60
76 Arian Foster .25 .60
77 Brian Cushing .20 .50
78 J.J. Watt .30 .75
79 Matt Schaub .20 .50
80 Owen Daniels .20 .50
81 Austin Collie .20 .50
82 Delone Carter .20 .50
83 Donald Brown .20 .50
84 Dwight Freeney .20 .50
85 Reggie Wayne .25 .60
86 Robert Mathis .20 .50
87 Blaine Gabbert .20 .50
88 Laurent Robinson .20 .50
89 Mike Thomas .25 .60
90 Marcedes Lewis .20 .50
91 Maurice Jones-Drew .20 .50
92 Paul Posluszny .20 .50
93 Dwayne Bowe .25 .60
94 Steve Breaston .20 .50
95 Jamaal Charles .25 .60
96 Matt Cassel .20 .50
97 Peyton Hillis .20 .50
98 Tamba Hali .20 .50
99 Anthony Fasano .20 .50
100 Matt Moore .20 .50
101 Davone Bess .20 .50
102 Karlos Dansby .20 .50
103 Daniel Thomas .20 .50
104 Reggie Bush .20 .50
105 Adrian Peterson .30 .75
106 Chad Greenway .25 .60
107 Christian Ponder .20 .50
108 Jared Allen .20 .50
109 Percy Harvin .20 .50
110 Toby Gerhart .20 .50
111 Aaron Hernandez .25 .60
112 Brandon Lloyd .20 .50
113 Stevan Ridley .20 .50
114 Jerod Mayo .20 .50
115 Rob Gronkowski .30 .75
116 Tom Brady .75 2.00
117 Wes Welker .25 .60
118 Darren Sproles .25 .60
119 Drew Brees .30 .75
120 Jimmy Graham .30 .75
121 Mark Ingram .25 .60
122 Marques Colston .20 .50
123 Pierre Thomas .20 .50
124 Ahmad Bradshaw .20 .50
125 Eli Manning .25 .60
126 Hakeem Nicks .20 .50
127 Jason Pierre-Paul .20 .50
128 Justin Tuck .20 .50
129 Victor Cruz .25 .60
130 Darrelle Revis .20 .50
131 Plaxico Burress .20 .50
132 Dustin Keller .20 .50
133 Mark Sanchez .20 .50
134 Santonio Holmes .20 .50
135 Shonn Greene .20 .50
136 Tim Tebow .30 .75
137 Carson Palmer .25 .60
138 Darren McFadden .20 .50
139 Darrius Heyward-Bey .20 .50
140 Denarius Moore .20 .50
141 Marcel Reece RC .30 .75
142 Jacoby Ford .20 .50
143 Brent Celek .20 .50
144 DeSean Jackson .25 .60
145 Jeremy Maclin .20 .50
146 LeSean McCoy .30 .75
147 Michael Vick .25 .60
148 Nnamdi Asomugha .20 .50
149 Antonio Brown .30 .75
150 Ben Roethlisberger .30 .75
151 James Harrison .25 .60
152 Heath Miller .20 .50
153 Mike Wallace .20 .50
154 Rashard Mendenhall .20 .50
155 Antonio Gates .25 .60
156 Troy Polamalu .30 .75
157 Malcom Floyd .20 .50
158 Philip Rivers .30 .75
159 Eddie Royal .20 .50
160 Robert Meachem .20 .50
161 Ryan Mathews .25 .60
162 Aldon Smith .20 .50
163 Alex Smith QB .25 .60
164 Frank Gore .25 .60
165 Michael Crabtree .20 .50
166 Patrick Willis .25 .60
167 Randy Moss .25 .60
168 Vernon Davis .20 .50
169 Braylon Edwards .20 .50
170 Golden Tate .20 .50
171 Marshawn Lynch .25 .60
172 Matt Flynn .20 .50
173 Doug Baldwin .30 .75
174 Sidney Rice .20 .50
175 Austin Pettis .20 .50
176 Chris Long .20 .50
177 Lance Kendricks .20 .50
178 James Laurinaitis .20 .50
179 Sam Bradford .20 .50
180 Danny Amendola .25 .60
181 Steven Jackson .20 .50
182 Ronde Barber .20 .50
183 Dallas Clark .20 .50
184 Josh Freeman .25 .60
185 Mike Williams .25 .60
186 LeGarrette Blount .25 .60
187 Vincent Jackson .20 .50
188 Chris Johnson .20 .50
189 Jake Locker .30 .75
190 Kenny Britt .20 .50
191 Matt Hasselbeck .20 .50
192 Jared Cook .20 .50
193 Nate Washington .20 .50
194 Brian Orakpo .25 .60
195 Leonard Hankerson .20 .50
196 Fred Davis .20 .50
197 Pierre Garcon .25 .60
198 Ryan Kerrigan .20 .50
199 Santana Moss .25 .60
200 Roy Helu Jr. .20 .50
201 Alfred Morris RC .60 1.50
202 Adrien Robinson RC .60 1.50
203 Andre Branch RC .60 1.50
204 B.J. Coleman RC .60 1.50
205 B.J. Cunningham RC .60 1.50
206 Bobby Rainey RC .60 1.50
207 Bobby Wagner RC 1.00 2.50
208 Brandon Hardin RC .75 2.00
209 Brandon Taylor RC .60 1.50
210 Bruce Irvin RC .75 2.00
211 Bryce Brown RC .60 1.50
212 Case Keenum RC 1.25 3.00
213 Casey Hayward RC .60 1.50
214 Chandler Harnish RC .60 1.50
215 Chandler Jones RC .60 1.50
216 Chris Polk RC .60 1.50
217 Chris Rainey RC .60 1.50
218 Cory Harkey RC .75 2.00
219 Coty Sensabaugh RC .75 2.00
220 Courtney Upshaw RC .75 2.00
221 Cyrus Gray RC .60 1.50
222 Dan Herron RC .60 1.50
223 Danny Coale RC .60 1.50
224 David DeCastro RC .60 1.50
225 Davin Meggett RC .60 1.50
226 Deangelo Peterson RC .60 1.50
227 Demario Davis RC .60 1.50
228 Derek Wolfe RC .75 2.00
229 Devon Still RC .75 2.00
230 Devon Wylie RC .60 1.50
231 Dont'a Hightower RC 1.00 2.50
232 Dontari Poe RC .60 1.50
233 Dre Kirkpatrick RC .60 1.50
234 Bill Bentley RC .75 2.00
235 Dwight Jones RC .60 1.50
236 Eric Page RC .75 2.00
237 Fletcher Cox RC 1.00 2.50
238 George Iloka RC .60 1.50
239 Gerell Robinson RC .60 1.50
240 Greg Childs RC .60 1.50
241 Harrison Smith RC .60 1.50
242 Jamell Fleming RC .60 1.50
243 James Hanna RC .60 1.50
244 Janoris Jenkins RC .75 2.00
245 Jared Crick RC .60 1.50
246 Jeff Fuller RC .60 1.50
247 Jerel Worthy RC .60 1.50
248 Jonathan Martin RC .60 1.50
249 Josh Robinson RC 1.00 2.50
250 Juron Criner RC .60 1.50
251 Kellen Moore RC .75 2.00
252 Kendall Reyes RC .60 1.50
253 Keshawn Martin RC .75 2.00
254 Kevin Zeitler RC .60 1.50
255 Kirk Cousins RC 2.50 6.00
256 Ladarius Green RC .60 1.50
257 LaVon Brazill RC 1.00 2.50
258 Lavonte David RC 1.00 2.50
259 Luke Kuechly RC 1.50 4.00
260 Marc Tyler RC .60 1.50
261 Mark Barron RC .60 1.50
262 Marquis Maze RC .60 1.50
263 Marvin Jones RC .60 1.50
264 Marvin McNutt RC .60 1.50
265 Matt Kalil RC .60 1.50
266 Melvin Ingram RC .60 1.50
267 Michael Brockers RC .60 1.50
268 Michael Smith RC .75 2.00
269 Mike Martin RC .75 2.00
270 Morris Claiborne RC .60 1.50
271 Mychal Kendricks RC 1.00 2.50
272 Najee Goode RC .60 1.50
273 Nick Perry RC .75 2.00
274 Olivier Vernon RC 1.00 2.50
275 Omar Bolden RC .75 2.00
276 Orson Charles RC .60 1.50
277 Quinton Coples RC .60 1.50
278 Rhett Ellison RC .75 2.00
279 Riley Reiff RC .60 1.50
280 Rishard Matthews RC .60 1.50
281 Ronnell Lewis RC .60 1.50
282 Ryan Lindley RC .60 1.50
283 Sean Spence RC .75 2.00
284 Shea McClellin RC .75 2.00
285 Stephon Gilmore RC .75 2.00
286 T.Y. Hilton RC 1.25 3.00
287 Tauren Poole RC .60 1.50
288 Tavon Wilson RC .75 2.00
289 Terrance Ganaway RC .75 2.00
290 Tim Benford RC .60 1.50
291 Tommy Streeter RC .60 1.50
292 Travis Benjamin RC .60 1.50
293 Trumaine Johnson RC .60 1.50
294 Tyrone Crawford RC .60 1.50
295 Vick Ballard RC .75 2.00
296 Vinny Curry RC .75 2.00
297 Vontaze Burfict RC .75 2.00
298 Whitney Mercilus RC .60 1.50
299 Zach Brown RC .60 1.50
300 Brandon Bolden RC .60 1.50
301 R.Griffin III JSY AU/149* RC 5.00 12.00
302 Alshon Jeffery JSY AU/152* RC 12.00 30.00
303 Dwayne Allen JSY AU/249* RC 4.00 10.00
304 L.James JSY AU/249* RC 4.00 10.00
305 R.Turbin JSY AU/249* RC 4.00 10.00
306 T.Richardson JSY AU/149* RC 4.00 10.00
307 Brian Quick JSY AU/249* RC 4.00 10.00
308 Joe Adams JSY AU/249* RC 4.00 10.00
309 Nick Foles JSY AU/249* RC 25.00 60.00
310 R.Hillman JSY AU/249* RC 4.00 10.00
311 D.Wilson JSY AU/249* RC 4.00 10.00
312 Lamar Miller JSY AU/249* RC 6.00 15.00
313 M.Floyd JSY AU/249* RC 4.00 10.00
314 Doug Martin JSY AU/249* RC 6.00 15.00
315 Chris Givens JSY AU/249* RC 4.00 10.00
316 B.Weeden JSY AU/149* RC 4.00 10.00
317 R.Tannehill JSY AU/149* RC 6.00 15.00
318 Kendall Wright JSY AU/249* RC 4.00 10.00
319 DeVier Posey JSY AU/249* RC 4.00 10.00
320 R.Wilson JSY AU/249* RC 60.00 100.00
321 T.J. Graham JSY AU/249* RC 4.00 10.00
322 Andrew Luck JSY AU/149* RC 75.00 150.00
323 A.J. Jenkins JSY AU/249* RC 4.00 10.00
324 Nick Toon JSY AU/249* RC 4.00 10.00
325 Ryan Broyles JSY AU/249* RC 4.00 10.00
326 Isaiah Pead JSY AU/249* RC 4.00 10.00
327 B.Pierce JSY AU/249* RC 4.00 10.00
328 Michael Egnew JSY AU/249* RC 4.00 10.00
329 Rueben Randle JSY AU/249* RC 4.00 10.00
330 Mohamed Sanu JSY AU/249* RC 6.00 15.00
331 B.Osweiler JSY AU/249* RC 4.00 10.00
332 Jarius Wright JSY AU/249* RC 4.00 10.00
333 Coby Fleener JSY AU/249* RC 4.00 10.00
334 Stephen Hill JSY AU/249* RC 4.00 10.00
335 J.Blackmon JSY AU/149* RC 4.00 10.00

2012 Gridiron Gold O's

*1-200 VETS/100: 2.5X TO 6X BASIC CARDS
*201-300 ROOKIES/100: .8X TO 2X BASIC RC

2012 Gridiron Gold X's

*1-200 VETS/100: 2.5X TO 6X BASIC CARDS
*201-300 ROOKIES/100: .8X TO 2X BASIC RC

2012 Gridiron Platinum O's

*1-200 VETS/25: 5X TO 12X BASIC CARDS
*201-300 ROOKIES/25: 1.5X TO 4X BASIC RC

2012 Gridiron Platinum X's

*1-200 VETS/25: 5X TO 12X BASIC CARDS
*201-300 ROOKIES/25: 1.5X TO 4X BASIC RC

2012 Gridiron Rookie Gridiron Gems Jersey Autographs Gold Ink

GOLD INK/50: .5X TO 1.2X JSY AU/199-299
FIRST 50 CARDS SIGNED IN GOLD INK

2012 Gridiron Silver O's

*1-200 VETS/250: 2X TO 5X BASIC CARDS
*201-300 ROOKIES/250: .6X TO 1.5X BASIC RC

2012 Gridiron Silver X's

-200 VETS/250: 2X TO 5X BASIC CARDS
*201-300 ROOKIES/250: .6X TO 1.5X BASIC RC

2012 Gridiron Air Command

OLD/100: .6X TO 1.5X BASIC INSERTS
*PLATINUM/25: 1X TO 2.5X BASIC INSERTS
*SILVER/250: .5X TO 1.2X BASIC INSERTS
1 Calvin Johnson 1.00 2.50
2 Andre Johnson .75 2.00
3 Larry Fitzgerald .75 2.00
4 Hakeem Nicks .60 1.50
5 Victor Cruz .75 2.00
6 Roddy White .60 1.50
7 Wes Welker .75 2.00
8 Greg Jennings .60 1.50
9 Mike Wallace .60 1.50
10 A.J. Green 1.00 2.50
11 Jordy Nelson .75 2.00
12 Julio Jones 1.00 2.50
13 Brandon Marshall .75 2.00
14 Steve Smith WR .75 2.00
15 Miles Austin .60 1.50
16 Dez Bryant 1.00 2.50
17 Percy Harvin .60 1.50
18 Vincent Jackson .60 1.50
19 Jeremy Maclin .60 1.50
20 Dwayne Bowe .75 2.00
21 Kenny Britt .60 1.50
22 Anquan Boldin .60 1.50
23 Steve Johnson .75 2.00
24 DeSean Jackson .75 2.00
25 Reggie Wayne .75 2.00

2012 Gridiron Arms Race

OLD/100: .6X TO 1.5X BASIC INSERTS
*PLATINUM/25: 1X TO 2.5X BASIC INSERTS
*SILVER/250: .5X TO 1.2X BASIC INSERTS
1 Aaron Rodgers 1.50 4.00
2 Michael Vick .75 2.00
3 Tom Brady 2.50 6.00
4 Drew Brees 1.00 2.50
5 Andy Dalton .75 2.00
6 Ben Roethlisberger 1.00 2.50
7 Matt Schaub .60 1.50
8 Ryan Fitzpatrick .60 1.50
9 Mark Sanchez .60 1.50
10 Peyton Manning 2.00 5.00
11 Matthew Stafford .75 2.00
12 Matt Cassel .60 1.50
13 Carson Palmer .75 2.00
14 Philip Rivers 1.00 2.50
15 Jay Cutler .60 1.50
16 Christian Ponder .60 1.50
17 Matt Ryan .75 2.00
18 Cam Newton 1.00 2.50
19 Tony Romo .75 2.00
20 Eli Manning .75 2.00
21 Kevin Kolb .60 1.50
22 Josh Freeman .75 2.00
23 Sam Bradford .60 1.50
24 Joe Flacco .75 2.00
25 Blaine Gabbert .60 1.50

2012 Gridiron Crash Course

OLD/100: .6X TO 1.5X BASIC INSERTS
*PLATINUM/25: 1X TO 2.5X BASIC INSERTS
*SILVER/250: .5X TO 1.2X BASIC INSERTS
1 Ray Lewis 1.00 2.50
2 Jon Beason .60 1.50
3 Patrick Willis .75 2.00
4 Dwight Freeney .60 1.50
5 James Harrison .75 2.00
6 J.J. Watt 1.00 2.50
7 Lance Briggs .75 2.00
8 DeMarcus Ware 1.00 2.50
9 Clay Matthews 1.00 2.50
10 Jason Pierre-Paul .60 1.50
11 DeMeco Ryans .60 1.50
12 James Laurinaitis .60 1.50
13 Takeo Spikes .60 1.50
14 Von Miller .75 2.00
15 Aaron Curry .60 1.50
16 Paul Posluszny .60 1.50
17 D'Qwell Jackson .60 1.50
18 Adrian Clayborn .60 1.50
19 Sean Weatherspoon .60 1.50
20 NaVorro Bowman .75 2.00
21 Brian Orakpo .75 2.00
22 Karlos Dansby .60 1.50
23 Tamba Hali .60 1.50
24 Jerod Mayo .60 1.50
25 Mario Williams .60 1.50

2012 Gridiron Gamebreakers Jerseys

*PRIME/49: .6X TO 1.5X BASIC JSY/99
*PRIME/20-25: .8X TO 2X BASIC JSY/99
1 Ray Rice/99 3.00 8.00
4 Drew Brees/49 5.00 12.00
5 Tom Brady/99 12.00 30.00
6 Darren McFadden/49 3.00 8.00
8 Devin Hester/20 5.00 12.00
9 Dwayne Bowe/25 5.00 12.00
11 Eli Manning/99 4.00 10.00
12 Michael Vick/20 5.00 12.00
13 DeSean Jackson/99 4.00 10.00
14 Dez Bryant/99 5.00 12.00
15 Troy Polamalu/49 5.00 12.00

2012 Gridiron Gridiron Kings Jerseys

*PRIME/49: .6X TO 1.5X BASIC JSY/99
*PRIME/20: .8X TO 2X BASIC JSY/99
1 Emmitt Smith/99 10.00 25.00
2 Walter Payton/99 12.00 30.00
3 Boomer Esiason/99 5.00 12.00
4 Troy Aikman/99 8.00 20.00
5 Jim Brown/49 8.00 20.00
6 John Elway/99 10.00 25.00
7 Barry Sanders/99 10.00 25.00
8 Earl Campbell/25 6.00 15.00
9 Warren Moon/49 8.00 20.00
10 Joe Montana/49 15.00 40.00
11 Marcus Allen/99 6.00 15.00
12 Joe Namath/99 12.00 30.00
13 Randall Cunningham/99 5.00 12.00
14 Jerry Rice/99 10.00 25.00
15 Eric Dickerson/99 5.00 12.00

2012 Gridiron Gridiron Signatures

STATED PRINT RUN 5-49
1 Ray Rice/25 EXCH 15.00 40.00
2 Cam Newton/15
5 Michael Turner/25 10.00 25.00
6 Anquan Boldin/25 10.00 25.00
7 Steve Johnson/49 10.00 25.00
8 Matt Forte/25 10.00 25.00
9 A.J. Green/25
10 Andy Dalton/49 10.00 25.00
11 DeMarco Murray/25 12.00 30.00
12 DeMarcus Ware/49 15.00 40.00
13 Dez Bryant/25 15.00 40.00
14 Tony Romo/25 12.00 30.00
15 Peyton Manning/15 125.00 200.00
17 Clay Matthews/49 25.00 50.00
18 Greg Jennings/25 10.00 25.00
19 Jermichael Finley/15 [illegible] [illegible]
20 Jordy Nelson/49 10.00 25.00
21 Arian Foster/25 EXCH
22 J.J. Watt/49 30.00 60.00
23 Matt Schaub/25 10.00 25.00
24 Reggie Wayne/15 12.00 30.00
25 Tamba Hali/49 8.00 20.00
26 Brandon Lloyd/25 10.00 25.00
27 Fred Jackson/49 15.00 40.00
28 Frank Gore/25 10.00 25.00
29 Adrian Peterson/15 60.00 100.00
30 Rob Gronkowski/25 25.00 50.00
32 Drew Brees/25 25.00 60.00
33 Jimmy Graham/25 EXCH 15.00 40.00
34 Eli Manning/15
35 Jason Pierre-Paul/49 12.00 30.00
37 Santonio Holmes/25 10.00 25.00
39 Darren McFadden/25 12.00 30.00
41 LeSean McCoy/25 15.00 40.00
42 Michael Vick/15 25.00 50.00
43 Percy Harvin/25 10.00 25.00
44 Mike Wallace/25 10.00 25.00
45 Antonio Gates/25 12.00 30.00
46 Roddy White/25 10.00 25.00
47 Philip Rivers/15 EXCH
48 Ryan Mathews/25 12.00 30.00
49 Santana Moss/49 10.00 25.00
50 Patrick Willis/25 12.00 30.00
51 Vernon Davis/25 EXCH 10.00 25.00
52 Marshawn Lynch/25 12.00 30.00
53 James Laurinaitis/49 8.00 20.00
54 Pierre Garcon/49 10.00 25.00
55 Nnamdi Asomugha/49 8.00 20.00
56 Mario Williams/49 8.00 20.00
57 LeGarrette Blount/49 10.00 25.00
58 Vincent Jackson/49 8.00 20.00
59 Kenny Britt/25 10.00 25.00
60 Brian Orakpo/49 10.00 25.00
61 Von Miller/25 12.00 30.00
62 Brent Celek/49 8.00 20.00
63 Darren Sproles/25 12.00 30.00
64 Ahmad Bradshaw/49 8.00 20.00
65 Miles Austin/25

2012 Gridiron Jerseys X's

1 Antonio Gates/18 5.00 12.00
3 Larry Fitzgerald/25 5.00 12.00
4 Adrian Wilson/199 2.50 6.00
6 Matt Ryan/25 5.00 12.00
7 Matt Hasselbeck/25 4.00 10.00
10 Joe Flacco/49 4.00 10.00
11 Ray Lewis/49 5.00 12.00
12 Ray Rice/99 3.00 8.00
13 Terrell Suggs/99 3.00 8.00
14 Haloti Ngata/99 3.00 8.00
16 Ryan Fitzpatrick/25 4.00 10.00
17 Steve Johnson/49 4.00 10.00
19 Jon Beason/25 4.00 10.00
20 Steve Smith WR/199 3.00 8.00
22 Devin Hester/20 5.00 12.00
23 Lance Briggs/49 5.00 12.00
24 Jay Cutler/49 3.00 8.00
26 Brian Urlacher/199 4.00 10.00
29 Jermaine Gresham/25 4.00 10.00
30 Jordan Shipley/49 3.00 8.00
33 Dez Bryant/99 5.00 12.00
34 Jason Witten/199 3.00 8.00
35 Miles Austin/99 3.00 8.00
36 Tony Romo/199 3.00 8.00
38 Michael Griffin/99 3.00 8.00
39 Santana Moss/49 4.00 10.00
41 Matthew Stafford/25 5.00 12.00
44 Charles Woodson/49 6.00 15.00
47 Andre Johnson/199 3.00 8.00
48 Arian Foster/25 5.00 12.00
52 Maurice Jones-Drew/20 4.00 10.00
53 Marcedes Lewis/20 4.00 10.00
54 Dwayne Bowe/25 5.00 12.00
55 Jamaal Charles/49 4.00 10.00
56 Matt Cassel/99 3.00 8.00
58 Reggie Bush/25 4.00 10.00
61 Percy Harvin/99 3.00 8.00
62 Jerod Mayo/49 3.00 8.00
63 Tom Brady/99 12.00 30.00
65 Drew Brees/49 5.00 12.00
66 Marques Colston/99 3.00 8.00
68 Devery Henderson/99 3.00 8.00
69 Eli Manning/199 3.00 8.00
70 Ahmad Bradshaw/199 2.50 6.00
71 Hakeem Nicks/99 3.00 8.00
72 Darrelle Revis/199 2.50 6.00
73 Mark Sanchez/20 4.00 10.00
75 Shonn Greene/25 4.00 10.00
77 Darren McFadden/49 3.00 8.00
81 Michael Vick/20 5.00 12.00
82 James Harrison/49 5.00 12.00
84 Troy Polamalu/49 5.00 12.00
85 Malcom Floyd/25 4.00 10.00
86 Philip Rivers/75 5.00 12.00
87 Ryan Mathews/25 5.00 12.00
89 Frank Gore/25 5.00 12.00
90 Michael Crabtree/15 4.00 10.00
93 Steven Jackson/99 3.00 8.00
94 James Laurinaitis/25 4.00 10.00
95 Sam Bradford/25 4.00 10.00
96 Josh Freeman/25 5.00 12.00

2012 Gridiron Monday Night Heroes

*GOLD/100: .6X TO 1.5X BASIC INSERTS
*PLATINUM/25: 1X TO 2.5X BASIC INSERTS
*SILVER/250: .5X TO 1.2X BASIC INSERTS
1 Drew Brees 1.00 2.50
2 Tom Brady 2.50 6.00
3 Darren McFadden .60 1.50
4 Eli Manning .75 2.00
5 Josh Freeman .75 2.00
6 LeGarrette Blount .75 2.00
7 Calvin Johnson 1.00 2.50
8 Jahvid Best .60 1.50
9 Santonio Holmes .60 1.50
10 Maurice Jones-Drew .60 1.50
11 Matt Cassel .60 1.50
12 Jay Cutler .60 1.50
13 Aaron Rodgers 1.50 4.00
14 Jordy Nelson .75 2.00
15 Rob Gronkowski 1.00 2.50
16 Jimmy Graham 1.00 2.50
17 Victor Cruz .75 2.00
18 Philip Rivers 1.00 2.50
19 Ryan Mathews .75 2.00
20 Marshawn Lynch .75 2.00
21 Vernon Davis .60 1.50
22 Frank Gore .75 2.00
23 Julio Jones 1.00 2.50
24 Marques Colston .60 1.50
25 Felix Jones .60 1.50

2012 Gridiron NFL Nation Jerseys

1 Jamaal Charles/25 5.00 12.00
2 Brian Cushing/99 3.00 8.00
4 Felix Jones/99 3.00 8.00
6 Lance Briggs/49 5.00 12.00
7 Marcedes Lewis/20 4.00 10.00
8 Mark Sanchez/15 4.00 10.00
9 Matt Cassel/49 3.00 8.00
10 Michael Crabtree/15 4.00 10.00
11 Owen Daniels/25 4.00 10.00
12 Plaxico Burress/15 4.00 10.00
14 Sidney Rice/25 4.00 10.00
19 Donald Brown/99 3.00 8.00
20 Donald Driver/49 4.00 10.00

2012 Gridiron NFL Nation Jerseys Prime

1 Jamaal Charles/20 8.00 20.00
4 Felix Jones/49 5.00 12.00
5 Chris Johnson/49 5.00 12.00
15 Tony Gonzalez/20 8.00 20.00

2012 Gridiron Rookie Autographs X's

CH EXPIRATION: 4/24/2014
*AUTO O/25: .8X TO 2X AUTO X/499
*AUTO O/25: .5X TO 1.2X AUTO X/99
201 Alfred Morris/99 4.00 10.00
202 Adrien Robinson/99 4.00 10.00
203 Andre Branch/99 4.00 10.00
204 B.J. Coleman/99 4.00 10.00
205 B.J. Cunningham/499 2.50 6.00
206 Bobby Rainey/99 4.00 10.00
207 Bobby Wagner/499 4.00 10.00
208 Brandon Hardin/499 3.00 8.00
209 Brandon Taylor/499 2.50 6.00
210 Bruce Irvin/499 3.00 8.00
211 Bryce Brown/99 12.00 30.00
212 Case Keenum/99 8.00 20.00
213 Casey Hayward/499 2.50 6.00
214 Chandler Harnish/99 4.00 10.00
215 Chandler Jones/99 EXCH 4.00 10.00
216 Chris Polk/499 2.50 6.00
217 Chris Rainey/499 2.50 6.00
218 Cory Harkey/499 3.00 8.00
219 Coty Sensabaugh/499 3.00 8.00
220 Courtney Upshaw/499 3.00 8.00
221 Cyrus Gray/499 2.50 6.00
222 Dan Herron/99 4.00 10.00
223 Danny Coale/499 2.50 6.00
224 David DeCastro/499 2.50 6.00
225 Davin Meggett/499 2.50 6.00
226 Deangelo Peterson/499 2.50 6.00
227 Demario Davis/499 2.50 6.00
228 Derek Wolfe/99 EXCH 5.00 12.00
229 Devon Still/499 3.00 8.00
230 Devon Wylie/499 2.50 6.00
231 Dont'a Hightower/499 4.00 10.00
232 Dontari Poe/99 4.00 10.00
233 Dre Kirkpatrick/99 4.00 10.00
234 Bill Bentley/499 3.00 8.00
235 Dwight Jones/499 2.50 6.00
236 Eric Page/499 3.00 8.00
237 Fletcher Cox/499 4.00 10.00
238 George Iloka/499 2.50 6.00
239 Gerell Robinson/499 2.50 6.00
240 Greg Childs/499 2.50 6.00
241 Harrison Smith/499 2.50 6.00
242 Jamell Fleming/499 2.50 6.00
243 James Hanna/99 4.00 10.00
244 Janoris Jenkins/499 3.00 8.00
245 Jared Crick/99 EXCH 4.00 10.00
246 Jeff Fuller/499 2.50 6.00
247 Jerel Worthy/99 4.00 10.00
248 Jonathan Martin/499 2.50 6.00
249 Josh Robinson/499 4.00 10.00
250 Juron Criner/499 2.50 6.00
251 Kellen Moore/499 3.00 8.00
252 Kendall Reyes/499 2.50 6.00
253 Keshawn Martin/99 EXCH 5.00 12.00
254 Kevin Zeitler/499 2.50 6.00
255 Kirk Cousins/499 10.00 25.00
256 Ladarius Green/499 2.50 6.00
257 LaVon Brazill/499 4.00 10.00
258 Lavonte David/499 4.00 10.00
259 Luke Kuechly/499 8.00 20.00
260 Marc Tyler/499 2.50 6.00
261 Mark Barron/99 4.00 10.00
262 Marquis Maze/499 2.50 6.00
263 Marvin Jones/499 2.50 6.00
264 Marvin McNutt/499 2.50 6.00
265 Matt Kalil/99 EXCH 4.00 10.00
266 Melvin Ingram/99 EXCH 4.00 10.00
267 Michael Brockers/99 EXCH 4.00 10.00
268 Michael Smith/99 EXCH 5.00 12.00
269 Mike Martin/499 3.00 8.00
270 Morris Claiborne/99 4.00 10.00
271 Mychal Kendricks/499 4.00 10.00
272 Najee Goode/499 2.50 6.00
273 Nick Perry/99 EXCH 5.00 12.00
274 Olivier Vernon/499 4.00 10.00
275 Omar Bolden/499 3.00 8.00
276 Orson Charles/499 2.50 6.00
277 Quinton Coples/99 4.00 10.00
278 Rhett Ellison/499 3.00 8.00
279 Riley Reiff/499 2.50 6.00
280 Rishard Matthews/499 2.50 6.00
281 Ronnell Lewis/499 2.50 6.00
282 Ryan Lindley/499 2.50 6.00
283 Sean Spence/499 3.00 8.00
284 Shea McClellin/99 10.00 25.00
285 Stephon Gilmore/99 EXCH 5.00 12.00
286 T.Y. Hilton/99 8.00 20.00
287 Tauren Poole/499 2.50 6.00
288 Tavon Wilson/499 3.00 8.00
289 Terrance Ganaway/99 5.00 12.00
290 Tim Benford/499 2.50 6.00
291 Tommy Streeter/99 4.00 10.00
292 Travis Benjamin/499 2.50 6.00
293 Trumaine Johnson/499 2.50 6.00
294 Tyrone Crawford/499 2.50 6.00
295 Vick Ballard/99 5.00 12.00
296 Vinny Curry/499 3.00 8.00
297 Vontaze Burfict/99 5.00 12.00
298 Whitney Mercilus/99 4.00 10.00
299 Zach Brown/499 2.50 6.00
300 Brandon Bolden/99 EXCH 4.00 10.00

2012 Gridiron Rookie Gridiron Gems Jerseys

STATED PRINT RUN 49-199
*JUMBO/99: .5X TO 1.2X JSY/199
*JUMBO/98: .3X TO .8X BASIC JSY/49
*JUMBO/49: .4X TO 1X BASIC JSY/49
*JMB PRIME/49: .8X TO 2X BASIC JSY/199
*JMB PRIME/49: .6X TO 1.5X BASIC JSY/49
*PRIME/49: .6X TO 1.5X BASIC JSY/199
*PRIME/49: .5X TO 1.2X BASIC JSY/49
*RETAIL/250: .4X TO 1X BASIC JSY/199
*RETAIL/49: .4X TO 1X BASIC JSY/49
*COMBO/249: .4X TO 1X JSY/199
*COMBO/99: .4X TO 1X JSY/49
*COMBO/49: .4X TO 1X JSY/49
*CMB PRIME/49: .6X TO 1.5X JSY/199
*CMB PRIME/49: .5X TO 1.2X JSY/49
*TRIO/199: .4X TO 1X JSY/199
*TRIO/199: .3X TO .8X JSY/49
*TRIO/99: .4X TO 1X JSY/49
*TRIO PRIME/49: .6X TO 1.5X JSY/199
*TRIO PRIME/49: .5X TO 1.2X JSY/49
301 Robert Griffin III/199 1.50 4.00
302 Alshon Jeffery/199 2.50 6.00
303 Dwayne Allen/199 1.25 3.00
304 LaMichael James/199 1.25 3.00
305 Robert Turbin/199 1.25 3.00
306 Trent Richardson/199 1.25 3.00
307 Brian Quick/199 1.25 3.00
308 Joe Adams/199 1.25 3.00
309 Nick Foles/199 3.00 8.00
310 Ronnie Hillman/199 1.25 3.00
311 David Wilson/49 1.50 4.00
312 Lamar Miller/49 2.50 6.00
313 Michael Floyd/199 1.25 3.00
314 Doug Martin/199 2.00 5.00
315 Chris Givens/199 1.25 3.00
316 Brandon Weeden/199 1.25 3.00
317 Ryan Tannehill/199 2.00 5.00
318 Kendall Wright/199 1.25 3.00
319 DeVier Posey/49 1.50 4.00
320 Russell Wilson/199 8.00 20.00
321 T.J. Graham/199 1.25 3.00
322 Andrew Luck/199 12.00 30.00
323 A.J. Jenkins/199 1.25 3.00
324 Nick Toon/199 1.25 3.00
325 Ryan Broyles/199 1.25 3.00
326 Isaiah Pead/199 1.25 3.00
327 Bernard Pierce/199 1.25 3.00
328 Michael Egnew/199 1.25 3.00
329 Rueben Randle/49 1.50 4.00
330 Mohamed Sanu/199 2.00 5.00
331 Brock Osweiler/199 1.25 3.00
332 Jarius Wright/199 1.25 3.00
333 Coby Fleener/199 1.25 3.00
334 Stephen Hill/199 1.25 3.00
335 Justin Blackmon/199 1.25 3.00

2012 Gridiron Rookie Gridiron Gems Jerseys Combos Autographs

*COMBO AU/49: .5X TO 1.2X JSY AU/199-299
*COMBO AU/15: .5X TO 1.5X JSY AU/299
STATED PRINT RUN 5-49
301 Robert Griffin III/49 6.00 15.00
320 Russell Wilson/49 100.00 175.00
322 Andrew Luck/49 125.00 250.00

2012 Gridiron Rookie Gridiron Gems Jerseys Combos Autographs Prime

*PRIME/25: .6X TO 1.5X BASIC JSY AU/199-299
STATED PRINT RUN 25 SER.#'d SETS
EXCH EXPIRATION: 4/24/2014
301 Robert Griffin III 8.00 20.00
320 Russell Wilson 125.00 200.00
322 Andrew Luck 175.00 300.00

2012 Gridiron Rookie Gridiron Gems Jerseys Trios Autographs

1 Robert Griffin III/49 6.00 15.00
17 Russell Wilson/49 60.00 125.00
18 Andrew Luck 100.00 200.00

2012 Gridiron Rookie Gridiron Gems Jerseys Trios Autographs Prime

*PRIME/25: .6X TO 1.5X BASIC JSY AU/199-299
STATED PRINT RUN 25 SER.#'d SETS
1 Robert Griffin III 8.00 20.00
17 Russell Wilson 125.00 200.00
18 Andrew Luck 150.00 300.00

2012 Gridiron Rookie Gridiron Kings Autographs

Andrew Luck 75.00 150.00
2 Robert Griffin III 4.00 10.00
3 Trent Richardson EXCH 3.00 8.00
4 Justin Blackmon 3.00 8.00
5 Michael Floyd 3.00 8.00
6 Ryan Tannehill 5.00 12.00
7 Kendall Wright 3.00 8.00
8 Brandon Weeden 3.00 8.00
9 A.J. Jenkins 3.00 8.00
10 Joe Adams 3.00 8.00
11 LaMichael James 3.00 8.00
12 Russell Wilson 40.00 80.00
13 Ryan Broyles 3.00 8.00
14 Andre Branch 3.00 8.00
15 Bobby Wagner 5.00 12.00
16 Bruce Irvin 4.00 10.00
17 Case Keenum 6.00 15.00
18 Chandler Harnish 3.00 8.00
19 Chandler Jones EXCH 3.00 8.00
20 Chris Rainey 3.00 8.00
21 Courtney Upshaw 4.00 10.00
22 Dan Herron 3.00 8.00
23 Danny Coale 3.00 8.00
24 David DeCastro 3.00 8.00
25 Devon Still 4.00 10.00
26 Dont'a Hightower 5.00 12.00
27 Dontari Poe 3.00 8.00
28 Dre Kirkpatrick 3.00 8.00
29 Fletcher Cox 6.00 15.00
30 George Iloka 3.00 8.00
31 Janoris Jenkins 4.00 10.00
32 Jared Crick EXCH 3.00 8.00
33 Juron Criner 3.00 8.00
34 Kellen Moore 4.00 10.00
35 Kirk Cousins 12.00 30.00
36 Ladarius Green 3.00 8.00
37 LaVon Brazill 5.00 12.00
38 Lavonte David 5.00 12.00
39 Luke Kuechly 15.00 30.00
40 Mark Barron 3.00 8.00
41 Marquis Maze 3.00 8.00
42 Matt Kalil EXCH 3.00 8.00
43 Melvin Ingram 3.00 8.00
44 Michael Brockers EXCH 3.00 8.00
45 Mychal Kendricks 5.00 12.00
46 Nick Perry EXCH 4.00 10.00
47 Quinton Coples 3.00 8.00
48 Riley Reiff 3.00 8.00
49 Stephon Gilmore EXCH 4.00 10.00
50 Whitney Mercilus 3.00 8.00

2012 Gridiron Rookie Gridiron Kings Jerseys Prime

*BASE JSY/299: .25X TO .6X PRIME/49
*BASE JSY/25: .4X TO 1X PRIME/49
1 Andrew Luck 15.00 40.00
2 Robert Griffin III 2.50 6.00
3 Trent Richardson 2.00 5.00
4 Justin Blackmon 2.00 5.00
5 Ryan Tannehill 3.00 8.00
6 Michael Floyd 2.00 5.00
7 Kendall Wright 2.00 5.00
8 Brandon Weeden 2.00 5.00
9 A.J. Jenkins 2.00 5.00
10 Doug Martin 3.00 8.00
11 David Wilson 2.00 5.00
12 Alshon Jeffery 4.00 10.00
13 Bernard Pierce 2.00 5.00
14 Brian Quick 2.00 5.00
15 Brock Osweiler 2.00 5.00
16 Coby Fleener 2.00 5.00
17 DeVier Posey 2.00 5.00
18 Dwayne Allen 2.00 5.00
19 Isaiah Pead 2.00 5.00
20 Chris Givens 2.00 5.00
21 Joe Adams 2.00 5.00
22 Lamar Miller 3.00 8.00
23 LaMichael James 2.00 5.00
24 Michael Egnew 2.00 5.00
25 Mohamed Sanu 3.00 8.00
26 Nick Foles 5.00 12.00
27 Nick Toon 2.00 5.00
28 Robert Turbin 2.00 5.00
29 Ronnie Hillman 2.00 5.00
30 Rueben Randle 2.00 5.00
31 Russell Wilson 10.00 25.00
32 Ryan Broyles 2.00 5.00
33 Stephen Hill 2.00 5.00
34 T.J. Graham 2.00 5.00
35 Jarius Wright 2.00 5.00

1939 Gridiron Greats Blotters

is set of 12 ink blotters was produced by the Louis F. Dow Company in honor of great college football players. These blotters were issued in two different sizes: legal sized blotter at approximately 9" by 3 7/8" and a smaller version at 3 3/8" by 6 1/4." They were issued in a brown paper sleeve as a complete set. The left portion of the blotter front has a head and shoulders sepia-toned drawing, with the player wearing either a red or a blue jersey. The right portion of the blotter has a brief player profile and one or more or even none of the following: a sponsor advertisement and/or monthly calendar (a different month on each of the 12 blotters). The backs are blank with just the felt-like blotter material and each is numbered in small print on the front. Many of these player blotters were issued over a period of years as some have been found with different calendar years, no calendar at all, and/or various advertisors such as Syracuse Letter Co., Famous Energy, or Pyott Foundry. Louis Dow also produced larger wall type calendars for some, or all, of these player works of art as well as bound notebooks using the player images on the covers.

COMPLETE SET (12) 7000.00 10000.00
B3941 Jim Thorpe 900.00 1500.00
B3942 Walter Eckersall 300.00 500.00
B3943 Edward Mahan 300.00 500.00
B3944 Sammy Baugh 750.00 1250.00
B3945 Thomas Shevlin 300.00 500.00
B3946 Red Grange 900.00 1500.00
B3947 Ernie Nevers 400.00 750.00
B3948 George Gipp 600.00 1000.00
B3949 Pudge Heffelfinger 300.00 500.00
B3950 Bronko Nagurski 900.00 1500.00
B3951 Willie Heston 300.00 500.00
B3952 Jay Berwanger 300.00 500.00

1939 Gridiron Greats Notebooks

These notebook covers were produced by the Louis F. Dow Company in honor of great college football players. Each measures slightly smaller than 8" by 10" and was blank backed. They can be found bound with pages or with the pages carefully removed.

1 Jay Berwanger 300.00 500.00
2 George Gipp 600.00 1000.00
3 Willie Heston 300.00 500.00
4 Bronko Nagurski 900.00 1500.00

1941 Gridiron Greats Blotters

These oversized blotters are virtually identical to the 1939 Gridiron Greats Blotters and were produced by Louis F. Dow Company. The artwork featured for each player is the same but the calendar is for the year 1941. It is believed that there are likely a number of different advertising sponsors used on the calendars as well as the full complement of players.

1 Red Grange 900.00 1500.00

1943 Gridiron Greats Calendars

ese oversized calendars are very similar to the 1939 Gridiron Greats Blotters and were produced by Louis F. Dow Company. The artwork featured for each player is the same but these calendars are vertically oriented. The fronts contain a small attached calendar for the year 1943 along with sponsor advertising. It is believed that there are likely a number of different advertising sponsors used on the calendars as well as the full complement of players.

M3902 Walter Eckersall 250.00 400.00
M3910 Bronko Nagurski 600.00 1000.00
M3952 Jay Berwanger 250.00 400.00

2002 Gridiron Kings Chicago Collection

T PRICED DUE TO SCARCITY

2002 Gridiron Kings National Promos

stributed at the 2002 National Convention in Chicago, the first 6-cards of this set were distributed to promote the 2002 Donruss Gridiron Kings release. A seventh autographed card of Gale Sayers was made available to select members of the press who attended the Playoff press conference.

COMPLETE SET (7) 20.00 35.00
N1 Anthony Thomas 1.25 3.00
N2 Brian Urlacher 1.50 4.00
N3 Brett Favre 3.00 8.00
N4 Tom Brady 8.00 20.00
N5 Jeff Garcia 1.00 2.50
N6 Joey Harrington 1.00 2.50
N7 Gale Sayers AU/150 25.00 50.00

2002 Gridiron Kings Samples

*SAMPLES: .8X TO 2X BASE CARDS

2002 Gridiron Kings

leased in October 2002, this 175-card set includes 100 veterans, 50 rookies and 25 retired legends. Boxes contained 24 packs of 4 cards. The complete set was comprised of reprints from original oil paintings.

COMPLETE SET (175) 60.00 120.00
COMP.SET w/o SP's (100) 15.00 40.00
1 David Boston .30 .75
2 Jake Plummer .30 .75
3 Michael Vick .40 1.00
4 Warrick Dunn .30 .75
5 Jamal Lewis .40 1.00
6 Ray Lewis .50 1.25
7 Drew Bledsoe .40 1.00
8 Travis Henry .30 .75
9 Eric Moulds .30 .75
10 Chris Weinke .30 .75
11 Lamar Smith .30 .75
12 Anthony Thomas .40 1.00
13 Chris Chandler .40 1.00
14 Brian Urlacher .50 1.25
15 Corey Dillon .30 .75
16 Peter Warrick .30 .75
17 Tim Couch .30 .75
18 James Jackson .30 .75
19 Kevin Johnson .30 .75
20 Quincy Carter .30 .75
21 Emmitt Smith .75 2.00
22 Joey Galloway .40 1.00
23 Brian Griese .30 .75
24 Terrell Davis .40 1.00
25 Ed McCaffrey .40 1.00
26 Rod Smith .40 1.00
27 Mike McMahon .30 .75
28 Az-Zahir Hakim .30 .75
29 Germane Crowell .30 .75
30 Brett Favre 1.00 2.50
31 Terry Glenn .40 1.00
32 Ahman Green .40 1.00
33 James Allen .30 .75
34 Tony Simmons .30 .75
35 Peyton Manning 1.25 3.00
36 Edgerrin James .40 1.00
37 Marvin Harrison .40 1.00
38 Dominic Rhodes .30 .75
39 Mark Brunell .40 1.00
40 Jimmy Smith .40 1.00
41 Keenan McCardell .40 1.00
42 Fred Taylor .30 .75
43 Priest Holmes .30 .75
44 Snoop Minnis .30 .75
45 Trent Green .30 .75
46 Tony Gonzalez .40 1.00
47 Chris Chambers .30 .75
48 Ricky Williams .40 1.00
49 Jay Fiedler .40 1.00
50 Zach Thomas .40 1.00
51 Randy Moss .40 1.00
52 Cris Carter .50 1.25
53 Daunte Culpepper .40 1.00
54 Michael Bennett .30 .75
55 Tom Brady 2.50 6.00
56 Antowain Smith .40 1.00
57 Troy Brown .30 .75
58 Aaron Brooks .30 .75
59 Deuce McAllister .40 1.00
60 Joe Horn .30 .75
61 Kerry Collins .30 .75
62 Ron Dayne .40 1.00
63 Michael Strahan .40 1.00
64 Vinny Testaverde .30 .75
65 Curtis Martin .40 1.00
66 Wayne Chrebet .30 .75
67 Rich Gannon .40 1.00
68 Tim Brown .50 1.25
69 Jerry Rice 1.00 2.50
70 Charlie Garner .40 1.00
71 Donovan McNabb .40 1.00
72 Duce Staley .30 .75
73 Freddie Mitchell .30 .75
74 Kordell Stewart .30 .75
75 Jerome Bettis .50 1.25
76 Plaxico Burress .30 .75
77 Kendrell Bell .30 .75
78 LaDainian Tomlinson .50 1.25
79 Drew Brees 1.00 2.50
80 Doug Flutie .40 1.00
81 Junior Seau .40 1.00
82 Jeff Garcia .30 .75
83 Terrell Owens .40 1.00
84 Garrison Hearst .30 .75
85 Trent Dilfer .30 .75
86 Shaun Alexander .30 .75
87 Koren Robinson .30 .75
88 Marshall Faulk .40 1.00
89 Kurt Warner .10 1.00
90 Torry Holt .40 1.00
91 Isaac Bruce .50 1.25
92 Brad Johnson .40 1.00

93 Keyshawn Johnson .40 1.00
94 Mike Alstott .30 .75
95 Warren Sapp .40 1.00
96 Steve McNair .40 1.00
97 Eddie George .40 1.00
98 Jevon Kearse .30 .75
99 Stephen Davis .30 .75
100 Rod Gardner .30 .75
101 David Carr RC 1.00 2.50
102 Joey Harrington RC 1.00 2.50
103 Patrick Ramsey RC 1.25 3.00
104 Josh McCown RC 1.50 4.00
105 David Garrard RC 1.25 3.00
106 Rohan Davey RC 1.50 4.00
107 Randy Fasani RC 1.00 2.50
108 Kurt Kittner RC 1.00 2.50
109 William Green RC 1.25 3.00
110 T.J. Duckett RC 1.00 2.50
111 DeShaun Foster RC 1.50 4.00
112 Clinton Portis RC 1.50 4.00
113 Maurice Morris RC 1.25 3.00
114 Ladell Betts RC 1.50 4.00
115 Lamar Gordon RC 1.25 3.00
116 Brian Westbrook RC 2.00 5.00
117 Jonathan Wells RC 1.25 3.00
118 Travis Stephens RC 1.00 2.50
119 Josh Scobey RC 1.25 3.00
120 Donte Stallworth RC 1.50 4.00
121 Ashley Lelie RC 1.00 2.50
122 Javon Walker RC 1.50 4.00
123 Jabar Gaffney RC 1.00 2.50
124 Josh Reed RC 1.25 3.00
125 Tim Carter RC 1.25 3.00
126 Andre Davis RC 1.00 2.50
127 Reche Caldwell RC 1.25 3.00
128 Antwaan Randle El RC 1.25 3.00
129 Antonio Bryant RC 1.50 4.00
130 Deion Branch RC 1.50 4.00
131 Marquise Walker RC 1.00 2.50
132 Cliff Russell RC 1.00 2.50
133 Eric Crouch RC 1.50 4.00
134 Ron Johnson RC 1.25 3.00
135 Terry Charles RC 1.00 2.50
136 Jeremy Shockey RC 1.50 4.00
137 Daniel Graham RC 1.25 3.00
138 Julius Peppers RC 2.50 6.00
139 Dwight Freeney RC 2.00 5.00
140 Ryan Sims RC 1.50 4.00
141 John Henderson RC 1.25 3.00
142 Wendell Bryant RC 1.00 2.50
143 Albert Haynesworth RC 1.50 4.00
144 Quentin Jammer RC 1.50 4.00
145 Phillip Buchanon RC 1.50 4.00
146 Lito Sheppard RC 1.50 4.00
147 Roy Williams RC 1.00 2.50
148 Ed Reed RC 6.00 15.00
149 Napoleon Harris RC 1.25 3.00
150 Mike Williams RC 1.00 2.50
151 Art Monk 1.25 3.00
152 Barry Sanders 2.00 5.00
153 Bob Griese 1.25 3.00
154 Dan Marino 2.50 6.00
155 Dick Butkus 1.50 4.00
156 Earl Campbell 1.25 3.00
157 Eric Dickerson 1.00 2.50
158 Fran Tarkenton 1.25 3.00
159 Franco Harris 1.25 3.00
160 Herschel Walker 1.25 3.00
161 Joe Montana 4.00 10.00
162 Ronnie Lott 1.00 2.50
163 Joe Theismann 1.25 3.00
164 John Elway 2.00 5.00
165 John Riggins 1.00 2.50
166 Ken Stabler 1.50 4.00
167 Len Dawson 1.25 3.00
168 Marcus Allen 1.25 3.00
169 Mike Singletary 1.25 3.00
170 Roger Staubach 1.50 4.00
171 Walter Payton 5.00 12.00
172 Steve Largent 1.25 3.00
173 Terry Bradshaw 1.50 4.00
174 Thurman Thomas 1.00 2.50
175 Tony Dorsett 1.25 3.00

2002 Gridiron Kings Bronze

*VETS 1-100: 1.5X TO 4X BASIC CARDS
*ROOKIES 101-150: .5X TO 1.2X
*RETIRED 151-175: .6X TO 1.5X
OVERALL PARALLEL ODDS 1:6

2002 Gridiron Kings Gold

*VETS 1-100: 5X TO 12X BASIC CARDS
*ROOKIES 101-150: 1.5X TO 4X
*RETIRED 151-175: 2X TO 5X
GOLD PRINT RUN 100 SER.#'d SETS

2002 Gridiron Kings Silver

*VETS 1-100: 2.5X TO 6X BASIC CARDS
*ROOKIES 101-150: .8X TO 2X
*RETIRED 151-175: 1X TO 2.5X
SILVER PRINT RUN 400 SER.#'d SETS

2002 Gridiron Kings DK Originals

Randomly inserted in packs, this set features current NFL stars with a color framed portrait along with a smaller color action shot. Cards were serial numbered on back to 1000.
STATED PRINT RUN 1000 SER.#'d SETS
DK1 Emmitt Smith 3.00 8.00
DK2 Brett Favre 4.00 10.00
DK3 Shaun Alexander 1.25 3.00
DK4 Tom Brady 10.00 25.00
DK5 Chris Chambers 1.25 3.00
DK6 Mark Brunell 1.50 4.00
DK7 Jeff Garcia 1.25 3.00
DK8 Marvin Harrison 1.50 4.00
DK9 Ahman Green 1.50 4.00
DK10 LaDainian Tomlinson 2.00 5.00
DK11 Brian Griese 1.25 3.00
DK12 Jerome Bettis 2.00 5.00
DK13 Quincy Carter 1.25 3.00
DK14 Tim Couch 1.25 3.00
DK15 Donovan McNabb 1.50 4.00
DK16 Corey Dillon 1.25 3.00
DK17 Chris Weinke 1.25 3.00
DK18 Rich Gannon 1.50 4.00
DK19 Drew Bledsoe 1.50 4.00
DK20 Terrell Davis 1.50 4.00
DK21 Travis Henry 1.25 3.00
DK22 Curtis Martin 1.50 4.00
DK23 Aaron Brooks 1.25 3.00
DK24 Ray Lewis 2.00 5.00
DK25 Michael Vick 1.50 4.00

2002 Gridiron Kings Donruss 1894

Randomly inserted in packs,this set features current and retired NFL stars produced in the style of the 1894 Mayo set. The cards were serial numbered on back to 1000.
STATED PRINT RUN 1000 SER.#'d SETS
MC1 Anthony Thomas 1.50 4.00
MC2 Randy Moss 1.50 4.00
MC3 Tom Brady 10.00 25.00
MC4 Jerry Rice 4.00 10.00
MC5 Jerome Bettis 2.00 5.00
MC6 Junior Seau 1.50 4.00
MC7 Emmitt Smith 3.00 8.00
MC8 Marshall Faulk 1.50 4.00
MC9 Eddie George 1.50 4.00
MC10 Barry Sanders 4.00 10.00
MC11 Kurt Warner 1.50 4.00
MC12 Peyton Manning 5.00 12.00
MC13 Dan Marino 5.00 12.00
MC14 Ricky Williams 1.50 4.00
MC15 Dick Butkus 3.00 8.00
MC16 Brett Favre 4.00 10.00
MC17 Earl Campbell 2.50 6.00
MC18 Zach Thomas 1.50 4.00
MC19 John Elway 4.00 10.00
MC20 Edgerrin James 1.50 4.00
MC21 Joey Harrington 1.25 3.00
MC22 William Green 1.50 4.00
MC23 Donte Stallworth 2.00 5.00
MC24 Roy Williams 1.25 3.00
MC25 Brian Urlacher 2.00 5.00

2002 Gridiron Kings Gridiron Cut Collection

ndomly inserted in packs, this 110 card set features game and event worn jerseys, footballs, and authentic autographs printed in various quantities.
GC1-GC40 AUTO PRINT RUN 50-400
GC41-GC90/GC101-GC110 JSY PRINT RUN 400
GC91-GC100 FB PRINT RUN 550
GC1 Art Monk AU/219 12.00 30.00
GC2 Barry Sanders AU/83 75.00 150.00
GC3 Bob Griese AU/50 30.00 80.00
GC4 Dick Butkus AU/125 30.00 80.00
GC5 Earl Campbell AU/50 30.00 80.00
GC6 Eric Dickerson AU/50 25.00 60.00
GC7 Fran Tarkenton AU/50 30.00 80.00
GC8 Franco Harris AU/50 40.00 100.00
GC9 Herschel Walker AU/50 30.00 80.00
GC10 Joe Montana AU/50 75.00 150.00
GC11 Ronnie Lott AU/82 20.00 50.00
GC12 Joe Theismann AU/50 25.00 60.00
GC13 John Riggins AU/50 25.00 60.00
GC14 Ken Stabler AU/50 40.00 100.00
GC15 Len Dawson AU/50 25.00 60.00
GC16 Marcus Allen AU/50 30.00 80.00
GC17 Mike Singletary AU/50 30.00 80.00
GC18 Roger Staubach AU/83 60.00 120.00
GC19 Steve Largent AU/50 30.00 80.00
GC20 Terry Bradshaw AU/160 25.00 60.00
GC21 Thurman Thomas AU/400 10.00 25.00
GC22 Tony Dorsett AU/50 30.00 80.00
GC23 Brian Urlacher AU/197 30.00 60.00
GC24 Chris Weinke AU/300 8.00 20.00
GC25 David Boston AU/266 8.00 20.00
GC26 Deuce McAllister AU/310 10.00 25.00
GC27 Drew Brees AU/400 30.00 60.00
GC28A Zach Thomas AU/400 10.00 25.00
GC28B Z.Thomas Buddy Lee AU 15.00 40.00
GC29 Quincy Carter AU/400 8.00 20.00
GC30 Ray Lewis AU/245 40.00 80.00
GC31 Terrell Owens AU/200 10.00 25.00
GC32 Garrison Hearst AU/400 8.00 20.00
GC33 DeShaun Foster AU/400 12.00 30.00
GC34 Dwight Freeney AU/400 10.00 25.00
GC35 Lito Sheppard AU/400 12.00 30.00
GC36 Reche Caldwell AU/350 10.00 25.00
GC37 Rohan Davey AU/350 12.00 30.00
GC38 Maurice Morris AU/382 10.00 25.00
GC39 Phillip Buchanon No Auto 5.00 12.00
GC40 Travis Stephens AU/400 8.00 20.00
GC41 Dan Marino JSY/400 10.00 25.00
GC42 John Elway JSY/400 8.00 20.00
GC43 Daunte Culpepper JSY/400 4.00 10.00
GC44 Kordell Stewart JSY/400 3.00 8.00
GC45 Steve McNair JSY/400 4.00 10.00
GC46 Jeff Garcia JSY/400 3.00 8.00
GC47 Kurt Warner JSY/400 4.00 10.00
GC48 Jake Plummer JSY/400 3.00 8.00
GC49 D.McNabb JSY/400 4.00 10.00
GC50 Tim Couch JSY/400 3.00 8.00
GC51 Rich Gannon JSY/400 4.00 10.00
GC52 Quincy Carter JSY/400 3.00 8.00
GC53 Tom Brady JSY/400 25.00 60.00
GC54 Brian Griese JSY/400 3.00 8.00
GC55 Mark Brunell JSY/400 4.00 10.00
GC56 Brett Favre JSY/400 10.00 25.00
GC57 Peyton Manning JSY/400 12.00 30.00
GC58 Emmitt Smith JSY/400 8.00 20.00
GC59 Mike Alstott JSY/400 3.00 8.00
GC60 Jerome Bettis JSY/400 6.00 15.00
GC61 Marshall Faulk JSY/400 4.00 10.00
GC62 L.Tomlinson JSY/400 5.00 12.00
GC63 Terrell Davis JSY/400 4.00 10.00
GC64 Antowain Smith JSY/400 4.00 10.00
GC65 Fred Taylor JSY/400 3.00 8.00
GC66 Edgerrin James JSY/400 4.00 10.00
GC67 Ron Dayne JSY/400 4.00 10.00
GC68 Curtis Martin JSY/400 4.00 10.00
GC69 Stephen Davis JSY/400 3.00 8.00
GC70 Walter Payton JSY/400 15.00 40.00
GC71 Freddie Mitchell JSY/400 3.00 8.00
GC72 Cris Carter JSY/400 5.00 12.00
GC73 David Boston JSY/400 3.00 8.00
GC74 Tony Gonzalez JSY/400 4.00 10.00
GC75 Marvin Harrison JSY/400 4.00 10.00
GC76 Torry Holt JSY/400 4.00 10.00
GC77 Jerry Rice JSY/400 10.00 25.00
GC78 Randy Moss JSY/400 4.00 10.00
GC79 Jimmy Smith JSY/400 4.00 10.00
GC80 Ed McCaffrey JSY/400 4.00 10.00
GC81 Eric Moulds JSY/400 3.00 8.00
GC82 Keyshawn Johnson JSY/400 4.00 10.00
GC83 Isaac Bruce JSY/400 5.00 12.00
GC84 Tim Brown JSY/400 5.00 12.00
GC85 Peter Warrick JSY/400 3.00 8.00
GC86 Zach Thomas JSY/400 4.00 10.00
GC87 Warren Sapp JSY/400 4.00 10.00
GC88 Junior Seau JSY/400 4.00 10.00
GC89 Jevon Kearse JSY/400 3.00 8.00
GC90 Ray Lewis JSY/400 5.00 12.00
GC91 Donovan McNabb FB/550 4.00 10.00
GC92 Eddie George FB/550 4.00 10.00
GC93 Curtis Martin FB/550 4.00 10.00
GC94 Anthony Thomas FB/550 4.00 10.00
GC95 Jeff Garcia FB/550 3.00 8.00
GC96 Shaun Alexander FB/550 3.00 8.00
GC97 Rod Smith FB/550 4.00 10.00
GC98 Aaron Brooks FB/550 3.00 8.00
GC99 Peyton Manning FB/550 12.00 30.00
GC100 Brett Favre FB/550 10.00 25.00
GC101 David Carr JSY/400 3.00 8.00
GC102 J.Harrington JSY/400 3.00 8.00
GC103 William Green JSY/400 4.00 10.00
GC104 T.J. Duckett JSY/400 3.00 8.00
GC105 Clinton Portis JSY/400 5.00 12.00
GC106 DeShaun Foster JSY/400 5.00 12.00
GC107 Donte Stallworth JSY/400 5.00 12.00
GC108 Ashley Lelie JSY/400 3.00 8.00
GC109 Antw Randle El JSY/400 4.00 10.00
GC110 Jeremy Shockey JSY/400 5.00 12.00

2002 Gridiron Kings Heritage Collection

Inserted at a rate of 1:23, this set features retired NFL greats done with a grey background and player headshot framed with a gold border.
COMPLETE SET (25) 40.00 100.00
STATED ODDS 1:23
HC1 Art Monk 2.00 5.00
HC2 Barry Sanders 3.00 8.00
HC3 Bob Griese 2.00 5.00
HC4 Dan Marino 4.00 10.00
HC5 Dick Butkus 2.50 6.00
HC6 Earl Campbell 2.00 5.00
HC7 Eric Dickerson 1.50 4.00
HC8 Fran Tarkenton 2.00 5.00
HC9 Franco Harris 2.00 5.00
HC10 Herschel Walker 2.00 5.00
HC11 Joe Montana 6.00 15.00
HC12 Ronnie Lott 1.50 4.00
HC13 Joe Theismann 2.00 5.00
HC14 John Elway 3.00 8.00
HC15 John Riggins 1.50 4.00
HC16 Ken Stabler 2.50 6.00
HC17 Len Dawson 2.00 5.00
HC18 Marcus Allen 2.00 5.00
HC19 Mike Singletary 2.00 5.00
HC20 Roger Staubach 2.50 6.00
HC21 Walter Payton 8.00 20.00
HC22 Steve Largent 2.00 5.00
HC23 Terry Bradshaw 2.50 6.00
HC24 Thurman Thomas 1.50 4.00
HC25 Tony Dorsett 2.00 5.00

2002 Gridiron Kings Team Duos

serted at a rate of 1:72, this set features retired and active NFL teammates with a headshot of each player produced in each team's respective colors.
COMPLETE SET (10) 30.00 80.00
STATED ODDS 1:72
TD1 A.Thomas/B.Urlacher 2.50 6.00
TD2 P.Manning/E.James 6.00 15.00
TD3 R.Williams/Z.Thomas 2.00 5.00
TD4 D.Culpepper/R.Moss 2.00 5.00
TD5 D.Carr/J.Gaffney 1.50 4.00
TD6 T.Bradshaw/F.Harris 4.00 10.00
TD7 K.Warner/M.Faulk 2.00 5.00
TD8 R.Staubach/T.Dorsett 4.00 10.00
TD9 S.McNair/E.George 2.00 5.00
TD10 J.Rice/T.Brown 5.00 12.00

2003 Gridiron Kings

Released in October of 2003, this set consists of 175 cards including 100 veterans, 50 rookies, and 25 retired players. Boxes contained 24 packs of 5 cards. Pack SRP was $4.
COMPLETE SET (175) 75.00 150.00
COMP.SET w/o SP's (100) 10.00 25.00
1 David Boston .25 .60
2 Marcel Shipp .25 .60
3 Jake Plummer .25 .60
4 Michael Vick .30 .75
5 T.J. Duckett .25 .60
6 Warrick Dunn .25 .60
7 Ray Lewis .40 1.00
8 Jamal Lewis .30 .75
9 Todd Heap .25 .60
10 Drew Bledsoe .30 .75
11 Eric Moulds .25 .60
12 Travis Henry .25 .60
13 Julius Peppers .40 1.00
14 Steve Smith .40 1.00
15 Muhsin Muhammad .25 .60
16 Anthony Thomas .30 .75
17 David Terrell .25 .60
18 Brian Urlacher .40 1.00
19 Corey Dillon .25 .60
20 Chad Johnson .25 .60
21 William Green .25 .60
22 Tim Couch .25 .60
23 Quincy Morgan .25 .60
24 Roy Williams .25 .60
25 Emmitt Smith .60 1.50
26 Antonio Bryant .25 .60
27 Clinton Portis .25 .60
28 Ashley Lelie .25 .60
29 Rod Smith .30 .75
30 Brian Griese .25 .60
31 Joey Harrington .25 .60
32 James Stewart .25 .60
33 Az-Zahir Hakim .25 .60
34 Brett Favre .75 2.00
35 Ahman Green .30 .75
36 Donald Driver .30 .75
37 Javon Walker .30 .75
38 David Carr .25 .60
39 Jabar Gaffney .25 .60
40 Jonathan Wells .25 .60
41 Edgerrin James .30 .75
42 Marvin Harrison .30 .75
43 Peyton Manning 1.00 2.50
44 Mark Brunell .30 .75
45 Jimmy Smith .30 .75
46 Fred Taylor .25 .60
47 Priest Holmes .25 .60
48 Tony Gonzalez .30 .75
49 Trent Green .25 .60
50 Jay Fiedler .25 .60
51 Chris Chambers .25 .60
52 Zach Thomas .30 .75
53 Ricky Williams .30 .75
54 Randy Moss .30 .75
55 Daunte Culpepper .30 .75
56 Michael Bennett .25 .60
57 Tom Brady 1.50 4.00
58 Deion Branch .25 .60
59 Antowain Smith .30 .75
60 Donte Stallworth .25 .60
61 Deuce McAllister .30 .75
62 Aaron Brooks .25 .60
63 Kerry Collins .25 .60
64 Jeremy Shockey .25 .60
65 Tiki Barber .30 .75
66 Curtis Martin .30 .75
67 Chad Pennington .25 .60
68 Santana Moss .30 .75
69 Jerry Rice .75 2.00
70 Rich Gannon .30 .75
71 Tim Brown .40 1.00
72 Charlie Garner .30 .75
73 Donovan McNabb .30 .75
74 Duce Staley .25 .60
75 Antonio Freeman .30 .75
76 Tommy Maddox .25 .60
77 Jerome Bettis .40 1.00
78 Antwaan Randle El .25 .60
79 Plaxico Burress .25 .60
80 LaDainian Tomlinson .40 1.00
81 Junior Seau .30 .75
82 Drew Brees .40 1.00
83 Terrell Owens .30 .75
84 Jeff Garcia .25 .60
85 Garrison Hearst .25 .60
86 Koren Robinson .30 .75
87 Shaun Alexander .25 .60
88 Trent Dilfer .25 .60
89 Marshall Faulk .30 .75
90 Kurt Warner .30 .75
91 Isaac Bruce .40 1.00
92 Brad Johnson .30 .75
93 Keyshawn Johnson .40 1.00
94 Warren Sapp .30 .75
95 Steve McNair .30 .75
96 Derrick Mason .25 .60
97 Eddie George .30 .75
98 Bruce Smith .30 .75
99 Rod Gardner .25 .60
100 Patrick Ramsey .30 .75
101 Carson Palmer RC 1.25 3.00
102 Byron Leftwich RC .75 2.00
103 Kyle Boller RC .60 1.50
104 Chris Simms RC .60 1.50
105 Dave Ragone RC .60 1.50
106 Rex Grossman RC .75 2.00
107 Brian St.Pierre RC .60 1.50
108 Kliff Kingsbury RC 1.00 2.50
109 Seneca Wallace RC .75 2.00
110 Larry Johnson RC .75 2.00
111 Lee Suggs RC .60 1.50
112 Justin Fargas RC 1.00 2.50
113 Onterrio Smith RC .60 1.50
114 Willis McGahee RC .75 2.00
115 Chris Brown RC .60 1.50
116 Musa Smith RC .60 1.50
117 Artose Pinner RC .60 1.50
118 Domanick Davis RC .75 2.00
119 Charles Rogers RC .75 2.00
120 Andre Johnson RC 1.50 4.00
121 Taylor Jacobs RC .60 1.50
122 Bryant Johnson RC 1.00 2.50
123 Kelley Washington RC .60 1.50
124 Brandon Lloyd RC 1.00 2.50
125 Tyrone Calico RC .60 1.50
126 Kevin Curtis RC .60 1.50
127 Bethel Johnson RC .60 1.50
128 Anquan Boldin RC 1.00 2.50
129 Nate Burleson RC .75 2.00
130 Jason Witten RC 2.50 6.00
131 Bennie Joppru RC .60 1.50
132 Teyo Johnson RC .75 2.00
133 Dallas Clark RC 1.00 2.50
134 Terrell Suggs RC .75 2.00
135 Chris Kelsay RC .75 2.00
136 Jerome McDougle RC .60 1.50
137 Michael Haynes RC .60 1.50
138 Calvin Pace RC .60 1.50
139 Jimmy Kennedy RC .75 2.00
140 Kevin Williams RC 1.00 2.50
141 DeWayne Robertson RC .75 2.00
142 William Joseph RC .60 1.50
143 Johnathan Sullivan RC .60 1.50
144 Boss Bailey RC .75 2.00
145 E.J. Henderson RC .75 2.00
146 Terence Newman RC 1.00 2.50
147 Marcus Trufant RC .75 2.00
148 Andre Woolfolk RC .60 1.50
149 Troy Polamalu RC 10.00 25.00
150 Mike Doss RC 1.00 2.50
151 Andre Reed .75 2.00
152 Bo Jackson 1.25 3.00
153 Dan Marino 2.00 5.00
154 Deacon Jones .75 2.00
155 Deion Sanders .75 2.00
156 Doak Walker 1.00 2.50
157 Don Maynard .75 2.00
158 Frank Gifford 1.00 2.50
159 Fred Biletnikoff 1.00 2.50
160 Gale Sayers 1.00 2.50
161 Jack Lambert 1.00 2.50
162 Jim Brown 1.25 3.00
163 Jim Kelly 1.00 2.50
164 Joe Greene 1.00 2.50
165 Joe Montana 3.00 8.00
166 John Elway 1.50 4.00
167 John Riggins .75 2.00
168 Johnny Unitas 2.00 5.00
169 Larry Csonka 1.00 2.50
170 Lawrence Taylor 1.00 2.50
171 Mike Ditka 1.00 2.50
172 Ozzie Newsome .75 2.00
173 Red Grange 1.00 2.50
174 Troy Aikman 1.25 3.00
175 Warren Moon 1.00 2.50

2003 Gridiron Kings Bronze

*VETS 1-100: 1.5X TO 4X BASIC CARDS
*ROOKIES 101-150: .6X TO 1.5X
*RETIRED 151-175: .8X TO 2X
STATED ODDS 1:6

2003 Gridiron Kings Gold

*VETS 1-100: 6X TO 15X BASIC CARDS
*ROOKIES 101-150: 2X TO 5X
*RETIRED 151-175: 3X TO 8X
STATED PRINT RUN 75 SER.#'d SETS

2003 Gridiron Kings Silver

ETS 1-100: 2.5X TO 6X BASIC CARDS
*ROOKIES 101-150: .8X TO 2X
*RETIRED 151-175: 1.2X TO 3X
STATED PRINT RUN 150 SER.#'d SETS

2003 Gridiron Kings Donruss 1894

ndomly inserted in packs,this set features current and retired NFL stars produced in the style of the 1894 Mayo set. Each card is serial numbered to 600.
COMPLETE SET (25) 40.00 100.00
STATED PRINT RUN 600 SER.#'d SETS
MC26 Michael Vick 1.50 4.00
MC27 Drew Bledsoe 1.50 4.00
MC28 Julius Peppers 2.00 5.00
MC29 Clinton Portis 1.25 3.00
MC30 Ahman Green 1.50 4.00
MC31 David Carr 1.25 3.00
MC32 Marvin Harrison 1.50 4.00
MC33 Priest Holmes 1.25 3.00
MC34 Michael Bennett 1.25 3.00
MC35 Deuce McAllister 1.50 4.00
MC36 Jeremy Shockey 1.25 3.00
MC37 Chad Pennington 1.25 3.00
MC38 Rich Gannon 1.50 4.00
MC39 Donovan McNabb 1.50 4.00
MC40 LaDainian Tomlinson 2.00 5.00
MC41 Jeff Garcia 1.25 3.00
MC42 Steve McNair 1.50 4.00
MC43 Doak Walker 2.00 5.00
MC44 Jim Brown 2.50 6.00
MC45 Jim Kelly 2.00 5.00
MC46 Joe Montana 6.00 15.00
MC47 Carson Palmer 1.25 3.00
MC48 Byron Leftwich .75 2.00
MC49 Charles Rogers 1.50 4.00
MC50 Andre Johnson 1.50 4.00

2003 Gridiron Kings GK Evolution

serted at a rate of 1:23, this set features cards that blend present Gridiron King artwork with the photo that inspired it using lenticular technology similar to past brands of Sportflix.
COMPLETE SET (25) 25.00 60.00
STATED ODDS 1:23
GE1 Michael Vick .75 2.00
GE2 Travis Henry .60 1.50
GE3 Emmitt Smith 1.50 4.00
GE4 Clinton Portis .60 1.50
GE5 Joey Harrington .60 1.50
GE6 Brett Favre 2.00 5.00
GE7 David Carr .60 1.50
GE8 Peyton Manning 2.50 6.00
GE9 Priest Holmes .60 1.50
GE10 Ricky Williams .75 2.00
GE11 Randy Moss .75 2.00
GE12 Deuce McAllister .75 2.00
GE13 Jeremy Shockey .60 1.50
GE14 Chad Pennington .60 1.50
GE15 Jerry Rice 2.00 5.00
GE16 Donovan McNabb .75 2.00
GE17 Plaxico Burress .60 1.50
GE18 LaDainian Tomlinson 1.00 2.50
GE19 Terrell Owens .75 2.00
GE20 Shaun Alexander .60 1.50
GE21 Marshall Faulk .75 2.00
GE22 Warren Sapp .75 2.00
GE23 Eddie George .75 2.00
GE24 Dan Marino 2.00 5.00
GE25 John Elway 1.50 4.00

2003 Gridiron Kings Gridiron Cut Collection

ndomly inserted in packs, this set features cards with either an authentic player autograph, game used material, or both. Cards GC1-GC40 feature authentic player autograph stickers with silver foil and are serial numbered to varying quantities. Cards GC41-GC80 feature game worn jersey swatches with silver foil and are serial numbered to varying quantities. Cards GC81-GC90 feature game used football swatches with silver foil and are serial numbered to 275. Cards GC91-GC100 feature a game worn jersey swatch, an authentic player autograph sticker, and are serial numbered to 50.
GC1-GC23 RETIRED AU PRINT RUN 24-200
GC26-GC40 ROOKIE AU PRINT RUN 25-250
GC41-GC80 JSY PRINT RUN 225-475
GC81-GC90 FB PRINT RUN 275
GC91-GC100 JSY AU PRINT RUN 50
GC1 Andre Reed AU/200 10.00 25.00
GC2 Bo Jackson AU/100 40.00 80.00
GC3 Dan Marino AU/25 60.00 150.00
GC4 Deacon Jones AU/100 12.00 30.00
GC5 Deion Sanders AU/25 40.00 100.00
GC6 Don Maynard AU/100 12.00 30.00
GC7 Frank Gifford AU/100 20.00 50.00
GC8 Fred Biletnikoff AU/100 20.00 50.00
GC9 Gale Sayers AU/100 25.00 50.00
GC10 Jack Lambert AU/150 50.00 100.00
GC11 Jim Brown AU/50 40.00 80.00
GC12 Jim Kelly AU/25 60.00 120.00
GC13 Joe Greene AU/150 25.00 50.00
GC14 Joe Montana AU/50 75.00 150.00
GC15 John Elway AU/24 60.00 150.00
GC16 John Riggins AU/50 40.00 80.00
GC17 Johnny Unitas AU/40 200.00 350.00
GC18 Larry Csonka AU/100 25.00 60.00
GC19 Lawrence Taylor AU/100 30.00 50.00
GC20 Mike Ditka AU/100 20.00 40.00
GC21 Ozzie Newsome AU/100 10.00 25.00
GC22 Troy Aikman AU/25 60.00 120.00
GC23 Warren Moon AU/100 12.00 30.00
GC25 Bennie Joppru AU/250 5.00 12.00
GC26 Boss Bailey AU/250 6.00 15.00
GC27 Brian St.Pierre AU/250 5.00 12.00
GC28 Bryant Johnson AU/150 8.00 20.00
GC29 Jimmy Kennedy AU/250 6.00 15.00
GC30 Chris Kelsay AU/250 6.00 15.00
GC31 Dallas Clark AU/250 8.00 20.00
GC33 Brandon Lloyd AU/250 8.00 20.00
GC34 Kelley Washington AU/107 5.00 12.00
GC35 Lee Suggs AU/250 5.00 12.00
GC36 Mike Doss AU/250 8.00 20.00
GC37 Onterrio Smith AU/150 5.00 12.00
GC38 Terrell Suggs AU/100 15.00 30.00
GC39 Tyrone Calico AU/150 5.00 12.00
GC40 Carson Palmer AU/25 60.00 120.00
GC41 David Boston JSY/475 2.50 6.00
GC42 T.J. Duckett JSY/275 2.50 6.00
GC43 Jamal Lewis JSY/375 3.00 8.00
GC44 Eric Moulds JSY/375 2.50 6.00
GC45 Travis Henry JSY/375 2.50 6.00
GC46 David Terrell JSY/375 2.50 6.00
GC47 Anthony Thomas JSY/375 3.00 8.00
GC48 Corey Dillon JSY/475 2.50 6.00
GC49 Tim Couch JSY/475 2.50 6.00
GC50 Emmitt Smith JSY/375 6.00 15.00
GC51 Antonio Bryant JSY/375 2.50 6.00
GC52 Clinton Portis JSY/275 2.50 6.00
GC53 Joey Harrington JSY/375 2.50 6.00
GC54 Brett Favre JSY/275 8.00 20.00
GC55 Javon Walker JSY/475 3.00 8.00
GC56 Edgerrin James JSY/375 3.00 8.00
GC57 Peyton Manning JSY/375 10.00 25.00
GC58 Fred Taylor JSY/475 2.50 6.00
GC59 Priest Holmes JSY/375 2.50 6.00
GC60 Trent Green JSY/475 2.50 6.00
GC61 Ricky Williams JSY/275 3.00 8.00
GC62 Randy Moss JSY/275 3.00 8.00
GC63 Jeremy Shockey JSY/375 2.50 6.00
GC64 Tiki Barber JSY/475 3.00 8.00
GC65 Santana Moss JSY/375 3.00 8.00
GC66 Curtis Martin JSY/375 3.00 8.00
GC67 Rich Gannon JSY/275 3.00 8.00
GC68 Donovan McNabb JSY/475 3.00 8.00
GC69 Duce Staley JSY/475 2.50 6.00
GC70 Jerome Bettis JSY/475 5.00 12.00
GC71 Antwaan Randle El JSY/375 2.50 6.00
GC72 LaD Tomlinson JSY/375 4.00 10.00
GC73 Junior Seau JSY/475 3.00 8.00
GC74 Terrell Owens JSY/375 3.00 8.00
GC75 Jeff Garcia JSY/275 2.50 6.00
GC76 Marshall Faulk JSY/275 3.00 8.00
GC77 Kurt Warner JSY/375 3.00 8.00
GC78 Warren Sapp JSY/375 3.00 8.00
GC79 Troy Aikman JSY/225 12.50 25.00
GC80 Joe Montana JSY/225 15.00 40.00
GC81 LaD Tomlinson FB/275 4.00 10.00
GC82 Jeremy Shockey FB/275 2.50 6.00
GC83 Antonio Bryant FB/275 2.50 6.00
GC84 Marshall Faulk FB/275 3.00 8.00
GC85 Jerry Rice FB/275 8.00 20.00
GC86 Joey Harrington FB/275 2.50 6.00
GC87 Jeff Garcia FB/275 2.50 6.00
GC88 Marvin Harrison FB/275 3.00 8.00
GC89 Rod Smith FB/275 3.00 8.00
GC90 Charlie Garner FB/275 3.00 8.00
GC91 Deacon Jones JSY AU/50 20.00 50.00
GC92 Don Maynard JSY AU/50 25.00 60.00
GC93 Fred Biletnikoff JSY AU/50 40.00 80.00
GC94 Jim Brown JSY AU/50 60.00 120.00
GC95 Jim Kelly JSY AU/50 50.00 100.00
GC96 Joe Montana JSY AU/50 75.00 150.00
GC97 John Riggins JSY AU/50 40.00 80.00
GC98 Ozzie Newsome JSY AU/50 15.00 40.00
GC99 Warren Moon JSY AU/50 20.00 50.00
GC100 Kurt Warner JSY AU/50 40.00 80.00

2003 Gridiron Kings Heritage Collection

serted at a rate of 1:23, this set highlights retired superstars. Each card features silver holofoil on canvas.
COMPLETE SET (25) 25.00 60.00
STATED ODDS 1:23
HC1 Andre Reed .75 2.00
HC2 Bo Jackson 1.25 3.00
HC3 Dan Marino 2.00 5.00
HC4 Deacon Jones .75 2.00
HC5 Deion Sanders .75 2.00
HC6 Doak Walker 1.00 2.50
HC7 Don Maynard .75 2.00
HC8 Frank Gifford 1.00 2.50
HC9 Fred Biletnikoff 1.00 2.50
HC10 Gale Sayers 1.00 2.50
HC11 Jack Lambert 1.00 2.50
HC12 Jim Brown 1.25 3.00
HC13 Jim Kelly 1.00 2.50
HC14 Joe Greene 1.00 2.50
HC15 Joe Montana 3.00 8.00
HC16 John Elway 1.50 4.00
HC17 John Riggins .75 2.00
HC18 Johnny Unitas 2.00 5.00
HC19 Larry Csonka 1.00 2.50
HC20 Lawrence Taylor 1.00 2.50
HC21 Mike Ditka 1.00 2.50
HC22 Ozzie Newsome .75 2.00
HC23 Red Grange 1.00 2.50
HC24 Troy Aikman 1.25 3.00
HC25 Warren Moon 1.00 2.50

2003 Gridiron Kings Royal Expectations

Inserted 1:23, this set highlights top 2003 rookies. Each cards features gold foil on canvas.
COMPLETE SET (15) 20.00 50.00
STATED ODDS 1:23
RE1 Andre Johnson 1.50 4.00
RE2 Byron Leftwich .75 2.00
RE3 Carson Palmer 1.25 3.00
RE4 Bryant Johnson 1.00 2.50
RE5 Chris Brown .60 1.50
RE6 Dallas Clark 1.00 2.50
RE7 Justin Fargas 1.00 2.50
RE8 Kelley Washington .60 1.50
RE9 Kyle Boller .60 1.50
RE10 Larry Johnson .75 2.00
RE11 Willis McGahee .75 2.00
RE12 Terence Newman 1.00 2.50
RE13 Rex Grossman .75 2.00
RE14 Taylor Jacobs .60 1.50
RE15 Terrell Suggs .75 2.00

2003 Gridiron Kings Royal Expectations Materials Gold

Inserted 1:52, this set highlights top 2003 rookies. Each card features crown shaped event worn jersey swatches
STATED ODDS 1:52
*SILVER: .4X TO 1X GOLD
SILVERS FEATURE SQUARE SWATCHES
RE1 Andre Johnson 5.00 12.00
RE2 Byron Leftwich 2.50 6.00
RE3 Carson Palmer 4.00 10.00
RE4 Bryant Johnson 3.00 8.00
RE5 Chris Brown 2.00 5.00
RE6 Dallas Clark 3.00 8.00
RE7 Justin Fargas 3.00 8.00
RE8 Kelley Washington 2.00 5.00
RE9 Kyle Boller 2.00 5.00
RE10 Larry Johnson 2.50 6.00
RE11 Willis McGahee 2.50 6.00
RE12 Terence Newman 3.00 8.00
RE13 Rex Grossman 2.50 6.00
RE14 Taylor Jacobs 2.00 5.00
RE15 Terrell Suggs 2.50 6.00

2003 Gridiron Kings Team Timeline

Randomly inserted in packs, this set features two players from different eras who starred for the same team. Each card features silver foil on canvas and is serial numbered to 600.
COMPLETE SET (10) 20.00 50.00
PRINT RUN 600 SERIAL #'d SETS
TT1 D.Marino/J.Fiedler 3.00 8.00
TT2 D.Sanders/Roy.Williams 1.25 3.00
TT3 D.Walker/J.Harrington 1.50 4.00
TT4 F.Biletnikoff/T.Brown 1.50 4.00
TT5 G.Sayers/A.Thomas 1.50 4.00
TT6 J.Brown/W.Green 2.00 5.00
TT7 J.Montana/J.Garcia 5.00 12.00
TT8 J.Unitas/P.Manning 4.00 10.00
TT9 L.Csonka/Ric.Williams 1.50 4.00
TT10 W.Moon/D.Carr 1.50 4.00

2003 Gridiron Kings Team Timeline Materials

Randomly inserted in packs, this set features two game worn swatches. Each card is serial numbered to 100.
PRINT RUN 100 SERIAL #'d SETS
TT1 D.Marino/J.Fiedler 12.00 30.00
TT2 D.Sanders/Roy.Williams 10.00 25.00
TT3 D.Walker/J.Harrington 15.00 40.00
TT4 F.Biletnikoff/T.Brown 6.00 15.00
TT5 G.Sayers/A.Thomas 6.00 15.00
TT6 J.Brown/W.Green 8.00 20.00
TT7 J.Montana/J.Garcia 20.00 50.00
TT8 J.Unitas/P.Manning 15.00 40.00
TT9 L.Csonka/Ric.Williams 6.00 15.00
TT10 W.Moon/D.Carr 6.00 15.00

2015 Gridiron Kings

1 Chris Ivory .25 .60
2 Mark Ingram .25 .60
3A Odell Beckham Jr. .30 .75
3B Odell Beckham Jr. SP 8.00 20.00
4 Johnny Manziel .25 .60
5 Ryan Tannehill .25 .60
6 Andre Johnson .25 .60
7 Anquan Boldin .20 .50
8A Peyton Manning .60 1.50
8B Peyton Manning SP 10.00 25.00
9 LeGarrette Blount .25 .60
10 Delanie Walker .20 .50
11A Tom Brady .75 2.00
11B Tom Brady SP 12.00 30.00
12 Ndamukong Suh .25 .60
13 Demaryius Thomas .25 .60
14 Frank Gore .25 .60
15 Philip Rivers .30 .75
16 Ben Roethlisberger .30 .75
17 DeMarco Murray .25 .60
18 Sammy Watkins .25 .60
19 Luke Kuechly .25 .60
20 Eddie Lacy .20 .50
21 Geno Smith .20 .50
22A Dez Bryant .30 .75
22B Dez Bryant SP
23 Matthew Stafford .25 .60
24 Jeremy Hill .20 .50
25 Kelvin Benjamin .25 .60
26 Jordy Nelson .25 .60
27 Tavon Austin .20 .50
28 Justin Forsett .25 .60
29 Isaiah Crowell .20 .50
30 Russell Wilson .40 1.00
31 Antonio Gates .20 .50
32 Latavius Murray .20 .50
33 Kendall Wright .20 .50
34 Alex Smith .25 .60
35 Keenan Allen .25 .60
36A Julio Jones .30 .75
36B Julio Jones SP
37 DeMarcus Ware .25 .60
38 Jarvis Landry .25 .60
39 Andy Dalton .25 .60
40 Jason Witten .25 .60
41A J.J. Watt .30 .75
41B J.J. Watt SP 4.00 10.00
42 Nick Foles .25 .60
43 Eli Manning .25 .60
44 Matt Ryan .25 .60
45 Mike Wallace .20 .50
46 Mike Evans .25 .60
47 Julian Edelman .30 .75
48 Rob Gronkowski .30 .75
49 Larry Fitzgerald .25 .60
50 Joseph Randle .20 .50
51 Le'Veon Bell .25 .60
52 Adrian Peterson .30 .75
53 Robert Griffin III .20 .50
54 Steve Smith .25 .60
55 Richard Sherman .30 .75
56 Marqise Lee .20 .50
57 Bishop Sankey .20 .50
58 Matt Forte .20 .50
59 Calvin Johnson .30 .75
60 DeSean Jackson .25 .60
61 Derek Carr .30 .75
62 Marshawn Lynch .25 .60
63A Aaron Rodgers .60 1.50
63B Aaron Rodgers SP 8.00 20.00
64 A.J. Green .30 .75
65 Arian Foster .25 .60
66 Tony Romo .25 .60
67 Doug Martin .25 .60
68 Alshon Jeffery .25 .60
69 Andre Ellington .20 .50
70 Teddy Bridgewater .25 .60
71 Jason Pierre-Paul .20 .50
72 Jeremy Maclin .20 .50
73 Carlos Hyde .20 .50
74 LeSean McCoy .30 .75
75 Jay Cutler .20 .50
76 Carson Palmer .25 .60
77 Taylor Gabriel .20 .50
78 Devonta Freeman .25 .60
79 Antonio Brown .30 .75
80 Sam Bradford .20 .50
81 Mario Williams .20 .50
82 Jamaal Charles .25 .60
83 T.Y. Hilton .25 .60
84A Andrew Luck .40 1.00
84B Andrew Luck SP
85 Marques Colston .20 .50
86 Colin Kaepernick .25 .60
87 Brandon Marshall .20 .50
88 Robert Quinn .25 .60
89 Joe Flacco .25 .60
90 Joique Bell .20 .50
91 DeAndre Hopkins .25 .60
92 Drew Brees .30 .75
93 Blake Bortles .20 .50
94 Gerald McCoy .20 .50
95A Cam Newton .30 .75
95B Cam Newton SP
96 Jordan Matthews .25 .60
97 Alfred Morris .20 .50
98 Paul Posluszny .20 .50
99A Charles Woodson .30 .75
99B Charles Woodson SP 4.00 10.00
100 C.J. Anderson .25 .60
101 Jameis Winston RC .60 1.50
102 Todd Gurley RC 1.00 2.50
103 Kevin White RC .30 .75
104 Nelson Agholor RC .30 .75
105 Phillip Dorsett RC .25 .60
106 Bryce Petty RC .25 .60
107 T.J. Yeldon RC .25 .60
108 Devin Funchess RC .40 1.00
109 Dorial Green-Beckham RC .25 .60
110 Jaelen Strong RC .30 .75
111 Garrett Grayson RC .25 .60
112 Tevin Coleman RC .30 .75
113 Jay Ajayi RC .40 1.00
114 Matt Jones RC .25 .60
115 Sammie Coates RC .30 .75
116 Leonard Williams RC .25 .60
117 Buck Allen RC .30 .75
118 Ty Montgomery RC .25 .60
119 Vince Mayle RC .30 .75
120 Rashad Greene RC .25 .60
121 Maxx Williams RC .25 .60
122 Mike Davis RC .25 .60
123 Jamison Crowder RC .30 .75
124 Justin Hardy RC .25 .60
125 Stefon Diggs RC .60 1.50
126 Sean Mannion RC .25 .60
127 David Johnson RC .60 1.50
128 Duke Johnson RC .40 1.00
129 Jeremy Langford RC .25 .60
130 Chris Conley RC .25 .60
131 Brett Hundley RC .25 .60
132 Ameer Abdullah RC .40 1.00
133 David Cobb RC .25 .60
134 Devin Smith RC .25 .60
135 Tyler Lockett RC .40 1.00
136 Marcus Mariota RC 1.00 2.50
137 Melvin Gordon RC .60 1.50
138 Amari Cooper RC .75 2.00
139 DeVante Parker RC .40 1.00
140 Breshad Perriman RC .25 .60
141 Karlos Williams RC .25 .60
142 Kevin Johnson RC .25 .60
143 Cameron Artis-Payne RC .25 .60
144 Marcus Peters RC .40 1.00
145 Shane Ray RC .25 .60
146 Shaq Thompson RC .30 .75
147 Stephone Anthony RC .25 .60
148 Trae Waynes RC .25 .60
149 Vic Beasley Jr. RC .30 .75
150 Clive Walford RC .25 .60
151 Markus Golden RC .25 .60
152 Nate Orchard RC .25 .60
153 Preston Smith RC .30 .75
154 Quinten Rollins RC .50 1.25
155 Randy Gregory RC .25 .60
156 Nick O'Leary RC .25 .60
157 Bud Dupree RC .30 .75
158 Kenny Bell RC .40 1.00
159 Tony Lippett RC .25 .60
160 Tre McBride RC .25 .60
161 Michael Irvin LL .60 1.50
162 Terry Bradshaw LL .75 2.00
163 Earl Campbell LL .60 1.50
164 Gale Sayers LL .60 1.50
165 Joe Greene LL .60 1.50
166 Bo Jackson LL .75 2.00
167 Jim Kelly LL .60 1.50
168 John Elway LL 1.00 2.50
169 Joe Namath LL .75 2.00
170 Jerome Bettis LL .60 1.50
171 Barry Sanders LL 1.00 2.50
172 John Stallworth LL .50 1.25
173 Marshall Faulk LL .50 1.25
174 Dan Marino LL 1.25 3.00
175 Tim Brown LL .60 1.50
176 Steve Young LL .75 2.00
177 Tony Dorsett LL .60 1.50
178 Troy Aikman LL .75 2.00
179 Deion Sanders LL .50 1.25
180 Walter Payton LL 1.25 3.00
181 Peyton Manning SK 1.25 3.00
182 Marcus Allen SK .60 1.50
183 Warren Moon SK .60 1.50
184 Joe Theismann SK .60 1.50
185 Steve Largent SK .60 1.50
186 Steve Young SK .75 2.00
187 Marshall Faulk SK .50 1.25
188 Troy Aikman SK .75 2.00
189 Barry Sanders SK 1.00 2.50
190 Eric Dickerson SK .50 1.25
191 Franco Harris SK .60 1.50
192 Don Majkowski SK .50 1.25
193 Fran Tarkenton SK .60 1.50
194 Rod Woodson SK .50 1.25
195 Paul Hornung SK .60 1.50
196 Joe Montana SK 1.50 4.00
197 Brett Favre SK 1.25 3.00
198 Andrew Luck SK .75 2.00
199 Jerry Rice SK 1.00 2.50
200 Tom Brady SK 1.50 4.00

2015 Gridiron Kings Framed Blue

*VETS (1-100): 1X TO 2.5X BASIC CARDS
*ROOKIES (101-160): 1X TO 2.5X BASIC CARDS
*VETS (161-200): .8X TO 2X BASIC CARDS

2015 Gridiron Kings Framed Green

*VETS (1-100): 2X TO 5X BASIC CARDS
*ROOKIES (101-160): 1.5X TO 4X BASIC CARDS
*VETS (161-200): 1.2X TO 3X BASIC CARDS

2015 Gridiron Kings Framed Red

*VETS (1-100): .6X TO 1.5X BASIC CARDS
*ROOKIES (101-160): .75X TO 2X BASIC CARDS
*LEGENDS (161-200): .6X TO 1.5X BASIC CARDS

2015 Gridiron Kings Aficionado

A1 DeMarco Murray .50 1.25
A2 Drew Brees .60 1.50
A3 Odell Beckham Jr. .60 1.50
A4 J.J. Watt .60 1.50
A5 Jeremy Hill .40 1.00
A6 Emmanuel Sanders .50 1.25
A7 Mike Evans .50 1.25
A8 Richard Sherman .60 1.50
A9 Jordy Nelson .50 1.25
A10 Cordarrelle Patterson .40 1.00
A11 Devin Hester .50 1.25
A12 Fred Jackson .50 1.25
A13 Ryan Tannehill .50 1.25
A14 Matt Forte .40 1.00
A15 Antonio Brown .60 1.50
A16 Larry Fitzgerald .50 1.25
A17 Knile Davis .40 1.00
A18 Steve Smith .50 1.25
A19 Dez Bryant .60 1.50
A20 Amari Cooper 1.25 3.00

2015 Gridiron Kings AKA

AKA1 Walter Payton 1.25 3.00
AKA2 Deion Sanders .50 1.25
AKA3 Joe Namath .75 2.00
AKA4 Calvin Johnson .60 1.50
AKA5 Peyton Manning 1.25 3.00
AKA6 Ben Roethlisberger .60 1.50
AKA7 Tyrann Mathieu .50 1.25
AKA8 Rob Gronkowski .60 1.50
AKA9 Matt Ryan .50 1.25
AKA10 Mario Williams .40 1.00
AKA11 Tom Brady 1.50 4.00
AKA12 LeSean McCoy .60 1.50
AKA13 Adrian Peterson .60 1.50

AKA14 Robert Griffin III .40 1.00
AKA15 Jerome Bettis .60 1.50
AKA16 Joe Montana 1.50 4.00
AKA17 Johnny Manziel .50 1.25
AKA18 Cam Newton .60 1.50
AKA19 Marshawn Lynch .50 1.25
AKA20 Jameis Winston 1.00 2.50

2015 Gridiron Kings All Time Stat Kings Autographs

1 Peyton Manning/15
5 Steve Largent/25 20.00 40.00
10 Eric Dickerson/15 20.00 40.00
11 Franco Harris/15 30.00 60.00
13 Fran Tarkenton/25
14 Rod Woodson/26 15.00 30.00
15 Paul Hornung/49 10.00 25.00

2015 Gridiron Kings Art Nouveau Materials

*PRIME/49: .6X TO 1.5X BASIC JSY/249
ANAA Ameer Abdullah 2.00 5.00
ANAC Amari Cooper 4.00 10.00
ANBA Buck Allen 1.50 4.00
ANBG Brett Hundley 1.25 3.00
ANBR Bryce Petty 1.25 3.00
ANBP Breshad Perriman 1.25 3.00
ANCC Chris Conley 1.25 3.00
ANDC David Cobb 1.25 3.00
ANDF Devin Funchess 2.00 5.00
ANDGB Dorial Green-Beckham 1.25 3.00
ANDJ David Johnson 3.00 8.00
ANDP DeVante Parker 2.00 5.00
ANDS Devin Smith 1.25 3.00
ANDU Duke Johnson 2.00 5.00
ANGG Garrett Grayson 1.25 3.00
ANJA Jay Ajayi 2.00 5.00
ANJC Jamison Crowder 1.50 4.00
ANJH Justin Hardy 1.25 3.00
ANJL Jeremy Langford 1.25 3.00
ANJS Jaelen Strong 1.50 4.00
ANJW Jameis Winston 3.00 8.00
ANKA Karlos Williams 1.25 3.00
ANKW Kevin White 1.50 4.00
ANLW Leonard Williams 1.25 3.00
ANMD Mike Davis 1.25 3.00
ANMG Melvin Gordon 3.00 8.00
ANMJ Matt Jones 1.25 3.00
ANMM Marcus Mariota 5.00 12.00
ANMW Maxx Williams 1.25 3.00
ANNA Nelson Agholor 1.50 4.00
ANPD Phillip Dorsett 1.25 3.00
ANRD Rashad Greene 1.25 3.00
ANSC Sammie Coates 1.50 4.00
ANSD Stefon Diggs 3.00 8.00
ANSM Sean Mannion 1.25 3.00
ANTC Tevin Coleman 1.50 4.00
ANTG Todd Gurley 4.00 10.00
ANTL Tyler Lockett 2.00 5.00
ANTM Ty Montgomery 1.25 3.00
ANTY T.J. Yeldon 1.25 3.00
ANVM Vince Mayle 1.50 4.00

2015 Gridiron Kings Expressionists

EX1 J.J. Watt .60 1.50
EX2 Cam Newton .60 1.50
EX3 Johnny Manziel .50 1.25
EX4 Jameis Winston 1.00 2.50
EX5 Terrell Davis .50 1.25
EX6 Tom Brady 1.50 4.00
EX7 Aaron Rodgers 1.25 3.00
EX8 Deion Sanders .50 1.25
EX9 Amari Cooper 1.25 3.00
EX10 Tim Tebow .50 1.25
EX11 Antonio Brown .60 1.50
EX12 Devin Hester .50 1.25
EX13 Leonard Williams .40 1.00
EX14 Odell Beckham Jr. .60 1.50
EX15 Dez Bryant .60 1.50
EX16 Colin Kaepernick .50 1.25
EX17 Clay Matthews .60 1.50
EX18 LaDainian Tomlinson .50 1.25
EX19 Andrew Luck .75 2.00
EX20 Russell Wilson .75 2.00

2015 Gridiron Kings Gridiron Art Autographs

GAAA Ameer Abdullah/25 5.00 12.00
GACC Chris Conley/125 2.00 5.00
GADC Tevin Coleman/125 2.50 6.00
GADF Devin Funchess/25 5.00 12.00
GADJ David Johnson/99 5.00 12.00
GADP DeVante Parker/99 3.00 8.00
GADS Devin Smith/99 2.00 5.00
GAMJ Matt Jones/125 2.00 5.00
GANA Nelson Agholor/49 3.00 8.00
GATL Tyler Lockett/125 3.00 8.00
GATY T.J. Yeldon/125 2.00 5.00
GAVM Vince Mayle/125 2.50 6.00

2015 Gridiron Kings Gridiron Art Autographs Framed Red

*RED/49: .5X TO 1.2X BASIC AU/99-125
*RED/25: .6X TO 1.5X BASIC AU/99-125
*RED/25: .5X TO 1.2X BASIC AU/49
*RED/15: .5X TO 1.2X BASIC AU/25
GAAA Ameer Abdullah/15 6.00 15.00
GAJW Jameis Winston/35
GAMM Marcus Mariota/25 30.00 60.00

2015 Gridiron Kings Gridiron Kings Dual Jerseys

*PRIME/49: .6X TO 1.5X BASIC JSY/249
*PRIME/20: .8X TO 2X BASIC JSY/249
*PRIME/99: .6X TO 1.5X BASIC JSY/99
DJAABS A.Abdullah/B.Sanders/49 6.00 15.00
DJAEDJ A.Ellington/D.Johnson/249 4.00 10.00
DJALTY A.Luck/T.Hilton/199 3.00 8.00
DJARTM A.Rodgers/T.Montgomery/25 30.00 60.00
DJBPSS B.Perriman/S.Smith/85 2.50 6.00
DJCNDF C.Newton/D.Funchess/249 2.50 6.00
DJESTA E.Smith/T.Aikman/50 20.00 40.00
DJJEPM J.Elway/P.Manning/99 15.00 30.00
DJJKTT J.Kelly/T.Thomas/99 10.00 25.00
DJJMJR J.Rice/J.Montana/50 30.00 60.00
DJJTJR J.Theismann/J.Riggins/99 12.00 30.00
DJJWME J.Winston/M.Evans/249 4.00 10.00
DJLTMG L.Tomlinson/M.Gordon/99 5.00 12.00
DJMFTG M.Faulk/T.Gurley/149
DJMMDJB D.Green-Beckham/M.Mariota/249 6.00 15.00
DJTBAC A.Cooper/T.Brown/249 5.00 12.00
DJWMEC E.Campbell/W.Moon/99 3.00 8.00

2015 Gridiron Kings Heir Apparent Autographs

HAAA Arik Armstead/99 2.00 5.00
HABM Barkevious Mingo/49 5.00 12.00
HABO Branden Oliver/99 5.00 12.00
HACAP Cameron Artis-Payne/99 2.00 5.00
HADC Derek Carr/25 10.00 25.00
HADH Danielle Hunter/99 2.50 6.00
HAEK Eric Kendricks/99 4.00 10.00
HAJG Jimmy Garoppolo/99 8.00 20.00
HAJM Jordan Matthews/25 8.00 20.00
HAJT Julius Thomas/25 6.00 15.00
HALM Latavius Murray/99 4.00 10.00
HAMB Martavis Bryant/49 5.00 12.00
HAMP Marcus Peters/25 10.00 25.00
HAPD Paul Dawson/49 6.00 15.00
HASA Stephone Anthony/99 4.00 10.00
HASR Shane Ray/99 2.00 5.00
HAST Shaq Thompson/99 2.50 6.00
HAVB Vic Beasley Jr./99 2.50 6.00

2015 Gridiron Kings Impressionist Ink

*BLUE/49: .6X TO 1.5X BASIC AU/199-249
*BLUE/49: .5X TO 1.2X BASIC AU/99
*BLUE/25: .8X TO 2X BASIC AU/199
IIBB Bryce Petty/15 50.00
IIDP DeVante Parker/99 6.00 15.00
IIDS Devin Smith/199 1.50 4.00
IIDU Duke Johnson/199 2.50 6.00
IIJA Jay Ajayi/99 3.00 8.00
IIJL Jeremy Langford/249 1.50 4.00
IIJH Justin Hardy/249 1.50 4.00
IIMJ Matt Jones/199 8.00 20.00
IIMD Mike Davis/249 1.50 4.00
IIRG Rashad Greene/249 1.50 4.00
IISC Sammie Coates/199 2.00 5.00
IISM Sean Mannion/199 1.50 4.00
IITY T.J. Yeldon/199 1.50 4.00
IITL Tyler Lockett/199 2.50 6.00
IIVM Vince Mayle/249 2.00 5.00
IIAG Antwan Goodley/199 1.50 4.00
IIBD Bud Dupree/249 2.00 5.00
IITH Taylor Heinicke/249 2.50 6.00
IISH Shane Carden/199 1.50 4.00
IIDA Dres Anderson/249 1.50 4.00
IILC Landon Collins/249 2.00 5.00
IIBB Bryan Bennett/249 6.00 15.00
IIDF Devin Funchess/99 3.00 8.00
IICC Chris Conley/199 3.00 8.00

2015 Gridiron Kings Masters of the Game Materials

*PRIME/49: .6X TO 1.5X BASIC JSY/249
*PRIME/25-28: .8X TO 2X BASIC JSY/149-249
*PRIME/49: .3X TO .8X BASIC JSY/18
MOGAB Antonio Brown/249 4.00 10.00
MOGAB Anthony Barr/249 2.50 6.00
MOGAD Andy Dalton/249 3.00 8.00
MOGAG A.J. Green/49 6.00 15.00
MOGAJ Alshon Jeffery/249 3.00 8.00
MOGAM Alfred Morris/249 2.50 6.00
MOGAP Adrian Peterson/125 5.00 12.00
MOGAW Andre Williams/249 2.50 6.00
MOGBB Blake Bortles/249 2.50 6.00
MOGBC Brandin Cooks/249 3.00 8.00
MOGCH Carlos Hyde/249 2.50 6.00
MOGCK Colin Kaepernick/35 5.00 12.00
MOGDA Davante Adams/249 3.00 8.00
MOGDC Derek Carr/249 4.00 10.00
MOGDH Devin Hester/249 3.00 8.00
MOGDM Donte Moncrief/249 3.00 8.00
MOGDP Dontari Poe/249 2.50 6.00
MOGDT Demaryius Thomas/18 6.00 15.00
MOGDW Delanie Walker/249 2.50 6.00
MOGED Eric Decker/249 2.50 6.00
MOGEE Eric Ebron/249 2.50 6.00
MOGES Emmanuel Sanders/249 3.00 8.00
MOGJH Jeremy Hill/249 2.50 6.00
MOGJM Jordan Matthews/249 3.00 8.00
MOGJR Joseph Randle/249 2.50 6.00
MOGKB Kelvin Benjamin/249 3.00 8.00
MOGKD Knile Davis/249 2.50 6.00
MOGKM Khalil Mack/249 4.00 10.00
MOGLB Le'Veon Bell/199 3.00 8.00
MOGME Mike Evans/249 3.00 8.00
MOGMI Mark Ingram/49 5.00 12.00
MOGMS Matthew Stafford/25 6.00 15.00
MOGOBJ Odell Beckham Jr./249 4.00 10.00
MOGPM Peyton Manning/249 8.00 20.00
MOGRT Ryan Tannehill/99 4.00 10.00
MOGSW Sammy Watkins/249 3.00 8.00
MOGTB Teddy Bridgewater/249 3.00 8.00
MOGTR Tony Romo/149 3.00 8.00
MOGVM Von Miller/249 3.00 8.00

2015 Gridiron Kings New Aesthetic

1 Jeremy Hill .40 1.00
2 Jason Witten .50 1.25
3 Eddie Lacy .40 1.00
4 T.Y. Hilton .50 1.25
5 Todd Gurley 1.50 4.00
6 Jamaal Charles .50 1.25
7 Teddy Bridgewater .50 1.25
8 Melvin Gordon 1.00 2.50
9 Rob Gronkowski .60 1.50
10 Odell Beckham Jr. .60 1.50
11 Amari Cooper 1.25 3.00
12 Le'Veon Bell .50 1.25
13 Demaryius Thomas .50 1.25
14 Golden Tate .40 1.00
15 Arian Foster .50 1.25
16 Justin Forsett .50 1.25
17 Alshon Jeffery .50 1.25
18 Sammy Watkins .50 1.25
19 Cam Newton .60 1.50
20 Ryan Tannehill .50 1.25

2015 Gridiron Kings Performance Art Materials

*PRIME/45-49: .6X TO 1.5X BASIC JSY/199-249
*PRIME/25: .6X TO 1.5X BASIC JSY/99
*PRIME/25: .5X TO 1.2X BASIC JSY/49
*PRIME/17: X TO X BASIC JSY/50
*PRIME/15: .8X TO 2X BASIC JSY/99
*PRIME/15: .5X TO 1.2X BASIC JSY/25
PAAB Antonio Brown/25 6.00 15.00
PAAD Andy Dalton/99 3.00 8.00
PAAJ Alshon Jeffery/249 2.50 6.00
PAAL Andrew Luck/25 8.00 20.00
PACJ Calvin Johnson/25 6.00 15.00
PACK Colin Kaepernick/249 2.50 6.00
PACN Cam Newton/149 3.00 8.00
PADC Derek Carr/249 3.00 8.00
PAJJ Julio Jones/49 5.00 12.00
PAOBJ Odell Beckham Jr./249 3.00 8.00
PAPM Peyton Manning/99 12.00 30.00
PAPR Philip Rivers/50 5.00 12.00
PATB Teddy Bridgewater/199 2.50 6.00
PATW Terrance Williams/49 3.00 8.00

2015 Gridiron Kings Rookie Portraits Materials

*PRIME/49: .6X TO 1.5X BASIC JSY/249
RPMAA Ameer Abdullah 2.00 5.00
RPMBH Brett Hundley 1.25 3.00
RPMBP Breshad Perriman 1.25 3.00
RPMBR Bryce Petty 1.25 3.00
RPMDF Devin Funchess 2.00 5.00
RPMDJ Duke Johnson 2.00 5.00
RPMDS Devin Smith 1.25 3.00
RPMJA Jay Ajayi 2.00 5.00
RPMJW Jameis Winston 3.00 8.00
RPMKW Kevin White 1.50 4.00
RPMMG Melvin Gordon 3.00 8.00
RPMMM Marcus Mariota 5.00 12.00
RPMPD Phillip Dorsett 1.25 3.00
RPMSC Sammie Coates 1.50 4.00
RPMTC Tevin Coleman 1.50 4.00
RPMTG Todd Gurley 4.00 10.00
RPMTL Tyler Lockett 2.00 5.00
SPMAC Amari Cooper 4.00 10.00

2015 Gridiron Kings Rookie Studio Signatures

RSSAA Ameer Abdullah/35 4.00 10.00
RSSAC Amari Cooper/15
RSSBH Brett Hundley/99 10.00 25.00
RSSBP Bryce Petty/15 4.00 10.00
RSSBR Breshad Perriman/49
RSSCC Chris Conley/199 1.50 4.00
RSSDC David Cobb/249 1.50 4.00
RSSDF Devin Funchess/199 2.50 6.00
RSSDJ David Johnson/149 4.00 10.00
RSSDP DeVante Parker/99 3.00 8.00
RSSDS Devin Smith/149 1.50 4.00
RSSDU Duke Johnson/199 2.50 6.00
RSSJA Jay Ajayi/199 2.50 6.00
RSSJH Justin Hardy/249 1.50 4.00
RSSJL Jeremy Langford/249 1.50 4.00
RSSJS Jaelen Strong/175 2.00 5.00
RSSJW Jameis Winston/75 5.00 12.00
RSSKW Kevin White/35 3.00 8.00
RSSMD Mike Davis/249 1.50 4.00
RSSMJ Matt Jones/199 1.50 4.00
RSSMM Marcus Mariota/75 25.00 50.00
RSSMW Maxx Williams/249 1.50 4.00
RSSNA Nelson Agholor/25 4.00 10.00
RSSRG Rashad Greene/249 1.50 4.00
RSSSC Sammie Coates/199 2.00 5.00
RSSSM Sean Mannion/175 1.50 4.00
RSSTC Tevin Coleman/199 2.00 5.00
RSSTG Todd Gurley/35 20.00 50.00
RSSTL Tyler Lockett/199 2.50 6.00
RSSTM Ty Montgomery/175 1.50 4.00
RSSTY T.J. Yeldon/199 1.50 4.00
RSSVM Vince Mayle/149 2.00 5.00

2015 Gridiron Kings Rookie Studio Signatures Blue

*BLUE/23-25: .6X TO 1.5X BASIC AU/99
*BLUE/15: .6X TO 1.5X BASIC AU/35-49
*BLUE/23-25: .8X TO 2X BASIC AU/149-249

2015 Gridiron Kings Royal Performances

1 Franco Harris .60 1.50
2 Devin Hester .50 1.25
3 Roger Staubach .75 2.00
4 Peyton Manning 1.25 3.00
5 Herman Edwards .40 1.00
6 Dwight Clark .50 1.25
7 Malcolm Butler .60 1.50
8 Dave Casper .40 1.00
9 James Harrison .50 1.25
10 Terrell Owens .50 1.25
11 John Elway 1.00 2.50
12 DeMarco Murray .50 1.25
13 Emmitt Smith 1.00 2.50
14 Adam Vinatieri .40 1.00
15 John Elway 1.00 2.50
16 Marshawn Lynch .50 1.25
17 John Riggins .50 1.25
18 Jacoby Jones .40 1.00
19 Odell Beckham Jr. .60 1.50
20 Adrian Peterson .60 1.50

2015 Gridiron Kings Sketches and Swatches Autographs

1 Jameis Winston/75 8.00 20.00
2 Marcus Mariota/75 25.00 50.00
3 Amari Cooper/15 20.00 50.00
5 Kevin White/149 3.00 8.00
6 Todd Gurley/149 30.00 60.00
7 DeVante Parker/249 4.00 10.00
8 Melvin Gordon/75 8.00 20.00
9 Nelson Agholor/199 3.00 8.00
10 Breshad Perriman/249 2.50 6.00
12 T.J. Yeldon/249 2.50 6.00
13 Devin Smith/249 2.50 6.00
15 Devin Funchess/249 4.00 10.00
16 Ameer Abdullah/199 4.00 10.00
17 Maxx Williams/249 2.50 6.00
18 Tyler Lockett/249 4.00 10.00
19 Jaelen Strong/249 3.00 8.00
20 Tevin Coleman/249 3.00 8.00
22 Chris Conley/249 2.50 6.00
23 Duke Johnson/249 4.00 10.00
24 David Johnson/249 10.00 25.00
25 Sammie Coates/249 3.00 8.00
26 Sean Mannion/249 2.50 6.00
27 Ty Montgomery/249 2.50 6.00
28 Matt Jones/249 2.50 6.00
29 Bryce Petty/249 2.50 6.00
31 Jeremy Langford/249 2.50 6.00
32 Justin Hardy/249 2.50 6.00
33 Vince Mayle/249 3.00 8.00
35 Mike Davis/249 2.50 6.00
36 David Cobb/249 2.50 6.00
37 Rashad Greene/249 2.50 6.00
39 Brett Hundley/99 3.00 8.00
40 Jay Ajayi/249 4.00 10.00

2015 Gridiron Kings Sketches and Swatches Autographs Prime

*PRIME/49: .6X TO 1.5X BASIC JSY AU/149
*PRIME/25: .8X TO 2X BASIC JSY AU/249
*PRIME/25: .6X TO 1.5X BASIC JSY AU/75-99
6 Todd Gurley/49 40.00 100.00

2015 Gridiron Kings Sovereign Signatures Materials

1 Bo Jackson/15
5 Jerome Bettis/15
9 Dan Hampton/49 5.00 12.00
11 Steve Largent/25 10.00 25.00
16 Tim Brown/15 25.00 50.00
17 LaDainian Tomlinson/50 6.00 15.00
19 Wilbert Montgomery/99 6.00 15.00

2015 Gridiron Kings Stat Kings Autographs

3 DeMarco Murray/29 8.00 20.00
6 J.J. Watt/25 30.00 60.00
7 Antonio Brown/25 25.00 50.00
8 Demaryius Thomas/15 10.00 25.00
9 Dez Bryant/50 25.00 50.00
12 Antonio Gates/25 6.00 15.00
13 Derek Carr/25 10.00 25.00
14 Richard Sherman/35 25.00 50.00
15 Randall Cobb/99 10.00 20.00
18 Devin Hester/23 8.00 20.00
19 Kelvin Benjamin/99 5.00 12.00
23 Mike Evans/99 5.00 12.00
24 Eddie Lacy/27 15.00 30.00

2015 Gridiron Kings Stat Kings Autographs Framed Red

*RED/49: .5X TO 1.2X BASIC AU/99
*RED/25: .4X TO 1X BASIC AU/23-29
*RED/25: .5X TO 1.2X BASIC AU/50
*RED/15: .5X TO 1.2X BASIC AU/25
6 J.J. Watt/15 40.00 80.00
11 Teddy Bridgewater/15 20.00 40.00
14 Richard Sherman/25 30.00 60.00

2015 Gridiron Kings Studio Signatures

1 Jimmy Garoppolo/49 10.00 25.00
2 Ricky Williams/49 10.00 25.00
5 Jordan Matthews/25 8.00 20.00
6 Kelvin Benjamin/99 5.00 12.00
15 Doug Martin/49 6.00 15.00
17 Randall Cobb/49 6.00 15.00
18 Ryan Tannehill/17 10.00 25.00
21 Jason Witten/25 15.00 40.00
22 Mike Evans/25 8.00 20.00

1991 GTE Super Bowl Theme Art

This limited edition set of approximately 4 5/8" by 6" cards was issued on the occasion of Super Bowl XXV and sponsored by GTE, whose company logo appears at the bottom on the front of each card above a full color reproduction of the Super Bowl program cover enframed by black borders. The back includes information on the Super Bowl for that particular year, including location, teams, score, winning coach, MVP, and a GTE Super Bowl Telefact.

COMPLETE SET (25) 3.20 8.00
COMMON CARD (1-25) .16 .40
1 Super Bowl I .25 .60
25 Super Bowl XXV .25 .60

1995 GTE Super Bowl XXIX Phone Cards

GTE produced and distributed these two cards for the 1995 NFL Experience Super Bowl Card Show in Miami. Each measures 3 3/8" by 2 1/8" and has rounded corners. Card #1 originally could be purchased for $8.85 and provided 15-units of long distance. Card #2 sold initially for $17.11 and provided 29-units. Each one was issued in a clear cellophane pack. The backs have instructions on how to use the calling card feature. Each is numbered of 3000 produced and expired on 12/31/95.

COMPLETE SET (2) 1.20 3.00
1 Super Bowl XXIX Teams/49ers Chargers .60 1.50
2 Super Bowl XXIX Logo .60 1.50

1995 GTE Shell Super Bowl Phone Cards

GTE produced this phone card set sponsored and distributed by Shell Oil Co. Each card was valued at 5-units of GTE phone time that expired on January 31, 1996. Five previous Super Bowl game scores are included on each of the first five cards and four games on the last card.

COMPLETE SET (6) 3.20 8.00
COMMON CARD (1-6) .60 1.50

1995-96 Hallmark Ornament Cards

1 Troy Aikman (1995 Classic) 1.00 2.50
HK3 Joe Namath (1996 Score Board) 2.00 5.00

1963 Hall of Fame Postcards

Sammy Baugh 10.00 20.00
2 Dutch Clark 7.50 15.00
3 Fats Henry 7.50 15.00
4 Johnny Blood McNally 7.50 15.00
5 Ernie Nevers 7.50 15.00
6 Jim Thorpe 12.50 25.00

1982-2013 Hall of Fame Metallics

This set features Pro Football Hall of Fame enshrinees and was distributed in separate series with each series containing the inductees for specific years. Only 2,000 of each series were produced and a purchase of a complete run of series' included a Letter of Authenticity. Each 10 mil 2 1/2" by 3 1/2" silver-toned metallic card carries an imprinted reproduction of the enshrinee's bust from the Hall of Fame along with appropriate statistical data of the enshrinee's football career along with a blank back. The first fifteen series' were produced together in 1982-83 and sold separately as 8-card series. Subsequent series' were sold as that year's enshrinees were announced, therefore they vary in number of cards. We've assigned numbers to the cards below according to alphabetical order within series. Note that Lynn Swann was not produced for the set.

COMPLETE SET (225) 600.00 1200.00
1 Sammy Baugh 5.00 10.00
2 Joe Carr 2.00 4.00
3 George Halas 4.00 8.00
4 Mel Hein 2.00 4.00
5 Dick Lane 2.50 5.00
6 Bob Lilly 4.00 8.00
7 Marion Motley 3.00 6.00
8 Jim Thorpe 5.00 10.00
9 Herb Adderley 2.50 5.00
10 Dutch Clark 2.00 4.00
11 Red Grange 5.00 10.00
12 Vince Lombardi 7.50 15.00
13 Joe Perry 3.00 6.00
14 Art Rooney 2.50 5.00
15 Joe Schmidt 2.50 5.00
16 Bill Willis 2.50 5.00
17 Paul Brown 3.00 6.00
18 Fats Henry 2.00 4.00
19 Elroy Hirsch 3.00 6.00
20 Bronko Nagurski 6.00 12.00
21 Leo Nomellini 2.50 5.00
22 Jim Ringo 2.50 5.00
23 Joe Stydahar 2.00 4.00
24 Y.A. Tittle 4.00 8.00
25 Guy Chamberlin 2.00 4.00
26 George Connor 2.50 5.00
27 Willie Davis 2.50 5.00
28A Frank Gifford ERR 3.00 6.00
28B Frank Gifford COR 3.00 6.00
29 Clarke Hinkle 2.00 4.00
30 Lamar Hunt 2.00 4.00
31 Bruiser Kinard 2.00 4.00
32 Curly Lambeau 2.50 5.00
33 Weeb Ewbank 2.00 4.00
34 Dan Fortmann 2.00 4.00
35 Yale Lary 2.50 5.00
36 Sid Luckman 4.00 8.00
37 Lenny Moore 4.00 8.00
38 Ernie Nevers 2.50 5.00
39 Jim Parker 2.50 5.00
40 Ernie Stautner 3.00 6.00
41 Lance Alworth 4.00 8.00
42 Red Badgro 2.00 4.00
43 Chuck Bednarik 3.00 6.00
44 Roosevelt Brown 2.50 5.00
45 Bill Dudley 2.00 4.00
46 Bobby Layne 4.00 8.00
47 Link Lyman 2.00 4.00
48 Steve Owen 2.00 4.00
49 Paddy Driscoll 2.00 4.00
50 Len Ford 2.50 5.00
51 Sam Huff 3.00 6.00
52 Deacon Jones 3.00 6.00
53 Dante Lavelli 2.50 5.00
54 Tuffy Leemans 2.00 4.00
55 Dan Reeves 2.00 4.00
56 Bulldog Turner 2.50 5.00
57 Doug Atkins 2.50 5.00
58 George Blanda 5.00 10.00
59 Dick Butkus 5.00 10.00
60 Joe Guyon 2.00 4.00
61 Arnie Herber 2.00 4.00
62 Don Hutson 3.00 6.00
63 Walt Kiesling 2.00 4.00
64 Ron Mix 2.00 4.00
65 Cliff Battles 2.00 4.00
66 Jim Brown 6.00 12.00
67 Lou Groza 3.00 6.00
68 Ed Healey 2.00 4.00
69 Jim Otto 2.50 5.00
70 Pete Pihos 2.50 5.00
71 Hugh Shorty Ray 2.00 4.00
72 Bob Waterfield 3.00 6.00
73 Raymond Berry 3.00 6.00
74 Turk Edwards 2.00 4.00
75 Johnny Blood McNally 2.00 4.00
76 Greasy Neale 2.00 4.00
77 Ace Parker 2.00 4.00
78 Andy Robustelli 2.50 5.00
79 Charley Trippi 2.00 4.00
80 Larry Wilson 2.00 4.00
81 Art Donovan 2.50 5.00
82 Forrest Gregg 2.50 5.00
83 Tim Mara 2.00 4.00
84 Mike Michalske 2.00 4.00
85 Wayne Millner 2.00 4.00
86 Gale Sayers 5.00 10.00
87 Ken Strong 2.50 5.00
88 Norm Van Brocklin 3.00 6.00
89 Charles Bidwill 2.00 4.00
90 Bill George 2.50 5.00
91 Bill Hewitt 2.00 4.00
92 Hugh McElhenny [illegible] [illegible]
93 Bart Starr 7.50 15.00
94 George Trafton 2.00 4.00
95 Steve Van Buren 3.00 6.00
96 Alex Wojciechowicz 2.00 4.00
97 Tony Canadeo 2.50 5.00
98 Jack Christiansen 2.00 4.00
99 Gino Marchetti 2.50 5.00
100 George Preston Marshall 2.00 4.00
101 Ollie Matson 2.50 5.00
102 George Musso 2.00 4.00
103 Ray Nitschke 4.00 8.00
104 Johnny Unitas 6.00 12.00
105 Bert Bell 2.00 4.00
106 Tom Fears 2.50 5.00
107 Ray Flaherty 2.00 4.00
108 Otto Graham 5.00 10.00
109 Cal Hubbard 2.00 4.00
110 George McAfee 2.00 4.00
111 Merlin Olsen 3.00 6.00
112 Jim Taylor 3.00 6.00
113 Bobby Bell 2.50 5.00
114 Jimmy Conzelman 2.00 4.00
115 Sid Gillman 2.00 4.00
116 Sonny Jurgensen 3.00 8.00
117 Bobby Mitchell 3.00 6.00
118 Emlen Tunnell 2.50 5.00
119 Paul Warfield 3.00 6.00
120 Hall of Fame logo 2.00 4.00
121 Willie Brown 2.00 4.00
122 Mike McCormack 2.00 4.00
123 Charley Taylor 2.50 5.00
124 Arnie Weinmeister 2.00 4.00
125 Frank Gatski 2.00 4.00
126 Joe Namath 10.00 20.00
127 Pete Rozelle 2.00 4.00
128 O.J. Simpson 5.00 10.00
129 Roger Staubach 7.50 15.00
130 Paul Hornung 5.00 10.00
131 Ken Houston 2.50 5.00
132 Willie Lanier 2.50 5.00
133 Fran Tarkenton 4.00 8.00
134 Doak Walker 3.00 6.00
135 Larry Csonka 4.00 8.00
136 Len Dawson 3.00 8.00
137 Joe Greene 3.00 6.00
138 John Henry Johnson 2.00 4.00
139 Jim Langer 2.00 4.00
140 Don Maynard 3.00 6.00
141 Gene Upshaw 2.50 5.00
142 Fred Biletnikoff 3.00 8.00
143 Mike Ditka 6.00 12.00
144 Jack Ham 3.00 6.00
145 Alan Page 2.50 5.00
146 Mel Blount 3.00 6.00
147 Terry Bradshaw 7.50 15.00
148 Art Shell 3.00 6.00
149 Willie Wood 2.50 5.00
150 Buck Buchanan 2.50 5.00
151 Bob Griese 4.00 8.00
152 Franco Harris 4.00 8.00
153 Ted Hendricks 2.50 5.00
154 Jack Lambert 3.00 6.00
155 Tom Landry 4.00 8.00
156 Bob St. Clair 2.50 5.00
157 Earl Campbell 3.00 6.00
158 John Hannah 2.50 5.00
159 Stan Jones 2.00 4.00
160 Tex Schramm 2.00 4.00
161 Jan Stenerud 2.50 5.00
162 Lem Barney 2.00 4.00
163 Al Davis 3.00 6.00
164 John Mackey 2.00 4.00
165 John Riggins 2.00 4.00
166 Dan Fouts 3.00 8.00
167 Larry Little 2.00 4.00
168 Chuck Noll 3.00 6.00
169 Walter Payton 15.00 30.00
170 Bill Walsh 3.00 6.00
171 Tony Dorsett 4.00 8.00
172 Bud Grant 3.00 6.00
173 Jim Johnson 2.00 4.00
174 Leroy Kelly 3.00 6.00
175 Jackie Smith 2.00 4.00
176 Randy White 3.00 6.00
177 Jim Finks 2.00 4.00
178 Hank Jordan 2.50 5.00
179 Steve Largent 3.00 6.00
180 Lee Roy Selmon 2.00 4.00
181 Kellen Winslow 2.00 4.00
182 Lou Creekmur 2.50 5.00
183 Dan Dierdorf 2.50 5.00
184 Joe Gibbs 2.50 5.00
185 Charlie Joiner 2.50 5.00
186 Mel Renfro 2.50 5.00
187 Mike Haynes 3.00 6.00
188 Wellington Mara 3.00 6.00
189 Don Shula 3.00 8.00
190 Mike Webster 3.00 6.00
191 Paul Krause 2.00 4.00
192 Tommy McDonald 2.00 4.00
193 Anthony Munoz 2.00 4.00
194 Mike Singletary 2.50 5.00
195 Dwight Stephenson 2.00 4.00
196 Eric Dickerson 2.50 5.00
197 Tom Mack 2.00 4.00
198 Ozzie Newsome 2.50 5.00
199 Billy Shaw 2.00 4.00
200 Lawrence Taylor 3.00 6.00
201 Howie Long 2.50 5.00
202 Ronnie Lott 2.50 5.00
203 Joe Montana 6.00 15.00
204 Dan Rooney 2.00 4.00
205 Dave Wilcox 2.00 4.00
206 Nick Buoniconti 2.50 5.00
207 Marv Levy 2.00 4.00
208 Mike Munchak 2.00 4.00
209 Jackie Slater 2.00 4.00
210 Ron Yary 2.00 4.00
211 Jack Youngblood 2.50 5.00
212 George Allen 2.50 5.00
213 Dave Casper 2.00 4.00
214 Dan Hampton 2.00 4.00
215 Jim Kelly 3.00 8.00
216 John Stallworth 2.50 5.00
217 Marcus Allen 3.00 6.00
218 Elvin Bethea 2.00 4.00
219 Joe DeLamielleure 2.00 4.00
220 James Lofton 2.50 5.00
221 Hank Stram 2.50 5.00
222 Bob Brown 2.00 4.00
223 Carl Eller 2.50 5.00
224 John Elway 3.00 8.00
225 Barry Sanders 3.00 8.00
226 Benny Friedman 1.50 4.00
227 Dan Marino 5.00 10.00
228 Fritz Pollard 1.50 4.00
229 Steve Young 2.50 6.00
230 Troy Aikman 2.50 6.00
231 Harry Carson 1.50 4.00
232 John Madden 1.50 4.00
233 Warren Moon 1.50 4.00
234 Reggie White 2.00 5.00
235 Rayfield Wright 1.50 4.00
236 Gene Hickerson 1.50 4.00
237 Michael Irvin 2.00 5.00
238 Bruce Matthews 1.50 4.00
239 Charlie Sanders 1.50 4.00
240 Thurman Thomas 2.00 5.00
241 Roger Wehrli 1.50 4.00
242 Fred Dean 1.50 4.00
243 Darrell Green 1.50 4.00
244 Art Monk 1.50 4.00
245 Emmitt Thomas 1.50 4.00
246 Andre Tippett 1.50 4.00
247 Gary Zimmerman 1.50 4.00
248 Bob Hayes 5.00 10.00
249 Randall McDaniel 4.00 8.00
250 Bruce Smith 5.00 10.00
251 Derrick Thomas 5.00 10.00
252 Ralph Wilson, Jr. 4.00 8.00
253 Rod Woodson 5.00 10.00
254 Russ Grimm 4.00 8.00
255 Rickey Jackson 4.00 8.00
256 Dick LeBeau 4.00 8.00
257 Floyd Little 4.00 8.00
258 John Randle 4.00 8.00
259 Jerry Rice 6.00 12.00
260 Emmitt Smith 6.00 12.00
261 Richard Dent 4.00 8.00
262 Marshall Faulk 5.00 10.00
263 Chris Hanburger 4.00 8.00
264 Les Richter 4.00 8.00
265 Ed Sabol 4.00 8.00
266 Deion Sanders 5.00 10.00
267 Shannon Sharpe 5.00 10.00
268 Jack Butler 4.00 8.00
269 Dermontti Dawson 4.00 8.00
270 Chris Doleman 4.00 8.00
271 Cortez Kennedy 4.00 8.00
272 Curtis Martin 4.00 8.00
273 Willie Roaf 4.00 8.00
274 Larry Allen 5.00 10.00
275 Cris Carter 6.00 12.00
276 Curley Culp 5.00 10.00
277 Jonathan Ogden 5.00 10.00
278 Bill Parcells 5.00 10.00
279 Dave Robinson 5.00 10.00
280 Warren Sapp 5.00 10.00

1990 Hall of Fame Stickers

This 80-sticker set is actually part of a book; the individual stickers in the book measure approximately 1 7/8" by 2 1/8". The book was entitled "The Official Pro Football Hall of Fame Fun and Fact Sticker Book." The original artwork from which the stickers were derived was performed by noted hobbyist Mark Rucker and featured 80 members of the Pro Football Hall of Fame.

COMPLETE SET (80) 20.00 35.00
1 Fats Henry .25 .60
2 George Trafton .25 .60
3 Mike Michalske .25 .60
4 Turk Edwards .25 .60
5 Bill Hewitt .25 .60
6 Mel Hein .25 .60
7 Joe Stydahar .25 .60
8 Dan Fortmann .25 .60
9 Alex Wojciechowicz .25 .60
10 George Connor .25 .60
11 Jim Thorpe .50 1.25
12 Ernie Nevers .25 .60
13 Johnny Blood McNally .25 .60
14 Ken Strong .25 .60
15 Bronko Nagurski .50 1.25
16 Clarke Hinkle .25 .60
17 Clarence(Ace) Parker .25 .60
18 Bill Dudley .25 .60
19 Don Hutson .30 1.00
20 Dante Lavelli .30 .75
21 Elroy Hirsch .30 1.00
22 Raymond Berry .30 1.00
23 Bobby Mitchell .30 .75
24 Don Maynard .30 1.00
25 Mike Ditka .50 1.25
26 Lance Alworth .30 1.00
27 Charley Taylor .30 .75
28 Paul Warfield .30 .75
29 Lou Groza .30 .75
30 Art Donovan .30 .75
31 Leo Nomellini .25 .60
32 Andy Robustelli .25 .60
33 Gino Marchetti .30 .75
34 Forrest Gregg .30 .75
35 Jim Otto .30 .75
36 Ron Mix .30 .75
37 Deacon Jones .30 1.00
38 Bob Lilly .30 1.00
39 Merlin Olsen .30 1.00
40 Alan Page .30 .75
41 Joe Greene .30 1.00
42 Art Shell .30 .75
43 Sammy Baugh .50 1.25
44 Sid Luckman .20 .75
45 Bob Waterfield .30 .75
46 Bobby Layne .40 1.00
47 Norm Van Brocklin .30 .75
48 Y.A. Tittle .50 1.25
49 Johnny Unitas 1.50 4.00
50 Bart Starr 1.50 4.00
51 Sonny Jurgensen .30 1.00
52 Joe Namath 1.25 3.00
53 Roger Staubach 1.00 2.50
54 Terry Bradshaw 1.00 2.50
55 Steve Van Buren .25 .60
56 Marion Motley .30 .75
57 Joe Perry .30 .75
58 Hugh McElhenny .30 .75
59 Frank Gifford .40 1.00
60 Jim Brown .75 2.00
61 Jim Taylor .30 1.00
62 Gale Sayers .60 1.50
63 Larry Csonka .30 1.00
64 Emlen Tunnell .25 .60
65 Jack Christiansen .25 .60
66 Dick(Night Train) Lane .25 .60
67 Sam Huff .30 .75
68 Ray Nitschke .30 1.00
69 Larry Wilson .25 .60
70 Willie Wood .30 .75
71 Bobby Bell .30 .75
72 Willie Brown .30 .75
73 Dick Butkus .60 1.50
74 Jack Ham .30 1.00
75 George Halas .40 1.00
76 Steve Owen .25 .60
77 Art Rooney .30 .75
78 Bert Bell .25 .60
79 Paul Brown .30 .75
80 Pete Rozelle .25 .60

1974 Hawaii Hawaiians WFL Team Issue

These photos were issued by the team for promotional purposes and fan mail requests. Each includes a black and white image printed above the subject's name and team logo. Each measures 5 1/2" by 7."

COMPLETE SET (9) 25.00 60.00
1 Gary Baccus 3.00 8.00
2 Damone Bame CO 3.00 8.00
3 Lem Burnham 3.00 8.00
4 Ron East 3.00 8.00
5 John Kelsey 3.00 8.00
6 Al Oliver 3.00 8.00
7 Greg Slough 3.00 8.00
8 Levi Stanley 3.00 8.00
9 Norris Weese 3.00 8.00

1993 Heads and Tails SB XXVII

Designed and produced by Heads and Tails Inc., this 25-card standard-size set features the best past and current players that the Super Bowl has to offer as well as some 1993 NFL Pro Bowl picks. The production run was reportedly 200,000 sets, and these sets were sold through Wal-Mart and other retailers. Randomly inserted throughout the product were 10,000 sets featuring gold foil stamping on the words "Rose Bowl" and on the stem of the Rose Bowl insignia. The remaining 190,000 sets have silver foil stamping instead of gold. Gold sets are valued at two to three times the values listed below. Each set was packed in a special box that contained foil packs with over 200 cards from other NFL licensed trading card producers (Topps, Fleer Ultra, GameDay, Proline, and Wild Card). The cards feature full-bleed color action player photos. The Pro Bowl picks have the player's name embossed in foil at the bottom. The Super Bowl player cards display the player's name in white printed vertically down one edge, a Rose Bowl foil embossed emblem, and an icon showing the Super Bowl they played in. On a background consisting of a ghosted picture of the Rose Bowl, the backs summarize the player's performance. After a checklist/header card, the set is arranged as follows: NFL Salutes (2-3), '93 Pro Bowl Picks (4-7), Super Bowl MVP's of the Past (8-11), AFC Champions Buffalo Bills (12-18), and NFC Champions Dallas Cowboys (19-25). The cards are numbered with an "SB" prefix.

COMPLETE SET (25) 5.00 12.00
COMP.GOLD SET (25) 10.00 25.00
*GOLD CARDS: .8X TO 2X SILVERS
SB1 Title Card CL .08 .25
SB2 L.Taylor/M.Singletary .15 .40
SB3 Dennis Byrd .08 .25
SB4 Junior Seau .20 .50
SB5 Steve Young .40 1.00
SB6 Sterling Sharpe .15 .40
SB7 Cortez Kennedy .15 .40
SB8 Terry Bradshaw .40 1.00
SB9 Fred Biletnikoff .15 .40
SB10 John Riggins .15 .40
SB11 Phil Simms .15 .40
SB12 Cornelius Bennett .15 .40
SB13 Jim Kelly .25 .60
SB14 Bruce Smith .15 .40
SB15 Andre Reed .15 .40
SB16 Keith McKeller .08 .25
SB17 James Lofton .15 .40
SB18 Thurman Thomas .25 .60
SB19 Emmitt Smith 1.00 2.50
SB20 Kelvin Martin .08 .25
SB21 Troy Aikman .60 1.50
SB22 Charles Haley .08 .25
SB23 Alvin Harper .15 .40
SB24 Michael Irvin .25 .60
SB25 Jay Novacek .15 .40

1970 Hi-C Mini-Posters

is set of ten posters were the insides of the Hi-C drink can labels. They are numbered very subtly below the player's picture but they are listed below in alphabetical order. The players selected for the set were leaders at their positions during the 1969 season. The mini-posters measure approximately 6 5/8" by 13 3/4".

COMPLETE SET (10) 300.00 600.00
1 Greg Cook 30.00 60.00
2 Fred Cox 30.00 60.00
3 Sonny Jurgensen 50.00 100.00
4 David Lee 25.00 50.00
5 Dennis Partee 25.00 50.00
6 Dick Post 25.00 50.00
7 Mel Renfro 50.00 100.00
8 Gale Sayers 75.00 150.00
9 Emmitt Thomas 30.00 60.00
10 Jim Turner 25.00 50.00

1997 Highland Mint Football Shaped Medallions

These football-shaped medallions are 1 7/8 inches wide and 1 1/8 inches at their greatest width and manufactured with silver. Each medallion was numbered of either 5000 or 7500 and is housed with an astroturf-like holder in a pigskin textured box. The original suggested retail price for these medallions was $29.95. Many players were also produced with a real diamond piece included. The diamond version pieces were numbered of 500.

1 Dan Marino S/7500 20.00 30.00
2 Troy Aikman S/5000 20.00 30.00
3 Troy Aikman DIAM/500 65.00 125.00
4 Brett Favre S/5000 20.00 30.00
5 Brett Favre DIAM/500 65.00 125.00
6 Jerry Rice S/7500 20.00 30.00
7 Jerry Rice DIA/500 65.00 125.00
8 Emmitt Smith S/7500 20.00 30.00
9 Emmitt Smith DIA/500 65.00 125.00

1995 Highland Mint Legends Mint-Cards

The Highland Mint Legends Collection features NFL greats in a newly designed Mint-Card format. These standard-sized bronze metal cards are enclosed in a plastic display holder case with each being serial numbered of either 2500 or 5000. Silver versions of these cards (20% of total of bronzes) were produced as well.

1 Joe Namath S/1000 90.00 160.00
2 Joe Namath B/5000 20.00 35.00
3 Roger Staubach S/500 90.00 160.00
4 Roger Staubach B/2500 20.00 35.00
5 Johnny Unitas S/500 90.00 160.00
6 Johnny Unitas B/2500 20.00 35.00

1997 Highland Mint Mint-Cards Pinnacle/Score/UD

These cards are replicas of previously-issued Pinnacle, Score or Upper Deck cards. The silver and bronze cards contain 4.25 ounces of metal; the gold cards are 24-karat gold-plate on 4.25 ounces of silver. Each card is individually numbered, packaged in a lucite display holder and accompanied by a certificate of authenticity. The production mintage according to Highland Mint is listed below.

1 Troy Aikman 89 S/1000 125.00 175.00
2 Troy Aikman 89 B/5000 12.50 25.00
3 Drew Bledsoe 94 S/1000 125.00 175.00
4 Drew Bledsoe 94 B/5000 12.50 25.00
5 Brett Favre 93 S/250 125.00 200.00
6 Brett Favre 93 B/1500 25.00 50.00
7 Dan Marino 94 G/500 150.00 250.00
8 Dan Marino 94 S/1000 125.00 175.00
9 Dan Marino 94 B/5000 17.50 35.00
10 Joe Montana 92 G/500 175.00 300.00
11 Joe Montana 92 S/1000 125.00 175.00
12 Joe Montana 92 B/5000 20.00 40.00
13 Errict Rhett 94 S/500 125.00 175.00
14 Errict Rhett 94 B/2500 7.50 15.00
15 Jerry Rice 95 S/500 125.00 175.00
16 Jerry Rice 95 B/2500 15.00 30.00
17 Rashaan Salaam 95 S/500 125.00 175.00
18 Rashaan Salaam 95 B/2500 7.50 15.00
19 Barry Sanders 93 S/250 125.00 175.00
20 Barry Sanders 89 B/1500 20.00 40.00
21 Heath Shuler 94 S/500 125.00 175.00

22 Heath Shuler 94 B/2500 7.50 15.00
23 Emmitt Smith 90 G/500 150.00 250.00
24 Emmitt Smith 90 S/1000 125.00 175.00
25 Emmitt Smith 90 B/5000 15.00 30.00
26 Kordell Stewart 95 S/500 125.00 175.00
27 Kordell Stewart 95 B/2500 10.00 20.00

1997 Highland Mint Mint-Cards Topps

Produced by Highland Mint, these cards measure the standard size and are metal reproductions of Topps football cards. The reported .999 fine silver content for both the silver and gold plated cards was 4.25 troy ounces. The reported final mintage figures for each card are listed below. Highland Mint also issued 40 bronze promos of the Smith card. Each card bears a serial number on its bottom edge. These cards were available only through direct distributors, and were packaged in a lucite display case within an album. Each card came with a sequentially numbered Certificate of Authenticity. The numbering on the card backs reflects the actual card numbers from the original Topps issues; however the listing below is ordered alphabetically for convenience.

1 Troy Aikman 89 G/375 125.00 250.00
2 Troy Aikman 89 S/500 125.00 175.00
3 Troy Aikman 89 B/2500 20.00 50.00
4 Marcus Allen 83 S/88 125.00 175.00
5 Marcus Allen 83 B/549 15.00 30.00
6 Jerome Bettis 93 S/301 125.00 175.00
7 Jerome Bettis 93 B/1566 12.50 25.00
8 Drew Bledsoe 93 G/375 125.00 200.00
9 Drew Bledsoe 93 S/500 125.00 175.00
10 Drew Bledsoe 93 B/2500 12.50 25.00
11 John Elway 84 S/500 125.00 175.00
12 John Elway 84 B/2020 20.00 40.00
13 Marshall Faulk 94 S/530 125.00 175.00
14 Marshall Faulk 94 B/2500 12.50 25.00
15 Brett Favre 92 S/110 125.00 200.00
16 Brett Favre 92 B/714 30.00 60.00
17 Michael Irvin 89 S/509 125.00 175.00
18 Michael Irvin 89 B/1633 12.50 25.00
19 Jim Kelly 87 S/419 125.00 175.00
20 Jim Kelly 87 B/1165 15.00 30.00
21 Dan Marino 84 G/375 150.00 300.00
22 Dan Marino 84 S/500 125.00 200.00
23 Dan Marino 84 B/2500 20.00 40.00
24 Natrone Means 93 S/136 125.00 175.00
25 Natrone Means 93 B/1026 12.50 25.00
26 Rick Mirer 93 S/384 125.00 175.00
27 Rick Mirer 93 B/1982 12.50 25.00
28 Jerry Rice 86 G/375 150.00 300.00
29 Jerry Rice 86 S/750 125.00 175.00
30 Jerry Rice 86 B/2500 15.00 30.00
31 Barry Sanders 89 G/375 150.00 300.00
32 Barry Sanders 89 S/750 125.00 175.00
33 Barry Sanders 89 B/2500 15.00 30.00
34 Deion Sanders 89 S/191 125.00 175.00
35 Deion Sanders 89 B/1033 12.50 30.00
36 Sterling Sharpe 89 S/171 125.00 175.00
37 Sterling Sharpe 89 B/901 12.50 25.00
38 Emmitt Smith 90 G/375 150.00 300.00
39 Emmitt Smith 90 S/750 125.00 175.00
40 Emmitt Smith 90 B/2500 17.50 35.00
41 Lawrence Taylor 84 S/585 125.00 175.00
42 Lawrence Taylor 84 B/1630 12.50 25.00
43 Steve Young 86 G/375 125.00 200.00
44 Steve Young 86 S/500 125.00 175.00
45 Steve Young 86 B/2500 12.50 25.00

1997-00 Highland Mint Mint-Coins

Each medallion weighs one-troy ounce and is individually numbered. The fronts feature a player likeness as well as name, uniform number, and signature. The backs display the team logo and statistics. The medallions were packaged in a hard plastic capsule and a velvet jewelry box. Unless noted below, the unpriced solid gold coins were produced in quantities of 100, the bronze coins were printed in quantities of 25,000 and the silvers 7500. Highland Mint also produced two-tone "Signature Series" silver medallions with gold plate highlights and a production run of 1500 of each piece.

1 Troy Aikman B 5.00 12.00
2 Troy Aikman S 30.00 40.00
3 Troy Aikman SS 35.00 60.00
4 Jerome Bettis Rams S/2100 30.00 40.00
5 Jerome Bettis Steelers S/5400 30.00 40.00
6 J.Bettis K.Stewart S 30.00 40.00
7 Drew Bledsoe B 5.00 12.00
8 Drew Bledsoe S 30.00 40.00
9 Drew Bledsoe SS 30.00 50.00
10 Mark Brunell B 5.00 12.00
11 Mark Brunell S 30.00 40.00
12 Ki-Jana Carter S 30.00 40.00
13 Kerry Collins S 30.00 40.00
14 Tim Couch S 30.00 40.00
15 Randall Cunningham B 5.00 12.00
16 Terrell Davis B 5.00 12.00
17 Terrell Davis S 30.00 40.00
18 Trent Dilfer S 30.00 40.00
19 Warrick Dunn S 30.00 40.00
20 John Elway B 6.00 15.00
21 John Elway S 30.00 40.00
22 John Elway RET S 30.00 40.00
23 John Elway SS 45.00 80.00
24 Marshall Faulk B 5.00 12.00
25 Marshall Faulk S 20.00 40.00
26 Brett Favre B 6.00 15.00
27 Brett Favre S 30.00 40.00
28 Favre B.Sanders S 30.00 40.00
29 Eddie George S/5000 30.00 40.00
30 Terry Glenn S 30.00 40.00
31 Michael Irvin S 30.00 40.00
32 Jim Kelly S 30.00 40.00
33 Ryan Leaf S 30.00 40.00
34 Peyton Manning B 6.00 15.00
35 Peyton Manning S 15.00 40.00
36 Dan Marino B 6.00 15.00
37 Dan Marino G/100
38 Dan Marino S 30.00 40.00
39 Dan Marino SS 60.00 100.00
40 Curtis Martin S 30.00 40.00
41 Natrone Means S 30.00 40.00
42 Rick Mirer S 30.00 40.00
43 Joe Montana B 6.00 15.00
44 Montana Rice B 6.00 15.00
45 Joe Montana G/100
46 Joe Montana S 30.00 40.00
47 Randy Moss B 6.00 15.00
48 Randy Moss S 30.00 40.00
49 Joe Namath S 30.00 40.00
50 Jake Plummer S 30.00 40.00
51 Jerry Rice B 5.00 12.00
52 Jerry Rice S 30.00 40.00
53 Jerry Rice SS 35.00 60.00
54 Rashaan Salaam S 30.00 40.00
55 Barry Sanders B 6.00 15.00
56 Barry Sanders S 30.00 40.00
57 Deion Sanders B 4.00 10.00
58 Deion Sanders Cowboys S/4810 30.00 40.00
59 Deion Sanders 49ers S/2690 30.00 40.00
60 Junior Seau S 30.00 40.00
61 Heath Shuler S 30.00 40.00
62 Emmitt Smith B 6.00 15.00
63 Emmitt Smith G/100
64 Emmitt Smith S 30.00 40.00
65 Emmitt Smith SS 45.00 80.00
66 Kordell Stewart B 5.00 12.00
67 Kordell Stewart S 30.00 40.00
68 Reggie White S 30.00 40.00
69 Ricky Williams S 30.00 40.00
70 Steve Young B 4.00 10.00
71 Steve Young S 30.00 40.00
72 Cowboys Set B/2500 6.00 15.00
73 49ers B/2500 6.00 15.00

1991 Homers

This six-card standard-size set was sponsored by Legend Food Products in honor of the listed Hall of Famers. One free card was randomly inserted in either 3 1/2 or 10 oz. boxes of QB's Cookies. The vanilla-flavored cookies came in six player shapes (wide receiver, kicker, linebacker, tackle, running back, and quarterback), with a trivia quiz and secret message featured on each box. The card fronts display sepia-toned photos enclosed by bronze borders on a white card face. The player's name appears in a bronze bar at the lower left corner. The backs present year of induction into the Pro Football Hall of Fame, biography, career highlights, and a checklist for the set.

COMPLETE SET (6) 75.00 135.00
1 Vince Lombardi CO 15.00 30.00
2 Hugh McElhenny 7.50 15.00
3 Elroy Hirsch 7.50 15.00
4 Jim Thorpe 12.50 25.00
5 Dick Lane 6.00 12.00
6 Bart Starr 20.00 40.00

2001 Hot Prospects

In August of 2001 Fleer released Hot Prospects as a 100-card base set in hobby packs. The cardfronts use a partial foilboard and glossy design highlighted with silver-foil lettering and team logos. The cardbacks use a 3-color design, brown, black, and one of the featured players' team colors. While the hobby version of this product contained no rookie cards, please note that cards 101-135 were available only in retail packs at the rate of 1:10.

COMP.SET w/o SP's (100) 10.00 25.00
1 Aaron Brooks .20 .50
2 Tim Couch .20 .50
3 Jeff George .25 .60
4 Brett Favre .60 1.50
5 Donovan McNabb .25 .60
6 Ray Lucas .20 .50
7 Doug Flutie .25 .60
8 Mark Brunell .25 .60
9 Steve McNair .25 .60
10 Trent Green .20 .50
11 Daunte Culpepper .25 .60
12 Rich Gannon .25 .60
13 Kurt Warner .50 1.25
14 Brian Griese .20 .50
15 Kerry Collins .20 .50
16 Vinny Testaverde .20 .50
17 David Boston .20 .50
18 Peyton Manning .75 2.00
19 Keyshawn Johnson .25 .60
20 Tim Biakabutuka .20 .50
21 J.R. Redmond .20 .50
22 Emmitt Smith .50 1.25
23 Terry Glenn .25 .60
24 Tony Gonzalez .25 .60
25 Charlie Garner .25 .60
26 Lamar Smith .25 .60
27 Eddie George .30 .75
28 Fred Taylor .20 .50
29 Marvin Harrison .25 .60
30 Terrell Davis .25 .60
31 Marcus Robinson .25 .60
32 Edgerrin James .25 .60
33 Ed McCaffrey .25 .60
34 Ricky Williams .25 .60
35 Todd Pinkston .20 .50
36 Jerome Bettis .30 .75
37 Shaun Alexander .20 .50
38 Mike Anderson .20 .50
39 Keenan McCardell .25 .60
40 Mike Alstott .20 .50
41 Terrell Fletcher .20 .50
42 Kevin Johnson .20 .50
43 Wesley Walls .20 .50
44 Derrick Mason .20 .50
45 Sammy Morris .20 .50
46 Joey Galloway .25 .60
47 Sylvester Morris .20 .50
48 Stephen Davis .20 .50
49 Terrell Owens .25 .60
50 Troy Edwards .20 .50
51 Amani Toomer .20 .50
52 Ray Lewis .30 .75
53 Terance Mathis .20 .50
54 Brian Urlacher .40 1.00
55 Junior Seau .25 .60
56 Rocket Ismail .25 .60
57 Wayne Chrebet .20 .50
58 Peter Warrick .20 .50
59 Andre Rison .25 .60
60 Desmond Howard .25 .60
61 Eric Moulds .20 .50
62 Jerry Rice .60 1.50
63 Stephen Alexander .20 .50
64 Isaac Bruce .30 .75
65 Travis Prentice .20 .50
66 James Stewart .20 .50
67 Jamal Anderson .25 .60
68 Ricky Watters .25 .60
69 Jamal Lewis .30 .75
70 Priest Holmes .20 .50
71 Ahman Green .25 .60
72 Marshall Faulk .25 .60
73 Warrick Dunn .20 .50
74 Curtis Martin .25 .60
75 Corey Dillon .20 .50
76 Ron Dayne .25 .60
77 Thomas Jones .20 .50
78 Duce Staley .20 .50
79 Tiki Barber .25 .60
80 Cris Carter .30 .75
81 Tim Brown .30 .75
82 Jimmy Smith .25 .60
83 Elvis Grbac .25 .60
84 Randy Moss .25 .60
85 Tim Dwight .25 .60
86 Antonio Freeman .30 .75
87 Muhsin Muhammad .20 .50
88 Torry Holt .25 .60
89 Frank Wycheck .20 .50
90 Jake Plummer .20 .50
91 Brad Johnson .25 .60
92 Chris Chandler .25 .60
93 Drew Bledsoe .25 .60
94 Rob Johnson .25 .60
95 Matt Hasselbeck .20 .50
96 Jon Kitna .20 .50
97 Kordell Stewart .20 .50
98 Charlie Batch .20 .50
99 Cade McNown .25 .60
100 Jeff Garcia .20 .50
101 Quincy Morgan RC .75 2.00
102 Jesse Palmer RC .75 2.00
103 Reggie Wayne RC 1.25 3.00
104 Deuce McAllister RC 1.00 2.50
105 Chad Johnson RC 1.00 2.50
106 Chris Weinke RC .75 2.00
107 Michael Bennett RC .75 2.00
108 Rod Gardner RC .75 2.00
109 Michael Vick RC 1.50 4.00
110 Anthony Thomas RC 1.00 2.50
111 Santana Moss RC 1.00 2.50
112 Kevan Barlow RC .75 2.00
113 Koren Robinson RC .75 2.00
114 Rudi Johnson RC 1.00 2.50
115 Josh Heupel RC 1.00 2.50
116 James Jackson RC .60 1.50
117 Freddie Mitchell RC .60 1.50
118 LaDainian Tomlinson RC 3.00 8.00
119 Marques Tuiasosopo RC .75 2.00
120 Drew Brees RC 4.00 10.00
121 David Terrell RC .75 2.00
122 Chris Chambers RC .60 1.50
123 Mike McMahon RC .75 2.00
124 Robert Ferguson RC 1.00 2.50
125 Justin Smith RC 1.25 3.00
126 Leonard Davis RC 1.00 2.50
127 Todd Heap RC .75 2.00
128 Dan Morgan RC .75 2.00
129 Gerard Warren RC .75 2.00
130 Travis Henry RC .75 2.00
131 Travis Minor RC .75 2.00
132 Richard Seymour RC 1.00 2.50
133 Quincy Carter RC .75 2.00
134 Snoop Minnis RC .60 1.50
135 Sage Rosenfels RC .75 2.00
CL1 Checklist .02 .10

2001 Hot Prospects Draft Day Postmarks

Draft Day Postmarks were random inserts in packs of Fleer Hot Prospects. This 21-card set featured the players taken in the 2001 NFL Draft. The cards were serial numbered and featured a postmark from the location and date of the draft. The cards contained no numbers on the back and are arranged below in alphabetical order.

1 Kevan Barlow/1975 1.00 2.50
2 Michael Bennett/1825 1.00 2.50
3 Drew Brees/1775 5.00 12.00
4 Rod Gardner/1875 1.00 2.50
5 Josh Heupel/1825 1.25 3.00
6 James Jackson/1975 .75 2.00
7 Chad Johnson/1875 1.25 3.00
8 Rudi Johnson/1975 1.25 3.00
9 Deuce McAllister/1825 1.25 3.00
10 Freddie Mitchell/1875 .75 2.00
11 Quincy Morgan/1875 1.00 2.50
12 Santana Moss/1750 1.25 3.00
13 Jesse Palmer/1875 1.00 2.50
14 Koren Robinson/1825 1.00 2.50
15 David Terrell/1825 1.00 2.50
16 Anthony Thomas/1875 1.25 3.00
17 LaDainian Tomlinson/1775 4.00 10.00
18 Marques Tuiasosopo/1875 1.00 2.50
19 Michael Vick/1775 2.00 5.00
20 Reggie Wayne/1875 1.50 4.00
21 Chris Weinke/1775 1.00 2.50

2001 Hot Prospects Draft Day Postmarks Autographs

aft Day Postmarks were random inserts in packs of Fleer Hot Prospects. This 21-card set featured the players taken in the 2001 NFL Draft. The cards were serial numbered and featured a postmark from the location and date of the draft. Each card was autographed, and please note there were 7 exchange cards at the time of this products release. The cards contained no numbers on the back and are arranged below in alphabetical order.

2 Michael Bennett 8.00 20.00
3 Drew Brees SP 100.00 175.00
5 Josh Heupel 10.00 25.00
7 Chad Johnson 15.00 40.00
8 Rudi Johnson 10.00 25.00
11 Quincy Morgan 8.00 20.00
12 Santana Moss SP 12.00 30.00
13 Jesse Palmer 8.00 20.00
14 Koren Robinson 8.00 20.00
15 David Terrell 8.00 20.00
16 Anthony Thomas 10.00 25.00
17 LaDainian Tomlinson SP 60.00 125.00
18 Marques Tuiasosopo 8.00 20.00
21 Chris Weinke SP 10.00 25.00

2001 Hot Prospects Honor Guard

Honor Guard was randomly inserted in packs of 2001 Fleer Hot Prospects at a rate of 1:5. This 49-card set featured some of the top NFL stars past and present. The cardfronts are highlighted with silver-foil lettering and logo. The card numbering carried an 'of 49 HG' suffix.

COMPLETE SET (49) 40.00 80.00
STATED ODDS 1:5
1 Troy Aikman 1.00 2.50
2 Marcus Allen .75 2.00
3 Mike Alstott .50 1.25
4 Jerome Bettis .75 2.00
5 Drew Bledsoe .60 1.50
6 Isaac Bruce .75 2.00
7 Mark Brunell .60 1.50
8 Wayne Chrebet .50 1.25
9 Daunte Culpepper .60 1.50
10 Randall Cunningham .60 1.50
11 Terrell Davis .60 1.50
12 Stephen Davis .50 1.25
13 Corey Dillon .50 1.25
14 Warrick Dunn .50 1.25
15 Marshall Faulk .60 1.50
16 Brett Favre 1.50 4.00
17 Doug Flutie .60 1.50
18 Jeff Garcia .50 1.25
19 Eddie George .75 2.00
20 Brian Griese .50 1.25
21 Bo Jackson 1.00 2.50
22 Jamal Lewis .75 2.00
23 Dan Marino 1.50 4.00
24 Donovan McNabb .60 1.50
25 Steve McNair .60 1.50
26 Joe Montana 2.50 6.00
27 Randy Moss .60 1.50
28 Jerry Rice 1.50 4.00
29 Jerry Rice 1.50 4.00
30 Deion Sanders .60 1.50
31 Emmitt Smith 1.25 3.00
32 Fred Taylor .50 1.25
33 John Elway 1.25 3.00
34 Kurt Warner 1.25 3.00
35 Ricky Williams .60 1.50
36 Marvin Harrison .60 1.50
37 Edgerrin James .60 1.50
38 Curtis Martin .60 1.50
39 Vinny Testaverde .50 1.25
40 Rod Smith .60 1.50
41 Warren Moon .75 2.00
42 Steve Young 1.00 2.50
43 Jamal Anderson .60 1.50
44 Tim Brown .75 2.00
45 Plaxico Burress .50 1.25
46 Tim Couch .50 1.25
47 Az-Zahir Hakim .50 1.25
48 Ed McCaffrey .60 1.50
49 Ron Dayne .60 1.50

2001 Hot Prospects Pigskin Prospects

Pigskin Prospects were randomly inserted in packs of 2001 Fleer Hot Prospects at a rate of 1:15. This 15-card set featured top draft picks from the 2001 NFL Draft. These unique cards take on the shape of a football. The card fronts are highlighted with silver-foil lettering and logo. The card numbers carried an 'of 15 PP' suffix.

COMPLETE SET (15) 25.00 50.00
STATED ODDS 1:15
PP1 Drew Brees 8.00 20.00
PP2 Koren Robinson .60 1.50
PP3 Robert Ferguson .75 2.00
PP4 Rod Gardner .60 1.50
PP5 Chad Johnson .75 2.00
PP6 Reggie Wayne 1.00 2.50
PP7 Chris Weinke .60 1.50
PP8 Deuce McAllister .75 2.00
PP9 Chris Chambers .50 1.25
PP10 Freddie Mitchell .50 1.25
PP11 Quincy Carter .60 1.50
PP12 LaDainian Tomlinson 2.50 6.00
PP13 Santana Moss .75 2.00
PP14 David Terrell .60 1.50
PP15 Michael Vick 1.25 3.00

2001 Hot Prospects Pigskin Prospects Jerseys

Pigskin Prospects were randomly inserted in packs of 2001 Fleer Hot Prospects at a rate of 1:51. These unique cards take on the shape of a football. The card fronts are highlighted with silver-foil lettering and logo, and had a jersey swatch on them.

STATED ODDS 1:51
1 Drew Brees 15.00 40.00
3 Robert Ferguson 2.50 6.00
4 Chad Johnson 2.50 6.00
5 Reggie Wayne 3.00 8.00
6 Chris Weinke 2.00 5.00

2001 Hot Prospects Rookie Premiere Postmarks Jerseys

Rookie Premiere Postmarks Jerseys were inserted into packs of Fleer Hot Prospects. Fleer announced that 1500 of each jersey card existed, but please note the cards had different stated serial numbers on them. The serial numbers on each card varied from 1500 to 1975, with the remaining cards from the 1500 existing as Draft Day Postmarks or Draft Day Postmark Autographs.

STATED PRINT RUN 1500 SETS
1 Kevan Barlow 2.00 5.00
2 Michael Bennett 2.00 5.00
3 Drew Brees 15.00 40.00
4 Quincy Carter 2.00 5.00
5 Chris Chambers 1.50 4.00
6 Leonard Davis 2.50 6.00
7 Robert Ferguson 2.50 6.00
8 Rod Gardner 2.00 5.00
9 Todd Heap 2.00 5.00
10 Travis Henry 2.00 5.00
11 Josh Heupel 2.50 6.00
12 James Jackson 1.50 4.00
13 Chad Johnson 2.50 6.00
14 Rudi Johnson 2.50 6.00
15 Deuce McAllister 2.50 6.00
16 Mike McMahon 2.00 5.00
17 Snoop Minnis 1.50 4.00
18 Travis Minor 2.00 5.00
19 Freddie Mitchell 1.50 4.00
20 Dan Morgan 2.00 5.00
21 Quincy Morgan 2.00 5.00
22 Santana Moss 2.50 6.00
23 Jesse Palmer 2.00 5.00
24 Koren Robinson 2.00 5.00
25 Sage Rosenfels 2.00 5.00
26 Richard Seymour 2.50 6.00
27 Justin Smith 3.00 8.00
28 David Terrell 2.00 5.00
29 Anthony Thomas 2.50 6.00
30 LaDainian Tomlinson 8.00 20.00
31 Marques Tuiasosopo 2.00 5.00
32 Michael Vick 4.00 10.00
33 Gerard Warren 2.00 5.00
34 Reggie Wayne 3.00 8.00
35 Chris Weinke 2.00 5.00

2001 Hot Prospects Scoring King Jerseys

Scoring Kings were randomly inserted in packs of 2001 Fleer Hot Prospects at a rate of 1:12. This 48-card set featured players from the past and present who seemed to find their way to the endzone quite frequently. The card featured a a small jersey swatch cut into the shape of a crown on the cardfronts. The cards were highlighted with silver-foil for the logo and the lettering.

STATED ODDS 1:12
1 Troy Aikman SP 5.00 12.00
2 Marcus Allen 3.00 8.00
3 Mike Alstott 2.00 5.00
4 Jamal Anderson SP 3.00 8.00
5 Jerome Bettis 3.00 8.00
6 Drew Bledsoe SP 3.00 8.00
7 Tim Brown SP 4.00 10.00
8 Isaac Bruce SP 4.00 10.00
9 Mark Brunell SP 3.00 8.00
10 Plaxico Burress 2.00 5.00
11 Wayne Chrebet SP 2.50 6.00
12 Tim Couch SP 2.50 6.00
13 Daunte Culpepper SP 3.00 8.00
14 Randall Cunningham 2.50 6.00
15 Stephen Davis SP 2.50 6.00
16 Terrell Davis SP 3.00 8.00
17 Ron Dayne 2.50 6.00
18 Corey Dillon SP 2.50 6.00
19 Warrick Dunn 2.00 5.00
20 John Elway SP 6.00 15.00
21 Marshall Faulk 2.50 6.00
22 Brett Favre SP 8.00 20.00
23 Doug Flutie 2.50 6.00
24 Jeff Garcia SP 2.50 6.00
25 Eddie George 3.00 8.00
26 Brian Griese SP 2.50 6.00
27 Az-Zahir Hakim 2.00 5.00
28 Marvin Harrison SP 3.00 8.00
29 Bo Jackson 4.00 10.00
30 Edgerrin James SP 3.00 8.00
31 Jamal Lewis SP 4.00 10.00
32 Dan Marino SP 8.00 20.00
33 Curtis Martin SP 3.00 8.00
34 Ed McCaffrey 2.50 6.00
35 Donovan McNabb SP 3.00 8.00
36 Steve McNair 2.50 6.00
37 Joe Montana 10.00 25.00
38 Warren Moon SP 4.00 10.00
39 Randy Moss SP 3.00 8.00
40 Jerry Rice SP 8.00 20.00
41 Deion Sanders 2.50 6.00
42 Emmitt Smith SP 6.00 15.00
43 Rod Smith 2.50 6.00
44 Fred Taylor SP 2.50 6.00
45 Vinny Testaverde 2.00 5.00
46 Kurt Warner SP 6.00 15.00
47 Ricky Williams SP 3.00 8.00
48 Steve Young 4.00 10.00

2001 Hot Prospects TD Fever

Randomly inserted into packs of 2001 Fleer Hot Prospects at a rate of 1:21, this 14-card set featured a piece of the game-used goal post cover from the RCA Dome in Indianapolis. The theme to these cards were players who have seen time in the Indianapolis endzone in the 2000 NFL season.

STATED ODDS 1:21
1 Drew Bledsoe 2.00 5.00
2 Daunte Culpepper 2.00 5.00
3 Oronde Gadsden 1.50 4.00
4 Rich Gannon 2.00 5.00
5 Marvin Harrison 2.00 5.00
6 Edgerrin James 2.00 5.00
7 Peyton Manning 6.00 15.00
8 Curtis Martin 2.00 5.00
9 Randy Moss 2.00 5.00
10 Peerless Price 1.50 4.00
11 J.R. Redmond 1.50 4.00
12 Jimmy Smith 2.00 5.00
13 James Stewart 1.50 4.00
14 Tyrone Wheatley 2.00 5.00

2002 Hot Prospects

Released in July 2002, this 112-card base set includes 80 veterans and 32 rookies. The rookie cards offer swatches of game-worn jersey and are serial #'d to 1000. The product contains 15 packs per box, 5 cards per pack. The David Carr RC never made it into packs and was mailed out by Fleer to top dealers across the country. It does not feature a jersey swatch like the other Rookie Cards, and is serial numbered to 250.

COMP.SET w/o SP's (80) 10.00 25.00
ROOKIE JSY PRINT RUN 1000
1 Donovan McNabb .30 .75
2 Drew Brees .75 2.00
3 Curtis Martin .30 .75
4 Priest Holmes .25 .60
5 Quincy Carter .25 .60
6 Chris Weinke .25 .60
7 Marshall Faulk .30 .75
8 Jake Plummer .25 .60
9 Tom Brady 2.00 5.00
10 Ahman Green .30 .75
11 Brian Urlacher .40 1.00
12 Keyshawn Johnson .30 .75
13 Jerome Bettis .40 1.00
14 Tiki Barber .30 .75
15 Edgerrin James .30 .75
16 Jamal Lewis .30 .75
17 Terrell Owens .30 .75
18 Joe Horn .25 .60
19 Daunte Culpepper .30 .75
20 Terrell Davis .30 .75
21 Fred Taylor .25 .60
22 Emmitt Smith .60 1.50
23 Jamal Anderson .30 .75
24 Garrison Hearst .25 .60
25 Chad Pennington .25 .60
26 Michael Bennett .25 .60
27 James Allen .25 .60
28 Marty Booker .25 .60
29 Warren Sapp .30 .75
30 Jerry Rice .75 2.00
31 Antowain Smith .30 .75
32 Marvin Harrison .30 .75
33 Tim Couch .25 .60
34 Stephen Davis .25 .60
35 Kordell Stewart .25 .60
36 Tony Gonzalez .30 .75
37 Mike McMahon .25 .60
38 Eric Moulds .25 .60
39 Kurt Warner .30 .75
40 Ricky Williams .30 .75
41 Michael Strahan .30 .75
42 Trent Green .25 .60
43 Brian Griese .25 .60
44 David Boston .25 .60
45 LaDainian Tomlinson .40 1.00
46 Tim Brown .40 1.00
47 Deuce McAllister .30 .75
48 Jamie Sharper .30 .75
49 Rod Gardner .25 .60
50 Isaac Bruce .40 1.00
51 Freddie Mitchell .25 .60
52 Kerry Collins .25 .60
53 Mark Brunell .30 .75
54 Corey Dillon .25 .60
55 Steve McNair .30 .75
56 Aaron Brooks .25 .60
57 Chris Chambers .25 .60
58 Bill Schroeder .25 .60
59 Ray Lewis .40 1.00
60 Shaun Alexander .25 .60
61 Kevin Johnson .25 .60
62 Michael Vick .30 .75
63 Jeff Garcia .25 .60
64 Laveranues Coles .30 .75
65 Jimmy Smith .30 .75
66 Brett Favre .75 2.00
67 Anthony Thomas .30 .75
68 Torry Holt .30 .75
69 Duce Staley .25 .60
70 Randy Moss .30 .75
71 Peyton Manning 1.00 2.50
72 Peter Warrick .25 .60
73 Eddie George .30 .75
74 Plaxico Burress .25 .60
75 Troy Brown .25 .60
76 Rod Smith .30 .75
77 Drew Bledsoe .30 .75
78 Darrell Jackson .30 .75
79 Rich Gannon .30 .75
80 Jay Fiedler .30 .75
81 David Carr/250 RC 8.00 20.00
82 Andre Davis JSY RC 2.00 5.00
83 Daniel Graham JSY RC 2.50 6.00
84 Ron Johnson JSY RC 2.50 6.00
85 Julius Peppers JSY RC 5.00 12.00
86 Josh Reed JSY RC 2.50 6.00
87 Travis Stephens JSY RC 2.00 5.00
88 Mike Williams JSY RC 2.00 5.00
89 Antonio Bryant JSY RC 3.00 8.00
90 Eric Crouch JSY RC 3.00 8.00
91 DeShaun Foster JSY RC 3.00 8.00
92 Joey Harrington JSY RC 2.00 5.00
93 Josh McCown JSY RC 3.00 8.00
94 Patrick Ramsey JSY RC 2.50 6.00
95 Jeremy Shockey JSY RC 3.00 8.00
96 Marquise Walker JSY RC
97 Reche Caldwell JSY RC 2.50 6.00
98 Rohan Davey JSY RC 3.00 8.00
99 Jabar Gaffney JSY RC 2.00 5.00
100 David Garrard JSY RC 2.50 6.00
101 Maurice Morris JSY RC 2.50 6.00
102 Antwaan Randle El JSY RC 2.50 6.00
103 Donte Stallworth JSY RC 3.00 8.00
104 Roy Williams JSY RC 2.00 5.00
105 Ladell Betts JSY RC 3.00 8.00
106 Tim Carter JSY RC 2.50 6.00
107 T.J. Duckett JSY RC 2.00 5.00
108 William Green JSY RC 2.50 6.00
109 Ashley Lelie JSY RC 2.00 5.00
110 Clinton Portis JSY RC 3.00 8.00
111 Cliff Russell JSY RC 2.00 5.00
112 Javon Walker JSY RC 3.00 8.00

2002 Hot Prospects Class Of

This 20-card set is serially #'d to 750. The set offers two players from the same draft class on one card.

STATED PRINT RUN 750 SER.#'d SETS
1 T.Couch/D.McNabb 1.25 3.00
2 T.Holt/D.Boston 1.25 3.00
3 F.Taylor/A.Green 1.25 3.00
4 J.Plummer/C.Dillon 1.00 2.50
5 K.Johnson/M.Harrison 1.25 3.00
6 W.Sapp/C.Martin 1.25 3.00
7 A.Brooks/D.Culpepper 1.25 3.00
8 M.Faulk/I.Bruce 1.50 4.00
9 B.Griese/P.Manning 4.00 10.00
10 S.Davis/E.George 1.25 3.00
11 E.James/R.Williams 1.25 3.00
12 R.Moss/H.Ward 1.25 3.00
13 M.Strahan/J.Bettis 1.50 4.00
14 T.Owens/M.Alstott 1.25 3.00
15 B.Favre/R.Watters 3.00 8.00
16 R.Dayne/S.Alexander 1.25 3.00
17 P.Warrick/T.Jones 1.00 2.50
18 T.Brady/C.Pennington 8.00 20.00
19 M.Vick/D.Brees 3.00 8.00
20 L.Tomlinson/A.Thomas 1.50 4.00

2002 Hot Prospects Class Of Memorabilia

This set is serially #'d to 375, and features two players from the same draft class with memorabilia swatches from each.

STATED PRINT RUN 375 SER.#'d SETS
ABDC A.Brooks/D.Culpepper 2.50 6.00
EJRW E.James/R.Williams 2.50 6.00
FTAG F.Taylor/A.Green 2.50 6.00
JPCD J.Plummer/C.Dillon 2.00 5.00
KJMH K.Johnson/M.Harrison 2.50 6.00
LTAT L.Tomlinson/A.Thomas 3.00 8.00
MFIB M.Faulk/I.Bruce 3.00 8.00
MSJB M.Strahan/J.Bettis 3.00 8.00
MVDB M.Vick/D.Brees 6.00 15.00
PWTJ P.Warrick/T.Jones 2.00 5.00
RDSA R.Dayne/S.Alexander 2.50 6.00
RMHW R.Moss/H.Ward 2.50 6.00
SDEG S.Davis/E.George 2.50 6.00
TBCP T.Brady/C.Pennington 15.00 40.00
TCDM T.Couch/D.McNabb 2.50 6.00
THDB T.Holt/D.Boston 2.50 6.00
TOMA T.Owens/M.Alstott 2.50 6.00
WSCM W.Sapp/C.Martin 2.50 6.00

2002 Hot Prospects Hat Trick

is 10-card set was inserted at a rate of 1:7. The set features a unique tri-player card that offers photos of three of the NFL's best at their position.

STATED ODDS 1:7
HTAMD Alxndr/McAllstr/Ducket 1.25 3.00
HTBMS Burress/Mitchll/Stllwrth 1.50 4.00
HTDTF Dayne/Thomas/Foster 1.50 4.00
HTFHS Franks/Heap/Shockey 1.50 4.00
HTLTG Lewis/Tomlinson/Green 1.50 4.00
HTRBH Redman/Brees/Harring 3.00 8.00
HTTRG Taylor/Robinson/Gaffney 1.00 2.50
HTUMP Urlach/Morgan/Pepp. 2.50 6.00
HTWGL Warrick/Gardner/Lelie 1.00 2.50

2002 Hot Prospects Hat Trick Memorabilia

This 10-card set is serially #'d to 150. The set features a unique tri-swatch card that offers pieces of hats worn by three former attendees of the annual NFL Players Rookie Premiere.

STATED PRINT RUN 150 SER.#'d SETS
HTAMD Alxndr/McAllstr/Ducket 3.00 8.00
HTBMS Burress/Mitchll/Stllwrth 4.00 10.00
HTDTF Dayne/Thomas/Foster 4.00 10.00
HTFHS Franks/Heap/Shockey 4.00 10.00
HTLTG Lewis/Tomlinson/Green 4.00 10.00
HTRBH Redman/Brees/Harring 8.00 20.00
HTTRG Taylor/Robins/Gaffney 2.50 6.00
HTUMP Urlach/Morgan/Peppers 6.00 15.00
HTWGL Warrick/Gardner/Lelie 2.50 6.00

2002 Hot Prospects Hot Materials

Inserted in packs at a rate of 1:6, this 45-card insert set includes game-worn jersey swatches from both veteran and rookie players.

STATED ODDS 1:6
*RED HOT/50: .6X TO 1.5X BASIC JSY
RED HOT PRINT RUN 50 SER.#'d SETS
HMAB Aaron Brooks 2.00 5.00
HMAB2 Antonio Bryant 3.00 8.00
HMAG Ahman Green 2.50 6.00
HMAL Ashley Lelie 2.00 5.00
HMAR Antwaan Randle El 2.50 6.00
HMAT Anthony Thomas 2.50 6.00
HMBF Brett Favre 6.00 15.00
HMBU Brian Urlacher 3.00 8.00
HMCD Corey Dillon SP/361 2.00 5.00
HMCM Curtis Martin 2.50 6.00
HMCP Clinton Portis 3.00 8.00
HMDB Drew Brees SP/124 6.00 15.00
HMDC Daunte Culpepper 2.50 6.00
HMDC2 Reche Caldwell 2.50 6.00
HMDF DeShaun Foster 3.00 8.00
HMDM Donovan McNabb 2.50 6.00
HMDS Donte Stallworth 3.00 8.00
HMEG Eddie George 2.50 6.00
HMES Emmitt Smith 5.00 12.00
HMIB Isaac Bruce 3.00 8.00
HMJG Jabar Gaffney 2.00 5.00
HMJG2 Jeff Garcia 2.00 5.00
HMJH Joey Harrington 2.00 5.00
HMJR Jerry Rice 6.00 15.00
HMJR2 Josh Reed 2.50 6.00
HMJW Javon Walker 3.00 8.00
HMKJ Keyshawn Johnson 2.50 6.00
HMKS Kordell Stewart SP/161 2.00 5.00
HMKW Kurt Warner 2.50 6.00
HMLC Laveranues Coles 2.50 6.00
HMLT LaDainian Tomlinson 3.00 8.00
HMMF Marshall Faulk 2.50 6.00
HMMW Marquise Walker 2.00 5.00
HMPR Patrick Ramsey SP/331 2.50 6.00
HMPW Peter Warrick 2.00 5.00
HMRM Randy Moss SP/62 2.50 6.00
HMRW Ricky Williams 2.50 6.00
HMSD Stephen Davis 2.00 5.00
HMTB Tom Brady 15.00 40.00
HMTC Tim Couch 2.00 5.00
HMTC2 Trung Canidate 2.00 5.00
HMTD T.J. Duckett 2.00 5.00
HMTH Torry Holt 2.50 6.00
HMTO Terrell Owens 2.50 6.00
HMWG William Green 2.50 6.00

2002 Hot Prospects Hot Tandems Memorabilia

This 44-card set includes dual player cards that offer dual game-worn jersey swatches. The set is serially #'d to 100.

STATED PRINT RUN 100 SER.#'d SETS
UNPRICED RED HOT PRINT RUN 10
ABJR A.Bryant/J.Reed 4.00 10.00
ABRW A.Brooks/R.Williams 3.00 8.00
AGCD A.Green/C.Dillon 3.00 8.00
ALJR A.Lelie/J.Reed 3.00 8.00
ALTC A.Lelie/T.Canidate 2.50 6.00
ARJW A.Randle El/J.Walker 4.00 10.00
ATBU A.Thomas/B.Urlacher 4.00 10.00
BFCM B.Favre/C.Martin 8.00 20.00
CPDF C.Portis/D.Foster 4.00 10.00
DCRM D.Culpepper/R.Moss 3.00 8.00
DFCM D.Foster/C.Martin 4.00 10.00
DMAB D.McNabb/A.Brooks 3.00 8.00
DMDC D.McNabb/D.Culpepper 3.00 8.00
DMTC D.McNabb/T.Couch 3.00 8.00
DSMW D.Stallworth/M.Walker 4.00 10.00
EGTD E.George/T.J.Duckett 3.00 8.00
ESMF E.Smith/M.Faulk 6.00 15.00
ESWG E.Smith/W.Green 6.00 15.00
JGAB J.Gaffney/A.Bryant 4.00 10.00
JGAG J.Garcia/A.Green 3.00 8.00
JGLT J.Garcia/L.Tomlinson 4.00 10.00
JRBU J.Rice/B.Urlacher 8.00 20.00
JRDS J.Rice/D.Stallworth 8.00 20.00
KJMW K.Johnson/M.Walker 3.00 8.00
KSAR K.Stewart/A.Randle El 3.00 8.00
KSTC K.Stewart/T.Couch 2.50 6.00
LCJB L.Coles/J.Gaffney 3.00 8.00
LTMM L.Tomlinson/M.Morris 4.00 10.00
PWCD P.Warrick/C.Dillon 2.50 6.00
RCJW R.Caldwell/J.Walker 4.00 10.00
RCPR R.Caldwell/P.Ramsey 3.00 8.00
RMTO R.Moss/T.Owens 3.00 8.00
RWAT R.Williams/A.Thomas 3.00 8.00
SDEG S.Davis/E.George 3.00 8.00
SDLC S.Davis/L.Coles 3.00 8.00
TBJH T.Brady/J.Harrington 20.00 50.00
TBKW T.Brady/K.Warner 20.00 50.00
TCPR T.Couch/P.Ramsey 3.00 8.00
THMF T.Holt/M.Faulk 3.00 8.00
THTC T.Holt/T.Canidate 3.00 8.00
TOBF T.Owens/B.Favre 8.00 20.00
WGTD W.Green/T.J.Duckett 3.00 8.00

2002 Hot Prospects Sweet Selections

This 10-card set is randomly inserted in packs at a rate of 1:15, and features some of this year's top rookies.

STATED ODDS 1:15
1 David Carr .60 1.50
2 Julius Peppers 1.50 4.00
3 Joey Harrington .60 1.50
4 Donte Stallworth 1.00 2.50
5 William Green .75 2.00
6 T.J. Duckett .60 1.50
7 Ashley Lelie .60 1.50
8 Javon Walker 1.00 2.50
9 Patrick Ramsey .75 2.00
10 Jabar Gaffney .60 1.50

2003 Hot Prospects

Released in November of 2003, this set originally consisted of 120-cards, including 80-veterans and 40-rookies. The overall rookie odds were 1:4. Rookies 81-91 were issued as exchange cards in packs redeemable for a card featuring an authentic player autograph serial numbered to 400. Rookies 92-103 featured game worn jersey swatches and were serial numbered to 750. Rookies 104-109 were issued as exchange cards in packs redeemable for a card featuring an authentic player autograph serial numbered to 400. Rookies 110-120 were serial numbered to 1250. Boxes contained 15 packs of 4 cards and the SRP was $4.99. Ultimately Fleer never redeemed any of the signed rookies from the set so those have been removed from the checklist below leaving a complete skip-numbered set of 103-cards.

COMP.SET w/o SP's (80) 7.50 20.00
92-103 JSY ROOKIE PRINT RUN 750
110-120 ROOKIE PRINT RUN 1250
OVERALL ROOKIE STATED ODDS 1:4
1 Emmitt Smith .60 1.50
2 Terrell Owens .30 .75
3 Tiki Barber .30 .75
4 Trent Green .25 .60
5 Quincy Morgan .25 .60
6 Eric Moulds .25 .60
7 Simeon Rice .25 .60
8 Hines Ward .30 .75
9 Michael Bennett .25 .60
10 Donald Driver .30 .75
11 Stephen Davis .25 .60
12 Steve McNair .30 .75
13 David Boston .25 .60
14 Deuce McAllister .30 .75
15 Marvin Harrison .30 .75
16 Peerless Price .25 .60
17 Matt Hasselbeck .25 .60
18 Jerry Rice .75 2.00
19 Junior Seau .30 .75
20 Clinton Portis .25 .60
21 Fred Taylor .25 .60
22 William Green .25 .60
23 Warrick Dunn .25 .60
24 Koren Robinson .30 .75
25 Jeremy Shockey .25 .60
26 Chris Chambers .25 .60
27 Brett Favre .75 2.00
28 Julius Peppers .40 1.00
29 Eddie George .30 .75
30 Todd Pinkston .25 .60
31 Tom Brady 1.50 4.00
32 Edgerrin James .30 .75
33 Chad Johnson .25 .60
34 Laveranues Coles .25 .60
35 LaDainian Tomlinson .40 1.00
36 Priest Holmes .25 .60
37 Shannon Sharpe .30 .75
38 Jamal Lewis .30 .75
39 Warren Sapp .30 .75
40 Tim Brown .40 1.00
41 Kerry Collins .25 .60
42 Jimmy Smith .30 .75
43 Chad Hutchinson .25 .60
44 Marcel Shipp .25 .60
45 Jeff Garcia .25 .60
46 Donovan McNabb .30 .75
47 Randy Moss .30 .75
48 Ahman Green .30 .75
49 Travis Henry .25 .60
50 Brad Johnson .30 .75
51 Tommy Maddox .25 .60
52 Aaron Brooks .25 .60
53 Peyton Manning 1.00 2.50
54 Brian Urlacher .40 1.00
55 Rod Gardner .25 .60
56 Chad Pennington .25 .60
57 Ricky Williams .30 .75
58 James Stewart .25 .60
59 Todd Heap .25 .60
60 Marshall Faulk .30 .75
61 Corey Dillon .25 .60
62 Michael Vick .30 .75
63 Shaun Alexander .25 .60
64 Curtis Martin .30 .75
65 Mark Brunell .30 .75
66 Joey Harrington .25 .60
67 Drew Bledsoe .30 .75
68 Keyshawn Johnson .40 1.00
69 Jerome Bettis .40 1.00
70 Daunte Culpepper .30 .75
71 David Carr .25 .60
72 Marty Booker .25 .60
73 Patrick Ramsey .30 .75
74 Drew Brees .40 1.00
75 Donte Stallworth .25 .60
76 Jake Plummer .25 .60
77 Ray Lewis .40 1.00
78 Kurt Warner .30 .75
79 Rich Gannon .30 .75
80 Tony Gonzalez .30 .75
92 Dallas Clark JSY RC 3.00 8.00
93 Terence Newman JSY RC 3.00 8.00
94 Rex Grossman JSY RC 2.50 6.00
95 Kelley Washington JSY RC 2.00 5.00
96 Kyle Boller JSY RC 2.00 5.00
97 Carson Palmer JSY RC 4.00 10.00
98 Charles Rogers JSY RC 2.50 6.00
99 Chris Simms JSY RC 2.00 5.00
100 Larry Johnson JSY RC 2.50 6.00

101 Andre Johnson JSY RC 5.00 12.00
102 Taylor Jacobs JSY RC 2.00 5.00
103 Byron Leftwich JSY RC 2.50 6.00
110 Tyrone Calico RC 1.00 2.50
111 Billy McMullen RC 1.00 2.50
112 Jerome McDougle RC 1.00 2.50
113 Willis McGahee RC 1.25 3.00
114 Anquan Boldin RC 1.50 4.00
115 Artose Pinner RC 1.00 2.50
116 Kevin Williams RC 1.50 4.00
117 Bethel Johnson RC 1.00 2.50
118 Quentin Griffin RC 1.25 3.00
119 Nate Burleson RC 1.25 3.00
120 DeWayne Robertson RC 1.25 3.00

2003 Hot Prospects Cream of the Crop

COMPLETE SET (15) 15.00 40.00
STATED ODDS 1:5
1 Byron Leftwich .60 1.50
2 Charles Rogers .60 1.50
3 Carson Palmer 1.00 2.50
4 Taylor Jacobs .50 1.25
5 Bryant Johnson .75 2.00
6 Kyle Boller .50 1.25
7 Rex Grossman .60 1.50
8 Andre Johnson 1.25 3.00
9 Kelley Washington .50 1.25
10 Larry Johnson .60 1.50
11 Willis McGahee .60 1.50
12 Chris Simms .50 1.25
13 Jason Witten 2.00 5.00
14 Anquan Boldin .75 2.00
15 Quentin Griffin .60 1.50

2003 Hot Prospects Hot Materials

Randomly inserted in packs, this set features game worn jersey swatches. Each card is serial numbered to 150.
STATED PRINT RUN 150 SER.#'d SETS
*RED HOT/50: .6X TO 1.5X JSY/150
RED HOT PRINT RUN 50 SER.#'d SETS
OVERALL MEMORABILIA ODDS 1:6
HMBF Brett Favre 8.00 20.00
HMBU Brian Urlacher 4.00 10.00
HMCP Clinton Portis 2.50 6.00
HMCP2 Chad Pennington 2.50 6.00
HMDB Drew Bledsoe 3.00 8.00
HMDB2 Drew Brees 4.00 10.00
HMDC Daunte Culpepper 3.00 8.00
HMDC2 David Carr 2.50 6.00
HMDM Deuce McAllister 3.00 8.00
HMDM2 Donovan McNabb 3.00 8.00
HMDS Donte Stallworth 2.50 6.00
HMEJ Edgerrin James 3.00 8.00
HMJG Jeff Garcia 2.50 6.00
HMJH Joey Harrington 2.50 6.00
HMJL Jamal Lewis 3.00 8.00
HMJR Jerry Rice 8.00 20.00
HMJS Jeremy Shockey 2.50 6.00
HMKW Kurt Warner 3.00 8.00
HMLT LaDainian Tomlinson 4.00 10.00
HMMF Marshall Faulk 3.00 8.00
HMMV Michael Vick 3.00 8.00
HMPM Peyton Manning 10.00 25.00
HMPR Patrick Ramsey 3.00 8.00
HMRG Rod Gardner 2.50 6.00
HMRG Rich Gannon 3.00 8.00
HMRM Randy Moss 3.00 8.00
HMRW Ricky Williams 3.00 8.00
HMSA Shaun Alexander 2.50 6.00
HMTB Tom Brady 15.00 40.00
HMTO Terrell Owens 3.00 8.00

2003 Hot Prospects Hot Tandems

Randomly inserted in packs, this set pairs two NFL superstars with a game used jersey swatch of each player. Each card is serial numbered to 100. A Red parallel of this set exists, with cards numbered to 10. Red parallels are not priced due to scarcity.
STATED PRINT RUN 100 SER.#'d SETS
UNPRICED RED HOTS SER.#'d TO 10
OVERALL MEMORABILIA ODDS 1:6
BFTB B.Favre/T.Brady 20.00 50.00
BUJR B.Urlacher/J.Rice 12.00 30.00
CPJL C.Portis/J.Lewis 5.00 12.00
CPMV C.Pennington/M.Vick 5.00 12.00
CPRW C.Pennington/R.Williams 5.00 12.00
DBDB D.Bledsoe/D.Brees 6.00 15.00
DCDC D.Culpepper/D.Carr 5.00 12.00
DCPR D.Carr/P.Ramsey 5.00 12.00
DMRM D.McNabb/R.Moss 5.00 12.00
DMSA D.McAllister/S.Alexander 5.00 12.00
EJLT E.James/L.Tomlinson 6.00 15.00
JGDM J.Garcia/D.McNabb 5.00 12.00
JHDB J.Harrington/D.Bledsoe 5.00 12.00
JHDC J.Harrington/D.Culpepper 5.00 12.00
JRRM J.Rice/R.Moss 12.00 30.00
JSBF J.Shockey/B.Favre 12.00 30.00
JSRG J.Shockey/R.Gardner 4.00 10.00
KWRG K.Warner/R.Gannon 5.00 12.00
LTJL L.Tomlinson/J.Lewis 6.00 15.00
MFMV M.Faulk/M.Vick 5.00 12.00
PMBU P.Manning/B.Urlacher 15.00 40.00
PMKW P.Manning/K.Warner 15.00 40.00
RWMF R.Williams/M.Faulk 5.00 12.00
TODM T.Owens/D.McAllister 5.00 12.00
TODS T.Owens/D.Stallworth 5.00 12.00

2003 Hot Prospects Hot Triple Patches

Randomly inserted in packs, this set features cards with three game used jersey swatches of NFL superstars. Each card is serial numbered to 50.
STATED PRINT RUN 50 SERIAL #'d SETS
OVERALL MEMORABILIA ODDS 1:6
BGP Brady/Garcia/Penning 50.00 125.00
CRB Carr/Ramsey/Brees 12.00 30.00
FMM Favre/Manning/McNbb 30.00 80.00
HBC Harring/Bledsoe/Culp 10.00 25.00
JLA James/Lewis/Alexander 10.00 25.00
JTL James/Tomlinson/Lewis 12.00 30.00
MMM McNabb/R.Moss/Mann 30.00 80.00
MPT McAllister/Portis/Tomlin 12.00 30.00
ORM Owens/Rice/R.Moss 25.00 60.00
SFB Shockey/Favre/Brady 50.00 125.00
SSG Shockey/Stallw/Gardner 8.00 20.00
UWF Urlach/Ric.Will/M.Faulk 12.00 30.00
VHC Vick/Harrington/Culpep 10.00 25.00
WFV Ric.Williams/Faulk/Vick 10.00 25.00
WGB Warner/Gannon/Bleds 10.00 25.00

2003 Hot Prospects Playergraphs Redemption

Randomly inserted in packs, all of the cards in this set were issued as exchange cards in packs to be redeemed for authentic player autographs. Each redeemed card is numbered to 200. A Red parallel of this set exists, featuring cards serial numbered to 50.
STATED PRINT RUN 200 SER.#'d SETS
*REDS: .6X TO 1.5X BASIC AUTOS
RED HOT PRINT RUN 50 SER.#'d SETS
OVERALL AUTOGRAPH ODDS 1:60
PDM Donovan McNabb AU 15.00 40.00
PJH Joey Harrington AU 20.00 50.00
PMB Michael Bennett AU 10.00 25.00
PPB Plaxico Burress AU 10.00 25.00

2003 Hot Prospects Sweet Selections

COMPLETE SET (10) 12.00 30.00
STATED ODDS 1:15
1 C.Palmer/D.Carr 1.00 2.50
2 L.Tomlinson/J.Lewis 1.25 3.00
3 J.Harrington/S.McNair 1.00 2.50
4 B.Urlacher/F.Taylor 1.25 3.00
5 M.Vick/P.Manning 3.00 8.00
6 T.Holt/T.Brown 1.25 3.00
7 R.Williams/J.Seau 1.00 2.50
8 D.McNabb/M.Faulk 1.00 2.50
9 P.Burress/D.Boston .75 2.00
10 Key.Johnson/Bledsoe 1.25 3.00

2003 Hot Prospects Sweet Selections Jerseys

Randomly inserted in packs, these cards feature two game used jersey swatches. Each card is serial numbered to 325.
STATED PRINT RUN 325 SER.#'d SETS
OVERALL MEMORABILIA ODDS 1:6
BUFT B.Urlacher/F.Taylor 4.00 10.00
DMMF D.McNabb/M.Faulk 3.00 8.00
JHSM J.Harrington/S.McNair 3.00 8.00
KJDB Key.Johnson/Bledsoe 4.00 10.00
LTJL L.Tomlinson/J.Lewis 4.00 10.00
MVPM M.Vick/P.Manning 10.00 25.00
PBDB P.Burress/D.Boston 2.50 6.00
PMDC C.Palmer/D.Carr 3.00 8.00
RWJS R.Williams/J.Seau 3.00 8.00
THTB T.Holt/T.Brown 4.00 10.00

2004 Hot Prospects

Fleer Hot Prospects initially released in early August 2004. The base set consists of 112-cards including 24-jersey autographed rookie cards, 8-jersey rookie cards, and 10-rookies serial numbered of 1000. Hobby boxes contained 15-packs of 5-cards and carried an S.R.P. of $7.99 per pack while retail boxes contained 24-packs of 5-cards and carried an S.R.P. of $2.99. Two parallel sets and a variety of inserts can be found seeded in hobby and retail packs highlighted by the Notable Notations Autograph inserts. Some signed cards were issued via mail-in exchange or redemption cards. Card #92 Luke McCown was one of those exchange cards in packs, but the live card was never released.
COMP.SET w/o SP's (70) 7.50 20.00
71-94 AU JSY RC ODDS 1:20H, 1:840R
95-102 JSY RC ODDS 1:42H, 1:420R
95-102 JSY RC PRINT RUN 350 #'d SETS
103-112 ROOKIE ODDS 1:18H, 1:1440R
103-112 RC PRINT RUN 1000 SER. #'d SETS
UNPRICED WHITE HOT PRINT RUN 1
1 Donovan McNabb .25 .60
2 Charlie Garner .25 .60
3 Tim Rattay .20 .50
4 Drew Brees .30 .75
5 Jerry Rice .60 1.50
6 Aaron Brooks .20 .50
7 Chris Chambers .20 .50
8 Byron Leftwich .20 .50
9 Andre Johnson .25 .60
10 Edgerrin James .25 .60
11 Charles Rogers .20 .50
12 Quentin Griffin .20 .50
13 Carson Palmer .25 .60
14 Ray Lewis .30 .75
15 Clinton Portis .20 .50
16 Marc Bulger .20 .50
17 Matt Hasselbeck .20 .50
18 Plaxico Burress .20 .50
19 Priest Holmes .20 .50
20 David Carr .20 .50
21 Ahman Green .25 .60
22 Roy Williams S .20 .50
23 Travis Henry .20 .50
24 Michael Vick .25 .60
25 Eddie George .25 .60
26 Marshall Faulk .25 .60
27 Kevan Barlow .20 .50
28 Shaun Alexander .20 .50
29 Hines Ward .25 .60
30 Anquan Boldin .20 .50
31 Chad Pennington .20 .50
32 Randy Moss .25 .60
33 Fred Taylor .20 .50
34 Marvin Harrison .25 .60
35 Joey Harrington .20 .50
36 Rich Gannon .25 .60
37 Deuce McAllister .25 .60
38 Deion Branch .20 .50
39 Tony Gonzalez .25 .60
40 Brett Favre .60 1.50
41 Keyshawn Johnson .25 .60
42 Lee Suggs .25 .60
43 Jake Delhomme .20 .50
44 Rex Grossman .20 .50
45 Drew Bledsoe .25 .60
46 Warrick Dunn .20 .50
47 Steve McNair .25 .60
48 Torry Holt .25 .60
49 Brian Westbrook .20 .50
50 Santana Moss .25 .60
51 Jeremy Shockey .20 .50
52 Daunte Culpepper .25 .60
53 Jeff Garcia .20 .50
54 Stephen Davis .20 .50
55 Eric Moulds .20 .50
56 Emmitt Smith .50 1.25
57 Keenan McCardell .20 .50
58 LaDainian Tomlinson .30 .75
59 Terrell Owens .25 .60
60 Curtis Martin .25 .60
61 Joe Horn .20 .50
62 Tiki Barber .25 .60
63 Tom Brady 1.25 3.00
64 Ricky Williams .25 .60
65 Peyton Manning .75 2.00
66 Jake Plummer .20 .50
67 Chad Johnson .20 .50
68 Brian Urlacher .30 .75
69 Jamal Lewis .25 .60
70 Laveranues Coles .20 .50
71 Tatum Bell JSY AU/350 RC 8.00 20.00
72 B.Berrian JSY AU/344 RC 20.00 40.00
73 M.Clayton JSY AU/350 RC 8.00 20.00
74 Lee Evans JSY AU/350 RC 12.00 30.00
75 Fitzgerald JSY AU/140 RC 60.00 120.00
76 Henderson JSY AU/350 RC 8.00 20.00
77 D.Henson JSY AU/331 RC 8.00 20.00
78 St.Jackson JSY AU/300 RC 12.00 30.00
80 Greg Jones JSY AU/289 RC 8.00 20.00
81 Kev.Jones JSY AU/278 RC 8.00 20.00
82 J.Losman JSY AU/350 RC 8.00 20.00
83 Eli Manning JSY AU/350 RC 60.00 120.00
84 Chris Perry JSY AU/350 RC 8.00 20.00
85 Phil.Rivers JSY AU/350 RC 50.00 100.00
86 Roethlis.JSY AU/150 RC 100.00 200.00
87 Reg.Williams JSY AU/350 RC 8.00 20.00
88 Ro.Williams JSY AU/350 RC 8.00 20.00
89 Kell.Winslow JSY AU/50 RC 40.00 100.00
90 R.Woods JSY AU/350 RC 8.00 20.00
91 Jul.Jones JSY AU/350 RC 8.00 20.00
93 K.Colbert JSY AU/349 RC 8.00 20.00
94 M.Schaub JSY AU/120 RC 12.00 30.00
95 Cedric Cobbs JSY RC 3.00 8.00
96 Darius Watts JSY RC 3.00 8.00
97 DeAngelo Hall JSY RC 5.00 12.00
98 Derrick Hamilton JSY RC 3.00 8.00
99 Devard Darling JSY RC 3.00 8.00
100 Ben Troupe JSY RC 3.00 8.00
101 Mewelde Moore JSY RC 4.00 10.00
102 Ben Watson JSY RC 4.00 10.00
103 Sean Taylor RC 6.00 15.00
104 Ricky Ray RC 1.50 4.00
105 Carlos Francis RC 1.00 2.50
106 Samie Parker RC 1.00 2.50
107 Jerricho Cotchery RC 1.25 3.00
108 Ernest Wilford RC 1.25 3.00
109 Craig Krenzel RC 1.00 2.50
110 Robert Gallery RC 1.25 3.00
111 Dunta Robinson RC 1.00 2.50
112 Jonathan Vilma RC 1.25 3.00

2004 Hot Prospects Red Hot

*VETS 1-72: 6X TO 15X BASIC CARDS
*ROOK.71-94: .5X TO 1.2X AU RC/278-350
*ROOK.71-94: .4X TO 1X AU RC/50-150
*ROOKIES 95-102: .8X TO 2X
*ROOKIES 103-112: 1.2X TO 3X
OVERALL PARALLEL ODDS 1:26H, 1:420R
RED HOT PRINT RUN 50 SER.#'d SETS
89 Kellen Winslow JSY AU 40.00 100.00

2004 Hot Prospects Alumni Ink

STATED PRINT RUN 50 SER.#'d SETS
UNPRICED RED HOT PRINT RUN 10
UNPRICED WHITE HOT PRINT RUN 1
CPBL Pennington/Leftwich 20.00 50.00
DHMC D.Henderson/M.Clayton 12.00 30.00
DHTB D.Henson/T.Brady 100.00 175.00
DMEM D.McAllister/E.Manning 60.00 120.00
LECC L.Evans/C.Chambers 10.00 25.00
TBRW T.Bell/R.Woods 8.00 20.00

2004 Hot Prospects Double Team Autograph Patches

AUTO PRINT RUN 25 SER.#'d SETS
UNPRICED RED HOT PRINT RUN 5
UNPRICED WHITE HOT PRINT RUN 1
DTKJ Kevin Jones 15.00 40.00
DTMS Matt Schaub 20.00 50.00
DTRW Roy Williams WR 12.00 30.00
DTSJ Steven Jackson 20.00 50.00

2004 Hot Prospects Double Team Jersey

STATED PRINT RUN 100 SER.#'d SETS
*RED HOT/25: .8X TO 2X BASIC JSY/100
RED HOT PRINT RUN 25 SER.#'d SETS
UNPRICED WHITE HOT PRINT RUN 1
*PATCH/50: .6X TO 1.5X BASIC JSY/100
PATCH PRINT RUN 50 SER.#'d SETS
*RH PATCH/10: 1X TO 2.5X JSY/100
UNPRICED WHITE HOT PATCH PRINT RUN 1
DTDF DeShaun Foster 2.50 6.00
DTDH Drew Henson 2.00 5.00
DTEM Eli Manning 10.00 25.00
DTKJ Kevin Jones 2.50 6.00
DTKW Kellen Winslow Jr. 2.00 5.00
DTLE Lee Evans 3.00 8.00
DTMS Matt Schaub 2.00 5.00
DTQG Quentin Griffin 2.00 5.00
DTRW Roy Williams WR 2.00 5.00
DTSJ Steven Jackson 3.00 8.00

2004 Hot Prospects Draft Rewind

COMPLETE SET (30) 25.00 60.00
STATED ODDS 1:5
1DR Donovan McNabb .75 2.00
2DR Jerry Rice 2.00 5.00
3DR Andre Johnson .75 2.00
4DR Edgerrin James .75 2.00
5DR Charles Rogers .60 1.50
6DR Carson Palmer .75 2.00
7DR David Carr .60 1.50
8DR Roy Williams S .60 1.50
9DR Michael Vick .75 2.00
10DR Eddie George .75 2.00
11DR Marshall Faulk .75 2.00
12DR Anquan Boldin .60 1.50
13DR Chad Pennington .60 1.50
14DR Randy Moss .75 2.00
15DR Marvin Harrison .75 2.00
16DR Joey Harrington .60 1.50
17DR Deuce McAllister .75 2.00
18DR Brett Favre 2.00 5.00
19DR Steve McNair .75 2.00
20DR Jeremy Shockey .60 1.50
21DR Daunte Culpepper .75 2.00
22DR Emmitt Smith 1.50 4.00
23DR LaDainian Tomlinson 1.00 2.50
24DR Terrell Owens .75 2.00
25DR Eli Manning 3.00 8.00
26DR Ricky Williams .75 2.00
27DR Peyton Manning 2.50 6.00
28DR Chad Johnson .60 1.50
29DR Brian Urlacher 1.00 2.50
30DR Jamal Lewis .75 2.00

2004 Hot Prospects Draft Rewind Jersey

ATED PRINT RUN 101-189
*RED HOT/10: .8X TO 2X BASIC JSY
UNPRICED WHITE HOT PRINT RUN 1
*PATCH/43-99: .5X TO 1.2X BASIC JSY
*PATCH/31-33: .6X TO 1.5X BASIC JSY
*PATCH/21-29: .8X TO 2X BASIC JSY
*PATCH/11-19: 1X TO 2.5X BASIC JSY
UNPRICED RED HOT PATCH PRINT RUN 5
DRAB Anquan Boldin/154 3.00 8.00
DRAJ Andre Johnson/103 4.00 10.00
DRBF Brett Favre/133 10.00 25.00
DRBU Brian Urlacher/109 6.00 15.00
DRCJ Chad Johnson/136 3.00 8.00
DRCP Carson Palmer/101 4.00 10.00
DRCP2 Chad Pennington/118 3.00 8.00
DRCR Charles Rogers/102 3.00 8.00
DRDC David Carr/101 3.00 8.00
DRDC2 Daunte Culpepper/111 4.00 10.00
DRDM Deuce McAllister/123 4.00 10.00
DRDM2 Donovan McNabb/102 4.00 10.00
DREG Eddie George/114 4.00 10.00
DREJ Edgerrin James/104 4.00 10.00
DREM Eli Manning/101 15.00 40.00
DRES Emmitt Smith/117 10.00 25.00
DRJH Joey Harrington/103 3.00 8.00
DRJL Jamal Lewis/105 4.00 10.00
DRJR Jerry Rice/116 10.00 25.00
DRJS Jeremy Shockey/114 3.00 8.00
DRLT LaDainian Tomlinson/105 5.00 12.00
DRMF Marshall Faulk/102 4.00 10.00
DRMH Marvin Harrison/119 4.00 10.00
DRMV Michael Vick/101 6.00 15.00
DRPM Peyton Manning/101 12.00 30.00
DRRM Randy Moss/121 4.00 10.00
DRRW Ricky Williams/105 4.00 10.00
DRRW2 Roy Williams S/108 3.00 8.00
DRSM Steve McNair/103 4.00 10.00
DRTO Terrell Owens/189 4.00 10.00

2004 Hot Prospects Hot Materials

ATED PRINT RUN 500 SER.#'d SETS
*RED HOT/50: .8X TO 2X BASIC JSY/500
RED HOT PRINT RUN 50 SER.#'d SETS
UNPRICED WHITE HOT PRINT RUN 1
HMAB Anquan Boldin 2.00 5.00
HMBF Brett Favre 6.00 15.00
HMBR Ben Roethlisberger 12.00 30.00
HMBU Brian Urlacher 3.00 8.00
HMCP Carson Palmer 2.50 6.00
HMCP2 Chad Pennington 2.00 5.00
HMDC David Carr 2.00 5.00
HMDC2 Daunte Culpepper 2.50 6.00
HMDH Drew Henson 2.00 5.00
HMDM Donovan McNabb 2.50 6.00
HMDM2 Deuce McAllister 2.50 6.00
HMEJ Edgerrin James 2.50 6.00
HMEM Eli Manning 12.00 30.00
HMES Emmitt Smith 5.00 12.00
HMJH Joey Harrington 2.00 5.00
HMJL Jamal Lewis 2.50 6.00
HMJR Jerry Rice 6.00 15.00
HMJS Jeremy Shockey 2.00 5.00
HMKJ Kevin Jones 2.50 6.00
HMKW Kellen Winslow Jr. 2.00 5.00
HMLE Lee Evans 3.00 8.00
HMLF Larry Fitzgerald 6.00 15.00
HMLT LaDainian Tomlinson 3.00 8.00
HMMF Marshall Faulk 2.50 6.00
HMMH Marvin Harrison 2.50 6.00
HMMV Michael Vick 5.00 12.00
HMPM Peyton Manning 8.00 20.00
HMPR Philip Rivers 5.00 12.00
HMRM Randy Moss 2.50 6.00
HMRW Ricky Williams 2.50 6.00
HMRW2 Roy Williams WR 1.50 4.00
HMRW3 Reggie Williams 2.00 5.00
HMSM Steve McNair 2.50 6.00
HMTB Tom Brady 12.00 30.00
HMTO Terrell Owens 2.50 6.00

2004 Hot Prospects Notable Newcomers

MPLETE SET (15) 20.00 50.00
STATED ODDS 1:15
1NN Eli Manning 5.00 12.00
2NN Larry Fitzgerald 2.50 6.00
3NN Ben Roethlisberger 5.00 12.00
4NN Roy Williams WR .60 1.50
5NN Kellen Winslow Jr. .60 1.50
6NN Kevin Jones .75 2.00
7NN Reggie Williams .60 1.50
8NN Michael Clayton .75 2.00
9NN Phillip Rivers 2.00 5.00
10NN Lee Evans 1.00 2.50
11NN Drew Henson .60 1.50
12NN Steven Jackson 1.00 2.50
13NN Chris Perry .60 1.50
14NN Greg Jones .60 1.50
15NN J.P. Losman .60 1.50

2004 Hot Prospects Notable Notations Autographs

STATED PRINT RUN 50 SER.#'d SETS
1NN Eli Manning 60.00 120.00
2NN Larry Fitzgerald 40.00 80.00
3NN Ben Roethlisberger 75.00 150.00
4NN Roy Williams WR 8.00 20.00
7NN Reggie Williams 8.00 20.00
8NN Michael Clayton
9NN Philip Rivers 40.00 80.00
10NN Lee Evans 12.00 30.00
11NN Drew Henson 8.00 20.00
12NN Steven Jackson 12.00 30.00
13NN Chris Perry 8.00 20.00
15NN J.P. Losman 8.00 20.00

2006 Hot Prospects

is 224-card set was released in October, 2006. The set was issued into the hobby five-card packs, with a $9.99 SRP which came 15 packs to a box. Cards numbered 1-100 feature veterans in team alphabetical order while cards numbered 101-224 feature 2006 rookies. Those Rookie Cards are broken into the follwing groupings: Cards numbered 101-160 were issued to a stated print run of 1150 serial numbered sets; cards numbered 161-190 which were signed by the player were issued to a stated print run of 299 serial numbered sets. Cards numbered 201-222 contained both player-worn swatches and an signature were issued to a stated print of 999 serial numbered sets and the set concludes with cards 223 and 224 which also had player-worn swatches and autographs and those two cards were issued to a stated print run of 399 serial numbered sets.
COMP.SET w/o RC's (100) 10.00 25.00
101-160 PRINT RUN 1150 SER.#'d SETS
161-190 AU PRINT RUN 299 SER.#'d SETS
191-200 JSY AU PRINT RUN 175 SETS
201-222 JSY AU PRINT RUN 999 SETS
223-224 JSY AU PRINT RUN 399 SETS
1 Edgerrin James .25 .60
2 Larry Fitzgerald .25 .60
3 Anquan Boldin .20 .50
4 Michael Vick .25 .60
5 Warrick Dunn .20 .50
6 Roddy White .20 .50
7 Jamal Lewis .25 .60
8 Steve McNair .25 .60
9 Mark Clayton .20 .50
10 Willis McGahee .20 .50
11 Lee Evans .25 .60
12 J.P. Losman .25 .60
13 Jake Delhomme .20 .50
14 Steve Smith .30 .75
15 DeShaun Foster .25 .60
16 Rex Grossman .20 .50
17 Thomas Jones .20 .50
18 Brian Urlacher .30 .75
19 Carson Palmer .25 .60
20 Chad Johnson .20 .50
21 Rudi Johnson .20 .50
22 T.J. Houshmandzadeh .20 .50
23 Braylon Edwards .20 .50
24 Charlie Frye .25 .60
25 Reuben Droughns .25 .60
26 Julius Jones .20 .50
27 Terrell Owens .25 .60
28 Drew Bledsoe .25 .60
29 Jake Plummer .20 .50
30 Tatum Bell .20 .50
31 Javon Walker .25 .60
32 Kevin Jones .20 .50
33 Roy Williams WR .20 .50
34 Mike Williams .20 .50
35 Brett Favre .60 1.50
36 Donald Driver .25 .60
37 Ahman Green .25 .60
38 David Carr .20 .50
39 Domanick Davis .20 .50
40 Andre Johnson .25 .60
41 Peyton Manning .75 2.00
42 Reggie Wayne .25 .60
43 Marvin Harrison .25 .60
44 Matt Jones .20 .50
45 Greg Jones .20 .50
46 Byron Leftwich .20 .50
47 Larry Johnson .20 .50
48 Trent Green .20 .50
49 Eddie Kennison .20 .50
50 Tony Gonzalez .25 .60
51 Daunte Culpepper .25 .60
52 Ronnie Brown .25 .60
53 Chris Chambers .20 .50
54 Troy Williamson .20 .50
55 Chester Taylor .25 .60
56 Koren Robinson .20 .50
57 Tom Brady 1.00 2.50
58 Corey Dillon .20 .50
59 Deion Branch .20 .50
60 Drew Brees .30 .75
61 Donte Stallworth .20 .50
62 Deuce McAllister .25 .60
63 Tiki Barber .25 .60
64 Eli Manning .25 .60
65 Plaxico Burress .20 .50
66 Chad Pennington .20 .50
67 Curtis Martin .25 .60
68 Justin McCareins .20 .50
69 Randy Moss .25 .60
70 LaMont Jordan .25 .60
71 Aaron Brooks .20 .50
72 Jerry Porter .20 .50
73 Donovan McNabb .25 .60
74 Brian Westbrook .20 .50
75 Reggie Brown .20 .50
76 Ben Roethlisberger .40 1.00
77 Hines Ward .25 .60
78 Willie Parker .25 .60
79 LaDainian Tomlinson .30 .75
80 Philip Rivers .30 .75
81 Antonio Gates .30 .75
82 Alex Smith QB .25 .60
83 Frank Gore .25 .60
84 Antonio Bryant .20 .50
85 Shaun Alexander .20 .50
86 Matt Hasselbeck .20 .50
87 Nate Burleson .20 .50
88 Torry Holt .25 .60
89 Marc Bulger .20 .50
90 Steven Jackson .20 .50
91 Kevin Curtis .25 .60
92 Cadillac Williams .25 .60
93 Chris Simms .20 .50
94 Joey Galloway .25 .60
95 Drew Bennett .25 .60
96 David Givens .25 .60
97 Billy Volek .20 .50
98 Clinton Portis .20 .50
99 Santana Moss .25 .60
100 Antwaan Randle El .20 .50
101 Donte Whitner RC 2.50 6.00
102 Haloti Ngata RC 2.50 6.00
103 Kamerion Wimbley RC 2.50 6.00
104 Jason Allen RC 2.50 6.00
105 Bobby Carpenter RC 2.00 5.00
106 Antonio Cromartie RC 2.50 6.00
107 Tamba Hali RC 3.00 8.00
108 Manny Lawson RC 2.50 6.00
109 Davin Joseph RC 2.50 6.00
110 Johnathan Joseph RC 2.50 6.00
111 John McCargo RC 2.00 5.00
112 Nick Mangold RC 2.50 6.00
113 Marcus Vick RC 2.00 5.00
114 Rocky McIntosh RC 2.00 5.00
115 Tim Day RC 2.50 6.00
116 Danieal Manning RC 3.00 8.00
117 Roman Harper RC 2.50 6.00
118 Josh Lay RC 2.00 5.00
119 Chris Gocong RC 2.50 6.00
120 Greg Blue RC 2.50 6.00
121 Bernard Pollard RC 2.50 6.00
122 Richard Marshall RC 2.00 5.00
123 Tony Scheffler RC 3.00 8.00
124 Dawan Landry RC 3.00 8.00
125 Darryl Tapp RC 2.50 6.00
126 Anthony Schlegel RC 2.50 6.00
127 Jon Alston RC 2.00 5.00
128 Pat Watkins RC 2.50 6.00
129 Anthony Smith RC 3.00 8.00
130 David Thomas RC 2.00 5.00
131 David Pittman RC 2.50 6.00
132 Frostee Rucker RC 2.50 6.00
133 Troy Bergeron RC 2.50 6.00
134 Freddie Keiaho RC 2.50 6.00
135 Stephen Tulloch RC 2.50 6.00
136 Gerris Wilkinson RC 2.00 5.00
137 Eric Smith RC 2.50 6.00
138 Garrett Mills RC 2.50 6.00
139 Skyler Green RC 2.00 5.00
140 Brodie Croyle RC 2.00 5.00
141 P.J. Daniels RC 2.00 5.00
142 Marques Hagans RC 2.00 5.00
143 Jamar Williams RC 2.50 6.00
144 Ingle Martin RC 2.50 6.00
145 Charles Spencer RC 2.00 5.00
146 Andrew Whitworth RC 2.00 5.00
147 Jeff King RC 2.50 6.00
148 Taitusi Lutui RC 2.50 6.00
149 Quinn Sypniewski RC 2.50 6.00
150 P.J. Pope RC 3.00 8.00
151 Wali Lundy RC 2.00 5.00
152 Jonathan Orr RC 2.50 6.00
153 Jonathan Lewis RC 2.00 5.00
154 Adam Jennings RC 2.50 6.00
155 Jeff Webb RC 2.50 6.00
156 Cedric Humes RC 2.00 5.00
157 T.J. Williams RC 3.00 8.00
158 Todd Watkins RC 2.00 5.00
159 Bennie Brazell RC 2.50 6.00
160 Marques Colston RC 3.00 8.00
161 DonTrell Moore AU RC 5.00 12.00
162 Brad Smith AU RC 5.00 12.00
163 Gerald Riggs AU RC 5.00 12.00
164 Chad Greenway AU RC 6.00 15.00
165 Cory Rodgers AU RC 4.00 10.00
166 Darrell Hackney AU RC 5.00 12.00
167 D.J. Shockley AU RC 5.00 12.00
168 Dominique Byrd AU RC 4.00 10.00
169 Joseph Addai AU RC 4.00 10.00
170 Darnell Bing AU RC 5.00 12.00
171 Mike Bell AU RC 4.00 10.00
172 Ernie Sims AU RC 4.00 10.00
173 Brodrick Bunkley AU RC 5.00 12.00
174 Hank Baskett AU RC 4.00 10.00
175 Jerome Harrison AU RC 4.00 10.00
176 Jimmy Williams AU RC 4.00 10.00
177 D'Brickashaw Ferguson AU RC 4.00 10.00
178 Josh Betts AU RC 5.00 12.00
179 Leonard Pope AU RC 6.00 15.00
180 Terrence Whitehead AU RC 5.00 12.00
181 Mathias Kiwanuka AU RC 6.00 15.00
182 Ashton Youboty AU RC 4.00 10.00
183 DeMeco Ryans AU RC 5.00 12.00
184 Thomas Howard AU RC 4.00 10.00
185 Owen Daniels AU RC 6.00 15.00
186 Reggie McNeal AU RC 4.00 10.00
187 Tye Hill AU RC 4.00 10.00
188 Will Blackmon AU RC 4.00 10.00
189 Winston Justice AU RC 5.00 12.00
190 Greg Jennings AU RC 6.00 15.00
191 M.Leinart AU/175 RC 6.00 15.00
192 V.Young AU/175 RC 6.00 15.00
193 Jay Cutler AU/175 RC 8.00 20.00
194 R.Bush AU/175 RC 10.00 25.00
195 L.Maroney AU/175 RC 6.00 15.00
196 L.White AU/175 RC 6.00 15.00
197 DeA.Williams AU/175 RC 8.00 20.00
198 V.Davis AU/175 RC 8.00 20.00
199 S.Holmes AU/175 RC 8.00 20.00
200 Sin.Moss AU/175 RC 6.00 15.00
201 Jason Avant JSY AU RC 4.00 10.00
202 Brian Calhoun JSY AU RC 4.00 10.00
203 Kellen Clemens JSY AU RC 4.00 10.00
204 Dem.Williams JSY AU RC 4.00 10.00
205 Br.Williams JSY AU RC 4.00 10.00
206 Maurice Drew JSY AU RC 6.00 15.00
207 Travis Wilson JSY AU RC 4.00 10.00
208 Joe Klopfenstein JSY AU RC 4.00 10.00
209 Derek Hagan JSY AU RC 5.00 12.00
210 A.J. Hawk JSY AU RC 5.00 12.00
211 Michael Huff JSY AU RC 5.00 12.00
212 T.Jackson JSY AU RC 4.00 10.00
213 Omar Jacobs JSY AU RC 4.00 10.00
214 Mario Williams JSY AU RC 6.00 15.00
215 Marcedes Lewis JSY AU RC 4.00 10.00
216 B.Marshall JSY AU RC 10.00 25.00
217 Chad Jackson JSY AU RC 4.00 10.00
218 Jerious Norwood JSY AU RC 4.00 10.00
219 M.Robinson JSY AU RC 4.00 10.00
220 Maurice Stovall JSY AU RC 4.00 10.00
221 Leon Washington JSY AU RC 4.00 10.00
222 Charlie Whitehurst JSY AU RC 4.00 10.00
223 K.Jennings JSY AU/399 RC 6.00 15.00
224 M.McNeill JSY AU/399 RC 5.00 12.00

2006 Hot Prospects Red Hot

*VETERANS 1-100: 6X TO 15X BASIC CARDS
*ROOKIES 101-160: .8X TO 2X BASIC CARDS
AU ROOK.161-190: .8X TO 2X
1-190 PRINT RUN 50
*FB AU ROOK.191-199: .4X TO 1X
*FB AU ROOK.201-222: .6X TO 1.5X
191-222 FB AUTO PRINT RUN 99

2006 Hot Prospects Red Hot Autographed Rookie Material Letters

STATED PRINT RUN 25 SER.#'d SETS
UNPRICED SET REDEMPTION #'d TO 5
191 Matt Leinart 12.00 30.00
192 Vince Young 12.00 30.00
193 Jay Cutler 30.00 60.00
194 Reggie Bush 20.00 50.00
195 Laurence Maroney 12.00 30.00
196 LenDale White 12.00 30.00
197 DeAngelo Williams 15.00 40.00
198 Vernon Davis 15.00 40.00
199 Santonio Holmes 15.00 40.00
200 Sinorice Moss

2006 Hot Prospects Endorsements

UNPRICED WHITE HOT PRINT RUN 1
HPAC Alge Crumpler 4.00 10.00
HPAG Antonio Gates 6.00 15.00
HPAH A.J. Hawk SP 25.00 50.00
HPBA Ronde Barber 6.00 15.00
HPBB Brodrick Bunkley SP 6.00 15.00
HPBC Brian Calhoun 6.00 15.00
HPBE Braylon Edwards 6.00 15.00
HPBF Brett Favre SP 75.00 150.00
HPBG Bruce Gradkowski 6.00 15.00
HPBL Byron Leftwich SP
HPBM Brandon Marshall SP 10.00 25.00
HPBR Ben Roethlisberger SP 40.00 80.00
HPBS Brad Smith 6.00 15.00
HPBU Reggie Bush SP 10.00 25.00
HPBW Brandon Williams SP 6.00 15.00
HPCF Charlie Frye 6.00 15.00
HPCG Chad Greenway 6.00 15.00
HPCI Clint Ingram 6.00 15.00
HPCJ Chad Jackson SP 8.00 20.00
HPCP Carson Palmer SP 15.00 40.00
HPCR Cory Rodgers 4.00 10.00
HPCS Chris Simms 6.00 15.00
HPCU Kevin Curtis 4.00 10.00
HPCW Cadillac Williams SP
HPDB Drew Bennett 4.00 10.00
HPDF D'Brickashaw Ferguson 6.00 15.00
HPDG David Givens 4.00 10.00
HPDH Darrell Hackney 3.00 8.00
HPDM Deuce McAllister 4.00 10.00
HPDO Drew Olson 3.00 8.00
HPDR Drew Bledsoe SP 15.00 30.00
HPDS D.J. Shockley 6.00 15.00
HPDW DeAngelo Williams SP 20.00 50.00
HPEM Eli Manning SP
HPFO DeShaun Foster 4.00 10.00
HPGJ Greg Jennings 6.00 15.00
HPGL Greg Lee 3.00 8.00
HPGR Gerald Riggs 4.00 10.00
HPHA Andre Hall 4.00 10.00
HPHB Hank Baskett 6.00 15.00
HPHI Tye Hill SP 6.00 15.00
HPJA Joseph Addai SP 12.00 30.00
HPJB Josh Betts 4.00 10.00
HPJC Jay Cutler SP 8.00 20.00
HPJH Jerome Harrison 6.00 15.00
HPJI Jimmy Williams 4.00 10.00
HPJJ Julius Jones SP
HPJN Jerious Norwood SP 12.00 30.00
HPJO Greg Jones 3.00 8.00
HPJW Jason Witten 15.00 30.00
HPKC Kellen Clemens SP
HPKJ Keyshawn Johnson 10.00 25.00
HPKO Kyle Orton 3.00 8.00
HPLA LaMont Jordan 4.00 10.00
HPLJ Larry Johnson SP 12.00 30.00
HPLM Laurence Maroney SP 8.00 20.00
HPLP Leonard Pope 4.00 10.00
HPLT LaDainian Tomlinson SP 30.00 80.00
HPLW LenDale White SP
HPMA Derrick Mason 4.00 10.00
HPMC Michael Clayton 4.00 10.00
HPMI Mike Williams 4.00 10.00
HPML Matt Leinart SP 12.00 30.00
HPMM Muhsin Muhammad 4.00 10.00
HPMN Martin Nance 3.00 8.00
HPMV Michael Vick SP 15.00 40.00
HPMW Mario Williams SP
HPOD Owen Daniels 6.00 15.00
HPPM Peyton Manning 50.00 100.00
HPPR Philip Rivers SP 12.00 30.00
HPRB Reggie Brown 4.00 10.00
HPRJ Rudi Johnson 6.00 15.00
HPRM Ryan Moats 4.00 10.00
HPRO Ronnie Brown SP
HPRW Reggie Wayne 6.00 15.00
HPSH Santonio Holmes SP 15.00 40.00
HPSM Sinorice Moss SP
HPTA Lofa Tatupu 10.00 25.00
HPTG Trent Green SP
HPTH T.J. Houshmandzadeh 6.00 15.00
HPTI Tiki Barber SP 15.00 30.00
HPTJ Thomas Jones 6.00 15.00
HPVD Vernon Davis SP 8.00 20.00
HPVY Vince Young SP 15.00 40.00
HPWI Demetrius Williams SP
HPWJ Winston Justice 4.00 10.00
HPWP Willie Parker SP 15.00 40.00

2006 Hot Prospects Endorsements Red Hot

ED HOT: 1X TO 2.5X BASE AUTO
*RED HOT: .6X TO 1.5X BASE AUTO SP
RED HOT PRINT RUN 25 SER.#'d SETS
HPPM Peyton Manning 100.00 175.00

2006 Hot Prospects Dual Endorsements

ATED PRINT RUN 25 SER.#'d SETS
UNPRICED RED HOT PRINT RUN 10
UNPRICED WHITE HOT PRINT RUN 1
AC B.Calhoun/J.Addai 20.00 50.00
BA Re.Brown/J.Avant 15.00 40.00
BH Ro.Brown/D.Hagan 20.00 50.00
CF D.Ferguson/K.Clemens 20.00 50.00
DG A.Gates/V.Davis 20.00 50.00
EF J.Elway/B.Favre 175.00 300.00
FW D.Foster/D.Williams 20.00 50.00
GJ C.Greenway/T.Jackson 20.00 50.00
HB D.Bing/M.Huff
HS A.Hawk/E.Sims 15.00 40.00
HW J.Williams/T.Hill
JD G.Jones/M.Drew 15.00 40.00
JH O.Jacobs/S.Holmes 15.00 40.00
JJ T.Jones/J.Jones 15.00 40.00
JS K.Johnson/S.Smith 15.00 40.00
JT L.Johnson/L.Tomlinson 50.00 120.00
KB D.Byrd/J.Klopfenstein 12.00 30.00
KM M.Kiwanuka/S.Moss 15.00 40.00
LP C.Palmer/M.Leinart 15.00 40.00
MB Br.Williams/M.Robinson 15.00 40.00
MJ Jackson/Maroney 15.00 40.00
MM P.Manning/E.Manning 150.00 250.00
OM M.Muhammad/K.Orton 15.00 40.00
RW P.Rivers/C.Whitehurst 25.00 60.00
SC M.Clayton/M.Stovall
SW B.Smith/L.Washington 20.00 50.00
WB M.Williams/R.Bush 12.00 30.00
WF J.Witten/A.Fasano 30.00 60.00
WR D.Ryans/M.Williams 15.00 40.00
YW L.White/V.Young 15.00 40.00

2006 Hot Prospects Triple Endorsements

COMMON CARD 25.00 50.00
UNLISTED STARS 30.00 60.00
STATED PRINT RUN 25 SER.#'d SETS
UNPRICED RED HOT PRINT RUN 10
UNPRICED WHITE HOT PRINT RUN 1
CJW Whthrst/Clem/Jackson 25.00 50.00
CMJ Jcksn/Cutler/Maroney 10.00 25.00
HTI Ismail/Hornung/Theismann 50.00 80.00
JWB Jhnsn/Ro.Brown/Williams 25.00 50.00
MBM Barber/Manning/Moss 50.00 120.00
RPH Roeth/Parker/Holmes 60.00 120.00
SRO Simms/Rivers/Orton 30.00 60.00
WAW Williams/Addai/White 40.00 100.00
WHH Hawk/Williams/Huff 30.00 60.00
YLC Cutler/Leinart/Young 10.00 25.00

2006 Hot Prospects Prospectus

ATED PRINT RUN 299 SER.#'d SETS
PRAH A.J. Hawk .75 2.00
PRBC Brian Calhoun .60 1.50
PRBM Brandon Marshall 1.25 3.00
PRBW Brandon Williams .60 1.50
PRCJ Chad Jackson .60 1.50
PRCW Charlie Whitehurst .60 1.50
PRDH Derek Hagan .75 2.00
PRDW DeAngelo Williams .75 2.00
PRJA Jason Avant .60 1.50
PRJK Joe Klopfenstein .60 1.50
PRKC Kellen Clemens .60 1.50
PRLE Matt Leinart .60 1.50
PRLM Laurence Maroney .60 1.50
PRLW Leon Washington .60 1.50
PRMD Maurice Drew 1.00 2.50
PRMH Michael Huff .75 2.00
PRML Marcedes Lewis .60 1.50
PRMR Michael Robinson .60 1.50
PRMS Maurice Stovall .60 1.50
PRMW Mario Williams 1.00 2.50
PROJ Omar Jacobs .60 1.50
PRRB Reggie Bush 1.00 2.50
PRSH Santonio Holmes .75 2.00
PRSM Sinorice Moss .60 1.50
PRTJ Tarvaris Jackson .60 1.50
PRTW Travis Wilson .60 1.50
PRVD Vernon Davis .75 2.00
PRVY Vince Young .60 1.50
PRWH LenDale White .60 1.50
PRWI Demetrius Williams .60 1.50

2006 Hot Prospects Prospectus Jerseys

AH A.J. Hawk/275 6.00 15.00
PRBC Brian Calhoun/250 2.00 5.00
PRBM Brandon Marshall/200 4.00 10.00
PRBW Brandon Williams/250 2.00 5.00
PRCJ Chad Jackson/250 2.00 5.00
PRCW Charlie Whitehurst/275 2.00 5.00
PRDH Derek Hagan/275 2.50 6.00
PRDW DeAngelo Williams/250 6.00 15.00
PRJA Jason Avant/250 2.00 5.00
PRJK Joe Klopfenstein/250 2.00 5.00
PRKC Kellen Clemens/200 2.00 5.00
PRLE Matt Leinart/199 2.00 5.00
PRLM Laurence Maroney/250 2.00 5.00
PRLW Leon Washington/250 2.00 5.00
PRMD Maurice Drew/250 3.00 8.00
PRMH Michael Huff/275 2.50 6.00
PRML Marcedes Lewis/250 2.00 5.00
PRMR Michael Robinson/250 2.00 5.00
PRMS Maurice Stovall/275 2.00 5.00
PRMW Mario Williams/250 3.00 8.00
PROJ Omar Jacobs/275 2.00 5.00
PRRB Reggie Bush/100 4.00 10.00
PRSH Santonio Holmes/250 2.50 6.00
PRSM Sinorice Moss/250 2.00 5.00
PRTJ Tarvaris Jackson/250 2.00 5.00
PRTW Travis Wilson/250 2.00 5.00
PRVD Vernon Davis/250 2.50 6.00
PRVY Vince Young/100 2.50 6.00
PRWH LenDale White/250 2.00 5.00
PRWI Demetrius Williams/400 2.00 5.00

2006 Hot Prospects Retrospective

ATED PRINT RUN 699 SER.#'d SETS
REAG Antonio Gates 1.50 4.00
REAR Aaron Rodgers 4.00 10.00
REAS Alex Smith QB 1.25 3.00
REBA Tiki Barber 1.25 3.00
REBE Braylon Edwards 1.00 2.50
REBF Brett Favre 3.00 8.00
REBJ Brad Johnson 1.25 3.00
REBL Byron Leftwich 1.00 2.50
REBR Ben Roethlisberger 2.00 5.00
REBU Brian Urlacher 1.50 4.00
RECB Cedric Benson 1.00 2.50
RECJ Chad Johnson 1.00 2.50
RECP Carson Palmer 1.25 3.00
RECR Charles Rogers 1.25 3.00
RECS Chris Simms 1.00 2.50
RECW Cadillac Williams 1.25 3.00
REDB Drew Bledsoe 1.25 3.00
REDC Daunte Culpepper 1.25 3.00
REDF DeShaun Foster 1.25 3.00
REDH Dante Hall 1.00 2.50
REDM Donovan McNabb 1.25 3.00
REDR Drew Brees 1.50 4.00
REEJ Edgerrin James 1.25 3.00
REEM Eli Manning 1.25 3.00
REGR Trent Green 1.00 2.50
REHM Heath Miller 1.00 2.50
REIB Isaac Bruce 1.50 4.00
REJD Jake Delhomme 1.00 2.50
REJH Joey Harrington 1.00 2.50
REJO LaMont Jordan 1.25 3.00
REJP Jerry Porter 1.00 2.50
REJS Junior Seau 1.50 4.00
REKJ Kevin Jones 1.00 2.50
REKM Keenan McCardell 1.25 3.00
REKO Kyle Orton 1.00 2.50
RELF Larry Fitzgerald 1.25 3.00
RELJ Larry Johnson 1.00 2.50
RELO Lofa Tatupu 1.00 2.50
RELT LaDainian Tomlinson 1.50 4.00
REMB Mark Brunell 1.25 3.00
REMC Deuce McAllister 1.25 3.00
REMO Ryan Moats 1.00 2.50
REMV Michael Vick 1.25 3.00
REMW Mike Williams 1.00 2.50
REPH Priest Holmes 1.00 2.50
REPM Peyton Manning 4.00 10.00
RERB Ronnie Brown 1.25 3.00
RERM Randy Moss 1.25 3.00
RERS Rod Smith 1.25 3.00
RESA Shaun Alexander 1.00 2.50
RESH Jeremy Shockey 1.00 2.50
RESJ Steven Jackson 1.00 2.50
RETA Tatum Bell 1.00 2.50
RETB Tom Brady 5.00 12.00
RETD T.J. Duckett 1.00 2.50
RETG Tony Gonzalez 1.25 3.00
RETO Terrell Owens 1.25 3.00
RETW Troy Williamson 1.00 2.50
REWM Willis McGahee 1.00 2.50

2006 Hot Prospects Retrospective Jerseys

AG Antonio Gates 4.00 10.00
REAR Aaron Rodgers 15.00 40.00
REAS Alex Smith QB 4.00 10.00
REBA Tiki Barber SP 4.00 10.00
REBE Braylon Edwards SP 4.00 10.00
REBF Brett Favre 8.00 20.00
REBJ Brad Johnson 3.00 8.00
REBL Byron Leftwich 3.00 8.00
REBR Ben Roethlisberger 8.00 20.00
REBU Brian Urlacher 4.00 10.00
RECB Cedric Benson 4.00 10.00
RECJ Chad Johnson 3.00 8.00
RECP Carson Palmer 4.00 10.00
RECR Charles Rogers [illegible] [illegible]
RECS Chris Simms 3.00 8.00
RECW Cadillac Williams SP 4.00 10.00
REDB Drew Bledsoe 4.00 10.00
REDC Daunte Culpepper 4.00 10.00

REDF DeShaun Foster SP 3.00 8.00
REDH Dante Hall 3.00 8.00
REDM Donovan McNabb 4.00 10.00
REDR Drew Brees 3.00 8.00
REEJ Edgerrin James 4.00 10.00
REEM Eli Manning 5.00 12.00
REGR Trent Green SP 3.00 8.00
REHM Heath Miller 4.00 10.00
REIB Isaac Bruce 3.00 8.00
REJD Jake Delhomme 3.00 8.00
REJH Joey Harrington 3.00 8.00
REJO LaMont Jordan SP 3.00 8.00
REJP Jerry Porter 3.00 8.00
REJS Junior Seau 4.00 10.00
REKJ Kevin Jones 4.00 10.00
REKM Keenan McCardell 2.50 6.00
REKO Kyle Orton SP 3.00 8.00
RELF Larry Fitzgerald 4.00 10.00
RELJ Larry Johnson SP 4.00 10.00
RELO Lofa Tatupu SP 3.00 8.00
RELT LaDainian Tomlinson SP 4.00 10.00
REMB Mark Brunell 3.00 8.00
REMC Deuce McAllister 3.00 8.00
REMO Ryan Moats 2.50 6.00
REMV Michael Vick SP 3.00 8.00
REMW Mike Williams SP 4.00 10.00
REPH Priest Holmes 3.00 8.00
REPM Peyton Manning SP 6.00 15.00
RERB Ronnie Brown SP 4.00 10.00
RERM Randy Moss 4.00 10.00
RERS Rod Smith 3.00 8.00
RESA Shaun Alexander 4.00 10.00
RESH Jeremy Shockey 4.00 10.00
RESJ Steven Jackson 4.00 10.00
RETA Tatum Bell 3.00 8.00
RETB Tom Brady 6.00 15.00
RETD T.J. Duckett 2.50 6.00
RETG Tony Gonzalez 3.00 8.00
RETO Terrell Owens 4.00 10.00
RETW Troy Williamson 3.00 8.00
REWM Willis McGahee 4.00 10.00

1974 Houston Texans WFL Team Issue 8X10

The photos measure roughly 8" x 10" and include black and white images with the player's name in the lower left below the photo, his position centered, and the team name on the right side below the photo. The backs are blank.

1 Garland Boyette 7.50 15.00
2 Joe Robb 7.50 15.00

1999 Houston ThunderBears AFL

MPLETE SET (27) 7.50 15.00
1 Hunter Adams .30 .75
2 Rodney Blackshear .30 .75
3 Marcus Bradley .30 .75
4 Ben Bronson .30 .75
5 David Caldwell .30 .75
6 Joe Carollo .30 .75
7 Terence Davis .30 .75
8 Clint Dolezel .60 1.50
9 Murray Garrett .30 .75
10 Dietrich Griffin .30 .75
11 Robert Hall .30 .75
12 Michael Harrison .30 .75
13 Lucas Yarnell .30 .75
14 Bernard Holmes .30 .75
15 Ed Howard .30 .75
16 Conrad Lewis .30 .75
17 Steve Thonn CO .30 .75
18 Junior Soli .30 .75
19 Shawn Washington .30 .75
20 Jeff Mitchell .30 .75
21 Walter Shelton .30 .75
22 Justin Skinner .30 .75
23 Verone McKinley .30 .75
24 Clayton Baker .30 .75
25 Larry Jones .30 .75
26 Team Photo .30 .75
27 Cover Card .30 .75

1938 Huskies Cereal

These cards are actually entire backs of Huskies cereal boxes from the late 1930s. Each box back features an artist's rendering of the University of Washington Huskies coach Jimmy Phelan and one NFL player (or just a single player) at the top along with brief bios on each. A series of smaller drawings appears below the two that were intended to be cut out and used to form a moving picture simulating football action when flipped by the collector.

1 J.Phelan 350.00 600.00
S.Baugh
2 Dutch Clark 300.00 500.00
3 J.Phelan 350.00 600.00
D.Hutson

1994 Images

is premier edition of Classic Images features 125 standard-size cards. Production was limited to 1,994 cases. The full-bleed color action photos on the fronts have a metallic sheen to them. The player's name is printed toward the bottom, with the "Images" logo between the first and last name. A second black-and-white photo appears on the back, along with the player's name, position, team name and statistics, as well as a small color headshot on the left side. The cards were sold six cards to a pack, with no jumbo or periodical versions produced. Rookie Cards in this set include Derrick Alexander, Isaac Bruce, Trent Dilfer, Marshall Faulk, William Floyd, Greg Hill, Charles Johnson, Byron Bam Morris, Errict Rhett, Darnay Scott and Heath Shuler. The Emmitt Smith (one per box chiptopper) and Drew Bledsoe Throwbacks (random insert in packs) NFL Experience preview cards were included in the Images product. An Emmitt Smith Images promo card was produced as well and is priced below.

COMPLETE SET (125) 15.00 40.00
1 Emmitt Smith 1.25 3.00
2 Reggie White .30 .75
3 Michael Haynes .15 .40
4 Chris Warren .15 .40
5 Jeff George .30 .75
6 Sean Gilbert .07 .20
7 Ricky Watters .15 .40
8 Eric Metcalf .15 .40
9 Randall Cunningham .30 .75
10 Tim Brown .30 .75
11 Trent Dilfer RC .75 2.00
12 Marshall Faulk RC 3.00 8.00
13 David Klingler .07 .20
14 Barry Foster .07 .20
15 John Elway 1.50 4.00
16 Joe Montana 1.50 4.00
17 Rodney Hampton .15 .40
18 Todd Steussie RC .15 .40
19 Bruce Smith .30 .75
20 Wayne Gandy RC .07 .20
21 Anthony Miller .15 .40
22 Reggie Brooks .15 .40
23 Johnny Johnson .07 .20
24 Byron Bam Morris RC .15 .40
25 Drew Bledsoe .75 2.00
26 Jeff Hostetler .15 .40
27 Alvin Harper .15 .40
28 Cris Carter .40 1.00
29 Bert Emanuel RC .30 .75
30 Errict Rhett RC .30 .75
31 Scott Mitchell .15 .40
32 Deion Sanders .40 1.00
33 Lewis Tillman .07 .20
34 Tim Bowens RC .15 .40
35 Charles Haley .15 .40
36 Stan Humphries .15 .40
37 Haywood Jeffires .15 .40
38 Andre Reed .15 .40
39 Charles Johnson RC .30 .75
40 Ronald Moore .07 .20
41 Jim Everett .15 .40
42 Greg Hill RC .30 .75
43 Thurman Thomas .30 .75
44 Willie McGinest RC .30 .75
45 Aaron Glenn RC .30 .75
46 Erric Pegram .07 .20
47 Terry Kirby .30 .75
48 Warren Moon .30 .75
49 Clyde Simmons .07 .20
50 Eric Turner .07 .20
51 Heath Shuler RC .30 .75
52 Rickey Jackson .07 .20
53 Johnnie Morton RC .75 2.00
54 Charlie Garner RC .75 2.00
55 Mark Collins .07 .20
56 Mike Pritchard .07 .20
57 Bryant Young RC .50 1.25
58 Joe Johnson RC .07 .20
59 Erik Kramer .15 .40
60 Barry Sanders 1.25 3.00
61 Rod Woodson .15 .40
62 Dave Brown .15 .40
63 Gary Brown .07 .20
64 Brett Favre 1.50 4.00
65 Isaac Bruce RC 2.50 6.00
66 Boomer Esiason .15 .40
67 Jim Harbaugh .30 .75
68 Jackie Harris .07 .20
69 Art Monk .15 .40
70 Jamir Miller RC .15 .40
71 Neil O'Donnell .30 .75
72 Neil Smith .15 .40
73 Junior Seau .30 .75
74 Jerome Bettis .50 1.25
75 Bernard Williams RC .07 .20
76 Jeff Burris RC .15 .40
77 Henry Ellard .15 .40
78 Reggie Cobb .07 .20
79 Shante Carver RC .07 .20
80 Terry Allen .15 .40
81 Cortez Kennedy .15 .40
82 Trev Alberts RC .15 .40
83 Michael Irvin .30 .75
84 Herschel Walker .15 .40
85 Dan Marino 1.50 4.00
86 Dave Meggett .07 .20
87 Herman Moore .30 .75
88 Darnay Scott RC .40 1.00
89 Dewayne Washington RC .15 .40
90 Rob Fredrickson RC .15 .40
91 Rick Mirer .30 .75
92 Thomas Lewis RC .15 .40
93 Chris Miller .07 .20
94 Marion Butts .07 .20
95 Sam Adams RC .15 .40
96 Jerry Rice .75 2.00
97 Ben Coates .15 .40
98 David Palmer RC .30 .75
99 Antonio Langham RC .15 .40
100 Curtis Conway .30 .75
101 Derrick Thomas .30 .75
102 Ken Norton Jr. .15 .40
103 Ronnie Lott .15 .40
104 Sterling Sharpe .15 .40
105 Troy Aikman .75 2.00
106 Shannon Sharpe .15 .40
107 Natrone Means .30 .75
108 Derek Brown RBK .07 .20
109 Dan Wilkinson RC .15 .40
110 Andre Rison .15 .40
111 Quentin Coryatt .07 .20
112 Cody Carlson .07 .20
113 William Floyd RC .30 .75
114 Marcus Allen .30 .75
115 Steve Young .60 1.50
116 Jim Kelly .30 .75
117 LeShon Johnson RC .15 .40
118 Irving Fryar .15 .40
119 Carl Pickens .15 .40
120 Keith Jackson .07 .20
121 John Thierry RC .07 .20
122 Vinny Testaverde .15 .40
123 Derrick Alexander WR RC .30 .75
124 Seth Joyner .07 .20
125 Checklist .07 .20
IF1 Emmitt Smith Promo 1.00 2.50
TP1 D.Bledsoe NFL Exp/1994 25.00 50.00
NNO Emmitt Smith NFL Exp. 4.00 10.00

1994 Images All-Pro

Featuring Perennial All-Pros and All-Pro Prospects, this 25-card set measures the standard size. Two All-Pro insert packs containing six cards were inserted in every case, while two additional All-Pro cards were inserted in every box. Just 2,600 of each insert card were produced. The first 12 cards of this set highlight AFC players, while the last 13 showcase NFC players. The fronts are foil stamped in either red or blue to designate the AFC or NFC. The full-bleed color action photos on the front have a metallic sheen to them. The player's name is printed toward the bottom. A second photo appears on the back, along with the player's name and his accomplishment which establishes his place as a Perennial All-Pro or All-Pro Prospect, as well as a smaller, black-and-white version of this photo underneath.

COMPLETE SET (25) 100.00 200.00
STATED ODDS 1:12
A1 Heath Shuler 1.00 2.50
A2 Steve Young 3.00 8.00
A3 Trent Dilfer 2.50 6.00
A4 Troy Aikman 4.00 10.00
A5 Emmitt Smith 6.00 15.00
A6 Barry Sanders 6.00 15.00
A7 Jerome Bettis 2.50 6.00
A8 Errict Rhett 1.00 2.50
A9 Jerry Rice 4.00 10.00
A10 Michael Irvin 1.50 4.00
A11 Andre Rison .75 2.00
A12 Sterling Sharpe .75 2.00
A13 Reggie White 1.50 4.00
A14 Rick Mirer 1.50 4.00
A15 Drew Bledsoe 4.00 10.00
A16 John Elway 8.00 20.00
A17 Joe Montana 8.00 20.00
A18 Dan Marino 8.00 20.00
A19 Thurman Thomas 1.50 4.00
A20 Marshall Faulk 10.00 25.00
A21 Marcus Allen 1.50 4.00
A22 Charles Johnson 1.00 2.50
A23 Tim Brown 1.50 4.00
A24 Anthony Miller .75 2.00
A25 Derrick Thomas 1.50 4.00

1994-95 Images Update

ese ten standard-size cards were randomly inserted in retail packs of 1995 Classic Images 4-Sport. These cards feature some leading NFL players and were numbered in continuation of the 1994 Classic Images set.

COMPLETE SET (10) 30.00 60.00
126 Emmitt Smith 8.00 15.00
127 Troy Aikman 5.00 10.00
128 Steve Young 4.00 8.00
129 Deion Sanders 2.50 5.00
130 Ben Coates 2.00 4.00
131 Natrone Means 2.00 4.00
132 Drew Bledsoe 6.00 12.00
133 Cris Carter 2.50 5.00
134 Marshall Faulk 6.00 12.00
135 Errict Rhett 1.50 3.00

1995 Images Limited

assic issued Images NFL as a 125-card set in two separate releases: Live (retail) and Limited (hobby). Each set had different action photos of the same players on 24-point micro-lined foil-board cards. A few cards at the end of each set were changed. Card fronts have a silver background with the player's name along the bottom of the card. The Live version also contains the word "Live!" along the left side of the card. Limited card backs feature a full bleed shot with the player's name on the left of the card and statistical information at the bottom. Live card backs contain a player shot in a diagonal photo with the player's name and statistics at the bottom. Rookie Cards in this set include Jeff Blake, Ki-Jana Carter, Kerry Collins, Joey Galloway, Curtis Martin, Steve McNair, Rashaan Salaam, Kordell Stewart, J.J. Stokes and Michael Westbrook. Another bonus feature was Hot Boxes, where each pack contained approximately 50% inserts. Hot Boxes were specially marked and could be found in every five cases. Drew Bledsoe Promo cards were produced and priced below.

COMPLETE SET (125) 10.00 25.00
1 Emmitt Smith .75 2.00
2 Steve Young .40 1.00
3 Drew Bledsoe .30 .75
4 Dan Marino 1.00 2.50
5 John Elway 1.00 2.50
6 Barry Sanders .75 2.00
7 Brett Favre 1.00 2.50
8 Troy Aikman .50 1.25
9 Jim Kelly .15 .40
10 Marshall Faulk .60 1.50
11 Jerry Rice .50 1.25
12 Warren Moon .07 .20
13 Jim Everett .02 .10
14 Rodney Hampton .07 .20
15 Jeff Hostetler .07 .20
16 Errict Rhett .07 .20
17 Jerome Bettis .15 .40
18 Byron Bam Morris .02 .10
19 Randall Cunningham .15 .40
20 Rick Mirer .07 .20
21 Natrone Means .07 .20
22 Jeff George .07 .20
23 Garrison Hearst .15 .40
24 Michael Irvin .15 .40
25 Cris Carter .15 .40
26 Irving Fryar .07 .20
27 Jeff Blake RC .30 .75
28 Bruce Smith .15 .40
29 Shannon Sharpe .07 .20
30 Steve Beuerlein .07 .20
31 Stan Humphries .07 .20
32 Chris Warren .07 .20
33 Ben Coates .07 .20
34 Boomer Esiason .07 .20
35 Trent Dilfer .15 .40
36 Chris Miller .02 .10
37 Dave Brown .07 .20
38 Herman Moore .15 .40
39 Anthony Miller .07 .20
40 Andre Reed .07 .20
41 Reggie White .15 .40
42 Darnay Scott .07 .20
43 Erik Kramer .02 .10
44 Leroy Hoard .02 .10
45 Fred Barnett .07 .20
46 Junior Seau .15 .40
47 Vinny Testaverde .07 .20
48 Gus Frerotte .07 .20
49 William Floyd .07 .20
50 Mo Lewis .02 .10
51 Tim Brown .15 .40
52 Greg Lloyd .07 .20
53 Chester McGlockton .07 .20
54 Heath Shuler .07 .20
55 Rod Woodson .07 .20
56 Don Beebe .02 .10
57 Carl Pickens .07 .20
58 Charles Haley .07 .20
59 Steve Bono .07 .20
60 Harvey Williams .02 .10
61 Greg Hill .07 .20
62 Eric Metcalf .07 .20
63 Mario Bates .07 .20
64 Terry Allen .07 .20
65 Michael Timpson .02 .10
66 Mark Stepnoski .02 .10
67 Jeff Lageman .02 .10
68 Robert Smith .15 .40
69 Eric Allen .02 .10
70 Ricky Watters .07 .20
71 Derek Loville .02 .10
72 Bernie Parmalee .07 .20
73 Bryce Paup .07 .20
74 Frank Reich .02 .10
75 Henry Thomas .02 .10
76 Craig Erickson .02 .10
77 Eric Green .02 .10
78 Dave Meggett .02 .10
79 Deion Sanders .30 .75
80 Herschel Walker .07 .20
01 Andre Rison .07 .20
82 Ki-Jana Carter RC .15 .40
83 Tony Boselli RC .15 .40
84 Steve McNair RC 1.25 3.00
85 Michael Westbrook RC .15 .40
86 Kerry Collins RC .75 2.00
87 Kevin Carter RC .15 .40
88 Warren Sapp RC .60 1.50
89 Joey Galloway RC .60 1.50
90 J.J. Stokes RC .15 .40
92 Kyle Brady RC .15 .40
93 Napoleon Kaufman RC .40 1.00
94 Tyrone Wheatley RC .40 1.00
95 Mike Mamula RC .02 .10
96 Desmond Howard .07 .20
97 James O. Stewart RC .40 1.00
98 Craig Newsome RC .02 .10
99 Ty Law RC 1.00 2.50
100 Ellis Johnson RC .02 .10
101 Hugh Douglas RC .15 .40
102 Mark Bruener RC .07 .20
103 Tyrone Poole .15 .40
104 Luther Elliss .02 .10
105 Mark Fields RC .15 .40
106 Frank Sanders RC .15 .40
107 Rashaan Salaam RC .07 .20
108 Craig Powell RC .02 .10
109 Sherman Williams RC .02 .10
110 Chad May RC .02 .10
111 Rob Johnson RC .30 .75
112 Todd Collins RC .50 1.25
113 Terrell Davis RC 1.00 2.50
114 Eric Zeier RC .15 .40
115 Curtis Martin RC 1.25 3.00
116 Kordell Stewart RC .60 1.50
117 Troy Vincent .02 .10
118 Ray Zellars RC .07 .20
119 Dave Krieg .02 .10
120 Mike Sherrard .02 .10
121 Willie Davis .02 .10
122 Robert Brooks .07 .20
123 Chris Sanders RC .07 .20
124 Drew Bledsoe CL .15 .40
125 Emmitt Smith CL .25 .60
LT1 Drew Bledsoe Promo .60 1.50

1995 Images Limited/Live Die Cuts

is 30 card set was randomly inserted into both Limited and Live packs at a rate of one in 99 packs. Cards DC1-DC15 were randomly inserted in Limited packs, while cards DC16-DC30 were found in Live packs. There are no other differences between the cards. Card fronts are die cut on the right side on a black background and have a silver-foil background on the rest. Card backs are numbered out of 965 at the top with a black and green background. A brief statistical summary is also included.

COMPLETE SET (30) 80.00 200.00
COMP.SERIES 1 (15) 30.00 80.00
COMP.SERIES 2 (15) 50.00 120.00
DC1-DC15 ODDS 1:99 LIMITED
DC16-DC30 ODDS 1:99 LIVE
DC1 Jim Kelly 2.50 6.00
DC2 Kerry Collins 3.00 8.00
DC3 Michael Irvin 2.00 5.00
DC4 Troy Aikman 6.00 15.00
DC5 John Elway 12.50 30.00
DC6 Barry Sanders 10.00 25.00
DC7 Marshall Faulk 2.50 6.00
DC8 James O. Stewart .75 2.00
DC9 Drew Bledsoe 2.00 5.00
DC10 Herman Moore 1.25 3.00
DC11 Byron Bam Morris .75 2.00
DC12 Jerry Rice 8.00 20.00
DC13 Joey Galloway 2.00 5.00
DC14 Rick Mirer 1.25 3.00
DC15 Errict Rhett 1.25 3.00
DC16 Rob Moore .75 2.00
DC17 Jeff George 1.25 3.00
DC18 Rashaan Salaam .75 2.00
DC19 Andre Rison 1.25 3.00
DC20 Emmitt Smith 12.50 30.00
DC21 Brett Favre 15.00 40.00
DC22 Dan Marino 15.00 40.00
DC23 Warren Moon 1.25 3.00
DC24 Dave Brown .75 2.00
DC25 Napoleon Kaufman .75 2.00
DC26 Natrone Means 1.25 3.00
DC27 Steve Young 5.00 12.00
DC28 Reggie White 2.00 5.00
DC29 Jerome Bettis 2.00 5.00
DC30 Michael Westbrook .75 2.00

1995 Images Limited Focused Gold

is 30 card set was inserted as a special one-card pack in both products at a rate of one in every box. The cards feature two star players from the same team and are printed on 24-point acetate material. Card fronts from the Limited set have two gold gears in the background with a photo of each player over a gear. The player's names are listed at the bottom of the card on a white and blue background with the "Focused" logo between them. The Live version card fronts feature the gear background in a clear holographic pattern against a blue background.

COMPLETE SET (30) 40.00 80.00
*LIVE BLUE: .4X TO 1X LIMITED GOLD
ONE PER BOX LIMITED/LIVE
F1 R.Salaam .60 1.50
E.Kramer
F2 K.Collins 1.00 2.50
F.Reich
F3 J.Kelly 1.25 3.00
A.Reed
F4 J.George .60 1.50
C.Heyward
F5 G.Hearst .75 2.00
D.Krieg
F6 C.Pickens 1.25 3.00
J.Blake
F7 A.Rison .60 1.50
L.Hoard
F8 E.Smith 4.00 10.00
T.Aikman
F9 J.Elway 5.00 12.00
Sh.Sharpe
F10 B.Sanders 4.00 10.00
H.Moore
F11 W.Davis .60 1.50
S.Bono
F12 J.O.Stewart 1.25 3.00
Beuerlein
F13 M.Faulk 3.00 8.00
C.Erickson
F14 S.McNair 2.50 6.00
C.Chandler
F15 B.Favre 6.00 12.00
R.White
F16 R.Hampton .60 1.50
D.Brown
F17 M.Bates .60 1.50
J.Everett
F18 D.Bledsoe 1.50 4.00
B.Coates
F19 W.Moon 1.25 3.00
C.Carter
F20 D.Marino 5.00 12.00
I.Fryar
F21 N.Means .75 2.00
S.Humphries
F22 B.Morris .60 1.50
K.Greene
F23 R.Watters .75 2.00
R.Cunningham
F24 T.Brown .60 1.50
J.Hostetler
F25 B.Esiason .60 1.50
K.Brady
F26 J.Galloway 1.25 3.00
R.Mirer
F27 S.Young 4.00 8.00
J.Rice
F28 J.Bettis 1.25 3.00
K.Carter
F29 E.Rhett .75 2.00
T.Dilfer
F30 M.Westbrook .75 2.00
T.Allen

1995 Images Limited Icons

This 20 card set was randomly inserted in Limited packs only at a rate of one in 20 packs. The card fronts have a fabric backgound with the player's name and "Icons" logo in foil. Card backs are numbered with an "I" prefix and have a brief commentary surrounded by an orange border.

COMPLETE SET (20) 50.00 120.00
STATED ODDS 1:20 LIMITED
I1 Jim Kelly 1.25 2.50
I2 Rashaan Salaam .30 .75
I3 Andre Rison .60 1.25
I4 Troy Aikman 4.00 8.00
I5 Emmitt Smith 6.00 12.00
I6 John Elway 8.00 15.00
I7 Barry Sanders 6.00 12.00
I8 Brett Favre 8.00 15.00
I9 Marshall Faulk 5.00 10.00
I10 Irving Fryar .60 1.25
I11 Dan Marino 8.00 15.00
I12 Drew Bledsoe 2.50 5.00
I13 Rodney Hampton .60 1.25
I14 Ricky Watters .60 1.25
I15 Byron Bam Morris .25 .60
I16 Natrone Means .60 1.25
I17 Steve Young 3.00 6.00
I18 Jerry Rice 4.00 8.00
I19 Errict Rhett .60 1.25
I20 Michael Westbrook .75 1.50

1995 Images Limited Sculpted Previews

is five card set was randomly inserted in Limited packs only at a rate of 24 packs. The cards are preview cards of the "Sculpted" insert set that was released in the 1996 Classic NFL Experience product. Card fronts are die cut at the top with the word "Sculpted" across the top and a wood grain background. The photo of the player is in the center of the card with the team's logo in the background. The word "preview" runs along the left side of the card and the player's name is located on the bottom right side. Card backs have an NFL logo in the background with the phrase "Congratulations! You have received a limited edition 1996 NFL Experience Preview Card. Card backs also have a "NX" prefix.

COMPLETE SET (5) 12.50 25.00
STATED ODDS 1:24 LIMITED
NX1 Emmitt Smith 5.00 10.00
NX2 Drew Bledsoe 2.00 4.00
NX3 Steve Young 2.50 5.00
NX4 Rashaan Salaam .40 1.00
NX5 Marshall Faulk 4.00 8.00

1995 Images Limited/Live Silks

is 10 card set was randomly inserted in both Limited and Live packs at a rate of one in 375 packs. Card numbers S1-S5 were inserted in Live packs and numbers S6-S10 were inserted in Limited packs. Card fronts have an orange die cut background surrounded by a black background. The image of the player is made with a silk material. The player's name is in white at the bottom of the card. Card backs contain a statistical summary and the cards are numbered with a "S" prefix.

COMPLETE SET (10) 40.00 100.00
COMP.SERIES 1 (5) 20.00 50.00
COMP.SERIES 2 (5) 20.00 50.00
S1-S5 ODDS 1:375 LIVE
S6-S10 ODDS 1:375 LIMITED
S1 Troy Aikman 10.00 25.00
S2 Marshall Faulk 5.00 12.00
S3 Drew Bledsoe 4.00 10.00
S4 Byron Bam Morris 2.00 5.00
S5 James O. Stewart 2.50 6.00
S6 Emmitt Smith 20.00 50.00
S7 Steve Young 8.00 20.00
S8 Rashaan Salaam 2.00 5.00
S9 Natrone Means 2.50 6.00
S10 Michael Westbrook 2.00 5.00

1995 Images Live

COMPLETE SET (125) 10.00 25.00
UNLESS LISTED LIMITED/LIVE SAME PRICE
119 Mark Brunell .30 .75
120 Keenan McCardell .07 .20
121 Terry Kirby .07 .20
122 Marcus Allen .15 .40
123 Charlie Garner .07 .20
LV1 Drew Bledsoe Promo .60 1.50
numbered LT1, ad back

1995 Images Live Untouchables

is 25 card set was randomly inserted into Live packs only and is printed on three-dimensional holographic foil board. Card fronts contain the player's name on the left side with the "NFL Untouchables" logo underneath it. A full shot of the player is shown with an additional head shot in the bottom right corner. Card backs have mostly a black background with bullet-point information about the player on the left side. Cards are numbered with a "U" prefix.

COMPLETE SET (25) 100.00 200.00
STATED ODDS 1:20 LIVE
U1 Jim Kelly 2.50 5.00
U2 Kerry Collins 3.00 6.00
U3 Rashaan Salaam .30 .75
U4 Troy Aikman 8.00 15.00
U5 Emmitt Smith 12.50 25.00
U6 John Elway 15.00 30.00
U7 Barry Sanders 12.50 25.00
U8 Reggie White 2.50 5.00
U9 Steve McNair 6.00 12.00
U10 Marshall Faulk 10.00 20.00
U11 Dan Marino 15.00 30.00
U12 Drew Bledsoe 5.00 10.00
U13 Ben Coates 1.25 2.50
U14 Tyrone Wheatley 2.00 4.00
U15 Chester McGlockton 1.25 2.50
U16 Ricky Watters 1.25 2.50
U17 Junior Seau 2.50 5.00
U18 Natrone Means 1.25 2.50
U19 Steve Young 6.00 12.00
U20 Jerry Rice 8.00 15.00
U21 Rick Mirer 1.25 2.50
U22 Jerome Bettis 2.50 5.00
U23 Warren Sapp 3.00 6.00
U24 Michael Westbrook .75 1.50
U25 Heath Shuler 1.25 2.50

2013-14 Immaculate Collection Multisport Autographs

RANDOM INSERTS IN PACKS
STATED PRINT RUN 10-25
EXCHANGE DEADLINE 3/3/2016
7 Johnny Manziel EXCH 30.00 80.00
8 Brett Favre EXCH 125.00 250.00
9 Peyton Manning EXCH 150.00 250.00
10 Bo Jackson/10 100.00 200.00

2014 Immaculate Collection

1-100 VETERAN PRINT RUN 99
102-141 ROOKIE JSY AU PRINT RUN 99
142-200 ROOKIE AU PRINT RUN 49
1 Marshawn Lynch 2.50 6.00
2 Aaron Rodgers 8.00 20.00
3 Frank Gore 2.50 6.00
4 EJ Manuel 2.00 5.00
5 Geno Smith 2.00 5.00
6 Ryan Tannehill 2.50 6.00
7 Ndamukong Suh 2.50 6.00
8 Tom Brady 10.00 25.00
9 Fred Jackson 2.50 6.00
10 Lamar Miller 2.00 5.00
11 Vincent Jackson 2.00 5.00
12 Steve Smith 2.50 6.00
13 Eric Decker 2.00 5.00
14 Andy Dalton 2.50 6.00
15 Julian Edelman 3.00 8.00
16 Joe Flacco 2.50 6.00
17 Ben Tate 2.00 5.00
18 Ben Roethlisberger 4.00 10.00
19 Giovani Bernard 2.00 5.00
20 LeSean McCoy 3.00 8.00
21 Torrey Smith 2.00 5.00
22 Jordan Cameron 2.00 5.00
23 Alfred Morris 2.00 5.00
24 Dwayne Bowe 2.50 6.00
25 Kendall Wright 2.00 5.00
26 Trent Richardson 2.00 5.00
27 Matthew Stafford 2.50 6.00
28 Andre Johnson 2.50 6.00
29 Andrew Luck 8.00 20.00
30 Shonn Greene 2.00 5.00
31 Arian Foster 2.50 6.00
32 Reggie Wayne 2.50 6.00
33 Jeremy Maclin 2.00 5.00
34 Troy Polamalu 3.00 8.00
35 Jake Locker 2.50 6.00
36 Cecil Shorts 2.00 5.00
37 Hakeem Nicks 2.00 5.00
38 Keenan Allen 2.50 6.00
39 Jamaal Charles 2.50 6.00
40 Maurice Jones-Drew 2.00 5.00
41 Philip Rivers 3.00 8.00
42 Wes Welker 2.50 6.00
43 Alex Smith 2.50 6.00
44 Ryan Mathews 2.50 6.00
45 Peyton Manning 8.00 20.00
46 Darren McFadden 2.00 5.00
47 Montee Ball 2.00 5.00
48 Le'Veon Bell 2.50 6.00
49 Robert Griffin III 2.00 5.00
50 Antonio Brown 3.00 8.00
51 DeMarco Murray 2.50 6.00
52 Riley Cooper 2.50 6.00
53 Eli Manning 2.50 6.00
54 C.J. Spiller 2.00 5.00
55 A.J. Green 3.00 8.00
56 Tony Romo 4.00 10.00
57 Nick Foles 2.50 6.00
58 Victor Cruz 2.50 6.00
59 Pierre Garcon 2.50 6.00
60 Rashad Jennings 2.00 5.00
61 DeSean Jackson 2.50 6.00
62 Jay Cutler 2.00 5.00
63 Adrian Peterson 4.00 10.00
64 Eddie Lacy 2.00 5.00
65 Matt Forte 2.00 5.00
66 Toby Gerhart 2.00 5.00
67 Brandon Marshall 2.00 5.00
68 Alshon Jeffery 2.50 6.00
69 Chris Johnson 2.00 5.00
70 Calvin Johnson 3.00 8.00
71 DeMarcus Ware 2.50 6.00
72 Jordy Nelson 2.50 6.00
73 Reggie Bush 2.00 5.00
74 Clay Matthews 2.00 5.00
75 Cam Newton 3.00 8.00
76 Doug Martin 2.50 6.00
77 Steven Jackson 2.00 5.00
78 Drew Brees 3.00 8.00
79 Brian Hartline 2.00 5.00
80 Julio Jones 3.00 8.00
81 DeAngelo Williams 2.00 5.00
82 Josh McCown 2.00 5.00
83 Matt Ryan 2.50 6.00
84 Marques Colston 2.00 5.00
85 Jerricho Cotchery 2.00 5.00
86 Pierre Thomas 2.00 5.00
87 Andre Ellington 2.00 5.00
88 Mike Wallace 2.00 5.00
89 Zac Stacy 2.00 5.00
90 Carson Palmer 2.50 6.00
91 Rob Gronkowski 3.00 8.00
92 Michael Crabtree 2.00 5.00
93 Richard Sherman 5.00 12.00
94 Sam Bradford 2.00 5.00
95 Larry Fitzgerald 2.50 6.00
96 Colin Kaepernick 2.50 6.00
97 Russell Wilson 5.00 12.00
98 Dez Bryant 3.00 8.00
99 Greg Jennings 2.00 5.00
100 J.J. Watt 3.00 8.00
102 Blake Bortles JSY AU RC 8.00 20.00
103 Sammy Watkins JSY AU RC 10.00 25.00
105 Mike Evans JSY AU RC 25.00 60.00
106 Eric Ebron JSY AU RC 8.00 20.00
107 Odell Beckham Jr. JSY AU RC 75.00 150.00
108 Brandin Cooks JSY AU RC 10.00 25.00
109 Johnny Manziel JSY AU RC 10.00 25.00
110 Kelvin Benjamin JSY AU RC 10.00 25.00
111 Teddy Bridgewater JSY AU RC 10.00 25.00
113 Austin Seferian-Jenkins JSY AU RC 6.00 15.00
114 Marqise Lee JSY AU RC 8.00 20.00
115 Jordan Matthews JSY AU RC 10.00 25.00
118 Davante Adams JSY AU RC 20.00 50.00
119 Bishop Sankey JSY AU RC 10.00 25.00
121 Cody Latimer JSY AU RC 8.00 20.00
122 Carlos Hyde JSY AU RC 8.00 20.00
123 Allen Robinson JSY AU RC 10.00 25.00
124 Jimmy Garoppolo JSY AU RC 100.00 200.00
125 Jarvis Landry JSY AU RC 12.00 30.00
126 Charles Sims JSY AU RC 6.00 15.00
127 Tre Mason JSY AU RC 25.00 50.00
128 Donte Moncrief JSY AU RC 6.00 15.00
129 Terrance West JSY AU RC 6.00 15.00
130 Dri Archer JSY AU RC 6.00 15.00
131 Devonta Freeman JSY AU RC 25.00 50.00
132 Andre Williams JSY AU RC 10.00 25.00
133 Ka'Deem Carey JSY AU RC 6.00 15.00
134 Logan Thomas JSY AU RC 6.00 15.00
136 Tom Savage JSY AU RC 6.00 15.00
137 Aaron Murray JSY AU RC 6.00 15.00
138 A.J. McCarron JSY AU RC 6.00 15.00
139 Tajh Boyd JSY AU RC 6.00 15.00
140 Asa Watson JSY AU RC 6.00 15.00
141 Connor Shaw JSY AU RC 6.00 15.00
142 Greg Robinson AU RC 5.00 12.00
143 Jake Matthews AU RC 5.00 12.00
144 Anthony Barr AU RC 5.00 12.00
145 Isaiah Crowell AU RC 6.00 15.00
146 Martavis Bryant AU RC 20.00 50.00
147 Kyle Fuller AU RC 5.00 12.00
148 Ryan Shazier AU RC 8.00 20.00
149 Branden Oliver AU RC 8.00 20.00
151 Calvin Pryor AU RC 5.00 12.00
152 Crockett Gillmore AU RC 6.00 15.00
153 Ha Ha Clinton-Dix AU RC 6.00 15.00
154 Dee Ford AU RC 5.00 12.00
155 Darqueze Dennard AU RC 6.00 15.00
156 Jason Verrett AU RC 5.00 12.00
157 Marcus Smith AU RC 5.00 12.00
168 Doono Bucannon AU RC 5.00 12.00
159 Chris Borland AU RC 5.00 12.00
160 Jimmie Ward AU RC 6.00 15.00
161 Bradley Roby AU RC 5.00 12.00
162 Trevor Reilly AU RC 5.00 12.00
163 Kyle Van Noy AU RC 6.00 15.00
164 Lamarcus Joyner AU RC 6.00 15.00
165 Garrett Gilbert AU RC 5.00 12.00
166 Trent Murphy AU RC 5.00 12.00
167 Telvin Smith AU RC 5.00 12.00
168 Troy Niklas AU RC 5.00 12.00
169 Kony Ealy AU RC 6.00 15.00
170 C.J. Fiedorowicz AU RC 5.00 12.00
171 Preston Brown AU RC 5.00 12.00
172 Josh Huff AU RC 6.00 15.00
173 John Brown AU RC 8.00 20.00
174 Jerick McKinnon AU RC 6.00 15.00
175 Richard Rodgers AU RC 8.00 20.00
178 Shaq Evans AU RC 5.00 12.00
179 Kevin Norwood AU RC 5.00 12.00
180 James White AU RC 10.00 25.00
181 Lorenzo Taliaferro AU RC 5.00 12.00
182 Devin Street AU RC 5.00 12.00
183 Jared Abbrederis AU RC 15.00 30.00
184 Zach Mettenberger AU RC 5.00 12.00
185 David Fales AU RC 5.00 12.00
186 Robert Herron AU RC 5.00 12.00
187 Lache Seastrunk AU RC 5.00 12.00
189 Matt Hazel AU RC 5.00 12.00
190 Keith Wenning AU RC 6.00 15.00
191 Marion Grice AU RC 5.00 12.00
192 Tyler Gaffney AU RC 5.00 12.00
193 Jordan Lynch AU RC 6.00 15.00
194 Michael Campanaro AU RC 5.00 12.00
195 Jeff Janis AU RC 10.00 25.00
196 Tevin Reese AU RC 5.00 12.00
197 Michael Sam AU RC 5.00 12.00
198 Rajion Neal AU RC 5.00 12.00
199 L'Damian Washington AU RC 6.00 15.00
200 Mike Davis AU RC 5.00 12.00

2014 Immaculate Collection Gold

*1-100 VETS/25: .6X TO 1.5X BASIC CARDS/99
*101-141 ROOKIE JSY AU/25: .6X TO 1.5X JSY AU/99
1-141 STATED PRINT RUN 25
142-200 UNPRICED AUTO PRINT RUN 10
124 Jimmy Garoppolo JSY AU 200.00 400.00

2014 Immaculate Collection Veteran Patch Autographs

1 Peyton Manning/14
2 Andrew Luck/25 150.00 300.00
3 Barry Sanders/25 125.00 250.00
4 Bo Jackson/25 100.00 200.00
5 Jerry Rice/25 150.00 250.00
6 Jamaal Charles/25 25.00 50.00
8 Adrian Peterson/25 75.00 150.00
9 Jay Cutler/25 30.00 60.00
10 Emmitt Smith/25 175.00 300.00
11 Wes Welker/25 25.00 50.00
12 Joe Flacco/25 40.00 80.00
13 LeSean McCoy/25 25.00 50.00
15 Tony Romo/25 50.00 100.00
16 Dez Bryant/25
18 Matt Ryan/25 30.00 60.00
19 Philip Rivers/25 40.00 80.00
21 Demaryius Thomas/25 15.00 40.00
26 Richard Sherman/13
29 Ryan Tannehill/25 50.00 100.00
30 Von Miller/25 15.00 40.00

2014 Immaculate Collection Gloves Logos

IGAM Aaron Murray/30 10.00 25.00
IGAM A.J. McCarron/30 10.00 25.00
IGAR Allen Robinson/30 15.00 40.00
IGAS Austin Seferian-Jenkins/30 10.00 25.00
IGAW Andre Williams/30 12.00 30.00
IGBB Blake Bortles/30 12.00 30.00
IGBC Brandin Cooks/30 15.00 40.00
IGBS Bishop Sankey/30 10.00 25.00
IGCH Carlos Hyde/30 12.00 30.00
IGCL Cody Latimer/30 12.00 30.00
IGCS Charles Sims/30 10.00 25.00
IGDA Davante Adams/30 15.00 40.00
IGDA Dri Archer/30 10.00 25.00
IGDC Derek Carr/30 60.00 150.00
IGDF Devonta Freeman/30 25.00 50.00
IGDM Donte Moncrief/30 10.00 25.00
IGDT De'Anthony Thomas/30
IGEE Eric Ebron/30 12.00 30.00
IGJC Jadeveon Clowney/30
IGJG Jimmy Garoppolo/30 40.00 80.00
IGJH Jeremy Hill/30 12.00 30.00
IGJL Jarvis Landry/30 20.00 50.00
IGJM Jordan Matthews/30 15.00 40.00
IGJM Johnny Manziel/30 15.00 40.00
IGKB Kelvin Benjamin/30 15.00 40.00
IGKC Ka'Deem Carey/30 25.00 50.00
IGKM Khalil Mack/30
IGLT Logan Thomas/30 10.00 25.00
IGME Mike Evans/30 30.00 60.00
IGML Marqise Lee/30 12.00 30.00
IGOB Odell Beckham Jr./30 30.00 60.00
IGSW Sammy Watkins/30 15.00 40.00
IGTB Teddy Bridgewater/30 15.00 40.00
IGTB Tajh Boyd/30 10.00 25.00
IGTM Tre Mason/30 10.00 25.00
IGTS Tom Savage/30 10.00 25.00
IGTW Terrance West/30 10.00 25.00

2014 Immaculate Collection Immaculate Moments Autographs

2 Emmitt Smith 150.00 250.00
3 Tony Dorsett 40.00 80.00
4 John Elway 125.00 200.00
7 Tom Brady 350.00 500.00
10 Kellen Winslow 40.00 80.00

2014 Immaculate Collection Immaculate Standard

ISAB Antonio Brown/25 8.00 20.00
ISAD Andy Dalton/25 6.00 15.00
ISAG Antonio Gates/25 5.00 12.00
ISAG A.J. Green/25 8.00 20.00
ISAM Aaron Murray/49 3.00 8.00
ISAM A.J. McCarron/49 3.00 8.00
ISAR Allen Robinson/49 5.00 12.00
ISAS Austin Seferian-Jenkins/49 3.00 8.00
ISAW Andre Williams/49 3.00 8.00
ISBB Blake Bortles/49 4.00 10.00
ISBC Brandin Cooks/49 5.00 12.00
ISBS Bishop Sankey/49 3.00 8.00
ISCH Carlos Hyde/49 4.00 10.00
ISCL Cody Latimer/49 4.00 10.00
ISCP Cordarrelle Patterson/25 5.00 12.00
ISCS Connor Shaw/49 3.00 8.00
ISCS Charles Sims/49 3.00 8.00
ISCS C.J. Spiller/25 5.00 12.00
ISCW Cameron Wake/25 5.00 12.00
ISDA Davante Adams/49 5.00 12.00
ISDA Dri Archer/49 3.00 8.00
ISDB Dwayne Bowe/25 6.00 15.00
ISDC Derek Carr/49 8.00 20.00
ISDF Devonta Freeman/49 5.00 12.00
ISDH DeAngelo Hall/25 5.00 12.00
ISDJ Derrick Johnson/25 8.00 20.00
ISDM DeMarco Murray/25 6.00 15.00
ISDM Donte Moncrief/49 10.00 25.00
ISDT De'Anthony Thomas/49 3.00 8.00
ISDT Demaryius Thomas/25 6.00 15.00
ISDW DeMarcus Ware/25 6.00 15.00
ISDW Delanie Walker/25 5.00 12.00
ISEB Eric Berry/25 6.00 15.00
ISED Elvis Dumervil/25 5.00 12.00
ISEE Eric Ebron/49 4.00 10.00
ISEM EJ Manuel/25 5.00 12.00
ISER Eddie Royal/25 5.00 12.00
ISES Emmanuel Sanders/25 6.00 15.00
ISGA Geno Atkins/25 5.00 12.00
ISGB Giovani Bernard/25 5.00 12.00
ISJC Jordan Cameron/25 5.00 12.00
ISJC Jadeveon Clowney/49 4.00 10.00
ISJC Jared Cook/25 5.00 12.00
ISJF Joe Flacco/25 6.00 15.00
ISJG Jimmy Garoppolo/49 25.00 60.00
ISJG Jermaine Gresham/25 5.00 12.00
ISJH Jeremy Hill/49 4.00 10.00
ISJH Joe Haden/25 5.00 12.00
ISJJ Jacoby Jones/25 5.00 12.00
ISJL Jarvis Landry/49 6.00 15.00
ISJL Jake Locker/25 6.00 15.00
ISJM Johnny Manziel/49 5.00 12.00
ISJM Jordan Matthews/49 5.00 12.00
ISJR Jordan Reed/25 5.00 12.00
ISJT Jacob Tamme/25 5.00 12.00
ISJU Johnny Unitas/25 30.00 60.00
ISKB Kelvin Benjamin/49 5.00 12.00
ISKC Ka'Deem Carey/49 3.00 8.00
ISKM Knowshon Moreno/25 5.00 12.00
ISKM Khalil Mack/49 12.00 30.00
ISKS Kenny Stills/25 5.00 12.00
ISKW Kendall Wright/25 5.00 12.00
ISLF Larry Fitzgerald/25 6.00 15.00
ISLT Logan Thomas/49 3.00 8.00
ISMB Montee Ball/25 5.00 12.00
ISMC Morris Claiborne/25 5.00 12.00
ISMC Marques Colston/25 5.00 12.00
ISME Mike Evans/49 8.00 20.00
ISML Marqise Lee/49 4.00 10.00
ISMS Michael Sam/49 3.00 8.00
ISMW Mario Williams/25 5.00 12.00
ISMW Mike Wallace/25 5.00 12.00
ISNW Nate Washington/25 5.00 12.00
ISOB Odell Beckham Jr./49 8.00 20.00
ISPM Peyton Manning/25 30.00 60.00
ISPP Patrick Peterson/25 5.00 12.00
ISPR Paul Richardson/49 4.00 10.00
ISPR Philip Rivers/25 8.00 20.00
ISRW Robert Woods/25 6.00 15.00
ISSG Shonn Greene/25 5.00 12.00
ISSS Steve Smith/25 8.00 20.00
ISSW Sammy Watkins/49 5.00 12.00
ISTB Tajh Boyd/49 3.00 8.00
ISTB Teddy Bridgewater/49 5.00 12.00
ISTG Toby Gerhart/25 5.00 12.00
ISTH Tamba Hali/25 5.00 12.00
ISTM Tre Mason/49 3.00 8.00
ISTR Tony Romo/25 6.00 15.00
ISTS Torrey Smith/25 5.00 12.00
ISTS Terrell Suggs/25 5.00 12.00
ISTS Tom Savage/49 3.00 8.00
ISTW Terrance West/49 3.00 8.00
ISTW Terrance Williams/25 5.00 12.00
ISVJ Vincent Jackson/25 5.00 12.00
ISVM Von Miller/25 6.00 15.00
ISWW Wesley Woodyard/25 8.00 20.00
ISWW Wes Welker/25 6.00 15.00

2014 Immaculate Collection Ink

1 Joe Montana 100.00 175.00
3 Troy Aikman 40.00 80.00
4 Arian Foster 12.00 30.00
5 Andre Ellington 8.00 20.00

6 Paul Posluszny 8.00 20.00
8 Zach Ertz 10.00 25.00
9 Sean Lee 10.00 25.00
10 Rob Gronkowski 30.00 60.00
14 Dick Butkus 30.00 60.00
15 Gale Sayers 30.00 60.00
16 Paul Warfield 12.00 30.00
18 Emmitt Smith 100.00 175.00
19 Barry Sanders 100.00 175.00
20 Thurman Thomas 25.00 50.00
22 Mike Ditka 20.00 40.00
23 Tim Brown
24 Warren Moon 25.00 50.00
25 Mike James 8.00 20.00
26 Rod Woodson 25.00 50.00
27 Terrell Davis 25.00 50.00
28 Kellen Winslow 15.00 40.00
31 James Lofton 12.00 30.00
34 Brett Favre 100.00 175.00
35 Steve Largent 25.00 50.00
36 Dwight Clark
39 Gavin Escobar 10.00 25.00
40 Rod Streater 8.00 20.00

2014 Immaculate Collection Logos

IMAM A.J. McCarron/20 12.00 30.00
IMAS Austin Seferian-Jenkins/11 15.00 40.00
IMAW Andre Williams/15
IMBB Blake Bortles/14
IMBC Brandin Cooks/11 15.00 40.00
IMBS Bishop Sankey/18 10.00 25.00
IMCH Carlos Hyde/12 12.00 30.00
IMCS Connor Shaw/17 10.00 25.00
IMDA Dri Archer/18 10.00 25.00
IMDF Devonta Freeman/16 15.00 40.00
IMDT De'Anthony Thomas/14 10.00 25.00
IMEE Eric Ebron/12 12.00 30.00
IMJC Jadeveon Clowney/19 12.00 30.00
IMJH Jeremy Hill/52 8.00 20.00
IMJL Jarvis Landry/20 20.00 50.00
IMJM Jordan Matthews/12 15.00 40.00
IMJM Johnny Manziel/17 15.00 40.00
IMKB Kelvin Benjamin/32 10.00 25.00
IMKC Ka'Deem Carey/15
IMKM Khalil Mack/20 40.00 100.00
IMLT Logan Thomas/18 10.00 25.00
IMME Mike Evans/13 25.00 50.00
IMML Marqise Lee/13 12.00 30.00
IMOB Odell Beckham Jr./15 60.00 120.00
IMSW Sammy Watkins/12 15.00 40.00
IMTB Teddy Bridgewater/13
IMTM Tre Mason/19 10.00 25.00
IMTS Tom Savage/18 10.00 25.00
IMTW Terrance West/17

2014 Immaculate Collection Nameplate Nobility

NNTB Teddy Bridgewater/11 30.00 60.00
NNASJ Austin Seferian-Jenkins/15 20.00 40.00

2014 Immaculate Collection Numbers Jumbo Patches

1 Jeremy Hill/50 6.00 15.00
2 Marques Colston/17 10.00 25.00
3 Dri Archer/50 5.00 12.00
4 Ryan Mathews/43 10.00 25.00
5 Jason Witten/14 30.00 60.00
6 Alex Smith/23 12.00 30.00
7 Jadeveon Clowney/50 6.00 15.00
8 Doug Martin/22 12.00 30.00
9 Kelvin Benjamin/50 8.00 20.00
10 Jake Locker/29 10.00 25.00
11 Cody Latimer/50 6.00 15.00
12 Matt Forte/36 25.00 50.00
13 Devonta Freeman/50 8.00 20.00
14 Ryan Tannehill/31 12.00 30.00
15 Dez Bryant/29 12.00 30.00
16 Anquan Boldin/29 8.00 20.00
17 Blake Bortles/50 6.00 15.00
18 Dwayne Bowe/50 8.00 20.00
19 Teddy Bridgewater/50 8.00 20.00
20 Jamaal Charles/50 25.00 50.00
21 Carlos Hyde/50 6.00 15.00
23 Andre Williams/50 5.00 12.00
24 Shonn Greene/50 6.00 15.00
25 Tony Romo/15
26 Antonio Brown/50 10.00 25.00
27 Sammy Watkins/50 8.00 20.00
29 Derek Carr/50 15.00 40.00
30 Jeremy Maclin/16 10.00 25.00
31 Allen Robinson/50 8.00 20.00
32 Morris Claiborne/39 8.00 20.00
33 Ka'Deem Carey/50 5.00 12.00
34 Steve Smith/50 15.00 30.00
35 DeMarco Murray/50 10.00 25.00
36 Bernard Pierce/50 6.00 15.00
37 Khalil Mack/50 20.00 50.00
38 Elvis Dumervil/44 10.00 25.00
39 Austin Seferian-Jenkins/50 5.00 12.00
40 Jimmy Graham/13 30.00 80.00
41 Jimmy Garoppolo/50 20.00 50.00
42 Nate Washington/50 6.00 15.00
43 Logan Thomas/50 5.00 12.00
44 Terrell Suggs/20 15.00 40.00
45 Wes Welker/15
46 Brian Hartline/50 6.00 15.00
47 Mike Evans/50 12.00 30.00
48 Eric Berry/50 15.00 30.00
49 Marqise Lee/50 6.00 15.00
50 Joe Flacco/17 15.00 40.00
51 Jarvis Landry/50 12.00 30.00
52 Owen Daniels/42 8.00 20.00
53 De'Anthony Thomas/50 6.00 15.00
54 Thurman Thomas/25 10.00 25.00
55 Von Miller/38 10.00 25.00
56 C.J. Spiller/50 6.00 15.00
57 Eric Ebron/50 6.00 15.00
58 Fred Jackson/50 15.00 30.00
59 Jordan Matthews/50 8.00 20.00
60 Jonathan Stewart/50 6.00 15.00
61 Charles Sims/50 5.00 12.00
63 Tom Savage/50 5.00 12.00
66 Cameron Wake/50 20.00 40.00
67 Odell Beckham Jr./50 25.00 60.00
68 Gavin Escobar/25 8.00 20.00
69 Paul Richardson/50 12.00 30.00
70 Kendall Wright/38 8.00 20.00
71 Tre Mason/50 5.00 12.00
72 Pierre Thomas/25 15.00 40.00
73 Aaron Murray/50 5.00 12.00
74 Vincent Jackson/15 10.00 25.00
75 Demaryius Thomas/31 15.00 40.00
76 DeAngelo Williams/26 8.00 20.00
77 Brandin Cooks/50 8.00 20.00
80 Lamar Miller/50 10.00 25.00
81 Donte Moncrief/50 5.00 12.00
82 Robert Woods/50 10.00 25.00
83 A.J. McCarron/50 5.00 12.00
85 A.J. Green/36 20.00 50.00
86 Delanie Walker/50 6.00 15.00
87 Johnny Manziel/50 8.00 20.00
88 Haloti Ngata/50 12.00 30.00
89 Davante Adams/50 8.00 20.00
90 Larry Fitzgerald/15 12.00 30.00
91 Terrance West/50 5.00 12.00
92 Roddy White/32 8.00 20.00
95 Giovani Bernard/36 8.00 20.00
96 Derrick Johnson/50 20.00 40.00
97 Mario Williams/50 10.00 25.00
98 Jacoby Jones/50 6.00 15.00
99 Bishop Sankey/50 5.00 12.00

2014 Immaculate Collection Numbers Patch

IMAB Antonio Brown/84 10.00 25.00
IMAD Andy Dalton/14
IMAF Arian Foster/23 12.00 30.00
IMAG A.J. Green/18 15.00 40.00
IMAJ Andre Johnson/80 8.00 20.00
IMAL Andrew Luck/12
IMAM Alfred Morris/46 8.00 20.00
IMAP Adrian Peterson/28 12.00 30.00
IMAS Alex Smith/11
IMBJ Bo Jackson/34 15.00 40.00
IMBR Bill Romanowski/53 12.00 30.00
IMBS Barry Sanders/20 25.00 60.00
IMCC Cris Carter/80 15.00 40.00
IMCJ Calvin Johnson/81 25.00 50.00
IMCP Cordarrelle Patterson/84 6.00 15.00
IMCS Cecil Shorts/84 6.00 15.00
IMCT Charles Tillman/33 10.00 25.00
IMDB Dez Bryant/88 12.00 30.00
IMDM Dan Marino/13
IMDM Darren McFadden/20 10.00 25.00
IMED Eric Dickerson/29 20.00 40.00
IMED Eric Decker/87 6.00 15.00
IMEL Eddie Lacy/27 8.00 20.00
IMES Emmitt Smith/22
IMHL Howie Long/75 15.00 30.00
IMJC Jamaal Charles/25 10.00 25.00
IMJG Jimmy Graham/80 10.00 25.00
IMJG Josh Gordon/12 10.00 25.00
IMJJ Julio Jones/11 15.00 40.00
IMJK Jim Kelly/12
IMJM Joe Montana/16 40.00 100.00
IMJR Jerry Rice/80 20.00 50.00
IMJW Jason Witten/82 8.00 20.00
IMKA Keenan Allen/13 12.00 30.00
IMLC Larry Csonka/39 12.00 30.00
IMLF Larry Fitzgerald/11
IMLM LeSean McCoy/25
IMMB Montee Ball/28 8.00 20.00
IMME Mike Evans/13 25.00 60.00
IMMF Marshall Faulk/28 10.00 25.00
IMMF Matt Forte/22 10.00 25.00
IMML Marshawn Lynch/24 12.00 30.00
IMPM Peyton Manning/18 50.00 100.00
IMPR Philip Rivers/17 15.00 40.00
IMPW Paul Warfield/42 10.00 25.00
IMRL Ronnie Lott/42 10.00 25.00
IMRS Richard Sherman/25 25.00 60.00
IMRT Ryan Tannehill/17 20.00 50.00
IMSR Sheldon Richardson/91 6.00 15.00
IMSW Sammy Watkins/14 15.00 40.00
IMTA Tavon Austin/11 10.00 25.00
IMTB Tom Brady/12 40.00 100.00
IMTD Terrell Davis/30 15.00 40.00
IMTE Tyler Eifert/85 6.00 15.00
IMTR Trent Richardson/34 8.00 20.00
IMTS Torrey Smith/82 6.00 15.00
IMTT Thurman Thomas/34 10.00 25.00
IMVC Victor Cruz/80 8.00 20.00
IMVJ Vincent Jackson/83 6.00 15.00
IMWD Warrick Dunn/28 12.00 30.00
IMWP Walter Payton/34 50.00 120.00
IMWW Wes Welker/83 8.00 20.00
IMZM Zach Miller/86 6.00 15.00
IMZS Zac Stacy/30 8.00 20.00

2014 Immaculate Collection Numbers Rookie Autographs

142 Greg Robinson/79 4.00 10.00
143 Jake Matthews/70 4.00 10.00
144 Anthony Barr/55 4.00 10.00
145 Isaiah Crowell/34 6.00 15.00
147 Kyle Fuller/23 6.00 15.00
148 Ryan Shazier/50 6.00 15.00
149 Arthur Lynch/88 4.00 10.00
151 Calvin Pryor/25 6.00 15.00
152 Crockett Gillmore/80 5.00 12.00
153 Ha Ha Clinton-Dix/21 8.00 20.00
154 Dee Ford/55 4.00 10.00
155 Darqueze Dennard/21 8.00 20.00
156 Jason Verrett/22 6.00 15.00
157 Marcus Smith/90 4.00 10.00
158 Deone Bucannon/36 5.00 12.00
159 Chris Borland/50 4.00 10.00
160 Jimmie Ward/25
162 Trevor Reilly/49 4.00 10.00
163 Kyle Van Noy/95 5.00 12.00
164 Lamarcus Joyner/20 8.00 20.00
166 Trent Murphy/93 4.00 10.00
168 Troy Niklas/87 4.00 10.00
169 Kony Ealy/94 5.00 12.00
170 C.J. Fiedorowicz/87 4.00 10.00
171 Preston Brown/52 4.00 10.00
174 Jerick McKinnon/31 6.00 15.00
175 Richard Rodgers/89 6.00 15.00
178 Shaq Evans/81 4.00 10.00
179 Kevin Norwood/81 4.00 10.00
180 James White/28 12.00 30.00
181 Lorenzo Taliaferro/34 10.00 25.00
182 Devin Street/15 6.00 15.00
183 Jared Abbrederis/84 8.00 20.00
187 Lache Seastrunk/35 5.00 12.00
189 Matt Hazel/83 4.00 10.00
191 Marion Grice/26 6.00 15.00
192 Tyler Gaffney/27 6.00 15.00
193 Jordan Lynch/36 6.00 15.00
195 Jeff Janis/83 8.00 20.00
196 Tevin Reese/84 4.00 10.00
197 Michael Sam/96 4.00 10.00
198 Rajion Neal/34 5.00 12.00
200 Mike Davis/19 6.00 15.00

2014 Immaculate Collection Numbers Rookie Patch Autographs

106 Eric Ebron/85 8.00 20.00
113 Austin Seferian-Jenkins/87 6.00 15.00
115 Jordan Matthews/81 10.00 25.00
118 Davante Adams/17 15.00 40.00
119 Bishop Sankey/20 10.00 25.00
122 Carlos Hyde/28 12.00 30.00
123 Allen Robinson/80 10.00 25.00
126 Charles Sims/34 8.00 20.00
127 Tre Mason/27 25.00 60.00
129 Terrance West/20 10.00 25.00
131 Devonta Freeman/33 30.00 60.00
132 Andre Williams/44 8.00 20.00
133 Ka'Deem Carey/25 10.00 25.00
140 Asa Watson/86 6.00 15.00

2014 Immaculate Collection Premium Patch Autographs

PAB Anquan Boldin 15.00 40.00
PAB Antonio Brown 50.00 100.00
PAD Andy Dalton 20.00 50.00
PAG A.J. Green 25.00 60.00
PAM Alfred Morris 15.00 40.00
PAS Alex Smith 20.00 50.00
PCB Champ Bailey 20.00 50.00
PCS C.J. Spiller 15.00 40.00
PDB Dwayne Bowe 20.00 50.00
PDM Doug Martin 20.00 50.00
PDM Dan Marino 100.00 200.00
PDM DeMarco Murray 20.00 50.00
PDT De'Anthony Thomas 15.00 40.00
PDT Demaryius Thomas 20.00 50.00
PDW Danny Woodhead 20.00 50.00
PDW DeAngelo Williams 15.00 40.00
PED Eric Decker 15.00 40.00
PET Earl Thomas 25.00 60.00
PFJ Fred Jackson 20.00 50.00
PGB Giovani Bernard 15.00 40.00
PJC Jamaal Charles 20.00 50.00
PJC Jay Cutler 15.00 40.00
PJH Jeremy Hill 20.00 50.00
PKA Kiko Alonso 15.00 40.00
PLB Lance Briggs 20.00 50.00
PLM LeSean McCoy 25.00 60.00
PLM Lamar Miller 15.00 40.00
PMB Montee Ball 15.00 40.00
PMC Marques Colston 15.00 40.00
PPM Peyton Manning 250.00 450.00
PPR Philip Rivers 30.00 60.00
PSJ Steve Johnson 20.00 50.00
PTB Tom Brady 400.00 600.00
PTR Tony Romo 40.00 80.00

2014 Immaculate Collection Quad Jerseys

*PRIME/25: .6X TO 1.5X BASIC QUAD/99
1 Brtls/Crr/Mnzl/Brdgwtr/99 12.00 30.00
2 Hyde/Snky/Wst/Msn/99 2.50 6.00
3 Cks/Bnjmn/Mthws/Wtk/99 3.00 8.00
5 Sms/Evns/Glnn/SfrnJnk/99 5.00 12.00
6 Mrry/Svge/Grplo/Thms/99 15.00 40.00
7 Archr/Frmn/Hll/Cry/99 3.00 8.00
8 Adms/Evns/Ltmr/Mncrf/99 5.00 12.00
9 Clwny/Brtls/Mck/Wtkns/99 8.00 20.00
10 Lndry/Lee/Bckhm/Rchrd/99 5.00 12.00
11 Wlms/Thms/Ebrn/SfrnJnk/99 4.00 10.00
12 Smth/Sndrs/Cmpbll/Pytn/25 50.00 100.00
13 Mntna/Nmth/Brdy/Elwy/25 75.00 150.00
14 Cks/Clstn/Evns/Jcksn/49 5.00 12.00
15 Crr/Crr/Mnng/Mnng/35 30.00 80.00
16 Flcco/Smth/Prce/Sggs/49 8.00 20.00
17 Smth/Chrls/Dvs/Hll/49 8.00 20.00
18 Dltn/Brnrd/McCrrn/Hill/99 8.00 20.00
19 Spllr/Mnl/Jcksn/Wtkns/99 3.00 8.00
20 Brdy/Mrno/Brs/Mnng/25 75.00 150.00
21 Ptrsn/Dckrsn/Sndrs/Dvs/25 25.00 60.00
22 Tte/Mrno/Thms/Lynch/49 4.00 10.00
23 Kprnck/Sggs/Flcco/Wlls/49 8.00 20.00
24 Brdy/Mnng/Ncks/Wlkr/49 15.00 40.00
25 Nwtn/Lcy/Grffnlll/Brdfrd/25 8.00 20.00
26 Smth/Grpplo/Tnnhll/Mnl/99 15.00 40.00
28 Lck/Brtls/Lckr/Svge/99 4.00 10.00
29 Mrry/Crr/Mnng/Rvrs/99 20.00 50.00
30 Mnng/Rmo/Fles/Grffnlll/49 10.00 25.00
31 Nlsn/Brdgwtr/Ctlr/Stffrd/49 3.00 8.00
32 Nwtn/Brs/Ryn/Glnn/49 8.00 20.00
33 Thms/Kprnck/Shrmn/Brad/49 5.00 12.00
34 Cks/Hyde/Bnjmn/Brdgwtr/99 3.00 8.00
35 Crr/Clwny/Wtkns/Wst/99 12.00 30.00
36 Clwny/Jcksn/Mnng/Akmn/25
37 Dckrsn/Mllr/Bsh/Grffnlll/25
38 Sndrs/Brtls/Jhnsn/Ftzgrld/49 12.00 30.00
39 Grn/McFddn/Wtkns/Rvers/99 3.00 8.00

2014 Immaculate Collection Rookie Helmets Team Logo

2 Sammy Watkins/12 15.00 40.00
3 Jadeveon Clowney/14 12.00 30.00
5 Mike Evans/16 40.00 80.00
7 Tre Mason/14 10.00 25.00
15 Austin Seferian-Jenkins/16 10.00 25.00
23 Charles Sims/16 10.00 25.00
30 Eric Ebron/14
33 Tom Savage/14

2014 Immaculate Collection Rookie Ink

1 Johnny Manziel EXCH 6.00 15.00
2 Mike Evans 30.00 60.00
3 Sammy Watkins 6.00 15.00
4 Teddy Bridgewater 6.00 15.00
5 Blake Bortles 5.00 12.00
6 Cody Latimer 5.00 12.00
8 Chris Borland 4.00 10.00
9 Jason Verrett 4.00 10.00
10 Lamarcus Joyner 5.00 12.00
11 Martavis Bryant 5.00 12.00
12 Aaron Murray 4.00 10.00
13 John Brown 6.00 15.00
15 Bruce Ellington 4.00 10.00
16 Deone Bucannon 4.00 10.00
17 Dri Archer 4.00 10.00
18 Jerick McKinnon 5.00 12.00
19 Jimmie Ward 6.00 15.00
20 Josh Huff 5.00 12.00
21 Lorenzo Taliaferro 4.00 10.00
22 Crockett Gillmore 5.00 12.00
23 Arthur Lynch 4.00 10.00
24 Tom Savage 4.00 10.00
25 Connor Shaw 4.00 10.00
26 Calvin Pryor 4.00 10.00
27 C.J. Fiedorowicz 4.00 10.00
28 Austin Seferian-Jenkins 4.00 10.00
29 Asa Watson 4.00 10.00
31 Kyle Fuller 4.00 10.00
32 Michael Sam 4.00 10.00
35 Shaq Evans 4.00 10.00
36 Isaiah Crowell 5.00 12.00
37 Terrance West 4.00 10.00
38 Odell Beckham Jr. 75.00 150.00
39 Allen Robinson 6.00 15.00
40 A.J. McCarron 12.00 30.00
42 Kevin Norwood 4.00 10.00
43 Jake Matthews 4.00 10.00
44 Anthony Barr 4.00 10.00
45 Devonta Freeman 20.00 40.00
46 Brandin Cooks 10.00 25.00
47 Ka'Deem Carey 4.00 10.00
48 Jimmy Garoppolo 60.00 125.00
49 Telvin Smith 4.00 10.00
50 Tajh Boyd 4.00 10.00
51 Kelvin Benjamin 8.00 20.00
52 Derek Carr 75.00 135.00
53 David Fales 4.00 10.00
54 Jace Amaro 4.00 10.00
56 Davante Adams 15.00 40.00
57 Jared Abbrederis 10.00 25.00
58 James White 8.00 20.00
59 Tre Mason 20.00 40.00
60 Bishop Sankey 4.00 10.00

2014 Immaculate Collection Rookie Player Caps

RPCAM A.J. McCarron/49 3.00 8.00
RPCAM Aaron Murray/49 3.00 8.00
RPCAR Allen Robinson/43 5.00 12.00
RPCAS Austin Seferian-Jenkins/21 4.00 10.00
RPCAW Andre Williams/49 10.00 25.00
RPCAW Asa Watson/22 4.00 10.00
RPCBB Blake Bortles/40 4.00 10.00
RPCBC Brandin Cooks/49 12.00 30.00
RPCBS Bishop Sankey/49 8.00 20.00
RPCCH Carlos Hyde/49 4.00 10.00
RPCCL Cody Latimer/49 4.00 10.00
RPCCS Connor Shaw/22 4.00 10.00
RPCCS Charles Sims/32 3.00 8.00
RPCDA Davante Adams/49 15.00 40.00
RPCDA Dri Archer/49 3.00 8.00
RPCDC Derek Carr/49 20.00 50.00
RPCDF Devonta Freeman/49 8.00 20.00
RPCDM Donte Moncrief/49 3.00 8.00
RPCDT De'Anthony Thomas/49 3.00 8.00
RPCEE Eric Ebron/36 4.00 10.00
RPCJC Jadeveon Clowney/49 4.00 10.00
RPCJG Jimmy Garoppolo/41 20.00 40.00
RPCJH Jeremy Hill/49 4.00 10.00
RPCJL Jarvis Landry/11 12.00 30.00
RPCJM Jordan Matthews/49 5.00 12.00
RPCJM Johnny Manziel/49 5.00 12.00
RPCKB Kelvin Benjamin/49 5.00 12.00
RPCKC Ka'Deem Carey/49 3.00 8.00
RPCKM Khalil Mack/49 12.00 30.00
RPCLT Logan Thomas/49 3.00 8.00
RPCME Mike Evans/49 8.00 20.00
RPCML Marqise Lee/39 4.00 10.00
RPCOB Odell Beckham Jr./49 20.00 50.00
RPCSW Sammy Watkins/49 5.00 12.00
RPCTB Tajh Boyd/49 3.00 8.00
RPCTB Teddy Bridgewater/49 5.00 12.00
RPCTM Tre Mason/49 10.00 25.00
RPCTS Tom Savage/49 8.00 20.00
RPCTW Terrance West/30 3.00 8.00

2014 Immaculate Collection Rookie Premium Patch Autographs

PRAM Aaron Murray 8.00 20.00
PRAMC A.J. McCarron 8.00 20.00
PRAR Allen Robinson 12.00 30.00
PRASJ Austin Seferian-Jenkins 8.00 20.00
PRAW Andre Williams 8.00 20.00
PRAWA Asa Watson 8.00 20.00
PRBB Blake Bortles 10.00 25.00
PRBC Brandin Cooks 50.00 100.00
PRBS Bishop Sankey 8.00 20.00
PRCL Cody Latimer 10.00 25.00
PRCS Charles Sims 8.00 20.00
PRDA Davante Adams 30.00 60.00
PRDAR Dri Archer 10.00 25.00
PRDC Derek Carr 75.00 150.00
PRDF Devonta Freeman 25.00 50.00
PRDT De'Anthony Thomas 8.00 20.00
PREE Eric Ebron 10.00 25.00
PRJG Jimmy Garoppolo 200.00 300.00
PRJL Jarvis Landry 40.00 80.00
PRJM Johnny Manziel 12.00 30.00
PRJMA Jordan Matthews 12.00 30.00
PRKB Kelvin Benjamin 50.00 100.00
PRKC Ka'Deem Carey 15.00 40.00
PRLT Logan Thomas 8.00 20.00
PRME Mike Evans 20.00 50.00
PRML Marqise Lee 10.00 25.00
PROB Odell Beckham Jr. 100.00 200.00
PRSW Sammy Watkins 12.00 30.00
PRTB Tajh Boyd 8.00 20.00
PRTBR Teddy Bridgewater 12.00 30.00
PRTM Tre Mason 25.00 60.00
PRTS Tom Savage 8.00 20.00
PRTW Terrance West 8.00 20.00

2014 Immaculate Collection Rookie Signature Patches

*PATCH AU/49: .5X TO 1.2X JSY AU/99 RC
107 Odell Beckham Jr. 50.00 100.00

2014 Immaculate Collection Signature Patches

AB Antonio Brown/60 25.00 50.00
AD Andy Dalton/60 10.00 25.00
AG Ahman Green/60 20.00 40.00
AG Antonio Gates/60 20.00 40.00
AG A.J. Green/60 12.00 30.00
AM Alfred Morris/60 8.00 20.00
AP Adrian Peterson/60 60.00 100.00
AS Alex Smith/60 30.00 60.00
CC Cris Carter/60 40.00 80.00
CS C.J. Spiller/60 8.00 20.00
DC Dallas Clark/60 8.00 20.00
DW DeAngelo Williams/60 8.00 20.00
FG Frank Gore/60 12.00 30.00
FJ Fred Jackson/60 12.00 30.00
GB Giovani Bernard/60 8.00 20.00
JC Jay Cutler/60 25.00 50.00
JK Jeremy Kerley/48 8.00 20.00
KW Kendall Wright/60 8.00 20.00
LM Lamar Miller/60 8.00 20.00
MB Montee Ball/60 8.00 20.00
MC Marques Colston/60 8.00 20.00
MF Marshall Faulk/60 30.00 60.00
MG Mike Gillislee/60 8.00 20.00
MT Manti Te'o/60 10.00 25.00
PR Philip Rivers/60 15.00 40.00
TR Tony Romo/60 40.00 80.00

2014 Immaculate Collection Multisport Autographs

109A Jose Abreu BB 50.00 120.00
109B Javier Baez BB 10.00 25.00
109C Kris Bryant BB 125.00 250.00
109D George Gervin BK 15.00 40.00
109E Kyrie Irving BK 60.00 120.00
109F Max Scherzer BB 12.00 30.00
109G George Springer BB 15.00 40.00
109H Bill Walton BK

2014 Immaculate Collection Multisport Patch Autographs

109A Kevin Durant BK/25 150.00 250.00
109B Ken Griffey Jr. BB/25 100.00 200.00
109D Mark Messier HK/25 40.00 80.00
109E David Robinson BK/25 50.00 100.00
109F Dominque Wilkins BK/25 30.00 80.00

2014 Immaculate Collection Trios Jerseys

*PRIME/25: .8X TO 2X BASIC TRIO/99
*PRIME/25: .6X TO 1.5X BASIC TRIO/49
1 Shw/Mnzl/Wst/99 4.00 10.00
2 SfrnJnkns/Evns/Sms/99 6.00 15.00
3 Brtls/Brdgwtr/Mnzl/99 4.00 10.00
4 Clwny/Brtls/Wtkns/99 4.00 10.00
5 Lck/Fshr/Clwny/49 15.00 40.00
6 Wtkns/Evns/Bckhm/99 6.00 15.00
7 Cks/Bnjmn/Evns/99 6.00 15.00
8 Snky/Hyde/Hll/99 3.00 8.00
9 Grpplo/Crr/Thms/99 20.00 50.00
10 Rbnsn/Lee/Brtls/99 4.00 10.00
11 Wllms/Frmn/Cry/99 4.00 10.00
12 Msn/Sms/Wst/99 2.50 6.00
13 Rbnsn/Lndry/Ltmr/99 5.00 12.00
14 Chrls/Dvs/Thms/49 4.00 10.00
15 Mtthws/Lee/Rchrdsn/99 4.00 10.00
16 SfrnJnkns/Ebrn/Amro/99 3.00 8.00
17 Evns/Mnzl/Mllr/49 8.00 20.00
18 Frmn/Bnjmn/Bldn/49 8.00 20.00
19 Lcy/Jns/McCrrn/49 5.00 12.00
20 Jcksn/Nwtn/Msn/49 25.00 50.00
21 Gre/Mllr/Bnjmn/49 4.00 10.00
22 Brdgwtr/Pwll/Dgls/49 10.00 25.00
23 Lndry/Hll/Bckhm./99 6.00 15.00
24 Hrtlne/Hlmes/Hyde/49 6.00 15.00
25 Mrry/Brdfrd/Ptrsn/49 10.00 25.00
26 Wtkns/Ellngtn/Hpkns/99 8.00 20.00
27 Cks/Rdgrs/Jcksn/49 6.00 15.00
28 Thmas/Wrd/Stwrt/49 3.00 8.00
29 Mthws/Adms/Crr/49 10.00 25.00
30 Jffry/Clwny/Cook/49 4.00 10.00
31 Plmr/Lee/Brkly/49 4.00 10.00
32 SfrnJnkns/Snky/Lckr/49 4.00 10.00
33 Ctlr/Mtthws/Stcy/25 8.00 20.00
34 Chncllr/Thms/Ryl/49 5.00 12.00
35 Wlkr/Amndla/Crbtree/49 6.00 15.00
36 Wke/Rbnsn/Hll/49 10.00 25.00
37 Mrry/Brynt/Rmo/49 20.00 40.00
38 Sndrs/Pytn/Smth/25
39 Fvre/Nmth/Mntna/25 40.00 80.00
40 Rce/Lrgnt/Crtr/25 25.00 50.00
41 Sndrs/Tylr/Ltt/25 25.00 50.00
42 Stbch/Rmo/Akmn/25
43 Mntna/Yng/Kprnck/25 60.00 120.00
44 Cry/Frte/Pytn/25 15.00 40.00
45 Jcksn/McFddn/Crr/25 40.00 80.00
46 Mnng/Elwy/Dvs/25 40.00 80.00
47 Moon/Snky/Cmpbll/25 8.00 20.00
48 Crtr/Trkntn/Brdgwtr/25 8.00 20.00
49 Dckrsn/Flk/Msn/25 20.00 40.00
50 Jcksn/Klly/Wtkns/25 15.00 40.00
51 Archr/Brdshw/Plmlu/25 10.00 25.00
52 Sndrs/Ebrn/Stffrd/25 20.00 40.00
53 Sms/Mrtn/Dnn/25 6.00 15.00
54 Mnng/Brdy/Brs/25 30.00 60.00
55 Jhnsn/Thms/Brynt/25 25.00 50.00
56 Ptrsn/Gre/Jcksn/25 8.00 20.00
57 Mnng/Fvre/Mrno/25 50.00 100.00
58 Dly/Cndro/Ltt/25 30.00 60.00
59 Smth/Alln/Tylr/25 10.00 25.00
60 Rce/Fvre/Smth/25 40.00 80.00

2015 Immaculate Collection

EXCH EXPIRATION 5/25/2017
1 Jamaal Charles 2.50 6.00
2 Tony Romo 2.50 6.00
3 Eric Dickerson 2.50 6.00
4 Arian Foster 2.50 6.00
5 Russell Wilson 4.00 10.00
6 DeMarco Murray 2.50 6.00
7 Michael Irvin 3.00 8.00
8 Andy Dalton 2.50 6.00
9 Calvin Johnson 3.00 8.00
10 Joe Montana 8.00 20.00
11 Julio Jones 3.00 8.00
12 Tom Brady 8.00 20.00
13 Odell Beckham Jr. 3.00 8.00
14 Blake Bortles 2.00 5.00
15 Terry Bradshaw 4.00 10.00
16 Carson Palmer 2.50 6.00
17 Alfred Morris 2.00 5.00
18 Peyton Manning 6.00 15.00
19 Dwayne Bowe 2.50 6.00
20 Aaron Rodgers 6.00 15.00
21 Joe Namath 4.00 10.00
22 Derek Carr 3.00 8.00
23 Len Dawson 3.00 8.00
24 LeSean McCoy 3.00 8.00
25 Marshall Faulk 2.50 6.00
26 Bishop Sankey 2.00 5.00
27 Drew Brees 3.00 8.00
28 Ndamukong Suh 2.50 6.00
29 Mike Evans 2.50 6.00
30 Tre Mason 2.50 6.00
31 Steve Smith 2.50 6.00
32 Teddy Bridgewater 2.50 6.00
33 Philip Rivers 3.00 8.00
34 Walter Payton 6.00 15.00
35 Eli Manning 2.50 6.00
36 J.J. Watt 3.00 8.00
37 Dez Bryant 3.00 8.00
38 Matt Forte 2.00 5.00
39 Luke Kuechly 2.50 6.00
40 Le'Veon Bell 2.50 6.00
41 Marshawn Lynch 2.50 6.00
42 A.J. Green 3.00 8.00
43 Jerry Rice 5.00 12.00
44 DeSean Jackson 2.50 6.00
45 Barry Sanders 5.00 12.00
46 Brett Favre 6.00 15.00
47 Terrell Suggs 2.00 5.00
48 Derrick Brooks 2.00 5.00
49 Fred Taylor 2.00 5.00
50 Bo Jackson 4.00 10.00
51 Brandon Marshall 2.00 5.00
52 Larry Fitzgerald 2.50 6.00
53 Andrew Luck 4.00 10.00
54 Torrey Smith 2.00 5.00
55 Sam Bradford 2.00 5.00
56 Jeremy Maclin 2.00 5.00
57 Dan Marino 6.00 15.00
58 Adrian Peterson 3.00 8.00
59 Ozzie Newsome 2.50 6.00
60 Matt Ryan 2.50 6.00
61 Warren Moon 3.00 8.00
62 Sammy Watkins 2.50 6.00
63 John Elway 5.00 12.00
64 Kelvin Benjamin 2.50 6.00
65 Rob Gronkowski 3.00 8.00
66 Marques Colston 2.00 5.00
67 Emmitt Smith 5.00 12.00
68 Colin Kaepernick 2.50 6.00
69 Tim Brown 3.00 8.00
70 Joe Flacco 2.50 6.00
71 Jordy Nelson 2.50 6.00
72 Julius Thomas 2.00 5.00
73 Nick Foles 2.50 6.00
74 Harold Carmichael 2.00 5.00
75 Kurt Warner 2.50 6.00
76 Antonio Gates 2.00 5.00
77 Ickey Woods 2.00 5.00
78 Fran Tarkenton 3.00 8.00
79 Johnny Manziel 2.50 6.00
80 Vincent Jackson 2.00 5.00
81 Michael Strahan 2.50 6.00
82 Matthew Stafford 2.50 6.00
83 DeAndre Hopkins 2.50 6.00
84 Darrelle Revis 2.00 5.00
85 Demaryius Thomas 2.50 6.00
86 Kendall Wright 2.00 5.00
87 Troy Aikman 4.00 10.00
88 LaDainian Tomlinson 2.50 6.00
89 T.Y. Hilton 2.50 6.00
90 Roddy White 2.00 5.00
91 Curtis Martin 2.50 6.00
92 Cam Newton 3.00 8.00
93 Jim Kelly 3.00 8.00
94 Fred Biletnikoff 3.00 8.00
95 Mark Ingram 2.50 6.00
96 Ben Roethlisberger 3.00 8.00
97 Brian Urlacher 3.00 8.00
98 Joe Theismann 3.00 8.00
99 Steve Largent 3.00 8.00
100 Ryan Tannehill 2.50 6.00
102 Randy Gregory AU RC 4.00 10.00
104 Cameron Artis-Payne AU RC 4.00 10.00
107 Shaq Thompson AU RC 5.00 12.00
108 Trae Waynes AU RC 4.00 10.00
109 Vic Beasley Jr. AU RC 5.00 12.00
110 Stephone Anthony AU RC 4.00 10.00
111 Marcus Peters AU RC 6.00 15.00
113 Kenny Bell AU RC 6.00 15.00
114 Jesse James AU RC 5.00 12.00
115 Deontay Greenberry AU RC 4.00 10.00
116 Clive Walford AU RC 4.00 10.00
119 Byron Jones AU RC 6.00 15.00
120 Mario Alford AU RC 4.00 10.00
121 Tony Lippett AU RC 4.00 10.00
122 Tre McBride AU RC 4.00 10.00
123 Landon Collins AU RC 5.00 12.00
124 Benardrick McKinney AU RC 4.00 10.00
125 K.Williams JSY AU RC EXCH 6.00 15.00
126 Jay Ajayi JSY AU RC 10.00 25.00
127 Brett Hundley JSY AU RC 6.00 15.00
128 S.Diggs JSY AU RC EXCH 15.00 40.00
129 Rashad Greene JSY AU RC 6.00 15.00
130 David Cobb JSY AU RC 6.00 15.00
131 Mike Davis JSY AU RC 6.00 15.00
132 Buck Allen JSY AU RC EXCH 8.00 20.00
133 Vince Mayle JSY AU RC 8.00 20.00
134 Justin Hardy JSY AU RC 6.00 15.00
135 J.Langford JSY AU RC EXCH 6.00 15.00
136 Jamison Crowder JSY AU RC 8.00 20.00
137 Bryce Petty JSY AU RC 6.00 15.00
138 Matt Jones JSY AU RC 6.00 15.00
139 Ty Montgomery JSY AU RC 6.00 15.00
140 Sean Mannion JSY AU RC 6.00 15.00
141 Sammie Coates JSY AU RC 8.00 20.00
142 David Johnson JSY AU RC 15.00 40.00
143 Duke Johnson JSY AU RC 10.00 25.00
144 Chris Conley JSY AU RC 6.00 15.00
145 Garrett Grayson JSY AU RC 6.00 15.00
146 T.Coleman JSY AU RC EXCH 8.00 20.00
147 Jaelen Strong JSY AU RC 8.00 20.00
148 Tyler Lockett JSY AU RC 10.00 25.00
149 Maxx Williams JSY AU RC 6.00 15.00
150 Ameer Abdullah JSY AU RC 10.00 25.00
151 Devin Funchess JSY AU RC 10.00 25.00
152 D.Green-Beckham JSY AU RC EXCH 6.00 15.00
153 Devin Smith JSY AU RC 6.00 15.00
154 T.J. Yeldon JSY AU RC 6.00 15.00
155 Phillip Dorsett JSY AU RC EXCH 6.00 15.00
156 Breshad Perriman JSY AU RC 6.00 15.00
157 Nelson Agholor JSY AU RC 8.00 20.00
158 Melvin Gordon JSY AU RC 15.00 40.00
159 D.Parker JSY AU RC EXCH 10.00 25.00
160 Todd Gurley JSY AU RC 25.00 60.00
161 Kevin White JSY AU RC 8.00 20.00
162 L.Williams JSY AU RC EXCH 6.00 15.00
163 A.Cooper JSY AU RC EXCH 50.00 100.00
164 Marcus Mariota JSY AU RC 40.00 80.00
165 J.Winston JSY AU RC EXCH 15.00 40.00

2015 Immaculate Collection Gold

*VETS/25: .6X TO 1.5X BASIC CARDS/99
*ROOK AU/25: .6X TO 1.5X BASIC AU RC/99
*ROOK JSY AU/25: .6X TO 1.5X BASIC JSY AU RC/99
160 Todd Gurley JSY AU/25 40.00 100.00
164 Marcus Mariota JSY AU/25 60.00 150.00
165 J.Winston JSY AU/25 EXCH 25.00 60.00

2015 Immaculate Collection Acetate Jerseys

1 Jamaal Charles/25 10.00 25.00
3 Eric Dickerson/29 10.00 25.00
4 Arian Foster/23 12.00 30.00
6 DeMarco Murray/29 10.00 25.00
7 Jason Witten/82 8.00 20.00
9 Calvin Johnson/80 10.00 25.00
10 Joe Montana/16 50.00 100.00
17 Alfred Morris/46 8.00 20.00
18 Peyton Manning/18
19 Dwayne Bowe/80 8.00 20.00
23 Len Dawson/16 15.00 40.00
24 LeSean McCoy/25 12.00 30.00
25 Marshall Faulk/28 10.00 25.00
26 Bishop Sankey/20 10.00 25.00
28 Ndamukong Suh/93 8.00 20.00
30 Tre Mason/27 10.00 25.00
31 Steve Smith/89 8.00 20.00
33 Philip Rivers/17 15.00 40.00
34 Walter Payton/34 25.00 60.00
36 J.J. Watt/99 12.00 30.00
37 Dez Bryant/88 10.00 25.00
38 Matt Forte/22 10.00 25.00
39 Jonathan Stewart/28 8.00 20.00
40 Le'Veon Bell/26 10.00 25.00
41 Marshawn Lynch/24 12.00 30.00
42 A.J. Green/18 15.00 40.00
43 Jerry Rice/80 15.00 40.00
45 Barry Sanders/20 40.00 80.00
47 Terrell Suggs/55 8.00 20.00
48 Derrick Brooks/55 8.00 20.00
49 Fred Taylor/28 8.00 20.00
50 Bo Jackson/34 15.00 40.00
51 Eric Decker/87 6.00 15.00
54 Torrey Smith/82 6.00 15.00
56 Jeremy Maclin/19 10.00 25.00
58 Adrian Peterson/28
59 Ozzie Newsome/82 8.00 20.00
65 Rob Gronkowski/87 12.00 30.00
67 Emmitt Smith/22
69 Tim Brown/81 12.00 30.00
71 Jordy Nelson/87 8.00 20.00
72 Julius Thomas/80 6.00 15.00
74 Jordan Matthews/81 8.00 20.00
76 Antonio Gates/85 6.00 15.00
77 Devon Still/75 10.00 25.00
80 Doug Martin/22 12.00 30.00
81 Michael Strahan/92 8.00 20.00
83 Cecil Shorts/85 6.00 15.00
84 Darrelle Revis/24 10.00 25.00
85 Demaryius Thomas/88 8.00 20.00
88 LaDainian Tomlinson/21 12.00 30.00
90 Roddy White/84 6.00 15.00
91 Curtis Martin/28 10.00 25.00
94 Fred Biletnikoff/25 12.00 30.00
95 Mark Ingram/22 12.00 30.00
97 Brian Urlacher/54 12.00 30.00
99 Steve Largent/80 10.00 25.00
100 Ryan Tannehill/17 12.00 30.00

2015 Immaculate Collection Acetate Rookie Patch Autographs

125 Karlos Williams/40 8.00 20.00
126 Jay Ajayi/33 12.00 30.00
130 David Cobb/44 8.00 20.00
131 Mike Davis/20 10.00 25.00
132 Buck Allen/37 EXCH 10.00 25.00
133 Vince Mayle/85 8.00 20.00
134 Justin Hardy/16 10.00 25.00
135 Jeremy Langford/36 20.00 50.00
136 Jamison Crowder/80 8.00 20.00
138 Matt Jones/31 8.00 20.00
139 Ty Montgomery/88 6.00 15.00
142 David Johnson/31 75.00 150.00
143 Duke Johnson/29 12.00 30.00
144 Chris Conley/17 10.00 25.00
145 Garrett Grayson/18 10.00 25.00
146 Tevin Coleman/26 EXCH 10.00 25.00
148 Tyler Lockett/16 15.00 40.00
149 Maxx Williams/87 6.00 15.00
150 Ameer Abdullah/21 15.00 40.00
151 Devin Funchess/17 15.00 40.00
152 Dorial Green-Beckham/17 EXCH
153 Devin Smith/84 6.00 15.00
154 T.J. Yeldon/24 10.00 25.00
155 Phillip Dorsett/16
156 Breshad Perriman/18 10.00 25.00
157 Nelson Agholor/17 12.00 30.00
158 Melvin Gordon/28 40.00 80.00
160 Todd Gurley/30 40.00 100.00
162 Leonard Williams/62 6.00 15.00
163 Amari Cooper/89 60.00 125.00

2015 Immaculate Collection Dual Jerseys

*GOLD/25: .6X TO 1.5X BASIC JSY/99
*GOLD/15: .6X TO 1.5X BASIC JSY/49
*GOLD/15: .8X TO 2X BASIC JSY/99
1 A.Cooper/T.Yeldon/99 5.00 12.00
2 J.Winston/R.Greene/99 6.00 15.00
3 C.Conley/T.Gurley/99 6.00 15.00
4 D.Johnson/P.Dorsett/99 2.50 6.00
5 D.Cobb/M.Williams/99 1.50 4.00
6 M.Mariota/J.Winston/99 8.00 20.00
7 K.White/A.Cooper/99 5.00 12.00
8 M.Gordon/T.Gurley/99 6.00 15.00
9 J.Langford/K.White/99 2.00 5.00
10 V.Mayle/D.Johnson/99 2.50 6.00
11 J.Ajayi/D.Parker/99 2.50 6.00
12 J.Hardy/T.Coleman/99 2.00 5.00
13 T.Yeldon/R.Greene/99 1.50 4.00
14 B.Petty/D.Smith/99 1.50 4.00
15 B.Hundley/T.Montgomery/99 1.50 4.00
16 S.Mannion/T.Gurley/99 6.00 15.00
17 B.Perriman/B.Allen/99 2.00 5.00
18 M.Jones/J.Crowder/99 2.00 5.00
19 M.Mariota/D.Green-Beckham/99 8.00 20.00
20 D.Funchess/K.Benjamin/99 2.50 6.00
21 B.Bortles/T.Yeldon/99 1.50 4.00
22 J.Winston/M.Evans/99 6.00 15.00
23 B.Cooks/G.Grayson/99 2.00 5.00
24 J.Matthews/N.Agholor/99 2.00 5.00
25 J.Landry/D.Parker/99 2.50 6.00
26 D.Adams/T.Montgomery/99 2.00 5.00
27 D.Freeman/T.Coleman/99 2.00 5.00
28 D.Moncrief/P.Dorsett/99 2.00 5.00
29 A.Cooper/D.Carr/99 5.00 12.00
30 E.Sanders/P.Manning/25 8.00 20.00
31 R.Gronkowski/T.Brady/25 25.00 50.00
32 A.Cooper/T.Brown/49 6.00 15.00
33 M.Gordon/L.Tomlinson/49 10.00 25.00
34 B.Carr/O.Beckham Jr./99 2.50 6.00
35 D.Green-Beckham/O.Beckham Jr./99 2.50 6.00
36 S.Coates/A.Brown/49 3.00 8.00
37 A.Jeffery/K.White/99 2.00 5.00
38 M.Williams/K.Williams/99 1.50 4.00
39 C.Shorts/J.Strong/99 2.00 5.00
40 D.Still/J.Hill/99 2.50 6.00

2015 Immaculate Collection Gloves Logos

1 David Johnson 20.00 50.00
2 Tevin Coleman 10.00 25.00
3 Breshad Perriman 8.00 20.00
4 Karlos Williams 8.00 20.00
5 Devin Funchess 12.00 30.00
6 Kevin White 10.00 25.00
7 Duke Johnson 12.00 30.00
8 Ameer Abdullah 12.00 30.00
9 Ty Montgomery 8.00 20.00
10 Jaelen Strong 10.00 25.00
11 Phillip Dorsett 8.00 20.00
12 T.J. Yeldon 8.00 20.00
13 Chris Conley 8.00 20.00
14 DeVante Parker 12.00 30.00
15 Stefon Diggs 20.00 50.00
16 Garrett Grayson 8.00 20.00
17 Devin Smith 8.00 20.00
18 Bryce Petty
19 Amari Cooper 25.00 60.00
20 Nelson Agholor 10.00 25.00
21 Sammie Coates 10.00 25.00
22 Melvin Gordon 20.00 50.00
23 Mike Davis 8.00 20.00
24 Sean Mannion 8.00 20.00
25 Todd Gurley 30.00 80.00
26 Tyler Lockett 12.00 30.00
27 Jameis Winston 20.00 50.00
28 Dorial Green-Beckham 8.00 20.00
29 Marcus Mariota 30.00 80.00
30 Matt Jones 8.00 20.00

2015 Immaculate Collection Immaculate Draft Autographs

24 Melvin Gordon/15 30.00 60.00
25 Johnny Manziel/22 25.00 50.00
26 Dez Bryant/24 60.00 120.00
27 Breshad Perriman/26 6.00 15.00
28 Dan Marino/27 100.00 200.00
29 Kelvin Benjamin/28 12.00 30.00
31 Teddy Bridgewater/32 25.00 50.00
32 Paul Posluszny/34 6.00 15.00
33 Jordy Nelson/36 30.00 60.00
34 Devin Funchess/41 10.00 25.00
35 Jaelen Strong/70 6.00 15.00

2015 Immaculate Collection Immaculate Fours Patches

2 Snky/GrnBckhm/Wrght/Mrta 20.00 50.00
3 Abdllh/Whte/Dggs/Mntgmry 12.00 30.00
4 Dvs/Grly/Lcktt/Jhnsn 15.00 40.00
5 Clmn/Fnchss/Grysn/Wnstn 15.00 40.00
6 Strt/Aghlr/Bckhm/Crwdr 10.00 25.00
7 Grpplo/Wllms/Wllms/Prkr 12.00 30.00
8 Prrmn/Cts/Jhnsn/Hll 10.00 25.00
9 Drstt/Strng/Mrta/Yldn 20.00 50.00
10 Cpr/Ltmr/Grdn/Cnly 12.00 30.00
11 Grysn/Wnstn/Mrta/Mnn 20.00 50.00
12 Abdllh/Yldn/Grly/Grdn 15.00 40.00
13 Jhnsn/Jns/Clmn/Jhnsn 12.00 30.00
14 Aghlr/Cpr/Prkr/Whte 12.00 30.00
15 GrnBckhm/Prmn/Smth/Drstt 6.00 15.00
16 Cnly/Fnchss/Strng/Lcktt 10.00 25.00
17 Crwdr/Hrdy/Cts/Mntgmry 8.00 20.00
18 Alln/Cbb/Lngfrd/Dvs 8.00 20.00
19 Wnstn/Mnzl/Mrta/Grffn 20.00 50.00
20 Frmn/Wnstn/Grne/Bnjmn 15.00 40.00
21 Wllms/Bckhm/Smth/Wllms 10.00 25.00
22 Alln/Wllms/Lee/Aghlr 8.00 20.00
23 Cpr/Yldn/Msly/ClntnDx 12.00 30.00
24 Prmn/Alln/Wllms/Tlfrro 8.00 20.00
25 Jhnsn/Myle/Mnzl/Wst 10.00 25.00
26 Hrns/Grne/Brtls/Yldn 6.00 15.00
27 Hndly/Lngfrd/Mntgmry/White 8.00 20.00
28 Prkr/Lndry/Ajyi/Mllr 10.00 25.00
29 Brwn/Mnl/Wllms/Wtkns 8.00 20.00
30 Cnly/Dvs/Fshr/Hll 6.00 15.00
31 Clbrne/Crr/Scndrck/Crwfrd 6.00 15.00
32 Cks/Grysn/Ingrm/Clstn 8.00 20.00
33 Tte/Abdllh/Pttgrw/Ebrn 10.00 25.00
34 Cpr/Crr/Mck/Crbtree 12.00 30.00
35 Chncllr/Dvs/Lcktt/Hyde 10.00 25.00
36 GrnBckhm/Cpr/Evns/Bckhm 12.00 30.00
37 Prkr/Wnstn/Wtkns/Wllms 15.00 40.00
38 Te'o/Grdn/Jns/Alln 12.00 30.00
39 Ptty/Smth/Dckr/Ivry 8.00 20.00
40 Grly/Msn/Brtt/Mnn 15.00 40.00
41 Hndly/Adms/Khn/Mntgmry 8.00 20.00
42 Brwn/Mtthws/Aghlr/Cts 10.00 25.00
43 Jcksn/Crwdr/Jns/Grcn 8.00 20.00
44 Bnjmn/Fnchss/Olsn/Tdmn 10.00 25.00
45 Pttrsn/Wllce/Dggs/Brdgwtr 12.00 30.00
46 Mncrf/Jcksn/Drstt/Mths 8.00 20.00
47 Clmn/Frmn/Jns/Hrdy 10.00 25.00
48 Grn/Dltn/Hll/Snu 10.00 25.00
49 Hllmn/Oswlr/Ltmr/Sndrs 8.00 20.00
50 Wshngtn/Shrts/Hpkns/Strng 8.00 20.00
51 Wnstn/Whte/Aghlr/Grly 15.00 40.00
52 Cpr/Prkr/Mrta/Grdn 20.00 50.00
53 McCrrn/Cts/Cpr/Msn 12.00 30.00
54 Jffry/White/Lngfrd/Frte 8.00 20.00
55 Mnng/Wllms/Hrrs/Bckhm 10.00 25.00
56 Cpr/Mrta/Grdn/Clmn 20.00 50.00
57 Wtsn/Grly/Grn/Cnly 15.00 40.00
58 Hrtlne/Hwk/Hyde/Smth 8.00 20.00
59 Pwll/Prkr/Dmrvl/Brdgwtr 10.00 25.00

2015 Immaculate Collection Immaculate Moments Autographs

6 Eli Manning/25 75.00 150.00
7 Franco Harris/25 20.00 50.00
10 Ben Roethlisberger/25 100.00 200.00
11 Roger Staubach/25 60.00 120.00
13 Bo Jackson/25 50.00 100.00
15 Steve Young/25 60.00 120.00

2015 Immaculate Collection Immaculate Jersey Numbers

1 David Johnson/32 12.00 30.00
2 Justin Hardy/50 5.00 12.00
3 Tevin Coleman/50 6.00 15.00
4 Breshad Perriman/47 5.00 12.00
5 Maxx Williams/47 5.00 12.00
6 Buck Allen/48 6.00 15.00
7 Karlos Williams/48 5.00 12.00
8 Devin Funchess/50 8.00 20.00
9 Jeremy Langford/41 5.00 12.00
10 Kevin White/40 6.00 15.00
11 Duke Johnson/44 8.00 20.00
12 Vince Mayle/44 6.00 15.00
13 Ameer Abdullah/45 8.00 20.00
14 Ty Montgomery/47 5.00 12.00
15 Brett Hundley/46 5.00 12.00
16 Jaelen Strong/46 6.00 15.00
17 Phillip Dorsett/48 5.00 12.00
18 T.J. Yeldon/50 5.00 12.00
19 Rashad Greene/49 5.00 12.00
20 Chris Conley/50 5.00 12.00
21 DeVante Parker/44 8.00 20.00
22 Jay Ajayi/41 8.00 20.00
23 Stefon Diggs/35 12.00 30.00
24 Garrett Grayson/42 5.00 12.00
25 Leonard Williams/45 5.00 12.00
26 Devin Smith/40 5.00 12.00
27 Bryce Petty/43 5.00 12.00
28 Amari Cooper/41 15.00 40.00
29 Nelson Agholor/41 6.00 15.00
30 Sammie Coates/34 6.00 15.00
31 Melvin Gordon/49 12.00 30.00
32 Mike Davis/45 5.00 12.00
33 Sean Mannion/50 5.00 12.00
34 Todd Gurley/49 30.00 80.00
35 Tyler Lockett/50 8.00 20.00
36 Jameis Winston/50 12.00 30.00
37 Dorial Green-Beckham/43 5.00 12.00
38 David Cobb/47 5.00 12.00
39 Marcus Mariota/40 20.00 50.00
40 Jamison Crowder/49 6.00 15.00
41 Matt Jones/49 5.00 12.00
43 Lorenzo Taliaferro/36 8.00 20.00
44 C.J. Mosley/33 8.00 20.00
45 Michael Campanaro/19 10.00 25.00

46 Tamba Hali/30	8.00	20.00
47 Justin Hunter/18	25.00	50.00
50 Nick Foles/24	12.00	30.00
51 LeSean McCoy/32	12.00	30.00
54 Blake Bortles/22	10.00	25.00
55 Allen Hurns/37	8.00	20.00
56 Marqise Lee/18	10.00	25.00
58 Devon Still/18	15.00	40.00
60 Kiko Alonso/18	10.00	25.00
67 D'Qwell Jackson/20	10.00	25.00
68 Dan Bailey/20	10.00	25.00
69 Demaryius Thomas/18	12.00	30.00
73 Kenny Britt/16	10.00	25.00
74 Malcolm Smith/31	5.00	12.00
78 Nate Washington/19	10.00	25.00
83 Robert Woods/31	10.00	25.00
86 Vincent Jackson/20	10.00	25.00
87 Andre Ellington/23	10.00	25.00
88 Anthony Fasano/35	8.00	20.00
91 Jarvis Landry/18	12.00	30.00
92 Jeremy Hill/31	8.00	20.00
93 Barry Church/38	10.00	25.00
94 Lamar Miller/20	10.00	25.00
95 Malcom Floyd/20	10.00	25.00
96 Mark Ingram/17	15.00	40.00
97 Martellus Bennett/22	10.00	25.00
99 Steve Smith/17	12.00	30.00

2015 Immaculate Collection Immaculate Standard

1 Odell Beckham Jr./49	5.00	12.00
3 Peyton Manning/25	25.00	50.00
4 Antonio Brown/25	6.00	15.00
5 Teddy Bridgewater/49	4.00	10.00
6 Joe Montana/25		
7 Ryan Tannehill/25	5.00	12.00
8 A.J. Green/25	6.00	15.00
9 Julio Jones/25	6.00	15.00
10 Tamba Hali/25	4.00	10.00
11 Robert Woods/49	4.00	10.00
12 Devon Still/49	4.00	10.00
13 Larry Fitzgerald/25	5.00	12.00
14 Walter Payton/25	25.00	50.00
15 Bart Starr/15	25.00	50.00
16 Brian Urlacher/25	6.00	15.00
17 Matt Ryan/25	5.00	12.00
18 Andrew Luck/15	10.00	25.00
20 Robert Griffin III/25	4.00	10.00
21 Terrance Williams/25	4.00	10.00
22 DeSean Jackson/25	5.00	12.00
23 Eli Manning/15	6.00	15.00
24 Cam Newton/25	6.00	15.00
25 Marshawn Lynch/15	6.00	15.00
26 Matthew Stafford/25	5.00	12.00
27 Colin Kaepernick/15	6.00	15.00
28 Joe Flacco/15	6.00	15.00
29 Jerry Rice/25	25.00	50.00
30 Devin McCourty/25	4.00	10.00
31 Andy Dalton/25	5.00	12.00
33 Barry Sanders/15	25.00	50.00
34 T.Y. Hilton/25	5.00	12.00
35 Joe Namath/15	40.00	80.00
36 Tim Brown/25	20.00	40.00
37 Philip Rivers/25	6.00	15.00
38 Lawrence Taylor/25	10.00	25.00
39 Troy Aikman/25	10.00	25.00
40 Stefon Diggs/49	6.00	15.00
41 Ty Montgomery/49	2.50	6.00
42 Sammie Coates/49	3.00	8.00
43 David Johnson/49	6.00	15.00
44 Garrett Grayson/49	2.50	6.00
45 Tevin Coleman/49	3.00	8.00
46 Ameer Abdullah/49	4.00	10.00
47 Devin Funchess/49	4.00	10.00
48 Dorial Green-Beckham/49	2.50	6.00
49 Devin Smith/49	2.50	6.00
50 T.J. Yeldon/49	2.50	6.00
51 Phillip Dorsett/49	2.50	6.00
52 Breshad Perriman/49	2.50	6.00
53 Nelson Agholor/49	3.00	8.00
54 Melvin Gordon/49	6.00	15.00
55 DeVante Parker/49	4.00	10.00
56 Todd Gurley/49	12.00	30.00
57 Kevin White/49	3.00	8.00
58 Amari Cooper/49	10.00	25.00
59 Marcus Mariota/49	10.00	25.00
60 Jameis Winston/49	10.00	25.00

2015 Immaculate Collection Ink

7 Deion Sanders/49	30.00	60.00
8 Troy Aikman/49	40.00	80.00
9 Cris Collinsworth/99	10.00	25.00
10 Tony Dorsett/49	30.00	60.00
13 Tim Brown/49	20.00	40.00
15 Richard Sherman/49	30.00	60.00
16 Kenny Stills/99	6.00	15.00
17 Kendall Wright/99	6.00	15.00
19 Matthew Stafford/49	20.00	40.00
20 Jason Witten/49	25.00	50.00
22 Lamar Miller/99	6.00	15.00
23 Darren Sproles/99	8.00	20.00
25 Bo Jackson/49	50.00	100.00
26 Dan Hampton/99	8.00	20.00
27 Derrick Brooks/99	6.00	15.00
28 Mark Chmura/99	8.00	20.00
29 Don Majkowski/99	10.00	25.00
30 Doug Flutie/99	10.00	25.00
31 Fran Tarkenton/99	12.00	30.00
32 Fred Biletnikoff/99	20.00	40.00
34 Paul Hornung/99	12.00	30.00
35 Steve Grogan/99	8.00	20.00
36 Troy Brown/99	8.00	20.00
37 Andrew Luck/49	100.00	200.00
40 Earl Thomas/99	15.00	30.00
45 Eric Decker/99	6.00	15.00
48 Blake Bortles/49	8.00	20.00
49 Teddy Bridgewater/49	20.00	40.00
50 Isaiah Crowell/99	6.00	15.00

2015 Immaculate Collection Past and Present Signatures

3 Jameis Winston/25	25.00	60.00
4 Marcus Mariota/25	50.00	100.00
5 Johnny Manziel/49	10.00	25.00
7 Russell Wilson/25 EXCH	50.00	100.00
8 Tony Romo/25	40.00	80.00
9 Brett Hundley/99	4.00	10.00
10 Melvin Gordon/25	25.00	60.00
12 Jason Witten/49	40.00	80.00
13 Richard Sherman/49	25.00	50.00
14 Kevin White/49	10.00	25.00
16 Joe Flacco/25	12.00	30.00
17 Matthew Stafford/25	12.00	30.00
18 Jordy Nelson/99	20.00	40.00
19 Kendall Wright/99	6.00	15.00
20 Andrew Luck/25	75.00	150.00
21 Ameer Abdullah/49	12.00	30.00
22 Bryce Petty/99	4.00	10.00
25 Jay Ajayi/49	12.00	30.00
27 Sammie Coates/25	12.00	30.00
28 T.J. Yeldon/25		
29 Lamar Miller/99	6.00	15.00
30 Teddy Bridgewater/99	25.00	50.00
31 Mike Evans/99	8.00	20.00
32 Sean Mannion/49	8.00	20.00
33 Todd Gurley/25	40.00	80.00
35 Breshad Perriman/49	8.00	20.00

2015 Immaculate Collection Premium Patch Autographs

4 Dan Marino/25	200.00	300.00
5 Tony Romo/25	30.00	60.00
6 Russell Wilson/25 EXCH	75.00	150.00
7 Marshawn Lynch/49	40.00	80.00
10 Richard Sherman/49	40.00	80.00
11 Kendall Wright/99	6.00	15.00
12 Ryan Tannehill/99	12.00	30.00
13 Marques Colston/99	15.00	40.00
14 Teddy Bridgewater/49	25.00	60.00
16 Danny Amendola/99	15.00	40.00
18 Lamar Miller/99	6.00	15.00
20 Blake Bortles/49	20.00	40.00
21 DeSean Jackson/49	10.00	25.00
22 Derek Carr/99	30.00	60.00
23 Barry Sanders/25	90.00	150.00
24 Alex Smith/49	10.00	25.00
25 Eli Manning/49	50.00	100.00
26 Matt Ryan/49	25.00	50.00
29 Fred Jackson/99	8.00	20.00
30 Antonio Gates/49	8.00	20.00
33 Brian Urlacher/25	75.00	150.00
34 Deion Sanders/25	50.00	100.00
35 Doug Flutie/25	25.00	60.00
36 Dwight Clark/75	10.00	25.00
37 Earl Campbell/49	30.00	60.00
38 Eric Dickerson/49	30.00	80.00
39 Michael Strahan/25	25.00	50.00
41 Dez Bryant/49	50.00	100.00
42 Steve Largent/49	25.00	50.00
43 Tim Brown/25	50.00	100.00
45 Cameron Wake/99	25.00	50.00
47 Danny Woodhead/99	15.00	40.00
48 Jordan Matthews/99	8.00	20.00
50 Montee Ball/49	8.00	20.00

2015 Immaculate Collection Quad Jerseys

*GOLD/25: .5X TO 1.2X BASIC JSY/49

1 Brtls/Wnstn/Brdgwtr/Mrta/49		
2 Cpr/Crr/Wnstn/Evns/49	8.00	20.00
3 Mnn/Grysn/Wnstn/Mrta/49	10.00	25.00
4 Prkr/White/Cpr/Aghlr/49	8.00	20.00
5 Prrmn/Smth/Drstt/GrnBckhm/49	2.50	6.00
6 Lcktt/Cnly/Strng/Cts/49	4.00	10.00
7 Abdllh/Grdn/Yldn/Grly/49	8.00	20.00
8 Jhnsn/Jhnsn/Jnes/Clmn/49	6.00	15.00
9 Alln/Cbb/Lngfrd/Dvs/49	3.00	8.00
11 Brynt/Wllms/Rmo/McFddn/25		
12 Gts/Alln/Rvrs/Grdn/25		
13 Wllms/Mnng/Bckhm/Crz/49	4.00	10.00
14 Mrry/Brdfrd/Mtthws/Aghlr/49	3.00	8.00
15 Jffry/Bnntt/Frte/White/49	8.00	20.00
16 Ptrsn/Pttrsn/Brdgwtr/Wllce/49	4.00	10.00
17 Jhnsn/Abdllh/Ebrn/Stffrd/49	4.00	10.00
18 Frmn/Jns/Ryn/White/49	4.00	10.00
19 Nwtn/Stwrt/Bnjmn/Fnchss/49	4.00	10.00
20 Crmrte/Rvs/Wllms/Rchrdsn/49	2.50	6.00
21 McCy/Cly/Hrvn/Wtkns/25		
22 Lck/Hltn/Mncrf/Drstt/49	5.00	12.00
23 Wllms/Wnstn/Mnzl/Mrta/49	10.00	25.00
24 Crwdr/Jns/Mrrs/Jcksn/25		
25 Gts/Grhm/Thms/Grnkwski/25		
26 Sndrs/Pytn/Mrtn/Smth/25		
27 Rdgrs/Brynt/Bll/Grnkwski/25		
28 Wtt/Sh/Drs/Wllms/25		
29 Rvs/Thms/Wddle/Shrmn/25		
30 Fvre/Brdy/Mnng/Yng/25	75.00	150.00

2015 Immaculate Collection Rookie Cleats

1 David Johnson/25	10.00	25.00
2 Justin Hardy/25	4.00	10.00
3 Tevin Coleman/18	5.00	12.00
4 Breshad Perriman/25	4.00	10.00
5 Maxx Williams/25	4.00	10.00
6 Buck Allen/18	5.00	12.00
7 Karlos Williams/25	4.00	10.00
8 Devin Funchess/22	6.00	15.00
9 Jeremy Langford/18	4.00	10.00
10 Kevin White/18	5.00	12.00
13 Ameer Abdullah/18	6.00	15.00
14 Ty Montgomery/18	4.00	10.00
15 Brett Hundley/25	4.00	10.00
16 Jaelen Strong/25	5.00	12.00
18 T.J. Yeldon/25	4.00	10.00
19 Rashad Greene/25	4.00	10.00
20 Chris Conley/25	4.00	10.00
21 DeVante Parker/18	6.00	15.00
22 Jay Ajayi/18	6.00	15.00
23 Stefon Diggs/25	10.00	25.00
24 Garrett Grayson/25	4.00	10.00
25 Leonard Williams/25	4.00	10.00
26 Devin Smith/25	4.00	10.00
27 Bryce Petty/22	4.00	10.00
28 Amari Cooper/25	12.00	30.00
30 Sammie Coates/18	5.00	12.00
31 Melvin Gordon/25	10.00	25.00
32 Mike Davis/25	4.00	10.00
33 Sean Mannion/25	4.00	10.00
34 Todd Gurley/25	25.00	50.00
36 Jameis Winston/25	10.00	25.00
37 Dorial Green-Beckham/22	4.00	10.00
38 David Cobb/25	4.00	10.00
39 Marcus Mariota/25	15.00	40.00
41 Matt Jones/18	4.00	10.00

2015 Immaculate Collection Rookie Helmet

1 David Johnson	12.00	30.00
2 Tevin Coleman	6.00	15.00
3 Breshad Perriman	5.00	12.00
4 Karlos Williams	5.00	12.00
5 Devin Funchess	8.00	20.00
6 Kevin White	6.00	15.00
7 Duke Johnson	8.00	20.00
8 Ameer Abdullah		
9 Ty Montgomery	5.00	12.00
10 Jaelen Strong	6.00	15.00
11 Phillip Dorsett	5.00	12.00
12 T.J. Yeldon	5.00	12.00
13 Rashad Greene	5.00	12.00
14 Chris Conley	5.00	12.00
15 DeVante Parker	8.00	20.00
16 Stefon Diggs	12.00	30.00
17 Garrett Grayson	5.00	12.00
18 Leonard Williams	5.00	12.00
19 Amari Cooper	15.00	40.00
20 Nelson Agholor	6.00	15.00
21 Sammie Coates	6.00	15.00
22 Melvin Gordon	12.00	30.00
23 Mike Davis	5.00	12.00
24 Todd Gurley	25.00	60.00
25 Tyler Lockett	8.00	20.00
26 Jameis Winston	12.00	30.00
27 Dorial Green-Beckham	5.00	12.00
28 Marcus Mariota	50.00	100.00
29 Matt Jones	5.00	12.00

2015 Immaculate Collection Rookie Ink

1 Antwan Goodley/99	3.00	8.00
3 Ben Koyack/99	5.00	12.00
4 Bryan Bennett/99	3.00	8.00
5 Danielle Hunter/99	4.00	10.00
6 Darren Waller/99	4.00	10.00
7 DaVaris Daniels/99	3.00	8.00
10 Deiron Smith/99	3.00	8.00
11 Dezmin Lewis/99	3.00	8.00
12 Dres Anderson/99	3.00	8.00
13 Eddie Goldman/99	3.00	8.00
14 Eli Harold/99	3.00	8.00
15 Eric Rowe/99	3.00	8.00
16 Byron Jones/99	5.00	12.00
17 Jalen Collins/99	3.00	8.00
18 Josh Harper/99	3.00	8.00
19 Josh Shaw/99	5.00	12.00
21 Mario Edwards Jr./99	3.00	8.00
22 Markus Golden/99	3.00	8.00
23 MyCole Pruitt/99	3.00	8.00
24 Nick O'Leary/99	3.00	8.00
25 P.J. Williams/99	4.00	10.00
26 Paul Dawson/99	4.00	10.00
27 Rannell Hall/99	3.00	8.00
29 Shane Carden/99	3.00	8.00
30 Taylor Heinicke/99	5.00	12.00
31 Terrence Magee/99	5.00	12.00
32 Titus Davis/99	4.00	10.00
33 Trey Williams/99	4.00	10.00
34 Marcus Mariota/49	75.00	150.00
36 Sammie Coates/49	5.00	12.00
37 Todd Gurley/25	50.00	100.00
39 Ameer Abdullah/25	8.00	20.00
41 Melvin Gordon/25	25.00	60.00
42 Mike Davis/49	10.00	25.00
44 T.J. Yeldon/25	5.00	12.00
45 Vince Mayle/49	5.00	12.00
46 Sean Mannion/49	4.00	10.00
47 Jamison Crowder/49	5.00	12.00
48 Justin Hardy/49	4.00	10.00
49 Matt Jones/49	4.00	10.00
50 Randy Gregory/49	4.00	10.00

2015 Immaculate Collection Rookie Player Caps

1 David Johnson	6.00	15.00
2 Justin Hardy	2.50	6.00
3 Tevin Coleman	3.00	8.00
4 Breshad Perriman	2.50	6.00
5 Maxx Williams	2.50	6.00
6 Buck Allen	3.00	8.00
7 Karlos Williams	2.50	6.00
8 Devin Funchess	4.00	10.00
9 Jeremy Langford	2.50	6.00
10 Kevin White	3.00	8.00
11 Duke Johnson	4.00	10.00
12 Vince Mayle	3.00	8.00
13 Ameer Abdullah	4.00	10.00
14 Ty Montgomery	2.50	6.00
15 Brett Hundley	2.50	6.00
16 Jaelen Strong	3.00	8.00
17 Phillip Dorsett	2.50	6.00
18 T.J. Yeldon	2.50	6.00
19 Rashad Greene	2.50	6.00
20 Chris Conley	2.50	6.00
21 DeVante Parker	4.00	10.00
22 Jay Ajayi	4.00	10.00
23 Stefon Diggs	6.00	15.00
24 Garrett Grayson	2.50	6.00
25 Leonard Williams	2.50	6.00
26 Devin Smith	2.50	6.00
27 Bryce Petty	2.50	6.00
28 Amari Cooper	8.00	20.00
29 Nelson Agholor	3.00	8.00
30 Sammie Coates	3.00	8.00
31 Melvin Gordon	6.00	15.00
32 Mike Davis	2.50	6.00
33 Sean Mannion	2.50	6.00
34 Todd Gurley	12.00	30.00
35 Tyler Lockett	4.00	10.00
36 Jameis Winston	6.00	15.00
37 Dorial Green-Beckham	2.50	6.00
38 Marcus Mariota	12.00	30.00
39 Jamison Crowder	3.00	8.00
40 Matt Jones	2.50	6.00

2015 Immaculate Collection Rookie Premium Patch Autographs

*GOLD/25: .6X TO 1.5X BASIC JSY AU/99
*GOLD/25: .5X TO 1.2X BASIC JSY AU/49
EXCH EXPIRATION 5/25/2017

1 Jameis Winston/49	20.00	50.00
2 Marcus Mariota/49	75.00	150.00
3 Amari Cooper/15 EXCH	75.00	150.00
4 Kevin White/49	10.00	25.00
5 Todd Gurley/49	50.00	100.00
6 Jay Ajayi/99	10.00	25.00
7 Melvin Gordon/49	20.00	50.00
8 DeVante Parker/49 EXCH	12.00	30.00
9 Nelson Agholor/49	10.00	25.00
10 Phillip Dorsett/49	8.00	20.00
11 T.J. Yeldon/99	6.00	15.00
12 Ameer Abdullah/49	12.00	30.00
13 Devin Funchess/49	12.00	30.00
14 Jaelen Strong/49	10.00	25.00
15 Chris Conley/49	8.00	20.00
16 Tevin Coleman/99 EXCH	8.00	20.00
17 David Johnson/49	25.00	60.00
18 Sammie Coates/49	10.00	25.00
19 Bryce Petty/99	6.00	15.00
20 Stefon Diggs/99 EXCH	15.00	40.00
21 Brett Hundley/99	6.00	15.00
22 Justin Hardy/99	6.00	15.00
23 Matt Jones/99	6.00	15.00
24 Duke Johnson/99	10.00	25.00
25 Garrett Grayson/49	8.00	20.00
26 Tyler Lockett/99	10.00	25.00
27 Maxx Williams/99	6.00	15.00
28 D.Green-Beckham/99 EXCH	6.00	15.00
29 Devin Smith/49	8.00	20.00
30 Breshad Perriman/49	8.00	20.00

2015 Immaculate Collection Rookie Signature Patches

*GOLD/25: .6X TO 1.5X BASIC JSY AU/99
*GOLD/25: .5X TO 1.2X BASIC JSY AU/49
EXCH EXPIRATION 5/25/2017

1 David Johnson/49	25.00	60.00
2 Tevin Coleman/49 EXCH	10.00	25.00
3 Buck Allen/99 EXCH	8.00	20.00
4 Breshad Perriman/49	8.00	20.00
5 Devin Funchess/49	12.00	30.00
6 Kevin White/49	10.00	25.00
7 Jeremy Langford/99 EXCH	25.00	50.00
8 Vince Mayle/49	10.00	25.00
9 Ameer Abdullah/49	12.00	30.00
10 Ty Montgomery/99	6.00	15.00
11 Jaelen Strong/49	10.00	25.00
12 Phillip Dorsett/49 EXCH	8.00	20.00
13 Rashad Greene/99	6.00	15.00
14 Chris Conley/49	8.00	20.00
15 DeVante Parker/49 EXCH	12.00	30.00
16 Garrett Grayson/49	8.00	20.00
17 Devin Smith/49	8.00	20.00
18 Leonard Williams/49 EXCH	8.00	20.00
19 Amari Cooper/15	75.00	150.00
20 Nelson Agholor/49	10.00	25.00
21 Sammie Coates/49	10.00	25.00
22 Melvin Gordon/49	30.00	80.00
23 Mike Davis/99	6.00	15.00
24 Tyler Lockett/49	12.00	30.00
25 Todd Gurley/49	50.00	100.00
26 Sean Mannion/49	15.00	40.00
27 Jameis Winston/49	20.00	50.00
28 Marcus Mariota/49	75.00	150.00
29 David Cobb/99	6.00	15.00

2015 Immaculate Collection Signature Moves

5 Victor Cruz/25	20.00	50.00
6 Terrell Davis/25	60.00	125.00
10 Dez Bryant/25	75.00	150.00
11 Tim Tebow/25	60.00	120.00
12 Steve Smith/25	20.00	50.00
14 J.J. Watt/25	50.00	100.00
16 Jordy Nelson/25	100.00	200.00
18 Ickey Woods/25	15.00	40.00
20 Richard Sherman/25	60.00	120.00
21 Joe Namath/25	100.00	200.00
23 Marshawn Lynch/25	40.00	80.00
25 Michael Strahan/25	40.00	80.00

2015 Immaculate Collection Signature Patches

2 Thurman Thomas/49	12.00	30.00
3 Torry Holt/49	12.00	30.00
4 Cordarrelle Patterson/25	10.00	25.00
5 Russell Wilson/25 EXCH	90.00	150.00
8 Kendall Wright/99	6.00	15.00
9 Ryan Tannehill/49	10.00	25.00
10 Marques Colston/99	6.00	15.00
11 Demaryius Thomas/49	10.00	25.00
15 Lamar Miller/99	6.00	15.00
18 DeSean Jackson/49	10.00	25.00
19 Derek Carr/99	40.00	80.00
20 Joe Namath/25	60.00	100.00
21 Alex Smith/99	8.00	20.00
22 Bishop Sankey/49	8.00	20.00
23 Teddy Bridgewater/99	25.00	50.00
25 Dez Bryant/49	30.00	80.00
26 Fred Jackson/99	8.00	20.00
29 Matthew Stafford/49	20.00	40.00
30 Earl Campbell/49	30.00	60.00
31 Marqise Lee/99	6.00	15.00
33 Johnny Manziel/49	15.00	40.00
35 Cameron Wake/99	25.00	50.00
37 Isaiah Crowell/99	6.00	15.00
38 Joe Montana/25	150.00	250.00
39 Michael Floyd/50	8.00	20.00
40 Montee Ball/99	6.00	15.00
42 Andrew Luck/25	75.00	150.00
44 Emmitt Smith/25	100.00	200.00
45 Marshawn Lynch/49	40.00	80.00
47 Mike Evans/99	8.00	20.00
49 Jordan Matthews/99	8.00	20.00
50 Jordy Nelson/99	25.00	50.00

2015 Immaculate Collection The College Standard

1 Odell Beckham Jr.	6.00	15.00
2 Jameis Winston	10.00	25.00
3 Johnny Manziel	5.00	12.00
4 Marcus Mariota	30.00	60.00
5 Mike Evans	5.00	12.00
6 Amari Cooper	12.00	30.00
7 A.J. McCarron	4.00	10.00
8 Kevin White	5.00	12.00
9 Teddy Bridgewater	5.00	12.00
10 Melvin Gordon	10.00	25.00
11 Jeremy Hill	4.00	10.00
12 Bryce Petty	4.00	10.00
13 Sammy Watkins	5.00	12.00
14 Sammie Coates	5.00	12.00
15 Derek Carr	6.00	15.00
16 Brett Hundley	10.00	25.00
17 Kelvin Benjamin	5.00	12.00
18 Todd Gurley	15.00	40.00
19 Jarvis Landry	5.00	12.00
20 Ameer Abdullah	6.00	15.00
21 Brandin Cooks	5.00	12.00
22 Garrett Grayson	4.00	10.00
23 Nelson Agholor	5.00	12.00
24 Breshad Perriman	4.00	10.00
25 DeVante Parker	6.00	15.00
26 Phillip Dorsett	4.00	10.00
27 Tre Mason	5.00	12.00
28 Devonta Freeman	5.00	12.00
29 Ty Montgomery	4.00	10.00
30 Sean Mannion	4.00	10.00
31 T.J. Yeldon	4.00	10.00
32 Rashad Greene	4.00	10.00
33 Leonard Williams	4.00	10.00
34 Khalil Mack	6.00	15.00
35 Duke Johnson	6.00	15.00
36 Buck Allen	5.00	12.00
37 Bishop Sankey	4.00	10.00
38 Devin Funchess	6.00	15.00
39 Matt Jones	4.00	10.00
40 Chris Conley	4.00	10.00

2015 Immaculate Collection Trios Jerseys

*GOLD/25: .5X TO 1.2X BASIC JSY/49
*GOLD/15: .6X TO 1.5X BASIC JSY/49

1 Jhnsn/Wst/Crwll/49	3.00	8.00
2 Brtls/Lee/Yldn/49	2.00	5.00
3 Wllms/Ptty/Smth/49	2.00	5.00
4 Cbb/GrnBckhm/Mrta/49		
5 Prrmn/Alln/Wllms/49	2.50	6.00
6 Prkr/Lndry/Stlls/49	3.00	8.00
7 Grn/Dltn/Hll/49	5.00	12.00
8 Flcco/Wllms/Prrmn/49	4.00	10.00
9 Stbch/Rmo/Akmn/15	30.00	60.00
11 Abdllh/Sndrs/Bll/15	8.00	20.00
12 Flk/Msn/Grley/49	10.00	25.00
13 Lngfrd/Frte/Pytn/15	30.00	60.00
14 Thms/Klce/Cnly/49	3.00	8.00
15 Ltmr/Thms/Sndrs/25	3.00	8.00
16 Stwrt/Alnso/Mrta/49	6.00	15.00
17 Ptrsn/Ellngtn/Jhnsn/49	8.00	20.00
18 Lcktt/Bldwn/Wlsn/15	15.00	40.00
19 Wnstn/Wllms/Grne/49	8.00	20.00
20 Wllms/Alln/Aghlr/49	2.50	6.00
21 Bckhm/Lndry/Hll/49	3.00	8.00
22 Lck/Mntgmry/Shrmn/15	6.00	15.00
23 Mrry/Bll/McCy/25	4.00	10.00
24 Brwn/Jns/Thms/25	4.00	10.00
25 Brynt/Nlsn/Brwn/25	10.00	25.00
27 Wllms/Wllms/Wllms/49	2.00	5.00
28 Lee/Cpr/Cks/49	6.00	15.00
29 Wllms/Grdn/Bll/49	8.00	20.00
30 Dmrvl/Tmmns/Kchly/25	10.00	25.00

2016 Immaculate Collection

1 Joe Flacco	2.50	6.00
2 Ray Lewis	3.00	8.00
3 Jim Kelly	3.00	8.00
4 LeSean McCoy	3.00	8.00
5 Thurman Thomas	2.50	6.00
6 Andy Dalton	2.50	6.00
7 A.J. Green	3.00	8.00
8 Robert Griffin III	2.00	5.00
9 Duke Johnson	2.00	5.00
10 John Elway	5.00	12.00
11 Von Miller	2.50	6.00
12 Demaryius Thomas	2.50	6.00
13 Brock Osweiler	2.00	5.00
14 DeAndre Hopkins	2.50	6.00
15 J.J. Watt	3.00	8.00
16 Earl Campbell	3.00	8.00
17 Andrew Luck	4.00	10.00
18 Peyton Manning	6.00	15.00
19 Marvin Harrison	2.50	6.00
20 Blake Bortles	2.00	5.00
21 T.J. Yeldon	2.00	5.00
22 Allen Robinson	2.50	6.00
23 Joe Montana	8.00	20.00
24 Jamaal Charles	2.50	6.00
25 Jeremy Maclin	2.00	5.00
26 Ryan Tannehill	2.50	6.00
27 Jarvis Landry	2.50	6.00
28 Dan Marino	6.00	15.00
29 Tom Brady	8.00	20.00
30 Rob Gronkowski	3.00	8.00
31 Joe Namath	4.00	10.00
32 Matt Forte	2.00	5.00
33 Johnny Unitas	5.00	12.00
34 Darrelle Revis	2.00	5.00
35 Derek Carr	3.00	8.00
36 Amari Cooper	3.00	8.00
37 Khalil Mack	3.00	8.00
38 Bo Jackson	4.00	10.00
39 Ben Roethlisberger	3.00	8.00
40 Antonio Brown	3.00	8.00
41 Terry Bradshaw	4.00	10.00
42 Rod Woodson	2.50	6.00
43 Philip Rivers	3.00	8.00
44 Melvin Gordon	2.50	6.00
45 LaDainian Tomlinson	2.50	6.00
46 Marcus Mariota	3.00	8.00
47 DeMarco Murray	2.50	6.00
48 Delanie Walker	2.00	5.00
49 Carson Palmer	2.50	6.00
50 David Johnson	3.00	8.00
51 Larry Fitzgerald	2.50	6.00
52 Michael Floyd	2.00	5.00
53 Matt Ryan	2.50	6.00
54 Julio Jones	3.00	8.00
55 Devonta Freeman	2.50	6.00
56 Cam Newton	3.00	8.00
57 Jonathan Stewart	2.00	5.00
58 Luke Kuechly	2.50	6.00
59 Jay Cutler	2.00	5.00
60 Jeremy Langford	2.50	6.00
61 Walter Payton	6.00	15.00
62 Brian Urlacher	3.00	8.00
63 Tony Romo	2.50	6.00
64 Troy Aikman	4.00	10.00
65 Emmitt Smith	5.00	12.00
66 Dez Bryant	3.00	8.00
67 Matthew Stafford	2.50	6.00
68 Ameer Abdullah	2.00	5.00
69 Barry Sanders	5.00	12.00
70 Aaron Rodgers	6.00	15.00
71 Eddie Lacy	2.00	5.00
72 Clay Matthews	3.00	8.00
73 Bart Starr	5.00	12.00
74 Brett Favre	6.00	15.00
75 Todd Gurley	3.00	8.00
76 Eric Dickerson	2.50	6.00
77 Kurt Warner	2.50	6.00
78 Teddy Bridgewater	2.50	6.00
79 Adrian Peterson	3.00	8.00
80 Cris Carter	3.00	8.00
81 Drew Brees	3.00	8.00
82 Mark Ingram	2.50	6.00
83 Ricky Williams	2.50	6.00
84 Eli Manning	2.50	6.00
85 Odell Beckham Jr.	3.00	8.00
86 Lawrence Taylor	3.00	8.00
87 Jordan Matthews	2.50	6.00
88 Ryan Mathews	2.50	6.00
89 Randall Cunningham	2.50	6.00
90 Jerry Rice	5.00	12.00
91 Carlos Hyde	2.00	5.00
92 Steve Young	4.00	10.00
93 Russell Wilson	4.00	10.00
94 Thomas Rawls	2.00	5.00
95 Steve Largent	3.00	8.00
96 Richard Sherman	3.00	8.00
97 Jameis Winston	3.00	8.00
98 Doug Martin	2.50	6.00
99 Kirk Cousins	3.00	8.00
100 Jordan Reed	2.00	5.00
101 Jared Goff JSY AU RC	50.00	100.00
102 Carson Wentz JSY AU RC	75.00	150.00
103 Paxton Lynch JSY AU RC	6.00	15.00
104 Christian Hackenberg JSY AU RC	6.00	15.00
105 Cody Kessler JSY AU RC	6.00	15.00
106 Connor Cook JSY AU RC	8.00	20.00
107 Dak Prescott JSY AU RC	50.00	100.00
108 Cardale Jones JSY AU RC	6.00	15.00
109 Kevin Hogan JSY AU RC	8.00	20.00
110 DeAndre Washington JSY AU RC	6.00	15.00
111 Ezekiel Elliott JSY AU RC	60.00	125.00
112 Derrick Henry JSY AU RC	15.00	40.00
113 Kenyan Drake JSY AU RC	10.00	25.00
114 C.J. Prosise JSY AU RC	6.00	15.00
115 Tyler Ervin JSY AU RC	6.00	15.00
116 Kenneth Dixon JSY AU RC	6.00	15.00
117 Devontae Booker JSY AU RC	8.00	20.00
118 Paul Perkins JSY AU RC	6.00	15.00
119 Jordan Howard JSY AU RC EXCH	15.00	40.00
120 Wendell Smallwood JSY AU RC	6.00	15.00
121 Jonathan Williams JSY AU RC	8.00	20.00
122 Alex Collins JSY AU RC	8.00	20.00
123 Keenan Reynolds JSY AU RC	8.00	20.00
124 Corey Coleman JSY AU RC	10.00	25.00
125 Laquon Treadwell JSY AU RC	8.00	20.00
126 Josh Doctson JSY AU RC	8.00	20.00
127 Will Fuller JSY AU RC	10.00	25.00
128 Sterling Shepard JSY AU RC	8.00	20.00
129 Michael Thomas JSY AU RC	12.00	30.00
130 Tyler Boyd JSY AU RC	8.00	20.00
131 Braxton Miller JSY AU RC	6.00	15.00
132 Leonte Carroo JSY AU RC	6.00	15.00
133 Chris Moore JSY AU RC	8.00	20.00
134 Ricardo Louis JSY AU RC	6.00	15.00
135 Pharoh Cooper JSY AU RC	6.00	15.00
136 Demarcus Robinson JSY AU RC	6.00	15.00
137 Trevor Davis JSY AU RC	6.00	15.00
138 Hunter Henry JSY AU RC	8.00	20.00
139 Joey Bosa JSY AU RC	12.00	30.00
140 Moritz Bohringer JSY AU RC	6.00	15.00
141 Brandon Allen AU RC	4.00	10.00
142 Brandon Doughty AU RC	4.00	10.00
143 Jake Rudock AU RC	4.00	10.00
144 Jeff Driskel AU RC	4.00	10.00
145 Nate Sudfeld AU RC	4.00	10.00
146 Artie Burns AU RC	5.00	12.00
148 Keith Marshall AU RC	4.00	10.00
149 Kelvin Taylor AU RC	4.00	10.00
150 Nick Vannett AU RC	4.00	10.00
151 Cody Core AU RC	4.00	10.00
152 Jordan Payton AU RC	4.00	10.00
153 William Jackson III AU RC	5.00	12.00
154 Rashard Higgins AU RC	4.00	10.00
155 Tajae Sharpe AU RC	5.00	12.00
156 Jaylon Smith AU RC	4.00	10.00
157 Eli Apple AU RC	5.00	12.00
158 Jacoby Brissett AU RC	5.00	12.00
159 Vernon Hargreaves III AU RC	6.00	15.00
160 DeForest Buckner AU RC	4.00	10.00
161 Shaq Lawson AU RC	4.00	10.00
162 Vernon Butler AU RC	4.00	10.00
164 Malcolm Mitchell AU RC	4.00	10.00
165 Myles Jack AU RC	5.00	12.00

2016 Immaculate Collection Gold

*ROOK JSY AU/25: .6X TO 1.5X BASIC JSY AU/99
*ROOK AU/25: .6X TO 1.5X BASIC AU/99

2016 Immaculate Collection Dual Jerseys

1 P.Cooper/J.Goff/99	8.00	20.00
2 W.Smallwood/C.Wentz/99	12.00	30.00
3 D.Booker/P.Lynch/99	3.00	8.00
4 C.Kessler/R.Louis/99	2.50	6.00
5 C.Coleman/C.Kessler/99	4.00	10.00
6 E.Elliott/D.Prescott/99	12.00	30.00
7 C.Jones/J.Williams/99	3.00	8.00
8 D.Robinson/K.Hogan/99	3.00	8.00
9 K.Drake/L.Carroo/99	4.00	10.00
10 A.Collins/C.Prosise/99	3.00	8.00
11 B.Miller/W.Fuller/99	4.00	10.00
12 H.Henry/J.Bosa/99	5.00	12.00
13 C.Moore/K.Dixon/99	3.00	8.00
14 P.Perkins/S.Shepard/99	3.00	8.00
15 L.Treadwell/M.Bohringer/99	3.00	8.00
16 C.Cook/D.Washington/99	3.00	8.00
17 D.Henry/M.Mariota/49	8.00	20.00
18 J.Goff/T.Gurley/49	20.00	50.00
19 C.Cook/A.Cooper/49	5.00	12.00
20 J.Doctson/M.Jones/49	4.00	10.00
21 C.Prosise/T.Lockett/49	4.00	10.00
22 J.Hill/T.Boyd/49	4.00	10.00
23 J.Langford/J.Howard/49	8.00	20.00
24 T.Bridgewater/L.Treadwell/49	4.00	10.00
25 C.Cook/D.Carr/49	5.00	12.00
26 B.Cooks/M.Thomas/25	8.00	20.00
27 O.Beckham Jr./S.Shepard/25	6.00	15.00
28 C.Jones/S.Watkins/25	6.00	15.00
29 D.Funchess/K.Benjamin/25	5.00	12.00
30 M.Singletary/W.Payton/15	40.00	80.00
31 D.Hopkins/J.Watt/15	8.00	20.00
32 A.Rodgers/J.Nelson/15	25.00	50.00
33 R.Gronkowski/T.Brady/15	25.00	50.00
34 D.Bryant/T.Romo/15	25.00	50.00
35 A.Brown/B.Roethlisberger/15	30.00	60.00

2016 Immaculate Collection Eye Black Autographs

1 Drew Brees/15	20.00	50.00
2 Tim Tebow/15	20.00	50.00
3 J.J. Watt/25	75.00	150.00
4 Ray Lewis/25	60.00	120.00
5 Todd Gurley/99	10.00	25.00
6 Joe Namath/15	25.00	60.00
7 Darren McFadden/68	8.00	20.00
8 Derek Carr/99	10.00	25.00
9 Stefon Diggs/99	8.00	20.00
10 Jordy Nelson/99	12.00	30.00
11 Matthew Stafford/15	15.00	40.00
13 Ameer Abdullah/99	6.00	15.00
14 Travis Kelce/99	10.00	25.00
15 Darrelle Revis/16	12.00	30.00
16 Russell Wilson/25	75.00	150.00
17 Matt Jones/99	8.00	20.00
18 LeSean McCoy/99	10.00	25.00
20 Alex Smith/24	12.00	30.00
21 Marcus Mariota/25	75.00	150.00
22 Allen Hurns/99	6.00	15.00
23 Carlos Hyde/99	6.00	15.00
24 Devonta Freeman/99	8.00	20.00
25 Jameis Winston/24	15.00	40.00
26 Troy Aikman/25	100.00	200.00
27 Jerry Rice/25	75.00	150.00
29 Doug Baldwin/41	25.00	50.00
30 Doug Flutie/95	8.00	20.00
31 LaDainian Tomlinson/50	15.00	40.00
32 Carl Eller/75	6.00	15.00
34 Matt Forte/99	6.00	15.00
35 Charlie Joiner/75	6.00	15.00
36 Charcandrick West/85	6.00	15.00
37 Eddie George/99	25.00	50.00
38 Antonio Brown/15	20.00	50.00
39 Tyler Eifert/99	8.00	20.00
40 David Johnson/99	15.00	40.00
41 Brock Osweiler/50	8.00	20.00
42 Blake Bortles/15	12.00	30.00
43 Earl Campbell/50	20.00	40.00
44 Ben Roethlisberger/25	75.00	150.00
45 Doug Martin/25	12.00	30.00
46 Jeremy Langford/99	8.00	20.00
48 Gary Barnidge/99	6.00	15.00
49 Thomas Rawls/99	6.00	15.00
50 Zach Ertz/99	8.00	20.00
51 Marshall Faulk/15	15.00	40.00
52 Tyrod Taylor/99	8.00	20.00
53 John Brown/99	8.00	20.00
54 Devin Funchess/99	6.00	15.00
55 Steve Smith/50	10.00	25.00
56 Danny Woodhead/99	8.00	20.00
57 Golden Tate III/50	8.00	20.00
59 Bo Jackson/95	50.00	100.00
60 Charles Haley/99	10.00	25.00

2016 Immaculate Collection Immaculate Numbers

2 Marcus Mariota/50	5.00	12.00
6 Ameer Abdullah/50	3.00	8.00
8 Karlos Williams/50	3.00	8.00
18 Kevin White/25	4.00	10.00
21 Devin Funchess/25	4.00	10.00
24 Melvin Gordon/25	5.00	12.00
27 Devonta Freeman/25	5.00	12.00
29 Stefon Diggs/50	4.00	10.00
33 Jeremy Langford/50	4.00	10.00
35 Jameis Winston/50	12.00	30.00
36 Demaryius Thomas/25	5.00	12.00
37 Kelvin Benjamin/25	5.00	12.00
39 T.J. Yeldon/25	4.00	10.00
42 Tyler Lockett/25	5.00	12.00
50 Odell Beckham Jr./25	6.00	15.00
55 Matt Jones/25	5.00	12.00
56 Sammie Coates/25	4.00	10.00
57 Todd Gurley/25	6.00	15.00
59 Moritz Bohringer/50	3.00	8.00
60 Teddy Bridgewater/15		
61 Alex Collins/50	4.00	10.00
62 Braxton Miller/50	3.00	8.00
63 C.J. Prosise/50	3.00	8.00
64 Cardale Jones/50	3.00	8.00
65 Carson Wentz/50	20.00	50.00
66 Chris Moore/50	4.00	10.00
67 Christian Hackenberg/50	3.00	8.00
68 Cody Kessler/50	3.00	8.00
69 Connor Cook/50	4.00	10.00
70 Corey Coleman/50	5.00	12.00
71 Dak Prescott/50	15.00	40.00
72 Demarcus Robinson/50	3.00	8.00
73 Derrick Henry/50	8.00	20.00
74 Devontae Booker/50	4.00	10.00
75 Ezekiel Elliott/50	40.00	80.00
76 Hunter Henry/50	4.00	10.00
77 DeAndre Washington/50	3.00	8.00
78 Jared Goff/50	10.00	25.00
79 Joey Bosa/50	8.00	20.00
80 Jonathan Williams/50	4.00	10.00
81 Jordan Howard/50	8.00	20.00
82 Josh Doctson/50	4.00	10.00
83 Keenan Reynolds/50	4.00	10.00
84 Kenneth Dixon/50	3.00	8.00
85 Kenyan Drake/50	5.00	12.00
86 Kevin Hogan/50	4.00	10.00
87 Laquon Treadwell/50	4.00	10.00
88 Leonte Carroo/50	3.00	8.00
90 Michael Thomas/50	6.00	15.00
91 Paul Perkins/50	3.00	8.00
92 Paxton Lynch/50	3.00	8.00
93 Pharoh Cooper/50	3.00	8.00
94 Ricardo Louis/50	3.00	8.00
95 Sterling Shepard/50	8.00	20.00
96 Trevor Davis/50	3.00	8.00
97 Tyler Boyd/50	4.00	10.00
98 Tyler Ervin/50	3.00	8.00
99 Wendell Smallwood/50	3.00	8.00
100 Will Fuller/50	5.00	12.00

2016 Immaculate Collection Immaculate Numbers Memorabilia

2 Ray Lewis/52	12.00	30.00
4 LeSean McCoy/25	6.00	15.00
5 Thurman Thomas/34	4.00	10.00
7 A.J. Green/18	8.00	20.00
8 Ozzie Newsome/82	3.00	8.00
9 Duke Johnson/29	4.00	10.00
11 Von Miller/58	8.00	20.00
12 Demaryius Thomas/88	3.00	8.00
15 J.J. Watt/99	4.00	10.00
16 Earl Campbell/34	12.00	30.00
18 Peyton Manning/18	40.00	80.00
19 Marvin Harrison/88	3.00	8.00
21 T.J. Yeldon/24	4.00	10.00
22 Allen Robinson/15	6.00	15.00
23 Joe Montana/19	30.00	60.00
24 Jamaal Charles/25	5.00	12.00
25 Jeremy Maclin/19	5.00	12.00
26 Ryan Tannehill/17	6.00	15.00
30 Rob Gronkowski/87	10.00	25.00
32 Curtis Martin/28	5.00	12.00
33 Brandon Marshall/15	5.00	12.00
34 Darrelle Revis/24	4.00	10.00
36 Amari Cooper/89	4.00	10.00
37 Khalil Mack/52	5.00	12.00
38 Bo Jackson/34	12.00	30.00
40 Antonio Brown/84	15.00	40.00
42 Rod Woodson/26	10.00	25.00
43 Philip Rivers/17	8.00	20.00
44 Melvin Gordon/28	5.00	12.00
45 LaDainian Tomlinson/21	8.00	20.00
47 Eddie George/27	10.00	25.00
48 Delanie Walker/82	2.50	6.00
50 David Johnson/31	5.00	12.00
52 Michael Floyd/15	5.00	12.00
55 Devonta Freeman/24	5.00	12.00
57 Jonathan Stewart/28	4.00	10.00
60 Jeremy Langford/33	4.00	10.00
61 Walter Payton/34	25.00	50.00
62 Brian Urlacher/54	5.00	12.00
65 Emmitt Smith/22	15.00	40.00
66 Dez Bryant/88	12.00	30.00
67 Ameer Abdullah/21	4.00	10.00
69 Barry Sanders/20	25.00	50.00
71 Eddie Lacy/28	4.00	10.00
72 Clay Matthews/52	5.00	12.00
73 Bart Starr/15	25.00	50.00
75 Todd Gurley/30	5.00	12.00
76 Eric Dickerson/29	12.00	30.00
79 Adrian Peterson/28	6.00	15.00
80 Cris Carter/80	4.00	10.00
82 Mark Ingram/22	5.00	12.00
83 Ricky Williams/34	4.00	10.00
86 Lawrence Taylor/56	5.00	12.00
87 Johnny Unitas/19	25.00	50.00
88 Ryan Mathews/24	5.00	12.00
90 Jerry Rice/80	10.00	25.00
95 Steve Largent/80	4.00	10.00
96 Richard Sherman/25	6.00	15.00
100 Jordan Reed/86	2.50	6.00

2016 Immaculate Collection Immaculate Seasons Autographs

2 Ray Lewis/17		
12 Darrell Green/20	50.00	100.00
18 Andre Reed/15	12.00	30.00

2016 Immaculate Collection Immaculate Standard Jerseys

1 Ezekiel Elliott/49	15.00	40.00
2 Joey Bosa/49	6.00	15.00
3 Josh Doctson/49	4.00	10.00
4 Jared Goff/49	10.00	25.00
5 Corey Coleman/49	5.00	12.00
6 Carson Wentz/49	15.00	40.00
7 Laquon Treadwell/49	4.00	10.00
8 Will Fuller/49	5.00	12.00
9 Derrick Henry/49	10.00	25.00
10 Paxton Lynch/49	3.00	8.00
11 Moritz Bohringer/25	4.00	10.00
12 Michael Thomas/25	8.00	20.00
13 Devontae Booker/25	5.00	12.00
14 Kenyan Drake/25	6.00	15.00
15 Braxton Miller/25	4.00	10.00
16 Cody Kessler/25	4.00	10.00
17 Christian Hackenberg/25	4.00	10.00
18 Kenneth Dixon/25	4.00	10.00
19 Sterling Shepard/25	5.00	12.00
20 Connor Cook/25	5.00	12.00
21 Antonio Brown/15	8.00	20.00
22 Julio Jones/15	8.00	20.00
23 Barry Sanders/15	20.00	40.00
24 Tom Brady/15	30.00	60.00
25 Troy Aikman/15	10.00	25.00
26 Matt Ryan/15	6.00	15.00
27 Todd Gurley/15	8.00	20.00
28 Peyton Manning/15	30.00	60.00
29 Andy Dalton/15	6.00	15.00
30 Larry Fitzgerald/15	6.00	15.00
31 Joe Namath/15	10.00	25.00
32 Odell Beckham Jr./15	8.00	20.00
33 Amari Cooper/15	8.00	20.00
34 Ray Lewis/15	8.00	20.00
35 Walter Payton/15	30.00	60.00
37 Joe Montana/15	30.00	60.00
38 DeAndre Hopkins/15	6.00	15.00
39 Roger Staubach/15	10.00	25.00
40 Teddy Bridgewater/15	6.00	15.00
41 T.Y. Hilton/15	6.00	15.00
42 Brian Urlacher/15	8.00	20.00
43 Marcus Mariota/15	8.00	20.00
44 Eli Manning/15	6.00	15.00
45 John Elway/15	12.00	30.00
46 Andrew Luck/15	10.00	25.00
47 Joe Flacco/15	6.00	15.00
48 Jerry Rice/15	25.00	50.00
49 Ryan Tannehill/15	6.00	15.00
50 Marvin Harrison/15	6.00	15.00
51 Jameis Winston/15	8.00	20.00
52 Aaron Rodgers/15	30.00	60.00
53 Philip Rivers/15	8.00	20.00
54 A.J. Green/15	8.00	20.00
55 Blake Bortles/15	5.00	12.00
56 J.J. Watt/15	8.00	20.00
57 Cam Newton/15	8.00	20.00

2016 Immaculate Collection League Leaders Autographs

1 Drew Brees/15	100.00	200.00
2 Philip Rivers/15	20.00	50.00
8 Antonio Brown/15		

2016 Immaculate Collection Logos

2 Marcus Mariota/15	8.00	20.00
6 Ameer Abdullah/15	5.00	12.00
14 Amari Cooper/15	8.00	20.00
19 Derek Carr/15	8.00	20.00
21 Devin Funchess/15	5.00	12.00
24 Melvin Gordon/15	6.00	15.00
27 Devonta Freeman/15	6.00	15.00
29 Stefon Diggs/15	6.00	15.00
33 Jeremy Langford/15	6.00	15.00
39 T.J. Yeldon/15	5.00	12.00
42 Tyler Lockett/15	6.00	15.00
55 Matt Jones/15	6.00	15.00
56 Sammie Coates/15	5.00	12.00
59 Moritz Bohringer/20	5.00	12.00
61 Alex Collins/20	6.00	15.00
62 Braxton Miller/20	5.00	12.00
63 C.J. Prosise/20	5.00	12.00
64 Cardale Jones/20	5.00	12.00
65 Carson Wentz/20	50.00	125.00
66 Chris Moore/20	6.00	15.00
67 Christian Hackenberg/20	5.00	12.00
68 Cody Kessler/20	5.00	12.00
69 Connor Cook/20	6.00	15.00
70 Corey Coleman/20	8.00	20.00
71 Dak Prescott/20	25.00	60.00
72 Demarcus Robinson/20	5.00	12.00
73 Derrick Henry/20	12.00	30.00
74 Devontae Booker/20	6.00	15.00
75 Ezekiel Elliott/20	25.00	60.00
76 Hunter Henry/20	6.00	15.00
77 DeAndre Washington/20	5.00	12.00
78 Jared Goff/20	30.00	80.00
79 Joey Bosa/20	10.00	25.00
80 Jonathan Williams/20	6.00	15.00
81 Jordan Howard/20	12.00	30.00
82 Josh Doctson/20	6.00	15.00
83 Keenan Reynolds/20	6.00	15.00
84 Kenneth Dixon/20	5.00	12.00
85 Kenyan Drake/20	8.00	20.00
86 Kevin Hogan/20	6.00	15.00
87 Laquon Treadwell/20	6.00	15.00
88 Leonte Carroo/20	5.00	12.00
90 Michael Thomas/20	10.00	25.00
91 Paul Perkins/20	5.00	12.00
92 Paxton Lynch/20	5.00	12.00
93 Pharoh Cooper/20	5.00	12.00
94 Ricardo Louis/20	5.00	12.00
95 Sterling Shepard/20	6.00	15.00
96 Trevor Davis/20	5.00	12.00
97 Tyler Boyd/20	6.00	15.00
98 Tyler Ervin/20	5.00	12.00
99 Wendell Smallwood/20	5.00	12.00
100 Will Fuller/20	8.00	20.00

2016 Immaculate Collection NFL Honors Autographs

1 Todd Gurley	20.00	50.00
2 Jameis Winston	40.00	80.00
3 Drew Brees	60.00	120.00
4 Charles Woodson	75.00	150.00
5 Antonio Brown		
6 Adrian Peterson	50.00	100.00
7 J.J. Watt	50.00	100.00

2016 Immaculate Collection Past and Present Signatures

3 Jonathan Williams/50	10.00	25.00
4 Michael Thomas/25	20.00	50.00

7 Joey Bosa/25 20.00 50.00
8 Ezekiel Elliott/25 100.00 200.00
9 Sterling Shepard/50 10.00 25.00
10 Austin Hooper/50 8.00 20.00
11 Laquon Treadwell/15 15.00 40.00
12 Braxton Miller/25 10.00 25.00
13 Kenyan Drake/50 12.00 30.00
17 Corey Coleman/15 20.00 50.00
18 Hunter Henry/50 10.00 25.00
19 Devontae Booker/25 12.00 30.00
22 Dak Prescott/15 75.00 150.00
23 Myles Jack/20 15.00 40.00

2016 Immaculate Collection Players Collection Materials Autographs

1 David Johnson/99 10.00 25.00
2 Devonta Freeman/50 10.00 25.00
3 Karlos Williams/99 6.00 15.00
4 Sammy Watkins/15 20.00 50.00
5 Devin Funchess/50 8.00 20.00
6 Kelvin Benjamin/25 12.00 30.00
7 Jeremy Langford/50 10.00 25.00
8 Allen Robinson/99
10 Ameer Abdullah/99 6.00 15.00
12 Blake Bortles/25 10.00 25.00
13 Jarvis Landry/50 10.00 25.00
14 Stefon Diggs/99 8.00 20.00
15 Teddy Bridgewater/25 EXCH 12.00 30.00
16 Brandin Cooks/25 12.00 30.00
18 Derek Carr/25 15.00 40.00
19 Nelson Agholor/50 8.00 20.00
20 Zach Ertz/15 15.00 40.00
21 Sammie Coates/99 6.00 15.00
22 Melvin Gordon/25 EXCH 12.00 30.00
23 Carlos Hyde/50 8.00 20.00
25 Todd Gurley/50 12.00 30.00
26 Jameis Winston/25 30.00 60.00
27 Mike Evans/50 10.00 25.00
28 Dorial Green-Beckham/99 6.00 15.00
29 Marcus Mariota/25 15.00 40.00
30 Jamison Crowder/99 6.00 15.00
31 Matt Jones/99 8.00 20.00
32 Jared Goff/15 60.00 120.00
33 Carson Wentz/15 200.00 400.00
34 Paxton Lynch/15 12.00 30.00
35 Connor Cook/50 10.00 25.00
36 Christian Hackenberg/50 8.00 20.00
37 Dak Prescott/50 50.00 100.00
38 Cardale Jones/25 10.00 25.00
39 Ezekiel Elliott/15 75.00 150.00
40 Derrick Henry/15 30.00 80.00
41 C.J. Prosise/35 8.00 20.00
42 Devontae Booker/50 10.00 25.00
43 Laquon Treadwell/25 12.00 30.00
44 Corey Coleman/50 12.00 30.00
45 Josh Doctson/50 10.00 25.00
46 Will Fuller/50 12.00 30.00
47 Michael Thomas/50 15.00 40.00
48 Braxton Miller/50 8.00 20.00
49 Kenyan Drake/50 12.00 30.00
50 Joey Bosa/50 15.00 40.00

2016 Immaculate Collection Premium Patch Autographs

1 A.J. Green/75 10.00 25.00
2 Deion Sanders/25 12.00 30.00
3 Allen Hurns/75 6.00 15.00
4 Earl Thomas
5 Ameer Abdullah/99 6.00 15.00
6 Andy Dalton/50 10.00 25.00
7 Blake Bortles/25 10.00 25.00
8 Brian Urlacher/25 40.00 80.00
10 Clay Matthews/50 40.00 80.00
11 Darren McFadden/50 8.00 20.00
12 J.J. Watt/50 60.00 120.00
13 Demaryius Thomas/25 12.00 30.00
14 Derek Carr/75 30.00 60.00
15 DeSean Jackson/25 12.00 30.00
16 Devin Funchess/50 8.00 20.00
17 Devonta Freeman/75 8.00 20.00
18 Dez Bryant/50 20.00 50.00
20 Ed Reed/75 60.00 120.00
22 Giovani Bernard/99 6.00 15.00
23 Jameis Winston/25 40.00 80.00
24 Jarvis Landry/50 EXCH 10.00 25.00
25 Jeremy Hill/50 8.00 20.00
26 Jeremy Langford/99 8.00 20.00
28 Jerome Bettis/15 60.00 125.00
29 Brett Favre/15 100.00 200.00
30 Joe Montana/15 250.00 400.00
32 Karlos Williams/99 6.00 15.00
33 Kelvin Benjamin/50 EXCH 10.00 25.00
34 LaDainian Tomlinson/25 12.00 30.00
35 LeSean McCoy/50 EXCH 15.00 40.00
36 Marcus Mariota/50 40.00 80.00
37 Marvin Harrison/25 30.00 60.00
38 Matt Jones/75 8.00 20.00
39 Maurice Jones-Drew/50
41 Ray Lewis/28 EXCH 150.00 300.00
42 Russell Wilson/15 250.00 400.00
43 Sammy Watkins/75 10.00 25.00
44 Stefon Diggs/50 EXCH 10.00 25.00
45 Teddy Bridgewater/25 12.00 30.00
46 Tim Tebow/15 EXCH 50.00 100.00
47 Todd Gurley/50 25.00 50.00
48 Tyler Eifert/99 8.00 20.00
50 Zach Ertz/90 8.00 20.00

2016 Immaculate Collection Pro Bowl Swatches

1 Derek Carr/49 5.00 12.00
2 Eli Manning/49 4.00 10.00
3 Russell Wilson/49 6.00 15.00
4 Jameis Winston/49 10.00 25.00
5 Teddy Bridgewater/49 4.00 10.00
6 Adrian Peterson/49 5.00 12.00
7 Doug Martin/25 5.00 12.00
8 Devonta Freeman/49 4.00 10.00
9 Todd Gurley/49 5.00 12.00
10 Richard Sherman/49 5.00 12.00
11 Amari Cooper/49 5.00 12.00
12 Odell Beckham Jr./49 5.00 12.00
13 Tyler Lockett/49 4.00 10.00
14 Jarvis Landry/25 5.00 12.00
15 Allen Robinson/25 5.00 12.00
16 DeAndre Hopkins/49 4.00 10.00
17 A.J. Green/49 5.00 12.00
18 Julio Jones/49 5.00 12.00
19 T.Y. Hilton/25 5.00 12.00
20 Travis Kelce/25 6.00 15.00
21 Khalil Mack/35 5.00 12.00
22 Clay Matthews/49 5.00 12.00
23 Charles Woodson/49 10.00 25.00
24 Marcus Peters/49 3.00 8.00
25 Tyrod Taylor/25 5.00 12.00
26 Andrew Luck/49 6.00 15.00
28 Drew Brees/49 8.00 20.00
29 Antonio Brown/49 5.00 12.00
30 Jamaal Charles/49 4.00 10.00
31 DeMarco Murray/49 4.00 10.00
32 Matt Ryan/49 4.00 10.00
33 C.J. Anderson/49 4.00 10.00
34 Greg Olsen/25 5.00 12.00
37 Patrick Peterson/25 4.00 10.00
39 Joe Haden/25 4.00 10.00
42 DeMarcus Ware/49 4.00 10.00

2016 Immaculate Collection Quad Jerseys

1 Gff/Lnch/Wntz/Hcknbrg/49 12.00 30.00
2 Jns/Ksslr/Ck/Prsctt/49 12.00 30.00
3 Hnry/Ellt/Prse/Drke/49 12.00 30.00
4 Bkr/Dxn/Ervn/Prkns/30 3.00 8.00
5 Dctsn/Fllr/Clmn/Trdwll/49 4.00 10.00
6 Mllr/Thms/Shprd/Byd/49 5.00 12.00

2016 Immaculate Collection Rookie Cleats

1 Jared Goff/15 12.00 30.00
2 Carson Wentz/15 40.00 100.00
3 Paxton Lynch/15 4.00 10.00
4 Christian Hackenberg/15 4.00 10.00
5 Dak Prescott/15 30.00 60.00
6 Cody Kessler/15 4.00 10.00
7 Connor Cook/15 5.00 12.00
8 DeAndre Washington/15 4.00 10.00
9 Ezekiel Elliott/15 75.00 150.00
10 Derrick Henry/15 10.00 25.00
11 Kenyan Drake/15 15.00 40.00
12 C.J. Prosise/15 4.00 10.00
15 Devontae Booker/15 5.00 12.00
18 Corey Coleman/15 6.00 15.00
19 Laquon Treadwell/15 5.00 12.00
20 Josh Doctson/15 15.00 40.00
21 Will Fuller/15 6.00 15.00
22 Sterling Shepard/15 5.00 12.00
23 Michael Thomas/15 8.00 20.00
24 Tyler Boyd/15 5.00 12.00
25 Braxton Miller/15 4.00 10.00
26 Chris Moore/15 5.00 12.00
27 Trevor Davis/15 4.00 10.00
28 Ricardo Louis/15 4.00 10.00
29 Joey Bosa/15 8.00 20.00
30 Keenan Reynolds/15 5.00 12.00

2016 Immaculate Collection Rookie Eye Black Autographs

1 Jared Goff/25 50.00 100.00
2 Carson Wentz/25 75.00 150.00
3 Paxton Lynch/25 6.00 15.00
4 Connor Cook/40 6.00 15.00
5 Christian Hackenberg/50 5.00 12.00
6 Cardale Jones/48 5.00 12.00
7 Dak Prescott/99 40.00 80.00
8 Cody Kessler/99 4.00 10.00
9 Derrick Henry/25 15.00 40.00
10 Ezekiel Elliott/25 100.00 200.00
11 C.J. Prosise/75 4.00 10.00
12 Paul Perkins/75 4.00 10.00
13 Jordan Howard/99 10.00 25.00
14 Alex Collins/99 5.00 12.00
15 Devontae Booker/99 5.00 12.00
16 Kenneth Dixon/99 4.00 10.00
17 Kenyan Drake/99 6.00 15.00
18 Kevin Hogan/99 5.00 12.00
19 Jonathan Williams/99 5.00 12.00
20 DeAndre Washington/99 4.00 10.00
21 Laquon Treadwell/50 6.00 15.00
22 Corey Coleman/75 6.00 15.00
23 Josh Doctson/50 6.00 15.00
24 Will Fuller/50 8.00 20.00
25 Michael Thomas/50 10.00 25.00
26 Braxton Miller/99 4.00 10.00
27 Leonte Carroo/99 4.00 10.00
28 Sterling Shepard/99 5.00 12.00
29 Tyler Ervin/99 4.00 10.00
30 Pharoh Cooper/99 4.00 10.00
31 Wendell Smallwood/99 4.00 10.00
32 Keenan Reynolds/99 5.00 12.00
33 Chris Moore/99 5.00 12.00
34 Tyler Boyd/75 5.00 12.00
35 Hunter Henry/99 5.00 12.00
36 Ricardo Louis/99 4.00 10.00
37 Demarcus Robinson/49 5.00 12.00
38 Joey Bosa/50 10.00 25.00
39 Trevor Davis/99 4.00 10.00
40 Moritz Bohringer/50 5.00 12.00

2016 Immaculate Collection Rookie Premium Patch Autographs

1 Laquon Treadwell/49 10.00 25.00
2 Michael Thomas/49 15.00 40.00
3 DeAndre Washington/99 6.00 15.00
4 Christian Hackenberg/49 8.00 20.00
5 Cody Kessler/49 8.00 20.00
6 Alex Collins/99 8.00 20.00
7 Cardale Jones/49 8.00 20.00
8 Connor Cook/49 10.00 25.00
9 Moritz Bohringer/99 6.00 15.00
10 Dak Prescott/99 60.00 125.00
11 Carson Wentz/49 125.00 250.00
12 Paxton Lynch/49 8.00 20.00
13 Braxton Miller/99 6.00 15.00
14 Paul Perkins/99 6.00 15.00
15 Will Fuller/49 12.00 30.00
16 Jared Goff/49 60.00 125.00
17 Corey Coleman/49 12.00 30.00
18 Josh Doctson/49 10.00 25.00
19 Sterling Shepard/99 8.00 20.00
20 Devontae Booker/49 10.00 25.00
21 Ezekiel Elliott/99 100.00 200.00
22 Kenyan Drake/99 10.00 25.00
23 Kenneth Dixon/49 8.00 20.00
24 Wendell Smallwood/99 6.00 15.00
25 C.J. Prosise/49 15.00 40.00
26 Pharoh Cooper/49 8.00 20.00
27 Derrick Henry/99 15.00 40.00
28 Trevor Davis/99 6.00 15.00
29 Leonte Carroo/49 8.00 20.00
30 Joey Bosa/49 15.00 40.00

2016 Immaculate Collection Rookie Signature Patches

1 Ezekiel Elliott/49 200.00 300.00
2 Carson Wentz/49 100.00 200.00
3 Corey Coleman/99 10.00 25.00
4 Cardale Jones/49 8.00 20.00
5 C.J. Prosise/99 12.00 30.00
6 Will Fuller/99 10.00 25.00
7 Derrick Henry/49 20.00 50.00
8 Paxton Lynch/49 8.00 20.00
9 Sterling Shepard/49 10.00 25.00
10 Jonathan Williams/99 8.00 20.00
11 Jordan Howard/99 EXCH 15.00 40.00
12 Jared Goff/49 60.00 125.00
13 Kenyan Drake/99 10.00 25.00
14 Laquon Treadwell/49 10.00 25.00
15 Kenneth Dixon/49 8.00 20.00
16 Joey Bosa/49 15.00 40.00
17 Dak Prescott/49 60.00 125.00
18 Keenan Reynolds/99 8.00 20.00
19 Devontae Booker/49 10.00 25.00
20 Tyler Ervin/99 6.00 15.00
21 Christian Hackenberg/99 6.00 15.00
22 Ricardo Louis/49 8.00 20.00
23 Josh Doctson/99 8.00 20.00
24 Kevin Hogan/49 10.00 25.00
25 Hunter Henry/49 10.00 25.00
26 Tyler Boyd/49 10.00 25.00
27 Cody Kessler/49 8.00 20.00
28 Demarcus Robinson/99 6.00 15.00
29 Braxton Miller/49 8.00 20.00
30 Leonte Carroo/99 6.00 15.00

2016 Immaculate Collection Signature Moves

1 Michael Irvin 60.00 120.00
2 Clay Matthews 50.00 100.00
3 Andrew Luck 60.00 120.00
4 Antonio Brown
5 Tom Brady 400.00 800.00
6 DeMarcus Ware 15.00 40.00
7 Ray Lewis
8 John Brown
9 Von Miller 30.00 60.00
10 Randall Cobb 15.00 40.00

2016 Immaculate Collection Triple Jerseys

1 Cpr/Gff/Grly/49 8.00 20.00
2 Bker/Lnch/Wre/49 6.00 15.00
3 Ksslr/Clmn/Lous/49 4.00 10.00
4 Trdwll/Bhrngr/Brdgwtr/49 3.00 8.00
5 Hnry/Wrght/Mrta/49 6.00 15.00
6 Mllr/Ervn/Fllr/49 4.00 10.00
7 Dltn/Byd/Grn/25 5.00 12.00
8 Mre/Rynlds/Dxn/49 3.00 8.00
9 Drke/Tnhll/Lndry/49 4.00 10.00
11 Hrns/Rbnsn/Brtls/25 4.00 10.00
12 Wlsn/Lcktt/Prsse/25 6.00 15.00
13 Bckhm/Mnng/Shprd/49 6.00 15.00
14 Hnry/Bsa/Rvrs/25 6.00 15.00
15 Prsctt/Brnt/Elltt/49 40.00 80.00

2017 Immaculate Collection

1 David Johnson 3.00 8.00
2 Larry Fitzgerald 2.50 6.00
3 Kurt Warner 2.50 6.00
4 Matt Ryan 2.50 6.00
5 Julio Jones 3.00 8.00
6 Deion Sanders 2.50 6.00
7 Joe Flacco 2.50 6.00
8 Breshad Perriman 2.00 5.00
9 Ray Lewis 3.00 8.00
10 LeSean McCoy 3.00 8.00
11 Sammy Watkins 3.00 8.00
12 Thurman Thomas 2.50 6.00
13 Cam Newton 3.00 8.00
14 Kelvin Benjamin 2.50 6.00
15 Julius Peppers 2.50 6.00
16 Jordan Howard 3.00 8.00
17 Kevin White 2.00 5.00
18 Walter Payton 6.00 15.00
19 Andy Dalton 2.50 6.00
20 A.J. Green 3.00 8.00
21 Ken Anderson 2.00 5.00
22 Isaiah Crowell 2.00 5.00
23 Corey Coleman 2.00 5.00
24 Paul Warfield 2.50 6.00
25 Dak Prescott 3.00 8.00
26 Ezekiel Elliott 4.00 10.00
27 Jason Witten 2.50 6.00
28 Troy Aikman 4.00 10.00
29 Trevor Siemian 2.00 5.00
30 Jamaal Charles 2.50 6.00
31 John Elway 5.00 12.00
32 Matthew Stafford 2.50 6.00
33 Barry Sanders 5.00 12.00
34 Calvin Johnson 3.00 8.00
35 Aaron Rodgers 6.00 15.00
36 Jordy Nelson 2.50 6.00
37 Davante Adams 2.50 6.00
38 Brett Favre 6.00 15.00
39 Lamar Miller 2.00 5.00
40 DeAndre Hopkins 2.50 6.00
41 J.J. Watt 3.00 8.00
42 Andrew Luck 4.00 10.00
43 T.Y. Hilton 2.50 6.00
44 Peyton Manning 6.00 15.00
45 Blake Bortles 2.00 5.00
46 Marqise Lee 2.00 5.00
47 Mark Brunell 2.50 6.00
48 Alex Smith 2.50 6.00
49 Tyreek Hill 3.00 8.00
50 Joe Montana 8.00 20.00
51 Philip Rivers 3.00 8.00
52 Melvin Gordon 2.50 6.00
53 Lance Alworth 2.50 6.00
54 Jared Goff 3.00 8.00
55 Todd Gurley II 3.00 8.00
56 Eric Dickerson 3.00 8.00
57 Jay Cutler 2.00 5.00
58 Jay Ajayi 2.50 6.00
59 Dan Marino 6.00 15.00
60 Sam Bradford 2.00 5.00
61 Stefon Diggs 2.50 6.00
62 Warren Moon 3.00 8.00
63 Tom Brady 8.00 20.00
64 Rob Gronkowski 3.00 8.00
65 Randy Moss 2.50 6.00
66 Ty Law 3.00 8.00
67 Drew Brees 3.00 8.00
68 Adrian Peterson 3.00 8.00
69 Michael Thomas 3.00 8.00
70 Eli Manning 2.50 6.00
71 Odell Beckham Jr. 3.00 8.00
72 Brandon Marshall 2.00 5.00
73 Matt Forte 2.00 5.00
74 Leonard Williams 2.00 5.00
75 Joe Namath 4.00 10.00
76 Derek Carr 3.00 8.00
77 Marshawn Lynch 2.50 6.00
78 Amari Cooper 3.00 8.00
79 Carson Wentz 4.00 10.00
80 LeGarrette Blount 2.50 6.00
81 Alshon Jeffery 2.50 6.00
82 Ben Roethlisberger 3.00 8.00
83 Le'Veon Bell 2.50 6.00
84 Antonio Brown 3.00 8.00
85 Terry Bradshaw 5.00 12.00
86 Carlos Hyde 2.00 5.00
87 Navorro Bowman 2.50 6.00
88 Jerry Rice 5.00 12.00
89 Russell Wilson 4.00 10.00
90 Doug Baldwin 2.50 6.00
91 Eddie Lacy 2.00 5.00
92 Jameis Winston 2.50 6.00
93 Mike Evans 2.50 6.00
94 DeSean Jackson 2.50 6.00
95 Marcus Mariota 3.00 8.00
96 DeMarco Murray 2.50 6.00
97 Derrick Henry 2.50 6.00
98 Kirk Cousins 3.00 8.00
99 Robert Kelley 2.00 5.00
100 Terrelle Pryor Sr. 2.00 5.00
101 Mitchell Trubisky JSY AU RC 50.00 100.00
102 Deshaun Watson JSY AU RC 75.00 150.00
103 DeShone Kizer JSY AU RC 5.00 12.00
104 Patrick Mahomes II JSY AU RC 250.00 500.00
105 Nathan Peterman JSY AU RC 6.00 15.00
106 Davis Webb JSY AU RC 5.00 12.00
107 R. Joshua Dobbs JSY AU RC 6.00 15.00
108 C.J. Beathard JSY AU RC 5.00 12.00
109 Dalvin Cook JSY AU RC 40.00 80.00
110 Leonard Fournette JSY AU RC 40.00 80.00
111 Christian McCaffrey JSY AU RC 50.00 100.00
112 Joe Mixon JSY AU RC 10.00 25.00
113 Alvin Kamara JSY AU RC 30.00 60.00
114 Marlon Mack JSY AU RC 8.00 20.00
115 Samaje Perine JSY AU RC 5.00 12.00
116 Wayne Gallman JSY AU RC 6.00 15.00
117 Kareem Hunt JSY AU RC 15.00 40.00
118 D'Onta Foreman JSY AU RC 6.00 15.00
120 James Conner JSY AU RC 10.00 25.00
121 Jamaal Williams JSY AU RC 5.00 12.00
122 Joe Williams JSY AU RC 5.00 12.00
123 O.J. Howard JSY AU RC 6.00 15.00
124 Evan Engram JSY AU RC 6.00 15.00
125 Mike Williams JSY AU RC 8.00 20.00
126 John Ross III JSY AU RC 6.00 15.00
127 Corey Davis JSY AU RC 8.00 20.00
128 JuJu Smith-Schuster JSY AU RC 30.00 60.00
129 Dede Westbrook JSY AU RC 5.00 12.00
130 Curtis Samuel JSY AU RC 6.00 15.00
131 Amara Darboh JSY AU RC 5.00 12.00
132 Carlos Henderson JSY AU RC 5.00 12.00
133 Zay Jones JSY AU RC 6.00 15.00
134 Cooper Kupp JSY AU RC 8.00 20.00
135 ArDarius Stewart JSY AU RC 5.00 12.00
136 Chris Godwin JSY AU RC 6.00 15.00
137 Taywan Taylor JSY AU RC 5.00 12.00
138 Kenny Golladay JSY AU RC 8.00 20.00
139 Mack Hollins JSY AU RC 5.00 12.00
140 Josh Reynolds JSY AU RC 5.00 12.00
141 Ryan Switzer AU RC 5.00 12.00
142 Josh Malone AU RC 3.00 8.00
143 Brad Kaaya AU RC 3.00 8.00
144 Chad Hansen AU RC 3.00 8.00
145 Shelton Gibson AU RC 3.00 8.00
146 Marlon Humphrey AU RC 3.00 8.00
147 Brian Hill AU RC 3.00 8.00
148 Jehu Chesson AU RC 4.00 10.00
149 Gerald Everett AU RC 3.00 8.00
150 Adam Shaheen AU RC 3.00 8.00
151 Marshon Lattimore AU RC 4.00 10.00
152 Malik Hooker AU RC 3.00 8.00
153 Jamal Adams AU RC 3.00 8.00
154 Jonathan Allen AU RC 4.00 10.00
155 Solomon Thomas AU RC 3.00 8.00
156 Tarik Cohen AU RC 6.00 15.00
157 Donnel Pumphrey AU RC 4.00 10.00
158 Taco Charlton AU RC 3.00 8.00
159 Adoree' Jackson AU RC EXCH 4.00 10.00
160 David Njoku AU RC 4.00 10.00
161 Gareon Conley AU RC 3.00 8.00
162 Tre'Davious White AU RC 3.00 8.00
163 Derek Barnett AU RC 10.00 25.00
164 Jabrill Peppers AU RC 5.00 12.00
165 T.J. Watt AU RC 20.00 50.00

2017 Immaculate Collection Dual Jerseys

1 D.Prescott/E.Elliott/99 5.00 12.00
2 E.Smith/T.Aikman/15 12.00 30.00
3 O.Beckham/E.Manning/25 6.00 15.00
4 C.Wentz/Z.Ertz/99 12.00 30.00
5 J.Reed/K.Cousins/99 4.00 10.00
6 J.Riggins/J.Theismann/15 8.00 20.00
7 L.McCoy/T.Taylor/99 4.00 10.00
8 R.Tannehill/J.Ajayi/99 3.00 8.00
9 D.Marino/L.Csonka/15 15.00 40.00
10 R.Grnkwski/T.Brady/25 15.00 40.00
11 L.Ftzgrld/D.Johnson/99 4.00 10.00
12 J.Goff/T.Gurley/99 4.00 10.00
13 K.Warner/M.Faulk/49 4.00 10.00
14 J.Montana/J.Rice/25 15.00 40.00
15 J.Elway/P.Manning/25 20.00 50.00
16 R.Sherman/R.Wilson/99 5.00 12.00
17 M.Allen/J.Montana/99 10.00 25.00
18 T.Hill/A.Smith/99 4.00 10.00
19 L.Tmlnsn/P.Rivers/99 4.00 10.00
20 A.Cooper/D.Carr/99 4.00 10.00
21 W.Payton/M.Singletary/25 12.00 30.00
22 B.Sanders/C.Johnson/15 12.00 30.00
23 A.Rodgers/B.Favre/49 25.00 50.00
24 D.Adams/J.Nelson/99 8.00 20.00
25 E.Reed/R.Lewis/99 6.00 15.00
26 A.Green/A.Dalton/99 4.00 10.00
27 B.Rthlsbrgr/L.Bell/99 20.00 50.00
28 H.Ward/J.Bettis/99 6.00 15.00
29 J.Jones/M.Ryan/99 4.00 10.00
30 C.Newton/K.Benjamin/99 4.00 10.00
31 D.Brees/M.Thomas/99 4.00 10.00
32 J.Winston/M.Evans/99 3.00 8.00
33 F.Taylor/M.Brunell/15 6.00 15.00
34 A.Luck/P.Manning/25 25.00 50.00
35 D.Murray/M.Mariota/99 4.00 10.00

2017 Immaculate Collection Eye Black Autographs

1 Randy Moss/25 75.00 150.00
2 Jason Taylor/49 25.00 50.00
3 Lance Alworth/25 40.00 100.00
4 Jason Witten/99 30.00 60.00
5 Jerry Rice/15 50.00 100.00
6 Bill Bates/99 6.00 15.00
7 Christian Okoye/99 6.00 15.00
8 Hines Ward/99 25.00 50.00
9 Joe Theismann/99 10.00 25.00
10 Larry Csonka/25 EXCH 12.00 30.00
11 Mike Ditka/25 20.00 50.00
12 Priest Holmes/99 6.00 15.00
13 Dont'a Hightower/99 6.00 15.00
14 Andre Reed/99 8.00 20.00
15 Mike Vrabel/49 12.00 30.00
16 Roger Craig/99 8.00 20.00
17 Barry Sanders/15 75.00 150.00
18 Fred Biletnikoff/99 10.00 25.00
19 Kyle Rudolph/84 6.00 15.00
20 Sterling Sharpe/99 8.00 20.00
22 Brett Keisel/99 6.00 15.00
23 Earl Thomas III/99 8.00 20.00
24 Matt Ryan/25 30.00 60.00
25 Jerome Bettis/25 40.00 80.00
26 Marcus Mariota/25
27 DeMarco Murray/99 8.00 20.00
28 Tyler Lockett/99 8.00 20.00
29 Chris Spielman/99 8.00 20.00
30 Brian Urlacher/25
31 Robert Kelley/99 6.00 15.00
33 Troy Aikman/15 40.00 80.00
34 Richard Sherman/49 25.00 50.00
35 Jamaal Charles/99 8.00 20.00
37 Terrelle Pryor Sr./99 6.00 15.00
38 Tevin Coleman/99 8.00 20.00
39 Mark Ingram/99 8.00 20.00
40 Heath Miller/99 20.00 50.00
41 Aaron Rodgers/15 200.00 300.00
42 Troy Brown/99 6.00 15.00
43 Ryan Shazier/99 6.00 15.00
44 Ron Jaworski/99 8.00 20.00
46 Michael Irvin/15 30.00 60.00
47 Reggie Wayne/99 8.00 20.00
48 Cole Beasley/99 10.00 25.00
49 Brett Favre/15 75.00 150.00
50 Blake Bortles/25 10.00 25.00

2017 Immaculate Collection Honors Signatures

1 Dak Prescott 50.00 100.00
2 Joey Bosa 25.00 50.00
3 Matt Ryan 40.00 80.00
5 Jordy Nelson 40.00 80.00

2017 Immaculate Collection Immaculate Numbers

101 Mitchell Trubisky/25 15.00 40.00
102 Deshaun Watson/25 25.00 60.00
103 DeShone Kizer/25 4.00 10.00
104 Patrick Mahomes II/25 50.00 100.00
105 Nathan Peterman/50 4.00 10.00
106 Davis Webb/50 3.00 8.00
107 R. Joshua Dobbs/25 5.00 12.00
108 C.J. Beathard/50 3.00 8.00
109 Dalvin Cook/50 6.00 15.00
110 Leonard Fournette/25 15.00 40.00
111 Christian McCaffrey/25 15.00 40.00
112 Joe Mixon/25 8.00 20.00
113 Alvin Kamara/25 10.00 25.00
114 Marlon Mack/50 5.00 12.00
115 Samaje Perine/50 3.00 8.00
116 Wayne Gallman/25 5.00 12.00
117 Kareem Hunt/25 8.00 20.00
118 D'Onta Foreman/25 5.00 12.00
119 Jeremy McNichols/50 3.00 8.00
120 James Conner/25 8.00 20.00
121 Jamaal Williams/25 4.00 10.00
122 Joe Williams/50 3.00 8.00
123 O.J. Howard/25 5.00 12.00
124 Evan Engram/25 5.00 12.00
125 Mike Williams/25 6.00 15.00
126 John Ross III/25 5.00 12.00
127 Corey Davis/25 6.00 15.00
128 JuJu Smith-Schuster/25 8.00 20.00
129 Dede Westbrook/50 3.00 8.00
130 Curtis Samuel/50 4.00 10.00
131 Amara Darboh/50 3.00 8.00
132 Carlos Henderson/50 3.00 8.00
133 Zay Jones/25 5.00 12.00
134 Cooper Kupp/25 6.00 15.00
135 ArDarius Stewart/50 3.00 8.00
136 Chris Godwin/50 4.00 10.00
137 Taywan Taylor/50 3.00 8.00
138 Kenny Golladay/25 6.00 15.00
139 Mack Hollins/50 3.00 8.00
140 Josh Reynolds/50 3.00 8.00
150 Adam Jones/20 5.00 12.00
151 C.J. Anderson/20 6.00 15.00
153 A.J. Green/20 8.00 20.00
160 DeMarcus Lawrence/20 5.00 12.00
164 Reshad Jones/25 4.00 10.00
165 Blake Bortles/15 5.00 12.00
169 Justin Houston/25 4.00 10.00
182 Byron Jones/25 4.00 10.00
183 Jordan Matthews/15 5.00 12.00
186 Dwight Clark/18 10.00 25.00
189 Ameer Abdullah/25 4.00 10.00

2017 Immaculate Collection Immaculate Numbers Memorabilia

1 David Johnson/31 6.00 15.00
6 Devonta Freeman/24 6.00 15.00
9 Ray Lewis/52 5.00 12.00
10 LeSean McCoy/25 6.00 15.00
12 Thurman Thomas/34 5.00 12.00
15 Julius Peppers/90 3.00 8.00
16 Jordan Howard/24 8.00 20.00
18 Walter Payton/34 30.00 60.00
20 A.J. Green/18 8.00 20.00
23 Corey Coleman/19 5.00 12.00
24 Ozzie Newsome/82 3.00 8.00
26 Ezekiel Elliott/21
27 Jason Witten/82 3.00 8.00
28 Mike Ditka/89 4.00 10.00
30 Von Miller/58 4.00 10.00
33 Barry Sanders/20 20.00 50.00
34 Ameer Abdullah/21 5.00 12.00
36 Jordy Nelson/87 3.00 8.00
37 Davante Adams/17 6.00 15.00
39 Earl Campbell/34 6.00 15.00
41 J.J. Watt/99 4.00 10.00
44 Peyton Manning/18
46 Allen Robinson/15 6.00 15.00
50 Joe Montana/19 20.00 50.00
51 Philip Rivers/17 8.00 20.00
52 Melvin Gordon/28 5.00 12.00
53 Joey Bosa/99 4.00 10.00
54 Jared Goff/16 8.00 20.00
55 Todd Gurley II/30 6.00 15.00
56 Eric Dickerson/29 10.00 25.00
57 Ryan Tannehill/17 6.00 15.00
58 Jay Ajayi/23 6.00 15.00
64 Rob Gronkowski/87 4.00 10.00
65 Randy Moss/81 3.00 8.00
66 James White/28 5.00 12.00
68 Mark Ingram/22 6.00 15.00
72 Sterling Shepard/87 3.00 8.00
73 Matt Forte/22 5.00 12.00
74 Leonard Williams/92 2.50 6.00
77 Khalil Mack/52 5.00 12.00
78 Amari Cooper/89 4.00 10.00
80 Ryan Mathews/24 6.00 15.00
81 Jordan Matthews/81 2.50 6.00
83 Le'Veon Bell/26 15.00 40.00
84 Antonio Brown/84 8.00 20.00
86 Carlos Hyde/28 4.00 10.00
87 Navorro Bowman/53 4.00 10.00
88 Jerry Rice/80 8.00 20.00
90 Doug Baldwin/89 3.00 8.00
91 Thomas Rawls/34 4.00 10.00
94 Doug Martin/22 6.00 15.00
96 DeMarco Murray/29 5.00 12.00
97 Derrick Henry/22 6.00 15.00
99 Robert Kelley/32 4.00 10.00
100 Jordan Reed/86 2.50 6.00

2017 Immaculate Collection Immaculate Patches

101 Mitchell Trubisky/15 20.00 50.00
102 Deshaun Watson/15 25.00 60.00
103 DeShone Kizer/15 6.00 15.00
104 Patrick Mahomes II/15 40.00 80.00
105 Nathan Peterman/15 8.00 20.00
106 Davis Webb/15 6.00 15.00
107 R. Joshua Dobbs/15 8.00 20.00
108 C.J. Beathard/15 6.00 15.00
109 Dalvin Cook/15 15.00 40.00
110 Leonard Fournette/15 20.00 50.00
111 Christian McCaffrey/15 15.00 40.00
114 Marlon Mack/15 10.00 25.00
117 Kareem Hunt/15 12.00 30.00
119 Jeremy McNichols/15 6.00 15.00
121 Jamaal Williams/15 6.00 15.00
122 Joe Williams/15 6.00 15.00
126 John Ross III/15 8.00 20.00
127 Corey Davis/15 10.00 25.00
128 JuJu Smith-Schuster/15 15.00 40.00
129 Dede Westbrook/15 6.00 15.00
130 Curtis Samuel/15 8.00 20.00
131 Amara Darboh/15 6.00 15.00
132 Carlos Henderson/15 6.00 15.00
133 Zay Jones/15 8.00 20.00
134 Cooper Kupp/15 10.00 25.00
135 ArDarius Stewart/15 6.00 15.00
136 Chris Godwin/15 8.00 20.00
137 Taywan Taylor/15 6.00 15.00
138 Kenny Golladay/15 10.00 25.00
139 Mack Hollins/15 6.00 15.00
140 Josh Reynolds/15 6.00 15.00
151 C.J. Anderson/20 8.00 20.00
172 Terrance Williams/25 5.00 12.00
186 Dwight Clark/25 6.00 15.00
189 Ameer Abdullah/20 6.00 15.00
195 Cardale Jones/20 6.00 15.00

2017 Immaculate Collection Immaculate Standard Jerseys

2 Dak Prescott/25 6.00 15.00
3 Ezekiel Elliott/25 8.00 20.00
4 Hunter Henry/30 4.00 10.00
5 Joey Bosa/25 6.00 15.00
6 Cody Kessler/30 4.00 10.00
7 Paul Perkins/30 4.00 10.00
8 Carson Wentz/25 8.00 20.00
9 Sterling Shepard/30 5.00 12.00
10 Melvin Gordon/25 5.00 12.00
11 Derrick Henry/25 5.00 12.00
12 Marcus Mariota/25 6.00 15.00
13 Jameis Winston/25 5.00 12.00
14 Jordan Howard/30 6.00 15.00
15 Michael Thomas/30 6.00 15.00
16 Jay Ajayi/30 5.00 12.00
17 Jimmy Garoppolo/30 8.00 20.00
18 Rich Gannon/25 4.00 10.00
19 Jerry Rice/25 10.00 25.00
20 Jim Kelly/25 6.00 15.00
21 J.J. Watt/25 6.00 15.00
22 Julio Jones/25 6.00 15.00
23 Ryan Tannehill/30 5.00 12.00
25 Tony Romo/30 5.00 12.00
26 Edgerrin James/25 5.00 12.00
27 Tony Dorsett/25 6.00 15.00
28 Antonio Brown/25 6.00 15.00
29 Earl Thomas III/25 5.00 12.00
30 Marshall Faulk/25 5.00 12.00
31 Von Miller/30 5.00 12.00
32 Curtis Martin/25 5.00 12.00
33 Andrew Luck/30 8.00 20.00
34 Mark Brunell/25 5.00 12.00
36 Tyreek Hill/30 6.00 15.00
37 Ed Reed/25 5.00 12.00
38 Darren McFadden/49 3.00 8.00
39 David Johnson/30 6.00 15.00
40 Martavis Bryant/25 4.00 10.00
41 James White/25 5.00 12.00
42 T.Y. Hilton/25 5.00 12.00
43 Jordan Reed/25 4.00 10.00
44 Doug Martin/25 5.00 12.00
45 Allen Hurns/25 4.00 10.00
46 Joe Montana/25 15.00 40.00
47 Keenan Allen/30 5.00 12.00
48 DeMarco Murray/25 5.00 12.00
49 Mike Evans/21 6.00 15.00
50 Derrick Johnson/25 4.00 10.00
51 Davante Adams/25 5.00 12.00
52 LeSean McCoy/25 6.00 15.00
53 Devonta Freeman/30 5.00 12.00
54 Sammy Watkins/25 6.00 15.00
55 Allen Robinson/25 5.00 12.00
56 Eric Berry/25 5.00 12.00
58 Jeremy Langford/25 5.00 12.00
60 Jonathan Stewart/20 5.00 12.00
61 Ndamukong Suh/25 5.00 12.00
63 Rob Gronkowski/25 6.00 15.00
64 Malcolm Mitchell/25 5.00 12.00
65 Delanie Walker/25 4.00 10.00
66 Cardale Jones/25 4.00 10.00
67 Laquon Treadwell/25 4.00 10.00
68 Teddy Bridgewater/25 5.00 12.00
69 Tevin Coleman/25 5.00 12.00
70 Sammie Coates/25 4.00 10.00

2017 Immaculate Collection Logos

103 DeShone Kizer/17 5.00 12.00
107 R. Joshua Dobbs/25 5.00 12.00
108 C.J. Beathard/18 5.00 12.00
110 Leonard Fournette/16 15.00 40.00
112 Joe Mixon/17 10.00 25.00
115 Samaje Perine/19 5.00 12.00
117 Kareem Hunt/15 10.00 25.00
119 Jeremy McNichols/23 5.00 12.00
120 James Conner/25 8.00 20.00
121 Jamaal Williams/16 5.00 12.00
122 Joe Williams/17 5.00 12.00
123 O.J. Howard/23 6.00 15.00
128 JuJu Smith-Schuster/22 12.00 30.00
129 Dede Westbrook/16 5.00 12.00
130 Curtis Samuel/26 5.00 12.00
135 ArDarius Stewart/16 5.00 12.00
136 Chris Godwin/23 6.00 15.00
137 Taywan Taylor/16 5.00 12.00
138 Kenny Golladay/16 8.00 20.00
140 Josh Reynolds/17 5.00 12.00

2017 Immaculate Collection Past and Present Jerseys

1 Deshaun Watson 20.00 50.00
2 Mitchell Trubisky 12.00 30.00
3 DeShone Kizer 4.00 10.00
4 Patrick Mahomes II 30.00 60.00
5 C.J. Beathard 4.00 10.00
6 Davis Webb 4.00 10.00
7 Nathan Peterman 5.00 12.00
8 R. Joshua Dobbs 5.00 12.00
9 Leonard Fournette 15.00 40.00
10 Dalvin Cook 8.00 20.00
11 Christian McCaffrey 12.00 30.00
12 D'Onta Foreman 5.00 12.00
13 Alvin Kamara 10.00 25.00
14 Samaje Perine 4.00 10.00
15 Wayne Gallman 5.00 12.00
16 Kareem Hunt 8.00 20.00
17 Jeremy McNichols 4.00 10.00
18 James Conner 8.00 20.00
19 Joe Mixon 8.00 20.00
20 Marlon Mack 6.00 15.00
21 O.J. Howard 5.00 12.00
22 Mike Williams 8.00 20.00
23 Corey Davis 6.00 15.00
24 John Ross III 5.00 12.00
25 JuJu Smith-Schuster 8.00 20.00
26 Zay Jones 5.00 12.00
27 Curtis Samuel 5.00 12.00
28 Dede Westbrook 4.00 10.00
29 Carlos Henderson 4.00 10.00
30 Chris Godwin 5.00 12.00
31 Joe Williams 4.00 10.00
32 Cooper Kupp 8.00 20.00
33 Amara Darboh 4.00 10.00
34 Jamaal Williams 4.00 10.00
35 ArDarius Stewart 4.00 10.00
36 Kenny Golladay 6.00 15.00
37 Josh Reynolds 4.00 10.00
38 Taywan Taylor 4.00 10.00
39 Mack Hollins 4.00 10.00
40 Evan Engram 5.00 12.00

2017 Immaculate Collection Players Collection Materials Autographs

1 Mitchell Trubisky/25 50.00 100.00
2 Deshaun Watson/25 100.00 200.00
3 DeShone Kizer/25 10.00 25.00
4 Patrick Mahomes II/25 400.00 800.00
5 Nathan Peterman/25 12.00 30.00
6 Davis Webb/25 10.00 25.00
7 R. Joshua Dobbs/99 8.00 20.00
8 C.J. Beathard/25 10.00 25.00
9 Dalvin Cook/25 25.00 60.00
10 Leonard Fournette/25
11 Christian McCaffrey/25 50.00 100.00
12 Joe Mixon/49 15.00 40.00
13 Alvin Kamara/25
14 Marlon Mack/99 10.00 25.00
15 Samaje Perine/25 10.00 25.00
16 Wayne Gallman/99 8.00 20.00
17 Kareem Hunt/99 12.00 30.00
18 D'Onta Foreman/25 12.00 30.00
20 James Conner/99 12.00 30.00
21 Jamaal Williams/99 6.00 15.00
22 Joe Williams/99 6.00 15.00
23 O.J. Howard/25 12.00 30.00
24 Evan Engram/99 8.00 20.00
25 Mike Williams/25 15.00 40.00
26 John Ross III/25 12.00 30.00
27 Corey Davis/25 15.00 40.00
28 JuJu Smith-Schuster/25 25.00 60.00
29 Dede Westbrook/25 10.00 25.00
30 Curtis Samuel/25 12.00 30.00
31 Amara Darboh/99 6.00 15.00
32 Carlos Henderson/99 6.00 15.00
33 Zay Jones/25 12.00 30.00
34 Cooper Kupp/99 10.00 25.00
35 ArDarius Stewart/99 6.00 15.00
36 Chris Godwin/99 8.00 20.00
37 Taywan Taylor/99 6.00 15.00
38 Kenny Golladay/99 10.00 25.00
39 Mack Hollins/99 6.00 15.00
40 Josh Reynolds/99 6.00 15.00
41 Carson Wentz/15 125.00 250.00
42 Jordan Howard/15 20.00 50.00
43 Ezekiel Elliott/15 50.00 100.00
44 Sterling Shepard/15 15.00 40.00
45 Jared Goff/15 30.00 60.00
46 Derrick Henry/15 15.00 40.00
47 Paxton Lynch/15 12.00 30.00
48 Michael Thomas/15 20.00 50.00

2017 Immaculate Collection Pro Bowl Swatches

*PRIME/15-20: .5X TO 1.2X BASIC JSY/25
*PRIME/25: .4X TO 1X BASIC JSY/30
1 Andy Dalton/15 6.00 15.00
2 Alex Smith/15 6.00 15.00
3 Philip Rivers/25 6.00 15.00
4 Kirk Cousins/25 6.00 15.00
5 Drew Brees/25 6.00 15.00
6 Dak Prescott/25 6.00 15.00
7 DeMarco Murray/25 5.00 12.00
8 Jay Ajayi/25 5.00 12.00
9 Patrick Peterson/25 4.00 10.00
10 Jordan Howard/25 6.00 15.00
11 Ezekiel Elliott/25 8.00 20.00
12 T.Y. Hilton/25 5.00 12.00
13 Demaryius Thomas/25 5.00 12.00
14 Travis Kelce/25 6.00 15.00
15 Delanie Walker/15 5.00 12.00
16 Tyreek Hill/30 6.00 15.00
17 Emmanuel Sanders/25 6.00 15.00
18 Odell Beckham Jr./25 6.00 15.00
19 Doug Baldwin/25 5.00 12.00
20 Dez Bryant/25 6.00 15.00
21 Jimmy Graham/25 6.00 15.00
22 Greg Olsen/25 5.00 12.00
23 Michael Bennett/25 4.00 10.00
24 Harrison Smith/25 4.00 10.00
25 Bobby Wagner/25 4.00 10.00
26 Sean Lee/25 5.00 12.00
27 Richard Sherman/25 6.00 15.00
28 Ryan Shazier/25 4.00 10.00
29 Von Miller/30 5.00 12.00
30 Justin Tucker/25 4.00 10.00

2017 Immaculate Collection Quad Jerseys

1 Wtsn/Kzr/Trbsky/Mhms/49 15.00 40.00
2 Bthrd/Dbbs/Wbb/Ptrmn/25 5.00 12.00
3 Frntte/Gllmn/McCffry/Ck/49 15.00 40.00
4 Wllms/Hnt/Mxn/Wllms/49 10.00 25.00
5 Kmra/Frmn/Prne/Mck/25 10.00 25.00
6 Wllms/Dvs/Rss/Hwrd/49 10.00 25.00
7 Wstbrk/SmthSchstr/Jns/Engrm/25 10.00 25.00

2017 Immaculate Collection Rookie Cleats

2 Deshaun Watson 20.00 50.00
3 DeShone Kizer 5.00 12.00
4 Patrick Mahomes II 100.00 200.00
5 Nathan Peterman 6.00 15.00
6 Davis Webb 5.00 12.00
7 R. Joshua Dobbs 6.00 15.00
8 C.J. Beathard 5.00 12.00
9 Dalvin Cook 10.00 25.00
10 Leonard Fournette 12.00 30.00
11 Christian McCaffrey 10.00 25.00
12 Joe Mixon 10.00 25.00
13 Alvin Kamara 15.00 40.00
14 Marlon Mack 8.00 20.00
15 Samaje Perine 5.00 12.00
16 Wayne Gallman 6.00 15.00
17 Kareem Hunt 12.00 30.00
18 D'Onta Foreman 6.00 15.00
19 Jeremy McNichols 5.00 12.00
20 Jamaal Williams 5.00 12.00
21 Joe Williams 5.00 12.00
22 O.J. Howard 6.00 15.00
23 Mike Williams 8.00 20.00
24 John Ross III 6.00 15.00
25 Corey Davis 10.00 25.00
26 ArDarius Stewart 5.00 12.00
27 Curtis Samuel 6.00 15.00
28 Zay Jones 6.00 15.00
29 JuJu Smith-Schuster 10.00 25.00
30 Cooper Kupp 8.00 20.00

2017 Immaculate Collection Rookie Eye Black Autographs

1 Deshaun Watson/24 100.00 200.00
2 Mitchell Trubisky/25 100.00 200.00
3 DeShone Kizer/49 6.00 15.00
4 Patrick Mahomes II/49 200.00 400.00
5 C.J. Beathard/49 6.00 15.00
6 Davis Webb/49 6.00 15.00
7 Nathan Peterman/99 6.00 15.00
8 R. Joshua Dobbs/99 6.00 15.00
9 Leonard Fournette/25 25.00 60.00
10 Dalvin Cook/49 15.00 40.00
11 Christian McCaffrey/49 15.00 40.00
12 D'Onta Foreman/99 6.00 15.00
13 Alvin Kamara/99 20.00 50.00
14 Samaje Perine/99 5.00 12.00
15 Wayne Gallman/99 6.00 15.00
16 Kareem Hunt/99 10.00 25.00
17 Jeremy McNichols/99 5.00 12.00
18 James Conner/99 10.00 25.00
19 Joe Mixon/99 10.00 25.00
20 Marlon Mack/99 8.00 20.00
21 O.J. Howard/49 8.00 20.00
22 Mike Williams/48 10.00 25.00
23 Corey Davis/99 8.00 20.00
24 John Ross III/99 6.00 15.00
25 JuJu Smith-Schuster/99 12.00 30.00
26 Zay Jones/99 6.00 15.00
27 Curtis Samuel/84 6.00 15.00
28 Dede Westbrook/99 5.00 12.00
29 Carlos Henderson/99 5.00 12.00
30 Chris Godwin/99 6.00 15.00
31 Joe Williams/99 5.00 12.00
32 Cooper Kupp/99 8.00 20.00
33 Amara Darboh/99 5.00 12.00
34 Jamaal Williams/99 5.00 12.00
35 ArDarius Stewart/99 5.00 12.00
36 Kenny Golladay/99 8.00 20.00
37 Josh Reynolds/99 5.00 12.00
38 Taywan Taylor/99 5.00 12.00
39 Mack Hollins/99 5.00 12.00
40 Evan Engram/99 6.00 15.00

2017 Immaculate Collection Rookie Premium Patch Autographs

*PRIME/25: .6X TO 1.5X BASIC JSY AU/99
*PRIME/15: .8X TO 2X BASIC JSY AU/99
1 Deshaun Watson/49 150.00 300.00
2 Mitchell Trubisky/49 75.00 150.00
3 DeShone Kizer/49 8.00 20.00
4 Patrick Mahomes II/49 200.00 400.00
5 Dalvin Cook/49 30.00 80.00
6 Leonard Fournette/49 75.00 150.00
7 Christian McCaffrey/49 60.00 125.00
8 O.J. Howard/49 10.00 25.00
9 Mike Williams/49 12.00 30.00
10 John Ross III/49 10.00 25.00
11 Corey Davis/49 12.00 30.00
12 JuJu Smith-Schuster/49 30.00 60.00
13 Zay Jones/49 10.00 25.00
14 Kareem Hunt/99 15.00 40.00
15 D'Onta Foreman/99 8.00 20.00
17 Joe Mixon/99 12.00 30.00
18 Jamaal Williams/99 6.00 15.00
19 ArDarius Stewart/99 6.00 15.00
20 Kenny Golladay/99 10.00 25.00
21 R. Joshua Dobbs/99 8.00 20.00
22 Dede Westbrook/99 6.00 15.00
23 Amara Darboh/99 6.00 15.00
24 Taywan Taylor/99 6.00 15.00
25 Cooper Kupp/99 10.00 25.00
26 Davis Webb/99 6.00 15.00
27 Joe Williams/99 6.00 15.00
28 Curtis Samuel/99 8.00 20.00
29 Chris Godwin/99 8.00 20.00
30 James Conner/99 30.00 60.00

2017 Immaculate Collection Rookie Signature Patches

*PRIME/25: .6X TO 1.5X BASIC JSY AU/99
*PRIME/15: .8X TO 2X BASIC JSY AU/99
1 Deshaun Watson/49 150.00 300.00
2 Mitchell Trubisky/49 75.00 150.00
3 DeShone Kizer/49 8.00 20.00
4 Patrick Mahomes II/49 200.00 400.00
5 Dalvin Cook/49 30.00 80.00
6 Leonard Fournette/49 75.00 150.00
7 Christian McCaffrey/49 60.00 125.00
8 O.J. Howard/49 10.00 25.00
9 Mike Williams/49 12.00 30.00
10 John Ross III/49 10.00 25.00
11 Corey Davis/49 12.00 30.00
12 JuJu Smith-Schuster/49 20.00 50.00
13 Zay Jones/49 10.00 25.00
14 Kareem Hunt/49 20.00 50.00
15 D'Onta Foreman/49 10.00 25.00
17 Joe Mixon/49 15.00 40.00
18 Jamaal Williams/49 8.00 20.00
19 ArDarius Stewart/49 8.00 20.00
20 Kenny Golladay/99 10.00 25.00
21 Nathan Peterman/99 8.00 20.00
22 C.J. Beathard/99 6.00 15.00
23 Alvin Kamara/99 25.00 60.00

24 Marlon Mack/99 10.00 25.00
25 Samaje Perine/99 6.00 15.00
26 Wayne Gallman/99 8.00 20.00
27 Evan Engram/99 8.00 20.00
28 Carlos Henderson/99 6.00 15.00
29 Mack Hollins/99 6.00 15.00
30 Josh Reynolds/99 6.00 15.00

2017 Immaculate Collection Shadowbox Autographs

1 Bob Lilly/99 12.00 30.00
2 Robert Kelley/99 6.00 15.00
3 Eric Dickerson/15 30.00 60.00
4 Jim McMahon/25 25.00 50.00
5 Tony Romo/15 40.00 80.00
6 Joe Theismann/49 12.00 30.00
7 Steve Atwater/99 12.00 30.00
8 Ty Law/49 12.00 30.00
10 Jevon Kearse/49 8.00 20.00
11 Marshawn Lynch/25 25.00 50.00
12 Mark Brunell/99 8.00 20.00
13 Rich Gannon/99 6.00 15.00
14 Ricky Williams/99 8.00 20.00
15 Sterling Sharpe/49 10.00 25.00
17 Jeff Garcia/99 6.00 15.00
18 Archie Manning/49 10.00 25.00
19 Doug Baldwin/49 10.00 25.00
20 Mike Evans/49 10.00 25.00
22 James Harrison/49 40.00 80.00
23 Tyreek Hill/99 10.00 25.00
24 J.J. Watt/15 30.00 60.00
25 Kirk Cousins/25 40.00 80.00
29 Ezekiel Elliott/25 60.00 125.00

2017 Immaculate Collection Triple Jerseys

1 Dvs/Hnry/Mrta/25 8.00 20.00
2 Prsctt/Brynt/Elltt/49 25.00 50.00
3 Jns/Ryn/Frmn/25 6.00 15.00
4 McCffry/Nwtn/Bnjmn/25 12.00 30.00
5 Evns/Wnstn/Hwrd/25 5.00 12.00
6 Hwrd/Whte/Trbsky/49 10.00 25.00
7 Brwn/Rthlsbrgr/Bll/25 30.00 60.00
8 Grn/Dltn/Mxn/49 6.00 15.00
9 Thms/Lnch/Mllr/25 5.00 12.00
10 Gff/Grly/Kpp/49 5.00 12.00
11 Drbh/Rwls/Wlsn/15 10.00 25.00
12 Hnt/Mhms/Hll/49 8.00 20.00
13 Bsa/Grdn/Wllms/49 5.00 12.00
14 Bckhm/Gllmn/Shprd/15 8.00 20.00
15 Rbnsn/Brtls/Frntte/25 12.00 30.00

2018 Immaculate Collection

1 Tom Brady 8.00 20.00
2 Julian Edelman 3.00 8.00
3 Rob Gronkowski 3.00 8.00
4 LeSean McCoy 3.00 8.00
5 Kelvin Benjamin 2.50 6.00
6 Ryan Tannehill 2.50 6.00
7 Frank Gore 2.50 6.00
8 DeVante Parker 2.50 6.00
9 LaDainian Tomlinson 2.50 6.00
10 Jermaine Kearse 2.00 5.00
11 Robby Anderson 2.00 5.00
12 Ben Roethlisberger 3.00 8.00
13 Le'Veon Bell 2.50 6.00
14 Antonio Brown 3.00 8.00
15 Joe Flacco 2.50 6.00
16 Michael Crabtree 2.00 5.00
17 Terrell Suggs 2.00 5.00
18 Andy Dalton 2.50 6.00
19 A.J. Green 3.00 8.00
20 Joe Mixon 2.50 6.00
21 Tyrod Taylor 2.50 6.00
22 Josh Gordon 2.00 5.00
23 Jarvis Landry 2.50 6.00
24 Blake Bortles 2.00 5.00
25 Jalen Ramsey 2.50 6.00
26 Leonard Fournette 3.00 8.00
27 Marcus Mariota 3.00 8.00
28 Derrick Henry 3.00 8.00
29 Corey Davis 2.50 6.00
30 Andrew Luck 4.00 10.00
31 T.Y. Hilton 2.50 6.00
32 Peyton Manning 6.00 15.00
33 Deshaun Watson 4.00 10.00
34 D'Onta Foreman 2.00 5.00
35 DeAndre Hopkins 2.50 6.00
36 Patrick Mahomes II 8.00 20.00
37 Kareem Hunt 2.50 6.00
38 Tyreek Hill 3.00 8.00
39 Philip Rivers 3.00 8.00
40 Melvin Gordon 2.50 6.00
41 Joey Bosa 3.00 8.00
42 Derek Carr 3.00 8.00
43 Amari Cooper 3.00 8.00
44 Khalil Mack 3.00 8.00
45 Case Keenum 2.50 6.00
46 Von Miller 2.50 6.00
47 Chris Harris Jr. 2.00 5.00
48 Carson Wentz 4.00 10.00
49 Malcolm Jenkins 2.00 5.00
50 Zach Ertz 2.50 6.00
51 Dak Prescott 3.00 8.00
52 Ezekiel Elliott 4.00 10.00
53 Alex Smith 2.50 6.00
54 Jamison Crowder 2.00 5.00
55 Eli Manning 2.50 6.00
56 Odell Beckham Jr. 3.00 8.00
57 Evan Engram 2.00 5.00
58 Kirk Cousins 3.00 8.00
59 Adam Thielen 3.00 8.00
60 Dalvin Cook 2.50 6.00
61 Harrison Smith 3.00 8.00
62 Matthew Stafford 2.50 6.00
63 Golden Tate III 2.00 5.00
64 Aaron Rodgers 6.00 15.00
65 Davante Adams 2.50 6.00
66 Jimmy Graham 3.00 8.00
67 Mitchell Trubisky 3.00 8.00
68 Jordan Howard 3.00 8.00
69 Allen Robinson 2.50 6.00
70 Drew Brees 3.00 8.00
71 Alvin Kamara 2.50 6.00
72 Marshon Lattimore 2.00 5.00
73 Cam Newton 3.00 8.00
74 Christian McCaffrey 3.00 8.00
75 Devin Funchess 2.00 5.00
76 Matt Ryan 2.50 6.00
77 Julio Jones 3.00 8.00
78 Devonta Freeman 2.50 6.00
79 Jameis Winston 2.50 6.00
80 Mike Evans 2.50 6.00
81 Jared Goff 3.00 8.00
82 Todd Gurley II 3.00 8.00
83 Brandin Cooks 2.50 6.00
84 Russell Wilson 4.00 10.00
85 Doug Baldwin 2.50 6.00
86 Kam Chancellor 3.00 8.00
87 David Johnson 3.00 8.00
88 Larry Fitzgerald 2.50 6.00
89 Patrick Peterson 2.00 5.00
90 Jimmy Garoppolo 4.00 10.00
91 Jerick McKinnon 2.00 5.00
92 Pierre Garcon 2.50 6.00
93 Brian Dawkins 3.00 8.00
94 Ed Reed 2.50 6.00
95 Michael Vick 2.50 6.00
96 Joe Montana 8.00 20.00
97 Emmitt Smith 5.00 12.00
98 Jerry Rice 5.00 12.00
99 Barry Sanders 5.00 12.00
100 Randy Moss 2.50 6.00
101 Baker Mayfield JSY AU RC 125.00 250.00
102 Saquon Barkley JSY AU RC EXCH 125.00 250.00
103 Josh Rosen JSY AU RC 40.00 80.00
104 Josh Allen JSY AU RC EXCH 60.00 125.00
105 Bradley Chubb JSY AU RC 8.00 20.00
106 Sam Darnold JSY AU RC 75.00 150.00
107 Mason Rudolph JSY AU RC 12.00 30.00
108 Derrius Guice JSY AU RC 10.00 25.00
109 Calvin Ridley JSY AU RC 12.00 30.00
110 Ronald Jones II JSY AU RC 5.00 12.00
111 Nick Chubb JSY AU RC 30.00 60.00
112 Sony Michel JSY AU RC 30.00 60.00
113 Courtland Sutton JSY AU RC EXCH 8.00 20.00
114 Christian Kirk JSY AU RC 8.00 20.00
115 Anthony Miller JSY AU RC 8.00 20.00
116 Lamar Jackson JSY AU RC 75.00 150.00
117 D.J. Chark Jr. JSY AU RC 6.00 15.00
118 D.J. Moore JSY AU RC 15.00 40.00
119 Mike Gesicki JSY AU RC 6.00 15.00
120 Kyle Lauletta JSY AU RC 10.00 25.00
121 Mike White JSY AU RC 6.00 15.00
122 Mark Walton JSY AU RC 6.00 15.00
123 Royce Freeman JSY AU RC 6.00 15.00
124 Rashaad Penny JSY AU RC 8.00 20.00
125 Kalen Ballage JSY AU RC 6.00 15.00
126 Nyheim Hines JSY AU RC EXCH 6.00 15.00
127 Ito Smith JSY AU RC 6.00 15.00
128 James Washington JSY AU RC 10.00 25.00
129 Keke Coutee JSY AU RC EXCH 6.00 15.00
130 J'Mon Moore JSY AU RC 5.00 12.00
131 Michael Gallup JSY AU RC 15.00 40.00
132 Dante Pettis JSY AU RC 8.00 20.00
133 Jaylen Samuels JSY AU RC 10.00 25.00
134 DaeSean Hamilton JSY AU RC 6.00 15.00
135 Tre'Quan Smith JSY AU RC 8.00 20.00
136 Jaleel Scott JSY AU RC 5.00 12.00
137 Marquez Valdes-Scantling JSY AU RC 6.00 15.00
138 Daurice Fountain JSY AU RC 6.00 15.00
139 Hayden Hurst JSY AU RC EXCH 6.00 15.00
140 Kerryon Johnson JSY AU RC 15.00 40.00
141 Marcell Ateman AU RC 4.00 10.00
142 Braxton Berrios AU RC 3.00 8.00
143 Cedrick Wilson Jr. AU RC 3.00 8.00
144 Jordan Lasley AU RC 3.00 8.00
145 Justin Watson AU RC 4.00 10.00
147 Mark Andrews AU RC 5.00 12.00
148 Dallas Goedert AU RC 4.00 10.00
149 Jordan Wilkins AU RC 4.00 10.00
150 Chase Edmonds AU RC 3.00 8.00
151 John Kelly AU RC 4.00 10.00
152 Logan Woodside AU RC 5.00 12.00
153 Daron Payne AU RC 5.00 12.00
154 Luke Falk AU RC 4.00 10.00
155 Denzel Ward AU RC 8.00 20.00
156 Jaire Alexander AU RC 12.00 30.00
157 Joshua Jackson AU RC 6.00 15.00
158 Duke Dawson AU RC 3.00 8.00
159 Marcus Davenport AU RC EXCH 6.00 15.00
160 Vita Vea AU RC 5.00 12.00
161 Minkah Fitzpatrick AU RC 6.00 15.00
162 Derwin James AU RC 25.00 50.00
163 Leighton Vander Esch AU RC 50.00 100.00
164 Roquan Smith AU RC 10.00 25.00
165 Shaquem Griffin AU RC 12.00 30.00

2018 Immaculate Collection Chad Pennington Shadowbox Autograph

1 Chad Pennington 10.00 25.00

2018 Immaculate Collection Dual Jersey Numbers

1 L.Bell/S.Barkley 15.00 40.00
2 A.Dalton/S.Darnold 12.00 30.00
3 A.Green/C.Ridley 6.00 15.00
4 J.Allen/P.Rivers 8.00 20.00
5 B.Chubb/C.Jones 5.00 12.00
6 J.Reed/M.Gesicki 4.00 10.00
7 M.Rudolph/M.Ryan 6.00 15.00
8 A.Luck/D.Moore 6.00 15.00
9 J.Rosen/R.Wilson 8.00 20.00
10 J.Winston/M.White 4.00 10.00
11 S.Diggs/C.Sutton 5.00 12.00
12 L.Fournette/R.Jones II 5.00 12.00
13 D.Johnson/N.Chubb 6.00 15.00
14 C.Kirk/M.Evans 5.00 12.00
15 N.Hines/P.DiMarco 4.00 10.00
16 L.Jackson/M.Mariota 12.00 30.00
17 D.Chark Jr./D.Funchess 4.00 10.00
18 D.Guice/E.Berry 6.00 15.00
19 M.Gallup/M.Thomas 6.00 15.00
20 C.Newton/S.Michel 6.00 15.00
21 K.Drake/M.Walton 4.00 10.00
22 B.Allen/R.Freeman 4.00 10.00
23 R.Kelley/R.Penny 5.00 12.00
24 D.Cook/K.Ballage 4.00 10.00
25 A.Miller/D.Adams 5.00 12.00
26 I.Smith/T.Gurley II 5.00 12.00
27 J.Washington/N.Agholor 6.00 15.00
28 J.Moore/J.Nelson 4.00 10.00
29 K.Lauletta/R.Tannehill 5.00 12.00
30 D.Pettis/C.Kupp 5.00 12.00

2018 Immaculate Collection Dual Jerseys

1 J.Houston/E.Berry 4.00 10.00
2 A.Kamara/M.Thomas 5.00 12.00
3 R.Williams/K.Ballage 4.00 10.00
4 S.Diggs/A.Thielen 5.00 12.00
5 R.Jones II/W.Dunn 3.00 8.00
6 C.Beasley/M.Gallup 6.00 15.00
7 M.White/D.Prescott 5.00 12.00
8 A.Gates/J.Witten 4.00 10.00
9 D.Johnson/J.Rosen 8.00 20.00
10 M.Trubisky/A.Miller 6.00 15.00
11 E.Manning/S.Barkley 15.00 40.00
12 L.Fournette/F.Taylor 5.00 12.00
13 M.Lynch/R.Penny 5.00 12.00
14 D.Funchess/D.Moore 6.00 15.00
15 C.Ridley/J.Jones 6.00 15.00
16 B.Mayfield/B.Favre 12.00 30.00
17 J.Allen/L.McCoy 8.00 20.00
18 B.Chubb/V.Miller 5.00 12.00
19 D.Thomas/C.Sutton 5.00 12.00
20 A.Luck/D.Fountain 6.00 15.00
21 C.Portis/D.Guice 6.00 15.00
22 J.Moore/D.Adams 4.00 10.00
23 K.Coutee/D.Watson 6.00 15.00
24 D.Prescott/E.Elliott 6.00 15.00
25 K.Johnson/B.Sanders 6.00 15.00
26 J.Flacco/L.Jackson 12.00 30.00
27 A.Dalton/M.Walton 4.00 10.00
28 M.Thomas/T.Smith 5.00 12.00
29 T.Kelce/P.Mahomes II 12.00 30.00
30 R.Penny/R.Wilson 6.00 15.00
31 B.Bortles/D.Chark Jr. 4.00 10.00
32 M.Trubisky/A.Robinson 5.00 12.00
33 J.Flacco/J.Scott 4.00 10.00
34 A.Brown/J.Washington 6.00 15.00
35 T.Watt/B.Keisel 4.00 10.00

2018 Immaculate Collection Eye Black Autographs

1 Tom Brady/15 800.00 1200.00
2 Gilbert Brown/99 6.00 15.00
3 Jackie Slater/99 6.00 15.00
4 Jermaine Kearse/49 8.00 20.00
5 Adam Vinatieri/25 10.00 25.00
6 Drew Pearson/99 8.00 20.00
7 Plaxico Burress/99 6.00 15.00
8 Marshawn Lynch/25 12.00 30.00
9 Lynn Dickey/15 15.00 40.00
10 Steve Bartkowski/15 15.00 40.00
11 Vince Ferragamo/15 50.00 100.00
12 Randall Cunningham/25 25.00 50.00
13 Rod Woodson/25 15.00 40.00
14 Jay Ajayi/25 12.00 30.00
15 Bob Lilly/49 10.00 25.00
16 Dan Bailey/99 6.00 15.00
17 Jack Youngblood/99 6.00 15.00
18 Vinny Testaverde/39 8.00 20.00
19 Tedy Bruschi/25 15.00 40.00
20 Curtis Martin/25 12.00 30.00
21 Ty Law/25 15.00 40.00
22 Mike Singletary/25 15.00 40.00
24 Brian Dawkins/15 40.00 80.00
25 Alejandro Villanueva/25 50.00 100.00
26 Jim Jeffcoat/99 6.00 15.00
27 Emmitt Thomas/99 6.00 15.00
28 Leon Lett/99 6.00 15.00
29 Cris Carter/25 30.00 60.00
30 Deion Sanders/25 25.00 50.00

2018 Immaculate Collection Eye Black Dual Autographs

1 J.Taylor/P.Hornung/15 75.00 150.00
6 K.Warner/I.Bruce/15 50.00 100.00
7 R.Cunningham/R.Jaworski/15
8 E.Elliott/D.Prescott/15 100.00 200.00

2018 Immaculate Collection Eye Black Jersey Autographs

1 Josh Gordon/99 8.00 20.00
2 Melvin Gordon/20 20.00 50.00
3 Vance Johnson/99 8.00 20.00
5 Andre Reed/95 10.00 25.00
6 Paul Hornung/99 12.00 30.00
7 Tony Gonzalez/15 40.00 80.00
10 Ezekiel Elliott/35 60.00 125.00
13 Terrell Davis/25 15.00 40.00
15 Leonard Fournette/15 25.00 60.00
16 LaDainian Tomlinson/15 60.00 125.00
17 Ed Reed/15 50.00 100.00
18 Clay Matthews/15 20.00 50.00
19 Kurt Warner/15 20.00 50.00
20 Larry Johnson/99 8.00 20.00

2018 Immaculate Collection HOF Jerseys

1 Jerry Rice 8.00 20.00
2 Andre Reed 4.00 10.00
3 Brian Dawkins 5.00 12.00
4 Cris Carter 5.00 12.00
5 Dan Marino 10.00 25.00
6 Earl Campbell 5.00 12.00
7 Fran Tarkenton 5.00 12.00
8 Harry Carson 3.00 8.00
9 Howie Long 5.00 12.00
10 Jerome Bettis 5.00 12.00
11 Jim Kelly 5.00 12.00
12 Joe Montana 12.00 30.00
13 Joe Namath 6.00 15.00
14 Dan Hampton 4.00 10.00
15 John Elway 8.00 20.00
16 John Riggins 4.00 10.00
17 Kurt Warner 4.00 10.00
18 LaDainian Tomlinson 4.00 10.00
19 Lance Alworth 4.00 10.00
20 Len Dawson 5.00 12.00
21 Marcus Allen 5.00 12.00
22 Michael Irvin 5.00 12.00
23 Ozzie Newsome 4.00 10.00
24 Marshall Faulk 4.00 10.00
25 Terrell Davis 4.00 10.00
26 Terry Bradshaw 8.00 20.00
27 Thurman Thomas 4.00 10.00

2018 Immaculate Collection Honors Signatures

2 Deshaun Watson 40.00 80.00
3 Drew Brees 150.00 300.00
4 Carson Wentz EXCH 75.00 150.00
5 Luke Kuechly 15.00 40.00

2018 Immaculate Collection Immaculate Moments Autographs

1 Kareem Hunt/25 20.00 50.00
2 Stefon Diggs/25 25.00 50.00
3 Jake Elliott/25 12.00 30.00
4 Tarik Cohen/25 20.00 50.00
5 Patrick Mahomes II/15 200.00 300.00
6 Chris Long/25 15.00 40.00
7 Terrell Davis/15 40.00 80.00
9 LaDainian Tomlinson/15 50.00 100.00
10 Jason Taylor/15 30.00 60.00
11 Morten Andersen/25 10.00 25.00
15 Delanie Walker/25 10.00 25.00
16 Travis Kelce/25 15.00 40.00
18 Matthew Stafford/15 25.00 50.00
19 J.J. Watt/15 75.00 150.00
20 Kyle Rudolph/25 10.00 25.00
21 Eric Berry/25 12.00 30.00
25 Len Dawson/20 20.00 50.00
27 Trent Dilfer/25 10.00 25.00
28 Justin Tucker/25 20.00 50.00
29 Clinton Portis/20 12.00 30.00
30 Adam Vinatieri/20 12.00 30.00
34 Hines Ward/15 30.00 60.00
35 Desmond Howard/15 30.00 60.00
37 Marcus Allen/15 20.00 50.00
41 Bruce Smith/20 15.00 40.00

2018 Immaculate Collection Immaculate Numbers

1 Baker Mayfield/25 25.00 50.00
2 Saquon Barkley/25 20.00 50.00
3 Josh Rosen/25 10.00 25.00
4 Josh Allen/25 10.00 25.00
5 Bradley Chubb/25 6.00 15.00
6 Sam Darnold/25 15.00 40.00
7 Mason Rudolph/25 10.00 25.00
8 Derrius Guice/25 8.00 20.00
9 Calvin Ridley/25 8.00 20.00
10 Ronald Jones II/25 4.00 10.00
11 Nick Chubb/25 12.00 30.00
12 Sony Michel/25 8.00 20.00
13 Courtland Sutton/25 6.00 15.00
14 Christian Kirk/25 6.00 15.00
15 Anthony Miller/25 8.00 20.00
16 Lamar Jackson/25 15.00 40.00
17 D.J. Chark Jr./25 5.00 12.00
18 D.J. Moore/25 8.00 20.00
19 Mike Gesicki/25 5.00 12.00
20 Kyle Lauletta/25 6.00 15.00
21 Mike White/25 5.00 12.00
22 Mark Walton/25 5.00 12.00
23 Royce Freeman/25 5.00 12.00
24 Rashaad Penny/25 6.00 15.00
25 Kalen Ballage/25 5.00 12.00
26 Nyheim Hines/25 5.00 12.00
27 Ito Smith/25 5.00 12.00
28 James Washington/25 8.00 20.00
29 Keke Coutee/25 5.00 12.00
30 J'Mon Moore/25 4.00 10.00
31 Michael Gallup/25 8.00 20.00
32 Dante Pettis/25 6.00 15.00
33 Jaylen Samuels/25 5.00 12.00
34 DaeSean Hamilton/25 5.00 12.00
35 Tre'Quan Smith/25 6.00 15.00
36 Jaleel Scott/25 4.00 10.00
37 Marquez Valdes-Scantling/25 5.00 12.00
38 Daurice Fountain/25 5.00 12.00
39 Hayden Hurst/25 5.00 12.00
40 Kerryon Johnson/25 6.00 15.00
41 Carson Wentz/50 10.00 25.00
42 Cooper Kupp/50 4.00 10.00
43 Mike Williams/50 3.00 8.00
44 Kenyan Drake/50 3.00 8.00
45 Christian McCaffrey/50 5.00 12.00
46 Curtis Samuel/50 3.00 8.00
47 DeVante Parker/50 4.00 10.00
48 Nelson Agholor/50 3.00 8.00
49 Devin Funchess/50 3.00 8.00
50 Corey Davis/47 4.00 10.00
51 LaDainian Tomlinson/50 4.00 10.00
52 Demarcus Robinson/50 3.00 8.00
53 DeSean Jackson/29 5.00 12.00
54 Joey Bosa/50 5.00 12.00
55 Ezekiel Elliott/50 6.00 15.00
56 Alvin Kamara/25 5.00 12.00
57 Kareem Hunt/50 4.00 10.00
58 Jared Goff/50 5.00 12.00
59 Zay Jones/50 3.00 8.00
60 Patrick Mahomes II/50 12.00 30.00
61 Joe Mixon/50 4.00 10.00
62 Ryan Tannehill/50 4.00 10.00
63 Stefon Diggs/50 4.00 10.00
64 Dede Westbrook/50 3.00 8.00
65 O.J. Howard/50 3.00 8.00
66 Marcus Mariota/50 5.00 12.00
67 D'Onta Foreman/50 3.00 8.00
68 David Johnson/50 5.00 12.00
69 Mitchell Trubisky/50 5.00 12.00
70 Devontae Booker/50 3.00 8.00
71 Mike Evans/50 4.00 10.00
72 Tyler Boyd/50 3.00 8.00
73 Sterling Shepard/50 4.00 10.00
74 Jason Witten/50 4.00 10.00
75 Dak Prescott/50 5.00 12.00
76 Reshad Jones/50 3.00 8.00
77 Laquon Treadwell/50 3.00 8.00
78 JuJu Smith-Schuster/50 5.00 12.00
79 Zach Ertz/50 4.00 10.00
80 Ameer Abdullah/49 3.00 8.00
81 Cameron Wake/50 3.00 8.00
82 Josh Doctson/50 3.00 8.00
83 Tevin Coleman/50 3.00 8.00
84 Evan Engram/50 3.00 8.00
85 Jordan Howard/50 5.00 12.00
86 Marqise Lee/50 3.00 8.00
88 Leonard Fournette/50 5.00 12.00
89 Will Fuller V/50 3.00 8.00
90 Tyler Lockett/50 4.00 10.00
91 Duke Johnson Jr./50 3.00 8.00
92 Michael Thomas/50 5.00 12.00
93 James Conner/50 5.00 12.00
94 Dalvin Cook/50 4.00 10.00
95 Davante Adams/50 4.00 10.00
96 Ty Montgomery/50 3.00 8.00
97 Amari Cooper/37 5.00 12.00
98 Jabrill Peppers/32 4.00 10.00
99 Jim Kelly/22 6.00 15.00
100 Pharoh Cooper/50 3.00 8.00

2018 Immaculate Collection Immaculate Numbers Memorabilia

2 Rob Gronkowski/87 4.00 10.00
3 LeSean McCoy/25 6.00 15.00
4 Ryan Tannehill/17 6.00 15.00
5 LaDainian Tomlinson/21 6.00 15.00
7 Le'Veon Bell/26 5.00 12.00
8 Antonio Brown/84 4.00 10.00
10 Terrell Suggs/55 3.00 8.00
12 A.J. Green/18 8.00 20.00
16 Jalen Ramsey/20 6.00 15.00
17 Leonard Fournette/27 6.00 15.00
19 Derrick Henry/22 8.00 20.00
21 Peyton Manning/18 15.00 40.00
24 Patrick Mahomes II/15 20.00 50.00
25 Kareem Hunt/27 5.00 12.00
27 Philip Rivers/17 8.00 20.00
28 Melvin Gordon/28 5.00 12.00
29 Joey Bosa/99 4.00 10.00
31 Khalil Mack/52 5.00 12.00
32 Alejandro Villanueva/78 3.00 8.00
33 Von Miller/58 4.00 10.00
36 Ezekiel Elliott/21 10.00 25.00
41 Adam Thielen/19 8.00 20.00
42 Dalvin Cook/33 5.00 12.00
43 Harrison Smith/22 8.00 20.00
46 Davante Adams/17 6.00 15.00
49 Alvin Kamara/41 5.00 12.00
50 Marshon Lattimore/23 5.00 12.00
52 Christian McCaffrey/22 8.00 20.00
57 Jared Goff/16 8.00 20.00
58 Todd Gurley II/30 6.00 15.00
60 Doug Baldwin/89 3.00 8.00
62 Patrick Peterson/21 5.00 12.00
64 Brian Dawkins/20 8.00 20.00
65 Ed Reed/20 6.00 15.00
67 Joe Montana/16 20.00 50.00
68 Emmitt Smith/22 12.00 30.00
69 Jerry Rice/80 6.00 15.00
70 Barry Sanders/20 12.00 30.00

2018 Immaculate Collection Immaculate Patches

1 Baker Mayfield/23 20.00 50.00
2 Saquon Barkley/25 20.00 50.00
3 Josh Rosen/22 12.00 30.00
4 Josh Allen/22 12.00 30.00
5 Bradley Chubb/25 6.00 15.00
6 Sam Darnold/22 20.00 50.00
7 Mason Rudolph/25 10.00 25.00
8 Derrius Guice/22 10.00 25.00
9 Calvin Ridley/22 10.00 25.00
10 Ronald Jones II/25 4.00 10.00
11 Nick Chubb/23 15.00 40.00
12 Sony Michel/22 10.00 25.00
13 Courtland Sutton/25 6.00 15.00
14 Christian Kirk/22 8.00 20.00
15 Anthony Miller/25 8.00 20.00
16 Lamar Jackson/22 20.00 50.00
18 D.J. Moore/25 8.00 20.00
19 Mike Gesicki/22 6.00 15.00
20 Kyle Lauletta/25 6.00 15.00
21 Mike White/25 5.00 12.00
22 Mark Walton/25 5.00 12.00
23 Royce Freeman/22 6.00 15.00
24 Rashaad Penny/22 8.00 20.00
25 Kalen Ballage/25 5.00 12.00
26 Nyheim Hines/25 5.00 12.00
27 Ito Smith/25 5.00 12.00
28 James Washington/25 8.00 20.00
29 Keke Coutee/25 5.00 12.00
30 J'Mon Moore/25 4.00 10.00
31 Michael Gallup/22 10.00 25.00
32 Dante Pettis/25 6.00 15.00
33 Jaylen Samuels/22 6.00 15.00
34 DaeSean Hamilton/22 6.00 15.00
35 Tre'Quan Smith/25 6.00 15.00
36 Jaleel Scott/22 5.00 12.00
37 Marquez Valdes-Scantling/22 6.00 15.00
38 Daurice Fountain/25 5.00 12.00
39 Hayden Hurst/22 6.00 15.00
40 Kerryon Johnson/25 6.00 15.00
45 Christian McCaffrey/25 6.00 15.00
46 Curtis Samuel/25 4.00 10.00
52 Demarcus Robinson/25 4.00 10.00
55 Ezekiel Elliott/25 8.00 20.00
57 Kareem Hunt/25 5.00 12.00
59 Zay Jones/25 4.00 10.00
60 Patrick Mahomes II/25 15.00 40.00
63 Stefon Diggs/25 5.00 12.00
68 David Johnson/25 6.00 15.00
69 Mitchell Trubisky/25 6.00 15.00
72 Tyler Boyd/25 4.00 10.00
74 Jason Witten/25 5.00 12.00
75 Dak Prescott/25 6.00 15.00
77 Laquon Treadwell/25 4.00 10.00
78 JuJu Smith-Schuster/25 6.00 15.00
82 Josh Doctson/25 4.00 10.00
85 Jordan Howard/25 6.00 15.00
90 Tyler Lockett/25 5.00 12.00
91 Duke Johnson Jr./25 4.00 10.00
93 James Conner/25 6.00 15.00
94 Dalvin Cook/25 5.00 12.00
95 Davante Adams/25 5.00 12.00
96 Ty Montgomery/25 4.00 10.00

2018 Immaculate Collection Immaculate Standard Jerseys

1 Kiko Alonso/49 3.00 8.00
2 Mike Tolbert/49 3.00 8.00
3 Cameron Wake/49 3.00 8.00
4 Cordrea Tankersley/49 3.00 8.00
5 Xavien Howard/49 3.00 8.00
6 Demaryius Thomas/49 4.00 10.00
7 Maliek Collins/49 3.00 8.00
8 Jourdan Lewis/19 5.00 12.00
9 Noah Brown/49 3.00 8.00
10 Terrance Williams/49 3.00 8.00
11 Chidobe Awuzie/34 3.00 8.00
12 Tre'Davious White/49 3.00 8.00
13 Patrick DiMarco/49 3.00 8.00
14 Micah Hyde/49 3.00 8.00
15 Jordan Poyer/44 3.00 8.00
16 Stephon Gilmore/49 3.00 8.00
17 Garett Bolles/49 3.00 8.00
19 DeMarcus Walker/49 3.00 8.00
20 Zay Jones/49 3.00 8.00
21 Kyle Williams/49 3.00 8.00
22 Sammy Watkins/49 5.00 12.00
23 DeVante Parker/49 4.00 10.00
24 Ryan Tannehill/49 4.00 10.00
25 Charles Clay/49 3.00 8.00
26 Kenyan Drake/49 3.00 8.00
27 Giovani Bernard/49 3.00 8.00
28 Blake Bortles/49 3.00 8.00
29 Geno Atkins/49 3.00 8.00
30 Joe Flacco/49 4.00 10.00
31 Tyler Eifert/49 4.00 10.00
32 Willis McGahee/49 3.00 8.00
33 Devontae Booker/49 3.00 8.00
34 LeSean McCoy/49 5.00 12.00
35 Shaq Lawson/49 3.00 8.00
36 Reshad Jones/49 3.00 8.00
37 Joe Mixon/49 4.00 10.00
38 Marqise Lee/49 3.00 8.00
39 Derek Wolfe/49 3.00 8.00
40 Byron Jones/49 3.00 8.00
41 Jeff Heath/49 3.00 8.00
42 Travis Frederick/49 3.00 8.00
43 Brandon McManus/49 3.00 8.00
44 Emmanuel Sanders/49 5.00 12.00
46 Darqueze Dennard/49 3.00 8.00
47 Lorenzo Alexander/49 3.00 8.00
48 Julio Jones/49 5.00 12.00
49 Jerry Hughes/49 3.00 8.00
50 Matt Ryan/49 4.00 10.00
51 Philip Rivers/49 5.00 12.00
53 Telvin Smith/49 3.00 8.00
54 Tyron Smith/49 3.00 8.00
55 Cole Beasley/49 4.00 10.00
56 Nathan Peterman/49 3.00 8.00
57 A.J. Green/49 5.00 12.00
58 Jordan Reed/49 3.00 8.00
59 Charles Harris/49 3.00 8.00
60 Nick Foles/49 4.00 10.00
61 Zack Martin/49 3.00 8.00
62 Myles Jack/49 3.00 8.00
63 Adam Vinatieri/49 3.00 8.00
64 Dan Bailey/49 3.00 8.00
66 Andrew Billings/49 3.00 8.00
67 Bradley Roby/49 3.00 8.00
68 Carlos Dunlap/49 3.00 8.00
69 Chris Hogan/21 5.00 12.00
70 Jarvis Landry/49 4.00 10.00

2018 Immaculate Collection Past and Present Jerseys

1 Baker Mayfield 15.00 40.00
2 Saquon Barkley 20.00 50.00
3 Josh Rosen 10.00 25.00
4 Josh Allen 10.00 25.00
5 Bradley Chubb 6.00 15.00
6 Sam Darnold 15.00 40.00
7 Mason Rudolph 10.00 25.00
8 Derrius Guice 8.00 20.00
9 Calvin Ridley 8.00 20.00
10 Ronald Jones II 4.00 10.00
11 Nick Chubb 12.00 30.00
12 Sony Michel 8.00 20.00
13 Courtland Sutton 6.00 15.00
14 Christian Kirk 6.00 15.00
15 Anthony Miller 8.00 20.00
16 Lamar Jackson 15.00 40.00
17 D.J. Chark Jr. 5.00 12.00
18 D.J. Moore 8.00 20.00
19 Mike Gesicki 5.00 12.00
20 Kyle Lauletta 6.00 15.00
21 Mike White 5.00 12.00
22 Mark Walton 5.00 12.00
24 Rashaad Penny 6.00 15.00
25 Kalen Ballage 5.00 12.00
26 Nyheim Hines 5.00 12.00
27 Ito Smith 5.00 12.00
28 James Washington 8.00 20.00
29 Keke Coutee 5.00 12.00
30 J'Mon Moore 4.00 10.00
31 Michael Gallup 8.00 20.00
32 Dante Pettis 6.00 15.00
33 Jaylen Samuels 5.00 12.00
34 DaeSean Hamilton 5.00 12.00
35 Tre'Quan Smith 6.00 15.00
36 Jaleel Scott 4.00 10.00
37 Marquez Valdes-Scantling 5.00 12.00
38 Daurice Fountain 5.00 12.00
39 Hayden Hurst 5.00 12.00
40 Kerryon Johnson 6.00 15.00

2018 Immaculate Collection Players Collection Material Autographs

1 Baker Mayfield/25 150.00 300.00
2 Saquon Barkley/25 60.00 350.00
3 Josh Rosen/25 50.00 100.00
4 Josh Allen/25 EXCH 75.00 150.00
5 Bradley Chubb/25 12.00 30.00
7 Mason Rudolph/49 15.00 40.00
8 Derrius Guice/25 15.00 40.00
9 Calvin Ridley/15 25.00 60.00
10 Ronald Jones II/99 5.00 12.00
11 Nick Chubb/49 20.00 50.00
12 Sony Michel/49 20.00 50.00
13 Courtland Sutton/49 EXCH 10.00 25.00
14 Christian Kirk/25 12.00 30.00
15 Anthony Miller/99 8.00 20.00
17 D.J. Chark Jr./49 8.00 20.00
18 D.J. Moore/25 15.00 40.00
19 Mike Gesicki/25 10.00 25.00
20 Kyle Lauletta/25 12.00 30.00
21 Mike White/25 10.00 25.00
22 Mark Walton/99 6.00 15.00
23 Royce Freeman/25 10.00 25.00
24 Rashaad Penny/49 10.00 25.00
25 Kalen Ballage/99 6.00 15.00
26 Nyheim Hines/99 EXCH 6.00 15.00
27 Ito Smith/99 6.00 15.00
28 James Washington/99 10.00 25.00
29 Keke Coutee/99 6.00 15.00
30 J'Mon Moore/99 5.00 12.00
31 Michael Gallup/25 15.00 40.00
32 Dante Pettis/49 10.00 25.00
33 Jaylen Samuels/99 6.00 15.00
34 DaeSean Hamilton/25 10.00 25.00
35 Tre'Quan Smith/99 8.00 20.00
36 Jaleel Scott/99 5.00 12.00
37 Marquez Valdes-Scantling/25 10.00 25.00
38 Daurice Fountain/99 6.00 15.00
39 Hayden Hurst/25 EXCH 10.00 25.00
40 Kerryon Johnson/99 8.00 20.00
41 Patrick Mahomes II/25 150.00 300.00
43 O.J. Howard/49 10.00 25.00
44 Kareem Hunt/49 20.00 50.00
45 JuJu Smith-Schuster/49 30.00 60.00
46 T.J. Watt/49 20.00 50.00
47 Stefon Diggs/25 15.00 40.00
48 Ezekiel Elliott/49 60.00 125.00
49 Joe Mixon/49 12.00 30.00
50 Corey Davis/49 12.00 30.00

2018 Immaculate Collection Premium Patch Autographs

1 Ozzie Newsome/99 10.00 25.00
2 Adam Thielen/25 75.00 150.00
4 Patrick Mahomes II/25 150.00 300.00
8 David Johnson/25 20.00 50.00
9 Mitchell Trubisky/25 50.00 100.00
10 Chris Thompson/59 10.00 25.00
11 Rod Woodson/49 15.00 40.00
12 Devin Funchess/49 10.00 25.00
16 Travis Kelce/49 15.00 40.00
18 Lamar Miller/49 10.00 25.00
19 Eric Dickerson/49 40.00 80.00
21 Dan Bailey/49 10.00 25.00
22 Warren Moon/25 30.00 60.00
23 Dak Prescott/25
25 Tedy Bruschi/25 20.00 50.00
27 John Randle/25 30.00 60.00
28 O.J. Howard/99 8.00 20.00
29 T.J. Watt/99 15.00 40.00
30 Devin Hester/19 30.00 60.00
31 Harry Carson/99 8.00 20.00
32 Ezekiel Elliott/25 75.00 150.00
33 Deshaun Watson/25 50.00 100.00
35 Marlon Mack/99 8.00 20.00
37 Plaxico Burress/46 10.00 25.00
38 Stefon Diggs/49 12.00 30.00
41 Jurrell Casey/99 8.00 20.00
42 Nelson Agholor/99 8.00 20.00
43 Derrick Henry/25 20.00 50.00
46 Greg Olsen/49
49 Terry Bradshaw/25 60.00 125.00

2018 Immaculate Collection Quad Jerseys

1 Sttn/Hmltn/Frmn/Chbb 8.00 20.00
2 Rsn/Drnld/Myfld/Alln 15.00 40.00
3 Hnt/Mhms/Hll/Klce 15.00 40.00
4 Cpr/Crr/Mck/Lnch 6.00 15.00
5 Chbb/Pnny/Mchl/Brkly 20.00 50.00
6 Sttn/Ptts/Rdly/Mre 8.00 20.00
7 Chbb/Drnld/Myfld/Brkly 20.00 50.00
8 Kmra/Elltt/Frntte/Brkly 20.00 50.00
9 Gff/Wntz/Mrta/Drnld 15.00 40.00
10 Smls/Jcksn/Hrst/Rdlph 15.00 40.00

2018 Immaculate Collection Records Autographs

1 Chandler Jones/25 10.00 25.00
2 Christian McCaffrey/25 30.00 60.00
7 JuJu Smith-Schuster/25 20.00 40.00
10 Eric Dickerson/15 30.00 60.00
11 LaDainian Tomlinson/15 50.00 100.00
14 Bruce Smith/15 15.00 40.00
15 Paul Krause/25 10.00 25.00
16 Kareem Hunt/25 20.00 50.00
19 Kyle Rudolph/25 10.00 25.00

2018 Immaculate Collection Rookie Eye Black Jersey Autographs

1 Derrius Guice/99 10.00 25.00
2 Ronald Jones II/99 5.00 12.00
3 Rashaad Penny/99 8.00 20.00
4 Dante Pettis/99 8.00 20.00
5 James Washington/99 10.00 25.00
6 Jaylen Samuels/99 6.00 15.00
7 Mason Rudolph/99 12.00 30.00
8 Sam Darnold/25 75.00 350.00
9 Kyle Lauletta/99 8.00 20.00
10 Saquon Barkley/25 60.00 350.00
11 Tre'Quan Smith/99 8.00 20.00
12 Sony Michel/99 15.00 40.00
13 Kalen Ballage/99 6.00 15.00
14 Mike Gesicki/99 6.00 15.00
15 D.J. Chark Jr./99 6.00 15.00
16 Daurice Fountain/99 6.00 15.00
17 Nyheim Hines/99 EXCH 6.00 15.00
18 Keke Coutee/99 6.00 15.00
19 J'Mon Moore/99 5.00 12.00
20 Marquez Valdes-Scantling/99 6.00 15.00
21 Kerryon Johnson/99 8.00 20.00
22 Bradley Chubb/99 8.00 20.00
23 Courtland Sutton/99 8.00 20.00
24 DaeSean Hamilton/99 6.00 15.00
25 Royce Freeman/99 6.00 15.00
26 Michael Gallup/99 10.00 25.00
27 Mike White/99 6.00 15.00
28 Baker Mayfield/20 150.00 300.00
29 Nick Chubb/94 15.00 40.00
30 Mark Walton/99 6.00 15.00
31 Anthony Miller/99 8.00 20.00
32 D.J. Moore/99 10.00 25.00
33 Josh Allen/25 75.00 150.00
34 Hayden Hurst/99 6.00 15.00
35 Jaleel Scott/99 5.00 12.00
36 Lamar Jackson/25 75.00 150.00
37 Calvin Ridley/45 15.00 40.00
38 Ito Smith/99 6.00 15.00
39 Christian Kirk/99 8.00 20.00
40 Josh Rosen/25 50.00 100.00

2018 Immaculate Collection Rookie Premium Patch Autographs

1 Saquon Barkley/99 40.00 250.00
2 Sam Darnold/35 60.00 300.00
3 Calvin Ridley/35 15.00 40.00
4 Josh Allen/99 EXCH 50.00 100.00
5 Bradley Chubb/35 10.00 25.00
6 Baker Mayfield/99 125.00 200.00
7 Mason Rudolph/99 12.00 30.00
8 D.J. Moore/99 10.00 25.00
9 Josh Rosen/99 30.00 60.00
10 Mike White/35 8.00 20.00
11 Courtland Sutton/99 EXCH 8.00 20.00
12 Ronald Jones II/99 5.00 12.00
13 Nick Chubb/99 15.00 40.00
14 Christian Kirk/35 10.00 25.00
15 Nyheim Hines/99 EXCH 6.00 15.00
16 Lamar Jackson/35 60.00 125.00
17 D.J. Chark Jr./35 8.00 20.00
18 Derrius Guice/35 12.00 30.00
19 Michael Gallup/35 12.00 30.00
20 Sony Michel/99 15.00 40.00
21 Mark Walton/99 6.00 15.00
22 Royce Freeman/35 8.00 20.00
23 Rashaad Penny/99 8.00 20.00
24 Kalen Ballage/99 6.00 15.00
25 Anthony Miller/99 8.00 20.00
26 Ito Smith/99 6.00 15.00
27 James Washington/99 10.00 25.00
28 J'Mon Moore/99 5.00 12.00
29 Kyle Lauletta/35 10.00 25.00
30 Dante Pettis/99 8.00 20.00

2018 Immaculate Collection Rookie Signature Patches

1 Ronald Jones II/99 5.00 12.00
2 Nick Chubb/99 15.00 40.00
3 Josh Rosen/99 30.00 60.00
4 Josh Allen/99 EXCH 50.00 100.00
5 Baker Mayfield/99 125.00 200.00
6 Sam Darnold/35 60.00 300.00
7 Mason Rudolph/99 12.00 30.00
8 Derrius Guice/35 12.00 30.00
9 Tre'Quan Smith/99 8.00 20.00
10 Bradley Chubb/35 10.00 25.00
11 Saquon Barkley/99 40.00 250.00
12 Sony Michel/99 15.00 40.00
13 Courtland Sutton/99 EXCH 8.00 20.00
14 J'Mon Moore/99 5.00 12.00
15 Royce Freeman/35 8.00 20.00
16 D.J. Moore/99 10.00 25.00
17 Kyle Lauletta/35 10.00 25.00
18 Anthony Miller/99 8.00 20.00
19 Calvin Ridley/35 15.00 40.00
20 Rashaad Penny/99 8.00 20.00
21 Kalen Ballage/99 6.00 15.00
22 James Washington/99 10.00 25.00
23 Keke Coutee/99 6.00 15.00
24 Christian Kirk/35 10.00 25.00
25 Michael Gallup/35 12.00 30.00
26 Dante Pettis/99 8.00 20.00
27 Jaylen Samuels/99 6.00 15.00
28 DaeSean Hamilton/35 8.00 20.00
29 Mike White/35 8.00 20.00
30 Marquez Valdes-Scantling/35 8.00 20.00

2018 Immaculate Collection Shadowbox Autographs

1 Patrick Mahomes II/25 150.00 250.00
4 T.J. Watt/99 12.00 30.00
5 Tedy Bruschi/15 20.00 50.00
6 Trent Dilfer/99 6.00 15.00
7 Adam Thielen/25 60.00 125.00
8 Rodney Harrison/15 15.00 40.00
9 Stefon Diggs/25 12.00 30.00
10 Fletcher Cox/99 6.00 15.00
11 Ken Anderson/99 6.00 15.00
12 Joe Mixon/99 8.00 20.00
13 Deion Branch/15 12.00 30.00
22 Eric Berry/99 8.00 20.00
25 Travis Kelce/25 15.00 40.00
27 JuJu Smith-Schuster/25 20.00 50.00
28 Kyle Rudolph/99 6.00 15.00
30 Marvin Jones Jr./25 10.00 25.00

2018 Immaculate Collection Signature Moves

1 Ezekiel Elliott 100.00 200.00
2 Tyreek Hill EXCH 15.00 40.00
3 Antonio Brown EXCH 40.00 80.00
4 Ty Law 15.00 40.00
5 Devin Hester 30.00 60.00

2018 Immaculate Collection Triple Jerseys

1 Smls/Wshngtn/Rdlph 10.00 25.00
2 Chbb/Sttn/Frmn 8.00 20.00
3 Hrst/Sctt/Jcksn 15.00 40.00
4 Myfld/Rsn/Drnld 15.00 40.00
5 Mchl/Pnny/Brkly 20.00 50.00
6 Rdly/Sttn/Mre 8.00 20.00
7 Smth/Smth/Jns 6.00 15.00
8 Elltt/Brkly/Gce 20.00 50.00
9 Wltn/Cnnr/Chbb 12.00 30.00
10 Elltt/Prsctt/Gllp 8.00 20.00
11 Hwrd/Trbsky/Mllr 8.00 20.00
12 Krk/Jhnsn/Rsn 10.00 25.00
13 McCy/Alln/Bnjmn 10.00 25.00
14 Drke/Prkr/Tnnhll 5.00 12.00
15 Bldwn/Pnny/Wlsn 8.00 20.00

2016 Immaculate Collection Collegiate

1 A.J. Green 2.50 6.00
2 Aaron Rodgers 5.00 12.00
3 Adrian Peterson 2.50 6.00
4 Amari Cooper 2.50 6.00
5 Ameer Abdullah 1.50 4.00
6 Andrew Luck 3.00 8.00
7 Andy Dalton 2.00 5.00
8 Barry Sanders 4.00 10.00
9 Ben Roethlisberger 2.50 6.00
10 Bo Jackson 3.00 8.00
11 Cam Newton 2.50 6.00
12 Cameron Artis-Payne 1.50 4.00
13 Charles Woodson 2.50 6.00
14 Colin Kaepernick 2.00 5.00
15 Dan Marino 5.00 12.00
16 David Johnson 2.50 6.00
17 Deion Sanders 2.00 5.00
18 DeMarco Murray 2.00 5.00
19 Devin Funchess 1.50 4.00
20 Devin Smith 1.50 4.00
21 Dez Bryant 2.50 6.00
22 Drew Brees 2.50 6.00
23 Duke Johnson 1.50 4.00
24 Earl Campbell 2.50 6.00
25 Eddie Lacy 1.50 4.00
26 Eli Manning 2.00 5.00
27 J.J. Watt 2.50 6.00
28 Jamaal Charles 2.00 5.00
29 Jameis Winston 2.50 6.00
30 Jamison Crowder 1.50 4.00
31 Jason Witten 2.00 5.00
32 Jeremy Langford 2.00 5.00
33 Jimmy Graham 2.50 6.00
34 Joe Flacco 2.00 5.00
35 Joe Namath 3.00 8.00
36 John Elway 4.00 10.00
37 Karlos Williams 1.50 4.00
38 LeSean McCoy 2.50 6.00
39 Le'Veon Bell 2.00 5.00
40 Marcus Mariota 2.50 6.00
41 Matt Jones 2.00 5.00
42 Melvin Gordon 2.00 5.00
43 Nelson Agholor 1.50 4.00
44 Odell Beckham Jr. 2.50 6.00
45 Peyton Manning 5.00 12.00
46 Phillip Dorsett 1.50 4.00
47 Rob Gronkowski 2.50 6.00
48 Russell Wilson 3.00 8.00
49 T.J. Yeldon 1.50 4.00
50 Thomas Rawls 1.50 4.00
51 Tim Tebow 2.50 6.00
52 Todd Gurley 2.50 6.00
53 Tom Brady 6.00 15.00
54 Tony Romo 2.00 5.00
55 Tyler Lockett 2.00 5.00
56 Allen Hurns/25 AU 5.00 12.00
57 Cody Kessler/99 AU 3.00 8.00
58 Anquan Boldin/25 AU 5.00 12.00
60 Brian Bosworth/44 AU 12.00 30.00
62 Bob Lilly/72 AU 5.00 12.00
64 DeAndre Washington/99 AU 3.00 8.00
65 Kevin Hogan/99 AU 4.00 10.00
67 Devin Hester/25 AU 6.00 15.00
68 Drew Brees/15 AU 30.00 60.00
69 Wendell Smallwood/99 AU 3.00 8.00
70 Earl Campbell/25 AU 30.00 60.00
72 Emmanuel Sanders/25 AU 8.00 20.00
73 Emmitt Smith/22 AU 100.00 200.00
75 Fred Biletnikoff/25 AU 10.00 25.00
78 Chris Moore/99 AU 4.00 10.00
81 Keenan Reynolds/99 AU 4.00 10.00
82 Kellen Winslow/83 AU 4.00 10.00
83 Kelvin Benjamin/25 AU 6.00 15.00
84 Lance Alworth/23 AU 50.00 100.00
85 Demarcus Robinson/99 AU 3.00 8.00
86 Latavius Murray/28 AU 5.00 12.00
87 Lawrence Taylor/25 AU 8.00 20.00
88 Lenny Moore/25 AU 5.00 12.00
89 Floyd Little/44 AU 4.00 10.00
90 George Rogers/25 AU 5.00 12.00
94 Melvin Gordon/25 AU 6.00 15.00
96 Philip Rivers/17 AU 12.00 30.00
98 Ricky Williams/25 AU 15.00 40.00
99 Russell Wilson/16 AU 40.00 80.00
100 T.J. Yeldon/25 AU 5.00 12.00
101 Joey Bosa AU RC 6.00 15.00
102 Jared Goff AU RC 30.00 60.00
103 Laquon Treadwell AU RC 4.00 10.00
104 Carson Wentz AU RC 50.00 100.00
105 Ezekiel Elliott AU RC 75.00 150.00
106 Paxton Lynch AU RC 3.00 8.00
107 Corey Coleman AU RC 5.00 12.00
108 Connor Cook AU RC 4.00 10.00
109 Hunter Henry AU RC 4.00 10.00
110 Michael Thomas AU RC 6.00 15.00
111 Josh Doctson AU RC 4.00 10.00
112 Derrick Henry AU RC 8.00 20.00
113 Tyler Boyd AU RC 4.00 10.00
114 Austin Hooper AU RC 3.00 8.00
115 Pharoh Cooper AU RC 3.00 8.00

116 Alex Collins AU RC 4.00 10.00
118 Kenneth Dixon AU RC 3.00 8.00
119 Christian Hackenberg AU RC 3.00 8.00
120 Sterling Shepard AU RC 4.00 10.00
121 Devontae Booker AU RC 4.00 10.00
122 Braxton Miller AU RC 3.00 8.00
123 Jordan Howard AU RC 8.00 20.00
124 Kenny Lawler AU RC 5.00 12.00
125 Kenyan Drake AU RC 5.00 12.00
126 Leonte Carroo AU RC 3.00 8.00
127 De'Runnya Wilson AU RC 3.00 8.00
128 Nick Vannett AU RC 3.00 8.00
129 Paul Perkins AU RC 3.00 8.00
130 Bralon Addison AU RC 3.00 8.00
131 Aaron Burbridge AU RC 3.00 8.00
132 Dak Prescott AU RC 50.00 100.00
133 Jonathan Williams AU RC 4.00 10.00
134 Keyarris Garrett AU RC 3.00 8.00
135 Kelvin Taylor AU RC 3.00 8.00
136 Malcolm Mitchell AU RC 3.00 8.00
137 Ricardo Louis AU RC 3.00 8.00
138 Cardale Jones AU RC 6.00 15.00
139 Jeff Driskel AU RC 3.00 8.00
140 Josh Ferguson AU RC 3.00 8.00
141 Kolby Listenbee AU RC 3.00 8.00
142 Aaron Green AU RC 3.00 8.00
143 Keith Marshall AU RC 3.00 8.00
145 Jordan Payton AU RC 3.00 8.00
146 Daniel Lasco AU RC 3.00 8.00
147 Tyler Ervin AU RC 3.00 8.00
148 Daniel Braverman AU RC 3.00 8.00
149 Jalen Ramsey AU RC 5.00 12.00
151 Teddy Bridgewater/25 AU 6.00 15.00
155 Trevor Davis/99 AU 3.00 8.00
157 Y.A. Tittle/25 AU 8.00 20.00

2016 Immaculate Collection Collegiate Gold

*GOLD/25: .6X TO 1.5X BASIC AU/99

2016 Immaculate Collection Collegiate Red

*VETS/25: .6X TO 1.5X BASIC CARDS/99
*GOLD AU/25: .6X TO 1.5X BASIC AU/99
*GOLD AU/25: .5X TO 1.2X BASIC AU/44-72

2016 Immaculate Collection Collegiate Immaculate Gloves

2 Jared Goff/26 15.00 40.00
3 Ezekiel Elliott/26 20.00 50.00
4 Paxton Lynch/25 3.00 8.00
5 Will Fuller V/26 4.00 10.00
6 Laquon Treadwell/16 5.00 12.00
7 Josh Doctson/25 4.00 10.00
8 Connor Cook/42 3.00 8.00
9 Corey Coleman/32 4.00 10.00
10 Michael Thomas/26 5.00 12.00
11 Derrick Henry/26 6.00 15.00
12 Sterling Shepard/36 3.00 8.00
13 Cardale Jones/20 4.00 10.00
14 Hunter Henry/16 5.00 12.00
15 Christian Hackenberg/32 2.50 6.00
16 Kenneth Dixon/34 2.50 6.00
17 Alex Collins/36 3.00 8.00
18 C.J. Prosise/26 2.50 6.00
19 Braxton Miller/26 2.50 6.00
20 Pharoh Cooper/16 4.00 10.00
21 Wendell Smallwood/36 2.50 6.00
22 Devontae Booker/16 5.00 12.00
23 Dak Prescott/16 20.00 50.00
24 Leonte Carroo/16 4.00 10.00
25 Jordan Howard/23 8.00 20.00
26 Trevor Davis/38 2.50 6.00
27 Tyler Ervin/16 4.00 10.00
28 Malcolm Mitchell/26 2.50 6.00
29 Paul Perkins/16 4.00 10.00
31 Cody Kessler/46 2.50 6.00
32 Jonathan Williams/16 5.00 12.00
33 Kevin Hogan/25 4.00 10.00
34 Kenyan Drake/23 5.00 12.00
35 Ricardo Louis/42 2.50 6.00
36 Tyler Boyd/38 3.00 8.00
37 Demarcus Robinson/36 2.50 6.00
38 Keenan Reynolds/42 3.00 8.00
39 Chris Moore/27 3.00 8.00
40 Joey Bosa/26 5.00 12.00

2016 Immaculate Collection Collegiate Immaculate Helmets

1 Jared Goff 15.00 40.00
2 Carson Wentz 25.00 60.00
3 Ezekiel Elliott 12.00 30.00
4 Laquon Treadwell 3.00 8.00
5 Paxton Lynch 2.50 6.00
6 Josh Doctson 3.00 8.00
7 Michael Thomas 5.00 12.00
8 Corey Coleman 4.00 10.00
9 Derrick Henry 6.00 15.00
11 Sterling Shepard 3.00 8.00
12 Kenneth Dixon 2.50 6.00
13 Braxton Miller 2.50 6.00
14 Alex Collins 3.00 8.00
15 Paul Perkins 2.50 6.00
16 Hunter Henry 3.00 8.00
17 Jacoby Brissett 3.00 8.00
18 Dak Prescott 12.00 30.00
19 Pharoh Cooper 2.50 6.00
20 Devontae Booker 3.00 8.00

2016 Immaculate Collection Collegiate Immaculate INK

4 John Elway 50.00 100.00
5 Aaron Rodgers 125.00 250.00
7 Brett Favre 50.00 100.00
12 Jerry Rice 40.00 80.00
13 Dan Marino 50.00 100.00
16 Troy Aikman 40.00 80.00
17 Barry Sanders
18 Peyton Manning 100.00 200.00
19 Bo Jackson 40.00 80.00
23 Tim Tebow 60.00 125.00
24 Andrew Luck
26 Drew Brees
ES Emmitt Smith 75.00 150.00
Issued in '17 Immaculate Collegiate

2016 Immaculate Collection Collegiate Immaculate Jumbo Jerseys

*NUMBERS/25: .6X TO 1.5X BASIC JSY/99
*NUMBERS/25: .8X TO 2X BASIC JSY/99
1 Carson Wentz 20.00 50.00
2 Jared Goff 12.00 30.00
3 Ezekiel Elliott 10.00 25.00
5 Will Fuller V 3.00 8.00
6 Laquon Treadwell 2.50 6.00
7 Josh Doctson 2.50 6.00
8 Connor Cook 2.50 6.00
9 Corey Coleman 3.00 8.00
10 Michael Thomas 4.00 10.00
11 Derrick Henry 5.00 12.00
12 Sterling Shepard 2.50 6.00
13 Cardale Jones 2.00 5.00
14 Hunter Henry 2.50 6.00
15 Christian Hackenberg 2.00 5.00
16 Kenneth Dixon 2.00 5.00
17 Alex Collins 2.50 6.00
18 C.J. Prosise 2.00 5.00
19 Braxton Miller 2.00 5.00
20 Pharoh Cooper 2.00 5.00
21 Wendell Smallwood 2.00 5.00
22 Devontae Booker 2.50 6.00
23 Dak Prescott 10.00 25.00
24 Leonte Carroo 2.00 5.00
25 Jordan Howard 5.00 12.00
26 Trevor Davis 2.00 5.00
27 Ricardo Louis 2.00 5.00
28 Malcolm Mitchell 2.00 5.00
29 Paul Perkins 2.00 5.00
30 Jacoby Brissett 2.50 6.00
31 Cody Kessler 2.00 5.00
32 Jonathan Williams 2.50 6.00
33 Kevin Hogan 2.50 6.00
34 Kenyan Drake 3.00 8.00
35 Kelvin Taylor 2.00 5.00
36 Tyler Boyd 2.50 6.00
37 Demarcus Robinson 2.00 5.00
38 Keenan Reynolds 2.50 6.00
39 Chris Moore 2.50 6.00
40 Joey Bosa 4.00 10.00

2016 Immaculate Collection Collegiate Immaculate Signature Patches Gold

*GOLD/25: .6X TO 1.5X BASIC JSY AU/99
*GOLD/25: .5X TO 1.2X BASIC JSY AU/49
105 Ezekiel Elliott 150.00 300.00
132 Dak Prescott 60.00 150.00

2016 Immaculate Collection Collegiate Material Combos

*PRIME/25: .6X TO 1.5X BASIC JSY/99
1 D.Henry/K.Drake/99 6.00 15.00
2 A.McCarron/A.Cooper/99 4.00 10.00
3 J.Jones/A.Cooper/49 5.00 12.00
4 N.Foles/R.Gronkowski/25 6.00 15.00
5 C.Jones/S.Wright/25 4.00 10.00
6 B.Petty/C.Coleman/99 4.00 10.00
7 A.Rodgers/J.Goff/25 25.00 60.00
8 A.Ellington/D.Hopkins/25 5.00 12.00
9 G.Grayson/R.Higgins/99 2.50 6.00
10 K.Taylor/M.Jones/99 3.00 8.00
11 D.Parker/T.Brdgwtr/99 3.00 8.00
12 J.Hill/O.Beckham/99 4.00 10.00
13 G.Olsen/J.Graham/25 6.00 15.00
14 P.Dorsett/D.Johnson/99 2.50 6.00
15 A.Burbridge/C.Cook/99 3.00 8.00
16 D.Funchess/T.Rawls/49 3.00 8.00
17 D.Prescott/D.Wilson/99 12.00 30.00
18 J.Bellino/R.Staubach/25 8.00 20.00
19 C.Jones/E.Elliott/99 12.00 30.00
20 D.Moncrief/L.Treadwell/99 3.00 8.00
21 M.Mariota/V.Adams/20 8.00 20.00
22 A.Robinson/C.Hcknbrg/99 3.00 8.00
23 M.Faulk/R.Hillman/99 3.00 8.00
24 E.Sanders/E.Dickerson/99 4.00 10.00
25 A.Luck/J.Elway/25 10.00 25.00
26 A.Luck/R.Sherman/25 8.00 20.00
27 B.Allen/N.Agholor/99 2.50 6.00
29 J.Payton/P.Perkins/99 2.50 6.00
30 C.Kessler/T.Madden/99 2.50 6.00
31 N.Sudfeld/J.Howard/99 6.00 15.00
32 D.Robinson/K.Taylor/99 2.50 6.00
33 A.Hooper/K.Hogan/99 3.00 8.00
34 D.Smith/M.Thomas/99 5.00 12.00
35 J.Winston/J.Goff/99 15.00 40.00
36 C.Wentz/M.Mariota/99 25.00 60.00
37 E.Elliott/T.Gurley/99 12.00 30.00
39 D.Henry/M.Gordon/99 6.00 15.00
40 L.Treadwell/ACooper/99 4.00 10.00
41 A.Cooper/D.Carr/99 4.00 10.00
42 B.Osweiler/D.Hopkins/25 5.00 12.00
43 S.Watkins/T.Taylor/99 4.00 10.00
44 M.Evans/J.Winston/99 4.00 10.00
45 S.Diggs/T.Bridgewater/99 3.00 8.00
46 J.Goff/T.Gurley/99 15.00 40.00
47 E.Lacy/A.Rodgers/25 12.00 30.00

2016 Immaculate Collection Collegiate Material Quads

*PRIME/25: .6X TO 1.5X BASIC JSY/99
1 Lcy/Drke/Hnry/Yldn/25 8.00 20.00
2 Cllns/Alln/Wllms/Hnry/99 3.00 8.00
3 Sdfld/Ltmr/Hwrd/Clmn/99 6.00 15.00
4 Brbrdge/Lngfrd/Ck/Bll/99 3.00 8.00
5 Jns/Ellt/Thms/Mllr/99 12.00 30.00
6 Addsn/Mrta/Mrshll/Bcknr/99 4.00 10.00
7 Dctsn/Lstnbe/Bykn/Grn/99 3.00 8.00
8 Plmr/Ksslr/Brkly/Snchz/99 3.00 8.00
9 Mllr/Drke/Prkns/Clmn/99 4.00 10.00
10 Wntz/Wnstn/Gff/Mrta/99 25.00 60.00
11 Hnry/ Elltt/Grdn/Grly/99 12.00 30.00
12 Whte/Whte/Trdwll/Cpr/99 4.00 10.00

2016 Immaculate Collection Collegiate Material Trios

*PRIME/25: .6X TO 1.5X BASIC JSY/99
*PRIME/25: .5X TO 1.2X BASIC JSY/49
1 Hnry/Yldn/Lcy/25 10.00 25.00
2 Oswlr/Fstr/Strng/99 3.00 8.00
3 Lsco/Gff/Lwlr/99 15.00 40.00
4 Alln/Jcksn/Lwlr/49 5.00 12.00
5 Frmn/Bnjmn/Wllms/99 3.00 8.00
6 Crr/Wllr/Adms/99 4.00 10.00
7 Cnly/Grly/Mtchll/99 4.00 10.00
8 Hnry/Wnstn/Mrta/99 6.00 15.00
9 Bllno/Rynlds/Stbch/25 8.00 20.00
10 Jns/Thms/Smth/99 5.00 12.00
11 Addsn/Mrta/Mrshll/99 4.00 10.00
12 Hpr/Cjste/Hgn/99 3.00 8.00
13 Lck/Elwy/Shrmn/25 10.00 25.00
14 Hgn/Lck/Elwy/25 10.00 25.00
15 Hndly/Pytn/Prkns/99 2.50 6.00
16 Clmn/Bckhm/Lcktt/99 4.00 10.00

2016 Immaculate Collection Collegiate Patch Autographs

101 Joey Bosa/99 10.00 25.00
102 Jared Goff/99 30.00 80.00
103 Laquon Treadwell/99 6.00 15.00
104 Carson Wentz/99 50.00 100.00
105 Ezekiel Elliott/99 100.00 200.00
106 Will Fuller V/99 8.00 20.00
107 Corey Coleman/99 8.00 20.00
108 Connor Cook/99 6.00 15.00
109 Hunter Henry/99 6.00 15.00
110 Michael Thomas/99 10.00 25.00
111 Josh Doctson/99 6.00 15.00
112 Derrick Henry/49 15.00 40.00
114 Austin Hooper/49 6.00 15.00
115 Pharoh Cooper/99 5.00 12.00
116 Alex Collins/99 6.00 15.00
118 Kenneth Dixon/99 5.00 12.00
119 Christian Hackenberg/99 5.00 12.00
120 Sterling Shepard/99 6.00 15.00
121 Devontae Booker/99 6.00 15.00
122 Braxton Miller/99 5.00 12.00
123 Jordan Howard/99 12.00 30.00
125 Kenyan Drake/99 8.00 20.00
126 Leonte Carroo/99 5.00 12.00
127 De'Runnya Wilson/99 5.00 12.00
128 Kolby Listenbee/99 5.00 12.00
129 Paul Perkins/99 5.00 12.00
130 Daniel Lasco/99 5.00 12.00
131 Aaron Burbridge/99 5.00 12.00
132 Dak Prescott/99 60.00 125.00
133 Jonathan Williams/99 6.00 15.00
134 Keyarris Garrett/99 5.00 12.00
135 Kelvin Taylor/99 5.00 12.00
136 Malcolm Mitchell/99 5.00 12.00
137 Jordan Payton/99 5.00 12.00
138 Cardale Jones/99 5.00 12.00
139 C.J. Prosise/99 5.00 12.00
140 Josh Ferguson/99 5.00 12.00

2016 Immaculate Collection Collegiate Patch Autographs Gold

*GOLD/25: .6X TO 1.5X BASIC JSY AU/99
*GOLD/25: .5X TO 1.2X BASIC JSY AU/49
105 Ezekiel Elliott 150.00 150.00

2016 Immaculate Collection Collegiate Premium Patches Autographs

101 Devontae Booker/99 6.00 15.00
102 Jared Goff/99 30.00 80.00
103 Laquon Treadwell/99 6.00 15.00
104 Carson Wentz/99 50.00 100.00
105 Ezekiel Elliott/99 150.00 250.00
106 Will Fuller V/99 8.00 20.00
107 Corey Coleman/99 8.00 20.00
108 Connor Cook/99 6.00 15.00
109 Hunter Henry/99 6.00 15.00
110 Michael Thomas/99 10.00 25.00
111 Josh Doctson/99 6.00 15.00
112 Derrick Henry/25 20.00 50.00
114 Austin Hooper/25 8.00 20.00
115 Pharoh Cooper/99 5.00 12.00
116 Alex Collins/99 6.00 15.00
118 Kenneth Dixon/99 5.00 12.00
119 Christian Hackenberg/99 5.00 12.00
120 Sterling Shepard/99 6.00 15.00

2017 Immaculate Collection Collegiate

1 Aaron Rodgers 5.00 12.00
2 Andrew Luck 3.00 8.00
3 Barry Sanders 4.00 10.00
4 Bo Jackson 3.00 8.00
5 Brett Favre 5.00 12.00
6 Carson Wentz 3.00 8.00
7 Dak Prescott 2.50 6.00
8 Dan Marino 5.00 12.00
9 Derrick Henry 2.00 5.00
10 Emmitt Smith 4.00 10.00
11 Ezekiel Elliott 3.00 8.00
12 Jared Goff 2.50 6.00
13 Jerry Rice 4.00 10.00
14 Jim Thorpe 3.00 8.00
15 Joe Namath 3.00 8.00
16 Joey Bosa 2.50 6.00
17 John Elway 4.00 10.00
18 Marcus Mariota 2.50 6.00
19 Odell Beckham Jr. 2.50 6.00
20 Paxton Lynch 1.50 4.00
21 Peyton Manning 5.00 12.00
22 Red Grange 3.00 8.00
23 Russell Wilson 3.00 8.00
24 Tim Tebow 2.50 6.00
25 Tom Brady 6.00 15.00
27 Adrian Peterson JSY/28 5.00 12.00
30 Bobby Layne JSY/22 6.00 15.00
34 Elroy Crazy Legs Hirsch JSY/40 3.00 8.00
35 Eric Dickerson JSY/19 8.00 20.00
36 Ernie Davis JSY/44 15.00 40.00
37 Gale Sayers JSY/48 8.00 20.00
38 Ezekiel Elliott JSY/15 10.00 25.00
40 Jared Goff JSY/16 8.00 20.00
41 Joey Bosa JSY/97 3.00 8.00
42 John Hannah JSY/73 2.00 5.00
45 Knute Rockne JSY/25 25.00 50.00
47 Le'Veon Bell JSY/24 6.00 15.00
48 Marcus Allen JSY/33 4.00 10.00
50 Marshall Faulk JSY/28 4.00 10.00
51 Norm Van Brocklin JSY/25 5.00 12.00
52 Peyton Manning JSY/16 40.00 80.00
54 Rob Gronkowski JSY/48 4.00 10.00
55 Rod Woodson JSY/26 4.00 10.00
56 Roger Staubach JSY/12
57 Thomas Rawls JSY/38 2.50 6.00
58 Thurman Thomas JSY/34 4.00 10.00
84 Thomas Rawls AU/49 15.00 40.00
101 David Njoku AU/99 RC 4.00 10.00
102 Alvin Kamara AU/99 RC 30.00 60.00
103 Marlon Mack AU/99 RC 5.00 12.00
104 Taywan Taylor AU/99 RC 3.00 8.00
105 Carlos Henderson AU/99 RC 3.00 8.00
106 Nathan Peterman AU/99 RC 4.00 10.00
107 Matthew Dayes AU/99 RC 3.00 8.00
108 Josh Malone AU/99 RC 3.00 8.00
109 Brian Hill AU/99 RC 3.00 8.00
110 KD Cannon AU/99 RC 3.00 8.00
111 Dalvin Cook JSY AU/99 RC 60.00 125.00
112 Mike Williams JSY AU/99 RC 8.00 20.00
113 Leonard Fournette JSY AU/99 RC 40.00 80.00
114 Mitchell Trubisky JSY AU/99 RC 50.00 100.00
115 Deshaun Watson JSY AU/99 RC 100.00 200.00
116 Corey Davis JSY AU/99 RC 8.00 20.00
117 John Ross III JSY AU/99 RC 6.00 15.00
118 Christian McCaffrey JSY AU/49 RC 50.00 100.00
119 JuJu Smith-Schuster JSY AU/99 RC 12.00 30.00
120 DeShone Kizer JSY AU/99 RC 12.00 30.00
121 Dede Westbrook JSY AU/99 RC 5.00 12.00
122 Cooper Kupp JSY AU/99 RC 8.00 20.00
123 Curtis Samuel JSY AU/99 RC 6.00 15.00
124 D'Onta Foreman JSY AU/99 RC 6.00 15.00
125 Amara Darboh JSY AU/99 RC 5.00 12.00
126 Isaiah Ford JSY AU/99 RC 5.00 12.00
127 Zay Jones JSY AU/99 RC 6.00 15.00
128 Malachi Dupre JSY AU/99 RC 5.00 12.00
129 Patrick Mahomes II JSY AU/99 RC 200.00 400.00
130 Samaje Perine JSY AU/99 RC 5.00 12.00
131 Brad Kaaya JSY AU/99 RC 5.00 12.00
132 Chris Godwin JSY AU/99 RC 6.00 15.00
133 Joe Mixon JSY AU/99 RC 10.00 25.00
134 Noah Brown JSY AU/99 RC 6.00 15.00
135 Artavis Scott JSY AU/99 RC 5.00 12.00
136 Wayne Gallman JSY AU/99 RC 6.00 15.00
137 Kareem Hunt JSY AU/99 RC 15.00 40.00
138 Stacy Coley JSY AU/99 RC 5.00 12.00
139 Jeremy McNichols JSY AU/99 RC 5.00 12.00
140 Corey Clement JSY AU/99 RC 6.00 15.00
141 Davis Webb JSY AU/99 RC 5.00 12.00
142 Ryan Switzer JSY AU/99 RC 6.00 15.00
143 James Conner JSY AU/99 RC 10.00 25.00
144 Donnel Pumphrey JSY AU/99 RC 6.00 15.00
145 Chad Kelly JSY AU/99 RC 5.00 12.00
146 O.J. Howard JSY AU/99 RC 6.00 15.00
148 Evan Engram JSY AU/99 RC 6.00 15.00
149 Jordan Leggett JSY AU/99 RC 5.00 12.00
150 Jake Butt JSY AU/99 RC 12.00 30.00
151 Alvin Kamara JSY AU/99 RC 40.00 80.00
152 Elijah McGuire JSY AU/99 RC 5.00 12.00
153 Travis Rudolph JSY AU/99 RC 5.00 12.00
154 Travin Dural JSY AU/99 RC 6.00 15.00
155 Josh Reynolds JSY AU/99 RC 5.00 12.00
156 Jerod Evans JSY AU/99 RC 6.00 15.00
157 R. Joshua Dobbs JSY AU/99 RC 6.00 15.00
158 Chad Hansen JSY AU/99 RC 10.00 25.00
159 ArDarius Stewart JSY AU/99 RC 5.00 12.00

2017 Immaculate Collection Collegiate Red

*RED/30: .6X TO 1.5X BASIC CARDS/99
*RED/25: .5X TO 1.2X BASIC AU/49

2017 Immaculate Collection Collegiate Premium Rookie Patch Autographs

*PATCH/99: .4X TO 1X BASIC JSY AU/99
*PATCH/25: .6X TO 1.5X BASIC JSY AU/99
*PATCH/25: .5X TO 1.2X BASIC JSY AU/49
118 Christian McCaffrey/25 75.00 150.00
129 Patrick Mahomes II/99 200.00 400.00

2017 Immaculate Collection Collegiate Premium Rookie Patch Autographs Gold

*GOLD/25: .6X TO 1.5X BASIC JSY AU/99
113 Leonard Fournette/25 100.00 200.00
115 Deshaun Watson/25 150.00 250.00

2017 Immaculate Collection Collegiate Helmets Team Logos

3 Leonard Fournette/42 50.00 100.00
4 Mitchell Trubisky/23 25.00 60.00
7 Christian McCaffrey/17 12.00 30.00
13 Alvin Kamara/19 25.00 50.00
18 C.J. Beathard/18 30.00 60.00

2017 Immaculate Collection Collegiate Immaculate Dual Autographs

1 D.Watson/M.Williams 75.00 150.00
2 M.Dupre/L.Fournette 40.00 80.00
3 M.Trubisky/R.Switzer 75.00 150.00
4 J.Watt/T.Watt 100.00 200.00
5 B.Sims/S.Perine 50.00 100.00

2017 Immaculate Collection Collegiate Immaculate Helmets

1 Dalvin Cook 8.00 20.00
2 Mike Williams 5.00 12.00
3 Leonard Fournette 15.00 40.00
4 Mitchell Trubisky 15.00 40.00
5 Corey Davis 5.00 12.00
6 John Ross III 4.00 10.00
7 Christian McCaffrey 8.00 20.00
8 Deshaun Watson 25.00 50.00
10 Dede Westbrook 3.00 8.00
11 Cooper Kupp 5.00 12.00
12 Joe Mixon 6.00 15.00
13 Alvin Kamara 12.00 30.00
14 D'Onta Foreman 4.00 10.00
15 Patrick Mahomes II 40.00 100.00
16 JuJu Smith-Schuster 8.00 20.00
17 Amara Darboh 40.00 80.00
18 C.J. Beathard 3.00 8.00
20 Samaje Perine 3.00 8.00

2017 Immaculate Collection Collegiate Immaculate INK

2 Dak Prescott 30.00 80.00
3 Brett Favre 50.00 100.00
4 Peyton Manning 90.00 150.00
5 Emmitt Smith

2017 Immaculate Collection Collegiate Immaculate Jumbo Jerseys

*NUMBER/25: .5X TO 1.2X BASIC JSY/49
1 Dalvin Cook 5.00 12.00
2 Mike Williams 3.00 8.00
3 Leonard Fournette 10.00 25.00
4 O.J. Howard 2.50 6.00
5 Mitchell Trubisky 10.00 25.00
6 Jabrill Peppers 3.00 8.00
7 Corey Davis 3.00 8.00
8 John Ross III 2.50 6.00
9 DeShone Kizer 2.00 5.00
10 Christian McCaffrey 5.00 12.00
11 Deshaun Watson 12.00 30.00
12 Evan Engram 2.50 6.00
13 Curtis Samuel 2.50 6.00
14 Dede Westbrook 2.00 5.00
15 Cooper Kupp 3.00 8.00
16 Malachi Dupre 2.00 5.00
17 Alvin Kamara 8.00 20.00
18 Isaiah Ford 2.00 5.00
19 Patrick Mahomes II 25.00 60.00
20 JuJu Smith-Schuster 5.00 12.00

2017 Immaculate Collection Collegiate Immaculate Signature Patches

4 Adrian Peterson 40.00 100.00

2017 Immaculate Collection Collegiate Immaculate Triple Autographs

1 McCffry/Ck/Frntte 200.00 350.00
2 Wtsn/Trbsky/Kzr 200.00 300.00
3 Dvs/Rss/Wllms 50.00 100.00
4 Prne/Wstbrk/Mxn 200.00 300.00
5 Ellt/Wtsn/Hwrd 200.00 300.00

2017 Immaculate Collection Collegiate Material Combos

*PRIME/25: .6X TO 1.5X BASIC JSY/99
1 A.Stewart/O.Howard 3.00 8.00
2 C.Samuel/N.Brown 3.00 8.00
3 C.Kelly/E.Engram 3.00 8.00
4 A.Kamara/R.Dobbs 10.00 25.00
5 C.Hansen/D.Webb 2.50 6.00
6 J.Conner/N.Peterman 5.00 12.00
7 D.Cook/T.Rudolph 6.00 15.00
8 E.Elliott/D.Prescott 12.00 30.00
9 E.Elliott/J.Bosa 5.00 12.00
10 C.Samuel/E.Elliott 5.00 12.00

2017 Immaculate Collection Collegiate Material Quads

1 Sctt/Wtsn/Lggtt/Wllms 15.00 40.00
2 Drbh/Btt/Ppprs/Chssn 25.00 60.00
3 Ck/Wnstn/Bnjmn/Rdlph 6.00 15.00
4 Drl/Frntte/Dpre/Bckhm 15.00 40.00
5 Cpr/Hnry/Hwrd/Stwrt 4.00 10.00
6 McCffry/Hgn/Mntgmry/Hpr 6.00 15.00
7 Bsa/Brwn/Sml/Ellt 5.00 12.00
8 Wstbrk/Mxn/Prne/Shprd 5.00 12.00
9 Kzr/Wtsn/Trbsky/Mhms 15.00 40.00
10 Kmra/Ck/McCffry/Frntte 15.00 40.00

2017 Immaculate Collection Collegiate Material Trios

*PRIME/25: .6X TO 1.5X BASIC JSY/99
1 Frntte/Dpre/Drl 15.00 40.00
2 Wstbrk/Mxn/Prne 5.00 12.00
3 Swtzr/Hd/Trbsky 12.00 30.00
6 Hnsn/Gff/Wbb 4.00 10.00
7 Engrm/Trdwll/Klly 3.00 8.00
8 Cnnr/Ptrmn/Byd 5.00 12.00
9 Rss/Dvs/Wllms 4.00 10.00
10 Wstbrk/Kpp/Sml 4.00 10.00

2017 Immaculate Collection Collegiate Rookie Premiere Player Caps

3 Leonard Fournette/19
6 Corey Davis/16 10.00 25.00

2018 Immaculate Collection Collegiate

1 Aaron Rodgers 5.00 12.00
2 Lamar Jackson 10.00 25.00
3 Barry Sanders 4.00 10.00
4 Brett Favre 5.00 12.00
5 Brian Bosworth 2.00 5.00
6 Brian Urlacher 2.50 6.00
7 Calvin Johnson 2.50 6.00
8 Charles Woodson 2.50 6.00
9 Clay Matthews 2.00 5.00
10 Dak Prescott 2.50 6.00
11 Dan Marino 5.00 12.00
12 Equanimeous St. Brown 2.50 6.00
13 Derek Carr 2.50 6.00
14 Derrick Henry 2.50 6.00
15 Earl "Dutch" Clark 2.00 5.00
16 Eddie George 2.00 5.00
17 Ezekiel Elliott 3.00 8.00
18 Emmitt Smith 4.00 10.00
19 Herschel Walker 2.50 6.00
20 J.J. Watt 2.50 6.00
21 Jerry Rice 4.00 10.00
22 Joe Namath 3.00 8.00
23 John Elway 4.00 10.00
24 Julio Jones 2.50 6.00
25 LaDainian Tomlinson 2.00 5.00
26 Leonard Fournette 2.50 6.00
27 Marcus Allen 2.50 6.00
28 Nick Foles 2.00 5.00
29 Odell Beckham Jr. 2.50 6.00
30 Peyton Manning 5.00 12.00
31 Red Grange 3.00 8.00
32 Russell Wilson 3.00 8.00
33 Tim Tebow 2.50 6.00
34 Todd Gurley II 2.50 6.00
35 Tom Brady 6.00 15.00
41 Eric Dickerson JSY/19 8.00 20.00
42 Ezekiel Elliott JSY/15 10.00 25.00
43 Herschel Walker JSY/34 10.00 25.00
44 Jared Goff JSY/16 8.00 20.00
45 Joey Bosa JSY/97 3.00 8.00
47 John Hannah JSY/73 2.00 5.00
50 Le'Veon Bell JSY/24 6.00 15.00
52 Marcus Allen JSY/33 5.00 12.00
54 Marshall Faulk JSY/28 4.00 10.00
57 Ricky Williams JSY/34 4.00 10.00
58 Rob Gronkowski JSY/48 4.00 10.00
74 Kyle Lauletta AU/49 6.00 15.00
75 Lamar Jackson AU/25 100.00 200.00
85 Tre'Quan Smith AU/49 6.00 15.00
101 Josh Rosen JSY AU/49 RC 20.00 50.00
102 Sam Darnold JSY AU/49 RC 40.00 100.00
103 Josh Allen JSY AU/49 RC 25.00 60.00
105 Baker Mayfield JSY AU/49 RC 75.00 150.00
106 Saquon Barkley JSY AU/25 RC 225.00 350.00
107 Derrius Guice JSY AU/49 RC 12.00 30.00
108 D.J. Moore JSY AU/99 RC 10.00 25.00
109 Mike White JSY AU/99 RC 6.00 15.00
110 Nick Chubb JSY AU/99 RC 15.00 40.00
111 Mason Rudolph JSY AU/49 RC 15.00 40.00
112 Ronald Jones II JSY AU/99 RC 5.00 12.00
113 Christian Kirk JSY AU/49 RC 10.00 25.00
114 Calvin Ridley JSY AU/49 RC 15.00 40.00
115 James Washington JSY AU/99 RC 10.00 25.00
116 Courtland Sutton JSY AU/99 RC 8.00 20.00
117 Deon Cain JSY AU/99 RC 6.00 15.00
119 Dante Pettis JSY AU/99 RC 8.00 20.00
120 D.J. Chark JSY AU/99 RC 6.00 15.00
121 Allen Lazard JSY AU/99 RC 5.00 12.00
122 Anthony Miller JSY AU/99 RC 8.00 20.00
123 Luke Falk JSY AU/99 RC 6.00 15.00
124 Rashaad Penny JSY AU/99 RC 8.00 20.00
126 Nyheim Hines JSY AU/99 RC 6.00 15.00
127 Deontay Burnett JSY AU/99 RC 6.00 15.00
128 Michael Gallup JSY AU/99 RC 10.00 25.00
129 Josh Adams JSY AU/49 RC 12.00 30.00
130 Kerryon Johnson JSY AU/99 RC 8.00 20.00
131 Trey Quinn JSY AU/99 RC 5.00 12.00
132 Sony Michel JSY AU/99 RC 15.00 40.00
133 Auden Tate JSY AU/99 RC 5.00 12.00
134 Royce Freeman JSY AU/99 RC 6.00 15.00
135 John Kelly JSY AU/99 RC 6.00 15.00
136 Bo Scarbrough JSY AU/99 RC 6.00 15.00
138 Marcell Ateman JSY AU/99 RC 6.00 15.00
139 Akrum Wadley JSY AU/99 RC 5.00 12.00
140 Justin Jackson JSY AU/99 RC 6.00 15.00
142 Jaylen Samuels JSY AU/99 RC 6.00 15.00
143 Kalen Ballage JSY AU/99 RC 6.00 15.00
144 Kamryn Pettway JSY AU/99 RC 8.00 20.00
145 J'Mon Moore JSY AU/99 RC 5.00 12.00
147 Robert Foster JSY AU/99 RC 5.00 12.00
148 Kurt Benkert JSY AU/99 RC 6.00 15.00
149 Riley Ferguson JSY AU/99 RC 8.00 20.00
151 Jaleel Scott AU/99 RC 3.00 8.00
152 Dallas Goedert AU/99 RC 4.00 10.00
154 Mike Gesicki AU/99 RC 4.00 10.00
155 Jordan Lasley AU/99 RC 3.00 8.00
156 Mike White AU/99 RC 4.00 10.00
157 Jake Wieneke AU/99 RC 4.00 10.00
158 Quadree Henderson AU/99 RC 4.00 10.00
159 Cedrick Wilson Jr. AU/99 RC 3.00 8.00
160 Javon Wims AU/99 RC 3.00 8.00
161 Richie James AU/99 RC 3.00 8.00
162 DaeSean Hamilton AU/99 RC 4.00 10.00
163 Darren Carrington II AU/99 RC 4.00 10.00
164 Kyle Lauletta AU/99 RC 5.00 12.00
165 Keke Coutee AU/99 RC 4.00 10.00

2018 Immaculate Collection Collegiate Premium Rookie Patch Autographs

*PREMIUM/99: .3X TO .8X BASIC JSY AU/49
*PREMIUM/99: .4X TO 1X BASIC JSY AU/99
*PREMIUM/49: .5X TO 1.2X BASIC JSY AU/99
*PREMIUM/25: .5X TO 1.2X BASIC JSY AU/49
*PREMIUM/25: .4X TO 1X BASIC JSY AU/25
105 Baker Mayfield/99 75.00 150.00

2018 Immaculate Collection Collegiate Premium Rookie Patch Autographs Gold

*PREM GOLD/25: .6X TO 1.5X BASIC JSY AU/99
*PREM GOLD/25: .5X TO 1.2X BASIC JSY AU/49
103 Josh Allen/25 75.00 150.00

2018 Immaculate Collection Collegiate Red

*VETS/49: .5X TO 1.2X BASIC CARDS/99
*RED AU/25: .5X TO 1.2X BASIC AU/49
*RED AU/15: .5X TO 1.2X BASIC AU/25
75 Lamar Jackson AU/15 125.00 250.00

2018 Immaculate Collection Collegiate '17 Update

1 Aaron Rodgers/25 8.00 20.00
4 Ezekiel Elliott/25 5.00 12.00
7 Emmitt Smith/25 6.00 15.00
10 Herschel Walker/49 3.00 8.00
11 Herschel Walker/25 4.00 10.00
13 Herschel Walker/25 4.00 10.00
16 Herschel Walker/25 4.00 10.00
19 DeMarco Murray/25 3.00 8.00
22 Jim Brown/24 6.00 15.00

2018 Immaculate Collection Collegiate Combo Materials

1 K.Pettway/K.Johnson 4.00 10.00
2 N.Chubb/S.Michel 6.00 15.00
3 D.Guice/D.Chark 5.00 12.00
4 A.Miller/R.Ferguson 4.00 10.00
5 J.Samuels/N.Hines 3.00 8.00
6 B.Mayfield/M.Andrews 10.00 25.00
7 S.Barkley/D.Hamilton 12.00 30.00
8 C.Sutton/T.Quinn 4.00 10.00
9 A.Kamara/J.Kelly 3.00 8.00
10 D.Guice/L.Fournette 5.00 12.00
11 D.Pettis/J.Ross 4.00 10.00
12 P.Mahomes/N.Shimonek 10.00 25.00
13 A.Tate/D.Cook 3.00 8.00
14 C.Beathard/A.Wadley 2.50 6.00
15 C.Kirk/J.Reynolds 4.00 10.00
16 D.Pumphrey/R.Penny 4.00 10.00

2018 Immaculate Collection Collegiate Immaculate Cleats

1 Sam Darnold/19 20.00 50.00
2 Josh Rosen/26 12.00 30.00
3 Baker Mayfield/22 20.00 50.00
4 Josh Allen/18 15.00 40.00
8 Christian Kirk/16 8.00 20.00
9 Derrius Guice/16 10.00 25.00
10 Ronald Jones II/16 5.00 12.00
11 Courtland Sutton/18 8.00 20.00
12 Mason Rudolph/15 12.00 30.00
13 Kerryon Johnson/22 8.00 20.00
14 Sony Michel/18 12.00 30.00
15 Rashaad Penny/18 8.00 20.00
16 James Washington/40 8.00 20.00
17 D.J. Chark/17 6.00 15.00
18 Anthony Miller/22 8.00 20.00
19 D.J. Moore/16 15.00 40.00
20 Mike White/31 5.00 12.00
21 Nick Chubb/20 12.00 30.00
22 Nyheim Hines/16 6.00 15.00
25 Kalen Ballage/22 6.00 15.00
26 Jaylen Samuels/18 6.00 15.00
27 Dante Pettis/20 8.00 20.00
29 DaeSean Hamilton/20 12.00 30.00
30 Kyle Lauletta/16 8.00 20.00
31 Mark Walton/26 5.00 12.00
34 Hayden Hurst/22 12.00 30.00
35 Royce Freeman/18 12.00 30.00

2018 Immaculate Collection Collegiate Immaculate Dual Autographs

1 S.Michel/N.Chubb 40.00 100.00
2 D.Guice/D.Chark 25.00 60.00
3 K.Pettway/K.Johnson 20.00 50.00
5 J.Washington/M.Rudolph 30.00 80.00
6 C.Sutton/T.Quinn 20.00 50.00
7 J.Rosen/J.Lasley 40.00 100.00
8 A.Miller/R.Ferguson 20.00 50.00
9 J.Samuels/N.Hines 15.00 40.00
10 B.Scarbrough/C.Ridley 30.00 80.00

2018 Immaculate Collection Collegiate Immaculate Gloves

*PRIME/72-92: .4X TO 1X BASIC GLOVE/60
*PRIME/72-92: .3X TO .8X BASIC GLOVE/40-52
*PRIME/54: .4X TO 1X BASIC GLOVE/39
*PRIME/32: .6X TO 1.5X BASIC GLOVE/99
*PRIME/20: .8X TO 2X BASIC GLOVE/99
1 Sam Darnold/99 15.00 40.00
2 Josh Rosen/48 10.00 25.00
3 Baker Mayfield/48 12.00 30.00
4 Josh Allen/99 10.00 25.00
5 Lamar Jackson/40 20.00 50.00
6 Saquon Barkley/52 25.00 60.00
7 Calvin Ridley/48 8.00 20.00
8 Christian Kirk/99 4.00 10.00
9 Derrius Guice/48 6.00 15.00
10 Ronald Jones II/99 2.50 6.00
11 Courtland Sutton/52 5.00 12.00
12 Mason Rudolph/52 8.00 20.00
13 Kerryon Johnson/48 5.00 12.00
14 Sony Michel/48 8.00 20.00
15 Rashaad Penny/78 4.00 10.00
16 James Washington/39 6.00 15.00
17 D.J. Chark/48 4.00 10.00
18 Anthony Miller/52 5.00 12.00
19 D.J. Moore/99 5.00 12.00
20 Mike White/44 4.00 10.00
21 Nick Chubb/48 8.00 20.00
22 Nyheim Hines/44 4.00 10.00
23 Keke Coutee/48 4.00 10.00
24 Jaleel Scott/48 3.00 8.00
25 Kalen Ballage/99 3.00 8.00
26 Jaylen Samuels/41 4.00 10.00
27 Dante Pettis/48 5.00 12.00
28 Michael Gallup/52 6.00 15.00
29 DaeSean Hamilton/99 3.00 8.00
30 Kyle Lauletta/40 5.00 12.00
31 Mark Walton/40 4.00 10.00
32 J'Mon Moore/32 3.00 8.00
33 Tre'Quan Smith/32 5.00 12.00
34 Hayden Hurst/99 3.00 8.00
35 Royce Freeman/60 3.00 8.00

2018 Immaculate Collection Collegiate Immaculate Helmets Team Logo

5 Lamar Jackson/30 25.00 60.00
7 Calvin Ridley/19 12.00 30.00
9 Derrius Guice/28 8.00 20.00
11 Courtland Sutton/20 8.00 20.00
13 Kerryon Johnson/22 8.00 20.00
14 Sony Michel/18 15.00 40.00
17 D.J. Chark/26 5.00 12.00
19 D.J. Moore/28 8.00 20.00
21 Nick Chubb/18 15.00 40.00
22 Nyheim Hines/15 6.00 15.00
23 Dante Pettis/22 8.00 20.00
25 Hayden Hurst/22 6.00 15.00

2018 Immaculate Collection Collegiate Immaculate INK

2 Peyton Manning 100.00 200.00
6 Emmitt Smith 60.00 125.00
7 Jerry Rice 50.00 100.00
8 Ed Reed 12.00 30.00
9 Brett Favre 50.00 100.00
10 Cris Carter 15.00 40.00
11 John Elway EXCH 50.00 100.00
13 Barry Sanders 50.00 100.00
15 Bo Jackson 50.00 100.00

2018 Immaculate Collection Collegiate Immaculate Jumbo Jerseys

*NUMBER/25: .6X TO 1.5X BASIC JSY/99
1 Sam Darnold 10.00 25.00
2 Josh Rosen 10.00 25.00
3 Baker Mayfield 12.00 30.00
4 Josh Allen 8.00 20.00
5 Lamar Jackson 10.00 25.00
6 Saquon Barkley 12.00 30.00
7 Calvin Ridley 6.00 15.00
8 Christian Kirk 4.00 10.00
9 Derrius Guice 5.00 12.00
10 Ronald Jones II 2.50 6.00
11 Courtland Sutton 4.00 10.00
12 Mason Rudolph 6.00 15.00
13 Kerryon Johnson 4.00 10.00
14 Sony Michel 6.00 15.00
15 Rashaad Penny 4.00 10.00
16 James Washington 5.00 12.00
17 D.J. Chark 3.00 8.00
18 Anthony Miller 4.00 10.00
19 D.J. Moore 5.00 12.00
20 Mike White 3.00 8.00
21 Nick Chubb 6.00 15.00
22 Nyheim Hines 3.00 8.00
23 Keke Coutee 3.00 8.00
24 Kalen Ballage 3.00 8.00
25 John Kelly 3.00 8.00
26 Jaylen Samuels 3.00 8.00
27 Dante Pettis 4.00 10.00
28 Michael Gallup 5.00 12.00
29 DaeSean Hamilton 3.00 8.00
30 Kyle Lauletta 4.00 10.00
31 Mark Walton 3.00 8.00
32 J'Mon Moore 2.50 6.00
33 Tre'Quan Smith 4.00 10.00
34 Luke Falk 3.00 8.00
35 Royce Freeman 3.00 8.00

2018 Immaculate Collection Collegiate Immaculate Signature Patches

1 Deshaun Watson 60.00 125.00
2 Leonard Fournette 30.00 60.00
4 Carson Wentz 60.00 125.00
5 Dan Marino 100.00 200.00

2018 Immaculate Collection Collegiate Quad Jerseys

1 Stwrt/Rdly/Scrbrgh/Hwrd 8.00 20.00
2 Cn/Gllmn/Wtsn/Wllms 6.00 15.00
3 Myfld/Prne/Wstbrk/Mxn 12.00 30.00
4 Brntt/Jns/SthSchtr/Drnld 12.00 30.00
5 Myfld/Wstbrk/Wtsn/Jcksn 12.00 30.00
6 Myfld/McCffry/Hnry/Wtsn 12.00 30.00
7 Mrta/Grdn/Cpr/Brrtt 5.00 12.00
8 Myfld/Hnry/Jcksn/Mrta 12.00 30.00

2018 Immaculate Collection Collegiate Triple Jerseys

1 Fstr/Scrbrgh/Rdly 8.00 20.00
2 Wshngtn/Atmn/Rdlph 8.00 20.00
3 Brntt/Drnld/Jns 12.00 30.00
4 Hmltn/Gdwn/Brkly 15.00 40.00
5 Sml/Ellt/Brrtt 6.00 15.00
6 Klly/Dbbs/Kmra 4.00 10.00

2015 Immaculate Collection Collegiate Multisport Premium Patches Autographs

1 Aaron Murray/99 5.00 12.00
3 A.J. McCarron/99 5.00 12.00
4 Allen Robinson/99
5 Andre Williams/75
6 Austin Seferian-Jenkins/99 5.00 12.00
9 Carson Palmer/25
10 Charles Sims/99 5.00 12.00
11 Cody Latimer/99 5.00 12.00
12 Connor Shaw/49
20 Doug Flutie/25
22 Eric Dickerson/25
23 Eric Ebron/99 5.00 12.00
30 Johnny Manziel/99 8.00 20.00
31 Jordan Matthews/49 6.00 15.00
33 Kelvin Benjamin/99
38 Lawrence Taylor/25
41 Marcus Allen/25
43 Marqise Lee/99 5.00 12.00
44 Mike Evans/99 8.00 20.00
49 Rod Woodson/25
54 Tajh Boyd/99 5.00 12.00
55 Teddy Bridgewater/99
58 Tom Savage/99 5.00 12.00
59 Tre Mason/99 5.00 12.00

2015 Immaculate Collection Collegiate Multisport Rookie Patch Autographs

*GOLD/25: .6X TO 1.5X BASIC JSY AU/99
301 Jameis Winston 60.00 125.00
302 Marcus Mariota 40.00 800.00
303 Brett Hundley 25.00 50.00
304 Bryce Petty 6.00 15.00
305 Garrett Grayson 6.00 15.00
306 Sean Mannion 6.00 15.00
307 Todd Gurley 15.00 40.00
308 Melvin Gordon 25.00 50.00
309 Ameer Abdullah 25.00 50.00
310 T.J. Yeldon 5.00 12.00
312 Duke Johnson 5.00 12.00
313 David Johnson 15.00 40.00
314 Matt Jones 8.00 20.00
317 Mike Davis 5.00 12.00
318 David Cobb 5.00 12.00
319 Jay Ajayi 15.00 40.00
320 Amari Cooper 30.00 80.00
321 Kevin White 10.00 25.00
323 Jaelen Strong 6.00 15.00
324 Devin Smith 8.00 20.00
326 Nelson Agholor 5.00 12.00
327 Breshad Perriman 5.00 12.00
328 Devin Funchess 6.00 15.00
329 Maxx Williams 5.00 12.00
330 Tyler Lockett 8.00 20.00
331 Chris Conley 5.00 12.00
332 Sammie Coates 5.00 12.00
333 Ty Montgomery 6.00 15.00
334 Jamison Crowder 6.00 15.00
335 Justin Hardy 5.00 12.00
336 Vince Mayle 5.00 12.00
337 Rashad Greene 6.00 15.00
340 Dorial Green-Beckham 5.00 12.00

2015 Immaculate Collection Collegiate Multisport Rookie Signature Patches

*GOLD/25: .6X TO 1.5X BASIC JSY AU/99
301 Jameis Winston 60.00 125.00
302 Marcus Mariota 50.00 100.00
303 Brett Hundley 25.00 50.00
304 Bryce Petty 6.00 15.00
305 Garrett Grayson 6.00 15.00
306 Sean Mannion 6.00 15.00
307 Todd Gurley 15.00 40.00
308 Melvin Gordon 25.00 50.00
309 Ameer Abdullah 25.00 50.00
310 T.J. Yeldon 5.00 12.00
312 Duke Johnson 5.00 12.00
313 David Johnson 15.00 40.00
314 Matt Jones 8.00 20.00
317 Mike Davis 5.00 12.00
318 David Cobb 5.00 12.00
319 Jay Ajayi 15.00 40.00
320 Amari Cooper
321 Kevin White 10.00 25.00
323 Jaelen Strong 6.00 15.00
324 Devin Smith 8.00 20.00
326 Nelson Agholor 5.00 12.00
327 Breshad Perriman 5.00 12.00
328 Devin Funchess 6.00 15.00
329 Maxx Williams 5.00 12.00
330 Tyler Lockett 8.00 20.00
331 Chris Conley 5.00 12.00
332 Sammie Coates 5.00 12.00
333 Ty Montgomery 6.00 15.00
334 Jamison Crowder 6.00 15.00
335 Justin Hardy 5.00 12.00
336 Vince Mayle 5.00 12.00
337 Rashad Greene 6.00 15.00
340 Dorial Green-Beckham 5.00 12.00

2015 Immaculate Collection Multisport Autographs

RANDOM INSERTS IN PACKS
PRINT RUNS B/WN 5-25 COPIES PER
NO PRICING ON QTY 10 OR LESS
EXCHANGE DEADLINE 2/26/2017
9 Kevin White/25 12.00 30.00
10 DeVante Parker/25 12.00 30.00

2000 Impact

leased as a 199-card set, this set was numbered 1-200 due to the last minute pulling of card number 137. Base cards are white bordered and feature full color action photos. Impact was packaged in 36-pack boxes with packs containing 10 cards and carried a suggested retail price of $.99.

COMPLETE SET (199) 12.50 30.00
1 Kurt Warner .30 .75
2 Dan Marino .40 1.00
3 Sedrick Irvin .12 .30
4 Chris Redman RC .20 .50
5 Robert Smith .12 .30
6 Amani Toomer .12 .30
7 Richard Huntley .12 .30
8 Ahman Green .15 .40
9 Fred Lane .12 .30
10 Eddie George .15 .40
11 Rocket Ismail .15 .40
12 Shannon Sharpe .15 .40
13 Shawn Jefferson .12 .30
14 Michael Wiley RC .20 .50
15 Jeff Graham .12 .30
16 Steve Beuerlein .15 .40
17 Tim Biakabutuka .15 .40
18 Chris Watson .12 .30
19 Kevin Faulk .12 .30
20 Emmitt Smith .30 .75
21 Plaxico Burress RC .25 .60
22 Hines Ward .15 .40
23 Jacquez Green .12 .30
24 Doug Flutie .15 .40
25 Leslie Shepherd .12 .30
26 Johnnie Morton .15 .40
27 Tom Brady RC 30.00 60.00
28 Jeff George .15 .40
29 Derrick Mason .12 .30
30 Marshall Faulk .15 .40
31 Derrick Mayes .12 .30
32 Jerome Bettis .20 .50
33 Adrian Murrell .12 .30
34 Curtis Enis .12 .30
35 Kimble Anders .12 .30
36 Travis Prentice RC .20 .50
37 Curtis Martin .15 .40
38 Ronnie Powell .12 .30
39 Steve Christie .12 .30
40 Brett Favre .40 1.00
41 Michael Bates .12 .30
42 Rondell Mealey RC .20 .50
43 Randall Cunningham .15 .40
44 Kerry Collins .12 .30
45 William Thomas .12 .30
46 Ricky Watters .15 .40
47 Marvin Harrison .15 .40
48 Corey Bradford .12 .30

49 Terry Kirby .12 .30
50 Troy Aikman .25 .60
51 Cris Carter .20 .50
52 Jamal Lewis RC .30 .75
53 Duce Staley .12 .30
54 Isaac Bruce .20 .50
55 Yancey Thigpen .12 .30
56 R.Jay Soward RC .20 .50
57 Jermaine Lewis .12 .30
58 Zach Thomas .15 .40
59 Sylvester Morris RC .20 .50
60 Steve McNair .15 .40
61 Tiki Barber .15 .40
62 Torrance Small .12 .30
63 Champ Bailey .15 .40
64 Tim Dwight .15 .40
65 Willie Jackson .12 .30
66 Edgerrin James .15 .40
67 Ron Dayne RC .30 .75
68 Rich Gannon .15 .40
69 Junior Seau .15 .40
70 Warren Sapp .15 .40
71 Rob Johnson .15 .40
72 Antonio Freeman .15 .40
73 O.J. McDuffie .15 .40
74 Tamarick Vanover .12 .30
75 Courtney Brown RC .25 .60
76 Donovan McNabb .15 .40
77 Az-Zahir Hakim .12 .30
78 Albert Connell .12 .30
79 Qadry Ismail .12 .30
80 Terrell Davis .15 .40
81 Dorsey Levens .15 .40
82 Tony Martin .15 .40
83 Laveranues Coles RC .25 .60
84 Karim Abdul-Jabbar .12 .30
85 Charles Johnson .12 .30
86 Torry Holt .15 .40
87 Stephen Davis .12 .30
88 Tony Banks .12 .30
89 Akili Smith .12 .30
90 Tim Couch .15 .40
91 Bill Schroeder .15 .40
92 Andre Hastings .12 .30
93 Eddie Kennison .12 .30
94 Randy Moss .15 .40
95 Tony Horne .12 .30
96 Sherrod Gideon RC .20 .50
97 Wesley Walls .12 .30
98 Brian Griese .12 .30
99 Jake Delhomme RC .25 .60
100 Peyton Manning .50 1.25
101 Brad Johnson .15 .40
102 Trung Canidate RC .20 .50
103 Freddie Jones .12 .30
104 Muhsin Muhammad .12 .30
105 Eric Moulds .12 .30
106 Ed McCaffrey .15 .40
107 Joe Montgomery .12 .30
108 Olandis Gary .15 .40
109 J.J. Stokes .15 .40
110 Ricky Williams .15 .40
111 Jim Harbaugh .15 .40
112 Mike Alstott .12 .30
113 Errict Rhett .15 .40
114 Terance Mathis .12 .30
115 Kevin Johnson .12 .30
116 Tremain Mack .12 .30
117 Peter Warrick RC .20 .50
118 Lamont Warren .12 .30
119 Damon Huard .12 .30
120 Cade McNown .12 .30
121 Natrone Means .15 .40
122 Ken Oxendine .12 .30
123 J.R. Redmond RC .20 .50
124 Ken Dilger .12 .30
125 James Johnson .12 .30
126 Napoleon Kaufman .15 .40
127 Ryan Leaf .15 .40
128 Michael Westbrook .12 .30
129 Mario Bates .12 .30
130 Jake Plummer .12 .30
131 James Jett .15 .40
132 Darnay Scott .15 .40
133 Curtis Conway .15 .40
134 Fred Taylor .12 .30
135 Wayne Chrebet .12 .30
136 Sean Dawkins .12 .30
138 Keenan McCardell .15 .40
139 Donnell Bennett .12 .30
140 Jerry Rice .50 1.25
141 Vinny Testaverde .12 .30
142 Chad Pennington RC .25 .60
143 Jonathan Linton .12 .30
144 Herman Moore .12 .30
145 David Patten .12 .30
146 Troy Edwards .12 .30
147 Jon Kitna .12 .30
148 Jimmy Smith .15 .40
149 Tee Martin RC .20 .50
150 Jevon Kearse .12 .30
151 Frank Sanders .12 .30
152 Marcus Robinson .15 .40
153 Mike Hollis .12 .30
154 Frank Wycheck .15 .40
155 Tim Rattay RC .25 .60
156 Dedric Ward .12 .30
157 Terrell Owens .15 .40
158 Chris Chandler .15 .40
159 Damon Griffin .12 .30
160 Mike Vanderjagt .12 .30
161 Elvis Grbac .12 .30
162 Rickey Dudley .12 .30
163 Jeff Garcia .12 .30
164 Thomas Jones RC .25 .60
165 Tyrone Wheatley .12 .30
166 Rod Smith .15 .40
167 Bubba Franks RC .20 .50
168 Chris Warren .12 .30
169 Anthony Lucas RC .20 .50
170 Terry Glenn .15 .40
171 John Carney .12 .30
172 Warrick Dunn .12 .30
173 Shaun Alexander RC .30 .75
174 David Boston .12 .30
175 Bobby Engram .12 .30
176 Travis Taylor RC .20 .50
177 Derrick Alexander .12 .30
178 Keyshawn Johnson .15 .40
179 Steve Young .25 .60
180 Deion Sanders .15 .40
181 Charlie Batch .12 .30
182 Drew Bledsoe .15 .40
183 Reuben Droughns RC .20 .50
184 Ray Lucas .12 .30
185 Shaun King .12 .30
186 Jamal Anderson .15 .40
187 Corey Dillon .12 .30
188 Joe Hamilton RC .20 .50
189 Terrence Wilkins .12 .30
190 Mark Brunell .15 .40
191 Tony Gonzalez .15 .40
192 Tim Brown .20 .50
193 Charlie Garner .15 .40
194 Antowain Smith .15 .40
195 David LaFleur .12 .30
196 Germane Crowell .12 .30
197 Terry Allen .15 .40
198 Marc Bulger RC .25 .60
199 Kevin Dyson .15 .40
200 Kordell Stewart .12 .30

2000 Impact Hats Off

Randomly inserted in Hobby packs at the rate of one in 720 and retail packs at one in 1444, this 21-card set features swatches of hats worn by each respective player.

STATED ODDS 1:720H/1:1444R
1 Karim Abdul-Jabbar 8.00 20.00
2 Jamal Anderson 10.00 25.00
3 David Boston 8.00 20.00
4 Isaac Bruce 12.00 30.00
5 Chris Chandler 10.00 25.00
6 Curtis Conway 10.00 25.00
7 Tim Couch 10.00 25.00
8 Tim Dwight 10.00 25.00
9 Curtis Enis 8.00 20.00
10 Marshall Faulk 15.00 40.00
11 Az-Zahir Hakim 8.00 20.00
12 Torry Holt 10.00 25.00
13 Kevin Johnson 8.00 20.00
14 Terry Kirby 8.00 20.00
15 Terance Mathis 8.00 20.00
16 Shane Matthews 8.00 20.00
17 Cade McNown 8.00 20.00
18 Rob Moore 8.00 20.00
19 Jake Plummer 8.00 20.00
20 Marcus Robinson 10.00 25.00
21 Frank Sanders 8.00 20.00

2000 Impact Point of Impact

ndomly inserted in packs at the rate of one in 30, this 10-card set features die cut cards with silver foil highlights of some of the NFL's top point scorers.

COMPLETE SET (10) 12.50 30.00
STATED ODDS 1:30
PI1 Peyton Manning 2.50 6.00
PI2 Edgerrin James .75 2.00
PI3 Brett Favre 2.00 5.00
PI4 Marshall Faulk .75 2.00
PI5 Fred Taylor .60 1.50
PI6 Tim Couch .75 2.00
PI7 Emmitt Smith 1.50 4.00
PI8 Eddie George .75 2.00
PI9 Randy Moss .75 2.00
PI10 Terrell Davis .75 2.00

2000 Impact Rewind '99

Randomly inserted in packs at the rate of one in one, this 40-card set showcases top moments form the 1999 season. Cards are enhanced with foil set to match the team colors of each featured player.

COMPLETE SET (40) 6.00 15.00
ONE PER PACK
1 Jake Plummer .15 .40
2 Tim Dwight .20 .50
3 Tony Banks .15 .40
4 Doug Flutie .20 .50
5 Tim Biakabutuka .20 .50
6 Marcus Robinson .20 .50
7 Corey Dillon .15 .40
8 Tim Couch .20 .50
9 Troy Aikman .30 .75
10 Olandis Gary .20 .50
11 Germane Crowell .15 .40
12 Brett Favre .50 1.25
13 Peyton Manning .60 1.50
14 Mark Brunell .20 .50
15 Tony Gonzalez .20 .50
16 Dan Marino .50 1.25
17 Randy Moss .20 .50
18 Drew Bledsoe .20 .50
19 Ricky Williams .20 .50
20 Amani Toomer .15 .40
21 Keyshawn Johnson .20 .50
22 Rich Gannon .20 .50
23 Duce Staley .15 .40
24 Jerome Bettis .25 .60
25 Kenny Bynum .15 .40
26 Charlie Garner .20 .50
27 Jon Kitna .15 .40
28 Kurt Warner .40 1.00
29 Mike Alstott .15 .40
30 Eddie George .20 .50
31 Stephen Davis .15 .40
32 Kurt Warner .40 1.00
33 Edgerrin James .20 .50
34 Jevon Kearse .15 .40
35 Marshall Faulk .20 .50
36 Edgerrin James .20 .50
37 Marvin Harrison .20 .50
38 Jimmy Smith .20 .50
39 Steve Beuerlein .20 .50
40 Kurt Warner .40 1.00

2000 Impact Team Tattoos

Randomly inserted in packs at the rate of one in four, this 31-card set features temporary tattoos of all the NFL's team logos.

COMPLETE SET (31) 10.00 25.00
COMMON TATTOO .40 1.00
STATED ODDS 1:4

2011 In The Game Canadiana Authentic Patch Silver

ANNOUNCED PRINT RUN 30
AP2 Dave Cutler 25.00 50.00

2011 In The Game Canadiana Autographs

OVERALL AUTO/MEM ODDS THREE PER BOX
ADCU1 Dave Cutler 10.00 20.00
ADCU2 Dave Cutler 10.00 20.00

2011 In The Game Canadiana Autographs Blue

*BLUE: .75X TO 1.5X BLACK AUTOS
OVERALL AUTO ODDS ONE PER BOX

2011 In The Game Canadiana Mega Memorabilia Silver

MM3 Dave Cutler L 10.00 20.00

2011 In The Game Canadiana Red

BLUE/50: .75X TO 2X BASIC RED
UNPRICED ONYX ANNOUNCED RUN 5
ANNOUNCED PRINT RUN 180 SETS
10 Bronko Nagurski .75 2.00
17 Dave Cutler .60 1.50

1992-93 Intimidator Bio Sheets

Produced by Intimidator, each of these bio sheets measures approximately 8 1/2" by 11" and is printed on card stock. The fronts display a large glossy color player photo framed by black and white inner borders. The right side of the photo is edged by a gold foil stripe that presents the player's name, team name, Intimidator logo, and uniform number. The surrounding card face, which constitutes the outer border, is team color-coded. The backs carry two black-and-white player photos, pro career summary, college career summary, and personal as well as biographical information. An autograph slot at the lower right corner and a date (1/93) rounds out the back. The bio sheets are unnumbered and checklisted below in alphabetical order. Two Derrick Thomas promos were also produced.

COMPLETE SET (36) 40.00 100.00
1 Troy Aikman 4.00 10.00
2 Jerry Ball .60 1.50
3 Cornelius Bennett .80 2.00
4 Earnest Byner .60 1.50
5 Randall Cunningham 1.20 3.00
6 Chris Doleman .80 2.00
7 John Elway 6.00 15.00
8 Jim Everett .80 2.00
9 Michael Irvin 1.20 3.00
10 Jim Kelly 1.20 3.00
11 James Lofton .80 2.00
12 Howie Long 1.20 3.00
13 Ronnie Lott .80 2.00
14 Nick Lowery .60 1.50
15 Charles Mann .60 1.50
16 Dan Marino 6.00 15.00
17 Art Monk .80 2.00
18 Joe Montana 10.00 20.00
19 Warren Moon 1.20 3.00
20 Christian Okoye .80 2.00
21 Leslie O'Neal .80 2.00
22 Andre Reed .80 2.00
23 Jerry Rice 4.00 10.00
24 Andre Rison .80 2.00
25 Deion Sanders 2.00 5.00
26 Junior Seau 1.20 3.00
27 Mike Singletary .80 2.00
28 Bruce Smith .80 2.00
29 Emmitt Smith 6.00 15.00
30 Neil Smith .80 2.00
31 Pat Swilling .80 2.00
32 Lawrence Taylor .80 2.00
33 Broderick Thomas .60 1.50
34 Derrick Thomas 1.20 3.00
35 Thurman Thomas 1.20 3.00
36 Lorenzo White .80 2.00
P1 Derrick Thomas Promo 1.60 4.00
P2 Derrick Thomas Promo 1.60 4.00

1995 Iowa Barnstormers AFL

The Iowa Barnstormers Arena Football League team issued this set of cards in conjunction with Taco John's stores. Two cards were distributed each week of the season at participating stores and complete team sets reportedly were sold through the team. The cards are not numbered but have been arranged alphabetically below with players and coaches first and mascot and cheerleaders last. This was Kurt Warner's first football card.

COMPLETE SET (42) 75.00 150.00
1 Mike Black 1.25 3.00
2 Larry Blue 1.25 3.00
3 Lester Brinkley 1.25 3.00
4 Jim Burrow ACO 1.25 3.00
5 Toney Catchings 1.25 3.00
6 Andy Chilcote 1.25 3.00
7 Leonard Conley 1.25 3.00
8 Jim Foster OWN 1.25 3.00
9 John Gregory CO 1.25 3.00
10 Art Haege ACO 1.25 3.00
11 Weylan Harding 1.25 3.00
12 Todd Harrington 1.25 3.00
13 Willis Jacox 1.25 3.00
14 Carlos James 1.25 3.00
15 Brian Krulikowski 1.25 3.00
16 Jeff Loots 1.25 3.00
17 Ron Lopez 1.25 3.00
18 Adrian Lunsford 1.25 3.00
19 Ron Moran 1.25 3.00
20 Ryan Murray 1.25 3.00
21 Bob Rees 1.25 3.00
22 Jon Roehlk CO 1.25 3.00
23 Rick Schaaf 1.25 3.00
24 Mike Sunvold 1.25 3.00
25 Reggie Sutton 1.25 3.00
26 Kurt Warner 40.00 80.00
27 Ralph Young ACO 1.25 3.00
28 Tony Young 1.25 3.00
29 Jim Zabel ANN 1.25 3.00
30 Billy Barnstormer 1.25 3.00
31 Cheerleaders 1.25 3.00
32 Cheerleaders 1.25 3.00
33 Cheerleaders 1.25 3.00
34 Cheerleaders 1.25 3.00
35 Cheerleaders 1.25 3.00
36 Cheerleaders 1.25 3.00
37 Cheerleaders 1.25 3.00
38 Cheerleaders 1.25 3.00
39 Cheerleaders 1.25 3.00
40 Cheerleaders 1.25 3.00
41 Cheerleaders 1.25 3.00
42 Cheerleaders 1.25 3.00

1996 Iowa Barnstormers AFL

r the second year, the Iowa Barnstormers Arena Football League team issued a set of cards. Complete team sets reportedly were sold through the team. The cards were numbered on the backs.

COMPLETE SET (42) 60.00 120.00
1 Mike Black 1.25 3.00
2 Matthew Steeple 1.25 3.00
3 Ron Lopez 1.25 3.00
4 Ryan Murray 1.25 3.00
5 David Bush 1.25 3.00
6 Kurt Warner 30.00 60.00
7 Andy Chilcote 1.25 3.00
8 Mark Friday 1.25 3.00
9 Leonard Conley 1.25 3.00
10 Steve Houghton 1.25 3.00
11 Toney Catchings 1.25 3.00
12 Lamart Cooper 1.25 3.00
13 Chris Spencer 1.25 3.00
14 Todd Harrington 1.25 3.00
15 Carlos James 1.25 3.00
16 Larry Blue 1.25 3.00
17 Harold Jasper 1.25 3.00
18 Weylan Harding 1.25 3.00
19 Garry Howe 1.25 3.00
20 Matt Eller 1.25 3.00
21 Willis Jacox 1.25 3.00
22 Calvin Shakoor 1.25 3.00
23 Jim Burrow ACO 1.25 3.00
24 George Asleson ACO 1.25 3.00
25 Art Haege ACO 1.25 3.00
26 John Gregory CO 1.25 3.00
27 Jim Foster OWN 1.25 3.00
28 Cheerleaders 1.25 3.00
29 Cheerleaders 1.25 3.00
30 Cheerleaders 1.25 3.00
31 Cheerleaders 1.25 3.00
32 Cheerleaders 1.25 3.00
33 Cheerleaders 1.25 3.00
34 Cheerleaders 1.25 3.00
35 Cheerleaders 1.25 3.00
36 Cheerleaders 1.25 3.00
37 Cheerleaders 1.25 3.00
38 Cheerleaders 1.25 3.00
39 Cheerleaders 1.25 3.00
40 Barnstormer Billy 1.25 3.00
41 Harvie Herrington ANN 1.25 3.00
42 Ron Moran ANN 1.25 3.00

1997 Iowa Barnstormers AFL

r the third year, the Iowa Barnstormers Arena Football League team issued a set of cards that included Kurt Warner. Complete team sets were sold through the team with portions of the proceeds going to local charities. The cards were numbered on the backs.

COMPLETE SET (50) 60.00 120.00
1 John Gregory CO 1.25 3.00
2 Art Haege ACO 1.25 3.00
3 Jim Burrow ACO 1.25 3.00
4 George Asleson ACO 1.25 3.00
5 Jim Foster OWN 1.25 3.00
6 Mike Black 1.25 3.00
7 Carlos James 1.25 3.00
8 Larry Blue 1.25 3.00
9 Lamart Cooper 1.25 3.00
10 Andre Allen 1.25 3.00
11 Jarrod DeGeorgia 1.25 3.00
12 Kurt Warner 30.00 60.00
13 Mike Horacek 1.25 3.00
14 Charles Puleri 2.00 5.00
15 Todd Harrington 1.25 3.00
16 Hiawatha Phifer 1.25 3.00
17 Greg Eaglin 1.25 3.00
18 John Anderson S 1.25 3.00
19 Leonard Conley 1.25 3.00
20 John Motton 1.25 3.00
21 Ron Moran 1.25 3.00
22 Steve Houghton 1.25 3.00
23 David Witthun 1.25 3.00
24 David Bush 1.25 3.00
25 Garry Howe 1.25 3.00
26 Vernon Broughton 1.25 3.00
27 Matt Eller 1.25 3.00
28 Anthony Hutch 1.25 3.00
29 Chris Spencer 1.25 3.00
30 Willis Jacox 1.25 3.00
31 Toney Catchings 1.25 3.00
32 Evan Matautia 1.25 3.00
33 Barnyard Bob 1.25 3.00
Barnstormer Billy
34 Cheerleaders 1.25 3.00
35 Cheerleaders 1.25 3.00
36 Cheerleaders 1.25 3.00
37 Cheerleaders 1.25 3.00
38 Cheerleaders 1.25 3.00
39 Cheerleaders 1.25 3.00
40 Cheerleaders 1.25 3.00
41 Cheerleaders 1.25 3.00
42 Cheerleaders 1.25 3.00
43 Cheerleaders 1.25 3.00
44 Cheerleaders 1.25 3.00
45 Cheerleaders 1.25 3.00
46 Cheerleaders 1.25 3.00
47 Cheerleaders 1.25 3.00
48 Team Support Staff 1.25 3.00
49 Front Office Team 1.25 3.00
50 Broadcast Team 1.25 3.00

1999 Iowa Barnstormers AFL

The Iowa Barnstormers Arena Football League team issued this set of cards. Complete sets were sold through the team and at the arena with portions of the proceeds going to local charities.

COMPLETE SET (42) 20.00 40.00
1 George Asleson ACO .75 2.00
2 Larry Blue .75 2.00
3 Jim Burrow ACO .75 2.00
4 Toney Catchings .75 2.00
5 Scott Cloman .75 2.00
6 Leonard Conley .75 2.00
7 Rodney Filer .75 2.00
8 John Fisher .75 2.00
9 Jim Foster OWN .75 2.00
10 Aaron Garcia .75 2.00
11 Eric Gohlstin .75 2.00
12 Marvin Graves .75 2.00
13 John Gregory CO .75 2.00
14 Art Haege ACO .75 2.00
15 Todd Harrington .75 2.00
16 Mike Horacek .75 2.00
17 Garry Howe .75 2.00
18 Anthony Hutch .75 2.00
19 Carlos James .75 2.00
20 Kevin Kaesviharn .75 2.00
21 Skip McClendon .75 2.00
22 John Motton .75 2.00
23 Basil Proctor .75 2.00
24 Matt Sherman .75 2.00
25 Shea Showers .75 2.00
26 Chris Spencer .75 2.00
27 Kevin Swayne .75 2.00
28 Geoff Turner .75 2.00
29 Mathias Vavao .75 2.00
30 Jack Walker .75 2.00
31 Jim Zabel .75 2.00
Gary Fletcher ANN
32 Chearleaders .75 2.00
33 Chearleaders .75 2.00
34 Chearleaders .75 2.00
35 Chearleaders .75 2.00
36 Chearleaders .75 2.00
37 Chearleaders .75 2.00
38 Chearleaders .75 2.00
39 Chearleaders .75 2.00
40 Chearleaders .75 2.00
41 Chearleaders .75 2.00
42 Chearleaders .75 2.00

2007 Iowa Blackhawks APFL

MPLETE SET (39) 6.00 12.00
1 Black Jack (Mascot) .20 .50
2 George Patterson III .20 .50
3 Paul Kosel .20 .50
4 Chris Moore .20 .50
5 Mike Wolff CO .20 .50
6 Justin Kammrad .20 .50
7 Ted Hennings .20 .50
8 Shawn Ronk .20 .50
9 Kurt Ferguson .20 .50
10 Mike Reynolds .20 .50
11 Tony Doremus Asst.CO .20 .50
12 Chuck Wright .20 .50
13 Mike Stuart .20 .50
14 Ray Rose .20 .50
15 Brett Ryan Asst.CO .20 .50
16 Elijah Simmons .20 .50
17 Dave Coberly Asst.CO .20 .50
18 Dedric Washington .20 .50
19 Burton Bosan .20 .50
20 Mike Paulson Asst.CO .20 .50
21 Eric Smith .20 .50
22 Ryan Dennhardt .20 .50
23 Dontae Allen .20 .50
24 Steve Rush .20 .50
25 Cameron Gales .20 .50
26 Yano Jones .20 .50
27 Matt Smoyer .20 .50
28 Scott Yates .20 .50
29 Djuan Johnson .20 .50
30 Jeremy Glynn .20 .50
31 Travis Kleinbeck .20 .50
32 Taylor Wallin .20 .50
33 Tyrice Ellebb .20 .50
34 Ryan Kauffman .20 .50
35 Ryan Hoden .20 .50
36 Dave Liebentritt .20 .50
37 Kaylon Price .20 .50
38 Jerry Lakin .20 .50
39 Team Picture .20 .50

2008 Iowa Blackhawks APFL

MPLETE SET (32) 6.00 12.00
1 Mike Wolff and Staff .20 .50
2 Chuck Wright .20 .50
3 Dave Liebentritt .20 .50
4 Rich Rylee .20 .50
5 Jeremy Glynn .20 .50
6 Greg Ernster .20 .50
7 Djuan Johnson .20 .50
8 Jon Helget .20 .50
9 Elijah Simmons .20 .50
10 Eric Johnson .20 .50
11 Ryan Kauffman .20 .50
12 Brad Triplett .20 .50
13 Kurt Ferguson .20 .50
14 Mike Neville .20 .50
15 Mike Stuart .20 .50
16 Matt Smoyer .20 .50
17 Jerry Lakin .20 .50
18 Tyrice Ellebb .20 .50
19 Cameron Gales .20 .50
20 Marty Wolff .20 .50
21 Ryan Hoden .20 .50
22 Burton Bosan .20 .50
23 Ryan Dennhardt .20 .50
24 Josh Hayes .20 .50
25 Dontae Allen .20 .50
26 Jared Isenhart .20 .50
27 Chris Moore .20 .50
28 Travis Hines .20 .50
29 Scott Yates .20 .50
30 Brandon Carrera .20 .50
31 Eric Smith .20 .50
32 Iowa Hot Wings .20 .50

1997 Iron Kids Bread

These cards were issued in packages of Iron Kids Bread in 1997. Each includes a color photo of the featured player on the front along with the "Iron Kids Bread" sponsorship logo in the lower right corner. Any additions to the list below are appreciated.

NNO Dot Richardson
NNO Grant Fuhr
NNO Isaac Bruce
NNO Ivan Rodriguez
NNO Janet Evans
NNO Jennifer Azzi
NNO Juan Gonzalez
NNO Ken Norton .75 2.00
NNO Kerri Strug
NNO Mia Hamm
NNO Mitch Richmond
NNO Shannon Miller
NNO Sheryl Swoopes

2007-08 ITG Ultimate Memorabilia Cityscapes

STATED PRINT RUN 24 SERIAL #'d SETS
3 D.Hasek/D.Flutie 15.00 40.00
4 M.Turco/D.Sanders 10.00 25.00
9 P.Roy/J.Elway 20.00 50.00
10 Datsyuk/Sanders 15.00 40.00
15 M.Modano/M.Irvin 15.00 40.00

1974 Jacksonville Sharks WFL Team Issue

These black and white photos were issued by the team and measure roughly 3 1/2" x 4 3/4." The backs are blank but the fronts include a large amount of information within the space below the player image: jersey number, player's name, team logo, position initials, height, and weight.

1 Tommy Durrance 6.00 12.00
2 Dennis Hughes 6.00 12.00
3 Grant Guthrie 6.00 12.00
4 Kay Stephenson 6.00 12.00

1975 Jacksonville Express Team Issue

The Jacksonville Express of the World Football League distributed this set of player photos. Each photo measures approximately 4 1/2" by 5" and features a black and white player picture with a blank cardback. The photos contain no player names nor any other identifying text. We've listed the photos below according to the player's jersey number.

COMPLETE SET (38) 450.00 900.00
2 Johnny Osborne 12.50 25.00
3 Lee McGriff 12.50 25.00
6 Dan Callahan 12.50 25.00
7 Steve Barrios 12.50 25.00
8 Steve Foley 15.00 30.00
10 George Mira 15.00 30.00
12 David Fowler 12.50 25.00
16 Ron Coppenbarger 12.50 25.00
18 Abb Ansley 12.50 25.00
20 Jimmy Poulos 12.50 25.00
21 Tommy Reamon 12.50 25.00
23 Alfred Haywood 12.50 25.00
30 Jeff Davis RB 12.50 25.00
31 Fletcher Smith 12.50 25.00
32 Brian Duncan 12.50 25.00
42 Canary Simmons 12.50 25.00
44 Skip Johns 12.50 25.00
46 Willie Jackson DB 15.00 30.00
50 Rick Thomann 12.50 25.00
Ted Jarnov
51 Jay Casey 12.50 25.00
52 Glen Gaspard 12.50 25.00
54 Howard Kindig 12.50 25.00
55 Fred Abbott 12.50 25.00
57 Ted Jarnov 12.50 25.00
58 Chip Myrtle 15.00 30.00
59 Sherman Miller 12.50 25.00
63 Tom Walker 12.50 25.00
68 Carleton Oats 12.50 25.00
70 Buck Baker 12.50 25.00
76 Carl Taibi 12.50 25.00
77 Joe Jackson 12.50 25.00
78 Kenny Moore 12.50 25.00
79 Larry Gagner 12.50 25.00
80 Dennis Hughes 12.50 25.00
81 Charles Hall 12.50 25.00
82 Don Brumm 15.00 30.00
87 Mike Creaney 12.50 25.00
88 Witt Beckman 12.50 25.00

1997 Jaguars Collector's Choice

Upper Deck released several team sets in 1997 in a blister pack wrapper. Each of the 14-cards in this set are very similar to the base Collector's Choice cards except for the card numbering on the cardback. A cover/checklist card was added featuring the team helmet.

COMPLETE SET (14) 1.20 3.00
JA1 Jimmy Smith .08 .25
JA2 Pete Mitchell .02 .10
JA3 Natrone Means .05 .15
JA4 Mark Brunell .50 1.25
JA5 Kevin Hardy .05 .15
JA6 Tony Brackens .05 .15
JA7 Aaron Beasley .02 .10
JA8 Chris Hudson .02 .10
JA9 Renaldo Wynn .02 .10
JA10 John Jurkovic .02 .10
JA11 Keenan McCardell .08 .25
JA12 James O. Stewart .05 .15
JA13 Deon Figures .02 .10
JA14 Jaguars Logo .20 .50
Checklist

1997 Jaguars Team Issue

This 37-card set features black-and-white player photos in blue borders measuring approximately 5" by 8". The set was sponsored by Champion Health Care and displays a "Jaguars Don't Smoke" logo in the bottom right. The backs are blank. The cards are unnumbered and checklisted below in alphabetical order.

COMPLETE SET (37) 32.00 80.00
1 Bryan Barker .80 2.00
2 Aaron Beasley .80 2.00
3 Tony Boselli 1.00 2.50
4 Brant Boyer .80 2.00
5 Tony Brackens 1.00 2.50
6 Mark Brunell 4.80 12.00
7 Michael Cheever .80 2.00
8 Ben Coleman .80 2.00
9 Don Davey .80 2.00
10 Travis Davis .80 2.00
11 Brian DeMarco .80 2.00
12 Deon Figures .80 2.00
13 Dana Hall .80 2.00
14 James Hamilton .80 2.00
15 Kevin Hardy 1.00 2.50
16 Mike Hollis .80 2.00
17 Willie Jackson 1.00 2.50
18 John Jurkovic .80 2.00
19 Jeff Lageman .80 2.00
20 Mike Logan .80 2.00
21 Keenan McCardell 1.60 4.00
22 Tom McManus .80 2.00
23 Pete Mitchell 1.00 2.50
24 Will Moore .80 2.00
25 Jeff Novak .80 2.00
26 Chris Parker .80 2.00
27 Seth Payne .80 2.00
28 Kelvin Pritchett .80 2.00
29 Eddie Robinson .80 2.00
30 Bryan Schwartz .80 2.00
31 Leon Searcy .80 2.00
32 Joel Smeenge .80 2.00
33 Jimmy Smith 1.60 4.00
34 James Stewart 1.00 2.50
35 Dave Thomas .80 2.00
36 Rich Tylski .80 2.00
37 Renaldo Wynn .80 2.00

2005 Jaguars Super Bowl XXXIX

ch card manufacturer produced 2-cards to be distributed at the Super Bowl Card Show XXXIX in Jacksonville via wrapper redemption programs. The design varies from manufacturer and from card-to-card but each is numbered on the back as part of the 8-card set.

COMPLETE SET (8) 10.00 20.00
1 Greg Jones 1.00 2.50
(Topps)
2 Reggie Williams 1.25 3.00
(Upper Deck)
3 Ernest Wilford .75 2.00
(Fleer)
4 Marcus Stroud .75 2.00
(Donruss Playoff)
5 Byron Leftwich 1.50 4.00
(Donruss Playoff)
6 David Garrard .75 2.00
(Upper Deck)
7 Fred Taylor 1.25 3.00
(Fleer)
8 Jimmy Smith 1.00 2.50
(Topps)

2006 Jaguars Topps

COMPLETE SET (12) 3.00 6.00
JAC1 Greg Jones .25 .60
JAC2 Fred Taylor .25 .60
JAC3 Ernest Wilford .25 .60
JAC4 David Garrard .25 .60
JAC5 Byron Leftwich .25 .60
JAC6 Matt Jones .25 .60
JAC7 Alvin Pearman .25 .60
JAC8 Jimmy Smith .30 .75
JAC9 Mike Peterson .25 .60
JAC10 Daryl Smith .20 .50
JAC11 Maurice Drew .40 1.00
JAC12 Marcedes Lewis .25 .60

2007 Jaguars Topps

COMPLETE SET (12) 2.50 5.00
1 Fred Taylor .40 1.00
2 Matt Jones .50 1.25
3 Reggie Williams .50 1.25
4 Ernest Wilford .40 1.00
5 Jermaine Wiggins .40 1.00
6 Reggie Nelson .40 1.00
7 David Garrard .40 1.00
8 Maurice Jones-Drew .40 1.00
9 Rashean Mathis .40 1.00
10 Byron Leftwich .40 1.00
11 Dennis Northcutt .40 1.00
12 Mike Peterson .40 1.00

2008 Jaguars Topps

COMPLETE SET (12) 2.00 4.00
1 Maurice Jones-Drew .40 1.00
2 Fred Taylor .40 1.00
3 Cleo Lemon .40 1.00
4 David Garrard .40 1.00
5 Reggie Nelson .40 1.00
6 Jerry Porter .40 1.00
7 Reggie Williams .50 1.25
8 Dennis Northcutt .40 1.00
9 Marcedes Lewis .40 1.00
10 Rashean Mathis .40 1.00
11 Derrick Harvey .40 1.00
12 Mike Peterson .40 1.00

1985 Jeno's Pizza Logo Stickers

is set of stickers was originally issued in complete sheet form. Since the stickers are often found individually cut, we've cataloged them this way. Each is blankbacked and features either an NFL team helmet or Super Bowl logo on the fronts.

COMPLETE SET (48) 60.00 150.00
1 Atlanta Falcons 1.25 3.00
2 Buffalo Bills 1.25 3.00
3 Chicago Bears 1.25 3.00
4 Cincinnati Bengals 1.25 3.00
5 Cleveland Browns 1.25 3.00
6 Dallas Cowboys 2.00 5.00
7 Denver Broncos 1.25 3.00
8 Detroit Lions 1.25 3.00
9 Green Bay Packers 2.00 5.00
10 Houston Oilers 1.25 3.00
11 Indianapolis Colts 1.25 3.00
12 Kansas City Chiefs 1.25 3.00
13 Los Angeles Raiders 2.00 5.00
14 Los Angeles Rams 1.25 3.00
15 Miami Dolphins 2.00 5.00
16 Minnesota Vikings 1.25 3.00
17 New England Patriots 1.25 3.00
18 New Orleans Saints 1.25 3.00
19 New York Giants 1.25 3.00
20 New York Jets 1.25 3.00
21 Philadelphia Eagles 1.25 3.00
22 Pittsburgh Steelers 2.00 5.00
23 St. Louis Cardinals 1.25 3.00
24 San Diego Chargers 1.25 3.00
25 San Francisco 49ers 2.00 5.00
26 Seattle Seahawks 1.25 3.00
27 Tampa Bay Buccaneers 1.25 3.00
28 Washington Redskins 2.00 5.00
29 Super Bowl I 1.25 3.00
30 Super Bowl II 1.25 3.00
31 Super Bowl III 1.25 3.00
32 Super Bowl IV 1.25 3.00
33 Super Bowl V 1.25 3.00
34 Super Bowl VI 1.25 3.00
35 Super Bowl VII 1.25 3.00
36 Super Bowl VIII 1.25 3.00
37 Super Bowl IX 1.25 3.00
38 Super Bowl X 1.25 3.00
39 Super Bowl XI 1.25 3.00
40 Super Bowl XII 1.25 3.00
41 Super Bowl XIII 1.25 3.00
42 Super Bowl XIV 1.25 3.00
43 Super Bowl XV 1.25 3.00
44 Super Bowl XVI 1.25 3.00
45 Super Bowl XVII 1.25 3.00
46 Super Bowl XVIII 1.25 3.00
47 Super Bowl XIX 1.25 3.00
48 Super Bowl XX 1.25 3.00

1986 Jeno's Pizza

The 1986 Jeno's Pizza football set contains 56 cards (two for each of the 28 teams). The two cards for each team typically represent a retired star and a current player. The cards are standard sized (2 1/2" by 3 1/2") and were printed horizontally (most of them) on thin card stock. The cards were distributed as a promotion with one card, sealed in plastic, contained in each special Jeno's box. Reportedly 10,000 sets were produced. There was also a Terry Bradshaw Action Play Book to house the cards issued via a mail redemption coupon.

COMPLETE SET (56) 10.00 25.00
1 Duane Thomas .15 .40
2 Butch Johnson .15 .40
3 Andy Headen .40 1.00
4 Joe Morris .12 .30
5 Wilbert Montgomery .12 .30
6 Harold Carmichael .15 .40
7 Ottis Anderson .15 .40
8 Roy Green .10 .25
9 Mark Murphy .10 .25
10 Joe Theismann .30 .75
11 Jim McMahon .30 .75
12 Walter Payton 2.00 5.00
13 Billy Sims .15 .40
14 James Jones FB .10 .25
15 Willie Davis .15 .40
16 Eddie Lee Ivery .10 .25
17 Fran Tarkenton .40 1.00
18 Alan Page .15 .40
19 Ricky Bell .12 .30
20 Cecil Johnson .10 .25
21 Bubba Bean .10 .25
22 Gerald Riggs .10 .25
23 Eric Dickerson and .25 .60
24 Jack Reynolds .12 .30
25 Archie Manning .15 .40
26 Wayne Wilson .12 .30
27 Dan Bunz and .10 .25
28 Roger Craig 1.25 3.00
29 O.J. Simpson .40 1.00
30 Joe Cribbs .12 .30
31 Rick Volk and .15 .40
32 Earl Morrall .12 .30
33 Jim Kiick .12 .30
34 Dan Marino 2.50 6.00
35 Craig James .15 .40
36 Julius Adams .10 .25
37 Joe Namath 1.25 3.00
38 Freeman McNeil .12 .30
39 Pete Johnson .10 .25
40 Larry Kinnebrew .10 .25
41 Brian Sipe .12 .30
42 Kevin Mack and .12 .30
43 Dan Pastorini .12 .30
44 Elvin Bethea .15 .40
C.Hartwig
45 Fran Tarkenton and .40 1.00
46 Terry Bradshaw 1.00 2.50
47 Randy Gradishar and .12 .30
48 Sammy Winder .10 .25
49 Robert Holmes .10 .25
50 Buck Buchanan and .15 .40
51 Willie Jones and .10 .25
52 Marcus Allen .50 1.25
53 Dan Fouts and .25 .60
54 Dan Fouts .50 1.25
55 Blair Bush .10 .25
56 Steve Largent .50 1.25
NNO Play Book 1.25 3.00

1963 Jets Team Issue

These 4" by 5" Black and White cards were issued by the New York Jets in their first season as the Jets. They had been the Titans for the previous three seasons. There are small facsimile autographs on the bottom of the cardfronts. As these cards are not numbered we have sequenced them in alphabetical order.

COMPLETE SET (8) 60.00 120.00
1 Weeb Ewbank CO 10.00 20.00
2 Larry Grantham 7.50 15.00
3 Gene Heeter 7.50 15.00
4 Bill Mathis 7.50 15.00
5 Don Maynard 12.50 25.00
6 Mark Smolinski 7.50 15.00
7 Bake Turner 7.50 15.00
8 Dick Wood 7.50 15.00

1963 Jets Team Issue 5x7

This set of the New York Jets measures approximately 5" by 7" and look very similar to the Jay Publishing issues of the early 1960s and the 1965-66 Jets set listings. The fronts feature black-and-white player photos with just the player's name and team name below the photo. It is very likely that the Jets issued these photos in groups over a number of years as they can be found in 6 or 8-card envelopes. The backs are blank. The cards are unnumbered and checklisted below in alphabetical order.

1 Bill Atkins 6.00 12.00
2 Dick Christy 6.00 12.00
3 Larry Grantham 6.00 12.00
4 Dick Guesman 6.00 12.00
5 Mike Hudock 6.00 12.00
6 Charlie Janerette 6.00 12.00
7 Don Maynard 10.00 20.00
8 Bill Mathis 6.00 12.00
9 LaVerne Torczon 6.00 12.00

1965 Jets Team Issue 8x10

This set of the New York Jets photos measures approximately 8 1/2" by 10 1/4" and are very similar in design to other Jets photos issued in the 1960s and 1970s. The fronts feature black and white player photos with just the player's name and position (spelled out on most) below the photo along with the team's logo. This year can be identified by the slightly slanted position of the Jets' logo below the player image. The blankbacked photos are unnumbered and checklisted below in alphabetical order.

COMPLETE SET (10) 125.00 200.00
1 Emerson Boozer 7.50 15.00
2 Larry Grantham 6.00 12.00
4 Bill Mathis 6.00 12.00
3 John Huarte 6.00 12.00
5 Don Maynard 12.50 25.00
6 Wahoo McDaniel 7.50 15.00
7 Joe Namath 50.00 100.00
8 George Sauer 6.00 12.00
9 Matt Snell 7.50 15.00
10 Bake Turner 6.00 12.00

1965-66 Jets Team Issue 5x7

This set of the New York Jets measures approximately 5" by 7" and look very similar to the Jay Publishing issues of the early 1960s. The fronts feature black-and-white player photos with just the player's name and team name below the photo. It is very likely that the Jets issued these photos in groups over a number of years as they can be found in 6 or 8-card envelopes. The backs are blank. The cards are unnumbered and checklisted below in alphabetical order.

COMPLETE SET (10) 100.00 175.00
1 Ralph Baker 6.00 12.00
2 Dan Ficca 6.00 12.00
3 Wahoo McDaniel 7.50 15.00
4 Joe Namath 45.00 80.00
5 Dainard Paulson 6.00 12.00
6 Gerry Philbin 6.00 12.00
7 Mark Smolinski 6.00 12.00
8 Matt Snell 7.50 15.00
9 Bake Turner 6.00 12.00
10 Dick Wood 6.00 12.00

1969 Jets Tasco Prints

Tasco Associates produced this set of New York Jets prints. The fronts feature a large color artist's rendering of the player along with the player's name and position. The backs are blank. The prints measure approximately 11" by 16."

COMPLETE SET (6) 75.00 125.00
1 Winston Hill 7.50 15.00
2 Joe Namath 35.00 60.00
3 Gerry Philbin 7.50 15.00
4 Johnny Sample 7.50 15.00
5 Matt Snell 10.00 20.00
6 Jim Turner 7.50 15.00

1969 Jets Team Issue 8x10

This set of the New York Jets photos measures approximately 8" by 10" and are very similar in design to the 1965 issue except for the logo. The fronts feature black and white player photos with just the player's name and position (spelled out on most in all caps) below the photo along with the team's logo. This year can be identified by the horizontal position of the Jets' logo below the player image. The blankbacked photos are unnumbered and checklisted below in alphabetical order.

1 Al Atkinson 6.00 12.00
2 Verlon Biggs 6.00 12.00
3 Emerson Boozer 7.50 15.00
4 Earl Christy 6.00 12.00
5 Mike D'Amato 6.00 12.00
6 John Dockery 7.50 15.00
7 John Elliott 6.00 12.00
8 Roger Finnie 6.00 12.00
9 Dave Foley 6.00 12.00
10 Karl Henke 6.00 12.00
11 Billy Joe 7.50 15.00

12 Cecil Leonard 6.00 12.00
13 Bill Mathis 6.00 12.00
14 Carl McAdams 6.00 12.00
15 George Nock 6.00 12.00
16 Bill Rademacher 6.00 12.00
17 Randy Rasmussen 6.00 12.00
18 Jeff Richardson 6.00 12.00
19 Paul Rochester 6.00 12.00
20 Johnny Sample 7.50 15.00
21 George Sauer 6.00 12.00
22 John Schmitt 6.00 12.00
23 Mark Smolinski 6.00 12.00
24 Wayne Stewart 6.00 12.00
25 Mike Stromberg 6.00 12.00
26 Bob Talamini 6.00 12.00
27 Bake Turner 7.50 15.00
28 Sam Walton 6.00 12.00
29 Lee White 6.00 12.00
30 Al Woodall 7.50 15.00

1973-76 Jets Team Issue

The Jets issued these 8 " by 10" photos over the course of several years in the mid-1970s. Each includes a black and white photo of a Jets player with the older style (JETS within an oval) team logo, his name, and his position listed below the image. The type style and size varies slightly from photo to photo and several players were likely issued in differing styles. The backs are blank. Any additions to this list are appreciated.

1 Mike Adamle 5.00 10.00
4 Ralph Baker 5.00 10.00
6 Carl Barzilauskas 5.00 10.00
7 Mike Battle 5.00 10.00
9 Roger Bernhardt 5.00 10.00
10 Hank Bjorklund 5.00 10.00
11 Emerson Boozer 6.00 12.00
12 Willie Brister 5.00 10.00
13 Gordon Brown 5.00 10.00
14 Bob Burns 5.00 10.00
15 Greg Buttle 5.00 10.00
16 Duane Carrell 5.00 10.00
18 Bill Demory 5.00 10.00
19 John Dockery 5.00 10.00
21 Bill Ferguson 5.00 10.00
23 Richmond Flowers 5.00 10.00
25 Ed Galigher 5.00 10.00
26 Greg Gantt 5.00 10.00
27 Bruce Harper 5.00 10.00
28 Dave Herman 5.00 10.00
29 Winston Hill 5.00 10.00
2A Al Atkinson 5.00 10.00
(jersey number fully visible)
2B Al Atkinson 5.00 10.00
(half of jersey number visible)
30 Lou Holtz CO 7.50 15.00
(press conference holding ball)
31 Delles Howell 5.00 10.00
32 Bobby Howfield 5.00 10.00
33 Clarence Jackson 5.00 10.00
34 J.J. Jones 5.00 10.00
35 Larry Keller 5.00 10.00
36 David Knight 5.00 10.00
37 Warren Koegel 5.00 10.00
38 Pete Lammons 5.00 10.00
39 Pat Leahy 5.00 10.00
3A Darrell Austin 5.00 10.00
(with neck pad)
3B Darrell Austin 5.00 10.00
(without neck pad)
40 John Little 5.00 10.00
41 Mark Lomas 5.00 10.00
42 Bob Martin 5.00 10.00
43 Don Maynard 10.00 20.00
44 Wayne Mulligan 5.00 10.00
45 Joe Namath Action 20.00 35.00
46 Jim Nance 6.00 12.00
47 Richard Neal 5.00 10.00
48 Burgess Owens 5.00 10.00
49 Gerry Philbin 5.00 10.00
(all-pro defensive end)
50 Lou Piccone 5.00 10.00
51 Lawrence Pillers 5.00 10.00
52 Garry Puetz 5.00 10.00
53 Randy Rasmussen 5.00 10.00
54 Steve Reese 5.00 10.00
56 Jamie Rivers 5.00 10.00
57 Travis Roach 5.00 10.00
58 Joe Schmiesing 5.00 10.00
59 John Schmitt 5.00 10.00
5A Jerome Barkum 5.00 10.00
(photo from waist up)
5B Jerome Barkum 5.00 10.00
(close-up of face)
60 Richard Sowells 5.00 10.00
61 Shafer Suggs 5.00 10.00
62 Bob Svihus 5.00 10.00
63 Steve Tannen 5.00 10.00
64 Ed Taylor 5.00 10.00
65 Earlie Thomas 5.00 10.00
67 Godwin Turk 5.00 10.00
68 Phil Wise 5.00 10.00
70 Larry Woods 5.00 10.00
71 Robert Woods 5.00 10.00
72 Roscoe Word 5.00 10.00
8A Ed Bell 5.00 10.00
(facing straight forward)
8B Ed Bell 5.00 10.00
(turned to his side)
17A Richard Caster 6.00 12.00
(listed as Richard)
17B Richard Caster 6.00 12.00
(listed as Rich)
20A John Ebersole Port 5.00 10.00
20B John Ebersole Port 5.00 10.00
20C John Ebersole On field 5.00 10.00
22A Joe Fields mustache 5.00 10.00
22B Joe Fields smiling 5.00 10.00
24A Clark Gaines Action 5.00 10.00
24B Clark Gaines Jacket 5.00 10.00
55A John Riggins 10.00 20.00
(close up portrait)
55B John Riggins Action 10.00 20.00
66A Richard Todd 7.50 15.00
(action photo)
66B Richard Todd 7.50 15.00
(portrait)
69A Al Woodall 5.00 10.00
(green jersey)
69B Al Woodall 5.00 10.00
(white jersey)

1981 Jets Police

This unnumbered Police issue is complete at ten cards. Cards measure approximately 2 5/8" by 4 1/8" and have a green border around the photo on the front of the cards. The set was sponsored by New York City Crime Prevention Section, Frito-Lay, Kiwanis Club, and the New York Jets. The backs each contain a safety tip printed in red ink. The 1981 date is printed on the card backs. Apparently these Jets Police cards were printed on a sheet such that six of the cards were double printed and four of the cards were single printed. The single-printed cards, which are more difficult to find, are indicated below by SP.

COMPLETE SET (10) 14.00 35.00
14 Richard Todd SP 3.00 8.00
42 Bruce Harper .60 1.50
51 Greg Buttle .60 1.50
73 Joe Klecko 1.00 2.50
79 Marvin Powell .60 1.50
80 Johnny Lam Jones SP 1.50 4.00
85 Wesley Walker SP 4.00 10.00
93 Marty Lyons 1.00 2.50
99 Mark Gastineau 1.00 2.50
NNO Team Effort SP 1.50 4.00

1987 Jets Ace Fact Pack

is 33-card set was made in West Germany (by Ace Fact Pack) for sale in England. This set measures approximately 2 1/4" by 3 5/8" and features members of the New York Jets. This set features cards with rounded corners; the card backs have a design for "Ace" like a playing card. We have checklisted the 22 players in the set in alphabetical order.

COMPLETE SET (33) 40.00 100.00
1 Dan Alexander 1.25 3.00
2 Tom Baldwin 1.25 3.00
3 Barry Bennett 1.25 3.00
4 Russell Carter 2.00 5.00
5 Kyle Clifton 2.00 5.00
6 Bob Crable 1.25 3.00
7 Joe Fields 2.00 5.00
8 Rusty Guilbeau 1.25 3.00
9 Harry Hamilton 1.25 3.00
10 Johnny Hector 2.00 5.00
11 Jerry Holmes 1.25 3.00
12 Gordon King 1.25 3.00
13 Lester Lyles 1.25 3.00
14 Marty Lyons 2.00 5.00
15 Kevin McArthur 1.25 3.00
16 Freeman McNeil 2.50 6.00
17 Ken O'Brien 2.50 6.00
18 Tony Paige 2.00 5.00
19 Mickey Shuler 2.00 5.00
20 Jim Sweeney 1.25 3.00
21 Al Toon 3.00 8.00
22 Wesley Walker 3.00 8.00
23 Jets Helmet 1.25 3.00
24 Jets Information 1.25 3.00
25 Jets Uniform 1.25 3.00
26 Game Record Holders 1.25 3.00
27 Season Record Holders 1.25 3.00
28 Career Record Holders 1.25 3.00
29 Record 1967-86 1.25 3.00
30 1986 Team Statistics 1.25 3.00
31 All-Time Greats 1.25 3.00
32 Roll of Honour 1.25 3.00
33 Giants Stadium 1.25 3.00

1988 Jets Ace Fact Pack

Cards from this 33-card set measure approximately 2 1/4" by 3 5/8". This set consists of 22-player cards and 11-additional informational cards about the Jets team. We've checklisted the cards alphabetically beginning with the 22-players. The cards have square corners (as opposed to rounded like the 1987 sets) and a playing card design on the back. These cards were manufactured in West Germany (by Ace Fact Pack) and released primarily in Great Britain.

COMPLETE SET (33) 60.00 120.00
1 Dan Alexander 1.50 4.00
2 Tom Baldwin 1.50 4.00
3 Kyle Clifton 1.50 4.00
4 Bob Crable 1.50 4.00
5 Mark Gastineau 3.00 8.00
6 Alex Gordon 1.50 4.00
7 Harry Hamilton 1.50 4.00
8 Johnny Hector 1.50 4.00
9 Jerry Holmes 1.50 4.00
10 Bobby Humphery 1.50 4.00
11 Lester Lyles 1.50 4.00
12 Marty Lyons 1.50 4.00
13 Kevin McArthur 1.50 4.00
14 Freeman McNeil 3.00 8.00
15 Matt Monger 1.50 4.00
16 Ken O'Brien 2.00 5.00
17 Mickey Shuler 1.50 4.00
18 Kurt Sohn 1.50 4.00
19 Jim Sweeney 1.50 4.00
20 Al Toon 2.00 5.00
21 Roger Vick 1.50 4.00
22 Wesley Walker 2.00 5.00
23 1987 Team Statistics 1.50 4.00
24 All-Time Greats 1.50 4.00
25 Career Record Holders 1.50 4.00
26 Game Record Holders 1.50 4.00
27 Giants Stadium 1.50 4.00
28 Jets Helmet 1.50 4.00
29 Jets Helmet 1.50 4.00
30 Jets Uniform 1.50 4.00
31 Record 1968-87 1.50 4.00
32 Roll Of Honour 1.50 4.00
33 Season Record Holders 1.50 4.00

2004 Jets NY Post Stickers

This set of stickers was issued over a series of weeks within the NY Post newspaper. Each sheet features stickers of a number of Jets players intended to be pasted into an album.

COMPLETE SET (6) 5.00 12.00
1 Sheet 1 1.25 3.00
Kevin Mawae
Chad Pennington
Sam Cowart
Santana Moss
Shaun Ellis (2)
Curtis Martin
Justin McCareins
Giants Stadium
Jets Logo
2 Sheet 2 1.25 3.00
Kevin Mawae
Wayne Chrebet
Ray Mickens
Curtis Martin
Shaun Ellis
Jason Fabini
Santana Moss
Jets Logo
3 Sheet 3 1.25 3.00
Santana Moss
Kevin Mawae
Shaun Ellis
Wayne Chrebet
Curtis Martin
Ray Mickens
Jason Fabini
Jets Logo
4 Sheet 4 1.25 3.00
Jason Fabini
Wayne Chrebet
John Abraham
Justin McCareins
Sam Cowart (2)
Santana Moss
Ray Mickens
Kevin Mawae
5 Sheet 5 1.25 3.00
Wayne Chrebet
Jason Fabini
Justin McCareins
John Abraham (2)
Sam Cowart
Ray Mickens
Chad Pennington (2)
Curtis Martin
NNO Album .60 1.50

2006 Jets Topps

COMPLETE SET (12) 3.00 6.00
NYJ1 Jonathan Vilma .25 .60
NYJ2 Cedric Houston .25 .60
NYJ3 Laveranues Coles .25 .60
NYJ4 Chad Pennington .25 .60
NYJ5 Patrick Ramsey .30 .75
NYJ6 Curtis Martin .30 .75
NYJ7 Tim Dwight .20 .50
NYJ8 Justin Miller .25 .60
NYJ9 B. J. Askew .25 .60
NYJ10 Justin McCareins .25 .60
NYJ11 D'Brickashaw Ferguson .25 .60
NYJ12 Kellen Clemens .25 .60

2007 Jets Delta

These cards were sponsored by Delta and Channel 2 and feature members of the Jets. Each was issued as part of a perforated 4-card sheet and measures roughly 4 14" by 5 1/4" when separated.

COMPLETE SET (16) 7.50 15.00
1 Laveranues Coles .40 1.00
2 Jerricho Cotchery .40 1.00
3 Shaun Ellis .40 1.00
4 D'Brickashaw Ferguson .40 1.00
5 David Harris .40 1.00
6 Victor Hobson .40 1.00
7 Thomas Jones .40 1.00
8 Eric Mangini CO .40 1.00
9 Nick Mangold .40 1.00
10 Mike Nugent .40 1.00
11 Chad Pennington .40 1.00
12 Darrelle Revis .50 1.25
13 Kerry Rhodes .40 1.00
14 Dewayne Robertson .40 1.00
15 Jonathan Vilma .40 1.00
16 Leon Washington .40 1.00

2007 Jets Topps

COMPLETE SET (12) 2.50 6.00
1 Chad Pennington .40 1.00
2 Thomas Jones .40 1.00
3 Laveranues Coles .40 1.00
4 Leon Washington .40 1.00
5 Jerricho Cotchery .40 1.00
6 Kerry Rhodes .40 1.00
7 Justin Miller .40 1.00
8 Jonathan Vilma .40 1.00
9 Cedric Houston .40 1.00
10 Bryan Thomas .40 1.00
11 David Harris .40 1.00
12 Darrelle Revis .50 1.25

2008 Jets Topps

COMPLETE SET (12) 2.50 5.00
1 Chad Pennington .40 1.00
2 Thomas Jones .40 1.00
3 Jerricho Cotchery .40 1.00
4 Kellen Clemens .40 1.00
5 David Harris .40 1.00
6 Jesse Chatman .40 1.00
7 Kerry Rhodes .40 1.00
8 Leon Washington .40 1.00
9 Laveranues Coles .40 1.00
10 Chris Baker .40 1.00
11 Dustin Keller .50 1.25
12 Vernon Gholston .40 1.00

2009 Jets Breast Cancer Awareness

is three card set was issued at a Jets game in 2009. Each unnumbered card was created by one of the three NFL licensed manufacturers and features the pink ribbon breast cancer awareness logo on the fronts.

COMPLETE SET (3) 3.00 6.00
1 Trent Edwards Panini .60 1.50
2 Lee Evans Upper Deck .60 1.50
3 Paul Posluszny Topps .30 .75

2014 Jets Panini Super Bowl XLVIII

COMPLETE SET (10) 2.00 5.00
ISSUED AS PART OF 40-CARD FACT.SET
1 Geno Smith .40 1.00
2 Chris Ivory .50 1.25
3 Bilal Powell .40 1.00
4 Jeremy Kerley .40 1.00
5 Santonio Holmes .40 1.00
6 Muhammad Wilkerson .40 1.00
7 Sheldon Richardson .40 1.00
8 Nick Mangold .40 1.00
9 Dee Milliner .40 1.00
10 Nick Folk .40 1.00

1963 Jewish Sports Champions

The 16 cards in this set, measuring roughly 2 2/3" x 3", are cut out of an "Activity Funbook" entitled Jewish Sports Champions. The set pays tribute to famous Jewish athletes from baseball, football, bull fighting to chess. The cards have a green border with a yellow background and a player close-up illustration. Cards that are still attached carry a premium over those that have been cut-out. The cards are unnumbered and listed below in alphabetical order with an assigned sport prefix (BB-baseball, BK- basketball, BX-boxing, FB- football, OT- other).

COMPLETE SET (16) 100.00 200.00
FB1 Benny Friedman FB 6.00 12.00
FB2 Sid Luckman FB 10.00 20.00

1996 Jimmy Dean All-Time Greats

These cards were issued one per package of various Jimmy Dean products in 1996. The cards include a color photo of the player on the front and biographical information on the back. A mail order offer was included for obtaining a signed card from each player for $7.95 each.

COMPLETE SET (4) 1.60 4.00
1 Tony Dorsett .40 1.00
2 Steve Largent .40 1.00
3 Gale Sayers .60 1.50
4 Bart Starr .80 2.00

1996 Jimmy Dean All-Time Greats Autographs

ese cards were distributed via a mail order offer included with 1996 Jimmy Dean cards. Each card could be originally obtained for $7.95 each and was issued along with a separate paper certificate of authenticity.

COMPLETE SET (4) 45.00 80.00
1 Tony Dorsett 10.00 20.00
2 Steve Largent 7.50 15.00
3 Gale Sayers 10.00 20.00
4 Bart Starr 25.00 40.00

1994-96 John Deere

Over a three year period, the John Deere tractor company used professional athletes to promote their products and included cards of these athletes in their set. These five cards were issued in 1994 (Ryan and Novacek), 1995 (Jackson and Petty) and 1996 (Larry Bird). For our cataloguing purposes we are sequencing these cards in alphabetical order. Larry Bird signed some cards for this promotion but these cards are so thinly traded that no pricing is available

COMPLETE SET (5) 15.00 40.00
3 Jay Novacek 1.00 2.50

1959 Kahn's

e 1959 Kahn's football set of 31 black and white cards features players from the Cleveland Browns and the Pittsburgh Steelers. The cards measure approximately 3 1/4" by 3 15/16". The backs contain height, weight and short football career data. The statistics on the back are single spaced. The cards are unnumbered and hence are listed below alphabetically for convenience.

COMPLETE SET (31) 3000.00 5000.00
1 Dick Alban 75.00 125.00
2 Jim Brown 800.00 1200.00
3 Jack Butler 75.00 125.00
4 Lew Carpenter 75.00 125.00
5 Preston Carpenter 75.00 125.00
6 Vince Costello 75.00 125.00
7 Dale Dodrill 75.00 125.00
8 Bob Gain 75.00 125.00
9 Gary Glick 75.00 125.00
10 Lou Groza 125.00 200.00
11 Gene Hickerson 150.00 250.00
12 Bill Howton 90.00 150.00
13 Art Hunter 75.00 125.00
14 Joe Krupa 75.00 125.00
15 Bobby Layne 175.00 300.00
16 Joe Lewis 75.00 125.00
17 Jack McClairen 75.00 125.00
18 Mike McCormack 100.00 175.00
19 Walt Michaels 90.00 150.00
20 Bobby Mitchell 150.00 250.00
21 Jim Ninowski 75.00 125.00
22 Chuck Noll 500.00 800.00
23 Jimmy Orr 75.00 125.00
24 Milt Plum 90.00 150.00
25 Ray Renfro 90.00 150.00
26 Mike Sandusky 75.00 125.00
27 Billy Ray Smith 75.00 125.00
28 Jim Ray Smith 75.00 125.00
29 Ernie Stautner 150.00 250.00
30 Tom Tracy 90.00 150.00
31 Frank Varrichione 75.00 125.00

1960 Kahn's

e 1960 Kahn's football set of 38 cards features Cleveland Browns and Pittsburgh Steelers. The cards measure approximately 3 1/4" by 3 15/16". In addition to data similar to the backs of the 1959 Kahn's cards, the backs of the 1960 Kahn's cards contain an ad for a free professional album and instruction booklet, which could be obtained by sending two labels to Kahn's. The cards are unnumbered and hence are listed below alphabetically for convenience. Willie Davis' card predates his 1964 Philadelphia Rookie Card by four years.

COMPLETE SET (38) 3500.00 6000.00
1 Sam Baker 50.00 80.00
2 Jim Brown SP 900.00 1500.00
3 Ray Campbell 50.00 80.00
4 Preston Carpenter 50.00 80.00
5 Vince Costello 50.00 80.00
6 Willie Davis 75.00 125.00
7 Galen Fiss 50.00 80.00
8 Bob Gain 50.00 80.00
9 Lou Groza 90.00 150.00
10 Gene Hickerson 100.00 175.00
11 John Henry Johnson 75.00 125.00
12 Rich Kreitling 50.00 80.00
13 Joe Krupa 50.00 80.00
14 Bobby Layne 150.00 250.00
15 Jack McClairen 50.00 80.00
16 Mike McCormack 75.00 125.00
17 Walt Michaels 50.00 100.00
18 Bobby Mitchell 90.00 150.00
19 Dick Moegle 50.00 100.00
20 John Morrow 50.00 80.00
21 Gern Nagler 50.00 80.00
22 John Nisby 50.00 80.00
23 Jimmy Orr 50.00 100.00
24 Bernie Parrish 50.00 80.00
25 Milt Plum 50.00 100.00
26 John Reger 50.00 80.00
27 Ray Renfro 50.00 100.00
28 Will Renfro 50.00 80.00
29 Mike Sandusky 50.00 80.00
30 Dick Schafrath 50.00 80.00
31 Jim Ray Smith 50.00 80.00
32 Billy Ray Smith 50.00 100.00
33 Ernie Stautner 90.00 150.00
34 George Tarasovic 50.00 80.00
35 Tom Tracy 50.00 100.00
36 Frank Varrichione 50.00 80.00
37 John Wooten 50.00 80.00
38 Lowe Wren 50.00 80.00

1961 Kahn's

e 1961 Kahn's football set of 36 cards features Cleveland and Pittsburgh players. The cards measure approximately 3 1/4" by 4 1/16". The backs are the same as the 1960 Kahn's cards; however, the free booklet ad requires but one label to be sent in rather than the two labels required for the 1960 offer. Pictures of Larry Krutko and Tom Tracy are reversed. The cards are unnumbered and hence are listed below alphabetically for convenience.

COMPLETE SET (36) 1200.00 2000.00
1 Sam Baker 25.00 40.00
2 Jim Brown 250.00 400.00
3 Preston Carpenter 25.00 40.00
4 Vince Costello 25.00 40.00
5 Dean Derby 25.00 40.00
6 Buddy Dial 25.00 40.00
7 Don Fleming 25.00 40.00
8 Bob Gain 25.00 40.00
9 Bobby Joe Green 25.00 40.00
10 Gene Hickerson 60.00 100.00
11 Jim Houston 25.00 40.00
12 Dan James 25.00 40.00
13 John Henry Johnson 60.00 100.00
14 Rich Kreitling 25.00 40.00
15 Joe Krupa 25.00 40.00
16 Larry Krutko UER 25.00 40.00
17 Bobby Layne 100.00 175.00
18 Joe Lewis 25.00 40.00
19 Gene Lipscomb 40.00 80.00
20 Mike McCormack 60.00 100.00
21 Bobby Mitchell 75.00 125.00
22 John Morrow 25.00 40.00
23 John Nisby 25.00 40.00
24 Jimmy Orr 25.00 40.00
25 Milt Plum 30.00 50.00
26 John Reger 25.00 40.00
27 Ray Renfro 30.00 50.00
28 Will Renfro 25.00 40.00
29 Mike Sandusky 25.00 40.00
30 Dick Schafrath 25.00 40.00
31 Jim Ray Smith 25.00 40.00
32 Ernie Stautner 60.00 100.00
33 George Tarasovic 25.00 40.00
34 Tom Tracy UER 30.00 50.00
35 Frank Varrichione 25.00 40.00
36 John Wooten 25.00 40.00

1962 Kahn's

e 1962 Kahn's football card set contains 38 players from eight different teams. New teams added in this year's set are the Chicago Bears, Detroit Lions, and Minnesota Vikings. The cards measure approximately 3 1/4" by 4 3/16". The backs contain information comparable to the backs of previous years; however, the statistics are double spaced, and the player's name on the back is in bold-faced type. The cards are unnumbered and hence are listed below alphabetically for conveniencee. An album was also issued to house the set.

COMPLETE SET (38) 1200.00 2000.00
1 Maxie Baughan 25.00 40.00
2 Charley Britt 25.00 40.00
3 Jim Brown 200.00 350.00
4 Preston Carpenter 25.00 40.00
5 Pete Case 25.00 40.00
6 Howard Cassady 25.00 50.00
7 Vince Costello 25.00 40.00
8 Buddy Dial 25.00 50.00
9 Gene Hickerson 40.00 80.00
10 Jim Houston 25.00 40.00
11 Dan James 25.00 40.00
12 Rich Kreitling 25.00 40.00
13 Joe Krupa 25.00 40.00
14 Bobby Layne 90.00 150.00
15 Ray Lemek 25.00 40.00
16 Gene Lipscomb 30.00 60.00
17 Dave Lloyd 25.00 40.00
18 Lou Michaels 25.00 40.00
19 Larry Morris 25.00 40.00
20 John Morrow 25.00 40.00
21 Jim Ninowski 25.00 40.00
22 Buzz Nutter 25.00 40.00
23 Jimmy Orr 25.00 40.00
24 Bernie Parrish 25.00 40.00
25 Milt Plum 25.00 50.00
26 Myron Pottios 25.00 40.00
27 John Reger 25.00 40.00
28 Ray Renfro 25.00 50.00
29 Frank Ryan 25.00 50.00
30 Johnny Sample 25.00 40.00
31 Mike Sandusky 25.00 40.00
32 Dick Schafrath 25.00 40.00
33 Jim Shofner 25.00 50.00
34 Jim Ray Smith 25.00 40.00
35 Ernie Stautner 40.00 80.00
36 Fran Tarkenton 150.00 250.00
37 Paul Wiggin 25.00 40.00
38 John Wooten 25.00 40.00

1963 Kahn's

The 1963 Kahn's football card set includes players from six new teams not appearing in previous Kahn sets. All 14 NFL teams are represented in this set. The new teams are Dallas Cowboys, Green Bay Packers, New York Giants, St. Louis Cardinals, San Francisco 49ers and Washington Redskins. The cards measure approximately 3 1/4" by 4 3/16". The backs contain player statistics comparable to previous years; however, this set may be distinguished from Kahn's sets of other years because it is the only Kahn's football card set that has a distinct white border surrounding the picture on the obverse. With a total of 92 different cards, this is the largest Kahn's football issue. The cards are unnumbered and hence are listed below alphabetically for convenience.

COMPLETE SET (92) 1800.00 3000.00
1 Bill Barnes 15.00 25.00
2 Erich Barnes 15.00 25.00
3 Dick Bass 18.00 30.00
4 Don Bosseler 15.00 25.00
5 Jim Brown 175.00 300.00
6 Roger Brown 15.00 25.00
7 Roosevelt Brown 25.00 40.00
8 Ronnie Bull 18.00 30.00
9 Preston Carpenter 15.00 25.00
10 Frank Clarke 25.00 40.00
11 Gail Cogdill 15.00 25.00
12 Bobby Joe Conrad 15.00 25.00
13 John David Crow 18.00 30.00
14 Dan Currie 18.00 30.00
15 Buddy Dial 18.00 30.00
16 Mike Ditka 90.00 150.00
17 Fred Dugan 15.00 25.00
18 Galen Fiss 15.00 25.00
19 Bill Forester 18.00 30.00
20 Bob Gain 15.00 25.00
21 Willie Galimore 18.00 30.00
22 Bill George 25.00 40.00
23 Frank Gifford 60.00 100.00
24 Bill Glass 18.00 30.00
25 Forrest Gregg 25.00 40.00
26 Fred Hageman 15.00 25.00
27 Jimmy Hill 15.00 25.00
28 Sam Huff 35.00 60.00
29 Dan James 15.00 25.00
30 John Henry Johnson 25.00 40.00
31 Sonny Jurgensen 35.00 60.00
32 Jim Katcavage 18.00 30.00
33 Ron Kostelnik 15.00 25.00
34 Jerry Kramer 25.00 40.00
35 Ron Kramer 18.00 30.00
36 Dick Lane 25.00 40.00
37 Yale Lary 25.00 40.00
38 Eddie LeBaron 25.00 40.00
39 Dick Lynch 15.00 25.00
40 Tommy Mason 18.00 30.00
41 Tommy McDonald 25.00 40.00
42 Lou Michaels 18.00 30.00
43 Bobby Mitchell 30.00 50.00
44 Dick Modzelewski 15.00 25.00
45 Lenny Moore 35.00 60.00
46 John Morrow 15.00 25.00
47 John Nisby 15.00 25.00
48 Ray Nitschke 50.00 80.00
49 Leo Nomellini 25.00 40.00
50 Jimmy Orr 15.00 25.00
51 John Paluck 15.00 25.00
52 Jim Parker 25.00 40.00
53 Bernie Parrish 15.00 25.00
54 Jim Patton 15.00 25.00
55 Don Perkins 25.00 40.00
56 Richie Petitbon 18.00 30.00
57 Jim Phillips 15.00 25.00
58 Nick Pietrosante 15.00 25.00
59 Milt Plum 18.00 30.00
60 Myron Pottios 15.00 25.00
61 Sonny Randle 18.00 30.00
62 John Reger 15.00 25.00
63 Ray Renfro 18.00 30.00
64 Pete Retzlaff 18.00 30.00
65 Pat Richter 15.00 25.00
66 Jim Ringo 25.00 40.00
67 Andy Robustelli 30.00 50.00
68 Joe Rutgens 15.00 25.00
69 Bob St. Clair 25.00 40.00
70 Johnny Sample 18.00 30.00
71 Lonnie Sanders 15.00 25.00
72 Dick Schafrath 15.00 25.00
73 Joe Schmidt 30.00 50.00
74 Del Shofner 18.00 30.00
75 J.D. Smith 15.00 25.00
76 Norm Snead 25.00 40.00
77 Bill Stacy 15.00 25.00
78 Bart Starr 125.00 225.00
79 Ernie Stautner 30.00 50.00
80 Jim Steffen 15.00 25.00
81 Andy Stynchula 15.00 25.00
82 Fran Tarkenton 60.00 100.00
83 Jim Taylor 50.00 80.00
84 Clendon Thomas 15.00 25.00
85 Fuzzy Thurston 25.00 40.00
86 Y.A. Tittle 60.00 100.00
87 Bob Toneff 15.00 25.00
88 Jerry Tubbs 25.00 40.00
89 Johnny Unitas 150.00 250.00
90 Bill Wade 18.00 30.00
91 Willie Wood 25.00 40.00
92 Abe Woodson 18.00 30.00

1964 Kahn's

e 1964 Kahn's football card set of 53 is the only Kahn's football card set in full color. It is also the only set which does not contain the statement "Compliments of Kahn's, the Wiener the World Awaited" on the cardfront. This slogan is contained on the back of the card which also contains player data similar to cards of other years. The cards measure approximately 3" by 3 5/8". The cards are unnumbered and hence are listed below alphabetically for convenience. Paul Warfield's card holds special interest in that it was issued very early in his career.

COMPLETE SET (53) 900.00 1500.00
1 Doug Atkins 18.00 30.00
2 Terry Barr 10.00 20.00
3 Dick Bass 15.00 25.00
4 Ordell Braase 10.00 20.00
5 Ed Brown 15.00 25.00
6 Jimmy Brown 90.00 150.00
7 Gary Collins 15.00 25.00
8 Bobby Joe Conrad 10.00 20.00
9 Mike Ditka 60.00 100.00
10 Galen Fiss 10.00 20.00
11 Paul Flatley 15.00 25.00
12 Joe Fortunato 10.00 20.00
13 Bill George 18.00 30.00
14 Bill Glass 15.00 25.00
15 Ernie Green 15.00 25.00
16 Dick Hoak 10.00 20.00
17 Paul Hornung 30.00 50.00
18 Sam Huff 20.00 35.00
19 Charley Johnson 15.00 25.00
20 John Henry Johnson 18.00 30.00
21 Alex Karras 18.00 30.00
22 Jim Katcavage 15.00 25.00
23 Joe Krupa 10.00 20.00
24 Dick Lane 18.00 30.00
25 Tommy Mason 15.00 25.00
26 Don Meredith 50.00 80.00
27 Bobby Mitchell 20.00 35.00
28 Larry Morris 10.00 20.00
29 Jimmy Orr 15.00 25.00
30 Jim Parker 18.00 30.00
31 Bernie Parrish 10.00 20.00
32 Don Perkins 15.00 25.00
33 Jim Phillips 10.00 20.00
34 Sonny Randle 10.00 20.00
35 Pete Retzlaff 15.00 25.00
36 Jim Ringo 18.00 30.00
37 Frank Ryan 15.00 25.00
38 Dick Schafrath 10.00 20.00
39 Joe Schmidt 18.00 30.00
40 Del Shofner 15.00 25.00
41 J.D. Smith 10.00 20.00
42 Norm Snead 15.00 25.00
43 Bart Starr 60.00 100.00
44 Fran Tarkenton 50.00 80.00
45 Jim Taylor 25.00 40.00
46 Clendon Thomas 10.00 20.00
47 Y.A. Tittle 30.00 50.00
48 Jerry Tubbs 15.00 25.00
49 Johnny Unitas 60.00 100.00
50 Bill Wade 15.00 25.00
51 Paul Warfield 35.00 60.00
52 Alex Webster 15.00 25.00
53 Abe Woodson 10.00 20.00

1971 Keds KedKards

This set is composed of crude artistic renditions of popular subjects from various sports from 1971 who were apparently celebrity endorsers of Keds shoes. The cards actually form a complete panel on the Keds tennis shoes box. The three different panels are actually different sizes; the Bing panel contains smaller cards. The smaller Bubba Smith shows him without beard and standing straight; the large Bubba shows him leaning over, with beard, and jersey number partially visible. The individual player card portions of the card panels measure approximately 2 15/16" by 2 3/4" and 2 5/16" by 2 3/16" respectively, although it should noted that there are slight size differences among the individual cards even on the same panel. The panel background is colored in black and yellow. On the Bench/Reed card (number 3 below) each player measures approximately 5 1/4" by 3 1/2". A facsimile autograph appears in the upper left corner of each player's drawing. The Bench/Reed was issued with the Keds Champion boys basketball shoe box, printed on the box top with a black broken line around the card to follow when cutting the card out.

COMPLETE SET (3) 112.50 225.00
1FB Bubba Smith with beard 30.00 60.00
2FB Bubba Smith no beard 30.00 60.00

1937 Kellogg's Pep Stamps

Kellogg's distributed these multi-sport stamps inside specially marked Pep brand cereal boxes in 1937. They were originally issued in four-stamp blocks along with an instructional type tab at the top. The tab contained the sheet number. We've noted the sheet number after each athlete's name below. Note that six athletes appear on two sheets, thereby making those six double prints. There were 24-different sheets produced. We've catalogued the unnumbered stamps below in single loose form according to sport (AR- auto racing, AV- aviation, BB- baseball, BX-boxing, FB- football, GO- golf, HO- horses, SW- swimming, TN- tennis). Stamps can often be found intact in blocks of four along with the tab. Complete blocks of stamps are valued at roughly 50 percent more than the total value of the four individual stamps as priced below. An album was also produced to house the set.

COMPLETE SET (90) 1000.00 2000.00
FB1 Bill Alexander 2 12.00 20.00
FB2 Matty Bell 3 12.00 20.00
FB3 Fritz Crisler 14 25.00 40.00
FB4 Bill Cunningham 23 12.00 20.00
FB5 Red Grange 16/22 125.00 200.00
FB6 Howard Jones 18 15.00 25.00
FB7 Andy Kerr 4 15.00 25.00
FB8 Harry Kipke 19 12.00 20.00
FB9 Lou Little 8 25.00 40.00
FB10 Ed Madigan 12 12.00 20.00
FB11 Bronko Nagurski 15 125.00 200.00
FB12 Ernie Nevers 21 35.00 60.00
FB13 Jimmy Phelan 20 12.00 20.00
FB14 Bill Shakespeare 10 15.00 25.00
FB15 Frank Thomas 5 15.00 25.00
FB16 Tiny Thornhill 9 12.00 20.00
FB17 Jim Thorpe 17 125.00 200.00
FB18 Wallace Wade 11 12.00 20.00

1948 Kellogg's All Wheat Sport Tips Series 1

Football: Punting 3.00 8.00
22 Football: Passing 3.00 8.00
23 Football: Placement Kick 3.00 8.00
24 Football: Ball Carrying 3.00 8.00

1948 Kellogg's All Wheat Sport Tips Series 2

12 Football: Shoulder Block 3.00 8.00
26 Football: Cross Body Block 3.00 8.00
27 Football: Holding the Ball 3.00 8.00
28 Football: Punt 3.00 8.00

1948 Kellogg's Pep

These small cards measure approximately 1 7/16" by 1 5/8". The card front presents a black and white head-and-shoulders shot of the player, with a white border. The back has the player's name and a brief description of his accomplishments. The cards are unnumbered, but have been assigned numbers below using a sport (BB- baseball, FB-football, BK- basketball, OT- other) prefix. Other Movie Star Kellogg's Pep cards exist, but they are not listed below. The catalog designation for this set is F273-19. An album was also produced to house the set.

COMPLETE SET (20) 700.00 1400.00
FB1 Lou Groza 80.00 120.00
FB2 George McAfee 25.00 40.00
FB3 Norm Standlee 18.00 30.00
FB4A Charley Trippi 50.00 80.00
FB4B Charley Trippi 50.00 80.00
FB5 Bob Waterfield 80.00 120.00

1970 Kellogg's

e 1970 Kellogg's football set of 60 cards was Kellogg's first football issue. The cards have a 3D effect and are approximately 2 1/4" by 3 1/2". The cards could be obtained from boxes of cereal or as a set from a box top offer. The 1970 Kellogg's set can easily be distinguished from the 1971 Kellogg's set by recognizing the color of the helmet logo on the front of each card. In the 1970 set this helmet logo is blue, whereas with the 1971 set the helmet logo is red. The 1971 set also is distinguished by its thick blue (with white spots) border on each card front as well as by the small inset photo in the upper left corner of each reverse. The key card in the set is O.J. Simpson as 1970 was O.J.'s rookie year for cards.

COMPLETE SET (60) 50.00 100.00
1 Carl Eller .60 1.50
2 Jim Otto .60 1.50
3 Tom Matte .40 1.00
4 Bill Nelsen .30 .75
5 Travis Williams .30 .75
6 Len Dawson 2.00 4.00
7 Gene Washington Vik .30 .75
8 Jim Nance .30 .75
9 Norm Snead .40 1.00
10 Dick Butkus 4.00 8.00
11 George Sauer Jr. .40 1.00
12 Billy Kilmer .50 1.25
13 Alex Karras 1.25 2.50
14 Larry Wilson .60 1.50
15 Dave Robinson .40 1.00
16 Bill Brown .30 .75
17 Bob Griese 3.00 6.00
18 Al Denson .30 .75
19 Dick Post .30 .75
20 Jan Stenerud .60 1.50
21 Paul Warfield 2.00 4.00
22 Mel Farr .30 .75
23 Mel Renfro .60 1.50
24 Roy Jefferson .30 .75
25 Mike Garrett .30 .75
26 Harry Jacobs .30 .75
27 Carl Garrett .30 .75
28 Dave Wilcox .50 1.25
29 Matt Snell .40 1.00
30 Tom Woodeshick .30 .75
31 Leroy Kelly .75 2.00
32 Floyd Little .40 1.00
33 Ken Willard .30 .75
34 John Mackey .75 2.00
35 Merlin Olsen 1.50 3.00
36 Dave Grayson .30 .75
37 Lem Barney 1.25 2.50
38 Deacon Jones 1.25 2.50
39 Bob Hayes 1.25 2.50
40 Lance Alworth 2.00 4.00
41 Larry Csonka 3.00 6.00
42 Bobby Bell .75 2.00
43 George Webster .30 .75
44 Johnny Roland .30 .75
45 Dick Shiner .30 .75
46 Bubba Smith 1.25 2.50
47 Daryle Lamonica .50 1.25
48 O.J. Simpson 5.00 10.00
49 Calvin Hill .50 1.25
50 Fred Biletnikoff 2.00 4.00
51 Gale Sayers 4.00 8.00
52 Homer Jones .30 .75
53 Sonny Jurgensen 2.00 4.00
54 Bob Lilly 1.50 3.00
55 Johnny Unitas 6.00 12.00
56 Tommy Nobis .50 1.25
57 Ed Meador .30 .75
58 Spider Lockhart .30 .75
59 Don Maynard 2.00 4.00
60 Greg Cook .30 .75

1971 Kellogg's

e 1971 Kellogg's set of 60 cards could be obtained only from boxes of cereal. One card was inserted in each specially marked box of Kellogg's Corn Flakes and Kellogg's Raisin Bran cereals. The cards measure approximately 2 1/4" by 3 1/2". This set is much more difficult to obtain than the previous Kellogg's set since no box top offer was available. The 1971 Kellogg's set can easily be distinguished from the 1970 Kellogg's set by recognizing the color of the helmet logo on the front of each card. In the 1970 set this helmet logo is blue, whereas with the 1971 set the helmet logo is red. The 1971 set also is distinguished by its thick blue (with white spots) border on each card front as well as by the small inset photo in the uppper left corner of each reverse. Among the key cards in the set is Joe Greene as 1971 was "Mean" Joe's rookie year for cards.

COMPLETE SET (60) 200.00 400.00
1 Tom Barrington 2.50 5.00
2 Chris Hanburger 3.00 6.00
3 Frank Nunley 2.50 5.00
4 Houston Antwine 2.50 5.00
5 Ron Johnson 3.00 6.00
6 Craig Morton 4.00 8.00
7 Jack Snow 3.00 6.00
8 Mel Renfro 5.00 10.00
9 Les Josephson 2.50 5.00
10 Gary Garrison 2.50 5.00
11 Dave Herman 2.50 5.00
12 Fred Dryer 4.00 8.00
13 Larry Brown 3.00 6.00
14 Gene Washington 49er 3.00 6.00
15 Joe Greene 10.00 20.00
16 Marlin Briscoe 2.50 5.00
17 Bob Grant 2.50 5.00
18 Dan Conners 2.50 5.00
19 Mike Curtis 3.00 6.00
20 Harry Schuh 2.50 5.00
21 Rich Jackson 2.50 5.00
22 Clint Jones 2.50 5.00
23 Hewritt Dixon 2.50 5.00
24 Jess Phillips 2.50 5.00
25 Gary Cuozzo 2.50 5.00
26 Bo Scott 2.50 5.00
27 Glen Ray Hines 2.50 5.00
28 Johnny Unitas 17.50 35.00
29 John Gilliam 2.50 5.00
30 Harmon Wages 2.50 5.00
31 Walt Sweeney 2.50 5.00
32 Bruce Taylor 2.50 5.00
33 George Blanda 10.00 20.00
34 Ken Bowman 2.50 5.00
35 Johnny Robinson 3.00 6.00
36 Ed Podolak 2.50 5.00
37 Curley Culp 2.50 5.00
38 Jim Hart 3.00 6.00
39 Dick Butkus 12.50 25.00
40 Floyd Little 3.00 6.00
41 Nick Buoniconti 4.00 8.00
42 Larry Smith RB 2.50 5.00
43 Wayne Walker 3.00 6.00
44 MacArthur Lane 2.50 5.00
45 John Brodie 6.00 12.00
46 Dick LeBeau 2.50 5.00
47 Claude Humphrey 2.50 5.00
48 Jerry LeVias 2.50 5.00
49 Erich Barnes 2.50 5.00
50 Andy Russell 3.00 6.00
51 Donny Anderson 3.00 6.00
52 Mike Reid 4.00 8.00
53 Al Atkinson 2.50 5.00
54 Tom Dempsey 2.50 5.00
55 Bob Griese 10.00 20.00
56 Dick Gordon 2.50 5.00
57 Charlie Sanders 3.00 6.00
58 Doug Cunningham 2.50 5.00
59 Cyril Pinder 2.50 5.00
60 Dave Osborn 2.50 5.00

1978 Kellogg's Stickers

These stickers measure approximately 2 1/2" by 2 5/8". The fronts feature color team helmets with the team's name below. The backs carry a short team history and a quiz about referee's signals. The stickers are numbered on the back "X of 28."

COMPLETE SET (28) 60.00 100.00
1 Atlanta Falcons 3.00 6.00
2 Baltimore Colts 3.00 6.00
3 Buffalo Bills 3.00 6.00
4 Chicago Bears 4.00 8.00
5 Cincinnati Bengals 3.00 6.00
6 Cleveland Browns 4.00 8.00
7 Dallas Cowboys 4.00 8.00
8 Denver Broncos 3.00 6.00
9 Detroit Lions 3.00 6.00
10 Green Bay Packers 4.00 8.00
11 Houston Oilers 3.00 6.00
12 Kansas City Chiefs 3.00 6.00
13 Los Angeles Rams 3.00 6.00
14 Miami Dolphins 4.00 8.00
15 Minnesota Vikings 3.00 6.00
16 New England Patriots 3.00 6.00
17 New Orleans Saints 3.00 6.00

18 New York Giants	3.00	6.00
19 New York Jets	3.00	6.00
20 Oakland Raiders	4.00	8.00
21 Philadelphia Eagles	3.00	6.00
22 Pittsburgh Steelers	4.00	8.00
23 St. Louis Cardinals	3.00	6.00
24 San Diego Chargers	3.00	6.00
25 San Francisco 49ers	3.00	6.00
26 Seattle Seahawks	3.00	6.00
27 Tampa Bay Buccaneers	3.00	6.00
28 Washington Redskins	4.00	8.00

1982 Kellogg's Panels

e 1982 Kellogg's National Football League set of 24 cards was issued in eight panels of three cards each. The cards measure 2 1/2" by 3 1/2" and the panels are approximately 4 1/8" by 7 1/2". The cards came with Kellogg's Raisin Bran cereal and contain statistics on the back. Cards are in color and contain the Kellogg's logo in the lower right corner of the front of the card. While not numbered, the cards have been listed in the checklist below alphabetically according to the left hand side player, when the panel is viewed from the front. Prices below are for full panels of three. It is possible (but not recommended) to separate the cards at the perforation marks. Sharp-eyed Cowboy fans will notice that the photos for Harvey Martin and Billy Joe DuPree were erroneously switched.

COMPLETE SET (8)	4.00	10.00
1 Ken Anderson	.40	1.00
Frank Lewis		
Gifford Nielsen		
2 Ottis Anderson	.75	2.00
Cris Collinsworth		
Franco Harris		
3 William Andrews	.40	1.00
Brian Sipe		
Fred Smerlas		
4 Steve Bartkowski	.40	1.00
Robert Brazile		
Jack Rudnay		
5 Tony Dorsett	.75	2.00
Eric Hipple		
Pat McInally		
6 Billy Joe DuPree UER	.60	1.50
(Photo actually		
Harvey Martin)		
David Hill		
John Stallworth		
7 Harvey Martin UER	.40	1.00
(Photo actually		
Billy Joe DuPree)		
Mike Pruitt		
Joe Senser		
8 Art Still	.40	1.00
Mel Gray		
Tommy Kramer		

1982 Kellogg's Team Posters

These 28 NFL team posters were inserted in specially marked boxes of Kellogg's Raisin Bran cereal. Each poster measures approximately 8" by 10 1/2" and is printed on thin paper stock. Inside a thin black border, the fronts feature a color painting of an action scene, with a smaller painting of another scene placed over to the side. The team name appears inside a bar at the bottom of the picture. The back carries the official contest rules and an entry form for the Kellogg's "Raisin Bran Super Bowl Sweepstakes". If the team pictured on the poster was the winning team in the 1983 Super Bowl, the collector was to print his name and address on the entry form and mail in the entire poster so that it would be received between January 30 and March 19, 1983. From the entries, the winners would be selected in a random drawing to receive one of four trips for two to the 1984 Super Bowl (1st prize) or one of 500 Spalding leather footballs (2nd prize). The posters are unnumbered and checklisted below alphabetically according to the team's city name. The NFL properties logo is prominently displayed on the card front. The posters are typically found with fold marks as they were folded into three parts both horizontally and vertically. The posters are copyrighted 1982 on the front. No players are explicitly identified on the cards. The poster backs are printed in light blue ink.

COMPLETE SET (28)	100.00	250.00
1 Atlanta Falcons	4.00	10.00
2 Buffalo Bills	4.00	10.00
3 Chicago Bears	4.00	10.00
4 Cincinnati Bengals	4.00	10.00
5 Cleveland Browns	4.00	10.00
6 Dallas Cowboys	6.00	15.00
7 Denver Broncos	6.00	15.00
8 Detroit Lions	4.00	10.00
9 Green Bay Packers	8.00	20.00
10 Houston Oilers	4.00	10.00
11 Indianapolis Colts	4.00	10.00
12 Kansas City Chiefs	4.00	10.00
13 Los Angeles Raiders	12.00	30.00
14 Los Angeles Rams	4.00	10.00
15 Miami Dolphins	6.00	15.00
16 Minnesota Vikings	4.00	10.00
17 New England Patriots	4.00	10.00
18 New Orleans Saints	4.00	10.00
19 New York Giants	4.00	10.00
20 New York Jets	4.00	10.00
21 Philadelphia Eagles	4.00	10.00
22 Pittsburgh Steelers	6.00	15.00
23 St. Louis Cardinals	4.00	10.00
24 San Diego Chargers	4.00	10.00
25 San Francisco 49ers	6.00	15.00
26 Seattle Seahawks	4.00	10.00
27 Tampa Bay Buccaneers	4.00	10.00
28 Washington Redskins	12.00	30.00

1983 Kellogg's Stickers

Similar to the 1978 Kellogg's Stickers, these measure approximately 2 1/2" by 2 5/8" with the fronts featuring color team helmets with the team's name below. The backs carry a football game called "Touchdown" that could be played with the cards. A blankbacked version of the stickers was also released.

COMPLETE SET (28)	40.00	80.00
1 Atlanta Falcons	2.00	5.00
2 Baltimore Colts	2.00	5.00
3 Buffalo Bills	2.00	5.00
4 Chicago Bears	2.50	6.00
5 Cincinnati Bengals	2.00	5.00
6 Cleveland Browns	2.50	6.00
7 Dallas Cowboys	2.50	6.00
8 Denver Broncos	2.00	5.00
9 Detroit Lions	2.00	5.00
10 Green Bay Packers	2.50	6.00
11 Houston Oilers	2.00	5.00
12 Kansas City Chiefs	2.00	5.00
13 Los Angeles Raiders	2.50	6.00
14 Los Angeles Rams	2.00	5.00
15 Miami Dolphins	2.50	6.00
16 Minnesota Vikings	2.00	5.00
17 New England Patriots	2.00	5.00
18 New Orleans Saints	2.00	5.00
19 New York Giants	2.00	5.00
20 New York Jets	2.00	5.00
21 Philadelphia Eagles	2.00	5.00
22 Pittsburgh Steelers	2.50	6.00
23 St. Louis Cardinals	2.00	5.00
24 San Diego Chargers	2.00	5.00
25 San Francisco 49ers	2.00	5.00
26 Seattle Seahawks	2.00	5.00
27 Tampa Bay Buccaneers	2.00	5.00
28 Washington Redskins	2.50	6.00

1969 Kelly's Chips Zip Stickers

is set of small stickers was inserted one per package in Kelly's Brand Chips in 1969. Each includes a black and white head photo of the player against a red/orange (cards #1-6), green (#7-12), or blue (#13-20) colored background along with the word "ZIP" on the fronts. The backs contain the sticker number and instructions on obtaining a full color action signed photo of a player. Each sticker measures roughly 2" by 3" and often are found in slightly varying sizes and miscuts.

1 Dave Williams UER	50.00	80.00
2 Johnny Roland	50.00	80.00
3 Willis Crenshaw	50.00	80.00
4 Jim Bakken	50.00	80.00
5 Chuck Walker	50.00	80.00
6 Larry Wilson	60.00	100.00
7 Bart Starr	300.00	500.00
8 John Mackey	60.00	100.00
9 Joe Namath	300.00	500.00
10 Ray Nitschke UER	100.00	175.00
11 Jim Grabowski	60.00	100.00
12 Bob Hayes	90.00	150.00
13 Gale Sayers	175.00	300.00
14 Dick Butkus	175.00	300.00
15 Ed O'Bradovich	50.00	80.00
16 Brian Piccolo	175.00	300.00
17 Mike Pyle	50.00	80.00
19 Roman Gabriel	60.00	100.00
20 Bill Brown	60.00	100.00

1993 Kemper Walter Payton

Kemper Mutual Funds sponsored this card and pin set featuring Walter Payton. The card and pin together were given away at a 1993 Bears game honoring Walter Payton's induction into the Hall of Fame.

COMPLETE SET (2)	3.20	8.00
1 Walter Payton Card	2.00	5.00
2 Walter Payton Pin	1.20	3.00

1989 King B Discs

e 1989 King B Football Discs set has 24 red-bordered 2 3/8" diameter round discs. The fronts have helmetless color mug shots; the backs are white and have sparse bio and stats. One disc was included in each specially marked can of King B beef jerky. The discs are numbered on the back. The set is arranged alphabetically by teams, one player per team, with only 24 of the 28 NFL teams represented. The set, which was produced by Michael Schechter Associates, was apparently endorsed only by the NFLPA. There are many quarterbacks included in the set. The discs are referred to as "1st Annual Collectors Edition." It has been estimated that 500,000 total discs were produced for this issue.

COMPLETE SET (24)	40.00	80.00
1 Chris Miller	1.00	2.50
2 Shane Conlan	.60	1.50
3 Richard Dent	1.00	2.50
4 Boomer Esiason	1.00	2.50
5 Frank Minnifield	.60	1.50
6 Herschel Walker	1.00	2.50
7 Karl Mecklenburg	.60	1.50
8 Mike Cofer	.60	1.50
9 Warren Moon	1.50	4.00
10 Chris Chandler	1.50	4.00
11 Deron Cherry	.60	1.50
12 Bo Jackson	2.00	5.00
13 Jim Everett	1.00	2.50
14 Dan Marino	10.00	25.00
15 Anthony Carter	1.00	2.50
16 Andre Tippett	.60	1.50
17 Bobby Hebert	.60	1.50
18 Phil Simms	1.00	2.50
19 Al Toon	1.00	2.50
20 Gary Anderson RB	.60	1.50
21 Joe Montana	10.00	25.00
22 Dave Krieg	.60	1.50
23 Randall Cunningham	1.50	4.00
24 Bubby Brister	1.00	2.50

1990 King B Discs

e 1990 King B Discs set contains 24 discs each measuring approximately 2 3/8" in diameter. The fronts have color head shots of the players (without helmets), encircled by a red border on a yellow background. The year "1990" in green block lettering and a King B football icon overlay the bottom of the picture. On the backs, the biographical and statistical information is encircled by a ring of stars. The style of the set is very similar to the previous year.

COMPLETE SET (24)	30.00	75.00
1 Jim Everett	.50	1.25
2 Marcus Allen	1.20	3.00
3 Brian Blades	.50	1.25
4 Bubby Brister	.80	2.00
5 Mark Carrier WR	.80	2.00
6 Steve Jordan	.50	1.25
7 Barry Sanders	10.00	25.00
8 Ronnie Lott	.80	2.00
9 Howie Long	1.20	3.00
10 Steve Atwater	.50	1.25
11 Dan Marino	10.00	25.00
12 Boomer Esiason	.80	2.00
13 Dalton Hilliard	.50	1.25
14 Phil Simms	.80	2.00
15 Jim Kelly	1.20	3.00
16 Mike Singletary	.80	2.00
17 John Stephens	.50	1.25
18 Christian Okoye	.50	1.25
19 Art Monk	.80	2.00
20 Chris Miller	.80	2.00
21 Roger Craig	.80	2.00
22 Duane Bickett	.50	1.25
23 Don Majkowski	.50	1.25
24 Eric Metcalf	.80	2.00
NNO Uncut Sheet	35.00	60.00

1991 King B Discs

This set of 24 discs was produced by Michael Schechter Associates, and each one measures approximately 2 5/8" in diameter. One disc was included in each specially marked can of King B beef jerky. The front features a head shot of the player, his name, position, and team name printed in gold in the magenta border. The year and the King B logo are printed at the base of each picture. The circular backs are printed in scarlet and carry biographical and statistical information encircled by stars.

COMPLETE SET (24)	20.00	50.00
1 Mark Rypien	.60	1.50
2 Art Monk	.60	1.50
3 Sean Jones	.40	1.00
4 Bubby Brister	.60	1.50
5 Warren Moon	.80	2.00
6 Andre Rison	.60	1.50
7 Emmitt Smith	5.00	12.00
8 Mervyn Fernandez	.40	1.00
9 Rickey Jackson	.40	1.00
10 Bruce Armstrong	.40	1.00
11 Neal Anderson	.60	1.50
12 Christian Okoye	.40	1.00
13 Thurman Thomas	.80	2.00
14 Bruce Smith	.80	2.00
15 Jeff Hostetler	.60	1.50
16 Barry Sanders	6.00	15.00
17 Andre Reed	.60	1.50
18 Derrick Thomas	.80	2.00
19 Jim Everett	.60	1.50
20 Boomer Esiason	.60	1.50
21 Merril Hoge	.40	1.00
22 Steve Atwater	.40	1.00
23 Dan Marino	6.00	15.00
24 Mark Collins	.40	1.00
NNO Uncut Sheet	8.00	20.00

1992 King B Discs

r the fourth consecutive year, Mike Schechter Associates produced a 24-disc set for King B. One disc was included in each specially marked can of King B beef jerky. The discs measure approximately 2 3/8" in diameter. The fronts feature posed color player photos edged by a bright yellow border on a black face. The player's name appears in white at the top with his position and team name immediately below. The year in white block lettering and a bright yellow King B helmet icon are at the base of the picture. The backs are white with black print, and they carry biography, statistics, the player's name, and the King B helmet icon. The left and right edges are detailed with solid black and black outline stars.

COMPLETE SET (24)	12.00	30.00
1 Derrick Thomas	.40	1.00
2 Wilber Marshall	.30	.75
3 Andre Rison	.40	1.00
4 Thurman Thomas	.50	1.25
5 Emmitt Smith	3.20	8.00
6 Charles Mann	.30	.75
7 Michael Irvin	.50	1.25
8 Jim Everett	.40	1.00
9 Gary Anderson RB	.30	.75
10 Trace Armstrong	.30	.75
11 John Elway	3.20	8.00
12 Chip Lohmiller	.30	.75
13 Bobby Hebert	.30	.75
14 Cornelius Bennett	.40	1.00
15 Chris Miller	.30	.75
16 Warren Moon	.50	1.25
17 Charles Haley	.30	.75
18 Mark Rypien	.30	.75
19 Darrell Green	.30	.75
20 Barry Sanders	3.20	8.00
21 Rodney Hampton	.40	1.00
22 Shane Conlan	.30	.75
23 Jerry Ball	.30	.75
24 Morten Andersen	.30	.75
NNO Uncut Sheet	8.00	20.00

1993 King B Discs

This Fifth Annual Collectors Edition of the King B Discs set was produced by Michael Schechter Associates. One disc was included in each specially marked can of King B beef jerky. Each disc measures approximately 2 3/8" in diameter and features on its front a posed color player head shot bordered on the sides by a green gridiron design. The player's name, position, and team appear in orange and white lettering within the black margin above the photo. The year of the set, 1993, and a blue football helmet icon bearing the King B logo rest in the black margin at the bottom. The backs are white with black print, and they carry the player's name, team, position, biography, statistics (or highlights), and the King B helmet icon. The left and right edges are detailed with solid black and black outline stars. This set was also issued in an uncut sheet measuring 17 1/4" by 12 3/4".

COMPLETE SET (24)	12.50	25.00
1 Luis Sharpe	.40	1.00
2 Erik McMillan	.40	1.00
3 Chris Doleman	.40	1.00
4 Cortez Kennedy	.40	1.00
5 Howie Long	.50	1.25
6 Bill Romanowski	.40	1.00
7 Andre Tippett	.40	1.00
8 Simon Fletcher	.40	1.00
9 Derrick Thomas	.50	1.25
10 Rodney Peete	.40	1.00
11 Ronnie Lott	.50	1.25
12 Duane Bickett	.40	1.00
13 Steve Walsh	.40	1.00
14 Stan Humphries	.50	1.25
15 Jeff George	.50	1.25
16 Jay Novacek	.50	1.25
17 Andre Reed	.50	1.25
18 Andre Rison	.50	1.25
19 Emmitt Smith	4.00	8.00
20 Neal Anderson	.50	1.25
21 Ricky Sanders	.40	1.00
22 Thurman Thomas	1.00	2.50
23 Lorenzo White	.40	1.00
24 Barry Foster	.40	1.00

1994 King B Discs

oduced by Michael Schechter Associates, this was the Sixth Annual Collectors Edition of 1994 King B discs. One disc was included in each specially-marked can of King B beef jerky. The discs measure approximately 2 3/8" in diameter. On a green background, the fronts feature posed color closeups. The player's name, position and the team name appear inside a yellow ochre bar across the bottom part of the photo. The year 1994 and the King B logo are below. The backs are white with green print and carry player biography and statistics. The discs are basically arranged alphabetically and numbered on the back as "X of 24."

COMPLETE SET (24)	12.50	25.00
1 Marcus Allen	.60	1.50
2 Jerome Bettis	1.00	2.50
3 Terrell Buckley	.40	1.00
4 Craig Erickson	.40	1.00
5 Brett Favre	4.00	8.00
6 Barry Foster	.40	1.00
7 Irving Fryar	.40	1.00
8 Gary Brown	.40	1.00
9 Rodney Hampton	.40	1.00
10 Qadry Ismail	.50	1.25
11 Jim Jeffcoat	.40	1.00
12 Jim Lachey	.40	1.00
13 Natrone Means	.50	1.25
14 Tony Meola	.40	1.00
15 Pete Metzelaars	.40	1.00
16 Scott Mitchell	.40	1.00
17 Ronald Moore	.40	1.00
18 Andre Rison	.50	1.25
19 Jay Schroeder	.40	1.00
20 Junior Seau	.50	1.25
21 Shannon Sharpe	.50	1.25
22 Sterling Sharpe	.50	1.25
23 Tim Brown	.60	1.50
24 Chris Warren	.40	1.00

1995 King B Discs

Produced by Michael Schechter Associates, the "7th Annual Collectors Edition" was issued both as a 17 1/4" by 12 1/2" collector sheet and as individual discs in shredded beef jerky containers. The discs measure 2 5/8" in diameter and feature on their fronts color closeup photos on a white back picturing in gray a running back pursued by two defenders. The left side of the disc is dark brown with thin vertical gold stripes. Inside a circle formed by the player's name and alternating football and star icons, the backs present biography and statistics. The discs are numbered on the back "X of 24."

COMPLETE SET (24)	12.50	25.00
1 Errict Rhett	.40	1.00
2 Andre Reed	.50	1.25
3 Rodney Hampton	.40	1.00
4 Kevin Greene	.40	1.00
5 Merton Hanks	.40	1.00
6 Jerome Bettis	.75	2.00
7 Johnny Johnson	.40	1.00
8 Ricky Watters	.40	1.00
9 Harvey Williams	.40	1.00
10 Mel Gray	.40	1.00
11 Craig Erickson	.40	1.00
12 Stan Humphries	.40	1.00
13 Natrone Means	.40	1.00
14 Terance Mathis	.40	1.00
15 Ken Harvey	.40	1.00
16 Brian Mitchell	.40	1.00
17 Cris Carter	.60	1.50
18 Tim Brown	.60	1.50
19 Marshall Faulk	3.00	6.00
20 Eric Turner	.40	1.00
21 Terry Allen	.40	1.00
22 Chris Warren	.40	1.00
23 Randy Baldwin	.40	1.00
24 Ben Coates	.40	1.00

1996 King B Discs

Michael Schechter Associates again produced a King B Discs set in 1996. This "8th Annual Collectors Edition" was issued both as a 17 1/4" by 12 1/2" collector sheet and as individual discs in shredded beef jerky containers. The discs measure 2 5/8" in diameter and feature on their fronts color closeup photos on white paper stock. Only top NFL defensive players were included in the set. The backs present a player biography and statistics as well as the card's number "X of 24."

COMPLETE SET (24)	12.50	25.00
1 Reggie White	1.00	2.50
2 Rickey Jackson	.40	1.00
3 Kevin Greene	.50	1.25
4 Tony Bennett	.40	1.00
5 Bryce Paup	.40	1.00
6 John Copeland	.40	1.00
7 Pat Swilling	.40	1.00
8 Willie McGinest	.40	1.00
9 Charles Haley	.50	1.25
10 Chris Doleman	.40	1.00
11 Clyde Simmons	.40	1.00
12 Hugh Douglas	.40	1.00
13 Henry Thomas	.40	1.00
14 John Randle	.50	1.25
15 Phil Hansen	.40	1.00
16 Bruce Smith	.60	1.50
17 Jim Flanigan	.40	1.00
18 D'Marco Farr	.40	1.00
19 Ray Seals	.40	1.00
20 Neil Smith	.40	1.00
21 Andy Harmon	.40	1.00
22 William Fuller	.40	1.00
23 Tracy Scroggins	.40	1.00
24 Leslie O'Neal	.40	1.00

1997 King B Discs

chael Schechter Associates produced a King B Discs set in 1997 for the 9th time. This set was issued both as a 17 1/4" by 12 1/2" collector sheet and as individual discs in shredded beef jerky containers. The discs measure 2 5/8" in diameter and feature on their fronts color closeup photos on white paper stock. Only top NFL rookies were included in the set. The backs present a player biography and college statistics as well as the card's number "X of 24."

COMPLETE SET (24)	40.00	75.00
1 Orlando Pace	1.00	2.50
2 Darrell Russell	1.00	2.50
3 Shawn Springs	.75	2.00
4 Peter Boulware	1.25	3.00
5 Bryant Westbrook	.75	2.00
6 Walter Jones	1.25	3.00
7 Ike Hilliard	1.25	3.00
8 James Farrior	1.00	2.50
9 Tom Knight	.75	2.00
10 Chris Naeole	.75	2.00
11 Warrick Dunn	3.00	8.00
12 Tony Gonzalez	3.00	8.00
13 Reinard Wilson	.75	2.00
14 Yatil Green	1.25	3.00
15 Reidel Anthony	1.25	3.00
16 Dwayne Rudd	.75	2.00
17 Renaldo Wynn	.75	2.00
18 David LaFleur	.75	2.00
19 Antowain Smith	2.50	6.00
20 Chad Scott	.75	2.00
21 Jim Druckenmiller	1.25	3.00
22 Rae Carruth	.75	2.00
23 Ronnie McAda	.75	2.00
24 Jake Plummer	3.00	8.00

1998 King B Discs

oduced by Michael Schechter Associates, the "10th Annual Collectors Edition" was issued both as a 17 1/4" by 12 1/2" collector sheet and as individual discs in shredded beef jerky containers. The discs measure 2 5/8" in diameter and feature on their fronts color closeup photos with an art drawing of a generic player in the background. Again, the set featured only NFL draft picks and was subtitled Hot Picks. The disc backs feature player vital statistics and career college stats. Each is numbered on the back "X of 24."

COMPLETE SET (24)	25.00	50.00
1 Grant Wistrom	.50	1.25
2 Jerome Pathon	.75	2.00
3 Skip Hicks	.50	1.25
4 Charles Woodson	1.50	4.00
5 Joe Jurevicius	.75	2.00
6 Ira Thomas	.40	1.00
7 Andre Wadsworth	.50	1.25
8 Fred Taylor	3.00	6.00
9 Duane Starks	.50	1.25
10 Takeo Spikes	.75	2.00
11 Anthony Simmons	.40	1.00
12 Brian Simmons	.40	1.00
13 Kevin Dyson	1.00	2.50
14 Curtis Enis	.75	2.00
15 Robert Edwards	1.00	2.50
16 Greg Ellis	.40	1.00
17 Marcus Nash	.40	1.00
18 Jason Peter	.50	1.25
19 Keith Brooking	.75	2.00
20 John Avery	.50	1.25
21 Ahman Green	1.50	4.00
22 Jacquez Green	.50	1.25
23 Brian Griese	3.00	6.00
24 Randy Moss	5.00	12.00

1999 King B Discs

Produced by Michael Schechter Associates (MSA), the "11th Annual Collectors Edition" was issued as individual discs in shredded beef jerky containers. The discs measure 2 5/8" in diameter and feature on their fronts color closeup photos of a top 1998 NFL Draft Pick. The disc backs feature player vital statistics and career college stats. Each is numbered on the back "X of 24."

COMPLETE SET (24)	25.00	50.00
1 Jevon Kearse	1.50	4.00
2 Kevin Johnson	1.50	4.00
3 Torry Holt	1.25	3.00
4 Jermaine Fazande	.50	1.25
5 Shaun King	.50	1.25
6 Edgerrin James	5.00	10.00
7 James Johnson	.50	1.25
8 Chris McAlister	.40	1.00
9 Antoine Winfield	.40	1.00
10 D'Wayne Bates	.40	1.00
11 Peerless Price	1.50	4.00
12 Troy Edwards	.50	1.25
13 Ebenezer Ekuban	.40	1.00
14 Andy Katzenmoyer	.50	1.25
15 Kevin Faulk	.75	2.00
16 David Boston	1.50	4.00
17 Brock Huard	.75	2.00
18 Daunte Culpepper	4.00	8.00
19 Akili Smith	.40	1.00
20 Mike Cloud	.50	1.25
21 Champ Bailey	.75	2.00
22 Rob Konrad	.50	1.25
23 Chris Claiborne	.40	1.00
24 Donovan McNabb	5.00	10.00

2000 King B Discs

is set is titled "Stars of the New Millennium" on the fronts and includes only 2000 NFL Draft picks. The discs were issued one per King B Jerky package. A color image of the player is included on the cardfronts with a simple blue and white cardback.

COMPLETE SET (24)	25.00	50.00
1 Ron Dayne	1.25	3.00
2 Trung Canidate	1.00	2.50
3 Plaxico Burress	1.50	4.00
4 Courtney Brown	.75	2.00
5 Anthony Becht	.60	1.50
6 Shaun Alexander	1.50	4.00
7 Sylvester Morris	.75	2.00
8 Jamal Lewis	2.50	6.00
9 Thomas Jones	.75	2.00
10 Bubba Franks	.75	2.00
11 Ron Dugans	.40	1.00
12 Reuben Droughns	.60	1.50
13 J.R. Redmond	.60	1.50
14 Travis Prentice	.60	1.50
15 Jerry Porter	1.00	2.50
16 Todd Pinkston	.60	1.50
17 Chad Pennington	2.50	6.00
18 Dennis Northcutt	.75	2.00
19 Peter Warrick	1.25	3.00
20 Brian Urlacher	2.50	6.00
21 Travis Taylor	1.00	2.50
22 R.Jay Soward	.60	1.50
23 Corey Simon	.75	2.00
24 Chris Samuels	.40	1.00
NNO Uncut Sheet	7.50	20.00

2001 King B Discs

r the 13th straight year, King B Jerky issued a set of NFL player discs. This set is titled "Prime Pros" as printed on the cardfronts and includes NFL stars licensed by Player's Inc. The discs were issued one per King B Jerky package. A color image of the player is included on the cardfronts with a standard black and white cardback.

COMPLETE SET (24)	25.00	50.00
1 Ray Lewis	.75	2.00
2 Emmitt Smith	2.00	5.00
3 Ed McCaffrey	.75	2.00
4 Dorsey Levens	.60	1.50
5 Edgerrin James	2.00	5.00
6 Mark Brunell	.75	2.00
7 Terrell Owens	.75	2.00
8 Randy Moss	1.50	4.00
9 Daunte Culpepper	.75	2.00
10 Ty Law	.60	1.50
11 Tony Gonzalez	.75	2.00
12 Jason Sehorn	.40	1.00
13 Tiki Barber	.60	1.50
14 Zach Thomas	.75	2.00
15 Kurt Warner	1.50	4.00
16 Marshall Faulk	1.00	2.50
17 Eddie George	.75	2.00
18 Stephen Davis	.60	1.50
19 Jamal Anderson	.60	1.50
20 Tony Siragusa	.40	1.00
21 Corey Dillon	.75	2.00
22 Wayne Chrebet	.60	1.50
23 Curtis Martin	.75	2.00
24 Marvin Harrison	.75	2.00
NNO Uncut Sheet	7.50	20.00

2002 King B Discs

For the 14th straight year, King B Jerky issued a set of NFL player discs. This set is titled "Team Stars" as printed on the cardfronts and includes NFL stars licensed by Player's Inc. The discs were issued one per King B Jerky package. A color image of the player is included on the cardfronts with a standard black and white cardback. A collectible uncut sheet of the entire set was also produced. Please note that two players were incorrectly numbered 21 and that no disc #23 was produced.

COMPLETE SET (24)	25.00	50.00
1 Corey Dillon	.60	1.50
2 Rod Smith	.60	1.50
3 Ahman Green	.75	2.00
4 Edgerrin James	1.25	3.00
5 Tony Gonzalez	.75	2.00
6 Tom Brady	2.50	6.00
7 Michael Strahan	.60	1.50
8 Curtis Martin	.75	2.00
9 Tim Brown	.75	2.00
10 Jerome Bettis	.75	2.00
11 Marshall Faulk	1.00	2.50
12 Kurt Warner	1.50	4.00
13 Terrell Owens	.75	2.00
14 Shaun Alexander	1.00	2.50
15 Warren Sapp	.60	1.50
16 Eddie George	.75	2.00
17 Brett Favre	2.50	6.00
18 Jeff Garcia	.75	2.00
19 Rich Gannon	.60	1.50
20 Jerry Rice	2.00	5.00
21A Kordell Stewart	.60	1.50
21B Adam Vinatieri	.75	2.00
22 Brian Griese	.75	2.00
23 Marvin Harrison	.75	2.00
NNO Uncut Sheet	7.50	20.00

1991 Knudsen

is 18-card set (of bookmarks) produced by Knudsen's Dairy in California measures approximately 2" by 8". They were presented to youngsters who checked out library books during the 1991 football season in order to promote reading. The fronts feature a player photo superimposed on the page of a book, with biography and career summary below. Card numbers appear in circles in the lower right corner of each card. The backs have logos of the sponsors and describe two books that are available at the public library. The bookmarks were distributed in the team's respective areas, San Diego Chargers (1-6), Los Angeles Rams (7-12), and San Francisco 49ers (13-18).

COMPLETE SET (18)	32.00	80.00
1 Gill Byrd	.80	2.00
2 Courtney Hall	.80	2.00
3 Ronnie Harmon	.80	2.00
4 Anthony Miller	.80	2.00
5 Joe Phillips	.80	2.00
6 Junior Seau	1.60	4.00
7 Jim Everett	1.20	3.00
8 Kevin Greene	1.20	3.00
9 Damone Johnson	.80	2.00
10 Tom Newberry	.80	2.00
11 John Robinson CO	.80	2.00
12 Michael Stewart	.80	2.00
13 Michael Carter	.80	2.00
14 Charles Haley	1.20	3.00
15 Joe Montana	14.00	35.00
16 Tom Rathman	.80	2.00
17 Jerry Rice	10.00	25.00
18 George Seifert CO	1.20	3.00

1971 Lake County Rifles Milk Cartons

ese cards were cut from milk cartons and feature a small single color player image from the Lake County (Illinois) semi-pro football team. Each card also include a very short bio of the player as well as the team's season schedule. A coupon good for a discounted game ticket was also included at the bottom, but presumably would be removed from most cards. The cardbacks are blank.

1 Clifford Boyd	5.00	10.00
2 Bruce Hart	5.00	10.00
3 Terry Stanger	5.00	10.00

1993 Lakers Forum

This set features great sports and entertainment personalities who have appeared at the Great Western Forum in Los Angeles during the past 25 years. The set was sponsored by the Los Angeles Times and "Rebuild LA" and celebrates the 25th Anniversary of the Forum with 25,000 sets produced. The set includes one randomly inserted bonus card in each pack of an outstanding Laker basketball player. The bonus cards were numbered on the back with the prefix "BC". The bonus cards were randomly inserted; one could buy five regular sets and still not guarantee a complete insert set. Noted sports artist Terry Smith designed the set. Proceeds from the 12-card sets, originally priced at 25.00 each, were intended to benefit Los Angeles-area Boys and Girls Clubs. The sets were sold at the Forum's box office and concession stands during all Forum events. Sets could also be ordered through Ticketmaster outlets. The cards measure approximately 2 1/2" by 5". The black card fronts have an inner blue border on the left, right, and upper edges. Across the top is a 25th Anniversary design printed on the border with black points along the upper border edge. The name of the highlighted athlete is printed in white with the first name along the left edge and the last name appearing on the bottom edge. The horizontal backs carry a close-up posed shot on the left with a colored panel on the right giving career highlights and significant information pertaining to their appearances at the Great Western Forum.

COMPLETE SET (11)	6.00	15.00
7 Ken Norton	.20	.50

1976 Sports Deck Landsman Playing Cards

ese decks of playing cards were released in the mid-1970s and feature a Landsman black and white artwork image of one player per deck of cards. We've listed only one player name below although each player can be found in all 54-card versions of a standard deck of playing cards. Any additions to this list are appreciated.

COMP.FOREMAN DECK (54)	15.00	30.00
COMP.NAMATH DECK (54)	20.00	50.00
COMP.SAYERS DECK (54)	15.00	40.00
COMP.STABLER DECK (54)	15.00	40.00
COMP.STARR DECK (54)	20.00	50.00
COMP.TARKENTON (54)	15.00	40.00
1 Chuck Foreman	.40	1.00
2 Joe Namath	1.00	2.50
3 Gale Sayers	.60	1.50
4 Ken Stabler	.75	2.00
5 Bart Starr	.75	2.00
6 Fran Tarkenton	.60	1.50

1976 Landsman Portraits

These 8 1/2" by 11" black-and-white portraits were issued around 1976 and feature art by Landsman. The checklist below is thought to be incomplete, however any additional information would be appreciated.

COMPLETE SET (3)	25.00	50.00
1 Chuck Foreman	5.00	10.00
2 Ken Stabler	12.50	25.00
3 Fran Tarkenton	7.50	15.00

1996 Laser View

The 1996 Laser View set was issued in one series totalling 40 cards and features 3.5 seconds of actual game footage printed on super premium 20pt. card stock with full-motion hologram technology. The one-card packs originally retailed for $4.99 each.

COMPLETE SET (40)	15.00	40.00
1 Jim Kelly	.50	1.25
2 Troy Aikman	1.25	3.00
3 Michael Irvin	.50	1.25
4 Emmitt Smith	2.00	5.00
5 John Elway	2.50	6.00
6 Barry Sanders	2.00	5.00
7 Brett Favre	2.50	6.00
8 Jim Harbaugh	.25	.60
9 Dan Marino	2.50	6.00
10 Warren Moon	.25	.60
11 Drew Bledsoe	.75	2.00
12 Jim Everett	.10	.30
13 Jeff Hostetler	.10	.30
14 Neil O'Donnell	.25	.60
15 Junior Seau	.50	1.25
16 Jerry Rice	1.25	3.00
17 Steve Young	1.00	2.50
18 Rick Mirer	.25	.60
19 Boomer Esiason	.25	.60
20 Bernie Kosar	.10	.30
21 Heath Shuler	.25	.60
22 Dave Brown	.10	.30
23 Jeff Blake	.50	1.25
24 Kerry Collins	.50	1.25
25 Kordell Stewart	.50	1.25
26 Scott Mitchell	.25	.60
27 Kerry Collins PE	.50	1.25
28 Troy Aikman PE	.75	2.00
29 Kordell Stewart PE	.50	1.25
30 Michael Irvin PE	.25	.60
31 Emmitt Smith PE	1.25	3.00
32 John Elway PE	1.50	4.00
33 Barry Sanders PE	1.25	3.00
34 Brett Favre PE	1.50	4.00
35 Dan Marino PE	1.50	4.00
36 Drew Bledsoe PE	.50	1.25
37 Neil O'Donnell PE	.25	.60
38 Jerry Rice PE	.75	2.00
39 Steve Young PE	.75	2.00
40 Jeff Blake PE	.25	.60
P5 John Elway Promo	1.25	3.00

1996 Laser View Gold

COMPLETE SET (40)	50.00	100.00
*GOLDS: 1X TO 2.5X BASIC CARDS		
STATED ODDS 1:12		

1996 Laser View Eye on the Prize

Randomly inserted in packs at a rate of one in 24, this 12-card set spotlights on the league's superstar elite as they compete for the coveted Lombardi Trophy.

COMPLETE SET (12)	30.00	80.00
STATED ODDS 1:24		
1 Troy Aikman	4.00	10.00
2 Emmitt Smith	6.00	15.00
3 Michael Irvin	1.50	4.00
4 Steve Young	3.00	8.00
5 Jerry Rice	4.00	10.00
6 Dan Marino	8.00	20.00
7 John Elway	8.00	20.00
8 Junior Seau	1.50	4.00
9 Neil O'Donnell	.75	2.00
10 Jeff Hostetler	.40	1.00
11 Jim Kelly	1.50	4.00
12 Kordell Stewart	1.50	4.00

1996 Laser View Inscriptions

ndomly inserted in packs at a rate of one in 24, this set is a 25-card, sequentially numbered set featuring autographs of some of the top players in the NFL. The cards are unnumbered and listed below alphabetically. The number of autographs that each player signed is listed after his name. There were hand-numbered Promo versions of some signed cards that were released. These Promos typically sell at discounted levels over the below prices.

AUTO/900-4900 ODDS 1:24		
1 Jeff Blake/3125	8.00	20.00
2 Drew Bledsoe/2775	12.00	30.00
3 Dave Brown/3100	8.00	20.00
4 Mark Brunell/3200	10.00	25.00
5 Kerry Collins/3000	10.00	25.00
6 John Elway/3100	30.00	80.00
7 Boomer Esiason/1500	15.00	40.00
8 Jim Everett/3100	8.00	20.00
9 Brett Favre/4850	40.00	100.00
10 Jeff George/2900	8.00	20.00
11 Jim Harbaugh/3500	10.00	25.00
12 Jeff Hostetler/3750	8.00	20.00
13 Michael Irvin/3050	10.00	25.00
14 Jim Kelly/3100	15.00	40.00
15 Bernie Kosar/3200	12.00	30.00
16 Erik Kramer/3150	30.00	80.00
17 Rick Mirer/3150	10.00	25.00
18 Scott Mitchell/4900	8.00	20.00
19 Warren Moon/2800	10.00	25.00
20 Neil O'Donnell/1600	8.00	20.00
21 Jerry Rice/900	60.00	120.00
22 Barry Sanders/2900	40.00	80.00
23 Junior Seau/3000	20.00	40.00
24 Heath Shuler/3100	10.00	25.00
25 Steve Young/1950	25.00	50.00

1983 Latrobe Police

is 30-card standard-size set is subtitled "The Birth of Professional Football" in Latrobe, Pennsylvania. Cards were not printed in full color, rather either sepia or black and white. The set is not attractive and, hence, has never been very aggressively pursued by collectors. The set is available with two kinds of backs. There is no difference in value between the two sets of backs although the set with safety tips on the back seems to be more in demand due to the many collectors of police issues.

COMPLETE SET (30)	6.00	12.00
1 John Kinport Brallier	.40	1.00
2 John K. Brallier	.20	.50
3 Latrobe YMCA Team 1895	.20	.50
4 Brallier and Team	.20	.50
5 Latrobe A.A. Team 1896	.20	.50
6 Latrobe A.A. 1897	.20	.50
7 1st All Pro Team 1897	.20	.50
8 David J. Berry Mgr.	.20	.50
9 Harry Cap Ryan RT	.20	.50
10 Walter Okeson LE	.20	.50
11 Edward Wood RE	.20	.50
12 E.Big Bill Hammer C	.20	.50
13 Marcus Saxman LH	.20	.50
14 Charles Shumaker SUB	.20	.50
15 Charles McDyre LE	.20	.50
16 Edward Abbaticchio FB	.20	.50
17 George Flickinger C LT	.20	.50
18 Walter Howard RH	.20	.50
19 Thomas Trenchard	.20	.50
20 John Kinport Brallier	.40	1.00
21 Jack Gass LH	.20	.50
22 Dave Campbell LT	.20	.50
23 Edward Blair RH	.20	.50
24 John Johnston RG	.20	.50
25 Sam Johnston LG	.20	.50
26 Alex Laird SUB	.20	.50
27 Latrobe A.A. 1897 Team	.20	.50
28 Pro Football	.20	.50
29 Commemorative	.20	.50
30 Birth of Pro Football	.20	.50

1975 Laughlin Flaky Football

is 26-card set measures approximately 2 1/2" by 3 3/8". The title card indicates that the set was copyrighted in 1975 by noted artist, R.G. Laughlin. The typical orientation of the cards is that the city name is printed on the top of the card, with the mock team name running from top to bottom down the left side. The cartoon pictures are oriented horizontally inside the right angle formed by these two lines of text. The cards are numbered in the lower right hand corner (usually) and the backs of the cards are blank.

COMPLETE SET (27)	125.00	225.00
1 Pittsburgh Stealers	8.00	12.00
2 Minnesota Spikings	8.00	12.00
3 Cincinnati Bungles	6.00	10.00
4 Chicago Bares	8.00	12.00
5 Miami Dullfins	8.00	12.00
6 Philadelphia Eggles	6.00	10.00
7 Cleveland Brawns	8.00	12.00
8 New York Gianuts	8.00	12.00
9 Buffalo Bulls	6.00	10.00
10 Dallas Plowboys	8.00	12.00
11 New England Pastry Nuts	6.00	10.00
12 Green Bay Porkers	8.00	12.00
13 Denver Bongos	6.00	10.00
14 St. Louis Cigardinals	6.00	10.00
15 New York Jests	8.00	12.00
16 Washington Redshins	8.00	12.00
17 Oakland Waders	8.00	12.00
18 Los Angeles Yams	6.00	10.00
19 Baltimore Kilts	6.00	10.00
20 New Orleans Scents	6.00	10.00
21 San Diego Charges	6.00	10.00
22 Detroit Loins	6.00	10.00
23 Kansas City Chefs	6.00	10.00
24 Atlanta Fakin's	6.00	10.00
25 Houston Owlers	6.00	10.00
26 San Francisco 40 Miners	8.00	12.00
NNO Title Card	8.00	12.00

1948 Leaf

e 1948 Leaf set of 98-cards features black and white player portraits against a solid colored background. The player's uniforms were also colored and quite a number of variations have been reported in the player's uniform and background colors. We've included the most collected/recognized variations in the listing below but any additions to the variations list are appreciated. The cards measure approximately 2 3/8" by 2 7/8" and can be found on gray or cream colored card stock or a lighter, nearly white, stock. These differences in paper stock may account for the large number of color variations discovered. The second series (50-98) cards are much more difficult to obtain than the first series (1-49). This set features the Rookie Cards of many football stars since it was, along with the 1948 Bowman set, the first major post-war set. The set included then current NFL players as well as current college players.

COMPLETE SET (98)	4500.00	6000.00
WRAPPER (5-CENT)	110.00	160.00
1A Sid Luckman YB RC	250.00	400.00
1B Sid Luckman WB RC		
2 Steve Suhey RC	20.00	30.00
3A Bull.Turner RB BYP RC	75.00	135.00
3B Bull.Turner RB DYP RC	75.00	135.00
3C Bull.Turner WB RC	100.00	175.00
4A Doak Walker BYB RC	125.00	200.00
4B Doak Walker WB RC		
5A Levi Jackson BJ RC	25.00	40.00
5B Levi Jackson WJ RC	30.00	50.00
6A Bobby Layne YP RC	250.00	400.00
6B Bobby Layne RP RC	300.00	500.00
7A Bill Fischer RB BYP RC	20.00	30.00
7B Bill Fischer RB DYP RC	20.00	30.00
7C Bill Fischer WB RC	25.00	40.00
8A Vince Banonis BL RC	20.00	30.00
8B Vince Banonis WL RC	30.00	50.00
8C Vince Banonis WB RC		
9A Tommy Thompson YJN RC	25.00	40.00
9B Tommy Thompson BJN RC	40.00	80.00
9C Tommy Thompson GJN RC	40.00	80.00
10A Perry Moss BFB RC	20.00	30.00
10B Perry Moss TFB RC	20.00	30.00
11A Terry Brennan BYP RC	25.00	40.00
11B Terry Brennan DYP RC	25.00	40.00
12A Bill Swiacki BL RC	20.00	30.00
12B Bill Swiacki WL RC	30.00	50.00
13A Johnny Lujack RC	125.00	200.00
13B Johnny Lujack ERR RC	175.00	300.00
14A Mal Kutner BL RC	20.00	30.00
14B Mal Kutner WL RC	30.00	50.00
15 Charlie Justice RC	50.00	90.00
16A Pete Pihos YJN RC	90.00	150.00
16B Pete Pihos BJN RC	125.00	200.00
17A Kenny Washington BL RC	35.00	60.00
17B Kenny Washington WL RC	50.00	80.00
18A Harry Gilmer MJ RC	30.00	50.00
18B Harry Gilmer PJ RC	30.00	50.00
18C Harry Gilmer RJ RC	30.00	50.00
19A George McAfee RC	90.00	150.00
19B George McAfee ERR RC	125.00	200.00
20A George Taliaferro YB RC	25.00	40.00
20B George Taliaferro WB RC	30.00	50.00
21 Paul Christman RC	30.00	50.00
22A Steve Van Buren GJ RC	150.00	250.00
22B Steve Van Buren YJ RC	175.00	300.00
22C Steve Van Buren GJ BS RC	200.00	350.00
22D Steve Van Buren BJ GS RC	200.00	350.00
22E Steve Van Buren GJ GS RC		
23A Ken Kavanaugh YS RC	25.00	40.00
23B Ken Kavanaugh RS RC		
24A Jim Martin RB BYP RC	25.00	40.00
24B Jim Martin RB DYP RC	25.00	40.00
24C Jim Martin WB RC	30.00	50.00
25A Bud Angsman BL RC	25.00	40.00
25B Bud Angsman WL RC	35.00	60.00
25C Bud Angsman WB RC		
26A Bob Waterfield BL RC	150.00	250.00
26B Bob Waterfield WL RC	300.00	450.00
27A Fred Davis YB RC	20.00	30.00
27B Fred Davis WB RC	30.00	50.00
28A Whitey Wistert YJ RC	25.00	40.00
28B Whitey Wistert GJ RC	30.00	50.00
29 Charley Trippi RC	65.00	110.00
30A Paul Governali BRH RC	25.00	40.00
30B Paul Governali TH RC	25.00	40.00
30C Paul Governali BH RC	30.00	50.00
31A Tom McWilliams MJ RC	20.00	30.00
31B Tom McWilliams RJ RC	25.00	40.00
32A Leroy Zimmerman GNN RC	20.00	30.00
32B Leroy Zimmerman YN RC	20.00	30.00
32C Leroy Zimmerman GYN RC	20.00	30.00
33 Pat Harder UER RC	30.00	50.00
34A Sammy Baugh MJ RC	400.00	600.00
34B Sammy Baugh RJ RC	400.00	600.00
35A Ted Fritsch Sr. DJN RC	25.00	40.00
35B Ted Fritsch Sr. FJN RC	25.00	40.00
36 Bill Dudley RC	75.00	125.00
37A George Connor BYP RC	50.00	100.00
37B George Connor DYP RC	50.00	100.00
38A Frank Dancewicz GNN RC	20.00	30.00
38B Frank Dancewicz BN RC	20.00	40.00
38C Frank Dancewicz GYN RC	20.00	40.00

39 Billy Dewell RC 20.00 30.00
40A John Nolan GN RC 20.00 30.00
40B John Nolan BN RC 20.00 40.00
40C John Nolan YN RC 20.00 40.00
41A Harry Szulborski OP RC 20.00 30.00
41B Harry Szulborski YP RC 30.00 50.00
41C Harry Szulborski YP RC
Orange Pants, bright yellow jersey)
42 Tex Coulter RC 25.00 40.00
43A Robert Nussbaumer MJ RC 20.00 30.00
43B Robert Nussbaumer RJ RC 30.00 50.00
43C Robert Nussbaumer WB RC
44 Bob Mann RC 20.00 30.00
45A Jim White BB RC 25.00 40.00
45B Jim White WB RC
46A Jack Jacobs JN RC 20.00 30.00
46B Jack Jacobs NJN RC 30.00 50.00
47A John Clement BFB BYJ RC 20.00 30.00
47B John Clement BFB DYJ RC 20.00 30.00
47C John Clement YFB RC 60.00 100.00
48 Frank Reagan RC 20.00 30.00
49 Frank Tripucka RC 25.00 40.00
50 John Rauch RC 100.00 175.00
51A Mike DiMitro BYP RC 100.00 175.00
51B Mike DiMitro DYP RC 100.00 175.00
52A Leo Nomellini BBMJ RC 300.00 450.00
52B Leo Nomellini BBRJ RC 350.00 500.00
52C Leo Nomellini WB RC 350.00 500.00
53 Charley Conerly BB RC 300.00 450.00
53B Charley Conerly WB RC
54A Chuck Bednarik YB RC 350.00 500.00
54B Chuck Bednarik WB RC 350.00 500.00
55 Chick Jagade RC 100.00 175.00
56A Bob Folsom BB RC 125.00 200.00
56B Bob Folsom WB RC
57 Gene Rossides RC 125.00 200.00
58 Art Weiner RC 100.00 175.00
59 Alex Sarkistian RC 100.00 175.00
60 Dick Harris RC 100.00 175.00
61 Len Younce RC 100.00 175.00
62 Gene Derricotte RC 100.00 175.00
63A Roy Rebel Steiner RJ RC 100.00 175.00
63B Roy Rebel Steiner WJ RC 125.00 200.00
64A Frank Seno YN RC 100.00 175.00
64B Frank Seno GN RC 100.00 175.00
65A Bob Hendren BYP RC 100.00 175.00
65B Bob Hendren DYP RC 100.00 175.00
66A Jack Cloud BB YJ RC 100.00 175.00
66B Jack Cloud BB GJ RC 100.00 175.00
66C Jack Cloud WB RC 125.00 200.00
67 Harrell Collins RC 100.00 175.00
68A Clyde LeForce RB RC 100.00 175.00
68B Clyde LeForce WB RC 125.00 200.00
69 Larry Joe RC 100.00 175.00
70 Phil O'Reilly RC 100.00 175.00
71 Paul Campbell RC 100.00 175.00
72A Ray Evans RC 100.00 175.00
72B Ray Evans RC 100.00 175.00
73A Jackie Jensen RB RC 250.00 400.00
73B Jackie Jensen WB RC 300.00 450.00
74 Russ Steger RC 100.00 175.00
75 Tony Minisi RC 100.00 175.00
76A Clayton Tonnemaker BYP RC 100.00 175.00
76B Clayton Tonnemaker DYP RC 100.00 175.00
77A George Savitsky GS BYP RC 100.00 175.00
77B George Savitsky GS DYP RC 100.00 175.00
77C George Savitsky NGS RC 125.00 200.00
78 Clarence Self RC 100.00 175.00
79 Rod Franz RC 100.00 175.00
80A Jim Youle RB BYP RC 100.00 175.00
80B Jim Youle RB DYP RC 100.00 175.00
80C Jim Youle WB RC 125.00 200.00
81A Billy Bye YPMJ RC 100.00 175.00
81B Billy Bye YPRJ RC 125.00 200.00
81C Billy Bye WPMJ RC 125.00 200.00
82 Fred Enke RC 100.00 175.00
83A Fred Folger GJ RC 100.00 175.00
83B Fred Folger WJ RC 125.00 200.00
84 Jug Girard RC 125.00 200.00
85 Joe Scott RC 100.00 175.00
86A Bob DeMoss BYP RC 100.00 175.00
86B Bob DeMoss DYP RC 100.00 175.00
87 Dave Templeton RC 100.00 175.00
88A Herb Siegert BYP RC 100.00 175.00
88B Herb Siegert DYP RC 100.00 175.00
89A Bucky O'Conner BJ RC 100.00 175.00
89B Bucky O'Conner WJ RC 150.00 250.00
90 Joe Whisler RC 100.00 175.00
91 Leon Hart RC 150.00 250.00
92 Earl Banks RC 100.00 175.00
93A Frank Aschenbrenner PJ RC 100.00 175.00
93B Frank Aschenbrenner BJ RC 100.00 175.00
94 John Goldsberry RC 100.00 175.00
95 Porter Payne RC 100.00 175.00
96A Pete Perini BB RC 100.00 175.00
96B Pete Perini WB RC
97A Jay Rhodemyre BYJ RC 100.00 175.00
97B Jay Rhodemyre DYJ RC 100.00 175.00
98A Al DiMarco BYP RC 125.00 250.00
98B Al DiMarco DYP RC 125.00 250.00

1949 Leaf

asuring approximately 2 3/8" by 2 7/8", the 1949 Leaf set contains 49 cards that are skip-numbered from 1 to 150. Designed much like the 1948 issue (use of many of the same portraits), the fronts feature player portraits againts a solid background. The player's name is at the bottom. The backs carry career highlights and a bio. The cards can be found on either gray or cream colored card stock. The card backs detail an offer to send in five wrappers and a dime for a 12" by 6" felt pennant of one of the teams listed on the different card backs including college and pro teams. Unlike the 1948 set, all the players portrayed were in the NFL. There are no key Rookie Cards in this set as virtually all of the players in the 1949 set were also in the 1948 Leaf set.

COMPLETE SET (49) 1500.00 2200.00
WRAPPER (5-CENT) 250.00 300.00
1 Bob Hendren 40.00 80.00
2 Joe Scott 18.00 30.00
3 Frank Reagan 18.00 30.00
4 John Rauch 18.00 30.00
7 Bill Fischer 18.00 30.00
9 Elmer Bud Angsman 20.00 35.00
10 Billy Dewell 18.00 30.00
13 Tommy Thompson QB 25.00 35.00
15 Sid Luckman 75.00 125.00
16 Charley Trippi 35.00 60.00
17 Bob Mann 18.00 30.00
19 Paul Christman 25.00 35.00
22 Bill Dudley 35.00 60.00
23 Clyde LeForce 18.00 30.00
26 Sammy Baugh 200.00 350.00
28 Pete Pihos 50.00 70.00
31 Tex Coulter 25.00 35.00
32 Mal Kutner 25.00 35.00
35 Whitey Wistert 25.00 35.00
37 Ted Fritsch Sr. 25.00 35.00
38 Vince Banonis 18.00 30.00
39 Jim White 18.00 30.00
40 George Connor 35.00 60.00
41 George McAfee 35.00 60.00
43 Frank Tripucka 30.00 50.00
47 Fred Enke 18.00 30.00
49 Charley Conerly 60.00 100.00
51 Ken Kavanaugh 25.00 35.00
52 Bob Demoss 18.00 30.00
56 Johnny Lujack 60.00 100.00
57 Jim Youle 18.00 30.00
62 Harry Gilmer 25.00 35.00
65 Robert Nussbaumer 18.00 30.00
67 Bobby Layne 125.00 200.00
70 Herb Siegert 18.00 30.00
74 Tony Minisi 18.00 30.00
79 Steve Van Buren 90.00 150.00
81 Perry Moss 18.00 30.00
89 Bob Waterfield 75.00 125.00
90 Jack Jacobs 18.00 30.00
95 Kenny Washington 30.00 50.00
101 Pat Harder UER 25.00 35.00
110 Bill Swiacki 25.00 35.00
118 Fred Davis 18.00 30.00
126 Jay Rhodemyre 18.00 30.00
127 Frank Seno 18.00 30.00
134 Chuck Bednarik 110.00 175.00
144 George Savitsky 18.00 30.00
150 Bulldog Turner 90.00 150.00

1983 Leaf Football Facts Booklets

One Football Facts Booklet for each NFL team was produced by Leaf in 1983. They were distributed one per small box of Leaf bubble gum and unfold to reveal team history and statistics. The booklets are unnumbered.

COMPLETE SET (28) 30.00 75.00
1 Atlanta Falcons 1.25 3.00
2 Baltimore Colts 1.25 3.00
3 Buffalo Bills 1.25 3.00
4 Chicago Bears 2.00 5.00
5 Cincinnati Bengals 1.25 3.00
6 Cleveland Browns 1.25 3.00
7 Dallas Cowboys 2.50 6.00
8 Denver Broncos 1.25 3.00
9 Detroit Lions 1.25 3.00
10 Green Bay Packers 2.50 6.00
11 Houston Oilers 1.25 3.00
12 Kansas City Chiefs 1.25 3.00
13 Los Angeles Rams 1.25 3.00
14 Miami Dolphins 2.50 6.00
15 Minnesota Vikings 1.25 3.00
16 New England Patriots 1.25 3.00
17 New Orleans Saints 1.25 3.00
18 New York Giants 1.25 3.00
19 New York Jets 1.25 3.00
20 Oakland Raiders 2.50 6.00
21 Philadelphia Eagles 1.25 3.00
22 Pittsburgh Steelers 2.50 6.00
23 St. Louis Cardinals 1.25 3.00
24 San Diego Chargers 1.25 3.00
25 San Francisco 49ers 2.50 6.00
26 Seattle Seahawks 1.25 3.00
27 Tampa Bay Buccaneers 1.25 3.00
28 Washington Redskins 2.50 6.00

1996 Leaf

This 190-card set was distributed in 10-card packs with a suggested retail price of $2.99. The fronts feature borderless action color player photos with silver foil highlights. The backs carry another player photo with career statistics.

COMPLETE SET (190) 7.50 20.00
1 Troy Aikman .40 1.00
2 Ricky Watters .07 .20
3 Robert Brooks .15 .40
4 Ki-Jana Carter .07 .20
5 Drew Bledsoe .25 .60
6 Eric Swann .02 .10
7 Hardy Nickerson .02 .10
8 Tony Martin .07 .20
9 Garrison Hearst .07 .20
10 Bernie Parmalee .02 .10
11 Neil Smith .07 .20
12 Aaron Craver .02 .10
13 Rashaan Salaam .07 .20
14 Greg Hill .07 .20
15 Charlie Garner .07 .20
16 Kimble Anders .07 .20
17 Steve McNair .30 .75
18 Neil O'Donnell .07 .20
19 Greg Lloyd .07 .20
20 Warren Moon .07 .20
21 Bernie Kosar .02 .10
22 Derrick Thomas .15 .40
23 Andre Hastings .02 .10
24 Wayne Chrebet .25 .60
25 Mark Seay .02 .10
26 Eric Metcalf .02 .10
27 Shawn Jefferson .02 .10
28 Napoleon Kaufman .15 .40
29 Steve Walsh .02 .10
30 Derrick Alexander DE .02 .10
31 Rodney Peete .02 .10
32 Terance Mathis .02 .10
33 Michael Westbrook .15 .40
34 Kevin Carter .02 .10
35 Aaron Hayden RC .02 .10
36 J.J. Stokes .15 .40
37 Andre Reed .07 .20
38 Chris Warren .07 .20
39 Jerry Rice .40 1.00
40 Ben Coates .07 .20
41 Reggie White .15 .40
42 Joey Galloway .15 .40
43 Sean Dawkins .02 .10
44 Brett Favre .75 2.00
45 Jeff George .07 .20
46 Robert Smith .07 .20
47 Ken Dilger .07 .20
48 Larry Centers .07 .20
49 Jackie Harris .02 .10
50 Hugh Douglas .07 .20
51 Herschel Walker .07 .20
52 Kerry Collins .15 .40
53 Michael Irvin .15 .40
54 Willie McGinest .02 .10
55 Herman Moore .07 .20
56 Leroy Hoard .02 .10
57 Scott Mitchell .07 .20
58 Terrell Davis .30 .75
59 Kevin Greene .07 .20
60 Yancey Thigpen .07 .20
61 Kevin Smith .02 .10
62 Trent Dilfer .15 .40
63 Cortez Kennedy .02 .10
64 Carnell Lake .02 .10
65 Quinn Early .02 .10
66 Kyle Brady .02 .10
67 Marshall Faulk .20 .50
68 Fred Barnett .02 .10
69 Quentin Coryatt .02 .10
70 Dan Marino .75 2.00
71 Junior Seau .15 .40
72 Andre Coleman .02 .10
73 Terry Kirby .07 .20
74 Curtis Martin .30 .75
75 Isaac Bruce .15 .40
76 Mark Chmura .07 .20
77 Edgar Bennett .07 .20
78 Mario Bates .07 .20
79 Eric Zeier .02 .10
80 Adrian Murrell .07 .20
81 Mark Brunell .25 .60
82 Mark Rypien .02 .10
83 Erric Pegram .02 .10
84 Bryan Cox .02 .10
85 Heath Shuler .07 .20
86 Lake Dawson .02 .10
87 O.J. McDuffie .07 .20
88 Emmitt Smith .60 1.50
89 Jim Harbaugh .07 .20
90 Aaron Bailey .02 .10
91 Jim Kelly .15 .40
92 Rodney Hampton .07 .20
93 Cris Carter .15 .40
94 Henry Ellard .02 .10
95 Darnay Scott .07 .20
96 Daryl Johnston .07 .20
97 Tamarick Vanover .07 .20
98 Jeff Blake .15 .40
99 Anthony Miller .07 .20
100 Darren Woodson .07 .20
101 Irving Fryar .07 .20
102 Craig Heyward .02 .10
103 Derek Loville .02 .10
104 Ernie Mills .02 .10
105 Brian Blades .02 .10
106 Gus Frerotte .07 .20
107 Alvin Harper .02 .10
108 Tyrone Wheatley .07 .20
109 John Elway .75 2.00
110 Charles Haley .07 .20
111 Terrell Fletcher .02 .10
112 Vincent Brisby .02 .10
113 Jerome Bettis .15 .40
114 Barry Sanders .60 1.50
115 Ken Norton Jr. .02 .10
116 Sherman Williams .02 .10
117 Antonio Freeman .15 .40
118 Bert Emanuel .07 .20
119 Marcus Allen .15 .40
120 Stan Humphries .07 .20
121 Chris Sanders .07 .20
122 Jeff Graham .02 .10
123 Jay Novacek .02 .10
124 Aeneas Williams .02 .10
125 Kordell Stewart .15 .40
126 Steve Young .30 .75
127 Jake Reed .07 .20
128 Rick Mirer .07 .20
129 Jeff Hostetler .02 .10
130 Tim Brown .15 .40
131 Shannon Sharpe .07 .20
132 Dave Brown .02 .10
133 Harvey Williams .02 .10
134 Rodney Thomas .02 .10
135 Frank Sanders .07 .20
136 Brett Perriman .02 .10
137 Steve Bono .02 .10
138 Steve Atwater .02 .10
139 Andre Rison .07 .20
140 Orlando Thomas .02 .10
141 Terry Allen .07 .20
142 Carl Pickens .07 .20
143 William Floyd .07 .20
144 Bryce Paup .02 .10
145 James O. Stewart .07 .20
146 Eric Bjornson .02 .10
147 Errict Rhett .07 .20
148 Darick Holmes .02 .10
149 Brian Mitchell .02 .10
150 Brent Jones .02 .10
151 Natrone Means .07 .20
152 Rod Woodson .07 .20
153 Bruce Smith .07 .20
154 Deion Sanders .25 .60
155 Kevin Williams .02 .10
156 Erik Kramer .02 .10
157 Jim Everett .02 .10
158 Vinny Testaverde .07 .20
159 Boomer Esiason .07 .20
160 Leslie O'Neal .02 .10
161 Curtis Conway .15 .40
162 Thurman Thomas .15 .40
163 Tony Brackens RC .15 .40
164 Steptret Williams RC .07 .20
165 Alex Van Dyke RC .07 .20
166 Cedric Jones RC .02 .10
167 Stanley Pritchett RC .07 .20
168 Willie Anderson RC .02 .10
169 Regan Upshaw RC .02 .10
170 Daryl Gardener RC .02 .10
171 Alex Molden RC .02 .10
172 John Mobley RC .02 .10
173 Danny Kanell RC .15 .40
174 Marco Battaglia RC .02 .10
175 Simeon Rice RC .40 1.00
176 Tony Banks RC .15 .40
177 Stephen Davis RC .60 1.50
178 Walt Harris RC .02 .10
179 Amani Toomer RC .40 1.00
180 Derrick Mayes RC .15 .40
181 Jeff Lewis RC .07 .20
182 Chris Darkins RC .02 .10
183 Rickey Dudley RC .15 .40
184 Jonathan Ogden RC .40 1.00
185 Mike Alstott RC .50 1.25
186 Eric Moulds RC .60 1.50
187 Karim Abdul-Jabbar RC .15 .40
188 Jerry Rice CL .15 .40
189 Dan Marino CL .15 .40
190 Emmitt Smith CL .15 .40

1996 Leaf Collector's Edition

COMP.FACT SET (191) 12.50 30.00
COMPLETE SET (190) 7.50 20.00
*COLLECTOR EDITION: .4X TO 1X BASIC CARDS

1996 Leaf Press Proofs

COMPLETE SET (190) 100.00 200.00
*STARS: 4X TO 10X BASIC CARDS
*RCs: 2.5X TO 6X BASIC CARDS
ANNOUNCED PRINT RUN 2000 SETS

1996 Leaf Red

*STARS: .6X TO 1.5X BASIC CARDS
*ROOKIES: .4X TO 1X BASIC CARDS

1996 Leaf American All-Stars

This 20-card set features color player photos of top former All-American NFL players printed on simulated sail cloth card stock with the look and feel of a real American flag. Only 5000 of this set were produced, and each card is sequentially numbered. A Gold parallel version numbered of 1000 set produced was also randomly seeded in packs.

COMPLETE SET (20) 75.00 150.00
STATED PRINT RUN 5000 SERIAL #'d SETS
*GOLDS: .8X TO 2X BASIC INSERTS
GOLDS PRINT RUN 1000 SERIAL #'d SETS
1 Emmitt Smith 5.00 12.00
2 Drew Bledsoe 2.00 5.00
3 Jerry Rice 3.00 8.00
4 Kerry Collins 1.25 3.00
5 Eddie George .60 1.50
6 Keyshawn Johnson 2.50 6.00
7 Lawrence Phillips 1.00 2.50
8 Rashaan Salaam .60 1.50
9 Deion Sanders 2.00 5.00
10 Marshall Faulk 1.50 4.00
11 Steve Young 2.50 6.00
12 Ki-Jana Carter .60 1.50
13 Curtis Martin 2.50 6.00
14 Joey Galloway 1.25 3.00
15 Troy Aikman 3.00 8.00
16 Barry Sanders 5.00 12.00
17 Dan Marino 6.00 15.00
18 John Elway 6.00 15.00
19 Steve McNair 2.50 6.00
20 Tim Biakabutuka 1.00 2.50

1996 Leaf Collector's Edition Autographs

ndomly inserted at the rate of at least one per factory set, this 9-card set features authentic player autographs. Reportedly, no more than 2000 autographs were produced of any of the players. The original checklist from Pinnacle listed 11 players, but only 9 were ever confirmed to exist. The cards are checklisted below alphabetically.

COMPLETE SET (9) 75.00 150.00
ONE PER COLL.EDITION FACT.SET
ANNOUNCED PRINT RUN 2000 SETS
1 Karim Abdul-Jabbar 5.00 12.00
2 Isaac Bruce 6.00 15.00
3 Terrell Davis 15.00 40.00
4 Bobby Engram 4.00 10.00
5 Joey Galloway 6.00 15.00
6 Marvin Harrison 30.00 50.00
7 Eddie Kennison 5.00 12.00
8 Leeland McElroy 4.00 10.00
9 Tamarick Vanover 5.00 12.00

1996 Leaf Gold Leaf Rookies

This 10-card set features color photos of ten standout newcomers with gold foil triangular side borders. The backs carry another player photo with team color triangular side borders and a paragraph about the player.

COMPLETE SET (10) 7.50 20.00
1 Leeland McElroy .60 1.50
2 Marvin Harrison 2.50 6.00
3 Lawrence Phillips 1.00 2.50
4 Bobby Engram .60 1.50
5 Kevin Hardy .60 1.50
6 Keyshawn Johnson 1.00 2.50
7 Eddie Kennison .60 1.50
8 Tim Biakabutuka 1.00 2.50
9 Eddie George 1.25 3.00
10 Terry Glenn 1.00 2.50

1996 Leaf Gold Leaf Stars

Randomly inserted in retail packs only, this 15-card set features color player photos on a gold foil background with a 22 karat gold seal. The backs carry a small player photo and a paragraph about the player. Only 2500 of this set were produced.

COMPLETE SET (15) 100.00 200.00
RANDOM INSERTS IN RETAIL PACKS
STATED PRINT RUN 2500 SERIAL #'d SETS
1 Drew Bledsoe 4.00 10.00
2 Jerry Rice 6.00 15.00
3 Emmitt Smith 10.00 25.00
4 Dan Marino 12.50 30.00
5 Isaac Bruce 2.50 6.00
6 Kerry Collins 2.50 6.00
7 Barry Sanders 10.00 25.00
8 Keyshawn Johnson 3.00 8.00
9 Errict Rhett 1.25 3.00
10 Joey Galloway 2.50 6.00
11 Brett Favre 12.50 30.00
12 Curtis Martin 5.00 12.00
13 Steve Young 5.00 12.00
14 Troy Aikman 6.00 15.00
15 John Elway 12.50 30.00

1996 Leaf Grass Roots

is 20-card set features color images of some of the NFL's top running backs on a simulated artificial turf look and feel background. The backs carry another player photo and a paragraph about the player's running ability. Only 5000 of this set were produced with each card being sequentially numbered.

COMPLETE SET (20) 25.00 50.00
STATED PRINT RUN 5000 SERIAL #'d SETS
*PROMOS: .4X TO 1X BASIC INSERTS
1 Thurman Thomas 1.00 2.50
2 Eddie George 3.00 8.00
3 Rodney Hampton .50 1.25
4 Rashaan Salaam .50 1.25
5 Natrone Means .50 1.25
6 Errict Rhett .50 1.25
7 Leeland McElroy .25 .60
8 Emmitt Smith 4.00 10.00
9 Marshall Faulk 1.25 3.00
10 Ricky Watters .50 1.25
11 Chris Warren .50 1.25
12 Tim Biakabutuka 1.00 2.50
13 Barry Sanders 4.00 10.00
14 Karim Abdul-Jabbar 1.00 2.50
15 Darick Holmes .25 .60
16 Terrell Davis 2.00 5.00
17 Lawrence Phillips 1.00 2.50
18 Ki-Jana Carter .50 1.25
19 Curtis Martin 2.00 5.00
20 Kordell Stewart 1.00 2.50

1996 Leaf Grass Roots Promos

Emmitt Smith 4.00 10.00
13 Barry Sanders 3.00 8.00
20 Kordell Stewart 1.00 2.50

1996 Leaf Shirt Off My Back

ndomly inserted in magazine packs only, this 10-card set features color images of the league's top quarterbacks with each team jersey and number as a background and is printed on card stock that simulates jersey material. Only 2500 of each card were produced and are sequentially numbered.

COMPLETE SET (10) 50.00 125.00
RANDOM INS.IN MAGAZINE PACKS
STATED PRINT RUN 2500 SETS
1 Steve Young 5.00 12.00
2 Jeff Blake 2.50 6.00
3 Drew Bledsoe 3.00 8.00
4 Kordell Stewart 2.50 6.00
5 Troy Aikman 6.00 15.00
6 Steve McNair 5.00 12.00
7 John Elway 10.00 25.00
8 Dan Marino 10.00 25.00
9 Kerry Collins 2.50 6.00
10 Brett Favre 12.50 30.00

1996 Leaf Statistical Standouts

ndomly inserted in hobby packs only, this 15-card set features color player images printed on a simulated leather football die-cut card. The backs carry a small player circular head photo with season and career statistics. Only 2500 of each card were produced and are sequentially numbered.

COMPLETE SET (15) 75.00 150.00
RANDOM INSERTS IN HOBBY PACKS
STATED PRINT RUN 2500 SERIAL #'d SETS
1 John Elway 10.00 25.00
2 Jerry Rice 5.00 12.00
3 Reggie White 2.00 5.00
4 Drew Bledsoe 3.00 8.00
5 Chris Warren 1.00 2.50
6 Bruce Smith 1.00 2.50
7 Barry Sanders 8.00 20.00
8 Greg Lloyd 1.00 2.50
9 Emmitt Smith 8.00 20.00
10 Dan Marino 10.00 25.00
11 Steve Young 4.00 10.00
12 Steve Atwater .50 1.25
13 Isaac Bruce 2.00 5.00
14 Deion Sanders 3.00 8.00
15 Brett Favre 10.00 25.00

1997 Leaf

is 200-card set features color action player photos and was distributed in 10-card packs with a suggested retail price of $2.99. The set contains the following subsets: Gold Leaf Rookies (#153-182) and Legacy (#183-197).

COMPLETE SET (200) 10.00 25.00
1 Steve Young .30 .75
2 Brett Favre 1.00 2.50
3 Barry Sanders .75 2.00
4 Drew Bledsoe .30 .75
5 Troy Aikman .50 1.25
6 Kerry Collins .25 .60
7 Dan Marino 1.00 2.50
8 Jerry Rice .50 1.25
9 John Elway 1.00 2.50
10 Emmitt Smith .75 2.00
11 Tony Banks .15 .40
12 Gus Frerotte .08 .25
13 Elvis Grbac .15 .40
14 Neil O'Donnell .15 .40
15 Michael Irvin .25 .60
16 Marshall Faulk .30 .75
17 Todd Collins .08 .25
18 Scott Mitchell .15 .40
19 Trent Dilfer .25 .60
20 Rick Mirer .08 .25
21 Frank Sanders .15 .40
22 Larry Centers .15 .40
23 Brad Johnson .25 .60
24 Garrison Hearst .15 .40
25 Steve McNair .30 .75
26 Dorsey Levens .25 .60
27 Eric Metcalf .15 .40
28 Jeff George .15 .40
29 Rodney Hampton .15 .40
30 Michael Westbrook .15 .40
31 Cris Carter .25 .60
32 Heath Shuler .08 .25
33 Warren Moon .25 .60
34 Rod Woodson .15 .40
35 Ken Dilger .08 .25
36 Ben Coates .15 .40
37 Andre Reed .15 .40
38 Terrell Owens .30 .75
39 Jeff Blake .15 .40
40 Vinny Testaverde .15 .40
41 Robert Brooks .15 .40
42 Shannon Sharpe .15 .40
43 Terry Allen .25 .60
44 Terance Mathis .15 .40
45 Bobby Engram .15 .40
46 Rickey Dudley .15 .40
47 Alex Molden .08 .25
48 Lawrence Phillips .08 .25
49 Curtis Martin .30 .75
50 Jim Harbaugh .15 .40
51 Wayne Chrebet .25 .60
52 Quentin Coryatt .08 .25
53 Eddie George .25 .60
54 Michael Jackson .15 .40
55 Greg Lloyd .08 .25
56 Natrone Means .15 .40
57 Marcus Allen .25 .60
58 Desmond Howard .15 .40
59 Stan Humphries .15 .40
60 Reggie White .25 .60
61 Brett Perriman .08 .25
62 Warren Sapp .15 .40
63 Adrian Murrell .15 .40
64 Mark Brunell .30 .75
65 Carl Pickens .15 .40
66 Kordell Stewart .25 .60
67 Ricky Watters .15 .40
68 Tyrone Wheatley .15 .40
69 Stanley Pritchett .08 .25
70 Kevin Greene .15 .40
71 Karim Abdul-Jabbar .15 .40
72 Ki-Jana Carter .08 .25
73 Rashaan Salaam .08 .25
74 Simeon Rice .15 .40
75 Napoleon Kaufman .25 .60
76 Muhsin Muhammad .15 .40
77 Bruce Smith .15 .40
78 Eric Moulds .25 .60
79 O.J. McDuffie .15 .40
80 Danny Kanell .08 .25
81 Harvey Williams .08 .25
82 Greg Hill .08 .25
83 Terrell Davis .30 .75
84 Dan Wilkinson .08 .25
85 Yancey Thigpen .15 .40
86 Darrell Green .15 .40
87 Tamarick Vanover .15 .40
88 Mike Alstott .25 .60
89 Johnnie Morton .15 .40
90 Dale Carter .08 .25
91 Jerome Bettis .25 .60
92 James O.Stewart .15 .40
93 Irving Fryar .15 .40
94 Junior Seau .25 .60
95 Sean Dawkins .08 .25
96 J.J. Stokes .15 .40
97 Tim Biakabutuka .15 .40
98 Bert Emanuel .15 .40
99 Eddie Kennison .15 .40
100 Ray Zellars .08 .25
101 Dave Brown .08 .25
102 Leeland McElroy .08 .25
103 Chris Warren .15 .40
104 Byron Bam Morris .08 .25
105 Thurman Thomas .25 .60
106 Kyle Brady .08 .25
107 Anthony Miller .08 .25
108 Derrick Thomas .25 .60
109 Mark Chmura .15 .40
110 Deion Sanders .25 .60
111 Eric Swann .08 .25
112 Amani Toomer .15 .40
113 Raymont Harris .08 .25
114 Jake Reed .15 .40
115 Bryant Young .08 .25
116 Keenan McCardell .15 .40
117 Herman Moore .25 .60
118 Errict Rhett .08 .25
119 Henry Ellard .08 .25
120 Bobby Hoying .15 .40
121 Robert Smith .15 .40
122 Keyshawn Johnson .25 .60
123 Zach Thomas .25 .60
124 Charlie Garner .15 .40
125 Terry Kirby .15 .40
126 Darren Woodson .08 .25
127 Darnay Scott .15 .40
128 Chris Sanders .08 .25
129 Charles Johnson .15 .40
130 Joey Galloway .15 .40
131 Curtis Conway .15 .40
132 Isaac Bruce .25 .60
133 Bobby Taylor .08 .25
134 Jamal Anderson .25 .60
135 Ken Norton .08 .25
136 Darick Holmes .08 .25
137 Tony Brackens .08 .25
138 Tony Martin .15 .40
139 Antonio Freeman .25 .60
140 Neil Smith .15 .40
141 Terry Glenn .25 .60
142 Marvin Harrison .25 .60
143 Daryl Johnston .15 .40
144 Tim Brown .25 .60
145 Kimble Anders .15 .40
146 Derrick Alexander WR .15 .40
147 LeShon Johnson .08 .25
148 Anthony Johnson .08 .25
149 Leslie Shepherd .08 .25
150 Chris T. Jones .08 .25
151 Edgar Bennett .15 .40
152 Ty Detmer .15 .40
153 Ike Hilliard RC .40 1.00
154 Jim Druckenmiller RC .15 .40
155 Warrick Dunn RC .75 2.00
156 Yatil Green RC .15 .40
157 Reidel Anthony RC .25 .60
158 Antowain Smith RC .60 1.50
159 Rae Carruth RC .08 .25
160 Tiki Barber RC 1.50 4.00
161 Byron Hanspard RC .15 .40
162 Jake Plummer RC 1.00 2.50
163 Joey Kent RC .25 .60
164 Corey Dillon RC 1.00 2.50
165 Kevin Lockett RC .15 .40
166 Will Blackwell RC .15 .40
167 Troy Davis RC .15 .40
168 James Farrior RC .25 .60
169 Danny Wuerffel RC .25 .60
170 Pat Barnes RC .25 .60
171 Darnell Autry RC .15 .40
172 Tom Knight RC .08 .25
173 David LaFleur RC .08 .25
174 Tony Gonzalez RC 1.00 2.50
175 Kenny Holmes RC .25 .60
176 Reinard Wilson RC .15 .40
177 Renaldo Wynn RC .08 .25
178 Bryant Westbrook RC .08 .25
179 Darrell Russell RC .08 .25
180 Orlando Pace RC .25 .60
181 Shawn Springs RC .15 .40
182 Peter Boulware RC .25 .60
183 Dan Marino L .50 1.25
184 Brett Favre L .50 1.25
185 Emmitt Smith L .40 1.00
186 Eddie George L .25 .60
187 Curtis Martin L .15 .40
188 Tim Brown L .15 .40
189 Mark Brunell L .25 .60
190 Isaac Bruce L .15 .40
191 Deion Sanders L .15 .40
192 John Elway L .50 1.25
193 Jerry Rice L .25 .60
194 Barry Sanders L .40 1.00
195 Herman Moore L .15 .40
196 Carl Pickens L .15 .40
197 Karim Abdul-Jabbar L .15 .40
198 Drew Bledsoe CL .25 .60
199 Troy Aikman CL .25 .60
200 Terrell Davis CL .25 .60

1997 Leaf Fractal Matrix

1 Steve Young GZ 6.00 15.00
2 Brett Favre GX 20.00 50.00
3 Barry Sanders GZ 12.50 30.00
4 Drew Bledsoe GZ 5.00 12.00
5 Troy Aikman GZ 5.00 12.00
6 Kerry Collins GZ 4.00 10.00
7 Dan Marino GX 20.00 50.00
8 Jerry Rice GZ 7.50 20.00
9 John Elway GZ 15.00 40.00
10 Emmitt Smith GX 15.00 40.00
11 Tony Banks GY 4.00 10.00
12 Gus Frerotte SX 1.25 3.00
13 Elvis Grbac SX 3.00 8.00
14 Neil O'Donnell BX .40 1.00
15 Michael Irvin SY 2.00 5.00
16 Marshall Faulk SY 2.00 5.00
17 Todd Collins SX 1.25 3.00
18 Scott Mitchell BX .40 1.00
19 Trent Dilfer SY 1.50 4.00
20 Rick Mirer SX 1.25 3.00
21 Frank Sanders SX 2.00 5.00
22 Larry Centers BX .40 1.00
23 Brad Johnson BX 1.25 3.00
24 Garrison Hearst SY 1.50 4.00
25 Steve McNair GZ 5.00 12.00
26 Dorsey Levens BX 1.25 3.00
27 Eric Metcalf BX .40 1.00
28 Jeff George SX 2.00 5.00
29 Rodney Hampton BX .40 1.00
30 Michael Westbrook SY 1.50 4.00
31 Cris Carter SY 2.00 5.00
32 Heath Shuler SX 1.25 3.00
33 Warren Moon BX 1.25 3.00
34 Rod Woodson SX 1.25 3.00
35 Ken Dilger BX .60 1.50
36 Ben Coates BX .60 1.50
37 Andre Reed BX .60 1.50
38 Terrell Owens SZ 2.00 5.00
39 Jeff Blake SY 1.50 4.00
40 Vinny Testaverde BX .60 1.50
41 Robert Brooks SY 1.00 2.50
42 Shannon Sharpe SX 2.00 5.00
43 Terry Allen SY 1.50 4.00
44 Terance Mathis BX .60 1.50
45 Bobby Engram BZ .30 .75
46 Rickey Dudley BX 1.25 3.00
47 Alex Molden BX .40 1.00
48 Lawrence Phillips SY 1.00 2.50
49 Curtis Martin GZ 5.00 12.00
50 Jim Harbaugh BX .60 1.50
51 Wayne Chrebet BX 1.25 3.00
52 Quentin Coryatt BX .40 1.00
53 Eddie George GX 5.00 12.00
54 Michael Jackson BX .40 1.00
55 Greg Lloyd BX .40 1.00
56 Natrone Means SZ 1.50 4.00
57 Marcus Allen GY 4.00 10.00
58 Desmond Howard BX .60 1.50
59 Stan Humphries BX .40 1.00
60 Reggie White GY 4.00 10.00
61 Brett Perriman SY 1.00 2.50
62 Warren Sapp BX 1.25 3.00
63 Adrian Murrell SZ 1.50 4.00
64 Mark Brunell GZ 4.00 10.00
65 Carl Pickens GY 2.50 6.00
66 Kordell Stewart GZ 4.00 10.00
67 Ricky Watters GY 2.50 6.00
68 Tyrone Wheatley BX 1.25 3.00
69 Stanley Pritchett BX .40 1.00
70 Kevin Greene BX .40 1.00
71 Karim Abdul-Jabbar GZ 2.50 6.00
72 Ki-Jana Carter SY 1.50 4.00
73 Rashaan Salaam SY 1.00 2.50
74 Simeon Rice BX .60 1.50
75 Napoleon Kaufman SY 2.00 5.00
76 Muhsin Muhammad SZ 2.00 5.00
77 Bruce Smith GY 2.50 6.00
78 Eric Moulds SX 3.00 8.00
79 O.J. McDuffie BX .60 1.50
80 Danny Kanell BZ .30 .75
81 Harvey Williams BX .40 1.00
82 Greg Hill SY 1.00 2.50
83 Terrell Davis GZ 5.00 12.00
84 Dan Wilkinson BX .40 1.00
85 Yancey Thigpen BX .60 1.50
86 Darrell Green SX 1.25 3.00
87 Tamarick Vanover SX 2.00 5.00
88 Mike Alstott BX 1.25 3.00
89 Johnnie Morton SX 2.00 5.00
90 Dale Carter BX .40 1.00
91 Jerome Bettis GY 4.00 10.00
92 James O.Stewart BX .60 1.50
93 Irving Fryar SX 2.00 5.00
94 Junior Seau SY 2.00 5.00
95 Sean Dawkins BX .40 1.00
96 J.J. Stokes BZ 2.50 6.00
97 Tim Biakabutuka SY 1.50 4.00
98 Bert Emanuel BX .60 1.50
99 Eddie Kennison GY 2.50 6.00
100 Ray Zellars BX .40 1.00
101 Dave Brown BX .60 1.50
102 Leeland McElroy SY 1.00 2.50
103 Chris Warren SY 1.00 2.50
104 Byron Bam Morris BX .40 1.00
105 Thurman Thomas GY 2.50 6.00
106 Kyle Brady BX 1.25 3.00
107 Anthony Miller GY 2.50 6.00
108 Derrick Thomas SY 2.00 5.00
109 Mark Chmura BX .60 1.50
110 Deion Sanders GZ 4.00 10.00
111 Eric Swann BX .60 1.50
112 Amani Toomer SX 3.00 8.00
113 Raymont Harris BX .40 1.00
114 Jake Reed BX .60 1.50
115 Bryant Young BX .60 1.50
116 Keenan McCardell SX 2.00 5.00
117 Herman Moore GZ 2.50 6.00
118 Errict Rhett SZ 1.50 4.00
119 Henry Ellard BX .60 1.50
120 Bobby Hoying SX 3.00 8.00
121 Robert Smith BX 1.25 3.00
122 Keyshawn Johnson GZ 4.00 10.00
123 Zach Thomas BX 1.25 3.00
124 Charlie Garner BX .60 1.50
125 Terry Kirby BX .60 1.50
126 Darren Woodson BX .40 1.00
127 Darnay Scott SX 2.00 5.00
128 Chris Sanders SY 1.00 2.50
129 Charles Johnson SX 1.25 3.00
130 Joey Galloway SZ 1.50 4.00
131 Curtis Conway SY 1.50 4.00
132 Isaac Bruce GZ 4.00 10.00
133 Bobby Taylor BX .40 1.00
134 Jamal Anderson SY 2.00 5.00
135 Ken Norton BX .40 1.00
136 Darick Holmes BX .40 1.00
137 Tony Brackens BX .60 1.50
138 Tony Martin BX .60 1.50
139 Antonio Freeman SZ 2.00 5.00
140 Neil Smith BX .40 1.00
141 Terry Glenn GZ 2.50 6.00
142 Marvin Harrison SY 2.00 5.00
143 Daryl Johnston BX .60 1.50
144 Tim Brown GY 4.00 10.00
145 Kimble Anders BX .60 1.50
146 Derrick Alexander SX 2.00 5.00
147 LeShon Johnson BX .40 1.00
148 Anthony Johnson BX .40 1.00
149 Leslie Shepherd BX .60 1.50
150 Chris T. Jones BX .40 1.00
151 Edgar Bennett BX .40 1.00
152 Ty Detmer BX .60 1.50
153 Ike Hilliard GX 4.00 10.00
154 Jim Druckenmiller SZ 1.00 2.50
155 Warrick Dunn GZ 4.00 10.00
156 Yatil Green GZ 1.50 4.00
157 Reidel Anthony GZ 2.50 6.00
158 Antowain Smith GZ 4.00 10.00
159 Rae Carruth SY 1.00 2.50
160 Tiki Barber GZ 6.00 15.00
161 Byron Hanspard SZ 1.50 4.00
162 Jake Plummer SY 4.00 10.00
163 Joey Kent SZ 1.00 2.50
164 Corey Dillon SY 4.00 10.00
165 Kevin Lockett BZ 1.50 4.00
166 Will Blackwell BY .30 .75
167 Troy Davis GZ 1.50 4.00
168 James Farrior BX .60 1.50
169 Danny Wuerffel SY 2.00 5.00
170 Pat Barnes SY 1.00 2.50
171 Darnell Autry SY 2.00 5.00
172 Tom Knight BX .40 1.00
173 David LaFleur BY .30 .75
174 Tony Gonzalez BY 2.50 6.00
175 Kenny Holmes BX .40 1.00
176 Reinard Wilson BX .40 1.00
177 Renaldo Wynn BX .40 1.00
178 Bryant Westbrook BX .60 1.50
179 Darrell Russell BX .60 1.50
180 Orlando Pace BX 1.25 3.00
181 Shawn Springs BX .60 1.50
182 Peter Boulware BX 1.25 3.00
183 Dan Marino L BY 7.50 20.00
184 Brett Favre L BY 7.50 20.00
185 Emmitt Smith L BY 6.00 15.00
186 Eddie George L BY 1.00 2.50
187 Curtis Martin L BY 1.50 4.00
188 Tim Brown L BZ 1.00 2.50
189 Mark Brunell L BY 2.50 6.00
190 Isaac Bruce L BY 1.00 2.50
191 Deion Sanders L BY 1.00 2.50
192 John Elway L BY 7.50 20.00
193 Jerry Rice L BY 4.00 10.00
194 Barry Sanders L BY 6.00 15.00
195 Herman Moore L BY .50 1.25
196 Carl Pickens L BY .50 1.25
197 Karim Abdul-Jabbar L BY .50 1.25
198 Drew Bledsoe CL BY 1.50 4.00
199 Troy Aikman CL BY 2.50 6.00
200 Terrell Davis CL BY 1.50 4.00

1997 Leaf Fractal Matrix Die-Cuts

1 Steve Young GZ 20.00 50.00
2 Brett Favre GX 25.00 60.00
3 Barry Sanders GZ 40.00 100.00
4 Drew Bledsoe GZ 15.00 40.00
5 Troy Aikman GZ 15.00 40.00
6 Kerry Collins GZ 7.50 20.00
7 Dan Marino GX 30.00 80.00
8 Jerry Rice GZ 25.00 60.00
9 John Elway GZ 50.00 120.00
10 Emmitt Smith GX 25.00 60.00
11 Tony Banks GY 7.50 20.00
12 Gus Frerotte SX 2.50 6.00
13 Elvis Grbac SX 4.00 10.00
14 Neil O'Donnell BX 1.00 2.50
15 Michael Irvin SY 7.50 20.00
16 Marshall Faulk SY 7.50 20.00
17 Todd Collins SX 2.00 5.00
18 Scott Mitchell BX 1.00 2.50
19 Trent Dilfer SY 5.00 12.00
20 Rick Mirer SX 2.00 5.00
21 Frank Sanders SX 2.50 6.00
22 Larry Centers BX 1.00 2.50
23 Brad Johnson BX 2.00 5.00
24 Garrison Hearst SY 5.00 12.00
25 Steve McNair GZ 15.00 40.00
26 Dorsey Levens BX 2.00 5.00
27 Eric Metcalf BX 1.00 2.50
28 Jeff George SX 2.50 6.00
29 Rodney Hampton BX 1.00 2.50
30 Michael Westbrook SY 5.00 12.00
31 Cris Carter SY 7.50 20.00
32 Heath Shuler SX 2.50 6.00
33 Warren Moon BX 2.00 5.00
34 Rod Woodson SX 2.00 5.00
35 Ken Dilger BX 1.50 4.00
36 Ben Coates BX 1.50 4.00
37 Andre Reed BX 1.50 4.00
38 Terrell Owens SZ 12.50 30.00
39 Jeff Blake SY 7.50 20.00
40 Vinny Testaverde BX 1.50 4.00
41 Robert Brooks SY 5.00 12.00
42 Shannon Sharpe SX 4.00 10.00
43 Terry Allen SY 5.00 12.00
44 Terance Mathis BX 1.50 4.00
45 Bobby Engram BZ 3.00 8.00
46 Rickey Dudley BX 1.50 4.00
47 Alex Molden BX 1.00 2.50
48 Lawrence Phillips SY 3.00 8.00
49 Curtis Martin GZ 15.00 40.00
50 Jim Harbaugh BX 1.50 4.00
51 Wayne Chrebet BX 2.00 5.00
52 Quentin Coryatt BX 1.00 2.50
53 Eddie George GX 7.50 20.00
54 Michael Jackson BX 1.50 4.00
55 Greg Lloyd BX 1.00 2.50
56 Natrone Means SZ 7.50 20.00
57 Marcus Allen GY 7.50 20.00
58 Desmond Howard BX 1.50 4.00
59 Stan Humphries BX 1.50 4.00
60 Reggie White GY 5.00 12.00
61 Brett Perriman SY 3.00 8.00
62 Warren Sapp BX 2.00 5.00
63 Adrian Murrell SZ 7.50 20.00
64 Mark Brunell GZ 15.00 40.00
65 Carl Pickens GY 5.00 12.00
66 Kordell Stewart GZ 12.50 30.00
67 Ricky Watters GY 5.00 12.00
68 Tyrone Wheatley BX 2.00 5.00

1949 Leaf

69 Stanley Pritchett BX 1.00 2.50
70 Kevin Greene BX 1.00 2.50
71 Karim Abdul-Jabbar GZ 7.50 20.00
72 Ki-Jana Carter SY 5.00 12.00
73 Rashaan Salaam SY 3.00 8.00
74 Simeon Rice BX 1.50 4.00
75 Napoleon Kaufman SY 7.50 20.00
76 Muhsin Muhammad SZ 12.50 30.00
77 Bruce Smith GY 5.00 12.00
78 Eric Moulds SX 4.00 10.00
79 O.J. McDuffie BX 1.50 4.00
80 Danny Kanell BZ 5.00 12.00
81 Harvey Williams BX 1.00 2.50
82 Greg Hill SY 3.00 8.00
83 Terrell Davis GZ 15.00 40.00
84 Dan Wilkinson BX 1.00 2.50
85 Yancey Thigpen BX 1.50 4.00
86 Darrell Green SX 2.00 5.00
87 Tamarick Vanover SX 2.50 6.00
88 Mike Alstott BX 2.00 5.00
89 Johnnie Morton SX 2.50 6.00
90 Dale Carter BX 1.00 2.50
91 Jerome Bettis GY 7.50 20.00
92 James O.Stewart BX 1.50 4.00
93 Irving Fryar SX 2.50 6.00
94 Junior Seau SY 7.50 20.00
95 Sean Dawkins BX 1.50 4.00
96 J.J. Stokes BZ 5.00 12.00
97 Tim Biakabutuka SY 5.00 12.00
98 Bert Emanuel BX 1.50 4.00
99 Eddie Kennison GY 5.00 12.00
100 Ray Zellars BX 1.00 2.50
101 Dave Brown BX 1.50 4.00
102 Leeland McElroy SY 3.00 8.00
103 Chris Warren SY 3.00 8.00
104 Byron Bam Morris BX 1.00 2.50
105 Thurman Thomas GY 5.00 12.00
106 Kyle Brady BX 2.00 5.00
107 Anthony Miller GY 3.00 8.00
108 Derrick Thomas SY 7.50 20.00
109 Mark Chmura BX 1.50 4.00
110 Deion Sanders GZ 12.50 30.00
111 Eric Swann BX 1.00 2.50
112 Amani Toomer SX 4.00 10.00
113 Raymont Harris BX 1.00 2.50
114 Jake Reed BX 1.50 4.00
115 Bryant Young BX 1.50 4.00
116 Keenan McCardell SX 2.50 6.00
117 Herman Moore GZ 7.50 20.00
118 Errict Rhett SZ 5.00 12.00
119 Henry Ellard BX 1.50 4.00
120 Bobby Hoying SX 2.50 6.00
121 Robert Smith BX 2.00 5.00
122 Keyshawn Johnson GZ 12.50 30.00
123 Zach Thomas BX 2.00 5.00
124 Charlie Garner BX 1.50 4.00
125 Terry Kirby BX 1.50 4.00
126 Darren Woodson BX 1.00 2.50
127 Darnay Scott SX 2.50 6.00
128 Chris Sanders SY 3.00 8.00
129 Charles Johnson SX 2.00 5.00
130 Joey Galloway SZ 7.50 20.00
131 Curtis Conway SY 5.00 12.00
132 Isaac Bruce GZ 12.50 30.00
133 Bobby Taylor BX 1.00 2.50
134 Jamal Anderson SY 7.50 20.00
135 Ken Norton BX 1.00 2.50
136 Darick Holmes BX 1.00 2.50
137 Tony Brackens BX 1.50 4.00
138 Tony Martin BX 1.50 4.00
139 Antonio Freeman SZ 12.50 30.00
140 Neil Smith BX 1.00 2.50
141 Terry Glenn GZ 7.50 20.00
142 Marvin Harrison SY 7.50 20.00
143 Daryl Johnston BX 1.50 4.00
144 Tim Brown GY 7.50 20.00
145 Kimble Anders BX 1.50 4.00
146 Derrick Alexander SX 2.50 6.00
147 LeShon Johnson BX 1.00 2.50
148 Anthony Johnson BX 1.00 2.50
149 Leslie Shepherd BX 1.50 4.00
150 Chris T. Jones BX 1.00 2.50
151 Edgar Bennett BX 1.50 4.00
152 Ty Detmer BX 1.50 4.00
153 Ike Hilliard GX 4.00 10.00
154 Jim Druckenmiller SZ 5.00 12.00
155 Warrick Dunn GZ 12.50 30.00
156 Yatil Green GZ 5.00 12.00
157 Reidel Anthony GZ 7.50 20.00
158 Antowain Smith GZ 12.50 30.00
159 Rae Carruth GY 3.00 8.00
160 Tiki Barber GZ 15.00 40.00
161 Byron Hanspard SZ 7.50 20.00
162 Jake Plummer SY 8.00 20.00
163 Joey Kent SZ 5.00 12.00
164 Corey Dillon SY 8.00 20.00
165 Kevin Lockett BZ 3.00 8.00
166 Will Blackwell BY 2.00 5.00
167 Troy Davis GZ 5.00 12.00
168 James Farrior BX 1.50 4.00
169 Danny Wuerffel SY 7.50 20.00
170 Pat Barnes SY 3.00 8.00
171 Darnell Autry SY 7.50 20.00
172 Tom Knight BX 1.00 2.50
173 David LaFleur BY 2.00 5.00
174 Tony Gonzalez BY 8.00 20.00
175 Kenny Holmes BX 1.00 2.50
176 Reinard Wilson BX 1.00 2.50
177 Renaldo Wynn BX 1.00 2.50
178 Bryant Westbrook BX 1.00 2.50
179 Darrell Russell BX 1.00 2.50
180 Orlando Pace BX 2.00 5.00
181 Shawn Springs BX 1.50 4.00
182 Peter Boulware BX 2.00 5.00
183 Dan Marino L BY 20.00 50.00
184 Brett Favre L BY 20.00 50.00
185 Emmitt Smith L BY 15.00 40.00
186 Eddie George L BY 4.00 10.00
187 Curtis Martin L BY 6.00 15.00
188 Tim Brown L BZ 7.50 20.00
189 Mark Brunell L BY 6.00 15.00
190 Isaac Bruce L BY 4.00 10.00
191 Deion Sanders L BY 4.00 10.00
192 John Elway L BY 20.00 50.00
193 Jerry Rice L BY 10.00 25.00
194 Barry Sanders L BY 15.00 40.00
195 Herman Moore L BY 2.50 6.00
196 Carl Pickens L BY 2.50 6.00
197 Karim Abdul-Jabbar L BY 2.50 6.00
198 Drew Bledsoe CL BY 4.00 10.00
199 Troy Aikman CL BY 6.00 15.00
200 Terrell Davis CL BY 6.00 15.00

1997 Leaf Signature Proofs

COMPLETE SET (200) 300.00 600.00
*STARS: 8X TO 20X BASIC CARDS
*RCs: 4X TO 10X BASIC CARDS
STATED PRINT RUN 200 SER.#'d SETS

1997 Leaf Hardwear

ndomly inserted in packs, this 20-card set features color player head photos printed on plastic die-cut helmet-shaped cards. Only 3500 of each card were produced and sequentially numbered.

COMPLETE SET (20) 75.00 150.00
STATED PRINT RUN 3500 SERIAL #'d SETS
1 Dan Marino 8.00 20.00
2 Brett Favre 8.00 20.00
3 Emmitt Smith 6.00 15.00
4 Jerry Rice 4.00 10.00
5 Barry Sanders 6.00 15.00
6 Deion Sanders 2.00 5.00
7 Reggie White 2.00 5.00
8 Tim Brown 2.00 5.00
9 Steve McNair 2.50 6.00
10 Steve Young 2.50 6.00
11 Mark Brunell 2.50 6.00
12 Ricky Watters 1.25 3.00
13 Eddie Kennison 1.25 3.00
14 Kordell Stewart 2.00 5.00
15 Kerry Collins 2.00 5.00
16 Joey Galloway 1.25 3.00
17 Terrell Owens 2.50 6.00
18 Terry Glenn 2.00 5.00
19 Keyshawn Johnson 2.00 5.00
20 Eddie George 2.00 5.00

1997 Leaf Lettermen

Randomly inserted in packs, this 15-card set features color action player images on a background of the first letter of their team's name with an embossed, holographic foil stamped design printed on a flocking material for the look and feel of an actual letter jacket. Only 1000 of this set were produced and sequentially numbered.

COMPLETE SET (15) 125.00 250.00
STATED PRINT RUN 1000 SERIAL #'d SETS
1 Brett Favre 12.50 30.00
2 Emmitt Smith 10.00 25.00
3 Dan Marino 12.50 30.00
4 Jerry Rice 6.00 15.00
5 Mark Brunell 4.00 10.00
6 Barry Sanders 10.00 25.00
7 John Elway 12.50 30.00
8 Eddie George 3.00 8.00
9 Troy Aikman 6.00 15.00
10 Curtis Martin 4.00 10.00
11 Karim Abdul-Jabbar 2.00 5.00
12 Terrell Davis 4.00 10.00
13 Ike Hilliard 5.00 12.00
14 Terry Glenn 3.00 8.00
15 Drew Bledsoe 4.00 10.00

1997 Leaf Reproductions

Randomly inserted in packs, this 24-card set honors 12 current and 12 former NFL greats with color action player photos printed in the original 1948 Leaf design on old-time styled card stock. Only 1948 of each card were produced and are sequentially numbered. The final 500-cards of the 12-former NFL greats were actually autographed by the featured player. Sid Luckman seems to have signed a limited number of cards shortly before his death. It's uncertain if any of these cards actually made it into packs.

COMPLETE SET (24) 125.00 250.00
STATED PRINT RUN 1948 SERIAL #'d SETS
*PROMO: .2X TO .5X BASIC INSERTS
1 Emmitt Smith 12.50 30.00
2 Brett Favre 15.00 40.00
3 Dan Marino 15.00 40.00
4 Barry Sanders 12.50 30.00
5 Jerry Rice 8.00 20.00
6 Terrell Davis 5.00 12.00
7 Curtis Martin 5.00 12.00
8 Troy Aikman 8.00 20.00
9 Drew Bledsoe 5.00 12.00
10 Herman Moore 4.00 10.00
11 Isaac Bruce 4.00 10.00
12 Carl Pickens 2.50 6.00
13 Len Dawson 4.00 10.00
14 Dan Fouts 4.00 10.00
15 Jim Plunkett 4.00 10.00
16 Ken Stabler 4.00 10.00
17 Joe Theismann 4.00 10.00
18 Billy Kilmer 4.00 10.00
19 Danny White 4.00 10.00
20 Archie Manning 4.00 10.00
21 Ron Jaworski 2.50 6.00
22 Y.A. Tittle 4.00 10.00
23 Sid Luckman 4.00 10.00
24 Sammy Baugh 4.00 10.00

1997 Leaf Reproductions Autographs

This set features a signed version of the cards of the former NFL greats found in the Leaf 1948 Leaf Reproduction set. Each player signed the last 500 of his cards to create this limited edition insert set. The autographs were inserted into packs and also available via inserted mail redemption cards. Sid Luckman signed cards surfaced after the product had been live for some time and may or may not have been inserted into packs. It has been speculated that the signed cards were released after his death quite possibly by his family. A Gold Holofoil version of the Sammy Baugh and Billy Kilmer cards were signed, numbered of 500, and released via wrapper redemptions at various Pinnacle sponsored events.

STATED PRINT RUN 500 SETS
13 Len Dawson 15.00 40.00
14 Dan Fouts 15.00 40.00
15 Jim Plunkett 10.00 25.00
16 Ken Stabler 12.00 30.00
17 Joe Theismann 10.00 25.00
18 Billy Kilmer 10.00 25.00
18P Billy Kilmer GH 10.00 25.00
19 Danny White 10.00 25.00
20 Archie Manning 10.00 25.00
21 Ron Jaworski 10.00 25.00
22 Y.A. Tittle 10.00 25.00
23 Sid Luckman 50.00 100.00
24 Sammy Baugh 75.00 150.00
24P Sammy Baugh GH 75.00 150.00

1997 Leaf Run and Gun

ndomly inserted in packs, this 18-card set consists of a double-front card with color images of a top running back on one side and a top quarterback from the same team on the other. One side features full holographic foil stock with foil stamping on the other. The set is sequentially numbered to just 3500.

COMPLETE SET (18) 100.00 200.00
STATED PRINT RUN 3500 SERIAL #'d SETS
1 D.Marino / K.Abdul-Jabbar 10.00 25.00
2 T.Aikman / E.Smith 10.00 25.00
3 J.Elway / T.Davis 12.50 30.00
4 D.Bledsoe / C.Martin 5.00 12.00
5 K.Stewart / J.Bettis 6.00 15.00
6 M.Brunell / N.Means 6.00 15.00
7 K.Collins / T.Biakabutuka 3.00 8.00
8 R.Mirer / R.Salaam 2.00 5.00
9 S.Mitchell / B.Sanders 10.00 25.00
10 S.McNair / E.George 3.00 8.00
11 T.Dilfer / W.Dunn 4.00 10.00
12 J.Blake / K.Carter 3.00 8.00
13 T.Banks / L.Phillips 3.00 8.00
14 S.Young / G.Hearst 5.00 12.00
15 J.Harbaugh / M.Faulk 4.00 10.00
16 E.Grbac / M.Allen 3.00 8.00
17 N.O'Donnell / A.Murrell 2.00 5.00
18 G.Frerotte / T.Allen 3.00 8.00

2012 Leaf Best of Football Autographs

ONE AUTO OR SKETCH PER PACK
BAAT1 Andre Tippett 8.00 20.00
BABG2 Bob Griese 12.00 30.00
BABL1 Bob Lilly 8.00 20.00
BABM1 Bobby Mitchell 8.00 20.00
BABS1 Billy Shaw 8.00 20.00
BABS2 Barry Sanders
BABSC Bob St. Clair 8.00 20.00
BACE1 Carl Eller 6.00 15.00
BACH1 Chris Hanburger 6.00 15.00
BACS1 Charlie Sanders 6.00 15.00
BACT1 Charley Taylor 6.00 15.00
BADD1 Dan Dierdorf 6.00 15.00
BADH1 Dan Hampton 6.00 15.00
BADJ1 Deacon Jones 15.00 30.00
BADM2 Don Maynard 8.00 20.00
BADS1 Dwight Stephenson 6.00 15.00
BADS2 Deion Sanders
BADS3 Don Shula
BADW1 Dave Wilcox 6.00 15.00
BAEB1 Elvin Bethea 6.00 15.00
BAEC1 Earl Campbell 15.00 30.00
BAED1 Eric Dickerson
BAFB1 Fred Biletnikoff 10.00 25.00
BAFD1 Fred Dean 6.00 15.00
BAFG1 Frank Gifford
BAGM1 Gino Marchetti 6.00 15.00
BAHC1 Harry Carson 6.00 15.00
BAHM1 Hugh McElhenny 8.00 20.00
BAJB1 Jerome Bettis
BAJDL Joe DeLamielleure 6.00 15.00
BAJH1 John Hannah 8.00 20.00
BAJJ1 Jimmy Johnson 8.00 20.00
BAJK1 Jim Kelly 20.00 40.00
BAJL1 James Lofton 6.00 15.00
BAJL2 Jim Langer 10.00 25.00
BAJO1 Jim Otto 6.00 15.00
BAJR1 Jerry Rice
BAJS1 Jackie Smith 6.00 15.00
BAJS2 Jan Stenerud 6.00 15.00
BAJS3 Joe Schmidt 12.00 30.00
BAJY1 Jack Youngblood 6.00 15.00
BAKW1 Kellen Winslow 8.00 20.00
BALB1 Lem Barney 6.00 15.00
BALK1 Leroy Kelly 8.00 20.00
BALL1 Larry Little 6.00 15.00
BALM1 Lenny Moore 6.00 15.00
BALT1 Lawrence Taylor
BALW1 Larry Wilson 6.00 15.00
BAMD1 Mike Ditka 12.00 30.00
BAMF1 Marshall Faulk 20.00 40.00
BAMH1 Mike Haynes 8.00 20.00
BAML1 Marv Levy 20.00 40.00
BAMR1 Mel Renfro 8.00 20.00
BAPK1 Paul Krause 6.00 15.00
BAPW1 Paul Warfield 8.00 20.00
BARJ1 Rickey Jackson 6.00 15.00
BARL1 Ronnie Lott 20.00 40.00
BARW1 Rayfield Wright 6.00 15.00
BARW2 Roger Wehrli 6.00 15.00
BARW3 Randy White
BARW4 Rod Woodson
BARY1 Ron Yary 6.00 15.00
BASH1 Sam Huff 8.00 20.00
BASL1 Steve Largent 10.00 25.00
BASY1 Steve Young
BATB1 Tim Brown
BATD1 Tony Dorsett 20.00 40.00
BATM1 Tom Mack 6.00 15.00
BAWB1 Willie Brown 6.00 15.00
BAWM1 Warren Moon 15.00 30.00
BAYAT Y.A. Tittle 10.00 25.00

2015 Leaf Best of Football

ANNOUNCED PRINT RUN 146
BLUE/16: X TO X BASIC CARDS/146*
GREEN/36: X TO X BASIC CARD/146*
1 Amari Cooper
2 Ameer Abdullah
3 Bryce Petty
4 David Johnson
5 DeVante Parker
6 Dorial Green-Beckham
7 Duke Johnson
8 Jameis Winston
9 Kevin White
10 Marcus Mariota
11 Matt Jones
12 Melvin Gordon
13 Nelson Agholor
14 Phillip Dorsett
15 Stefon Diggs
16 T.J. Yeldon
17 Tevin Coleman
18 Todd Gurley
19 Ty Montgomery
20 Tyler Lockett

1999 Leaf Certified

The 1999 Leaf Certified set was released as a 225 card set. The set was broken down in four card groups as folows: the first 100 cards in the set were done with one blue star on card front and were available four cards in each pack. The two star level was a 50 card set inserted one in each pack. The three star level was done as a 25 card set and inserted one in three packs. The four star level was a 50 card short printed set of the 1999 rookies and was inserted at a rate of one in five packs. Only the rookie cards were available in the four star format.

COMPLETE SET (225) 100.00 200.00
COMP.SET w/o RCs 175) 15.00 40.00
1 Simeon Rice .25 .60
2 Frank Sanders .25 .60
3 Andre Wadsworth .25 .60
4 Larry Centers .25 .60
5 Byron Hanspard .25 .60
6 Terance Mathis .25 .60
7 O.J. Santiago .25 .60
8 Chris Calloway .25 .60
9 Michael Jackson .25 .60
10 Rod Woodson .40 1.00
11 Pat Johnson .25 .60
12 Rob Johnson .30 .75
13 Andre Reed .40 1.00
14 Tim Biakabutuka .30 .75
15 Rae Carruth .25 .60
16 Fred Lane .25 .60
17 Muhsin Muhammad .25 .60
18 Wesley Walls .30 .75
19 Edgar Bennett .30 .75
20 Curtis Conway .30 .75
21 Bobby Engram .25 .60
22 Jeff Blake .30 .75
23 Darnay Scott .25 .60
24 Ty Detmer .25 .60
25 Sedrick Shaw .25 .60
26 Leslie Shepherd .25 .60
27 Terry Kirby .25 .60
28 Chris Warren .30 .75
29 Rocket Ismail .30 .75
30 Marcus Nash .25 .60
31 Neil Smith .25 .60
32 Bubby Brister .25 .60
33 Brian Griese .25 .60
34 Germane Crowell .25 .60
35 Johnnie Morton .30 .75
36 Gus Frerotte .25 .60
37 Robert Brooks .30 .75
38 Mark Chmura .25 .60
39 Derrick Mayes .25 .60
40 Jerome Pathon .25 .60
41 Jimmy Smith .30 .75
42 James Stewart .25 .60
43 Tavian Banks .25 .60
44 Derrick Alexander WR .25 .60
45 Kimble Anders .25 .60
46 Elvis Grbac .25 .60
47 Derrick Thomas .40 1.00
48 Byron Bam Morris .25 .60
49 Tony Gonzalez .30 .75
50 John Avery .25 .60
51 Tyrone Wheatley .30 .75
52 Zach Thomas .30 .75
53 Lamar Thomas .25 .60
54 Jeff George .25 .60
55 John Randle .40 1.00
56 Jake Reed .30 .75
57 Leroy Hoard .25 .60
58 Robert Edwards .25 .60
59 Ben Coates .30 .75
60 Tony Simmons .25 .60
61 Shawn Jefferson .25 .60
62 Eddie Kennison .30 .75
63 Lamar Smith .25 .60
64 Tiki Barber .30 .75
65 Kerry Collins .25 .60
66 Ike Hilliard .25 .60
67 Gary Brown .25 .60
68 Joe Jurevicius .25 .60
69 Kent Graham .25 .60
70 Dedric Ward .25 .60
71 Terry Allen .30 .75
72 Neil O'Donnell .30 .75
73 Desmond Howard .30 .75
74 James Jett .25 .60
75 Jon Ritchie .25 .60
76 Rickey Dudley .25 .60
77 Charles Johnson .25 .60
78 Chris Fuamatu-Ma'afala .25 .60
79 Hines Ward .30 .75
80 Ryan Leaf .30 .75
81 Jim Harbaugh .30 .75
82 Junior Seau .30 .75
83 Mikhael Ricks .25 .60
84 J.J. Stokes .25 .60
85 Ahman Green .30 .75
86 Tony Banks .30 .75
87 Robert Holcombe .25 .60
88 Az-Zahir Hakim .25 .60
89 Greg Hill .25 .60
90 Trent Green .25 .60
91 Eric Zeier .25 .60
92 Reidel Anthony .25 .60
93 Bert Emanuel .30 .75
94 Warren Sapp .30 .75
95 Kevin Dyson .25 .60
96 Yancey Thigpen .25 .60
97 Frank Wycheck .30 .75
98 Michael Westbrook .25 .60
99 Albert Connell .25 .60
100 Darrell Green .40 1.00
101 Rob Moore .30 .75
102 Adrian Murrell .30 .75
103 Jake Plummer .30 .75
104 Chris Chandler .40 1.00
105 Jamal Anderson .40 1.00
106 Tim Dwight .40 1.00
107 Jermaine Lewis .30 .75
108 Priest Holmes .30 .75
109 Bruce Smith .40 1.00
110 Eric Moulds .30 .75
111 Antowain Smith .30 .75
112 Curtis Enis .30 .75
113 Corey Dillon .30 .75
114 Michael Irvin .50 1.25
115 Ed McCaffrey .40 1.00
116 Shannon Sharpe .40 1.00
117 Terrell Davis .40 1.00
118 Charlie Batch .30 .75
119 Antonio Freeman .40 1.00
120 Dorsey Levens .40 1.00
121 Marvin Harrison .40 1.00
122 Peyton Manning 1.50 4.00
123 Keenan McCardell .40 1.00
124 Fred Taylor .30 .75
125 Andre Rison .40 1.00
126 O.J. McDuffie .40 1.00
127 Karim Abdul-Jabbar .30 .75
128 Randy Moss .40 1.00
129 Terry Glenn .40 1.00
130 Vinny Testaverde .30 .75
131 Keyshawn Johnson .40 1.00
132 Curtis Martin .40 1.00
133 Wayne Chrebet .30 .75
134 Napoleon Kaufman .30 .75
135 Charles Woodson .50 1.25
136 Duce Staley .30 .75
137 Kordell Stewart .30 .75
138 Terrell Owens .40 1.00
139 Ricky Watters .40 1.00
140 Joey Galloway .40 1.00
141 Jon Kitna .30 .75
142 Isaac Bruce .50 1.25
143 Jacquez Green .30 .75
144 Warrick Dunn .30 .75
145 Mike Alstott .30 .75
146 Trent Dilfer .30 .75
147 Steve McNair .40 1.00
148 Eddie George .40 1.00
149 Skip Hicks .30 .75
150 Brad Johnson .40 1.00
151 Doug Flutie .75 2.00
152 Thurman Thomas .60 1.50
153 Carl Pickens .60 1.50
154 Emmitt Smith 1.25 3.00
155 Troy Aikman 1.00 2.50
156 Deion Sanders .60 1.50
157 John Elway 1.25 3.00
158 Rod Smith .60 1.50
159 Barry Sanders 1.25 3.00
160 Herman Moore .60 1.50
161 Brett Favre 1.50 4.00
162 Mark Brunell .60 1.50
163 Warren Moon .75 2.00
164 Dan Marino 1.50 4.00
165 Randall Cunningham .60 1.50
166 Robert Smith .50 1.25
167 Cris Carter .75 2.00
168 Drew Bledsoe .60 1.50
169 Tim Brown .75 2.00
170 Jerome Bettis .75 2.00
171 Natrone Means .60 1.50
172 Jerry Rice 2.00 5.00
173 Steve Young 1.00 2.50
174 Garrison Hearst .50 1.25
175 Marshall Faulk .60 1.50
176 David Boston RC 1.00 2.50
177 Jeff Paulk RC 1.00 2.50
178 Reginald Kelly RC 1.00 2.50
179 Scott Covington RC 1.00 2.50
180 Chris McAlister RC 1.00 2.50
181 Shawn Bryson RC 1.00 2.50
182 Peerless Price RC 1.00 2.50
183 Cade McNown RC 1.00 2.50
184 Michael Bishop RC 1.25 3.00
185 D'Wayne Bates RC 1.00 2.50
186 Marty Booker RC 1.00 2.50
187 Akili Smith RC 1.00 2.50
188 Craig Yeast RC 1.00 2.50
189 Tim Couch RC 1.25 3.00
190 Kevin Johnson RC 1.25 3.00
191 Wane McGarity RC 1.00 2.50
192 Olandis Gary RC 1.50 4.00
193 Travis McGriff RC 1.00 2.50
194 Sedrick Irvin RC 1.00 2.50
195 Chris Claiborne RC 1.00 2.50
196 De'Mond Parker RC 1.00 2.50
197 Dee Miller RC 1.00 2.50
198 Edgerrin James RC 1.50 4.00
199 Mike Cloud RC 1.00 2.50
200 Larry Parker RC 1.25 3.00
201 Cecil Collins RC 1.00 2.50
202 James Johnson RC 1.00 2.50
203 Rob Konrad RC 1.00 2.50
204 Daunte Culpepper RC 1.50 4.00
205 Jim Kleinsasser RC 1.50 4.00
206 Kevin Faulk RC 1.00 2.50
207 Andy Katzenmoyer RC 1.25 3.00
208 Ricky Williams RC 1.50 4.00
209 Joe Montgomery RC 1.00 2.50
210 Sean Bennett RC 1.00 2.50
211 Dameane Douglas RC 1.00 2.50
212 Donovan McNabb RC 3.00 8.00
213 Na Brown RC 1.00 2.50
214 Amos Zereoue RC 1.00 2.50
215 Troy Edwards RC 1.00 2.50
216 Jermaine Fazande RC 1.00 2.50
217 Tai Streets RC 1.25 3.00
218 Brock Huard RC 1.00 2.50
219 Charlie Rogers RC 1.00 2.50
220 Karsten Bailey RC 1.00 2.50
221 Joe Germaine RC 1.25 3.00
222 Torry Holt RC 2.00 5.00
223 Shaun King RC 1.00 2.50
224 Jevon Kearse RC 1.25 3.00
225 Champ Bailey RC 2.00 5.00

1999 Leaf Certified Mirror Gold

*1-100 1-STAR/45: 10X TO 25X BASIC CARD
*101-150 2-STAR/35: 8X TO 20X BASIC CARD
*151-175 3-STAR/25: 6X TO 15X BASIC CARD
*176-225 4-STAR/30: 2.5X TO 6X BASIC RC

1999 Leaf Certified Mirror Red

*1-100 1-STAR: 6X TO 15X BASIC CARDS
1-100 1-STAR STATED ODDS 1:17
*101-150 2-STAR: 6X TO 15X BASIC CARDS
101-150 2-STAR STATED ODDS 1:53
*151-175 3-STAR: 5X TO 12X BASIC CARDS
151-175 3-STAR ODDS 1:125
*176-225 4-STAR: 1.2X TO 3X BASIC RC
176-225 4-STAR ODDS 1:89

1999 Leaf Certified Skills

ndomly inserted at a rate of one in 35 packs, This 20 card insert set features a dual player design with one player on the card front and back. Also available was a mirror black parallel version which had a print run of 25 sets made.

STATED ODDS 1:35
*MIRROR BLACK/25: 2X TO 5X BASIC INSERTS
CS1 D.Sanders / C.Bailey 2.50 6.00
CS2 J.Elway / C.McNown 3.00 8.00
CS3 C.Carter / D.Boston 2.00 5.00
CS4 M.Faulk / E.James 2.00 5.00
CS5 J.Rice / R.Moss 5.00 12.00
CS6 A.Freeman / T.Owens 1.50 4.00
CS7 T.Davis / R.Williams 2.00 5.00
CS8 D.Bledsoe / D.Flutie 2.00 5.00
CS9 E.George / J.Anderson 1.50 4.00
CS10 T.Aikman / P.Manning 6.00 15.00
CS11 B.Sanders / W.Dunn 3.00 8.00
CS12 Cunningham / Culpepper 2.00 5.00
CS13 D.Marino / T.Couch 4.00 10.00
CS14 E.Smith / F.Taylor 3.00 8.00
CS15 K.Johnson / E.Moulds 1.50 4.00
CS16 S.Young / M.Brunell 2.50 6.00
CS17 D.McNabb / A.Smith 4.00 10.00
CS18 B.Favre / J.Plummer 4.00 10.00
CS19 K.Stewart / S.McNair 1.50 4.00
CS20 T.Holt / T.Edwards 2.50 6.00

1999 Leaf Certified Fabric of the Game

Randomly inserted in packs this insert set was done in a three level format with 25 cards done for each level. The 3 levels comprised of Pro Bowl appearences done on nylon, Carreer TD'S done on an all leather card, and career yards which were done on an all plastic card. Cards were individually serial numbered between 100 and 1000.

FG1 John Elway/100 30.00 80.00
FG2 Barry Sanders/100 30.00 80.00
FG3 Jerry Rice/100 20.00 50.00
FG4 Brett Favre/250 15.00 40.00
FG5 Steve Young/250 10.00 25.00
FG6 Troy Aikman/250 15.00 40.00
FG7 Deion Sanders/250 5.00 12.00
FG8 Terrell Davis/500 4.00 10.00
FG9 Mark Brunell/500 4.00 10.00
FG10 Drew Bledsoe/500 6.00 15.00
FG11 Randall Cunningham/500 4.00 10.00
FG12 Eddie George/500 4.00 10.00
FG13 Jamal Anderson/750 3.00 8.00
FG14 Doug Flutie/750 3.00 8.00
FG15 Robert Smith/750 3.00 8.00
FG16 Garrison Hearst/750 3.00 8.00
FG17 Keyshawn Johnson/750 3.00 8.00
FG18 Randy Moss/750 6.00 15.00
FG19 Eric Moulds/1000 2.50 6.00
FG20 Curtis Enis/1000 2.50 6.00
FG21 Ricky Williams/1000 4.00 10.00
FG22 Peyton Manning/1000 10.00 25.00
FG23 Tim Couch/1000 3.00 8.00
FG24 Cade McNown/1000 3.00 8.00
FG25 Akili Smith/1000 2.50 6.00
FG26 Dan Marino/100 30.00 80.00
FG27 Jerry Rice/100 20.00 50.00
FG28 Emmitt Smith/100 20.00 50.00
FG29 Cris Carter/250 5.00 12.00
FG30 Steve Young/250 10.00 25.00
FG31 Herman Moore/250 5.00 12.00
FG32 Tim Brown/250 5.00 12.00
FG33 Jerome Bettis/500 6.00 15.00
FG34 Natrone Means/500 4.00 10.00
FG35 Antonio Freeman/500 4.00 10.00
FG36 Terrell Davis/500 4.00 10.00
FG37 Carl Pickens/500 2.00 5.00
FG38 Karim Abdul-Jabbar/750 3.00 8.00
FG39 Mike Alstott/750 3.00 8.00
FG40 Jake Plummer/750 3.00 8.00
FG41 Steve McNair/750 3.00 8.00
FG42 Terrell Owens/750 3.00 8.00
FG43 Kordell Stewart/750 3.00 8.00
FG44 Randy Moss/1000 6.00 15.00
FG45 Fred Taylor/1000 3.00 8.00
FG46 Peyton Manning/1000 10.00 25.00
FG47 Tim Couch/1000 3.00 8.00
FG48 Akili Smith/1000 2.50 6.00
FG49 Torry Holt/1000 6.00 15.00
FG50 Donovan McNabb/1000 12.50 25.00
FG51 Barry Sanders/100 30.00 80.00
FG52 Dan Marino/100 30.00 80.00
FG53 Jerry Rice/100 20.00 50.00
FG54 John Elway/250 20.00 50.00
FG55 Brett Favre/250 15.00 40.00
FG56 Emmitt Smith/250 15.00 30.00
FG57 Mark Brunell/250 5.00 12.00
FG58 Jake Plummer/500 4.00 10.00
FG59 Ricky Watters/500 2.00 5.00
FG60 Dorsey Levens/500 4.00 10.00
FG61 Curtis Martin/500 4.00 10.00
FG62 Marshall Faulk/500 6.00 15.00
FG63 Eddie George/750 3.00 8.00
FG64 Corey Dillon/750 3.00 8.00
FG65 Warrick Dunn/750 3.00 8.00
FG66 Antowain Smith/750 3.00 8.00
FG67 Napoleon Kaufman/750 3.00 8.00
FG68 Joey Galloway/750 3.00 8.00
FG69 Fred Taylor/1000 3.00 8.00
FG70 Charlie Batch/1000 3.00 8.00
FG71 Ricky Williams/1000 4.00 10.00
FG72 Edgerrin James/1000 7.50 20.00
FG73 Jon Kitna/1000 3.00 8.00
FG74 Daunte Culpepper/1000 7.50 20.00
FG75 Skip Hicks/1000 2.50 6.00

1999 Leaf Certified Gold Future

Randomly inserted at a rate of one in 17 packs, This 30 card insert set featured color action shots of key rookies for the 1999 class.

COMPLETE SET (30) 60.00 120.00
STATED ODDS 1:17
*MIRROR BLACK/25: 2.5X TO 6X BASIC INSERT
1 Travis McGriff .75 2.00
2 Jermaine Fazande .75 2.00
3 Kevin Faulk .75 2.00
4 Edgerrin James 1.25 3.00
5 Ricky Williams 1.25 3.00
6 Tim Couch 1.00 2.50
7 Torry Holt 1.50 4.00
8 Kevin Johnson 1.00 2.50
9 Amos Zereoue .75 2.00
10 Joe Germaine 1.00 2.50
11 Shawn Bryson .75 2.00
12 D'Wayne Bates .75 2.00
13 Akili Smith .75 2.00
14 Shaun King .75 2.00
15 Joe Montgomery .75 2.00
16 Troy Edwards .75 2.00
17 Rob Konrad .75 2.00
18 David Boston .75 2.00
19 Reginald Kelly .75 2.00
20 Donovan McNabb 2.50 6.00
21 Champ Bailey 1.50 4.00
22 Craig Yeast .75 2.00
23 Daunte Culpepper 1.25 3.00
24 Peerless Price .75 2.00
25 Cecil Collins .75 2.00
26 Cade McNown .75 2.00
27 Karsten Bailey .75 2.00
28 James Johnson .75 2.00
29 Brock Huard .75 2.00
30 Mike Cloud .75 2.00

1999 Leaf Certified Gold Team

ndomly inserted at a rate of one in 17 packs, This 30 card insert set features star players with a color action photo and a gold background.

STATED ODDS 1:17
*MIRROR BLACK/25: 2X TO 5X BASIC INSERT
CGT1 Randy Moss 1.50 4.00
CGT2 Terrell Davis 1.50 4.00
CGT3 Peyton Manning 6.00 15.00
CGT4 Fred Taylor 1.25 3.00
CGT5 Jake Plummer 1.25 3.00
CGT6 Drew Bledsoe 1.50 4.00
CGT7 John Elway 3.00 8.00
CGT8 Mark Brunell 1.50 4.00
CGT9 Joey Galloway 1.50 4.00
CGT10 Troy Aikman 2.50 6.00
CGT11 Jerome Bettis 2.00 5.00
CGT12 Tim Brown 2.00 5.00
CGT13 Dan Marino 4.00 10.00
CGT14 Antonio Freeman 1.50 4.00
CGT15 Steve Young 2.50 6.00
CGT16 Jamal Anderson 1.50 4.00
CGT17 Brett Favre 4.00 10.00
CGT18 Jerry Rice 5.00 12.00
CGT19 Corey Dillon 1.25 3.00
CGT20 Barry Sanders 3.00 8.00
CGT21 Doug Flutie 2.00 5.00
CGT22 Emmitt Smith 3.00 8.00
CGT23 Curtis Martin 1.50 4.00
CGT24 Dorsey Levens 1.50 4.00
CGT25 Kordell Stewart 1.25 3.00
CGT26 Eddie George 1.50 4.00
CGT27 Terrell Owens 1.50 4.00
CGT28 Keyshawn Johnson 1.50 4.00
CGT29 Steve McNair 1.50 4.00
CGT30 Cris Carter 2.00 5.00

1999 Leaf Certified Gridiron Gear

ndomly inserted in packs, this insert set featured 72 different players with an actual piece of a game used NFL worn jersey on the card front. Cards were individually serial numbered to 300 of each on card back.

STATED PRINT RUN 300 SER.#'d SETS
AF86 Antonio Freeman 6.00 15.00
BC87 Ben Coates 6.00 15.00
BF4A Brett Favre White 15.00 40.00
BF4H Brett Favre Green 15.00 40.00
BS20 Barry Sanders 12.00 30.00
CC80 Curtis Conway 6.00 15.00
CM28 Curtis Martin 6.00 15.00
CS81 Chris Sanders 5.00 12.00
CW24 Charles Woodson 10.00 25.00
DB11 Drew Bledsoe 6.00 15.00
DF7A Doug Flutie White 8.00 20.00
DF7H Doug Flutie Blue 8.00 20.00
DG28 Darrell Green 8.00 20.00
DH80 Desmond Howard 6.00 15.00
DL25A Dorsey Levens White 6.00 15.00
DL25H Dorsey Levens Green 6.00 15.00
DM13A Dan Marino White 15.00 40.00
DM13H Dan Marino Teal 15.00 40.00
DS21 Deion Sanders 6.00 15.00
DT58 Derrick Thomas 40.00 80.00
EG27 Eddie George 6.00 15.00
ES22 Emmitt Smith 12.00 30.00
HM84 Herman Moore 6.00 15.00
IB80 Isaac Bruce 8.00 20.00
JA32 Jamal Anderson 6.00 15.00
JB36 Jerome Bettis 12.00 30.00
JE7H John Elway Blue 12.00 30.00
JE7HC John Elway Orange 12.00 30.00
JJ82 James Jett 5.00 12.00
JK12 Jim Kelly 8.00 20.00
JM19 Joe Montana 25.00 60.00
JP16 Jake Plummer 5.00 12.00
JR80A Jerry Rice White 20.00 50.00
JR80H Jerry Rice Red 20.00 50.00
JS33 James Stewart 5.00 12.00
JS55 Junior Seau 6.00 15.00
JS82 Jimmy Smith 6.00 15.00
KA33 Karim Abdul-Jabbar 5.00 12.00
KJ19 Keyshawn Johnson 6.00 15.00
KM87 Keenan McCardell 6.00 15.00
KS10 Kordell Stewart 5.00 12.00
MB8A Mark Brunell White 6.00 15.00
MB8H Mark Brunell Teal 6.00 15.00
MC89 Mark Chmura 5.00 12.00
MH88 Marvin Harrison 6.00 15.00
MI88 Michael Irvin 8.00 20.00
NK26A Nap.Kaufman White 5.00 12.00
NK26H Nap.Kaufman Black 5.00 12.00
NM20 Natrone Means 6.00 15.00
NS90 Neil Smith 5.00 12.00
OM81 O.J. McDuffie 6.00 15.00
PM18 Peyton Manning 20.00 50.00
PS12 Phil Simms 8.00 20.00
RB87 Robert Brooks 6.00 15.00
RC7 Randall Cunningham 6.00 15.00
RL16 Ryan Leaf 6.00 15.00
RM84A Randy Moss White 6.00 15.00
RM84H Randy Moss Purple 6.00 15.00
SM9 Steve McNair 6.00 15.00
SY8 Steve Young 10.00 25.00
TA8 Troy Aikman 10.00 25.00
TB71 Tony Boselli 6.00 15.00
TB81 Tim Brown 8.00 20.00
TD12 Trent Dilfer 5.00 12.00
TD30A Terrell Davis White 6.00 15.00
TD30H Terrell Davis Blue 6.00 15.00
TT34 Thurman Thomas 6.00 15.00
VT12 Vinny Testaverde 5.00 12.00
WD28 Warrick Dunn 5.00 12.00
WM1 Warren Moon 8.00 20.00
WS99 Warren Sapp 6.00 15.00
ZT54 Zach Thomas 6.00 15.00

2000 Leaf Certified

leased as a 250-card original set, Leaf Certified contained 150-veteran player cards and 100 Rookie cards. Base cards have blue borders with a holographic fractal foil stock. Leaf Certified was packaged in 18-pack boxes with packs containing five cards each.

COMP.SET w/o RC's (150) 15.00 40.00
151-190 RC 3-STAR PRINT RUN 2000
221-250 RC 5-STAR PRINT RUN 1000
1 Frank Sanders .25 .60
2 Rob Moore .25 .60
3 Simeon Rice .30 .75
4 David Boston .25 .60
5 Tim Dwight .30 .75
6 Jamal Anderson .30 .75
7 Chris Chandler .30 .75
8 Terance Mathis .25 .60
9 Priest Holmes .25 .60
10 Rod Woodson .40 1.00
11 Tony Banks .25 .60
12 Jermaine Lewis .25 .60
13 Shannon Sharpe .30 .75
14 Qadry Ismail .25 .60
15 Doug Flutie .30 .75
16 Antowain Smith .30 .75
17 Peerless Price .30 .75
18 Rob Johnson .30 .75
19 Muhsin Muhammad .25 .60
20 Wesley Walls .25 .60
21 Tim Biakabutuka .30 .75
22 Steve Beuerlein .30 .75
23 Patrick Jeffers .25 .60
24 Natrone Means .30 .75
25 Curtis Enis .25 .60
26 Bobby Engram .25 .60
27 Marcus Robinson .30 .75
28 Eddie Kennison .25 .60
29 Marty Booker .25 .60
30 Darnay Scott .30 .75
31 Carl Pickens .30 .75
32 Karim Abdul-Jabbar .25 .60
33 Errict Rhett .30 .75
34 Darrin Chiaverini .25 .60
35 Randall Cunningham .30 .75
36 Michael Irvin .40 1.00
37 Rocket Ismail .30 .75
38 Ed McCaffrey .30 .75
39 Rod Smith .30 .75
40 Herman Moore .25 .60
41 Johnnie Morton .30 .75
42 James Stewart .25 .60
43 Bill Schroeder .30 .75
44 Ahman Green .30 .75
45 Terrence Wilkins .25 .60
46 Keenan McCardell .30 .75
47 Derrick Alexander .25 .60
48 Elvis Grbac .25 .60
49 Tony Gonzalez .30 .75
50 O.J. McDuffie .30 .75
51 Tony Martin .30 .75
52 James Johnson .25 .60
53 Thurman Thomas .30 .75
54 Jay Fiedler .30 .75
55 Damon Huard .25 .60
56 Leroy Hoard .25 .60
57 Terry Glenn .30 .75
58 Kevin Faulk .25 .60
59 Jeff Blake .30 .75
60 Jake Reed .30 .75
61 Amani Toomer .25 .60
62 Kerry Collins .25 .60
63 Ike Hilliard .25 .60
64 Joe Montgomery .25 .60
65 Vinny Testaverde .25 .60
66 Wayne Chrebet .25 .60
67 Ray Lucas .25 .60
68 Napoleon Kaufman .30 .75
69 Charles Woodson .40 1.00
70 Tyrone Wheatley .25 .60
71 Rich Gannon .30 .75
72 Duce Staley .25 .60
73 Kordell Stewart .25 .60
74 Jerome Bettis .40 1.00
75 Troy Edwards .25 .60
76 Junior Seau .30 .75
77 Jim Harbaugh .30 .75
78 Curtis Conway .30 .75
79 Jermaine Fazande .25 .60
80 Terrell Owens .30 .75
81 Charlie Garner .30 .75
82 Garrison Hearst .25 .60
83 Jeff Garcia .25 .60
84 Derrick Mayes .25 .60
85 Az-Zahir Hakim .25 .60
86 Mike Alstott .25 .60
87 Warrick Dunn .25 .60
88 Jacquez Green .25 .60
89 Warren Sapp .30 .75
90 Yancey Thigpen .25 .60
91 Kevin Dyson .30 .75
92 Frank Wycheck .30 .75
93 Jevon Kearse .25 .60
94 Adrian Murrell .25 .60
95 Bruce Smith .30 .75
96 Michael Westbrook .25 .60
97 Albert Connell .25 .60
98 Champ Bailey .30 .75
99 Jeff George .30 .75
100 Deion Sanders .30 .75
101 Jake Plummer .30 .75
102 Eric Moulds .30 .75
103 Cade McNown .30 .75
104 Corey Dillon .30 .75
105 Akili Smith .30 .75
106 Tim Couch .40 1.00
107 Kevin Johnson .30 .75
108 Emmitt Smith .75 2.00
109 Troy Aikman .60 1.50
110 Joey Galloway .40 1.00
111 John Elway .75 2.00
112 Terrell Davis .40 1.00
113 Olandis Gary .40 1.00
114 Brian Griese .30 .75
115 Charlie Batch .30 .75
116 Barry Sanders .75 2.00
117 Germane Crowell .30 .75
118 Brett Favre 1.00 2.50
119 Dorsey Levens .40 1.00
120 Antonio Freeman .40 1.00
121 Peyton Manning 1.25 3.00
122 Edgerrin James .40 1.00
123 Marvin Harrison .40 1.00
124 Mark Brunell .40 1.00
125 Fred Taylor .30 .75
126 Jimmy Smith .40 1.00
127 Dan Marino 1.00 2.50
128 Randy Moss .40 1.00
129 Daunte Culpepper .40 1.00
130 Cris Carter .50 1.25
131 Robert Smith .30 .75
132 Drew Bledsoe .40 1.00
133 Ricky Williams .40 1.00
134 Curtis Martin .40 1.00
135 Tim Brown .50 1.25
136 Donovan McNabb .40 1.00
137 Jerry Rice 1.25 3.00
138 Steve Young .60 1.50
139 Jon Kitna .30 .75
140 Ricky Watters .40 1.00
141 Kurt Warner .75 2.00
142 Marshall Faulk .40 1.00
143 Torry Holt .40 1.00

144 Isaac Bruce .50 1.25
145 Shaun King .30 .75
146 Keyshawn Johnson .40 1.00
147 Eddie George .40 1.00
148 Steve McNair .40 1.00
149 Stephen Davis .30 .75
150 Brad Johnson .40 1.00
151 Rogers Beckett RC 1.25 3.00
152 Erik Flowers RC 1.25 3.00
153 Demario Brown RC 1.25 3.00
154 Doug Johnson RC 1.25 3.00
155 Deon Grant RC 1.25 3.00
156 Ian Gold RC 1.25 3.00
157 Brian Urlacher RC 6.00 15.00
158 Frank Murphy RC 1.25 3.00
159 James Whalen RC 1.25 3.00
160 JaJuan Dawson RC 1.25 3.00
161 William Bartee RC 1.25 3.00
162 Aaron Shea RC 1.50 4.00
163 Deltha O'Neal RC 1.25 3.00
164 Jarious Jackson RC 1.50 4.00
165 Muneer Moore RC 1.25 3.00
166 Hank Poteat RC 1.25 3.00
167 Jacoby Shepherd RC 1.25 3.00
168 Ben Kelly RC 1.25 3.00
169 Orantes Grant RC 1.25 3.00
170 Chris Hovan RC 1.50 4.00
171 Leon Murray RC 1.25 3.00
172 Marc Bulger RC 1.50 4.00
173 Chad Morton RC 1.50 4.00
174 Na'il Diggs RC 1.25 3.00
175 Shaun Ellis RC 1.50 4.00
176 John Abraham RC 2.00 5.00
177 Fred Robbins RC 1.25 3.00
178 Marcus Knight RC 1.25 3.00
179 Thomas Hamner RC 1.25 3.00
180 Cornelius Griffin RC 1.25 3.00
181 Raynoch Thompson RC 1.25 3.00
182 Paul Smith RC 1.25 3.00
183 Ahmed Plummer RC 1.25 3.00
184 John Engelberger RC 1.25 3.00
185 Darren Howard RC 1.25 3.00
186 Corey Moore RC 1.25 3.00
187 Joe Hamilton RC 1.25 3.00
188 Rob Morris RC 1.50 4.00
189 Keith Bulluck RC 1.50 4.00
190 Todd Husak RC 1.25 3.00
191 Mareno Philyaw RC 1.50 4.00
192 Kwame Cavil RC 1.50 4.00
193 Sammy Morris RC 1.50 4.00
194 Avion Black RC 1.50 4.00
195 Bashir Yamini RC 1.50 4.00
196 Curtis Keaton RC 1.50 4.00
197 Mike Anderson RC 1.50 4.00
198 Bubba Franks RC 1.50 4.00
199 Anthony Lucas RC 1.50 4.00
200 Rondell Mealey RC 1.50 4.00
201 Terrelle Smith RC 1.50 4.00
202 Frank Moreau RC 1.50 4.00
203 Deon Dyer RC 1.50 4.00
204 Quinton Spotwood RC 1.50 4.00
205 Troy Walters RC 1.50 4.00
206 Doug Chapman RC 1.50 4.00
207 Tom Brady RC 250.00 500.00
208 Sherrod Gideon RC 1.50 4.00
209 Ron Dixon RC 1.50 4.00
210 Anthony Becht RC 1.50 4.00
211 James Williams RC 1.50 4.00
212 Sebastian Janikowski RC 2.50 6.00
213 Corey Simon RC 2.00 5.00
214 Gari Scott RC 1.50 4.00
215 Dante Hall RC 1.50 4.00
216 Tim Rattay RC 2.00 5.00
217 Chafie Fields RC 1.50 4.00
218 Trung Canidate RC 1.50 4.00
219 Chris Coleman RC 1.50 4.00
220 Erron Kinney RC 1.50 4.00
221 Thomas Jones RC 2.50 6.00
222 Travis Taylor RC 2.00 5.00
223 Chris Redman RC 2.00 5.00
224 Jamal Lewis RC 3.00 8.00
225 Dez White RC 2.00 5.00
226 Peter Warrick RC 2.00 5.00
227 Ron Dugans RC 2.00 5.00
228 Courtney Brown RC 2.50 6.00
229 Travis Prentice RC 2.00 5.00
230 Dennis Northcutt RC 2.00 5.00
231 Michael Wiley RC 2.00 5.00
232 Chris Cole RC 2.50 6.00
233 Reuben Droughns RC 2.00 5.00
234 R.Jay Soward RC 2.00 5.00
235 Shyrone Stith RC 2.00 5.00
236 Sylvester Morris RC 2.00 5.00
237 J.R. Redmond RC 2.00 5.00
238 Ron Dayne RC 3.00 8.00
239 Chad Pennington RC 2.50 6.00
240 Laveranues Coles RC 2.50 6.00
241 Jerry Porter RC 3.00 8.00
242 Todd Pinkston RC 2.00 5.00
243 Plaxico Burress RC 2.50 6.00
244 Danny Farmer RC 2.00 5.00
245 Tee Martin RC 2.00 5.00
246 Trevor Gaylor RC 2.00 5.00
247 Giovanni Carmazzi RC 2.00 5.00
248 Darrell Jackson RC 2.00 5.00
249 Shaun Alexander RC 3.00 8.00
250 Chris Samuels RC 3.00 8.00

2000 Leaf Certified Mirror Gold

*VETS 1-100: 12X TO 30X BASIC CARDS
1-100 1-STAR PRINT RUN 20
*VETS 101-150: 10X TO 25X BASIC CARD
101-150 2-STAR PRINT RUN 25
*ROOKIES 151-190: 1.2X TO 5X
151-190 3-STAR ROOKIE PRINT RUN 30
*ROOKIES 191-220: 1.5X TO 4X
191-220 4-STAR ROOKIE PRINT RUN 35
*ROOKIES 221-250: 1X TO 2.5X
221-250 5-STAR ROOKIE PRINT RUN 40
207 Tom Brady 2000.00 3000.00

2000 Leaf Certified Mirror Red

ETS 1-100: 2X TO 5X BASIC CARD
1-100 1-STAR VETERAN ODDS 1:17
*VETS 101-150: 1.5X TO 4X BASIC CARD
101-150 2-STAR VETERAN ODDS 1:53
*ROOKIES 151-190: .6X TO 1.5X
151-190 3-STAR ROOKIE ODDS 1:89
*ROOKIES 191-220: .5X TO 1.2X
191-220 4-STAR ROOKIE ODDS 1:125
*ROOKIES 221-250: .4X TO 1X
221-250 5-STAR ROOKIE ODDS 1:161
207 Tom Brady 400.00 800.00

2000 Leaf Certified Rookie Die Cuts

-STAR 151-190: 1X TO 2.5X HI COL.
*4-STAR 191-220: .75X TO 2X HI COL.
*5-STAR 221-250: .4X TO 1X HI COL.
FIRST 250 CARDS OF PRINT RUN DIE CUT
207 Tom Brady 300.00 600.00

2000 Leaf Certified Fabric of the Game

Randomly inserted in packs, this 75-card set is divided into five tiers: Legendary Material sequentially numbered to 100, Hall of Fame Material sequentially numbered to 250, Superstar Material sequentially numbered to 500, Star Material sequentially numbered to 750, and Professional Material sequentially numbered to 1000. Despite the set name, these cards do not feature game used material yet are produced with a variety of different material, such as plastic, simulated leather, and cardboard.

STATED PRINT RUN 100-1000
FG1 Barry Sanders/100 10.00 25.00
FG2 John Elway/100 10.00 25.00
FG3 Jerry Rice/100 15.00 40.00
FG4 Cris Carter/250 4.00 10.00
FG5 Emmitt Smith/250 6.00 15.00
FG6 Troy Aikman/250 5.00 12.00
FG7 Deion Sanders/250 3.00 8.00
FG8 Terrell Davis/500 2.50 6.00
FG9 Marshall Faulk/500 2.50 6.00
FG10 Mark Brunell/500 2.50 6.00
FG11 Randy Moss/500 2.50 6.00
FG12 Peyton Manning/500 8.00 20.00
FG13 Kurt Warner/750 4.00 10.00
FG14 Jamal Anderson/750 2.00 5.00
FG15 Edgerrin James/750 2.00 5.00
FG16 Isaac Bruce/750 2.50 6.00
FG17 Jimmy Smith/750 2.00 5.00
FG18 Keyshawn Johnson/750 2.00 5.00
FG19 Brian Griese/1000 1.50 4.00
FG20 Cade McNown/1000 1.50 4.00
FG21 Shaun King/1000 1.50 4.00
FG22 Chad Pennington/1000 2.00 5.00
FG23 Plaxico Burress/1000 2.00 5.00
FG24 Thomas Jones/1000 2.00 5.00
FG25 Peter Warrick/1000 1.50 4.00
FG26 Dan Marino/100 12.00 30.00
FG27 John Elway/100 12.00 30.00
FG28 Emmitt Smith/100 10.00 25.00
FG29 Brett Favre/250 8.00 20.00
FG30 Steve Young/250 5.00 12.00
FG31 Cris Carter/250 4.00 10.00
FG32 Michael Irvin/250 4.00 10.00
FG33 Eddie George/500 2.50 6.00
FG34 Drew Bledsoe/500 2.50 6.00
FG35 Antonio Freeman/500 2.50 6.00
FG36 Steve McNair/500 2.50 6.00
FG37 Randy Moss/500 2.50 6.00
FG38 Kurt Warner/750 4.00 10.00
FG39 Eric Moulds/750 1.50 4.00
FG40 Fred Taylor/750 1.50 4.00
FG41 Charlie Batch/750 1.50 4.00
FG42 Marvin Harrison/750 2.00 5.00
FG43 Joey Galloway/750 2.00 5.00
FG44 Tim Couch/1000 2.00 5.00
FG45 Ricky Williams/1000 2.00 5.00
FG46 Donovan McNabb/1000 2.00 5.00
FG47 Akili Smith/1000 1.50 4.00
FG48 Kevin Johnson/1000 1.50 4.00
FG49 Thomas Jones/1000 2.00 5.00
FG50 Ron Dayne/1000 2.50 6.00
FG51 Dan Marino/100 12.00 30.00
FG52 Barry Sanders/100 10.00 25.00
FG53 Jerry Rice/100 15.00 40.00
FG54 Brett Favre/250 8.00 20.00
FG55 Tim Brown/250 4.00 10.00
FG56 Steve Young/250 5.00 12.00
FG57 Thurman Thomas/250 3.00 8.00
FG58 Jeff George/500 2.50 6.00
FG59 Curtis Martin/500 2.50 6.00
FG60 Terrell Davis/500 2.50 6.00
FG61 Peyton Manning/500 8.00 20.00
FG62 Ricky Watters/500 2.50 6.00
FG63 Edgerrin James/750 2.00 5.00
FG64 Fred Taylor/750 1.50 4.00
FG65 Stephen Davis/750 1.50 4.00
FG66 Jake Plummer/750 1.50 4.00
FG67 Brad Johnson/750 2.00 5.00
FG68 Jon Kitna/750 1.50 4.00
FG69 Tim Couch/1000 2.00 5.00
FG70 Daunte Culpepper/1000 2.00 5.00
FG71 Olandis Gary/1000 2.00 5.00
FG72 Jamal Lewis/1000 2.50 6.00
FG73 Peter Warrick/1000 1.50 4.00
FG74 Stephen Alexander/1000 1.50 4.00
FG75 Travis Taylor/1000 1.50 4.00

2000 Leaf Certified Gold Future

ndomly inserted in packs at the rate of one in 17, this 30-card set features a mirror foil card stock with gold foil highlights.

COMPLETE SET (30) 20.00 50.00
STATED ODDS 1:17
*MIRROR BLACK/25: 5X TO 12X BASIC INSERTS
MIRROR BLACK PRINT RUN 25 SER.#'D SETS
CGF1 Peter Warrick .50 1.25
CGF2 Chad Pennington .60 1.50
CGF3 Thomas Jones .60 1.50
CGF4 Plaxico Burress .60 1.50
CGF5 Jamal Lewis .75 2.00
CGF6 Travis Taylor .50 1.25
CGF7 Chris Redman .50 1.25
CGF8 Dez White .50 1.25
CGF9 Shaun Alexander .75 2.00
CGF10 Sylvester Morris .50 1.25
CGF11 Ron Dayne .75 2.00
CGF12 R.Jay Soward .50 1.25
CGF13 Travis Prentice .50 1.25
CGF14 Giovanni Carmazzi .50 1.25
CGF15 Todd Pinkston .50 1.25
CGF16 J.R. Redmond .50 1.25
CGF17 Trevor Gaylor .50 1.25
CGF18 Trung Canidate .50 1.25
CGF19 Danny Farmer .50 1.25
CGF20 Tee Martin .50 1.25
CGF21 Darrell Jackson .50 1.25
CGF22 Gari Scott .50 1.25
CGF23 Dennis Northcutt .50 1.25
CGF24 Jerry Porter .75 2.00
CGF25 Reuben Droughns .50 1.25
CGF26 Laveranues Coles .60 1.50
CGF27 Bubba Franks .50 1.25
CGF28 Doug Chapman .50 1.25
CGF29 Chris Cole .60 1.50
CGF30 Ron Dugans .50 1.25

2000 Leaf Certified Gold Team

ndomly inserted in packs at the rate of one in 17, this 40-card set features players on mirror foil board with gold foil highlights.

COMPLETE SET (40) 40.00 100.00
STATED ODDS 1:17
*MIRROR BLACKS: 5X TO 12X BASIC INSERTS
MIRROR BLACKS PRINT RUN 25 SER.#'d SETS
CGT1 Randy Moss 1.00 2.50
CGT2 Brett Favre 2.50 6.00
CGT3 Dan Marino 2.50 6.00
CGT4 Barry Sanders 2.00 5.00
CGT5 John Elway 2.00 5.00
CGT6 Peyton Manning 3.00 8.00
CGT7 Terrell Davis 1.00 2.50
CGT8 Emmitt Smith 2.00 5.00
CGT9 Troy Aikman 1.50 4.00
CGT10 Jerry Rice 3.00 8.00
CGT11 Fred Taylor .75 2.00
CGT12 Jake Plummer .75 2.00
CGT13 Charlie Batch .75 2.00
CGT14 Drew Bledsoe 1.00 2.50
CGT15 Mark Brunell 1.00 2.50
CGT16 Steve Young 1.50 4.00
CGT17 Eddie George 1.00 2.50
CGT18 Tim Brown 1.25 3.00
CGT19 Cris Carter 1.25 3.00
CGT20 Stephen Davis .75 2.00
CGT21 Marshall Faulk 1.00 2.50
CGT22 Antonio Freeman 1.00 2.50
CGT23 Marvin Harrison 1.00 2.50
CGT24 Brad Johnson 1.00 2.50
CGT25 Keyshawn Johnson 1.00 2.50
CGT26 Jon Kitna .75 2.00
CGT27 Curtis Martin 1.00 2.50
CGT28 Steve McNair 1.00 2.50
CGT29 Isaac Bruce 1.25 3.00
CGT30 Kurt Warner 2.00 5.00
CGT31 Edgerrin James 1.00 2.50
CGT32 Tim Couch 1.00 2.50
CGT33 Ricky Williams 1.00 2.50
CGT34 Donovan McNabb 1.00 2.50
CGT35 Cade McNown .75 2.00
CGT36 Daunte Culpepper 1.00 2.50
CGT37 Torry Holt 1.00 2.50
CGT38 Robert Smith .75 2.00
CGT39 Mike Alstott .75 2.00
CGT40 Dorsey Levens 1.00 2.50

2000 Leaf Certified Gridiron Gear

ndomly inserted in packs, this 76-card set features swatches from game worn jerseys. Each card is sequentially numbered to either 100 or 300.

AF86H Antonio Freeman/300 3.00 8.00
BF4A Brett Favre W/300 8.00 20.00
BF4H Brett Favre G/100 10.00 25.00
BG14H Brian Griese/100 3.00 8.00
BS20H Barry Sanders/100 8.00 20.00
CB12H Charlie Batch/300 2.50 6.00
CB24H Champ Bailey/300 3.00 8.00
CC80H Cris Carter/100 5.00 12.00
CD28H Corey Dillon/300 2.50 6.00
CE44A Curtis Enis W/300 2.50 6.00
CE44H Curtis Enis Blu/300 2.50 6.00
CM8A Cade McNown/300 2.50 6.00
CM28H Curtis Martin/100 4.00 10.00
CW24H Charles Woodson/300 4.00 10.00
DB11H Drew Bledsoe/100 4.00 10.00
DF7H Doug Flutie/300 3.00 8.00
DH11H Damon Huard/300 2.50 6.00
DL25A Dorsey Levens W/300 3.00 8.00
DL25H Dorsey Levens G/300 3.00 8.00
DM5A Donovan McNabb/300 3.00 8.00
DM13A Dan Marino W/300 8.00 20.00
DM13H Dan Marino Teal/100 10.00 25.00
DS21H Deion Sanders/300 3.00 8.00
EG27A Eddie George/100 4.00 10.00
EJ32H Edg.James Blu/100 4.00 10.00
EJ32PB Edg.James PB/300 3.00 8.00
EM80A Eric Moulds/300 2.50 6.00
EM87H Ed McCaffrey/300 3.00 8.00
ES22H Emmitt Smith/100 8.00 20.00
FT28A Fred Taylor W/300 2.50 6.00
FT28H Fred Taylor Teal/100 3.00 8.00
IB80A Isaac Bruce W/100 5.00 12.00
IB80H Isaac Bruce Blu/300 4.00 10.00
JB36H Jerome Bettis/100 5.00 12.00
JE7A John Elway/100 8.00 20.00
JH4A Jim Harbaugh/300 3.00 8.00
JK90A Jevon Kearse/300 2.50 6.00
JM87A Johnnie Morton/300 3.00 8.00
JP16A Jake Plummer/300 2.50 6.00
JR80A Jerry Rice W/100 12.00 30.00
JR80H Jerry Rice R/300 10.00 25.00
JS82A Jimmy Smith W/100 4.00 10.00
JS82H Jimmy Smith Teal/300 3.00 8.00
KM87H Keenan McCardell/300 3.00 8.00
KS10A Kordell Stewart/300 2.50 6.00
KW13A Kurt Warner W/300 6.00 15.00
KW13H Kurt Warner Blu/100 8.00 20.00
MA40H Mike Alstott/300 2.50 6.00
MB8A Mark Brunell W/100 4.00 10.00
MB8H Mark Brunell Teal/300 3.00 8.00
MF28A Marshall Faulk W/100 4.00 10.00
MF28H Marshall Faulk Blu/300 3.00 8.00
MH88H Marvin Harrison/300 3.00 8.00
NK26A Napoleon Kaufman/100 4.00 10.00
OG22H Olandis Gary/100 4.00 10.00
PM18A Peyton Manning/100 12.00 30.00
RC7H Randall Cunningham/300 3.00 8.00
RL6A Ray Lucas/100 3.00 8.00
RM84H Randy Moss/100 4.00 10.00
RS80H Rod Smith/300 3.00 8.00
RW32A Ricky Watters/300 3.00 8.00
RW34A Ricky Williams W/100 4.00 10.00
RW34H Ricky Williams Blk/100 4.00 10.00
SK10H Shaun King/100 3.00 8.00
SM9H Steve McNair/100 4.00 10.00
SY8H Steve Young/100 6.00 15.00
TA8H Troy Aikman/100 6.00 15.00
TB81A Tim Brown W/300 4.00 10.00
TB81H Tim Brown Blk/300 4.00 10.00
TC2H Tim Couch/100 4.00 10.00
TD30A Terrell Davis/100 4.00 10.00
TO81H Terrell Owens/300 3.00 8.00
TW47H Tyrone Wheatley/300 2.50 6.00
WC80H Wayne Chrebet/300 2.50 6.00
WD28A Warrick Dunn/300 2.50 6.00

2000 Leaf Certified Gridiron Gear Century

NSIGNED CENTURY: 1X TO 2.5X JSY/300
*UNSIGNED CENTURY: .8X TO 2X JSY/100
BF4A Brett Favre W AU 150.00 300.00
DM13A Dan Marino W AU 100.00 200.00
EJ32H Edgerrin James Blu AU 40.00 80.00
JE7A John Elway AU 75.00 150.00
JP16A Jake Plummer AU 20.00 50.00
KW13A Kurt Warner W AU 60.00 120.00
KW13H Kurt Warner B AU 60.00 120.00
RW34A Ricky Williams W AU 25.00 60.00
RW34H Ricky Williams Blk AU 25.00 60.00
SY8H Steve Young AU 60.00 120.00
TA8H Troy Aikman AU 60.00 120.00

2000 Leaf Certified Heritage Collection

ndomly inserted in packs, this set showcases NFL legends with a swatch of an authentic jersey. 48-cards were issued in packs with each card sequentially numbered to 100. Larry Csonka was released later in 2001 Leaf Certified Materials packs.

STATED PRINT RUN 100 SER.#'d SETS
BE7H Boomer Esiason 5.00 12.00
BG12A Bob Griese 5.00 12.00
BJ7H Bert Jones 3.00 8.00
BK19H Bernie Kosar 4.00 10.00
BS15H Bart Starr 20.00 50.00
CJ32A Craig James 4.00 10.00
DF14A Dan Fouts W 4.00 10.00
DF14H Dan Fouts Blu 4.00 10.00
DM13H Don Maynard 4.00 10.00
DT58H Derrick Thomas 20.00 50.00
EC34A Earl Campbell 5.00 12.00
ED29A Eric Dickerson W 4.00 10.00
ED29H Eric Dickerson Blu 4.00 10.00
FG16H Frank Gifford 5.00 12.00
FT10H Fran Tarkenton 5.00 12.00
GS40H Gale Sayers 5.00 12.00
HL75A Howie Long 5.00 12.00
HW34 Herschel Walker 5.00 12.00
JB12H John Brodie 4.00 10.00
JB32H Jim Brown 6.00 15.00
JK12A Jim Kelly 5.00 12.00
JM16A Joe Montana 49ers 15.00 40.00
JM19A Joe Montana Chiefs 15.00 40.00
JN12A Joe Namath 10.00 25.00
JP16H Jim Plunkett 4.00 10.00
JT7H Joe Theismann 5.00 12.00
JU19H Johnny Unitas 20.00 50.00
KJ88H Keith Jackson 3.00 8.00
KS12A Ken Stabler 6.00 15.00
LS39A Larry Csonka 5.00 12.00
LT56A Lawrence Taylor 5.00 12.00
MA32A Marcus Allen W 5.00 12.00
MA32H Marcus Allen R 5.00 12.00
MO74H Merlin Olsen 3.00 8.00
ON82A Ozzie Newsome 3.00 8.00
PS11H Phil Simms 5.00 12.00
RB82A Raymond Berry 4.00 10.00
RL42H Ronnie Lott 5.00 12.00
RN66H Ray Nitschke 25.00 60.00
RW92H Reggie White 15.00 40.00
SJ9H Sonny Jurgensen 5.00 12.00
SL80A Steve Largent 5.00 12.00
TB12A Terry Bradshaw W 12.00 30.00
TB12P Terry Bradshaw PB 12.00 30.00
TD33H Tony Dorsett 15.00 40.00
TH83A Ted Hendricks 4.00 10.00
WM1A Warren Moon 5.00 12.00
WP34A Walter Payton W 20.00 50.00
WP34H Walter Payton Blu 20.00 50.00

2000 Leaf Certified Heritage Collection Century

BE7H Boomer Esiason 8.00 20.00
BG12A Bob Griese AU 60.00 120.00
BJ7H Bert Jones 5.00 12.00
BK19H Bernie Kosar 6.00 15.00
BS15H Bart Starr AU 150.00 250.00
CJ32A Craig James 6.00 15.00
DF14A Dan Fouts W AU 50.00 100.00
DF14H Dan Fouts Blue AU 50.00 100.00
DM13H Don Maynard 6.00 15.00
DT58H Derrick Thomas 30.00 80.00
EC0034 Earl Campbell AU 60.00 120.00
ED29A E.Dickerson W AU 60.00 120.00
ED29H E.Dickerson Blue AU 60.00 120.00
FG16H Frank Gifford 8.00 20.00
FT10H Fran Tarkenton AU 60.00 120.00
GS40H Gale Sayers 8.00 20.00
HL75A Howie Long AU 75.00 150.00
HW34 Herschel Walker 8.00 20.00
JB12H John Brodie 6.00 15.00
JB32A Jim Brown 10.00 25.00
JK12A Jim Kelly 8.00 20.00
JM16A Joe Montana 49er AU 125.00 250.00
JM19A Joe Montana Chiefs AU 100.00 200.00
JN12A Joe Namath AU 100.00 200.00
JP16H Jim Plunkett 6.00 15.00
JT7H Joe Theismann 8.00 20.00
JU19H Johnny Unitas AU 300.00 550.00
KJ88H Keith Jackson 5.00 12.00
KS12A Ken Stabler AU 75.00 150.00
LT56A Lawrence Taylor AU 75.00 150.00
MA32A Marcus Allen W AU 60.00 120.00
MA32H Marcus Allen R AU 60.00 120.00
MO74H Merlin Olsen 5.00 12.00
ON82A Ozzie Newsome 5.00 12.00
PS11H Phil Simms 8.00 20.00
RB82A Raymond Berry 6.00 15.00
RL42H Ronnie Lott AU 50.00 100.00
RN66H Ray Nitschke 40.00 100.00
RW92H Reggie White 25.00 60.00
SJ9H Sonny Jurgensen AU 50.00 100.00
SL80A Steve Largent 8.00 20.00
TB12A Terry Bradshaw W AU 100.00 200.00
TB12P Terry Bradshaw PB AU 100.00 200.00
TD33H Tony Dorsett 25.00 60.00
TH83A Ted Hendricks 6.00 15.00
WM1A Warren Moon 8.00 20.00
WP34A Walter Payton W 30.00 80.00
WP34H Walter Payton Blue 30.00 80.00

2000 Leaf Certified Skills

ndomly inserted in packs at the rate of one in 35, this 30-card set features dual player cards with mirror foil fronts and enhanced foil stamping on the back.

COMPLETE SET (30) 40.00 100.00
STATED ODDS 1:35
*MIRROR BLACK/25: 3X TO 8X BASIC INSERTS
MIRROR BLACK PRINT RUN 25 SER.#'d SETS
CS1 J.Anderson / T.Jones 1.00 2.50
CS2 R.Moss / G.Crowell 1.00 2.50
CS3 B.Favre / D.McNabb 2.50 6.00
CS4 D.Marino / T.Couch 2.50 6.00
CS5 B.Sanders / J.Stewart 2.00 5.00
CS6 J.Elway / B.Griese 2.00 5.00
CS7 P.Manning / C.Pennington 3.00 8.00
CS8 T.Davis / O.Gary 1.00 2.50
CS9 E.Smith / D.Staley 2.00 5.00
CS10 T.Aikman / C.McNown 1.50 4.00
CS11 J.Rice / I.Bruce 3.00 8.00
CS12 F.Taylor / S.Davis .75 2.00
CS13 D.Bledsoe / B.Johnson 1.00 2.50
CS14 M.Brunell / S.King 1.00 2.50
CS15 S.Young / A.Smith 1.50 4.00
CS16 E.George / R.Williams 1.00 2.50
CS17 K.Warner / J.Kitna 2.00 5.00
CS18 E.James / C.Dillon 1.00 2.50
CS19 C.Carter / T.Brown 1.25 3.00
CS20 K.Johnson / P.Burress 1.00 2.50
CS21 M.Faulk / R.Smith 1.00 2.50
CS22 A.Freeman / T.Taylor 1.00 2.50
CS23 M.Harrison / K.Johnson 1.00 2.50
CS24 D.Levens / J.Lewis 1.25 3.00
CS25 C.Martin / S.Alexander 1.25 3.00
CS26 S.McNair / D.Culpepper 1.00 2.50
CS27 J.Smith / P.Warrick 1.00 2.50
CS28 J.Bettis / R.Dayne 1.25 3.00
CS29 J.Galloway / T.Holt 1.00 2.50
CS30 E.Moulds / T.Owens 1.00 2.50

2001 Leaf Certified Materials

is 145 card set was issued in five card packs which were issued 12 packs per box and six boxes per case. The SRP on these packs was $11.99 per pack. Cards number 1-100 feature veterans while cards 101-145 feature rookies. Of the rookies, cards number 111-145 feature rookie cards with pieces of memorabilia and are serial numbered to 400. A variety of different swatches were used on some cards with the value being the same on all versions.

COMP.SET w/o SPs (100) 12.50 30.00
1 Aaron Brooks .25 .60
2 Ahman Green .30 .75
3 Akili Smith .25 .60
4 Amani Toomer .25 .60
5 Antonio Freeman .40 1.00
6 Barry Sanders .60 1.50
7 Brad Johnson .30 .75
8 Brett Favre .75 2.00
9 Brian Griese .25 .60
10 Brian Urlacher .50 1.25
11 Bruce Smith .30 .75
12 Cade McNown .30 .75
13 Chad Pennington .25 .60
14 Charlie Batch .25 .60
15 Charlie Garner .30 .75
16 Corey Dillon .25 .60
17 Cris Carter .40 1.00
18 Curtis Martin .30 .75
19 Dan Marino .75 2.00
20 Darrell Jackson .30 .75
21 Daunte Culpepper .30 .75
22 David Boston .25 .60
23 Derrick Alexander .25 .60
24 Donovan McNabb .30 .75
25 Dorsey Levens .30 .75
26 Doug Flutie .30 .75
27 Drew Bledsoe .30 .75
28 Ed McCaffrey .30 .75
29 Eddie George .40 1.00
30 Edgerrin James .30 .75
31 Elvis Grbac .30 .75
32 Emmitt Smith .60 1.50
33 Eric Moulds .25 .60
34 Frank Wycheck .25 .60
35 Fred Taylor .25 .60
36 Ike Hilliard .25 .60
37 Isaac Bruce .40 1.00
38 Jacquez Green .25 .60
39 Jake Plummer .25 .60
40 Jamal Anderson .30 .75
41 Jamal Lewis .40 1.00
42 James Stewart .25 .60
43 Jay Fiedler .30 .75
44 Jeff Garcia .25 .60
45 Jeff George .30 .75
46 Jerome Bettis .40 1.00
47 Jerry Rice .75 2.00
48 Jevon Kearse .25 .60
49 Jimmy Smith .30 .75
50 Joe Horn .25 .60
51 Joey Galloway .30 .75
52 John Elway .60 1.50
53 Junior Seau .30 .75
54 Keenan McCardell .30 .75
55 Kerry Collins .25 .60
56 Keyshawn Johnson .30 .75
57 Kurt Warner .60 1.50
58 Lamar Smith .30 .75
59 Laveranues Coles .30 .75
60 Marcus Robinson .30 .75
61 Mark Brunell .30 .75
62 Marshall Faulk .30 .75
63 Marvin Harrison .30 .75
64 Matt Hasselbeck .25 .60
65 Mike Alstott .25 .60
66 Mike Anderson .25 .60
67 Muhsin Muhammad .25 .60
68 Peter Warrick .25 .60
69 Peyton Manning 1.00 2.50
70 Plaxico Burress .25 .60
71 Randy Moss .30 .75
72 Ray Lewis .40 1.00
73 Rich Gannon .30 .75
74 Ricky Watters .30 .75
75 Ricky Williams .30 .75
76 Rob Johnson .30 .75
77 Rod Smith .30 .75
78 Ron Dayne .30 .75
79 Shannon Sharpe .30 .75
80 Shaun Alexander .25 .60
81 Stephen Davis .25 .60
82 Steve McNair .30 .75
83 Steve Young .50 1.25
84 Sylvester Morris .25 .60
85 Terrell Davis .30 .75
86 Terrell Owens .30 .75
87 Terry Glenn .30 .75
88 Thomas Jones .25 .60
89 Tiki Barber .30 .75
90 Tim Brown .40 1.00
91 Tim Couch .25 .60
92 Tony Gonzalez .30 .75
93 Torry Holt .30 .75
94 Travis Taylor .25 .60
95 Troy Aikman .50 1.25
96 Tyrone Wheatley .30 .75
97 Vinny Testaverde .25 .60
98 Warren Sapp .30 .75
99 Warrick Dunn .25 .60
100 Wayne Chrebet .25 .60
101 Chris Taylor RC 1.25 3.00
102 Ken-Yon Rambo RC 1.25 3.00
103 Correll Buckhalter RC 1.25 3.00
104 A.J. Feeley RC 1.50 4.00
105 Josh Booty RC 1.50 4.00
106 LaMont Jordan RC 2.00 5.00
107 Alge Crumpler RC 2.00 5.00
108 Jamal Reynolds RC 1.25 3.00
109 Nate Clements RC 1.50 4.00
110 Will Allen RC 2.00 5.00
111 Santana Moss FF RC 3.00 8.00
112 Chad Johnson FF RC 3.00 8.00
113 Chris Chambers FF RC 2.00 5.00
114 David Terrell FF RC 2.50 6.00
115 Freddie Mitchell FF RC 2.00 5.00
116 Koren Robinson FF RC 2.50 6.00
117 Quincy Morgan FF RC 2.50 6.00
118 Reggie Wayne FF RC 4.00 10.00
119 Robert Ferguson FF RC 3.00 8.00
120 Rod Gardner FF RC 2.50 6.00
121 Snoop Minnis FF RC 2.00 5.00
122 Josh Heupel FF RC 3.00 8.00
123 Anthony Thomas FF RC 3.00 8.00
124 Deuce McAllister FF RC 3.00 8.00
125 James Jackson FF RC 2.00 5.00
126 Travis Minor FF RC 2.50 6.00
127 Kevan Barlow FF RC 2.50 6.00
128 LaDain Tomlinson FF RC 10.00 25.00
129 Todd Heap FF RC 2.50 6.00
130 Michael Bennett FF RC 2.50 6.00
131 Rudi Johnson FF RC 3.00 8.00
132 Travis Henry FF RC 2.50 6.00
133 Michael Vick FF RC 5.00 12.00
134 Drew Brees FF RC 15.00 40.00
135 Chris Weinke FF RC 2.50 6.00
136 Quincy Carter FF RC 2.50 6.00
137 Mike McMahon FF RC 2.50 6.00
138 Jesse Palmer FF RC 2.50 6.00
139 M.Tuiasosopo FF RC 2.50 6.00
140 Dan Morgan FF RC 2.50 6.00
141 Gerard Warren FF RC 2.50 6.00
142 Leonard Davis FF RC 3.00 8.00
143 Andre Carter FF RC 2.50 6.00
144 Justin Smith FF RC 4.00 10.00
145 Sage Rosenfels FF RC 2.50 6.00

2001 Leaf Certified Materials Mirror Gold

ETS 1-110: 10X TO 25X BASIC CARDS
*ROOKIES 101-110: 2X TO 5X
*ROOKIE FF 111-145: 2X TO 5X
STATED PRINT RUN 25 SER.#'d SETS
OVERALL INSERT ODDS 1:4

2001 Leaf Certified Materials Mirror Red

*VETS 1-100: 5X TO 12X BASIC CARDS
*ROOKIES 101-110: 1X TO 2.5X
1-110 VET/ROOKIE PRINT RUN 75
111-145 FF AUTO PRINT RUN 150
OVERALL INSERT ODDS 1:4
111 Santana Moss FF AU 10.00 25.00
112 Chad Johnson FF AU 4.00 10.00
113 Chris Chambers FF AU 6.00 15.00
114 David Terrell FF AU 8.00 20.00
115 Freddie Mitchell FF AU 6.00 15.00
116 Koren Robinson FF AU 8.00 20.00
117 Quincy Morgan FF AU 8.00 20.00
118 Reggie Wayne FF AU 30.00 80.00
119 Robert Ferguson FF AU 10.00 25.00
120 Rod Gardner FF AU 8.00 20.00
121 Snoop Minnis FF AU 6.00 15.00
122 Josh Heupel FF AU 10.00 25.00
123 Anthony Thomas FF AU 10.00 25.00
124 Deuce McAllister FF AU 10.00 25.00
125 James Jackson FF AU 6.00 15.00
126 Travis Minor FF AU 8.00 20.00
127 Kevan Barlow FF AU 8.00 20.00
128 L.Tomlinson FF AU 40.00 100.00
129 Todd Heap FF AU 8.00 20.00
130 Michael Bennett FF AU 8.00 20.00
131 Rudi Johnson FF AU 10.00 25.00
132 Travis Henry FF AU 8.00 20.00
133 Michael Vick FF AU 15.00 40.00
134 Drew Brees FF AU 75.00 150.00
135 Chris Weinke FF AU 8.00 20.00
136 Quincy Carter FF AU 8.00 20.00
137 Mike McMahon FF AU 8.00 20.00
138 Jesse Palmer FF AU 8.00 20.00
139 M.Tuiasosopo FF AU 8.00 20.00
140 Dan Morgan FF AU 8.00 20.00
141 Gerard Warren FF AU 8.00 20.00
143 Andre Carter FF AU 8.00 20.00
144 Justin Smith FF AU 12.00 30.00
145 Sage Rosenfels FF AU 8.00 20.00

2001 Leaf Certified Materials Fabric of the Game

This set, which features 150 different player cards, was randomly inserted in packs. The cards are broken down into these categories: Base (unnumbered, Bronze), Career (serial numbered to a career stat, Silver), Season (serial numbered to a season stat, Gold), Jersey Number (serial numbered to the player's jersey number, Platinum Blue foil logo), and Century (serial numbered to 21, Platinum Holofoil logo). Several players signed some or all of one specific card. Those were issued via mail redemption cards that carried an expiration date of 11/14/2003.

OVERALL INSERT ODDS 1:4
1BA Art Monk 3.00 8.00
1CE Art Monk/21 8.00 20.00
1CR Art Monk/68 4.00 10.00
1JN Art Monk/81 4.00 10.00
2BA Barry Sanders 5.00 12.00
2CE Barry Sanders/21 AU 100.00 200.00
2CR Barry Sanders/109 5.00 12.00
2JN Barry Sanders/20 12.00 30.00
3BA Bart Starr 6.00 15.00
3CE Bart Starr/21 AU 100.00 200.00
3CR Bart Starr/57 10.00 25.00
3SN Bart Starr/105 6.00 15.00
4BA Bob Griese 3.00 8.00
4CE Bob Griese/21 8.00 20.00
4CR Bob Griese/56 5.00 12.00
4SN Bob Griese/90 4.00 10.00
5BA Dan Fouts W 2.50 6.00
5CE Dan Fouts W/21 6.00 15.00
5CR Dan Fouts W/58 4.00 10.00
5SN Dan Fouts W/93 3.00 8.00
6BA Dan Fouts B 2.50 6.00
6CE Dan Fouts B/21 6.00 15.00
6CR Dan Fouts B/58 4.00 10.00
6SN Dan Fouts B/93 3.00 8.00
7BA Dan Marino T 6.00 15.00
7CE Dan Marino T/21 AU 250.00 400.00
7CR Dan Marino T/86 8.00 20.00
7SN Dan Marino T/48 10.00 25.00
8BA Dan Marino W 6.00 15.00
8CE Dan Marino W/21 15.00 40.00
8CR Dan Marino W/86 8.00 20.00
8SN Dan Marino W/48 10.00 25.00
9BA Deacon Jones 2.50 6.00
9CE Deacon Jones/21 6.00 15.00
9JN Deacon Jones/75 3.00 8.00
9SN Deacon Jones/21 6.00 15.00
10BA Don Maynard 2.50 6.00
10CE Don Maynard/21 6.00 15.00
10CR Don Maynard/88 3.00 8.00
10SN Don Maynard/22 6.00 15.00
11BA Earl Campbell 3.00 8.00
11CE Earl Campbell/21 8.00 20.00
11CR Earl Campbell/74 4.00 10.00
11JN Earl Campbell/34 6.00 15.00
11SN Earl Campbell/36 5.00 12.00
12BA Eric Dickerson 2.50 6.00
12CE Eric Dickerson/21 6.00 15.00
12CR Eric Dickerson/96 3.00 8.00
12JN Eric Dickerson/29 5.00 12.00
12SN Eric Dickerson/20 6.00 15.00
13BA Fran Tarkenton 3.00 8.00
13CE Fran Tarkenton/21 8.00 20.00
13CR Fran Tarkenton/80 4.00 10.00
13SN Fran Tarkenton/31 6.00 15.00
14BA Frank Gifford 3.00 8.00
14CE Frank Gifford/21 8.00 20.00
14CR Frank Gifford/77 4.00 10.00
14SN Frank Gifford/51 5.00 12.00
15BA Gale Sayers 3.00 8.00
15CE Gale Sayers/21 8.00 20.00
15CR Gale Sayers/56 5.00 12.00
15SN Gale Sayers/37 5.00 12.00
15JNAU Gale Sayers/40 AU 40.00 80.00
16BA George Blanda SP 2.50 6.00
16CE George Blanda/21 6.00 15.00
16CR George Blanda/135 2.50 6.00
16SN George Blanda/47 4.00 10.00
17BA Jim Brown SP 4.00 10.00
17CE Jim Brown/21 10.00 25.00
17CR Jim Brown/126 4.00 10.00
17JN Jim Brown AU/32 75.00 150.00
17SN Jim Brown/21 10.00 25.00
18BA Joe Montana W 10.00 25.00
18CE Joe Montana W/21 25.00 60.00
18CR Joe Montana W/63 12.00 30.00
18SN Joe Montana W/87 12.00 30.00
19BA Joe Montana R SP 10.00 25.00
19CE Joe Montana R/21 25.00 60.00
19CR Joe Montana R/63 12.00 30.00
19JN Joe Montana R/16 AU 250.00 500.00
19SN Joe Montana R/112 10.00 25.00
20BA Joe Namath 5.00 12.00
20CE Joe Namath/21 12.00 30.00
20CR Joe Namath/50 8.00 20.00
20SN Joe Namath/26 10.00 25.00
21BA John Elway O 5.00 12.00
21CE John Elway O/21 AU 100.00 200.00
21CR John Elway O/56 8.00 20.00
21SN John Elway O/93 6.00 15.00
22BA John Elway B 5.00 12.00
22CE John Elway B/21 12.00 30.00
22CR John Elway B/56 8.00 20.00
22SN John Elway B/93 6.00 15.00
23BA Johnny Unitas 6.00 15.00
23CE Johnny Unitas/21 AU 250.00 500.00
23CR Johnny Unitas/54 10.00 25.00
23SN Johnny Unitas/97 8.00 20.00
24BA Larry Csonka SP 3.00 8.00
24CE Larry Csonka/21 8.00 20.00
24CR Larry Csonka/68 4.00 10.00
24JN Larry Csonka/39 5.00 12.00
24SN Larry Csonka/118 3.00 8.00
25BA Lawrence Taylor SP 3.00 8.00
25CE Lawrence Taylor/21 8.00 20.00
25CR Lawrence Taylor/132 3.00 8.00
25JN Lawrence Taylor/56 5.00 12.00
25SN Lawrence Taylor/20 8.00 20.00
27BA Marcus Allen R SP 3.00 8.00
27CE Marcus Allen R/21 8.00 20.00
27CR Marcus Allen R/123 3.00 8.00
27JN Marcus Allen R/32 6.00 15.00
27SN Marcus Allen R/68 4.00 10.00
28BA Marcus Allen W SP 3.00 8.00
28CE Marcus Allen W/21 8.00 20.00
28CR Marcus Allen W/123 3.00 8.00
28JN Marcus Allen W/32 6.00 15.00
28SN Marcus Allen W/68 4.00 10.00
29BA Ozzie Newsome SP 2.50 6.00
29CE Ozzie Newsome/21 6.00 15.00
29CR Ozzie Newsome/47 4.00 10.00
29JN Ozzie Newsome/82 3.00 8.00
29SN Ozzie Newsome/89 3.00 8.00
30BA Raymond Berry SP 2.50 6.00
30CE Raymond Berry/21 6.00 15.00
30CR Raymond Berry/68 3.00 8.00
30JN Raymond Berry/82 3.00 8.00
30SN Raymond Berry/75 3.00 8.00
31BA Roger Staubach SP 4.00 10.00
31CE Roger Staubach/21 10.00 25.00
31CR Roger Staubach/153 4.00 10.00
31SN Roger Staubach/62 5.00 12.00
32BA Sonny Jurgensen 3.00 8.00
32CE Sonny Jurgensen/21 8.00 20.00
32CR Sonny Jurgensen/57 5.00 12.00
32SN Sonny Jurgensen/32 6.00 15.00
33BA Steve Largent SP 3.00 8.00
33CE Steve Largent/21 8.00 20.00
33CR Steve Largent/100 3.00 8.00
33JN Steve Largent/80 4.00 10.00
34BA Steve Young W 4.00 10.00
34CE Steve Young W/21 10.00 25.00
34CR Steve Young W/96 5.00 12.00
34SN Steve Young W/36 6.00 15.00
35BA Steve Young R 4.00 10.00
35CE Steve Young R/21 10.00 25.00
35CR Steve Young R/96 5.00 12.00
35SN Steve Young R/36 6.00 15.00
36BA Terry Bradshaw W 4.00 10.00
36CE Terry Bradshaw W/21 10.00 25.00
36CR Terry Bradshaw W/51 6.00 15.00
36SN Terry Bradshaw W/28 8.00 20.00
37BA Terry Bradshaw PB 4.00 10.00
37CE Terry Bradshaw PB/21 10.00 25.00
37CR Terry Bradshaw PB/51 6.00 15.00
37SN Terry Bradshaw PB/28 8.00 20.00
38BA Tony Dorsett 3.00 8.00
38CE Tony Dorsett/21 8.00 20.00
38CR Tony Dorsett/91 4.00 10.00
38JN Tony Dorsett/33 6.00 15.00
38SN Tony Dorsett/51 5.00 12.00
39BA Walter Payton W SP 8.00 20.00
39CE Walter Payton W/21 20.00 50.00
39CR Walter Payton W/125 8.00 20.00
39JN Walter Payton W/34 15.00 40.00
39SN Walter Payton W/53 12.00 30.00
40BA Walter Payton B SP 8.00 20.00
40CE Walter Payton B/21 20.00 50.00
40CR Walter Payton B/125 8.00 20.00
40JN Walter Payton B/34 15.00 40.00
40SN Walter Payton B/53 12.00 30.00
41BA Brett Favre G SP 6.00 15.00
41CE Brett Favre G/21 15.00 40.00
41CR Brett Favre G/266 6.00 15.00
41SN Brett Favre G/20 15.00 40.00
42BA Brett Favre W SP 6.00 15.00
42CE Brett Favre W/21 15.00 40.00
42CR Brett Favre W/266 6.00 15.00
42SN Brett Favre W/20 15.00 40.00
43BA Brian Griese 2.00 5.00
43CE Brian Griese/21 5.00 12.00
43CR Brian Griese/36 3.00 8.00
43SN Brian Griese/102 2.00 5.00
44BA Charley Taylor 2.00 5.00
44CE Charley Taylor/21 5.00 12.00
44CR Charley Taylor/90 2.50 6.00
44JN Charley Taylor/42 3.00 8.00
44SN Charley Taylor/72 2.50 6.00
45BA Daunte Culpepper P 2.50 6.00
45CE Daunte Culpepper P/21 6.00 15.00
45CR Daunte Culpepper P/40 4.00 10.00
45SN Daunte Culpepper P/98 3.00 8.00
46BA Daunte Culpepper W 2.50 6.00
46CE Daunte Culpepper W/21 6.00 15.00
46CR Daunte Culpepper W/40 4.00 10.00
46SN Daunte Culpepper W/98 3.00 8.00
47BA Donovan McNabb G 2.50 6.00
47CE Donovan McNabb G/21 6.00 15.00
47CR Donovan McNabb G/133 2.50 6.00
47SN Donovan McNabb G/77 3.00 8.00
48BA Donovan McNabb W 2.50 6.00
48CE Donovan McNabb W/21 6.00 15.00
48CR Donovan McNabb W/133 2.50 6.00
48SN Donovan McNabb W/77 3.00 8.00
49BA Drew Bledsoe 2.50 6.00
49CE Drew Bledsoe/21 6.00 15.00
49CR Drew Bledsoe/166 2.50 6.00
49SN Drew Bledsoe/77 3.00 8.00
50BA Eddie George 3.00 8.00
50CE Eddie George/21 8.00 20.00
50CR Eddie George/164 3.00 8.00
50JN Eddie George/27 6.00 15.00
51BA Edgerrin James B 2.50 6.00
51CE Edgerrin James B/21 6.00 15.00
51CR Edgerrin James B/72 3.00 8.00
51JN Edgerrin James B/32 5.00 12.00
51SN Edgerrin James B/63 3.00 8.00
52BA Edgerrin James W 2.50 6.00
52CE Edgerrin James W/21 6.00 15.00
52CR Edgerrin James W/72 3.00 8.00
52JN Edgerrin James W/32 5.00 12.00
52SN Edgerrin James W/63 3.00 8.00
53BA Emmitt Smith W 5.00 12.00
53CE Emmitt Smith W/21 12.00 30.00
53CR Emmitt Smith W/145 5.00 12.00
53JN Emmitt Smith W/22 12.00 30.00
53SN Emmitt Smith W/79 6.00 15.00
54BA Emmitt Smith B 5.00 12.00
54CE Emmitt Smith B/21 12.00 30.00
54CR Emmitt Smith B/145 5.00 12.00
54JN Emmitt Smith B/22 12.00 30.00
54SN Emmitt Smith B/79 6.00 15.00
55BA Jamal Lewis 3.00 8.00
55CE Jamal Lewis/21 8.00 20.00
55CR Jamal Lewis/27 6.00 15.00
55JN Jamal Lewis/31 6.00 15.00
55SN Jamal Lewis/45 5.00 12.00
56BA Jerry Rice R 6.00 15.00
56CE Jerry Rice R/21 15.00 40.00
56CR Jerry Rice R/96 8.00 20.00
56JN Jerry Rice R/80 8.00 20.00
56SN Jerry Rice R/75 8.00 20.00
57BA Jerry Rice W 6.00 15.00
57CE Jerry Rice W/21 15.00 40.00
57CR Jerry Rice W/96 8.00 20.00
57JN Jerry Rice W/80 8.00 20.00
57SN Jerry Rice W/75 8.00 20.00
58BA Kurt Warner W 5.00 12.00
58CE Kurt Warner W/21 12.00 30.00
58CR Kurt Warner W/104 5.00 12.00
58SN Kurt Warner W/21 12.00 30.00
59BA Kurt Warner B 5.00 12.00
59CE Kurt Warner B/21 12.00 30.00
59CR Kurt Warner B/104 5.00 12.00
59SN Kurt Warner B/21 12.00 30.00
60BA Marshall Faulk W 2.50 6.00
60CE Marshall Faulk W/21 6.00 15.00
60CR Marshall Faulk W/89 3.00 8.00
60JN Marshall Faulk W/28 5.00 12.00
60SN Marshall Faulk W/81 3.00 8.00
61BA Marshall Faulk B 2.50 6.00
61CE Marshall Faulk B/21 6.00 15.00
61CR Marshall Faulk B/89 3.00 8.00
61JN Marshall Faulk B/28 5.00 12.00
61SN Marshall Faulk B/81 3.00 8.00
62BA Mike Anderson 2.00 5.00
62CE Mike Anderson/21 5.00 12.00
62CR Mike Anderson/80 2.50 6.00
62JN Mike Anderson/38 3.00 8.00
63BA Peyton Manning W 8.00 20.00
63CE Peyton Manning W/21 20.00 50.00

63CR Peyton Manning W/88 10.00 25.00
63JN Peyton Manning W/18 20.00 50.00
63SN Peyton Manning W/94 10.00 25.00
64BA Peyton Manning B 8.00 20.00
64CE Peyton Manning B/21 20.00 50.00
64CR Peyton Manning B/88 10.00 25.00
64JN Peyton Manning B/18 20.00 50.00
64SN Peyton Manning B/94 10.00 25.00
65BA Randy Moss W 2.50 6.00
65CE Randy Moss W/21 6.00 15.00
65CR Randy Moss W/43 4.00 10.00
65JN Randy Moss W/84 3.00 8.00
65SN Randy Moss W/78 3.00 8.00
66BA Randy Moss P 2.50 6.00
66CE Randy Moss P/21 6.00 15.00
66CR Randy Moss P/43 4.00 10.00
66JN Randy Moss P/84 3.00 8.00
66SN Randy Moss P/78 3.00 8.00
67BA Ricky Williams SP 2.50 6.00
67CE Ricky Williams/21 6.00 15.00
67JN Ricky Williams/34 5.00 12.00
67SN Ricky Williams/248 2.50 6.00
68BA Terrell Davis SP 2.50 6.00
68CE Terrell Davis/21 6.00 15.00
68CR Terrell Davis/157 2.50 6.00
68JN Terrell Davis/30 5.00 12.00
68SN Terrell Davis/78 3.00 8.00
69BA Troy Aikman 4.00 10.00
69CE Troy Aikman/21 10.00 25.00
69CR Troy Aikman/167 4.00 10.00
69SN Troy Aikman/69 5.00 12.00
70BA Warren Moon 3.00 8.00
70CE Warren Moon/21 8.00 20.00
70CR Warren Moon/80 4.00 10.00
70SN Warren Moon/33 6.00 15.00
71BA Antonio Freeman W SP 3.00 8.00
71CE Antonio Freeman W/21 8.00 20.00
71CR Antonio Freeman W/365 3.00 8.00
71JN Antonio Freeman W/86 4.00 10.00
72BA Antonio Freeman G SP 3.00 8.00
72CE Antonio Freeman G/21 8.00 20.00
72CR Antonio Freeman G/365 3.00 8.00
72JN Antonio Freeman G/86 4.00 10.00
73BA Bernie Kosar 2.50 6.00
73CE Bernie Kosar/21 6.00 15.00
73CR Bernie Kosar/124 2.50 6.00
73SN Bernie Kosar/102 2.50 6.00
74BA Boomer Esiason 2.50 6.00
74CE Boomer Esiason/21 6.00 15.00
74CR Boomer Esiason/247 2.50 6.00
74SN Boomer Esiason/63 3.00 8.00
75BA Cade McNown 2.50 6.00
75CE Cade McNown/21 6.00 15.00
75CR Cade McNown/281 2.50 6.00
75SN Cade McNown/68 3.00 8.00
76BA Charlie Batch 2.00 5.00
76CE Charlie Batch/21 5.00 12.00
76CR Charlie Batch/76 2.50 6.00
76SN Charlie Batch/221 2.00 5.00
77BA Corey Dillon SP 2.00 5.00
77CE Corey Dillon/21 5.00 12.00
77CR Corey Dillon/104 2.00 5.00
77JN Corey Dillon/28 4.00 10.00
77SN Corey Dillon/315 2.00 5.00
78BA Cris Carter 3.00 8.00
78CE Cris Carter/21 8.00 20.00
78CR Cris Carter/123 3.00 8.00
78JN Cris Carter/80 4.00 10.00
78SN Cris Carter/96 4.00 10.00
79BA Curtis Martin 2.50 6.00
79CE Curtis Martin/21 6.00 15.00
79CR Curtis Martin/275 2.50 6.00
79JN Curtis Martin/28 5.00 12.00
79SN Curtis Martin/55 4.00 10.00
80BA Deion Sanders 2.50 6.00
80CE Deion Sanders/21 6.00 15.00
80CR Deion Sanders/48 4.00 10.00
80JN Deion Sanders/21 6.00 15.00
80SN Deion Sanders/91 3.00 8.00
81BA Duce Staley 2.00 5.00
81CE Duce Staley/21 5.00 12.00
81CR Duce Staley/125 2.00 5.00
81JN Duce Staley/22 5.00 12.00
81SN Duce Staley/201 2.00 5.00
82BA Ed McCaffrey 2.50 6.00
82CE Ed McCaffrey/21 6.00 15.00
82CR Ed McCaffrey/52 4.00 10.00
82JN Ed McCaffrey/87 3.00 8.00
82SN Ed McCaffrey/101 2.50 6.00
83BA Eric Moulds 2.00 5.00
83CE Eric Moulds/21 5.00 12.00
83CR Eric Moulds/84 2.50 6.00
83JN Eric Moulds/80 2.50 6.00
83SN Eric Moulds/94 2.50 6.00
84BA Fred Taylor 2.00 5.00
84CE Fred Taylor/21 5.00 12.00
84CR Fred Taylor/77 2.50 6.00
84JN Fred Taylor/28 4.00 10.00
84SN Fred Taylor/240 2.00 5.00
85BA Isaac Bruce B 3.00 8.00
85CE Isaac Bruce B/21 8.00 20.00
85CR Isaac Bruce B/80 4.00 10.00
85JN Isaac Bruce B/80 4.00 10.00
85SN Isaac Bruce B/87 4.00 10.00
86BA Isaac Bruce W 3.00 8.00
86CE Isaac Bruce W/21 8.00 20.00
86CR Isaac Bruce W/80 4.00 10.00
86JN Isaac Bruce W/80 4.00 10.00
86SN Isaac Bruce W/87 4.00 10.00
87BA Jake Plummer SP 2.00 5.00
87CE Jake Plummer/21 5.00 12.00
87CR Jake Plummer/166 2.00 5.00
87SN Jake Plummer/270 2.00 5.00
88BA Jamal Anderson SP 2.50 6.00
88CE Jamal Anderson/21 6.00 15.00
88CR Jamal Anderson/39 4.00 10.00
88JN Jamal Anderson/32 5.00 12.00
88SN Jamal Anderson/382 2.50 6.00
89BA Jerome Bettis B SP 3.00 8.00
89CE Jerome Bettis B/21 8.00 20.00
89CR Jerome Bettis B/52 5.00 12.00
89JN Jerome Bettis B/36 5.00 12.00
89SN Jerome Bettis B/355 3.00 8.00
90BA Jerome Bettis W SP 3.00 8.00
90CE Jerome Bettis W/21 8.00 20.00
90CR Jerome Bettis W/52 5.00 12.00
90JN Jerome Bettis W/36 5.00 12.00
90SN Jerome Bettis W/355 3.00 8.00
91BA Jevon Kearse 2.00 5.00
91CE Jevon Kearse/21 5.00 12.00
91CR Jevon Kearse/110 2.00 5.00
91JN Jevon Kearse/90 2.50 6.00
92BA Jim Kelly 3.00 8.00
92CE Jim Kelly/21 8.00 20.00
92CR Jim Kelly/237 3.00 8.00
92SN Jim Kelly/64 4.00 10.00
93BA Keyshawn Johnson SP 2.50 6.00
93CE Keyshawn Johnson/21 6.00 15.00
93CR Keyshawn Johnson/376 2.50 6.00
93SN Keyshawn Johnson/71 3.00 8.00
94BA Mark Brunell W SP 2.50 6.00
94CE Mark Brunell W/21 6.00 15.00
94CR Mark Brunell W/119 2.50 6.00
94SN Mark Brunell W/311 2.50 6.00
95BA Mark Brunell T SP 2.50 6.00
95CE Mark Brunell T/21 6.00 15.00
95CR Mark Brunell T/119 2.50 6.00
95SN Mark Brunell T/311 2.50 6.00
96BA Marvin Harrison 2.50 6.00
96CE Marvin Harrison/21 6.00 15.00
96CR Marvin Harrison/78 3.00 8.00
96JN Marvin Harrison/88 3.00 8.00
96SN Marvin Harrison/102 2.50 6.00
97BA Michael Irvin 3.00 8.00
97CE Michael Irvin/21 8.00 20.00
97CR Michael Irvin/65 4.00 10.00
97JN Michael Irvin/88 4.00 10.00
97SN Michael Irvin/111 3.00 8.00
98BA Mike Alstott 2.00 5.00
98CE Mike Alstott/21 5.00 12.00
98CR Mike Alstott/150 2.00 5.00
98JN Mike Alstott/40 3.00 8.00
98SN Mike Alstott/131 2.00 5.00
99BA Olandis Gary 2.00 5.00
99CE Olandis Gary/21 5.00 12.00
99CR Olandis Gary/289 2.00 5.00
99JN Olandis Gary/22 5.00 12.00
99SN Olandis Gary/80 2.50 6.00
100BA Peter Warrick 2.00 5.00
100CE Peter Warrick/21 5.00 12.00
100CR Peter Warrick/148 2.00 5.00
100JN Peter Warrick/80 2.50 6.00
100SN Peter Warrick/51 3.00 8.00
101BA Ron Dayne 2.50 6.00
101CE Ron Dayne/21 6.00 15.00
101CR Ron Dayne/228 2.50 6.00
101JN Ron Dayne/27 5.00 12.00
101SN Ron Dayne/50 4.00 10.00
102BA Shaun Alexander SP 2.00 5.00
102CE Shaun Alexander/21 5.00 12.00
102CR Shaun Alexander/313 2.00 5.00
102JN Shaun Alexander/37 3.00 8.00
102SN Shaun Alexander/41 3.00 8.00
103BA Stephen Davis SP 2.00 5.00
103CE Stephen Davis/21 5.00 12.00
103CR Stephen Davis/76 2.50 6.00
103JN Stephen Davis/48 3.00 8.00
103SN Stephen Davis/313 2.00 5.00
104BA Steve McNair B SP 2.50 6.00
104CE Steve McNair B/21 6.00 15.00
104CR Steve McNair B/362 2.50 6.00
104SN Steve McNair B/83 3.00 8.00
105BA Steve McNair W SP 2.50 6.00
105CE Steve McNair W/21 6.00 15.00
105CR Steve McNair W/362 2.50 6.00
105SN Steve McNair W/83 3.00 8.00
106BA Terrell Owens SP 2.50 6.00
106CE Terrell Owens/21 6.00 15.00
106CR Terrell Owens/319 2.50 6.00
106JN Terrell Owens/81 3.00 8.00
106SN Terrell Owens/69 3.00 8.00
107BA Tim Brown 3.00 8.00
107CE Tim Brown/21 8.00 20.00
107CR Tim Brown/87 4.00 10.00
107JN Tim Brown/81 4.00 10.00
107SN Tim Brown/76 4.00 10.00
108BA Tim Couch 2.00 5.00
108CE Tim Couch/21 5.00 12.00
108CR Tim Couch/360 2.00 5.00
108SN Tim Couch/77 2.50 6.00
109BA Torry Holt 2.50 6.00
109CE Torry Holt/21 6.00 15.00
109CR Torry Holt/134 2.50 6.00
109JN Torry Holt/88 3.00 8.00
109SN Torry Holt/85 3.00 8.00
110BA Warrick Dunn SP 2.00 5.00
110CE Warrick Dunn/21 5.00 12.00
110CR Warrick Dunn/191 2.00 5.00
110JN Warrick Dunn/28 4.00 10.00
110SN Warrick Dunn/248 2.00 5.00
111BA Akili Smith 2.00 5.00
111CE Akili Smith/21 5.00 12.00
111CR Akili Smith/198 2.00 5.00
111SN Akili Smith/41 3.00 8.00
112BA Amani Toomer 2.00 5.00
112CE Amani Toomer/21 5.00 12.00
112CR Amani Toomer/201 2.00 5.00
112JN Amani Toomer/81 2.50 6.00
112SN Amani Toomer/91 2.50 6.00
113BA Az-Zahir Hakim 2.00 5.00
113CE Az-Zahir Hakim/21 5.00 12.00
113CR Az-Zahir Hakim/109 2.00 5.00
113JN Az-Zahir Hakim/81 2.50 6.00
113SN Az-Zahir Hakim/80 2.50 6.00
114BA Champ Bailey 2.50 6.00
114CE Champ Bailey/21 6.00 15.00
114CR Champ Bailey/123 2.50 6.00
114JN Champ Bailey/24 6.00 15.00
114SN Champ Bailey/103 2.50 6.00
115BA Charles Woodson 3.00 8.00
115CE Charles Woodson/21 8.00 20.00
115CR Charles Woodson/169 3.00 8.00
115JN Charles Woodson/24 8.00 20.00
115SN Charles Woodson/79 4.00 10.00
116BA Chris Redman 3.00 8.00
116CE Chris Redman/21 8.00 20.00
116CR Chris Redman/84 4.00 10.00
116SN Chris Redman/66 4.00 10.00
117BA Courtney Brown 2.00 5.00
117CE Courtney Brown/21 5.00 12.00
117CR Courtney Brown/69 2.50 6.00
117JN Courtney Brown/92 2.50 6.00
117SN Courtney Brown/61 2.50 6.00
118BA Darrell Green 3.00 8.00
118CE Darrell Green/21 8.00 20.00
118CR Darrell Green/121 3.00 8.00
118FG Darrell Green/28 6.00 15.00
118SN Darrell Green/23 8.00 20.00
119BA Dorsey Levens 2.50 6.00
119CE Dorsey Levens/21 6.00 15.00
119CR Dorsey Levens/247 2.50 6.00
119JN Dorsey Levens/25 5.00 12.00
119SN Dorsey Levens/77 3.00 8.00
120BA Frank Sanders 2.00 5.00
120CE Frank Sanders/21 5.00 12.00
120CR Frank Sanders/70 2.50 6.00
120JN Frank Sanders/81 2.50 6.00
120SN Frank Sanders/54 3.00 8.00
121BA Herman Moore 2.00 5.00
121CE Herman Moore/21 5.00 12.00
121CR Herman Moore/93 2.50 6.00
121JN Herman Moore/84 2.50 6.00
121SN Herman Moore/40 3.00 8.00
122BA J.J. Stokes 2.00 5.00
122CE J.J. Stokes/21 5.00 12.00
122CR J.J. Stokes/241 2.00 5.00
122JN J.J. Stokes/83 2.50 6.00
122SN J.J. Stokes/53 3.00 8.00
123BA James Allen 2.00 5.00
123CE James Allen/21 5.00 12.00
123CR James Allen/56 3.00 8.00
123JN James Allen/20 5.00 12.00
123SN James Allen/290 2.00 5.00
124BA Jason Sehorn 2.50 6.00
124CE Jason Sehorn/21 6.00 15.00
124CR Jason Sehorn/163 2.50 6.00
124JN Jason Sehorn/31 5.00 12.00
124SN Jason Sehorn/73 3.00 8.00
125BA Jay Fiedler 2.50 6.00
125CE Jay Fiedler/21 6.00 15.00
125CR Jay Fiedler/268 2.50 6.00
125SN Jay Fiedler/74 3.00 8.00
126BA Jimmy Smith 2.50 6.00
126CE Jimmy Smith/21 6.00 15.00
126CR Jimmy Smith/75 3.00 8.00
126JN Jimmy Smith/82 3.00 8.00
126SN Jimmy Smith/91 3.00 8.00
127BA Johnnie Morton 2.50 6.00
127CE Johnnie Morton/21 6.00 15.00
127CR Johnnie Morton/98 3.00 8.00
127JN Johnnie Morton/87 3.00 8.00
127SN Johnnie Morton/61 3.00 8.00
128BA Junior Seau 2.50 6.00
128CE Junior Seau/21 6.00 15.00
128CR Junior Seau/45 4.00 10.00
128JN Junior Seau/55 4.00 10.00
128SN Junior Seau/123 2.50 6.00
129BA Keenan McCardell 2.50 6.00
129CE Keenan McCardell/21 6.00 15.00
129CR Keenan McCardell/32 5.00 12.00
129JN Keenan McCardell/87 3.00 8.00
129SN Keenan McCardell/94 3.00 8.00
130BA Kevin Johnson 2.00 5.00
130CE Kevin Johnson/21 5.00 12.00
130CR Kevin Johnson/123 2.00 5.00
130JN Kevin Johnson/85 2.50 6.00
130SN Kevin Johnson/79 2.50 6.00
131BA Kordell Stewart SP 2.00 5.00
131CE Kordell Stewart/21 5.00 12.00
131CR Kordell Stewart/357 2.00 5.00
131SN Kordell Stewart/73 2.50 6.00
132BA Lamar Smith SP 2.50 6.00
132CE Lamar Smith/21 6.00 15.00
132CR Lamar Smith/108 2.50 6.00
132JN Lamar Smith/26 5.00 12.00
132SN Lamar Smith/309 2.50 6.00
133BA Laveranues Coles SP 2.50 6.00
133CE Laveranues Coles/21 6.00 15.00
133CR Laveranues Coles/370 2.50 6.00
133JN Laveranues Coles/87 3.00 8.00
134BA Michael Strahan 2.50 6.00
134CE Michael Strahan/21 6.00 15.00
134CR Michael Strahan/327 2.50 6.00
134JN Michael Strahan/92 3.00 8.00
135BA Rich Gannon SP 2.50 6.00
135CE Rich Gannon/21 6.00 15.00
135CR Rich Gannon/134 2.50 6.00
135SN Rich Gannon/284 2.50 6.00
136BA Ricky Watters 2.50 6.00
136CE Ricky Watters/21 6.00 15.00
136CR Ricky Watters/90 3.00 8.00
136JN Ricky Watters/32 5.00 12.00
136SN Ricky Watters/278 2.50 6.00
137BA Rob Johnson 2.50 6.00
137CE Rob Johnson/21 6.00 15.00
137CR Rob Johnson/89 3.00 8.00
137SN Rob Johnson/307 2.50 6.00
138BA Rod Smith 2.50 6.00
138CE Rod Smith/21 6.00 15.00
138CR Rod Smith/78 3.00 8.00
138JN Rod Smith/80 3.00 8.00
138SN Rod Smith/100 2.50 6.00
139BA Sebastian Janikowski 2.00 5.00
139CE Sebastian Janikowski/21 5.00 12.00
139CR Sebastian Janikowski/112 2.00 5.00
139SN Sebastian Janikowski/68 2.50 6.00
140BA Shaun King 2.00 5.00
140CE Shaun King/21 5.00 12.00
140CR Shaun King/322 2.00 5.00
140SN Shaun King/78 2.50 6.00
141BA Terry Glenn SP 2.50 6.00
141CE Terry Glenn/21 6.00 15.00
141CR Terry Glenn/315 2.50 6.00
141JN Terry Glenn/86 3.00 8.00
141SN Terry Glenn/39 4.00 10.00
142BA Thurman Thomas 2.50 6.00
142CE Thurman Thomas/21 6.00 15.00
142CR Thurman Thomas/65 3.00 8.00
142JN Thurman Thomas/34 5.00 12.00
142SN Thurman Thomas/136 2.50 6.00
143BA Tony Gonzalez 2.50 6.00
143CE Tony Gonzalez/21 6.00 15.00
143CR Tony Gonzalez/261 2.50 6.00
143JN Tony Gonzalez/88 3.00 8.00
143SN Tony Gonzalez/39 4.00 10.00
144BA Travis Prentice 2.00 5.00
144CE Travis Prentice/21 5.00 12.00
144CR Travis Prentice/173 2.00 5.00
144JN Travis Prentice/41 3.00 8.00
144SN Travis Prentice/191 2.00 5.00
145BA Tyrone Wheatley 2.50 6.00
145CE Tyrone Wheatley/21 6.00 15.00
145CR Tyrone Wheatley/80 3.00 8.00
145JN Tyrone Wheatley/47 4.00 10.00
145SN Tyrone Wheatley/232 2.50 6.00
146BA Vinny Testaverde 2.00 5.00
146CE Vinny Testaverde/21 5.00 12.00
146CR Vinny Testaverde/226 2.00 5.00
146SN Vinny Testaverde/69 2.50 6.00
147BA Warren Sapp 2.50 6.00
147CE Warren Sapp/21 6.00 15.00
147CR Warren Sapp/274 2.50 6.00
147JN Warren Sapp/99 3.00 8.00
148BA Wayne Chrebet 2.00 5.00
148CE Wayne Chrebet/21 5.00 12.00
148CR Wayne Chrebet/70 2.50 6.00
148JN Wayne Chrebet/80 2.50 6.00
148SN Wayne Chrebet/69 2.50 6.00
149BA Wesley Walls SP 2.00 5.00
149CE Wesley Walls/21 5.00 12.00
149CR Wesley Walls/368 2.00 5.00
149JN Wesley Walls/85 2.50 6.00
150BA JaJuan Dawson 2.00 5.00
150CE JaJuan Dawson/21 5.00 12.00
150CR JaJuan Dawson/97 2.50 6.00
150JN JaJuan Dawson/88 2.50 6.00
150SN JaJuan Dawson/26 4.00 10.00

2002 Leaf Certified

Released in late September, 2002, this set contains 100 veterans and 32 rookies. Each rookie features a piece of event worn jersey, except for William Green, who features event worn football. The rookies are serial #'d to 800. Each box contained 16 packs of 5 cards. SRP for this product was $9.99 per pack.

COMP.SET w/o SP's (100) 10.00 25.00
ROOKIE JERSEY PRINT RUN 800
1 David Boston .25 .60
2 Jake Plummer .25 .60
3 Michael Vick .30 .75
4 Jamal Anderson .30 .75
5 Chris Redman .25 .60
6 Ray Lewis .40 1.00
7 Eric Moulds .25 .60
8 Travis Henry .25 .60
9 Nate Clements .25 .60
10 Chris Weinke .25 .60
11 Muhsin Muhammad .25 .60
12 Wesley Walls .30 .75
13 Anthony Thomas .30 .75
14 Brian Urlacher .40 1.00
15 Dez White .25 .60
16 Corey Dillon .25 .60
17 Peter Warrick .25 .60
18 Tim Couch .25 .60
19 Kevin Johnson .25 .60
20 James Jackson .25 .60
21 Emmitt Smith .60 1.50
22 Quincy Carter .25 .60
23 Brian Griese .25 .60
24 Ed McCaffrey .30 .75
25 Rod Smith .30 .75
26 Terrell Davis .30 .75
27 Mike Anderson .25 .60
28 Germane Crowell .25 .60
29 James Stewart .25 .60
30 Charlie Batch .25 .60
31 Antonio Freeman .40 1.00
32 Brett Favre .75 2.00
33 Ahman Green .30 .75
34 LeRoy Butler .30 .75
35 Edgerrin James .30 .75
36 Marvin Harrison .30 .75
37 Peyton Manning 1.00 2.50
38 Fred Taylor .25 .60
39 Jimmy Smith .30 .75
40 Mark Brunell .30 .75
41 Keenan McCardell .30 .75
42 Tony Gonzalez .30 .75
43 Priest Holmes .25 .60
44 Jay Fiedler .30 .75
45 Chris Chambers .25 .60
46 Zach Thomas .30 .75
47 Travis Minor .25 .60
48 Cris Carter .40 1.00
49 Daunte Culpepper .30 .75
50 Randy Moss .30 .75
51 Drew Bledsoe .30 .75
52 Tom Brady 2.00 5.00
53 Antowain Smith .30 .75
54 Troy Brown .25 .60
55 Aaron Brooks .25 .60
56 Ricky Williams .30 .75
57 Ron Dayne .30 .75
58 Kerry Collins .25 .60
59 Michael Strahan .30 .75
60 Amani Toomer .25 .60
61 Chad Pennington .25 .60
62 Curtis Martin .30 .75
63 Vinny Testaverde .25 .60
64 Wayne Chrebet .25 .60
65 Charles Woodson .40 1.00
66 Rich Gannon .30 .75
67 Tim Brown .40 1.00
68 Jerry Rice .75 2.00
69 Tyrone Wheatley .30 .75
70 Donovan McNabb .30 .75
71 Duce Staley .25 .60
72 Todd Pinkston .25 .60
73 Correll Buckhalter .25 .60
74 Jerome Bettis .40 1.00
75 Kordell Stewart .25 .60
76 Plaxico Burress .25 .60
77 Hines Ward .30 .75
78 Junior Seau .30 .75
79 LaDainian Tomlinson .40 1.00
80 Doug Flutie .30 .75
81 Terrell Owens .30 .75
82 Jeff Garcia .25 .60
83 Ricky Watters .30 .75
84 Shaun Alexander .25 .60
85 Koren Robinson .25 .60
86 Isaac Bruce .40 1.00
87 Kurt Warner .30 .75
88 Marshall Faulk .30 .75
89 Torry Holt .30 .75
90 Keyshawn Johnson .30 .75
91 Mike Alstott .25 .60
92 Warren Sapp .30 .75
93 Brad Johnson .30 .75
94 Eddie George .30 .75
95 Jevon Kearse .25 .60
96 Steve McNair .30 .75
97 Derrick Mason .25 .60
98 Frank Wycheck .25 .60
99 Champ Bailey .30 .75
100 Stephen Davis .25 .60
101 Ladell Betts JSY RC 3.00 8.00
102 Antonio Bryant JSY RC 3.00 8.00
103 Reche Caldwell JSY RC 2.50 6.00
104 David Carr JSY RC 2.00 5.00
105 Tim Carter JSY RC 2.50 6.00
106 Eric Crouch JSY RC 3.00 8.00
107 Rohan Davey JSY RC 3.00 8.00
108 Andre Davis JSY RC 2.00 5.00
109 T.J. Duckett JSY RC 2.00 5.00
110 DeShaun Foster JSY RC 3.00 8.00
111 Jabar Gaffney JSY RC 2.00 5.00
112 Daniel Graham JSY RC 2.50 6.00
113 William Green FB RC 2.50 6.00
114 Joey Harrington JSY RC 2.00 5.00
115 David Garrard JSY RC 2.50 6.00
116 Ron Johnson JSY RC 2.50 6.00
117 Ashley Lelie JSY RC 2.00 5.00
118 Josh McCown JSY RC 3.00 8.00
119 Maurice Morris JSY RC 2.50 6.00
120 Julius Peppers JSY RC 5.00 12.00
121 Clinton Portis JSY RC 3.00 8.00
122 Patrick Ramsey JSY RC 2.50 6.00
123 Antwaan Randle El JSY RC 2.50 6.00
124 Josh Reed JSY RC 2.50 6.00
125 Cliff Russell JSY RC 2.00 5.00
126 Jeremy Shockey JSY RC 3.00 8.00
127 Donte Stallworth JSY RC 3.00 8.00
128 Travis Stephens JSY RC 2.00 5.00
129 Javon Walker JSY RC 3.00 8.00
130 Marquise Walker JSY RC 2.00 5.00
131 Roy Williams JSY RC 2.00 5.00
132 Mike Williams JSY RC 2.00 5.00

2002 Leaf Certified Mirror Blue Materials

*VETS 1-100: .6X TO 1.5X MIRROR RED
*ROOKIE 101-132: .6X TO 1.5X MIR.RED
1-100 VET JERSEY PRINT RUN 50
101-132 ROOKIE HELMET PRINT RUN 100

2002 Leaf Certified Mirror Gold Materials

ETS 1-100: 1X TO 2.5X MIRROR RED
*ROOKIES 101-132: 1X TO 2.5X MIR.RED
MIRROR GOLD PRINT RUN 25

2002 Leaf Certified Mirror Red Materials

1-100 VETERAN PRINT RUN 100
101-132 ROOKIE JSY/FB PRINT RUN 250
1 David Boston 4.00 10.00
2 Jake Plummer 4.00 10.00
3 Michael Vick 5.00 12.00
4 Jamal Anderson 5.00 12.00
5 Chris Redman 4.00 10.00
6 Ray Lewis 6.00 15.00
7 Eric Moulds 4.00 10.00
8 Travis Henry 4.00 10.00
9 Nate Clements 4.00 10.00
10 Chris Weinke 4.00 10.00
11 Muhsin Muhammad 4.00 10.00
12 Wesley Walls 5.00 12.00
13 Anthony Thomas 5.00 12.00
14 Brian Urlacher 6.00 15.00
15 Dez White 4.00 10.00
16 Corey Dillon 4.00 10.00
17 Peter Warrick 4.00 10.00
18 Tim Couch 4.00 10.00
19 Kevin Johnson 4.00 10.00
20 James Jackson 4.00 10.00
21 Emmitt Smith 10.00 25.00
22 Quincy Carter 4.00 10.00
23 Brian Griese 4.00 10.00
24 Ed McCaffrey 5.00 12.00
25 Rod Smith 5.00 12.00
26 Terrell Davis 5.00 12.00
27 Mike Anderson 4.00 10.00
28 Germane Crowell 4.00 10.00
29 James Stewart 4.00 10.00
30 Charlie Batch 4.00 10.00
31 Antonio Freeman 6.00 15.00
32 Brett Favre 12.00 30.00
33 Ahman Green 5.00 12.00
34 LeRoy Butler 5.00 12.00
35 Edgerrin James 5.00 12.00
36 Marvin Harrison 5.00 12.00
37 Peyton Manning 15.00 40.00
38 Fred Taylor 4.00 10.00
39 Jimmy Smith 5.00 12.00
40 Mark Brunell 5.00 12.00
41 Keenan McCardell 5.00 12.00
42 Tony Gonzalez 5.00 12.00
43 Priest Holmes 4.00 10.00
44 Jay Fiedler 5.00 12.00
45 Chris Chambers 4.00 10.00
46 Zach Thomas 5.00 12.00
47 Travis Minor 4.00 10.00
48 Cris Carter 6.00 15.00
49 Daunte Culpepper 5.00 12.00
50 Randy Moss 5.00 12.00
51 Drew Bledsoe 5.00 12.00
52 Tom Brady 30.00 80.00
53 Antowain Smith 5.00 12.00
54 Troy Brown 4.00 10.00
55 Aaron Brooks 4.00 10.00
56 Ricky Williams 5.00 12.00
57 Ron Dayne 5.00 12.00
58 Kerry Collins 4.00 10.00
59 Michael Strahan 5.00 12.00
60 Amani Toomer 4.00 10.00
61 Chad Pennington 4.00 10.00
62 Curtis Martin 5.00 12.00
63 Vinny Testaverde 4.00 10.00
64 Wayne Chrebet 4.00 10.00
65 Charles Woodson 6.00 15.00
66 Rich Gannon 5.00 12.00
67 Tim Brown 6.00 15.00
68 Jerry Rice 12.00 30.00
69 Tyrone Wheatley 5.00 12.00
70 Donovan McNabb 5.00 12.00
71 Duce Staley 4.00 10.00
72 Todd Pinkston 4.00 10.00
73 Correll Buckhalter 4.00 10.00
74 Jerome Bettis 6.00 15.00
75 Kordell Stewart 4.00 10.00
76 Plaxico Burress 4.00 10.00
77 Hines Ward 5.00 12.00
78 Junior Seau 5.00 12.00
79 LaDainian Tomlinson 6.00 15.00
80 Doug Flutie 5.00 12.00
81 Terrell Owens 5.00 12.00
82 Jeff Garcia 4.00 10.00
83 Ricky Watters 5.00 12.00
84 Shaun Alexander 4.00 10.00
85 Koren Robinson 4.00 10.00
86 Isaac Bruce 6.00 15.00
87 Kurt Warner 5.00 12.00
88 Marshall Faulk 5.00 12.00
89 Torry Holt 5.00 12.00
90 Keyshawn Johnson 5.00 12.00
91 Mike Alstott 4.00 10.00
92 Warren Sapp 5.00 12.00
93 Brad Johnson 5.00 12.00
94 Eddie George 5.00 12.00
95 Jevon Kearse 4.00 10.00
96 Steve McNair 5.00 12.00
97 Derrick Mason 4.00 10.00
98 Frank Wycheck 4.00 10.00
99 Champ Bailey 5.00 12.00
100 Stephen Davis 4.00 10.00
101 Ladell Betts 5.00 12.00
102 Antonio Bryant 5.00 12.00
103 Reche Caldwell 4.00 10.00
104 David Carr 3.00 8.00
105 Tim Carter 4.00 10.00
106 Eric Crouch 5.00 12.00
107 Rohan Davey 5.00 12.00
108 Andre Davis 3.00 8.00
109 T.J. Duckett 3.00 8.00
110 DeShaun Foster 5.00 12.00
111 Jabar Gaffney 3.00 8.00
112 Daniel Graham 4.00 10.00
113 William Green 4.00 10.00
114 Joey Harrington 3.00 8.00
115 David Garrard 4.00 10.00
116 Ron Johnson 4.00 10.00
117 Ashley Lelie 3.00 8.00
118 Josh McCown 5.00 12.00
119 Maurice Morris 4.00 10.00
120 Julius Peppers 8.00 20.00
121 Clinton Portis 5.00 12.00
122 Patrick Ramsey 4.00 10.00
123 Antwaan Randle El 4.00 10.00
124 Josh Reed 4.00 10.00
125 Cliff Russell 3.00 8.00
126 Jeremy Shockey 5.00 12.00
127 Donte Stallworth 5.00 12.00
128 Travis Stephens 3.00 8.00
129 Javon Walker 5.00 12.00
130 Marquise Walker 3.00 8.00
131 Roy Williams 3.00 8.00
132 Mike Williams 3.00 8.00

2002 Leaf Certified Fabric of the Game

ndomly inserted into packs, this set features a swatch of game used memorabilia from some of the NFL's current and past stars. Each card is serial #'d to 100. There is also a team logo parallel that is serial #'d to 50. It features a team logo die cut over a jersey swatch.

STATED PRINT RUN 100 SER.#'d SETS
*TEAM LOGO/50: .5X TO 1.2X BASIC JSY
TEAM LOGO PRINT RUN 50 SER.#'d SETS
1 Andre Reed 8.00 20.00
2 Art Monk 15.00 40.00
3 Barry Sanders 15.00 40.00
4 Bert Jones 6.00 15.00
5 Bob Griese 10.00 25.00
6 Craig Morton 8.00 20.00
7 Deacon Jones 8.00 20.00
8 Dick Butkus 12.00 30.00
9 Don Maynard 8.00 20.00
10 Earl Campbell 10.00 25.00
11 Eric Dickerson 8.00 20.00
12 Fran Tarkenton 10.00 25.00
13 Franco Harris 10.00 25.00
14 Gale Sayers 10.00 25.00
15 Henry Ellard 6.00 15.00
16 Herschel Walker 10.00 25.00
17 Howie Long 12.00 30.00
18 Jim McMahon 10.00 25.00
19 Joe Theismann 10.00 25.00
20 John Riggins 8.00 20.00
21 Ken Stabler 12.00 30.00
22 L.C. Greenwood 6.00 15.00
23 Marcus Allen 10.00 25.00
24 Ozzie Newsome 8.00 20.00
25 Raymond Berry 8.00 20.00
26 Roger Staubach 12.00 30.00
27 Sterling Sharpe 8.00 20.00
28 Steve Bartkowski 8.00 20.00
29 Steve Largent 10.00 25.00
30 Terry Bradshaw 12.00 30.00
31 Tony Dorsett 10.00 25.00
32 Joe Montana 30.00 80.00
33 Joe Namath 15.00 40.00
34 Ronnie Lott 8.00 20.00
35 Thurman Thomas 8.00 20.00
36 Boomer Esiason 8.00 20.00
37 Dan Marino 20.00 50.00
38 Jim Kelly 10.00 25.00
39 John Elway 15.00 40.00
40 Phil Simms 8.00 20.00
41 Steve Young 12.00 30.00
42 Troy Aikman 12.00 30.00
43 Warren Moon 10.00 25.00
44 Daunte Culpepper 8.00 20.00
45 Edgerrin James 8.00 20.00
46 Emmitt Smith 15.00 40.00
47 Kurt Warner 8.00 20.00
48 Marshall Faulk 8.00 20.00
49 Tim Brown 10.00 25.00
50 Terrell Owens 8.00 20.00

2002 Leaf Certified Fabric of the Game Autographs

This set is a signed parallel version of the Fabric of the Game set. Each card is serial numbered to the player's jersey number. Some cards were only available via exchange cards.

STATED PRINT RUN 1-84
1 Andre Reed/83 20.00 50.00
2 Art Monk/81 25.00 60.00
3 Barry Sanders/20 100.00 200.00
7 Deacon Jones/75 25.00 60.00
8 Dick Butkus/51 60.00 100.00
10 Earl Campbell/34 75.00 125.00
11 Eric Dickerson/29 40.00 100.00
13 Franco Harris/32 75.00 150.00
14 Gale Sayers/40 60.00 120.00
15 Henry Ellard/80 20.00 50.00
16 Herschel Walker/34 25.00 60.00
17 Howie Long/75 30.00 80.00
20 John Riggins/44 40.00 100.00
22 L.C. Greenwood/68 25.00 60.00
23 Marcus Allen/32 40.00 80.00
24 Ozzie Newsome/82 20.00 50.00
25 Raymond Berry/82 20.00 50.00
27 Sterling Sharpe/84 25.00 60.00
29 Steve Largent/80 25.00 60.00
31 Tony Dorsett/33 30.00 80.00
34 Ronnie Lott/42 40.00 80.00
35 Thurman Thomas/34 50.00 100.00
45 Edgerrin James/32 40.00 80.00
46 Emmitt Smith/22 125.00 200.00
48 Marshall Faulk/28 60.00 120.00
49 Tim Brown/81 40.00 80.00
50 Terrell Owens/81 20.00 50.00

2002 Leaf Certified Future

Inserted into packs at a rate of 1:15, this set highlights some of the best of the 2002 rookie class.

COMPLETE SET (20) 25.00 60.00
STATED ODDS 1:15
CF1 David Carr .60 1.50
CF2 Joey Harrington .60 1.50
CF3 Kurt Kittner .60 1.50
CF4 Patrick Ramsey .75 2.00
CF5 William Green .75 2.00
CF6 T.J. Duckett .60 1.50
CF7 Clinton Portis 1.00 2.50
CF8 DeShaun Foster 1.00 2.50
CF9 Brian Westbrook 1.25 3.00
CF10 Javon Walker 1.00 2.50
CF11 Donte Stallworth 1.00 2.50
CF12 Antonio Bryant 1.00 2.50
CF13 Ashley Lelie .60 1.50
CF14 Jabar Gaffney .60 1.50
CF15 Reche Caldwell .75 2.00
CF16 Josh Reed .75 2.00
CF17 Julius Peppers 1.50 4.00
CF18 Albert Haynesworth 1.00 2.50
CF19 Quentin Jammer 1.00 2.50
CF20 Roy Williams .60 1.50

2002 Leaf Certified Gold Team

Inserted into packs at a rate of 1:15, this set showcases many of the NFL's best and brightest.

COMPLETE SET (20) 20.00 50.00
STATED ODDS 1:15
GT1 Kurt Warner 1.00 2.50
GT2 Brett Favre 2.50 6.00
GT3 Jeff Garcia .75 2.00
GT4 Rich Gannon 1.00 2.50
GT5 Steve McNair 1.00 2.50
GT6 Tom Brady 6.00 15.00
GT7 Edgerrin James 1.00 2.50
GT8 Curtis Martin 1.00 2.50
GT9 Marshall Faulk 1.00 2.50
GT10 Emmitt Smith 2.00 5.00
GT11 Ricky Williams 1.00 2.50
GT12 Garrison Hearst .75 2.00
GT13 David Boston .75 2.00
GT14 Jerry Rice 2.50 6.00
GT15 Randy Moss 1.00 2.50
GT16 Keyshawn Johnson 1.00 2.50
GT17 Tim Brown 1.25 3.00
GT18 Marvin Harrison 1.00 2.50
GT19 Michael Strahan 1.00 2.50
GT20 Brian Urlacher 1.25 3.00

2002 Leaf Certified Mirror Red Signatures

Randomly inserted into packs, this set features authentic autographs, with each card serial #'d to 50. In addition, there is a Blue and Gold parallel set. The Blue version is serial #'d to 25, and the Gold version is serial #'d to 10. Please note that some players were only available via exchange cards.

STATED PRINT RUN 50 SER.#'d SETS
*BLUE/25: .6X TO 1.5X RED AUTO/50
BLUE PRINT RUN 25 SER.#'d SETS
UNPRICED GOLD PRINT RUN 10 SETS
1 Joe Montana 50.00 120.00
2 Joe Namath 50.00 100.00
3 Ronnie Lott 20.00 40.00
4 Thurman Thomas 12.00 30.00
5 John Riggins 20.00 50.00
6 Barry Sanders 50.00 100.00
7 Phil Simms 12.00 30.00
8 Steve Young 20.00 40.00
9 Troy Aikman 40.00 80.00
10 Deuce McAllister 10.00 25.00
11 Justin Smith 7.50 20.00
12 Eric Moulds 6.00 15.00
13 Chris Weinke 7.50 20.00
14 Aaron Brooks 7.50 20.00
15 Kurt Warner 25.00 60.00
16 Drew Brees 40.00 80.00
17 Edgerrin James 12.00 30.00
18 Correll Buckhalter 7.50 20.00
19 Jimmy Smith 6.00 15.00
20 Elvis Grbac 6.00 15.00
21 Tim Brown 10.00 25.00
22 Stephen Davis 7.50 20.00
23 Dan Morgan 6.00 15.00
24 Robert Ferguson 10.00 25.00
25 Peter Warrick 10.00 25.00
26 Kerry Collins 10.00 25.00
27 Isaac Bruce 10.00 25.00
28 David Terrell 7.50 20.00
29 Jamal Lewis 10.00 25.00
30 Jeff Blake 6.00 15.00
31 Santana Moss 10.00 25.00
32 Mark Brunell 10.00 25.00
33 Gerard Warren 6.00 15.00
34 Marcus Robinson 6.00 15.00
35 Randall Cunningham 10.00 25.00
36 Quincy Carter 7.50 20.00
37 Marshall Faulk 25.00 50.00
38 LaMont Jordan 10.00 25.00

2002 Leaf Certified Skills

Inserted into packs at a rate of 1:15, this set highlights players who exhibit top notch skills at their position.

COMPLETE SET (20) 12.50 30.00
STATED ODDS 1:15
CS1 Donovan McNabb .75 2.00
CS2 Kordell Stewart .60 1.50
CS3 Mark Brunell .75 2.00
CS4 Peyton Manning 2.50 6.00
CS5 Daunte Culpepper .75 2.00
CS6 Brian Griese .60 1.50
CS7 Eddie George .75 2.00
CS8 Ahman Green .75 2.00
CS9 Shaun Alexander .60 1.50
CS10 LaDainian Tomlinson 1.00 2.50
CS11 Anthony Thomas .75 2.00
CS12 Priest Holmes .60 1.50
CS13 Torry Holt .75 2.00
CS14 Rod Smith .75 2.00
CS15 Terrell Owens .75 2.00
CS16 Troy Brown .60 1.50
CS17 Derrick Mason .60 1.50
CS18 Jimmy Smith .75 2.00
CS19 Jevon Kearse .60 1.50
CS20 Zach Thomas .75 2.00

2002 Leaf Certified Samples

*SAMPLES: .8X TO 2X BASIC CARDS

2002 Leaf Certified Samples Gold

*GOLD SAMPLES: .6X TO 1.5X SILVER

2003 Leaf Certified Materials

Released in September of 2003, this set consists of 180 cards including 150 veterans and 30 rookies. The rookies were serial numbered to 1250 and featured a swatch of event worn jersey from the 2003 Rookie Photo Shoot. Boxes contained 10 packs of 5 cards.

COMP.SET w/o SP's (150) 12.50 30.00
151-180 ROOKIE PRINT RUN 1250
1 Jake Plummer .25 .60
2 David Boston .25 .60
3 MarTay Jenkins .25 .60
4 Marcel Shipp .25 .60
5 Michael Vick .30 .75
6 T.J. Duckett .25 .60
7 Chris Redman .25 .60
8 Ray Lewis .40 1.00
9 Jamal Lewis .30 .75
10 Eric Moulds .25 .60
11 Nate Clements .30 .75
12 Travis Henry .25 .60
13 Drew Bledsoe .30 .75
14 Peerless Price .25 .60
15 Josh Reed .25 .60
16 Wesley Walls .30 .75
17 Muhsin Muhammad .25 .60
18 Julius Peppers .40 1.00
19 Dez White .25 .60
20 Mike Brown .25 .60
21 Brian Urlacher .40 1.00
22 Anthony Thomas .30 .75
23 David Terrell .25 .60
24 Corey Dillon .25 .60
25 Peter Warrick .25 .60
26 Josh McCown .30 .75
27 Dennis Northcutt .25 .60
28 Kevin Johnson .25 .60
29 Tim Couch .25 .60
30 Gerard Warren .25 .60
31 William Green .25 .60
32 Antonio Bryant .25 .60
33 Darren Woodson .30 .75
34 Emmitt Smith .60 1.50
35 Quincy Carter .25 .60
36 Roy Williams .25 .60
37 Brian Griese .25 .60
38 Ed McCaffrey .30 .75
39 Mike Anderson .25 .60
40 Rod Smith .30 .75
41 Clinton Portis .25 .60
42 Ashley Lelie .25 .60
43 Cory Schlesinger .25 .60
44 Germane Crowell .25 .60
45 James Stewart .25 .60
46 Scotty Anderson .25 .60
47 Joey Harrington .25 .60
48 Brett Favre .75 2.00
49 Terry Glenn .30 .75
50 Ahman Green .30 .75
51 Donald Driver .30 .75
52 Javon Walker .30 .75
53 David Carr .25 .60
54 Ron Dayne .30 .75
55 Terrell Davis .30 .75
56 Edgerrin James .30 .75
57 Marvin Harrison .30 .75
58 Peyton Manning 1.00 2.50
59 Fred Taylor .30 .75
60 Jimmy Smith .30 .75
61 Kyle Brady .25 .60
62 Mark Brunell .30 .75
63 Tony Gonzalez .30 .75
64 Priest Holmes .25 .60
65 Trent Green .25 .60
66 Jason Taylor .30 .75
67 Jay Fiedler .25 .60
68 Zach Thomas .30 .75
69 Chris Chambers .25 .60
70 Ricky Williams .30 .75
71 Randy McMichael .25 .60
72 Daunte Culpepper .30 .75
73 Randy Moss .30 .75
74 Michael Bennett .25 .60
75 Ty Law .40 1.00
76 Tom Brady 1.50 4.00
77 Troy Brown .25 .60
78 Antowain Smith .30 .75
79 Aaron Brooks .25 .60
80 Donte Stallworth .25 .60
81 Joe Horn .25 .60
82 Deuce McAllister .30 .75
83 Amani Toomer .25 .60
84 Kerry Collins .30 .75
85 Michael Strahan .30 .75
86 Tiki Barber .30 .75
87 Jeremy Shockey .25 .60
88 Chad Pennington .25 .60
89 Curtis Martin .30 .75
90 Laveranues Coles .25 .60
91 Vinny Testaverde .25 .60
92 Santana Moss .30 .75
93 Charles Woodson .40 1.00
94 Sebastian Janikowski .25 .60
95 Tim Brown .40 1.00
96 Rich Gannon .30 .75
97 Jerry Rice .75 2.00
98 Donovan McNabb .30 .75
99 Duce Staley .25 .60
100 Todd Pinkston .25 .60
101 Chad Lewis .30 .75
102 A.J. Feeley .25 .60
103 Jerome Bettis .40 1.00
104 Plaxico Burress .25 .60
105 Hines Ward .30 .75
106 Antwaan Randle El .25 .60
107 Kendrell Bell .25 .60
108 Junior Seau .30 .75
109 LaDainian Tomlinson .40 1.00
110 Doug Flutie .30 .75
111 Drew Brees .40 1.00
112 Terrell Owens .30 .75
113 Jeff Garcia .25 .60
114 Garrison Hearst .25 .60
115 Koren Robinson .30 .75
116 Shaun Alexander .25 .60
117 Isaac Bruce .40 1.00
118 Kurt Warner .30 .75
119 Marshall Faulk .30 .75
120 Torry Holt .30 .75
121 Keyshawn Johnson .40 1.00
122 Warren Sapp .30 .75
123 Mike Alstott .25 .60
124 Brad Johnson .30 .75
125 Eddie George .30 .75
126 Jevon Kearse .25 .60
127 Steve McNair .30 .75

128 Derrick Mason .25 .60
129 Keith Bulluck .25 .60
130 Champ Bailey .30 .75
131 Darrell Green .40 1.00
132 Stephen Davis .25 .60
133 Rod Gardner .25 .60
134 Barry Sanders .75 2.00
135 Cris Carter .50 1.25
136 Dan Marino 1.00 2.50
137 Deion Sanders .40 1.00
138 Jim Kelly .50 1.25
139 Joe Montana 1.50 4.00
140 John Elway .75 2.00
141 Marcus Allen .50 1.25
142 Reggie White .50 1.25
143 Sterling Sharpe .50 1.25
144 Steve Young .60 1.50
145 Thurman Thomas .50 1.25
146 Troy Aikman .60 1.50
147 Warren Moon .50 1.25
148 Drew Bledsoe .30 .75
149 Jerry Rice .75 2.00
150 Ricky Williams .30 .75
151 Carson Palmer JSY RC 4.00 10.00
152 Byron Leftwich JSY RC 2.50 6.00
153 Kyle Boller JSY RC 2.00 5.00
154 Rex Grossman JSY RC 2.50 6.00
155 Dave Ragone JSY RC 2.00 5.00
156 Kliff Kingsbury JSY RC 3.00 8.00
157 Seneca Wallace JSY RC 2.50 6.00
158 Larry Johnson JSY RC 2.50 6.00
159 Willis McGahee JSY RC 3.00 8.00
160 Justin Fargas JSY RC 3.00 8.00
161 Onterrio Smith JSY RC 2.00 5.00
162 Chris Brown JSY RC 2.00 5.00
163 Musa Smith JSY RC 2.00 5.00
164 Artose Pinner JSY RC 2.00 5.00
165 Andre Johnson JSY RC 5.00 12.00
166 Kelley Washington JSY RC 2.00 5.00
167 Taylor Jacobs JSY RC 2.00 5.00
168 Bryant Johnson JSY RC 3.00 8.00
169 Tyrone Calico JSY RC 2.00 5.00
170 Anquan Boldin JSY RC 3.00 8.00
171 Bethel Johnson JSY RC 2.00 5.00
172 Nate Burleson JSY RC 2.50 6.00
173 Kevin Curtis JSY RC 2.00 5.00
174 Dallas Clark JSY RC 3.00 8.00
175 Teyo Johnson JSY RC 2.50 6.00
176 Terrell Suggs JSY RC 2.50 6.00
177 DeWayne Robertson JSY RC 2.50 6.00
178 Brian St.Pierre JSY RC 2.00 5.00
179 Terence Newman JSY RC 3.00 8.00
180 Marcus Trufant JSY RC 2.50 6.00

2003 Leaf Certified Materials Mirror Black

STATED PRINT RUN 1 SER.#'d SET
NOT PRICED DUE TO SCARCITY

2003 Leaf Certified Materials Mirror Blue

*BLUE VETS: 10X TO 25X BASIC CARDS
*BLUE RETIRED: 8X TO 20X
*BLUE ROOKIES: 1X TO 2.5X
STATED PRINT RUN 50 SER.#'d SETS

2003 Leaf Certified Materials Mirror Emerald

ATED PRINT RUN 5 SER.#'d SETS
NOT PRICED DUE TO SCARCITY

2003 Leaf Certified Materials Mirror Gold

*GOLD VETS: 20X TO 50X BASIC CARDS
*GOLD RETIRED: 15X TO 40X
*GOLD ROOKIES: 2.5X TO 6X
STATED PRINT RUN 25 SER.#'d SETS

2003 Leaf Certified Materials Mirror Red

ED VETS: 6X TO 15X BASIC CARDS
*RED RETIRED: 5X TO 12X
*RED ROOKIES: .6X TO 1.5X
STATED PRINT RUN 150 SER.#'d SETS

2003 Leaf Certified Materials Fabric of the Game

Randomly inserted into packs, this set consists of 400 cards featuring jersey swatches, with some also featuring sticker autographs. Each card is serial numbered to various quantities. This set is actually four sets in one with BA being the base cards, DE representing debut year cards, JN representing jersey number cards, and LO representing the logo cards. Please note that several cards were only issued in packs as exchange cards
SER.#'d UNDER 25 NOT PRICED

1BA Art Monk/50 10.00 25.00
1DE Art Monk/80 8.00 20.00
1JN Art Monk AU/81 25.00 60.00
1LO Art Monk/25 15.00 40.00
2BA Barry Sanders/50 15.00 40.00
2DE Barry Sanders/89 12.00 30.00
2JN Barry Sanders AU/20 150.00 300.00
2LO Barry Sanders/25 25.00 60.00
3BA Bart Starr/50 15.00 40.00
3DE Bart Starr/56 15.00 40.00
3LO Bart Starr/25 25.00 60.00
4BA Bob Griese/50 10.00 25.00
4DE Bob Griese/67 10.00 25.00
4LO Bob Griese/25 15.00 40.00
5BA Charley Taylor/50 6.00 15.00
5DE Charley Taylor/64 6.00 15.00
5JN Charley Taylor AU/42 20.00 50.00
5LO Charley Taylor/25 10.00 25.00
6BA Cris Carter/50 10.00 25.00
6DE Cris Carter/87 8.00 20.00
6JN Cris Carter AU/80 60.00 120.00
6LO Cris Carter/25 15.00 40.00
7BA Dan Fouts/50 8.00 20.00
7DE Dan Fouts/73 6.00 15.00
7LO Dan Fouts/25 12.00 30.00
8BA Dan Marino/50 20.00 50.00
8DE Dan Marino/83 15.00 40.00
8LO Dan Marino/25 30.00 80.00
9BA Daryl Johnston/50 8.00 20.00
9DE Daryl Johnston/89 6.00 15.00
9JN Daryl Johnston AU/48 100.00 175.00
9LO Daryl Johnston/25 12.00 30.00
10BA Daryle Lamonica/50 6.00 15.00
10DE Daryle Lamonica/63 6.00 15.00
10LO Daryle Lamonica/25 10.00 25.00
11BA Deacon Jones/50 8.00 20.00
11DE Deacon Jones/61 8.00 20.00
11JN Deacon Jones AU/75 25.00 60.00
11LO Deacon Jones/25 12.00 30.00
12BA Deion Sanders/50 8.00 20.00
12DE Deion Sanders/89 6.00 15.00
12JN Deion Sanders AU/21 75.00 150.00
12LO Deion Sanders/25 12.00 30.00
13BA Dick Butkus/50 12.00 30.00
13DE Dick Butkus/65 12.00 30.00
13JN Dick Butkus AU/51 75.00 150.00
13LO Dick Butkus/25 20.00 50.00
14BA Doak Walker BA/50 15.00 40.00
14DE Doak Walker DE/50 15.00 40.00
14JN Doak Walker/37 40.00 80.00
14LO Doak Walker/25 25.00 60.00
15BA Don Maynard/50 8.00 20.00
15DE Don Maynard/58 8.00 20.00
15LO Don Maynard/25 12.00 30.00
16BA Earl Campbell/50 10.00 25.00
16DE Earl Campbell/78 8.00 20.00
16JN Earl Campbell AU/34 40.00 100.00
16LO Earl Campbell/25 15.00 40.00
17BA Eric Dickerson/50 8.00 20.00
17DE Eric Dickerson/83 6.00 15.00
17JN Eric Dickerson AU/29 40.00 100.00
17LO Eric Dickerson/25 12.00 30.00
18BA Franco Harris/50 12.00 30.00
18DE Franco Harris/72 10.00 25.00
18JN Franco Harris AU/32 60.00 150.00
18LO Franco Harris/25 20.00 50.00
19BA Frank Gifford/50 10.00 25.00
19DE Frank Gifford/52 10.00 25.00
19LO Frank Gifford/25 15.00 40.00
20BA Fred Biletnikoff/50 10.00 25.00
20DE Fred Biletnikoff/65 10.00 25.00
20JN Fred Biletnikoff AU/25 30.00 80.00
20LO Fred Biletnikoff/25 15.00 40.00
21BA Gale Sayers/50 10.00 25.00
21DE Gale Sayers/65 10.00 25.00
21JN Gale Sayers AU/40 75.00 150.00
21LO Gale Sayers/25 15.00 40.00
22BA George Blanda/50 8.00 20.00
22DE George Blanda/49 8.00 20.00
22LO George Blanda/25 12.00 30.00
23BA Herman Edwards/50 8.00 20.00
23DE Herman Edwards/77 6.00 15.00
23JN Herman Edwards AU/46 20.00 50.00
23LO Herman Edwards/25 12.00 30.00
24BA Irving Fryar/50 6.00 15.00
24DE Irving Fryar/84 5.00 12.00
24JN Irving Fryar AU/80 20.00 50.00
24LO Irving Fryar/25 10.00 25.00
25BA James Lofton/50 6.00 15.00
25DE James Lofton/78 5.00 12.00
25JN James Lofton AU/80 20.00 50.00
25LO James Lofton/25 10.00 25.00
26BA Jay Novacek/50 10.00 25.00
26DE Jay Novacek/85 10.00 25.00
26JN Jay Novacek AU/84 40.00 100.00
26LO Jay Novacek/25 12.00 30.00
27BA Jim Brown/50 12.00 30.00
27DE Jim Brown/57 12.00 30.00
27JN Jim Brown AU/32 125.00 250.00
27LO Jim Brown/25 20.00 50.00
28BA Jim Kelly/50 15.00 40.00
28DE Jim Kelly/86 8.00 20.00
28LO Jim Kelly/25 15.00 40.00
29BA Jim McMahon/50 10.00 25.00
29DE Jim McMahon/82 8.00 20.00
29LO Jim McMahon/25 15.00 40.00
30BA Jim Plunkett/50 8.00 20.00
30DE Jim Plunkett/71 6.00 15.00
30LO Jim Plunkett/25 12.00 30.00
31BA Jim Thorpe/50 60.00 120.00
31LO Jim Thorpe/25 75.00 150.00
32BA Joe Greene/50 10.00 25.00
32DE Joe Greene/69 10.00 25.00
32JN Joe Greene AU/75 60.00 100.00
32LO Joe Greene/25 15.00 40.00
33BA Joe Montana/50 30.00 80.00
33DE Joe Montana/79 25.00 60.00
33LO Joe Montana/25 50.00 125.00
34BA Joe Theismann/50 10.00 25.00
34DE Joe Theismann/74 8.00 20.00
34LO Joe Theismann/25 15.00 40.00
35BA John Elway/50 15.00 40.00
35DE John Elway/83 12.00 30.00
35LO John Elway/25 25.00 60.00
36BA John Riggins/50 8.00 20.00
36DE John Riggins/71 6.00 15.00
36JN John Riggins AU/44 30.00 80.00
36LO John Riggins/25 12.00 30.00
37BA John Taylor/50 8.00 20.00
37DE John Taylor/87 6.00 15.00
37JN John Taylor AU/82 15.00 40.00
37LO John Taylor/25 12.00 30.00
38BA Johnny Unitas/50 20.00 50.00
38DE Johnny Unitas/56 20.00 50.00
38LO Johnny Unitas/25 30.00 80.00
39BA Ken Stabler/50 12.00 30.00
39DE Ken Stabler/70 10.00 25.00
39LO Ken Stabler/25 20.00 50.00
40BA L.C. Greenwood/50 6.00 15.00
40DE L.C. Greenwood/69 6.00 15.00
40JN L.C. Greenwood AU/68 30.00 80.00
40LO L.C. Greenwood/25 10.00 25.00
41BA Larry Csonka/50 10.00 25.00
41DE Larry Csonka/68 10.00 25.00
41JN Larry Csonka AU/39 40.00 100.00
41LO Larry Csonka/25 15.00 40.00
42BA Lawrence Taylor/50 10.00 25.00
42DE Lawrence Taylor/81 8.00 20.00
42JN Lawrence Taylor AU/56 50.00 100.00
42LO Lawrence Taylor/25 15.00 40.00
43BA Marcus Allen/50 10.00 25.00
43DE Marcus Allen/82 8.00 20.00
43JN Marcus Allen AU/32 40.00 100.00
43LO Marcus Allen/25 15.00 40.00
44BA Mark Bavaro/50 8.00 20.00
44DE Mark Bavaro/85 6.00 15.00
44JN Mark Bavaro AU/89 25.00 60.00
44LO Mark Bavaro/25 12.00 30.00
45BA Mel Blount/50 8.00 20.00
45DE Mel Blount/70 6.00 15.00
45JN Mel Blount AU/47 60.00 120.00
45LO Mel Blount/25 12.00 30.00
46BA Ozzie Newsome/50 8.00 20.00
46DE Ozzie Newsome/78 6.00 15.00
46JN Ozzie Newsome AU/82 20.00 50.00
46LO Ozzie Newsome/25 12.00 30.00
47BA Ray Nitschke/50 20.00 50.00
47DE Ray Nitschke/58 20.00 50.00
47JN Ray Nitschke/66 20.00 50.00
47LO Ray Nitschke/25 25.00 60.00
48BA Raymond Berry/50 8.00 20.00
48DE Raymond Berry/55 8.00 20.00
48JN Raymond Berry AU/82 20.00 50.00
48LO Raymond Berry/25 12.00 30.00
49BA Reggie White/50 15.00 40.00
49DE Reggie White/85 12.00 30.00
49JN Reggie White AU/92 200.00 400.00
49LO Reggie White/25 25.00 60.00
50BA Richard Dent/50 8.00 20.00
50DE Richard Dent/83 6.00 15.00
50JN Richard Dent AU/95 25.00 60.00
50LO Richard Dent/25 12.00 30.00
51BA Roger Staubach/50 12.00 30.00
51DE Roger Staubach/69 12.00 30.00
51LO Roger Staubach/25 20.00 50.00
52BA Sonny Jurgensen/50 8.00 20.00
52DE Sonny Jurgensen/57 8.00 20.00
52LO Sonny Jurgensen/25 12.00 30.00
53BA Sterling Sharpe/50 10.00 25.00
53DE Sterling Sharpe/88 6.00 15.00
53JN Sterling Sharpe AU/84 25.00 60.00
53LO Sterling Sharpe/25 15.00 40.00
54BA Steve Largent/50 10.00 25.00
54DE Steve Largent/76 8.00 20.00
54JN Steve Largent AU/80 25.00 60.00
54LO Steve Largent/25 15.00 40.00
55BA Steve Young/50 12.00 30.00
55DE Steve Young/85 10.00 25.00
55LO Steve Young/25 20.00 50.00
56BA Ted Hendricks/50 8.00 20.00
56DE Ted Hendricks/69 8.00 20.00
56JN Ted Hendricks AU/83 20.00 50.00
56LO Ted Hendricks/25 12.00 30.00
57BA Terrell Davis/50 8.00 20.00
57DE Terrell Davis/95 5.00 12.00
57JN Terrell Davis AU/30 40.00 100.00
57LO Terrell Davis/25 12.00 30.00
58BA Terry Bradshaw/50 12.00 30.00
58DE Terry Bradshaw/70 10.00 25.00
58LO Terry Bradshaw/25 20.00 50.00
59BA Thurman Thomas/50 10.00 25.00
59DE Thurman Thomas/88 6.00 15.00
59JN Thurman Thomas AU/34 30.00 80.00
59LO Thurman Thomas/25 15.00 40.00
60BA Tony Dorsett/50 10.00 25.00
60DE Tony Dorsett/77 8.00 20.00
60JN Tony Dorsett AU/33 40.00 100.00
60LO Tony Dorsett/25 15.00 40.00
61BA Troy Aikman/50 12.00 30.00
61DE Troy Aikman/89 8.00 20.00
61LO Troy Aikman/25 20.00 50.00
62BA Walter Payton/50 30.00 80.00
62DE Walter Payton/75 25.00 60.00
62JN Walter Payton/34 40.00 100.00
62LO Walter Payton/25 50.00 125.00
63BA Warren Moon/50 10.00 25.00
63DE Warren Moon/84 8.00 20.00
63LO Warren Moon/25 15.00 40.00
64BA Michael Vick/50 6.00 15.00
64LO Michael Vick/25 10.00 25.00
65BA Emmitt Smith/50 12.00 30.00
65DE Emmitt Smith/90 10.00 25.00
65JN Emmitt Smith/22 20.00 50.00
65LO Emmitt Smith/25 20.00 50.00
66BA Brett Favre/50 15.00 40.00
66DE Brett Favre/91 12.00 30.00
66LO Brett Favre/25 25.00 60.00
67BA Edgerrin James/50 6.00 15.00
67DE Edgerrin James/99 5.00 12.00
67JN Edgerrin James/32 8.00 20.00
67LO Edgerrin James/25 10.00 25.00
68BA Peyton Manning/50 20.00 50.00
68DE Peyton Manning/98 15.00 40.00
68LO Peyton Manning/25 30.00 80.00
69BA Priest Holmes/50 5.00 12.00
69DE Priest Holmes/98 4.00 10.00
69JN Priest Holmes AU/31 30.00 80.00
69LO Priest Holmes/25 8.00 20.00
70BA Randy Moss/50 6.00 15.00
70DE Randy Moss/98 5.00 12.00
70JN Randy Moss/84 5.00 12.00
70LO Randy Moss/25 10.00 25.00
71BA Jerry Rice/50 15.00 40.00
71DE Jerry Rice/85 12.00 30.00
71JN Jerry Rice/80 12.00 30.00
71LO Jerry Rice/25 25.00 60.00
72BA Donovan McNabb/50 6.00 15.00
72DE Donovan McNabb/99 5.00 12.00
72LO Donovan McNabb/25 10.00 25.00
73BA LaDainian Tomlinson/50 8.00 20.00
73JN LaDainian Tomlinson/21 12.00 30.00
73LO LaDainian Tomlinson/25 12.00 30.00
74BA Marshall Faulk/50 6.00 15.00
74DE Marshall Faulk/94 5.00 12.00
74JN Marshall Faulk/28 10.00 25.00
74LO Marshall Faulk/25 10.00 25.00
75BA Kurt Warner/50 6.00 15.00
75DE Kurt Warner/99 5.00 12.00
75LO Kurt Warner/25 10.00 25.00
76BA David Carr/50 5.00 12.00
76LO David Carr/25 8.00 20.00
77BA Joey Harrington/50 5.00 12.00
77LO Joey Harrington/25 8.00 20.00
78BA Clinton Portis/50 5.00 12.00
78JN Clinton Portis AU/26 30.00 80.00
78LO Clinton Portis/25 8.00 20.00
79BA Roy Williams/50 5.00 12.00
79JN Roy Williams/31 6.00 15.00
79LO Roy Williams/25 8.00 20.00
80BA Jerome Bettis/50 12.00 30.00
80DE Jerome Bettis/93 10.00 25.00
80JN Jerome Bettis AU/36 100.00 200.00
80LO Jerome Bettis/25 20.00 50.00
81BA Tim Brown/50 8.00 20.00
81DE Tim Brown/88 6.00 15.00
81JN Tim Brown/81 6.00 15.00
81LO Tim Brown/25 12.00 30.00
82BA Jeff Garcia/50 5.00 12.00
82DE Jeff Garcia/99 4.00 10.00
82LO Jeff Garcia/25 8.00 20.00
83BA Eddie George/50 6.00 15.00
83DE Eddie George/96 5.00 12.00
83JN Eddie George/27 10.00 25.00
83LO Eddie George/25 10.00 25.00
84BA Ahman Green/50 6.00 15.00
84DE Ahman Green/98 5.00 12.00
84JN Ahman Green/30 8.00 20.00
84LO Ahman Green/25 10.00 25.00
85BA Ed McCaffrey/50 6.00 15.00
85DE Ed McCaffrey/91 5.00 12.00
85JN Ed McCaffrey/87 5.00 12.00
85LO Ed McCaffrey/25 10.00 25.00
86BA Steve McNair/50 6.00 15.00
86DE Steve McNair/95 5.00 12.00
86LO Steve McNair/25 10.00 25.00
87BA Terrell Owens/50 6.00 15.00
87DE Terrell Owens/96 5.00 12.00
87JN Terrell Owens/81 5.00 12.00
87LO Terrell Owens/25 10.00 25.00
88BA Zach Thomas/50 6.00 15.00
88DE Zach Thomas/96 5.00 12.00
88JN Zach Thomas AU/54 30.00 80.00
88LO Zach Thomas/25 10.00 25.00
89BA Michael Bennett/50 5.00 12.00
89JN Michael Bennett AU/23 20.00 50.00
89LO Michael Bennett/25 8.00 20.00
90BA Rich Gannon/50 6.00 15.00
90DE Rich Gannon/87 5.00 12.00
90LO Rich Gannon/25 10.00 25.00
91BA Tony Gonzalez/50 6.00 15.00
91DE Tony Gonzalez/97 5.00 12.00
91JN Tony Gonzalez/88 5.00 12.00
91LO Tony Gonzalez/25 10.00 25.00
92BA Garrison Hearst/50 5.00 12.00
92DE Garrison Hearst/93 4.00 10.00
92JN Garrison Hearst/20 8.00 20.00
92LO Garrison Hearst/25 8.00 20.00
93BA Jevon Kearse/50 5.00 12.00
93DE Jevon Kearse/99 4.00 10.00
93JN Jevon Kearse/90 4.00 10.00
93LO Jevon Kearse/25 8.00 20.00
94BA Santana Moss/50 6.00 15.00
94JN Santana Moss AU/83 12.00 30.00
94LO Santana Moss/25 10.00 25.00
95BA Eric Moulds/50 5.00 12.00
95DE Eric Moulds/96 4.00 10.00
95JN Eric Moulds/80 4.00 10.00
95LO Eric Moulds/25 8.00 20.00
96BA Mike Alstott/50 5.00 12.00
96DE Mike Alstott/96 4.00 10.00
96JN Mike Alstott/40 6.00 15.00
96LO Mike Alstott/25 8.00 20.00
97BA Anthony Thomas/50 6.00 15.00
97JN Anthony Thomas/35 8.00 20.00
97LO Anthony Thomas/25 10.00 25.00
98BA Daunte Culpepper/50 6.00 15.00
98DE Daunte Culpepper/99 5.00 12.00
98LO Daunte Culpepper/25 10.00 25.00
99BA Junior Seau/50 6.00 15.00
99DE Junior Seau/90 5.00 12.00
99JN Junior Seau/55 6.00 15.00
99LO Junior Seau/25 10.00 25.00
100BA Warren Sapp/50 6.00 15.00
100DE Warren Sapp/96 5.00 12.00
100JN Warren Sapp/99 5.00 12.00
100LO Warren Sapp/25 10.00 25.00

2003 Leaf Certified Materials Mirror Signatures

Randomly inserted into packs, this set features authentic player autographs on foil stickers. Each card is serial numbered to various quantities. Please note that Terry Bradshaw, Larry Johnson, Terrell Suggs, and cards MS14 and MS17 were only issued in packs as exchange cards.
STATED PRINT RUN 25-100

MS1 Jim Brown/100 40.00 80.00
MS2 Joe Montana/100 75.00 150.00
MS3 John Riggins/100 15.00 40.00
MS4 Randy White/100 15.00 40.00
MS5 Terry Bradshaw/100 [illegible]
MS6 Deion Branch/50 12.00 30.00
MS7 Jeff Garcia/25 15.00 40.00
MS8 Joe Horn/50 10.00 25.00
MS9 Joey Harrington/25 15.00 40.00
MS10 Kurt Warner/100 20.00 40.00
MS11 Randy Moss/25 50.00 100.00
MS12 Tim Brown/25 20.00 50.00
MS13 Torry Holt/25 15.00 40.00
MS14 Zach Thomas/25 15.00 40.00
MS15 Byron Leftwich/25 25.00 60.00
MS16 Carson Palmer/25 100.00 200.00
MS17 Charles Rogers/25 10.00 25.00
MS18 Larry Johnson/25 25.00 60.00
MS19 Bryant Johnson/50 12.00 30.00
MS20 Kelley Washington/50 12.00 30.00
MS21 Terrell Suggs/50 20.00 40.00
MS22 Terence Newman/100 12.00 30.00
MS23 Musa Smith/100 8.00 20.00
MS24 Dave Ragone/100 8.00 20.00
MS25 Chris Brown/100 8.00 20.00

2003 Leaf Certified Materials Potential

ndomly inserted into packs, this set features authentic game worn jersey swatches. Each card is serial numbered to 125.
STATED PRINT RUN 125 SER.#'d SETS

CP1 Antonio Bryant 3.00 8.00
CP2 Antwaan Randle El 3.00 8.00
CP3 Ashley Lelie 3.00 8.00
CP4 Chris Chambers 3.00 8.00
CP5 Clinton Portis 3.00 8.00
CP6 David Carr 3.00 8.00
CP7 Drew Brees 5.00 12.00
CP8 Javon Walker 4.00 10.00
CP9 Jeremy Shockey 3.00 8.00
CP10 Joey Harrington 3.00 8.00
CP11 Josh Reed 3.00 8.00
CP12 Julius Peppers 5.00 12.00
CP13 Koren Robinson 4.00 10.00
CP14 LaDainian Tomlinson 5.00 12.00
CP15 Marcel Shipp 3.00 8.00
CP16 Roy Williams 3.00 8.00
CP17 T.J. Duckett 3.00 8.00
CP18 Travis Henry 3.00 8.00

2003 Leaf Certified Materials Skills

ndomly inserted into packs, this set features authentic game worn jersey swatches. Each card is serial numbered to 100.
STATED PRINT RUN 100 SER.#'d SETS

CS1 Rich Gannon 4.00 10.00
CS2 Drew Bledsoe 4.00 10.00
CS3 Peyton Manning 12.00 30.00
CS4 Kerry Collins 3.00 8.00
CS5 Daunte Culpepper 4.00 10.00
CS6 Tom Brady 20.00 50.00
CS7 Trent Green 3.00 8.00
CS8 Brett Favre 10.00 25.00
CS9 Aaron Brooks 3.00 8.00
CS10 Steve McNair 4.00 10.00
CS11 Jeff Garcia 3.00 8.00
CS12 Drew Brees 5.00 12.00
CS13 Brian Griese 3.00 8.00
CS14 Chad Pennington 3.00 8.00
CS15 Brad Johnson 4.00 10.00
CS16 Ricky Williams 4.00 10.00
CS17 LaDainian Tomlinson 5.00 12.00
CS18 Priest Holmes 3.00 8.00
CS19 Clinton Portis 3.00 8.00
CS20 Travis Henry 3.00 8.00
CS21 Deuce McAllister 4.00 10.00
CS22 Tiki Barber 4.00 10.00
CS23 Jamal Lewis 4.00 10.00
CS24 Fred Taylor 3.00 8.00
CS25 Corey Dillon 3.00 8.00
CS26 Michael Bennett 3.00 8.00
CS27 Ahman Green 4.00 10.00
CS28 Shaun Alexander 3.00 8.00
CS29 Eddie George 4.00 10.00
CS30 Curtis Martin 4.00 10.00
CS31 Duce Staley 3.00 8.00
CS32 James Stewart 3.00 8.00
CS33 Marvin Harrison 4.00 10.00
CS34 Randy Moss 4.00 10.00
CS35 Amani Toomer 3.00 8.00
CS36 Hines Ward 4.00 10.00
CS37 Plaxico Burress 3.00 8.00
CS38 Torry Holt 4.00 10.00
CS39 Terrell Owens 4.00 10.00
CS40 Eric Moulds 3.00 8.00
CS41 Laveranues Coles 3.00 8.00
CS42 Peerless Price 3.00 8.00
CS43 Koren Robinson 4.00 10.00
CS44 Jerry Rice 10.00 25.00
CS45 Emmitt Smith 8.00 20.00
CS46 Keyshawn Johnson 5.00 12.00
CS47 Isaac Bruce 5.00 12.00
CS48 Donald Driver 4.00 10.00
CS49 Jimmy Smith 4.00 10.00
CS50 Rod Smith 4.00 10.00

2003 Leaf Certified Materials Samples

Inserted one per Beckett Football Card Monthly, these cards parallel the basic Certified Materials cards. Each can be noted by the word "Sample" stamped in silver on the back.
*SAMPLES: .8X TO 2X BASIC CARDS

2004 Leaf Certified Materials

Leaf Certified Materials initially released in early October 2004. The base set consists of 233-cards including 50-rookie or rookie autographs serial numbered of 1000 and 33-jersey rookie cards. Hobby boxes contained 10-packs of 5-cards and carried an S.R.P. of $15 per pack. Six parallel sets and a variety of inserts can be found seeded in hobby and retail packs highlighted by the multi-tiered Material game used jerseys and Signatures autographed inserts.
COMP.SET w/o SP's (150) 12.50 30.00
151-200 ROOKIE AU PRINT RUN 1000
201-233 ROOKIE JSY PRINT RUN 1250
UNPRICED MIRROR BLACK PRINT RUN 1
UNPRICED MIRR.EMERALD PRINT RUN 5

1 Anquan Boldin .25 .60
2 Emmitt Smith .60 1.50
3 Josh McCown .30 .75
4 Marcel Shipp .25 .60
5 Michael Vick .30 .75
6 Peerless Price .25 .60
7 T.J. Duckett .25 .60
8 Warrick Dunn .25 .60
9 Jamal Lewis .30 .75
10 Kyle Boller .25 .60
11 Ray Lewis .40 1.00
12 Terrell Suggs .25 .60
13 Todd Heap .25 .60
14 Drew Bledsoe .30 .75
15 Eric Moulds .25 .60
16 Travis Henry .25 .60
17 Julius Peppers .30 .75
18 Muhsin Muhammad .25 .60
19 Stephen Davis .25 .60
20 Anthony Thomas .30 .75
21 Brian Urlacher .40 1.00
22 Rex Grossman .25 .60
23 Chad Johnson .25 .60
24 Corey Dillon .25 .60
25 Peter Warrick .25 .60
26 Jeff Garcia .25 .60
27 Tim Couch .30 .75
28 William Green .25 .60
29 Antonio Bryant .30 .75
30 Keyshawn Johnson .30 .75
31 Quincy Carter .25 .60
32 Roy Williams S .25 .60
33 Terence Newman .30 .75
34 Ashley Lelie .25 .60
35 Ed McCaffrey .40 1.00
36 Jake Plummer .25 .60
37 Mike Anderson .25 .60
38 Rod Smith .30 .75
39 Charles Rogers .25 .60
40 Joey Harrington .25 .60
41 Ahman Green .30 .75
42 Brett Favre .75 2.00
43 Donald Driver .30 .75
44 Javon Walker .25 .60
45 Robert Ferguson .25 .60
46 Andre Johnson .30 .75
47 David Carr .25 .60
48 Edgerrin James .30 .75
49 Marvin Harrison .30 .75
50 Peyton Manning 1.00 2.50
51 Reggie Wayne .30 .75
52 Byron Leftwich .25 .60
53 Fred Taylor .25 .60
54 Jimmy Smith .30 .75
55 Dante Hall .25 .60
56 Priest Holmes .25 .60
57 Tony Gonzalez .30 .75
58 Trent Green .25 .60
59 A.J. Feeley .25 .60
60 Chris Chambers .25 .60
61 David Boston .25 .60
62 Jason Taylor .30 .75
63 Jay Fiedler .25 .60
64 Junior Seau .40 1.00
65 Randy McMichael .25 .60
66 Ricky Williams .30 .75
67 Zach Thomas .30 .75
68 Daunte Culpepper .30 .75
69 Michael Bennett .25 .60
70 Randy Moss .30 .75
71 Tom Brady 1.50 4.00
72 Troy Brown .25 .60
73 Ty Law .40 1.00
74 Aaron Brooks .25 .60
75 Deuce McAllister .30 .75
76 Donte Stallworth .25 .60
77 Amani Toomer .25 .60
78 Jeremy Shockey .25 .60
79 Kerry Collins .25 .60
80 Michael Strahan .30 .75
81 Tiki Barber .30 .75
82 Chad Pennington .25 .60
83 Curtis Martin .30 .75
84 Justin McCareins .25 .60
85 Santana Moss .30 .75
86 Charles Woodson .40 1.00
87 Jerry Rice .75 2.00
88 Rich Gannon .30 .75
89 Tim Brown .40 1.00
90 Warren Sapp .30 .75
91 Correll Buckhalter .25 .60
92 Donovan McNabb .30 .75
93 Freddie Mitchell .25 .60
94 Jevon Kearse .25 .60
95 Terrell Owens .30 .75
96 Antwaan Randle El .25 .60
97 Duce Staley .25 .60
98 Hines Ward .30 .75
99 Jerome Bettis .40 1.00
100 Plaxico Burress .25 .60
101 Doug Flutie .30 .75
102 LaDainian Tomlinson .40 1.00
103 Koren Robinson .25 .60
104 Matt Hasselbeck .25 .60
105 Shaun Alexander .25 .60
106 Isaac Bruce .40 1.00
107 Kurt Warner .30 .75
108 Marc Bulger .25 .60
109 Marshall Faulk .30 .75
110 Torry Holt .30 .75
111 Brad Johnson .30 .75
112 Mike Alstott .25 .60
113 Derrick Mason .25 .60
114 Drew Bennett .30 .75
115 Eddie George .30 .75
116 Frank Wycheck .30 .75
117 Keith Bulluck .25 .60
118 Steve McNair .30 .75
119 Tyrone Calico .30 .75
120 Clinton Portis .25 .60
121 LaVar Arrington .25 .60
122 Laveranues Coles .25 .60
123 Mark Brunell .30 .75
124 Patrick Ramsey .30 .75
125 Rod Gardner .25 .60
126 Jake Plummer FLB .25 .60
127 Thomas Jones FLB .25 .60
128 Priest Holmes FLB .25 .60
129 Jim Kelly FLB .60 1.50
130 Doug Flutie FLB .30 .75
131 Walter Payton FLB 2.50 6.00
132 Troy Aikman FLB .75 2.00
133 John Elway FLB 1.00 2.50
134 Barry Sanders FLB 1.00 2.50
135 Mark Brunell FLB .30 .75
136 Earl Campbell FLB .60 1.50
137 Joe Montana FLB 2.00 5.00
138 Dan Marino FLB 1.25 3.00
139 Curtis Martin FLB .30 .75
140 Drew Bledsoe FLB .30 .75
141 Ricky Williams FLB .30 .75
142 Junior Seau FLB .40 1.00
143 Charlie Garner FLB .30 .75
144 Jerry Rice FLB .75 2.00
145 Ahman Green FLB .30 .75
146 Jerome Bettis FLB .40 1.00
147 Trent Green FLB .25 .60
148 Warrick Dunn FLB .25 .60
149 Deion Sanders FLB .30 .75
150 Stephen Davis FLB .25 .60
151 Adimchinobe Echemandu AU RC 3.00 8.00
152 Ahmad Carroll RC 1.25 3.00
153 Andy Hall AU RC 2.50 6.00
154 B.J. Johnson AU RC 2.50 6.00
155 B.J. Symons AU RC 2.50 6.00
156 Bradlee Van Pelt AU RC 3.00 8.00
157 Brandon Miree AU RC 2.50 6.00
158 Bruce Perry AU RC 2.50 6.00
159 Carlos Francis AU RC 2.50 6.00
160 Casey Bramlet AU RC 2.50 6.00
161 Chris Gamble RC 1.25 3.00
162 Clarence Moore AU RC 2.50 6.00
163 Cody Pickett AU RC 2.50 6.00
164 Craig Krenzel AU RC 2.50 6.00
165 D.J. Hackett RC 1.25 3.00
166 D.J. Williams RC 2.00 5.00
167 Derrick Ward AU RC 4.00 10.00
168 Drew Carter AU RC 3.00 8.00
169 Ernest Wilford RC 1.50 4.00
170 Drew Henson RC 1.25 3.00
171 Jamaar Taylor AU RC 2.50 6.00
172 Jared Lorenzen AU RC 3.00 8.00
173 Jarrett Payton AU RC 3.00 8.00
174 Jason Babin AU RC 4.00 10.00
175 Jeff Smoker AU RC 3.00 8.00
176 Jeris McIntyre AU RC 2.50 6.00
177 Jerricho Cotchery RC 1.50 4.00
178 Jim Sorgi AU RC 3.00 8.00
179 John Navarre AU RC 2.50 6.00
180 Patrick Crayton AU RC 4.00 10.00
181 Johnnie Morant RC 1.25 3.00
182 Sean Taylor RC 8.00 20.00
183 Jonathan Vilma RC 1.50 4.00
184 Josh Harris RC 1.25 3.00
185 Kenechi Udeze RC 1.50 4.00
186 Mark Jones AU RC 2.50 6.00
187 Matt Mauck AU RC 2.50 6.00
188 Maurice Mann AU RC 2.50 6.00
189 Michael Turner RC 1.25 3.00
190 P.K. Sam RC 1.25 3.00
191 Quincy Wilson RC 1.25 3.00
192 Ran Carthon AU RC 2.50 6.00
193 Ryan Krause AU RC 2.50 6.00
194 Samie Parker RC 1.25 3.00
195 Sloan Thomas AU RC 3.00 8.00
196 Tommie Harris RC 1.50 4.00
197 Triandos Luke AU RC 2.50 6.00
198 Troy Fleming AU RC 2.50 6.00
199 Vince Wilfork RC 2.00 5.00
200 Will Smith RC 1.50 4.00
201 Larry Fitzgerald JSY RC 6.00 15.00
202 DeAngelo Hall JSY RC 2.50 6.00
203 Matt Schaub JSY RC 1.50 4.00
204 Michael Jenkins JSY RC 1.50 4.00
205 Devard Darling JSY RC 1.50 4.00
206 J.P. Losman JSY RC 1.50 4.00
207 Lee Evans JSY RC 2.50 6.00
208 Keary Colbert JSY RC 1.50 4.00
209 Bernard Berrian JSY RC 1.50 4.00
210 Chris Perry JSY RC 1.50 4.00
211 Kellen Winslow JSY RC 1.50 4.00
212 Luke McCown JSY RC 1.50 4.00
213 Julius Jones JSY RC 1.50 4.00
214 Darius Watts JSY RC 1.50 4.00
215 Tatum Bell JSY RC 1.50 4.00
216 Kevin Jones JSY RC 2.00 5.00
217 Roy Williams JSY RC 1.50 4.00
218 Dunta Robinson JSY RC 1.50 4.00
219 Greg Jones JSY RC 1.50 4.00
220 Reggie Williams JSY RC 1.50 4.00
221 Mewelde Moore JSY RC 2.00 5.00
222 Ben Watson JSY RC 2.00 5.00
223 Cedric Cobbs JSY RC 1.50 4.00
224 Devery Henderson JSY RC 1.50 4.00
225 Eli Manning JSY RC 12.00 30.00
226 Robert Gallery JSY RC 2.00 5.00
227 Ben Roethlisberger JSY RC 12.00 30.00
228 Philip Rivers JSY RC 5.00 12.00
229 Derrick Hamilton JSY RC 1.50 4.00
230 Rashaun Woods JSY RC 1.50 4.00
231 Steven Jackson JSY RC 2.50 6.00
232 Michael Clayton JSY RC 2.00 5.00
233 Ben Troupe JSY RC 1.50 4.00

2004 Leaf Certified Materials Mirror Blue

ETS 1-150: 1X TO 2.5X MIRROR WHITE
*ROOKIES 151-200: 1X TO 2.5X MIR.WHITE
STATED PRINT RUN 50 SER.#'d SETS

2004 Leaf Certified Materials Mirror Gold

ETS 1-150: 1.5X TO 4X MIRROR WHITE
*ROOKIES 151-200: 1.5X TO 4X MIRR.WHITE
STATED PRINT RUN 25 SER.#'d SETS

2004 Leaf Certified Materials Mirror Red

ETS 1-150: .5X TO 1.2X MIRROR WHITE
*ROOKIES 151-200: .5X TO 1.2X MIR.WHITE
STATED PRINT RUN 100 SER.#'d SETS

2004 Leaf Certified Materials Mirror White

ETS 1-150: 2X TO 5X BASIC CARDS
COMMON ROOKIE (151-200) 1.25 3.00
ROOKIE SEMISTARS 151-200 1.50 4.00
ROOKIE UNL.STARS 151-200 2.00 5.00
STATED PRINT RUN 150 SER.#'d SETS
189 Michael Turner 1.25 3.00

2004 Leaf Certified Materials Certified Potential Jersey

ATED PRINT RUN 150 SER.#'d SETS
*INFINITE/75: .5X TO 1.2X BASIC JSY
INFINITE PRINT RUN 75 SER.#'d SETS
*INFINITE PRIME/25: 1.2X TO 3X BASIC JSY
INFIN.PRIME PRINT RUN 25 SER.#'d SETS
UNPRICED BLACK PRINT RUN 1 SET

CP1 A.J. Feeley 2.50 6.00
CP2 Andre Johnson 3.00 8.00
CP3 Anquan Boldin 2.50 6.00
CP4 Antonio Bryant 3.00 8.00
CP5 Antwaan Randle El 2.50 6.00
CP6 Ashley Lelie 2.50 6.00
CP7 Bryant Johnson 2.50 6.00
CP8 Byron Leftwich 2.50 6.00
CP9 Charles Rogers 2.50 6.00
CP10 Correll Buckhalter 2.50 6.00
CP11 Dallas Clark 2.50 6.00
CP12 David Carr 2.50 6.00
CP13 Donte Stallworth 2.50 6.00
CP14 Drew Bennett 3.00 8.00
CP15 Javon Walker 2.50 6.00
CP16 Joey Harrington 2.50 6.00
CP17 Josh McCown 3.00 8.00
CP18 Justin McCareins 2.50 6.00
CP19 Kyle Boller 2.50 6.00
CP20 Marcel Shipp 2.50 6.00
CP21 Nick Barnett 2.50 6.00
CP22 Rex Grossman 2.50 6.00
CP23 Terence Newman 3.00 8.00
CP24 Terrell Suggs 2.50 6.00
CP25 Tyrone Calico 3.00 8.00

2004 Leaf Certified Materials Certified Skills Jersey

ATED PRINT RUN 175 SER.#'d SETS
*POSITION/75: .5X TO 1.2X BASIC JSY
POSITION PRINT RUN 75 SER.#'d SETS
*POSITION PRIME/25: 1.2X TO 3X BASIC JSY
POSIT.PRIME PRINT RUN 25 SER.#'d SETS
UNPRICED BLACK PRINT RUN 1 SET

CS1 Peyton Manning 12.00 30.00
CS2 Trent Green 3.00 8.00
CS3 Marc Bulger 3.00 8.00
CS4 Matt Hasselbeck 3.00 8.00
CS5 Brad Johnson 4.00 10.00
CS6 Tom Brady 20.00 50.00
CS7 Aaron Brooks 3.00 8.00
CS8 Daunte Culpepper 4.00 10.00
CS9 Brett Favre 10.00 25.00
CS10 Quincy Carter 3.00 8.00
CS11 Donovan McNabb 4.00 10.00
CS12 Steve McNair 4.00 10.00
CS13 Kerry Collins 3.00 8.00
CS14 Dan Marino 10.00 25.00
CS15 John Elway 8.00 20.00
CS16 Warren Moon 5.00 12.00
CS17 Fran Tarkenton 5.00 12.00
CS18 Brett Favre 10.00 25.00
CS19 Joe Montana 15.00 40.00
CS20 Jamal Lewis 4.00 10.00
CS21 Ahman Green 4.00 10.00
CS22 LaDainian Tomlinson 5.00 12.00
CS23 Deuce McAllister 4.00 10.00
CS24 Clinton Portis 3.00 8.00
CS25 Fred Taylor 3.00 8.00
CS26 Stephen Davis 3.00 8.00
CS27 Shaun Alexander 3.00 8.00
CS28 Priest Holmes 3.00 8.00
CS29 Ricky Williams 4.00 10.00
CS30 Travis Henry 3.00 8.00
CS31 Curtis Martin 4.00 10.00
CS32 Edgerrin James 4.00 10.00
CS33 Tiki Barber 4.00 10.00
CS34 Eddie George 4.00 10.00
CS35 Anthony Thomas 4.00 10.00
CS36 Emmitt Smith [illegible]
CS37 Walter Payton 20.00 50.00
CS38 Barry Sanders 8.00 20.00
CS39 Torry Holt 4.00 10.00
CS40 Randy Moss 4.00 10.00
CS41 Anquan Boldin 3.00 8.00
CS42 Chad Johnson 3.00 8.00
CS43 Derrick Mason 3.00 8.00
CS44 Marvin Harrison 4.00 10.00
CS45 Laveranues Coles 3.00 8.00
CS46 Hines Ward 4.00 10.00
CS47 Santana Moss 4.00 10.00
CS48 Terrell Owens 4.00 10.00
CS49 Jerry Rice 10.00 25.00
CS50 Tim Brown 5.00 12.00

2004 Leaf Certified Materials Fabric of the Game

STATED PRINT RUN 100 SER.#'d SETS
*21st CENT/21: 1X TO 2.5X BASIC JSY
21st CENTURY PRINT RUN 21
*DEBUT YEAR/70-103: .4X TO 1X
*DEBUT YEAR/50-69: .5X TO 1.2X
*DEBUT YEAR/15: 1.2X TO 3X
UNPRICED TEAM LOGO PRINT RUN 5

FG1 Aaron Brooks 3.00 8.00
FG2 Ahman Green 4.00 10.00
FG3 Andre Johnson 4.00 10.00
FG4 Anquan Boldin 3.00 8.00
FG5 Antwaan Randle El 3.00 8.00
FG6 Barry Sanders 10.00 25.00
FG7 Bart Starr 15.00 40.00
FG8 Bob Griese 6.00 15.00
FG9 Brett Favre 10.00 25.00
FG10 Brian Urlacher 5.00 12.00
FG11 Bruce Smith 5.00 12.00
FG12 Byron Leftwich 3.00 8.00
FG13 Chad Johnson 3.00 8.00
FG14 Chad Pennington 3.00 8.00
FG15 Charles Rogers 3.00 8.00
FG16 Charles Woodson 5.00 12.00
FG17 Chris Chambers 3.00 8.00
FG18 Clinton Portis 3.00 8.00
FG19 Dan Marino 12.00 30.00
FG20 Daryl Johnston 5.00 12.00
FG21 Daunte Culpepper 4.00 10.00
FG22 David Carr 3.00 8.00
FG23 Deacon Jones 5.00 12.00
FG24 Deion Sanders 4.00 10.00
FG25 Derrick Mason 3.00 8.00
FG26 Deuce McAllister 4.00 10.00
FG27 Doak Walker 10.00 25.00
FG28 Don Maynard 5.00 12.00
FG29 Don Shula 6.00 15.00
FG30 Donovan McNabb 4.00 10.00
FG31 Drew Bledsoe 4.00 10.00
FG32 Earl Campbell 6.00 15.00
FG33 Eddie George 4.00 10.00
FG34 Edgerrin James 4.00 10.00
FG35 Emmitt Smith 8.00 20.00
FG36 Fran Tarkenton 6.00 15.00
FG37 Franco Harris 8.00 20.00
FG38 Fred Biletnikoff 6.00 15.00
FG39 George Blanda 6.00 15.00
FG40 Harvey Martin 4.00 10.00
FG41 Herman Edwards 5.00 12.00
FG42 Hines Ward 4.00 10.00
FG43 Jake Plummer 3.00 8.00
FG44 Jamal Lewis 4.00 10.00
FG45 James Lofton 4.00 10.00
FG46 Javon Walker 3.00 8.00
FG47 Jeremy Shockey 3.00 8.00
FG48 Jerry Rice 10.00 25.00
FG49 Jim Brown 8.00 20.00
FG50 Jim Kelly 6.00 15.00
FG51 Jim Plunkett 5.00 12.00
FG52 Jim Thorpe 60.00 120.00
FG53 Joe Greene 6.00 15.00
FG54 Joe Montana 15.00 40.00
FG55 Joe Namath 12.00 30.00
FG56 Joey Harrington 3.00 8.00
FG57 John Elway 10.00 25.00
FG58 John Riggins 5.00 12.00
FG59 Kendrell Bell 3.00 8.00
FG60 L.C. Greenwood 4.00 10.00
FG61 LaDainian Tomlinson 5.00 12.00
FG62 Lawrence Taylor 6.00 15.00
FG63 Leroy Kelly 5.00 12.00
FG64 Lynn Swann 12.00 30.00
FG65 Marc Bulger 3.00 8.00
FG66 Mark Bavaro 4.00 10.00
FG67 Marshall Faulk 4.00 10.00
FG68 Matt Hasselbeck 3.00 8.00
FG69 Mel Blount 5.00 12.00
FG70 Michael Irvin 6.00 15.00
FG71 Michael Vick 8.00 20.00
FG72 Mike Singletary 6.00 15.00
FG73 Ozzie Newsome 5.00 12.00
FG74 Paul Warfield 5.00 12.00
FG75 Peyton Manning 12.00 30.00
FG76 Priest Holmes 3.00 8.00
FG77 Quincy Carter 3.00 8.00
FG78 Randy Moss 4.00 10.00
FG79 Ray Nitschke 12.00 25.00
FG80 Reggie White 6.00 15.00
FG81 Rex Grossman 3.00 8.00
FG82 Richard Dent 4.00 10.00
FG83 Ricky Williams 4.00 10.00
FG84 Roger Staubach 8.00 20.00
FG85 Roy Williams S 3.00 8.00
FG86 Santana Moss 4.00 10.00
FG87 Shaun Alexander 3.00 8.00
FG88 Sterling Sharpe 5.00 12.00
FG89 Steve McNair 4.00 10.00
FG90 Terrell Davis 5.00 12.00
FG91 Terry Bradshaw 8.00 20.00
FG92 Thurman Thomas 5.00 12.00
FG93 Tiki Barber 4.00 10.00
FG94 Todd Heap 3.00 8.00
FG95 Tom Brady 20.00 50.00
FG96 Tony Dorsett 6.00 15.00
FG97 Trent Green 3.00 8.00
FG98 Troy Aikman 8.00 20.00
FG99 Walter Payton 20.00 50.00
FG100 Warren Moon 6.00 15.00

2004 Leaf Certified Materials Fabric of the Game Jersey Number

ERSEY/66-99: .5X TO 1.2X BASIC INSERTS
*JERSEY/32-37: .8X TO 2X BASIC INSERTS
*JERSEY/22-28: 1X TO 2.5X BASIC INSERTS
*JERSEY/10-18: 1.2X TO 3X BASIC INSERTS
STATED PRINT RUN 1-97
JSY's #'d UNDER 10 NOT PRICED
JSY AU's #'d UNDER 20 NOT PRICED

FG2 Ahman Green AU/30 20.00 50.00
FG4 Anquan Boldin AU/81 15.00 40.00
FG5 Antwaan Randle El AU/82 12.00 30.00
FG6 Barry Sanders AU/20 75.00 150.00
FG10 Brian Urlacher AU/54 30.00 60.00
FG13 Chad Johnson AU/85 12.00 30.00
FG17 Chris Chambers AU/84 15.00 40.00
FG18 Clinton Portis AU/26 15.00 40.00
FG20 Daryl Johnston AU/48 20.00 50.00
FG23 Deacon Jones AU/75 15.00 40.00
FG24 Deion Sanders AU/21 30.00 80.00
FG25 Derrick Mason AU/85 12.00 30.00
FG26 Deuce McAllister AU/26 15.00 40.00
FG29 Don Shula AU/25 25.00 60.00
FG32 Earl Campbell AU/34 30.00 80.00
FG33 Eddie George AU/27 25.00 50.00
FG34 Edgerrin James/32 8.00 20.00
FG35 Emmitt Smith/22 [illegible]
FG37 Franco Harris AU/32 50.00 100.00
FG38 Fred Biletnikoff AU/25 25.00 60.00
FG40 Harvey Martin/79 5.00 12.00
FG41 Herman Edwards AU/46 12.00 30.00
FG42 [illegible]

FG44 Jamal Lewis AU/31 20.00 50.00
FG45 James Lofton AU/80 12.00 30.00
FG46 Javon Walker AU/84 12.00 30.00
FG49 Jim Brown AU/32 60.00 120.00
FG53 Joe Greene AU/75 20.00 50.00
FG58 John Riggins AU/44 25.00 60.00
FG59 Kendrell Bell AU/97 12.00 30.00
FG60 L.C. Greenwood AU/68 40.00 80.00
FG61 LaDainian Tomlinson AU/21 40.00 100.00
FG62 Lawrence Taylor AU/56 60.00 100.00
FG63 Leroy Kelly AU/44 20.00 50.00
FG66 Mark Bavaro AU/89 20.00 50.00
FG69 Mel Blount AU/47 25.00 60.00
FG70 Michael Irvin AU/88 30.00 60.00
FG72 Mike Singletary AU/50 20.00 50.00
FG73 Ozzie Newsome AU/82 15.00 40.00
FG74 Paul Warfield AU/42 25.00 60.00
FG76 Priest Holmes AU/31 20.00 50.00
FG80 Reggie White AU/92 250.00 400.00
FG82 Richard Dent AU/95 12.00 30.00
FG85 Roy Williams S AU/31 20.00 50.00
FG86 Santana Moss AU/83 12.00 30.00
FG87 Shaun Alexander AU/37 25.00 60.00
FG88 Sterling Sharpe AU/84 20.00 50.00
FG90 Terrell Davis AU/30 30.00 80.00
FG92 Thurman Thomas AU/34 30.00 80.00
FG93 Tiki Barber AU/21 30.00 80.00
FG94 Todd Heap AU/86 15.00 40.00
FG96 Tony Dorsett AU/33 30.00 80.00

2004 Leaf Certified Materials Gold Team Jersey

ATED PRINT RUN 150 SER.#'d SETS
*24K/75: .5X TO 1.2X BASIC JSY
24K PRINT RUN 75 SER.#'d SETS
*24K PRIME/25: 1X TO 2.5X BASIC JSY
24K PRIME PRINT RUN 25 SER.#'d SETS
UNPRICED BLACK PRINT RUN 1 SET
GT1 Barry Sanders 6.00 15.00
GT2 Brett Favre 8.00 20.00
GT3 Brian Urlacher 4.00 10.00
GT4 Byron Leftwich 2.50 6.00
GT5 Chad Pennington 2.50 6.00
GT6 Dan Marino 8.00 20.00
GT7 Daunte Culpepper 3.00 8.00
GT8 David Carr 2.50 6.00
GT9 Deuce McAllister 3.00 8.00
GT10 Donovan McNabb 3.00 8.00
GT11 Emmitt Smith 6.00 15.00
GT12 Jerry Rice 8.00 20.00
GT13 Joe Montana 12.00 30.00
GT14 Joey Harrington 2.50 6.00
GT15 John Elway 6.00 15.00
GT16 LaDainian Tomlinson 4.00 10.00
GT17 Michael Vick 3.00 8.00
GT18 Peyton Manning 10.00 25.00
GT19 Priest Holmes 2.50 6.00
GT20 Randy Moss 3.00 8.00
GT21 Ricky Williams 3.00 8.00
GT22 Steve McNair 3.00 8.00
GT23 Tom Brady 15.00 40.00
GT24 Troy Aikman 5.00 12.00
GT25 Walter Payton 15.00 40.00

2004 Leaf Certified Materials Mirror Red Materials

ED ROOK.201-233: .6X TO 1.5X BASE JSY
MIRROR RED PRINT RUN 150
UNPRICED BLACK PRINT RUN 1
*BLUE/50: .8X TO 2X MIRROR RED
BLUE PRINT RUN 50 SER.#'d SETS
UNPRICED EMERALD PRINT RUN 5
*GOLD/25: 1X TO 2.5X MIRROR RED
MIRROR GOLD PRINT RUN 25
*WHITE/250: .3X TO .8X MIRROR RED
*WHITE/75: .5X TO 1.2X MIRROR RED
MIRROR WHITE PRINT RUN 75-250
1 Anquan Boldin 2.50 6.00
2 Emmitt Smith 6.00 15.00
3 Josh McCown 3.00 8.00
4 Marcel Shipp 2.50 6.00
5 Michael Vick 3.00 8.00
6 Peerless Price 2.50 6.00
7 T.J. Duckett 2.50 6.00
8 Warrick Dunn 2.50 6.00
9 Jamal Lewis 3.00 8.00
10 Kyle Boller 2.50 6.00
11 Ray Lewis 4.00 10.00
12 Terrell Suggs 2.50 6.00
13 Todd Heap 2.50 6.00
14 Drew Bledsoe 3.00 8.00
15 Eric Moulds 2.50 6.00
16 Travis Henry 2.50 6.00
17 Julius Peppers 3.00 8.00
18 Muhsin Muhammad 2.50 6.00
19 Stephen Davis 2.50 6.00
20 Anthony Thomas 3.00 8.00
21 Brian Urlacher 4.00 10.00
22 Rex Grossman 2.50 6.00
23 Chad Johnson 2.50 6.00
24 Corey Dillon 2.50 6.00
25 Peter Warrick 2.50 6.00
26 Jeff Garcia 2.50 6.00
27 Tim Couch 3.00 8.00
28 William Green 2.50 6.00
29 Antonio Bryant 3.00 8.00
30 Keyshawn Johnson 3.00 8.00
31 Quincy Carter 2.50 6.00
32 Roy Williams S 2.50 6.00
33 Terence Newman 3.00 8.00
34 Ashley Lelie 2.50 6.00
35 Ed McCaffrey 4.00 10.00
36 Jake Plummer 2.50 6.00
37 Mike Anderson 2.50 6.00
38 Rod Smith 3.00 8.00
39 Charles Rogers 2.50 6.00
40 Joey Harrington 2.50 6.00
41 Ahman Green 3.00 8.00
42 Brett Favre 8.00 20.00
43 Donald Driver 3.00 8.00
44 Javon Walker 2.50 6.00
45 Robert Ferguson 2.50 6.00
46 Andre Johnson 3.00 8.00
47 David Carr 2.50 6.00
48 Edgerrin James 3.00 8.00
49 Marvin Harrison 3.00 8.00
50 Peyton Manning 10.00 25.00
51 Reggie Wayne 3.00 8.00
52 Byron Leftwich 2.50 6.00
53 Fred Taylor 2.50 6.00
54 Jimmy Smith 3.00 8.00
55 Dante Hall 2.50 6.00
56 Priest Holmes 2.50 6.00
57 Tony Gonzalez 3.00 8.00
58 Trent Green 2.50 6.00
59 A.J. Feeley 2.50 6.00
60 Chris Chambers 2.50 6.00
61 David Boston 2.50 6.00
62 Jason Taylor 3.00 8.00
63 Jay Fiedler 2.50 6.00
64 Junior Seau 4.00 10.00
65 Randy McMichael 2.50 6.00
66 Ricky Williams 3.00 8.00
67 Zach Thomas 3.00 8.00
68 Daunte Culpepper 3.00 8.00
69 Michael Bennett 2.50 6.00
70 Randy Moss 3.00 8.00
71 Tom Brady 15.00 40.00
72 Troy Brown 2.50 6.00
73 Ty Law 4.00 10.00
74 Aaron Brooks 2.50 6.00
75 Deuce McAllister 3.00 8.00
76 Donte Stallworth 2.50 6.00
77 Amani Toomer 2.50 6.00
78 Jeremy Shockey 2.50 6.00
79 Kerry Collins 2.50 6.00
80 Michael Strahan 3.00 8.00
81 Tiki Barber 3.00 8.00
82 Chad Pennington 2.50 6.00
83 Curtis Martin 3.00 8.00
84 Justin McCareins 2.50 6.00
85 Santana Moss 3.00 8.00
86 Charles Woodson 4.00 10.00
87 Jerry Rice 8.00 20.00
88 Rich Gannon 3.00 8.00
89 Tim Brown 4.00 10.00
90 Warren Sapp 3.00 8.00
91 Correll Buckhalter 2.50 6.00
92 Donovan McNabb 3.00 8.00
93 Freddie Mitchell 2.50 6.00
94 Jevon Kearse 2.50 6.00
95 Terrell Owens 3.00 8.00
96 Antwaan Randle El 2.50 6.00
97 Duce Staley 2.50 6.00
98 Hines Ward 3.00 8.00
99 Jerome Bettis 4.00 10.00
100 Plaxico Burress 2.50 6.00
101 Doug Flutie 3.00 8.00
102 LaDainian Tomlinson 4.00 10.00
103 Koren Robinson 2.50 6.00
104 Matt Hasselbeck 2.50 6.00
105 Shaun Alexander 2.50 6.00
106 Isaac Bruce 4.00 10.00
107 Kurt Warner 3.00 8.00
108 Marc Bulger 2.50 6.00
109 Marshall Faulk 3.00 8.00
110 Torry Holt 3.00 8.00
111 Brad Johnson 3.00 8.00
112 Mike Alstott 2.50 6.00
113 Derrick Mason 2.50 6.00
114 Drew Bennett 3.00 8.00
115 Eddie George 3.00 8.00
116 Frank Wycheck 3.00 8.00
117 Keith Bulluck 2.50 6.00
118 Steve McNair 3.00 8.00
119 Tyrone Calico 3.00 8.00
120 Clinton Portis 2.50 6.00
121 LaVar Arrington 2.50 6.00
122 Laveranues Coles 2.50 6.00
123 Mark Brunell 3.00 8.00
124 Patrick Ramsey 3.00 8.00
125 Rod Gardner 2.50 6.00
126 Jake Plummer FLB 2.50 6.00
127 Thomas Jones FLB 2.50 6.00
128 Priest Holmes FLB 2.50 6.00
129 Jim Kelly FLB 5.00 12.00
130 Doug Flutie FLB 3.00 8.00
131 Walter Payton FLB 20.00 50.00
132 Troy Aikman FLB 6.00 15.00
133 John Elway FLB 8.00 20.00
134 Barry Sanders FLB 8.00 20.00
135 Mark Brunell FLB 3.00 8.00
136 Earl Campbell FLB 5.00 12.00
137 Joe Montana FLB 15.00 40.00
138 Dan Marino FLB 10.00 25.00
139 Curtis Martin FLB 3.00 8.00
140 Drew Bledsoe FLB 3.00 8.00
141 Ricky Williams FLB 3.00 8.00
142 Junior Seau FLB 4.00 10.00
143 Charlie Garner FLB 3.00 8.00
144 Jerry Rice FLB 8.00 20.00
145 Ahman Green FLB 3.00 8.00
146 Jerome Bettis FLB 6.00 15.00
147 Trent Green FLB 2.50 6.00
148 Warrick Dunn FLB 2.50 6.00
149 Deion Sanders FLB 6.00 15.00
150 Stephen Davis FLB 2.50 6.00

2004 Leaf Certified Materials Mirror Blue Signatures

UE STATED PRINT RUN 15-100
BLUES #'d UNDER 20 NOT PRICED
UNPRICED BLACK PRINT RUN 1 SET
UNPRICED EMERALD PRINT RUN 5 SETS
1 Anquan Boldin/50 8.00 20.00
3 Josh McCown/100 8.00 20.00
5 Michael Vick/100 12.00 30.00
21 Brian Urlacher/40 25.00 60.00
22 Rex Grossman/100 6.00 15.00
30 Keyshawn Johnson/20 12.00 30.00
32 Roy Williams S/89 6.00 15.00
40 Joey Harrington/20 10.00 25.00
41 Ahman Green/60 10.00 25.00
44 Javon Walker/20 10.00 25.00
56 Priest Holmes/25 10.00 25.00
60 Chris Chambers/20 10.00 25.00
69 Michael Bennett/84 6.00 15.00
74 Aaron Brooks/28 10.00 25.00
75 Deuce McAllister/50 10.00 25.00
80 Michael Strahan/25 12.00 30.00
82 Chad Pennington/20 10.00 25.00
85 Santana Moss/100 8.00 20.00
96 Antwaan Randle El/38 10.00 25.00
98 Hines Ward/25 30.00 60.00
102 LaDainian Tomlinson/25 25.00 60.00
104 Matt Hasselbeck/87 6.00 15.00
105 Shaun Alexander/25 10.00 25.00
129 Jim Kelly FLB/25 30.00 80.00
137 Joe Montana FLB/25 60.00 120.00
152 Ahmad Carroll/25 10.00 25.00
161 Chris Gamble/75 6.00 15.00
165 D.J. Hackett/75 6.00 15.00
166 D.J. Williams/100 10.00 25.00
169 Ernest Wilford/25 12.00 30.00
177 Jerricho Cotchery/75 8.00 20.00
181 Johnnie Morant/50 8.00 20.00
183 Jonathan Vilma/75 8.00 20.00
184 Josh Harris/25 10.00 25.00
185 Kenechi Udeze/100 8.00 20.00
189 Michael Turner/100 6.00 15.00
190 P.K. Sam/100 6.00 15.00
191 Quincy Wilson/50 8.00 20.00
194 Samie Parker/75 6.00 15.00
196 Tommie Harris/50 10.00 25.00
199 Vince Wilfork/100 10.00 25.00
200 Will Smith/75 8.00 20.00

2004 Leaf Certified Materials Mirror Gold Signatures

LD PRINT RUN 10-25
GOLD SER.#'d LESS THAN 25 UNPRICED
1 Anquan Boldin/25 10.00 25.00
3 Josh McCown/25 12.00 30.00
5 Michael Vick/25 20.00 50.00
22 Rex Grossman/25 10.00 25.00
23 Chad Johnson/25 10.00 25.00
32 Roy Williams S/25 10.00 25.00
41 Ahman Green/25 12.00 30.00
42 Brett Favre/20 150.00 250.00
47 David Carr/25 10.00 25.00
54 Jimmy Smith/20 12.00 30.00
55 Dante Hall/25 10.00 25.00
69 Michael Bennett/25 10.00 25.00
85 Santana Moss/25 12.00 30.00
96 Antwaan Randle El/25 10.00 25.00
104 Matt Hasselbeck/25 10.00 25.00
113 Derrick Mason/25 10.00 25.00
122 Laveranues Coles/25 10.00 25.00
161 Chris Gamble/25 10.00 25.00
165 D.J. Hackett/25 10.00 25.00
166 D.J. Williams/25 15.00 40.00
177 Jerricho Cotchery/25 12.00 30.00
181 Johnnie Morant/25 10.00 25.00
183 Jonathan Vilma/25 12.00 30.00
185 Kenechi Udeze/25 12.00 30.00
189 Michael Turner/25 10.00 25.00
190 P.K. Sam/25 10.00 25.00
191 Quincy Wilson/25 10.00 25.00
194 Samie Parker/25 10.00 25.00
196 Tommie Harris/25 12.00 30.00
199 Vince Wilfork/25 15.00 40.00
200 Will Smith/25 12.00 30.00

2004 Leaf Certified Materials Mirror Red Signatures

D STATED PRINT RUN 20-250
RED SER. #'d UNDER 20 NOT PRICED
1 Anquan Boldin/89 6.00 15.00
3 Josh McCown/135 6.00 15.00
5 Michael Vick/120 12.00 30.00
14 Drew Bledsoe/20 12.00 30.00
21 Brian Urlacher/50 25.00 60.00
22 Rex Grossman/237 5.00 12.00
30 Keyshawn Johnson/40 10.00 25.00
32 Roy Williams S/125 5.00 12.00
40 Joey Harrington/32 10.00 25.00
41 Ahman Green/60 10.00 25.00
44 Javon Walker/31 10.00 25.00
49 Marvin Harrison/20 12.00 30.00
50 Peyton Manning/20 75.00 150.00
56 Priest Holmes/63 8.00 20.00
60 Chris Chambers/31 10.00 25.00
69 Michael Bennett/125 5.00 12.00
71 Tom Brady/20 125.00 200.00
75 Deuce McAllister/85 8.00 20.00
80 Michael Strahan/60 10.00 25.00
82 Chad Pennington/30 10.00 25.00
85 Santana Moss/250 6.00 15.00
96 Antwaan Randle El/50 8.00 20.00
98 Hines Ward/49 15.00 40.00
102 LaDainian Tomlinson/60 20.00 50.00
105 Shaun Alexander/60 8.00 20.00
115 Eddie George/20 12.00 30.00
120 Clinton Portis/20 10.00 25.00
129 Jim Kelly FLB/48 20.00 50.00
132 Troy Aikman FLB/20 40.00 80.00
136 Earl Campbell FLB/20 20.00 50.00
137 Joe Montana FLB/60 60.00 100.00
145 Ahman Green FLB/100 8.00 20.00
152 Ahmad Carroll/90 6.00 15.00
161 Chris Gamble/100 6.00 15.00
165 D.J. Hackett/90 6.00 15.00
166 D.J. Williams/250 8.00 20.00
169 Ernest Wilford/55 10.00 25.00
177 Jerricho Cotchery/90 8.00 20.00
181 Johnnie Morant/90 6.00 15.00
183 Jonathan Vilma/225 6.00 15.00
185 Kenechi Udeze/165 6.00 15.00
189 Michael Turner/130 5.00 12.00
190 P.K. Sam/215 5.00 12.00
191 Quincy Wilson/90 6.00 15.00
194 Samie Parker/140 5.00 12.00
196 Tommie Harris/75 8.00 20.00
199 Vince Wilfork/225 8.00 20.00
200 Will Smith/100 8.00 20.00

2005 Leaf Certified Materials

is 229-card set was released in September, 2005. The set was issued through the hobby in five-card packs with an $10 SRP which came 10 packs to a box. Cards numbered 151-229 all feature 2005 rookies with cards numbered 201-229 also including a player-worn jersey swatch. Those cards from 151-200 were all issued to a stated print run of 1000 serial numbered sets while the cards 201-229 were issued to stated print runs between 499 and 1499 serial numbered sets.

COMP.SET w/o RCs (150) 15.00 40.00
151-200 ROOKIE PRINT RUN 1000
1 Anquan Boldin .25 .60
2 Josh McCown .30 .75
3 Larry Fitzgerald .40 1.00
4 Michael Vick .30 .75
5 Peerless Price .25 .60
6 T.J. Duckett .25 .60
7 Warrick Dunn .25 .60
8 Jamal Lewis .30 .75
9 Kyle Boller .25 .60
10 Todd Heap .25 .60
11 Ray Lewis .40 1.00
12 Terrell Suggs .25 .60
13 Drew Bledsoe .30 .75
14 Eric Moulds .25 .60
15 J.P. Losman .25 .60
16 Lee Evans .30 .75
17 Willis McGahee .25 .60
18 DeShaun Foster .30 .75
19 Jake Delhomme .25 .60
20 Steve Smith .40 1.00
21 Brian Urlacher .40 1.00
22 Rex Grossman .25 .60
23 Carson Palmer .30 .75
24 Chad Johnson .25 .60
25 Rudi Johnson .25 .60
26 Kellen Winslow Jr. .25 .60
27 Kelly Holcomb .25 .60
28 Lee Suggs .25 .60
29 William Green .25 .60
30 Julius Jones .25 .60
31 Keyshawn Johnson .30 .75
32 Roy Williams S .25 .60
33 Terence Newman .25 .60
34 Ashley Lelie .25 .60
35 Champ Bailey .30 .75
36 Darius Watts .25 .60
37 Jake Plummer .25 .60
38 Tatum Bell .25 .60
39 Charles Rogers .25 .60
40 Joey Harrington .25 .60
41 Kevin Jones .25 .60
42 Roy Williams WR .25 .60
43 Ahman Green .30 .75
44 Brett Favre .75 2.00
45 Javon Walker .25 .60
46 Robert Ferguson .25 .60
47 Andre Johnson .30 .75
48 David Carr .25 .60
49 Domanick Davis .25 .60
50 Dallas Clark .25 .60
51 Edgerrin James .30 .75
52 Marvin Harrison .30 .75
53 Peyton Manning 1.00 2.50
54 Reggie Wayne .30 .75
55 Byron Leftwich .25 .60
56 Fred Taylor .25 .60
57 Jimmy Smith .30 .75
58 Reggie Williams .25 .60
59 Priest Holmes .25 .60
60 Tony Gonzalez .30 .75
61 Trent Green .25 .60
62 Chris Chambers .25 .60
63 Jason Taylor .30 .75
64 Junior Seau .30 .75
65 Zach Thomas .30 .75
66 Daunte Culpepper .30 .75
67 Michael Bennett .25 .60
68 Randy Moss .30 .75
69 Corey Dillon .25 .60
70 Tom Brady 1.50 4.00
71 Deion Branch .25 .60
72 Aaron Brooks .25 .60
73 Deuce McAllister .30 .75
74 Donte Stallworth .25 .60
75 Joe Horn .25 .60
76 Eli Manning .60 1.50
77 Jeremy Shockey .25 .60
78 Michael Strahan .30 .75
79 Tiki Barber .30 .75
80 Anthony Becht .25 .60
81 Chad Pennington .25 .60
82 Curtis Martin .30 .75
83 Justin McCareins .25 .60
84 Laveranues Coles .25 .60
85 Santana Moss .30 .75
86 Shaun Ellis .25 .60
87 Jerry Porter .25 .60
88 Brian Westbrook .25 .60
89 Chad Lewis .25 .60
90 Donovan McNabb .30 .75
91 Freddie Mitchell .25 .60
92 Hugh Douglas .25 .60
93 Jevon Kearse .25 .60
94 Terrell Owens .30 .75
95 Todd Pinkston .25 .60
96 Antwaan Randle El .25 .60
97 Ben Roethlisberger .60 1.50
98 Duce Staley .25 .60
99 Hines Ward .30 .75
100 Jerome Bettis .40 1.00
101 Antonio Gates .40 1.00
102 Drew Brees .40 1.00
103 LaDainian Tomlinson .40 1.00
104 Kevan Barlow .25 .60
105 Darrell Jackson .25 .60
106 Koren Robinson .25 .60
107 Matt Hasselbeck .25 .60
108 Shaun Alexander .25 .60
109 Marc Bulger .25 .60
110 Steven Jackson .25 .60
111 Torry Holt .30 .75
112 Michael Clayton .25 .60
113 Chris Brown .25 .60
114 Drew Bennett .30 .75
115 Keith Bulluck .25 .60
116 Steve McNair .30 .75
117 Clinton Portis .25 .60
118 LaVar Arrington .25 .60
119 John Riggins .40 1.00
120 Sean Taylor .40 1.00
121 Jake Plummer .25 .60
122 Thomas Jones .25 .60
123 Doug Flutie .30 .75
124 Walter Payton 1.25 3.00
125 Corey Dillon .25 .60
126 Troy Aikman .60 1.50
127 Terrell Davis .30 .75
128 Marshall Faulk .30 .75
129 Dan Marino 1.00 2.50
130 Thurman Thomas .40 1.00
131 Warren Moon .50 1.25
132 Curtis Martin .30 .75
133 Drew Bledsoe .30 .75
134 Kerry Collins .25 .60
135 Keyshawn Johnson .30 .75
136 A.J. Feeley .25 .60
137 Duce Staley .25 .60
138 Junior Seau .30 .75
139 Jerry Rice .75 2.00
140 Steve Young .60 1.50
141 Jerome Bettis .40 1.00
142 Kurt Warner .30 .75
143 Trent Green .25 .60
144 Keyshawn Johnson .30 .75
145 Warren Sapp .30 .75
146 Warrick Dunn .25 .60
147 Jevon Kearse .25 .60
148 Deion Sanders .40 1.00
149 Laveranues Coles .25 .60
150 Stephen Davis .25 .60
151 Cedric Benson RC 1.25 3.00
152 Mike Williams 1.50 4.00
153 DeMarcus Ware RC 4.00 10.00
154 Shawne Merriman RC 2.00 5.00
155 Thomas Davis RC 1.25 3.00
156 Derrick Johnson RC 1.50 4.00
157 Travis Johnson RC 1.25 3.00
158 David Pollack RC 1.25 3.00
159 Erasmus James RC 1.25 3.00
160 Marcus Spears RC 1.25 3.00
161 Fabian Washington RC 1.25 3.00
162 Aaron Rodgers RC 20.00 40.00
163 Marlin Jackson RC 1.25 3.00
164 Heath Miller RC 2.50 6.00
165 Matt Roth RC 1.25 3.00
166 Dan Cody RC 1.25 3.00
167 Bryant McFadden RC 1.50 4.00
168 Chris Henry RC 1.50 4.00
169 David Greene RC 1.25 3.00
170 Brandon Jones RC 1.50 4.00
171 Marion Barber RC 1.25 3.00
172 Brandon Jacobs RC 1.50 4.00
173 Jerome Mathis RC 2.00 5.00
174 Craphonso Thorpe RC 1.25 3.00
175 Alvin Pearman RC 1.25 3.00
176 Darren Sproles RC 2.00 5.00
177 Fred Gibson RC 1.25 3.00
178 Roydell Williams RC 1.50 4.00
179 Airese Currie RC 1.25 3.00
180 Damien Nash RC 1.50 4.00
181 Dan Orlovsky RC 1.25 3.00
182 Adrian McPherson RC 1.25 3.00
183 Larry Brackins RC 1.25 3.00
184 Rasheed Marshall RC 1.50 4.00
185 Cedric Houston RC 2.00 5.00
186 Chad Owens RC 1.25 3.00
187 Tab Perry RC 1.25 3.00
188 Dante Ridgeway RC 1.25 3.00
189 Craig Bragg RC 1.25 3.00
190 Deandra Cobb RC 1.25 3.00
191 Derek Anderson RC 1.50 4.00
192 Paris Warren RC 1.50 4.00
193 Lionel Gates RC 1.25 3.00
194 Anthony Davis RC 1.25 3.00
195 Ryan Fitzpatrick RC 2.00 5.00
196 J.R. Russell RC 1.25 3.00
197 Jason White RC 2.00 5.00
198 Kay-Jay Harris RC 1.25 3.00
199 T.A. McLendon RC 1.25 3.00
200 Taylor Stubblefield RC 1.25 3.00
201 Adam Jones JSY/1499 RC 2.00 5.00
202 Alex Smith QB JSY/499 RC 12.50 30.00
203 Andrew Walter JSY/1249 RC 2.00 5.00
204 Antrel Rolle JSY/999 RC 3.00 8.00
205 Braylon Edwards JSY/499 RC 2.50 6.00
206 Cadillac Williams JSY/499 RC 2.50 6.00
207 Carlos Rogers JSY/1499 RC 2.00 5.00
208 Charlie Frye JSY/1499 RC 1.25 3.00
209 Ciatrick Fason JSY/1499 RC 2.00 5.00
210 Courtney Roby JSY/1249 RC 2.00 5.00
211 Eric Shelton JSY/999 RC 2.00 5.00
212 Frank Gore JSY/999 RC 5.00 12.00
213 J.J. Arrington JSY/499 RC 3.00 8.00
214 Kyle Orton JSY/1499 RC 2.00 5.00
215 Jason Campbell JSY/749 RC 2.00 5.00
216 Mark Bradley JSY/999 RC 2.00 5.00
217 Mark Clayton JSY/499 RC 2.50 6.00
218 Matt Jones JSY/749 RC 2.00 5.00
219 Maurice Clarett JSY/999 2.00 5.00
220 Reggie Brown JSY/999 RC 2.00 5.00
221 Roddy White JSY/749 RC 3.00 8.00
222 Ronnie Brown JSY/499 RC 3.00 8.00
223 Roscoe Parrish JSY/999 RC 2.00 5.00
224 Ryan Moats JSY/999 RC 2.00 5.00
225 Stefan LeFors JSY/1499 RC 2.00 5.00
226 Terrence Murphy JSY/1499 RC 2.00 5.00
227 Troy Williamson JSY/749 RC 2.00 5.00
228 Vernand Morency JSY/1499 RC 2.00 5.00
229 Vincent Jackson JSY/1499 RC 3.00 8.00

2005 Leaf Certified Materials Mirror Blue

*VETERANS: 5X TO 12X BASIC CARDS
*ROOKIES: 1X TO 2.5X BASIC CARDS
MIRROR BLUE PRINT RUN 50 SER.#'d SETS
162 Aaron Rodgers 100.00 200.00

2005 Leaf Certified Materials Mirror Gold

*VETERANS: 8X TO 20X BASIC CARDS
*ROOKIES: 2X TO 5X BASIC CARDS
MIRROR GOLD PRINT RUN 25 SER.#'d SETS
162 Aaron Rodgers 100.00 200.00

2005 Leaf Certified Materials Mirror Red

*VETERANS: 3X TO 8X BASIC CARDS
*ROOKIES: .8X TO 2X BASIC CARDS
MIRROR RED PRINT RUN 100 SER.#'d SETS
162 Aaron Rodgers 75.00 150.00

2005 Leaf Certified Materials Mirror White

*VETERANS: 2X TO 5X BASIC CARDS
*ROOKIES: .5X TO 1.2X BASIC CARDS
MIRR.WHITE PRINT RUN 150 SER.#'d SETS
162 Aaron Rodgers 50.00 100.00

2005 Leaf Certified Materials Certified Potential

STATED PRINT RUN 750 SER.#'d SETS
UNPRICED BLACK PRINT RUN 10 SETS
*BLUE/100: .8X TO 2X BASIC INSERTS
*EMERALD/25: 2X TO 5X BASIC INSERTS
*GOLD/50: 1.2X TO 3X BASIC INSERTS
*MIRROR/500: .5X TO 1.2X BASIC INSERTS
*RED/250: .6X TO 1.5X BASIC INSERTS
1 Anquan Boldin .75 2.00
2 Larry Fitzgerald 1.25 3.00
3 Kyle Boller .75 2.00
4 Lee Evans 1.00 2.50
5 Willis McGahee .75 2.00
6 DeShaun Foster 1.00 2.50
7 Rex Grossman .75 2.00
8 Carson Palmer 1.00 2.50
9 Julius Jones .75 2.00
10 Ashley Lelie .75 2.00
11 Kevin Jones .75 2.00
12 Roy Williams WR .75 2.00
13 Javon Walker .75 2.00
14 Andre Johnson 1.00 2.50
15 Domanick Davis .75 2.00
16 Byron Leftwich .75 2.00
17 Reggie Williams .75 2.00
18 Nate Burleson .75 2.00
19 Eli Manning 2.00 5.00
20 Ben Roethlisberger 2.00 5.00
21 Antonio Gates 1.25 3.00
22 Steven Jackson .75 2.00
23 Michael Clayton .75 2.00
24 Sean Taylor 1.25 3.00
25 Kellen Winslow .75 2.00

2005 Leaf Certified Materials Certified Potential Jersey

STATED PRINT RUN 150 SER.#'d SETS
*INFINITE/75: .5X TO 1.2X BASIC JSY/150
*PRIME/25: 1X TO 2.5X BASIC JSY/150
UNPRICED BLACK PRINT RUN 1 SET
1 Anquan Boldin 2.50 6.00
2 Larry Fitzgerald 4.00 10.00
3 Kyle Boller 2.50 6.00
4 Lee Evans 3.00 8.00
5 Willis McGahee 2.50 6.00
6 DeShaun Foster 3.00 8.00
7 Rex Grossman 2.50 6.00
8 Carson Palmer 3.00 8.00
9 Julius Jones 2.50 6.00
10 Ashley Lelie 2.50 6.00
11 Kevin Jones 2.50 6.00
12 Roy Williams WR 2.50 6.00
13 Javon Walker 2.50 6.00
14 Andre Johnson 3.00 8.00
15 Domanick Davis 2.50 6.00
16 Byron Leftwich 2.50 6.00
17 Reggie Williams 2.50 6.00
18 Nate Burleson 2.50 6.00
19 Eli Manning 6.00 15.00
20 Ben Roethlisberger 6.00 15.00
21 Antonio Gates 4.00 10.00
22 Steven Jackson 2.50 6.00
23 Michael Clayton 2.50 6.00
24 Sean Taylor 10.00 25.00
25 Kellen Winslow 2.50 6.00

2005 Leaf Certified Materials Certified Skills

STATED PRINT RUN 750 SER.#'d SETS
UNPRICED BLACK PRINT RUN 10 SETS
*BLUE/100: .8X TO 2X BASIC INSERTS
*EMERALD/25: 2X TO 5X BASIC INSERTS
*GOLD/50: 1.2X TO 3X BASIC INSERTS
*MIRROR/500: .5X TO 1.2X BASIC INSERTS
*RED/250: .6X TO 1.5X BASIC INSERTS
1 Daunte Culpepper 1.00 2.50
2 Trent Green .75 2.00
3 Peyton Manning 3.00 8.00
4 Jake Plummer .75 2.00
5 Brett Favre 2.50 6.00
6 Marc Bulger .75 2.00
7 Jake Delhomme .75 2.00
8 Donovan McNabb 1.00 2.50
9 Aaron Brooks .75 2.00
10 Tom Brady 5.00 12.00
11 David Carr .75 2.00
12 Matt Hasselbeck .75 2.00
13 Drew Brees 1.25 3.00
14 Joey Harrington .75 2.00
15 Curtis Martin 1.00 2.50
16 Shaun Alexander .75 2.00
17 Corey Dillon .75 2.00
18 Edgerrin James 1.00 2.50
19 Tiki Barber 1.00 2.50
20 Rudi Johnson .75 2.00
21 LaDainian Tomlinson 1.25 3.00
22 Clinton Portis .75 2.00
23 Domanick Davis .75 2.00
24 Ahman Green 1.00 2.50
25 Kevin Jones .75 2.00
26 Willis McGahee .75 2.00
27 Deuce McAllister 1.00 2.50
28 Chris Brown .75 2.00
29 Jamal Lewis 1.00 2.50
30 Jerome Bettis 1.25 3.00
31 Priest Holmes .75 2.00
32 Joe Horn .75 2.00
33 Javon Walker .75 2.00
34 Torry Holt 1.00 2.50
35 Chad Johnson .75 2.00
36 Drew Bennett 1.00 2.50
37 Reggie Wayne 1.00 2.50
38 Terrell Owens 1.00 2.50
39 Darrell Jackson .75 2.00
40 Michael Clayton .75 2.00
41 Jimmy Smith 1.00 2.50
42 Rod Smith 1.00 2.50
43 Andre Johnson 1.00 2.50
44 Marvin Harrison 1.00 2.50
45 Ashley Lelie .75 2.00
46 Eric Moulds .75 2.00
47 Nate Burleson .75 2.00
48 Hines Ward 1.00 2.50
49 Antonio Gates 1.25 3.00
50 Laveranues Coles .75 2.00

2005 Leaf Certified Materials Certified Skills Jersey

STATED PRINT RUN 175 SER.#'d SETS
UNPRICED BLACK PRINT RUN 1 SET
*POSITION/75: .5X TO 1.2X BASIC JSY/175
*PRIME/25: 1X TO 2.5X BASIC JSY/175
1 Daunte Culpepper 3.00 8.00
2 Trent Green 2.50 6.00
3 Peyton Manning 10.00 25.00
4 Jake Plummer 2.50 6.00
5 Brett Favre 8.00 20.00
6 Marc Bulger 2.50 6.00
7 Jake Delhomme 2.50 6.00
8 Donovan McNabb 3.00 8.00
9 Aaron Brooks 2.50 6.00
10 Tom Brady 15.00 40.00
11 David Carr 2.50 6.00
12 Matt Hasselbeck 2.50 6.00
13 Drew Brees 4.00 10.00
14 Joey Harrington 2.50 6.00
15 Curtis Martin 3.00 8.00
16 Shaun Alexander 2.50 6.00
17 Corey Dillon 2.50 6.00
18 Edgerrin James 3.00 8.00
19 Tiki Barber 3.00 8.00
20 Rudi Johnson 2.50 6.00
21 LaDainian Tomlinson 4.00 10.00
22 Clinton Portis 2.50 6.00
23 Domanick Davis 2.50 6.00
24 Ahman Green 3.00 8.00
25 Kevin Jones 2.50 6.00
26 Willis McGahee 2.50 6.00
27 Deuce McAllister 3.00 8.00
28 Chris Brown 2.50 6.00
29 Jamal Lewis 3.00 8.00
30 Jerome Bettis 5.00 12.00
31 Priest Holmes 2.50 6.00
32 Joe Horn 2.50 6.00
33 Javon Walker 2.50 6.00
34 Torry Holt 3.00 8.00
35 Chad Johnson 2.50 6.00
36 Drew Bennett 3.00 8.00
37 Reggie Wayne 3.00 8.00
38 Terrell Owens 3.00 8.00
39 Darrell Jackson 2.50 6.00
40 Michael Clayton 2.50 6.00
41 Jimmy Smith 3.00 8.00
42 Rod Smith 3.00 8.00
43 Andre Johnson 3.00 8.00
44 Marvin Harrison 3.00 8.00
45 Ashley Lelie 2.50 6.00
46 Eric Moulds 2.50 6.00
47 Nate Burleson 2.50 6.00
48 Hines Ward 3.00 8.00
49 Antonio Gates 4.00 10.00
50 Laveranues Coles 2.50 6.00

2005 Leaf Certified Materials Fabric of the Game

STATED PRINT RUN 100 SER.#'d SETS
UNPRICED TEAM LOGO PRINT RUN 5 SETS
1 Barry Sanders 12.00 30.00
2 Bart Starr 12.00 30.00
3 Ben Roethlisberger 8.00 20.00
4 Bo Jackson 10.00 25.00
5 Bob Griese 8.00 20.00
6 Boomer Esiason 6.00 15.00
7 Brett Favre 10.00 25.00
8 Brian Urlacher 5.00 12.00
9 Byron Leftwich 3.00 8.00
10 Carson Palmer 4.00 10.00
11 Chad Johnson 3.00 8.00
12 Chad Pennington 3.00 8.00
13 Clinton Portis 3.00 8.00
14 Corey Dillon 3.00 8.00
15 Cris Collinsworth 6.00 15.00
16 Dan Marino 12.00 30.00
17 Dan Fouts 6.00 15.00
18 Eli Manning 8.00 20.00
19 Daryl Johnston 8.00 20.00
20 David Carr 3.00 8.00
21 Deacon Jones 6.00 15.00
22 Deion Sanders 6.00 15.00
23 Don Maynard 6.00 15.00
24 Don Meredith 15.00 40.00
25 Don Shula 8.00 20.00
26 Donovan McNabb 4.00 10.00
27 Earl Campbell 8.00 20.00
28 Fran Tarkenton 8.00 20.00
29 Gale Sayers 8.00 20.00
30 Gene Upshaw 6.00 15.00
31 Herman Edwards 5.00 12.00
32 Herschel Walker 8.00 20.00
33 Hines Ward 4.00 10.00
34 Ickey Woods 5.00 12.00
35 James Lofton 5.00 12.00
36 Jerry Rice 10.00 25.00
37 Jevon Kearse 3.00 8.00
38 Jim Brown 10.00 25.00
39 Jim Kelly 8.00 20.00
40 Joe Greene 8.00 20.00
41 Joe Montana 25.00 60.00
42 Joe Namath 12.00 30.00
43 John Elway 12.00 30.00
44 John Riggins 6.00 15.00
45 John Taylor 5.00 12.00
46 L.C. Greenwood 5.00 12.00
47 Julius Jones 3.00 8.00
48 Lawrence Taylor 8.00 20.00
49 Leroy Kelly 6.00 15.00
50 Marcus Allen 8.00 20.00
51 Michael Irvin 8.00 20.00
52 Michael Vick 6.00 15.00
53 Mike Ditka 8.00 20.00
54 Mike Singletary 8.00 20.00
55 Ozzie Newsome 6.00 15.00
56 Paul Warfield 6.00 15.00
57 Peyton Manning 12.00 30.00
58 Priest Holmes 3.00 8.00
59 Randall Cunningham 6.00 15.00
60 Roger Craig 8.00 20.00
61 Richard Dent 6.00 15.00
62 Roger Staubach 10.00 25.00
63 Rudi Johnson 3.00 8.00
64 Domanick Davis 3.00 8.00
65 Sonny Jurgensen 6.00 15.00
66 Steve Largent 8.00 20.00
67 Sterling Sharpe 6.00 15.00
68 Steve Young 10.00 25.00
69 Steven Jackson 3.00 8.00
70 Tatum Bell 3.00 8.00
71 Terrell Davis 6.00 15.00
72 Andre Johnson 4.00 10.00
73 Terry Bradshaw 10.00 25.00
74 Thurman Thomas 6.00 15.00
75 Tom Brady 20.00 50.00
76 Tony Dorsett 8.00 20.00
77 Troy Aikman 10.00 25.00
78 Walter Payton 15.00 40.00
79 Warren Moon 8.00 20.00
80 Willis McGahee 3.00 8.00
81 J.Unitas/J.Thorpe 60.00 120.00
82 L.Arrington/R.Lewis 6.00 15.00
83 T.Barber/J.Lewis 5.00 12.00
84 A.Brooks/J.Harrington 4.00 10.00
85 B.Westbrook/A.Green 5.00 12.00
86 T.Owens/A.Boldin 5.00 12.00
87 A.Gates/T.Heap 6.00 15.00
88 M.Hasselbeck/T.Green 4.00 10.00
89 C.Martin/S.Alexander 5.00 12.00
90 M.Clayton/R.Williams WR 4.00 10.00
91 D.Culpepper/S.McNair 5.00 12.00
92 L.Fitzgerald/J.Walker 6.00 15.00
93 L.Tomlinson/K.Jones 6.00 15.00
94 D.Brees/M.Bulger 6.00 15.00
95 R.Nitschke/Reg.White 20.00 50.00
96 R.Moss/M.Harrison 5.00 12.00
97 J.Shockey/T.Gonzalez 5.00 12.00
98 S.Smith/T.Holt 6.00 15.00
99 C.Brown/D.McAllister 5.00 12.00
100 J.Plummer/J.Delhomme 4.00 10.00

2005 Leaf Certified Materials Fabric of the Game 21st Century

*21st CENT/21: 1X TO 2.5X BASIC JSY/100
81 J.Unitas/J.Thorpe 125.00 250.00

2005 Leaf Certified Materials Fabric of the Game Debut Year

EBUT YEAR/70-104: .4X TO 1X
*DEBUT YEAR/51-69: .5X TO 1.2X
DEBUT YEAR PRINT RUN 51-104
81 J.Unitas/J.Thorpe 90.00 150.00

2005 Leaf Certified Materials Fabric of the Game Jersey Number

ERSEY/56-89: .5X TO 1.2X BASIC JSY
*JERSEY/31-37: .8X TO 2X BASIC JSY
*JERSEY/17-29: 1X TO 2.5X BASIC JSY
SERIAL #'d UNDER 15 NOT PRICED
1 Barry Sanders AU/20 90.00 175.00
2 Bart Starr AU/15 100.00 200.00
4 Bo Jackson AU/34 90.00 150.00
8 Brian Urlacher AU/54 30.00 60.00
11 Chad Johnson AU/85 15.00 40.00
13 Clinton Portis AU/26 15.00 40.00
15 Cris Collinsworth AU/80 12.50 30.00
19 Daryl Johnston AU/48 30.00 60.00
21 Deacon Jones AU/75 12.50 30.00
22 Deion Sanders AU/21 50.00 100.00
24 Don Meredith AU/17 90.00 150.00
25 Don Shula AU/25 30.00 80.00
27 Earl Campbell AU/34 25.00 60.00
29 Gale Sayers AU/40 40.00 80.00
30 Gene Upshaw AU/63 25.00 50.00
31 Herman Edwards AU/46 10.00 25.00
32 Herschel Walker AU/34 15.00 40.00
33 Hines Ward AU/86 40.00 100.00
34 Ickey Woods AU/30 12.50 30.00
35 James Lofton AU/80 12.50 30.00
37 Jevon Kearse AU/93 10.00 25.00
38 Jim Brown AU/32 60.00 120.00
40 Joe Greene AU/75 40.00 80.00
41 Joe Montana AU/16 75.00 150.00
44 John Riggins AU/44 30.00 60.00
45 John Taylor AU/82 15.00 40.00
46 L.C. Greenwood AU/68 25.00 50.00
47 Julius Jones AU/21 12.50 30.00
48 Lawrence Taylor AU/56 50.00 100.00
49 Leroy Kelly AU/44 15.00 40.00
50 Marcus Allen AU/32 75.00 125.00
53 Mike Ditka AU/89 40.00 80.00
54 Mike Singletary AU/50 15.00 40.00
55 Ozzie Newsome AU/82 10.00 25.00
56 Paul Warfield AU/42 20.00 50.00
58 Priest Holmes AU/31 30.00 60.00
60 Roger Craig AU/33 30.00 60.00
61 Richard Dent AU/95 12.50 30.00
63 Rudi Johnson AU/32 15.00 40.00
64 Domanick Davis AU/37 15.00 40.00
66 Steve Largent AU/80 25.00 60.00
67 Sterling Sharpe AU/84 15.00 40.00
69 Steven Jackson AU/39 20.00 50.00
70 Tatum Bell AU/26 15.00 40.00
71 Terrell Davis AU/30 20.00 50.00
72 Andre Johnson AU/80 10.00 25.00
74 Thurman Thomas AU/34 15.00 40.00
76 Tony Dorsett AU/33 40.00 80.00
80 Willis McGahee AU/21 12.50 30.00
81 J.Unitas/J.Thorpe 125.00 250.00

2005 Leaf Certified Materials Gold Team

ATED PRINT RUN 750 SER.#'d SETS
*MIRROR/500: .5X TO 1.2X BASIC INSERTS
1 Anquan Boldin .75 2.00
2 Antonio Gates 1.25 3.00
3 LaVar Arrington .75 2.00
4 Brett Favre 2.50 6.00
5 Brian Urlacher 1.25 3.00
6 Byron Leftwich .75 2.00
7 Chad Pennington .75 2.00
8 Deuce McAllister 1.00 2.50
9 Dan Marino 2.50 6.00
10 Daunte Culpepper 1.00 2.50
11 Donovan McNabb 1.00 2.50
12 Drew Brees 1.25 3.00
13 Earl Campbell 1.25 3.00
14 Edgerrin James 1.00 2.50
15 Gale Sayers 1.25 3.00
16 Michael Clayton .75 2.00
17 Jerry Rice 2.50 6.00
18 John Elway 2.00 5.00
19 LaDainian Tomlinson 1.25 3.00
20 Larry Fitzgerald 1.25 3.00
21 Michael Vick 1.00 2.50
22 Peyton Manning 3.00 8.00
23 Priest Holmes .75 2.00
24 Tom Brady 5.00 12.00
25 Troy Aikman 1.50 4.00

2005 Leaf Certified Materials Gold Team Jersey

ATED PRINT RUN 150 SER.#'d SETS
*24K/75: .5X TO 1.2X BASIC JSY/150
UNPRICED BLACK PRINT RUN 1 SET
*PRIME/25: 1X TO 2.5X BASIC JSY/150
1 Anquan Boldin 2.50 6.00
2 Antonio Gates 4.00 10.00
3 LaVar Arrington 2.50 6.00
4 Brett Favre 8.00 20.00
5 Brian Urlacher 4.00 10.00
6 Byron Leftwich 2.50 6.00
7 Chad Pennington 2.50 6.00
8 Deuce McAllister 3.00 8.00
9 Dan Marino 10.00 25.00
10 Daunte Culpepper 3.00 8.00
11 Donovan McNabb 3.00 8.00
12 Drew Brees 4.00 10.00
13 Earl Campbell 5.00 12.00
14 Edgerrin James 3.00 8.00
15 Gale Sayers 5.00 12.00
16 Michael Clayton 2.50 6.00
17 Jerry Rice 8.00 20.00
18 John Elway 8.00 20.00
19 LaDainian Tomlinson 4.00 10.00
20 Larry Fitzgerald 4.00 10.00
21 Michael Vick 5.00 12.00
22 Peyton Manning 10.00 25.00
23 Priest Holmes 2.50 6.00
24 Tom Brady 15.00 40.00
25 Troy Aikman 6.00 15.00

2005 Leaf Certified Materials Mirror Red Materials

150 VET RED PRINT RUN 100
201-229 ROOKIE RED PRINT RUN 150
UNPRICED MIR.BLACK PRINT RUN 1 SET
UNPRICED MIR.EMERALD PRINT RUN 5 SETS
1 Anquan Boldin 2.50 6.00
2 Josh McCown 3.00 8.00
3 Larry Fitzgerald 4.00 10.00
4 Michael Vick 3.00 8.00
5 Peerless Price 2.50 6.00
6 T.J. Duckett 2.50 6.00
7 Warrick Dunn 2.50 6.00
8 Jamal Lewis 3.00 8.00
9 Kyle Boller 2.50 6.00
10 Todd Heap 2.50 6.00
11 Ray Lewis 4.00 10.00
12 Terrell Suggs 2.50 6.00
13 Drew Bledsoe 3.00 8.00
14 Eric Moulds 2.50 6.00
15 J.P. Losman 2.50 6.00
16 Lee Evans 3.00 8.00
17 Willis McGahee 2.50 6.00
18 DeShaun Foster 3.00 8.00
19 Jake Delhomme 2.50 6.00
20 Steve Smith 4.00 10.00
21 Brian Urlacher 4.00 10.00
22 Rex Grossman 2.50 6.00
23 Carson Palmer 3.00 8.00
24 Chad Johnson 2.50 6.00
25 Rudi Johnson 2.50 6.00
26 Kellen Winslow 2.50 6.00
27 Kelly Holcomb 2.50 6.00
28 Lee Suggs 2.50 6.00
29 William Green 2.50 6.00
30 Julius Jones 2.50 6.00
31 Keyshawn Johnson 3.00 8.00

32 Roy Williams S 2.50 6.00
33 Terence Newman 2.50 6.00
34 Ashley Lelie 2.50 6.00
35 Champ Bailey 3.00 8.00
36 Darius Watts 2.50 6.00
37 Jake Plummer 2.50 6.00
38 Tatum Bell 2.50 6.00
39 Charles Rogers 2.50 6.00
40 Joey Harrington 2.50 6.00
41 Kevin Jones 2.50 6.00
42 Roy Williams WR 2.50 6.00
43 Ahman Green 3.00 8.00
44 Brett Favre 8.00 20.00
45 Javon Walker 2.50 6.00
46 Robert Ferguson 2.50 6.00
47 Andre Johnson 3.00 8.00
48 David Carr 2.50 6.00
49 Domanick Davis 2.50 6.00
50 Dallas Clark 2.50 6.00
51 Edgerrin James 3.00 8.00
52 Marvin Harrison 3.00 8.00
53 Peyton Manning 10.00 25.00
54 Reggie Wayne 3.00 8.00
55 Byron Leftwich 2.50 6.00
56 Fred Taylor 2.50 6.00
57 Jimmy Smith 3.00 8.00
58 Reggie Williams 2.50 6.00
59 Priest Holmes 2.50 6.00
60 Tony Gonzalez 3.00 8.00
61 Trent Green 2.50 6.00
62 Chris Chambers 2.50 6.00
63 Jason Taylor 3.00 8.00
64 Junior Seau 3.00 8.00
65 Zach Thomas 3.00 8.00
66 Daunte Culpepper 3.00 8.00
67 Michael Bennett 2.50 6.00
68 Randy Moss 3.00 8.00
69 Corey Dillon 2.50 6.00
70 Tom Brady 15.00 40.00
71 Deion Branch 2.50 6.00
72 Aaron Brooks 2.50 6.00
73 Deuce McAllister 3.00 8.00
74 Donte Stallworth 2.50 6.00
75 Joe Horn 2.50 6.00
76 Eli Manning 6.00 15.00
77 Jeremy Shockey 2.50 6.00
78 Michael Strahan 3.00 8.00
79 Tiki Barber 3.00 8.00
80 Anthony Becht 2.50 6.00
81 Chad Pennington 2.50 6.00
82 Curtis Martin 3.00 8.00
83 Justin McCareins 2.50 6.00
84 Laveranues Coles 2.50 6.00
85 Santana Moss 3.00 8.00
86 Shaun Ellis 2.50 6.00
87 Jerry Porter 2.50 6.00
88 Brian Westbrook 2.50 6.00
89 Chad Lewis 2.50 6.00
90 Donovan McNabb 3.00 8.00
91 Freddie Mitchell 2.50 6.00
92 Hugh Douglas 2.50 6.00
93 Jevon Kearse 2.50 6.00
94 Terrell Owens 3.00 8.00
95 Todd Pinkston 2.50 6.00
96 Antwaan Randle El 2.50 6.00
97 Ben Roethlisberger 6.00 15.00
98 Duce Staley 2.50 6.00
99 Hines Ward 3.00 8.00
100 Jerome Bettis 6.00 15.00
101 Antonio Gates 4.00 10.00
102 Drew Brees 4.00 10.00
103 LaDainian Tomlinson 4.00 10.00
104 Kevan Barlow 2.50 6.00
105 Darrell Jackson 2.50 6.00
106 Koren Robinson 2.50 6.00
107 Matt Hasselbeck 2.50 6.00
108 Shaun Alexander 2.50 6.00
109 Marc Bulger 2.50 6.00
110 Steven Jackson 2.50 6.00
111 Torry Holt 3.00 8.00
112 Michael Clayton 2.50 6.00
113 Chris Brown 2.50 6.00
114 Drew Bennett 3.00 8.00
115 Keith Bulluck 2.50 6.00
116 Steve McNair 3.00 8.00
117 Clinton Portis 2.50 6.00
118 LaVar Arrington 2.50 6.00
119 John Riggins 4.00 10.00
120 Sean Taylor 12.00 30.00
121 Jake Plummer 2.50 6.00
122 Thomas Jones 2.50 6.00
123 Doug Flutie 4.00 10.00
124 Walter Payton 12.00 30.00
125 Corey Dillon 2.50 6.00
126 Troy Aikman 6.00 15.00
127 Terrell Davis 4.00 10.00
128 Marshall Faulk 3.00 8.00
129 Dan Marino 10.00 25.00
130 Thurman Thomas 4.00 10.00
131 Warren Moon 5.00 12.00
132 Curtis Martin 3.00 8.00
133 Drew Bledsoe 3.00 8.00
134 Kerry Collins 2.50 6.00
135 Keyshawn Johnson 3.00 8.00
136 A.J. Feeley 2.50 6.00
137 Duce Staley 2.50 6.00
138 Junior Seau 3.00 8.00
139 Jerry Rice 8.00 20.00
140 Steve Young 6.00 15.00
141 Jerome Bettis 8.00 20.00
142 Kurt Warner 6.00 15.00
143 Trent Green 2.50 6.00
144 Keyshawn Johnson 3.00 8.00
145 Warren Sapp 3.00 8.00
146 Warrick Dunn 2.50 6.00
147 Jevon Kearse 2.50 6.00
148 Deion Sanders 4.00 10.00
149 Laveranues Coles 2.50 6.00
150 Stephen Davis 2.50 6.00
201 Adam Jones 2.00 5.00
202 Alex Smith QB 8.00 20.00
203 Andrew Walter 2.00 5.00
204 Antrel Rolle 3.00 8.00
205 Braylon Edwards 2.00 5.00
206 Cadillac Williams 2.00 5.00
207 Carlos Rogers 3.00 8.00
208 Charlie Frye 2.00 5.00
209 Ciatrick Fason 2.00 5.00
210 Courtney Roby 2.00 5.00
211 Eric Shelton 2.00 5.00
212 Frank Gore 4.00 10.00
213 J.J. Arrington 2.50 6.00
214 Kyle Orton 2.00 5.00
215 Jason Campbell 2.00 5.00
216 Mark Bradley 2.00 5.00
217 Mark Clayton 2.00 5.00
218 Matt Jones 2.00 5.00
219 Maurice Clarett 2.00 5.00
220 Reggie Brown 2.00 5.00
221 Roddy White 3.00 8.00
222 Ronnie Brown 2.50 6.00
223 Roscoe Parrish 2.00 5.00
224 Ryan Moats 2.00 5.00
225 Stefan LeFors 2.00 5.00
226 Terrence Murphy 2.00 5.00
227 Troy Williamson 2.00 5.00
228 Vernand Morency 2.00 5.00
229 Vincent Jackson 3.00 0.00

2005 Leaf Certified Materials Mirror Blue Materials

ETERANS: .8X TO 2X MIR.RED MATER.
*ROOKIES: 1.2X TO 3X MIRROR RED MATER.
BLUE PRINT RUN 50 SER.#'d SETS

2005 Leaf Certified Materials Mirror Gold Materials

ETERANS: 1.2X TO 3X MIR.RED MATER.
*ROOKIE: 2X TO 5X MIRROR RED MAT.
GOLD PRINT RUN 25 SER.#'d SETS

2005 Leaf Certified Materials Mirror White Materials

INGLES: .3X TO .8X MIRROR RED MATER.
MIR.WHITE PRINT RUN 175 SER.#'d SETS

2005 Leaf Certified Materials Mirror White Signatures

PRICED MIR.BLACK PRINT RUN 1 SET
UNPRICED MIR.EMER.PRINT RUN 5 SETS
4 Michael Vick/100 12.00 30.00
10 Todd Heap/50 6.00 15.00
15 J.P. Losman/50 6.00 15.00
16 Lee Evans/50 8.00 20.00
17 Willis McGahee/50 6.00 15.00
20 Steve Smith/100 8.00 20.00
30 Julius Jones/100 5.00 12.00
31 Keyshawn Johnson/25 10.00 25.00
33 Terence Newman/100 5.00 12.00
34 Ashley Lelie/50 6.00 15.00
38 Tatum Bell/50 6.00 15.00
40 Joey Harrington/25 8.00 20.00
54 Reggie Wayne/50 8.00 20.00
55 Byron Leftwich/50 6.00 15.00
57 Jimmy Smith/75 6.00 15.00
71 Deion Branch/75 5.00 12.00
72 Aaron Brooks/100 5.00 12.00
73 Deuce McAllister/50 8.00 20.00
75 Joe Horn/75 5.00 12.00
76 Eli Manning/125 40.00 80.00
79 Tiki Barber/50 20.00 40.00
93 Jevon Kearse/50 6.00 15.00
98 Duce Staley/50 6.00 15.00
99 Hines Ward/39 35.00 60.00
101 Antonio Gates/75 10.00 25.00
107 Matt Hasselbeck/75 5.00 12.00
110 Steven Jackson/79 5.00 12.00
112 Michael Clayton/100 5.00 12.00
113 Chris Brown/100 5.00 12.00
114 Drew Bennett/75 6.00 15.00
119 John Riggins/50 30.00 60.00
131 Warren Moon/50 15.00 40.00
140 Steve Young/50 40.00 80.00
153 DeMarcus Ware/100 25.00 50.00
154 Shawne Merriman/50 10.00 25.00
155 Thomas Davis/100 5.00 12.00
156 Derrick Johnson/50 8.00 20.00
157 Travis Johnson/100 5.00 12.00
158 David Pollack/50 6.00 15.00
159 Erasmus James/50 6.00 15.00
162 Aaron Rodgers/50 150.00 300.00
163 Marlin Jackson/100 5.00 12.00
164 Heath Miller/50 12.50 30.00
165 Matt Roth/100 5.00 12.00
166 Dan Cody/100 5.00 12.00
167 Bryant McFadden/100 6.00 15.00
168 Chris Henry/100 6.00 15.00
169 David Greene/100 5.00 12.00
170 Brandon Jones/100 6.00 15.00
171 Marion Barber/100 5.00 12.00
172 Brandon Jacobs/100 12.00 30.00
173 Jerome Mathis/100 8.00 20.00
174 Craphonso Thorpe/100 5.00 12.00
175 Alvin Pearman/100 5.00 12.00
176 Darren Sproles/100 20.00 40.00
177 Fred Gibson/100 5.00 12.00
178 Roydell Williams/100 6.00 15.00
179 Airese Currie/100 5.00 12.00
180 Damien Nash/100 6.00 15.00
181 Dan Orlovsky/100 5.00 12.00
182 Adrian McPherson/100 5.00 12.00
183 Larry Brackins/100 5.00 12.00
184 Rasheed Marshall/100 6.00 15.00
185 Cedric Houston/100 8.00 20.00
186 Chad Owens/100 5.00 12.00
187 Tab Perry/100 5.00 12.00
188 Dante Ridgeway/100 5.00 12.00
189 Craig Bragg/100 5.00 12.00
190 Deandra Cobb/100 5.00 12.00
191 Derek Anderson/100 6.00 15.00
192 Paris Warren/100 6.00 15.00
193 Lionel Gates/100 5.00 12.00
194 Anthony Davis/100 5.00 12.00
195 Ryan Fitzpatrick/100 8.00 20.00
196 J.R. Russell/100 5.00 12.00
197 Jason White/100 8.00 20.00
198 Kay-Jay Harris/100 5.00 12.00
199 T.A. McLendon/100 5.00 12.00
200 Taylor Stubblefield/100 5.00 12.00

2005 Leaf Certified Materials Mirror Blue Signatures

ETS/30-50: .6X TO 1.5X MIR.WHITE/100
*VETERANS/30: .6X TO 1.5X MIR.WHITE/75
*VETERANS/25: .6X TO 1.5X MIR.WHITE/100
*ROOKIES/30: .8X TO 2X MIR.WHITE/100
BLUE SER.#'d UNDER 25 NOT PRICED

2005 Leaf Certified Materials Mirror Gold Signatures

*GOLD/15-25: .6X TO 1.5X WHITE/75-100
97 Ben Roethlisberger/20 60.00 120.00

2005 Leaf Certified Materials Mirror Red Signatures

ED/70-75: .4X TO 1X WHITE/100
*RED/50: .5X TO 1.2X WHITE/75-100
*RED/25: .5X TO 1.2X WHITE/39-50
*RED/25: .6X TO 1.5X WHITE/100
RED STATED PRINT RUN 20-100
9 Kyle Boller/25 8.00 20.00
43 Ahman Green/25 15.00 40.00
71 Deion Branch/50 6.00 15.00
151 Cedric Benson/25 30.00 80.00
162 Aaron Rodgers/25 250.00 500.00

2006 Leaf Certified Materials

This 251-card set was released in September, 2006. The set was issued into the hobby in September, 2006. The set was five-card packs which came 10 packs to a box. Cards numbered 1-150 feature veterans in team alphabetical order while cards numbered 151-231 feature rookies and cards numbered 232-251 feature retired greats. Cards numbered 151-200 were issued to a stated print run of either 500 or 1000 copies, while cards numbered 201-232 all had player-worn swatches and those cards were issued to various print runs, which we have notated in our checklists and cards numbered 233-251 all feature game-worn swatches and those cards were issued to stated print runs of between 75 and 150 serial numbered copies.

COMP.SET w/o SP's (150) 15.00 40.00
1 Anquan Boldin .25 .60
2 Edgerrin James .30 .75
3 Kurt Warner .30 .75
4 Larry Fitzgerald .30 .75
5 Alge Crumpler .30 .75
6 Brian Finneran .25 .60
7 Michael Jenkins .25 .60
8 Michael Vick .30 .75
9 Warrick Dunn .25 .60
10 Derrick Mason .25 .60
11 Jamal Lewis .30 .75
12 Kyle Boller .25 .60
13 Todd Heap .25 .60
14 Mark Clayton .25 .60
15 Eric Moulds .25 .60
16 J.P. Losman .30 .75
17 Josh Reed .25 .60
18 Lee Evans .30 .75
19 Willis McGahee .25 .60
20 DeShaun Foster .30 .75
21 Jake Delhomme .25 .60
22 Stephen Davis .25 .60
23 Keary Colbert .25 .60
24 Steve Smith .40 1.00
25 Brian Urlacher .40 1.00
26 Cedric Benson .25 .60
27 Muhsin Muhammad .25 .60
28 Rex Grossman .25 .60
29 Thomas Jones .25 .60
30 Carson Palmer .30 .75
31 Chad Johnson .25 .60
32 Rudi Johnson .25 .60
33 T.J. Houshmandzadeh .25 .60
34 Charlie Frye .30 .75
35 Dennis Northcutt .25 .60
36 Braylon Edwards .25 .60
37 Reuben Droughns .30 .75
38 Drew Bledsoe .30 .75
39 Julius Jones .25 .60
40 Terrell Owens .30 .75
41 Jason Witten .30 .75
42 Terry Glenn .30 .75
43 Roy Williams S .25 .60
44 Jake Plummer .25 .60
45 Rod Smith .30 .75
46 Tatum Bell .25 .60
47 Ashley Lelie .25 .60
48 Josh McCown .25 .60
49 Kevin Jones .25 .60
50 Mike Williams .25 .60
51 Roy Williams WR .25 .60
52 Ahman Green .30 .75
53 Brett Favre .75 2.00
54 Aaron Rodgers 1.00 2.50
55 Samkon Gado .25 .60
56 Donald Driver .30 .75
57 Robert Ferguson .25 .60
58 Andre Johnson .30 .75
59 David Carr .25 .60
60 Domanick Davis .25 .60
61 Dallas Clark .25 .60
62 Marvin Harrison .30 .75
63 Peyton Manning 1.00 2.50
64 Reggie Wayne .30 .75
65 Brandon Stokley .25 .60
66 Byron Leftwich .25 .60
67 Fred Taylor .25 .60
68 Jimmy Smith .30 .75
69 Matt Jones .25 .60
70 Larry Johnson .25 .60
71 Tony Gonzalez .30 .75
72 Trent Green .25 .60
73 Eddie Kennison .25 .60
74 Samie Parker .25 .60
75 Chris Chambers .25 .60
76 Daunte Culpepper .30 .75
77 Randy McMichael .25 .60
78 Ronnie Brown .30 .75
79 Marty Booker .25 .60
80 Zach Thomas .30 .75
81 Brad Johnson .30 .75
82 Mewelde Moore .25 .60
83 Nate Burleson .25 .60
84 Troy Williamson .25 .60
85 Deion Branch .25 .60
86 Tom Brady 1.25 3.00
87 Corey Dillon .25 .60
88 Daniel Graham .25 .60
89 Troy Brown .25 .60
90 Deuce McAllister .30 .75
91 Donte Stallworth .25 .60
92 Drew Brees .40 1.00
93 Joe Horn .25 .60
94 Devery Henderson .25 .60
95 Eli Manning .30 .75
96 Jeremy Shockey .25 .60
97 Plaxico Burress .25 .60
98 Amani Toomer .25 .60
99 Tiki Barber .30 .75
100 Chad Pennington .25 .60
101 Curtis Martin .30 .75
102 Laveranues Coles .25 .60
103 Justin McCareins .25 .60
104 Jerry Porter .25 .60
105 LaMont Jordan .30 .75
106 Doug Gabriel .25 .60
107 Randy Moss .30 .75
108 Brian Westbrook .25 .60
109 Donovan McNabb .30 .75
110 Reggie Brown .25 .60
111 Chad Lewis .25 .60
112 Ryan Moats .25 .60
113 Jevon Kearse .25 .60
114 Ben Roethlisberger .50 1.25
115 Heath Miller .25 .60
116 Hines Ward .30 .75
117 Willie Parker .30 .75
118 Troy Polamalu .40 1.00
119 Antonio Gates .40 1.00
120 Eric Parker .25 .60
121 Keenan McCardell .30 .75
122 LaDainian Tomlinson .40 1.00
123 Philip Rivers .40 1.00
124 Alex Smith QB .30 .75
125 Antonio Bryant .25 .60
126 Frank Gore .30 .75
127 Kevan Barlow .25 .60
128 Darrell Jackson .30 .75
129 Jerramy Stevens .30 .75
130 Matt Hasselbeck .25 .60
131 Shaun Alexander .25 .60
132 Isaac Bruce .40 1.00
133 Marc Bulger .25 .60
134 Marshall Faulk .30 .75
135 Steven Jackson .25 .60
136 Torry Holt .30 .75
137 Cadillac Williams .30 .75
138 Chris Simms .25 .60
139 Joey Galloway .30 .75
140 Michael Clayton .25 .60
141 Brandon Jones .25 .60
142 Chris Brown .25 .60
143 Drew Bennett .30 .75
144 Tyrone Calico .25 .60
145 Steve McNair .30 .75
146 Antwaan Randle El .25 .60
147 Clinton Portis .25 .60
148 Mark Brunell .30 .75
149 Santana Moss .30 .75
150 Jason Campbell .25 .60
151 Brodie Croyle/500 RC 2.00 5.00
152 Greg Jennings/500 RC 3.00 8.00
153 Joseph Addai/500 RC 2.00 5.00
154 Bennie Brazell/1000 RC 1.50 4.00
155 David Thomas/500 RC 2.00 5.00
156 Marques Colston/1000 RC 2.00 5.00
157 Reggie McNeal/500 RC 2.00 5.00
158 D.J. Shockley/1000 RC 1.50 4.00
159 Dominique Byrd/500 RC 2.00 5.00
160 Antonio Cromartie/1000 RC 1.50 4.00
161 Donte Whitner/1000 RC 1.50 4.00
162 Anwar Phillips/1000 RC 1.50 4.00
163 A.J. Nicholson/1000 RC 1.25 3.00
164 De'Arrius Howard/500 RC 3.00 8.00
165 Erik Meyer/500 RC 2.00 5.00
166 Darrell Hackney/1000 RC 1.50 4.00
167 Paul Pinegar/500 RC 2.00 5.00
168 Brandon Kirsch/500 RC 2.50 6.00
169 Quinton Ganther/1000 RC 1.25 3.00
170 Andre Hall/1000 RC 1.50 4.00
171 Derrick Ross/1000 RC 1.50 4.00
172 Mike Bell/1000 RC 2.00 5.00
173 Wendell Mathis/500 RC 2.50 6.00
174 Garrett Mills/500 RC 2.50 6.00
175 David Anderson/1000 RC 1.50 4.00
176 Kevin McMahan/1000 RC 1.50 4.00
177 Martin Nance/1000 RC 1.25 3.00
178 Greg Lee/500 RC 2.00 5.00
179 Anthony Mix/500 RC 2.50 6.00
180 D.Ferguson/500 RC 2.00 5.00
181 Tamba Hali/500 RC 3.00 8.00
182 Haloti Ngata/1000 RC 1.50 4.00
183 Claude Wroten/1000 RC 1.25 3.00
184 Gabe Watson/1000 RC 1.25 3.00
185 D'Qwell Jackson/1000 RC 1.25 3.00
186 Abdul Hodge/500 RC 2.00 5.00
187 Chad Greenway/500 RC 3.00 8.00
188 Bobby Carpenter/1000 RC 1.25 3.00
189 DeMeco Ryans/500 RC 2.50 6.00
190 Rocky McIntosh/500 RC 2.00 5.00
191 Thomas Howard/1000 RC 1.25 3.00
192 Jon Alston/500 RC 2.00 5.00
193 Jimmy Williams/1000 RC 1.25 3.00
194 Ashton Youboty/500 RC 2.00 5.00
195 Alan Zemaitis/1000 RC 1.25 3.00
196 Cedric Griffin/500 RC 2.50 6.00
197 Ko Simpson/1000 RC 1.50 4.00
198 Pat Watkins/500 RC 2.50 6.00
199 Bernard Pollard/1000 RC 1.50 4.00
200 Jay Cutler/500 RC 1.50 4.00
201 Chad Jackson JSY/1400 RC 3.00 8.00
202 L.Maroney JSY/550 RC 2.00 5.00
203 Tar.Jackson JSY/1400 RC 1.50 4.00
204 Michael Huff JSY/1400 RC 2.00 5.00
205 Mario Williams JSY/1400 RC 2.50 6.00
206 Mar.Lewis JSY/1400 RC 1.50 4.00
207 Maurice Drew JSY/1400 RC 2.50 6.00
208 Vince Young JSY/550 RC 2.00 5.00
209 LenDale White JSY/550 RC 4.00 10.00
210 Reggie Bush JSY/550 RC 3.00 8.00
211 Matt Leinart JSY/550 RC 2.00 5.00
212 M.Robinson JSY/1400 RC 3.00 8.00
213 Vernon Davis JSY/550 RC 2.50 6.00
214 Br.Williams JSY/1400 RC 1.50 4.00
215 Derek Hagan JSY/1400 RC 3.00 8.00
216 Jason Avant JSY/1400 RC 1.50 4.00
217 B.Marshall JSY/1400 RC 3.00 8.00
218 Omar Jacobs JSY/1400 RC 3.00 8.00
219 S.Holmes JSY/550 RC 6.00 15.00
220 J.Norwood JSY/1400 RC 1.50 4.00
221 Dem.Williams JSY/1400 RC 3.00 8.00
222 Sinorice Moss JSY/1400 RC 3.00 8.00
223 L.Washington JSY/1400 RC 1.50 4.00
224 Kellen Clemens JSY/900 RC 1.50 4.00
225 A.J. Hawk JSY/550 RC 2.50 6.00
226 Maurice Stovall JSY/1400 RC 3.00 8.00
227 DeA.Williams JSY/550 RC 2.50 6.00
228 C.Whitehurst JSY/1400 RC 1.50 4.00
229 Travis Wilson JSY/1400 RC 3.00 8.00
230 J.Klopfenstein JSY/1400 RC 3.00 8.00
231 Brian Calhoun JSY/1400 RC 3.00 8.00
232 Barry Sanders JSY/150 10.00 25.00
233 Jerry Rice JSY/150 8.00 20.00
234 Dan Marino JSY/150 12.00 30.00
235 Earl Campbell JSY/150 6.00 15.00
236 Jim Brown JSY/100 10.00 25.00
237 Joe Montana JSY/125 10.00 25.00
238 Troy Aikman JSY/150 8.00 20.00
239 Walter Payton JSY/100 15.00 40.00
240 Terry Bradshaw JSY/150 10.00 25.00
241 John Elway JSY/150 10.00 25.00
242 Fred Biletnikoff JSY/100 6.00 15.00
243 Lance Alworth JSY/125 6.00 15.00
244 Ronnie Lott JSY/150 6.00 15.00
245 Yale Lary JSY/125 6.00 15.00
246 Bart Starr JSY/80 12.00 30.00
247 Doak Walker JSY/75 10.00 25.00
248 Gale Sayers JSY/100 8.00 20.00
249 Bo Jackson JSY/150 6.00 15.00
250 Roger Staubach JSY/125 10.00 25.00
251 Dick Butkus JSY/150 8.00 20.00

2006 Leaf Certified Materials Mirror Red

*RED VETS 1-150: 4X TO 10X BASIC CARDS
*ROOKIES: 1X TO 2.5X BASIC RC/1000
*ROOKIES: .6X TO 1.5X BASIC RC/500
RED PRINT RUN 100 SER.#'d SETS
UNPRICED MIRROR BLACK #'d TO 1
UNPRICED MIRROR EMERALD #'d TO 5

2006 Leaf Certified Materials Mirror Blue

*BLUE VETS 1-150: 5X TO 12X BASIC CARDS
*ROOKIES: 1.2X TO 3X BASIC RC/1000
*ROOKIES: .8X TO 2X BASIC RC/500
BLUE PRINT RUN 50 SER.#'d SETS

2006 Leaf Certified Materials Mirror Gold

*GOLD VETS 1-150: 8X TO 20X BASIC CARDS
*ROOKIES: 2X TO 5X BASIC RC/1000
*ROOKIES: 1.2X TO 3X BASIC RC/500
GOLD PRINT RUN 25 SER.#'d SETS

2006 Leaf Certified Materials Certified Potential Gold

*MIRROR/500: .5X TO 1.2X GOLD/800
MIRROR PRINT RUN 500 SER.#'d SETS
*RED/250: .6X TO 1.5X GOLD/800
RED PRINT RUN 250 SER.#'d SETS
*BLUE/100: .8X TO 2X GOLD/800
BLUE PRINT RUN 100 SER.#'d SETS
*HOLOGOLD/25: 1.2X TO 3X GOLD/800
HOLOGOLD PRINT RUN 25 SER.#'d SETS
UNPRICED EMERALD PRINT RUN 5 SETS
UNPRICED BLACK PRINT RUN 1 SET
1 Alex Smith QB 1.00 2.50
2 Andre Johnson 1.00 2.50
3 Braylon Edwards .75 2.00
4 Cadillac Williams 1.00 2.50
5 Cedric Benson .75 2.00
6 Charlie Frye 1.00 2.50
7 Chris Brown .75 2.00
8 Chris Chambers .75 2.00
9 Darrell Jackson 1.00 2.50
10 Kevin Jones .75 2.00
11 Lee Evans 1.00 2.50
12 Mark Clayton .75 2.00
13 Matt Jones .75 2.00
14 Nate Burleson .75 2.00
15 Reggie Brown .75 2.00
16 Ronnie Brown 1.00 2.50
17 Samkon Gado .75 2.00
18 Santana Moss 1.00 2.50
19 Steven Jackson .75 2.00

2006 Leaf Certified Materials Certified Potential Materials

STATED PRINT RUN 100 SER.#'d SETS
PRIME BLACK PRINT RUN 1 SER.#'d SETS
1 Alex Smith QB 4.00 10.00
2 Andre Johnson 3.00 8.00
3 Braylon Edwards 3.00 8.00
4 Cadillac Williams 4.00 10.00
5 Cedric Benson 3.00 8.00
7 Chris Brown 2.50 6.00
8 Chris Chambers 3.00 8.00
9 Darrell Jackson 3.00 8.00
10 Kevin Jones 4.00 10.00
11 Lee Evans 2.50 6.00
12 Mark Clayton 3.00 8.00
13 Matt Jones 3.00 8.00
14 Nate Burleson 3.00 8.00
15 Reggie Brown 3.00 8.00
16 Ronnie Brown 4.00 10.00
17 Samkon Gado/51 3.00 8.00
18 Santana Moss 3.00 8.00
19 Steven Jackson 4.00 10.00

2006 Leaf Certified Materials Certified Skills Gold

GOLD PRINT RUN 800 SER.#'d SETS
*MIRROR/500: .5X TO 1.2X GOLD/800
MIRROR PRINT RUN 500 SER.#'d SETS
*RED/250: .6X TO 1.5X GOLD/800
RED PRINT RUN 250 SER.#'d SETS
*BLUE/100: .8X TO 2X GOLD/800
BLUE PRINT RUN 100 SER.#'d SETS
*HOLOGOLD/25: 1.2X TO 3X GOLD/800
EMERALD PRINT RUN 5 SER.#'d SETS
BLACK PRINT RUN 1 SER.#'d SETS
1 Anquan Boldin .75 2.00
2 Antonio Gates 1.25 3.00
3 Byron Leftwich .75 2.00
4 Chad Johnson .75 2.00
5 Clinton Portis .75 2.00
6 Domanick Davis .75 2.00
7 Donovan McNabb 1.00 2.50
8 Drew Bennett 1.00 2.50
9 Edgerrin James 1.00 2.50
10 Hines Ward 1.00 2.50
11 Javon Walker 1.00 2.50
12 Larry Johnson .75 2.00
13 Marvin Harrison 1.00 2.50
14 Roy Williams WR .75 2.00
15 Rudi Johnson .75 2.00
16 Tatum Bell .75 2.00
17 Tiki Barber 1.00 2.50
18 Torry Holt 1.00 2.50
19 Willie Parker 1.00 2.50
20 Willis McGahee .75 2.00

2006 Leaf Certified Materials Certified Skills Materials

STATED PRINT RUN 100 SER.#'d SETS
UNPRICED PRIME PRINT RUN 5 SETS
UNPRICED PRIME BLACK PRINT RUN 1 SET
1 Anquan Boldin 3.00 8.00
2 Antonio Gates 3.00 8.00
3 Byron Leftwich 3.00 8.00
4 Chad Johnson 3.00 8.00
5 Clinton Portis 4.00 10.00
6 Domanick Davis 2.50 6.00
7 Donovan McNabb 4.00 10.00
8 Drew Bennett 2.50 6.00
9 Edgerrin James 4.00 10.00
10 Hines Ward 4.00 10.00
11 Javon Walker 3.00 8.00
12 Larry Johnson 4.00 10.00
14 Roy Williams WR 4.00 10.00
15 Rudi Johnson 3.00 8.00
16 Tatum Bell 3.00 8.00
17 Tiki Barber 4.00 10.00
18 Torry Holt 3.00 8.00
20 Willis McGahee 3.00 8.00

2006 Leaf Certified Materials Fabric of the Game

STATED PRINT RUN 100 SER.#'d SETS
SERIAL #'d UNDER 25 NOT PRICED
1 Barry Sanders 10.00 25.00
2 Bart Starr/75 12.00 30.00
3 Bo Jackson 10.00 25.00
4 Bob Griese 5.00 12.00
5 Deuce McAllister 3.00 8.00
6 Charley Taylor 4.00 10.00
7 Cliff Branch 5.00 12.00
8 Craig Morton 4.00 10.00
9 Cris Carter 6.00 15.00
10 Dan Marino 12.00 30.00
11 Deacon Jones 4.00 10.00
12 Deion Sanders 5.00 12.00
13 Dick Butkus 8.00 20.00
14 Don Maynard 4.00 10.00
15 Earl Campbell 5.00 12.00
16 Eric Dickerson 5.00 12.00
17 Fran Tarkenton 5.00 12.00
18 Fred Biletnikoff 5.00 12.00
19 Gale Sayers/75 8.00 20.00
20 George Blanda 8.00 20.00
21 Harvey Martin 5.00 12.00
22 Henry Ellard 4.00 10.00
23 Herman Edwards 3.00 8.00
24 Ickey Woods 4.00 10.00
25 Jack Lambert 8.00 20.00
26 Jackie Smith 4.00 10.00
27 Jim Brown/50 12.00 30.00
28 Jim Otto 5.00 12.00
29 Joe Montana/80 12.00 30.00
30 Joe Theismann 5.00 12.00
31 John Elway 10.00 25.00
32 John Riggins 5.00 12.00
33 Lance Alworth/75 8.00 20.00
34 Len Dawson 6.00 15.00
35 Marcus Allen 5.00 12.00
36 Mark Gastineau 5.00 12.00
37 Mike Singletary 5.00 12.00
38 Paul Krause 4.00 10.00
39 Paul Warfield 4.00 10.00
40 Phil Simms 5.00 12.00
41 Roger Staubach 10.00 25.00
42 Ronnie Lott 6.00 15.00
43 Steve Largent 5.00 12.00
44 Terrell Davis/75 5.00 12.00
45 Terry Bradshaw 10.00 25.00
46 Thurman Thomas 4.00 10.00
47 Tony Dorsett 6.00 15.00
48 Troy Aikman 8.00 20.00
49 Walter Payton/75 15.00 40.00
50 Warren Moon 5.00 12.00
51 Willie Brown 4.00 10.00
52 Y.A. Tittle 8.00 20.00
53 Yale Lary 4.00 10.00
54 Doak Walker/50 20.00 40.00
55 Jerry Rice 8.00 20.00
57 Red Grange/50 75.00 135.00
60 Ahman Green 4.00 10.00
61 Alex Smith QB 4.00 10.00
62 Alge Crumpler 3.00 8.00
63 Andre Johnson 3.00 8.00
64 Anquan Boldin 3.00 8.00
65 Jimmy Smith 3.00 8.00
66 Antonio Gates 3.00 8.00
67 Ashley Lelie 2.50 6.00
68 Ben Roethlisberger 8.00 20.00
69 Deion Branch 3.00 8.00
70 Brandon Jones 2.50 6.00
71 Braylon Edwards 3.00 8.00
72 Brett Favre 8.00 20.00
73 Brian Urlacher 4.00 10.00
74 Brian Westbrook/75 3.00 8.00
75 Byron Leftwich 3.00 8.00
76 Cadillac Williams 4.00 10.00
77 Carson Palmer 4.00 10.00
78 Cedric Benson 3.00 8.00
79 Chad Johnson 3.00 8.00
80 Chad Pennington 3.00 8.00
82 Chris Brown 2.50 6.00
83 Chris Chambers 3.00 8.00
84 Clinton Portis 4.00 10.00
85 Corey Dillon 3.00 8.00
86 Curtis Martin 4.00 10.00
87 Dallas Clark 2.50 6.00
88 Darrell Jackson 3.00 8.00
89 David Carr 3.00 8.00
91 Domanick Davis 2.50 6.00
93 Donovan McNabb 4.00 10.00
94 Donte Stallworth 3.00 8.00
95 Daunte Culpepper 4.00 10.00
97 Edgerrin James 4.00 10.00
98 Eli Manning 6.00 15.00
99 Fred Taylor 3.00 8.00
100 Hines Ward 4.00 10.00
101 Jake Delhomme 3.00 8.00
102 Javon Walker 3.00 8.00
103 Jeremy Shockey 4.00 10.00
104 Julius Jones 4.00 10.00
105 Keenan McCardell 2.50 6.00
106 Kevin Jones 4.00 10.00
107 LaDainian Tomlinson 4.00 10.00
108 LaMont Jordan 3.00 8.00
109 Larry Fitzgerald 3.00 8.00
110 Larry Johnson 4.00 10.00
111 Laveranues Coles 3.00 8.00
112 Lee Evans 2.50 6.00
113 Marc Bulger/75 3.00 8.00
114 Mark Clayton 3.00 8.00
115 Marvin Harrison 4.00 10.00
116 Matt Hasselbeck 3.00 8.00
117 Matt Jones 3.00 8.00
118 Michael Clayton 2.50 6.00
119 Michael Vick 4.00 10.00
120 Peyton Manning 8.00 20.00
121 Philip Rivers 4.00 10.00
122 Plaxico Burress 3.00 8.00
123 Priest Holmes 3.00 8.00
124 Randy Moss 4.00 10.00
125 Reggie Brown 3.00 8.00
126 Reggie Wayne 3.00 8.00
127 Reuben Droughns 2.50 6.00
128 Robert Ferguson 2.50 6.00
129 Rod Smith 3.00 8.00
130 Ronnie Brown 4.00 10.00
131 Roy Williams S 4.00 10.00
132 Roy Williams WR 4.00 10.00
133 Rudi Johnson 3.00 8.00
134 Samkon Gado 3.00 8.00
135 Santana Moss 3.00 8.00
136 Shaun Alexander 5.00 12.00
137 Steve McNair 3.00 8.00
138 Steve Smith 4.00 10.00
139 Steven Jackson 4.00 10.00
140 Stephen Davis 2.50 6.00
142 Thomas Jones 3.00 8.00
143 Tiki Barber 4.00 10.00
144 Tom Brady 6.00 15.00
145 Tony Gonzalez 3.00 8.00
146 Torry Holt 3.00 8.00
147 Trent Green 3.00 8.00
149 Willis McGahee 3.00 8.00

2006 Leaf Certified Materials Fabric of the Game Prime

RIME/15-25: 1X TO 2.5X BASIC JSY/75-100
*PRIME/15-25: .8X TO 2X BASIC JSY/50
59 Aaron Rodgers 25.00 60.00
92 Donald Driver 6.00 15.00
96 Drew Bledsoe 10.00 25.00
141 T.J. Houshmandzadeh 6.00 15.00
148 Willie Parker 10.00 25.00
150 Zach Thomas 10.00 25.00

2006 Leaf Certified Materials Fabric of the Game College

ATED PRINT RUN 100 SER.#'d SETS
*PRIME/25: 1X TO 2.5X BASIC INSERTS
PRIME PRINT RUN 25 SER.#'d SETS
PRIME SER.#'d UNDER 25 NOT PRICED
1 Roy Williams WR 6.00 15.00
2 LenDale White 8.00 20.00
3 Reggie Bush 5.00 12.00
4 Matt Leinart 3.00 8.00
5 Cadillac Williams 6.00 15.00
6 Ronnie Brown 6.00 15.00
7 Reggie Wayne/65 4.00 10.00
8 Braylon Edwards 4.00 10.00
9 Dan Marino 15.00 40.00
10 Eric Dickerson 8.00 20.00
11 Peyton Manning 20.00 50.00
12 A.J. Hawk 10.00 25.00
13 Laurence Maroney 3.00 8.00
14 Maurice Drew 8.00 20.00
15 Maurice Stovall 6.00 15.00
16 Travis Wilson 6.00 15.00
17 Marcedes Lewis 5.00 12.00
18 Jay Cutler 4.00 10.00
19 Mario Williams 5.00 12.00
20 Joseph Addai 3.00 8.00

2006 Leaf Certified Materials Fabric of the Game College Combos

STATED PRINT RUN 50 SER.#'d SETS
UNPRICED PRIME PRINT RUN 10 SETS
1 R.Will.WR/C.Benson 10.00 25.00
2 P.Manning/M.Leinart 25.00 60.00
3 B.Sanders/T.Thomas 25.00 60.00
4 Staubach/Bradshaw 15.00 40.00
5 M.Williams/A.Hawk 10.00 25.00

2006 Leaf Certified Materials Fabric of the Game Combos

ATED PRINT RUN 1-50 SER.#'d SETS
SERIAL #'d UNDER 25 NOT PRICED
UNPRICED PRIME PRINT RUN 10 SETS
1 B.Starr/A.Rodgers 30.00 80.00
2 T.Thomas/W.McGahee 5.00 12.00
3 I.Woods/R.Johnson 5.00 12.00
5 D.Walker/D.Clark/25 50.00 100.00
6 E.Dickerson/M.Allen 8.00 20.00
7 T.Gonzalez/J.Shockey 5.00 12.00
8 Roeth/Hasselbeck 15.00 40.00
10 J.Jones/T.Jones 10.00 25.00
11 C.Benson/R.Williams WR 6.00 15.00
12 P.Manning/C.Palmer 15.00 40.00
13 B.Jackson/S.Gado 8.00 20.00
14 J.Smith/S.Smith 5.00 12.00
15 J.Montana/B.Favre 25.00 60.00
16 R.Lott/R.Williams S 10.00 25.00
18 T.Dorsett/B.Sanders 15.00 40.00
19 C.Williams/R.Brown 6.00 15.00
20 D.Marino/T.Aikman 30.00 80.00
21 L.Johnson/L.Tomlinson 8.00 20.00
22 J.Elway/T.Brady 15.00 40.00
24 Bradshaw/Theismann 12.00 30.00
25 J.Rice/L.Alworth 15.00 40.00

2006 Leaf Certified Materials Fabric of the Game Football Die Cut

*FB/66-100: .4X TO 1X BASIC FOTG/75-100
*FB/40-58: .5X TO 1.2X BASIC FOTG/75-100
STATED PRINT RUN 1-100 SER.#'d SETS
SERIAL #'d UNDER 25 NOT PRICED
57 Red Grange/25 90.00 150.00

2006 Leaf Certified Materials Fabric of the Game Jersey Number

*JN/75-99: .4X TO 1X BASIC FOTG/75-100
*JN/40-60: .5X TO 1.2X BASIC FOTG/75-100
*JN/30-39: .6X TO 1.5X BASIC FOTG/75-100
*JN/30-39: .5X TO 1.2X BASIC FOTG/50
*JN/20-29: .8X TO 2X BASIC FOTG/75-100
STATED PRINT RUN 1-99 SER.#'d SETS
SERIAL #'d UNDER 25 NOT PRICED

2006 Leaf Certified Materials Fabric of the Game Jersey Number Autographs

ATED PRINT RUN 1-89 SER.#'d SETS
SERIAL #'d UNDER 25 NOT PRICED
1 Barry Sanders/20 75.00 150.00
3 Bo Jackson/34 60.00 120.00
6 Charley Taylor/42 15.00 40.00
11 Deacon Jones/75 20.00 40.00
15 Earl Campbell/34 30.00 60.00
16 Eric Dickerson/29 40.00 80.00
18 Fred Biletnikoff/25 30.00 60.00
19 Gale Sayers/40 40.00 80.00
22 Henry Ellard/80 10.00 25.00
23 Herman Edwards/46 10.00 25.00
24 Ickey Woods/30 15.00 30.00
25 Jack Lambert/58 40.00 80.00
27 Jim Brown/32 60.00 120.00
28 Jim Otto/60 15.00 40.00
32 John Riggins/44 30.00 60.00
35 Marcus Allen/32 40.00 80.00
37 Mike Singletary/50 20.00 40.00
39 Paul Warfield/42 20.00 40.00
42 Ronnie Lott/42 40.00 80.00
43 Steve Largent/80 25.00 50.00
44 Terrell Davis/30 20.00 50.00
46 Thurman Thomas/34 15.00 40.00
47 Tony Dorsett/33 30.00 80.00
53 Yale Lary/28 30.00 60.00
55 Jerry Rice/80 90.00 150.00
62 Alge Crumpler/83 10.00 30.00
64 Anquan Boldin/81 12.00 30.00
69 Deion Branch/83 12.00 30.00
78 Cedric Benson/32 20.00 50.00
82 Chris Brown/29 10.00 25.00
87 Dallas Clark/44 12.00 30.00
91 Domanick Davis/37 12.00 30.00
97 Edgerrin James/32 20.00 50.00
100 Hines Ward/86 30.00 60.00
106 Kevin Jones/34 15.00 40.00
108 LaMont Jordan/34 20.00 40.00
110 Larry Johnson/27 20.00 50.00
112 Lee Evans/83 10.00 25.00
118 Michael Clayton/80 10.00 25.00
123 Priest Holmes/31 20.00 50.00
125 Reggie Brown/86 12.00 30.00
126 Reggie Wayne/87 20.00 40.00
131 Roy Williams S/31 30.00 60.00
133 Rudi Johnson/32 15.00 40.00
134 Samkon Gado/35 15.00 40.00
135 Santana Moss/89 20.00 40.00
136 Shaun Alexander/37 40.00 80.00
138 Steve Smith/89 20.00 40.00
139 Steven Jackson/39 20.00 40.00
146 Torry Holt/81 12.00 30.00

2006 Leaf Certified Materials Fabric of the Game Position

*POS/40-50: .5X TO 1.2X FOTG/75-100
*POS/30-39: .6X TO 1.5X FOTG/75-100
STATED PRINT RUN 24-50 SER.#'d SETS
SERIAL #'d UNDER 25 NOT PRICED
59 Aaron Rodgers/30 20.00 40.00

2006 Leaf Certified Materials Fabric of the Game Team Logo

L/25: 1X TO 2.5X FOTG/75-100
STATED PRINT RUN 5-25 SER.#'d SETS
SERIAL #'d UNDER 25 NOT PRICED
UNPRICED AUTO PRINT RUN 2-5
58 Aaron Brooks 6.00 15.00
59 Aaron Rodgers 20.00 50.00
90 DeShaun Foster 8.00 20.00
92 Donald Driver 8.00 20.00
141 T.J. Houshmandzadeh 8.00 20.00
148 Willie Parker 10.00 25.00
150 Zach Thomas 8.00 20.00

2006 Leaf Certified Materials Gold Team

STATED PRINT RUN 500 SER.#'d SETS
*MIRROR/100: .6X TO 1.5X GOLD/500
MIRROR PRINT RUN 100 SER.#'d SETS
1 Ben Roethlisberger 2.00 5.00
2 Brett Favre 3.00 8.00
3 Carson Palmer 1.25 3.00
4 Eli Manning 1.25 3.00
5 LaDainian Tomlinson 1.50 4.00
6 Larry Johnson 1.00 2.50
7 Peyton Manning 4.00 10.00
8 Shaun Alexander 1.00 2.50
9 Steve Smith 1.50 4.00
10 Tom Brady 5.00 12.00

2006 Leaf Certified Materials Gold Team Materials

STATED PRINT RUN 85-100 SER.#'d SETS
UNPRICED PRIME PRINT RUN 5 SETS
UNPRICED PRIME BLACK PRINT RUN 1
1 Ben Roethlisberger 8.00 20.00
2 Brett Favre 8.00 20.00
3 Carson Palmer 4.00 10.00
4 Eli Manning 6.00 15.00
5 LaDainian Tomlinson 4.00 10.00
6 Larry Johnson 4.00 10.00
7 Peyton Manning/85 8.00 20.00
8 Shaun Alexander 5.00 12.00
9 Steve Smith 4.00 10.00
10 Tom Brady 6.00 15.00

2006 Leaf Certified Materials Mirror Red Signatures

D PRINT RUN 30-250 SER.#'d SETS
UNPRICED EMERALD PRINT RUN 5 SETS
UNPRICED BLACK PRINT RUN 1 SET
13 Todd Heap/172 6.00 15.00
18 Lee Evans/75 5.00 12.00
21 Jake Delhomme/75 8.00 20.00
32 Rudi Johnson/50 6.00 15.00
46 Tatum Bell/50 6.00 15.00
60 Domanick Davis/30 8.00 20.00
63 Peyton Manning/50 60.00 100.00
64 Reggie Wayne/50 8.00 20.00
69 Matt Jones/75 6.00 15.00
70 Larry Johnson/100 15.00 40.00
83 Nate Burleson/50 8.00 20.00
110 Reggie Brown/75 8.00 20.00
113 Jevon Kearse/100 6.00 15.00
154 Bennie Brazell/250 4.00 10.00
155 David Thomas/250 5.00 12.00
156 Marques Colston/150 5.00 12.00
157 Reggie McNeal/125 4.00 10.00
158 D.J. Shockley/125 4.00 10.00
159 Dominique Byrd/250 5.00 12.00
160 Antonio Cromartie/125 5.00 12.00
161 Donte Whitner/125 5.00 12.00
162 Anwar Phillips/169 4.00 10.00
163 A.J. Nicholson/194 4.00 10.00
165 Erik Meyer/250 4.00 10.00
166 Darrell Hackney/250 4.00 10.00
167 Paul Pinegar/250 4.00 10.00
168 Brandon Kirsch/244 5.00 12.00
169 Quinton Ganther/250 4.00 10.00
170 Andre Hall/250 5.00 12.00
171 Derrick Ross/250 4.00 10.00
172 Mike Bell/250 8.00 20.00
173 Wendell Mathis/250 4.00 10.00
174 Garrett Mills/250 5.00 12.00
175 David Anderson/250 4.00 10.00
176 Kevin McMahan/118 4.00 10.00
177 Martin Nance/250 4.00 10.00
178 Greg Lee/250 4.00 10.00
180 D'Brickashaw Ferguson/250 5.00 12.00
181 Tamba Hali/250 5.00 12.00
182 Haloti Ngata/250 5.00 12.00
183 Claude Wroten/250 4.00 10.00
184 Gabe Watson/250 4.00 10.00
185 D'Qwell Jackson/250 4.00 10.00
188 Abdul Hodge/250 5.00 12.00
187 Chad Greenway/250 6.00 15.00
188 Bobby Carpenter/250 4.00 10.00
189 DeMeco Ryans/250 6.00 15.00
190 Rocky McIntosh/250 5.00 12.00
191 Thomas Howard/250 5.00 12.00
192 Jon Alston/250 5.00 12.00
193 Jimmy Williams/250 5.00 12.00

194 Ashton Youboty/250 5.00 12.00
195 Alan Zemaitis/234 5.00 12.00
196 Cedric Griffin/250 4.00 10.00
197 Ko Simpson/250 4.00 10.00
198 Pat Watkins/250 5.00 12.00
199 Bernard Pollard/250 5.00 12.00

2006 Leaf Certified Materials Mirror Blue Signatures

13 Todd Heap/100 8.00 20.00
14 Mark Clayton/25 15.00 40.00
18 Lee Evans/25 10.00 25.00
21 Jake Delhomme/50 12.00 30.00
32 Rudi Johnson/50 8.00 20.00
43 Roy Williams S/40 12.00 30.00
46 Tatum Bell/25 12.00 30.00
60 Domanick Davis/25 10.00 25.00
63 Peyton Manning/25 75.00 150.00
64 Reggie Wayne/25 15.00 40.00
69 Matt Jones/50 10.00 25.00
70 Larry Johnson/50 15.00 40.00
83 Nate Burleson/25 12.00 30.00
110 Reggie Brown/25 12.00 30.00
113 Jevon Kearse/75 8.00 20.00
143 Drew Bennett/50 8.00 20.00
151 Brodie Croyle/50 6.00 15.00
152 Greg Jennings/50 10.00 25.00
153 Joseph Addai/75 20.00 50.00
154 Bennie Brazell/100 5.00 12.00
155 David Thomas/100 6.00 15.00
156 Marques Colston/50 10.00 25.00
157 Reggie McNeal/75 5.00 12.00
158 D.J. Shockley/75 6.00 15.00
159 Dominique Byrd/100 6.00 15.00
160 Antonio Cromartie/75 6.00 15.00
161 Donte Whitner/75 6.00 15.00
162 Anwar Phillips/100 5.00 12.00
163 A.J. Nicholson/100 5.00 12.00
164 De'Arrius Howard/70 5.00 12.00
165 Erik Meyer/100 5.00 12.00
166 Darrell Hackney/100 5.00 12.00
167 Paul Pinegar/100 5.00 12.00
168 Brandon Kirsch/100 6.00 15.00
169 Quinton Ganther/100 5.00 12.00
170 Andre Hall/100 6.00 15.00
171 Derrick Ross/100 5.00 12.00
172 Mike Bell/100 6.00 15.00
173 Wendell Mathis/100 5.00 12.00
174 Garrett Mills/100 5.00 12.00
175 David Anderson/100 5.00 12.00
176 Kevin McMahan/100 5.00 12.00
177 Martin Nance/100 5.00 12.00
178 Greg Lee/100 5.00 12.00
179 Anthony Mix/100 5.00 12.00
180 D'Brickashaw Ferguson/100 6.00 15.00
181 Tamba Hali/100 6.00 15.00
182 Haloti Ngata/100 6.00 15.00
183 Claude Wroten/100 5.00 12.00
184 Gabe Watson/100 5.00 12.00
185 D'Qwell Jackson/100 5.00 12.00
186 Abdul Hodge/100 6.00 15.00
187 Chad Greenway/100 6.00 15.00
188 Bobby Carpenter/100 6.00 15.00
189 DeMeco Ryans/100 8.00 20.00
190 Rocky McIntosh/100 6.00 15.00
191 Thomas Howard/100 6.00 15.00
192 Jon Alston/100 6.00 15.00
193 Jimmy Williams/100 6.00 15.00
194 Ashton Youboty/100 6.00 15.00
195 Alan Zemaitis/100 6.00 15.00
196 Cedric Griffin/100 5.00 12.00
197 Ko Simpson/100 5.00 12.00
198 Pat Watkins/100 6.00 15.00
199 Bernard Pollard/100 6.00 15.00
200 Jay Cutler/50 30.00 60.00

2006 Leaf Certified Materials Mirror Gold Signatures

GOLD PRINT RUN 6-25 SER.#'d SETS
SERIAL NUMBERED UNDER 25 NOT PRICED
5 Alge Crumpler/25 10.00 25.00
13 Todd Heap/25 12.00 30.00
21 Jake Delhomme/25 15.00 40.00
29 Thomas Jones/25 12.00 30.00
32 Rudi Johnson/25 12.00 30.00
36 Braylon Edwards/25 12.00 30.00
43 Roy Williams S/24 15.00 40.00
51 Roy Williams WR/25 15.00 40.00
55 Samkon Gado/25 12.00 30.00
62 Marvin Harrison/25 20.00 50.00
66 Byron Leftwich/25 15.00 40.00
68 Jimmy Smith/25 12.00 30.00
69 Matt Jones/25 12.00 30.00
70 Larry Johnson/25 15.00 40.00
113 Jevon Kearse/25 12.00 30.00
117 Willie Parker/25 15.00 40.00
130 Matt Hasselbeck/25 15.00 40.00
138 Chris Simms/25 12.00 30.00
143 Drew Bennett/25 10.00 25.00
151 Brodie Croyle/25 10.00 25.00
152 Greg Jennings/25 12.00 30.00
153 Joseph Addai/25 30.00 80.00
154 Bennie Brazell/25 8.00 20.00
155 David Thomas/25 10.00 25.00
156 Marques Colston/25 12.00 30.00
157 Reggie McNeal/25 8.00 20.00
158 D.J. Shockley/25 8.00 20.00
159 Dominique Byrd/25 10.00 25.00
160 Antonio Cromartie/25 10.00 25.00
161 Donte Whitner/25 10.00 25.00
162 Anwar Phillips/25 8.00 20.00
163 A.J. Nicholson/25 8.00 20.00
164 De'Arrius Howard/25 8.00 20.00
165 Erik Meyer/25 8.00 20.00
166 Darrell Hackney/25 8.00 20.00
167 Paul Pinegar/25 8.00 20.00
168 Brandon Kirsch/25 10.00 25.00
169 Quinton Ganther/25 8.00 20.00
170 Andre Hall/25 12.00 30.00
171 Derrick Ross/25 8.00 20.00
172 Mike Bell/25 10.00 25.00
173 Wendell Mathis/25 8.00 20.00
174 Garrett Mills/25 8.00 20.00
175 David Anderson/25 8.00 20.00
176 Kevin McMahan/25 8.00 20.00
177 Martin Nance/25 8.00 20.00
178 Greg Lee/25 8.00 20.00
179 Anthony Mix/25 8.00 20.00
180 D'Brickashaw Ferguson/25 10.00 25.00
181 Tamba Hali/25 10.00 25.00
182 Haloti Ngata/25 10.00 25.00
183 Claude Wroten/25 8.00 20.00
184 Gabe Watson/25 8.00 20.00
185 D'Qwell Jackson/25 8.00 20.00
186 Abdul Hodge/25 10.00 25.00
187 Chad Greenway/25 10.00 25.00
188 Bobby Carpenter/25 10.00 25.00
189 DeMeco Ryans/25 12.00 30.00
190 Rocky McIntosh/25 10.00 25.00
191 Thomas Howard/25 10.00 25.00
192 Jon Alston/25 10.00 25.00
193 Jimmy Williams/25 10.00 25.00
194 Ashton Youboty/25 10.00 25.00
195 Alan Zemaitis/25 10.00 25.00
196 Cedric Griffin/25 8.00 20.00
197 Ko Simpson/25 8.00 20.00
198 Pat Watkins/25 10.00 25.00
199 Bernard Pollard/25 10.00 25.00
200 Jay Cutler/25 25.00 60.00

2006 Leaf Certified Materials Mirror Red Materials

ETIRED 232-251: .5X TO 1.2 BASE JSY
RED PRINT RUN 40-150
UNPRICED MIRROR BLACK #'d TO 1
UNPRICED MIRROR EMERALD #'d TO 5
1 Anquan Boldin 2.50 6.00
2 Edgerrin James 3.00 8.00
4 Larry Fitzgerald 3.00 8.00
5 Alge Crumpler 3.00 8.00
7 Michael Jenkins 2.50 6.00
8 Michael Vick 3.00 8.00
9 Warrick Dunn 2.50 6.00
11 Jamal Lewis 3.00 8.00
12 Kyle Boller/125 2.50 6.00
13 Todd Heap 2.50 6.00
14 Mark Clayton 2.50 6.00
16 J.P. Losman 3.00 8.00
17 Josh Reed 2.50 6.00
18 Lee Evans 3.00 8.00
19 Willis McGahee 2.50 6.00
21 Jake Delhomme 2.50 6.00
22 Stephen Davis 2.50 6.00
23 Keary Colbert 2.50 6.00
24 Steve Smith 4.00 10.00
25 Brian Urlacher 4.00 10.00
26 Cedric Benson 2.50 6.00
27 Muhsin Muhammad 2.50 6.00
28 Rex Grossman 2.50 6.00
29 Thomas Jones 2.50 6.00
30 Carson Palmer 3.00 8.00
31 Chad Johnson 2.50 6.00
32 Rudi Johnson 2.50 6.00
35 Dennis Northcutt 2.50 6.00
36 Braylon Edwards 2.50 6.00
37 Reuben Droughns 3.00 8.00
39 Julius Jones 2.50 6.00
42 Terry Glenn 3.00 8.00
43 Roy Williams S 2.50 6.00
44 Jake Plummer 2.50 6.00
45 Rod Smith 3.00 8.00
46 Tatum Bell 2.50 6.00
47 Ashley Lelie 2.50 6.00
49 Kevin Jones 2.50 6.00
50 Mike Williams 2.50 6.00
51 Roy Williams WR 2.50 6.00
52 Ahman Green/81 3.00 8.00
53 Brett Favre/100 8.00 20.00
54 Aaron Rodgers/50 20.00 50.00
55 Samkon Gado 2.50 6.00
57 Robert Ferguson 2.50 6.00
58 Andre Johnson 3.00 8.00
59 David Carr 2.50 6.00
60 Domanick Davis/100 2.50 6.00
61 Dallas Clark 2.50 6.00
62 Marvin Harrison 3.00 8.00
63 Peyton Manning 10.00 25.00
64 Reggie Wayne 3.00 8.00
65 Brandon Stokley 2.50 6.00
66 Byron Leftwich 2.50 6.00
67 Fred Taylor 2.50 6.00
68 Jimmy Smith 3.00 8.00
69 Matt Jones 2.50 6.00
70 Larry Johnson 2.50 6.00
71 Tony Gonzalez 3.00 8.00
72 Trent Green 2.50 6.00
75 Chris Chambers 2.50 6.00
76 Daunte Culpepper 3.00 8.00
78 Ronnie Brown 3.00 8.00
81 Brad Johnson 3.00 8.00
84 Troy Williamson 2.50 6.00
85 Deion Branch 2.50 6.00
86 Tom Brady 12.00 30.00
87 Corey Dillon 2.50 6.00
89 Troy Brown 2.50 6.00
90 Deuce McAllister 3.00 8.00
91 Donte Stallworth 2.50 6.00
93 Joe Horn 2.50 6.00
95 Eli Manning 3.00 8.00
96 Jeremy Shockey 2.50 6.00
97 Plaxico Burress 2.50 6.00
98 Amani Toomer 2.50 6.00
99 Tiki Barber 3.00 8.00
100 Chad Pennington 2.50 6.00
101 Curtis Martin 3.00 8.00
102 Laveranues Coles 2.50 6.00
104 Jerry Porter/100 2.50 6.00
105 LaMont Jordan 3.00 8.00
107 Randy Moss 3.00 8.00
108 Brian Westbrook/75 2.50 6.00
109 Donovan McNabb 3.00 8.00
110 Reggie Brown 2.50 6.00
111 Chad Lewis 2.50 6.00
113 Jevon Kearse 2.50 6.00
114 Ben Roethlisberger 5.00 12.00
116 Hines Ward 3.00 8.00
117 Willie Parker/63 4.00 10.00
118 Troy Polamalu 4.00 10.00
119 Antonio Gates 4.00 10.00
121 Keenan McCardell 3.00 8.00
122 LaDainian Tomlinson 4.00 10.00
123 Philip Rivers 4.00 10.00
124 Alex Smith QB 3.00 8.00
125 Antonio Bryant/40 3.00 8.00
127 Kevan Barlow 2.50 6.00
128 Darrell Jackson 3.00 8.00
130 Matt Hasselbeck 2.50 6.00
131 Shaun Alexander 2.50 6.00
132 Isaac Bruce 4.00 10.00
133 Marc Bulger 2.50 6.00
134 Marshall Faulk 3.00 8.00
135 Steven Jackson 2.50 6.00
136 Torry Holt 3.00 8.00
137 Cadillac Williams 3.00 8.00
138 Chris Simms 2.50 6.00
140 Michael Clayton 2.50 6.00
141 Brandon Jones 2.50 6.00
142 Chris Brown 2.50 6.00
143 Drew Bennett 3.00 8.00
144 Tyrone Calico 2.50 6.00
145 Steve McNair 3.00 8.00
147 Clinton Portis 2.50 6.00
148 Mark Brunell 3.00 8.00
149 Santana Moss 3.00 8.00
150 Jason Campbell 2.50 6.00
201 Chad Jackson 2.50 6.00
202 Laurence Maroney 2.50 6.00
203 Tarvaris Jackson 2.50 6.00
204 Michael Huff 3.00 8.00
205 Mario Williams 4.00 10.00
206 Marcedes Lewis 2.50 6.00
207 Maurice Drew 4.00 10.00
208 Vince Young 2.50 6.00
209 LenDale White 2.50 6.00
210 Reggie Bush 4.00 10.00
211 Matt Leinart 2.50 6.00
212 Michael Robinson 2.50 6.00
213 Vernon Davis 3.00 8.00
214 Brandon Williams 2.50 6.00
215 Derek Hagan 3.00 8.00
216 Jason Avant 2.50 6.00
217 Brandon Marshall 5.00 12.00
218 Omar Jacobs 2.50 6.00
219 Santonio Holmes 3.00 8.00
220 Jerious Norwood 2.50 6.00
221 Demetrius Williams 2.50 6.00
222 Sinorice Moss 2.50 6.00
223 Leon Washington 2.50 6.00
224 Kellen Clemens 2.50 6.00
225 A.J. Hawk 3.00 8.00
226 Maurice Stovall 2.50 6.00
227 DeAngelo Williams 3.00 8.00
228 Charlie Whitehurst 2.50 6.00
229 Travis Wilson 2.50 6.00
230 Joe Klopfenstein 2.50 6.00
231 Brian Calhoun 2.50 6.00

2006 Leaf Certified Materials Mirror Blue Materials

UE PRINT RUN 15-50
SERIAL #'d UNDER 25 NOT PRICED
201 Chad Jackson AU 12.00 30.00
202 Laurence Maroney AU 12.00 30.00
203 Tarvaris Jackson AU 12.00 30.00
204 Michael Huff AU 15.00 40.00
205 Mario Williams AU 20.00 50.00
206 Marcedes Lewis AU 12.00 30.00
207 Maurice Drew AU 20.00 50.00
208 Vince Young AU 12.00 30.00
209 LenDale White AU 12.00 30.00
210 Reggie Bush AU 20.00 50.00
211 Matt Leinart AU 12.00 30.00
212 Michael Robinson AU 12.00 30.00
213 Vernon Davis AU 15.00 40.00
214 Brandon Williams AU 12.00 30.00
215 Derek Hagan AU 15.00 40.00
216 Jason Avant AU 12.00 30.00
217 Brandon Marshall AU 25.00 60.00
218 Omar Jacobs AU 12.00 30.00
219 Santonio Holmes AU 15.00 40.00
220 Jerious Norwood AU 12.00 30.00
221 Demetrius Williams AU 12.00 30.00
222 Sinorice Moss AU 12.00 30.00
223 Leon Washington AU 12.00 30.00
224 Kellen Clemens AU 12.00 30.00
225 A.J. Hawk AU 15.00 40.00
226 Maurice Stovall AU 12.00 30.00
227 DeAngelo Williams AU 15.00 40.00
228 Charlie Whitehurst AU 12.00 30.00
229 Travis Wilson ERR AU 12.00 30.00
230 Joe Klopfenstein AU 12.00 30.00
231 Brian Calhoun AU 12.00 30.00

2006 Leaf Certified Materials Mirror Gold Materials

OLD/15-25: .8X TO 2X RED MATERIAL
*GOLD AU/25: .6X TO 1.2X BLUE MAT.AU

2007 Leaf Certified Materials

This 253-card set was released in September, 2007. The set was issued into the hobby in five-card packs, with a $10 SRP, which came 10 packs to a box. Cards numbered 1-150 are veterans sequenced in alphabetical team order by division while cards numbered 151-234 feature 2007 NFL rookies and cards numbered 235-254 honor retired greats. Within the Rookie Cards groupings; Cards numbered 151-175 were issued to a stated print run of 1000 serial numbered sets, while cards 176-200, signed by the player, were issued to a stated print run of 399 serial numbered sets and cards numbered 201-234 which had a player-worn jersey swatch were issued to stated print runs between 849 and 1499 serial numbered sets. The retired greats all have game-worn jersey swatches and those cards were issued to a stated print run of 75 serial numbered copies. Card number 245 was never issued for this set.

COMP.SET w/o SP's (150) 15.00 40.00
ROOKIE PRINT RUN 1500 SER.#'d SETS
AU ROOKIE PRINT RUN 399 SER.#'d SETS
JSY ROOKIE PRINT RUN 849-1499
JSY LEGEND PRINT RUN 75 SER.#'d SETS
UNPRICED MIRR.BLACK PRINT RUN 1
UNPRICED MIRR.EMERALD PRINT RUN 5
1 Tony Romo .50 1.25
2 Julius Jones .25 .60
3 Terry Glenn .30 .75
4 Terrell Owens .30 .75
5 Jason Witten .30 .75
6 Patrick Crayton .25 .60
7 Eli Manning .30 .75
8 Plaxico Burress .25 .60
9 Jeremy Shockey .25 .60
10 Brandon Jacobs .25 .60
11 Sinorice Moss .30 .75
12 Donovan McNabb .30 .75
13 Brian Westbrook .25 .60
14 Reggie Brown .25 .60
15 Hank Baskett .30 .75
16 Jason Campbell .25 .60
17 Clinton Portis .25 .60
18 Santana Moss .30 .75
19 Chris Cooley .25 .60
20 Ladell Betts .25 .60
21 Rex Grossman .25 .60
22 Cedric Benson .25 .60
23 Bernard Berrian .25 .60
24 Devin Hester .30 .75
25 Brian Urlacher .40 1.00
26 Jon Kitna .25 .60
27 Roy Williams WR .25 .60
28 Mike Furrey .30 .75
29 Tatum Bell .25 .60
30 Brett Favre .75 2.00
31 Donald Driver .30 .75
32 Greg Jennings .25 .60
33 Nick Barnett .25 .60
34 Tarvaris Jackson .25 .60
35 Chester Taylor .25 .60
36 Troy Williamson .25 .60
37 Michael Vick .30 .75
38 Warrick Dunn .25 .60
39 Joe Horn .25 .60
40 Michael Jenkins .25 .60
41 Alge Crumpler .30 .75
42 Jerious Norwood .25 .60
43 Jake Delhomme .25 .60
44 DeShaun Foster .30 .75
45 Steve Smith .30 .75
46 DeAngelo Williams .25 .60
47 Drew Brees .40 1.00
48 Deuce McAllister .30 .75
49 Marques Colston .25 .60
50 Devery Henderson .25 .60
51 Reggie Bush .25 .60
52 Cadillac Williams .30 .75
53 Joey Galloway .30 .75
54 Michael Clayton .25 .60
55 Derrick Brooks .25 .60
56 Matt Leinart .25 .60
57 Edgerrin James .30 .75
58 Anquan Boldin .25 .60
59 Larry Fitzgerald .30 .75
60 Marc Bulger .25 .60
61 Steven Jackson .25 .60
62 Torry Holt .30 .75
63 Isaac Bruce .40 1.00
64 Randy McMichael .25 .60
65 Drew Bennett .25 .60
66 Alex Smith QB .30 .75
67 Frank Gore .30 .75
68 Vernon Davis .25 .60
69 Darrell Jackson .25 .60
70 Matt Hasselbeck .25 .60
71 Shaun Alexander .25 .60
72 Deion Branch .25 .60
73 Nate Burleson .25 .60
74 J.P. Losman .25 .60
75 Anthony Thomas .25 .60
76 Lee Evans .30 .75
77 Josh Reed .25 .60
78 Daunte Culpepper .30 .75
79 Ronnie Brown .25 .60
80 Chris Chambers .25 .60
81 Marty Booker .25 .60
82 Jason Taylor .30 .75
83 Zach Thomas .30 .75
84 Tom Brady 1.25 3.00
85 Laurence Maroney .30 .75
86 Randy Moss .30 .75
87 Ben Watson .25 .60
88 Donte Stallworth .30 .75
89 Tedy Bruschi .30 .75
90 Chad Pennington .25 .60
91 Thomas Jones .25 .60
92 Laveranues Coles .25 .60
93 Jerricho Cotchery .25 .60
94 Leon Washington .25 .60
95 Steve McNair .30 .75
96 Willis McGahee .25 .60
97 Demetrius Williams .25 .60
98 Todd Heap .25 .60
99 Ray Lewis .40 1.00
100 Mark Clayton .25 .60
101 Carson Palmer .30 .75
102 Rudi Johnson .25 .60
103 Chad Johnson .25 .60
104 T.J. Houshmandzadeh .25 .60
105 Charlie Frye .30 .75
106 Braylon Edwards .25 .60
107 Kellen Winslow .25 .60
108 Jamal Lewis .30 .75
109 Ben Roethlisberger .40 1.00
110 Willie Parker .30 .75
111 Hines Ward .30 .75
112 Heath Miller .25 .60
113 Troy Polamalu .40 1.00
114 Ahman Green .30 .75
115 Andre Johnson .30 .75
116 Matt Schaub .25 .60
117 DeMeco Ryans .30 .75
118 Peyton Manning 1.00 2.50
119 Joseph Addai .25 .60
120 Marvin Harrison .30 .75
121 Reggie Wayne .30 .75
122 Dallas Clark .30 .75
123 Byron Leftwich .25 .60
124 Fred Taylor .25 .60
125 Matt Jones .30 .75
126 Reggie Williams .30 .75
127 Marcedes Lewis .25 .60
128 Maurice Jones-Drew .25 .60
129 Ernest Wilford .25 .60
130 Vince Young .25 .60
131 LenDale White .30 .75
132 Brandon Jones .25 .60
133 Jay Cutler .25 .60
134 Travis Henry .30 .75
135 Javon Walker .30 .75
136 Rod Smith .30 .75
137 Champ Bailey .30 .75
138 Mike Bell .30 .75
139 Brandon Marshall .30 .75
140 Larry Johnson .25 .60
141 Eddie Kennison .25 .60
142 Tony Gonzalez .30 .75
143 Brodie Croyle .30 .75
144 LaMont Jordan .30 .75
145 Ronald Curry .25 .60
146 Philip Rivers .40 1.00
147 LaDainian Tomlinson .40 1.00
148 Michael Turner .25 .60
149 Antonio Gates .40 1.00
150 Shawne Merriman .25 .60
151 Aaron Ross RC 1.25 3.00
152 Adam Carriker RC 1.25 3.00
153 Ahmad Bradshaw RC 2.00 5.00
154 Alan Branch RC 1.25 3.00
155 Chansi Stuckey RC 1.50 4.00
156 Charles Johnson RC 1.25 3.00
157 Chris Leak RC 1.25 3.00
158 Jarvis Moss RC 1.25 3.00
159 Dan Bazuin RC 1.50 4.00
160 David Harris RC 1.25 3.00
161 Dwayne Wright RC 1.25 3.00
162 Eric Frampton RC 1.50 4.00
163 Eric Wright RC 1.25 3.00
164 Jared Zabransky RC 1.25 3.00
165 Jason Snelling RC 1.25 3.00
166 Jordan Palmer RC 1.50 4.00
167 Kenneth Darby RC 1.25 3.00
168 LaMarr Woodley RC 2.50 6.00
169 LaRon Landry RC 2.00 5.00
170 Lawrence Timmons RC 2.00 5.00
171 Leon Hall RC 1.25 3.00
172 Michael Griffin RC 1.25 3.00
173 Mike Walker RC 2.00 5.00
174 Paul Posluszny RC 1.25 3.00
175 Thomas Clayton RC 1.50 4.00
176 Amobi Okoye AU RC 4.00 10.00
177 Anthony Spencer AU RC 4.00 10.00
178 Aundrae Allison AU RC 3.00 8.00
179 Ben Patrick AU RC 4.00 10.00
180 Brandon Meriweather AU RC 4.00 10.00
181 Chris Davis AU RC 3.00 8.00
182 Chris Houston AU RC 3.00 8.00
184 Dallas Baker AU RC 3.00 8.00
185 Darius Walker AU RC 3.00 8.00
186 Darrelle Revis AU RC 8.00 20.00
187 David Clowney AU RC 3.00 8.00
188 DeShawn Wynn AU RC 3.00 8.00
189 Ikaika Alama-Francis AU RC 5.00 12.00
190 Isaiah Stanback AU RC 3.00 8.00
191 Jacoby Jones AU RC 3.00 8.00
192 Jamaal Anderson AU RC 4.00 10.00
193 James Jones AU RC 3.00 8.00
194 Courtney Taylor AU RC 3.00 8.00
195 Jon Beason AU RC 3.00 8.00
196 Jonathan Wade AU RC 3.00 8.00
197 Josh Wilson AU RC 4.00 10.00
198 Kolby Smith AU RC 3.00 8.00
199 Laurent Robinson AU RC 5.00 12.00
200 Reggie Nelson AU RC 3.00 8.00
201 Dwayne Jarrett JSY RC 2.50 6.00
202 Johnnie Lee Higgins JSY RC 2.00 5.00
203 Michael Bush JSY RC 2.00 5.00
204 Antonio Pittman JSY RC 2.00 5.00
205 Patrick Willis JSY RC 3.00 8.00
206 Gaines Adams JSY RC 2.50 6.00
207 Tony Hunt JSY RC 2.00 5.00
208 Chris Henry RB JSY RC 2.00 5.00
209 John Beck JSY RC 2.00 5.00
210 Dwayne Bowe JSY RC 2.00 5.00
211 Brian Leonard JSY RC 2.00 5.00
212 Anthony Gonzalez JSY RC 2.00 5.00
213 Trent Edwards JSY RC 2.00 5.00
214 Jason Hill JSY RC 2.00 5.00
215 JaMarcus Russell JSY/849 RC 2.00 5.00
216 Ted Ginn Jr. JSY RC 2.50 6.00
217 Paul Williams JSY RC 2.00 5.00
218 Garrett Wolfe JSY RC 2.00 5.00
219 A.Peterson JSY/849 RC 12.00 30.00
220 Kevin Kolb JSY RC 2.50 6.00
221 M.Lynch JSY/849 RC 4.00 10.00
222 Steve Smith USC JSY RC 2.00 5.00
223 Greg Olsen JSY RC 3.00 8.00
224 Kenny Irons JSY RC 2.00 5.00
225 Brandon Jackson JSY RC 2.00 5.00
226 Yamon Figurs JSY RC 2.00 5.00
227 Lorenzo Booker JSY RC 2.50 6.00
228 Drew Stanton JSY RC 2.00 5.00
229 Brady Quinn JSY/849 RC 2.00 5.00
230 Joe Thomas JSY RC 3.00 8.00
231 Robert Meachem JSY RC 2.50 6.00
232 Troy Smith JSY RC 2.00 5.00
233 Sidney Rice JSY RC 2.50 6.00
234 C.Johnson JSY/849 RC 10.00 25.00
235 Bart Starr JSY 12.00 30.00
236 Bob Griese JSY 8.00 20.00
237 Bobby Layne JSY/50 10.00 25.00
238 Bulldog Turner JSY 8.00 20.00
239 Earl Campbell JKT 8.00 20.00
240 Franco Harris JSY 8.00 20.00
241 James Lofton JSY 5.00 12.00
242 Jim McMahon JSY 10.00 25.00
243 Jim Thorpe JSY 60.00 100.00
244 Joe Namath JSY 10.00 25.00
246 Lou Groza JSY 6.00 15.00
247 Ray Nitschke JSY 10.00 25.00
248 Ron Mix JSY 5.00 12.00
249 Roosevelt Brown JSY 5.00 12.00
250 Sam Huff JSY 6.00 15.00
251 Sammy Baugh JSY 20.00 40.00
252 Sid Luckman JSY 15.00 30.00
253 Otto Graham JSY 15.00 30.00
254 Y.A. Tittle JSY 8.00 20.00

2007 Leaf Certified Materials Mirror Black

UNPRICED MIRROR BLACK PRINT RUN 1

2007 Leaf Certified Materials Mirror Blue

*VETS 1-150: 5X TO 12X BASIC CARDS
*BLUE ROOKIES: .5X TO 1.2X MIRROR RED
STATED PRINT RUN 50 SER.#'d SETS

2007 Leaf Certified Materials Mirror Emerald

UNPRICED EMERALD PRINT RUN 5

2007 Leaf Certified Materials Mirror Gold

*VET 1-150: 8X TO 20X BASIC CARDS
*GOLD ROOKIES: .8X TO 2X MIRROR RED
STATED PRINT RUN 25 SER.#'d SETS

2007 Leaf Certified Materials Mirror Red

ETS 1-150: 4X TO 10X BASIC CARDS
COMMON ROOKIE (151-200) 3.00 8.00
ROOKIE SEMISTARS 4.00 10.00
ROOKIE UNL.STARS 5.00 12.00
STATED PRINT RUN 100 SER.#'d SETS
169 LaRon Landry 5.00 12.00
174 Paul Posluszny 3.00 8.00
188 DeShawn Wynn 3.00 8.00
191 Jacoby Jones 3.00 8.00
193 James Jones 3.00 8.00

2007 Leaf Certified Materials Certified Potential

ATED PRINT RUN 1000 SER.#'d SETS
*MIRROR/500: .5X TO 1.2X BASIC INSERTS
MIRROR PRINT RUN 500 SER.#'d SETS
*RED/250: .6X TO 1.5X BASIC INSERTS
RED PRINT RUN 250 SER.#'d SETS
*BLUE/100: .8X TO 2X BASIC INSERTS
BLUE PRINT RUN 100 SER.#'d SETS
*GOLD/25: 1.2X TO 3X BASIC INSERTS
GOLD PRINT RUN 25 SER.#'d SETS
UNPRICED EMERALD PRINT RUN 5
UNPRICED BLACK PRINT RUN 1
1 Brandon Marshall .60 1.50
2 DeAngelo Williams .50 1.25
3 Demetrius Williams .50 1.25
4 Laurence Maroney .60 1.50
5 LenDale White .60 1.50
6 Joseph Addai .50 1.25
7 Marcedes Lewis .50 1.25
8 Maurice Jones-Drew .50 1.25
9 Santonio Holmes .50 1.25
10 Sinorice Moss .60 1.50
11 Tarvaris Jackson .50 1.25
12 Reggie Bush .50 1.25
13 Matt Leinart .50 1.25
14 Vince Young .50 1.25
15 Vernon Davis .50 1.25

2007 Leaf Certified Materials Certified Potential Materials

STATED PRINT RUN 10-250
UNPRICED PRIME PRINT RUN 5
UNPRICED PRIME BLACK PRINT RUN 1
SERIAL #'d UNDER 25 NOT PRICED
1 Brandon Marshall 2.50 6.00
3 Demetrius Williams 2.00 5.00
4 Laurence Maroney 2.50 6.00
5 LenDale White 2.50 6.00
6 Joseph Addai 2.00 5.00
8 Maurice Jones-Drew 2.00 5.00
9 Santonio Holmes 2.00 5.00
10 Sinorice Moss 2.50 6.00
12 Reggie Bush 2.00 5.00
13 Matt Leinart 2.00 5.00
14 Vince Young 2.00 5.00

2007 Leaf Certified Materials Certified Skills

ATED PRINT RUN 1000 SER.#'d SETS
*MIRROR/500: .5X TO 1.2X BASIC INSERTS
MIRROR PRINT RUN 500 SER.#'d SETS
*RED/250: .6X TO 1.5X BASIC INSERTS
RED PRINT RUN 250 SER.#'d SETS
*BLUE/100: .8X TO 2X BASIC INSERTS
BLUE PRINT RUN 100 SER.#'d SETS
*GOLD/25: 1.2X TO 3X BASIC INSERTS
GOLD PRINT RUN 25 SER.#'d SETS
UNPRICED EMERALD PRINT RUN 5
UNPRICED BLACK PRINT RUN 1
1 Carson Palmer .60 1.50
2 Brett Favre 1.50 4.00
3 Tom Brady 2.50 6.00
4 Eli Manning .60 1.50
5 Tony Romo 1.00 2.50
6 Philip Rivers .75 2.00
7 Steven Jackson .50 1.25
8 Willie Parker .60 1.50
9 Rudi Johnson .50 1.25
10 Brian Westbrook .50 1.25
11 Edgerrin James .60 1.50
12 Deuce McAllister .60 1.50
13 Shaun Alexander .50 1.25
14 Reggie Wayne .60 1.50
15 Donald Driver .60 1.50
16 Lee Evans .60 1.50
17 Torry Holt .60 1.50
18 Steve Smith .60 1.50
19 Terrell Owens .60 1.50
20 T.J. Houshmandzadeh .50 1.25

2007 Leaf Certified Materials Certified Skills Materials

STATED PRINT RUN 5-100
UNPRICED PRIME PRINT RUN 5
UNPRICED PRIME BLACK PRINT RUN 1
SERIAL #'d UNDER 25 NOT PRICED
1 Carson Palmer/60 2.50 6.00
2 Brett Favre 6.00 15.00
3 Tom Brady 10.00 25.00
4 Eli Manning/50 4.00 10.00
5 Tony Romo/50 4.00 10.00
6 Philip Rivers/50 3.00 8.00
7 Steven Jackson 2.00 5.00
8 Willie Parker/50 2.50 6.00
9 Rudi Johnson 2.00 5.00
11 Edgerrin James 2.50 6.00
12 Deuce McAllister 2.50 6.00
13 Shaun Alexander 2.00 5.00
14 Reggie Wayne 2.50 6.00
16 Lee Evans 2.50 6.00
18 Steve Smith 2.50 6.00

2007 Leaf Certified Materials Fabric of the Game

STATED PRINT RUN 1-40
SERIAL #'d UNDER 40 NOT PRICED
3 Andre Johnson 3.00 8.00
5 Antonio Gates 4.00 10.00
9 Brandon Marshall 3.00 8.00
11 Brett Favre 8.00 20.00
12 Brian Urlacher 4.00 10.00
14 Byron Leftwich 2.50 6.00
15 Cadillac Williams 3.00 8.00
16 Carson Palmer 3.00 8.00
17 Cedric Benson 2.50 6.00
18 Chad Johnson 2.50 6.00
19 Chad Pennington 2.50 6.00
21 Clinton Portis 2.50 6.00
25 DeAngelo Williams 2.50 6.00
27 DeShaun Foster 3.00 8.00
28 Deuce McAllister 3.00 8.00
29 Devin Hester 3.00 8.00
30 Donald Driver 3.00 8.00
31 Donovan McNabb 3.00 8.00
32 Drew Brees 4.00 10.00
34 Edgerrin James 3.00 8.00
35 Eli Manning 3.00 8.00
36 Frank Gore 3.00 8.00
38 Hines Ward 3.00 8.00
43 Javon Walker 3.00 8.00
44 Jay Cutler 2.50 6.00
50 Joseph Addai 2.50 6.00
51 Julius Jones 2.50 6.00
52 LaDainian Tomlinson 4.00 10.00
54 Larry Fitzgerald 3.00 8.00
55 Larry Johnson 2.50 6.00
56 Laurence Maroney 3.00 8.00
59 LenDale White 3.00 8.00
60 Leon Washington 2.50 6.00
64 Marques Colston 2.50 6.00
65 Marvin Harrison 3.00 8.00
66 Matt Hasselbeck 2.50 6.00
67 Matt Leinart 2.50 6.00
68 Maurice Jones-Drew 2.50 6.00
71 Mike Bell 3.00 8.00
73 Peyton Manning 10.00 25.00
74 Philip Rivers 4.00 10.00
77 Reggie Bush 2.50 6.00
78 Reggie Wayne 3.00 8.00
79 Rex Grossman 2.50 6.00
80 Ronnie Brown 2.50 6.00
82 Roy Williams WR 2.50 6.00
83 Rudi Johnson 2.50 6.00
85 Shaun Alexander 2.50 6.00
86 Shawne Merriman 2.50 6.00
87 Sinorice Moss 3.00 8.00
89 Steve Smith 3.00 8.00
90 Steven Jackson 2.50 6.00
91 T.J. Houshmandzadeh 2.50 6.00
93 Terrell Owens 3.00 8.00
96 Tom Brady 12.00 30.00
97 Tony Gonzalez 3.00 8.00
99 Torry Holt 3.00 8.00
101 Vince Young 2.50 6.00
103 Warrick Dunn 2.50 6.00
104 Willie Parker 3.00 8.00
106 Jan Stenerud 4.00 10.00
107 Barry Sanders 10.00 25.00
108 Bart Starr 10.00 25.00
109 Bill Bates 4.00 10.00
110 Bob Griese 6.00 15.00
111 Charlie Joiner 4.00 10.00
112 Dan Hampton 5.00 12.00
113 Dan Marino 12.00 30.00
114 Earl Campbell JKT 6.00 15.00
115 Franco Harris 6.00 15.00
116 Cliff Harris 4.00 10.00
117 Gale Sayers 6.00 15.00
118 Jack Lambert 6.00 15.00
119 James Lofton 4.00 10.00
120 Jerry Rice 12.00 30.00
121 Jim Brown 8.00 20.00
122 Jim Kelly 6.00 15.00
124 Joe Montana 20.00 50.00
125 Joe Namath 8.00 20.00
126 Joe Theismann 6.00 15.00
127 John Elway 10.00 25.00
128 John Riggins 5.00 12.00
130 Johnny Unitas 25.00 60.00
131 Lance Alworth 5.00 12.00
132 Lee Roy Selmon 4.00 10.00
133 Len Dawson 6.00 15.00
134 Lou Groza 5.00 12.00
135 Mike Singletary 6.00 15.00
136 Ozzie Newsome 5.00 12.00
138 Paul Warfield 5.00 12.00
139 Ray Nitschke 12.00 30.00
140 Ron Mix 4.00 10.00
141 Roosevelt Brown 4.00 10.00
142 Sam Huff 5.00 12.00
143 Sammy Baugh 20.00 50.00
144 Ted Hendricks 5.00 12.00
145 Tiki Barber 5.00 12.00
146 Troy Aikman 8.00 20.00
147 Walter Payton 12.00 30.00
148 Warren Moon 6.00 15.00
149 Y.A. Tittle 6.00 15.00
150 Sid Luckman 15.00 40.00

2007 Leaf Certified Materials Fabric of the Game NFL Die Cut

MMON CARD 8.00 20.00
SEMISTARS 10.00 25.00
UNLISTED STARS 12.00 30.00
*NFL DC/20-25: .8X TO 2X BASIC FOTG
STATED PRINT RUN 5-25
6 Ben Roethlisberger 12.00 30.00
98 Tony Romo 15.00 40.00

2007 Leaf Certified Materials Fabric of the Game Jersey Number

ER.NO/31-99: .4X TO 1X BASE FOTG
*JER.NO/20-29: .5X TO 1.2X BASE FOTG
STATED PRINT RUN 1-99
SERIAL #'d UNDER 20 NOT PRICED
2 Alge Crumpler/83 5.00 12.00
3 Andre Johnson/80 5.00 12.00
4 Anquan Boldin/81 4.00 10.00
5 Antonio Gates/85 6.00 15.00
7 Ben Watson/84 4.00 10.00
8 Bernard Berrian/80 4.00 10.00
12 Brian Urlacher/54 6.00 15.00
15 Cadillac Williams/24 6.00 15.00
17 Cedric Benson/32 4.00 10.00
20 Chris Chambers/84 4.00 10.00
21 Clinton Portis/26 5.00 12.00
22 Correll Buckhalter/28 5.00 12.00
23 Dallas Clark/44 5.00 12.00
25 DeAngelo Williams/34 4.00 10.00
27 DeShaun Foster/26 6.00 15.00
28 Deuce McAllister/26 6.00 15.00
29 Devin Hester/23 6.00 15.00
30 Donald Driver/80 5.00 12.00
34 Edgerrin James/32 5.00 12.00
36 Frank Gore/21 6.00 15.00
37 Fred Taylor/28 5.00 12.00
38 Hines Ward/86 5.00 12.00
39 Isaac Bruce/80 6.00 15.00
43 Javon Walker/84 5.00 12.00
45 Jeremy Shockey/80 4.00 10.00
46 Jerious Norwood/32 4.00 10.00
48 Jerry Porter/84 5.00 12.00
49 Joey Galloway/84 5.00 12.00
50 Joseph Addai/29 5.00 12.00
51 Julius Jones/21 5.00 12.00
52 LaDainian Tomlinson/21 8.00 20.00
53 LaMont Jordan/34 5.00 12.00
55 Larry Johnson/27 5.00 12.00
56 Laurence Maroney/39 5.00 12.00
58 Lee Evans/83 5.00 12.00
59 LenDale White/25 6.00 15.00
60 Leon Washington/29 5.00 12.00
62 Marion Barber/24 6.00 15.00
65 Marvin Harrison/88 5.00 12.00
68 Maurice Jones-Drew/32 4.00 10.00
69 Michael Clayton/80 4.00 10.00
71 Mike Bell/20 6.00 15.00
72 Muhsin Muhammad/87 4.00 10.00
73 Peyton Manning/18 5.00 12.00
75 Ray Lewis/52 6.00 15.00
77 Reggie Bush/25 5.00 12.00
78 Reggie Wayne/87 5.00 12.00
80 Ronnie Brown/23 5.00 12.00
81 Roy Williams S/31 4.00 10.00
83 Rudi Johnson/32 4.00 10.00
84 Santana Moss/89 5.00 12.00
85 Shaun Alexander/37 4.00 10.00
86 Shawne Merriman/56 4.00 10.00
87 Sinorice Moss/83 5.00 12.00
89 Steve Smith/89 5.00 12.00
90 Steven Jackson/39 4.00 10.00
91 T.J. Houshmandzadeh/84 4.00 10.00
92 Tedy Bruschi/54 5.00 12.00
94 Terry Glenn/83 5.00 12.00
95 Todd Heap/86 4.00 10.00
97 Tony Gonzalez/88 5.00 12.00
102 Vincent Jackson/83 4.00 10.00
103 Warrick Dunn/28 5.00 12.00
104 Willie Parker/39 5.00 12.00
105 Zach Thomas/54 5.00 12.00
107 Barry Sanders/20 20.00 50.00
109 Bill Bates/40 6.00 15.00
112 Dan Hampton/99 8.00 20.00
114 Earl Campbell/34 10.00 25.00
115 Franco Harris/32 10.00 25.00
116 Cliff Harris/43 6.00 15.00
117 Gale Sayers/40 10.00 25.00
118 Jack Lambert/58 10.00 25.00
119 James Lofton/80 6.00 15.00
120 Jerry Rice/80 20.00 50.00
121 Jim Brown/32 8.00 20.00
128 John Riggins/44 8.00 20.00
132 Lee Roy Selmon/63 6.00 15.00
134 Lou Groza/76 8.00 20.00
135 Mike Singletary/50 10.00 25.00
136 Ozzie Newsome/82 5.00 12.00
138 Paul Warfield/42 5.00 12.00
139 Ray Nitschke/66 12.00 30.00
140 Ron Mix/74 6.00 15.00
141 Roosevelt Brown/79 6.00 15.00
142 Sam Huff/70 8.00 20.00
143 Sammy Baugh/33 20.00 50.00
144 Ted Hendricks/83 8.00 20.00
145 Tiki Barber/21 10.00 25.00
147 Walter Payton/34 20.00 50.00
150 Sid Luckman/42 15.00 40.00

2007 Leaf Certified Materials Fabric of the Game Position

OSITION/40-50: .4X TO 1X BASE FOTG
*POSITION/25-30: .5X TO 1.2X BASE FOTG
STATED PRINT RUN 9-50
1 Alex Smith QB 5.00 12.00
2 Alge Crumpler 5.00 12.00
3 Andre Johnson 5.00 12.00
4 Anquan Boldin 4.00 10.00
5 Antonio Gates 6.00 15.00
7 Ben Watson 4.00 10.00
8 Bernard Berrian 4.00 10.00
9 Brandon Marshall 5.00 12.00
11 Brett Favre 12.00 30.00
12 Brian Urlacher 6.00 15.00
14 Byron Leftwich 4.00 10.00
15 Cadillac Williams 5.00 12.00
16 Carson Palmer 5.00 12.00
18 Chad Johnson 4.00 10.00
19 Chad Pennington 4.00 10.00
20 Chris Chambers 4.00 10.00
21 Clinton Portis 4.00 10.00
22 Correll Buckhalter 4.00 10.00
23 Dallas Clark 5.00 12.00
24 Daunte Culpepper 5.00 12.00
27 DeShaun Foster 5.00 12.00
28 Deuce McAllister 5.00 12.00
29 Devin Hester 5.00 12.00
31 Donovan McNabb 5.00 12.00
32 Drew Brees 6.00 15.00
34 Edgerrin James 5.00 12.00
35 Eli Manning/25 6.00 15.00
36 Frank Gore 5.00 12.00
37 Fred Taylor 4.00 10.00
38 Hines Ward 5.00 12.00
41 Jake Delhomme 4.00 10.00
42 Jason Campbell 4.00 10.00
43 Javon Walker 5.00 12.00
44 Jay Cutler 4.00 10.00
45 Jeremy Shockey 4.00 10.00
46 Jerious Norwood 4.00 10.00
48 Jerry Porter 5.00 12.00
49 Joey Galloway 5.00 12.00
50 Joseph Addai 4.00 10.00
51 Julius Jones 4.00 10.00
52 LaDainian Tomlinson 6.00 15.00
53 LaMont Jordan/25 6.00 15.00
54 Larry Fitzgerald 5.00 12.00
55 Larry Johnson 4.00 10.00
56 Laurence Maroney 5.00 12.00
58 Lee Evans 5.00 12.00
59 LenDale White 5.00 12.00
60 Leon Washington/49 4.00 10.00
61 Marc Bulger 4.00 10.00
62 Marion Barber 6.00 15.00
65 Marvin Harrison 5.00 12.00
66 Matt Hasselbeck 4.00 10.00
67 Matt Leinart 4.00 10.00
68 Maurice Jones-Drew 4.00 10.00
69 Michael Clayton 4.00 10.00
70 Michael Vick 5.00 12.00
71 Mike Bell 5.00 12.00
72 Muhsin Muhammad 4.00 10.00
73 Peyton Manning/25 20.00 50.00
74 Philip Rivers/25 8.00 20.00
75 Ray Lewis 6.00 15.00
77 Reggie Bush 4.00 10.00
78 Reggie Wayne 5.00 12.00
79 Rex Grossman 4.00 10.00
80 Ronnie Brown 4.00 10.00
81 Roy Williams S 4.00 10.00
82 Roy Williams WR 4.00 10.00
83 Rudi Johnson 4.00 10.00
84 Santana Moss/45 5.00 12.00
85 Shaun Alexander 4.00 10.00
87 Sinorice Moss 5.00 12.00
88 Steve McNair/25 6.00 15.00
89 Steve Smith 5.00 12.00
90 Steven Jackson 4.00 10.00
92 Tedy Bruschi 5.00 12.00
94 Terry Glenn 5.00 12.00
95 Todd Heap 4.00 10.00
96 Tom Brady 20.00 50.00
97 Tony Gonzalez/25 6.00 15.00
101 Vince Young/25 5.00 12.00
102 Vincent Jackson/25 5.00 12.00
103 Warrick Dunn 4.00 10.00
105 Zach Thomas 5.00 12.00
106 Jan Stenerud 6.00 15.00
107 Barry Sanders 15.00 40.00
108 Bart Starr 15.00 40.00
109 Bill Bates 6.00 15.00
111 Charlie Joiner 6.00 15.00
112 Dan Hampton 8.00 20.00
113 Dan Marino 20.00 50.00
114 Earl Campbell 10.00 25.00
115 Franco Harris 10.00 25.00
116 Cliff Harris 6.00 15.00
117 Gale Sayers 10.00 25.00
118 Jack Lambert 10.00 25.00
119 James Lofton 6.00 15.00
120 Jerry Rice 20.00 50.00
121 Jim Brown/30 15.00 40.00
122 Jim Kelly/25 12.00 30.00
123 Jim McMahon/25 15.00 40.00
124 Joe Montana 30.00 80.00

125 Joe Namath 12.00 30.00
126 Joe Theismann 10.00 25.00
127 John Elway 15.00 40.00
128 John Riggins 8.00 20.00
130 Johnny Unitas 25.00 60.00
131 Lance Alworth/25 10.00 25.00
132 Lee Roy Selmon 6.00 15.00
133 Len Dawson 10.00 25.00
134 Lou Groza/25 10.00 25.00
135 Mike Singletary/25 12.00 30.00
136 Ozzie Newsome 8.00 20.00
138 Paul Warfield/25 8.00 20.00
139 Ray Nitschke/25 15.00 40.00
140 Ron Mix 6.00 15.00
141 Roosevelt Brown/30 8.00 20.00
142 Sam Huff/25 10.00 25.00
144 Ted Hendricks 8.00 20.00
145 Tiki Barber 8.00 20.00
146 Troy Aikman 12.00 30.00
147 Walter Payton 20.00 50.00
148 Warren Moon 10.00 25.00
149 Y.A. Tittle 10.00 25.00
150 Sid Luckman/25 20.00 50.00

2007 Leaf Certified Materials Fabric of the Game Prime

RIME/20-25: .5X TO 1.2X BASE FOTG
PRIME PRINT RUN 1-25
1 Alex Smith QB 6.00 15.00
2 Alge Crumpler 6.00 15.00
3 Andre Johnson 6.00 15.00
5 Antonio Gates 8.00 20.00
6 Ben Roethlisberger 8.00 20.00
7 Ben Watson 5.00 12.00
8 Bernard Berrian 5.00 12.00
9 Brandon Marshall 6.00 15.00
10 Braylon Edwards 5.00 12.00
12 Brian Urlacher 8.00 20.00
13 Brian Westbrook 5.00 12.00
14 Byron Leftwich 5.00 12.00
15 Cadillac Williams 6.00 15.00
16 Carson Palmer 6.00 15.00
17 Cedric Benson 5.00 12.00
18 Chad Johnson 5.00 12.00
19 Chad Pennington 5.00 12.00
20 Chris Chambers 5.00 12.00
21 Clinton Portis 5.00 12.00
22 Correll Buckhalter 5.00 12.00
23 Dallas Clark 6.00 15.00
24 Daunte Culpepper 6.00 15.00
25 DeAngelo Williams 5.00 12.00
26 Deion Branch 5.00 12.00
27 DeShaun Foster 6.00 15.00
28 Deuce McAllister 6.00 15.00
29 Devin Hester 6.00 15.00
30 Donald Driver 6.00 15.00
31 Donovan McNabb 6.00 15.00
32 Drew Brees 8.00 20.00
33 Eddie Kennison 5.00 12.00
34 Edgerrin James 6.00 15.00
35 Eli Manning 6.00 15.00
36 Frank Gore 6.00 15.00
37 Fred Taylor 5.00 12.00
38 Hines Ward 6.00 15.00
40 J.P. Losman 5.00 12.00
41 Jake Delhomme 5.00 12.00
42 Jason Campbell 5.00 12.00
43 Javon Walker 6.00 15.00
44 Jay Cutler 5.00 12.00
45 Jeremy Shockey/20 5.00 12.00
46 Jerious Norwood 5.00 12.00
47 Jerricho Cotchery 5.00 12.00
48 Jerry Porter 6.00 15.00
49 Joey Galloway 6.00 15.00
50 Joseph Addai 5.00 12.00
51 Julius Jones 5.00 12.00
52 LaDainian Tomlinson 8.00 20.00
53 LaMont Jordan 6.00 15.00
55 Larry Johnson 5.00 12.00
56 Laurence Maroney 6.00 15.00
57 Laveranues Coles 5.00 12.00
58 Lee Evans 6.00 15.00
59 LenDale White 6.00 15.00
60 Leon Washington 5.00 12.00
61 Marc Bulger 5.00 12.00
62 Marion Barber 6.00 15.00
63 Mark Clayton 5.00 12.00
64 Marques Colston 5.00 12.00
65 Marvin Harrison 6.00 15.00
66 Matt Hasselbeck 5.00 12.00
68 Maurice Jones-Drew 5.00 12.00
69 Michael Clayton 5.00 12.00
70 Michael Vick 6.00 15.00
71 Mike Bell 6.00 15.00
72 Muhsin Muhammad 5.00 12.00
73 Peyton Manning 20.00 50.00
74 Philip Rivers 8.00 20.00
75 Ray Lewis 10.00 25.00
76 Reggie Brown 5.00 12.00
77 Reggie Bush 5.00 12.00
78 Reggie Wayne 6.00 15.00
79 Rex Grossman 5.00 12.00
80 Ronnie Brown 5.00 12.00
81 Roy Williams S 5.00 12.00
82 Roy Williams WR 5.00 12.00
83 Rudi Johnson 5.00 12.00
84 Santana Moss 6.00 15.00
85 Shaun Alexander 5.00 12.00
86 Shawne Merriman 5.00 12.00
87 Sinorice Moss 6.00 15.00
89 Steve Smith 6.00 15.00
90 Steven Jackson 5.00 12.00
91 T.J. Houshmandzadeh 5.00 12.00
92 Tedy Bruschi 6.00 15.00
93 Terrell Owens 6.00 15.00
94 Terry Glenn 6.00 15.00
95 Todd Heap 5.00 12.00
96 Tom Brady 25.00 60.00
97 Tony Gonzalez 6.00 15.00
98 Tony Romo 10.00 25.00
99 Torry Holt 6.00 15.00
100 Vernon Davis 5.00 12.00
103 Warrick Dunn 5.00 12.00
104 Willie Parker 6.00 15.00
105 Zach Thomas 6.00 15.00
107 Barry Sanders 20.00 50.00
108 Bart Starr 20.00 50.00
109 Bill Bates 8.00 20.00
111 Charlie Joiner 8.00 20.00
112 Dan Hampton 10.00 25.00
113 Dan Marino 25.00 60.00
114 Earl Campbell 12.00 30.00
115 Franco Harris 12.00 30.00
116 Cliff Harris 8.00 20.00
117 Gale Sayers 12.00 30.00
118 Jack Lambert 12.00 30.00
119 James Lofton 8.00 20.00
120 Jerry Rice 25.00 60.00
121 Jim Brown 15.00 40.00
122 Jim Kelly 12.00 30.00
123 Jim McMahon 15.00 40.00
124 Joe Montana 40.00 100.00
125 Joe Namath 15.00 40.00
127 John Elway 20.00 50.00
128 John Riggins 10.00 25.00
130 Johnny Unitas 30.00 80.00
131 Lance Alworth 10.00 25.00
132 Lee Roy Selmon 8.00 20.00
133 Len Dawson 12.00 30.00
135 Mike Singletary 12.00 30.00
136 Ozzie Newsome 10.00 25.00
138 Paul Warfield 10.00 25.00
140 Ron Mix 8.00 20.00
145 Tiki Barber 10.00 25.00
146 Troy Aikman 15.00 40.00
147 Walter Payton 25.00 60.00

2007 Leaf Certified Materials Fabric of the Game Team Logo

EAM LOGO/20-25: .5X TO 1.2X BASE FOTG
STATED PRINT RUN 2-25
1 Alex Smith QB 6.00 15.00
2 Alge Crumpler 6.00 15.00
3 Andre Johnson 6.00 15.00
5 Antonio Gates 8.00 20.00
6 Ben Roethlisberger 8.00 20.00
7 Ben Watson 5.00 12.00
8 Bernard Berrian 5.00 12.00
9 Brandon Marshall 6.00 15.00
10 Braylon Edwards 5.00 12.00
12 Brian Urlacher 8.00 20.00
13 Brian Westbrook 5.00 12.00
14 Byron Leftwich 5.00 12.00
15 Cadillac Williams 6.00 15.00
16 Carson Palmer 6.00 15.00
18 Chad Johnson 5.00 12.00
19 Chad Pennington 5.00 12.00
20 Chris Chambers 5.00 12.00
21 Clinton Portis 5.00 12.00
22 Correll Buckhalter 5.00 12.00
23 Dallas Clark 6.00 15.00
25 DeAngelo Williams 5.00 12.00
26 Delon Branch/22 5.00 12.00
27 DeShaun Foster 6.00 15.00
28 Deuce McAllister 6.00 15.00
29 Devin Hester 6.00 15.00
30 Donald Driver 6.00 15.00
31 Donovan McNabb 6.00 15.00
32 Drew Brees 8.00 20.00
33 Eddie Kennison 5.00 12.00
34 Edgerrin James 6.00 15.00
35 Eli Manning 6.00 15.00
36 Frank Gore 6.00 15.00
37 Fred Taylor 5.00 12.00
38 Hines Ward 6.00 15.00
40 J.P. Losman 5.00 12.00
41 Jake Delhomme 5.00 12.00
42 Jason Campbell 5.00 12.00
43 Javon Walker/20 6.00 15.00
44 Jay Cutler 5.00 12.00
45 Jeremy Shockey 5.00 12.00
46 Jerious Norwood 5.00 12.00
47 Jerricho Cotchery 5.00 12.00
48 Jerry Porter 6.00 15.00
49 Joey Galloway 6.00 15.00
51 Julius Jones 5.00 12.00
52 LaDainian Tomlinson 8.00 20.00
53 LaMont Jordan 6.00 15.00
55 Larry Johnson 5.00 12.00
56 Laurence Maroney 6.00 15.00
57 Laveranues Coles 5.00 12.00
58 Lee Evans 6.00 15.00
59 LenDale White 6.00 15.00
60 Leon Washington 5.00 12.00
61 Marc Bulger 5.00 12.00
62 Marion Barber 8.00 20.00
63 Mark Clayton 5.00 12.00
65 Marvin Harrison 6.00 15.00
66 Matt Hasselbeck 5.00 12.00
68 Maurice Jones-Drew 5.00 12.00
69 Michael Clayton 5.00 12.00
71 Mike Bell 6.00 15.00
72 Muhsin Muhammad 5.00 12.00
73 Peyton Manning 20.00 50.00
74 Philip Rivers 8.00 20.00
75 Ray Lewis 8.00 20.00
76 Reggie Brown 5.00 12.00
77 Reggie Bush 5.00 12.00
78 Reggie Wayne 6.00 15.00
79 Rex Grossman 5.00 12.00
80 Ronnie Brown 5.00 12.00
81 Roy Williams S 5.00 12.00
82 Roy Williams WR 5.00 12.00
83 Rudi Johnson 5.00 12.00
84 Santana Moss 6.00 15.00
85 Shaun Alexander 5.00 12.00
86 Shawne Merriman 5.00 12.00
87 Sinorice Moss 6.00 15.00
89 Steve Smith 6.00 15.00
90 Steven Jackson 5.00 12.00
91 T.J. Houshmandzadeh 5.00 12.00
92 Tedy Bruschi 6.00 15.00
93 Terrell Owens 6.00 15.00
94 Terry Glenn 6.00 15.00
95 Todd Heap 5.00 12.00
96 Tom Brady 25.00 60.00
97 Tony Gonzalez 6.00 15.00
98 Tony Romo 10.00 25.00
99 Torry Holt 6.00 15.00
100 Vernon Davis 5.00 12.00
103 Warrick Dunn 5.00 12.00
104 Willie Parker 6.00 15.00
105 Zach Thomas 6.00 15.00
107 Barry Sanders 20.00 50.00
108 Bart Starr 20.00 50.00
109 Bill Bates 8.00 20.00
111 Charlie Joiner 8.00 20.00
112 Dan Hampton 10.00 25.00
113 Dan Marino 25.00 60.00
114 Earl Campbell 12.00 30.00
115 Franco Harris 12.00 30.00
116 Cliff Harris 8.00 20.00
117 Gale Sayers 12.00 30.00
118 Jack Lambert 12.00 30.00
119 James Lofton 8.00 20.00
120 Jerry Rice 25.00 60.00
121 Jim Brown 15.00 40.00
122 Jim Kelly 12.00 30.00
124 Joe Montana 40.00 100.00
125 Joe Namath 15.00 40.00
127 John Elway 20.00 50.00
128 John Riggins 10.00 25.00
129 John Stallworth 12.00 30.00
130 Johnny Unitas 30.00 80.00
131 Lance Alworth 10.00 25.00
132 Lee Roy Selmon 8.00 20.00
133 Len Dawson 12.00 30.00
135 Mike Singletary 12.00 30.00
136 Ozzie Newsome 10.00 25.00
137 Paul Krause/22 8.00 20.00
138 Paul Warfield 10.00 25.00
145 Tiki Barber 10.00 25.00
146 Troy Aikman 15.00 40.00
147 Walter Payton 25.00 60.00

2007 Leaf Certified Materials Fabric of the Game Autographs Jersey Number

STATED PRINT RUN 1-63
UNPRICED BASE AU FOTG SER.#'d 5-10
UNPRICED AU FB DIE CUT SER.#'d 1-10
UNPRICED AU POSITION SER.#'d 4-10
UNPRICED AU TEAM LOGO SER.#'d 4-5
15 Cadillac Williams/24 25.00 50.00
17 Cedric Benson/32 12.00 30.00
25 DeAngelo Williams/34 15.00 40.00
36 Frank Gore/21 20.00 40.00
37 Fred Taylor/28 12.00 30.00
46 Jerious Norwood/32 12.00 30.00
50 Joseph Addai/29 25.00 60.00
52 LaDainian Tomlinson/21
55 Larry Johnson/27 25.00 50.00
59 LenDale White/25
62 Marion Barber/24 40.00 80.00
68 Maurice Jones-Drew/32 20.00 40.00
71 Mike Bell/20
77 Reggie Bush/25 25.00 60.00
80 Ronnie Brown/23 25.00 50.00
83 Rudi Johnson/32 15.00 40.00
90 Steven Jackson/39 20.00 40.00
104 Willie Parker/39 25.00 50.00
107 Barry Sanders/20 75.00 150.00
109 Bill Bates/40 25.00 50.00
114 Earl Campbell/34 25.00 50.00
116 Cliff Harris/43 25.00 50.00
117 Gale Sayers/40 40.00 80.00
121 Jim Brown/32 40.00 80.00
128 John Riggins/44 20.00 50.00
132 Lee Roy Selmon/63 15.00 40.00
138 Paul Warfield/42 15.00 40.00
145 Tiki Barber/21

2007 Leaf Certified Materials Fabric of the Game College

STATED PRINT RUN 100 SER.#'d SETS
*PRIME/25: 1X TO 2.5X BASIC INSERTS
PRIME PRINT RUN 5-25
UNPRICED AUTO PRINT RUN 5
1 Frank Gore 2.50 6.00
2 Kenny Irons 2.00 5.00
3 Robert Meachem 2.50 6.00
4 Courtney Taylor 2.00 5.00
5 Dwayne Jarrett 2.50 6.00
6 Steve Smith USC 2.00 5.00
7 Adrian Peterson 10.00 25.00
8 Brandon Meriweather 2.50 6.00
9 Greg Olsen 3.00 8.00
10 Brady Quinn 2.00 5.00
11 Jon Beason 2.00 5.00
12 JaMarcus Russell 2.00 5.00
13 Dwayne Bowe 2.00 5.00
14 Craig Buster Davis 2.00 5.00
15 LaRon Landry 3.00 8.00
16 Zach Miller 2.00 5.00
17 Jordan Palmer 2.50 6.00
18 Johnnie Lee Higgins 2.00 5.00
19 Vince Young 2.00 5.00
20 Michael Bush 2.00 5.00

2007 Leaf Certified Materials Fabric of the Game College Combos

ATED PRINT RUN 50 SER.#'d SETS
UNPRICED PRIME PRINT RUN 2-10
1 V.Young/A.Peterson 30.00 60.00
2 C.Palmer/J.Palmer 10.00 25.00
3 J.Russell/D.Bowe 4.00 10.00
4 B.Quinn/M.Stovall 4.00 10.00
5 S.Smith USC/D.Jarrett 5.00 12.00

2007 Leaf Certified Materials Fabric of the Game Combos

STATED PRINT RUN 1-100
*PRIME/25: .8X TO 2X BASE COMBO/75-100
*PRIME/25: .5X TO 1.2X BASE COMBO/25-45
PRIME PRINT RUN 5-25
2 B.Layne/Y.Lary/25 25.00 50.00
3 S.Luckman/B.Turner/75 20.00 40.00
4 O.Graham/L.Groza 12.00 30.00
5 J.Thorpe/S.Baugh/75 60.00 120.00
6 J.Unitas/J.Namath 20.00 40.00
7 J.Otto/R.Nitschke 15.00 30.00
9 W.Payton/D.Walker 20.00 40.00
11 T.Aikman/T.Romo 20.00 40.00
12 W.Moon/V.Young 15.00 30.00
13 J.Lofton/D.Driver/45 10.00 25.00
14 B.Sanders/R.Bush 20.00 40.00
15 B.Bates/R.Williams S 8.00 20.00
16 J.Rice/C.Johnson 8.00 20.00
17 F.Harris/W.Parker 10.00 25.00
18 J.Elway/J.Cutler 15.00 40.00
19 J.Montana/P.Manning 25.00 60.00
20 M.Singletary/J.Lambert 8.00 20.00
21 J.Brown/L.Tomlinson 12.00 30.00
22 D.Marino/B.Favre 30.00 60.00
23 G.Sayers/C.Benson 15.00 30.00
24 J.Riggins/L.Johnson 8.00 20.00
25 T.Brady/M.Leinart 12.00 30.00

2007 Leaf Certified Materials Gold Team

STATED PRINT RUN 500 SER.#'d SETS
*MIRROR/100: .5X TO 1.2X BASIC INSERTS
MIRROR PRINT RUN 100 SER.#'d SETS
1 LaDainian Tomlinson 1.50 4.00
2 Larry Johnson 1.00 2.50
3 Frank Gore 1.25 3.00
4 Tiki Barber 1.25 3.00
5 Chad Johnson 1.00 2.50
6 Marvin Harrison 1.25 3.00
7 Roy Williams WR 1.00 2.50
8 Drew Brees 1.50 4.00
9 Peyton Manning 4.00 10.00
10 Marc Bulger 1.00 2.50

2007 Leaf Certified Materials Gold Team Materials

STATED PRINT RUN 50-250
UNPRICED PRIME PRINT RUN 5
UNPRICED PRIME BLK PRINT RUN 1
1 LaDainian Tomlinson 3.00 8.00
2 Larry Johnson 2.00 5.00
3 Frank Gore/180 2.50 6.00
4 Tiki Barber 2.50 6.00
6 Marvin Harrison 2.50 6.00
7 Roy Williams WR/50 3.00 8.00
8 Drew Brees 3.00 8.00
9 Peyton Manning/125 8.00 20.00
10 Marc Bulger 2.00 5.00

2007 Leaf Certified Materials Mirror Blue Materials

IRROR BLUE: .5X TO 1.2X MIRROR RED
COMMON ROOKIE JSY AU 12.00 30.00
ROOKIE JSY AU SEMISTARS 15.00 40.00
ROOKIE JSY AU UNL.STARS 20.00 50.00
MIRROR BLUE PRINT RUN 12-50
SERIAL #'d UNDER 25 NOT PRICED
205 Patrick Willis FF AU 20.00 50.00
210 Dwayne Bowe FF AU 12.00 30.00
215 JaMarcus Russell FF AU 12.00 30.00
219 Adrian Peterson FF AU 125.00 250.00
220 Kevin Kolb FF AU 15.00 40.00
221 Marshawn Lynch FF AU 30.00 60.00
222 Steve Smith FF USC AU 12.00 30.00
223 Greg Olsen FF AU 20.00 50.00
229 Brady Quinn FF AU 12.00 30.00
234 Calvin Johnson FF AU 50.00 120.00

2007 Leaf Certified Materials Mirror Gold Materials

IRR.GOLD: .8X TO 2X MIRR.RED/90-150
*MIRR.GOLD: .6X TO 1.5X MIRR.RED/30-35
*ROOK.JSY AU/25: .6X TO 1.5X MIRR.BLUE/50
*RETIRED: .6X TO 1.5X MIRR.RED
MIRROR GOLD PRINT RUN 8-25
SERIAL #'d UNDER 20 NOT PRICED
219 Adrian Peterson FF AU 300.00 500.00
234 Calvin Johnson FF AU 150.00 250.00

2007 Leaf Certified Materials Mirror Red Materials

ETIRED: .5X TO 1.2X BASE JSYs
STATED PRINT RUN 25-250
UNPRICED MIRROR BLACK #'d TO 1
UNPRICED MIRROR EMERALD #'d TO 5
1 Tony Romo/100 5.00 12.00
2 Julius Jones/125 2.50 6.00
3 Terry Glenn/125 3.00 8.00
4 Terrell Owens/100 3.00 8.00
5 Jason Witten/150 3.00 8.00
7 Eli Manning/100 3.00 8.00
8 Plaxico Burress/125 2.50 6.00
9 Jeremy Shockey/125 2.50 6.00
10 Brandon Jacobs/125 2.50 6.00
11 Sinorice Moss/125 3.00 8.00
12 Donovan McNabb/100 3.00 8.00
13 Brian Westbrook/90 2.50 6.00
14 Reggie Brown/125 2.50 6.00
15 Hank Baskett/125 3.00 8.00
16 Jason Campbell/125 2.50 6.00
17 Clinton Portis/100 2.50 6.00
18 Santana Moss/125 3.00 8.00
21 Rex Grossman/125 2.50 6.00
22 Cedric Benson/125 2.50 6.00
23 Bernard Berrian/100 2.50 6.00
24 Devin Hester/125 3.00 8.00
25 Brian Urlacher/125 4.00 10.00
26 Jon Kitna/125 2.50 6.00
27 Roy Williams WR/100 2.50 6.00
29 Tatum Bell/125 2.50 6.00
30 Brett Favre/100 8.00 20.00
31 Donald Driver/100 3.00 8.00
33 Nick Barnett/125 2.50 6.00
35 Chester Taylor/100 2.50 6.00
36 Troy Williamson/125 2.50 6.00
37 Michael Vick/35 4.00 10.00
38 Warrick Dunn/125 2.50 6.00
39 Joe Horn/125 2.50 6.00
40 Michael Jenkins/100 2.50 6.00
41 Alge Crumpler/100 3.00 8.00
42 Jerious Norwood/100 2.50 6.00
43 Jake Delhomme/125 2.50 6.00
44 DeShaun Foster/100 3.00 8.00
45 Steve Smith/100 3.00 8.00
46 DeAngelo Williams/100 2.50 6.00
47 Drew Brees/100 4.00 10.00
48 Deuce McAllister/100 3.00 8.00
49 Marques Colston/100 2.50 6.00
51 Reggie Bush/100 2.50 6.00
52 Cadillac Williams/100 3.00 8.00
53 Joey Galloway/125 3.00 8.00
54 Michael Clayton/125 2.50 6.00
55 Derrick Brooks/125 2.50 6.00
56 Matt Leinart/100 2.50 6.00
57 Edgerrin James/100 3.00 8.00
58 Anquan Boldin/100 2.50 6.00
59 Larry Fitzgerald/100 3.00 8.00
60 Marc Bulger/125 2.50 6.00
61 Steven Jackson/100 2.50 6.00
62 Torry Holt/100 3.00 8.00
63 Isaac Bruce/115 4.00 10.00
66 Alex Smith QB/125 3.00 8.00
67 Frank Gore/100 3.00 8.00
68 Vernon Davis/100 2.50 6.00
70 Matt Hasselbeck/100 2.50 6.00
71 Shaun Alexander/100 2.50 6.00
72 Deion Branch/125 2.50 6.00
74 J.P. Losman/125 2.50 6.00
75 Anthony Thomas/125 2.50 6.00
76 Lee Evans/125 3.00 8.00
77 Josh Reed/125 2.50 6.00
78 Daunte Culpepper/125 3.00 8.00
79 Ronnie Brown/100 2.50 6.00
80 Chris Chambers/100 2.50 6.00
82 Jason Taylor/125 3.00 8.00
83 Zach Thomas/125 3.00 8.00
84 Tom Brady/100 12.00 30.00
85 Laurence Maroney/125 3.00 8.00
86 Randy Moss/100 3.00 8.00
87 Ben Watson/110 2.50 6.00
89 Tedy Bruschi/125 3.00 8.00
90 Chad Pennington/125 2.50 6.00
91 Thomas Jones/125 2.50 6.00
92 Laveranues Coles/125 2.50 6.00
93 Jerricho Cotchery/125 2.50 6.00
94 Leon Washington/100 2.50 6.00
95 Steve McNair/100 3.00 8.00
96 Willis McGahee/125 2.50 6.00
98 Todd Heap/125 2.50 6.00
99 Ray Lewis/125 4.00 10.00
100 Mark Clayton/125 2.50 6.00
101 Carson Palmer/100 3.00 8.00
102 Rudi Johnson/125 2.50 6.00
103 Chad Johnson/100 2.50 6.00
104 T.J. Houshmandzadeh/125 2.50 6.00
105 Charlie Frye/125 3.00 8.00
106 Braylon Edwards/125 2.50 6.00
107 Kellen Winslow/125 2.50 6.00
108 Jamal Lewis/125 3.00 8.00
109 Ben Roethlisberger/125 4.00 10.00
110 Willie Parker/125 3.00 8.00
111 Hines Ward/100 3.00 8.00
112 Heath Miller/125 2.50 6.00
114 Ahman Green/110 3.00 8.00
115 Andre Johnson/125 3.00 8.00
117 DeMeco Ryans/125 3.00 8.00
118 Peyton Manning/100 10.00 25.00
119 Joseph Addai/100 2.50 6.00
120 Marvin Harrison/125 3.00 8.00
121 Reggie Wayne/125 3.00 8.00
122 Dallas Clark/125 3.00 8.00
123 Byron Leftwich/125 2.50 6.00
124 Fred Taylor/125 2.50 6.00
125 Matt Jones/125 3.00 8.00
128 Maurice Jones-Drew/125 2.50 6.00
130 Vince Young/100 2.50 6.00
131 LenDale White/125 3.00 8.00
132 Brandon Jones/100 2.50 6.00
133 Jay Cutler/100 2.50 6.00
135 Javon Walker/30 4.00 10.00
136 Rod Smith/125 3.00 8.00
137 Champ Bailey/100 3.00 8.00
138 Mike Bell/125 3.00 8.00
139 Brandon Marshall/125 3.00 8.00
140 Larry Johnson/125 2.50 6.00
141 Eddie Kennison/125 2.50 6.00
142 Tony Gonzalez/125 3.00 8.00
143 Brodie Croyle/125 3.00 8.00
144 LaMont Jordan/100 3.00 8.00
146 Philip Rivers/125 4.00 10.00
147 LaDainian Tomlinson/125 4.00 10.00
149 Antonio Gates/125 4.00 10.00
150 Shawne Merriman/125 2.50 6.00
201 Dwayne Jarrett/250 2.50 6.00
202 Johnnie Lee Higgins/250 2.00 5.00
203 Michael Bush/250 2.00 5.00
204 Antonio Pittman/250 2.00 5.00
205 Patrick Willis/250 3.00 8.00
206 Gaines Adams/250 2.50 6.00
207 Tony Hunt/250 2.00 5.00
208 Chris Henry RB/250 2.00 5.00
209 John Beck/250 2.00 5.00
210 Dwayne Bowe/250 2.00 5.00
211 Brian Leonard/250 2.00 5.00
212 Anthony Gonzalez/250 2.00 5.00
213 Trent Edwards/250 2.00 5.00
214 Jason Hill/250 2.00 5.00
215 JaMarcus Russell/250 2.00 5.00
216 Ted Ginn Jr./250 2.50 6.00
217 Paul Williams/250 2.00 5.00
218 Garrett Wolfe/250 2.00 5.00
219 Adrian Peterson/250 6.00 15.00
220 Kevin Kolb/250 2.50 6.00
221 Marshawn Lynch/250 4.00 10.00
222 Steve Smith USC/250 2.00 5.00
223 Greg Olsen/250 3.00 8.00
224 Kenny Irons/250 2.00 5.00
225 Brandon Jackson/250 2.00 5.00
226 Yamon Figurs/250 2.00 5.00
227 Lorenzo Booker/250 2.50 6.00
228 Drew Stanton/250 2.00 5.00
229 Brady Quinn/250 2.00 5.00
230 Joe Thomas/250 3.00 8.00
231 Robert Meachem/250 2.50 6.00
232 Troy Smith/250 2.00 5.00
233 Sidney Rice/250 2.50 6.00
234 Calvin Johnson/250 6.00 15.00
235 Bart Starr/50 15.00 40.00
236 Bob Griese/50 10.00 25.00
237 Bobby Layne/25 12.00 30.00
238 Bulldog Turner/50 10.00 26.00
239 Earl Campbell/50 10.00 25.00
240 Franco Harris/50 10.00 25.00
241 James Lofton/50 6.00 15.00
242 Jim McMahon/25 12.00 30.00
243 Jim Thorpe/25 60.00 120.00
244 Joe Namath/50 12.00 30.00
245 John Stallworth/50 8.00 20.00
246 Lou Groza/50 8.00 20.00
247 Ray Nitschke/50 12.00 30.00
248 Ron Mix/50 6.00 15.00
249 Roosevelt Brown/50 6.00 15.00
250 Sam Huff/50 8.00 20.00
251 Sammy Baugh/50 20.00 50.00
252 Sid Luckman/25 15.00 40.00
253 Otto Graham/25 15.00 40.00
254 Y.A. Tittle/50 10.00 25.00

2007 Leaf Certified Materials Mirror Blue Signatures

MIRROR BLUE PRINT RUN 50 SER.#'d SETS
*MIRR.GOLD/25: .5X TO 1.2X MIRR.BLUE/50
MIRROR GOLD PRINT RUN 10-25
*MIRR.RED/100: .3X TO .8X MIRR.BLUE/50
MIRROR RED PRINT RUN 100
UNPRICED MIRROR BLACK PRINT RUN 1
UNPRICED MIRROR EMERALD PRINT RUN 5
151 Aaron Ross 4.00 10.00
153 Ahmad Bradshaw 6.00 15.00
155 Chansi Stuckey 5.00 12.00
159 Dan Bazuin 5.00 12.00
160 David Harris 4.00 10.00
161 Dwayne Wright 4.00 10.00
162 Eric Frampton 5.00 12.00
165 Jason Snelling 4.00 10.00
167 Kenneth Darby 4.00 10.00
168 LaMarr Woodley 10.00 25.00
172 Michael Griffin 4.00 10.00
173 Mike Walker 6.00 15.00
177 Anthony Spencer 5.00 12.00
178 Aundrae Allison 4.00 10.00
179 Ben Patrick 5.00 12.00
180 Brandon Meriweather 5.00 12.00
181 Chris Davis 4.00 10.00
182 Chris Houston 4.00 10.00
184 Dallas Baker 4.00 10.00
187 David Clowney 4.00 10.00
188 DeShawn Wynn 8.00 20.00
189 Ikaika Alama-Francis 6.00 15.00
190 Isaiah Stanback 4.00 10.00
194 Courtney Taylor 4.00 10.00
196 Jonathan Wade 4.00 10.00
197 Josh Wilson 5.00 12.00
198 Kolby Smith 4.00 10.00

2007 Leaf Certified Materials Souvenir Stamps Autographs Pro Team Logos

UNPRICED 1969 STAMP AU PRINT RUN 5-10
UNPRICED PRO TEAM AU PRINT RUN 5-15
UNPRICED USA FLAG AU #'d TO 1

2007 Leaf Certified Materials Souvenir Stamps Material Pro Team Logos

ATED PRINT RUN 50 SER.#'d SETS
*1969 STAMP/25: .5X TO 1.2X TEAM LOGO
UNPRICED POP WARNER PRINT RUN 5
UNPRICED USA FLAG PRINT RUN 10
UNPRICED AUTOs PRINT RUN 1
1 Trent Edwards 3.00 8.00
2 Marshawn Lynch 6.00 15.00
3 Chris Henry RB 3.00 8.00
4 Paul Williams 3.00 8.00
5 Sidney Rice 4.00 10.00
6 Adrian Peterson 10.00 25.00
7 Drew Stanton 3.00 8.00
8 Calvin Johnson 10.00 25.00
9 Yamon Figurs 3.00 8.00
10 Brian Leonard 3.00 8.00
11 Garrett Wolfe 3.00 8.00
12 Kenny Irons 3.00 8.00
13 Joe Thomas 5.00 12.00
14 Brady Quinn 3.00 8.00
15 Brandon Jackson 3.00 8.00
16 Steve Smith USC 3.00 8.00
17 Dwayne Jarrett 4.00 10.00
18 Troy Smith 3.00 8.00
19 Ted Ginn Jr. 4.00 10.00
20 John Beck 3.00 8.00
21 Lorenzo Booker 4.00 10.00
22 Antonio Pittman 3.00 8.00
23 Robert Meachem 4.00 10.00
24 Dwayne Bowe 3.00 8.00
25 Greg Olsen 5.00 12.00
26 Anthony Gonzalez 3.00 8.00
27 JaMarcus Russell 3.00 8.00
28 Michael Bush 3.00 8.00
29 Johnnie Lee Higgins 3.00 8.00
30 Kevin Kolb 4.00 10.00
31 Tony Hunt 3.00 8.00
32 Patrick Willis 5.00 12.00
33 Jason Hill 3.00 8.00
34 Gaines Adams 4.00 10.00

2007 Leaf Certified Materials Souvenir Stamps College Autographs College Logo

PRICED AU COLLEGE PRINT RUN 5-9
UNPRICED AU 1969 STAMP PRINT RUN 5
UNPRICED AU USA FLAG PRINT RUN 1

2007 Leaf Certified Materials Souvenir Stamps College Material College Logo

STATED PRINT RUN 50 SER.#'d SETS
*1969 STAMP/25: .5X TO 1.2X BASE INSERTS
UNPRICED AUTOs PRINT RUN 1
UNPRICED POP WARNER PRINT RUN 5
UNPRICED USA FLAG PRINT RUN 10
1 Kenny Irons 6.00 15.00
2 Robert Meachem 8.00 20.00
3 Adrian Peterson 25.00 60.00
4 Greg Olsen 5.00 12.00
5 Michael Bush 3.00 8.00
6 JaMarcus Russell 3.00 8.00
7 Dwayne Bowe 3.00 8.00

2008 Leaf Certified Materials

This set was released on September 24, 2008. The base set consists of 255 cards. Cards 1-150 feature veterans, cards 151-200 are a mix of rookies serial numbered of 1500 and autographed rookie cards serial numbered of 249-999. Cards 201-234 are jersey rookie cards serial numbered of 599, and cards 235-255 are jersey legend cards serial numbered of 100.

COMP.SET w/o SP's (150) 15.00 40.00
UNSIGNED ROOKIE PRINT RUN 1500
AU ROOKIE PRINT RUN 249-999
JSY ROOKIE PRINT RUN 599
JSY LEGEND PRINT RUN 100
1 Matt Leinart .25 .60
2 Larry Fitzgerald .30 .75
3 Anquan Boldin .25 .60
4 Edgerrin James .30 .75
5 Jerious Norwood .25 .60
6 Roddy White .25 .60
7 Joe Horn .25 .60
8 Michael Turner .25 .60
9 Willis McGahee .25 .60
10 Derrick Mason .25 .60
11 Mark Clayton .25 .60
12 Demetrius Williams .25 .60
13 Trent Edwards .25 .60
14 Marshawn Lynch .30 .75
15 Lee Evans .30 .75
16 Steve Smith .30 .75
17 DeAngelo Williams .25 .60
18 Julius Peppers .30 .75
19 Jake Delhomme .25 .60
20 Adrian Peterson .25 .60
21 Greg Olsen .30 .75
22 Devin Hester .30 .75
23 Brian Urlacher .40 1.00
24 Rex Grossman .25 .60
25 Carson Palmer .30 .75
26 Chad Johnson .25 .60
27 T.J. Houshmandzadeh .25 .60
28 Rudi Johnson .25 .60
29 Derek Anderson .25 .60
30 Jamal Lewis .30 .75
31 Kellen Winslow .25 .60
32 Braylon Edwards .25 .60
33 Tony Romo .30 .75
34 Terrell Owens .30 .75
35 Marion Barber .25 .60
36 Jason Witten .30 .75
37 Jay Cutler .25 .60
38 Selvin Young .25 .60
39 Brandon Marshall .30 .75
40 Brandon Stokley .25 .60
41 Jon Kitna .25 .60
42 Roy Williams WR .25 .60
43 Calvin Johnson .40 1.00
44 Mike Furrey .30 .75
45 Aaron Rodgers .75 2.00
46 Ryan Grant .30 .75
47 Greg Jennings .25 .60
48 Donald Driver .30 .75
49 Matt Schaub .25 .60
50 Ahman Green .30 .75
51 Andre Johnson .30 .75
52 Kevin Walter .30 .75
53 DeMeco Ryans .30 .75
54 Peyton Manning 1.00 2.50
55 Joseph Addai .25 .60
56 Marvin Harrison .30 .75
57 Reggie Wayne .30 .75
58 Dallas Clark .25 .60
59 Anthony Gonzalez .25 .60
60 David Garrard .25 .60
61 Fred Taylor .25 .60
62 Maurice Jones-Drew .25 .60
63 Reggie Williams .30 .75
64 Marcedes Lewis .25 .60
65 Matt Jones .30 .75
66 Jerry Porter .25 .60
67 Brodie Croyle .30 .75
68 Larry Johnson .25 .60
69 Kolby Smith .25 .60
70 Tony Gonzalez .30 .75
71 Dwayne Bowe .30 .75
72 John Beck .25 .60
73 Ronnie Brown .25 .60
74 Ted Ginn Jr. .25 .60
75 Derek Hagan .25 .60
76 Jason Taylor .30 .75
77 Bernard Berrian .25 .60
78 Tarvaris Jackson .25 .60
79 Adrian Peterson .40 1.00
80 Chester Taylor .25 .60
81 Sidney Rice .25 .60
82 Tom Brady 1.25 3.00
83 Randy Moss .30 .75
84 Laurence Maroney .30 .75
85 Wes Welker .30 .75
86 Drew Brees .40 1.00
87 Reggie Bush .25 .60
88 Deuce McAllister .30 .75
89 Marques Colston .25 .60
90 Eli Manning .30 .75
91 Plaxico Burress .25 .60
92 Brandon Jacobs .25 .60
93 Amani Toomer .25 .60
94 Jeremy Shockey .25 .60
95 Steve Smith USC .30 .75
96 Michael Strahan .30 .75
97 Kellen Clemens .25 .60
98 Leon Washington .25 .60
99 Jerricho Cotchery .25 .60
100 Laveranues Coles .25 .60
101 Thomas Jones .25 .60
102 Javon Walker .30 .75
103 JaMarcus Russell .25 .60
104 Justin Fargas .25 .60
105 Michael Bush .25 .60
106 Zach Miller .25 .60
107 Donovan McNabb .30 .75
108 Brian Westbrook .25 .60
109 Kevin Curtis .25 .60
110 Reggie Brown .25 .60
111 Greg Lewis .25 .60
112 Ben Roethlisberger .40 1.00
113 Willie Parker .30 .75
114 Hines Ward .30 .75
115 Santonio Holmes .25 .60
116 Philip Rivers .40 1.00
117 LaDainian Tomlinson .40 1.00
118 Vincent Jackson .25 .60
119 Antonio Gates .30 .75
120 Brett Favre .75 2.00
121 Alex Smith QB .30 .75
122 Frank Gore .30 .75
123 Michael Robinson .25 .60
124 Vernon Davis .25 .60
125 Isaac Bruce .40 1.00
126 Patrick Willis .30 .75
127 Matt Hasselbeck .25 .60
128 Nate Burleson .25 .60
129 Deion Branch .25 .60
130 Julius Jones .25 .60
131 Marc Bulger .25 .60
132 Steven Jackson .25 .60
133 Torry Holt .30 .75
134 Warrick Dunn .25 .60
135 Jeff Garcia .25 .60
136 Cadillac Williams .30 .75
137 Earnest Graham .25 .60
138 Joey Galloway .30 .75
139 Michael Clayton .25 .60
140 Vince Young .25 .60
141 LenDale White .25 .60
142 Justin Gage .25 .60
143 Roydell Williams .25 .60
144 Alge Crumpler .25 .60
145 Brandon Jones .25 .60
146 Jason Campbell .25 .60
147 Clinton Portis .25 .60
148 Ladell Betts .25 .60
149 Santana Moss .25 .60
150 Chris Cooley .25 .60
151 Adrian Arrington AU/999 RC 2.50 6.00
152 Andre Woodson RC 1.00 2.50
153 Antoine Cason AU/749 RC 3.00 8.00
154 Aqib Talib AU/999 RC 4.00 10.00
155 Brad Cottam AU/999 RC 2.50 6.00
156 Brandon Flowers AU/899 RC 3.00 8.00
157 Chauncey Washington AU/799 RC 3.00 8.00
158 Chevis Jackson RC 1.00 2.50
159 Colt Brennan RC 1.25 3.00
160 Curtis Lofton AU/999 RC 3.00 8.00
161 Dan Connor RC 1.00 2.50
162 Dennis Dixon RC 1.00 2.50
163 Derrick Harvey RC 1.00 2.50
164 D.Rodgers-Cromartie RC 1.25 3.00
165 Erik Ainge AU/699 RC 2.50 6.00
166 Fred Davis AU/999 RC 2.50 6.00
167 Jacob Hester AU/399 RC 3.00 8.00
168 Jermichael Finley RC 1.00 2.50
169 Jerod Mayo RC 1.50 4.00
170 John Carlson RC 1.00 2.50
171 Josh Johnson RC 1.00 2.50
172 Jordon Dizon AU/299 RC 3.00 8.00
173 Josh Morgan RC 1.00 2.50
174 Justin Forsett AU/649 RC 3.00 8.00
175 Keenan Burton RC 1.00 2.50
176 Keith Rivers RC 1.00 2.50
177 Kenny Phillips RC 1.00 2.50
178 Kevin Robinson AU/999 RC 2.50 6.00
179 Lavelle Hawkins RC 1.25 3.00
180 Leodis McKelvin AU/999 RC 3.00 8.00
181 Marcus Smith RC 1.25 3.00
182 Marcus Thomas AU/499 RC 4.00 10.00
183 Martellus Bennett RC 1.25 3.00
184 Matt Flynn RC 1.00 2.50
185 Mike Jenkins RC 1.00 2.50
186 Mike Hart RC 1.00 2.50
187 Paul Hubbard RC 1.00 2.50
188 Peyton Hillis AU/499 RC 5.00 12.00
189 Quentin Groves AU/275 RC 4.00 10.00
190 Reggie Smith RC 1.00 2.50
191 Ryan Torain AU/299 RC 4.00 10.00
192 Sedrick Ellis RC 1.00 2.50
193 Shawn Crable RC 1.00 2.50
194 Tashard Choice AU/999 RC 2.50 6.00
195 Terrell Thomas AU/999 RC 2.50 6.00
196 Thomas Brown AU/999 RC 2.50 6.00
197 Tim Hightower AU/499 RC 4.00 10.00
198 Tracy Porter AU/999 RC 3.00 8.00
199 Vernon Gholston AU/999 RC 2.50 6.00
200 Will Franklin AU/249 RC 4.00 10.00
201 Andre Caldwell JSY RC 1.50 4.00
202 Dustin Keller JSY RC 2.00 5.00
203 Earl Bennett JSY RC 2.50 6.00
204 Early Doucet JSY RC 1.50 4.00
205 Glenn Dorsey JSY RC 1.50 4.00
206 Harry Douglas JSY RC 2.00 5.00
207 John David Booty JSY RC 1.50 4.00
208 Kevin O'Connell JSY RC 1.50 4.00
209 Darren McFadden JSY RC 1.50 4.00
210 Jonathan Stewart JSY RC 2.50 6.00
211 Felix Jones JSY RC 1.50 4.00
212 R.Mendenhall JSY RC 1.50 4.00
213 Chris Johnson JSY RC 2.00 5.00
214 Matt Forte JSY RC 2.50 6.00
215 Ray Rice JSY RC 1.50 4.00
216 Kevin Smith JSY RC 1.50 4.00
217 Jamaal Charles JSY RC 2.50 6.00
218 Steve Slaton JSY RC 1.50 4.00
219 Matt Ryan JSY RC 5.00 12.00
220 Joe Flacco JSY RC 3.00 8.00
221 Brian Brohm JSY RC 1.50 4.00
222 Chad Henne JSY RC 2.00 5.00
223 Donnie Avery JSY RC 2.00 5.00
224 Devin Thomas JSY RC 1.50 4.00
225 Jordy Nelson JSY RC 5.00 12.00
226 James Hardy JSY RC 1.50 4.00
227 Eddie Royal JSY RC 1.50 4.00
228 DeSean Jackson JSY RC 3.00 8.00
229 Malcolm Kelly JSY RC 1.50 4.00
230 Limas Sweed JSY RC 1.50 4.00
231 Mario Manningham JSY RC 1.50 4.00
232 Jerome Simpson JSY RC 2.00 5.00
233 Dexter Jackson JSY RC 2.50 6.00
234 Jake Long JSY RC 2.50 6.00
235 Bart Starr JSY 10.00 25.00
236 Johnny Unitas JSY/75 12.00 30.00
237 Brett Favre JSY 10.00 25.00
238 Tom Landry JSY 12.00 30.00
239 Hank Stram JSY 6.00 15.00
240 Chuck Foreman JSY 4.00 10.00
241 Dan Marino JSY 12.00 30.00
242 Andre Reed JSY 5.00 12.00
243 Frank Gifford JSY/50 6.00 15.00
244 John Riggins JSY 5.00 12.00
245 John Stallworth JSY 5.00 12.00
246 John Elway JSY 10.00 25.00
247 Emmitt Smith JSY 10.00 25.00
248 Randall Cunningham JSY 5.00 12.00
249 Reggie White JSY 6.00 15.00
250 John Matuszak JSY 6.00 15.00
251 Troy Aikman JSY 8.00 20.00
252 Billy Sims JSY 5.00 12.00
253 Willie Brown JSY 4.00 10.00
254 Barry Sanders JSY 10.00 25.00
255 Walter Payton JSY 12.00 30.00

2008 Leaf Certified Materials Mirror Black

UNPRICED MIRROR BLACK PRINT RUN 1

2008 Leaf Certified Materials Mirror Blue

*VETS 1-150: 5X TO 12X BASIC CARDS
*ROOKIES 151-200: .5X TO 1.2X MIRR.RED
STATED PRINT RUN 50 SER.#'d SETS

2008 Leaf Certified Materials Mirror Emerald

UNPRICED MIRROR EMERALD PRINT RUN 5

2008 Leaf Certified Materials Mirror Gold

*VETS 1-150: 8X TO 20X BASIC CARDS
*ROOKIES 151-200: .8X TO 2X MIRR.RED
STATED PRINT RUN 25 SER.#'d SETS

2008 Leaf Certified Materials Mirror Red

*VETS 1-150: 4X TO 10X BASIC CARDS
COMMON ROOKIE (151-200) 3.00 8.00
ROOKIE UNL.STARS 4.00 10.00
STATED PRINT RUN 100 SER.#'d SETS

2008 Leaf Certified Materials Certified Potential

ATED PRINT RUN 1000 SER.#'d SETS
*MIRROR/500: .4X TO 1X BASIC INSERTS
MIRROR PRINT RUN 500 SER.#'d SETS
*RED/250: .5X TO 1.2X BASIC INSERTS
RED PRINT RUN 250 SER.#'d SETS
*BLUE/100: .6X TO 1.5X BASIC INSERTS
BLUE PRINT RUN 100 SER.#'d SETS
*GOLD/25: 1X TO 2.5X BASIC INSERTS
GOLD PRINT RUN 25 SER.#'d SETS
UNPRICED EMERALD PRINT RUN 5
UNPRICED BLACK PRINT RUN 1
1 Darren McFadden .50 1.25
2 Jonathan Stewart .75 2.00
3 Felix Jones .50 1.25
4 Rashard Mendenhall .50 1.25
5 Chris Johnson .60 1.50
6 Matt Forte .75 2.00
7 Ray Rice .50 1.25
8 Kevin Smith .50 1.25
9 Jamaal Charles .75 2.00
10 Steve Slaton .50 1.25
11 Matt Ryan 1.50 4.00
12 Joe Flacco 1.00 2.50
13 Brian Brohm .50 1.25
14 Chad Henne .60 1.50
15 Donnie Avery .60 1.50
16 Devin Thomas .50 1.25
17 Jordy Nelson 1.50 4.00
18 James Hardy .50 1.25
19 Eddie Royal .50 1.25
20 DeSean Jackson 1.00 2.50
21 Malcolm Kelly .50 1.25
22 Limas Sweed .50 1.25
23 Mario Manningham .50 1.25
24 Jerome Simpson .60 1.50
25 Dexter Jackson .75 2.00

2008 Leaf Certified Materials Certified Potential Autographs
STATED PRINT RUN 50-100
1 Darren McFadden/50 4.00 10.00
2 Jonathan Stewart/50 6.00 15.00
3 Felix Jones/50 4.00 10.00
4 Rashard Mendenhall/50 6.00 15.00
5 Chris Johnson 5.00 12.00
6 Matt Forte 12.00 30.00
7 Ray Rice 4.00 10.00
8 Kevin Smith 4.00 10.00
9 Jamaal Charles 6.00 15.00
10 Steve Slaton 4.00 10.00
11 Matt Ryan/50 50.00 100.00
12 Joe Flacco 8.00 20.00
13 Brian Brohm/50 4.00 10.00
14 Chad Henne/50 5.00 12.00
15 Donnie Avery 5.00 12.00
16 Devin Thomas 4.00 10.00
17 Jordy Nelson 20.00 50.00
18 James Hardy 4.00 10.00
19 Eddie Royal 4.00 10.00
20 DeSean Jackson 10.00 25.00
21 Malcolm Kelly 4.00 10.00
22 Limas Sweed 4.00 10.00
23 Mario Manningham 4.00 10.00
24 Jerome Simpson 5.00 12.00
25 Dexter Jackson 6.00 15.00

2008 Leaf Certified Materials Certified Potential Materials
STATED PRINT RUN 250 SER.#'d SETS
*PRIME/25: 1X TO 2.5X BASIC JSY/250
PRIME PRINT RUN 25 SER.#'d SETS
UNPRICED PRIME BLACK PRINT RUN 1
1 Darren McFadden 2.00 5.00
2 Jonathan Stewart 2.00 5.00
3 Felix Jones 2.00 5.00
4 Rashard Mendenhall 1.25 3.00
5 Chris Johnson 1.50 4.00
6 Matt Forte 2.00 5.00
7 Ray Rice 1.25 3.00
8 Kevin Smith 1.25 3.00
9 Jamaal Charles 2.00 5.00
10 Steve Slaton 1.25 3.00
11 Matt Ryan 4.00 10.00
12 Joe Flacco 2.50 6.00
13 Brian Brohm 1.25 3.00
14 Chad Henne 1.50 4.00
15 Donnie Avery 2.00 5.00
16 Devin Thomas 1.25 3.00
17 Jordy Nelson 4.00 10.00
18 James Hardy 1.25 3.00
19 Eddie Royal 1.25 3.00
20 DeSean Jackson 2.50 6.00
21 Malcolm Kelly 1.25 3.00
22 Limas Sweed 1.25 3.00
23 Mario Manningham 2.00 5.00
24 Jerome Simpson 2.50 6.00
25 Dexter Jackson 2.50 6.00

2008 Leaf Certified Materials Certified Skills
STATED PRINT RUN 1000 SER.#'d SETS
*MIRROR/500: .4X TO 1X BASIC INSERTS
MIRROR PRINT RUN 500 SER.#'d SETS
*RED/250: .5X TO 1.2X BASIC INSERTS
RED PRINT RUN 250 SER.#'d SETS
*BLUE/100: .6X TO 1.5X BASIC INSERTS
BLUE PRINT RUN 100 SER.#'d SETS
*GOLD/25: 1X TO 2.5X BASIC INSERTS
GOLD PRINT RUN 25 SER.#'d SETS
UNPRICED EMERALD PRINT RUN 5
UNPRICED BLACK PRINT RUN 1
1 Adrian Peterson .75 2.00
2 Greg Jennings .50 1.25
3 Marion Barber .50 1.25
4 LaRon Landry .60 1.50
5 Brandon Marshall .60 1.50
6 Brandon Jacobs .50 1.25
7 T.J. Houshmandzadeh .50 1.25
8 Reggie Wayne .60 1.50
9 Braylon Edwards .50 1.25
10 Brian Westbrook .50 1.25

2008 Leaf Certified Materials Certified Skills Materials Prime
PRIME PRINT RUN 25 SER.#'d SETS
*BASE JSY/250: .2X TO .5X PRIME/25
UNPRICED PRIME BLACK PRINT RUN 1
1 Adrian Peterson/24 6.00 15.00
6 Brandon Jacobs 4.00 10.00
7 T.J. Houshmandzadeh 4.00 10.00
8 Reggie Wayne 5.00 12.00
10 Brian Westbrook 4.00 10.00

2008 Leaf Certified Materials Fabric of the Game
ATED PRINT RUN 25-99
UNPRICED TEAM LOGO AUTO PRINT RUN 1-5
1 Alan Page 4.00 10.00
2 Andre Reed 5.00 12.00
3 Barry Sanders 10.00 25.00
4 Bart Starr 10.00 25.00
5 Billy Sims 5.00 12.00
6 Bo Jackson 8.00 20.00
7 Bob Griese 6.00 15.00
8 Bob Lilly 5.00 12.00
9 Brett Favre 8.00 20.00
11 Charley Taylor 4.00 10.00
12 Charlie Joiner 4.00 10.00
13 Chuck Foreman 4.00 10.00
14 Cliff Harris 4.00 10.00
15 Cris Collinsworth 5.00 12.00
16 Dan Marino 12.00 30.00
17 Danny White 4.00 10.00
18 Daryl Johnston/25 5.00 12.00
19 Daryle Lamonica 5.00 12.00
20 Deacon Jones 5.00 12.00
21 Dick Butkus 8.00 20.00
22 Don Maynard 5.00 12.00
23 Emmitt Smith 10.00 25.00
24 Eric Dickerson 5.00 12.00
25 Fran Tarkenton 6.00 15.00
26 Franco Harris 6.00 15.00
28 Fred Biletnikoff 6.00 15.00
29 Gene Upshaw 4.00 10.00
30 Garo Yepremian 4.00 10.00
31 Hank Stram 5.00 12.00
34 James Lofton 4.00 10.00
35 Jan Stenerud/75 4.00 10.00
36 Jerry Rice 12.00 30.00
37 Jim Brown/50 8.00 20.00
38 Jim Kelly/50 6.00 15.00
39 Jim McMahon 6.00 15.00
40 Jim Otto 4.00 10.00
41 John Matuszak 6.00 15.00
42 Joe Montana 20.00 50.00
43 John Riggins 5.00 12.00
44 John Elway 10.00 25.00
45 John Stallworth 5.00 12.00
46 Ken Stabler 6.00 15.00
47 Lance Alworth/33 5.00 12.00
49 Lenny Moore 4.00 10.00
50 Marcus Allen 6.00 15.00
51 Mark Duper 4.00 10.00
52 Mark Gastineau/50 4.00 10.00
53 Merlin Olsen/35 4.00 10.00
54 Michael Irvin 6.00 15.00
55 Ozzie Newsome 5.00 12.00
56 Paul Warfield/50 5.00 12.00
57 Phil Simms 5.00 12.00
58 Randall Cunningham 5.00 12.00
59 Randy White 5.00 12.00
60 Reggie White 6.00 15.00
61 Ronnie Lott 5.00 12.00
62 Rosey Grier 4.00 10.00
63 Sammy Baugh/50 6.00 15.00
64 Steve Largent 6.00 15.00
66 Steve Young 8.00 20.00
67 Ted Hendricks 4.00 10.00
68 Tiki Barber 5.00 12.00
69 Tom Landry 8.00 20.00
70 Troy Aikman 8.00 20.00
71 Walter Payton 12.00 30.00
72 Warren Moon 6.00 15.00
74 Y.A. Tittle/50 6.00 15.00
75 LaDainian Tomlinson 4.00 10.00
76 Adrian Peterson/40 4.00 10.00
78 Willie Parker 3.00 8.00
79 Clinton Portis 2.50 6.00
80 Edgerrin James 3.00 8.00
81 Willis McGahee 2.50 6.00
82 Fred Taylor/80 2.50 6.00
83 Marshawn Lynch 3.00 8.00
84 Frank Gore 3.00 8.00
85 Joseph Addai 2.50 6.00
86 Marion Barber 2.50 6.00
89 Brandon Jacobs 2.50 6.00
90 Tom Brady/70 12.00 30.00
91 Peyton Manning 10.00 25.00
92 Drew Brees 4.00 10.00
93 Tony Romo 3.00 8.00
94 Carson Palmer 3.00 8.00
95 Jon Kitna 2.50 6.00
96 Matt Hasselbeck 2.50 6.00
98 Jay Cutler 2.50 6.00
99 Eli Manning 3.00 8.00
100 Donovan McNabb 3.00 8.00
103 Philip Rivers 4.00 10.00
106 Chad Johnson 2.50 6.00
107 Larry Fitzgerald 3.00 8.00
111 Marques Colston 2.50 6.00
113 Torry Holt 3.00 8.00
114 Wes Welker 3.00 8.00
117 T.J. Houshmandzadeh/70 2.50 6.00
118 Santonio Holmes 2.50 6.00
119 Derrick Mason 2.50 6.00
121 Steve Smith 3.00 8.00
123 Dwayne Bowe/40 3.00 8.00

2008 Leaf Certified Materials Fabric of the Game Prime
*PRIME/20-25: .6X TO 1.5X BASIC FOTG
PRIME PRINT RUN 1-25
10 Carl Eller 8.00 20.00
65 Sterling Sharpe 8.00 20.00

2008 Leaf Certified Materials Fabric of the Game College
STATED PRINT RUN 6-100
SERIAL #'d UNDER 20 NOT PRICED
UNPRICED AUTO PRINT RUN 10
1 Malcolm Kelly 2.00 5.00
2 Allen Patrick 2.00 5.00
3 Shawn Crable 2.00 5.00
4 Chris Long 2.50 6.00
5 Felix Jones/50 2.00 5.00
6 Darren McFadden 2.00 5.00
7 Marcus Monk 2.50 6.00
8 Matt Ryan/20 12.00 30.00
9 Dan Connor 2.00 5.00
11 Jamaal Charles 3.00 8.00
12 Limas Sweed 2.00 5.00
13 Sedrick Ellis 2.00 5.00
14 Keith Rivers 2.00 5.00
15 Fred Davis 2.00 5.00
16 John David Booty 2.00 5.00
17 Terrell Thomas 2.00 5.00
19 Brandon Flowers 2.50 6.00
21 Colt Brennan 2.50 6.00
22 Aqib Talib 3.00 8.00
23 Brian Brohm 2.00 5.00
24 Glenn Dorsey 2.00 5.00
25 Early Doucet 2.00 5.00
26 Chevis Jackson 2.00 5.00
27 Craig Steltz 2.00 5.00
28 Kenny Phillips 2.00 5.00
29 Calais Campbell 2.50 6.00
30 Mike Hart 2.00 5.00
31 Chad Henne 2.50 6.00
32 Mario Manningham 2.00 5.00
33 Lawrence Jackson 2.00 5.00
34 Steve Largent 5.00 12.00
35 Simeon Castille 2.00 5.00
36 Ali Highsmith 2.50 6.00
37 Ernie Wheelwright 2.50 6.00
38 Jonathan Hefney 2.00 5.00
39 Robert Killebrew 2.50 6.00

2008 Leaf Certified Materials Fabric of the Game College Prime
*PRIME/25: .8X TO 2X FOTG/100
*PRIME/25: .6X TO 1.5X FOTG/50
*PRIME/20: .5X TO 1.2X FOTG/20
PRIME PRINT RUN 20-25
10 Erik Ainge 4.00 10.00
18 Xavier Adibi 4.00 10.00

2008 Leaf Certified Materials Fabric of the Game College Combos
STATED PRINT RUN 25-50
1 V.Young/J.Charles 5.00 12.00
2 F.Jones/D.McFadden/25 3.00 8.00
3 M.Bush/H.Douglas 4.00 10.00
4 M.Manningham/M.Hart 3.00 8.00
5 A.Peterson/M.Kelly 5.00 12.00
6 M.Leinart/J.Booty 3.00 8.00
7 J.Russell/E.Doucet 3.00 8.00
9 S.Smith USC/F.Davis 4.00 10.00
10 J.Shockey/K.Winslow 3.00 8.00

2008 Leaf Certified Materials Fabric of the Game College Combos Prime
*PRIME/25: .5X TO 1.2X BASIC COMBO
PRIME PRINT RUN 5-25
8 X.Adibi/B.Flowers 5.00 12.00

2008 Leaf Certified Materials Fabric of the Game Combos
STATED PRINT RUN 50-100
3 E.Manning/P.Burress/80 4.00 10.00
4 L.Fitzgerald/E.James 4.00 10.00
6 T.Jackson/A.Peterson 8.00 20.00
9 J.Garcia/J.Galloway/50 4.00 10.00
10 T.Landry/H.Stram 12.00 30.00
11 R.White/B.Lilly 8.00 20.00
12 B.Sanders/A.Peterson 12.00 30.00

2008 Leaf Certified Materials Fabric of the Game Combos Prime
PRIME PRINT RUN 3-25
1 T.Brady/R.Moss 25.00 60.00
2 P.Rivers/L.Tomlinson 8.00 20.00
3 E.Manning/P.Burress 6.00 15.00
5 R.Moss/T.Owens 6.00 15.00
7 C.Portis/S.Moss 5.00 12.00
8 J.Kitna/R.Williams WR 5.00 12.00
9 J.Garcia/J.Galloway 6.00 15.00
11 R.White/B.Lilly 10.00 25.00
12 B.Sanders/A.Peterson 15.00 40.00
13 E.Manning/T.Brady 25.00 60.00

2008 Leaf Certified Materials Fabric of the Game Jersey Number
*JER NUM/50-99: .5X TO 1.2X BASIC JSY
*JER NUM/20-44: .6X TO 1.5X BASIC JSY
STATED PRINT RUN 1-99
SERIAL #'d UNDER 20 NOT PRICED
77 Brian Westbrook/36 5.00 12.00

2008 Leaf Certified Materials Fabric of the Game NFL Die Cut
*NFL DC/50: .5X TO 1.2X BASIC FOTG
*NFL DC/20-25: .6X TO 1.5X BASIC FOTG
NFL DIE CUT PRINT RUN 10-50
10 Carl Eller 6.00 15.00
77 Brian Westbrook/25 4.00 10.00

2008 Leaf Certified Materials Fabric of the Game NFL Die Cut Prime
*NFL DC PRIME/20-25: .8X TO 2X BASIC FOTG
NFL DIE CUT PRIME PRINT RUN 1-25
65 Sterling Sharpe 10.00 25.00

2008 Leaf Certified Materials Fabric of the Game Position
*POSITION/25-50: .4X TO 1X BASIC JSY
STATED PRINT RUN 10-50
10 Carl Eller/25 6.00 15.00
27 Frank Gifford/25 8.00 20.00
77 Brian Westbrook/25 3.00 8.00

2008 Leaf Certified Materials Fabric of the Game Team Die Cut
EAM DC/15-25: .8X TO 2X BASIC FOTG
TEAM DIE CUT PRINT RUN 10-25
UNPRICED PRIME TEAM DC PRINT RUN 1-10

2008 Leaf Certified Materials Fabric of the Game Team Logo Prime
COMMON ACTIVE/25 5.00 12.00
ACTIVE UNL.STARS/25 6.00 15.00
*TEAM LOGO/25: .6X TO 1.5X BASIC FOTG
STATED PRINT RUN 3-25
65 Sterling Sharpe 8.00 20.00

2008 Leaf Certified Materials Gold Team
STATED PRINT RUN 1000 SER.#'d SETS
*MIRROR/100: .8X TO 2X BASIC INSERTS
MIRROR PRINT RUN 100 SER.#'d SETS
1 Tom Brady 2.50 6.00
2 Peyton Manning 2.00 5.00
3 Tony Romo .60 1.50
4 LaDainian Tomlinson .75 2.00
5 Terrell Owens .60 1.50
6 Randy Moss .60 1.50
7 Joseph Addai .50 1.25
8 Ben Roethlisberger .75 2.00
9 Eli Manning .60 1.50
10 Drew Brees .75 2.00

2008 Leaf Certified Materials Gold Team Materials
STATED PRINT RUN 10-250
SERIAL #'d UNDER 10 NOT PRICED
UNPRICED PRIME BLACK PRINT RUN 1
1 Tom Brady/125 10.00 25.00
3 Tony Romo/250 2.50 6.00
10 Drew Brees/180 3.00 8.00

2008 Leaf Certified Materials Gold Team Materials Prime
COMMON CARD 8.00 20.00
PRIME PRINT RUN 25 SER.#'d SETS
1 Tom Brady 20.00 50.00
4 LaDainian Tomlinson 6.00 15.00
5 Terrell Owens 5.00 12.00
6 Randy Moss 5.00 12.00
9 Eli Manning 5.00 12.00

2008 Leaf Certified Materials Mirror Blue Materials
MMON ACTIVE/20-50 3.00 8.00
ACTIVE SEMISTARS/20-50 4.00 10.00
ACTIVE UNL.STARS/20-50 5.00 12.00
*BLUE ROOKIES: .4X TO 1X MIR.RED
*BLUE RETIRED: .5X TO 1.2X MIR.RED
MIRROR BLUE PRINT RUN 20-50
45 Aaron Rodgers/40 10.00 25.00
54 Peyton Manning 12.00 30.00
79 Adrian Peterson 5.00 12.00
82 Tom Brady 15.00 40.00

2008 Leaf Certified Materials Mirror Blue Signatures
MIRROR BLUE PRINT RUN 50-100
UNPRICED MIRR.BLACK PRINT RUN 1
UNPRICED MIRR.EMERALD PRINT RUN 5
151 Adrian Arrington/100 3.00 8.00
152 Andre Woodson/50 4.00 10.00
153 Antoine Cason/50 5.00 12.00
154 Aqib Talib/100 5.00 12.00
155 Brad Cottam/100 3.00 8.00
156 Brandon Flowers/50 5.00 12.00
157 Chauncey Washington/50 5.00 12.00
159 Colt Brennan/50 5.00 12.00
160 Curtis Lofton/100 4.00 10.00
161 Dan Connor/50 4.00 10.00
162 Dennis Dixon/50 10.00 25.00
163 Derrick Harvey/50 4.00 10.00
164 Dominique Rodgers-Cromartie/100 4.00 10.00
165 Erik Ainge/50 4.00 10.00
166 Fred Davis/100 3.00 8.00
167 Jacob Hester/50 4.00 10.00
168 Jermichael Finley/100 3.00 8.00
169 Jerod Mayo/100 5.00 12.00
170 John Carlson/100 3.00 8.00
171 Josh Johnson/50 4.00 10.00
172 Jordon Dizon/50 4.00 10.00
173 Josh Morgan/100 3.00 8.00
174 Justin Forsett/50 5.00 12.00
175 Keenan Burton/100 3.00 8.00
176 Keith Rivers/50 4.00 10.00
177 Kenny Phillips/100 3.00 8.00
178 Kevin Robinson/100 3.00 8.00
179 Lavelle Hawkins/100 4.00 10.00
180 Leodis McKelvin/100 4.00 10.00
182 Marcus Thomas/50 5.00 12.00
183 Martellus Bennett/100 4.00 10.00
184 Matt Flynn/50 4.00 10.00
185 Mike Jenkins/100 3.00 8.00
186 Mike Hart/100 3.00 8.00
188 Peyton Hillis/50 6.00 15.00
189 Quentin Groves/50 5.00 12.00
190 Reggie Smith/100 3.00 8.00
191 Ryan Torain/50 5.00 12.00
192 Sedrick Ellis/100 3.00 8.00
194 Tashard Choice/100 3.00 8.00
195 Terrell Thomas/100 3.00 8.00
196 Thomas Brown/100 3.00 8.00
197 Tim Hightower/50 5.00 12.00
198 Tracy Porter/100 4.00 10.00
199 Vernon Gholston/100 3.00 8.00
200 Will Franklin/50 5.00 12.00
201 Andre Caldwell FF 6.00 15.00
202 Dustin Keller FF 8.00 20.00
203 Earl Bennett FF 10.00 25.00
204 Early Doucet FF 6.00 15.00
205 Glenn Dorsey FF EXCH
206 Harry Douglas FF
207 John David Booty FF 6.00 15.00
208 Kevin O'Connell FF 6.00 15.00
209 Darren McFadden FF 8.00 20.00
210 Jonathan Stewart FF 12.00 30.00
211 Felix Jones FF 8.00 20.00
212 Rashard Mendenhall FF 8.00 20.00
213 Chris Johnson FF 8.00 20.00
214 Matt Forte FF 10.00 25.00
215 Ray Rice FF 6.00 15.00
216 Kevin Smith FF 6.00 15.00
217 Jamaal Charles FF 10.00 25.00
218 Steve Slaton FF 6.00 15.00
219 Matt Ryan FF 40.00 100.00
220 Joe Flacco FF 15.00 40.00
221 Brian Brohm FF 8.00 20.00
222 Chad Henne FF 10.00 25.00
223 Donnie Avery FF 8.00 20.00
224 Devin Thomas FF 6.00 15.00
225 Jordy Nelson FF 25.00 60.00
226 James Hardy FF 6.00 15.00
227 Eddie Royal FF 6.00 15.00
228 DeSean Jackson FF 15.00 40.00
229 Malcolm Kelly FF 6.00 15.00
230 Limas Sweed FF 6.00 15.00
231 Mario Manningham FF 6.00 15.00
232 Jerome Simpson FF 8.00 20.00
233 Dexter Jackson FF 10.00 25.00
234 Jake Long FF 10.00 25.00

2008 Leaf Certified Materials Mirror Gold Materials
COMMON ACTIVE/15-25 5.00 12.00
ACTIVE SEMISTARS/15-25 6.00 15.00
ACTIVE UNL.STARS/15-25 8.00 20.00
*GOLD ROOKIES: .8X TO 2X MIR.RED
*GOLD RETIRED: .8X TO 2X MIR.RED
MIRROR GOLD PRINT RUN 15-25
54 Peyton Manning 20.00 50.00
79 Adrian Peterson 8.00 20.00
82 Tom Brady 25.00 60.00

2008 Leaf Certified Materials Mirror Gold Signatures
*FF AU GOLD/25: .8X TO 2X BLUE/100
*FF AU GOLD/25: .6X TO 1.5X BLUE/50
MIRROR GOLD PRINT RUN 10-25
SERIAL #'d UNDER 25 NOT PRICED
168 Jermichael Finley 5.00 12.00
169 Jerod Mayo 8.00 20.00
173 Josh Morgan 5.00 12.00
184 Matt Flynn 5.00 12.00
185 Mike Jenkins 5.00 12.00
186 Mike Hart 5.00 12.00
188 Peyton Hillis 8.00 20.00
213 Chris Johnson FF 15.00 40.00
214 Matt Forte FF 20.00 50.00
215 Ray Rice FF 12.00 30.00
219 Matt Ryan FF 100.00 200.00
220 Joe Flacco FF 20.00 50.00
222 Chad Henne FF 15.00 40.00

2008 Leaf Certified Materials Mirror Red Materials
COMMON ROOKIE/100 3.00 8.00
ROOKIE SEMIS/100 4.00 10.00
ROOKIE UNL.STAR/100 5.00 12.00
*RETIRED: .5X TO 1.2X BASIC JSY
MIRROR RED PRINT RUN 20-150
UNPRICED MIRROR EMERALD PRINT RUN 5
UNPRICED MIRROR BLACK PRINT RUN 1
1 Matt Leinart 2.50 6.00
2 Larry Fitzgerald 3.00 8.00
3 Anquan Boldin 2.50 6.00
4 Edgerrin James 3.00 8.00
5 Jerious Norwood 2.50 6.00
7 Joe Horn/50 3.00 8.00
8 Michael Turner 2.50 6.00
9 Willis McGahee 2.50 6.00
10 Derrick Mason 2.50 6.00
11 Mark Clayton 2.50 6.00
12 Demetrius Williams 2.50 6.00
13 Trent Edwards 2.50 6.00
14 Marshawn Lynch 3.00 8.00
15 Lee Evans 3.00 8.00
16 Steve Smith 3.00 8.00
17 DeAngelo Williams/75 3.00 8.00
18 Julius Peppers 3.00 8.00
22 Devin Hester 3.00 8.00
23 Brian Urlacher/70 5.00 12.00
24 Rex Grossman 2.50 6.00
25 Carson Palmer 3.00 8.00
26 Chad Johnson 2.50 6.00
27 T.J. Houshmandzadeh 2.50 6.00
28 Rudi Johnson 2.50 6.00
29 Derek Anderson/120 2.50 6.00
31 Kellen Winslow Jr/65 3.00 8.00
33 Tony Romo 3.00 8.00
34 Terrell Owens 3.00 8.00
35 Marion Barber 2.50 6.00
36 Jason Witten/125 3.00 8.00
37 Jay Cutler 2.50 6.00
39 Brandon Marshall/100 3.00 8.00
40 Brandon Stokley 2.50 6.00
41 Jon Kitna 2.50 6.00
42 Roy Williams WR 2.50 6.00
43 Calvin Johnson 4.00 10.00
47 Greg Jennings/125 2.50 6.00
48 Donald Driver 3.00 8.00
51 Andre Johnson/50 4.00 10.00
53 DeMeco Ryans 3.00 8.00
54 Peyton Manning 10.00 25.00
55 Joseph Addai 2.50 6.00
56 Marvin Harrison/50 4.00 10.00
57 Reggie Wayne 3.00 8.00
58 Dallas Clark 2.50 6.00
59 Anthony Gonzalez 2.50 6.00
60 David Garrard/75 3.00 8.00
61 Fred Taylor 2.50 6.00
62 Maurice Jones-Drew/110 2.50 6.00
63 Reggie Williams 3.00 8.00
65 Matt Jones 3.00 8.00
67 Brodie Croyle 3.00 8.00
68 Larry Johnson 2.50 6.00
70 Tony Gonzalez/125 3.00 8.00
71 Dwayne Bowe 3.00 8.00
73 Ronnie Brown 2.50 6.00
74 Ted Ginn Jr./105 2.50 6.00
76 Jason Taylor 3.00 8.00
77 Bernard Berrian 2.50 6.00
78 Tarvaris Jackson 2.50 6.00
79 Adrian Peterson 4.00 10.00
80 Chester Taylor 2.50 6.00
82 Tom Brady 12.00 30.00
83 Randy Moss/125 3.00 8.00
84 Laurence Maroney 3.00 8.00
85 Wes Welker 3.00 8.00
86 Drew Brees 4.00 10.00
87 Reggie Bush 2.50 6.00
88 Deuce McAllister 3.00 8.00
89 Marques Colston 2.50 6.00
90 Eli Manning 3.00 8.00
91 Plaxico Burress 2.50 6.00
92 Brandon Jacobs/125 2.50 6.00
93 Amani Toomer 2.50 6.00
94 Jeremy Shockey 2.50 6.00
95 Steve Smith USC/110 3.00 8.00
96 Michael Strahan 3.00 8.00
98 Leon Washington 2.50 6.00
99 Jerricho Cotchery 2.50 6.00
100 Laveranues Coles 2.50 6.00
101 Thomas Jones/20 4.00 10.00
102 Javon Walker 3.00 8.00
104 Justin Fargas/145 2.50 6.00
107 Donovan McNabb 3.00 8.00
108 Brian Westbrook 2.50 6.00
111 Greg Lewis 2.50 6.00
112 Ben Roethlisberger/130 4.00 10.00
113 Willie Parker 3.00 8.00
114 Hines Ward 3.00 8.00
115 Santonio Holmes 2.50 6.00
116 Philip Rivers 4.00 10.00
117 LaDainian Tomlinson 4.00 10.00
118 Vincent Jackson 2.50 6.00
121 Alex Smith QB 3.00 8.00
122 Frank Gore 3.00 8.00
123 Michael Robinson 2.50 6.00
124 Vernon Davis 2.50 6.00
125 Isaac Bruce/60 5.00 12.00
126 Patrick Willis 3.00 8.00
127 Matt Hasselbeck 2.50 6.00
129 Deion Branch/20 4.00 10.00
130 Julius Jones 2.50 6.00
132 Steven Jackson/20 4.00 10.00
133 Torry Holt 3.00 8.00
134 Warrick Dunn 2.50 6.00
135 Jeff Garcia 2.50 6.00
136 Cadillac Williams 3.00 8.00
139 Michael Clayton 2.50 6.00
140 Vince Young 2.50 6.00
141 LenDale White 2.50 6.00
144 Alge Crumpler 2.50 6.00
145 Brandon Jones 2.50 6.00
146 Jason Campbell/65 3.00 8.00
147 Clinton Portis 2.50 6.00
148 Ladell Betts 2.50 6.00
150 Chris Cooley/20 4.00 10.00
201 Andre Caldwell 2.50 6.00
202 Dustin Keller 3.00 8.00
203 Earl Bennett 4.00 10.00
204 Early Doucet 2.50 6.00
205 Glenn Dorsey 2.50 6.00
206 Harry Douglas 3.00 8.00
207 John David Booty 2.50 6.00
208 Kevin O'Connell 2.50 6.00
209 Darren McFadden 2.50 6.00
210 Jonathan Stewart 4.00 10.00
211 Felix Jones 2.50 6.00
212 Rashard Mendenhall 2.50 6.00
213 Chris Johnson 3.00 8.00
214 Matt Forte 4.00 10.00
215 Ray Rice 2.50 6.00
216 Kevin Smith 2.50 6.00
217 Jamaal Charles 4.00 10.00
218 Steve Slaton 2.50 6.00
219 Matt Ryan 8.00 20.00
220 Joe Flacco 5.00 12.00
221 Brian Brohm 2.50 6.00
222 Chad Henne 3.00 8.00
223 Donnie Avery 3.00 8.00
224 Devin Thomas 2.50 6.00
225 Jordy Nelson 8.00 20.00
226 James Hardy 2.50 6.00
227 Eddie Royal 2.50 6.00
228 DeSean Jackson 5.00 12.00
229 Malcolm Kelly 2.50 6.00
230 Limas Sweed 2.50 6.00
231 Mario Manningham 2.50 6.00
232 Jerome Simpson 3.00 8.00
233 Dexter Jackson 4.00 10.00
234 Jake Long 4.00 10.00
235 Bart Starr 12.00 30.00
236 Johnny Unitas 15.00 40.00
237 Brett Favre 12.00 30.00
238 Tom Landry 10.00 25.00
239 Hank Stram 6.00 15.00
240 Chuck Foreman 5.00 12.00
241 Dan Marino 15.00 40.00
242 Andre Reed 6.00 15.00
243 Frank Gifford/25 10.00 25.00
244 John Riggins 6.00 15.00
245 John Stallworth 6.00 15.00
246 John Elway 12.00 30.00
247 Emmitt Smith 12.00 30.00
248 Randall Cunningham 6.00 15.00
249 Reggie White 8.00 20.00
250 John Matuszak 8.00 20.00
251 Troy Aikman 10.00 25.00
252 Billy Sims 6.00 15.00
253 Willie Brown 5.00 12.00
254 Barry Sanders 12.00 30.00
255 Walter Payton 15.00 40.00

2008 Leaf Certified Materials Mirror Red Signatures
*RED/250: .25X TO .6X MIR.BLUE/100
*RED/100: .3X TO .8X MIR.BLUE/50
MIRROR RED PRINT RUN 100-250
213 Chris Johnson FF/250 5.00 12.00
219 Matt Ryan FF/100 40.00 100.00
220 Joe Flacco FF/100 12.00 30.00

2008 Leaf Certified Materials Rookie Fabric of the Game
STATED PRINT RUN 250 SER.#'d SETS
UNPRICED AUTO PRINT RUN 5
*JER NUM/72-89: .5X TO 1.2X FOTG/250
*JER NUM/34-39: .6X TO 1.5X FOTG/250
*JER NUM/20-29: .8X TO 2X FOTG/250
JERSEY NUMBER PRINT RUN 1-89
*NFL DC/99: .5X TO 1.2X FOTG/250
*POSITION/100: .5X TO 1.2X FOTG/250
*TEAM DC/25: .8X TO 2X FOTG/250
*TEAM PRIME/25: 1X TO 2.5X FOTG/250
1 Earl Bennett 2.50 6.00
2 Harry Douglas 2.00 5.00
3 Dustin Keller 2.00 5.00
4 Jake Long 2.50 6.00
5 Early Doucet 1.50 4.00
6 Malcolm Kelly 1.50 4.00
7 Dexter Jackson 2.50 6.00
8 Rashard Mendenhall 1.50 4.00
9 Steve Slaton 1.50 4.00
10 Joe Flacco 3.00 8.00
11 Donnie Avery 2.00 5.00
12 James Hardy 1.50 4.00
13 Kevin Smith 1.50 4.00
14 DeSean Jackson 3.00 8.00
15 Kevin O'Connell 1.50 4.00
16 Ray Rice 1.50 4.00
17 Andre Caldwell 1.50 4.00
18 Chris Johnson 2.00 5.00
19 Jonathan Stewart 5.00 12.00
20 Matt Ryan 6.00 15.00
21 Matt Forte 5.00 12.00
22 Jamaal Charles 2.50 6.00
23 Eddie Royal 1.50 4.00
24 Darren McFadden 1.50 4.00
25 Brian Brohm 1.50 4.00
26 Felix Jones 1.50 4.00
27 Jordy Nelson 5.00 12.00
28 Jerome Simpson 2.00 5.00
29 Chad Henne 2.00 5.00
30 John David Booty 1.50 4.00
31 Mario Manningham 1.50 4.00
32 Glenn Dorsey 1.50 4.00
33 Devin Thomas 1.50 4.00
34 Limas Sweed 1.50 4.00

2008 Leaf Certified Materials Souvenir Stamps Autographs Pro Team Logos
PRO LOGO PRINT RUN 1-21
UNPRICED COLLEGE LOGO PRINT RUN 2-10
UNPRICED 1969 STAMP PRINT RUN 2-5
UNPRICED USA FLAG PRINT RUN 2-5
2 Jerome Simpson/21 8.00 20.00
5 James Hardy/21 6.00 15.00
8 Devin Thomas/21 6.00 15.00
9 Dustin Keller/21 8.00 20.00
11 Jake Long/21 10.00 25.00
14 Donnie Avery/21 8.00 20.00
16 Ray Rice/21 6.00 15.00
18 Earl Bennett/21 10.00 25.00
19 Steve Slaton/21 6.00 15.00
20 Kevin O'Connell/21 6.00 15.00
22 Jordy Nelson/21 20.00 50.00
25 Joe Flacco/21 12.00 30.00
27 Dexter Jackson/21 10.00 25.00
30 Matt Forte/21 10.00 25.00
32 Chris Johnson/21 8.00 20.00
33 Kevin Smith/21 6.00 15.00
34 Andre Caldwell/21 6.00 15.00

2008 Leaf Certified Materials Souvenir Stamps College Material College Logo
COLLEGE LOGO PRINT RUN 20-50
*PRIME/25: .6X TO 1.5X COLL.LOGO/30-50
*PRIME/25: .5X TO 1.2X COLL.LOGO/20
PRIME PRINT RUN 1-25
*1969 STAMP/25: .5X TO 1.2X COLL.LOGO
1969 STAMP PRINT RUN 5-25
UNPRICED POP WARNER PRINT RUN 1-5
UNPRICED USA FLAG PRINT RUN 5-10
1 Brian Brohm 2.50 6.00
2 Chad Henne 8.00 20.00
3 Darren McFadden 2.50 6.00
4 DeSean Jackson/45 8.00 20.00
5 Early Doucet 5.00 12.00
6 Eddie Royal 2.50 6.00
7 Felix Jones 2.50 6.00
8 Glenn Dorsey 6.00 15.00
10 Jamaal Charles 6.00 15.00
11 John David Booty 2.50 6.00
13 Limas Sweed 2.50 6.00
14 Malcolm Kelly 5.00 12.00
15 Mario Manningham 2.50 6.00
16 Matt Ryan 12.00 30.00
18 Sedrick Ellis 4.00 10.00
19 Dan Connor 6.00 15.00
20 Kenny Phillips 4.00 10.00
21 Fred Davis 4.00 10.00
22 Mike Hart 8.00 20.00
23 Allen Patrick 5.00 12.00
24 Erik Ainge 5.00 12.00
25 Dennis Dixon/20 6.00 15.00
26 Matt Flynn/30 2.50 6.00
27 Vernon Gholston 5.00 12.00
28 Aqib Talib 4.00 10.00
29 Chris Long 3.00 8.00
30 Brandon Flowers 5.00 12.00

2008 Leaf Certified Materials Souvenir Stamps Material Pro Team Logos
PRO TEAM LOGO PRINT RUN 50
*PRIME/25: .6X TO 1.5X PRO TEAM/50
PRIME PRINT RUN 25
*1969 STAMP/25: .5X TO 1.2X PRO LOGO
1969 STAMP PRINT RUN 25
UNPRICED POP WARNER PRINT RUN 5
UNPRICED USA FLAG PRINT RUN 10
1 Malcolm Kelly 2.50 6.00
2 Jerome Simpson 3.00 8.00
3 Jamaal Charles 4.00 10.00
4 Limas Sweed 2.50 6.00
5 James Hardy 2.50 6.00
6 Felix Jones 2.50 6.00
7 Rashard Mendenhall 2.50 6.00
8 Devin Thomas 2.50 6.00
9 Dustin Keller 3.00 8.00
10 Brian Brohm 2.50 6.00
11 Jake Long 4.00 10.00
12 John David Booty 2.50 6.00
13 Eddie Royal 2.50 6.00
14 Donnie Avery 3.00 8.00
15 Early Doucet 2.50 6.00
16 Ray Rice 2.50 6.00
17 Chad Henne 3.00 8.00
18 Earl Bennett 4.00 10.00
19 Steve Slaton 2.50 6.00
20 Kevin O'Connell 2.50 6.00
21 Darren McFadden 2.50 6.00
22 Jordy Nelson 8.00 20.00
23 Matt Ryan 8.00 20.00
24 Harry Douglas 3.00 8.00
25 Joe Flacco 5.00 12.00
26 Mario Manningham 2.50 6.00
27 Dexter Jackson 4.00 10.00
28 DeSean Jackson 5.00 12.00
29 Glenn Dorsey 2.50 6.00
30 Matt Forte 4.00 10.00
31 Jonathan Stewart 4.00 10.00
32 Chris Johnson 3.00 8.00
33 Kevin Smith 2.50 6.00
34 Andre Caldwell 2.50 6.00

2008 Leaf Certified Materials Souvenir Stamps Material Autographs Pro Team Logos
UNPRICED PRO LOGO PRINT RUN 2-5
NINE DIFF.UNPRICED PARALLELS
SERIAL NUMBERED FROM 1-5

2012 Leaf Inscriptions
IBG1 Bob Griese 30.00 60.00
IRG3 Robert Griffin III 8.00 20.00

2011 Leaf Legends of Sport
STATED PRINT RUN 6-50
NO PRICING ON CARDS #'d TO 12 OR LESS
BA18 Cam Newton/15 50.00 100.00
BA39 Joe Greene/6
BA40 Joe Montana/14 75.00 150.00
BA47 Len Dawson/40 15.00 40.00
BA50 Mark Ingram/50 10.00 25.00
BA52 Mel Renfro/25 10.00 25.00
BA54 Mike Ditka/21 15.00 40.00
BA61 Ozzie Newsome/20 10.00 25.00
BA80 Ted Hendricks/20 10.00 25.00

2011 Leaf Legends of Sport Award Winners Autographs Bronze
STATED PRINT RUN 10-50
AW5 Cam Newton/18 60.00 150.00
AW15 Mark Ingram/50 10.00 25.00

2011 Leaf Legends of Sport Cut Signatures
GS Gale Sayers 20.00 50.00
JN6 Joe Namath
BB14 Bert Bell

2011 Leaf Legends of Sport Moments of Greatness Autographs Bronze
STATED PRINT RUN 10-50
MG7 Cam Newton/18 60.00 150.00
MG19 Mark Ingram/45 10.00 25.00
MG20 Mark Ingram/44 10.00 25.00
MG21 Mike Ditka/20 15.00 40.00
MG24 Ozzie Newsome/19 10.00 25.00

2011 Leaf Legends of Sport Numeration Autographs
STATED PRINT RUN 4-30
NO PRICING ON CARDS #'d TO 12 OR LESS
NU9 Joe Montana/16 75.00 150.00
NU11 Mark Ingram/22 10.00 25.00
NU25 Mel Renfro/20 10.00 25.00

2011 Leaf Legends of Sport Perennial All-Stars Autographs
STATED PRINT RUN 5-24
NO PRICING ON CARDS #'d TO 13 OR LESS
PE19 Joe Montana/8
PE25 Mike Ditka/5
PE29 Ozzie Newsome/7

2012 Leaf Legends of Sport
BAAT1 Andre Tippett 8.00 20.00
BABG2 Bob Griese 10.00 25.00
BABL1 Bob Lilly 6.00 15.00
BABS2 Barry Sanders 40.00 80.00
BABS3 Billy Shaw 6.00 15.00
BABSC Bob St. Clair 10.00 25.00
BACH1 Chris Hanburger 10.00 25.00
BACS1 Charlie Sanders 6.00 15.00
BACT1 Charley Taylor 8.00 20.00
BADD1 Dan Dierdorf 8.00 20.00
BADH1 Dan Hampton 6.00 15.00
BADJ1 Deacon Jones 8.00 20.00
BADM2 Don Maynard 8.00 20.00
BADM3 Doug Martin 8.00 20.00
BADS1 Dwight Stephenson 6.00 15.00
BADS2 Deion Sanders 30.00 60.00
BADW2 Dave Wilcox 8.00 20.00
BAEB3 Elvin Bethea 6.00 15.00
BAEC1 Earl Campbell 20.00 40.00
BAED1 Eric Dickerson 10.00 25.00
BAFB1 Fred Biletnikoff 8.00 20.00
BAFD1 Fred Dean 6.00 15.00
BAFG1 Frank Gifford 10.00 25.00
BAGM2 Gino Marchetti 6.00 15.00
BAHC1 Harry Carson 8.00 20.00
BAHM1 Hugh McElhenny 6.00 15.00
BAHM1 Bobby Mitchell 8.00 20.00
BAJDL Joe DeLamielleure 6.00 15.00
BAJJ1 Jimmy Johnson 6.00 15.00
BAJK1 Jim Kelly 12.00 30.00
BAJL1 James Lofton 8.00 20.00
BAJL2 Jim Langer 12.00 30.00
BAJM1 Joe Montana 40.00 80.00
BAJO1 Jim Otto 8.00 20.00
BAJR1 Jerry Rice 60.00 120.00
BAJS2 Jan Stenerud 6.00 15.00
BAJS3 Joe Schmidt 8.00 20.00
BAJS4 Jackie Smith 6.00 15.00
BAJY1 Jack Youngblood 8.00 20.00
BAKW1 Kellen Winslow 6.00 15.00
BALL1 Larry Little 6.00 15.00
BALM1 Lenny Moore 6.00 15.00
BALT1 Lawrence Taylor 20.00 40.00
BALW1 Larry Wilson 6.00 15.00
BAMD1 Mike Ditka 10.00 25.00
BAMF1 Marshall Faulk 20.00 40.00
BAMH1 Mike Haynes 8.00 20.00
BAML1 Marv Levy 8.00 20.00
BAMR1 Mel Renfro 8.00 20.00
BAPK1 Paul Krause 8.00 20.00
BAPW1 Paul Warfield 6.00 15.00
BARB1 Raymond Berry 6.00 15.00
BARG3 Robert Griffin III 15.00 40.00
BARJ3 Rickey Jackson 8.00 20.00
BARL2 Ronnie Lott 20.00 40.00
BARW1 Rayfield Wright 8.00 20.00
BARW2 Roger Wehrli 6.00 15.00
BARW3 Randy White 10.00 25.00
BARW4 Rod Woodson 12.00 30.00
BARY1 Ron Yary 8.00 20.00
BASH1 Sam Huff 8.00 20.00
BASL1 Steve Largent 12.00 30.00
BASY1 Steve Young 25.00 50.00
BATB1 Tim Brown 10.00 25.00
BATD1 Tony Dorsett 20.00 40.00
BATM1 Tom Mack 6.00 15.00
BATR1 Trent Richardson 10.00 25.00
BATT1 Thurman Thomas 8.00 20.00
BAWB2 Willie Brown 6.00 15.00
BAWM1 Warren Moon 12.00 30.00
BAYAT Y.A. Tittle 8.00 20.00

2012 Leaf Legends of Sport Unsigned Bronze
ANNOUNCED PRINT RUN 70
ONLINE EXCLUSIVE

2012 Leaf Legends of Sport AKA Autographs
AKABSC Bob St. Clair 10.00 25.00
AKADH1 Dan Hampton 6.00 15.00
AKADS2 Deion Sanders 30.00 60.00
AKAJB1 Jerome Bettis 35.00 70.00
AKAJH1 John Hannah 8.00 20.00
AKALM1 Lenny Moore 6.00 15.00
AKAYAT Y.A. Tittle 8.00 20.00

2012 Leaf Legends of Sport Award Winners Autographs
AWBG2 Bob Griese 10.00 25.00
AWEC1 Earl Campbell 15.00 40.00
AWJR1 Jerry Rice 60.00 120.00
AWJS4 Jackie Smith 6.00 15.00
AWYAT Y.A. Tittle 8.00 20.00

2012 Leaf Legends of Sport Numerations Autographs
PRINT RUN 5-45
NABS2 Barry Sanders/20 40.00 80.00
NADM2 Don Maynard/13 8.00 20.00
NADS2 Deion Sanders/21 30.00 60.00
NAEC1 Earl Campbell/34 12.00 30.00
NAJK1 Jim Kelly/12 25.00 50.00
NAMF1 Marshall Faulk/28 20.00 40.00
NASY1 Steve Young/8
NATT1 Thurman Thomas/34 10.00 25.00
NAYAT Y.A. Tittle/14 8.00 20.00

2012 Leaf Legends of Sport Perennial All-Stars Autographs
PASBG2 Bob Griese 10.00 25.00
PASCH1 Chris Hanburger 10.00 25.00
PASCS1 Charlie Sanders 6.00 15.00
PASCT1 Charley Taylor 8.00 20.00
PASDD1 Dan Dierdorf 8.00 20.00
PASDJ1 Deacon Jones 8.00 20.00
PASDS1 Dwight Stephenson 6.00 15.00
PASDW2 Dave Wilcox 8.00 20.00
PASEB3 Elvin Bethea 6.00 15.00
PASJY1 Jack Youngblood 8.00 20.00
PASKW1 Kellen Winslow 6.00 15.00
PASPW1 Paul Warfield 6.00 15.00
PASRJ3 Rickey Jackson 8.00 20.00
PASRW2 Roger Wehrli 6.00 15.00
PASWM1 Warren Moon 12.00 30.00
PASYAT Y.A. Tittle 8.00 20.00

2012 Leaf Legends of Sport Signature Swatches
SSJM1 Joe Montana JSY 75.00 150.00

2012 Leaf Legends of Sport We Are the Champions Autographs
WCBG2 Bob Griese 10.00 25.00
WCBL1 Bob Lilly 6.00 15.00
WCDM2 Don Maynard 8.00 20.00
WCDS3 Don Shula 12.00 30.00
WCFB1 Fred Biletnikoff 8.00 20.00
WCFD1 Fred Dean 6.00 15.00
WCGM2 Gino Marchetti 6.00 15.00
WCJM3 Jim McMahon 12.00 30.00
WCMR1 Mel Renfro 8.00 20.00
WCRW1 Rayfield Wright 8.00 20.00
WCRW3 Randy White 10.00 25.00
WCRY1 Ron Yary 8.00 20.00
WCSY1 Steve Young 25.00 50.00
WCWB2 Willie Brown 6.00 15.00

2000 Leaf Limited

Released in early February 2001, Leaf Limited features all foil base cards with a player action shot set against a striped background in each respective player's team colors with the team logo in the upper left hand corner. A black bordered diamond is centered behind the player and contains an action photo shaded in the color of the card's background. Card numbers 1-200 picture veteran players and are sequentially numbered as follows: 1-50 are sequentially numbered to 5000, 51-100 are sequentially numbered to 4000, 101-150 are sequentially numbered to 3000, 151-200 are sequentially numbered to 2000. Rookie and prospect cards are numbered in lower quantities as follows: 201-250 are sequentially numbered to 1500, 251-300 are sequentially numbered to 1000, 301-350 are sequentially numbered to 500, and 351-400 are sequentially numbered to 350. Card numbers 401-425 contain both swatches of game worn jerseys and game used footballs. The design differs from the base set in that cards are enhanced with gold foil and feature player action shots on the left side of the card front and two rectangular swatches of memorabilia on the right side of the card. A portrait style shaded photo of the featured player appears in a diamond behind the color action shot, and each respective player's team logo appears above the memorabilia swatches. These cards are inserted in packs at the rate of one in 17.

COMP.SET w/o SPs (200) 60.00 120.00
201-250 ROOKIE PRINT RUN 1500
251-300 ROOKIE PRINT RUN 1000
301-350 ROOKIE PRINT RUN 500
351-400 ROOKIE PRINT RUN 350
401-425 RC JSY-FB/100-1000 ODDS 1:17
1 Ben Coates .30 .75
2 Joe Horn .40 1.00
3 Jonathan Linton .30 .75
4 Derrick Mason .30 .75
5 Ray Lucas .30 .75
6 Brock Huard .30 .75
7 Frank Wycheck .40 1.00
8 Michael Strahan .40 1.00
9 Jessie Armstead .30 .75
10 Stephen Alexander .30 .75
11 Larry Centers .30 .75
12 Michael Pittman .30 .75
13 Priest Holmes .30 .75
14 Jermaine Lewis .30 .75
15 Jay Riemersma .30 .75
16 Wesley Walls .30 .75
17 Curtis Enis .30 .75
18 Bobby Engram .30 .75
19 Jim Miller .30 .75
20 Eddie Kennison .30 .75
21 Errict Rhett .40 1.00
22 Chris Warren .30 .75
23 Byron Chamberlain .30 .75
24 Desmond Howard .40 1.00
25 Lamar Smith .30 .75
26 Robert Porcher .30 .75
27 Corey Bradford .30 .75
28 Donald Driver .60 1.50
29 Ahman Green .40 1.00
30 Ken Dilger .30 .75
31 James McKnight .30 .75
32 Kimble Anders .30 .75
33 Zach Thomas .40 1.00
34 James Johnson .30 .75
35 Lawyer Milloy .30 .75
36 Ty Law .50 1.25
37 Willie McGinest .40 1.00
38 Jason Sehorn .30 .75
39 Andre Rison .40 1.00
40 Rickey Dudley .30 .75
41 Patrick Jeffers .30 .75
42 Darrell Russell .30 .75
43 Charles Johnson .30 .75
44 Michael Westbrook .30 .75
45 Levon Kirkland .30 .75
46 Ryan Leaf .40 1.00
47 Sean Dawkins .30 .75
48 Todd Lyght .30 .75
49 Kevin Carter .30 .75
50 Neil O'Donnell .30 .75
51 Randall Cunningham .40 1.00
52 Oronde Gadsden .40 1.00
53 O.J. McDuffie .40 1.00
54 Jake Reed .40 1.00
55 Brian Mitchell .30 .75
56 Kordell Stewart .30 .75
57 Derrick Mayes .30 .75
58 Az-Zahir Hakim .30 .75
59 Jacquez Green .30 .75
60 Andre Reed .50 1.25
61 Deion Sanders .40 1.00
62 Frank Sanders .30 .75
63 Rob Moore .30 .75
64 Shawn Jefferson .30 .75
65 Pat Johnson .30 .75
66 Peter Boulware .30 .75
67 Donald Hayes .30 .75
68 Marty Booker .30 .75
69 Leslie Shepherd .30 .75
70 Jason Tucker .30 .75
71 Johnnie Morton .40 1.00
72 Germane Crowell .30 .75
73 Herman Moore .30 .75
74 Bill Schroeder .40 1.00
75 E.G. Green .30 .75
76 Jerome Pathon .30 .75
77 Tony Brackens .30 .75
78 Tony Richardson RC .30 .75
79 Sam Madison .30 .75
80 Jeff George .40 1.00
81 Matthew Hatchette .30 .75
82 Kevin Faulk .30 .75
83 Jeff Blake .40 1.00
84 Ike Hilliard .30 .75
85 Napoleon Kaufman .40 1.00
86 Charles Woodson .50 1.25
87 Na Brown .30 .75
88 Hines Ward .40 1.00
89 Troy Edwards .30 .75
90 Curtis Conway .40 1.00
91 Junior Seau .40 1.00
92 Jim Harbaugh .40 1.00
93 J.J. Stokes .40 1.00
94 Jon Kitna .30 .75
95 Reidel Anthony .30 .75
96 Warrick Dunn .30 .75
97 Carl Pickens .40 1.00
98 Yancey Thigpen .30 .75
99 Albert Connell .30 .75
100 Irving Fryar .40 1.00
101 Qadry Ismail .40 1.00
102 Shannon Sharpe .50 1.25
103 Joey Galloway .50 1.25
104 Ed McCaffrey .50 1.25
105 Rod Smith .50 1.25
106 Terrell Owens .50 1.25
107 Warren Sapp .50 1.25
108 Jevon Kearse .40 1.00
109 Bruce Smith .50 1.25
110 Champ Bailey .50 1.25
111 David Boston .40 1.00
112 Tim Dwight .50 1.25
113 Terance Mathis .40 1.00
114 Tony Banks .40 1.00
115 Shawn Bryson .40 1.00
116 Peerless Price .50 1.25
117 Muhsin Muhammad .40 1.00
118 Tim Biakabutuka .50 1.25
119 Steve Beuerlein .50 1.25
120 Corey Dillon .40 1.00
121 Kevin Johnson .40 1.00
122 Rocket Ismail .50 1.25
123 Charlie Batch .40 1.00
124 James Stewart .40 1.00
125 Terrence Wilkins .40 1.00
126 Keenan McCardell .50 1.25
127 Mark Brunell .50 1.25
128 Fred Taylor .40 1.00
129 Derrick Alexander .40 1.00
130 Tony Gonzalez .50 1.25
131 Warren Moon .60 1.50
132 Thurman Thomas .50 1.25
133 Tony Martin .50 1.25
134 Jay Fiedler .50 1.25
135 John Randle .60 1.50
136 Troy Brown .40 1.00
137 Amani Toomer .40 1.00
138 Kerry Collins .40 1.00
139 Tiki Barber .50 1.25
140 Wayne Chrebet .40 1.00
141 Tyrone Wheatley .40 1.00
142 Duce Staley .40 1.00
143 Jermaine Fazande .40 1.00
144 Charlie Garner .50 1.25
145 Torry Holt .50 1.25
146 Mike Alstott .40 1.00
147 Shaun King .40 1.00
148 Darrell Green .50 1.25
149 Brad Johnson .50 1.25
150 Olandis Gary .50 1.25
151 Jake Plummer .50 1.25
152 Chris Chandler .60 1.50
153 Jamal Anderson .60 1.50
154 Eric Moulds .50 1.25
155 Doug Flutie .60 1.50
156 Rob Johnson .60 1.50
157 Marcus Robinson .60 1.50
158 Cade McNown .50 1.25
159 Akili Smith .50 1.25
160 Tim Couch .60 1.50
161 Emmitt Smith 1.25 3.00
162 Troy Aikman 1.00 2.50
163 Brian Griese .50 1.25
164 John Elway 1.25 3.00
165 Terrell Davis .60 1.50
166 Dorsey Levens .60 1.50
167 Antonio Freeman .60 1.50
168 Brett Favre 1.50 4.00
169 Marvin Harrison .60 1.50
170 Peyton Manning 2.00 5.00
171 Edgerrin James .60 1.50
172 Jimmy Smith .60 1.50
173 Elvis Grbac .50 1.25
174 Dan Marino 1.50 4.00
175 Randy Moss .60 1.50
176 Cris Carter .75 2.00
177 Robert Smith .50 1.25
178 Daunte Culpepper .60 1.50
179 Terry Glenn .60 1.50
180 Drew Bledsoe .60 1.50
181 Ricky Williams .60 1.50
182 Jake Delhomme RC .60 1.50
183 Curtis Martin .60 1.50
184 Vinny Testaverde .50 1.25
185 Tim Brown .75 2.00
186 Rich Gannon .60 1.50
187 Donovan McNabb .60 1.50
188 Jerome Bettis .75 2.00
189 Bobby Shaw RC .50 1.25
190 Jerry Rice 2.00 5.00
191 Steve Young 1.00 2.50
192 Jeff Garcia .50 1.25
193 Ricky Watters .60 1.50
194 Isaac Bruce .75 2.00
195 Marshall Faulk .60 1.50
196 Kurt Warner 1.25 3.00
197 Keyshawn Johnson .60 1.50
198 Eddie George .60 1.50
199 Steve McNair .60 1.50
200 Stephen Davis .50 1.25
201 Bobby Brooks RC 1.25 3.00
202 Cornelius Griffin RC 1.25 3.00
203 Danny Clark RC 1.25 3.00
204 Pat Dennis RC 1.25 3.00
205 Tommy Hendricks RC 1.25 3.00
206 Fred Jones RC 1.25 3.00
207 Isaiah Kacyvenski RC 1.25 3.00
208 Keith Miller RC 1.25 3.00
209 Andre O' Neal RC 1.25 3.00
210 Justin Snow RC 1.25 3.00
211 Armegis Spearman RC 1.25 3.00
212 Lester Towns RC 1.25 3.00
213 Antonio Wilson RC 1.25 3.00
214 Greg Wesley RC 1.25 3.00
215 Jabari Issa RC 1.25 3.00
216 Darwin Walker RC 1.25 3.00
217 Reggie Grimes RC 1.25 3.00
218 Rian Lindell RC 1.25 3.00
219 Chris Combs RC 1.25 3.00
220 Rashard Anderson RC 1.25 3.00
221 Erik Flowers RC 1.25 3.00
222 Corey Moore RC 1.25 3.00
223 Rob Meier RC 1.25 3.00
224 John Milem RC 1.25 3.00
225 Jeremiah Parker RC 1.25 3.00
226 Neil Rackers RC 1.25 3.00
227 Josh Taves RC 1.25 3.00
228 Mao Tosi RC 1.25 3.00
229 Gary Berry RC 1.25 3.00
230 Matt Bowen RC 1.25 3.00
231 Ralph Brown RC 1.25 3.00
232 Tony Darden RC 1.25 3.00
233 Arturo Freeman RC 1.25 3.00
234 David Gibson RC 1.25 3.00
235 Demario Brown RC 1.25 3.00
236 Deveron Harper RC 1.25 3.00
237 Johnnie Harris RC 1.25 3.00
238 Marcus Knight RC 1.25 3.00
239 Ronnie Heard RC 1.25 3.00
240 Eric Johnson RC 1.50 4.00
241 John Keith RC 1.25 3.00
242 Anthony Malbrough RC 1.25 3.00
243 Anthony Mitchell RC 1.25 3.00
244 Aric Morris RC 1.25 3.00
245 Bobby Myers RC 1.25 3.00
246 Erik Olson RC 1.25 3.00
247 Lewis Sanders RC 1.25 3.00
248 Tony Scott RC 1.25 3.00
249 David Terrell RC 1.25 3.00
250 Travares Tillman RC 1.25 3.00
251 David Stachelski RC 1.50 4.00
252 Darren Howard RC 1.50 4.00
253 Frank Chamberlin RC 1.50 4.00
254 Na'il Diggs RC 1.50 4.00
255 Orantes Grant RC 1.50 4.00
256 Barrett Green RC 1.50 4.00
257 Kory Minor RC 1.50 4.00
258 Deon Grant RC 1.50 4.00
259 Mark Simoneau RC 1.50 4.00
260 Raynoch Thompson RC 1.50 4.00
261 Kenyatta Wright RC 1.50 4.00
262 Marcus Bell LB RC 1.50 4.00
263 Jack Golden RC 1.50 4.00
264 Thomas Hamner RC 1.50 4.00
265 Sekou Sanyika RC 1.50 4.00
266 Marcus Washington RC 2.00 5.00
267 Tim Seder RC 1.50 4.00
268 Paul Edinger RC 2.50 6.00
269 Michael Boireau RC 1.50 4.00
270 Byron Frisch RC 1.50 4.00
271 Ketric Sanford RC 1.50 4.00
272 Frank Murphy RC 1.50 4.00
273 Robaire Smith RC 1.50 4.00
274 Adalius Thomas RC 5.00 12.00
275 William Bartee RC 1.50 4.00
276 Robert Bean RC 1.50 4.00
277 Tyrone Carter RC 2.00 5.00
278 Ike Charlton RC 1.50 4.00
279 Mario Edwards RC 1.50 4.00
280 Dwayne Goodrich RC 1.50 4.00
281 Michael Hawthorne RC 1.50 4.00
282 Kareem Larrimore RC 1.50 4.00
283 Mark Roman RC 1.50 4.00
284 Jacoby Shepherd RC 1.50 4.00
285 Jason Webster RC 1.50 4.00
286 Jimmy Wyrick RC 1.50 4.00
287 Rashidi Barnes RC 1.50 4.00
288 David Barrett RC 1.50 4.00
289 Ainsley Battles RC 1.50 4.00
290 Lamar Chapman RC 1.50 4.00
291 Todd Franz RC 1.50 4.00
292 Michael Green RC 1.50 4.00
293 Antwan Harris RC 1.50 4.00
294 Brandon Jennings RC 1.50 4.00
295 Darrick Vaughn RC 1.50 4.00
296 David Macklin RC 1.50 4.00
297 [illegible] RC [illegible]
298 Reggie Stephens RC 1.50 4.00
299 Kenoy Kennedy RC 1.50 4.00
300 Raion Hill RC 1.50 4.00
301 Windrell Hayes RC 2.50 6.00
302 DaShon Polk RC 2.50 6.00
303 Tywan Mitchell RC 2.50 6.00
304 Casey Crawford RC 2.50 6.00
305 Hank Poteat RC 2.50 6.00
306 Mondriel Fulcher RC 2.50 6.00
307 Cory Geason RC 2.50 6.00
308 James Hill RC 2.50 6.00
309 Brian Jennings RC 2.50 6.00
310 John Jones RC 2.50 6.00
311 Anthony Lucas RC 2.50 6.00
312 Mike Leach RC 2.50 6.00
313 Dustin Lyman RC 2.50 6.00
314 Derek Rackley RC 2.50 6.00
315 Sebastian Janikowski RC 6.00 15.00
316 Brad St.Louis RC 2.50 6.00
317 Jay Tant RC 2.50 6.00
318 Austin Wheatley RC 2.50 6.00
319 Jermaine Wiggins RC 3.00 8.00
320 Todd Yoder RC 2.50 6.00
321 Deon Dyer RC 2.50 6.00
322 Jim Finn RC 2.50 6.00
323 Herbert Goodman RC 2.50 6.00
324 Mike Green RC 3.00 8.00
325 Dante Hall RC 2.50 6.00
326 Thabiti Davis RC 2.50 6.00
327 Kevin Houser RC 2.50 6.00
328 Jonas Lewis RC 2.50 6.00
329 Chad Morton RC 3.00 8.00
330 Patrick Pass RC 2.50 6.00
331 Maurice Smith RC 2.50 6.00
332 Paul Smith RC 2.50 6.00
333 Terrelle Smith RC 2.50 6.00
334 Craig Walendy RC 2.50 6.00
335 Jamel White RC 2.50 6.00
336 Jarious Jackson RC 3.00 8.00
337 Matt Lytle RC 2.50 6.00
338 Ron Powlus RC 4.00 10.00
339 Ian Gold RC 2.50 6.00
340 Brandon Short RC 2.50 6.00
341 T.J. Slaughter RC 2.50 6.00
342 Nate Webster RC 2.50 6.00
343 John Engelberger RC 2.50 6.00
344 Rogers Beckett RC 2.50 6.00
345 Mike Brown RC 2.50 6.00
346 Anthony Wright RC 3.00 8.00
347 Danny Farmer RC 2.50 6.00
348 Clint Stoerner RC 4.00 10.00
349 Julian Peterson RC 4.00 10.00
350 Ahmed Plummer RC 2.50 6.00
351 Avion Black RC 3.00 8.00
352 Kwame Cavil RC 3.00 8.00
353 Chris Cole RC 4.00 10.00
354 Chris Coleman RC 3.00 8.00
355 Trevor Gaylor RC 3.00 8.00
356 Damon Hodge RC 4.00 10.00
357 Darrell Jackson RC 3.00 8.00
358 Reggie Jones RC 3.00 8.00
359 Charles Lee RC 3.00 8.00
360 Jerry Porter RC 5.00 12.00
361 Bobby Shaw 3.00 8.00
362 Ron Dugans RC 3.00 8.00
363 James Williams RC 3.00 8.00
364 Bashir Yamini RC 3.00 8.00
365 Anthony Becht RC 3.00 8.00
366 Erron Kinney RC 3.00 8.00
367 Aaron Shea RC 4.00 10.00
368 Chris Samuels RC 5.00 12.00
369 Trung Canidate RC 3.00 8.00
370 Obafemi Ayanbadejo RC 4.00 10.00
371 Doug Chapman RC 3.00 8.00
372 Ronney Jenkins RC 3.00 8.00
373 Curtis Keaton RC 3.00 8.00
374 Kevin McDougal RC 3.00 8.00
375 Frank Moreau RC 3.00 8.00
376 Aaron Stecker RC 3.00 8.00
377 Shyrone Stith RC 3.00 8.00
378 Tom Brady RC 500.00 1000.00
379 Giovanni Carmazzi RC 3.00 8.00
380 Joe Hamilton RC 3.00 8.00
381 Todd Husak RC 3.00 8.00
382 Doug Johnson RC 3.00 8.00
383 Tee Martin RC 3.00 8.00
384 Chad Pennington RC 4.00 10.00
385 Tim Rattay RC 4.00 10.00
386 Chris Redman RC 3.00 8.00
387 Billy Volek RC 5.00 12.00
388 Spergon Wynn RC 3.00 8.00
389 John Abraham RC 5.00 12.00
390 Keith Bulluck RC 4.00 10.00
391 Rob Morris RC 4.00 10.00
392 JaJuan Dawson RC 3.00 8.00
393 Chris Hovan RC 4.00 10.00
394 Shaun Ellis RC 4.00 10.00
395 Deltha O'Neal RC 3.00 8.00
396 Gari Scott RC 3.00 8.00
397 Dialleo Burks RC 3.00 8.00
398 Shockmain Davis RC 3.00 8.00
399 Brad Hoover RC 4.00 10.00
400 Brian Finneran RC 5.00 12.00
401 Sylvester Morris J FB/750 RC 2.50 6.00
402 Denn Northcutt J FB/500 RC 2.50 6.00
403 Todd Pinkston J FB/100 RC 4.00 10.00
404 Larry Foster J FB/500 RC 2.50 6.00
405 R.Jay Soward J FB/1000 RC 2.50 6.00
406 Travis Taylor J FB/250 RC 4.00 10.00
407 Peter Warrick J FB/1000 RC 2.50 6.00
408 Dez White J FB/1000 RC 2.50 6.00
409 Ron Dayne J FB/1000 RC 4.00 10.00
410 Thomas Jones J FB/500 RC 3.00 8.00
411 Jamal Lewis J FB/1000 RC 4.00 10.00
412 Sammy Morris J FB/500 RC 2.50 6.00
413 Travis Prentice J FB/500 RC 2.50 6.00
414 J.R. Redmond J FB/250 RC 4.00 10.00
415 Michael Wiley FB/1000 RC 2.50 6.00
416 Laver Coles J/FB/250 RC 5.00 12.00
417 Bubba Franks J FB/500 RC 2.50 6.00
418 Mike Anderson J FB/250 RC 4.00 10.00
419 Plaxico Burress J FB/250 RC 5.00 12.00
420 Ron Dixon J FB/1000 RC 2.50 6.00
421 Troy Walters J FB/1000 RC 2.50 6.00
422 Sha Alexander J/FB/1000 RC 4.00 10.00
423 Brian Urlacher J FB/1000 RC 12.00 30.00
424 Corey Simon J FB/1000 RC 3.00 8.00
425 Courtney Brown J FB/500 RC 3.00 8.00

2000 Leaf Limited Limited Series

*VETS 1-50: 6X TO 15X BASIC CARDS
*VETS 51-100: 6X TO 15X BASIC CARDS
*VETS 101-150: 5X TO 12X BASIC CARDS
*VETS 151-200: 4X TO 10X BASIC CARDS
*ROOKIE 151-200: 2X TO 5X BASIC CARD
1-200 VETERAN LS PRINT RUN 35
*ROOKIES 201-250: 1.5X TO 4X
*ROOKIES 251-300: 1.2X TO 3X
*ROOKIES 301-350: .8X TO 2X
*ROOKIES 351-400: .6X TO 1.5X
201-400 ROOKIE LS PRINT RUN 50
401-425 ROOK. JSY-FB PRINT RUN 25
LIM.SERIES OVERALL STATED ODDS 1:17
378 Tom Brady 1300.00 2000.00

2000 Leaf Limited Piece of the Game Previews

Randomly seeded in packs, this 25-card set features players in action coupled with a swatch of game worn memorabilia. Card stock placed action player photography over a football field background on the left with a down marker on the right side against a green and white marble background. The swatch of memorabilia is circular and is set at the top of the "down marker." The 4th down marker card is the base, and 1st through 3rd down are serial numbered parallels.

AKA 4TH DOWN BASE CARDS
*THIRD DOWN/300: .5X TO 1.2X FOURTH
THIRD DOWN PRINT RUN 300
*SECOND DOWN/100: .6X TO 1.5X FOURTH
SECOND DOWN PRINT RUN 100
*FIRST DOWN/25: 1.2X TO 3X FOURTH
FIRST DOWN PRINT RUN 25
BF4G Brett Favre 10.00 25.00
RG14N Brian Griese 3.00 8.00
BS20B Barry Sanders 8.00 20.00
DC11P Daunte Culpepper 4.00 10.00
DF7W Doug Flutie 4.00 10.00
DM5W Donovan McNabb 4.00 10.00
DM13W Dan Marino 12.00 30.00
DS22G Duce Staley 3.00 8.00
EJ32R Edgerrin James 4.00 10.00
EM87N Ed McCaffrey 4.00 10.00
FT28W Fred Taylor 3.00 8.00
IB80W Isaac Bruce 5.00 12.00
JB36B Jerome Bettis 8.00 20.00
JE7W John Elway 8.00 20.00
JK12W Jim Kelly 5.00 12.00
JP16R Jake Plummer 3.00 8.00
JR80R Jerry Rice 12.00 30.00
JS82B Jimmy Smith 4.00 10.00
KW13W Kurt Warner 8.00 20.00
MB8W Mark Brunell 4.00 10.00
RM84P Randy Moss 4.00 10.00
RS26P Robert Smith 3.00 8.00
SD48W Stephen Davis 3.00 8.00
SY8R Steve Young 6.00 15.00
TC2B Tim Couch 4.00 10.00

2003 Leaf Limited

Released in December of 2003, this set features 150 cards, including 100 active and retired veterans and 50 rookies. Cards 1-100 are serial numbered to 999, and rookies 101-125 are serial numbered to 750. Rookies 126-150 are serial numbered to 150, and feature an authentic player autograph on a silver foil sticker. Please note that Charles Rogers, Nate Burleson, Onterrio Smith, and Willis McGahee were issued as exchange cards in packs. The exchange deadline is 7/1/2006. Boxes contained 4 packs of 4 cards. The pack SRP was $70.

COMP.SET w/o SP's (100) 100.00 250.00
101-125 ROOKIE PRINT RUN 750
126-150 ROOKIE AU PRINT RUN 150
1 Emmitt Smith 2.50 6.00
2 Michael Vick 1.25 3.00
3 Peerless Price 1.00 2.50
4 T.J. Duckett 1.00 2.50
5 Jamal Lewis 1.25 3.00
6 Drew Bledsoe 1.25 3.00
7 Eric Moulds 1.00 2.50
8 Travis Henry 1.00 2.50
9 Jim Kelly 1.50 4.00
10 Julius Peppers 1.50 4.00
11 Dick Butkus 2.00 5.00
12 Mike Singletary 1.50 4.00
13 Walter Payton 5.00 12.00
14 Anthony Thomas 1.25 3.00
15 Brian Urlacher 1.50 4.00
16 Marty Booker 1.00 2.50
17 Corey Dillon 1.00 2.50
18 Jim Thorpe 2.00 5.00
19 Jim Brown 2.00 5.00
20 Tim Couch 1.00 2.50
21 William Green 1.00 2.50
22 Deion Sanders 1.25 3.00
23 Michael Irvin 1.50 4.00
24 Roger Staubach 2.00 5.00
25 Troy Aikman 2.00 5.00
26 Tony Dorsett 1.50 4.00
27 Antonio Bryant 1.00 2.50
28 Clinton Portis 1.00 2.50
29 Jake Plummer 1.00 2.50
30 Rod Smith 1.25 3.00
31 Barry Sanders 2.50 6.00
32 Doak Walker 1.50 4.00
33 Joey Harrington 1.00 2.50
34 Bart Starr 2.50 6.00
35 Ahman Green 1.25 3.00
36 Brett Favre 3.00 8.00
37 Donald Driver 1.25 3.00
38 David Carr 1.00 2.50
39 Don Shula 1.50 4.00
40 Johnny Unitas 3.00 8.00
41 Edgerrin James 1.25 3.00
42 Marvin Harrison 1.25 3.00
43 Peyton Manning 4.00 10.00
44 Fred Taylor 1.00 2.50
45 Jimmy Smith 1.25 3.00
46 Mark Brunell 1.25 3.00
47 Marcus Allen 1.50 4.00
48 Priest Holmes 1.00 2.50
49 Tony Gonzalez 1.25 3.00
50 Trent Green 1.00 2.50
51 Dan Marino 3.00 8.00
52 Bob Griese 1.50 4.00
53 Chris Chambers 1.00 2.50
54 Ricky Williams 1.25 3.00
55 Fran Tarkenton 1.50 4.00
56 Daunte Culpepper 1.25 3.00
57 Michael Bennett 1.00 2.50
58 Randy Moss 1.25 3.00
59 Tom Brady 6.00 15.00
60 Aaron Brooks 1.00 2.50
61 Deuce McAllister 1.25 3.00
62 Donte Stallworth 1.00 2.50
63 Mark Bavaro 1.25 3.00
64 Jeremy Shockey 1.00 2.50
65 Kerry Collins 1.00 2.50
66 Tiki Barber 1.25 3.00
67 Joe Namath 2.50 6.00
68 Chad Pennington 1.00 2.50
69 Curtis Martin 1.25 3.00
70 Jerry Porter 1.00 2.50
71 Jerry Rice 3.00 8.00
72 Rich Gannon 1.25 3.00
73 Tim Brown 1.50 4.00
74 Donovan McNabb 1.25 3.00
75 Terry Bradshaw 2.00 5.00
76 Antwaan Randle El 1.00 2.50
77 Plaxico Burress 1.00 2.50
78 Tommy Maddox 1.00 2.50
79 David Boston 1.00 2.50
80 Drew Brees 1.50 4.00
81 LaDainian Tomlinson 1.50 4.00
82 Joe Montana 5.00 12.00
83 Steve Young 2.00 5.00
84 Jeff Garcia 1.00 2.50
85 Terrell Owens 1.25 3.00
86 Koren Robinson 1.25 3.00
87 Matt Hasselbeck 1.00 2.50
88 Shaun Alexander 1.50 3.50
89 Isaac Bruce [illegible] 4.00
90 Kurt Warner 1.25 3.00
91 Marshall Faulk 1.25 3.00
92 Torry Holt 1.25 3.00
93 Brad Johnson 1.25 3.00
94 Keyshawn Johnson 1.50 4.00
95 Earl Campbell 1.50 4.00
96 Eddie George 1.25 3.00
97 Steve McNair 1.25 3.00
98 John Riggins 1.25 3.00
99 Laveranues Coles 1.00 2.50
100 Patrick Ramsey 1.25 3.00
101 LaTarence Dunbar RC 1.50 4.00
102 Sam Aiken RC 2.00 5.00
103 Bobby Wade RC 2.00 5.00
104 Justin Gage RC 2.00 5.00
105 Lee Suggs RC 1.50 4.00
106 Jason Witten RC 6.00 15.00
107 Quentin Griffin RC 2.00 5.00
108 Domanick Davis RC 2.00 5.00
109 LaBrandon Toefield RC 1.50 4.00
110 J.R. Tolver RC 2.00 5.00
111 Kliff Kingsbury RC 2.50 6.00
112 Talman Gardner RC 1.50 4.00
113 Teyo Johnson RC 2.00 5.00
114 Billy McMullen RC 1.50 4.00
115 L.J. Smith RC 2.50 6.00
116 Brian St.Pierre RC 1.50 4.00
117 Brandon Lloyd RC 2.50 6.00
118 Seneca Wallace RC 2.00 5.00
119 Kevin Curtis RC 1.50 4.00
120 Shaun McDonald RC 2.00 5.00
121 Terrell Suggs RC 2.00 5.00
122 Terence Newman RC 2.50 6.00
123 Tony Romo RC 15.00 40.00
124 DeWayne Robertson RC 2.00 5.00
125 Marcus Trufant RC 2.00 5.00
126 Artose Pinner AU RC 6.00 15.00
127 Bryant Johnson AU RC 10.00 25.00
128 Kelley Washington AU RC 6.00 15.00
129 Dallas Clark AU RC 10.00 25.00
130 Onterrio Smith AU RC 6.00 15.00
131 Tony Hollings AU RC 8.00 20.00
132 Tyrone Calico AU RC 6.00 15.00
133 Carson Palmer AU RC 20.00 50.00
134 Byron Leftwich AU RC 8.00 20.00
135 Rex Grossman AU RC 8.00 20.00
136 Kyle Boller AU RC 6.00 15.00
137 Chris Simms AU RC 6.00 15.00
138 Dave Ragone AU RC 6.00 15.00
139 Ken Dorsey AU RC 8.00 20.00
140 Willis McGahee AU RC 10.00 25.00
141 Larry Johnson AU RC 8.00 20.00
142 Musa Smith AU RC 6.00 15.00
143 Chris Brown AU RC 6.00 15.00
144 Charles Rogers AU RC 8.00 20.00
145 Andre Johnson AU RC 40.00 80.00
146 Taylor Jacobs AU RC 6.00 15.00
147 Anquan Boldin AU RC 10.00 25.00
148 Bethel Johnson AU RC 6.00 15.00
149 Justin Fargas AU RC 10.00 25.00
150 Nate Burleson AU RC 8.00 20.00

2003 Leaf Limited Bronze Spotlight

*VETS 1-100: .8X TO 2X BASIC CARDS
*ROOKIES 101-125: .6X TO 1.5X
1-125 STATED PRINT RUN 150
*ROOKIE AU/25 126-150: .6X TO 1.5X
126-150 ROOKIE AU PRINT RUN 25

2003 Leaf Limited Gold Spotlight

*VETS 1-100: 3X TO 8X BASIC CARDS
*ROOKIES 101-125: 2.5X TO 6X
1-125 STATED PRINT RUN 25
UNPRICED 126-150 AU PRINT RUN 10
123 Tony Romo 250.00 400.00

2003 Leaf Limited Platinum Spotlight

STATED PRINT RUN 1 SER.#'d SETS
NOT PRICED DUE TO SCARCITY

2003 Leaf Limited Silver Spotlight

*VETS 1-100: 1.2X TO 3X BASIC CARDS
*ROOKIES 101-125: 1X TO 2.5X
1-125 STATED PRINT RUN 75
UNPRICED 126-150 AU PRINT RUN 15

2003 Leaf Limited Contenders Preview Autographs

Randomly inserted in packs, this set is a preview of the 2003 Playoff Contenders Rookie Tickets. Each card features an authentic autograph on a silver foil sticker. The words "Preview Ticket" appear along the top border of the card fronts.

STATED PRINT RUN 10-25
SER.#'d TO 10 NOT PRICED
111 Mike Doss/25 15.00 40.00
112 Chris Simms/25 10.00 25.00
114 Justin Gage/25 12.00 30.00
117 Jason Witten/25 60.00 120.00
126 Carson Palmer/25 200.00 400.00
127 Byron Leftwich/25 12.00 30.00
128 Kyle Boller/25 10.00 25.00
129 Rex Grossman/25 20.00 50.00
133 Seneca Wallace/25 12.00 30.00
134 Larry Johnson/25 25.00 60.00
136 Justin Fargas/25 15.00 40.00
138 Chris Brown/25 10.00 25.00
139 Musa Smith/25 10.00 25.00
140 Artose Pinner/25 10.00 25.00
141 Andre Johnson/25 125.00 200.00
142 Kelley Washington/25 10.00 25.00
143 Taylor Jacobs/25 10.00 25.00
144 Bryant Johnson/25 15.00 40.00
145 Tyrone Calico/25 10.00 25.00
146 Anquan Boldin/25 15.00 40.00
147 Bethel Johnson/25 10.00 25.00
149 Kevin Curtis/25 10.00 25.00
150 Dallas Clark/25 15.00 40.00
151 Teyo Johnson/25 12.00 30.00
152 Terrell Suggs/25 25.00 60.00
154 Terence Newman/25 15.00 40.00
155 Marcus Trufant/25 12.00 30.00
157 Brooks Bollinger/25 12.00 30.00
158 Ken Dorsey/25 12.00 30.00
163 Avon Cobourne/25 10.00 25.00
165 Tony Hollings/25 12.00 30.00
167 Arlen Harris/25 10.00 25.00
170 L.J. Smith/25 15.00 40.00
196 Mike Sherman/25 15.00 40.00
197 Dave Wannstedt/25 12.00 30.00
198 Dick Vermeil/25 15.00 40.00
199 Tony Dungy/25 50.00 100.00
200 Mike Martz/25 12.00 30.00

2003 Leaf Limited Cuts Autographs

Randomly inserted in packs, this set features an authentic player autograph cut from an authentic jersey number.

LC1 John Elway/75 100.00 200.00
LC2 Michael Vick/94 20.00 50.00
LC3 Warren Moon/100 30.00 60.00
LC4 Aaron Brooks/100 12.00 30.00

2003 Leaf Limited Double Threads

Randomly inserted in packs, this set features two game worn jersey swatches from two teammates. Double Threads Prime, a parallel of this set, features two premium game worn jersey swatches from two teammates. Double Threads Prime cards are serial numbered to 10 and are not priced due to scarcity.

PRINT RUN 100 SER.#'d SETS
UNPRICED PRIME PRINT RUN 10
DT1 J.Unitas/P.Manning/25 60.00 100.00
DT2 D.Shula/E.James 15.00 40.00
DT3 J.Kelly/D.Bledsoe 5.00 12.00
DT4 J.Kelly/B.Smith 5.00 12.00
DT5 D.Butkus/B.Urlacher 25.00 60.00
DT6 W.Payton/M.Singletary 30.00 80.00
DT7 D.Butkus/M.Singletary [illegible]
DT8 J.Brown/B.Kosar 6.00 15.00
DT9 R.Staubach/T.Aikman 20.00 50.00
DT10 T.Dorsett/E.Smith 8.00 20.00
DT11 M.Irvin/A.Bryant 5.00 12.00
DT12 D.Sanders/R.Williams 4.00 10.00
DT13 T.Davis/C.Portis 3.00 8.00
DT14 J.Elway/T.Davis 8.00 20.00
DT15 T.Dorsett/C.Portis 5.00 12.00
DT16 D.Walker/B.Sanders 20.00 40.00
DT17 B.Starr/B.Favre 25.00 60.00
DT18 E.Campbell/E.George 5.00 12.00
DT19 J.Montana/R.Gannon 15.00 40.00
DT20 M.Allen/P.Holmes 5.00 12.00
DT21 B.Griese/D.Marino 15.00 40.00
DT22 F.Tarkenton/D.Culpepper 5.00 12.00
DT23 D.Bledsoe/T.Brady 20.00 50.00
DT24 R.Williams/D.McAllister 4.00 10.00
DT25 M.Bavaro/J.Shockey 4.00 10.00
DT26 J.Namath/C.Pennington 8.00 20.00
DT27 J.Namath/J.Riggins 8.00 20.00
DT28 M.Allen/J.Rice 10.00 25.00
DT29 T.Bradshaw/A.Randle El 6.00 15.00
DT30 D.Brees/L.Tomlinson 5.00 12.00
DT31 J.Montana/J.Garcia 20.00 50.00
DT32 S.Young/J.Rice 10.00 25.00
DT33 J.Montana/J.Rice 20.00 50.00
DT34 J.Rice/T.Owens 10.00 25.00
DT35 K.Warner/M.Faulk 4.00 10.00
DT36 J.Riggins/D.Sanders 4.00 10.00
DT37 M.Vick/D.McNabb 4.00 10.00
DT38 J.Harrington/D.Carr 3.00 8.00
DT39 J.Elway/B.Favre 15.00 40.00
DT40 J.Kelly/D.Marino 12.00 30.00
DT41 J.Montana/D.McNabb 15.00 40.00
DT42 S.Young/M.Vick 6.00 15.00
DT43 W.Payton/E.Smith 25.00 50.00
DT44 J.Brown/B.Sanders 8.00 20.00
DT45 R.Williams/P.Holmes 4.00 10.00
DT46 E.Smith/L.Tomlinson 8.00 20.00
DT47 M.Faulk/E.James 4.00 10.00
DT48 E.Campbell/R.Williams 5.00 12.00
DT49 E.James/C.Portis 4.00 10.00
DT50 J.Shockey/A.Johnson 8.00 20.00

2003 Leaf Limited Hardwear

Randomly inserted in packs, this set features game worn helmet pieces. There are two parallels of this set: Limited Hardwear and Limited Hardwear Shield. The Limited Hardwear set features holofoil cards with game worn helmet pieces imbedded on the card fronts. Limited Hardwear cards are serial numbered to 25 and are not priced due to scarcity. The Limited Hardwear Shield set features holofoil cards along with the NFL Shield logo taken from game worn helmets imbedded on the card fronts. Hardward Shields are serial numbered to 1 and are not priced due to scarcity.

STATED PRINT RUN 100 SER.#'d SETS
*LIMITED/25: .8X TO 2X BASIC HEL/100
UNPRICED SHIELD PRINT RUN 1
H1 Jeremy Shockey 3.00 8.00
H2 Dan Marino 20.00 50.00
H3 Joe Montana 30.00 80.00
H4 Emmitt Smith 15.00 40.00
H5 Brian Urlacher 10.00 25.00
H6 Brett Favre 20.00 50.00
H7 Ricky Williams 8.00 20.00
H8 Earl Campbell 10.00 25.00
H9 Jerry Rice 20.00 50.00
H10 John Elway 15.00 40.00
H11 Marcus Allen Chiefs 10.00 25.00
H12 Randy Moss 8.00 20.00
H13 Steve Young 12.00 30.00
H14 Troy Aikman 12.00 30.00
H15 Tony Dorsett 10.00 25.00
H16 Jim Kelly 10.00 25.00
H17 Marshall Faulk 8.00 20.00
H18 Jeff Garcia 6.00 15.00
H19 Tom Brady 40.00 100.00
H20 Chad Pennington 6.00 15.00
H21 Deuce McAllister 8.00 20.00
H22 Marcus Allen Raiders 10.00 25.00
H23 Travis Henry 6.00 15.00
H24 Roger Staubach 12.00 30.00
H25 Terrell Owens 8.00 20.00

2003 Leaf Limited Legends Jerseys

Randomly inserted in packs, this set features game worn jersey swatches. The Don Shula, Fran Tarkenton, and Jim Brown cards also feature an authentic player autograph on a silver foil sticker. Each card is serial numbered to 50.

STATED PRINT RUN 50 SER.#'d SETS
UNPRICED PRIME PRINT RUN 5
UNPRICED SEASONS PRINT RUN 6-19
LL1 Barry Sanders 15.00 40.00
LL2 Bart Starr 15.00 40.00
LL3 Brett Favre 15.00 40.00
LL4 Dan Marino 20.00 50.00
LL5 Doak Walker 20.00 50.00
LL6 Don Shula AU 30.00 60.00
LL7 Earl Campbell 10.00 25.00
LL8 Emmitt Smith 12.00 30.00
LL9 Fran Tarkenton AU 30.00 60.00
LL10 Jerry Rice 15.00 40.00
LL11 Jim Brown AU 70.00 120.00
LL12 Jim Kelly 10.00 25.00
LL13 Jim Thorpe 90.00 150.00
LL14 Joe Montana 30.00 80.00
LL15 Joe Namath 15.00 40.00
LL16 John Elway 20.00 50.00
LL17 John Riggins 8.00 20.00
LL18 Roger Staubach 12.00 30.00
LL19 Terry Bradshaw 12.00 30.00
LL20 Walter Payton 30.00 80.00

2003 Leaf Limited Material Monikers

Randomly inserted in packs, this set features single and double-sided cards with game used jersey swatches along with authentic player autographs on silver foil stickers. Please note that the Joe Namath, J.Namath/C.Pennington, and S.McNair/E.George cards were issued as exchange cards in packs. The exchange deadline is 7/1/2006. Cards are serial numbered to varying quantities.

STATED PRINT RUN 5-25
SER.#'d UNDER 15 NOT PRICED
UNPRICED LIMITED PRINT RUN 1
M1 Dan Marino/15 75.00 150.00
M3 Jim Brown/25 60.00 120.00
M4 Jim Kelly/25 30.00 80.00
M5 Joe Montana/25 100.00 200.00
M6 Joe Montana/15 75.00 150.00
M8 John Riggins/25 20.00 50.00
M9 John Riggins/25 20.00 50.00
M10 Mark Bavaro/25 40.00 80.00
M13 Daunte Culpepper/25 20.00 50.00
M14 Troy Aikman/15 50.00 100.00
M16 Michael Vick/25 30.00 80.00
M17 Roger Staubach/25 50.00 100.00
M18 Drew Bledsoe/25 20.00 50.00
M19 Brian Urlacher/25 50.00 100.00
M22 Joey Harrington/20 15.00 40.00
M25 David Carr/20 15.00 40.00
M26 Marvin Harrison/15 20.00 50.00
[illegible] Priest Holmes/15 [illegible]
M30 Ricky Williams/20 20.00 50.00
M31 Earl Campbell/25 25.00 60.00
M33 Tom Brady/20 175.00 300.00
M36 Jerry Rice/20 90.00 150.00
M37 Dick Butkus/25 60.00 100.00
M38 Jeff Garcia/20 15.00 40.00
M39 Joe Namath/15 60.00 120.00
M40 Kurt Warner/25 20.00 50.00
M41 J.Brown/J.Lewis/20 60.00 120.00
M42 K.Warner/T.Holt/20 60.00 100.00
M43 K.Warner/I.Bruce/25 60.00 100.00
M44 J.Montana/M.Allen/25 100.00 200.00
M45 J.Montana/J.Garcia/25 100.00 200.00
M48 S.McNair/E.George/25 50.00 100.00

2003 Leaf Limited Player Threads

Randomly inserted in packs, this set features single, double, and triple game worn jersey swatches. Each card is serial numbered to 50. There are two parallels of this set: Player Threads Prime and Player Threads Limited. The Threads Prime set features holofoil cards and two or three premium game worn jersey swatches. Threads Prime cards are serial numbered to 10 and are not priced due to scarcity. The Threads Limited set features holofoil cards and two or three premium game worn jersey swatches. Threads Limited cards are serial numbered to 1 and are not priced due to scarcity.

STATED PRINT RUN 34-50
UNPRICED LIMITED PRINT RUN 1
UNPRICED PRIME PRINT RUN 10
PT1 Barry Sanders 15.00 40.00
PT2 Brett Favre 20.00 50.00
PT3 Dan Marino 20.00 50.00
PT4 Donovan McNabb 8.00 20.00
PT5 Earl Campbell/34 10.00 25.00
PT6 Emmitt Smith 15.00 40.00
PT7 Fran Tarkenton 10.00 25.00
PT8 Jeremy Shockey 6.00 15.00
PT9 Jim Kelly 10.00 25.00
PT10 John Riggins 8.00 20.00
PT11 LaDanian Tomlinson 10.00 25.00
PT12 Mike Singletary 10.00 25.00
PT13 Peyton Manning 25.00 60.00
PT14 Priest Holmes 6.00 15.00
PT15 Randy Moss 8.00 20.00
PT16 Roger Staubach 12.00 30.00
PT17 Steve Young 12.00 30.00
PT18 Terry Bradshaw 12.00 30.00
PT19 Tom Brady 40.00 100.00
PT20 Tony Dorsett 10.00 25.00
PT21 Troy Aikman 12.00 30.00
PT22 Walter Payton 30.00 80.00
PT23 Clinton Portis 6.00 15.00
PT24 Drew Bledsoe 8.00 20.00
PT25 Edgerrin James 8.00 20.00
PT26 Jerry Rice 20.00 50.00
PT27 Joe Montana 30.00 80.00
PT28 John Elway 15.00 40.00
PT29 Marshall Faulk 8.00 20.00
PT30 Ricky Williams 8.00 20.00

2003 Leaf Limited Team Trademarks Autographs

Randomly inserted in packs, this set features game worn jersey swatches die cut in the shape of the player's team logo. The cards also feature authentic player autographs on silver foil stickers. Please note that Clinton Portis, Ashley Lelie, Joe Namath, Priest Holmes, and Terrell Owens were issued as exchange cards in packs. The exchange deadline is 7/1/2006. Unless noted below, each card is serial numbered to 50.

STATED PRINT RUN 5-50
*LIMITED/25: .5X TO 1.2X BASE AU/50
LT1 Aaron Brooks 12.00 30.00
LT2 Ahman Green 15.00 40.00
LT4 Bob Griese 20.00 50.00
LT5 Brian Urlacher 25.00 60.00
LT6 Chad Pennington 12.00 30.00
LT7 Chris Chambers 12.00 30.00
LT8 Clinton Portis 12.00 30.00
LT9 Dan Marino 100.00 200.00
LT10 David Carr 12.00 30.00
LT11 Deion Sanders 40.00 80.00
LT12 Deuce McAllister 15.00 40.00
LT13 Dick Butkus 50.00 100.00
LT14 Don Shula 20.00 50.00
LT15 Drew Bledsoe 15.00 40.00
LT16 Earl Campbell 20.00 50.00
LT17 Ashley Lelie 12.00 30.00
LT18 Eric Moulds 12.00 30.00
LT19 Fran Tarkenton 20.00 50.00
LT20 Isaac Bruce 20.00 50.00
LT21 Jamal Lewis 15.00 40.00
LT22 Jim Kelly 40.00 80.00
LT23 Joe Namath 75.00 150.00
LT24 Joey Harrington 12.00 30.00
LT26 Kendrell Bell 12.00 30.00
LT27 Kurt Warner 20.00 50.00
LT28 Antwaan Randle El 12.00 30.00
LT29 Marcus Allen 20.00 50.00
LT30 Marvin Harrison 15.00 40.00
LT31 Michael Irvin 30.00 60.00
LT32 Michael Vick 30.00 60.00
LT33 Mike Alstott 12.00 30.00
LT34 Mike Singletary 20.00 50.00
LT35 Priest Holmes 12.00 30.00
LT36 Ricky Williams 15.00 40.00
LT37 Roger Staubach 60.00 100.00
LT38 Roy Williams 12.00 30.00
LT39 Santana Moss 15.00 40.00
LT40 Shaun Alexander 12.00 30.00
LT41 Steve Largent 20.00 50.00
LT42 Steve McNair 15.00 40.00
LT43 Steve Young 40.00 80.00
LT44 Terrell Owens 15.00 40.00
LT45 Tim Brown 20.00 50.00
LT46 Tom Brady 150.00 300.00
LT47 Tony Dorsett 20.00 50.00
LT48 Quincy Carter 12.00 30.00
LT49 Troy Aikman 60.00 120.00
LT50 Warren Moon 20.00 50.00

2003 Leaf Limited Threads

Randomly inserted in packs, this set features game worn jersey swatches. Please note that the Don Shula, Earl Campbell, Fran Tarkenton, and Kurt Warner cards also feature authentic autographs on silver foil stickers. Each card is serial numbered to 100.

STATED PRINT RUN 100 SER.#'d SETS
*POSITION/75: .5X TO 1.2X BASIC JSY
POSITION STATED PRINT RUN 75
LT1 Aaron Brooks 2.50 6.00
LT2 Aaron Brooks 2.50 6.00
LT3 Ahman Green 3.00 8.00
LT4 Ahman Green 3.00 8.00
LT5 Barry Sanders 6.00 15.00
LT6 Barry Sanders 6.00 15.00
LT7 Bart Starr 6.00 15.00
LT8 Bob Griese 4.00 10.00
LT9 Brett Favre 8.00 20.00
LT10 Brett Favre 8.00 20.00
LT11 Brian Urlacher 4.00 10.00
LT12 Chad Pennington 2.50 6.00
LT13 Clinton Portis 2.50 6.00
LT14 Clinton Portis 2.50 6.00
LT15 Clinton Portis Miami 2.50 6.00
LT16 Dan Marino 8.00 20.00
LT17 Dan Marino 8.00 20.00
LT18 Daunte Culpepper 3.00 8.00
LT19 Daunte Culpepper 3.00 8.00
LT20 Daunte Culpepper 3.00 8.00
LT21 David Carr 2.50 6.00
LT22 Deion Sanders 3.00 8.00
LT23 Deion Sanders 3.00 8.00
LT24 Deuce McAllister 3.00 8.00
LT25 Dick Butkus 5.00 12.00
LT26 Doak Walker 15.00 40.00
LT27 Don Shula AU [illegible]
LT28 Donovan McNabb 3.00 8.00
LT29 Donovan McNabb 3.00 8.00
LT30 Drew Bledsoe 3.00 8.00
LT31 Drew Bledsoe 3.00 8.00
LT32 Drew Bledsoe 3.00 8.00
LT33 Drew Bledsoe 3.00 8.00

LT34 Drew Brees 4.00 10.00
LT35 Earl Campbell/66* 8.00 20.00
LT35AU Earl Campbell AU/34* 30.00 50.00
LT36 Earl Campbell 4.00 10.00
LT37 Edgerrin James 3.00 8.00
LT38 Edgerrin James 3.00 8.00
LT39 Edgerrin James 3.00 8.00
LT40 Emmitt Smith 6.00 15.00
LT41 Fran Tarkenton AU 25.00 50.00
LT42 Jeff Garcia 2.50 6.00
LT43 Jeff Garcia 2.50 6.00
LT44 Jeremy Shockey 2.50 6.00
LT45 Jeremy Shockey 2.50 6.00
LT46 Jerry Rice 8.00 20.00
LT47 Jerry Rice 8.00 20.00
LT48 Jerry Rice 8.00 20.00
LT49 Jim Brown 5.00 12.00
LT50 Jim Kelly 4.00 10.00
LT51 Jim Thorpe 40.00 100.00
LT52 Joe Montana 15.00 40.00
LT53 Joe Montana 12.00 30.00
LT54 Joe Montana 12.00 30.00
LT55 Joe Namath 6.00 15.00
LT56 Joey Harrington 2.50 6.00
LT57 John Elway 12.00 30.00
LT58 John Elway 12.00 30.00
LT59 John Elway 12.00 30.00
LT60 John Elway 12.00 30.00
LT61 John Riggins Redskins 3.00 8.00
LT62 John Riggins Jets 3.00 8.00
LT63 Johnny Unitas 8.00 20.00
LT64 Kurt Warner AU 30.00 60.00
LT65 LaDainian Tomlinson 4.00 10.00
LT66 Shaun Alexander 2.50 6.00
LT67 Marcus Allen 4.00 10.00
LT68 Marcus Allen 4.00 10.00
LT69 Mark Bavaro 3.00 8.00
LT70 Marshall Faulk 3.00 8.00
LT71 Marshall Faulk 3.00 8.00
LT72 Marshall Faulk SDSU 3.00 8.00
LT73 Marvin Harrison 3.00 8.00
LT74 Marvin Harrison 3.00 8.00
LT75 Michael Vick 3.00 8.00
LT76 Mike Singletary 4.00 10.00
LT77 Mike Singletary 4.00 10.00
LT78 Peyton Manning 10.00 25.00
LT79 Peyton Manning 10.00 25.00
LT80 Peyton Manning 10.00 25.00
LT81 Priest Holmes 2.50 6.00
LT82 Priest Holmes 2.50 6.00
LT83 Randy Moss 3.00 8.00
LT84 Randy Moss 3.00 8.00
LT85 Ricky Williams 3.00 8.00
LT86 Ricky Williams 3.00 8.00
LT87 Ricky Williams 3.00 8.00
LT88 Ricky Williams 3.00 8.00
LT89 Roger Staubach 5.00 12.00
LT90 Steve Young 5.00 12.00
LT91 Terrell Owens 3.00 8.00
LT92 Terry Bradshaw 5.00 12.00
LT93 Tom Brady 15.00 40.00
LT94 Tom Brady 15.00 40.00
LT95 Tony Dorsett 4.00 10.00
LT96 Tony Dorsett 4.00 10.00
LT97 Troy Aikman 5.00 12.00
LT98 Troy Aikman 5.00 12.00
LT99 Walter Payton 12.00 30.00
LT100 Walter Payton 12.00 30.00

2003 Leaf Limited Threads At the Half

*HALF/50: .6X TO 1.5X BASE JSY/100
LT1 Aaron Brooks AU 15.00 40.00
LT2 Aaron Brooks AU 15.00 40.00
LT24 Deuce McAllister AU 20.00 50.00
LT56 Joey Harrington AU 20.00 50.00
LT64 Kurt Warner AU 30.00 80.00
LT67 Marcus Allen AU 30.00 80.00
LT68 Marcus Allen AU 30.00 80.00
LT69 Mark Bavaro AU 25.00 60.00
LT76 Mike Singletary AU 25.00 60.00
LT81 Priest Holmes AU 25.00 60.00
LT82 Priest Holmes AU 25.00 60.00
LT96 Tony Dorsett AU 20.00 50.00

2003 Leaf Limited Threads Jersey Numbers

*JSY/80-89: .4X TO 1X BASE JSY/100
*JSY/44-63: .6X TO 1.5X BASE JSY/100
*JSY/32-37: .8X TO 2X BASE JSY/100
*JSY/21-28: 1X TO 2.5X BASE JSY/100
STATED PRINT RUN 1-89
LT3 Ahman Green AU/30 20.00 50.00
LT4 Ahman Green AU/30 20.00 50.00
LT5 Barry Sanders AU/20 125.00 200.00
LT6 Barry Sanders AU/20 125.00 200.00
LT11 Brian Urlacher AU/54 30.00 80.00
LT13 Clinton Portis AU/26 25.00 60.00
LT14 Clinton Portis AU/26 25.00 60.00
LT15 Clinton Portis AU/28 25.00 60.00
LT22 Deion Sanders AU/21 50.00 100.00
LT23 Deion Sanders AU/21 50.00 100.00
LT24 Deuce McAllister AU/26 30.00 80.00
LT25 Dick Butkus AU/51 40.00 100.00
LT27 Don Shula AU/25 30.00 80.00
LT35 Earl Campbell AU/34 30.00 80.00
LT36 Earl Campbell AU/20 30.00 80.00
LT66 Shaun Alexander AU/37 20.00 50.00
LT69 Mark Bavaro AU/89 20.00 50.00
LT81 Priest Holmes AU/31 30.00 80.00
LT82 Priest Holmes AU/33 30.00 80.00
LT95 Tony Dorsett AU/33 30.00 80.00
LT96 Tony Dorsett AU/33 30.00 80.00

2003 Leaf Limited Threads Prime

RIME/25: .8X TO 2X BASE JSY/100
LT1 Aaron Brooks AU 15.00 40.00
LT2 Aaron Brooks AU 15.00 40.00
LT3 Ahman Green AU 20.00 50.00
LT4 Ahman Green AU 20.00 50.00
LT8 Bob Griese AU 25.00 60.00
LT9 Brett Favre AU 150.00 250.00
LT10 Brett Favre AU 150.00 250.00
LT12 Chad Pennington AU 15.00 40.00
LT15 Clinton Portis AU 15.00 40.00
LT19 Daunte Culpepper AU 20.00 50.00
LT30 Drew Bledsoe AU 20.00 50.00
LT31 Drew Bledsoe AU 20.00 50.00
LT32 Drew Bledsoe AU 20.00 50.00
LT33 Drew Bledsoe AU 20.00 50.00
LT41 Fran Tarkenton AU 25.00 60.00
LT56 Joey Harrington AU 15.00 40.00
LT61 John Riggins AU 20.00 50.00
LT62 John Riggins AU 20.00 50.00
LT64 Kurt Warner AU 20.00 50.00
LT66 Shaun Alexander AU 15.00 40.00
LT75 Michael Vick AU 20.00 50.00
LT81 Priest Holmes AU 15.00 40.00
LT85 Ricky Williams AU 20.00 50.00
LT86 Ricky Williams AU 20.00 50.00
LT87 Ricky Williams AU 20.00 50.00
LT88 Ricky Williams AU 20.00 50.00
LT92 Terry Bradshaw AU 75.00 150.00
LT97 Troy Aikman AU 75.00 150.00

2004 Leaf Limited

Leaf Limited initially released in early December 2004 and was one of the most well-received products of the year due to the large number of game used and autographed card inserts. The base set consists of 233-cards including 50-retired players serial numbered of 799, 50-rookies numbered of 350, and 33-rookie jersey autograph cards numbered of 150. Hobby boxes contained 4-packs of 4-cards and carried an S.R.P. of $70 per pack.
201-233 ROOK.JSY AU PRINT RUN 150
UNPRICED PLATINUM PRINT RUN 1
1 A.J. Feeley 1.00 2.50
2 Aaron Brooks 1.00 2.50
3 Ahman Green 1.25 3.00
4 Andre Johnson 1.25 3.00
5 Anquan Boldin 1.00 2.50
6 Antwaan Randle El 1.00 2.50
7 Ashley Lelie 1.00 2.50
8 Brad Johnson 1.25 3.00
9 Brett Favre 3.00 8.00
10 Brian Urlacher 1.50 4.00
11 Brian Westbrook 1.00 2.50
12 Byron Leftwich 1.00 2.50
13 Carson Palmer 1.25 3.00
14 Chad Johnson 1.00 2.50
15 Chad Pennington 1.00 2.50
16 Charlie Garner 1.25 3.00
17 Charles Rogers 1.00 2.50
18 Chris Brown 1.00 2.50
19 Chris Chambers 1.00 2.50
20 Clinton Portis 1.00 2.50
21 Corey Dillon 1.00 2.50
22 Deion Sanders 1.25 3.00
23 Curtis Martin 1.25 3.00
24 Daunte Culpepper 1.25 3.00
25 David Terrell 1.00 2.50
26 David Carr 1.00 2.50
27 Deion Branch 1.00 2.50
28 Derrick Mason 1.00 2.50
29 DeShaun Foster 1.25 3.00
30 Deuce McAllister 1.25 3.00
31 Domanick Davis 1.00 2.50
32 Donovan McNabb 1.25 3.00
33 Donte Stallworth 1.00 2.50
34 Drew Bledsoe 1.25 3.00
35 Duce Staley 1.00 2.50
36 Eddie George 1.25 3.00
37 Edgerrin James 1.25 3.00
38 Emmitt Smith 2.50 6.00
39 Eric Moulds 1.00 2.50
40 Fred Taylor 1.00 2.50
41 Hines Ward 1.25 3.00
42 Isaac Bruce 1.50 4.00
43 Jake Delhomme 1.00 2.50
44 Jake Plummer 1.00 2.50
45 Javon Walker 1.00 2.50
46 Jeff Garcia 1.00 2.50
47 Jeremy Shockey 1.00 2.50
48 Jerome Bettis 1.50 4.00
49 Jerry Porter 1.00 2.50
50 Jerry Rice 3.00 8.00
51 Jevon Kearse 1.00 2.50
52 Jimmy Smith 1.25 3.00
53 Joe Horn 1.00 2.50
54 Joey Harrington 1.00 2.50
55 Josh McCown 1.25 3.00
56 Kevan Barlow 1.00 2.50
57 Koren Robinson 1.00 2.50
58 Kyle Boller 1.00 2.50
59 LaDainian Tomlinson 1.50 4.00
60 LaVar Arrington 1.00 2.50
61 Laveranues Coles 1.00 2.50
62 Lee Suggs 1.25 3.00
63 Marc Bulger 1.00 2.50
64 Mark Brunell 1.25 3.00
65 Marshall Faulk 1.25 3.00
66 Marvin Harrison 1.25 3.00
67 Matt Hasselbeck 1.00 2.50
68 Michael Bennett 1.00 2.50
69 Michael Strahan 1.25 3.00
70 Michael Vick 1.25 3.00
71 Peerless Price 1.00 2.50
72 Peter Warrick 1.00 2.50
73 Peyton Manning 4.00 10.00
74 Priest Holmes 1.00 2.50
75 Quentin Griffin 1.00 2.50
76 Randy Moss 1.25 3.00
77 Ray Lewis 1.50 4.00
78 Rex Grossman 1.00 2.50
79 Lamar Gordon 1.00 2.50
80 Rod Smith 1.25 3.00
81 Roy Williams S 1.00 2.50
82 Rudi Johnson 1.00 2.50
83 Santana Moss 1.25 3.00
84 Shaun Alexander 1.00 2.50
85 Stephen Davis 1.00 2.50
86 Steve McNair 1.25 3.00
87 Steve Smith 1.50 4.00
88 T.J. Duckett 1.00 2.50
89 Terrell Owens 1.25 3.00
90 Thomas Jones 1.00 2.50
91 Tiki Barber 1.25 3.00
92 Tim Brown 1.50 4.00
93 Tom Brady 6.00 15.00
94 Tony Gonzalez 1.25 3.00
95 Torry Holt 1.25 3.00
96 Travis Henry 1.00 2.50
97 Trent Green 1.00 2.50
98 Warren Sapp 1.25 3.00
99 William Green 1.00 2.50
100 Willis McGahee 1.00 2.50
101 Barry Sanders 3.00 8.00
102 Bart Starr 5.00 12.00
103 Bo Jackson 2.50 6.00
104 Bob Griese 2.00 5.00
105 Bronko Nagurski 2.00 5.00
106 Dan Marino 4.00 10.00
107 Deion Sanders 1.50 4.00
108 Dick Butkus 2.50 6.00
109 Doak Walker 2.00 5.00
110 Don Maynard 1.50 4.00
111 Don Shula 2.00 5.00
112 Earl Campbell 2.00 5.00
113 Fran Tarkenton 2.00 5.00
114 Franco Harris 2.50 6.00
115 Fred Biletnikoff 2.00 5.00
116 Gale Sayers 2.00 5.00
117 Herman Edwards 1.50 4.00
118 Jim Brown 2.50 6.00
119 Jim Kelly 2.00 5.00
120 Jim Thorpe 2.00 5.00
121 Jimmy Johnson 1.50 4.00
122 Joe Greene 2.00 5.00
123 Joe Montana 6.00 15.00
124 Joe Namath 3.00 8.00
125 John Elway 3.00 8.00
126 John Riggins 1.50 4.00
127 Johnny Unitas 5.00 12.00
128 Larry Csonka 2.00 5.00
129 Lawrence Taylor 2.00 5.00
130 Marcus Allen 2.00 5.00
131 Mark Bavaro 1.25 3.00
132 Michael Irvin 2.00 5.00
133 Mike Ditka 2.00 5.00
134 Mike Singletary 2.00 5.00
135 Ozzie Newsome 1.50 4.00
136 Paul Warfield 1.50 4.00
137 Randall Cunningham 1.50 4.00
138 Ray Nitschke 2.00 5.00
139 Red Grange 2.00 5.00
140 Reggie White 2.00 5.00
141 Roger Staubach 2.50 6.00
142 Sterling Sharpe 1.50 4.00
143 Steve Largent 2.00 5.00
144 Terrell Davis 1.50 4.00
145 Terry Bradshaw 2.50 6.00
146 Thurman Thomas 1.50 4.00
147 Tony Dorsett 2.00 5.00
148 Troy Aikman 2.50 6.00
149 Walter Payton 8.00 20.00
150 Warren Moon 2.00 5.00
151 Ahmad Carroll RC 2.00 5.00
152 Andy Hall RC 2.00 5.00
153 Antwan Odom RC 2.00 5.00
154 B.J. Symons RC 2.00 5.00
155 Carlos Francis RC 2.00 5.00
156 Casey Bramlet RC 2.00 5.00
157 Chris Cooley RC 2.50 6.00
158 Chris Gamble RC 2.00 5.00
159 Clarence Moore RC 2.00 5.00
160 Cody Pickett RC 2.00 5.00
161 Courtney Watson RC 2.00 5.00
162 Craig Krenzel RC 2.00 5.00
163 D.J. Hackett RC 2.00 5.00
164 D.J. Williams RC 3.00 8.00
165 Derrick Strait RC 2.00 5.00
166 Dontarrious Thomas RC 2.50 6.00
167 Drew Henson RC 2.00 5.00
168 Ernest Wilford RC 2.50 6.00
169 Jamaar Taylor RC 2.00 5.00
170 Jason Babin RC 3.00 8.00
171 Jeff Smoker RC 2.50 6.00
172 Jerricho Cotchery RC 2.50 6.00
173 Jim Sorgi RC 2.50 6.00
174 Joey Thomas RC 2.00 5.00
175 John Navarre RC 2.00 5.00
176 Johnnie Morant RC 2.00 5.00
177 Jonathan Vilma RC 2.50 6.00
178 Josh Harris RC 2.00 5.00
179 Keiwan Ratliff RC 2.00 5.00
180 Kenechi Udeze RC 2.50 6.00
181 Kris Wilson RC 2.50 6.00
182 Marcus Tubbs RC 2.00 5.00
183 Marquise Hill RC 2.00 5.00
184 Matt Mauck RC 2.00 5.00
185 Maurice Mann RC 2.00 5.00
186 Michael Boulware RC 3.00 8.00
187 Michael Turner RC 2.00 5.00
188 P.K. Sam RC 2.00 5.00
189 Patrick Crayton RC 3.00 8.00
190 Ricardo Colclough RC 2.00 5.00
191 Richard Smith RC 2.00 5.00
192 Samie Parker RC 2.00 5.00
193 Sean Taylor RC 12.00 30.00
194 Teddy Lehman RC 2.00 5.00
195 Thomas Tapeh RC 2.50 6.00
196 Tommie Harris RC 2.50 6.00
197 Triandos Luke RC 2.00 5.00
198 Troy Fleming RC 2.00 5.00
199 Vince Wilfork RC 3.00 8.00
200 Will Smith RC 2.50 6.00
201 Larry Fitzgerald JSY AU RC 75.00 150.00
202 DeAngelo Hall JSY AU RC 12.00 30.00
203 Matt Schaub JSY AU RC 8.00 20.00
204 Michael Jenkins JSY AU RC 8.00 20.00
205 Devard Darling JSY AU RC 8.00 20.00
206 J.P. Losman JSY AU RC 8.00 20.00
207 Lee Evans JSY AU RC 12.00 30.00
208 Keary Colbert JSY AU RC 8.00 20.00
209 Bernard Berrian JSY AU RC 8.00 20.00
210 Chris Perry JSY AU RC 8.00 20.00
211 K.Winslow JSY AU RC 8.00 20.00
212 Luke McCown JSY AU RC 8.00 20.00
213 Julius Jones JSY AU RC 8.00 20.00
214 Darius Watts JSY AU RC 8.00 20.00
215 Tatum Bell JSY AU RC 8.00 20.00
216 Kevin Jones JSY AU RC 10.00 25.00
217 Roy Will.WR JSY AU RC 8.00 20.00
218 Dunta Robinson JSY AU RC 8.00 20.00
219 Greg Jones JSY AU RC 8.00 20.00
220 Reggie Williams JSY AU RC 8.00 20.00
221 Mewelde Moore JSY AU RC 10.00 25.00
222 Ben Watson JSY AU RC 10.00 25.00
223 Cedric Cobbs JSY AU RC 8.00 20.00
224 Devery Henderson JSY AU RC 8.00 20.00
225 Eli Manning JSY AU RC 60.00 120.00
226 Robert Gallery JSY AU RC 10.00 25.00
227 Roethlisberger JSY AU RC 75.00 150.00
228 Philip Rivers JSY AU RC 50.00 100.00
229 Derrick Hamilton JSY AU RC 8.00 20.00
230 Rashaun Woods JSY AU RC 8.00 20.00
231 Stev.Jackson JSY AU RC 12.00 30.00
232 Michael Clayton JSY AU RC 10.00 25.00
233 Ben Troupe JSY AU RC 8.00 20.00

2004 Leaf Limited Bronze Spotlight

*VETS 1-100: .8X TO 2X BASIC CARDS
*RETIRED 101-150: .8X TO 2X
*ROOKIES 151-200: .5X TO 1.2X
1-200 PRINT RUN 100 SER.#'d SETS
*ROOKIE JSY AU: .5X TO 1.2X
201-233 ROOK.JSY AU PRINT RUN 25
225 Eli Manning JSY AU 125.00 250.00
227 Ben Roethlisberger JSY AU 150.00 300.00

2004 Leaf Limited Gold Spotlight

*VETS 1-100: 2X TO 5X BASIC CARDS
*RETIRED 101-150: 2X TO 5X
*ROOKIES 151-200: 1X TO 2.5X
1-200 PRINT RUN 25 SER.#'d SETS
UNPRICED ROOK.JSY AU PRINT RUN 10

2004 Leaf Limited Silver Spotlight

ETS 1-100: 1.2X TO 3X BASIC CARDS
*RETIRED 101-150: 1.2X TO 3X
*ROOKIES 151-200: .6X TO 1.5X
1-150 PRINT RUN 50 SER.#'d SETS
*ROOKIE JSY AU: .6X TO 1.5X
151-233 ROOK.JSY AU PRINT RUN 15
225 Eli Manning JSY AU 125.00 250.00
227 Ben Roethlisberger JSY AU 150.00 300.00

2004 Leaf Limited Bound by Round Jerseys

ATED PRINT RUN 50 SER.#'d SETS
*PRIME/25: .6X TO 1.5X BASIC DUAL/50
PRIME PRINT RUN 25 SER.#'d SETS
BR1 B.Favre/A.Boldin 20.00 50.00
BR2 D.Marino/B.Sanders 20.00 50.00
BR3 J.Elway/E.Smith 20.00 50.00
BR4 W.Payton/J.Rice 25.00 60.00
BR5 B.Jackson/M.Vick 15.00 40.00
BR6 M.Allen/T.Brown 10.00 25.00
BR7 J.Montana/T.Owens 20.00 50.00
BR8 T.Brady/M.Hasselbeck 15.00 40.00
BR9 D.McNabb/M.Harrison 10.00 25.00
BR10 Ri.Williams/D.McAllister 7.50 20.00
BR11 C.Portis/A.Randle El 7.50 20.00
BR12 H.Ward/A.Green 7.50 20.00
BR13 M.Faulk/E.James 7.50 20.00
BR14 T.Davis/M.Bulger 10.00 25.00
BR15 M.Bavaro/St.Davis 6.00 15.00
BR16 A.Brooks/R.Johnson 7.50 20.00
BR17 McCaffrey/S.Largent 10.00 25.00
BR18 Ch.Johnson/T.Henry 7.50 20.00
BR19 C.Chambers/Biletnikoff 10.00 25.00
BR20 Singletary/Cunningham 10.00 25.00
BR21 F.Tarkenton/Nitschke 15.00 40.00
BR22 T.Green/L.Kelly 10.00 25.00
BR23 M.Irvin/St.Sharpe 7.50 20.00
BR24 J.Lewis/R.Lewis 7.50 20.00
BR25 B.Urlacher/D.Culpepper 10.00 25.00
BR26 J.Namath/C.Pennington 12.00 30.00
BR27 B.Leftwich/R.Moss 10.00 25.00
BR28 J.Kelly/D.Bledsoe 10.00 25.00
BR29 T.Dorsett/L.Tomlinson 10.00 25.00
BR30 D.Butkus/L.Taylor 15.00 40.00
BR31 G.Sayers/S.Alexander 10.00 25.00
BR32 E.Campbell/D.Carr 7.50 20.00
BR33 D.Sanders/Ro.Williams S 12.00 30.00
BR34 O.Newsome/J.Shockey 7.50 20.00
BR35 J.Harrington/Bo.Griese 7.50 20.00
BR36 R.White/P.Manning 15.00 40.00
BR37 J.Riggins/L.Csonka 10.00 25.00
BR38 J.Lofton/T.Holt 7.50 20.00
BR39 J.Greene/J.Peppers 10.00 25.00
BR40 P.Warfield/S.Moss 6.00 15.00
BR41 T.Aikman/S.McNair 10.00 25.00
BR42 W.Payton/M.Vick 25.00 60.00
BR43 C.Portis/B.Favre 15.00 40.00
BR44 D.Marino/E.Smith 20.00 50.00
BR45 B.Jackson/J.Rice 15.00 40.00
BR46 J.Namath/T.Aikman 15.00 40.00
BR47 J.Elway/B.Sanders 20.00 50.00
BR48 P.Manning/D.Carr 12.00 30.00
BR49 B.Urlacher/R.Moss 12.00 30.00
BR50 Ri.Williams/D.McNabb 10.00 25.00

2004 Leaf Limited Common Threads

STATED PRINT RUN 50 SER.#'d SETS
*PRIME/10: 1.2X TO 3X BASIC DUAL/50
PRIME PRINT RUN 10 SETS
CT1 D.Culpepper/S.McNair 8.00 20.00
CT2 Cunningham/D.McNabb 10.00 25.00
CT3 B.Leftwich/A.Brooks 8.00 20.00
CT4 J.Elway/D.Carr 15.00 40.00
CT5 Montana 49rs/T.Brady 25.00 60.00
CT6 Montana Chfs/T.Green 20.00 50.00
CT7 T.Aikman/J.Harrington 12.00 30.00
CT8 J.Namath/C.Pennington 12.00 30.00
CT9 F.Tarkenton/M.Vick 12.00 30.00
CT10 M.Bulger/M.Hasselbeck 6.00 15.00
CT11 D.Marino/P.Manning 25.00 60.00
CT12 B.Starr/B.Favre 40.00 80.00
CT13 J.Kelly/D.Bledsoe 10.00 25.00
CT14 E.Campbell/Ri.Williams 8.00 20.00
CT15 M.Allen/P.Holmes 10.00 25.00
CT16 W.Payton/L.Tomlinson 20.00 50.00
CT17 B.Sanders/C.Portis 20.00 50.00
CT18 B.Jackson/J.Lewis 12.00 30.00
CT19 T.Davis/E.James 10.00 25.00
CT20 L.Csonka/D.McAllister 10.00 25.00
CT21 G.Sayers/S.Alexander 12.00 30.00
CT22 T.Dorsett/A.Green 10.00 25.00
CT23 L.Kelly/J.Riggins 10.00 25.00
CT24 E.Smith/T.Henry 12.00 30.00
CT25 B.Jackson/Ru.Johnson 12.00 30.00
CT26 J.Rice/A.Boldin 12.00 30.00
CT27 J.Rice/M.Harrison 12.00 30.00
CT28 R.Moss/C.Chambers 10.00 25.00
CT29 M.Irvin/T.Owens 10.00 25.00
CT30 Biletnikoff/T.Brown 8.00 20.00
CT31 T.Holt/Ch.Johnson 8.00 20.00
CT32 J.Lofton/St.Sharpe 8.00 20.00
CT33 S.Largent/L.Coles 10.00 25.00
CT34 P.Warfield/S.Moss 6.00 15.00
CT35 Re.White/J.Peppers 10.00 25.00
CT36 M.Singletary/R.Lewis 15.00 40.00
CT37 D.Butkus/B.Urlacher 15.00 40.00
CT38 L.Taylor/L.Arrington 10.00 25.00
CT39 D.Sanders/T.Newman 12.00 30.00
CT40 M.Bavaro/J.Shockey 8.00 20.00
CT41 M.Vick/D.McNabb 12.00 30.00
CT42 J.Elway/B.Favre 20.00 50.00
CT43 Montana 49rs/Marino 20.00 50.00
CT44 T.Aikman/T.Brady 15.00 40.00
CT45 Montana Chfs/Pennington 20.00 50.00
CT46 J.Kelly/P.Manning 15.00 40.00
CT47 D.Marino/J.Elway 25.00 60.00
CT48 W.Payton/B.Sanders 25.00 60.00
CT49 W.Payton/E.Smith 25.00 60.00
CT50 J.Rice/R.Moss 15.00 40.00

2004 Leaf Limited Contenders Preview Autographs

ATED PRINT RUN 15-25
102 Ahmad Carroll/25 10.00 25.00
106 Ben Roethlisberger/15 250.00 400.00
107 Ben Troupe/25 10.00 25.00
108 Ben Watson/25 12.00 30.00
109 Bernard Berrian/25 25.00 50.00
114 Cedric Cobbs/25 10.00 25.00
116 Chris Perry/25 10.00 25.00
117 Clarence Moore/25 10.00 25.00
119 Craig Krenzel/25 10.00 25.00
121 D.J. Williams/25 15.00 40.00
123 DeAngelo Hall/20 15.00 40.00
124 Derrick Hamilton/25 10.00 25.00
126 Devard Darling/25 10.00 25.00
127 Devery Henderson/25 10.00 25.00
129 Drew Henson/15 10.00 25.00
131 Eli Manning/15 250.00 400.00
132 Ernest Wilford/25 12.00 30.00
133 Greg Jones/25 10.00 25.00
134 J.P. Losman/25 10.00 25.00
135 Jamaar Taylor/25 10.00 25.00
138 Jason Babin/25 15.00 40.00
144 Jonathan Vilma/25 12.00 30.00
146 Julius Jones/25 10.00 25.00
147 Keary Colbert/25 10.00 25.00
149 Kenechi Udeze/25 12.00 30.00
150 Kevin Jones/20 12.00 30.00
152 Lee Evans/25 15.00 40.00
153 Luke McCown/25 10.00 25.00
154 Matt Mauck/25 10.00 25.00
155 Matt Schaub/25 30.00 80.00
157 Mewelde Moore/25 12.00 30.00
158 Michael Clayton/25 12.00 30.00
159 Michael Jenkins/25 10.00 25.00
162 Philip Rivers/25 125.00 250.00
165 Rashaun Woods/25 10.00 25.00
166 Reggie Williams/20 10.00 25.00
167 Ricardo Colclough/25 10.00 25.00
169 Roy Williams WR/25 10.00 25.00
174 Steven Jackson/25 15.00 40.00
175 Tatum Bell/25 10.00 25.00
178 Troy Fleming/25 10.00 25.00
182 Michael Boulware/25 15.00 40.00
186 Chris Cooley/20 25.00 50.00
188 Willie Parker/25 25.00 50.00
194 Erik Coleman/25 12.00 30.00
196 Andy Reid CO/15 15.00 40.00
197 Brian Billick CO/15 15.00 40.00
198 Jeff Fisher CO/15 15.00 40.00
199 Jon Gruden CO/15 15.00 40.00
200 Marvin Lewis CO/15 15.00 40.00

2004 Leaf Limited Cuts Autographs

ATED PRINT RUN 25-100
LC1 Tom Brady/50 175.00 300.00
LC2 Priest Holmes/50 20.00 50.00
LC3 Dan Marino/50 100.00 200.00
LC4 L.Tomlinson/50 25.00 60.00
LC5 Jake Plummer/100 15.00 40.00
LC6 Bronko Nagurski/30 200.00 350.00
LC7 Vince Lombardi/25 350.00 550.00
LC8 Aaron Brooks/55 12.00 30.00
LC9 Warren Moon/55 20.00 50.00

2004 Leaf Limited Hardwear

ATED PRINT RUN 100 SER.#'d SETS
UNPRICED SHIELD PRINT RUN 1 SET
H1 Anquan Boldin 5.00 12.00
H2 Ahman Green 6.00 15.00
H3 Brian Urlacher 8.00 20.00
H4 Chad Johnson 5.00 12.00
H5 Chad Pennington 5.00 12.00
H6 Chris Chambers 5.00 12.00
H7 Eddie George 6.00 15.00
H8 Jake Plummer 5.00 12.00
H9 Jerry Rice 15.00 40.00
H10 Larry Csonka 8.00 20.00
H11 LaDainian Tomlinson 8.00 20.00
H12 Lawrence Taylor 8.00 20.00
H13 Marc Bulger 5.00 12.00
H14 Marcus Allen 8.00 20.00
H15 Matt Hasselbeck 5.00 12.00
H16 Michael Bennett 5.00 12.00
H17 Marvin Harrison 6.00 15.00
H18 Michael Irvin 8.00 20.00
H19 Peyton Manning 20.00 50.00
H20 Randy Moss 6.00 15.00
H21 Ray Lewis 8.00 20.00
H22 Ricky Williams 6.00 15.00
H23 Shaun Alexander 5.00 12.00
H24 Steve McNair 6.00 15.00
H25 Torry Holt 6.00 15.00

2004 Leaf Limited Hardwear Limited

NSIGNED LIMITED: .8X TO 2X
LIMITED PRINT RUN 25 SER.#'d SETS
H1 Anquan Boldin AU 25.00 60.00
H3 Brian Urlacher AU 60.00 100.00
H15 Matt Hasselbeck AU 30.00 80.00
H23 Shaun Alexander AU 75.00 135.00
H25 Torry Holt AU 30.00 80.00

2004 Leaf Limited Legends Jerseys

ATED PRINT RUN 50 SER.#'d SETS
UNPRICED PRIME PRINT RUN 5 SETS
UNPRICED SEASON PRINT RUN 6-18 SETS
LL1 Barry Sanders 15.00 40.00
LL2 Bart Starr 20.00 50.00
LL3 Brett Favre 20.00 50.00
LL4 Dick Butkus 12.00 30.00
LL5 Doak Walker 10.00 25.00
LL6 Fran Tarkenton 10.00 25.00
LL7 Franco Harris 12.00 30.00
LL8 Fred Biletnikoff 10.00 25.00
LL9 Gale Sayers 10.00 25.00
LL10 Jim Brown AU 60.00 120.00
LL11 Jim Kelly 10.00 25.00
LL12 Jim Thorpe 100.00 200.00
LL13 Joe Montana 49ers 20.00 50.00
LL14 Joe Namath AU 50.00 100.00
LL15 John Elway 15.00 40.00
LL16 John Riggins 8.00 20.00
LL17 Johnny Unitas 20.00 50.00
LL18 Steve Largent 10.00 25.00
LL19 Terry Bradshaw 12.00 30.00
LL20 Walter Payton 25.00 60.00

2004 Leaf Limited Lettermen

PRICED LETTERMEN PRINT RUN 4-10

2004 Leaf Limited Material Monikers

RDS #'d UNDER 20 NOT PRICED
UNPRICED LIMITED PRINT RUN 1 SET
MM1 Ahman Green/25 20.00 50.00
MM2 Barry Sanders/25 125.00 250.00
MM3 Bart Starr/31 90.00 150.00
MM8 Joe Namath/50 50.00 100.00
MM9 Byron Leftwich/25 15.00 40.00
MM10 Donovan McNabb/25 40.00 80.00
MM11 Daunte Culpepper/40 15.00 40.00
MM12 Fran Tarkenton/50 20.00 50.00
MM13 Jamal Lewis/25 20.00 50.00
MM14 Jim Brown/25 60.00 120.00
MM16 Anquan Boldin/25 15.00 40.00
MM20 Tom Brady/25 175.00 300.00
MM22 Jim Kelly/25 40.00 80.00
MM23 Clinton Portis/25 20.00 50.00
MM24 John Riggins/25 20.00 50.00
MM25 Roy Williams S/25 15.00 40.00
MM26 Deion Sanders/25 50.00 100.00
MM27 Earl Campbell/20 25.00 60.00
MM28 Priest Holmes/50 12.00 30.00
MM29 Larry Csonka/25 25.00 60.00
MM31 LaDainian Tomlinson/25 50.00 100.00
MM33 Steve McNair/50 15.00 40.00
MM34 Peyton Manning/45 60.00 120.00
MM36 Terry Bradshaw/50 50.00 100.00
MM37 Bo Jackson/25 90.00 150.00
MM42 J.Brown/J.Lewis/25 60.00 120.00
MM45 J.Riggins/C.Portis/25 40.00 80.00
MM46 D.Sanders/R.Will.S/25 50.00 100.00

2004 Leaf Limited Player Threads

READS PRINT RUN 50 SER.#'d SETS
*PRIME/25: .6X TO 1.5X BASIC INSERT
PRIME PRINT RUN 25 SER.#'d SETS
UNPRICED LIMITED PRINT RUN 1 SET
PT1 Ahman Green Tri 8.00 20.00
PT2 Barry Sanders Tri 20.00 50.00
PT3 Brett Favre Dual 15.00 40.00
PT4 Brian Urlacher Dual 10.00 25.00
PT5 Carson Palmer Dual 6.00 15.00
PT6 Clinton Portis Tri 6.00 15.00
PT7 Dan Marino Tri 25.00 60.00
PT8 Daunte Culpepper Tri 8.00 20.00
PT9 Donovan McNabb Dual 6.00 15.00
PT10 Drew Bledsoe Tri 8.00 20.00
PT11 Edgerrin James Tri 8.00 20.00
PT12 Emmitt Smith Tri 15.00 40.00
PT13 Fran Tarkenton Dual 10.00 25.00
PT14 Jeremy Shockey Tri 6.00 15.00
PT15 Jerry Rice Tri 20.00 50.00
PT16 Joe Montana Tri 40.00 100.00
PT17 John Elway Tri 25.00 60.00
PT18 Marcus Allen Tri 12.00 30.00
PT19 Marshall Faulk Tri 8.00 20.00
PT20 Michael Vick Dual 12.00 30.00
PT21 Mike Singletary Dual 10.00 25.00
PT22 Peyton Manning Dual 20.00 50.00
PT23 Priest Holmes Tri 6.00 15.00
PT24 Randy Moss Dual 6.00 15.00
PT25 Ricky Williams Tri 8.00 20.00
PT26 Roger Staubach Dual 12.00 30.00
PT27 Terry Bradshaw Dual 12.00 30.00
PT28 Tom Brady Dual 30.00 80.00
PT29 Troy Aikman Dual 12.00 30.00
PT30 Walter Payton Dual 30.00 80.00

2004 Leaf Limited Team Threads Dual

ATED PRINT RUN 50 SER.#'d SETS
*PRIME/10: .8X TO 2X BASIC DUAL/50
PRIME PRINT RUN 10 SETS
TT1 A.Boldin/L.Fitzgerald 10.00 25.00
TT2 M.Vick/P.Price 6.00 15.00
TT3 J.Lewis/R.Lewis 8.00 20.00
TT4 D.Bledsoe/J.Kelly 10.00 25.00
TT5 B.Urlacher/W.Payton 30.00 80.00
TT6 C.Palmer/Ch.Johnson 6.00 15.00
TT7 E.Smith/T.Aikman 12.00 30.00
TT8 J.Elway/T.Davis 12.00 30.00
TT9 B.Sanders/J.Harrington 12.00 30.00
TT10 B.Favre/St.Sharpe 15.00 40.00
TT11 A.Johnson/D.Carr 6.00 15.00
TT12 E.James/P.Manning 20.00 50.00
TT13 B.Leftwich/F.Taylor 5.00 12.00
TT14 P.Holmes/J.Montana 25.00 60.00
TT15 D.Marino/Ri.Williams 15.00 40.00
TT16 Culpepper/R.Moss 6.00 15.00
TT17 T.Brady/D.Bledsoe 30.00 80.00
TT18 L.Taylor/J.Shockey 10.00 25.00
TT19 Pennington/J.Namath 12.00 30.00
TT20 J.Rice/B.Jackson 15.00 40.00
TT21 McNabb/Cunningham 6.00 15.00
TT22 J.Rice/J.Montana 30.00 80.00
TT23 M.Hasselbeck/S.Largent 8.00 20.00
TT24 S.McNair/E.Campbell 8.00 20.00
TT25 C.Portis/L.Coles 5.00 12.00

2004 Leaf Limited Team Threads Quad

UNPRICED QUAD PRINT RUN 10
UNPRICED AUTOS PRINT RUN 1

2004 Leaf Limited Team Threads Triple

STATED PRINT RUN 25 SER.#'d SETS
UNPRICED PRIME PRINT RUN 5
TT1 Vick/P.Price/W.Dunn 12.00 30.00
TT2 Bledsoe/Kelly/B.Smith 15.00 40.00
TT3 Urlacher/Butkus/Payton 50.00 120.00
TT4 E.Smith/Irvin/Aikman 40.00 100.00
TT5 Plummer/Elway/T.Davis 30.00 80.00
TT6 B.Sand/Harring/Doak 40.00 100.00
TT7 A.Green/Favre/St.Sharpe 50.00 120.00
TT8 James/Harrison/P.Mann 25.00 60.00
TT9 Montana/Holmes/M.Allen 40.00 100.00
TT10 Griese/Marino/Ri.Williams 40.00 100.00
TT11 Culpepper/Tarken/Moss 15.00 40.00
TT12 Shockey/LT/Bavaro 15.00 40.00
TT13 Namath/Pennin/Martin 25.00 60.00
TT14 B.Jackson/M.Allen/Rice 30.00 80.00
TT15 Portis/Coles/Riggins 12.00 30.00

2004 Leaf Limited Team Trademarks Autographs

TO PRINT RUN 50 SER.#'d SETS
*LIMITED/25: .5X TO 1.2X BASIC AU
LIMITED PRINT RUN 25 SER.#'d SETS
TT1 Ahman Green 12.00 30.00
TT2 Anquan Boldin 10.00 25.00
TT3 Bo Jackson 30.00 80.00
TT4 Bob Griese 15.00 40.00
TT5 Brian Urlacher 25.00 60.00
TT6 Chad Johnson 10.00 25.00
TT7 Chad Pennington 10.00 25.00
TT8 Clinton Portis 10.00 25.00
TT9 Dan Marino 75.00 150.00
TT10 Deuce McAllister 12.00 30.00
TT11 Domanick Davis 10.00 25.00
TT12 Don Shula 20.00 50.00
TT13 Drew Bledsoe 12.00 30.00
TT14 Fran Tarkenton 20.00 50.00
TT15 Franco Harris 25.00 60.00
TT16 Fred Biletnikoff 15.00 40.00
TT17 Gale Sayers 25.00 60.00
TT18 Herman Edwards 12.00 30.00
TT19 Jake Delhomme 10.00 25.00
TT20 Jim Brown 60.00 120.00
TT21 Jimmy Johnson 20.00 50.00
TT22 Joe Montana 49ers 60.00 120.00
TT23 Joe Namath 50.00 100.00
TT24 Joey Harrington 10.00 25.00
TT25 John Riggins 20.00 50.00
TT26 LaDainian Tomlinson 25.00 60.00
TT27 Lawrence Taylor 25.00 60.00
TT28 Marvin Harrison 12.00 30.00
TT29 Matt Hasselbeck 10.00 25.00
TT30 Michael Irvin 15.00 40.00
TT31 Michael Strahan 12.00 30.00
TT32 Michael Vick 15.00 40.00
TT33 Mike Singletary 15.00 40.00
TT34 Ozzie Newsome 12.00 30.00
TT35 Priest Holmes 12.00 30.00
TT36 Steve Smith 15.00 40.00
TT37 Rex Grossman 10.00 25.00
TT38 Earl Campbell 25.00 50.00
TT39 Roger Staubach 40.00 100.00
TT40 Roy Williams S 10.00 25.00
TT41 Santana Moss 12.00 30.00
TT42 Shaun Alexander 10.00 25.00
TT43 Stephen Davis 10.00 25.00
TT44 Steve Largent 15.00 40.00
TT45 Thurman Thomas 12.00 30.00
TT46 Tom Brady 150.00 250.00
TT47 Tony Dorsett 25.00 50.00
TT48 Torry Holt 12.00 30.00
TT49 Trent Green 10.00 25.00
TT50 Troy Aikman 40.00 100.00

2004 Leaf Limited Threads

STATED PRINT RUN 75-100
LT1 Aaron Brooks/75 3.00 8.00
LT2 Ahman Green Sea./75 4.00 10.00
LT3 Ahman Green GB/75 4.00 10.00
LT4 Andre Johnson Mia./75 4.00 10.00
LT5 Andre Johnson/75 4.00 10.00
LT6 Anquan Boldin FSU/75 3.00 8.00
LT7 Anquan Boldin/75 3.00 8.00
LT8 Barry Sanders OSU/100 10.00 25.00
LT9 Barry Sanders/100 10.00 25.00
LT10 Bart Starr/100 15.00 40.00
LT11 Bo Jackson/100 8.00 20.00
LT12 Bob Griese/75 6.00 15.00
LT13 Brett Favre/100 10.00 25.00
LT14 Brian Urlacher/75 8.00 20.00
LT15 Byron Leftwich/75 3.00 8.00
LT16 Carson Palmer USC/75 4.00 10.00
LT17 Carson Palmer/75 4.00 10.00
LT18 Chad Pennington/75 3.00 8.00
LT19 Clinton Portis Mia./75 3.00 8.00
LT20 Clinton Portis/75 3.00 8.00
LT21 David Carr/75 4.00 10.00
LT22 Dan Marino/100 12.00 30.00
LT23 Dan Marino PB/100 12.00 30.00
LT24 Daunte Culpepper/75 4.00 10.00
LT25 Daunte Culpepper PB/75 4.00 10.00
LT26 Deion Sanders 'Boys/75 8.00 20.00
LT27 Deion Sanders 'Skins/75 5.00 12.00
LT28 Deuce McAllister AU/100 10.00 25.00
LT29 Dick Butkus/75 8.00 20.00
LT30 Domanick Davis AU/100 8.00 20.00
LT31 Don Maynard/75 5.00 12.00
LT32 Donovan McNabb/75 8.00 20.00
LT33 Drew Bledsoe WSU/75 6.00 15.00
LT34 Drew Bledsoe/75 4.00 10.00
LT35 Earl Campbell/75 6.00 15.00
LT36 Edgerrin James Mia./75 4.00 10.00
LT37 Edgerrin James/75 4.00 10.00
LT38 Emmitt Smith/100 10.00 25.00
LT39 Fran Tarkenton Vikes/75 6.00 15.00
LT40 Fran Tarkenton NYG/75 6.00 15.00
LT41 George Blanda/75 6.00 15.00
LT42 Jake Delhomme AU/100 8.00 20.00
LT43 Jamal Lewis/75 4.00 10.00
LT44 Jeremy Shockey Mia./75 3.00 8.00
LT45 Jeremy Shockey/75 3.00 8.00
LT46 Jerry Rice/100 10.00 25.00
LT47 Jevon Kearse Flor./75 3.00 8.00
LT48 Jim Kelly/75 8.00 20.00
LT49 Joe Greene/75 6.00 15.00
LT50 Joe Greene SB/75 6.00 15.00
LT51 Joe Montana 49ers/100 12.00 30.00
LT52 Joe Montana Chiefs/100 12.00 30.00
LT53 Joe Namath/100 10.00 25.00
LT54 Joey Harrington/75 3.00 8.00
LT55 John Elway Stan./100 10.00 25.00
LT56 John Elway/100 10.00 25.00
LT57 John Riggins NYJ/75 5.00 12.00
LT58 John Riggins 'Skins/75 5.00 12.00
LT59 Josh McCown/75 4.00 10.00
LT60 Kellen Winslow Jr. Mia./75 3.00 8.00
LT61 Kyle Boller Cal./75 3.00 8.00
LT62 Michael Vick VT/100 8.00 20.00
LT63 LaDainian Tomlinson/75 5.00 12.00
LT64 Larry Fitzgerald/75 12.00 30.00
LT65 Lawrence Taylor/75 6.00 15.00
LT66 Marc Bulger/75 3.00 8.00
LT67 Marcus Allen Raid./75 6.00 15.00
LT68 Marcus Allen Chiefs/75 6.00 15.00
LT69 Marshall Faulk SDSU/75 4.00 10.00
LT70 Marshall Faulk Rams/75 4.00 10.00
LT71 Matt Hasselbeck AU/100 8.00 20.00
LT72 Michael Clayton LSU/75 4.00 10.00
LT73 Michael Irvin/75 6.00 15.00
LT74 Michael Irvin PB/75 6.00 15.00
LT75 Michael Vick/100 8.00 20.00
LT76 Mike Singletary Bay./75 6.00 15.00
LT77 Ozzie Newsome/75 5.00 12.00
LT78 Peyton Manning/75 12.00 30.00
LT79 Peyton Manning PB/75 12.00 30.00
LT80 Priest Holmes Chiefs/75 3.00 8.00
LT81 Priest Holmes Rav./75 3.00 8.00
LT82 Randy Moss/75 4.00 10.00
LT83 Reggie White/75 6.00 15.00
LT84 Reggie Williams Wash./75 3.00 8.00
LT85 Rex Grossman/75 3.00 8.00
LT86 Ricky Williams/75 4.00 10.00
LT87 Roger Staubach/75 8.00 20.00
LT88 Shaun Alexander/75 3.00 8.00
LT89 Steve Largent/75 6.00 15.00
LT90 Steve McNair/75 4.00 10.00
LT91 Sonny Jurgensen/75 5.00 12.00
LT92 Steve Smith AU/100 12.00 30.00
LT93 Terrell Davis/75 5.00 12.00
LT94 Terry Bradshaw/100 8.00 20.00
LT95 Tom Brady/100 20.00 50.00
LT96 Tom Brady PB/100 20.00 50.00
LT97 Tony Dorsett/75 6.00 15.00
LT98 Trent Green/75 3.00 8.00
LT99 Troy Aikman/75 8.00 20.00
LT100 Walter Payton/100 25.00 60.00

2004 Leaf Limited Threads At the Half

*UNSIGNED: .5X TO 1.2X BASIC THREADS
LT3 Ahman Green GB AU/50 12.00 30.00
LT6 Anquan Boldin FSU AU/50 10.00 25.00
LT7 Anquan Boldin AU/50 10.00 25.00
LT28 Deuce McAllister AU/50 12.00 30.00
LT30 Domanick Davis AU/50 10.00 25.00
LT35 Earl Campbell AU/50 20.00 50.00
LT42 Jake Delhomme AU/50 10.00 25.00
LT49 Joe Greene AU/50 20.00 50.00
LT53 Joe Namath AU/50 30.00 80.00
LT63 LaDainian Tomlinson AU/50 30.00 80.00
LT71 Matt Hasselbeck AU/50 10.00 25.00
LT83 Re.White AU/50 ERR 75.00 150.00
LT85 Rex Grossman AU/50 10.00 25.00
LT91 Sonny Jurgensen AU/50 15.00 40.00
LT92 Steve Smith AU/50 15.00 40.00
LT98 Trent Green AU/50 10.00 25.00

2004 Leaf Limited Threads Jersey Numbers

NSIGNED/63-92: .5X TO 1.2X THREADS
*UNSIGNED/42-56: .6X TO 1.5X THREADS
*UNSIGNED/30-37: .8X TO 2X BASIC THREADS
*UNSIGNED/21-28: 1X TO 2.5X BASIC THREADS
*UNSIGNED/10-19: 1.2X TO 3X BASIC THREADS
STATED PRINT RUN 1-92
AUTOs #'d UNDER 20 NOT PRICED
LT2 Ahman Green Sea. AU/30 15.00 40.00
LT9 Barry Sanders AU/20 100.00 175.00
LT14 Brian Urlacher AU/54 25.00 60.00
LT19 C.Portis Mia. AU/28 25.00 60.00
LT20 Clinton Portis AU/26 25.00 60.00
LT26 Deion Sanders 'Boys AU/21 50.00 100.00
LT28 Deuce McAllister AU/26 25.00 60.00
LT30 Domanick Davis AU/37 15.00 40.00
LT35 Earl Campbell AU/34 25.00 60.00
LT57 John Riggins NYJ AU/44 40.00 80.00
LT58 J.Riggins 'Skins AU/44 30.00 80.00
LT63 LaDainian Tomlinson AU/21 40.00 80.00
LT80 P.Holmes Chiefs AU/31 25.00 60.00
LT92 Steve Smith AU/89 15.00 40.00
LT93 Terrell Davis AU/30 15.00 40.00
LT97 Tony Dorsett AU/33 25.00 60.00

2004 Leaf Limited Threads Positions

*UNSIGNED: .5X TO 1.2X BASIC THREADS
LT7 Anquan Boldin AU/75 8.00 20.00
LT28 Deuce McAllister AU/75 10.00 25.00
LT30 Domanick Davis AU/75 8.00 20.00
LT42 Jake Delhomme AU/75 8.00 20.00
LT71 Matt Hasselbeck AU/75 8.00 20.00
LT92 Steve Smith AU/75 12.00 30.00

2004 Leaf Limited Threads Prime

*UNSIGNED: .8X TO 2X BASIC THREADS
PRIME PRINT RUN 25 SER.#'d SETS
LT2 Ahman Green Sea. AU 15.00 40.00
LT3 Ahman Green GB AU 15.00 40.00
LT6 Anquan Boldin FSU AU 12.00 30.00
LT7 Anquan Boldin AU 12.00 30.00
LT8 Barry Sanders OSU AU 100.00 200.00
LT14 Brian Urlacher AU 30.00 80.00
LT15 Byron Leftwich AU 12.00 30.00
LT19 Clinton Portis Mia. AU 12.00 30.00
LT20 Clinton Portis AU 12.00 30.00
LT21 David Carr AU 12.00 30.00
LT28 Deuce McAllister AU 15.00 40.00
LT30 Domanick Davis AU 12.00 30.00
LT35 Earl Campbell AU 40.00 80.00
LT39 Fran Tarkenton Vikes AU 25.00 60.00
LT40 Fran Tarkenton NYG AU 25.00 60.00
LT41 George Blanda AU 40.00 80.00
LT42 Jake Delhomme AU 12.00 30.00
LT46 Jerry Rice AU 150.00 250.00
LT53 Joe Namath AU 60.00 120.00
LT54 Joey Harrington AU 12.00 30.00
LT57 John Riggins NYJ AU 20.00 50.00
LT58 John Riggins 'Skins AU 40.00 80.00
LT63 LaDainian Tomlinson AU 40.00 100.00
LT65 Lawrence Taylor AU 40.00 80.00
LT67 Marcus Allen Raid. AU 40.00 100.00
LT68 Marcus Allen Chiefs AU 40.00 80.00
LT71 Matt Hasselbeck AU 12.00 30.00
LT75 Michael Vick AU 50.00 100.00
LT76 Mike Singletary Bay. AU 25.00 60.00
LT78 Peyton Manning AU 100.00 200.00
LT79 Peyton Manning PB AU 100.00 200.00
LT83A Re.White AU ERR 30.00 80.00
LT83B Reggie White AU COR 200.00 350.00
LT85 Rex Grossman AU 12.00 30.00
LT87 Roger Staubach AU 60.00 120.00
LT88 Shaun Alexander AU 12.00 30.00
LT89 Steve Largent AU 40.00 80.00
LT92 Steve Smith AU 20.00 50.00
LT93 Terrell Davis AU 20.00 50.00
LT94 Terry Bradshaw AU 75.00 150.00
LT97 Tony Dorsett AU 25.00 60.00

2005 Leaf Limited

This 229-card set was released in November, 2005. The set was issued in the hobby in four-card hobby packs with an $70 SRP. Cards numbered 1-100 feature veterans in team alphabetical order while cards numbered 101-150 feature veterans in first name alphabetical order and the set concludes with rookies from 151-229. Within the rookie subset, the final 29 cards (201-229) feature both autographs and player-worn jersey pieces. All cards 1-150 were issued to a stated print run of 599 serial numbered sets while cards numbered 151-200 were issued to a stated print run of 250 copies and cards numbered 201-229 were issued to a stated print run of 100 copies. A few players did not return their signatures in time for pack out and those cards could be redeemed until June 1, 2007.
1-150 PRINT RUN 599 SER.#'d SETS
151-200 ROOKIE PRINT RUN 250
201-229 JSY AU PRINT RUN 100 SETS
UNPRICED PLATINUM SER.#'d TO 1
1 Anquan Boldin 1.00 2.50
2 Kurt Warner 1.25 3.00
3 Larry Fitzgerald 1.50 4.00
4 Alge Crumpler 1.25 3.00
5 Michael Vick 1.25 3.00
6 Warrick Dunn 1.00 2.50
7 Jamal Lewis 1.25 3.00
8 Kyle Boller 1.00 2.50
9 Ray Lewis 1.50 4.00
10 Derrick Mason 1.00 2.50
11 J.P. Losman 1.00 2.50
12 Lee Evans 1.25 3.00
13 Willis McGahee 1.00 2.50
14 DeShaun Foster 1.25 3.00
15 Jake Delhomme 1.00 2.50
16 Steve Smith 1.50 4.00
17 Brian Urlacher 1.50 4.00
18 Rex Grossman 1.00 2.50
19 Muhsin Muhammad 1.00 2.50
20 Carson Palmer 1.25 3.00
21 Chad Johnson 1.00 2.50
22 Rudi Johnson 1.00 2.50
23 Antonio Bryant 1.00 2.50
24 Lee Suggs 1.00 2.50
25 Trent Dilfer 1.00 2.50
26 Drew Bledsoe 1.25 3.00
27 Julius Jones 1.00 2.50
28 Keyshawn Johnson 1.25 3.00
29 Roy Williams S 1.00 2.50
30 Ashley Lelie 1.00 2.50
31 Jake Plummer 1.00 2.50
32 Tatum Bell 1.00 2.50
33 Rod Smith 1.25 3.00
34 Joey Harrington 1.00 2.50
35 Kevin Jones 1.00 2.50
36 Roy Williams WR 1.00 2.50
37 Ahman Green 1.25 3.00
38 Brett Favre 3.00 8.00
39 Javon Walker 1.00 2.50

40 Andre Johnson 1.25 3.00
41 David Carr 1.00 2.50
42 Domanick Davis 1.00 2.50
43 Edgerrin James 1.25 3.00
44 Marvin Harrison 1.25 3.00
45 Peyton Manning 4.00 10.00
46 Reggie Wayne 1.25 3.00
47 Byron Leftwich 1.00 2.50
48 Fred Taylor 1.00 2.50
49 Jimmy Smith 1.25 3.00
50 Priest Holmes 1.00 2.50
51 Tony Gonzalez 1.25 3.00
52 Trent Green 1.00 2.50
53 Chris Chambers 1.00 2.50
54 Ricky Williams 1.25 3.00
55 Daunte Culpepper 1.25 3.00
56 Nate Burleson 1.00 2.50
57 Michael Bennett 1.00 2.50
58 Corey Dillon 1.00 2.50
59 Deion Branch 1.00 2.50
60 Tom Brady 6.00 15.00
61 Aaron Brooks 1.00 2.50
62 Deuce McAllister 1.25 3.00
63 Joe Horn 1.00 2.50
64 Eli Manning 2.50 6.00
65 Jeremy Shockey 1.00 2.50
66 Plaxico Burress 1.00 2.50
67 Tiki Barber 1.25 3.00
68 Chad Pennington 1.00 2.50
69 Curtis Martin 1.25 3.00
70 Laveranues Coles 1.00 2.50
71 Kerry Collins 1.00 2.50
72 LaMont Jordan 1.25 3.00
73 Randy Moss 1.25 3.00
74 Brian Westbrook 1.00 2.50
75 Donovan McNabb 1.25 3.00
76 Terrell Owens 1.25 3.00
77 Ben Roethlisberger 2.50 6.00
78 Duce Staley 1.00 2.50
79 Hines Ward 1.25 3.00
80 Jerome Bettis 1.50 4.00
81 Antonio Gates 1.50 4.00
82 Drew Brees 1.50 4.00
83 LaDainian Tomlinson 1.50 4.00
84 Brandon Lloyd 1.00 2.50
85 Kevan Barlow 1.00 2.50
86 Darrell Jackson 1.00 2.50
87 Matt Hasselbeck 1.00 2.50
88 Shaun Alexander 1.00 2.50
89 Marc Bulger 1.00 2.50
90 Steven Jackson 1.00 2.50
91 Torry Holt 1.25 3.00
92 Brian Griese 1.00 2.50
93 Michael Clayton 1.00 2.50
94 Chris Brown 1.00 2.50
95 Drew Bennett 1.25 3.00
96 Steve McNair 1.25 3.00
97 Clinton Portis 1.00 2.50
98 LaVar Arrington 1.00 2.50
99 Patrick Ramsey 1.25 3.00
100 Santana Moss 1.25 3.00
101 Barry Sanders 3.00 8.00
102 Bart Starr 3.00 8.00
103 Bo Jackson 2.50 6.00
104 Brian Piccolo 2.50 6.00
105 Bob Griese 2.00 5.00
106 Dan Fouts 1.50 4.00
107 Dan Marino 4.00 10.00
108 Deacon Jones 1.50 4.00
109 Doak Walker 2.00 5.00
110 Don Maynard 1.50 4.00
111 Don Meredith 2.00 5.00
112 Don Shula 2.00 5.00
113 Earl Campbell 2.00 5.00
114 Eric Dickerson 1.50 4.00
115 Fran Tarkenton 2.00 5.00
116 Franco Harris 2.00 5.00
117 Gale Sayers 2.00 5.00
118 Jack Lambert 2.00 5.00
119 James Lofton 1.25 3.00
120 Jim Brown 2.50 6.00
121 Jim Kelly 2.00 5.00
122 Jim Thorpe 2.50 6.00
123 Joe Greene 2.00 5.00
124 Joe Montana 6.00 15.00
125 Joe Namath 3.00 8.00
126 John Elway 3.00 8.00
127 John Riggins 1.50 4.00
128 Johnny Unitas 3.00 8.00
129 Lawrence Taylor 2.00 5.00
130 Leroy Kelly 1.50 4.00
131 Marcus Allen 2.00 5.00
132 Michael Irvin 2.00 5.00
133 Mike Ditka 2.00 5.00
134 Mike Singletary 2.00 5.00
135 Ozzie Newsome 1.50 4.00
136 Paul Hornung 2.00 5.00
137 Paul Warfield 1.50 4.00
138 Randall Cunningham 1.50 4.00
139 Red Grange 2.50 6.00
140 Roger Staubach 2.50 6.00
141 Sammy Baugh 2.00 5.00
142 Sonny Jurgensen 1.50 4.00
143 Steve Largent 2.00 5.00
144 Steve Young 2.50 6.00
145 Terrell Davis 1.50 4.00
146 Terry Bradshaw 2.50 6.00
147 Tony Dorsett 2.00 5.00
148 Troy Aikman 2.50 6.00
149 Walter Payton 5.00 12.00
150 Warren Moon 2.00 5.00
151 Aaron Rodgers RC 40.00 80.00
152 Adrian McPherson RC 2.00 5.00
153 Airese Currie RC 2.00 5.00
154 Alvin Pearman RC 2.00 5.00
155 Anthony Davis RC 2.00 5.00
156 Brandon Jacobs RC 2.50 6.00
157 Brandon Jones RC 2.50 6.00
158 Cedric Benson RC 2.00 5.00
159 Cedric Houston RC 3.00 8.00
160 Chad Owens RC 2.00 5.00
161 Chris Henry RC 2.50 6.00
162 Nate Washington RC 3.00 8.00
163 Craig Bragg RC 2.00 5.00
164 Craphonso Thorpe RC 2.00 5.00
165 Damien Nash RC 2.50 6.00
166 Dan Orlovsky RC 2.00 5.00
167 Dante Ridgeway RC 2.00 5.00
168 Darren Sproles RC 3.00 8.00
169 David Greene RC 2.00 5.00
170 David Pollack RC 2.00 5.00
171 Deandra Cobb RC 2.00 5.00
172 DeMarcus Ware RC 6.00 15.00
173 Derek Anderson RC 2.50 6.00
174 Derrick Johnson RC 2.50 6.00
175 Erasmus James RC 2.00 5.00
176 Fabian Washington RC 2.00 5.00
177 Fred Gibson RC 2.00 5.00
178 Harry Williams RC 2.50 6.00
179 Heath Miller RC 4.00 10.00
180 J.R. Russell RC 2.00 5.00
181 James Kilian RC 2.00 5.00
182 Jerome Mathis RC 3.00 8.00
183 Larry Brackins RC 2.00 5.00
184 LeRon McCoy RC 2.00 5.00
185 Lionel Gates RC 2.00 5.00
186 Marcus Spears RC 2.00 5.00
187 Marion Barber RC 2.00 5.00
188 Marlin Jackson RC 2.00 5.00
189 Matt Cassel RC 2.00 5.00
190 Mike Williams 2.50 6.00
191 Noah Herron RC 2.00 5.00
192 Paris Warren RC 2.50 6.00
193 Rasheed Marshall RC 2.50 6.00
194 Roscoe Crosby RC 2.00 5.00
195 Roydell Williams RC 2.50 6.00
196 Ryan Fitzpatrick RC 3.00 8.00
197 Shawne Merriman RC 3.00 8.00
198 Tab Perry RC 2.00 5.00
199 Thomas Davis RC 2.00 5.00
200 Travis Johnson RC 2.00 5.00
201 Adam Jones JSY AU RC 6.00 15.00
202 Alex Smith QB JSY AU RC 20.00 50.00
203 Andrew Walter JSY AU RC 6.00 15.00
204 Antrel Rolle JSY AU RC 10.00 25.00
205 Braylon Edwards JSY AU RC 6.00 15.00
206 Cadillac Williams JSY AU RC 6.00 15.00
207 Carlos Rogers JSY AU RC 10.00 25.00
208 Charlie Frye JSY AU RC 6.00 15.00
209 Ciatrick Fason JSY AU RC 6.00 15.00
210 Courtney Roby JSY AU RC 6.00 15.00
211 Eric Shelton JSY AU RC 6.00 15.00
212 Frank Gore JSY AU RC 12.00 30.00
213 J.J. Arrington JSY AU RC 8.00 20.00
214 Kyle Orton JSY AU RC 6.00 15.00
215 Jason Campbell JSY AU RC 6.00 15.00
216 Mark Bradley JSY AU RC 6.00 15.00
217 Mark Clayton JSY AU RC 6.00 15.00
218 Matt Jones JSY AU RC 6.00 15.00
219 Maurice Clarett JSY AU 6.00 15.00
220 Reggie Brown JSY AU RC 6.00 15.00
221 Ronnie Brown JSY AU RC 8.00 20.00
222 Roddy White JSY AU RC 10.00 25.00
223 Ryan Moats JSY AU RC 6.00 15.00
224 Roscoe Parrish JSY AU RC 6.00 15.00
225 Stefan LeFors JSY AU RC 6.00 15.00
226 Terrence Murphy JSY AU RC 6.00 15.00
227 Troy Williamson JSY AU RC 6.00 15.00
228 Vernand Morency JSY AU RC 6.00 15.00
229 Vincent Jackson JSY AU RC 10.00 25.00

2005 Leaf Limited Bronze Spotlight

ETS 1-100: .8X TO 2X BASIC CARDS
*RETIRED 101-150: .6X TO 1.5X BASIC CARD
*ROOKIES 151-200: .4X TO 1X BASIC CARD
1-200 STATED PRINT RUN 100
*ROOKIE AU 201-229: .6X TO 1.5X BASIC AU
201-229 AU STATED PRINT RUN 25
151 Aaron Rodgers 75.00 125.00
202 Alex Smith QB JSY AU 60.00 150.00

2005 Leaf Limited Gold Spotlight

*VETS 1-100: 2X TO 5X BASIC CARDS
*RETIRED 101-150: 1.5X TO 4X BASIC CARD
*ROOKIES 151-200: 1X TO 2.5X BASIC CARD
1-200 STATED PRINT RUN 25
UNPRICED 201-229 AU PRINT RUN 10
142 Sonny Jurgensen AU 15.00 40.00
151 Aaron Rodgers 125.00 250.00

2005 Leaf Limited Silver Spotlight

*VETS 1-100: 1.2X TO 3X BASIC CARDS
*RETIRED 101-150: 1X TO 2.5X BASIC CARD
*ROOKIES 151-200: .6X TO 1.5X BASIC CARD
1-200 STATED PRINT RUN 50
*ROOKIES 201-299: .5X TO 1.2X BASIC AU RC
201-299 AU STATED PRINT RUN 15
142 Sonny Jurgensen AU 12.00 30.00
151 Aaron Rodgers 125.00 200.00
202 Alex Smith QB JSY AU 60.00 150.00

2005 Leaf Limited Bound by Round Jerseys

STATED PRINT RUN 75 SER.#'d SETS
*PRIME/25: .8X TO 2X BASIC DUAL/75
BR1 P.Manning/D.Marino 12.00 30.00
BR2 L.Taylor/J.Shockey 5.00 12.00
BR3 D.Sanders/R.Williams S 4.00 10.00
BR4 S.McNair/B.Leftwich 4.00 10.00
BR5 J.Namath/C.Pennington 8.00 20.00
BR6 L.Tomlinson/S.Alexander 5.00 12.00
BR7 D.Culpepper/D.McNabb 4.00 10.00
BR8 J.Rice/T.Holt 10.00 25.00
BR9 E.James/J.Lewis 4.00 10.00
BR10 G.Sayers/T.Dorsett 5.00 12.00
BR11 E.Campbell/B.Jackson 6.00 15.00
BR12 J.Elway/M.Vick 8.00 20.00
BR13 J.Rice/S.Young 10.00 25.00
BR14 R.Lewis/B.Urlacher 5.00 12.00
BR15 J.Namath/J.Riggins 8.00 20.00
BR16 T.Aikman/D.Carr 6.00 15.00
BR17 P.Manning/M.Harrison 12.00 30.00
BR18 M.Allen/B.Jackson 6.00 15.00
BR19 J.Brown/W.Payton 12.00 30.00
BR20 O.Newsome/P.Warfield 4.00 10.00
BR21 J.Lofton/J.Walker 3.00 8.00
BR22 J.Kelly/J.Losman 5.00 12.00
BR23 Bo.Griese/D.Marino 10.00 25.00
BR24 S.Young/D.McNabb 6.00 15.00
BR25 B.Sanders/W.Payton 25.00 60.00
BR26 M.Irvin/T.Aikman 6.00 15.00
BR27 D.Marino/J.Elway 10.00 25.00
BR28 R.Moss/R.Williams WR 4.00 10.00
BR29 M.Irvin/Mi.Clayton 5.00 12.00
BR30 J.Rice/L.Fitzgerald 10.00 25.00
BR31 E.Manning/P.Manning 12.00 30.00
BR32 Roethlis/T.Bradshaw 20.00 50.00
BR33 E.Dickerson/S.Jackson 4.00 10.00
BR34 B.Sanders/K.Jones 8.00 20.00
BR35 S.Sharpe/J.Walker 4.00 10.00
BR36 B.Jackson/W.McGahee 6.00 15.00
BR37 S.Young/M.Vick 6.00 15.00
BR38 E.Manning/Roethlisberger 8.00 20.00
BR39 M.Singletary/J.Lambert 5.00 12.00
BR40 C.Portis/R.Cunningham 4.00 10.00
BR41 A.Randle El/C.Johnson 3.00 8.00
BR42 A.Boldin/J.Plummer 3.00 8.00
BR43 B.Favre/J.Jones 10.00 25.00
BR44 J.Montana/F.Tarkenton 15.00 40.00
BR45 T.Owens/H.Ward 4.00 10.00
BR46 R.Nitschke/A.Green 4.00 10.00
BR47 D.Davis/R.Johnson 3.00 8.00
BR48 S.Largent/A.Brooks 5.00 12.00
BR49 T.Brady/T.Davis 20.00 50.00
BR50 Hasselbeck/M.Bulger 3.00 8.00

2005 Leaf Limited Common Threads

STATED PRINT RUN 25 SER.#'d SETS
UNPRICED PRIME PRINT RUN 10 SETS
CT1 S.Young/M.Vick 10.00 25.00
CT2 D.Marino/P.Manning 20.00 50.00
CT3 Bradshaw/Roethlisberger 12.00 30.00
CT4 J.Montana/T.Brady 30.00 80.00
CT5 J.Namath/C.Pennington 12.00 30.00
CT6 B.Starr/B.Favre 15.00 40.00
CT7 D.Culpepper/D.McNabb 6.00 15.00
CT8 S.McNair/W.Moon 8.00 20.00
CT9 J.Elway/J.Plummer 12.00 30.00
CT10 R.Staubach/T.Aikman 10.00 25.00
CT11 J.Kelly/J.Losman 8.00 20.00
CT12 J.Montana/T.Green 25.00 60.00
CT13 R.Cunningham/A.Brooks 6.00 15.00
CT14 M.Bulger/M.Hasselbeck 5.00 12.00
CT15 D.Carr/B.Leftwich 5.00 12.00
CT16 E.Campbell/D.Davis 8.00 20.00
CT17 T.Dorsett/J.Jones 8.00 20.00
CT18 M.Allen/P.Holmes 8.00 20.00
CT19 J.Brown/L.Kelly 10.00 25.00
CT20 B.Sanders/K.Jones 12.00 30.00
CT21 J.Riggins/C.Portis 6.00 15.00
CT22 W.Payton/G.Sayers 20.00 50.00
CT23 T.Davis/J.Lewis 6.00 15.00
CT24 E.Dickerson/S.Jackson 6.00 15.00
CT25 B.Jackson/W.McGahee 10.00 25.00
CT26 L.Tomlinson/E.James 8.00 20.00
CT27 S.Alexander/A.Green 6.00 15.00
CT28 D.McAllister/R.Johnson 6.00 15.00
CT29 M.Irvin/K.Johnson 8.00 20.00
CT30 T.Owens/A.Johnson 6.00 15.00
CT31 M.Harrison/R.Wayne 6.00 15.00
CT32 R.Moss/R.Williams WR 6.00 15.00
CT33 T.Holt/C.Johnson 6.00 15.00
CT34 S.Sharpe/J.Walker 6.00 15.00
CT35 J.Rice/L.Fitzgerald 15.00 40.00
CT36 S.Largent/P.Warfield 8.00 20.00
CT37 J.Lambert/B.Urlacher 8.00 20.00
CT38 M.Singletary/R.Lewis 8.00 20.00
CT39 L.Taylor/L.Arrington 8.00 20.00
CT40 O.Newsome/J.Shockey 6.00 15.00
CT41 B.Starr/J.Unitas 40.00 80.00
CT42 P.Manning/E.Manning 20.00 50.00
CT43 J.Montana/S.Young 25.00 60.00
CT44 T.Bradshaw/T.Brady 10.00 25.00
CT45 J.Montana/T.Aikman 25.00 60.00
CT46 J.Elway/B.Favre 15.00 40.00
CT47 D.Marino/J.Kelly 15.00 40.00
CT48 M.Vick/D.McNabb 6.00 15.00
CT49 J.Brown/B.Sanders 12.00 30.00
CT50 W.Payton/J.Rice 20.00 50.00

2005 Leaf Limited Contenders Preview Autographs

102 Adam Jones/25 10.00 25.00
103 Adrian McPherson/25 10.00 25.00
104 Alvin Pearman/25 10.00 25.00
109 Antrel Rolle/25 15.00 40.00
110 Brandon Jacobs/25 12.00 30.00
111 Brandon Jones/25 12.00 30.00
119 Charlie Frye/25 10.00 25.00
121 Ciatrick Fason/25 10.00 25.00
122 Courtney Roby/25 10.00 25.00
127 Dan Orlovsky/25 10.00 25.00
129 Darren Sproles/25 15.00 40.00
130 David Greene/25 10.00 25.00
131 David Pollack/25 10.00 25.00
133 DeMarcus Ware/25 30.00 80.00
135 Derrick Johnson/25 12.00 30.00
137 Eric Shelton/25 10.00 25.00
141 Heath Miller/25 20.00 50.00
146 Jerome Mathis/25 15.00 40.00
152 Marion Barber/25 25.00 60.00
153 Mark Bradley/25 10.00 25.00
162 Reggie Brown/25 10.00 25.00
163 Roddy White/25 15.00 40.00
165 Roscoe Parrish/25 10.00 25.00
168 Ryan Moats/25 12.00 30.00
170 Shawne Merriman/25 15.00 40.00
171 Stefan LeFors/25 10.00 25.00
176 Terrence Murphy/25 10.00 25.00
179 Troy Williamson/25 10.00 25.00
180 Vernand Morency/25 10.00 25.00
181 Vincent Jackson/25 15.00 40.00

2005 Leaf Limited Cuts Autographs

LC1 Brett Favre/25 125.00 250.00
LC2 Jim Brown/50 40.00 100.00
LC3 Joe Montana/50 75.00 150.00
LC5 Terry Bradshaw/25 75.00 150.00
LC6 Willis McGahee/100 15.00 40.00

2005 Leaf Limited Hardwear

STATED PRINT RUN 100 SER.#'d SETS
UNPRICED LIMITED SHIELD #'d TO 1
H1 Boomer Esiason 8.00 20.00
H2 Curtis Martin 3.00 8.00
H3 Daunte Culpepper 3.00 8.00
H4 Donovan McNabb 3.00 8.00
H5 Drew Brees 4.00 10.00
H6 Edgerrin James 3.00 8.00
H7 Eric Dickerson 3.00 8.00
H8 Hines Ward 3.00 8.00
H9 Jake Delhomme 2.50 6.00
H10 Jamal Lewis 3.00 8.00
H11 Jerome Bettis 10.00 25.00
H12 Jerry Rice 8.00 20.00
H13 Marcus Allen 4.00 10.00
H14 Marvin Harrison 3.00 8.00
H15 Michael Vick 8.00 20.00
H16 Priest Holmes 2.50 6.00
H17 Randall Cunningham AU 20.00 40.00
H18 Randy Moss 3.00 8.00
H19 Reggie White 15.00 40.00
H20 Steve Young 5.00 12.00
H21 Tom Brady 30.00 60.00
H22 Eli Manning 6.00 15.00
H23 Clinton Portis 2.50 6.00
H24 Brett Favre 8.00 20.00
H25 Thurman Thomas 3.00 8.00

2005 Leaf Limited Hardwear Limited

*UNSIGNED/25: .8X TO 2X BASIC INSERTS
LIMITED PRINT RUN 25 SER.#'d SETS
H1 Boomer Esiason AU 30.00 80.00
H7 Eric Dickerson AU 40.00 100.00
H9 Jake Delhomme AU 25.00 60.00
H12 Jerry Rice AU 100.00 175.00
H17 Randall Cunningham AU 30.00 80.00
H20 Steve Young AU 75.00 135.00
H23 Clinton Portis AU 30.00 80.00

2005 Leaf Limited Legends Jerseys

STATED PRINT RUN 50 SER.#'d SETS
UNPRICED PRIME SER.#'d TO 5
*SEASON/14-20: .6X TO 1.5X BASIC JSY
SEASON PRINT RUN 6-20
LL1 Bart Starr 10.00 25.00
LL2 Brett Favre 12.00 30.00
LL3 Dan Marino 12.00 30.00
LL4 Don Meredith AU 50.00 100.00
LL5 Fran Tarkenton AU 25.00 50.00
LL6 Franco Harris AU 30.00 60.00
LL7 Gale Sayers AU 30.00 60.00
LL8 Jerry Rice 12.00 30.00
LL9 Jack Lambert 6.00 15.00
LL10 Jim Brown 8.00 20.00
LL11 Jim Thorpe 60.00 125.00
LL12 Joe Montana 20.00 50.00
LL13 Joe Namath 10.00 25.00
LL14 John Elway 10.00 25.00
LL15 Johnny Unitas 10.00 25.00
LL16 Terry Bradshaw 8.00 20.00
LL17 Doak Walker 6.00 15.00
LL18 Don Shula AU 20.00 50.00
LL19 John Riggins 5.00 12.00
LL20 Steve Largent 6.00 15.00

2005 Leaf Limited Lettermen

UNPRICED LETTERMEN PRINT RUN 4-14

2005 Leaf Limited Material Monikers

MATERIAL MONIKERS SER.#'d FROM 10-50
UNPRICED LIMITED SER.#'d TO 1
CARDS SER.#'d UNDER 15 NOT PRICED
MM1 Barry Sanders/35 100.00 200.00
MM2 Bart Starr/25 100.00 175.00
MM3 Ben Roethlisberger/35 50.00 120.00
MM4 Bo Jackson/50 40.00 80.00
MM5 Brett Favre/25 125.00 250.00
MM6 Dan Marino/25 100.00 200.00
MM7 Don Meredith/50 50.00 100.00
MM8 Earl Campbell/35 25.00 60.00
MM9 Eli Manning/25 40.00 100.00
MM10 Jack Lambert/50 60.00 100.00
MM11 Jerry Rice/35 100.00 200.00
MM12 Jim Brown/50 40.00 100.00
MM13 Jim Kelly/25 40.00 100.00
MM14 Joe Montana/15 100.00 200.00
MM15 Joe Namath/50 50.00 120.00
MM16 John Elway/50 75.00 150.00
MM17 Julius Jones/25 40.00 80.00
MM18 Marcus Allen/25 40.00 80.00
MM19 Michael Vick/25 40.00 80.00
MM20 Priest Holmes/25 25.00 60.00
MM21 Roger Staubach/15 60.00 120.00
MM22 Steve Young/25 60.00 120.00
MM23 Terry Bradshaw/35 60.00 120.00
MM24 Tom Brady/15 150.00 300.00
MM25 Tony Dorsett/25 40.00 80.00
MM26 J.Brown/B.Sanders/15 150.00 250.00
MM27 B.Starr/B.Favre/25 175.00 300.00
MM28 M.Allen/B.Jackson/25 100.00 175.00
MM29 Bo.Griese/D.Marino/25 125.00 250.00
MM30 B.Esiason/C.Palmer/17 30.00 80.00
MM31 Marino/P.Mann/25 250.00 400.00
MM33 Dickerson/Jackson/50 30.00 80.00
MM34 J.Lambert/J.Greene/50 90.00 175.00
MM35 J.Kelly/J.Losman/50 30.00 80.00
MM37 Namath/Penning/25 60.00 150.00
MM38 J.Riggins/C.Portis/50 25.00 60.00
MM39 J.Elway/T.Davis/25 100.00 200.00
MM40 Staubach/Ditka/25 60.00 120.00
MM41 Singletary/Urlacher/50 40.00 80.00
MM42 Montana/S.Young/25 150.00 300.00
MM43 Bradshaw/Roethlis/15 200.00 350.00
MM44 Dorsett/J.Jones/25 50.00 100.00
MM45 T.Aikman/M.Irvin/50 60.00 120.00
MM46 Deion/Ro.Will.S/25 60.00 100.00
MM47 L.Taylor/Eli/40 60.00 120.00
MM48 J.Rice/M.Harrison/15 150.00 250.00
MM49 T.Thomas/McGahee/50 25.00 60.00
MM50 T.Davis/T.Bell/20 40.00 80.00

2005 Leaf Limited Player Threads

STATED PRINT RUN 50 SER.#'d SETS
*PRIME/25: .6X TO 1.5X BASIC JSY/50
UNPRICED LIMITED PRINT RUN 1
PT1 Ahman Green 5.00 12.00
PT2 Barry Sanders 10.00 25.00
PT3 Brett Favre 12.00 30.00
PT4 Carson Palmer 5.00 12.00
PT5 Clinton Portis 4.00 10.00
PT6 Corey Dillon 4.00 10.00
PT7 Curtis Martin 5.00 12.00
PT8 Dan Marino 12.00 30.00
PT9 Daunte Culpepper 5.00 12.00
PT10 Donovan McNabb 5.00 12.00
PT11 Edgerrin James 5.00 12.00
PT12 Deion Sanders 5.00 12.00
PT13 Jamal Lewis 5.00 12.00
PT14 Joe Montana 20.00 50.00
PT15 Joe Namath 10.00 25.00
PT16 John Elway 10.00 25.00
PT17 Julius Jones 4.00 10.00
PT18 Jerome Bettis 6.00 15.00
PT19 Marcus Allen 6.00 15.00
PT20 Michael Vick 5.00 12.00
PT21 Peyton Manning 15.00 40.00
PT22 Priest Holmes 4.00 10.00
PT23 Terry Bradshaw 8.00 20.00
PT24 Tom Brady 25.00 60.00
PT25 Troy Aikman 8.00 20.00
PT26 Walter Payton 15.00 40.00
PT27 Willis McGahee 4.00 10.00
PT28 Joe Greene 6.00 15.00
PT29 Steven Jackson 4.00 10.00
PT30 Lawrence Taylor 6.00 15.00

2005 Leaf Limited Prime Pairings Autographs

UNPRICED PAIRINGS PRINT RUN 5 SETS

2005 Leaf Limited Team Threads Dual

ATED PRINT RUN 75 SER.#'d SETS
TT1 M.Vick/W.Dunn 5.00 12.00
TT2 J.Kelly/W.McGahee 6.00 15.00
TT3 W.Payton/G.Sayers 15.00 40.00
TT4 B.Esiason/C.Palmer 5.00 12.00
TT5 J.Brown/O.Newsome 8.00 20.00
TT6 T.Aikman/M.Irvin 8.00 20.00
TT7 J.Elway/T.Davis 10.00 25.00
TT8 D.Walker/B.Sanders 10.00 25.00
TT9 B.Starr/B.Favre 12.00 30.00
TT10 E.Campbell/W.Moon 6.00 15.00
TT11 J.Unitas/P.Manning 15.00 40.00
TT12 J.Montana/M.Allen 20.00 50.00
TT13 M.Allen/B.Jackson 8.00 20.00
TT14 E.Dickerson/S.Jackson 5.00 12.00
TT15 Bo.Griese/D.Marino 12.00 30.00
TT16 D.Culpepper/R.Moss 5.00 12.00
TT17 T.Brady/C.Dillon 25.00 60.00
TT18 L.Taylor/E.Manning 10.00 25.00
TT19 J.Namath/C.Pennington 10.00 25.00
TT20 D.McNabb/T.Owens 5.00 12.00
TT21 T.Bradshaw/Roethlis 10.00 25.00
TT22 D.Fouts/L.Tomlinson 6.00 15.00
TT23 J.Montana/J.Rice 20.00 50.00
TT24 S.Largent/M.Hasselbeck 6.00 15.00
TT25 J.Riggins/C.Portis 5.00 12.00

2005 Leaf Limited Team Threads Triple

STATED PRINT RUN 50 SER.#'d SETS
TT1 Lewis/Lewis/Boller 8.00 20.00
TT2 Payton/Sayers/Singletary 20.00 50.00
TT3 Brown/Newsome/Warfield 10.00 25.00
TT4 Aikman/Irvin/Dorsett 10.00 25.00
TT5 Walker/Sanders/Jones 12.00 30.00
TT6 Starr/Favre/Sharpe 15.00 40.00
TT7 Campbell/Moon/McNair 8.00 20.00
TT8 Unitas/P.Mann/James 20.00 50.00
TT9 Montana/Allen/Holmes 25.00 60.00
TT10 Allen/Bo/Rice 15.00 40.00
TT11 Dickerson/Jackson/Bulger 6.00 15.00
TT12 Brady/Dillon/Bledsoe 30.00 80.00
TT13 Bradshaw/Roeth/Lambert 25.00 60.00
TT14 Fouts/Tomlinson/Brees 8.00 20.00
TT15 Montana/Rice/Young 25.00 60.00

2005 Leaf Limited Team Threads Quad

STATED PRINT RUN 25 SER.#'d SETS
TT1 Vick/Dunn/Crump/Duck 8.00 20.00
TT2 Kelly/McG/Losman/Thomas 10.00 25.00
TT3 Pay/Say/Single/Urlacher 30.00 60.00
TT4 Aikman/Irvin/Dorsett/Stau 12.00 30.00
TT5 Walk/Sand/Jones/Will WR 15.00 40.00
TT6 Unitas/P.Mann/Jms/Harrs 25.00 60.00
TT7 Culp/Moss/Fran/Bennett 10.00 25.00
TT8 Taylor/Barber/Eli/Shockey 15.00 40.00
TT9 Namath/Penn/Martin/Coles 15.00 40.00
TT10 Brad/Roeth/Lamb/Franco 15.00 40.00

2005 Leaf Limited Team Trademarks Autographs

1-TT31 PRINT RUN 50 SER.#'d SETS
TT32-TT46 PRINT RUN 25 SER.#'d SETS
*LIMITED/25: .5X TO 1.2X AUTOS/50
LIMITED SER.#'d TO 10 NOT PRICED
TT1 Barry Sanders 75.00 150.00
TT2 Bo Jackson 40.00 80.00
TT3 Bob Griese 15.00 40.00
TT4 Dan Fouts 12.00 30.00
TT5 Don Maynard 12.00 30.00
TT6 Don Meredith 50.00 100.00
TT7 Don Shula 15.00 40.00
TT8 Earl Campbell 15.00 40.00
TT9 Eric Dickerson 15.00 40.00
TT10 L.C. Greenwood 15.00 40.00
TT11 Franco Harris 25.00 60.00
TT12 Gene Upshaw 15.00 40.00
TT13 Jack Lambert 50.00 100.00
TT14 Jim Brown 50.00 100.00
TT15 Jim Kelly 25.00 60.00
TT16 Joe Montana 50.00 120.00
TT17 Joe Namath 50.00 100.00
TT18 John Riggins 12.00 30.00
TT19 Marcus Allen 15.00 40.00
TT20 Michael Irvin 40.00 80.00
TT21 Mike Ditka 30.00 60.00
TT22 Mike Singletary 15.00 40.00
TT23 Paul Warfield 10.00 25.00
TT24 Richard Dent 12.00 30.00
TT25 Roger Staubach 50.00 100.00
TT26 Sonny Jurgensen 15.00 40.00
TT27 James Lofton 10.00 25.00
TT28 Steve Largent 15.00 40.00
TT29 Steve Young 40.00 80.00
TT30 Tony Dorsett 15.00 40.00
TT31 Warren Moon 15.00 40.00
TT32 Aaron Brooks/25 12.00 30.00
TT33 Ahman Green/25 15.00 40.00
TT34 Ben Roethlisberger/25 75.00 150.00
TT35 Brian Urlacher/25 30.00 80.00
TT37 Chris Brown/25 12.00 30.00
TT38 David Carr/25 12.00 30.00
TT39 Deion Sanders/25 30.00 80.00
TT41 Eli Manning/25 75.00 125.00
TT42 Hines Ward/25 30.00 60.00
TT43 Julius Jones/25 12.00 30.00
TT44 Matt Hasselbeck/25 12.00 30.00
TT45 Michael Clayton/25 12.00 30.00
TT46 Michael Vick/25 50.00 80.00
TT48 Roy Williams S/25 12.00 30.00
TT49 Steven Jackson/25 12.00 30.00

2005 Leaf Limited Threads

STATED PRINT RUN 25-100
LT1 Aaron Brooks/25 6.00 15.00
LT2 Ahman Green 4.00 10.00
LT3 Andre Johnson/25 8.00 20.00
LT4 Barry Sanders 12.00 320.00
LT5 Ben Roethlisberger 8.00 20.00
LT6 Bo Jackson 8.00 20.00
LT7 Bob Griese 6.00 15.00
LT8 Boomer Esiason 5.00 12.00
LT9 Brett Favre 10.00 25.00
LT10 Brian Urlacher 5.00 12.00
LT11 Byron Leftwich 3.00 8.00
LT12 Cadillac Williams 3.00 8.00
LT13 Carson Palmer 4.00 10.00
LT14 Cedric Benson 3.00 8.00
LT15 Chad Johnson 3.00 8.00
LT16 Chad Pennington 3.00 8.00
LT17 Clinton Portis 3.00 8.00
LT18 Corey Dillon 3.00 8.00
LT19 Dan Fouts 5.00 12.00
LT20 Dan Marino Pitt 20.00 50.00
LT21 Dan Marino 10.00 25.00
LT22 Dan Marino 10.00 25.00
LT23 Daunte Culpepper 4.00 10.00
LT24 David Carr 3.00 8.00
LT25 Deuce McAllister 4.00 10.00
LT26 Domanick Davis/25 6.00 15.00
LT27 Don Maynard AU 12.50 30.00
LT28 Donovan McNabb 4.00 10.00
LT29 Earl Campbell 6.00 15.00
LT30 Edgerrin James 4.00 10.00
LT31 Eli Manning 8.00 20.00
LT32 Eric Dickerson Rams 5.00 12.00
LT33 Eric Dickerson Colts 5.00 12.00
LT34 Gale Sayers 6.00 15.00
LT35 Hines Ward 4.00 10.00
LT36 J.P. Losman 3.00 8.00
LT37 Jack Lambert 6.00 15.00
LT38 Jake Delhomme 3.00 8.00
LT39 James Lofton 4.00 10.00
LT40 Jerry Rice 49ers 10.00 25.00
LT41 Jerry Rice Raid. 10.00 25.00
LT42 Jim Kelly 6.00 15.00
LT43 Joe Greene 6.00 15.00
LT44 Joe Montana 49ers 15.00 40.00
LT45 Joe Montana Chiefs 15.00 40.00
LT46 Joe Namath 10.00 25.00
LT47 John Elway 8.00 20.00
LT48 John Elway 8.00 20.00
LT49 John Riggins 5.00 12.00
LT50 Julius Jones 3.00 8.00
LT51 Julius Jones ND 5.00 12.00
LT52 Kevin Jones 3.00 8.00
LT53 Keyshawn Johnson 4.00 10.00
LT54 LaDainian Tomlinson 5.00 12.00
LT55 Larry Fitzgerald 5.00 12.00
LT56 Lawrence Taylor 6.00 15.00
LT57 Lawrence Taylor NC 10.00 25.00
LT58 Marcus Allen Raid. 6.00 15.00
LT59 Marcus Allen Chiefs 6.00 15.00
LT60 Marvin Harrison 4.00 10.00
LT61 Matt Hasselbeck 3.00 8.00
LT62 Michael Clayton 3.00 8.00
LT63 Michael Clayton LSU 3.00 8.00
LT64 Michael Irvin 6.00 15.00
LT65 Michael Vick 6.00 15.00
LT66 Michael Vick VT 6.00 15.00
LT67 Mike Singletary 6.00 15.00
LT68 Mike Singletary Bay. 6.00 15.00
LT69 Ozzie Newsome 5.00 12.00
LT70 Leroy Kelly AU 12.50 30.00
LT71 Peyton Manning 12.00 30.00
LT72 Priest Holmes 3.00 8.00
LT73 Randy Moss 4.00 10.00
LT74 Reggie Wayne AU/25 20.00 40.00
LT75 Roger Staubach 8.00 20.00
LT76 Roy Williams S 3.00 8.00
LT77 Roy Williams S Okl 6.00 15.00
LT78 Roy Williams WR 3.00 8.00
LT79 Rudi Johnson 3.00 8.00
LT80 Sonny Jurgensen AU/100 12.50 30.00
LT81 Sterling Sharpe 5.00 12.00
LT82 Steve Largent 6.00 15.00
LT83 Steve Young 8.00 20.00
LT84 Steven Jackson 3.00 8.00
LT85 Steven Jackson Ore.St. 3.00 8.00
LT86 Tatum Bell 3.00 8.00
LT87 Terrell Davis 5.00 12.00
LT88 Terrell Owens 4.00 10.00
LT89 Terry Bradshaw SB 8.00 20.00
LT90 Terry Bradshaw PB 8.00 20.00
LT91 Tiki Barber AU/25 25.00 50.00
LT92 Tom Brady 20.00 50.00
LT93 Tom Brady PB 20.00 50.00
LT94 Tony Dorsett 6.00 15.00
LT95 Tony Dorsett Pitt 6.00 15.00
LT96 Trent Green AU/25 15.00 40.00
LT97 Troy Aikman 8.00 20.00
LT98 Walter Payton 15.00 40.00
LT99 Warren Moon 6.00 15.00
LT100 Willis McGahee 3.00 8.00

2005 Leaf Limited Threads At the Half

NSIGNED/50: .5X TO 1.2X THREADS/75
*UNSIGNED/25: .6X TO 1.5X THREADS/75
STATED PRINT RUN 25-50
LT2 Ahman Green AU/25 20.00 50.00
LT7 Bob Griese AU/50 15.00 40.00
LT8 Boomer Esiason AU/50 15.00 40.00
LT11 Byron Leftwich AU/25 20.00 50.00
LT15 Chad Johnson AU/25 20.00 50.00
LT18 Corey Dillon AU/25 15.00 40.00
LT19 Dan Fouts AU/50 20.00 50.00
LT27 Don Maynard 6.00 15.00
LT53 Keyshawn Johnson AU/25 15.00 40.00
LT61 Matt Hasselbeck AU/25 20.00 50.00
LT69 Ozzie Newsome AU/50 12.00 30.00
LT70 Leroy Kelly AU/50 12.00 30.00
LT74 Reggie Wayne AU/25 20.00 50.00
LT78 Roy Williams WR AU/25 15.00 40.00
LT80 Sonny Jurgensen AU/50 20.00 50.00
LT81 Sterling Sharpe AU/50 15.00 40.00
LT91 Tiki Barber AU/25 20.00 50.00
LT96 Trent Green AU/25 15.00 40.00

2005 Leaf Limited Threads Jersey Numbers

*UNSIGNED/80-88: .4X TO 1X BASE THREADS
*UNSIGNED/32-56: .5X TO 1.2X BASE THREAD
*UNSIGNED/18-29: .6X TO 1.5X
CARDS SER.#'d UNDER 15 NOT PRICED
LT2 Ahman Green AU/30 20.00 50.00
LT6 Bo Jackson AU/34 30.00 80.00
LT10 Brian Urlacher AU/54 60.00 100.00
LT12 Cadillac Williams AU/24 60.00 120.00
LT14 Cedric Benson AU/32 25.00 60.00
LT15 Chad Johnson AU/85 12.00 30.00
LT17 Clinton Portis AU/28 20.00 50.00
LT25 Deuce McAllister AU/26 20.00 50.00
LT29 Earl Campbell AU/34 25.00 60.00
LT34 Gale Sayers AU/40 50.00 100.00
LT35 Hines Ward AU/86 50.00 80.00
LT37 Jack Lambert AU/58 60.00 120.00
LT38 Jake Delhomme AU/17 15.00 40.00
LT39 James Lofton AU/80 12.00 30.00
LT43 Joe Greene AU/75 30.00 80.00
LT44 Joe Montana 49ers AU/16 100.00 200.00
LT45 Joe Montana Chiefs AU/19 100.00 200.00
LT49 John Riggins AU/44 20.00 50.00
LT50 Julius Jones AU/21 20.00 50.00
LT51 Julius Jones ND AU/22 15.00 40.00
LT53 Keyshawn Johnson AU/19 20.00 50.00
LT57 L.Taylor NC AU/98 60.00 120.00
LT58 Marcus Allen Raid.AU/32 40.00 80.00
LT59 M.Allen Chiefs AU/32 25.00 60.00
LT62 Michael Clayton AU/80 12.00 30.00
LT67 Mike Singletary AU/50 20.00 50.00
LT68 M.Singletary Bay.AU/63 20.00 50.00
LT69 Ozzie Newsome AU/82 15.00 40.00
LT70 Leroy Kelly AU/44 15.00 40.00
LT72 Priest Holmes AU/31 30.00 80.00
LT74 Reggie Wayne AU/87 15.00 40.00
LT76 Roy Williams S AU/31 30.00 80.00
LT77 Roy Will.S Okl.AU/38 60.00 100.00
LT79 Rudi Johnson AU/32 20.00 50.00
LT81 Sterling Sharpe AU/84 15.00 40.00
LT84 Steven Jackson AU/39 25.00 60.00
LT85 S.Jackson Ore.St.AU/34 20.00 50.00
LT86 Tatum Bell AU/26 15.00 40.00
LT87 Terrell Davis AU/30 25.00 60.00
LT91 Tiki Barber AU/21 20.00 50.00
LT95 Tony Dorsett Pitt AU/33 30.00 80.00
LT100 Willis McGahee AU/21 15.00 40.00

2005 Leaf Limited Threads Prime

*PRIME/25: .8X TO 2X BASIC THREAD/75
STATED PRINT RUN 10-25
PRIME SER.#'d UNDER 25 NOT PRICED
LT6 Bo Jackson AU/25 60.00 120.00
LT7 Bob Griese AU/25 25.00 60.00
LT19 Dan Fouts AU/25 25.00 60.00
LT27 Don Maynard AU/25 15.00 40.00
LT29 Earl Campbell AU/25 25.00 60.00
LT34 Gale Sayers AU/25 50.00 100.00
LT37 Jack Lambert AU/25 90.00 150.00
LT39 James Lofton AU/25 20.00 50.00
LT42 Jim Kelly AU/25 40.00 100.00
LT46 Joe Namath AU/25 50.00 120.00
LT57 L.Taylor NC AU/25 100.00 175.00
LT69 Ozzie Newsome AU/25 15.00 40.00
LT70 Leroy Kelly AU/25 15.00 40.00
LT80 Sonny Jurgensen AU/25 25.00 60.00
LT81 Sterling Sharpe AU/25 20.00 50.00
LT82 Steve Largent AU/25 20.00 50.00
LT83 Steve Young AU/25 40.00 100.00
LT87 Terrell Davis AU/25 25.00 60.00
LT99 Warren Moon AU/25 20.00 50.00

2006 Leaf Limited

This 305-card set was released in November, 2006. The set was issued into the hobby in four-card packs with an $70 SRP. Cards numbered 1-150, which include a retired greats subset from cards 118-150, were issued to a stated print run of 799 serial numbered sets. Cards numbered 151-305 feature 2006 rookies and they are broken down into the following subsets: Cards numbered 151-250 were issued to a stated print run of 299 serial numbered sets while cards numbered 251-295 were signed by the player and those cards were issued to a stated print run of 100 serial numbered sets and the set concludes with multi-player signed cards, some of which have player-worn jersey swatches as well. Those cards between 296 and 305 were issed to stated print runs between 25 and 100 serial numbered sets.

1-150 PRINT RUN 799 SER.#'d SETS
151-250 RC PRINT RUN 299 SER.#'d SETS
AU RC PRINT RUN 100 SETS
296-305 JSY AU PRINT RUN 25-100
1 Alex Smith QB 1.25 3.00
2 Antonio Bryant 1.00 2.50
3 Frank Gore 1.25 3.00
4 Rex Grossman 1.00 2.50
5 Thomas Jones 1.00 2.50
6 Cedric Benson 1.00 2.50
7 Carson Palmer 1.25 3.00
8 Chad Johnson 1.00 2.50
9 Rudi Johnson 1.00 2.50
10 T.J. Houshmandzadeh 1.00 2.50
11 J.P. Losman 1.25 3.00
12 Lee Evans 1.25 3.00
13 Willis McGahee 1.00 2.50
14 Jake Plummer 1.00 2.50
15 Javon Walker 1.25 3.00
16 Rod Smith 1.25 3.00
17 Tatum Bell 1.00 2.50
18 Braylon Edwards 1.00 2.50
19 Charlie Frye 1.25 3.00
20 Reuben Droughns 1.25 3.00
21 Cadillac Williams 1.25 3.00
22 Chris Simms 1.00 2.50
23 Joey Galloway 1.25 3.00
24 Anquan Boldin 1.00 2.50
25 Edgerrin James 1.25 3.00
26 Kurt Warner 1.25 3.00
27 Larry Fitzgerald 1.25 3.00
28 Antonio Gates 1.50 4.00
29 Keenan McCardell 1.25 3.00
30 LaDainian Tomlinson 1.50 4.00
31 Philip Rivers 1.50 4.00
32 Eddie Kennison 1.00 2.50
33 Larry Johnson 1.00 2.50
34 Priest Holmes 1.00 2.50
35 Trent Green 1.00 2.50
36 Tony Gonzalez 1.25 3.00
37 Dallas Clark 1.00 2.50
38 Marvin Harrison 1.25 3.00
39 Peyton Manning 4.00 10.00
40 Reggie Wayne 1.25 3.00
41 Drew Bledsoe 1.25 3.00
42 Julius Jones 1.00 2.50
43 Roy Williams S 1.00 2.50
44 Terrell Owens 1.25 3.00
45 Terry Glenn 1.25 3.00
46 Chris Chambers 1.00 2.50
47 Daunte Culpepper 1.25 3.00
48 Marty Booker 1.00 2.50
49 Ronnie Brown 1.25 3.00
50 Brian Westbrook 1.00 2.50
51 Donovan McNabb 1.25 3.00
52 Jevon Kearse 1.00 2.50
53 Reggie Brown 1.00 2.50
54 Alge Crumpler 1.25 3.00
55 Michael Vick 1.25 3.00
56 Warrick Dunn 1.00 2.50
57 Eli Manning 1.25 3.00
58 Jeremy Shockey 1.00 2.50
59 Plaxico Burress 1.00 2.50
60 Tiki Barber 1.25 3.00
61 Byron Leftwich 1.00 2.50
62 Fred Taylor 1.00 2.50
63 Jimmy Smith 1.25 3.00
64 Matt Jones 1.00 2.50
65 Josh McCown 1.00 2.50
66 Roy Williams WR 1.00 2.50
67 Kevin Jones 1.00 2.50
68 Aaron Rodgers 4.00 10.00
69 Brett Favre 3.00 8.00
70 Robert Ferguson 1.00 2.50
71 Samkon Gado 1.00 2.50
72 Ahman Green 1.25 3.00
73 DeShaun Foster 1.25 3.00
74 Jake Delhomme 1.00 2.50
75 Keary Colbert 1.00 2.50
76 Steve Smith 1.50 4.00
77 Corey Dillon 1.00 2.50
78 Deion Branch 1.00 2.50
79 Tedy Bruschi 1.25 3.00
80 Tom Brady 5.00 12.00
81 Jerry Porter 1.00 2.50
82 Randy Moss 1.25 3.00
83 LaMont Jordan 1.25 3.00
84 Isaac Bruce 1.50 4.00
85 Marc Bulger 1.00 2.50
86 Steven Jackson 1.00 2.50
87 Torry Holt 1.25 3.00
88 Derrick Mason 1.00 2.50
89 Mark Clayton 1.00 2.50
90 Steve McNair 1.25 3.00
91 Jamal Lewis 1.25 3.00
92 Antwaan Randle El 1.00 2.50
93 Clinton Portis 1.00 2.50
94 Santana Moss 1.25 3.00
95 Chad Pennington 1.00 2.50
96 Laveranues Coles 1.00 2.50
97 Curtis Martin 1.25 3.00
98 Mewelde Moore 1.00 2.50
99 Troy Williamson 1.00 2.50
100 Brad Johnson 1.25 3.00
101 Darrell Jackson 1.25 3.00
102 Matt Hasselbeck 1.00 2.50
103 Nate Burleson 1.00 2.50
104 Shaun Alexander 1.00 2.50
105 Ben Roethlisberger 2.00 5.00
106 Hines Ward 1.25 3.00
107 Willie Parker 1.25 3.00
108 Donte Stallworth 1.00 2.50
109 Drew Brees 1.50 4.00
110 Deuce McAllister 1.25 3.00
111 Andre Johnson 1.25 3.00
112 David Carr 1.00 2.50
113 Domanick Davis 1.00 2.50
114 Eric Moulds 1.00 2.50
115 David Givens 1.25 3.00
116 Drew Bennett 1.25 3.00
117 Chris Brown 1.00 2.50
118 Bob Griese 2.00 5.00
119 Daryle Lamonica 1.25 3.00
120 Dave Casper 1.25 3.00
121 Don Meredith 2.00 5.00
122 Herschel Walker 2.00 5.00
123 Jack Lambert 2.00 5.00
124 Jackie Smith 1.25 3.00
125 Jim Otto 1.25 3.00
126 John Riggins 1.50 4.00
127 John Stallworth 1.50 4.00
128 Lawrence Taylor 2.00 5.00
129 Lester Hayes 1.25 3.00
130 L.C. Greenwood 1.25 3.00
131 Paul Warfield 1.50 4.00
132 Barry Sanders 3.00 8.00
133 Bart Starr 3.00 8.00
134 Billy Sims 1.50 4.00
135 Bulldog Turner 1.50 4.00
136 Deion Sanders 1.50 4.00
137 Dutch Clark 1.50 4.00
138 Forrest Gregg 1.25 3.00
139 Gale Sayers 2.00 5.00
140 Jim Brown 2.50 6.00
141 Jim Thorpe 2.50 6.00
142 Joe Montana 6.00 15.00
143 John Elway 3.00 8.00
144 Johnny Unitas 3.00 8.00
145 Lance Alworth 1.50 4.00
146 Raymond Berry 1.50 4.00
147 Doak Walker 2.00 5.00
148 Red Grange 2.50 6.00
149 Walter Payton 4.00 10.00
150 Yale Lary 1.25 3.00
151 Adam Jennings RC 2.50 6.00
152 Alan Zemaitis RC 2.00 5.00
153 Patrick Cobbs RC 2.50 6.00
154 Anthony Schlegel RC 2.50 6.00
155 Anthony Smith RC 3.00 8.00
156 Antonio Cromartie RC 2.50 6.00
157 Ashton Youboty RC 2.00 5.00
158 Bennie Brazell RC 2.50 6.00
159 Bernard Pollard RC 2.50 6.00
160 Brodrick Bunkley RC 2.50 6.00
161 Calvin Lowry RC 3.00 8.00
162 Cedric Griffin RC 2.50 6.00
163 Cedric Humes RC 2.00 5.00
164 Charles Davis RC 2.50 6.00
165 Chris Gocong RC 2.50 6.00
166 Claude Wroten RC 2.00 5.00
167 Clint Ingram RC 3.00 8.00
168 D.J. Shockley RC 2.50 6.00
169 Danieal Manning RC 3.00 8.00
170 Daniel Bullocks RC 2.00 5.00
171 Darnell Bing RC 2.50 6.00
172 Chris Hannon RC 2.50 6.00
173 Darryl Tapp RC 2.50 6.00
174 David Anderson RC 2.50 6.00
175 David Kirtman RC 2.50 6.00
176 David Pittman RC 2.50 6.00
177 Davin Joseph RC 2.50 6.00
178 Sam Hurd RC 2.00 5.00
179 Delanie Walker RC 4.00 10.00
180 DeMeco Ryans RC 2.50 6.00
181 Derrick Ross RC 2.50 6.00
182 Devin Hester RC 4.00 10.00
183 Domenik Hixon RC 3.00 8.00
184 Dominique Byrd RC 2.00 5.00
185 Donte Whitner RC 2.50 6.00
186 D'Qwell Jackson RC 2.00 5.00
187 Dusty Dvoracek RC 3.00 8.00
188 Eric Smith RC 2.50 6.00
189 Fred Evans RC 2.50 6.00
190 Ernie Sims RC 2.00 5.00
191 Ethan Kilmer RC 2.50 6.00
192 Freddie Keiaho RC 2.50 6.00
193 Frostee Rucker RC 2.50 6.00
194 Gabe Watson RC 2.00 5.00
195 Garrett Mills RC 2.50 6.00
196 Dawan Landry RC 3.00 8.00
197 Gerris Wilkinson RC 2.00 5.00
198 Jarrad Page RC 3.00 8.00
199 Haloti Ngata RC 2.50 6.00
200 Hank Baskett RC 2.00 5.00
201 Jai Lewis RC 2.50 6.00
202 Jamar Williams RC 2.50 6.00
203 James Anderson RC 2.00 5.00
204 Jason Allen RC 2.50 6.00
205 Jason Hatcher RC 3.00 8.00
206 Chris Barclay RC 2.50 6.00
207 J.D. Runnels RC 2.50 6.00
208 Jeff King RC 2.50 6.00
209 Jeffrey Webb RC 2.50 6.00
210 Jerome Harrison RC 2.00 5.00
211 Jimmy Williams RC 2.00 5.00
212 John David Washington RC 2.00 5.00
213 Jon Alston RC 2.00 5.00
214 Johnathan Joseph RC 2.50 6.00
215 Kamerion Wimbley RC 2.50 6.00
216 Kelly Jennings RC 2.50 6.00
217 Charles Sharon RC 2.50 6.00
218 Ko Simpson RC 2.50 6.00
219 Lawrence Vickers RC 2.50 6.00

220 Leon Williams RC 2.50 6.00
221 Leonard Pope RC 3.00 8.00
222 Marques Colston RC 3.00 8.00
223 Martin Nance RC 2.00 5.00
224 Mathias Kiwanuka RC 3.00 8.00
225 Mike Bell RC 2.00 5.00
226 Mike Hass RC 2.00 5.00
227 Miles Austin RC 2.50 6.00
228 Nate Salley RC 2.50 6.00
229 Nick Mangold RC 2.50 6.00
230 Owen Daniels RC 3.00 8.00
231 Shaun Bodiford RC 2.50 6.00
232 Quinn Sypniewski RC 2.50 6.00
233 Quinton Ganther RC 2.00 5.00
234 Richard Marshall RC 2.00 5.00
235 Rocky McIntosh RC 2.00 5.00
236 Roman Harper RC 2.50 6.00
237 Stephen Tulloch RC 2.50 6.00
238 Brett Basanez RC 3.00 8.00
239 Tamba Hali RC 3.00 8.00
240 Brett Elliott RC 3.00 8.00
241 Thomas Howard RC 2.00 5.00
242 Tim Jennings RC 3.00 8.00
243 Jason Carter RC 2.50 6.00
244 Todd Watkins RC 2.00 5.00
245 Tony Scheffler RC 3.00 8.00
246 Tye Hill RC 2.00 5.00
247 Victor Adeyanju RC 2.50 6.00
248 Wendell Mathis RC 2.50 6.00
249 Will Blackmon RC 2.00 5.00
250 Willie Reid RC 2.50 6.00
251 Mario Williams JSY AU RC 8.00 20.00
252 Reggie Bush JSY AU RC 8.00 20.00
253 Vince Young JSY AU RC 5.00 12.00
254 A.J. Hawk JSY AU RC 6.00 15.00
255 Vernon Davis JSY AU RC 6.00 15.00
256 Michael Huff JSY AU RC 6.00 15.00
257 Matt Leinart JSY AU RC 5.00 12.00
258 Jay Cutler AU RC 6.00 15.00
259 L.Maroney JSY AU RC 5.00 12.00
260 Santonio Holmes JSY AU RC 6.00 15.00
261 DeA.Williams JSY AU RC 6.00 15.00
262 Marcedes Lewis JSY AU RC 5.00 12.00
263 Joseph Addai AU RC 5.00 12.00
264 Chad Jackson JSY AU RC 5.00 12.00
265 Sinorice Moss JSY AU RC 5.00 12.00
266 LenDale White JSY AU RC 5.00 12.00
267 Kellen Clemens JSY AU RC 5.00 12.00
268 Greg Jennings AU RC 8.00 20.00
269 Joe Klopfenstein JSY AU RC 5.00 12.00
270 Maurice Drew JSY AU RC 12.00 30.00
271 Tarvaris Jackson JSY AU RC 5.00 12.00
272 Brian Calhoun JSY AU RC 5.00 12.00
273 Travis Wilson JSY AU RC 5.00 12.00
274 Jerious Norwood JSY AU RC 5.00 12.00
275 C.Whitehurst JSY AU RC 5.00 12.00
276 Derek Hagan JSY AU RC 6.00 15.00
277 Brandon Williams JSY AU RC 5.00 12.00
278 Brodie Croyle AU RC 5.00 12.00
279 Maurice Stovall JSY AU RC 5.00 12.00
280 Michael Robinson JSY AU RC 5.00 12.00
281 Jason Avant JSY AU RC 5.00 12.00
282 Dem.Williams JSY AU RC 5.00 12.00
283 Leon Washington JSY AU RC 5.00 12.00
284 B.Marshall JSY AU RC 10.00 25.00
285 Omar Jacobs JSY AU RC 5.00 12.00
286 Anthony Fasano AU RC 5.00 12.00
287 Ingle Martin AU RC 6.00 15.00
288 Reggie McNeal AU RC 5.00 12.00
289 Brad Smith AU RC 6.00 15.00
290 Jeremy Bloom AU RC 5.00 12.00
291 Bruce Gradkowski AU RC 6.00 15.00
292 P.J. Daniels AU RC 5.00 12.00
293 Cory Rodgers AU RC 5.00 12.00
294 Skyler Green AU RC 5.00 12.00
295 Bobby Carpenter AU RC 5.00 12.00
296 Arom/Obom/Mix AU/100 10.00 25.00
297 Hodge/Greenway AU/100 10.00 25.00
298 M.Will/McCar/Lwsn AU/100 20.00 40.00
299 Fasano/Stovall AU/50 20.00 40.00
300 Hawk/Carpenter AU/50 20.00 50.00
301 Leinart/Bush/Wht AU/25 15.00 40.00
302 Young/Thomas AU/50 12.00 30.00
303 Olson/Drew/Lewis AU/100 15.00 40.00
304 Hagans/Lundy/Ferg AU/100 10.00 25.00
305 Calhn/Willms/Orr AU/100 10.00 25.00
TC Steve Smith TC/500 2.50 6.00
TCA Steve Smith TC AU/50 20.00 40.00

2006 Leaf Limited Bronze Spotlight

*VETS/50 1-117: .8X TO 2X BASIC CARDS
*RETIRED/50 118-150: .6X TO 1.5X
*ROOKIE/50 151-250: .6X TO 1.5X
STATED PRINT RUN 50 SER.#'d SETS

2006 Leaf Limited Gold Spotlight

UNPRICED GOLD SPOTLIGHT PRINT RUN 5-10

2006 Leaf Limited Platinum Spotlight

UNPRICED PLATINUM PRINT RUN 1

2006 Leaf Limited Silver Spotlight

ETS/25 1-117: 1.2X TO 3X BASIC CARDS
*RETIRED/25 118-150: 1X TO 2.5X
*ROOKIE/25 151-250: 1X TO 2.5X
*ROOKIE AU/25 251-295: .6X TO 1.2X
*COMBO AU/25 296-305: .6X TO 1.2X
SILVER PRINT RUN 10-25
SERIAL #'d TO 10 NOT PRICED

2006 Leaf Limited College Phenoms Autographs

*ROOKIES: .4X TO 1X BASIC CARDS
STATED PRINT RUN 50 SER.#'d SETS
UNPRICED GOLD PRINT RUN 10
UNPRICED PLATINUM PRINT RUN 1
*SILVER/25: .5X TO 1.2X BASIC CARDS

2006 Leaf Limited Contenders Preview Autographs

STATED PRINT RUN 50-100
1 Brodie Croyle/100 5.00 12.00
2 Santonio Holmes/100 25.00 50.00
3 Tim Jennings/100 8.00 20.00
4 Travis Wilson/100 5.00 12.00
5 Leon Washington/100 5.00 12.00
6 Brad Smith/100 6.00 15.00
7 Jerome Harrison/100 5.00 12.00
8 Joe Klopfenstein/100 5.00 12.00
9 Matt Leinart/50 15.00 40.00
10 Chad Greenway/100 8.00 20.00
11 Dominique Byrd/100 5.00 12.00
12 A.J. Hawk/50 10.00 25.00
13 Greg Jennings/100 8.00 20.00
14 Johnathan Joseph /100 6.00 15.00
15 Mike Bell/50 8.00 20.00
16 Willie Reid/100 6.00 15.00
17 Haloti Ngata/100 6.00 15.00
18 Marques Hagans/100 5.00 12.00
19 Will Blackmon/100 5.00 12.00
20 Reggie Bush/50 12.00 30.00
21 Domenik Hixon/100 8.00 20.00
22 Leonard Pope /100 8.00 20.00
23 John McCargo/100 5.00 12.00
24 Daniel Bullocks/100 5.00 12.00
25 Rocky McIntosh/100 5.00 12.00
26 Jason Allen/100 6.00 15.00
27 Jay Cutler/50 10.00 25.00
28 Richard Marshall/100 6.00 15.00
29 LenDale White/50 8.00 20.00
30 Roman Harper/100 6.00 15.00
31 Vernon Davis/50 10.00 25.00
32 Danieal Manning/100 8.00 20.00
33 Cory Rodgers/100 5.00 12.00
34 David Thomas/100 5.00 12.00
35 Derek Hagan/100 6.00 15.00
36 Jerious Norwood/100 5.00 12.00
37 Vince Young/50 8.00 20.00
38 Joseph Addai/100 5.00 12.00
39 Skyler Green/100 5.00 12.00
40 Omar Jacobs/100 5.00 12.00

2006 Leaf Limited Cuts Autographs

ATED PRINT RUN 30 SER.#'d SETS
1 A.J. Hawk 20.00 50.00
2 Brandon Marshall 20.00 50.00
3 Brandon Williams 10.00 25.00
4 Brian Calhoun 10.00 25.00
5 Chad Jackson 10.00 25.00
6 Charlie Whitehurst 10.00 25.00
7 DeAngelo Williams 15.00 40.00
8 Demetrius Williams 10.00 25.00
9 Derek Hagan 12.00 30.00
10 Jason Avant 10.00 25.00
11 Jerious Norwood 10.00 25.00
12 Joe Klopfenstein 10.00 25.00
13 Kellen Clemens 10.00 25.00
14 Laurence Maroney 10.00 25.00
15 LenDale White 10.00 25.00
16 Leon Washington 10.00 25.00
17 Marcedes Lewis 10.00 25.00
18 Mario Williams 15.00 40.00
19 Matt Leinart 10.00 25.00
20 Maurice Drew 25.00 60.00
21 Maurice Stovall 10.00 25.00
22 Michael Huff 12.00 30.00
23 Michael Robinson 10.00 25.00
24 Omar Jacobs 10.00 25.00
25 Reggie Bush 15.00 40.00
26 Santonio Holmes 12.00 30.00
27 Sinorice Moss 10.00 25.00
28 Tarvaris Jackson 10.00 25.00
29 Travis Wilson 10.00 25.00
30 Vernon Davis 12.00 30.00
31 Vince Young 10.00 25.00
32 Greg Jennings 15.00 40.00
33 Brodie Croyle 10.00 25.00
34 Joseph Addai 10.00 25.00
35 Jay Cutler 12.00 30.00

2006 Leaf Limited Hardwear

HARDWEAR PRINT RUN 24-100
*LTD/27-39: .6X TO 1.5X HARDWEAR/100
*LTD/27-39: .5X TO 1.2X HARDWEAR/49
LIMITED PRINT RUN 2-39
1 Brian Urlacher/58 8.00 20.00
2 Carson Palmer/24 8.00 20.00
3 Curtis Martin 6.00 15.00
4 Derrick Thomas 15.00 30.00
5 Priest Holmes/28 6.00 15.00
6 Eric Dickerson 5.00 12.00
7 Herman Edwards 5.00 12.00
8 Jerry Rice/49 12.00 30.00
9 Jim Kelly 8.00 20.00
10 John Elway 10.00 25.00
11 Marcus Allen 6.00 15.00
12 Marshall Faulk 5.00 12.00
13 Marvin Harrison 6.00 15.00
14 Michael Vick 6.00 15.00
15 Mike Singletary/86 6.00 15.00
16 Steve Young 8.00 20.00
17 Terrell Davis 6.00 15.00
18 Thurman Thomas 5.00 12.00
19 Reggie White 8.00 20.00
20 Willis McGahee 6.00 15.00

2006 Leaf Limited Legends

STATED PRINT RUN 100 SER.#'d SETS
*HOLOFOIL/50: .5X TO 1.2X BASIC INSERTS
HOLOFOIL PRINT RUN 50 SER.#'d SETS
1 Bart Starr 4.00 10.00
2 Dobby Layne 2.00 5.00
3 Gale Sayers 2.50 6.00
4 Doak Walker 2.50 6.00
5 Red Grange 3.00 8.00
6 Johnny Unitas 4.00 10.00
7 Y.A. Tittle 2.50 6.00
8 Yale Lary 1.50 4.00
9 Walter Payton 5.00 12.00
10 Jim Thorpe 3.00 8.00
11 Jim Brown 3.00 8.00
12 Bulldog Turner 2.00 5.00
13 Lance Alworth 2.00 5.00
14 Sonny Jurgensen 2.00 5.00
15 Ray Nitschke 2.50 6.00
16 Bob Lilly 2.00 5.00
17 Dutch Clark 2.00 5.00
18 Lee Roy Selmon 1.50 4.00
19 Craig Morton 1.50 4.00
20 Forrest Gregg 1.50 4.00

2006 Leaf Limited Legends Materials

ATED PRINT RUN 5-100
*PRIME/25: .6X TO 1.5X BASIC JSYs
PRIME PRINT RUN 2-25
SERIAL #'d UNDER 25 NOT PRICED
1 Bart Starr 12.00 30.00
2 Bobby Layne 8.00 20.00
3 Gale Sayers 8.00 20.00
4 Doak Walker 8.00 20.00
5 Red Grange Hel/75 50.00 100.00
6 Johnny Unitas 12.00 30.00
7 Y.A. Tittle 8.00 20.00
8 Yale Lary 6.00 15.00
9 Walter Payton 12.00 30.00
10 Jim Thorpe 40.00 100.00
11 Jim Brown 10.00 25.00
12 Bulldog Turner 8.00 20.00
13 Lance Alworth/55 10.00 25.00
14 Sonny Jurgensen 6.00 15.00
15 Ray Nitschke 12.00 30.00
16 Bob Lilly 6.00 15.00
18 Lee Roy Selmon 6.00 15.00
19 Craig Morton 6.00 15.00
20 Forrest Gregg 8.00 20.00

2006 Leaf Limited Legends Signature Materials

ATED PRINT RUN 25-100 SER.#'d SETS
*PRIME/25: .6X TO 1.5X BASIC JSY AUTOs
PRIME PRINT RUN 5-25 SER.#'d SETS
1 Bart Starr/50 75.00 135.00
3 Gale Sayers/25 30.00 60.00
7 Y.A. Tittle/100 20.00 50.00
8 Yale Lary/100 12.00 30.00
11 Jim Brown/25 50.00 100.00
13 Lance Alworth/25 40.00 80.00
14 Sonny Jurgensen/100 12.00 30.00
16 Bob Lilly/100 12.00 30.00
18 Lee Roy Selmon/100 15.00 40.00
19 Craig Morton/50 12.00 30.00
20 Forrest Gregg/50 30.00 60.00

2006 Leaf Limited Lettermen

PRICED LETTERMEN PRINT RUN 4-12

2006 Leaf Limited Matching Numbers Jerseys

STATED PRINT RUN 100 SER.#'d SETS
*PRIME/25: .6X TO 1.5X BASIC JSYs
PRIME PRINT RUN 10-25
*POSITION/100: .4X TO 1X NUMBER JSYs
*POSIT.PRIME/25: .6X TO 1.5X BASIC JSYs
1 J.Kelly/T.Brady 12.00 30.00
2 B.Sims/B.Sanders 12.00 30.00
3 R.Staubach/T.Bradshaw 12.00 30.00
4 J.Brown/M.Allen 10.00 25.00
5 S.Largent/J.Rice 12.00 30.00
6 R.Berry/O.Newsome/50 6.00 15.00
7 L.Dawson/J.Montana 12.00 30.00
8 D.Maynard/D.Marino 15.00 40.00
9 F.Gregg/J.Greene/30 20.00 50.00
10 E.Campbell/W.Payton 15.00 40.00
11 J.Unitas/L.Alworth 15.00 40.00
12 Z.Thomas/B.Urlacher 8.00 20.00
13 L.Tomlinson/J.Jones 8.00 20.00
14 P.Manning/R.Moss 10.00 25.00
15 T.Barber/W.McGahee 6.00 15.00
16 C.Johnson/A.Gates 6.00 15.00
17 S.Smith/S.Moss 8.00 20.00
18 L.Fitzgerald/R.Williams WR 6.00 15.00
19 S.Alexander/D.Davis 8.00 20.00
20 T.Holt/A.Boldin 5.00 12.00

2006 Leaf Limited Material Monikers Jersey Number

ATED PRINT RUN 1-89
SERIAL #'d UNDER 20 NOT PRICED
6 Chad Johnson/85 15.00 30.00
7 Chris Chambers/84 10.00 25.00
8 Darrell Jackson/82
9 Domanick Davis/37 10.00 25.00
12 Clinton Portis/26 20.00 40.00
14 Jerry Porter/84 10.00 25.00
15 Julius Jones/21 15.00 30.00
16 Kevin Jones/34 20.00 40.00
17 LaDainian Tomlinson/21 40.00 80.00
18 Larry Johnson/27 20.00 50.00
21 Mark Clayton/89 10.00 25.00
23 Marvin Harrison/88 25.00 50.00
28 Priest Holmes/31 15.00 30.00
30 Reggie Wayne/87 15.00 30.00
31 Ronnie Brown/23 20.00 40.00
33 Rudi Johnson/32 15.00 30.00
34 Samkon Gado/35 10.00 25.00
35 Santana Moss/89 10.00 25.00
36 Shaun Alexander/37 25.00 50.00
37 Steve Smith/89 20.00 40.00
38 T.J. Houshmandzadeh/84 10.00 25.00
39 Tatum Bell/26 15.00 40.00
40 Tiki Barber/21 30.00 60.00
41 Torry Holt/81 15.00 30.00
42 Willie Parker/39 15.00 40.00
43 Willis McGahee/21 15.00 30.00
44 Barry Sanders/20 100.00 175.00
45 Bo Jackson/34 40.00 80.00
46 Charley Taylor/42 15.00 30.00
47 Cliff Branch/21 20.00 40.00
48 Cris Carter/80
49 Deion Sanders/21 40.00 80.00
51 Henry Ellard/80 10.00 25.00
53 Paul Krause/22
54 Tony Dorsett/33 25.00 50.00
56 Billy Sims/20 15.00 30.00
58 Deacon Jones/75 15.00 40.00
59 Fred Biletnikoff/25 30.00 60.00
61 Willie Brown/24 20.00 40.00

2006 Leaf Limited Material Monikers Jersey Number Prime

IME PRINT RUN 5-25 SER.#'d SETS
SERIAL #'d UNDER 25 NOT PRICED
1 Alex Smith QB/25 40.00 80.00
4 Byron Leftwich/25 15.00 40.00
19 Roger Staubach/25 75.00 135.00
20 Marc Bulger/25 15.00 40.00
42 Willie Parker/25 25.00 60.00
46 Charley Taylor/25 15.00 40.00
47 Cliff Branch/25 15.00 40.00
48 Cris Carter/25 75.00 135.00
49 Deion Sanders/25 30.00 60.00
50 Fran Tarkenton/25 30.00 60.00
51 Henry Ellard/25 15.00 40.00
52 Joe Theismann/25 30.00 60.00
53 Paul Krause/25 15.00 40.00
54 Tony Dorsett/25 30.00 60.00
55 Warren Moon/25 25.00 60.00
56 Billy Sims/25 15.00 40.00
57 Boomer Esiason/25 15.00 40.00
58 Deacon Jones/25 30.00 60.00
59 Fred Biletnikoff/25 30.00 60.00
61 Willie Brown/25 15.00 40.00
62 Troy Aikman/25 60.00 120.00
64 John Elway/25 100.00 175.00
65 Steve Young/25 75.00 135.00

2006 Leaf Limited Monikers Autographs Gold

GOLD STATED PRINT RUN 1-100
UNPRICED PLATINUM PRINT RUN 1
3 Frank Gore/50 15.00 30.00
4 Rex Grossman/50 6.00 15.00
5 Thomas Jones/20 8.00 20.00
9 Rudi Johnson/32 6.00 15.00
10 T.J. Houshmandzadeh/50 6.00 15.00
11 J.P. Losman/50 8.00 20.00
12 Lee Evans/83
13 Willis McGahee/21 8.00 20.00
19 Charlie Frye/50 8.00 20.00
25 Edgerrin James/32 8.00 20.00
28 Antonio Gates/85 10.00 25.00
30 LaDainian Tomlinson/21 30.00 60.00
34 Priest Holmes/31 10.00 25.00
37 Dallas Clark/44 6.00 15.00
38 Marvin Harrison/25 15.00 40.00
39 Peyton Manning/25 75.00 150.00
46 Chris Chambers/25 8.00 20.00
49 Ronnie Brown/23 10.00 25.00
51 Donovan McNabb/25 20.00 50.00
52 Jevon Kearse/50 6.00 15.00
54 Alge Crumpler/50 8.00 20.00
57 Eli Manning/25 60.00 100.00
61 Byron Leftwich/25 8.00 20.00
63 Jimmy Smith/50 8.00 20.00
64 Matt Jones/50 6.00 15.00
67 Kevin Jones/34 6.00 15.00
71 Samkon Gado/50 6.00 15.00
72 Ahman Green/30 10.00 25.00
76 Steve Smith/50 15.00 30.00
78 Deion Branch/50 6.00 15.00
79 Tedy Bruschi/54 30.00 60.00
81 Jerry Porter/84 5.00 12.00
83 LaMont Jordan/34 8.00 20.00
86 Steven Jackson/39 6.00 15.00
88 Derrick Mason/50 6.00 15.00
93 Clinton Portis/26 12.00 30.00
95 Chad Pennington/50 6.00 15.00
96 Laveranues Coles/22 8.00 20.00
101 Darrell Jackson/82 6.00 15.00
102 Matt Hasselbeck/25 12.00 30.00
104 Shaun Alexander/37 10.00 25.00
107 Willie Parker/39 10.00 25.00
110 Deuce McAllister/50 8.00 20.00
111 Andre Johnson/50 8.00 20.00
112 David Carr/49 6.00 15.00
113 Domanick Davis/50 6.00 15.00
116 Drew Bennett/50 8.00 20.00
117 Chris Brown/50 6.00 15.00
118 Bob Griese/50 12.00 30.00
119 Daryle Lamonica/100 8.00 20.00
120 Dave Casper/87 12.00 30.00
121 Don Meredith/50 50.00 80.00
122 Herschel Walker/100 10.00 25.00
123 Jack Lambert/58 30.00 50.00
124 Jackie Smith/25 12.00 30.00
125 Jim Otto/50 20.00 40.00
126 John Riggins/44 20.00 40.00
127 John Stallworth/50 20.00 40.00
128 Lawrence Taylor/56 25.00 50.00
129 Lester Hayes/50 12.00 30.00
130 L.C. Greenwood/68 15.00 30.00
131 Paul Warfield/42 15.00 30.00
132 Barry Sanders/20 50.00 100.00
134 Billy Sims/100 8.00 20.00
136 Deion Sanders/21 30.00 60.00
138 Forrest Gregg/75 25.00 50.00
139 Gale Sayers/40 40.00 80.00
140 Jim Brown/32 40.00 80.00
146 Raymond Berry/82 8.00 20.00
150 Yale Lary/75 12.00 30.00
151 Adam Jennings/50 8.00 20.00
152 Alan Zemaitis/25 8.00 20.00
155 Anthony Smith/25 12.00 30.00
156 Antonio Cromartie/50 8.00 20.00
157 Ashton Youboty/25 8.00 20.00
158 Bennie Brazell/25 10.00 25.00
159 Bernard Pollard/25 10.00 25.00
160 Brodrick Bunkley/25 10.00 25.00
161 Calvin Lowry/25 12.00 30.00
162 Cedric Griffin/25 10.00 25.00
163 Cedric Humes/100 5.00 12.00
166 Claude Wroten/25 8.00 20.00
168 D.J. Shockley/25 10.00 25.00
169 Danieal Manning/25 12.00 30.00
170 Daniel Bullocks/25 8.00 20.00
171 Darnell Bing/25 10.00 25.00
173 Darryl Tapp/25 10.00 25.00
174 David Anderson/25 10.00 25.00
175 David Kirtman/25 10.00 25.00
176 David Pittman/25 10.00 25.00
179 Delanie Walker/50 12.00 30.00
180 DeMeco Ryans/25 10.00 25.00
182 Devin Hester/100 10.00 25.00
183 Domenik Hixon/50 10.00 25.00
184 Dominique Byrd/100 5.00 12.00
185 Donte Whitner/50 8.00 20.00
186 D'Qwell Jackson/25 8.00 20.00
187 Dusty Dvoracek/25 12.00 30.00
188 Eric Smith/25 10.00 25.00
190 Ernie Sims/25 8.00 20.00
191 Ethan Kilmer/25 10.00 25.00
194 Gabe Watson/25 8.00 20.00
195 Garrett Mills/50 8.00 20.00
199 Haloti Ngata/25 10.00 25.00
201 Jai Lewis/25 10.00 25.00
204 Jason Allen/50 8.00 20.00
209 Jeffrey Webb/50 8.00 20.00
210 Jerome Harrison/100 5.00 12.00
211 Jimmy Williams/25 8.00 20.00
213 Jon Alston/25 8.00 20.00
214 Johnathan Joseph/50 8.00 20.00
215 Kamerion Wimbley/25 10.00 25.00
216 Kelly Jennings/50 8.00 20.00
218 Ko Simpson/25 10.00 25.00
221 Leonard Pope/50 10.00 25.00
222 Marques Colston/25 12.00 30.00
224 Mathias Kiwanuka/25 12.00 30.00
225 Mike Bell/40 6.00 15.00
226 Mike Hass/100 5.00 12.00
228 Nate Salley/25 10.00 25.00
230 Owen Daniels/50 10.00 25.00
233 Quinton Ganther/100 5.00 12.00
234 Richard Marshall/25 10.00 25.00
235 Rocky McIntosh/25 8.00 20.00
236 Roman Harper/50 8.00 20.00
239 Tamba Hali/25 12.00 30.00
241 Thomas Howard/25 8.00 20.00
242 Tim Jennings/25 12.00 30.00
244 Todd Watkins/25 8.00 20.00
245 Tony Scheffler/100 8.00 20.00
248 Tye Hill/50 6.00 15.00
249 Will Blackmon/50 6.00 15.00
250 Willie Reid/100 6.00 15.00

2006 Leaf Limited Player Threads

ATED PRINT RUN 100 SER.#'d SETS
*PRIME/25-30: .8X TO 2X BASIC INSERTS
PRIME PRINT RUN 5-30
1 Sinorice Moss 4.00 10.00
2 Mario Williams 5.00 12.00
3 Demetrius Williams 4.00 10.00
4 Marcedes Lewis 4.00 10.00
5 Matt Leinart 2.00 5.00
6 Reggie Bush 3.00 8.00
7 LenDale White 6.00 15.00
8 A.J. Hawk 8.00 20.00
9 Laurence Maroney 2.00 5.00
10 Maurice Drew 8.00 20.00
11 Maurice Stovall 4.00 10.00
12 Travis Wilson 4.00 10.00
13 Cedric Benson 5.00 12.00
14 Roy Williams S 4.00 10.00
15 Roy Williams WR 5.00 12.00
16 Ronnie Brown 5.00 12.00
17 Cadillac Williams 4.00 10.00
18 Dan Marino 15.00 40.00
19 Thurman Thomas 6.00 15.00
20 Tony Dorsett 8.00 20.00
21 Peyton Manning 12.00 30.00
22 Laveranues Coles 4.00 10.00
23 Hines Ward 5.00 12.00
24 Michael Clayton 4.00 10.00
25 Andre Johnson 4.00 10.00
26 Jeremy Shockey 5.00 12.00
27 Carson Palmer 5.00 12.00
28 Willis McGahee 5.00 12.00
29 Santana Moss 4.00 10.00
30 Curtis Martin 5.00 12.00
31 Roger Staubach 12.00 30.00
32 Eric Dickerson 6.00 15.00
33 Earl Campbell 8.00 20.00
34 Drew Bledsoe 5.00 12.00
35 Kevin Jones 5.00 12.00
36 Lawrence Taylor 8.00 20.00
37 DeShaun Foster 4.00 10.00
38 Terry Bradshaw 12.00 30.00
39 Terrell Davis 8.00 20.00
40 Mike Singletary 6.00 15.00

2006 Leaf Limited Prime Pairings Autographs

ATED PRINT RUN 25 SER.#'d SETS
1 Rose Bowl Rookies 30.00 60.00
2 Dallas Cowboys 250.00 400.00
3 Oakland Raiders 150.00 250.00
4 Pittsburgh Steelers 300.00 450.00
5 Retired QBs and RBs 500.00 750.00

2006 Leaf Limited Team Threads Dual

ATED PRINT RUN 100 SER.#'d SETS
*PRIME/30: .8X TO 2X BASIC INSERTS
PRIME PRINT RUN 5-30
1 T.Thomas/W.McGahee 6.00 15.00
2 B.Turner/B.Urlacher 10.00 25.00
3 B.Starr/B.Favre 15.00 40.00
4 R.Staubach/D.Bledsoe 10.00 25.00
5 E.Dickerson/M.Faulk 6.00 15.00
6 Y.Tittle/S.Young 10.00 25.00
7 S.Jurgensen/J.Theismann 8.00 20.00
8 J.Brown/R.Droughns 8.00 20.00
9 L.Dawson/J.Montana 12.00 30.00
10 P.Warfield/C.Chambers 6.00 15.00
11 C.Morton/J.Elway 10.00 25.00
12 M.Allen/L.Jordan 8.00 20.00
13 H.Ellard/I.Bruce 5.00 12.00
14 D.Maynard/C.Pennington 5.00 12.00
15 L.Alworth/A.Gates 8.00 20.00

2006 Leaf Limited Team Threads Triples

STATED PRINT RUN 100 SER.#'d SETS
*PRIME/25-30: .8X TO 2X BASIC INSERTS
PRIME PRINT RUN 25-30
1 Walker/Sims/Sanders 12.00 30.00
2 Staubach/Dorsett/Martin 12.00 30.00
3 Tittle/Montana/Young 20.00 40.00
4 Bradshaw/Lambert/Stallworth 12.00 30.00
5 Starr/Gregg/Nitschke 20.00 40.00
6 Lamonica/Blanda/Plunkett 10.00 25.00
7 Turner/Butkus/Singletary 20.00 40.00
8 Theismann/Taylor/Riggins 10.00 25.00
9 Elway/Davis/Smith 12.00 30.00
10 Dickerson/Ellard/Jones 6.00 15.00

2006 Leaf Limited Team Threads Quads

QUAD PRINT RUN 25-50
*PRIME/25: .5X TO 1.2X BASIC QUAD/50
*PRIME/25: .4X TO 1X QUAD/25-30
PRIME PRINT RUN 5-25
1 Walk/Lary/Layne/Clark/25 60.00 150.00
2 Unitas/Berry/Mann/Harr/50 40.00 80.00
3 Grng/Turner/Syrs/Pytn/30 150.00 250.00
4 Starr/Nits/Grgg/Wht/50 40.00 80.00
5 Staub/Drstt/Lilly/Mrtn/50 40.00 80.00

2006 Leaf Limited Team Trademarks

STATED PRINT RUN 100 SER.#'d SETS
*HOLOFOIL/50: .5X TO 1.2X BASIC INSERTS
HOLOFOIL PRINT RUN 50 SER.#'d SETS
1 Alex Smith QB 1.50 4.00
2 Anquan Boldin 1.25 3.00
3 Antonio Gates 2.00 5.00
4 Ben Roethlisberger 2.50 6.00
5 Brett Favre 4.00 10.00
6 Michael Vick 1.50 4.00
7 Willis McGahee 1.25 3.00
8 Jake Delhomme 1.25 3.00
9 Cedric Benson 1.25 3.00
10 Chad Johnson 1.25 3.00
11 Drew Bledsoe 1.50 4.00
12 Julius Jones 1.25 3.00
13 Tatum Bell 1.25 3.00
14 Roy Williams WR 1.25 3.00
15 Samkon Gado 1.25 3.00
16 Andre Johnson 1.50 4.00
17 Peyton Manning 5.00 12.00
18 Byron Leftwich 1.25 3.00
19 Larry Johnson 1.25 3.00
20 Ronnie Brown 1.50 4.00
21 Chris Chambers 1.25 3.00
22 Reggie Wayne 1.50 4.00
23 Tom Brady 6.00 15.00
24 Deion Branch 1.25 3.00
25 Donte Stallworth 1.25 3.00
26 Eli Manning 1.50 4.00
27 Tiki Barber 1.50 4.00
28 Curtis Martin 1.50 4.00
29 Randy Moss 1.50 4.00
30 Donovan McNabb 1.50 4.00
31 Reggie Brown 1.25 3.00
32 Willie Parker 1.50 4.00
33 Hines Ward 1.50 4.00
34 Philip Rivers 2.00 5.00
35 LaDainian Tomlinson 2.00 5.00
36 Shaun Alexander 1.25 3.00
37 Marc Bulger 1.25 3.00
38 Torry Holt 1.50 4.00
39 Cadillac Williams 1.50 4.00
40 Clinton Portis 1.25 3.00

2006 Leaf Limited Team Trademarks Materials

STATED PRINT RUN 100 SER.#'d SETS
*PRIME/30: .8X TO 2X BASIC JSYs
PRIME PRINT RUN 30 SER.#'d SETS
1 Alex Smith QB 4.00 10.00
2 Anquan Boldin 3.00 8.00
3 Antonio Gates 4.00 10.00
4 Ben Roethlisberger 6.00 15.00
5 Brett Favre 8.00 20.00
6 Michael Vick 4.00 10.00
7 Willis McGahee 4.00 10.00
8 Jake Delhomme 3.00 8.00
9 Cedric Benson 4.00 10.00
10 Chad Johnson 3.00 8.00
11 Drew Bledsoe 4.00 10.00
12 Julius Jones 4.00 10.00
13 Tatum Bell 3.00 8.00
14 Roy Williams WR 4.00 10.00
15 Samkon Gado 4.00 10.00
16 Andre Johnson 3.00 8.00
17 Peyton Manning 6.00 15.00
18 Byron Leftwich 3.00 8.00
19 Larry Johnson 4.00 10.00
20 Ronnie Brown 4.00 10.00
21 Chris Chambers 3.00 8.00
22 Reggie Wayne 3.00 8.00
23 Tom Brady 6.00 15.00
24 Deion Branch 3.00 8.00
25 Donte Stallworth 3.00 8.00
26 Eli Manning 5.00 12.00
27 Tiki Barber 4.00 10.00
28 Curtis Martin 4.00 10.00
29 Randy Moss 4.00 10.00
30 Donovan McNabb 4.00 10.00
31 Reggie Brown 3.00 8.00
32 Willie Parker 3.00 8.00
33 Hines Ward 4.00 10.00
34 Philip Rivers 4.00 10.00
35 LaDainian Tomlinson 4.00 10.00
36 Shaun Alexander 4.00 10.00
37 Marc Bulger 3.00 8.00
38 Torry Holt 3.00 8.00
39 Cadillac Williams 3.00 8.00
40 Clinton Portis 4.00 10.00

2006 Leaf Limited Team Trademarks Autograph Materials

TRADEMARK AU PRINT RUN 2-100
*PRIME/25: .6X TO 1.5X BASIC JSY AUs
PRIME PRINT RUN 3-25
SERIAL #'d UNDER 25 NOT PRICED
1 Alex Smith QB/50 10.00 25.00
2 Anquan Boldin/30 8.00 20.00
3 Antonio Gates/50 12.00 30.00
4 Ben Roethlisberger/50 60.00 120.00
7 Willis McGahee/25 8.00 20.00
9 Cedric Benson/40 8.00 20.00
10 Chad Johnson/50 8.00 20.00
11 Drew Bledsoe/50 10.00 25.00
12 Julius Jones/40 8.00 20.00
13 Tatum Bell/25 8.00 20.00
15 Samkon Gado/50 8.00 20.00
16 Andre Johnson/50 10.00 25.00
17 Peyton Manning/40 75.00 125.00
18 Byron Leftwich/100 8.00 20.00
19 Larry Johnson/35 8.00 20.00
21 Chris Chambers/50 8.00 20.00
22 Reggie Wayne/25 10.00 25.00
24 Deion Branch/50 8.00 20.00
26 Eli Manning/45 50.00 80.00
30 Donovan McNabb/40 25.00 50.00
31 Reggie Brown/50 8.00 20.00
32 Willie Parker/50 12.00 30.00
34 Philip Rivers/40 25.00 50.00
35 LaDainian Tomlinson/40 25.00 60.00
36 Shaun Alexander/40 25.00 50.00
39 Cadillac Williams/50 10.00 25.00
40 Clinton Portis/50 8.00 20.00

2006 Leaf Limited Threads

HREADS/50: .3X TO .8X PRIME/30
THREADS PRINT RUN 5-50
SERIAL #'d UNDER 25 NOT PRICED
119 Daryle Lamonica 5.00 12.00
146 Raymond Berry 6.00 15.00
147 Doak Walker 8.00 20.00

2006 Leaf Limited Threads Prime

*TEAM LOGO/30: .4X TO 1X PRIME/30
1 Alex Smith QB 8.00 20.00
3 Frank Gore 8.00 20.00
4 Rex Grossman 8.00 20.00
5 Thomas Jones 6.00 15.00
6 Cedric Benson 8.00 20.00
7 Carson Palmer 8.00 20.00
8 Chad Johnson 6.00 15.00
9 Rudi Johnson 6.00 15.00
10 T.J. Houshmandzadeh 6.00 15.00
11 J.P. Losman 6.00 15.00
12 Lee Evans 6.00 15.00
13 Willis McGahee 8.00 20.00
14 Jake Plummer 6.00 15.00
16 Rod Smith 6.00 15.00
17 Tatum Bell 6.00 15.00
18 Braylon Edwards 8.00 20.00
19 Charlie Frye 8.00 20.00
20 Reuben Droughns 6.00 15.00
21 Cadillac Williams 6.00 15.00
22 Chris Simms 6.00 15.00
23 Joey Galloway 6.00 15.00
24 Anquan Boldin 6.00 15.00
26 Kurt Warner 6.00 15.00
27 Larry Fitzgerald 8.00 20.00
28 Antonio Gates 8.00 20.00
29 Keenan McCardell 5.00 12.00
30 LaDainian Tomlinson 8.00 20.00
31 Philip Rivers 8.00 20.00
32 Eddie Kennison 5.00 12.00
33 Larry Johnson 8.00 20.00
34 Priest Holmes 6.00 15.00
35 Trent Green 6.00 15.00
36 Tony Gonzalez 6.00 15.00
37 Dallas Clark 5.00 12.00
38 Marvin Harrison 8.00 20.00
39 Peyton Manning 12.00 30.00
40 Reggie Wayne 6.00 15.00
41 Drew Bledsoe 8.00 20.00
42 Julius Jones 8.00 20.00
43 Roy Williams S 6.00 15.00
45 Terry Glenn 6.00 15.00
46 Chris Chambers 6.00 15.00
47 Daunte Culpepper 8.00 20.00
49 Ronnie Brown 8.00 20.00
50 Brian Westbrook 6.00 15.00
51 Donovan McNabb 8.00 20.00
52 Jevon Kearse 6.00 15.00
53 Reggie Brown 6.00 15.00
54 Alge Crumpler 6.00 15.00
55 Michael Vick 8.00 20.00
56 Warrick Dunn 6.00 15.00
57 Eli Manning 10.00 25.00
58 Jeremy Shockey 8.00 20.00
59 Plaxico Burress 6.00 15.00
60 Tiki Barber 8.00 20.00
61 Byron Leftwich 6.00 15.00
62 Fred Taylor 6.00 15.00
63 Jimmy Smith 6.00 15.00
64 Matt Jones 6.00 15.00
66 Roy Williams WR 8.00 20.00
67 Kevin Jones 8.00 20.00
68 Aaron Rodgers 20.00 50.00
69 Brett Favre 15.00 40.00
70 Robert Ferguson 5.00 12.00
72 Ahman Green 6.00 15.00
73 DeShaun Foster 6.00 15.00
74 Jake Delhomme 6.00 15.00
75 Keary Colbert 5.00 12.00
76 Steve Smith 8.00 20.00
77 Corey Dillon 6.00 15.00
79 Tedy Bruschi 10.00 25.00
80 Tom Brady 12.00 30.00
81 Jerry Porter 6.00 15.00
82 Randy Moss 8.00 20.00
83 LaMont Jordan 6.00 15.00
84 Isaac Bruce 6.00 15.00
85 Marc Bulger 6.00 15.00
86 Steven Jackson 8.00 20.00
87 Torry Holt 6.00 15.00
88 Derrick Mason 5.00 12.00
89 Mark Clayton 6.00 15.00
91 Jamal Lewis 6.00 15.00
93 Clinton Portis 8.00 20.00
94 Santana Moss 6.00 15.00
95 Chad Pennington 6.00 15.00
96 Laveranues Coles 6.00 15.00
97 Curtis Martin 8.00 20.00
98 Mewelde Moore 5.00 12.00
99 Troy Williamson 6.00 15.00
101 Darrell Jackson 6.00 15.00
102 Matt Hasselbeck 6.00 15.00
104 Shaun Alexander 8.00 20.00
105 Ben Roethlisberger 12.00 30.00
106 Hines Ward 8.00 20.00
107 Willie Parker 6.00 15.00
110 Deuce McAllister 6.00 15.00
111 Andre Johnson 6.00 15.00
112 David Carr 6.00 15.00
113 Domanick Davis 6.00 15.00
116 Drew Bennett 5.00 12.00
117 Chris Brown 6.00 15.00
118 Bob Griese 8.00 20.00
120 Dave Casper 6.00 15.00
122 Herschel Walker/25 6.00 15.00
123 Jack Lambert 8.00 20.00
124 Jackie Smith 6.00 15.00
125 Jim Otto 8.00 20.00
126 John Riggins 8.00 20.00
127 John Stallworth 8.00 20.00
128 Lawrence Taylor 8.00 20.00
130 L.C. Greenwood 6.00 15.00
131 Paul Warfield 6.00 15.00
132 Barry Sanders 12.00 30.00
133 Bart Starr 12.00 30.00
134 Billy Sims 6.00 15.00
135 Bulldog Turner/25 20.00 40.00
136 Deion Sanders 10.00 25.00
137 Dutch Clark/20 6.00 15.00
138 Forrest Gregg 8.00 20.00
139 Gale Sayers 10.00 25.00
140 Jim Brown 10.00 25.00
142 Joe Montana 12.00 30.00
143 John Elway 12.00 30.00
144 Johnny Unitas 12.00 30.00
145 Lance Alworth 8.00 20.00
149 Walter Payton 15.00 40.00

2007 Leaf Limited

This 355-card set was released in November, 2007. The set was issued into the hobby in a seven-card pack (box) with an $125 SRP. Cards numbered 1-100 feature veterans in alphabetical team order issued to a stated print run of 659 serial numbered sets while cards numbered 101-200 feature retired greats in first name alphabetical order issued to a stated print run of 249 serial numbered sets. The set concludes with 2007 NFL rookies (Cards 201-355). Cards numbered 201-250 were issued to a stated print run of 399 serial numbered sets; cards numbered 251-300 were signed by the player and were issued to stated print runs of between 194 and 299 serial numbered sets and the set concludes with more signed cards from 301-355 all of which were issued to a stated print run of 99 serial numbered sets.

1-100 PRINT RUN 659 SER.#'d SETS
101-200 LEGEND PRINT RUN 249
201-250 ROOKIE PRINT RUN 399
251-300 ROOKIE AU PRINT RUN 194-299
301-355 ROOKIE AU PRINT RUN 99
1 Anquan Boldin 1.00 2.50
2 Edgerrin James 1.25 3.00
3 Larry Fitzgerald 1.25 3.00
4 Matt Leinart 1.00 2.50
5 Alge Crumpler 1.25 3.00
6 Warrick Dunn 1.00 2.50
7 Jerious Norwood 1.00 2.50
8 Willis McGahee 1.00 2.50
9 Steve McNair 1.25 3.00
10 Mark Clayton 1.00 2.50
11 Anthony Thomas 1.00 2.50
12 J.P. Losman 1.00 2.50
13 Lee Evans 1.25 3.00
14 Jake Delhomme 1.00 2.50
15 Steve Smith 1.25 3.00
16 DeAngelo Williams 1.00 2.50
17 Rex Grossman 1.00 2.50
18 Cedric Benson 1.00 2.50
19 Bernard Berrian 1.00 2.50
20 Carson Palmer 1.25 3.00
21 Chad Johnson 1.00 2.50
22 Rudi Johnson 1.00 2.50
23 T.J. Houshmandzadeh 1.00 2.50
24 Kellen Winslow 1.00 2.50
25 Braylon Edwards 1.00 2.50
26 Jamal Lewis 1.25 3.00
27 Julius Jones 1.00 2.50
28 Terrell Owens 1.25 3.00
29 Tony Romo 2.00 5.00
30 Jay Cutler 1.00 2.50
31 Javon Walker 1.25 3.00
32 Travis Henry 1.25 3.00
33 Tatum Bell 1.00 2.50
34 Roy Williams WR 1.00 2.50
35 Jon Kitna 1.00 2.50
36 Brett Favre 3.00 8.00
37 Donald Driver 1.25 3.00
38 Greg Jennings 1.00 2.50
39 Matt Schaub 1.00 2.50
40 Andre Johnson 1.25 3.00
41 Ahman Green 1.25 3.00
42 Peyton Manning 4.00 10.00
43 Marvin Harrison 1.25 3.00
44 Reggie Wayne 1.25 3.00
45 Joseph Addai 1.00 2.50
46 David Garrard 1.00 2.50
47 Fred Taylor 1.00 2.50
48 Maurice Jones-Drew 1.00 2.50
49 Brodie Croyle 1.25 3.00
50 Larry Johnson 1.00 2.50
51 Tony Gonzalez 1.25 3.00
52 Trent Green 1.00 2.50
53 Ronnie Brown 1.00 2.50
54 Chris Chambers 1.00 2.50
55 Tarvaris Jackson 1.00 2.50
56 Troy Williamson 1.00 2.50
57 Chester Taylor 1.00 2.50
58 Tom Brady 5.00 12.00
59 Randy Moss 1.25 3.00
60 Laurence Maroney 1.25 3.00
61 Donte Stallworth 1.25 3.00
62 Drew Brees 1.50 4.00
63 Deuce McAllister 1.25 3.00
64 Reggie Bush 1.00 2.50
65 Marques Colston 1.00 2.50
66 Eli Manning 1.25 3.00
67 Jeremy Shockey 1.00 2.50
68 Brandon Jacobs 1.00 2.50
69 Chad Pennington 1.00 2.50
70 Thomas Jones 1.00 2.50
71 Laveranues Coles 1.00 2.50
72 Jerry Porter 1.25 3.00
73 LaMont Jordan 1.25 3.00
74 Donovan McNabb 1.25 3.00
75 Brian Westbrook 1.00 2.50
76 Reggie Brown 1.00 2.50
77 Ben Roethlisberger 1.50 4.00
78 Hines Ward 1.25 3.00
79 Willie Parker 1.25 3.00
80 Philip Rivers 1.50 4.00
81 Antonio Gates 1.50 4.00
82 LaDainian Tomlinson 1.50 4.00
83 Alex Smith QB 1.25 3.00
84 Darrell Jackson 1.00 2.50
85 Frank Gore 1.25 3.00
86 Matt Hasselbeck 1.00 2.50
87 Shaun Alexander 1.00 2.50
88 Deion Branch 1.00 2.50
89 Marc Bulger 1.00 2.50
90 Steven Jackson 1.00 2.50
91 Torry Holt 1.25 3.00
92 Jeff Garcia 1.00 2.50
93 Cadillac Williams 1.25 3.00
94 Joey Galloway 1.25 3.00
95 Vince Young 1.00 2.50
96 Brandon Jones 1.00 2.50
97 LenDale White 1.25 3.00
98 Jason Campbell 1.00 2.50
99 Clinton Portis 1.00 2.50
100 Santana Moss 1.25 3.00
101 Alan Page 2.00 5.00
102 Barry Sanders 5.00 12.00
103 Bart Starr 5.00 12.00
104 Bill Dudley 2.50 6.00
105 Billy Howton 2.00 5.00
106 Bob Griese 3.00 8.00
107 Bobby Layne 2.50 6.00
108 Boyd Dowler 2.00 5.00
109 Charley Taylor 2.00 5.00
110 Charley Trippi 2.00 5.00
111 Charlie Joiner 2.00 5.00
112 Chuck Bednarik 2.50 6.00
113 Cris Collinsworth 2.50 6.00
114 Dan Fouts 2.50 6.00
115 Dan Hampton 2.50 6.00
116 Dan Marino 6.00 15.00
117 Dante Lavelli 2.00 5.00
118 Darrell Green 2.50 6.00
119 Daryle Lamonica 2.00 5.00
120 Deacon Jones 2.50 6.00
121 Dick Butkus 4.00 10.00
122 Doak Walker 2.50 6.00
123 Don Maynard 2.50 6.00
124 Don Perkins 2.00 5.00
125 Dutch Clark 2.50 6.00
126 Earl Campbell 3.00 8.00
127 Forrest Gregg 2.00 5.00
128 Fran Tarkenton 3.00 8.00
129 Franco Harris 3.00 8.00
130 Fred Biletnikoff 3.00 8.00
131 Gale Sayers 3.00 8.00
132 Gene Upshaw 2.00 5.00
133 George Blanda 2.50 6.00
134 Harlon Hill 2.00 5.00
135 Jack Lambert 3.00 8.00
136 Jack Youngblood 2.50 6.00
137 James Lofton 2.00 5.00
138 Jan Stenerud 2.00 5.00
139 Jethro Pugh 2.00 5.00
140 Jim Brown 4.00 10.00
141 Jim Kelly 3.00 8.00
142 Jim McMahon 4.00 10.00
143 Jim Otto 2.00 5.00
144 Jim Thorpe 4.00 10.00
145 Jimmy Orr 2.00 5.00
146 Joe Greene 3.00 8.00
147 Joe Montana 10.00 25.00
148 Joe Namath 4.00 10.00
149 Joe Theismann 3.00 8.00
150 John Elway 5.00 12.00
151 John Mackey 2.50 6.00
152 John Riggins 2.50 6.00
153 John Stallworth 2.50 6.00
154 Johnny Morris 2.00 5.00
155 Johnny Unitas 5.00 12.00
156 Kellen Winslow Sr. 2.50 6.00
157 Ken Stabler 4.00 10.00
158 Lance Alworth 2.50 6.00
159 Larry Csonka 3.00 8.00
160 Larry Little 2.00 5.00
161 Lee Roy Selmon 2.00 5.00
162 Len Dawson 3.00 8.00
163 Lou Groza 2.50 6.00
164 Lydell Mitchell 2.00 5.00
165 Marcus Allen 3.00 8.00
166 Mark Duper 2.00 5.00
167 Merlin Olsen 2.00 5.00

168 Mike Singletary 3.00 8.00
169 Ollie Matson 2.50 6.00
170 Otto Graham 2.50 6.00
171 Ozzie Newsome 2.50 6.00
172 Paul Hornung 3.00 8.00
173 Paul Warfield 2.50 6.00
174 Phil Simms 2.50 6.00
175 Randall Cunningham 2.50 6.00
176 Ray Nitschke 3.00 8.00
177 Raymond Berry 2.50 6.00
178 Red Grange 4.00 10.00
179 Rick Casares 2.00 5.00
180 Ron Mix 2.00 5.00
181 Roger Craig 2.50 6.00
182 Roger Staubach 4.00 10.00
183 Rosey Brown 2.00 5.00
184 Rosey Grier 2.00 5.00
185 Ronnie Lott 2.50 6.00
186 Sam Huff 2.50 6.00
187 Sammy Baugh 3.00 8.00
188 Sid Luckman 3.00 8.00
189 Sonny Jurgensen 2.50 6.00
190 Sterling Sharpe 2.50 6.00
191 Steve Largent 3.00 8.00
192 Steve Young 4.00 10.00
193 Ted Hendricks 2.50 6.00
194 Thurman Thomas 2.50 6.00
195 Tim Brown 3.00 8.00
196 Tiki Barber 2.50 6.00
197 Troy Aikman 4.00 10.00
198 Walter Payton 6.00 15.00
199 Willie Brown 2.00 5.00
200 Elroy Hirsch 2.50 6.00
201 Brandon McDonald RC 2.00 5.00
202 David Irons RC 2.00 5.00
203 Fred Bennett RC 2.00 5.00
204 Nick Graham RC 2.50 6.00
205 Rashad Barksdale RC 2.00 5.00
206 Tanard Jackson RC 2.00 5.00
207 Tarell Brown RC 3.00 8.00
208 Usama Young RC 2.50 6.00
209 William Gay RC 2.50 6.00
210 Jarvis Moss RC 2.00 5.00
211 Le'Ron McClain RC 3.00 8.00
212 Kevin Payne RC 2.00 5.00
213 Adam Hayward RC 2.50 6.00
214 Brandon Siler RC 2.00 5.00
215 Chad Nkang RC 2.00 5.00
216 Clint Session RC 2.50 6.00
217 Desmond Bishop RC 3.00 8.00
218 Edmond Miles RC 2.50 6.00
219 H.B. Blades RC 2.00 5.00
220 Justin Durant RC 3.00 8.00
221 Justin Rogers RC 3.00 8.00
222 Nate Harris RC 2.50 6.00
223 Quincy Black RC 3.00 8.00
224 Quinton Culberson RC 2.00 5.00
225 Ramon Guzman RC 2.00 5.00
226 Stephen Nicholas RC 2.50 6.00
227 Tim Shaw RC 2.50 6.00
228 Tony Taylor RC 2.50 6.00
229 Zak DeOssie RC 2.50 6.00
230 Mason Crosby RC 2.50 6.00
231 Nick Folk RC 3.00 8.00
232 Matt Gutierrez RC 3.00 8.00
233 Matt Moore RC 3.00 8.00
234 Tyler Thigpen RC 3.00 8.00
235 Clifton Dawson RC 3.00 8.00
236 Gary Russell RC 2.50 6.00
237 Kenton Keith RC 2.50 6.00
238 Pierre Thomas RC 3.00 8.00
239 Gerald Alexander RC 2.00 5.00
240 John Wendling RC 2.50 6.00
241 Eric Frampton RC 2.50 6.00
242 Eric Weddle RC 2.50 6.00
243 Daniel Coats RC 2.50 6.00
244 Michael Matthews RC 2.50 6.00
245 Biren Ealy RC 2.50 6.00
246 Bobby Sippio RC 2.50 6.00
247 Glenn Holt RC 2.50 6.00
248 John Broussard RC 2.50 6.00
249 Legedu Naanee RC 2.50 6.00
250 Syndric Steptoe RC 2.50 6.00
251 Levi Brown AU RC 3.00 8.00
252 Jamaal Anderson AU RC 4.00 10.00
253 Amobi Okoye AU RC 4.00 10.00
254 Adam Carriker AU RC 3.00 8.00
255 Darrelle Revis AU RC 4.00 10.00
256 Michael Griffin AU RC 3.00 8.00
257 Aaron Ross AU RC 3.00 8.00
258 Brandon Meriweather AU RC 4.00 10.00
259 Jon Beason AU RC 3.00 8.00
260 Anthony Spencer AU RC 6.00 15.00
261 Alan Branch No AU RC 2.00 5.00
262 Chris Houston AU RC 3.00 8.00
263 LaMarr Woodley AU RC 8.00 20.00
264 David Harris AU RC 3.00 8.00
265 Eric Wright No AU RC 2.00 5.00
266 Josh Wilson AU RC 4.00 10.00
267 Tim Crowder AU RC 4.00 10.00
268 Victor Abiamiri AU RC 3.00 8.00
269 Ikaika Alama-Francis AU RC 5.00 12.00
270 Dan Bazuin AU RC 4.00 10.00
271 Sabby Piscitelli AU RC 3.00 8.00
272 Quentin Moses AU RC 3.00 8.00
273 Buster Davis AU RC 4.00 10.00
274 Marcus McCauley AU RC 3.00 8.00
275 Matt Spaeth AU RC 5.00 12.00
276 Demarcus Tank Tyler No AU RC 2.00 5.00
277 Charles Johnson No AU RC 2.00 5.00
278 Jonathan Wade AU RC 3.00 8.00
279 Stewart Bradley AU RC 3.00 8.00
280 Aaron Rouse AU RC 3.00 8.00
281 Michael Okwo AU RC 4.00 10.00
282 Daymeion Hughes AU RC 3.00 8.00
283 Ray McDonald AU RC 4.00 10.00
284 Thomas Clayton AU RC 4.00 10.00
285 DeShawn Wynn AU RC 3.00 8.00
286 Jason Snelling AU RC 6.00 15.00
287 Kenneth Darby AU RC 3.00 8.00
288 A.Bradshaw AU/291 RC 5.00 12.00
289 Nate Ilaoa AU/203 RC 4.00 10.00
290 Joel Filani AU RC 3.00 8.00
291 Courtney Taylor AU RC 3.00 8.00
292 Jordan Kent AU/245 RC 4.00 10.00
293 Dallas Baker AU RC 3.00 8.00
294 Roy Hall AU RC 5.00 12.00
295 Chansi Stuckey AU RC 4.00 10.00
296 Scott Chandler AU RC 5.00 12.00
297 Ben Patrick AU RC 4.00 10.00
298 Chris Leak AU RC 3.00 8.00
299 Jared Zabransky AU RC 3.00 8.00
300 Selvin Young AU/194 RC 3.00 8.00
301 A.Peterson JSY AU RC 150.00 250.00
302 Anthony Gonzalez JSY AU RC 5.00 12.00
303 Antonio Pittman JSY AU RC 5.00 12.00
304 Aundrae Allison AU RC 5.00 12.00
305 Brady Quinn JSY AU RC 5.00 12.00
306 Brandon Jackson JSY AU RC 5.00 12.00
307 Brian Leonard JSY AU RC 5.00 12.00
308 Calvin Johnson JSY AU RC 90.00 150.00
309 Chris Davis AU RC 5.00 12.00
310 Chris Henry RB JSY AU RC 5.00 12.00
312 David Clowney AU RC 5.00 12.00
313 Drew Stanton JSY AU RC 5.00 12.00
314 Dwayne Bowe JSY AU RC 12.00 30.00
315 Dwayne Jarrett JSY AU RC 6.00 15.00
316 Dwayne Wright AU RC 5.00 12.00
317 Gaines Adams JSY AU RC 6.00 15.00
318 Garrett Wolfe JSY AU RC 5.00 12.00
319 Greg Olsen JSY AU RC 8.00 20.00
320 Isaiah Stanback AU RC 5.00 12.00
321 Jacoby Jones AU RC 5.00 12.00
322 JaMarcus Russell JSY AU RC 5.00 12.00
323 James Jones AU RC 5.00 12.00
324 Jason Hill JSY AU RC 3.00 12.00
325 Jeff Rowe AU RC 5.00 12.00
326 Joe Thomas JSY AU RC 15.00 40.00
327 John Beck JSY AU RC 5.00 12.00
328 J.Lee Higgins JSY AU RC 5.00 12.00
329 Jordan Palmer AU RC 6.00 15.00
330 Kenny Irons JSY No AU RC 5.00 12.00
331 Kevin Kolb JSY AU RC 6.00 15.00
332 Kolby Smith AU RC 5.00 12.00
333 LaRon Landry AU RC 8.00 20.00
334 Laurent Robinson AU RC 8.00 20.00
335 Lawrence Timmons AU RC 8.00 20.00
336 Leon Hall AU RC 5.00 12.00
337 Lorenzo Booker JSY AU RC 6.00 15.00
338 M.Lynch JSY AU RC 25.00 50.00
339 Michael Bush JSY AU RC 5.00 12.00
340 Mike Walker AU RC 8.00 20.00
341 Patrick Willis JSY AU RC 15.00 40.00
342 Paul Posluszny AU RC 5.00 12.00
343 Paul Williams JSY AU RC 5.00 12.00
344 Reggie Nelson AU RC 5.00 12.00
345 Robert Meachem JSY AU RC 6.00 15.00
346 Ryne Robinson AU RC 6.00 15.00
347 Sidney Rice JSY AU RC 6.00 15.00
348 Steve Breaston AU RC 5.00 12.00
349 S.Smith USC JSY AU RC 12.00 30.00
350 Ted Ginn Jr. JSY AU RC 12.00 30.00
351 Tony Hunt JSY AU RC 5.00 12.00
352 Trent Edwards JSY AU RC 5.00 12.00
353 Troy Smith JSY AU RC 5.00 12.00
354 Yamon Figurs JSY AU RC 5.00 12.00
355 Zach Miller AU RC 5.00 12.00

2007 Leaf Limited Bronze Spotlight

*VETS 1-100: 1X TO 2.5X BASIC CARDS
*LEGENDS 101-200: .8X TO 2X BASIC CARDS
COMMON ROOKIE (201-300) 4.00 10.00
ROOKIE SEMISTARS 5.00 12.00
ROOKIE UNL.STARS 6.00 15.00
STATED PRINT RUN 32 SER.#'d SETS
238 Pierre Thomas 6.00 15.00

2007 Leaf Limited Gold Spotlight

*VETS 1-100: 2.5X TO 6X BASIC CARDS
*LEGENDS 101-200: 1.5X TO 4X BASIC CARDS
COMMON ROOKIE (201-300) 6.00 15.00
ROOKIE SEMISTARS 8.00 20.00
ROOKIE UNL.STARS 10.00 25.00
1-300 UNPRICED GOLD PRINT RUN 10
*ROOKIE AU: .5X TO 1.2X BASIC CARDS
301-355 AU PRINT RUN 25
238 Pierre Thomas 10.00 25.00
301 Adrian Peterson JSY AU 125.00 250.00
308 Calvin Johnson JSY AU 100.00 175.00
322 JaMarcus Russell JSY AU 15.00 40.00
338 Marshawn Lynch JSY AU 40.00 80.00

2007 Leaf Limited Platinum Spotlight

UNPRICED PLATINUM PRINT RUN 1

2007 Leaf Limited Silver Spotlight

*VETS 1-100: 1.5X TO 4X BASIC CARDS
*LEGENDS 101-200: 1.2X TO 3X BASIC CARDS
COMMON ROOKIE (201-300) 5.00 12.00
ROOKIE SEMISTARS 6.00 15.00
ROOKIE UNL.STARS 8.00 20.00
1-300 PRINT RUN 20 SER.#'d SETS
*ROOKIE AU: .4X TO 1X BASIC CARDS
301-355 AU PRINT RUN 49
234 Tyler Thigpen 8.00 20.00
238 Pierre Thomas 8.00 20.00
301 Adrian Peterson JSY AU 150.00 250.00
308 Calvin Johnson JSY AU 60.00 120.00
322 JaMarcus Russell JSY AU 12.00 30.00
338 Marshawn Lynch JSY AU 25.00 60.00

2007 Leaf Limited Banner Season Materials

STATED PRINT RUN 100 SER.#'d SETS
*PRIME/25: 1X TO 2.5X BASIC JSYs
PRIME PRINT RUN 25 SER.#'d SETS
1 LaDainian Tomlinson 4.00 10.00
2 Larry Johnson 2.50 6.00
3 Frank Gore 3.00 8.00
4 Tiki Barber 3.00 8.00
5 Steven Jackson 2.50 6.00
6 Willie Parker 3.00 8.00
7 Drew Brees 4.00 10.00
8 Peyton Manning 10.00 25.00
9 Carson Palmer 3.00 8.00
10 Brett Favre 8.00 20.00
11 Tom Brady 12.00 30.00
12 Ben Roethlisberger 4.00 10.00
13 Philip Rivers 4.00 10.00
14 Chad Johnson 2.50 6.00
15 Marvin Harrison 3.00 8.00
16 Reggie Wayne 3.00 8.00
17 Roy Williams WR 2.50 6.00
18 Lee Evans 3.00 8.00
19 Anquan Boldin 2.50 6.00
20 Torry Holt 3.00 8.00
21 Terrell Owens 3.00 8.00
22 Steve Smith 3.00 8.00
23 Reggie Bush 2.50 6.00
24 Vince Young 2.50 6.00
25 Maurice Jones-Drew 2.50 6.00

2007 Leaf Limited Banner Season Autograph Materials

STATED PRINT RUN 25 SER.#'d SETS
*PRIME/15: .6X TO 1.5X BASIC JSY AU/25
PRIME AU PRINT RUN 5-15
1 LaDainian Tomlinson 30.00 80.00
2 Larry Johnson 20.00 50.00
3 Frank Gore 15.00 40.00
4 Tiki Barber
5 Steven Jackson 20.00 50.00
6 Willie Parker 20.00 50.00
7 Drew Brees 40.00 80.00
8 Peyton Manning 75.00 150.00
10 Brett Favre 125.00 200.00
12 Ben Roethlisberger 50.00 100.00
14 Chad Johnson 15.00 40.00
15 Marvin Harrison 20.00 50.00
16 Reggie Wayne 15.00 40.00
17 Roy Williams WR 15.00 40.00
19 Anquan Boldin 12.00 30.00
20 Torry Holt 15.00 40.00
22 Steve Smith 15.00 40.00
23 Reggie Bush 20.00 50.00
24 Vince Young 15.00 40.00
25 Maurice Jones-Drew 15.00 40.00

2007 Leaf Limited College Phenoms Autographs

STATED PRINT RUN 25 SER.#'d SETS
UNPRICED SILVER PRINT RUN 10
UNPRICED GOLD PRINT RUN 5
UNPRICED PLATINUM PRINT RUN 1
301 Adrian Peterson 150.00 300.00
302 Anthony Gonzalez 6.00 15.00
303 Antonio Pittman 6.00 15.00
304 Aundrae Allison 6.00 15.00
305 Brady Quinn JSY 6.00 15.00
306 Brandon Jackson 6.00 15.00
307 Brian Leonard 6.00 15.00
308 Calvin Johnson 75.00 150.00
313 Drew Stanton 6.00 15.00
314 Dwayne Bowe 6.00 15.00
315 Dwayne Jarrett JSY 8.00 20.00
317 Gaines Adams 8.00 20.00
318 Garrett Wolfe 6.00 15.00
319 Greg Olsen 10.00 25.00
321 Jacoby Jones 6.00 15.00
322 JaMarcus Russell JSY 6.00 15.00
323 James Jones 6.00 15.00
324 Jason Hill 6.00 15.00
327 John Beck 6.00 15.00
328 Johnnie Lee Higgins 6.00 15.00
329 Jordan Palmer JSY 8.00 20.00
331 Kevin Kolb 8.00 20.00
332 Kolby Smith 6.00 15.00
333 LaRon Landry 10.00 25.00
335 Lawrence Timmons 10.00 25.00
336 Leon Hall 6.00 15.00
337 Lorenzo Booker 8.00 20.00
338 Marshawn Lynch 30.00 60.00
339 Michael Bush JSY 6.00 15.00
341 Patrick Willis 10.00 25.00
342 Paul Posluszny 6.00 15.00
344 Reggie Nelson 6.00 15.00
345 Robert Meachem 8.00 20.00
347 Sidney Rice 25.00 50.00
348 Steve Breaston 6.00 15.00
349 Steve Smith USC 6.00 15.00
350 Ted Ginn Jr. 8.00 20.00
351 Tony Hunt 6.00 15.00
352 Trent Edwards 6.00 15.00
353 Troy Smith 6.00 15.00
354 Yamon Figurs 6.00 15.00
355 Zach Miller 6.00 15.00

2007 Leaf Limited Contenders Preview Autographs

STATED PRINT RUN 25-50
RTP1 Marshawn Lynch/25 60.00 120.00
RTP2 Adrian Peterson/25 250.00 400.00
RTP3 Sidney Rice/50 25.00 50.00
RTP4 Brandon Jackson/50 6.00 15.00
RTP5 Kenny Irons/50 6.00 15.00
RTP6 Brady Quinn/25 8.00 20.00
RTP7 Calvin Johnson/25 75.00 150.00
RTP8 Steve Smith USC/25 15.00 40.00
RTP9 Dwayne Jarrett/50 8.00 20.00
RTP10 Ted Ginn/50 8.00 20.00
RTP11 Dwayne Bowe/50 20.00 50.00
RTP12 Greg Olsen/50 10.00 25.00
RTP13 Anthony Gonzalez/50 6.00 15.00
RTP14 JaMarcus Russell/25 8.00 20.00
RTP15 Michael Bush/50 6.00 15.00
RTP16 Kevin Kolb/50 8.00 20.00
RTP17 Patrick Willis/50 40.00 80.00
RTP18 Jason Hill/50 6.00 15.00

2007 Leaf Limited Cuts Autographs

STATED PRINT RUN 5-150
SER.#'d UNDER 20 NOT PRICED
1 Red Badgro/60 50.00 120.00
2 Tony Canadeo/150 30.00 80.00
3 George Connor/100 25.00 60.00
4 Weeb Ewbank/50 30.00 80.00
5 Ray Flaherty/74 40.00 100.00
6 Lou Groza/68 30.00 80.00
7 Mel Hein/75 50.00 120.00
8 Bulldog Turner/75 50.00 100.00
9 Roosevelt Brown/150 20.00 50.00
10 Ernie Stautner/150 25.00 60.00
11 Ken Strong/100 30.00 80.00
12 Elroy Hirsch/50 30.00 80.00
13 Doak Walker/30 125.00 250.00
15 Sammy Baugh/33 75.00 200.00
18 Otto Graham/30 125.00 250.00
23 Jim Parker/73 25.00 60.00
24 Ace Parker/50 50.00 120.00

2007 Leaf Limited Hardwear

STATED PRINT RUN 93-150
*LIMITED/22-44: 1X TO 2.5X BASIC INSERTS
LIMITED PRINT RUN 22-44
1 Phil Simms/110 8.00 20.00
2 Roger Craig/100 10.00 25.00
3 Ted Hendricks/150 6.00 15.00
4 Ronnie Lott/105 8.00 20.00
5 Darrell Green/93 10.00 25.00

2007 Leaf Limited Hardwear Autographs

ATED PRINT RUN 25 SER.#'d SETS
*LIMITED/25: .8X TO 2X BASIC AUTOs
LIMITED PRINT RUN 25 SER.#'d SETS
1 Phil Simms 40.00 80.00
2 Roger Craig 40.00 80.00
4 Ronnie Lott 50.00 100.00
5 Darrell Green 60.00 120.00

2007 Leaf Limited Jumbo Jerseys

STATED PRINT RUN 50 SER.#'d SETS
*PRIME/10: .8X TO 2X BASIC JSY/50
PRIME PRINT RUN 10 SER.#'d SETS
*NUMBERS/80-87: .3X TO .8X BASIC JSY/50
*NUMBERS/32-39: .5X TO 1.2X BASIC JSY/50
*NUMBERS/21-25: .6X TO 1.5X BASIC JSY/50
*NUMBERS/10-18: .8X TO 2X BASIC JSY/50
NUMBERS STATED PRINT RUN 4-87
*NUM.PRIME/10: .8X TO 2X BASIC JSY/50
NUMBERS PRIME STATED PRINT RUN 10
*TEAM LOGO/50: .4X TO 1X BASIC JSY/50
TEAM LOGO PRINT RUN 50 SER.#'d SETS
*TM LOGO PRIME/10: .8X TO 2X BASIC JSY/50
TEAM LOGO PRIME PRINT RUN 10
1 Carson Palmer 4.00 10.00
2 Tom Brady 15.00 40.00
3 Marc Bulger 3.00 8.00
4 Chad Pennington 3.00 8.00
5 J.P. Losman 3.00 8.00
6 Alex Smith QB 4.00 10.00
7 Matt Hasselbeck 3.00 8.00
8 Edgerrin James 4.00 10.00
9 Shaun Alexander 3.00 8.00
10 Lee Evans 4.00 10.00
11 Terrell Owens 4.00 10.00
12 Andre Johnson 4.00 10.00
13 Laveranues Coles 3.00 8.00
14 Brett Favre 10.00 25.00
15 Peyton Manning 12.00 30.00
16 Donovan McNabb 4.00 10.00
17 Drew Brees 5.00 12.00
18 LaDainian Tomlinson 5.00 12.00
19 Frank Gore 4.00 10.00
20 Steven Jackson 3.00 8.00
21 Brian Westbrook 3.00 8.00
22 Reggie Bush 3.00 8.00
23 Vince Young 3.00 8.00
24 Torry Holt 4.00 10.00
25 Eli Manning 4.00 10.00

2007 Leaf Limited Lettermen

PRICED LETTERMEN PRINT RUN 4-9

2007 Leaf Limited Matching Numbers Jerseys

STATED PRINT RUN 100 SER.#'d SETS
*PRIME/25: .8X TO 2X BASIC JSYs
PRIME PRINT RUN 25 SER.#'d SETS
*POSITION/100: .4X TO 1X BASIC JSYs
POSITIONS PRINT RUN 100 SER.#'d SETS
*POS.PRIME/25: .8X TO 2X BASIC JSYs
POSITIONS PRIME PRINT RUN 25
1 M.Bulger/V.Young 2.50 6.00
2 J.McMahon/D.Brees 5.00 12.00
3 J.Namath/T.Brady 15.00 40.00
4 J.Elway/M.Leinart 6.00 15.00
5 B.Griese/R.Cunningham 4.00 10.00
6 T.Brown/T.Owens 4.00 10.00
7 F.Harris/M.Jones-Drew 4.00 10.00
8 T.Barber/L.Tomlinson 4.00 10.00
9 T.Gonzalez/M.Harrison 3.00 8.00
10 M.Hasselbeck/S.Young 5.00 12.00
11 L.Coles/R.Wayne 3.00 8.00
12 S.Largent/D.Driver 4.00 10.00
13 R.Bush/L.White 3.00 8.00
14 S.Jurgensen/T.Romo 5.00 12.00
15 P.Hornung/D.McNabb 4.00 10.00
16 F.Tarkenton/E.Manning 4.00 10.00
17 C.Joiner/P.Manning 10.00 25.00
18 L.Csonka/W.Parker 4.00 10.00
19 A.Gates/V.Davis 4.00 10.00
20 B.Jacobs/L.Johnson 2.50 6.00

2007 Leaf Limited Material Monikers Jersey Number

*MAT.MONIKER/66-99: .25X TO .6X PRIME/25
*MAT.MONIKER/34-60: .3X TO .8X PRIME/25
*MAT.MONIKER/21-32: .4X TO 1X PRIME/25
*MAT.MONIKER/10-18: .5X TO 1.2X PRIME/25
STATED PRINT RUN 1-99 SER.#'d SETS
1 Marques Colston/12 25.00 60.00
2 Larry Johnson/27 20.00 50.00
3 Raymond Berry/82 12.00 30.00
4 Cedric Benson/32 20.00 50.00
5 Dan Fouts/14 30.00 80.00
6 Maurice Jones-Drew/32 15.00 40.00
7 Peyton Manning/18 100.00 200.00
8 Frank Gore/21 20.00 50.00
9 Steven Jackson/39 15.00 40.00
10 Rudi Johnson/32 15.00 40.00
11 Joe Montana/16 150.00 300.00
12 Joe Namath/12 60.00 150.00
13 Steve Largent/80 15.00 40.00
15 Jim Brown/32 50.00 120.00
16 John Riggins/44 15.00 40.00
17 Marion Barber/24 25.00 60.00
18 Chuck Bednarik/60 20.00 50.00
19 Cris Collinsworth/80 12.00 30.00
20 Randall Cunningham/12 25.00 60.00
22 A.J. Hawk/50 15.00 40.00
24 Ladell Betts/46 10.00 25.00
25 Thurman Thomas/34 15.00 40.00
26 Reggie Bush/25 20.00 50.00
27 Roger Staubach/12 60.00 150.00
28 Tim Brown/81 15.00 40.00
29 Dan Marino/13 150.00 300.00
30 Dan Hampton/99 12.00 30.00
31 Larry Little/66 10.00 25.00
34 Deacon Jones/75 12.00 30.00
36 Charley Taylor/42 15.00 40.00
37 Hank Baskett/84 10.00 25.00
38 Charlie Joiner/18 20.00 50.00
39 Don Maynard/13 15.00 40.00
40 Gale Sayers/40 30.00 80.00
41 Steve Smith/89 10.00 25.00
42 James Lofton/80 10.00 25.00
43 Chad Johnson/85 10.00 25.00
44 Bart Starr/15 175.00 350.00
46 Brian Westbrook/36 12.00 30.00
47 Ozzie Newsome/82 12.00 30.00
48 LaDainian Tomlinson/21 40.00 100.00
49 Reggie Wayne/87 10.00 25.00

2007 Leaf Limited Material Monikers Jersey Number Prime

PRIME PRINT RUN 4-25
1 Marques Colston 12.00 30.00
2 Larry Johnson 12.00 30.00
4 Cedric Benson 12.00 30.00
5 Dan Fouts 20.00 50.00
6 Maurice Jones-Drew 15.00 40.00
7 Peyton Manning 75.00 150.00
8 Frank Gore 15.00 40.00
9 Steven Jackson 12.00 30.00
10 Rudi Johnson 12.00 30.00
11 Joe Montana 125.00 250.00
12 Joe Namath 60.00 120.00
13 Steve Largent 25.00 60.00
15 Jim Brown 60.00 120.00
16 John Riggins 20.00 50.00
17 Marion Barber 15.00 40.00
18 Chuck Bednarik 25.00 60.00
19 Cris Collinsworth 20.00 50.00
20 Randall Cunningham 20.00 50.00
21 Sonny Jurgensen 20.00 50.00
22 A.J. Hawk 12.00 30.00
23 Eli Manning 15.00 40.00
24 Ladell Betts 12.00 30.00
25 Thurman Thomas 20.00 50.00
26 Reggie Bush 30.00 80.00
27 Roger Staubach 60.00 120.00
28 Tim Brown 25.00 60.00
29 Dan Marino 125.00 250.00
30 Dan Hampton 20.00 50.00
31 Larry Little 15.00 40.00
33 Jan Stenerud 15.00 40.00
34 Deacon Jones 20.00 50.00
35 Steve Young 50.00 100.00
36 Charley Taylor 15.00 40.00
37 Hank Baskett 15.00 40.00
39 Don Maynard 20.00 50.00
40 Gale Sayers 50.00 100.00
41 Steve Smith 15.00 40.00
42 James Lofton 15.00 40.00
43 Chad Johnson 12.00 30.00
44 Bart Starr 150.00 300.00
45 Brett Favre 125.00 200.00
46 Brian Westbrook 12.00 30.00
47 Ozzie Newsome 20.00 50.00
48 LaDainian Tomlinson 40.00 100.00
49 Reggie Wayne 15.00 40.00

2007 Leaf Limited Monikers Autographs Silver

*SILVER/99: .5X TO 1.2X BASIC AU/194-299
SILVER PRINT RUN 99 SER.#'d SETS
*GOLD/49: .6X TO 1.5X BASIC AU/194-299
GOLD PRINT RUN 49 SER.#'d SETS
UNPRICED PLATINUM PRINT RUN 1

2007 Leaf Limited Prime Pairings Autographs

ATED PRINT RUN 10-100
SERIAL #'d UNDER 25 NOT PRICED
1 F.Harris/W.Parker/25 75.00 125.00
2 P.Manning/E.Manning/25 100.00 200.00
3 McMahon/Grossman/25 30.00 60.00
4 J.Kelly/T.Thomas/25 60.00 100.00
5 R.Craig/F.Gore/25 20.00 50.00
6 D.Marino/M.Duper/25 100.00 200.00
7 J.Namath/D.Maynard/25 60.00 100.00
10 B.Griese/L.Csonka/25 60.00 100.00
11 Collinsworth/C.Johnson/25 30.00 60.00
12 Hill/Casares/Morris/100 30.00 60.00
13 Fts/Jnr/Wnslw/25 60.00 100.00
14 M.Allen/L.Johnson/25
15 J.Mackey/J.Orr/25 20.00 50.00
16 J.Stallworth/H.Ward/25 75.00 125.00
17 M.Harrison/R.Wayne/25 50.00 100.00
19 P.Simms/J.Kelly/25 30.00 80.00
20 S.Jurgensen/J.Theismann/25 40.00 80.00
21 T.Brown/J.Lofton/25 30.00 60.00
22 R.Lott/D.Green/25 60.00 120.00
24 Jones/Olsen/Grier/25 60.00 100.00
25 Hwtn/Dwlr/Lftn/Shrpe/25 75.00 150.00
26 Brown/Sndrs/Tomlin/15 150.00 300.00

2007 Leaf Limited Rookie Jumbo Jersey Numbers

STATED PRINT RUN 2-90
UNPRICED PRIME PRINT RUN 2-10
SERIAL #'d UNDER 15 NOT PRICED
1 Sidney Rice/18 4.00 10.00
2 Kenny Irons/30 2.00 5.00
4 Calvin Johnson/81 5.00 12.00
6 Joe Thomas/73 2.50 6.00
7 Marshawn Lynch/23 5.00 12.00
9 Antonio Pittman/24 2.50 6.00
11 Adrian Peterson/28 8.00 20.00
12 Brandon Jackson/32 2.00 5.00
13 Chris Henry RB/42 2.00 5.00
14 Yamon Figurs/16 3.00 8.00
15 Robert Meachem/17 4.00 10.00
16 Garrett Wolfe/25 2.50 6.00
17 Brian Leonard/23 2.50 6.00
18 Tony Hunt/29 2.50 6.00
21 Greg Olsen/82 2.50 6.00
24 Dwayne Jarrett/80 2.00 5.00
25 Johnnie Lee Higgins/15 3.00 8.00
27 Ted Ginn Jr./19 4.00 10.00
28 Patrick Willis/52 2.50 6.00
29 Lorenzo Booker/20 3.00 8.00
31 Gaines Adams/90 2.00 5.00
32 Jason Hill/89 1.50 4.00
33 Dwayne Bowe/82 1.50 4.00
34 Michael Bush/43 2.00 5.00

2007 Leaf Limited Rookie Jumbo Jersey Numbers Autographs

ATED PRINT RUN 25 SER.#'d SETS
UNPRICED PRIME PRINT RUN 5
1 Sidney Rice 8.00 20.00
2 Kenny Irons No AU 6.00 15.00
3 Trent Edwards 6.00 15.00
4 Calvin Johnson 60.00 120.00
5 Drew Stanton 6.00 15.00
6 Joe Thomas 10.00 25.00
7 Marshawn Lynch 30.00 80.00
8 Brady Quinn 6.00 15.00
9 Antonio Pittman 6.00 15.00
10 Paul Williams 6.00 15.00
11 Adrian Peterson 250.00 400.00
12 Brandon Jackson 6.00 15.00
13 Chris Henry RB 6.00 15.00
14 Yamon Figurs 6.00 15.00
15 Robert Meachem 8.00 20.00
16 Garrett Wolfe 6.00 15.00
17 Brian Leonard 6.00 15.00
18 Tony Hunt 6.00 15.00
19 Kevin Kolb 8.00 20.00
20 Steve Smith USC 15.00 40.00
21 Greg Olsen 10.00 25.00
22 JaMarcus Russell 15.00 40.00
23 Anthony Gonzalez 6.00 15.00
24 Dwayne Jarrett 8.00 20.00
25 Johnnie Lee Higgins 6.00 15.00
26 Troy Smith 6.00 15.00
27 Ted Ginn Jr. 15.00 40.00
28 Patrick Willis 25.00 60.00
29 Lorenzo Booker 8.00 20.00
30 John Beck 6.00 15.00
31 Gaines Adams 8.00 20.00
32 Jason Hill 6.00 15.00
33 Dwayne Bowe 12.00 30.00
34 Michael Bush 6.00 15.00

2007 Leaf Limited Slideshow Autographs

STATED PRINT RUN 30 SER.#'d SETS
1 Trent Edwards 6.00 15.00
2 Marshawn Lynch 15.00 40.00
3 Chris Henry RB 6.00 15.00
4 Paul Williams 6.00 15.00
5 Sidney Rice 8.00 20.00
6 Adrian Peterson 250.00 400.00
7 Drew Stanton 6.00 15.00
8 Calvin Johnson 60.00 150.00
9 Yamon Figurs 6.00 15.00
10 Brian Leonard 6.00 15.00
11 Garrett Wolfe 6.00 15.00
12 Kenny Irons 6.00 15.00
13 Joe Thomas 10.00 25.00
14 Brady Quinn 6.00 15.00
15 Brandon Jackson 6.00 15.00
16 Steve Smith USC 12.00 30.00
17 Dwayne Jarrett 8.00 20.00
18 Troy Smith 6.00 15.00
19 Ted Ginn Jr. 8.00 20.00
20 John Beck 6.00 15.00
21 Lorenzo Booker 8.00 20.00
22 Antonio Pittman 6.00 15.00
23 Robert Meachem 8.00 20.00
24 Dwayne Bowe 6.00 15.00
25 Greg Olsen 10.00 25.00
26 Anthony Gonzalez 6.00 15.00
27 JaMarcus Russell 6.00 15.00
28 Michael Bush 6.00 15.00
29 Johnnie Lee Higgins 6.00 15.00
30 Kevin Kolb 8.00 20.00
31 Tony Hunt 6.00 15.00
32 Patrick Willis 20.00 50.00
33 Jason Hill 6.00 15.00
34 Gaines Adams 8.00 20.00

2007 Leaf Limited Team Threads Dual

STATED PRINT RUN 100 SER.#'d SETS
*PRIME/20-25: .8X TO 2X BASIC DUAL/100
PRIME PRINT RUN 4-25
1 S.Young/R.Lott 6.00 15.00
2 D.Butkus/M.Singletary 6.00 15.00
3 J.Kelly/T.Thomas 5.00 12.00
4 J.Brown/L.Groza 6.00 15.00
5 D.Fouts/K.Winslow Sr. 4.00 10.00
6 L.Dawson/J.Stenerud 5.00 12.00
7 B.Griese/L.Csonka 5.00 12.00
8 R.Brown/S.Huff 4.00 10.00
9 J.Namath/D.Maynard 6.00 15.00
10 B.Starr/P.Hornung 25.00 50.00
11 G.Blanda/F.Biletnikoff 5.00 12.00
12 M.Allen/T.Brown 5.00 12.00
13 M.Olsen/R.Grier 3.00 8.00
14 J.Theismann/J.Riggins 5.00 12.00
15 J.Lambert/J.Greene 12.00 30.00

2007 Leaf Limited Team Threads Triples

STATED PRINT RUN 65-100
*PRIME/25: .8X TO 2X BASIC TRIPLE/65-100
PRIME PRINT RUN 5-25
1 Young/Lott/Craig/65 12.00 30.00
2 McMahon/Singletary/Hampton 12.00 30.00
3 Brown/Graham/Groza 12.00 30.00
4 Fouts/Alworth/Winslow Sr. 12.00 30.00
5 Griese/Csonka/Little 10.00 25.00
6 Starr/Hornung/Nitschke 15.00 40.00
7 Blanda/Lamonica/Stabler 12.00 30.00
8 Olsen/Grier/Youngblood 8.00 20.00
9 Baugh/Jurgensen/Theismann 20.00 50.00
10 Harris/Greene/Lambert 15.00 40.00
11 Staubach/Aikman/Romo 12.00 30.00

2007 Leaf Limited Team Threads Quads

STATED PRINT RUN 100 SER.#'d SETS
*PRIME/25: .6X TO 1.5X BASIC QUAD/100
PRIME PRINT RUN 1-25
1 Young/Lott/Smith QB/Gore 20.00 50.00
2 Butkus/Single/Hamp/Urlacher 25.00 60.00
3 Kelly/Thomas/Losman/Evans 12.00 30.00
4 Fouts/Wins Sr/Rivers/Gates 12.00 30.00
5 Griese/Csonka/Chamb/Brown 12.00 30.00
6 Brown/Huff/Manning/Shockey 10.00 25.00
7 Namath/Maynard/Penn/Coles 15.00 40.00
8 Starr/Hornung/Favre/Driver 25.00 60.00
9 Blanda/Biletnikoff/Allen/Brown 12.00 30.00
10 Lambert/Greene/Ward/Parker 15.00 40.00

2007 Leaf Limited Team Trademarks

ATED PRINT RUN 100 SER.#'d SETS
*HOLOFOIL/25: .8X TO 2X BASIC INSERTS
HOLOFOIL PRINT RUN 25 SER.#'d SETS
1 John Elway 5.00 10.00
2 Vince Young 1.50 4.00
3 Merlin Olsen 2.00 5.00
4 Brandon Jacobs 1.50 4.00
5 Vernon Davis 1.50 4.00
6 Mark Duper 2.00 5.00
7 Chester Taylor 1.50 4.00
8 Sterling Sharpe 2.50 6.00
9 Carson Palmer 2.00 5.00
10 T.J. Houshmandzadeh 1.50 4.00
11 Lee Roy Selmon 2.00 5.00
12 Torry Holt 2.00 5.00
13 Jack Youngblood 2.50 6.00
14 Barry Sanders 5.00 12.00
15 Cadillac Williams 2.00 5.00
16 Matt Leinart 1.50 4.00
17 Kellen Winslow Sr. 2.50 6.00
18 Jim Kelly 3.00 8.00
19 Ron Mix 2.00 5.00
20 Sam Huff 2.50 6.00
21 Franco Harris 3.00 8.00
22 Dick Butkus 4.00 10.00
23 Joe Greene 3.00 8.00
24 Paul Hornung 3.00 8.00
25 Rosey Grier 2.00 5.00
26 Fran Tarkenton 3.00 8.00
27 Marvin Harrison 2.00 5.00
28 George Blanda 2.50 6.00
29 Ronnie Lott 2.50 6.00
30 Jack Lambert 3.00 8.00
31 Bob Griese 3.00 8.00
32 Daryle Lamonica 2.00 5.00
33 Len Dawson 3.00 8.00
34 Mike Singletary 3.00 8.00
35 Tom Brady 8.00 20.00
36 Larry Csonka 3.00 8.00
37 Jim McMahon 4.00 10.00
38 Marcus Allen 3.00 8.00
39 Earl Campbell 3.00 8.00
40 Drew Brees 2.50 6.00

2007 Leaf Limited Team Trademarks Materials

STATED PRINT RUN 99 SER.#'d SETS
*PRIME/50: .6X TO 1.5X BASIC JSY/99
*PRIME/25: .8X TO 2X BASIC JSY/99
PRIME PRINT RUN 25-50
*TEAM LOGO/50: .5X TO 1.2X BASIC JSY/99
TEAM LOGO PRINT RUN 50
1 John Elway 8.00 20.00
2 Vince Young 2.50 6.00
3 Merlin Olsen 3.00 8.00
4 Brandon Jacobs 2.50 6.00
5 Vernon Davis 2.50 6.00
6 Mark Duper 3.00 8.00
7 Chester Taylor 2.50 6.00
8 Sterling Sharpe 4.00 10.00
9 Carson Palmer 3.00 8.00
10 T.J. Houshmandzadeh 2.50 6.00
11 Lee Roy Selmon 3.00 8.00
12 Torry Holt 3.00 8.00
13 Jack Youngblood 4.00 10.00
14 Barry Sanders 8.00 20.00
15 Cadillac Williams 3.00 8.00
16 Matt Leinart 2.50 6.00
17 Kellen Winslow Sr. 4.00 10.00
18 Jim Kelly 5.00 12.00
19 Ron Mix 3.00 8.00
20 Sam Huff 4.00 10.00
21 Franco Harris 5.00 12.00
22 Dick Butkus 6.00 15.00
23 Joe Greene 5.00 12.00
24 Paul Hornung 5.00 12.00
25 Rosey Grier 3.00 8.00
26 Fran Tarkenton 5.00 12.00
27 Marvin Harrison 3.00 8.00
28 George Blanda 4.00 10.00
30 Jack Lambert 5.00 12.00
31 Bob Griese 5.00 12.00
32 Daryle Lamonica 3.00 8.00
33 Len Dawson 5.00 12.00
34 Mike Singletary 5.00 12.00
35 Tom Brady 12.00 30.00
36 Larry Csonka 5.00 12.00
37 Jim McMahon 6.00 15.00
38 Marcus Allen 5.00 12.00
39 Earl Campbell 5.00 12.00
40 Drew Brees 4.00 10.00

2007 Leaf Limited Team Trademarks Autograph Materials

STATED PRINT RUN 25 SER.#'d SETS
*PRIME/15: .5X TO 1.2X BASIC JSY AU/25
PRIME PRINT RUN 5-15
*TEAM LOGO/25: .4X TO 1X BASE JSY AU/25
TEAM LOGO PRINT RUN 25 SER.#'d SETS
1 John Elway 60.00 120.00
2 Vince Young 12.00 30.00
3 Merlin Olsen 15.00 40.00
4 Brandon Jacobs 12.00 30.00
5 Vernon Davis 12.00 30.00
6 Mark Duper 15.00 40.00
7 Chester Taylor 12.00 30.00
8 Sterling Sharpe 20.00 50.00
10 T.J. Houshmandzadeh 12.00 30.00
11 Lee Roy Selmon 25.00 60.00
12 Torry Holt 6.00 15.00
13 Jack Youngblood 20.00 50.00
14 Barry Sanders 75.00 150.00
15 Cadillac Williams 15.00 40.00
17 Kellen Winslow Sr. 20.00 50.00
18 Jim Kelly 25.00 60.00
19 Ron Mix 15.00 40.00
20 Sam Huff 20.00 50.00
21 Franco Harris 25.00 60.00
23 Joe Greene 25.00 60.00
24 Paul Hornung 30.00 80.00
25 Rosey Grier 15.00 40.00
26 Fran Tarkenton 25.00 60.00
27 Marvin Harrison 15.00 40.00
28 George Blanda 25.00 60.00
29 Ronnie Lott 20.00 50.00
30 Jack Lambert 40.00 80.00
31 Bob Griese 20.00 50.00
32 Daryle Lamonica 15.00 40.00
33 Len Dawson 20.00 50.00
34 Mike Singletary 20.00 50.00
36 Larry Csonka 25.00 60.00
37 Jim McMahon 20.00 50.00
38 Marcus Allen 25.00 60.00
39 Earl Campbell 20.00 50.00
40 Drew Brees 50.00 100.00

2007 Leaf Limited Threads

STATED PRINT RUN 100 SER.#'d SETS
*PRIME/25: .8X TO 2X BASIC JSY/100
*PRIME/10-15: 1.2X TO 3X BASIC JSY/100
PRIME PRINT RUN 2-25
*PRIM JSY #/58-99: .6X TO 1.5X BASIC JSY/100
*PRIM JSY #/32-51: 1X TO 2.5X BASIC JSY/100
*PRIM JSY #/20-29: 1.2X TO 3X BASIC JSY/100
*PRIM JSY #/10-19: 1.5X TO 4X BASIC JSY/100
PRIME JERSEY NUMBER PRINT RUN 1-99
*PRIME TEAM LOGO/10: 1.2X TO 3X BASIC JSY/100
PRIME TEAM LOGO PRINT RUN 5-10
UNPRICED SUPER PRIME PRINT RUN 1
1 Anquan Boldin 2.50 6.00
2 Edgerrin James 3.00 8.00
3 Larry Fitzgerald 3.00 8.00
4 Matt Leinart 2.50 6.00
5 Alge Crumpler 3.00 8.00
6 Warrick Dunn 2.50 6.00
7 Jerious Norwood 2.50 6.00
9 Steve McNair 3.00 8.00
10 Mark Clayton 2.50 6.00
12 J.P. Losman 2.50 6.00
13 Lee Evans 3.00 8.00
14 Jake Delhomme 2.50 6.00
15 Steve Smith 3.00 8.00
16 DeAngelo Williams 2.50 6.00
17 Rex Grossman 2.50 6.00
18 Cedric Benson 2.50 6.00
19 Bernard Berrian 2.50 6.00
20 Carson Palmer 3.00 8.00
21 Chad Johnson 2.50 6.00
22 Rudi Johnson 2.50 6.00
23 T.J. Houshmandzadeh 2.50 6.00
24 Kellen Winslow 2.50 6.00
25 Braylon Edwards 2.50 6.00
27 Julius Jones 2.50 6.00
28 Terrell Owens 3.00 8.00
29 Tony Romo 5.00 12.00
30 Jay Cutler 2.50 6.00
31 Javon Walker 3.00 8.00
34 Roy Williams WR 2.50 6.00
35 Jon Kitna 2.50 6.00
36 Brett Favre 8.00 20.00
37 Donald Driver 3.00 8.00
38 Greg Jennings 2.50 6.00
40 Andre Johnson 3.00 8.00
42 Peyton Manning 8.00 20.00
43 Marvin Harrison 3.00 8.00
44 Reggie Wayne 3.00 8.00
45 Joseph Addai 2.50 6.00
47 Fred Taylor 2.50 6.00
48 Maurice Jones-Drew 2.50 6.00
49 Brodie Croyle 3.00 8.00
50 Larry Johnson 2.50 6.00
51 Tony Gonzalez 3.00 8.00
53 Ronnie Brown 2.50 6.00
54 Chris Chambers 2.50 6.00
55 Tarvaris Jackson 2.50 6.00
56 Troy Williamson 2.50 6.00
57 Chester Taylor 2.50 6.00
58 Tom Brady 8.00 20.00
59 Randy Moss 6.00 15.00
60 Laurence Maroney 3.00 8.00
62 Drew Brees 4.00 10.00
63 Deuce McAllister 3.00 8.00
64 Reggie Bush 2.50 6.00
65 Marques Colston 2.50 6.00
66 Eli Manning 3.00 8.00
67 Jeremy Shockey 2.50 6.00
68 Brandon Jacobs 2.50 6.00
69 Chad Pennington 2.50 6.00
71 Laveranues Coles 2.50 6.00
72 Jerry Porter 3.00 8.00
73 LaMont Jordan 3.00 8.00
74 Donovan McNabb 3.00 8.00
75 Brian Westbrook 2.50 6.00
76 Reggie Brown 2.50 6.00
77 Ben Roethlisberger 4.00 10.00
78 Hines Ward 3.00 8.00
79 Willie Parker 3.00 8.00
80 Philip Rivers 4.00 10.00
81 Antonio Gates 4.00 10.00
82 LaDainian Tomlinson 4.00 10.00
83 Alex Smith QB 3.00 8.00
85 Frank Gore 3.00 8.00
86 Matt Hasselbeck 2.50 6.00
87 Shaun Alexander 2.50 6.00
88 Deion Branch 2.50 6.00
89 Marc Bulger 2.50 6.00
90 Steven Jackson 2.50 6.00
91 Torry Holt 3.00 8.00
93 Cadillac Williams 3.00 8.00
94 Joey Galloway 3.00 8.00
95 Vince Young 2.50 6.00
96 Brandon Jones 2.50 6.00
97 LenDale White 3.00 8.00
98 Jason Campbell 2.50 6.00
99 Clinton Portis 2.50 6.00
100 Santana Moss 3.00 8.00
101 Alan Page 4.00 10.00
102 Barry Sanders 10.00 25.00
103 Bart Starr 10.00 25.00
106 Bob Griese 6.00 15.00
107 Bobby Layne 5.00 12.00
109 Charley Taylor 4.00 10.00
111 Charlie Joiner 4.00 10.00
112 Chuck Bednarik 8.00 20.00
113 Cris Collinsworth 5.00 12.00
114 Dan Fouts 5.00 12.00
115 Dan Hampton 6.00 15.00
116 Dan Marino 12.00 30.00
118 Darrell Green 5.00 12.00
119 Daryle Lamonica 4.00 10.00
120 Deacon Jones 5.00 12.00
121 Dick Butkus 8.00 20.00
122 Doak Walker 8.00 20.00
123 Don Maynard 5.00 12.00
126 Earl Campbell 6.00 15.00
127 Forrest Gregg 5.00 12.00
128 Fran Tarkenton 6.00 15.00
129 Franco Harris 6.00 15.00
130 Fred Biletnikoff 6.00 15.00
131 Gale Sayers 10.00 25.00
133 George Blanda 5.00 12.00
135 Jack Lambert 8.00 20.00
136 Jack Youngblood 5.00 12.00
137 James Lofton 4.00 10.00
138 Jan Stenerud 4.00 10.00
140 Jim Brown 8.00 20.00
141 Jim Kelly 6.00 15.00
142 Jim McMahon 6.00 15.00
143 Jim Otto 4.00 10.00
144 Jim Thorpe 60.00 100.00
146 Joe Greene 6.00 15.00
147 Joe Montana 20.00 50.00
148 Joe Namath 8.00 20.00
149 Joe Theismann 6.00 15.00
150 John Elway 10.00 25.00
152 John Riggins 5.00 12.00
155 Johnny Unitas 6.00 15.00
156 Kellen Winslow Sr. 5.00 12.00
157 Ken Stabler 8.00 20.00
158 Lance Alworth 8.00 20.00
159 Larry Csonka 6.00 15.00
160 Larry Little 4.00 10.00
161 Lee Roy Selmon 4.00 10.00
162 Len Dawson 6.00 15.00
163 Lou Groza 5.00 12.00
165 Marcus Allen 6.00 15.00
166 Mark Duper 4.00 10.00
167 Merlin Olsen 4.00 10.00
168 Mike Singletary 6.00 15.00
170 Otto Graham 8.00 20.00
171 Ozzie Newsome 5.00 12.00
172 Paul Hornung 6.00 15.00
173 Paul Warfield 5.00 12.00
174 Phil Simms 5.00 12.00
175 Randall Cunningham 5.00 12.00
176 Ray Nitschke 8.00 20.00
177 Raymond Berry 5.00 12.00
180 Ron Mix 4.00 10.00
182 Roger Staubach 8.00 20.00
183 Rosey Brown 4.00 10.00
184 Rosey Grier 4.00 10.00
186 Sam Huff 5.00 12.00
187 Sammy Baugh 12.00 30.00
188 Sid Luckman 12.00 30.00
189 Sonny Jurgensen 5.00 12.00
190 Sterling Sharpe 5.00 12.00
191 Steve Largent 6.00 15.00
192 Steve Young 8.00 20.00
193 Ted Hendricks 5.00 12.00
194 Thurman Thomas 5.00 12.00
195 Tim Brown 6.00 15.00
196 Tiki Barber 5.00 12.00
197 Troy Aikman 8.00 20.00
198 Walter Payton 15.00 40.00
199 Willie Brown 4.00 10.00
200 Elroy Hirsch 12.00 30.00

2008 Leaf Limited

This set was released on October 29, 2008. The base set consists of 333 cards. Cards 1-100 feature veterans, while cards 101-200 feature legends serial numbered of 499. Cards 201-300 have rookies serial numbered of 999 as well as some autographed rookies serial numbered of 99-299. Cards 301-334 are rookie jersey cards serial numbered of 99.

COMP.SET w/o SP's (100) 8.00 20.00
101-200 LEGEND PRINT RUN 499
BASE ROOKIE PRINT RUN 999
AU ROOKIE PRINT RUN 99-299
JSY ROOKIE PRINT RUN 99 SER.#'d SETS
1 Anquan Boldin .25 .60
2 Edgerrin James .30 .75
3 Larry Fitzgerald .30 .75
4 Kurt Warner .30 .75
5 Michael Turner .25 .60
6 Roddy White .25 .60
7 Joe Horn .25 .60
8 Derrick Mason .25 .60
9 Mark Clayton .25 .60
10 Willis McGahee .25 .60
11 Trent Edwards .25 .60
12 Marshawn Lynch .30 .75
13 Lee Evans .30 .75
14 Jake Delhomme .25 .60
15 Steve Smith .30 .75
16 DeAngelo Williams .25 .60
17 Rex Grossman .25 .60
18 Adrian Peterson Bears .25 .60
19 Devin Hester .30 .75
20 Carson Palmer .30 .75
21 Chris Perry .25 .60
22 T.J. Houshmandzadeh .25 .60
23 Chad Johnson .25 .60
24 Braylon Edwards .25 .60
25 Derek Anderson .25 .60
26 Jamal Lewis .30 .75
27 Tony Romo .30 .75
28 Terrell Owens .30 .75
29 Marion Barber .25 .60
30 Jason Witten .30 .75
31 Jay Cutler .25 .60
32 Selvin Young .25 .60
33 Brandon Marshall .30 .75
34 Jon Kitna .25 .60
35 Calvin Johnson .40 1.00
36 Roy Williams WR .25 .60
37 Aaron Rodgers .75 2.00
38 Donald Driver .30 .75
39 Greg Jennings .25 .60
40 Matt Schaub .25 .60
41 Andre Johnson .30 .75
42 Kevin Walter .30 .75
43 Peyton Manning 1.00 2.50
44 Joseph Addai .25 .60
45 Reggie Wayne .30 .75
46 David Garrard .25 .60
47 Fred Taylor .25 .60
48 Maurice Jones-Drew .25 .60
49 Reggie Williams .30 .75
50 Brodie Croyle .30 .75
51 Larry Johnson .25 .60
52 Tony Gonzalez .30 .75
53 Chad Pennington .25 .60
54 Ronnie Brown .25 .60
55 Ted Ginn Jr. .25 .60
56 Tarvaris Jackson .25 .60
57 Adrian Peterson .40 1.00
58 Chester Taylor .25 .60
59 Tom Brady 1.25 3.00
60 Randy Moss .30 .75
61 Laurence Maroney .30 .75
62 Drew Brees .40 1.00
63 Marques Colston .25 .60
64 Reggie Bush .25 .60
65 Eli Manning .30 .75
66 Plaxico Burress .25 .60
67 Brandon Jacobs .25 .60
68 Brett Favre 3.00 8.00
69 Jerricho Cotchery .25 .60
70 Laveranues Coles .25 .60
71 JaMarcus Russell .25 .60
72 Justin Fargas .25 .60
73 Ronald Curry .25 .60
74 Donovan McNabb .30 .75
75 Brian Westbrook .25 .60
76 Kevin Curtis .25 .60
77 Ben Roethlisberger .40 1.00
78 Willie Parker .30 .75
79 Santonio Holmes .25 .60
80 Philip Rivers .40 1.00
81 LaDainian Tomlinson .40 1.00
82 Antonio Gates .30 .75
83 J.T. O'Sullivan .25 .60
84 Frank Gore .30 .75
85 Isaac Bruce .40 1.00
86 Matt Hasselbeck .25 .60
87 Julius Jones .25 .60
88 Deion Branch .25 .60
89 Marc Bulger .25 .60
90 Steven Jackson .25 .60
91 Torry Holt .30 .75
92 Jeff Garcia .25 .60
93 Earnest Graham .25 .60
94 Joey Galloway .30 .75
95 Vince Young .25 .60
96 LenDale White .25 .60
97 Roydell Williams .25 .60
98 Jason Campbell .25 .60
99 Santana Moss .25 .60
100 Clinton Portis .25 .60
101 Alan Page 1.25 3.00
102 Bart Starr 3.00 8.00
103 Bert Jones 1.25 3.00
104 Bill Dudley 1.25 3.00
105 Billy Howton 1.25 3.00
106 Red Grange 2.50 6.00
107 Billy Sims 1.50 4.00
108 Bo Jackson 2.50 6.00
109 Bob Griese 2.00 5.00
110 Bob Lilly 1.50 4.00
111 Bob Waterfield 1.50 4.00
112 Bobby Bell 1.25 3.00
113 Brett Favre 4.00 10.00
114 Carl Eller 1.25 3.00
115 Charley Taylor 1.25 3.00
116 Charley Trippi 1.25 3.00
117 Chuck Foreman 1.25 3.00
118 Cliff Harris 1.25 3.00
119 Cris Collinsworth 1.50 4.00
120 Danny White 1.25 3.00
121 Dante Lavelli 1.25 3.00
122 Daryl Johnston 1.50 4.00
123 Daryle Lamonica 1.50 4.00
124 Deacon Jones 1.50 4.00
125 Del Shofner 1.25 3.00
126 Dick Butkus 2.50 6.00
127 Doak Walker 2.00 5.00
128 Don Perkins 1.25 3.00
129 Dub Jones 1.25 3.00
130 Forrest Gregg 1.25 3.00
131 Fran Tarkenton 2.00 5.00
132 Frank Gifford 2.00 5.00
133 Fred Biletnikoff 2.00 5.00
134 Fred Dryer 1.25 3.00
135 Fred Williamson 1.25 3.00
136 Gale Sayers 2.00 5.00
137 Gary Collins 1.25 3.00
138 Hugh McElhenny 1.25 3.00
139 Jack Lambert 2.00 5.00
140 James Lofton 1.25 3.00
141 Jan Stenerud 1.25 3.00
142 Jim McMahon 2.00 5.00
143 Jim Otto 1.25 3.00
144 Jim Taylor 2.00 5.00
145 Jim Thorpe 2.50 6.00
146 Joe Montana 6.00 15.00
147 John Riggins 1.50 4.00
148 John Matuszak 2.00 5.00
149 Johnny Unitas 3.00 8.00
150 Ken Stabler 2.00 5.00
152 Lance Alworth 1.50 4.00
153 Larry Little 1.25 3.00
154 Lee Roy Selmon 1.25 3.00
155 Lem Barney 1.25 3.00
156 Len Dawson 2.00 5.00
157 Lenny Moore 1.25 3.00
158 Leroy Kelly 1.50 4.00
159 Lydell Mitchell 1.25 3.00
160 Marcus Allen 2.00 5.00
161 Mark Duper 1.25 3.00
162 Mark Gastineau 1.25 3.00
163 Merlin Olsen 1.25 3.00
164 Mike Curtis 1.25 3.00
165 Norm Van Brocklin 1.50 4.00
166 Ollie Matson 1.50 4.00
167 Ozzie Newsome 1.50 4.00
168 Paul Hornung 2.00 5.00
169 Paul Krause 1.25 3.00
170 Paul Warfield 1.50 4.00
171 Pete Retzlaff 1.25 3.00
172 Phil Simms 1.50 4.00
173 Ace Parker 1.25 3.00
174 Randy White 1.50 4.00
175 Reggie White 2.00 5.00
176 Roger Craig 1.50 4.00
177 Ronnie Lott 1.50 4.00
178 Rosey Grier 1.25 3.00
179 Sammy Baugh 2.00 5.00
180 Sid Luckman 1.50 4.00
181 Sonny Jurgensen 1.50 4.00
182 Sterling Sharpe 1.50 4.00
183 Steve Largent 2.00 5.00
184 Ted Hendricks 1.25 3.00
185 Tiki Barber 1.50 4.00
186 Tim Brown 2.00 5.00
187 Tom Fears 1.25 3.00
188 Tommy McDonald 1.50 4.00
189 Tony Canadeo 1.25 3.00
190 Tony Dorsett 2.00 5.00
191 Troy Aikman 2.50 6.00
192 Walter Payton 4.00 10.00
193 Warren Moon 2.00 5.00
194 William Perry 1.25 3.00
195 Willie Lanier 1.25 3.00
196 Willie Brown 1.25 3.00
197 Willie Davis 1.25 3.00
198 Willie Wood 1.25 3.00
199 Y.A. Tittle 2.00 5.00
200 Yale Lary 1.25 3.00
201 Adrian Arrington AU/99 RC 3.00 8.00
202 Alex Brink RC 2.00 5.00
203 Ali Highsmith AU/99 RC 3.00 8.00
204 Allen Patrick RC 1.50 4.00
205 Andre Woodson AU/99 RC 3.00 8.00
206 Anthony Alridge RC 1.50 4.00
207 Antoine Cason AU/99 RC 4.00 10.00
208 Aqib Talib AU/199 RC 4.00 10.00
209 Arman Shields RC 2.00 5.00
210 Brad Cottam AU/99 RC 3.00 8.00
211 Brandon Flowers RC 2.00 5.00
212 Bruce Davis RC 2.00 5.00
213 Calais Campbell AU/299 RC 3.00 8.00
214 Caleb Campbell AU/99 RC 5.00 12.00
215 Chauncey Washington RC 2.00 5.00
216 Chevis Jackson RC 1.50 4.00
217 Chris Long AU/99 RC 10.00 25.00
218 Colt Brennan AU/99 RC 4.00 10.00
219 Cory Boyd RC 1.50 4.00
220 Craig Steltz RC 1.50 4.00
221 Craig Stevens RC 1.50 4.00
222 Curtis Lofton AU/99 RC 4.00 10.00
223 Dan Connor AU/299 RC 2.50 6.00
224 Dantrell Savage RC 2.00 5.00
225 Darius Reynaud AU/99 RC 3.00 8.00
226 Darrell Strong RC 2.00 5.00
227 Davone Bess AU/299 RC 6.00 15.00
228 Dennis Dixon AU/99 RC 8.00 20.00
229 Derek Fine RC 1.50 4.00
230 Derrick Harvey AU/299 RC 2.50 6.00
231 DJ Hall RC 1.50 4.00
232 Rodgers-Cromartie AU/299 RC 3.00 8.00
233 Erik Ainge AU/299 RC 2.50 6.00
234 Erin Henderson AU/99 RC 4.00 10.00
235 Ernie Wheelwright RC 2.00 5.00
236 Fred Davis AU/299 RC 2.50 6.00
237 Joe Jon Finley RC 1.50 4.00
238 Jacob Hester AU/99 RC 3.00 8.00
239 Jacob Tamme AU/299 RC 3.00 8.00
240 Jalen Parmele RC 2.00 5.00
241 Jamar Adams RC 1.50 4.00
242 Jason Rivers RC 1.50 4.00
243 Jaymar Johnson RC 1.50 4.00
244 Jed Collins RC 2.00 5.00
245 Jermichael Finley AU/99 RC 3.00 8.00
246 Jerod Mayo AU/99 RC 5.00 12.00
247 John Carlson AU/299 RC 2.50 6.00
248 Jonathan Hefney RC 1.50 4.00
249 Jordon Dizon AU/99 RC 3.00 8.00
250 Josh Johnson AU/299 RC 2.50 6.00
251 Josh Morgan RC 1.50 4.00
252 Justin Forsett RC 2.00 5.00
253 Kalvin McRae RC 1.50 4.00
254 Keenan Burton AU/299 RC 2.50 6.00
255 Keith Rivers AU/299 RC 2.50 6.00
256 Kellen Davis AU/99 RC 3.00 8.00
257 Kenneth Moore RC 1.50 4.00
258 Kenny Phillips AU/299 RC 2.50 6.00
259 Kentwan Balmer AU/299 RC 2.50 6.00
260 Kevin Robinson RC 1.50 4.00
261 Lavelle Hawkins AU/299 RC 3.00 8.00
262 L.Jackson AU/299 RC 2.50 6.00
263 Leodis McKelvin AU/299 RC 3.00 8.00
264 Marcus Henry RC 1.50 4.00
265 Marcus Monk RC 2.00 5.00
266 Marcus Smith RC 2.00 5.00
267 Marcus Thomas RC 2.00 5.00
268 Mark Bradford RC 1.50 4.00
269 M.Bennett AU/299 RC 5.00 12.00
270 Martin Rucker AU/299 RC 2.50 6.00
271 Matt Flynn AU/299 RC 2.50 6.00
272 Mike Jenkins AU/299 RC 2.50 6.00
273 Mike Hart AU/299 RC 2.50 6.00
274 Owen Schmitt RC 1.50 4.00
275 Pat Sims AU/299 RC 3.00 8.00
276 Patrick Lee RC 1.50 4.00
277 Paul Hubbard RC 1.50 4.00
278 Paul Smith RC 1.50 4.00
279 Peyton Hillis RC 2.50 6.00
280 Phillip Merling AU/299 RC 2.50 6.00
281 Pierre Garcon RC 5.00 12.00
282 Quentin Groves RC 2.00 5.00
283 Reggie Smith AU/99 RC 3.00 8.00
284 Ryan Grice-Mullen RC 1.50 4.00
285 Ryan Torain AU/99 RC 4.00 10.00
286 Sam Keller RC 1.50 4.00
287 Sedrick Ellis AU/299 RC 2.50 6.00
288 Shawn Crable RC 1.50 4.00
289 Simeon Castille RC 1.50 4.00
290 Tashard Choice AU/299 RC 2.50 6.00
291 Tavares Gooden RC 1.50 4.00
292 Terrell Thomas AU/99 RC 3.00 8.00
293 Terrence Wheatley RC 1.50 4.00
294 Thomas Brown AU/99 RC 3.00 8.00
295 Tim Hightower RC 2.00 5.00
296 Tracy Porter RC 2.00 5.00
297 V.Gholston AU/299 RC 2.50 6.00
298 Will Franklin RC 2.00 5.00
299 Xavier Adibi AU/299 RC 2.50 6.00
300 Xavier Omon RC 1.50 4.00
301 Andre Caldwell JSY AU RC 6.00 15.00
302 Brian Brohm JSY AU RC 6.00 15.00
303 Chad Henne JSY AU RC 8.00 20.00
304 Chris Johnson JSY AU RC 8.00 20.00
305 D.McFadden JSY AU RC 6.00 15.00
306 De.Jackson JSY AU RC 12.00 30.00
307 Devin Thomas JSY AU RC 6.00 15.00
308 Dexter Jackson JSY AU RC 10.00 25.00
309 Donnie Avery JSY AU RC 8.00 20.00
310 Dustin Keller JSY AU RC 8.00 20.00
311 Earl Bennett JSY AU RC 10.00 25.00
312 Early Doucet JSY AU RC 6.00 15.00
313 Eddie Royal JSY AU RC 6.00 15.00
314 Felix Jones JSY AU RC 6.00 15.00
315 G.Dorsey JSY AU RC EXCH 6.00 15.00
316 Harry Douglas JSY AU RC 8.00 20.00
317 Jake Long JSY AU RC 10.00 25.00
318 Jamaal Charles JSY AU RC 10.00 25.00
319 James Hardy JSY AU RC 6.00 15.00
320 Jerome Simpson JSY AU RC 8.00 20.00
321 Joe Flacco JSY AU RC 12.00 30.00
322 J.David Booty JSY AU RC 6.00 15.00
323 J.Stewart JSY AU RC 10.00 25.00
324 Jordy Nelson JSY AU RC 20.00 40.00
325 Kevin O'Connell JSY AU RC 6.00 15.00
326 Kevin Smith JSY AU RC 6.00 15.00
327 Limas Sweed JSY AU RC 6.00 15.00
328 Malcolm Kelly JSY AU RC 6.00 15.00
329 M.Manningham JSY AU RC 12.00 30.00
330 Matt Forte JSY AU RC 15.00 40.00
331 Matt Ryan JSY AU RC 30.00 80.00
332 R.Mendenhall JSY AU RC 6.00 15.00
333 Ray Rice JSY AU RC 6.00 15.00
334 Steve Slaton JSY AU RC 6.00 15.00

2008 Leaf Limited Bronze Spotlight

*VETS 1-100: 2.5X TO 6X BASIC CARDS
*LEGENDS 101-200: .6X TO 1.5X BASIC CARDS
COMMON ROOKIE (201-300) 1.50 4.00
ROOKIE SEMISTARS 2.00 5.00
ROOKIE UNL.STARS 2.50 6.00
STATED PRINT RUN 125 SER.#'d SETS
68 Brett Favre 5.00 12.00
217 Chris Long 2.00 5.00
218 Colt Brennan 2.00 5.00
227 Davone Bess 2.00 5.00
246 Jerod Mayo 2.50 6.00
271 Matt Flynn 1.50 4.00
273 Mike Hart 1.50 4.00
279 Peyton Hillis 2.50 6.00
295 Tim Hightower 2.00 5.00

2008 Leaf Limited Gold Spotlight

*VETS 1-100: 3X TO 8X BASIC CARDS
*LEGENDS 101-200: .8X TO 2X BASIC CARDS
*ROOKIES 201-300: .5X TO 1.2X BASIC CARDS
1-300 PRINT RUN 49 SER.#'d SETS
*JSY AU 301-334: .5X TO 1.2X BASE JSY AU
301-334 PRINT RUN 25 SER.#'d SETS
68 Brett Favre 6.00 15.00
321 Joe Flacco JSY 15.00 40.00
331 Matt Ryan JSY 40.00 100.00

2008 Leaf Limited Platinum Spotlight

UNPRICED PLATINUM PRINT RUN 1

2008 Leaf Limited Silver Spotlight

ETS 1-100: 2.5X TO 6X BASIC CARDS
*LEGENDS 101-200: .6X TO 1.5X BASIC CARDS
*ROOKIES 201-300: .4X TO 1X BRONZE
1-300 PRINT RUN 99 SER.#'d SETS
*JSY AU 301-334: .4X TO 1X BASE JSY AU
301-334 PRINT RUN 49 SER.#'d SETS
68 Brett Favre 5.00 12.00
304 Chris Johnson JSY 8.00 20.00
321 Joe Flacco JSY 12.00 30.00
331 Matt Ryan JSY 50.00 120.00

2008 Leaf Limited Banner Season

ATED PRINT RUN 999 SER.#'d SETS
*HOLOFOIL/100: .6X TO 1.5X BASIC INSERTS
HOLOFOIL PRINT RUN 100 SER.#'d SETS
1 Adrian Peterson .75 2.00
2 Anthony Gonzalez .50 1.25
3 Brandon Jacobs .50 1.25
4 Brandon Marshall .60 1.50
5 Brian Westbrook .50 1.25
6 Willie Parker .60 1.50
7 LaDainian Tomlinson .75 2.00
8 Reggie Wayne .60 1.50
9 Randy Moss .60 1.50
10 Chad Johnson .50 1.25
11 Larry Fitzgerald .60 1.50
12 Terrell Owens .60 1.50
13 Braylon Edwards .50 1.25
14 Marques Colston .50 1.25
15 Roddy White .50 1.25
16 Santonio Holmes .50 1.25
17 Tom Brady 2.50 6.00
18 Drew Brees .75 2.00
19 Tony Romo .60 1.50
20 Eli Manning .60 1.50
21 Joseph Addai .50 1.25
22 Patrick Crayton .60 1.50
23 Tony Gonzalez .60 1.50
24 Clinton Portis .50 1.25
25 Greg Jennings .50 1.25

2008 Leaf Limited Banner Season Autograph Materials

STATED PRINT RUN 5-25
*PRIME/16-25: .5X TO 1.2X BASIC JSY AU/25
PRIME PRINT RUN 1-25
SERIAL #'d UNDER 15 NOT PRICED
2 Anthony Gonzalez 10.00 25.00
3 Brandon Jacobs 10.00 25.00
4 Brandon Marshall 12.00 30.00
5 Brian Westbrook 10.00 25.00
6 Willie Parker 12.00 30.00
8 Reggie Wayne 12.00 30.00
10 Chad Johnson 10.00 25.00
13 Braylon Edwards 10.00 25.00
14 Marques Colston 10.00 25.00
15 Roddy White 10.00 25.00
18 Drew Brees 40.00 80.00
19 Tony Romo 50.00 100.00
21 Joseph Addai 10.00 25.00
22 Patrick Crayton 12.00 30.00
25 Greg Jennings 10.00 25.00

2008 Leaf Limited Banner Season Materials

STATED PRINT RUN 60-100
*PRIME/25: .8X TO 2X BASIC JSY
PRIME PRINT RUN 25 SER.#'d SETS
1 Adrian Peterson 3.00 8.00
2 Anthony Gonzalez 2.00 5.00
3 Brandon Jacobs 2.00 5.00
4 Brandon Marshall 2.50 6.00
5 Brian Westbrook 2.00 5.00
6 Willie Parker 2.50 6.00
7 LaDainian Tomlinson 3.00 8.00
8 Reggie Wayne 2.50 6.00
9 Randy Moss 2.50 6.00
10 Chad Johnson 2.00 5.00
11 Larry Fitzgerald/78 2.50 6.00
12 Terrell Owens 2.50 6.00
13 Braylon Edwards 2.00 5.00
14 Marques Colston 2.00 5.00
15 Roddy White 2.00 5.00
16 Santonio Holmes 2.00 5.00
17 Tom Brady 10.00 25.00
18 Drew Brees 3.00 8.00
19 Tony Romo 2.50 6.00
20 Eli Manning 2.50 6.00
21 Joseph Addai 2.00 5.00
22 Patrick Crayton/60 2.50 6.00
23 Tony Gonzalez 2.50 6.00
24 Clinton Portis 2.00 5.00
25 Greg Jennings 2.00 5.00

2008 Leaf Limited College Phenoms Jersey Autographs

STATED PRINT RUN 45-99
*SILVER/25-50: .5X TO 1.2X BASIC JSY AU
SILVER SPOTLIGHT PRINT RUN 25-50
*GOLD-10-25: .6X TO 1.5X BASIC JSY AU
GOLD SPOTLIGHT PRINT RUN 10-25
UNPRICED PLATINUM PRINT RUN 1
204 Allen Patrick/99 5.00 12.00
218 Colt Brennan/99 8.00 20.00
223 Dan Connor/99 5.00 12.00
233 Erik Ainge/99 12.00 30.00
255 Keith Rivers/99 5.00 12.00
273 Mike Hart/99 5.00 12.00
297 Vernon Gholston/50 6.00 15.00
302 Brian Brohm/99 5.00 12.00
305 Darren McFadden/50 8.00 20.00
312 Early Doucet/50 6.00 15.00
314 Felix Jones/45 6.00 15.00
315 Glenn Dorsey/50 EXCH 6.00 15.00
316 Harry Douglas/50 8.00 20.00
318 Jamaal Charles/50 10.00 25.00
327 Limas Sweed/50 6.00 15.00
328 Malcolm Kelly/50 6.00 15.00

2008 Leaf Limited Cuts Autographs

STATED PRINT RUN 1-100
SERIAL #'d UNDER 15 NOT PRICED
1 Bert Bell/50 40.00 80.00
2 Ace Parker/29 40.00 80.00
4 Tom Fears/15 60.00 120.00
5 Bulldog Turner/75 40.00 80.00
6 Bob Waterfield/40 60.00 120.00
7 Doak Walker/25 150.00 250.00
9 Ernie Stautner/100 25.00 60.00
10 Bruiser Kinard/40 100.00 200.00
11 Hank Stram/85 30.00 80.00
15 Sammy Baugh/30 60.00 120.00
17 Tony Canadeo/72 40.00 80.00
18 Walter Payton/100 150.00 300.00
20 Elroy Hirsch/23 50.00 100.00
21 Otto Graham/21 40.00 80.00
22 Jim Brown/25 60.00 100.00
23 Gale Sayers/25 40.00 80.00
24 Hugh McElhenny/25 25.00 60.00
25 Ozzie Newsome/25 25.00 60.00

2008 Leaf Limited Jumbo Jerseys

STATED PRINT RUN 25-50
*PRIME/10: 1X TO 2.5X BASIC JSY
PRIME PRINT RUN 10
*JER NUM/25-30: .4X TO 1X BASIC JSY
JERSEY NUMBER PRINT RUN 25-30
*JER NUM PRIME/10: 1X TO 2.5X BASIC JSY
JSY NUMBER PRIME PRINT RUN 5-10
*TEAM LOGO/25-50: .4X TO 1X BASIC JSY
TEAM LOGO PRINT RUN 4-50
*TM LOGO PRIME/2-10: 1X TO 2.5X BASIC JSY
TEAM LOGO PRIME PRINT RUN 2-10
1 Philip Rivers 4.00 10.00
2 Torry Holt/45 3.00 8.00
3 Steven Jackson 2.50 6.00
4 Adrian Peterson 4.00 10.00
5 Brandon Jacobs 2.50 6.00
6 Calvin Johnson 4.00 10.00
7 DeAngelo Williams 2.50 6.00
8 Derrick Mason 2.50 6.00
9 Marion Barber 2.50 6.00
10 Steve Smith 3.00 8.00
11 LaRon Landry 3.00 8.00
12 Marques Colston 2.50 6.00
13 Larry Johnson/30 2.50 6.00
14 Ronnie Brown 2.50 6.00
15 Rudi Johnson 2.50 6.00
16 Sidney Rice/25 2.50 6.00
17 Randy Moss 3.00 8.00
18 Tony Romo 3.00 8.00
19 Clinton Portis 2.50 6.00
20 LaDainian Tomlinson 4.00 10.00
21 Brian Westbrook 2.50 6.00
22 Laurence Maroney 3.00 8.00
23 T.J. Houshmandzadeh 2.50 6.00
24 Antonio Gates 3.00 8.00
25 Andre Johnson 3.00 8.00

2008 Leaf Limited Jumbo Jerseys Autographs

STATED PRINT RUN 5-25
UNPRICED PRIME PRINT RUN 1-5
*JSY NUM AU/15-25: .4X TO 1X BASIC JSY AU
JERSEY NUMBER PRINT RUN 5-25
UNPRICED JSY NUM PRIME PRINT RUN 1-5
*TM LOGO AU/15-25: .4X TO 1X BASE JSY AU
TEAM LOGO PRINT RUN 5-25
UNPRICED TEAM LOGO PRIME PRINT RUN 1-5
7 DeAngelo Williams/15 10.00 25.00
11 LaRon Landry/25 12.00 30.00
12 Marques Colston/25 10.00 25.00
14 Ronnie Brown/25 10.00 25.00
21 Brian Westbrook/25 15.00 40.00

2008 Leaf Limited Lettermen

UNPRICED LETTERMEN PRINT RUN 4-10

2008 Leaf Limited Matching Numbers Jerseys

STATED PRINT RUN 100 SER.#'d SETS
*PRIME/25: .8X TO 2X BASIC DUAL/100
PRIME PRINT RUN 25
*POSITION/100: .4X TO 1X BASIC DUAL/100
POSITION PRINT RUN 100 SER.#'d SETS
*POS.PRIME/25: .8X TO 2X BASIC DUAL/100
POSITION PRIME PRINT RUN 25
1 T.Edwards/D.McNabb 4.00 10.00
2 B.Roethlisberger/M.Leinart 5.00 12.00
3 M.Schaub/M.Hasselbeck 3.00 8.00
4 C.Palmer/T.Romo 8.00 20.00
5 S.Holmes/V.Young 3.00 8.00
6 L.Fitzgerald/R.Williams WR 4.00 10.00
7 A.Rodgers/M.Colston 10.00 25.00
8 B.Edwards/P.Burress 3.00 8.00
9 P.Rivers/J.Campbell 5.00 12.00
10 M.Lynch/D.Hester 6.00 15.00
11 F.Taylor/A.Peterson 8.00 20.00
12 J.Addai/C.Taylor 3.00 8.00
13 E.James/R.Johnson 4.00 10.00
14 W.Parker/L.Maroney 4.00 10.00
15 D.Driver/A.Johnson 4.00 10.00
16 T.Owens/R.Moss 4.00 10.00
17 L.Evans/D.Branch 4.00 10.00
18 T.Houshmandzadeh/J.Galloway 4.00 10.00
19 C.Johnson/G.Jennings 3.00 8.00
20 S.Smith/J.Cotchery 4.00 10.00

2008 Leaf Limited Material Monikers Jersey Number

ATED PRINT RUN 15-50
*PRIME/25: .6X TO 1.5X JSY AU/45-50
*PRIME/15-25: .5X TO 1.2X JSY AU/45-50
PRIME PRINT RUN 4-25
1 Ben Roethlisberger 50.00 100.00
2 A.J. Hawk 8.00 20.00
3 Calvin Johnson/20 30.00 60.00
4 Chris Henry RB 10.00 25.00
5 Dallas Clark/16 10.00 25.00
6 DeAngelo Williams 8.00 20.00
7 DeMeco Ryans 10.00 25.00
8 Derrick Mason/15 10.00 25.00
9 Derrick Ward 8.00 20.00
10 Donald Driver 10.00 25.00
11 Frank Gore 10.00 25.00
12 Fred Taylor 8.00 20.00
13 Greg Lewis 8.00 20.00
14 James Jones 8.00 20.00
15 Jerious Norwood/25 10.00 25.00
17 Justin Fargas 8.00 20.00
19 Kevin Curtis 8.00 20.00
21 Ladell Betts 8.00 20.00
22 LaMont Jordan 10.00 25.00
23 LaRon Landry 10.00 25.00
24 Larry Johnson 8.00 20.00
25 Marion Barber 20.00 40.00
26 Marques Colston 8.00 20.00
27 Mike Bell 8.00 20.00
28 Mike Furrey 10.00 25.00
29 Patrick Crayton 10.00 25.00
30 Patrick Willis/15 12.00 30.00
31 Peyton Manning/18 50.00 100.00
32 Jason Witten 20.00 40.00
33 Hank Baskett 8.00 20.00
34 Ronnie Brown 8.00 20.00
35 Rudi Johnson/24 10.00 25.00
36 Ryan Grant 10.00 25.00
37 Santonio Holmes 8.00 20.00
38 Selvin Young/44 8.00 20.00
39 Sidney Rice 8.00 20.00
40 Tarvaris Jackson/15 10.00 25.00
41 T.J. Houshmandzadeh 8.00 20.00
42 Tony Romo 50.00 80.00
43 Trent Edwards 8.00 20.00
44 Vincent Jackson 8.00 20.00
45 Wes Welker 15.00 40.00
46 Willie Parker 12.00 30.00
47 Jim Brown 40.00 80.00
49 Adrian Peterson/25 60.00 120.00
50 Braylon Edwards 8.00 20.00

2008 Leaf Limited Monikers Autographs Gold

UNPRICED GOLD AU PRINT RUN 10
UNPRICED PLATINUM AU PRINT RUN 1

2008 Leaf Limited Prime Pairings Autographs

STATED PRINT RUN 25-75
PP1 Klecko/Gastineau/25 15.00 40.00
PP2 E.Smith/Jhnstn/25 EXCH 75.00 150.00
PP3 R.Berry/L.Moore/75 15.00 40.00
PP4 J.McMahon/W.Perry/50 25.00 50.00
PP5 D.Jones/B.Jones/25 12.00 30.00
PP6 Long/Stblr/Ups/25 60.00 100.00
PP7 Tarkent/Foreman/25 25.00 50.00
PP8 Jones/Olsen/Grier/25 30.00 60.00
PP9 Willimsn/Bell/Lanier/25 40.00 80.00
PP10 McDonald/P.Retzlaff/25 12.00 30.00
PP11 McFad/Fargas/Bush/25 20.00 50.00
PP12 L.Johnson/K.Smith/75 15.00 40.00
PP13 T.Romo/M.Barber/25 40.00 100.00
PP14 A.Page/C.Eller/25 25.00 50.00
PP15 R.Johnson/Watson/25 10.00 25.00
PP16 Roeth/Holmes/25 60.00 120.00
PP17 M.Lynch/F.Jackson/25 40.00 80.00
PP18 W.Davis/W.Wood/25 50.00 100.00
PP19 Starr/Taylor/Gregg/25 125.00 200.00
PP20 L.Barney/A.Karras/25 15.00 40.00
PP21 G.Collins/P.Warfield/25 25.00 50.00
PP22 Y.Tittle/D.Shofner/25 25.00 50.00
PP23 Brown/Lamon/Bilet/25 40.00 100.00
PP24 Jurgensen/C.Taylor/25 30.00 60.00
PP25 B.Jackson/M.Allen/25 75.00 135.00
PP26 J.Brown/L.Kelly/25 60.00 100.00

2008 Leaf Limited Rookie Jumbo Jerseys

STATED PRINT RUN 50 SER.#'d SETS
*PRIME/10: 1.2X TO 3X BASIC JSY
PRIME PRINT RUN 10 SER.#'d SETS
*JSY NUM/50: .4X TO 1X BASIC JSY
JERSEY NUMBER PRINT RUN 50
*JSY NUM PRIME/10: 1.2X TO 3X BASIC JSY
JERSEY NUMBER PRIME PRINT RUN 2-10
*TEAM LOGO/50: .4X TO 1X BASIC JSY
TEAM LOGO PRINT RUN 50
*TEAM LOGO PRIME/10: 1.2X TO 3X BASIC JSY
TEAM LOGO PRIME PRINT RUN 2-10
1 Jordy Nelson 5.00 12.00
2 Rashard Mendenhall 1.50 4.00
3 Steve Slaton 1.50 4.00
4 DeSean Jackson 3.00 8.00
5 Donnie Avery 2.00 5.00
6 Felix Jones 1.50 4.00
7 Dustin Keller 2.00 5.00
8 Earl Bennett 2.50 6.00
9 Devin Thomas 1.50 4.00
10 Kevin O'Connell 1.50 4.00
11 John David Booty 1.50 4.00
12 Joe Flacco 3.00 8.00
13 Darren McFadden 1.50 4.00
14 Malcolm Kelly 1.50 4.00
15 Jake Long 2.50 6.00
16 Jerome Simpson 2.00 5.00
17 Brian Brohm 1.50 4.00
18 Glenn Dorsey 1.50 4.00
19 Mario Manningham 1.50 4.00
20 Limas Sweed 1.50 4.00
21 Matt Ryan 5.00 12.00
22 Eddie Royal 1.50 4.00
23 Jonathan Stewart 2.50 6.00
24 Jamaal Charles 2.50 6.00
25 Dexter Jackson 2.50 6.00
26 Harry Douglas 2.00 5.00
27 James Hardy 1.50 4.00
28 Chris Johnson 2.00 5.00
29 Early Doucet 1.50 4.00
30 Kevin Smith 1.50 4.00
31 Ray Rice 1.50 4.00
32 Chad Henne 2.00 5.00
33 Andre Caldwell 2.50 6.00
34 Matt Forte 2.50 6.00

2008 Leaf Limited Rookie Jumbo Jerseys Autographs

STATED PRINT RUN 5-15
UNPRICED PRIME PRINT RUN 1-5
*JSY NUM/15: .4X TO 1X BASIC JSY AU/15
JERSEY NUMBER PRINT RUN 2-15
UNPRICED JSY NUM.PRIME PRINT RUN 1-5
*TEAM LOGO/15: .4X TO 1X BASIC JSY AU/15
TEAM LOGO PRINT RUN 3-15
UNPRICED TEAM LOGO PRIME PRINT RUN 1-5
1 Jordy Nelson 25.00 50.00
2 Rashard Mendenhall 8.00 20.00
3 Steve Slaton 8.00 20.00
4 DeSean Jackson 15.00 40.00
5 Donnie Avery 10.00 25.00
6 Felix Jones 8.00 20.00
7 Dustin Keller 10.00 25.00
8 Earl Bennett 12.00 30.00
9 Devin Thomas/10 8.00 20.00
10 Kevin O'Connell 8.00 20.00
11 John David Booty 8.00 20.00
12 Joe Flacco 15.00 40.00
13 Darren McFadden 8.00 20.00
15 Jake Long 12.00 30.00
16 Jerome Simpson 10.00 25.00
17 Brian Brohm 8.00 20.00
19 Mario Manningham 8.00 20.00
20 Limas Sweed 8.00 20.00
21 Matt Ryan 40.00 100.00
22 Eddie Royal 8.00 20.00
23 Jonathan Stewart 12.00 30.00
24 Jamaal Charles 12.00 30.00
25 Dexter Jackson 12.00 30.00
27 James Hardy 8.00 20.00
28 Chris Johnson 10.00 25.00
29 Early Doucet 8.00 20.00
30 Kevin Smith 8.00 20.00
31 Ray Rice 8.00 20.00
32 Chad Henne/10 10.00 25.00
33 Andre Caldwell 8.00 20.00
34 Matt Forte 12.00 30.00

2008 Leaf Limited Slideshow Autographs

ATED PRINT RUN 50 SER.#'d SETS
1 Steve Slaton 8.00 20.00
2 Ray Rice 8.00 20.00
3 Rashard Mendenhall 8.00 20.00
4 Matt Ryan 30.00 80.00
5 Matt Forte 12.00 30.00
6 Mario Manningham 8.00 20.00
7 Malcolm Kelly 8.00 20.00
8 Limas Sweed 8.00 20.00
9 Kevin Smith 8.00 20.00
10 Kevin O'Connell 8.00 20.00
11 Jordy Nelson 25.00 50.00
12 Jonathan Stewart 10.00 25.00
13 John David Booty 8.00 20.00
14 Joe Flacco 15.00 40.00
15 Jerome Simpson 10.00 25.00
16 James Hardy 8.00 20.00
17 Jamaal Charles 12.00 30.00
18 Jake Long 12.00 30.00
19 Harry Douglas 10.00 25.00
20 Glenn Dorsey 8.00 20.00
21 Felix Jones 8.00 20.00
22 Eddie Royal 8.00 20.00
23 Early Doucet 8.00 20.00
24 Earl Bennett 12.00 30.00
25 Dustin Keller 10.00 25.00
26 Donnie Avery 10.00 25.00
27 Dexter Jackson 12.00 30.00
28 Devin Thomas 8.00 20.00
29 DeSean Jackson 15.00 40.00
30 Darren McFadden 6.00 15.00
31 Chris Johnson 10.00 25.00
32 Chad Henne 10.00 25.00
33 Brian Brohm 8.00 20.00
34 Andre Caldwell 8.00 20.00

2008 Leaf Limited Team Threads Dual

STATED PRINT RUN 100 SER.#'d SETS
*PRIME/25: .8X TO 2X BASIC DUAL JSY
PRIME PRINT RUN 25 SER.#'d SETS
1 L.Evans/M.Lynch 4.00 10.00
2 D.Anderson/B.Edwards 3.00 8.00
3 M.Schaub/A.Johnson 4.00 10.00
4 F.Taylor/M.Jones-Drew 3.00 8.00
5 V.Young/L.White 3.00 8.00
6 J.Cutler/B.Stokley 3.00 8.00
7 L.Johnson/T.Gonzalez 4.00 10.00
8 B.Westbrook/C.Buckhalter 3.00 8.00
9 R.Williams WR/C.Johnson 5.00 12.00
10 S.Jackson/T.Holt 4.00 10.00

2008 Leaf Limited Team Threads Triples

STATED PRINT RUN 100 SER.#'d SETS
*PRIME/25: .8X TO 2X BASIC TRIO JSY
PRIME PRINT RUN 25 SER.#'d SETS
1 Garrard/Taylor/Jones 5.00 12.00
2 Garcia/Williams/Galloway 5.00 12.00
3 Delhomme/Smith/Williams 5.00 12.00
4 Manning/Burress/Jacobs 5.00 12.00
5 Smith QB/Gore/Davis 5.00 12.00
6 McGahee/Clayton/Lewis 6.00 15.00
7 Hasselbeck/Branch/Burleson 4.00 10.00
8 Jones/Cotchery/Coles 4.00 10.00
9 Jackson/Peterson/Taylor 10.00 25.00
10 McNabb/Westbrook/Brown 5.00 12.00

2008 Leaf Limited Team Threads Quads

STATED PRINT RUN 100 SER.#'d SETS
*PRIME/25: .6X TO 1.5X BASIC QUAD JSY
PRIME PRINT RUN 25 SER.#'d SETS
1 Brady/Moss/Maroney/Welker 25.00 60.00
2 Manning/Addai/Wayne/Clark 20.00 50.00
3 Rodgers/Driver/Jennings/Grant 15.00 40.00
4 Palmer/Johnsn/Johnsn/Housh 6.00 15.00
5 Roeth/Parkr/Holmes/Ward 8.00 20.00
6 Brees/McAllister/Bush/Colston 8.00 20.00
7 Leinart/James/Boldin/Fitzgrld 6.00 15.00
8 Rivers/Tomlin/Gates/Jacksn 8.00 20.00
9 Campbell/Portis/Cooley/Moss 8.00 20.00
10 Romo/Owens/Barber/Witten 6.00 15.00

2008 Leaf Limited Team Trademarks

ATED PRINT RUN 999 SER.#'d SETS
*HOLOFOIL/100: .5X TO 1.2X BASIC INSERTS
HOLOFOIL PRINT RUN 100 SER.#'d SETS
1 Alex Karras 1.25 3.00
2 Dan Marino 3.00 8.00
3 Emmitt Smith 2.50 6.00
4 Gene Upshaw 1.00 2.50
5 Joe Klecko 1.00 2.50
6 Roger Staubach 2.00 5.00
7 Raymond Berry 1.25 3.00
8 Eric Dickerson 1.25 3.00
9 Earl Campbell 1.50 4.00
10 Howie Long 1.50 4.00
11 John Mackey 1.00 2.50
12 Jim Brown 2.00 5.00
13 Franco Harris 1.50 4.00
14 Steve Young 2.00 5.00
15 Barry Sanders 2.50 6.00
16 Billy Sims 1.25 3.00
17 Brett Favre 2.50 6.00
18 Carl Eller 1.00 2.50
19 Charley Taylor 1.00 2.50
20 Chuck Foreman 1.00 2.50
21 Dallas Clark .75 2.00
22 Alan Page 1.00 2.50
23 Danny White 1.00 2.50
24 Deacon Jones 1.25 3.00
25 Dick Butkus 2.00 5.00
26 Fran Tarkenton 1.50 4.00
27 Fred Dryer 1.00 2.50
28 Hank Baskett .75 2.00
29 John Matuszak 1.50 4.00
30 Len Dawson 1.50 4.00
31 Mark Gastineau 1.00 2.50
32 Ladell Betts .75 2.00
33 Paul Warfield 1.25 3.00
34 Randall Cunningham 1.25 3.00
35 Ronnie Lott 1.25 3.00
36 Sonny Jurgensen 1.25 3.00
37 Tiki Barber 1.25 3.00
38 Willie Brown 1.00 2.50
39 Willie Lanier 1.00 2.50
40 Kenny Watson .75 2.00

2008 Leaf Limited Team Trademarks Autograph Materials Prime

STATED PRINT RUN 1-25
SERIAL #'d UNDER 15 NOT PRICED
2 Dan Marino 90.00 150.00
5 Joe Klecko 12.00 30.00
6 Roger Staubach 40.00 80.00
7 Raymond Berry 15.00 40.00
10 Howie Long 30.00 60.00
11 John Mackey 12.00 30.00
12 Jim Brown 50.00 100.00
13 Franco Harris 40.00 80.00
14 Steve Young 30.00 60.00
15 Barry Sanders/15 60.00 120.00
16 Billy Sims 15.00 40.00
17 Brett Favre 100.00 175.00
18 Carl Eller 12.00 30.00
22 Alan Page 12.00 30.00
28 Hank Baskett 10.00 25.00
30 Len Dawson 20.00 50.00
31 Mark Gastineau 12.00 30.00
32 Ladell Betts 10.00 25.00
34 Randall Cunningham 30.00 60.00
35 Ronnie Lott 15.00 40.00
37 Tiki Barber 15.00 40.00
38 Willie Brown 12.00 30.00
39 Willie Lanier 12.00 30.00

2008 Leaf Limited Team Trademarks Materials

STATED PRINT RUN 100 SER.#'d SETS
*PRIME/50: .6X TO 1.5X BASIC JSY/100
*PRIME/50: .4X TO 1X BASIC JSY/44
*PRIME/20-30: .8X TO 2X BASIC JSY/100
PRIME PRINT RUN 5-50
*TEAM LOGO/50: .4X TO 1X BASIC JSY/100
*TEAM LOGO/15-25: .5X TO 1.2X BASIC JSY/100
TEAM LOGO PRINT RUN 15-50
1 Alex Karras 4.00 10.00
2 Dan Marino 10.00 25.00
3 Emmitt Smith Pants/44 12.00 30.00
4 Gene Upshaw 3.00 8.00
5 Joe Klecko 3.00 8.00
6 Roger Staubach 6.00 15.00
7 Raymond Berry 4.00 10.00
8 Eric Dickerson 4.00 10.00
9 Earl Campbell 5.00 12.00
10 Howie Long 6.00 15.00
11 John Mackey 3.00 8.00
12 Jim Brown 6.00 15.00
13 Franco Harris 5.00 12.00
14 Steve Young 6.00 15.00
15 Barry Sanders 8.00 20.00
17 Brett Favre 8.00 20.00
18 Carl Eller 3.00 8.00
19 Charley Taylor 3.00 8.00
20 Chuck Foreman 5.00 12.00
22 Alan Page 3.00 8.00
23 Danny White 4.00 10.00
24 Deacon Jones 4.00 10.00
25 Dick Butkus 6.00 15.00
26 Fran Tarkenton 5.00 12.00
27 Fred Dryer 3.00 8.00
28 Hank Baskett 3.00 8.00
29 John Matuszak 5.00 12.00
30 Len Dawson 5.00 12.00
31 Mark Gastineau 3.00 8.00
32 Ladell Betts 3.00 8.00
33 Paul Warfield 4.00 10.00
34 Randall Cunningham 4.00 10.00
35 Ronnie Lott 4.00 10.00
36 Sonny Jurgensen 4.00 10.00
37 Tiki Barber 4.00 10.00
38 Willie Brown 3.00 8.00
39 Willie Lanier 3.00 8.00

2008 Leaf Limited Threads

STATED PRINT RUN 15-100
UNPRICED SUPER PRIME PRINT RUN 1
1 Anquan Boldin 2.00 5.00
2 Edgerrin James 2.50 6.00
3 Larry Fitzgerald 2.50 6.00
5 Michael Turner/55 2.00 5.00
6 Roddy White 2.00 5.00
8 Derrick Mason 2.00 5.00
9 Mark Clayton 2.00 5.00
10 Willis McGahee 2.00 5.00
11 Trent Edwards 2.00 5.00
12 Marshawn Lynch 2.50 6.00
13 Lee Evans 2.50 6.00
15 Steve Smith 2.50 6.00
16 DeAngelo Williams 2.00 5.00
17 Rex Grossman/35 3.00 8.00
19 Devin Hester 2.50 6.00
20 Carson Palmer 2.50 6.00
22 T.J. Houshmandzadeh 2.00 5.00
23 Chad Johnson 2.00 5.00
24 Braylon Edwards 2.00 5.00
25 Derek Anderson 2.00 5.00
26 Jamal Lewis 2.50 6.00
27 Tony Romo 2.50 6.00
28 Terrell Owens 2.50 6.00
29 Marion Barber 2.00 5.00
30 Jason Witten 2.50 6.00
31 Jay Cutler 2.00 5.00
32 Selvin Young 2.00 5.00
33 Brandon Marshall 2.50 6.00
34 Jon Kitna 2.00 5.00
35 Calvin Johnson 3.00 8.00
36 Roy Williams WR 2.00 5.00
37 Aaron Rodgers 6.00 15.00
38 Donald Driver 2.50 6.00
39 Greg Jennings 2.00 5.00
40 Matt Schaub 2.00 5.00
41 Andre Johnson 2.50 6.00
43 Peyton Manning 8.00 20.00
44 Joseph Addai 2.00 5.00
45 Reggie Wayne 2.50 6.00
46 David Garrard 2.00 5.00
47 Fred Taylor 2.00 5.00
48 Maurice Jones-Drew 2.00 5.00
49 Reggie Williams 2.50 6.00
50 Brodie Croyle/33 4.00 10.00
51 Larry Johnson 2.00 5.00
52 Tony Gonzalez/25 5.00 12.00
54 Ronnie Brown 2.00 5.00
56 Tarvaris Jackson 2.00 5.00
57 Adrian Peterson 3.00 8.00
58 Chester Taylor 2.00 5.00
59 Tom Brady 10.00 25.00
60 Randy Moss 2.50 6.00
61 Laurence Maroney 2.50 6.00
62 Drew Brees 3.00 8.00
63 Marques Colston 2.00 5.00
64 Reggie Bush/65 2.00 5.00
65 Eli Manning 2.50 6.00
66 Plaxico Burress 2.00 5.00
67 Brandon Jacobs 2.00 5.00
69 Jerricho Cotchery 2.00 5.00
70 Laveranues Coles/50 2.00 5.00
71 JaMarcus Russell 2.00 5.00
72 Justin Fargas 2.00 5.00
74 Donovan McNabb 2.50 6.00
75 Brian Westbrook 2.00 5.00
76 Kevin Curtis 2.00 5.00
77 Ben Roethlisberger 3.00 8.00
78 Willie Parker 2.50 6.00
79 Santonio Holmes 2.00 5.00
80 Philip Rivers 3.00 8.00
81 LaDainian Tomlinson 3.00 8.00
82 Antonio Gates 2.50 6.00
84 Frank Gore 2.50 6.00
86 Matt Hasselbeck 2.00 5.00
87 Julius Jones/60 2.00 5.00
88 Deion Branch 2.00 5.00
89 Marc Bulger 2.00 5.00
90 Steven Jackson 2.00 5.00
91 Torry Holt 2.50 6.00
92 Jeff Garcia 2.00 5.00
94 Joey Galloway 2.50 6.00
95 Vince Young 2.00 5.00
96 LenDale White 2.00 5.00
97 Roydell Williams 2.00 5.00
98 Jason Campbell 2.00 5.00
99 Santana Moss 2.00 5.00
100 Clinton Portis 2.00 5.00
101 Alan Page 2.50 6.00
102 Bart Starr 6.00 15.00
103 Bert Jones 2.50 6.00
108 Bo Jackson 5.00 12.00

109 Bob Griese 4.00 10.00
110 Bob Lilly 3.00 8.00
111 Bob Waterfield 8.00 20.00
113 Brett Favre 6.00 15.00
114 Carl Eller 2.50 6.00
115 Charley Taylor 2.50 6.00
117 Chuck Foreman 2.50 6.00
118 Cliff Harris/40 4.00 10.00
119 Cris Collinsworth/40 5.00 12.00
120 Danny White 2.50 6.00
124 Deacon Jones 3.00 8.00
126 Dick Butkus 5.00 12.00
127 Doak Walker 8.00 20.00
130 Forrest Gregg 2.50 6.00
131 Fran Tarkenton/30 6.00 15.00
132 Frank Gifford 4.00 10.00
133 Fred Biletnikoff 4.00 10.00
134 Fred Dryer 2.50 6.00
136 Gale Sayers 4.00 10.00
139 Jack Lambert 4.00 10.00
140 James Lofton 2.50 6.00
141 Jan Stenerud/15 5.00 12.00
142 Jim McMahon 4.00 10.00
143 Jim Otto 2.50 6.00
145 Jim Thorpe/24 100.00 175.00
146 Joe Montana 12.00 30.00
147 John Riggins 3.00 8.00
148 John Matuszak 4.00 10.00
149 Johnny Unitas 6.00 15.00
152 Lance Alworth/40 5.00 12.00
153 Larry Little 2.50 6.00
154 Lee Roy Selmon 2.50 6.00
155 Lem Barney 2.50 6.00
156 Len Dawson 4.00 10.00
157 Lenny Moore 2.50 6.00
160 Marcus Allen 4.00 10.00
162 Mark Gastineau 2.50 6.00
165 Norm Van Brocklin 3.00 8.00
166 Ollie Matson 3.00 8.00
167 Ozzie Newsome 3.00 8.00
168 Paul Hornung 4.00 10.00
170 Paul Warfield 3.00 8.00
172 Phil Simms 3.00 8.00
174 Randy White 3.00 8.00
175 Reggie White 4.00 10.00
176 Roger Craig/85 4.00 10.00
177 Ronnie Lott 3.00 8.00
178 Rosey Grier/49 3.00 8.00
179 Sammy Baugh 10.00 25.00
180 Sid Luckman 10.00 25.00
181 Sonny Jurgensen 3.00 8.00
183 Steve Largent 4.00 10.00
184 Ted Hendricks 2.50 6.00
185 Tiki Barber 3.00 8.00
186 Tim Brown 4.00 10.00
187 Tom Fears 2.50 6.00
188 Tommy McDonald 3.00 8.00
190 Tony Dorsett 4.00 10.00
191 Troy Aikman 5.00 12.00
192 Walter Payton 8.00 20.00
193 Warren Moon 4.00 10.00
194 William Perry/19 5.00 12.00
195 Willie Lanier 2.50 6.00
196 Willie Brown 2.50 6.00
199 Y.A. Tittle 4.00 10.00

2008 Leaf Limited Threads Prime

*PRIME/35-50: .6X TO 1.5X BASIC JSY/49-100
*PRIME/50: .5X TO 1.2X BASIC JSY/25-35
*PRIME/15-29: .8X TO 2X BASIC JSY/49-100
*PRIME/25: .6X TO 1.5X BASIC JSY/30-40
PRIME PRINT RUN 1-50 SER.#'d SETS
14 Jake Delhomme/50 3.00 8.00
55 Ted Ginn Jr./29 4.00 10.00
161 Mark Duper/35 5.00 12.00
182 Sterling Sharpe/25 8.00 20.00

2008 Leaf Limited Threads Prime Jersey Number

COMMON ACTIVE/80-89 3.00 8.00
ACTIVE SEMISTARS/80-89 4.00 10.00
ACTIVE UNL.STARS/80-89 5.00 12.00
COMMON ACTIVE/31-39 5.00 12.00
ACTIVE UNL.STARS/31-39 6.00 15.00
COMMON ACTIVE/15-29 5.00 12.00
ACTIVE SEMISTARS/15-29 6.00 15.00
ACTIVE UNL.STARS/15-29 8.00 20.00
COMMON RETIRED/54-84 6.00 15.00
COMMON RETIRED/32-42 8.00 20.00
RETIRED UNL.STARS/32-42 10.00 25.00
COMMON RETIRED/15-24 8.00 20.00
RETIRED SEMISTARS/15-24 10.00 25.00
RETIRED UNL.STARS/15-24 12.00 30.00
STATED PRINT RUN 2-89
SERIAL #'d UNDER 15 NOT PRICED
14 Jake Delhomme/17 4.00 10.00
43 Peyton Manning/18 15.00 40.00
55 Ted Ginn Jr./19 4.00 10.00
57 Adrian Peterson/28 6.00 15.00
64 Reggie Bush/25 4.00 10.00
81 LaDainian Tomlinson/21 6.00 15.00
102 Bart Starr/15 15.00 40.00
136 Gale Sayers/40 8.00 20.00
146 Joe Montana/16 30.00 80.00
149 Johnny Unitas/19 15.00 40.00
182 Sterling Sharpe/84 5.00 12.00
192 Walter Payton/34 15.00 40.00

2008 Leaf Limited Threads Prime Team Logo

*PRIME/25: .8X TO 2X BASIC JSY/49-100
*PRIME/25: .6X TO 1.5X BASIC JSY/25-35
STATED PRINT RUN 1-25
SERIAL #'d UNDER 25 NOT PRICED
55 Ted Ginn Jr./25 4.00 10.00

2011 Leaf Metal National Convention

STATED PRINT RUN 300 SER. #'d SETS
*PRISM BLUE/25: 1.5X TO 4X BASIC CARDS
*PRISM SILVER/70: 1X TO 2.5X BASIC CARDS
PR2 Cam Newton 3.00 8.00
PR4 Vince Lombardi 2.50 6.00

2011 Leaf Metal National Convention Prismatic Silver

*PRISM SILVER/70: 1X TO 2.5X BASIC CARDS
STATED PRINT RUN 70 SER. #'d SETS

2011 Leaf Muhammad Ali Metal Fans of Ali Autographs

FAUM7 Joe Montana 40.00 80.00

2012 Leaf National Convention

BG2 Bob Griese .30 .75
BL1 Bob Lilly .25 .60
BS2 Barry Sanders .50 1.25
DD1 Dan Dierdorf .20 .50
DH1 Dan Hampton .20 .50
DM2 Don Maynard .25 .60
DS2 Deion Sanders .30 .75
DS3 Don Shula .30 .75
EC1 Earl Campbell .30 .75
ED1 Eric Dickerson .25 .60
FG1 Frank Gifford .25 .60
JK1 Jim Kelly .40 1.00
JL1 James Lofton .25 .60
JM1 Joe Montana .60 1.50
JO1 Jim Otto .20 .50
JR1 Jerry Rice .50 1.25
LD1 Len Dawson .30 .75
MD1 Mike Ditka .30 .75
MF1 Marshall Faulk .30 .75
MR1 Mel Renfro .25 .60
ON1 Ozzie Newsome .25 .60
RL1 Ronnie Lott .30 .75
SY1 Steve Young .40 1.00
TH1 Ted Hendricks .20 .50
TT1 Thurman Thomas .30 .75
WM1 Warren Moon .30 .75
YAT Y.A. Tittle .25 .60

2012 Leaf National Convention VIP

COMPLETE SET (5) 5.00 12.00
VIP2 Robert Griffin III 2.00 5.00

2014 Leaf National Convention

COMPLETE SET (10) 4.00 10.00
2 Johnny Manziel FB .75 2.00
3 Teddy Bridgewater FB .60 1.50
4 Tre Mason FB .50 1.25
5 Blake Bortles FB .60 1.50
6 Sammy Watkins FB .50 1.25
10 Jadeveon Clowney FB .50 1.25

2015 Leaf National Convention '90 Leaf Acetate

AC1 Amari Cooper 1.25 3.00
DJ1 Duke Johnson .75 2.00
JW1 Jameis Winston 1.50 4.00
KW1 Kevin White .75 2.00
MG1 Melvin Gordon 1.25 3.00
MM1 Marcus Mariota 2.00 5.00
TG1 Todd Gurley 1.00 2.50

2015 Leaf National Convention VIP

COMPLETE SET (11)
4 Brett Hundley
5 Bryce Petty
6 Marcus Mariota
7 Jameis Winston
8 Todd Gurley
9 Melvin Gordon

2014 Leaf Originals '48 Autographs

*ALTERNATE ART: .4X TO 1X BASIC AU
AB1 Anthony Barr 2.00 5.00
AJM A.J. McCarron/51* 2.50 6.00
AM1 Aaron Murray/57* 2.50 6.00
AR1 Allen Robinson 3.00 8.00
ASJ Austin Seferian-Jenkins 2.00 5.00
AW1 Andre Williams 2.00 5.00
BR1 Bradley Roby 4.00 10.00
BS1 Bishop Sankey 8.00 20.00
CH1 Carlos Hyde/51* 3.00 8.00
CJM C.J. Mosley 2.50 6.00
CK1 Cyrus Kouandjio 2.50 6.00
CS1 Charles Sims/66* 2.50 6.00
DAT De'Anthony Thomas 2.00 5.00
DC1 Derek Carr/50* 12.00 30.00
DW1 Damien Williams 3.00 8.00
EE1 Eric Ebron 2.50 6.00
HCD Ha Ha Clinton-Dix 2.50 6.00
JA1 Jared Abbrederis/36* 2.50 6.00
JA2 Jace Amaro/61* 2.50 6.00
JC1 Jadeveon Clowney 2.50 6.00
JH1 Josh Huff 2.50 6.00
JL1 Jarvis Landry/66* 5.00 12.00
JM1 Johnny Manziel 3.00 8.00
JM2 Jordan Matthews 3.00 8.00
JM3 Jake Matthews/30* 4.00 10.00
JWJ James Wilder Jr. 2.50 6.00
KDC Ka'Deem Carey 4.00 10.00
LN3 Louis Nix III 2.00 5.00
LS1 Lache Seastrunk 4.00 10.00
MD1 Mike Davis 2.00 5.00
ME1 Mike Evans 8.00 20.00
MG2 Marion Grice 2.00 5.00
ML1 Marqise Lee 2.50 6.00
OBJ Odell Beckham Jr. 30.00 60.00
PR1 Paul Richardson 4.00 10.00
SM1 Stephen Morris 2.00 5.00
SR1 Silas Redd/25* 4.00 10.00
SW1 Sammy Watkins 3.00 8.00
TB1 Teddy Bridgewater 15.00 30.00
TB2 Tajh Boyd/25* 3.00 8.00
TL1 Taylor Lewan 2.00 5.00
ZM1 Zach Mettenberger/36* 2.50 6.00
RED Hot Rookie EXCH 50.00 80.00

2014 Leaf Originals '48 Autographs Blue

*BLUE/25: .8X TO 2X BASIC AU

2014 Leaf Originals '48 Autographs Yellow

*YELLOW/99: .5X TO 1.2X BASIC AU
YELLOW/99: .4X TO 1X BASIC AU/30-66
YELLOW/99: .3X TO .8X BASIC AU/25

2014 Leaf Originals '48 Autographs Alternate Art Yellow

*YELLOW/85: .5X TO 1.2X BASIC AU
YELLOW/85: .4X TO 1X BASIC AU/36-57
*YELLOW/25: .6X TO 1.5X BASIC AU
YELLOW/25: .5X TO 1.2X BASIC AU/30-66
YELLOW/25: .4X TO 1X BASIC AU/25

2014 Leaf Originals '60 Autographs

*PURPLE/50: .5X TO 1.2X BASIC AU
PURPLE/25: .5X TO 1.2X BASIC AU/45
*SILVER/25: .6X TO 1.5X BASIC AU
SILVER/15: .8X TO 2X BASIC AU/45
AA1 Antonio Andrews 2.00 5.00
AJ1 Anthony Johnson 2.50 6.00
BB1 Blake Bortles 2.50 6.00
BC1 Brandin Cooks 3.00 8.00
BC2 Brandon Coleman 2.50 6.00
BE1 Bruce Ellington 2.00 5.00
BS1 Brett Smith 2.00 5.00
DA1 Davante Adams 3.00 8.00
DF1 David Fales/130* 2.50 6.00
DF2 Devonta Freeman 8.00 20.00
DM1 Donte Moncrief 2.00 5.00
DS1 Devin Street 2.50 6.00
IC1 Isaiah Crowell 2.50 6.00
JG1 Jimmy Garoppolo/155* 40.00 80.00
JG2 Justin Gilbert
JH1 Jeremy Hill 2.50 6.00
KB1 Kelvin Benjamin 3.00 8.00
KM1 Khalil Mack 8.00 20.00
LT1 Logan Thomas/45* 2.50 6.00
RS1 Ryan Shazier 3.00 8.00
SE1 Shaquelle Evans 2.00 5.00
ST1 Stephon Tuitt 3.00 8.00
TG1 Tyler Gaffney 2.00 5.00
TJ1 Timmy Jernigan 2.00 5.00
TM1 Trent Murphy 2.00 5.00
TM2 Tre Mason EXCH 20.00 40.00
TW1 Terrance West 2.00 5.00
ZM1 Zack Martin 4.00 10.00

2014 Leaf Peck and Snyder Promos

COMPLETE SET (45) 25.00 60.00
2 A.J. McCarron FB 1.00 2.50
4 Bishop Sankey FB 1.00 2.50
5 Blake Bortles FB 2.00 5.00
7 Brandin Cooks FB .75 2.00
12 Derek Carr FB 1.25 3.00
13Â•Eric Ebron FB 1.00 2.50
19Â•Jadeveon Clowney FB 1.50 4.00
21Â•Johnny Manziel FB 2.50 6.00
30 Mike Evans FB .75 2.00
38Â•Sammy Watkins FB 1.50 4.00
41Â•Teddy Bridgewater FB 2.00 5.00
43Â•Tre Mason FB 1.25 3.00

2011 Leaf Previews National Convention

PR2 Cam Newton 2.60 6.00
PR4 Vince Lombardi 1.50 4.00
PR6 Mark Ingram 1.50 4.00

2014 Leaf Q Autographs Silver

*GOLD/25: .5X TO 1.2X BASIC
AJC1 Jadeveon Clowney SP 5.00 12.00

2014 Leaf Q Memorabilia Autographs Gold

*GOLD: .6X TO 1.5X BASIC
*GOLD BAT: .4X TO 1X BASIC
*GOLD JKT: .4X TO 1X BASIC
*GOLD SHOE: .4X TO 1X BASIC
RANDOM INSERTS IN PACKS
STATED PRINT RUN 25 SER.#'d SETS
SOME NOT PRICED DUE TO LACK OF INFO

2014 Leaf Q Memorabilia Autographs Silver

MTB1 Teddy Bridgewater SP 25.00 60.00
AMJM1 Joe Montana 60.00 150.00

2014 Leaf Q Pure Autographs Charcoal

*BLUE/22-25: .5X TO 1.2X BASIC
PJC1 Jadeveon Clowney 4.00 10.00
PJM2 Johnny Manziel 6.00 15.00
PJR1 Jerry Rice 30.00 80.00

1998 Leaf Rookies and Stars

The 1998 Leaf Rookies and Stars set was issued in one series totalling 300 cards. The fronts feature color action palyer photos. The backs carry player information. The set includes the following short-printed subsets with an insertion rate of 1:2: Rookies (171-240) and Power Tools (241-270). Also inclued in the set are Team Lineup cards (271-300).

COMPLETE SET (300) 125.00 250.00
1 Keyshawn Johnson .25 .60
2 Marvin Harrison .25 .60
3 Eddie Kennison .15 .40
4 Bryant Young .08 .25
5 Darren Woodson .08 .25
6 Tyrone Wheatley .15 .40
7 Michael Westbrook .15 .40
8 Charles Way .08 .25
9 Ricky Watters .15 .40
10 Chris Warren .15 .40
11 Wesley Walls .15 .40
12 Tamarick Vanover .08 .25
13 Zach Thomas .25 .60
14 Derrick Thomas .25 .60
15 Yancey Thigpen .08 .25
16 Vinny Testaverde .15 .40
17 Dana Stubblefield .08 .25
18 J.J. Stokes .15 .40
19 James Stewart .15 .40
20 Jeff George .15 .40
21 John Randle .15 .40
22 Gary Brown .08 .25
23 Ed McCaffrey .15 .40
24 James Jett .15 .40
25 Rob Johnson .15 .40
26 Daryl Johnston .15 .40
27 Jermaine Lewis .15 .40
28 Tony Martin .15 .40
29 Derrick Mayes .15 .40
30 Keenan McCardell .15 .40
31 O.J. McDuffie .15 .40
32 Chris Chandler .15 .40
33 Doug Flutie .25 .60
34 Scott Mitchell .15 .40
35 Warren Moon .25 .60
36 Rob Moore .15 .40
37 Johnnie Morton .15 .40
38 Neil O'Donnell .15 .40
39 Rich Gannon .25 .60
40 Andre Reed .15 .40
41 Jake Reed .15 .40
42 Errict Rhett .15 .40
43 Simeon Rice .15 .40
44 Andre Rison .15 .40
45 Eric Moulds .25 .60
46 Frank Sanders .15 .40
47 Darnay Scott .15 .40
48 Junior Seau .25 .60
49 Shannon Sharpe .15 .40
50 Bruce Smith .15 .40
51 Jimmy Smith .15 .40
52 Robert Smith .25 .60
53 Derrick Alexander .15 .40
54 Kimble Anders .15 .40
55 Jamal Anderson .25 .60
56 Mario Bates .15 .40
57 Edgar Bennett .08 .25
58 Tim Biakabutuka .15 .40
59 Ki-Jana Carter .08 .25
60 Larry Centers .08 .25
61 Mark Chmura .15 .40
62 Wayne Chrebet .25 .60
63 Ben Coates .15 .40
64 Curtis Conway .15 .40
65 Randall Cunningham .25 .60
66 Rickey Dudley .08 .25
67 Bert Emanuel .15 .40
68 Bobby Engram .15 .40
69 William Floyd .08 .25
70 Irving Fryar .15 .40
71 Elvis Grbac .15 .40
72 Kevin Greene .15 .40
73 Jim Harbaugh .15 .40
74 Raymont Harris .08 .25
75 Garrison Hearst .25 .60
76 Greg Hill .08 .25
77 Desmond Howard .15 .40
78 Bobby Hoying .15 .40
79 Michael Jackson .08 .25
80 Terry Allen .25 .60
81 Jerome Bettis .25 .60
82 Jeff Blake .15 .40
83 Robert Brooks .15 .40
84 Tim Brown .25 .60
85 Isaac Bruce .25 .60
86 Cris Carter .25 .60
87 Ty Detmer .15 .40
88 Trent Dilfer .25 .60
89 Marshall Faulk .30 .75
90 Antonio Freeman .25 .60
91 Gus Frerotte .08 .25
92 Joey Galloway .15 .40
93 Michael Irvin .25 .60
94 Brad Johnson .25 .60
95 Danny Kanell .15 .40
96 Napoleon Kaufman .25 .60
97 Dorsey Levens .25 .60
98 Natrone Means .15 .40
99 Herman Moore .15 .40
100 Adrian Murrell .15 .40
101 Carl Pickens .15 .40
102 Rod Smith .15 .40
103 Thurman Thomas .25 .60
104 Reggie White .25 .60
105 Jim Druckenmiller .08 .25
106 Antowain Smith .25 .60
107 Reidel Anthony .15 .40
108 Ike Hilliard .15 .40
109 Rae Carruth .08 .25
110 Troy Davis .08 .25
111 Terance Mathis .15 .40
112 Brett Favre 1.00 2.50
113 Dan Marino 1.00 2.50
114 Emmitt Smith .75 2.00
115 Barry Sanders .75 2.00
116 Eddie George .25 .60
117 Drew Bledsoe .40 1.00
118 Troy Aikman .50 1.25
119 Terrell Davis .25 .60
120 John Elway 1.00 2.50
121 Mark Brunell .25 .60
122 Jerry Rice .50 1.25
123 Kordell Stewart .25 .60
124 Steve McNair .25 .60
125 Curtis Martin .25 .60
126 Steve Young .30 .75
127 Kerry Collins .15 .40
128 Terry Glenn .25 .60
129 Deion Sanders .25 .60
130 Mike Alstott .25 .60
131 Tony Banks .15 .40
132 Karim Abdul-Jabbar .25 .60
133 Terrell Owens .25 .60
134 Yatil Green .08 .25
135 Tony Gonzalez .25 .60
136 Byron Hanspard .08 .25
137 David LaFleur .08 .25
138 Danny Wuerffel .15 .40
139 Tiki Barber .25 .60
140 Peter Boulware .08 .25
141 Will Blackwell .08 .25
142 Warrick Dunn .25 .60
143 Corey Dillon .25 .60
144 Jake Plummer .25 .60
145 Neil Smith .15 .40
146 Charles Johnson .08 .25
147 Fred Lane .08 .25
148 Dan Wilkinson .08 .25
149 Ken Norton Jr. .08 .25
150 Stephen Davis .08 .25
151 Gilbert Brown .08 .25
152 Kenny Bynum RC .08 .25
153 Derrick Cullors .08 .25
154 Charlie Garner .15 .40
155 Jeff Graham .08 .25
156 Warren Sapp .15 .40
157 Jerald Moore .08 .25
158 Sean Dawkins .08 .25
159 Charlie Jones .08 .25
160 Kevin Lockett .08 .25
161 James McKnight .25 .60
162 Chris Penn .08 .25
163 Leslie Shepherd .08 .25
164 Karl Williams .08 .25
165 Mark Bruener .08 .25
166 Ernie Conwell .08 .25
167 Ken Dilger .08 .25
168 Troy Drayton .08 .25
169 Freddie Jones .08 .25
170 Dale Carter .08 .25
171 Charles Woodson RC 5.00 12.00
172 Alonzo Mayes RC 1.00 2.50
173 Andre Wadsworth RC 1.50 4.00
174 Grant Wistrom RC 1.50 4.00
175 Greg Ellis RC 1.00 2.50
176 Chris Howard RC 1.00 2.50
177 Keith Brooking RC 2.50 6.00
178 Takeo Spikes RC 2.50 6.00
179 Anthony Simmons RC 1.50 4.00
180 Brian Simmons RC 1.50 4.00
181 Sam Cowart RC 1.50 4.00
182 Ken Oxendine RC 1.00 2.50
183 Vonnie Holliday RC 1.50 4.00
184 Terry Fair RC 1.50 4.00
185 Shaun Williams RC 1.50 4.00
186 Tremayne Stephens RC 1.00 2.50
187 Duane Starks RC 1.00 2.50
188 Jason Peter RC 1.00 2.50
189 Tebucky Jones RC 1.00 2.50
190 Donovin Darius RC 1.50 4.00
191 R.W. McQuarters RC 1.50 4.00
192 Corey Chavous RC 2.50 6.00
193 Cameron Cleeland RC 1.00 2.50
194 Stephen Alexander RC 1.50 4.00
195 Rod Rutledge RC 1.00 2.50
196 Scott Frost RC 1.00 2.50
197 Fred Beasley RC 1.00 2.50
198 Dorian Boose RC 1.00 2.50
199 Randy Moss RC 10.00 25.00
200 Jacquez Green RC 1.50 4.00
201 Marcus Nash RC 1.00 2.50
202 Hines Ward RC 12.50 25.00
203 Kevin Dyson RC 2.50 6.00
204 E.G. Green RC 1.50 4.00
205 Germane Crowell RC 1.50 4.00
206 Joe Jurevicius RC 2.50 6.00
207 Tony Simmons RC 1.50 4.00
208 Tim Dwight RC 2.50 6.00
209 Az-Zahir Hakim RC 2.50 6.00
210 Jerome Pathon RC 2.50 6.00
211 Pat Johnson RC 1.50 4.00
212 Mikhael Ricks RC 1.50 4.00
213 Donald Hayes RC 1.50 4.00
214 Jammi German RC 1.00 2.50
215 Larry Shannon RC 1.00 2.50
216 Brian Alford RC 1.00 2.50
217 Curtis Enis RC 1.00 2.50
218 Fred Taylor RC 4.00 10.00
219 Robert Edwards RC 1.50 4.00
220 Ahman Green RC 5.00 12.00
221 Tavian Banks RC 1.50 4.00
222 Skip Hicks RC 1.50 4.00
223 Robert Holcombe RC 1.50 4.00
224 John Avery RC 1.50 4.00
225 Chris Fuamatu-Ma'afala RC 1.50 4.00
226 Michael Pittman RC 4.00 8.00
227 Rashaan Shehee RC 1.50 4.00
228 Jonathan Linton RC 1.50 4.00
229 Jon Ritchie RC 1.50 4.00
230 Chris Floyd RC 1.00 2.50
231 Wilmont Perry RC 1.00 2.50
232 Raymond Priester RC 1.00 2.50
233 Peyton Manning RC 20.00 50.00
234 Ryan Leaf RC 2.50 6.00
235 Brian Griese RC 5.00 12.00
236 Jeff Ogden RC 2.50 6.00
237 Charlie Batch RC 2.50 6.00
238 Moses Moreno RC 1.00 2.50
239 Jonathan Quinn RC 2.50 6.00
240 Flozell Adams RC 1.00 2.50
241 Brett Favre PT 5.00 12.00
242 Dan Marino PT 5.00 12.00
243 Emmitt Smith PT 4.00 10.00
244 Barry Sanders PT 4.00 10.00
245 Eddie George PT 1.00 2.50
246 Drew Bledsoe PT 2.00 5.00
247 Troy Aikman PT 2.50 6.00
248 Terrell Davis PT 1.00 2.50
249 John Elway PT 5.00 12.00
250 Carl Pickens PT 1.00 2.50
251 Jerry Rice PT 2.50 6.00
252 Kordell Stewart PT 1.00 2.50
253 Steve McNair PT 1.00 2.50
254 Curtis Martin PT 1.00 2.50
255 Steve Young PT 1.50 4.00
256 Herman Moore PT 1.00 2.50
257 Dorsey Levens PT 1.00 2.50
258 Deion Sanders PT 1.00 2.50
259 Napoleon Kaufman PT 1.00 2.50
260 Warrick Dunn PT 1.00 2.50
261 Corey Dillon PT 1.00 2.50
262 Jerome Bettis PT 1.00 2.50
263 Tim Brown PT 1.00 2.50
264 Cris Carter PT 1.00 2.50
265 Antonio Freeman PT 1.00 2.50
266 Randy Moss PT 6.00 15.00
267 Curtis Enis PT 1.00 2.50
268 Fred Taylor PT 1.50 4.00
269 Robert Edwards PT 1.00 2.50
270 Peyton Manning PT 10.00 25.00
271 Barry Sanders TL .40 1.00
272 Eddie George TL .15 .40
273 Troy Aikman TL .25 .60
274 Mark Brunell TL .25 .60
275 Kordell Stewart TL .25 .60
276 Tim Biakabutuka TL .08 .25
277 Terry Glenn TL .08 .25
278 Mike Alstott TL .08 .25
279 Tony Banks TL .08 .25
280 Karim Abdul-Jabbar TL .08 .25
281 Terrell Owens TL .15 .40
282 Byron Hanspard TL .08 .25
283 Jake Plummer TL .15 .40
284 Terry Allen TL .08 .25
285 Jeff Blake TL .08 .25
286 Brad Johnson TL .08 .25
287 Danny Kanell TL .08 .25
288 Natrone Means TL .08 .25
289 Rod Smith TL .08 .25
290 Thurman Thomas TL .08 .25
291 Reggie White TL .08 .25
292 Troy Davis TL .08 .25
293 Curtis Conway TL .08 .25
294 Irving Fryar TL .08 .25
295 Jim Harbaugh TL .08 .25
296 Andre Rison TL .08 .25
297 Ricky Watters TL .08 .25
298 Keyshawn Johnson TL .08 .25
299 Jeff George TL .08 .25
300 Marshall Faulk TL .25 .60

1998 Leaf Rookies and Stars Longevity

*LONGEVITY STARS: 20X TO 50X BASIC
*LONGEVITY RC STARS: 1.5X TO 4X BASIC
*LONGEV.PT STARS: 4X TO 10X BASIC PT's
*LONGEV.PT ROOKIES: 1.2X TO 3X PT's
STATED PRINT RUN 50 SERIAL #'d SETS
202 Hines Ward 75.00 150.00
233 Peyton Manning 175.00 300.00

1998 Leaf Rookies and Stars True Blue

MPLETE SET (300) 400.00 800.00
*TRUE BLUE STARS: 4X TO 10X HI COL.
*TRUE BLUE RCs: .3X TO .8X BASIC CARDS
*TRUE BLUE PT's: .8X TO 2X BASIC CARDS
STATED PRINT RUN 500 SETS

1998 Leaf Rookies and Stars Cross Training

Randomly inserted in packs, this 10-card set features action color photos of players that excel at mutiple aspects of the game. Each card highlights the same player on front and back demonstrating the different skills that make him great. The set is printed on foil board and sequentially numbered to only 1,000.

COMPLETE SET (10) 40.00 80.00
STATED PRINT RUN 1000 SERIAL #'d SETS
1 Brett Favre 10.00 25.00
2 Mark Brunell 2.50 6.00
3 Barry Sanders 8.00 20.00
4 John Elway 10.00 25.00
5 Jerry Rice 5.00 12.00
6 Kordell Stewart 2.50 6.00
7 Steve McNair 2.50 6.00
8 Deion Sanders 2.50 6.00
9 Jake Plummer 2.50 6.00
10 Steve Young 3.00 8.00

1998 Leaf Rookies and Stars Crusade Green

Randomly inserted in sets, this 30-card set features color player images with simulated Crusade shields as the background printed using Spectra-tech holographic technology. This limited insert set is sequentially numbered to 250. Two parallel sets were also produced: a Purple (sequentailly numbered to 100) and a Red (sequentially numbered to 25).

COMPLETE SET (30) 250.00 500.00
GREEN PRINT RUN 250 SERIAL #'d SETS
*PURPLE/100: .8X TO 2X GREEN/250
PURPLE PRINT RUN 100 SERIAL #'d SETS
*RED/25: 1.5X TO 4X GREEN/250
RED PRINT RUN 25 SERIAL #'d SETS
1 Brett Favre 20.00 50.00
2 Dan Marino 20.00 50.00
3 Emmitt Smith 15.00 40.00
4 Barry Sanders 15.00 40.00
5 Eddie George 4.00 12.00
6 Drew Bledsoe 6.00 15.00
7 Troy Aikman 10.00 25.00
8 Terrell Davis 5.00 12.00
9 John Elway 20.00 50.00
10 Mark Brunell 4.00 10.00
11 Jerry Rice 10.00 25.00
12 Kordell Stewart 4.00 10.00
13 Steve McNair 5.00 12.00
14 Curtis Martin 5.00 12.00
16 Steve Young 6.00 15.00
18 Deion Sanders 5.00 12.00
22 Terrell Owens 5.00 12.00
23 Jamal Anderson 4.00 10.00
25 Jerome Bettis 5.00 12.00
30 Cris Carter 5.00 12.00
32 Marshall Faulk 6.00 15.00
33 Antonio Freeman 4.00 10.00
40 Dorsey Levens 3.00 8.00
49 Garrison Hearst 3.00 8.00
57 Warrick Dunn 4.00 10.00
59 Jake Plummer 4.00 10.00
66 Peyton Manning 50.00 120.00
69 Randy Moss 12.00 30.00
77 Fred Taylor 5.00 12.00
78 Robert Edwards 3.00 8.00

1998 Leaf Rookies and Stars Extreme Measures

ndomly inserted in packs, this 10-card set features color action photos of top players highlighting an outstanding but extreme statistic for each. The set was printed on foil board and sequentially numberd to only 1000. A limited die-cut parallel version was produced using the first xxx# of each player's cards according to their highlighted statistic. For example, Brett Favre threw 35 TDs in 1998-99 season so the first 35 of his cards were die-cut.

COMPLETE SET (10) 60.00 120.00
OVERALL PRINT RUN 1000 SER.#'d SETS
1 Barry Sanders/918* 7.50 20.00
2 Warrick Dunn/941* 2.50 6.00
3 Curtis Martin/930* 2.50 6.00
4 Terrell Davis/419* 2.50 6.00
5 Troy Aikman/929* 5.00 12.00
6 Drew Bledsoe/972* 4.00 10.00
7 Eddie George/191* 6.00 15.00
8 Emmitt Smith/888* 7.50 20.00
9 Dan Marino/615* 12.50 30.00
10 Brett Favre/965* 10.00 25.00

1998 Leaf Rookies and Stars Extreme Measures Die Cuts

COMPLETE SET (10) 300.00 600.00
1 Barry Sanders/82* 40.00 100.00
2 Warrick Dunn/59* 10.00 25.00
3 Curtis Martin/70* 10.00 25.00
4 Terrell Davis/581* 5.00 12.00
5 Troy Aikman/71* 15.00 40.00
6 Drew Bledsoe/28* 40.00 100.00
7 Eddie George/809* 5.00 12.00
8 Emmitt Smith/112* 30.00 80.00
9 Dan Marino/385* 20.00 50.00
10 Brett Favre/35* 75.00 200.00

1998 Leaf Rookies and Stars Freshman Orientation

ndomly inserted in packs, this 20-card set features color action photos of the future stars of the game highlighting which round and overall number each player was selected in the NFL draft. Each card is sequentially numbered to 2,500 and highlighted with holographic foil.

COMPLETE SET (20) 30.00 80.00
STATED PRINT RUN 2500 SERIAL #'d SETS
1 Peyton Manning 12.00 30.00
2 Kevin Dyson 1.25 3.00
3 Joe Jurevicius 1.25 3.00
4 Tony Simmons 1.00 2.50
5 Marcus Nash .60 1.50
6 Ryan Leaf 1.25 3.00
7 Curtis Enis .60 1.50
8 Skip Hicks 1.25 3.00
9 Brian Griese 2.50 6.00
10 Jerome Pathon 1.25 3.00
11 John Avery 1.00 2.50
12 Fred Taylor 2.00 5.00
13 Robert Edwards 1.00 2.50
14 Robert Holcombe 1.00 2.50
15 Ahman Green 3.00 8.00
16 Hines Ward 6.00 12.00
17 Jacquez Green 1.25 3.00
18 Germane Crowell 1.25 3.00
19 Randy Moss 8.00 20.00
20 Charles Woodson 3.00 8.00

1998 Leaf Rookies and Stars Game Plan

ndomly inserted in packs, this 20-card set features color action player images on a game plan background drawing with a silver border. Each card is printed on foil board and sequentially numbered to 5,000. The first 500 of each card was treated with a "Master Game Plan" logo and unique color coating to form a parallel set to this insert.

COMPLETE SET (20) 15.00 40.00
STATED PRINT RUN 5000 SERIAL #'d SETS
*MASTERS: 1.2X TO 3X BASIC INSERTS
MASTERS PRINT RUN FIRST 500 SER.#'d SETS
1 Ryan Leaf .60 1.25
2 Peyton Manning 4.00 10.00
3 Brett Favre 2.50 6.00
4 Mark Brunell .60 1.50
5 Isaac Bruce .60 1.50
6 Dan Marino 2.50 6.00
7 Jerry Rice 1.25 3.00
8 Cris Carter .60 1.50
9 Emmitt Smith 2.00 5.00
10 Kordell Stewart .60 1.50
11 Corey Dillon .60 1.50
12 Barry Sanders 2.00 5.00
13 Curtis Martin .60 1.50
14 Carl Pickens .40 1.00
15 Eddie George .60 1.50
16 Warrick Dunn .60 1.50
17 Jake Plummer .60 1.50
18 Curtis Enis .20 .50
19 Drew Bledsoe 1.00 2.50
20 Terrell Davis .60 1.50

1998 Leaf Rookies and Stars Great American Heroes

ndomly inserted in packs, this 20-card set features color photos of players who have made the game great. Each card is stamped with holographic foil and sequentially numberd to 2,500.

COMPLETE SET (20) 40.00 80.00
STATED PRINT RUN 2500 SERIAL #'d SETS
1 Brett Favre 4.00 10.00
2 Dan Marino 4.00 10.00
3 Emmitt Smith 3.00 8.00
4 Barry Sanders 3.00 8.00
5 Eddie George 1.00 2.50
6 Drew Bledsoe 1.50 4.00
7 Troy Aikman 2.00 5.00
8 Terrell Davis 1.00 2.50
9 John Elway 4.00 10.00
10 Mark Brunell 1.00 2.50
11 Jerry Rice 2.00 5.00
12 Kordell Stewart 1.00 2.50
13 Steve McNair 1.00 2.50
14 Curtis Martin 1.00 2.50
15 Steve Young 1.25 3.00
16 Dorsey Levens 1.00 2.50
17 Herman Moore .60 1.50
18 Deion Sanders 1.00 2.50
19 Thurman Thomas 1.00 2.50
20 Peyton Manning 5.00 12.00

1998 Leaf Rookies and Stars Greatest Hits

Randomly inserted in packs, this 20-card set features color action player photos and is sequentially numbered to 2,500.

COMPLETE SET (20) 25.00 60.00
STATED PRINT RUN 2500 SERIAL #'d SETS
1 Brett Favre 4.00 10.00
2 Eddie George 1.00 2.50
3 John Elway 4.00 10.00
4 Steve Young 1.25 3.00
5 Napoleon Kaufman 1.00 2.50
6 Dan Marino 4.00 10.00
7 Drew Bledsoe 1.50 4.00
8 Mark Brunell 1.00 2.50
9 Warrick Dunn 1.00 2.50
10 Dorsey Levens 1.00 2.50
11 Emmitt Smith 3.00 8.00
12 Troy Aikman 2.00 5.00
13 Jerry Rice 2.00 5.00
14 Jake Plummer 1.00 2.50
15 Herman Moore .60 1.50
16 Barry Sanders 3.00 8.00
17 Terrell Davis 1.00 2.50
18 Kordell Stewart 1.00 2.50
19 Jerome Bettis 1.00 2.50
20 Isaac Bruce 1.00 2.50

1998 Leaf Rookies and Stars MVP Contenders

Randomly inserted in packs, this 20-card set features action color photos of the league's top players who will contend for the MVP award. Each card is accented with holographic foil stamping and sequentially numbered to 2,500.

COMPLETE SET (20) 25.00 60.00
STATED PRINT RUN 2500 SERIAL #'d SETS
1 Tim Brown 1.00 2.50
2 Herman Moore .60 1.50
3 Jake Plummer 1.00 2.50
4 Warrick Dunn 1.00 2.50
5 Dorsey Levens 1.00 2.50
6 Steve McNair 1.00 2.50
7 John Elway 4.00 10.00
8 Troy Aikman 2.00 5.00
9 Steve Young 1.25 3.00
10 Curtis Martin 1.00 2.50
11 Kordell Stewart 1.00 2.50
12 Jerry Rice 2.00 5.00
13 Mark Brunell 1.00 2.50
14 Terrell Davis 1.00 2.50
15 Drew Bledsoe 1.50 4.00
16 Eddie George 1.00 2.50
17 Barry Sanders 3.00 8.00
18 Emmitt Smith 3.00 8.00
19 Dan Marino 4.00 10.00
20 Brett Favre 4.00 10.00

1998 Leaf Rookies and Stars Standing Ovation

Randomly inserted in packs, this 10-card set features color action photos of top players printed with holographic foil stamping and sequentially numbed to 5,000.

COMPLETE SET (10) 12.50 30.00
STATED PRINT RUN 5000 SERIAL #'d SETS
1 Brett Favre 2.50 6.00
2 Dan Marino 2.50 6.00
3 Emmitt Smith 2.00 5.00
4 Barry Sanders 2.00 5.00
5 Terrell Davis .60 1.50
6 Jerry Rice 1.25 3.00
7 Steve Young .75 2.00
8 Reggie White .60 1.50
9 John Elway 2.50 6.00
10 Eddie George .60 1.50

1998 Leaf Rookies and Stars Ticket Masters

Randomly inserted in packs, this 20-card set features color action photos of top players from the same team printed on double sided foil board. Each card is sequentially numbered to 2,500 with the first 250 die-cut like a ticket.

COMPLETE SET (20) 50.00 100.00
STATED PRINT RUN 2500 SERIAL #'d SETS
*DIE CUT/250: 1.2X TO 3X BASIC INSERT
1 B.Favre/D.Levens 5.00 12.00
2 D.Marino/K.Abdul-Jabbar 5.00 12.00
3 T.Aikman/D.Sanders 2.50 6.00
4 B.Sanders/H.Moore 4.00 10.00
5 S.McNair/E.George 1.50 4.00
6 D.Bledsoe/R.Edwards 2.00 5.00
7 T.Davis/J.Elway 5.00 12.00
8 J.Rice/S.Young 3.00 8.00
9 K.Stewart/J.Bettis 1.50 4.00
10 C.Martin/K.Johnson 1.00 2.50
11 W.Dunn/T.Dilfer 1.50 4.00
12 C.Dillon/C.Pickens 1.50 4.00
13 T.Brown/N.Kaufman 1.50 4.00
14 J.Plummer/F.Sanders 1.50 4.00
15 R.Leaf/N.Means 1.50 4.00
16 P.Manning/M.Faulk 12.00 30.00
17 M.Brunell/F.Taylor 1.50 4.00
18 C.Enis/C.Conway 1.00 2.50
19 C.Carter/R.Moss 10.00 25.00
20 I.Bruce/T.Banks 1.00 2.50

1998 Leaf Rookies and Stars Touchdown Club

Randomly inserted in packs, this 20-card set features color action photos of players who are know to score a lot of touchdowns. Each card is printed on foil board and sequentially numbered to 5,000.

COMPLETE SET (20) 20.00 50.00
STATED PRINT RUN 5000 SERIAL #'d SETS
1 Brett Favre 2.50 6.00
2 Dan Marino 2.50 6.00
3 Emmitt Smith 2.00 5.00
4 Barry Sanders 2.00 5.00
5 Eddie George .60 1.50
6 Drew Bledsoe 1.00 2.50
7 Terrell Davis .60 1.50
8 Mark Brunell .60 1.50
9 Jerry Rice 1.25 3.00
10 Kordell Stewart .60 1.50
11 Curtis Martin .60 1.50
12 Karim Abdul-Jabbar .60 1.50
13 Warrick Dunn .60 1.50
14 Corey Dillon .60 1.50
15 Jerome Bettis .60 1.50
16 Antonio Freeman .60 1.50
17 Keyshawn Johnson .60 1.50
18 John Elway 2.50 6.00
19 Steve Young .75 2.00
20 Jake Plummer .60 1.50

1999 Leaf Rookies and Stars

leased as a 300-card set, 1999 Leaf Rookies and Stars features 200 veteran players and 100 rookies inserted at one in two packs. Base cards are highlighted with silver foil and rookie cards are highlighted with blue foil.

COMPLETE SET (300) 75.00 150.00
COMP.SET w/o SP's (200) 15.00 30.00
1 Frank Sanders .15 .40
2 Adrian Murrell .15 .40
3 Rob Moore .15 .40
4 Simeon Rice .15 .40
5 Michael Pittman .15 .40
6 Jake Plummer .15 .40
7 Chris Chandler .20 .50
8 Tim Dwight .20 .50
9 Chris Calloway .15 .40
10 Terance Mathis .15 .40
11 Jamal Anderson .20 .50
12 Byron Hanspard .15 .40
13 O.J. Santiago .15 .40
14 Ken Oxendine .15 .40
15 Priest Holmes .15 .40
16 Scott Mitchell .15 .40
17 Tony Banks .20 .50
18 Patrick Johnson .15 .40
19 Rod Woodson .25 .60
20 Jermaine Lewis .15 .40
21 Errict Rhett .15 .40
22 Stoney Case .15 .40
23 Andre Reed .25 .60
24 Eric Moulds .15 .40
25 Rob Johnson .20 .50
26 Doug Flutie .25 .60
27 Bruce Smith .20 .50
28 Jay Riemersma .15 .40
29 Antowain Smith .15 .40
30 Thurman Thomas .20 .50
31 Jonathan Linton .15 .40
32 Muhsin Muhammad .15 .40
33 Rae Carruth .15 .40
34 Wesley Walls .20 .50
35 Fred Lane .15 .40
36 Kevin Greene .25 .60
37 Tim Biakabutuka .20 .50
38 Curtis Enis .15 .40
39 Shane Matthews .15 .40
40 Bobby Engram .15 .40
41 Curtis Conway .20 .50
42 Marcus Robinson .20 .50
43 Darnay Scott .15 .40
44 Carl Pickens .20 .50
45 Corey Dillon .15 .40
46 Jeff Blake .20 .50
47 Terry Kirby .15 .40
48 Ty Detmer .15 .40
49 Leslie Shepherd .15 .40
50 Karim Abdul-Jabbar .15 .40
51 Emmitt Smith .40 1.00
52 Deion Sanders .20 .50
53 Michael Irvin .25 .60
54 Rocket Ismail .20 .50
55 David LaFleur .15 .40
56 Troy Aikman .30 .75
57 Ed McCaffrey .20 .50
58 Rod Smith .20 .50
59 Shannon Sharpe .20 .50
60 Brian Griese .15 .40
61 John Elway .40 1.00
62 Bubby Brister .15 .40
63 Neil Smith .15 .40
64 Terrell Davis .20 .50
65 John Avery .15 .40
66 Derek Loville .15 .40
67 Ron Rivers .15 .40
68 Herman Moore .20 .50
69 Johnnie Morton .20 .50
70 Charlie Batch .15 .40
71 Barry Sanders .40 1.00
72 Germane Crowell .15 .40
73 Greg Hill .15 .40
74 Gus Frerotte .15 .40
75 Corey Bradford .20 .50
76 Dorsey Levens .20 .50
77 Antonio Freeman .20 .50
78 Mark Chmura .15 .40
79 Brett Favre .50 1.25
80 Bill Schroeder .20 .50
81 Matt Hasselbeck .15 .40
82 E.G. Green .15 .40

83 Ken Dilger .15 .40
84 Jerome Pathon .15 .40
85 Marvin Harrison .20 .50
86 Peyton Manning .75 2.00
87 Tavian Banks .15 .40
88 Keenan McCardell .20 .50
89 Mark Brunell .20 .50
90 Fred Taylor .15 .40
91 Jimmy Smith .20 .50
92 James Stewart .15 .40
93 Kyle Brady .15 .40
94 Derrick Thomas .25 .60
95 Rashaan Shehee .15 .40
96 Derrick Alexander WR .15 .40
97 Byron Bam Morris .15 .40
98 Andre Rison .20 .50
99 Elvis Grbac .15 .40
100 Tony Gonzalez .20 .50
101 Donnell Bennett .15 .40
102 Warren Moon .25 .60
103 Zach Thomas .20 .50
104 Oronde Gadsden .15 .40
105 Dan Marino .50 1.25
106 O.J. McDuffie .20 .50
107 Tony Martin .20 .50
108 Randy Moss .20 .50
109 Cris Carter .25 .60
110 Robert Smith .15 .40
111 Randall Cunningham .20 .50
112 Jake Reed .20 .50
113 John Randle .25 .60
114 Leroy Hoard .15 .40
115 Jeff George .15 .40
116 Ty Law .25 .60
117 Shawn Jefferson .15 .40
118 Troy Brown .15 .40
119 Robert Edwards .15 .40
120 Tony Simmons .15 .40
121 Terry Glenn .20 .50
122 Ben Coates .20 .50
123 Drew Bledsoe .20 .50
124 Terry Allen .20 .50
125 Cameron Cleeland .15 .40
126 Eddie Kennison .20 .50
127 Amani Toomer .15 .40
128 Kerry Collins .15 .40
129 Joe Jurevicius .15 .40
130 Tiki Barber .20 .50
131 Ike Hilliard .15 .40
132 Michael Strahan .20 .50
133 Gary Brown .15 .40
134 Jason Sehorn .20 .50
135 Curtis Martin .20 .50
136 Vinny Testaverde .15 .40
137 Dedric Ward .15 .40
138 Keyshawn Johnson .20 .50
139 Wayne Chrebet .15 .40
140 Tyrone Wheatley .20 .50
141 Napoleon Kaufman .15 .40
142 Tim Brown .25 .60
143 Rickey Dudley .15 .40
144 Jon Ritchie .15 .40
145 James Jett .15 .40
146 Rich Gannon .20 .50
147 Charles Woodson .25 .60
148 Charles Johnson .15 .40
149 Duce Staley .15 .40
150 Will Blackwell .15 .40
151 Kordell Stewart .15 .40
152 Jerome Bettis .25 .60
153 Hines Ward .20 .50
154 Richard Huntley .15 .40
155 Natrone Means .20 .50
156 Mikhael Ricks .15 .40
157 Junior Seau .20 .50
158 Jim Harbaugh .20 .50
159 Ryan Leaf .20 .50
160 Erik Kramer .20 .50
161 Terrell Owens .20 .50
162 J.J. Stokes .15 .40
163 Lawrence Phillips .20 .50
164 Charlie Garner .20 .50
165 Jerry Rice .60 1.50
166 Garrison Hearst .15 .40
167 Steve Young .30 .75
168 Derrick Mayes .15 .40
169 Ahman Green .20 .50
170 Joey Galloway .20 .50
171 Ricky Watters .20 .50
172 Jon Kitna .15 .40
173 Sean Dawkins .15 .40
174 Az-Zahir Hakim .15 .40
175 Robert Holcombe .15 .40
176 Isaac Bruce .25 .60
177 Amp Lee .15 .40
178 Marshall Faulk .20 .50
179 Trent Green .15 .40
180 Eric Zeier .15 .40
181 Bert Emanuel .20 .50
182 Jacquez Green .15 .40
183 Reidel Anthony .15 .40
184 Warren Sapp .20 .50
185 Mike Alstott .15 .40
186 Warrick Dunn .15 .40
187 Trent Dilfer .15 .40
188 Neil O'Donnell .20 .50
189 Eddie George .20 .50
190 Yancey Thigpen .15 .40
191 Steve McNair .20 .50
192 Kevin Dyson .15 .40
193 Frank Wycheck .20 .50
194 Stephen Davis .15 .40
195 Stephen Alexander .15 .40
196 Darrell Green .25 .60
197 Skip Hicks .15 .40
198 Brad Johnson .20 .50
199 Michael Westbrook .15 .40
200 Albert Connell .15 .40
201 David Boston RC .75 2.00
202 Joel Makovicka RC .75 2.00
203 Chris Greisen RC .75 2.00
204 Jeff Paulk RC .75 2.00
205 Reginald Kelly RC .75 2.00
206 Chris McAlister RC .75 2.00
207 Brandon Stokley RC 1.00 2.50
208 Antoine Winfield RC .75 2.00
209 Bobby Collins RC .75 2.00
210 Peerless Price RC .75 2.00
211 Shawn Bryson RC .75 2.00
212 Sheldon Jackson RC .75 2.00
213 Kamil Loud RC .75 2.00
214 D'Wayne Bates RC .75 2.00
215 Jerry Azumah RC .75 2.00
216 Marty Booker RC .75 2.00
217 Cade McNown RC .75 2.00
218 James Allen RC .75 2.00
219 Nick Williams RC .75 2.00
220 Akili Smith RC .75 2.00
221 Craig Yeast RC .75 2.00
222 Damon Griffen RC 1.25 3.00
223 Scott Covington RC .75 2.00
224 Michael Basnight RC .75 2.00
225 Ronnie Powell RC .75 2.00
226 Rahim Abdullah RC .75 2.00
227 Tim Couch RC 1.00 2.50
228 Kevin Johnson RC 1.00 2.50
229 Darrin Chiaverini RC .75 2.00
230 Mark Campbell RC .75 2.00
231 Mike Lucky RC .75 2.00
232 Robert Thomas RC .75 2.00
233 Ebenezer Ekuban RC .75 2.00
234 Dat Nguyen RC 1.25 3.00
235 Wane McGarity RC .75 2.00
236 Jason Tucker RC 1.00 2.50
237 Olandis Gary RC 1.25 3.00
238 Al Wilson RC 1.25 3.00
239 Travis McGriff RC .75 2.00
240 Desmond Clark RC 1.00 2.50
241 Andre Cooper RC .75 2.00
242 Chris Watson RC .75 2.00
243 Sedrick Irvin RC .75 2.00
244 Chris Claiborne RC .75 2.00
245 Cory Sauter RC .75 2.00
246 Brock Olivo RC .75 2.00
247 De'Mond Parker RC .75 2.00
248 Aaron Brooks RC 1.00 2.50
249 Antuan Edwards RC .75 2.00
250 Basil Mitchell RC .75 2.00
251 Terrence Wilkins RC 1.00 2.50
252 Edgerrin James RC 1.25 3.00
253 Fernando Bryant RC .75 2.00
254 Mike Cloud RC .75 2.00
255 Larry Parker RC 1.00 2.50
256 Rob Konrad RC .75 2.00
257 Cecil Collins RC .75 2.00
258 James Johnson RC .75 2.00
259 Jim Kleinsasser RC 1.25 3.00
260 Daunte Culpepper RC 1.25 3.00
261 Michael Bishop RC 1.00 2.50
262 Andy Katzenmoyer RC 1.00 2.50
263 Kevin Faulk RC .75 2.00
264 Brett Bech RC .75 2.00
265 Ricky Williams RC 1.25 3.00
266 Sean Bennett RC .75 2.00
267 Joe Montgomery RC .75 2.00
268 Dan Campbell RC 1.25 3.00
269 Ray Lucas RC 1.00 2.50
270 Scott Dreisbach RC .75 2.00
271 Jed Weaver RC .75 2.00
272 Dameane Douglas RC .75 2.00
273 Cecil Martin RC .75 2.00
274 Donovan McNabb RC 6.00 15.00
275 Na Brown RC .75 2.00
276 Jerame Tuman RC .75 2.00
277 Amos Zereoue RC .75 2.00
278 Troy Edwards RC .75 2.00
279 Jermaine Fazande RC .75 2.00
280 Steve Heiden RC .75 2.00
281 Jeff Garcia RC 5.00 12.00
282 Terry Jackson RC .75 2.00
283 Charlie Rogers RC .75 2.00
284 Brock Huard RC .75 2.00
285 Karsten Bailey RC .75 2.00
286 Lamar King RC .75 2.00
287 Justin Watson RC .75 2.00
288 Kurt Warner RC 6.00 15.00
289 Torry Holt RC 1.50 4.00
290 Joe Germaine RC 1.00 2.50
291 Dre Bly RC 1.25 3.00
292 Martin Gramatica RC .75 2.00
293 Rabih Abdullah RC .75 2.00
294 Shaun King RC .75 2.00
295 Anthony McFarland RC 1.00 2.50
296 Darnell McDonald RC .75 2.00
297 Kevin Daft RC .75 2.00
298 Jevon Kearse RC 1.00 2.50
299 Mike Sellers 1.00 2.50
300 Champ Bailey RC 1.50 4.00

1999 Leaf Rookies and Stars Longevity

*STARS: 20X TO 50X HI COL.
1-200 STATED PRINT RUN 50 SER.#'d SETS
*RCs: 2X TO 5X
201-300 STATED PRINT RUN 30 SER.#'d SETS

1999 Leaf Rookies and Stars Cross Training

Ranomly inserted in packs, this 25-card set features full color action shots set against a background of concentric rays. Each card is sequentially numbered to 1250, and card backs carry a "CT" prefix.

COMPLETE SET (25) 60.00 120.00
STATED PRINT RUN 1250 SER.#'d SETS
CT1 Champ Bailey 2.00 5.00
CT2 Mark Brunell 2.00 5.00
CT3 Daunte Culpepper 5.00 12.00
CT4 Randall Cunningham 2.00 5.00
CT5 Terrell Davis 2.00 5.00
CT6 Charlie Batch 2.00 5.00
CT7 Dorsey Levens 2.00 5.00
CT8 John Elway 6.00 15.00
CT9 Marshall Faulk 2.50 6.00
CT10 Brett Favre 6.00 15.00
CT11 Doug Flutie 2.00 5.00
CT12 Edgerrin James 5.00 12.00
CT13 Curtis Martin 2.00 5.00
CT14 Donovan McNabb 6.00 15.00
CT15 Steve McNair 2.00 5.00
CT16 Cade McNown .75 2.00
CT17 Randy Moss 5.00 12.00
CT18 Jake Plummer 1.25 3.00
CT19 Barry Sanders 6.00 15.00
CT20 Deion Sanders 2.00 5.00
CT21 Akili Smith .75 2.00
CT22 Kordell Stewart 1.25 3.00
CT23 Ricky Williams 2.50 6.00
CT24 Charles Woodson 2.00 5.00
CT25 Steve Young 2.50 6.00

1999 Leaf Rookies and Stars Dress For Success

ndomly seeded in packs, this 30-card set features action player shots coupled with one or two swatches of game-worn jerseys. Single jersey cards are numbered out of 200 and dual jersey cards are numbered out of 100.

SINGLE JERSEY PRINT RUN 200 SER.#'d SETS
DUAL JERSEYS PRINT RUN 100 SER.#'d SETS
1 Barry Sanders 30.00 80.00
2 Emmitt Smith 30.00 80.00
3 B.Sanders/E.Smith 60.00 150.00
4 Eddie George 10.00 25.00
5 Terrell Davis 10.00 25.00
6 E.George/T.Davis 15.00 40.00
7 Tim Couch 10.00 25.00
8 Dan Marino 30.00 80.00
9 T.Couch/D.Marino 50.00 120.00
10 Brett Favre 40.00 100.00
11 Troy Aikman 20.00 50.00
12 B.Favre/T.Aikman 60.00 120.00
13 Drew Bledsoe 12.50 30.00
14 Mark Brunell 10.00 25.00
15 D.Bledsoe/M.Brunell 15.00 40.00
16 Randy Moss 25.00 60.00
17 Jerry Rice 25.00 60.00
18 R.Moss/J.Rice 40.00 100.00
19 Antonio Freeman 7.50 20.00
20 Terry Glenn 7.50 20.00
21 A.Freeman/T.Glenn 12.00 30.00
22 Steve Young 15.00 40.00
23 Kordell Stewart 7.50 20.00
24 S.Young/K.Stewart 25.00 60.00
25 Fred Taylor 7.50 20.00
26 Dorsey Levens 6.00 15.00
27 T.Taylor/D.Levens 10.00 25.00
28 Keyshawn Johnson 10.00 25.00
29 Herman Moore 6.00 15.00
30 K.Johnson/H.Moore 10.00 25.00

1999 Leaf Rookies and Stars John Elway Collection

Randomly inserted in packs, this 5-card set pays tribute to John Elway and places swatches of game-used jerseys, shoes, and helmets on the card front. Helmet/shoe cards are numbered to 125 and jersey cards are numbered to 300.

HELMET/SHOES PRINT RUN 125 CARDS
JERSEY PRINT RUN 300 SERIAL #'d CARDS
JEC1 John Elway Home Jer. 12.00 30.00
JEC2 John Elway Away Jer. 20.00 50.00
JEC3 John Elway Shoe 25.00 60.00
JEC4 John Elway Blue Helmet 40.00 100.00
JEC5 John Elway Orange Hel. 40.00 120.00

1999 Leaf Rookies and Stars Freshman Orientation

Randomly inserted in packs, this 25-card set focues on top rookies. Card fronts feature action photos with colored borders on the left and right of the card. Each card is sequentially numbered to 2500 and card backs carry an "FO" prefix.

COMPLETE SET (25) 40.00 80.00
STATED PRINT RUN 2500 SER.#'d SETS
FO1 Champ Bailey 1.25 3.00
FO2 D'Wayne Bates .50 1.25
FO3 David Boston .60 1.50
FO4 Kurt Warner 4.00 10.00
FO5 Cecil Collins .30 .75
FO6 Tim Couch .60 1.50
FO7 Daunte Culpepper 3.00 8.00
FO8 Troy Edwards .50 1.25
FO9 Kevin Faulk .60 1.50
FO10 Joe Germaine .50 1.25
FO11 Torry Holt 2.50 6.00
FO12 Brock Huard .60 1.50
FO13 Sedrick Irvin .30 .75
FO14 Edgerrin James 3.00 8.00
FO15 Kevin Johnson .60 1.50
FO16 Shaun King .50 1.25
FO17 Rob Konrad .60 1.50
FO18 Sean Bennett .30 .75
FO19 Donovan McNabb 4.00 10.00
FO20 Cade McNown .50 1.25
FO21 Peerless Price .60 1.50
FO22 Akili Smith .50 1.25
FO23 Ricky Williams 1.50 4.00
FO24 James Johnson .50 1.25
FO25 Olandis Gary .60 1.50

1999 Leaf Rookies and Stars Game Plan

Randomly inserted in packs, this 25-card set showcases NFL playmakers on this all-foil card. Each card is sequentially numbered to 2500 and card backs carry a "GP" prefix.

COMPLETE SET (25) 40.00 80.00
STATED PRINT RUN 2500 SER.#'d SETS
*MASTERS: 3X TO 8X BASIC INSERTS
MASTERS PRINT RUN 50 SER.#'d SETS
GP1 Jamal Anderson 1.25 3.00
GP2 Jerome Bettis 1.25 3.00
GP3 Drew Bledsoe 1.50 4.00
GP4 Tim Brown 1.25 3.00
GP5 Mark Brunell 1.25 3.00
GP6 Tim Couch .60 1.50
GP7 Terrell Davis 1.25 3.00
GP8 Corey Dillon 1.25 3.00
GP9 Warrick Dunn 1.25 3.00
GP10 Brad Johnson 1.25 3.00
GP11 Brett Favre 4.00 10.00
GP12 Doug Flutie 1.25 3.00
GP13 Joey Galloway .75 2.00
GP14 Eddie George 1.25 3.00
GP15 Keyshawn Johnson 1.25 3.00
GP16 Peyton Manning 4.00 10.00
GP17 Dan Marino 4.00 10.00
GP18 Donovan McNabb 4.00 10.00
GP19 Cade McNown .50 1.25
GP20 Randy Moss 3.00 8.00
GP21 Jake Plummer .75 2.00
GP22 Barry Sanders 4.00 10.00
GP23 Emmitt Smith 2.50 6.00
GP24 Ricky Williams 1.50 4.00
GP25 Steve Young 1.50 4.00

1999 Leaf Rookies and Stars Great American Heroes

ndomly inserted in packs, this 25 card set places action photos inside a bordered oval on the left side of the card. The right side of the card contains a Great American Heroes logo. Cards are sequentially numbered to 2500 and card backs carry a "GAH" prefix.

COMPLETE SET (25) 40.00 80.00
STATED PRINT RUN 2500 SER.#'d SETS
1 Troy Aikman 2.50 6.00
2 Jamal Anderson 1.25 3.00
3 Drew Bledsoe 1.50 4.00
4 Mark Brunell 1.25 3.00
5 Cris Carter 1.25 3.00
6 Randall Cunningham 1.25 3.00
7 Terrell Davis 1.25 3.00
8 John Elway 4.00 10.00
9 Brett Favre 4.00 10.00
10 Doug Flutie 1.25 3.00
11 Antonio Freeman 1.25 3.00
12 Eddie George 1.25 3.00
13 Peyton Manning 4.00 10.00
14 Dan Marino 4.00 10.00
15 Curtis Martin 1.25 3.00
16 Warren Moon 1.25 3.00
17 Randy Moss 3.00 8.00
18 Jake Plummer .75 2.00
19 Jerry Rice 2.50 6.00
20 Barry Sanders 4.00 10.00
21 Deion Sanders 1.25 3.00
22 Emmitt Smith 2.50 6.00
23 Fred Taylor 1.25 3.00
24 Ricky Williams 4.00 10.00
25 Steve Young 1.50 4.00

1999 Leaf Rookies and Stars Greatest Hits

ndomly seeded in packs, this 25-card set places full color action photos on a colored background with a silver foil Greatest Hits logo on the card front. Each card is sequentially numbered to 2500 and card backs carry a "GH" prefix.

COMPLETE SET (25) 30.00 60.00
STATED PRINT RUN 2500 SER.#'d SETS
GH1 Troy Aikman 2.50 6.00
GH2 Terry Glenn 1.25 3.00
GH3 Jamal Anderson 1.25 3.00
GH4 Drew Bledsoe 1.50 4.00
GH5 Cris Carter 1.25 3.00
GH6 Terrell Davis 1.25 3.00
GH7 John Elway 4.00 10.00
GH8 Brett Favre 4.00 10.00
GH9 Antonio Freeman 1.25 3.00
GH10 Eddie George 1.25 3.00
GH11 Priest Holmes 2.00 5.00
GH12 Keyshawn Johnson 1.25 3.00
GH13 Dorsey Levens 1.25 3.00
GH14 Dan Marino 4.00 10.00
GH15 Curtis Martin 1.25 3.00
GH16 Randy Moss 3.00 8.00
GH17 Eric Moulds .75 2.00
GH18 Terrell Owens 1.25 3.00
GH19 Carl Pickens .75 2.00
GH20 Jake Plummer .75 2.00
GH21 Jerry Rice 2.50 6.00
GH22 Barry Sanders 2.50 6.00
GH23 Marvin Harrison 1.25 3.00
GH24 Robert Smith 1.25 3.00
GH25 Fred Taylor 1.25 3.00

1999 Leaf Rookies and Stars Prime Cuts

ndomly inserted in packs, this 15-card set features prime jersey cut swatches, such as logos, numbers, and patches, on the card front. Card backs carry a "PC" prefix.

PC1 Tim Couch 20.00 50.00
PC2 Fred Taylor 20.00 50.00
PC3 Terry Glenn 15.00 40.00
PC4 Drew Bledsoe 25.00 60.00
PC5 Dan Marino 60.00 150.00
PC6 Jerry Rice 40.00 100.00
PC7 Barry Sanders 40.00 100.00
PC8 Mark Brunell 20.00 50.00
PC9 Brett Favre 50.00 120.00
PC10 Steve Young 30.00 80.00
PC11 Keyshawn Johnson 20.00 50.00
PC12 Antonio Freeman 20.00 50.00
PC13 Randy Moss 30.00 80.00
PC14 Troy Aikman 30.00 80.00
PC15 Emmitt Smith 50.00 120.00

1999 Leaf Rookies and Stars Signature Series

Randomly seeded in packs, this 30-card set showcases one or two player action photos coupled with autographs of those appearing on the card front. Single autograph cards are numbered out of 150 and double autograph cards are numbered out of 50. Some cards were issued via mail redemptions that carried an expiration date of 12/31/2000. Please note that card number SS6 Eddie George/Ricky Williams dual auto was signed by Eddie George only and serial numbered to 90.

SINGLE SIGNED PRINT RUN 150 SER.#'d SETS
DUAL SIGNED PRINT RUN 50 SER.#'d SETS
SS1 Terrell Davis 15.00 40.00
SS2 Edgerrin James 15.00 40.00
SS3 T.Davis/E.James 60.00 120.00
SS4 Eddie George 15.00 40.00
SS5 Ricky Williams 15.00 40.00
SS6 E.George AU R.Will/90 20.00 50.00
SS7 Jake Plummer 15.00 40.00
SS8 Donovan McNabb 30.00 80.00
SS9 Plummer/McNabb 40.00 80.00
SS10 Randall Cunningham 15.00 40.00
SS11 Daunte Culpepper 15.00 40.00
SS12 R.Cunning/D.Culpepper 40.00 100.00
SS13 Fred Taylor 12.00 30.00
SS14 Cecil Collins 10.00 25.00
SS15 F.Taylor/O.Gary 15.00 40.00
SS16 Randy Moss 30.00 60.00
SS17 Torry Holt 15.00 40.00
SS18 R.Moss/T.Holt 40.00 80.00
SS19 Steve Young 40.00 80.00
SS20 Cade McNown 12.00 30.00
SS21 S.Young/C.McNown 40.00 100.00
SS22 Jerry Rice 60.00 120.00
SS23 David Boston 12.00 30.00
SS24 J.Rice/D.Boston 40.00 100.00
SS25 Doug Flutie 15.00 40.00
SS26 Akili Smith 10.00 25.00
SS27 D.Flutie/Ak.Smith 30.00 60.00
SS28 Dan Marino 75.00 150.00
SS29 Tim Couch 12.00 30.00
SS30 D.Marino/T.Couch 75.00 150.00

1999 Leaf Rookies and Stars SlideShow

ndomly inserted in packs, this 25-card set features transparent cell technology that places an action slide of the featured player in the center of this card. Base slide show cards have a red border around the cell and are sequentially numbered to 100.

COMP.RED SET (25) 250.00 500.00
RED STATED PRINT RUN 100 SER.#'d CARDS
*GREEN STARS: .8X TO 2X REDS
*GREEN ROOKIES: .6X TO 1.5X REDS
GREEN STATED PRINT RUN 50 SER.#'d CARDS
*BLUE STARS: 1.5X TO 4X REDS
*BLUE ROOKIES: 1X TO 2.5X REDS
BLUE STATED PRINT RUN 25 SER.#'d CARDS
UNPRICED STUDIOS SERIAL #'d OF 1 SET
1 Troy Aikman 12.50 30.00
2 Drew Bledsoe 7.50 20.00
3 Mark Brunell 6.00 15.00
4 Tim Couch 6.00 15.00
5 Terrell Davis 6.00 15.00
6 John Elway 20.00 50.00
7 Brett Favre 20.00 50.00
8 Antonio Freeman 6.00 15.00
9 Eddie George 6.00 15.00
10 Torry Holt 7.50 20.00
11 Edgerrin James 12.00 30.00
12 Keyshawn Johnson 6.00 15.00
13 Jon Kitna 6.00 15.00
14 Dorsey Levens 6.00 15.00
15 Peyton Manning 15.00 40.00
16 Dan Marino 20.00 50.00
17 Randy Moss 12.50 30.00
18 Jake Plummer 6.00 15.00
19 Jerry Rice 12.50 30.00
20 Barry Sanders 20.00 50.00
21 Marvin Harrison 6.00 15.00
22 Emmitt Smith 12.50 30.00
23 Fred Taylor 6.00 15.00
24 Ricky Williams 7.50 20.00
25 Steve Young 7.50 20.00

1999 Leaf Rookies and Stars Statistical Standouts

ndomly inserted in packs, this 25-card set showcases the top 25 producers for rushing, receiving, and passing. Cards place action photos on a simulated leather football background highlighted with white foil. Each card is sequentially numbered to 1250 and card backs carry an "SS" prefix.

COMPLETE SET (25) 50.00 100.00
STATED PRINT RUN 1250 SER.#'d SETS
SS1 Jamal Anderson 1.50 4.00
SS2 Jerome Bettis 1.50 4.00
SS3 Drew Bledsoe 2.00 5.00
SS4 Cris Carter 1.50 4.00
SS5 Randall Cunningham 1.50 4.00
SS6 Terrell Davis 1.50 4.00
SS7 John Elway 5.00 12.00
SS8 Marshall Faulk 2.00 5.00
SS9 Brett Favre 5.00 12.00
SS10 Antonio Freeman 1.50 4.00
SS11 Joey Galloway 1.00 2.50
SS12 Eddie George 1.50 4.00
SS13 Garrison Hearst 1.00 2.50
SS14 Keyshawn Johnson 1.50 4.00
SS15 Peyton Manning 5.00 12.00
SS16 Steve McNair 1.50 4.00
SS17 Randy Moss 4.00 10.00
SS18 Eric Moulds 1.00 2.50
SS19 Terrell Owens 1.50 4.00
SS20 Jake Plummer 1.00 2.50
SS21 Barry Sanders 5.00 12.00
SS22 Emmitt Smith 3.00 8.00
SS23 Fred Taylor 1.50 4.00
SS24 Vinny Testaverde 1.00 2.50
SS25 Steve Young 2.00 5.00

1999 Leaf Rookies and Stars Statistical Standouts Die Cuts

COMPLETE SET (25) 600.00 1200.00
CARDS #'d UNDER 26 NOT PRICED
SS2 Jerome Bettis/71 6.00 15.00
SS3 Drew Bledsoe/37 15.00 40.00
SS5 Randall Cunningham/52 10.00 25.00
SS7 John Elway/47 30.00 80.00
SS8 Marshall Faulk/86 10.00 25.00
SS9 Brett Favre/63 30.00 80.00
SS12 Eddie George/76 7.50 20.00
SS13 Garrison Hearst/51 6.00 15.00
SS14 Keyshawn Johnson/60 6.00 15.00
SS15 Peyton Manning/26 40.00 100.00
SS16 Steve McNair/71 7.50 20.00
SS17 Randy Moss/17 60.00 150.00
SS21 Barry Sanders/76 25.00 60.00
SS22 Emmitt Smith/25 40.00 100.00
SS23 Fred Taylor/77 7.50 20.00
SS24 Vinny Testaverde/29 7.50 20.00
SS25 Steve Young/34 20.00 50.00

1999 Leaf Rookies and Stars Ticket Masters

ndomly inserted in packs, this 25-card set places action player photos on a ticket stub background. Each card is sequentially numbered to 2500 and card backs carry a "TM" prefix.

COMPLETE SET (25) 50.00 100.00
STATED PRINT RUN 2500 SER.#'d SETS
*EXECUTIVES: 4X TO 10X HI COL.
TM1 R.Moss C.Carter 5.00 12.00
TM2 B.Favre A.Freeman 5.00 12.00
TM3 C.Collins D.Marino 5.00 12.00
TM4 B.Griese T.Davis 2.00 5.00
TM5 E.James P.Manning 12.50 25.00
TM6 E.Smith T.Aikman 3.00 8.00
TM7 J.Rice S.Young 3.00 8.00
TM8 M.Brunell F.Taylor 1.25 3.00
TM9 D.Boston J.Plummer 1.25 3.00
TM10 T.Glenn D.Bledsoe 2.00 5.00
TM11 C.Batch H.Moore 1.25 3.00
TM12 M.Alstott W.Dunn 1.25 3.00
TM13 E.George S.McNair 1.25 3.00
TM14 K.Stewart J.Bettis 1.25 3.00
TM15 C.Chandler J.Anderson 1.25 3.00
TM16 A.Smith C.Dillon 1.25 3.00
TM17 C.Enis C.McNown 1.25 3.00
TM18 I.Bruce M.Faulk 1.25 3.00
TM19 E.Moulds D.Flutie 1.25 3.00
TM20 J.Galloway R.Watters 1.25 3.00
TM21 M.Westbrook B.Johnson 1.25 3.00
TM22 C.Martin K.Johnson 1.25 3.00
TM23 N.Kaufman T.Brown 1.25 3.00
TM24 K.Johnson T.Couch 1.25 3.00
TM25 D.Staley D.McNabb 4.00 10.00

1999 Leaf Rookies and Stars Touchdown Club

ndomly inserted in packs, this 20-card set highlights top touchdown scorers. Card fronts contain the total number of touchdowns in a black oval on the top. Each card is sequentially numbered to 1000 and card backs carry a "TC" prefix.

COMPLETE SET (20) 75.00 150.00
STATED PRINT RUN 1000 SER.#'d SETS
*DIE CUTS: 2X TO 5X BASIC INSERTS
DIE CUT STATED PRINT RUN 60 SER.#'d SETS
TC1 Randy Moss 6.00 15.00
TC2 Brett Favre 8.00 20.00
TC3 Dan Marino 8.00 20.00
TC4 Barry Sanders 8.00 20.00
TC5 John Elway 8.00 20.00
TC6 Terrell Davis 2.50 6.00
TC7 Peyton Manning 8.00 20.00
TC8 Emmitt Smith 5.00 12.00
TC9 Jerry Rice 5.00 12.00
TC10 Fred Taylor 2.50 6.00
TC11 Drew Bledsoe 3.00 8.00
TC12 Steve Young 3.00 8.00
TC13 Eddie George 2.50 6.00
TC14 Cris Carter 2.50 6.00
TC15 Antonio Freeman 2.50 6.00
TC16 Marvin Harrison 2.50 6.00
TC17 Kurt Warner 6.00 15.00
TC18 Stephen Davis 2.50 6.00
TC19 Terry Glenn 2.50 6.00
TC20 Brad Johnson 2.50 6.00

2000 Leaf Rookies and Stars

leased in late December 2000, Leaf Rookies and Stars features a 300-card base set divided up into 100 veteran cards, 160 rookies sequentially numbered to 1000, and 40 NFL Europe Prospects sequentially numbered to 3000. Base cards showcase full color player action shots with a border along the left side and bottom of the card. Rookie cards have the word "Rookie" along the left card border, and the words "NFLE Prospects" appear along the left edge of the NFL Europe Prospect cards. In addition, several rookies and all of the NFL Europe Prospects autographed the first 200 serial numbered sets out of the stated print run which are broken out into a separate listing. Leaf Rookies and Stars was packaged five cards per pack and carried a suggested retail price of $2.99.

COMP.SET w/o SP's (100) 6.00 15.00
1 Jake Plummer .15 .40
2 David Boston .15 .40
3 Tim Dwight .20 .50
4 Jamal Anderson .20 .50
5 Chris Chandler .20 .50
6 Tony Banks .15 .40
7 Qadry Ismail .15 .40
8 Eric Moulds .15 .40
9 Doug Flutie .20 .50
10 Lamar Smith .15 .40
11 Peerless Price .20 .50
12 Rob Johnson .20 .50
13 Reggie White .25 .60
14 Muhsin Muhammad .15 .40
15 Steve Beuerlein .20 .50
16 Cade McNown .15 .40
17 Derrick Alexander .15 .40
18 Marcus Robinson .20 .50
19 Corey Dillon .15 .40
20 Akili Smith .15 .40
21 Tim Couch .20 .50
22 Kevin Johnson .15 .40
23 Emmitt Smith .40 1.00
24 Troy Aikman .30 .75
25 Joey Galloway .20 .50
26 Rocket Ismail .20 .50
27 John Elway .40 1.00
28 Terrell Davis .20 .50
29 Brian Griese .15 .40
30 Olandis Gary .20 .50
31 Ed McCaffrey .20 .50
32 Rod Smith .20 .50
33 Barry Sanders .40 1.00
34 Charlie Batch .15 .40
35 Germane Crowell .15 .40
36 James Stewart .15 .40
37 Brett Favre .50 1.25
38 Dorsey Levens .20 .50
39 Antonio Freeman .20 .50
40 Peyton Manning .60 1.50
41 Edgerrin James .20 .50
42 Marvin Harrison .20 .50
43 Fred Taylor .15 .40
44 Mark Brunell .20 .50
45 Jimmy Smith .20 .50
46 Elvis Grbac .15 .40
47 Tony Gonzalez .20 .50
48 Dan Marino .50 1.25
49 Joe Horn .20 .50
50 Jay Fiedler .20 .50
51 James Allen .15 .40
52 Randy Moss .20 .50
53 Daunte Culpepper .20 .50
54 Cris Carter .25 .60
55 Robert Smith .15 .40
56 Drew Bledsoe .20 .50
57 Terry Glenn .20 .50
58 Ricky Williams .20 .50
59 Amani Toomer .15 .40
60 Kerry Collins .15 .40
61 Curtis Martin .20 .50
62 Vinny Testaverde .15 .40
63 Wayne Chrebet .15 .40
64 Tim Brown .25 .60
65 Tyrone Wheatley .15 .40
66 Rich Gannon .20 .50
67 Donovan McNabb .20 .50
68 Duce Staley .15 .40
69 Jerome Bettis .25 .60
70 Donald Hayes .15 .40
71 Junior Seau .20 .50
72 Jermaine Fazande .15 .40
73 Jerry Rice .60 1.50
74 Steve Young .30 .75
75 Terrell Owens .20 .50
76 Charlie Garner .20 .50
77 Jeff Garcia .15 .40
78 Tim Biakabutuka .20 .50
79 Tiki Barber .20 .50
80 Ricky Watters .20 .50
81 Kurt Warner .40 1.00
82 Marshall Faulk .20 .50
83 Isaac Bruce .25 .60
84 Torry Holt .20 .50
85 Mike Alstott .15 .40
86 Warrick Dunn .15 .40
87 Shaun King .15 .40
88 Keyshawn Johnson .20 .50
89 Warren Sapp .20 .50
90 Eddie George .20 .50
91 Jevon Kearse .15 .40
92 Steve McNair .20 .50
93 Carl Pickens .20 .50
94 Deion Sanders .20 .50
95 Stephen Davis .15 .40
96 Brad Johnson .20 .50
97 Bruce Smith .20 .50
98 Michael Westbrook .15 .40
99 Albert Connell .15 .40
100 Jeff George .20 .50
101 Thomas Jones RC 2.50 6.00
102 Bashir Yamini RC 2.00 5.00
103 Jamal Lewis RC 3.00 8.00
104 Travis Taylor RC 2.00 5.00
105 Chris Redman RC 2.00 5.00
106 Avion Black RC 2.00 5.00
107 Sammy Morris RC 2.00 5.00
108 Dez White RC 2.00 5.00
109 Peter Warrick RC 2.00 5.00
110 Ron Dugans RC 2.00 5.00
111 Curtis Keaton RC 2.00 5.00
112 Danny Farmer RC 2.00 5.00
113 Courtney Brown RC 2.50 6.00
114 Dennis Northcutt RC 2.00 5.00
115 Travis Prentice RC 2.00 5.00
116 JaJuan Dawson RC 2.00 5.00
117 Spergon Wynn RC 2.00 5.00
118 Michael Wiley RC 2.00 5.00
119 Chris Cole RC 2.50 6.00
120 Mike Anderson RC 2.00 5.00
121 Muneer Moore RC 2.00 5.00
122 Reuben Droughns RC 2.00 5.00
123 Bubba Franks RC 2.00 5.00
124 Anthony Lucas RC 2.00 5.00
125 Charles Lee RC 2.00 5.00
126 R.Jay Soward RC 2.00 5.00
127 Shyrone Stith RC 2.00 5.00
128 Sylvester Morris RC 2.00 5.00
129 Frank Moreau RC 2.00 5.00
130 Dante Hall RC 2.00 5.00
131 Doug Chapman RC 2.00 5.00
132 Troy Walters RC 2.00 5.00
133 J.R. Redmond RC 2.00 5.00
134 Tom Brady RC 300.00 600.00
135 Terrelle Smith RC 2.00 5.00
136 Chad Morton RC 2.50 6.00
137 Ron Dayne RC 3.00 8.00
138 Ron Dixon RC 2.00 5.00
139 Chad Pennington RC 2.50 6.00
140 Anthony Becht RC 2.00 5.00
141 Laveranues Coles RC 2.50 6.00
142 Windrell Hayes RC 2.00 5.00
143 Sebastian Janikowski RC 3.00 8.00
144 Jerry Porter RC 3.00 8.00
145 Corey Simon RC 2.50 6.00
146 Todd Pinkston RC 2.00 5.00
147 Gari Scott RC 2.00 5.00
148 Plaxico Burress RC 2.50 6.00
149 Tee Martin RC 2.00 5.00
150 Trevor Gaylor RC 2.00 5.00
151 Ronney Jenkins RC 2.00 5.00
152 Giovanni Carmazzi RC 2.00 5.00
153 Tim Rattay RC 2.50 6.00
154 Shaun Alexander RC 3.00 8.00
155 Darrell Jackson RC 2.00 5.00
156 James Williams RC 2.00 5.00
157 Trung Canidate RC 2.00 5.00
158 Joe Hamilton RC 2.00 5.00
159 Erron Kinney RC 2.00 5.00
160 Todd Husak RC 2.00 5.00
161 Raynoch Thompson RC 2.00 5.00
162 Darwin Walker RC 2.00 5.00
163 Jay Tant RC 2.00 5.00
164 Doug Johnson RC 2.00 5.00
165 Robert Bean RC 2.00 5.00
166 Mark Simoneau RC 2.00 5.00
167 John Jones RC 2.00 5.00
168 Obafemi Ayanbadejo RC 2.50 6.00
169 Mike Brown RC 2.00 5.00
170 Shockmain Davis RC 2.00 5.00
171 Erik Flowers RC 2.00 5.00
172 Corey Moore RC 2.00 5.00
173 Drew Haddad RC 2.00 5.00
174 Kwame Cavil RC 2.00 5.00
175 Pat Dennis RC 2.00 5.00
176 Rashard Anderson RC 2.00 5.00
177 Brian Finneran RC 3.00 8.00
178 Na'il Diggs RC 2.00 5.00
179 Marc Bulger RC 2.50 6.00
180 Mondriel Fulcher RC 2.00 5.00
181 Dwayne Carswell 2.00 5.00
182 Brian Urlacher RC 10.00 25.00
183 Paul Edinger RC 3.00 8.00
184 Karon Coleman RC 2.00 5.00
185 Aaron Shea RC 2.50 6.00
186 Fabien Bownes RC 2.00 5.00
187 Damon Hodge RC 2.50 6.00
188 Dwayne Goodrich RC 2.00 5.00
189 Clint Stoerner RC 3.00 8.00
190 James Whalen RC 2.00 5.00
191 Deltha O'Neal RC 2.00 5.00
192 Ian Gold RC 2.00 5.00
193 Kenoy Kennedy RC 2.00 5.00
194 Jarious Jackson RC 2.50 6.00
195 Leroy Fields RC 2.00 5.00
196 Barrett Green RC 2.00 5.00
197 Joey Jamison RC 2.00 5.00
198 Rondell Mealey RC 2.00 5.00
199 Rob Morris RC 2.50 6.00
200 Marcus Washington RC 2.50 6.00
201 Trevor Insley RC 2.00 5.00
202 Jamel White RC 2.00 5.00
203 Kevin McDougal RC 2.00 5.00
204 Ibn Green RC 2.00 5.00
205 T.J. Slaughter RC 2.00 5.00
206 Emanuel Smith RC 2.00 5.00
207 Herbert Goodman RC 2.00 5.00
208 William Bartee RC 2.00 5.00
209 Orantes Grant RC 2.00 5.00
210 Brad Hoover RC 2.50 6.00
211 Deon Dyer RC 2.00 5.00
212 Jonas Lewis RC 2.00 5.00
213 Chris Hovan RC 2.50 6.00
214 Fred Robbins RC 2.00 5.00
215 Michael Boireau RC 2.00 5.00
216 Giles Cole RC 2.00 5.00
217 Dave Stachelski RC 2.00 5.00
218 Patrick Pass RC 2.00 5.00
219 Darren Howard RC 2.00 5.00
220 Austin Wheatley RC 2.00 5.00
221 Kevin Houser RC 2.00 5.00
222 Rian Lindell RC 2.00 5.00
223 Jake Delhomme RC 2.50 6.00
224 Cornelius Griffin RC 2.00 5.00
225 Shaun Ellis RC 2.50 6.00
226 John Abraham RC 3.00 8.00
227 Travares Tillman RC 2.00 5.00
228 Julian Peterson RC 3.00 8.00
229 Marcus Knight RC 2.00 5.00
230 Thomas Hamner RC 2.00 5.00
231 Hank Poteat RC 2.00 5.00
232 Neil Rackers RC 2.00 5.00
233 Bobby Shaw RC 2.00 5.00
234 Rogers Beckett RC 2.00 5.00
235 Reggie Jones RC 2.00 5.00
236 Tim Seder RC 2.00 5.00
237 Durell Price RC 2.00 5.00
238 Ahmed Plummer RC 2.00 5.00
239 John Engelberger RC 2.00 5.00
240 Paul Smith RC 2.00 5.00
241 Chafie Fields RC 2.00 5.00
242 Kevin Feterik RC 2.00 5.00
243 Jacoby Shepherd RC 2.00 5.00
244 Nate Webster RC 2.00 5.00
245 Ketric Sanford RC 2.00 5.00
246 Tavarus Hogans RC 2.00 5.00
247 Keith Bulluck RC 2.50 6.00
248 Mike Green RC 2.50 6.00
249 Chris Coleman RC 2.00 5.00
250 Demario Brown RC 2.00 5.00
251 Billy Volek RC 3.00 8.00
252 Mareno Philyaw RC 2.00 5.00
253 Ethan Howell RC 2.00 5.00
254 Chris Samuels RC 3.00 8.00
255 Brandon Short RC 2.00 5.00
256 Maurice Smith RC 2.50 6.00
257 Frank Murphy RC 2.00 5.00
258 Darrick Vaughn RC 2.00 5.00
259 Payton Williams RC 2.00 5.00
260 JaJuan Seider RC 2.00 5.00
261 Antonio Banks EP RC .60 1.50
262 Jonathan Brown EP RC .60 1.50
263 Ontiwaun Carter EP RC .60 1.50
264 Jeremaine Copeland EP .60 1.50
265 Ralph Dawkins EP RC .60 1.50
266 Marques Douglas EP RC .60 1.50
267 Kevin Drake EP RC .60 1.50
268 Damon Dunn EP RC .60 1.50
269 Todd Floyd EP RC .60 1.50
270 Tony Graziani EP .75 2.00
271 Derrick Ham EP RC .75 2.00
272 Duane Hawthorne EP RC .60 1.50
273 Alonzo Johnson EP RC .60 1.50
274 Mark Kacmarynski EP RC .60 1.50
275 Eric Kresser EP .60 1.50
276 Jim Kubiak EP RC .60 1.50
277 Blaine McElmurry EP RC .60 1.50
278 Scott Milanovich EP .60 1.50
279 Norman Miller EP RC .60 1.50
280 Sean Morey EP RC .60 1.50
281 Jeff Ogden EP .60 1.50
282 Pepe Pearson EP RC .60 1.50
283 Ron Powlus EP RC 1.00 2.50
284 Jason Shelley EP RC .60 1.50
285 Ben Snell EP RC .60 1.50
286 Aaron Stecker EP RC .60 1.50
287 L.C. Stevens EP .60 1.50
288 Mike Sutton EP RC .60 1.50
289 Damian Vaughn EP RC .60 1.50
290 Ted White EP .60 1.50
291 Marcus Crandell EP RC .60 1.50
292 Darryl Daniel EP RC .60 1.50
293 Jesse Haynes EP .60 1.50
294 Matt Lytle EP RC .60 1.50
295 Deon Mitchell EP RC .60 1.50
296 Kendrick Nord EP RC .60 1.50
297 Ronnie Powell EP .60 1.50
298 Selucio Sanford EP RC .60 1.50
299 Corey Thomas EP .60 1.50
300 Vershan Jackson EP RC .60 1.50
301 Michael Vick XRC 8.00 20.00
302 Drew Brees XRC 30.00 60.00
303 Quincy Carter XRC 3.00 8.00
304 Marques Tuiasosopa XRC 3.00 8.00
305 Chris Weinke XRC 3.00 8.00
306 LaDainian Tomlinson XRC 6.00 15.00
307 Deuce McAllister XRC 4.00 10.00
308 Michael Bennett XRC 4.00 10.00
309 Anthony Thomas XRC 4.00 10.00
310 LaMont Jordan XRC 4.00 10.00
311 David Terrell XRC 3.00 8.00
312 Koren Robinson XRC 3.00 8.00
313 Rod Gardner XRC 3.00 8.00
314 Santana Moss XRC 4.00 10.00
315 Freddie Mitchell XRC 2.50 6.00
316 Gerard Warren XRC 2.50 6.00
317 Justin Smith XRC 5.00 12.00
318 Richard Seymour XRC 3.00 8.00
319 Andre Carter XRC 2.50 6.00
320 Jamal Reynolds XRC 2.50 6.00

2000 Leaf Rookies and Stars Longevity

*VETS 1-100: 10X TO 25X BASIC CARDS
1-100 VETERAN PRINT RUN 50
*ROOKIES 101-260: 1X TO 2.5X
*EP 261-300: 2X TO 5X BASIC CARDS
*ROOKIES 301-320: .8X TO 2X
101-320 ROOKIE/EP PRINT RUN 30
134 Tom Brady 900.00 1500.00
302 Drew Brees 75.00 125.00
306 LaDainian Tomlinson 30.00 80.00

2000 Leaf Rookies and Stars Rookie Autographs

Randomly inserted in packs, this set features the first 200 serial numbered copies of some Draft Picks and NFL Europe Prospect cards from the base set. Each card contains an authentic player autograph. Most cards were issued as exchanges with an expiration date of 8/31/2002.
FIRST 200 SER.#'d ROOKIE CARDS SIGNED
103 Jamal Lewis 8.00 20.00
104 Travis Taylor 5.00 12.00
105 Chris Redman 5.00 12.00
108 Dez White 5.00 12.00
109 Peter Warrick 5.00 12.00
112 Danny Farmer 5.00 12.00
113 Courtney Brown 6.00 15.00
115 Travis Prentice 5.00 12.00
116 JaJuan Dawson 5.00 12.00
120 Mike Anderson 5.00 12.00
123 Bubba Franks 5.00 12.00
126 R.Jay Soward 5.00 12.00
127 Shyrone Stith 5.00 12.00
128 Sylvester Morris 5.00 12.00
137 Ron Dayne 8.00 20.00
139 Chad Pennington 6.00 15.00
141 Laveranues Coles 6.00 15.00
144 Jerry Porter 8.00 20.00
145 Corey Simon 6.00 15.00
146 Todd Pinkston 5.00 12.00
148 Plaxico Burress 6.00 15.00
154 Shaun Alexander 8.00 20.00
155 Darrell Jackson 5.00 12.00
157 Trung Canidate 5.00 12.00
261 Antonio Banks 5.00 12.00
262 Jonathan Brown 5.00 12.00
263 Ontiwaun Carter 5.00 12.00
264 Jeremaine Copeland 5.00 12.00
266 Marques Douglas 5.00 12.00
267 Kevin Drake 5.00 12.00
268 Damon Dunn 5.00 12.00
269 Todd Floyd 5.00 12.00
270 Tony Graziani 6.00 15.00
272 Duane Hawthorne 5.00 12.00
273 Alonzo Johnson 5.00 12.00
274 Mark Kacmarynski 5.00 12.00
275 Eric Kresser 5.00 12.00
276 Jim Kubiak 5.00 12.00
277 Blaine McElmurry 5.00 12.00
278 Scott Milanovich 5.00 12.00
279 Norman Miller 5.00 12.00
280 Sean Morey 5.00 12.00
281 Jeff Ogden 5.00 12.00
282 Pepe Pearson 5.00 12.00
283 Ron Powlus 8.00 20.00
284 Jason Shelley 5.00 12.00
285 Ben Snell 5.00 12.00
286 Aaron Stecker 5.00 12.00
287 L.C. Stevens 5.00 12.00
288 Mike Sutton 5.00 12.00
290 Ted White 5.00 12.00
292 Darryl Daniel 5.00 12.00
293 Jesse Haynes 5.00 12.00
294 Matt Lytle 5.00 12.00
295 Deon Mitchell 5.00 12.00
296 Kendrick Nord 5.00 12.00
298 Selucio Sanford 5.00 12.00
299 Corey Thomas 5.00 12.00
300 Vershan Jackson 5.00 12.00
114 Dennis Northcutt 5.00 12.00

2000 Leaf Rookies and Stars Dress Four Success

Randomly inserted in packs, this 50-card set features player action photography and swatches of memorabilia. For each player, a card with a jersey swatch, shoe swatch, helmet swatch, football or pants swatch, and a combination of all four were produced. Card backs carry a "D4S" prefix.
STATED PRINT RUN 25-300
1C Jerry Rice Combo/25 60.00 150.00
1H Jerry Rice Helmet/100 25.00 60.00
1J Jerry Rice Jersey/300 15.00 40.00
1P Jerry Rice Pants/300 15.00 40.00
1S Jerry Rice Shoe/50 30.00 80.00
2C Eddie George Combo/25 20.00 50.00
2F Eddie George FB/100 8.00 20.00
2J Eddie George Jersey/200 5.00 12.00
2S Eddie George Shoe/50 10.00 25.00
3C Troy Aikman Combo/25 30.00 80.00
3F Troy Aikman FB/100 12.00 30.00
3H Troy Aikman Helmet/100 12.00 30.00
3J Troy Aikman Jersey/300 8.00 20.00
3S Troy Aikman Shoe/50 15.00 40.00
4F Mark Brunell FB/100 8.00 20.00
4J Mark Brunell Jersey/300 5.00 12.00
4S Mark Brunell Shoe/50 10.00 25.00
5C Barry Sanders Combo/25 40.00 100.00
5F Barry Sanders FB/100 15.00 40.00
5H Barry Sanders Helmet 15.00 40.00
5J Barry Sanders Jersey/300 10.00 25.00
5S Barry Sanders Shoe/50 20.00 50.00
6C Marshall Faulk Combo/25 20.00 50.00
6J Marshall Faulk Jersey/300 5.00 12.00
6P Marshall Faulk Pants/300 5.00 12.00
6S Marshall Faulk Shoe/50 10.00 25.00
7C Dan Marino Combo/25 50.00 125.00
7H Dan Marino Helmet/100 20.00 50.00
7J Dan Marino Jersey/300 12.00 30.00
7P Dan Marino Pants/300 12.00 30.00
7S Dan Marino Shoe/50 30.00 80.00
8C Stephen Davis Combo/25 15.00 40.00
8F Stephen Davis FB/100 6.00 15.00
8H Stephen Davis Helmet 6.00 15.00
8J Stephen Davis Jersey/300 4.00 10.00
8S Stephen Davis Shoe/50 8.00 20.00
9C Terrell Davis Combo/25 20.00 50.00
9H Terrell Davis Helmet/100 8.00 20.00
9J Terrell Davis Jersey/225 5.00 12.00
9S Terrell Davis Shoe/50 10.00 25.00
10C Brett Favre Combo/25 50.00 125.00
10F Brett Favre FB/100 20.00 50.00
10H Brett Favre Helmet/100 20.00 50.00
10J Brett Favre Jersey/175 15.00 40.00
10S Brett Favre Shoe/50 25.00 60.00

2000 Leaf Rookies and Stars Freshman Orientation

Randomly inserted in packs, this 30-card set features top rookies from the 2000 season showcased on a card with a banner carrying the respective player's team logo along the bottom and a border resembling a jersey along the left side of the card. Each card is sequentially numbered to 2000.
COMPLETE SET (30) 50.00 100.00
STATED PRINT RUN 2000 SER.#'d SETS
F01 Peter Warrick .75 2.00
F02 Jamal Lewis 1.25 3.00
F03 Thomas Jones 1.00 2.50
F04 Plaxico Burress 1.00 2.50
F05 Travis Taylor .75 2.00
F06 Ron Dayne 1.25 3.00
F07 Bubba Franks .75 2.00
F08 Chad Pennington 1.00 2.50
F09 Shaun Alexander 1.25 3.00
F010 Sylvester Morris .75 2.00
F011 R.Jay Soward .75 2.00
F012 Trung Canidate .75 2.00
F013 Dennis Northcutt .75 2.00
F014 Todd Pinkston .75 2.00
F015 Jerry Porter 1.25 3.00
F016 Travis Prentice .75 2.00
F017 Giovanni Carmazzi .75 2.00
F018 Ron Dugans .75 2.00
F019 Dez White .75 2.00
F020 Mike Anderson .75 2.00
F021 Ron Dixon .75 2.00
F022 Chris Redman .75 2.00
F023 J.R. Redmond .75 2.00
F024 Laveranues Coles 1.00 2.50
F025 JaJuan Dawson .75 2.00
F026 Darrell Jackson .75 2.00
F027 Sammy Morris .75 2.00
F028 Doug Chapman .75 2.00
F029 Tim Rattay 1.00 2.50
F030 Gari Scott .75 2.00

2000 Leaf Rookies and Stars Game Plan

Randomly seeded in packs, this 30-card set features NFL's top playmakers on an all foil board card with silver foil highlights. Each card is sequentially numbered to 2000.
COMPLETE SET (30) 30.00 60.00
STATED PRINT RUN 2000 SER.#'d SETS
*MASTERS/50: 2X TO 5X BASIC INSERTS
MASTERS PRINT RUN 50 SER.#'d SETS
GP1 Charlie Garner .60 1.50
GP2 Jerome Bettis .75 2.00
GP3 Jamal Lewis .75 2.00
GP4 Eric Moulds .50 1.25
GP5 Cade McNown .50 1.25
GP6 Peter Warrick .50 1.25
GP7 Tim Couch .60 1.50
GP8 Emmitt Smith 1.25 3.00
GP9 Troy Aikman 1.00 2.50
GP10 Terrell Davis .60 1.50
GP11 Brett Favre 1.50 4.00
GP12 Peyton Manning 2.00 5.00
GP13 Edgerrin James .60 1.50
GP14 Fred Taylor .50 1.25
GP15 Randy Moss .60 1.50
GP16 Daunte Culpepper .60 1.50
GP17 Drew Bledsoe .60 1.50
GP18 Ricky Williams .60 1.50
GP19 Ron Dayne .75 2.00
GP20 Curtis Martin .60 1.50
GP21 Donovan McNabb .60 1.50
GP22 Plaxico Burress .60 1.50
GP23 Jerry Rice 2.00 5.00
GP24 Shaun Alexander .75 2.00
GP25 Kurt Warner 1.25 3.00
GP26 Marshall Faulk .60 1.50
GP27 Keyshawn Johnson .60 1.50
GP28 Eddie George .60 1.50
GP29 Steve McNair .60 1.50
GP30 Stephen Davis .50 1.25

2000 Leaf Rookies and Stars Great American Heroes

Randomly inserted in packs, this 10-card set features top players on a foil board card. Base insert frames players with an oval and has silver foil highlights. Each card is sequentially numbered to 1000.
COMPLETE SET (10) 20.00 40.00
STATED PRINT RUN 1000 SER.#'d SETS
GAH1 John Elway 1.50 4.00
GAH2 Terrell Davis .75 2.00
GAH3 Barry Sanders 1.50 4.00
GAH4 Edgerrin James .75 2.00
GAH5 Dan Marino 2.00 5.00
GAH6 Randy Moss .75 2.00
GAH7 Ricky Williams .75 2.00
GAH8 Jerry Rice 2.50 6.00
GAH9 Steve Young 1.25 3.00
GAH10 Kurt Warner 1.50 4.00

2000 Leaf Rookies and Stars Great American Signatures

Randomly inserted in packs, this 10-card set parallels the base Great American Heroes insert set enhanced with an authentic player autograph. Each card was sequentially numbered to 100.
AUTO.PRINT RUN 100 SER.#'d SETS
GAS1 John Elway 60.00 120.00
GAS2 Terrell Davis 15.00 40.00
GAS3 Barry Sanders 50.00 100.00
GAS4 Edgerrin James 15.00 40.00
GAS5 Dan Marino 75.00 150.00
GAS7 Ricky Williams 15.00 40.00
GAS8 Jerry Rice 75.00 135.00
GAS10 Kurt Warner 30.00 60.00

2000 Leaf Rookies and Stars Great American Treasures

Randomly inserted in packs, this 10-card set parallels the base Great American Heroes insert set enhanced with an authentic game worn jersey. Each card was sequentially numbered to 100. The first 25 serial numbered sets were autographed.
JERSEY PRINT RUN 100 SER.#'d SETS
GAT1 John Elway 15.00 40.00
GAT2 Terrell Davis 8.00 20.00
GAT3 Barry Sanders 15.00 40.00
GAT4 Edgerrin James 8.00 20.00
GAT5 Dan Marino 20.00 50.00
GAT6 Randy Moss 8.00 20.00
GAT7 Ricky Williams 8.00 20.00
GAT8 Jerry Rice 25.00 60.00
GAT9 Steve Young 12.00 30.00
GAT10 Kurt Warner 15.00 40.00

2000 Leaf Rookies and Stars Great American Treasures Autographs

Randomly inserted in packs, this 10-card set parallels the base Great American Heroes set and consists of the first 25 serial numbered Great American Heroes Jerseys set. Each card is autographed and sequentially numbered from 001/100 to 025/100. Some cards were issued via mail redemptions in packs that expired on 8/31/2002.
GATA1 John Elway 100.00 200.00
GATA2 Terrell Davis 25.00 60.00
GATA3 Barry Sanders 100.00 200.00
GATA4 Edgerrin James 25.00 60.00
GATA5 Dan Marino 125.00 250.00
GATA7 Ricky Williams 25.00 60.00
GATA8 Jerry Rice 125.00 200.00
GATA9 Steve Young 75.00 150.00
GATA10 Kurt Warner 60.00 120.00

2000 Leaf Rookies and Stars Joe Montana Collection

Randomly inserted in Hobby packs, this five card set features sequentially numbered cards with an action photograph of Joe Montana and a swatch of game used memorabilia. The first 25 serial numbered sets of each card were autographed.
STATED PRINT RUN 125-300
MC1 Joe Montana SF Jer/275* 15.00 40.00
MC2 Joe Montana KC Jer/275* 15.00 40.00
MC3 Joe Montana Helmet/100* 30.00 80.00
MC4 Joe Montana FB/100* 30.00 80.00
MC5 Joe Montana Shoe/100* 25.00 60.00

2000 Leaf Rookies and Stars Joe Montana Collection Autographs

ndomly inserted Hobby in packs, this 5-card set parallels the base Joe Montana Collection insert set. This set consists of the first 26 serial numbered copies of each card. All cards are autogrpahed by Joe Montana.
COMMON CARD (MC1-MC5) 75.00 200.00
FIRST 25 SER.#'d SETS SIGNED
MC1 Joe Montana SF JSY 75.00 200.00
MC2 Joe Montana KC JSY 75.00 200.00
MC3 J.Montana Helmet 75.00 200.00
MC4 J.Montana FB 75.00 200.00
MC5 J.Montana Shoe 75.00 200.00

2000 Leaf Rookies and Stars Prime Cuts

ndomly inserted in Hobby Packs, this 30-card set features a full color action photograph of each player coupled with a premium swatch of a game worn jersey. Swatches include patches, numbers and logos. Each card is sequentially numbered to 25.
STATED PRINT RUN 25 SER.#'d SETS
PC1 Eric Moulds 6.00 15.00
PC2 Cade McNown 6.00 15.00
PC3 Tim Couch 8.00 20.00
PC4 Emmitt Smith 15.00 40.00
PC5 John Elway 15.00 40.00
PC6 Terrell Davis 8.00 20.00
PC7 Brian Griese 6.00 15.00
PC8 Barry Sanders 15.00 40.00
PC9 Brett Favre 20.00 50.00
PC10 Antonio Freeman 8.00 20.00
PC11 Peyton Manning 25.00 60.00
PC12 Edgerrin James 8.00 20.00
PC13 Marvin Harrison 8.00 20.00
PC14 Fred Taylor 6.00 15.00
PC15 Mark Brunell 8.00 20.00
PC16 Jimmy Smith 8.00 20.00
PC17 Dan Marino 20.00 50.00
PC18 Randy Moss 8.00 20.00
PC19 Cris Carter 10.00 25.00
PC20 Ricky Williams 8.00 20.00
PC21 Curtis Martin 8.00 20.00
PC22 Donovan McNabb 8.00 20.00
PC23 Jerry Rice 25.00 60.00
PC24 Steve Young 12.00 30.00
PC25 Kurt Warner 15.00 40.00
PC26 Marshall Faulk 8.00 20.00
PC27 Isaac Bruce 10.00 25.00
PC28 Shaun King 6.00 15.00
PC29 Eddie George 8.00 20.00
PC30 Steve McNair 8.00 20.00

2000 Leaf Rookies and Stars SlideShow

Randomly inseretd in packs, this 60-card set features an on field action photograph of a player framed by a border set to match each player's respective team colors. Cards are sequentially numbered to 1000.
COMPLETE SET (60) 60.00 120.00
STATED PRINT RUN 1000 SER.#'d SETS
*STUDIO/25: 3X TO 8X BASIC INSERTS
S1 Jake Plummer .60 1.50
S2 Thomas Jones .60 1.50
S3 Jamal Anderson .75 2.00
S4 Jamal Lewis .75 2.00
S5 Travis Taylor .50 1.25
S6 Eric Moulds .60 1.50
S7 Cade McNown .60 1.50
S8 Marcus Robinson .75 2.00
S9 Corey Dillon .60 1.50
S10 Akili Smith .60 1.50
S11 Peter Warrick .50 1.25
S12 Tim Couch .75 2.00
S13 Travis Prentice .50 1.25
S14 Emmitt Smith 1.50 4.00
S15 Troy Aikman 1.25 3.00
S16 Mike Anderson .50 1.25
S17 John Elway 1.50 4.00
S18 Terrell Davis .75 2.00
S19 Brian Griese .60 1.50
S20 Terrell Owens .75 2.00
S21 Barry Sanders 1.50 4.00
S22 Charlie Batch .60 1.50
S23 Brett Favre 2.00 5.00
S24 Dorsey Levens .75 2.00
S25 Antonio Freeman .75 2.00
S26 Peyton Manning 2.50 6.00
S27 Edgerrin James .75 2.00
S28 Marvin Harrison .75 2.00
S29 Fred Taylor .60 1.50
S30 Mark Brunell .75 2.00
S31 Jimmy Smith .75 2.00
S32 Sylvester Morris .60 1.50
S33 Dan Marino 2.00 5.00
S34 Randy Moss .75 2.00
S35 Daunte Culpepper .75 2.00
S36 Cris Carter 1.00 2.50
S37 Robert Smith .60 1.50
S38 Drew Bledsoe .75 2.00
S39 Ricky Williams .75 2.00
S40 Ron Dayne .75 2.00
S41 Curtis Martin .75 2.00
S42 Chad Pennington .60 1.50
S43 Tim Brown 1.00 2.50
S44 Donovan McNabb .75 2.00
S45 Torry Holt .75 2.00
S46 Plaxico Burress .60 1.50
S47 Jerry Rice 2.50 6.00
S48 Steve Young 1.25 3.00
S49 Shaun Alexander .75 2.00
S50 Kurt Warner 1.50 4.00
S51 Marshall Faulk .75 2.00
S52 Isaac Bruce 1.00 2.50
S53 Shaun King .60 1.50
S54 Keyshawn Johnson .75 2.00
S55 Mike Alstott .60 1.50
S56 Eddie George .75 2.00
S57 Steve McNair .75 2.00
S58 Jevon Kearse .60 1.50
S59 Stephen Davis .60 1.50
S60 Brad Johnson .75 2.00

2000 Leaf Rookies and Stars Statistical Standouts

Randomly inserted in packs, this 40-card set features color player action photography on a card with a background colored to resemble the leather of a football and foil highlights. Each card is sequentially numbered to 500.
COMPLETE SET (40) 75.00 150.00
STATED PRINT RUN 500 SER.#'d SETS
SS1 Thomas Jones 1.00 2.50
SS2 Jamal Lewis 1.25 3.00
SS3 Travis Taylor .75 2.00
SS4 Cade McNown 1.00 2.50
SS5 Corey Dillon 1.00 2.50
SS6 Akili Smith 1.00 2.50
SS7 Peter Warrick .75 2.00
SS8 Tim Couch 1.25 3.00
SS9 Emmitt Smith 2.50 6.00
SS10 Troy Aikman 2.00 5.00
SS11 John Elway 2.50 6.00
SS12 Terrell Davis 1.25 3.00
SS13 Barry Sanders 2.50 6.00
SS14 Brett Favre 3.00 8.00
SS15 Dorsey Levens 1.25 3.00
SS16 Antonio Freeman 1.25 3.00
SS17 Peyton Manning 4.00 10.00
SS18 Edgerrin James 1.00 2.50
SS19 Marvin Harrison 1.25 3.00
SS20 Fred Taylor 1.00 2.50
SS21 Dan Marino 3.00 8.00
SS22 Randy Moss 1.25 3.00
SS23 Daunte Culpepper 1.25 3.00
SS24 Cris Carter 1.50 4.00
SS25 Drew Bledsoe 1.25 3.00
SS26 Ricky Williams 1.25 3.00
SS27 Ron Dayne 1.25 3.00
SS28 Curtis Martin 1.25 3.00
SS29 Chad Pennington 1.00 2.50
SS30 Plaxico Burress 1.00 2.50
SS31 Jerry Rice 4.00 10.00
SS32 Steve Young 2.00 5.00
SS33 Shaun Alexander 1.50 4.00
SS34 Kurt Warner 2.50 6.00
SS35 Marshall Faulk 1.25 3.00
SS36 Isaac Bruce 1.50 4.00
SS37 Eddie George 1.25 3.00
SS38 Steve McNair 1.25 3.00
SS39 Stephen Davis 1.00 2.50
SS40 Brad Johnson 1.25 3.00

2000 Leaf Rookies and Stars Ticket Masters

Randomly inserted in packs, this 30-card set features back-to-back dual player cards. Team standouts are paired on a foil enhanced base card that is sequentially numbered to 2000.
COMPLETE SET (30) 30.00 60.00
STATED PRINT RUN 2000 SER.#'d SETS
TM1 T.Jones .60 1.50
J.Plummer
TM2 J.Anderson .60 1.50
C.Chandler
TM3 T.Taylor .75 2.00
J.Lewis
TM4 E.Moulds .60 1.50
R.Johnson
TM5 M.Muhammad .60 1.50
S.Beuerlein
TM6 C.McNown .60 1.50
M.Robinson
TM7 P.Warrick .50 1.25
Ak.Smith
TM8 T.Couch .60 1.50
Kv.Johnson
TM9 E.Smith 1.25 3.00
T.Aikman
TM10 T.Davis .60 1.50
B.Griese
TM11 C.Batch .50 1.25
J.Stewart
TM12 B.Favre 1.50 4.00
A.Freeman
TM13 P.Manning 2.00 5.00
E.James
TM14 M.Brunell .60 1.50
F.Taylor
TM15 J.Fiedler .60 1.50
L.Smith
TM16 R.Moss .60 1.50
D.Culpepper
TM17 D.Bledsoe .60 1.50
T.Glenn
TM18 R.Williams .60 1.50
J.Blake
TM19 K.Collins .75 2.00
R.Dayne
TM20 C.Pennington .60 1.50
C.Martin
TM21 T.Brown .75 2.00
R.Gannon
TM22 D.McNabb .60 1.50
D.Staley
TM23 P.Burress .75 2.00
J.Bettis
TM24 R.Leaf .60 1.50
J.Fazande
TM25 J.Rice 2.00 5.00
T.Owens
TM26 S.Alexander .75 2.00
R.Watters
TM27 K.Warner 1.25 3.00
M.Faulk
TM28 S.King .60 1.50
Ky.Johnson
TM29 E.George .60 1.50
S.McNair
TM30 S.Davis .60 1.50
B.Johnson

2001 Leaf Rookies and Stars Chicago Collection

T PRICED DUE TO SCARCITY

2001 Leaf Rookies and Stars

This 300 card set was issued in December, 2001. The cards were issued in five card packs which came 24 to a box. Cards numbered 1-100 honored leading veterans while cards numbered 101-300 featured rookies.
COMP.SET w/o SP's (100) 7.50 20.00
201-300 ROOKIE ODDS 1:24
1 Aaron Brooks .15 .40
2 Ahman Green .20 .50
3 Antonio Freeman .25 .60
4 Brad Johnson .20 .50
5 Brett Favre .50 1.25
6 Brian Griese .15 .40
7 Brian Urlacher .30 .75
8 Bruce Smith .20 .50
9 Cade McNown .20 .50
10 Chad Pennington .15 .40
11 Champ Bailey .20 .50
12 Charles Woodson .25 .60
13 Charlie Batch .15 .40
14 Charlie Garner .20 .50
15 Corey Dillon .15 .40
16 Cris Carter .25 .60
17 Curtis Martin .20 .50
18 Dan Marino .50 1.25
19 Daunte Culpepper .20 .50
20 David Boston .15 .40
21 Deion Sanders .20 .50
22 Donovan McNabb .20 .50
23 Doug Flutie .20 .50
24 Drew Bledsoe .20 .50
25 Duce Staley .15 .40
26 Ed McCaffrey .20 .50
27 Eddie George .25 .60
28 Edgerrin James .20 .50
29 Elvis Grbac .20 .50
30 Emmitt Smith .40 1.00
31 Eric Moulds .15 .40
32 Fred Taylor .15 .40
33 Germane Crowell .15 .40
34 Ike Hilliard .15 .40
35 Isaac Bruce .25 .60
36 Jake Plummer .15 .40
37 Jamal Anderson .20 .50
38 Jamal Lewis .25 .60
39 James Allen .15 .40
40 James Stewart .15 .40
41 Jay Fiedler .20 .50
42 Jeff Garcia .15 .40
43 Jeff George .20 .50
44 Jeff Lewis .15 .40
45 Jerome Bettis .25 .60
46 Jerry Rice .50 1.25
47 Jevon Kearse .15 .40
48 Jimmy Smith .20 .50
49 Joey Galloway .20 .50
50 John Elway .40 1.00
51 Junior Seau .20 .50
52 Keenan McCardell .20 .50
53 Kerry Collins .15 .40
54 Kevin Johnson .15 .40
55 Keyshawn Johnson .20 .50
56 Kordell Stewart .15 .40
57 Kurt Warner .40 1.00
58 Lamar Smith .20 .50
59 Marcus Robinson .20 .50
60 Mark Brunell .20 .50
61 Marshall Faulk .20 .50
62 Marvin Harrison .20 .50
63 Matt Hasselbeck .15 .40
64 Mike Alstott .15 .40
65 Mike Anderson .15 .40
66 Muhsin Muhammad .15 .40
67 Peter Warrick .15 .40
68 Peyton Manning .60 1.50
69 Priest Holmes .15 .40
70 Randy Moss .20 .50
71 Ray Lewis .25 .60
72 Rich Gannon .20 .50
73 Ricky Watters .20 .50
74 Ricky Williams .20 .50
75 Rob Johnson .20 .50
76 Rod Smith .20 .50
77 Ron Dayne .20 .50
78 Shannon Sharpe .20 .50
79 Shaun Alexander .15 .40
80 Stephen Davis .15 .40
81 Steve McNair .20 .50
82 Steve Young .30 .75
83 Sylvester Morris .15 .40
84 Terrell Davis .20 .50
85 Terrell Owens .20 .50
86 Thomas Jones .15 .40
87 Tim Brown .25 .60
88 Tim Couch .15 .40
89 Tony Banks .15 .40
90 Tony Gonzalez .20 .50
91 Torry Holt .20 .50
92 Travis Taylor .15 .40
93 Trent Green .15 .40
94 Troy Aikman .30 .75
95 Tyrone Wheatley .20 .50
96 Vinny Testaverde .15 .40
97 Warren Sapp .20 .50
98 Warrick Dunn .15 .40
99 Wayne Chrebet .15 .40
100 Zach Thomas .20 .50
101 A.J. Feeley RC 1.50 4.00
102 Josh Booty RC 1.50 4.00
103 Roderick Robinson RC 1.25 3.00
104 Renaldo Hill RC 1.50 4.00
105 Harold Blackmon RC 1.25 3.00
106 Rudi Johnson RC 2.00 5.00
107 Curtis Fuller RC 1.25 3.00
108 Dan Alexander RC 1.50 4.00
109 Anthony Thomas RPS 2.00 5.00
110 Travis Minor RPS 1.50 4.00
111 Heath Evans RC 1.50 4.00
112 Joe Walker RC 1.25 3.00
113 Moran Norris RC 1.25 3.00
114 Quincy Carter RPS 1.50 4.00
115 Michael Vick RPS 2.00 5.00
116 Vinny Sutherland RC 1.25 3.00
117 Scotty Anderson RC 1.25 3.00
118 Eddie Berlin RC 1.25 3.00
119 Jonathan Carter RC 1.25 3.00
120 Monty Beisel RC 1.25 3.00
121 T.J. Houshmandzadeh RC 1.50 4.00
122 Rodney Bailey RC 1.25 3.00
123 Reggie Germany RC 1.25 3.00
124 Ellis Wyms RC 1.25 3.00
125 Koren Robinson RPS 1.50 4.00
126 Antonio Pierce RC 4.00 10.00
127 Arnold Jackson RC 1.25 3.00
128 Andre Rone RC 1.25 3.00
129 Richard Newsome RC 1.25 3.00
130 Ifeanyi Ohalete RC 1.25 3.00
131 Dan O'Leary RC 1.25 3.00
132 Shad Meier RC 1.25 3.00
133 Jay Feely RC 2.00 5.00
134 B.Manumaleuna RC 1.50 4.00
135 Riall Johnson RC 1.25 3.00
136 Snoop Minnis RPS 1.25 3.00
137 Jermaine Hampton RC 1.25 3.00
138 Johnny Huggins RC 1.25 3.00
139 Marcellus Rivers RC 1.25 3.00
140 Andre Carter RPS 1.50 4.00
141 Michael Stone RC 1.25 3.00
142 Tony Dixon RC 1.25 3.00
143 Bhawoh Jue RC 1.50 4.00
144 Will Peterson RC 1.50 4.00
145 Anthony Henry RC 2.00 5.00
146 M.Tuiasosopo RPS 1.50 4.00
147 Reggie Swinton RC 1.25 3.00
148 Robert Carswell RC 1.25 3.00
149 Freddie Mitchell RPS 1.25 3.00
150 Idrees Bashir RC 1.25 3.00
151 James Boyd RC 1.25 3.00
152 Chris Chambers RPS .75 2.00
153 Aaron Schobel RC 2.00 5.00
154 Dominic Raiola RC 1.25 3.00
155 Derrick Burgess RC 2.00 5.00
156 DeLawrence Grant RC 1.25 3.00
157 Karon Riley RC 1.25 3.00
158 Cedric Scott RC 1.25 3.00
159 Patrick Washington RC 1.25 3.00
160 Eric Johnson RC 2.00 5.00
161 Tevita Ofahengaue RC 1.25 3.00
162 Chris Cooper RC 1.25 3.00
163 Fred Wakefield RC 1.25 3.00
164 Kenny Smith RC 1.25 3.00
165 Marcus Bell RC 1.25 3.00
166 Mario Fatafehi RC 1.25 3.00
167 Anthony Herron RC 1.25 3.00
168 Joe Tafoya RC 1.25 3.00
169 Morlon Greenwood RC 1.25 3.00
170 Orlando Huff RC 1.25 3.00
171 Carlos Polk RC 1.25 3.00
172 Edgerton Hartwell RC 1.25 3.00
173 Zeke Moreno RC 1.50 4.00
174 Alex Lincoln RC 1.25 3.00
175 Quinton Caver RC 1.25 3.00
176 Matt Stewart RC 1.25 3.00
177 Markus Steele RC 1.25 3.00
178 Dwight Smith RC 1.25 3.00
179 Reggie Wayne RPS 1.50 4.00
180 Jerametrius Butler RC 1.25 3.00
181 Jason Doering RC 1.25 3.00
182 John Howell RC 1.25 3.00
183 Alvin Porter RC 1.25 3.00
184 Eric Downing RC 1.25 3.00
185 John Nix RC 1.25 3.00
186 Tim Baker RC 1.25 3.00
187 Robert Garza RC 1.25 3.00
188 Randy Chevrier RC 1.25 3.00
189 Drew Brees RPS 25.00 50.00
190 Shawn Worthen RC 1.25 3.00
191 Drew Bennett RC 2.00 5.00
192 Marlon McCree RC 1.25 3.00
193 David Terrell RPS 1.50 4.00
194 Jeff Backus RC 1.25 3.00
195 Otis Leverette RC 1.25 3.00
196 Jason Glenn RC 1.25 3.00
197 Rashad Holman RC 1.25 3.00
198 T.J. Turner RC 1.25 3.00
199 Lynn Scott RC 1.25 3.00
200 Bill Gramatica RC 1.25 3.00
201 Michael Vick RC 5.00 12.00
202 Drew Brees RC 50.00 100.00
203 Quincy Carter RC 2.50 6.00
204 Jesse Palmer RC 2.50 6.00
205 Mike McMahon RC 2.50 6.00
206 Dave Dickenson RC 2.50 6.00
207 Jameel Cook RC 2.50 6.00
208 Marques Tuiasosopo RC 2.50 6.00
209 Chris Weinke RC 2.50 6.00
210 Sage Rosenfels RC 2.50 6.00
211 Josh Heupel RC 3.00 8.00
212 LaDainian Tomlinson RC 10.00 25.00
213 Michael Bennett RC 2.50 6.00
214 Anthony Thomas RC 3.00 8.00
215 Travis Henry RC 2.50 6.00
216 James Jackson RC 2.00 5.00
217 Correll Buckhalter RC 2.00 5.00
218 Derrick Blaylock RC 2.50 6.00
219 Dee Brown RC 2.00 5.00
220 LeVar Woods RC 2.50 6.00
221 Deuce McAllister RC 3.00 8.00
222 LaMont Jordan RC 3.00 8.00
223 Kevan Barlow RC 2.50 6.00
224 Travis Minor RC 2.50 6.00
225 David Terrell RC 2.50 6.00
226 Koren Robinson RC 2.50 6.00
227 Rod Gardner RC 2.50 6.00
228 Santana Moss RC 3.00 8.00
229 Freddie Mitchell RC 2.00 5.00
230 Reggie Wayne RC 4.00 10.00
231 Quincy Morgan RC 2.50 6.00
232 Chris Chambers RC 2.00 5.00
233 Steve Smith RC 6.00 15.00
234 Snoop Minnis RC 2.00 5.00
235 Justin McCareins RC 2.50 6.00
236 Onome Ojo RC 2.00 5.00
237 Darnerien McCants RC 2.50 6.00
238 Mike McMahon RPS 2.50 6.00
239 Cedrick Wilson RC 2.50 6.00
240 Kevin Kasper RC 2.00 5.00
241 Chris Taylor RC 2.00 5.00
242 Ken-Yon Rambo RC 2.00 5.00
243 Richmond Flowers RC 2.00 5.00
244 Andre King RC 2.00 5.00
245 Boo Williams RC 2.00 5.00
246 Adrian Wilson RC 8.00 20.00
247 Cory Bird RC 2.50 6.00
248 Alex Bannister RC 2.00 5.00
249 Elvis Joseph RC 2.00 5.00
250 Chad Johnson RC 3.00 8.00
251 Robert Ferguson RC 3.00 8.00
252 David Martin RC 2.00 5.00
253 Quentin McCord RC 2.50 6.00
254 Todd Heap RC 2.50 6.00
255 Alge Crumpler RC 3.00 8.00
256 Nate Clements RC 2.50 6.00
257 Will Allen RC 3.00 8.00
258 Willie Middlebrooks RC 2.50 6.00
259 Fred Smoot RC 2.50 6.00
260 Andre Dyson RC 2.00 5.00
261 Gary Baxter RC 2.00 5.00
262 Jamar Fletcher RC 2.00 5.00
263 Ken Lucas RC 2.50 6.00
264 Tay Cody RC 2.00 5.00
265 Eric Kelly RC 2.00 5.00
266 Adam Archuleta RC 2.50 6.00
267 Derrick Gibson RC 2.00 5.00
268 Jarrod Cooper RC 2.50 6.00
269 Hakim Akbar RC 2.00 5.00
270 Tony Driver RC 2.50 6.00
271 Justin Smith RC 4.00 10.00
272 Andre Carter RC 2.50 6.00
273 Jamal Reynolds RC 2.00 5.00
274 Gerard Warren RC 2.50 6.00
275 Richard Seymour RC 3.00 8.00
276 Damione Lewis RC 2.50 6.00
277 Casey Hampton RC 3.00 8.00
278 Marcus Stroud RC 2.50 6.00
279 Benjamin Gay RC 2.50 6.00
280 Shaun Rogers RC 3.00 8.00
281 Dan Morgan RC 2.50 6.00
282 Kendrell Bell RC 3.00 8.00
283 Tommy Polley RC 2.00 5.00
284 Jamie Winborn RC 2.50 6.00
285 Sedrick Hodge RC 2.00 5.00
286 Torrance Marshall RC 2.00 5.00
287 Eric Westmoreland RC 2.00 5.00
288 Brian Allen RC 2.00 5.00
289 Brandon Spoon RC 2.50 6.00
290 Henry Burris RC 3.00 8.00
291 Leonard Davis RC 3.00 8.00
292 Kenyatta Walker RC 2.00 5.00
293 Cedric James RC 2.00 5.00
294 Sean Brewer RC 2.00 5.00
295 Jason Brookins RC 3.00 8.00
296 Kyle Vanden Bosch RC 3.00 8.00
297 Nick Goings RC 3.00 8.00
298 Kris Jenkins RC 3.00 8.00
299 Dominic Rhodes RC 2.50 6.00
300 Leonard Myers RC 2.00 5.00

2001 Leaf Rookies and Stars Longevity

ETS 1-100: 10X TO 25X BASIC CARDS
1-100 VETERAN PRINT RUN 50
*ROOKIES 101-200: 2.5X TO 6X
*ROOKIES 201-300: 1.5X TO 4X
101-200 ROOKIE PRINT RUN 25

2001 Leaf Rookies and Stars Rookie Autographs

Randomly inserted in packs, these 50 cards have signatures of leading rookie prospects. These cards are skip numbered since not every rookie signed cards for this product. These cards had a stated print run of 230. Some players did not sign their cards in time for inclusion in this product and those cards could be redeemed until May 1, 2003.
ANNOUNCED PRINT RUN 230 SETS
106 Rudi Johnson 10.00 25.00
111 Heath Evans 8.00 20.00
113 Moran Norris 6.00 15.00
118 Eddie Berlin 6.00 15.00
119 Jonathan Carter 6.00 15.00
121 T.J. Houshmandzadeh 8.00 20.00
123 Reggie Germany 6.00 15.00
201 Michael Vick 15.00 40.00
202 Drew Brees 600.00 1000.00
204 Jesse Palmer 8.00 20.00
205 Mike McMahon 8.00 20.00
206 Dave Dickenson 8.00 20.00
209 Chris Weinke 8.00 20.00
212 LaDainian Tomlinson 60.00 120.00
213 Michael Bennett 8.00 20.00
214 Anthony Thomas 10.00 25.00
215 Travis Henry 8.00 20.00
216 James Jackson 6.00 15.00
217 Correll Buckhalter 6.00 15.00
218 Derrick Blaylock 8.00 20.00
219 Dee Brown 6.00 15.00
221 Deuce McAllister 10.00 25.00
222 LaMont Jordan 10.00 25.00
223 Kevan Barlow 8.00 20.00
224 Travis Minor 8.00 20.00
225 David Terrell 8.00 20.00
226 Koren Robinson 8.00 20.00
228 Santana Moss 10.00 25.00
229 Freddie Mitchell 6.00 15.00
231 Quincy Morgan 8.00 20.00
233 Steve Smith 40.00 80.00
234 Snoop Minnis 6.00 15.00
235 Justin McCareins 8.00 20.00
236 Onome Ojo 6.00 15.00
239 Cedrick Wilson 8.00 20.00
240 Kevin Kasper 6.00 15.00
242 Ken-Yon Rambo 6.00 15.00
248 Alex Bannister 6.00 15.00
250 Chad Johnson 15.00 40.00
251 Robert Ferguson 10.00 25.00
254 Todd Heap 8.00 20.00
255 Alge Crumpler 10.00 25.00
256 Nate Clements No Auto 8.00 20.00
257 Will Allen 10.00 25.00
271 Justin Smith 12.00 30.00
273 Jamal Reynolds 6.00 15.00
275 Richard Seymour No Auto 10.00 25.00
276 Damione Lewis 8.00 20.00
277 Casey Hampton No Auto 15.00 40.00
280 Shaun Rogers 10.00 25.00

2001 Leaf Rookies and Stars Cross Training

ndomly inserted in packs, these 25 cards feature two players (one a veteran and one a rookie) of the same position and are serial numbered to 100
STATED PRINT RUN 100 SER.#'d SETS
CT1 T.Davis/M.Bennett 4.00 10.00
CT2 T.Aikman/Q.Carter 6.00 15.00
CT3 D.McNabb/M.Vick 8.00 20.00
CT4 R.Moss/R.Gardner 4.00 10.00
CT5 C.Dillon/K.Barlow 3.00 8.00
CT6 W.Sapp/G.Warren 4.00 10.00
CT7 M.Faulk/D.McAllister 4.00 10.00
CT8 E.James/J.Jackson 4.00 10.00
CT9 C.Carter/R.Wayne 6.00 15.00
CT10 B.Sanders/L.Tomlinson 15.00 40.00
CT11 T.Couch/D.Brees 20.00 50.00
CT12 P.Warrick/S.Minnis 3.00 8.00
CT13 T.Holt/K.Robinson 4.00 10.00
CT14 I.Bruce/S.Moss 5.00 12.00
CT15 J.Rice/D.Terrell 10.00 25.00
CT16 T.Brown/C.Chambers 5.00 12.00
CT17 E.Smith/T.Henry 8.00 20.00
CT18 E.George/A.Thomas 5.00 12.00
CT19 D.Bledsoe/C.Weinke 4.00 10.00
CT20 D.Marino/J.Heupel 10.00 25.00
CT21 J.Bettis/Rud.Johnson 5.00 12.00
CT22 Key.Johnson/C.Johnson 5.00 12.00
CT23 M.Brunell/M.Tuiasosopo 4.00 10.00
CT24 J.Kearse/A.Carter 4.00 10.00
CT25 S.Young/M.McMahon 6.00 15.00

2001 Leaf Rookies and Stars Dress For Success

Inserted in packs at stated odds of one in 96, these 25 cards feature game-worn uniform swatches from these past and present NFL stars.
STATED ODDS 1:96
*PRIME CUT/50: .8X TO 2X BASIC INSERT
PRIME CUT PRINT RUN 50 SER.#'d SETS
DFS1 Tim Brown 4.00 10.00
DFS2 Lamar Smith 3.00 8.00
DFS3 Boomer Esiason 3.00 8.00
DFS4 Dan Marino 8.00 20.00
DFS5 Lawrence Taylor 4.00 10.00
DFS6 Marshall Faulk 3.00 8.00
DFS7 Isaac Bruce 4.00 10.00
DFS8 Stephen Davis 2.50 6.00
DFS9 Marvin Harrison 3.00 8.00
DFS10 Michael Strahan 3.00 8.00
DFS11 Jerome Bettis 4.00 10.00
DFS12 Cris Carter 4.00 10.00
DFS13 Emmitt Smith 6.00 15.00
DFS14 Jevon Kearse 2.50 6.00
DFS15 Eric Moulds 2.50 6.00
DFS16 Curtis Martin 3.00 8.00
DFS17 Randy Moss 3.00 8.00
DFS18 Peyton Manning 10.00 25.00
DFS19 John Elway 6.00 15.00
DFS20 Warrick Dunn 2.50 6.00
DFS21 Steve Young 5.00 12.00
DFS22 Donovan McNabb 3.00 8.00
DFS23 Keyshawn Johnson 3.00 8.00
DFS24 Ron Dayne 3.00 8.00
DFS25 Rich Gannon 3.00 8.00

2001 Leaf Rookies and Stars Dress For Success Autographs

Randomly inserted in packs, these 13 cards partially parallel the Dress for Success insert set. Donruss Playoff announced that each player signed 25 of these cards for inclusion in this set.
ANNOUNCED PRINT RUN 25 SETS
DFS1 Tim Brown 40.00 100.00
DFS4 Dan Marino 175.00 300.00
DFS6 Marshall Faulk 40.00 100.00
DFS7 Isaac Bruce 50.00 125.00
DFS8 Stephen Davis 30.00 80.00
DFS9 Marvin Harrison 40.00 100.00
DFS12 Cris Carter 50.00 125.00
DFS13 Emmitt Smith 175.00 300.00
DFS15 Eric Moulds
DFS19 John Elway 100.00 200.00
DFS21 Steve Young 75.00 150.00
DFS24 Ron Dayne 40.00 100.00

2001 Leaf Rookies and Stars Freshman Orientation

serted in packs at stated odds of one in 96, these 25 cards feature some of the leading rookie prospects of the 2001 season. Each card includes a swatch of the featured player's jersey.
STATED ODDS 1:96
*CLASS OFFICER/50: .8X TO 2X BASIC INSERTS
CLASS OFFICERS PRINT RUN 50 SER.#'d SETS
F01 Michael Vick 5.00 12.00
F02 Drew Brees 12.00 30.00
F03 Quincy Carter 2.50 6.00
F04 Chris Weinke 2.50 6.00
F05 Santana Moss 3.00 8.00
F06 Mike McMahon 2.50 6.00
F07 Jesse Palmer 2.50 6.00
F08 Deuce McAllister 3.00 8.00
F09 LaDainian Tomlinson 10.00 25.00
F010 Anthony Thomas 3.00 8.00
F011 Michael Bennett 2.50 6.00
F012 Travis Henry 2.50 6.00
F013 James Jackson 2.00 5.00
F014 Kevan Barlow 2.50 6.00
F015 Rudi Johnson 3.00 8.00
F016 Travis Minor 2.50 6.00
F017 David Terrell 2.50 6.00
F018 Rod Gardner 2.50 6.00
F019 Quincy Morgan 2.50 6.00
F020 Freddie Mitchell 2.00 5.00
F021 Reggie Wayne 4.00 10.00
F022 Koren Robinson 2.50 6.00
F023 Chris Chambers 2.00 5.00
F024 Snoop Minnis 2.00 5.00
F025 Chad Johnson 3.00 8.00

2001 Leaf Rookies and Stars Freshman Orientation Autographs

Randomly inserted in packs, these four cards feature 25 autographed cards of players in the freshmen orientation insert set.
ANNOUNCED PRINT RUN 25 SETS
F04 Chris Weinke 25.00 60.00
F09 LaDainian Tomlinson 125.00 250.00
F019 Quincy Morgan 25.00 60.00
F025 Chad Johnson 25.00 60.00

2001 Leaf Rookies and Stars Player's Collection

Randomly inserted in packs, these 15 cards feature swatches of game-worn memorabilia from three football superstars. A card with a single memorabilia swatch is serial numbered to 100 while the cards with more than one swatch are serial numbered to 25.
SINGLE MEM PRINT RUN 100
COMBO PRINT RUN 25
PC1 Eddie George Glove 12.50 30.00
PC2 Eddie George JSY 12.50 30.00
PC3 Eddie George Helmet 12.50 30.00
PC4 Eddie George Shoes 12.50 30.00
PC5 Eddie George Combo 30.00 80.00
PC6 Troy Aikman FB 20.00 50.00
PC7 Troy Aikman JSY 20.00 50.00
PC8 Troy Aikman Helmet 25.00 60.00
PC9 Troy Aikman Shoes 20.00 50.00
PC10 Troy Aikman Combo 75.00 150.00
PC11 Kurt Warner Pants 15.00 40.00
PC12 Kurt Warner JSY 15.00 40.00
PC13 Kurt Warner Helmet 15.00 40.00
PC14 Kurt Warner Shoes 15.00 40.00
PC15 Kurt Warner Combo 40.00 100.00

2001 Leaf Rookies and Stars Player's Collection Autographs

ndomly inserted in packs, these two cards feature autographs of players who signed their personal collection cards. These two cards have a stated print run of 25 serial numbered sets.
STATED PRINT RUN 25 SER.#'d SETS
PC8 Troy Aikman 60.00 120.00
PC13 Kurt Warner 50.00 100.00

2001 Leaf Rookies and Stars Slideshow

ndomly inserted in packs, these cards feature action highlights of the featured players along with a swatch of game used jersey. These cards are serial numbered to 100.
STATED PRINT RUN 100 SER.#'d SETS
*VIEWMASTER/25: .6X TO 1.5X BASIC INSERTS

VIEWMASTER PRINT RUN 25 SER.#'d SETS
SS1 Barry Sanders 6.00 15.00
SS2 Brett Favre 8.00 20.00
SS3 Brian Griese 2.50 6.00
SS4 Cris Carter 4.00 10.00
SS5 Dan Marino 8.00 20.00
SS6 Daunte Culpepper 3.00 8.00
SS7 Donovan McNabb 3.00 8.00
SS8 Drew Bledsoe 3.00 8.00
SS9 Eddie George 4.00 10.00
SS10 Edgerrin James 3.00 8.00
SS11 Emmitt Smith 6.00 15.00
SS12 Fred Taylor 2.50 6.00
SS13 John Elway 6.00 15.00
SS14 Kurt Warner 6.00 15.00
SS15 Marshall Faulk 3.00 8.00
SS16 Peyton Manning 10.00 25.00
SS17 Randy Moss 3.00 8.00
SS18 Ricky Williams 3.00 8.00
SS19 Ron Dayne 3.00 8.00
SS20 Steve McNair 3.00 8.00
SS21 Steve Young 5.00 12.00
SS22 Terrell Davis 3.00 8.00
SS23 Tim Brown 4.00 10.00
SS24 Tim Couch 2.50 6.00
SS25 Troy Aikman 5.00 12.00

2001 Leaf Rookies and Stars Slideshow Autographs

ndomly inserted in packs, these five cards partially parallel the Slideshow insert set. Each of these players signed 25 cards for inclusion in this product.
STATED PRINT RUN 25 SER.#'d SETS
UNPRICED VIEW MASTER AU PRINT RUN 5
SS3 Brian Griese 25.00 60.00
SS4 Cris Carter 50.00 120.00
SS18 Ricky Williams 40.00 100.00
SS21 Steve Young 125.00 250.00
SS23 Tim Brown 50.00 120.00

2001 Leaf Rookies and Stars Statistical Standouts

Inserted in packs at stated odds of one in 96, these 25 cards feature players who put up outstanding totals on the field. Each card is enhanced with a swatch of game used football.
STATED ODDS 1:96
*SUPER/50: .8X TO 2X BASIC INSERTS
SUPER SS PRINT RUN 50 SER.#'d SETS
SS1 Peyton Manning 8.00 20.00
SS2 Jeff Garcia 2.00 5.00
SS3 Donovan McNabb 2.50 6.00
SS4 Daunte Culpepper 2.50 6.00
SS5 Kurt Warner 5.00 12.00
SS6 Vinny Testaverde 2.00 5.00
SS7 Mark Brunell 2.50 6.00
SS8 Edgerrin James 2.50 6.00
SS9 Eddie George 3.00 8.00
SS10 Mike Anderson 2.00 5.00
SS11 Corey Dillon 2.00 5.00
SS12 Fred Taylor 2.00 5.00
SS13 Marshall Faulk 2.50 6.00
SS14 Stephen Davis 2.00 5.00
SS15 Torry Holt 2.50 6.00
SS16 Rod Smith 2.50 6.00
SS17 Isaac Bruce 3.00 8.00
SS18 Terrell Owens 2.50 6.00
SS19 Randy Moss 2.50 6.00
SS20 Marvin Harrison 2.50 6.00
SS21 Kerry Collins 2.00 5.00
SS22 Junior Seau 2.50 6.00
SS23 Warren Sapp 2.50 6.00
SS24 Donnie Abraham 2.00 5.00
SS25 Dexter McCleon 2.00 5.00

2001 Leaf Rookies and Stars Statistical Standouts Autographs

ndomly inserted in packs, these 13 cards partially parallel the Statistical Standout set. Each of these players listed signed 25 cards for inclusion in this product.
STATED PRINT RUN 25 SER.#'d SETS
SS4 Daunte Culpepper 25.00 60.00
SS5 Kurt Warner 50.00 100.00
SS6 Vinny Testaverde 20.00 50.00
SS7 Mark Brunell 25.00 60.00
SS8 Edgerrin James 25.00 60.00
SS10 Mike Anderson 20.00 50.00
SS11 Corey Dillon 20.00 50.00
SS13 Marshall Faulk 25.00 60.00
SS14 Stephen Davis 20.00 50.00
SS15 Torry Holt 25.00 60.00
SS17 Isaac Bruce 30.00 80.00
SS18 Terrell Owens 25.00 60.00
SS20 Marvin Harrison 25.00 60.00

2001 Leaf Rookies and Stars Triple Threads

ndomly inserted in packs, these cards feature three players from the same franchise. These cards are serial numbered to 100.
STATED PRINT RUN 100 SER.#'d SETS
TT1 Carter/Culpepper/Moss 15.00 40.00
TT2 Taylor/Smith/Brunell 12.00 30.00
TT3 James/Harrison/Manning 30.00 80.00
TT4 Freeman/Favre/Levens 30.00 80.00
TT5 Griese/McCaffrey/Davis 12.00 30.00
TT6 Bruce/Warner/Faulk 25.00 60.00
TT7 Aikman/Smith/Irvin 25.00 60.00
TT8 Johnson/Sapp/Dunn 10.00 25.00
TT9 Kelly/Thomas/Reed 12.00 30.00
TT10 George/Kearse/McNair 15.00 40.00

2002 Leaf Rookies and Stars

leased in December 2002, this set contains 100 veterans and 200 rookies. Rookies were inserted approximately one per pack. Boxes contained 24 packs of 6 cards.
COMPLETE SET (300) 100.00 250.00
COMP.SET w/o SP's (100) 10.00 25.00
1 Jake Plummer .20 .50
2 David Boston .20 .50
3 Thomas Jones .20 .50
4 Michael Vick .25 .60
5 Warrick Dunn .20 .50
6 Jamal Lewis .25 .60
7 Chris Redman .20 .50
8 Ray Lewis .30 .75
9 Drew Bledsoe .25 .60
10 Travis Henry .20 .50
11 Eric Moulds .20 .50
12 Steve Smith .30 .75
13 Chris Weinke .20 .50
14 Lamar Smith .20 .50
15 Anthony Thomas .25 .60
16 David Terrell .20 .50
17 Brian Urlacher .30 .75
18 Corey Dillon .20 .50
19 Michael Westbrook .20 .50
20 Peter Warrick .20 .50
21 Tim Couch .20 .50
22 James Jackson .20 .50
23 Kevin Johnson .20 .50
24 Quincy Carter .20 .50
25 Joey Galloway .25 .60
26 Emmitt Smith .50 1.25
27 Terrell Davis .25 .60
28 Brian Griese .20 .50
29 Ed McCaffrey .25 .60
30 Rod Smith .25 .60
31 Mike McMahon .20 .50
32 Germane Crowell .20 .50
33 Az-Zahir Hakim .20 .50
34 Terry Glenn .25 .60
35 Brett Favre .60 1.50
36 Ahman Green .25 .60
37 James Allen .20 .50
38 Corey Bradford .20 .50
39 Peyton Manning .75 2.00
40 Edgerrin James .25 .60
41 Marvin Harrison .25 .60
42 Qadry Ismail .20 .50
43 Fred Taylor .20 .50
44 Mark Brunell .25 .60
45 Jimmy Smith .25 .60
46 Priest Holmes .20 .50
47 Tony Gonzalez .25 .60
48 Trent Green .20 .50
49 Johnnie Morton .25 .60
50 Chris Chambers .20 .50
51 Ricky Williams .25 .60
52 Zach Thomas .25 .60
53 Randy Moss .25 .60
54 Michael Bennett .20 .50
55 Derrick Alexander .20 .50
56 Daunte Culpepper .25 .60
57 Tom Brady 1.50 4.00
58 Troy Brown .20 .50
59 Antowain Smith .25 .60
60 Joe Horn .20 .50
61 Aaron Brooks .20 .50
62 Deuce McAllister .25 .60
63 Kerry Collins .20 .50
64 Amani Toomer .20 .50
65 Michael Strahan .25 .60
66 Laveranues Coles .25 .60
67 Vinny Testaverde .20 .50
68 Curtis Martin .25 .60
69 Rich Gannon .25 .60
70 Tim Brown .30 .75
71 Jerry Rice .60 1.50
72 Donovan McNabb .25 .60
73 Freddie Mitchell .20 .50
74 Duce Staley .20 .50
75 Kordell Stewart .20 .50
76 Jerome Bettis .30 .75
77 Plaxico Burress .20 .50
78 Drew Brees .60 1.50
79 LaDainian Tomlinson .30 .75
80 Junior Seau .25 .60
81 Jeff Garcia .20 .50
82 Garrison Hearst .20 .50
83 Terrell Owens .25 .60
84 Shaun Alexander .20 .50
85 Koren Robinson .20 .50
86 Kurt Warner .25 .60
87 Marshall Faulk .25 .60
88 Isaac Bruce .30 .75
89 Torry Holt .25 .60
90 Rob Johnson .25 .60
91 Brad Johnson .25 .60
92 Keyshawn Johnson .25 .60
93 Mike Alstott .20 .50
94 Eddie George .25 .60
95 Steve McNair .25 .60
96 Derrick Mason .20 .50
97 Jevon Kearse .20 .50
98 Stephen Davis .20 .50
99 Sage Rosenfels .25 .60
100 Rod Gardner .20 .50
101 Adrian Peterson RC 1.25 3.00
102 Nick Rolovich RC 1.00 2.50
103 Lew Thomas RC 1.00 2.50
104 David Carr RC 1.00 2.50
105 Daryl Jones RC 1.00 2.50
106 Brandon Doman RC 1.00 2.50
107 Ed Reed RC 6.00 15.00
108 Tellis Redmon RC 1.00 2.50
109 Andra Davis RC 1.00 2.50
110 Kendall Newson RC 1.00 2.50
111 Joe Burns RC 1.00 2.50
112 Maurice Morris RC 1.25 3.00
113 Craig Nall RC 1.25 3.00
114 Phillip Buchanon RC 1.50 4.00
115 Mike Echols RC 1.00 2.50
116 Terry Jones Jr. RC 1.00 2.50
117 Anthony Weaver RC 1.00 2.50
118 Jeb Putzier RC 1.50 4.00
119 Tony Fisher RC 1.00 2.50
120 Joey Harrington RC 1.00 2.50
121 Lamar Gordon RC 1.25 3.00
122 Tracey Wistrom RC 1.25 3.00
123 Ashley Lelie RC 1.00 2.50
124 Will Witherspoon RC 1.50 4.00
125 Travis Stephens RC 1.00 2.50
126 J.T. O'Sullivan RC 1.25 3.00
127 Brian Westbrook RC 2.00 5.00
128 James Mungro RC 1.50 4.00
129 Lamont Thompson RC 1.25 3.00
130 Jarrod Baxter RC 1.00 2.50
131 Andre Lott RC 1.00 2.50
132 Steve Bellisari RC 1.00 2.50
133 David Garrard RC 1.25 3.00
134 Michael Lewis RC 1.25 3.00
135 James Allen RC 1.00 2.50
136 Bryant McKinnie RC 1.00 2.50
137 Marques Anderson RC 1.25 3.00
138 Rohan Davey RC 1.50 4.00
139 Kyle Johnson RC 1.00 2.50
140 Dusty Bonner RC 1.00 2.50
141 DeShaun Foster RC 1.50 4.00
142 Chad Hutchinson RC 1.00 2.50
143 Jack Brewer RC 1.00 2.50
144 Eddie Freeman RC 1.00 2.50
145 Seth Burford RC 1.00 2.50
146 Roosevelt Williams RC 1.00 2.50
147 Jamin Elliott RC 1.00 2.50
148 Charles Grant RC 1.50 4.00
149 Jeff Kelly RC 1.00 2.50
150 Cliff Russell RC 1.00 2.50
151 Josh Scobey RC 1.25 3.00
152 Tank Williams RC 1.25 3.00
153 Larry Tripplett RC 1.00 2.50
154 Clinton Portis RC 1.50 4.00
155 Javin Hunter RC 1.00 2.50
156 Deveren Johnson RC 1.00 2.50
157 Reche Caldwell RC 1.25 3.00
158 Ronald Curry RC 1.00 2.50
159 Chris Hope RC 1.50 4.00
160 Damien Anderson RC 1.00 2.50
161 Saleem Rasheed RC 1.00 2.50
162 Albert Haynesworth RC 1.50 4.00
163 Bryan Gilmore RC 1.00 2.50
164 Wes Pate RC 1.00 2.50
165 Deion Branch RC 1.50 4.00
166 Ben Leber RC 1.00 2.50
167 Andre Davis RC 1.00 2.50
168 Darrell Hill RC 1.00 2.50
169 Rodney Wright RC 1.00 2.50
170 Demontray Carter RC 1.00 2.50
171 Zak Kustok RC 1.00 2.50
172 James Wofford RC 1.00 2.50
173 David Priestley RC 1.00 2.50
174 Donte Stallworth RC 1.50 4.00
175 Marc Boerigter RC 1.50 4.00
176 Freddie Milons RC 1.00 2.50
177 John Simon RC 1.00 2.50
178 Josh Norman RC 1.00 2.50
179 Jabar Gaffney RC 1.00 2.50
180 Doug Jolley RC 1.00 2.50
181 Preston Parsons RC 1.00 2.50
182 Chris Baker RC 1.00 2.50
183 Javon Walker RC 1.50 4.00
184 Justin Peelle RC 1.00 2.50
185 Josh Reed RC 1.25 3.00
186 Omar Easy RC 1.25 3.00
187 Jerramy Stevens RC 1.50 4.00
188 Shaun Hill RC 1.50 4.00
189 David Thornton RC 1.00 2.50
190 John Henderson RC 1.25 3.00
191 Verron Haynes RC 1.00 2.50
192 Dennis Johnson RC 1.00 2.50
193 Napoleon Harris RC 1.25 3.00
194 Jonathan Wells RC 1.25 3.00
195 Howard Green RC 1.00 2.50
196 Travis Fisher RC 1.25 3.00
197 Anton Palepoi RC 1.00 2.50
198 Ed Stansbury RC 1.00 2.50
199 Josh McCown RC 1.50 4.00
200 Alex Brown RC 1.50 4.00
201 Joseph Jefferson RC 1.00 2.50
202 Julius Peppers RC 2.50 6.00
203 Larry Ned RC 1.00 2.50
204 Rock Cartwright RC 1.50 4.00
205 Kalimba Edwards RC 1.25 3.00
206 Matt Schobel RC 1.25 3.00
207 Maurice Jackson RC 1.00 2.50
208 Kelly Campbell RC 1.25 3.00
209 Mel Mitchell RC 1.00 2.50
210 Ken Simonton RC 1.00 2.50
211 Brian Allen RC 1.00 2.50
212 Darnell Sanders RC 1.00 2.50
213 Jesse Chatman RC 1.00 2.50
214 Keyuo Craver RC 1.00 2.50
215 Chester Taylor RC 1.50 4.00
216 Kurt Kittner RC 1.00 2.50
217 Derek Ross RC 1.25 3.00
218 Charles Hill RC 1.00 2.50
219 Jarvis Green RC 1.00 2.50
220 Mike Jenkins RC 1.00 2.50
221 Robert Royal RC 1.50 4.00
222 Ladell Betts RC 1.50 4.00
223 Antwoine Womack RC 1.00 2.50
224 Raonall Smith RC 1.00 2.50
225 Charles Stackhouse RC 1.00 2.50
226 Quinn Gray RC 1.25 3.00
227 Lito Sheppard RC 1.50 4.00
228 Ryan Van Dyke RC 1.00 2.50
229 Will Overstreet RC 1.00 2.50
230 Leonard Henry RC 1.00 2.50
231 Dorsett Davis RC 1.00 2.50
232 Marquand Manuel RC 1.00 2.50
233 Luke Staley RC 1.00 2.50
234 Carlos Hall RC 1.00 2.50
235 Marcus Brady RC 1.00 2.50
236 Ryan Denney RC 1.00 2.50
237 Eric McCoo RC 1.00 2.50
238 Major Applewhite RC 1.50 4.00
239 Adam Tate RC 1.00 2.50
240 Marquise Walker RC 1.00 2.50
241 John Flowers RC 1.00 2.50
242 Levar Fisher RC 1.00 2.50
243 Ricky Williams RC 1.25 3.00
244 Mike Rumph RC 1.00 2.50
245 Delvin Joyce RC 1.00 2.50
246 Bryan Thomas RC 1.00 2.50
247 Mike Williams RC 1.00 2.50
248 Sam Brandon RC 1.00 2.50
249 Eddie Drummond RC 1.00 2.50
250 Najeh Davenport RC 1.00 2.50
251 Brian Williams RC 1.00 2.50
252 Scott Fujita RC 1.50 4.00
253 Dwight Freeney RC 2.00 5.00
254 Herb Haygood RC 1.00 2.50
255 Patrick Ramsey RC 1.25 3.00
256 Atnaf Harris RC 1.00 2.50
257 Jason McAddley RC 1.25 3.00
258 Pete Rebstock RC 1.00 2.50
259 Quentin Jammer RC 1.50 4.00
260 Luke Butkus RC 1.00 2.50
261 Jeremy Allen RC 1.00 2.50
262 Jake Schifino RC 1.00 2.50
263 Randy Fasani RC 1.00 2.50
264 Bryan Fletcher RC 1.00 2.50
265 Jeremy Shockey RC 1.50 4.00
266 Kevin Bentley RC 1.00 2.50
267 Jon McGraw RC 1.00 2.50
268 Robert Thomas RC 1.00 2.50
269 Coy Wire RC 1.25 3.00
270 Brian Poli-Dixon RC 1.00 2.50
271 Willie Offord RC 1.00 2.50
272 Rocky Calmus RC 1.25 3.00
273 Sheldon Brown RC 1.50 4.00
274 Terry Charles RC 1.00 2.50
275 Ron Johnson RC 1.25 3.00
276 Roy Williams RC 1.00 2.50
277 Sam Simmons RC 1.00 2.50
278 Andre Goodman RC 1.00 2.50
279 Ryan Sims RC 1.50 4.00
280 Antwaan Randle El RC 1.25 3.00
281 Alan Harper RC 1.00 2.50
282 Tavon Mason RC 1.00 2.50
283 Kahlil Hill RC 1.00 2.50
284 Antonio Bryant RC 1.50 4.00
285 Akin Ayodele RC 1.25 3.00
286 T.J. Duckett RC 1.00 2.50
287 Kenyon Coleman RC 1.00 2.50
288 Tim Carter RC 1.25 3.00
289 Lamont Brightful RC 1.00 2.50
290 Trev Faulk RC 1.00 2.50
291 Randy McMichael RC 1.50 4.00
292 Daniel Graham RC 1.25 3.00
293 Wendell Bryant RC 1.00 2.50
294 Jamar Martin RC 1.25 3.00
295 Chris Luzar RC 1.00 2.50
296 William Green RC 1.25 3.00
297 Lee Mays RC 1.00 2.50
298 Eric Crouch RC 1.50 4.00
299 Steve Smith RC 1.00 2.50
300 Woody Dantzler RC 1.25 3.00

2002 Leaf Rookies and Stars Longevity

ETS 1-100: 10X TO 25X BASIC CARDS
*ROOKIES 101-200: 2X TO 5X
STATED PRINT RUN 50 SER.#'d SETS

2002 Leaf Rookies and Stars Rookie Autographs

ndomly inserts into packs, this set features autographs of some of the NFL's 2002 rookies. Each card has an announced print run of 150. This is a skip numbered set. Please note that some cards were issued only as redemptions with an expiration date of 6/1/2004.
ANNOUNCED PRINT RUN 150
101 Adrian Peterson 8.00 20.00
109 Andra Davis 6.00 15.00
117 Anthony Weaver 6.00 15.00
123 Ashley Lelie 6.00 15.00
127 Brian Westbrook 12.00 30.00
131 Andre Lott 6.00 15.00
136 Bryant McKinnie 6.00 15.00
142 Chad Hutchinson 6.00 15.00
148 Charles Grant 10.00 25.00
150 Cliff Russell 6.00 15.00
154 Clinton Portis 10.00 25.00
160 Damien Anderson 6.00 15.00
165 Deion Branch 12.50 30.00
170 Demontray Carter 6.00 15.00
174 Donte Stallworth 10.00 25.00
176 Freddie Milons 6.00 15.00
179 Jabar Gaffney 6.00 15.00
183 Javon Walker 10.00 25.00
190 John Henderson 8.00 20.00
199 Josh McCown 10.00 25.00
202 Julius Peppers 40.00 100.00
205 Kalimba Edwards 8.00 20.00
208 Kelly Campbell 8.00 20.00
210 Ken Simonton 6.00 15.00
214 Keyuo Craver 6.00 15.00
216 Kurt Kittner 6.00 15.00
222 Ladell Betts 10.00 25.00
227 Lito Sheppard 10.00 25.00
233 Luke Staley 6.00 15.00
240 Marquise Walker 6.00 15.00
244 Mike Rumph 6.00 15.00
247 Mike Williams 6.00 15.00
250 Najeh Davenport 6.00 15.00
255 Patrick Ramsey 8.00 20.00
259 Quentin Jammer 10.00 25.00
263 Randy Fasani 6.00 15.00
268 Robert Thomas 6.00 15.00
272 Rocky Calmus 8.00 20.00
275 Ron Johnson 8.00 20.00
276 Roy Williams 6.00 15.00
282 Tavon Mason 6.00 15.00
284 Antonio Bryant 10.00 25.00
286 T.J. Duckett 6.00 15.00
288 Tim Carter 8.00 20.00
290 Trev Faulk 6.00 15.00
293 Wendall Bryant 6.00 15.00
296 William Green 8.00 20.00
300 Woody Dantzler 8.00 20.00

2002 Leaf Rookies and Stars Action Packed Bronze

is set brings back the look and feel of the old Action Packed sets. Each card has an embossed front and is serial #'d to 1850. There is also a silver parallel #'d to 500, and a gold parallel #'d to 150.
COMPLETE SET (20) 25.00 60.00
BRONZE PRINT RUN 1850 SER.#'d SETS
*SILVER/500: .8X TO 2X BRONZE/1850
SILVER PRINT RUN 500 SER.#'d SETS
*GOLD/150: 1.5X TO 4X BRONZE/1850
GOLD PRINT RUN 150 SER.#'d SETS
1 Brian Urlacher 1.00 2.50
2 Randy Moss .75 2.00
3 T.J. Duckett .60 1.50
4 Peyton Manning 2.50 6.00
5 Edgerrin James .75 2.00
6 Donte Stallworth 1.00 2.50
7 Joey Harrington .60 1.50
8 Drew Brees 2.00 5.00
9 Anthony Thomas .75 2.00
10 William Green .75 2.00
11 LaDainian Tomlinson 1.00 2.50
12 Donovan McNabb .75 2.00
13 Patrick Ramsey .75 2.00
14 Shaun Alexander .60 1.50
15 Kurt Warner .75 2.00
16 Michael Vick .75 2.00
17 Antonio Bryant 1.00 2.50
18 Jeff Garcia .60 1.50
19 David Carr .60 1.50
20 Chris Chambers .60 1.50

2002 Leaf Rookies and Stars Dress for Success

is set features two jersey swatches from each player, and is serial #'d to 400.
STATED PRINT RUN 400 SER.#'d SETS
DS1 LaDainian Tomlinson 3.00 8.00
DS2 Quincy Carter 2.00 5.00
DS3 Freddie Mitchell 2.00 5.00
DS4 Anthony Thomas 2.50 6.00
DS5 Quincy Morgan 2.00 5.00
DS6 Chris Weinke 2.00 5.00

2002 Leaf Rookies and Stars Freshman Orientation Jerseys

is set features event worn swatches from many of the NFL's top 2002 rookies. Each card is serial #'d to 650. The first 25-copies for the first ten players were issued signed.
STATED PRINT RUN 650 SER.#'d SETS
FO1 Ashley Lelie 2.00 5.00
FO2 David Garrard 2.50 6.00
FO3 Javon Walker 3.00 8.00
FO4 Jeremy Shockey 3.00 8.00
FO5 Josh McCown 3.00 8.00
FO6 Josh Reed 2.50 6.00
FO7 Ladell Betts 3.00 8.00
FO8 Patrick Ramsey 2.50 6.00
FO9 Tim Carter 2.50 6.00
FO10 Joey Harrington 2.00 5.00
FO11 Roy Williams 2.00 5.00
FO12 David Carr 2.00 5.00
FO13 Antonio Bryant 3.00 8.00
FO14 T.J. Duckett 2.00 5.00
FO15 Reche Caldwell 2.50 6.00
FO16 Julius Peppers 5.00 12.00
FO17 Maurice Morris 2.50 6.00
FO18 Clinton Portis 3.00 8.00
FO19 DeShaun Foster 3.00 8.00
FO20 Donte Stallworth 3.00 8.00
FO21 Eric Crouch 3.00 8.00
FO22 Andre Davis 2.00 5.00
FO23 Marquise Walker 2.00 5.00
FO24 Rohan Davey 3.00 8.00
FO25 Antwaan Randle El 2.50 6.00
FO26 Jabar Gaffney 2.00 5.00
FO27 Travis Stephens 2.00 5.00
FO28 Ron Johnson 2.50 6.00
FO29 Daniel Graham 2.50 6.00
FO30 Cliff Russell 2.00 5.00
FO31 Mike Williams 2.00 5.00
FO32 William Green 2.50 6.00

2002 Leaf Rookies and Stars Freshman Orientation Autographs

This set contains jersey swatches and authentic autographs from ten 2002 rookies. Each card is serial #'d to 25. Some cards were issued only as redemptions with an expiration date of 6/1/2004.
STATED PRINT RUN 25 SER.#'d SETS
FO1 Ashley Lelie 12.00 30.00
FO2 David Garrard 75.00 150.00
FO3 Javon Walker 20.00 50.00
FO4 Jeremy Shockey 30.00 80.00
FO5 Josh McCown 20.00 50.00
FO6 Josh Reed 15.00 40.00
FO7 Ladell Betts 20.00 50.00
FO8 Patrick Ramsey 15.00 40.00
FO9 Tim Carter
FO10 Joey Harrington 12.00 30.00

2002 Leaf Rookies and Stars Great American Heroes

This set highlights 40 Great American Hereoes who either play or have played in the NFL. Each card is serial #'d to 2000.
COMPLETE SET (40) 40.00 100.00
STATED PRINT RUN 2000 SER.#'d SETS
GAH1 Steve Young 1.00 2.50
GAH2 Troy Aikman 1.00 2.50
GAH3 Daunte Culpepper .60 1.50
GAH4 Correll Buckhalter .50 1.25
GAH5 Marshall Faulk .60 1.50
GAH6 Kevan Barlow .50 1.25
GAH7 Marvin Harrison .60 1.50
GAH8 Peter Warrick .50 1.25
GAH9 LaMont Jordan .60 1.50
GAH10 Rod Gardner .50 1.25
GAH11 Charlie Batch .50 1.25
GAH12 Reggie Wayne .60 1.50
GAH13 Ricky Watters .60 1.50
GAH14 Ken-Yon Rambo .50 1.25
GAH15 Kurt Warner .60 1.50
GAH16 Ahman Green .60 1.50
GAH17 Dan Morgan .50 1.25
GAH18 Isaac Bruce .75 2.00
GAH19 Chad Pennington .50 1.25
GAH20 Josh Heupel .60 1.50
GAH21 Tony Stewart .50 1.25
GAH22 Rudi Johnson .50 1.25
GAH23 Michael Bennett .50 1.25
GAH24 Quincy Carter .50 1.25
GAH25 Aaron Brooks .50 1.25
GAH26 Jesse Palmer .50 1.25
GAH27 Cade McNown .60 1.50
GAH28 Jeff Garcia .50 1.25
GAH29 Jevon Kearse .50 1.25
GAH30 Justin Smith .60 1.50
GAH31 Kerry Collins .50 1.25
GAH32 Kordell Stewart .50 1.25
GAH33 Michael Vick .60 1.50
GAH34 Ricky Williams .60 1.50
GAH35 Vinny Testaverde .50 1.25
GAH36 Terrell Davis .60 1.50
GAH37 Jake Plummer .50 1.25
GAH38 Drew Bledsoe .60 1.50
GAH39 Santana Moss .60 1.50
GAH40 Elvis Grbac .50 1.25

2002 Leaf Rookies and Stars Great American Heroes Autographs

This set of 40 cards features authentic signatures from many of the cards in the basic Great American Heroes insert set. Each card is serial numbered from 10-242.
STATED PRINT RUN 10-242
GAH3 Daunte Culpepper/33
GAH5 Marshall Faulk/67 20.00 40.00
GAH6 Kevan Barlow/30 12.00 30.00
GAH7 Marvin Harrison/25 20.00 50.00
GAH8 Peter Warrick/110 6.00 15.00
GAH9 LaMont Jordan/40 15.00 40.00
GAH10 Rod Gardner/25
GAH11 Charlie Batch/20
GAH12 Reggie Wayne/35 20.00 40.00
GAH13 Ricky Watters/100 7.50 20.00
GAH14 Ken-Yon Rambo/20
GAH18 Isaac Bruce/25 15.00 40.00
GAH19 Chad Pennington/50 25.00 60.00
GAH20 Josh Heupel/120 10.00 25.00
GAH21 Tony Stewart/199 6.00 15.00
GAH22 Rudi Johnson/59 10.00 25.00
GAH23 Michael Bennett/242 7.50 20.00
GAH24 Quincy Carter/106 10.00 25.00
GAH25 Aaron Brooks/25 12.00 30.00
GAH26 Jesse Palmer/25
GAH27 Cade McNown/25
GAH28 Jeff Garcia/25 15.00 40.00
GAH29 Jevon Kearse/25
GAH30 Justin Smith/40
GAH31 Kerry Collins/25 15.00 40.00
GAH32 Kordell Stewart/25 12.00 30.00
GAH33 Michael Vick/57 30.00 80.00
GAH34 Ricky Williams/25
GAH37 Jake Plummer/25 15.00 40.00
GAH38 Drew Bledsoe/25 15.00 40.00
GAH39 Santana Moss/200 7.50 20.00
GAH40 Elvis Grbac/40 10.00 25.00

2002 Leaf Rookies and Stars Initial Steps

is set features jersey swatches from 25 top rookies from 2002. Each card is serial #'d to 125.
STATED PRINT RUN 125 SER.#'d SETS
IS1 Jabar Gaffney 2.50 6.00
IS2 Cliff Russell 2.50 6.00
IS3 T.J. Duckett 2.50 6.00
IS4 Josh Reed 3.00 8.00
IS5 Daniel Graham 3.00 8.00
IS6 Antonio Bryant 4.00 10.00
IS7 Ashley Lelie 2.50 6.00
IS8 Mike Williams 2.50 6.00
IS9 Ladell Betts 4.00 10.00
IS10 Jeremy Shockey 4.00 10.00
IS11 Josh McCown 4.00 10.00
IS12 Andre Davis 2.50 6.00
IS13 Travis Stephens 2.50 6.00
IS14 Roy Williams 2.50 6.00
IS15 Rohan Davey 4.00 10.00
IS16 Julius Peppers 6.00 15.00
IS17 Javon Walker 4.00 10.00
IS18 Reche Caldwell 3.00 8.00
IS19 Clinton Portis 4.00 10.00
IS20 Antwaan Randle El 3.00 8.00
IS21 Eric Crouch 4.00 10.00
IS22 Patrick Ramsey 3.00 8.00
IS23 Marquise Walker 2.50 6.00
IS24 David Carrard 3.00 8.00
IS25 David Carr 2.50 6.00

2002 Leaf Rookies and Stars Pinnacle

ndomly inserted into retail packs at the rate of 1:670, this set highlights 10 NFL superstars who are at the Pinnacle of their careers. The card design was modeled after the 1991 Pinnacle base set.
STATED ODDS 1:670 RETAIL
1 Brett Favre 6.00 15.00
2 Emmitt Smith 5.00 12.00
3 Kurt Warner 2.50 6.00
4 Jerry Rice 6.00 15.00
5 Michael Vick 2.50 6.00
6 LaDainian Tomlinson 3.00 8.00
7 Eddie George 2.50 6.00
8 Tom Brady 15.00 40.00
9 Marshall Faulk 2.50 6.00
10 Peyton Manning 8.00 20.00

2002 Leaf Rookies and Stars Rookie Masks

is set features authentic chunks of face masks from 32 top 2002 rookies. Each card is serial #'d to 250.
STATED PRINT RUN 250 SER.#'d SETS
RM1 Ladell Betts 4.00 10.00
RM2 Antonio Bryant 4.00 10.00
RM3 Reche Caldwell 3.00 8.00
RM4 David Carr 2.50 6.00
RM5 Tim Carter 3.00 8.00
RM6 Eric Crouch 4.00 10.00
RM7 Rohan Davey 4.00 10.00
RM8 Andre Davis 2.50 6.00
RM9 T.J. Duckett 2.50 6.00
RM10 DeShaun Foster 4.00 10.00
RM11 Jabar Gaffney 2.50 6.00
RM12 Daniel Graham 3.00 8.00
RM13 William Green 3.00 8.00
RM14 Joey Harrington 2.50 6.00
RM15 Ron Johnson 3.00 8.00
RM16 Ashley Lelie 2.50 6.00
RM17 Josh McCown 4.00 10.00
RM18 Maurice Morris 3.00 8.00
RM19 Julius Peppers 6.00 15.00
RM20 Clinton Portis 4.00 10.00
RM21 Patrick Ramsey 3.00 8.00
RM22 Antwaan Randle El 3.00 8.00
RM23 Josh Reed 3.00 8.00
RM24 Cliff Russell 2.50 6.00
RM25 Jeremy Shockey 4.00 10.00
RM26 Donte Stallworth 4.00 10.00
RM27 Travis Stephens 2.50 6.00
RM28 Javon Walker 4.00 10.00
RM29 Marquise Walker 2.50 6.00
RM30 Roy Williams 2.50 6.00
RM31 Mike Williams 2.50 6.00
RM32 David Garrard 3.00 8.00

2002 Leaf Rookies and Stars Run With History

This set commemorates the brilliant career of Emmitt Smith. Each of the 12 cards is serial #'d to the number of rushing yards achieved that season.
RH1 Emmitt Smith/937 4.00 10.00
RH2 Emmitt Smith/1563 4.00 10.00
RH3 Emmitt Smith/1713 4.00 10.00
RH4 Emmitt Smith/1486 4.00 10.00
RH5 Emmitt Smith/1484 4.00 10.00
RH6 Emmitt Smith/1773 4.00 10.00
RH7 Emmitt Smith/1204 4.00 10.00
RH8 Emmitt Smith/1074 4.00 10.00
RH9 Emmitt Smith/1332 4.00 10.00
RH10 Emmitt Smith/1397 4.00 10.00
RH11 Emmitt Smith/1203 4.00 10.00
RH12 Emmitt Smith/1021 4.00 10.00

2002 Leaf Rookies and Stars Run With History Autographs

This set commemorates Emmitt Smith's brilliant career. Each card features Emmitt's autograph and is serial #'d to 22.
STATED PRINT RUN 22 SERIAL #'d SETS
RH1 Emmitt Smith 175.00 300.00
RH3 Emmitt Smith 175.00 300.00
RH4 Emmitt Smith 175.00 300.00
RH6 Emmitt Smith 175.00 300.00

2002 Leaf Rookies and Stars Slideshow

is set was created to resemble a slide, and when held to the light, a full color picture is visible. Each card is serial #'d to 1500.
STATED PRINT RUN 1500 SER.#'d SETS
SS1 Anthony Thomas 1.00 2.50
SS2 Eddie George 1.00 2.50
SS3 Kurt Warner 1.00 2.50
SS4 Ricky Williams 1.00 2.50
SS5 Donovan McNabb 1.00 2.50
SS6 Jeff Garcia .75 2.00
SS7 Randy Moss 1.00 2.50
SS8 Shaun Alexander .75 2.00
SS9 Brett Favre 2.50 6.00
SS10 Jerry Rice 2.50 6.00
SS11 Emmitt Smith 2.00 5.00
SS12 Marshall Faulk 1.00 2.50
SS13 Michael Vick 1.00 2.50
SS14 Zach Thomas 1.00 2.50
SS15 Peyton Manning 3.00 8.00

2002 Leaf Rookies and Stars Standing Ovation

This set highlights several top performers, and each card is serial #'d to 2500.
COMPLETE SET (13) 10.00 25.00
STATED PRINT RUN 2500 SER.#'d SETS
SO1 Tom Brady 5.00 12.00
SO2 Kordell Stewart .60 1.50
SO3 Kurt Warner .75 2.00
SO4 Jeff Garcia .60 1.50
SO5 Priest Holmes .60 1.50
SO6 Shaun Alexander .60 1.50
SO7 Marshall Faulk .75 2.00
SO8 Anthony Thomas .75 2.00
SO9 Jerry Rice 2.00 5.00
SO10 David Boston .60 1.50
SO11 Terrell Owens .75 2.00
SO12 Michael Strahan .75 2.00
SO13 New England Patriots .75 2.50

2002 Leaf Rookies and Stars Ticket Masters

is set pairs up teammates in a card design similar to a ticket. Each card is serial #'d to 2500.
COMPLETE SET (20) 25.00 60.00
STATED PRINT RUN 2500 SER.#'d SETS
TM1 M.Vick/T.J.Duckett .75 2.00
TM2 J.Lewis/R.Lewis 1.00 2.50
TM3 D.Bledsoe/T.Henry .75 2.00
TM4 C.Weinke/D.Foster 1.00 2.50
TM5 A.Thomas/B.Urlacher 1.00 2.50
TM6 T.Couch/W.Green .75 2.00
TM7 Q.Carter/E.Smith 1.50 4.00
TM8 B.Griese/A.Lelie .60 1.50
TM9 J.Harrington/G.Crowell .60 1.50
TM10 B.Favre/A.Green 2.00 5.00
TM11 D.Carr/J.Gaffney .60 1.50
TM12 P.Manning/E.James 2.50 6.00
TM13 R.Williams/C.Chambers .75 2.00
TM14 R.Moss/D.Culpepper .75 2.00
TM15 A.Brooks/D.Stallworth 1.00 2.50
TM16 J.Rice/T.Brown 2.00 5.00
TM17 D.Brees/L.Tomlinson 2.00 5.00
TM18 J.Garcia/G.Hearst .60 1.50
TM19 K.Warner/M.Faulk .75 2.00
TM20 S.McNair/E.George .75 2.00

2002 Leaf Rookies and Stars Triple Threads

is set features three jersey swatches from top NFL superstars. Each card is serial #'d to 50.
STATED PRINT RUN 50 SER.#'d SETS
TT1 Stewart/Bettis/Burress 15.00 40.00
TT2 Garcia/Owens/Hearst 6.00 15.00
TT3 Brown/Rice/Gannon 25.00 50.00
TT4 Thomas/Urlacher/Terrell 20.00 50.00
TT5 Favre/Green/Glenn 30.00 60.00

2003 Leaf Rookies and Stars

leased in December of 2003, this set contains 295 cards, including 96 veterans and 199 rookies. Rookies 201-250 are serial numbered to 750. Rookies 251-280 feature event worn jersey swatches and are serial numbered to 550. Rookies 281-295 feature event worn jersey swatches and are serial numbered to 400. Boxes contained 24 packs of 6 cards. SRP was $4.
COMP.SET w/o SP's (100) 7.50 20.00
201-250 PRINT RUN 750 SER.#'d SETS
1 Emmitt Smith .50 1.25
2 Michael Vick .25 .60
3 Peerless Price .20 .50
4 T.J. Duckett .20 .50
5 Warrick Dunn .20 .50
6 Jamal Lewis .25 .60
7 Ray Lewis .30 .75
8 Drew Bledsoe .25 .60
9 Eric Moulds .20 .50
10 Josh Reed .20 .50
11 Travis Henry .20 .50
12 Julius Peppers .30 .75
13 Anthony Thomas .25 .60
14 Brian Urlacher .30 .75
15 Marty Booker .20 .50
16 Kordell Stewart .20 .50
17 Corey Dillon .20 .50
18 Chad Johnson .20 .50
19 Tim Couch .20 .50
20 William Green .20 .50
21 Antonio Bryant .20 .50
22 Roy Williams .20 .50
23 Ashley Lelie .20 .50
24 Clinton Portis .20 .50
25 Ed McCaffrey .25 .60
26 Jake Plummer .20 .50
27 Rod Smith .25 .60
28 Joey Harrington .20 .50
29 Ahman Green .25 .60
30 Brett Favre .60 1.50
31 Donald Driver .25 .60
32 Javon Walker .25 .60
33 David Carr .20 .50
34 Edgerrin James .25 .60
35 Marvin Harrison .25 .60
36 Peyton Manning .75 2.00
37 Fred Taylor .20 .50
38 Jimmy Smith .25 .60
39 Mark Brunell .25 .60
40 Priest Holmes .20 .50
41 Tony Gonzalez .25 .60
42 Trent Green .20 .50
43 Chris Chambers .20 .50
44 Jay Fiedler .20 .50
45 Junior Seau .25 .60
46 Ricky Williams .25 .60
47 Zach Thomas .25 .60
48 Daunte Culpepper .25 .60
49 Michael Bennett .20 .50
50 Randy Moss .25 .60
51 Tom Brady 1.25 3.00
52 Troy Brown .20 .50
53 Aaron Brooks .20 .50
54 Deuce McAllister .25 .60
55 Donte Stallworth .20 .50
56 Joe Horn .20 .50
57 Jeremy Shockey .20 .50
58 Kerry Collins .20 .50
59 Michael Strahan .25 .60
60 Tiki Barber .25 .60
61 Chad Pennington .20 .50
62 Curtis Martin .25 .60
63 Santana Moss .25 .60
64 Charles Woodson .30 .75
65 Jerry Rice .60 1.50
66 Rich Gannon .25 .60
67 Tim Brown .30 .75
68 Donovan McNabb .25 .60
69 Antwaan Randle El .20 .50
70 Tommy Maddox .20 .50
71 Jerome Bettis .30 .75
72 Kendrell Bell .20 .50
73 Plaxico Burress .20 .50
74 David Boston .20 .50
75 Drew Brees .30 .75
76 LaDainian Tomlinson .30 .75
77 Kevan Barlow .20 .50
78 Jeff Garcia .20 .50
79 Terrell Owens .25 .60
80 Matt Hasselbeck .20 .50
81 Koren Robinson .25 .60
82 Shaun Alexander .20 .50
83 Isaac Bruce .30 .75
84 Kurt Warner .25 .60
85 Marshall Faulk .25 .60
86 Torry Holt .25 .60
87 Brad Johnson .25 .60
88 Keyshawn Johnson .30 .75
89 Mike Alstott .20 .50
90 Warren Sapp .25 .60
91 Eddie George .25 .60
92 Jevon Kearse .20 .50
93 Steve McNair .25 .60
94 Laveranues Coles .20 .50
95 Rod Gardner .20 .50
96 Patrick Ramsey .25 .60
97 Boller/Suggs/Smith CL .15 .40
98 R.Grossman/T.Jacobs CL .07 .20
99 A.Boldin/B.Johnson CL .10 .25
100 T.Calico/C.Brown CL .12 .30
101 Charles Tillman RC 5.00 12.00
102 Justin Griffith RC 1.25 3.00
103 Ovie Mughelli RC 1.25 3.00
104 Chris Edmonds RC 1.00 2.50
105 Jeremi Johnson RC 1.00 2.50
106 Malaefou MacKenzie RC 1.00 2.50
107 James Lynch RC 1.00 2.50
108 B.J. Askew RC 1.25 3.00
109 Andrew Pinnock RC 1.25 3.00
110 Chris Davis RC 1.25 3.00
111 Dan Curley RC 1.00 2.50
112 Lenny Walls RC 1.00 2.50
113 Travis Fisher 1.25 3.00
114 Ahmaad Galloway RC 1.25 3.00
115 Joe Smith RC 1.25 3.00
116 Reno Mahe RC 1.25 3.00
117 Torrie Cox RC 1.00 2.50
118 Kerry Carter RC 1.00 2.50
119 Dwone Hicks RC 1.00 2.50
120 Cato June RC 2.00 5.00
121 Terry Pierce RC 1.00 2.50
122 Eddie Moore RC 1.00 2.50
123 Mike Seidman RC 1.00 2.50
124 Michael Nattiel RC 1.00 2.50
125 Casey Fitzsimmons RC 1.25 3.00
126 George Wrighster RC 1.00 2.50
127 Mike Pinkard RC 1.00 2.50
128 Donald Lee RC 1.25 3.00
129 Sean Berton RC 1.00 2.50
130 Soloman Bates RC 1.00 2.50
131 Zach Hilton RC 1.25 3.00
132 Antonio Gates RC 15.00 40.00
133 Aaron Walker RC 1.25 3.00
134 Richard Angulo RC 1.00 2.50
135 Will Heller RC 1.25 3.00
136 Theo Sanders RC 1.00 2.50
137 Jimmy Farris RC 1.00 2.50
138 Ryan Nece RC 1.25 3.00
139 Antonio Brown RC 1.00 2.50
140 Clarence Coleman RC 1.00 2.50
141 Lawrence Hamilton RC 1.00 2.50
142 C.J. Jones RC 1.00 2.50
143 Frisman Jackson RC 1.25 3.00
144 Antonio Chatman RC 1.50 4.00
145 Rocky Boiman RC 1.25 3.00
146 Tron LaFavor RC 1.00 2.50
147 Derick Armstrong RC 1.25 3.00
148 J.J. Moses RC 1.00 2.50
149 Aaron Moorehead RC 1.25 3.00
150 Brad Pyatt RC 1.00 2.50
151 Arland Bruce RC 1.00 2.50
152 Chris Horn RC 1.25 3.00
153 Kareem Kelly RC 1.00 2.50
154 Talman Gardner RC 1.00 2.50
155 David Tyree RC 1.25 3.00
156 Willie Ponder RC 1.00 2.50
157 Greg Lewis RC 3.00 8.00
158 Eric Parker RC 1.50 4.00
159 Kassim Osgood RC 1.50 4.00
160 Jason Willis RC 1.00 2.50
161 Akbar Gbaja-Biamila RC 1.25 3.00
162 Mike Furrey RC 4.00 10.00
163 Chris Kelsay RC 1.25 3.00
164 Cory Redding RC 1.25 3.00
165 Kenny Peterson RC 1.25 3.00
166 Osi Umenyiora RC 2.00 5.00
167 Tyler Brayton RC 1.25 3.00
168 DeWayne White RC 1.00 2.50
169 Kevin Williams RC 1.50 4.00
170 Dan Klecko RC 1.25 3.00
171 Johnathan Sullivan RC 1.00 2.50
172 William Joseph RC 1.00 2.50
173 Rien Long RC 1.00 2.50
174 Angelo Crowell RC 1.25 3.00
175 Chaun Thompson RC 1.00 2.50
176 Bradie James RC 1.50 4.00
177 Antwan Peek RC 1.00 2.50
178 Kawika Mitchell RC 1.50 4.00
179 Cie Grant RC 1.25 3.00
180 E.J. Henderson RC 1.25 3.00
181 Victor Hobson RC 1.00 2.50
182 Alonzo Jackson RC 1.00 2.50
183 Matt Wilhelm RC 1.25 3.00
184 Pisa Tinoisamoa RC 1.50 4.00
185 Ricky Manning RC 1.25 3.00
186 Dennis Weathersby RC 1.00 2.50
187 Donald Strickland RC 1.00 2.50
188 Asante Samuel RC 2.50 6.00
189 Eugene Wilson RC 1.50 4.00
190 Nnamdi Asomugha RC 1.50 4.00
191 Ike Taylor RC 1.50 4.00
192 Drayton Florence RC 1.50 4.00
193 DeJuan Groce RC 1.50 4.00
194 Shane Walton RC 1.00 2.50
195 Terrence Holt RC 1.25 3.00
196 Rashean Mathis RC 1.00 2.50
197 Julian Battle RC 1.25 3.00
198 Hanik Milligan RC 1.00 2.50
199 Terrence Kiel RC 1.25 3.00
200 Ken Hamlin RC 1.50 4.00
201 Lee Suggs RC 1.25 3.00
202 Charles Rogers RC 1.50 4.00
203 Brandon Lloyd RC 2.00 5.00
204 Terrence Edwards RC 1.25 3.00
205 Tony Romo RC 12.00 30.00
206 Brooks Bollinger RC 1.50 4.00
207 Jerome McDougle RC 1.25 3.00
208 Jimmy Kennedy RC 1.50 4.00
209 Ken Dorsey RC 1.50 4.00
210 Kirk Farmer RC 1.50 4.00

211 Mike Doss RC 2.00 5.00
212 Chris Simms RC 1.25 3.00
213 Cecil Sapp RC 1.25 3.00
214 Justin Gage RC 1.50 4.00
215 Sam Aiken RC 1.50 4.00
216 Doug Gabriel RC 1.50 4.00
217 Jason Witten RC 5.00 12.00
218 Bennie Joppru RC 1.25 3.00
219 Jason Gesser RC 1.50 4.00
220 Brock Forsey RC 1.50 4.00
221 Quentin Griffin RC 1.50 4.00
222 Avon Cobourne RC 1.25 3.00
223 Domanick Davis RC 1.50 4.00
224 Boss Bailey RC 1.50 4.00
225 Tony Hollings RC 1.50 4.00
226 LaBrandon Toefield RC 1.25 3.00
227 Arlen Harris RC 1.25 3.00
228 Sultan McCullough RC 1.25 3.00
229 Visanthe Shiancoe RC 2.00 5.00
230 L.J. Smith RC 2.00 5.00
231 LaTarence Dunbar RC 1.25 3.00
232 Walter Young RC 1.25 3.00
233 Bobby Wade RC 1.50 4.00
234 Zuriel Smith RC 1.25 3.00
235 Adrian Madise RC 1.25 3.00
236 Ken Hamlin RC 2.00 5.00
237 Carl Ford RC 1.25 3.00
238 Cortez Hankton RC 1.50 4.00
239 J.R. Tolver RC 1.50 4.00
240 Keenan Howry RC 1.25 3.00
241 Billy McMullen RC 1.25 3.00
242 Arnaz Battle RC 2.00 5.00
243 Shaun McDonald RC 1.50 4.00
244 Andre Woolfolk RC 1.25 3.00
245 Sammy Davis RC 1.50 4.00
246 Calvin Pace RC 1.25 3.00
247 Michael Haynes RC 1.25 3.00
248 Ty Warren RC 1.50 4.00
249 Nick Barnett RC 2.00 5.00
250 Troy Polamalu RC 15.00 30.00
251 Carson Palmer JSY RC 4.00 10.00
252 Byron Leftwich JSY RC 2.50 6.00
253 Kyle Boller JSY RC 2.00 5.00
254 Rex Grossman JSY RC 2.50 6.00
255 Dave Ragone JSY RC 2.00 5.00
256 Brian St.Pierre JSY RC 2.00 5.00
257 Kliff Kingsbury JSY RC 3.00 8.00
258 Seneca Wallace JSY RC 2.50 6.00
259 Larry Johnson JSY RC 2.50 6.00
260 Willis McGahee JSY RC 2.50 6.00
261 Justin Fargas JSY RC 3.00 8.00
262 Onterrio Smith JSY RC 2.00 5.00
263 Chris Brown JSY RC 2.00 5.00
264 Musa Smith JSY RC 2.00 5.00
265 Artose Pinner JSY RC 2.00 5.00
266 Andre Johnson JSY RC 5.00 12.00
267 Kelley Washington JSY RC 2.00 5.00
268 Taylor Jacobs JSY RC 2.00 5.00
269 Bryant Johnson JSY RC 3.00 8.00
270 Tyrone Calico JSY RC 2.00 5.00
271 Anquan Boldin JSY RC 3.00 8.00
272 Bethel Johnson JSY RC 2.00 5.00
273 Nate Burleson JSY RC 2.50 6.00
274 Kevin Curtis JSY RC 2.00 5.00
275 Dallas Clark JSY RC 3.00 8.00
276 Teyo Johnson JSY RC 2.50 6.00
277 Terrell Suggs JSY RC 2.50 6.00
278 DeWayne Robertson JSY RC 2.50 6.00
279 Terence Newman JSY RC 3.00 8.00
280 Marcus Trufant JSY RC 2.50 6.00
281 C.Palmer/B.Leftwich JSY 4.00 10.00
282 R.Grossman/B.St.Pierre JSY 2.50 6.00
283 K.Boller/D.Ragone JSY 2.00 5.00
284 K.Kingsbury/S.Wallace JSY 3.00 8.00
285 L.Johnson/W.McGahee JSY 2.50 6.00
286 J.Fargas/O.Smith JSY 3.00 8.00
287 C.Brown/M.Smith JSY 2.00 5.00
288 A.Pinner/A.Johnson JSY 5.00 12.00
289 K.Washington/T.Jacobs JSY 2.00 5.00
290 B.Johnson/T.Calico JSY 3.00 8.00
291 A.Boldin/B.Johnson JSY 3.00 8.00
292 N.Burleson/K.Curtis JSY 2.50 6.00
293 D.Clark/T.Johnson JSY 3.00 8.00
294 T.Suggs/D.Robertson JSY 2.50 6.00
295 T.Newman/M.Trufant JSY 3.00 8.00

2003 Leaf Rookies and Stars Longevity

*1-100 VETS/100: 5X TO 12X BASIC CARDS
1-100 PRINT RUN 100 SER.#'d SETS
*101-200 ROOKIES/50: 2.5X TO 6X
101-200 PRINT RUN 50
201-250 AUTO PRINT RUN 25
UNPRICED 251-280 JSY AU PRINT RUN 10
*DUAL JSY 181-295: .6X TO 1.5X
281-295 DUAL JSY PRINT RUN 25
SERIAL #'d UNDER 25 NOT PRICED
201 Lee Suggs AU 12.00 30.00
202 Charles Rogers AU 15.00 40.00
203 Brandon Lloyd AU 20.00 50.00
204 Terrence Edwards AU 12.00 30.00
205 Tony Romo AU 600.00 1000.00
206 Brooks Bollinger AU 15.00 40.00
207 Jerome McDougle AU 12.00 30.00
208 Jimmy Kennedy AU 15.00 40.00
209 Ken Dorsey AU 15.00 40.00
210 Kirk Farmer AU 15.00 40.00
211 Mike Doss AU 20.00 50.00
212 Chris Simms AU 12.00 30.00
213 Cecil Sapp AU 12.00 30.00
214 Justin Gage AU 15.00 40.00
215 Sam Aiken AU 15.00 40.00
216 Doug Gabriel AU 15.00 40.00
217 Jason Witten AU 75.00 125.00
218 Bennie Joppru AU 12.00 30.00
219 Jason Gesser AU 15.00 40.00
220 Brock Forsey AU 15.00 40.00
222 Avon Cobourne AU 12.00 30.00
223 Domanick Davis AU 15.00 40.00
224 Boss Bailey AU 15.00 40.00
225 Tony Hollings AU 15.00 40.00
227 Arlen Harris AU 12.00 30.00
228 Sultan McCullough AU 12.00 30.00
229 Visanthe Shiancoe AU 20.00 50.00
230 L.J. Smith AU 20.00 50.00
231 LaTarence Dunbar AU 12.00 30.00
232 Walter Young AU 12.00 30.00
234 Zuriel Smith AU 12.00 30.00
235 Adrian Madise AU 12.00 30.00
236 Ken Hamlin AU 20.00 50.00
237 Carl Ford AU 12.00 30.00
238 Cortez Hankton AU 15.00 40.00
239 J.R. Tolver AU 15.00 40.00
242 Arnaz Battle AU 20.00 50.00
243 Shaun McDonald AU 15.00 40.00
244 Andre Woolfolk AU 12.00 30.00
245 Sammy Davis AU 15.00 40.00
246 Calvin Pace AU 12.00 30.00
247 Michael Haynes AU 12.00 30.00
248 Ty Warren AU 15.00 40.00
240 Nick Barnett AU 20.00 50.00
250 Troy Polamalu AU 300.00 500.00

2003 Leaf Rookies and Stars Rookie Autographs

Randomly inserted in packs, this set features authentic player autographs on silver foil stickers. The first 150 cards of rookies 201-250 feature autographs. Rookies 251-280 feature an event worn jersey swatch in addition to the autograph. The first 50 cards of rookies 251-280 feature autographs. Please note that B.McMullen, B.Wade, C.Rogers, D.Davis, D.Robertson, K.Howry, L.Suggs, L.Toefield, N.Barnett, N.Burleson, O.Smith, Q.Griffin, T.Romo, T. Warren, and W.McGahee were all issued as exchange cards in packs. The exchange deadline is 6/1/2006.

201-250 AUTO PRINT RUN 150
201-250 FIRST 150 BASE CARDS SIGNED
251-280 JSY AUTO PRINT RUN 50
251-280 FIRST 50 BASE CARDS SIGNED
201 Lee Suggs 6.00 15.00
202 Charles Rogers 8.00 20.00
203 Brandon Lloyd 10.00 25.00
204 Terrence Edwards 6.00 15.00
205 Tony Romo 300.00 600.00
206 Brooks Bollinger 8.00 20.00
207 Jerome McDougle 6.00 15.00
208 Jimmy Kennedy 8.00 20.00
209 Ken Dorsey 8.00 20.00
210 Kirk Farmer 8.00 20.00
211 Mike Doss 10.00 25.00
212 Chris Simms 6.00 15.00
213 Cecil Sapp 6.00 15.00
214 Justin Gage 8.00 20.00
215 Sam Aiken 8.00 20.00
216 Doug Gabriel 8.00 20.00
217 Jason Witten 40.00 80.00
218 Bennie Joppru 6.00 15.00
219 Jason Gesser 8.00 20.00
220 Brock Forsey 8.00 20.00
221 Quentin Griffin 8.00 20.00
222 Avon Cobourne 6.00 15.00
223 Domanick Davis 8.00 20.00
224 Boss Bailey 8.00 20.00
225 Tony Hollings 8.00 20.00
226 LaBrandon Toefield 6.00 15.00
227 Arlen Harris 6.00 15.00
228 Sultan McCullough 6.00 15.00
229 Visanthe Shiancoe 10.00 25.00
230 L.J. Smith 10.00 25.00
231 LaTarence Dunbar 6.00 15.00
232 Walter Young 6.00 15.00
233 Bobby Wade 8.00 20.00
234 Zuriel Smith 6.00 15.00
235 Adrian Madise 6.00 15.00
236 Ken Hamlin 10.00 25.00
237 Carl Ford 6.00 15.00
238 Cortez Hankton 8.00 20.00
239 J.R. Tolver 8.00 20.00
242 Arnaz Battle 10.00 25.00
243 Shaun McDonald 8.00 20.00
244 Andre Woolfolk 6.00 15.00
245 Sammy Davis 8.00 20.00
246 Calvin Pace 6.00 15.00
247 Michael Haynes 6.00 15.00
248 Ty Warren 8.00 20.00
249 Nick Barnett 10.00 25.00
250 Troy Polamalu 150.00 300.00
251 Carson Palmer JSY 90.00 150.00
252 Byron Leftwich JSY 12.00 30.00
253 Kyle Boller JSY 10.00 25.00
254 Rex Grossman JSY 12.00 30.00
255 Dave Ragone JSY 10.00 25.00
256 Brian St.Pierre JSY 10.00 25.00
257 Kliff Kingsbury JSY 15.00 40.00
258 Seneca Wallace JSY 12.00 30.00
259 Larry Johnson JSY 12.00 30.00
260 Willis McGahee JSY 12.00 30.00
261 Justin Fargas JSY 15.00 40.00
262 Onterrio Smith JSY 10.00 25.00
263 Chris Brown JSY 10.00 25.00
264 Musa Smith JSY 10.00 25.00
265 Artose Pinner JSY 10.00 25.00
266 Andre Johnson JSY 50.00 100.00
267 Kelley Washington JSY 10.00 25.00
268 Taylor Jacobs JSY 10.00 25.00
269 Bryant Johnson JSY 15.00 40.00
270 Tyrone Calico JSY 10.00 25.00
271 Anquan Boldin JSY 15.00 40.00
272 Bethel Johnson JSY 10.00 25.00
273 Nate Burleson JSY 12.00 30.00
274 Kevin Curtis JSY 10.00 25.00
275 Dallas Clark JSY 15.00 40.00
276 Teyo Johnson JSY 12.00 30.00
277 Terrell Suggs JSY 25.00 60.00
279 Terence Newman JSY 15.00 40.00
280 Marcus Trufant JSY 12.00 30.00

2003 Leaf Rookies and Stars Freshman Orientation Jersey

Randomly inserted in packs, this set features event worn jersey swatches. Each card is serial numbered to 600. Class Officers, a parallel of this set, are serial numbered to 25 and feature event worn jersey swatches. Class Officers are not priced due to scarcity.

PRINT RUN 600 SERIAL #'d SETS
*CLASS OFFICER/25: 1.2X TO 3X JSY/600
CL.OFFICERS PRINT RUN 25 SER.#'d SETS
FO1 Carson Palmer 3.00 8.00
FO2 Byron Leftwich 2.00 5.00
FO3 Kyle Boller 1.50 4.00
FO4 Rex Grossman 2.00 5.00
FO5 Dave Ragone 1.50 4.00
FO6 Brian St.Pierre 1.50 4.00
FO7 Kliff Kingsbury 2.50 6.00
FO8 Seneca Wallace 2.00 5.00
FO9 Larry Johnson 2.00 5.00
FO10 Willis McGahee 2.00 5.00
FO11 Justin Fargas 2.50 6.00
FO12 Onterrio Smith 1.50 4.00
FO13 Chris Brown 1.50 4.00
FO14 Musa Smith 1.50 4.00
FO15 Artose Pinner 1.50 4.00
FO16 Andre Johnson 4.00 10.00
FO17 Kelley Washington 1.50 4.00
FO18 Taylor Jacobs 1.50 4.00
FO19 Bryant Johnson 2.50 6.00
FO20 Tyrone Calico 1.50 4.00
FO21 Anquan Boldin 2.50 6.00
FO22 Bethel Johnson 1.50 4.00
FO23 Nate Burleson 2.00 5.00
FO24 Kevin Curtis 1.50 4.00
FO25 Dallas Clark 2.50 6.00
FO26 Teyo Johnson 2.00 5.00
FO27 Terrell Suggs 2.00 5.00
FO28 DeWayne Robertson 2.00 5.00
FO29 Terence Newman 2.50 6.00
FO30 Marcus Trufant 2.00 5.00

2003 Leaf Rookies and Stars Great American Heroes

Randomly inserted in packs, this set features past and present stars of the NFL printed on clear plastic. Each card is serial numbered to 1325.

COMPLETE SET (20) 20.00 50.00
PRINT RUN 1325 SERIAL #'d SETS
GA1 Brian Urlacher 1.25 3.00
GA2 Bob Griese 1.25 3.00
GA3 Mel Blount 1.00 2.50
GA4 Ahman Green 1.00 2.50
GA5 Aaron Brooks .75 2.00
GA6 Chad Pennington .75 2.00
GA7 Clinton Portis .75 2.00
GA8 Isaac Bruce 1.25 3.00
GA9 Jamal Lewis 1.00 2.50
GA10 Jeff Garcia .75 2.00
GA11 Jerry Rice 2.50 6.00
GA12 Joey Harrington .75 2.00
GA13 Kurt Warner 1.00 2.50
GA14 LaDainian Tomlinson 1.25 3.00
GA15 Rod Smith 1.00 2.50
GA16 Tommy Maddox .75 2.00
GA17 Rex Grossman 1.00 2.50
GA18 Cecil Sapp .75 2.00
GA19 Byron Leftwich 1.00 2.50
GA20 Kenny Peterson 1.00 2.50

2003 Leaf Rookies and Stars Great American Heroes Autographs

Randomly inserted in packs, this set features authentic player autographs on silver foil stickers with cards serial numbered between 17-150. Please note that Kenny Peterson was issued as an exchange card in packs but never signed for the set. Instead his card was issued with "No Autogrpah" printed on the front. The exchange deadline was 6/1/2006.

STATED PRINT RUN 17-150
SERIAL #'d UNDER 25 NOT PRICED
GA1 Brian Urlacher/25 30.00 80.00
GA3 Mel Blount/53 15.00 40.00
GA4 Ahman Green/25 25.00 60.00
GA5 Aaron Brooks/75 10.00 25.00
GA7 Clinton Portis/30 20.00 50.00
GA8 Isaac Bruce/75 12.50 30.00
GA9 Jamal Lewis/25 20.00 50.00
GA10 Jeff Garcia/25 20.00 50.00
GA11 Jerry Rice/25 100.00 200.00
GA12 Joey Harrington/30 20.00 50.00
GA13 Kurt Warner/25 30.00 80.00
GA14 LaDainian Tomlinson/25 75.00 125.00
GA15 Rod Smith/150 12.50 30.00
GA16 Tommy Maddox/50 12.50 30.00
GA17 Rex Grossman/50 5.00 12.00
GA18 Cecil Sapp/100 6.00 15.00
GA19 Byron Leftwich/25 25.00 60.00
GA20 Kenny Peterson No Auto 6.00 15.00

2003 Leaf Rookies and Stars Initial Steps Shoe

Randomly inserted in packs, this set features event worn shoe swatches. Each card is serial numbered to 100.

PRINT RUN 100 SERIAL #'d SETS
IS1 Carson Palmer 5.00 12.00
IS2 Byron Leftwich 3.00 8.00
IS3 Kyle Boller 2.50 6.00
IS4 Rex Grossman 3.00 8.00
IS5 Dave Ragone 2.50 6.00
IS6 Brian St.Pierre 2.50 6.00
IS7 Kliff Kingsbury 4.00 10.00
IS8 Seneca Wallace 3.00 8.00
IS9 Larry Johnson 3.00 8.00
IS10 Willis McGahee 3.00 8.00
IS11 Justin Fargas 4.00 10.00
IS12 Onterrio Smith 2.50 6.00
IS13 Chris Brown 2.50 6.00
IS14 Musa Smith 2.50 6.00
IS15 Artose Pinner 2.50 6.00
IS16 Andre Johnson 6.00 15.00
IS17 Kelley Washington 2.50 6.00
IS18 Taylor Jacobs 2.50 6.00
IS19 Bryant Johnson 4.00 10.00
IS20 Tyrone Calico 2.50 6.00
IS21 Anquan Boldin 4.00 10.00
IS22 Bethel Johnson 2.50 6.00
IS23 Nate Burleson 3.00 8.00
IS24 Kevin Curtis 2.50 6.00
IS25 Dallas Clark 4.00 10.00
IS26 Teyo Johnson 3.00 8.00
IS27 Terrell Suggs 3.00 8.00
IS28 DeWayne Robertson 3.00 8.00
IS29 Terence Newman 4.00 10.00
IS30 Marcus Trufant 3.00 8.00

2003 Leaf Rookies and Stars Masks

Randomly inserted in packs, this set features single pieces of event worn facemasks. Each card is serial numbered to 350. The first 100 cards of the print run feature two pieces of event worn facemask, and make up the Masks Dual set.

STATED PRINT RUN 350 SER. #'d SETS
*DUAL MASK/100: .8X TO 2X FO JSY/600
DUAL PRINT RUN 100 SER.#'d SETS
FIRST 100 CARDS FEATURE DUAL SWATCHES
RM1 Carson Palmer 4.00 10.00
RM2 Byron Leftwich 2.50 6.00
RM3 Kyle Boller 2.00 5.00
RM4 Rex Grossman 2.50 6.00
RM5 Dave Ragone 2.00 5.00
RM6 Brian St.Pierre 2.00 5.00
RM7 Kliff Kingsbury 3.00 8.00
RM8 Seneca Wallace 2.50 6.00
RM9 Larry Johnson 2.50 6.00
RM10 Willis McGahee 2.50 6.00
RM11 Justin Fargas 3.00 8.00
RM12 Onterrio Smith 2.00 5.00
RM13 Chris Brown 2.00 5.00
RM14 Musa Smith 2.00 5.00
RM15 Artose Pinner 2.00 5.00
RM16 Andre Johnson 5.00 12.00
RM17 Kelley Washington 2.00 5.00
RM18 Taylor Jacobs 2.00 5.00
RM19 Bryant Johnson 3.00 8.00
RM20 Tyrone Calico 2.00 5.00
RM21 Anquan Boldin 3.00 8.00
RM22 Bethel Johnson 2.00 5.00
RM23 Nate Burleson 2.50 6.00
RM24 Kevin Curtis 2.00 5.00
RM25 Dallas Clark 3.00 8.00
RM26 Teyo Johnson 2.50 6.00
RM27 Terrell Suggs 2.50 6.00
RM28 DeWayne Robertson 2.50 6.00
RM29 Terence Newman 3.00 8.00
RM30 Marcus Trufant 2.50 6.00

2003 Leaf Rookies and Stars Prime Cuts

ndomly inserted in packs, this set features premium game used jersey swatches. Each card is serial numbered to 25.

STATED PRINT RUN 25 SER.#'d SETS
PC1 Aaron Brooks 8.00 20.00
PC2 Ahman Green 10.00 25.00
PC3 Antonio Bryant 8.00 20.00
PC4 Antwaan Randle El 8.00 20.00
PC5 Ashley Lelie 8.00 20.00
PC6 Brett Favre 25.00 60.00
PC7 Brian Urlacher 12.00 30.00
PC8 Chad Pennington 8.00 20.00
PC9 Chris Chambers 8.00 20.00
PC10 Clinton Portis 8.00 20.00
PC11 Daunte Culpepper 10.00 25.00
PC12 David Carr 8.00 20.00
PC13 Deuce McAllister 10.00 25.00
PC14 Donovan McNabb 10.00 25.00
PC15 Donte Stallworth 8.00 20.00
PC16 Drew Bledsoe 10.00 25.00
PC17 Drew Brees 12.00 30.00
PC18 Edgerrin James 10.00 25.00
PC19 Jeff Garcia 8.00 20.00
PC20 Jeremy Shockey 8.00 20.00
PC21 Jerry Rice 25.00 60.00
PC22 Joey Harrington 8.00 20.00
PC23 Julius Peppers 12.00 30.00
PC24 Kurt Warner 10.00 25.00
PC25 LaDainian Tomlincon 12.00 30.00
PC26 Marshall Faulk 10.00 25.00
PC27 Marvin Harrison 10.00 25.00
PC28 Michael Vick 10.00 25.00
PC29 Peyton Manning 30.00 80.00
PC30 Priest Holmes 8.00 20.00
PC31 Randy Moss 10.00 25.00
PC32 Ricky Williams 10.00 25.00
PC33 Shaun Alexander 8.00 20.00
PC34 Steve McNair 10.00 25.00
PC35 Tom Brady 50.00 125.00
PC36 William Green 8.00 20.00

2003 Leaf Rookies and Stars Slideshow

ndomly inserted in packs, this set features the stars of the NFL printed on clear plastic. Each card is serial numbered to 1500.

COMPLETE SET (10) 10.00 25.00
PRINT RUN 1500 SER. #'d SETS
SS1 Clinton Portis .75 2.00
SS2 Drew Bledsoe 1.00 2.50
SS3 Michael Vick 1.00 2.50
SS4 Donovan McNabb 1.00 2.50
SS5 Brett Favre 2.50 6.00
SS6 Deuce McAllister 1.00 2.50
SS7 Ricky Williams 1.00 2.50
SS8 Jeremy Shockey .75 2.00
SS9 Brian Urlacher 1.25 3.00
SS10 Chad Pennington .75 2.00

2003 Leaf Rookies and Stars Ticket Masters

COMPLETE SET (20) 25.00 60.00
STATED PRINT RUN 1325 SER.#'d SETS
TM1 B.Favre/A.Green 2.50 6.00
TM2 J.Harrington/C.Rogers 1.00 2.50
TM3 B.Urlacher/A.Thomas 1.25 3.00
TM4 R.Moss/D.Culpepper 1.00 2.50
TM5 K.Warner/M.Faulk 1.00 2.50
TM6 J.Garcia/T.Owens 1.00 2.50
TM7 R.Williams/Z.Thomas 1.00 2.50
TM8 L.Tomlinson/D.Brees 1.25 3.00
TM9 J.Rice/R.Gannon 2.50 6.00
TM10 P.Holmes/T.Gonzalez 1.00 2.50
TM11 C.Portis/R.Smith 1.00 2.50
TM12 D.Bledsoe/T.Henry 1.00 2.50
TM13 C.Johnson/C.Palmer 1.25 3.00
TM14 C.Pennington/C.Martin 1.00 2.50
TM15 S.McNair/E.George 1.00 2.50
TM16 P.Manning/M.Harrison 3.00 8.00
TM17 D.McAllister/A.Brooks 1.00 2.50
TM18 D.McNabb/D.Staley 1.00 2.50
TM19 M.Vick/P.Price 1.00 2.50
TM20 J.Shockey/T.Barber 1.00 2.50

2003 Leaf Rookies and Stars Triple Threads

Randomly inserted in packs, this set features three game used jersey swatches from three teammates. Each card is serial numbered to 100.

STATED PRINT RUN 100 SER.#'d SETS
TT1 Vick/Duckett/Dunn 6.00 15.00
TT2 Warner/Faulk/Holt 6.00 15.00
TT3 Bledsoe/Moulds/Henry 6.00 15.00
TT4 Urlacher/Thomas/Brown 15.00 40.00
TT5 Portis/McCaffrey/Smith 6.00 15.00
TT6 Favre/Green/Driver 15.00 40.00
TT7 Manning/James/Harrison 20.00 50.00
TT8 Brunell/Taylor/J.Smith 6.00 15.00
TT9 Green/Holmes/Gonzalez 6.00 15.00
TT10 Ri.Willms/Chmbrs/Z.Thmas 6.00 15.00
TT11 Culpepper/Bennett/Moss 6.00 15.00
TT12 Brady/A.Smith/T.Brown 30.00 80.00
TT13 Brooks/McAllist/Stallworth 6.00 15.00
TT14 Collins/Shockey/Strahan 6.00 15.00
TT15 Pennington/Martin/Moss 6.00 15.00
TT16 Gannon/Rice/T.Brown 15.00 40.00
TT17 McNabb/Staley/Pinkston 6.00 15.00
TT18 Bettis/Bell/Burress 8.00 20.00
TT19 Brees/Flutie/Tomlinson 8.00 20.00
TT20 Garcia/Hearst/Owens 6.00 15.00

2004 Leaf Rookies and Stars

Leaf Rookies and Stars initially released in mid-November 2004. The base set consists of 299-cards including 100-rookies non-serial numbered, 50-rookies numbered of 750, 33-rookie jersey cards numbered of 750, and 16-dual rookie jersey cards numbered of 500. Hobby boxes contained 24-packs of 6-cards and carried an S.R.P. of $4 per pack. Three parallel sets and a variety of inserts can be found seeded in hobby and retail packs highlighted by the Fans of the Game Autograph and Rookie Autograph inserts.

COMP.SET w/o SP's (200) 30.00 60.00
COMP.SET w/o RC's (100) 7.50 20.00
201-250 RC PRINT RUN 750 SER.#'d SETS
251-283 JSY PRINT RUN 750 SER.#'d SETS
284-299 PRINT RUN 500 SER.#'d SETS
1 Anquan Boldin .20 .50
2 Emmitt Smith .50 1.25
3 Josh McCown .25 .60
4 Michael Vick .25 .60
5 Peerless Price .20 .50
6 T.J. Duckett .20 .50
7 Warrick Dunn .20 .50
8 Jamal Lewis .25 .60
9 Kyle Boller .20 .50
10 Ray Lewis .30 .75
11 Drew Bledsoe .25 .60
12 Eric Moulds .20 .50
13 Travis Henry .20 .50
14 Jake Delhomme .20 .50
15 Stephen Davis .20 .50
16 Steve Smith .30 .75
17 Brian Urlacher .30 .75
18 Rex Grossman .20 .50
19 Thomas Jones .20 .50
20 Carson Palmer .25 .60
21 Chad Johnson .20 .50
22 Rudi Johnson .20 .50
23 Jeff Garcia .20 .50
24 William Green .20 .50
25 Keyshawn Johnson .25 .60
26 Terence Newman .25 .60
27 Roy Williams S .20 .50
28 Jake Plummer .20 .50
29 Quentin Griffin .20 .50
30 Rod Smith .25 .60
31 Charles Rogers .20 .50
32 Joey Harrington .20 .50
33 Ahman Green .25 .60
34 Brett Favre .60 1.50
35 Javon Walker .20 .50
36 Andre Johnson .25 .60
37 David Carr .20 .50
38 Domanick Davis .20 .50
39 Edgerrin James .25 .60
40 Marvin Harrison .25 .60
41 Peyton Manning .75 2.00
42 Byron Leftwich .20 .50
43 Fred Taylor .20 .50
44 Jimmy Smith .25 .60
45 Priest Holmes .20 .50
46 Tony Gonzalez .25 .60
47 Trent Green .20 .50
48 A.J. Feeley .20 .50
49 Chris Chambers .20 .50
50 Deion Sanders .25 .60
51 Daunte Culpepper .25 .60
52 Michael Bennett .20 .50
53 Randy Moss .25 .60
54 Corey Dillon .20 .50
55 Deion Branch .20 .50
56 Tom Brady 1.25 3.00
57 Aaron Brooks .20 .50
58 Deuce McAllister .25 .60
59 Joe Horn .20 .50
60 Jeremy Shockey .20 .50
61 Michael Strahan .25 .60
62 Tiki Barber .25 .60
63 Chad Pennington .20 .50
64 Curtis Martin .25 .60
65 Santana Moss .25 .60
66 Jerry Porter .20 .50
67 Jerry Rice .60 1.50
68 Warren Sapp .25 .60
69 Donovan McNabb .25 .60
70 Jevon Kearse .20 .50
71 Terrell Owens .25 .60
72 Duce Staley .20 .50
73 Hines Ward .25 .60
74 Jerome Bettis .30 .75
75 LaDainian Tomlinson .30 .75
76 Kevan Barlow .20 .50
77 Tim Rattay .20 .50
78 Koren Robinson .20 .50
79 Matt Hasselbeck .20 .50
80 Shaun Alexander .20 .50
81 Isaac Bruce .30 .75
82 Marc Bulger .20 .50
83 Marshall Faulk .25 .60
84 Torry Holt .25 .60
85 Brad Johnson .25 .60
86 Derrick Brooks .20 .50
87 Chris Brown .20 .50
88 Derrick Mason .20 .50
89 Eddie George .25 .60
90 Steve McNair .25 .60
91 Clinton Portis .20 .50
92 LaVar Arrington .20 .50
93 Laveranues Coles .20 .50
94 Mark Brunell .25 .60
95 Hall/Schaub/Jenkins CL .20 .50
96 Losman/L.Evans CL .20 .50
97 Winslow Jr./L.McCown CL .12 .30
98 D.Watts/T.Bell CL .12 .30
99 K.Jones/Ro.Will. CL .15 .40
100 G.Jones/Re.Will. CL .12 .30
101 Darnell Dockett RC 1.50 4.00
102 Karlos Dansby RC 1.25 3.00
103 Larry Croom RC 1.00 2.50
104 Chad Lavalais RC 1.00 2.50
105 Demorrio Williams RC 1.50 4.00
106 B.J. Sams RC 1.00 2.50
107 Dwan Edwards RC 1.00 2.50
108 Jason Peters RC 1.25 3.00
109 Shaud Williams RC 1.25 3.00
110 Tim Anderson RC 1.25 3.00
111 Tim Euhus RC 1.00 2.50
112 Michael Gaines RC 1.00 2.50
113 Rod Rutherford RC 1.00 2.50
114 Leon Joe RC 1.00 2.50
115 Nathan Vasher RC 1.50 4.00
116 Caleb Miller RC 1.00 2.50
117 Jamall Broussard RC 1.00 2.50
118 Keiwan Ratliff RC 1.00 2.50
119 Landon Johnson RC 1.00 2.50
120 Madieu Williams RC 1.00 2.50
121 Matthias Askew RC 1.00 2.50
122 Robert Geathers RC 1.00 2.50
123 Richard Alston RC 1.00 2.50
124 Bruce Thornton RC 1.00 2.50
125 Patrick Crayton RC 1.50 4.00
126 Bradlee Van Pelt RC 1.25 3.00
127 Charlie Adams RC 1.00 2.50
128 Nate Jackson RC 1.00 2.50
129 Roc Alexander RC 1.00 2.50
130 Romar Crenshaw RC 1.00 2.50
131 Keith Smith RC 1.00 2.50
132 Joey Thomas RC 1.00 2.50
133 Kelvin Kight RC 1.00 2.50
134 Scott McBrien RC 1.25 3.00
135 Andrae Thurman RC 1.00 2.50
136 Derick Armstrong 1.00 2.50
137 Glenn Earl RC 1.00 2.50
138 Kendrick Starling RC 1.00 2.50
139 Ben Hartsock RC 1.00 2.50
140 Gilbert Gardner RC 1.00 2.50
141 Jason David RC 1.00 2.50
142 Daryl Smith RC 1.00 2.50
143 Jared Allen RC 5.00 12.00
144 Jeris McIntyre RC 1.00 2.50
145 John Booth RC 1.00 2.50
146 Jonathan Smith RC 1.00 2.50
147 Junior Siavii RC 1.00 2.50
148 Keyaron Fox RC 1.25 3.00
149 Kris Wilson RC 1.25 3.00
150 Doug Easlick RC 1.00 2.50
151 Fred Russell RC 1.25 3.00
152 Tony Bua RC 1.00 2.50
153 Will Poole RC 1.50 4.00
154 Ben Nelson RC 1.00 2.50
155 Brock Lesnar RC 8.00 20.00
156 Butchie Wallace RC 1.00 2.50
157 Darrion Scott RC 1.25 3.00
158 Dontarrious Thomas RC 1.25 3.00
159 Richard Owens RC 1.00 2.50
160 Rod Davis RC 1.00 2.50
161 Dexter Reid RC 1.00 2.50
162 Kory Chapman RC 1.00 2.50
163 Marquise Hill RC 1.00 2.50
164 Courtney Watson RC 1.00 2.50
165 Mike Karney RC 1.25 3.00
166 Gibril Wilson RC 1.50 4.00
167 Reggie Torbor RC 1.00 2.50
168 Darrell McClover RC 1.00 2.50
169 Derrick Strait RC 1.00 2.50
170 Erik Coleman RC 1.25 3.00
171 Johnathan Reese RC 1.00 2.50
172 Rashad Washington RC 1.00 2.50
173 Courtney Anderson RC 1.00 2.50
174 Stuart Schweigert RC 1.25 3.00
175 J.R. Reed RC 1.00 2.50
176 Justin Jenkins RC 1.00 2.50
177 Matt Ware RC 1.50 4.00
178 Nate Lawrie RC 1.00 2.50
179 Thomas Tapeh RC 1.25 3.00
180 Matt Kranchick RC 1.25 3.00
181 Willie Parker RC 1.50 4.00
182 Igor Olshansky RC 1.25 3.00
183 Ryan Krause RC 1.00 2.50
184 Shaun Phillips RC 1.25 3.00
185 Wes Welker RC 6.00 15.00
186 Richard Seigler RC 1.00 2.50
187 Shawntae Spencer RC 1.00 2.50
188 Marcus Tubbs RC 1.00 2.50
189 Niko Koutouvides RC 1.00 2.50
190 Brandon Chillar RC 1.25 3.00
191 Tony Hargrove RC 1.00 2.50
192 Mark Jones RC 1.00 2.50
193 Marquis Cooper RC 1.00 2.50
194 Antwan Odom RC 1.00 2.50
195 Michael Waddell RC 1.00 2.50
196 Randy Starks RC 1.00 2.50
197 Rich Gardner RC 1.25 3.00
198 Travis Laboy RC 1.25 3.00
199 Vick King RC 1.00 2.50
200 Chris Cooley RC 1.25 3.00
201 Adimchinobe Echemandu RC 2.00 5.00
202 Ahmad Carroll RC 1.50 4.00
203 Andy Hall RC 1.50 4.00
204 B.J. Johnson RC 1.50 4.00
205 B.J. Symons RC 1.50 4.00
206 Brandon Miree RC 1.50 4.00
207 Bruce Perry RC 1.50 4.00
208 Carlos Francis RC 1.50 4.00
209 Casey Bramlet RC 1.50 4.00
210 Chris Gamble RC 1.50 4.00
211 Clarence Moore RC 1.50 4.00
212 Cody Pickett RC 1.50 4.00
213 Craig Krenzel RC 1.50 4.00
214 D.J. Hackett RC 1.50 4.00
215 D.J. Williams RC 2.50 6.00
216 Derrick Ward RC 2.50 6.00
217 Drew Carter RC 2.00 5.00
218 Drew Henson RC 1.50 4.00
219 Ernest Wilford RC 2.00 5.00
220 Jamaar Taylor RC 1.50 4.00
221 Jared Lorenzen RC 2.00 5.00
222 Jarrett Payton RC 2.00 5.00
223 Jason Babin RC 2.50 6.00
224 Jeff Smoker RC 2.00 5.00
225 Jerricho Cotchery RC 2.00 5.00
226 Jim Sorgi RC 2.00 5.00
227 John Navarre RC 1.50 4.00
228 Johnnie Morant RC 1.50 4.00
229 Jonathan Vilma RC 2.00 5.00
230 Josh Harris RC 1.50 4.00
231 Kenechi Udeze RC 2.00 5.00
232 Matt Mauck RC 1.50 4.00
233 Maurice Mann RC 1.50 4.00
234 Michael Turner RC 1.50 4.00
235 P.K. Sam RC 1.50 4.00
236 Quincy Wilson RC 1.50 4.00
237 Ran Carthon RC 1.50 4.00
238 Ricardo Colclough RC 1.50 4.00
239 Samie Parker RC 1.50 4.00
240 Sean Jones RC 1.50 4.00
241 Sean Taylor RC 10.00 25.00
242 Sloan Thomas RC 2.00 5.00
243 Tommie Harris RC 2.00 5.00
244 Triandos Luke RC 1.50 4.00
245 Troy Fleming RC 1.50 4.00
246 Vince Wilfork RC 2.50 6.00
247 Will Smith RC 2.00 5.00
248 Michael Boulware RC 2.50 6.00
249 Richard Smith RC 1.50 4.00
250 Teddy Lehman RC 1.50 4.00
251 Larry Fitzgerald JSY RC 8.00 20.00
252 DeAngelo Hall JSY RC 3.00 8.00
253 Matt Schaub JSY RC 2.00 5.00
254 Michael Jenkins JSY RC 2.00 5.00
255 Devard Darling JSY RC 2.00 5.00
256 J.P. Losman JSY RC 2.00 5.00
257 Lee Evans JSY RC 3.00 8.00
258 Keary Colbert JSY RC 2.00 5.00
259 Bernard Berrian JSY RC 2.00 5.00
260 Chris Perry JSY RC 2.00 5.00
261 Kellen Winslow Jr. JSY RC 2.00 5.00
262 Luke McCown JSY RC 2.00 5.00
263 Julius Jones JSY RC 2.00 5.00
264 Darius Watts JSY RC 2.00 5.00
265 Tatum Bell JSY RC 2.00 5.00
266 Kevin Jones JSY RC 2.50 6.00
267 Roy Williams JSY RC 2.00 5.00
268 Dunta Robinson JSY RC 2.00 5.00
269 Greg Jones JSY RC 2.00 5.00
270 Reggie Williams JSY RC 2.00 5.00
271 Mewelde Moore JSY RC 2.50 6.00
272 Ben Watson JSY RC 2.50 6.00
273 Cedric Cobbs JSY RC 2.00 5.00
274 Devery Henderson JSY RC 2.00 5.00
275 Eli Manning JSY RC 15.00 40.00
276 Robert Gallery JSY RC 2.50 6.00
277 Ben Roethlisberger JSY RC 15.00 40.00
278 Philip Rivers JSY RC 6.00 15.00
279 Derrick Hamilton JSY RC 2.00 5.00
280 Rashaun Woods JSY RC 2.00 5.00
281 Steven Jackson JSY RC 3.00 8.00
282 Michael Clayton JSY RC 2.50 6.00
283 Ben Troupe JSY RC 2.00 5.00
284 E.Manning/Rivers JSY 15.00 40.00
285 Fitzgerald/Ro.Williams JSY 8.00 20.00
286 Winslow Jr./G.Jones JSY 2.00 5.00
287 D.Hall/D.Robinson JSY 3.00 8.00
288 Re.Williams/Darling JSY 2.00 5.00
289 Roethlisberger/Losman JSY 15.00 40.00
290 Clayton/Henderson JSY 2.50 6.00
291 S.Jackson/Perry JSY 3.00 8.00
292 L.Evans/M.Jenkins JSY 3.00 8.00
293 R.Woods/T.Bell JSY 2.00 5.00
294 K.Jones/Berrian JSY 2.00 5.00
295 Watson/Troupe JSY 2.50 6.00
296 J.Jones/M.Moore JSY 2.50 6.00
297 M.Schaub/Hamilton JSY 2.00 5.00
298 L.McCown/Watts JSY 2.00 5.00
299 Colbert/Cobbs JSY 2.00 5.00

2004 Leaf Rookies and Stars Longevity Parallel

*VETS 1-100: 3X TO 8X BASIC CARDS
1-100 PRINT RUN 125
*ROOKIES 101-200: 1.2X TO 3X
101-200 STATED PRINT RUN 75
201-250 AU PRINT RUN 50
UNPRICED 251-283 AU PRINT RUN 10
*ROOKIES JSY 284-299: 1.2X TO 3X
284-299 JSY PRINT RUN 25
216 Derrick Ward AU 12.00 30.00
234 Michael Turner AU 20.00 50.00
241 Sean Taylor No Auto 8.00 20.00

2004 Leaf Rookies and Stars Longevity Holofoil Parallel

ETS 1-100: 4X TO 10X BASE CARD HI
1-100 PRINT RUN 75 SER.#'d SETS
*ROOKIES 101-200: 2X TO 5X
101-200 PRINT RUN 25 SER.#'d SETS
UNPRICED 201-250 AU PRINT RUN 10 SETS
UNPRICED 251-283 JSY AU PRINT RUN 5
UNPRICED 284-299 JSY PRINT RUN 10 SETS

2004 Leaf Rookies and Stars Longevity True Blue Parallel

ETS 1-100: 2X TO 5X BASE CARD HI
1-100 PRINT RUN 249 SER.#'d SETS
*ROOKIES 101-200: 1.2X TO 3X
101-200 PRINT RUN 75 SER.#'d SETS
*ROOKIES 201-250: 2.5X TO 6X
201-250 PRINT RUN 25 SER.#'d SETS

2004 Leaf Rookies and Stars Crusade Red

RED PRINT RUN 1250 SER.#'d SETS
*GREEN/750: .5X TO 1.2X RED/1250
GREEN PRINT RUN 750 SER.#'d SETS
*GREEN DC/25: 2X TO 5X RED/1250
GREEN DIE CUT PRINT RUN 25
*PURPLE/250: .6X TO 1.5X RED/1250
PURPLE PRINT RUN 250 SER.#'d SETS
*PRPL DC/50: 1.2X TO 3X RED/1250
PURPLE DIE CUT PRINT RUN 50
*RED DC/10: 3X TO 8X RED/1250
RED DC PRINT RUN 10 SETS
C1 Brett Favre 2.50 6.00
C2 Brian Urlacher 1.25 3.00
C3 Byron Leftwich .75 2.00
C4 Carson Palmer 1.00 2.50
C5 Chad Pennington .75 2.00
C6 Clinton Portis .75 2.00
C7 Daunte Culpepper 1.00 2.50
C8 David Carr .75 2.00
C9 Deuce McAllister 1.00 2.50
C10 Donovan McNabb 1.00 2.50
C11 Emmitt Smith 2.00 5.00
C12 Jamal Lewis 1.00 2.50
C13 Jeremy Shockey .75 2.00
C14 Jerry Rice 2.50 6.00
C15 Joe Namath 2.00 5.00
C16 Joey Harrington .75 2.00
C17 LaDainian Tomlinson 1.25 3.00
C18 LaVar Arrington .75 2.00
C19 Michael Vick 1.00 2.50
C20 Peyton Manning 3.00 8.00
C21 Priest Holmes .75 2.00
C22 Randy Moss 1.00 2.50
C23 Ricky Williams 1.00 2.50
C24 Steve McNair 1.00 2.50
C25 Tom Brady 5.00 12.00

2004 Leaf Rookies and Stars Fans of the Game

MPLETE SET (6) 12.00 30.00
STATED ODDS 1:24 HOBBY
FG1 Tony Hawk 1.00 2.50
FG2 Michael Phelps 10.00 25.00
FG3 Damien Fahey .75 2.00
FG4 Jackie Mason .75 2.00
FG5 Bob Saget .75 2.00
FG6 Linda Cohn 1.00 2.50

2004 Leaf Rookies and Stars Fans of the Game Autographs

1 Tony Hawk SP 40.00 80.00
FG2 Michael Phelps SP 300.00 500.00
FG3 Damien Fahey 8.00 20.00
FG4 Jackie Mason 12.00 30.00
FG5 Bob Saget 12.00 30.00
FG6 Linda Cohn 12.00 30.00

2004 Leaf Rookies and Stars Freshman Orientation Jersey

ATED PRINT RUN 500 SER.#'d SETS
*CLASS OFFICERS/100: .6X TO 1.5X
CLASS OFFICERS PRINT RUN 100 SETS
FO1 Eli Manning 12.00 30.00
FO2 Robert Gallery 2.00 5.00
FO3 Larry Fitzgerald 6.00 15.00
FO4 Philip Rivers 5.00 12.00
FO5 Kellen Winslow Jr. 1.50 4.00
FO6 Roy Williams WR 1.50 4.00
FO7 DeAngelo Hall 2.50 6.00
FO8 Reggie Williams 1.50 4.00
FO9 Dunta Robinson 1.50 4.00
FO10 Ben Roethlisberger 12.00 30.00
FO11 Lee Evans 2.50 6.00
FO12 Michael Clayton 2.00 5.00
FO13 J.P. Losman 1.50 4.00
FO14 Steven Jackson 2.50 6.00
FO15 Chris Perry 1.50 4.00
FO16 Michael Jenkins 1.50 4.00
FO17 Kevin Jones 2.00 5.00
FO18 Rashaun Woods 1.50 4.00
FO19 Ben Watson 2.00 5.00
FO20 Ben Troupe 1.50 4.00
FO21 Tatum Bell 1.50 4.00
FO22 Julius Jones 1.50 4.00
FO23 Devery Henderson 1.50 4.00
FO24 Darius Watts 1.50 4.00
FO25 Greg Jones 1.50 4.00
FO26 Keary Colbert 1.50 4.00
FO27 Derrick Hamilton 1.50 4.00
FO28 Bernard Berrian 1.50 4.00
FO29 Devard Darling 1.50 4.00
FO30 Matt Schaub 1.50 4.00
FO31 Luke McCown 1.50 4.00
FO32 Mewelde Moore 2.00 5.00
FO33 Cedric Cobbs 1.50 4.00

2004 Leaf Rookies and Stars Great American Heroes Red

D PRINT RUN 1250 SER.#'d SETS
*BLUE/250: .6X TO 1.5X RED/1250
BLUE PRINT RUN 250 SER.#'d SETS
*WHITE/750: .5X TO 1.2X RED/1250
WHITE PRINT RUN 750 SER.#'d SETS
GAH1 Anquan Boldin .75 2.00
GAH2 Chad Pennington .75 2.00
GAH3 Christian Okoye .75 2.00
GAH4 Dante Hall .75 2.00
GAH5 Derrick Mason .75 2.00
GAH6 Domanick Davis .75 2.00
GAH7 Hines Ward 1.00 2.50
GAH8 Joe Horn .75 2.00
GAH9 Joe Namath 2.00 5.00
GAH10 Laveranues Coles .75 2.00
GAH11 Matt Hasselbeck .75 2.00
GAH12 Patrick Ramsey 1.00 2.50
GAH13 Rex Grossman .75 2.00
GAH14 Rudi Johnson .75 2.00
GAH15 Sammy Baugh 1.25 3.00
GAH16 Steve Smith 1.25 3.00
GAH17 Terrell Suggs .75 2.00
GAH18 Todd Heap .75 2.00
GAH19 Tom Brady 5.00 12.00
GAH20 Adam Vinatieri .75 2.00
GAH21 Craig Krenzel .60 1.50
GAH22 DeAngelo Hall 1.00 2.50
GAH23 Matt Mauck .60 1.50
GAH24 Philip Rivers 2.00 5.00
GAH25 Tatum Bell .60 1.50

2004 Leaf Rookies and Stars Great American Heroes Autographs

STATED PRINT RUN 25-100
GAH1 Anquan Boldin/50 6.00 15.00
GAH2 Chad Pennington/25 10.00 25.00
GAH3 Christian Okoye/100 6.00 15.00
GAH4 Dante Hall/50 6.00 15.00
GAH5 Derrick Mason/50 6.00 15.00
GAH6 Domanick Davis/75 6.00 15.00
GAH7 Hines Ward/50 25.00 60.00
GAH8 Joe Horn/100 6.00 15.00
GAH9 Joe Namath/100 50.00 100.00
GAH10 Laveranues Coles/25 10.00 25.00
GAH11 Matt Hasselbeck/25 10.00 25.00
GAH12 Patrick Ramsey/25 12.00 30.00
GAH13 Rex Grossman/25 10.00 25.00
GAH14 Rudi Johnson/50 6.00 15.00
GAH16 Steve Smith/75 10.00 25.00
GAH18 Todd Heap -
GAH19 Tom Brady/25 175.00 300.00
GAH20 Adam Vinatieri/75 30.00 60.00
GAH21 Craig Krenzel/25 10.00 25.00
GAH22 DeAngelo Hall/25 15.00 40.00
GAH23 Matt Mauck/25 10.00 25.00
GAH24 Philip Rivers/25 50.00 80.00

2004 Leaf Rookies and Stars Initial Steps Shoe

ATED PRINT RUN 100 SER.#'d SETS
IS1 Eli Manning 12.00 30.00
IS2 Robert Gallery 2.00 5.00
IS3 Larry Fitzgerald 6.00 15.00
IS4 Philip Rivers 5.00 12.00
IS5 Kellen Winslow Jr. 1.50 4.00
IS6 Roy Williams WR 1.50 4.00
IS7 DeAngelo Hall 2.50 6.00
IS8 Reggie Williams 1.50 4.00
IS9 Dunta Robinson 1.50 4.00
IS10 Ben Roethlisberger 12.00 30.00
IS11 Lee Evans 2.50 6.00
IS12 Michael Clayton 2.00 5.00
IS13 J.P. Losman 1.50 4.00
IS14 Steven Jackson 2.50 6.00
IS15 Chris Perry 1.50 4.00
IS16 Michael Jenkins 1.50 4.00
IS17 Kevin Jones 2.00 5.00
IS18 Rashaun Woods 1.50 4.00
IS19 Ben Watson 2.00 5.00
IS20 Ben Troupe 1.50 4.00
IS21 Tatum Bell 1.50 4.00
IS22 Julius Jones 1.50 4.00
IS23 Devery Henderson 1.50 4.00
IS24 Darius Watts 1.50 4.00
IS25 Greg Jones 1.50 4.00
IS26 Keary Colbert 1.50 4.00
IS27 Derrick Hamilton 1.50 4.00
IS28 Bernard Berrian 1.50 4.00
IS29 Devard Darling 1.50 4.00
IS30 Matt Schaub 1.50 4.00
IS31 Luke McCown 1.50 4.00
IS32 Mewelde Moore 2.00 5.00
IS33 Cedric Cobbs 1.50 4.00

2004 Leaf Rookies and Stars Masks

ATED PRINT RUN 325 SER.#'d SETS
M1 Eli Manning 12.00 30.00
M2 Robert Gallery 2.00 5.00
M3 Larry Fitzgerald 6.00 15.00
M4 Philip Rivers 5.00 12.00
M5 Kellen Winslow Jr. 1.50 4.00
M6 Roy Williams WR 1.50 4.00
M7 DeAngelo Hall 2.50 6.00
M8 Reggie Williams 1.50 4.00

M9 Dunta Robinson 1.50 4.00
M10 Ben Roethlisberger 12.00 30.00
M11 Lee Evans 2.50 6.00
M12 Michael Clayton 2.00 5.00
M13 J.P. Losman 1.50 4.00
M14 Steven Jackson 2.50 6.00
M15 Chris Perry 1.50 4.00
M16 Michael Jenkins 1.50 4.00
M17 Kevin Jones 2.00 5.00
M18 Rashaun Woods 1.50 4.00
M19 Ben Watson 2.00 5.00
M20 Ben Troupe 1.50 4.00
M21 Tatum Bell 1.50 4.00
M22 Julius Jones 1.50 4.00
M23 Devery Henderson 1.50 4.00
M24 Darius Watts 1.50 4.00
M25 Greg Jones 1.50 4.00
M26 Keary Colbert 1.50 4.00
M27 Derrick Hamilton 1.50 4.00
M28 Bernard Berrian 1.50 4.00
M29 Devard Darling 1.50 4.00
M30 Matt Schaub 1.50 4.00
M31 Luke McCown 1.50 4.00
M32 Mewelde Moore 2.00 5.00
M33 Cedric Cobbs 1.50 4.00

2004 Leaf Rookies and Stars Prime Cuts

STATED PRINT RUN 25 SER.#'d SETS
PC1 Brett Favre 30.00 80.00
PC2 Brian Urlacher 15.00 40.00
PC3 Byron Leftwich 10.00 25.00
PC4 Chad Pennington 10.00 25.00
PC5 Daunte Culpepper 12.00 30.00
PC6 David Carr 10.00 25.00
PC7 Deuce McAllister 12.00 30.00
PC8 Donovan McNabb 12.00 30.00
PC9 Emmitt Smith 25.00 60.00
PC10 Jamal Lewis 12.00 30.00
PC11 Jeremy Shockey 10.00 25.00
PC12 Jerry Rice 30.00 80.00
PC13 Joe Namath 30.00 80.00
PC14 Joey Harrington 10.00 25.00
PC15 LaDainian Tomlinson 15.00 40.00
PC16 LaVar Arrington 15.00 40.00
PC17 Marc Bulger 10.00 25.00
PC18 Matt Hasselbeck 10.00 25.00
PC19 Michael Vick 12.00 30.00
PC20 Peyton Manning 40.00 100.00
PC21 Priest Holmes 10.00 25.00
PC22 Randy Moss 12.00 30.00
PC23 Ricky Williams 12.00 30.00
PC24 Steve McNair 12.00 30.00
PC25 Tom Brady 60.00 150.00

2004 Leaf Rookies and Stars Rookie Autographs

201-250 PRINT RUN 150 SER.#'d SETS
251-283 PRINT RUN 50 SER.#'d SETS
CARDS SER.#'d UNDER 20 NOT PRICED
201 Adimchinobe Echemandu 6.00 15.00
202 Ahmad Carroll 5.00 12.00
203 Andy Hall 5.00 12.00
204 B.J. Johnson 5.00 12.00
205 B.J. Symons 5.00 12.00
206 Brandon Miree 5.00 12.00
207 Bruce Perry 5.00 12.00
208 Carlos Francis 5.00 12.00
209 Casey Bramlet 5.00 12.00
210 Chris Gamble 5.00 12.00
211 Clarence Moore 5.00 12.00
212 Cody Pickett 5.00 12.00
213 Craig Krenzel 5.00 12.00
214 D.J. Hackett 5.00 12.00
215 D.J. Williams 8.00 20.00
216 Derrick Ward 8.00 20.00
217 Drew Carter 6.00 15.00
218 Drew Henson 5.00 12.00
219 Ernest Wilford 6.00 15.00
220 Jamaar Taylor 5.00 12.00
221 Jared Lorenzen 6.00 15.00
222 Jarrett Payton 6.00 15.00
223 Jason Babin 8.00 20.00
224 Jeff Smoker 6.00 15.00
225 Jerricho Cotchery 6.00 15.00
226 Jim Sorgi 6.00 15.00
227 John Navarre 5.00 12.00
228 Johnnie Morant 5.00 12.00
229 Jonathan Vilma 6.00 15.00
230 Josh Harris 5.00 12.00
231 Kenechi Udeze 6.00 15.00
232 Matt Mauck 5.00 12.00
233 Maurice Mann 5.00 12.00
234 Michael Turner 10.00 25.00
235 P.K. Sam 5.00 12.00
236 Quincy Wilson 5.00 12.00
237 Ran Carthon 5.00 12.00
238 Ricardo Colclough 5.00 12.00
239 Samie Parker 5.00 12.00
240 Sean Jones 5.00 12.00
241 Sean Taylor No Auto 6.00 15.00
242 Sloan Thomas 6.00 15.00
243 Tommie Harris 6.00 15.00
244 Triandos Luke 5.00 12.00
245 Troy Fleming 5.00 12.00
246 Vince Wilfork 8.00 20.00
247 Will Smith 6.00 15.00
248 Michael Boulware 8.00 20.00
249 Richard Smith 5.00 12.00
250 Teddy Lehman 5.00 12.00
252 DeAngelo Hall JSY 12.00 30.00
253 Matt Schaub JSY 8.00 20.00
254 Michael Jenkins JSY 8.00 20.00
255 Devard Darling JSY 8.00 20.00
256 J.P. Losman JSY 8.00 20.00
257 Lee Evans JSY 12.00 30.00
258 Keary Colbert JSY 8.00 20.00
259 Bernard Berrian JSY 8.00 20.00
260 Chris Perry JSY 8.00 20.00
261 Kellen Winslow JSY 8.00 20.00
262 Luke McCown JSY 8.00 20.00
263 Julius Jones JSY 8.00 20.00
264 Darius Watts JSY 8.00 20.00
265 Tatum Bell JSY 8.00 20.00
266 Kevin Jones JSY 10.00 25.00
267 Roy Williams WR JSY 8.00 20.00
268 Dunta Robinson JSY 8.00 20.00
269 Greg Jones JSY 8.00 20.00
270 Reggie Williams JSY 8.00 20.00
271 Mewelde Moore JSY 10.00 25.00
272 Ben Watson JSY 10.00 25.00
273 Cedric Cobbs JSY 8.00 20.00
274 Devery Henderson JSY 8.00 20.00
275 Eli Manning JSY 175.00 300.00
276 Robert Gallery JSY 10.00 25.00
277 Ben Roethlisberger JSY 125.00 250.00
278 Philip Rivers JSY 75.00 150.00
279 Derrick Hamilton JSY 8.00 20.00
280 Rashaun Woods JSY 8.00 20.00
281 Steven Jackson JSY 12.00 30.00
282 Michael Clayton JSY 10.00 25.00
283 Ben Troupe JSY 8.00 20.00

2004 Leaf Rookies and Stars Slideshow Bronze

ONZE PRINT RUN 1250 SER.#'d SETS
*VIEW MASTER/250: .6X TO 1.5X BRNZ
VIEW MASTER PRINT RUN 250
*SILVER STUDIO/750: .5X TO 1.2X BRNZ
SILVER STUDIO PRINT RUN 750
SS1 Aaron Brooks .75 2.00
SS2 Ahman Green 1.00 2.50
SS3 Anquan Boldin .75 2.00
SS4 Chad Johnson .75 2.00
SS5 Chris Chambers .75 2.00
SS6 Drew Bledsoe 1.00 2.50
SS7 Edgerrin James 1.00 2.50
SS8 Jake Delhomme .75 2.00
SS9 Jake Plummer .75 2.00
SS10 Joe Namath 2.00 5.00
SS11 Kevan Barlow .75 2.00
SS12 Kyle Boller .75 2.00
SS13 LaVar Arrington .75 2.00
SS14 Marc Bulger .75 2.00
SS15 Marshall Faulk 1.00 2.50
SS16 Marvin Harrison 1.00 2.50
SS17 Matt Hasselbeck .75 2.00
SS18 Roy Williams S .75 2.00
SS19 Rudi Johnson .75 2.00
SS20 Shaun Alexander .75 2.00
SS21 Stephen Davis .75 2.00
SS22 Tom Brady 5.00 12.00
SS23 Travis Henry .75 2.00
SS24 Trent Green .75 2.00
SS25 Donovan McNabb 1.00 2.50

2004 Leaf Rookies and Stars Ticket Masters Bronze

ONZE PRINT RUN 1250 SER.#'d SETS
*GOLD/250: .6X TO 1.5X BRONZE/1250
GOLD CHAMPIONSHIP PRINT RUN 250
*SILVER/750: .5X TO 1.2X BRONZE/1250
SILVER STATED PRINT RUN 750
TM1 Em.Smith/A.Boldin 2.00 5.00
TM2 M.Vick/M.Jenkins 1.00 2.50
TM3 J.Lewis/R.Lewis 1.25 3.00
TM4 D.Bledsoe/T.Henry 1.00 2.50
TM5 J.Delhomme/J.Peppers 1.00 2.50
TM6 B.Urlacher/R.Grossman 1.25 3.00
TM7 C.Palmer/C.Johnson 1.00 2.50
TM8 K.Winslow Jr./J.Garcia .75 2.00
TM9 Harrington/Ro.Will.WR .50 1.25
TM10 B.Favre/A.Green 2.50 6.00
TM11 D.Carr/A.Johnson 1.00 2.50
TM12 P.Manning/E.James 3.00 8.00
TM13 B.Leftwich/F.Taylor .75 2.00
TM14 P.Holmes/T.Green .75 2.00
TM15 Ri.Williams/Chambers 1.00 2.50
TM16 D.Culpepper/R.Moss 1.00 2.50
TM17 T.Brady/C.Dillon 5.00 12.00
TM18 E.Manning/J.Shockey 4.00 10.00
TM19 C.Pennington/C.Martin 1.00 2.50
TM20 J.Rice/T.Brown 2.50 6.00
TM21 D.McNabb/T.Owens 1.00 2.50
TM22 Roethlisberger/Ward 4.00 10.00
TM23 P.Rivers/L.Tomlinson 1.50 4.00
TM24 M.Bulger/M.Faulk 1.00 2.50
TM25 C.Portis/L.Arrington .75 2.00

2004 Leaf Rookies and Stars Triple Threads

STATED PRINT RUN 100 SER.#'d SETS
1 Boldin/J.McCown/Fitzgerald 10.00 25.00
2 Vick/Dunn/Price 6.00 15.00
3 J.Lewis/Boller/R.Lewis 8.00 20.00
4 Bledsoe/Moulds/Henry 6.00 15.00
5 Delh/S.Davis/S.Smith 8.00 20.00
6 Urlacher/Gross/A.Thomas 8.00 20.00
7 C.John/R.John/Warrick 5.00 12.00
8 Woodson/Ro.Will/Newman 10.00 25.00
9 Plummer/R.Smith/Sharpe 6.00 15.00
10 Favre/A.Green/Walker 25.00 50.00
11 Ramsey/Coles/Arrington 10.00 25.00
12 P.Manning/James/Harris. 20.00 50.00
13 Leftwich/Taylor/J.Smith 6.00 15.00
14 T.Green/Holmes/Hall 5.00 12.00
15 Ri.Will/Chamb/Z.Thomas 6.00 15.00
16 Culpepper/Bennett/R.Moss 6.00 15.00
17 Brady/B.Johnson/Law 30.00 80.00
18 Brooks/McAllis/Stallworth 5.00 12.00
19 Barber/Shockey/Toomer 6.00 15.00
20 Penning/Martin/S.Moss 6.00 15.00
21 J.Rice/Gannon/T.Brown 15.00 40.00
22 Bettis/Ward/Burress 8.00 20.00
23 Hassel/Alex/Robinson 5.00 12.00
24 Bulger/M.Faulk/Bruce 8.00 20.00
25 McNair/C.Brown/Mason 6.00 15.00
26 Carr/D.Davis/A.Johnson 6.00 15.00

2004 Leaf Rookies and Stars Longevity

af Rookies and Stars Longevity initially released in late-February 2005. The base set closely resembles the Leaf Rookies and Stars product and consists of 283-cards including 100-rookies serial numbered to 999, 50-rookies numbered to 499 and 33-rookie jersey cards numbered of 299. Boxes contained 24-packs of 5-cards each. Five parallel sets and a variety of inserts can be found seeded in hobby packs highlighted by the multi-tiered Material game used jersey inserts.

COMP.SET w/o RCs (100) 10.00 25.00
*VETS 1-100: .6X TO 1.5X BASIC CARDS
*ROOKIES 101-200: .5X TO 1.2X
101-200 RC PRINT RUN 999
*ROOKIES 201-250: .5X TO 1.2X
201-250 RC STATED PRINT RUN 499
*ROOKIES 251-283: .5X TO 1.2X
251-283 JSY RC PRINT RUN 299

2004 Leaf Rookies and Stars Longevity Black

*VETS 1-100: 3X TO 8X BASIC CARDS
1-100 PRINT RUN 75 SER.#'d SETS
*ROOKIES 101-200: 1.5X TO 4X BASIC CARDS
101-200 PRINT RUN 50 SER.#'d SETS
*ROOKIES 201-250: 1.5X TO 4X BASIC CARDS
201-250 PRINT RUN 25 SER.#'d SETS
251-283 UNPRICED JSY PRINT RUN 10 SETS

2004 Leaf Rookies and Stars Longevity Emerald

*VETS 1-100: 2.5X TO 6X BASIC CARDS
1-100 PRINT RUN 99 SER.#'d SETS
*ROOKIES 101-200: 1.2X TO 3X BASIC CARDS
101-200 PRINT RUN 75 SER.#'d SETS
*ROOKIES 201-250: 1X TO 2.5X BASIC CARDS
201-250 PRINT RUN 50 SER.#'d SETS
*ROOKIES 251-283: 1.2X TO 3X BASIC CARDS
251-283 JSY PRINT RUN 25 SER.#'d SETS

2004 Leaf Rookies and Stars Longevity Gold

ETS 1-100: 1.5X TO 4X BASIC CARDS
1-100 STATED PRINT RUN 150
*ROOKIES 101-200: 1X TO 2.5X BASIC CARDS
101-200 STATED PRINT RUN 99
*ROOKIES 201-250: .8X TO 2X BASIC CARDS
201-250 STATED PRINT RUN 75
*ROOKIES 251-283: .6X TO 1.5X BASIC JSY
251-283 JSY PRINT RUN 50

2004 Leaf Rookies and Stars Longevity Ruby

*VETS 1-100: 1X TO 2.5X BASIC CARDS
1-100 STATED PRINT RUN 250
*ROOKIES 101-200: .6X TO 1.5X BASIC CARDS
101-200 STATED PRINT RUN 199
*ROOKIES 201-250: .5X TO 1.2X BASIC CARDS
201-250 STATED PRINT RUN 150
*ROOKIES 251-283: .5X TO 1.2X BASIC JSY
251-283 JSY PRINT RUN 99

2004 Leaf Rookies and Stars Longevity Sapphire

*VETS 1-100: 1.2X TO 3X BASIC CARDS
1-100 STATED PRINT RUN 199
*ROOKIES 101-200: .8X TO 2X BASIC CARDS
101-200 STATED PRINT RUN 150
*ROOKIES 201-250: .6X TO 1.5X BASIC CARDS
201-250 STATED PRINT RUN 99
*ROOKIES 251-283: .5X TO 1.2X BASIC JSY
251-283 JSY PRINT RUN 75

2004 Leaf Rookies and Stars Longevity Draft Class of 2001 Autographs

STATED ODDS 1:233
301 Michael Vick 35.00 60.00
302 Drew Brees 50.00 100.00
304 Marques Tuiasosopo 7.50 20.00
305 Chris Weinke 7.50 20.00
307 Deuce McAllister 50.00 100.00
309 Anthony Thomas 6.00 15.00
311 David Terrell 7.50 20.00
312 Koren Robinson 7.50 20.00
314 Santana Moss 7.50 20.00
315 Freddie Mitchell 7.50 20.00
316 Gerard Warren 7.50 20.00
317 Justin Smith 7.50 20.00
320 Jamal Reynolds 6.00 15.00

2004 Leaf Rookies and Stars Longevity Materials Black

COMMON CARD/20-25 8.00 20.00
SEMISTARS/20-25 10.00 25.00
UNL.STARS/20-25 12.00 30.00
BLACK SER.#'d TO 5 OR 10 NOT PRICED

2004 Leaf Rookies and Stars Longevity Materials Emerald

1 Anquan Boldin/35 6.00 15.00
2 Emmitt Smith/50 12.00 30.00
3 Josh McCown/35 8.00 20.00
4 Michael Vick/50 6.00 15.00
5 Peerless Price/25 8.00 20.00
6 T.J. Duckett/35 6.00 15.00
7 Warrick Dunn/35 6.00 15.00
8 Jamal Lewis/25 10.00 25.00
9 Kyle Boller/25 8.00 20.00
10 Ray Lewis/25 12.00 30.00
11 Drew Bledsoe/25 10.00 25.00
12 Eric Moulds/35 6.00 15.00
13 Travis Henry/35 6.00 15.00
14 Jake Delhomme/35 6.00 15.00
15 Stephen Davis/35 6.00 15.00
16 Steve Smith/35 10.00 25.00
17 Brian Urlacher/35 10.00 25.00
18 Rex Grossman/35 6.00 15.00
19 Thomas Jones/35 6.00 15.00
20 Carson Palmer/25 10.00 25.00
21 Chad Johnson/35 6.00 15.00
22 Rudi Johnson/35 6.00 15.00
23 Jeff Garcia/35 6.00 15.00
24 William Green/25 8.00 20.00
25 Keyshawn Johnson/35 8.00 20.00
26 Terence Newman/25 10.00 25.00
27 Roy Williams S/35 6.00 15.00
28 Jake Plummer/35 6.00 15.00
29 Quentin Griffin/25 8.00 20.00
30 Rod Smith/25 10.00 25.00
31 Charles Rogers/35 6.00 15.00
32 Joey Harrington/35 6.00 15.00
33 Ahman Green/35 8.00 20.00
34 Brett Favre/50 15.00 40.00
35 Javon Walker/35 6.00 15.00
36 Andre Johnson/35 8.00 20.00
37 David Carr/25 8.00 20.00
38 Domanick Davis/35 6.00 15.00
39 Edgerrin James/35 8.00 20.00
40 Marvin Harrison/35 8.00 20.00
41 Peyton Manning/50 20.00 50.00
43 Fred Taylor/35 6.00 15.00
44 Jimmy Smith/25 10.00 25.00
45 Priest Holmes/40 6.00 15.00
46 Tony Gonzalez/35 8.00 20.00
47 Trent Green/35 6.00 15.00
49 Chris Chambers/35 6.00 15.00
51 Daunte Culpepper/40 8.00 20.00
52 Michael Bennett/35 6.00 15.00
53 Randy Moss/40 8.00 20.00
54 Corey Dillon/40 6.00 15.00
56 Tom Brady/50 30.00 80.00
57 Aaron Brooks/35 6.00 15.00
58 Deuce McAllister/35 8.00 20.00
60 Jeremy Shockey/35 6.00 15.00
61 Michael Strahan/35 8.00 20.00
62 Tiki Barber/35 8.00 20.00
63 Chad Pennington/35 6.00 15.00
64 Curtis Martin/35 8.00 20.00
65 Santana Moss/35 8.00 20.00
66 Jerry Porter/35 6.00 15.00
67 Jerry Rice/50 15.00 40.00
69 Donovan McNabb/50 6.00 15.00
70 Jevon Kearse/25 8.00 20.00
71 Terrell Owens/35 8.00 20.00
72 Duce Staley/25 8.00 20.00
73 Hines Ward/35 8.00 20.00
74 Jerome Bettis/35 10.00 25.00
75 LaDainian Tomlinson/40 10.00 25.00
78 Koren Robinson/35 6.00 15.00
79 Matt Hasselbeck/35 6.00 15.00
80 Shaun Alexander/35 6.00 15.00
81 Isaac Bruce/25 12.00 30.00
82 Marc Bulger/35 6.00 15.00
83 Marshall Faulk/35 8.00 20.00
84 Torry Holt/35 8.00 20.00
85 Brad Johnson/25 10.00 25.00
87 Chris Brown/35 6.00 15.00
88 Derrick Mason/25 8.00 20.00
89 Eddie George/35 8.00 20.00
90 Steve McNair/35 8.00 20.00
91 Clinton Portis/35 6.00 15.00
92 LaVar Arrington/35 6.00 15.00
93 Laveranues Coles/25 8.00 20.00

2004 Leaf Rookies and Stars Longevity Materials Gold

1 Anquan Boldin/75 5.00 12.00
4 Michael Vick/75 6.00 15.00
6 T.J. Duckett/75 5.00 12.00
8 Jamal Lewis/50 6.00 15.00
9 Kyle Boller/65 5.00 12.00
10 Ray Lewis/50 8.00 20.00
11 Drew Bledsoe/75 6.00 15.00
13 Travis Henry/75 5.00 12.00
14 Jake Delhomme/50 5.00 12.00
16 Steve Smith/75 8.00 20.00
17 Brian Urlacher/75 8.00 20.00
18 Rex Grossman/75 5.00 12.00
19 Thomas Jones/75 5.00 12.00
21 Chad Johnson/50 5.00 12.00
23 Jeff Garcia/50 5.00 12.00
24 William Green/75 5.00 12.00
25 Keyshawn Johnson/50 6.00 15.00
26 Terence Newman/75 6.00 15.00
28 Jake Plummer/50 5.00 12.00
29 Quentin Griffin/50 5.00 12.00
32 Joey Harrington/50 5.00 12.00
36 Andre Johnson/50 6.00 15.00
37 David Carr/75 5.00 12.00
38 Domanick Davis/75 5.00 12.00
40 Marvin Harrison/75 6.00 15.00
42 Byron Leftwich/75 5.00 12.00
43 Fred Taylor/25 6.00 15.00
46 Tony Gonzalez/75 6.00 15.00
48 A.J. Feeley/50 5.00 12.00
50 Deion Sanders/75 6.00 15.00
53 Randy Moss/50 6.00 15.00
54 Corey Dillon/75 5.00 12.00
57 Aaron Brooks/75 5.00 12.00
58 Deuce McAllister/50 6.00 15.00
59 Joe Horn/25 6.00 15.00
60 Jeremy Shockey/75 5.00 12.00
61 Michael Strahan/75 6.00 15.00
62 Tiki Barber/75 6.00 15.00
63 Chad Pennington/75 5.00 12.00
64 Curtis Martin/75 6.00 15.00
65 Santana Moss/50 6.00 15.00
66 Jerry Porter/75 5.00 12.00
67 Jerry Rice/75 15.00 40.00
68 Warren Sapp/75 6.00 15.00
69 Donovan McNabb/75 6.00 15.00
70 Jevon Kearse/75 5.00 12.00
72 Duce Staley/60 5.00 12.00
73 Hines Ward/75 6.00 15.00
78 Koren Robinson/75 5.00 12.00
79 Matt Hasselbeck/75 5.00 12.00
81 Isaac Bruce/50 8.00 20.00
82 Marc Bulger/75 5.00 12.00
83 Marshall Faulk/75 6.00 15.00
84 Torry Holt/50 6.00 15.00
85 Brad Johnson/50 6.00 15.00
88 Derrick Mason/50 5.00 12.00
89 Eddie George/50 6.00 15.00
93 Laveranues Coles/50 5.00 12.00
94 Mark Brunell/50 6.00 15.00

2004 Leaf Rookies and Stars Longevity Materials Ruby

4 Michael Vick/150 4.00 10.00
6 T.J. Duckett/125 3.00 8.00
11 Drew Bledsoe/150 4.00 10.00
14 Jake Delhomme/150 3.00 8.00
15 Stephen Davis/99 3.00 8.00
16 Steve Smith/150 5.00 12.00
18 Rex Grossman/150 3.00 8.00
19 Thomas Jones/150 3.00 8.00
20 Carson Palmer/99 4.00 10.00
23 Jeff Garcia/99 3.00 8.00
24 William Green/125 3.00 8.00
26 Terence Newman/125 4.00 10.00
29 Quentin Griffin/99 3.00 8.00
32 Joey Harrington/99 3.00 8.00
36 Andre Johnson/99 4.00 10.00
37 David Carr/150 3.00 8.00
38 Domanick Davis/150 3.00 8.00
40 Marvin Harrison/150 4.00 10.00
42 Byron Leftwich/150 3.00 8.00
43 Fred Taylor/135 3.00 8.00
44 Jimmy Smith/99 4.00 10.00
46 Tony Gonzalez/150 4.00 10.00
48 A.J. Feeley/99 3.00 8.00
50 Deion Sanders/150 4.00 10.00
52 Michael Bennett/99 3.00 8.00
53 Randy Moss/125 4.00 10.00
54 Corey Dillon/99 3.00 8.00
57 Aaron Brooks/150 3.00 8.00
58 Deuce McAllister/99 4.00 10.00
60 Jeremy Shockey/125 3.00 8.00
61 Michael Strahan/125 4.00 10.00
62 Tiki Barber/125 4.00 10.00
63 Chad Pennington/150 3.00 8.00
64 Curtis Martin/125 4.00 10.00
66 Jerry Porter/150 3.00 8.00
67 Jerry Rice/150 10.00 25.00
68 Warren Sapp/125 4.00 10.00
69 Donovan McNabb/150 4.00 10.00
70 Jevon Kearse/150 3.00 8.00
72 Duce Staley/99 3.00 8.00
73 Hines Ward/150 4.00 10.00
74 Jerome Bettis/50 6.00 15.00
75 LaDainian Tomlinson/50 6.00 15.00
78 Koren Robinson/150 3.00 8.00
79 Matt Hasselbeck/150 3.00 8.00
80 Shaun Alexander/50 4.00 10.00
81 Isaac Bruce/75 6.00 15.00
82 Marc Bulger/150 3.00 8.00
85 Brad Johnson/99 4.00 10.00
87 Chris Brown/80 4.00 10.00
88 Derrick Mason/99 3.00 8.00
90 Steve McNair/150 4.00 10.00
92 LaVar Arrington/99 3.00 8.00
93 Laveranues Coles/125 3.00 8.00
94 Mark Brunell/125 4.00 10.00

2004 Leaf Rookies and Stars Longevity Materials Sapphire

Anquan Boldin/99 4.00 10.00
3 Josh McCown/84 5.00 12.00
4 Michael Vick/99 5.00 12.00
6 T.J. Duckett/99 4.00 10.00
8 Jamal Lewis/75 6.00 15.00
9 Kyle Boller/99 4.00 10.00
11 Drew Bledsoe/99 5.00 12.00
13 Travis Henry/99 4.00 10.00
14 Jake Delhomme/75 5.00 12.00
16 Steve Smith/99 6.00 15.00
17 Brian Urlacher/99 6.00 15.00
18 Rex Grossman/99 4.00 10.00
19 Thomas Jones/99 4.00 10.00
24 William Green/99 4.00 10.00
25 Keyshawn Johnson/50 6.00 15.00
26 Terence Newman/99 5.00 12.00
27 Roy Williams S/50 5.00 12.00
28 Jake Plummer/50 5.00 12.00
29 Quentin Griffin/75 5.00 12.00
36 Andre Johnson/75 6.00 15.00
37 David Carr/99 4.00 10.00
38 Domanick Davis/99 4.00 10.00
40 Marvin Harrison/99 5.00 12.00
41 Peyton Manning/50 20.00 50.00
42 Byron Leftwich/99 4.00 10.00
44 Jimmy Smith/50 6.00 15.00
46 Tony Gonzalez/99 5.00 12.00
48 A.J. Feeley/75 5.00 12.00
50 Deion Sanders/99 5.00 12.00
51 Daunte Culpepper/50 6.00 15.00
52 Michael Bennett/50 5.00 12.00
53 Randy Moss/75 6.00 15.00
54 Corey Dillon/99 4.00 10.00
56 Tom Brady/75 30.00 80.00
57 Aaron Brooks/99 4.00 10.00
58 Deuce McAllister/75 6.00 15.00
60 Jeremy Shockey/99 4.00 10.00
61 Michael Strahan/99 5.00 12.00
62 Tiki Barber/99 5.00 12.00
63 Chad Pennington/99 4.00 10.00
64 Curtis Martin/99 5.00 12.00
65 Santana Moss/25 10.00 25.00
66 Jerry Porter/99 4.00 10.00
67 Jerry Rice/99 12.00 30.00
68 Warren Sapp/99 5.00 12.00
69 Donovan McNabb/99 5.00 12.00
70 Jevon Kearse/99 4.00 10.00
72 Duce Staley/75 5.00 12.00
73 Hines Ward/99 5.00 12.00
78 Koren Robinson/99 4.00 10.00
79 Matt Hasselbeck/99 4.00 10.00
81 Isaac Bruce/50 8.00 20.00
82 Marc Bulger/99 4.00 10.00
85 Brad Johnson/75 6.00 15.00
89 Eddie George/75 6.00 15.00
91 Clinton Portis/50 5.00 12.00
92 LaVar Arrington/50 5.00 12.00
93 Laveranues Coles/75 5.00 12.00
94 Mark Brunell/75 6.00 15.00

2005 Leaf Rookies and Stars

is 293-card set was released in December, 2005. The set was issued in six-card packs with an $4 SRP which came 24 packs to a box. The set begins with veterans in alphabetical order by team (Cards 1-96); Checklists (97-100); Rookies (101-250); Rookies with a player-worn jersey piece (251-279) and concludes with multi-player rookie jersey cards (280-293). Cards numbered 201 through 250 were issued to a stated print run of 799 serial numbered sets, while cards numbered 251-279 were issued to a stated print run of 750 serial numbered seta and cards numbered 280-293 were issued to a stated print run of 500 serial numbered sets.

COMP.SET w/o RC's (100) 7.50 20.00
201-250 RC PRINT RUN 799 SER.#'d SETS
251-279 JSY PRINT RUN 750 SER.#'d SETS
280-293 JSY DUAL PRINT RUN 500 SER.#'d SETS
1 Anquan Boldin .20 .50
2 Kurt Warner .25 .60
3 Larry Fitzgerald .30 .75
4 Michael Vick .25 .60
5 T.J. Duckett .20 .50
6 Warrick Dunn .20 .50
7 Jamal Lewis .25 .60
8 Kyle Boller .20 .50
9 Ray Lewis .30 .75
10 Derrick Mason .20 .50
11 J.P. Losman .20 .50
12 Lee Evans .25 .60
13 Willis McGahee .20 .50
14 DeShaun Foster .25 .60
15 Jake Delhomme .20 .50
16 Steve Smith .30 .75
17 Brian Urlacher .30 .75
18 Rex Grossman .20 .50
19 Muhsin Muhammad .20 .50
20 Carson Palmer .25 .60
21 Chad Johnson .20 .50
22 Rudi Johnson .20 .50
23 Lee Suggs .20 .50
24 Drew Bledsoe .25 .60
25 Julius Jones .20 .50
26 Keyshawn Johnson .25 .60
27 Roy Williams S .20 .50
28 Ashley Lelie .20 .50
29 Jake Plummer .20 .50
30 Rod Smith .25 .60
31 Tatum Bell .25 .60
32 Joey Harrington .20 .50
33 Kevin Jones .20 .50
34 Roy Williams WR .20 .50
35 Ahman Green .25 .60
36 Brett Favre .60 1.50
37 Javon Walker .20 .50
38 Andre Johnson .25 .60
39 David Carr .20 .50
40 Domanick Davis .20 .50
41 Edgerrin James .25 .60
42 Marvin Harrison .25 .60
43 Peyton Manning .75 2.00
44 Reggie Wayne .25 .60
45 Byron Leftwich .20 .50
46 Fred Taylor .20 .50
47 Jimmy Smith .25 .60
48 Priest Holmes .20 .50
49 Tony Gonzalez .25 .60
50 Trent Green .20 .50
51 Chris Chambers .20 .50
52 Daunte Culpepper .25 .60
53 Michael Bennett .20 .50
54 Nate Burleson .20 .50
55 Corey Dillon .20 .50
56 Deion Branch .20 .50
57 Tom Brady 1.25 3.00
58 Aaron Brooks .20 .50
59 Deuce McAllister .25 .60
60 Joe Horn .20 .50
61 Eli Manning .50 1.25
62 Jeremy Shockey .20 .50
63 Tiki Barber .25 .60
64 Plaxico Burress .20 .50
65 Chad Pennington .20 .50
66 Curtis Martin .25 .60
67 Laveranues Coles .20 .50
68 Jerry Porter .20 .50
69 Kerry Collins .20 .50
70 LaMont Jordan .25 .60
71 Randy Moss .25 .60
72 Brian Westbrook .20 .50
73 Donovan McNabb .25 .60
74 Terrell Owens .25 .60
75 Ben Roethlisberger .50 1.25
76 Duce Staley .20 .50
77 Hines Ward .25 .60
78 Jerome Bettis .30 .75
79 Antonio Gates .30 .75
80 Drew Brees .30 .75
81 LaDainian Tomlinson .30 .75
82 Kevan Barlow .20 .50
83 Darrell Jackson .20 .50
84 Matt Hasselbeck .20 .50
85 Shaun Alexander .20 .50
86 Marc Bulger .20 .50
87 Steven Jackson .20 .50
88 Torry Holt .25 .60
89 Brian Griese .20 .50
90 Michael Clayton .20 .50
91 Chris Brown .20 .50
92 Drew Bennett .25 .60
93 Steve McNair .25 .60
94 Clinton Portis .20 .50
95 LaVar Arrington .20 .50
96 Santana Moss .25 .60
97 A.Smith QB CL/F.Gore .75 2.00
98 B.Edwards CL/C.Frye .20 .50
99 C.Fason CL/T.Williamson .20 .50
100 C.Rogers CL/J.Campbell .30 .75
101 Travis Johnson RC 1.00 2.50
102 Alex Smith TE RC 1.00 2.50
103 Channing Crowder RC 1.25 3.00
104 Craig Bragg RC 1.00 2.50
105 Darrent Williams RC 1.50 4.00
106 Derrick Wimbush RC 1.25 3.00
107 Josh Cribbs RC 5.00 12.00
108 Luis Castillo RC 1.25 3.00
109 Matt Roth RC 1.00 2.50
110 Mike Patterson RC 1.00 2.50
111 Fred Gibson RC 1.00 2.50
112 Marcus Spears RC 1.00 2.50
113 Brodney Pool RC 1.25 3.00
114 Barrett Ruud RC 1.25 3.00
115 Stanford Routt RC 1.25 3.00
116 Josh Bullocks RC 1.25 3.00
117 Kevin Burnett RC 1.25 3.00
118 Corey Webster RC 1.25 3.00
119 Lofa Tatupu RC 1.25 3.00
120 Mike Nugent RC 1.25 3.00
121 Jim Leonhard RC 1.25 3.00
122 Ronald Bartell RC 1.25 3.00
123 Nick Collins RC 1.50 4.00
124 Justin Miller RC 1.00 2.50
125 Jonathan Babineaux RC 1.00 2.50
126 Kelvin Hayden RC 1.25 3.00
127 Matt McCoy RC 1.25 3.00
128 Oshiomogho Atogwe RC 1.25 3.00
129 Stanley Wilson RC 1.25 3.00
130 Justin Tuck RC 1.25 3.00
131 Eric Green RC 1.00 2.50
132 Karl Paymah RC 1.25 3.00
133 Kirk Morrison RC 1.50 4.00
134 Dustin Fox RC 1.25 3.00
135 Alfred Fincher RC 1.25 3.00
136 Chris Henry RC 1.25 3.00
137 Ellis Hobbs RC 1.50 4.00
138 Scott Starks RC 1.25 3.00
139 Jordan Beck RC 1.25 3.00
140 Vincent Burns RC 1.00 2.50
141 Darryl Blackstock RC 1.00 2.50
142 Domonique Foxworth RC 1.25 3.00
143 Leroy Hill RC 1.50 4.00
144 Cedric Killings RC 1.00 2.50
145 Leonard Weaver RC 1.00 2.50
146 Sean Considine RC 1.00 2.50
147 Antonio Perkins RC 1.25 3.00
148 Travis Daniels RC 1.25 3.00
149 Vincent Fuller RC 1.25 3.00
150 Manuel White RC 1.25 3.00
151 Kerry Rhodes RC 1.25 3.00
152 Brady Poppinga RC 1.50 4.00
153 Chris Canty RC 1.50 4.00
154 James Sanders RC 1.00 2.50
155 Matt Giordano RC 1.25 3.00
156 Boomer Grigsby RC 1.50 4.00
157 Donte Nicholson RC 1.00 2.50
158 Jerome Collins RC 1.25 3.00
159 Trent Cole RC 1.50 4.00
160 Alphonso Hodge RC 1.00 2.50
161 Jonathan Welsh RC 1.00 2.50
162 Adam Seward RC 1.25 3.00
163 Robert McCune RC 1.25 3.00
164 Eric King RC 1.00 2.50
165 Gerald Sensabaugh RC 1.50 4.00
166 Justin Green RC 1.50 4.00
167 Jeb Huckeba RC 1.25 3.00
168 Michael Boley RC 1.50 4.00
169 Andre Maddox RC 1.00 2.50
170 Rian Wallace RC 1.25 3.00
171 Michael Hawkins RC 1.00 2.50
172 Lance Mitchell RC 1.25 3.00
173 Ryan Claridge RC 1.00 2.50
174 James Butler RC 1.25 3.00
175 Ryan Riddle RC 1.00 2.50
176 Bo Scaife RC 1.25 3.00
177 Chris Harris RC 1.00 2.50
178 C.C. Brown RC 1.00 2.50
179 Pat Thomas RC 1.00 2.50
180 Derrick Johnson CB RC 1.00 2.50
181 Joel Dreessen RC 1.25 3.00
182 Rick Razzano RC 1.00 2.50
183 Nehemiah Broughton RC 1.25 3.00
184 Marcus Maxwell RC 1.00 2.50
185 Harry Williams RC 1.25 3.00
186 Patrick Estes RC 1.00 2.50
187 Billy Bajema RC 1.00 2.50
188 Madison Hedgecock RC 1.50 4.00
189 Manuel Wright RC 1.25 3.00
190 Roscoe Crosby RC 1.00 2.50
191 Wesley Duke RC 1.25 3.00
192 Ronnie Cruz RC 1.00 2.50
193 Adam Bergen RC 1.00 2.50
194 B.J. Ward RC 1.00 2.50
195 Stephen Spach RC 1.00 2.50
196 Marviel Underwood RC 1.25 3.00
197 John Bronson RC 1.00 2.50
198 Zak Keasey RC 1.25 3.00
199 Gregg Guenther RC 1.00 2.50
200 Jerome Carter RC 1.00 2.50
201 Aaron Rodgers RC 25.00 50.00
202 Adrian McPherson RC 1.25 3.00
203 Alvin Pearman RC 1.25 3.00
204 Airese Currie RC 1.25 3.00
205 Anthony Davis RC 1.25 3.00
206 Brandon Jacobs RC 1.50 4.00
207 Brandon Jones RC 1.50 4.00
208 Bryant McFadden RC 1.50 4.00
209 Cedric Benson RC 1.25 3.00
210 Cedric Houston RC 2.00 5.00
211 Chad Owens RC 1.25 3.00
212 Chris Henry 1.50 4.00
213 Craphonso Thorpe RC 1.25 3.00
214 Damien Nash RC 1.50 4.00
215 Dan Cody RC 1.25 3.00
216 Dan Orlovsky RC 1.25 3.00
217 Dante Ridgeway RC 1.25 3.00
218 Darren Sproles RC 2.00 5.00
219 David Greene RC 1.25 3.00
220 David Pollack RC 1.25 3.00
221 Deandra Cobb RC 1.25 3.00
222 DeMarcus Ware RC 4.00 10.00
223 Derek Anderson RC 1.50 4.00
224 Derrick Johnson RC 1.50 4.00
225 Fabian Washington RC 1.25 3.00
226 Roydell Williams RC 1.50 4.00
227 Heath Miller RC 2.50 6.00
228 J.R. Russell RC 1.25 3.00
229 James Kilian RC 1.25 3.00
230 Jerome Mathis RC 2.00 5.00
231 Larry Brackins RC 1.25 3.00
232 LeRon McCoy RC 1.25 3.00
233 Lionel Gates RC 1.25 3.00
234 Marion Barber RC 1.25 3.00
235 Marlin Jackson RC 1.25 3.00
236 Matt Cassel RC 1.25 3.00
237 Mike Williams 1.50 4.00
238 Nate Washington RC 2.00 5.00
239 Noah Herron RC 1.25 3.00
240 Fred Amey RC 1.50 4.00
241 Paris Warren RC 1.50 4.00
242 Rasheed Marshall RC 1.50 4.00
243 Ryan Fitzpatrick RC 2.00 5.00
244 Shaun Cody RC 1.50 4.00
245 Shawne Merriman RC 2.00 5.00
246 Tab Perry RC 1.25 3.00
247 Thomas Davis RC 1.25 3.00
248 Tyson Thompson RC 2.00 5.00
249 Chris Carr RC 1.50 4.00
250 Odell Thurman RC 2.00 5.00
251 Adam Jones JSY RC 2.00 5.00
252 Alex Smith QB JSY RC 6.00 15.00
253 Andrew Walter JSY RC 1.50 4.00
254 Antrel Rolle JSY RC 2.50 6.00
255 Braylon Edwards JSY RC 1.50 4.00
256 Carlos Rogers JSY RC 2.50 6.00
257 Cadillac Williams JSY RC 1.50 4.00
258 Charlie Frye JSY RC 1.50 4.00
259 Ciatrick Fason JSY RC 1.50 4.00
260 Courtney Roby JSY RC 1.50 4.00
261 Eric Shelton JSY RC 1.50 4.00
262 Frank Gore JSY RC 3.00 8.00
263 J.J. Arrington JSY RC 2.00 5.00
264 Jason Campbell JSY RC 1.50 4.00
265 Kyle Orton JSY RC 1.50 4.00
266 Mark Clayton JSY RC 1.50 4.00
267 Mark Bradley JSY RC 1.50 4.00
268 Matt Jones JSY RC 1.50 4.00
269 Maurice Clarett JSY 2.00 5.00
270 Reggie Brown JSY RC 1.50 4.00
271 Roddy White JSY RC 2.50 6.00
272 Ronnie Brown JSY RC 2.00 5.00
273 Roscoe Parrish JSY RC 1.50 4.00
274 Ryan Moats JSY RC 2.00 5.00
275 Stefan LeFors JSY RC 1.50 4.00
276 Terrence Murphy JSY RC 2.00 5.00
277 Troy Williamson JSY RC 1.50 4.00
278 Vernand Morency JSY RC 1.50 4.00
279 Vincent Jackson JSY RC 2.50 6.00
280 A.Smith QB J/J.Campbell J 6.00 15.00
281 R.Brown J/C.Williams J 2.00 5.00
282 B.Edwards J/T.Williamson J 1.50 4.00
283 A.Jones J/A.Rolle J 2.50 6.00
284 R.Parrish J/F.Gore J 3.00 8.00
285 C.Frye J/A.Walter J 1.50 4.00
286 J.Arrington J/E.Shelton J 2.00 5.00
287 C.Rogers J/K.Orton J 2.50 6.00
288 M.Clayton J/M.Bradley J 1.50 4.00
289 R.White J/Re.Brown J 2.50 6.00
290 T.Murphy J/C.Roby J 1.50 4.00
291 M.Clarett J/C.Fason J 1.50 4.00
292 R.Moats J/S.LeFors J 1.50 4.00
293 M.Jones J/V.Jackson J 2.50 6.00

2005 Leaf Rookies and Stars Longevity Parallel

*VETERANS: 2.5X TO 6X BASIC CARDS
1-100 VET PRINT RUN 150 SER.#'d SETS
*ROOKIES 101-200: 1X TO 2.5X BASIC CARDS
101-200 ROOKIE PRINT RUN 99 SER.#'d SETS
201-250 ROOKIE AUTO PRINT RUN 50
UNPRICED 251-279 JSY AU PRINT RUN 10
*DUAL JSY: 1X TO 2.5X BASIC CARDS
280-293 DUAL JSY PRINT RUN 25 SETS
201 Aaron Rodgers AU 350.00 500.00
202 Adrian McPherson AU 6.00 15.00
203 Alvin Pearman AU 6.00 15.00
204 Airese Currie AU 6.00 15.00
205 Anthony Davis AU 6.00 15.00
206 Brandon Jacobs AU 8.00 20.00
207 Brandon Jones AU 8.00 20.00
208 Bryant McFadden AU 8.00 20.00
209 Cedric Benson AU 15.00 40.00
210 Cedric Houston AU 10.00 25.00
211 Chad Owens AU 6.00 15.00
212 Chris Henry AU 8.00 20.00
213 Craphonso Thorpe AU 6.00 15.00
214 Damien Nash AU 8.00 20.00
215 Dan Cody AU 6.00 15.00
216 Dan Orlovsky AU 6.00 15.00
217 Dante Ridgeway AU 6.00 15.00
218 Darren Sproles AU 20.00 50.00
219 David Greene AU 6.00 15.00
220 David Pollack AU 6.00 15.00
221 Deandra Cobb AU 6.00 15.00
222 DeMarcus Ware AU 30.00 60.00
223 Derek Anderson AU 8.00 20.00
224 Derrick Johnson AU 8.00 20.00
225 Fabian Washington AU 6.00 15.00
226 Roydell Williams AU 8.00 20.00
227 Heath Miller AU 12.00 30.00
228 J.R. Russell AU 6.00 15.00
229 James Kilian AU 6.00 15.00
230 Jerome Mathis AU 10.00 25.00
231 Larry Brackins AU 6.00 15.00
232 LeRon McCoy AU 6.00 15.00
233 Lionel Gates AU 6.00 15.00
234 Marion Barber AU 15.00 40.00
235 Marlin Jackson AU 6.00 15.00
236 Matt Cassel AU 25.00 60.00
237 Mike Williams AU 8.00 20.00
238 Nate Washington AU 15.00 30.00
239 Noah Herron AU 6.00 15.00
240 Fred Amey AU 6.00 15.00
241 Paris Warren AU 8.00 20.00
242 Rasheed Marshall AU 8.00 20.00
243 Ryan Fitzpatrick AU 10.00 25.00
244 Shaun Cody AU 8.00 20.00
245 Shawne Merriman AU 10.00 25.00
246 Tab Perry AU 6.00 15.00
247 Thomas Davis AU 6.00 15.00
248 Tyson Thompson AU 6.00 15.00
249 Chris Carr AU 6.00 15.00
250 Odell Thurman AU 10.00 25.00

2005 Leaf Rookies and Stars Longevity Holofoil Parallel

*VETERANS 1-100: 3X TO 8X BASIC CARDS
1-100 VET PRINT RUN 99 SER.#'d SETS
*ROOKIES 101-200: 2.5X TO 6X BASIC CARDS
101-200 ROOKIE PRINT RUN 25 SER.#'d SETS
UNPRICED 201-250 AU PRINT RUN 10
UNPRICED 251-279 JSY AU PRINT RUN 5
UNPRICED 280-293 DUAL JSY PRINT RUN 10

2005 Leaf Rookies and Stars Longevity True Blue Parallel

ETERANS 1-100: 3X TO 8X BASIC CARDS
1-100 PRINT RUN 99 SER.#'d SETS
*ROOKIES 101-200: 1.5X TO 4X BASIC CARDS
101-200 ROOKIE PRINT RUN 50 SER.#'d SETS
UNPRICED 201-250 PRINT RUN 10 SETS
INSERTS IN SPECIAL RETAIL BOXES

2005 Leaf Rookies and Stars Longevity True Green Parallel

ETERANS 1-100: 2.5X TO 6X BASIC CARDS
1-100 PRINT RUN 200 SER.#'d SETS
*ROOKIES 101-200: 1X TO 2.5X BASIC CARDS
101-200 ROOKIE PRINT RUN 100 SER.#'d SETS
*ROOKIES 201-250: 1.5X TO 4X BASIC CARDS
201-250 ROOKIE PRINT RUN 25 SER.#'d SETS
201 Aaron Rodgers 150.00 250.00

2005 Leaf Rookies and Stars Crusade Red

D PRINT RUN 1250 SER.#'d SETS
*GREEN: .5X TO 1.2X RED
GREEN PRINT RUN 750 SER.#'d SETS
*GREEN DIE CUT: 2X TO 5X RED
GREEN DIE CUT PRINT RUN 25 SER.#'d SETS
*PURPLE: .6X TO 1.5X RED
PURPLE PRINT RUN 250 SER.#'d SETS
*PURPLE DIE CUT: 1.2X TO 3X RED
PURPLE DIE CUT PRINT RUN 50 SER.#'d SETS
UNPRICED RED DIE CUT PRINT RUN 10 SETS
C1 Aaron Brooks .75 2.00
C2 Ahman Green 1.00 2.50
C3 Andre Johnson 1.00 2.50
C4 Ben Roethlisberger 2.00 5.00
C5 Brian Urlacher 1.25 3.00
C6 Byron Leftwich .75 2.00
C7 Carson Palmer 1.00 2.50
C8 Chad Pennington .75 2.00
C9 Domanick Davis .75 2.00
C10 Donovan McNabb 1.00 2.50
C11 Eli Manning 2.00 5.00
C12 Jake Plummer .75 2.00
C13 Jamal Lewis 1.00 2.50
C14 Julius Jones .75 2.00
C15 Jerome Bettis 1.25 3.00
C16 Larry Fitzgerald 1.25 3.00
C17 Marvin Harrison 1.00 2.50
C18 Michael Vick 1.00 2.50
C19 Peyton Manning 3.00 8.00
C20 Priest Holmes .75 2.00
C21 Ray Lewis 1.25 3.00
C22 Steve McNair 1.00 2.50
C23 Terrell Owens 1.00 2.50
C24 Tiki Barber 1.00 2.50
C25 Willis McGahee .75 2.00

2005 Leaf Rookies and Stars Crusade Materials

TERIAL PRINT RUN 250 SER.#'d SETS
*DIE CUT/150: .5X TO 1.2X BASIC JSY
*PRIME/25: 1X TO 2.5X BASIC JSY
C1 Aaron Brooks 2.50 6.00
C2 Ahman Green 3.00 8.00
C3 Andre Johnson 3.00 8.00
C4 Ben Roethlisberger 8.00 20.00
C5 Brian Urlacher 4.00 10.00
C6 Byron Leftwich 2.50 6.00
C7 Carson Palmer 3.00 8.00
C8 Chad Pennington 2.50 6.00
C9 Domanick Davis 2.50 6.00
C10 Donovan McNabb 3.00 8.00
C11 Eli Manning 8.00 20.00
C12 Jake Plummer 2.50 6.00
C13 Jamal Lewis 3.00 8.00
C14 Julius Jones 2.50 6.00
C15 Jerome Bettis 10.00 25.00
C16 Larry Fitzgerald 4.00 10.00
C17 Marvin Harrison 3.00 8.00
C18 Michael Vick 3.00 8.00
C19 Peyton Manning 10.00 25.00
C20 Priest Holmes 2.50 6.00
C21 Ray Lewis 4.00 10.00
C22 Steve McNair 3.00 8.00
C23 Terrell Owens 3.00 8.00
C24 Tiki Barber 3.00 8.00
C25 Willis McGahee 2.50 6.00

2005 Leaf Rookies and Stars Freshman Orientation Jersey

ATED PRINT RUN 350 SER.#'d SETS
*CLASS OFFICE: .6X TO 1.5X BASIC JSYs
CLASS OFFICER PRINT RUN 100 SER.#'d SETS
F01 Adam Jones 1.50 4.00
F02 Alex Smith QB 6.00 15.00
F03 Andrew Walter 1.50 4.00
F04 Antrel Rolle 2.50 6.00
F05 Braylon Edwards 1.50 4.00
F06 Carlos Rogers 2.50 6.00
F07 Cadillac Williams 1.50 4.00
F08 Charlie Frye 1.50 4.00
F09 Ciatrick Fason 1.50 4.00
F010 Courtney Roby 1.50 4.00
F011 Eric Shelton 1.50 4.00
F012 Frank Gore 3.00 8.00
F013 J.J. Arrington 2.00 5.00
F014 Jason Campbell 1.50 4.00
F015 Kyle Orton 1.50 4.00
F016 Mark Clayton 1.50 4.00
F017 Mark Bradley 1.50 4.00
F018 Matt Jones 1.50 4.00
F019 Maurice Clarett 1.50 4.00
F020 Reggie Brown 1.50 4.00
F021 Roddy White 2.50 6.00
F022 Ronnie Brown 2.00 5.00
F023 Roscoe Parrish 1.50 4.00
F024 Ryan Moats 1.50 4.00
F025 Stefan LeFors 1.50 4.00
F026 Terrence Murphy 2.00 5.00
F027 Troy Williamson 1.50 4.00
F028 Vernand Morency 1.50 4.00
F029 Vincent Jackson 2.50 6.00

2005 Leaf Rookies and Stars Great American Heroes Red

RED PRINT RUN 1250 SER.#'d SETS
*BLUE: .6X TO 1.5X RED
BLUE PRINT RUN 250 SER.#'d SETS
*WHITE: .5X TO 1.2X RED
WHITE PRINT RUN 750 SER.#'d SETS
GAH1 Aaron Brooks 1.00 2.50
GAH2 Alge Crumpler 1.25 3.00
GAH3 Antonio Gates 1.50 4.00
GAH4 Jevon Kearse 1.00 2.50
GAH5 Byron Leftwich 1.00 2.50
GAH6 Chad Johnson 1.00 2.50
GAH7 Chad Pennington 1.00 2.50
GAH8 Chris Brown 1.00 2.50
GAH9 Cris Collinsworth 1.50 4.00
GAH10 Daryl Johnston 1.50 4.00
GAH11 Derrick Brooks 1.00 2.50
GAH12 Domanick Davis 1.00 2.50
GAH13 Herschel Walker 2.00 5.00
GAH14 J.P. Losman 1.00 2.50
GAH15 Jim Plunkett 1.50 4.00
GAH16 John Taylor 1.25 3.00
GAH17 Julius Jones 1.00 2.50
GAH18 Leroy Kelly 1.50 4.00
GAH19 Michael Vick 1.25 3.00
GAH20 Nate Burleson 1.00 2.50
GAH21 Richard Dent 1.50 4.00
GAH22 Roger Craig 2.00 5.00
GAH23 Rudi Johnson 1.00 2.50
GAH24 Steve Smith 1.50 4.00
GAH25 Terence Newman 1.00 2.50

2005 Leaf Rookies and Stars Great American Heroes Autographs

STATED PRINT RUN 50-300
GAH1 Aaron Brooks/150 6.00 15.00
GAH2 Alge Crumpler/100 7.50 20.00
GAH3 Antonio Gates/100 12.00 30.00
GAH4 Jevon Kearse/100 7.50 20.00
GAH5 Byron Leftwich/50 12.50 30.00
GAH6 Chad Johnson/50 8.00 30.00
GAH7 Chad Pennington/50 12.50 30.00
GAH8 Chris Brown/150 7.50 20.00
GAH9 Cris Collinsworth/70 7.50 20.00
GAH10 Daryl Johnston/202 15.00 40.00
GAH11 Derrick Brooks/300 12.50 30.00
GAH12 Domanick Davis/50 7.50 20.00
GAH13 Herschel Walker/100 15.00 40.00
GAH14 J.P. Losman/75 7.50 20.00
GAH15 Jim Plunkett/100 12.50 30.00
GAH16 John Taylor/75 7.50 20.00
GAH17 Julius Jones/50 25.00 50.00
GAH18 Leroy Kelly/75 12.50 30.00
GAH19 Michael Vick/50 12.00 30.00
GAH20 Nate Burleson/100 7.50 20.00
GAH21 Richard Dent/105 15.00 40.00
GAH22 Roger Craig/212 12.50 30.00
GAH23 Rudi Johnson/100 12.50 30.00
GAH24 Steve Smith/100 12.50 30.00
GAH25 Terence Newman/150 12.50 30.00

2005 Leaf Rookies and Stars Great American Heroes Jerseys

JERSEY PRINT RUN 250 SER.#'d SETS
*PRIME: 1X TO 2.5X BASIC JERSEYS
PRIME PRINT RUN 25 SER.#'d SETS
GAH1 Aaron Brooks 3.00 8.00
GAH2 Alge Crumpler 3.00 8.00
GAH3 Antonio Gates 4.00 10.00
GAH4 Jevon Kearse 3.00 8.00
GAH5 Byron Leftwich 4.00 10.00
GAH6 Chad Johnson 4.00 10.00
GAH7 Chad Pennington 4.00 10.00
GAH8 Chris Brown 3.00 8.00
GAH9 Cris Collinsworth 4.00 10.00
GAH10 Daryl Johnston/135 6.00 15.00
GAH11 Derrick Brooks 4.00 10.00
GAH12 Domanick Davis 3.00 8.00
GAH13 Herschel Walker 4.00 10.00
GAH14 J.P. Losman 3.00 8.00
GAH15 Jim Plunkett 5.00 12.00
GAH16 John Taylor 4.00 10.00
GAH17 Julius Jones 5.00 12.00
GAH18 Leroy Kelly 4.00 10.00
GAH19 Michael Vick 6.00 15.00
GAH20 Nate Burleson 3.00 8.00
GAH21 Richard Dent 4.00 10.00
GAH22 Roger Craig 5.00 12.00
GAH23 Rudi Johnson 3.00 8.00
GAH24 Steve Smith 3.00 8.00
GAH25 Terence Newman 3.00 8.00

2005 Leaf Rookies and Stars Initial Steps Shoe

STATED PRINT RUN 100 SER.#'d SETS
IS1 Adam Jones 5.00 12.00
IS2 Alex Smith QB 12.50 30.00
IS3 Andrew Walter 5.00 12.00
IS4 Antrel Rolle 5.00 12.00
IS5 Braylon Edwards 6.00 15.00
IS6 Carlos Rogers 5.00 12.00
IS7 Cadillac Williams 8.00 20.00
IS8 Charlie Frye 5.00 12.00
IS9 Ciatrick Fason 5.00 12.00
IS10 Courtney Roby 5.00 12.00
IS11 Eric Shelton 5.00 12.00
IS12 Frank Gore 8.00 20.00
IS13 J.J. Arrington 5.00 12.00
IS14 Jason Campbell 6.00 15.00
IS15 Kyle Orton 5.00 12.00
IS16 Mark Clayton 5.00 12.00
IS17 Mark Bradley 5.00 12.00
IS18 Matt Jones
IS19 Maurice Clarett 5.00 12.00
IS20 Reggie Brown 5.00 12.00
IS21 Roddy White 6.00 15.00
IS22 Ronnie Brown 12.50 30.00
IS23 Roscoe Parrish 5.00 12.00
IS24 Ryan Moats 5.00 12.00
IS25 Stefan LeFors 5.00 12.00
IS26 Terrence Murphy 5.00 12.00
IS27 Troy Williamson 5.00 12.00
IS28 Vernand Morency 5.00 12.00
IS29 Vincent Jackson 4.00 10.00

2005 Leaf Rookies and Stars Masks

ATED PRINT RUN 325 SER.#'d SETS
M1 Adam Jones 4.00 10.00
M2 Alex Smith QB 10.00 25.00
M3 Andrew Walter 4.00 10.00
M4 Antrel Rolle 4.00 10.00
M5 Braylon Edwards 6.00 15.00
M6 Carlos Rogers 5.00 12.00
M7 Cadillac Williams 8.00 20.00
M8 Charlie Frye 4.00 10.00
M9 Ciatrick Fason 4.00 10.00
M10 Courtney Roby 4.00 10.00
M11 Eric Shelton 4.00 10.00
M12 Frank Gore 6.00 15.00
M13 J.J. Arrington 4.00 10.00
M14 Jason Campbell 5.00 12.00
M15 Kyle Orton 5.00 12.00
M16 Mark Clayton 4.00 10.00
M17 Mark Bradley 4.00 10.00
M18 Matt Jones 4.00 10.00
M19 Maurice Clarett 4.00 10.00
M20 Reggie Brown 4.00 10.00
M21 Roddy White 5.00 12.00
M22 Ronnie Brown 10.00 25.00
M23 Roscoe Parrish 4.00 10.00
M24 Ryan Moats 4.00 10.00
M25 Stefan LeFors 4.00 10.00
M26 Terrence Murphy 4.00 10.00
M27 Troy Williamson 4.00 10.00
M28 Vernand Morency 4.00 10.00
M29 Vincent Jackson 5.00 12.00

2005 Leaf Rookies and Stars Prime Cuts

STATED PRINT RUN 25 SER.#'d SETS
PC1 Peyton Manning 30.00 80.00
PC2 Michael Vick 10.00 25.00
PC3 Tom Brady 50.00 125.00
PC4 Daunte Culpepper 10.00 25.00
PC5 Brett Favre 25.00 60.00
PC6 Ben Roethlisberger 25.00 60.00
PC7 Byron Leftwich 8.00 20.00
PC8 Steve McNair 10.00 25.00
PC9 Chad Pennington 8.00 20.00
PC10 Eli Manning 25.00 60.00
PC11 LaDainian Tomlinson 12.00 30.00
PC12 Priest Holmes 8.00 20.00
PC13 Shaun Alexander 8.00 20.00
PC14 Clinton Portis 8.00 20.00
PC15 Julius Jones 8.00 20.00
PC16 Ahman Green 10.00 25.00
PC17 Corey Dillon 8.00 20.00
PC18 Edgerrin James 10.00 25.00
PC19 Marvin Harrison 10.00 25.00
PC20 Chad Johnson 8.00 20.00
PC21 Hines Ward 10.00 25.00
PC22 Torry Holt 10.00 25.00
PC23 Andre Johnson 10.00 25.00
PC24 Michael Clayton 8.00 20.00
PC25 Randy Moss 10.00 25.00

2005 Leaf Rookies and Stars Rookie Autographs

201-250 AUTO PRINT RUN 150
251-279 JSY AUTO PRINT RUN 50
201 Aaron Rodgers 250.00 400.00
202 Adrian McPherson 5.00 12.00
203 Alvin Pearman 5.00 12.00
204 Airese Currie 5.00 12.00
205 Anthony Davis 5.00 12.00
206 Brandon Jacobs 12.00 30.00
207 Brandon Jones 6.00 15.00
208 Bryant McFadden 6.00 15.00
209 Cedric Benson 5.00 12.00
210 Cedric Houston 8.00 20.00
211 Chad Owens 5.00 12.00
212 Chris Henry 6.00 15.00
213 Craphonso Thorpe 5.00 12.00
214 Damien Nash 6.00 15.00
215 Dan Cody 5.00 12.00
216 Dan Orlovsky 5.00 12.00
217 Dante Ridgeway 5.00 12.00
218 Darren Sproles 8.00 20.00
219 David Greene 5.00 12.00
220 David Pollack 5.00 12.00
221 Deandra Cobb 5.00 12.00
222 DeMarcus Ware 25.00 50.00
223 Derek Anderson 6.00 15.00
224 Derrick Johnson 6.00 15.00
225 Fabian Washington 5.00 12.00
226 Roydell Williams 6.00 15.00
227 Heath Miller 10.00 25.00
228 J.R. Russell 5.00 12.00
229 James Kilian 5.00 12.00
230 Jerome Mathis 8.00 20.00
231 Larry Brackins 5.00 12.00
232 LeRon McCoy 5.00 12.00
233 Lionel Gates 5.00 12.00
234 Marion Barber 12.00 30.00
235 Marlin Jackson 5.00 12.00
236 Matt Cassel 15.00 40.00
237 Mike Williams 10.00 25.00
238 Nate Washington 8.00 20.00
239 Noah Herron 5.00 12.00
240 Fred Amey 5.00 12.00
241 Paris Warren 6.00 15.00
242 Rasheed Marshall 6.00 15.00
243 Ryan Fitzpatrick 8.00 20.00
244 Shaun Cody 6.00 15.00
245 Shawne Merriman 8.00 20.00
246 Tab Perry 5.00 12.00
247 Thomas Davis 5.00 12.00
248 Tyson Thompson 5.00 12.00
249 Chris Carr 5.00 12.00
250 Odell Thurman 8.00 20.00
251 Adam Jones JSY 10.00 25.00
252 Alex Smith QB JSY 60.00 120.00
253 Andrew Walter JSY 10.00 25.00
254 Antrel Rolle JSY 15.00 40.00
255 Braylon Edwards JSY 20.00 50.00
256 Carlos Rogers JSY 15.00 40.00
257 Cadillac Williams JSY 12.00 30.00
258 Charlie Frye JSY 10.00 25.00
259 Ciatrick Fason JSY 10.00 25.00
260 Courtney Roby JSY 10.00 25.00
261 Eric Shelton JSY 10.00 25.00
262 Frank Gore JSY 30.00 60.00
263 J.J. Arrington JSY 12.00 30.00
264 Jason Campbell JSY 30.00 60.00
265 Kyle Orton JSY 25.00 50.00
266 Mark Clayton JSY 10.00 25.00
267 Mark Bradley JSY 10.00 25.00
268 Matt Jones JSY 10.00 25.00
269 Maurice Clarett JSY 10.00 25.00
270 Reggie Brown JSY 10.00 25.00
271 Roddy White JSY 15.00 40.00
272 Ronnie Brown JSY 40.00 100.00
273 Roscoe Parrish JSY 10.00 25.00
274 Ryan Moats JSY 10.00 25.00
275 Stefan LeFors JSY 10.00 25.00
276 Terrence Murphy JSY 10.00 25.00
277 Troy Williamson JSY 10.00 25.00
278 Vernand Morency JSY 10.00 25.00
279 Vincent Jackson JSY 15.00 40.00

2005 Leaf Rookies and Stars Slideshow Bronze

BRONZE PRINT RUN 1250 SER.#'d SETS
*SILVER: .5X TO 1.2X BRONZE
SILVER PRINT RUN 750 SER.#'d SETS
*VIEW MASTER: .6X TO 1.5X BRONZE
VIEW MASTER PRINT RUN 250 SER.#'d SETS
SS1 Brett Favre 2.50 6.00
SS2 Michael Vick 1.00 2.50
SS3 Deion Sanders 1.00 2.50
SS4 J.P. Losman .75 2.00
SS5 Julius Jones .75 2.00
SS6 Eli Manning 2.00 5.00
SS7 Kevin Jones .75 2.00
SS8 Domanick Davis .75 2.00
SS9 Edgerrin James 1.00 2.50
SS10 Byron Leftwich .75 2.00
SS11 Priest Holmes .75 2.00
SS12 Tom Brady 5.00 12.00
SS13 Tedy Bruschi 1.00 2.50
SS14 Deuce McAllister 1.00 2.50
SS15 Jeremy Shockey .75 2.00
SS16 Chad Pennington .75 2.00
SS17 Randy Moss 1.00 2.50
SS18 Terrell Owens 1.00 2.50
SS19 Ben Roethlisberger 2.00 5.00
SS20 Antonio Gates 1.25 3.00
SS21 Alex Smith QB 3.00 8.00
SS22 Steven Jackson .75 2.00
SS23 Clinton Portis .75 2.00
SS24 Steve McNair 1.00 2.50
SS25 Willis McGahee .75 2.00

2005 Leaf Rookies and Stars Ticket Masters Bronze

BRONZE PRINT RUN 1250 SER.#'d SETS
*GOLD: .6X TO 1.5X BRONZE
GOLD PRINT RUN 250 SER.#'d SETS
*SILVER: .5X TO 1.2X BRONZE
SILVER PRINT RUN 750 SER.#'d SETS
TM1 L.Fitzgerald/A.Boldin 2.00 5.00
TM2 A.Crumpler/M.Vick 3.00 8.00
TM3 W.McGahee/J.Losman 2.00 5.00
TM4 S.Alexander/M.Hasselbeck 2.50 6.00
TM5 B.Urlacher/C.Benson 2.00 5.00
TM6 C.Palmer/R.Johnson 2.00 5.00
TM7 J.Jones/D.Bledsoe 2.50 6.00
TM8 J.Plummer/J.Rice 3.00 8.00
TM9 K.Jones/R.Williams WR 2.00 5.00
TM10 B.Favre/J.Walker 5.00 12.00
TM11 D.Carr/D.Davis 2.00 5.00
TM12 P.Manning/M.Harrison 3.00 8.00
TM13 T.Gonzalez/P.Holmes 2.00 5.00
TM14 Ro.Brown/C.Chambers 3.00 8.00
TM15 T.Williamson/D.Culpepper 2.00 5.00
TM16 T.Brady/D.Branch 6.00 15.00
TM17 E.Manning/P.Burress 4.00 10.00
TM18 C.Pennington/L.Coles 2.00 5.00
TM19 R.Moss/L.Jordan 2.00 5.00
TM20 D.McNabb/J.Kearse 2.50 6.00
TM21 Roethlis/J.Bettis 5.00 12.00
TM22 L.Tomlinson/A.Gates 2.50 6.00
TM23 T.Holt/S.Jackson 2.50 6.00
TM24 S.McNair/D.Bennett 2.00 5.00
TM25 Mi.Clayton/C.Williams 2.50 6.00

2005 Leaf Rookies and Stars Triple Threads

ATED PRINT RUN 150 SER.#'d SETS
*PRIME: .8X TO 2X BASIC JERSEYS
PRIME PRINT RUN 25 SER.#'d SETS
TT1 Losman/Moulds/McGahee 7.50 20.00
TT2 Grossman/Jones/Urlacher 12.50 30.00
TT3 Palmer/Johnson/Johnson 8.00 30.00
TT4 J.Jones/Roy Will.S/Key. 12.50 30.00
TT5 Plummer/Bell/Lelie 7.50 20.00
TT6 Harrington/Jones/Will WR 7.50 20.00
TT7 Favre/Green/Walker 15.00 40.00
TT8 Carr/Davis/Johnson 7.50 20.00
TT9 Manning/Wayne/Harrison 15.00 40.00
TT10 Leftwich/Taylor/Smith 7.50 20.00
TT11 Green/Holmes/Gonzalez 10.00 25.00
TT12 Culp/Bennett/Burleson 10.00 25.00
TT13 Brady/Dillon/Branch 12.50 30.00
TT14 Brooks/McAllister/Horn 7.50 20.00
TT15 Manning/Shockey/Barber 20.00 40.00
TT16 Pennington/Martin/Coles 10.00 25.00
TT17 Delhomme/Davis/Peppers 10.00 25.00
TT18 McNabb/Westbrook/Owens 12.50 30.00
TT19 Ben/Bettis/Ward 20.00 50.00
TT20 Brees/Tomlinson/Gates 12.50 30.00
TT21 Hassel/Alexan/Jackson 15.00 30.00
TT22 Bulger/Jackson/Holt 10.00 25.00
TT23 McNair/Brown/Bennett 10.00 25.00
TT24 Portis/Arrington/Gardner 10.00 25.00
TT25 Boller/Lewis/Lewis 7.50 20.00

2005 Leaf Rookies and Stars Longevity

This 279-card set was released in January, 2006. The set was issued in the hobby in five-card packs which came 24 packs to a box. The first 96 cards in the set feature veterans sequenced in team alphabetical order while cards numbered 97-100 feature two rookie teammate checklists and cards 101-279 all feature rookies. In the rookie subset, cards numbered 251-279 all have a player-worn relic piece attached. Cards numbered 101-200 were issued to a stated print run of 999 serial numbered sets while cards numbered 201-250 were issued to a stated print run of 599 serial numbered sets and cards numbered 251-279 were issued to a stated print run of 299 serial numbered sets.

COMP.SET w/o RC's (100) 10.00 25.00
*VETS 1-100: .5X TO 1.2X BASIC LR&S
*ROOKIES 101-200: .4X TO 1X
101-200 PRINT RUN 999 SER.#'d SETS
*ROOKIES 201-250: .4X TO 1X
201-250 PRINT RUN 599 SER.#'d SETS
*ROOKIE JSYs 251-279: .4X TO 1X
251-279 JSY PRINT RUN 299 SER.#'d SETS
201 Aaron Rodgers RC 25.00 50.00

2005 Leaf Rookies and Stars Longevity Black

*VETERANS 1-100: 2.5X TO 6X BASIC CARDS
1-100 PRINT RUN 99 SER.#'d SETS
*ROOKIES 101-200: 1.5X TO 4X BASIC CARDS
101-200 PRINT RUN 50 SER.#'d SETS
*ROOKIES 201-250: 1.5X TO 4X BASIC CARDS
201-250 PRINT RUN 25 SER.#'d SETS
251-279 UNPRICED JSY PRINT RUN 10 SETS
201 Aaron Rodgers 150.00 250.00

2005 Leaf Rookies and Stars Longevity Emerald

*VETERANS 1-100: 2X TO 5X BASIC CARDS
1-100 PRINT RUN 150 SER.#'d SETS
*ROOKIES: 1X TO 2.5X BASIC CARDS
101-200 PRINT RUN 99 SER.#'d SETS
*ROOKIES 201-250: 1.2X TO 3X BASIC CARDS
201-250 PRINT RUN 50 SER.#'d SETS
*ROOKIE JSYs 251-279: 1.2X TO 3X
251-279 JSY PRINT RUN 25 SER.#'d SETS
201 Aaron Rodgers 125.00 200.00

2005 Leaf Rookies and Stars Longevity Gold

ETS 1-100: 1.5X TO 4X BASIC CARDS
1-100 PRINT RUN 199 SER.#'d SETS
*ROOKIES 101-200: .8X TO 2X BASIC CARDS
101-200 PRINT RUN 150 SER.#'d SETS
*ROOKIES 201-250: .8X TO 2X BASIC CARDS
201-250 PRINT RUN 99 SER.#'d SETS
*ROOKIE JSYs 201-250: .8X TO 2X
251-279 JSY PRINT RUN 50 SER.#'d SETS
201 Aaron Rodgers 100.00 175.00

2005 Leaf Rookies and Stars Longevity Ruby

*VETERANS 1-100: 1.2X TO 3X BASIC CARDS
1-100 PRINT RUN 299 SER.#'d SETS
*ROOKIES 101-200: .6X TO 1.5X
101-200 PRINT RUN 250 SER.#'d SETS
*ROOKIES 201-250: .6X TO 1.5X
201-250 PRINT RUN 199 SER.#'d SETS
*ROOKIE JSYs 251-2790: .6X TO 1.5X
251-279 JSY PRINT RUN 99 SER.#'d SETS
201 Aaron Rodgers 40.00 100.00

2005 Leaf Rookies and Stars Longevity Sapphire

*VETERANS 1-100: 1.2X TO 3X BASIC CARDS
1-100 PRINT RUN 250 SER.#'d SETS
*ROOKIES 101-200: .8X TO 2X
101-200 PRINT RUN 199 SER.#'d SETS
*ROOKIES 201-250: .8X TO 2X
201-250 PRINT RUN 150 SER.#'d SETS
*ROOKIE JSYs 251-279: .8X TO 2X
251-279 JSY PRINT RUN 75 SER.#'d SETS
201 Aaron Rodgers 75.00 150.00

2005 Leaf Rookies and Stars Longevity Materials Black

MMON CARD/25 7.50 20.00
SEMISTARS/25 10.00 25.00
UNL.STARS/25 12.50 30.00
BLACK STATED PRINT RUN 5-25
36 Brett Favre/15 25.00 60.00
43 Peyton Manning/25 30.00 80.00
57 Tom Brady/25 50.00 125.00
78 Jerome Bettis/25 20.00 50.00

2005 Leaf Rookies and Stars Longevity Materials Emerald

COMMON CARD/39-50 5.00 12.00
SEMISTARS/39-50 6.00 15.00
UNL.STARS/39-50 8.00 20.00
COMMON CARD/20-30 8.00 20.00
UNL.STARS/20-30 10.00 25.00
EMERALD STATED PRINT RUN 9-50
4 Michael Vick/20 8.00 20.00
36 Brett Favre/30 20.00 50.00
43 Peyton Manning/50 20.00 50.00
57 Tom Brady/50 30.00 80.00
61 Eli Manning/25 15.00 40.00
78 Jerome Bettis/50 12.00 30.00

2005 Leaf Rookies and Stars Longevity Materials Gold

COMMON CARD/80-99 4.00 10.00
SEMISTARS/80-99 5.00 12.00
UNL.STARS/80-99 6.00 15.00
COMMON CARD/55-79 6.00 15.00
UNL.STARS/55-79 8.00 20.00
COMMON CARD/30-50 6.00 15.00
SEMISTARS/30-50 8.00 20.00
UNL.STARS/30-50 10.00 25.00
COMMON CARD/15-25 10.00 25.00
UNL.STARS/15-25 12.00 30.00
GOLD STATED PRINT RUN 13-99
36 Brett Favre/99 12.00 30.00
43 Peyton Manning/99 15.00 40.00
57 Tom Brady/99 25.00 60.00
61 Eli Manning/99 10.00 25.00
75 Ben Roethlisberger/99 10.00 25.00
78 Jerome Bettis/99 10.00 25.00

2005 Leaf Rookies and Stars Longevity Materials Ruby

COMMON CARD/150-199 2.50 6.00
SEMISTARS/150-199 3.00 8.00
UNL.STARS/150-199 4.00 10.00
COMMON CARD/100-130 3.00 8.00
SEMISTARS/100-130 4.00 10.00
UNL.STARS/100-130 5.00 12.00
COMMON CARD/50-79 5.00 12.00
UNL.STARS/50-79 7.50 20.00
RUBY STATED PRINT RUN 55-199
36 Brett Favre/199 8.00 20.00
43 Peyton Manning/199 10.00 25.00
61 Eli Manning/165 6.00 15.00
75 Ben Roethlisberger/199 6.00 15.00

2005 Leaf Rookies and Stars Longevity Materials Sapphire

MMON CARD/90-150 3.00 8.00
SEMISTARS/90-150 4.00 10.00
UNL.STARS/90-150 5.00 12.00
COMMON CARD/50-77 4.00 10.00
SEMISTARS/50-77 5.00 12.00
UNL.STARS/50-77 6.00 15.00
COMMON CARD/25 6.00 15.00
SAPPHIRE STATED PRINT RUN 25-150
36 Brett Favre/150 10.00 25.00
43 Peyton Manning/150 12.00 30.00
61 Eli Manning/105 8.00 20.00
75 Ben Roethlisberger/150 8.00 20.00
78 Jerome Bettis/77 10.00 25.00

2005 Leaf Rookies and Stars Longevity Sunday Signatures

*GOLD: .5X TO 1.2X BASIC AUTOS
GOLDS SER.#'d UNDER 20 NOT PRICED
1 Aaron Brooks/150 6.00 15.00
3 Antonio Gates/75 10.00 25.00
4 Ashley Lelie/175 10.00 25.00
6 Chris Brown/125
7 Christian Okoye/50 10.00 25.00
8 Daryl Johnston/175 15.00 40.00
9 Deion Branch/100 10.00 25.00
11 Derrick Brooks/299 10.00 25.00
12 Nate Burleson/251 6.00 15.00
13 Donnie Edwards/299 6.00 15.00
14 Drew Bennett/276 6.00 15.00
15 Domanick Davis/75 6.00 15.00
17 Fran Tarkenton/99 15.00 40.00
19 Gene Upshaw/107 10.00 25.00
20 Herschel Walker/99 15.00 40.00
21 Hines Ward/63 20.00 50.00
23 Jevon Kearse/299 10.00 25.00
24 Jimmy Smith/100 6.00 15.00
25 John Taylor/99 10.00 25.00
27 L.C. Greenwood/50 15.00 40.00
28 LaMont Jordan/299 10.00 25.00
29 Lee Evans/299 6.00 15.00
30 Leroy Kelly/57 12.50 30.00
33 Mike Ditka/150 20.00 40.00
34 Mike Singletary/15 15.00 40.00
35 Paul Hornung/75 12.50 30.00
36 Paul Warfield/179 10.00 25.00
37 Randall Cunningham/75 15.00 40.00
38 Reggie Wayne/150 12.50 30.00
39 Rex Grossman/125 15.00 30.00
40 Richard Dent/95 10.00 25.00
41 Rudi Johnson/50 10.00 25.00
42 Sonny Jurgensen/79 15.00 40.00
43 Sterling Sharpe/75 12.50 30.00
45 Tatum Bell/97 10.00 25.00
49 Warren Moon/50 12.50 30.00
50 Y.A. Tittle/100 12.00 30.00

2006 Leaf Rookies and Stars

This 281-card set was released in October, 2006. The set was issued into the hobby in five-card packs which came 24 to a box. Cards numbered 1-100 feature players in team alphabetical order while cards numbered 101-281 feature 2006 rookies. The Rookie Cards are broken into the following subsets: Cards numbered 101-200 were issued to a stated print run of 999 serial numbered sets, while cards 201-250 were issued to a stated print run of 599 serial numbered sets. Cards numbered 251-270 have a player-worn jersey swatch and those cards were issued to a stated print run of 799 serial numbered sets and the set concludes with cards numbered 271-281 which have both player-worn swatches and an autograph and those cards were issued to stated print runs betwwn 99 and 449 serial numbered copies. For those cards, we have explicitly notated the print runs in our checklist.

COMP.SET w/o RC's (100) 8.00 20.00
101-200 ROOKIE PRINT RUN 999
201-250 ROOKIE PRINT RUN 599
251-270 JSY ROOKIE PRINT RUN 799
JSY AU ROOKIE PRINT RUN 99-449
1 Anquan Boldin .15 .40
2 Edgerrin James .20 .50
3 Kurt Warner .20 .50
4 Larry Fitzgerald .20 .50
5 Alge Crumpler .20 .50
6 Michael Vick .20 .50
7 Warrick Dunn .15 .40
8 Derrick Mason .15 .40
9 Jamal Lewis .20 .50
10 Mike Anderson .15 .40
11 Josh Reed .15 .40
12 Lee Evans .20 .50
13 Willis McGahee .15 .40
14 DeShaun Foster .20 .50
15 Jake Delhomme .15 .40
16 Keyshawn Johnson .20 .50
17 Steve Smith .25 .60
18 Cedric Benson .15 .40
19 Muhsin Muhammad .15 .40
20 Rex Grossman .15 .40
21 Carson Palmer .20 .50
22 Chad Johnson .15 .40
23 Rudi Johnson .15 .40
24 T.J. Houshmandzadeh .15 .40
25 Charlie Frye .20 .50
26 Joe Jurevicius .15 .40
27 Reuben Droughns .20 .50
28 Drew Bledsoe .20 .50
29 Julius Jones .15 .40
30 Terrell Owens .20 .50
31 Terry Glenn .20 .50
32 Jake Plummer .15 .40
33 Rod Smith .20 .50
34 Tatum Bell .15 .40
35 Josh McCown .15 .40
36 Kevin Jones .15 .40
37 Roy Williams WR .15 .40
38 Ahman Green .20 .50
39 Brett Favre .50 1.25
40 Donald Driver .20 .50
41 Robert Ferguson .15 .40
42 Samkon Gado .15 .40
43 Andre Johnson .20 .50
44 David Carr .15 .40
45 Domanick Davis .15 .40
46 Eric Moulds .15 .40
47 Marvin Harrison .20 .50
48 Peyton Manning .60 1.50
49 Reggie Wayne .20 .50
50 Dallas Clark .15 .40
51 Fred Taylor .15 .40
52 Byron Leftwich .15 .40
53 Jimmy Smith .20 .50
54 Larry Johnson .15 .40
55 Tony Gonzalez .20 .50
56 Trent Green .15 .40
57 Eddie Kennison .15 .40
58 Chris Chambers .15 .40
59 Daunte Culpepper .20 .50
60 Ronnie Brown .20 .50
61 Chester Taylor .20 .50
62 Brad Johnson .20 .50
63 Deion Branch .15 .40
64 Corey Dillon .15 .40
65 Tom Brady .75 2.00
66 Deuce McAllister .20 .50
67 Donte Stallworth .15 .40
68 Drew Brees .25 .60
69 Eli Manning .20 .50
70 Plaxico Burress .15 .40
71 Tiki Barber .20 .50
72 Chad Pennington .15 .40
73 Curtis Martin .20 .50
74 Laveranues Coles .15 .40
75 Aaron Brooks .15 .40
76 LaMont Jordan .20 .50
77 Randy Moss .20 .50
78 Brian Westbrook .15 .40
79 Donovan McNabb .20 .50
80 Jabar Gaffney .15 .40
81 Hines Ward .20 .50
82 Ben Roethlisberger .30 .75
83 Willie Parker .20 .50
84 Antonio Gates .25 .60
85 LaDainian Tomlinson .25 .60
86 Philip Rivers .25 .60
87 Alex Smith QB .20 .50
88 Antonio Bryant .15 .40
89 Kevan Barlow .15 .40
90 Darrell Jackson .20 .50
91 Matt Hasselbeck .15 .40
92 Shaun Alexander .15 .40
93 Torry Holt .20 .50
94 Steven Jackson .15 .40
95 Cadillac Williams .20 .50
96 Joey Galloway .20 .50
97 David Givens .20 .50
98 Drew Bennett .20 .50
99 Antwaan Randle El .15 .40
100 Clinton Portis .15 .40
101 Kamerion Wimbley RC 1.25 3.00
102 Mathias Kiwanuka RC 1.50 4.00
103 Reggie McNeal RC 1.00 2.50
104 Claude Wroten RC 1.00 2.50
105 Gabe Watson RC 1.00 2.50
106 D'Qwell Jackson RC 1.00 2.50
107 Todd Watkins RC 1.00 2.50
108 Bennie Brazell RC 1.25 3.00
109 David Anderson RC 1.25 3.00
110 John David Washington RC 1.00 2.50
111 Marques Hagans RC 1.00 2.50
112 Kevin Youngblood RC 1.00 2.50
113 Ben Obomanu RC 1.25 3.00
114 Jamal Jones RC 1.00 2.50
115 Nick Mangold RC 1.25 3.00
116 Davin Joseph RC 1.25 3.00
117 Erik Meyer RC 1.00 2.50
118 Taurean Henderson RC 1.00 2.50
119 A.J. Nicholson RC 1.00 2.50
120 Thomas Howard RC 1.00 2.50
121 Jon Alston RC 1.00 2.50
122 Ashton Youboty RC 1.00 2.50
123 Alan Zemaitis RC 1.00 2.50
124 Lawrence Vickers RC 1.25 3.00
125 J.D. Runnels RC 1.25 3.00
126 Ray Perkins RC 1.25 3.00
127 Jeff King RC 1.25 3.00
128 Quinn Sypniewski RC 1.25 3.00
129 Jason Carter RC 1.25 3.00
130 Malcom Floyd RC 1.25 3.00
131 Mike Jennings RC 1.25 3.00
132 Chris Gocong RC 1.25 3.00
133 Frostee Rucker RC 1.25 3.00
134 Jason Hatcher RC 1.50 4.00
135 Victor Adeyanju RC 1.25 3.00
136 Elvis Dumervil RC 1.50 4.00
137 Ray Edwards RC 1.50 4.00
138 Anthony Schlegel RC 1.25 3.00
139 Freddie Keiaho RC 1.25 3.00
140 Gerris Wilkinson RC 1.00 2.50
141 Leon Williams RC 1.25 3.00
142 Stephen Tulloch RC 1.25 3.00
143 Jamar Williams RC 1.25 3.00
144 Clint Ingram RC 1.50 4.00
145 James Anderson RC 1.00 2.50
146 Darrell Hackney RC 1.25 3.00
147 Paul Pinegar RC 1.00 2.50
148 Brandon Kirsch RC 1.25 3.00
149 Andre Hall RC 1.25 3.00
150 De'Arrius Howard RC 1.50 4.00
151 Cedric Humes RC 1.00 2.50
152 Wendell Mathis RC 1.25 3.00
153 Gerald Riggs RC 1.25 3.00
154 Quinton Ganther RC 1.00 2.50
155 Martin Nance RC 1.00 2.50
156 Greg Lee RC 1.00 2.50
157 Jai Lewis RC 1.25 3.00
158 Cory Rodgers RC 1.00 2.50
159 Mike Espy RC 1.25 3.00
160 Chris Barclay RC 1.25 3.00
161 DeMeco Ryans RC 1.25 3.00
162 Rocky McIntosh RC 1.00 2.50
163 David Kirtman RC 1.25 3.00
164 Skyler Green RC 1.00 2.50
165 Will Blackmon RC 1.00 2.50
166 Darryl Tapp RC 1.25 3.00
167 Dusty Dvoracek RC 1.50 4.00
168 Richard Marshall RC 1.00 2.50
169 Tim Jennings RC 1.50 4.00
170 David Pittman RC 1.25 3.00
171 DeMario Minter RC 1.25 3.00
172 Marcus Maxey RC 1.25 3.00
173 Roman Harper RC 1.25 3.00
174 Anthony Smith RC 1.50 4.00
175 Nate Salley RC 1.25 3.00
176 Mike Hass RC 1.00 2.50
177 Greg Blue RC 1.25 3.00
178 Daniel Bullocks RC 1.00 2.50
179 Danieal Manning RC 1.50 4.00
180 Calvin Lowry RC 1.50 4.00
181 Eric Smith RC 1.25 3.00
182 Jimmy Williams RC 1.00 2.50
183 Cedric Griffin RC 1.25 3.00
184 Ko Simpson RC 1.25 3.00
185 Pat Watkins RC 1.25 3.00
186 Marcus Vick RC 1.00 2.50
187 Bernard Pollard RC 1.25 3.00
188 Darnell Bing RC 1.25 3.00
189 Cory Ross RC 1.50 4.00
190 Patrick Cobbs RC 1.25 3.00
191 Montell Owens RC 1.25 3.00
192 Chris Hannon RC 1.25 3.00
193 John Madsen RC 1.25 3.00
194 Shaun Bodiford RC 1.25 3.00
195 Fred Evans RC 1.25 3.00
196 Cletis Gordon RC .75 2.00
197 Jarrad Page RC 1.50 4.00
198 Brett Elliott RC 1.50 4.00
199 Brett Basanez RC 1.50 4.00
200 Drew Olson RC 1.00 2.50
201 Jay Cutler RC 1.50 4.00
202 Brodie Croyle RC 1.25 3.00
203 Ingle Martin RC 1.50 4.00
204 Derrick Ross RC 1.50 4.00
205 Bruce Gradkowski RC 1.50 4.00
206 D.J. Shockley RC 1.50 4.00
207 Joseph Addai RC 1.25 3.00
208 P.J. Daniels RC 1.25 3.00
209 Marques Colston RC 2.00 5.00
210 Jerome Harrison RC 1.25 3.00
211 Wali Lundy RC 1.25 3.00
212 Mike Bell RC 1.25 3.00
213 Miles Austin RC 1.50 4.00
214 Anthony Fasano RC 1.25 3.00
215 Tony Scheffler RC 2.00 5.00
216 Leonard Pope RC 2.00 5.00
217 David Thomas RC 1.25 3.00
218 Dominique Byrd RC 1.25 3.00
219 Garrett Mills RC 1.50 4.00
220 Hank Baskett RC 1.25 3.00
221 Greg Jennings RC 2.00 5.00
222 Devin Hester RC 2.50 6.00
223 Willie Reid RC 1.50 4.00
224 Brad Smith RC 1.50 4.00
225 Sam Hurd RC 1.25 3.00
226 Owen Daniels RC 2.00 5.00
227 Domenik Hixon RC 2.00 5.00
228 Jeremy Bloom RC 1.25 3.00
229 Dawan Landry RC 2.00 5.00
230 Jonathan Orr RC 1.50 4.00
231 Delanie Walker RC 2.50 6.00
232 Adam Jennings RC 1.50 4.00
233 Jeffrey Webb RC 1.50 4.00
234 Ethan Kilmer RC 1.50 4.00
235 Tye Hill RC 1.25 3.00
236 Jason Allen RC 1.50 4.00
237 Antonio Cromartie RC 1.50 4.00
238 D'Brickashaw Ferguson RC 1.25 3.00
239 Tamba Hali RC 2.00 5.00
240 Haloti Ngata RC 1.50 4.00
241 Brodrick Bunkley RC 1.50 4.00
242 John McCargo RC 1.25 3.00
243 Johnathan Joseph RC 1.50 4.00
244 Kelly Jennings RC 1.50 4.00
245 Donte Whitner RC 1.50 4.00
246 Abdul Hodge RC 1.25 3.00
247 Ernie Sims RC 1.25 3.00
248 Chad Greenway RC 2.00 5.00
249 Bobby Carpenter RC 1.25 3.00
250 Manny Lawson RC 1.50 4.00
251 Matt Leinart JSY/599 RC 2.00 5.00
252 Kellen Clemens JSY RC 1.50 4.00
253 Tarvaris Jackson JSY RC 1.50 4.00
254 Charlie Whitehurst JSY RC 1.50 4.00
255 DeAn.Williams JSY/599 RC 2.50 6.00
256 Maurice Drew JSY RC 2.50 6.00
257 Brian Calhoun JSY RC 1.50 4.00
258 Jerious Norwood JSY RC 1.50 4.00
259 Vernon Davis JSY RC 2.00 5.00
260 Joe Klopfenstein JSY RC 1.50 4.00
261 Sinorice Moss JSY RC 1.50 4.00
262 Derek Hagan JSY RC 2.00 5.00
263 Brandon Williams JSY RC 1.50 4.00
264 Michael Robinson JSY RC 1.50 4.00
265 Jason Avant JSY RC 1.50 4.00
266 Brandon Marshall JSY RC 3.00 8.00
267 Demetrius Williams JSY RC 1.50 4.00
268 Mario Williams JSY RC 2.50 6.00
269 Michael Huff JSY RC 2.00 5.00
270 Chad Jackson JSY RC 1.50 4.00
271 V.Young JSY AU/249 RC 6.00 15.00
272 Omar Jacobs JSY AU/449 RC 6.00 15.00
273 Reggie Bush JSY AU/99 RC 6.00 15.00
274 L.Maroney JSY AU/99 RC 15.00 40.00
275 L.White JSY AU/249 RC 15.00 40.00
276 Washington JSY AU/199 RC 12.00 30.00
277 M.Lewis JSY AU/449 RC 4.00 10.00
278 S.Holmes JSY AU/449 RC 12.00 30.00
279 Travis Wilson JSY AU/449 RC 4.00 10.00
280 M.Stovall JSY AU/99 RC 5.00 12.00
281 A.J. Hawk JSY AU/99 RC 12.00 30.00

2006 Leaf Rookies and Stars Gold

ETERANS 1-100: 2X TO 5X BASIC CARDS
*ROOKIES 101-200: 1X TO 2.5X BASIC CARDS
*ROOKIES 201-250: .8X TO 2X BASIC CARDS
STATED PRINT RUN 299 SER.#'d SETS

2006 Leaf Rookies and Stars Longevity Black Parallel

*VETS 1-100: 10X TO 25X BASIC CARDS
VETERANS PRINT RUN 25 SER.#'d SETS
UNPRICED ROOKIE 101-250 PRINT RUN 10
UNPRICED ROOKIE JSY PRINT RUN 10

2006 Leaf Rookies and Stars Longevity Gold Parallel

*VETS 1-100: 6X TO 15X BASIC CARDS
VETERANS PRINT RUN 49 SER.#'d SETS
*ROOKIES 101-200: 2.5X TO 6X BASIC CARDS
*ROOKIES 201-250: 2X TO 5X BASIC CARDS
101-250 PRINT RUN 25 SER.#'d SETS
*JSY ROOKIES 251-270: 1X TO 2.5X
JSY ROOKIES PRINT RUN 25 SER.#'d SETS

2006 Leaf Rookies and Stars Longevity Holofoil Parallel

*VETS 1-100: 4X TO 10X BASIC CARDS
VETERANS PRINT RUN 99 SER.#'d SETS
*ROOKIES 101-250: 1.5X TO 4X BASIC CARDS
*ROOKIES 201-250: 1.2X TO 3X BASIC CARDS
101-250 PRINT RUN 49 SER.#'d SETS
*JSY ROOKIES 251-270: .6X TO 1.5X
JSY ROOKIES PRINT RUN 50 SER.#'d SETS

2006 Leaf Rookies and Stars Longevity Silver Parallel

*VETS 1-100: 2.5X TO 6X BASIC CARDS
VETERANS PRINT RUN 199 SER.#'d SETS
*ROOKIES 101-200: 1.2X TO 3X BASIC CARDS
*ROOKIES 201-250: 1X TO 2.5X BASIC CARDS
101-250 PRINT RUN 99 SER.#'d SETS
*JSY ROOKIES 251-270: .5X TO 1.2X
JSY ROOKIES PRINT RUN 100 SER.#'d SETS

2006 Leaf Rookies and Stars 1948 Leaf Blue

*ORANGE: .5X TO 1.2X BASIC INSERTS
*YELLOW: .8X TO 2X BASIC INSERTS
INSERTS IN WALMART BLASTER BOXES
1 Vince Young .75 2.00
2 LenDale White .75 2.00
3 Reggie Bush 1.25 3.00
4 Matt Leinart .75 2.00
5 Michael Robinson .75 2.00
6 Vernon Davis 1.00 2.50
7 Chad Jackson .75 2.00
8 Tarvaris Jackson .75 2.00
9 Jason Avant .75 2.00
10 Brandon Marshall 1.50 4.00
11 Santonio Holmes 1.00 2.50
12 Jerious Norwood .75 2.00
13 Sinorice Moss .75 2.00
14 Leon Washington .75 2.00
15 Charlie Whitehurst .75 2.00
16 Travis Wilson .75 2.00
17 Joe Klopfenstein .75 2.00
18 Brian Calhoun .75 2.00
19 Mario Williams 1.25 3.00
20 Maurice Stovall .75 2.00
21 Brodie Croyle .75 2.00
22 Greg Jennings 1.25 3.00
23 Demetrius Williams .75 2.00
24 A.J. Hawk 1.00 2.50
25 Omar Jacobs .75 2.00
26 Brandon Williams .75 2.00
27 Kellen Clemens .75 2.00
28 Maurice Drew 1.25 3.00
29 Michael Huff 1.00 2.50
30 Jay Cutler 1.00 2.50
31 Laurence Maroney .75 2.00
32 Derek Hagan 1.00 2.50
33 Joseph Addai .75 2.00
34 DeAngelo Williams 1.00 2.50
35 Marcedes Lewis .75 2.00

2006 Leaf Rookies and Stars Cross Training Red

D PRINT RUN 1000 SER.#'d SETS
*BLUE/500: .5X TO 1.2X RED/1000
BLUE PRINT RUN 500 SER.#'d SETS
*GREEN/100: .8X TO 2X RED/1000
GREEN PRINT RUN 100 SER.#'d SETS
*PURPLE/25: 1.5X TO 4X RED/1000
PURPLE PRINT RUN 25 SER.#'d SETS
1 Laurence Maroney .50 1.25
2 Brandon Marshall 1.00 2.50
3 Santonio Holmes .60 1.50
4 DeAngelo Williams .60 1.50
5 Leon Washington .50 1.25
6 Mario Williams .75 2.00
7 LenDale White .50 1.25
8 Brian Calhoun .50 1.25
9 Charlie Whitehurst .50 1.25
10 Kellen Clemens .50 1.25
11 A.J. Hawk .60 1.50
12 Joe Klopfenstein .50 1.25
13 Maurice Drew .75 2.00
14 Omar Jacobs .50 1.25
15 Jason Avant .50 1.25
16 Matt Leinart .50 1.25
17 Marcedes Lewis .50 1.25
18 Jerious Norwood .50 1.25
19 Demetrius Williams .50 1.25
20 Vince Young .50 1.25
21 Brandon Williams .50 1.25
22 Maurice Stovall .50 1.25
23 Sinorice Moss .50 1.25
24 Michael Huff .60 1.50
25 Reggie Bush .75 2.00
26 Michael Robinson .50 1.25
27 Chad Jackson .50 1.25
28 Derek Hagan .60 1.50
29 Vernon Davis .60 1.50

2006 Leaf Rookies and Stars Cross Training Materials

STATED PRINT RUN 125 SER.#'d SETS
*PRIME/25: .6X TO 1.5X BASIC INSERTS
PRIME PRINT RUN 25 SER.#'d SETS
1 Laurence Maroney 1.25 3.00
2 Brandon Marshall 3.00 8.00
3 Santonio Holmes 1.50 4.00
4 DeAngelo Williams 1.50 4.00
5 Leon Washington 3.00 8.00
6 Mario Williams 2.00 5.00
7 LenDale White 4.00 10.00
8 Brian Calhoun 2.50 6.00
9 Charlie Whitehurst 2.50 6.00
10 Kellen Clemens 3.00 8.00
11 A.J. Hawk 6.00 15.00
12 Joe Klopfenstein 2.50 6.00
13 Maurice Drew 5.00 12.00
14 Omar Jacobs 2.50 6.00
15 Jason Avant 1.25 3.00
16 Matt Leinart 1.25 3.00
17 Marcedes Lewis 2.50 6.00
18 Jerious Norwood 3.00 8.00
19 Demetrius Williams 2.50 6.00
20 Vince Young 1.25 3.00
21 Brandon Williams 2.50 6.00
22 Maurice Stovall 2.50 6.00
23 Sinorice Moss 2.50 6.00
24 Michael Huff 1.50 4.00
25 Reggie Bush 2.00 5.00
26 Michael Robinson 2.50 6.00
27 Chad Jackson 2.50 6.00
28 Derek Hagan 2.50 6.00
29 Vernon Davis 1.50 4.00

2006 Leaf Rookies and Stars Crusade Red

RED PRINT RUN 1000 SER.#'d SETS
*BLUE/500: .5X TO 1.2X RED/1000
BLUE PRINT RUN 500 SER.#'d SETS
*GREEN/100: 1X TO 2.5X RED/1000
GREEN PRINT RUN 100 SER.#'d SETS
*PURPLE/25: 1.5X TO 4X RED/1000
PURPLE PRINT RUN 25 SER.#'d SETS

UNPRICED AUTO PRINT RUN 1-5
1 Ben Roethlisberger 1.50 4.00
2 Brett Favre 2.50 6.00
3 LaDainian Tomlinson 1.25 3.00
4 Michael Vick 1.00 2.50
5 Peyton Manning 3.00 8.00
6 Chad Johnson .75 2.00
7 Eli Manning 1.00 2.50
8 Marvin Harrison 1.00 2.50
9 Steve Smith 1.25 3.00
10 Shaun Alexander .75 2.00
11 Philip Rivers 1.25 3.00
12 Willie Parker 1.00 2.50
13 Tom Brady 4.00 10.00
14 Donovan McNabb 1.00 2.50
15 Larry Johnson .75 2.00

2006 Leaf Rookies and Stars Crusade Materials

ATED PRINT RUN 250 SER.#'d SETS
*PRIME/25: 1X TO 2.5X JSY/250
PRIME PRINT RUN 25 SER.#'d SETS
1 Ben Roethlisberger 6.00 15.00
2 Brett Favre 8.00 20.00
3 LaDainian Tomlinson 4.00 10.00
4 Michael Vick 4.00 10.00
5 Peyton Manning 6.00 15.00
6 Chad Johnson 3.00 8.00
7 Eli Manning 5.00 12.00
8 Marvin Harrison 4.00 10.00
9 Steve Smith 4.00 10.00
10 Shaun Alexander/200 4.00 10.00
11 Philip Rivers 4.00 10.00
12 Willie Parker 3.00 8.00
13 Tom Brady 12.00 30.00
14 Donovan McNabb 4.00 10.00
15 Larry Johnson 4.00 10.00

2006 Leaf Rookies and Stars Dress for Success Jerseys

BASE JSY PRINT RUN 100 SER.#'d SETS
*PRIME/25: .6X TO 1.5X JSY/100
PRIME PRINT RUN 25 SER.#'d SETS
*SHOES/115: .4X TO 1X BASIC JSYs
SHOE PRINT RUN 115 SER.#'d SETS
*HELMET/110: .5X TO 1.2X JSY/100
HELMET PRINT RUN 110 SER.#'d SETS
*FACE MASK/335-350: .4X TO 1X JSY/100
PRINT RUN 335-350 SER.#'d SETS
UNPRICED JSY AU PRINT RUN 10
UNPRICED PRIME AU PRINT RUN 5
1 Demetrius Williams 2.50 6.00
2 Leon Washington 1.25 3.00
3 A.J. Hawk 6.00 15.00
4 Brian Calhoun 2.50 6.00
5 Omar Jacobs 2.50 6.00
6 Reggie Bush 10.00 25.00
7 Michael Robinson 2.50 6.00
8 Brandon Williams 2.50 6.00
9 Jason Avant 1.25 3.00
10 Jerious Norwood 3.00 8.00
11 Kellen Clemens 3.00 8.00
12 Sinorice Moss 2.50 6.00
13 Maurice Stovall 2.50 6.00
14 Mario Williams 2.00 5.00
15 Maurice Drew 5.00 12.00
16 LenDale White 4.00 10.00
17 Matt Leinart 4.00 10.00
18 Vernon Davis 1.50 4.00
19 Derek Hagan 2.50 6.00
20 Brandon Marshall 3.00 8.00
21 Santonio Holmes 1.50 4.00
22 DeAngelo Williams 6.00 15.00
23 Joe Klopfenstein 2.50 6.00
24 Charlie Whitehurst 2.50 6.00
25 Travis Wilson 2.50 6.00
26 Marcedes Lewis 2.50 6.00
27 Chad Jackson 2.50 6.00
28 Vince Young 1.25 3.00
29 Michael Huff 1.50 4.00
30 Tarvaris Jackson 1.25 3.00
31 Laurence Maroney 1.25 3.00

2006 Leaf Rookies and Stars Elements

*FOIL: .6X TO 1.5X BASIC INSERTS
*HOLOFOIL: .8X TO 2X BASIC INSERTS
1 Ben Roethlisberger 2.00 5.00
2 Zach Thomas 1.25 3.00
3 Troy Polamalu 1.50 4.00
4 Tedy Bruschi 1.25 3.00
5 Ray Lewis 1.50 4.00
6 Tom Brady 5.00 12.00
7 Chad Johnson 1.00 2.50
8 Fred Taylor 1.00 2.50
9 Byron Leftwich 1.00 2.50
10 Rudi Johnson 1.00 2.50
11 Chad Pennington 1.00 2.50
12 Hines Ward 1.25 3.00
13 Brian Urlacher 1.50 4.00
14 Peyton Manning 4.00 10.00
15 LaDainian Tomlinson 1.50 4.00
16 Shaun Alexander 1.00 2.50
17 Trent Green 1.00 2.50
18 Curtis Martin 1.25 3.00
19 Willis McGahee 1.00 2.50

2006 Leaf Rookies and Stars Elements Materials

STATED PRINT RUN 250 SER.#'d SETS
*FOIL/100: .5X TO 1.2X JSY/250
FOIL PRINT RUN 100 SER.#'d SETS
*HOLOFOIL/25: 1X TO 2.5X JSY/250
HOLOFOIL PRINT RUN 25 SER.#'d SETS
1 Ben Roethlisberger 6.00 15.00
2 Zach Thomas 4.00 10.00
3 Troy Polamalu 4.00 10.00
4 Tedy Bruschi 4.00 10.00
5 Ray Lewis 4.00 10.00
6 Tom Brady 6.00 15.00
7 Chad Johnson 3.00 8.00
8 Fred Taylor 3.00 8.00
9 Byron Leftwich 3.00 8.00
10 Rudi Johnson 3.00 8.00
11 Chad Pennington 3.00 8.00
12 Hines Ward 4.00 10.00
13 Brian Urlacher 4.00 10.00
14 Peyton Manning 6.00 15.00
15 LaDainian Tomlinson 4.00 10.00
16 Shaun Alexander 4.00 10.00
17 Trent Green 3.00 8.00
18 Curtis Martin 4.00 10.00
19 Willis McGahee 4.00 10.00

2006 Leaf Rookies and Stars Freshman Orientation Materials Jerseys

STATED PRINT RUN 125 SER.#'d SETS
*PRIME/25: .6X TO 1.5X JSY/125
PRIME PRINT RUN 25 SER.#'d SETS
*FOOTBALL/150-175: .4X TO 1X JSY/125
FOOTBALLS PRINT RUN 150-175
UNPRICED JSY AU PRINT RUN 10
UNPRICED JSY PRIME AU PRINT RUN 5
1 DeAngelo Williams 1.50 4.00
2 Reggie Bush 2.00 5.00
3 LenDale White 4.00 10.00
4 Charlie Whitehurst 3.00 8.00
5 Travis Wilson 2.50 6.00
6 Vince Young 1.25 3.00
7 Brandon Marshall 3.00 8.00
8 Joe Klopfenstein 2.50 6.00
9 Mario Williams 2.00 5.00
10 Omar Jacobs 2.50 6.00
11 Michael Huff 1.50 4.00
12 Sinorice Moss 2.50 6.00
13 Brian Calhoun 2.50 6.00
14 Demetrius Williams 2.50 6.00
15 Brandon Williams 3.00 8.00
16 Maurice Drew 4.00 10.00
17 Derek Hagan 2.50 6.00
18 Jerious Norwood 3.00 8.00
19 Leon Washington 1.25 3.00
20 Kellen Clemens 3.00 8.00
21 Santonio Holmes 1.50 4.00
22 Jason Avant 1.25 3.00
23 A.J. Hawk 6.00 15.00
24 Maurice Stovall 2.50 6.00
25 Vernon Davis 1.50 4.00
26 Marcedes Lewis 2.50 6.00
27 Tarvaris Jackson 1.25 3.00
28 Laurence Maroney 1.25 3.00
29 Chad Jackson 2.50 6.00
30 Michael Robinson 2.50 6.00
31 Matt Leinart 1.25 3.00

2006 Leaf Rookies and Stars Materials Gold

*LONG.GOLD/250: .5X TO 1.2X BASIC JSYs
LONG.GOLD PRINT RUN 250 SER.#'d SETS
*LONG.BLACK/25: 1.2X TO 3X BASIC JSYs
LONG.BLACK PRINT RUN 25 SER.#'d SETS
1 Anquan Boldin 2.50 6.00
3 Kurt Warner 2.50 6.00
4 Larry Fitzgerald 3.00 8.00
5 Alge Crumpler 2.50 6.00
6 Michael Vick 3.00 8.00
7 Warrick Dunn 2.50 6.00
11 Josh Reed 2.00 5.00
12 Lee Evans 2.50 6.00
13 Willis McGahee 3.00 8.00
14 DeShaun Foster 2.50 6.00
15 Jake Delhomme 2.50 6.00
17 Steve Smith 3.00 8.00
18 Cedric Benson 3.00 8.00
20 Rex Grossman 3.00 8.00
21 Carson Palmer 3.00 8.00
25 Charlie Frye 3.00 8.00
27 Reuben Droughns 2.50 6.00
28 Drew Bledsoe 3.00 8.00
29 Julius Jones 3.00 8.00
31 Terry Glenn 2.50 6.00
32 Jake Plummer 2.50 6.00
33 Rod Smith 2.50 6.00
34 Tatum Bell 2.50 6.00
36 Kevin Jones 3.00 8.00
37 Roy Williams WR 3.00 8.00
38 Ahman Green 2.50 6.00
39 Brett Favre 6.00 15.00
40 Donald Driver 2.50 6.00
41 Robert Ferguson 2.00 5.00
42 Samkon Gado 3.00 8.00
43 Andre Johnson 2.50 6.00
44 David Carr 2.50 6.00
45 Domanick Davis 2.50 6.00
47 Marvin Harrison 3.00 8.00
48 Peyton Manning 5.00 12.00
49 Reggie Wayne 2.50 6.00
50 Dallas Clark 2.00 5.00
51 Fred Taylor 2.50 6.00
52 Byron Leftwich 2.50 6.00
53 Jimmy Smith 2.50 6.00
54 Larry Johnson 3.00 8.00
57 Eddie Kennison 2.00 5.00
58 Chris Chambers 2.50 6.00
60 Ronnie Brown 3.00 8.00
63 Deion Branch 2.50 6.00
64 Corey Dillon 2.50 6.00
65 Tom Brady 5.00 12.00
69 Eli Manning 4.00 10.00
71 Tiki Barber 3.00 8.00
72 Chad Pennington 2.50 6.00
73 Curtis Martin 3.00 8.00
74 Laveranues Coles 2.50 6.00
76 LaMont Jordan 2.50 6.00
78 Brian Westbrook 2.50 6.00
79 Donovan McNabb 3.00 8.00
81 Hines Ward 3.00 8.00
82 Ben Roethlisberger 5.00 12.00
83 Willie Parker 2.50 6.00
84 Antonio Gates 3.00 8.00
85 LaDainian Tomlinson 3.00 8.00
86 Philip Rivers 3.00 8.00
87 Alex Smith QB 3.00 8.00
90 Darrell Jackson 2.50 6.00
91 Matt Hasselbeck 2.50 6.00
92 Shaun Alexander 3.00 8.00
93 Torry Holt 2.50 6.00
94 Steven Jackson 3.00 8.00
95 Cadillac Williams 2.50 6.00
96 Joey Galloway 2.50 6.00
98 Drew Bennett 2.00 5.00
100 Clinton Portis 3.00 8.00

2006 Leaf Rookies and Stars NFL Kickoff Classic

1 Brett Favre 3.00 8.00
2 Ben Roethlisberger 2.00 5.00
3 Peyton Manning 4.00 10.00
4 Tom Brady 5.00 12.00
5 Eli Manning 1.25 3.00
6 Shaun Alexander 1.00 2.50
7 LaDainian Tomlinson 1.50 4.00
8 Larry Johnson 1.00 2.50
9 Ronnie Brown 1.25 3.00
10 Cadillac Williams 1.25 3.00

2006 Leaf Rookies and Stars Rookie Material Autographs

STATED PRINT RUN 25-85
UNPRICED LONG.HOLOFOIL PRINT RUN 10
UNPRICED LONG.GOLD PRINT RUN 5
UNPRICED BLACK PRIME PRINT RUN 1
251 Matt Leinart/85 20.00 50.00
252 Kellen Clemens/25 6.00 15.00
253 Tarvaris Jackson/25 6.00 15.00
254 Charlie Whitehurst/25 6.00 15.00
255 DeAngelo Williams/25 30.00 80.00
256 Maurice Drew/85 25.00 60.00
257 Brian Calhoun/25 6.00 15.00
258 Jerious Norwood/25 6.00 15.00
259 Vernon Davis/25 8.00 20.00
260 Joe Klopfenstein/85 5.00 12.00
261 Sinorice Moss/25 6.00 15.00
262 Derek Hagan/85 6.00 15.00
263 Brandon Williams/25 6.00 15.00
264 Michael Robinson/25 6.00 15.00
265 Jason Avant/85 5.00 12.00
266 Brandon Marshall/25 12.00 30.00
267 Demetrius Williams/25 6.00 15.00
268 Mario Williams/25 10.00 25.00
269 Michael Huff/25 8.00 20.00
270 Chad Jackson/85 5.00 12.00

2006 Leaf Rookies and Stars Rookie Material Autographs Longevity

LONGEVITY PRINT RUN 15-25 SER.#'d SETS
271 Vince Young/25 25.00 60.00
272 Omar Jacobs/25 8.00 20.00
273 Reggie Bush/25 20.00 50.00
274 Laurence Maroney/25 20.00 50.00
275 LenDale White/25 20.00 50.00
276 Leon Washington/25 20.00 50.00
277 Marcedes Lewis/25 8.00 20.00
278 Santonio Holmes/25 30.00 60.00
279 Travis Wilson/25 8.00 20.00
280 Maurice Stovall/25 8.00 20.00
281 A.J. Hawk/25 40.00 80.00

2006 Leaf Rookies and Stars Prime Cuts

STATED PRINT RUN 50 SER.#'d SETS
*COMBO/25: .6X TO 1.5X PRIME CUT/50
COMBO PRINT RUN 25 SER.#'d SETS
1 Alge Crumpler 6.00 15.00
2 Antonio Gates 8.00 20.00
3 Peyton Manning 12.00 30.00
4 Chad Johnson 6.00 15.00
5 Julius Jones 8.00 20.00
6 Shaun Alexander 8.00 20.00
7 Marvin Harrison 8.00 20.00
8 Larry Johnson 8.00 20.00
9 Torry Holt 6.00 15.00
10 Curtis Martin 8.00 20.00
11 Tom Brady 12.00 30.00
12 Anquan Boldin 6.00 15.00
13 Michael Vick 8.00 20.00

2006 Leaf Rookies and Stars Rookie Autographs Longevity

STATED PRINT RUN 15-50 SETS
*HOLOFOIL/19-25: .6X TO 1.5X BASIC AU/50
HOLOFOIL PRINT RUN 7-25 SER.#'d SETS
SER.#'d UNDER 25 NOT PRICED
103 Reggie McNeal/25 6.00 15.00
104 Claude Wroten 4.00 10.00
105 Gabe Watson 4.00 10.00
107 Todd Watkins 4.00 10.00
108 Bennie Brazell 5.00 12.00
109 David Anderson 5.00 12.00
110 John David Washington 4.00 10.00
111 Marques Hagans/25 6.00 15.00
117 Erik Meyer 4.00 10.00
118 Taurean Henderson 4.00 10.00
119 A.J. Nicholson 4.00 10.00
122 Ashton Youboty 4.00 10.00
123 Alan Zemaitis 4.00 10.00
146 Darrell Hackney 5.00 12.00
147 Paul Pinegar 4.00 10.00
148 Brandon Kirsch/40 5.00 12.00
149 Andre Hall 5.00 12.00
151 Cedric Humes/25 6.00 15.00
152 Wendell Mathis/45 5.00 12.00
153 Gerald Riggs 5.00 12.00
154 Quinton Ganther/25 6.00 15.00
155 Martin Nance/25 6.00 15.00
156 Greg Lee/25 6.00 15.00
157 Jai Lewis 5.00 12.00
158 Cory Rodgers 4.00 10.00
161 DeMeco Ryans 5.00 12.00
162 Rocky McIntosh 4.00 10.00
163 David Kirtman 5.00 12.00
164 Skyler Green 4.00 10.00
165 Will Blackmon 4.00 10.00
166 Darryl Tapp 5.00 12.00
167 Dusty Dvoracek 6.00 15.00
168 Richard Marshall 4.00 10.00
169 Tim Jennings 6.00 15.00
170 David Pittman 5.00 12.00
171 DeMario Minter 5.00 12.00
172 Marcus Maxey 5.00 12.00
173 Roman Harper 5.00 12.00
174 Anthony Smith 6.00 15.00
175 Nate Salley 5.00 12.00
176 Mike Hass 4.00 10.00
177 Greg Blue 5.00 12.00
178 Daniel Bullocks 4.00 10.00
179 Danieal Manning 6.00 15.00
180 Calvin Lowry 6.00 15.00
181 Eric Smith 5.00 12.00
182 Jimmy Williams 4.00 10.00
183 Cedric Griffin 5.00 12.00
184 Ko Simpson 5.00 12.00
185 Pat Watkins 5.00 12.00
187 Bernard Pollard 5.00 12.00
188 Darnell Bing/34 5.00 12.00
201 Jay Cutler/25 8.00 20.00
202 Brodie Croyle/25 6.00 15.00
203 Ingle Martin/25 8.00 20.00
204 Derrick Ross 5.00 12.00
205 Bruce Gradkowski/25 8.00 20.00
206 D.J. Shockley/25 8.00 20.00
207 Joseph Addai/25 6.00 15.00
208 P.J. Daniels/25 6.00 15.00
209 Marques Colston 6.00 15.00
210 Jerome Harrison/25 6.00 15.00
211 Wali Lundy/25 6.00 15.00
212 Mike Bell/40 4.00 10.00
213 Miles Austin/25 20.00 50.00
214 Anthony Fasano 4.00 10.00
215 Tony Scheffler 6.00 15.00
216 Leonard Pope 6.00 15.00
217 David Thomas 4.00 10.00
218 Dominique Byrd 4.00 10.00
219 Garrett Mills 5.00 12.00
220 Hank Baskett 4.00 10.00
221 Greg Jennings 6.00 15.00
222 Devin Hester 8.00 20.00
223 Willie Reid 5.00 12.00
224 Brad Smith 5.00 12.00
225 Sam Hurd 4.00 10.00
226 Owen Daniels 6.00 15.00
227 Domenik Hixon 6.00 15.00
228 Jeremy Bloom 4.00 10.00
229 Dawan Landry 6.00 15.00
230 Jonathan Orr 5.00 12.00
231 Delanie Walker 8.00 20.00
232 Adam Jennings 5.00 12.00
233 Jeffrey Webb 5.00 12.00
234 Ethan Kilmer 5.00 12.00
235 Tye Hill 4.00 10.00
236 Jason Allen 5.00 12.00
237 Antonio Cromartie 5.00 12.00
238 D'Brickashaw Ferguson 4.00 10.00
239 Tamba Hali 6.00 15.00
240 Haloti Ngata 5.00 12.00
241 Brodrick Bunkley 5.00 12.00
242 John McCargo 4.00 10.00
243 Johnathan Joseph 5.00 12.00
244 Kelly Jennings 5.00 12.00
245 Donte Whitner 5.00 12.00
246 Abdul Hodge 4.00 10.00
247 Ernie Sims 4.00 10.00
248 Chad Greenway 6.00 15.00
249 Bobby Carpenter 4.00 10.00
250 Manny Lawson 5.00 12.00

2006 Leaf Rookies and Stars Rookie Crusade Red

RED PRINT RUN 1000 SER.#'d SETS
*BLUE/500: .5X TO 1.2X RD/1000
BLUE PRINT RUN 500 SER.#'d SETS
*GREEN/100: .8X TO 2X RED/1000
GREEN PRINT RUN 100 SER.#'d SETS
*PURPLE/25: 1.5X TO 4X RED/1000
PURPLE PRINT RUN 25 SER.#'d SETS
1 Chad Jackson .50 1.25
2 Laurence Maroney .50 1.25
3 Tarvaris Jackson .50 1.25
4 Michael Huff .60 1.50
5 Mario Williams .75 2.00
6 Marcedes Lewis .50 1.25
7 Maurice Drew .75 2.00
8 Vince Young .50 1.25
9 LenDale White .50 1.25
10 Reggie Bush .75 2.00
11 Matt Leinart .50 1.25
12 Michael Robinson .50 1.25
13 Vernon Davis .60 1.50
14 Brandon Williams .50 1.25
15 Derek Hagan .60 1.50
16 Jason Avant .50 1.25
17 Brandon Marshall 1.00 2.50
18 Omar Jacobs .50 1.25
19 Santonio Holmes .60 1.50
20 Jerious Norwood .50 1.25
21 Demetrius Williams .50 1.25
22 Sinorice Moss .50 1.25
23 Leon Washington .50 1.25
24 Kellen Clemens .50 1.25
25 A.J. Hawk .60 1.50
26 Maurice Stovall .50 1.25
27 DeAngelo Williams .60 1.50
28 Charlie Whitehurst .50 1.25
29 Travis Wilson .50 1.25
30 Joe Klopfenstein .50 1.25
31 Brian Calhoun .50 1.25

2006 Leaf Rookies and Stars Rookie Crusade Materials

STATED PRINT RUN 175 SER.#'d SETS
*PRIME/25: .6X TO 1.5X JSY/175
PRIME PRINT RUN 25 SER.#'d SETS
1 Chad Jackson 2.50 6.00
2 Laurence Maroney 1.25 3.00
3 Tarvaris Jackson 3.00 8.00
4 Michael Huff 3.00 8.00
5 Mario Williams 2.00 5.00
6 Marcedes Lewis 2.50 6.00
7 Maurice Drew 5.00 12.00
8 Vince Young 1.25 3.00
9 LenDale White 4.00 10.00
10 Reggie Bush 2.00 5.00
11 Matt Leinart 1.25 3.00
12 Michael Robinson 2.50 6.00
13 Vernon Davis 1.50 4.00
14 Brandon Williams 2.50 6.00
15 Derek Hagan 2.50 6.00
16 Jason Avant 2.50 6.00
17 Brandon Marshall 2.50 6.00
18 Omar Jacobs 2.50 6.00
19 Santonio Holmes 4.00 10.00
20 Jerious Norwood 3.00 8.00
21 Demetrius Williams 2.50 6.00
22 Sinorice Moss 2.50 6.00
23 Leon Washington 1.25 3.00
24 Kellen Clemens 3.00 8.00
25 A.J. Hawk 6.00 15.00
26 Maurice Stovall 2.50 6.00
27 DeAngelo Williams 1.50 4.00
28 Charlie Whitehurst 2.50 6.00
29 Travis Wilson 2.50 6.00
30 Joe Klopfenstein 2.50 6.00
31 Brian Calhoun 2.50 6.00

2006 Leaf Rookies and Stars Standing Ovation Red

RED/1000 PRINT RUN 1000 SER.#'d SETS
*BLUE/500: .5X TO 1.2X RED/1000
BLUE PRINT RUN 500 SER.#'d SETS
*GREEN/100: 1X TO 2.5X RED/1000
GREEN PRINT RUN 100 SER.#'d SETS
*PURPLE/25: 1.5X TO 4X RED/1000
PURPLE PRINT RUN 25 SER.#'d SETS
1 Alex Smith QB 1.00 2.50
2 Brian Urlacher 1.25 3.00
3 Chris Brown .75 2.00
4 Darrell Jackson 1.00 2.50
5 Domanick Davis .75 2.00
6 Jerry Porter .75 2.00
7 Jevon Kearse .75 2.00
8 LaMont Jordan 1.00 2.50
9 Lee Evans 1.00 2.50
10 Mark Clayton .75 2.00
11 Marc Bulger .75 2.00
12 Reggie Brown .75 2.00
13 Reggie Wayne 1.00 2.50
14 Roy Williams S .75 2.00
15 Rudi Johnson .75 2.00
16 T.J. Houshmandzadeh .75 2.00
17 Tedy Bruschi 1.00 2.50
18 Willis McGahee .75 2.00
19 Torry Holt 1.00 2.50
20 Alge Crumpler 1.00 2.50
21 Andre Johnson 1.00 2.50
22 Zach Thomas 1.00 2.50
23 Warrick Dunn .75 2.00
24 Priest Holmes .75 2.00
25 Derrick Mason .75 2.00

2006 Leaf Rookies and Stars Standing Ovation Autographs

ATED PRINT RUN 25 SER.#'d SETS
SER.#'d UNDER 25 NOT PRICED
5 Domanick Davis 8.00 20.00
7 Jevon Kearse 8.00 20.00
8 LaMont Jordan 8.00 20.00
12 Reggie Brown 8.00 20.00
13 Reggie Wayne 12.00 30.00
14 Roy Williams S 12.00 30.00
15 Rudi Johnson 15.00 40.00
16 T.J. Houshmandzadeh 12.00 30.00
17 Tedy Bruschi 40.00 80.00
18 Willis McGahee 12.00 30.00

2006 Leaf Rookies and Stars Standing Ovation Materials

STATED PRINT RUN 250 SER.#'d SETS
*PRIME/25: 1X TO 2.5X JSY/250
PRIME PRINT RUN 25 SER.#'d SETS
1 Alex Smith QB 5.00 12.00
2 Brian Urlacher 4.00 10.00
3 Chris Brown 3.00 8.00
4 Darrell Jackson 3.00 8.00
5 Domanick Davis 3.00 8.00
6 Jerry Porter 3.00 8.00
7 Jevon Kearse 3.00 8.00
8 LaMont Jordan 3.00 8.00
9 Lee Evans 3.00 8.00
10 Mark Clayton 3.00 8.00
11 Marc Bulger 3.00 8.00
12 Reggie Brown 3.00 8.00
13 Reggie Wayne 3.00 8.00
14 Roy Williams S 3.00 8.00
15 Rudi Johnson 3.00 8.00
16 T.J. Houshmandzadeh 3.00 8.00
17 Tedy Bruschi 4.00 10.00
18 Willis McGahee 4.00 10.00
19 Torry Holt 3.00 8.00
20 Alge Crumpler 3.00 8.00
21 Andre Johnson 3.00 8.00
22 Zach Thomas 4.00 10.00
23 Warrick Dunn 3.00 8.00
24 Priest Holmes 3.00 8.00
25 Derrick Mason 2.50 6.00

2006 Leaf Rookies and Stars Statistical Standouts Autographs

UNPRICED AUTO PRINT RUN 2-10

2006 Leaf Rookies and Stars Statistical Standouts Materials

STATED PRINT RUN 250 SER.#'d SETS
*PRIME/25: 1X TO 2.5X JSY/250
PRIME PRINT RUN 25 SER.#'d SETS
1 Tom Brady 6.00 15.00
2 Trent Green 3.00 8.00
3 Brett Favre 8.00 20.00
4 Carson Palmer 4.00 10.00
5 Eli Manning 5.00 12.00
6 Peyton Manning 6.00 15.00
7 Drew Bledsoe 4.00 10.00
8 Matt Hasselbeck 3.00 8.00
9 Jake Delhomme 3.00 8.00
10 Steve Smith 4.00 10.00
11 Santana Moss 3.00 8.00
12 Chad Johnson 3.00 8.00
13 Larry Fitzgerald 4.00 10.00
14 Torry Holt 3.00 8.00
15 Joey Galloway 3.00 8.00
16 Marvin Harrison 4.00 10.00
17 Shaun Alexander 4.00 10.00
18 Tiki Barber 4.00 10.00
19 Larry Johnson 4.00 10.00
20 Clinton Portis 4.00 10.00
21 LaDainian Tomlinson 4.00 10.00
22 Rudi Johnson 3.00 8.00
23 Warrick Dunn 3.00 8.00
24 Willie Parker 3.00 8.00
25 Chris Chambers 3.00 8.00

2006 Leaf Rookies and Stars Statistical Standouts Material Autographs Prime

PRIME PRINT RUN 4-27 SER.#'d SETS
UNPRICED JSY AU PRINT RUN 5-20
SER.#'d UNDER 25 NOT PRICED
11 Santana Moss/25 12.00 30.00
12 Chad Johnson/25 12.00 30.00
16 Marvin Harrison/25 25.00 50.00
17 Shaun Alexander/25 15.00 40.00
18 Tiki Barber/21
19 Larry Johnson/27 20.00 50.00
20 Clinton Portis/26 15.00 40.00
21 LaDainian Tomlinson/21 25.00 60.00
24 Willie Parker/25 15.00 40.00
25 Chris Chambers/25 12.00 30.00

2006 Leaf Rookies and Stars Longevity Target

MP.SET w/o RC's (100) 8.00 20.00
*VETERANS 1-100: .4X TO 1X BASIC CARDS
*ROOKIES/999 101-200: .4X TO 1X
101-200 PRINT RUN 999 SER.#'d SETS
*ROOKIES/599 201-250: .4X TO 1X
201-250 PRINT RUN 599 SER.#'d SETS

2006 Leaf Rookies and Stars Longevity Target Emerald Parallel

*VETS 1-100: 6X TO 15X BASIC CARDS
VETERANS PRINT RUN 49 SER.#'d SETS
*ROOKIES 101-200: 2.5X TO 6X BASIC CARDS
*ROOKIES 201-250: 2X TO 5X BASIC CARDS
101-250 PRINT RUN 29 SER.#'d SETS

2006 Leaf Rookies and Stars Longevity Target Ruby Parallel

*VETS 1-100: 2X TO 5X BASIC CARDS
VETERANS PRINT RUN 249 SER.#'d SETS
*ROOKIES 101-200: 1X TO 2.5X BASIC CARDS
*ROOKIES 201-250: .8X TO 2X BASIC CARDS
ROOKIES PRINT RUN 199 SER.#'d SETS
*ROOKIE JSY 251-270: .4X TO 1X
JSY ROOKIES PRINT RUN 499 SER.#'d SETS

2006 Leaf Rookies and Stars Longevity Target Sapphire Parallel

*VETS 1-100: 3X TO 8X BASIC CARDS
1-100 PRINT RUN 149 SER.#'d SETS
*ROOKIES 101-200: 1.22X TO 3X
*ROOKIES 201-250: 1X TO 2.5X BASIC CARDS
101-200 PRINT RUN 99 SER.#'d SETS
*ROOKIE JSY 251-270: .5X TO 1.2X
JSY ROOKIES PRINT RUN 249 SER.#'d SETS

2006 Leaf Rookies and Stars Longevity Target Materials Ruby

*LONG.RUBY/150-250: .5X TO 1.2X
*LONG.RUBY/82-100: .6X TO 1.5X MAT.GOLD
*LONG.RUBY/55: .8X TO 2X MAT.GOLD
*LONG.RUBY/25: 1.2X TO 3X MAT.GOLD
STATED PRINT RUN 1-250 SER.#'d SETS
*EMER.PRIME/25: 1.2X TO 3X MAT.GOLD
EMERALD PRIME PRINT RUN 10-25
*SAPPHIRE/88-100: .6X TO 1.5X MAT.GOLD
*SAPPHIRE/50: .8X TO 2X MAT.GOLD
SAPPHIRE PRINT RUN 100 SER.#'d SETS
SER.#'d UNDER 25 NOT PRICED
1 Anquan Boldin/250 3.00 8.00
4 Larry Fitzgerald/250 4.00 10.00
6 Michael Vick/250 5.00 12.00
9 Jamal Lewis/250 3.00 8.00
15 Jake Delhomme/250 3.00 8.00
19 Muhsin Muhammad/82 4.00 10.00
32 Jake Plummer/250 3.00 8.00
38 Ahman Green/175 3.00 8.00
39 Brett Favre/55 12.00 30.00
44 David Carr/250 3.00 8.00
48 Peyton Manning/250 6.00 15.00
52 Byron Leftwich/250 3.00 8.00
53 Jimmy Smith/250 3.00 8.00
55 Tony Gonzalez/100 4.00 10.00
64 Corey Dillon/150 3.00 8.00
67 Donte Stallworth/180 3.00 8.00
69 Eli Manning/250 5.00 12.00
72 Chad Pennington/250 3.00 8.00
73 Curtis Martin/250 4.00 10.00
79 Donovan McNabb/100 5.00 12.00
82 Ben Roethlisberger/25 15.00 40.00
98 Drew Bennett/250 2.50 6.00
100 Clinton Portis/250 4.00 10.00

2006 Leaf Rookies and Stars Longevity Target Rookie Autographs

STATED PRINT RUN 5-250 SER.#'d SETS
SER.#'d UNDER 25 NOT PRICED
104 Claude Wroten/125 3.00 8.00
105 Gabe Watson/70 5.00 12.00
107 Todd Watkins/125 4.00 10.00
108 Bennie Brazell/125 4.00 10.00
109 David Anderson/125 4.00 10.00
110 John David Washington/125 4.00 10.00
111 Marques Hagans/90 4.00 10.00
117 Erik Meyer/250 3.00 8.00
118 Taurean Henderson/59 6.00 15.00
121 Jon Alston/50 6.00 15.00
122 Ashton Youboty/95 5.00 12.00
146 Darrell Hackney/54 5.00 12.00
147 Paul Pinegar/61 5.00 12.00
148 Brandon Kirsch/45 8.00 20.00
149 Andre Hall/100 6.00 15.00
150 De'Arrius Howard/100 5.00 12.00
152 Wendell Mathis/100 4.00 10.00
154 Quinton Ganther/40 6.00 15.00
155 Martin Nance/104 4.00 10.00
156 Greg Lee/102 4.00 10.00
157 Jai Lewis/142 3.00 8.00
162 Rocky McIntosh/125 5.00 12.00
163 David Kirtman/125 4.00 10.00
164 Skyler Green/40 8.00 20.00
165 Will Blackmon/125 4.00 10.00
166 Darryl Tapp/125 4.00 10.00
167 Dusty Dvoracek/125 5.00 12.00
168 Richard Marshall/125 4.00 10.00
169 Tim Jennings/125 4.00 10.00
170 David Pittman/125 4.00 10.00
171 DeMario Minter/125 4.00 10.00
172 Marcus Maxey/125 4.00 10.00
173 Roman Harper/125 4.00 10.00
174 Anthony Smith/125 6.00 15.00
175 Nate Salley/125 4.00 10.00
176 Mike Hass/40 8.00 20.00
177 Greg Blue/125 4.00 10.00
178 Daniel Bullocks/125 5.00 12.00
179 Danieal Manning/125 5.00 12.00
180 Calvin Lowry/125 5.00 12.00
181 Eric Smith/125 4.00 10.00
182 Jimmy Williams/62 8.00 20.00
183 Cedric Griffin/125 4.00 10.00
185 Pat Watkins/125 5.00 12.00
187 Bernard Pollard/125 4.00 10.00
204 Derrick Ross/125 5.00 12.00
207 Joseph Addai/50 25.00 60.00
211 Wali Lundy/40 8.00 20.00
213 Miles Austin/105 4.00 10.00
219 Garrett Mills/40 8.00 20.00
225 Sam Hurd/125 3.00 8.00
226 Owen Daniels/125 5.00 12.00
227 Domenik Hixon/40 8.00 20.00
229 Dawan Landry/125 5.00 12.00
230 Jonathan Orr/40 6.00 15.00
231 Delanie Walker/40 6.00 15.00
233 Jeffrey Webb/40 6.00 15.00
234 Ethan Kilmer/125 5.00 12.00
236 Jason Allen/40 8.00 20.00
240 Haloti Ngata/125 6.00 15.00
241 Brodrick Bunkley/40 8.00 20.00
242 John McCargo/125 4.00 10.00
246 Abdul Hodge/25 1.00 25.00
248 Chad Greenway/125 5.00 12.00
250 Manny Lawson/125 5.00 12.00

2006 Leaf Rookies and Stars Longevity Target Rookie Material Autographs Ruby

STATED PRINT RUN 25-50 SER.#'d SETS
UNPRICED TARGET EMERALD PRINT RUN 1
UNPRICED TARGET SAPP.PRINT RUN 5-10
251 Matt Leinart/25 30.00 80.00
252 Kellen Clemens/50 12.00 30.00
253 Tarvaris Jackson/50 10.00 25.00
254 Charlie Whitehurst/50 8.00 20.00
255 DeAngelo Williams/25 30.00 80.00
256 Maurice Drew/50 35.00 60.00
257 Brian Calhoun/25 10.00 25.00
258 Jerious Norwood/50 15.00 40.00
259 Vernon Davis/25 15.00 40.00
260 Joe Klopfenstein/50 6.00 15.00
261 Sinorice Moss/25 10.00 25.00
262 Derek Hagan/50 8.00 20.00
263 Brandon Williams/50 8.00 20.00
264 Michael Robinson/50 8.00 20.00
265 Jason Avant/50 8.00 20.00
266 Brandon Marshall/50 15.00 30.00
267 Demetrius Williams/50 8.00 20.00
268 Mario Williams/50 12.00 30.00
269 Michael Huff/50 10.00 25.00
270 Chad Jackson/25 10.00 25.00
271 Vince Young/25 25.00 60.00
272 Omar Jacobs/50 6.00 15.00
273 Reggie Bush/25 15.00 40.00
274 Laurence Maroney/25 20.00 50.00
275 LenDale White/25 30.00 60.00
276 Leon Washington/50 20.00 40.00
277 Marcedes Lewis/50 8.00 20.00
278 Santonio Holmes/25 25.00 60.00
279 Travis Wilson/50 8.00 20.00
280 Maurice Stovall/50 8.00 20.00
281 A.J. Hawk/25 20.00 50.00

2007 Leaf Rookies and Stars

is 266-card set was released in November, 2007. The set was issued into the hobby in five-card packs, with a $4 SRP, which came 24 packs to a box. Cards 1-115 feature veterans while cards 116-266 feature 2007 NFL rookies. The Rookie Cards are broken down thusly: Cards numbered 116-200 were issued to a stated print run of 999 serial numbered sets while cards numbered 201-266 were all signed by the player and were issued to stated print runs of between 99 and 299 serial numbered sets. A few players did not return their cards in time for pack out and those cards could be redeemed until June 1, 2009.

COMP.SET w/o SP's (100) 10.00 25.00
116-200 ROOKIE PRINT RUN 999
201-266 ROOKIE AU PRINT RUN 99-299
1 Tony Romo .40 1.00
2 Julius Jones .20 .50
3 Terrell Owens .25 .60
4 Eli Manning .25 .60
5 Plaxico Burress .20 .50
6 Jeremy Shockey .20 .50
7 Brandon Jacobs .20 .50
8 Donovan McNabb .25 .60
9 Brian Westbrook .20 .50
10 Reggie Brown .20 .50
11 Jason Campbell .20 .50
12 Clinton Portis .20 .50
13 Santana Moss .25 .60
14 Rex Grossman .20 .50
15 Cedric Benson .20 .50
16 Muhsin Muhammad .20 .50
17 Jon Kitna .20 .50
18 Roy Williams WR .20 .50
19 Tatum Bell .20 .50
20 Brett Favre .60 1.50
21 Vernand Morency .25 .60
22 Donald Driver .25 .60
23 Tarvaris Jackson .20 .50
24 Chester Taylor .20 .50
25 Troy Williamson .20 .50
26 Jerious Norwood .20 .50
27 Warrick Dunn .20 .50
28 Alge Crumpler .25 .60
29 Jake Delhomme .20 .50
30 DeShaun Foster .25 .60
31 Steve Smith .25 .60
32 Drew Brees .30 .75
33 Deuce McAllister .25 .60
34 Marques Colston .20 .50
35 Reggie Bush .20 .50
36 Jeff Garcia .20 .50
37 Cadillac Williams .25 .60
38 Joey Galloway .25 .60
39 Matt Leinart .20 .50
40 Edgerrin James .25 .60
41 Anquan Boldin .20 .50
42 Larry Fitzgerald .25 .60
43 Marc Bulger .20 .50
44 Steven Jackson .20 .50
45 Torry Holt .25 .60
46 Alex Smith QB .25 .60
47 Frank Gore .25 .60
48 Vernon Davis .20 .50
49 Matt Hasselbeck .20 .50
50 Shaun Alexander .20 .50
51 Deion Branch .20 .50
52 J.P. Losman .20 .50
53 Anthony Thomas .20 .50
54 Lee Evans .25 .60
55 Trent Green .20 .50
56 Ronnie Brown .20 .50
57 Chris Chambers .20 .50
58 Tom Brady 1.00 2.50
59 Laurence Maroney .25 .60
60 Randy Moss .25 .60
61 Chad Pennington .20 .50
62 Jerricho Cotchery .20 .50
63 Leon Washington .20 .50
64 Steve McNair .25 .60
65 Willis McGahee .20 .50
66 Mark Clayton .20 .50
67 Carson Palmer .25 .60
68 Rudi Johnson .20 .50
69 Chad Johnson .20 .50
70 T.J. Houshmandzadeh .20 .50
71 Charlie Frye .25 .60
72 Braylon Edwards .20 .50
73 Jamal Lewis .25 .60
74 Ben Roethlisberger .30 .75
75 Willie Parker .25 .60
76 Hines Ward .25 .60
77 Ahman Green .25 .60
78 Andre Johnson .25 .60
79 Matt Schaub .20 .50
80 Peyton Manning .75 2.00
81 Joseph Addai .20 .50
82 Marvin Harrison .25 .60
83 Reggie Wayne .25 .60
84 Byron Leftwich .20 .50
85 Fred Taylor .20 .50
86 Maurice Jones-Drew .20 .50
87 Vince Young .20 .50
88 LenDale White .25 .60
89 Brandon Jones .20 .50
90 Jay Cutler .20 .50
91 Javon Walker .25 .60
92 Mike Bell .25 .60
93 Larry Johnson .20 .50
94 Tony Gonzalez .25 .60
95 Brodie Croyle .25 .60
96 LaMont Jordan .25 .60
97 Dominic Rhodes .20 .50
98 Philip Rivers .30 .75
99 LaDainian Tomlinson .30 .75
100 Antonio Gates .30 .75
101 Drew Brees ELE 1.50 4.00
102 Reggie Bush ELE 1.00 2.50
103 Brett Favre ELE 3.00 8.00
104 Marvin Harrison ELE 1.25 3.00
105 Eli Manning ELE 1.25 3.00
106 Willie Parker ELE 1.25 3.00
107 Brian Westbrook ELE 1.00 2.50
108 Tom Brady ELE 5.00 12.00
109 Jay Cutler ELE 1.00 2.50
110 Rudi Johnson ELE 1.00 2.50
111 J.P. Losman ELE 1.00 2.50
112 Laurence Maroney ELE 1.25 3.00
113 Carson Palmer ELE 1.25 3.00
114 Ben Roethlisberger ELE 1.50 4.00
115 Brian Urlacher ELE 1.50 4.00
116 A.J. Davis RC 1.25 3.00
117 Usama Young RC 1.50 4.00
118 Aaron Rouse RC 1.25 3.00
119 Ahmad Bradshaw RC 2.00 5.00
120 Alan Branch RC 1.25 3.00
121 Alonzo Coleman RC 1.50 4.00
122 Amobi Okoye RC 1.50 4.00
123 Anthony Spencer RC 1.50 4.00
124 Deon Anderson RC 1.50 4.00
125 Justin Durant RC 2.00 5.00
126 Brandon Siler RC 1.25 3.00
127 Buster Davis RC 1.50 4.00
128 Charles Johnson RC 1.25 3.00
129 Courtney Taylor RC 1.25 3.00
130 Dallas Baker RC 1.25 3.00
131 Dan Bazuin RC 1.50 4.00
132 Danny Ware RC 2.00 5.00
133 Darius Walker RC 1.25 3.00
134 David Ball RC 1.25 3.00
135 David Harris RC 1.25 3.00
136 David Irons RC 1.25 3.00
137 Daymeion Hughes RC 1.25 3.00
138 Anthony Waters RC 1.50 4.00
139 Antwan Barnes RC 2.00 5.00
140 Eric Frampton RC 1.50 4.00
141 Eric Weddle RC 1.50 4.00
142 Eric Wright RC 1.25 3.00
143 Fred Bennett RC 1.25 3.00
144 Gary Russell RC 1.50 4.00
145 H.B. Blades RC 1.25 3.00
146 Jacoby Jones RC 1.25 3.00
147 Clifton Dawson RC 2.00 5.00
148 Kevin Boss RC 2.00 5.00
149 Jarvis Moss RC 1.25 3.00
150 Gerald Alexander RC 1.25 3.00
151 Jeff Rowe RC 1.25 3.00
152 Tanard Jackson RC 1.25 3.00
153 Joel Filani RC 1.25 3.00
154 Jon Abbate RC 1.25 3.00
155 Jon Beason RC 1.25 3.00
156 Marcus Mason RC 2.00 5.00
157 Jonathan Wade RC 1.25 3.00
158 Dante Rosario RC 2.00 5.00
159 Josh Wilson RC 1.50 4.00
160 Kenneth Darby RC 1.25 3.00
161 Biren Ealy RC 1.50 4.00
162 LaMarr Woodley RC 2.50 6.00
163 Levi Brown RC 1.25 3.00
164 Marcus McCauley RC 1.25 3.00
165 Matt Spaeth RC 2.00 5.00
166 Michael Okwo RC 1.50 4.00
167 Mike Walker RC 2.00 5.00
168 Quentin Moses RC 1.25 3.00
169 Ray McDonald RC 1.50 4.00
170 Reggie Ball RC 1.50 4.00
171 Justin Harrell RC 1.25 3.00
172 Ed Johnson RC 1.50 4.00
173 Rufus Alexander RC 1.25 3.00
174 Ryan McBean RC 2.00 5.00
175 Ryne Robinson RC 1.50 4.00
176 Sabby Piscitelli RC 1.25 3.00
177 Scott Chandler RC 2.00 5.00
178 Selvin Young RC 1.25 3.00
179 Steve Breaston RC 1.25 3.00
180 Stewart Bradley RC 1.25 3.00
181 Turk McBride RC 1.50 4.00
182 Demarcus Tank Tyler RC 1.25 3.00
183 Tim Crowder RC 1.50 4.00
184 Tim Shaw RC 1.50 4.00
185 Kenton Keith RC 1.50 4.00
186 Tyler Palko RC 2.00 5.00
187 Mason Crosby RC 1.50 4.00
188 Pierre Thomas RC 2.00 5.00
189 Victor Abiamiri RC 1.25 3.00
190 Zak DeOssie RC 1.50 4.00
191 Tyler Thigpen RC 2.00 5.00
192 Tony Ugoh RC 1.25 3.00
193 Michael Allan RC 1.25 3.00
194 Martrez Milner RC 1.25 3.00
195 John Broussard RC 1.50 4.00
196 Roy Hall RC 2.00 5.00
197 Matt Gutierrez RC 2.00 5.00
198 Legedu Naanee RC 1.50 4.00
199 Derek Stanley RC 1.50 4.00
200 Quincy Black RC 2.00 5.00
201 Trent Edwards/99 AU RC 8.00 20.00
202 Marshawn Lynch/99 AU RC 20.00 40.00
203 Chris Henry/99 AU RC 8.00 20.00
204 Paul Williams/299 AU RC 5.00 12.00
205 Sidney Rice/99 AU RC 10.00 25.00
206 Adrian Peterson/99 AU RC 100.00 200.00
207 Drew Stanton/99 AU RC 8.00 20.00
208 Calvin Johnson/99 AU RC 60.00 120.00
209 Yamon Figurs/99 AU RC 8.00 20.00
210 Troy Smith/99 AU RC 8.00 20.00
211 Garrett Wolfe/249 AU RC 5.00 12.00
212 Greg Olsen/99 AU RC 12.00 30.00
213 Joe Thomas/99 AU RC 12.00 30.00
214 Brady Quinn/99 AU RC 8.00 20.00
215 Ted Ginn Jr./99 AU RC 10.00 25.00
216 John Beck/99 AU RC 8.00 20.00
218 Robert Meachem/99 AU RC 10.00 25.00
219 JaMarcus Russell/99 AU RC 8.00 20.00
220 Michael Bush/99 AU RC 8.00 20.00
221 Kevin Kolb/99 AU RC 10.00 25.00
223 Patrick Willis/99 AU RC 12.00 30.00
224 Jason Hill/249 AU RC 5.00 12.00
225 Brandon Jackson/99 AU RC 8.00 20.00
226 David Clowney/299 AU RC 5.00 12.00
228 Leon Hall/99 AU RC 8.00 20.00
229 Dwayne Bowe/99 AU RC 8.00 20.00
230 Kolby Smith/299 AU RC 6.00 15.00
232 Dwayne Jarrett/99 AU RC 10.00 25.00
233 Lorenzo Booker/99 AU RC 10.00 25.00
234 Anthony Gonzalez/99 AU RC 8.00 20.00
235 J.Lee Higgins/99 AU RC 8.00 20.00
236 Isaiah Stanback/299 AU RC 5.00 12.00
237 LaRon Landry/249 AU RC 8.00 20.00
238 Paul Posluszny/99 AU RC 8.00 20.00
239 Brian Leonard/99 AU RC 8.00 20.00
242 Aundrae Allison/249 AU RC 5.00 12.00
244 Jamaal Anderson/249 AU RC 6.00 15.00
245 Adam Carriker/99 AU RC 8.00 20.00
246 Darrelle Revis/99 AU RC 10.00 25.00
247 Lawrence Timmons/99 AU RC 12.00 30.00
248 Michael Griffin/299 AU RC 5.00 12.00

250 Reggie Nelson/99 AU RC 8.00 20.00
252 Zach Miller/99 AU RC 10.00 25.00
253 Chris Houston/299 AU RC 5.00 12.00
255 Laurent Robinson/299 AU RC 8.00 20.00
256 James Jones/246 AU RC 5.00 12.00
258 Chris Davis/249 AU RC 5.00 12.00
259 Thomas Clayton/299 AU RC 6.00 15.00
260 Jordan Palmer/99 AU RC 10.00 25.00
261 Jordan Kent/299 AU RC 6.00 15.00
262 Chansi Stuckey/299 AU RC 6.00 15.00
263 Nate Ilaoa/299 AU RC 6.00 15.00
264 Chris Leak/99 AU RC 8.00 20.00
265 Jared Zabransky/99 AU RC 8.00 20.00
266 Syndric Steptoe/299 AU RC 6.00 15.00

2007 Leaf Rookies and Stars Gold Retail

*1-100 VETS/349: 1.5X TO 4X BASIC CARDS
*101-115 VETS/349: .4X TO 1X BASIC CARDS
*ROOKIES/349: .5X TO 1.2X BASIC CARDS
STATED PRINT RUN 349 SER.#'d SETS

2007 Leaf Rookies and Stars Black Holofoil

-100 VETS/25: 8X TO 20X BASIC CARDS
*101-115 VETS/10: 2.5X TO 6X BASIC CARDS
1-100 VETERAN PRINT RUN 25
*117-200 ROOKIE/10: 2.5X TO 6X BASIC CARD
101-200 STATED PRINT RUN 10

2007 Leaf Rookies and Stars Gold

*1-100 VETS/49: 5X TO 12X BASIC CARDS
*101-115 VETS/25: 1.5X TO 4X BASIC CARDS
1-115 VETERAN STATED PRINT RUN 49
*ROOKIES/25: 1.5X TO 4X BASIC CARDS
116-200 ROOKIE STATED PRINT RUN 25

2007 Leaf Rookies and Stars Silver Holofoil

-100 VETS/99: 3X TO 8X BASIC CARDS
*101-115 VETS/49: .8X TO 2X BASIC CARDS
1-115 VETERAN PRINT RUN 99
*ROOKIES/49: 1X TO 2.5X BASIC CARDS
116-200 ROOKIE PRINT RUN 49

2007 Leaf Rookies and Stars Silver

-100 VETS/249: 2X TO 5X BASIC CARDS
*101-115 VETS/199: .6X TO 1.5X BASIC CARDS
1-115 VETERAN PRINT RUN 199-249
*ROOKIES/199: .8X TO 2X BASIC CARDS
116-200 ROOKIE PRINT RUN 199

2007 Leaf Rookies and Stars Crosstraining Red

RED PRINT RUN 1000 SER.#'d SETS
*BLUE/500: .5X TO 1.2X RED/1000
BLUE PRINT RUN 500 SER.#'d SETS
*GREEN/100: .6X TO 1.5X RED/1000
GREEN PRINT RUN 100 SER.#'d SETS
*PURPLE/25: 1.5X TO 4X RED/1000
PURPLE PRINT RUN 25 SER.#'d SETS
1 Yamon Figurs .50 1.25
2 Marshawn Lynch 1.00 2.50
3 Dwayne Jarrett .60 1.50
4 Greg Olsen .75 2.00
5 Brady Quinn .50 1.25
6 Calvin Johnson 3.00 8.00
7 Drew Stanton .50 1.25
8 Brandon Jackson .50 1.25
9 Anthony Gonzalez .50 1.25
10 Dwayne Bowe .50 1.25
11 John Beck .50 1.25
12 Ted Ginn Jr. .60 1.50
13 Adrian Peterson 1.50 4.00
14 Robert Meachem .60 1.50
15 JaMarcus Russell .50 1.25
16 Michael Bush .50 1.25
17 Kevin Kolb .60 1.50
18 Jason Hill .50 1.25
19 Brian Leonard .50 1.25
20 Paul Williams .50 1.25

2007 Leaf Rookies and Stars Crosstraining Materials Green

STATED PRINT RUN 250 SER.#'d SETS
*PURPLE PRIME/25: .8X TO 2X BASIC JSYs
PURPLE PRIME PRINT RUN 25 SER.#'d SETS
1 Yamon Figurs 2.50 6.00
2 Marshawn Lynch 2.50 6.00
3 Dwayne Jarrett 1.50 4.00
4 Greg Olsen 2.00 5.00
5 Brady Quinn 1.25 3.00
6 Calvin Johnson 4.00 10.00
7 Drew Stanton 1.25 3.00
8 Brandon Jackson 1.25 3.00
9 Anthony Gonzalez 1.25 3.00
10 Dwayne Bowe 1.25 3.00
11 John Beck 1.25 3.00
12 Ted Ginn Jr. 1.50 4.00
13 Adrian Peterson 12.00 30.00
14 Robert Meachem 2.50 6.00
15 JaMarcus Russell 1.25 3.00
16 Michael Bush 1.25 3.00
17 Kevin Kolb 1.50 4.00
18 Jason Hill 2.50 6.00
19 Brian Leonard 2.50 6.00
20 Paul Williams 2.50 6.00

2007 Leaf Rookies and Stars Crusade Red

D PRINT RUN 1000 SER.#'d SETS
*BLUE/500: .5X TO 1.2X RED/1000
BLUE PRINT RUN 500 SER.#'d SETS
*GREEN/100: .8X TO 2X RED/1000
GREEN PRINT RUN 100 SER.#'d SETS
*PURPLE/25: 1.5X TO 4X RED/1000
PURPLE PRINT RUN 25 SER.#'d SETS
1 Hines Ward .60 1.50
2 Andre Johnson .60 1.50
3 Joey Galloway .60 1.50
4 Terry Glenn .60 1.50
5 Jerricho Cotchery .50 1.25
6 Mark Clayton .50 1.25
7 Brandon Marshall .60 1.50
8 Braylon Edwards .50 1.25
9 Brett Favre 1.50 4.00
10 Tom Brady 2.50 6.00
11 LaDainian Tomlinson .75 2.00
12 Larry Johnson .50 1.25
13 Chad Johnson .50 1.25
14 Torry Holt .60 1.50
15 Vincent Jackson .50 1.25

2007 Leaf Rookies and Stars Crusade Materials Green

STATED PRINT RUN 250 SER.#'d SETS
*PURPLE PRIME/25: 1X TO 2.5X BASIC JSYs
PURPLE PRIME PRINT RUN 8-25
1 Hines Ward 2.50 6.00
2 Andre Johnson 2.50 6.00
3 Joey Galloway 2.50 6.00
4 Terry Glenn 2.50 6.00
5 Jerricho Cotchery 2.00 5.00
6 Mark Clayton 2.00 5.00
7 Brandon Marshall 2.50 6.00
8 Braylon Edwards 2.00 5.00
9 Brett Favre 6.00 15.00
10 Tom Brady 10.00 25.00
11 LaDainian Tomlinson 3.00 8.00
12 Larry Johnson 2.00 5.00
13 Chad Johnson 2.00 5.00
14 Torry Holt 2.50 6.00
16 Vincent Jackson 2.00 5.00

2007 Leaf Rookies and Stars Dress for Success Jerseys

STATED PRINT RUN 175 SER.#'d SETS
*PRIME/25: .8X TO 2X JSY/175
*FACE MASK/287-300: .4X TO 1X JSY/175
*HELMET/55: .8X TO 2X JSY/175
*SHOE/55: .6X TO 1.5X JSY/175
*LONGEVITY JSY/100: .5X TO 1.2X BASIC JSY/175
*LONG.HELMET/55: .6X TO 1.5X JSY/175
*LONG.SHOE/55: .6X TO 1.5X JSY/175
*LONG.FACE MASK/50: .6X TO 1.5X JSY/175
UNPRICED AUTO PRINT RUN 10
UNPRICED PRIME AU PRINT RUN 5
1 Troy Smith 1.25 3.00
2 Yamon Figurs 1.25 3.00
3 Trent Edwards 1.25 3.00
4 Marshawn Lynch 2.50 6.00
5 Dwayne Jarrett 1.50 4.00
6 Garrett Wolfe 1.25 3.00
7 Greg Olsen 2.00 5.00
8 Kenny Irons 1.25 3.00
9 Joe Thomas 2.00 5.00
10 Brady Quinn 1.25 3.00
11 Calvin Johnson 4.00 10.00
12 Drew Stanton 1.25 3.00
13 Brandon Jackson 1.25 3.00
14 Anthony Gonzalez 1.25 3.00
15 Dwayne Bowe 1.25 3.00
16 John Beck 1.25 3.00
17 Lorenzo Booker 1.50 4.00
18 Ted Ginn Jr. 1.50 4.00
19 Adrian Peterson 4.00 10.00
20 Sidney Rice 1.50 4.00
21 Antonio Pittman 1.25 3.00
22 Robert Meachem 1.50 4.00
23 Steve Smith USC 1.25 3.00
24 JaMarcus Russell 1.25 3.00
25 Johnnie Lee Higgins 2.00 5.00
26 Michael Bush 1.25 3.00
27 Kevin Kolb 1.50 4.00
28 Tony Hunt 1.25 3.00
29 Patrick Willis 2.00 5.00
30 Jason Hill 1.25 3.00
31 Brian Leonard 1.25 3.00
32 Gaines Adams 1.50 4.00
33 Chris Henry RB 1.25 3.00
34 Paul Williams 1.25 3.00

2007 Leaf Rookies and Stars Elements Materials

ATED PRINT RUN 250 SER.#'d SETS
*FOIL/100: .5X TO 1.2X BASIC JSYs
FOIL PRINT RUN 100 SER.#'d SETS
*HOLOFOIL/25: 1X TO 2.5X BASIC JSYs
HOLOFOIL PRINT RUN 25 SER.#'d SETS
101 Drew Brees 4.00 10.00
102 Reggie Bush 2.50 6.00
103 Brett Favre 8.00 20.00
104 Marvin Harrison 3.00 8.00
105 Eli Manning 3.00 8.00
106 Willie Parker 3.00 8.00
107 Brian Westbrook 2.50 6.00
108 Tom Brady 12.00 30.00
109 Jay Cutler 2.50 6.00
110 Rudi Johnson 2.50 6.00
111 J.P. Losman 2.50 6.00
112 Laurence Maroney 3.00 8.00
113 Carson Palmer 3.00 8.00
114 Ben Roethlisberger 4.00 10.00
115 Brian Urlacher 4.00 10.00

2007 Leaf Rookies and Stars Freshman Orientation Materials Jerseys

JERSEY PRINT RUN 175 SER.#'d SETS
*PRIME/25: .8X TO 2X BASIC JSY/175
*FOOTBALL/49-107: .6X TO 1.5X JSY/175
*LONG.JSY/100: .5X TO 1.2X BASIC JSY/175
*LONG.BALL/25: .8X TO 2X BASIC JSY/175
UNPRICED AUTO PRINT RUN 10
UNPRICED PRIME AU PRINT RUN 5
1 Yamon Figurs 1.25 3.00
2 Marshawn Lynch 2.50 6.00
3 Garrett Wolfe 1.25 3.00
4 Kenny Irons 1.25 3.00
5 Brady Quinn 1.25 3.00
6 Drew Stanton 1.25 3.00
7 Anthony Gonzalez 1.25 3.00
8 John Beck 1.25 3.00
9 Ted Ginn Jr. 1.50 4.00
10 Sidney Rice 1.50 4.00
11 Robert Meachem 1.50 4.00
12 JaMarcus Russell 1.25 3.00
13 Michael Bush 1.25 3.00
14 Tony Hunt 1.25 3.00
15 Jason Hill 1.25 3.00
16 Gaines Adams 1.50 4.00
17 Paul Williams 1.25 3.00
18 Troy Smith 1.25 3.00
19 Trent Edwards 1.25 3.00
20 Dwayne Jarrett 1.50 4.00
21 Greg Olsen 2.00 5.00
22 Joe Thomas 2.00 5.00
23 Calvin Johnson 8.00 20.00
24 Brandon Jackson 1.25 3.00
25 Dwayne Bowe 1.25 3.00
26 Lorenzo Booker 1.50 4.00
27 Adrian Peterson 4.00 10.00
28 Antonio Pittman 1.25 3.00
29 Steve Smith USC 1.25 3.00
30 Johnnie Lee Higgins 2.00 5.00
31 Kevin Kolb 1.50 4.00
32 Patrick Willis 2.00 5.00
33 Brian Leonard 1.25 3.00
34 Chris Henry RB 1.25 3.00

2007 Leaf Rookies and Stars Materials Gold Retail

UNNUMBERED INSERTS IN RETAIL PACKS
*GOLD HOB/185-200: .4X TO 1X GOLD RET
*GOLD HOB/100-125: .5X TO 1.2X GOLD RET
*GOLD HOB/50-65: .6X TO 1.5X GOLD RET
*GOLD HOB/15-25: .8X TO 2X GOLD RET
GOLD HOBBY PRINT RUN 1-250
*BLACK PRIME/10: 1.5X TO 4X GOLD RET
BLACK PRIME PRINT RUN 10
*EMERALD PRIME/25: 1X TO 2.5X GOLD RET
EMERALD PRIME PRINT RUN 25
*LONG.RUBY/150-250: .4X TO 1X GOLD RET
LONGEVITY RUBY PRINT RUN 150-250
*LONG.SAPPHIRE/100: .5X TO 1.2X GOLD RET
*LONG.SAPPHIRE/15: .8X TO 2X GOLD RET
LONGEVITY SAPPHIRE PRINT RUN 15-100
1 Tony Romo 5.00 12.00
2 Julius Jones 2.50 6.00
4 Eli Manning 3.00 8.00
5 Plaxico Burress 2.50 6.00
6 Jeremy Shockey 2.50 6.00
7 Brandon Jacobs 2.50 6.00
8 Donovan McNabb 3.00 8.00
9 Brian Westbrook 2.50 6.00
10 Reggie Brown 2.50 6.00
11 Jason Campbell 2.50 6.00
12 Clinton Portis 2.50 6.00
13 Santana Moss 3.00 8.00
14 Rex Grossman 2.50 6.00
15 Cedric Benson 2.50 6.00
16 Muhsin Muhammad 2.50 6.00
17 Jon Kitna 2.50 6.00
18 Roy Williams WR 2.50 6.00
19 Tatum Bell 2.50 6.00
20 Brett Favre 8.00 20.00
22 Donald Driver 3.00 8.00
23 Tarvaris Jackson 2.50 6.00
24 Chester Taylor 2.50 6.00
25 Troy Williamson 2.50 6.00
26 Jerious Norwood 2.50 6.00
27 Warrick Dunn 2.50 6.00
28 Alge Crumpler 3.00 8.00
29 Jake Delhomme 2.50 6.00
30 DeShaun Foster 3.00 8.00
31 Steve Smith 3.00 8.00
32 Drew Brees 4.00 10.00
33 Deuce McAllister 3.00 8.00
34 Marques Colston 2.50 6.00
35 Reggie Bush 2.50 6.00
36 Jeff Garcia 2.50 6.00
37 Cadillac Williams 3.00 8.00
38 Joey Galloway 3.00 8.00
39 Matt Leinart 2.50 6.00
40 Edgerrin James 3.00 8.00
41 Anquan Boldin 2.50 6.00
42 Larry Fitzgerald 3.00 8.00
43 Marc Bulger 2.50 6.00
44 Steven Jackson 2.50 6.00
45 Torry Holt 3.00 8.00
46 Alex Smith QB 3.00 8.00
47 Frank Gore 3.00 8.00
48 Vernon Davis 2.50 6.00
49 Matt Hasselbeck 2.50 6.00
50 Shaun Alexander 2.50 6.00
51 Deion Branch 2.50 6.00
52 J.P. Losman 2.50 6.00
53 Anthony Thomas 2.50 6.00
54 Lee Evans 3.00 8.00
55 Trent Green 2.50 6.00
56 Ronnie Brown 2.50 6.00
57 Chris Chambers 2.50 6.00
58 Tom Brady 12.00 30.00
59 Laurence Maroney 3.00 8.00
60 Randy Moss 3.00 8.00
61 Chad Pennington 2.50 6.00
62 Jerricho Cotchery 2.50 6.00
63 Leon Washington 2.50 6.00
64 Steve McNair 3.00 8.00
65 Willis McGahee 2.50 6.00
66 Mark Clayton 2.50 6.00
67 Carson Palmer 3.00 8.00
68 Rudi Johnson 2.50 6.00
69 Chad Johnson 2.50 6.00
70 T.J. Houshmandzadeh 2.50 6.00
71 Charlie Frye 3.00 8.00
72 Braylon Edwards 2.50 6.00
73 Jamal Lewis 3.00 8.00
74 Ben Roethlisberger 4.00 10.00
75 Willie Parker 3.00 8.00
76 Hines Ward 3.00 8.00
78 Andre Johnson 3.00 8.00
80 Peyton Manning 10.00 25.00
81 Joseph Addai 2.50 6.00
82 Marvin Harrison 3.00 8.00
83 Reggie Wayne 3.00 8.00
84 Byron Leftwich 2.50 6.00
86 Maurice Jones-Drew 2.50 6.00
87 Vince Young 2.50 6.00
88 LenDale White 3.00 8.00
89 Brandon Jones 2.50 6.00
90 Jay Cutler 2.50 6.00
91 Javon Walker 3.00 8.00
92 Mike Bell 3.00 8.00
93 Larry Johnson 2.50 6.00
94 Tony Gonzalez 3.00 8.00
95 Brodie Croyle 3.00 8.00
96 LaMont Jordan 3.00 8.00
98 Philip Rivers 4.00 10.00
99 LaDainian Tomlinson 4.00 10.00
100 Antonio Gates 4.00 10.00

2007 Leaf Rookies and Stars Prime Cuts

STATED PRINT RUN 50 SER.#'d SETS
*COMBOS/25: .6X TO 1.5X BASIC JSYs
COMBOS PRINT RUN 25 SER.#'d SETS
1 Vince Young 5.00 12.00
2 LaDainian Tomlinson 8.00 20.00
3 Chad Johnson 5.00 12.00
4 Tom Brady 25.00 60.00
5 Brett Favre 15.00 40.00
6 Marvin Harrison 6.00 15.00
7 Larry Johnson 5.00 12.00

2007 Leaf Rookies and Stars Rookie Autographs Holofoil

HOLOFOIL PRINT RUN 50-75
UNPRICED GOLD AUTO PRINT RUN 8-20
UNPRICED EMERALD AUTO PRINT RUN 5
UNPRICED BLACK AUTO PRINT RUN 1
*LONGEVITY/50: .4X TO 1X HOLO.AU/50-75
*LONGEVITY/25: .5X TO 1.2X HOLO.AU/50-75
LONGEVITY PRINT RUN 9-50
UNPRICED LONG.RUBY PRINT RUN 5-10
UNPRICED LONG.SAPPHIRE PRINT RUN 1
116 A.J. Davis 5.00 12.00
118 Aaron Rouse 5.00 12.00
121 Alonzo Coleman 6.00 15.00
122 Amobi Okoye 6.00 15.00
123 Anthony Spencer 6.00 15.00
129 Courtney Taylor 5.00 12.00
130 Dallas Baker 5.00 12.00
131 Dan Bazuin 6.00 15.00
132 Danny Ware 8.00 20.00
133 Darius Walker 5.00 12.00
134 David Ball 5.00 12.00
135 David Harris 5.00 12.00
136 David Irons 5.00 12.00
137 Daymeion Hughes 5.00 12.00
140 Eric Frampton 6.00 15.00
143 Fred Bennett 5.00 12.00
144 Gary Russell 6.00 15.00
145 H.B. Blades 5.00 12.00
146 Jacoby Jones 5.00 12.00
149 Jarvis Moss 5.00 12.00
151 Jeff Rowe 5.00 12.00
153 Joel Filani 5.00 12.00
155 Jon Beason 5.00 12.00
157 Jonathan Wade 5.00 12.00
159 Josh Wilson 6.00 15.00
160 Kenneth Darby 5.00 12.00
162 LaMarr Woodley 12.00 30.00
163 Levi Brown 5.00 12.00
164 Marcus McCauley 5.00 12.00
165 Matt Spaeth 8.00 20.00
166 Michael Okwo 6.00 15.00
167 Mike Walker 8.00 20.00
168 Quentin Moses 5.00 12.00
169 Ray McDonald 6.00 15.00
170 Reggie Ball 6.00 15.00
173 Rufus Alexander 5.00 12.00
174 Ryan McBean 8.00 20.00
175 Ryne Robinson 6.00 15.00
176 Sabby Piscitelli/75 5.00 12.00
177 Scott Chandler 8.00 20.00
179 Steve Breaston 5.00 12.00
180 Stewart Bradley 5.00 12.00
183 Tim Crowder 6.00 15.00
184 Tim Shaw/75 6.00 15.00
186 Tyler Palko 8.00 20.00
189 Victor Abiamiri 5.00 12.00

2007 Leaf Rookies and Stars Rookie Autographs College

*COLLEGE/12-25: .8X TO 2X BASIC AU/246-299
*COLLEGE/12-25: .5X TO 1.2X BASIC AU/99
COLLEGE SWATCH PRINT RUN 12-25
UNPRICED GOLD PRINT RUN 10
UNPRICED EMERALD PRINT RUN 5
UNPRICED BLACK PRINT RUN 1
UNPRICED LONGEVITY PRINT RUN 10
UNPRICED LONGEVITY RUBY PRINT RUN 5
UNPRICED LONG.SAPPHIRE PRINT RUN 1
206 Adrian Peterson/15 150.00 300.00
208 Calvin Johnson/15 100.00 200.00
214 Brady Quinn/15 10.00 25.00

2007 Leaf Rookies and Stars Rookie Crusade Red

STATED PRINT RUN 1000 SER.#'d SETS
*BLUE: .5X TO 1.2X BASIC INSERTS
BLUE PRINT RUN 500 SER.#'d SETS
*GREEN: .6X TO 1.5X BASIC INSERTS
GREEN PRINT RUN 100 SER.#'d SETS
*PURPLE: 1.5X TO 4X BASIC INSERTS
PURPLE PRINT RUN 25 SER.#'d SETS
1 Troy Smith .50 1.25
2 Yamon Figurs .50 1.25
3 Trent Edwards .50 1.25
4 Marshawn Lynch 1.00 2.50
5 Dwayne Jarrett .60 1.50
6 Garrett Wolfe .50 1.25
7 Greg Olsen .75 2.00
8 Kenny Irons .50 1.25
9 Joe Thomas .75 2.00
10 Brady Quinn .50 1.25
11 Calvin Johnson 1.50 4.00
12 Drew Stanton .50 1.25
13 Brandon Jackson .50 1.25
14 Anthony Gonzalez .50 1.25
15 Dwayne Bowe .50 1.25
16 John Beck .50 1.25
17 Lorenzo Booker .60 1.50
18 Ted Ginn Jr. .60 1.50
19 Adrian Peterson 1.50 4.00
20 Sidney Rice .60 1.50
21 Antonio Pittman .50 1.25
22 Robert Meachem .60 1.50
23 Steve Smith USC .50 1.25
24 JaMarcus Russell .50 1.25
25 Johnnie Lee Higgins .50 1.25
26 Michael Bush .50 1.25
27 Kevin Kolb .60 1.50
28 Tony Hunt .50 1.25
29 Patrick Willis .75 2.00
30 Jason Hill .50 1.25
31 Brian Leonard .50 1.25
32 Gaines Adams .60 1.50
33 Chris Henry RB .50 1.25
34 Paul Williams .50 1.25

2007 Leaf Rookies and Stars Rookie Crusade Materials Green

ATED PRINT RUN 250 SER.#'d SETS
*PURPLE/25: .8X TO 2X GREEN/250
PURPLE PRIME PRINT RUN 25 SER.#'d SETS
1 Troy Smith 1.25 3.00
2 Yamon Figurs 1.25 3.00
3 Trent Edwards 1.25 3.00
4 Marshawn Lynch 2.50 6.00
5 Dwayne Jarrett 1.50 4.00
6 Garrett Wolfe 1.25 3.00
7 Greg Olsen 2.00 5.00
8 Kenny Irons 1.25 3.00
9 Joe Thomas 2.00 5.00
10 Brady Quinn 1.25 3.00
11 Calvin Johnson 4.00 10.00
12 Drew Stanton 1.25 3.00
13 Brandon Jackson 1.25 3.00
14 Anthony Gonzalez 1.25 3.00
15 Dwayne Bowe 1.25 3.00
16 John Beck 1.25 3.00
17 Lorenzo Booker 1.50 4.00
18 Ted Ginn Jr. 1.50 4.00
19 Adrian Peterson 4.00 10.00
20 Sidney Rice 1.50 4.00
21 Antonio Pittman 1.25 3.00
22 Robert Meachem 1.50 4.00
23 Steve Smith USC 1.25 3.00
24 JaMarcus Russell 1.25 3.00
25 Johnnie Lee Higgins 2.00 5.00
26 Michael Bush 1.25 3.00
27 Kevin Kolb 1.50 4.00
28 Tony Hunt 1.25 3.00
29 Patrick Willis 2.00 5.00
30 Jason Hill 1.25 3.00
31 Brian Leonard 1.25 3.00
32 Gaines Adams 1.50 4.00
33 Chris Henry RB 1.25 3.00
34 Paul Williams 1.25 3.00

2007 Leaf Rookies and Stars Rookie Jerseys Jumbo Swatch

STATED PRINT RUN 50 SER.#'d SETS
*GOLD/25: .6X TO 1.5X BASIC JSY/50
GOLD PRINT RUN 25 SER.#'d SETS
UNPRICED EMERALD PRINT RUN 2-5
UNPRICED BLACK PRINT RUN 1
*LONGEVITY/50: .4X TO 1X BASIC JUMBO/50
LONGEVITY PRINT RUN 50 SER.#'d SETS
UNPRICED LONGEVITY RUBY PRINT RUN 2-5
UNPRICED LONGEVITY SAPPHIRE PRINT RUN 1
201 Trent Edwards 2.50 6.00
202 Marshawn Lynch 5.00 12.00
203 Chris Henry RB 2.50 6.00
204 Paul Williams 2.50 6.00
205 Sidney Rice 3.00 8.00
206 Adrian Peterson 8.00 20.00
207 Drew Stanton 2.50 6.00
208 Calvin Johnson 8.00 20.00
209 Yamon Figurs 2.50 6.00
210 Troy Smith 2.50 6.00
211 Garrett Wolfe 2.50 6.00
212 Greg Olsen 4.00 10.00
213 Joe Thomas 4.00 10.00
214 Brady Quinn 2.50 6.00
215 Ted Ginn Jr. 3.00 8.00
216 John Beck 2.50 6.00
217 Antonio Pittman 2.50 6.00
218 Robert Meachem 3.00 8.00
219 JaMarcus Russell 2.50 6.00
220 Michael Bush 2.50 6.00
221 Kevin Kolb 3.00 8.00
222 Tony Hunt 2.50 6.00
223 Patrick Willis 4.00 10.00
224 Jason Hill 2.50 6.00
225 Brandon Jackson 2.50 6.00
227 Kenny Irons 2.50 6.00
229 Dwayne Bowe 2.50 6.00
231 Steve Smith USC 2.50 6.00
232 Dwayne Jarrett 3.00 8.00
233 Lorenzo Booker 3.00 8.00
234 Anthony Gonzalez 2.50 6.00
235 Johnnie Lee Higgins 2.50 6.00
239 Brian Leonard 2.50 6.00
240 Gaines Adams 3.00 8.00

2007 Leaf Rookies and Stars Rookie Jerseys Jumbo Swatch College

COLLEGE PRINT RUN 5-15
*GOLD/10: .5X TO 1.2X BASIC JSY/15
COLLEGE GOLD PRINT RUN 2-10
UNPRICED EMERALD PRINT RUN 2-3
UNPRICED BLACK PRINT RUN 1
206 Adrian Peterson 100.00 200.00
212 Greg Olsen 10.00 25.00
214 Brady Quinn 6.00 15.00
219 JaMarcus Russell 6.00 15.00
220 Michael Bush 6.00 15.00
229 Dwayne Bowe 6.00 15.00
232 Dwayne Jarrett 8.00 20.00
237 LaRon Landry 10.00 25.00
241 Craig Buster Davis 6.00 15.00

2007 Leaf Rookies and Stars Standing Ovation Red

RED PRINT RUN 1000 SER.#'d SETS
*BLUE/500: .5X TO 1.2X RED/1000
BLUE PRINT RUN 500 SER.#'d SETS
*GREEN/100: .8X TO 2X RED/1000
GREEN PRINT RUN 100 SER.#'d SETS
*PURPLE/25: 1.5X TO 4X RED/1000
PURPLE PRINT RUN 25 SER.#'d SETS
1 Tiki Barber 1.00 2.50
2 Ladell Betts .75 2.00
3 Fred Taylor .75 2.00
4 Warrick Dunn .75 2.00
5 Julius Jones .75 2.00
6 Deuce McAllister 1.00 2.50
7 Ronnie Brown .75 2.00
8 Maurice Jones-Drew .75 2.00
9 Shaun Alexander .75 2.00
10 Steve Smith 1.00 2.50
11 Isaac Bruce 1.25 3.00
12 T.J. Houshmandzadeh .75 2.00
13 Marques Colston .75 2.00
14 Devin Hester 1.00 2.50
15 Larry Fitzgerald 1.00 2.50
16 Antonio Gates 1.25 3.00
17 Tony Gonzalez 1.00 2.50
18 Muhsin Muhammad .75 2.00
19 Eli Manning 1.00 2.50
20 Rex Grossman .75 2.00
21 Peyton Manning 3.00 8.00
22 Steve McNair 1.00 2.50
23 Tony Romo 1.50 4.00
24 Alex Smith QB 1.00 2.50
25 Donovan McNabb 1.00 2.50
26 Matt Leinart .75 2.00
27 Lee Evans 1.00 2.50
28 Matt Hasselbeck .75 2.00
29 Jay Cutler .75 2.00
30 Vince Young .75 2.00
31 Reggie Bush .75 2.00

2007 Leaf Rookies and Stars Standing Ovation Materials Green

GREEN PRINT RUN 150-250
*PURPLE PRIME/25: 1X TO 2.5X GRN/150-250
PURPLE PRIME PRINT RUN 25 SER.#'d SETS
1 Tiki Barber/150 3.00 8.00
2 Ladell Betts 2.50 6.00
3 Fred Taylor/192 2.50 6.00
4 Warrick Dunn/245 2.50 6.00
5 Julius Jones 2.50 6.00
6 Deuce McAllister 3.00 8.00
7 Ronnie Brown 2.50 6.00
8 Maurice Jones-Drew 2.50 6.00
9 Shaun Alexander 2.50 6.00
10 Steve Smith 3.00 8.00
11 Isaac Bruce 4.00 10.00
12 T.J. Houshmandzadeh 2.50 6.00
13 Marques Colston 2.50 6.00
14 Devin Hester 6.00 15.00
15 Larry Fitzgerald 3.00 8.00
16 Antonio Gates 4.00 10.00
17 Tony Gonzalez 3.00 8.00
18 Muhsin Muhammad 2.50 6.00
19 Eli Manning 3.00 8.00
20 Rex Grossman 2.50 6.00
21 Peyton Manning 10.00 25.00
22 Steve McNair 3.00 8.00
23 Tony Romo 5.00 12.00
24 Alex Smith QB 3.00 8.00
25 Donovan McNabb 3.00 8.00
26 Matt Leinart 2.50 6.00
27 Lee Evans 3.00 8.00
28 Matt Hasselbeck 2.50 6.00
29 Jay Cutler 2.50 6.00
30 Vince Young 2.50 6.00
31 Reggie Bush 2.50 6.00

2007 Leaf Rookies and Stars Statistical Standouts Materials

STATED PRINT RUN 245-250
*PRIME/25: 1X TO 2.5X BASIC JSYs
UNPRICED AUTO PRINT RUN 5
UNPRICED PRIME AU PRINT RUN 1
1 Drew Brees 4.00 10.00
2 Peyton Manning 10.00 25.00
3 Marc Bulger 2.50 6.00
4 Carson Palmer 3.00 8.00
5 Brett Favre 8.00 20.00
6 Tom Brady 12.00 30.00
7 Philip Rivers 4.00 10.00
8 Chad Johnson 2.50 6.00
9 Marvin Harrison 3.00 8.00
10 Reggie Wayne 3.00 8.00
11 Roy Williams WR 2.50 6.00
12 Donald Driver 3.00 8.00
13 Anquan Boldin 2.50 6.00
14 Torry Holt 3.00 8.00
15 Terrell Owens/245 3.00 8.00
16 LaDainian Tomlinson 4.00 10.00
17 Larry Johnson 2.50 6.00
18 Frank Gore 3.00 8.00
19 Steven Jackson 2.50 6.00
20 Willie Parker 3.00 8.00
21 Rudi Johnson 2.50 6.00
22 Brian Westbrook 2.50 6.00
23 Joseph Addai 2.50 6.00
24 Reggie Bush 2.50 6.00
25 Vince Young 2.50 6.00

2007 Leaf Rookies and Stars Studio Rookies

INSERTS IN WAL-MART BLASTER BOXES
1 Adrian Peterson 1.50 4.00
2 Anthony Gonzalez .50 1.25
3 Antonio Pittman .50 1.25
4 Brady Quinn .50 1.25
5 Brandon Jackson .50 1.25
6 Brian Leonard .50 1.25
7 Calvin Johnson 1.50 4.00
8 Chris Henry RB .50 1.25
9 Drew Stanton .50 1.25
10 Dwayne Bowe .50 1.25
11 Dwayne Jarrett .60 1.50
12 Gaines Adams .60 1.50
13 Garrett Wolfe .50 1.25
14 Greg Olsen .75 2.00
15 JaMarcus Russell .50 1.25
16 Jason Hill .50 1.25
17 Joe Thomas .75 2.00
18 John Beck .50 1.25
19 Johnnie Lee Higgins .50 1.25
20 Kenny Irons .50 1.25
21 Kevin Kolb .60 1.50
22 Lorenzo Booker .60 1.50
23 Marshawn Lynch 1.00 2.50
24 Michael Bush .50 1.25
25 Patrick Willis .75 2.00
26 Paul Williams .50 1.25
27 Robert Meachem .60 1.50
28 Sidney Rice .60 1.50
29 Steve Smith USC .50 1.25
30 Ted Ginn Jr. .60 1.50
31 Tony Hunt .50 1.25
32 Trent Edwards .50 1.25
33 Troy Smith .50 1.25
34 Yamon Figurs .50 1.25
35 J.Russell/D.Bowe .50 1.25
36 S.Smith USC/D.Jarrett .60 1.50
37 T.Smith/Y.Figurs .50 1.25
38 M.Lynch/T.Edwards 1.00 2.50
39 G.Wolfe/G.Olsen .75 2.00
40 B.Quinn/J.Thomas .75 2.00
41 D.Stanton/C.Johnson 1.50 4.00
42 A.Peterson/S.Rice 1.50 4.00
43 A.Pittman/R.Meachem .60 1.50
44 T.Hunt/K.Kolb .60 1.50
45 J.Hill/P.Willis .75 2.00
46 C.Henry RB/P.Williams .50 1.25
47 M.Lynch/A.Peterson 1.50 4.00
48 P.Willis/G.Adams .75 2.00
49 J.Russell/B.Quinn .50 1.25
50 D.Bowe/T.Hunt .50 1.25
51 Booker/Beck/Ginn Jr. .60 1.50
52 Bush/Russell/Higgins .50 1.25
53 Quinn/Petrsn/Johnsn/Russ 8.00 20.00
54 Pittman/Ginn/Smith/Gonzal .60 1.50

2007 Leaf Rookies and Stars Thanksgiving Classic

SERTS IN DICK'S SPORTING GOODS PACKS
TC1 Tony Romo 1.00 2.50
TC2 Calvin Johnson 1.50 4.00
TC3 Warrick Dunn .50 1.25
TC4 Brett Favre 1.50 4.00
TC5 Chad Pennington .50 1.25
TC6 Peyton Manning 2.00 5.00
TC7 Adrian Peterson 1.25 3.00
TC8 Vince Young .50 1.25
TC9 Reggie Bush .50 1.25
TC10 Brady Quinn .40 1.00
TC11 JaMarcus Russell .40 1.00
TC12 Marshawn Lynch 1.00 2.50

2007 Leaf Rookies and Stars Longevity

COMP.SET w/o RC's (115) 8.00 20.00
*1-115 VETS: .4X TO 1X BASIC CARDS
*ROOKIES/999: .4X TO 1X BASIC CARDS
116-200 ROOKIE PRINT RUN 999

2007 Leaf Rookies and Stars Longevity Emerald

*1-100 VETS/49: 6X TO 15X BASIC CARDS
*101-115 VETS/29: 1.5X TO 4X BASIC CARDS
1-115 VETERAN PRINT RUN 49
*ROOKIES/29: 2X TO 5X BASIC CARDS
116-200 ROOKIE PRINT RUN 29

2007 Leaf Rookies and Stars Longevity Ruby

-100 VETS/249: 2X TO 5X BASIC CARDS
*101-115 VETS/199: .6X TO 1.5X BASIC CARDS
1-115 VETERAN PRINT RUN 199-249
*ROOKIES/199: .8X TO 2X BASIC CARDS
161-200 ROOKIE PRINT RUN 199

2007 Leaf Rookies and Stars Longevity Sapphire

*1-100 VETS/149: 2.5X TO 6X BASIC CARDS
*101-115 VETS/99: .8X TO 2X BASIC CARDS
1-115 VETERAN PRINT RUN 99-149
*ROOKIES/99: 1.2X TO 3X BASIC CARDS
116-200 ROOKIE PRINT RUN 99

2008 Leaf Rookies and Stars

is set was released on November 12, 2008. The base set consists of 249 cards. Cards 1-115 feature veterans, and cards 116-200 are rookies serial numbered of 999. Cards 201-250 are autographed rookie cards, with serial numbers ranging from 52-273.

COMP.SET w/o SP's (100) 10.00 25.00
116-200 ROOKIE PRINT RUN 999
AU ROOKIE PRINT RUN 52-273
1 Matt Leinart .20 .50
2 Larry Fitzgerald .25 .60
3 Anquan Boldin .20 .50
4 Edgerrin James .25 .60
5 Roddy White .20 .50
6 Michael Turner .20 .50
7 Willis McGahee .20 .50
8 Derrick Mason .20 .50
9 Demetrius Williams .20 .50
10 Trent Edwards .20 .50
11 Marshawn Lynch .25 .60
12 Lee Evans .25 .60
13 Steve Smith .25 .60
14 DeAngelo Williams .20 .50
15 Julius Peppers .25 .60
16 Greg Olsen .25 .60
17 Devin Hester .25 .60
18 Rex Grossman .20 .50
19 Carson Palmer .25 .60
20 Chad Johnson .20 .50
21 T.J. Houshmandzadeh .20 .50
22 Chris Perry .20 .50
23 Derek Anderson .20 .50
24 Kellen Winslow .20 .50
25 Braylon Edwards .20 .50
26 Tony Romo .25 .60
27 Terrell Owens .25 .60
28 Marion Barber .20 .50
29 Jay Cutler .20 .50
30 Brandon Stokley .20 .50
31 Jon Kitna .20 .50
32 Roy Williams WR .20 .50
33 Calvin Johnson .30 .75
34 Aaron Rodgers .60 1.50
35 Ryan Grant .25 .60
36 Donald Driver .25 .60
37 Matt Schaub .20 .50
38 Andre Johnson .25 .60
39 Kevin Walter .25 .60
40 Peyton Manning .75 2.00
41 Joseph Addai .20 .50
42 Reggie Wayne .25 .60
43 Dallas Clark .20 .50
44 David Garrard .20 .50
45 Fred Taylor .20 .50
46 Maurice Jones-Drew .20 .50
47 Reggie Williams .25 .60
48 Brodie Croyle .25 .60
49 Larry Johnson .20 .50
50 Tony Gonzalez .25 .60
51 Chad Pennington .20 .50
52 Ronnie Brown .20 .50
53 Ted Ginn Jr. .20 .50
54 Tarvaris Jackson .20 .50
55 Adrian Peterson .30 .75
56 Sidney Rice .20 .50
57 Tom Brady 1.00 2.50
58 Randy Moss .25 .60
59 Laurence Maroney .25 .60
60 Drew Brees .30 .75
61 Reggie Bush .20 .50
62 Deuce McAllister .25 .60
63 Eli Manning .25 .60
64 Plaxico Burress .20 .50
65 Brandon Jacobs .20 .50
66 Brett Favre 2.00 5.00
67 Leon Washington .20 .50
68 Laveranues Coles .20 .50
69 JaMarcus Russell .20 .50
70 Justin Fargas .20 .50
71 Zach Miller .20 .50
72 Donovan McNabb .25 .60
73 Brian Westbrook .20 .50
74 Reggie Brown .20 .50
75 Ben Roethlisberger .30 .75
76 Willie Parker .25 .60
77 Santonio Holmes .20 .50
78 Philip Rivers .30 .75
79 LaDainian Tomlinson .30 .75
80 Vincent Jackson .20 .50
81 Antonio Gates .25 .60
82 J.T. O'Sullivan .20 .50
83 Frank Gore .25 .60
84 Vernon Davis .20 .50
85 Matt Hasselbeck .20 .50
86 Deion Branch .20 .50
87 Julius Jones .20 .50
88 Marc Bulger .20 .50
89 Steven Jackson .20 .50
90 Torry Holt .25 .60
91 Warrick Dunn .20 .50
92 Jeff Garcia .20 .50
93 Joey Galloway .25 .60
94 Vince Young .20 .50
95 LenDale White .20 .50
96 Roydell Williams .20 .50
97 Jason Campbell .20 .50
98 Clinton Portis .20 .50
99 Santana Moss .20 .50
100 Ladell Betts .20 .50
101 Trent Edwards ELE 1.00 2.50
102 Marshawn Lynch ELE 1.25 3.00
103 Braylon Edwards ELE 1.00 2.50
104 Carson Palmer ELE 1.25 3.00
105 Tom Brady ELE 5.00 12.00
106 Matt Hasselbeck ELE 1.00 2.50
107 Nate Burleson ELE 1.00 2.50
108 Fred Taylor ELE 1.00 2.50
109 David Garrard ELE 1.00 2.50
110 Maurice Jones-Drew ELE 1.00 2.50
111 Devin Hester ELE 1.25 3.00
112 Willie Parker ELE 1.25 3.00
113 Ben Roethlisberger ELE 1.50 4.00
114 Ryan Grant ELE 1.25 3.00
115 Eli Manning ELE 1.25 3.00
116 Adrian Arrington RC 1.25 3.00
117 Ali Highsmith RC 1.25 3.00
118 Anthony Alridge RC 1.25 3.00
119 Antoine Cason RC 1.50 4.00
120 Aqib Talib RC 2.00 5.00
121 Brad Cottam RC 1.25 3.00
122 Brandon Flowers RC 1.50 4.00
123 Calais Campbell RC 1.50 4.00
124 Chauncey Washington RC 1.50 4.00
125 Chevis Jackson RC 1.25 3.00
126 Cory Boyd RC 1.25 3.00
127 Craig Steltz RC 1.25 3.00
128 Curtis Lofton RC 1.50 4.00
129 DJ Hall RC 1.25 3.00
130 Dantrell Savage RC 1.50 4.00
131 Darius Reynaud RC 1.25 3.00
132 Darrell Strong RC 1.50 4.00
133 Davone Bess RC 1.50 4.00
134 Derrick Harvey RC 1.25 3.00
135 D.Rodgers-Cromartie RC 1.50 4.00
136 Erin Henderson RC 1.50 4.00
137 Ernie Wheelwright RC 1.50 4.00
138 Fred Davis RC 1.25 3.00
139 Joe Jon Finley RC 1.25 3.00
140 Jacob Hester RC 1.25 3.00
141 Jacob Tamme RC 1.50 4.00
142 Jamar Adams RC 1.25 3.00
143 Jason Rivers RC 1.25 3.00
144 Jed Collins RC 1.50 4.00
145 Jermichael Finley RC 1.25 3.00
146 John Carlson RC 1.25 3.00
147 Jonathan Hefney RC 1.25 3.00
148 Jordon Dizon RC 1.25 3.00
149 Josh Morgan RC 1.25 3.00
150 Justin Forsett RC 1.50 4.00
151 Kalvin McRae RC 1.25 3.00
152 Keenan Burton RC 1.25 3.00
153 Kellen Davis RC 1.25 3.00
154 Kentwan Balmer RC 1.25 3.00
155 Kevin Robinson RC 1.25 3.00
156 Lawrence Jackson RC 1.25 3.00
157 Leodis McKelvin RC 1.50 4.00
158 Marcus Monk RC 1.50 4.00
159 Marcus Smith RC 1.50 4.00
160 Marcus Thomas RC 1.50 4.00
161 Mark Bradford RC 1.25 3.00
162 Martellus Bennett RC 1.50 4.00
163 Martin Rucker RC 1.25 3.00
164 Mike Jenkins RC 1.25 3.00
165 Owen Schmitt RC 1.25 3.00
166 Pat Sims RC 1.50 4.00
167 Paul Hubbard RC 1.25 3.00
168 Paul Smith RC 1.25 3.00
169 Peyton Hillis RC 2.00 5.00
170 Phillip Merling RC 1.25 3.00
171 Quentin Groves RC 1.50 4.00
172 Reggie Smith RC 1.25 3.00
173 Ryan Grice-Mullen RC 1.25 3.00
174 Ryan Torain RC 1.50 4.00
175 Sam Keller RC 1.25 3.00
176 Sedrick Ellis RC 1.25 3.00
177 Shawn Crable RC 1.25 3.00
178 Simeon Castille RC 1.25 3.00
179 Terrell Thomas RC 1.25 3.00
180 Thomas Brown RC 1.25 3.00
181 Tim Hightower RC 1.50 4.00
182 Tracy Porter RC 1.50 4.00
183 Vernon Gholston RC 1.25 3.00
184 Will Franklin RC 1.50 4.00
185 Xavier Adibi RC 1.25 3.00
186 Alex Brink RC 1.50 4.00
187 Jalen Parmele RC 1.50 4.00
188 Xavier Omon RC 1.25 3.00
189 Craig Stevens RC 1.25 3.00
190 Derek Fine RC 1.25 3.00
191 Gary Barnidge RC 2.00 5.00
192 Arman Shields RC 1.50 4.00
193 Kenneth Moore RC 1.25 3.00
194 Marcus Henry RC 1.25 3.00
195 Jaymar Johnson RC 1.25 3.00
196 Pierre Garcon RC 2.50 6.00
197 Patrick Lee RC 1.25 3.00
198 Terrence Wheatley RC 1.25 3.00
199 Tavares Gooden RC 1.25 3.00
200 Bruce Davis RC 1.50 4.00
201 Allen Patrick AU/268 RC 5.00 12.00
202 Andre Caldwell AU/116 RC 6.00 15.00
203 Andre Woodson AU/219 RC 5.00 12.00
204 Brian Brohm AU/99 RC 12.00 30.00
206 Chad Henne AU/99 RC 10.00 25.00
207 Chris Johnson AU/166 RC 8.00 20.00
208 Chris Long AU/99 RC EXCH 12.00 30.00
209 Colt Brennan AU/213 RC 6.00 15.00
210 Dan Connor AU/270 RC 5.00 12.00
211 Darren McFadden AU/99 RC 8.00 20.00
212 Dennis Dixon AU/218 RC 5.00 12.00
213 DeSean Jackson AU/119 RC 12.00 30.00
214 Devin Thomas AU/118 RC 6.00 15.00
215 Dexter Jackson AU/132 RC 10.00 25.00
216 Donnie Avery AU/129 RC 8.00 20.00
217 Dustin Keller AU/115 RC 8.00 20.00
218 Earl Bennett AU/118 RC 15.00 30.00
219 Early Doucet AU/106 RC 6.00 15.00
220 Eddie Royal AU/126 RC 6.00 15.00
221 Erik Ainge AU/271 RC 5.00 12.00
222 Felix Jones AU/99 RC 8.00 20.00
223 Glenn Dorsey AU/99 RC 8.00 20.00
224 Harry Douglas AU/99 RC 10.00 25.00
225 Jake Long AU/99 RC 12.00 30.00
226 Jamaal Charles AU/118 RC 12.00 30.00
227 James Hardy AU/118 RC 6.00 15.00
228 Jerod Mayo AU/52 RC 30.00 60.00
229 Jerome Simpson AU/117 RC 8.00 20.00
230 Joe Flacco AU/99 RC 15.00 40.00
231 John David Booty AU/118 RC 6.00 15.00
232 Jonathan Stewart AU/99 RC 12.00 30.00
233 Jordy Nelson AU/99 RC 30.00 60.00
234 Josh Johnson AU/268 RC 5.00 12.00
235 Keith Rivers AU/263 RC 6.00 15.00
236 Kenny Phillips AU/99 RC 10.00 25.00
237 Kevin O'Connell AU/142 RC 6.00 15.00
238 Kevin Smith AU/117 RC 6.00 15.00
239 Lavelle Hawkins AU/273 RC 6.00 15.00
240 Limas Sweed AU/103 RC 6.00 15.00
241 Malcolm Kelly AU/108 RC 6.00 15.00
242 M.Manningham AU/118 RC 15.00 30.00
243 Matt Flynn AU/263 RC 5.00 12.00
244 Matt Forte AU/107 RC 15.00 40.00
245 Matt Ryan AU/99 RC 40.00 100.00
246 Mike Hart AU/263 RC 5.00 12.00
247 R.Mendenhall AU/99 RC 8.00 20.00
248 Ray Rice AU/105 RC 6.00 15.00
249 Steve Slaton AU/118 RC 6.00 15.00
250 Tashard Choice AU/270 RC 5.00 12.00

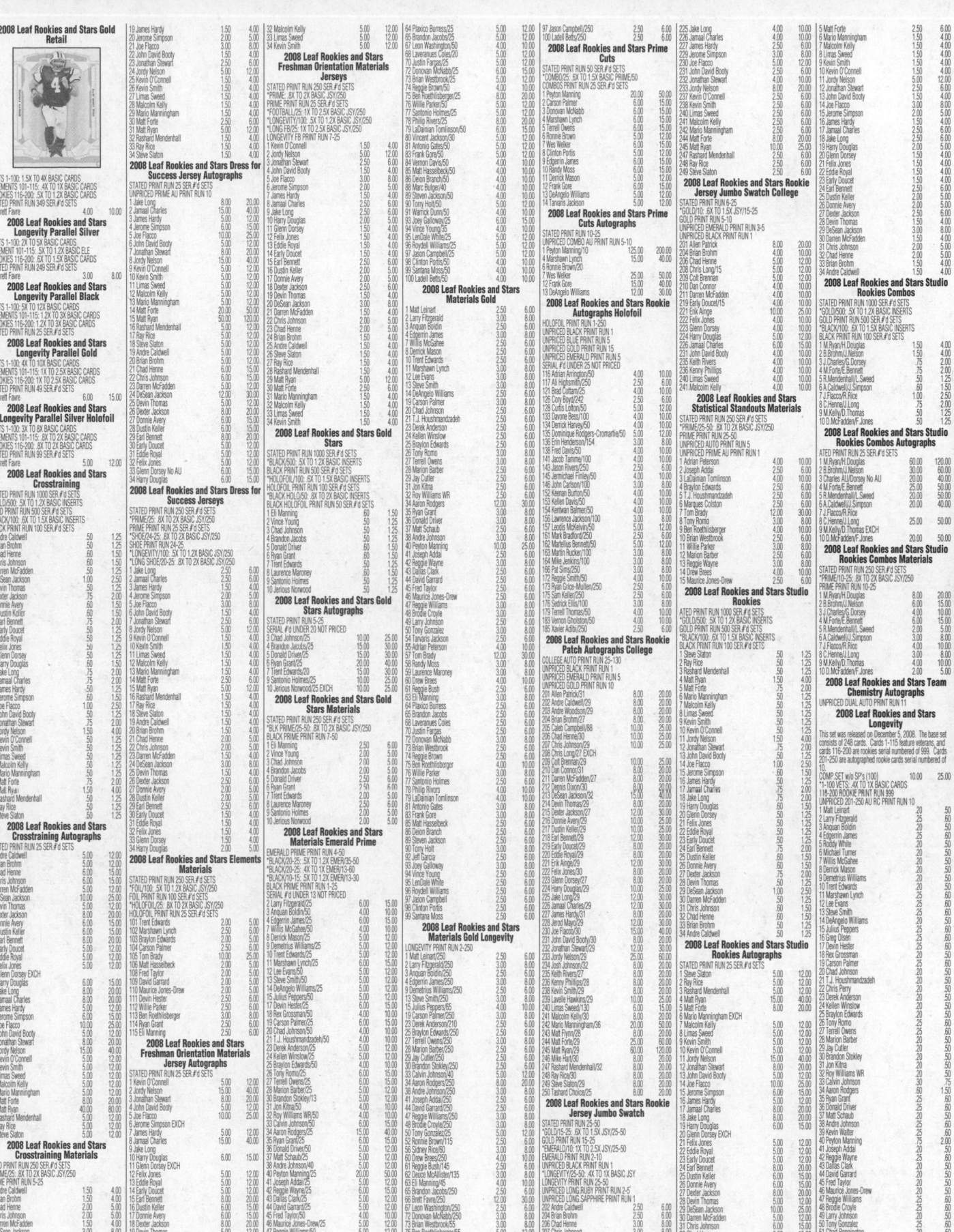

2008 Leaf Rookies and Stars Gold Retail

*VETS 1-100: 1.5X TO 4X BASIC CARDS
*ELEMENTS 101-115: .4X TO 1X BASIC CARDS
*ROOKIES 116-200: .5X TO 1.2X BASIC CARDS
STATED PRINT RUN 349 SER.#'d SETS
66 Brett Favre 4.00 10.00

2008 Leaf Rookies and Stars Longevity Parallel Silver

*VETS 1-100: 2X TO 5X BASIC CARDS
*ELEMENT 101-115: .5X TO 1.2X BASIC ELE
*ROOKIES 116-200: .6X TO 1.5X BASIC CARDS
STATED PRINT RUN 249 SER.#'d SETS
66 Brett Favre 3.00 8.00

2008 Leaf Rookies and Stars Longevity Parallel Black

*VETS 1-100: 5X TO 12X BASIC CARDS
*ELEMENTS 101-115: 1.2X TO 3X BASIC CARDS
*ROOKIES 116-200: 1.2X TO 3X BASIC CARDS
STATED PRINT RUN 25 SER.#'d SETS

2008 Leaf Rookies and Stars Longevity Parallel Gold

*VETS 1-100: 4X TO 10X BASIC CARDS
*ELEMENTS 101-115: 1X TO 2.5X BASIC CARDS
*ROOKIES 116-200: 1X TO 2.5X BASIC CARDS
STATED PRINT RUN 49 SER.#'d SETS
66 Brett Favre 6.00 15.00

2008 Leaf Rookies and Stars Longevity Parallel Silver Holofoil

*VETS 1-100: 3X TO 8X BASIC CARDS
*ELEMENTS 101-115: .8X TO 2X BASIC CARDS
*ROOKIES 116-200: .8X TO 2X BASIC CARDS
STATED PRINT RUN 99 SER.#'d SETS
66 Brett Favre 5.00 12.00

2008 Leaf Rookies and Stars Crosstraining

STATED PRINT RUN 1000 SER.#'d SETS
*GOLD/500: .5X TO 1.2X BASIC INSERTS
GOLD PRINT RUN 500 SER.#'d SETS
*BLACK/100: .6X TO 1.5X BASIC INSERTS
BLACK PRINT RUN 100 SER.#'d SETS
1 Andre Caldwell .50 1.25
2 Brian Brohm .50 1.25
3 Chad Henne .60 1.50
4 Chris Johnson .60 1.50
5 Darren McFadden .50 1.25
6 DeSean Jackson 1.00 2.50
7 Devin Thomas .50 1.25
8 Dexter Jackson .75 2.00
9 Donnie Avery .60 1.50
10 Dustin Keller .60 1.50
11 Earl Bennett .75 2.00
12 Early Doucet .50 1.25
13 Eddie Royal .50 1.25
14 Felix Jones .50 1.25
15 Glenn Dorsey .50 1.25
16 Harry Douglas .60 1.50
17 Jake Long .75 2.00
18 Jamaal Charles .75 2.00
19 James Hardy .50 1.25
20 Jerome Simpson .60 1.50
21 Joe Flacco 1.00 2.50
22 John David Booty .50 1.25
23 Jonathan Stewart .75 2.00
24 Jordy Nelson 1.50 4.00
25 Kevin O'Connell .50 1.25
26 Kevin Smith .50 1.25
27 Limas Sweed .50 1.25
28 Malcolm Kelly .50 1.25
29 Mario Manningham .50 1.25
30 Matt Forte .75 2.00
31 Matt Ryan 1.50 4.00
32 Rashard Mendenhall .50 1.25
33 Ray Rice .50 1.25
34 Steve Slaton .50 1.25

2008 Leaf Rookies and Stars Crosstraining Autographs

STATED PRINT RUN 25 SER.#'d SETS
1 Andre Caldwell 5.00 12.00
2 Brian Brohm 5.00 12.00
3 Chad Henne 6.00 15.00
4 Chris Johnson 6.00 15.00
5 Darren McFadden 5.00 12.00
6 DeSean Jackson 10.00 25.00
7 Devin Thomas 5.00 12.00
8 Dexter Jackson 8.00 20.00
9 Donnie Avery 6.00 15.00
10 Dustin Keller 6.00 15.00
11 Earl Bennett 8.00 20.00
12 Early Doucet 5.00 12.00
13 Eddie Royal 5.00 12.00
14 Felix Jones 5.00 12.00
15 Glenn Dorsey EXCH
16 Harry Douglas 6.00 15.00
17 Jake Long 8.00 20.00
18 Jamaal Charles 8.00 20.00
19 James Hardy 5.00 12.00
20 Jerome Simpson 6.00 15.00
21 Joe Flacco 10.00 25.00
22 John David Booty 5.00 12.00
23 Jonathan Stewart 8.00 20.00
24 Jordy Nelson 15.00 40.00
25 Kevin O'Connell 5.00 12.00
26 Kevin Smith 5.00 12.00
27 Limas Sweed 5.00 12.00
28 Malcolm Kelly 5.00 12.00
29 Mario Manningham 5.00 12.00
30 Matt Forte 8.00 20.00
31 Matt Ryan 40.00 80.00
32 Rashard Mendenhall 5.00 12.00
33 Ray Rice 5.00 12.00
34 Steve Slaton 5.00 12.00

2008 Leaf Rookies and Stars Crosstraining Materials

ATED PRINT RUN 250 SER.#'d SETS
*PRIME/25: .8X TO 2X BASIC JSY/250
PRIME PRINT RUN 5-25
1 Andre Caldwell 1.50 4.00
2 Brian Brohm 1.50 4.00
3 Chad Henne 2.00 5.00
4 Chris Johnson 2.00 5.00
5 Darren McFadden 1.50 4.00
6 DeSean Jackson 3.00 8.00
7 Devin Thomas 1.50 4.00
8 Dexter Jackson 2.50 6.00
9 Donnie Avery 2.00 5.00
10 Dustin Keller 2.00 5.00
11 Earl Bennett 2.50 6.00
12 Early Doucet 1.50 4.00
13 Eddie Royal 1.50 4.00
14 Felix Jones 1.50 4.00
15 Glenn Dorsey 2.00 5.00
16 Harry Douglas 2.00 5.00
17 Jake Long 2.50 6.00
18 Jamaal Charles 2.50 6.00
19 James Hardy 1.50 4.00
20 Jerome Simpson 2.00 5.00
21 Joe Flacco 3.00 8.00
22 John David Booty 1.50 4.00
23 Jonathan Stewart 2.50 6.00
24 Jordy Nelson 5.00 12.00
25 Kevin O'Connell 1.50 4.00
26 Kevin Smith 1.50 4.00
27 Limas Sweed 1.50 4.00
28 Malcolm Kelly 1.50 4.00
29 Mario Manningham 1.50 4.00
30 Matt Forte 2.50 6.00
31 Matt Ryan 5.00 12.00
32 Rashard Mendenhall 1.50 4.00
33 Ray Rice 1.50 4.00
34 Steve Slaton 1.50 4.00

2008 Leaf Rookies and Stars Dress for Success Jersey Autographs

STATED PRINT RUN 25 SER.#'d SETS
UNPRICED PRIME AU PRINT RUN 10
1 Jake Long 8.00 20.00
2 Jamaal Charles 15.00 40.00
3 James Hardy 5.00 12.00
4 Jerome Simpson 6.00 15.00
5 Joe Flacco 10.00 25.00
6 John David Booty 5.00 12.00
7 Jonathan Stewart 8.00 20.00
8 Jordy Nelson 15.00 40.00
9 Kevin O'Connell 5.00 12.00
10 Kevin Smith 5.00 12.00
11 Limas Sweed 5.00 12.00
12 Malcolm Kelly 5.00 12.00
13 Mario Manningham 5.00 12.00
14 Matt Forte 20.00 50.00
15 Matt Ryan 50.00 120.00
16 Rashard Mendenhall 5.00 12.00
17 Ray Rice 5.00 12.00
18 Steve Slaton 5.00 12.00
19 Andre Caldwell 5.00 12.00
20 Brian Brohm 5.00 12.00
21 Chad Henne 6.00 15.00
22 Chris Johnson 6.00 15.00
23 Darren McFadden 5.00 12.00
24 DeSean Jackson 12.00 30.00
25 Devin Thomas 5.00 12.00
26 Dexter Jackson 8.00 20.00
27 Donnie Avery 6.00 15.00
28 Dustin Keller 6.00 15.00
29 Earl Bennett 8.00 20.00
30 Early Doucet 5.00 12.00
31 Eddie Royal 5.00 12.00
32 Felix Jones 5.00 12.00
33 Glenn Dorsey No AU 6.00 15.00
34 Harry Douglas 6.00 15.00

2008 Leaf Rookies and Stars Dress for Success Jerseys

STATED PRINT RUN 250 SER.#'d SETS
*PRIME/25: .8X TO 2X BASIC JSY/250
PRIME PRINT RUN 25 SER.#'d SETS
*SHOE/24-25: .8X TO 2X BASIC JSY/250
SHOE PRINT RUN 24-25
*LONGEVITY/100: .5X TO 1.2X BASIC JSY/250
*LONG SHOE/20-25: .8X TO 2X BASIC JSY/250
1 Jake Long 2.50 6.00
2 Jamaal Charles 2.50 6.00
3 James Hardy 1.50 4.00
4 Jerome Simpson 2.00 5.00
5 Joe Flacco 3.00 8.00
6 John David Booty 1.50 4.00
7 Jonathan Stewart 2.50 6.00
8 Jordy Nelson 5.00 12.00
9 Kevin O'Connell 1.50 4.00
10 Kevin Smith 1.50 4.00
11 Limas Sweed 1.50 4.00
12 Malcolm Kelly 1.50 4.00
13 Mario Manningham 1.50 4.00
14 Matt Forte 2.50 6.00
15 Matt Ryan 5.00 12.00
16 Rashard Mendenhall 1.50 4.00
17 Ray Rice 1.50 4.00
18 Steve Slaton 1.50 4.00
19 Andre Caldwell 1.50 4.00
20 Brian Brohm 1.50 4.00
21 Chad Henne 2.00 5.00
22 Chris Johnson 2.00 5.00
23 Darren McFadden 1.50 4.00
24 DeSean Jackson 3.00 8.00
25 Devin Thomas 1.50 4.00
26 Dexter Jackson 2.50 6.00
27 Donnie Avery 2.00 5.00
28 Dustin Keller 2.00 5.00
29 Earl Bennett 2.50 6.00
30 Early Doucet 1.50 4.00
31 Eddie Royal 1.50 4.00
32 Felix Jones 1.50 4.00
33 Glenn Dorsey 1.50 4.00
34 Harry Douglas 2.00 5.00

2008 Leaf Rookies and Stars Elements Materials

STATED PRINT RUN 250 SER.#'d SETS
*FOIL/100: .5X TO 1.2X BASIC JSY/250
FOIL PRINT RUN 100 SER.#'d SETS
*HOLOFOIL/25: .8X TO 2X BASIC JSY/250
HOLOFOIL PRINT RUN 25 SER.#'d SETS
101 Trent Edwards 2.00 5.00
102 Marshawn Lynch 2.50 6.00
103 Braylon Edwards 2.00 5.00
104 Carson Palmer 2.50 6.00
105 Tom Brady 10.00 25.00
106 Matt Hasselbeck 2.00 5.00
108 Fred Taylor 2.00 5.00
109 David Garrard 2.00 5.00
110 Maurice Jones-Drew 2.00 5.00
111 Devin Hester 2.50 6.00
112 Willie Parker 2.50 6.00
113 Ben Roethlisberger 3.00 8.00
114 Ryan Grant 2.50 6.00
115 Eli Manning 2.50 6.00

2008 Leaf Rookies and Stars Freshman Orientation Materials Jersey Autographs

STATED PRINT RUN 25 SER.#'d SETS
1 Kevin O'Connell 5.00 12.00
2 Jordy Nelson 15.00 40.00
3 Jonathan Stewart 8.00 20.00
4 John David Booty 5.00 12.00
5 Joe Flacco 10.00 25.00
6 Jerome Simpson EXCH
7 James Hardy 5.00 12.00
8 Jamaal Charles 15.00 40.00
9 Jake Long
10 Harry Douglas 6.00 15.00
11 Glenn Dorsey EXCH
12 Felix Jones 5.00 12.00
13 Eddie Royal 5.00 12.00
14 Early Doucet 5.00 12.00
15 Earl Bennett 8.00 20.00
16 Dustin Keller 6.00 15.00
17 Donnie Avery 6.00 15.00
18 Dexter Jackson 8.00 20.00
19 Devin Thomas 5.00 12.00
20 DeSean Jackson 10.00 25.00
21 Darren McFadden 5.00 12.00
22 Chris Johnson 6.00 15.00
23 Chad Henne 6.00 15.00
24 Brian Brohm 5.00 12.00
25 Andre Caldwell 5.00 12.00
26 Steve Slaton 5.00 12.00
27 Ray Rice 5.00 12.00
28 Rashard Mendenhall 8.00 20.00
29 Matt Ryan 60.00 120.00
30 Matt Forte 20.00 50.00
31 Mario Manningham 5.00 12.00
32 Malcolm Kelly 5.00 12.00
33 Limas Sweed 5.00 12.00
34 Kevin Smith 5.00 12.00

2008 Leaf Rookies and Stars Freshman Orientation Materials Jerseys

STATED PRINT RUN 250 SER.#'d SETS
*PRIME: .8X TO 2X BASIC JSY/250
PRIME PRINT RUN 25 SER.#'d SETS
*FOOTBALL/25: 1X TO 2.5X BASIC JSY/250
*LONGEVITY/100: .5X TO 1.2X BASIC JSY/250
*LONG FB/25: 1X TO 2.5X BASIC JSY/250
LONGEVITY FB PRINT RUN 7-25
1 Kevin O'Connell 1.50 4.00
2 Jordy Nelson 5.00 12.00
3 Jonathan Stewart 2.50 6.00
4 John David Booty 1.50 4.00
5 Joe Flacco 3.00 8.00
6 Jerome Simpson 2.00 5.00
7 James Hardy 1.50 4.00
8 Jamaal Charles 2.50 6.00
9 Jake Long 2.50 6.00
10 Harry Douglas 2.00 5.00
11 Glenn Dorsey 1.50 4.00
12 Felix Jones 1.50 4.00
13 Eddie Royal 1.50 4.00
14 Early Doucet 1.50 4.00
15 Earl Bennett 2.50 6.00
16 Dustin Keller 2.00 5.00
17 Donnie Avery 2.00 5.00
18 Dexter Jackson 2.50 6.00
19 Devin Thomas 1.50 4.00
20 DeSean Jackson 3.00 8.00
21 Darren McFadden 1.50 4.00
22 Chris Johnson 2.00 5.00
23 Chad Henne 2.00 5.00
24 Brian Brohm 1.50 4.00
25 Andre Caldwell 1.50 4.00
26 Steve Slaton 1.50 4.00
27 Ray Rice 1.50 4.00
28 Rashard Mendenhall 1.50 4.00
29 Matt Ryan 5.00 12.00
30 Matt Forte 2.50 6.00
31 Mario Manningham 1.50 4.00
32 Malcolm Kelly 1.50 4.00
33 Limas Sweed 1.50 4.00
34 Kevin Smith 1.50 4.00

2008 Leaf Rookies and Stars Gold Stars

STATED PRINT RUN 1000 SER.#'d SETS
*BLACK/500: .5X TO 1.2X BASIC INSERTS
BLACK PRINT RUN 500 SER.#'d SETS
*HOLOFOIL/100: .6X TO 1.5X BASIC INSERTS
HOLOFOIL PRINT RUN 100 SER.#'d SETS
*BLACK HOLO/50: .8X TO 2X BASIC INSERTS
BLACK HOLOFOIL PRINT RUN 50 SER.#'d SETS
1 Eli Manning .60 1.50
2 Vince Young .50 1.25
3 Chad Johnson .50 1.25
4 Brandon Jacobs .50 1.25
5 Donald Driver .60 1.50
6 Ryan Grant .60 1.50
7 Trent Edwards .50 1.25
8 Laurence Maroney .60 1.50
9 Santonio Holmes .50 1.25
10 Jerious Norwood .50 1.25

2008 Leaf Rookies and Stars Gold Stars Autographs

STATED PRINT RUN 5-25
SERIAL #'d UNDER 20 NOT PRICED
3 Chad Johnson/25 10.00 25.00
4 Brandon Jacobs/25 15.00 30.00
5 Donald Driver/25 15.00 30.00
6 Ryan Grant/25 20.00 40.00
7 Trent Edwards/20 15.00 30.00
9 Santonio Holmes/25 10.00 25.00
10 Jerious Norwood/25 EXCH 10.00 25.00

2008 Leaf Rookies and Stars Gold Stars Materials

STATED PRINT RUN 250 SER.#'d SETS
*BLK PRIME/25-50: .8X TO 2X BASIC JSY/250
BLACK PRIME PRINT RUN 7-50
1 Eli Manning 2.50 6.00
2 Vince Young 2.00 5.00
3 Chad Johnson 2.00 5.00
4 Brandon Jacobs 2.00 5.00
5 Donald Driver 2.50 6.00
6 Ryan Grant 2.50 6.00
7 Trent Edwards 2.00 5.00
8 Laurence Maroney 2.50 6.00
9 Santonio Holmes 2.00 5.00
10 Jerious Norwood 2.00 5.00

2008 Leaf Rookies and Stars Materials Emerald Prime

EMERALD PRIME PRINT RUN 4-50
*BLACK/20-25: .5X TO 1.2X EMER/35-50
*BLACK/20-25: .4X TO 1X EMER/13-60
*BLACK/10-15: .5X TO 1.2X EMER/13-30
BLACK PRIME PRINT RUN 1-25
SERIAL #'d UNDER 13 NOT PRICED
2 Larry Fitzgerald/25 6.00 15.00
3 Anquan Boldin/50 4.00 10.00
4 Edgerrin James/25 6.00 15.00
7 Willis McGahee/50 4.00 10.00
8 Derrick Mason/25 5.00 12.00
9 Demetrius Williams/25 5.00 12.00
10 Trent Edwards/25 5.00 12.00
11 Marshawn Lynch/25 6.00 15.00
12 Lee Evans/50 5.00 12.00
13 Steve Smith/50 5.00 12.00
14 DeAngelo Williams/25 5.00 12.00
15 Julius Peppers/50 5.00 12.00
17 Devin Hester/25 6.00 15.00
18 Rex Grossman/50 4.00 10.00
19 Carson Palmer/25 6.00 15.00
20 Chad Johnson/50 4.00 10.00
21 T.J. Houshmandzadeh/50 4.00 10.00
23 Derek Anderson/25 5.00 12.00
24 Kellen Winslow/25 5.00 12.00
25 Braylon Edwards/50 4.00 10.00
26 Tony Romo/25 6.00 15.00
27 Terrell Owens/25 6.00 15.00
28 Marion Barber/25 5.00 12.00
30 Brandon Stokley/13 5.00 12.00
31 Jon Kitna/50 4.00 10.00
32 Roy Williams WR/50 4.00 10.00
33 Calvin Johnson/50 6.00 15.00
34 Aaron Rodgers/25 15.00 40.00
35 Ryan Grant/25 6.00 15.00
36 Donald Driver/50 5.00 12.00
37 Matt Schaub/25 5.00 12.00
38 Andre Johnson/40 5.00 12.00
40 Peyton Manning/25 20.00 50.00
41 Joseph Addai/25 5.00 12.00
42 Reggie Wayne/25 6.00 15.00
43 Dallas Clark/25 5.00 12.00
44 David Garrard/25 5.00 12.00
45 Fred Taylor/50 4.00 10.00
46 Maurice Jones-Drew/25 5.00 12.00
47 Reggie Williams/50 5.00 12.00
49 Larry Johnson/50 4.00 10.00
50 Tony Gonzalez/50 5.00 12.00
52 Ronnie Brown/50 4.00 10.00
54 Tarvaris Jackson/25 5.00 12.00
55 Adrian Peterson/30 20.00 50.00
57 Tom Brady/50 20.00 50.00
58 Randy Moss/25 6.00 15.00
59 Laurence Maroney/50 5.00 12.00
60 Drew Brees/25 8.00 20.00
61 Reggie Bush/25 5.00 12.00
62 Deuce McAllister/25 5.00 12.00
63 Eli Manning/25 6.00 15.00
64 Plaxico Burress/25 5.00 12.00
65 Brandon Jacobs/25 5.00 12.00
67 Leon Washington/50 4.00 10.00
68 Laveranues Coles/20 5.00 12.00
70 Justin Fargas/25 5.00 12.00
72 Donovan McNabb/25 6.00 15.00
73 Brian Westbrook/25 5.00 12.00
74 Reggie Brown/50 4.00 10.00
75 Ben Roethlisberger/25 8.00 20.00
76 Willie Parker/50 5.00 12.00
77 Santonio Holmes/25 5.00 12.00
78 Philip Rivers/25 8.00 20.00
79 LaDainian Tomlinson/50 6.00 15.00
80 Vincent Jackson/30 5.00 12.00
81 Antonio Gates/50 5.00 12.00
83 Frank Gore/50 5.00 12.00
84 Vernon Davis/50 4.00 10.00
85 Matt Hasselbeck/50 4.00 10.00
86 Deion Branch/50 4.00 10.00
88 Marc Bulger/40 4.00 10.00
89 Steven Jackson/50 4.00 10.00
90 Torry Holt/50 5.00 12.00
91 Warrick Dunn/50 4.00 10.00
93 Joey Galloway/25 6.00 15.00
94 Vince Young/35 4.00 10.00
95 LenDale White/25 5.00 12.00
96 Roydell Williams/25 5.00 12.00
97 Jason Campbell/25 5.00 12.00
98 Clinton Portis/50 4.00 10.00
99 Santana Moss/50 4.00 10.00
100 Ladell Betts/50 4.00 10.00

2008 Leaf Rookies and Stars Materials Gold

1 Matt Leinart 2.50 6.00
2 Larry Fitzgerald 3.00 8.00
3 Anquan Boldin 2.50 6.00
4 Edgerrin James 3.00 8.00
7 Willis McGahee 2.50 6.00
8 Derrick Mason 2.50 6.00
10 Trent Edwards 2.50 6.00
11 Marshawn Lynch 3.00 8.00
12 Lee Evans 3.00 8.00
13 Steve Smith 3.00 8.00
14 DeAngelo Williams 2.50 6.00
19 Carson Palmer 3.00 8.00
20 Chad Johnson 2.50 6.00
21 T.J. Houshmandzadeh 2.50 6.00
23 Derek Anderson 2.50 6.00
24 Kellen Winslow 2.50 6.00
25 Braylon Edwards 2.50 6.00
26 Tony Romo 3.00 8.00
27 Terrell Owens 3.00 8.00
28 Marion Barber 2.50 6.00
29 Jay Cutler 2.50 6.00
31 Jon Kitna 2.50 6.00
32 Roy Williams WR 2.50 6.00
34 Aaron Rodgers 12.00 30.00
35 Ryan Grant 3.00 8.00
36 Donald Driver 3.00 8.00
37 Matt Schaub 2.50 6.00
38 Andre Johnson 3.00 8.00
40 Peyton Manning 10.00 25.00
41 Joseph Addai 2.50 6.00
42 Reggie Wayne 3.00 8.00
43 Dallas Clark 2.50 6.00
44 David Garrard 2.50 6.00
45 Fred Taylor 2.50 6.00
46 Maurice Jones-Drew 2.50 6.00
47 Reggie Williams 3.00 8.00
48 Brodie Croyle 3.00 8.00
49 Larry Johnson 2.50 6.00
50 Tony Gonzalez 3.00 8.00
54 Tarvaris Jackson 2.50 6.00
55 Adrian Peterson 4.00 10.00
57 Tom Brady 12.00 30.00
58 Randy Moss 3.00 8.00
59 Laurence Maroney 3.00 8.00
60 Drew Brees 4.00 10.00
61 Reggie Bush 2.50 6.00
63 Eli Manning 3.00 8.00
64 Plaxico Burress 2.50 6.00
65 Brandon Jacobs 2.50 6.00
68 Laveranues Coles 2.50 6.00
70 Justin Fargas 2.50 6.00
72 Donovan McNabb 3.00 8.00
73 Brian Westbrook 2.50 6.00
74 Reggie Brown 2.50 6.00
75 Ben Roethlisberger 4.00 10.00
76 Willie Parker 3.00 8.00
77 Santonio Holmes 2.50 6.00
78 Philip Rivers 4.00 10.00
79 LaDainian Tomlinson 4.00 10.00
81 Antonio Gates 3.00 8.00
83 Frank Gore 3.00 8.00
85 Matt Hasselbeck 2.50 6.00
86 Deion Branch 2.50 6.00
89 Steven Jackson 2.50 6.00
90 Torry Holt 3.00 8.00
92 Jeff Garcia 2.50 6.00
93 Joey Galloway 3.00 8.00
94 Vince Young 2.50 6.00
95 LenDale White 2.50 6.00
96 Roydell Williams 2.50 6.00
97 Jason Campbell 2.50 6.00
98 Clinton Portis 2.50 6.00
99 Santana Moss 2.50 6.00

2008 Leaf Rookies and Stars Materials Gold Longevity

LONGEVITY PRINT RUN 2-250
1 Matt Leinart/250 2.50 6.00
2 Larry Fitzgerald/250 3.00 8.00
3 Anquan Boldin/250 2.50 6.00
4 Edgerrin James/250 3.00 8.00
9 Demetrius Williams/250 2.50 6.00
13 Steve Smith/250 3.00 8.00
15 Julius Peppers/65 4.00 10.00
19 Carson Palmer/250 3.00 8.00
23 Derek Anderson/210 2.50 6.00
25 Braylon Edwards/250 2.50 6.00
27 Terrell Owens/250 3.00 8.00
28 Marion Barber/250 2.50 6.00
29 Jay Cutler/250 2.50 6.00
30 Brandon Stokley/250 2.50 6.00
33 Calvin Johnson/40 5.00 12.00
34 Aaron Rodgers/250 8.00 20.00
38 Andre Johnson/250 3.00 8.00
41 Joseph Addai/250 2.50 6.00
44 David Garrard/250 2.50 6.00
47 Reggie Williams/250 3.00 8.00
48 Brodie Croyle/250 3.00 8.00
50 Tony Gonzalez/25 5.00 12.00
52 Ronnie Brown/115 2.50 6.00
56 Sidney Rice/60 3.00 8.00
60 Drew Brees/250 4.00 10.00
61 Reggie Bush/145 2.50 6.00
62 Deuce McAllister/135 3.00 8.00
63 Eli Manning/45 4.00 10.00
65 Brandon Jacobs/250 2.50 6.00
66 Brett Favre/250 12.00 30.00
67 Leon Washington/250 2.50 6.00
72 Donovan McNabb/250 3.00 8.00
73 Brian Westbrook/55 3.00 8.00
75 Ben Roethlisberger/55 5.00 12.00
76 Willie Parker/30 5.00 12.00
80 Vincent Jackson/250 2.50 6.00
81 Antonio Gates/49 4.00 10.00
83 Frank Gore/60 4.00 10.00
84 Vernon Davis/80 2.50 6.00
86 Deion Branch/18 4.00 10.00
88 Marc Bulger/250 2.50 6.00
89 Steven Jackson/250 3.00 8.00
90 Torry Holt/250 3.00 8.00
91 Warrick Dunn/215 2.50 6.00
92 Jeff Garcia/250 2.50 6.00
94 Vince Young/250 3.00 8.00
95 LenDale White/250 2.50 6.00
96 Roydell Williams/100 2.50 6.00
97 Jason Campbell/250 2.50 6.00
100 Ladell Betts/250 2.50 6.00

2008 Leaf Rookies and Stars Prime Cuts

STATED PRINT RUN 50 SER.#'d SETS
*COMBO/25: .6X TO 1.5X BASIC PRIME/50
COMBOS PRINT RUN 25 SER.#'d SETS
1 Peyton Manning 20.00 50.00
2 Carson Palmer 6.00 15.00
3 Donovan McNabb 6.00 15.00
4 Marshawn Lynch 6.00 15.00
5 Terrell Owens 6.00 15.00
6 Ronnie Brown 5.00 12.00
7 Wes Welker 6.00 15.00
8 Clinton Portis 5.00 12.00
9 Edgerrin James 6.00 15.00
10 Randy Moss 6.00 15.00
11 Derrick Mason 5.00 12.00
12 Frank Gore 6.00 15.00
13 DeAngelo Williams 5.00 12.00
14 Tarvaris Jackson 5.00 12.00

2008 Leaf Rookies and Stars Prime Cuts Autographs

STATED PRINT RUN 10-25
UNPRICED COMBO AU PRINT RUN 5-10
1 Peyton Manning/10 125.00 200.00
4 Marshawn Lynch 15.00 40.00
6 Ronnie Brown/20
7 Wes Welker 25.00 50.00
12 Frank Gore 15.00 40.00
13 DeAngelo Williams 12.00 30.00

2008 Leaf Rookies and Stars Rookie Autographs Holofoil

HOLOFOIL PRINT RUN 1-250
UNPRICED BLACK PRINT RUN 1
UNPRICED BLUE PRINT RUN 5
UNPRICED GOLD PRINT RUN 15
UNPRICED EMERALD PRINT RUN 5
SERIAL #'d UNDER 25 NOT PRICED
116 Adrian Arrington/50 4.00 10.00
117 Ali Highsmith/250 2.50 6.00
121 Brad Cottam/25 4.00 10.00
126 Cory Boyd/242 2.50 6.00
128 Curtis Lofton/50 5.00 12.00
133 Davone Bess/100 4.00 10.00
134 Derrick Harvey/50 4.00 10.00
135 Dominique Rodgers-Cromartie/50 5.00 12.00
136 Erin Henderson/154 3.00 8.00
138 Fred Davis/50 4.00 10.00
141 Jacob Tamme/100 4.00 10.00
143 Jason Rivers/250 2.50 6.00
145 Jermichael Finley/50 4.00 10.00
146 John Carlson/100 3.00 8.00
152 Keenan Burton/50 4.00 10.00
153 Kellen Davis/50 4.00 10.00
154 Kentwan Balmer/50 4.00 10.00
156 Lawrence Jackson/100 3.00 8.00
157 Leodis McKelvin/50 5.00 12.00
161 Mark Bradford/250 2.50 6.00
162 Martellus Bennett/50 5.00 12.00
163 Martin Rucker/100 3.00 8.00
164 Mike Jenkins/100 3.00 8.00
166 Pat Sims/250 3.00 8.00
172 Reggie Smith/50 4.00 10.00
173 Ryan Grice-Mullen/250 2.50 6.00
175 Sam Keller/250 2.50 6.00
176 Sedrick Ellis/100 3.00 8.00
179 Terrell Thomas/50 4.00 10.00
183 Vernon Gholston/50 4.00 10.00
185 Xavier Adibi/250 2.50 6.00

2008 Leaf Rookies and Stars Rookie Patch Autographs College

COLLEGE AUTO PRINT RUN 25-130
UNPRICED BLACK PRINT RUN 1
UNPRICED EMERALD PRINT RUN 5
UNPRICED GOLD PRINT RUN 10
201 Allen Patrick/31 8.00 20.00
202 Andre Caldwell/29 8.00 20.00
203 Andre Woodson/29 8.00 20.00
204 Brian Brohm/27 8.00 20.00
205 Caleb Campbell/88 10.00 25.00
206 Chad Henne/30 10.00 25.00
207 Chris Johnson/29 10.00 25.00
208 Chris Long/27 EXCH
209 Colt Brennan/29 10.00 25.00
210 Dan Connor/31 8.00 20.00
211 Darren McFadden/27 8.00 20.00
212 Dennis Dixon/30 8.00 20.00
213 DeSean Jackson/32 15.00 40.00
214 Devin Thomas/29 8.00 20.00
215 Dexter Jackson/27 12.00 30.00
216 Donnie Avery/29 10.00 25.00
217 Dustin Keller/29 10.00 25.00
218 Earl Bennett/29 12.00 30.00
219 Early Doucet/29 8.00 20.00
220 Eddie Royal/29 8.00 20.00
221 Erik Ainge/29 12.00 30.00
222 Felix Jones/30 8.00 20.00
223 Glenn Dorsey/27 8.00 20.00
224 Harry Douglas/29 10.00 25.00
225 Jake Long/29 12.00 30.00
226 Jamaal Charles/29 12.00 30.00
227 James Hardy/31 8.00 20.00
228 Jerod Mayo/29 12.00 30.00
230 Joe Flacco/30 15.00 40.00
231 John David Booty/30 8.00 20.00
232 Jonathan Stewart/29 12.00 30.00
233 Jordy Nelson/29 25.00 60.00
234 Josh Johnson/32 8.00 20.00
235 Keith Rivers/27 8.00 20.00
236 Kenny Phillips/28 8.00 20.00
238 Kevin Smith/29 8.00 20.00
239 Lavelle Hawkins/29 10.00 25.00
240 Limas Sweed/130 6.00 15.00
241 Malcolm Kelly/30 8.00 20.00
242 Mario Manningham/36 20.00 50.00
243 Matt Flynn/28 8.00 20.00
244 Matt Forte/29 25.00 60.00
245 Matt Ryan/29 60.00 120.00
246 Mike Hart/30 8.00 20.00
247 Rashard Mendenhall/32 8.00 20.00
248 Ray Rice/30 8.00 20.00
249 Steve Slaton/29 8.00 20.00
250 Tashard Choice/25 8.00 20.00

2008 Leaf Rookies and Stars Rookie Jersey Jumbo Swatch

STATED PRINT RUN 25-50
*GOLD/15-25: .6X TO 1.5X JSY/25-50
GOLD PRINT RUN 15-25
*EMERALD/10: 1X TO 2.5X JSY/25-50
EMERALD PRINT RUN 2-10
UNPRICED BLACK PRINT RUN 1
*LONGEVITY/25-50: .4X TO 1X BASIC JSY
LONGEVITY PRINT RUN 25-50
UNPRICED LONG.RUBY PRINT RUN 2-5
UNPRICED LONG.SAPPHIRE PRINT RUN 1
202 Andre Caldwell 2.50 6.00
204 Brian Brohm 2.50 6.00
206 Chad Henne 3.00 8.00
207 Chris Johnson 3.00 8.00
211 Darren McFadden 2.50 6.00
213 DeSean Jackson 5.00 12.00
214 Devin Thomas 2.50 6.00
215 Dexter Jackson 4.00 10.00
216 Donnie Avery 3.00 8.00
217 Dustin Keller 3.00 8.00
218 Earl Bennett 4.00 10.00
219 Early Doucet 2.50 6.00
220 Eddie Royal 2.50 6.00
222 Felix Jones 2.50 6.00
223 Glenn Dorsey 2.50 6.00
224 Harry Douglas 3.00 8.00
225 Jake Long 4.00 10.00
226 Jamaal Charles 4.00 10.00
227 James Hardy 2.50 6.00
229 Jerome Simpson 3.00 8.00
230 Joe Flacco 5.00 12.00
231 John David Booty 2.50 6.00
232 Jonathan Stewart 4.00 10.00
233 Jordy Nelson 8.00 20.00
237 Kevin O'Connell 2.50 6.00
238 Kevin Smith 2.50 6.00
240 Limas Sweed 2.50 6.00
241 Malcolm Kelly 2.50 6.00
242 Mario Manningham 2.50 6.00
244 Matt Forte 8.00 20.00
245 Matt Ryan 10.00 25.00
247 Rashard Mendenhall 2.50 6.00
248 Ray Rice 2.50 6.00
249 Steve Slaton 2.50 6.00

2008 Leaf Rookies and Stars Rookie Jersey Jumbo Swatch College

STATED PRINT RUN 6-25
*GOLD/10: .6X TO 1.5X JSY/15-25
GOLD PRINT RUN 5-10
UNPRICED EMERALD PRINT RUN 3-5
UNPRICED BLACK PRINT RUN 1
201 Allen Patrick 8.00 20.00
204 Brian Brohm 4.00 10.00
206 Chad Henne 5.00 12.00
208 Chris Long/15 5.00 12.00
209 Colt Brennan 5.00 12.00
210 Dan Connor 4.00 10.00
211 Darren McFadden 4.00 10.00
219 Early Doucet/15 4.00 10.00
221 Erik Ainge 10.00 25.00
222 Felix Jones 4.00 10.00
223 Glenn Dorsey 4.00 10.00
224 Harry Douglas 5.00 12.00
226 Jamaal Charles 6.00 15.00
231 John David Booty 4.00 10.00
235 Keith Rivers 4.00 10.00
236 Kenny Phillips 4.00 10.00
240 Limas Sweed 4.00 10.00
241 Malcolm Kelly 4.00 10.00

2008 Leaf Rookies and Stars Statistical Standouts Materials

STATED PRINT RUN 250 SER.#'d SETS
*PRIME/25-50: .8X TO 2X BASIC JSY/250
PRIME PRINT RUN 25-50
UNPRICED AUTO PRINT RUN 5
UNPRICED PRIME AU PRINT RUN 1
1 Adrian Peterson 4.00 10.00
2 Joseph Addai 2.50 6.00
3 LaDainian Tomlinson 4.00 10.00
4 Braylon Edwards 2.50 6.00
5 T.J. Houshmandzadeh 2.50 6.00
6 Marques Colston 2.50 6.00
7 Tom Brady 12.00 30.00
8 Tony Romo 3.00 8.00
9 Ben Roethlisberger 4.00 10.00
10 Brian Westbrook 2.50 6.00
11 Willie Parker 3.00 8.00
12 Marion Barber 2.50 6.00
13 Reggie Wayne 3.00 8.00
14 Drew Brees 4.00 10.00
15 Maurice Jones-Drew 2.50 6.00

2008 Leaf Rookies and Stars Studio Rookies

ATED PRINT RUN 1000 SER.#'d SETS
*GOLD/500: .5X TO 1.2X BASIC INSERTS
GOLD PRINT RUN 500 SER.#'d SETS
*BLACK/100: .6X TO 1.5X BASIC INSERTS
BLACK PRINT RUN 100 SER.#'d SETS
1 Steve Slaton .50 1.25
2 Ray Rice .50 1.25
3 Rashard Mendenhall .50 1.25
4 Matt Ryan 1.50 4.00
5 Matt Forte .75 2.00
6 Mario Manningham .50 1.25
7 Malcolm Kelly .50 1.25
8 Limas Sweed .50 1.25
9 Kevin Smith .50 1.25
10 Kevin O'Connell .50 1.25
11 Jordy Nelson 1.50 4.00
12 Jonathan Stewart .75 2.00
13 John David Booty .50 1.25
14 Joe Flacco 1.00 2.50
15 Jerome Simpson .60 1.50
16 James Hardy .50 1.25
17 Jamaal Charles .75 2.00
18 Jake Long .75 2.00
19 Harry Douglas .60 1.50
20 Glenn Dorsey .50 1.25
21 Felix Jones .50 1.25
22 Eddie Royal .50 1.25
23 Early Doucet .50 1.25
24 Earl Bennett .75 2.00
25 Dustin Keller .60 1.50
26 Donnie Avery .60 1.50
27 Dexter Jackson .75 2.00
28 Devin Thomas .50 1.25
29 DeSean Jackson 1.00 2.50
30 Darren McFadden .50 1.25
31 Chris Johnson .60 1.50
32 Chad Henne .60 1.50
33 Brian Brohm .50 1.25
34 Andre Caldwell .50 1.25

2008 Leaf Rookies and Stars Studio Rookies Autographs

STATED PRINT RUN 25 SER.#'d SETS
1 Steve Slaton 5.00 12.00
2 Ray Rice 5.00 12.00
3 Rashard Mendenhall 5.00 12.00
4 Matt Ryan 15.00 40.00
5 Matt Forte 8.00 20.00
6 Mario Manningham EXCH
7 Malcolm Kelly 5.00 12.00
8 Limas Sweed 5.00 12.00
9 Kevin Smith 5.00 12.00
10 Kevin O'Connell 5.00 12.00
11 Jordy Nelson 15.00 40.00
12 Jonathan Stewart 8.00 20.00
13 John David Booty 5.00 12.00
14 Joe Flacco 10.00 25.00
15 Jerome Simpson 6.00 15.00
16 James Hardy 5.00 12.00
17 Jamaal Charles 8.00 20.00
18 Jake Long 8.00 20.00
19 Harry Douglas 6.00 15.00
20 Glenn Dorsey EXCH
21 Felix Jones 5.00 12.00
22 Eddie Royal 5.00 12.00
23 Early Doucet 5.00 12.00
24 Earl Bennett 8.00 20.00
25 Dustin Keller 6.00 15.00
26 Donnie Avery 6.00 15.00
27 Dexter Jackson 8.00 20.00
28 Devin Thomas 5.00 12.00
29 DeSean Jackson 10.00 25.00
30 Darren McFadden 5.00 12.00
31 Chris Johnson 6.00 15.00
32 Chad Henne 6.00 15.00
33 Brian Brohm 5.00 12.00
34 Andre Caldwell 5.00 12.00

2008 Leaf Rookies and Stars Studio Rookies Materials

STATED PRINT RUN 250 SER.#'d SETS
*PRIME/25: .8X TO 2X BASIC JSY/250
PRIME PRINT RUN 5-25
1 Steve Slaton 1.50 4.00
2 Ray Rice 1.50 4.00
3 Rashard Mendenhall 1.50 4.00
4 Matt Ryan 5.00 12.00
5 Matt Forte 2.50 6.00
6 Mario Manningham 1.50 4.00
7 Malcolm Kelly 1.50 4.00
8 Limas Sweed 1.50 4.00
9 Kevin Smith 1.50 4.00
10 Kevin O'Connell 1.50 4.00
11 Jordy Nelson 5.00 12.00
12 Jonathan Stewart 2.50 6.00
13 John David Booty 1.50 4.00
14 Joe Flacco 3.00 8.00
15 Jerome Simpson 2.00 5.00
16 James Hardy 1.50 4.00
17 Jamaal Charles 2.50 6.00
18 Jake Long 2.50 6.00
19 Harry Douglas 2.00 5.00
20 Glenn Dorsey 1.50 4.00
21 Felix Jones 1.50 4.00
22 Eddie Royal 1.50 4.00
23 Early Doucet 1.50 4.00
24 Earl Bennett 2.50 6.00
25 Dustin Keller 2.00 5.00
26 Donnie Avery 2.00 5.00
27 Dexter Jackson 2.50 6.00
28 Devin Thomas 1.50 4.00
29 DeSean Jackson 3.00 8.00
30 Darren McFadden 1.50 4.00
31 Chris Johnson 2.00 5.00
32 Chad Henne 2.00 5.00
33 Brian Brohm 1.50 4.00
34 Andre Caldwell 1.50 4.00

2008 Leaf Rookies and Stars Studio Rookies Combos

STATED PRINT RUN 1000 SER.#'d SETS
*GOLD/500: .5X TO 1.2X BASIC INSERTS
GOLD PRINT RUN 500 SER.#'d SETS
*BLACK/100: .6X TO 1.5X BASIC INSERTS
BLACK PRINT RUN 100 SER.#'d SETS
1 M.Ryan/H.Douglas 1.50 4.00
2 B.Brohm/J.Nelson 1.50 4.00
3 J.Charles/G.Dorsey .75 2.00
4 M.Forte/E.Bennett .75 2.00
5 R.Mendenhall/L.Sweed .50 1.25
6 A.Caldwell/J.Simpson .60 1.50
7 J.Flacco/R.Rice 1.00 2.50
8 C.Henne/J.Long .75 2.00
9 M.Kelly/D.Thomas .50 1.25
10 D.McFadden/F.Jones .50 1.25

2008 Leaf Rookies and Stars Studio Rookies Combos Autographs

ATED PRINT RUN 25 SER.#'d SETS
1 M.Ryan/H.Douglas 60.00 120.00
2 B.Brohm/J.Nelson 30.00 60.00
3 Charles AU/Dorsey No AU 20.00 40.00
4 M.Forte/E.Bennett 25.00 50.00
5 R.Mendenhall/L.Sweed 20.00 50.00
6 A.Caldwell/J.Simpson 20.00 40.00
7 J.Flacco/R.Rice
8 C.Henne/J.Long 25.00 50.00
9 M.Kelly/D.Thomas EXCH
10 D.McFadden/F.Jones 20.00 50.00

2008 Leaf Rookies and Stars Studio Rookies Combos Materials

STATED PRINT RUN 250 SER.#'d SETS
*PRIME/10-25: .8X TO 2X BASIC JSY/250
PRIME PRINT RUN 10-25
1 M.Ryan/H.Douglas 8.00 20.00
2 B.Brohm/J.Nelson 6.00 15.00
3 J.Charles/G.Dorsey 4.00 10.00
4 M.Forte/E.Bennett 6.00 15.00
5 R.Mendenhall/L.Sweed 2.00 5.00
6 A.Caldwell/J.Simpson 3.00 8.00
7 J.Flacco/R.Rice 4.00 10.00
8 C.Henne/J.Long 3.00 8.00
9 M.Kelly/D.Thomas 4.00 10.00
10 D.McFadden/F.Jones 2.00 5.00

2008 Leaf Rookies and Stars Team Chemistry Autographs

UNPRICED DUAL AUTO PRINT RUN 11

2008 Leaf Rookies and Stars Longevity

This set was released on December 5, 2008. The base set consists of 248 cards. Cards 1-115 feature veterans, and cards 116-200 are rookies serial numbered of 999. Cards 201-250 are autographed rookie cards serial numbered of 10.

COMP.SET w/o SP's (100) 10.00 25.00
*1-100 VETS: .4X TO 1X BASIC CARDS
116-200 ROOKIE PRINT RUN 999
UNPRICED 201-250 AU RC PRINT RUN 10
1 Matt Leinart .20 .50
2 Larry Fitzgerald .25 .60
3 Anquan Boldin .20 .50
4 Edgerrin James .25 .60
5 Roddy White .20 .50
6 Michael Turner .20 .50
7 Willis McGahee .20 .50
8 Derrick Mason .20 .50
9 Demetrius Williams .20 .50
10 Trent Edwards .20 .50
11 Marshawn Lynch .25 .60
12 Lee Evans .25 .60
13 Steve Smith .25 .60
14 DeAngelo Williams .20 .50
15 Julius Peppers .25 .60
16 Greg Olsen .25 .60
17 Devin Hester .25 .60
18 Rex Grossman .20 .50
19 Carson Palmer .25 .60
20 Chad Johnson .20 .50
21 T.J. Houshmandzadeh .20 .50
22 Chris Perry .20 .50
23 Derek Anderson .20 .50
24 Kellen Winslow .20 .50
25 Braylon Edwards .20 .50
26 Tony Romo .25 .60
27 Terrell Owens .25 .60
28 Marion Barber .20 .50
29 Jay Cutler .20 .50
30 Brandon Stokley .20 .50
31 Jon Kitna .20 .50
32 Roy Williams WR .20 .50
33 Calvin Johnson .30 .75
34 Aaron Rodgers .60 1.50
35 Ryan Grant .25 .60
36 Donald Driver .25 .60
37 Matt Schaub .20 .50
38 Andre Johnson .25 .60
39 Kevin Walter .25 .60
40 Peyton Manning .75 2.00
41 Joseph Addai .20 .50
42 Reggie Wayne .25 .60
43 Dallas Clark .20 .50
44 David Garrard .20 .50
45 Fred Taylor .20 .50
46 Maurice Jones-Drew .20 .50
47 Reggie Williams .25 .60
48 Brodie Croyle .25 .60
49 Larry Johnson .20 .50
50 Tony Gonzalez .25 .60
51 Chad Pennington .20 .50
52 Ronnie Brown .20 .50
53 Ted Ginn Jr. .20 .50
54 Tarvaris Jackson .20 .50
55 Adrian Peterson .30 .75
56 Sidney Rice .20 .50
57 Tom Brady 1.00 2.50
58 Randy Moss .25 .60
59 Laurence Maroney .25 .60
60 Drew Brees .30 .75
61 Reggie Bush .25 .60
62 Deuce McAllister .20 .50
63 Eli Manning .25 .60

64 Plaxico Burress .20 .50
65 Brandon Jacobs .20 .50
66 Brett Favre 2.00 5.00
67 Leon Washington .20 .50
68 Laveranues Coles .20 .50
69 JaMarcus Russell .20 .50
70 Justin Fargas .20 .50
71 Zach Miller .20 .50
72 Donovan McNabb .25 .60
73 Brian Westbrook .20 .50
74 Reggie Brown .20 .50
75 Ben Roethlisberger .30 .75
76 Willie Parker .25 .60
77 Santonio Holmes .20 .50
78 Philip Rivers .30 .75
79 LaDainian Tomlinson .30 .75
80 Vincent Jackson .20 .50
81 Antonio Gates .25 .60
82 J.T. O'Sullivan .20 .50
83 Frank Gore .25 .60
84 Vernon Davis .20 .50
85 Matt Hasselbeck .20 .50
86 Deion Branch .20 .50
87 Julius Jones .20 .50
88 Marc Bulger .20 .50
89 Steven Jackson .20 .50
90 Torry Holt .25 .60
91 Warrick Dunn .20 .50
92 Jeff Garcia .20 .50
93 Joey Galloway .25 .60
94 Vince Young .20 .50
95 LenDale White .20 .50
96 Roydell Williams .20 .50
97 Jason Campbell .20 .50
98 Clinton Portis .20 .50
99 Santana Moss .20 .50
100 Ladell Betts .20 .50
101 Trent Edwards ELE .60 1.50
102 Marshawn Lynch ELE .75 2.00
103 Braylon Edwards ELE .60 1.50
104 Carson Palmer ELE .75 2.00
105 Tom Brady ELE 3.00 8.00
106 Matt Hasselbeck ELE .60 1.50
107 Nate Burleson ELE .60 1.50
108 Fred Taylor ELE .60 1.50
109 David Garrard ELE .60 1.50
110 Maurice Jones-Drew ELE .60 1.50
111 Devin Hester ELE .75 2.00
112 Willie Parker ELE .75 2.00
113 Ben Roethlisberger ELE 1.00 2.50
114 Ryan Grant ELE .75 2.00
115 Eli Manning ELE .75 2.00
116 Adrian Arrington RC 1.25 3.00
117 Ali Highsmith RC 1.25 3.00
118 Anthony Alridge RC 1.25 3.00
119 Antoine Cason RC 1.50 4.00
120 Aqib Talib RC 2.00 5.00
121 Brad Cottam RC 1.25 3.00
122 Brandon Flowers RC 1.50 4.00
123 Calais Campbell RC 1.50 4.00
124 Chauncey Washington RC 1.50 4.00
125 Chevis Jackson RC 1.25 3.00
126 Cory Boyd RC 1.25 3.00
127 Craig Steltz RC 1.25 3.00
128 Curtis Lofton RC 1.50 4.00
129 DJ Hall RC 1.25 3.00
130 Dantrell Savage RC 1.50 4.00
131 Darius Reynaud RC 1.25 3.00
132 Darrell Strong RC 1.50 4.00
133 Davone Bess RC 1.50 4.00
134 Derrick Harvey RC 1.25 3.00
135 D.Rodgers-Cromartie RC 1.50 4.00
136 Erin Henderson RC 1.50 4.00
137 Ernie Wheelwright RC 1.50 4.00
138 Fred Davis RC 1.25 3.00
139 Joe Jon Finley RC 1.25 3.00
140 Jacob Hester RC 1.25 3.00
141 Jacob Tamme RC 1.50 4.00
142 Jamar Adams RC 1.25 3.00
143 Jason Rivers RC 1.25 3.00
144 Jed Collins RC 1.50 4.00
145 Jermichael Finley RC 1.25 3.00
146 John Carlson RC 1.25 3.00
147 Jonathan Hefney RC 1.25 3.00
148 Jordon Dizon RC 1.25 3.00
149 Josh Morgan RC 1.25 3.00
150 Justin Forsett RC 1.50 4.00
151 Kalvin McRae RC 1.25 3.00
152 Keenan Burton RC 1.25 3.00
153 Kellen Davis RC 1.25 3.00
154 Kentwan Balmer RC 1.25 3.00
155 Kevin Robinson RC 1.25 3.00
156 Lawrence Jackson RC 1.25 3.00
157 Leodis McKelvin RC 1.50 4.00
158 Marcus Monk RC 1.50 4.00
159 Marcus Smith RC 1.50 4.00
160 Marcus Thomas RC 1.50 4.00
161 Mark Bradford RC 1.25 3.00
162 Martellus Bennett RC 1.50 4.00
163 Martin Rucker RC 1.25 3.00
164 Mike Jenkins RC 1.25 3.00
165 Owen Schmitt RC 1.25 3.00
166 Pat Sims RC 1.50 4.00
167 Paul Hubbard RC 1.25 3.00
168 Paul Smith RC 1.25 3.00
169 Peyton Hillis RC 2.00 5.00
170 Phillip Merling RC 1.25 3.00
171 Quentin Groves RC 1.50 4.00
172 Reggie Smith RC 1.25 3.00
173 Ryan Grice-Mullen RC 1.25 3.00
174 Ryan Torain RC 1.50 4.00
175 Sam Keller RC 1.25 3.00
176 Sedrick Ellis RC 1.25 3.00
177 Shawn Crable RC 1.25 3.00
178 Simeon Castille RC 1.25 3.00
179 Terrell Thomas RC 1.25 3.00
180 Thomas Brown RC 1.25 3.00
181 Tim Hightower RC 1.50 4.00
182 Tracy Porter RC 1.50 4.00
183 Vernon Gholston RC 1.25 3.00
184 Will Franklin RC 1.50 4.00
185 Xavier Adibi RC 1.25 3.00
186 Alex Brink RC 1.50 4.00
187 Jalen Parmele RC 1.50 4.00
188 Xavier Omon RC 1.25 3.00
189 Craig Stevens RC 1.25 3.00
190 Derek Fine RC 1.25 3.00
191 Gary Barnidge RC 2.00 5.00
192 Arman Shields RC 1.50 4.00
193 Kenneth Moore RC 1.25 3.00
194 Marcus Henry RC 1.25 3.00
195 Jaymar Johnson RC 1.25 3.00
196 Pierre Garcon RC 2.50 6.00
197 Patrick Lee RC 1.25 3.00
198 Terrence Wheatley RC 1.25 3.00
199 Tavares Gooden RC 1.25 3.00
200 Bruce Davis RC 1.50 4.00

2008 Leaf Rookies and Stars Longevity Emerald

*VETS 1-100: 4X TO 10X BASIC CARDS
*ELEMENTS 101-115: 1.5X TO 4X BASIC CARDS
*ROOKIES 116-200: 1X TO 2.5X BASIC CARDS
EMERALD PRINT RUN 49 SER.#'d SETS
66 Brett Favre 6.00 15.00

2008 Leaf Rookies and Stars Longevity Ruby

*VETS 1-100: 2X TO 5X BASIC CARDS
*ELEMENTS 101-115: .8X TO 2X BASIC CARDS
*ROOKIES 116-200: .5X TO 1.2X BASIC CARDS
RUBY PRINT RUN 249 SER.#'d SETS
66 Brett Favre 3.00 8.00

2008 Leaf Rookies and Stars Longevity Sapphire

ETS 1-100: 2.5X TO 6X BASIC CARDS
*ELEMENT 101-115: 1X TO 2.5X BASIC CARDS
*ROOKIES 116-200: .6X TO 1.5X BASIC CARDS
SAPPHIRE PRINT RUN 149 SER.#'d SETS
66 Brett Favre 4.00 10.00

2008 Leaf Rookies and Stars Longevity Materials Sapphire

PPHIRE PRINT RUN 100 SER.#'d SETS
*RUBY/250-350: .3X TO .8X BASIC INSERTS
*RUBY/97-175: .4X TO 1X BASIC INSERTS
RUBY PRINT RUN 97-350
1 Matt Leinart 3.00 8.00
2 Larry Fitzgerald 4.00 10.00
3 Anquan Boldin 3.00 8.00
4 Edgerrin James 4.00 10.00
7 Willis McGahee 3.00 8.00
8 Derrick Mason 3.00 8.00
9 Demetrius Williams 3.00 8.00
10 Trent Edwards 3.00 8.00
11 Marshawn Lynch 4.00 10.00
12 Lee Evans 4.00 10.00
13 Steve Smith 4.00 10.00
14 DeAngelo Williams 3.00 8.00
15 Julius Peppers 4.00 10.00
17 Devin Hester 4.00 10.00
19 Carson Palmer 4.00 10.00
20 Chad Johnson 3.00 8.00
21 T.J. Houshmandzadeh 3.00 8.00
23 Derek Anderson 3.00 8.00
24 Kellen Winslow 3.00 8.00
25 Braylon Edwards 3.00 8.00
26 Tony Romo 4.00 10.00
27 Terrell Owens 4.00 10.00
28 Marion Barber 3.00 8.00
29 Jay Cutler 3.00 8.00
30 Brandon Stokley 3.00 8.00
31 Jon Kitna 3.00 8.00
32 Roy Williams WR 3.00 8.00
34 Aaron Rodgers 10.00 25.00
35 Ryan Grant 4.00 10.00
36 Donald Driver 4.00 10.00
37 Matt Schaub 3.00 8.00
38 Andre Johnson 4.00 10.00
40 Peyton Manning 12.00 30.00
41 Joseph Addai 3.00 8.00
42 Reggie Wayne 4.00 10.00
43 Dallas Clark 3.00 8.00
44 David Garrard 3.00 8.00
45 Fred Taylor 3.00 8.00
46 Maurice Jones-Drew 3.00 8.00
47 Reggie Williams 4.00 10.00
48 Brodie Croyle 4.00 10.00
49 Larry Johnson 3.00 8.00
50 Tony Gonzalez 4.00 10.00
54 Tarvaris Jackson 3.00 8.00
55 Adrian Peterson 5.00 12.00
57 Tom Brady 15.00 40.00
58 Randy Moss 4.00 10.00
59 Laurence Maroney 4.00 10.00
60 Drew Brees 5.00 12.00
61 Reggie Bush 3.00 8.00
63 Eli Manning 4.00 10.00
64 Plaxico Burress 3.00 8.00
65 Brandon Jacobs 3.00 8.00
67 Leon Washington/60 3.00 8.00
68 Laveranues Coles 3.00 8.00
70 Justin Fargas 3.00 8.00
72 Donovan McNabb 4.00 10.00
73 Brian Westbrook 3.00 8.00
74 Reggie Brown 3.00 8.00
75 Ben Roethlisberger 5.00 12.00
76 Willie Parker 4.00 10.00
77 Santonio Holmes 3.00 8.00
78 Philip Rivers 5.00 12.00
79 LaDainian Tomlinson 5.00 12.00
81 Antonio Gates 4.00 10.00
83 Frank Gore 4.00 10.00
85 Matt Hasselbeck 3.00 8.00
86 Deion Branch 3.00 8.00
88 Marc Bulger/50 3.00 8.00
89 Steven Jackson 3.00 8.00
90 Torry Holt 4.00 10.00
92 Jeff Garcia 3.00 8.00
93 Joey Galloway 4.00 10.00
94 Vince Young 3.00 8.00
95 LenDale White 3.00 8.00
96 Roydell Williams 3.00 8.00
97 Jason Campbell 3.00 8.00
98 Clinton Portis 3.00 8.00
99 Santana Moss 3.00 8.00
100 Ladell Betts 3.00 8.00

2008 Leaf Rookies and Stars Longevity Rookie Autographs

LONGEVITY PRINT RUN 9-500
UNPRICED RUBY PRINT RUN 5
UNPRICED SAPPHIRE PRINT RUN 1
UNPRICED COLLEGE PRINT RUN 5
UNPRICED COLLEGE RUBY PRINT RUN 1
UNPRICED COLL.SAPPHIRE PRINT RUN 1
117 Ali Highsmith/500 2.00 5.00
123 Calais Campbell/250 3.00 8.00
126 Cory Boyd/500 2.00 5.00
130 Dantrell Savage/314 3.00 8.00
131 Darius Reynaud/50 3.00 8.00
136 Erin Henderson/500 2.50 6.00
143 Jason Rivers/500 2.00 5.00
145 Jermichael Finley/100 3.00 8.00
153 Kellen Davis/125 3.00 8.00
154 Kentwan Balmer/250 2.50 6.00
161 Mark Bradford/500 2.00 5.00
166 Pat Sims/450 2.50 6.00
173 Ryan Grice-Mullen/500 2.00 5.00
175 Sam Keller/500 2.00 5.00
185 Xavier Adibi/450 2.00 5.00

1997 Leaf Signature

The 1997 Leaf Signature set was issued in one series totalling 117 cards and features UV coated borderless color player photos measuring approximately 8" by 10". The cards are unnumberd and checklisted below alphabetically.

COMPLETE SET (117) 90.00 150.00
1 Karim Abdul-Jabbar 1.00 2.50
2 Troy Aikman 2.00 5.00
3 Derrick Alexander WR .60 1.50
4 Terry Allen 1.00 2.50
5 Mike Alstott 1.00 2.50
6 Jamal Anderson 1.00 2.50
7 Reidel Anthony RC 1.00 2.50
8 Darnell Autry RC .60 1.50
9 Tony Banks .60 1.50
10 Tiki Barber RC 4.00 10.00
11 Pat Barnes RC 1.00 2.50
12 Jerome Bettis 1.00 2.50
13 Tim Biakabutuka .60 1.50
14 Will Blackwell RC .60 1.50
15 Jeff Blake .60 1.50
16 Drew Bledsoe 1.25 3.00
17 Peter Boulware RC 1.00 2.50
18 Robert Brooks .60 1.50
19 Dave Brown .60 1.50
20 Tim Brown 1.00 2.50
21 Isaac Bruce 1.00 2.50
22 Mark Brunell 1.25 3.00
23 Rae Carruth RC .40 1.00
24 Ki-Jana Carter .40 1.00
25 Cris Carter 1.00 2.50
26 Larry Centers .60 1.50
27 Ben Coates .60 1.50
28 Kerry Collins 1.00 2.50
29 Todd Collins .40 1.00
30 Albert Connell RC 1.00 2.50
31 Curtis Conway .60 1.50
32 Terrell Davis 1.25 3.00
33 Troy Davis RC .60 1.50
34 Corey Dillon RC 2.50 6.00
35 Jim Druckenmiller RC .60 1.50
36 Warrick Dunn RC 2.00 5.00
37 John Elway 4.00 10.00
38 Bert Emanuel .60 1.50
39 Bobby Engram .60 1.50
40 Boomer Esiason .60 1.50
41 Jim Everett .40 1.00
42 Marshall Faulk 1.25 3.00
43 Brett Favre 4.00 10.00
44 Antonio Freeman 1.00 2.50
45 Gus Frerotte .40 1.00
46 Irving Fryar .60 1.50
47 Joey Galloway .60 1.50
48 Eddie George 1.00 2.50
49 Jeff George .60 1.50
50 Tony Gonzalez RC 2.50 6.00
51 Jay Graham .60 1.50
52 Elvis Grbac .60 1.50
53 Darrell Green .60 1.50
54 Yatil Green RC .60 1.50
55 Rodney Hampton .60 1.50
56 Byron Hanspard RC .60 1.50
57 Jim Harbaugh .60 1.50
58 Marvin Harrison 1.00 2.50
59 Garrison Hearst .60 1.50
60 Greg Hill .40 1.00
61 Ike Hilliard RC 1.00 2.50
62 Jeff Hostetler .40 1.00
63 Brad Johnson 1.00 2.50
64 Keyshawn Johnson 1.00 2.50
65 Daryl Johnston .60 1.50
66 Napoleon Kaufman 1.00 2.50
67 Jim Kelly 1.00 2.50
68 Eddie Kennison .60 1.50
69 Joey Kent 1.00 2.50
70 Bernie Kosar .40 1.00
71 Erik Kramer .40 1.00
72 Dorsey Levens 1.00 2.50
73 Kevin Lockett RC .60 1.50
74 Dan Marino 4.00 10.00
75 Curtis Martin 1.25 3.00
76 Tony Martin .60 1.50
77 Leeland McElroy .40 1.00
78 Steve McNair 1.25 3.00
79 Natrone Means .60 1.50
80 Eric Metcalf .60 1.50
81 Anthony Miller .40 1.00
82 Rick Mirer .40 1.00
83 Scott Mitchell .60 1.50
84 Warren Moon 1.00 2.50
85 Herman Moore .60 1.50
86 Muhsin Muhammad .60 1.50
87 Adrian Murrell .60 1.50
88 Neil O'Donnell .60 1.50
89 Terrell Owens 1.25 3.00
90 Brett Perriman .40 1.00
91 Lawrence Phillips .40 1.00
92 Jake Plummer RC 2.50 6.00
93 Andre Reed .60 1.50
94 Jerry Rice 2.00 5.00
95 Darrell Russell RC .40 1.00
96 Rashaan Salaam .40 1.00
97 Barry Sanders 3.00 8.00
98 Chris Sanders .40 1.00
99 Deion Sanders 1.00 2.50
100 Frank Sanders .60 1.50
101 Darnay Scott .60 1.50
102 Junior Seau 1.00 2.50
103 Shannon Sharpe .60 1.50
104 Sedrick Shaw RC .60 1.50
105 Heath Shuler .40 1.00
106 Antowain Smith RC 1.50 4.00
107 Bruce Smith .60 1.50
108 Emmitt Smith 3.00 8.00
109 Kordell Stewart 1.00 2.50
110 J.J. Stokes .60 1.50
111 Vinny Testaverde .60 1.50
112 Thurman Thomas 1.00 2.50
113 Tamarick Vanover .60 1.50
114 Herschel Walker .60 1.50
115 Michael Westbrook .60 1.50
116 Danny Wuerffel RC 1.00 2.50
117 Steve Young 1.25 3.00

1997 Leaf Signature Autographs

Randomly inserted one in every pack, this set features borderless color player photos measuring 8" by 10" and printed on super-premium card stock with foil treatment and a signable UV coating. Each card is autographed and displays an "Authentic Signature" designation. The cards are unnumbered and checklisted below in alphabetical order. A few cards, such as Jerry Rice, appeared on the secondary market after Pinnacle folded. Presumably these cards were never inserted in packs.

UNL.STARS/1000-2500 10.00 25.00
ONE AUTOGRAPH PER PACK
*FD MARKERS/1000-5000: .8X TO 2X
*FD MARKERS/200-500: .6X TO 1.5X
*FD MARK SP #64/87: 1X TO 2.5X
FIRST DOWN PRINT RUN 100 SETS
1 K.Abdul-Jabbar/2500 6.00 15.00
2 D.Alexander WR/4000 5.00 12.00
3 Terry Allen/3000 5.00 12.00
4 Mike Alstott/4000 8.00 20.00
5 Jamal Anderson/4000 8.00 20.00
6 Reidel Anthony/2000 6.00 15.00
7 Darnell Autry/4000 3.00 8.00
8 Tony Banks/500 15.00 40.00
9 Tiki Barber/4000 12.00 30.00
10 Pat Barnes/4000 3.00 8.00
11 Jerome Bettis/500 40.00 80.00
12 T.Biakabutuka/3000 5.00 12.00
13 Will Blackwell/2500 4.00 10.00
14 Jeff Blake/500 12.00 25.00
15 Drew Bledsoe/500 30.00 60.00
16 Peter Boulware/4000 8.00 20.00
17 Robert Brooks/1000 6.00 15.00
18 Dave Brown/500 12.00 25.00
19 Tim Brown/2500 12.00 30.00
20 Isaac Bruce/2500 10.00 25.00
21 Mark Brunell/500 15.00 40.00
22 Rae Carruth/5000 8.00 20.00
23 Cris Carter/2500 12.00 30.00
24 Larry Centers/4000 5.00 12.00
25 Ben Coates/4000 3.00 8.00
26 Todd Collins/4000 8.00 20.00
27 Albert Connell/4000 3.00 8.00
28 Curtis Conway/3000 5.00 12.00
29 Terrell Davis/2500 15.00 30.00
30 Troy Davis/4000 3.00 8.00
31 Trent Dilfer/500 20.00 50.00
32 Corey Dillon/4000 8.00 20.00
33 J.Druckenmiller/5000 3.00 8.00
34 Warrick Dunn/2000 12.00 30.00
35 John Elway/500 60.00 120.00
36 Bert Emanuel/4000 5.00 12.00
37 Bobby Engram/3000 5.00 12.00
38 Boomer Esiason/500 20.00 50.00
39 Jim Everett/500 12.00 25.00
40 Marshall Faulk/3000 15.00 30.00
41 Antonio Freeman/2000 10.00 25.00
42 Gus Frerotte/500 15.00 40.00
43 Irving Fryar/3000 5.00 12.00
44 Joey Galloway/3000 5.00 12.00
45 Eddie George/300 20.00 50.00
46 Jeff George/500 12.50 25.00
47 Tony Gonzalez/4000 15.00 40.00
48 Jay Graham/1000 4.00 10.00
49 Elvis Grbac/500 15.00 40.00
50 Darrell Green/2500 12.00 30.00
51 Yatil Green/5000 3.00 8.00
52 Rodney Hampton/4000 3.00 8.00
53 Byron Hanspard/4000 3.00 8.00
54 Jim Harbaugh/500 15.00 40.00
55 Marvin Harrison/3000 25.00 40.00
56 Garrison Hearst/4000 8.00 20.00
57 Greg Hill/4000 3.00 8.00
58 Ike Hilliard/2000 6.00 15.00
59 Jeff Hostetler/500 12.00 25.00
60 Brad Johnson/2000 6.00 15.00
61 K.Johnson/1000 12.00 25.00
62 Daryl Johnston/3000 8.00 20.00
63 Jim Kelly/500 40.00 80.00
64 Eddie Kennison/3000 5.00 12.00
65 Joey Kent/4000 3.00 8.00
66 Bernie Kosar/500 15.00 40.00
67 Erik Kramer/500 12.00 25.00
68 Dorsey Levens/3000 8.00 20.00
69 Kevin Lockett/4000 3.00 8.00
70 Tony Martin/4000 5.00 12.00
71 Leeland McElroy/4000 3.00 8.00
72 Natrone Means/3000 5.00 12.00
73 Eric Metcalf/4000 5.00 12.00
74 Anthony Miller/3000 3.00 8.00
75 Rick Mirer/500 12.00 25.00
76 Scott Mitchell/500 15.00 40.00
77 Warren Moon/500 20.00 50.00
78 Herman Moore/2500 5.00 12.00
79 M.Muhammad/3000 8.00 20.00
80 Adrian Murrell/3000 3.00 8.00
81 Neil O'Donnell/500 12.00 25.00
82 Terrell Owens/3000 20.00 40.00
83 Brett Perriman/1000 4.00 10.00
84 Lawrence Phillips/1000 4.00 10.00
85 Jake Plummer/5000 15.00 30.00
86 Andre Reed/3000 8.00 20.00
87 Jerry Rice 60.00 120.00
88 Darrell Russell/2000 4.00 10.00
89 Rashaan Salaam/3000 3.00 8.00
90 Barry Sanders/400 60.00 120.00
91 Chris Sanders/3000 3.00 8.00
92 Frank Sanders/3000 5.00 12.00
93 Darnay Scott/2000 5.00 12.00
94 Junior Seau/500 30.00 60.00
95 Shannon Sharpe/1000 20.00 40.00
96 Sedrick Shaw/4000 3.00 8.00
97 Heath Shuler/500 12.00 25.00
98 Antowain Smith/5000 8.00 20.00
99 Emmitt Smith/200 150.00 250.00
100 Kordell Stewart/500 15.00 40.00
101 J.J. Stokes/3000 5.00 12.00
102 Vinny Testaverde/200 20.00 50.00
103 Thurman Thomas/2500 15.00 30.00
104 Tamarick Vanover/4000 5.00 12.00
105 Herschel Walker/3000 15.00 30.00
106 M.Westbrook/3000 5.00 12.00
107 Danny Wuerffel/4000 5.00 12.00
108 Steve Young/500 50.00 100.00

1997 Leaf Signature Old School Drafts Autographs

This 11-card set features autographed borderless photos of retired NFL stars. Only 1,000 of each card were produced and are sequentially numbered. Card #10 Sid Luckman was never signed.

STATED PRINT RUN 1000 SERIAL #'d SETS
1 Joe Theismann 15.00 40.00
2 Archie Manning 20.00 50.00
3 Len Dawson 12.00 30.00
4 Sammy Baugh 40.00 80.00
5 Dan Fouts 15.00 40.00
6 Danny White 15.00 40.00
7 Ron Jaworski 12.00 30.00
8 Jim Plunkett 12.00 30.00
9 Y.A. Tittle 20.00 50.00
11 Ken Stabler 20.00 50.00
12 Billy Kilmer 12.00 30.00

2013 Leaf Sports Heroes

BAAT1 Andre Tippett 5.00 12.00
BABG2 Bob Griese 10.00 25.00
BABS1 Barry Sanders/5*
BACJ1 Charlie Joiner 5.00 12.00
BACT1 Charley Taylor 4.00 10.00
BACT2 Charley Trippi 6.00 15.00
BADD1 Dan Dierdorf 5.00 12.00
BADJ1 Deacon Jones 8.00 20.00
BADM2 Don Maynard 4.00 10.00
BADS1 Don Shula 12.00 30.00
BADS2 Dwight Stephenson 4.00 10.00
BADW1 Dave Wilcox 6.00 15.00
BAEC1 Earl Campbell 12.00 30.00
BAED1 Eric Dickerson 12.00 30.00
BAFB1 Fred Biletnikoff 8.00 20.00
BAFD1 Fred Dean 6.00 15.00
BAFG1 Frank Gifford/19* 8.00 20.00
BAJDL Joe DeLamielleure 5.00 12.00
BAJK1 Jim Kelly/6*
BAJM1 Joe Montana 40.00 80.00
BAJO1 Jim Otto 6.00 15.00
BAJS1 Jackie Smith 4.00 10.00
BAJT1 Joe Theismann 8.00 20.00
BAJY1 Jack Youngblood 6.00 15.00
BAKW1 Kellen Winslow 8.00 20.00
BALD1 Len Dawson 8.00 20.00
BALM1 Lenny Moore 6.00 15.00
BAMD1 Mike Ditka 12.00 30.00
BAMF1 Marshall Faulk/18* 8.00 20.00
BAML1 Marv Levy 10.00 25.00
BARJ3 Rickey Jackson 5.00 12.00
BARL1 Ronnie Lott 10.00 25.00
BARW1 Randy White 8.00 20.00
BARW2 Rod Woodson 12.00 30.00
BASL1 Steve Largent 8.00 20.00
BAWM1 Warren Moon/15*
BAYAT Y.A. Tittle 8.00 20.00
CMOQA M.Oher/Q.Aaron 10.00 25.00

2013 Leaf Sports Heroes Canton's Finest Autographs

*SILVER/25: .5X TO 1.2X BASIC CARDS
CFAT1 Andre Tippett 5.00 12.00
CFBG2 Bob Griese 8.00 20.00
CFBL1 Bob Lilly 8.00 20.00
CFBM2 Bobby Mitchell 8.00 20.00
CFBS4 Billy Shaw 6.00 15.00
CFBSC Bob St. Clair/10*
CFCH2 Chris Hanburger 6.00 15.00
CFCJ1 Charlie Joiner 5.00 12.00
CFCS1 Charlie Sanders 5.00 12.00
CFCT1 Charley Taylor 6.00 15.00
CFCT2 Charley Trippi 6.00 15.00
CFDH1 Dan Hampton 6.00 15.00
CFDS2 Dwight Stephenson 5.00 12.00
CFEB2 Elvin Bethea 6.00 15.00
CFFB1 Fred Biletnikoff 8.00 20.00
CFFD1 Fred Dean 5.00 12.00
CFGM2 Gino Marchetti 6.00 15.00
CFHC1 Harry Carson 6.00 15.00
CFHM1 Hugh McElhenny 6.00 15.00
CFJDL Joe DeLamielleure 5.00 12.00
CFJH1 Jack Ham 12.00 30.00
CFJH2 John Hannah/5*
CFJL2 James Lofton 6.00 15.00
CFJL3 Jim Langer 6.00 15.00
CFJO1 Jim Otto 6.00 15.00
CFJS1 Jackie Smith 5.00 12.00
CFJS2 Jackie Slater 6.00 15.00
CFJS3 Jan Stenerud 5.00 12.00
CFKW1 Kellen Winslow 10.00 25.00
CFLL1 Larry Little 5.00 12.00
CFLW1 Larry Wilson 8.00 20.00
CFMD1 Mike Ditka 12.00 30.00
CFMH2 Mike Haynes 8.00 20.00
CFML1 Marv Levy 10.00 25.00
CFMR1 Mel Renfro 5.00 12.00
CFPK1 Paul Krause 5.00 12.00
CFPW1 Paul Warfield 6.00 15.00
CFRJ3 Rickey Jackson 5.00 12.00
CFRW3 Rayfield Wright 6.00 15.00
CFRW4 Roger Wehrli 5.00 12.00
CFRY1 Ron Yary 6.00 15.00
CFTM1 Tom Mack 5.00 12.00
CFWB2 Willie Brown 5.00 12.00
CFYAT Y.A. Tittle 6.00 15.00

2013 Leaf Sports Heroes Canton's Finest Autographs Silver

STATED PRINT RUN 25 SER. #'d SETS

2013 Leaf Sports Heroes Loyalty Autographs

*SILVER/25: .5X TO 1.2X BASIC CARDS
LAT1 Andre Tippett 5.00 12.00
LBG2 Bob Griese 8.00 20.00
LCT2 Charley Trippi 5.00 12.00
LDS2 Dwight Stephenson 5.00 12.00
LFB1 Fred Biletnikoff 6.00 15.00
LKW1 Kellen Winslow 8.00 20.00

2013 Leaf Sports Heroes Loyalty Autographs Silver

*SILVER: .5X TO 1.2X BASIC CARDS
STATED PRINT RUN 25 SER.#'d SETS

2017 Leaf Valiant

*ORANGE/25: .5X TO 1.2X BASIC AU/50
*PURPLE/15: .6X TO 1.5X BASIC AU
BAAD1 Amara Darboh 4.00 10.00
BAAK1 Alvin Kamara 15.00 40.00
BAAS1 ArDarius Stewart 4.00 10.00
BAAS2 Artavis Scott 4.00 10.00
BABH1 Bucky Hodges 4.00 10.00
BABH2 Brian Hill 4.00 10.00
BABK1 Brad Kaaya 4.00 10.00
BACC1 Corey Clement 5.00 12.00
BACD1 Corey Davis 6.00 15.00
BACG1 Chris Godwin 5.00 12.00
BACH1 Carlos Henderson 4.00 10.00
BACJB C.J. Beathard 4.00 10.00
BACK1 Chad Kelly 4.00 10.00
BACK2 Cooper Kupp 6.00 15.00
BACM1 Christian McCaffrey 10.00 25.00
BACR1 Cam Robinson 4.00 10.00
BACR2 Cooper Rush 5.00 12.00
BADB1 Derek Barnett 5.00 12.00
BADC1 Dalvin Cook 10.00 25.00
BADF1 D'Onta Foreman 5.00 12.00
BADK1 DeShone Kizer 4.00 10.00
BADN1 David Njoku 5.00 12.00
BADP1 Donnel Pumphrey 5.00 12.00
BADS1 Damore'ea Stringfellow 5.00 12.00
BADVS De'Veon Smith 10.00 25.00
BADW1 Davis Webb 4.00 10.00
BADW2 Deshaun Watson 40.00 80.00
BADW3 Dede Westbrook 4.00 10.00
BAEE1 Evan Engram 5.00 12.00
BAEH1 Elijah Hood 4.00 10.00
BAIF1 Isaiah Ford 4.00 10.00
BAJB1 Jake Butt 5.00 12.00
BAJC1 James Conner 8.00 20.00
BAJC2 Jehu Chesson 5.00 12.00
BAJD1 Joshua Dobbs 5.00 12.00
BAJE1 Jerod Evans 5.00 12.00
BAJJS JuJu Smith-Schuster 10.00 25.00
BAJL1 Jordan Leggett 4.00 10.00
BAJM1 Jeremy McNichols 4.00 10.00
BAJM2 Joe Mixon 8.00 20.00
BAJP1 Jabrill Peppers 6.00 15.00
BAJQ1 James Quick 5.00 12.00
BAJR1 John Ross 5.00 12.00
BAJR2 Josh Reynolds 4.00 10.00
BAJW1 Jamaal Williams 4.00 10.00
BAKDC KD Cannon 4.00 10.00
BAKH1 Kareem Hunt 8.00 20.00
BAMD1 Malachi Dupre 4.00 10.00
BAMT1 Mitch Trubisky 40.00 80.00
BAMW1 Mike Williams 6.00 15.00
BANP1 Nathan Peterman 5.00 12.00
BAOJH O.J. Howard 5.00 12.00
BAPM1 Pat Mahomes II 150.00 300.00
BASC1 Stacy Coley 4.00 10.00
BASJ1 Sidney Jones 4.00 10.00
BASP1 Samaje Perine 4.00 10.00
BATC1 Taco Charlton 4.00 10.00
BATD1 Travin Dural 5.00 12.00
BATF1 Tarean Folston 6.00 15.00
BATJW T.J. Watt 12.00 30.00
BATR1 Travis Rudolph 4.00 10.00
BAWG1 Wayne Gallman 5.00 12.00

2017 Leaf Valiant Big Targets

*ORANGE/25: .5X TO 1.2X BASIC AU/50
*PURPLE/15: .6X TO 1.5X BASIC AU
BTBH1 Bucky Hodges 4.00 10.00
BTDN1 David Njoku 5.00 12.00
BTEE1 Evan Engram 5.00 12.00
BTJB1 Jake Butt 5.00 12.00
BTJL1 Jordan Leggett 4.00 10.00
BTOJH O.J. Howard 5.00 12.00

2017 Leaf Valiant Field Generals

*ORANGE/25: .5X TO 1.2X BASIC AU/50
*PURPLE/15: .6X TO 1.5X BASIC AU
FG1CJB C.J. Beathard 4.00 10.00
FG1CK1 Chad Kelly 4.00 10.00
FG1DW1 Davis Webb 4.00 10.00
FG1DW2 Deshaun Watson 40.00 80.00
FG1JD1 Joshua Dobbs 5.00 12.00
FG1JE1 Jerod Evans 5.00 12.00
FG1MT1 Mitch Trubisky 40.00 80.00
FG1NP1 Nathan Peterman 5.00 12.00

2017 Leaf Valiant Speed Kills

*ORANGE/25: .5X TO 1.2X BASIC AU/50
*PURPLE/15: .6X TO 1.5X BASIC AU
SKCG1 Chris Godwin 5.00 12.00
SKCM1 Christian McCaffrey 10.00 25.00
SKCS1 Curtis Samuel EXCH 5.00 12.00
SKDC1 Dalvin Cook 10.00 25.00
SKDP1 Donnel Pumphrey 5.00 12.00
SKJR1 John Ross 5.00 12.00

2017 Leaf Valiant TD Machines

*ORANGE/25: .5X TO 1.2X BASIC AU/50
*PURPLE/15: .6X TO 1.5X BASIC AU
TDMAK1 Alvin Kamara 15.00 40.00
TDMCC1 Corey Clement 5.00 12.00
TDMCD1 Corey Davis 6.00 15.00
TDMCK1 Cooper Kupp 6.00 15.00
TDMDF1 D'Onta Foreman 5.00 12.00
TDMDW1 Dede Westbrook 4.00 10.00
TDMJJS JuJu Smith-Schuster 10.00 25.00
TDMJM1 Joe Mixon 8.00 20.00
TDMKH1 Kareem Hunt 8.00 20.00
TDMMW1 Mike Williams 6.00 15.00

2017 Leaf Valiant Tenacious D

*ORANGE/25: .5X TO 1.2X BASIC AU/50
*PURPLE/15: .6X TO 1.5X BASIC AU
TDDB1 Derek Barnett 5.00 12.00
TDJA1 Jonathan Allen 5.00 12.00
TDMH1 Marlon Humphrey 4.00 10.00
TDTC1 Taco Charlton 4.00 10.00
TDTJW T.J. Watt 12.00 30.00
TDTW1 Tim Williams 5.00 12.00

2018 Leaf Valiant

*GREEN/60: .5X TO 1.2X BASIC AU
*ORANGE/35: .5X TO 1.2X BASIC AU
*NAVY/25: .6X TO 1.5X BASIC AU
*PURPLE/15: .8X TO 2X BASIC AU
BAAK1 Arden Key 2.50 6.00
BAAL1 Allen Lazard 2.50 6.00
BAAM1 Anthony Miller 4.00 10.00
BAAT1 Auden Tate 2.50 6.00
BAAW1 Akrum Wadley 2.50 6.00
BABB1 Braxton Berrios 2.50 6.00
BABC1 Bradley Chubb 4.00 10.00
BABM1 Baker Mayfield 25.00 60.00
BABS1 Bo Scarbrough 3.00 8.00
BACD1 Carlton Davis 3.00 8.00
BACK1 Christian Kirk 4.00 10.00
BACR1 Calvin Ridley 6.00 15.00
BACS1 Courtland Sutton 4.00 10.00
BACS2 Cam Serigne 2.50 6.00
BACW1 Cedrick Wilson Jr. 2.50 6.00
BADB1 Deontay Burnett 3.00 8.00
BADC1 Deon Cain 3.00 8.00
BADC2 Darren Carrington II 3.00 8.00
BADG1 Derrius Guice 5.00 12.00
BADG2 DeAndre Goolsby 2.50 6.00
BADG3 Dallas Goedert 3.00 8.00
BADJC D.J. Chark 3.00 8.00
BADJM D.J. Moore 5.00 12.00
BADP1 Dante Pettis 4.00 10.00
BADRP Daron Payne 4.00 10.00
BADS2 Durham Smythe 2.50 6.00
BADS3 Dalton Schultz 3.00 8.00
BADW1 Denzel Ward 6.00 15.00
BAHH1 Hayden Hurst 3.00 8.00
BAIS1 Ito Smith 3.00 8.00
BAIT1 Ian Thomas 2.50 6.00
BAJA1 Josh Allen 10.00 25.00
BAJA2 Josh Adams 5.00 12.00
BAJJ1 Justin Jackson 3.00 8.00
BAJK1 John Kelly 3.00 8.00
BAJMM J'Mon Moore 2.50 6.00
BAJR1 Josh Rosen 8.00 20.00
BAJW1 Jake Wieneke 3.00 8.00
BAJW2 James Washington 5.00 12.00
BAJW3 Javon Wims 2.50 6.00
BAKB1 Kurt Benkert 3.00 8.00
BAKC1 Keke Coutee 3.00 8.00
BAKH1 Kenny Hill 3.00 8.00
BAKJ1 Kerryon Johnson 4.00 10.00
BALF1 Luke Falk 3.00 8.00
BALW1 Logan Woodside 4.00 10.00
BAMA1 Mark Andrews 4.00 10.00
BAMA2 Marcell Ateman 3.00 8.00
BAMB1 Marcus Baugh 2.50 6.00
BAMC1 Martez Carter 2.50 6.00
BAMF1 Minkah Fitzpatrick 5.00 12.00
BAMG1 Michael Gallup 5.00 12.00
BAMG2 Mike Gesicki 3.00 8.00
BAMH1 Maurice Hurst 3.00 8.00
BAMR1 Mason Rudolph 6.00 15.00
BAMW1 Mark Walton 3.00 8.00
BAMW2 Mike White 3.00 8.00
BANC1 Nick Chubb 8.00 20.00
BAQF1 Quinton Flowers 2.50 6.00
BARE1 Rashaan Evans 4.00 10.00
BARF1 Royce Freeman 3.00 8.00
BARF2 Riley Ferguson 4.00 10.00
BARJ2 Ronald Jones II 2.50 6.00
BARP1 Rashaad Penny 4.00 10.00
BARS1 Roquan Smith 8.00 20.00
BARW1 Ralph Webb 3.00 8.00
BASC1 Simmie Cobbs Jr. 4.00 10.00
BASD1 Sam Darnold 15.00 40.00
BASH1 Sam Hubbard 3.00 8.00
BASM1 Sony Michel 8.00 20.00
BATF1 Troy Fumagalli 3.00 8.00
BATT1 Trenton Thompson 2.50 6.00
BAVV1 Vita Vea 4.00 10.00

2018 Leaf Valiant Big Targets

*GREEN/60: .5X TO 1.2X BASIC AU
*ORANGE/35: .5X TO 1.2X BASIC AU
*NAVY/25: .6X TO 1.5X BASIC AU
*PURPLE/15: .8X TO 2X BASIC AU
BTCS2 Cam Serigne 2.50 6.00
BTDG2 DeAndre Goolsby 2.50 6.00
BTDG3 Dallas Goedert 3.00 8.00
BTDS2 Durham Smythe 2.50 6.00
BTDS3 Dalton Schultz 3.00 8.00
BTHH1 Hayden Hurst 3.00 8.00
BTIT1 Ian Thomas 2.50 6.00
BTMA1 Mark Andrews 4.00 10.00
BTMB1 Marcus Baugh 2.50 6.00
BTMG2 Mike Gesicki 3.00 8.00
BTTF1 Troy Fumagalli 3.00 8.00

2018 Leaf Valiant Here Comes the Boom

*GREEN/60: .5X TO 1.2X BASIC AU
*ORANGE/35: .5X TO 1.2X BASIC AU
*NAVY/25: .6X TO 1.5X BASIC AU
*PURPLE/15: .8X TO 2X BASIC AU
HBAK1 Arden Key 2.50 6.00
HBBC1 Bradley Chubb 4.00 10.00
HBCD1 Carlton Davis 3.00 8.00
HBDRP Daron Payne 4.00 10.00
HBDW1 Denzel Ward 6.00 15.00
HBMF1 Minkah Fitzpatrick 5.00 12.00
HBMH1 Maurice Hurst 3.00 8.00
HBRE1 Rashaan Evans 4.00 10.00
HBRS1 Roquan Smith 8.00 20.00
HBSH1 Sam Hubbard 3.00 8.00
HBTT1 Trenton Thompson 2.50 6.00
HBVV1 Vita Vea 4.00 10.00

2018 Leaf Valiant Midas Touch

*GREEN/60: .5X TO 1.2X BASIC AU
*ORANGE/35: .5X TO 1.2X BASIC AU
*NAVY/25: .6X TO 1.5X BASIC AU
*PURPLE/15: .8X TO 2X BASIC AU
MTBM1 Baker Mayfield 25.00 60.00
MTJA1 Josh Allen 10.00 25.00
MTJR1 Josh Rosen 8.00 20.00
MTKB1 Kurt Benkert 3.00 8.00
MTKH1 Kenny Hill 3.00 8.00
MTLF1 Luke Falk 3.00 8.00
MTLW1 Logan Woodside 4.00 10.00
MTMR1 Mason Rudolph 6.00 15.00
MTMW2 Mike White 3.00 8.00
MTQF1 Quinton Flowers 2.50 6.00
MTRF2 Riley Ferguson 4.00 10.00
MTSD1 Sam Darnold 15.00 40.00

2018 Leaf Valiant Rising Stock

*GREEN/60: .5X TO 1.2X BASIC AU
*ORANGE/35: .5X TO 1.2X BASIC AU
*NAVY/25: .6X TO 1.5X BASIC AU
*PURPLE/15: .8X TO 2X BASIC AU
RSAW1 Akrum Wadley 2.50 6.00
RSDJC D.J. Chark 3.00 8.00
RSJW2 James Washington 5.00 12.00
RSLF1 Luke Falk 3.00 8.00
RSNC1 Nick Chubb 8.00 20.00
RSRF2 Riley Ferguson 4.00 10.00
RSRP1 Rashaad Penny 4.00 10.00
RSSM1 Sony Michel 8.00 20.00

2018 Leaf Valiant Take it to the House

*GREEN/60: .5X TO 1.2X BASIC AU
*ORANGE/35: .5X TO 1.2X BASIC AU
*NAVY/25: .6X TO 1.5X BASIC AU
*PURPLE/15: .8X TO 2X BASIC AU
THAL1 Allen Lazard 2.50 6.00
THAM1 Anthony Miller 4.00 10.00
THAT1 Auden Tate 2.50 6.00
THAW1 Akrum Wadley 2.50 6.00
THBB1 Braxton Berrios 2.50 6.00
THBS1 Bo Scarbrough 3.00 8.00
THCK1 Christian Kirk 4.00 10.00
THCR1 Calvin Ridley 6.00 15.00
THCS1 Courtland Sutton 4.00 10.00
THCW1 Cedrick Wilson Jr. 2.50 6.00
THDB1 Deontay Burnett 3.00 8.00
THDC1 Deon Cain 3.00 8.00
THDC2 Darren Carrington II 3.00 8.00
THDG1 Derrius Guice 5.00 12.00
THDJC D.J. Chark 3.00 8.00
THDJM D.J. Moore 5.00 12.00
THDP1 Dante Pettis 4.00 10.00
THIS1 Ito Smith 3.00 8.00
THJA2 Josh Adams 5.00 12.00
THJJ1 Justin Jackson 3.00 8.00
THJK1 John Kelly 3.00 8.00
THJMM J'Mon Moore 2.50 6.00
THJW1 Jake Wieneke 3.00 8.00
THJW2 James Washington 5.00 12.00
THJW3 Javon Wims 2.50 6.00
THKC1 Keke Coutee 3.00 8.00
THKJ1 Kerryon Johnson 4.00 10.00
THMA2 Marcell Ateman 3.00 8.00
THMC1 Martez Carter 2.50 6.00
THMG1 Michael Gallup 5.00 12.00
THMW1 Mark Walton 3.00 8.00
THNC1 Nick Chubb 8.00 20.00
THRF1 Royce Freeman 3.00 8.00
THRJ2 Ronald Jones II 2.50 6.00
THRP1 Rashaad Penny 4.00 10.00
THRW1 Ralph Webb 3.00 8.00
THSC1 Simmie Cobbs Jr. 4.00 10.00
THSM1 Sony Michel 8.00 20.00

2018 Leaf Valiant We Are the Champions

*GREEN/60: .5X TO 1.2X BASIC AU
*ORANGE/35: .5X TO 1.2X BASIC AU
*NAVY/25: .6X TO 1.5X BASIC AU
*PURPLE/15: .8X TO 2X BASIC AU
WCBS1 Bo Scarbrough 3.00 8.00
WCCR1 Calvin Ridley 6.00 15.00
WCDRP Daron Payne 4.00 10.00
WCMF1 Minkah Fitzpatrick 5.00 12.00
WCRE1 Rashaan Evans 4.00 10.00

2019 Leaf Valiant

*BLUE/25: .8X TO 2X BASIC AU
*GREEN/75: .5X TO 1.2X BASIC AU
*ORANGE/50: .6X TO 1.5X BASIC AU
*PINK/15: 1X TO 2.5X BASIC AU
*PURPLE/20: 1X TO 2.5X BASIC AU
BAAB1 Alex Barnes 3.00 8.00
BAAJ1 Anthony Johnson 3.00 8.00
BAAJB A.J. Brown 6.00 15.00
BAAO1 Amani Oruwariye 3.00 8.00
BAAW1 Antoine Wesley 2.50 6.00
BAAW2 Aeris Williams 3.00 8.00
BABB3 Brian Burns 3.00 8.00
BABL1 Bryce Love 4.00 10.00
BABSJ Benny Snell Jr. 8.00 20.00
BACF1 Clelin Ferrell 4.00 10.00
BACW1 Caleb Wilson 2.50 6.00
BACW3 Chase Winovich 8.00 20.00
BADB1 Deandre Baker 6.00 15.00
BADH1 Damien Harris 6.00 15.00
BADH2 Dwayne Haskins EXCH
BADJ1 Daniel Jones 12.00 30.00
BADJ2 Diontae Johnson 3.00 8.00
BADKM D.K. Metcalf 8.00 20.00
BADL1 Drew Lock 12.00 30.00
BADL2 DaMarkus Lodge 2.50 6.00
BADL3 Dexter Lawrence 4.00 10.00
BADM1 David Montgomery 10.00 25.00
BADS1 Deebo Samuel 6.00 15.00
BADS2 Devin Singletary 3.00 8.00
BADSV David Sills V 8.00 20.00
BADT1 Deionte Thompson 3.00 8.00
BAEH1 Emanuel Hall 2.50 6.00
BAGJJ Gary Jennings Jr. 4.00 10.00
BAHB1 Hakeem Butler 5.00 12.00
BAIB1 Isaiah Buggs 6.00 15.00
BAISJ Irv Smith Jr. 5.00 12.00
BAJD1 Johnnie Dixon 3.00 8.00
BAJJ3 Josh Jacobs 12.00 30.00
BAJJW JJ Arcega-Whiteside 4.00 10.00
BAJP1 Jachai Polite 3.00 8.00
BAJS1 Jarrett Stidham 8.00 20.00
BAJS2 Jeffery Simmons 2.50 6.00
BAJS3 Jace Sternberger 3.00 8.00
BAJS4 Jordan Scarlett 2.50 6.00
BAJS5 Jaylen Smith 2.50 6.00
BAJT1 Jerry Tillery 3.00 8.00
BAJW1 Jamarius Way 3.00 8.00
BAKH1 Kelvin Harmon 4.00 10.00
BAKH2 Karan Higdon 3.00 8.00
BAKK1 Kyle Kempt 4.00 10.00
BAKM1 Kyler Murray 25.00 60.00
BAKS1 Kaden Smith 2.50 6.00
BAKS2 Kyle Shurmur 5.00 12.00
BAKSJ KeeSean Johnson 2.50 6.00
BALJH Lil'Jordan Humphrey 3.00 8.00
BALJS L.J. Scott 4.00 10.00
BAMB1 Marquise Brown 8.00 20.00
BAMB2 Miles Boykin 3.00 8.00
BAMG3 Myles Gaskin 5.00 12.00
BAMS2 Miles Sanders 6.00 15.00
BAMW1 Mike Weber 4.00 10.00
BANB1 Nick Bosa 8.00 20.00
BANF1 Noah Fant 5.00 12.00
BANKH N'Keal Harry 8.00 20.00
BAPC1 Parris Campbell 6.00 15.00
BAQW1 Quinnen Williams 2.50 6.00
BARA1 Rodney Anderson 3.00 8.00
BARF1 Ryan Finley 5.00 12.00
BARR1 Riley Ridley 4.00 10.00
BASM1 Stanley Morgan Jr. 4.00 10.00
BATB1 Tyre Brady 2.50 6.00
BATH1 Travis Homer 2.50 6.00
BATL1 Tre Lamar 4.00 10.00
BATW1 Trayveon Williams 3.00 8.00
BAWG1 Will Grier 8.00 20.00

2019 Leaf Valiant All American

*BLUE/25: .8X TO 2X BASIC AU
*GREEN/75: .5X TO 1.2X BASIC AU
*ORANGE/50: .6X TO 1.5X BASIC AU
*PINK/15: 1X TO 2.5X BASIC AU
*PURPLE/20: 1X TO 2.5X BASIC AU
AAAJB A.J. Brown 6.00 15.00
AABSJ Benny Snell Jr. 8.00 20.00
AADH1 Damien Harris 6.00 15.00
AADH2 Dwayne Haskins EXCH
AADJ1 Daniel Jones 12.00 30.00
AADL1 Drew Lock 12.00 30.00
AAJJ3 Josh Jacobs 12.00 30.00
AAKM1 Kyler Murray 25.00 60.00
AAMB1 Marquise Brown 8.00 20.00
AATW1 Trayveon Williams 3.00 8.00

2019 Leaf Valiant Rising Stock

*BLUE/25: .8X TO 2X BASIC AU
*GREEN/75: .5X TO 1.2X BASIC AU
*ORANGE/50: .6X TO 1.5X BASIC AU
*PINK/15: 1X TO 2.5X BASIC AU
*PURPLE/20: 1X TO 2.5X BASIC AU
RSAI1 Andy Isabella 4.00 10.00
RSARW Anthony Ratliff-Williams 5.00 12.00
RSBR1 Brett Rypien 3.00 8.00
RSCT1 Clayton Thorson 4.00 10.00
RSDH3 Darrell Henderson 6.00 15.00
RSEH2 Elijah Holyfield 4.00 10.00
RSJH1 Justice Hill 4.00 10.00
RSJH3 Jalen Hurd 3.00 8.00
RSMH1 Mecole Hardman 6.00 15.00
RSTJ1 Tyree Jackson 6.00 15.00

2019 Leaf Valiant Tenacious D

*BLUE/25: .8X TO 2X BASIC AU
*GREEN/75: .5X TO 1.2X BASIC AU
*ORANGE/50: .6X TO 1.5X BASIC AU
*PINK/15: 1X TO 2.5X BASIC AU
*PURPLE/20: 1X TO 2.5X BASIC AU
TDCW2 Christian Wilkins 10.00 25.00
TDDBJ Devin Bush II 10.00 25.00
TDDMJ Dre'Mont Jones 3.00 8.00
TDDW1 Devin White 8.00 20.00
TDEO1 Ed Oliver 4.00 10.00
TDGW1 Greedy Williams 8.00 20.00
TDJA1 Josh Allen 10.00 25.00
TDJJ1 Jalen Jelks 3.00 8.00
TDMW2 Mack Wilson 3.00 8.00
TDZA1 Zach Allen 4.00 10.00

2012 Leaf Vince Lombardi Legacy

COMPLETE SET (40) 75.00 150.00
COMMON CARD 2.00 5.00

2012 Leaf Vince Lombardi Legacy Autographs Blue Ink
*RED INK/50: .5X TO 1.2X BLUE INK
*GREEN INK/25: .6X TO 1.5X BLUE INK
OAAD1 Art Donovan 10.00 25.00
OADL1 Daryle Lamonica EXCH 8.00 20.00
OAFW1 Fred Williamson 8.00 20.00
OALD1 Len Dawson 12.00 30.00
OAMR1 Mel Renfro 10.00 25.00
OAYAT Y.A. Tittle 12.00 30.00
PABD1 Boyd Dowler 10.00 25.00
PABS1 Bart Starr 50.00 100.00
PABS1 Bob Skoronski 8.00 20.00
PADA1 Donny Anderson 8.00 20.00
PADR1 Dave Robinson 10.00 25.00
PAFG1 Forrest Gregg 12.00 30.00
PAJG1 Jim Grabowski 8.00 20.00
PAJK1 Jerry Kramer 10.00 25.00
PAMF1 Marv Fleming 10.00 25.00
PAWD1 Willie Davis 12.00 30.00
PAZB1 Zeke Bratkowski 10.00 25.00

2012 Leaf Vince Lombardi Legacy Jacket Swatches
COMMON CARD
ONE JACKET SWATCH PER BOX
UNPRICED GOLD PRINT RUN 5
UNPRICED SILVER PRINT RUN 10
UNPRICED PURPLE PRINT RUN 1

2015 Leaf Welcome to
*GOLD/40: .6X TO 1.5X BASIC BRONZE
*GREEN/30: .6X TO 1.5X BASIC BRONZE
*SILVER/100: .5X TO 1.2X BASIC BRONZE
WTTMM1 Marcus Mariota .60 1.50
WTTBJW1 Jameis Winston .40 1.00

1993-94 Legendary Foils
e Legendary Foils Sport Series was intended to be a monthly series featuring Pro Football Hall of Famers. The cards measure approximately 3 1/2" by 5" and were issued in a green and black custom designed folder. The embossed fronts carry the players portrait and a short career summary. The gold edition cards are completely gold foil layered on a matte gold background, while the colored edition cards have a green background. Production was limited to no more than 95,000 for the colored edition and 5,000 for the gold edition. The serial number also appears on the front. The backs are silver and carry Legendary Foil logos. There were no card numbers. We've included single card prices below for the colored version.
1 Morris Red Badgro .80 2.00
2 Terry Bradshaw 1.60 4.00
P1 Terry Bradshaw Promo 1.60 4.00

2006 Lehigh Valley Outlawz GLIFL
COMPLETE SET (36) 6.00 12.00
1 Corey Adderley .20 .50
2 Mark Barrionette .20 .50
3 Lloyd C. Brooks Jr. .20 .50
4 Damien Ciecwisz .20 .50
5 Steve Cook .20 .50
6 Doug Folger .20 .50
7 Drew DeRogatis .20 .50
8 T.K. Ford .20 .50
9 Larry Koch .20 .50
10 Keith McConnell .20 .50
11 Sean McGinley .20 .50
12 Andrew Nelson .20 .50
13 Billy Parker .20 .50
14 Mike Ramos .20 .50
15 Chris Reed .20 .50
16 Chad Schwenk .20 .50
17 Brian Smith .20 .50
18 James Spence .20 .50
19 Keeno Theadford .20 .50
20 Joe Wooten .20 .50
21 Coaches .20 .50
Owner
Jim DePaul Own
Mike DePaul GM
Al Forsythe Asst.CO
Clayton
22 Outkast Mascot .20 .50
23 Lady Outlawz - Amber .20 .50
24 Lady Outlawz - Andrea .20 .50
25 Lady Outlawz - Brittany .20 .50
26 Lady Outlawz - Chrissy .20 .50
27 Lady Outlawz - Gabrielle .20 .50
28 Lady Outlawz - Genie .20 .50
29 Lady Outlawz - Jessie .20 .50
30 Lady Outlawz - Kate .20 .50
31 Lady Outlawz - Kelly .20 .50
32 Lady Outlawz - Amanda .20 .50
33 Lady Outlawz - Michele .20 .50
34 Lady Outlawz - Monica .20 .50
35 Lady Outlawz - Valerie .20 .50
36 Lady Outlawz Group Photo .20 .50

2007 Lehigh Valley Outlawz CIFL
COMPLETE SET (40) 6.00 12.00
1 Marc Barionnette .20 .50
2 Kevin Bliss .20 .50
3 Lloyd Brooks .20 .50
4 Ed Chan .20 .50
5 Phil DeCecco .20 .50
6 Joe DeLuise .20 .50
7 Drew DeRogatis .20 .50
8 Ryan Harrison .20 .50
9 Barry Helverson .20 .50
10 Omar Johnson .20 .50
11 Collis Martin .20 .50
12 Keith McConnell .20 .50
13 Mike Merritt .20 .50
14 Allen Neal .20 .50
15 Billy Parker .20 .50
16 Mike Ramos .20 .50
17 Zikoma Richards .20 .50
18 Eddie Scipio .20 .50
19 Ray Simmons .20 .50
20 Brian Smith .20 .50
21 Dom Stewart .20 .50
22 Al Stokes .20 .50
23 Sal Tubbs .20 .50
24 Joe Wooten .20 .50
25 Devon White .20 .50
26 Coaches .20 .50
Mike DePaul Asst.CO
James DePaul CO
Al Forsythe Ast.CO
Trev Mar
27 Team Card .20 .50
28 Lady Outlawz - Amber .20 .50
29 Lady Outlawz - Genie .20 .50
30 Lady Outlawz - Jes .20 .50
31 Lady Outlawz - Julie .20 .50
32 Lady Outlawz - Kasey .20 .50
33 Lady Outlawz - Kate .20 .50
34 Lady Outlawz - Michele .20 .50
35 Lady Outlawz - Robyn .20 .50
36 Lady Outlawz - Sarah .20 .50
37 Lady Outlawz - Shaina .20 .50
38 Lady Outlawz - Shannon .20 .50
39 Lady Outlawz - Valerie .20 .50
40 Lady Outlawz Group Photo .20 .50

2008 Lehigh Valley Outlawz CIFL
COMPLETE SET (40) 6.00 12.00
1 Dom Stewart .20 .50
2 Desmond Maul .20 .50
3 Joe Wooten .20 .50
4 Steve Cook .20 .50
5 BJ Hall .20 .50
6 Brandon Simmons .20 .50
7 Dave Carter .20 .50
8 Eddie Scipio .20 .50
9 Billy Parker .20 .50
10 Mark Sedlock .20 .50
11 Jermaine Thaxton .20 .50
12 Mark Barrionette .20 .50
13 Jaime Sellers .20 .50
14 Adwela Dawes .20 .50
15 Sal Byron .20 .50
16 Devon White .20 .50
17 Brian Smith .20 .50
18 Scott Blum .20 .50
19 Greg Hammond .20 .50
20 Wendell Bates .20 .50
21 Sal Tubbs .20 .50
22 Drew DeRogotis .20 .50
23 Mike Ramos .20 .50
24 Gene Rich .20 .50
25 Al Stokes .20 .50
26 Outlawz Team CL .20 .50
27 Outkast Mascot .20 .50
28 Bethany CHEER .20 .50
29 Gabrielle CHEER .20 .50
30 Genie CHEER .20 .50
31 Jackie CHEER .20 .50
32 Jes CHEER .20 .50
33 Julie CHEER .20 .50
34 Kate CHEER .20 .50
35 Marci CHEER .20 .50
36 Michele CHEER .20 .50
37 Robyn CHEER .20 .50
38 Shannon CHEER .20 .50
39 Valerie CHEER .20 .50
40 Lady Outlawz Photo .20 .50

2013 Lehigh Valley Steel Hawks PIFL
COMPLETE SET (28) 10.00 20.00
1 Alex Ajayi .40 1.00
2 Adam Bednarik .40 1.00
3 David Castillo .40 1.00
4 Tyrone Collins .40 1.00
5 Clarence Curry .40 1.00
6 Devin Duggan .40 1.00
7 John Esposito .40 1.00
8 Larry Ford .40 1.00
9 Torieal Gibson .40 1.00
10 Tom Gilson .40 1.00
11 Chad Hounshell .40 1.00
12 Chris Johnson .40 1.00
13 John Kennedy .40 1.00
14 Travis Miller .40 1.00
15 Troy Pascley .40 1.00
16 Evan Selman .40 1.00
17 Ian Simon .40 1.00
18 Michael Simons .40 1.00
19 Eddie Smith .40 1.00
20 Justin Smith .40 1.00
21 Terence Thomas .40 1.00
22 Hunter Wanket .40 1.00
23 E.J. Wood .40 1.00
24 Elliott White .40 1.00
25 Rich White .40 1.00
26 Stefaun Whitehead .40 1.00
27 Bryan Wick .40 1.00
28 Jeff Willis .40 1.00

2009 Limited
1-150 STATED PRINT RUN 399
AUTO ROOKIE PRINT RUN 99-399
JSY AUTO ROOKIE PRINT RUN 149
1 Kurt Warner 1.25 3.00
2 Larry Fitzgerald 1.25 3.00
3 Tim Hightower 1.00 2.50
4 Matt Ryan 1.25 3.00
5 Michael Turner 1.00 2.50
6 Roddy White 1.00 2.50
7 Tony Gonzalez 1.25 3.00
8 Mark Clayton 1.00 2.50
9 Joe Flacco 1.25 3.00
10 Willis McGahee 1.00 2.50
11 Lee Evans 1.25 3.00
12 Marshawn Lynch 1.25 3.00
13 Terrell Owens 1.25 3.00
14 DeAngelo Williams 1.00 2.50
15 Jake Delhomme 1.00 2.50
16 Steve Smith 1.25 3.00
17 Brian Urlacher 1.50 4.00
18 Greg Olsen 1.25 3.00
19 Jay Cutler 1.00 2.50
20 Matt Forte 1.00 2.50
21 Carson Palmer 1.25 3.00
22 Cedric Benson 1.00 2.50
23 Chad Ochocinco 1.00 2.50
24 Brady Quinn 1.00 2.50
25 Braylon Edwards 1.00 2.50
26 Jamal Lewis 1.25 3.00
27 Marion Barber 1.25 3.00
28 Roy Williams WR 1.00 2.50
29 Tony Romo 1.25 3.00
30 Eddie Royal 1.00 2.50
31 Kyle Orton 1.00 2.50
32 LaMont Jordan 1.00 2.50
33 Calvin Johnson 1.50 4.00
34 Daunte Culpepper 1.25 3.00
35 Kevin Smith 1.00 2.50
36 Aaron Rodgers 3.00 8.00
37 Greg Jennings 1.00 2.50
38 Ryan Grant 1.25 3.00
39 Andre Johnson 1.25 3.00
40 Matt Schaub 1.00 2.50
41 Steve Slaton 1.00 2.50
42 Anthony Gonzalez 1.00 2.50
43 Joseph Addai 1.00 2.50
44 Peyton Manning 4.00 10.00
45 Reggie Wayne 1.25 3.00
46 David Garrard 1.00 2.50
47 Maurice Jones-Drew 1.00 2.50
48 Torry Holt 1.25 3.00
49 Dwayne Bowe 1.25 3.00
50 Larry Johnson 1.00 2.50
51 Matt Cassel 1.00 2.50
52 Chad Pennington 1.00 2.50
53 Ronnie Brown 1.00 2.50
54 Ricky Williams 1.25 3.00
55 Adrian Peterson 1.50 4.00
56 Bernard Berrian 1.00 2.50
57 Brett Favre Vikings 6.00 15.00
58 Laurence Maroney 1.25 3.00
59 Randy Moss 1.25 3.00
60 Tom Brady 5.00 12.00
61 Wes Welker 1.25 3.00
62 Drew Brees 1.50 4.00
63 Marques Colston 1.00 2.50
64 Reggie Bush 1.00 2.50
65 Brandon Jacobs 1.00 2.50
66 Eli Manning 1.25 3.00
67 Kevin Boss 1.00 2.50
68 Jerricho Cotchery 1.00 2.50
69 Leon Washington 1.00 2.50
70 Darren McFadden 1.50 4.00
71 JaMarcus Russell 1.00 2.50
72 Zach Miller 1.00 2.50
73 Brian Westbrook 1.00 2.50
74 DeSean Jackson 1.25 3.00
75 Donovan McNabb 1.25 3.00
76 Ben Roethlisberger 1.50 4.00
77 Santonio Holmes 1.00 2.50
78 Willie Parker 1.00 2.50
79 Antonio Gates 1.25 3.00
80 LaDainian Tomlinson 1.50 4.00
81 Philip Rivers 1.50 4.00
82 Vincent Jackson 1.00 2.50
83 Frank Gore 1.25 3.00
84 Isaac Bruce 1.50 4.00
85 Vernon Davis 1.00 2.50
86 Julius Jones 1.00 2.50
87 Matt Hasselbeck 1.00 2.50
88 T.J. Houshmandzadeh 1.00 2.50
89 Donnie Avery 1.00 2.50
90 Marc Bulger 1.00 2.50
91 Steven Jackson 1.00 2.50
92 Antonio Bryant 1.00 2.50
93 Derrick Ward 1.00 2.50
94 Kellen Winslow Jr. 1.00 2.50
95 Chris Johnson 1.00 2.50
96 Kerry Collins 1.00 2.50
97 LenDale White 1.00 2.50
98 Chris Cooley 1.00 2.50
99 Clinton Portis 1.00 2.50
100 Jason Campbell 1.00 2.50
101 Archie Manning 1.50 4.00
102 Bart Starr 3.00 8.00
103 Billy Howton 1.25 3.00
104 Bob Griese 2.00 5.00
105 Bob Lilly 1.50 4.00
106 Brett Favre Jets 3.00 8.00
107 Carl Eller 1.25 3.00
108 Charley Taylor 1.25 3.00
109 Charley Trippi 1.25 3.00
110 Chuck Bednarik 1.50 4.00
111 Dan Fouts 1.50 4.00
112 Dan Marino 3.00 8.00
113 Deacon Jones 1.50 4.00
114 Don Maynard 1.50 4.00
115 Emmitt Smith 2.50 6.00
116 Fran Tarkenton 2.00 5.00
117 Fred Biletnikoff 2.00 5.00
118 Garo Yepremian 1.25 3.00
119 George Blanda 1.50 4.00
120 Hugh McElhenny 1.25 3.00
121 Jack Lambert 2.00 5.00
122 James Lofton 1.25 3.00
123 Jan Stenerud 1.25 3.00
124 Jerry Rice 3.00 8.00
125 Jethro Pugh 1.25 3.00
126 Jim Brown 2.50 6.00
127 Jim Otto 1.25 3.00
128 Joe Greene 2.00 5.00
129 Joe Montana 5.00 12.00
130 Joe Namath 2.50 6.00
131 John Elway 2.50 6.00
132 John Stallworth 1.50 4.00
133 Lance Alworth 1.50 4.00
134 Lenny Moore 1.25 3.00
135 Phil Simms 1.50 4.00
136 Raymond Berry 1.50 4.00
137 Roger Staubach 2.50 6.00
138 Ted Hendricks 1.25 3.00
139 Tiki Barber 1.25 3.00
140 Troy Aikman 2.00 5.00
141 Willie Brown 1.25 3.00
142 Walter Payton 3.00 8.00
143 Jim Thorpe 2.50 6.00
144 Doak Walker 2.00 5.00
145 Ace Parker 1.25 3.00
146 Don Perkins 1.25 3.00
147 Sammy Baugh 2.00 5.00
148 Jim McMahon 1.50 4.00
149 Jim Kelly 1.50 4.00
150 Barry Sanders 2.50 6.00
151 Aaron Brown RC/399 1.50 4.00
152 Aaron Kelly AU/399 RC 3.00 8.00
153 Aaron Maybin AU/99 RC 5.00 12.00
154 Austin Collie AU/399 RC 3.00 8.00
155 B.J. Raji AU/399 RC 4.00 10.00
156 Bernard Scott RC/399 2.00 5.00
157 Brandon Gibson AU/399 RC 4.00 10.00
158 Brandon Tate AU/399 RC 4.00 10.00
159 Brian Cushing AU/199 RC 3.00 8.00
160 Brian Hartline RC/399 2.00 5.00
161 Brian Orakpo AU/249 RC 4.00 10.00
162 Brooks Foster AU/399 RC 3.00 8.00
163 Cameron Morrah AU/399 RC 3.00 8.00
164 Cedric Peerman AU/199 RC 3.00 8.00
165 Chase Coffman AU/399 RC 3.00 8.00
166 Chris Ogbonnaya RC/399 1.50 4.00
167 Clay Matthews AU/299 RC 30.00 60.00
168 Clint Sintim AU/149 RC 4.00 10.00
160 Cornelius Ingram AU/300 RC 3.00 8.00
170 Demetrius Byrd AU/99 RC 5.00 12.00
171 Devin Moore AU/299 RC 3.00 8.00
172 D.Edison AU/399 RC 3.00 8.00
173 Everette Brown AU/399 RC 3.00 8.00
174 Gartrell Johnson RC/399 1.25 3.00
175 Hunter Cantwell AU/149 RC 4.00 10.00
176 James Casey AU/399 RC 4.00 10.00
177 J.Laurinaitis AU/299 RC 5.00 12.00
178 Jared Cook AU/399 RC 4.00 10.00
179 Jarett Dillard AU/399 RC 3.00 8.00
180 Johnny Knox AU/399 RC 4.00 10.00
181 Kenny McKinley AU/399 RC 3.00 8.00
182 Kevin Ogletree AU/249 RC 4.00 10.00
183 Kory Sheets AU/99 RC 5.00 12.00
184 Larry English AU/249 RC 4.00 10.00
185 Louis Murphy AU/99 RC 4.00 10.00
186 Malcolm Jenkins AU/249 RC 3.00 8.00
187 Mike Goodson AU/299 RC 4.00 10.00
188 Nathan Brown AU/399 RC 4.00 10.00
189 P.J. Hill AU/399 RC 3.00 8.00
190 Quan Cosby AU/249 RC 3.00 8.00
191 Quinn Johnson AU/399 RC 3.00 8.00
192 Rashad Jennings AU/199 RC 4.00 10.00
193 Rey Maualuga AU/399 RC 5.00 12.00
194 S.Nelson AU/99 RC EXCH
195 Tiquan Underwood RC/399 1.25 3.00
196 Tom Brandstater AU/149 RC 5.00 12.00
197 T.Fiammetta AU/399 RC 3.00 8.00
198 Travis Beckum AU/399 RC 3.00 8.00
199 Tyrell Sutton AU/399 RC 3.00 8.00
200 Vontae Davis AU/399 RC 3.00 8.00
201 Glen Coffee JSY AU RC 5.00 12.00
202 M.Crabtree JSY AU RC 8.00 20.00
203 Nate Davis JSY AU RC 5.00 12.00
204 Javon Ringer JSY AU RC 5.00 12.00
205 Kenny Britt JSY AU RC 8.00 20.00
206 Mike Wallace JSY AU RC 8.00 20.00
207 Jeremy Maclin JSY AU RC 6.00 15.00
208 LeSean McCoy JSY AU RC 25.00 60.00
209 Donald Brown JSY AU RC 5.00 12.00
210 Mike Thomas JSY AU RC 5.00 12.00
211 Tyson Jackson JSY AU RC 5.00 12.00
212 Josh Freeman JSY AU RC 5.00 12.00
213 D.Heyward-Bey JSY AU RC 8.00 20.00
214 Aaron Curry JSY AU RC 8.00 20.00
215 Deon Butler JSY AU RC 5.00 12.00
216 Jason Smith JSY AU RC 5.00 12.00
217 Juaquin Iglesias JSY AU RC 5.00 12.00
218 Stephen McGee JSY AU RC 5.00 12.00
219 Andre Brown JSY AU RC 6.00 15.00
220 H.Nicks JSY AU RC EXCH 6.00 15.00
221 Ramses Barden JSY AU RC 5.00 12.00
222 Rhett Bomar JSY AU RC 5.00 12.00
223 Percy Harvin JSY AU RC 5.00 12.00
224 Pat White JSY AU RC 6.00 15.00
225 Patrick Turner JSY AU RC 5.00 12.00
226 Chris Wells JSY AU RC 12.00 30.00
227 Mark Sanchez JSY AU RC 20.00 50.00
228 Shonn Greene JSY AU RC 5.00 12.00
229 Brian Robiskie JSY AU RC 5.00 12.00
230 Massaquoi JSY AU RC 5.00 12.00
231 B.Pettigrew JSY AU RC 5.00 12.00
232 Derrick Williams JSY AU RC 5.00 12.00
233 M.Stafford JSY AU RC 40.00 100.00
234 K.Moreno JSY AU RC 5.00 12.00

2009 Limited Gold Spotlight
1-200 UNPRICED GOLD PRINT RUN 5
201-234 UNPRICED GOLD JSY AU PRINT RUN 10

2009 Limited Silver Spotlight
1-200 UNPRICED SILVER PRINT RUN 10
*201-234 JSY AU/25: .5X TO 1.2X BASE JSY AU
201-234 ROOKIE JSY AU PRINT RUN 25
212 Josh Freeman JSY AU 6.00 15.00
227 Mark Sanchez JSY AU 60.00 150.00
233 Matthew Stafford JSY AU 75.00 150.00

2009 Limited Banner Season Autograph Materials
JSY AUTO PRINT RUN 2-25
4 Bernard Berrian/20 8.00 20.00
12 Drew Brees/25 50.00 100.00
19 Matt Ryan/25 30.00 60.00

2009 Limited Banner Season Autograph Materials Prime
PRIME AUTO PRINT RUN 1-25
19 Matt Ryan/25 40.00 80.00

2009 Limited Banner Season Materials
STATED PRINT RUN 50 SER.#'d SETS
4 Bernard Berrian 3.00 8.00
7 Brian Westbrook 3.00 8.00
12 Drew Brees 5.00 12.00
19 Matt Ryan 4.00 10.00
25 Willis McGahee 3.00 8.00

2009 Limited Banner Season Materials Prime
STATED PRINT RUN 2-25
2 Andre Johnson/25 5.00 12.00
7 Brian Westbrook/25 4.00 10.00
10 Clinton Portis/25 4.00 10.00
11 DeAngelo Williams/25 4.00 10.00
17 LenDale White/25 4.00 10.00
19 Matt Ryan/25 5.00 12.00
20 Maurice Jones-Drew/25 4.00 10.00
22 Steve Smith/25 5.00 12.00

2009 Limited Cuts Autographs
CUT AUTO STATED PRINT RUN 3-26
2 Bert Bell/20 25.00 50.00
4 Dante Lavelli/22 12.00 30.00
7 Frank Gatski/25 25.00 50.00
10 George McAfee/26 25.00 50.00
11 Jay Berwanger/16 30.00 60.00
16 Red Badgro/25 25.00 50.00
17 Ollie Matson/16 30.00 60.00
20 Roosevelt Brown/25 30.00 60.00
21 Sammy Baugh/25 50.00 100.00
23 Tony Canadeo/25 30.00 60.00
25 Weeb Ewbank/25 25.00 50.00

2009 Limited Draft Day Jerseys Autographs Prime
PRIME AUTO PRINT RUN 25
1 Josh Freeman 5.00 12.00
2 Brian Cushing 5.00 12.00
3 Aaron Curry 8.00 20.00
4 Michael Crabtree 8.00 20.00
5 Jason Smith 5.00 12.00

2009 Limited Draft Day Lids
ATED PRINT RUN 50 SER.#'d SETS
*JSY/100: .3X TO .8X BASIC LID/50
*JSY PRIME/84-100: 4X TO 1X LID/50
*COMBO/50: .4X TO 1X BASIC LID/50
*COMBO PRIME/17-25: .6X TO 1.5X LID/50
1 Josh Freeman 2.00 5.00
2 Brian Cushing 2.00 5.00
3 Matthew Stafford 10.00 25.00
4 Aaron Curry 3.00 8.00
5 Michael Crabtree 3.00 8.00
6 Jason Smith 2.00 5.00
7 Eugene Monroe 2.00 5.00
8 Michael Oher 12.50 25.00
9 Brian Orakpo 2.50 6.00

2009 Limited Jumbo Jerseys Jersey Number
JUMBO JSY NUMBER PRINT RUN 10-50
*JUMBO JSY/10-50: .4X TO 1X JUM.JSY NUM
2 Antonio Gates/25 4.00 10.00
4 Brian Urlacher/50 5.00 12.00
9 Mark Clayton/50 3.00 8.00
12 Earnest Graham/50 3.00 8.00
14 Jamal Lewis/50 4.00 10.00
15 Jim Brown/10 15.00 40.00
19 Ray Lewis/50 6.00 15.00
20 Reggie Brown/15 4.00 10.00
22 Ricky Williams/50 4.00 10.00

2009 Limited Jumbo Jerseys Autographs
JUMBO JSY AUTO PRINT RUN 1-25
*JSY NUM AU/25: .4X TO 1X BASIC JSY AU/25
15 Jim Brown/25 60.00 125.00
23 Ryan Grant/25 15.00 40.00

2009 Limited Material Monikers
STATED PRINT RUN 9-50
SERIAL #'d UNDER 15 NOT PRICED
1 Andre Johnson/25 12.00 30.00
2 Barry Sanders/15 60.00 120.00
4 Chuck Bednarik/50 12.00 30.00
6 Dan Fouts/25 15.00 40.00
7 Dan Marino/25 100.00 175.00
8 Deacon Jones/50 12.00 30.00
13 Fran Tarkenton/25 20.00 50.00
16 Jack Lambert/20 40.00 80.00
20 Jerry Rice/25 75.00 150.00
21 Jim Brown/50 30.00 80.00
22 Jim Kelly/25 25.00 50.00
23 Jim McMahon/50 12.00 30.00
25 Joe Montana/15 100.00 175.00
26 Joe Namath/50 40.00 80.00
31 LaRon Landry/50 8.00 20.00
32 Larry Johnson/20 10.00 25.00
38 Joe Greene/25 25.00 50.00
39 Phil Simms/25 15.00 40.00
42 Santonio Holmes/20 10.00 25.00
43 Raymond Berry/50 12.00 30.00
44 Steve Slaton/50 8.00 20.00
45 Roger Staubach/25 30.00 60.00
46 Ryan Grant/50 12.00 30.00
47 Tiki Barber/25 12.00 30.00
48 Tony Romo/15 40.00 80.00
49 Vincent Jackson/50 8.00 20.00

2009 Limited Monikers Autographs Gold
LD STATED PRINT RUN 4-50
SERIAL #'d UNDER 16 NOT PRICED
3 Tim Hightower/28 6.00 15.00
4 Matt Ryan/25 30.00 60.00
20 Matt Forte/25 6.00 15.00
22 Cedric Benson/19 6.00 15.00
30 Eddie Royal/33 5.00 12.00
41 Steve Slaton/25 6.00 15.00
62 Drew Brees/30 40.00 80.00
82 Vincent Jackson/33 5.00 12.00
88 T.J. Houshmandzadeh/22 6.00 15.00
93 Derrick Ward/50 5.00 12.00
101 Archie Manning/25 12.00 30.00
103 Billy Howton/50 8.00 20.00
104 Bob Griese/25 15.00 40.00
105 Bob Lilly/50 12.00 30.00
106 Brett Favre/25 100.00 200.00
107 Carl Eller/50 8.00 20.00
108 Charley Taylor/50 8.00 20.00
109 Charley Trippi/50 10.00 25.00
110 Chuck Bednarik/50 10.00 25.00
111 Dan Fouts/25 30.00 60.00
112 Dan Marino/25 100.00 175.00
113 Deacon Jones/50 12.00 30.00
114 Don Maynard/50 10.00 25.00
115 Emmitt Smith/22 75.00 150.00
116 Fran Tarkenton/25 15.00 40.00
117 Fred Biletnikoff/25 15.00 40.00
118 Garo Yepremian/50 8.00 20.00
119 George Blanda/25 20.00 50.00
120 Hugh McElhenny/50 8.00 20.00
122 James Lofton/50 8.00 20.00
123 Jan Stenerud/50 8.00 20.00
125 Jethro Pugh/50 8.00 20.00
126 Jim Brown/50 30.00 80.00
127 Jim Otto/50 8.00 20.00
129 Joe Montana/16 75.00 150.00
132 John Stallworth/25 12.00 30.00
133 Lance Alworth/25 30.00 60.00
134 Lenny Moore /50 8.00 20.00
136 Raymond Berry/50 10.00 25.00
138 Ted Hendricks/25 10.00 25.00
139 Tiki Barber/25 12.00 30.00
141 Willie Brown/50 8.00 20.00
145 Ace Parker/25 10.00 25.00
146 Don Perkins/50 8.00 20.00
148 Jim McMahon/25 12.00 30.00

2009 Limited Prime Pairings Autographs
STATED PRINT RUN 5-20
SERIAL #'d UNDER 15 NOT PRICED
1 J.Stenerud/Yepremian/50 12.00 30.00
2 B.Howton/B.Starr/25 60.00 120.00
3 G.Blanda/Jim Otto/25 30.00 60.00
4 F.Tarkenton/C.Eller/31 40.00 80.00
5 C.Trippi/A.Parker/25 25.00 50.00
6 W.Brown/T.Hendricks/25 15.00 40.00
7 J.Montana/P.Simms/15 60.00 120.00
8 J.Namath/M.Sanchez/50 75.00 150.00
9 McElhenny/J.Brown/50 40.00 80.00
10 E.Smith/T.Barber/25 75.00 150.00
12 D.Maynard/L.Alworth/25 30.00 60.00
13 R.Berry/L.Moore /50 12.00 30.00
14 J.McMahon/J.Elway/25 75.00 150.00
15 Biletnikoff/W.Brown/25 20.00 50.00
16 D.Jones/J.Greene/20 25.00 50.00
17 Staubach/B.Griese/25 50.00 100.00
19 A.Manning/D.Fouts/25 40.00 80.00
21 J.Lofton/J.Stallworth/25 20.00 40.00
22 C.Tylr/Biletnikoff/25 20.00 50.00
23 Prkns/Lilly/Pugh/50 30.00 60.00
25 Bednarik/Maybin/50 20.00 40.00
26 T.Jackson/B.Orakpo/50 EXCH 10.00 25.00
27 M.Jenkins/V.Davis/50 8.00 20.00
28 Cush/Mtthws/Mluga/50 40.00 80.00
29 P.Harvin/L.Murphy/50 8.00 20.00
30 D.Williams/D.Butler/50 12.00 30.00

2009 Limited Pro Bowl Materials
STATED PRINT RUN 100
*PRIME/25: .6X TO 1.5X BASIC JSY/100
1 Chris Cooley 4.00 10.00
2 DeMarcus Ware 4.00 10.00
3 Anquan Boldin 2.50 6.00
4 Kurt Warner 3.00 8.00
5 Wes Welker 3.00 8.00

2009 Limited Pro Bowl Materials Combo
STATED PRINT RUN 100 SER.#'d SETS
*PRIME/25: .6X TO 1.5X BASIC COMBO/100
1 P.Manning/Cutler 12.00 30.00
2 P.Manning/E.Manning 10.00 25.00
3 M.Turner/Peterson 5.00 12.00
4 T.Jones/R.Brown 3.00 8.00
5 P.Manning/Brees 12.00 30.00
6 P.Mann/Gonzalez 12.00 30.00
7 Brees/L.Fitzgerald 5.00 12.00
8 Eli/L.Fitzgerald 4.00 10.00
9 M.Turner/R.White 3.00 8.00
10 Sellers/Cooley 3.00 8.00
11 A.Peterson/J.Allen 12.00 30.00
12 T.Jones/Faneca 3.00 8.00
13 A.Johnson/M.Williams 4.00 10.00
14 Peppers/J.Allen 6.00 15.00
15 Polamalu/A.Wilson 8.00 20.00

2009 Limited Pro Bowl Materials Quad
ATED PRINT RUN 100 SER.#'d SETS
*PRIME/25: .6X TO 1.5X BASIC QUAD/100
1 Trnr/Ptrsn/T.Jns/Brwn 6.00 15.00
2 Fitz/S.Smth/Bldn/R.Whte 5.00 12.00
3 A.Jhnsn/Wyne/Wlkr/T.Gnz 5.00 12.00
4 S.Smth/Fitz/T.Gnz/Wyne 5.00 12.00
5 Ptrsn/Fitz/McClain/T.Gnz 6.00 15.00
6 Wrnr/Fitz/Bldn/A.Wilsn 10.00 25.00
7 P.Mnn/Wyne/Mthis/Frney 15.00 40.00
8 M.Will/Frney/Mthis/Hynsw 5.00 12.00
9 Wre/Briggs/Willis/Beasn 5.00 12.00
10 Hrrisn/Sggs/Lwis/Frrior 12.00 30.00

2009 Limited Pro Bowl Materials Trios
TRIO JSY STATED PRINT RUN 100
*PRIME/25: .6X TO 1.5X BASIC TRIO/100
1 Warner/Eli/Brees 6.00 15.00
2 P.Mann/Brees/Eli 12.00 30.00
3 S.Smith/Pppers/Bsn 4.00 10.00
4 McClain/R.Lws/Sggs 8.00 20.00
5 Farrior/J.Hrrsn/Pola 12.00 30.00

2009 Limited Rookie Jumbo Jerseys
ATED PRINT RUN 50 SER.#'d SETS
*JSY NUM/50: .4X TO 1X BASIC JSY/50
*JSY NUM PRIME/25: .6X TO 1.5X BASIC JSY/50
*PRIME/25: .6X TO 1.5X BASIC JSY/50
1 Knowshon Moreno 1.50 4.00
2 Derrick Williams 1.50 4.00
3 Brandon Pettigrew 1.50 4.00
4 Mark Sanchez 1.50 4.00
5 Brian Robiskie 1.50 4.00
6 Patrick Turner 1.50 4.00
7 Percy Harvin 1.50 4.00
8 Ramses Barden 2.00 5.00
9 Andre Brown 2.00 5.00
10 Matthew Stafford 8.00 20.00
11 Juaquin Iglesias 1.50 4.00
12 Deon Butler 1.50 4.00
13 Darrius Heyward-Bey 2.50 6.00
14 Tyson Jackson 1.50 4.00
15 Donald Brown 1.50 4.00
16 Jeremy Maclin 2.00 5.00
17 Kenny Britt 2.50 6.00
18 Michael Crabtree 2.50 6.00
19 Josh Freeman 1.50 4.00
20 Mike Wallace 2.50 6.00
21 Hakeem Nicks 2.00 5.00
22 Rhett Bomar 1.50 4.00
23 Mohamed Massaquoi 1.50 4.00
24 Aaron Curry 2.50 6.00
25 Pat White 2.00 5.00
26 Jason Smith 1.50 4.00
27 Mike Thomas 1.50 4.00
28 Chris Wells 1.50 4.00
29 Stephen McGee 1.50 4.00
30 Shonn Greene 1.50 4.00
31 LeSean McCoy 4.00 10.00
32 Javon Ringer 1.50 4.00
33 Nate Davis 1.50 4.00
34 Glen Coffee 1.50 4.00

2009 Limited Rookie Jumbo Jerseys Autographs Prime
PRIME AUTO PRINT RUN 25 SER.#'d SETS
1 Knowshon Moreno 6.00 15.00
2 Derrick Williams 6.00 15.00
3 Brandon Pettigrew 6.00 15.00
4 Mark Sanchez 40.00 100.00
5 Brian Robiskie 6.00 15.00
6 Patrick Turner 6.00 15.00
7 Percy Harvin 6.00 15.00
8 Ramses Barden 6.00 15.00
9 Andre Brown 8.00 20.00
10 Matthew Stafford 75.00 150.00
11 Juaquin Iglesias 6.00 15.00
12 Deon Butler 6.00 15.00
13 Darrius Heyward-Bey 10.00 25.00
14 Tyson Jackson 6.00 15.00
15 Donald Brown 6.00 15.00
16 Jeremy Maclin 8.00 20.00
17 Kenny Britt 10.00 25.00
18 Michael Crabtree 10.00 25.00
19 Josh Freeman 6.00 15.00
20 Mike Wallace 10.00 25.00
21 Hakeem Nicks 8.00 20.00
22 Rhett Bomar 6.00 15.00
23 Mohamed Massaquoi 6.00 15.00
24 Aaron Curry 10.00 25.00
25 Pat White 8.00 20.00
26 Jason Smith 6.00 15.00
27 Mike Thomas 6.00 15.00
28 Chris Wells 6.00 15.00
29 Stephen McGee 6.00 15.00
30 Shonn Greene 6.00 15.00
31 LeSean McCoy 30.00 80.00
32 Javon Ringer 6.00 15.00
33 Nate Davis 6.00 15.00
34 Glen Coffee 6.00 15.00

2009 Limited Slideshow Autographs
STATED PRINT RUN 50 SER.#'d SETS
1 Donald Brown 5.00 12.00
2 Tyson Jackson 5.00 12.00
3 Darrius Heyward-Bey 8.00 20.00
4 Deon Butler 5.00 12.00
5 Juaquin Iglesias 5.00 12.00
6 Andre Brown 6.00 15.00
7 Ramses Barden 5.00 12.00
8 Percy Harvin 5.00 12.00
9 Patrick Turner 5.00 12.00
10 Mark Sanchez 8.00 20.00
11 Brian Robiskie 5.00 12.00
12 Brandon Pettigrew 5.00 12.00
13 Matthew Stafford 40.00 80.00
14 Knowshon Moreno 5.00 12.00
15 LeSean McCoy 20.00 50.00
16 Mike Wallace 8.00 20.00
17 Javon Ringer 5.00 12.00
18 Michael Crabtree 8.00 20.00
19 Glen Coffee 5.00 12.00
20 Nate Davis 5.00 12.00
21 Derrick Williams 5.00 12.00
22 Mohamed Massaquoi 5.00 12.00
23 Shonn Greene 5.00 12.00
24 Chris Wells 5.00 12.00
25 Pat White 6.00 15.00
26 Rhett Bomar 5.00 12.00
27 Hakeem Nicks 6.00 15.00
28 Stephen McGee 5.00 12.00
29 Jason Smith 5.00 12.00
30 Aaron Curry 8.00 20.00
31 Josh Freeman 5.00 12.00
32 Jeremy Maclin 6.00 15.00
33 Mike Thomas 5.00 12.00
34 Kenny Britt 8.00 20.00

2009 Limited Super Bowl Materials Combo
COMBO PRINT RUN 50 SER.#'d SETS
*BASE MATERIAL/35: .4X TO 1X COMBO MAT/50
1 Kurt Warner 6.00 15.00
2 Larry Fitzgerald 6.00 15.00
3 Anquan Boldin 5.00 12.00
4 Ben Patrick 5.00 12.00
5 Steve Breaston 6.00 15.00
6 Ben Roethlisberger 15.00 40.00
7 Santonio Holmes 10.00 25.00
8 Willie Parker 5.00 12.00
9 James Harrison 15.00 40.00
10 Gary Russell 5.00 12.00

2009 Limited Team Trademarks Autograph Materials
STATED PRINT RUN 4-25
*PRIME/18: .5X TO 1.2X JSY AU/25
SERIAL #'d UNDER 25 NOT PRICED
9 Donald Driver/25 20.00 40.00

2009 Limited Team Trademarks Materials
STATED PRINT RUN 30-50
7 Carson Palmer/50 4.00 10.00
10 Donovan McNabb/50 4.00 10.00
11 Felix Jones/50 3.00 8.00
13 Jake Delhomme/50 3.00 8.00
18 Marshawn Lynch/50 4.00 10.00
20 Matt Schaub/30 3.00 8.00
21 Peyton Manning/50 12.00 30.00
24 Tom Brady/50 15.00 40.00
25 Walter Payton/50 12.00 30.00

2009 Limited Team Trademarks Materials Prime
STATED PRINT RUN 25 SER.#'d SETS
6 Cadillac Williams 6.00 15.00
9 Donald Driver 6.00 15.00
11 Felix Jones 5.00 12.00
12 Hines Ward 6.00 15.00
13 Jake Delhomme 5.00 12.00
14 Jason Campbell 5.00 12.00
15 Jason Witten 6.00 15.00
17 Marion Barber 6.00 15.00
18 Marshawn Lynch 6.00 15.00
19 Matt Hasselbeck 5.00 12.00
22 Reggie Bush 5.00 12.00
24 Tom Brady 25.00 60.00
25 Walter Payton 20.00 50.00

2009 Limited Threads Prime
PRIME STATED PRINT RUN 1-50
4 Matt Ryan/15 6.00 15.00
8 Mark Clayton/50 4.00 10.00
11 Lee Evans/50 5.00 12.00
12 Marshawn Lynch/50 5.00 12.00
14 DeAngelo Williams/50 4.00 10.00
16 Steve Smith/50 5.00 12.00
17 Brian Urlacher/49 6.00 15.00
23 Chad Ochocinco/50 4.00 10.00
24 Brady Quinn/50 4.00 10.00
26 Jamal Lewis/25 6.00 15.00
27 Marion Barber/50 5.00 12.00
38 Ryan Grant/25 6.00 15.00
39 Andre Johnson/50 5.00 12.00
47 Maurice Jones-Drew/50 4.00 10.00
49 Dwayne Bowe/20 6.00 15.00
50 Larry Johnson/50 4.00 10.00
53 Ronnie Brown/50 4.00 10.00
54 Ricky Williams/50 5.00 12.00
58 Laurence Maroney/50 5.00 12.00
60 Tom Brady/50 20.00 50.00
64 Reggie Bush/50 4.00 10.00
73 Brian Westbrook/50 4.00 10.00
77 Santonio Holmes/50 4.00 10.00
78 Willie Parker/50 4.00 10.00
79 Antonio Gates/50 5.00 12.00
82 Vincent Jackson/50 4.00 10.00
83 Frank Gore/50 5.00 12.00
87 Matt Hasselbeck/50 4.00 10.00
90 Marc Bulger/50 4.00 10.00
91 Steven Jackson/50 4.00 10.00
97 LenDale White/25 5.00 12.00
98 Chris Cooley/50 4.00 10.00
99 Clinton Portis/50 4.00 10.00
100 Jason Campbell/50 4.00 10.00
105 Bob Lilly/15 10.00 25.00
106 Brett Favre/35 12.00 30.00
108 Charley Taylor/50 6.00 15.00
111 Dan Fouts/50 8.00 20.00
112 Dan Marino/50 15.00 40.00
113 Deacon Jones/25 10.00 25.00
114 Don Maynard/25 10.00 25.00
116 Fran Tarkenton/50 10.00 25.00
117 Fred Biletnikoff/50 10.00 25.00
121 Jack Lambert/25 12.00 30.00
122 James Lofton/50 6.00 15.00
123 Jan Stenerud/50 6.00 15.00
124 Jerry Rice/50 15.00 40.00
126 Jim Brown/25 15.00 40.00
127 Jim Otto/25 8.00 20.00
129 Joe Montana/25 30.00 80.00
132 John Stallworth/25 10.00 25.00
136 Raymond Berry/50 8.00 20.00
137 Roger Staubach/50 12.00 30.00
138 Ted Hendricks/50 6.00 15.00
139 Tiki Barber/50 6.00 15.00
141 Willie Brown/50 6.00 15.00
142 Walter Payton/50 15.00 40.00
149 Jim Kelly/50 8.00 20.00
150 Barry Sanders/50 12.00 30.00

2010 Limited
1-150 STATED PRINT RUN 499
151-200 ROOKIE PRINT RUN 499
201-235 JSY AU RC PRINT RUN 199
EXCH EXPIRATION: 5/24/2012
1 Chris Wells 1.00 2.50
2 Larry Fitzgerald 1.25 3.00
3 Steve Breaston 1.00 2.50
4 Matt Ryan 1.25 3.00
5 Michael Turner 1.00 2.50
6 Roddy White 1.00 2.50
7 Anquan Boldin 1.00 2.50
8 Joe Flacco 1.25 3.00
9 Ray Rice 1.00 2.50
10 Ryan Fitzpatrick 1.00 2.50
11 Lee Evans 1.25 3.00
12 Marshawn Lynch 1.25 3.00
13 DeAngelo Williams 1.00 2.50
14 Jonathan Stewart 1.00 2.50
15 Steve Smith 1.25 3.00
16 Devin Hester 1.25 3.00
17 Jay Cutler 1.00 2.50
18 Matt Forte 1.00 2.50
19 Carson Palmer 1.25 3.00
20 Cedric Benson 1.00 2.50
21 Chad Ochocinco 1.00 2.50
22 Terrell Owens 1.25 3.00
23 Mohamed Massaquoi 1.25 3.00
24 Jerome Harrison 1.00 2.50
25 Josh Cribbs 1.00 2.50
26 Jason Witten 1.25 3.00
27 Miles Austin 1.00 2.50
28 Tony Romo 1.25 3.00
29 Eddie Royal 1.00 2.50
30 Knowshon Moreno 1.00 2.50
31 Kyle Orton 1.00 2.50
32 Calvin Johnson 1.50 4.00
33 Matthew Stafford 1.25 3.00
34 Nate Burleson 1.00 2.50
35 Aaron Rodgers 3.00 8.00
36 Greg Jennings 1.00 2.50
37 Ryan Grant 1.25 3.00
38 Andre Johnson 1.25 3.00
39 Matt Schaub 1.00 2.50
40 Owen Daniels 1.00 2.50
41 Dallas Clark 1.00 2.50
42 Peyton Manning 4.00 10.00
43 Joseph Addai 1.00 2.50
44 Reggie Wayne 1.25 3.00
45 David Garrard 1.00 2.50
46 Maurice Jones-Drew 1.00 2.50
47 Mike Sims-Walker 1.00 2.50
48 Dwayne Bowe 1.25 3.00
49 Jamaal Charles 1.25 3.00
50 Matt Cassel 1.00 2.50
51 Chad Henne 1.25 3.00
52 Ronnie Brown 1.00 2.50
53 Brandon Marshall 1.25 3.00
54 Adrian Peterson 1.50 4.00
55 Brett Favre 3.00 8.00
56 Percy Harvin 1.00 2.50
57 Visanthe Shiancoe 1.25 3.00
58 Randy Moss 1.25 3.00
59 Tom Brady 4.00 10.00
60 Wes Welker 1.25 3.00
61 Devery Henderson 1.00 2.50
62 Drew Brees 1.50 4.00
63 Reggie Bush 1.00 2.50
64 Brandon Jacobs 1.00 2.50
65 Eli Manning 1.25 3.00
66 Steve Smith USC 1.00 2.50
67 Braylon Edwards 1.00 2.50
68 Mark Sanchez 1.00 2.50
69 Shonn Greene 1.00 2.50
70 Darren McFadden 1.00 2.50
71 Jason Campbell 1.00 2.50
72 Louis Murphy 1.00 2.50
73 Kevin Kolb 1.00 2.50
74 DeSean Jackson 1.25 3.00
75 LeSean McCoy 1.50 4.00
76 Ben Roethlisberger 1.50 4.00
77 Rashard Mendenhall 1.00 2.50
78 Hines Ward 1.25 3.00
79 Antonio Gates 1.25 3.00
80 Darren Sproles 1.25 3.00
81 Philip Rivers 1.50 4.00
82 Alex Smith QB 1.25 3.00
83 Frank Gore 1.25 3.00
84 Vernon Davis 1.00 2.50
85 Leon Washington 1.00 2.50
86 Matt Hasselbeck 1.00 2.50
87 Deion Branch 1.00 2.50
88 James Laurinaitis 1.25 3.00
89 Steven Jackson 1.00 2.50
90 Donnie Avery 1.00 2.50
91 Cadillac Williams 1.00 2.50
92 Josh Freeman 1.25 3.00
93 Kellen Winslow Jr. 1.00 2.50
94 Chris Johnson 1.00 2.50
95 Kenny Britt 1.00 2.50
96 Vince Young 1.00 2.50
97 Donovan McNabb 1.25 3.00
98 Chris Cooley 1.00 2.50
99 Clinton Portis 1.00 2.50
100 Santana Moss 1.25 3.00
101 Alan Page 1.50 4.00
102 Alex Karras 1.50 4.00
103 Andre Reed 1.50 4.00
104 Archie Manning 1.50 4.00
105 Art Monk 2.00 5.00
106 Billy Howton 1.25 3.00
107 Bobby Bell 1.25 3.00
108 Boyd Dowler 1.25 3.00
109 Charley Taylor 1.25 3.00
110 Charley Trippi 1.25 3.00
111 Charlie Joiner 1.25 3.00
112 Dante Lavelli 1.25 3.00
113 Daryle Lamonica 1.25 3.00
114 Dave Casper 1.25 3.00
115 Deacon Jones 1.50 4.00
116 Del Shofner 1.25 3.00
117 Doug Flutie 1.50 4.00
118 Dub Jones 1.25 3.00
119 Earl Campbell 2.00 5.00
120 Ernie Davis 4.00 10.00
121 Floyd Little 1.25 3.00
122 Forrest Gregg 1.25 3.00
123 Jan Stenerud 1.25 3.00
124 George Blanda 1.50 4.00
125 Harlon Hill 1.25 3.00
126 Hank Jordan 1.25 3.00
127 Jack Youngblood 1.25 3.00
128 Jackie Slater 1.25 3.00
129 Jim McMahon 1.50 4.00
130 Jim Otto 1.25 3.00
131 Jim Plunkett 1.50 4.00
132 Jim Taylor 2.00 5.00
133 Jimmy Orr 1.25 3.00
134 Larry Little 1.25 3.00
135 Lee Roy Selmon 1.50 4.00
136 Lem Barney 1.25 3.00
137 Lenny Moore 1.25 3.00
138 Leroy Kelly 1.50 4.00
139 Lydell Mitchell 1.25 3.00
140 Mark Duper 1.25 3.00
141 Merlin Olsen 1.25 3.00
142 Mike Curtis 1.25 3.00
143 Ozzie Newsome 1.50 4.00
144 Paul Krause 1.25 3.00
145 Priest Holmes 1.25 3.00
146 Randy White 1.50 4.00
147 Raymond Berry 1.50 4.00
148 Roger Craig 1.50 4.00
149 Ronnie Lott 1.50 4.00

150 Walter Payton 4.00 10.00
151 Aaron Hernandez RC 1.25 3.00
152 Anthony Dixon RC 1.25 3.00
153 Anthony McCoy RC 1.25 3.00
154 Antonio Brown RC 10.00 25.00
155 Brandon Graham RC 1.50 4.00
156 Brandon Spikes RC 1.25 3.00
157 Bryan Bulaga RC 1.25 3.00
158 Carlos Dunlap RC 1.25 3.00
159 Carlton Mitchell RC 1.25 3.00
160 Chris Cook RC 1.25 3.00
161 Corey Wootton RC 1.25 3.00
162 David Gettis RC 1.25 3.00
163 David Reed RC 1.25 3.00
164 Deji Karim RC 1.50 4.00
165 Derrick Morgan RC 1.25 3.00
166 Devin McCourty RC 1.50 4.00
167 Dominique Franks RC 1.25 3.00
168 Earl Thomas RC 3.00 8.00
169 Ed Dickson RC 1.25 3.00
170 Everson Griffen RC 1.25 3.00
171 Garrett Graham RC 1.25 3.00
172 Jacoby Ford RC 1.25 3.00
173 Jason Pierre-Paul RC 2.00 5.00
174 Jason Worilds RC 1.25 3.00
175 Javier Arenas RC 1.25 3.00
176 Jerry Hughes RC 1.25 3.00
177 Jimmy Graham RC 3.00 8.00
178 Joe Haden RC 2.00 5.00
179 Joe Webb RC 1.25 3.00
180 John Skelton RC 1.50 4.00
181 Kareem Jackson RC 1.25 3.00
182 Marc Mariani RC 2.00 5.00
183 Max Hall RC 2.00 5.00
184 Michael Hoomanawanui RC 2.00 5.00
185 Morgan Burnett RC 1.50 4.00
186 Nate Allen RC 2.00 5.00
187 NaVorro Bowman RC 2.50 6.00
188 Patrick Robinson RC 1.50 4.00
189 Perrish Cox RC 1.50 4.00
190 Ricky Sapp RC 1.25 3.00
191 Riley Cooper RC 1.25 3.00
192 Russell Okung RC 1.25 3.00
193 Sean Lee RC 2.50 6.00
194 Sean Weatherspoon RC 1.25 3.00
195 Stephen Williams RC 2.00 5.00
196 Taylor Mays RC 1.25 3.00
197 Tony Moeaki RC 1.50 4.00
198 Tony Pike RC 1.25 3.00
199 Trent Williams RC 1.50 4.00
200 Victor Cruz RC 2.50 6.00
201 Sam Bradford JSY AU RC 15.00 40.00
202 N.Suh JSY AU RC 10.00 25.00
203 Gerald McCoy JSY AU RC 5.00 12.00
204 Eric Berry JSY AU RC 8.00 20.00
205 R.McClain JSY AU RC 5.00 12.00
206 C.J. Spiller JSY AU RC 5.00 12.00
207 R.Mathews JSY AU RC 5.00 12.00
208 J.Gresham JSY AU RC 5.00 12.00
209 D.Thomas JSY AU RC 12.00 30.00
210 Dez Bryant JSY AU RC 30.00 60.00
211 Tim Tebow JSY AU RC 30.00 60.00
212 Jahvid Best JSY AU RC 5.00 12.00
213 D.McCluster JSY AU RC 6.00 15.00
214 Arrelious Benn JSY AU RC 5.00 12.00
215 R.Gronkowski JSY AU RC 40.00 80.00
216 Jimmy Clausen JSY AU RC 5.00 12.00
217 Toby Gerhart JSY AU RC 5.00 12.00
218 Ben Tate JSY AU RC 5.00 12.00
219 Montario Hardesty JSY AU RC 5.00 12.00
220 Golden Tate JSY AU RC 6.00 15.00
221 Damian Williams JSY AU RC 5.00 12.00
222 Brandon LaFell JSY AU RC 8.00 20.00
223 E.Sanders JSY AU RC 8.00 20.00
224 Jordan Shipley JSY AU RC 5.00 12.00
225 Colt McCoy JSY AU RC 6.00 15.00
226 Eric Decker JSY AU RC 6.00 15.00
227 Andre Roberts JSY AU RC 6.00 15.00
228 Armanti Edwards JSY AU RC 6.00 15.00
229 Taylor Price JSY AU RC 5.00 12.00
230 Mardy Gilyard JSY AU RC 5.00 12.00
231 Mike Williams JSY AU RC 5.00 12.00
232 Marcus Easley JSY AU RC 5.00 12.00
233 Joe McKnight JSY AU RC 5.00 12.00
234 Mike Kafka JSY AU RC 6.00 15.00
235 J.Dwyer JSY AU RC 5.00 12.00

2010 Limited Gold Spotlight

*VETS 1-100: 1X TO 2.5X BASIC CARDS
*LEGENDS 101-150: .8X TO 2X BASIC CARDS
*ROOKIES 151-200: .8X TO 2X BASIC CARDS
1-200 STATED PRINT RUN 25
201-235 UNPRICED JSY AU PRINT RUN 10

2010 Limited Silver Spotlight

*VETS 1-100: .8X TO 2X BASIC CARDS
*LEGENDS 101-150: .6X TO 1.5X BASIC CARDS
*ROOKIES 151-200: .6X TO 1.5X BASIC CARDS
1-200 STATED PRINT RUN 50
*ROOK.JSY AU 201-235: .5X TO 1.2X JSY AU RC
201-235 JSY AU PRINT RUN 25

2010 Limited America's Team

STATED PRINT RUN 50 SER.#'d SETS
1 Bill Bates 4.00 10.00
2 Bob Hayes 6.00 15.00
3 Bob Lilly 5.00 12.00
4 Chuck Howley 4.00 10.00
5 Cliff Harris 4.00 10.00
6 D.D. Lewis 4.00 10.00
7 Danny White 5.00 12.00
8 Darren Woodson 5.00 12.00
9 Deion Sanders 5.00 12.00
10 DeMarcus Ware 4.00 10.00
11 Don Perkins 4.00 10.00
12 Ed Too Tall Jones 4.00 10.00
13 Emmitt Smith 8.00 20.00
14 Everson Walls 4.00 10.00
15 Felix Jones 4.00 10.00
16 Harvey Martin 4.00 10.00
17 Jason Witten 3.00 8.00
18 Lee Roy Jordan 5.00 12.00
19 Mark Stepnoski 4.00 10.00
20 Mel Renfro 4.00 10.00
21 Michael Irvin 6.00 15.00
22 Rayfield Wright 4.00 10.00
23 Roger Staubach 8.00 20.00
24 Tony Dorsett 6.00 15.00
25 Tony Romo 3.00 8.00

2010 Limited America's Team Autographs

STATED PRINT RUN 1-50
EXCH EXPIRATION: 5/24/2012
1 Bill Bates/50 15.00 40.00
3 Bob Lilly/50 15.00 40.00
5 Cliff Harris/50 15.00 40.00
6 D.D. Lewis/20 20.00 50.00
8 Darren Woodson/50 15.00 40.00
9 Deion Sanders/21 30.00 60.00
10 DeMarcus Ware/50 15.00 40.00
11 Don Perkins/50 15.00 40.00
14 Everson Walls/50 15.00 40.00
18 Lee Roy Jordan/50 15.00 40.00
19 Mark Stepnoski/50 15.00 40.00
20 Mel Renfro/50 20.00 50.00
21 Michael Irvin/15 30.00 60.00
22 Rayfield Wright/50 20.00 50.00
24 Tony Dorsett/33 30.00 60.00

2010 Limited America's Team Threads

STATED PRINT RUN 50 SER.#'d SETS
*PRIME/15-25: .5X TO 1.2X BASIC JSY/50
1 Bill Bates 8.00 20.00
2 Bob Hayes 8.00 20.00
3 Bob Lilly 8.00 20.00
4 Chuck Howley 8.00 20.00
5 Cliff Harris 6.00 15.00
6 D.D. Lewis 6.00 15.00
7 Danny White 8.00 20.00
8 Darren Woodson 8.00 20.00
9 Deion Sanders 8.00 20.00
10 DeMarcus Ware 6.00 15.00
12 Ed Too Tall Jones 6.00 15.00
13 Emmitt Smith 12.00 30.00
15 Felix Jones 5.00 12.00
16 Harvey Martin 8.00 20.00
17 Jason Witten 6.00 15.00
21 Michael Irvin 10.00 25.00
23 Roger Staubach 12.00 30.00
24 Tony Dorsett 8.00 20.00
25 Tony Romo 6.00 15.00

2010 Limited America's Team Threads Autographs

STATED PRINT RUN 5-25
*PRIME/15: .5X TO 1.2X JSY AU/22-25
1 Bill Bates/25 25.00 50.00
3 Bob Lilly/25 25.00 50.00
4 Chuck Howley/25 25.00 50.00
6 D.D. Lewis/25 25.00 50.00
7 Danny White/25 25.00 50.00
8 Darren Woodson/25 25.00 50.00
9 Deion Sanders/25 40.00 80.00
10 DeMarcus Ware/25 25.00 50.00
12 Ed Too Tall Jones/25 30.00 60.00
13 Emmitt Smith/22 100.00 175.00
21 Michael Irvin/25 40.00 80.00
24 Tony Dorsett/25 30.00 60.00

2010 Limited Banner Season Autograph Materials

STATED PRINT RUN 15-25
1 LeSean McCoy/25 15.00 40.00
2 Aaron Rodgers/15 150.00 250.00
3 Vernon Davis/25 12.00 25.00
4 Mark Sanchez/25 25.00 50.00
7 Calvin Johnson/25 15.00 40.00
8 Maurice Jones-Drew/25 10.00 25.00
10 Matt Ryan/25 30.00 60.00
13 DeSean Jackson/25 12.00 30.00
14 Andre Johnson/15
15 Brett Favre/25 100.00 200.00
16 Dallas Clark/25 15.00 40.00
18 Rashard Mendenhall/25 10.00 25.00
19 Philip Rivers/15 15.00 40.00
20 Percy Harvin/15
21 Matt Forte/25 10.00 25.00
22 Vince Young/15 10.00 25.00
23 Knowshon Moreno/25 10.00 25.00
24 Visanthe Shiancoe/25 12.00 30.00
25 Brent Celek/25 10.00 25.00

2010 Limited Banner Season Autograph Materials Prime

STATED PRINT RUN 5-15
1 LeSean McCoy/15 20.00 50.00
3 Vernon Davis/15 15.00 40.00
4 Mark Sanchez/15 30.00 60.00
6 Chad Ochocinco/15 12.00 30.00
7 Calvin Johnson/15 20.00 50.00
8 Maurice Jones-Drew/15 12.00 30.00
10 Matt Ryan/15 40.00 80.00
13 DeSean Jackson/15 15.00 40.00
15 Brett Favre/15 125.00 250.00
16 Dallas Clark/14 12.00 30.00
17 Lee Evans/15 15.00 40.00
18 Rashard Mendenhall/15 12.00 30.00
21 Matt Forte/15 12.00 30.00
23 Knowshon Moreno/15 12.00 30.00
24 Visanthe Shiancoe/10 15.00 40.00
25 Brent Celek/15 12.00 30.00

2010 Limited Banner Season Materials

STATED PRINT RUN 100 SER.#'d SETS
1 LeSean McCoy 4.00 10.00
2 Aaron Rodgers 12.50 25.00
3 Vernon Davis 2.50 6.00
4 Mark Sanchez 2.50 6.00
7 Calvin Johnson 4.00 10.00
8 Maurice Jones-Drew 2.50 6.00
9 Chris Johnson 2.50 6.00
10 Matt Ryan 3.00 8.00
13 DeSean Jackson 3.00 8.00
14 Andre Johnson 3.00 8.00
15 Brett Favre 8.00 20.00
16 Dallas Clark 2.50 6.00
18 Rashard Mendenhall 2.50 6.00
19 Philip Rivers 4.00 10.00
20 Percy Harvin 2.50 6.00
21 Matt Forte 2.50 6.00
22 Vince Young 2.50 6.00
23 Knowshon Moreno 2.50 6.00
24 Visanthe Shiancoe 3.00 8.00
25 Brent Celek 2.50 6.00

2010 Limited Banner Season Materials Prime

*PRIME/45-50: .6X TO 1.5X BASIC JSY/100
*PRIME/25: .8X TO 2X BASIC JSY/100
PRIEM STATED PRINT RUN 25-50
6 Chad Ochocinco/50 4.00 10.00
17 Lee Evans/45 5.00 12.00

2010 Limited Cuts Autographs

STATED PRINT RUN 1-50
4 Bill Dudley/50 12.00 30.00
10 Bulldog Turner/20 40.00 80.00

2010 Limited Draft Day Duos

STATED PRINT RUN 25-75
*PRIME/25: .8X TO 2X BASIC DUO/75-100
1 C.Spiller/J.Best/100 2.00 5.00
2 E.Berry/D.Williams/75 3.00 8.00
3 D.Thomas/D.Morgan/100 5.00 12.00
4 S.Bradford/N.Suh/25 5.00 12.00
5 T.Williams/R.Okung/100 2.50 6.00

2010 Limited Draft Day Quads

STATED PRINT RUN 25-100
*PRIME/25: .8X TO 2X BASIC QUAD/100
1 Brdfrd/Suh/G.McC/Will/25 6.00 15.00
2 Brry/Okng/Hadn/Spillr/100 8.00 20.00
3 Brdfrd/Spillr/Thms/Best/25 8.00 20.00
4 Suh/G.McC/Will/Odrck/100 5.00 12.00

2010 Limited Draft Day Jerseys Autographs Prime

1 Bryan Bulaga 8.00 20.00
2 C.J. Spiller 8.00 20.00
3 Demaryius Thomas 20.00 50.00
4 Derrick Morgan 8.00 20.00
5 Eric Berry 12.00 30.00
6 Gerald McCoy 10.00 25.00
7 Jahvid Best 8.00 20.00
8 Joe Haden 12.00 30.00
9 Ndamukong Suh 15.00 40.00
10 Russell Okung 8.00 20.00
11 Trent Williams
13 Dan Williams 8.00 20.00
14 Jared Odrick 10.00 25.00

2010 Limited Draft Day Lids

LIDS PRINT RUN 50 SER.#'d SETS
*COMBO/50: .4X TO 1X LID/50
*COMBO PRIME/18-25: .8X TO 2X LID/50
*JERSEY/100: .3X TO .8X LID/50
*JSY PRIME/50: .5X TO 1.2X LID/50
1 Bryan Bulaga 2.00 5.00
2 C.J. Spiller 2.00 5.00
3 Demaryius Thomas 5.00 12.00
4 Derrick Morgan 2.00 5.00
5 Eric Berry 3.00 8.00
6 Gerald McCoy 2.00 5.00
7 Jahvid Best 2.00 5.00
8 Joe Haden 3.00 8.00
9 Ndamukong Suh 4.00 10.00
10 Russell Okung 2.00 5.00
11 Trent Williams 2.50 6.00
12 Sam Bradford 2.50 6.00
13 Dan Williams 2.00 5.00
14 Jared Odrick 3.00 8.00

2010 Limited Draft Day Trios

STATED PRINT RUN 25-100
*PRIME/25: .8X TO 2X BASIC TRIO/100
1 Bradford/Suh/McCoy/25 6.00 15.00
2 Williams/Berry/Okung/100 4.00 10.00
3 Spiller/Best/Thomas/100 6.00 15.00
4 Bradford/McCoy/Williams/25 4.00 10.00

2010 Limited Initial Steps Autographs

STATED PRINT RUN 10-99
EXCH EXPIRATION: 5/24/2012
1 Eric Berry/99 6.00 15.00
2 Montario Hardesty/99 4.00 10.00
3 Joe McKnight/99 4.00 10.00
5 Demaryius Thomas/99 10.00 25.00
6 Jonathan Dwyer /99 4.00 10.00
7 Colt McCoy/99 5.00 12.00
8 Rob Gronkowski/99 25.00 50.00
9 Jermaine Gresham/99 4.00 10.00
10 Sam Bradford/99 15.00 40.00
11 Eric Decker/99 5.00 12.00
12 Toby Gerhart/99 4.00 10.00
13 Mike Williams/99 4.00 10.00
15 Dexter McCluster No AU/99 2.00 5.00
16 Brandon LaFell/99 6.00 15.00
17 Mike Kafka/99 5.00 12.00
18 Armanti Edwards/99 5.00 12.00
19 Ryan Mathews/99 4.00 10.00
20 Tim Tebow/99 30.00 80.00
21 Emmanuel Sanders/99 6.00 15.00
22 Taylor Price/99 4.00 10.00
23 C.J. Spiller/10
24 Jahvid Best/99 4.00 10.00
25 Golden Tate/99 5.00 12.00
26 Jordan Shipley/99 4.00 10.00
27 Dez Bryant/99 30.00 60.00
28 Rolando McClain/99 4.00 10.00
29 Arrelious Benn/99 4.00 10.00
30 Ben Tate/99 4.00 10.00
31 Jimmy Clausen/99 4.00 10.00
32 Damian Williams/99 4.00 10.00
33 Andre Roberts/99 5.00 12.00
34 Marcus Easley/99 4.00 10.00
35 Mardy Gilyard/99 4.00 10.00

2010 Limited Initial Steps Jerseys

JERSEY PRINT RUN 99 SER.#'d SETS
*PRIME/25: .8X TO 2X BASIC JSY/99
*SHOES/80: .5X TO 1.2X BASIC JSY/99
1 Eric Berry 2.50 6.00
2 Montario Hardesty 1.50 4.00
3 Joe McKnight 1.50 4.00
4 Ndamukong Suh 3.00 8.00
5 Demaryius Thomas 4.00 10.00
6 Jonathan Dwyer 1.50 4.00
7 Colt McCoy 2.00 5.00
8 Rob Gronkowski 5.00 12.00
9 Jermaine Gresham 1.50 4.00
10 Sam Bradford 2.00 5.00
11 Eric Decker 2.00 5.00
12 Toby Gerhart 1.50 4.00
13 Mike Williams 1.50 4.00
14 Gerald McCoy 1.50 4.00
15 Dexter McCluster 2.00 5.00
16 Brandon LaFell 2.50 6.00
17 Mike Kafka 2.00 5.00
18 Armanti Edwards 2.00 5.00
19 Ryan Mathews 1.50 4.00
20 Tim Tebow 5.00 12.00
21 Emmanuel Sanders 2.50 6.00
22 Taylor Price 1.50 4.00
23 C.J. Spiller 1.50 4.00
24 Jahvid Best 1.50 4.00
25 Golden Tate 2.00 5.00
26 Jordan Shipley 1.50 4.00
27 Dez Bryant 4.00 10.00
28 Rolando McClain 1.50 4.00
29 Arrelious Benn 1.50 4.00
30 Ben Tate 1.50 4.00
31 Jimmy Clausen 1.50 4.00
32 Damian Williams 1.50 4.00
33 Andre Roberts 2.00 5.00
34 Marcus Easley 1.50 4.00
35 Mardy Gilyard 1.50 4.00

2010 Limited Jumbo Jerseys

STATED PRINT RUN 25 SER.#'d SETS
3 Willis McGahee 4.00 10.00
4 Clinton Portis 4.00 10.00
6 Brian Orakpo 4.00 10.00
8 Marion Barber 5.00 12.00
9 Heath Miller 4.00 10.00
10 Patrick Willis 5.00 12.00
11 Darrelle Revis 6.00 15.00
12 Eddie Royal 4.00 10.00
13 Dwayne Bowe 5.00 12.00
14 Sidney Rice 4.00 10.00
15 Randy Moss 5.00 12.00
16 Shonn Greene 4.00 10.00
19 Darren McFadden 4.00 10.00
20 Kyle Orton 4.00 10.00
21 Will Smith 4.00 10.00
22 Joseph Addai 4.00 10.00
23 Bernard Berrian 4.00 10.00
24 Santana Moss 5.00 12.00
25 Ray Lewis 8.00 20.00
26 Felix Jones 4.00 10.00
28 Jay Cutler 4.00 10.00
29 Steven Jackson 4.00 10.00
30 Devin Hester 5.00 12.00
31 Cedric Benson 4.00 10.00
33 Reggie Bush 4.00 10.00
34 DeMarcus Ware 5.00 12.00
35 Devery Henderson 4.00 10.00

2010 Limited Jumbo Jerseys Jersey Number

STATED PRINT RUN 12-25
1 Greg Jennings/25 4.00 10.00
2 Charles Woodson/10
3 Willis McGahee/25 4.00 10.00
4 Clinton Portis/25 4.00 10.00
6 Brian Orakpo/25 4.00 10.00
8 Marion Barber/25 5.00 12.00
9 Heath Miller/25 4.00 10.00
10 Patrick Willis/25 5.00 12.00
11 Darrelle Revis/25 6.00 15.00
12 Eddie Royal/25 4.00 10.00
13 Dwayne Bowe/25 5.00 12.00
14 Sidney Rice/25 4.00 10.00
15 Randy Moss/25 5.00 12.00
16 Shonn Greene/25 4.00 10.00
19 Darren McFadden/25 4.00 10.00
20 Kyle Orton/25 4.00 10.00
21 Will Smith/25 4.00 10.00
22 Joseph Addai/25 4.00 10.00
23 Bernard Berrian/25 4.00 10.00
24 Santana Moss/25 5.00 12.00
25 Ray Lewis/25 8.00 20.00
26 Felix Jones/25 4.00 10.00
28 Jay Cutler/25 4.00 10.00
29 Steven Jackson/25 4.00 10.00
30 Devin Hester/10
31 Cedric Benson/25 4.00 10.00
33 Reggie Bush/12
34 DeMarcus Ware/25 5.00 12.00
35 Devery Henderson/25 4.00 10.00

2010 Limited Jumbo Jerseys Jersey Number Prime

STATED PRINT RUN 1-15
1 Greg Jennings/15 6.00 15.00
4 Clinton Portis/15 6.00 15.00
5 Hines Ward/15 8.00 20.00
6 Brian Orakpo/15 6.00 15.00
7 Cadillac Williams/15 6.00 15.00
8 Marion Barber/15 8.00 20.00
9 Heath Miller/15 6.00 15.00
10 Patrick Willis/15 8.00 20.00
11 Darrelle Revis/15 6.00 15.00
12 Eddie Royal/15 6.00 15.00
13 Dwayne Bowe/15 8.00 20.00
14 Sidney Rice/15 6.00 15.00
15 Randy Moss/15 8.00 20.00
17 Donald Driver/15 8.00 20.00
19 Darren McFadden/15 6.00 15.00
21 Will Smith/15 6.00 15.00
22 Joseph Addai/15 6.00 15.00
23 Bernard Berrian/15 6.00 15.00
24 Santana Moss/15 8.00 20.00
25 Ray Lewis/15 12.00 30.00
26 Felix Jones/15 6.00 15.00
28 Jay Cutler/15 6.00 15.00
29 Steven Jackson/15 6.00 15.00
30 Devin Hester/15 8.00 20.00
31 Cedric Benson/15 6.00 15.00
34 DeMarcus Ware/15 8.00 20.00
35 Devery Henderson/15 6.00 15.00

2010 Limited Jumbo Jerseys Prime

STATED PRINT RUN 1-15
1 Greg Jennings/15 6.00 15.00
2 Charles Woodson/15 10.00 25.00
3 Willis McGahee/15 6.00 15.00
4 Clinton Portis/15 6.00 15.00
5 Hines Ward/15 8.00 20.00
6 Brian Orakpo/15 6.00 15.00
7 Cadillac Williams/15 6.00 15.00
8 Marion Barber/15 8.00 20.00
9 Heath Miller/15 6.00 15.00
10 Patrick Willis/15 8.00 20.00
11 Darrelle Revis/15 10.00 25.00
12 Eddie Royal/15 6.00 15.00
13 Dwayne Bowe/15 8.00 20.00
14 Sidney Rice/15 6.00 15.00
15 Randy Moss/15 8.00 20.00
17 Donald Driver/15 8.00 20.00
19 Darren McFadden/15 6.00 15.00
21 Will Smith/15 6.00 15.00
22 Joseph Addai/15 6.00 15.00
23 Bernard Berrian/15 6.00 15.00
24 Santana Moss/15 8.00 20.00
25 Ray Lewis/15 12.00 30.00
26 Felix Jones/15 6.00 15.00
28 Jay Cutler/15 6.00 15.00
29 Steven Jackson/15 6.00 15.00
30 Devin Hester/15 8.00 20.00
31 Cedric Benson/15 6.00 15.00
33 Reggie Bush/15 6.00 15.00
34 DeMarcus Ware/15 8.00 20.00
35 Devery Henderson/15 6.00 15.00

2010 Limited Material Monikers

STATED PRINT RUN 15-50
*PRIME/15: .6X TO 1.5X JSY AU/50
*PRIME/14-15: .5X TO 1.2X JSY AU/15-25
1 Barry Sanders/25 60.00 120.00
2 Bart Starr/25 90.00 150.00
3 Bernie Kosar/25 20.00 50.00
4 Bo Jackson/25 40.00 80.00
5 Bob Griese/25 20.00 50.00
6 Boomer Esiason/25 25.00 60.00
7 Bruce Smith/25 20.00 50.00
8 Chuck Bednarik/15 15.00 40.00
9 Craig James/25 12.00 30.00
10 Curtis Martin/25 20.00 50.00
11 Dan Marino/50 60.00 120.00
12 Dick Butkus/25 30.00 60.00
13 Don Maynard/25 15.00 40.00
14 Ed McCaffrey/25 30.00 60.00
15 Eddie George/12 15.00 40.00
16 Fran Tarkenton/25 20.00 50.00
17 Fred Biletnikoff/25 20.00 50.00
18 Gale Sayers/25 25.00 60.00
19 Henry Ellard/25 12.00 30.00
20 Howie Long/25 20.00 50.00
21 Irving Fryar/25 15.00 40.00
23 Jerry Rice/25 75.00 150.00
24 Jim Brown/25 40.00 80.00
25 Jim Kelly/25 20.00 50.00
27 Joe Montana/50 60.00 100.00
28 Joe Namath/50 40.00 80.00
29 John Elway/50 60.00 120.00
30 John Randle/25 15.00 40.00
31 Junior Seau/25 50.00 100.00
32 Keyshawn Johnson/25 12.00 30.00
33 L.C. Greenwood/25 20.00 50.00
34 Len Dawson/25 20.00 50.00
35 Michael Strahan/25 15.00 40.00
36 Mike Alstott/25 20.00 50.00
37 Mike Singletary/25 20.00 50.00
38 Paul Warfield/25 15.00 40.00
39 Phil Simms/25 15.00 40.00
40 Randall Cunningham/25 25.00 50.00
41 Rod Smith/25 12.00 30.00
42 Steve Largent/25 20.00 50.00
43 Steve Young/25 40.00 80.00
44 Terry Bradshaw/25 60.00 120.00
45 Tiki Barber/25 15.00 40.00
46 Wayne Chrebet/25 15.00 40.00
47 Brent Jones/25 12.00 30.00
48 Terrell Davis/25 15.00 40.00
49 Thurman Thomas/25 15.00 40.00
50 Tom Rathman/25 15.00 40.00

2010 Limited Monikers Autographs Gold

1-100 GOLD VET PRINT RUN 4-25
101-150 GOLD LEGEND PRINT RUN 5-25
151-199 GOLD ROOKIE PRINT RUN 25
*SILVER/199: .25X TO .6X GOLD/25
1 Chris Wells/25
6 Roddy White/25 8.00 20.00
9 Ray Rice/25 15.00 40.00
13 DeAngelo Williams/25
14 Jonathan Stewart/25 8.00 20.00
15 Steve Smith/25
20 Cedric Benson/15 8.00 20.00
25 Josh Cribbs/25 20.00 40.00
33 Matthew Stafford/25 25.00 50.00
39 Matt Schaub/25 8.00 20.00
41 Dallas Clark/15 20.00 40.00
42 Peyton Manning/18 60.00 120.00
49 Jamaal Charles/25 10.00 25.00
67 Braylon Edwards/25 8.00 20.00
68 Mark Sanchez/25 20.00 40.00
72 Louis Murphy/25 8.00 20.00
73 Kevin Kolb/25 8.00 20.00
77 Rashard Mendenhall/25 12.00 30.00
80 Darren Sproles/25 10.00 25.00
81 Philip Rivers/17
95 Kenny Britt/25 10.00 25.00
97 Donovan McNabb/25 15.00 40.00
101 Alan Page/25 10.00 25.00
102 Alex Karras/25 10.00 25.00
103 Andre Reed/15 10.00 25.00
104 Archie Manning/25 15.00 40.00
105 Art Monk/25 50.00 80.00
106 Billy Howton/25 8.00 20.00
107 Bobby Bell/25 8.00 20.00
108 Boyd Dowler/25 8.00 20.00
109 Charley Taylor/25 8.00 20.00
110 Charley Trippi/25 10.00 25.00
111 Charlie Joiner/25 10.00 25.00
113 Daryle Lamonica/25 8.00 20.00
114 Dave Casper/25 10.00 25.00
115 Deacon Jones/25 10.00 25.00
116 Del Shofner/25 8.00 20.00
117 Doug Flutie/25 EXCH 12.00 30.00
118 Dub Jones/25 8.00 20.00
119 Earl Campbell/25 12.00 30.00
121 Floyd Little/25 8.00 20.00
122 Forrest Gregg/25 12.00 30.00
123 Jan Stenerud/25 8.00 20.00
124 George Blanda/25 25.00 50.00
125 Harlon Hill/25 8.00 20.00
127 Jack Youngblood/25 8.00 20.00
128 Jackie Slater/25 8.00 20.00
129 Jim McMahon/25 10.00 25.00
130 Jim Otto/25 8.00 20.00
131 Jim Plunkett/25 12.00 30.00
132 Jim Taylor/25 25.00 50.00
133 Jimmy Orr/25 8.00 20.00
134 Larry Little/25 8.00 20.00
135 Lee Roy Selmon/25 12.00 30.00
136 Lem Barney/25 8.00 20.00
137 Lenny Moore/25 8.00 20.00
138 Leroy Kelly/25 12.00 30.00
139 Lydell Mitchell/25 8.00 20.00
140 Mark Duper/25 10.00 25.00
142 Mike Curtis/25 10.00 25.00
143 Ozzie Newsome/25 10.00 25.00
144 Paul Krause/25 10.00 25.00
145 Priest Holmes/25 10.00 25.00
146 Randy White/25 12.00 30.00
147 Raymond Berry/25 12.00 30.00
149 Ronnie Lott/25 20.00 40.00
151 Aaron Hernandez/25 5.00 12.00
152 Anthony Dixon/25 5.00 12.00
153 Anthony McCoy/25 5.00 12.00
154 Antonio Brown/25 60.00 125.00
155 Brandon Graham/25 6.00 15.00
156 Brandon Spikes/25 5.00 12.00
157 Bryan Bulaga/25 5.00 12.00
158 Carlos Dunlap/25 5.00 12.00
159 Carlton Mitchell/25 5.00 12.00
160 Chris Cook/25 5.00 12.00
161 Corey Wootton/25 5.00 12.00
162 David Gettis/25 5.00 12.00
165 Derrick Morgan/25 5.00 12.00
166 Devin McCourty/25 6.00 15.00
167 Dominique Franks/25 5.00 12.00
168 Earl Thomas/25 12.00 30.00
169 Ed Dickson/25 5.00 12.00
170 Everson Griffen/25 5.00 12.00
171 Garrett Graham/25 5.00 12.00
172 Jacoby Ford/25 5.00 12.00
173 Jason Pierre-Paul/25 8.00 20.00
174 Jason Werilds/25 5.00 12.00
176 Jerry Hughes/25 5.00 12.00
177 Jimmy Graham/25 25.00 50.00
178 Joe Haden/25 8.00 20.00
180 John Skelton/25 6.00 15.00
181 Kareem Jackson/25 5.00 12.00
185 Morgan Burnett/25 6.00 15.00
186 Nate Allen/25 8.00 20.00
187 NaVorro Bowman/25 10.00 25.00
188 Patrick Robinson/25 EXCH 6.00 15.00
189 Perrish Cox/25 6.00 15.00
190 Ricky Sapp/25 5.00 12.00
191 Riley Cooper/25 10.00 25.00
192 Russell Okung/25 10.00 25.00
193 Sean Lee/25 10.00 25.00
194 Sean Weatherspoon/25 5.00 12.00
196 Taylor Mays/25 5.00 12.00
198 Tony Pike/25 5.00 12.00
199 Trent Williams/25 6.00 15.00

2010 Limited Rookie Jumbo Jerseys

STATED PRINT RUN 100 SER.#'d SETS
*JSY NUMBER/50: .5X TO 1.2X JSY/100
1 C.J. Spiller 1.50 4.00
2 Tim Tebow 5.00 12.00
3 Brandon LaFell 2.50 6.00
4 Jonathan Dwyer 1.50 4.00
5 Damian Williams 1.50 4.00
6 Sam Bradford 2.00 5.00
7 Andre Roberts 2.00 5.00
8 Mike Williams 1.50 4.00
9 Jermaine Gresham 1.50 4.00
10 Rob Gronkowski 5.00 12.00
11 Taylor Price 1.50 4.00
12 Gerald McCoy 1.50 4.00
13 Jahvid Best 1.50 4.00
14 Eric Decker 2.00 5.00
15 Toby Gerhart 1.50 4.00
16 Joe McKnight 1.50 4.00
17 Dexter McCluster 2.00 5.00
18 Ndamukong Suh 3.00 8.00
19 Marcus Easley 1.50 4.00
20 Jordan Shipley 1.50 4.00
21 Dez Bryant 4.00 10.00
22 Golden Tate 2.00 5.00
23 Mardy Gilyard 1.50 4.00
24 Jimmy Clausen 1.50 4.00
25 Rolando McClain 1.50 4.00
26 Mike Kafka 2.00 5.00
27 Colt McCoy 2.00 5.00
28 Ben Tate 1.50 4.00
29 Emmanuel Sanders 2.50 6.00
30 Eric Berry 2.50 6.00
31 Ryan Mathews 1.50 4.00
32 Montario Hardesty 1.50 4.00
33 Armanti Edwards 2.00 5.00
34 Demaryius Thomas 4.00 10.00
35 Arrelious Benn 1.50 4.00

2010 Limited Rookie Jumbo Jerseys Autographs Prime

PRIME PRINT RUN 25 SER.#'d SETS
*BASIC JSY AU/10: .5X TO 1.2X PRIME AU/25
*JSY # AU/10: .5X TO 1.2X PRIME AU/25
EXCH EXPIRATION: 5/24/2012
1 C.J. Spiller 6.00 15.00
2 Tim Tebow 50.00 120.00
3 Brandon LaFell 10.00 25.00
4 Jonathan Dwyer 6.00 15.00
5 Damian Williams 6.00 15.00
6 Sam Bradford 8.00 20.00
7 Andre Roberts 8.00 20.00
8 Mike Williams 6.00 15.00
9 Jermaine Gresham 6.00 15.00
10 Rob Gronkowski 40.00 80.00
11 Taylor Price 6.00 15.00
12 Gerald McCoy 6.00 15.00
13 Jahvid Best 6.00 15.00
14 Eric Decker 8.00 20.00
15 Toby Gerhart 6.00 15.00
16 Joe McKnight 6.00 15.00
18 Ndamukong Suh 25.00 60.00
19 Marcus Easley 6.00 15.00
20 Jordan Shipley 6.00 15.00
21 Dez Bryant 40.00 80.00
22 Golden Tate 8.00 20.00
23 Mardy Gilyard 6.00 15.00
24 Jimmy Clausen 6.00 15.00
25 Rolando McClain 6.00 15.00
26 Mike Kafka 8.00 20.00
27 Colt McCoy 8.00 20.00
28 Ben Tate 6.00 15.00
29 Emmanuel Sanders 10.00 25.00
30 Eric Berry 10.00 25.00
31 Ryan Mathews 6.00 15.00
32 Montario Hardesty 6.00 15.00
33 Armanti Edwards 8.00 20.00
34 Demaryius Thomas 15.00 40.00
35 Arrelious Benn 6.00 15.00

2010 Limited Team Trademarks Autograph Materials

STATED PRINT RUN 5-15
1 Kevin Kolb/15
2 Brandon Jacobs/15
3 Adrian Peterson/15 75.00 150.00
5 Darren Sproles/15 12.00 30.00
6 Drew Brees/15 40.00 80.00
8 Chris Cooley/15 30.00 60.00
10 Eli Manning/15 40.00 80.00
12 Jamaal Charles/15 15.00 40.00
13 Peyton Manning/15
14 Ryan Grant/15 15.00 40.00
16 Carson Palmer/15 12.00 30.00
18 Ben Roethlisberger/15 50.00 100.00
20 Tom Brady/15 125.00 200.00
22 Frank Gore/15 12.00 30.00
24 Antonio Gates/15 12.00 30.00
25 Joe Flacco/15 30.00 60.00

2010 Limited Team Trademarks Materials

STATED PRINT RUN 100 SER.#'d SETS
1 Kevin Kolb 2.50 6.00
2 Brandon Jacobs 2.50 6.00
3 Adrian Peterson 4.00 10.00
5 Darren Sproles 3.00 8.00
6 Drew Brees 4.00 10.00
8 Chris Cooley 2.50 6.00
9 Jason Witten 3.00 8.00
12 Jamaal Charles 3.00 8.00
13 Peyton Manning 10.00 25.00
14 Ryan Grant 3.00 8.00
15 Larry Fitzgerald 3.00 8.00
16 Carson Palmer 3.00 8.00
17 Wes Welker 3.00 8.00
18 Ben Roethlisberger 4.00 10.00
20 Tom Brady 10.00 25.00
21 Jeremy Shockey 2.50 6.00
22 Frank Gore 3.00 8.00
23 Brian Urlacher 4.00 10.00
24 Antonio Gates 3.00 8.00
25 Joe Flacco 3.00 8.00

2010 Limited Team Trademarks Materials Prime

*PRIME/30-50: .6X TO 1.5X BASIC JSY
*PRIME/25: .8X TO 2X BASIC JSY
PRIME PRINT RUN 10-50
7 Troy Polamalu/50 10.00 25.00
19 Ronnie Brown/50 4.00 10.00

2010 Limited Threads

STATED PRINT RUN 1-199
1 Chris Wells/199 2.50 6.00
2 Larry Fitzgerald/199 3.00 8.00
4 Matt Ryan/199 3.00 8.00
6 Roddy White/199 2.50 6.00
11 Lee Evans/199 3.00 8.00
16 Devin Hester/199 3.00 8.00
17 Jay Cutler/199 2.50 6.00
18 Matt Forte/199 2.50 6.00
19 Carson Palmer/199 3.00 8.00
20 Cedric Benson/199 2.50 6.00
21 Chad Ochocinco/199 2.50 6.00
22 Terrell Owens/199 3.00 8.00
26 Jason Witten/95 3.00 8.00
28 Tony Romo/199 3.00 8.00
29 Eddie Royal/199 2.50 6.00
30 Knowshon Moreno/199 2.50 6.00
31 Kyle Orton/199 2.50 6.00
32 Calvin Johnson/199 4.00 10.00
33 Matthew Stafford/199 3.00 8.00
35 Aaron Rodgers/199 12.00 30.00
36 Greg Jennings/199 2.50 6.00
37 Ryan Grant/115 3.00 8.00
38 Andre Johnson/199 3.00 8.00
39 Matt Schaub/199 2.50 6.00
40 Owen Daniels/195 2.50 6.00
41 Dallas Clark/115 2.50 6.00
42 Peyton Manning/199 10.00 25.00
43 Joseph Addai/199 2.50 6.00
45 David Garrard/199 2.50 6.00
46 Maurice Jones-Drew/199 2.50 6.00
47 Mike Sims-Walker/199 2.50 6.00
48 Dwayne Bowe/199 3.00 8.00
49 Jamaal Charles/199 3.00 8.00
50 Matt Cassel/199 2.50 6.00
54 Adrian Peterson/199 4.00 10.00
55 Brett Favre/199 8.00 20.00
57 Visanthe Shiancoe/199 3.00 8.00
59 Tom Brady/199 12.00 30.00
61 Devery Henderson/100 2.50 6.00
62 Drew Brees/199 4.00 10.00
63 Reggie Bush/199 2.50 6.00
64 Brandon Jacobs/199 2.50 6.00
65 Eli Manning/199 3.00 8.00
66 Steve Smith USC/199 2.50 6.00
67 Braylon Edwards/199 2.50 6.00
68 Mark Sanchez/199 2.50 6.00
69 Shonn Greene/185 2.50 6.00
70 Darren McFadden/199 2.50 6.00
71 Jason Campbell/199 2.50 6.00
72 Louis Murphy/199 2.50 6.00
73 Kevin Kolb/199 2.50 6.00
74 DeSean Jackson/199 3.00 8.00
75 LeSean McCoy/199 4.00 10.00
76 Ben Roethlisberger/199 4.00 10.00
77 Rashard Mendenhall/100 2.50 6.00
79 Antonio Gates/199 3.00 8.00
80 Darren Sproles/199 3.00 8.00
81 Philip Rivers/199 4.00 10.00
82 Alex Smith QB/150 3.00 8.00
83 Frank Gore/199 3.00 8.00
84 Vernon Davis/199 2.50 6.00
86 Matt Hasselbeck/199 2.50 6.00
89 Steven Jackson/85 2.50 6.00
94 Chris Johnson/195 2.50 6.00
96 Vince Young/199 2.50 6.00
97 Donovan McNabb/199 3.00 8.00
98 Chris Cooley/199 2.50 6.00
99 Clinton Portis/199 2.50 6.00
100 Santana Moss/199 3.00 8.00
101 Alan Page/199 5.00 12.00
102 Alex Karras/199 5.00 12.00
103 Andre Reed/199 5.00 12.00
104 Archie Manning/100 5.00 12.00
105 Art Monk/199 6.00 15.00
109 Charley Taylor/199 4.00 10.00
111 Charlie Joiner/199 4.00 10.00
113 Daryle Lamonica/199 4.00 10.00
115 Deacon Jones/199 5.00 12.00
117 Doug Flutie/199 5.00 12.00
119 Earl Campbell/199 6.00 15.00
120 Ernie Davis/199 10.00 25.00
122 Forrest Gregg/199 5.00 12.00
124 George Blanda/199 5.00 12.00
126 Hank Jordan/199 6.00 15.00
127 Jack Youngblood/199 4.00 10.00
128 Jackie Slater/199 4.00 10.00
129 Jim McMahon/199 5.00 12.00
130 Jim Otto/199 4.00 10.00
131 Jim Plunkett/199 5.00 12.00
134 Larry Little/199 4.00 10.00
135 Lee Roy Selmon/199 5.00 12.00
137 Lenny Moore/30 6.00 15.00
140 Mark Duper/130 4.00 10.00
141 Merlin Olsen/199 4.00 10.00
143 Ozzie Newsome/199 5.00 12.00
145 Priest Holmes/199 4.00 10.00
147 Raymond Berry/199 5.00 12.00
148 Roger Craig/199 5.00 12.00
149 Ronnie Lott/199 5.00 12.00
150 Walter Payton/199 12.00 30.00

2010 Limited Threads Prime

PRIME STATED PRINT RUN 2-50
1 Chris Wells/25 4.00 10.00
2 Larry Fitzgerald/25 5.00 12.00
4 Matt Ryan/25 5.00 12.00
6 Roddy White/50 3.00 8.00
11 Lee Evans/50 4.00 10.00
14 Jonathan Stewart/50 3.00 8.00
16 Devin Hester/50 4.00 10.00
17 Jay Cutler/30 3.00 8.00
18 Matt Forte/50 3.00 8.00
19 Carson Palmer/50 4.00 10.00
20 Cedric Benson/50 3.00 8.00
21 Chad Ochocinco/50 3.00 8.00
26 Jason Witten/50 4.00 10.00
20 Tony Romo/50 4.00 10.00
29 Eddie Royal/50 3.00 8.00
30 Knowshon Moreno/50 3.00 8.00
31 Kyle Orton/40 3.00 8.00
32 Calvin Johnson/50 5.00 12.00
35 Aaron Rodgers/50 15.00 40.00
36 Greg Jennings/50 3.00 8.00
38 Andre Johnson/50 4.00 10.00
42 Peyton Manning/50 12.00 30.00
43 Joseph Addai/50 3.00 8.00
45 David Garrard/50 3.00 8.00
46 Maurice Jones-Drew/50 3.00 8.00
47 Mike Sims-Walker/50 3.00 8.00
48 Dwayne Bowe/50 4.00 10.00
49 Jamaal Charles/50 4.00 10.00
50 Matt Cassel/50 3.00 8.00
52 Ronnie Brown/50 3.00 8.00
54 Adrian Peterson/50 5.00 12.00
55 Brett Favre/25 12.00 30.00
56 Percy Harvin/50 3.00 8.00
58 Randy Moss/35 4.00 10.00
59 Tom Brady/50 20.00 40.00
60 Wes Welker/50 4.00 10.00
61 Devery Henderson/50 3.00 8.00
64 Brandon Jacobs/50 3.00 8.00
67 Braylon Edwards/50 3.00 8.00
68 Mark Sanchez/50 3.00 8.00
70 Darren McFadden/50 3.00 8.00
72 Louis Murphy/50 3.00 8.00
73 Kevin Kolb/50 3.00 8.00
74 DeSean Jackson/50 4.00 10.00
75 LeSean McCoy/50 5.00 12.00
76 Ben Roethlisberger/25 6.00 15.00
77 Rashard Mendenhall/50 3.00 8.00
78 Hines Ward/50 4.00 10.00
79 Antonio Gates/50 4.00 10.00
80 Darren Sproles/50 4.00 10.00
81 Philip Rivers/50 5.00 12.00
82 Alex Smith QB/50 4.00 10.00
83 Frank Gore/30 4.00 10.00
84 Vernon Davis/50 3.00 8.00
89 Steven Jackson/50 3.00 8.00
91 Cadillac Williams/50 3.00 8.00
94 Chris Johnson/50 3.00 8.00
95 Kenny Britt/20 4.00 10.00
98 Chris Cooley/50 3.00 8.00
99 Clinton Portis/50 3.00 8.00
100 Santana Moss/50 4.00 10.00
101 Alan Page/50 6.00 15.00
105 Art Monk/50 8.00 20.00
109 Charley Taylor/25 8.00 20.00
113 Daryle Lamonica/20 8.00 20.00
117 Doug Flutie/50 6.00 15.00
120 Ernie Davis/50 15.00 40.00
126 Hank Jordan/15 10.00 25.00
128 Jackie Slater/50 5.00 12.00
129 Jim McMahon/50 6.00 15.00
130 Jim Otto/50 5.00 12.00
131 Jim Plunkett/15 10.00 25.00
134 Larry Little/50 5.00 12.00
135 Lee Roy Selmon/50 6.00 15.00
140 Mark Duper/30 5.00 12.00
145 Priest Holmes/50 5.00 12.00
148 Roger Craig/25 10.00 25.00
149 Ronnie Lott/50 6.00 15.00
150 Walter Payton/50 15.00 40.00

2011 Limited

1-200 STATED PRINT RUN 499
201-236 ROOK.JSY AU PRINT RUN 199-299
EXCH EXPIRATION: 6/28/2013
1 Beanie Wells 1.00 2.50
2 Kevin Kolb 1.00 2.50
3 Larry Fitzgerald 1.25 3.00
4 Matt Ryan 1.25 3.00
5 Michael Turner 1.00 2.50
6 Roddy White 1.00 2.50
7 Anquan Boldin 1.00 2.50
8 Joe Flacco 1.25 3.00
9 Ray Rice 1.25 3.00
10 C.J. Spiller 1.00 2.50
11 Ryan Fitzpatrick 1.00 2.50
12 Steve Johnson 1.00 2.50
13 DeAngelo Williams 1.00 2.50
14 Jonathan Stewart 1.00 2.50
15 Steve Smith 1.25 3.00
16 Jay Cutler 1.00 2.50
17 Matt Forte 1.00 2.50
18 Roy Williams WR 1.00 2.50
19 Bo Scaife 1.00 2.50
20 Cedric Benson 1.00 2.50
21 Jordan Shipley 1.00 2.50
22 Colt McCoy 1.00 2.50
23 Josh Cribbs 1.00 2.50
24 Peyton Hillis 1.00 2.50
25 Felix Jones 1.00 2.50
26 Jason Witten 1.25 3.00
27 Miles Austin 1.00 2.50
28 Tony Romo 1.25 3.00
29 Brandon Lloyd 1.00 2.50
30 Knowshon Moreno 1.00 2.50
31 Kyle Orton 1.00 2.50
32 Calvin Johnson 1.50 4.00
33 Jahvid Best 1.00 2.50
34 Matthew Stafford 1.25 3.00
35 Aaron Rodgers 2.50 6.00
36 Greg Jennings 1.00 2.50
37 Jordy Nelson 1.25 3.00
38 Andre Johnson 1.25 3.00
39 Arian Foster 1.00 2.50
40 Matt Schaub 1.00 2.50
41 Dallas Clark 1.00 2.50
42 Peyton Manning 3.00 8.00
43 Reggie Wayne 1.25 3.00
44 Mike Thomas 1.25 3.00
45 Marcedes Lewis 1.00 2.50
46 Maurice Jones-Drew 1.00 2.50
47 Dwayne Bowe 1.25 3.00
48 Jamaal Charles 1.25 3.00
49 Matt Cassel 1.00 2.50
50 Brian Hartline 1.25 3.00
51 Chad Henne 1.25 3.00
52 Reggie Bush 1.00 2.50
53 Adrian Peterson 1.50 4.00
54 Donovan McNabb 1.25 3.00
55 Percy Harvin 1.00 2.50
56 BenJarvus Green-Ellis 1.00 2.50
57 Chad Ochocinco 1.00 2.50
58 Tom Brady 3.00 8.00
59 Wes Welker 1.25 3.00
60 Devery Henderson 1.00 2.50
61 Drew Brees 1.50 4.00
62 Marques Colston 1.00 2.50
63 Ahmad Bradshaw 1.00 2.50
64 Eli Manning 1.25 3.00
65 Hakeem Nicks 1.00 2.50
66 Mark Sanchez 1.00 2.50
67 Santonio Holmes 1.00 2.50
68 Shonn Greene 1.00 2.50
69 Darren McFadden 1.00 2.50
70 Jacoby Ford 1.25 3.00
71 Jason Campbell 1.00 2.50
72 DeSean Jackson 1.25 3.00
73 LeSean McCoy 1.50 4.00
74 Michael Vick 1.25 3.00
75 Nnamdi Asomugha 1.00 2.50
76 Ben Roethlisberger 1.50 4.00
77 Mike Wallace 1.00 2.50
78 Rashard Mendenhall 1.00 2.50
79 Antonio Gates 1.00 2.50
80 Philip Rivers 1.50 4.00
81 Ryan Mathews 1.25 3.00
82 Frank Gore 1.25 3.00
83 Michael Crabtree 1.00 2.50

84 Vernon Davis 1.00 2.50
85 Marshawn Lynch 1.25 3.00
86 Zach Miller 1.00 2.50
87 Sidney Rice 1.00 2.50
88 Tarvaris Jackson 1.00 2.50
89 Danny Amendola 1.25 3.00
90 Sam Bradford 1.00 2.50
91 Steven Jackson 1.00 2.50
92 Josh Freeman 1.25 3.00
93 LeGarrette Blount 1.25 3.00
94 Mike Williams 1.25 3.00
95 Chris Johnson 1.00 2.50
96 Kenny Britt 1.00 2.50
97 Matt Hasselbeck 1.00 2.50
98 Chris Cooley 1.00 2.50
99 Rex Grossman 1.00 2.50
100 Ryan Torain 1.00 2.50
101 Ozzie Newsome 1.50 4.00
102 Andre Reed 1.50 4.00
103 Doug Flutie 1.50 4.00
104 Franco Harris 2.00 5.00
105 Jack Lambert 2.00 5.00
106 Jay Novacek 1.50 4.00
107 Jerry Rice 3.00 8.00
108 Jim Kelly 2.00 5.00
109 Jim Otto 1.25 3.00
110 Ken Stabler 2.00 5.00
111 Terrell Davis 1.50 4.00
112 Willie Brown 1.25 3.00
113 Joe Namath 2.50 6.00
114 Junior Seau 1.50 4.00
115 Rod Woodson 1.50 4.00
116 Sam Huff 1.50 4.00
117 Steve Bartkowski 1.50 4.00
118 Steve Young 2.50 6.00
119 Troy Aikman 2.50 6.00
120 Y.A. Tittle 2.00 5.00
121 Cris Collinsworth 1.50 4.00
122 Dick Butkus 2.50 6.00
123 Earl Campbell 2.00 5.00
124 Fred Biletnikoff 2.00 5.00
125 Jerome Bettis 2.00 5.00
126 Bo Jackson 2.50 6.00
127 Brett Favre 4.00 10.00
128 Alan Page 1.25 3.00
129 Art Monk 2.00 5.00
130 Barry Sanders 3.00 8.00
131 Bernie Kosar 1.50 4.00
132 Bob Griese 2.00 5.00
133 Bob Hayes 2.00 5.00
134 Boyd Dowler 1.25 3.00
135 Bruce Smith 1.50 4.00
136 Charley Taylor 1.25 3.00
137 Charlie Joiner 1.25 3.00
138 Billy Sims 1.50 4.00
139 Boomer Esiason 1.50 4.00
140 Chuck Bednarik 1.50 4.00
141 Chuck Foreman 1.25 3.00
142 Cliff Harris 1.25 3.00
143 Dan Fouts 1.50 4.00
144 Dave Casper 1.25 3.00
145 Derrick Thomas 5.00 12.00
146 Don Maynard 1.50 4.00
147 Doug Williams 1.50 4.00
148 Eddie George 1.50 4.00
149 Emmitt Smith 3.00 8.00
150 Fred Williamson 1.25 3.00
151 Aaron Williams RC 1.25 3.00
152 Adrian Clayborn RC 1.25 3.00
153 Akeem Ayers RC 1.25 3.00
154 Aldon Smith RC 1.25 3.00
155 Terrelle Pryor RC 2.00 5.00
156 Brandon Harris RC 1.25 3.00
157 Cameron Heyward RC 1.50 4.00
158 Cameron Jordan RC 1.50 4.00
159 Cecil Shorts RC 1.25 3.00
160 Corey Liuget RC 1.25 3.00
161 D.J. Williams RC 1.25 3.00
162 Da'Quan Bowers RC 1.25 3.00
163 Denarius Moore RC 1.25 3.00
164 Dion Lewis RC 1.50 4.00
165 Dwayne Harris RC 1.25 3.00
166 Evan Royster RC 1.25 3.00
167 Greg McElroy RC 2.00 5.00
168 Greg Salas RC 1.25 3.00
169 J.J. Watt RC 6.00 15.00
170 Jacquizz Rodgers RC 1.25 3.00
171 Jeremy Kerley RC 2.00 5.00
172 Jimmy Smith RC 1.25 3.00
173 Johnny White RC 1.25 3.00
174 Jordan Cameron RC 1.50 4.00
175 Julius Thomas RC 1.50 4.00
176 Justin Houston RC 1.50 4.00
177 Kealoha Pilares RC 1.25 3.00
178 Kris Durham RC 1.25 3.00
179 Lance Kendricks RC 1.25 3.00
180 Luke Stocker RC 1.25 3.00
181 Martez Wilson RC 1.25 3.00
182 Chris Neild RC 3.00 8.00
183 Niles Paul RC 1.25 3.00
184 Owen Marecic RC 1.25 3.00
185 Patrick Peterson RC 2.50 6.00
186 Phil Taylor RC 1.25 3.00
187 Prince Amukamara RC 1.25 3.00
188 Quinton Carter RC 1.25 3.00
189 Rahim Moore RC 1.25 3.00
190 Ricky Stanzi RC 1.25 3.00
191 Robert Housler RC 1.25 3.00
192 Robert Quinn RC 1.25 3.00
193 Roy Helu RC 1.25 3.00
194 Ryan Kerrigan RC 1.50 4.00
195 Ryan Whalen RC 1.25 3.00
196 Stephen Paea RC 1.25 3.00
197 T.J. Yates RC 1.25 3.00
198 Tandon Doss RC 1.25 3.00
199 Tyrod Taylor RC 2.50 6.00
200 Tyron Smith RC 1.50 4.00
201 Cam Newton JSY AU/199 RC 60.00 120.00
202 V.Miller JSY AU/299 RC 15.00 40.00
203 Dareus JSY AU/299 RC EXCH
204 A.J. Green JSY AU/199 RC 25.00 60.00
205 J.Jones JSY AU/299 RC EXCH 30.00 80.00
206 Jake Locker JSY AU/199 RC 6.00 15.00
207 B.Gabbert JSY AU/199 RC 6.00 15.00
208 Ponder JSY AU/199 RC 6.00 15.00
209 Baldwin JSY AU/299 RC 6.00 15.00
210 Mark Ingram JSY AU/199 RC 10.00 25.00
211 Andy Dalton JSY AU/299 RC 12.00 30.00
212 Kaepernick JSY AU/299 RC 10.00 25.00
213 R.Williams JSY AU/299 RC 6.00 15.00
214 Rudolph JSY AU/299 RC EXCH 6.00 15.00
215 Titus Young JSY AU/299 RC 6.00 15.00
216 Shane Vereen JSY AU/299 RC 8.00 20.00
217 Mikel Leshoure JSY AU/299 RC 15.00 30.00
218 Torrey Smith JSY AU/299 RC 6.00 15.00
219 Greg Little JSY AU/299 RC 8.00 20.00
220 D.Thomas JSY AU/299 RC EXCH 6.00 15.00
221 Randall Cobb JSY AU/299 RC 10.00 25.00
222 D.Murray JSY AU/299 RC 12.00 30.00
223 S.Ridley JSY AU/299 RC 6.00 15.00
224 Ryan Mallett JSY AU/199 RC 6.00 15.00
225 Austin Pettis JSY AU/299 RC 6.00 15.00
226 Hankerson JSY AU/299 RC 6.00 15.00
227 Vincent Brown JSY AU/299 RC 6.00 15.00
228 Jerrel Jernigan JSY AU/299 RC 6.00 15.00
229 Alex Green JSY AU/299 RC 8.00 20.00
230 Clyde Gates JSY AU/299 RC 6.00 15.00
231 K. Hunter JSY AU/299 RC 6.00 15.00
232 Delone Carter JSY AU/299 RC 6.00 15.00
233 Taiwan Jones JSY AU/299 RC 6.00 15.00
234 Bilal Powell JSY AU/299 RC 8.00 20.00
235 J.Harper JSY AU/299 RC 8.00 20.00
236 Jordan Todman JSY AU/299 RC 6.00 15.00

2011 Limited Gold Spotlight
*1-100 VETS/25: 1X TO 2.5X BASIC CARDS
*101-150 LEGEND/25: 1X TO 2.5X BASIC CARDS
*151-200 ROOKIES/25: .8X TO 2X BASIC RC
1-200 STATED PRINT RUN 25
UNPRICED 201-236 JSY AU PRINT RUN 10

2011 Limited Silver Spotlight
*1-100 VETS/50: .8X TO 2X BASIC CARDS
*101-150 LEGEND/50: .8X TO 2X BASIC CARDS
*151-200 ROOKIES/50: .6X TO 1.5X BASIC RC
1-200 STATED PRINT RUN 50
*201-236 ROOKIE JSY AU/25: .5X TO 1.2X
201-236 STATED PRINT RUN 25
201 Cam Newton JSY AU 125.00 250.00
206 Jake Locker JSY AU 8.00 20.00
210 Mark Ingram JSY AU 12.00 30.00
222 DeMarco Murray JSY AU 15.00 40.00

2011 Limited Banner Season Materials Prime
STATED PRINT RUN 4-50
3 Dwayne Bowe/50 5.00 12.00
4 Aaron Rodgers/50 15.00 40.00
5 Matt Ryan/50 5.00 12.00
6 Ed Reed/50 6.00 15.00
7 Maurice Jones-Drew/50 4.00 10.00
8 Philip Rivers/50 6.00 15.00
9 Santana Moss/50 5.00 12.00
10 Roddy White/50 4.00 10.00
11 DeMarcus Ware/50 5.00 12.00
13 Brandon Lloyd/50 4.00 10.00
14 Michael Vick/44 5.00 12.00
15 Jamaal Charles/50 5.00 12.00
16 Eli Manning/50 5.00 12.00
17 Calvin Johnson/50 6.00 15.00
18 Michael Turner/50 4.00 10.00
20 Chris Johnson/50 4.00 10.00
22 Matt Schaub/50 4.00 10.00
23 Adrian Peterson/50 6.00 15.00

2011 Limited Draft Day Duos
STATED PRINT RUN 100 SER.#'d SETS
*PRIME/25: .8X TO 2X BASIC DUO/100
1 Newton/Gabbert 10.00 25.00
2 A.Green/J.Jones 8.00 20.00
3 V.Miller/A.Smith 3.00 8.00
4 A.Green/M.Ingram 5.00 12.00
5 J.Jones/M.Ingram 6.00 15.00

2011 Limited Draft Day Jerseys
STATED PRINT RUN 100 SER.#'d SETS
*PRIME/50: .5X TO 1.2X JSY/100
*LIDS/50: .5X TO 1.2X JSY/100
*COMBOS/50: .5X TO 1.2X JSY/100
*COMBO PRIME/25: .8X TO 2X JSY/100
1 Cam Newton 12.00 30.00
2 Von Miller 3.00 8.00
3 A.J. Green 5.00 12.00
4 Julio Jones 6.00 15.00
5 Aldon Smith 2.00 5.00
6 Tyron Smith 5.00 12.00
7 Blaine Gabbert 2.00 5.00
8 J.J. Watt 10.00 25.00
9 Nick Fairley 2.00 5.00
10 Corey Liuget 2.00 5.00
11 Adrian Clayborn 4.00 10.00
12 Phil Taylor 2.00 5.00
13 Mark Ingram 3.00 8.00

2011 Limited Draft Day Jerseys Autographs Prime
STATED PRINT RUN 15 SER.#'d SETS
*BASE JSY AU/10: .4X TO 1X PRIME/15
1 Cam Newton 125.00 250.00
2 Von Miller 25.00 60.00
3 A.J. Green 60.00 120.00
4 Julio Jones 50.00 100.00
5 Aldon Smith EXCH 10.00 25.00
6 Tyron Smith 30.00 60.00
7 Blaine Gabbert 10.00 25.00
8 J.J. Watt 75.00 135.00
10 Corey Liuget 10.00 25.00
11 Adrian Clayborn 10.00 25.00
12 Phil Taylor 10.00 25.00
13 Mark Ingram 15.00 40.00

2011 Limited Draft Day Quads
STATED PRINT RUN 100 SER.#'d SETS
*PRIME/25: .8X TO 2X BASIC QUAD/100
1 Newton/Miller/Green/Jones 15.00 40.00
2 Newton/Green/Jones/Gabbert 15.00 40.00
3 Miller/Smith/Watt/Fairley 8.00 20.00
4 Smith/Liuget/Clayborn/Taylor 6.00 15.00

2011 Limited Draft Day Trios
STATED PRINT RUN 100 SER.#'d SETS
*PRIME/25: .8X TO 2X BASIC TRIO/100
1 Ingram/Green/Jones 8.00 20.00
2 Fairley/Liuget/Taylor 2.50 6.00
3 Miller/Smith/Gabbert 4.00 10.00
4 Newton/Green/Ingram 10.00 25.00

2011 Limited Initial Steps Autographs
STATED PRINT RUN 25-50
1 Mikel Leshoure/50 4.00 10.00
4 Vincent Brown/50 5.00 12.00
6 Jerrel Jernigan/50 4.00 10.00
7 Mark Ingram/25 8.00 20.00
8 Von Miller/50 10.00 25.00
9 Titus Young/50 4.00 10.00
10 Leonard Hankerson/50 4.00 10.00
11 Cam Newton/25 40.00 100.00
13 Alex Green/50 4.00 10.00
14 Christian Ponder/25 5.00 12.00
15 Colin Kaepernick/50 6.00 15.00
17 Jonathan Baldwin/50 4.00 10.00
20 Jake Locker/25 5.00 12.00
21 DeMarco Murray/50 8.00 20.00
22 Randall Cobb/50 6.00 15.00
23 A.J. Green/25 12.00 30.00
25 Ryan Mallett/25 5.00 12.00
26 Delone Carter/50 4.00 10.00
27 Blaine Gabbert/25 5.00 12.00
28 Austin Pettis/50 4.00 10.00
32 Torrey Smith/50 4.00 10.00
33 Andy Dalton/50 8.00 20.00
34 Shane Vereen/50 5.00 12.00
36 Jordan Todman/50 4.00 10.00

2011 Limited Initial Steps Jerseys
JERSEY PRINT RUN 99 SER.#'d SETS
*PRIME/25: .6X TO 1.5X BASIC JSY/99
SHOE/99: .4X TO 1X BASIC JSY/99
1 Mikel Leshoure/99 2.00 5.00
2 Bilal Powell/99 2.50 6.00
3 Jamie Harper/99 2.00 5.00
4 Vincent Brown/99 2.00 5.00
5 Clyde Gates/99 2.00 5.00
6 Jerrel Jernigan/99 2.00 5.00
7 Mark Ingram/99 3.00 8.00
8 Von Miller/99 3.00 8.00
9 Titus Young/99 2.00 5.00
10 Leonard Hankerson/99 2.00 5.00
11 Cam Newton/99 10.00 25.00
12 Julio Jones/99 6.00 15.00
13 Alex Green/99 2.00 5.00
14 Christian Ponder/99 2.00 5.00
15 Colin Kaepernick/99 3.00 8.00
16 Taiwan Jones/99 2.00 5.00
17 Jonathan Baldwin/99 2.00 5.00
18 Ryan Williams/99 2.00 5.00
19 Marcell Dareus/99 2.00 5.00
20 Jake Locker/99 2.00 5.00
21 DeMarco Murray/99 4.00 10.00
22 Randall Cobb/99 3.00 8.00
23 A.J. Green/75 5.00 12.00
24 Daniel Thomas/99 2.00 5.00
25 Ryan Mallett/99 2.00 5.00
26 Delone Carter/99 2.00 5.00
27 Blaine Gabbert/99 2.00 5.00
28 Austin Pettis/99 2.00 5.00
29 Stevan Ridley/99 2.00 5.00
30 Kyle Rudolph/99 2.00 5.00
31 Greg Little/99 2.50 6.00
32 Torrey Smith/99 2.00 5.00
33 Andy Dalton/99 4.00 10.00
34 Shane Vereen/99 2.50 6.00
35 Kendall Hunter/99 2.00 5.00
36 Jordan Todman/99 2.00 5.00

2011 Limited Jumbo Jerseys Autographs
UNPRICED JUMBO AU PRINT RUN 10

2011 Limited Jumbo Jerseys Jersey Number
STATED PRINT RUN 25 SER.#'d SETS
*PRIME/13-15: .6X TO 1.5X JUMBO JSY/25
*JSY # PRIME/15: .6X TO 1.5X JUM.JSY/25
1 Johnny Knox 4.00 10.00
2 Jordan Shipley 4.00 10.00
3 Steve Johnson 4.00 10.00
4 Dexter McCluster 4.00 10.00
5 Santana Moss 5.00 12.00
6 Brian Hartline 5.00 12.00
7 Marcedes Lewis 4.00 10.00
8 Jason Campbell 4.00 10.00
9 London Fletcher 5.00 12.00
10 Jon Beason 4.00 10.00
11 Jared Allen 8.00 20.00
12 Jacoby Ford 5.00 12.00
13 Jermaine Gresham 4.00 10.00
14 James Harrison 8.00 20.00
16 DeAngelo Hall 4.00 10.00
17 Marc Mariani 5.00 12.00
18 Cedric Benson 4.00 10.00
19 Patrick Willis 5.00 12.00
20 Matt Cassel 4.00 10.00
21 Antonio Gates 4.00 10.00
23 Shonn Greene 4.00 10.00
24 Marques Colston 4.00 10.00
25 Tamba Hali 6.00 15.00
26 Tony Romo 5.00 12.00
27 Tony Gonzalez 5.00 12.00
28 Julius Peppers 5.00 12.00
29 Chad Greenway 10.00 25.00
30 Knowshon Moreno 4.00 10.00
32 Chris Cooley 4.00 10.00
34 Eddie Royal 4.00 10.00
35 Brian Orakpo 5.00 12.00

2011 Limited Limitless
STATED PRINT RUN 249 SER.#'d SETS
1 Colt McCoy 1.00 2.50
2 Tim Tebow 4.00 10.00
3 Michael Vick 1.25 3.00
4 Danny Woodhead 2.00 5.00
5 Darren McFadden 1.00 2.50
6 DeAngelo Williams 1.00 2.50
7 Jacoby Ford 1.25 3.00
8 Vernon Davis 1.00 2.50
9 Ryan Mathews 1.25 3.00
10 DeSean Jackson 1.25 3.00
11 Dez Bryant 1.50 4.00
12 Mark Sanchez 1.00 2.50
13 Steven Jackson 1.00 2.50
14 Joe Flacco 1.25 3.00
15 Sam Bradford 1.00 2.50
16 Darrelle Revis 1.00 2.50
17 Miles Austin 1.00 2.50
18 Adrian Peterson 1.50 4.00
19 Tom Brady 4.00 10.00
20 Kenny Britt 1.00 2.50
21 Percy Harvin 1.00 2.50
22 Ryan Torain 1.00 2.50
23 Jason Witten 1.25 3.00
24 Devin Hester 1.25 3.00
25 Santonio Holmes 1.00 2.50

2011 Limited Limitless Threads Autographs
STATED PRINT RUN 10-25
*PRIME/10-20: .5X TO 1.2X JSY AU/15-25
1 Colt McCoy/25 10.00 25.00
2 Tim Tebow/25 40.00 100.00
3 Michael Vick/15 30.00 60.00
5 Darren McFadden/20 15.00 40.00
6 DeAngelo Williams/20 10.00 25.00
7 Jacoby Ford/10 EXCH
8 Vernon Davis/20 10.00 25.00
9 Ryan Mathews/25
10 DeSean Jackson/20 12.00 30.00
11 Dez Bryant/20 20.00 50.00
12 Mark Sanchez/20 12.00 30.00
13 Steven Jackson/25 10.00 25.00
14 Joe Flacco/20 25.00 50.00
15 Sam Bradford/25 10.00 25.00
16 Darrelle Revis/20 15.00 40.00
17 Miles Austin/20 15.00 40.00
18 Adrian Peterson/10
19 Tom Brady/15 EXCH
21 Percy Harvin/20 15.00 40.00
22 Ryan Torain/25 12.00 30.00
23 Jason Witten/20 20.00 50.00
25 Santonio Holmes/25 10.00 25.00

2011 Limited Material Monikers
STATED PRINT RUN 10-50
*PRIME/10: .6X TO 1.5X JSY AU/30-50
*PRIME/10: .5X TO 1.2X JSY AU/20-25
1 Arian Foster/50 20.00 50.00
2 Jim Kelly/35 25.00 50.00
3 Dwayne Bowe/20
4 Aaron Rodgers/20 150.00 300.00
5 Matt Ryan/20 20.00 50.00
6 Jim Otto/50 12.00 30.00
7 Maurice Jones-Drew/30 12.00 30.00
8 Doug Flutie/25 15.00 40.00
9 Terrell Davis/35 25.00 50.00
10 Andre Reed/25 15.00 40.00
12 Jack Lambert/25 30.00 60.00
13 Brandon Lloyd/25 10.00 25.00
14 Willie Brown/50 10.00 25.00
15 Jamaal Charles/20 12.00 30.00
16 Ken Stabler/50 15.00 40.00
17 Calvin Johnson/25 40.00 80.00
18 Michael Turner/20 10.00 25.00
20 Dan Marino/30 100.00 175.00
21 Drew Brees/10
22 Franco Harris/25 20.00 50.00
23 Adrian Peterson/10
24 Jerry Rice/25 75.00 150.00
25 Mike Wallace/25 15.00 40.00
26 Cris Collinsworth/25 15.00 40.00
27 Junior Seau/35 30.00 60.00
28 Fred Biletnikoff/25 20.00 50.00
29 Michael Vick/20 40.00 80.00
30 Earl Campbell/25 20.00 50.00
31 Bo Jackson/25 40.00 80.00
32 Steve Young/30 40.00 80.00
33 Philip Rivers/25 15.00 40.00
35 Jerome Bettis/25 75.00 150.00
36 Roddy White/25 10.00 25.00
37 Steve Bartkowski/35 12.00 30.00
38 Brett Favre/20 90.00 150.00
39 Danny White/50 12.00 30.00
40 Rod Woodson/25 40.00 100.00
41 Y.A. Tittle/30 EXCH 20.00 50.00
42 Peyton Hillis/25 15.00 40.00
44 Joe Namath/35 50.00 100.00
45 Chuck Howley/50 EXCH 12.00 30.00
46 Dick Butkus/30 40.00 80.00
47 Eli Manning/20 50.00 100.00
48 Troy Aikman/30 EXCH 30.00 60.00
49 Jan Stenerud/50 10.00 25.00
50 Peyton Manning/20 60.00 120.00

2011 Limited Monikers Autographs Gold
GOLD STATED PRINT RUN 4-25
EXCH EXPIRATION: 6/28/2013
10 C.J. Spiller/25 8.00 20.00
19 Bo Scaife/25 8.00 20.00
25 Felix Jones/15 8.00 20.00
33 Jahvid Best/25 8.00 20.00
34 Matthew Stafford/25 25.00 60.00
36 Greg Jennings/15 8.00 20.00
39 Arian Foster/25 25.00 60.00
40 Matt Schaub/25 12.00 30.00
51 Chad Henne/25 10.00 25.00
54 Donovan McNabb/15 25.00 50.00
56 BenJarvus Green-Ellis/25 8.00 20.00
57 Chad Ochocinco/25 12.00 30.00
75 Nnamdi Asomugha/25 15.00 40.00
76 Ben Roethlisberger/25 40.00 80.00
83 Michael Crabtree/25 12.00 30.00
87 Sidney Rice/25 8.00 20.00
89 Danny Amendola/25 15.00 40.00
92 Josh Freeman/25 10.00 25.00
99 Rex Grossman/25 8.00 20.00
100 Ryan Torain/25 12.00 30.00
101 Ozzie Newsome/25 12.00 30.00
103 Doug Flutie/15 15.00 40.00
108 Jim Kelly/15 20.00 40.00
109 Jim Otto/25 10.00 25.00
112 Willie Brown/25 10.00 25.00
125 Jerome Bettis/15 50.00 100.00
128 Alan Page/15 12.00 30.00
129 Art Monk/25 30.00 60.00
130 Barry Sanders/25 60.00 120.00
131 Bernie Kosar/25 15.00 40.00
132 Bob Griese/25 25.00 50.00
134 Boyd Dowler/25 8.00 20.00
136 Charley Taylor/25 8.00 20.00
137 Charlie Joiner/25 8.00 20.00
139 Boomer Esiason/25 20.00 40.00
140 Chuck Bednarik/25 10.00 25.00
142 Cliff Harris/25 12.00 30.00
144 Dave Casper/25 12.00 30.00
147 Doug Williams/25 15.00 40.00
148 Eddie George/25 25.00 50.00
149 Emmitt Smith/22 100.00 200.00
150 Fred Williamson/25 12.00 30.00
151 Aaron Williams/25 5.00 12.00
152 Adrian Clayborn/25 5.00 12.00
153 Akeem Ayers/25 5.00 12.00
154 Aldon Smith/25 EXCH 5.00 12.00
155 Terrelle Pryor/25 10.00 25.00
156 Brandon Harris/25 5.00 12.00
157 Cameron Heyward/25 6.00 15.00
158 Cameron Jordan/25 6.00 15.00
159 Cecil Shorts/25 5.00 12.00
160 Corey Liuget/25 5.00 12.00
161 D.J. Williams/25 5.00 12.00
162 Da'Quan Bowers/25 5.00 12.00
163 Denarius Moore/25 5.00 12.00
164 Dion Lewis/25 6.00 15.00
165 Dwayne Harris/25 10.00 25.00
166 Evan Royster/25 12.00 30.00
167 Greg McElroy/25 8.00 20.00
168 Greg Salas/25 5.00 12.00
169 J.J. Watt/25 60.00 120.00
170 Jacquizz Rodgers/25 5.00 12.00
171 Jeremy Kerley/25 8.00 20.00
172 Jimmy Smith/25 5.00 12.00
173 Johnny White/25 5.00 12.00
174 Jordan Cameron/25 6.00 15.00
175 Julius Thomas/25 6.00 15.00
176 Justin Houston/25 6.00 15.00
177 Kealoha Pilares/25 5.00 12.00
178 Kris Durham/25 5.00 12.00
179 Lance Kendricks/25 5.00 12.00
180 Luke Stocker/25 5.00 12.00
181 Martez Wilson/25 5.00 12.00
183 Niles Paul/25 5.00 12.00
185 Patrick Peterson/25 10.00 25.00
186 Phil Taylor/25 5.00 12.00
187 Prince Amukamara/25 5.00 12.00
188 Quinton Carter/25 5.00 12.00
189 Rahim Moore/25 5.00 12.00
190 Ricky Stanzi/25 5.00 12.00
191 Robert Housler/25 5.00 12.00
193 Roy Helu/25 5.00 12.00
194 Ryan Kerrigan/25 6.00 15.00
195 Ryan Whalen/25 5.00 12.00
196 Stephen Paea/25 5.00 12.00
197 T.J. Yates/25 5.00 12.00
198 Tandon Doss/25 5.00 12.00
199 Tyrod Taylor/25 10.00 25.00

2011 Limited Monikers Autographs Silver
TERAN/LEGEND PRINT RUN 10-50
*SILVER ROOKIE/199: .25X TO .6X GOLD
ROOKIE STATED PRINT RUN 199
EXCH EXPIRATION: 6/28/2013
4 Matt Ryan/10
6 Roddy White/25 8.00 20.00
7 Anquan Boldin/35 6.00 15.00
8 Joe Flacco/10
10 C.J. Spiller/50 6.00 15.00
13 DeAngelo Williams/25 8.00 20.00
14 Jonathan Stewart/50
17 Matt Forte/25 12.00 30.00
19 Bo Scaife/50 6.00 15.00
22 Colt McCoy/25 8.00 20.00
24 Peyton Hillis/25 12.00 30.00
25 Felix Jones/35 6.00 15.00
26 Jason Witten/25 15.00 40.00
27 Miles Austin/25 12.00 30.00
29 Brandon Lloyd/25 8.00 20.00
30 Knowshon Moreno/50 6.00 15.00
33 Jahvid Best/50 6.00 15.00
34 Matthew Stafford/50 20.00 50.00
35 Aaron Rodgers/10
36 Greg Jennings/50 6.00 15.00
39 Arian Foster/50 20.00 50.00
40 Matt Schaub/50 10.00 25.00
42 Peyton Manning/25 60.00 120.00
43 Reggie Wayne/25 10.00 25.00
48 Jamaal Charles/25 10.00 25.00
49 Matt Cassel/25 8.00 20.00
50 Brian Hartline/25 10.00 25.00
51 Chad Henne/50 8.00 20.00
54 Donovan McNabb/25 25.00 50.00
55 Percy Harvin/25 8.00 20.00
56 BenJarvus Green-Ellis/50 6.00 15.00
57 Chad Ochocinco/50 10.00 25.00
61 Drew Brees/15 40.00 80.00
64 Eli Manning/15 75.00 125.00
66 Mark Sanchez/15 12.00 30.00
67 Santonio Holmes/25 8.00 20.00
68 Shonn Greene/50 6.00 15.00
69 Darren McFadden/25 12.00 30.00
72 DeSean Jackson/15
73 LeSean McCoy/25 12.00 30.00
80 Philip Rivers/15 15.00 40.00
83 Michael Crabtree/50 10.00 25.00
84 Vernon Davis/15
87 Sidney Rice/50 6.00 15.00
89 Danny Amendola/50 12.00 30.00
90 Sam Bradford/15 8.00 20.00
92 Josh Freeman/50 8.00 20.00
98 Chris Cooley/25 12.00 30.00
99 Rex Grossman/50 6.00 15.00
101 Ozzie Newsome/30 10.00 25.00
102 Andre Reed/15 12.00 30.00
104 Franco Harris/10
105 Jack Lambert/25 30.00 60.00
108 Jim Kelly/25 20.00 40.00
109 Jim Otto/30 10.00 25.00
111 Terrell Davis/20 15.00 40.00
112 Willie Brown/35
113 Joe Namath/25 50.00 100.00
117 Steve Bartkowski/50 8.00 20.00
128 Alan Page/50 10.00 25.00
132 Bob Griese/35 15.00 40.00
134 Boyd Dowler/50 12.00 30.00
139 Boomer Esiason/40 12.00 30.00
142 Cliff Harris/50 10.00 25.00
144 Dave Casper/50 10.00 25.00
147 Doug Williams/50 10.00 25.00
150 Fred Williamson/50 10.00 25.00

2011 Limited Rookie Jumbo Jerseys
STATED PRINT RUN 43-99
*JUMBO PRIME/10: 1.2X TO 3X JUM.JSY/43-99
*JSY #/36-49: .5X TO 1.2X JUM.JSY/43-99
*JSY # PRIME/10: 1.2X TO 3X JUM.JSY/43-99
1 Cam Newton/99 8.00 20.00
2 Jonathan Baldwin/99 1.50 4.00
3 Von Miller/99 2.50 6.00
4 Ryan Mallett/99 1.50 4.00
5 A.J. Green/60 4.00 10.00
6 Bilal Powell/99 2.00 5.00
7 Greg Little/99 2.00 5.00
8 Leonard Hankerson/99 1.50 4.00
9 Taiwan Jones/99 1.50 4.00
10 Shane Vereen/99 2.00 5.00
11 Jamie Harper/99 1.50 4.00
12 Daniel Thomas/99 1.50 4.00
13 Andy Dalton/99 3.00 8.00
14 Clyde Gates/99 1.50 4.00
15 Kendall Hunter/99 1.50 4.00
16 Mikel Leshoure/99 1.50 4.00
17 Torrey Smith/99 1.50 4.00
18 Blaine Gabbert/99 1.50 4.00
19 Alex Green/99 1.50 4.00
20 Delone Carter/99 1.50 4.00
22 Mark Ingram/99 2.50 6.00
23 Austin Pettis/99 1.50 4.00
24 Marcell Dareus/99 1.50 4.00
25 Titus Young/99 1.50 4.00
26 Randall Cobb/99 2.50 6.00
27 Christian Ponder/99 1.50 4.00
28 Julio Jones/99 5.00 12.00
29 Stevan Ridley/99 1.50 4.00
30 Vincent Brown/99 1.50 4.00
31 Jake Locker/99 1.50 4.00
32 Jordan Todman/99 1.50 4.00
33 Jerrel Jernigan/99 1.50 4.00
34 DeMarco Murray/99 3.00 8.00
35 Kyle Rudolph/43 1.50 4.00
36 Colin Kaepernick/99 2.50 6.00

2011 Limited Rookie Jumbo Jerseys Autographs Prime
STATED PRINT RUN 25 SER.#'d SETS
*BASIC JSY AU/10: .4X TO 1X PRIME AU/25
*JSY # AU/10: .4X TO 1X PRIME AU/25
EXCH EXPIRATION: 6/28/2013
1 Cam Newton 75.00 150.00
2 Jonathan Baldwin 8.00 20.00
3 Von Miller 20.00 50.00
4 Ryan Mallett 8.00 20.00
5 A.J. Green 40.00 80.00
6 Bilal Powell 10.00 25.00
7 Greg Little 10.00 25.00
8 Leonard Hankerson 8.00 20.00
9 Taiwan Jones 8.00 20.00
10 Shane Vereen 10.00 25.00
11 Jamie Harper EXCH 8.00 20.00
12 Daniel Thomas 8.00 20.00
13 Andy Dalton 15.00 40.00
14 Clyde Gates 8.00 20.00
15 Kendall Hunter 8.00 20.00
16 Mikel Leshoure 8.00 20.00
17 Torrey Smith 8.00 20.00
18 Blaine Gabbert 8.00 20.00
19 Alex Green 8.00 20.00
20 Delone Carter 8.00 20.00
21 Ryan Williams 8.00 20.00
22 Mark Ingram 12.00 30.00
23 Austin Pettis 8.00 20.00
24 Marcell Dareus EXCH
25 Titus Young 8.00 20.00
26 Randall Cobb 12.00 30.00
27 Christian Ponder 8.00 20.00
28 Julio Jones 40.00 80.00
29 Stevan Ridley 8.00 20.00
30 Vincent Brown 8.00 20.00
31 Jake Locker 8.00 20.00
32 Jordan Todman 8.00 20.00
33 Jerrel Jernigan 8.00 20.00
34 DeMarco Murray 15.00 40.00
35 Kyle Rudolph 8.00 20.00
36 Colin Kaepernick 12.00 30.00

2011 Limited Rookie Lettermen
UNPRICED LETTERMEN PRINT RUN 4-10

2011 Limited Team Trademarks Autograph Materials
STATED PRINT RUN 6-25
*PRIME/10: .5X TO 1.2X JSY AU/15-25
1 Larry Fitzgerald/20 15.00 40.00
2 Michael Turner/15 10.00 25.00
3 Anquan Boldin/20 10.00 25.00
4 Jonathan Stewart/6
5 Steve Smith/20 EXCH 12.00 30.00
7 Troy Polamalu/25 50.00 100.00
8 Matt Forte/20 15.00 40.00
9 Hakeem Nicks/20 10.00 25.00
10 Reggie Wayne/25 12.00 30.00
11 Matthew Stafford/25 30.00 80.00
12 Jay Cutler/20 10.00 25.00
14 Ray Rice/25 10.00 25.00
15 Hines Ward/20 40.00 80.00
17 Dallas Clark/25 10.00 25.00
18 LaDainian Tomlinson/25 15.00 40.00
19 LeSean McCoy/20 15.00 40.00
22 Frank Gore/25 12.00 30.00
23 Jeremy Maclin/25

2011 Limited Team Trademarks Materials Prime
STATED PRINT RUN 5-50
2 Michael Turner/50 4.00 10.00
3 Anquan Boldin/50 4.00 10.00
5 Steve Smith/50 5.00 12.00
6 Brian Urlacher/50 6.00 15.00
8 Matt Forte/50 4.00 10.00
9 Hakeem Nicks/50 4.00 10.00
10 Reggie Wayne/50 5.00 12.00
11 Matthew Stafford/50 5.00 12.00
12 Jay Cutler/50 4.00 10.00
13 Mike Thomas/50 5.00 12.00
14 Ray Rice/50 4.00 10.00
17 Dallas Clark/50 4.00 10.00
18 LaDainian Tomlinson/50 6.00 15.00
20 Ray Lewis/50 8.00 20.00
21 Wes Welker/50 8.00 20.00
22 Frank Gore/25 6.00 15.00
23 Jeremy Maclin/50 4.00 10.00
24 Chris Johnson/50 4.00 10.00
25 Visanthe Shiancoe/43 5.00 12.00

2011 Limited Threads
STATED PRINT RUN 13-99
1 Beanie Wells/99 2.50 6.00
2 Kevin Kolb/99 2.50 6.00
3 Larry Fitzgerald/48 3.00 8.00
4 Matt Ryan/99 3.00 8.00
5 Michael Turner/99 2.50 6.00
7 Anquan Boldin/99 2.50 6.00
8 Joe Flacco/99 3.00 8.00
9 Ray Rice/99 4.00 10.00
10 C.J. Spiller/99 2.50 6.00
11 Ryan Fitzpatrick/99 2.50 6.00
12 Steve Johnson/99 2.50 6.00
13 DeAngelo Williams/99 2.50 6.00
16 Jay Cutler/99 2.50 6.00
17 Matt Forte/99 2.50 6.00
18 Roy Williams WR/99 2.50 6.00
20 Cedric Benson/99 2.50 6.00
21 Jordan Shipley/99 2.50 6.00
22 Colt McCoy/99 2.50 6.00
23 Josh Cribbs/99 2.50 6.00
25 Felix Jones/99 2.50 6.00
26 Jason Witten/99 5.00 12.00
27 Miles Austin/99 2.50 6.00
28 Tony Romo/99 3.00 8.00
29 Brandon Lloyd/99 2.50 6.00
30 Knowshon Moreno/99 2.50 6.00
31 Kyle Orton/99 2.50 6.00
32 Calvin Johnson/99 4.00 10.00
33 Jahvid Best/99 2.50 6.00
34 Matthew Stafford/99 3.00 8.00
35 Aaron Rodgers/99 10.00 25.00
38 Andre Johnson/99 3.00 8.00
40 Matt Schaub/99 2.50 6.00
41 Dallas Clark/99 2.50 6.00
43 Reggie Wayne/99 3.00 8.00
45 Marcedes Lewis/50 2.50 6.00
46 Maurice Jones-Drew/99 2.50 6.00
47 Dwayne Bowe/99 3.00 8.00
48 Jamaal Charles/99 3.00 8.00
49 Matt Cassel/99 2.50 6.00
50 Brian Hartline/99 3.00 8.00
51 Chad Henne/99 3.00 8.00
54 Donovan McNabb/99 3.00 8.00
55 Percy Harvin/99 2.50 6.00
56 BenJarvus Green-Ellis/99 6.00 10.00
58 Tom Brady/99 12.00 30.00
59 Wes Welker/99 3.00 8.00
60 Devery Henderson/99 2.50 6.00
61 Drew Brees/99 4.00 10.00
62 Marques Colston/99 2.50 6.00
64 Eli Manning/99 3.00 8.00
65 Hakeem Nicks/99 2.50 6.00
66 Mark Sanchez/99 2.50 6.00
67 Santonio Holmes/99 2.50 6.00
68 Shonn Greene/99 2.50 6.00
69 Darren McFadden/99 2.50 6.00
70 Jacoby Ford/99 3.00 8.00
71 Jason Campbell/99 2.50 6.00
72 DeSean Jackson/99 3.00 8.00
73 LeSean McCoy/99 4.00 10.00
74 Michael Vick/99 3.00 8.00
76 Ben Roethlisberger/99 4.00 10.00
77 Mike Wallace/99 2.50 6.00
78 Rashard Mendenhall/25 3.00 8.00
79 Antonio Gates/99 2.50 6.00
80 Philip Rivers/99 4.00 10.00
81 Ryan Mathews/99 3.00 8.00
82 Frank Gore/99 3.00 8.00
83 Michael Crabtree/65 2.50 6.00
84 Vernon Davis/99 2.50 6.00
86 Zach Miller/99 2.50 6.00
89 Danny Amendola/99 3.00 8.00
90 Sam Bradford/99 2.50 6.00
91 Steven Jackson/99 2.50 6.00
95 Chris Johnson/99 2.50 6.00
96 Kenny Britt/99 2.50 6.00
97 Matt Hasselbeck/99 2.50 6.00
98 Chris Cooley/99 4.00 10.00
100 Ryan Torain/99 2.50 6.00
101 Ozzie Newsome/99 5.00 12.00
102 Andre Reed/30 6.00 15.00
103 Doug Flutie/99 5.00 12.00
104 Franco Harris/99 6.00 15.00
105 Jack Lambert/99 6.00 15.00
106 Jay Novacek/99 6.00 15.00
107 Jerry Rice/99 8.00 20.00
108 Jim Kelly/99 6.00 15.00
109 Jim Otto/99 4.00 10.00
110 Ken Stabler/99 6.00 15.00
111 Terrell Davis/99 5.00 12.00
112 Willie Brown/99 4.00 10.00
113 Joe Namath/23 10.00 25.00
114 Junior Seau/99 5.00 12.00
115 Rod Woodson/99 6.00 15.00
116 Sam Huff/99 5.00 12.00
117 Steve Bartkowski/99 5.00 12.00
118 Steve Young/99 8.00 20.00
119 Troy Aikman/99 8.00 20.00
120 Y.A. Tittle/99 6.00 15.00
121 Cris Collinsworth/99 5.00 12.00
122 Dick Butkus/99 8.00 20.00
123 Earl Campbell/93 6.00 15.00
124 Fred Biletnikoff/99 6.00 15.00
126 Bo Jackson/99 8.00 20.00
127 Brett Favre/99 12.00 30.00
128 Alan Page/99 4.00 10.00
131 Bernie Kosar/99 5.00 12.00
132 Bob Griese/99 6.00 15.00
133 Bob Hayes/99 8.00 20.00
135 Bruce Smith/99 5.00 12.00
136 Charley Taylor/99 4.00 10.00
137 Charlie Joiner/13 6.00 15.00
138 Billy Sims/46 5.00 12.00
139 Boomer Esiason/99 5.00 12.00
141 Chuck Foreman/99 5.00 12.00
143 Dan Fouts/99 5.00 12.00
145 Derrick Thomas/25 40.00 100.00
146 Don Maynard/99 5.00 12.00
148 Eddie George/99 5.00 12.00
149 Emmitt Smith/99 10.00 25.00

2011 Limited Threads Prime
STATED PRINT RUN 1-50
1 Beanie Wells/15 4.00 10.00
4 Matt Ryan/50 4.00 10.00
5 Michael Turner/50 3.00 8.00
6 Roddy White/50 3.00 8.00
7 Anquan Boldin/50 3.00 8.00
8 Joe Flacco/50 4.00 10.00
9 Ray Rice/50 5.00 12.00
10 C.J. Spiller/50 3.00 8.00
11 Ryan Fitzpatrick/50 3.00 8.00
12 Steve Johnson/50 3.00 8.00
13 DeAngelo Williams/50 3.00 8.00
15 Steve Smith/50 4.00 10.00
16 Jay Cutler/50 3.00 8.00
17 Matt Forte/50 3.00 8.00
20 Cedric Benson/25 4.00 10.00
21 Jordan Shipley/50 3.00 8.00
22 Colt McCoy/50 3.00 8.00
23 Josh Cribbs/50 3.00 8.00
25 Felix Jones/50 3.00 8.00
26 Jason Witten/50 6.00 15.00
27 Miles Austin/50 3.00 8.00
28 Tony Romo/50 4.00 10.00
29 Brandon Lloyd/50 3.00 8.00
30 Knowshon Moreno/40 3.00 8.00
32 Calvin Johnson/50 5.00 12.00
33 Jahvid Best/32 3.00 8.00
34 Matthew Stafford/50 4.00 10.00
35 Aaron Rodgers/50 12.00 30.00
40 Matt Schaub/50 3.00 8.00
41 Dallas Clark/21 4.00 10.00
43 Reggie Wayne/19 5.00 12.00
45 Marcedes Lewis/34 3.00 8.00
46 Maurice Jones-Drew/50 3.00 8.00
47 Dwayne Bowe/50 4.00 10.00
48 Jamaal Charles/60 4.00 10.00
49 Matt Cassel/50 3.00 8.00
50 Brian Hartline/50 4.00 10.00
53 Adrian Peterson/50 5.00 12.00
55 Percy Harvin/50 3.00 8.00
56 BenJarvus Green-Ellis/50 8.00 20.00
59 Wes Welker/50 4.00 10.00
60 Devery Henderson/50 3.00 8.00
62 Marques Colston/25 4.00 10.00
63 Ahmad Bradshaw/50 3.00 8.00
64 Eli Manning/50 4.00 10.00
65 Hakeem Nicks/50 3.00 8.00
66 Mark Sanchez/25 4.00 10.00
67 Santonio Holmes/50 3.00 8.00
68 Shonn Greene/50 3.00 8.00
69 Darren McFadden/50 3.00 8.00
70 Jacoby Ford/50 4.00 10.00
72 DeSean Jackson/50 4.00 10.00
79 Antonio Gates/50 3.00 8.00
80 Philip Rivers/50 5.00 12.00
81 Ryan Mathews/50 4.00 10.00
82 Frank Gore/25 5.00 12.00
86 Zach Miller/50 3.00 8.00
89 Danny Amendola/50 4.00 10.00
90 Sam Bradford/50 3.00 8.00
91 Steven Jackson/50 3.00 8.00
95 Chris Johnson/50 3.00 8.00
96 Kenny Britt/30 3.00 8.00
97 Matt Hasselbeck/25 4.00 10.00
98 Chris Cooley/50 5.00 12.00
100 Ryan Torain/50 3.00 8.00
101 Ozzie Newsome/50 6.00 15.00
103 Doug Flutie/50 6.00 15.00
104 Franco Harris/20 10.00 25.00
105 Jack Lambert/50 8.00 20.00
106 Jay Novacek/50 8.00 20.00
107 Jerry Rice/24 12.00 30.00
108 Jim Kelly/50 8.00 20.00
109 Jim Otto/50 5.00 12.00
111 Terrell Davis/50 6.00 15.00
114 Junior Seau/15 8.00 20.00
115 Rod Woodson/50 8.00 20.00
116 Sam Huff/50 6.00 15.00
117 Steve Bartkowski/50 6.00 15.00
118 Steve Young/50 10.00 25.00
119 Troy Aikman/50 10.00 25.00
120 Y.A. Tittle/50 8.00 20.00
121 Cris Collinsworth/50 6.00 15.00
125 Jerome Bettis/50 8.00 20.00
128 Alan Page/50 5.00 12.00
130 Barry Sanders/50 12.00 30.00
131 Bernie Kosar/50 6.00 15.00
132 Bob Griese/50 8.00 20.00
133 Bob Hayes/50 10.00 25.00
135 Bruce Smith/50 6.00 15.00
139 Boomer Esiason/50 6.00 15.00
141 Chuck Foreman/25 8.00 20.00
145 Derrick Thomas/50 40.00 100.00
146 Don Maynard/35 6.00 15.00
148 Eddie George/50 6.00 15.00
149 Emmitt Smith/50 12.00 30.00

2012 Limited
1-100 VETERAN PRINT RUN 399
101-150 LEGEND PRINT RUN 349
151-200 ROOKIE PRINT RUN 299
ROOKIE JSY AU PRINT RUN 98-299
1 Aaron Rodgers 2.50 6.00
2 Jordy Nelson 1.25 3.00
3 Greg Jennings 1.00 2.50
4 Kevin Kolb 1.00 2.50
5 Beanie Wells 1.00 2.50
6 Larry Fitzgerald 1.25 3.00
7 Matt Ryan 1.00 2.50
8 Michael Turner 1.00 2.50
9 Roddy White 1.00 2.50
10 Joe Flacco 1.25 3.00
11 Ray Lewis 1.50 4.00
12 Ray Rice 1.00 2.50
13 Torrey Smith 1.00 2.50
14 Ryan Fitzpatrick 1.00 2.50
15 Steve Johnson 1.25 3.00
16 Fred Jackson 1.25 3.00
17 Cam Newton 1.50 4.00
18 DeAngelo Williams 1.00 2.50
19 Steve Smith 1.25 3.00
20 Jay Cutler 1.00 2.50
21 Matt Forte 1.00 2.50
22 Brandon Marshall 1.25 3.00
23 Andy Dalton 1.25 3.00
24 BenJarvus Green-Ellis 1.25 3.00
25 A.J. Green 1.50 4.00
26 Greg Little 1.00 2.50
27 Josh Cribbs 1.00 2.50
28 Tony Romo 1.25 3.00
29 Miles Austin 1.00 2.50
30 Dez Bryant 1.50 4.00
31 DeMarco Murray 1.25 3.00
32 Peyton Manning 5.00 12.00
33 Willis McGahee 1.00 2.50
34 Demaryius Thomas 1.50 4.00
35 Matthew Stafford 1.25 3.00
36 Calvin Johnson 1.50 4.00
37 Ndamukong Suh 1.25 3.00
38 Matt Schaub 1.00 2.50
39 Andre Johnson 1.25 3.00
40 Arian Foster 1.25 3.00
41 Reggie Wayne 1.25 3.00
42 Donnie Avery 1.00 2.50
43 Donald Brown 1.00 2.50
44 Blaine Gabbert 1.00 2.50
45 Maurice Jones-Drew 1.00 2.50
46 Laurent Robinson 1.00 2.50
47 Matt Cassel 1.00 2.50
48 Jamaal Charles 1.25 3.00
49 Dwayne Bowe 1.25 3.00
50 Reggie Bush 1.00 2.50
51 Anthony Fasano 1.00 2.50
52 Karlos Dansby 1.00 2.50
53 Christian Ponder 1.00 2.50
54 Percy Harvin 1.00 2.50
55 Adrian Peterson 1.50 4.00
56 Tom Brady 4.00 10.00
57 Aaron Hernandez 1.25 3.00
58 Wes Welker 1.25 3.00
59 Rob Gronkowski 1.50 4.00
60 Drew Brees 1.50 4.00
61 Marques Colston 1.25 3.00
62 Jimmy Graham 1.50 4.00
63 Eli Manning 1.25 3.00
64 Ahmad Bradshaw 1.00 2.50
65 Victor Cruz 1.25 3.00
66 Hakeem Nicks 1.00 2.50
67 Mark Sanchez 1.00 2.50
68 Shonn Greene 1.00 2.50
69 Santonio Holmes 1.00 2.50
70 Tim Tebow 1.50 4.00
71 Carson Palmer 1.25 3.00
72 Darren McFadden 1.00 2.50
73 Darrius Heyward-Bey 1.00 2.50
74 Michael Vick 1.25 3.00
75 LeSean McCoy 1.50 4.00
76 DeSean Jackson 1.25 3.00
77 Ben Roethlisberger 1.50 4.00
78 Isaac Redman 1.00 2.50
79 Mike Wallace 1.00 2.50
80 Philip Rivers 1.50 4.00
81 Ryan Mathews 1.25 3.00
82 Antonio Gates 1.25 3.00
83 Alex Smith 1.25 3.00
84 Frank Gore 1.25 3.00
85 Vernon Davis 1.00 2.50
86 Randy Moss 1.25 3.00
87 Matt Flynn 1.25 3.00
88 Marshawn Lynch 1.25 3.00
89 Sidney Rice 1.00 2.50
90 Sam Bradford 1.00 2.50
91 Steven Jackson 1.00 2.50

92 James Laurinaitis 1.00 2.50
93 Josh Freeman 1.25 3.00
94 Dallas Clark 1.00 2.50
95 Vincent Jackson 1.00 2.50
96 Jake Locker 1.50 4.00
97 Chris Johnson 1.00 2.50
98 Kenny Britt 1.00 2.50
99 Pierre Garcon 1.25 3.00
100 Roy Helu 1.00 2.50
101 Ozzie Newsome 1.50 4.00
102 Andre Reed 1.50 4.00
103 Doug Flutie 1.50 4.00
104 Franco Harris 2.00 5.00
105 Jack Lambert 2.00 5.00
106 Jay Novacek 1.50 4.00
107 Jerry Rice 3.00 8.00
108 Jim Kelly 2.00 5.00
109 Jim Otto 1.25 3.00
110 Ken Stabler 2.00 5.00
111 Terrell Davis 1.50 4.00
112 Willie Brown 1.25 3.00
113 Joe Namath 3.00 8.00
114 Jim Brown 2.50 6.00
115 Rod Woodson 1.50 4.00
116 Sam Huff 1.50 4.00
117 Steve Bartkowski 1.50 4.00
118 Steve Young 2.50 6.00
119 Troy Aikman 2.50 6.00
120 Y.A. Tittle 2.00 5.00
121 Cris Collinsworth 1.50 4.00
122 Dick Butkus 2.50 6.00
123 Earl Campbell 2.00 5.00
124 Joe Montana 5.00 12.00
125 Jerome Bettis 2.00 5.00
126 Bo Jackson 2.50 6.00
127 Brett Favre 4.00 10.00
128 Alan Page 1.25 3.00
129 Art Monk 2.00 5.00
130 Barry Sanders 3.00 8.00
131 Bernie Kosar 1.50 4.00
132 Bob Griese 2.00 5.00
133 Bob Hayes 2.00 5.00
134 Boyd Dowler 1.25 3.00
135 Bruce Smith 1.50 4.00
136 Charley Taylor 1.25 3.00
137 Charlie Joiner 1.25 3.00
138 Billy Sims 1.50 4.00
139 Boomer Esiason 1.50 4.00
140 John Elway 3.00 8.00
141 Chuck Foreman 1.25 3.00
142 Cliff Harris 1.25 3.00
143 Dan Fouts 1.50 4.00
144 Jim Plunkett 1.50 4.00
145 Derrick Thomas 4.00 10.00
146 Don Maynard 1.50 4.00
147 Doug Williams 1.50 4.00
148 Eddie George 1.50 4.00
149 Emmitt Smith 3.00 8.00
150 Fred Williamson 1.25 3.00
151 Morris Claiborne RC 1.25 3.00
152 Alfred Morris RC 1.25 3.00
153 B.J. Cunningham RC 1.25 3.00
154 Bobby Rainey RC 1.25 3.00
155 Bobby Wagner RC 2.00 5.00
156 Case Keenum RC 2.50 6.00
157 Chandler Harnish RC 1.25 3.00
158 Chandler Jones RC 1.25 3.00
159 Chris Polk RC 1.25 3.00
160 Chris Rainey RC 1.25 3.00
161 Coty Sensabaugh RC 1.50 4.00
162 Courtney Upshaw RC 1.50 4.00
163 Cyrus Gray RC 1.25 3.00
164 Danny Coale RC 1.25 3.00
165 David DeCastro RC 1.25 3.00
166 Devon Wylie RC 1.25 3.00
167 Dont'a Hightower RC 2.00 5.00
168 Dontari Poe RC 1.25 3.00
169 Dre Kirkpatrick RC 1.25 3.00
170 Jeff Demps RC 1.50 4.00
171 Fletcher Cox RC 2.00 5.00
172 George Iloka RC 1.25 3.00
173 Gerell Robinson RC 1.25 3.00
174 Josh Cooper RC 1.50 4.00
175 James Hanna RC 1.25 3.00
176 Janoris Jenkins RC 1.50 4.00
177 Juron Criner RC 1.25 3.00
178 Kellen Moore RC 1.50 4.00
179 Keshawn Martin RC 1.50 4.00
180 Kirk Cousins RC 5.00 12.00
181 Ladarius Green RC 1.25 3.00
182 LaVon Brazill RC 2.00 5.00
183 Lavonte David RC 2.00 5.00
184 Luke Kuechly RC 3.00 8.00
185 Mark Barron RC 1.25 3.00
186 Josh Gordon RC 3.00 8.00
187 Marvin McNutt RC 1.25 3.00
188 Matt Kalil RC 1.25 3.00
189 Melvin Ingram RC 1.25 3.00
190 Michael Brockers RC 1.25 3.00
191 Michael Smith RC 1.50 4.00
192 Mychal Kendricks RC 2.00 5.00
193 Shea McClellin RC 1.50 4.00
194 Stephon Gilmore RC 1.50 4.00
195 Terrance Ganaway RC 1.50 4.00
196 Tim Benford RC 1.25 3.00
197 Tommy Streeter RC 1.25 3.00
198 Travis Benjamin RC 1.25 3.00
199 Tyrone Crawford RC 1.25 3.00
200 Whitney Mercilus RC 1.25 3.00
201 A.Luck JSY AU/199 RC 125.00 250.00
202 R.Griffin III JSY AU/199 RC 8.00 20.00
203 Richardson JSY AU/98 RC 6.00 15.00
204 R.Tannehill JSY AU/199 RC 10.00 25.00
205 Blackmon JSY AU/199 RC 6.00 15.00
206 B.Weeden JSY AU/199 RC 6.00 15.00
207 B.Osweiler JSY AU/199 RC 6.00 15.00
208 M.Floyd JSY AU/299 RC EX 15.00 40.00
209 K.Wright JSY AU/199 RC EX 6.00 15.00
210 A.J. Jenkins JSY AU/140 RC 6.00 15.00
211 D.Martin JSY AU/299 RC 8.00 20.00
212 L.Miller JSY AU/299 RC 8.00 20.00
213 Isaiah Pead JSY AU/299 RC 5.00 12.00
214 D.Wilson JSY AU/122 RC 6.00 15.00
215 S.Hill JSY AU/299 RC EXCH 5.00 12.00
216 M.Sanu JSY AU/299 RC 8.00 20.00
217 B.Pierce JSY AU/299 RC EXCH 5.00 12.00
218 N.Foles JSY AU/299 RC 30.00 60.00
219 L.James JSY AU/199 RC 6.00 15.00
220 Randle JSY AU/199 RC EXCH 6.00 15.00
221 Fleener JSY AU/299 RC 5.00 12.00
222 R.Broyles JSY AU/299 RC 5.00 12.00
223 D.Allen JSY AU/299 RC 5.00 12.00
224 R.Hillman JSY AU/140 RC 6.00 15.00
225 R.Wilson JSY AU/299 RC 90.00 150.00
226 M.Egnew JSY AU/299 RC 5.00 12.00
227 Givens JSY AU/299 RC EXCH 5.00 12.00
228 J.Adams JSY AU/299 RC 5.00 12.00
229 R.Turbin JSY AU/299 RC 5.00 12.00
230 N.Toon JSY AU/299 RC 5.00 12.00
231 Graham JSY AU/299 RC EXCH 5.00 12.00
232 Brian Quick JSY AU/299 RC 5.00 12.00
233 D.Posey JSY AU/299 RC 5.00 12.00
234 J.Wright JSY AU/299 RC 5.00 12.00
235 Alshon Jeffery JSY AU/299 RC 10.00 25.00

2012 Limited Gold Spotlight

ETS/25: .8X TO 2X BASIC VET/399
*LEGENDS/25: .8X TO 2X BASIC LEG/349
*ROOKIES/25: .6X TO 1.5X BASIC RC/299
*ROOK.JSY AU/25: .8X TO 2X JSY AU/299
*ROOK.JSY AU/25: .6X TO 1.5X JSY AU/98-199
STATED PRINT RUN 25 SER.#'d SETS
201 Andrew Luck JSY AU 200.00 400.00
225 Russell Wilson JSY AU 150.00 250.00

2012 Limited Silver Spotlight

*VETS/49: .6X TO 1.5X BASIC VET/399
*LEGENDS/49: .6X TO 1.5X BASIC LEG/349
*ROOKIES/49: .5X TO 1.2X BASIC RC/299
1-200 STATED PRINT RUN 49
*ROOK.JSY AU/49: .6X TO 1.5X JSY AU/299
*RK.JSY AU/40-49: .5X TO 1.2X JSY AU/98-199
201-235 JSY AU PRINT RUN 40-49
201 Andrew Luck JSY AU/49 125.00 250.00
225 R.Wilson JSY AU/49 75.00 150.00

2012 Limited Blast From The Past Materials

1 Anquan Boldin/25 2.50 6.00
2 Michael Vick/25 3.00 8.00
3 Willis McGahee/25 2.50 6.00
5 Greg Olsen/25 3.00 8.00
6 Louis Murphy/25 2.50 6.00
7 Roy Williams/25 2.50 6.00
8 Tim Tebow/25 4.00 10.00
9 DeMeco Ryans/25 2.50 6.00
12 Dallas Clark/25 2.50 6.00
13 David Garrard/25 2.50 6.00
15 Ronnie Brown/25 2.50 6.00
16 Randy Moss helmet/15 25.00 50.00
17 Sidney Rice/25 2.50 6.00
18 Robert Meachem/25 2.50 6.00
19 Mario Manningham/25 2.50 6.00
20 Santana Moss/25 3.00 8.00
21 Nnamdi Asomugha/25 2.50 6.00
22 Kevin Kolb/25 2.50 6.00
24 Vincent Jackson/25 2.50 6.00
25 Shawne Merriman/25 2.50 6.00
26 Matt Hasselbeck/25 2.50 6.00
27 Kellen Winslow Jr./25 3.00 8.00
28 Cortland Finnegan/25 2.50 6.00
29 Stephen Tulloch/25 2.50 6.00
30 Jason Campbell/25 2.50 6.00
31 Champ Bailey/25 3.00 8.00
32 Jay Cutler/25 2.50 6.00
34 Tarvaris Jackson/25 2.50 6.00
35 Steve Smith USC/25 3.00 8.00

2012 Limited Blue Chip Jerseys

*PRIME/25: .8X TO 2X BASIC JSY/60-99
*SHOES/49: .5X TO 1.2X BASIC JSY/60-99
1 Andrew Luck/99 12.00 30.00
2 Robert Griffin III/99 2.00 5.00
3 Trent Richardson/99 1.50 4.00
4 Ryan Tannehill/99 2.50 6.00
5 Justin Blackmon/99 1.50 4.00
6 Brandon Weeden/99 1.50 4.00
7 Brock Osweiler/99 1.50 4.00
8 Michael Floyd/99 1.50 4.00
9 Kendall Wright/99 1.50 4.00
10 A.J. Jenkins/99 1.50 4.00
11 Doug Martin/99 2.50 6.00
12 Lamar Miller/99 2.50 6.00
13 Isaiah Pead/99 1.50 4.00
14 David Wilson/99 1.50 4.00
15 Stephen Hill/99 1.50 4.00
16 Mohamed Sanu/99 2.50 6.00
17 Bernard Pierce/99 1.50 4.00
18 Nick Foles/99 4.00 10.00
19 LaMichael James/99 1.50 4.00
20 Rueben Randle/99 1.50 4.00
21 Coby Fleener/99 1.50 4.00
22 Ryan Broyles/99 1.50 4.00
23 Dwayne Allen/99 1.50 4.00
24 Ronnie Hillman/99 1.50 4.00
25 Russell Wilson/99 12.00 30.00
26 Michael Egnew/99 1.50 4.00
27 Chris Givens/99 1.50 4.00
28 Joe Adams/99 1.50 4.00
29 Robert Turbin/99 1.50 4.00
30 Nick Toon/60 1.50 4.00
31 T.J. Graham/99 1.50 4.00
32 Brian Quick/99 1.50 4.00
33 DeVier Posey/99 1.50 4.00
34 Jarius Wright/99 1.50 4.00
35 Alshon Jeffery/99 3.00 8.00

2012 Limited Game Day Materials

1 Darren McFadden/25 4.00 10.00
2 Ray Rice/27 4.00 10.00
6 Dez Bryant/49 5.00 12.00
7 Tony Romo/49 4.00 10.00
11 Jamaal Charles/49 4.00 10.00
12 Devery Henderson/33 3.00 8.00
13 Hakeem Nicks/49 3.00 8.00
14 Santana Moss/35 4.00 10.00
15 Ryan Mathews/46 4.00 10.00
18 London Fletcher/49 5.00 12.00
19 Marques Colston/24 4.00 10.00
20 Eli Manning/20 5.00 12.00
21 Miles Austin/49 3.00 8.00
23 Dwayne Bowe/49 4.00 10.00

2012 Limited Inked

EXCH EXPIRATION: 7/16/2014
2 Ahmad Bradshaw/49 6.00 15.00
3 Antonio Brown/49 10.00 25.00
4 Malcom Floyd/25 EXCH 8.00 20.00
6 Brandon Jacobs/49 6.00 15.00
7 Brian Hartline/25 10.00 25.00
11 Greg Little/25 8.00 20.00
12 Greg Olsen/25 10.00 25.00
14 Rob Gronkowski/25 25.00 50.00
15 Jermichael Finley/49 6.00 15.00
16 J.J. Watt/49 40.00 80.00
25 Tamba Hali/25 8.00 20.00
31 Paul Hornung/25 12.00 30.00
34 Doug Flutie/25 EXCH 12.00 30.00
36 Bo Jackson/25 EXCH 30.00 60.00
42 Alan Page/25 EXCH

2012 Limited Jumbo Jerseys

*JSY NUM/15-49: .4X TO 1X BASIC JSY/15-49
*PRIME/15-25: .6X TO 1.5X BASIC JSY/49
*PRME JSY#/15-25: .6X TO 1.5X BASIC JSY/49
1 Jake Plummer/25 4.00 10.00
2 Ryan Mathews/49 4.00 10.00
3 Roddy White/25 4.00 10.00
4 Joe Flacco/49 4.00 10.00
6 Steve Smith/49 4.00 10.00
7 Walter Payton/25 30.00 80.00
9 Dez Bryant/25 6.00 15.00
10 Jason Witten/25 8.00 20.00
11 John Elway/49 10.00 25.00
12 London Fletcher/49 5.00 12.00
14 Mike Wallace/15 4.00 10.00
15 Matt Cassel/49 3.00 8.00
16 Darren McFadden/49 3.00 8.00
17 Steven Jackson/49 3.00 8.00
18 Percy Harvin/49 3.00 8.00
19 Christian Ponder/25 4.00 10.00
20 Adrian Peterson/25 10.00 25.00
21 Eli Manning/49 4.00 10.00
23 Darren Sproles/25 5.00 12.00
24 Marques Colston/25 4.00 10.00
25 Mark Sanchez/49 3.00 8.00
26 Joe Namath/49 12.00 30.00
27 Michael Vick/49 4.00 10.00
28 DeSean Jackson/49 4.00 10.00
29 Santana Moss/25 5.00 12.00

2012 Limited Limitless Threads Autographs

*PRIME/20-25: .5X TO 1.2X JSY AU/25
3 C.J. Spiller/25 8.00 20.00
5 Mike Wallace/25 12.00 30.00
6 LeSean McCoy/15 12.00 30.00

2012 Limited Material Monikers

EXCH EXPIRATION: 7/16/2014
3 Ahmad Bradshaw/25 8.00 20.00
8 Jared Allen/25 20.00 40.00
9 Marques Colston/25 EXCH 8.00 20.00
10 Brian Orakpo/25 10.00 25.00
11 Kevin Walter/25 8.00 20.00
12 Matt Ryan/25 25.00 50.00
15 DeAngelo Williams/25 8.00 20.00
16 Jim Kelly/25 25.00 50.00
17 Sean Lee/25 12.00 30.00
18 DeSean Jackson/25 10.00 25.00
20 Donald Driver/25 20.00 40.00
23 Felix Jones/25 8.00 20.00
26 Heath Miller/25 20.00 40.00
27 Michael Turner/25 8.00 20.00
29 Jason Witten/15 25.00 50.00
31 Jeremy Maclin/25 8.00 20.00
32 Joe Flacco/25 25.00 50.00
34 Jonathan Stewart/25 8.00 20.00
36 London Fletcher/25 12.00 30.00
37 Matt Cassel/25 8.00 20.00
38 Matt Forte/25 8.00 20.00
45 Randall Cunningham/25 20.00 40.00
46 Santana Moss/25 10.00 25.00
47 Boomer Esiason/25 12.00 30.00

2012 Limited Membership Autographs

EXCH EXPIRATION: 7/16/2014
1 Andrew Luck/25 200.00 350.00
2 Brock Osweiler/25 6.00 15.00
3 Brandon Weeden/25 6.00 15.00
4 Robert Griffin III/25 8.00 20.00
5 Nick Foles/49 15.00 40.00
6 Russell Wilson/25 100.00 200.00
7 Ryan Tannehill/25 10.00 25.00
8 Coby Fleener/49 5.00 12.00
9 Dwayne Allen/99 4.00 10.00
10 Michael Egnew/99 4.00 10.00
11 LaMichael James/25 6.00 15.00
12 Ronnie Hillman/25 6.00 15.00
13 Robert Turbin/99 4.00 10.00
14 Trent Richardson/25 EXCH 6.00 15.00
15 Doug Martin/25 10.00 25.00
16 Lamar Miller/25 10.00 25.00
17 Isaiah Pead/49 5.00 12.00
18 David Wilson/49 5.00 12.00
19 Bernard Pierce/49 10.00 25.00
20 Rueben Randle/49 5.00 12.00
21 Ryan Broyles/99 4.00 10.00
22 Chris Givens/99 4.00 10.00
23 Joe Adams/25 6.00 15.00
24 Nick Toon/99 4.00 10.00
25 T.J. Graham/25 6.00 15.00
26 Brian Quick/99 4.00 10.00
27 DeVier Posey/25 6.00 15.00
28 Jarius Wright/99 4.00 10.00
29 Alshon Jeffery/99 8.00 20.00
30 Michael Floyd/25 6.00 15.00
31 Kendall Wright/25 6.00 15.00
32 A.J. Jenkins/99 4.00 10.00
33 Justin Blackmon/25 6.00 15.00
34 Stephen Hill/25 EXCH 6.00 15.00
35 Mohamed Sanu/49 8.00 20.00

2012 Limited Monikers Autographs Silver

OLD VET/25: .5X TO 1.2X SLVR/49-75
*GOLD VET/25: .4X TO 1X SLVR/20-25
*GOLD LEG/25: .5X TO 1.2X SILVER/49
*GOLD LEG/25: .4X TO 1X SILVER/25
*GLD ROOK/25: .8X TO 2X SILVER RK/249-299
*GLD ROOK/25: .6X TO 1.5X SILVER ROOK/99
*GLD ROOK/25: .4X TO 1X SILVER ROOK/25
EXCH EXPIRATION: 7/16/2014
13 Torrey Smith/25 6.00 15.00
18 DeAngelo Williams/15 6.00 15.00
23 Andy Dalton/15 12.00 30.00
24 BenJarvus Green-Ellis/25 8.00 20.00
25 A.J. Green/25
26 Greg Little/49 5.00 12.00
27 Josh Cribbs/25 6.00 15.00
34 Demaryius Thomas/25 10.00 25.00
38 Matt Schaub/20 6.00 15.00
41 Reggie Wayne/15 8.00 20.00
44 Blaine Gabbert/20 6.00 15.00
53 Christian Ponder/20 6.00 15.00
57 Aaron Hernandez/25 8.00 20.00
59 Rob Gronkowski/25 20.00 50.00
64 Ahmad Bradshaw/25 6.00 15.00
65 Victor Cruz/25 15.00 30.00
69 Santonio Holmes/20 6.00 15.00
73 Darrius Heyward-Bey/25 6.00 15.00
79 Mike Wallace/25 6.00 15.00
83 Alex Smith/15 8.00 20.00
87 Matt Flynn/75 5.00 12.00
92 James Laurinaitis/25 8.00 20.00
93 Josh Freeman/15 8.00 20.00
95 Vincent Jackson/25 6.00 15.00
98 Kenny Britt/25 6.00 15.00
99 Pierre Garcon/25 8.00 20.00
100 Roy Helu/49 5.00 12.00
106 Jay Novacek/25 12.00 30.00
112 Willie Brown/25 8.00 20.00
115 Rod Woodson/25 25.00 50.00
116 Sam Huff/25 10.00 25.00
117 Steve Bartkowski/49 8.00 20.00
132 Bob Griese/15 15.00 40.00
142 Cliff Harris/25 8.00 20.00
146 Don Maynard/25
147 Doug Williams/15 10.00 25.00
150 Fred Williamson/25 8.00 20.00
151 Morris Claiborne/25
152 Alfred Morris/299 2.50 6.00
153 B.J. Cunningham/299 2.50 6.00
154 Bobby Rainey/25 5.00 12.00
155 Bobby Wagner/299 4.00 10.00
156 Case Keenum/249 5.00 12.00
157 Chandler Harnish/299 2.50 6.00
158 Chandler Jones/249 2.50 6.00
159 Chris Polk/249 2.50 6.00
160 Chris Rainey/25
161 Coty Sensabaugh/299 3.00 8.00
162 Courtney Upshaw/299 3.00 8.00
163 Cyrus Gray/249 2.50 6.00
164 Danny Coale/299 2.50 6.00
165 David DeCastro/299 2.50 6.00
166 Devon Wylie/25 5.00 12.00
167 Dont'a Hightower/299 4.00 10.00
168 Dontari Poe/25 5.00 12.00
169 Dre Kirkpatrick/25 EXCH 5.00 12.00
170 Jeff Demps/249 3.00 8.00
171 Fletcher Cox/99 5.00 12.00
172 George Iloka/299 2.50 6.00
173 Gerell Robinson/299 2.50 6.00
174 Josh Cooper/25 6.00 15.00
175 James Hanna/25 EXCH 5.00 12.00
176 Janoris Jenkins/25 6.00 15.00
177 Juron Criner/299 2.50 6.00
178 Kellen Moore/249 3.00 8.00
179 Keshawn Martin/25 6.00 15.00
180 Kirk Cousins/249 6.00 15.00
181 Ladarius Green/299 2.50 6.00
182 LaVon Brazill/299 4.00 10.00
183 Lavonte David/25 8.00 20.00
184 Luke Kuechly/99 12.00 30.00
185 Mark Barron/25 5.00 12.00
186 Josh Gordon/299 6.00 15.00
187 Marvin McNutt/299 2.50 6.00
188 Matt Kalil/25 5.00 12.00
189 Melvin Ingram/25 5.00 12.00
190 Michael Brockers/25 EXCH 5.00 12.00
191 Michael Smith/25 EXCH 6.00 15.00
192 Mychal Kendricks/299 4.00 10.00
193 Shea McClellin/25 6.00 15.00
194 Stephon Gilmore/25 6.00 15.00
195 Terrance Ganaway/299 3.00 8.00
196 Tim Benford/299 2.50 6.00
197 Tommy Streeter/25 5.00 12.00
198 Travis Benjamin/299 2.50 6.00
199 Tyrone Crawford/299 2.50 6.00
200 Whitney Mercilus/299 2.50 6.00

2012 Limited Prime Colors

1 Darren Sproles/25 5.00 12.00
4 Warrick Dunn/25 4.00 10.00
8 Santonio Holmes/20 4.00 10.00
11 Dez Bryant/25 6.00 15.00
12 Emmitt Smith/25 15.00 40.00
15 Barry Sanders/25 12.00 30.00
16 Steven Jackson/25 4.00 10.00
19 Dwayne Bowe/25 5.00 12.00
20 Percy Harvin/25 4.00 10.00
21 Wes Welker/25 5.00 12.00
24 Ahmad Bradshaw/25 4.00 10.00
25 Curtis Martin/25
29 DeSean Jackson/25 5.00 12.00
30 Sam Bradford/25 4.00 10.00
31 Darren McFadden/25 4.00 10.00
32 Philip Rivers/25 6.00 15.00
34 Matt Ryan/15 8.00 20.00

2012 Limited Rookie Jumbo Jerseys

*JSY #/80-99: .5X TO 1.2X JUMBO JSY/99
*PRIME/49: 1X TO 2.5X JUMBO JSY/99
*PRIME/20-25: 1X TO 2.5X JUMBO JSY/99
*PRM JSY #/45-49: .8X TO 2X JUM JSY/99
*PRM JSY #/20-25: 1X TO 2.5X JUM JSY/99
1 Andrew Luck 12.00 30.00
2 Robert Griffin III 2.00 5.00
3 Trent Richardson 1.50 4.00
4 Ryan Tannehill 2.50 6.00
5 Justin Blackmon 1.50 4.00
6 Brandon Weeden 1.50 4.00
7 Brock Osweiler 1.50 4.00
8 Michael Floyd 1.50 4.00
9 Kendall Wright 1.50 4.00
10 A.J. Jenkins 1.50 4.00
11 Doug Martin 2.50 6.00
12 Lamar Miller 2.50 6.00
13 Isaiah Pead 1.50 4.00
15 Stephen Hill 1.50 4.00
17 Bernard Pierce 1.50 4.00
18 Nick Foles 4.00 10.00
19 LaMichael James 1.50 4.00
20 Rueben Randle 1.50 4.00
21 Coby Fleener 1.50 4.00
22 Ryan Broyles 1.50 4.00
23 Dwayne Allen 1.50 4.00
24 Ronnie Hillman 1.50 4.00
25 Russell Wilson 12.00 30.00
26 Michael Egnew 1.50 4.00
28 Joe Adams 1.50 4.00
29 Robert Turbin 1.50 4.00
31 T.J. Graham 1.50 4.00
32 Brian Quick 1.50 4.00
33 DeVier Posey 1.50 4.00
34 Jarius Wright 1.50 4.00
35 Alshon Jeffery 3.00 8.00

2012 Limited Rookie Jumbo Jerseys Autographs

*JSY NUM/49: .4X TO 1X JSY AU/30-49
1 Andrew Luck/49 150.00 300.00
2 Robert Griffin III/49 8.00 20.00
3 Trent Richardson/49 6.00 15.00
4 Ryan Tannehill/49 10.00 25.00
5 Justin Blackmon/49 6.00 15.00
6 Brandon Weeden/49 6.00 15.00
7 Brock Osweiler/49 6.00 15.00
8 Michael Floyd/49 8.00 20.00
9 Kendall Wright/49 6.00 15.00
10 A.J. Jenkins/49 6.00 15.00
11 Doug Martin/49 10.00 25.00
12 Lamar Miller/49 10.00 25.00
13 Isaiah Pead/49 6.00 15.00
15 Stephen Hill/49 EXCH 6.00 15.00
16 Mohamed Sanu/49 10.00 25.00
17 Bernard Pierce/49 6.00 15.00
18 Nick Foles/49 30.00 60.00
19 LaMichael James/49 6.00 15.00
20 Rueben Randle/30 8.00 20.00
21 Coby Fleener/49 6.00 15.00
22 Ryan Broyles/49 6.00 15.00
23 Dwayne Allen/49 6.00 15.00
24 Ronnie Hillman/49 10.00 25.00
25 Russell Wilson/49 75.00 150.00
26 Michael Egnew/49 6.00 15.00
27 Chris Givens/49 6.00 15.00
28 Joe Adams/49 6.00 15.00
29 Robert Turbin/49 6.00 15.00
30 Nick Toon/49 6.00 15.00
31 T.J. Graham/49 6.00 15.00
32 Brian Quick/49 6.00 15.00
33 DeVier Posey/49 6.00 15.00
34 Jarius Wright/49 6.00 15.00
35 Alshon Jeffery/49 12.00 30.00

2012 Limited Rookie Jumbo Jerseys Autographs Prime

*PRIME AU/18-25: .5X TO 1.2X JSY AU/30-49
*PRM JSY# AU/18-25: .4X TO 1X PRM AU/18-25
1 Andrew Luck/25 175.00 300.00
2 Robert Griffin III/25 10.00 25.00
4 Ryan Tannehill/25 12.00 30.00
14 David Wilson/25 8.00 20.00
25 Russell Wilson/25 150.00 250.00

2012 Limited Stadium Stars Helmets

1 Cris Carter/23 20.00 50.00
2 Darrell Green/99 10.00 25.00
3 Doak Walker/50 25.00 60.00
4 Doug Flutie/50 10.00 25.00
5 Ed Reed/99 10.00 25.00
6 Len Dawson/55 10.00 25.00
7 Marshall Faulk/99 6.00 15.00
8 Phil Simms/99 8.00 20.00
9 Priest Holmes/40 10.00 25.00
10 Steve McNair/70 6.00 15.00
11 Tom Brady/30 40.00 80.00
13 Wayne Chrebet/16 12.00 30.00
14 Eddie George/35 10.00 25.00
15 Edgerrin James/20 10.00 25.00
16 Jake Plummer/42 8.00 20.00
17 Jamal Lewis/24 12.00 30.00
18 Kurt Warner/75 8.00 20.00
19 Ron Jaworski/25 15.00 40.00
20 Warrick Dunn/99 6.00 15.00

2012 Limited Team Trademarks Autograph Materials

EXCH EXPIRATION: 7/16/2014
3 DeAngelo Williams/25 8.00 20.00
6 Heath Miller/25 20.00 40.00
8 Jonathan Stewart/25 8.00 20.00
10 LeSean McCoy/15 12.00 30.00
11 Marcedes Lewis/25 8.00 20.00
12 Fred Jackson/25 EXCH 10.00 25.00
13 Matt Forte/25 8.00 20.00
14 Tamba Hali/25 8.00 20.00
18 Ryan Mathews/25 10.00 25.00
28 C.J. Spiller/15 8.00 20.00
29 Jason Witten/15 25.00 50.00

2012 Limited Threads

1 Joe Flacco/99 3.00 8.00
2 Ray Lewis/99 5.00 12.00
3 Ray Rice/99 2.50 6.00
8 Troy Polamalu/99 4.00 10.00
9 Rashard Mendenhall/25 4.00 10.00
11 Mike Wallace/49 3.00 8.00
12 Heath Miller/25 6.00 15.00
14 Arian Foster/99 3.00 8.00
15 Andre Johnson/99 3.00 8.00
16 Owen Daniels/25 4.00 10.00
18 Ryan Fitzpatrick/49 3.00 8.00
20 Marcedes Lewis/99 2.50 6.00
21 Chris Johnson/99 2.50 6.00
22 Matt Hasselbeck/25 4.00 10.00
23 Eddie George/99 3.00 8.00
24 Warren Moon/25 6.00 15.00
25 Doug Flutie/99 3.00 8.00
26 Ronnie Lott/99 5.00 12.00
29 Tom Brady/99 8.00 20.00
30 Wes Welker/99 3.00 8.00
31 Jerod Mayo/99 2.50 6.00
32 Danny Woodhead/34 8.00 20.00
33 Mark Sanchez/99 2.50 6.00
34 Shonn Greene/99 2.50 6.00
35 Darrelle Revis/95 2.50 6.00
36 David Harris/99 2.50 6.00
37 Knowshon Moreno/99 2.50 6.00
38 Von Miller/49 4.00 10.00
39 Keyshawn Johnson/45 4.00 10.00
40 Matt Cassel/99 2.50 6.00
41 Dwayne Bowe/99 3.00 8.00
42 Jamaal Charles/99 3.00 8.00
43 Darren McFadden/99 2.50 6.00
45 Philip Rivers/99 4.00 10.00
46 Junior Seau/99 3.00 8.00
47 Ryan Mathews/99 3.00 8.00
48 Antonio Gates/99 3.00 8.00
49 Jay Cutler/99 2.50 6.00
50 Matt Forte/99 2.50 6.00
51 Brian Urlacher/43 5.00 12.00
52 Devin Hester/99 3.00 8.00
55 Barry Sanders/99 8.00 20.00
56 Steve Young/99 6.00 15.00
57 Michael Crabtree/99 2.50 6.00
58 Greg Jennings/49 3.00 8.00
59 Marshall Faulk/15 8.00 20.00
61 Adrian Peterson/99 4.00 10.00
63 Percy Harvin/99 2.50 6.00
64 Christian Ponder/99 2.50 6.00
65 Matt Ryan/99 3.00 8.00
66 Michael Turner/99 2.50 6.00
67 Roddy White/99 2.50 6.00
69 Steve Smith/99 3.00 8.00
72 DeAngelo Williams/99 2.50 6.00
73 Drew Brees/99 4.00 10.00
74 Devery Henderson/25 4.00 10.00
75 Marques Colston/99 2.50 6.00
78 Tony Romo/99 3.00 8.00
79 Dez Bryant/99 4.00 10.00
80 Miles Austin/15 4.00 10.00
81 Felix Jones/99 2.50 6.00
82 Eli Manning/99 3.00 8.00
84 Ahmad Bradshaw/99 2.50 6.00
85 Michael Vick/99 3.00 8.00
86 Jeremy Maclin/99 2.50 6.00
88 DeSean Jackson/99 3.00 8.00
89 Santana Moss/99 3.00 8.00
90 London Fletcher/99 4.00 10.00
91 Brian Orakpo/99 3.00 8.00
92 Larry Fitzgerald/99 3.00 8.00
93 Beanie Wells/99 2.50 6.00
95 Darren Sproles/49 4.00 10.00
96 Frank Gore/49 4.00 10.00
97 Vernon Davis/99 2.50 6.00
98 Sam Bradford/99 2.50 6.00
100 Zach Miller/99 2.50 6.00

2012 Limited Threads Prime

*PRIME/99: .5X TO 1.2X THREAD/99
*PRIME/49: .6X TO 1.5X THREAD/99
*PRIME/49: .4X TO 1X THREAD/15-25
*PRIME/30: .5X TO 1.2X THREAD/45
*PRIME/15-25: .8X TO 2X THREAD/99
*PRIME/25: .6X TO 1.5X THREAD/49
6 Steven Jackson/25 5.00 12.00
44 Randall Cunningham/20 6.00 15.00
62 Cris Carter/49 8.00 20.00
83 Hakeem Nicks/49 4.00 10.00

2013 Limited

1-100 VETERAN PRINT RUN 349
101-150 LEGEND PRINT RUN 349
151-200 ROOKIE PRINT RUN 249
201-240 ROOKIE PRINT RUN 249
1 Carson Palmer 1.25 3.00
2 Larry Fitzgerald 1.25 3.00
3 Patrick Peterson 1.00 2.50
4 Matt Ryan 1.25 3.00
5 Julio Jones 1.50 4.00
6 Steven Jackson 1.00 2.50
7 Joe Flacco 1.25 3.00
8 Torrey Smith 1.00 2.50
9 Ray Rice 1.00 2.50
10 Steve Johnson 1.25 3.00
11 C.J. Spiller 1.00 2.50
12 Fred Jackson 1.25 3.00
13 Cam Newton 1.50 4.00
14 Brandon LaFell 1.00 2.50
15 Jonathan Stewart 1.00 2.50
16 Jay Cutler 1.00 2.50
17 Brandon Marshall 1.25 3.00
18 Matt Forte 1.00 2.50
19 Andy Dalton 1.25 3.00
20 A.J. Green 1.50 4.00
21 Jermaine Gresham 1.25 3.00
22 Brandon Weeden 1.00 2.50
23 Greg Little 1.00 2.50
24 Trent Richardson 1.00 2.50
25 Tony Romo 1.25 3.00
26 Dez Bryant 1.50 4.00
27 Miles Austin 1.00 2.50
28 DeMarco Murray 1.25 3.00
29 Peyton Manning 3.00 8.00
30 Eric Decker 1.00 2.50
31 Wes Welker 1.25 3.00
32 Demaryius Thomas 1.25 3.00
33 Matthew Stafford 1.25 3.00
34 Calvin Johnson 1.50 4.00
35 Reggie Bush 1.00 2.50
36 Brandon Pettigrew 1.00 2.50
37 Aaron Rodgers 2.50 6.00
38 Jordy Nelson 1.25 3.00
39 Randall Cobb 1.25 3.00
40 Matt Schaub 1.00 2.50
41 Andre Johnson 1.00 2.50
42 Arian Foster 1.25 3.00
43 J.J. Watt 1.25 3.00
44 Andrew Luck 2.50 6.00
45 T.Y. Hilton 1.25 3.00
46 Ahmad Bradshaw 1.00 2.50
47 Justin Blackmon 1.00 2.50
48 Cecil Shorts 1.00 2.50
49 Maurice Jones-Drew 1.00 2.50
50 Alex Smith 1.25 3.00
51 Dwayne Bowe 1.25 3.00
52 Jamaal Charles 1.25 3.00
53 Ryan Tannehill 1.25 3.00
54 Mike Wallace 1.00 2.50
55 Lamar Miller 1.00 2.50
56 Christian Ponder 1.00 2.50
57 Greg Jennings 1.00 2.50
58 Adrian Peterson 1.50 4.00
59 Tom Brady 4.00 10.00
60 Rob Gronkowski 1.50 4.00
61 Danny Amendola 1.25 3.00
62 Drew Brees 1.50 4.00
63 Jimmy Graham 1.50 4.00
64 Pierre Thomas 1.25 3.00
65 Eli Manning 1.25 3.00
66 Victor Cruz 1.25 3.00
67 David Wilson 1.00 2.50
68 Mark Sanchez 1.00 2.50
69 Jeremy Kerley 1.00 2.50
70 Chris Ivory 1.25 3.00
71 Matt Flynn 1.00 2.50
72 Jacoby Ford 1.00 2.50
73 Darren McFadden 1.25 3.00
74 Michael Vick 1.25 3.00
75 DeSean Jackson 1.25 3.00
76 LeSean McCoy 1.50 4.00
77 Ben Roethlisberger 1.50 4.00
78 Antonio Brown 1.50 4.00
79 Heath Miller 1.00 2.50
80 Philip Rivers 1.50 4.00
81 Malcom Floyd 1.00 2.50
82 Ryan Mathews 1.25 3.00
83 Colin Kaepernick 1.25 3.00
84 Anquan Boldin 1.00 2.50
85 Frank Gore 1.25 3.00
86 Russell Wilson 3.00 8.00
87 Percy Harvin 1.00 2.50
88 Marshawn Lynch 1.25 3.00
89 Sam Bradford 1.00 2.50
90 Brian Quick 1.00 2.50
91 Jared Cook 1.00 2.50
92 Josh Freeman 1.25 3.00
93 Vincent Jackson 1.00 2.50
94 Doug Martin 1.25 3.00
95 Jake Locker 1.25 3.00
96 Kendall Wright 1.00 2.50
97 Chris Johnson 1.00 2.50
98 Robert Griffin III 1.00 2.50
99 Fred Davis 1.00 2.50
100 Alfred Morris 1.00 2.50
101 Andre Rison 1.50 4.00
102 Art Monk 2.00 5.00
103 Barry Sanders 3.00 8.00
104 Bart Starr 3.00 8.00
105 Bernie Kosar 1.50 4.00
106 Bo Jackson 2.50 6.00
107 Bob Griese 2.00 5.00
108 Boomer Esiason 1.50 4.00
109 Brett Favre 4.00 10.00
110 Cris Carter 2.00 5.00
111 Dan Fouts 1.50 4.00
112 Dan Marino 4.00 10.00
113 Dave Casper 1.25 3.00
114 Deion Sanders 1.50 4.00
115 Don Maynard 1.50 4.00
116 Doug Flutie 1.50 4.00
117 Doug Williams 1.50 4.00
118 Drew Bledsoe 1.50 4.00
119 Dwight Clark 1.50 4.00
120 Ed McCaffrey 1.25 3.00
121 Eddie George 2.50 6.00
122 Edgerrin James 1.50 4.00
123 Emmitt Smith 3.00 8.00
124 Eric Dickerson 1.50 4.00
125 Fran Tarkenton 2.00 5.00
126 Franco Harris 2.00 5.00
127 Fred Taylor 1.25 3.00
128 Gale Sayers 2.00 5.00
129 Howie Long 2.00 5.00
130 Isaac Bruce 2.00 5.00
131 Jack Ham 1.50 4.00
132 Jake Plummer 1.25 3.00
133 Jay Novacek 1.50 4.00
134 Jerome Bettis 2.00 5.00
135 Jerry Rice 3.00 8.00
136 Jim Kelly 2.00 5.00
137 Jim McMahon 1.50 4.00
138 Joe Montana 6.00 15.00
139 John Elway 3.00 8.00
140 Kellen Winslow 1.25 3.00
141 Kurt Warner 1.50 4.00
142 LaDainian Tomlinson 1.50 4.00
143 Lance Alworth 1.50 4.00
144 Marshall Faulk 1.50 4.00
145 Michael Irvin 2.00 5.00
146 Shannon Sharpe 1.50 4.00
147 Shaun Alexander 1.25 3.00
148 Steve Young 2.50 6.00
149 Tim Brown 2.00 5.00
150 Walter Payton 4.00 10.00
151 Alan Bonner RC 1.25 3.00
152 Aaron Mellette RC 1.25 3.00
153 Ace Sanders RC 1.25 3.00
154 Alec Ogletree RC 1.25 3.00
155 Alex Okafor RC 1.25 3.00
156 Arthur Brown RC 1.25 3.00
157 Barkevious Mingo RC 1.25 3.00
158 Bjoern Werner RC 1.25 3.00
159 Chris Gragg RC 1.25 3.00
160 Brad Sorensen RC 1.25 3.00
161 Brice Butler RC 1.25 3.00
162 D.J. Hayden RC 1.25 3.00
163 Damontre Moore RC 1.25 3.00
164 Da'Rick Rogers RC 1.25 3.00
165 Darius Slay RC 1.25 3.00
166 Datone Jones RC 1.25 3.00
167 Dee Milliner RC 1.25 3.00
168 Desmond Trufant RC 1.25 3.00
169 Dion Sims RC 1.25 3.00
170 Cornellius Carradine RC 1.25 3.00
171 Eric Reid RC 1.50 4.00
172 Ezekiel Ansah RC 1.25 3.00
173 Jamar Taylor RC 1.25 3.00
174 Jarvis Jones RC 1.25 3.00
175 Jawan Jamison RC 1.25 3.00
176 Chance Warmack RC 1.25 3.00
177 Johnthan Banks RC 1.25 3.00
178 Josh Boyce RC 1.25 3.00
179 Kenjon Barner RC 1.25 3.00
180 Kenny Vaccaro RC 1.25 3.00
181 Kevin Minter RC 1.25 3.00
182 Dustin Hopkins RC 1.25 3.00
183 Margus Hunt RC 1.25 3.00
184 Earl Wolff RC 2.00 5.00
185 Matt Elam RC 1.25 3.00
186 Jeff Tuel RC 1.25 3.00
187 Nick Kasa RC 1.25 3.00
188 Phillip Thomas RC 1.25 3.00
189 Rex Burkhead RC 1.50 4.00
190 Justin Brown RC 2.00 5.00
191 Kenbrell Thompkins RC 2.00 5.00
192 Mychal Rivera RC 1.25 3.00
193 Latavius Murray RC 1.50 4.00
194 Jon Bostic RC 1.25 3.00
195 Robert Alford RC 1.25 3.00
196 Tavarres King RC 1.25 3.00
197 Travis Kelce RC 3.00 8.00
198 Tyler Bray RC 1.25 3.00
199 Tyrann Mathieu RC 2.00 5.00
200 Xavier Rhodes RC 1.25 3.00
201 A.Dobson JSY AU/299 RC 4.00 10.00
202 A.Ellington JSY AU/299 RC 4.00 10.00
203 C.Michael JSY AU/299 RC 4.00 10.00
204 C.Patterson JSY AU/299 RC 4.00 10.00
205 D.Hopkins JSY AU/199 RC 10.00 25.00
206 D.Robinson JSY AU/299 RC 4.00 10.00
207 D.Jordan JSY AU/299 RC 4.00 10.00
208 E.Lacy JSY AU/199 RC 4.00 10.00
209 E.Manuel JSY AU/299 RC 4.00 10.00
210 G.Escobar JSY AU/299 RC 4.00 10.00
211 G.Smith JSY AU/199 RC 4.00 10.00
212 G.Bernard JSY AU/199 RC 4.00 10.00
213 J.Franklin JSY AU/199 RC 4.00 10.00
214 Jordan Reed JSY AU/299 RC 6.00 15.00
215 J.Randle JSY AU/299 RC 4.00 10.00
216 J.Hunter JSY AU/199 RC 4.00 10.00
217 K.Allen JSY AU/199 RC 10.00 25.00
218 Kenny Stills JSY AU/199 RC 4.00 10.00
219 K.Davis JSY AU/299 RC 4.00 10.00
220 L.Jones JSY AU/199 RC 4.00 10.00
221 L.Bell JSY AU/299 RC 12.00 30.00
222 M.Te'o JSY AU/199 RC 5.00 12.00
223 M.Lattimore JSY AU/299 RC 4.00 10.00
224 M.Wheaton JSY AU/199 RC 4.00 10.00
225 M.Goodwin JSY AU/299 RC 4.00 10.00
226 M.Barkley JSY AU/199 RC 4.00 10.00
227 M.Gillislee JSY AU/299 RC 4.00 10.00
228 M.Glennon JSY AU/199 RC 4.00 10.00
229 M.Ball JSY AU/299 RC 4.00 10.00
230 Q.Patton JSY AU/299 RC 4.00 10.00
231 R.Woods JSY AU/199 RC 6.00 15.00
232 R.Nassib JSY AU/299 RC 4.00 10.00
233 S.Bailey JSY AU/299 RC 4.00 10.00
234 S.Taylor JSY AU/299 RC 4.00 10.00
235 T.Austin JSY AU/199 RC 5.00 12.00
236 T.Williams JSY AU/299 RC 4.00 10.00
237 T.Eifert JSY AU/299 RC 4.00 10.00
238 T.Wilson JSY AU/199 RC 4.00 10.00
239 V.McDonald JSY AU/299 RC 5.00 12.00
240 Z.Ertz JSY AU/299 RC 8.00 20.00

2013 Limited Gold Spotlight

*VETS/25: 1X TO 2.5X BASIC CARDS
*LEGENDS/25: 1X TO 2.5X BASIC LEG
*ROOKIES/25: .6X TO 1.5X BASIC RC
*ROOK.JSY AU: .8X TO 2X JSY AU/199-299

2013 Limited Silver Spotlight

*VETS/49: .6X TO 1.5X BASIC CARDS
*LEGENDS/49: .6X TO 1.5X BASIC LEG
*ROOKIES/49: .5X TO 1.2X BASIC RC
*ROOK.JSY AU: .6X TO 1.5X JSY AU/199-299

2013 Limited Blue Chip Jerseys

*BLUE CHIP/99: .5X TO 1.2X JUMBO/199
*BC PRIME/25: .8X TO 2X JUMBO/199

2013 Limited Field Vision

1 Robert Griffin III 2.50 6.00
2 Lamar Miller 2.50 6.00
3 Stevan Ridley 2.50 6.00
4 Terrell Suggs 2.50 6.00
5 Ed Reed 3.00 8.00
6 Jacoby Jones 2.50 6.00
7 Anquan Boldin 2.50 6.00
8 Devin Hester 3.00 8.00
9 Andre Johnson 2.50 6.00
10 Chris Johnson 2.50 6.00
11 Jonathan Stewart 2.50 6.00
12 Denarius Moore 2.50 6.00
13 Ryan Mathews 3.00 8.00
14 Dez Bryant 4.00 10.00
15 Michael Vick 3.00 8.00
16 BenJarvus Green-Ellis 3.00 8.00
17 Matt Forte 2.50 6.00
18 Josh Gordon 2.50 6.00
19 Calvin Johnson 4.00 10.00
20 Randall Cobb 3.00 8.00
21 Cam Newton 4.00 10.00
22 Ronnie Hillman 2.50 6.00
23 Mark Ingram 3.00 8.00
24 Mark Barron 3.00 8.00
25 Lavonte David 2.50 6.00
26 Patrick Peterson 2.50 6.00
27 Darnell Dockett 2.50 6.00
28 Frank Gore 3.00 8.00
29 Aldon Smith 2.50 6.00
30 Marshawn Lynch 3.00 8.00
31 Joe Haden 2.50 6.00
32 Richard Sherman 8.00 20.00
33 Mario Williams 2.50 6.00
34 Jerod Mayo 3.00 8.00
35 Antonio Cromartie 2.50 6.00
36 Joe McKnight 2.50 6.00
37 Dre Kirkpatrick 2.50 6.00
38 Antoine Bethea 2.50 6.00
39 Michael Griffin 2.50 6.00
40 Kamerion Wimbley 2.50 6.00
41 Von Miller 3.00 8.00
42 Champ Bailey 3.00 8.00
43 Derrick Johnson 2.50 6.00
44 DeAngelo Hall 2.50 6.00
45 DeAngelo Williams 2.50 6.00
46 Patrick Willis 3.00 8.00
47 Willis McGahee 2.50 6.00
48 James Jones 2.50 6.00
49 Edgerrin James 3.00 8.00
50 LaDainian Tomlinson 3.00 8.00

2013 Limited Game Day Materials

*PRIME/15-25: .6X TO 1.5X BASIC JSY/49
1 Alfred Morris/49 3.00 8.00
2 Tony Romo/49 4.00 10.00
3 Steve Johnson/49 4.00 10.00
4 Michael Vick/49 4.00 10.00
5 Julio Jones/49 5.00 12.00
7 Robert Griffin III/49 3.00 8.00
8 Ray Rice/49 3.00 8.00
9 A.J. Green/49 5.00 12.00
10 Trent Richardson/49 3.00 8.00
11 Reggie Wayne/49 4.00 10.00
13 Demaryius Thomas/49 5.00 12.00
14 Arian Foster/49 4.00 10.00
15 Jamaal Charles/49 4.00 10.00
16 Ryan Tannehill/49 4.00 10.00
17 Marques Colston/49 3.00 8.00
18 Eli Manning/49 4.00 10.00
19 Darren McFadden/49 4.00 10.00
21 Sidney Rice/49 3.00 8.00
22 Sam Bradford/49 3.00 8.00
23 Elvis Dumervil/49 3.00 8.00
24 Reggie Bush/49 3.00 8.00
25 Anquan Boldin/49 3.00 8.00

2013 Limited Groundwork Materials

*PRIME/49: .5X TO 1.2X BASIC JSY/99
*PRIME/25: .5X TO 1.2X BASIC JSY/49
1 Adrian Peterson/49 5.00 12.00
2 Alfred Morris/49 3.00 8.00
3 Arian Foster/49 4.00 10.00
4 Chris Johnson/49 3.00 8.00
5 C.J. Spiller/49 3.00 8.00
6 Darren McFadden/99 4.00 10.00
7 DeMarco Murray/49 4.00 10.00
8 Doug Martin/99 4.00 10.00
10 Jamaal Charles/99 4.00 10.00
11 DeAngelo Williams/99 3.00 8.00
12 LeSean McCoy/25 6.00 15.00
13 Robert Turbin/99 3.00 8.00
14 Matt Forte/99 3.00 8.00
15 Maurice Jones-Drew/99 3.00 8.00
16 Ray Rice/99 3.00 8.00
17 Lamar Miller/99 3.00 8.00
19 Ronnie Hillman/99 3.00 8.00
20 Trent Richardson/99 3.00 8.00

2013 Limited Inked

12 David Wilson/49
15 Austin Pettis/19
20 Ted Ginn Jr./49 4.00 10.00
22 Rashard Mendenhall/25 25.00 60.00
23 Bryce Brown/49 4.00 10.00
24 T.Y. Hilton/25 12.00 30.00
35 Vinny Testaverde/25 10.00 25.00

2013 Limited Jumbo Jerseys

*JSY NUM/20-49: .4X TO 1X JSY/20-49
*JSY NUM/49: .3X TO .8X JSY/25
*PRIME/25: .6X TO 1.5X JSY/49
*PRIME/25: .5X TO 1.2X JSY/25
1 Bo Jackson/25 12.00 30.00
2 Carl Eller/25 6.00 15.00
3 Dan Marino/49 15.00 40.00
4 Boomer Esiason/49 6.00 15.00
5 Randall Cunningham/49 8.00 20.00
6 Fred Taylor/25 6.00 15.00
7 Steve Young/49 8.00 20.00
8 John Elway/25 15.00 40.00
11 Jerry Rice/20 15.00 40.00
12 Earl Campbell/25 8.00 20.00
13 Jerome Bettis/25 15.00 40.00
14 Marvin Harrison/49 6.00 15.00
15 Warrick Dunn/49 5.00 12.00
16 Arian Foster/20 6.00 15.00
17 Kam Chancellor/25 10.00 25.00
18 Jonathan Stewart/25 5.00 12.00
19 C.J. Spiller/25 5.00 12.00
20 Roddy White/25 5.00 12.00
21 DeMarcus Ware/25 8.00 20.00
23 Janoris Jenkins/25 5.00 12.00
24 Russell Wilson/49 12.00 30.00
25 Jason Witten/25 6.00 15.00
27 Larry Fitzgerald/25 6.00 15.00
29 Peyton Manning/25 15.00 40.00
30 Robert Turbin/25 5.00 12.00

31 Miles Austin/25 5.00 12.00
34 Dwayne Bowe/25 6.00 15.00
37 Trent Richardson/49 4.00 10.00
38 Demaryius Thomas/25 6.00 15.00
39 Matthew Stafford/25 6.00 15.00

2013 Limited Matching Numbers

*PRIME/25: .6X TO 1.5X BASIC JSY/49
*POSITION/25-49: .4X TO 1X NUM/25-49
*POSIT.PRM/25: .6X TO 1.5X JSY/49
1 J.Rice/S.Largent/49 8.00 20.00
3 Griese/Cunningham/25 8.00 20.00
4 E.Campbell/T.Thomas/49 5.00 12.00
5 Eli/R.Griffin III/49 4.00 10.00
6 F.Jackson/M.Forte/49 4.00 10.00
7 Peterson/C.Johnson/49 5.00 12.00
8 D.Bowe/T.Smith/49 4.00 10.00
9 D.Bryant/H.Nicks/25 6.00 15.00
10 J.Jones/Fitzgerald/49 5.00 12.00

2013 Limited Monikers Autographs Gold

*ROOKIE/25: .6X TO 1.5X SLVR/149-199

2013 Limited Rookie Jumbo Jerseys RC Logo

*PRIME/99: .6X TO 1.5X BASIC JSY/199
1 Aaron Dobson 1.25 3.00
2 Andre Ellington 1.25 3.00
3 Christine Michael 1.25 3.00
4 Cordarrelle Patterson 1.25 3.00
5 DeAndre Hopkins 3.00 8.00
6 Denard Robinson 1.25 3.00
7 Dion Jordan 1.25 3.00
8 Eddie Lacy 1.25 3.00
9 EJ Manuel 1.25 3.00
10 Gavin Escobar 1.25 3.00
11 Geno Smith 1.25 3.00
12 Giovani Bernard 1.25 3.00
13 Johnathan Franklin 1.25 3.00
14 Jordan Reed 2.00 5.00
15 Joseph Randle 1.25 3.00
16 Justin Hunter 1.25 3.00
17 Keenan Allen 2.50 6.00
18 Kenny Stills 1.25 3.00
19 Knile Davis 1.25 3.00
20 Landry Jones 1.25 3.00
21 Le'Veon Bell 4.00 10.00
22 Manti Te'o 1.50 4.00
23 Marcus Lattimore 1.25 3.00
24 Markus Wheaton 1.25 3.00
25 Marquise Goodwin 1.25 3.00
26 Matt Barkley 1.25 3.00
27 Mike Gillislee 1.25 3.00
28 Mike Glennon 1.25 3.00
29 Montee Ball 1.25 3.00
30 Quinton Patton 3.00 8.00
31 Robert Woods 2.00 5.00
32 Ryan Nassib 1.25 3.00
33 Stedman Bailey 1.25 3.00
34 Stepfan Taylor 1.25 3.00
35 Tavon Austin 1.50 4.00
36 Terrance Williams 1.25 3.00
37 Tyler Eifert 1.25 3.00
38 Tyler Wilson 1.25 3.00
39 Vance McDonald 1.50 4.00
40 Zach Ertz 2.50 6.00

2013 Limited Star Factor

*GOLD/25: .5X TO 1.2X BASIC INSERT
1 Colin Kaepernick 2.50 6.00
2 C.J. Spiller 2.00 5.00
3 Mike Wallace 2.00 5.00
4 Tom Brady 8.00 20.00
5 Santonio Holmes 2.00 5.00
6 Ray Rice 2.00 5.00
7 A.J. Green 3.00 8.00
8 Trent Richardson 2.00 5.00
9 Antonio Brown 3.00 8.00
10 Arian Foster 2.50 6.00
11 Andrew Luck 5.00 12.00
12 Justin Blackmon 2.00 5.00
13 Chris Johnson 2.00 5.00
14 Peyton Manning 6.00 15.00
15 Jamaal Charles 2.50 6.00
16 Darren McFadden 2.50 6.00
17 Antonio Gates 2.50 6.00
18 Dez Bryant 3.00 8.00
19 Victor Cruz 2.50 6.00
20 LeSean McCoy 3.00 8.00
21 Brandon Marshall 2.50 6.00
22 Calvin Johnson 3.00 8.00
23 Aaron Rodgers 6.00 15.00
24 Adrian Peterson 3.00 8.00
25 Julio Jones 3.00 8.00
26 Cam Newton 3.00 8.00
27 Drew Brees 3.00 8.00
28 Doug Martin 2.50 6.00
29 Eli Manning 2.50 6.00
30 Sam Bradford 2.00 5.00
31 Russell Wilson 6.00 15.00
32 Robert Griffin III 2.00 5.00
33 Tony Romo 2.50 6.00
34 Ben Roethlisberger 3.00 8.00
35 Larry Fitzgerald 2.50 6.00
36 Rob Gronkowski 3.00 8.00
37 Demaryius Thomas 2.50 6.00
38 Joe Flacco 2.50 6.00
39 Marshawn Lynch 2.50 6.00
40 Matt Ryan 2.50 6.00

2013 Limited Team Trademarks Autograph Materials

3 Colin Kaepernick/25 30.00 60.00
14 Golden Tate/25 6.00 15.00
18 Jeremy Kerley/25 6.00 15.00
19 Leonard Hankerson/25
23 Lamar Miller/25

2013 Limited Threads

*PRIME/40-49: .6X TO 1.5X BASIC JSY/99
*PRIME/20-25: .8X TO 2X BASIC JSY/99
*PRIME/25: .6X TO 1.5X BASIC JSY/49
1 A.J. Green/49 5.00 12.00
2 Adrian Peterson/49 5.00 12.00
3 Alfred Morris/49 3.00 8.00
4 Andy Dalton/99 3.00 8.00
5 Antonio Gates/99 3.00 8.00
6 Arian Foster/49 4.00 10.00
7 BenJarvus Green-Ellis/99 3.00 8.00
8 Brandon Marshall/49 4.00 10.00
9 Brandon Weeden/99 2.50 6.00
10 Brent Celek/99 2.50 6.00
11 Brian Hartline/99 2.50 6.00
12 Champ Bailey/99 3.00 8.00
13 Christian Ponder/99 2.50 6.00
14 C.J. Spiller/49 3.00 8.00
15 Darren McFadden/99 3.00 8.00
16 Colin Kaepernick/25
17 Chris Johnson/49 3.00 8.00
18 Darren Sproles/49 4.00 10.00
19 Jake Locker/99 3.00 8.00
20 DeAngelo Hall/99 2.50 6.00
21 DeMarco Murray/49 4.00 10.00
22 DeMarcus Ware/99 4.00 10.00
23 Demaryius Thomas/99 3.00 8.00
25 Derrick Johnson/99 2.50 6.00
26 DeSean Jackson/99 3.00 8.00
27 Dexter McCluster/99 3.00 8.00
28 Dez Bryant/49 5.00 12.00
29 D'Qwell Jackson/99 2.50 6.00
30 Drew Brees/99 4.00 10.00
31 Dwayne Bowe/99 3.00 8.00
32 Eli Manning/99 3.00 8.00
33 Eric Berry/99 3.00 8.00
34 Eric Decker/99 2.50 6.00
35 Fred Davis/99 2.50 6.00
36 Fred Jackson/99 3.00 8.00
37 Golden Tate/99 2.50 6.00
38 Greg Little/99 2.50 6.00
39 Greg Olsen/99 3.00 8.00
40 Hakeem Nicks/49 3.00 8.00
41 Haloti Ngata/99 2.50 6.00
42 Jacob Tamme/99 2.50 6.00
43 Jamaal Charles/99 3.00 8.00
44 Jason Witten/99 3.00 8.00
45 Jay Cutler/99 2.50 6.00
46 Jeremy Kerley/99 2.50 6.00
47 Jeremy Maclin/99 2.50 6.00
48 Jermaine Gresham/99 3.00 8.00
49 Jimmy Graham/49 5.00 12.00
50 Joe Flacco/99 3.00 8.00
51 Joe Haden/99 2.50 6.00
53 Jonathan Stewart/49 3.00 8.00
54 Josh Freeman/49 4.00 10.00
55 Josh Gordon/99 2.50 6.00
56 Julio Jones/49 5.00 12.00
57 Julius Peppers/99 3.00 8.00
58 Justin Blackmon/99 2.50 6.00
59 Kenny Britt/99 2.50 6.00
61 Lance Briggs/99 3.00 8.00
62 Larry Fitzgerald/99 3.00 8.00
63 Leonard Hankerson/99 2.50 6.00
64 LeSean McCoy/49 5.00 12.00
65 Malcom Floyd/99 2.50 6.00
66 Marcedes Lewis/99 2.50 6.00
67 Marques Colston/99 2.50 6.00
68 Matt Forte/99 2.50 6.00
69 Matt Ryan/99 3.00 8.00
70 Matt Schaub/99 2.50 6.00
71 Matthew Stafford/65 3.00 8.00
72 Maurice Jones-Drew/99 2.50 6.00
73 Michael Vick/99 3.00 8.00
74 Mike Williams/99 3.00 8.00
76 Peyton Manning/99 8.00 20.00
77 Philip Rivers/99 4.00 10.00
78 Ray Rice/99 2.50 6.00
79 Reggie Wayne/99 3.00 8.00
81 Robert Meachem/99 2.50 6.00
82 Roddy White/99 2.50 6.00
83 Ronnie Hillman/99 2.50 6.00
85 Ryan Tannehill/99 3.00 8.00
86 Sam Bradford/99 2.50 6.00
87 Santonio Holmes/99 2.50 6.00
88 Sidney Rice/99 2.50 6.00
89 Steve Johnson/99 3.00 8.00
90 Steve Smith/23
91 Tamba Hali/99 2.50 6.00
92 Terrell Suggs/99 2.50 6.00
93 Toby Gerhart/99 2.50 6.00
94 Tony Moeaki/99 2.50 6.00
95 Tony Romo/99 3.00 8.00
96 Torrey Smith/99 2.50 6.00
97 Trent Richardson/99 2.50 6.00
98 Vernon Davis/99 2.50 6.00
99 Vincent Jackson/99 2.50 6.00
100 Von Miller/99 3.00 8.00

2014 Limited

1-90 STATED PRINT RUN 399
91-100 STATED PRINT RUN 99
STATED ROOKIE PRINT RUN 99-199
LEGEND AU PRINT RUN 10-25
1 Mike Williams 1.25 3.00
2 C.J. Spiller 1.00 2.50
3 EJ Manuel 1.00 2.50
4 Ryan Tannehill 1.25 3.00
5 Knowshon Moreno 1.00 2.50
6 Mike Wallace 1.00 2.50
7 Tom Brady 4.00 10.00
8 Rob Gronkowski 1.50 4.00
9 Julian Edelman 1.50 4.00
10 Geno Smith 1.00 2.50
11 Chris Ivory 1.25 3.00
12 Jeremy Kerley 1.00 2.50
13 Joe Flacco 1.25 3.00
14 Steve Smith 1.25 3.00
15 Torrey Smith 1.00 2.50
16 Andy Dalton 1.25 3.00
17 BenJarvus Green-Ellis 1.25 3.00
18 A.J. Green 1.50 4.00
19 Joe Haden 1.00 2.50
20 Jordan Cameron 1.00 2.50
21 Ben Roethlisberger 1.50 4.00
22 Le'Veon Bell 1.25 3.00
23 Antonio Brown 1.50 4.00
24 Arian Foster 1.25 3.00
25 J.J. Watt 1.50 4.00
26 Andre Johnson 1.25 3.00
27 Andrew Luck 2.00 5.00
28 Trent Richardson 1.00 2.50
29 Jake Locker 1.25 3.00
30 Cecil Shorts III 1.00 2.50
31 Jordan Todman 1.00 2.50
32 Peyton Manning 3.00 8.00
33 Julius Thomas 1.00 2.50
34 Wes Welker 1.25 3.00
35 Demaryius Thomas 1.25 3.00
36 Jamaal Charles 1.25 3.00
37 Alex Smith 1.25 3.00
38 Dwayne Bowe 1.25 3.00
39 Maurice Jones-Drew 1.00 2.50
40 Matt Schaub 1.00 2.50
41 Philip Rivers 1.50 4.00
42 Ryan Mathews 1.25 3.00
43 Antonio Gates 1.00 2.50
44 Tony Romo 1.25 3.00
45 Dez Bryant 1.50 4.00
46 Jason Witten 1.25 3.00
47 DeMarco Murray 1.25 3.00
48 Eli Manning 1.25 3.00
49 Victor Cruz 1.25 3.00
50 Nick Foles 1.25 3.00
51 LeSean McCoy 1.50 4.00
52 Jeremy Maclin 1.00 2.50
53 Robert Griffin III 1.00 2.50
54 DeSean Jackson 1.25 3.00
55 Alfred Morris 1.00 2.50
56 Jay Cutler 1.00 2.50
57 Matt Forte 1.00 2.50
58 Alshon Jeffery 1.25 3.00
59 Matthew Stafford 1.25 3.00
60 Reggie Bush 1.00 2.50
61 Calvin Johnson 1.50 4.00
62 Aaron Rodgers 3.00 8.00
63 Eddie Lacy 1.00 2.50
64 Jordy Nelson 1.25 3.00
65 Adrian Peterson 1.50 4.00
66 Greg Jennings 1.00 2.50
67 Matt Ryan 1.25 3.00
68 Julio Jones 1.50 4.00
69 Steven Jackson 1.00 2.50
70 Cam Newton 1.50 4.00
71 DeAngelo Williams 1.00 2.50
72 Drew Brees 1.50 4.00
73 Jimmy Graham 1.50 4.00
74 Pierre Thomas 1.00 2.50
75 Josh McCown 1.00 2.50
76 Doug Martin 1.25 3.00
77 Vincent Jackson 1.00 2.50
78 Carson Palmer 1.25 3.00
79 Larry Fitzgerald 1.25 3.00
80 Tyrann Mathieu 1.25 3.00
81 Sam Bradford 1.00 2.50
82 Zac Stacy 1.00 2.50
83 Tavon Austin 1.00 2.50
84 Colin Kaepernick 1.25 3.00
85 Frank Gore 1.25 3.00
86 Anquan Boldin 1.00 2.50
87 Marshawn Lynch 1.25 3.00
88 Russell Wilson 2.50 6.00
89 Doug Baldwin 1.25 3.00
90 Richard Sherman 1.50 4.00
91 Emmitt Smith 3.00 8.00
92 Steve Young 2.50 6.00
93 Brett Favre 6.00 15.00
94 John Elway 3.00 8.00
95 Dan Marino 8.00 20.00
96 Barry Sanders 3.00 8.00
97 Jerry Rice 3.00 8.00
98 Joe Namath 2.50 6.00
99 Bo Jackson 2.50 6.00
100 Terry Bradshaw 6.00 15.00
101 Aaron Donald AU RC 6.00 15.00
102 Anthony Barr AU RC 2.50 6.00
103 Bradley Roby AU RC 2.50 6.00
104 Brandon Coleman AU RC 2.50 6.00
105 Brett Smith AU RC 2.50 6.00
106 Bruce Ellington AU RC 2.50 6.00
107 C.J. Fiedorowicz AU RC 2.50 6.00
108 Cyrus Kouandjio AU RC 3.00 8.00
109 Calvin Pryor AU RC 2.50 6.00
110 Chris Borland AU RC 2.50 6.00
111 Chris Smith AU RC 2.50 6.00
112 Jace Amaro AU RC 2.50 6.00
113 Cyril Richardson AU RC 2.50 6.00
114 Darqueze Dennard AU RC 3.00 8.00
115 David Fales AU RC 2.50 6.00
116 David Yankey AU RC 2.50 6.00
117 Dee Ford AU RC 2.50 6.00
118 Michael Sam AU RC 2.50 6.00
119 Deone Bucannon AU RC 2.50 6.00
120 Devin Street AU RC 2.50 6.00
121 Dominique Easley AU RC 2.50 6.00
122 Michael Campanaro AU RC 2.50 6.00
123 Ed Reynolds AU RC 2.50 6.00
124 Greg Robinson AU RC 2.50 6.00
125 Ha Ha Clinton-Dix AU RC 3.00 8.00
126 Isaiah Crowell AU RC 3.00 8.00
127 Jake Matthews AU RC 2.50 6.00
129 James Wilder Jr. AU RC 3.00 8.00
130 Jared Abbrederis AU RC 2.50 6.00
131 Jason Verrett AU RC 2.50 6.00
132 Jeff Janis AU RC 2.50 6.00
133 Jerick McKinnon AU RC 3.00 8.00
134 Jimmie Ward AU RC 3.00 8.00
135 John Brown AU RC 4.00 10.00
137 Kevin Norwood AU RC 2.50 6.00
138 Kony Ealy AU RC 3.00 8.00
139 Kyle Fuller AU RC 2.50 6.00
140 Kyle Van Noy AU RC 3.00 8.00
141 Lache Seastrunk AU RC 2.50 6.00
142 Lamarcus Joyner AU RC 3.00 8.00
143 L'Damian Washington AU RC 3.00 8.00
144 Louis Nix III AU RC 2.50 6.00
145 Marcus Smith AU RC 2.50 6.00
146 Marion Grice AU RC 2.50 6.00
147 Ra'Shede Hageman AU RC 2.50 6.00
148 Robert Herron AU RC 2.50 6.00
150 Scott Crichton AU RC 2.50 6.00
151 Shaq Evans AU RC 2.50 6.00
152 Shayne Skov AU RC 2.50 6.00
153 Taylor Lewan AU RC 2.50 6.00
154 Telvin Smith AU RC 2.50 6.00
155 Timmy Jernigan AU RC 2.50 6.00
156 Travis Swanson AU RC 2.50 6.00
157 Trent Murphy AU RC 2.50 6.00
158 Troy Niklas AU RC 2.50 6.00
161A Xavier Su'A-Filo AU RC 3.00 8.00
161B J.Garoppolo JSY AU/199 RC 50.00 100.00
162A Antonio Andrews AU RC 2.50 6.00
162B Tom Savage JSY AU/199 RC 4.00 10.00
163A Cody Hoffman AU RC 2.50 6.00
163B L.Thomas JSY AU/199 RC 4.00 10.00
164A Tevin Reese AU RC 2.50 6.00
164B A.Murray JSY AU/199 RC 4.00 10.00
165B A.McCarron JSY AU/199 RC 4.00 10.00
166A Marcus Roberson AU RC 3.00 8.00
166B Tajh Boyd JSY AU/199 RC 4.00 10.00
167A Ahmad Dixon AU RC 2.50 6.00
167B Jeremy Hill JSY AU/199 RC 5.00 12.00
168A Yawin Smallwood AU RC 2.50 6.00
168B Carlos Hyde JSY AU/199 RC 5.00 12.00
169A Rajion Neal AU RC 2.50 6.00
169B Dri Archer JSY AU/199 RC 4.00 10.00
170A Preston Brown AU RC 2.50 6.00
170B K.Carey JSY AU/199 RC 4.00 10.00
171A Matt Hazel AU RC 2.50 6.00
171B T.West JSY AU/199 RC 4.00 10.00
172A Trevor Reilly AU RC 2.50 6.00
172B C.Sims JSY AU/199 RC 10.00 25.00
173A Mike Davis AU RC 2.50 6.00
173B A.Williams JSY AU/199 RC 4.00 10.00
174A C.J. Mosley AU RC 3.00 8.00
174B D.Freeman JSY AU/199 RC 6.00 15.00
175A Tyler Gaffney AU RC 2.50 6.00
175B D.Thomas JSY AU/199 RC 4.00 10.00
176A John Taylor AU/25 6.00 15.00
176B T.Mason JSY AU/199 RC 4.00 10.00
177A Bill Romanowski AU/25 6.00 15.00
177B B.Cooks JSY AU/199 RC 10.00 25.00
178A Chuck Foreman AU/25 8.00 20.00
178B K.Benjamin JSY AU/125 RC 6.00 15.00
179A Warren Sapp AU/25 8.00 20.00
179B A.Robinson JSY AU/199 RC 6.00 15.00
180A Tom Rathman AU/25 6.00 15.00
180B D.Adams JSY AU/199 RC 8.00 20.00
181A Charlie Joiner AU/25 6.00 15.00
181B Cody Latimer JSY AU/199 RC 5.00 12.00
182A James Lofton AU/15 6.00 15.00
182B D.Moncrief JSY AU/199 RC 4.00 10.00
183A Bruce Matthews AU/25 12.00 30.00
183B P.Richardson JSY AU/199 RC 8.00 20.00
184A Ronde Barber AU/25 6.00 15.00
184B J.Matthews JSY AU/199 RC 6.00 15.00
185A L.C. Greenwood AU/15
185B Jarvis Landry JSY AU/199 RC 8.00 20.00
186A Cris Collinsworth AU/25 8.00 20.00
186B Eric Ebron JSY AU/199 RC 6.00 15.00
187A Ron Jaworski AU/25
187B Seferian-Jnkn JSY AU/199 RC 4.00 10.00
188A Steve Bartkowski AU/25 8.00 20.00
188B C.Shaw JSY AU/149 RC 4.00 10.00
189A Herman Moore AU/25 8.00 20.00
189B Khalil Mack JSY AU/199 RC 30.00 60.00
190B Asa Watson JSY AU/199 RC 4.00 10.00
191A Vinny Testaverde AU/25 8.00 20.00
191B Johnny Manziel JSY AU/99 RC 8.00 20.00
192B Blake Bortles JSY AU/99 RC 6.00 15.00
193A Kellen Winslow AU/25 8.00 20.00
193B T.Bridgewater JSY AU/99 RC 8.00 20.00
194B Sammy Watkins JSY AU/99 RC 8.00 20.00
195A John Randle AU/15 20.00 40.00
195B Mike Evans JSY AU/99 RC 12.00 30.00
196B J.Clowney JSY AU/99 RC EX 6.00 15.00
197B Derek Carr JSY AU/99 RC 40.00 80.00
198A Paul Warfield AU/25 8.00 20.00
198B O.Beckham JSY AU/99 RC 40.00 80.00
199B Bishop Sankey JSY AU/99 RC 10.00 25.00
200A Larry Little AU/15 6.00 15.00
200B Marqise Lee JSY AU/99 RC 6.00 15.00

2014 Limited Gold Spotlight

*VETS/25: 1X TO 2.5X BASIC CARDS/399
(1-90) STATED PRINT RUN 25
(91-200) UNPRICED PRINT RUN 3-10

2014 Limited Silver Spotlight

161B Jimmy Garoppolo JSY AU/49 60.00 125.00
198B Odell Beckham Jr. JSY AU/25 60.00 120.00

2014 Limited Dual Jersey Autographs

5 D.Carr/K.Mack/25 50.00 100.00
6 G.Escobar/J.Randle/25
10 A.Seferian-Jenkins/M.Evans/15 20.00 50.00
11 A.Watson/J.Garoppolo/15 40.00 80.00
13 C.Sims/K.Carey/25 6.00 15.00
14 E.Ebron/G.Bernard/15 10.00 25.00
15 A.McCarron/E.Lacy/15 25.00 50.00
21 A.Watson/M.Glennon/15 10.00 25.00
25 C.Palmer/M.Barkley/15 10.00 25.00
28 A.Morris/J.Reed/15 12.00 30.00
29 A.Robinson/M.Lee/15 12.00 30.00
30 J.Landry/R.Tannehill/15 15.00 40.00

2014 Limited Game Day Materials

*PRIME/25: .6X TO 1.5X BASIC JSY/99
*PRIME/25: .5X TO 1.2X BASIC JSY/49
*PRIME/25: .4X TO 1X BASIC JSY/25
1 A.J. Green/99 4.00 10.00
2 Alex Smith/25 6.00 15.00
3 Alfred Morris/99 2.50 6.00
4 Tyler Eifert/99 3.00 8.00
5 Marshawn Lynch/49 4.00 10.00
6 Dez Bryant/25 8.00 20.00
7 Knowshon Moreno/99 2.50 6.00
8 Antonio Gates/49 5.00 12.00
9 Larry Fitzgerald/25 5.00 12.00
10 Matt Forte/99 4.00 10.00
11 Matthew Stafford/49 4.00 10.00
12 EJ Manuel/99 2.50 6.00
13 C.J. Spiller/99 2.50 6.00
14 Dexter McCluster/99 3.00 8.00
15 Andy Dalton/99 3.00 8.00
16 Josh Gordon/99 2.50 6.00
17 Tony Romo/49 4.00 10.00
18 Demaryius Thomas/99 3.00 8.00
19 Jacob Tamme/99 2.50 6.00
20 Anthony Fasano/99 4.00 10.00
21 Dwayne Bowe/99 3.00 8.00
22 Jamaal Charles/99 3.00 8.00
23 Mike Wallace/99 2.50 6.00
24 Joe Haden/99 2.50 6.00
25 Vontaze Burfict/99 2.50 6.00
26 Jordan Cameron/99 2.50 6.00
27 Lamar Miller/99 2.50 6.00
28 Jermaine Gresham/99 2.50 6.00
29 Brian Hartline/99 2.50 6.00
30 Richard Sherman/25 6.00 15.00
31 D'Qwell Jackson/99 2.50 6.00
32 Nate Washington/99 2.50 6.00
33 Eric Berry/99 3.00 8.00
34 Colin Kaepernick/25
35 Eric Decker/99 2.50 6.00
36 Antonio Brown/49 6.00 15.00
37 Cecil Shorts III/99 2.50 6.00
38 Justin Houston/99 2.50 6.00
39 Tamba Hali/99 3.00 8.00
40 Russell Wilson/25 10.00 25.00

2014 Limited INK Autographs

*SILVER/35-50: .5X TO 1.2X BASIC AU/75-99
*SILVER/35-50: .4X TO 1X BASIC AU/35-50
*SILVER/20-25: .5X TO 1.2X BASIC AU/35-50
*GOLD/15-25: .6X TO 1.5X BASIC AU/75-99
*GOLD/15-25: .5X TO 1.2X BASIC AU/35-50
1 Charles Clay/40 2.50 6.00
2 Adrien Robinson/50 2.50 6.00
3 Nick Toon/50 2.50 6.00
4 Dwight Jones/50 2.50 6.00
5 Cory Harkey/99 2.00 5.00
6 Pat Devlin/50 2.50 6.00
7 Dwayne Harris/50 6.00 15.00
8 Jordan Todman/50 2.50 6.00
9 Yawin Smallwood/50 2.50 6.00
10 Janoris Jenkins/50 2.50 6.00
11 Bobby Rainey/50 2.50 6.00
12 David Fales/35 2.50 6.00
13 Bradley Roby/75 2.00 5.00
14 Brandon Coleman/75 2.00 5.00
15 David Yankey/50 2.50 6.00
16 Robert Herron/50 2.50 6.00
17 Mike James/50 2.50 6.00
18 Ahmad Dixon/50 2.50 6.00
19 Louis Nix III/50 2.50 6.00
20 Lamarcus Joyner/50 3.00 8.00
21 James Wilder Jr./50 3.00 8.00
22 Jerick McKinnon/50 3.00 8.00
23 Jimmy Smith/50 2.50 6.00
24 Robert Woods/50 3.00 8.00
25 Ed Reynolds/50 2.50 6.00
26 Michael Campanaro/50 2.50 6.00
27 Isaiah Crowell/50 3.00 8.00
28 Shayne Skov/50 2.50 6.00
29 Marion Grice/50 2.50 6.00
30 Tim Benford/50 3.00 8.00
31 Jim Kiick/50 2.50 6.00
32 Eric Page/50 2.50 6.00
33 Ryan Lindley/50 4.00 10.00
34 C.J. Fiedorowicz/99 2.00 5.00
35 C.J. Mosley/50 3.00 8.00
36 Jason Verrett/50 2.50 6.00
37 Deone Bucannon/50 2.50 6.00
38 Donte Moncrief/50 2.50 6.00
40 Matt Hazel/50 2.50 6.00
41 Scott Crichton/50 2.50 6.00
42 Jeff Janis/50 2.50 6.00
43 Michael Sam/50 2.50 6.00
44 Telvin Smith/50 2.50 6.00
45 Shaq Evans/50 2.50 6.00
46 Jared Abbrederis/50 2.50 6.00
48 L'Damian Washington/99 2.50 6.00
49 Keith Wenning/50 3.00 8.00
50 Jimmie Ward/50 3.00 8.00
52 Tevin Reese/50 2.50 6.00
53 Cody Latimer/50 3.00 8.00
54 Taylor Lewan/50 2.50 6.00
55 Rob Housler/50 2.50 6.00
56 Robert Turbin/35 2.50 6.00
57 Marcus Roberson/50 3.00 8.00
58 Antonio Andrews/99 2.00 5.00
59 Trevor Reilly/50 2.50 6.00
60 Tyler Gaffney/50 2.50 6.00
61 Rajion Neal/50 2.50 6.00
62 Chris Smith/50 2.50 6.00
63 Anthony Barr/35 2.50 6.00
64 Kyle Van Noy/50 3.00 8.00
65 Keshawn Martin/50 2.50 6.00
66 Clyde Gates/50 2.50 6.00
67 D.J. Williams/50 2.50 6.00
68 Adrian Clayborn/50 2.50 6.00
69 Dion Lewis/50 2.50 6.00
70 D.D. Lewis/50 8.00 20.00
72 Chimdi Chekwa/45 2.50 6.00
75 Connor Shaw/50 2.50 6.00
76 Lorenzo Taliaferro/50 2.50 6.00
78 Pierre Desir/50 2.50 6.00
79 Mike Davis/50 2.50 6.00
80 Asa Watson/50 2.50 6.00
82 Kyle Fuller/50 2.50 6.00
83 Kony Ealy/50 3.00 8.00
84 Kevin Norwood/50 2.50 6.00
86 Khalil Mack/50 30.00 60.00
89 Cyril Richardson/50 2.50 6.00
90 Devin Street/50 10.00 25.00
92 Austin Seferian-Jenkins/35 2.50 6.00
93 Tajh Boyd/35 2.50 6.00
94 Preston Brown/50 2.50 6.00
97 Jarvis Landry/50 5.00 12.00
98 Cyrus Kouandjio/50 3.00 8.00
99 Cody Hoffman/50 2.50 6.00

2014 Limited Jerseys

1 Marshawn Lynch/25 6.00 15.00
3 Golden Tate/25 6.00 15.00
4 Carson Palmer/25 6.00 15.00
5 Drew Brees/25 8.00 20.00
6 Matt Forte/25 5.00 12.00
7 Steve Johnson/25 6.00 15.00
8 Tony Romo/25 6.00 15.00
10 Knile Davis/25 5.00 12.00
14 Will Smith/25 5.00 12.00
15 Knowshon Moreno/25 5.00 12.00
17 BenJarvus Green-Ellis/25 6.00 15.00
18 Demaryius Thomas/25 6.00 15.00
20 Paul Posluszny/25 5.00 12.00

2014 Limited Partnership Dual Materials

*SILVER/25: .6X TO 1.5X BASIC JSY/99
*SILVER/25: .5X TO 1.2X BASIC JSY/49
1 B.Bortles/M.Lee/99 2.50 6.00
2 R.Woods/S.Watkins/99 6.00 15.00
3 J.Manziel/T.West/99 3.00 8.00
4 C.Sims/M.Evans/99 5.00 12.00
5 A.McCarron/J.Hill/99 2.50 6.00
6 J.Thomas/P.Manning/99 12.00 30.00
7 L.Fitzgerald/L.Thomas/99 2.50 6.00
8 J.Manziel/M.Evans/99 5.00 12.00
9 D.Freeman/M.Ryan/99 3.00 8.00
10 C.Newton/K.Benjamin/99 3.00 8.00
11 K.Carey/M.Forte/49 2.50 6.00
12 A.McCarron/A.Dalton/99 2.50 6.00
13 C.Shaw/J.Manziel/99 3.00 8.00
14 C.Latimer/D.Thomas/99 2.50 6.00
15 E.Ebron/M.Stafford/99 2.50 6.00
16 D.Adams/E.Lacy/99 3.00 8.00
17 J.Clowney/T.Savage/99 2.50 6.00
18 A.Luck/D.Moncrief/49 5.00 12.00
19 A.Robinson/B.Bortles/99 3.00 8.00
20 A.Murray/A.Smith/99 2.50 6.00
21 D.Thomas/J.Charles/99 2.50 6.00
22 J.Landry/R.Tannehill/99 4.00 10.00
23 G.Jennings/T.Bridgewater/99 3.00 8.00
24 J.Garoppolo/T.Brady/99 15.00 40.00
25 A.Watson/J.Garoppolo/99 10.00 25.00
26 B.Cooks/M.Colston/99 2.00 5.00
27 A.Williams/O.Beckham/99 5.00 12.00
28 G.Smith/T.Boyd/99 2.00 5.00
29 D.Carr/K.Mack/99 8.00 20.00
30 J.Matthews/N.Foles/99 3.00 8.00
31 D.Archer/L.Bell/49 3.00 8.00
32 C.Hyde/F.Gore/99 2.50 6.00
33 P.Richardson/Z.Miller/99 2.50 6.00
34 T.Mason/Z.Stacy/99 2.00 5.00
35 C.Sims/D.Martin/49 3.00 8.00
36 M.Evans/V.Jackson/99 5.00 12.00
37 A.Seferian-Jenkins/M.Glennon/99 2.50 6.00
38 B.Sankey/J.Locker/99 3.00 8.00
39 D.Bryant/T.Romo/99 5.00 12.00
40 A.Morris/R.Griffin III/49 2.50 6.00
41 P.Rivers/R.Mathews/99 3.00 8.00
42 J.Flacco/T.Smith/99 2.50 6.00
43 A.Johnson/A.Foster/25 4.00 10.00
44 E.Manuel/S.Watkins/99 2.00 5.00
45 D.Moore/D.Carr/99 8.00 20.00
46 A.McCarron/A.Dalton/99 2.50 6.00
47 C.Ponder/T.Bridgewater/99 3.00 8.00
48 D.Murray/J.Randle/99 8.00 20.00
49 J.Jones/R.White/49 4.00 10.00
50 C.Johnson/G.Tate/99 10.00 25.00

2014 Limited Partnership Quad Materials

1 Bortles/Carr/Manziel/Bridge 12.00 30.00
2 Sankey/Hyde/Sims/Hill 2.50 6.00
3 Cooks/Evans/Bckhm/Watkins 5.00 12.00
4 Shaw/Manziel/Camrn/Gordon 3.00 8.00
5 Sims/Martin/Evans/Jackson 5.00 12.00
6 McCarn/Daltn/Grn-Es/Hill 2.50 6.00
7 McCarron/Garop/Thms/Svge 15.00 40.00
8 Latimer/Adams/Matthews/Lee 3.00 8.00
9 Freeman/Archer/West/Mason 3.00 8.00
10 Johnsn/Foste/Clowny/Savge 2.50 6.00
11 Lynch/Richrd/Wilson/Miller 5.00 12.00
12 Luck/Newton/Fisher/Clowney 8.00 20.00
13 Bortles/Blackmon/Lewis/Lee 2.50 6.00
14 Newtn/Olsen/Stewart/Benjmn 3.00 8.00
15 Murray/Escobar/Willms/Romo 8.00 20.00
16 Jeffery/Marshall/Cutler/Carey 5.00 12.00
17 Latimer/Thomas/Ball/Manning 12.00 30.00
18 McCarn/Dalton/Shaw/Manziel 3.00 8.00
19 Spiller/Manuel/Jckon/Watkins 3.00 8.00
20 Ivory/Decker/Kerley/Boyd 5.00 12.00

2014 Limited Partnership Triple Materials

*PRIME/25: .6X TO 1.5X TRIPLE/49-75
LP3AC Fitzgerald/Thomas/Floyd/75 2.50 6.00
LP3AF Freeman/Jones/Ryan/75 6.00 15.00
LP3BB Manuel/Woods/Watkins/75 8.00 20.00
LP3BR Flacco/Suggs/Smith/75 6.00 15.00
LP3CB Shaw/Manziel/West/75 3.00 8.00
LP3CH Marshall/Cutler/Carey/75 4.00 10.00
LP3CP Newton/Williams/Benjmn/75 8.00 20.00
LP3DC Murray/Bryant/Romo/75 10.00 25.00
LP3DL Johnson/Ebron/Stafford/75 6.00 15.00
LP3HT Johnson/Foster/Clowney/75 2.50 6.00
LP3IC Luck/Moncrief/Richrdsn/49 8.00 20.00
LP3JJ Robinson/Bortles/Lee/75 3.00 8.00
LP3KC Murray/Smith/Bowe/75 2.50 6.00
LP3MD Thomas/Landry/Tannehill/75 8.00 20.00
LP3NE Watson/Garop/Ridley/75 15.00 40.00
LP3NG Williams/Eli/Beckham/75 5.00 12.00
LP3NJ Powell/Kerley/Boyd/75 4.00 10.00
LP3NO Cooks/Brees/Thomas/75 3.00 8.00
LP3OR Moore/Carr/Jones-Drew/75 12.00 30.00
LP3PE Matthews/McCoy/Foles/75 3.00 8.00
LP3PS Brown/Archer/Polamalu/75 10.00 25.00
LP3QB Bortles/Manziel/Bridge/75 3.00 8.00
LP3SF Boldin/Hyde/Kaepernick/75 8.00 20.00
LP3SR Bradford/Austin/Mason/75 2.00 5.00
LP3SS Richrdsn/Shermn/Wilson/75 10.00 25.00
LP3TB Sefern-Jen/Sims/Evans/75 5.00 12.00
LP3TE Watsn/Sefn-Jnkns/Ebrn/75 2.50 6.00
LP3CIN Green/McCarron/Hill/75 3.00 8.00
LP3WR1 Benjamin/Evans/Watkins/75 5.00 12.00
LP3WR2 Sankey/Hill/Mason/75 2.50 6.00

2014 Limited Rookie Jerseys

*PRIME/25: .8X TO 2X BASIC JSY/99
1 Jimmy Garoppolo 2.50 6.00
2 Tom Savage 1.25 3.00
3 Logan Thomas 1.25 3.00
4 Aaron Murray 1.25 3.00
5 A.J. McCarron 1.25 3.00
6 Tajh Boyd 1.25 3.00
7 Johnny Manziel 2.00 5.00
8 Blake Bortles 1.50 4.00
9 Teddy Bridgewater 2.00 5.00
10 Derek Carr 8.00 20.00
11 Jeremy Hill 1.50 4.00
12 Carlos Hyde 1.50 4.00
13 Dri Archer 1.25 3.00
14 Ka'Deem Carey 1.25 3.00
15 Terrance West 1.25 3.00
16 Charles Sims 1.25 3.00
17 Andre Williams 1.25 3.00
18 Devonta Freeman 2.00 5.00
19 De'Anthony Thomas 1.25 3.00
20 Tre Mason 1.25 3.00
21 Bishop Sankey 1.25 3.00
22 Brandin Cooks 2.00 5.00
23 Kelvin Benjamin 2.00 5.00
24 Allen Robinson 2.00 5.00
25 Davante Adams 2.00 5.00
26 Cody Latimer 1.50 4.00
27 Donte Moncrief 1.25 3.00
28 Paul Richardson 1.50 4.00
29 Jarvis Landry 2.50 6.00
30 Sammy Watkins 2.00 5.00
31 Mike Evans 3.00 8.00
32 Odell Beckham Jr. 3.00 8.00
33 Jordan Matthews 2.00 5.00
34 Marqise Lee 1.50 4.00
35 Eric Ebron 1.50 4.00
36 Austin Seferian-Jenkins 1.25 3.00
37 Asa Watson 1.25 3.00
38 Connor Shaw 1.25 3.00
39 Khalil Mack 5.00 12.00
40 Jadeveon Clowney 1.50 4.00

2014 Limited Rookie Jerseys Autographs

1 Jimmy Garoppolo 50.00 100.00
2 Tom Savage 5.00 12.00
3 Logan Thomas 5.00 12.00
4 Aaron Murray 5.00 12.00
5 A.J. McCarron 5.00 12.00
6 Tajh Boyd 5.00 12.00
7 Johnny Manziel 15.00 40.00
8 Blake Bortles 6.00 15.00
9 Teddy Bridgewater 8.00 20.00
10 Derek Carr 30.00 80.00
11 Jeremy Hill 6.00 15.00
12 Carlos Hyde 6.00 15.00
14 Ka'Deem Carey 5.00 12.00
15 Terrance West 5.00 12.00
16 Charles Sims 5.00 12.00
17 Andre Williams 8.00 20.00
20 Tre Mason 5.00 12.00
21 Bishop Sankey 5.00 12.00
22 Brandin Cooks 8.00 20.00
23 Kelvin Benjamin
24 Allen Robinson 8.00 20.00
25 Davante Adams 8.00 20.00
26 Cody Latimer 6.00 15.00
27 Donte Moncrief 5.00 12.00
28 Paul Richardson 6.00 15.00
29 Jarvis Landry
30 Sammy Watkins 8.00 20.00
31 Mike Evans
33 Jordan Matthews 8.00 20.00
34 Marqise Lee 6.00 15.00
35 Eric Ebron 6.00 15.00
36 Austin Seferian-Jenkins 5.00 12.00
37 Asa Watson 5.00 12.00
38 Connor Shaw 5.00 12.00
39 Khalil Mack 40.00 80.00

2014 Limited Rookie Star Factor Triple Material Autographs

RSFAM A.J. McCarron/15
RSFAR Allen Robinson/25 10.00 25.00
RSFAS Austin Seferian-Jenkins/25 6.00 15.00
RSFAW Asa Watson/25 6.00 15.00
RSFAW Andre Williams/25 6.00 15.00
RSFBB Blake Bortles/25 8.00 20.00
RSFBC Brandin Cooks/25 15.00 40.00
RSFCH Carlos Hyde/25 8.00 20.00
RSFCL Cody Latimer/25 8.00 20.00
RSFCS Charles Sims/25 6.00 15.00
RSFCS Connor Shaw/25 6.00 15.00
RSFDC Derek Carr/25 30.00 60.00
RSFDM Donte Moncrief/25 6.00 15.00
RSFEE Eric Ebron/25 8.00 20.00
RSFJA Jace Amaro/25 6.00 15.00
RSFJH Jeremy Hill/25
RSFJL Jarvis Landry/25
RSFJM Jordan Matthews/25
RSFJM Johnny Manziel/25 10.00 25.00
RSFKC Ka'Deem Carey/25 6.00 15.00
RSFKM Khalil Mack/25 15.00 40.00
RSFLT Logan Thomas/25
RSFSW Sammy Watkins/25 10.00 25.00
RSFTS Tom Savage/25 6.00 15.00
RSFTW Terrance West/25 6.00 15.00

2014 Limited Rookie Threads Autographs

1 Jace Amaro/25 4.00 10.00
2 Cody Latimer/25 5.00 12.00
3 Johnny Manziel/25 6.00 15.00
5 Eric Ebron/25 5.00 12.00
6 Ka'Deem Carey/25 4.00 10.00
7 Carlos Hyde/25 5.00 12.00
8 Austin Seferian-Jenkins/25 4.00 10.00
9 Derek Carr/25
10 Teddy Bridgewater/25 6.00 15.00

2014 Limited Star Factor Triple Material

STATED PRINT RUN 15-99
*SILVER/25: .6X TO 1.5X BASIC JSY/99
*SILVER/25: .5X TO 1.2X BASIC JSY/49
SFAL Andrew Luck/15 12.00 30.00
SFBJ Bo Jackson/25 8.00 20.00
SFBS Barry Sanders/25 10.00 25.00
SFDM Dan Marino/99 12.00 30.00
SFEM Eli Manning/25 5.00 12.00
SFGB Giovani Bernard/99 2.50 6.00
SFJE John Elway/99 8.00 20.00
SFJF Joe Flacco/49 4.00 10.00
SFJJ Julio Jones/15 6.00 15.00
SFLF Larry Fitzgerald/49 4.00 10.00
SFMS Matthew Stafford/25 5.00 12.00
SFNF Nick Foles/25 5.00 12.00
SFPM Peyton Manning/99 12.00 30.00
SFPR Philip Rivers/49 5.00 12.00
SFRB Reggie Bush/49 3.00 8.00
SFRG Robert Griffin III/25 4.00 10.00
SFSM Sam Bradford/99 2.50 6.00
SFVD Vernon Davis/99 2.50 6.00
SFWW Wes Welker/99 3.00 8.00
SFDMA Doug Martin/99 3.00 8.00

2014 Limited Star Factor Triple Material Autographs

SFAG A.J. Green
SFAM Alfred Morris
SFCP Carson Palmer 20.00 40.00
SFRB Reggie Bush 8.00 20.00
SFRL Ronnie Lott 10.00 25.00
SFRS Richard Sherman 40.00 80.00

2014 Limited Threads

*PRIME/25: .6X TO 1.5X BASIC JSY/99
*PRIME/25: .5X TO 1.2X BASIC JSY/49
THAL Andrew Luck/49 6.00 15.00
THBH Brian Hartline/99 2.50 6.00
THBJ Bo Jackson/25 10.00 25.00
THBS Barry Sanders/25 10.00 25.00
THCJ Calvin Johnson/99 4.00 10.00
THDM Doug Martin/49 4.00 10.00
THEM Eli Manning/49 4.00 10.00
THES Emmitt Smith/25 10.00 25.00
THJE John Elway/99 10.00 25.00
THJF Joe Flacco/99 3.00 8.00
THJJ Julio Jones/49 5.00 12.00
THJR Jerry Rice/99 6.00 15.00
THNF Nick Foles/25 5.00 12.00
THPM Peyton Manning/99 12.00 30.00
THRG Robert Griffin III/25 4.00 10.00
THRM Ryan Mathews/49 4.00 10.00
THRW Russell Wilson/25 10.00 25.00
THSB Sam Bradford/99 2.50 6.00
THTB Tom Brady/99 12.00 30.00
THTR Tony Romo/99 3.00 8.00

2014 Limited Triple Jersey Autographs

L3TB Seferian-Jenkins/Sims/Evans/25
L3TE Watson/Seferian-Jenkins/Ebron/25 10.00 25.00
L3CIN Green/Dalton/Bernard/15 30.00 60.00

2016 Limited

1 Marvin Jones Jr. 1.00 2.50
2 Demaryius Thomas 1.25 3.00
3 Matthew Stafford 1.25 3.00
4 T.Y. Hilton 1.25 3.00
5 Ben Roethlisberger 1.50 4.00
6 Blake Bortles 1.00 2.50
7 Jonathan Stewart 1.00 2.50
8 Mark Ingram 1.25 3.00
9 J.J. Watt 1.50 4.00
10 Philip Rivers 1.50 4.00
11 Alshon Jeffery 1.25 3.00
12 Ryan Tannehill 1.25 3.00
13 Terrance West 1.00 2.50
14 Julian Edelman 1.50 4.00
15 Trevor Siemian 1.00 2.50
16 Brock Osweiler 1.00 2.50
17 Alex Smith 1.25 3.00
18 Jerry Rice 2.50 6.00
19 Jordan Reed 1.00 2.50
20 Dez Bryant 1.50 4.00
21 Carson Palmer 1.25 3.00
22 Eli Manning 1.25 3.00
23 Vincent Jackson 1.00 2.50
24 Steve Smith 1.25 3.00
25 Latavius Murray 1.00 2.50
26 Tyrod Taylor 1.25 3.00
27 Antonio Brown 1.50 4.00
28 Duke Johnson 1.00 2.50
29 Rob Gronkowski 1.50 4.00
30 Sammy Watkins 1.50 4.00
31 Jay Cutler 1.00 2.50
32 Golden Tate III 1.00 2.50
33 Marshawn Lynch 1.25 3.00
34 Julio Jones 1.50 4.00
35 Doug Martin 1.25 3.00
36 Jeremy Langford 1.25 3.00
37 Brandon Marshall 1.00 2.50
38 Terrelle Pryor 1.00 2.50
39 C.J. Anderson 1.25 3.00
40 Jeremy Hill 1.00 2.50
41 Keenan Allen 1.25 3.00
42 A.J. Green 1.50 4.00
43 Tony Romo 1.25 3.00
44 Greg Olsen 1.25 3.00
45 Jeremy Kerley 1.00 2.50
46 Barry Sanders 2.50 6.00
47 Steve Young 2.00 5.00
48 Ryan Mathews 1.25 3.00
49 Matt Ryan 1.25 3.00
50 Drew Brees 1.50 4.00
51 Antonio Gates 1.00 2.50
52 Allen Robinson 1.25 3.00
53 Odell Beckham Jr. 1.50 4.00
54 Kirk Cousins 1.50 4.00
55 Tom Brady 4.00 10.00
56 DeMarco Murray 1.25 3.00
57 Jason Witten 1.25 3.00
58 David Johnson 1.50 4.00
59 Brandin Cooks 1.25 3.00
60 Joe Namath 2.00 5.00
61 LeSean McCoy 1.50 4.00
62 Le'Veon Bell 1.25 3.00
63 Aaron Rodgers 3.00 8.00
64 Tavon Austin 1.00 2.50
65 Stefon Diggs 1.25 3.00
66 Brett Favre 3.00 8.00
67 Frank Gore 1.25 3.00
68 DeSean Jackson 1.25 3.00
69 Andrew Luck 2.00 5.00
70 Jeremy Maclin 1.00 2.50
71 Jameis Winston 1.50 4.00
72 Jordy Nelson 1.25 3.00
73 Gary Barnidge 1.00 2.50
74 Jamaal Charles 1.25 3.00
75 Peyton Manning 3.00 8.00
76 Jordan Matthews 1.25 3.00
77 Todd Gurley II 1.50 4.00
78 DeAndre Hopkins 1.25 3.00
79 Marcus Mariota 1.50 4.00
80 Cam Newton 1.50 4.00
81 Delanie Walker 1.00 2.50
82 Richard Sherman 1.50 4.00
83 Matt Forte 1.00 2.50
84 Johnny Unitas 2.50 6.00
85 Eddie Lacy 1.00 2.50
86 Joe Flacco 1.25 3.00
87 Larry Fitzgerald 1.25 3.00
88 Amari Cooper 1.50 4.00
89 Dan Marino 3.00 8.00
90 Sam Bradford 1.00 2.50
91 Ray Lewis 1.50 4.00
92 Adrian Peterson 1.50 4.00
93 Terry Bradshaw 2.00 5.00
94 Andy Dalton 1.25 3.00
95 Devonta Freeman 1.25 3.00
96 Derek Carr 1.50 4.00
97 Russell Wilson 2.00 5.00
98 Allen Hurns 1.00 2.50
99 Jarvis Landry 1.25 3.00
100 Darrelle Revis 1.00 2.50
101 Connor Cook JSY AU/149 RC 4.00 10.00
102 Pharoh Cooper JSY AU/299 RC 3.00 8.00
103 Derrick Henry JSY AU/149 RC 8.00 20.00
104 Tyler Boyd JSY AU/299 RC 4.00 10.00
105 Jared Goff JSY AU/149 RC 40.00 80.00
106 Jordan Howard JSY AU/299 RC 12.00 30.00
107 Alex Collins JSY AU/299 RC 4.00 10.00
108 Kenyan Drake JSY AU/299 RC 5.00 12.00
109 Carson Wentz JSY AU/149 RC 50.00 100.00
110 Michael Thomas JSY AU/299 RC 6.00 15.00
111 Corey Coleman JSY AU/299 RC 5.00 12.00
112 Ricardo Louis JSY AU/299 RC 3.00 8.00
113 Devontae Booker JSY AU/299 RC 4.00 10.00
114 Tyler Ervin JSY AU/299 RC 3.00 8.00
115 DeAndre Washington JSY AU/299 RC 3.00 8.00
116 Josh Doctson JSY AU/299 RC 4.00 10.00
117 Braxton Miller JSY AU/299 RC 3.00 8.00
118 Kevin Hogan JSY AU/299 RC 4.00 10.00
119 Chris Moore JSY AU/299 RC 4.00 10.00
120 Moritz Bohringer JSY AU/299 RC 3.00 8.00
121 Dak Prescott JSY AU/299 RC 50.00 100.00
122 Sterling Shepard JSY AU/299 RC 4.00 10.00
123 Ezekiel Elliott JSY AU/149 RC 60.00 125.00
124 Wendell Smallwood JSY AU/299 RC 3.00 8.00
125 Joey Bosa JSY AU/299 RC 6.00 15.00
126 Keenan Reynolds JSY AU/299 RC 4.00 10.00
127 C.J. Prosise JSY AU/299 RC 3.00 8.00
128 Laquon Treadwell JSY AU/299 RC 4.00 10.00
129 Christian Hackenberg JSY AU/299 RC 3.00 8.00
130 Paul Perkins JSY AU/299 RC 3.00 8.00
131 Demarcus Robinson JSY AU/299 RC 3.00 8.00
132 Trevor Davis JSY AU/299 RC 3.00 8.00
133 Hunter Henry JSY AU/299 RC 4.00 10.00
134 Will Fuller V JSY AU/299 RC 5.00 12.00
135 Jonathan Williams JSY AU/299 RC 4.00 10.00
136 Kenneth Dixon JSY AU/299 RC 3.00 8.00
137 Cardale Jones JSY AU/299 RC 3.00 8.00
138 Leonte Carroo JSY AU/299 RC 3.00 8.00
139 Cody Kessler JSY AU/299 RC 3.00 8.00
140 Paxton Lynch JSY AU/149 RC 3.00 8.00
142 Jacoby Brissett AU/99 3.00 8.00
143 Jalen Ramsey AU/99 RC 4.00 10.00
144 Vernon Hargreaves III AU/99 RC 4.00 10.00
146 Blake Martinez AU/99 RC 3.00 8.00
148 Jeff Driskel AU/99 RC 2.50 6.00
149 Kenny Lawler AU/99 RC 4.00 10.00
150 Eli Apple AU/99 RC 3.00 8.00
151 Mackensie Alexander AU/99 RC 2.50 6.00
152 Jake Rudock AU/99 RC 2.50 6.00
153 Aaron Green AU/99 RC 2.50 6.00
154 A'Shawn Robinson AU/99 RC 2.50 6.00
155 Cody Core AU/99 RC 2.50 6.00
156 Brandon Allen AU/99 RC 2.50 6.00
157 Brandon Doughty AU/99 RC 2.50 6.00
158 Byron Marshall AU/99 RC 2.50 6.00
160 James Bradberry AU/45 RC 4.00 10.00
161 Jeremy Cash AU/99 RC 3.00 8.00
162 Keanu Neal AU/99 RC 2.50 6.00
163 KeiVarae Russell AU/99 RC 2.50 6.00
164 Kendall Fuller AU/99 RC 3.00 8.00
165 Nate Sudfeld AU/99 RC 2.50 6.00
166 Nick Vannett AU/99 RC 2.50 6.00
167 Reggie Ragland AU/99 RC 2.50 6.00
168 Darron Lee AU/99 RC 2.50 6.00
169 Su'a Cravens AU/99 RC 2.50 6.00
170 Vonn Bell AU/99 RC 3.00 8.00
171 Xavien Howard AU/99 RC 3.00 8.00
172 Myles Jack AU/99 RC 3.00 8.00
175 Austin Johnson AU/99 RC 2.50 6.00
170 Daniel Braverman AU/99 RC 2.50 6.00

178 Glenn Gronkowski AU/99 RC 2.50 6.00
179 Jaylon Smith AU/99 RC 2.50 6.00
180 Roberto Aguayo AU/99 RC 2.50 6.00
181 Jordan Payton AU/99 RC 2.50 6.00
183 Keyarris Garrett AU/99 RC 2.50 6.00
185 Shilique Calhoun AU/99 RC 2.50 6.00
186 Thomas Duarte AU/99 RC 2.50 6.00
187 Yannick Ngakoue AU/99 RC 4.00 10.00
188 Charone Peake AU/50 RC 3.00 8.00
189 Daryl Worley AU/99 RC 2.50 6.00
190 Emmanuel Ogbah AU/99 RC 3.00 8.00
191 Jalen Mills AU/99 RC 3.00 8.00
192 Jalin Marshall AU/99 RC 4.00 10.00
193 Keith Marshall AU/99 RC 2.50 6.00
194 Malcolm Mitchell AU/99 5.00 12.00
195 Maliek Collins AU/99 RC 2.50 6.00
197 Tajae Sharpe AU/99 3.00 8.00
198 Leonard Floyd AU/99 RC 3.00 8.00
199 D.J. White AU/99 RC 2.50 6.00
200 Kevin Byard AU/99 RC 2.50 6.00
201 Jacoby Brissett JSY AU/299 RC 10.00 25.00
202 Malcolm Mitchell JSY AU/299 RC 12.00 30.00
203 Tajae Sharpe JSY AU/299 RC 4.00 10.00

2016 Limited Gold Spotlight

*VETS/49: .8X TO 2X BASIC CARDS
*RC JSY AU/25: 1X TO 2.5X BASIC JSY AU/149-299
*RC AU/25: .6X TO 1.5X BASIC AU/99
121 Dak Prescott JSY AU 125.00 250.00
123 Ezekiel Elliott JSY AU 125.00 250.00

2016 Limited Silver Spotlight

*VETS/99: .6X TO 1.5X BASIC CARDS
*RC JSY AU/49: .8X TO 2X BASIC JSY AU/149-299
*RC AU/35: .5X TO 1.2X BASIC AU/99
121 Dak Prescott JSY AU 60.00 125.00
123 Ezekiel Elliott JSY AU 100.00 200.00

2016 Limited Draft Day Signatures Materials

1 Jack Conklin 8.00 20.00
2 Laquon Treadwell 6.00 15.00
3 Vernon Hargreaves III 8.00 20.00
4 Shaq Lawson 5.00 12.00
5 Eli Apple 6.00 15.00
6 Vernon Butler 5.00 12.00
7 Taylor Decker 6.00 15.00
8 Ezekiel Elliott 125.00 250.00
9 Laremy Tunsil 5.00 12.00
10 Darron Lee 5.00 12.00
11 Joey Bosa 25.00 50.00
12 Robert Nkemdiche 6.00 15.00
13 Corey Coleman 8.00 20.00
14 Jalen Ramsey 12.00 30.00
15 Josh Doctson 12.00 30.00
16 Jared Goff 30.00 80.00
17 Carson Wentz 75.00 150.00
18 Keanu Neal 5.00 12.00

2016 Limited Ink

*SILVER/35: .4X TO 1X BASIC AU/49
*GOLD/25: .5X TO 1.2X BASIC AU/49
2 Manti Te'o/25 8.00 20.00
3 Dan Hampton/25 8.00 20.00
5 Jace Amaro/49 6.00 15.00
7 Charcandrick West/49 6.00 15.00
9 Kony Ealy/49 6.00 15.00
10 Mike Evans/25 10.00 25.00
11 Ron Jaworski/25 10.00 25.00
13 Phil McConkey/49 8.00 20.00
15 Cameron Artis-Payne/49 6.00 15.00
17 John Hannah/49 6.00 15.00
19 Jim Kiick/49 6.00 15.00
20 Marqise Lee/25 8.00 20.00
21 Malcolm Smith/25 12.00 30.00
23 Dave Wilcox/49 6.00 15.00
25 Carl Eller/49 6.00 15.00
27 Steve Grogan/49 6.00 15.00
28 Lance Briggs/25 10.00 25.00
29 Brian Mitchell/49 6.00 15.00
30 Bob Lilly/25 10.00 25.00
31 Don Majkowski/25 10.00 25.00
33 Charlie Joiner/49 6.00 15.00
37 Troy Brown/49 6.00 15.00
38 Champ Bailey/25 10.00 25.00
39 Delvin Breaux/49 8.00 20.00
40 Latavius Murray/25 8.00 20.00

2016 Limited Monikers

*SILVER/25: .5X TO 1.2X BASIC AU/49
*GOLD/15: .6X TO 1.5X BASIC AU/49
1 Brandin Cooks/25 10.00 25.00
3 Joe Theismann/25 12.00 30.00
5 Ozzie Newsome/25 10.00 25.00
7 Julius Thomas/49 6.00 15.00
9 Troy Brown/49 6.00 15.00
11 Mike Evans/25 10.00 25.00
13 Paul Warfield/25 10.00 25.00
19 Charcandrick West/49 6.00 15.00
21 Antonio Freeman/25 10.00 25.00
25 Allen Hurns/49 6.00 15.00
27 Ickey Woods/49 6.00 15.00
29 Jim Kiick/49 6.00 15.00
MTE Tyler Eifert/25

2016 Limited Partnership Dual Autographs

1 P.Perkins/S.Shepard/25 12.00 30.00
2 S.Lawson/R.Ragland/49 8.00 20.00
3 K.Reynolds/K.Dixon/49 10.00 25.00
4 J.Ramsey/M.Jack/49 12.00 30.00
5 S.Calhoun/J.Ward/49 8.00 20.00
7 K.Fuller/S.Cravens/49 10.00 25.00
9 D.Robinson/K.Hogan/49 10.00 25.00
11 H.Henry/J.Bosa/25 20.00 50.00
12 C.Nassib/E.Ogbah/49 10.00 25.00
14 C.Jones/K.Russell/49 12.00 30.00
15 N.Spence/V.Hargreaves III/49 8.00 20.00
17 C.Jones/J.Williams/25 12.00 30.00
19 L.Carroo/K.Drake/49 12.00 30.00
21 A.Collins/C.Prosise/25 12.00 30.00
22 J.Smith/M.Collins/49 8.00 20.00
24 J.Brissett/M.Mitchell/49 10.00 25.00
25 A.Johnson/K.Dodd/49 8.00 20.00
27 D.Prescott/E.Elliott/25 150.00 300.00
29 M.Bohringer/L.Treadwell/25 12.00 30.00
30 J.Hannah/S.Grogan/49 8.00 20.00

2016 Limited Rookie Phenoms Jerseys

*SILVER/49: .5X TO 1.2X BASIC JSY/99
*GOLD/25: .6X TO 1.5X BASIC JSY/99
1 Paxton Lynch 2.00 5.00
2 Derrick Henry 5.00 12.00
3 Tyler Boyd 2.50 6.00
4 Jared Goff 6.00 15.00
5 Jordan Howard 4.00 10.00
6 Alex Collins 2.50 6.00
7 Kenyan Drake 3.00 8.00
8 Carson Wentz 8.00 20.00
9 Connor Cook 2.50 6.00
10 Pharoh Cooper 2.00 5.00
11 Devontae Booker 2.50 6.00
12 Tyler Ervin 2.00 5.00
13 DeAndre Washington 2.00 5.00
14 Josh Doctson 2.50 6.00
15 Braxton Miller 2.00 5.00
16 Kevin Hogan 2.50 6.00
17 Chris Moore 2.50 6.00
18 Michael Thomas 4.00 10.00
19 Corey Coleman 3.00 8.00
20 Ricardo Louis 2.00 5.00
21 Ezekiel Elliott 10.00 25.00
22 Wendell Smallwood 2.00 5.00
23 Joey Bosa 4.00 10.00
24 Keenan Reynolds 2.50 6.00
25 C.J. Prosise 2.00 5.00
26 Laquon Treadwell 2.50 6.00
27 Christian Hackenberg 2.00 5.00
[illegible]

29 Dak Prescott 10.00 25.00
30 Sterling Shepard 2.50 6.00
31 Hunter Henry 2.50 6.00
32 Will Fuller V 3.00 8.00
33 Jonathan Williams 2.50 6.00
34 Kenneth Dixon 2.00 5.00
35 Cardale Jones 2.00 5.00
36 Leonte Carroo 2.00 5.00
37 Cody Kessler 2.00 5.00
38 Paul Perkins 2.00 5.00
39 Demarcus Robinson 2.00 5.00
40 Trevor Davis 2.00 5.00

2016 Limited Spotlight Jerseys

*PRIME/25: .6X TO 1.5X BASIC JSY/125
1 Matt Ryan/49 3.00 8.00
2 Rod Woodson/49 3.00 8.00
3 Deion Sanders/49 3.00 8.00
4 Edgerrin James/49 3.00 8.00
5 Earl Campbell/49 4.00 10.00
6 Joe Flacco/49 3.00 8.00
7 Carson Wentz/125 20.00 50.00
8 Jordan Reed/49 2.50 6.00
9 Derrick Henry/125 5.00 12.00
10 Marshall Faulk/49 3.00 8.00
11 Rob Gronkowski/25 5.00 12.00
12 Brett Favre/25 10.00 25.00
13 Warren Moon/49 4.00 10.00
14 Dak Prescott/125 10.00 25.00
15 Jared Goff/125 12.00 30.00
16 Corey Coleman/125 3.00 8.00
17 Ezekiel Elliott/125 10.00 25.00
18 LaDainian Tomlinson/49 3.00 8.00
19 Paxton Lynch/125 2.00 5.00
20 Matthew Stafford/25 4.00 10.00

2016 Limited Star Factor Swatches

*PRIME/25: .6X TO 1.5X BASIC JSY/99-125
1 Jason Witten/49 3.00 8.00
2 Adrian Peterson/25 5.00 12.00
3 Julio Jones/25 5.00 12.00
4 Antonio Brown/25 5.00 12.00
5 Marvin Harrison/49 3.00 8.00
6 Buck Allen/99 2.00 5.00
7 Demaryius Thomas/49 3.00 8.00
8 Rob Gronkowski/25 5.00 12.00
9 Tim Tebow/49 4.00 10.00
10 Edgerrin James/49 3.00 8.00
11 Jeremy Hill/99 2.00 5.00
12 Jared Goff/125 6.00 15.00
13 Lance Briggs/49 3.00 8.00
14 Ben Roethlisberger/25 5.00 12.00
15 Matthew Stafford/25 4.00 10.00
16 Cam Newton/25 5.00 12.00
17 Carson Wentz/125 8.00 20.00
18 DeSean Jackson/49 3.00 8.00
19 Von Miller/49 3.00 8.00
20 Ezekiel Elliott/125 10.00 25.00
21 Emmanuel Sanders/49 4.00 10.00
22 Amari Cooper/99 3.00 8.00
23 LeSean McCoy/49 4.00 10.00
24 Boomer Esiason/99 2.50 6.00
25 Drew Brees/25 5.00 12.00
26 Darrelle Revis/25 3.00 8.00
27 Stefon Diggs/99 2.50 6.00
28 Fred Dryer/99 2.00 5.00
29 Tyler Eifert/99 2.50 6.00
30 Joe Flacco/25 4.00 10.00
31 Geno Atkins/99 2.00 5.00
32 Andrew Luck/25 6.00 15.00
33 Mark Ingram/25 4.00 10.00
34 Brett Favre/25 10.00 25.00
35 Peyton Manning/25 10.00 25.00
36 Darren Sproles/49 3.00 8.00
37 Dak Prescott/125 10.00 25.00
38 Ryan Tannehill/49 3.00 8.00
39 Jarvis Landry/99 2.50 6.00
40 Dez Bryant/49 4.00 10.00

2016 Limited Team Trademark Signatures

*SILVER/35: .4X TO 1X BASIC AU/49
*GOLD/25: .5X TO 1.2X BASIC AU/49
1 Charlie Joiner/49 6.00 15.00
3 Steve Grogan/49 6.00 15.00
5 Andre Reed/25 15.00 40.00
7 Ron Jaworski/25 10.00 25.00
9 Don Majkowski/49 8.00 20.00
11 Carl Eller/49 6.00 15.00
13 John Hannah/49 6.00 15.00
14 Jeremy Hill/25 8.00 20.00
15 Nelson Agholor/25 8.00 20.00
19 Dan Hampton/49 6.00 15.00
TSES Emmanuel Sanders/25

2016 Limited Threads

*PRIME/25: .6X TO 1.5X BASIC JSY/99-125
*PRIME/25: .5X TO 1.2X BASIC JSY/49
*PRIME/15: .8X TO 2X BASIC JSY/99
1 Tim Brown/99 3.00 8.00
2 Nelson Agholor/99 2.00 5.00
3 Jameis Winston/49 4.00 10.00
4 A.J. Green/49 4.00 10.00
5 John Kuhn/49 2.50 6.00
6 Andy Dalton/49 3.00 8.00
7 Marshall Faulk/25 4.00 10.00
8 Jared Goff/125 6.00 15.00
9 Ray Lewis/25 5.00 12.00
10 DeAngelo Hall/49 3.00 8.00
11 Todd Gurley II/99 3.00 8.00
12 Eli Manning/25 4.00 10.00
13 Jay Cutler/49 2.50 6.00
14 Carson Wentz/125 8.00 20.00
15 Ezekiel Elliott/125 10.00 25.00
16 Antonio Gates/49 2.50 6.00
17 Matt Ryan/25 4.00 10.00
18 C.J. Anderson/49 3.00 8.00
19 Russell Wilson/49 5.00 12.00
20 Derek Carr/49 4.00 10.00
21 Tony Romo/49 3.00 8.00
22 Eric Decker/49 2.50 6.00
23 Jeremy Langford/99 2.50 6.00
24 Allen Robinson/99 2.50 6.00
25 Larry Fitzgerald/49 3.00 8.00
26 Blake Bortles/99 2.00 5.00
27 Michael Strahan/49 3.00 8.00
28 Champ Bailey/99 2.50 6.00
29 Sammy Watkins/99 3.00 8.00
30 Devonta Freeman/99 2.50 6.00
31 Vontaze Burfict/99 2.00 5.00
32 Jadeveon Clowney/99 2.00 5.00
33 Jerome Bettis/49 4.00 10.00
34 Ameer Abdullah/99 2.00 5.00
35 Marcus Mariota/49 4.00 10.00
36 Brandin Cooks/99 2.50 6.00
37 Odell Beckham Jr./99 3.00 8.00
38 T.Y. Hilton/99 2.50 6.00
39 Dak Prescott/125 10.00 25.00
40 Donte Moncrief/99 2.50 6.00

2017 Limited

1 Joe Flacco 1.25 3.00
2 Terrell Suggs 1.00 2.50
3 Ray Lewis 1.50 4.00
4 Andy Dalton 1.25 3.00
5 A.J. Green 1.50 4.00
6 Ickey Woods 1.00 2.50
7 Isaiah Crowell 1.00 2.50
8 Jamie Collins 1.00 2.50
9 Jeff Garcia 1.00 2.50
10 Antonio Brown 1.50 4.00
11 Le'Veon Bell 1.25 3.00
12 Ben Roethlisberger 1.50 4.00
13 Heath Miller 1.00 2.50
14 J.J. Watt 1.50 4.00
15 DeAndre Hopkins 1.25 3.00
16 Ed Reed 1.25 3.00
[illegible]
18 T.Y. Hilton 1.25 3.00
19 Peyton Manning 3.00 8.00
20 Blake Bortles 1.00 2.50
21 Jalen Ramsey 1.00 2.50
22 Mark Brunell 1.25 3.00
23 Marcus Mariota 1.50 4.00
24 DeMarco Murray 1.25 3.00
25 Earl Campbell 1.50 4.00
26 Tyrod Taylor 1.25 3.00
27 LeSean McCoy 1.50 4.00
28 Jim Kelly 1.50 4.00
29 Jay Cutler 1.00 2.50
30 Jarvis Landry 1.25 3.00
31 Dan Marino 3.00 8.00
32 Tom Brady 4.00 10.00
33 Rob Gronkowski 1.50 4.00
34 Brandin Cooks 1.25 3.00
35 Tedy Bruschi 1.50 4.00
36 Matt Forte 1.00 2.50
37 Jermaine Kearse 1.00 2.50
38 Joe Namath 2.00 5.00
39 Von Miller 1.25 3.00
40 Emmanuel Sanders 1.50 4.00
41 John Elway 2.50 6.00
42 Travis Kelce 1.50 4.00
43 Alex Smith 1.25 3.00
44 Joe Montana 4.00 10.00
45 Philip Rivers 1.50 4.00
46 Melvin Gordon 1.25 3.00
47 Dan Fouts 1.25 3.00
48 Derek Carr 1.50 4.00
49 Marshawn Lynch 1.25 3.00
50 Amari Cooper 1.50 4.00
51 Jerry Rice 2.50 6.00
52 Jordan Howard 1.50 4.00
53 Leonard Floyd 1.00 2.50
54 Brian Urlacher 1.50 4.00
55 Matthew Stafford 1.25 3.00
56 Marvin Jones Jr. 1.00 2.50
57 Calvin Johnson 1.50 4.00
58 Aaron Rodgers 3.00 8.00
59 Clay Matthews 1.25 3.00
60 Brett Favre 3.00 8.00
61 Stefon Diggs 1.25 3.00
62 Harrison Smith 1.00 2.50
63 Randy Moss 1.25 3.00
64 Matt Ryan 1.25 3.00
65 Julio Jones 1.50 4.00
66 Michael Vick 1.25 3.00
67 Cam Newton 1.50 4.00
68 Luke Kuechly 1.25 3.00
69 Steve Smith 1.25 3.00
70 Drew Brees 1.50 4.00
71 Mark Ingram 1.25 3.00
72 Morten Andersen 1.00 2.50
73 Jameis Winston 1.25 3.00
74 Mike Evans 1.25 3.00
75 Warren Sapp 1.25 3.00
76 Dak Prescott 1.50 4.00
77 Ezekiel Elliott 2.00 5.00
78 Jason Witten 1.25 3.00
79 Troy Aikman 2.00 5.00
80 Eli Manning 1.25 3.00
81 Odell Beckham Jr. 1.50 4.00
82 Lawrence Taylor 1.50 4.00
83 Carson Wentz 2.00 5.00
84 Alshon Jeffery 1.25 3.00
85 Ron Jaworski 1.25 3.00
86 Kirk Cousins 1.50 4.00
87 Josh Norman 1.00 2.50
88 John Riggins 1.25 3.00
89 Larry Fitzgerald 1.25 3.00
90 Carson Palmer 1.25 3.00
91 Kurt Warner 1.25 3.00
92 Todd Gurley II 1.50 4.00
93 Aaron Donald 1.50 4.00
94 Marshall Faulk 1.25 3.00
95 Carlos Hyde 1.00 2.50
96 Pierre Garcon 1.25 3.00
97 Joe Montana 4.00 10.00
98 Russell Wilson 2.00 5.00
99 Richard Sherman 1.50 4.00
100 Steve Largent 1.50 4.00
101 Alvin Kamara JSY AU/299 RC 25.00 50.00
102 Amara Darboh JSY AU/299 RC 3.00 8.00
103 ArDarius Stewart JSY AU/299 RC 3.00 8.00
104 C.J. Beathard JSY AU/299 RC 3.00 8.00
105 Carlos Henderson JSY AU/299 RC 3.00 8.00
106 Chris Godwin JSY AU/299 RC 4.00 10.00
107 Christian McCaffrey JSY AU 225 RC EXCH 25.00 50.00
108 Cooper Kupp JSY AU/299 RC 5.00 12.00
109 Corey Davis JSY AU/299 RC EXCH 5.00 12.00
110 Curtis Samuel JSY AU/299 RC 4.00 10.00
111 Dalvin Cook JSY AU/225 RC EXCH 20.00 50.00
112 Davis Webb JSY AU/299 RC 3.00 8.00
113 Dede Westbrook JSY AU/299 RC EXCH 3.00 8.00
114 Deshaun Watson JSY AU/149 RC 50.00 100.00
115 DeShone Kizer JSY AU/149 RC 3.00 8.00
116 D'Onta Foreman JSY AU/299 RC 4.00 10.00
117 Evan Engram JSY AU/299 RC EXCH 4.00 10.00
118 Jamaal Williams JSY AU/299 RC EXCH 3.00 8.00
119 James Conner JSY AU/299 RC 10.00 25.00
120 Jeremy McNichols JSY AU/299 RC 3.00 8.00
121 Joe Mixon JSY AU/299 RC 6.00 15.00
122 Joe Williams JSY AU/299 RC 3.00 8.00
123 John Ross III JSY AU/299 RC 4.00 10.00
124 Josh Reynolds JSY AU/299 RC 3.00 8.00
125 R. Joshua Dobbs JSY AU/299 RC EXCH 4.00 10.00
126 JuJu Smith-Schuster JSY AU/299 RC 15.00 40.00
127 Kareem Hunt JSY AU/299 RC EXCH 10.00 25.00
128 Kenny Golladay JSY AU/299 RC 5.00 12.00
129 Leonard Fournette JSY AU/149 RC EXCH 30.00 60.00
130 Mack Hollins JSY AU/299 RC EXCH 3.00 8.00
131 Marlon Mack JSY AU/299 RC 5.00 12.00
132 Mike Williams JSY AU/199 RC 5.00 12.00
133 Mitchell Trubisky JSY AU/149 RC 50.00 100.00
134 Nathan Peterman JSY AU/299 RC 4.00 10.00
135 O.J. Howard JSY AU/299 RC 4.00 10.00
136 Patrick Mahomes II JSY AU/149 RC 250.00 500.00
137 Samaje Perine JSY AU/299 RC 3.00 8.00
138 Taywan Taylor JSY AU/299 RC 3.00 8.00
139 Wayne Gallman JSY AU/299 RC 4.00 10.00
140 Zay Jones JSY AU/299 RC EXCH 4.00 10.00
142 Justin Evans AU/99 RC 2.50 6.00
143 Jonnu Smith AU/99 RC 2.50 6.00
144 Jarrad Davis AU/99 RC 3.00 8.00
145 Tarik Cohen AU/99 RC 5.00 12.00
146 Chidobe Awuzie AU/99 RC 3.00 8.00
147 Charles Harris AU/99 RC 2.50 6.00
148 Josh Malone AU/99 RC 2.50 6.00
149 T.J. Watt AU/99 RC 8.00 20.00
150 Donnel Pumphrey AU/99 RC 3.00 8.00
151 Solomon Thomas AU/99 RC 2.50 6.00
152 Quincy Wilson AU/99 RC 2.50 6.00
153 Ryan Switzer AU/99 RC 3.00 8.00
154 Gareon Conley AU/99 RC 2.50 6.00
155 Jehu Chesson AU/25 RC 5.00 12.00
156 Jamal Adams AU/99 RC 2.50 6.00
159 Jake Butt AU/99 RC 3.00 8.00
160 Jabrill Peppers AU/49 RC 5.00 12.00
161 Zach Cunningham AU/99 RC 3.00 8.00
162 George Kittle AU/99 RC 6.00 15.00
163 Marshon Lattimore AU/99 RC 3.00 8.00
164 Chris Carson AU/99 RC 4.00 10.00
165 Jordan Leggett AU/99 RC 2.50 6.00
167 Jeremy Sprinkle AU/99 RC 2.50 6.00
168 Brian Hill AU/99 RC 2.50 6.00
169 Haason Reddick AU/99 RC 2.50 6.00
170 Budda Baker AU/99 RC 2.50 6.00
171 Shelton Gibson AU/99 RC 2.50 6.00
172 Tre'Davious White AU/99 RC 2.50 6.00
174 Raekwon McMillan AU/99 RC 2.50 6.00
175 Isaiah McKenzie AU/99 RC 2.50 6.00
177 DeAngelo Yancey AU/99 RC 2.50 6.00
178 Trent Taylor AU/99 RC 3.00 [illegible]
179 Taco Charlton AU/99 RC 2.50 6.00
180 Aaron Jones AU/99 RC 8.00 20.00
183 Sidney Jones AU/99 RC 2.50 6.00
184 De'Angelo Henderson AU/99 RC 2.50 6.00
185 Brad Kaaya AU/49 RC 3.00 8.00
186 Marlon Humphrey AU/99 RC 2.50 6.00
187 Stacy Coley AU/99 RC 2.50 6.00
188 Isaiah Ford AU/99 RC 2.50 6.00
190 Dalvin Tomlinson AU/99 RC 2.50 6.00
191 Noah Brown AU/99 RC 3.00 8.00
192 Jonathan Allen AU/49 RC 4.00 10.00
193 Elijah Hood AU/99 RC 2.50 6.00
194 Obi Melifonwu AU/99 RC 2.50 6.00
195 Adam Shaheen AU/99 RC 2.50 6.00
196 Malachi Dupre AU/99 RC 2.50 6.00
197 Matthew Dayes AU/99 RC 2.50 6.00
199 Chad Kelly AU/99 RC 12.00 30.00
200 DeMarcus Walker AU/99 RC 2.50 6.00

2017 Limited Gold Spotlight

*VETS: .8X TO 2X BASIC CARDS
*ROOK JSY AU/50: .8X TO 2X BASIC JSY AU
*ROOK AU/25: .6X TO 1.5X BASIC AU/99
114 Deshaun Watson JSY AU 75.00 150.00
136 Patrick Mahomes II JSY AU 400.00 800.00

2017 Limited Rookie Patch Autograph Variations

*ROOK JSY AU/25: 1X TO 2.5X BASIC JSY AU
133 Mitchell Trubisky 100.00 200.00
136 Patrick Mahomes II 400.00 800.00

2017 Limited Ruby Spotlight

*VETS/25: 1.5X TO 4X BASIC CARDS

2017 Limited Silver Spotlight

*VETS: .6X TO 1.5X BASIC CARDS
*ROOK JSY AU/75: .6X TO 1.5X BASIC JSY AU
*ROOK AU/35: .5X TO 1.2X BASIC AU/99
*ROOK AU/25: .5X TO 1.2X BASIC AU/49
*ROOK AU/15: .5X TO 1.2X BASIC AU/25
114 Deshaun Watson JSY AU 50.00 125.00
136 Patrick Mahomes II JSY AU 300.00 600.00

2017 Limited Combos Jersey Autographs

3 A.Stewart/C.Hackenberg/49 4.00 10.00
4 W.Gallman/P.Perkins/49 5.00 12.00
6 J.Ross III/A.Green/15
7 D.Kizer/C.Coleman/15
9 A.Kamara/M.Thomas/25 75.00 150.00

2017 Limited Draft Day Signatures Materials

1 Adoree' Jackson/55 10.00 25.00
2 Corey Davis/55 12.00 30.00
3 Derek Barnett/55 40.00 80.00
4 Deshaun Watson/54 75.00 150.00
5 Garett Bolles/55 8.00 20.00
6 Haason Reddick/55 8.00 20.00
7 Jamal Adams/55 8.00 20.00
8 John Ross III/55 10.00 25.00
9 Jonathan Allen/55 10.00 25.00
10 Leonard Fournette/55 60.00 125.00
11 Marshon Lattimore/55 10.00 25.00
12 Mitchell Trubisky/55 75.00 150.00
13 Ryan Ramczyk/55 8.00 20.00
14 Solomon Thomas/46 8.00 20.00
16 Tre'Davious White/55 8.00 20.00

2017 Limited Game Day Swatches

*PRIME/25: .6X TO 1.5X BASIC JSY/75
*PRIME/25: .5X TO 1.2X BASIC JSY/35-50
1 Travis Frederick/75 2.00 5.00
2 Adam Jones/75 2.00 5.00
3 Zack Martin/75 2.00 5.00
4 Vontaze Burfict/75 2.00 5.00
5 Trent Williams/75 2.00 5.00
6 Alex Smith/50 3.00 8.00
7 Andrew Luck/50 5.00 12.00
8 Andy Dalton/50 3.00 8.00
9 Antonio Brown/25 5.00 12.00
10 Antonio Gates/75 2.00 5.00
11 Aqib Talib/75 2.00 5.00
12 Blake Bortles/50 2.50 6.00
13 Cameron Wake/75 2.00 5.00
14 Carlos Dunlap/75 2.00 5.00
15 Champ Bailey/50 3.00 8.00
16 Clay Matthews/25 4.00 10.00
17 Cole Beasley/50 4.00 10.00
18 Dan Bailey/75 2.00 5.00
19 Demaryius Thomas/75 2.50 6.00
20 Dez Bryant/35 4.00 10.00
21 Eli Manning/75 2.50 6.00
22 Eric Fisher/75 2.00 5.00
23 Ezekiel Elliott/35 5.00 12.00
24 Geno Atkins/75 2.00 5.00
25 Jarvis Landry/50 3.00 8.00
26 Jay Ajayi/50 3.00 8.00
27 Tyler Boyd/75 2.00 5.00
28 Jordan Reed/35 2.50 6.00
29 Julio Jones/35 4.00 10.00
30 Kiko Alonso/75 2.00 5.00
31 LeSean McCoy/50 4.00 10.00
32 Matt Ryan/50 3.00 8.00
33 Matthew Stafford/25 4.00 10.00
34 Michael Vick/50 3.00 8.00
35 Mike Pouncey/75 2.00 5.00
36 Ryan Tannehill/50 3.00 8.00
37 Tony Romo/50 3.00 8.00
38 Tyler Eifert/75 2.50 6.00
39 Tyrod Taylor/50 3.00 8.00
40 Von Miller/35 3.00 8.00

2017 Limited Ink

*SILVER/35: .4X TO 1X BASIC AU/35-49
*SILVER/25: .5X TO 1.2X BASIC AU/35-49
*GOLD/25: .5X TO 1.2X BASIC AU/35-49
*GOLD/15: .6X TO 1.5X BASIC AU/35-49
2 Thomas Rawls/35 6.00 15.00
3 Greg Olsen/15 12.00 30.00
4 Kyle Rudolph/35 6.00 15.00
5 Alan Page/25 8.00 20.00
6 Hines Ward/15 12.00 30.00
9 Jamaal Charles/15 12.00 30.00
10 James White/49 8.00 20.00
11 Zach Ertz/49 8.00 20.00
12 Cameron Heyward/49 6.00 15.00
13 Mark Brunell/25 10.00 25.00
14 Christian Okoye/35 6.00 15.00
15 Michael Bennett/35 6.00 15.00
16 Rishard Matthews/49 6.00 15.00
17 Jason Verrett/49 6.00 15.00
19 Delvin Breaux/49 6.00 15.00
20 Steve Grogan/49 6.00 15.00
21 Maurkice Pouncey/49 6.00 15.00
22 Jimmy Johnson/49
23 Neil Smith/49 6.00 15.00
24 Ryan Shazier/49 6.00 15.00
25 Ron Yary/49 6.00 15.00
26 Mel Renfro/49 6.00 15.00
27 Lenny Moore/49 6.00 15.00
29 Jeremy Shockey/49 6.00 15.00
30 Rickey Jackson/49 6.00 15.00
31 Ahmad Rashad/49 8.00 20.00
32 Kordell Stewart/35 6.00 15.00
33 Tom Mack/35 6.00 15.00
34 Paul Krause/49 6.00 15.00
35 Mark Gastineau/25 8.00 20.00
36 Jason Taylor/15 10.00 25.00
37 Kabeer Gbaja-Biamila/25 8.00 20.00
38 Jevon Kearse/35 6.00 15.00
39 Drew Pearson/25 10.00 25.00
40 Golden Tate III/15 10.00 25.00

2017 Limited Limitless Materials

*PRIME/25: .6X TO 1.5X BASIC JSY/125
*PRIME/25: .5X TO 1.2X BASIC JSY/50
*PRIME/20: .8X TO 2X BASIC JSY/125
*PRIME/20: .6X TO 1.5X BASIC JSY/50
1 Dak Prescott/125 3.00 8.00
2 Ezekiel Elliott/125 4.00 10.00
3 Jordan Howard/125 3.00 8.00
4 Chris Conley/125 2.00 5.00
5 Aaron Rodgers/50 8.00 20.00
6 Corey Coleman/125 2.00 5.00
7 Devonta Freeman/125 2.50 6.00
8 David Johnson/125 3.00 8.00
9 Doug Baldwin/125 2.50 6.00
10 Matthew Stafford/50 3.00 8.00
11 Jay Ajayi/125 2.50 6.00
12 Joey Bosa/125 3.00 8.00
13 Khalil Mack/125 3.00 8.00
14 Luke Kuechly/125 2.50 6.00
15 Malcolm Mitchell/125 2.50 6.00
16 Marqise Lee/125 2.00 5.00
17 Paul Perkins/125 2.00 5.00
18 Trevor Siemian/50 2.50 6.00
19 Kirk Cousins/125 3.00 8.00
20 Travis Kelce/125 3.00 8.00
21 Ty Montgomery/125 2.00 5.00
22 Tyler Boyd/125 2.00 5.00
23 Tyler Lockett/125 2.50 6.00
24 Tyreek Hill/125 3.00 8.00
25 A.J. Green/50 4.00 10.00
26 Antonio Gates/125 2.00 5.00
27 Blake Bortles/125 2.00 5.00
28 Cam Newton/50 4.00 10.00
29 Zach Ertz/125 2.50 6.00
30 Will Fuller V/125 2.00 5.00
31 Cole Beasley/125 3.00 8.00
32 Dan Bailey/125 2.00 5.00
33 Danny Woodhead/125 2.50 6.00
34 Delanie Walker/125 2.00 5.00
35 Demaryius Thomas/125 2.50 6.00
36 Dez Bryant/125 3.00 8.00
37 Eli Manning/50 3.00 8.00
38 Emmanuel Sanders/50 4.00 10.00
39 Eric Berry/125 2.50 6.00
40 Geno Atkins/125 2.00 5.00

2017 Limited Partnership Dual Autographs

7 A.Page/C.Eller/49 25.00 50.00
12 B.Lilly/E.Jones/25
13 D.Hampton/M.Singletary/25 40.00 80.00
15 H.McElhenny/Y.Tittle/25 20.00 40.00
17 J.Zorn/S.Largent/25 40.00 80.00
18 R.Williams/R.Brown/15 20.00 50.00
19 L.Moore/T.Matte/49 12.00 30.00
20 F.Taylor/M.Brunell/15 20.00 50.00

2017 Limited Prime Time Jerseys

*PRIME/25: .5X TO 1.2X BASIC JSY/50
1 Marcus Allen/50 3.00 8.00
2 Bo Jackson/25 6.00 15.00
3 Barry Sanders/50 6.00 15.00
4 Brett Favre/25 10.00 25.00
5 Dan Marino/50 8.00 20.00
6 Howie Long/25 5.00 12.00
7 Fran Tarkenton/50 4.00 10.00
8 Lance Alworth/50 3.00 8.00
9 Ed Reed/50 3.00 8.00
10 Franco Harris/50 4.00 10.00
11 Maurice Jones-Drew/50 2.50 6.00
12 Paul Hornung/50 4.00 10.00
13 Ray Lewis/25 5.00 12.00
14 Terry Bradshaw/50 6.00 15.00
15 Tony Romo/50 3.00 8.00
16 Steve Young/50 5.00 12.00
17 Calvin Johnson/25 5.00 12.00
18 Champ Bailey/50 3.00 8.00
19 Deion Sanders/50 3.00 8.00
20 Curtis Martin/25 4.00 10.00

2017 Limited Ring of Honor Autographs

*SILVER/15: .5X TO 1.2X BASIC AU/25
2 Mike Singletary/25 12.00 30.00
6 Fran Tarkenton/25 40.00 80.00
7 Carl Eller/25 8.00 20.00
9 Archie Manning/15 20.00 50.00
11 Warren Sapp/15 12.00 30.00
15 Eric Dickerson/15 50.00 100.00
18 Ronnie Lott/15 40.00 80.00
19 Steve Largent/15 15.00 40.00
20 Jim Zorn/25 8.00 20.00
22 Randy White/25 10.00 25.00
27 Ron Jaworski/25 10.00 25.00
28 Joe Theismann/25 12.00 30.00
30 Doug Williams/15 12.00 30.00

2017 Limited Rookie Phenoms Jerseys

*SILVER/49: .5X TO 1.2X BASIC JSY/99
*GOLD/25: .6X TO 1.5X BASIC JSY/99
1 Alvin Kamara 8.00 20.00
2 Amara Darboh 2.00 5.00
3 ArDarius Stewart 2.00 5.00
4 C.J. Beathard 2.00 5.00
5 Carlos Henderson 2.00 5.00
6 Chris Godwin 2.50 6.00
7 Christian McCaffrey 6.00 15.00
8 Cooper Kupp 3.00 8.00
9 Corey Davis 3.00 8.00
10 Curtis Samuel 2.50 6.00
11 Dalvin Cook 4.00 10.00
12 Davis Webb 2.00 5.00
13 Dede Westbrook 2.00 5.00
14 Deshaun Watson 8.00 20.00
15 DeShone Kizer 2.00 5.00
16 D'Onta Foreman 2.50 6.00
17 Evan Engram 2.50 6.00
18 Jamaal Williams 2.00 5.00
19 James Conner 4.00 10.00
20 Jeremy McNichols 2.00 5.00
21 Joe Mixon 4.00 10.00
22 Joe Williams 2.00 5.00
23 John Ross III 2.50 6.00
24 Josh Reynolds 2.00 5.00
25 R. Joshua Dobbs 2.50 6.00
26 JuJu Smith-Schuster 5.00 12.00
27 Kareem Hunt 4.00 10.00
28 Kenny Golladay 3.00 8.00
29 Leonard Fournette 6.00 15.00
30 Mack Hollins 2.00 5.00
31 Marlon Mack 3.00 8.00
32 Mike Williams 3.00 8.00
33 Mitchell Trubisky 6.00 15.00
34 Nathan Peterman 2.50 6.00
35 O.J. Howard 2.50 6.00
36 Patrick Mahomes II 15.00 40.00
37 Samaje Perine 2.00 5.00
38 Taywan Taylor 2.00 5.00
39 Wayne Gallman 2.50 6.00
40 Zay Jones 2.50 6.00

2017 Limited Team Trademark Signatures

*SILVER/35: .4X TO 1X BASIC AU/35-49
*SILVER/25: .5X TO 1.2X BASIC AU/35-49
*SILVER/15: .5X TO 1.2X BASIC AU/25
*GOLD/25: .5X TO 1.2X BASIC AU/35-49
*GOLD/15: .6X TO 1.5X BASIC AU/35-49
2 Jordan Howard/25 12.00 30.00
3 LeSean McCoy/15 15.00 40.00
4 Derek Carr/15 40.00 80.00
5 Geno Atkins/49 6.00 15.00
6 Vic Beasley Jr./49 6.00 15.00
7 Melvin Gordon/25 10.00 25.00
8 Dont'a Hightower/35 6.00 15.00
9 Priest Holmes/25 8.00 20.00
11 Earl Thomas III/15 12.00 30.00
12 Gerald McCoy/49 6.00 15.00
13 Luke Kuechly/15 12.00 30.00
14 Fletcher Cox/35 6.00 15.00
15 Aaron Donald/35 10.00 25.00
16 Michael Vick/25 10.00 25.00
17 Landon Collins/35 6.00 15.00
18 Randall Cobb/25 10.00 25.00
20 Marcus Peters/49 6.00 15.00
TSAG A.J. Green/15
TSAR Allen Robinson/25

2018 Limited

1 Patrick Peterson 1.00 2.50
2 David Johnson 1.50 4.00
3 Larry Fitzgerald 1.25 3.00
4 Matt Ryan 1.25 3.00
5 Julio Jones 1.50 4.00
6 Devonta Freeman 1.25 3.00
7 Joe Flacco 1.25 3.00
8 Alex Collins 1.00 2.50
9 Terrell Suggs 1.00 2.50
10 Devin Funchess 1.00 2.50
11 LeSean McCoy 1.50 4.00
12 Kelvin Benjamin 1.25 3.00
13 Cam Newton 1.50 4.00
14 Christian McCaffrey 1.50 4.00
15 Greg Olsen 1.25 3.00
16 Mitchell Trubisky 1.50 4.00
17 Jordan Howard 1.50 4.00
18 Allen Robinson II 1.25 3.00
19 Andy Dalton 1.25 3.00
20 A.J. Green 1.50 4.00
21 Joe Mixon 1.25 3.00
22 David Njoku 1.25 3.00
23 Myles Garrett 1.50 4.00
24 Jarvis Landry 1.25 3.00
25 Dak Prescott 1.50 4.00
26 Ezekiel Elliott 2.00 5.00
27 Cole Beasley 1.25 3.00
28 Sean Lee 1.25 3.00
29 Case Keenum 1.25 3.00
30 Emmanuel Sanders 1.25 3.00
31 Von Miller 1.25 3.00
32 Matthew Stafford 1.25 3.00
33 Kenny Golladay 1.00 2.50
34 Marvin Jones Jr. 1.00 2.50
35 Aaron Rodgers 3.00 8.00
36 Jamaal Williams 1.00 2.50
37 Clay Matthews 1.00 2.50
38 Davante Adams 1.25 3.00
39 Deshaun Watson 2.00 5.00
40 Lamar Miller 1.00 2.50
41 DeAndre Hopkins 1.25 3.00
42 Andrew Luck 2.00 5.00
43 Marlon Mack 1.00 2.50
44 T.Y. Hilton 1.25 3.00
45 Blake Bortles 1.00 2.50
46 Leonard Fournette 1.50 4.00
47 Keelan Cole 1.00 2.50
48 Patrick Mahomes II 5.00 12.00
49 Kareem Hunt 1.50 4.00
50 Tyreek Hill 1.50 4.00
51 Jared Goff 1.50 4.00
52 Todd Gurley II 1.50 4.00
53 Brandin Cooks 1.25 3.00
54 Philip Rivers 1.25 3.00
55 Melvin Gordon III 1.50 4.00
56 Keenan Allen 1.25 3.00
57 Ryan Tannehill 1.25 3.00
58 Kenyan Drake 1.00 2.50
59 Kenny Stills 1.00 2.50
60 Kirk Cousins 1.50 4.00
61 Dalvin Cook 1.25 3.00
62 Stefon Diggs 1.25 3.00
63 Tom Brady 4.00 10.00
64 James White 1.25 3.00
65 Julian Edelman 1.25 3.00
66 Rob Gronkowski 1.50 4.00
67 Drew Brees 1.50 4.00
68 Alvin Kamara 1.50 4.00
69 Michael Thomas 1.50 4.00
70 Eli Manning 1.25 3.00
71 Odell Beckham Jr. 2.00 5.00
72 Evan Engram 1.00 2.50
73 Quincy Enunwa 1.00 2.50
74 Bilal Powell 1.00 2.50
75 Robby Anderson 1.00 2.50
76 Derek Carr 1.50 4.00
77 Marshawn Lynch 1.50 4.00
78 Amari Cooper 1.25 3.00
79 Carson Wentz 2.00 5.00
80 Zach Ertz 1.25 3.00
81 Alshon Jeffery 1.25 3.00
82 Ben Roethlisberger 1.50 4.00
83 James Conner 1.50 4.00
84 JuJu Smith-Schuster 1.50 4.00
85 Antonio Brown 1.50 4.00
86 Matt Breida 1.25 3.00
87 Richard Sherman 1.25 3.00
88 Marquise Goodwin 1.00 2.50
89 Russell Wilson 2.00 5.00
90 Chris Carson 1.25 3.00
91 Doug Baldwin 1.25 3.00
92 Jameis Winston 1.25 3.00
93 Mike Evans 1.50 4.00
94 O.J. Howard 1.00 2.50
95 Marcus Mariota 1.50 4.00
96 Derrick Henry 1.50 4.00
97 Dion Lewis 1.00 2.50
98 Alex Smith 1.25 3.00
99 Jordan Reed 1.00 2.50
100 Jamison Crowder 1.00 2.50
101 Baker Mayfield JSY AU/125 RC 150.00 300.00
102 Sam Darnold JSY AU/125 RC 40.00 80.00
103 Saquon Barkley JSY AU/175 RC EXCH 60.00 125.00
104 Josh Allen JSY AU/199 RC 30.00 60.00
105 Josh Rosen JSY AU/199 RC 30.00 60.00
106 Calvin Ridley JSY AU/125 RC 10.00 25.00
107 Sony Michel JSY AU/199 RC 15.00 40.00
108 Christian Kirk JSY AU/99 RC 8.00 20.00
109 Mason Rudolph JSY AU/299 RC 10.00 25.00
110 Courtland Sutton JSY AU/299 RC 8.00 20.00
111 D.J. Moore JSY AU/299 RC EXCH 6.00 15.00
112 Ronald Jones II JSY AU/299 RC 3.00 8.00
113 Anthony Miller JSY AU/299 RC 5.00 12.00
114 Kerryon Johnson JSY AU/299 RC EXCH 5.00 12.00
115 Kyle Lauletta JSY AU/199 RC 5.00 12.00
116 Royce Freeman JSY AU/299 RC 4.00 10.00
117 Michael Gallup JSY AU/225 RC 6.00 15.00
118 DaeSean Hamilton JSY AU/299 RC 4.00 10.00
119 D.J. Chark Jr. JSY AU/249 RC 4.00 10.00
120 Ito Smith JSY AU/299 RC 4.00 10.00
121 Kalen Ballage JSY AU/249 RC EXCH 4.00 10.00
122 Mark Walton JSY AU/299 RC 4.00 10.00
123 Mike White JSY AU/99 RC 6.00 15.00
124 Daurice Fountain JSY AU/299 RC 4.00 10.00
125 J'Mon Moore JSY AU/199 RC 3.00 8.00
126 Keke Coutee JSY AU/299 RC 4.00 10.00
127 Marquez Valdes-Scantling JSY AU/299 RC 4.00 10.00
128 Tre'Quan Smith JSY AU/199 RC 5.00 12.00
129 Jaylen Samuels JSY AU/299 RC EXCH 4.00 10.00
130 Lamar Jackson JSY AU/99 RC 50.00 100.00
131 Derrius Guice JSY AU/149 RC 10.00 25.00
132 Nick Chubb JSY AU/299 RC 10.00 25.00
133 Rashaad Penny JSY AU/299 RC 5.00 12.00
134 Dante Pettis JSY AU/299 RC 5.00 12.00
135 James Washington JSY AU/299 RC 6.00 15.00
136 Bradley Chubb JSY AU/299 RC 5.00 12.00
137 Hayden Hurst JSY AU/299 RC EXCH 4.00 10.00
138 Mike Gesicki JSY AU/299 RC 4.00 10.00
139 Nyheim Hines JSY AU/299 RC 4.00 10.00
140 Jaleel Scott JSY AU/299 RC 3.00 8.00
141 Baker Mayfield JSY AU/99 125.00 250.00
142 Sam Darnold JSY AU/99 50.00 100.00
143 Saquon Barkley JSY AU/99 EXCH 40.00 100.00
144 Josh Allen JSY AU/125 30.00 80.00
145 Josh Rosen JSY AU/125 30.00 80.00
146 Calvin Ridley JSY AU/60 16.00 40.00
147 Sony Michel JSY AU/99 25.00 60.00
148 Christian Kirk JSY AU/50 10.00 25.00
149 Mason Rudolph JSY AU/125 10.00 25.00
150 Courtland Sutton JSY AU/125 6.00 15.00
151 D.J. Moore JSY AU/199 EXCH 6.00 15.00
152 Ronald Jones IIJSY AU/199 6.00 15.00
153 Anthony Miller JSY AU/199 5.00 12.00
154 Kerryon Johnson JSY AU/199 5.00 12.00
155 Kyle Lauletta JSY AU/75 8.00 20.00
156 Royce Freeman JSY AU/125 5.00 12.00
157 Michael Gallup JSY AU/125 8.00 20.00
158 DaeSean Hamilton JSY AU/149 4.00 10.00
159 D.J. Chark Jr. JSY AU/199 4.00 10.00
160 Ito Smith JSY AU/199 4.00 10.00
161 Kalen Ballage JSY AU/149 EXCH 4.00 10.00
162 Mark Walton JSY AU/149 4.00 10.00
163 Mike White JSY AU/50 8.00 20.00
164 Daurice Fountain JSY AU/199 4.00 10.00
165 J'Mon Moore JSY AU/50 6.00 15.00
166 Keke Coutee JSY AU/199 4.00 10.00
167 Marquez Valdes-Scantling JSY AU/199 4.00 10.00
168 Tre'Quan Smith JSY AU/99 8.00 20.00
169 Jaylen Samuels JSY AU/199 EXCH 4.00 10.00
170 Lamar Jackson JSY AU/49 60.00 125.00
171 Chase Edmonds AU/60 RC 3.00 8.00
172 Josey Jewell AU/199 RC 2.50 6.00
173 Tremaine Edmunds AU/99 RC 5.00 12.00
175 Roquan Smith AU/99 RC 8.00 20.00
176 Denzel Ward AU/99 RC 10.00 25.00
177 Damion Ratley AU/199 RC 2.50 6.00
178 Will Dissly AU/199 RC 2.50 6.00
179 Phillip Lindsay AU/125 RC 10.00 25.00
180 Jaire Alexander AU/199 RC 3.00 8.00
181 Joshua Jackson AU/65 RC 6.00 15.00
182 Justin Reid AU/149 RC 2.00 5.00
183 Jordan Akins AU/199 RC 2.00 5.00
184 Jester Weah AU/199 RC 2.00 5.00
185 Steve Ishmael AU/199 RC 2.00 5.00
186 Jordan Wilkins AU/99 RC 3.00 8.00
187 Deon Cain AU/199 RC 2.50 6.00
188 Chad Thomas AU/199 RC 2.00 5.00
189 John Kelly AU/199 RC 2.50 6.00
190 Minkah Fitzpatrick AU/149 RC 4.00 10.00
191 Durham Smythe AU/99 RC 2.50 6.00
192 Mike Gesicki AU/149 RC 2.50 6.00
193 Mike Hughes AU/99 RC 4.00 10.00
194 Jake Wieneke AU/70 RC 3.00 8.00
195 Tyler Conklin AU/199 RC 2.00 5.00
196 Danny Etling AU/99 RC 8.00 20.00
197 Braxton Berrios AU/199 RC 2.00 5.00
198 Ronnie Harrison AU/70 RC 3.00 8.00
199 Boston Scott AU/199 RC 2.50 6.00
200 Marcell Ateman AU/199 RC 2.50 6.00
201 Josh Adams AU/60 RC 6.00 15.00
202 Dallas Goedert AU/199 RC 2.50 6.00
203 Terrell Edmunds AU/99 RC 8.00 20.00
204 Richie James AU/99 RC 2.50 6.00
205 Shaquem Griffin AU/99 RC 4.00 10.00
206 Justin Jackson AU/149 RC 2.50 6.00
207 Justin Watson AU/199 RC 2.50 6.00
208 Trey Quinn AU/199 RC 2.00 5.00
209 Rashaan Evans AU/99 RC 4.00 10.00
210 Harold Landry AU/199 RC EXCH 2.00 5.00
211 Simmie Cobbs Jr. AU/149 RC 3.00 8.00
212 Chase Litton AU/99 RC 3.00 8.00
213 Kyzir White AU/149 RC 3.00 8.00
214 Micah Kiser AU/99 RC 2.50 6.00
215 Rasheem Green AU/95 RC 2.50 6.00
216 Dalyn Dawkins AU/60 RC 3.00 8.00
217 Jaylen Samuels AU/50 RC EXCH 4.00 10.00
218 D.J. Moore AU/50 RC EXCH 6.00 15.00
219 Ronald Jones II AU/50 RC 3.00 8.00
220 Anthony Miller AU/50 RC 5.00 12.00
221 Kerryon Johnson AU/50 RC 5.00 12.00
222 Royce Freeman AU/50 RC 4.00 10.00
223 DaeSean Hamilton AU/50 RC 4.00 10.00
224 Ito Smith AU/50 RC 4.00 10.00
225 Kalen Ballage AU/50 RC EXCH 4.00 10.00
226 Mark Walton AU/50 RC 4.00 10.00
227 Nick Mullens AU/199 RC 6.00 15.00
229 Nyheim Hines AU/50 RC 4.00 10.00
230 Tre'Quan Smith AU/50 RC 5.00 12.00

2018 Limited Gold Spotlight

*VETS/49: .8X TO 2X BASIC CARDS
*ROOK JSY AU/50: .8X TO 2X BASIC JSY AU/149-299
*ROOK JSY AU/50: .6X TO 1.5X BASIC JSY AU/125
*ROOK JSY AU/50: .5X TO 1.2X BASIC JSY AU/75-99
*ROOK JSY AU/20: 1.2X TO 3X BASIC JSY AU/149-299
*ROOK JSY AU/20: 1X TO 2.5X BASIC JSY AU/125
*ROOK JSY AU/20: .8X TO 2X BASIC JSY AU/75-99
*ROOK JSY AU/20: .6X TO 1.5X BASIC JSY AU/49-50
*ROOK AU/35-50: .6X TO 1.5X BASIC AU/149-199
*ROOK AU/35-50: .5X TO 1.2X BASIC AU/70-125
*ROOK AU/35-50: .4X TO 1X BASIC AU/50-60
*ROOK AU/20: .5X TO 1.2X BASIC AU/50
101 Baker Mayfield JSY AU/50 200.00 400.00
141 Baker Mayfield JSY AU/20 250.00 500.00

2018 Limited Ruby Spotlight

*VETS: 1.2X TO 3X BASIC CARDS
*ROOK AU/25: .8X TO 2X BASIC AU/149-199
*ROOK AU/25: .6X TO 1.5X BASIC AU/70-125
*ROOK AU/25: .5X TO 1.2X BASIC AU/50-60
*ROOK AU/15: .6X TO 1.5X BASIC AU/50

2018 Limited Silver Spotlight

*VETS/99: .6X TO 1.5X BASIC CARDS
*ROOK JSY AU/75: .6X TO 1.5X BASIC JSY AU/149-299
*ROOK JSY AU/75: .5X TO 1.2X BASIC JSY AU/125
*ROOK JSY AU/75: .4X TO 1X BASIC JSY AU/75-99
*ROOK JSY AU/25: 1X TO 2.5X BASIC JSY AU/149-299
*ROOK JSY AU/25: .8X TO 2X BASIC JSY AU/125
*ROOK JSY AU/25: .6X TO 1.5X BASIC JSY AU/75-99
*ROOK JSY AU/25: .5X TO 1.2X BASIC JSY AU/50
101 Baker Mayfield JSY AU/75 125.00 250.00
103 Saquon Barkley JSY AU/75 EXCH 125.00 250.00
141 Baker Mayfield JSY AU/25 150.00 300.00
143 Saquon Barkley JSY AU/25 150.00 300.00

2018 Limited Combinations Patch Autographs

1 N.Hines/D.Fountain/75 8.00 20.00
2 K.Johnson/R.Freeman/75 25.00 50.00
3 A.Gates/P.Rivers/20 60.00 125.00
4 B.Mayfield/N.Chubb/25
5 C.Beasley/D.Prescott/25 30.00 60.00
6 J.Moore/M.Valdes-Scantling/75 8.00 20.00
7 D.Westbrook/M.Lee/35 8.00 20.00
8 J.Washington/J.Smith-Schuster/35 15.00 40.00
9 J.Allen/J.Rosen/15
10 N.Chubb/S.Michel/35 50.00 100.00

2018 Limited Combinations Patch Autographs Gold Spotlight

*GOLD/25: .6X TO 1.5X BASIC JSY AU/75
*GOLD/25: .5X TO 1.2X BASIC JSY AU/35
*GOLD/15: .6X TO 1.5X BASIC JSY AU/35
*GOLD/15: .4X TO 1X BASIC JSY AU/20
4 Baker Mayfield 250.00 350.00
Nick Chubb/15

2018 Limited Draft Day Signature Materials

1 Derwin James 40.00 80.00
2 Sam Darnold 75.00 150.00
3 Denzel Ward 50.00 100.00
4 Josh Allen 75.00 150.00
5 Bradley Chubb 12.00 30.00
6 Marcus Davenport 15.00 40.00
7 Taven Bryan 8.00 20.00
8 Kolton Miller 15.00 40.00
9 Tremaine Edmunds 15.00 40.00
10 Vita Vea 12.00 30.00
11 Jaire Alexander 12.00 30.00
12 Josh Rosen 25.00 60.00
13 Roquan Smith
14 Rashaan Evans 12.00 30.00
15 Minkah Fitzpatrick 15.00 40.00
16 Leighton Vander Esch 100.00 200.00
17 Lamar Jackson 100.00 200.00

2018 Limited Limitless Materials
*GOLD/50: .5X TO 1.2X BASIC JSY/99
*GOLD/50: .4X TO 1X BASIC JSY/50
*GOLD/50: .3X TO .8X BASIC JSY/25
*SILVER/75: .4X TO 1X BASIC JSY/99
*SILVER/75: .3X TO .8X BASIC JSY/50
*SILVER/75: .25X TO .6X BASIC JSY/25
1 Jordan Howard/99 3.00 8.00
2 Tyreek Hill/50 4.00 10.00
3 Alvin Kamara/50 3.00 8.00
4 Christian McCaffrey/50 4.00 10.00
5 Deshaun Watson/50 5.00 12.00
6 Marlon Mack/99 2.00 5.00
7 Devin Funchess/99 2.00 5.00
8 Kareem Hunt/50 3.00 8.00
9 John Ross III/99 2.50 6.00
10 D'Onta Foreman/99 2.00 5.00
11 Dede Westbrook/99 2.00 5.00
12 Cooper Kupp/50 3.00 8.00
13 Kenyan Drake/99 2.00 5.00
14 Patrick Mahomes II/50 10.00 25.00
15 Nelson Agholor/99 2.00 5.00
16 Evan Engram/99 2.00 5.00
17 Tyler Lockett/95 2.50 6.00
18 Corey Davis/99 2.50 6.00
19 Dalvin Cook/25 4.00 10.00
20 Jared Goff/25 5.00 12.00
21 O.J. Howard/99 2.00 5.00
22 Mike Williams/99 2.00 5.00
23 Zach Ertz/99 2.50 6.00
24 Will Fuller V/99 2.00 5.00
25 DeVante Parker/99 2.50 6.00

2018 Limited Partnership Dual Autographs
*GOLD/50: .5X TO 1.2X BASIC AU/75
*GOLD/25: .5X TO 1.2X BASIC AU/35-50
1 N.Hines/D.Fountain/75 6.00 15.00
2 B.Bates/E.Walls/35 25.00 50.00
3 H.Ward/K.Stewart/15
7 S.Griffin/S.Griffin/15 50.00 100.00
8 C.Sutton/D.Hamilton/35 10.00 25.00
9 D.Westbrook/K.Cole/35 6.00 15.00
10 J.Lasley/J.Scott/50 6.00 15.00

2018 Limited Partnership Trios Autographs
*GOLD/25: .5X TO 1.2X BASIC AU/35
1 Rd/Smth/Klly/15
2 Bnntt/Lng/Cx/15
5 Hrst/Sctt/Lsly/35 10.00 25.00

2018 Limited Prime Time Swatches
*GOLD/50: .5X TO 1.2X BASIC JSY/80-99
*SILVER/75: .4X TO 1X BASIC JSY/80-99
1 Dak Prescott/99 3.00 8.00
2 David Johnson/99 3.00 8.00
3 Christian McCaffrey/99 3.00 8.00
4 Mitchell Trubisky/99 3.00 8.00
5 Joe Mixon/99 2.50 6.00
6 Patrick Mahomes II/99 20.00 50.00
7 Davante Adams/99 2.50 6.00
8 Deshaun Watson/99 4.00 10.00
9 T.Y. Hilton/99 2.50 6.00
10 Leonard Fournette/99 3.00 8.00
11 Kareem Hunt/99 2.50 6.00
12 Jared Goff/99 3.00 8.00
13 Melvin Gordon III/99 2.50 6.00
14 Stefon Diggs/80 2.50 6.00
15 Michael Thomas/80 3.00 8.00
16 Carson Wentz/80 4.00 10.00
17 JuJu Smith-Schuster/85
18 Mike Evans/85 2.50 6.00
19 Derrick Henry/85 3.00 8.00
20 Jamison Crowder/99 2.00 5.00

2018 Limited Quad Signatures
7 Chbb/Hmltn/Sttn/Frmn 40.00 80.00
8 Jhnsn/Chbb/Jns/Frmn 40.00 80.00
12 Smth/Sml/Fnchss/Mre

2018 Limited Ring of Honor Autographs
*GOLD/25: .5X TO 1.2X BASIC AU/50
*SILVER/35: .4X TO 1X BASIC AU/50
*SILVER/15: .4X TO 1X BASIC AU/20
1 Edgerrin James/15
3 Mike Singletary/15 15.00 40.00
4 Mike Alsfott/20 25.00 50.00
5 Andre Reed/20
10 Neil Smith/50 6.00 15.00
11 Don Maynard/20 12.00 30.00
12 Brian Dawkins/15 15.00 40.00
15 Reggie Wayne/15 12.00 30.00

2018 Limited Rookie Phenoms Jerseys
*SILVER/75: .4X TO 1X BASIC JSY/99
*GOLD/50: .5X TO 1.2X BASIC JSY/99
1 Sam Darnold 8.00 20.00
2 Josh Rosen 5.00 12.00
3 Baker Mayfield 15.00 40.00
4 Josh Allen 5.00 12.00
5 Mason Rudolph 4.00 10.00
6 Saquon Barkley 12.00 30.00
7 Derrius Guice 4.00 10.00
8 Nick Chubb 4.00 10.00
9 Ronald Jones II 4.00 10.00
10 Sony Michel 4.00 10.00
11 Calvin Ridley 4.00 10.00
12 Courtland Sutton 3.00 8.00
13 Christian Kirk 3.00 8.00
14 Anthony Miller 3.00 8.00
15 D.J. Chark Jr. 2.50 6.00
16 D.J. Moore 4.00 10.00
17 Lamar Jackson 8.00 20.00
18 DaeSean Hamilton 2.50 6.00
19 Bradley Chubb 3.00 8.00
20 Kerryon Johnson 3.00 8.00
21 Dante Pettis 3.00 8.00
22 James Washington 4.00 10.00
23 Royce Freeman 2.50 6.00
24 Michael Gallup 4.00 10.00
25 Tre'Quan Smith 3.00 8.00
26 Keke Coutee 2.50 6.00
27 Nyheim Hines 2.50 6.00
28 Kyle Lauletta 3.00 8.00
29 Mark Walton 2.50 6.00
30 Kalen Ballage 2.50 6.00
31 Jaleel Scott 2.00 5.00
32 J'Mon Moore 2.00 5.00
33 Hayden Hurst 2.50 6.00
34 Jaylen Samuels 2.50 6.00
35 Mike Gesicki 2.50 6.00

2018 Limited Unlimited Signatures
*GOLD/25: .5X TO 1.2X BASIC AU/50
*GOLD/20: .6X TO 1.5X BASIC AU/50
*SILVER/35: .4X TO 1X BASIC AU/50
*SILVER/25: .5X TO 1.2X BASIC AU/50
1 Tarik Cohen/50 8.00 20.00
2 Luke Kuechly/20 EXCH 12.00 30.00
3 Gerald McCoy/35 6.00 15.00
4 James White/50 8.00 20.00
8 Aaron Donald/20 25.00 50.00

1950 Lions Matchbooks
Universal Match Corp. produced these Detroit Lions matchcovers. Each measures approximately 1 1/2" by 4 1/2" (when completely folded out) and features a blue bordered front with the player's photo in black and white along with an advertisement for either Mello Crisp Potato Chips or Ray Whyte Chevy. Backs contain the 1950 Lions' sesaon schedule. The prices given are for full covers (with strikers) missing the actual matches. This is the form in which the matchbooks are most commonly found. Complete books with matches typically carry a 50% premium. Books missing the striker are considered VG at best.
1 Leon Hart 12.50 25.00
2 Doak Walker 15.00 30.00

1953-59 Lions McCarthy Postcards

Photographer J.D. McCarthy released a number of postcards throughout the 1950s to the early 1980s with many issued over a number of years. This group was most likely released during the 1950s as most feature older photographs and follow the same format of featuring a facsimile autograph on the cardfronts. Several players are featured on more than one card type with the differences noted below. Most also include a typical postcard style cardback, but some were printed blankbacked and many do contain back variations. There are two slightly different sizes that were used as well: larger 3 5/8" by 5 1/2" and smaller 3 1/4" by 5 1/2". It is thought that many of the postcards were reprinted from time to time, thus the reasoning behind what may seem like undervalued prices.
COMPLETE SET (108) 500.00 1000.00
1A Charlie Ane 6.00 12.00
1B Charlie Ane (standing) 6.00 12.00
2A Vince Banonis 4.00 8.00
2B Vince Banonis 4.00 8.00
2C Vince Banonis 4.00 8.00
2D Vince Banonis 4.00 8.00
3 Terry Barr 6.00 12.00
4A Les Bingaman 6.00 12.00
4B Les Bingaman 6.00 12.00
4C Les Bingaman 6.00 12.00
5 Bill Bowman 4.00 8.00
6 Cloyce Box 7.50 15.00
7 Jim Cain DE 4.00 8.00
8 Stan Campbell 4.00 8.00
9 Lew Carpenter 4.00 8.00
10A Howard Cassady (With ball) 7.50 15.00
10B Howard Cassady (Standing) 7.50 15.00
11A Jack Christiansen 10.00 20.00
11B Jack Christiansen 10.00 20.00
11C Jack Christiansen 10.00 20.00
12A Ollie Cline 4.00 8.00
12B Ollie Cline 4.00 8.00
13A Lou Creekmur 10.00 20.00
13B Lou Creekmur 10.00 20.00
14 Gene Cronin 4.00 8.00
15A Jim David 6.00 12.00
15B Jim David 6.00 12.00
16A Dorne Dibble 4.00 8.00
16B Dorne Dibble 4.00 8.00
17A Don Doll 6.00 12.00
17B Don Doll 4.00 8.00
18A Jim Doran 6.00 12.00
18B Jim Doran 6.00 12.00
18C Jim Doran 6.00 12.00
19 Bob Dove 4.00 8.00
20 Tom Dublinski 4.00 8.00
21 Sonny Gandee 4.00 8.00
22 Gene Gedman 4.00 8.00
23A Jim Gibbons 4.00 8.00
23B Jim Gibbons 4.00 8.00
23C Jim Gibbons (catching pass) 4.00 8.00
24 Jug Girard 6.00 12.00
25 Bill Glass 4.00 8.00
26 Pat Harder 7.50 15.00
27 Leon Hart 12.50 25.00
28 Bob Hoernschemeyer 6.00 12.00
29 Doug Hogland 4.00 8.00
30A John Henry Johnson 12.50 25.00
30B John Henry Johnson 12.50 25.00
31 Steve Junker 4.00 8.00
32 Carl Karilivacz 4.00 8.00
33 Alex Karras 12.50 25.00
34 Ray Krouse 4.00 8.00
35A Dick Lane 10.00 20.00
35B Dick Lane 10.00 20.00
36A Yale Lary 10.00 20.00
36B Yale Lary 10.00 20.00
36C Yale Lary 10.00 20.00
37A Bobby Layne 20.00 40.00
37B Bobby Layne 20.00 40.00
38 Dan Lewis 4.00 8.00
39 Gary Lowe 4.00 8.00
40A Gil Mains 4.00 8.00
40B Gil Mains 4.00 8.00
41A Jim Martin (punting pose) 6.00 12.00
41B Jim Martin 6.00 12.00
41C Jim Martin 6.00 12.00
42 Darris McCord 4.00 8.00
43A Thurman McGraw 4.00 8.00
43B Thurman McGraw 6.00 12.00
43C Thurman McGraw 6.00 12.00
44 Don McIlhenny 6.00 12.00
45 Andy Miketa 4.00 8.00
46A Dave Middleton 4.00 8.00
46B Dave Middleton 4.00 8.00
47 Bob Miller 4.00 8.00
48A Earl Morrall 7.50 15.00
48B Earl Morrall 7.50 15.00
49 Buddy Parker CO 6.00 12.00
50 Gerry Perry 4.00 8.00
51 Nick Pietrosante 6.00 12.00
52A John Prchlik 4.00 8.00
53B John Prchlik 4.00 8.00
54 Jerry Reichow 4.00 8.00
55 Perry Richards 4.00 8.00
56 Lee Riley 4.00 8.00
57 Ken Russell 4.00 8.00
58 Tobin Rote 7.50 15.00
59 Tom Rychlec 4.00 8.00
60 Jim Salsbury 4.00 8.00
61A Joe Schmidt (hands on knees) 12.50 25.00
61B Joe Schmidt (kneeling pose) 12.50 25.00
62 Harley Sewell 6.00 12.00
63 Bob Smith RB 6.00 12.00
64 Oliver Spencer 4.00 8.00
65 Dick Stanfel 4.00 8.00
66 Bill Stits 4.00 8.00
67 Lavern Torgeson 4.00 8.00
68A Tom Tracy 4.00 8.00
68B Tom Tracy 4.00 8.00
69A Doak Walker (larger card) 17.50 35.00
69B Doak Walker (smaller card) 17.50 35.00
70A Wayne Walker (running pose) 6.00 12.00
70B Wayne Walker (portrait) 6.00 12.00
71 Ken Webb 4.00 8.00
72 Dave Whitsell 4.00 8.00
73A George Wilson CO 6.00 12.00
73B George Wilson CO 6.00 12.00
74 Roger Zatkoff 4.00 8.00

1960-85 Lions McCarthy Postcards
Photographer J.D. McCarthy released a number of postcards throughout the 1950s to the mid-1980s with many issued over a number of years. This group was most likely released gradually between 1960-1980 as most feature newer photographs and follow the similar format of including the player's name within a name plate below the photo. Several players are featured on more than one card type with the differences noted below. Most also include a typical postcard style cardback, but some were printed blankbacked and many do contain back variations. It is thought that many of the postcards were reprinted from time to time, thus the reasoning behind what may seem like undervalued prices.
COMPLETE SET (92) 200.00 400.00
1 Jimmy Allen 2.00 4.00
2 Al Baker 4.00 8.00
3 Larry Ball 2.00 4.00
4A Lem Barney ((portrait) 7.50 15.00
4B Lem Barney (kneeling pose) 7.50 15.00
5A Lynn Boden (standing) 2.00 4.00
5B Lynn Boden (kneeling) 2.00 4.00
6 Craig Cotton 2.00 4.00
7 Leon Crosswhite 2.00 4.00
8A Gary Danielson 3.00 6.00
8B Gary Danielson 3.00 6.00
8C Gary Danielson 2.00 4.00
8D Gary Danielson 3.00 6.00
9 Nick Eddy 2.00 4.00
10A Doug English (action photos) 3.00 6.00
10B Doug English (kneeling pose) 3.00 6.00
11A Mel Farr (standing) 3.00 6.00
11B Mel Farr (kneeling) 3.00 6.00
12 Bobby Felts 2.00 4.00
13 Ed Flanagan 2.00 4.00
14 Rockne Freitas 2.00 4.00
15 Frank Gallagher 2.00 4.00
16 Billy Gambrell 2.00 4.00
17A Jim Gibbons 2.00 4.00
17B Jim Gibbons (White background, Palmer Moving ad o 3.00 6.00
18 Bob Grottkau 2.00 4.00
19 Larry Hand 3.00 6.00
20 R.W. Hicks 2.00 4.00
21 Billy Howard 2.00 4.00
22 James Hunter 2.00 4.00
23 Ray Jarvis 2.00 4.00
24 Dick Jauron 4.00 8.00
25A Ron Jessie 3.00 6.00
25B Ron Jessie 3.00 6.00
26 Levi Johnson 2.00 4.00
27 Horace King 2.00 4.00
28A Bob Kowalkowski 2.00 4.00
28B Bob Kowalkowski 2.00 4.00
28C Bob Kowalkowski 2.00 4.00
29A Greg Landry 4.00 8.00
29B Greg Landry 4.00 8.00
29C Greg Landry 4.00 8.00
30 Dick Lane (kneeling pose) 5.00 10.00
31A Dick Lebeau 3.00 6.00
31B Dick Lebeau 3.00 6.00
32A Mike Lucci 3.00 6.00
32B Mike Lucci 3.00 6.00
32C Mike Lucci 3.00 6.00
32D Mike Lucci 3.00 6.00
32E Mike Lucci 3.00 6.00
33 Bruce Maher 2.00 4.00
34A Errol Mann (hands on hips) 2.00 4.00
34B Errol Mann (standing holding helmet) 2.00 4.00
35 Amos Marsh 2.00 4.00
36 Earl McCullouch 2.00 4.00
37 Jim Mitchell 2.00 4.00
38 Bill Munson 3.00 6.00
39 Eddie Murray 3.00 6.00
40 Paul Naumoff 2.00 4.00
41 Orlando Nelson 2.00 4.00
42 Herb Orvis 2.00 4.00
43A Steve Owens (right hand on helmet) 5.00 10.00
43B Steve Owens 5.00 10.00
43C Steve Owens 5.00 10.00
43D Steve Owens 5.00 10.00
43E Steve Owens 5.00 10.00
43F Steve Owens 2.00 4.00
44 Ernie Price 2.00 4.00
45 Wayne Rasmussen 2.00 4.00
46 Rudy Redmond 2.00 4.00
47A Charlie Sanders 4.00 8.00
47B Charlie Sanders 4.00 8.00
47C Charlie Sanders (squatting pose) 4.00 8.00
47D Charlie Sanders 4.00 8.00
47E Charlie Sanders ch 4.00 8.00
47F Charlie Sanders 4.00 8.00
47G Charlie Sanders 4.00 8.00
48 Freddie Scott 3.00 6.00
49 Bobby Thompson 2.00 4.00
50 Leonard Thompson 3.00 6.00
51A Bill Triplett 2.00 4.00
51B Bill Triplett 2.00 4.00
52A Wayne Walker 3.00 6.00
52B Wayne Walker 3.00 6.00
53 Jim Weatherall 2.00 4.00
54 Charlie Weaver 2.00 4.00
55 Herman Weaver 2.00 4.00
56A Mike Weger 2.00 4.00
56B Mike Weger 2.00 4.00
57 Bobby Williams 2.00 4.00
58 Jim Yarbrough 2.00 4.00
59 Garo Yepremian 4.00 8.00

1961 Lions Jay Publishing
This 12-card set features (approximately) 5" by 7" black-and-white player photos. The photos show players in traditional poses with the quarterback preparing to throw, the runner heading downfield, and the defenseman ready for the tackle. These cards were packaged 12 to a packet and originally sold for 25 cents. The backs are blank. The cards are unnumbered and checklisted below in alphabetical order.
COMPLETE SET (12) 50.00 100.00
1 Carl Brettschneider 4.00 8.00
2 Howard Cassady 5.00 10.00
3 Gail Cogdill 4.00 8.00
4 Jim Gibbons 4.00 8.00
5 Alex Karras 6.00 12.00
6 Yale Lary 6.00 12.00
7 Jim Martin 4.00 8.00
8 Earl Morrall 5.00 10.00
9 Jim Ninowski 5.00 10.00
10 Nick Pietrosante 4.00 8.00
11 Joe Schmidt 6.00 12.00
12 George Wilson CO 4.00 8.00

1961 Lions Team Issue
The Lions issued these photos around 1961. Each features a black and white player image, measures roughly 7 3/4" by 9 1/2" and is surrounded by a thin white border. The player's name and position is printed in a small box within the photo. The backs are blank and we've listed the photos alphabetically below.
COMPLETE SET (12) 75.00 125.00
1 Terry Barr 5.00 10.00
2 Howard Cassady 6.00 12.00
3 Gail Cogdill 5.00 10.00
4 Jim Gibbons 6.00 12.00
5 Dick Lane 7.50 15.00
6 Yale Lary 7.50 15.00
7 Dan Lewis 5.00 10.00
8 Jim Martin 5.00 10.00
9 Earl Morrall 7.50 15.00
10 Jim Ninowski 6.00 12.00
11 Nick Pietrosante 5.00 10.00
12 Joe Schmidt 10.00 20.00

1961-62 Lions Falstaff Beer Team Photos
These oversized (roughly 6 1/4" by 9") color team photos were sponsored by Falstaff Beer and distributed in the Detroit area. Each was printed on card stock and included advertising messages and the Lions season schedule on the back.
1961 Lions Team 18.00 30.00
1962 Lions Team 18.00 30.00

1963-67 Lions Team Issue 8x10
e Detroit Lions issued these photos printed on glossy photographic stock. Each measures approximately 8" by 10" and features a black and white photo. The player's name, position, and team name appear below the photo on most of the pictures. However, a few photos catalogued below do not include the player's position. Theretore it is likely that the photos were released over a period of years. A photographer's imprint can often be found on the backs.
COMPLETE SET (23) 100.00 200.00
1 Lem Barney 7.50 15.00
2 Charley Bradshaw 5.00 10.00
3 Roger Brown DT 5.00 10.00
4 Ernie Clark 5.00 10.00
5 Gail Cogdill 5.00 10.00
6 John Gordy 5.00 10.00
7 Wally Hilgenberg 6.00 12.00
8 Alex Karras 7.50 15.00
9 Alex Karras 7.50 15.00
10 Bob Kowalkowski 5.00 10.00
11 Dick LeBeau 5.00 10.00
12 Joe Don Looney 6.00 12.00
13 Mike Lucci 6.00 12.00
14 Bruce Maher 5.00 10.00
15 Paul Naumoff 5.00 10.00
16 Tom Nowatzke 5.00 10.00
17 Milt Plum 6.00 12.00
18 Pat Studstill 5.00 10.00
19 Pat Studstill 5.00 10.00
20 Pat Studstill 5.00 10.00
21 Karl Sweetan 5.00 10.00
22 Bobby Thompson 5.00 10.00
23 Wayne Walker 5.00 10.00

1964-65 Lions Team Issue
e Lions issued single photos and photo packs to fans throughout the mid 1960s. Each photo in this set is a black and white 7 3/8" by 9 3/8" posed action shot surrounded by a white border. The player's name, position, and team name are printed on a single line below the photo. The print type, style, and size are identical on each photo. However, some of the players were issued in one or more years as some of the cards can be found with a date (either Oct. 1, 1964 or Sep. 24, 1965) stamped in blue ink on the cardback while others have no stamp. Of those known to be stamped, we've included the year(s) below. The cards also look identical to the 1966 issue. Players found in both sets have the specific differences noted below.
COMPLETE SET (40) 150.00 300.00
1 Terry Barr 65 5.00 10.00
2 Roger Brown DT 65 5.00 10.00
3 Gail Cogdill 64 5.00 10.00
4 Dick Compton 64/65 5.00 10.00
5 Larry Ferguson 65 5.00 10.00
6 Dennis Gaubatz 64/65 5.00 10.00
7 Jim Gibbons 64/65 6.00 12.00
8 John Gonzaga 64/65 5.00 10.00
9 John Gordy 64/65 5.00 10.00
10 Tom Hall 65 5.00 10.00
11 Ron Kramer 5.00 10.00
12 Roger LaLonde 65 5.00 10.00
13 Dick Lane 64 7.50 15.00
14 Dan LaRose 65 5.00 10.00
15 Yale Lary 64/65 7.50 15.00
16 Dick LeBeau 65 5.00 10.00
17 Monte Lee 65 5.00 10.00
18 Dan Lewis 64/65 5.00 10.00
19 Gary Lowe 65 5.00 10.00
20 Bruce Maher 64 5.00 10.00
21 Darris McCord 64/65 5.00 10.00
22 Hugh McInnis 65 5.00 10.00
23 Max Messner 65 5.00 10.00
24 Floyd Peters 65 5.00 10.00
25 Nick Pietrosante 65 5.00 10.00
26 Milt Plum 65 6.00 12.00
27 Bill Quinlan 65 5.00 10.00
28 Nick Ryder 65 5.00 10.00
29 Daryl Sanders 65 5.00 10.00
30 Joe Schmidt 64/65 7.50 15.00
31 Bob Scholtz 65 5.00 10.00
32 James Simon 64 5.00 10.00
33 J.D. Smith T 65 5.00 10.00
34 Pat Studstill 65 5.00 10.00
35 Larry Vargo 65 5.00 10.00
36 Wayne Walker 64/65 5.00 10.00
37 Tom Watkins 64/65 5.00 10.00
38 Warren Wells 65 5.00 10.00
39 Bob Whitlow 65 5.00 10.00
40 Sam Williams 64 5.00 10.00

1966 Lions Marathon Oil
This set consists of seven photos measuring approximately 5" by 7" thought to have been released by Marathon Oil. The fronts feature black-and-white photos with white borders. The player's name, position, and team name are printed in the bottom border. The backs are blank. The cards are unnumbered and checklisted below in alphabetical order.
COMPLETE SET (7) 30.00 60.00
1 Gail Cogdill 5.00 10.00
2 John Gordy 5.00 10.00
3 Alex Karras 7.50 15.00
4 Ron Kramer 5.00 10.00
5 Milt Plum 6.00 12.00
6 Wayne Rasmussen 5.00 10.00
7 Daryl Sanders 5.00 10.00

1966 Lions Team Issue
The Detroit Lions issued this set of large photos to Lions' fans who requested player pictures in 1966. Each measures approximately 7 1/2" by 9 1/2" and features a black and white photo. The player's name, position, and team name appear below the photo. The cards look identical to the 1964-65 issue. Players found in both sets have the specific differences noted below.
COMPLETE SET (41) 150.00 300.00
1 Mike Alford 5.00 10.00
2 Roger Brown 5.00 10.00
3 Ernie Clark 5.00 10.00
4 Bill Cody 5.00 10.00
5 Gail Cogdill 5.00 10.00
6 Ed Flanagan 5.00 10.00
7 Jim Gibbons 5.00 10.00
8 John Gordy 5.00 10.00
9 Larry Hand 5.00 10.00
10 John Henderson 5.00 10.00
11 Wally Hilgenberg 6.00 12.00
12 Alex Karras 7.50 15.00
13 Bob Kowalkowski 5.00 10.00
14 Ron Kramer 5.00 10.00
15 Dick LeBeau 5.00 10.00
16 Joe Don Looney 6.00 12.00
17 Mike Lucci 6.00 12.00
18 Bruce Maher 5.00 10.00
19 Bill Malinchak 5.00 10.00
20 Amos Marsh 5.00 10.00
21 Jerry Mazzanti 5.00 10.00
22 Darris McCord 5.00 10.00
23 Bruce McLenna 5.00 10.00
24 Tom Nowatzke 5.00 10.00
25 Milt Plum 6.00 12.00
26 Wayne Rasmussen 5.00 10.00
27 Johnnie Robinson DB 5.00 10.00
28 Jerry Rush 5.00 10.00
29 Daryl Sanders 5.00 10.00
30 Bobby Smith 5.00 10.00
31 J.D. Smith 5.00 10.00
32 Pat Studstill 5.00 10.00
33 Karl Sweetan 5.00 10.00
34 Bobby Thompson 5.00 10.00
35 Jim Todd 5.00 10.00
36 Doug Van Horn 5.00 10.00
37 Tom Vaughn 5.00 10.00
38 Wayne Walker 5.00 10.00
39 Willie Walker 5.00 10.00
40 Tom Watkins 5.00 10.00
41 Coaching Staff 10.00 20.00

1968 Lions Tasco Prints
Tasco Associates produced this set of Detroit Lions prints. The fronts feature a large color artist's rendering of the player along with the player's name and position. The backs are blank. The prints measure approximately 11 1/2" by 16."
COMPLETE SET (7) 50.00 100.00
1 Lem Barney 7.50 15.00
2 Mel Farr 5.00 10.00
3 Alex Karras 15.00 25.00
4 Dick LeBeau 5.00 10.00
5 Mike Lucci 6.00 12.00
6 Earl McCullouch 5.00 10.00
7 Bill Munson 6.00 12.00
8 Wayne Rasmussen 5.00 10.00
9 Jerry Rush 5.00 10.00

1986 Lions Police
This 14-card set of Detroit Lions is numbered on the card backs, which are printed in black ink on white card stock. Cards measure approximately 2 5/8" by 4 1/8". The set was sponsored by the Detroit Lions, Oscar Mayer, Claussen, WJR/WHYT, the Detroit Crime Prevention Section, and the Pontiac Police Athletic League. Uniform numbers are printed on the card front along with the player's name and position.
COMPLETE SET (14) 2.50 6.00
1 William Gay .20 .50
2 Pontiac Silverdome .20 .50
3 Leonard Thompson .25 .60
4 Eddie Murray .30 .75
5 Eric Hipple .30 .75
6 James Jones FB .30 .75
7 Darryl Rogers CO .20 .50
8 Chuck Long .30 .75
9 Garry James .25 .60
10 Michael Cofer .25 .60
11 Jeff Chadwick .25 .60
12 Jimmy Williams .20 .50
13 Keith Dorney .20 .50
14 Bobby Watkins .20 .50

1987 Lions Ace Fact Pack
This 33 card set measures approximately 2 1/4" by 3 5/8". This set features members of the Detroit Lions and has rounded corners. The back of the cards features a design for "Ace" like a playing card. These cards were manufactured in West Germany (by Ace Fact Pack) and we have checklisted this set alphabetically.
COMPLETE SET (33) 30.00 80.00
1 Carl Bland 1.25 3.00
2 Lomas Brown 2.00 5.00
3 Jeff Chadwick 1.25 3.00
4 Michael Cofer 1.25 3.00
5 Keith Dorney 1.25 3.00
6 Keith Ferguson 1.25 3.00
7 William Gay 1.25 3.00
8 James Harrell 1.25 3.00
9 Eric Hipple 2.00 5.00
10 Garry James 2.00 5.00
11 Demetrious Johnson 1.25 3.00
12 James Jones FB 2.00 5.00
13 Chuck Long 2.00 5.00
14 Vernon Maxwell 1.25 3.00
15 Bruce McNorton 1.25 3.00
16 Devon Mitchell 1.25 3.00
17 Steve Mott 1.25 3.00
18 Eddie Murray 2.00 5.00
19 Harvey Salem 1.25 3.00
20 Rich Stenger 1.25 3.00
21 Eric Williams 2.00 5.00
22 Jimmy Williams 1.25 3.00
23 Lions Helmet 1.25 3.00
24 Lions Information 1.25 3.00
25 Lions Uniform 1.25 3.00
26 Game Record Holders 1.25 3.00
27 Season Record Holders 1.25 3.00
28 Career Record Holders 1.25 3.00
29 Record 1967-86 1.25 3.00
30 1986 Team Statistics 1.25 3.00
31 All-Time Greats 1.25 3.00
32 Championship Seasons 1.25 3.00
33 Pontiac Silverdome 1.25 3.00

1987 Lions Police
This 14-card set of Detroit Lions is numbered on the back. The card backs are printed in blue ink on white card stock and contain a safety tip entitled "Little Oscar Says". Cards measure approximately 2 5/8" by 4 1/8". The set was sponsored by the Detroit Lions, Oscar Mayer, Claussen Pickles, WJR/WHYT, the Detroit Crime Prevention Section, and the Pontiac Police Athletic League. Uniform numbers are printed on the card front along with the player's name and position. Reportedly, nearly three million cards were distributed through the participating police agencies. The Lions team name appears above the player photo which differentiates this set from the 1988 Police Lions set.
COMPLETE SET (14) 2.50 6.00
1 Michael Cofer .20 .50
2 Rich Strenger .15 .40
3 Keith Ferguson .15 .40
4 James Jones FB .25 .60
5 Jeff Chadwick .20 .50
6 Devon Mitchell .15 .40
7 Eddie Murray .25 .60
8 Reggie Rogers .20 .50
9 Chuck Long .25 .60
10 Jimmie Giles .25 .60
11 Eric Williams .15 .40
12 Lomas Brown .20 .50
13 Jimmy Williams .15 .40
14 Garry James .20 .50

1988 Lions Police
The 1988 Police Detroit Lions set contains 14 numbered cards measuring approximately 2 5/8" by 4 1/8". There are 13 single player cards plus one for Detroit's top three 1988 draft picks. The backs have career highlights and safety tips. The Lions team name appears below the player photo which differentiates this set from the similar-looking 1987 Police Lions set.
COMPLETE SET (14) 2.00 5.00
1 Rob Rubick .20 .50
2 Paul Butcher .20 .50
3 Pete Mandley .25 .60
4 Jimmy Williams .20 .50
5 Harvey Salem .20 .50
6 Chuck Long .25 .60
7 Pat Carter .25 .60
8 Jerry Ball .30 .75
9 Lomas Brown .25 .60
10 Dennis Gibson .20 .50
11 Jim Arnold .20 .50
12 Michael Cofer .20 .50
13 James Jones FB .25 .60
14 Steve Mott .20 .50

1989 Lions Police
e 1989 Police Detroit Lions set contains 12 numbered cards measuring approximately 2 5/8" by 4 1/8". The set was also sponsored by Oscar Mayer. The fronts have white borders and color action photos; some are horizontally oriented, others are vertically oriented. The horizontally oriented backs have safety tips and brief career highlights. These cards were printed on very thin stock. The set is notable for a card of Barry Sanders, showing a photo of him at his postdraft press conference. It has been reported that three million cards were given away during this program by police officers in Michigan and Ontario.
COMPLETE SET (12) 5.00 12.00
1 George Jamison .15 .40
2 Wayne Fontes CO .20 .50
3 Kevin Glover .15 .40
4 Chris Spielman .40 1.00
5 Eddie Murray .20 .50
6 Bennie Blades .30 .75
7 Joe Milinichik .15 .40
8 Michael Cofer .15 .40
9 Jerry Ball .20 .50
10 Dennis Gibson .15 .40
11 Barry Sanders 4.00 10.00
12 Jim Arnold .15 .40

1990 Lions Police
This 12-card set was issued by Oscar Mayer in conjunction with the Detroit Lions, Claussen, WWJ radio station, the Detroit Crime Prevention Society, and the Crime Prevention Association of Michigan. The fronts of the cards feature an action photo of the player on the front and a drawing of the player along with a brief note about the player on the back. In addition there is a safety tip from Little Oscar (the symbol for Oscar Mayer) on the back. The cards measure approximately 2 5/8" by 4 1/8".
COMPLETE SET (12) 3.20 8.00
1 William White .14 .35
2 Chris Spielman .30 .75
3 Rodney Peete .40 1.00
4 Jimmy Williams .14 .35
5 Bennie Blades .20 .50
6 Barry Sanders 2.00 5.00
7 Jerry Ball .20 .50
8 Richard Johnson .20 .50
9 Michael Cofer .14 .35
10 Lomas Brown .20 .50
11 Joe Schmidt GM& .30 .75
12 Eddie Murray .20 .50

1991 Lions Police
This 12-card Police Lions set was distributed during the season by participating Michigan police departments. The cards measure approximately 2 5/8" by 4 1/8" and feature color action shots of each player enclosed in a yellow border on thin card stock. Oscar Mayer's logo, player's name, and team helmet appearing at the bottom of each card are highlighted by blue lines above and below. Card backs, printed vertically, carry a black and white head shot of the player, player information, while a safety tip from the main sponsor appears at the bottom left half of card. The bottom right half lists card numbers and other sponsor names.
COMPLETE SET (12) 2.40 6.00
1 Mel Gray .25 .60
2 Ken Dallafior .14 .35
3 Chris Spielman .25 .60
4 Bennie Blades .20 .50
5 Robert Clark .20 .50
6 Eric Andolsek .20 .50
7 Rodney Peete .30 .75
8 William White .14 .35
9 Lomas Brown .20 .50
10 Jerry Ball .20 .50
11 Michael Cofer .14 .35
12 Barry Sanders 1.20 3.00

1993 Lions 60th Season Commemorative

These 16 standard-size 60th-season commemorative cards feature borderless player photos on their fronts. Some photos are color, others are black-and-white; some are action shots, others are posed. The player's name (or the card's title), the rectangle it appears in, and the 60th season logo, all appear in team colors. The white backs carry black-and-white head shots of the players. Also appearing are the players' names, the years they played for the Lions, position, and career highlights. The team color-coded 60th season logo reappears in a lower corner. The cards came with their own approximately 6" by 8" four page black vinyl card holder emblazoned with the Lions' 60th season logo.
COMPLETE SET (16) 10.00 25.00
1 Barry Sanders 4.80 12.00
2 Joe Schmidt .60 1.50
3 The Fearsome Foursome .30 .75
4 Chris Spielman .30 .75
5 Billy Sims .30 .75
6 '40s Phenoms .30 .75
7 Thunder and Lightning .20 .50
8 Bobby Layne 1.20 3.00
9 Dutch Clark .30 .75
10 Great Games .20 .50
11 Charlie Sanders .30 .75
12 Lomas Brown .20 .50
13 Doug English .30 .75
14 Doak Walker .80 2.00
15 Roaring '20s 1.60 4.00
16 Anniversary Card .20 .50

2005 Lions Activa Medallions
COMPLETE SET (21) 30.00 60.00
1 Jeff Backus 1.25 3.00
2 Boss Bailey 1.25 3.00
3 Dre Bly 1.25 3.00
4 Shaun Cody 1.25 3.00
5 Eddie Drummond 1.25 3.00
6 Jeff Garcia 1.50 4.00
7 James Hall 1.25 3.00
8 Jason Hanson 1.25 3.00
9 Joey Harrington 1.50 4.00
10 Kevin Jones 1.50 4.00
11 Kenoy Kennedy 1.25 3.00
12 Teddy Lehman 1.25 3.00
13 Marcus Pollard 1.25 3.00
14 Cory Redding 1.25 3.00
15 Charles Rogers 1.25 3.00
16 Shaun Rogers 1.25 3.00
17 Cory Schlesinger 1.25 3.00
18 Mike Williams .75 2.00
19 Roy Williams WR 1.50 4.00
20 Damien Woody 1.25 3.00
21 Lions Logo 1.00 2.50

2006 Lions Donruss Thanksgiving Classic
COMPLETE SET (7) 6.00 12.00
DT1 Jon Kitna .50 1.25
DT2 Kevin Jones .50 1.25
DT3 Roy Williams WR .50 1.25
DT4 Brian Calhoun .50 1.25
DT5 Ernie Sims .50 1.25
DT6 Billy Sims .75 2.00
NNO Cover Card CL .20 .50

2006 Lions Super Bowl XL
Each card manufacturer produced 3-cards to be distributed at the Super Bowl XL Card Show in Detroit via wrapper redemption programs. The design varies from manufacturer and slightly from card-to-card but each is numbered on the back as part of the 9-card set.
COMPLETE SET (9) 6.00 15.00
1 Barry Sanders Topps 1.25 3.00
2 Roy Williams WR Topps .60 1.50
3 Kevin Jones Topps .60 1.50
4 Joey Harrington Upper Deck .60 1.50
5 Dan Orlovsky Upper Deck .75 2.00
6 Boss Bailey Upper Deck .50 1.25
7 Mike Williams Donruss/Playoff .75 2.00
8 Shaun Rogers Donruss/Playoff .50 1.25
9 Marcus Pollard Donruss/Playoff .50 1.25

2006 Lions Topps
COMPLETE SET (12) 3.00 6.00
DET1 Charles Rogers .30 .75
DET2 Kevin Jones .25 .60
DET3 Roy Williams WR .25 .60
DET4 Mike Williams .25 .60
DET5 Scottie Vines .25 .60
DET6 Daniel Bullocks .25 .60
DET7 Dre Bly .25 .60
DET8 Marcus Pollard .25 .60
DET9 Josh McCown .25 .60
DET10 Jon Kitna .25 .60
DET11 Brian Calhoun .25 .60
DET12 Ernie Sims .25 .60

2007 Lions Donruss Thanksgiving Classic

COMPLETE SET (4) 3.00 8.00
1 Calvin Johnson 1.50 4.00
2 Roy Williams WR .40 1.00
3 Jon Kitna .40 1.00
4 Barry Sanders 1.00 2.50

2007 Lions Topps
COMPLETE SET (12) 3.00 6.00
1 Roy Williams WR .40 1.00
2 Kevin Jones .40 1.00
3 Mike Furrey .50 1.25
4 Jason Hanson .40 1.00
5 Ernie Sims .40 1.00
6 Jon Kitna .40 1.00
7 Shaun McDonald .40 1.00
8 T.J. Duckett .40 1.00
9 Tatum Bell .40 1.00
10 Shaun Rogers .40 1.00
11 Calvin Johnson 1.25 3.00
12 Drew Stanton .40 1.00

2008 Lions Topps
COMPLETE SET (12) 2.50 5.00
1 Roy Williams WR .40 1.00
2 Jon Kitna .40 1.00
3 Shaun McDonald .40 1.00
4 Ernie Sims .40 1.00
5 Kevin Jones .40 1.00
6 Calvin Johnson .60 1.50
7 Mike Furrey .50 1.25
8 Leigh Bodden .40 1.00
9 Tatum Bell .40 1.00
10 Paris Lenon .40 1.00
11 Kevin Smith .40 1.00
12 Jordon Dizon .40 1.00

1990 Little Big Leaguers
This 95-page book/album was published by Simon and Schuster and includes boyhood stories of today's pro football players. Moreover, five 8 1/2" by 11" sheets of cards (nine cards per sheet) are inserted at the end of the album; after perforation, the cards measure the standard size. The fronts feature black and white photos of these players as kids. The cards have blue and white borders, and in the thicker blue borders above and below the picture, one finds the player's name and the words "Little Football Big Leaguers" respectively. The backs have the same design, only with biography and career summary in place of the picture. The cards are unnumbered and checklisted below in alphabetical order.
COMPLETE SET (45) 24.00 60.00
1 Troy Aikman 4.00 10.00
2 Morten Andersen .30 .75
3 Jerry Ball .30 .75
4 Carl Banks .30 .75
5 Bennie Blades .30 .75
6 Brian Blades .40 1.00
7 Joey Browner .30 .75
8 Keith Byars .40 1.00
9 Anthony Carter .30 .75
10 Deron Cherry .30 .75
11 Roger Craig .40 1.00
12 John Elway 6.00 15.00
13 Doug Flutie 2.00 5.00
14 Tim Goad .30 .75
15 Bob Golic .30 .75
16 Dino Hackett .30 .75
17 Dan Hampton .30 .75
18 Bobby Hebert .30 .75
19 Darryl Henley .30 .75
20 Wes Hopkins .30 .75
21 Hank Ilesic .30 .75
22 Tunch Ilkin .30 .75
23 Perry Kemp .30 .75
24 Bernie Kosar .40 1.00
25 Mike Lansford .30 .75
26 Shawn Lee .30 .75
27 Charles Mann .30 .75
28 Dan Marino 6.00 15.00
29 Bruce Matthews .40 1.00
30 Clay Matthews .30 .75
31 Freeman McNeil .30 .75
32 Warren Moon 1.00 2.50
33 Anthony Munoz .40 1.00
34 Andre Reed .40 1.00
35 Andre Rison .40 1.00
36 Phil Simms 1.00 2.50
37 Mike Singletary .40 1.00
38 Rohn Stark .30 .75
39 Kelly Stouffer .30 .75
40 Vinny Testaverde .40 1.00
41 Doug Williams .30 .75
42 Marc Wilson .30 .75
43 Craig Wolfley .30 .75
44 Ron Wolfley .30 .75
45 Steve Young 3.20 8.00

2004 Los Angeles Avengers AFL
This 12-card set was issued by the team in a perforated sheet format and features several different sponsor logos on the cardfronts. The player's image is in color within a red border that features the words "Avenger Football" running down the left side.
COMPLETE SET (12) 6.00 12.00
1 Remy Hamilton .50 1.25
2 Chris Butterfield .50 1.25
3 Chris Jackson 1.00 2.50
4 Sean McNamara .50 1.25
5 Greg Hopkins 1.00 2.50
6 Damen Wheeler .50 1.25
7 Kevin Ingram .60 1.50

8 Henry Douglas .60 1.50
9 Lonnie Ford .60 1.50
10 Carlos Fowler .50 1.25
11 Al Lucas .50 1.25
12 Tony Graziani 1.00 2.50

2007 Los Angeles Avengers AFL

COMPLETE SET (12) 6.00 12.00
1 Sonny Cumbie .60 1.50
2 Silas Domary .40 1.00
3 Lonnie Ford .40 1.00
4 Remy Hamilton .50 1.25
5 Kevin Ingram .40 1.00
6 Lenzie Jackson .40 1.00
7 Sean McNamara .40 1.00
8 Brandon Perkins .40 1.00
9 Robert Quiroga .40 1.00
10 Jason Stewart .40 1.00
11 Rob Turner .40 1.00
12 Damen Wheeler .40 1.00

2008 Los Angeles Avengers AFL

COMPLETE SET (12) 5.00 10.00
1 Sonny Cumbie .60 1.50
2 Lonnie Ford .40 1.00
3 Tim Hicks .40 1.00
4 Kevin Ingram .40 1.00
5 Josh Jeffries .40 1.00
6 Ken Jones .40 1.00
7 Timon Marshall .40 1.00
8 Sean McNamara .40 1.00
9 Brandon Perkins .40 1.00
10 Jason Stewart .40 1.00
11 Lashaun Ward .40 1.00
12 Damen Wheeler .40 1.00

2001 Louisville Fire AF2

This set was produced for and distributed by the Louisville Fire Arena Football 2 team. The unnumbered cards are sponsored by SunCom and feature a color photo of the player on the front and a black and white cardback.

COMPLETE SET (12) 6.00 12.00
1 Alan Campos .40 1.00
2 Leroy Frederick .40 1.00
3 John Fuqua .50 1.25
4 Brian McDonald .40 1.00
5 Anthony Payton .40 1.00
6 Matt Pike .60 1.50
7 Ron Selesky CO .40 1.00
8 Charles Sheffield .40 1.00
9 Leland Taylor .40 1.00
10 Jabir Walker .40 1.00
11 Bobby Washington .50 1.25
12 Team Photo CL .40 1.00

2004 Louisville Fire AF2

This set was issued by the team and sponsored by Speedway. Each card was printed in full color and produced on very thin card stock. No year of issue or card number is provided on the cards. They are arranged alphabetically below for ease in cataloging.

COMPLETE SET (20) 10.00 20.00
1 Marvin Constant .40 1.00
2 Sam Crenshaw .50 1.25
3 Jason Ferguson .40 1.00
4 Demetrius Forney .40 1.00
5 Dennis Fryzel .40 1.00
6 Takuya Furutani .40 1.00
7 Tommy Johnson CO .50 1.25
8 Antwan Lawrence .40 1.00
9 Nick Myers .40 1.00
10 Anthony Payton .40 1.00
11 Marc Samuel .40 1.00
12 Matt Sauk .50 1.25
13 James Scott .40 1.00
14 Derrick Shephard .40 1.00
15 Tony Stallings .40 1.00
16 Vic Vrabel .40 1.00
17 Saru Wantanbe .40 1.00
18 Kenta Yagi .40 1.00
19 Axe (Mascot) .40 1.00
20 Team Photo CL .40 1.00

1968 MacGregor Advisory Staff

MacGregor released a number of player photos during the 1960s. Each measures roughly 8" by 10 1/2" and carries a black and white photo of the player. Included below the photo is a note that the player is a member of MacGregor's advisory staff. The photos are blankbacked and unnumbered and checklisted below in alphabetical order. Any additions to the list below are appreciated.

1 Mike Ditka 15.00 30.00
2 Joe Namath 30.00 60.00
3 Bart Starr 15.00 30.00
4 Johnny Unitas 20.00 40.00

1973-87 Mardi Gras Parade Doubloons

These Mardi Gras Parade Doubloons or coins were thrown into the crowds by passing floats during the celebration each year in New Orleans. Although many different subject matters appear on these types of coins, we've only listed the football players below. Each includes a sculpted portrait of the player on one side and the parade logo on the other on a gold or bronze colored coin; all are from the Gladiators Parade unless noted below. We've listed the coins by their year of issue. Any additions to the list below are appreciated.

COMPLETE SET (16) 15.00 30.00
1973 Danny Abramowicz 1.00 2.00
1974 George Blanda 1.50 3.00
1975 Ken Stabler 2.50 5.00
1977 Bert Jones 1.00 2.00
1978 Joe Ferguson 1.00 2.00
1979 Ray Guy 1.00 2.00
1980 Norris Weese 1.00 2.00
1981 Billy Kilmer 1.00 2.00
1982 Sonny Jurgensen 1.50 3.00
1983 Danny Abramowicz 1.00 2.00
1984 Archie Manning 1.50 3.00
1985 Richard Todd 1.00 2.00
1986 Brian Hansen 1.00 2.00
1987 Morten Andersen 1.00 2.00
1995 Jim Finks Green 1.00 2.00
1995 Jim Finks Silver 1.00 2.00

1997 Mark Brunell Tracard

This set of six-cards was printed specifically for Mark Brunell for use during signing sessions and fan mail requests. Each card was hand signed by Brunell and features a different photo on the front and religious message on the back along with the card number. No print year is given, but they were released throughout the late 1990s.

COMPLETE SET (6) 54.00 135.00
COMMON CARD (1-6) 10.00 25.00

1977 Marketcom Test

The 1977 Marketcom Test checklist below includes known mini-posters with each measuring approximately 5 1/2" by 8 1/2". They were printed on paper-thin stock and are virtually always found with fold creases. Marketcom is credited at the bottom of most of them along with the year 1977. Some are blankbacked while others include an advertisement for obtaining a large version of the poster. These posters are unnumbered and listed below in alphabetical order.

1 Otis Armstrong 20.00 40.00
2 Ken Burrough 20.00 40.00
3 Greg Pruitt 20.00 40.00
4 Jack Youngblood 20.00 40.00

1978-79 Marketcom Test

The 1978-79 Marketcom set includes mini-posters measuring approximately 5 1/2" by 8 1/2". They were printed on paper-thin stock and are virtually always found with fold creases. Marketcom is credited at the bottom of each poster front and some include a year designation while others do not. Most poster backs are blank but others have been found with an advertisement on the back for full sized posters. Finally, another version of many of the posters was also printed on thin cardboard stock without any folds. These cardboard versions are blankbacked and thicker than the paper version but slightly thinner than the 1980 posters. The posters are unnumbered and listed below in alphabetical order.

COMPLETE SET (34) 250.00 450.00
1 Otis Armstrong SP 5.00 10.00
2 Steve Bartkowski SP 6.00 12.00
3 Terry Bradshaw SP 20.00 40.00
4 Ken Burrough 3.00 6.00
5 Earl Campbell 15.00 30.00
6 Dave Casper 4.00 8.00
7 Gary Danielson 3.00 6.00
8 Dan Dierdorf SP 6.00 12.00
9 Tony Dorsett SP 20.00 40.00
10 Dan Fouts SP 12.50 25.00
11 Wallace Francis 4.00 8.00
12 Tony Galbreath 3.00 6.00
13 Randy Gradishar SP 5.00 10.00
14 Bob Griese SP 12.50 25.00
15 Steve Grogan 4.00 8.00
16 Ray Guy 4.00 8.00
17 Pat Haden SP 6.00 12.00
18 Jack Ham 6.00 12.00
19 Cliff Harris SP 5.00 10.00
20 Franco Harris 7.50 15.00
21 Jim Hart 4.00 8.00
22 Ron Jaworski 4.00 8.00
23 John Jefferson 5.00 10.00
24 Bert Jones SP 6.00 12.00
25 Jack Lambert SP 10.00 20.00
26 Archie Manning 6.00 12.00
27 Harvey Martin SP 5.00 10.00
28 Reggie McKenzie 3.00 6.00
29 Karl Mecklenburg SP 5.00 10.00
30 Craig Morton 4.00 8.00
31 Dan Pastorini 3.00 6.00
32 Walter Payton SP 20.00 40.00
33 Lee Roy Selmon 5.00 10.00
34 Roger Staubach SP 20.00 40.00
35 Joe Theismann UER 6.00 12.00
36 Wesley Walker SP 5.00 10.00
37 Randy White 6.00 12.00
38 Jack Youngblood SP 5.00 10.00
39 Jim Zorn 4.00 8.00

1980 Marketcom

In 1980, Marketcom issued a set of 50 Football Mini-Posters. These 5 1/2" by 8 1/2" cards are very attractive, featuring a large full color (action scene) picture of each player with a white border. The cards have the player's name on front at top and have a facsimile autograph on the picture as well; cards are numbered on the back at the bottom as "x of 50". A very tough to find Rocky Bleier card (numbered 51) was produced as well, but is not listed below due to lack of market information.

COMPLETE SET (50) 30.00 60.00
1 Ottis Anderson .75 2.00
2 Brian Sipe .40 1.00
3 Lawrence McCutcheon .40 1.00
4 Ken Anderson .75 2.00
5 Roland Harper .40 1.00
6 Chuck Foreman .40 1.00
7 Gary Danielson .40 1.00
8 Wallace Francis .40 1.00
9 John Jefferson .50 1.25
10 Charlie Waters .50 1.25
11 Jack Ham .75 2.00
12 Jack Lambert .75 2.00
13 Walter Payton 5.00 12.00
14 Bert Jones .50 1.25
15 Harvey Martin .50 1.25
16 Jim Hart .40 1.00
17 Craig Morton .50 1.25
18 Reggie McKenzie .40 1.00
19 Keith Wortman .40 1.00
20 Otis Armstrong .40 1.00
21 Steve Grogan .50 1.25
22 Jim Zorn .40 1.00
23 Bob Griese 1.25 3.00
24 Tony Dorsett 2.00 5.00
25 Wesley Walker .40 1.00
26 Dan Fouts 1.00 2.50
27 Dan Dierdorf .75 2.00
28 Steve Bartkowski .50 1.25
29 Archie Manning .50 1.25
30 Randy Gradishar .50 1.25
31 Randy White .75 2.00
32 Joe Theismann .75 2.00
33 Tony Galbreath .40 1.00
34 Cliff Harris .50 1.25
35 Ray Guy .50 1.25
36 Dave Casper .50 1.25
37 Ron Jaworski .50 1.25
38 Greg Pruitt .40 1.00
39 Ken Burrough .40 1.00
40 Robert Brazile .40 1.00
41 Pat Haden .50 1.25
42 Dan Pastorini .40 1.00
43 Lee Roy Selmon .75 2.00
44 Franco Harris 1.25 3.00
45 Jack Youngblood .50 1.25
46 Terry Bradshaw 3.00 8.00
47 Roger Staubach 3.00 8.00
48 Earl Campbell 2.00 5.00
49 Phil Simms 1.25 3.00
50 Delvin Williams .40 1.00

1981 Marketcom

In 1981, Marketcom issued a set of 50 Football Mini-Posters. These 5 1/2" by 8 1/2" cards are very attractive, featuring a large full color (action scene) picture of each player with a white border. The cards have player's name on front at top and have a facsimile autograph on the picture as well; cards are numbered on the back at the bottom. This set can be distinguished from the set of the previous year by the presence of statistics and text on the backs of this issue.

COMPLETE SET (50) 25.00 50.00
1 Ottis Anderson .60 1.50
2 Brian Sipe .40 1.00
3 Rocky Bleier .60 1.50
4 Ken Anderson .75 2.00
5 Roland Harper .30 .75
6 Steve Furness .30 .75
7 Gary Danielson .30 .75
8 Wallace Francis .40 1.00
9 John Jefferson .40 1.00
10 Charlie Waters .40 1.00
11 Jack Ham .60 1.50
12 Jack Lambert .75 2.00
13 Walter Payton 3.00 8.00
14 Bert Jones .60 1.50
15 Harvey Martin .40 1.00
16 Jim Hart .40 1.00
17 Craig Morton .60 1.50
18 Reggie McKenzie .30 .75
19 Keith Wortman .30 .75
20 Joe Greene .75 2.00
21 Steve Grogan .60 1.50
22 Jim Zorn .40 1.00
23 Bob Griese 1.00 2.50
24 Tony Dorsett 1.50 4.00
25 Wesley Walker .40 1.00
26 Dan Fouts 1.00 2.50
27 Dan Dierdorf .60 1.50
28 Steve Bartkowski .60 1.50
29 Archie Manning .60 1.50
30 Randy Gradishar .40 1.00
31 Randy White .75 2.00
32 Joe Theismann .75 2.00
33 Tony Galbreath .30 .75
34 Cliff Harris .40 1.00
35 Ray Guy .60 1.50
36 Joe Ferguson .40 1.00
37 Ron Jaworski .60 1.50
38 Greg Pruitt .40 1.00
39 Ken Burrough .30 .75
40 Robert Brazile .30 .75
41 Pat Haden .40 1.00
42 Ken Stabler 1.50 4.00
43 Lee Roy Selmon .60 1.50
44 Franco Harris 1.00 2.50
45 Jack Youngblood .60 1.50
46 Terry Bradshaw 2.50 6.00
47 Roger Staubach 2.50 6.00
48 Earl Campbell 1.50 4.00
49 Phil Simms .75 2.00
50 Delvin Williams .30 .75

1982 Marketcom

In 1982, Marketcom issued a set of 48 Football Mini-Posters. These 5 1/2" by 8 1/2" cards are very attractive, featuring a large full color (action scene) picture of each player with a white border. The cards have player's name on front at top and have a facsimile autograph on the picture as well; cards are numbered on the back at the bottom. The back carries biographical information, player profile, and statistics. The lower right corner of the card back indicates "St. Louis - Marketcom - Series C".

COMPLETE SET (48) 300.00 500.00
1 Joe Ferguson 2.50 6.00
2 Kellen Winslow 3.00 8.00
3 Jim Hart 2.50 6.00
4 Archie Manning 2.50 6.00
5 Earl Campbell 10.00 25.00
6 Wallace Francis 2.50 6.00
7 Randy Gradishar 2.50 6.00
8 Ken Stabler 10.00 25.00
9 Danny White 3.00 8.00
10 Jack Ham 3.00 8.00
11 Lawrence Taylor 12.00 30.00
12 Eric Hipple 2.00 5.00
13 Ron Jaworski 2.50 6.00
14 George Rogers 2.50 6.00
15 Jack Lambert 6.00 15.00
16 Randy White 5.00 12.00
17 Terry Bradshaw 15.00 40.00
18 Ray Guy 2.50 6.00
19 Rob Carpenter 2.00 5.00
20 Reggie McKenzie 2.00 5.00
21 Tony Dorsett 10.00 25.00
22 Wesley Walker 2.50 6.00
23 Tommy Kramer 2.50 6.00
24 Dwight Clark 2.50 6.00
25 Franco Harris 8.00 20.00
26 Craig Morton 2.50 6.00
27 Harvey Martin 2.50 6.00
28 Jim Zorn 2.50 6.00
29 Steve Bartkowski 2.50 6.00
30 Joe Theismann 4.00 10.00
31 Dan Dierdorf 3.00 8.00
32 Walter Payton 25.00 60.00
33 John Jefferson 2.50 6.00
34 Phil Simms 3.00 8.00
35 Lee Roy Selmon 4.00 10.00
36 Joe Montana 50.00 100.00
37 Robert Brazile 2.50 6.00
38 Steve Grogan 2.50 6.00
39 Dave Logan 2.00 5.00
40 Ken Anderson 3.00 8.00
41 Richard Todd 2.50 6.00
42 Jack Youngblood 3.00 8.00
43 Ottis Anderson 2.50 6.00
44 Brian Sipe 2.50 6.00
45 Mark Gastineau 2.50 6.00
46 Mike Pruitt 2.00 5.00
47 Cris Collinsworth 2.50 6.00
48 Dan Fouts 5.00 12.00

1987 Marketcom Sports Illustrated

This 20-card white-bordered, multi-sport set measures approximately 3 1/16" by 4 14/16" and features color action photos of players in various sports produced by Marketcom. Cards #1-13 display Baseball players; cards #14-17, Basketball players; cards #18-20, Football players. The backs are blank. The set was issued to promote the Sports Illustrated sticker line. The cards are unnumbered and checklisted below alphabetically within each sport.

COMPLETE SET (20) 60.00 150.00
18 John Elway 10.00 25.00
19 Lawrence Taylor 1.25 3.00
20 Herschel Walker 1.25 3.00

1971 Mattel Mini-Records

This set was designed to be played on a special Mattel mini-record player, which is not included in the complete set price. Each black plastic disc, approximately 2 1/2" in diameter, features a recording on one side and a color drawing of the player on the other. The picture appears on a paper disk that is glued onto the smooth unrecorded side of the mini-record. On the recorded side, the player's name and the set's subtitle appear in arcs stamped in the central portion of the mini-record. The hand-engraved player's name appears again along with a production number, copyright symbol, and the Mattel name and year of production in the ring between the central portion of the record and the grooves. The ivory discs are the ones which are double sided and are considered to be tougher than the black discs. They were also known as "Mattel Show 'N Tell". The discs are unnumbered and checklisted below in alphabetical order according to sport

COMPLETE SET (18) 200.00 400.00
FB1 Donny Anderson 1.25 3.00
FB2 Lem Barney 1.50 4.00
FB3 John Brodie DP 1.50 4.00
FB4 Dick Butkus DP 3.00 8.00
FB5 Bob Hayes DP 1.50 4.00
FB6 Sonny Jurgensen 2.50 6.00
FB7 Alex Karras 2.50 6.00
FB8 Leroy Kelly 2.00 5.00
FB9 Daryle Lamonica DP 1.25 3.00
FB10 John Mackey DP 1.50 4.00
FB11 Earl Morrall 1.25 3.00
FB12 Joe Namath 15.00 30.00
FB13 Merlin Olsen DP 1.50 4.00
FB14 Alan Page 2.00 5.00
FB15 Gale Sayers DP 3.00 8.00
FB16 O.J. Simpson DP 3.00 8.00
FB17 Bart Starr 12.50 25.00

1937 Mayfair Candies Touchdown 100 Yards

Mayfair Candies produced this perforated card set in 1937. Each unnumbered card features an unidentified football action photo on the front and a football play description on the back. The set involved a contest whereby the collector tried to accumulate "100 Yards" based on football plays described on the cardbacks. The offer expired on February 15, 1938 and winners could exchange the cards for an official sized football. The ACC designation is R343 and each card measures approximately 1 3/4" by 2 3/4" and was unnumbered. Since there are no card numbers and no identification of players, we have cataloged the cards below using the first several words found at the top of the cardbacks. We have also included the cardfront photo's background color and number of players featured in the image for each card to help catalog the cardfronts. Note that four cardfronts exist with two different cardbacks each. Red Grange is the only player of note that has been positively identified.

COMPLETE SET (24) 5000.00 8000.00
1 2 Yards to go!... 200.00 350.00
2 3 Yards to go... 200.00 350.00
3 Again the off tackle... 200.00 350.00
4 Being in perfect position... 200.00 350.00
5 Changing quickly from... 200.00 350.00
6 Charging hard... 200.00 350.00
7 Coming from in front... 200.00 350.00
8 Coming out of a... 200.00 350.00
9 Digging in their heels... 200.00 350.00
10 Early in the third... 200.00 350.00
11 Flipping a underhand... 200.00 350.00
12 Giving every ounce... 200.00 350.00
13 In a play that fizzled... 200.00 350.00
14 Indecision on the part... 200.00 350.00
15 Late in the same... 200.00 350.00
16 Left Tackle is called... 200.00 350.00
17 Line holds beautifully... (Red Grange pictured) 900.00 1500.00
18 Only intense rivalry... 200.00 350.00
19 Outmaneuvered.... 200.00 350.00
20 Quarterback runs... 200.00 350.00
21 Revealing for the first... 200.00 350.00
22 Same old story... 200.00 350.00
23 Smashing close behind... 200.00 350.00
24 Snapping out of their... 200.00 350.00
25 The fullback driving... 200.00 350.00
26 Three unsuccessful... 200.00 350.00
27 Trying the old... 200.00 350.00
28 What have we here?... 200.00 350.00

1894 Mayo

The 1894 Mayo college football series contains 35-cards of top Ivy League players. The cards feature sepia photos of the player surrounded by a black border, in which the player's name, his college, and a Mayo Cut Plug ad appears. The cards have solid black backs and measure approximately 1 5/8" by 2 7/8". Each card is unnumbered, but we've assigned card numbers alphabetically in the checklist below for your convenience. One of the cards has no specific identification of the player (John Dunlop of Harvard) and is listed below as being anonymous. It's one of the most highly sought after of all football cards and seldom seen. We've not included it in the complete set price due to its scarcity. Those players who were All-American selections are listed below with the year(s) of selection. The Poe (likely Neilson Poe) in the set is a direct descendant of the famous writer Edgar Allan Poe.

COMPLETE SET (34) 15000.00 25000.00
1 Robert Acton (Harvard) 500.00 800.00
2 George Adee (Yale) 500.00 800.00
3 Richard Armstrong (Yale) 500.00 800.00
4 H.W.Barnett (Princeton) 500.00 800.00
5 Art Beale (Harvard) 500.00 800.00
6 Anson Beard (Yale) 500.00 800.00
7 Charles Brewer (Harvard) 500.00 800.00
8 H.D.Brown (Princeton) 500.00 800.00
9 C.D. Burt (Princeton) 500.00 800.00
10 Frank Butterworth (Yale) 550.00 850.00
11 Eddie Crowdis (Princeton) 500.00 800.00
12 Robert Emmons (Harvard) 500.00 800.00
13 Madison Gonterman UER (Har) 500.00 800.00
14 George Gray (Harvard) 500.00 800.00
15 John Greenway (Yale) 550.00 850.00
16 William Hickok (Yale) 550.00 850.00
17 Frank Hinkey (Yale) 800.00 1200.00
18 Augustus Holly (Princeton) 500.00 800.00
19 Langdon Lea (Princeton) 550.00 850.00
20 William Mackie (Harvard) 500.00 800.00
21 Tom Manahan (Harvard) 500.00 800.00
22 Jim McCrea (Yale) 500.00 800.00
23 Frank Morse (Princeton) 500.00 800.00
24 Fred Murphy (Yale) 550.00 850.00
25 Neilson Poe (Princeton) 800.00 1200.00
26 Dudley Riggs (Princeton) 550.00 850.00
27 Phillip Stillman (Yale) 500.00 800.00
28 Knox Taylor (Princeton) 500.00 800.00
29 Brinck Thorne (Yale) 500.00 800.00
30 T.Trenchard (Princeton) 550.00 850.00
31 William Ward (Princeton) 500.00 800.00
32 Bert Waters (Harvard) 550.00 850.00
33 A. Wheeler (Princeton) 550.00 850.00
34 Edgar Wrightington (Har) 500.00 800.00
35 Anonymous (J.Dunlop) 12000.00 18000.00

1975 McDonald's Quarterbacks

The 1975 McDonald's Quarterbacks set contains four cards, each of which was used as a promotion for McDonald's hamburger restaurants. The cards measure 2 1/2" by 3 7/16". One might get a quarter back if the coupon at the bottom of the card were presented at one of McDonald's retail establishments. Each coupon was valid for only one week, that particular week clearly marked on the coupon. The cards themselves are in color with yellow borders on the front and statistics on the back. The back of each card is a different color. Statistics are given for each of the quarterback's previous seasons record passing and rushing. The prices below are for the cards with coupons intact as that is the way they are usually found.

COMPLETE SET (4) 12.50 25.00
1 Terry Bradshaw 7.50 15.00
2 Joe Ferguson 2.00 5.00
3 Ken Stabler 4.00 10.00
4 Al Woodall 1.50 4.00

1985 McDonald's Bears Orange Tab

This set of 32 cards featuring the Chicago Bears was available with three different tab colors. Yellow tabs referenced the Super Bowl. Orange tabs referenced the NFC Championship Game. Blue tabs referenced the Divisional Playoff game. All three sets contain the same 32 players. The cards measure approximately 4 1/2" by 5 7/8" with the tab intact and 4 1/2" by 4 3/8" without the tab, noticeably larger than the McDonald's cards of 1986. Apparently this set was a test market which evidently was successful enough for McDonald's to distribute all 28 teams (plus All-Stars) in 1986. The promotion was intended to last until the Bears were eliminated from the playoffs, but they never were; they won the Super Bowl in convincing fashion. Prices listed are for cards with tabs intact.

COMPLETE ORANGE SET (32) 12.00 30.00
COMP.BLUE SET (32) 15.00 40.00
*BLUE TAB: .5X TO 1.2X ORANGE
COMP.YELLOW SET (32) 12.00 30.00
*YELLOW TAB: .4X TO 1X ORANGE
4 Steve Fuller .30 .75
6 Kevin Butler .30 .75
8 Maury Buford .20 .50
9 Jim McMahon .75 2.00
21 Leslie Frazier .20 .50
22 Dave Duerson .20 .50
26 Matt Suhey .30 .75
27 Mike Richardson .20 .50
29 Dennis Gentry .20 .50
33 Calvin Thomas .20 .50
34 Walter Payton 3.00 8.00
45 Gary Fencik .30 .75
50 Mike Singletary 1.00 2.50
55 Otis Wilson .20 .50
58 Wilber Marshall .40 1.00
62 Mark Bortz .20 .50
63 Jay Hilgenberg .30 .75
72 William Perry .40 1.00
73 Mike Hartenstine .20 .50
74 Jim Covert .30 .75
75 Stefan Humphries .20 .50
76 Steve McMichael .40 1.00
78 Keith Van Horne .20 .50
80 Tim Wrightman .20 .50
82 Ken Margerum .20 .50
83 Willie Gault .40 1.00
85 Dennis McKinnon .30 .75
87 Emery Moorehead .20 .50
95 Richard Dent .75 2.00
99 Dan Hampton .75 2.00
NNO Mike Ditka CO .75 2.00
NNO Buddy Ryan ACO .40 1.00

1986 McDonald's All-Stars Green Tab

This 30-card set was issued in all of the cities that were not near NFL cities and hence is the easiest of the McDonald's subsets to find. The set was issued over a four-week period with blue tabs the first week, black (or gray) tabs the second week, gold (or orange) tabs the third week, and green tabs the fourth week. The cards measure approximately 3 1/16" by 4 11/16" with the tab intact and 3 1/16" by 3 5/8" without the tab. The value of cards without tabs or tabs scratched off is F-G at best. All-Stars were printed on a 30-card sheet; hence, there are no DP cards, unlike the situation with the team subsets, where six cards were double printed. Since the cards are unnumbered, they are listed below by uniform number; in several instances, players on different teams have the same number.

COMP.GREEN SET (30) 2.50 6.00
COMP.BLACK SET (30) 2.50 6.00
*BLACK: .4X TO 1X GREEN
COMP.BLUE SET (30) 2.50 6.00
*BLUE: .4X TO 1X GREEN
COMP.GOLD SET (30) 2.50 6.00
*GOLD: .4X TO 1X GREEN
9 Jim McMahon .15 .40
11 Phil Simms .15 .40
13 Dan Marino 1.00 2.50
14 Dan Fouts .15 .40
16 Joe Montana 1.00 2.50
20A Deron Cherry .06 .15
20B Joe Morris .06 .15
32 Marcus Allen .15 .40
33 Roger Craig .10 .25
34A Kevin Mack .06 .15
34B Walter Payton .60 1.50
42 Gerald Riggs .06 .15
45 Kenny Easley .06 .15
47A Joey Browner .06 .15
47B LeRoy Irvin .06 .15
52 Mike Webster .10 .25
54A E.J. Junior .06 .15
54B Randy White .10 .25
56 Lawrence Taylor .15 .40
63 Mike Munchak .06 .15
66 Joe Jacoby .06 .15
73 John Hannah .10 .25
75A Chris Hinton .06 .15
75B Rulon Jones .06 .15
75C Howie Long .10 .25
78 Anthony Munoz .10 .25
81 Art Monk .15 .40
82A Ozzie Newsome .15 .40
82B Mike Quick .06 .15
99 Mark Gastineau .06 .15

1986 McDonald's Bears Green Tab

This 24-card set was issued in McDonald's Hamburger restaurants around Chicago. The set was issued over a four-week period with blue tabs the first week, black (or gray) tabs the second week, gold (or orange) tabs the third week, and green tabs the fourth week. The cards measure approximately 3 1/16" by 4 11/16" with the tab intact and 3 1/16" by 3 5/8" without the tab. The cards are numbered below by uniform number. The value of cards without tabs or tabs scratched off is F-G at best. The cards were printed on a 30-card sheet; hence, there are six double-printed cards listed DP in the checklist below. For individual prices on the more expensive color tabs, merely apply the ratio of that color's set price to the base (cheapest) color set price and use the resulting multiple on the individual prices for that color.

COMP.GREEN SET (24) 3.00 8.00
COMP.BLACK SET (24) 3.00 8.00
*BLACK: .4X TO 1X GREEN
COMP.BLUE SET (24) 6.00 15.00
*BLUE: .8X TO 2X GREEN
COMP.GOLD SET (24) 3.00 8.00
*GOLD: .4X TO 1X GREEN
6 Kevin Butler DP .15 .40
8 Maury Buford .12 .30
9 Jim McMahon DP .40 1.00
22 Dave Duerson .12 .30
26 Matt Suhey .15 .40
27 Mike Richardson .12 .30
34 Walter Payton DP 1.00 2.50
45 Gary Fencik .15 .40
50 Mike Singletary DP .40 1.00
55 Otis Wilson .12 .30
57 Tom Thayer .12 .30
58 Wilber Marshall .20 .50
62 Mark Bortz DP .12 .30
63 Jay Hilgenberg .15 .40
72 William Perry DP .20 .50
74 Jim Covert .15 .40
76 Steve McMichael .20 .50
78 Keith Van Horne .12 .30
80 Tim Wrightman .12 .30
82 Ken Margerum .12 .30
83 Willie Gault .20 .50
87 Emery Moorehead .12 .30
95 Richard Dent .40 1.00
99 Dan Hampton .40 1.00

1986 McDonald's Bengals Green Tab

This 24-card set was issued in McDonald's Hamburger restaurants around Cincinnati. The set was issued over a four-week period with blue tabs the first week, black (or gray) tabs the second week, gold (or orange) tabs the third week, and green tabs the fourth week. The cards measure approximately 3 1/16" by 4 11/16" with the tab intact and 3 1/16" by 3 5/8" without the tab. The cards are numbered below by uniform number. The value of cards without tabs or tabs scratched off is F-G at best. The cards were printed on a 30-card sheet; hence, there are six double-printed cards listed DP in the checklist below. For individual prices on the more expensive color tabs, merely apply the ratio of that color's set price to the base (cheapest) color set price and use the resulting multiple on the individual prices for that color. Boomer Esiason appears in his Rookie Card year.

COMP.GREEN SET (24) 5.00 12.00
COMP.BLACK SET (24) 5.00 12.00
*BLACK: .4X TO 1X GREEN
COMP.BLUE SET (24) 10.00 25.00
*BLUE: .8X TO 2X GREEN
COMP.GOLD SET (24) 5.00 12.00
*GOLD: .4X TO 1X GREEN
7 Boomer Esiason 1.25 3.00
14 Ken Anderson DP .50 1.25
20 Ray Horton .25 .60
21 James Brooks DP .40 1.00
22 James Griffin .20 .50
28 Larry Kinnebrew .25 .60
34 Louis Breeden DP .20 .50
37 Robert Jackson .20 .50
40 Charles Alexander DP .20 .50
52 Dave Rimington .25 .60
57 Reggie Williams .40 1.00
65 Max Montoya .25 .60
69 Tim Krumrie .30 .75
73 Eddie Edwards .25 .60
74 Brian Blados DP .20 .50
77 Mike Wilson T .20 .50
78 Anthony Munoz .60 1.50
79 Ross Browner .25 .60
80 Cris Collinsworth .40 1.00
81 Eddie Brown DP .30 .75
82 Rodney Holman .25 .60
83 M.L. Harris .20 .50
90 Emanuel King .20 .50
91 Carl Zander .20 .50

1986 McDonald's Bills Green Tab

This 24-card set was issued in McDonald's Hamburger restaurants around Buffalo. The set was issued over a four-week period with blue tabs the first week, black (or gray) tabs the second week, gold (or orange) tabs the third week, and green tabs the fourth week. The cards measure approximately 3 1/16" by 4 11/16" with the tab intact and 3 1/16" by 3 5/8" without the tab. The cards are numbered below by uniform number. The value of cards without tabs or tabs scratched off is F-G at best. The cards were printed on a 30-card sheet; hence, there are six double-printed cards listed DP in the checklist below. For individual prices on the more expensive color tabs, merely apply the ratio of that color's set price to the base (cheapest) color set price and use the resulting multiple on the individual prices for that color. Andre Reed and Bruce Smith appear in their Rookie Card year.

COMP.GREEN SET (24) 6.00 15.00
COMP.BLACK SET (24) 12.00 30.00
*BLACK: .8X TO 2X GREEN
COMP.BLUE SET (24) 50.00 120.00
*BLUE: 3X TO 8X GREEN
COMP.GOLD SET (24) 6.00 15.00
*GOLD: .4X TO 1X GREEN
4 John Kidd .30 .75
7 Bruce Mathison .30 .75
11 Scott Norwood .40 1.00
22 Steve Freeman .30 .75
26 Charles Romes .30 .75
28 Greg Bell DP .40 1.00
29 Derrick Burroughs DP .30 .75
43 Martin Bayless DP .30 .75
51 Jim Ritcher .40 1.00
54 Eugene Marve .30 .75
55 Jim Haslett .30 .75
57 Lucius Sanford .30 .75
63 Justin Cross DP .30 .75
65 Tim Vogler .30 .75
70 Joe Devlin .30 .75
72 Ken Jones .30 .75
76 Fred Smerlas .40 1.00
77 Ben Williams .40 1.00
78 Bruce Smith 1.50 4.00
80 Jerry Butler DP .40 1.00
83 Andre Reed 1.50 4.00
85 Chris Burkett DP .40 1.00
87 Eason Ramson .30 .75
95 Sean McNanie .30 .75

1986 McDonald's Broncos Green Tab

This 24-card set was issued in McDonald's Hamburger restaurants around Denver. The set was issued over a four-week period with blue tabs the first week, black (or gray) tabs the second week, gold (or orange) tabs the third week, and green tabs the fourth week. The cards measure approximately 3 1/16" by 4 11/16" with the tab intact and 3 1/16" by 3 5/8" without the tab. The cards are numbered below by uniform number. The value of cards without tabs or tabs scratched off is F-G at best. The cards were printed on a 30-card sheet; hence, there are six double-printed cards listed DP in the checklist below. For individual prices on the more expensive color tabs, merely apply the ratio of that color's set price to the base (cheapest) color set price and use the resulting multiple on the individual prices for that color.

COMP.GREEN SET (24) 8.00 20.00
COMP.BLACK SET (24) 8.00 20.00
*BLACK: .4X TO 1X GREEN
COMP.BLUE SET (24) 15.00 40.00
*BLUE: .8X TO 2X GREEN
COMP.GOLD SET (24) 8.00 20.00
*GOLD: .4X TO 1X GREEN
3 Rich Karlis .20 .50
7 John Elway DP 4.00 10.00
20 Louis Wright .30 .75
22 Tony Lilly .20 .50
23 Sammy Winder .30 .75
30 Steve Sewell .30 .75
31 Mike Harden .30 .75
43 Steve Foley .30 .75
47 Gerald Willhite .30 .75
49 Dennis Smith .30 .75
50 Jim Ryan .20 .50
54 Keith Bishop DP .20 .50
55 Rick Dennison DP .20 .50
57 Tom Jackson .50 1.25
60 Paul Howard .20 .50
64 Bill Bryan DP .20 .50
68 Rubin Carter DP .20 .50
70 Dave Studdard .20 .50
75 Rulon Jones .30 .75
77 Karl Mecklenburg .20 .50
79 Barney Chavous DP .20 .50
81 Steve Watson .30 .75
82 Vance Johnson .20 .50
84 Clint Sampson .20 .50

1986 McDonald's Browns Green Tab

This 24-card set was issued in McDonald's Hamburger restaurants around Cleveland. The set was issued over a four-week period with blue tabs the first week, black (or gray) tabs the second week, gold (or orange) tabs the third week, and green tabs the fourth week. The cards measure approximately 3 1/16" by 4 11/16" with the tab intact and 3 1/16" by 3 5/8" without the tab. The cards are numbered below by uniform number. The value of cards without tabs or tabs scratched off is F-G at best. The cards were printed on a 30-card sheet; hence, there are six double-printed cards listed DP in the checklist below. For individual prices on the more expensive color tabs, merely apply the ratio of that color's set price to the base (cheapest) color set price and use the resulting multiple on the individual prices for that color. Bernie Kosar appears in his Rookie Card year.

COMP.GREEN SET (24) 2.50 6.00
COMP.BLACK SET (24) 3.00 8.00
*BLACK: .5X TO 1.2X GREEN
COMP.BLUE SET (24) 5.00 12.00
*BLUE .8X TO 2X GREEN
COMP.GOLD SET (24) 2.50 6.00
*GOLD: .4X TO 1X GREEN
9 Matt Bahr DP .10 .25
18 Gary Danielson .10 .25
19 Bernie Kosar DP .75 2.00
27 Al Gross .10 .25
29 Hanford Dixon .15 .40
31 Frank Minnifield .15 .40
34 Kevin Mack .20 .50
37 Chris Rockins .10 .25
44 Earnest Byner .30 .75
51 Eddie Johnson .10 .25
55 Curtis Weathers .10 .25
56 Chip Banks DP .10 .25
57 Clay Matthews .20 .50
60 Tom Cousineau .10 .25
61 Mike Baab DP .10 .25
63 Cody Risien .15 .40
77 Rickey Bolden DP .10 .25
78 Carl Hairston .10 .25
79 Bob Golic .15 .40
82 Ozzie Newsome .40 1.00
84 Glen Young .10 .25
85 Clarence Weathers .10 .25
86 Brian Brennan DP .15 .40
96 Reggie Camp .10 .25

1986 McDonald's Buccaneers Green Tab

This 24-card set was issued in McDonald's Hamburger restaurants in the Tampa Bay area. The set was issued over a four-week period with blue tabs the first week, black (or gray) tabs the second week, gold (or orange) tabs the third week, and green tabs the fourth week. The cards measure approximately 3 1/16" by 4 11/16" with the tab intact and 3 1/16" by 3 5/8" without the tab. The cards are numbered below by uniform number. The value of cards without tabs or tabs scratched off is F-G at best. The cards were printed on a 30-card sheet; hence, there are six double-printed cards listed DP in the checklist below. For individual prices on the more expensive color tabs, merely apply the ratio of that color's set price to the base (cheapest) color set price and use the resulting multiple on the individual prices for that color. Steve Young appears in his NFL Rookie Card year.

COMP.GREEN SET (24) 8.00 20.00
COMP.BLACK SET (24) 8.00 20.00
*BLACK: .4X TO 1X GREEN
COMP.BLUE SET (24) 8.00 20.00
*BLUE: .4X TO 1X GREEN
COMP.GOLD SET (24) 8.00 20.00
*GOLD: .4X TO 1X GREEN
1 Donald Igwebuike .12 .30
8 Steve Young 4.00 10.00
17 Steve DeBerg .30 .75
21 John Holt .12 .30
23 Jeremiah Castille DP .12 .30
30 David Greenwood .12 .30
32 James Wilder .20 .50
44 Ivory Sully .12 .30
51 Chris Washington .12 .30
52 Scot Brantley DP .12 .30
54 Ervin Randle .12 .30
58 Jeff Davis DP .12 .30
60 Randy Grimes .12 .30
62 Sean Farrell .15 .40
66 George Yarno .12 .30
73 Ron Heller .12 .30
76 David Logan .12 .30
78 John Cannon DP .12 .30
82 Jerry Bell DP .12 .30
86 Calvin Magee .12 .30
87 Gerald Carter DP .12 .30
88 Jimmie Giles .20 .50
89 Kevin House .20 .50
90 Ron Holmes .15 .40

1986 McDonald's Cardinals Green Tab

This 24-card set was issued in McDonald's Hamburger restaurants around St. Louis. The set was issued over a four-week period with blue tabs the first week, black (or gray) tabs the second week, gold (or orange) tabs the third week, and green tabs the fourth week. The cards measure approximately 3 1/16" by 4 11/16" with the tab intact and 3 1/16" by 3 5/8" without the tab. The cards are numbered below by uniform number. The value of cards without tabs or tabs scratched off is F-G at best. The cards were printed on a 30-card sheet; hence, there are six double-printed cards listed DP in the checklist below. For individual prices on the more expensive color tabs, merely apply the ratio of that color's set price to the base (cheapest) color set price and use the resulting multiple on the individual prices for that color.

COMP.GREEN SET (24) 2.50 6.00
COMP.BLACK SET (24) 2.50 6.00
*BLACK: .4X TO 1X GREEN
COMP.BLUE SET (24) 4.00 10.00
*BLUE: .6X TO 1.5X GREEN
COMP.GOLD SET (24) 2.50 6.00
*GOLD: .4X TO 1X GREEN
15 Neil Lomax .20 .50
18 Carl Birdsong DP .10 .25
30 Stump Mitchell .15 .40
32 Ottis Anderson DP .30 .75
43 Lonnie Young .10 .25
45 Leonard Smith .10 .25
47 Cedric Mack .10 .25
48 Lionel Washington .10 .25
53 Freddie Joe Nunn .15 .40
54 E.J. Junior .15 .40
57 Niko Noga .10 .25
60 Al Bubba Baker DP .15 .40
63 Tootie Robbins .10 .25
65 David Galloway .10 .25
66 Doug Dawson DP .10 .25
67 Luis Sharpe .10 .25
71 Joe Bostic DP .10 .25
73 Mark Duda DP .10 .25
75 Curtis Greer .10 .25
80 Doug Marsh .10 .25
81 Roy Green .20 .50
83 Pat Tilley .10 .25
84 J.T. Smith .15 .40
89 Greg LaFleur .10 .25

1986 McDonald's Chargers Green Tab

This 24-card set was issued in McDonald's Hamburger restaurants around San Diego. The set was issued over a four-week period with blue tabs the first week, black (or gray) tabs the second week, gold (or orange) tabs the third week, and green tabs the fourth week. The cards measure approximately 3 1/16" by 4 11/16" with the tab intact and 3 1/16" by 3 5/8" without the tab. The cards are numbered below by uniform number. The value of cards without tabs or tabs scratched off is F-G at best. The cards were printed on a 30-card sheet; hence, there are six double-printed cards listed DP in the checklist below. For individual prices on the more expensive color tabs, merely apply the ratio of that color's set price to the base (cheapest) color set price and use the resulting multiple on the individual prices for that color.

COMP.GREEN SET (24) 5.00 12.00
COMP.BLACK SET (24) 8.00 20.00
*BLACK: .6X TO 1.5X GREEN
COMP.BLUE SET (24) 10.00 25.00
*BLUE: .8X TO 2X GREEN
COMP.GOLD SET (24) 5.00 12.00
*GOLD: .4X TO 1X GREEN
9 Mark Herrmann .15 .40
14 Dan Fouts DP .60 1.50
18 Charlie Joiner .50 1.25
21 Buford McGee .15 .40
22 Gill Byrd DP .20 .50
26 Lionel James .20 .50
29 John Hendy .15 .40
37 Jeffery Dale DP .15 .40
40 Gary Anderson RB DP .30 .75
43 Tim Spencer .15 .40
51 Woodrow Lowe .15 .40
54 Billy Ray Smith .20 .50
60 Dennis McKnight .15 .40
62 Don Macek .15 .40
67 Ed White .15 .40
74 Jim Lachey .40 1.00
78 Chuck Ehin DP .15 .40
80 Kellen Winslow .60 1.50
83 Trumaine Johnson .15 .40
85 Eric Sievers .15 .40
88 Pete Holohan .20 .50
89 Wes Chandler DP .20 .50
93 Earl Wilson .15 .40
99 Lee Williams .20 .50

1986 McDonald's Chiefs Green Tab

This 24-card set was issued in McDonald's Hamburger restaurants around Kansas City. The set was issued over a four-week period with blue tabs the first week, black (or gray) tabs the second week, gold (or orange) tabs the third week, and green tabs the fourth week. The cards measure approximately 3 1/16" by 4 11/16" with the tab intact and 3 1/16" by 3 5/8" without the tab. The cards are numbered below by uniform number. The value of cards without tabs or tabs scratched off is F-G at best. The cards were printed on a 30-card sheet; hence, there are six double-printed cards listed DP in the checklist below. For individual prices on the more expensive color tabs, merely apply the ratio of that color's set price to the base (cheapest) color set price and use the resulting multiple on the individual prices for that color.

COMP.GREEN SET (24) 8.00 20.00
COMP.BLACK SET (24) 12.00 30.00
*BLACK: .6X TO 1.5X GREEN
COMP.BLUE SET (24) 8.00 20.00
*BLUE: .4X TO 1X GREEN
COMP.GOLD SET (24) 8.00 20.00
*GOLD: .4X TO 1X GREEN
6 Jim Arnold DP .30 .75
8 Nick Lowery .40 1.00
9 Bill Kenney .30 .75
14 Todd Blackledge DP .40 1.00
20 Deron Cherry DP .50 1.25
29 Albert Lewis .50 1.25
31 Kevin Ross .50 1.25
34 Lloyd Burruss DP .30 .75
41 Garcia Lane .30 .75
42 Jeff Smith RB .30 .75
43 Mike Pruitt .40 1.00
44 Herman Heard .30 .75
50 Calvin Daniels .30 .75
59 Gary Spani .30 .75
63 Bill Maas .30 .75
64 Bob Olderman .30 .75
66 Brad Budde DP .30 .75
67 Art Still .30 .75
72 David Lutz .30 .75
83 Stephone Paige .50 1.25
85 Jonathan Hayes .40 1.00
88 Carlos Carson DP .40 1.00
89 Henry Marshall .30 .75
97 Scott Radecic .30 .75

1986 McDonald's Colts Green Tab

This 24-card set was issued in McDonald's Hamburger restaurants around Indianapolis. The set was issued over a four-week period with blue tabs the first week, black (or gray) tabs the second week, gold (or orange) tabs the third week, and green tabs the fourth week. The cards measure approximately 3 1/16" by 4 11/16" with the tab intact and 3 1/16" by 3 5/8" without the tab. The cards are numbered below by uniform number. The value of cards without tabs or tabs scratched off is F-G at best. The cards were printed on a 30-card sheet; hence, there are six double-printed cards listed DP in the checklist below. For individual prices on the more expensive color tabs, merely apply the ratio of that color's set price to the base (cheapest) color set price and use the resulting multiple on the individual prices for that color.

COMP.GREEN SET (24) 8.00 20.00
COMP.BLACK SET (24) 8.00 20.00
*BLACK: .4X TO 1X GREEN
COMP.BLUE SET (24) 40.00 80.00
*BLUE: 1.5X TO 4X GREEN
COMP.GOLD SET (24) 6.00 15.00
*GOLD: .3X TO .8X GREEN
2 Raul Allegre DP .25 .60
3 Rohn Stark .30 .75
25 Nesby Glasgow .25 .60
27 Preston Davis .25 .60
32 Randy McMillan .30 .75
34 George Wonsley .25 .60
38 Eugene Daniel .30 .75
44 Owen Gill .25 .60
47 Leonard Coleman .25 .60
50 Duane Bickett DP .40 1.00
53 Ray Donaldson .30 .75
55 Barry Krauss .25 .60
64 Ben Utt .25 .60
66 Ron Solt .25 .60
72 Karl Baldischwiler DP .25 .60
75 Chris Hinton .30 .75
81 Pat Beach DP .25 .60
85 Matt Bouza DP .25 .60
87 Wayne Capers DP .25 .60
88 Robbie Martin .25 .60
92 Brad White .25 .60
93 Cliff Odom .25 .60
96 Blaise Winter .25 .60
98 Johnie Cooks .25 .60

1986 McDonald's Cowboys Green Tab

This 25-card set was issued in McDonald's Hamburger restaurants around Dallas. The set was issued over a four-week period with blue tabs the first week, black (or gray) tabs the second week, gold (or orange) tabs the third week, and green tabs the fourth week. The cards measure approximately 3 1/16" by 4 11/16" with the tab intact and 3 1/16" by 3 5/8" without the tab. The cards are numbered below by uniform number. The Herschel Walker card was produced later due to his popularity. Walker's card was produced only with a green tab without any coating on the tab to be scratched off; hence his cards are typically found in nice condition. The value of cards without tabs or tabs scratched off is F-G at best. The cards (other than Herschel Walker) were printed on a 30-card sheet; hence, there are six double-printed cards listed DP in the checklist below. For individual prices on the more expensive color tabs, merely apply the ratio of that color's set price to the base (cheapest) color set price and use the resulting multiple on the individual prices for that color.

COMP.GREEN SET (24) 4.00 10.00
COMP.BLACK SET (24) 4.00 10.00
*BLACK: .4X TO 1X GREEN
COMP.BLUE SET (24) 4.00 10.00
*BLUE: .4X TO 1X GREEN
COMP.GOLD SET (24) 4.00 10.00
*GOLD: .4X TO 1X GREEN
1 Rafael Septien .10 .25
11 Danny White .20 .50
24 Everson Walls .15 .40
26 Michael Downs DP .10 .25
27 Ron Fellows .10 .25
30 Timmy Newsome .10 .25
33 Tony Dorsett DP .50 1.25
34 Herschel Walker .75 2.00
40 Bill Bates DP .20 .50
47 Dextor Clinkscale DP .10 .25
50 Jeff Rohrer .10 .25
54 Randy White .30 .75
56 Eugene Lockhart .15 .40
58 Mike Hegman .10 .25
61 Jim Cooper DP .10 .25
63 Glen Titensor .10 .25
64 Tom Rafferty .10 .25
65 Kurt Petersen .10 .25
72 Ed Too Tall Jones .30 .75
75 Phil Pozderac .10 .25
77 Jim Jeffcoat .20 .50
78 John Dutton .15 .40
80 Tony Hill .15 .40
82 Mike Renfro .10 .25
84 Doug Cosbie DP .10 .25

1986 McDonald's Dolphins Green Tab

This 25-card set was issued in McDonald's Hamburger restaurants around Miami. The set was issued over a four-week period with blue tabs the first week, black (or gray) tabs the second week, gold (or orange) tabs the third week, and green tabs the fourth week. The cards measure approximately 3 1/16" by 4 11/16" with the tab intact and 3 1/16" by 3 5/8" without the tab. The cards are numbered below by uniform number. Joe Carter and Tony Nathan have photos reversed so that there are 25 different cards, but since this error happened on a double-printed player, no additional value is assigned. The value of cards without tabs or tabs scratched off is F-G at best. The cards were printed on a 30-card sheet; hence, there are five double-printed cards listed DP in the checklist below. For individual prices on the more expensive color tabs, merely apply the ratio of that color's set price to the base (cheapest) color set price and use the resulting multiple on the individual prices for that color.

COMP.GREEN SET (24) 10.00 25.00
COMP.BLACK SET (24) 10.00 25.00
*BLACK: .4X TO 1X GREEN
COMP.BLUE SET (24) 15.00 40.00
*BLUE: .6X TO 1.5X GREEN
COMP.GOLD SET (24) 10.00 25.00
*GOLD: .4X TO 1X GREEN
4 Reggie Roby .40 1.00
7 Fuad Reveiz .25 .60
10 Don Strock .40 1.00
13 Dan Marino 4.00 10.00
22 Tony Nathan .40 1.00
23A Joe Carter ERR .40 1.00
23B Joe Carter COR .25 .60
27 Lorenzo Hampton .25 .60
30 Ron Davenport .25 .60
43 Bud Brown DP .25 .60
47 Glenn Blackwood DP .25 .60
49 William Judson .25 .60
55 Hugh Green .40 1.00
57 Dwight Stephenson .75 2.00
58 Kim Bokamper DP .25 .60
59 Bob Brudzinski DP .25 .60
61 Roy Foster .25 .60
71 Mike Charles .25 .60
75 Doug Betters DP .25 .60
79 Jon Giesler .25 .60
83 Mark Clayton .60 1.50
84 Bruce Hardy .25 .60
85 Mark Duper .50 1.25
89 Nat Moore .40 1.00
91 Mack Moore .25 .60

1986 McDonald's Eagles Green Tab

This 24-card set was issued in McDonald's Hamburger restaurants around Philadelphia. The set was issued over a four-week period with blue tabs the first week, black (or gray) tabs the second week, gold (or orange) tabs the third week, and green tabs the fourth week. The cards measure approximately 3 1/16" by 4 11/16" with the tab intact and 3 1/16" by 3 5/8" without the tab. The cards are numbered below by uniform number. The value of cards without tabs or tabs scratched off is F-G at best. The cards were printed on a 30-card sheet; hence, there are six double-printed cards listed DP in the checklist below. For individual prices on the more expensive color tabs, merely apply the ratio of that color's set price to the base (cheapest) color set price and use the resulting multiple on the individual prices for that color. Randall Cunningham appears in this set, a year before his Topps Rookie Card.

COMP.GREEN SET (24) 6.00 15.00
COMP.BLACK SET (24) 8.00 20.00
*BLACK: .5X TO 1.2X GREEN
COMP.BLUE SET (24) 25.00 60.00
*BLUE: 1.5X TO 4X GREEN
COMP.GOLD SET (24) 6.00 15.00
*GOLD: .4X TO 1X GREEN
7 Ron Jaworski .20 .50
8 Paul McFadden .10 .25
12 Randall Cunningham DP 2.00 5.00
22 Brenard Wilson .10 .25
24 Ray Ellis .10 .25
29 Elbert Foules .10 .25
36 Herman Hunter .10 .25
41 Earnest Jackson .15 .40
43 Roynell Young .15 .40
48 Wes Hopkins .15 .40
50 Garry Cobb DP .10 .25
63 Ron Baker DP .10 .25
66 Ken Reeves .10 .25
71 Ken Clarke DP .10 .25
73 Steve Kenney .10 .25
74 Leonard Mitchell .10 .25
81 Kenny Jackson .15 .40
82 Mike Quick .15 .40
85 Ron Johnson WR .10 .25
88 John Spagnola .10 .25
91 Reggie White 2.00 5.00
93 Tom Strauthers .10 .25
94 Byron Darby DP .10 .25
98 Greg Brown DP .10 .25

1986 McDonald's Falcons Green Tab

This 24-card set was issued in McDonald's Hamburger restaurants around Atlanta. The set was issued over a four-week period with blue tabs the first week, black (or gray) tabs the second week, gold (or orange) tabs the third week, and green tabs the fourth week. The cards measure approximately 3 1/16" by 4 11/16" with the tab intact and 3 1/16" by 3 5/8" without the tab. The cards are numbered below by uniform number. The value of cards without tabs or tabs scratched off is F-G at best. The cards were printed on a 30-card sheet; hence, there are six double-printed cards listed DP in the checklist below. For individual prices on the more expensive color tabs, merely apply the ratio of that color's set price to the base (cheapest) color set price and use the resulting multiple on the individual prices for that color.

COMP.GREEN SET (24) 6.00 15.00
COMP.BLACK SET (24) 75.00 150.00
*BLACK: 4X TO 10X GREEN
COMP.BLUE SET (24) 20.00 50.00
*BLUE: 1.2X TO 3X GREEN
COMP.GOLD SET (24) 12.00 30.00
*GOLD: .8X TO 2X GREEN
3 Rick Donnelly .25 .60
16 David Archer DP .50 1.25
18 Mick Luckhurst .25 .60
23 Bobby Butler .25 .60
26 James Britt DP .25 .60
37 Kenny Johnson .25 .60
39 Cliff Austin DP .25 .60
42 Gerald Riggs .30 .75
50 Buddy Curry .25 .60
56 Al Richardson .25 .60
57 Jeff Van Note .30 .75
58 David Frye .25 .60
61 John Scully .25 .60
62 Brett Miller .25 .60
74 Mike Pitts .25 .60
76 Mike Gann .25 .60
77 Rick Bryan .25 .60
78 Mike Kenn .30 .75
79 Bill Fralic .30 .75
81 Billy Johnson .30 .75
82 Stacey Bailey DP .25 .60
87 Cliff Benson DP .25 .60
88 Arthur Cox .25 .60
89 Charlie Brown DP .30 .75

1986 McDonald's 49ers Green Tab

This 24-card set was issued in McDonald's Hamburger restaurants around San Francisco. The set was issued over a four-week period with blue tabs the first week, black (or gray) tabs the second week, gold (or orange) tabs the third week, and green tabs the fourth week. The cards measure approximately 3 1/16" by 4 11/16" with the tab intact and 3 1/16" by 3 5/8" without the tab. The cards are numbered below by uniform number. The value of cards without tabs or tabs scratched off is F-G at best. The cards were printed on a 30-card sheet; hence, there are six double-printed cards listed DP in the checklist below. For individual prices on the more expensive color tabs, merely apply the ratio of that color's set price to the base (cheapest) color set price and use the resulting multiple on the individual prices for that color. Jerry Rice appears in his Rookie Card year.

COMP.GREEN SET (24) 12.00 30.00
COMP.BLACK SET (24) 12.00 30.00
*BLACK: .4X TO 1X GREEN
COMP.BLUE SET (24) 20.00 50.00
*BLUE: .6X TO 1.5X GREEN
COMP.GOLD SET (24) 12.00 30.00
*GOLD: .4X TO 1X GREEN
16 Joe Montana 5.00 12.00
21 Eric Wright .40 1.00
26 Wendell Tyler .40 1.00
27 Carlton Williamson .25 .60
33 Roger Craig DP .50 1.25
42 Ronnie Lott .75 2.00
49 Jeff Fuller .25 .60
50 Riki Ellison .25 .60
51 Randy Cross DP .40 1.00
56 Fred Quillan .25 .60
58 Keena Turner .25 .60
62 Guy McIntyre .25 .60
68 John Ayers DP .25 .60
71 Keith Fahnhorst .25 .60
72 Jeff Stover .25 .60
76 Dwaine Board DP .25 .60
77 Bubba Paris .25 .60
78 Manu Tuiasosopo .25 .60
80 Jerry Rice 6.00 15.00
81 Russ Francis .40 1.00
86 John Frank .25 .60
87 Dwight Clark DP .40 1.00
90 Todd Shell .25 .60
95 Michael Carter DP .40 1.00

1986 McDonald's Giants Green Tab

This 24-card set was issued in McDonald's Hamburger restaurants around New York. The set was issued over a four-week period with blue tabs the first week, black (or gray) tabs the second week, gold (or orange) tabs the third week, and green tabs the fourth week. The cards measure approximately 3 1/16" by 4 11/16" with the tab intact and 3 1/16" by 3 5/8" without the tab. The cards are numbered below by uniform number. The value of cards without tabs or tabs scratched off is F-G at best. The cards were printed on a 30-card sheet; hence, there are six double-printed cards listed DP in the checklist below. For individual prices on the more expensive color tabs, merely apply the ratio of that color's set price to the base (cheapest) color set price and use the resulting multiple on the individual prices for that color.

COMP.GREEN SET (24) 2.50 6.00
COMP.BLACK SET (24) 3.00 8.00
*BLACK: .5X TO 1.2X GREEN
COMP.BLUE SET (24) 5.00 12.00
*BLUE: .8X TO 2X GREEN
COMP.GOLD SET (24) 2.50 6.00
*GOLD: .4X TO 1X GREEN
5 Sean Landeta .15 .40
11 Phil Simms .60 1.50
20 Joe Morris .20 .50
23 Perry Williams .10 .25
26 Rob Carpenter DP .10 .25
33 George Adams DP .10 .25
34 Elvis Patterson .15 .40
43 Terry Kinard .10 .25
44 Maurice Carthon .10 .25
48 Kenny Hill .10 .25
53 Harry Carson .15 .40
54 Andy Headen .10 .25
56 Lawrence Taylor .60 1.50
60 Brad Benson DP .10 .25
63 Karl Nelson .10 .25
64 Jim Burt DP .15 .40
67 Billy Ard DP .10 .25
70 Leonard Marshall .15 .40
75 George Martin .15 .40
80 Phil McConkey .15 .40
84 Zeke Mowatt .10 .25
85 Don Hasselbeck .10 .25
86 Lionel Manuel .15 .40
89 Mark Bavaro DP .15 .40

1986 McDonald's Jets Green Tab

This 24-card set was issued in McDonald's Hamburger restaurants around New York. The set was issued over a four-week period with blue tabs the first week, black (or gray) tabs the second week, gold (or orange) tabs the third week, and green tabs the fourth week. The cards measure approximately 3 1/16" by 4 11/16" with the tab intact and 3 1/16" by 3 5/8" without the tab. The cards are numbered below by uniform number. The value of cards without tabs or tabs scratched off is F-G at best. The cards were printed on a 30-card sheet; hence, there are six double-printed cards listed DP in the checklist below. For individual prices on the more expensive color tabs, merely apply the ratio of that color's set price to the base (cheapest) color set price and use the resulting multiple on the individual prices for that color.

COMP.GREEN SET (24) 15.00 40.00
COMP.BLACK SET (24) 40.00 80.00
*BLACK: .8X TO 2X GREEN
COMP.BLUE SET (24) 40.00 80.00
*BLUE: .8X TO 2X GREEN
COMP.GOLD SET (24) 15.00 40.00
*GOLD: .4X TO 1X GREEN
5 Pat Leahy .60 1.50
7 Ken O'Brien .75 2.00
21 Kirk Springs .60 1.50
24 Freeman McNeil 1.00 2.50
27 Russell Carter DP .60 1.50
29 Johnny Lynn .60 1.50
34 Johnny Hector .75 2.00
39 Harry Hamilton .60 1.50
49 Tony Paige .75 2.00
53 Jim Sweeney .60 1.50
56 Lance Mehl .60 1.50
59 Kyle Clifton DP .75 2.00
60 Dan Alexander DP .60 1.50
65 Joe Fields DP .60 1.50
73 Joe Klecko .75 2.00
78 Barry Bennett DP .60 1.50
80 Johnny Lam Jones .60 1.50
82 Mickey Shuler .60 1.50
85 Wesley Walker .75 2.00
87 Kurt Sohn .60 1.50
88 Al Toon 1.00 2.50
89 Rocky Klever .60 1.50
93 Marty Lyons .75 2.00
99 Mark Gastineau DP .75 2.00

1986 McDonald's Lions Green Tab

This 24-card set was issued in McDonald's Hamburger restaurants around Detroit. The set was issued over a four-week period with blue tabs the first week, black (or gray) tabs the second week, gold (or orange) tabs the third week, and green tabs the fourth week. The cards measure approximately 3 1/16" by 4 11/16" with the tab intact and 3 1/16" by 3 5/8" without the tab. The cards are numbered below by uniform number. The value of cards without tabs or tabs scratched off is F-G at best. The cards were printed on a 30-card sheet; hence, there are six double-printed cards listed DP in the checklist below. For individual prices on the more expensive color tabs, merely apply the ratio of that color's set price to the base (cheapest) color set price and use the resulting multiple on the individual prices for that color.

COMP.GREEN SET (24) 2.50 6.00
COMP.BLACK SET (24) 2.50 6.00
*BLACK: .4X TO 1X GREEN
COMP.BLUE SET (24) 2.50 6.00
*BLUE: .4X TO 1X GREEN
COMP.GOLD SET (24) 2.50 6.00
*GOLD: .4X TO 1X GREEN
3 Eddie Murray .15 .40
11 Mike Black DP .10 .25
17 Eric Hipple .15 .40
20 Billy Sims .20 .50
21 Demetrious Johnson .10 .25
27 Bobby Watkins .10 .25
29 Bruce McNorton .10 .25
30 James Jones FB .15 .40
33 William Graham .10 .25
35 Alvin Hall .10 .25
39 Leonard Thompson .15 .40
50 August Curley DP .10 .25
52 Steve Mott .10 .25
55 Mike Cofer DP .15 .40
59 Jimmy Williams .10 .25
70 Keith Dorney DP .10 .25
71 Rich Strenger .10 .25
75 Lomas Brown DP .15 .40
76 Eric Williams .10 .25
79 William Gay .10 .25
82 Pete Mandley .10 .25
86 Mark Nichols .10 .25
87 David Lewis TE .10 .25
89 Jeff Chadwick DP .10 .25

1986 McDonald's Oilers Green Tab

is 24-card set was issued in McDonald's Hamburger restaurants around Houston. The set was issued over a four-week period with blue tabs the first week, black (or gray) tabs the second week, gold (or orange) tabs the third week, and green tabs the fourth week. The cards measure approximately 3 1/16" by 4 11/16" with the tab intact and 3 1/16" by 3 5/8" without the tab. The cards are numbered below by uniform number. The value of cards without tabs or tabs scratched off is F-G at best. The cards were printed on a 30-card sheet; hence, there are six double-printed cards listed DP in the checklist below. For individual prices on the more expensive color tabs, merely apply the ratio of that color's set price to the base (cheapest) color set price and use the resulting multiple on the individual prices for that color.

COMP.GREEN SET (24) 3.00 8.00
COMP.BLACK SET (24) 3.00 8.00
*BLACK: .4X TO 1X GREEN
COMP.BLUE SET (24) 5.00 12.00
*BLUE: .6X TO 1.5X GREEN
COMP.GOLD SET (24) 3.00 8.00
*GOLD: .4X TO 1X GREEN
1 Warren Moon 1.50 4.00
7 Tony Zendejas .12 .30
10 Oliver Luck .12 .30
21 Bo Eason .12 .30
23 Richard Johnson .12 .30
24 Steve Brown DP .12 .30
25 Keith Bostic DP .12 .30
29 Patrick Allen DP .12 .30
33 Mike Rozier .20 .50
40 Butch Woolfolk .12 .30
53 Avon Riley .12 .30
56 Robert Abraham DP .12 .30
63 Mike Munchak .40 1.00
67 Mike Stensrud .12 .30
70 Dean Steinkuhler .12 .30
71 Richard Byrd DP .12 .30
73 Harvey Salem .12 .30
74 Bruce Matthews .30 .75
79 Ray Childress .30 .75
83 Tim Smith .12 .30
85 Drew Hill .30 .75
87 Jamie Williams .12 .30
91 Johnny Meads .12 .30
94 Frank Bush DP .12 .30

1986 McDonald's Packers Green Tab

This 24-card set was issued in McDonald's Hamburger restaurants around Green Bay and Milwaukee. The set was issued over a four-week period with blue tabs the first week, black (or gray) tabs the second week, gold (or orange) tabs the third week, and green tabs the fourth week. The cards measure approximately 3 1/16" by 4 11/16" with the tab intact and 3 1/16" by 3 5/8" without the tab. The cards are numbered below by uniform number. The value of cards without tabs or tabs scratched off is F-G at best. The cards were printed on a 30-card sheet; hence, there are six double-printed cards listed DP in the checklist below. For individual prices on the more expensive color tabs, merely apply the ratio of that color's set price to the base (cheapest) color set price and use the resulting multiple on the individual prices for that color.

COMP.GREEN SET (24) 2.50 6.00
COMP.BLACK SET (24) 2.50 6.00
*BLACK: .4X TO 1X GREEN
COMP.BLUE SET (24) 2.50 6.00
*BLUE: .4X TO 1X GREEN
COMP.GOLD SET (24) 2.50 6.00
*GOLD: .4X TO 1X GREEN
10 Al Del Greco DP .10 .25
12 Lynn Dickey .15 .40
16 Randy Wright .15 .40
18 Jim Zorn .15 .40
22 Mark Lee .10 .25
26 Tim Lewis .10 .25
31 Gerry Ellis .10 .25
33 Jessie Clark DP .10 .25
37 Mark Murphy .15 .40
41 Tom Flynn .10 .25
42 Gary Ellerson .10 .25
53 Mike Douglass .10 .25
55 Randy Scott .10 .25
59 John Anderson DP .10 .25
67 Karl Swanke .10 .25
75 Ken Ruettgers .10 .25
76 Alphonso Carreker DP .10 .25
77 Mike Butler DP .10 .25
79 Donnie Humphrey .10 .25
82 Paul Coffman DP .10 .25
85 Phillip Epps .15 .40
90 Ezra Johnson .10 .25
91 Brian Noble .15 .40
94 Charles Martin .10 .25

1986 McDonald's Patriots Green Tab

This 24-card set was issued in McDonald's Hamburger restaurants around New England. The set was issued over a four-week period with blue tabs the first week, black (or gray) tabs the second week, gold (or orange) tabs the third week, and green tabs the fourth week. The cards measure approximately 3 1/16" by 4 11/16" with the tab intact and 3 1/16" by 3 5/8" without the tab. The cards are numbered below by uniform number. The value of cards without tabs or tabs scratched off is F-G at best. The cards were printed on a 30-card sheet; hence, there are six double-printed cards listed DP in the checklist below. For individual prices on the more expensive color tabs, merely apply the ratio of that color's set price to the base (cheapest) color set price and use the resulting multiple on the individual prices for that color.

COMP.GREEN SET (24) 2.50 6.00
COMP.BLACK SET (24) 2.50 6.00
*BLACK: .4X TO 1X GREEN
COMP.BLUE SET (24) 2.50 6.00
*BLUE: .4X TO 1X GREEN
COMP.GOLD SET (24) 2.50 6.00
*GOLD: .4X TO 1X GREEN
3 Rich Camarillo DP .10 .25
11 Tony Eason DP .15 .40
14 Steve Grogan .20 .50
24 Robert Weathers .10 .25
26 Raymond Clayborn DP .10 .25
30 Mosi Tatupu .10 .25
31 Fred Marion .10 .25
32 Craig James .20 .50
33 Tony Collins DP .15 .40
38 Roland James .10 .25
42 Ronnie Lippett .10 .25
50 Larry McGrew .10 .25
55 Don Blackmon DP .10 .25
56 Andre Tippett .20 .50
57 Steve Nelson .10 .25
58 Pete Brock DP .10 .25
60 Garin Veris .10 .25
61 Ron Wooten .10 .25
73 John Hannah .20 .50
77 Kenneth Sims .10 .25
80 Irving Fryar .40 1.00
81 Stephen Starring .10 .25
83 Cedric Jones .10 .25
86 Stanley Morgan .20 .50

1986 McDonald's Raiders Green Tab

This 24-card set was issued in McDonald's Hamburger restaurants around Los Angeles. The set was issued over a four-week period with blue tabs the first week, black (or gray) tabs the second week, gold (or orange) tabs the third week, and green tabs the fourth week. The cards measure approximately 3 1/16" by 4 11/16" with the tab intact and 3 1/16" by 3 5/8" without the tab. The cards are numbered below by uniform number. The value of cards without tabs or tabs scratched off is F-G at best. The cards were printed on a 30-card sheet; hence, there are six double-printed cards listed DP in the checklist below. For individual prices on the more expensive color tabs, merely apply the ratio of that color's set price to the base (cheapest) color set price and use the resulting multiple on the individual prices for that color.

COMP.GREEN SET (24) 3.00 8.00
COMP.BLACK SET (24) 5.00 12.00
*BLACK: .6X TO 1.5X GREEN
COMP.BLUE SET (24) 6.00 15.00
*BLUE: .8X TO 2X GREEN
COMP.GOLD SET (24) 3.00 8.00
*GOLD: .4X TO 1X GREEN
1 Marc Wilson .15 .40
8 Ray Guy DP .20 .50
10 Chris Dahl DP .10 .25
16 Jim Plunkett .20 .50
22 Mike Haynes .15 .40
26 Vann McElroy .10 .25
27 Frank Hawkins .10 .25
32 Marcus Allen DP 1.00 2.50
36 Mike Davis DP .10 .25
37 Lester Hayes .15 .40
46 Todd Christensen DP .20 .50
53 Rod Martin .15 .40
54 Reggie McKenzie .10 .25
55 Matt Millen .15 .40
70 Henry Lawrence .10 .25
71 Bill Pickel .10 .25
72 Don Mosebar .15 .40
73 Charley Hannah .10 .25
75 Howie Long .60 1.50
79 Bruce Davis DP .10 .25
84 Jessie Hester .15 .40
85 Dokie Williams .10 .25
91 Brad Van Pelt .10 .25
99 Sean Jones .20 .50

1986 McDonald's Rams Green Tab

This 24-card set was issued in McDonald's Hamburger restaurants around Los Angeles. The set was issued over a four-week period with blue tabs the first week, black (or gray) tabs the second week, gold (or orange) tabs the third week, and green tabs the fourth week. The cards measure approximately 3 1/16" by 4 11/16" with the tab intact and 3 1/16" by 3 5/8" without the tab. The cards are numbered below by uniform number. The value of cards without tabs or tabs scratched off is F-G at best. The cards were printed on a 30-card sheet; hence, there are six double-printed cards listed DP in the checklist below. For individual prices on the more expensive color tabs, merely apply the ratio of that color's set price to the base (cheapest) color set price and use the resulting multiple on the individual prices for that color.

COMP.GREEN SET (24) 2.50 6.00
COMP.BLACK SET (24) 2.50 6.00
*BLACK: .4X TO 1X GREEN
COMP.BLUE SET (24) 3.00 8.00
*BLUE: .5X TO 1.2X GREEN
COMP.GOLD SET (24) 2.50 6.00
*GOLD: .4X TO 1X GREEN
1 Mike Lansford .10 .25
3 Dale Hatcher .10 .25
5 Dieter Brock DP .10 .25
20 Johnnie Johnson .10 .25
21 Nolan Cromwell DP .15 .40
22 Vince Newsome .10 .25
27 Gary Green .10 .25
29 Eric Dickerson DP .60 1.50
44 Mike Guman .10 .25
47 LeRoy Irvin .15 .40
50 Jim Collins DP .10 .25
54 Mike Wilcher .10 .25
55 Carl Ekern .10 .25
56 Doug Smith .10 .25
58 Mel Owens .10 .25
60 Dennis Harrah .10 .25
71 Reggie Doss DP .10 .25
72 Kent Hill .10 .25
75 Irv Pankey .10 .25
78 Jackie Slater .20 .50
80 Henry Ellard .40 1.00
81 David Hill .10 .25
87 Tony Hunter .10 .25
89 Ron Brown DP .15 .40

1986 McDonald's Redskins Green Tab

This 24-card set was issued in McDonald's Hamburger restaurants around Washington. The set was issued over a four-week period with blue tabs the first week, black (or gray) tabs the second week, gold (or orange) tabs the third week, and green tabs the fourth week. The cards measure approximately 3 1/16" by 4 11/16" with the tab intact and 3 1/16" by 3 5/8" without the tab. The cards are numbered below by uniform number. The value of cards without tabs or tabs scratched off is F-G at best. The cards were printed on a 30-card sheet; hence, there are six double-printed cards listed DP in the checklist below. For individual prices on the more expensive color tabs, merely apply the ratio of that color's set price to the base (cheapest) color set price and use the resulting multiple on the individual prices for that color.

COMP.GREEN SET (24) 2.50 6.00
COMP.BLACK SET (24) 2.50 6.00
*BLACK: .4X TO 1X GREEN
COMP.BLUE SET (24) 2.50 6.00
*BLUE: .4X TO 1X GREEN
COMP.GOLD SET (24) 2.50 6.00
*GOLD: .4X TO 1X GREEN
3 Mark Moseley .10 .25
10 Jay Schroeder .20 .50
22 Curtis Jordan .10 .25
28 Darrell Green .20 .50
32 Vernon Dean DP .10 .25
35 Keith Griffin .10 .25
37 Raphel Cherry DP .10 .25
38 George Rogers .15 .40
51 Monte Coleman DP .15 .40
52 Neal Olkewicz .10 .25
53 Jeff Bostic DP .10 .25
55 Mel Kaufman .10 .25
57 Rich Milot .10 .25
65 Dave Butz DP .15 .40
66 Joe Jacoby .15 .40
68 Russ Grimm .15 .40
71 Charles Mann .20 .50
72 Dexter Manley .15 .40
73 Mark May .15 .40
77 Darryl Grant .10 .25
81 Art Monk .60 1.50
84 Gary Clark DP .40 1.00
85 Don Warren .15 .40
86 Clint Didier .10 .25

1986 McDonald's Saints Green Tab

This 24-card set was issued in McDonald's Hamburger restaurants around New Orleans. The set was issued over a four-week period with blue tabs the first week, black (or gray) tabs the second week, gold (or orange) tabs the third week, and green tabs the fourth week. The cards measure approximately 3 1/16" by 4 11/16" with the tab intact and 3 1/16" by 3 5/8" without the tab. The cards are numbered below by uniform number. The value of cards without tabs or tabs scratched off is F-G at best. The cards were printed on a 30-card sheet; hence, there are six double-printed cards listed DP in the checklist below. For individual prices on the more expensive color tabs, merely apply the ratio of that color's set price to the base (cheapest) color set price and use the resulting multiple on the individual prices for that color.

COMP.GREEN SET (24) 8.00 20.00
COMP.BLACK SET (24) 12.00 30.00
*BLACK: .6X TO 1.5X GREEN
COMP.BLUE SET (24) 30.00 80.00
*BLUE: 1.5X TO 4X GREEN
COMP.GOLD SET (24) 6.00 15.00
*GOLD: .3X TO .8X GREEN
3 Bobby Hebert .50 1.25
7 Morten Andersen DP .60 1.50
10 Brian Hansen .30 .75
18 Dave Wilson .30 .75
20 Russell Gary .30 .75
25 Johnnie Poe .30 .75
30 Wayne Wilson .30 .75
44 Dave Waymer .40 1.00
46 Hokie Gajan .30 .75
49 Frank Wattelett .30 .75
50 Jack Del Rio DP .50 1.25
57 Rickey Jackson .50 1.25
60 Steve Korte .30 .75
61 Joel Hilgenberg .30 .75
63 Brad Edelman DP .30 .75
64 Dave Lafary .30 .75
67 Stan Brock DP .30 .75
73 Frank Warren .30 .75
75 Bruce Clark DP .30 .75
84 Eric Martin .50 1.25
85 Hoby Brenner DP .30 .75
88 Eugene Goodlow .30 .75
89 Tyrone Young .30 .75
99 Tony Elliott .30 .75

1986 McDonald's Seahawks Green Tab

This 24-card set was issued in McDonald's Hamburger restaurants around Seattle. The set was issued over a four-week period with blue tabs the first week, black (or gray) tabs the second week, gold (or orange) tabs the third week, and green tabs the fourth week. The cards measure approximately 3 1/16" by 4 11/16" with the tab intact and 3 1/16" by 3 5/8" without the tab. The cards are numbered below by uniform number. The value of cards without tabs or tabs scratched off is F-G at best. The cards were printed on a 30-card sheet; hence, there are six double-printed cards listed DP in the checklist below. For individual prices on the more expensive color tabs, merely apply the ratio of that color's set price to the base (cheapest) color set price and use the resulting multiple on the individual prices for that color.

COMP.GREEN SET (24) 2.50 6.00
COMP.BLACK SET (24) 2.50 6.00
*BLACK: .4X TO 1X GREEN
COMP.BLUE SET (24) 3.00 8.00
*BLUE: .5X TO 1.2X GREEN
COMP.GOLD SET (24) 2.50 6.00
*GOLD: .4X TO 1X GREEN
9 Norm Johnson .15 .40
17 Dave Krieg .20 .50
20 Terry Taylor .10 .25
22 Dave Brown DP .10 .25
28 Curt Warner .20 .50
33 Dan Doornink .10 .25
44 John Harris .10 .25
45 Kenny Easley .15 .40
46 David Hughes .10 .25
50 Fredd Young .10 .25
53 Keith Butler DP .10 .25
55 Michael Jackson .10 .25
58 Bruce Scholtz .10 .25
59 Blair Bush DP .10 .25
61 Robert Pratt .10 .25
64 Ron Essink .10 .25
65 Edwin Bailey DP .10 .25
72 Joe Nash .10 .25
77 Jeff Bryant DP .10 .25
78 Bob Cryder DP .10 .25
79 Jacob Green .15 .40
80 Steve Largent .75 2.00
81 Daryl Turner .10 .25
82 Paul Skansi .10 .25

1986 McDonald's Steelers Green Tab

This 24-card set was issued in McDonald's Hamburger restaurants around Pittsburgh. The set was issued over a four-week period with blue tabs the first week, black (or gray) tabs the second week, gold (or orange) tabs the third week, and green tabs the fourth week. The cards measure approximately 3 1/16" by 4 11/16" with the tab intact and 3 1/16" by 3 5/8" without the tab. The cards are numbered below by uniform number. The value of cards without tabs or tabs scratched off is F-G at best. The cards were printed on a 30-card sheet; hence, there are six double-printed cards listed DP in the checklist below. For individual prices on the more expensive color tabs, merely apply the ratio of that color's set price to the base (cheapest) color set price and use the resulting multiple on the individual prices for that color.

COMP.GREEN SET (24) 4.00 10.00
COMP.BLACK SET (24) 6.00 15.00
*BLACK: .6X TO 1.5X GREEN
COMP.BLUE SET (24) 10.00 25.00
*BLUE: 1X TO 2.5X GREEN
COMP.GOLD SET (24) 4.00 10.00
*GOLD: .4X TO 1X GREEN
1 Gary Anderson K DP .20 .50
16 Mark Malone .20 .50
21 Eric Williams S .15 .40
24 Rich Erenberg DP .15 .40
30 Frank Pollard .15 .40
31 Donnie Shell .20 .50
34 Walter Abercrombie DP .15 .40
49 Dwayne Woodruff .15 .40
50 David Little .15 .40
52 Mike Webster .20 .50
53 Bryan Hinkle .20 .50
56 Robin Cole DP .15 .40
57 Mike Merriweather .20 .50
62 Tunch Ilkin .15 .40
65 Ray Pinney .15 .40
67 Gary Dunn DP .15 .40
73 Craig Wolfley .15 .40
74 Terry Long .15 .40
82 John Stallworth .40 1.00
83 Louis Lipps .30 .75
87 Weegie Thompson .15 .40
92 Keith Gary DP .15 .40
93 Keith Willis .15 .40
99 Darryl Sims .15 .40

1986 McDonald's Vikings Green Tab

This 24-card set was issued in McDonald's Hamburger restaurants around Minneapolis and St. Paul. The set was issued over a four-week period with blue tabs the first week, black (or gray) tabs the second week, gold (or orange) tabs the third week, and green tabs the fourth week. The cards measure approximately 3 1/16" by 4 11/16" with the tab intact and 3 1/16" by 3 5/8" without the tab. The cards are numbered below by uniform number. The value of cards without tabs or tabs scratched off is F-G at best. The cards were printed on a 30-card sheet; hence, there are six double-printed cards listed DP in the checklist below. For individual prices on the more expensive color tabs, merely apply the ratio of that color's set price to the base (cheapest) color set price and use the resulting multiple on the individual prices for that color.

COMP.GREEN SET (24) 6.00 15.00
COMP.BLACK SET (24) 12.00 30.00
*BLACK: .8X TO 2X GREEN
COMP.BLUE SET (24) 15.00 40.00
*BLUE: 1X TO 2.5X GREEN
COMP.GOLD SET (24) 6.00 15.00
*GOLD: .4X TO 1X GREEN
8 Greg Coleman DP .25 .60
9 Tommy Kramer .30 .75
11 Wade Wilson .40 1.00
20 Darrin Nelson .30 .75
23 Ted Brown DP .25 .60
37 Willie Teal .25 .60
39 Carl Lee .30 .75
46 Alfred Anderson DP .25 .60
47 Joey Browner DP .40 1.00
55 Scott Studwell .25 .60
56 Chris Doleman .40 1.00
59 Matt Blair DP .30 .75
67 Dennis Swilley .25 .60
68 Curtis Rouse .25 .60
75 Keith Millard .40 1.00
76 Tim Irwin .25 .60
77 Mark Mullaney .25 .60
79 Doug Martin .25 .60
81 Anthony Carter DP .50 1.25
83 Steve Jordan .40 1.00
87 Leo Lewis .30 .75
89 Mike Jones WR .25 .60
96 Tim Newton .25 .60
99 David Howard .25 .60

1993 McDonald's GameDay

As part of the "McDonald's/NFL Kickoff Payoff" promotion, customers could win NFL Fantasy prizes, such as trips to Super Bowl XXVII, and McDonald's/GameDay trading cards featuring local NFL teams. Customers received a pull-tab gamepiece on packages of large and extra-large french fries, hash browns, 21- and 32-oz. soft drinks, and 16-oz. coffee. Every gamepiece won free food, an instant-win NFL Fantasy prize, or NFL Point Values of six (touchdown), three (field goal), or one (extra point). The Point Values could be collected and redeemed for trading cards or special discounts on merchandise. For ten points, customers received a six-card sheet at participating McDonald's restaurants while supplies lasted. Measuring approximately 2 1/2" by 4 3/4", the GameDay cards are similar to the regular issues, except that they have McDonald's logos on both sides, and on the backs are renumbered with a "McD" prefix. Three sheets make a complete team set. Most McDonald's restaurants in a region offered cards of the local NFL team(s). In addition, many restaurants offered an All-Star set of 18 NFL superstars. Each NFL team has 18 cards in total on three different sheets (A, B, and C), and the cards are listed below in alphabetical team order, preceded by the All-Star set. One sheet was distributed per week for three weeks during the promotion.

COMPLETE SET (87) 20.00 50.00
1 All-Stars A .80 2.00
2 All-Stars B .80 2.00
3 All-Stars C .40 1.00
4 Atlanta Falcons A .60 1.50
5 Atlanta Falcons B .40 1.00
6 Atlanta Falcons C .30 .75
7 Buffalo Bills A .40 1.00
8 Buffalo Bills B .40 1.00
9 Buffalo Bills C .50 1.25
10 Chicago Bears A .30 .75
11 Chicago Bears B .30 .75
12 Chicago Bears C .40 1.00
13 Cincinnati Bengals A .30 .75
14 Cincinnati Bengals B .50 1.25
15 Cincinnati Bengals C .30 .75
16 Cleveland Browns A .40 1.00
17 Cleveland Browns B .40 1.00
18 Cleveland Browns C .30 .75
19 Dallas Cowboys A .60 1.50
20 Dallas Cowboys B .40 1.00
21 Dallas Cowboys C 1.00 2.50
22 Denver Broncos A 1.00 2.50
23 Denver Broncos B .30 .75
24 Denver Broncos C .30 .75
25 Detroit Lions A .30 .75
26 Detroit Lions B .60 1.50
27 Detroit Lions C .40 1.00
28 Green Bay Packers A 1.00 2.50
29 Green Bay Packers B .40 1.00
30 Green Bay Packers C .50 1.25
31 Houston Oilers A .30 .75
32 Houston Oilers B .40 1.00
33 Houston Oilers C .30 .75
34 Indianapolis Colts A .30 .75
35 Indianapolis Colts B .40 1.00
36 Indianapolis Colts C .30 .75
37 Kansas City Chiefs A .30 .75
38 Kansas City Chiefs B .30 .75
39 Kansas City Chiefs C .60 1.50
40 Los Angeles Raiders A .30 .75
41 Los Angeles Raiders B .30 .75
42 Los Angeles Raiders C .40 1.00
43 Los Angeles Rams A .30 .75
44 Los Angeles Rams B .40 1.00
45 Los Angeles Rams C .60 1.50
46 Miami Dolphins A .30 .75
47 Miami Dolphins B 1.00 2.50
48 Miami Dolphins C .40 1.00
49 Minnesota Vikings A .40 1.00
50 Minnesota Vikings B .30 .75
51 Minnesota Vikings C .30 .75
52 New England Patriots A .30 .75
53 New England Patriots B .40 1.00
54 New England Patriots C 1.00 2.50
55 New Orleans Saints A .30 .75
56 New Orleans Saints B .30 .75
57 New Orleans Saints C .40 1.00
58 New York Giants A .40 1.00
59 New York Giants B .40 1.00
60 New York Giants C .40 1.00
61 New York Jets A .30 .75
62 New York Jets B .30 .75
63 New York Jets C .40 1.00
64 Philadelphia Eagles A .40 1.00
65 Philadelphia Eagles B .40 1.00
66 Philadelphia Eagles C .30 .75
67 Phoenix Cardinals A .30 .75
68 Phoenix Cardinals B .40 1.00
69 Phoenix Cardinals C .50 1.25
70 Pittsburgh Steelers A .50 1.25
71 Pittsburgh Steelers B .40 1.00
72 Pittsburgh Steelers C .40 1.00
73 San Diego Chargers A .30 .75
74 San Diego Chargers B .40 1.00
75 San Diego Chargers C .40 1.00
76 San Francisco 49ers A .40 1.00
77 San Francisco 49ers B .60 1.50
78 San Francisco 49ers C .60 1.50
79 Seattle Seahawks A .30 .75
80 Seattle Seahawks B .40 1.00
81 Seattle Seahawks C .40 1.00
82 Tampa Bay Buccaneers A .30 .75
83 Tampa Bay Buccaneers B .30 .75
84 Tampa Bay Buccaneers C .30 .75
85 Washington Redskins A .40 1.00
86 Washington Redskins B .40 1.00
87 Washington Redskins C .40 1.00

1996 McDonald's Looney Tunes Cups

These cups were available at participating McDonald's restaurants during the 1996 Season. Each player cup has a corresponding Looney Tunes character on the cup with them.

COMPLETE SET (4) 2.40 6.00
1 Drew Bledsoe .50 1.25
Wile E. Coyote
2 Dan Marino .80 2.00
Daffy Duck
3 Barry Sanders .50 1.25
Tazmanian Devil
4 Emmitt Smith .80 2.00
Bugs Bunny

2003 Merrick Mint Laser Line Gold

The Merrick Mint produced these licensed etched cards printed on gold foil stock in 2003. The set is commonly referred to as Laser Line Gold cards since that name is printed on the cardbacks.

1 Jerome Bettis 2.50 6.00
2 Drew Bledsoe 2.00 5.00
3 Tom Brady 10.00 25.00
4 David Carr 1.50 4.00
5 Daunte Culpepper 2.00 5.00
6 Marshall Faulk 2.00 5.00
7 Brett Favre 5.00 12.00
8 Rich Gannon 2.00 5.00
9 Eddie George 2.00 5.00
10 Edgerrin James 2.00 5.00
11 Peyton Manning 6.00 15.00
12 Donovan McNabb 2.00 5.00
13 Randy Moss 2.00 5.00
14 Chad Pennington 1.50 4.00
15 Carson Palmer 3.00 8.00
16 Jerry Rice 5.00 12.00
17 Warren Sapp 2.00 5.00
18 Jeremy Shockey 1.50 4.00
19 Emmitt Smith 4.00 10.00
20 Michael Strahan 2.00 5.00
21 LaDainian Tomlinson 2.50 6.00
22 Brian Urlacher 2.50 6.00
23 Kurt Warner 2.00 5.00

24 Ricky Williams 2.50 6.00
25 Michael Vick 2.00 5.00

2005 Merrick Mint Sculpted Gold Cards

1 Tom Brady 3.00 8.00

2006 Merrick Mint Draft Picks Silver Sig

This series of laser line foil cards was produced by Merrick Mint and relased in June 2006. Each card features a gold foil front and back etched in black with a player image from the 2006 NFL Draft. The backs include information about the laser line printing process as well as a stamped serial number. The cardfronts included a facsimile player autograph printed in one of three different foil colors. The Silver Sig version was produced in quantities of 2006, the Gold Sig version was 499-copies, and the Holographic Gold was printed in a quantity of 99-cards.

*GOLD SIG: .5X TO 1.2X SILVER SIG
*HOLO.GOLD: .6X TO 1.5X SILVER SIG
1 Reggie Bush 12.00 20.00
2 Jay Cutler 10.00 15.00
3 Matt Leinart 10.00 15.00
4 Vince Young 10.00 15.00

2006 Merrick Mint Feel the Game Sculpted Gold Cards

1 Brett Favre 7.50 15.00
2 Ben Roethlisberger 5.00 12.00
3 Brian Urlacher 3.00 8.00

2006 Merrick Mint Reggie Bush

This 3-card set issued by Merrick Mint in June 2006. Each card was printed in an all-gold foil front and back with a black etched design. The player's name and team name appear below the image and the backs are identical for the 3-cards. The cardfronts also feature a gold holofoil facsimile signature. Each is serial numbered of 619-cards made.

COMPLETE SET (3) 15.00 30.00
1 Reggie Bush 4.00 10.00
2 Reggie Bush 4.00 10.00
3 Reggie Bush 4.00 10.00

2007 Merrick Mint Laser Line Gold

1 Adrian Peterson 6.00 12.00
2 Brady Quinn 5.00 10.00
3 JaMarcus Russell 4.00 8.00

1995 Metal

This set marked the debut season for the 200 card all foil-etched stand[illegible]-size set. Cards were available in 8 card packs for the suggested retail price of $2.49. Card fronts feature different silver-etched backgrounds with the player's name and "Fleer Metal" logo at the bottom. Card backs are "machine-like" with player statistics and biographical information. The set is ordered by teams. Rookie Cards include Jeff Blake, Ki-Jana Carter, Kerry Collins, Joey Galloway, Steve McNair, Rashaan Salaam, J.J. Stokes and Michael Westbrook. Also included in random packs was an instant winner card for a trip to Super Bowl XXX. A Trent Dilfer Sample card was produced and priced below.

COMPLETE SET (200) 7.50 20.00
1 Garrison Hearst .15 .40
2 Seth Joyner .02 .10
3 Dave Krieg .02 .10
4 Lorenzo Lynch .02 .10
5 Rob Moore .07 .20
6 Eric Swann .07 .20
7 Aeneas Williams .02 .10
8 Chris Doleman .02 .10
9 Bert Emanuel .15 .40
10 Jeff George .07 .20
11 Craig Heyward .07 .20
12 Terance Mathis .07 .20
13 Eric Metcalf .07 .20
14 Cornelius Bennett .07 .20
15 Bucky Brooks .02 .10
16 Jeff Burris .02 .10
17 Jim Kelly .15 .40
18 Andre Reed .07 .20
19 Bruce Smith .15 .40
20 Don Beebe .02 .10
21 Kerry Collins RC .75 2.00
22 Barry Foster .07 .20
23 Lamar Lathon .02 .10
24 Sam Mills .07 .20
25 Tyrone Poole RC .15 .40
26 Frank Reich .02 .10
27 Joe Cain .02 .10
28 Curtis Conway .15 .40
29 Jeff Graham .02 .10
30 Erik Kramer .02 .10
31 Rashaan Salaam RC .07 .20
32 Lewis Tillman .02 .10
33 Chris Zorich .02 .10
34 Jeff Blake RC .30 .75
35 Ki-Jana Carter RC .15 .40
36 Carl Pickens .07 .20
37 Corey Sawyer .02 .10
38 Darnay Scott .07 .20
39 Dan Wilkinson .07 .20
40 Darryl Williams .02 .10
41 Derrick Alexander WR .15 .40
42 Leroy Hoard .02 .10
43 Michael Jackson .07 .20
44 Antonio Langham .02 .10
45 Andre Rison .07 .20
46 Vinny Testaverde .07 .20
47 Eric Turner .02 .10
48 Troy Aikman .40 1.00
49 Charles Haley .07 .20
50 Michael Irvin .15 .40
51 Daryl Johnston .07 .20
52 Jay Novacek .07 .20
53 Emmitt Smith .60 1.50
54 Kevin Williams WR .07 .20
55 Steve Atwater .02 .10
56 Rod Bernstine .02 .10
57 John Elway .75 2.00
58 Glyn Milburn .02 .10
59 Anthony Miller .07 .20
60 Mike Pritchard .02 .10
61 Shannon Sharpe .07 .20
62 Mike Johnson .02 .10
63 Scott Mitchell .07 .20
64 Herman Moore .15 .40
65 Brett Perriman .07 .20
66 Barry Sanders .60 1.50
67 Chris Spielman .07 .20
68 Edgar Bennett .07 .20
69 Robert Brooks .15 .40
70 Brett Favre .75 2.00
71 LeShon Johnson .07 .20
72 George Koonce .02 .10
73 Reggie White .15 .40
74 Gary Brown .02 .10
75 Cris Dishman .02 .10
76 Mel Gray .02 .10
77 Steve McNair RC 1.25 3.00
78 Webster Slaughter .02 .10
79 Rodney Thomas RC .07 .20
80 Trev Alberts .02 .10
81 Quentin Coryatt .07 .20
82 Sean Dawkins .07 .20
83 Craig Erickson .02 .10
84 Marshall Faulk .50 1.25
85 Stephen Grant RC .02 .10
86 Steve Beuerlein .07 .20
87 Tony Boselli RC .15 .40
88 Desmond Howard .07 .20
89 James O. Stewart RC .50 1.25
90 Marcus Allen .15 .40
91 Kimble Anders .07 .20
92 Steve Bono .07 .20
93 Lake Dawson .07 .20
94 Greg Hill .07 .20
95 Neil Smith .07 .20
96 William White .02 .10
97 Tim Bowens .02 .10
98 Bryan Cox .02 .10
99 Irving Fryar .07 .20
100 Eric Green .02 .10
101 Dan Marino .75 2.00
102 O.J. McDuffie .15 .40
103 Bernie Parmalee .07 .20
104 Cris Carter .15 .40
105 Jack Del Rio .02 .10
106 Rocket Ismail .07 .20
107 Warren Moon .07 .20
108 Jake Reed .07 .20
109 Dewayne Washington .07 .20
110 Bruce Armstrong .02 .10
111 Drew Bledsoe .25 .60
112 Vincent Brisby .02 .10
113 Ben Coates .07 .20
114 Willie McGinest .07 .20
115 Dave Meggett .02 .10
116 Chris Slade .02 .10
117 Mario Bates .07 .20
118 Quinn Early .07 .20
119 Jim Everett .02 .10
120 Michael Haynes .07 .20
121 Tyrone Hughes .07 .20
122 Renaldo Turnbull .02 .10
123 Ray Zellars RC .07 .20
124 Dave Brown .07 .20
125 Chris Calloway .02 .10
126 Rodney Hampton .07 .20
127 Thomas Lewis .07 .20
128 Phillippi Sparks .02 .10
129 Tyrone Wheatley RC .50 1.25
130 Kyle Brady RC .15 .40
131 Boomer Esiason .07 .20
132 Aaron Glenn .02 .10
133 Bobby Houston .02 .10
134 Mo Lewis .02 .10
135 Johnny Mitchell .02 .10
136 Ronald Moore .02 .10
137 Greg Biekert .02 .10
138 Tim Brown .15 .40
139 Jeff Hostetler .07 .20
140 Rocket Ismail .07 .20
141 Napoleon Kaufman RC .50 1.25
142 Chester McGlockton .07 .20
143 Harvey Williams .02 .10
144 Fred Barnett .07 .20
145 Randall Cunningham .15 .40
146 William Fuller .02 .10
147 Charlie Garner .15 .40
148 Andy Harmon .02 .10
149 Ricky Watters .07 .20
150 Calvin Williams .07 .20
151 Kevin Greene .07 .20
152 Charles Johnson .07 .20
153 Greg Lloyd .07 .20
154 Byron Bam Morris .02 .10
155 Neil O'Donnell .07 .20
156 Darren Perry .02 .10
157 Rod Woodson .07 .20
158 Jerome Bettis .15 .40
159 Isaac Bruce .25 .60
160 Troy Drayton .02 .10
161 Sean Gilbert .07 .20
162 Todd Lyght .02 .10
163 Chris Miller .02 .10
164 Andre Coleman .02 .10
165 Stan Humphries .07 .20
166 Shawn Jefferson .02 .10
167 Natrone Means .07 .20
168 Leslie O'Neal .07 .20
169 Junior Seau .15 .40
170 Mark Seay .07 .20
171 William Floyd .07 .20
172 Merton Hanks .02 .10
173 Brent Jones .02 .10
174 Jerry Rice .40 1.00
175 Deion Sanders UER .25 .60
176 J.J. Stokes RC .15 .40
177 Lee Woodall .02 .10
178 Bryant Young .07 .20
179 Steve Young .30 .75
180 Brian Blades .07 .20
181 Joey Galloway RC .60 1.50
182 Cortez Kennedy .07 .20
183 Kevin Mawae .02 .10
184 Rick Mirer .07 .20
185 Chris Warren .07 .20
186 Lawrence Dawsey .02 .10
187 Trent Dilfer .15 .40
188 Paul Gruber .02 .10
189 Hardy Nickerson .02 .10
190 Errict Rhett .07 .20
191 Warren Sapp RC .60 1.50
192 Tom Carter .02 .10
193 Henry Ellard .07 .20
194 Darrell Green .02 .10
195 Brian Mitchell .02 .10
196 Heath Shuler .07 .20
197 Michael Westbrook RC .15 .40
198 Checklist 1-96 .02 .10
199 Checklist 97-200 .02 .10
200 Checklist Inserts .02 .10
S1 Trent Dilfer Sample .40 1.00

1995 Metal Gold Blasters

This 18 card set was randomly inserted into packs at a rate of one in approximately six packs and highlights players who have had a major impact on the NFL. Card fronts have a gold-swirl background with some highlighting of the team's colors. Backs contain a melted yellow-orange background. In the melted area is a brief commentary on the featured player.

COMPLETE SET (18) 12.00 30.00
STATED ODDS 1:6
1 Troy Aikman 1.00 2.50
2 Jerome Bettis .40 1.00
3 Tim Brown .40 1.00
4 Ben Coates .20 .50
5 John Elway 2.00 5.00
6 Brett Favre 2.00 5.00
7 William Floyd .20 .50
8 Joey Galloway .75 1.50
9 Rodney Hampton .20 .50
10 Dan Marino 2.00 5.00
11 Steve McNair 1.50 3.00
12 Herman Moore .40 1.00
13 Errict Rhett .20 .50
14 Rashaan Salaam .07 .20
15 Chris Warren .20 .50
16 Michael Westbrook .15 .40
17 Rod Woodson .20 .50
18 Steve Young .75 2.00

1995 Metal Platinum Portraits

This 12 card set was randomly inserted at a rate of one in nine packs and is billed as a "serious heavy metal set" of 12 of the NFL's elite players. Card fronts contain a silver foil-etched background with a shot of the player and a circular-etched image of the player in action. Card backs have an orange and silver backgound with a player summary at the top of the card.

COMPLETE SET (12) 7.50 20.00
STATED ODDS 1:9
1 Drew Bledsoe 1.00 2.00
2 Ki-Jana Carter .60 1.25
3 Marshall Faulk 2.00 4.00
4 Natrone Means .25 .60
5 Byron Bam Morris .10 .30
6 Jerry Rice 1.50 3.00
7 Andre Rison .25 .60
8 Barry Sanders 2.50 5.00
9 Deion Sanders 1.00 2.00
10 Emmitt Smith 2.50 5.00
11 J.J. Stokes .60 1.25
12 Ricky Watters .25 .60

1995 Metal Silver Flashers

This 50 card set was randomly inserted at a rate of one in every two packs and features the NFL's flashiest performers. Card fronts have a silver foil-etched background with several different designs ranging from circular to squares to waves. The player's name is located at the bottom left corner of the card. Card backs feature the "Fleer Metal 1995" logo electrified with a melting orange and silver background. A brief player commentary is also on the back.

COMPLETE SET (50) 12.50 30.00
STATED ODDS 1:2
1 Troy Aikman 1.00 2.00
2 Marcus Allen .30 .75
3 Jerome Bettis .30 .75
4 Drew Bledsoe .60 1.25
5 Tim Brown .30 .75
6 Cris Carter .30 .75
7 Ki-Jana Carter .15 .40
8 Ben Coates .15 .40
9 Kerry Collins .75 2.00
10 Randall Cunningham .30 .75
11 Lake Dawson .15 .40
12 Trent Dilfer .30 .75
13 John Elway 2.00 4.00
14 Jim Everett .07 .20
15 Marshall Faulk 1.25 2.50
16 Brett Favre 2.00 4.00
17 William Floyd .15 .40
18 Jeff George .15 .40
19 Rodney Hampton .15 .40
20 Jeff Hostetler .15 .40
21 Stan Humphries .15 .40
22 Michael Irvin .30 .75
23 Cortez Kennedy .15 .40
24 Dan Marino 2.00 4.00
25 Terance Mathis .15 .40
26 Willie McGinest .15 .40
27 Natrone Means .15 .40
28 Rick Mirer .15 .40
29 Warren Moon .15 .40
30 Herman Moore .30 .75
31 Byron Bam Morris .07 .20
32 Carl Pickens .15 .40
33 Errict Rhett .15 .40
34 Jerry Rice 1.00 2.00
35 Andre Rison .15 .40
36 Rashaan Salaam .07 .20
37 Barry Sanders 1.50 3.00
38 Deion Sanders .60 1.25
39 Junior Seau .30 .75
40 Shannon Sharpe .15 .40
41 Heath Shuler .15 .40
42 Emmitt Smith 1.50 3.00
43 J.J. Stokes .15 .40
44 Chris Warren .15 .40
45 Ricky Watters .15 .40
46 Michael Westbrook .15 .40
47 Tyrone Wheatley .60 1.25
48 Reggie White .30 .75
49 Rod Woodson .15 .40
50 Steve Young .75 1.50

1996 Metal Samples

COMPLETE SET (3) 1.50 4.00
S1 Trent Dilfer .30 .75
S2 Brett Favre 1.00 2.50
S3 Dave Meggett .30 .75
NNO Uncut Panel 1.50 4.00

1996 Metal

The 1996 Fleer Metal set was issued in one series totalling 150 cards and features metallized foil engraved by hand on each card front making no two player cards alike. The eight-card packs retail for $2.49 each. The set contains the subset Rookies (124-148).

COMPLETE SET (150) 10.00 25.00
1 Garrison Hearst .07 .20
2 Rob Moore .07 .20
3 Frank Sanders .07 .20
4 Eric Swann .02 .10
5 Jeff George .07 .20
6 Craig Heyward .02 .10
7 Terance Mathis .02 .10
8 Eric Metcalf .02 .10
9 Derrick Alexander WR .07 .20
10 Andre Rison .07 .20
11 Vinny Testaverde .07 .20
12 Eric Turner .02 .10
13 Jim Kelly .15 .40
14 Bryce Paup .02 .10
15 Bruce Smith .07 .20
16 Thurman Thomas .15 .40
17 Bob Christian .02 .10
18 Kerry Collins .15 .40
19 Lamar Lathon .02 .10
20 Tyrone Poole .02 .10
21 Curtis Conway .15 .40
22 Bryan Cox .02 .10
23 Erik Kramer .02 .10
24 Rashaan Salaam .07 .20
25 Jeff Blake .15 .40
26 Ki-Jana Carter .07 .20
27 Carl Pickens .07 .20
28 Darnay Scott .07 .20
29 Troy Aikman .40 1.00
30 Michael Irvin .15 .40
31 Daryl Johnston .07 .20
32 Deion Sanders .25 .60
33 Emmitt Smith .60 1.50
34 Terrell Davis .30 .75
35 John Elway .75 2.00
36 Anthony Miller .07 .20
37 Shannon Sharpe .07 .20
38 Scott Mitchell .07 .20
39 Herman Moore .07 .20
40 Brett Perriman .02 .10
41 Barry Sanders .60 1.50
42 Edgar Bennett .07 .20
43 Robert Brooks .15 .40
44 Mark Chmura .07 .20
45 Brett Favre .75 2.00
46 Reggie White .15 .40
47 Mel Gray .02 .10
48 Steve McNair .30 .75
49 Chris Sanders .07 .20
50 Rodney Thomas .02 .10
51 Quentin Coryatt .02 .10
52 Sean Dawkins .02 .10
53 Ken Dilger .07 .20
54 Marshall Faulk .20 .50
55 Jim Harbaugh .07 .20
56 Tony Boselli .02 .10
57 Mark Brunell .25 .60
58 Natrone Means .07 .20
59 James O.Stewart .07 .20
60 Marcus Allen .15 .40
61 Steve Bono .02 .10
62 Neil Smith .07 .20
63 Tamarick Vanover .07 .20
64 Eric Green .02 .10
65 Terry Kirby .07 .20
66 Dan Marino .75 2.00
67 O.J. McDuffie .07 .20
68 Cris Carter .15 .40
69 Qadry Ismail .07 .20
70 Warren Moon .07 .20
71 Jake Reed .07 .20
72 Drew Bledsoe .25 .60
73 Ben Coates .07 .20
74 Curtis Martin .30 .75
75 Dave Meggett .02 .10
76 Mario Bates .07 .20
77 Jim Everett .02 .10
78 Michael Haynes .02 .10
79 Tyrone Hughes .02 .10
80 Dave Brown .02 .10
81 Rodney Hampton .07 .20
82 Thomas Lewis .02 .10
83 Tyrone Wheatley .07 .20
84 Kyle Brady .02 .10
85 Hugh Douglas .07 .20
86 Adrian Murrell .07 .20
87 Neil O'Donnell .07 .20
88 Tim Brown .15 .40
89 Jeff Hostetler .02 .10
90 Napoleon Kaufman .15 .40
91 Harvey Williams .02 .10
92 Charlie Garner .07 .20
93 Rodney Peete .02 .10
94 Ricky Watters .07 .20
95 Calvin Williams .02 .10
96 Jerome Bettis .15 .40
97 Greg Lloyd .07 .20
98 Kordell Stewart .15 .40
99 Yancey Thigpen .07 .20
100 Rod Woodson .07 .20
101 Isaac Bruce .15 .40
102 Kevin Carter .02 .10
103 Steve Walsh .02 .10
104 Aaron Hayden .02 .10
105 Stan Humphries .07 .20
106 Junior Seau .15 .40
107 William Floyd .07 .20
108 Brent Jones .02 .10
109 Jerry Rice .40 1.00
110 J.J. Stokes .15 .40
111 Steve Young .30 .75
112 Brian Blades .02 .10
113 Joey Galloway .15 .40
114 Rick Mirer .07 .20
115 Chris Warren .07 .20
116 Trent Dilfer .15 .40
117 Alvin Harper .02 .10
118 Hardy Nickerson .02 .10
119 Errict Rhett .07 .20
120 Terry Allen .07 .20
121 Brian Mitchell .02 .10
122 Heath Shuler .07 .20
123 Michael Westbrook .15 .40
124 Karim Abdul-Jabbar RC .15 .40
125 Tim Biakabutuka RC .15 .40
126 Duane Clemons RC .02 .10
127 Stephen Davis RC .75 2.00
128 Rickey Dudley RC .15 .40
129 Bobby Engram RC .15 .40
130 Daryl Gardener RC .02 .10
131 Eddie George RC .60 1.50
132 Terry Glenn RC .50 1.25
133 Kevin Hardy RC .15 .40
134 Walt Harris RC .02 .10
135 Marvin Harrison RC 1.25 3.00
136 Keyshawn Johnson RC .50 1.25
137 Cedric Jones RC .02 .10
138 Eddie Kennison RC .15 .40
139 Sam
Sean Manuel RC .02 .10
140 Leeland McElroy RC .07 .20
141 Ray Mickens RC .02 .10
142 Jonathan Ogden RC .40 1.00
143 Lawrence Phillips RC .15 .40
144 Kavika Pittman RC .02 .10
145 Simeon Rice RC .40 1.00
146 Regan Upshaw RC .02 .10
147 Alex Van Dyke RC .07 .20
148 Stepfret Williams RC .07 .20
149 Checklist .02 .10
150 Checklist .02 .10

1996 Metal Precious Metal

COMPLETE SET (148) 250.00 500.00
*VETS: 10X TO 25X BASIC CARDS
*ROOKIES: 6X TO 15X BASIC CARDS
ONE PER BOX

1996 Metal Freshly Forged

Randomly inserted in hobby packs only at a rate of one in 80, this 10-card set featues color player photos of second-year standouts and flashy rookies on acrylic cards. The backs carry a paragraph about the player.

COMPLETE SET (10) 15.00 40.00
STATED ODDS 1:80 HOBBY
1 Tim Biakabutuka .75 2.00
2 Jeff Blake 2.50 6.00
3 Ki-Jana Carter 1.25 3.00
4 Eddie George 3.00 8.00
5 Terry Glenn 2.50 6.00
6 Keyshawn Johnson 2.50 6.00
7 Curtis Martin 5.00 12.00
8 Leeland McElroy .40 1.00
9 Lawrence Phillips .75 2.00
10 Kordell Stewart 2.50 6.00

1996 Metal Goldfingers

Randomly inserted in packs at a rate of one in eight, this 12-card set is a 24-karat etched gold foil stamped collection of top-flight receivers. A color player image is set over a gold foil hand background. The backs carry another player photo and a paragraph about the player.

COMPLETE SET (12) 7.50 20.00
STATED ODDS 1:8
1 Isaac Bruce 1.25 3.00
2 Joey Galloway 1.25 3.00
3 Michael Irvin 1.25 3.00
4 Herman Moore .60 1.50
5 Carl Pickens .60 1.50
6 Jerry Rice 3.00 8.00
7 Chris Sanders .60 1.50
8 Frank Sanders .60 1.50
9 J.J. Stokes 1.25 3.00
10 Yancey Thigpen .60 1.50
11 Tamarick Vanover .60 1.50
12 Michael Westbrook 1.25 3.00

1996 Metal Goldflingers

Randomly inserted in retail packs only at the rate of one in 12, this 12-card set features color player images on a gold foil background of some of the NFL's best quarterbacks. The backs carry another player photo and a paragraph about the player.

COMPLETE SET (12) 10.00 25.00
STATED ODDS 1:12 RETAIL
1 Troy Aikman 1.50 4.00
2 Steve Bono .15 .40
3 Kerry Collins .60 1.50
4 Trent Dilfer .60 1.50
5 Brett Favre 3.00 8.00
6 Guo Frorotto .30 .75
7 Stan Humphries .30 .75
8 Dan Marino 3.00 8.00
9 Steve McNair 1.25 3.00
10 Scott Mitchell .30 .75
11 Steve Young 1.25 3.00
12 Eric Zeier .60 1.50

1996 Metal Molten Metal

Randomly inserted in packs at a rate of one in 120, this 10-card set features foil embossed cards of very hot players. The backs carry a paragraph about the player.

COMPLETE SET (10) 30.00 80.00
STATED ODDS 1:120
1 Troy Aikman 5.00 12.00
2 Ki-Jana Carter 1.00 2.50
3 Kerry Collins 2.00 5.00
4 Terrell Davis 4.00 10.00
5 Marshall Faulk 2.50 6.00
6 Brett Favre 10.00 25.00
7 Keyshawn Johnson 2.00 5.00
8 Curtis Martin 4.00 10.00
9 Deion Sanders 3.00 8.00
10 Emmitt Smith 8.00 20.00

1996 Metal Platinum Portraits

Fleer inserted the first 10-cards of the set into packs of 1996 Metal. The insertion ratio was one in 50. Additonally, the final two cards were later released via a mail redemption. They featured the two NFL Rookie of the Year Award winners. Both cards could be had for ten Metal wrappers plus $25. The offer expired June 30, 1997.

COMPLETE SET (10) 35.00 80.00
1-10: STATED ODDS 1:50
11-12: AVAIL.VIA WRAPPER OFFER
1 Isaac Bruce 1.50 4.00
2 Terrell Davis 3.00 8.00
3 John Elway 8.00 20.00
4 Joey Galloway 1.50 4.00
5 Steve McNair 3.00 8.00
6 Errict Rhett .75 2.00
7 Rashaan Salaam .75 2.00
8 Barry Sanders 6.00 15.00
9 Chris Warren .75 2.00
10 Steve Young 3.00 8.00
11 Eddie George 3.00 8.00
12 Simeon Rice 2.00 5.00

1997 Metal Universe

The 1997 Metal Universe set was issued in one series totalling 200-cards and was distributed in eight-card packs with a suggested retail price of $2.49. The fronts feature action photography with Marvel comic art backgrounds on etched foil card stock. The backs carry player information and career statistics with the player's best statistical category highlighted.

COMPLETE SET (200) 10.00 25.00
1 Terry Glenn .10 .30
2 Terry Kirby .10 .30
3 Thomas Lewis .07 .20
4 Tim Biakabutuka .10 .30
5 Tim Brown .20 .50
6 Todd Collins .07 .20
7 Tony Banks .10 .30
8 Tony Brackens .07 .20
9 Tony Martin .07 .20
10 Trent Dilfer .20 .50
11 Troy Aikman .40 1.00
12 Ty Detmer .10 .30
13 Tyrone Wheatley .10 .30
14 Vinny Testaverde .10 .30
15 Wayne Chrebet .20 .50
16 Wesley Walls .10 .30
17 William Floyd .10 .30
18 Willie McGinest .10 .30
19 Yancey Thigpen .10 .30
20 Zach Thomas .20 .50
21 Terry Allen .20 .50
22 Terrell Owens .25 .60
23 Terrell Davis .25 .60
24 Terance Mathis .10 .30
25 Ted Johnson .07 .20
26 Tamarick Vanover .07 .20
27 Steve Young .25 .60
28 Steve McNair .25 .60
29 Stan Humphries .10 .30
30 Simeon Rice .10 .30
31 Shannon Sharpe .20 .50
32 Sean Jones .07 .20
33 Scott Mitchell .10 .30
34 Sam Mills .10 .30
35 Rodney Hampton .10 .30
36 Rod Woodson .20 .50
37 Robert Smith .10 .30
38 Rob Moore .10 .30
39 Ricky Watters .10 .30
40 Rickey Dudley .10 .30
41 Rick Mirer .07 .20
42 Reggie White .20 .50
43 Ray Zellars .07 .20
44 Ray Lewis .30 .75
45 Rashaan Salaam .07 .20
46 Quentin Coryatt .07 .20
47 Qadry Ismail .10 .30
48 O.J. McDuffie .10 .30
49 Nilo Silvan .07 .20
50 Neil Smith .10 .30
51 Neil O'Donnell .10 .30
52 Natrone Means .10 .30
53 Napoleon Kaufman .10 .30
54 Mike Tomczak .07 .20
55 Mike Alstott .20 .50
56 Michael Westbrook .10 .30
57 Michael Jackson .10 .30
58 Michael Irvin .20 .50
59 Michael Haynes .07 .20
60 Michael Bates .07 .20
61 Mel Gray .07 .20
62 Marvin Harrison .20 .50
63 Marshall Faulk .20 .50
64 Mark Brunell .20 .50
65 Mario Bates .07 .20
66 Marcus Allen .20 .50
67 Lorenzo Neal .07 .20
68 Levon Kirkland .07 .20
69 Leonard Russell .07 .20
70 Leeland McElroy .07 .20
71 Lawyer Milloy .10 .30
72 Lawrence Phillips .07 .20
73 Larry Centers .10 .30
74 Lamar Lathon .07 .20
75 Kordell Stewart .20 .50
76 Kimble Anders .10 .30
77 Ki-Jana Carter .10 .30
78 Keyshawn Johnson .20 .50
79 Kevin Turner .07 .20
80 Jermaine Lewis .10 .30
81 Jerome Bettis .20 .50
82 Jerris McPhail .07 .20
83 Joey Galloway .10 .30
84 Jerry Rice .40 1.00
85 Jim Everett .07 .20
86 Jimmy Smith .10 .30
87 Jim Harbaugh .20 .50
88 John Elway .75 2.00
89 John Friesz .07 .20
90 John Mobley .07 .20
91 Johnnie Morton .10 .30
92 Junior Seau .20 .50
93 Karim Abdul-Jabbar .10 .30
94 Keenan McCardell .10 .30
95 Ken Dilger .07 .20
96 Ken Norton .07 .20
97 Kent Graham .07 .20
98 Kerry Collins .20 .50
99 Kevin Greene .10 .30
100 Kevin Hardy .07 .20
101 Jeff Lewis .07 .20
102 Jeff George .10 .30
103 Jeff Graham .07 .20
104 Jeff Blake .10 .30
105 Jason Sehorn .10 .30
106 Jason Dunn .07 .20
107 Jamie Asher .07 .20
108 Jamal Anderson .10 .30
109 Jake Reed .10 .30
110 Isaac Bruce .20 .50
111 Irving Fryar .10 .30
112 Iheanyi Uwaezuoke .07 .20
113 Hugh Douglas .07 .20
114 Herman Moore .10 .30
115 Harvey Williams .07 .20
116 Hardy Nickerson .07 .20
117 Gus Frerotte .07 .20
118 Greg Hill .07 .20
119 Glyn Milburn .07 .20
120 Frank Wycheck .07 .20
121 Frank Sanders .10 .30
122 Errict Rhett .07 .20
123 Erik Kramer .07 .20
124 Eric Moulds .10 .30
125 Eric Metcalf .10 .30
126 Emmitt Smith .60 1.50
127 Edgar Bennett .10 .30
128 Eddie Kennison .10 .30
129 Eddie George .20 .50
130 Drew Bledsoe .20 .50
131 Dorsey Levens .10 .30
132 Desmond Howard .10 .30
133 Derrick Thomas .20 .50
134 Derrick Alexander WR .10 .30
135 Deion Sanders .20 .50
136 Dave Brown .07 .20
137 Daryl Johnston .20 .50
138 Darnay Scott .10 .30
139 Darick Holmes .07 .20
140 Dan Marino .75 2.00
141 Curtis Martin .20 .50
142 Curtis Conway .10 .30
143 Cris Carter .20 .50
144 Chris Warren .10 .30
145 Chris T. Jones .07 .20
146 Chris Slade .07 .20
147 Chris Sanders .07 .20
148 Chester McGlockton .07 .20
149 Charlie Jones .07 .20
150 Charles Way .07 .20
151 Carl Pickens .10 .30
152 Bryan Still .07 .20
153 Bruce Smith .20 .50
154 Brian Mitchell .07 .20
155 Brett Perriman .07 .20
156 Brett Favre 1.00 2.50
157 Brad Johnson .10 .30
158 Thurman Thomas .20 .50
159 Bobby Engram .10 .30
160 Bert Emanuel .10 .30
161 Ben Coates .10 .30
162 Barry Sanders .60 1.50
163 Byron Bam Morris .07 .20
164 Ashley Ambrose .07 .20
165 Antonio Freeman .20 .50
166 Anthony Miller .07 .20
167 Anthony Johnson .07 .20
168 Andre Rison .10 .30
169 Andre Reed .10 .30
170 Alex Molden .07 .20
171 Aeneas Williams .07 .20
172 Adrian Murrell .10 .30
173 Aaron Hayden .07 .20
174 Darnell Autry RC .10 .30
175 Orlando Pace RC .20 .50
176 Darrell Russell RC .07 .20
177 Peter Boulware RC .20 .50
178 Shawn Springs RC .10 .30
179 Bryant Westbrook RC .07 .20
180 Dwayne Rudd RC .10 .30
181 Rae Carruth RC .07 .20
182 Troy Davis RC .10 .30
183 Antowain Smith RC .20 .50
184 James Farrior RC .20 .50
185 Walter Jones RC .20 .50
186 Sam Madison RC .20 .50
187 Tom Knight RC .07 .20
188 Reidel Anthony RC .10 .30
189 Warrick Dunn RC .50 1.25
190 Reinard Wilson RC .10 .30
191 Tyrus McCloud RC .07 .20
192 Michael Booker RC .07 .20
193 Tony Gonzalez RC .75 2.00
194 Pat Barnes RC .07 .20
195 Tiki Barber RC .75 2.00
196 Sedrick Shaw RC .10 .30
197 Corey Dillon RC .50 1.25
198 Danny Wuerffel RC .20 .50
199 Checklist (1-152) .07 .20
200 Checklist (153-200 inserts) .07 .20
S1 Terrell Davis Sample .75 2.00

1997 Metal Universe Precious Metal Gems

*PREC.METAL/150: 30X TO 80X BASIC CARDS
STATED PRINT RUN 150 SER.#'d SETS
140 Dan Marino 126.00 200.00
156 Brett Favre 150.00 250.00

1997 Metal Universe Precious Metal Gems Green

*VETS 1-173: 125X TO 250X BASIC CARDS
*ROOKIE STARS 174-198: 100X TO 200X
FIRST 15 SERIAL #'d CARDS ARE GREEN
84 Jerry Rice 175.00 300.00
88 John Elway 250.00 500.00
126 Emmitt Smith 250.00 400.00
140 Dan Marino 250.00 500.00
156 Brett Favre 300.00 600.00
162 Barry Sanders 250.00 400.00
193 Tony Gonzalez 200.00 400.00
195 Tiki Barber 200.00 400.00

1997 Metal Universe Body Shop

Randomly inserted in packs at a rate of one in 96, this 15-card set features sculpted cards that focus on the power anatomy of top players. Each player is chiseled out and his biggest strength is robotically enhanced with a unique mix of photography and technology.

COMPLETE SET (15) 50.00 120.00
STATED ODDS 1:96
1 Zach Thomas 6.00 15.00
2 Steve Young 8.00 20.00
3 Steve McNair 8.00 20.00
4 Simeon Rice 4.00 10.00
5 Shannon Sharpe 4.00 10.00
6 Napoleon Kaufman 6.00 15.00
7 Mike Alstott 6.00 15.00
8 Michael Westbrook 4.00 10.00
9 Kordell Stewart 6.00 15.00
10 Kevin Hardy 2.50 6.00
11 Kerry Collins 6.00 15.00
12 Junior Seau 6.00 15.00
13 Jamal Anderson 6.00 15.00
14 Drew Bledsoe 8.00 20.00
15 Deion Sanders 6.00 15.00

1997 Metal Universe Gold Universe

Randomly inserted in packs at a rate of one in 120, this 10-card retail exclusive set features color action photos of shining stars printed on gold holofoil card stock.

COMPLETE SET (10) 50.00 120.00
STATED ODDS 1:120 RETAIL
1 Dan Marino 20.00 50.00
2 Deion Sanders 5.00 12.00
3 Drew Bledsoe 6.00 15.00
4 Isaac Bruce 5.00 12.00
5 Joey Galloway 3.00 8.00
6 Karim Abdul-Jabbar 3.00 8.00
7 Lawrence Phillips 2.00 5.00
8 Marshall Faulk 6.00 15.00
9 Marvin Harrison 5.00 12.00
10 Steve Young 6.00 15.00

1997 Metal Universe Iron Rookies

Randomly inserted in packs at a rate of one in 24, this 15-card set features color action photos of the top 1997 draft choices. The cards were designed with an intricate die cut pattern and printed on foil stock.

COMPLETE SET (15) 40.00 80.00
STATED ODDS 1:24
1 Darnell Autry 1.50 3.00
2 Orlando Pace 2.00 4.00
3 Peter Boulware 2.00 4.00
4 Shawn Springs 1.50 3.00
5 Bryant Westbrook .60 1.50
6 Rae Carruth .60 1.50
7 Troy Davis 1.50 3.00
8 Antowain Smith 5.00 12.00
9 James Farrior 2.00 4.00
10 Dwayne Rudd .60 1.50
11 Darrell Russell .60 1.50
12 Warrick Dunn 6.00 15.00
13 Sedrick Shaw 1.50 3.00
14 Danny Wuerffel 2.00 4.00
15 Sam Madison 1.50 3.00

1997 Metal Universe Marvel Metal

ndomly inserted in packs at a rate of one in six, this 20-card set features color images of top young NFL superstars printed on a background of and compared to a Marvel Comic superhero, such as receivers with Spider-Man, heavy hitters with the Incredible Hulk, running backs with Wolverine, and quarterbacks with Captain America.

COMPLETE SET (20) 20.00 50.00
STATED ODDS 1:6
1 Barry Sanders 3.00 8.00
2 Bruce Smith .60 1.50
3 Desmond Howard .60 1.50
4 Eddie George 1.00 2.50
5 Eddie Kennison .60 1.50
6 Jerry Rice 2.00 5.00
7 Joey Galloway .60 1.50
8 John Elway 4.00 10.00
9 Karim Abdul-Jabbar .60 1.50
10 Kerry Collins 1.00 2.50
11 Kevin Hardy .40 1.00
12 Kordell Stewart 1.00 2.50
13 Mark Brunell 1.25 3.00
14 Marshall Faulk 1.25 3.00
15 Michael Westbrook .60 1.50
16 Simeon Rice .60 1.50
17 Steve McNair 1.25 3.00
18 Terry Glenn 1.00 2.50
19 Tony Brackens .40 1.00
20 Tony Martin .60 1.50

1997 Metal Universe Platinum Portraits

Randomly inserted in packs at a rate of one in 288, this 10-card set features portraits of the NFL's future Hall of Famers printed on an etched foil look card.

COMPLETE SET (10) 60.00 150.00
STATED ODDS 1:288
1 Troy Aikman 8.00 20.00
2 Terrell Davis 5.00 12.00
3 Marvin Harrison 4.00 10.00
4 Keyshawn Johnson 4.00 10.00
5 Jerry Rice 8.00 20.00
6 Emmitt Smith 12.50 30.00
7 Dan Marino 15.00 40.00
8 Curtis Martin 5.00 12.00
9 Brett Favre 15.00 40.00
10 Barry Sanders 12.50 30.00

1997 Metal Universe Titanium

Randomly inserted in hobby packs only at a rate of one in 72, this 20-card set features color images of some of the league's greatest players printed on a duel corner die-cut card over a titanium background.

COMPLETE SET (20) 60.00 150.00
STATED ODDS 1:72 HOBBY
1 Barry Sanders 8.00 20.00
2 Brett Favre 10.00 25.00
3 Curtis Martin 3.00 8.00
4 Eddie George 2.50 6.00
5 Eddie Kennison 1.50 4.00
6 Emmitt Smith 8.00 20.00
7 Herman Moore 1.50 4.00
8 Isaac Bruce 2.50 6.00
9 Jerry Rice 5.00 12.00
10 John Elway 10.00 25.00
11 Keyshawn Johnson 2.50 6.00
12 Lawrence Phillips 1.00 2.50
13 Mark Brunell 3.00 8.00
14 Mike Alstott 2.50 6.00
15 Steve McNair 3.00 8.00
16 Steve Young 3.00 8.00
17 Terrell Davis 3.00 8.00
18 Terry Glenn 2.50 6.00
19 Tony Banks 1.50 4.00
20 Troy Aikman 5.00 12.00

1998 Metal Universe Samples

1 Jake Plummer .40 1.00
2 Shannon Sharpe .50 1.25

1998 Metal Universe

The 1998 Metal Universe set was issued in one series totalling 200 cards. The 8-card packs retail for $2.69 each. The set contains the subset: Rookies (173-197), and Checklists (198-200). The fronts feature color action photography on flat foil and placed on a scenic background of the featured player's team state.

COMPLETE SET (200) 15.00 40.00
1 Jerry Rice .40 1.00
2 Muhsin Muhammad .15 .40
3 Ed McCaffrey .15 .40
4 Brett Favre 1.00 2.50
5 Troy Brown .15 .40
6 Brad Johnson .15 .40
7 John Elway .75 2.00
8 Herman Moore .15 .40
9 O.J. McDuffie .15 .40
10 Tim Brown .20 .50
11 Byron Hanspard .10 .30
12 Rae Carruth .10 .30
13 Rod Smith WR .15 .40
14 John Randle .15 .40
15 Karim Abdul-Jabbar .15 .40
16 Bobby Hoying .15 .40
17 Steve Young .25 .60
18 Andre Hastings .10 .30
19 Chidi Ahanotu .10 .30
20 Barry Sanders .60 1.50
21 Bruce Smith .15 .40
22 Kimble Anders .10 .30
23 Troy Davis .10 .30
24 Jamal Anderson .15 .40
25 Curtis Conway .15 .40
26 Mark Chmura .10 .30
27 Reggie White .20 .50
28 Jake Reed .15 .40
29 Willie McGinest .10 .30
30 Terrell Davis .20 .50

31 Joey Galloway .15 .40
32 Leslie Shepherd .10 .30
33 Peter Boulware .10 .30
34 Chad Lewis .10 .30
35 Marcus Allen .20 .50
36 Randal Hill .10 .30
37 Jerome Bettis .20 .50
38 William Floyd .10 .30
39 Warren Moon .20 .50
40 Mike Alstott .20 .50
41 Jay Graham .10 .30
42 Emmitt Smith .60 1.50
43 James O. Stewart .15 .40
44 Charlie Garner .15 .40
45 Merton Hanks .10 .30
46 Shawn Springs .10 .30
47 Chris Calloway .10 .30
48 Larry Centers .10 .30
49 Michael Jackson .10 .30
50 Deion Sanders .20 .50
51 Jimmy Smith .15 .40
52 Jason Sehorn .15 .40
53 Charles Johnson .10 .30
54 Garrison Hearst .15 .40
55 Chris Warren .15 .40
56 Warren Sapp .15 .40
57 Corey Dillon .15 .40
58 Marvin Harrison .20 .50
59 Chris Sanders .10 .30
60 Jamie Asher .10 .30
61 Yancey Thigpen .10 .30
62 Freddie Jones .10 .30
63 Rob Moore .15 .40
64 Jermaine Lewis .10 .30
65 Michael Irvin .20 .50
66 Natrone Means .15 .40
67 Charles Way .10 .30
68 Terry Kirby .10 .30
69 Tony Banks .15 .40
70 Steve McNair .20 .50
71 Vinny Testaverde .15 .40
72 Dexter Coakley .10 .30
73 Keenan McCardell .15 .40
74 Glenn Foley .10 .30
75 Isaac Bruce .20 .50
76 Terry Allen .15 .40
77 Todd Collins .10 .30
78 Troy Aikman .40 1.00
79 Damon Jones .10 .30
80 Leon Johnson .10 .30
81 James Jett .10 .30
82 Frank Wycheck .10 .30
83 Andre Reed .15 .40
84 Derrick Alexander WR .15 .40
85 Jason Taylor .15 .40
86 Wayne Chrebet .20 .50
87 Napoleon Kaufman .15 .40
88 Eddie George .20 .50
89 Ernie Conwell .10 .30
90 Antowain Smith .15 .40
91 Johnnie Morton .15 .40
92 Jerris McPhail .10 .30
93 Cris Carter .20 .50
94 Danny Kanell .10 .30
95 Stan Humphries .10 .30
96 Terrell Owens .20 .50
97 Willie Davis .10 .30
98 David Dunn .10 .30
99 Tony Brackens .10 .30
100 Kordell Stewart .15 .40
101 Rodney Thomas .10 .30
102 Keyshawn Johnson .20 .50
103 Carl Pickens .15 .40
104 Mark Brunell .20 .50
105 Jeff George .15 .40
106 Bert Emanuel .10 .30
107 Wesley Walls .15 .40
108 Bryant Westbrook .10 .30
109 Dorsey Levens .15 .40
110 Drew Bledsoe .20 .50
111 Adrian Murrell .10 .30
112 Aeneas Williams .10 .30
113 Raymont Harris .10 .30
114 Tony Gonzalez .20 .50
115 Sean Dawkins .10 .30
116 Billy Joe Hobert .10 .30
117 James McKnight .15 .40
118 Reidel Anthony .10 .30
119 Terance Mathis .10 .30
120 Darrien Gordon .10 .30
121 Dale Carter .10 .30
122 Duce Staley .20 .50
123 Jerald Moore .10 .30
124 Eric Swann .10 .30
125 Antonio Freeman .20 .50
126 Chris Penn .10 .30
127 Ken Dilger .10 .30
128 Robert Smith .15 .40
129 Tiki Barber .20 .50
130 Mark Bruener .10 .30
131 Junior Seau .20 .50
132 Trent Dilfer .20 .50
133 Gus Frerotte .10 .30
134 Jake Plummer .15 .40
135 Jeff Blake .15 .40
136 Jim Harbaugh .15 .40
137 Michael Strahan .15 .40
138 Gary Brown .10 .30
139 Tony Martin .15 .40
140 Stephen Davis .15 .40
141 Thurman Thomas .20 .50
142 Scott Mitchell .15 .40
143 Dan Marino .75 2.00
144 David Palmer .10 .30
145 J.J. Stokes .10 .30
146 Chris Chandler .15 .40
147 Darnell Autry .10 .30
148 Robert Brooks .15 .40
149 Derrick Mayes .10 .30
150 Curtis Martin .20 .50
151 Steve Broussard .10 .30
152 Eddie Kennison .15 .40
153 Kerry Collins .15 .40
154 Shannon Sharpe .20 .50
155 Andre Rison .15 .40
156 Dwayne Rudd .10 .30
157 Orlando Pace .10 .30
158 Terry Glenn .15 .40
159 Frank Sanders .10 .30
160 Ricky Proehl .10 .30
161 Marshall Faulk .20 .50
162 Irving Fryar .15 .40
163 Courtney Hawkins .10 .30
164 Eric Metcalf .10 .30
165 Warrick Dunn .20 .50
166 Cris Dishman .10 .30
167 Fred Lane .10 .30
168 John Mobley .10 .30
169 Elvis Grbac .15 .40
170 Ben Coates .15 .40
171 Rickey Dudley .10 .30
172 Ricky Watters .15 .40
173 Alonzo Mayes RC .10 .30
174 Andre Wadsworth RC .15 .40
175 Brian Simmons RC .10 .30
176 Charles Woodson RC .75 2.00
177 Curtis Enis RC .15 .40
178 Fred Taylor RC .60 1.50
179 Germane Crowell RC .15 .40
180 Greg Ellis RC .10 .30
181 Jacquez Green RC .15 .40
182 Jason Peter RC .10 .30
183 John Dutton RC .10 .30
184 Kevin Dyson RC .20 .50
185 Kivuusama Mays RC .10 .30
186 Marcus Nash RC .10 .30
187 Michael Myers RC .10 .30
188 Ahman Green RC .75 2.00
189 Peyton Manning RC 6.00 15.00
190 Randy Moss RC 2.00 5.00
191 Robert Edwards RC .15 .40
192 Robert Holcombe RC .10 .30
193 Ryan Leaf RC .20 .50
194 Takeo Spikes RC .30 .75
195 Tavian Banks RC .15 .40
196 Tim Dwight RC .20 .50
197 Vonnie Holliday RC .15 .40
198 Dorsey Levens CL .10 .30
199 Jerry Rice CL .20 .50
200 Dan Marino CL .30 .75

1998 Metal Universe Precious Metal Gems

*VETS: 60X TO 120X BASIC CARDS
*ROOKIE STARS: 25X TO 60X
STATED PRINT RUN 50 SER.#'d SETS
189 Peyton Manning 500.00 800.00

1998 Metal Universe Decided Edge

ndomly inserted in packs at a rate of one in 288, this 10-card set includes the top players of the game printed on foil card stock.

COMPLETE SET (10) 150.00 300.00
STATED ODDS 1:288
1 Terrell Davis 5.00 12.00
2 Brett Favre 20.00 50.00
3 John Elway 20.00 50.00
4 Barry Sanders 15.00 40.00
5 Eddie George 5.00 12.00
6 Jerry Rice 10.00 25.00
7 Emmitt Smith 15.00 40.00
8 Dan Marino 20.00 50.00
9 Troy Aikman 10.00 25.00
10 Marcus Allen 5.00 12.00

1998 Metal Universe E-X2001 Previews

ndomly inserted in packs at a rate of one in 144, this 15-card set previews the 1998 E-X2001 set. Each card is very similar in design to the base 1998 E-X2001 release except for the card numbering and different player photo.

COMPLETE SET (15) 125.00 250.00
STATED ODDS 1:144
1 Barry Sanders 15.00 40.00
2 Brett Favre 20.00 50.00
3 Corey Dillon 5.00 12.00
4 John Elway 20.00 50.00
5 Drew Bledsoe 8.00 20.00
6 Eddie George 5.00 12.00
7 Emmitt Smith 15.00 40.00
8 Joey Galloway 3.00 8.00
9 Karim Abdul-Jabbar 5.00 12.00
10 Kordell Stewart 5.00 12.00
11 Mark Brunell 5.00 12.00
12 Mike Alstott 5.00 12.00
13 Warrick Dunn 5.00 12.00
14 Antonio Freeman 5.00 12.00
15 Terrell Davis 5.00 12.00

1998 Metal Universe Planet Football

ndomly inserted in packs at a rate of one in eight, this 15-card set features players against a space age planet designed background.

COMPLETE SET (15) 25.00 50.00
STATED ODDS 1:8
1 Barry Sanders 3.00 8.00
2 Corey Dillon 1.00 2.50
3 Warrick Dunn 1.00 2.50
4 Jake Plummer 1.00 2.50
5 John Elway 4.00 10.00
6 Kordell Stewart 1.00 2.50
7 Curtis Martin 1.00 2.50
8 Mark Brunell 1.00 2.50
9 Dorsey Levens 1.00 2.50
10 Troy Aikman 2.00 5.00
11 Terry Glenn 1.00 2.50
12 Eddie George 1.00 2.50
13 Keyshawn Johnson 1.00 2.50
14 Steve McNair 1.00 2.50
15 Jerry Rice 2.00 5.00

1998 Metal Universe Quasars

asars was a random insert in packs. Each card featured a top 1998 NFL draft pick and was seeded at a rate of 1:20.

COMPLETE SET (15) 25.00 60.00
STATED ODDS 1:20
1 Peyton Manning 12.00 30.00
2 Ryan Leaf 1.25 3.00
3 Charles Woodson 3.00 8.00
4 Randy Moss 10.00 25.00
5 Curtis Enis .60 1.50
6 Tavian Banks 1.00 2.50
7 Germane Crowell 1.00 2.50
8 Kevin Dyson 1.25 3.00
9 Robert Edwards 1.00 2.50
10 Jacquez Green 1.00 2.50
11 Alonzo Mayes .60 1.50
12 Brian Simmons 1.00 2.50
13 Takeo Spikes 1.25 3.00
14 Andre Wadsworth 1.00 2.50
15 Ahman Green 3.00 8.00

1998 Metal Universe Titanium

ndomly inserted in packs at a rate of one in 96, this 10-card set included a mix of veteran NFL stars and young up-and-coming players.

COMPLETE SET (10) 30.00 80.00
STATED ODDS 1:96
1 Corey Dillon 2.50 6.00
2 Emmitt Smith 8.00 20.00
3 Terrell Davis 2.50 6.00
4 Brett Favre 10.00 25.00
5 Mark Brunell 2.50 6.00
6 Dan Marino 10.00 25.00
7 Curtis Martin 2.50 6.00
8 Kordell Stewart 2.50 6.00
9 Warrick Dunn 2.50 6.00
10 Steve McNair 2.50 6.00

1999 Metal Universe

is 250 card set was issued in eight card packs with a SRP of $2.69 and released in July, 1999. Subsets include Prominent and Dominant (183-207), Rookies (208-247) and Checklist (248-250). Notable Rookie Cards include Tim Couch, Edgerrin James and Ricky Williams. Before the set was released, a Promo Card of Doug Flutie was issued. This card is listed and priced at the end of these listings.

COMPLETE SET (250) 15.00 40.00
1 Eric Moulds .12 .30
2 David Palmer .12 .30
3 Ricky Watters .15 .40
4 Antonio Freeman .15 .40
5 Hugh Douglas .15 .40
6 Johnnie Morton .15 .40
7 Corey Fuller .12 .30
8 J.J. Stokes .12 .30
9 Keith Poole .12 .30
10 Steve Beuerlein .15 .40
11 Keenan McCardell .15 .40
12 Carl Pickens .15 .40
13 Mark Bruener .12 .30
14 Warren Sapp .15 .40
15 Rich Gannon .15 .40
16 Bruce Smith .15 .40
17 Mark Chmura .12 .30
18 Drew Bledsoe .15 .40
19 Charles Woodson .20 .50
20 Ahman Green .15 .40
21 Ricky Proehl .12 .30
22 Corey Dillon .12 .30
23 Terry Fair .12 .30
24 Mark Brunell .15 .40
25 Leroy Hoard .12 .30
26 La'Roi Glover RC .20 .50
27 Tim Brown .20 .50
28 Kevin Turner .12 .30
29 Terrell Owens .15 .40
30 Mike Alstott .12 .30
31 Rob Moore .12 .30
32 Troy Aikman .25 .60
33 Derrick Alexander .12 .30
34 Chris Calloway .12 .30
35 Kordell Stewart .12 .30
36 Reidel Anthony .12 .30
37 Michael Westbrook .12 .30
38 Ray Lewis .20 .50
39 Alonzo Mayes .12 .30
40 Rod Smith .15 .40
41 Reggie Barlow .12 .30
42 Sean Dawkins .12 .30
43 Duce Staley .12 .30
44 R.W. McQuarters .12 .30
45 Robert Holcombe .12 .30
46 Priest Holmes .12 .30
47 Erik Kramer .15 .40
48 Shannon Sharpe .15 .40
49 Mike Vanderjagt .12 .30
50 Cris Carter .20 .50
51 Billy Joe Tolliver .12 .30
52 Vinny Testaverde .12 .30
53 Antonio Langham .12 .30
54 Damon Gibson .12 .30
55 Garrison Hearst .12 .30
56 Brad Johnson .15 .40
57 Randall Cunningham .15 .40
58 Jim Harbaugh .15 .40
59 Curtis Enis .12 .30
60 Bill Romanowski .15 .40
61 Marcus Pollard .12 .30
62 Zach Thomas .15 .40
63 Cameron Cleeland .12 .30
64 Curtis Martin .15 .40
65 Charlie Garner .15 .40
66 Jerris McPhail .12 .30
67 Jon Kitna .12 .30
68 Chris Chandler .15 .40
69 Emmitt Smith .30 .75
70 Andre Rison .15 .40
71 Wayne Chrebet .12 .30
72 Mikhael Ricks .12 .30
73 Yancey Thigpen .12 .30
74 Peter Boulware .12 .30
75 Bobby Engram .12 .30
76 John Mobley .12 .30
77 Peyton Manning .60 1.50
78 O.J. McDuffie .15 .40
79 Tony Simmons .12 .30
80 Mo Lewis .12 .30
81 Bryan Still .12 .30
82 Eugene Robinson .15 .40
83 Curtis Conway .15 .40
84 Ed McCaffrey .15 .40
85 Marvin Harrison .15 .40
86 Dan Marino .40 1.00
87 Ty Law .20 .50
88 Leon Johnson .12 .30
89 Junior Seau .15 .40
90 Terance Mathis .12 .30
91 Wesley Walls .15 .40
92 John Elway .30 .75
93 Marshall Faulk .15 .40
94 Oronde Gadsden .12 .30
95 Keyshawn Johnson .15 .40
96 Muhsin Muhammad .12 .30
97 Dorsey Levens .15 .40
98 Shawn Jefferson .12 .30
99 Rocket Ismail .15 .40
100 Vonnie Holliday .12 .30
101 Terry Glenn .15 .40
102 Shawn Springs .12 .30
103 Tim Dwight .15 .40
104 Terrell Davis .15 .40
105 Karim Abdul-Jabbar .12 .30
106 Bryan Cox .15 .40
107 Steve McNair .15 .40
108 Tony Martin .15 .40
109 Jason Elam .12 .30
110 John Avery .12 .30
111 Aaron Glenn .12 .30
112 Eddie George .15 .40
113 Larry Centers .12 .30
114 Darnay Scott .12 .30
115 Jimmy Smith .15 .40
116 Tiki Barber .15 .40
117 Charles Johnson .12 .30
118 Mike Archie RC .20 .50
119 Adrian Murrell .12 .30
120 Dexter Coakley .12 .30
121 Dale Carter .12 .30
122 Kent Graham .12 .30
123 Hines Ward .15 .40
124 Greg Hill .12 .30
125 Skip Hicks .12 .30
126 Doug Flutie .20 .50
127 Leslie Shepherd .12 .30
128 Neil O'Donnell .15 .40
129 Herman Moore .15 .40
130 Kevin Hardy .12 .30
131 Randy Moss .15 .40
132 Andre Hastings .12 .30
133 Rickey Dudley .12 .30
134 Jerome Bettis .20 .50
135 Jerry Rice .50 1.25
136 Jake Plummer .12 .30
137 Billy Davis .12 .30
138 Tony Gonzalez .15 .40
139 Ike Hilliard .12 .30
140 Freddie Jones .12 .30
141 Isaac Bruce .20 .50
142 Darrell Green .20 .50
143 Trent Green .12 .30
144 Jamal Anderson .15 .40
145 Deion Sanders .15 .40
146 Byron Bam Morris .12 .30
147 Charles Way .12 .30
148 Natrone Means .15 .40
149 Frank Wycheck .15 .40
150 Brett Favre .40 1.00
151 Michael Bates .12 .30
152 Ben Coates .15 .40
153 Koy Detmer .12 .30
154 Eddie Kennison .15 .40
155 Eric Metcalf .12 .30
156 Takeo Spikes .12 .30
157 Fred Taylor .12 .30
158 Gary Brown .12 .30
159 Levon Kirkland .12 .30
160 Trent Dilfer .12 .30
161 Antowain Smith .12 .30
162 Robert Brooks .15 .40
163 Robert Smith .12 .30
164 Napoleon Kaufman .12 .30
165 Chad Brown .12 .30
166 Warrick Dunn .12 .30
167 Joey Galloway .15 .40
168 Frank Sanders .12 .30
169 Michael Irvin .20 .50
170 Elvis Grbac .12 .30
171 Michael Strahan .15 .40
172 Ryan Leaf .15 .40
173 Stephen Alexander .12 .30
174 Andre Reed .20 .50
175 Barry Sanders .30 .75
176 Jake Reed .15 .40
177 James Jett .12 .30
178 Steve Young .25 .60
179 Jermaine Lewis .12 .30
180 Charlie Batch .12 .30
181 Jacquez Green .12 .30
182 Kevin Dyson .12 .30
183 Roell Preston PD .12 .30
184 Randall Cunningham PD .15 .40
185 Charlie Batch PD .12 .30
186 Kordell Stewart PD .12 .30
187 Bennie Thompson PD .12 .30
188 Deion Sanders PD .15 .40
189 Jake Plummer PD .12 .30
190 Eric Moulds PD .12 .30
191 Derrick Brooks PD .20 .50
192 Steve McNair PD .15 .40
193 Ryan Leaf PD .15 .40
194 Keyshawn Johnson PD .15 .40
195 Eddie George PD .15 .40
196 Warrick Dunn PD .12 .30
197 Jessie Tuggle PD .12 .30
198 Rodney Harrison PD .12 .30
199 Vinny Testaverde PD .12 .30
200 Marshall Faulk PD .15 .40
201 Ray Buchanan PD .12 .30
202 Garrison Hearst PD .12 .30
203 John Randle PD .20 .50
204 Drew Bledsoe PD .15 .40
205 Sam Gash PD .12 .30
206 Troy Aikman PD .25 .60
207 Michael McCrary PD .12 .30
208 Chris Claiborne RC .20 .50
209 Ricky Williams RC .30 .75
210 Tim Couch RC .25 .60
211 Champ Bailey RC .40 1.00
212 Torry Holt RC .40 1.00
213 Donovan McNabb RC 1.50 4.00
214 David Boston RC .20 .50
215 Chris McAlister RC .20 .50
216 Aaron Gibson RC .20 .50
217 Daunte Culpepper RC .30 .75
218 Matt Stinchcomb RC .20 .50
219 Edgerrin James RC .30 .75
220 Jevon Kearse RC .25 .60
221 Ebenezer Ekuban RC .20 .50
222 Kris Farris RC .20 .50
223 Chris Terry RC .20 .50
224 Cecil Collins RC .20 .50
225 Akili Smith RC .20 .50
226 Shaun King RC .20 .50
227 Rahim Abdullah RC .20 .50
228 Peerless Price RC .20 .50
229 Antoine Winfield RC .20 .50
230 Antuan Edwards RC .20 .50
231 Rob Konrad RC .20 .50
232 Troy Edwards RC .20 .50
233 John Thornton RC .20 .50
234 Fred Vinson RC .20 .50
235 Gary Stills RC .20 .50
236 Desmond Clark RC .25 .60
237 Lamar King RC .20 .50
238 Jared DeVries RC .20 .50
239 Martin Gramatica RC .20 .50
240 Montae Reagor RC .20 .50
241 Andy Katzenmoyer RC .25 .60
242 Rufus French RC .20 .50
243 D'Wayne Bates RC .20 .50
244 Amos Zereoue RC .20 .50
245 Dre Bly RC .30 .75
246 Kevin Johnson RC .25 .60
247 Cade McNown RC .20 .50
248 Kordell Stewart CL .12 .30
249 Deion Sanders CL .15 .40
250 Vinny Testaverde CL .12 .30
P1 Doug Flutie Promo .40 1.00

1999 Metal Universe Precious Metal Gems

ETS 40X TO 100X
*ROOKIE STARS: 15X TO 40X
STATED PRINT RUN 50 SER.#'d SETS

1999 Metal Universe Linchpins

Inserted at a rate of one in 360 hobby and one in 480 retail packs, these 10 cards feature a laser die-cut design and featured players who are the key players on their teams. These cards have a "LP" prefix.

STATED ODDS 1:360 HOB, 1:480 RET
LP1 Emmitt Smith 20.00 50.00
LP2 Charlie Batch 6.00 15.00
LP3 Fred Taylor 8.00 20.00
LP4 Jake Plummer 8.00 20.00
LP5 Brett Favre 30.00 80.00
LP6 Barry Sanders 20.00 50.00
LP7 Mark Brunell 8.00 20.00
LP8 Peyton Manning 25.00 60.00
LP9 Randy Moss 12.00 30.00
LP10 Terrell Davis 10.00 25.00

1999 Metal Universe Planet Metal

Inserted at a rate of one in 36 hobby packs and one in 48 retail packs, these 15 cards feature leading players on die-cut cards with a metallic view of the planet behind pop-out action shots. The cards have a "PM" prefix.

COMPLETE SET (15) 75.00 150.00
STATED ODDS 1:36 HOB, 1:48 RET
PM1 Terrell Davis 2.50 6.00
PM2 Troy Aikman 5.00 12.00
PM3 Peyton Manning 8.00 20.00
PM4 Mark Brunell 2.50 6.00
PM5 John Elway 8.00 20.00
PM6 Doug Flutie 2.50 6.00
PM7 Dan Marino 8.00 20.00
PM8 Brett Favre 8.00 20.00
PM9 Barry Sanders 8.00 20.00
PM10 Emmitt Smith 5.00 12.00
PM11 Fred Taylor 2.50 6.00
PM12 Jerry Rice 5.00 12.00
PM13 Jamal Anderson 2.50 6.00
PM14 Randall Cunningham 2.50 6.00
PM15 Randy Moss 6.00 15.00

1999 Metal Universe Quasars

serted into packs at a rate of one in 18 hobby and one in 24 retail, these 15 cards feature leading rookies on a silver rainbow holofoil background. The cards have a "QS" prefix.

COMPLETE SET (15) 40.00 80.00
STATED ODDS 1:18 HOB, 1:24 RET
*PRISMS: .75X TO 2X HI COL.
PRISMS PRINT RUN 99 SERIAL #'d SETS
QS1 Ricky Williams 2.00 5.00
QS2 Tim Couch 1.00 2.50
QS3 Shaun King .60 1.50
QS4 Champ Bailey 1.25 3.00
QS5 Torry Holt 2.50 6.00
QS6 Donovan McNabb 5.00 12.00
QS7 David Boston 1.00 2.50
QS8 Andy Katzenmoyer .60 1.50
QS9 Daunte Culpepper 4.00 10.00
QS10 Edgerrin James 4.00 10.00
QS11 Cade McNown .60 1.50
QS12 Troy Edwards .60 1.50
QS13 Akili Smith .60 1.50
QS14 Peerless Price 1.00 2.50
QS15 Amos Zereoue 1.00 2.50

1999 Metal Universe Starchild

serted at a rate of one in six hobby packs and one in eight retail packs, this 20 card set feature young stars on foil stamped cards with a rainbow holofoil background. The cards have a "SC" prefix.

COMPLETE SET (20) 10.00 25.00
STATED ODDS 1:6 HOB, 1:8 RET
SC1 Skip Hicks .50 1.25
SC2 Mike Alstott 1.25 3.00
SC3 Joey Galloway .75 2.00
SC4 Tony Simmons .50 1.25
SC5 Jamal Anderson 1.25 3.00
SC6 John Avery .50 1.25
SC7 Charles Woodson 1.25 3.00
SC8 Jon Kitna 1.25 3.00
SC9 Marshall Faulk 1.50 4.00
SC10 Eric Moulds 1.25 3.00
SC11 Keyshawn Johnson 1.25 3.00
SC12 Ryan Leaf .60 1.25
SC13 Curtis Enis .50 1.25
SC14 Steve McNair 1.25 3.00
SC15 Corey Dillon 1.25 3.00
SC16 Tim Dwight 1.25 3.00
SC17 Brian Griese 1.25 3.00
SC18 Drew Bledsoe 1.50 4.00
SC19 Eddie George 1.25 3.00
SC20 Terrell Owens 1.25 3.00

2000 Metal

Released in early December 2000, Metal features a 300-card base set consisting of 200 veteran player cards, 50 rookie cards in vertical format, and 50 shortprinted rookies in horizontal format inserted in packs at the rate of one in two. Base cards feature a textured card with player names in silver ink and rookie cards with the same card stock but player names printed in bronze ink. Metal was packaged in 28-pack boxes with packs containing 10 cards each and carried a suggested retail price of $1.99.

COMPLETE SET (300) 40.00 80.00
COMP.SET w/o SP's (250) 6.00 15.00
251-300 ROOKIE SP ODDS 1:2
1 Tim Couch .15 .40
2 Olandis Gary .15 .40
3 Andre Hastings .12 .30
4 Donovan McNabb .15 .40
5 Bobby Engram .12 .30
6 Bert Emanuel .12 .30
7 Levon Kirkland .12 .30
8 Chris Chandler .15 .40
9 Herman Moore .12 .30
10 Jeff Blake .15 .40
11 Cortez Kennedy .15 .40
12 Antowain Smith .15 .40
13 Marvin Harrison .15 .40
14 Bryant Young .12 .30
15 Peerless Price .15 .40
16 Peyton Manning .50 1.25
17 Darrell Russell .12 .30
18 Darrell Green .15 .40
19 James Allen .12 .30
20 Tedy Bruschi .30 .75
21 Jon Kitna .12 .30
22 Doug Flutie .15 .40
23 Bill Schroeder .15 .40
24 Curtis Martin .15 .40
25 Kevin Lockett .12 .30
26 Errict Rhett .15 .40
27 Kevin Faulk .12 .30
28 J.J. Stokes .15 .40
29 Jonathan Linton .12 .30
30 Jimmy Smith .15 .40
31 Brian Dawkins .20 .50
32 Michael Westbrook .12 .30
33 Randall Cunningham .15 .40
34 Oronde Gadsden .15 .40
35 Shawn Springs .12 .30
36 Shannon Sharpe .15 .40
37 Terrence Wilkins .12 .30
38 Aaron Glenn .12 .30
39 Torrance Small .12 .30
40 Sean Dawkins .12 .30
41 Terrell Davis .15 .40
42 Ike Hilliard .12 .30
43 Warrick Dunn .12 .30
44 Jeremiah Trotter RC .40 1.00
45 O.J. McDuffie .15 .40
46 Richard Huntley .12 .30
47 Aeneas Williams .12 .30
48 Rocket Ismail .15 .40
49 Terry Glenn .15 .40
50 Derrick Mayes .12 .30
51 Wayne Chrebet .12 .30
52 Kevin Dyson .15 .40
53 Takeo Spikes .12 .30
54 Matthew Hatchette .12 .30
55 Shawn Bryson .12 .30
56 Qadry Ismail .12 .30
57 Jerome Pathon .12 .30
58 Rich Gannon .15 .40
59 Stephen Davis .12 .30
60 Marcus Robinson .15 .40
61 Damon Huard .12 .30
62 Junior Seau .15 .40
63 Curtis Enis .12 .30
64 Tony Richardson RC .12 .30
65 Troy Edwards .12 .30
66 Robert Brooks .15 .40
67 Antonio Freeman .15 .40
68 Kerry Collins .12 .30
69 Jacquez Green .12 .30
70 Akili Smith .12 .30
71 Zach Thomas .15 .40
72 Kordell Stewart .12 .30
73 Deion Sanders .15 .40
74 David Patten .12 .30
75 Drew Bledsoe .15 .40
76 Shaun King .12 .30
77 Eddie Kennison .12 .30
78 Stacey Mack .12 .30
79 Jim Harbaugh .15 .40
80 Shawn Jefferson .12 .30
81 James Stewart .12 .30
82 Pete Mitchell .12 .30
83 Mike Alstott .15 .40
84 Marty Booker .12 .30
85 Hardy Nickerson .12 .30
86 Charles Johnson .12 .30
87 Jeff George .15 .40
88 Jermaine Lewis .12 .30
89 Edgerrin James .15 .40
90 Rickey Dudley .12 .30
91 Eddie George .15 .40
92 Darren Woodson .15 .40
93 Willie McGinest .15 .40
94 Jeff Garcia .12 .30
95 Eric Moulds .12 .30
96 Tony Brackens .12 .30
97 Charles Woodson .20 .50
98 Warren Sapp .15 .40
99 Corey Dillon .12 .30
100 Tony Martin .15 .40
101 Bruce Smith .15 .40
102 Troy Aikman .25 .60
103 Daunte Culpepper .15 .40
104 Christian Fauria .12 .30
105 Steve Beuerlein .15 .40
106 Fred Taylor .12 .30
107 Ricky Watters .15 .40
108 Brian Mitchell .12 .30
109 Emmitt Smith .30 .75
110 Robert Smith .12 .30
111 Jerry Rice .50 1.25
112 Priest Holmes .12 .30
113 Jay Fiedler .15 .40
114 Curtis Conway .15 .40
115 Jamal Anderson .15 .40
116 E.G. Green .12 .30
117 Kent Graham .12 .30
118 Frank Wycheck .15 .40
119 Jake Plummer .12 .30
120 Randy Moss .15 .40
121 Charlie Garner .15 .40
122 Frank Sanders .12 .30
123 Germane Crowell .12 .30
124 Jason Sehorn .12 .30
125 Marshall Faulk .15 .40
126 David Sloan .12 .30
127 Cris Carter .20 .50
128 Robert Chancey .12 .30
129 Tony Banks .12 .30
130 Ken Dilger .12 .30
131 Dedric Ward .12 .30
132 Yancey Thigpen .12 .30
133 Jeremy McDaniel .12 .30
134 John Randle .20 .50
135 Jerome Bettis .20 .50
136 Tim Dwight .15 .40
137 Charlie Batch .12 .30
138 Mark Brunell .15 .40
139 Tyrone Wheatley .12 .30
140 Champ Bailey .15 .40
141 Brian Griese .12 .30
142 Keith Poole .12 .30
143 Kurt Warner .30 .75
144 Tim Biakabutuka .15 .40
145 Elvis Grbac .12 .30
146 Cade McNown .12 .30
147 Albert Connell .12 .30
148 Donald Driver .25 .60
149 Donald Hayes .12 .30
150 Terrell Owens .15 .40
151 Johnnie Morton .15 .40
152 Tiki Barber .15 .40
153 Keyshawn Johnson .15 .40
154 Carl Pickens .15 .40
155 Thurman Thomas .15 .40
156 Jeff Graham .12 .30
157 Peter Boulware .12 .30
158 Brett Favre .40 1.00
159 Vinny Testaverde .12 .30
160 Derrick Brooks .12 .30
161 Wesley Walls .12 .30
162 Derrick Alexander .12 .30
163 Duce Staley .12 .30
164 Troy Brown .12 .30
165 Keenan McCardell .15 .40
166 James Jett .15 .40
167 Simeon Rice .15 .40
168 Rod Smith .15 .40
169 Ricky Williams .15 .40
170 Az-Zahir Hakim .12 .30
171 Muhsin Muhammad .12 .30
172 Andre Rison .15 .40
173 Tim Brown .20 .50
174 Brad Johnson .15 .40
175 Darrin Chiaverini .12 .30
176 Jake Reed .15 .40
177 Kevin Carter .12 .30
178 Jay Riemersma .12 .30
179 Tony Gonzalez .15 .40
180 Hines Ward .15 .40
181 David Boston .12 .30
182 Ed McCaffrey .15 .40
183 Amani Toomer .12 .30
184 Torry Holt .15 .40
185 Rob Johnson .15 .40
186 Kevin Hardy .12 .30
187 Napoleon Kaufman .15 .40
188 Jevon Kearse .12 .30
189 Terance Mathis .12 .30
190 Dorsey Levens .15 .40
191 Kyle Brady .12 .30
192 Steve McNair .15 .40
193 Kevin Johnson .12 .30
194 Lamar Smith .12 .30
195 Ryan Leaf .15 .40
196 Rod Woodson .20 .50
197 Corey Bradford .12 .30
198 Joe Horn .15 .40
199 Isaac Bruce .20 .50
200 S.Young/D.Marino .40 1.00
201 DeMario Brown RC .25 .60
202 Chad Morton RC .30 .75
203 Quinton Spotwood RC .25 .60
204 Mike Anderson RC .25 .60
205 Jarlous Jackson RC .30 .75
206 Hank Poteat RC .25 .60
207 Rogers Beckett RC .25 .60
208 Deon Dyer RC .25 .60
209 Charles Lee RC .25 .60
210 Barrett Green RC .25 .60
211 T.J. Slaughter RC .25 .60
212 Chris Hovan RC .30 .75
213 Mark Simoneau RC .25 .60
214 Rashard Anderson RC .25 .60
215 Trevor Insley RC .25 .60
216 Paul Smith RC .25 .60
217 Doug Johnson RC .25 .60
218 Dwayne Goodrich RC .25 .60
219 Julian Peterson RC .40 1.00
220 Keith Bulluck RC .30 .75
221 Chris Samuels RC .40 1.00
222 Shaun Ellis RC .30 .75
223 Na'il Diggs RC .25 .60
224 William Bartee RC .25 .60
225 John Abraham RC .40 1.00
226 Trevor Gaylor RC .25 .60
227 Dante Hall RC .25 .60
228 Marcus Knight RC .25 .60
229 Patrick Pass RC .25 .60
230 Bashir Yamini RC .25 .60
231 Deltha O'Neal RC .25 .60
232 Vaughn Sanders RC .25 .60
233 Todd Husak RC .25 .60
234 Thomas Hamner RC .25 .60
235 Chafie Fields RC .25 .60
236 Orantes Grant RC .25 .60
237 Muneer Moore RC .25 .60
238 Kwame Cavil RC .25 .60
239 Spergon Wynn RC .25 .60
240 Leon Murray RC .25 .60
241 Rob Morris RC .30 .75
242 Ben Kelly RC .25 .60
243 Darren Howard RC .25 .60
244 Raynoch Thompson RC .25 .60
245 Mike Green RC .30 .75
246 Sammy Morris RC .25 .60
247 Ahmed Plummer RC .25 .60
248 Ian Gold RC .25 .60
249 Chris Coleman RC .25 .60
250 Ron Dixon RC .25 .60
251 Peter Warrick RC .50 1.25
252 Joe Hamilton RC .50 1.25
253 Dennis Northcutt RC .50 1.25
254 Laveranues Coles RC .60 1.50
255 Michael Wiley RC .50 1.25
256 Plaxico Burress RC .60 1.50
257 Danny Farmer RC .50 1.25
258 Aaron Shea RC .60 1.50
259 Sebastian Janikowski RC .75 2.00
260 Corey Simon RC .60 1.50
261 Frank Murphy RC .50 1.25
262 JaJuan Dawson RC .50 1.25
263 Ron Dayne RC .75 2.00
264 Tim Rattay RC .60 1.50
265 Troy Walters RC .50 1.25
266 J.R. Redmond RC .50 1.25
267 Tom Brady RC 100.00 200.00
268 Jamal Lewis RC .75 2.00
269 Anthony Lucas RC .50 1.25
270 Reuben Droughns RC .50 1.25
271 James Williams RC .50 1.25
272 Shyrone Stith RC .50 1.25
273 Jerry Porter RC .75 2.00
274 Brian Urlacher RC 2.50 6.00
275 Avion Black RC .50 1.25
276 Thomas Jones RC .60 1.50
277 Chad Pennington RC .60 1.50
278 Travis Prentice RC .50 1.25
279 Chris Redman RC .50 1.25
280 Travis Taylor RC .50 1.25
281 Giovanni Carmazzi RC .50 1.25
282 Sherrod Gideon RC .50 1.25
283 Bubba Franks RC .50 1.25
284 Sylvester Morris RC .50 1.25
285 Curtis Keaton RC .50 1.25
286 Frank Moreau RC .50 1.25
287 Terrelle Smith RC .50 1.25
288 Shaun Alexander RC .75 2.00
289 Tee Martin RC .50 1.25
290 R.Jay Soward RC .50 1.25
291 Dez White RC .50 1.25
292 Trung Canidate RC .50 1.25
293 Darrell Jackson RC .50 1.25
294 Marc Bulger RC .60 1.50
295 Courtney Brown RC .60 1.50
296 Todd Pinkston RC .50 1.25
297 Anthony Becht RC .50 1.25
298 Doug Chapman RC .50 1.25
299 Gari Scott RC .50 1.25
300 Chris Cole RC .60 1.50

2000 Metal Emerald

*VETS 1-200: 1.2X TO 3X BASIC CARDS
1-200 EMERALD VETERAN ODDS 1:4
*ROOKIES 201-250: .8X TO 2X RCs
*ROOKIES 251-300: .4X TO 1X RC SPs
201-300 EMERALD ROOKIE ODDS 1:7
267 Tom Brady 150.00 300.00

2000 Metal Heavy Metal

Randomly inserted in packs at the rate of one in 20, this 10-card set features player action photography set on a foil background with a bleached white cardboard letter box on both the left and right edge of the card with the respective player's name and team name.

COMPLETE SET (10) 10.00 25.00
STATED ODDS 1:20
1 Emmitt Smith 1.25 3.00
2 Randy Moss .60 1.50
3 Kurt Warner 1.25 3.00
4 Keyshawn Johnson .60 1.50
5 Ricky Williams .60 1.50
6 Peyton Manning 2.00 5.00
7 Edgerrin James .60 1.50
8 Peter Warrick .50 1.25
9 Brett Favre 1.50 4.00
10 Tim Couch .60 1.50

2000 Metal Hot Commodities

Randomly inserted in packs at the rate of one in 14, this 10-card set features player action photograpy on a die cut card with silver holo-foil highlights.

COMPLETE SET (10) 7.50 20.00
STATED ODDS 1:14
1 Kurt Warner 1.00 2.50
2 Jerry Rice 1.50 4.00
3 Terrell Davis .50 1.25
4 Peyton Manning 1.50 4.00
5 Stephen Davis .40 1.00
6 Brett Favre 1.25 3.00
7 Ron Dayne .60 1.50
8 Troy Aikman .75 2.00
9 Edgerrin James .50 1.25
10 Eddie George .50 1.25

2000 Metal Steel of the Draft

Randomly inserted in packs at the rate of one in 28, this 10-card set features top 2000 draft picks on an all foil card with a white border around 3/4 of the card. A foil area along the lower right hand corner appears with the respective player's name.

COMPLETE SET (10) 6.00 15.00
STATED ODDS 1:28
1 Peter Warrick .40 1.00
2 Ron Dayne .60 1.50
3 Plaxico Burress .50 1.25
4 Thomas Jones .50 1.25
5 Jamal Lewis .60 1.50
6 Shaun Alexander .60 1.50
7 Chad Pennington .50 1.25
8 Travis Taylor .40 1.00
9 Chris Redman .40 1.00
10 J.R. Redmond .40 1.00

2000 Metal Sunday Showdown

Randomly inserted in packs at the rate of one in four, this 15-card set features player combo cards with a silver "Sunday Showdown" stamp between them.

COMPLETE SET (15) 7.50 20.00
STATED ODDS 1:4
1 E.Smith / S.Davis .75 2.00
2 M.Brunell / T.Couch .40 1.00
3 R.Moss / I.Bruce .50 1.25
4 S.King / A.Smith .30 .75
5 P.Warrick / P.Burress .40 1.00
6 C.Pennington / P.Manning 1.25 3.00
7 R.Williams / E.James .40 1.00
8 M.Faulk / J.Anderson .40 1.00
9 T.Aikman / D.McNabb .60 1.50
10 D.Culpepper / C.McNown .40 1.00
11 T.Davis / S.Alexander .50 1.25
12 B.Favre / B.Johnson 1.00 2.50
13 J.Kearse / F.Taylor .30 .75
14 T.Jones / R.Dayne .50 1.25
15 J.Rice / Key.Johnson 1.25 3.00

1992 Metallic Images Tins

signed by Metallic Images Inc. and sold through participating 7-Eleven stores, these four collector tins each contained two decks of playing cards. The tins are unnumbered and listed below alphabetically.

COMPLETE SET (4) 12.50 30.00
1 Dan Marino 5.00 12.00
2 Warren Moon 2.00 5.00
3 Y.A. Tittle 2.00 5.00
4 Johnny Unitas 3.00 8.00

1993 Metallic Images QB Legends

An offshoot of CUI, a Wilmington-based maker of collectible ceramic and glassware products, Metallic Images Inc. produced these 20 metal cards to honor outstanding NFL quarterbacks. Only 49,000 numbered sets were produced, each accompanied by a certificate of authenticity and packaged in a collectors tin featuring graphics on the sides and lid. These metallic cards measure approximately 2 9/16" by 3 9/16" and have rolled metal edges. The fronts display a color action shot cutout and superimposed on a team color-coded background with gold pinstripes. A black-and-white headshot appears in an oval at the upper left corner, while the team logo and uniform number are below. On a pinstripe panel inside a team color-coded border, the backs present career summary.

COMPLETE SET (20) 20.00 50.00
1 Steve Bartkowski 2.50 6.00
2 John Brodie 2.50 6.00
3 Charley Conerly 2.00 5.00
4 Lynn Dickey 2.00 5.00
5 Tom Flores 2.00 5.00
6 Roman Gabriel 2.00 5.00
7 Bob Griese 2.50 6.00

8 Steve Grogan 2.50 6.00
9 James Harris 2.00 5.00
10 Jim Hart 2.00 5.00
11 Sonny Jurgensen 2.50 6.00
12 Billy Kilmer 2.50 6.00
13 Daryle Lamonica 2.50 6.00
14 Archie Manning 2.50 6.00
15 Craig Morton 2.50 6.00
16 Dan Pastorini 2.00 5.00
17 Jim Plunkett 2.50 6.00
18 Y.A. Tittle 2.50 6.00
19 Johnny Unitas 4.00 10.00
20 Danny White 2.50 6.00

1996 Metallic Impressions Golden Arm Greats

Released as a 5-card set, Metallic Impressions Golden Arm Greats showcases some of the best quarterbacks of the century. Base cards are thin metal and feature full color oval portrait shots in one of the upper corners and action shots across the majority of the card front. The set was released in factory set form within a colorful tin box.

COMPLETE SET (5) 12.50 25.00
1 Sonny Jurgensen 2.00 5.00
2 Jim Plunkett 2.00 5.00
3 Y.A. Tittle 2.00 5.00
4 Johnny Unitas 5.00 10.00
5 Danny White 2.00 5.00

2005 Mid Mon Valley Hall of Fame

This set was released in 2005 by the Mid Mon Valley Sports Hall of Fame. Each card features a local sport legend printed on white card stock with a black and white artist's rendering of the featured subject on the front. The cover card proclaims the set as "Series 1 (2001-2005)" inductees.

COMPLETE SET (36) 10.00 20.00
124 Henry Adams FB .30 .75
125 Tom Ballaban CO FB .30 .75
126 Gene Belczyk CO FB .30 .75
127 Dale Hamer OFF FB .30 .75
129 Joe Sarra CO FB .40 1.00
130 Jack Scarvel CO FB .30 .75
132 Bernie Galiffa FB .30 .75
133 Fred Mazurek FB .50 1.25
134 Bill Parkinson OFF FB .30 .75
135 Pete Rostosky FB .30 .75
136 Joe Rudolph FB .40 1.00
137 James Simms FB .30 .75
138 Bill Urbanik FB .50 1.25
139 John Bruno CO FB .30 .75
140 Don Croftcheck FB .50 1.25
141 Tony Romantino FB .30 .75
145 Fred Yuss FB .30 .75
146 Ron Yuss FB .30 .75
147 Melvin Bassi OFF FB .30 .75
149 Craig Cotton FB .50 1.25
152 Scott Zolak FB .50 1.25
154 Craig Fayak FB .30 .75
155 Steve Garban FB .40 1.00
156 Stan Kemp FB .30 .75

2006 Mid Mon Valley Hall of Fame

This set was released in 2006 by the Mid Mon Valley Sports Hall of Fame. Each card features a local sport legend printed on white card stock with a black and white artist's rendering of the featured subject on the front. The cover card proclaims the set as "Series 2 (1997-2000/2006)" inductees.

COMPLETE SET (36) 10.00 20.00
94 Rudy Andabaker FB .30 .75
98 Carl Crawley FB .30 .75
99 Doug Crusan FB .30 .75
100 Frank Lignelli FB .30 .75
101 Bill Malinchak FB .30 .75
102 Eric Crabtree FB .40 1.00
103 Dick Fields FB .30 .75
104 Pappy Johnson FB .30 .75
107 Jeff Petrucci FB .30 .75
111 Mike Buccianeri FB .30 .75
112 Bill Contz FB .40 1.00
113 Angelo DaBiero FB .30 .75
115 Sam Havrilak FB .40 1.00
116 John Popovich FB .30 .75
118 Tony Benjamin FB .30 .75
119 Auggie Bossu FB .30 .75
120 Julius Dawkins FB .30 .75
121 Val Jansante FB .30 .75
122 Joe Montana FB 2.00 5.00
159 Greg Paterra FB .30 .75
160 Anthony Peterson FB .30 .75

1985 Miller Lite Beer

These oversized cards measure approximately 4 3/4" by 7" and feature on their fronts white-bordered posed player photos. The player's name and position, along with logos for his team and Miller Lite appear within the wide bottom margin. The logos reappear on the white backs, along with the player's career highlights. The cards are unnumbered and checklisted below in alphabetical order.

COMPLETE SET (6) 60.00 150.00
1 Larry Csonka 10.00 25.00
2 John Hadl CO 6.00 15.00
3 Freeman McNeil 6.00 15.00
4 Jack Reynolds 6.00 15.00
5 Steve Young 30.00 80.00
6 1985 LA Express Cheerleaders (measures 6x9) 6.00 15.00

2012 Momentum

ROOKIE JSY AU PRINT RUN 399-599
ROOKIE AU PRINT RUN 99-799
EXCH EXPIRATION: 2/28/2014
1 Aaron Rodgers 1.25 3.00
2 Charles Woodson .75 2.00
3 Greg Jennings .50 1.25
4 Jordy Nelson .60 1.50
5 BenJarvus Green-Ellis .60 1.50
6 Rob Gronkowski .75 2.00
7 Tom Brady 2.00 5.00
8 Wes Welker .60 1.50
9 Frank Gore .60 1.50
10 Michael Crabtree .50 1.25
11 Vernon Davis .50 1.25
12 Darren Sproles .60 1.50
13 Drew Brees .75 2.00
14 Marques Colston .50 1.25
15 Anquan Boldin .50 1.25
16 Joe Flacco .60 1.50
17 Ray Rice .50 1.25
18 Ben Roethlisberger .75 2.00
19 Mike Wallace .50 1.25
20 Rashard Mendenhall .50 1.25
21 Troy Polamalu .75 2.00
22 Andre Johnson .60 1.50
23 Arian Foster .60 1.50
24 Matt Schaub .50 1.25
25 Matt Ryan .60 1.50
26 Michael Turner .50 1.25
27 Roddy White .50 1.25
28 Calvin Johnson .75 2.00
29 Matthew Stafford .60 1.50
30 Ndamukong Suh .60 1.50
31 A.J. Green .75 2.00
32 Andy Dalton .60 1.50
33 Austin Collie .50 1.25
34 Chris Johnson .50 1.25
35 Kenny Britt .50 1.25
36 Nate Washington .50 1.25
37 Ahmad Bradshaw .50 1.25
38 Eli Manning .60 1.50
39 Hakeem Nicks .50 1.25
40 Victor Cruz .60 1.50
41 Beanie Wells .50 1.25
42 Larry Fitzgerald .60 1.50
43 Patrick Peterson .50 1.25
44 Tim Tebow .75 2.00
45 Von Miller .60 1.50
46 Willis McGahee .50 1.25
47 Brian Urlacher .75 2.00
48 Jay Cutler .50 1.25
49 Matt Forte .50 1.25
50 Carson Palmer .60 1.50
51 Darren McFadden .50 1.25
52 Michael Bush .50 1.25
53 Philip Rivers .75 2.00
54 Ryan Mathews .60 1.50
55 Vincent Jackson .50 1.25
56 DeSean Jackson .60 1.50
57 LeSean McCoy .75 2.00
58 Michael Vick .60 1.50
59 Mark Sanchez .50 1.25
60 Santonio Holmes .50 1.25
61 Shonn Greene .50 1.25
62 Dez Bryant .75 2.00
63 Jason Witten .60 1.50
64 Tony Romo .60 1.50
65 Doug Baldwin .75 2.00
66 Marshawn Lynch .60 1.50
67 Sidney Rice .50 1.25
68 Dwayne Bowe .60 1.50
69 Jamaal Charles .60 1.50
70 Tamba Hali .50 1.25
71 Brandon Marshall .60 1.50
72 Karlos Dansby .50 1.25
73 Reggie Bush .50 1.25
74 Cam Newton .75 2.00
75 DeAngelo Williams .50 1.25
76 Steve Smith .60 1.50
77 Fred Jackson .60 1.50
78 Ryan Fitzpatrick .50 1.25
79 Steve Johnson .60 1.50
80 Fred Davis .50 1.25
81 Jabar Gaffney .50 1.25
82 Santana Moss .60 1.50
83 Blaine Gabbert .50 1.25
84 Marcedes Lewis .50 1.25
85 Maurice Jones-Drew .50 1.25
86 Josh Freeman .60 1.50
87 LeGarrette Blount .60 1.50
88 Mike Williams .60 1.50
89 Colt McCoy .60 1.50
90 Greg Little .50 1.25
91 Peyton Hillis .50 1.25
92 Adrian Peterson .75 2.00
93 Christian Ponder .50 1.25
94 Percy Harvin .50 1.25
95 Peyton Manning 1.50 4.00
96 Pierre Garcon .60 1.50
97 Reggie Wayne .60 1.50
98 Brandon Lloyd .50 1.25
99 Sam Bradford .50 1.25
100 Steven Jackson .50 1.25
101 A.Luck JSY AU/399 RC 60.00 125.00
102 R.Griffin III JSY AU/399 RC 4.00 10.00
103 T.Richardson JSY AU/399 RC 3.00 8.00
104 J.Blackmon JSY AU/399 RC 3.00 8.00
105 R.Tannehill JSY AU/399 RC 5.00 12.00
106 M.Floyd JSY AU/399 RC 3.00 8.00
107 K.Wright JSY AU/399 RC 3.00 8.00
108 B.Weeden JSY AU/399 RC 3.00 8.00
109 A.Jenkins JSY AU/499 RC 3.00 8.00
110 D.Martin JSY AU/399 RC 5.00 12.00
111 D.Wilson JSY AU/499 RC 3.00 8.00
112 A.Jeffery JSY AU/599 RC 6.00 15.00
113 B.Pierce JSY AU/499 RC 3.00 8.00
114 B.Quick JSY AU/599 RC 3.00 8.00
115 B.Osweiler JSY AU/399 RC 3.00 8.00
116 C.Fleener JSY AU/599 RC 3.00 8.00
117 D.Posey JSY AU/599 RC 3.00 8.00
118 D.Allen JSY AU/599 RC 3.00 8.00
119 I.Pead JSY AU/499 RC 3.00 8.00
120 C.Givens JSY AU/599 RC 3.00 8.00
121 J.Adams JSY AU/599 RC 3.00 8.00
122 L.Miller JSY AU/399 RC 5.00 12.00
123 L.James JSY AU/499 RC 3.00 8.00
124 M.Egnew JSY AU/599 RC 3.00 8.00
125 M.Sanu JSY AU/499 RC 5.00 12.00
126 N.Foles JSY AU/499 RC 25.00 50.00
127 N.Toon JSY AU/599 RC 3.00 8.00
128 R.Turbin JSY AU/599 RC 3.00 8.00
129 R.Hillman JSY AU/599 RC EXCH 3.00 8.00
130 R.Randle JSY AU/499 RC 3.00 8.00
131 R.Wilson JSY AU/599 RC 60.00 125.00
132 R.Broyles JSY AU/599 RC 3.00 8.00
133 S.Hill JSY AU/499 RC 3.00 8.00
134 T.Graham JSY AU/599 RC 3.00 8.00
135 J.Wright JSY AU/599 RC 3.00 8.00
136 T.Y. Hilton AU/299 RC 5.00 12.00
137 Alfred Morris AU/799 RC 2.00 5.00
138 Andre Branch AU/399 RC 2.50 6.00
139 B.J. Coleman AU/399 RC 2.50 6.00
140 B.J. Cunningham AU/799 RC 2.00 5.00
141 Bobby Wagner AU/399 RC 4.00 10.00
142 Bruce Irvin AU/799 RC 2.50 6.00
144 Case Keenum AU/299 RC 5.00 12.00
145 C.Harnish AU/799 RC 2.00 5.00
146 Chandler Jones AU/399 RC 2.50 6.00
147 Chris Rainey AU/299 RC 2.50 6.00
148 C.Upshaw AU/399 RC 3.00 8.00
149 Cyrus Gray AU/299 RC 2.50 6.00
150 Dan Herron AU/299 RC 2.50 6.00
151 Danny Coale AU/799 RC 2.00 5.00
152 David DeCastro AU/399 RC 2.50 6.00
153 Davin Meggett AU/399 RC 2.50 6.00
154 Devon Still AU/799 RC 2.50 6.00
155 Devon Wylie AU/399 RC 2.50 6.00
156 Dont'a Hightower AU/699 RC 3.00 8.00
157 Dontari Poe AU/399 RC 2.50 6.00
158 Kirkpatrick AU/799 RC EXCH 2.00 5.00
159 Fletcher Cox AU/399 RC 4.00 10.00
160 George Iloka AU/799 RC 2.00 5.00
161 Greg Childs AU/799 RC 2.00 5.00
162 Harrison Smith AU/799 RC 8.00 20.00
163 Janoris Jenkins AU/399 RC 3.00 8.00
164 Jared Crick AU/399 RC 2.50 6.00
165 Jonathan Martin AU/399 RC 2.50 6.00
166 Juron Criner AU/399 RC 2.50 6.00
167 Kellen Moore AU/299 RC 3.00 8.00
168 Keshawn Martin AU/799 RC 2.50 6.00
169 Kevin Zeitler AU/399 RC 2.50 6.00
170 Kirk Cousins AU/299 RC 12.00 30.00
171 Ladarius Green AU/399 RC 2.50 6.00
172 LaVon Brazill AU/799 RC 3.00 8.00
173 Lavonte David AU/799 RC 3.00 8.00
174 Luke Kuechly AU/399 RC 10.00 25.00
175 Mark Barron AU/399 RC 2.50 6.00
176 Marvin Jones AU/299 RC 2.50 6.00
177 Marvin McNutt AU/399 RC 2.50 6.00
178 Matt Kalil AU/399 RC 2.50 6.00
179 Melvin Ingram AU/299 RC 2.50 6.00
180 Michael Brockers AU/399 RC 2.50 6.00
182 Morris Claiborne AU/99 RC 5.00 12.00
183 Mychal Kendricks AU/799 RC 3.00 8.00
184 Nick Perry AU/399 RC 3.00 8.00
185 Orson Charles AU/399 RC 2.50 6.00
186 Quinton Coples AU/299 RC 2.50 6.00
187 Riley Reiff AU/699 RC 2.00 5.00
188 Rishard Matthews AU/399 RC 2.50 6.00
189 Ronnell Lewis AU/699 RC 2.00 5.00
190 Ryan Lindley AU/399 RC 2.50 6.00
191 Shea McClellin AU/799 RC 5.00 12.00
192 Stephon Gilmore AU/699 RC 2.50 6.00
193 Tauren Poole AU/299 RC 2.50 6.00
194 Terrance Ganaway AU/399 RC 3.00 8.00
195 T.Streeter AU/299 RC 2.50 6.00
196 Travis Benjamin AU/799 RC 2.00 5.00
197 Vick Ballard AU/399 RC 6.00 15.00
198 Vinny Curry AU/799 RC 2.50 6.00
199 Whitney Mercilus AU/699 RC 2.00 5.00
200 Zach Brown AU/699 RC 2.00 5.00
201 Marquis Maze AU/799 RC 2.00 5.00
202 A.Robinson AU/799 RC 2.00 5.00
203 Bobby Rainey AU/699 RC 2.00 5.00
204 B.Bolden AU/699 RC 2.00 5.00
205 Brandon Hardin AU/799 RC 2.50 6.00
206 Brandon Taylor AU/799 RC 2.00 5.00
207 Casey Hayward AU/799 RC 2.00 5.00
208 Chris Polk AU/299 RC 2.50 6.00
209 Cory Harkey AU/699 RC 2.50 6.00
210 Coty Sensabaugh AU/799 RC 2.50 6.00
211 Deangelo Peterson AU/799 RC 2.00 5.00
212 Demario Davis AU/799 RC 2.00 5.00
214 Dwight Bentley AU/799 RC 2.50 6.00
215 Dwight Jones AU/699 RC 2.00 5.00
216 Eric Page AU/699 RC 2.50 6.00
217 Gerell Robinson AU/399 RC 2.50 6.00
218 Jamell Fleming AU/799 RC 2.00 5.00
219 Jeff Fuller AU/399 RC 2.50 6.00
220 Jerel Worthy AU/799 RC 2.00 5.00
221 Josh Robinson AU/799 RC 3.00 8.00
222 Kendall Reyes AU/799 RC 2.00 5.00
223 Marc Tyler AU/399 RC 2.50 6.00
224 Mike Martin AU/799 RC 2.50 6.00
225 Najee Goode AU/799 RC 2.00 5.00
226 Olivier Vernon AU/799 RC 3.00 8.00
227 Omar Bolden AU/799 RC 2.50 6.00
228 Rhett Ellison AU/799 RC 2.50 6.00
229 Sean Spence AU/799 RC 2.50 6.00
230 Tavon Wilson AU/799 RC 2.50 6.00
231 Tim Benford AU/799 RC 2.00 5.00
232 Trumaine Johnson AU/799 RC 2.00 5.00
233 Tyrone Crawford AU/799 RC 2.00 5.00
234 Vontaze Burfict AU/799 RC 2.50 6.00
235 James Hanna AU/799 RC 2.00 5.00

2012 Momentum Gold

*1-100 VETS/99: .8X TO 2X BASIC CARDS
*101-135 ROOKIE JSY AU/49: .6X TO 1.5X
*ROOKIE AU/49: .6X TO 1.5X AU RC/699-799
*ROOKIE AU/49: .5X TO 1.2X AU RC/299-399
*ROOKIE AU/49: .5X TO 1.2X AU RC/99
EXCH EXPIRATION: 2/28/2014
101 Andrew Luck JSY AU 125.00 250.00
131 Russell Wilson JSY AU 100.00 200.00

2012 Momentum Platinum

*1-100 VETS/49: 1.2X TO 3X BASIC CARDS
1-100 VETERAN PRINT RUN 49
*101-135 ROOKIE JSY AU/25: .8X TO 2X
*ROOKIE AU/25: .8X TO 2X AU RC/699-799
*ROOKIE AU/25: .6X TO 1.5X AU RC/299-399
*ROOKIE AU/49: .6X TO 1.5X AU RC/99
101-235 ROOKIE PRINT RUN 25
101 Andrew Luck JSY AU 150.00 300.00
131 Russell Wilson JSY AU 150.00 250.00
137 Alfred Morris AU 4.00 10.00

2012 Momentum Double Feature Materials

*PRIME/25-49: .8X TO 2X BASIC JSY/149
*PRIME/49: .6X TO 1.5X BASIC JSY/49
1 D.Bryant/M.Austin/149 5.00 12.00
2 E.Reed/H.Ngata/49 6.00 15.00
3 B.Urlacher/J.Cutler/149 6.00 15.00
4 D.Murray/F.Jones/49 5.00 12.00
5 D.Clark/J.Addai/149 3.00 8.00
6 J.Charles/M.Cassel/149 4.00 10.00
7 D.Henderson/P.Thomas/149 3.00 8.00
8 E.Manning/H.Nicks/149 4.00 10.00
9 C.Johnson/K.Britt/149 3.00 8.00
10 M.Colston/R.Meachem/50 4.00 10.00
11 F.Biletnikoff/G.Blanda/149 5.00 12.00
12 B.Starr/F.Gregg/149 8.00 20.00
13 J.Montana/M.Allen/7
14 E.Dickerson/R.Lott/149 6.00 15.00
15 A.Page/C.Eller/149 3.00 8.00
16 C.Martin/W.Chrebet/149 6.00 15.00
17 Esiason/Collinsworth/149 6.00 15.00
18 F.Harris/J.Stallworth/85 8.00 20.00
19 H.Long/T.Brown/70 6.00 15.00
20 C.Carter/J.Randle/149 6.00 15.00

2012 Momentum Head of the Class Materials

STATED PRINT RUN 249 SER.#'d SETS
*PRIME/49: .6X TO 1.5X BASIC JSY/249
1 Ronnie Hillman 1.50 4.00
2 Joe Adams 1.50 4.00
3 David Wilson 1.50 4.00
4 Ryan Tannehill 2.50 6.00
5 Andrew Luck 12.00 30.00
6 Kendall Wright 1.50 4.00
7 Brock Osweiler 1.50 4.00
8 Michael Egnew 1.50 4.00
9 Isaiah Pead 1.50 4.00
10 Alshon Jeffery 3.00 8.00
11 Nick Foles 4.00 10.00
12 Trent Richardson 1.50 4.00
13 A.J. Jenkins 1.50 4.00
14 DeVier Posey 1.50 4.00
15 Russell Wilson 6.00 15.00
16 Ryan Broyles 1.50 4.00
17 Doug Martin 2.50 6.00
18 Bernard Pierce 1.50 4.00
19 Lamar Miller 2.50 6.00
20 Nick Toon 1.50 4.00
21 Coby Fleener 1.50 4.00
22 Justin Blackmon 1.50 4.00
23 Rueben Randle 1.50 4.00
24 Stephen Hill 1.50 4.00
25 Mohamed Sanu 2.50 6.00
26 Robert Griffin III 2.00 5.00
27 Michael Floyd 1.50 4.00
28 Chris Givens 1.50 4.00
29 Brian Quick 1.50 4.00
30 LaMichael James 1.50 4.00
31 Dwayne Allen 1.50 4.00
32 Brandon Weeden 1.50 4.00
33 T.J. Graham 1.50 4.00
34 Robert Turbin 1.50 4.00
35 Jarius Wright 1.50 4.00

2012 Momentum Head of the Class Materials Combo

STATED PRINT RUN 149 SER.#'d SETS
*PRIME/49: .6X TO 1.5X BASIC COMBO/149
1 A.Luck/R.Griffin III 10.00 25.00
2 T.Richardson/B.Weeden 1.50 4.00
3 D.Wilson/R.Randle 1.50 4.00
4 R.Wilson/R.Turbin 12.00 30.00
5 B.Weeden/J.Blackmon 1.50 4.00
6 T.Richardson/D.Martin 2.50 6.00
7 J.Blackmon/M.Floyd 1.50 4.00
8 R.Broyles/R.Randle 3.00 8.00
9 R.Griffin III/K.Wright 2.00 5.00
10 A.Luck/C.Fleener 6.00 15.00
11 M.Egnew/L.Miller 2.50 6.00
12 B.Osweiler/R.Hillman 1.50 4.00
13 N.Toon/R.Wilson 6.00 15.00
14 A.Jenkins/L.James 1.50 4.00
15 B.Quick/S.Hill 1.50 4.00

2012 Momentum Head of the Class Materials Quad

STATED PRINT RUN 49 SER.#'d SETS
*PRIME/25: .5X TO 1.2X BASIC QUAD/49
1 Tnne/Wdn/Wrght/Jnkns 5.00 12.00
2 Blckmn/Flyd/Wrght/Jnkns 3.00 8.00
3 Luck/RG3I/Tnnhll/Wdn 15.00 40.00
4 Tann/Wlsn/Martn/Pead 5.00 12.00
5 Lck/Rchrd/Blckmn/Flnr 6.00 15.00

2012 Momentum Head of the Class Materials Triple

STATED PRINT RUN 99 SER.#'d SETS
*PRIME/49: .6X TO 1.5X BASIC TRIPLE/99
1 Tannehill/Miller/Egnew 3.00 8.00
2 Pead/Givens/Quick 2.00 5.00
3 Luck/Richardson/Blackmon 10.00 25.00
4 Pead/James/Hillman 2.00 5.00
5 Weeden/Osweiler/Wilson 15.00 40.00
6 Jenkins/Quick/Hill 2.00 5.00
7 Blackmon/Floyd/Wright 2.00 5.00
8 Fleener/Allen/Egnew 2.00 5.00
9 Richardson/Martin/Wilson 3.00 8.00
10 Luck/Griffin III/Tannehill 10.00 25.00

2012 Momentum Materials

RIME/35-49: .8X TO 2X BASIC JSY/125-199
*PRIME/30-49: .6X TO 1.5X BASIC JSY/49-99
*PRIME/49: .4X TO 1X BASIC JSY/25
*PRIME/15-25: 1X TO 2.5X BASIC JSY/199
*PRIME/15: .8X TO 2X BASIC JSY/75
1 D.D. Lewis/99 4.00 10.00
2 Bob Cricse/199 4.00 10.00
3 Jim Plunkett/199 3.00 8.00
4 Kurt Warner/199 3.00 8.00
5 Charley Taylor/199 2.50 6.00
6 Barry Sanders/199 6.00 15.00
7 Mark Sanchez/149 2.50 6.00
8 Raymond Berry/199 3.00 8.00
9 C.J. Spiller/159 2.50 6.00
10 Amani Toomer/99 3.00 8.00
11 Emmitt Smith/199 6.00 15.00
12 Walter Payton/199 10.00 25.00
13 Daryle Lamonica/199 2.50 6.00
14 Keyshawn Johnson/199 3.00 8.00
15 Ryan Torain/199 2.50 6.00
16 Alex Karras/149 4.00 10.00
17 Shonn Greene/199 2.50 6.00
18 Bert Jones/199 3.00 8.00
19 Doug Flutie/199 3.00 8.00
20 Rocket Ismail/199 3.00 8.00
21 Danny White/199 4.00 10.00
22 Garo Yepremian/199 3.00 8.00
23 Jim Otto/199 2.50 6.00
24 Lee Roy Selmon/199 3.00 8.00
25 Santana Moss/99 4.00 10.00
26 Dick Lane/15 6.00 15.00
27 Art Monk/99 6.00 15.00
28 Jim Parker/199 2.50 6.00
29 Jim Kelly/199 4.00 10.00
30 Phil Simms/199 3.00 8.00
31 Ed Too Tall Jones/199 4.00 10.00
32 Irving Fryar/199 2.50 6.00
33 John Matuszak/199 4.00 10.00
34 Mike Alstott/199 2.50 6.00
35 Chris Cooley/199 2.50 6.00
36 Matthew Stafford/199 3.00 8.00
37 Don Maynard/199 3.00 8.00
38 Lenny Moore/199 2.50 6.00
39 Thurman Thomas/199 3.00 8.00
40 Y.A. Tittle/75 5.00 12.00
41 Jay Novacek/199 4.00 10.00
42 Larry Csonka/149 5.00 12.00
43 Ken Stabler/199 4.00 10.00
44 Warrick Dunn/99 3.00 8.00
45 Doug Williams/199 3.00 8.00
46 Yale Lary/99 3.00 8.00
47 Mark Gastineau/199 2.50 6.00
48 Jamaal Charles/149 3.00 8.00
49 Chris Johnson/99 3.00 8.00
50 Drew Bledsoe/199 4.00 10.00
51 Randy White/199 4.00 10.00
52 Larry Little/149 2.50 6.00
53 Sebastian Janikowski/199 3.00 8.00
54 John Elway/199 6.00 15.00
55 Junior Seau/199 3.00 8.00
56 Tom Rathman/175 3.00 8.00
57 Fred Taylor/49 3.00 8.00
58 Priest Holmes/175 2.50 6.00
59 Eddie George/25 6.00 15.00
60 Corey Dillon/149 2.50 6.00
61 Roger Staubach/199 6.00 15.00
62 Mark Duper/199 2.50 6.00
63 Ted Hendricks/199 2.50 6.00
64 Knowshon Moreno/199 2.50 6.00
65 Malcom Floyd/199 2.50 6.00
66 John Brodie/199 4.00 10.00
67 Maurice Jones-Drew/199 2.50 6.00
68 Dwayne Bowe/125 3.00 8.00
69 Steve McNair/199 3.00 8.00
70 Craig James/125 2.50 6.00
71 Tony Dorsett/199 5.00 12.00
72 Brent Celek/199 2.50 6.00
73 Brett Favre/199 8.00 20.00
74 Von Miller/199 3.00 8.00
75 Dan Fouts/199 3.00 8.00
76 Michael Turner/199 2.50 6.00
77 Andy Dalton/199 3.00 8.00
78 Matt Cassel/199 2.50 6.00
79 Anquan Boldin/199 2.50 6.00
80 Jerome Bettis/199 6.00 15.00
81 Tony Romo/199 3.00 8.00
82 Randall Cunningham/199 4.00 10.00
83 Fran Tarkenton/199 5.00 12.00
84 Henry Jordan/199 2.50 6.00
85 Jim McMahon/199 3.00 8.00
86 Steve Bartkowski/99 4.00 10.00
87 Ronnie Lott/199 3.00 8.00
88 Bernie Kosar/199 3.00 8.00
89 Joe Flacco/199 3.00 8.00
90 Jackie Slater/199 2.50 6.00
91 Troy Aikman/199 5.00 12.00
92 Warren Moon/199 4.00 10.00
93 Matt Schaub/199 2.50 6.00
94 Keith Jackson/199 2.50 6.00
95 Johnny Knox/99 3.00 8.00
96 Dez Bryant/99 5.00 12.00
97 Sam Bradford/95 3.00 8.00
98 Marques Colston/185 2.50 6.00
99 John Fuqua/199 3.00 8.00
100 Steve Largent/199 4.00 10.00

2012 Momentum Preferred Picks Jumbo

*PRIME/25: .8X TO 2X BASIC JSY/99
1 Rueben Randle 2.00 5.00
2 Alshon Jeffery 4.00 10.00
3 Michael Egnew 2.00 5.00
4 Ronnie Hillman 2.00 5.00
5 Robert Griffin III 2.50 6.00
6 Brandon Weeden 2.00 5.00
7 Chris Givens 2.00 5.00
8 Ryan Broyles 2.00 5.00
9 Nick Toon 2.00 5.00
10 David Wilson 2.00 5.00
11 Ryan Tannehill 3.00 8.00
12 Andrew Luck 20.00 50.00
13 A.J. Jenkins 2.00 5.00
14 Lamar Miller 3.00 8.00
15 Russell Wilson 8.00 20.00
16 Nick Foles 5.00 12.00
17 Brock Osweiler 2.00 5.00
18 Trent Richardson 2.00 5.00
19 Dwayne Allen 2.00 5.00
20 Mohamed Sanu 3.00 8.00
21 T.J. Graham 2.00 5.00
22 Robert Turbin 2.00 5.00
23 Brian Quick 2.00 5.00
24 Kendall Wright 2.00 5.00
25 Doug Martin 3.00 8.00
26 Coby Fleener 2.00 5.00
27 Joe Adams 2.00 5.00
28 LaMichael James 2.00 5.00
29 Stephen Hill 2.00 5.00
30 Justin Blackmon 2.00 5.00
31 Michael Floyd 2.00 5.00
32 Bernard Pierce 2.00 5.00
33 Isaiah Pead 2.00 5.00
34 DeVier Posey 2.00 5.00
35 Jarius Wright 2.00 5.00

2012 Momentum Rookie Salute Materials

STATED PRINT RUN 375 SER.#'d SETS
*PRIME/49: .6X TO 1.5X BASIC JSY/375
37 Jarius Wright 1.50 4.00
66 Andrew Luck 12.00 30.00
67 Justin Blackmon 1.50 4.00
68 Michael Floyd 1.50 4.00
69 Nick Toon 1.50 4.00
70 Robert Griffin III 2.00 5.00
71 Ryan Tannehill 2.50 6.00
72 Brandon Weeden 1.50 4.00
73 Nick Foles 4.00 10.00
74 Russell Wilson 8.00 20.00
75 Doug Martin 2.50 6.00
76 David Wilson 1.50 4.00
77 Lamar Miller 2.50 6.00
78 LaMichael James 1.50 4.00
79 Trent Richardson 1.50 4.00
80 Bernard Pierce 1.50 4.00
81 Isaiah Pead 1.50 4.00
82 Alshon Jeffery 3.00 8.00
83 Kendall Wright 1.50 4.00
84 Mohamed Sanu 2.50 6.00
85 Brian Quick 1.50 4.00
86 DeVier Posey 1.50 4.00
87 Ryan Broyles 1.50 4.00
88 Joe Adams 1.50 4.00
89 T.J. Graham 1.50 4.00
90 A.J. Jenkins 1.50 4.00
91 Dwayne Allen 1.50 4.00
92 Coby Fleener 1.50 4.00
93 Michael Egnew 1.50 4.00
94 Brock Osweiler 1.50 4.00
95 Ronnie Hillman 1.50 4.00
96 Robert Turbin 1.50 4.00
97 Rueben Randle 1.50 4.00
98 Chris Givens 1.50 4.00
99 Stephen Hill 1.50 4.00

2012 Momentum Rookie Salute Signatures

1 Matt Kalil/99 3.00 8.00
2 Morris Claiborne/25 5.00 12.00
3 Mark Barron/99 3.00 8.00
4 Luke Kuechly/99 8.00 20.00
5 Stephon Gilmore/99 4.00 10.00
6 Dontari Poe/99 3.00 8.00
7 Fletcher Cox/99 5.00 12.00
8 Michael Brockers/99 3.00 8.00
9 Bruce Irvin/99 4.00 10.00
10 Quinton Coples/99 3.00 8.00
11 Dre Kirkpatrick/99 EXCH 3.00 8.00
12 Melvin Ingram/99 3.00 8.00
13 Shea McClellin/99 4.00 10.00
14 Chandler Jones/99 3.00 8.00
15 Riley Reiff/99 3.00 8.00
16 David DeCastro/99 3.00 8.00
17 Dont'a Hightower/99 5.00 12.00
18 Whitney Mercilus/99 3.00 8.00
19 Kevin Zeitler/99 3.00 8.00
20 Nick Perry/99 4.00 10.00
21 Harrison Smith/99 3.00 8.00
22 Courtney Upshaw/50 4.00 10.00
23 Andre Branch/99 3.00 8.00
24 Janoris Jenkins/99 4.00 10.00
25 Jonathan Martin/99 3.00 8.00
26 Mychal Kendricks/99 5.00 12.00
27 Bobby Wagner/99 5.00 12.00
28 Zach Brown/99 3.00 8.00
29 Devon Still/99 4.00 10.00
30 Lavonte David/99 5.00 12.00
31 Vinny Curry/99 4.00 10.00
32 Travis Benjamin/99 3.00 8.00
33 Kirk Cousins/99 12.00 30.00
34 Devon Wylie/99 3.00 8.00
35 Ladarius Green/99 3.00 8.00
36 Orson Charles/99 3.00 8.00
37 Jarius Wright/25 5.00 12.00
38 Keshawn Martin/99 4.00 10.00
39 Ronnell Lewis/99 3.00 8.00
40 Jared Crick/99 3.00 8.00
41 Greg Childs/99 3.00 8.00
42 Danny Coale/99 3.00 8.00
43 Chris Rainey/99 3.00 8.00
44 Marvin Jones/99 3.00 8.00
45 George Iloka/99 3.00 8.00
46 Juron Criner/99 3.00 8.00
47 Vick Ballard/99 4.00 10.00
48 Alfred Morris/99 3.00 8.00
49 Cyrus Gray/99 3.00 8.00
50 B.J. Cunningham/99 3.00 8.00
51 Ryan Lindley/99 3.00 8.00
52 Dan Herron/99 3.00 8.00
53 Marvin McNutt/99 3.00 8.00
54 Tommy Streeter/99 3.00 8.00
55 Terrance Ganaway/99 4.00 10.00
56 LaVon Brazill/99 5.00 12.00
58 Rishard Matthews/99 3.00 8.00
60 B.J. Coleman/99 3.00 8.00
61 Chandler Harnish/99 3.00 8.00
62 Case Keenum/99 12.00 30.00
63 Kellen Moore/99 4.00 10.00
64 Davin Meggett/99 3.00 8.00
65 Chris Polk/99 3.00 8.00
66 Andrew Luck/25 75.00 150.00
67 Justin Blackmon/25 5.00 12.00
68 Michael Floyd/25 5.00 12.00
69 Nick Toon/25 5.00 12.00
70 Robert Griffin III/25 6.00 15.00
71 Ryan Tannehill/25 8.00 20.00
72 Brandon Weeden/25 5.00 12.00
73 Nick Foles/25 40.00 80.00
74 Russell Wilson/25 60.00 120.00
75 Doug Martin/25 8.00 20.00
76 David Wilson/25 5.00 12.00
77 Lamar Miller/25 8.00 20.00
78 LaMichael James/25 5.00 12.00
79 Trent Richardson/25 5.00 12.00
80 Bernard Pierce/25 EXCH 5.00 12.00
81 Isaiah Pead/25 5.00 12.00
82 Alshon Jeffery/25 10.00 25.00
83 Kendall Wright/25 5.00 12.00
84 Mohamed Sanu/25 8.00 20.00
85 Brian Quick/25 5.00 12.00
86 DeVier Posey/25 5.00 12.00
87 Ryan Broyles/25 5.00 12.00
88 Joe Adams/25 5.00 12.00
89 T.J. Graham/25 5.00 12.00
90 A.J. Jenkins/25 5.00 12.00
91 Dwayne Allen/25 5.00 12.00
92 Coby Fleener/25 5.00 12.00
93 Michael Egnew/25 5.00 12.00
94 Brock Osweiler/25 5.00 12.00
95 Ronnie Hillman/25 EXCH 5.00 12.00
96 Robert Turbin/25 5.00 12.00
97 Rueben Randle/25 5.00 12.00
98 Chris Givens/25 5.00 12.00
99 Stephen Hill/25 5.00 12.00
100 T.Y. Hilton/49 6.00 15.00

2012 Momentum Rookie Team Threads Dual Materials

STATED PRINT RUN 199 SER.#'d SETS
*PRIME/40: .6X TO 1.5X BASIC JSY/199
*TRIPLE/99: .5X TO 1.2X BASIC JSY/199
*TRIPLE PRIME/25: .8X TO 2X JSY/199
*QUAD/49: .8X TO 2X BASIC JSY/199
*QUAD PRIME/15: 1X TO 2.5X JSY/199
1 Andrew Luck 12.00 30.00
2 Robert Griffin III 2.00 5.00
3 Trent Richardson 1.50 4.00
4 Justin Blackmon 1.50 4.00
5 Ryan Tannehill 2.50 6.00
6 Michael Floyd 1.50 4.00
7 Kendall Wright 1.50 4.00
8 Brandon Weeden 1.50 4.00
9 A.J. Jenkins 1.50 4.00
10 Doug Martin 2.50 6.00
11 David Wilson 1.50 4.00
12 Alshon Jeffery 3.00 8.00
13 Bernard Pierce 1.50 4.00
14 Brian Quick 1.50 4.00
15 Brock Osweiler 1.50 4.00
16 Coby Fleener 1.50 4.00
17 DeVier Posey 1.50 4.00
18 Dwayne Allen 1.50 4.00
19 Isaiah Pead 1.50 4.00
20 Chris Givens 1.50 4.00
21 Joe Adams 1.50 4.00
22 Lamar Miller 2.50 6.00
23 LaMichael James 1.50 4.00
24 Michael Egnew 1.50 4.00
25 Mohamed Sanu 2.50 6.00
26 Nick Foles 4.00 10.00
27 Nick Toon 1.50 4.00
28 Robert Turbin 1.50 4.00
29 Ronnie Hillman 1.50 4.00
30 Rueben Randle 1.50 4.00
31 Russell Wilson 10.00 25.00
32 Ryan Broyles 1.50 4.00
33 Stephen Hill 1.50 4.00
34 T.J. Graham 1.50 4.00
35 Jarius Wright 1.50 4.00

2012 Momentum Rookie Team Threads Dual Materials Signatures

*PRIME/15: .6X TO 1.5X JSY AU/25
*TRIPLE JSY AU/15: .5X TO 1.2X JSY AU/25
1 Andrew Luck 125.00 250.00
2 Robert Griffin III 8.00 20.00
3 Trent Richardson 6.00 15.00
4 Justin Blackmon 6.00 15.00
5 Ryan Tannehill 10.00 25.00
6 Michael Floyd 6.00 15.00
7 Kendall Wright 6.00 15.00
8 Brandon Weeden 6.00 15.00
9 A.J. Jenkins 6.00 15.00
10 Doug Martin 10.00 25.00
11 David Wilson 6.00 15.00
12 Alshon Jeffery 12.00 30.00
13 Bernard Pierce EXCH 6.00 15.00
14 Brian Quick 6.00 15.00
15 Brock Osweiler 6.00 15.00
16 Coby Fleener 6.00 15.00
17 DeVier Posey 6.00 15.00
18 Dwayne Allen 6.00 15.00
19 Isaiah Pead 6.00 15.00
20 Chris Givens 6.00 15.00
21 Joe Adams 6.00 15.00
22 Lamar Miller 10.00 25.00
23 LaMichael James 6.00 15.00
24 Michael Egnew 6.00 15.00
25 Mohamed Sanu 10.00 25.00
26 Nick Foles 40.00 100.00
27 Nick Toon 6.00 15.00
28 Robert Turbin 6.00 15.00
29 Ronnie Hillman EXCH 6.00 15.00
30 Rueben Randle 6.00 15.00
31 Russell Wilson 100.00 175.00
32 Ryan Broyles 6.00 15.00
33 Stephen Hill 6.00 15.00
34 T.J. Graham 6.00 15.00
35 Jarius Wright 6.00 15.00

2012 Momentum Souvenir Signatures

EXCH EXPIRATION: 2/28/2014
1 Shannon Sharpe/15
2 Danny White/49 12.00 30.00
3 Andre Reed/75 6.00 15.00
4 Jack Lambert/30 25.00 50.00
5 Jim McMahon/49 15.00 30.00
6 Paul Warfield/75 8.00 20.00
7 Randall Cunningham/65 10.00 25.00
8 Billy Howton/25 10.00 25.00
9 Paul Krause/75 6.00 15.00
10 Jimmy Orr/75 6.00 15.00
11 Steve Largent/25 15.00 40.00
12 Sterling Sharpe/20 20.00 40.00
13 Thurman Thomas/25 10.00 25.00
14 Joe Klecko/75 6.00 15.00
15 Sonny Jurgensen/15
16 Don Perkins/34 8.00 20.00
17 Rod Smith/25 10.00 25.00
18 John Taylor/23 10.00 25.00
20 L.C. Greenwood/16 8.00 20.00
21 Fred Taylor/25 8.00 20.00
26 Jimmy Graham/99 6.00 15.00
27 Mike Williams/75 5.00 12.00
28 Dallas Clark/20 8.00 20.00
29 Asante Samuel/99 5.00 12.00
30 Steve Smith/20 20.00 40.00
31 Donald Driver/20 20.00 40.00
32 Kevin Walter/99 4.00 10.00
33 Cam Newton/25 30.00 60.00
34 Pierre Thomas/49 5.00 12.00
36 Tim Tebow/15 50.00 120.00
38 Clay Matthews/15 30.00 60.00
43 Ahmad Bradshaw/25 8.00 20.00
44 Darren Sproles/25 10.00 25.00
46 Jason Pierre-Paul/25 8.00 20.00
47 Jermichael Finley/25 8.00 20.00
48 Marshawn Lynch/25 25.00 50.00
49 Jabar Gaffney/50 4.00 10.00
50 Tamba Hali/25 8.00 20.00

2012 Momentum Souvenir Signatures Combo

1 C.Gates/J.Knox/25 8.00 20.00
6 D.Carter/M.Williams/25 10.00 25.00
7 N.Bowman/S.Lee/25 25.00 50.00
10 J.Graham/L.Hankerson/25 12.00 30.00
13 J.Nelson/J.Freeman/20 25.00 50.00

2012 Momentum Team Threads Triple Jerseys Signatures

3 Bernie Kosar/25 15.00 40.00
16 Alan Page/25 15.00 40.00

2012 Momentum Triple Feature Materials

*PRIME/25: .5X TO 1.2X BASIC TRIPLE/99
1 Bryant/Romo/Austin/99 8.00 20.00
2 Henderson/Thomas/Meachem/99 5.00 12.00
3 Nicks/Manning/Manningham/99 6.00 15.00
4 Reed/Lewis/Suggs/25
5 Urlacher/Cutler/Hester/99 10.00 25.00
6 Dawson/Stram/Stenerud/99 8.00 20.00
7 Dryer/Hadl/Olsen/99 8.00 20.00
8 Lilly/Meredith/Howley/99 12.00 30.00
9 Rice/Young/Sanders/50 15.00 40.00
10 Faulk/Warner/Holt/99 6.00 15.00

2013 Momentum

E ROOKIE PER PACK
1 Alfred Morris .50 1.25
2 Pierre Garcon .60 1.50
3 Robert Griffin III .50 1.25
4 Eli Manning .60 1.50
5 Jason Pierre-Paul .50 1.25
6 Victor Cruz .60 1.50
7 DeMarcus Ware .75 2.00
8 Miles Austin .50 1.25
9 Tony Romo .60 1.50
10 DeSean Jackson .60 1.50
11 Jeremy Maclin .50 1.25
12 LeSean McCoy .75 2.00
13 Aaron Rodgers 1.25 3.00
14 Clay Matthews .75 2.00
15 Jordy Nelson .60 1.50
16 Randall Cobb .60 1.50
17 Adrian Peterson .75 2.00
18 Christian Ponder .50 1.25
19 Greg Jennings .50 1.25
20 Brandon Marshall .60 1.50
21 Jay Cutler .50 1.25
22 Matt Forte .50 1.25
23 Calvin Johnson .75 2.00
24 Matthew Stafford .60 1.50
25 Reggie Bush .50 1.25
26 Asante Samuel .50 1.25
27 Julio Jones .75 2.00
28 Matt Ryan .60 1.50
29 Cam Newton .75 2.00
30 Luke Kuechly .60 1.50
31 Steve Smith .60 1.50
32 Drew Brees .75 2.00
33 Jimmy Graham .75 2.00
34 Marques Colston .50 1.25
35 Doug Martin .60 1.50
36 Josh Freeman .60 1.50
37 Vincent Jackson .50 1.25
38 Aldon Smith .50 1.25
39 Colin Kaepernick .60 1.50
40 Frank Gore .60 1.50
41 Michael Crabtree .50 1.25
42 Marshawn Lynch .60 1.50
43 Richard Sherman .75 2.00
44 Russell Wilson 1.50 4.00
45 James Laurinaitis .60 1.50
46 Sam Bradford .50 1.25
47 Isaiah Pead .50 1.25
48 Rashard Mendenhall .50 1.25
49 Larry Fitzgerald .60 1.50
50 Carson Palmer .60 1.50
52 Rob Gronkowski .75 2.00
53 Tom Brady 2.00 5.00
54 Danny Amendola .60 1.50
55 Mike Wallace .50 1.25
56 Dustin Keller .50 1.25
57 Ryan Tannehill .60 1.50
58 Antonio Cromartie .50 1.25
59 Mark Sanchez .50 1.25
60 Santonio Holmes .50 1.25
61 C.J. Spiller .50 1.25
62 Kevin Kolb .50 1.25
63 Steve Johnson .60 1.50
64 Torrey Smith .50 1.25
65 Joe Flacco .60 1.50
66 Ray Rice .50 1.25
67 A.J. Green .75 2.00
68 Andy Dalton .60 1.50
69 Jermaine Gresham .60 1.50
70 Ben Roethlisberger .75 2.00
71 Heath Miller .50 1.25
72 Antonio Brown .75 2.00
73 Brandon Weeden .50 1.25
74 Josh Gordon .50 1.25
75 Trent Richardson .50 1.25
76 Andre Johnson .50 1.25
77 Arian Foster .60 1.50
78 J.J. Watt .60 1.50
79 Matt Schaub .50 1.25
80 Andrew Luck 1.25 3.00
81 Reggie Wayne .60 1.50
82 T.Y. Hilton .60 1.50
83 Chris Johnson .50 1.25
84 Kendall Wright .50 1.25
85 Kenny Britt .50 1.25
86 Cecil Shorts .50 1.25
87 Justin Blackmon .50 1.25
88 Maurice Jones-Drew .50 1.25
89 Demaryius Thomas .60 1.50
90 Wes Welker .60 1.50
91 Peyton Manning 1.50 4.00
92 Malcom Floyd .50 1.25
93 Philip Rivers .75 2.00
94 Ryan Mathews .60 1.50
95 Jacoby Ford .50 1.25
96 Matt Flynn .50 1.25
97 Darren McFadden .60 1.50
98 Derrick Johnson .50 1.25
99 Dwayne Bowe .60 1.50
100 Jamaal Charles .60 1.50
101 Aaron Dobson RC .60 1.50
102 Aaron Mellette RC .60 1.50
103 Ace Sanders RC .60 1.50
104 Dennis Johnson RC .60 1.50
105 Alec Ogletree RC .60 1.50
106 Alex Okafor RC .60 1.50
107 Andre Ellington RC .60 1.50
108 Arthur Brown RC .60 1.50
109 Barkevious Mingo RC .60 1.50
110 Bjoern Werner RC .60 1.50
111 Chance Warmack RC .60 1.50
112 Chris Gragg RC .60 1.50
113 Chris Harper RC .60 1.50
114 Christine Michael RC .60 1.50
115 Johnathan Cyprien RC .60 1.50
116 Cobi Hamilton RC .60 1.50
117 Conner Vernon RC .60 1.50
118 Cordarrelle Patterson RC .60 1.50
119 Corey Fuller RC .60 1.50
120 Damontre Moore RC .60 1.50
121 Da'Rick Rogers RC .60 1.50
122 Darius Slay RC .60 1.50
123 Datone Jones RC .60 1.50
124 DeAndre Hopkins RC 1.50 4.00
125 Dee Milliner RC .60 1.50
126 Denard Robinson RC .60 1.50
127 Desmond Trufant RC .60 1.50
128 Dion Jordan RC .60 1.50
129 Dion Sims RC .60 1.50
130 Eddie Lacy RC .60 1.50
131 EJ Manuel RC .60 1.50
132 Eric Fisher RC .60 1.50
133 Eric Reid RC .75 2.00
134 Ezekiel Ansah RC .60 1.50
135 Gavin Escobar RC .60 1.50
136 Geno Smith RC .60 1.50
137 Giovani Bernard RC .60 1.50
138 Jamar Taylor RC .60 1.50
139 Jarvis Jones RC .60 1.50
140 Jawan Jamison RC .60 1.50
141 Johnathan Franklin RC .60 1.50
142 Jasper Collins RC .60 1.50
143 Johnthan Banks RC .60 1.50
144 Jordan Poyer RC .60 1.50
145 Jordan Reed RC 1.00 2.50
146 Joseph Randle RC .60 1.50
147 Josh Boyce RC .60 1.50
148 Justin Hunter RC .60 1.50
149 Keenan Allen RC 1.25 3.00
150 Kenjon Barner RC .60 1.50
151 Kenny Stills RC .60 1.50
152 Kenny Vaccaro RC .60 1.50
153 Kerwynn Williams RC .60 1.50
154 Kevin Minter RC .60 1.50
155 Knile Davis RC .60 1.50
156 Landry Jones RC .60 1.50
157 Le'Veon Bell RC 2.00 5.00
158 Onterio McCalebb RC .75 2.00
159 Luke Joeckel RC .60 1.50
160 Manti Te'o RC .75 2.00
161 Marcus Davis RC .60 1.50
162 Marcus Lattimore RC .60 1.50
163 Margus Hunt RC .60 1.50
164 Markus Wheaton RC .60 1.50
165 Marquess Wilson RC 1.00 2.50
166 Marquise Goodwin RC .60 1.50
167 Matt Barkley RC .60 1.50
168 Matt Elam RC .60 1.50
169 Matt Scott RC .60 1.50

170 Mike Gillislee RC .60 1.50
171 Mike Glennon RC .60 1.50
172 Montee Ball RC .60 1.50
173 Nick Kasa RC .60 1.50
174 Phillip Thomas RC .60 1.50
175 Quinton Patton RC .60 1.50
176 Sharrif Floyd RC .60 1.50
177 Rex Burkhead RC .75 2.00
178 Robert Woods RC 1.00 2.50
179 Rodney Smith RC .60 1.50
180 Ryan Nassib RC .60 1.50
181 Ryan Otten RC .60 1.50
182 Ryan Swope RC .60 1.50
183 Sam Montgomery RC .60 1.50
184 Sheldon Richardson RC .60 1.50
185 Star Lotulelei RC .75 2.00
186 Stedman Bailey RC .60 1.50
187 Stepfan Taylor RC .60 1.50
188 Tavarres King RC .60 1.50
189 Tavon Austin RC .75 2.00
190 Terrance Williams RC .60 1.50
191 Theo Riddick RC .60 1.50
192 Travis Kelce RC 1.50 4.00
193 Tyler Bray RC .60 1.50
194 Tyler Eifert RC .60 1.50
195 Tyler Wilson RC .60 1.50
196 Tyrann Mathieu RC 1.00 2.50
197 Vance McDonald RC .75 2.00
198 Xavier Rhodes RC .60 1.50
199 Zac Dysert RC .60 1.50
200 Zach Ertz RC 1.25 3.00

2013 Momentum Clear Cut

*VETS: 1.5X TO 4X BASIC CARDS
*ROOKIES: 1.2X TO 3X BASIC CARDS

2013 Momentum Gold

*1-100 VETS/99: .8X TO 2X BASIC CARDS
*101-200 ROOKIE/99: .6X TO 1.5X BASIC RC

2013 Momentum Platinum

-100 VETS/49: 1.2X TO 3X BASIC CARDS
*101-200 ROOKIE/49: 1X TO 2.5X BASIC RC

2013 Momentum Class Reunion Dual Autographs

6 J.Plummer/R.Barber/20 12.00 30.00

2013 Momentum Class Reunion Triple Autographs

1 Plmmr/Brbr/Dunn/15

2013 Momentum Double Feature Materials

1 Wells/Fitzgerald/149 3.00 8.00
2 J.Jones/M.Ryan/99 4.00 10.00
3 L.Webb/T.Suggs/25 6.00 15.00
4 Spiller/S.Johnson/149 3.00 8.00
5 D.Williams/J.Stewart/99 2.50 6.00
6 Green-Ellis/Gresham/99 3.00 8.00
7 D.Jackson/J.Haden/199 2.50 6.00
8 D.Bryant/M.Austin/49 5.00 12.00
9 D.Thomas/E.Decker/149 4.00 10.00
10 M.Lewis/Jones-Drew/99 2.50 6.00
11 D.Bowe/J.Charles/199 3.00 8.00
12 A.Peterson/C.Ponder/99 6.00 15.00
13 G.Tate/S.Rice/49 3.00 8.00
14 M.Colston/P.Thomas/199 3.00 8.00
15 E.Manning/H.Nicks/49 4.00 10.00
16 J.Kerley/M.Sanchez/49 3.00 8.00
19 A.Gates/M.Floyd/149 3.00 8.00
20 M.Crabtree/V.Davis/49 3.00 8.00

2013 Momentum Double Feature Materials Prime

*PRIME/49: .8X TO 2X BASIC JSY/99-199
*PRIME/49: .6X TO 1.5X BASIC JSY/49
*PRIME/25: 1X TO 2.5X BASIC JSY/99-199
*PRIME/25: .8X TO 2X BASIC JSY/49
*PRIME/25: .6X TO 1.5X BASIC JSY/25
17 D.McFadden/D.Moore/49 6.00 15.00

2013 Momentum Materials

RIME/49: .6X TO 1.5X BASIC JSY/99-199
*PRIME/49: .5X TO 1.2X BASIC JSY/49
*PRIME/25: .8X TO 2X BASIC JSY/99-199
*PRIME/25: .6X TO 1.5X BASIC JSY/49
*PRIME/25: .5X TO 1.2X BASIC JSY/25
1 BenJarvus Green-Ellis/49 4.00 10.00
2 Larry Fitzgerald/49 4.00 10.00
3 Marshall Faulk/199 3.00 8.00
4 Brandon Marshall/25 5.00 12.00
5 Derrick Johnson/99 2.50 6.00
6 Jason Witten/99 3.00 8.00
7 Matt Schaub/49 3.00 8.00
8 LeSean McCoy/199 4.00 10.00
9 DeMarcus Ware/99 4.00 10.00
10 Vincent Jackson/49 3.00 8.00
11 DeMarco Murray/99 3.00 8.00
12 Von Miller/49 4.00 10.00
13 Maurice Jones-Drew/99 2.50 6.00
14 Ray Lewis/199 4.00 10.00
15 Reggie Wayne/49 4.00 10.00
16 Joe Flacco/199 3.00 8.00
17 Eli Manning/199 3.00 8.00
18 Miles Austin/49 3.00 8.00
19 Fred Davis/99 2.50 6.00
20 Julio Jones/49 5.00 12.00
21 Malcom Floyd/99 2.50 6.00
22 Dexter McCluster/199 3.00 8.00
23 Donald Brown/199 2.50 6.00
24 Torrey Smith/49 3.00 8.00
25 Brian Hartline/199 2.50 6.00
26 Hakeem Nicks/49 3.00 8.00
27 Michael Vick/49 4.00 10.00
28 Marvin Harrison/99 3.00 8.00
29 Steve Johnson/199 3.00 8.00
30 Pierre Garcon/99 3.00 8.00
31 Julius Peppers/199 3.00 8.00
32 Robert Meachem/99 2.50 6.00
33 Eric Berry/199 3.00 8.00
34 Cameron Wake/149 2.50 6.00
35 Lardarius Webb/10
36 Mike Alstott/99 2.50 6.00
37 Ryan Kerrigan/199 2.50 6.00
38 D'Qwell Jackson/199 2.50 6.00
39 Philip Rivers/49 5.00 12.00
40 Tamba Hali/199 2.50 6.00
41 Justin Tuck/49 3.00 8.00
42 Ted Hendricks/199 2.50 6.00
43 Adrian Peterson/49 5.00 12.00
44 Jamaal Charles/149 3.00 8.00
45 Tom Brady/49 12.00 30.00
46 Ray Rice/199 2.50 6.00
47 Ryan Mathews/25 5.00 12.00
48 Darren Sproles/99 3.00 8.00
49 Arian Foster/49 4.00 10.00
50 Christian Ponder/199 2.50 6.00
51 Santonio Holmes/99 2.50 6.00
52 Vernon Davis/49 3.00 8.00
53 Darren McFadden/199 3.00 8.00
54 Matt Ryan/149 3.00 8.00
55 Brian Orakpo/99 3.00 8.00
56 Kurt Warner/99 3.00 8.00
57 Brent Celek/99 2.50 6.00
58 Jeremy Maclin/99 2.50 6.00
59 Antonio Gates/99 3.00 8.00
60 Chris Johnson/199 2.50 6.00
61 DeAngelo Hall/199 2.50 6.00
62 Jared Allen/25 4.00 10.00
63 Michael Crabtree/25 4.00 10.00
64 Alfred Morris/99 2.50 6.00
65 DeSean Jackson/199 3.00 8.00
66 Matthew Stafford/49 4.00 10.00
67 Josh Cribbs/199 2.50 6.00
68 Jonathan Baldwin/199 2.50 6.00
69 James Laurinaitis/199 3.00 8.00
70 A.J. Green/99 4.00 10.00
71 Jonathan Stewart/99 2.50 6.00
72 Michael Turner/199 2.50 6.00
73 Josh Gordon/99 2.50 6.00
75 Golden Tate/199 2.50 6.00
76 C.J. Spiller/99 2.50 6.00
77 Zach Miller/199 2.50 6.00
78 Justin Blackmon/99 2.50 6.00
79 Mike Singletary/199 4.00 10.00
80 Andy Dalton/99 3.00 8.00
81 Willis McGahee/99 2.50 6.00
82 Trent Richardson/99 2.50 6.00
83 Jermaine Gresham/199 3.00 8.00
84 Matt Forte/199 2.50 6.00
85 Marcedes Lewis/99 2.50 6.00
86 Josh Freeman/99 3.00 8.00
87 Sidney Rice/49 3.00 8.00
88 Santana Moss/199 3.00 8.00
89 Tony Moeaki/199 2.50 6.00
91 Eric Decker/99 2.50 6.00
92 Champ Bailey/199 3.00 8.00
93 LaDainian Tomlinson/199 3.00 8.00
94 Dez Bryant/99 4.00 10.00
95 Jay Cutler/49 3.00 8.00
96 Knowshon Moreno/199 2.50 6.00
97 Roddy White/49 3.00 8.00
98 Steve Largent/199 4.00 10.00
99 Greg Olsen/99 3.00 8.00
100 Amani Toomer/99 2.50 6.00

2013 Momentum Prized Signatures

1 Andre Rison/49 6.00 15.00
3 Bill Romanowski/49 40.00 100.00
17 Jim Kiick/99 8.00 20.00
18 Chuck Foreman/75 6.00 15.00
19 James Lofton/25 8.00 20.00
29 Brent Celek/49 5.00 12.00
32 Dustin Keller/49
33 Greg Olsen/49 8.00 20.00
35 London Fletcher/25 10.00 25.00
36 Patrick Willis/25 20.00 40.00
37 Paul Posluszny/99 5.00 12.00
39 Ronde Barber/49 6.00 15.00
41 Greg Jennings/20
44 Steve Smith/25 10.00 25.00
45 Amani Toomer/25
48 Maurice Jones-Drew/25 8.00 20.00
50 Ron Jaworski/49 12.50 25.00

2013 Momentum Rookie Initiation Materials

*PRIME/49: .6X TO 1.5X BASIC JSY/399
1 Aaron Dobson 1.50 4.00
7 Andre Ellington 1.50 4.00
14 Christine Michael 1.50 4.00
18 Cordarrelle Patterson 1.50 4.00
24 DeAndre Hopkins 4.00 10.00
26 Denard Robinson 1.50 4.00
28 Dion Jordan 1.50 4.00
30 Eddie Lacy 1.50 4.00
31 EJ Manuel 1.50 4.00
35 Gavin Escobar 1.50 4.00
36 Geno Smith 1.50 4.00
37 Giovani Bernard 1.50 4.00
42 Johnathan Franklin 1.50 4.00
46 Jordan Reed 2.50 6.00
47 Joseph Randle 1.50 4.00
49 Justin Hunter 1.50 4.00
50 Keenan Allen 3.00 8.00
52 Kenny Stills 1.50 4.00
56 Knile Davis 1.50 4.00
57 Landry Jones 1.50 4.00
58 Le'Veon Bell 5.00 12.00
61 Manti Te'o 2.00 5.00
63 Marcus Lattimore 1.50 4.00
65 Markus Wheaton 1.50 4.00
67 Marquise Goodwin 1.50 4.00
68 Matt Barkley 1.50 4.00
71 Mike Gillislee 1.50 4.00
72 Mike Glennon 1.50 4.00
73 Montee Ball 1.50 4.00
76 Quinton Patton 1.50 4.00
78 Robert Woods 2.50 6.00
80 Ryan Nassib 1.50 4.00
86 Stedman Bailey 1.50 4.00
87 Stepfan Taylor 1.50 4.00
89 Tavon Austin 2.00 5.00
90 Terrance Williams 1.50 4.00
94 Tyler Eifert 1.50 4.00
95 Tyler Wilson 1.50 4.00
97 Vance McDonald 2.00 5.00
100 Zach Ertz 3.00 8.00

2013 Momentum Rookie Initiation Signatures

1 Aaron Dobson/49 3.00 8.00
2 Aaron Mellette/299 2.50 6.00
3 Ace Sanders/299 6.00 15.00
5 Alec Ogletree/299 2.50 6.00
6 Alex Okafor/299 2.50 6.00
7 Andre Ellington/49 3.00 8.00
8 Arthur Brown/299 2.50 6.00
10 Bjoern Werner/299 2.50 6.00
11 Chance Warmack/299 2.50 6.00
12 Chris Gragg/299 2.50 6.00
14 Christine Michael/25 4.00 10.00
15 Cornellius Carradine/299 5.00 12.00
17 Conner Vernon/299 2.50 6.00
18 Cordarrelle Patterson/25 4.00 10.00
19 Corey Fuller/299 2.50 6.00
20 Damontre Moore/299 2.50 6.00
21 Da'Rick Rogers/49
22 Darius Slay/299 2.50 6.00
23 Datone Jones/299 2.50 6.00
24 DeAndre Hopkins/49 8.00 20.00
25 Dee Milliner/299 2.50 6.00
26 Denard Robinson/25
27 Desmond Trufant/299 2.50 6.00
28 Dion Jordan/49 3.00 8.00
29 Dion Sims/299 2.50 6.00
30 Eddie Lacy/49 3.00 8.00
31 EJ Manuel/25 4.00 10.00
32 Eric Fisher/299 2.50 6.00
33 Eric Reid/299 6.00 15.00
34 Ezekiel Ansah/99 3.00 8.00
35 Gavin Escobar/49
36 Geno Smith/25
37 Giovani Bernard/49 3.00 8.00
38 Jamar Taylor/299 2.50 6.00
39 Jarvis Jones/299 2.50 6.00
41 Johnathan Cyprien/299 2.50 6.00
42 Johnathan Franklin/49 3.00 8.00
43 Jasper Collins/299 2.50 6.00
44 Johnthan Banks/299 6.00 15.00
45 Jordan Poyer/299 2.50 6.00
46 Jordan Reed/49 5.00 12.00
47 Joseph Randle/49
48 Josh Boyce/299 2.50 6.00
49 Justin Hunter/49
50 Keenan Allen/49 6.00 15.00
51 Kenjon Barner/299 2.50 6.00
52 Kenny Stills/49 3.00 8.00
53 Kenny Vaccaro/299 2.50 6.00
54 Kerwynn Williams/299 2.50 6.00
55 Kevin Minter/299 2.50 6.00
56 Knile Davis/49 3.00 8.00
57 Landry Jones/49 3.00 8.00
58 Le'Veon Bell/49 25.00 50.00
59 Onterio McCalebb/299 3.00 8.00
61 Manti Te'o/49 4.00 10.00
62 Marcus Davis/299 2.50 6.00
63 Marcus Lattimore/49 3.00 8.00
64 Margus Hunt/299 2.50 6.00
65 Markus Wheaton/49
66 Marquess Wilson/299 6.00 15.00
67 Marquise Goodwin/49
68 Matt Barkley/49 3.00 8.00
69 Matt Elam/299 2.50 6.00
70 Matt Scott/99 3.00 8.00
71 Mike Gillislee/49 3.00 8.00
72 Mike Glennon/49
73 Montee Ball/49 3.00 8.00
74 Nick Kasa/299 2.50 6.00
75 Phillip Thomas/299 2.50 6.00
76 Quinton Patton/49 3.00 8.00
77 Rex Burkhead/299 10.00 25.00
78 Robert Woods/49
79 Rodney Smith/299 2.50 6.00
80 Ryan Nassib/25 4.00 10.00
81 Ryan Otten/299 2.50 6.00
82 Ryan Swope/299 2.50 6.00
83 Sam Montgomery/299 2.50 6.00
86 Stedman Bailey/25 4.00 10.00
87 Stepfan Taylor/49
88 Tavarres King/99 3.00 8.00
89 Tavon Austin/49 4.00 10.00
90 Terrance Williams/49 3.00 8.00
91 Theo Riddick/299 2.50 6.00
92 Travis Kelce/299 15.00 40.00
93 Tyler Bray/49 3.00 8.00
94 Tyler Eifert/49 3.00 8.00
95 Tyler Wilson/49
96 Tyrann Mathieu/299 15.00 30.00
97 Vance McDonald/49 6.00 15.00
98 Xavier Rhodes/299 6.00 15.00
99 Zac Dysert/49 3.00 8.00
100 Zach Ertz/49 6.00 15.00

2013 Momentum Rookie Signatures

CH EXPIRATION: 2/7/2015
101 Aaron Dobson/149 3.00 8.00
102 Aaron Mellette/499 2.00 5.00
103 Ace Sanders/599 4.00 10.00
104 Dennis Johnson/550 2.00 5.00
105 Alec Ogletree/99 3.00 8.00
106 Alex Okafor/499 2.00 5.00
107 Andre Ellington/399 5.00 12.00
108 Arthur Brown/599 2.00 5.00
109 Barkevious Mingo/599 5.00 12.00
110 Bjoern Werner/599 2.00 5.00
111 Chance Warmack/599 2.00 5.00
112 Chris Gragg/599 2.00 5.00
113 Chris Harper/99 EXCH 3.00 8.00
114 Christine Michael/49 4.00 10.00
115 Johnathan Cyprien/599 2.00 5.00
117 Conner Vernon/599 2.00 5.00
118 Cordarrelle Patterson/49 4.00 10.00
119 Corey Fuller/599 2.00 5.00
120 Damontre Moore/599 2.00 5.00
121 Da'Rick Rogers/499 4.00 10.00
122 Darius Slay/599 2.00 5.00
123 Datone Jones/599 2.00 5.00
124 DeAndre Hopkins/149 8.00 20.00
125 Dee Milliner/199 3.00 8.00
126 Denard Robinson/49 4.00 10.00
127 Desmond Trufant/599 2.00 5.00
128 Dion Jordan/399 2.50 6.00
129 Dion Sims/599 2.00 5.00
130 Eddie Lacy/199 3.00 8.00
131 EJ Manuel/49 4.00 10.00
132 Eric Fisher/599 2.00 5.00
133 Eric Reid/449 5.00 12.00
134 Ezekiel Ansah/199 3.00 8.00
135 Gavin Escobar/199 3.00 8.00
136 Geno Smith/49 4.00 10.00
137 Giovani Bernard/199 3.00 8.00
138 Jamar Taylor/399 2.50 6.00
139 Jarvis Jones/599 2.00 5.00
141 Johnathan Franklin/199 3.00 8.00
142 Jasper Collins/599 2.00 5.00
143 Johnthan Banks/399 6.00 15.00
144 Jordan Poyer/599 2.00 5.00
145 Jordan Reed/149 5.00 12.00
146 Joseph Randle/399 2.50 6.00
147 Josh Boyce/599 2.00 5.00
148 Justin Hunter/149 3.00 8.00
149 Keenan Allen/199 6.00 15.00
150 Kenjon Barner/599 2.00 5.00
151 Kenny Stills/199 3.00 8.00
152 Kenny Vaccaro/599 2.00 5.00
153 Kerwynn Williams/599 2.00 5.00
154 Kevin Minter/599 2.00 5.00
155 Knile Davis/199 3.00 8.00
156 Landry Jones/199 3.00 8.00
157 Le'Veon Bell/399 8.00 20.00
158 Onterio McCalebb/449 2.50 6.00
160 Manti Te'o/199 4.00 10.00
161 Marcus Davis/599 2.00 5.00
162 Marcus Lattimore/399 2.50 6.00
163 Margus Hunt/599 2.00 5.00
164 Markus Wheaton/199 3.00 8.00
165 Marquess Wilson/99 5.00 12.00
166 Marquise Goodwin/99 3.00 8.00
167 Matt Barkley/99 3.00 8.00
168 Matt Elam/599 2.00 5.00
169 Matt Scott/99 3.00 8.00
170 Mike Gillislee/75 3.00 8.00
171 Mike Glennon/199 3.00 8.00
172 Montee Ball/399 2.50 6.00
173 Nick Kasa/549 2.00 5.00
174 Phillip Thomas/599 2.00 5.00
175 Quinton Patton/199 3.00 8.00
177 Rex Burkhead/599 2.50 6.00
178 Robert Woods/199 5.00 12.00
179 Rodney Smith/599 2.00 5.00
180 Ryan Nassib/99 3.00 8.00
181 Ryan Otten/599 2.00 5.00
182 Ryan Swope/599 2.00 5.00
183 Sam Montgomery/599 2.00 5.00
186 Stedman Bailey/350 2.50 6.00
187 Stepfan Taylor/199 3.00 8.00
188 Tavarres King/599 2.00 5.00
189 Tavon Austin/199 4.00 10.00
190 Terrance Williams/199 3.00 8.00
191 Theo Riddick/599 2.00 5.00
192 Travis Kelce/449 12.00 30.00
193 Tyler Bray/599 2.00 5.00
194 Tyler Eifert/149 3.00 8.00
195 Tyler Wilson/199 3.00 8.00
196 Tyrann Mathieu/599 12.50 25.00
197 Vance McDonald/49 5.00 12.00
198 Xavier Rhodes/599 5.00 12.00
199 Zac Dysert/299 2.50 6.00
200 Zach Ertz/199 6.00 15.00
201 Aaron Dobson JSY/399 3.00 8.00
202 Andre Ellington JSY/399 3.00 8.00
203 Christine Michael JSY/199 8.00 20.00
204 C.Patterson JSY/199 4.00 10.00
205 DeAndre Hopkins JSY/199 10.00 25.00
206 Denard Robinson JSY/199 4.00 10.00
207 Eddie Lacy JSY/199 4.00 10.00
208 EJ Manuel JSY/199 4.00 10.00
209 Gavin Escobar JSY/399 3.00 8.00
210 Geno Smith JSY/199 4.00 10.00
211 Giovani Bernard JSY/199 4.00 10.00
212 Johnathan Franklin JSY/399 3.00 8.00
213 Jordan Reed JSY/399 5.00 12.00
214 Joseph Randle JSY/399 3.00 8.00
215 Justin Hunter JSY/199 4.00 10.00
216 Keenan Allen JSY/199 6.00 15.00
217 Kenny Stills JSY/399 3.00 8.00
218 Knile Davis JSY/399 3.00 8.00
219 Landry Jones JSY/199 4.00 10.00
220 Le'Veon Bell JSY/399 20.00 40.00
221 Manti Te'o JSY/199 5.00 12.00
222 Marcus Lattimore JSY/399 3.00 8.00
223 Markus Wheaton JSY/299 2.50 6.00
224 Marquise Goodwin JSY/399 3.00 8.00
225 Matt Barkley JSY/199 4.00 10.00
226 Mike Gillislee JSY/199 4.00 10.00
227 Mike Glennon JSY/199 4.00 10.00
228 Montee Ball JSY/399 3.00 8.00
229 Quinton Patton JSY/399 3.00 8.00
230 Robert Woods JSY/299 4.00 10.00
231 Ryan Nassib JSY/199 4.00 10.00
232 Stedman Bailey JSY/199 4.00 10.00
233 Stepfan Taylor JSY/399 3.00 8.00
234 Tavon Austin JSY/399 4.00 10.00
235 Terrance Williams JSY/199 4.00 10.00
236 Dion Jordan JSY/399 3.00 8.00
237 Tyler Eifert JSY/399 3.00 8.00
238 Tyler Wilson JSY/199 4.00 10.00
239 Vance McDonald JSY/199 6.00 15.00
240 Zach Ertz JSY/399 6.00 15.00

2013 Momentum Rookie Signatures Gold

*GOLD/49: .8X TO 2X BASIC AU/449-599
*GOLD/49: .6X TO 1.5X BASIC AU/299-399
*GOLD/49: .5X TO 1.2X BASIC AU/99-199
*GOLD/49: .4X TO 1X BASIC AU/49
*GOLD/15-25: 1X TO 2.5X BASIC AU/449-599
*GOLD/15-25: .8X TO 2X BASIC AU/299-350
*GOLD/15-25: .6X TO 1.5X BASIC AU/75-199
*GOLD/15-25: .5X TO 1.2X BASIC AU/49
130 Eddie Lacy/49 4.00 10.00
131 EJ Manuel/15 50.00 100.00
136 Geno Smith/15 5.00 12.00
208 EJ Manuel JSY/25 30.00 80.00
210 Geno Smith JSY/25 6.00 15.00

2013 Momentum Rookie Signatures Platinum

*PLAT/25: 1X TO 2.5X BASIC AU/449-599
*PLAT/25: .8X TO 2X BASIC AU/299-399
*PLAT/25:.6 X TO 1.5X BASIC AU/99-199
130 Eddie Lacy/25 5.00 12.00
189 Tavon Austin/25 6.00 15.00
234 Tavon Austin JSY/25 8.00 20.00

2013 Momentum Rookie Team Threads Dual Materials

*PRIME/49: .6X TO 1.5X BASIC JSY/399
*QUAD/299: .5X TO 1.2X DUAL JSY/399
*QUAD PRM/15: 1X TO 2.5X DUAL/399
*TRIPLE/299: .4X TO 1X DUAL/399
*TRIP PRM/25: .6X TO 1.5X DUAL/399
1 Tavon Austin 2.00 5.00
2 EJ Manuel 1.50 4.00
3 DeAndre Hopkins 4.00 10.00
4 Cordarrelle Patterson 1.50 4.00
5 Justin Hunter 1.50 4.00
6 Giovani Bernard 1.50 4.00
7 Geno Smith 1.50 4.00
8 Robert Woods 2.50 6.00
9 Montee Ball 1.50 4.00
10 Eddie Lacy 1.50 4.00
11 Mike Glennon 1.50 4.00
12 Terrance Williams 1.50 4.00
13 Keenan Allen 3.00 8.00
14 Markus Wheaton 1.50 4.00
15 Matt Barkley 1.50 4.00
16 Ryan Nassib 1.50 4.00
17 Tyler Wilson 1.50 4.00
18 Johnathan Franklin 1.50 4.00
19 Quinton Patton 1.50 4.00
20 Stepfan Taylor 1.50 4.00
21 Joseph Randle 1.50 4.00
22 Tyler Eifert 1.50 4.00
23 Zach Ertz 3.00 8.00
24 Le'Veon Bell 5.00 12.00
25 Aaron Dobson 1.50 4.00
26 Christine Michael 1.50 4.00
27 Stedman Bailey 1.50 4.00
28 Landry Jones 1.50 4.00
29 Marcus Lattimore 1.50 4.00
30 Vance McDonald 2.00 5.00
31 Marquise Goodwin 1.50 4.00
32 Denard Robinson 1.50 4.00
33 Knile Davis 1.50 4.00
34 Gavin Escobar 1.50 4.00
35 Kenny Stills 1.50 4.00

2013 Momentum Rookie Team Threads Dual Materials Signatures

*PRIME/25: .6X TO 1.5X BASIC AU/49
*TRIPLE/25-49: .4X TO 1X DUAL/25-49
*TRP PRM/15: .8X TO 2X DUAL/25-49
*QUAD/25-49: .5X TO 1.2X DUAL/25-49
1 Tavon Austin/49 5.00 12.00
2 EJ Manuel/25 5.00 12.00
3 DeAndre Hopkins/49 10.00 25.00
4 Cordarrelle Patterson/25 5.00 12.00
5 Justin Hunter/49 4.00 10.00
6 Giovani Bernard/49 4.00 10.00
7 Geno Smith/25 5.00 12.00
8 Robert Woods/49 6.00 15.00
9 Montee Ball/49 4.00 10.00
10 Eddie Lacy/49 4.00 10.00
11 Mike Glennon/49 4.00 10.00
12 Terrance Williams/49 4.00 10.00-
13 Keenan Allen/49 8.00 20.00
14 Markus Wheaton/49 4.00 10.00
15 Matt Barkley/49 4.00 10.00
16 Ryan Nassib/25 5.00 12.00
17 Tyler Wilson/49 4.00 10.00
18 Johnathan Franklin/49 4.00 10.00
19 Quinton Patton/49 4.00 10.00
20 Stepfan Taylor/49 4.00 10.00
21 Joseph Randle/49 4.00 10.00
22 Tyler Eifert/49 4.00 10.00
23 Zach Ertz/49 8.00 20.00
24 Le'Veon Bell/49 12.00 30.00
25 Aaron Dobson/49 4.00 10.00
26 Christine Michael/25 5.00 12.00
27 Stedman Bailey/25 5.00 12.00
28 Landry Jones/49 4.00 10.00
29 Marcus Lattimore/49 4.00 10.00
30 Vance McDonald/25 6.00 15.00
31 Marquise Goodwin/49 4.00 10.00
32 Denard Robinson/25 5.00 12.00
33 Knile Davis/49 4.00 10.00
34 Gavin Escobar/49 4.00 10.00
35 Kenny Stills/49 4.00 10.00

2013 Momentum Team Threads Jerseys

*PRIME/49: .6X TO 1.5X BASIC JSY/99
*PRIME/25: .8X TO 2X BASIC JSY/49
*PRIME/25: .6X TO 1.5X BASIC JSY/25
1 Darren Sproles/25 5.00 12.00
2 Brent Celek/49 3.00 8.00
3 Josh Cribbs/99 3.00 8.00
5 Matt Ryan/25 5.00 12.00
6 Vincent Jackson/20 4.00 10.00
7 Cam Newton/25 6.00 15.00
8 Jeremy Maclin/25 4.00 10.00
9 BenJarvus Green-Ellis/25 5.00 12.00
10 Larry Fitzgerald/25 5.00 12.00
11 Jason Witten/49 4.00 10.00
12 Matt Schaub/25 4.00 10.00
13 DeMarco Murray/49 4.00 10.00
14 Ray Lewis/25 8.00 20.00
15 Marshall Faulk/25 5.00 12.00
16 Hakeem Nicks/25 4.00 10.00
17 Jerry Rice/25 20.00 50.00
18 Santonio Holmes/25 4.00 10.00
19 Ray Rice/49 3.00 8.00
20 Julius Peppers/25 5.00 12.00
21 Von Miller/25 5.00 12.00
22 Brandon Marshall/25 5.00 12.00
23 Darren McFadden/25 5.00 12.00
25 Eric Decker/25 4.00 10.00
26 Roddy White/20 4.00 10.00
27 Marques Colston/25 4.00 10.00
28 Jay Cutler/49 3.00 8.00
30 Reggie Wayne/20 5.00 12.00
31 Dez Bryant/25 6.00 15.00
35 Jamaal Charles/25 5.00 12.00

2013 Momentum Team Threads Jerseys Signatures

2 Torrey Smith/25
3 Jonathan Stewart/25 8.00 20.00
9 Demaryius Thomas/25
10 Matthew Stafford/25
12 Warren Moon/20 25.00 50.00
16 Kyle Rudolph/49 6.00 15.00
19 Hakeem Nicks/25
20 Greg Olsen/20 10.00 25.00
21 Jeremy Maclin/25 8.00 20.00
23 Jonathan Baldwin/49
25 Michael Crabtree/25 8.00 20.00
26 Shaun Alexander/25
27 Sam Bradford/25
29 Kenny Britt/25
30 London Fletcher/25 15.00 40.00

2013 Momentum Team Threads Triple Jerseys Signatures

4 Frank Gore/25 15.00 40.00

2013 Momentum Triple Feature Materials

*PRIME/49: .8X TO 2X BASIC TRIPLE/99-199
*PRIME/20-25: .8X TO 2X BASIC TRIPLE/49-99
*PRIME/20-25: .6X TO 1.5X BASIC TRIPLE/25
1 Jcksn/McCy/Vck/199 6.00 15.00
2 Gtes/Rvrs/Mthws/149 6.00 15.00
3 Flcco/Rce/Smth/99 8.00 20.00
4 Orkpo/Fltchr/Krrgn/99 5.00 12.00
5 Ptrsn/Pndr/Alln/25 8.00 20.00
6 Gre/Crbtree/Dvis/25 12.00 30.00
7 Mrry/Brynt/Romo/99 8.00 20.00
8 Green/Dltn/Grn-Ells/149 6.00 15.00
9 Jnes/Ryan/Whte/49 8.00 20.00
10 Mrshll/Ctler/Frte/49 6.00 15.00

2013 Momentum Upside Jumbo Jerseys

*PRIME49: .6X TO 1.5X BASIC JSY/299
1 Tavon Austin 2.00 5.00
2 EJ Manuel 1.50 4.00
3 DeAndre Hopkins 4.00 10.00
4 Cordarrelle Patterson 1.50 4.00
5 Justin Hunter 1.50 4.00
6 Giovani Bernard 1.50 4.00
7 Geno Smith 1.50 4.00
8 Robert Woods 2.50 6.00
9 Montee Ball 1.50 4.00
10 Eddie Lacy 1.50 4.00
11 Mike Glennon 1.50 4.00
12 Terrance Williams 1.50 4.00
13 Keenan Allen 3.00 8.00
14 Markus Wheaton 1.50 4.00
15 Matt Barkley 1.50 4.00
16 Ryan Nassib 1.50 4.00
17 Tyler Wilson 1.50 4.00
18 Johnathan Franklin 1.50 4.00
19 Quinton Patton 1.50 4.00
20 Stepfan Taylor 1.50 4.00
21 Joseph Randle 1.50 4.00
22 Tyler Eifert 1.50 4.00
23 Zach Ertz 3.00 8.00
24 Le'Veon Bell 5.00 12.00
25 Aaron Dobson 1.50 4.00
26 Christine Michael 1.50 4.00
27 Stedman Bailey 1.50 4.00
28 Landry Jones 1.50 4.00
29 Marcus Lattimore 1.50 4.00
30 Vance McDonald 2.50 6.00
31 Marquise Goodwin 1.50 4.00
32 Denard Robinson 1.50 4.00
33 Knile Davis 1.50 4.00
34 Gavin Escobar 1.50 4.00
35 Kenny Stills 1.50 4.00

2005 Montgomery Maulers NIFL

This set was issued by the Montgomery Maulers of the National Indoor Football League. Each card features one or more players or coaches from the team.

COMPLETE SET (32) 5.00 10.00
1 Fred Barnett OL .20 .50
Jamaal Fletcher DB
2 Darian Chestnut .20 .50
3 Chrys Chukwuma .30 .75
4 Cliff Clark AC .20 .50
Mike Williams AC
Carlos Clayton AC
Kelvin Stokes AC
5 Undrae Crosby .20 .50
6 Cliff Darrington .20 .50
7 Pat Epkins .20 .50
8 Ray Fleming .20 .50
9 Eric Hall .20 .50
Corey Sears
10 Jonathan Harrell .20 .50
11 Antoine Hill .20 .50
12 Shaun Holmes .20 .50
13 Eric Hudson .20 .50
14 Kevin Jones K .20 .50
15 Jamie LaMunyon Owner .20 .50
16 Jesse Marsh .20 .50
17 Quincy McCall .20 .50
18 Nathan McDaniel .20 .50
19 David Philyaw .20 .50
20 Mareno Philyaw .30 .75
21 Andre Reed DL .20 .50
22 J.R. Richardson .20 .50
23 Richard Rowe .20 .50
24 Everette Rosette .20 .50
25 Machion Sanders .20 .50
26 James Shiver .20 .50
27 Archie Smith .20 .50
28 Tarsus Thomas .20 .50
29 Duke Vaiga .20 .50
30 Buffalo Wild Wings .20 .50
store photo
31 Buffalo Wild Wings Coupon/5 free wings .20 .50
32 Buffalo Wild Wings Coupon/10% off .20 .50

1988 Monty Gum

This 100-card set was made in Europe by Monty Gum. The cards measure approximately 1 15/16" by 2 3/4" and contain thick yellow borders around a color photo. There was also an album issued with the set. The cards do not feature specific players, only generic team action scenes; hence they are not very popular with collectors. The cards have blank backs. Each is numbered and subtitled at the bottom inside a black box. There is a blank-backed sticker version, a thin paper version and a white cardboard version of each card in the set. The sticker backs actually have a white paper cover that is removable. Otherwise, they are the same as the card versions; the stickers are considered the toughest version to find.

COMPLETE SET (100) 50.00 125.00
*STICKERS: 1X TO 2X CARDS
1 Atlanta Falcons .60 1.50
2 Atlanta Falcons .50 1.25
3 Atlanta Falcons .50 1.25
4 Buffalo Bills .50 1.25
5 Chicago Bears .50 1.25
6 Chicago Bears .50 1.25
7 Cincinnati Bengals .50 1.25
8 Cincinnati Bengals .50 1.25
9 Cincinnati Bengals 2.50 6.00
10 Cincinnati Bengals .50 1.25
11 Cincinnati Bengals .60 1.50
12 Cleveland Browns .50 1.25
13 Cleveland Browns .60 1.50
14 Cleveland Browns .50 1.25
15 Cleveland Browns .50 1.25
16 Dallas Cowboys .60 1.50
17 Dallas Cowboys .60 1.50
18 Dallas Cowboys .60 1.50
19 Denver Broncos .50 1.25
20 Denver Broncos .50 1.25
21 Denver Broncos .60 1.50
22 Detroit Lions .50 1.25
23 Green Bay Packers .50 1.25
24 Green Bay Packers .50 1.25
25 Houston Oilers .50 1.25
26 Houston Oilers .50 1.25
27 Indianapolis Colts .50 1.25
28 Kansas City Chiefs .50 1.25
29 Kansas City Chiefs .50 1.25
30 Kansas City Chiefs .60 1.50
31 Los Angeles Raiders .60 1.50
32 Los Angeles Raiders .60 1.50
33 Los Angeles Raiders .60 1.50
34 Los Angeles Raiders 1.25 3.00
35 Los Angeles Rams .50 1.25
36 Los Angeles Rams .60 1.50
37 Los Angeles Rams .50 1.25
38 Miami Dolphins 6.00 15.00
39 Miami Dolphins .60 1.50
40 Minnesota Vikings .50 1.25
41 Minnesota Vikings .50 1.25
42 New England Patriots .50 1.25
43 New England Patriots .60 1.50
44 New England Patriots 2.00 5.00
45 New Orleans Saints .75 2.00
46 New Orleans Saints UER .60 1.50
47 New York Giants .60 1.50
48 New York Giants .50 1.25
49 New York Jets .50 1.25
50 New York Jets .50 1.25
51 Philadelphia Eagles .50 1.25
52 Philadelphia Eagles .50 1.25
53 Philadelphia Eagles .50 1.25
54 Philadelphia Eagles .50 1.25
55 Pittsburgh Steelers .60 1.50
56 Pittsburgh Steelers .60 1.50
57 Pittsburgh Steelers .75 2.00
58 St.Louis Cardinals .50 1.25
59 St.Louis Cardinals .50 1.25
60 St.Louis Cardinals .50 1.25
61 St.Louis Cardinals UER .50 1.25
62 San Diego Chargers .50 1.25
63 San Diego Chargers .50 1.25
64 San Diego Chargers 1.00 2.50
65 San Diego Chargers .50 1.25
66 San Francisco 49ers .60 1.50
67 San Francisco 49ers .60 1.50
68 San Francisco 49ers 6.00 15.00
69 San Francisco 49ers 6.00 15.00
70 Seattle Seahawks .50 1.25
71 Seattle Seahawks .50 1.25
72 Tampa Bay Buccaneers .50 1.25
73 Tampa Bay Buccaneers .50 1.25
74 Tampa Bay Buccaneers .50 1.25
75 Tampa Bay Buccaneers .50 1.25
76 Washington Redskins .60 1.50
77 Washington Redskins .60 1.50
78 Washington Redskins .60 1.50
79 Washington Redskins .60 1.50
80 Official NFL Football .40 1.00
81 Helmets:Falcons .40 1.00
Bills
82 Helmets:Bears .40 1.00
Bengals
83 Helmets:Browns/ .40 1.00
84 Helmets:Broncos .40 1.00
Lions
85 Helmets:Packers/ .40 1.00
86 Helmets:Colts .40 1.00
Chiefs
87 Helmets:Raiders .40 1.00
Rams
88 Helmets:Dolphins/ .40 1.00
89 Helmets:Patriots/ .40 1.00
90 Helmets:Giants .40 1.00
Jets
91 Philadelphia Eagles .40 1.00
92 Pittsburgh Steelers .40 1.00
93 St. Louis Cardinals .40 1.00
94 San Diego Chargers .40 1.00
95 San Francisco 49ers .40 1.00
96 Seattle Seahawks .40 1.00
97 Tampa Bay Buccaneers .40 1.00
98 Washington Redskins .40 1.00
99 National Football .40 1.00
100 American Football Fans .50 1.25

1996 MotionVision

The 1996 MotionVision set was issued in two series of 12 cards each for a total of 24 cards and was distributed in one-card packs with a suggested retail price of $5.99 each. Only 25,000 of each player card was produced. Created on thick plastic, the cards feature Digital Film imaging technology which takes live actual game day footage from the NFL films, transfers them to a film emulsion, and plays back the action sequence on the card with the flick of a wrist. Each Digital Replay was individually packaged in its own see-through custom designed CD jewel case for maximum protection. A Super Bowl XXXI Promo card was distributed at the Super Bowl in New Orleans. It features NFC and AFC helmets crashing in action. An unnumbered Troy Aikman promo card was also distributed.

COMPLETE SET (24) 20.00 50.00
COMP.SERIES 1 (12) 10.00 25.00
COMP.SERIES 2 (12) 10.00 25.00
1 Troy Aikman 1.25 3.00
2 Dan Marino 2.50 6.00
3 Steve Young .75 2.00
4 Emmitt Smith 2.00 5.00
5 Drew Bledsoe 1.25 3.00
6 Kordell Stewart .75 2.00
7 Jerry Rice 1.25 3.00
8 Warren Moon .40 1.00
9 Junior Seau .75 2.00
10 Barry Sanders 2.00 5.00
11 Jim Harbaugh .30 .75
12 John Elway 2.50 6.00
13 Brett Favre 2.50 6.00
14 Brett Favre 2.50 6.00
15 Troy Aikman 1.25 3.00
16 Emmitt Smith 2.00 5.00
17 Dan Marino 2.50 6.00
18 Kordell Stewart .75 2.00
19 John Elway 2.50 6.00
20 Kerry Collins .40 1.00
21 Jim Kelly .40 1.00
22 Drew Bledsoe 1.25 3.00
23 Mark Brunell 1.25 3.00
24 Jerry Rice 1.25 3.00
P1 Troy Aikman Promo 1.20 3.00
NNO Super Bowl XXXI Promo 8.00 20.00

1996 MotionVision Limited Digital Replays

The MotionVision Limited Digital Replays were randomly inserted into packs. Series one cards were produced in quantities of 2500 each, with series two at 3500 of each. They are easily distinguishable from the regular cards by the addition of a standard card-like back

COMPLETE SET (10) 40.00 100.00
COMP.SERIES 1 (6) 20.00 50.00
COMP.SERIES 2 (4) 20.00 50.00
LDR1-LDR6: RANDOM INSERTS IN SER.1
LDR1-LDR6 PRINT RUN 2500 SETS
LDR7-LDR10: RANDOM INSERTS IN SER.2
LDR7-LDR10 PRINT RUN 3500 SETS
LDR1 Troy Aikman 4.00 10.00
LDR1A Troy Aikman AU 60.00 120.00
LDR2 Dan Marino 10.00 20.00
LDR3 Steve Young 3.00 8.00
LDR3A Steve Young AU 50.00 100.00
LDR4 Emmitt Smith 7.50 15.00
LDR5 Drew Bledsoe 3.00 8.00
LDR5A Drew Bledsoe AU 50.00 100.00
LDR6 Kordell Stewart 3.00 8.00
LDR6A Kordell Stewart AU 40.00 80.00
LDR7 Brett Favre 10.00 20.00
LDR8 Brett Favre 10.00 20.00
LDR9 Emmitt Smith 7.50 15.00
LDR10 Kerry Collins 2.50 6.00

1997 MotionVision

The 1997 MotionVision series one football set consisted of 20-cards and was distributed in one-card packs with a suggested retail price of $6.99. Series two was released later after the season and contained just 8-cards. Printed on thick plastic, the cards feature Digital Film imaging technology which takes live actual game day footage from NFL Films, transfers them to a film emulsion, and plays back the action sequence on the card with the flick of a wrist.

COMPLETE SET (28) 25.00 60.00
COMP.SERIES 1 (20) 12.50 30.00
COMP.SERIES 2 (8) 15.00 30.00
1 Terrell Davis .60 1.50
2 Curtis Martin .60 1.50
3 Joey Galloway .50 1.25
4 Eddie George .75 2.00
5 Isaac Bruce .75 2.00
6 Antonio Freeman .75 2.00
7 Terry Glenn .40 1.00
8 Deion Sanders .75 2.00
9 Jerome Bettis .75 2.00
10 Reggie White .75 2.00
11 Brett Favre 2.00 5.00
12 Dan Marino 2.00 5.00
13 Emmitt Smith 1.50 4.00
14 Mark Brunell .60 1.50
15 John Elway 2.00 5.00
16 Drew Bledsoe .60 1.50
17 Barry Sanders 1.50 4.00
18 Jeff Blake .40 1.00
19 Kerry Collins .75 2.00
20 Jerry Rice 1.00 2.50
21 Dan Marino 2.00 5.00
22 Troy Aikman 1.00 2.50
23 Brett Favre 2.00 5.00
24 Emmitt Smith 1.50 4.00
25 Kordell Stewart .75 2.00
26 Terrell Davis .60 1.50
27 Eddie George .75 2.00
28 Drew Bledsoe .60 1.50

1997 MotionVision Jumbos

These 4-jumbo cards (roughly 3 7/8" X 5 5/8") were inserted one per box in 1997 MotionVision series 2. They include the typical MotionVision card design along with unique card numbering.

COMPLETE SET (4) 10.00 25.00
SS1 Brett Favre 3.00 8.00
SS2 Dan Marino 3.00 8.00
SS3 John Elway 3.00 8.00
SS4 Steve Young 2.50 3.00

1997 MotionVision Limited Digital Replays

Randomly inserted in packs at the rate of one in 25, the four-card series 1 set featured motion sequences of top players found in the base set along with a printed cardback. The series 2 LDR inserts were both numbered XVRR for "Extra Value Rookie Redemption." Each of the two was accompanied by a free mail order redemption card that was exchangeable for a numbered LDR card of that player. The redemption offer expires 12/31/1998.

COMPLETE SET (8) 25.00 60.00
COMP.SERIES 1 (4) 50.00 50.00
COMP.SERIES 2 (4) 25.00 20.00
STATED ODDS 1:25
LDR1 Terrell Davis 6.00 15.00
LDR1A Terrell Davis AU 30.00 80.00
LDR2 Curtis Martin 3.00 8.00
LDR3 Brett Favre 7.50 20.00
LDR4 Barry Sanders 7.50 20.00
LDR5 Warrick Dunn 4.00 10.00
LDR6 Antowain Smith 3.00 8.00
XVRR Warrick Dunn EXCH 3.00 8.00
XVRR Antowain Smith EXCH 2.50 6.00

1997 MotionVision Super Bowl XXXI

These four cards were made available via a redemption offer in 1996 MotionVision series 2 packs, as well as 1997 series 1 packs. There was one card made commemorating each Conference Championship game and one for Super Bowl XXXI. The fourth card features Favre during the Super Bowl using a jumbo format (roughly 5 5/8" by 3 3/4"). Each is numbered of 5000 cards produced.

COMPLETE SET (4) 30.00 75.00
1 Drew Bledsoe 6.00 15.00
2 Brett Favre 8.00 20.00
3 Brett Favre 8.00 20.00
4 Brett Favre Jumbo 8.00 20.00

1976 MSA Cups

This set of cups was produced by MSA and distributed at various outlets and stores in 1976. Each features a photo of the player without the use of team logos. It is thought that two different 20-cup sets were released throughout the country. Any additions to this list are appreciated.

1 Ken Anderson 4.00 8.00
2 Lem Barney 4.00 8.00
3 Steve Bartkowski 3.00 6.00
4 Fred Biletnikoff 5.00 10.00
5 Terry Bradshaw 12.00 25.00
6 Gary Danielson 2.50 5.00
7 Joe Ferguson 3.00 6.00
8 Chuck Foreman 3.00 6.00
9 Dan Fouts 6.00 12.00
10 Randy Gradishar 3.00 6.00
11 Bob Griese 6.00 12.00
12 Archie Griffin 3.00 6.00
13 Steve Grogan 3.00 6.00
14 Pat Haden 3.00 6.00
15 Jim Hart 2.50 5.00
16 Gary Huff 2.50 5.00
17 Ron Jaworski 3.00 6.00
18 Billy Johnson 2.50 5.00
19 Essex Johnson 2.50 5.00
20 Bert Jones 3.00 6.00
21 Billy Kilmer 3.00 6.00
22 Mike Livingston 2.50 5.00
23 Archie Manning 2.50 5.00
24 Ed Marinaro 4.00 8.00
25 Lawrence McCutchen 2.50 5.00
26 Craig Morton 3.00 6.00
27 Dan Pastorini 3.00 6.00
28 Walter Payton 25.00 40.00
29 Jim Plunkett 5.00 10.00
30 Greg Pruitt 2.50 5.00
31 John Riggins 6.00 12.00
32 Brian Sipe 3.00 6.00
33 Steve Spurrier 10.00 20.00
34 Roger Staubach 12.50 25.00
35 Mark Van Eeghen 3.00 6.00
36 Brad Van Pelt 2.50 5.00
37 David Whitehurst 2.50 5.00

1981 MSA Holsum Discs

This 32-disc set was produced by MSA, but apparently not widely distributed. Several brands of bread (including Holsum and Gardner's in Wisconsin) carried one football disc per specially marked loaf during the promotion. The discs are blank backed and are approximately 2 3/4" in diameter. Since they are unnumbered, they are listed below in alphabetical order. The discs are licensed only by the NFL Players Association and carry no sponsor logos or identification. There were also two different posters (Holsum and Gardner's) produced for holding and displaying the set. The key card in the set depicts Joe Montana in his rookie year for cards.

COMPLETE SET (32) 125.00 250.00
1 Ken Anderson 2.00 5.00
2 Ottis Anderson 1.50 4.00
3 Steve Bartkowski 1.50 4.00
4 Ricky Bell 1.25 3.00
5 Terry Bradshaw 8.00 20.00
6 Harold Carmichael 1.50 4.00
7 Joe Cribbs 1.25 3.00

8 Gary Danielson 1.25 3.00
9 Lynn Dickey 1.25 3.00
10 Dan Doornink 1.25 3.00
11 Vince Evans 1.25 3.00
12 Joe Ferguson 1.50 4.00
13 Vagas Ferguson 1.25 3.00
14 Dan Fouts 3.00 8.00
15 Steve Fuller 1.25 3.00
16 Archie Griffin 1.50 4.00
17 Steve Grogan 1.50 4.00
18 Bruce Harper 1.25 3.00
19 Jim Hart 1.50 4.00
20 Jim Jensen 1.25 3.00
21 Bert Jones 1.50 4.00
22 Archie Manning 2.00 5.00
23 Ted McKnight 1.25 3.00
24 Joe Montana 40.00 80.00
25 Craig Morton 1.50 4.00
26 Robert Newhouse 1.50 4.00
27 Phil Simms 4.00 10.00
28 Billy Taylor 1.25 3.00
29 Joe Theismann 2.50 6.00
30 Mark Van Eeghen 1.25 3.00
31 Delvin Williams 1.25 3.00
32 Tim Wilson 1.25 3.00
NNO Display Poster 10.00 25.00

1982 MSA QB Super Series Icee Cups

This series of cups was licensed through MSA and features one quarterback from each NFL team - although not always the starting QB. They were sponsored by Icee and Coca-Cola and include a black and white photo of the player surrounded by a star design. There is an artist's rendering of a football scene on the back of the cups.

COMPLETE SET (28) 150.00 300.00
1 Craig Morton 5.00 12.00
2 Dan Fouts 10.00 25.00
3 Danny White 6.00 15.00
4 Gary Danielson 4.00 10.00
5 Tommy Kramer 5.00 12.00
6 Matt Robinson 4.00 10.00
7 Ken Anderson 6.00 15.00
8 Tom Flick 4.00 10.00
9 Pat Ryan 4.00 10.00
10 Phil Simms 6.00 15.00
11 Gifford Nielsen 4.00 10.00
12 Steve Grogan 5.00 12.00
13 Brian Sipe 5.00 12.00
14 Bob Avellini 4.00 10.00
15 Joe Pisarcik 4.00 10.00
16 Cliff Stoudt 4.00 10.00
17 Steve Fuller 4.00 10.00
18 Archie Manning 6.00 15.00
19 Bert Jones 5.00 12.00
20 Dave Krieg 4.00 10.00
21 Don Strock 5.00 12.00
22 Marc Wilson 5.00 12.00
23 Lynn Dickey 4.00 10.00
24 Steve Bartkowski 6.00 15.00
25 Guy Benjamin 4.00 10.00
26 Art Schlichter 4.00 10.00
27 Jim Hart 5.00 12.00
28 Doug Williams 6.00 15.00

1990 MSA Superstars

This 12-card, 2 1/2" by 3 3/8", set was issued in boxes of (Ralston Purina) Staff and Food Club Frosted Flakes cereal. The cards were released as two cards in every box and a coupon was also inserted that enabled collectors to mail away and receive the set for 2 UPC symbol codes and postage and handling. These cards are unnumbered so we have checklisted them alphabetically. The fronts of the cards have the word "Superstars" on top of the players photo and his name and team underneath. The back of the card features personal information about the player and statistical information in a textual style. There are no team logos on the card as the cards apparently were issued with only the permission of the National Football League Players Association. There is no mention of MSA on the cards, but they are very similar to the Mike Schechter baseball issue for Ralston Purina so they have been cataloged as such.

COMPLETE SET (12) 20.00 40.00
1 Carl Banks .60 1.50
2 Cornelius Bennett .80 2.00
3 Roger Craig .80 2.00
4 Jim Everett .80 2.00
5 Bo Jackson 1.50 4.00
6 Ronnie Lott .80 2.00
7 Don Majkowski .60 1.50
8 Dan Marino 12.50 25.00
9 Karl Mecklenburg .60 1.50
10 Christian Okoye .60 1.50
11 Mike Singletary 1.00 2.50
12 Herschel Walker 1.00 2.50

2000 MTA MetroCard

These 4-cards are actually New York subway tickets to be used at MTA. Each features a color image of the player printed on a thin plastic stock. The backs feature the MTA logo and an electronic strip.

COMPLETE SET (4) 2.40 6.00
1 Kevin Mawae .60 1.50
2 Wayne Chrebet .80 2.00
3 Jason Sehorn .60 1.50
4 Michael Strahan .80 2.00

1990 MVP Pins

This set of pins was produced by Ace Novelties and distributed along with a regular issue 1990 Score football card. Each die cut pin includes a color photo of the player along with the pin number and "Ace 1990" notation on the back. The pins were mounted on a thick backer board that featured the team's helmet logo and "MVP" at the top of the card.

COMPLETE PIN SET (67) 25.00 50.00
1 Troy Aikman .75 2.00
2 Flipper Anderson .30 .75
3 Neal Anderson .30 .75
4 Ottis Anderson .30 .75
5 Mark Bavaro .30 .75
6 Cornelius Bennett .30 .75
7 Albert Bentley .30 .75
8 Duane Bickett .30 .75
9 Brian Blades .30 .75
10 Bubby Brister .40 1.00
11 James Brooks .30 .75
12 Tim Brown .50 1.25
13 Mark Carrier WR .40 1.00
14 Anthony Carter .30 .75
15 Deron Cherry .30 .75
16 Mark Clayton .30 .75
17 Roger Craig .40 1.00
18 Henry Ellard .40 1.00
19 John Elway 1.25 3.00
20 Boomer Esiason .50 1.25
21 Jim Everett .40 1.00
22 Roy Green .30 .75
23 Drew Hill .30 .75
24 Dalton Hilliard .30 .75
25 Bobby Humphrey .30 .75
26 Bo Jackson .50 1.25
27 Keith Jackson .30 .75
28 Bernie Kosar .40 1.00
29 Louis Lipps .30 .75
30 Eugene Lockhart .30 .75
31 Howie Long .40 1.00
32 Ronnie Lott .40 1.00
33 Don Majkowski .30 .75
34 Charles Mann .30 .75
35 Dan Marino 1.25 3.00
36 Freeman McNeil .30 .75
37 Karl Mecklenburg .30 .75
38 Eric Metcalf .30 .75
39 Keith Millard .30 .75
40 Anthony Miller .40 1.00
41 Chris Miller .40 1.00
42 Art Monk .40 1.00
43 Joe Montana 1.50 4.00
44 Warren Moon .50 1.25
45 Ozzie Newsome .40 1.00
46 Christian Okoye .30 .75
47 Mike Quick .30 .75
48 Jerry Rice .75 2.00
49 Mark Rypien .40 1.00
50 Barry Sanders 1.25 3.00
51 Deion Sanders .60 1.50
52 Sterling Sharpe .50 1.25
53 Phil Simms .50 1.25
54 Mike Singletary .40 1.00
55 Billy Ray Smith .30 .75
56 Bruce Smith .40 1.00
57 Chris Spielman .30 .75
58 John Stephens .30 .75
59 Lawrence Taylor .50 1.25
60 Vinny Testaverde .50 1.25
61 Andre Tippett .30 .75
62 Mike Tomczak .30 .75
63 Al Toon .40 1.00
64 Herschel Walker .40 1.00
65 Reggie White .50 1.25
66 John L. Williams .30 .75
67 Ickey Woods .30 .75
L1 Bears Logo .08 .25
L2 Bengals Logo .08 .25
L3 Bills Logo .08 .25
L4 Broncos Logo .20 .50
L5 Browns Logo .08 .25
L6 Buccaneers Logo .08 .25
L7 Cardinals Logo .08 .25
L8 Chargers Logo .08 .25
L9 Chiefs Logo .08 .25
L10 Colts Logo .08 .25
L11 Cowboys Logo .20 .50
L12 Dolphins Logo .20 .50
L13 Eagles Logo .08 .25
L14 Falcons Logo .08 .25
L15 49ers Logo .20 .50
L16 Giants Logo .08 .25
L17 Jets Logo .08 .25
L18 Lions Logo .08 .25
L19 Oilers Logo .08 .25
L20 Packers Logo .20 .50
L21 Patriots Logo .08 .25
L22 Raiders Logo .20 .50
L23 Rams Logo .08 .25
L24 Redskins Logo .20 .50
L25 Saints Logo .08 .25
L26 Seahawks Logo .08 .25
L27 Steelers Logo .08 .25
L28 Vikings Logo .08 .25

1974 Nabisco Sugar Daddy

This set of 25 tiny (approximately 1 1/16" by 2 3/4") cards features athletes from a variety of popular pro sports. One card was included in specially marked Sugar Daddy and Sugar Mama candy bars. The cards were designed to be placed on a 18" by 24" poster, which could only be obtained through a mail-in offer direct from Nabisco. The set is referred to as "Pro Faces" as the cards show an enlarged head photo with a small caricature body. Cards 1-10 are football players, cards 11-16 and 22 are hockey players, and cards 17-21 and 23-25 are basketball players. Each card was produced in two printings. The first printing has a copyright date of 1973 printed on the backs (although the cards are thought to have been released in early 1974) and the second printing is missing a copyright date altogether.

COMPLETE SET (25) 75.00 150.00
1 Roger Staubach 15.00 30.00
2 Floyd Little 2.50 6.00
3 Steve Owens 2.50 6.00
4 Roman Gabriel 2.50 6.00
5 Bobby Douglass 2.00 5.00
6 John Gilliam 2.00 5.00
7 Bob Lilly 5.00 10.00
8 John Brockington 2.00 5.00
9 Jim Plunkett 2.50 6.00
10 Greg Landry 2.00 5.00

1975 Nabisco Sugar Daddy

This set of 25 tiny (approximately 1 1/16" by 2 3/4") cards features athletes from a variety of popular pro sports. One card was included in specially marked Sugar Daddy and Sugar Mama candy bars. The cards were designed to be placed on a 18" by 24" poster, which could only be obtained through a mail-in offer direct from Nabisco. The set is referred to as "Sugar Daddy All-Stars". As with the set of the previous year, the cards show an enlarged head photo with a small caricature body with a flag background of stars and stripes. This set is referred on the back as Series No. 2 and has a red, white, and blue background behind the picture on the front of the card. Cards 1-10 are pro football players and the remainder are pro basketball (17-21, 23-25) and hockey (11-16, 22) players.

COMPLETE SET (25) 75.00 150.00
1 Roger Staubach 12.00 30.00
2 Floyd Little 2.50 6.00
3 Alan Page 2.50 6.00
4 Merlin Olsen 4.00 8.00
5 Wally Chambers 2.00 5.00
6 John Gilliam 2.00 5.00
7 Bob Lilly 4.00 10.00
8 John Brockington 2.00 5.00
9 Jim Plunkett 2.50 6.00
10 Willie Lanier 2.50 6.00

1976 Nabisco Sugar Daddy 1

This set of 25 tiny (approximately 1 1/16" by 2 3/4") cards features action scenes from a variety of popular sports from around the world. One card was included in specially marked Sugar Daddy and Sugar Mama candy bars. The set is referred to as "Sugar Daddy Sports World - Series 1" on the backs of the cards. The cards are in color with a relatively wide white border around the front of the cards.

COMPLETE SET (25) 40.00 80.00
6 Football 5.00 12.00
Charley Johnson

1976 Nabisco Sugar Daddy 2

This set of 25 tiny (approximately 1 1/16" by 2 3/4") cards features action scenes from a variety of popular sports from around the world. One card was included in specially marked Sugar Daddy and Sugar Mama candy bars. The set is referred to as "Sugar Daddy Sports World - Series 2" on the backs of the cards. The cards are in color with a relatively wide white border around the front of the cards.

COMPLETE SET (25) 40.00 80.00
4 Football 7.50 15.00
(Sonny Jurgensen)

1935 National Chicle

The 1935 National Chicle set was the first nationally distributed bubble gum set dedicated exclusively to football players. The cards measure 2 3/8" by 2 7/8". Card numbers 25 to 36 are more difficult to obtain than other cards in this set. The Knute Rockne and Bronko Nagurski cards are two of the most valuable football cards in existence. The set features NFL players except for the Rockne card. There are variations on the backs of each of the first series (1-24) cards with respect to the size of Eddie Casey's facsimile signature. The variation of Casey's name printed in larger letters appears to be in shorter supply and that larger name is the only version appearing on the backs of the high series (25-36) cards. This leads us to believe that the first series large name variations were inserted into high series packs. Please note that many different reprints of these cards exist (particularly Rockne and Nagurski) so caution should be taken before paying a large sum for a card. The original cards were printed with blue ink on the back not green. Some reprints feature the word "reprint" on the front or back while others do not. A close look at the dot pattern on the front of the card is a tell tale sign of a reprint card. The originals do not show a dot pattern under magnification.

COMPLETE SET (36) 10000.00 15000.00
COMMON CARD (1-24) 100.00 175.00
COMMON CARD (25-36) 400.00 600.00
WRAPPER (1-CENT) 200.00 400.00
1A Dutch Clark SN RC 300.00 600.00
1B Dutch Clark LN 500.00 900.00
2A Bo Molenda SN RC 100.00 175.00
2B Bo Molenda LN 150.00 250.00
3A George Kenneally SN RC 100.00 175.00
3B George Kenneally LN 150.00 250.00
4A Ed Matesic SN RC 100.00 175.00
4B Ed Matesic LN 150.00 250.00
4C Ed Matesic LN ERR
5A Glenn Presnell SN RC 100.00 175.00
5B Glenn Presnell LN 150.00 250.00
6A Pug Rentner SN RC 100.00 175.00
6B Pug Rentner LN 150.00 250.00
7A Ken Strong SN RC 250.00 400.00
7B Ken Strong LN 350.00 600.00
8A Jim Zyntell SN RC 100.00 175.00
8B Jim Zyntell LN 150.00 250.00
9A Knute Rockne CO SN 1000.00 1600.00
9B Knute Rockne CO LN 1200.00 2200.00
10A Cliff Battles SN RC 250.00 400.00
10B Cliff Battles LN 350.00 600.00
11A Turk Edwards SN RC 250.00 400.00
11B Turk Edwards LN 350.00 600.00
12A Tom Hupke SN RC 100.00 175.00
12B Tom Hupke LN 150.00 250.00
13A Homer Griffiths SN RC 100.00 175.00
13B Homer Griffiths LN 150.00 250.00
14A Phil Sarboe SN RC UER 100.00 175.00
14B Phil Sarboe LN UER 150.00 250.00
15A Ben Ciccone SN RC UER 100.00 175.00
15B Ben Ciccone LN 150.00 250.00
16A Ben Smith SN RC UER 100.00 175.00
16B Ben Smith LN 150.00 250.00
17A Tom Jones SN RC 100.00 175.00
17B Tom Jones LN 150.00 250.00
18A Mike Mikulak SN RC 100.00 175.00
18B Mike Mikulak LN 150.00 250.00
19 Ralph Kercheval SN RC UER 100.00 175.00
19B Ralph Kercheval LN COR 150.00 250.00
20A Warren Heller SN RC UER 100.00 175.00
20B Warren Heller LN 150.00 250.00
21A Cliff Montgomery SN RC 100.00 175.00
21B Cliff Montgomery LN 150.00 250.00
22A Shipwreck Kelly SN RC UER 100.00 175.00
22B Shipwreck Kelly LN UER 150.00 250.00
23A Beattie Feathers SN RC UER 175.00 300.00
23B Beattie Feathers LN 250.00 450.00
24A Clarke Hinkle SN RC UER 400.00 600.00
24B Clarke Hinkle LN 500.00 900.00
25 Dale Burnett RC 400.00 600.00
26 John Dell Isola RC 400.00 600.00
27 Bull Tosi RC 600.00 1000.00
28 Stan Kostka RC 400.00 600.00
29 Jim MacMurdo RC 400.00 600.00
30 Ernie Caddel RC 400.00 600.00
31 Nic Niccola RC 400.00 600.00
32 Swede Johnston RC 400.00 600.00
33 Ernie Smith RC 400.00 600.00
34 Bronko Nagurski RC 3500.00 5000.00
35 Luke Johnsos RC 400.00 600.00
36 Bernie Masterson RC 350.00 800.00

2004 National Trading Card Day

This 53-card set (49 basic cards plus four cover cards) was given out in five separate sealed packs (one from each of the following manufacturers: Donruss, Fleer, Press Pass, Topps and Upper Deck). One of the five packs was distributed at no cost to each patron that visited a participating sports card shop on April 3rd, 2004 as part of the National Trading Card Day promotion in an effort to increase awareness of collecting sports cards. The 50-card set is composed of 16 baseball, 9 basketball, 10 football, 4 golf, 5 hockey and 4 NASCAR cards. Of note, first year cards of NBA rookie stars LeBron James and Carmelo Anthony were included respectively within the UD and Fleer packs. An early Alex Rodriguez Yankees card was also highlighted within the Fleer pack.

F1-F9 ISSUED IN FLEER PACK
T1-T12 ISSUED IN TOPPS PACK
DP1-DP6 ISSUED IN DONRUSS PACK
PP1-PP7 ISSUED IN PRESS PASS PACK
UD1-UD15 ISSUED IN UPPER DECK PACK
F5 Brett Favre .75 2.00
F6 Marshall Faulk .30 .75
T5 Michael Vick .50 1.25
T6 Charles Rogers .20 .50
DP5 Anquan Boldin .20 .50
DP6 Ricky Williams .30 .75
PP6 Eli Manning 1.50 4.00
PP7 Roy Williams WR .40 1.00
UD9 Michael Vick .50 1.25
UD11 Peyton Manning .75 2.00

1999 New Jersey Red Dogs AFL

COMPLETE SET (33) 7.50 15.00
1 Alvin Ashley .30 .75
2 Henry Baker .30 .75
3 Wilke Bazile .30 .75
4 Jerome Brown .30 .75
5 Kevin Clemens .30 .75
6 Keita Crespina .30 .75
7 Rickey Foggie .30 .75
8 Harvie Herrington .30 .75
9 Pierre Hixon .30 .75
10 Latish Kinsler .30 .75
11 Willie Latta .30 .75
12 Chad Lindsey .30 .75
13 Adrian Lunsford .30 .75
14 Ron Perry .30 .75
15 Manny Pina .30 .75
16 Charles Puleri .30 .75
17 John Robinson .30 .75
18 Dimitrious Stanley .30 .75
19 Matthew Steeple .30 .75
20 Robert Stewart .30 .75
21 Larry Thompson .30 .75
22 Steve Videtich .30 .75
23 Jason Walters .30 .75
24 Jermaine Younger .30 .75
25 Frank Mattiace CO .30 .75
26 Frank Haege AHC .30 .75
27 Pete Costanza AC .30 .75
28 Amod Field AC .30 .75
29 Jeff Hoffman AC .30 .75
30 Joe Moss AC .30 .75
31 Team Mascot .30 .75
32 Fans .30 .75
33 Dance Team .30 .75

1992 NewSport

This set of 32 glossy player photos was sponsored by NewSport and issued in France. The month when each card was issued is printed as a tagline on the card back; four cards were issued per month from November 1991 to June 1992. The set was also available in four-card uncut strips. The cards measure approximately 4" by 6" and display glossy color player photos with white borders. The player's name and position appear in the top border, while the NewSport and NFL logos adorn the bottom of the card face. In French, the backs present biography, complete statistics, and career summary. The cards are unnumbered and checklisted below in alphabetical order.

COMPLETE SET (32) 50.00 120.00
1 Bubby Brister 1.25 3.00
2 James Brooks .75 2.00
3 Joey Browner .75 2.00
4 Gill Byrd .75 2.00
5 Eric Dickerson 1.25 3.00
6 Henry Ellard 1.25 3.00
7 John Elway 7.50 20.00
8 Mervyn Fernandez .75 2.00
9 David Fulcher .75 2.00
10 Ernest Givins .75 2.00
11 Jay Hilgenberg .75 2.00
12 Michael Irvin 2.00 5.00
13 Dave Krieg .75 2.00
14 Albert Lewis .75 2.00
15 James Lofton 1.25 3.00
16 Dan Marino 7.50 20.00
17 Wilber Marshall .75 2.00
18 Freeman McNeil .75 2.00
19 Karl Mecklenburg .75 2.00
20 Joe Montana 10.00 25.00
21 Christian Okoye .75 2.00
22 Michael Dean Perry .75 2.00
23 Tom Rathman .75 2.00
24 Mark Rypien .75 2.00
25 Barry Sanders 6.00 15.00
26 Deion Sanders 2.50 6.00
27 Sterling Sharpe 1.25 3.00
28 Pat Swilling .75 2.00
29 Lawrence Taylor 1.25 3.00
30 Vinny Testaverde 1.25 3.00
31 Andre Tippett .75 2.00
32 Reggie White 2.00 5.00

2008 New York Dragons AFL Donruss

This set was produced by Donruss and issued at a regular season Dragons game in 2008.

NYD1 Aaron Garcia .50 1.25
NYD2 Kevin Swayne .40 1.00
NYD3 Joe Laudano .40 1.00
NYD4 Chris Anthony .40 1.00
NYD5 Billy Parker .40 1.00
NYD6 Jason Willis .40 1.00
NYD7 Greg Randall .40 1.00
NYD8 Weylan Harding CO .40 1.00

1974 New York News This Day in Sports

These cards are newspaper clippings of drawings by Hollreiser and are accompanied by textual description highlighting a player's unique sports feat. Cards are approximately 2" X 4 1/4". These are multisport cards and aranged in chronological order.

COMPLETE SET 50.00 120.00
25 Doc Blanchard 1.50 3.00
Glenn Davis
Sept. 30, 1944
27 Archie Manning 1.50 3.00
Oct. 4, 1969
31 Harold Jackson 1.00 2.00
Oct. 14, 1973
32 O.J. Simpson 1.50 3.00
Oct. 21, 1967
33 Doc Blanchard 1.00 2.00
Nov. 11, 1944
35 Bronko Nagurski 1.50 3.00
Nov. 23, 1929
37 New York Giants 1.00 2.00
Dec. 9, 1934
38 John Brodie 1.00 2.00
Dec. 20, 1970
39 Roger Staubach 2.00 4.00
Dec. 23, 1972
40 Paul Brown 1.50 3.00
Otto Graham
Dec. 26, 1954

1974 New York Stars WFL Team Issue 8X10

The photos measure roughly 8" x 10" and include black and white images with the player's name centered below the photo, the team logo to the left and the player's position to the right. The backs are blank.

1 Howard Baldwin Pres. 5.00 10.00
2 Robert Keating VP 5.00 10.00
3 Babe Parilli CO 7.50 15.00

1991-92 NFL Experience

This 28-card set measures approximately 2 1/2" by 4 3/4" and has black borders around each picture. Produced by the NFL, this stylized card set highlights Super Bowl players and scenes. Card fronts run either horizontally or vertically and carry the NFL Experience logo at the bottom center. The backs are printed horizontally with the words "The NFL Experience" and card number appearing in black in a light pink bar at the top. The bottom pink bar carries a description of front artwork, while the center portion describes some aspect of NFL life. Sponsors' logos appear on the right portion of each back.

COMPLETE SET (28) 1.60 4.00
1 NFL Experience .10 .30
2 Super Bowl I .07 .20
3 Super Bowl II .20 .50
4 Super Bowl III .30 .75
5 Super Bowl IV .07 .20
6 Super Bowl V .07 .20
7 Super Bowl VI .25 .60
8 Super Bowl VII .07 .20
9 Super Bowl VIII .10 .30
10 Super Bowl IX .07 .20
11 Super Bowl X .10 .30
12 Super Bowl XI .10 .30
13 Super Bowl XIII .10 .30
14 Super Bowl XIII .07 .20
15 Super Bowl XIV .25 .60
16 Super Bowl XV .07 .20
17 Super Bowl XVI .07 .20
18 Super Bowl XVII .10 .30
19 Super Bowl XVIII .10 .30
20 Super Bowl XIX .07 .20
21 Super Bowl XX .10 .30
22 Super Bowl XXI .07 .20
23 Super Bowl XXII .30 .75
24 Super Bowl XXIII .07 .20
25 Super Bowl XXIV .50 1.25
26 Super Bowl XXV .07 .20
27 Super Bowl XXVI .07 .20
28 Joe Theismann .10 .30

1998 NFL Films Magic Motion 5x7

1 Troy Aikman 3.00 8.00
2 Peyton Manning
3 Jerry Rice 4.00 10.00
4 Barry Sanders 4.00 10.00
5 Emmitt Smith 4.00 10.00
6 Steve Young 2.50 6.00

1997 NFL-Opoly

This set of cards was issued as part of a Monopoly style board game using the NFL and it's players as the pieces. Each card features a color player photo on the cardfront with basic team information and game point value on the cardbacks. The cards were not numbered.

COMPLETE SET (14) 10.00 25.00
1 Troy Aikman 1.60 4.00
2 Jeff Blake .40 1.00
3 Drew Bledsoe 1.20 3.00
4 Dave Brown .20 .50
5 Mark Brunell 1.20 3.00
6 Kerry Collins .40 1.00
7 John Elway 3.20 8.00
8 Brett Favre 3.20 8.00
9 Jim Harbaugh .40 1.00
10 Dan Marino 3.20 8.00
11 Neil O'Donnell .20 .50
12 Jerry Rice 1.60 4.00
13 Barry Sanders 3.20 8.00
14 Kordell Stewart 1.20 3.00

2005 NFL Players Inc

These cards were issued by Players Inc at various events to promote the players they represent. Each oversized (roughly 3 1/4" by 4 1/8") card includes a posed photo shoot image of a player with variations in the photography for some players. The cardbacks include specific information about the Players Inc and their licensees.

1 Chad Johnson 1.00 2.50
Player Marketing, close-up photo
Holding a football in both hands
2 Ben Roethlisberger 4.00 10.00
Fantasy Football
Photo crushing a football
3 Ben Roethlisberger 4.00 10.00
Reebok, full body photo
4 Roy Williams S 1.00 2.50
Marketing and Appearances
Holding up his hands
5 Roy Williams S 1.00 2.50
Trading Card Licensees
Full body photo
6 Brian Westbrook 1.00 2.50
Fantasy Football
Full body photo

1972 NFL Properties Cloth Patches

This set of team logos and team helmet stickers was produced by NFL Properties in 1972. Each measures roughly 1 1/2" by 1 3/4" and was printed on cloth sticker stock with a blank back. The stickers closely resemble the early cloth patches used in many of the Fleer releases from that era. It is thought by many hobbyists that this set was actually released in Schwebel Bread products in 1975.

COMPLETE SET (52) 150.00 300.00
1 Chicago Bears 3.00 6.00
2 Chicago Bears 3.00 6.00
3 Cincinnati Bengals 3.00 6.00
(logo)
4 Cincinnati Bengals 3.00 6.00
(helmet)
5 Buffalo Bills 3.00 6.00
(logo)
6 Buffalo Bills 3.00 6.00
(helmet)
7 Denver Broncos 3.00 6.00
(logo)
8 Denver Broncos 3.00 6.00
(helmet)
9 Cleveland Browns 5.00 10.00
(logo)
10 Cleveland Browns 4.00 8.00
(helmet)
11 St.Louis Cardinals 3.00 6.00
(logo)
12 St.Louis Cardinals 3.00 6.00
(helmet)
13 San Diego Chargers 3.00 6.00
(logo)
14 San Diego Chargers 3.00 6.00
(helmet)
15 Kansas City Chiefs 3.00 6.00
(logo)
16 Kansas City Chiefs 3.00 6.00
(helmet)
17 Baltimore Colts 3.00 6.00
(logo)
18 Baltimore Colts 3.00 6.00
(helmet)
19 Dallas Cowboys 5.00 10.00
(logo)
20 Dallas Cowboys 5.00 10.00
(helmet)
21 Miami Dolphins 5.00 10.00
(logo)
22 Miami Dolphins 5.00 10.00
(helmet)
23 Philadelphia Eagles 3.00 6.00
(logo)
24 Philadelphia Eagles 3.00 6.00
(helmet)
25 Atlanta Falcons 3.00 6.00
(logo)
26 Atlanta Falcons 3.00 6.00
(helmet)
27 San Francisco 49ers 4.00 8.00
(logo)
28 San Francisco 49ers 4.00 8.00
(helmet)
29 New York Giants 4.00 8.00
(logo)
30 New York Giants 4.00 8.00
(helmet)
31 New York Jets 3.00 6.00
(logo)
32 New York Jets 3.00 6.00
(helmet)
33 Detroit Lions 3.00 6.00
(logo)
34 Detroit Lions 3.00 6.00
(helmet)
35 Houston Oilers 3.00 6.00
(logo)
36 Houston Oilers 3.00 6.00
(helmet)
37 Green Bay Packers 4.00 8.00
(logo)
38 Green Bay Packers 4.00 8.00
(helmet)
39 New England Patriots 3.00 6.00
(logo)
40 New England Patriots 3.00 6.00
(helmet)
41 Oakland Raiders 5.00 10.00
(logo)
42 Oakland Raiders 5.00 10.00
{(helmet)
43 Los Angeles Rams 3.00 6.00
(logo)
44 Los Angeles Rams 3.00 6.00
(helmet)
45 Washington Redskins 5.00 10.00
(logo)
46 Washington Redskins 5.00 10.00
(helmet)
47 New Orleans Saints 3.00 6.00
(logo)
48 New Orleans Saints 3.00 6.00
(helmet)
49 Pittsburgh Steelers 4.00 8.00
(logo)
50 Pittsburgh Steelers 4.00 8.00
(helmet)
51 Minnesota Vikings 4.00 8.00
(logo)
52 Minnesota Vikings 4.00 8.00
(helmet)

1983 NFL Properties Huddles

These cards were produced by NFL Properties and distributed in various licensed products including Avon soaps. Each card features the Huddle character on the front along with the 1983 copyright line. The cardbacks provide a brief team history.

COMPLETE SET (28) 20.00 50.00
1 Atlanta Falcons .60 1.50
2 Buffalo Bills .75 2.00
3 Chicago Bears .75 2.00
4 Cincinnati Bengals .60 1.50
5 Cleveland Browns .75 2.00
6 Dallas Cowboys 1.25 3.00
7 Denver Broncos .75 2.00
8 Detroit Lions .60 1.50
9 Green Bay Packers 1.25 3.00
10 Houston Oilers .60 1.50
11 Indianapolis Colts .60 1.50
12 Kansas City Chiefs .60 1.50
13 Los Angeles Raiders 1.25 3.00
14 Los Angeles Rams .60 1.50
15 Miami Dolphins 1.25 3.00
16 Minnesota Vikings .75 2.00
17 New England Patriots .60 1.50
18 New Orleans Saints .60 1.50
19 New York Giants .75 2.00
20 New York Jets .75 2.00
21 Philadelphia Eagles .60 1.50
22 Pittsburgh Steelers 1.25 3.00
23 St. Louis Cardinals .60 1.50
24 San Diego Chargers .60 1.50
25 San Francisco 49ers 1.25 3.00
26 Seattle Seahawks .60 1.50
27 Tampa Bay Buccaneers .60 1.50
28 Washington Redskins .75 2.00

1987 NFL Properties Milk Cartons

3H Herschel Walker 3.00 8.00
4H John Elway 6.00 15.00

1993 NFL Properties Santa Claus

The first Santa Claus card produced by an NFL trading card licensee was in 1989. In 1993, each of the 12 trading card licensees produced an NFL Santa Claus Card, and the entire set, which included a checklist card issued by NFL Properties, was offered through a special mail-away offer for any 30 1993 NFL trading card wrappers and 1.50 for postage and handling. The cards were sent out to dealers along with a season's greeting card. All the cards measure the standard size and feature different artistic renderings of Santa Claus on their fronts and season's greetings on their backs. Although some cards are numbered while others are not, the cards are checklisted below alphabetically according to the licensee's name.

COMPLETE SET (13) 6.00 15.00
1 Santa Claus .50 1.25
2 Santa Claus .50 1.25
3 Santa Claus .50 1.25
4 Santa Claus .50 1.25
5 Santa Claus .50 1.25
6 Santa Claus .50 1.25
7 Santa Claus .50 1.25
8 Santa Claus .50 1.25
9 Santa Claus .50 1.25
10 Santa Claus .50 1.25
11 Santa Claus 2.00 5.00
Montana
12 Santa Claus .50 1.25
13 Checklist Card .50 1.25

1993-95 NFL Properties Show Redemption Cards

Produced by NFL Properties and handed out to attendees at card shows, these oversized cards measure approximately 3 1/2" by 5" and feature on their fronts collages of player portraits and/or photos. A banner at the top of each card carries the city and dates that the show was held. On the card given out at the National in Chicago, each of the honored players has signed the card in silver ink. The card given out in St. Louis, listed below as 4B, replaced 4A, which was done to commemorate the St. Louis Stallions NFL franchise that never materialized and so was not released. One thousand of 4B were distributed each of the three days of the show, making a total of 3,000. The white back of each card carries text about the players depicted on the front (except card number 2, the back of which carries the 49ers 1993 schedule) and the individual serial number out of the total produced. Card 4B also carries the date that the card was distributed next to the "X of 1000" production figure. Except for the first card, the cards are numbered on the back in Roman numerals. The 49ers card was available at the Team NFL booth at the 1993 San Francisco Labor Day Sports Collector's Convention in exchange for ten wrappers from any licensed 1993 NFL card product. Card number 6A was given to attendees of the Cocktail Reception sponsored by NFL Properties at the 15th National Sports Collectors Convention. The three featured players autographed the card in blue ink. Card number 6B was issued as part of a Back-to-School promotion; collectors redeemed two proofs-of-purchase for this oversized Elway card and an NFL FACT card.

COMPLETE SET (9) 360.00 900.00
1 Chicago Saluting 60.00 150.00
2 San Francisco Labor 12.00 30.00
3 San Francisco Labor 10.00 25.00
3AU Y.A. Tittle 80.00 200.00
Ken Stabler AUTO
4B St. Louis Saluting 4.00 10.00
5 Dallas Cowboys Champs 8.00 20.00
6A Houston Oilers 80.00 200.00
Stabler
Campbell
Pastor.
6B John Elway 80.00 200.00
7 Joe Namath 100.00 250.00
John Elway AUTO

1994 NFL Properties Back to School

The NFL developed this 11-card standard-size set for football fans and card collectors. The set was available to collectors who sent 20 wrappers from any NFL-licensed trading cards to the NFL '94 Back-to-School Offer address in Minnesota by Nov. 30, 1994. The set features one standard-size card from each of the major licensed football card manufacturers. As originally conceived, the set included a Brett Favre card by Pro Set, but NFL Properties was unable to include this card in the set since Pro Set went out of business. All cards feature on their backs the NFL Back-to-School logo and a message on the importance of staying in school. Only the Action Packed (BS1) and Upper Deck (#19) cards are numbered on the backs. The cards are checklisted below alphabetically according to card manufacturers.

COMPLETE SET (11) 6.00 15.00
1 NFL Quarterback Club .30 .75
2 Emmitt Smith 1.20 3.00
3 John Elway 1.20 3.00
4 Jerome Bettis .40 1.00
5 Sterling Sharpe .30 .75
6 Drew Bledsoe .80 2.00
7 Dana Stubblefield .20 .50
8 Jim Kelly .30 .75
9 Jerry Rice .80 2.00
10 Joe Montana 1.20 3.00
11 Checklist .20 .50

1994 NFL Properties Santa Claus

In 1994, each of the ten trading card licensees produced an NFL Santa Claus card. Collectors could obtain the set by sending in 20 wrappers of any participating football card manufacturer and 1.50 for postage and handling. The offer expired on March 31, 1995, or earlier should NFL Properties run out of cards. All the cards measure the standard-size and feature different artistic renderings of Santa Claus on their fronts and season's greetings on their backs. Though some cards are numbered while others are not, all the cards are listed below alphabetically according to licensee's name.

COMPLETE SET (11) 4.00 10.00
1 Santa Claus Action Packed .50 1.25
2 Santa Claus Classic .50 1.25
3 Santa Claus Collector's Edge .50 1.25
4 Santa Claus Fleer .50 1.25
5 Santa Claus Pacific .50 1.25
6 Santa Claus Pinnacle .50 1.25
7 Santa Claus Playoff .50 1.25
8 Santa Claus/J.Kelly 1.00 2.50
9 Santa Claus Topps .50 1.25
10 Santa Claus Upper Deck .50 1.25
11 Checklist NFL Properties .50 1.25

1995 NFL Properties Back to School

NFL Properties developed this set for football fans and card collectors. The set was available to collectors via a wrapper redemption prgram just like the 1994 set. The set features one standard-size card from each of the major licensed football card manufacturers. All cards feature on their backs the NFL Back-to-School logo and a message on the importance of staying in school. Some of the cards are numbered on the backs similar to that player's base set card. We've cataloged the cards below in alphabetical oder.

COMPLETE SET (9) 4.80 12.00
1 Troy Aikman .60 1.50
Drew Bledsoe
(Pinnacle)
2 John Elway 1.20 3.00
(NFL Properties)
3 Michael Irvin .30 .75
(Fleer)
4 Natrone Means .20 .50
(Pacific)
5 Rick Mirer .20 .50
(Playoff)
6 Joe Montana 1.20 3.00
(Collector's Choice)
7 Junior Seau .30 .75
(Collector's Edge)
8 Emmitt Smith 1.00 2.50
(Pro Line)
9 Steve Young .40 1.00
(Topps)

1995 NFL Properties Santa Claus

This nine-card set consists of Santa Claus cards produced by the eight NFL trading card licensees and features different artistic renderings of Santa Claus and season's greetings. The cards are listed below alphabetically according to the licensee's name. Collectors could obtain the set by sending in 20 wrappers of any participating football card manufacturer and $1.50 for postage and handling. The offer expired on March 31, 1996.

COMPLETE SET (9) 4.00 10.00
1 Title Card .40 1.00
Santa and friend
2 Santa Claus 1.00 2.50
Classic
3 Santa Claus .40 1.00
Collector's Edge
4 Santa Claus .40 1.00
Pacific
5 Santa Claus 1.20 3.00
Pinnacle
6 Santa Claus .40 1.00
Playoff
7 Santa Claus .40 1.00
Skybox
8 Santa Claus .40 1.00
Topps
9 Santa Claus .40 1.00
Upper Deck

1996 NFL Properties Back to School

The NFL developed this 9-card standard-size set to promote football card collecting. The set was available to collectors who sent 20 wrappers from any NFL-licensed trading card set and $1.50 postage to the NFL '96 Back-to-School Collector's Set address in Minnesota by Nov. 30, 1996. The set features one standard-size card from each of the major licensed football card manufacturers. The cards are checklisted below alphabetically.

COMPLETE SET (9) 4.80 12.00
1 Steve Bono .30 .75
Collector's Edge
2 John Elway 1.00 2.50
NFL Properties
3 Brett Favre 1.00 2.50
SkyBox Impact
4 Jerry Rice 1.00 2.50
Collector's Choice
5 Dan Marino .80 2.00
Steve Young
6 Deion Sanders .40 1.00
Playoff
7 Emmitt Smith .80 2.00
Classic
8 Chris Warren .20 .50
Pacific
9 Steve Young .40 1.00
Topps

1996 NFL Properties Santa Claus

This nine-card set consists of Santa Claus cards produced by the eight NFL trading card licensees and features different artistic renderings of Santa Claus and season's greetings. The cards are listed below alphabetically according to the licensee's name. Collectors could obtain the set by sending in 20 wrappers of any participating football card manufacturer and $1.50 for postage and handling. The offer expired on March 31, 1997.

COMPLETE SET (9) 4.00 10.00
1 Title Card .30 .75
Santa
2 S.Claus .30 .75
J.Blake
S.Bono
3 S.Claus 1.20 3.00
Favre
Fleer
Skybox
4 Santa Claus .30 .75
Pacific
5 S.Claus .80 2.00
Bledsoe
Harbaugh
Pinnacle
6 Santa Claus .30 .75
Playoff
7 San.Claus .80 2.00
Aikman
Score Board
8 Santa Claus .30 .75
Topps
9 Santa Claus .30 .75
Upper Deck

1996 NFL Properties 7-Eleven

NFL Properties and 7-Eleven stores teamed to distribute this 9-card set promoting football card collecting. Each card was available through 7-Eleven stores three per month (October-December) during the 1996 NFL season. A collector was required to send in two football card wrappers and a sales receipt from the 7-Eleven store along with $1 postage to receive one of the nine cards. A different NFL licensed trading card manufacturer produced each card.

COMPLETE SET (9) 10.00 25.00
1 John Elway 2.00 5.00
2 Jerry Rice 1.00 2.50
3 Dan Marino 2.00 5.00
4 Barry Sanders 2.00 5.00
5 Kordell Stewart .60 1.50
6 Steve Young .80 2.00
7 Joe Namath 1.00 2.50
8 Brett Favre 2.00 5.00
9 Trent Dilfer .30 .75

1997 NFL Properties Santa Claus

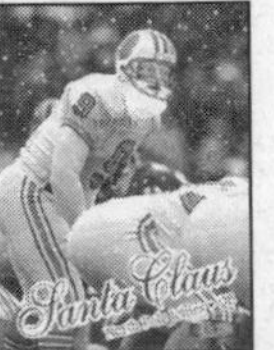

This eight card standard-size set continued the tradition of all the NFL card manufacturers combining to make a special holiday set. As with previous sets, one could receive this set in return for sending in wrappers and a small amount of money for a redemption.

COMPLETE SET (8) 3.20 8.00
1 Title Card .20 .50
Santa

2 S.Claus .20 .50
3 S.Claus 1.00 2.50
Bledsoe
K.Collins
Marino
4 Santa Claus .30 .75
Playoff
5 San.Claus 1.20 3.00
Favre
6 Santa Claus .20 .50
Topps
7 Santa Claus .30 .75
Ultra
S.McNair
8 Santa Claus .60 1.50
Upper Deck

2002 NFL Properties Punt, Pass, and Kick

This 10-card set was distributed as prizes at the NFL Properties Punt, Pass and Kick contest. Each card features color action photos, and the PPK logo. Each of the five major football manufacturers produced two cards for the set.

COMPLETE SET (10) 7.50 20.00
1 Troy Aikman/Fleer 1.25 3.00
2 Drew Bledsoe/Pacific 1.25 3.00
3 Randall Cunningham/Donruss .75 2.00
4 Brett Favre/Donruss 2.50 6.00
5 Bert Jones/Fleer .75 2.00
6 Jim Kelly/Topps .75 2.00
7 Bernie Kosar/Upper Deck .75 2.00
8 Dan Marino/Upper Deck 3.00 8.00
9 Vinny Testaverde/Topps .75 2.00
10 Danny White/Pacific .75 2.00

2001 NFL Showdown 1st Edition

The 2001 NFL Showdown product was released in mid-2001 as a 462-card football strategy game. Although the packaging and the cardbacks identifies the year of release as 2002, it is considered a 2001 year set. The 1st Edition cards were printed with a silver stamp on the front of the card reading 1st Edition. The set features 400-regular player cards and 62-foil cards that were short printed. The 1st Edition packs were released as eleven-card packs with seven player cards, two Strategy cards, and two Play cards per pack. The packs carried a suggested retail price of $2.99.

COMP.SET w/o FOILS (400) 20.00 50.00
1 Cary Blanchard .25 .60
2 David Boston .25 .60
3 Rob Fredrickson .25 .60
4 MarTay Jenkins .25 .60
5 Thomas Jones .25 .60
6 Tom Knight .25 .60
7 Kwamie Lassiter .25 .60
8 Ronald McKinnon FOIL .50 1.25
9 Michael Pittman .30 .75
10 Jake Plummer .25 .60
11 Frank Sanders .25 .60
12 L.J. Shelton .25 .60
13 Pat Tillman RC 6.00 15.00
14 Aeneas Williams .25 .60
15 Ashley Ambrose .25 .60
16 Morten Andersen .25 .60
17 Jamal Anderson .30 .75
18 Ronnie Bradford .25 .60
19 Ray Buchanan FOIL .50 1.25
20 Chris Chandler .30 .75
21 Henri Crockett .25 .60
22 Travis Hall .25 .60
23 Edward Jasper RC .25 .60
24 Shawn Jefferson .25 .60
25 Terance Mathis .25 .60
26 Ephraim Salaam RC .25 .60
27 Brady Smith .25 .60
28 Bob Whitfield .25 .60
29 Sam Adams .25 .60
30 Tony Banks .25 .60
31 Rob Burnett .25 .60
32 Trent Dilfer .25 .60
33 Kim Herring .25 .60
34 Priest Holmes .25 .60
35 Qadry Ismail .25 .60
36 Jamal Lewis FOIL .75 2.00
37 Ray Lewis FOIL .75 2.00
38 Michael McCrary FOIL .50 1.25
39 Edwin Mulitalo RC .25 .60
40 Jonathan Ogden FOIL .60 1.50
41 Shannon Sharpe .30 .75
42 Jamie Sharper .25 .60
43 Matt Stover .25 .60
44 Rod Woodson .40 1.00
45 Ruben Brown .25 .60
46 Keion Carpenter RC .25 .60
47 Steve Christie .25 .60
48 Sam Cowart FOIL .50 1.25
49 Doug Flutie FOIL .60 1.50
50 Rob Johnson .30 .75
51 Henry Jones .25 .60
52 Sammy Morris .25 .60
53 Eric Moulds .25 .60
54 Keith Newman RC .25 .60
55 Jay Riemersma .25 .60
56 Sam Rogers .25 .60
57 Ted Washington .25 .60
58 Marcellus Wiley .25 .60
59 Steve Beuerlein .30 .75
60 Tim Biakabutuka .25 .60
61 Isaac Byrd .25 .60
62 Eric Davis .25 .60
63 Doug Evans .25 .60
64 Sean Gilbert .25 .60
65 Donald Hayes .25 .60
66 Mike Minter FOIL RC .60 1.50
67 Muhsin Muhammad FOIL .50 1.25
68 Joe Nedney .25 .60
69 Chris Terry .25 .60
70 Wesley Walls .25 .60
71 Reggie White .40 1.00
72 Lee Woodall .25 .60
73 James Allen .25 .60
74 Mike Brown .25 .60
75 Phillip Daniels .25 .60
76 Paul Edinger .25 .60
77 Jim Flanigan .25 .60
78 Walt Harris .25 .60
79 Eddie Kennison .30 .75
80 Cade McNown .30 .75
81 Glyn Milburn .25 .60
82 Tony Parrish .25 .60
83 Marcus Robinson .30 .75
84 Brian Urlacher FOIL 1.00 2.50
85 Chris Villarrial RC .25 .60
86 James Williams .25 .60
87 Willie Anderson .25 .60
88 Chris Carter RC .25 .60
89 Tom Carter .25 .60
90 John Copeland .25 .60
91 Corey Dillon .25 .60
92 Steve Foley RC .25 .60
93 Oliver Gibson .25 .60
94 Tony McGee .25 .60
95 Matt O'Dwyer .25 .60
96 Akili Smith .25 .60
97 Armegis Spearman .25 .60
98 Takeo Spikes FOIL .50 1.25
99 Peter Warrick .25 .60
100 Darryl Williams .25 .60
101 Jim Bundren RC .25 .60
102 Stalin Colinet .25 .60
103 Tim Couch FOIL .50 1.25
104 Phil Dawson .25 .60
105 Percy Ellsworth .25 .60
106 Kevin Johnson .25 .60
107 Daylon McCutcheon .25 .60
108 Keith McKenzie .25 .60
109 Jamir Miller .25 .60
110 Roman Oben .25 .60
111 Doug Pederson .25 .60
112 Travis Prentice .25 .60
113 Wali Rainer .25 .60
114 Aaron Shea .25 .60
115 Troy Aikman .50 1.25
116 Larry Allen .40 1.00
117 Randall Cunningham .30 .75
118 Ebenezer Ekuban .25 .60
119 Jackie Harris .30 .75
120 Leon Lett .25 .60
121 James McKnight .25 .60
122 Solomon Page RC .25 .60
123 Izell Reese RC .25 .60
124 Tim Seder .25 .60
125 Emmitt Smith FOIL 1.25 3.00
126 Phillippi Sparks .25 .60
127 Mark Stepnoski .25 .60
128 Barron Wortham .25 .60
129 Mike Anderson FOIL .50 1.25
130 Eric Brown .25 .60
131 Dwayne Carswell FOIL .50 1.25
132 Desmond Clark .25 .60
133 Brian Griese FOIL .50 1.25
134 Billy Jenkins .25 .60
135 Tony Jones .25 .60
136 Ed McCaffrey .30 .75
137 John Mobley .25 .60
138 Tom Nalen .25 .60
139 Kavika Pittman .25 .60
140 Trevor Pryce .25 .60
141 Bill Romanowski .30 .75
142 Rod Smith .30 .75
143 Jimmy Spencer .25 .60
144 Al Wilson .25 .60
145 Charlie Batch .25 .60
146 Stephen Boyd .25 .60
147 Germane Crowell .25 .60
148 Luther Elliss .25 .60
149 Aaron Gibson .25 .60
150 Desmond Howard FOIL .60 1.50
151 James Jones .25 .60
152 Herman Moore .25 .60
153 Johnnie Morton .30 .75
154 Robert Porcher .25 .60
155 Kurt Schulz .25 .60
156 David Sloan .25 .60
157 James Stewart .25 .60
158 Bryant Westbrook .25 .60
159 LeRoy Butler .30 .75
160 Santana Dotson .25 .60
161 Brett Favre FOIL 1.50 4.00
162 Mike Flanagan RC .25 .60
163 Bubba Franks .25 .60
164 Antonio Freeman .40 1.00
165 Ahman Green .30 .75
166 Bernardo Harris .25 .60
167 Ryan Longwell .30 .75
168 Marco Rivera RC .25 .60
169 Bill Schroeder .30 .75
170 Darren Sharper FOIL .60 1.50
171 Nate Wayne RC .25 .60
172 Tyrone Williams .25 .60
173 Jason Belser .25 .60
174 Chad Bratzke .25 .60
175 Jeff Burris .25 .60
176 Ken Dilger .25 .60
177 Tarik Glenn .25 .60
178 Marvin Harrison FOIL .60 1.50
179 Waverly Jackson RC .25 .60
180 Edgerrin James FOIL .60 1.50
181 Ellis Johnson .25 .60
182 Peyton Manning FOIL 2.00 5.00
183 Adam Meadows RC .25 .60
184 Jerome Pathon .25 .60
185 Mike Peterson .25 .60
186 Marcus Pollard .25 .60
187 Terrence Wilkins .25 .60
188 Josh Williams RC .25 .60
189 Aaron Beasley .25 .60
190 Tony Boselli .30 .75
191 Tony Brackens .25 .60
192 Kyle Brady .25 .60
193 Mark Brunell .30 .75
194 Donovin Darius .25 .60
195 Todd Fordham RC .25 .60
196 Kevin Hardy .25 .60
197 Mike Hollis .25 .60
198 Keenan McCardell .30 .75
199 Jimmy Smith FOIL .60 1.50
200 Brendan Stai .25 .60
201 Fred Taylor FOIL .50 1.25
202 Gary Walker RC .25 .60
203 Derrick Alexander .25 .60
204 Kimble Anders .25 .60
205 Duane Clemons FOIL .50 1.25
206 Donnie Edwards .25 .60
207 Tony Gonzalez FOIL .60 1.50
208 Elvis Grbac .30 .75
209 James Hasty .25 .60
210 Eric Hicks RC .40 1.00
211 Sylvester Morris .25 .60
212 Marvcus Patton .25 .60
213 Tony Richardson .25 .60
214 John Tait .25 .60
215 Greg Wesley .25 .60
216 Dan Williams .25 .60
217 Trace Armstrong .25 .60
218 Mark Dixon RC .25 .60
219 Kevin Donnalley .25 .60
220 Jay Fiedler .30 .75
221 Oronde Gadsden .25 .60
222 Larry Izzo .25 .60
223 Sam Madison .25 .60
224 Olindo Mare .25 .60
225 Brock Marion .25 .60
226 Tim Ruddy .25 .60
227 Leslie Shepherd .25 .60
228 Lamar Smith .30 .75
229 Patrick Surtain .25 .60
230 Jason Taylor FOIL .75 2.00
231 Zach Thomas FOIL .60 1.50
232 Brian Walker .25 .60
233 Gary Anderson .25 .60
234 Matt Birk RC .25 .60
235 Cris Carter .40 1.00
236 Daunte Culpepper FOIL .60 1.50
237 Cris Dishman .25 .60
238 Robert Griffith .25 .60
239 Corbin Lacina .25 .60
240 Ed McDaniel .25 .60
241 Randy Moss FOIL .60 1.50
242 John Randle .30 .75
243 Talance Sawyer RC .25 .60
244 Robert Smith FOIL .50 1.25
245 Todd Steussie FOIL .50 1.25
246 Robert Tate .25 .60
247 Orlando Thomas .25 .60
248 Kailee Wong .25 .60
249 Drew Bledsoe .30 .75
250 Troy Brown .25 .60
251 Chad Eaton .25 .60
252 Kevin Faulk .25 .60
253 Terry Glenn .30 .75
254 Ty Law .40 1.00
255 Willie McGinest FOIL .50 1.25
256 Lawyer Milloy .25 .60
257 J.R. Redmond .25 .60
258 Chris Slade .25 .60
259 Greg Spires RC .25 .60
260 Henry Thomas .25 .60
261 Adam Vinatieri .25 .60
262 Grant Williams RC .25 .60
263 Jeff Blake FOIL .60 1.50
264 Andrew Glover .25 .60
265 La'Roi Glover FOIL .50 1.25
266 Joe Horn .25 .60
267 Darren Howard .25 .60
268 Willie Jackson .25 .60
269 Joe Johnson .25 .60
270 Sammy Knight .25 .60
271 Keith Mitchell RC .25 .60
272 Alex Molden .25 .60
273 Chris Naeole .25 .60
274 William Roaf .25 .60
275 Darrin Smith .25 .60
276 Kyle Turley .25 .60
277 Fred Weary .25 .60
278 Ricky Williams .30 .75
279 Jessie Armstead FOIL .50 1.25
280 Tiki Barber .30 .75
281 Micheal Barrow .25 .60
282 Lomas Brown .25 .60
283 Kerry Collins .25 .60
284 Ron Dayne .30 .75
285 Keith Hamilton .25 .60
286 Ike Hilliard .25 .60
287 Emmanuel McDaniel RC .25 .60
288 Pete Mitchell .25 .60
289 Ryan Phillips RC .25 .60
290 Jason Sehorn FOIL .60 1.50
291 Michael Strahan FOIL .60 1.50
292 Amani Toomer .25 .60
293 Shaun Williams .25 .60
294 Dusty Zeigler RC .25 .60
295 Richie Anderson .25 .60
296 Wayne Chrebet .25 .60
297 Marcus Coleman .25 .60
298 Bryan Cox .30 .75
299 Shaun Ellis .25 .60
300 Aaron Glenn .30 .75
301 Victor Green .25 .60
302 John Hall .25 .60
303 Marvin Jones .25 .60
304 Mo Lewis .25 .60
305 Curtis Martin .30 .75
306 Kevin Mawae .25 .60
307 Vinny Testaverde .25 .60
308 Randy Thomas RC .25 .60
309 Dedric Ward .25 .60
310 Ryan Young FOIL RC .50 1.25
311 Eric Allen .30 .75
312 Greg Biekert .25 .60
313 Tim Brown FOIL .75 2.00
314 Tony Bryant .25 .60
315 Mo Collins .25 .60
316 Rich Gannon FOIL .60 1.50
317 Grady Jackson RC .25 .60
318 Marquez Pope .25 .60
319 Andre Rison .30 .75
320 Barrett Robbins .25 .60
321 Darrell Russell .25 .60
322 Matt Stinchcomb .25 .60
323 William Thomas .25 .60
324 Tyrone Wheatley .30 .75
325 Steve Wisniewski .25 .60
326 Charles Woodson FOIL .75 2.00
327 Darnell Autry .25 .60
328 Mike Caldwell .25 .60
329 Brian Dawkins .25 .60
330 Hugh Douglas FOIL .50 1.25
331 Carlos Emmons .25 .60
332 Charles Johnson .25 .60
333 Chad Lewis .25 .60
334 Jermane Mayberry .25 .60
335 Donovan McNabb FOIL .60 1.50
336 Jon Runyan .25 .60
337 Corey Simon .25 .60
338 Torrance Small .25 .60
339 Dobby Taylor .25 .60
340 Hollis Thomas .25 .60
341 Jeremiah Trotter .25 .60
342 Troy Vincent FOIL .60 1.50
343 Brent Alexander .25 .60
344 Jerome Bettis .40 1.00
345 Kris Brown .25 .60
346 Mark Bruener .30 .75
347 Lethon Flowers .25 .60
348 Jason Gildon FOIL .50 1.25
349 Kent Graham .30 .75
350 Joey Porter RC .75 2.00
351 Chad Scott .25 .60
352 Bobby Shaw .25 .60
353 Kordell Stewart .25 .60
354 Rich Tylski .25 .60
355 Hines Ward .30 .75
356 Dewayne Washington .25 .60
357 Ben Coleman .25 .60
358 Curtis Conway .30 .75
359 Gerald Dixon .25 .60
360 Mike Dumas .25 .60
361 Terrell Fletcher .25 .60
362 Jeff Graham .25 .60
363 Jim Harbaugh .30 .75
364 Rodney Harrison FOIL .50 1.25
365 Freddie Jones .25 .60
366 Ryan Leaf .25 .60
367 John Parrella .25 .60
368 Raleigh Roundtree RC .25 .60
369 Orlando Ruff RC .25 .60
370 Junior Seau FOIL .60 1.50
371 Ray Brown .25 .60
372 Brentson Buckner .25 .60
373 Jeff Garcia .25 .60
374 Charlie Garner FOIL .60 1.50
375 Monty Montgomery RC .25 .60
376 Terrell Owens .30 .75
377 Julian Peterson .25 .60
378 Jerry Rice FOIL 1.50 4.00
379 Lance Schulters .25 .60
380 J.J. Stokes .25 .60
381 Winfred Tubbs .25 .60
382 Jason Webster .25 .60
383 Matt Willig .25 .60
384 Bryant Young .30 .75
385 Jay Bellamy .25 .60
386 Chad Brown .25 .60
387 Sean Dawkins .25 .60
388 Darrell Jackson .30 .75
389 Pete Kendall .25 .60
390 Cortez Kennedy .30 .75
391 Jon Kitna .25 .60
392 George Koonce .25 .60
393 Itula Mili .25 .60
394 Anthony Simmons .25 .60
395 Michael Sinclair .25 .60
396 Ricky Watters FOIL .60 1.50
397 Floyd Wedderburn RC .25 .60
398 Willie Williams .25 .60
399 Dre Bly .25 .60
400 Isaac Bruce .40 1.00
401 Marshall Faulk FOIL .60 1.50
402 London Fletcher FOIL .60 1.50
403 Trent Green .25 .60
404 Az-Zahir Hakim .25 .60
405 Torry Holt .30 .75
406 Mike A. Jones .25 .60
407 Keith Lyle .25 .60
408 Dexter McCleon .25 .60
409 Orlando Pace .25 .60
410 Ricky Proehl .25 .60
411 Ryan Tucker RC .25 .60
412 Kurt Warner FOIL 1.25 3.00
413 Grant Wistrom .25 .60
414 Jeff Zgonina RC .25 .60
415 Donnie Abraham .25 .60
416 Mike Alstott .25 .60
417 Ronde Barber FOIL .50 1.25
418 Derrick Brooks FOIL .50 1.25
419 Jeff Christy .25 .60
420 Jamie Duncan .25 .60
421 Warrick Dunn .25 .60
422 Martin Gramatica .25 .60
423 Jacquez Green .25 .60
424 Keyshawn Johnson .30 .75
425 Shaun King .25 .60
426 John Lynch .30 .75
427 Randall McDaniel .30 .75
428 Anthony McFarland .25 .60
429 Dave Moore .25 .60
430 Warren Sapp FOIL .60 1.50
431 Blaine Bishop .25 .60
432 Al Del Greco .25 .60
433 Eddie George FOIL .75 2.00
434 Randall Godfrey .25 .60
435 Kenny Holmes .25 .60
436 Brad Hopkins .25 .60
437 Jevon Kearse .25 .60
438 Derrick Mason FOIL .50 1.25
439 Bruce Matthews FOIL .50 1.25
440 Steve McNair .30 .75
441 Marcus Robertson .25 .60
442 Eddie Robinson .25 .60
443 Samari Rolle .25 .60
444 Chris Sanders .25 .60
445 John Thornton .25 .60
446 Frank Wycheck .25 .60
447 Stephen Alexander .25 .60
448 Champ Bailey .30 .75
449 Shawn Barber RC .25 .60
450 Marco Coleman .25 .60
451 Albert Connell .25 .60
452 Stephen Davis .25 .60
453 Irving Fryar .30 .75
454 Jeff George .30 .75
455 Andy Heck .25 .60
456 Brad Johnson .30 .75
457 Deion Sanders .30 .75
458 Sam Shade .25 .60
459 Keith Sims .25 .60
460 Bruce Smith FOIL .60 1.50
461 Dana Stubblefield .25 .60
462 James Thrash .30 .75

2001 NFL Showdown 1st Edition Monochrome

COMPLETE SET (62) 2.00 5.00
*MONOCHROMES: .1X TO .25X BASIC CARDS

2001 NFL Showdown 1st Edition Plays

These cards were issued 2-per 1st Edition pack. Each was to be used during game play and feature an outline of a football play with results of that play for the game. No player images appear on these cards.

COMPLETE SET (70) 1.50 4.00
COMMON CARD (1-70) .02 .10

2001 NFL Showdown 1st Edition Showdown Stars

These 9-cards were released as a promo set for the 2001 NFL Showdown 1ST Edition product. Each card includes a gold foil "Showdown Stars" notation on the front.

COMPLETE SET (9) 3.00 8.00
L1 Ray Lewis .30 .75
L2 Brian Urlacher .40 1.00
L3 Brett Favre .60 1.50
L4 Peyton Manning .75 2.00
L5 Tony Gonzalez .25 .60
L6 Randy Moss .25 .60
L7 Donovan McNabb .25 .60
L8 Marshall Faulk .25 .60
L9 Warren Sapp .25 .60

2001 NFL Showdown 1st Edition Strategy

rategy cards were issued 2-per 1st Edition Starter (S1-S25) or Booster (S26-S50) packs. Each card features a specific football strategy to be used during game play as well as a color action photo taken during an NFL game. The cardbacks include a red border instead of black and are identical to the 2002 Strategy cards in terms of design. The copyright date on the fron however is 2001. We've noted below key players that can be identified on each card.

COMPLETE SET (50) 5.00 12.00
S1 Keenan McCardell .15 .40
Afterburners
S2 Mark Brunell .25 .60
Air It Out
S3 Packers vs. Eagles .15 .40
Between the Hashes
S4 Browns vs. Titans .08 .25
Big Man
S5 Jackie Harris .08 .25
Big Play
S6 Panthers vs. Rams .08 .25
Great Block
S7 Brad Maynard .08 .25
Lucky Bounce
S8 Curtis Martin .25 .60
Second Effort
S9 Panthers vs. 49ers .08 .25
Thread the Needle
S10 Tiki Barber .15 .40
Tuck the Ball In
S11 Chiefs vs. Seahawks .08 .25
Back and Forth
S12 Kerry Collins .15 .40
Coverage Sack
S13 Bears vs. Lions .08 .25
Deep Blitz
S14 Warren Sapp .15 .40
Spy
S15 Jonathan Ogden .08 .25
Collision
S16 Browns Lineman .08 .25
Leg Trapped
S17 Buccaneers Lineman .08 .25
Speed Bump
S18 Falcons vs. Panthers .08 .25
Tangled Up
S19 Bears vs. Saints .08 .25
Defensive Holding
S20 Keyshawn Johnson .25 .60
Defensive Pass Interference
S21 Steve McNair .25 .60
Titans offensive line
False Start
S22 Tony Gonzalez .15 .40
Offensive Holding
S23 Colts vs. Jaguars .08 .25
Offsides
S24 Junior Seau .25 .60
Bert Emanuel
Bad Pass
S25 Sam Shade .08 .25
David LaFleur
Force Fumble
S26 Bears vs. Jaguars .08 .25
Battle for the Ball
S27 Emmitt Smith .60 1.50
Big Hole
S28 Derrick Alexander WR .15 .40
Burned
S29 Dave Wohlabaugh .08 .25
Clear the Middle
S30 Hines Ward .15 .40
Fingertips
S31 Marshall Faulk .40 1.00
Power Back
S32 Corey Dillon .25 .60
Spin Move
S33 Michael Westbrook .08 .25
Timing Pattern
S34 Colts vs. Packers .25 .60
Under Pressure
S35 Titans huddle .15 .40
Work the Clock
S36 Colts vs. Packers .08 .25
Deep Coverage
S37 Drew Bledsoe .30 .75
Deep in the Backfield
S38 Walt Harris .08 .25
Tony Parrish
Interceptor
S39 Stephen Davis .15 .40
Stuff
S40 Wesley Walls .08 .25
Gamer
S41 Tim Couch .25 .60
Walk It Off
S42 Chiefs vs. Seahawks .08 .25
Facemask
S43 Lions vs. Bears .08 .25
Personal Foul
S44 Browns vs. Titans .08 .25
Piling On
S45 Charlie Batch .15 .40
Roughing the Passer
S46 Redskins vs. Eagles .15 .40
Tripping
S47 Patriots vs. Buccaneers .08 .25
Blown Route
S48 Brett Favre 1.00 2.50
Piledriver
S49 Rams vs. Seahawks .08 .25
Quick Return
S50 Levon Kirkland .15 .40
Eric Warfield
Runback

2001 NFL Showdown First and Goal

This set marked the second release of NFL Showdown for 2001 and includes many of the top draft picks. Card #48 was intended to be Andy Katzenmoyer, but the card was never produced. The regular base cards do not feature the set name on the fronts but can be identified by the lack of the silver foil logo found on the "1st Edition" set. The foil cards feature the player's name printed in holofoil along with a holofoil printed set name "1st and Goal" near the bottom of the cardfront.

COMP.SET w/o FOILS (149) 15.00 40.00
1 Jason Elam .25 .60
2 Aaron Brooks FOIL .50 1.25
3 Anthony Wright .25 .60
4 David Akers RC .25 .60
5 John Kasay .25 .60
6 Chris Redman .40 1.00
7 Jeff Lewis .25 .60
8 Shane Matthews .25 .60
9 Chad Pennington .25 .60
10 Mike Vanderjagt .25 .60
11 Jeff Wilkins .25 .60
12 Todd Collins .25 .60
13 Dave Brown .25 .60
14 Autry Denson .25 .60
15 Chris Watson .25 .60
16 Duce Staley .25 .60
17 Aaron Stecker .25 .60
18 Rodney Heath .25 .60
19 Gerald McBurrows RC .25 .60
20 Deltha O'Neal .25 .60
21 Fakhir Brown RC .25 .60
22 Dorsey Levens .30 .75
23 Antoine Winfield .25 .60
24 Paul Smith .25 .60
25 Darren Woodson .30 .75
26 Chad Morton .25 .60
27 Brian Mitchell .30 .75
28 Terrell Davis .30 .75
29 George Teague .25 .60
30 Shyrone Stith .25 .60
31 Mike Cloud .25 .60
32 Tebucky Jones .25 .60
33 Brandon Bennett .25 .60
34 Shaun Alexander .25 .60
35 Carnell Lake .25 .60
36 Dainon Sidney RC .25 .60
37 Jon Witman .25 .60
38 Frank Moreau .25 .60
39 Zack Walz RC .25 .60
40 Ian Gold .25 .60
41 Warrick Holdman RC .25 .60
42 T.J. Slaughter .25 .60
43 Hardy Nickerson .25 .60
44 Brian Simmons .25 .60
45 Keith Brooking .30 .75
46 Peter Boulware .25 .60
47 Jessie Tuggle .25 .60
49 Kevin Long RC .25 .60
50 Damien Woody .25 .60
51 Shane Dronett .25 .60
52 Matt Lepsis RC .25 .60
53 Kenny Mixon RC .25 .60
54 Greg Jefferson .25 .60
55 Plaxico Burress .25 .60
56 Terry Hardy .25 .60
57 Troy Edwards .25 .60
58 Rocket Ismail .30 .75
59 O.J. McDuffie .25 .60
60 Tyrone Davis .25 .60
61 Bobby Engram .25 .60
62 Peerless Price .25 .60
63 Jed Weaver .25 .60
64 Michael Westbrook .25 .60
65 Patrick Jeffers FOIL .50 1.25
66 Jerry Porter .25 .60
67 Joey Galloway .30 .75
68 Rob Moore .25 .60
69 Cory Geason .25 .60
70 Cam Cleeland .25 .60
71 Andrew Jordan .25 .60
72 Greg Clark FOIL .50 1.25
73 Dennis Northcutt .25 .60
74 Jeremy McDaniel .25 .60
75 Ron Dixon .25 .60
76 Darnay Scott .30 .75
77 Kevin Dyson .25 .60
78 David Dunn .25 .60
79 JaJuan Dawson .25 .60
80 Damon Jones .25 .60
81 Travis Taylor .25 .60
82 David LaFleur .25 .60
83 Tai Streets .25 .60
84 Junior Bryant RC .25 .60
85 Chuck Smith .25 .60
86 Dimitrius Underwood .25 .60
87 Courtney Brown FOIL .50 1.25
88 Gilbert Brown .25 .60
89 John Abraham FOIL .50 1.25
90 Rob Morris .25 .60
91 Rick Lyle .25 .60
92 Brandon Whiting RC .25 .60
93 Raylee Johnson .25 .60
94 Alge Crumpler RC .75 2.00
95 Michael Vick FOIL RC 2.50 6.00
96 Todd Heap RC .60 1.50
97 Chris Weinke FOIL RC 1.25 3.00
98 David Terrell RC .60 1.50
99 Anthony Thomas RC .75 2.00
100 Chad Johnson RC .75 2.00
101 Justin Smith RC 1.00 2.50
102 Jeff Backus RC .50 1.25
103 Shaun Rogers RC .75 2.00
104 Reggie Wayne RC 1.00 2.50
105 Jamal Reynolds FOIL RC 1.00 2.50
106 Robert Ferguson RC .75 2.00
107 Chris Chambers RC .50 1.25
108 Jamar Fletcher RC .50 1.25
109 Deuce McAllister RC .75 2.00
110 Will Allen FOIL RC .75 2.00
111 Lamont Jordan RC .75 2.00
112 Santana Moss RC .75 2.00
113 Freddie Mitchell RC .50 1.25
114 Andre Carter FOIL RC 1.25 3.00
115 LaDainian Tomlinson FOIL RC 5.00 12.00
116 Drew Brees FOIL RC 6.00 15.00
117 Rod Gardner RC .60 1.50
118 Fred Smoot RC .60 1.50
119 Derrick Gibson RC .50 1.25
120 Adam Archuleta FOIL RC 1.25 3.00
121 Damione Lewis RC .60 1.50
122 Michael Bennett RC .60 1.50
123 Leonard Davis FOIL RC 1.50 4.00
124 Quincy Morgan RC .60 1.50
125 Marcus Stroud FOIL RC 1.25 3.00
126 Kenyatta Walker RC .50 1.25
127 Willie Middlebrooks RC .60 1.50
128 Kendrell Bell RC .75 2.00
129 Casey Hampton RC .75 2.00
130 Nate Clements RC .60 1.50
131 Steve Hutchinson RC 1.25 3.00
132 Koren Robinson FOIL RC 1.25 3.00
133 Brandon Stokley .25 .60
134 Jake Reed .30 .75
135 Kevin Donnalley .25 .60
136 Todd Steussie FOIL .25 .60
137 Ted Washington .25 .60
138 Jon Kitna .25 .60
139 Todd Lyght
140 Tony Horne .25 .60
141 Priest Holmes .25 .60
142 James McKnight .25 .60
143 Albert Connell .25 .60
144 Jay Bellamy .25 .60
145 James Darling
146 Matthew Hatchette .25 .60
147 James Thrash FOIL .30 .75
148 Alex Molden .25 .60
149 Ryan McNeil
150 Brad Johnson FOIL .30 .75
151 Simeon Rice .30 .75
152 Charlie Garner FOIL .30 .75
153 Trace Armstrong .25 .60
154 Mark Fields
155 Kim Herring .25 .60
156 Aeneas Williams .25 .60
157 Lance Johnstone .20 .50
158 Dwayne Rudd .20 .50
159 Rickey Dudley FOIL .40 1.00
160 Kenny Holmes .20 .50
161 Doug Flutie FOIL 1.00 2.50
162 Chester McGlockton .20 .50
163 Eddie Kennison .20 .50
164 Elvis Grbac FOIL .60 1.50
165 Ray Crockett .20 .50
166 Trent Green FOIL 1.00 2.50
167 Chad Eaton .20 .50
168 Matt Hasselbeck .30 .75
169 Levon Kirkland .20 .50
170 John Randle .30 .75
171 Marcus Robertson .20 .50
172 Pete Kendall .20 .50
173 Keith Traylor .20 .50
174 Jerry Rice FOIL 2.00 5.00
175 Dana Stubblefield .20 .50
CL1 Checklist Card 1 .02 .10
CL2 Checklist Card 2 .02 .10
CL3 Checklist Card 3 .02 .10

2001 NFL Showdown First and Goal Plays

These cards were issued 2-per pack. Each was to be used during game play and feature an outline of a football play with results of that play for the game. No player images appear on these cards.

COMPLETE SET (20) .60 1.50
COMMON CARD (P1-P20) .02 .10

2001 NFL Showdown First and Goal Strategy

Strategy cards were issued 2-per booster pack. Each card features a specific football strategy to be used during game play as well as a color action photo taken during an NFL game.

COMPLETE SET (10) 1.25 3.00
S1 Fake Handoff .10 .30
Akili Smith
S2 Force of Will .10 .30
S3 In Motion .30 .75
Tim Brown
S4 Long Routes .20 .50
Frank Sanders
S5 Shrug Them Off .10 .30
S6 Textbook Play .30 .75
Drew Bledsoe
Kenny Holmes
S7 Aggressive Coverage .10 .30
Darnay Scott
S8 Blind Side Rush .30 .75
S9 Support The Weak Side .10 .30
Browns vs. Colts
S10 Trick Plays .30 .75
Oakland Raiders sideline
Jon Gruden

2002 NFL Showdown

This 356-card set was available in packs found in starter kits and in 11-card booster packs. Despite the 2003 logo on the packaging and the cardbacks, this product was released in the Fall of 2002. The foil cards were produced with a gold foil player name at the top instead of a holofoil design like the 2001 release. A cover card featuring Brian Urlacher was also seeded into packs to promote the upcoming 1st and Goal second series.

COMP.SET w/o FOILS (300) 20.00 50.00
1 David Boston FOIL .60 1.50
2 Leonard Davis .25 .60
3 Rob Fredrickson .25 .60
4 MarTay Jenkins .25 .60
5 Kwamie Lassiter .25 .60
6 Ronald McKinnon .25 .60
7 Michael Pittman .30 .75
8 Scott Player .25 .60
9 Jake Plummer .25 .60
10 Frank Sanders .25 .60
11 Lonnie Shelton .25 .60
12 LeVar Woods .25 .60
13 Ashley Ambrose .25 .60
14 Ray Buchanan .25 .60
15 Chris Chandler .30 .75
16 Henri Crockett .25 .60
17 Kynan Forney .25 .60
18 Travis Hall .25 .60
19 Patrick Kerney .25 .60
20 Brady Smith .25 .60
21 Maurice Smith .25 .60
22 Darrick Vaughn .25 .60
23 Michael Vick FOIL .75 2.00
24 Bob Whitfield .25 .60
25 Peter Boulware .25 .60
26 Elvis Grbac .25 .60
27 Corey Harris .25 .60
28 Jermaine Lewis .25 .60
29 Ray Lewis FOIL 1.00 2.50
30 Chris McAlister .25 .60
31 Michael McCrary .25 .60
32 Edwin Mulitalo .25 .60
33 Jonathan Ogden .30 .75
34 Jamie Sharper .30 .75
35 Travis Taylor .25 .60
36 Rod Woodson FOIL 1.00 2.50
37 Ruben Brown .25 .60
38 Larry Centers .25 .60
39 Jay Foreman RC .25 .60
40 Phil Hansen .25 .60
41 Travis Henry .25 .60
42 Peerless Price FOIL .60 1.50
43 Brandon Spoon .25 .60
44 Alex Van Pelt .25 .60
45 Pat Williams RC .60 1.50
46 Doug Evans .25 .60
47 Richard Huntley .25 .60
48 Dan Morgan .25 .60
49 Muhsin Muhammad .25 .60
50 Todd Sauerbrun .25 .60
51 Steve Smith FOIL 1.00 2.50
52 Todd Steussie .25 .60
53 Chris Weinke .25 .60
54 Marty Booker .25 .60
55 Phillip Daniels .25 .60
56 Paul Edinger .25 .60
57 Warrick Holdman .25 .60
58 Olin Kreutz RC .50 1.25
59 Brad Maynard RC .25 .60
60 R.W. McQuarters FOIL .60 1.50
61 Jim Miller .25 .60
62 Tony Parrish .25 .60
63 Anthony Thomas FOIL .75 2.00
64 Keith Traylor .25 .60
65 Brian Urlacher FOIL 1.00 2.50
66 Larry Whigham .25 .60
67 James Williams .25 .60
68 Corey Dillon .25 .60
69 Oliver Gibson .25 .60
70 Jon Kitna .25 .60
71 Matt O'Dwyer .25 .60
72 Darnay Scott .30 .75
73 Brian Simmons .25 .60
74 Justin Smith .30 .75
75 Takeo Spikes FOIL .60 1.50
76 Roger Chanoine RC .25 .60
77 Tim Couch .25 .60
78 Corey Fuller .25 .60
79 Kevin Johnson .25 .60
80 Daylon McCutcheon .25 .60
81 Keith McKenzie .25 .60
82 Jamir Miller FOIL .60 1.50
83 Roman Oben .25 .60
84 Orpheus Roye .25 .60
85 Dwayne Rudd .25 .60
86 Gerard Warren .25 .60
87 Jamel White .25 .60
88 Larry Allen .40 1.00
89 Quincy Carter .25 .60
90 Michael Myers .25 .60
91 Dat Nguyen .25 .60
92 Emmitt Smith FOIL 1.50 4.00
93 Mark Stepnoski .25 .60
94 Reggie Swinton .25 .60
95 Darren Woodson .30 .75
96 Mike Anderson .25 .60
97 Eric Brown .25 .60
98 Desmond Clark .25 .60
99 Chris Cole .25 .60
100 Jason Elam .25 .60
101 Ian Gold .25 .60
102 Brian Griese .25 .60
103 Matt Lepsis .25 .60
104 John Mobley .25 .60
105 Deltha O'Neal FOIL .60 1.50
106 Trevor Pryce .25 .60
107 Rod Smith FOIL .75 2.00
108 Jeff Backus .25 .60
109 Charlie Batch .25 .60
110 Desmond Howard .30 .75
111 Johnnie Morton .30 .75
112 Robert Porcher .25 .60
113 Shaun Rogers FOIL .60 1.50
114 Brendan Stai .25 .60
115 James Stewart .25 .60
116 Corey Bradford .25 .60
117 Gilbert Brown .25 .60
118 LeRoy Butler .30 .75
119 Brett Favre FOIL 2.00 5.00
120 Mike Flanagan .25 .60
121 Bubba Franks .25 .60
122 Antonio Freeman .40 1.00
123 Ahman Green FOIL .75 2.00
124 Bernardo Harris .25 .60
125 Vonnie Holliday .25 .60
126 Mike McKenzie .25 .60
127 Marco Rivera .25 .60
128 Bill Schroeder .25 .60
129 Darren Sharper FOIL .60 1.50
130 Idrees Bashir .25 .60
131 Jeff Burris .25 .60
132 Ken Dilger .25 .60
133 Tarik Glenn .25 .60
134 Marvin Harrison FOIL .75 2.00
135 Peyton Manning 1.00 2.50
136 Mike Vanderjagt .25 .60
137 Terrence Wilkins .25 .60
138 Tony Brackens .25 .60
139 Mark Brunell .30 .75
140 Keenan McCardell .30 .75
141 Hardy Nickerson .25 .60
142 Seth Payne RC .25 .60
143 Jimmy Smith FOIL .75 2.00
144 Gary Walker .25 .60
145 Maurice Williams .25 .60
146 Donnie Edwards .25 .60
147 Tony Gonzalez .30 .75
148 Trent Green .25 .60
149 Priest Holmes FOIL .60 1.50
150 Marcus Patton .25 .60
151 Will Shields .25 .60
152 John Tait .25 .60
153 Greg Wesley .25 .60
154 Chris Chambers FOIL .60 1.50
155 Jay Fiedler .30 .75
156 Oronde Gadsden .25 .60
157 Sam Madison .25 .60
158 Olindo Mare .25 .60
159 Brock Marion FOIL .60 1.50
160 James McKnight .25 .60
161 Kenny Mixon .25 .60
162 Derrick Rodgers .25 .60
163 Tim Ruddy .25 .60
164 Lamar Smith .25 .60
165 Patrick Surtain .25 .60
166 Jason Taylor .30 .75
167 Zach Thomas FOIL .75 2.00
168 Gary Anderson .25 .60
169 Matt Birk .25 .60
170 Todd Bouman .25 .60
171 Cris Carter .40 1.00
172 Byron Chamberlain .25 .60
173 Daunte Culpepper FOIL .75 2.00
174 Chris Hovan .25 .60
175 Ed McDaniel .25 .60
176 Randy Moss .30 .75
177 Tom Brady 2.00 5.00
178 Troy Brown FOIL .60 1.50
179 Tedy Bruschi .30 .75
180 Mike Compton .25 .60
181 Bryan Cox .30 .75
182 Tebucky Jones .25 .60
183 Ty Law .40 1.00
184 Lawyer Milloy FOIL .60 1.50
185 David Patten .25 .60
186 Roman Phifer .25 .60
187 Richard Seymour .25 .60
188 Antowain Smith FOIL .75 2.00
189 Adam Vinatieri .25 .60
190 Grant Williams .25 .60
191 Jay Bellamy .25 .60
192 Aaron Brooks FOIL .60 1.50
193 John Carney .25 .60
194 Charlie Clemons .25 .60
195 Jerry Fontenot .25 .60
196 La'Roi Glover .25 .60
197 Joe Horn .25 .60
198 Darren Howard .25 .60
199 Willie Jackson .25 .60
200 Sammy Knight .25 .60
201 Deuce McAllister .30 .75
202 Kyle Turley .25 .60
203 Ricky Williams .30 .75
204 Will Allen .25 .60

205 Morten Andersen	.25	.60
206 Tiki Barber	.30	.75
207 Micheal Barrow	.25	.60
208 Kerry Collins	.25	.60
209 Ron Dayne	.30	.75
210 Keith Hamilton	.25	.60
211 Luke Petitgout	.25	.60
212 Jason Sehorn	.30	.75
213 Michael Strahan FOIL	.75	2.00
214 Amani Toomer	.25	.60
215 Shaun Williams	.25	.60
216 John Abraham FOIL	.75	2.00
217 Anthony Becht	.25	.60
218 Wayne Chrebet	.25	.60
219 Shaun Ellis	.25	.60
220 Victor Green	.25	.60
221 Marvin Jones	.25	.60
222 LaMont Jordan	.30	.75
223 Mo Lewis	.25	.60
224 Curtis Martin FOIL	.75	2.00
225 Steve Martin RC	.25	.60
226 Chad Pennington	.25	.60
227 Vinny Testaverde	.25	.60
228 Craig Yeast	.25	.60
229 Greg Biekert	.25	.60
230 Tim Brown FOIL	1.00	2.50
231 Tony Bryant	.25	.60
232 David Dunn	.25	.60
233 Rich Gannon FOIL	.75	2.00
234 Charlie Garner	.30	.75
235 Grady Jackson	.25	.60
236 Lincoln Kennedy	.25	.60
237 Shane Lechler	.25	.60
238 Marquez Pope	.25	.60
239 Jerry Rice FOIL	2.00	5.00
240 William Thomas	.25	.60
241 Tyrone Wheatley	.30	.75
242 Charles Woodson	.40	1.00
243 David Akers	.25	.60
244 Brian Dawkins	.40	1.00
245 Hugh Douglas FOIL	.60	1.50
246 Carlos Emmons	.25	.60
247 Chad Lewis	.25	.60
248 Jermane Mayberry	.25	.60
249 Donovan McNabb	.30	.75
250 Jon Runyan	.25	.60
251 Corey Simon	.25	.60
252 Duce Staley	.25	.60
253 Hollis Thomas	.25	.60
254 James Thrash	.30	.75
255 Jeremiah Trotter FOIL	.60	1.50
256 Troy Vincent FOIL	.75	2.00
257 Brent Alexander	.25	.60
258 Kendrell Bell FOIL	.60	1.50
259 Jerome Bettis FOIL	1.00	2.50
260 Kris Brown	.25	.60
261 Troy Edwards	.25	.60
262 Lethon Flowers	.25	.60
263 Jason Gildon	.30	.75
264 Jeff Hartings	.25	.60
265 Earl Holmes	.25	.60
266 Josh Miller RC	.25	.60
267 Kordell Stewart FOIL	.60	1.50
268 Hines Ward	.30	.75
269 Dewayne Washington	.25	.60
270 Amos Zereoue	.25	.60
271 Drew Brees	.75	2.00
272 Curtis Conway	.30	.75
273 Doug Flutie	.30	.75
274 Rodney Harrison	.25	.60
275 Vaughn Parker	.25	.60
276 Junior Seau	.30	.75
277 LaDainian Tomlinson FOIL	1.00	2.50
278 Marcellus Wiley	.25	.60
279 Kevan Barlow	.25	.60
280 Ray Brown	.25	.60
281 Jose Cortez RC	.25	.60
282 Dave Fiore	.25	.60
283 Jeff Garcia FOIL	.60	1.50
284 Garrison Hearst FOIL	.60	1.50
285 Eric Johnson	.25	.60
286 Terrell Owens FOIL	.75	2.00
287 Ahmed Plummer	.25	.60
288 Lance Schulters	.25	.60
289 J.J. Stokes	.25	.60
290 Dana Stubblefield	.25	.60
291 Jeff Ulbrich	.25	.60
292 Bryant Young	.25	.60
293 Shaun Alexander FOIL	.60	1.50
294 Chad Brown	.25	.60
295 Trent Dilfer	.25	.60
296 Chad Eaton	.25	.60
297 Jeff Feagles	.25	.60
298 Matt Hasselbeck	.25	.60
299 Steve Hutchinson	.30	.75
300 Darrell Jackson	.30	.75
301 Walter Jones	.25	.60
302 John Randle FOIL	.75	2.00
303 Koren Robinson	.25	.60
304 Anthony Simmons	.25	.60
305 Reggie Tongue	.25	.60
306 Dre Bly	.25	.60
307 Isaac Bruce	.40	1.00
308 Trung Canidate	.25	.60
309 Ernie Conwell	.25	.60
310 Marshall Faulk FOIL	.75	2.00
311 Mark Fields	.25	.60
312 London Fletcher	.30	.75
313 Az-Zahir Hakim	.25	.60
314 Torry Holt	.30	.75
315 Orlando Pace	.25	.60
316 Ryan Tucker	.25	.60
317 Kurt Warner FOIL	.75	2.00
318 Jeff Wilkins	.25	.60
319 Aeneas Williams FOIL	.60	1.50
320 Donnie Abraham	.25	.60
321 Mike Alstott FOIL	.60	1.50
322 Ronde Barber FOIL	.60	1.50
323 Derrick Brooks	.25	.60
324 Jamie Duncan	.25	.60
325 Martin Gramatica	.25	.60
326 Brad Johnson	.30	.75
327 Keyshawn Johnson	.30	.75
328 John Lynch	.30	.75
329 Randall McDaniel	.30	.75
330 Simeon Rice	.25	.60
331 Warren Sapp	.30	.75
332 Kevin Carter	.25	.60
333 Kevin Dyson	.30	.75
334 Eddie George	.30	.75
335 Randall Godfrey	.25	.60
336 Brad Hopkins	.25	.60
337 Jevon Kearse	.25	.60
338 Derrick Mason FOIL	.60	1.50
339 Bruce Matthews	.25	.60
340 Steve McNair FOIL	.75	2.00
341 Joe Nedney	.25	.60
342 Eddie Robinson	.25	.60
343 Frank Wycheck	.25	.60
344 Champ Bailey	.30	.75
345 Tony Banks	.25	.60
346 Bryan Barker	.25	.60
347 Marco Coleman	.25	.60
348 Stephen Davis	.25	.60
349 Kenard Lang FOIL	.60	1.50
350 Eric Metcalf	.25	.60
351 Kevin Mitchell	.25	.60
352 Chris Samuels	.25	.60
353 Sam Shade	.25	.60
354 Bruce Smith	.30	.75
355 Fred Smoot	.30	.75
356 David Terrell DB	.25	.60
NNO Brian Urlacher Cover	.40	1.00

2002 NFL Showdown Plays

Found in starter kits and booster packs, these cards allow game players to run plays, both offensively and defensively.

COMPLETE SET (70)	2.00	5.00
COMMON CARD (P1-P70)	.02	.10

2002 NFL Showdown Showdown Stars

These 6-cards were released as a promo set for the 2002 NFL Showdown product. Each card includes a gold foil "Showdown Stars" notation on the front. A "Training Camp" version of each card was also produced.

COMPLETE SET (6)	2.50	6.00
1 Brian Urlacher	.40	1.00
2 Curtis Martin	.30	.75
3 LaDainian Tomlinson	.40	1.00
4 Shaun Alexander	.25	.60
5 Michael Vick	.30	.75
6 Sammy Knight	.25	.60

2002 NFL Showdown Strategy

und in starter kits and booster packs, these cards allow game players to set up various strategies, both offensively and defensively. Each card features an unidentified color football action photo along with a play result to be used with the game. The cardbacks include a red border instead of black and are identical to the 2001 Strategy cards in terms of design. The copyright date on the front however is 2002. We've identified known players below in the otherwise generic photos.

COMPLETE SET (50)	3.00	8.00
S1 Trung Canidate	.10	.30
Burst of Speed		
S2 Kurt Warner	.30	.75
Clumsy Handoff		
S3 Brian Griese	.20	.50
Coverage Sack		
S4 Dorsey Levens	.10	.30
Deep Blitz		
S5 Colts vs. Packers	.07	.20
Deep in the Backfield		
S6 49ers vs. Saints	.07	.20
Great Coverage		
S7 Bengals vs. Ravens	.07	.20
Keepaway		
S8 Quarterback Hurry	.07	.20
S9 Matt Hasselbeck	.10	.30
Concussion		
S10 Falcons vs. Panthers	.07	.20
Deafening Collision		
S11 Steve Beuerlein	.10	.30
Leg Trapped		
S12 Stinger	.10	.30
S13 Thurman Thomas	.10	.30
Tangled Up		
S14 Muhsin Muhammad	.10	.30
Champ Bailey		
Afterburners		
S15 Chris Chandler	.10	.30
Aggressive Blocking		
S16 Giants vs. Chiefs	.07	.20
Battle for the Ball		
S17 Vinny Testaverde	.10	.30
Beat the Blitz		
S18 Matt Stover	.07	.20
Between the Hashes		
S19 Bengals vs. Ravens	.07	.20
Big Hole		
S20 Shaun Alexander	.10	.30
Burned		
S21 Germane Crowell	.07	.20
Cannon		
S22 Lamar Smith	.10	.30
Dodge		
S23 Bears vs. Panthers	.07	.20
Escape the Pressure		
S24 Jacquez Green	.07	.20
Fingertips		
S25 David Patten	.07	.20
Good Hands		
S26 Brett Favre	.20	.50
Marco Rivera		
William Henderson		
Great Block		
S27 Brad Johnson	.20	.50
Mike Alstott		
Grind the Clock		
S28 Shane Lechler	.07	.20
Hang Time		
S29 Cowboys vs. Raiders	.07	.20
Lucky Bounce		
S30 Brandon Bennett	.07	.20
Make Em Miss		
S31 Steve Christie	.07	.20
Off the Crossbar		
S32 Jets vs. Bills	.07	.20
Second Effort		
S33 Brian Griese	.20	.50
Thread the Needle		
S34 Doug Flutie	.20	.50
Work the Clock		
S35 Jeff Graham	.07	.20
Deltha O'Neal		
Yards After Catch		
S36 Curtis Conway	.07	.20
Defensive Holding		
S37 Bears vs. Jaguars	.07	.20
Defensive Pass Interference		
S38 49ers vs. Saints	.07	.20
Facemask		
S39 Cowboys vs. Raiders	.07	.20
False Start		
S40 Buccaneers vs. Vikings	.10	.30
Intentional Grounding		
(Brad Johnson)		
S41 Tony Gonzalez	.10	.30
Offensive Holding		
S42 Browns vs. Steelers	.07	.20
Offsides		
S43 Alex Van Pelt	.07	.20
Roughing the Passer		
S44 Cardinals vs. Redskins	.07	.20
Tripping		
S45 Todd Pinkston	.10	.30
James Thrash		
Bad Pass		
S46 Ty Law	.10	.30
Jacquez Green		
Blown Route		
S47 Forced Fumble	.07	.20
S48 Cardinals vs. Redskins	.07	.20
Into Traffic		
S49 Aeneas Williams	.07	.20
Open-Field Recovery		
S50 Buccaneers vs. Vikings	.07	.20
Pile Driver		

2002 NFL Showdown Training Camp

These 6-cards were released as a promo set for the 2002 NFL Showdown product. Each card includes a gold foil "Training Camp" notation on the front.

COMPLETE SET (6)	2.50	6.00
1 Brian Urlacher	.40	1.00
2 Curtis Martin	.30	.75
3 LaDainian Tomlinson	.40	1.00
4 Shaun Alexander	.25	.60
5 Michael Vick	.30	.75
6 Sammy Knight	.25	.60

2002 NFL Showdown First and Goal

This set marked the second series for 2002 which includes many of the top draft picks for that year. A total of 25-Foil cards were produced.

COMP.SET w/o FOILS (125)	20.00	40.00
1 John Henderson FOIL RC	1.25	3.00
2 Sean Moran	.25	.60
3 Bill Schroeder	.25	.60
4 Tony Simmons	.25	.60
5 Travis Fisher RC	.60	1.50
6 James Allen	.25	.60
7 Javon Walker FOIL RC	1.50	4.00
8 Robert Edwards	.25	.60
9 Jerome Pathon	.25	.60
10 Ryan Sims FOIL RC	1.50	4.00
11 Levar Fisher RC	.50	1.25
12 Bryant McKinnie FOIL RC	1.00	2.50
13 Larry Tripplett RC	.50	1.25
14 T.J. Duckett FOIL RC	1.00	2.50
15 Chris Sanders	.25	.60
16 Levi Jones RC	.50	1.25
17 Jon McGraw RC	.50	1.25
18 Quentin Jammer FOIL RC	1.50	4.00
19 Shannon Sharpe	.30	.75
20 Lito Sheppard FOIL RC	1.50	4.00
21 Mike Caldwell	.25	.60
22 Napoleon Harris RC	.60	1.50
23 Aaron Beasley	.25	.60
24 Brandon Mitchell RC	.50	1.25
25 Qadry Ismail	.25	.60
26 Wendell Bryant FOIL RC	1.00	2.50
27 Rabih Abdullah	.25	.60
28 Mike Pearson RC	.50	1.25
29 DeMingo Graham RC	.50	1.25
30 Steve White	.25	.60
31 Bryan Cox	.30	.75
32 Najeh Davenport RC	.50	1.25
33 Joey Harrington FOIL RC	1.00	2.50
34 Dennis Johnson RC	.50	1.25
35 Stalin Colinet	.25	.60
36 James Farrior FOIL	.25	.60
37 Marco Battaglia	.25	.60
38 Jerramy Stevens RC	.75	2.00
39 Duane Starks	.25	.60
40 Dorsett Davis RC	.50	1.25
41 James Cannida RC	.50	1.25
42 Ricky Williams FOIL	.75	2.00
43 Tank Williams RC	.60	1.50
44 Michael Lewis RC	.60	1.50
45 Omar Easy RC	.60	1.50
46 Sam Cowart	.25	.60
47 Albert Haynesworth FOIL RC	1.50	4.00
48 Tim Carter RC	.60	1.50
49 Chris Chandler	.30	.75
50 Freddie Jones	.25	.60
51 Brock Huard	.30	.75
52 Phillip Buchanon FOIL RC	1.50	4.00
53 Patrick Ramsey RC	.60	1.50
54 Jabar Gaffney RC	.50	1.25
55 Josh McCown RC	.75	2.00
56 Mikhael Ricks	.25	.60
57 William Roaf	.25	.60
58 Stephen Alexander	.25	.60
59 Reidel Anthony	.25	.60
60 Rick Mirer	.30	.75
61 William Green FOIL RC	1.25	3.00
62 Will Overstreet RC	.50	1.25
63 Dwight Freeney FOIL RC	2.00	5.00
64 Michael Pittman FOIL	.75	2.00
65 Spencer Folau RC	.50	1.25
66 Jamie Duncan	.25	.60
67 Robert Griffith	.25	.60
68 Rob Moore	.25	.60
69 Marquise Walker RC	.50	1.25
70 Doug Evans FOIL	.60	1.50
71 Ron Stone RC	.50	1.25
72 Ed Reed FOIL RC	6.00	15.00
73 Az-Zahir Hakim	.25	.60
74 Josh Reed RC	.60	1.50
75 Leonard Henry RC	.50	1.25
76 Rocky Calmus RC	.60	1.50
77 Jeremy Newberry RC	.50	1.25
78 Marques Anderson RC	.60	1.50
79 Kurt Kittner RC	.50	1.25
80 Clinton Portis RC	.75	2.00
81 Craig Nall RC	.60	1.50
82 Terrence Wilkins	.25	.60
83 Lance Schulters	.25	.60
84 Chris Carter	.25	.60
85 Raonall Smith	.25	.60
86 David Carr FOIL RC	1.00	2.50
87 Kerry Jenkins RC	.50	1.25
88 Bryan Thomas RC	.50	1.25
89 Alex Brown RC	.75	2.00
90 Donte Stallworth FOIL RC	1.50	4.00
91 Donnie Abraham	.25	.60
92 Rob Johnson	.30	.75
93 Donnie Edwards	.25	.60
94 Anthony Weaver RC	.50	1.25
95 Bill Romanowski	.30	.75
96 Pete Mitchell	.25	.60
97 Danny Wuerffel	.30	.75
98 Daryl Jones RC	.50	1.25
99 Chester Taylor RC	.75	2.00
100 Jamar Martin RC	.60	1.50
101 Robert Thomas RC	.50	1.25
102 Joe Jurevicius	.25	.60
103 Greg Comella	.25	.60
104 Eddie Freeman RC	.50	1.25
105 Drew Bledsoe	.30	.75
106 Andre Davis RC	.50	1.25
107 Kaseem Sinceno	.25	.60
108 Jumbo Elliott	.25	.60
109 Terrance Shaw	.25	.60
110 Barry Stokes RC	.50	1.25
111 Ken Dilger	.25	.60
112 Marc Colombo FOIL RC	1.00	2.50
113 Ashley Lelie FOIL RC	1.00	2.50
114 Brian Westbrook RC	1.00	2.50
115 Jeremiah Trotter FOIL	.60	1.50
116 Reche Caldwell RC	.60	1.50
117 Leon Searcy	.25	.60
118 Ryan Tucker	.25	.60
119 Corey Harris	.25	.60
120 Terry Glenn	.30	.75
121 Dale Carter	.25	.60
122 Blaine Bishop	.25	.60
123 Jamie Nails RC	.50	1.25
124 Ladell Betts RC	.75	2.00
125 Freddie Milons RC	.50	1.25
126 Corey Bradford	.25	.60
127 Kalimba Edwards RC	.60	1.50
128 Greg Favors	.25	.60
129 Walt Harris	.25	.60
130 Henri Crockett	.25	.60
131 Jeremy Shockey FOIL RC	1.50	4.00
132 Maurice Morris RC	.60	1.50
133 Antwaan Randle El RC	.60	1.50
134 Greg Jones	.25	.60
135 Chester Pitts RC	.50	1.25
136 Roosevelt Williams RC	.50	1.25
137 David Sloan	.25	.60
138 Sam Garnes	.25	.60
139 Jimmy Herndon RC	.50	1.25
140 Charles Grant RC	.75	2.00
141 Cory Raymer	.25	.60
142 D'Wayne Bates	.25	.60
143 Sam Simmons RC	.50	1.25
144 Victor Riley	.25	.60
145 Mike Rumph RC	.50	1.25
146 Kris Brown	.25	.60
147 Johnnie Morton FOIL	.75	2.00
148 Bobby Shaw	.25	.60
149 David Loverne RC	.50	1.25
150 Jake Schifino RC	.50	1.25

2002 NFL Showdown First and Goal Plays

These cards were issued 2-per pack. Each was to be used during game play and feature an outline of a football play with results of that play for the game. No player images appear on these cards.

COMPLETE SET (20)	.60	1.50
COMMON CARD (P1-P20)	.02	.10

2002 NFL Showdown First and Goal Strategy

Strategy cards were issued 2-per booster pack. Each card features a specific football strategy to be used during game play as well as a color action photo taken during an NFL game.

COMPLETE SET (10)	1.25	3.00
S1 Broncos vs. Dolphins	.07	.20
Bad Break		
S2 Broncos vs. Dolphins	.07	.20
Blocked Field Goal		
S3 Kevin Dyson	.10	.30
Serious Jets		
S4 Ray Lewis	.20	.50
Shadow		
S5 Tim Seder	.07	.20
Fake Field Goal		
S6 Jay Fiedler	.10	.30
Flushed from the Pocket		
S7 Kurt Warner	.30	.75
Golden Arm		
S8 Kurt Warner	.30	.75
Hurry-up Offense		
S9 Giants vs. Redskins	.07	.20
In the Trenches		
S10 Tom Brady	.40	1.00
Take a Chance		

1971 NFLPA Wonderful World Stamps

This set of 390 stamps was issued in both 1971 and 1972 under the auspices of the NFL Players Association in conjunction with an album entitled "The Wonderful World of Pro Football USA." The album features a photo of Earl Morrall and Mark Washington from Super Bowl V. The stamps are numbered and measure approximately 1 15/16" by 2 7/8". The team order of the album is arranged alphabetically according to the city name and then alphabetically by player name within each team The picture stamp album contains 30 pages measuring approximately 9 1/2" by 13 1/4". The text narrates the story of pro football in the United States. The album includes spaces for 390 color player stamps. The checklist and stamp numbering below is according to the album. There are some numbering and very slight text variations between the 1971 and 1972 issues on some stamps, as noted below.

COMPLETE SET (390)	350.00	600.00
1 Bob Berry	.40	1.00
2 Greg Brezina	.40	1.00
3 Ken Burrow	.40	1.00
4 Jim Butler	.40	1.00
5 Paul Gipson	.40	1.00
6 Claude Humphrey	.50	1.25
7 George Kunz	.40	1.00
8 Tom McCauley	.40	1.00
9 Jim Mitchell	.40	1.00
10 Tommy Nobis	.75	1.50
11 Ken Reaves	.40	1.00
12 Rudy Redmond	.40	1.00
13 John Small	.40	1.00
14 Harmon Wages	.40	1.00
15 John Zook	.40	1.00
16 Norm Bulaich	.40	1.00
17 Mike Curtis	.50	1.25
18 Jim Duncan	.40	1.00
19 Ted Hendricks	1.00	2.00
20 Roy Hilton	.40	1.00
21 Eddie Hinton	.40	1.00
22 David Lee	.40	1.00
23 Jerry Logan	.40	1.00
24 John Mackey	1.00	2.00
25 Tom Matte	.50	1.25
26 Jim O'Brien	.40	1.00
27 Glenn Ressler	.40	1.00
28 Johnny Unitas	6.00	12.00
29 Bob Vogel	.40	1.00
30 Rick Volk	.40	1.00
31 Butch Byrd	.40	1.00
32 Edgar Chandler	.40	1.00
33 Paul Costa	.40	1.00
34 Jim Dunaway	.40	1.00
35 Paul Guidry	.40	1.00
36 Jim Harris	.40	1.00
37 Robert James	.40	1.00
38 Mike McBath	.40	1.00
39 Haven Moses	.40	1.00
40 John Pitts	.40	1.00
41 Jim Reilly	.40	1.00
42 Dennis Shaw	.40	1.00
43 O.J. Simpson	5.00	10.00
44 Mike Stratton	.40	1.00
45 Bob Tatarek	.40	1.00
46 Craig Baynham	.40	1.00
47 Dick Butkus	5.00	10.00
48 Jim Cadile	.40	1.00
49 Lee Roy Caffey	.40	1.00
50 Jack Concannon	.50	1.25
51 Bobby Douglass	.50	1.25
52 Dick Gordon	.40	1.00
53 Bobby Joe Green	.40	1.00
54 Bob Hyland	.40	1.00
55 Ed O'Bradovich	.40	1.00
56 Mac Percival	.40	1.00
57 Gale Sayers	5.00	10.00
58 George Seals	.40	1.00
59 Bill Staley	.40	1.00
60 Cecil Turner	.40	1.00
61 Al Beauchamp	.40	1.00
62 Virgil Carter	.40	1.00
63 Vernon Holland	.40	1.00
64 Bob Johnson TE	.40	1.00
65 Ron Lamb	.40	1.00
66 Dave Lewis	.40	1.00
67 Rufus Mayes	.40	1.00
68 Horst Muhlmann	.40	1.00
69 Lemar Parrish	.50	1.25
70 Jess Phillips	.40	1.00
71 Mike Reid	.75	1.50
72 Ken Riley	.50	1.25
73 Paul Robinson	.40	1.00
74 Bob Trumpy	.50	1.25
75 Ernie Wright	.40	1.00
76 Don Cockroft	.40	1.00
77 Gary Collins	.50	1.25
78 Gene Hickerson	.40	1.00
79 Jim Houston	.40	1.00
80 Walter Johnson	.40	1.00
81 Joe Jones DE	.40	1.00
82 Leroy Kelly	1.00	2.00
83 Bob Matheson	.40	1.00
84 Milt Morin	.40	1.00
85 Bill Nelsen	.50	1.25
86 Mike Phipps	.50	1.25
87 Dick Schafrath	.50	1.25
88 Bo Scott	.50	1.25
89 Jerry Sherk	.40	1.00
90 Ron Snidow	.40	1.00
91 Herb Adderley	1.00	2.00
92 George Andrie	.40	1.00
93 Mike Clark	.40	1.00
94 Dave Edwards	.40	1.00
95 Walt Garrison	.50	1.25
96 Cornell Green	.50	1.25
97 Bob Hayes	1.00	2.00
98 Calvin Hill	.75	1.50
99 Chuck Howley	.50	1.25
100 Lee Roy Jordan	.75	1.50
101 Dave Manders	.40	1.00
102 Craig Morton	.75	1.50
103 Ralph Neely	.40	1.00
104 Mel Renfro	1.00	2.00
105 Roger Staubach	10.00	20.00
106 Bob Anderson	.40	1.00
107 Sam Brunelli	.40	1.00
108 Dave Costa	.40	1.00
109 Mike Current	.40	1.00
110 Pete Duranko	.40	1.00
111 Cornell Gordon	.40	1.00
112 Mike Haffner	.40	1.00
113 Don Horn	.40	1.00
114 Rich Jackson	.40	1.00
115 Floyd Little	.75	1.50
116 Dick Post	.50	1.25
117 Paul Smith	.40	1.00
118 Billy Thompson	.50	1.25
119 Dave Washington	.40	1.00
120 Jim Whalen	.40	1.00
121 Lem Barney	1.00	2.00
122 Nick Eddy	.40	1.00
123 Mel Farr	.40	1.00
124 Ed Flanagan	.40	1.00
125 Larry Hand	.40	1.00
126 Alex Karras	1.50	3.00
127 Greg Landry	.50	1.25
128 Dick LeBeau	.40	1.00
129 Mike Lucci	.50	1.25
130 Earl McCullouch	.40	1.00
131 Bill Munson	.50	1.25
132 Joe Robb	.40	1.00
133 Jerry Rush	.40	1.00
134 Altie Taylor	.40	1.00
135 Wayne Walker	.50	1.25
136 Lionel Aldridge	.40	1.00
137 Ken Bowman	.40	1.00
138 Fred Carr	.40	1.00
139 Carroll Dale	.50	1.25
140 Ken Ellis	.40	1.00
141 Gale Gillingham	.40	1.00
142 Dave Hampton	.40	1.00
143 Doug Hart	.40	1.00
144 John Hilton	.40	1.00
145 Mike McCoy	.40	1.00
146 Ray Nitschke	1.00	2.00
147 Frank Patrick	.40	1.00
148 Francis Peay	.40	1.00
149 Dave Robinson	.50	1.25
150 Bart Starr	6.00	12.00
151 Elvin Bethea	.75	1.50
152 Garland Boyette	.40	1.00
153 Ken Burrough	.50	1.25
154 Woody Campbell	.40	1.00
155 Joe Dawkins	.40	1.00
156 Lynn Dickey	.50	1.25
157 Elbert Drungo	.40	1.00
158 Gene Ferguson	.40	1.00
159 Willie Frazier	.40	1.00
160 Charley Johnson	.50	1.25
161 Charlie Joiner	1.25	2.50
162 Dan Pastorini	.75	1.50
163 Dave Rowe	.40	1.00
164 Walt Suggs	.40	1.00
165 Mike Tilleman	.40	1.00
166 Bobby Bell	1.00	2.00
167 Aaron Brown	.40	1.00
168 Buck Buchanan	1.00	2.00
169 Ed Budde	.40	1.00
170 Curley Culp	.50	1.25
171 Len Dawson	2.50	5.00
172 Robert Holmes	.40	1.00
173 Jim Lynch	.40	1.00
174 Jim Marsalis	.40	1.00
175 Mo Moorman	.40	1.00
176 Ed Podolak	.50	1.25
177 Johnny Robinson	.50	1.25
178 Jan Stenerud	.75	1.50
179 Otis Taylor	.75	1.50
180 Jim Tyrer	.40	1.00
181 Kermit Alexander	.40	1.00
182 Coy Bacon	.40	1.00
183 Roman Gabriel	.75	1.50
184 Ken Iman	.40	1.00
185 Deacon Jones	1.25	2.50
186 Les Josephson	.40	1.00
187 Marlin McKeever	.40	1.00
188 Merlin Olsen	2.00	4.00
189 Phil Olsen	.40	1.00
190 Richie Petitbon	.50	1.25
191 David Ray	.40	1.00
192 Lance Rentzel	.50	1.25
193 Isiah Robertson	.50	1.25
194 Larry Smith	.40	1.00
195 Jack Snow	.50	1.25
196 Nick Buoniconti	.75	1.50
197 Doug Crusan	.40	1.00
198 Larry Csonka	5.00	10.00
199 Bob DeMarco	.40	1.00
200 Marv Fleming	.50	1.25
201 Bob Griese	4.00	8.00
202 Jim Kiick	.75	1.50
203 Mercury Morris	.75	1.50
204 John Richardson	.40	1.00
205 Jim Riley	.40	1.00
206 Jake Scott	.75	1.50
207 Howard Twilley	.40	1.00
208 Paul Warfield	2.00	4.00
209 Ed Weisacosky	.40	1.00
210 Garo Yepremian	.50	1.25
211 Grady Alderman	.50	1.25
212 John Beasley	.40	1.00
213 Gary Cuozzo	.50	1.25
214 John Henderson	.40	1.00
215 Wally Hilgenberg	.40	1.00
216 Clinton Jones	.40	1.00
217 Karl Kassulke	.40	1.00
218 Paul Krause	.75	1.50
219 Dave Osborn	.50	1.25
220 Alan Page	1.00	2.00
221 Ed Sharockman	.40	1.00
222 Norm Snead	.50	1.25
223 Mick Tingelhoff	.50	1.25
224 Lon Warwick	.40	1.00
225 Gene Washington Vik.	.50	1.25
226 Hank Barton	.40	1.00
227 Larry Carwell	.40	1.00
228 Tom Funchess	.40	1.00
229 Carl Garrett	.50	1.25
230 Jim Hunt	.40	1.00
231 Daryle Johnson	.40	1.00
232 Joe Kapp	.50	1.25
233 Tim Kelly	.40	1.00
234 Jon Morris	.40	1.00
235 Jim Nance	.50	1.25
236 Jim Plunkett	1.50	3.00
237 Dan Schneiss	.40	1.00
238 Ron Sellers	.40	1.00
239 Ed Toner	.40	1.00
240 Gerald Warren	.40	1.00
241 Dan Abramowicz	.50	1.25
242 Tony Baker FB	.50	1.25
243 Leo Carroll	.40	1.00
244 Dick Davis	.40	1.00
245 Tom Dempsey	.50	1.25
246 Al Dodd	.40	1.00
247 Jim Flanigan LB	.40	1.00
248 Hoyle Granger	.40	1.00
249 Edd Hargett	.40	1.00
250 Gene Howard	.40	1.00
251 Jake Kupp	.40	1.00
252 Dave Long	.40	1.00
253 Dick Lyons	.40	1.00
254 Mike Morgan	.40	1.00
255 Del Williams	.40	1.00
256 Fred Dryer	.75	1.50
257 Bobby Duhon	.40	1.00
258 Jim Files	.40	1.00
259 Tucker Frederickson	.50	1.25
260 Pete Gogolak	.40	1.00
261 Don Herrmann	.40	1.00
262 Ron Johnson	.40	1.00
263 Jim Kanicki	.40	1.00
264 Ernie Koy	.40	1.00
265 Spider Lockhart	.40	1.00
266 Clifton McNeil	.40	1.00
267 Joe Morrison	.40	1.00
268 Fran Tarkenton	4.00	8.00
269 Willie Williams	.40	1.00
270 Willie Young	.40	1.00
271 Al Atkinson	.40	1.00
272 Ralph Baker	.40	1.00
273 Emerson Boozer	.50	1.25
274 Mike Battle	.40	1.00
275 John Elliott	.40	1.00
276 Dave Herman	.40	1.00
277 Winston Hill	.40	1.00
278 Gus Hollomon	.40	1.00
279 Bobby Howfield	.40	1.00
280 Pete Lammons	.40	1.00
281 Joe Namath	10.00	20.00
282 Gerry Philbin UER	.40	1.00
283 Matt Snell	.50	1.25
284 Steve Tannen	.40	1.00
285 Al Woodall	.40	1.00
286 Fred Biletnikoff	2.00	4.00
287 George Blanda	3.00	6.00
288 Willie Brown	1.00	2.00
289 Raymond Chester	.50	1.25
290 Tony Cline	.40	1.00
291 Dan Conners	.40	1.00
292 Ben Davidson	.50	1.25
293 Hewritt Dixon	.40	1.00
294 Bill Enyart	.40	1.00
295 Daryle Lamonica	.75	1.50
296 Gus Otto	.40	1.00
297 Jim Otto	1.00	2.00
298 Charlie Smith	.40	1.00
299 Gene Upshaw	1.00	2.00
300 Warren Wells	.40	1.00
301 Rick Arrington	.40	1.00
302 Gary Ballman	.40	1.00
303 Lee Bouggess	.40	1.00
304 Bill Bradley	.50	1.25
305 Richard Harris	.40	1.00
306 Ben Hawkins	.40	1.00
307 Harold Jackson	.75	1.50
308 Pete Liske	.40	1.00
309 Al Nelson	.40	1.00
310 Gary Pettigrew	.40	1.00
311 Cyril Pinder	.40	1.00
312 Tim Rossovich	.50	1.25
313 Tom Woodeshick	.50	1.25
314 Adrian Young	.40	1.00
315 Steve Zabel	.40	1.00
316 Chuck Allen	.40	1.00
317 Warren Bankston	.40	1.00
318 Chuck Beatty	.40	1.00
319 Terry Bradshaw	10.00	20.00
320 John Fuqua	.40	1.00
321 Terry Hanratty	.50	1.25
322 Chuck Hinton DT	.40	1.00
323 Ray Mansfield	.40	1.00
324 Ben McGee	.40	1.00
325 Andy Russell	.50	1.25
326 Ron Shanklin	.40	1.00
327 Bruce Van Dyke	.40	1.00
328 Lloyd Voss	.40	1.00
329 Bobby Walden	.40	1.00
330 Allen Watson	.40	1.00
331 Jim Bakken	.50	1.25
332 Pete Beathard	.40	1.00
333 Miller Farr	.40	1.00
334 Mel Gray	.75	1.50
335 Jim Hart	.75	1.50
336 MacArthur Lane	.50	1.25
337 Chuck Latourette	.40	1.00
338 Ernie McMillan	.40	1.00
339 Bob Reynolds	.40	1.00
340 Jackie Smith	1.00	2.00
341 Larry Stallings	.40	1.00
342 Jerry Stovall	.40	1.00
343 Chuck Walker	.40	1.00
344 Roger Wehrli	.50	1.25
345 Larry Wilson	1.00	2.00
346 Bob Babich	.40	1.00
347 Pete Barnes	.40	1.00
348 Marty Domres	.40	1.00
349 Steve DeLong	.40	1.00
350 Gary Garrison	.50	1.25
351 Walker Gillette	.40	1.00
352 Dave Grayson	.40	1.00
353 John Hadl	.75	1.50
354 Jim Hill	.40	1.00
355 Bob Howard DB	.40	1.00
356 Tony Liscio	.40	1.00
357 Dennis Partee	.40	1.00
358 Andy Rice	.40	1.00
359 Russ Washington	.40	1.00
360 Doug Wilkerson	.40	1.00
361 John Brodie	1.25	2.50
362 Doug Cunningham	.40	1.00
363 Bruce Gossett	.40	1.00
364 Stan Hindman	.40	1.00
365 John Isenbarger	.40	1.00
366 Charlie Krueger	.40	1.00
367 Frank Nunley	.40	1.00
368 Woody Peoples	.40	1.00
369 Len Rohde	.40	1.00
370 Steve Spurrier	6.00	12.00
371 Gene Washington 49er	.50	1.25
372 Dave Wilcox	.50	1.25
373 Ken Willard	.40	1.00
374 Bob Windsor	.40	1.00
375 Dick Witcher	.40	1.00
376 Maxie Baughan	.40	1.00
377 Larry Brown RB	.75	1.50
378 Boyd Dowler	.50	1.25
379 Chris Hanburger	.50	1.25
380 Charlie Harraway	.40	1.00
381 Rickie Harris	.40	1.00
382 Sonny Jurgensen	2.00	4.00
383 Billy Kilmer	.75	1.50
384 Tommy Mason	.50	1.25
385 Brig Owens	.40	1.00
386 Jack Pardee	.50	1.25
387 Myron Pottios	.40	1.00
388 Jerry Smith	.40	1.00
389 Diron Talbert	.40	1.00
390 Charley Taylor	1.50	3.00
NNO Wonderful World Album	50.00	100.00

1972 NFLPA Wonderful World Stamps

This set of 390 stamps was issued in both 1971 and 1972 under the auspices of the NFL Players Association in conjunction with an album entitled "The Wonderful World of Pro Football USA." The album pictures Walt Garrison being tackled during Super Bowl VI. The stamps are numbered and are approximately 1 15/16" by 2 7/8". The team order of the album is arranged alphabetically according to the city name and then alphabetically by player name within each team The picture stamp album contains 30 pages measuring approximately 9 1/2" by 13 1/4". The text narrates the story of pro football in the United States. The album includes spaces for 390 color player stamps. The checklist and stamp numbering below is according to the album. There are some numbering and very slight text variations between the 1971 and 1972 issues on some stamps, as noted below.

COMPLETE SET (390)	250.00	400.00
1 Bob Berry	.50	1.25
2 Greg Brezina	.40	1.00
3 Ken Burrow	.40	1.00
4 Jim Butler	.40	1.00
5 Wes Chesson	.40	1.00
6 Claude Humphrey	.40	1.00
7 George Kunz	.40	1.00
8 Tom McCauley	.40	1.00
9 Jim Mitchell TE	.40	1.00
10 Tommy Nobis	.75	1.50
11 Ken Reaves	.40	1.00
12 Bill Sandeman	.40	1.00
13 John Small	.40	1.00
14 Harmon Wages	.40	1.00
15 John Zook	.40	1.00
16 Norm Bulaich	.50	1.25
17 Bill Curry	.50	1.25
18 Mike Curtis	.50	1.25
19 Ted Hendricks	1.00	2.00
20 Roy Hilton	.40	1.00
21 Eddie Hinton	.40	1.00
22 David Lee	.40	1.00
23 Jerry Logan	.40	1.00
24 John Mackey	1.00	2.00
25 Tom Matte	.50	1.25
26 Jim O'Brien	.50	1.25
27 Glenn Ressler	.40	1.00
28 Johnny Unitas	6.00	12.00
29 Bob Vogel	.40	1.00
30 Rick Volk	.40	1.00
31 Paul Costa	.40	1.00
32 Jim Dunaway	.40	1.00
33 Paul Guidry	.40	1.00
34 Jim Harris	.40	1.00
35 Robert James	.40	1.00
36 Mike McBath	.40	1.00
37 Haven Moses	.50	1.25
38 Wayne Patrick	.40	1.00
39 John Pitts	.40	1.00
40 Jim Reilly T	.40	1.00
41 Pete Richardson	.40	1.00
42 Dennis Shaw	.50	1.25
43 O.J. Simpson	4.00	8.00
44 Mike Stratton	.40	1.00
45 Bob Tatarek	.40	1.00
46 Dick Butkus	5.00	10.00
47 Jim Cadile	.40	1.00
48 Jack Concannon	.50	1.25
49 Bobby Douglass	.50	1.25
50 George Farmer	.40	1.00
51 Dick Gordon	.40	1.00
52 Bobby Joe Green	.40	1.00
53 Ed O'Bradovich	.40	1.00
54 Mac Percival	.40	1.00
55 Gale Sayers	5.00	10.00
56 George Seals	.40	1.00
57 Jim Seymour	.40	1.00
58 Ron Smith	.40	1.00
59 Bill Staley	.40	1.00
60 Cecil Turner	.40	1.00
61 Al Beauchamp	.40	1.00
62 Virgil Carter	.40	1.00
63 Vern Holland	.40	1.00
64 Bob Johnson	.50	1.25
65 Ron Lamb	.40	1.00
66 Dave Lewis	.40	1.00
67 Rufus Mayes	.40	1.00
68 Horst Muhlmann	.40	1.00
69 Lemar Parrish	.50	1.25
70 Jess Phillips	.40	1.00
71 Mike Reid	1.00	2.00
72 Ken Riley	.50	1.25
73 Paul Robinson	.40	1.00
74 Bob Trumpy	.50	1.25
75 Fred Willis	.50	1.25
76 Don Cockroft	.40	1.00
77 Gary Collins	.40	1.00
78 Gene Hickerson	.40	1.00
79 Fair Hooker	.40	1.00
80 Jim Houston	.40	1.00
81 Walter Johnson	.40	1.00
82 Joe Jones DE	.40	1.00
83 Leroy Kelly	1.00	2.00
84 Milt Morin	.40	1.00
85 Reece Morrison	.40	1.00
86 Bill Nelsen	.50	1.25
87 Mike Phipps	.50	1.25
88 Bo Scott	.40	1.00
89 Jerry Sherk	.40	1.00
90 Ron Snidow	.40	1.00
91 Herb Adderley	1.00	2.00
92 George Andrie	.40	1.00
93 Mike Clark	.40	1.00
94 Dave Edwards	.40	1.00
95 Walt Garrison	.50	1.25
96 Cornell Green	.50	1.25
97 Bob Hayes	1.00	2.00
98 Calvin Hill	.75	1.50
99 Chuck Howley	.50	1.25
100 Lee Roy Jordan	1.00	2.00
101 Dave Manders	.40	1.00
102 Craig Morton	.75	1.50
103 Ralph Neely	.40	1.00
104 Mel Renfro	1.00	2.00
105 Roger Staubach	10.00	20.00
106 Bob Anderson	.40	1.00
107 Sam Brunelli	.40	1.00
108 Dave Costa	.40	1.00
109 Mike Current	.40	1.00
110 Pete Duranko	.40	1.00
111 George Goeddeke	.40	1.00
112 Cornell Gordon	.40	1.00
113 Don Horn	.40	1.00
114 Rich Jackson	.40	1.00
115 Larry Kaminski	.40	1.00
116 Floyd Little	.75	1.50
117 Marv Montgomery	.40	1.00
118 Steve Ramsey	.40	1.00
119 Paul Smith	.40	1.00
120 Bill Thompson	.40	1.00
121 Lem Barney	1.00	2.00
122 Nick Eddy	.40	1.00
123 Mel Farr	.40	1.00
124 Ed Flanagan	.40	1.00
125 Larry Hand	.40	1.00
126 Greg Landry	.50	1.25
127 Dick LeBeau	.50	1.25
128 Mike Lucci	.50	1.25
129 Earl McCullouch	.40	1.00
130 Bill Munson	.50	1.25
131 Wayne Rasmussen	.40	1.00
132 Joe Robb	.40	1.00
133 Jerry Rush	.40	1.00
134 Altie Taylor	.40	1.00
135 Wayne Walker	.50	1.25
136 Ken Bowman	.40	1.00
137 John Brockington	.50	1.25
138 Fred Carr	.40	1.00
139 Carroll Dale	.50	1.25
140 Ken Ellis	.40	1.00
141 Gale Gillingham	.40	1.00
142 Dave Hampton	.40	1.00
143 Doug Hart	.40	1.00
144 MacArthur Lane	.50	1.25
145 Mike McCoy DT	.40	1.00
146 Ray Nitschke	1.00	2.00
147 Frank Patrick	.40	1.00
148 Francis Peay	.40	1.00
149 Dave Robinson	.50	1.25
150 Bart Starr	6.00	12.00
151 Bob Atkins	.40	1.00
152 Elvin Bethea	.75	1.50
153 Garland Boyette	.40	1.00
154 Ken Burrough	.50	1.25
155 Woody Campbell	.40	1.00
156 John Charles	.40	1.00
157 Lynn Dickey	.50	1.25

158 Elbert Drungo .40 1.00
159 Gene Ferguson .40 1.00
160 Charley Johnson .50 1.25
161 Charlie Joiner 1.25 2.50
162 Dan Pastorini .75 1.50
163 Ron Pritchard .40 1.00
164 Walt Suggs .40 1.00
165 Mike Tilleman .40 1.00
166 Bobby Bell 1.00 2.00
167 Aaron Brown .40 1.00
168 Buck Buchanan 1.00 2.00
169 Ed Budde .40 1.00
170 Curley Culp .40 1.00
171 Len Dawson 2.50 5.00
172 Willie Lanier 1.25 2.50
173 Jim Lynch .40 1.00
174 Jim Marsalis .40 1.00
175 Mo Moorman .40 1.00
176 Ed Podolak .50 1.25
177 Johnny Robinson .50 1.25
178 Jan Stenerud .75 1.50
179 Otis Taylor .75 1.50
180 Jim Tyrer .40 1.00
181 Kermit Alexander .40 1.00
182 Coy Bacon .40 1.00
183 Dick Buzin .40 1.00
184 Roman Gabriel .75 1.50
185 Gene Howard .40 1.00
186 Ken Iman .40 1.00
187 Les Josephson .40 1.00
188 Marlin McKeever .40 1.00
189 Merlin Olsen 2.00 4.00
190 Phil Olsen .40 1.00
191 David Ray .40 1.00
192 Lance Rentzel .50 1.25
193 Isiah Robertson .50 1.25
194 Larry Smith RB .40 1.00
195 Jack Snow .50 1.25
196 Nick Buoniconti .75 1.50
197 Doug Crusan .40 1.00
198 Larry Csonka 5.00 10.00
199 Bob DeMarco .40 1.00
200 Marv Fleming .50 1.25
201 Bob Griese 4.00 8.00
202 Jim Kiick .75 1.50
203 Bob Kuechenberg .50 1.25
204 Mercury Morris .75 1.50
205 John Richardson .40 1.00
206 Jim Riley .40 1.00
207 Jake Scott .50 1.25
208 Howard Twilley .50 1.25
209 Paul Warfield 2.00 4.00
210 Garo Yepremian .50 1.25
211 Grady Alderman .40 1.00
212 John Beasley .40 1.00
213 John Henderson .40 1.00
214 Wally Hilgenberg .40 1.00
215 Clint Jones .40 1.00
216 Karl Kassulke .40 1.00
217 Paul Krause .75 1.50
218 Dave Osborn .40 1.00
219 Alan Page 1.00 2.00
220 Ed Sharockman .40 1.00
221 Fran Tarkenton 4.00 8.00
222 Mick Tingelhoff .50 1.25
223 Charlie West .40 1.00
224 Lonnie Warwick .40 1.00
225 Gene Washington Vik .50 1.25
226 Hank Barton .40 1.00
227 Ron Berger .40 1.00
228 Larry Carwell .40 1.00
229 Jim Cheyunski .40 1.00
230 Carl Garrett .40 1.00
231 Rickie Harris .40 1.00
232 Daryle Johnson .40 1.00
233 Steve Kiner .40 1.00
234 Jon Morris .40 1.00
235 Jim Nance .50 1.25
236 Tom Neville .40 1.00
237 Jim Plunkett 1.25 2.50
238 Ron Sellers .40 1.00
239 Len St. Jean .40 1.00
240 Don Webb .40 1.00
241 Dan Abramowicz .50 1.25
242 Dick Absher .40 1.00
243 Leo Carroll .40 1.00
244 Jim Duncan .40 1.00
245 Al Dodd .40 1.00
246 Jim Flanigan LB .40 1.00
247 Hoyle Granger .40 1.00
248 Edd Hargett .40 1.00
249 Glen Ray Hines .40 1.00
250 Hugo Hollas .40 1.00
251 Jake Kupp .40 1.00
252 Dave Long .40 1.00
253 Mike Morgan LB .40 1.00
254 Tom Roussel .40 1.00
255 Del Williams .40 1.00
256 Otto Brown .40 1.00
257 Bobby Duhon .40 1.00
258 Scott Eaton .40 1.00
259 Jim Files .40 1.00
260 Tucker Frederickson .50 1.25
261 Pete Gogolak .40 1.00
262 Bob Grim .40 1.00
263 Don Herrmann .40 1.00
264 Ron Johnson .50 1.25
265 Jim Kanicki .40 1.00
266 Spider Lockhart .50 1.25
267 Joe Morrison .50 1.25
268 Bob Tucker .50 1.25
269 Willie Williams .40 1.00
270 Willie Young .40 1.00
271 Al Atkinson .40 1.00
272 Ralph Baker .40 1.00
273 Emerson Boozer .50 1.25
274 John Elliott .40 1.00
275 Dave Herman .40 1.00
276 Winston Hill .40 1.00
277 Gus Hollomon .40 1.00
278 Bobby Howfield .40 1.00
279 Pete Lammons .40 1.00
280 Joe Namath 10.00 20.00
281 Gerry Philbin .40 1.00
282 Matt Snell .50 1.25
283 Steve Tannen .40 1.00
284 Earlie Thomas .40 1.00
285 Al Woodall .40 1.00
286 Fred Biletnikoff 2.00 4.00
287 George Blanda 3.00 6.00
288 Willie Brown 1.00 2.00
289 Raymond Chester .50 1.25
290 Tony Cline .40 1.00
291 Dan Conners .40 1.00
292 Ben Davidson .50 1.25
293 Hewritt Dixon .40 1.00
294 Tom Keating .40 1.00
295 Daryle Lamonica .75 1.50
296 Gus Otto .40 1.00
297 Jim Otto 1.00 2.00
298 Rod Sherman .40 1.00
299 Charlie Smith RB .40 1.00
300 Gene Upshaw 1.00 2.00
301 Rick Arrington .40 1.00
302 Gary Ballman .40 1.00
303 Lee Bouggess .40 1.00
304 Bill Bradley .50 1.25
305 Happy Feller .40 1.00
306 Richard Harris .40 1.00
307 Ben Hawkins .40 1.00
308 Harold Jackson .50 1.25
309 Pete Liske .40 1.00
310 Al Nelson .40 1.00
311 Gary Pettigrew .40 1.00
312 Tim Rossovich .40 1.00
313 Tom Woodeshick .40 1.00
314 Adrian Young .40 1.00
315 Steve Zabel .40 1.00
316 Chuck Allen .50 1.25
317 Warren Bankston .40 1.00
318 Chuck Beatty .40 1.00
319 Terry Bradshaw 10.00 20.00
320 John Fuqua .40 1.00
321 Terry Hanratty .50 1.25
322 Ray Mansfield .40 1.00
323 Ben McGee .40 1.00
324 John Rowser .40 1.00
325 Andy Russell .50 1.25
326 Ron Shanklin .40 1.00
327 Dave Smith WR .40 1.00
328 Bruce Van Dyke .40 1.00
329 Lloyd Voss .40 1.00
330 Bobby Walden .40 1.00
331 Donny Anderson .50 1.25
332 Jim Bakken .50 1.25
333 Pete Beathard .40 1.00
334 Miller Farr .40 1.00
335 Mel Gray .50 1.25
336 Jim Hart .75 1.50
337 Rolf Krueger .40 1.00
338 Chuck Latourette .40 1.00
339 Ernie McMillan .40 1.00
340 Bob Reynolds .40 1.00
341 Jackie Smith 1.00 2.00
342 Larry Stallings .40 1.00
343 Chuck Walker .40 1.00
344 Roger Wehrli .50 1.25
345 Larry Wilson 1.00 2.00
346 Bob Babich .40 1.00
347 Pete Barnes .40 1.00
348 Steve DeLong .40 1.00
349 Marty Domres .40 1.00
350 Gary Garrison .50 1.25
351 John Hadl .75 1.50
352 Kevin Hardy .40 1.00
353 Bob Howard .40 1.00
354 Deacon Jones 1.25 2.50
355 Terry Owens .40 1.00
356 Dennis Partee .40 1.00
357 Jeff Queen .40 1.00
358 Jim Tolbert .40 1.00
359 Russ Washington .40 1.00
360 Doug Wilkerson .40 1.00
361 John Brodie 1.25 2.50
362 Doug Cunningham .40 1.00
363 Bruce Gossett .40 1.00
364 Stan Hindman .40 1.00
365 John Isenbarger .40 1.00
366 Charlie Krueger .40 1.00
367 Frank Nunley .40 1.00
368 Woody Peoples .40 1.00
369 Len Rohde .40 1.00
370 Steve Spurrier 6.00 12.00
371 Gene Washington 49er .50 1.25
372 Dave Wilcox .50 1.25
373 Ken Willard .50 1.25
374 Bob Windsor .40 1.00
375 Dick Witcher .40 1.00
376 Verlon Biggs .40 1.00
377 Larry Brown .75 1.50
378 Speedy Duncan .50 1.25
379 Chris Hanburger .50 1.25
380 Charlie Harraway .40 1.00
381 Sonny Jurgensen 2.00 4.00
382 Billy Kilmer .75 1.50
383 Tommy Mason .50 1.25
384 Ron McDole .40 1.00
385 Brig Owens .40 1.00
386 Jack Pardee .50 1.25
387 Myron Pottios .40 1.00
388 Jerry Smith .40 1.00
389 Diron Talbert .40 1.00
390 Charley Taylor 1.50 3.00
NNO Wonderful World Album 10.00 20.00

1972 NFLPA Fabric Cards

The 1972 NFLPA Fabric Cards set includes 35 cards printed on cloth. These thin fabric cards measure approximately 2 1/4" by 3 1/2" and are blank backed. The cards are sometimes referred to as "Iron Ons" as they were intended to be semi-permanently ironed on to clothes. The full color portrait of the player is surrounded by a black border. Below the player's name at the bottom of the card is indicated copyright by the NFL Players Association in 1972. The cards may have been illegally reprinted. There is some additional interest in the Staubach card due to the fact that his 1972 Topps card (that same year) is considered his Rookie Card. Since they are unnumbered, they are listed below in alphabetical order according to the player's name. These fabric cards were originally available in vending machines at retail stores and other outlets.

COMPLETE SET (35) 75.00 150.00
1 Donny Anderson 1.00 2.50
2 George Blanda 3.00 6.00
3 Terry Bradshaw 7.50 15.00
4 John Brockington 1.00 2.50
5 John Brodie 2.00 4.00
6 Dick Butkus 5.00 10.00
7 Larry Csonka 3.00 6.00
8 Mike Curtis 1.00 2.50
9 Len Dawson 2.50 5.00
10 Carl Eller 1.25 3.00
11 Mike Garrett 1.00 2.50
12 Joe Greene 4.00 8.00
13 Bob Griese 3.00 6.00
14 Dick Gordon 1.00 2.50
15 John Hadl 1.25 3.00
16 Bob Hayes 1.50 4.00
17 Ron Johnson 1.00 2.50
18 Deacon Jones 1.50 4.00
19 Sonny Jurgensen 2.50 5.00
20 Leroy Kelly 1.50 4.00
21 Jim Kiick 1.25 3.00
22 Greg Landry 1.00 2.50
23 Floyd Little 1.25 3.00
24 Mike Lucci 1.00 2.50
25 Archie Manning 2.00 4.00
26 Joe Namath 10.00 20.00
27 Tommy Nobis 1.25 3.00
28 Alan Page 1.50 4.00
29 Jim Plunkett 2.00 4.00
30 Gale Sayers 5.00 10.00
31 O.J. Simpson 5.00 10.00
32 Roger Staubach 10.00 20.00
33 Duane Thomas 1.25 3.00
34 Johnny Unitas 10.00 20.00
35 Paul Warfield 3.00 6.00

1972 NFLPA Vinyl Stickers

The 1972 NFLPA Vinyl Stickers set contains 20 stand-up type stickers depicting the players in a caricature-like style with big heads. These irregularly shaped stickers are approximately 2 3/4" by 4 3/4". Below the player's name at the bottom of the card is indicated copyright by the NFL Players Association in 1972. The set is sometimes offered as a short set excluding the shorter-printed cards, i.e., those listed by SP in the checklist below. Since they are unnumbered, they are listed below in alphabetical order according to the player's name. The Roger Staubach card holds special interest in that 1972 represents Roger's rookie year for cards. These stickers were originally available in vending machines at retail stores and other outlets. The Dick Butkus and Joe Namath stickers exist as reverse negatives. The set is considered complete with either Butkus or Namath variation.

COMPLETE SET (20) 100.00 175.00
1 Donny Anderson 1.50 4.00
2 George Blanda 3.00 6.00
3 Terry Bradshaw 7.50 15.00
4 John Brockington 1.50 4.00
5 John Brodie 2.50 6.00
6A Dick Butkus 5.00 10.00
6B Dick Butkus 5.00 10.00
7 Dick Gordon 1.50 4.00
8 Joe Greene 2.50 6.00
9 John Hadl 2.00 5.00
10 Bob Hayes 2.50 6.00
11 Ron Johnson SP 4.00 8.00
12 Floyd Little 1.50 4.00
13A Joe Namath 10.00 20.00
13B Joe Namath 10.00 20.00
14 Tommy Nobis 2.00 5.00
15 Alan Page SP 6.00 12.00
16 Jim Plunkett 2.50 5.00
17 Gale Sayers 5.00 10.00
18 Roger Staubach 10.00 20.00
19 Johnny Unitas 10.00 20.00
20 Paul Warfield 2.50 6.00

1972 NFLPA Woodburning Kit

is Woodburning set was sold as an arts and crafts kit with 16-individual player wooden plaques measuring roughly 4" by 4 1/4", 2-generic football player plaques measuring 2 3/8" by 4 1/2" and two larger (roughly 8" by 10") plaques featuring 5-players on each. Each plaque is unnumbered and blankbacked with bright red or maroon printing on the front featuring a drawing of an NFL player. It is thought that each can be found with either the bright red printing or the darker maroon printing. The player image was supposed to be burning out with a tool and then painted by the collector.

1 Lance Alworth 10.00 25.00
2 Terry Bradshaw 15.00 40.00
3 Nick Buoniconti 8.00 20.00
4 Dick Butkus 12.00 30.00
5 Roy Jefferson 6.00 15.00
6 Ron Johnson 6.00 15.00
7 Sonny Jurgensen 10.00 25.00
8 Daryle Lamonica 8.00 20.00
9 Alan Page 8.00 20.00
10 O.J. Simpson 10.00 25.00
11 Matt Snell 8.00 20.00
12 Gene Washington Minn. 6.00 15.00
17 Generic Player 4.00 10.00
18 Quarterbacks 8.00 20.00
19 Running Backs 8.00 20.00

1979 NFLPA Pennant Stickers

The 1979 NFL Player's Association Pennant Stickers set contains stickers measuring approximately 2 1/2" by 5". The pennant-shaped stickers show a circular (black and white) photo of the player next to the NFL Players Association football logo. The set was apparently not approved by the NFL as the team logos are not shown on the cards. The player's name, position, and team are given at the bottom of the card. The backs are blank as it is a peel-off backing only. Some of the stickers can be found with more than one color background and have been listed accordingly below. The complete set price includes just one sticker for each player.

COMPLETE SET (55) 300.00 600.00
1 Lyle Alzado 3.00 6.00
2 Ken Anderson 4.00 8.00
3 Steve Bartkowski SP 12.50 25.00
4 Ricky Bell 3.00 6.00
5 Elvin Bethea 3.00 6.00
6A Tom Blanchard 2.50 5.00
6B Tom Blanchard (Red) 2.50 5.00
6C Tom Blanchard (Yellow) 2.50 5.00
7A Terry Bradshaw 25.00 50.00
7B Terry Bradshaw (Yellow) 25.00 50.00
8A Bob Breunig 2.50 5.00
8B Bob Breunig (Yellow) 2.50 5.00
9A Greg Brezina 2.50 5.00
9B Greg Brezina (Red) 2.50 5.00
9C Greg Brezina (Yellow) 2.50 5.00
10 Doug Buffone SP 12.50 25.00
11 Earl Campbell 15.00 30.00
12 John Cappelletti 4.00 8.00
13 Harold Carmichael 3.00 6.00
14 Chuck Crist SP 12.50 25.00
15 Sam Cunningham 2.50 5.00
16 Isaac Curtis SP (Blue) 12.50 25.00
17 Joe DeLamielleure 4.00 8.00
18A Tom Dempsey 2.50 5.00
18B Tom Dempsey (Red) 2.50 5.00
18C Tom Dempsey (Yellow) 2.50 5.00
19 Tony Dorsett 10.00 20.00
20 Dan Fouts SP 15.00 30.00
21A Roy Gerela 2.50 5.00
21B Roy Gerela (Yellow) 2.50 5.00
22 Bob Griese UER 10.00 20.00
23A Franco Harris Red 10.00 20.00
23B Franco Harris Yellow 10.00 20.00
23C Franco Harris SP Green 25.00 50.00
24 Jim Hart SP 12.50 25.00
25 Charlie Joiner 4.00 8.00
26 Doug Kotar SP 25.00 50.00
27 Paul Krause 4.00 8.00
28 Bob Kuechenberg 2.50 5.00
29 Greg Landry 3.00 6.00
30 Archie Manning 3.00 6.00
31 Chester Marcol 2.50 5.00
32A Harvey Martin 3.00 6.00
32B Harvey Martin Yellow 3.00 6.00
33 Lawrence McCutcheon SP 12.50 25.00
34 Craig Morton 3.00 6.00
35 Haven Moses 2.50 5.00
36 Steve Odom 2.50 5.00
37 Morris Owens 2.50 5.00
38 Dan Pastorini SP 12.50 25.00
39 Walter Payton 25.00 50.00
40 Greg Pruitt SP 12.50 25.00
41 John Riggins 6.00 12.00
42 Jake Scott 2.50 5.00
43 Jerry Sherk SP 12.50 25.00
44 Ken Stabler SP 30.00 60.00
45 Mike Siani SP 12.50 25.00
46 Roger Staubach 25.00 50.00
47 Jan Stenerud 3.00 6.00
48 Art Still SP 12.50 25.00
49 Mick Tingelhoff 2.50 5.00
50 Richard Todd 2.50 5.00
51 Brad Van Pelt SP 30.00 50.00
52 Phil Villapiano SP 12.50 25.00
53A Wesley Walker 3.00 6.00
53B Wesley Walker (Yellow) 3.00 6.00
54 Roger Wehrli SP 12.50 25.00
55 Jim Zorn SP 12.50 25.00

1983 NFLPA Player Pencils Series 1

This set was produced by NAPPCO and licensed by the NFL Player's Association. Each is an actual wooden pencil produced in the team colors with a one-color player image. Each pencil is numbered of 36-pencils in series 1.

COMPLETE SET (36) 125.00 200.00
1 Dan Fouts 3.00 8.00
2 LeRoy Irvin 1.50 4.00
3 Ray Guy 2.00 5.00
4 Steve Largent 3.00 8.00
5 Dwight Clark 2.00 5.00
6 Tom Jackson 2.00 5.00
7 Chuck Muncie 1.50 4.00
8 Ed Too Tall Jones 2.50 6.00
9 Joe Ferguson 1.50 4.00
10 Mark Gastineau 1.50 4.00
11 Stanley Morgan 1.50 4.00
12 Lawrence Taylor 2.50 6.00
13 Terry Bradshaw 8.00 20.00
14 Franco Harris 4.00 10.00
15 Vince Ferragamo 1.50 4.00
16 Mark Moseley 1.50 4.00
17 Mike Pagel 1.50 4.00
18 Ron Jaworski 2.00 5.00
19 Ozzie Newsome 2.50 6.00
20 Ken Anderson 2.00 5.00
21 Jack Lambert 2.50 6.00
22 Joe Klecko 1.50 4.00
23 Lee Roy Selmon 2.00 5.00
24 Steve Bartkowski 2.00 5.00
25 Tommy Vigorito 1.50 4.00
26 Russell Erxleben 1.50 4.00
27A Archie Manning 2.50 6.00
27B Carl Roaches 2.50 6.00
28 Danny White 2.50 6.00
29 William Andrews 2.00 5.00
30 Walter Payton 10.00 25.00
31 Billy Sims 2.00 5.00
32 Tommy Kramer 1.50 4.00
33 John Jefferson 2.00 5.00
34 Brad Budde 1.50 4.00
35 Ottis Anderson 2.00 5.00
36 Tony Dorsett 6.00 15.00

1983 NFLPA Player Pencils Series 2

This set was produced by NAPPCO and licensed by the NFL Player's Association. Each is an actual wooden pencil produced in the team colors with a one-color player image. Each pencil is numbered of 18-pencils in series 2.

3 Steve Largent 3.00 8.00
4 Ed Too Tall Jones 2.50 6.00
5 Lawrence Taylor 2.50 6.00
6 Franco Harris 4.00 10.00
7 Vince Ferragamo 1.50 4.00
9 Walter Payton 10.00 25.00
10 Billy Sims 2.00 5.00
13 Tony Dorsett 6.00 15.00
14 Joe Klecko 1.50 4.00

1986 NFLPA Player Pencils Series 3

13 William Perry 2.00 5.00

1987 NFLPA Player Pencils Series 3

This set was produced by Nappco and licensed by the NFL Player's Association. Each is an actual wooden pencil produced in the team colors with a one-color player image. Each pencil is numbered of 12 in the set and noted as part of the series 3. The year of issue is also included on the pencil.

1 John Elway 12.00 30.00
2 Jim McMahon 6.00 15.00
3 Dan Hampton 5.00 12.00
7 Marcus Allen 6.00 15.00
10 Joe Montana 12.00 30.00

1988 NFLPA Player Pencils

This set was licensed by the NFL Player's Association. Each is an actual wooden pencil produced with metallic paint highlights and a black and white player image. Most of the pencils were released in a numbered version (with NAPPCO logo) as well as unnumbered version. We've listed them below alphabetically. The year of issue is included on each pencil.

COMPLETE SET (18) 100.00 200.00
1 Eric Dickerson 4.00 10.00
2 John Elway 10.00 25.00
3 Jim Everett 3.00 8.00
4 Bobby Hebert 2.50 6.00
5 Jim Kelly 6.00 15.00
6 Bernie Kosar 3.00 8.00
7 Steve Largent 4.00 10.00
8 Howie Long 4.00 10.00
9 Dan Marino 10.00 25.00
10 Jim McMahon 3.00 8.00
11 Freeman McNeil 2.50 6.00
12 Joe Montana 15.00 40.00
13 Jerry Rice 8.00 20.00
14 Lawrence Taylor 4.00 10.00
15 Andre Tippett 2.50 6.00
16 Herschel Walker 3.00 8.00
17 Reggie White 4.00 10.00
18 Doug Williams 3.00 8.00

1995 NFLPA Super Bowl Player's Party

These ten standard-size cards were given away at a NFLPA Super Bowl XXIX player's party. Each card company produced one card; reportedly, the set was limited to 500 of each card. The cards are unnumbered and checklisted below in alphabetical order.

COMPLETE SET (10) 40.00 100.00
1 Marcus Allen 4.80 12.00
2 Jerome Bettis 4.80 12.00
3 Tim Brown 3.20 8.00
4 Trent Dilfer 3.20 8.00
5 Marshall Faulk 6.00 15.00
6 Ronnie Lott 2.40 6.00
7 Dan Marino 16.00 40.00
8 Junior Seau 2.40 6.00
9 Sterling Sharpe 2.40 6.00
10 Heath Shuler 2.40 6.00

1996 NFLPA Super Bowl Player's Party

is 12-card set was given away at a NFLPA Super Bowl XXX player's party. Each card company produced a card for one or more of their brands and each card carries the Players, Inc. logo. The cards are unnumbered and checklisted below in alphabetical order.

COMPLETE SET (12) 6.00 15.00
1 Marcus Allen Ronnie Lott .40 1.00
2 Steve Beuerlein .30 .75
3 Jeff Blake .60 1.50
4 Tim Brown .40 1.00
5 Kerry Collins .40 1.00
6 Kevin Greene .30 .75
7 Garrison Hearst .40 1.00
8 Daryl Johnston .30 .75
9 Joe Montana 2.00 5.00
10 Deion Sanders .60 1.50
11 Herschel Walker .30 .75
12 Logo Card CL .30 .75

1997 NFLPA Super Bowl Player's Party

This 11-card set was distributed at the NFL Player's Association Super Bowl XXXI player's party in New Orleans. Each card company produced one or two cards for the set with each carrying the Player's Party logo. The cards are unnumbered and checklisted below in alphabetical order.

COMPLETE SET (110 6.00 15.00
1 Morten Andersen .30 .75
2 Steve Bono .30 .75
3 Robert Brooks .40 1.00
4 Tony Dorsett .50 1.25
5 Gus Frerotte .40 1.00
6 Kevin Hardy .30 .75
7 Tyrone Hughes .30 .75
8 Dan Marino 2.00 5.00
9 Curtis Martin 1.00 2.50
10 Deion Sanders .50 1.25
11 Tim Brown SKED .40 1.00
12 Checklist Card .30 .75

1998 NFLPA Super Bowl Player's Party

This set was distributed at the NFL Player's Association Super Bowl player's party in San Diego. Each card company produced cards for the set with each carrying the Player's Party logo. The cards are unnumbered (except for the two Score Board issues) and checklisted below in alphabetical order.

COMPLETE SET (13) 4.00 10.00
1 Troy Aikman .80 2.00
2 Jerome Bettis .40 1.00
3 Tim Brown .40 1.00
4 Mark Brunell .60 1.50
5 Terrell Davis 1.20 3.00
6 Tony Dorsett .30 .75
7 Warrick Dunn .50 1.25
8 Eddie George .80 2.00
9 Stan Humphries .30 .75
10 Brent Jones .20 .50
11 Neil Smith .20 .50
12 Reggie White .40 1.00
13 Checklist Card .20 .50

1999 NFLPA Super Bowl Player's Party

This set was distributed at the NFL Player's Association Super Bowl Player's Party in Miami. Each card company produced cards for the set with each carrying the Player's Party logo. The cards feature various numbering schemes but have been listed below according to the checklist card order. Note that some of the cards carry a 1998 copyright line. The Daunte Culpepper card was issued by Press Pass and was signed by Culpepper at the event.

COMPLETE SET (11) 4.80 12.00
1 Cover Card CL .20 .50
2 Shannon Sharpe .30 .75
3 Mark Brunell .80 2.00
4 Warrick Dunn .40 1.00
5 Ray Lewis .20 .50
6 Trace Armstrong .20 .50
7 Zach Thomas .30 .75
8 Fuad Reveiz .20 .50
9 Jerome Bettis .40 1.00
10 Jacquez Green .20 .50
11 Emmitt Smith 1.60 4.00
NNO Daunte Culpepper AU 30.00 60.00

2000 NFLPA Super Bowl Player's Party

This set was distributed at the NFL Player's Association Super Bowl Player's Party in Atlanta in January 2000 in complete set form. The Tim Couch Press Pass card was inadvertently left out of the wrapped set and was distributed by hand later on. Each card company produced cards for the set with each carrying the Player's Inc. logo on the cardfronts. Each card is unnumbered but has been listed below according to the checklist card order. Note that some of the cards do carry a 1999 copyright line instead of 2000.

COMPLETE SET (14) 6.00 15.00
1 Edgerrin James 1.20 3.00
2 Curtis Martin .30 .75
3 Kurt Warner 2.00 5.00
4 Randy Moss .80 2.00
5 Tim Couch .80 2.00
6 Tim Couch .80 2.00
7 Emmitt Smith .60 1.50
8 Kevin Greene .10 .25
9 Dorsey Levens .16 .40
10 Mark Brunell .40 1.00
11 Herschel Walker .10 .25
12 Tim Dwight .16 .40
13 John Randle .16 .40
14 Checklist Card .10 .25

2001 NFLPA Stay Cool in School

This 11-card set was produced for the NFL Player's Association and sponsored by each of the licensed NFL card manufacturers. Cards and sets were given away during the 2001 NFL season to students in the New Orleans area as part of a larger Stay Cool in School program, sponsored by the NFL, that included a variety of prizes rewarding students for good grades and other achievements.

COMPLETE SET (11) 6.00 12.00
1 Mike Anderson (Topps) .50 1.25
2 Corey Dillon (Pacific) .30 .75
3 Ahman Green (Donruss/Playoff) .30 .75
4 Marvin Harrison .30 .75
5 Donovan McNabb (Fleer) .50 1.25
6 Shannon Sharpe (Fleer) .14 .40
7 LaDainian Tomlinson (Upper Deck) 1.25 3.00
8 Michael Vick 1.25 3.00
9 Kurt Warner (Donruss/Playoff) 1.00 2.50
10 Chris Weinke (Topps) .50 1.25
11 Cover Card CL .08 .25

2001 NFLPA Super Bowl Player's Party

This set was distributed at the NFL Player's Association Super Bowl Player's Party in Tampa in January 2001 in complete set form. Each card company produced cards for the set with each carrying the Player's Inc. logo on the cardfronts. Each card is unnumbered but has been listed below alphabetically. Note that some of the cards do carry a year 2000 copyright line instead of 2001.

COMPLETE SET (13) 4.00 10.00
1 Tony Boselli (Topps) .10 .25
2 Derrick Brooks (Collector's Edge) .30 .75
3 Isaac Bruce (Fleer) .30 .75
4 Plaxico Burress (Donruss) .16 .40
5 Tim Couch (Fleer) .40 1.00
6 Daunte Culpepper (Upper Deck) .60 1.50
7 Ron Dayne (Pacific) .60 1.50
8 Marshall Faulk (Collector's Edge) .30 .75
9 Edgerrin James (Topps) .80 2.00
10 Jon Kitna (Pacific) .16 .40
11 Kurt Warner (Playoff) .80 2.00
12 Peter Warrick (Upper Deck) .60 1.50
13 Cover Card CL .10 .25

2002 NFLPA Player of the Day

This set was released by the NFL Players Association to hobby shops participating in the Player of the Day contest in Fall 2002. Each NFL Players' licensed manufacturer issued one card representing one of their football brands. Each card featured the Player of the Day logo on the front.

COMPLETE SET (6) 6.00 15.00
1 Checklist Card .40 1.00
2 Jeff Garcia (Donruss/Playoff) .75 2.00
3 Donovan McNabb (Fleer Maximum) 1.00 2.50
4 Michael Vick (Pacific) 1.00 2.50
5 Brett Favre (Topps) 2.00 5.00
6 Peyton Manning (UD Game Gear) 1.50 4.00

2003 NFLPA Player of the Day

This set was released by the NFL Players Association to hobby shops participating in the Player of the Day contest in the Fall 2003. Each NFL Players' licensed manufacturer issued one card representing one of their football brands. Each card featured the Player of the Day logo on the front.

COMPLETE SET (4) 4.00 10.00
1 Peyton Manning 1.50 4.00
2 Jeff Garcia (Gridiron Kings) .75 2.00
3 David Carr (Fleer Platinum) 1.50 4.00
4 Clinton Portis (Topps) 1.25 3.00

2003 NFLPA Scholastic

is 6-card set was issued by the NFL Player's Association for the benefit of the national Scolastic education program. Each card was produced by one of the major NFL licensed trading card partners complete with a unique card number on the backs.

COMPLETE SET (6) 5.00 10.00
1 Brian Urlacher 1.00 2.50
2 Donovan McNabb (Ultra) 1.00 2.50
3 Jef Garcia (Score) .75 2.00
4 Peyton Manning 1.50 4.00
5 Michael Vick 1.25 3.00
NNO Cover Card .20 .50

2004 NFLPA Player of the Day

is 5-card set was released by NFL Players to hobby shops participating in the Player of the Day contest in Fall 2004. Each NFL Players' licensed manufacturer issued one card representing one of their 2004 football brands. Each card featured the 2004 Player of the Day logo on the front.

COMPLETE SET (5) 2.50 6.00
POD1 Eli Manning 1.50 4.00
POD2 Michael Vick .50 1.25
POD3 Larry Fitzgerald (Topps) .50 1.25
POD4 Tom Brady (SP Game Used Edition) .50 1.25
NNO Cover Card Checklist .08 .25

2005 NFLPA Player of the Day

This 4-card set was released by NFL Players to hobby shops participating in the Player of the Day contest in Fall 2005. Each NFL Players' licensed manufacturer issued one card representing one of their 2005 football brands.The cards feature the 2005 Player of the Day logo on the front.

COMPLETE SET (4) 2.00 4.00
POD1 Tom Brady (Topps) .50 1.25
POD2 Michael Vick (Playoff Prestige) .50 1.25
POD3 Cover Card CL .08 .25
POD4 Peyton Manning (Upper Deck) .60 1.50

2006 NFLPA Player of the Day

This 4-card set was released by NFL Players to hobby shops participating in the Player of the Day contest in Fall 2006. Each NFL Players' licensed manufacturer issued one card representing one of their 2006 football brands.The cards feature the 2006 Player of the Day logo on the front.

COMPLETE SET (4) 2.50 6.00
POD1 Tom Brady 1.50 4.00
POD2 Peyton Manning 1.25 3.00
POD3 Reggie Bush .40 1.00
POD4 Checklist Card .08 .25

2008 NFLPA Player of the Day

This 4-card set was released by NFL Players to hobby shops participating in the Player of the Day contest in Fall 2008. Each of the three NFL Players' licensed manufacturers issued one card representing one of their football brands.The cards feature the 2008 Player of the Day logo on the front.

COMPLETE SET (4) 2.50 6.00
POD1 Darren McFadden .25 .60
POD2 Adrian Peterson .50 1.25
POD3 Tom Brady 1.50 4.00
POD4 Checklist .08 .25

2009 NFLPA Player of the Day

This set was released by NFL Players to hobby shops participating in the Player of the Day contest in Fall 2009. Each of the three NFL Players' licensed manufacturers issued one card representing one of their football brands.The cards feature the 2009 Player of the Day logo on the front.

COMPLETE SET (3) 2.00 5.00
POD1 Larry Fitzgerald .40 1.00
POD2 Adrian Peterson .50 1.25
POD3 Peyton Manning 1.25 3.00

2012 NFLPA A&A Global Stickers

COMPLETE SET (15) 5.00 12.00
1 Ray Rice .25 .60
2 Adrian Peterson .40 1.00
3 Aaron Rodgers .60 1.50
4 Brian Urlacher .40 1.00
5 Calvin Johnson .40 1.00
6 Cam Newton .40 1.00
7 Darrelle Revis .25 .60
8 Darren McFadden .25 .60
9 Drew Brees .40 1.00
10 Eli Manning .30 .75
11 Michael Vick .30 .75
12 Philip Rivers .40 1.00
13 Tom Brady 1.00 2.50
14 Tony Romo .30 .75
15 Troy Polamalu .40 1.00

1983-85 Nike Poster Cards

The cards in this set measure approximately 5" by 7" and were produced for use by retailers of Nike full-size posters as a promotional counter display. The cards are plastic coated and feature color pictures of players posed in unique settings. The hole at the top was designed so that dealers could attach the cards to the display with a soft plastic fastener provided by Nike. The borders are black. Originally, 27-cards were issued together and others were added later as new posters were created. The backs are plain white and carry the poster name, item number, and the player names (except on group photos). The cards are numbered only by the item number on back and have been listed below according to the final two digits of that number.

COMPLETE SET (43) 125.00 225.00
26 Field Generals 5.00 10.00
27 Speedsters 6.00 12.00
40 Steeler Pounder 10.00 20.00
41 Atlanta Arsenal 3.00 6.00
42 Texas Thunder 6.00 12.00
46 No Passing 1.25 3.00
47 Lofton 2.00 5.00
59 Football L.Hayes L.Lipps 1.25 3.00
61 The Judge Lester Hayes 1.25 3.00

1985 Nike

This oversized (slightly larger than 3x5 cards) multisport set was issued by Nike to promote athletic shoe sales. Although the set contains an attractive rookie-season card of Michael Jordan, the fairly plentiful supply has kept the market value quite affordable. Sets were distributed in shrinkwrapped form. The cards are unnumbered and are listed here in alphabetical order.

COMP.FACTORY SET (5) 50.00 125.00
COMPLETE SET (5) 30.00 75.00
3 James Lofton .60 1.50

1984 Oakland Invaders Smokey

This five-card set features the Oakland Invaders of the USFL. The theme of the set is Forestry, i.e., Smokey the Bear is pictured on each card. The set commemorates the 40th birthday of Smokey Bear and is sponsored by the California Forestry Department in conjunction with the U.S. Forest Service. The cards measure approximately 5" by 7". The front features a color posed photo of the football player with Smokey Bear. The player's signature, jersey number, and a public service announcement concerning wildfire prevention occur below the picture. Biographical information is provided on the back.

COMPLETE SET (5) 30.00 60.00
1 Dupre Marshall 6.00 15.00
2 Gary Plummer 6.00 15.00
3 David Shaw 6.00 15.00
4 Kevin Shea 6.00 15.00
5 Smokey Bear 6.00 15.00

1985 Oakland Invaders Team Issue

These 5" by 7" black and white photos were issued by the Oakland Invaders USFL team. Each is blankbacked and features a player photo on the front with his name, position, and team name below the photo.

COMPLETE SET (15) 25.00 60.00
1 Ray Bentley 2.00 5.00
2 Fred Besana 1.50 4.00
3 Novo Bojovic 1.50 4.00
4 Anthony Carter 3.00 8.00
5 David Greenwood 1.50 4.00
6 Bobby Hebert 2.00 5.00
7 Derek Holloway 1.50 4.00
8 Jim Leonard 1.50 4.00
9 Ray Pinney 1.50 4.00
10 Gary Plummer 3.00 8.00
11 Charlie Sumner CO 1.50 4.00
12 Stan Talley 1.50 4.00
13 Ruben Vaughan 1.50 4.00
14 John Williams 2.00 5.00
15 Steve Wright 1.50 4.00

1992 Ocean Spray Frito Lay Posters

This set of posters, measuring 14 1/2"x 22" was sponsored by Ocean Spray and Frito Lay. Each includes a photo of one or more NFL stars as well as a brief list of all-time statistical leaders.

COMPLETE SET (5) 25.00 50.00
1 Bombs Away 7.50 15.00
2 Trench Warfare 6.00 12.00
3 Ground Assault 6.00 12.00
4 Air Strike 6.00 12.00
5 Sackers 4.00 8.00

2006 Odessa Roughnecks IFL

COMPLETE SET (28) 7.50 15.00
1 Ezequiel Arevalo .30 .75
2 Anthony Armstrong .30 .75
3 Joel Babb .30 .75
4 Arthur Berlanga .30 .75
5 Jermaine Blakley .30 .75
6 Andre Burns .30 .75
7 Ahmad Childress .30 .75
8 Marcus Dawson .30 .75
9 Aaron Dunklin .30 .75
10 Derin Graham .30 .75
11 Dewayne Hogan .30 .75
12 Tommy Jones .30 .75
13 Clint McNutt .30 .75
14 Jermaine Mills .30 .75
15 Sean Parker .30 .75
16 Jadhai Pickett .30 .75
17 David Robertson .30 .75
18 Joey Robinson .30 .75
19 Anthony Sapa .30 .75
20 Ryan Schneider .30 .75
21 Dominique Stoamer .30 .75
22 Larry Thompson .30 .75
23 Keith Turner .30 .75
24 Sikoti Uipi .30 .75
25 Chris Williams CO .30 .75
26 Levron Williams .30 .75
27 Digger - Mascot .30 .75
28 Roughneck Dancers .30 .75

2008 Odessa Roughnecks IFL

COMPLETE SET (15) 5.00 10.00
1 Rodney Allen .30 .75
2 Leonard Bell .30 .75
3 Jimmy Connor .30 .75
4 Brandon Douglas .30 .75
5 Shomari Earls .30 .75
6 Peter Fields .30 .75
7 Dennis Gile .30 .75
8 Mike Glover .30 .75
9 Sam Griffin .30 .75
10 DeWayne Hogan .30 .75
11 Michael Moore .30 .75
12 Thomas Parker .30 .75
13 Cameron Rodgers .30 .75
14 Earl Stephens .30 .75
15 Cover Card .30 .75

1960 Oilers Matchbooks

The 1960 Oilers Matchbook set was produced by Universal Match Corp. and features the team's logo and mascot on one side when flattened. The other side includes a small black and white player photo along with the Universal Match Corporation logo.

COMPLETE SET (10) 100.00 175.00
1 George Blanda 20.00 40.00
2 Johnny Carson 10.00 20.00
3 Doug Cline 10.00 20.00
4 Don Hitt 10.00 20.00
5 Mark Johnston 10.00 20.00
6 Dan Lanphear 10.00 20.00
7 Jacky Lee 10.00 20.00
8 Bill Mathis 10.00 20.00
9 Hogan Wharton 10.00 20.00
10 Bob White 10.00 20.00

1961 Oilers Jay Publishing

This 24-card set features (approximately) 5" by 7" black-and-white player photos. The photos show players in traditional poses with the quarterback preparing to throw, the runner heading downfield, and the defenseman ready for the tackle. These cards were packaged 12 to a packet and originally sold for 25 cents. The backs are blank. The cards are unnumbered and checklisted below in alphabetical order.

COMPLETE SET (24) 100.00 175.00
1 Dalva Allen 4.00 8.00
2 Tony Banfield 4.00 8.00
3 George Blanda 15.00 30.00
4 Billy Cannon 6.00 12.00
5 Doug Cline 4.00 8.00
6 Willard Dewveall 4.00 8.00
7 Mike Dukes 4.00 8.00
8 Don Floyd 4.00 8.00
9 Freddy Glick 4.00 8.00
10 Bill Groman 4.00 8.00
11 Charlie Hennigan 5.00 10.00
12 Ed Husmann 4.00 8.00
13 Al Jamison 4.00 8.00
14 Mark Johnston 4.00 8.00
15 Jacky Lee 4.00 8.00
16 Bob McLeod 4.00 8.00
17 Rich Michael 4.00 8.00
18 Dennit Morris 4.00 8.00
19 Jim Norton 4.00 8.00

20 Bob Schmidt 4.00 8.00
21 Dave Smith RB 4.00 8.00
22 Bob Talamini 4.00 8.00
23 Charley Tolar 4.00 8.00
24 Hogan Wharton 4.00 8.00

1965 Oilers Team Issue 8X10

These photos measure 8" by 10" and feature black-and-white player images with white borders. Most of the photos feature posed action shots. The player's position (spelled out completely), name, and team name are printed in the bottom white border in all caps. The backs are blank and the photos are unnumbered and checklisted below in alphabetical order.

COMPLETE SET (38) 200.00 350.00
1 Scott Appleton 6.00 12.00
2 Johnny Baker 6.00 12.00
3 Johnny Baker 6.00 12.00
4 Tony Banfield 6.00 12.00
5 Sonny Bishop 6.00 12.00
6A Sid Blanks 6.00 12.00
6B Sid Blanks 6.00 12.00
(position: Halfback)
7 Danny Brabham 6.00 12.00
8 Ode Burrell 6.00 12.00
9 Doug Cline 6.00 12.00
10 Gary Cutsinger 6.00 12.00
11 Norm Evans 6.00 12.00
12 Don Floyd 6.00 12.00
13 Wayne Frazier 6.00 12.00
14 Willie Frazier 6.00 12.00
15 John Frongillo 6.00 12.00
16 Freddy Glick 6.00 12.00
17 Tom Goode 6.00 12.00
18 Jim Hayes 6.00 12.00
19 Charlie Hennigan 6.00 12.00
20 W.K. Hicks 6.00 12.00
21 W.K. Hicks 6.00 12.00
22 Ed Husmann 6.00 12.00
23 Bobby Jancik 6.00 12.00
24 Pete Jacques 6.00 12.00
25 Bobby Maples 6.00 12.00
26 Bud McFadin 6.00 12.00
27 Bob McLeod 6.00 12.00
28 Bob McLeod 6.00 12.00
29 Jim Norton 6.00 12.00
30 Larry Onesti 6.00 12.00
31 Jack Spikes 6.00 12.00
32 Walt Suggs 6.00 12.00
33 Bob Talamini 6.00 12.00
34 Charley Tolar 6.00 12.00
35 Don Trull 6.00 12.00
36 Don Trull 6.00 12.00
37 Maxie Williams 6.00 12.00
38 John Wittenborn 6.00 12.00

1965 Oilers Team Issue Color

This team-issued set of 16 player photos measures approximately 7 3/4" by 9 3/4" and features color posed shots of players in uniform. Eight photos were grouped together as a set and packaged in plastic bags; set 1 and 2 each originally sold for 50 cents. The photos were printed on thin paper stock and white borders frame each picture. A facsimile autograph is inscribed across the pictures in black ink. The backs are blank. The photos are unnumbered and checklisted below in alphabetical order.

COMPLETE SET (16) 75.00 150.00
1 Scott Appleton 5.00 10.00
2 Tony Banfield 5.00 10.00
3 Sonny Bishop 5.00 10.00
4 George Blanda 15.00 30.00
5 Sid Blanks 5.00 10.00
6 Danny Brabham 5.00 10.00
7 Ode Burrell 5.00 10.00
8 Doug Cline 5.00 10.00
9 Don Floyd 5.00 10.00
10 Freddy Glick 5.00 10.00
11 Charlie Hennigan 5.00 10.00
12 Ed Husmann 5.00 10.00
13 Walt Suggs 5.00 10.00
14 Bob Talamini 5.00 10.00
15 Charley Tolar 5.00 10.00
16 Don Trull 5.00 10.00

1966 Oilers Team Issue 8X10

These photos measure 8" by 10" and feature black-and-white player images with white borders. Most of the photos feature posed action shots. The player's position (initials), name, and team name are printed in the bottom white border in all caps. The backs are blank and the photos are unnumbered and checklisted below in alphabetical order.

COMPLETE SET (5) 25.00 50.00
1 Scott Appleton 6.00 12.00
2 Ode Burrell 6.00 12.00
3 Jacky Lee 6.00 12.00
4 Walt Suggs 6.00 12.00
5 Charley Tolar 6.00 12.00

1967 Oilers Team Issue 5X7

This 14-card set of the Houston Oilers measures approximately 5 1/8" by 7" and features black-and-white player photos. The backs are blank. The cards are unnumbered and checklisted below in alphabetical order.

COMPLETE SET (14) 50.00 100.00
1 Pete Barnes 4.00 8.00
2 Sonny Bishop 4.00 8.00
3 Ode Burrell 4.00 8.00
4 Ronnie Caveness 4.00 8.00
5 Joe Childress CO 4.00 8.00
6 Glen Ray Hines 4.00 8.00
7 Pat Holmes 4.00 8.00
8 Bobby Jancik 4.00 8.00
9 Pete Johns 4.00 8.00
10 Jim Norton 4.00 8.00
11 Willie Parker 4.00 8.00
12 Bob Poole 4.00 8.00
13 Alvin Reed 4.00 8.00
14 Olen Underwood 4.00 8.00

1968 Oilers Team Issue 5X7

These 5" by 7" black-and-white photos have a 3/8" white border and include a facsimile signature of the featured player. The player's name, position (initials), and team name are printed in the bottom white border. The backs are blank and the photos are unnumbered, thus checklisted below in alphabetical order.

COMPLETE SET (12) 40.00 80.00
1 Pete Beathard 5.00 10.00
2 Garland Boyette 4.00 8.00
3 Ode Burrell 4.00 8.00
4 Miller Farr 4.00 8.00
5 Hoyle Granger 4.00 8.00
6 Pat Holmes 4.00 8.00
7 Bobby Maples 4.00 8.00
8 Jim Norton 4.00 8.00
9 George Rice 4.00 8.00
10 Walt Suggs 4.00 8.00
11 Bob Talamini 4.00 8.00
12 George Webster 5.00 10.00

1968-69 Oilers Team Issue 8X10

These approximately 8" by 10" black-and-white photos have white borders. Most of the photos feature posed action shots. The player's name, position (initials), and team name are printed in the bottom white border in all caps. The coaches photos feature a slightly different text style. The backs are blank and the photos are unnumbered and checklisted below in alphabetical order.

COMPLETE SET (40) 150.00 300.00
1A Jim Beirne 6.00 12.00
(position WR)
1B Jim Beirne
position SE
2 Elvin Bethea 7.50 15.00
3 Sonny Bishop 6.00 12.00
4 Garland Boyette 6.00 12.00
5 Ode Burrell 6.00 12.00
6 Ed Carrington 6.00 12.00
7 Joe Childress CO 6.00 12.00
8 Bob Davis QB 6.00 12.00
9 Hugh Devore CO 6.00 12.00
10 Tom Domres 6.00 12.00
11 F.A. Dry CO 6.00 12.00
12 Miller Farr 6.00 12.00
13 Charles Frazier 6.00 12.00
14 Hoyle Granger 6.00 12.00
15 Mac Haik 6.00 12.00
16 W.K. Hicks 6.00 12.00
17 Glen Ray Hines 6.00 12.00
18A Pat Holmes 6.00 12.00
(position: DE)
18B Pat Holmes 6.00 12.00
(position: DT)
19 Roy Hopkins 6.00 12.00
20 Wally Lemm CO 6.00 12.00
21 Jim LeMoine 6.00 12.00
22 Bobby Maples 6.00 12.00
23 Richard Marshall 6.00 12.00
24 Bud McFadin CO 6.00 12.00
25 Zeke Moore 6.00 12.00
26 Willie Parker DT 6.00 12.00
27 Johnny Peacock 6.00 12.00
28 Fran Polsfoot CO 6.00 12.00
29 Ron Pritchard 6.00 12.00
(Preparing to fend off blocker)
30 Alvin Reed 6.00 12.00
31 Tom Regner 6.00 12.00
32 George Rice 6.00 12.00
33 Bob Robertson 6.00 12.00
34 Walt Suggs 6.00 12.00
35 Don Trull 6.00 12.00
36 Olen Underwood 6.00 12.00
37 Loyd Wainscott 6.00 12.00
38 Wayne Walker 7.50 15.00
39 George Webster 7.50 15.00
40 Glenn Woods 6.00 12.00

1969 Oilers Postcards

These postcards were issued in the late 1960s or possibly early 1970s. Each features a black and white photo of an Oilers player on the front along with his name printed below the photo and to the left. The backs feature a postcard format with most also including a list of Oiler's souvenir items that could be ordered from the team. The postcards measure roughly 3 1/4" by 5 1/2." Any additions to this list are appreciated.

COMPLETE SET (6) 20.00 40.00
1 Jim Beirne 4.00 8.00
2 Woody Campbell 4.00 8.00
3 Alvin Reed 4.00 8.00
4 Tom Regner 4.00 8.00
5 Walt Suggs 4.00 8.00
6 George Webster 5.00 10.00

1971 Oilers Team Issue 4X5

This 23-card set measures approximately 4" by 5 1/2" and features black-and-white, close-up, player photos, bordered in white and printed on a textured paper stock. The team name appears at the top between an Oilers helmet and the NFL logo, while the player's name and position are printed in the bottom border. The cards are unnumbered and checklisted below in alphabetical order. The set's date is defined by the fact that Willie Alexander, Ron Billingsley, Ken Burrough, Lynn Dickey, Robert Holmes, Dan Pastorini, Floyd Rice, Mike Tilleman's first year with the Houston Oilers was 1971, and Charlie Johnson's last year with the Oilers was 1971.

COMPLETE SET (23) 75.00 150.00
1 Willie Alexander 4.00 8.00
2 Jim Beirne 4.00 8.00
3 Elvin Bethea 6.00 12.00
4 Ron Billingsley 4.00 8.00
5 Garland Boyette 4.00 8.00
6 Leo Brooks 4.00 8.00
7 Ken Burrough 5.00 10.00
8 Woody Campbell 4.00 8.00
9 Lynn Dickey 5.00 10.00
10 Elbert Drungo 4.00 8.00
11 Pat Holmes 4.00 8.00
12 Robert Holmes 4.00 8.00
13 Ken Houston 6.00 12.00
14 Charley Johnson 5.00 10.00
15 Charlie Joiner 10.00 20.00
16 Zeke Moore 4.00 8.00
17 Mark Moseley 5.00 10.00
18 Dan Pastorini 5.00 10.00
19 Alvin Reed 4.00 8.00
20 Tom Regner 4.00 8.00
21 Floyd Rice 4.00 8.00
22 Mike Tilleman 4.00 8.00
23 George Webster 5.00 10.00

1971 Oilers Team Issue 5X7

This set of the Houston Oilers measures approximately 5" by 7" and features borderless black-and-white player photos. The photos are very similar to the 1972 release but can be differentiated by the slight difference in the positioning of the player's name and team name below the photo. The 1972 photos feature both names much closer to the photos edge than the 1971 set. The cards are unnumbered and checklisted below in alphabetical order.

COMPLETE SET (15) 50.00 100.00
1 Allen Aldridge 4.00 8.00
2 Jim Beirne 4.00 8.00
3 Elvin Bethea 5.00 10.00
4 Ron Billingsley 4.00 8.00
5 Ken Burrough 5.00 10.00
6 John Charles 4.00 8.00
7 Joe Dawkins 4.00 8.00
8 Calvin Fox 4.00 8.00
9 Johnny Gonzalez Eq.Mgr. 4.00 8.00
10 Cleo Johnson 4.00 8.00
11 Spike Jones 4.00 8.00
12 Alvin Reed 4.00 8.00
13 Floyd Rice 4.00 8.00
14 Mike Tilleman 4.00 8.00
15 George Webster 5.00 10.00

1972 Oilers Team Issue 5X7

This set of the Houston Oilers measures approximately 5" by 7" and features borderless black-and-white player photos. The backs are blank. The cards are unnumbered and checklisted below in alphabetical order. The photos are very similar to the 1971 release but can be differentiated by the slight difference in the positioning of player's name and team name below the photo. The 1972 photos feature both names much closer to the photos edge than the 1971 set

COMPLETE SET (12) 40.00 80.00
1 Ron Billingsley 4.00 8.00
2 Garland Boyette 4.00 8.00
3 Levert Carr 4.00 8.00
4 Walter Highsmith 4.00 8.00
5 Al Johnson 4.00 8.00
6 Benny Johnson 4.00 8.00
7 Guy Murdock 4.00 8.00
8 Willie Rodgers 4.00 8.00
9 Ron Saul 4.00 8.00
10 Mike Tilleman 4.00 8.00
11 Ward Walsh 4.00 8.00
12 George Webster 5.00 10.00

1973 Oilers McDonald's

is set of photos was sponsored by McDonald's. Each photo measures approximately 8" by 10" and features a posed color close-up photo bordered in white. The player's name and team name are printed in black in the bottom white border. The top portion of the back has biographical information, career summary, and career statistics. The bottom portion carries the Oilers 1973 game schedule. The photos are unnumbered and are checklisted below alphabetically.

COMPLETE SET (4) 25.00 50.00
1 Bill Curry 5.00 10.00
2 John Matuszak 7.50 15.00
3 Zeke Moore 5.00 10.00
4 Dan Pastorini 7.50 15.00

1973 Oilers Team Issue

This 17-card set of the Houston Oilers measures approximately 5" by 8" and features black-and-white player photos with a white border. The backs are blank. The cards are unnumbered and checklisted below in alphabetical order.

COMPLETE SET (17) 50.00 100.00
1 Mack Alston 4.00 8.00
2 Bob Atkins 4.00 8.00
3 Skip Butler 4.00 8.00
4 Al Cowlings 4.00 8.00
5 Lynn Dickey 5.00 10.00
6 Mike Fanucci 4.00 8.00
7 Edd Hargett 4.00 8.00
8 Lewis Jolley 4.00 8.00
9 Clifton McNeil 4.00 8.00
10 Ralph Miller 4.00 8.00
11 Zeke Moore 4.00 8.00
12 Dave Parks 4.00 8.00
13 Willie Rodgers 4.00 8.00
14 Greg Sampson 4.00 8.00
15 Finn Seemann 4.00 8.00
16 Jeff Severson 4.00 8.00
17 Fred Willis 4.00 8.00

1974 Oilers Team Issue

These photos measure approximately 5" by 7" and contain black and white player shots on heavy paper stock. Each carries a facsimile signature and was produced around 1974. These cardbacks are blank. The Bethea, Bingham, Gresham, and Smith card are smaller in size than the rest of the series (approximately 5" by 6 1/2") and could possibly have been issued in another year.

COMPLETE SET (15) 50.00 100.00
1 Mack Alston 4.00 8.00
2 George Amundson 4.00 8.00
3 Elvin Bethea 6.00 12.00
4 Gregg Bingham UER 4.00 8.00
5 Ken Burrough 5.00 10.00
6 Skip Butler 4.00 8.00
7 Al Cowlings 4.00 8.00
8 Lynn Dickey 5.00 10.00
9 Bob Gresham 4.00 8.00
10 Zeke Moore 4.00 8.00
11 Billy Parks 4.00 8.00
12 Dan Pastorini 5.00 10.00
13 Greg Sampson 4.00 8.00
14 Jeff Severson 4.00 8.00
15 Tody Smith 4.00 8.00

1975 Oilers Team Issue

These photos measure approximately 5" by 7" and contain black and white player shots printed on heavy paper stock. Unlike the 1974 issue, these photos do not carry a facsimile signature. The cardbacks are blank and some of the photos are cropped smaller than others.

COMPLETE SET (12) 50.00 100.00
1 Willie Alexander 4.00 8.00
2 Elvin Bethea 6.00 12.00
3 Ken Burrough 5.00 10.00
4 Lynn Dickey 5.00 10.00
5 Fred Hoaglin 4.00 8.00
6 Billy Johnson 6.00 12.00
7 Steve Kiner 4.00 8.00
8 Zeke Moore 4.00 8.00
9 Guy Roberts 4.00 8.00
10 Willie Rodgers 4.00 8.00
11 Ted Washington 4.00 8.00
12 Fred Willis 4.00 8.00

1975 Oilers Team Sheets

This set consists of three 8" by 10" sheets that display a group of black-and-white player photos on each. The player's name is printed below each photo and the backs are blank. The sheets are unnumbered and checklisted below alphabetically according to the player featured in the upper left corner.

COMPLETE SET (3) 10.00 20.00
1 Sheet 1 4.00 8.00
2 Sheet 3 4.00 8.00
3 Sheet 2 3.00 6.00

1980 Oilers Police

The 14-card set of the 1980 Houston Oilers is unnumbered and checklist below in alphabetical order. The cards measure approximately 2 5/8" by 4 1/8". The Kiwanis Club, the local law enforcement agency, and the Houston Oilers sponsored this set. The backs feature "Oilers Tips" and a Kiwanis logo. The fronts feature logos of the Kiwanis and the City of Houston.

COMPLETE SET (14) 10.00 20.00
1 Gregg Bingham .40 1.00
2 Robert Brazile .50 1.25
3 Ken Burrough .60 1.50
4 Rob Carpenter .50 1.25
5 Ronnie Coleman .40 1.00
6 Curley Culp .50 1.25
7 Carter Hartwig .40 1.00
8 Billy Johnson .60 1.50
9 Carl Mauck .40 1.00
10 Gifford Nielsen .40 1.00
11 Cliff Parsley .40 1.00
12 Bum Phillips CO .75 2.00
13 Mike Renfro .40 1.00
14 Ken Stabler 3.00 8.00

1985 Oklahoma Outlaws Team Sheets

These 8" by 10" sheets were issued by the Oklahoma Outlaws primarily to the media for use as player images for print. Each features 8-players or coaches with the player's jersey number, name, and position beneath his picture. The sheets are blankbacked and unnumbered.

COMPLETE SET (6) 12.00 30.00
1 Selwyn Drain 2.50 6.00
Kelvin Middleton
Lance Shields
Fre
2 John Gillen 2.00 5.00
Ed Smith
Bruce Gheesling
Tom Thayer
3 Bruce Laird 2.00 5.00
Allan Clark
Mack Boatner
Daryl Good
4 Johnny Lewis 2.00 5.00
Kit Lathrop
Karl Lorch
Alvin Powel
5 W.R. Tatham Sr. 2.00 5.00
W.R. Tatham Jr.
Frank Kush
Roge
6 John Teerlinck 3.00 8.00
Tim Mills
Lonnie Harris
Case DeB

2001 Oklahoma Wranglers AFL

ese cards were released in 2001 by the Oklahoma Wranglers of the Arena Football League and sponsored by KWTV News. The cards are printed in color on the front and back and include the year of issue in the lower right hand corner of the cardfronts.

COMPLETE SET (22) 7.50 15.00
1 Kusanti Abdul-Salaam .40 1.00
2 Britt Bowen .40 1.00
3 Tom Briggs .40 1.00
4 Wes Caswell .40 1.00
5 Antonio Chandler .40 1.00
6 Lamart Cooper .50 1.25
7 Demetrius Crowder .40 1.00
8 Akaba Delaney .40 1.00
9 Darry Dillard .40 1.00
10 Shawn Foreman .40 1.00
11 Brian Goolsby .40 1.00
12 Lindsay Hassell .40 1.00
13 Josh Heskew .40 1.00
14 Carlos Johnson .40 1.00
15 Ron Lopez .75 2.00
16 Mike Mari .40 1.00
17 Travis McDonald .40 1.00
18 Bobby McGowins .40 1.00
19 Eric Miller .40 1.00
20 Tyrone Peace .40 1.00
21 Joe Phears .50 1.25
(No Photo on Front)
22 Chuck Reed .40 1.00

2008 Omaha Beef UIF

COMPLETE SET (30) 6.00 12.00
1 Javon Bell .20 .50
2 Reicko Jones .20 .50
3 James McNear .20 .50
4 Brent Hafford .20 .50
5 Chris Eads .20 .50
6 David Horne .20 .50
7 Kyle Whitehurst .20 .50
8 Ken Horton .20 .50
9 Ricky Lebeda .20 .50
10 Dustin Creager .20 .50
11 Chad Schmigel .20 .50
12 Jamar Day .20 .50
13 Diezeas Calbert .20 .50
14 R.J. Rollins .20 .50
15 James Poynter .20 .50
16 Dan Potmesil .20 .50
17 Ron Jackson .20 .50
18 Robert Moore .20 .50
19 Mike Nizzi .20 .50
20 Blake Fuchtman .20 .50
21 James Head .20 .50
22 Colin Bryant .20 .50
23 Demoine Adams .20 .50
24 Marques Salmond .20 .50
25 Steve Martin CO .20 .50
26 James Kerwin Asst. CO .20 .50
27 Tony Veland Def. Coor. .20 .50
28 Tommie Williams Off.Coor. .20 .50
29 Rival Game .20 .50
30 Schedule CL .20 .50

2010 Omaha Nighthawks UFL

COMPLETE SET (10) 15.00 30.00
1 Justin Brantly 1.00 2.50
2 Dusty Dvoracek 1.00 2.50
3 Robert Ferguson 1.50 4.00
4 George Foster 1.00 2.50
5 Jeff Garcia 2.50 6.00
6 Ahman Green 2.00 5.00
7 Cato June 1.50 4.00
8 Jay Moore 1.00 2.50
9 Gary Stills 1.00 2.50
10 Shaud Williams 1.00 2.50

1979 Open Pantry

This set is an unnumbered, 12-card issue featuring players from Milwaukee area professional sports teams with five Brewers baseball (1-5), five Bucks basketball (6-10), and two Packers football (11-12). Cards are black and white with red trim and measure approximately 5" by 6". Cards were sponsored by Open Pantry, Lake to Lake, and MACC (Milwaukee Athletes against Childhood Cancer). The cards are unnumbered and hence are listed and numbered below alphabetically within sport.

COMPLETE SET (12) 12.50 25.00
11 Rich McGeorge 1.00 2.00
12 Steve Wagner 1.00 2.00

1994 Orlando Predators AFL

The Orlando Predators of the Arena Football League issued this set for distribution through their consession stands and gift shop. Each card is unnumbered and measures the standard size. Reportedly, the set was limited to a production run of 2000.

COMPLETE SET (27) 6.00 12.00
1 Ben Bennett .30 .75
2 Henry Brown .20 .50
3 Webbie Burnett .20 .50
4 Jorge Cimadevilla .20 .50
5 Bernard Clark .20 .50
6 Wayne Dickson .20 .50
7 Eric Drakes .20 .50
8 Chris Ford .20 .50
9 Victor Hall .20 .50
10 Paul McGowan .20 .50
11 Perry Moss CO .30 .75
12 Jerry Odom .20 .50
13 Billy Owens WR .20 .50
14 Marshall Roberts .20 .50
15 Durwood Roquemore .20 .50
16 Rusty Russell DL .20 .50
17 Tony Scott .20 .50
18 Ricky Shaw .20 .50
19 Alex Shell .20 .50
20 Bill Stewart .20 .50
21 Duke Tobin .20 .50
22 Barry Wagner .40 1.00
23 Jackie Walker .20 .50
24 Herkie Walls .20 .50
25 Isaac Williams .20 .50
26 Coaches .30 .75
27 The Klaw (mascot) .20 .50

1998 Orlando Predators AFL

This set was released by the Predators in sealed factory set form. Each card includes a colorful border surrounding the player photo on the front with the players' name and jersey number above the image.

COMPLETE SET (28) 6.00 15.00
1 Chris Barber .20 .50
2 Webbie Burnett .20 .50
3 John Clark .20 .50
4 David Cool .20 .50
5 Bret Cooper .20 .50
6 Tommy Dorsey .20 .50
7 Eric Drakes .20 .50
8 Corris Ervin .20 .50
9 Kevin Gaines .20 .50
10 Robert Gordon .20 .50
11 Bill Hall .20 .50
12 Victor Hall .20 .50
13 Rick Hamilton .30 .75
14 Kelvin Ingram .20 .50
15 Chad Johnston .20 .50
16 Bruce LaSane .20 .50
17 Ty Law .20 .50
18 R.Lee .20 .50
J.Crockett
19 Damon Mason .20 .50
20 Connell Maynor .20 .50
21 Rich McKenzie .20 .50
22 Jerry Odom .20 .50
23 Pat O'Hara .30 .75
24 Howard Smothers .20 .50
25 Connell Spain .20 .50
26 Matt Storm .20 .50
27 Barry Wagner .50 1.25
28 Jay Gruden CO .50 1.25

1998 Orlando Predators AFL Champions

COMPLETE SET (27) 6.00 15.00
1 Connell Maynor .20 .50
2 Chris Barber .20 .50
3 Bruce Lasane .20 .50
4 Bret Cooper .20 .50
5 Bill Hall .20 .50
6 Barry Wagner .50 1.25
7 Howard Smothers .20 .50
8 Eric Drakes .20 .50
9 David Cool .20 .50
10 Damon Mason .20 .50
11 Corris Ervin .20 .50
12 Connell Spain .20 .50
13 Pat O'Hara .30 .75
14 Matt Storm .20 .50
15 Kevin Gaines .20 .50
16 Kenny McEntyre .20 .50
17 Kelvin Ingram .20 .50
18 Jay Gruden CO .50 1.25
19 Ty Law .20 .50
20 Tommy Dorsey .20 .50
21 Robert Gordon .20 .50
22 Rick Hamilton .30 .75
23 Rich McKenzie .20 .50
24 Reggie Lee .20 .50
25 Webbie Burnett .20 .50
26 Victor Hall .20 .50
27 Cover Card CL .20 .50

1999 Orlando Predators AFL

This set was produced by Mercury Printers Publications and released by the Predators in sealed factory set form. Each card includes a colorful border surrounding the player photo on the front with a bio on the back.

COMPLETE SET (27) 6.00 15.00
1 Keif Bryant .20 .50
2 Webbie Burnett .20 .50
3 William Carr .20 .50
4 B.J. Cohen .20 .50
5 David Cool .20 .50
6 Bret Cooper .20 .50
7 Jeff Cothran .20 .50
8 Cliff Dell .30 .75
9 Tommy Dorsey .20 .50
10 Eric Drakes .20 .50
11 Kevin Gaines .20 .50
12 Jay Gruden CO .50 1.25
13 Bill Hall .20 .50
14 Victor Hall .20 .50
15 Rick Hamilton .30 .75
16 Kevin Johnson OL .20 .50
17 Ty Law WR .20 .50
18 Reggie Lee .20 .50
19 Damon Mason .20 .50
20 Connell Maynor .20 .50
21 Kenny McEntyre .20 .50
22 Rich McKenzie .20 .50
23 Browning Nagle .50 1.25
24 Pat O'Hara .30 .75
25 Matt Storm .20 .50
26 Barry Wagner .50 1.25
27 Antwuan Wyatt .20 .50

2000 Orlando Predators AFL

COMPLETE SET (28) 10.00 20.00
1 Ernest Allen .40 1.00
2 Braniff Bonaventure .40 1.00
3 Rodney Brown .40 1.00
4 Webbie Burnett .40 1.00
5 B.J. Cohen .40 1.00
6 David Cool .40 1.00
7 Bret Cooper .40 1.00
8 Clif Dell .40 1.00
9 Tommy Dorsey .40 1.00
10 Joe Douglass .40 1.00
11 Curtis Eason .40 1.00
12 Jay Gruden CO .60 1.50
13 Bill Hall .40 1.00
14 Rick Hamilton .40 1.00
15 Ty Law .40 1.00
16 Reggie Lee .40 1.00
17 Damon Mason .40 1.00
18 Dedric Mathis .40 1.00
19 Connell Maynor .40 1.00
20 Kenny McEntyre .40 1.00
21 Rich McKenzie .40 1.00
22 Mark Nonsant .40 1.00
23 Pat O'Hara .60 1.50
24 Mike Osuna .40 1.00
25 Frederick Ray .40 1.00
26 Matt Storm .40 1.00
27 Team Card .40 1.00

1938-42 Overland All American Roll Candy Wrappers

These unnumbered candy wrappers measure roughly 5" by 5 1/4" and were issued over a period of time in the late 1930's and early 1940's. A drawing of the player is at the top of the wrapper with his name, team name, and a short biography below. All players known thus far are post college athletes with some playing in the NFL and some on the military teams which were so popular during World War II. The product name and price "All American Football Roll 1-cent" appears at the bottom with the Overland Candy Corporation mentioned below that. The backs are blank and the wrappers are nearly always found with multiple creases. Any additions to this list are appreciated.

1 Sammy Baugh 800.00 1200.00
2 Bill DeCorrevont 350.00 600.00
3 Rudy Mucha 350.00 600.00
4 Bruce Smith 500.00 800.00

1984 Pacific Legends

This 30-card set (produced by Pacific Trading Cards in 1984) has a yellowish tone to the front of the cards, similar to Cramer's Baseball Legends, but is entitled "Football Legends." The cards measure approximately 2 1/2" by 3 1/2". The set features prominent individuals who played football at universities in the Pac 10 conference (and its predecessors).

COMPLETE SET (30) 30.00 60.00
1 O.J. Simpson 2.50 6.00
2 Mike Garrett .75 2.00
3 Pop Warner CO .75 2.00
4 Bob Schloredt .60 1.50
5 Pat Haden .75 2.00
6 Ernie Nevers .75 2.00
7 Jackie Robinson 2.50 6.00
8 Arnie Weinmeister .75 2.00
9 Gary Beban 1.50 4.00
10 Jim Plunkett 1.50 4.00
11 Bobby Grayson .60 1.50
12 Craig Morton .75 2.00
13 Ben Davidson .75 2.00
14 Jim Hardy .60 1.50
15 Vern Burke .60 1.50
16 Hugh McElhenny 1.00 2.50
17 John Wayne 2.50 6.00
18 Ricky Bell .75 2.00
19 George Wilson RB .60 1.50
20 Bob Waterfield 1.00 2.50
21 Charlie Mitchell .60 1.50
22 Donn Moomaw .60 1.50
23 Don Heinrich .60 1.50
24 Terry Baker RB 1.50 4.00
25 Jack Thompson .75 2.00
26 Charles White 1.00 2.50
27 Frank Gifford 1.50 4.00
28 Lynn Swann 3.00 8.00
29 Brick Muller .60 1.50
30 Ron Yary .75 2.00

1989 Pacific Steve Largent

The 1989 Pacific Trading Cards Steve Largent set contains 110 standard-size cards, 85 of which are numbered. The numbered cards have silver borders on the fronts with photos of various career highlights; some are horizontally oriented, others are vertically oriented. The backs all are horizontally oriented and have light blue borders with information about the highlight shown on the front. The other 25 unnumbered cards are actually puzzle pieces which form a 12 1/2" by 17 1/2" poster of Largent in action. The cards were distributed as factory sets and in ten-card wax packs.

COMPLETE SET (110) 10.00 25.00
COMMON CARD (1-85) .08 .25
1 Title Card .30 .75
9 Coach Patera and .15 .40
10 Rookie 1976 .30 .75
13 First Team All Rookie .15 .40
16 Captains Largent and .15 .40
19 Jerry Rhome and Largent .30 .75
22 Zorn Connection .15 .40
23 Steve Largent and .15 .40
26 Seahawks MVP 1981 .15 .40
28 Chuck Knox Head Coach .15 .40
31 Tilley and Largent UER .30 .75
42 Seattle Sports Star .15 .40
45 Steve and Eugene .15 .40
51 Lane .15 .40
Brown
Largent
53 Krieg Connection .15 .40
55 NFL All-Time Leading .15 .40
57 Steve and Coach Knox .15 .40
58 1987 Seahawks MVP .15 .40
59 Largent at Quarterback .30 .75
60 NFL All-Time Great .15 .40
61 Travelers' NFL Man of .15 .40
63 Holding for Norm .15 .40
67 Tommie Agee .15 .40
Largent
Skansi
70 Largent 1.25 3.00
Elway
74 Jim Zorn and Largent .15 .40
75 Mr. Seahawk .15 .40
76 Sets NFL Career .15 .40
77 Two of the Greatest .30 .75
78 Steve Largent .30 .75
Rhome
Joiner
79 NFL All-Time Leader .15 .40
80 NFL All-Time Leader .15 .40
82 NFL All-Time Leader .15 .40
83 First Recipient of the .30 .75
84 Steve Largent .15 .40
85 Future Hall of Famer .40 1.00

1991 Pacific Prototypes

This five-card standard-size set was sent out by Pacific Trading Cards to prospective dealers prior to the general release of their debut set of NFL football cards. The cards are styled almost exactly like the regular issue Pacific cards that followed shortly thereafter. These prototype cards are distinguished from the regular issue cards by their different card numbers and the presence of zeroes for the stat totals on the prototype card backs. The cards are numbered on the back. The production run reportedly was approximately 5,000 sets, and these sets were distributed to dealers in the Pacific network with the rest being used as sales samples.

COMPLETE SET (5) 60.00 100.00
1 Joe Montana 25.00 40.00
32 Bo Jackson 4.00 8.00
66 Eric Metcalf 1.60 4.00
100 Barry Sanders 25.00 40.00
232 Troy Aikman 15.00 25.00

1991 Pacific

This 660-card standard size set was the first full football set issued by Pacific Trading Cards. The cards were issued in two series of 550 and 110 cards with packs containing 10 cards. Factory sets were also produced for each series. The cards feature a full-color glossy front with the name on the left hand side of the card. Rookie Cards include Mike Croel, Lawrence Dawsey, Craig Erickson (his only Rookie Card), Ricky Ervins, Brett Favre, Jeff Graham, Mark Higgs, Randal Hill, Michael Jackson, Herman Moore, Eric Pegram, Mike Pritchard, Leonard Russell and Harvey Williams.

COMPLETE SET (660) 7.50 15.00
COMP.SERIES 1 (550) 4.00 8.00
COMP.FACT.SER.1 (550) 5.00 10.00
COMP.SERIES 2 (110) 4.00 10.00
COMP.FACT.SER.2 (110) 6.00 12.00
COMP.CHECKLIST SET (5) 7.50 15.00
1 Deion Sanders .15 .40
2 Steve Broussard .01 .05
3 Aundray Bruce .01 .05
4 Rick Bryan .01 .05
5 John Rade .01 .05
6 Scott Case .01 .05
7 Tony Casillas .01 .05
8 Shawn Collins .01 .05
9 Darion Conner .01 .05
10 Tory Epps .01 .05
11 Bill Fralic .01 .05
12 Mike Gann .01 .05
13 Tim Green UER .01 .05
14 Chris Hinton .01 .05
15 Houston Hoover UER .01 .05
16 Chris Miller .02 .10
17 Andre Rison .02 .10
18 Mike Rozier .01 .05
19 Jessie Tuggle .01 .05
20 Don Beebe .01 .05
21 Ray Bentley .01 .05
22 Shane Conlan .01 .05
23 Kent Hull .01 .05
24 Mark Kelso .01 .05
25 James Lofton UER .02 .10
26 Scott Norwood .01 .05
27 Andre Reed .02 .10
28 Leonard Smith .01 .05
29 Bruce Smith .08 .25
30 Leon Seals .01 .05
31 Darryl Talley .01 .05
32 Steve Tasker .02 .10
33 Thurman Thomas .08 .25
34 James Williams .01 .05
35 Will Wolford .01 .05
36 Frank Reich .02 .10
37 Jeff Wright RC .01 .05
38 Neal Anderson .02 .10
39 Trace Armstrong .01 .05
40 Johnny Bailey UER .01 .05
41 Mark Bortz UER .01 .05
42 Cap Boso RC .01 .05
43 Kevin Butler .01 .05
44 Mark Carrier DB .02 .10
45 Jim Covert .01 .05
46 Wendell Davis .01 .05
47 Richard Dent .02 .10
48 Shaun Gayle .01 .05
49 Jim Harbaugh .08 .25
50 Jay Hilgenberg .01 .05
51 Brad Muster .01 .05
52 William Perry .02 .10
53 Mike Singletary UER .02 .10
54 Peter Tom Willis .01 .05
55 Donnell Woolford .01 .05
56 Steve McMichael .02 .10
57 Eric Ball .01 .05
58 Lewis Billups .01 .05
59 Jim Breech .01 .05
60 James Brooks .02 .10
61 Eddie Brown .01 .05
62 Rickey Dixon .01 .05
63 Boomer Esiason .02 .10
64 James Francis .01 .05
65 David Fulcher .01 .05
66 David Grant .01 .05
67 Harold Green UER .01 .05
68 Rodney Holman .01 .05
69 Stanford Jennings .01 .05
70A Tim Krumrie ERR .20 .50
70B Tim Krumrie COR .10 .30
71 Tim McGee .01 .05
72 Anthony Munoz .02 .10
73 Mitchell Price RC .01 .05
74 Eric Thomas .01 .05
75 Ickey Woods .01 .05
76 Mike Baab .01 .05
77 Thane Gash .01 .05
78 David Grayson .01 .05
79 Mike Johnson .01 .05
80 Reggie Langhorne .01 .05
81 Kevin Mack .01 .05
82 Clay Matthews .02 .10
83A Eric Metcalf ERR .20 .50
83B Eric Metcalf COR .10 .30
84 Frank Minnifield .01 .05
85 Mike Oliphant .01 .05
86 Mike Pagel .01 .05
87 John Talley .01 .05
88 Lawyer Tillman .01 .05
89 Gregg Rakoczy UER .01 .05
90 Bryan Wagner .01 .05
91 Rob Burnett RC .02 .10
92 Tommie Agee .01 .05
93 Troy Aikman UER .30 .75
94A Bill Bates ERR .20 .50
94B Bill Bates COR .10 .30
95 Jack Del Rio .02 .10
96 Issiac Holt UER .01 .05
(Photo on back Timmy Newsome)
97 Michael Irvin .08 .25
98 Jim Jeffcoat UER .01 .05
(red line has Jeff on back)
99 Jimmie Jones .01 .05
100 Kelvin Martin .01 .05
101 Nate Newton .02 .10
102 Danny Noonan .01 .05
103 Ken Norton Jr. .02 .10
104 Jay Novacek .08 .25
105 Mike Saxon .01 .05
106 Derrick Shepard .01 .05
107 Emmitt Smith 1.00 2.50
108 Daniel Stubbs .01 .05
109 Tony Tolbert .01 .05
110 Alexander Wright .01 .05
111 Steve Atwater .01 .05
112 Melvin Bratton .01 .05
113 Tyrone Braxton UER .01 .05
114 Alphonso Carreker .01 .05
115 John Elway .50 1.25
116 Simon Fletcher .01 .05
117 Bobby Humphrey .01 .05
118 Mark Jackson .01 .05
119 Vance Johnson .01 .05
120 Greg Kragen UER .01 .05
121 Karl Mecklenburg UER .01 .05
122A Orsen Mobley ERR .20 .50
122B Orson Mobley COR .02 .10
123 Alton Montgomery .01 .05
124 Ricky Nattiel .01 .05
125 Steve Sewell .01 .05
126 Shannon Sharpe .20 .50
127 Dennis Smith .01 .05
128A Andre Townsend ERR RC .20 .50
128B Andrew Townsend COR RC .02 .10
129 Mike Horan .01 .05
130 Jerry Ball .01 .05
131 Bennie Blades .01 .05
132 Lomas Brown .01 .05
133 Jeff Campbell UER .01 .05
134 Robert Clark .01 .05
135 Michael Cofer .01 .05
136 Dennis Gibson .01 .05
137 Mel Gray .02 .10
138 LeRoy Irvin UER .01 .05
139 George Jamison RC .01 .05
140 Richard Johnson .01 .05
141 Eddie Murray .01 .05
142 Dan Owens .01 .05
143 Rodney Peete .02 .10
144 Barry Sanders .50 1.25
145 Chris Spielman .02 .10
146 Marc Spindler .01 .05
147 Andre Ware .02 .10
148 William White .01 .05
149 Tony Bennett .02 .10
150 Robert Brown .01 .05
151 LeRoy Butler .02 .10
152 Anthony Dilweg .01 .05
153 Michael Haddix .01 .05
154 Ron Hallstrom .01 .05
155 Tim Harris .01 .05
156 Johnny Holland .01 .05
157 Chris Jacke .01 .05
158 Perry Kemp .01 .05
159 Mark Lee .01 .05
160 Don Majkowski .01 .05
161 Tony Mandarich UER .01 .05
162 Mark Murphy .01 .05
163 Brian Noble .01 .05
164 Shawn Patterson .01 .05
165 Jeff Query .01 .05
166 Sterling Sharpe .08 .25
167 Darrell Thompson .01 .05
168 Ed West .01 .05
169 Ray Childress UER .01 .05
170A Cris Dishman ERR RC .02 .10
170B Cris Dishman ERR/COR RC .02 .10
170C Cris Dishman COR RC .02 .10
171 Curtis Duncan .01 .05
172 William Fuller .02 .10
173 Ernest Givins UER .02 .10
174 Drew Hill .01 .05
175A Haywood Jeffires ERR .08 .25
175B Haywood Jeffires COR .08 .25
176 Sean Jones .02 .10
177 Lamar Lathon .01 .05
178 Bruce Matthews .02 .10
179 Bubba McDowell .01 .05
180 Johnny Meads .01 .05
181 Warren Moon UER .08 .25
182 Mike Munchak .02 .10
183 Allen Pinkett .01 .05
184 Dean Steinkuhler UER .01 .05
185 Lorenzo White UER .01 .05
186A John Grimsley ERR .20 .50
186B John Grimsley COR .02 .10
187 Pat Beach .01 .05
188 Albert Bentley .01 .05
189 Dean Biasucci .01 .05
190 Duane Bickett .01 .05
191 Bill Brooks .01 .05
192 Eugene Daniel .01 .05
193 Jeff George .08 .25
194 Jon Hand .01 .05
195 Jeff Herrod .01 .05
196A Jessie Hester ERR Jesse .10 .30
196B Jessie Hester ERR .02 .10
197 Mike Prior .01 .05
198 Stacey Simmons .01 .05
199 Rohn Stark .01 .05
200 Pat Tomberlin .01 .05
201 Clarence Verdin .01 .05
202 Keith Taylor .01 .05
203 Jack Trudeau .01 .05
204 Chip Banks .01 .05
205 John Alt .01 .05
206 Deron Cherry .01 .05
207 Steve DeBerg .01 .05
208 Tim Grunhard .01 .05
209 Albert Lewis .01 .05
210 Nick Lowery UER .01 .05
211 Bill Maas .01 .05
212 Chris Martin .01 .05
213 Todd McNair .01 .05
214 Christian Okoye .01 .05
215 Stephone Paige .01 .05
216 Steve Pelluer .01 .05
217 Kevin Porter .01 .05
218 Kevin Ross .01 .05
219 Dan Saleaumua .01 .05
220 Neil Smith .08 .25
221 David Szott RC UER .01 .05
222 Derrick Thomas .08 .25
223 Barry Word .01 .05
224 Percy Snow .01 .05
225 Marcus Allen .08 .25
226 Eddie Anderson UER .01 .05
227 Steve Beuerlein UER .02 .10
228A Tim Brown ERR NPO .08 .25
228B Tim Brown COR .08 .25
229 Scott Davis .01 .05
230 Mike Dyal .01 .05

231 Mervyn Fernandez UER .01 .05
232 Willie Gault UER .01 .05
233 Ethan Horton UER .01 .05
234 Bo Jackson UER .10 .30
235 Howie Long .08 .25
236 Terry McDaniel .01 .05
237 Max Montoya .01 .05
238 Don Mosebar .01 .05
239 Jay Schroeder .01 .05
240 Steve Smith .01 .05
241 Greg Townsend .01 .05
242 Aaron Wallace .01 .05
243 Lionel Washington .01 .05
244A Steve Wisniewski ERR .02 .10
244B Steve Wisniewski ERR/COR .30 .75
244C Steve Wisniewski COR .02 .10
245 Flipper Anderson .01 .05
246 Latin Berry RC .01 .05
247 Robert Delpino .01 .05
248 Marcus Dupree .08 .25
249 Henry Ellard .02 .10
250 Jim Everett .02 .10
251 Cleveland Gary .01 .05
252 Jerry Gray .01 .05
253 Kevin Greene .02 .10
254 Pete Holohan UER .01 .05
255 Buford McGee .01 .05
256 Tom Newberry .01 .05
257A Irv Pankey ERR .20 .50
257B Irv Pankey COR .02 .10
258 Jackie Slater .01 .05
259 Doug Smith .01 .05
260 Frank Stams .01 .05
261 Michael Stewart .01 .05
262 Fred Strickland .01 .05
263 J.B. Brown UER .01 .05
264 Mark Clayton .02 .10
265 Jeff Cross .01 .05
266 Mark Dennis RC .01 .05
267 Mark Duper .02 .10
268 Ferrell Edmunds .01 .05
269 Dan Marino .50 1.25
270 John Offerdahl .01 .05
271 Louis Oliver .01 .05
272 Tony Paige .01 .05
273 Reggie Roby .01 .05
274 Sammie Smith .01 .05
275 Keith Sims .01 .05
276 Brian Sochia .01 .05
277 Pete Stoyanovich .01 .05
278 Richmond Webb .01 .05
279 Jarvis Williams .01 .05
280 Tim McKyer .01 .05
281A Jim C. Jensen ERR .20 .50
281B Jim C. Jensen COR .02 .10
282 Scott Secules RC .01 .05
283 Ray Berry .01 .05
284 Joey Browner UER .01 .05
285 Anthony Carter .02 .10
286A Cris Carter ERR Chris .20 .50
286B Cris Carter ERR/COR Chris .60 1.50
286C Cris Carter COR .20 .50
287 Chris Doleman .01 .05
288 Mark Dusbabek UER .01 .05
289 Hassan Jones .01 .05
290 Steve Jordan .01 .05
291 Carl Lee .01 .05
292 Kirk Lowdermilk .01 .05
293 Randall McDaniel .02 .10
294 Mike Merriweather .01 .05
295A Keith Millard UER .07 .20
295B Keith Millard COR 1.00 2.50
296 Al Noga UER .01 .05
297 Scott Studwell UER .01 .05
298 Henry Thomas .01 .05
299 Herschel Walker .02 .10
300 Gary Zimmerman .02 .10
301 Rich Gannon .08 .25
302 Wade Wilson UER .02 .10
303 Vincent Brown .01 .05
304 Marv Cook .01 .05
305 Hart Lee Dykes .01 .05
306 Irving Fryar .02 .10
307 Tommy Hodson UER .01 .05
308 Maurice Hurst .01 .05
309 Ronnie Lippett UER .01 .05
310 Fred Marion .01 .05
311 Greg McMurtry .01 .05
312 Johnny Rembert .01 .05
313 Chris Singleton .01 .05
314 Ed Reynolds .01 .05
315 Andre Tippett .01 .05
316 Garin Veris .01 .05
317 Brent Williams .01 .05
318A John Stephens ERR .02 .10
318B John Stephens ERR/COR .30 .75
318C John Stephens COR .02 .10
319 Sammy Martin .01 .05
320 Bruce Armstrong .01 .05
321A Morten Andersen ERR .10 .30
321B Morten Andersen ERR/COR .30 .75
321C Morten Andersen COR .02 .10
322 Gene Atkins UER .01 .05
323 Vince Buck .01 .05
324 John Fourcade .01 .05
325 Kevin Haverdink .01 .05
326 Bobby Hebert .01 .05
327 Craig Heyward .02 .10
328 Dalton Hilliard .01 .05
329 Rickey Jackson .01 .05
330A Vaughan Johnson ERR .07 .20
330B Vaughan Johnson COR 1.00 2.50
331 Eric Martin .01 .05
332 Wayne Martin .01 .05
333 Rueben Mayes UER .01 .05
334 Sam Mills .01 .05
335 Brett Perriman .08 .25
336 Pat Swilling .02 .10
337 Renaldo Turnbull .01 .05
338 Lonzell Hill .01 .05
339 Steve Walsh UER .01 .05
340 Carl Banks UER .01 .05
341 Mark Bavaro UER .01 .05
342 Maurice Carthon .01 .05
343 Pat Harlow RC .01 .05
344 Eric Dorsey .01 .05
345 John Elliott .01 .05
346 Rodney Hampton .08 .25
347 Jeff Hostetler .02 .10
348 Erik Howard UER .01 .05
349 Pepper Johnson .01 .05
350A Sean Landeta ERR .02 .10
350B Sean Landeta COR .20 .50
351 Leonard Marshall .01 .05
352 Dave Meggett .02 .10
353A Bart Oates ERR .02 .10
353B Bart Oates ERR/COR .30 .75
353C Bart Oates COR .02 .10
354 Gary Reasons .01 .05
355 Phil Simms .02 .10
356 Lawrence Taylor .08 .25
357 Reyna Thompson .01 .05
358 Brian Williams OL UER .01 .05
359 Matt Bahr .01 .05
360 Mark Ingram .02 .10
361 Brad Baxter .01 .05
362 Mark Boyer .01 .05
363 Dennis Byrd .01 .05
364 Dave Cadigan UER .01 .05
365 Kyle Clifton .01 .05
366 James Hasty .01 .05
367 Joe Kelly UER .01 .05
368 Jeff Lageman .01 .05
369 Pat Leahy UER .01 .05
370 Terance Mathis .02 .10
371 Erik McMillan .01 .05
372 Rob Moore .08 .25
373 Ken O'Brien .01 .05
374 Tony Stargell .01 .05
375 Jim Sweeney UER .01 .05
376 Al Toon .02 .10
377 Johnny Hector .01 .05
378 Jeff Criswell .01 .05
379 Mike Haight RC .01 .05
380 Troy Benson .01 .05
381 Eric Allen .01 .05
382 Fred Barnett .08 .25
383 Jerome Brown .01 .05
384 Keith Byars .01 .05
385 Randall Cunningham .08 .25
386 Byron Evans .01 .05
387 Wes Hopkins .01 .05
388 Keith Jackson .02 .10
389 Seth Joyner UER .02 .10
390 Bobby Wilson RC .01 .05
391 Heath Sherman .01 .05
392 Clyde Simmons UER .01 .05
393 Ben Smith .01 .05
394 Andre Waters .01 .05
395 Reggie White UER .08 .25
396 Calvin Williams .02 .10
397 Al Harris .01 .05
398 Anthony Toney .01 .05
399 Mike Quick .01 .05
400 Anthony Bell .01 .05
401 Rich Camarillo .01 .05
402 Roy Green .01 .05
403 Ken Harvey .02 .10
404 Eric Hill .01 .05
405 Garth Jax UER RC .01 .05
406 Ernie Jones .01 .05
407A Cedric Mack ERR .07 .20
407B Cedric Mack COR 1.00 2.50
408 Dexter Manley .01 .05
409 Tim McDonald .01 .05
410 Freddie Joe Nunn .01 .05
411 Ricky Proehl .01 .05
412 Moe Gardner RC .01 .05
413 Timm Rosenbach .01 .05
414 Luis Sharpe UER .01 .05
415 Vai Sikahema UER .01 .05
416 Anthony Thompson .01 .05
417 Ron Wolfley UER .01 .05
418 Lonnie Young .01 .05
419 Gary Anderson K .01 .05
420 Bubby Brister .01 .05
421 Thomas Everett .01 .05
422 Eric Green .01 .05
423 Delton Hall .01 .05
424 Bryan Hinkle .01 .05
425 Merril Hoge .01 .05
426 Carnell Lake .01 .05
427 Louis Lipps .01 .05
428 David Little .01 .05
429 Greg Lloyd .08 .25
430 Mike Mularkey .01 .05
431 Keith Willis UER .01 .05
432 Dwayne Woodruff .01 .05
433 Rod Woodson .08 .25
434 Tim Worley .01 .05
435 Warren Williams .01 .05
436 Terry Long UER .01 .05
437 Martin Bayless .01 .05
438 Jarrod Bunch RC .01 .05
439 Marion Butts .02 .10
440 Gill Byrd UER .01 .05
441 Arthur Cox .01 .05
442 John Friesz .08 .25
443 Leo Goeas .01 .05
444 Burt Grossman .01 .05
445 Courtney Hall UER .01 .05
446 Ronnie Harmon .01 .05
447 Nate Lewis RC .01 .05
448 Anthony Miller .02 .10
449 Leslie O'Neal .02 .10
450 Gary Plummer .01 .05
451 Junior Seau .08 .25
452 Billy Ray Smith .01 .05
453 Billy Joe Tolliver .01 .05
454 Broderick Thompson .01 .05
455 Lee Williams .01 .05
456 Michael Carter .01 .05
457 Mike Cofer .01 .05
458 Kevin Fagan .01 .05
459 Charles Haley .02 .10
460 Pierce Holt .01 .05
461 Johnnie Jackson UER RC .01 .05
462 Brent Jones .08 .25
463 Guy McIntyre .01 .05
464 Joe Montana .50 1.25
465A Bubba Paris ERR .02 .10
465B Bubba Paris ERR/COR .20 .50
465C Bubba Paris COR .02 .10
466 Tom Rathman UER .01 .05
467 Jerry Rice UER .30 .75
468 Mike Sherrard .01 .05
469 John Taylor UER .02 .10
470 Steve Young .30 .75
471 Dennis Brown .01 .05
472 Dexter Carter .01 .05
473 Bill Romanowski .01 .05
474 Dave Waymer .01 .05
475 Robert Blackmon .01 .05
476 Derrick Fenner .01 .05
477 Nesby Glasgow UER .01 .05
478 Jacob Green .01 .05
479 Andy Heck .01 .05
480 Norm Johnson UER .01 .05
481 Tommy Kane .01 .05
482 Cortez Kennedy .08 .25
483A Dave Krieg ERR .07 .20
483B Dave Krieg COR 1.00 2.50
484 Bryan Millard .01 .05
485 Joe Nash .01 .05
486 Rufus Porter .01 .05
487 Eugene Robinson .01 .05
488 Mike Tice RC .01 .05
489 Chris Warren .08 .25
490 John L. Williams UER .01 .05
491 Terry Wooden .01 .05
492 Tony Woods .01 .05
493 Brian Blades .02 .10
494 Paul Skansi .01 .05
495 Gary Anderson RB .01 .05
496 Mark Carrier WR .08 .25
497 Chris Chandler .08 .25
498 Steve Christie .01 .05
499 Reggie Cobb .01 .05
500 Reuben Davis .01 .05
501 Willie Drewrey UER .01 .05
502 Randy Grimes .01 .05
503 Paul Gruber .01 .05
504 Wayne Haddix .01 .05
505 Ron Hall .01 .05
506 Harry Hamilton .01 .05
507 Bruce Hill .01 .05
508 Eugene Marve .01 .05
509 Keith McCants .01 .05
510 Winston Moss .01 .05
511 Kevin Murphy .01 .05
512 Mark Robinson .01 .05
513 Vinny Testaverde .02 .10
514 Broderick Thomas .01 .05
515A Jeff Bostic UER .02 .10
515B Jeff Bostic UER .02 .10
516 Todd Bowles .08 .25
517 Earnest Byner .01 .05
518 Gary Clark .08 .25
519 Craig Erickson RC .08 .25
520 Darryl Grant .01 .05
521 Darrell Green .01 .05
522 Russ Grimm .02 .10
523 Stan Humphries .08 .25
524 Joe Jacoby UER .01 .05
525 Jim Lachey .01 .05
526 Chip Lohmiller .01 .05
527 Charles Mann .01 .05
528 Wilber Marshall .01 .05
529A Art Monk .02 .10
529B Art Monk .02 .10
530 Tracy Rocker .01 .05
531 Mark Rypien .02 .10
532 Ricky Sanders UER .01 .05
533 Alvin Walton UER .01 .05
534 Todd Marinovich UER RC .01 .05
535 Mike Dumas RC .01 .05
536A Russell Maryland ERR RC .08 .25
536B Russell Maryland COR RC .08 .25
537 Eric Turner UER RC .02 .10
538 Ernie Mills RC .02 .10
539 Ed King RC .01 .05
540 Mike Stonebreaker RC .01 .05
541 Chris Zorich RC .08 .25
542A Mike Croel ERR RC .01 .05
542B Mike Croel COR RC .01 .05
543 Eric Moten RC .01 .05
544 Dan McGwire RC .01 .05
545 Keith Cash RC .01 .05
546 Kenny Walker UER RC .01 .05
547 Leroy Hoard UER .02 .10
548 Luis Cristobal UER .01 .05
549 Stacy Danley .01 .05
550 Todd Lyght RC .01 .05
551 Brett Favre RC 3.00 8.00
552 Mike Pritchard RC .08 .25
553 Moe Gardner .01 .05
554 Tim McKyer .01 .05
555 Erric Pegram RC .08 .25
556 Norm Johnson .01 .05
557 Bruce Pickens RC .01 .05
558 Henry Jones RC .02 .10
559 Phil Hansen RC .01 .05
560 Cornelius Bennett .02 .10
561 Stan Thomas .01 .05
562 Chris Zorich .02 .10
563 Anthony Morgan RC .01 .05
564 Darren Lewis RC .01 .05
565 Mike Stonebreaker .01 .05
566 Alfred Williams RC .01 .05
567 Lamar Rogers RC .01 .05
568 Erik Wilhelm UER RC .01 .05
569 Ed King .01 .05
570 Michael Jackson WR RC .08 .25
571 James Jones RC .01 .05
572 Russell Maryland .08 .25
573 Dixon Edwards RC .01 .05
574 Darrick Brownlow RC .01 .05
575 Larry Brown DB RC .02 .10
576 Mike Croel .01 .05
577 Keith Traylor RC .01 .05
578 Kenny Walker .01 .05
579 Reggie Johnson RC .01 .05
580 Herman Moore RC .08 .25
581 Kelvin Pritchett RC .02 .10
582 Kevin Scott RC .01 .05
583 Vinnie Clark RC .01 .05
584 Esera Tuaolo RC .01 .05
585 Don Davey .01 .05
586 Blair Kiel RC .01 .05
587 Mike Dumas .01 .05
588 Darryll Lewis RC .02 .10
589 John Flannery RC .01 .05
590 Kevin Donnalley RC .01 .05
591 Shane Curry .01 .05
592 Mark Vander Poel RC .01 .05
593 Dave McCloughan .01 .05
594 Mel Agee RC .01 .05
595 Kerry Cash RC .01 .05
596 Harvey Williams RC .08 .25
597 Joe Valerio RC .01 .05
598 Tim Barnett UER RC .01 .05
599 Todd Marinovich .02 .10
600 Nick Bell RC .01 .05
601 Roger Craig .02 .10
602 Ronnie Lott .02 .10
603 Mike Jones RC LB .01 .05
604 Todd Lyght .01 .05
605 Roman Phifer RC .01 .05
606 David Lang RC .01 .05
607 Aaron Craver RC .01 .05
608 Mark Higgs RC .01 .05
609 Chris Green .01 .05
610 Randy Baldwin RC .01 .05
611 Pat Harlow .01 .05
612 Leonard Russell RC .08 .25
613 Jerome Henderson RC .01 .05
614 Scott Zolak RC UER .01 .05
615 Jon Vaughn RC .01 .05
616 Harry Colon RC .01 .05
617 Wesley Carroll RC .01 .05
618 Quinn Early .02 .10
619 Reginald Jones RC .01 .05
620 Jarrod Bunch .01 .05
621 Kanavis McGhee RC .01 .05
622 Ed McCaffrey RC .75 2.00
623 Browning Nagle RC .01 .05
624 Mo Lewis RC .02 .10
625 Blair Thomas .01 .05
626 Antone Davis RC .01 .05
627 Jim McMahon .02 .10
628 Scott Kowalkowski RC .01 .05
629 Brad Goebel RC .01 .05
630 William Thomas RC .01 .05
631 Eric Swann RC .08 .25
632 Mike Jones DE RC .01 .05
633 Aeneas Williams RC .50 1.25
634 Dexter Davis RC .01 .05
635 Tom Tupa UER .01 .05
636 Johnny Johnson .01 .05
637 Randal Hill RC .02 .10
638 Jeff Graham RC .08 .25
639 Ernie Mills .01 .05
640 Adrian Cooper RC .01 .05
641 Stanley Richard RC .01 .05
642 Eric Bieniemy RC .01 .05
643 Eric Moten .01 .05
644 Shawn Jefferson RC .02 .10
645 Ted Washington RC .01 .05
646 John Johnson RC .01 .05
647 Dan McGwire .01 .05
648 Doug Thomas RC .01 .05
649 David Daniels RC .01 .05
650 John Kasay RC .02 .10
651 Jeff Kemp .01 .05
652 Charles McRae RC .01 .05
653 Lawrence Dawsey RC .02 .10
654 Robert Wilson RC .01 .05
655 Dexter Manley .01 .05
656 Chuck Weatherspoon .01 .05
657 Tim Ryan G RC .01 .05
658 Bobby Wilson .01 .05
659 Ricky Ervins RC .02 .10
660 Matt Millen .02 .10

1991 Pacific Picks The Pros

Randomly inserted in packs, this 25-card standard-size set features the best player for each offensive and defensive position. A card of first pick Russell Maryland is also included. The cards have color action player photos on the fronts, with either gold or silver foil borders. There were 10,000 cards produced with a gold foil border and an equal number with a silver foil border. The silver foil cards were randomly inserted into jumbo packs, while the gold foil cards were randomly inserted into the wax and foil packs. The words "Pacific Picks the Pros" are printed vertically in a blue and red colored stripe on the left side of the picture.

COMPLETE SET (25) 20.00 50.00
*GOLD/SILVER: SAME PRICE
GOLDS RANDOM INSERTS IN HOB/RET
SILVERS RANDOM INSERTS IN JUMBO
STATED PRINT RUN 10,000 SETS
1 Russell Maryland 1.00 2.50
2 Andre Reed .40 1.00
3 Jerry Rice 3.00 8.00
4 Keith Jackson .40 1.00
5 Jim Lachey .20 .50
6 Anthony Munoz .40 1.00
7 Randall McDaniel .20 .50
8 Bruce Matthews .40 1.00
9 Kent Hull .20 .50
10 Joe Montana 5.00 12.00
11 Barry Sanders 5.00 12.00
12 Thurman Thomas 1.00 2.50
13 Morten Andersen .40 1.00
14 Jerry Ball .20 .50
15 Jerome Brown .20 .50
16 Reggie White 1.00 2.50
17 Bruce Smith 1.00 2.50
18 Derrick Thomas 1.00 2.50
19 Lawrence Taylor 1.00 2.50
20 Charles Haley .40 1.00
21 Albert Lewis .20 .50
22 Rod Woodson 1.00 2.50
23 David Fulcher .20 .50
24 Joey Browner .20 .50
25 Sean Landeta .40 1.00

1991 Pacific Flash Cards

The 1991 Pacific Flash Cards football set contains 110 standard-size cards. The front design has brightly colored triangles on a white card face and a math problem involving addition, subtraction, multiplication, or division. By performing one of these operations on the two numbers, one arrives at the uniform number of the player featured on the backs. The back design is similar to the front but has a glossy color game shot of the player, with either career summary or last year's highlights below the picture.

COMPLETE SET (110) 4.00 10.00
1 Steve Young .30 .75
2 Hart Lee Dykes .01 .05
3 Timm Rosenbach .01 .06
4 Andre Collins .01 .05
5 Johnny Johnson .01 .05
6 Nick Lowery .01 .05
7 John Stephens .01 .05
8 Jim Arnold .01 .05
9 Steve DeBerg .01 .05
10 Christian Okoye .01 .05
11 Eric Swann .02 .10
12 Jerry Robinson .01 .05
13 Steve Wisniewski .01 .05
14 Jim Harbaugh .02 .10
15 Steve Broussard .01 .05
16 Mike Singletary UER .02 .10
17 Tim Green .01 .05
18 Roger Craig .02 .10
19 Maury Buford .01 .05
20 Marcus Allen .07 .20
21 Deion Sanders .20 .50
22 Chris Miller .02 .10
23 Joey Browner .01 .05
24 Bubby Brister .02 .10
25 Buford McGee .01 .05
26 Ed West .01 .05
27 Mark Murphy .01 .05
28 Tim Worley .01 .05
29 Keith Willis .01 .05
30 Rich Gannon .07 .20
31 Jim Everett .02 .10
32 Duval Love .01 .05
33 Bob Nelson NT .01 .05
34 Anthony Munoz .02 .10
35 Boomer Esiason .02 .10
36 Kenny Walker .01 .05
37 Mike Horan .01 .05
38 Gary Kubiak .01 .05
39 David Treadwell .01 .05
40 Robert Wilson .01 .05
41 Lewis Billups .01 .05
42 Kevin Mack .01 .05
43 John Elway .60 1.50
44 Lee Johnson .01 .05
45 Ken Willis .01 .05
46 Herman Moore .30 .75
47 Eddie Murray .01 .05
48 Mike Saxon .01 .05
49 John L. Williams .01 .05
50 Barry Sanders .60 1.50
51 Andre Ware .02 .10
52 Dave Krieg .02 .10
53 Cortez Kennedy .01 .05
54 Bo Jackson .07 .20
55 Derrick Fenner .01 .05
56 Steve Walsh .01 .05
57 Brett Maxie .01 .05
58 Stan Brock .01 .05
59 DeMond Winston .01 .05
60 Sam Mills .01 .05
61 Eric Martin .01 .05
62 Michael Carter .01 .05
63 Steve Wallace .01 .05
64 Jesse Sapolu .01 .05
65 Bill Romanowski .01 .05
66 Joe Montana .80 2.00
67 Sean Landeta .01 .05
68 Doug Riesenberg .01 .05
69 Myron Guyton .01 .05
70 Andre Reed .02 .10
71 John Elliott .01 .05
72 Jeff Hostetler .02 .10
73 Rohn Stark .01 .05
74 Jeff George .02 .10
75 Duane Bickett .01 .05
76 Emmitt Smith .75 2.00
77 Michael Irvin .07 .20
78 Tony Stargell .01 .05
79 Kyle Clifton .01 .05
80 John Booty .01 .05
81 Fred Barnett .02 .10
82 Blair Thomas .01 .05
83 Erik McMillan .01 .05
84 Broderick Thomas .01 .05
85 Jim Skow .01 .05
86 Gary Anderson RB .01 .05
87 Mark Robinson .01 .05
88 Steve Christie .01 .05
89 Cody Carlson .01 .05
90 Warren Moon .07 .20
91 Lorenzo White .01 .05
92 Reggie Roby .01 .05
93 Jim C. Jensen .01 .05
94 Mark Clayton .02 .10
95 Willie Gault .02 .10
96 Don Mosebar .01 .05
97 Gary Plummer .01 .05
98 Leslie O'Neal .01 .05
99 Neal Anderson .02 .10
100 Derrick Thomas .02 .10
101 Luis Sharpe .01 .05
102 D.J. Dozier .01 .05
103 Jarrod Bunch .01 .05
104 Mark Ingram .01 .05
105 James Lofton .02 .10
106 Jay Schroeder .01 .05
107 Ronnie Lott .07 .20
108 Todd Marinovich .01 .05
109 Chris Zorich .01 .05
110 Charles McRae .01 .05

1992 Pacific Prototypes

The 1992 Pacific prototypes were given away at the Super Bowl card show in Minneapolis and used as sales samples. The cards measure the standard size. The cards were intended to be a preview for the upcoming 1992 Pacific set since they used the new card design. The production run was approximately 5,000 sets. The fronts feature glossy color action player photos enclosed by white borders. The player's name is printed vertically in a color stripe running down the left side of the picture, with the team helmet in the lower left corner. In a horizontal format, the backs have a second color photo and player profile.

COMPLETE SET (6) 10.00 25.00
1 Warren Moon 2.00 5.00
2 Pat Swilling 1.60 4.00
3 Michael Irvin 2.00 5.00
4 Haywood Jeffires 1.60 4.00
5 Thurman Thomas 2.00 5.00
6 Leonard Russell 1.60 4.00

1992 Pacific

The 1992 Pacific set consists of 660 standard-size cards. The set was issued in two series of 330 cards. A factory set consisted of every card. Cards were issued in 14-card packs and 24-card jumbo packs for each series. Factory sets included a 30-card Statistical Leaders set. The cards are checklisted alphabetically according to teams. Cards 320-330 and 649-660 are Draft Picks. Rookie Cards include Steve Bono and Ben Coates (exclusive to Pacific). Separately numbered checklist cards were also randomly inserted in packs.

COMPLETE SET (660) 6.00 15.00
COMP.FACT.SET (690) 10.00 25.00
COMP.SERIES 1 (330) 3.00 8.00
COMP.SERIES 2 (330) 3.00 8.00
COMP.CHECKLIST SET (5) 1.25 3.00
1 Steve Broussard .01 .05
2 Darion Conner .01 .05
3 Tory Epps .01 .05
4 Michael Haynes .02 .10
5 Chris Hinton .01 .05
6 Mike Kenn .01 .05
7 Tim McKyer .01 .05
8 Chris Miller .02 .10
9 Erric Pegram .02 .10
10 Mike Pritchard .02 .10
11 Moe Gardner .01 .05
12 Tim Green .01 .05
13 Norm Johnson .01 .05
14 Don Beebe .01 .05
15 Cornelius Bennett .02 .10
16 Al Edwards .01 .05
17 Mark Kelso .01 .05
18 James Lofton .02 .10
19 Frank Reich .02 .10
20 Leon Seals .01 .05
21 Darryl Talley .01 .05
22 Thurman Thomas .08 .25
23 Kent Hull .01 .05
24 Jeff Wright .01 .05
25 Nate Odomes .01 .05
26 Carwell Gardner .01 .05
27 Neal Anderson .01 .05
28 Mark Carrier DB .01 .05
29 Johnny Bailey .01 .05
30 Jim Harbaugh .08 .25
31 Jay Hilgenberg .01 .05
32 William Perry .02 .10
33 Wendell Davis .01 .05
34 Donnell Woolford .01 .05
35 Keith Van Horne .01 .05
36 Shaun Gayle .01 .05
37 Tom Waddle .01 .05
38 Chris Zorich .02 .10
39 Tom Thayer .01 .05
40 Rickey Dixon .01 .05
41 James Francis .01 .05
42 David Fulcher .01 .05
43 Reggie Rembert .01 .05
44 Anthony Munoz .02 .10
45 Harold Green .01 .05
46 Mitchell Price .01 .05
47 Rodney Holman .01 .05
48 Bruce Kozerski .01 .05
49 Bruce Reimers .01 .05
50 Erik Wilhelm .01 .05
51 Harlon Barnett .01 .05
52 Mike Johnson .01 .05
53 Brian Brennan .01 .05
54 Ed King .01 .05
55 Reggie Langhorne .01 .05
56 James Jones DT .01 .05
57 Mike Baab .01 .05
58 Dan Fike .01 .05
59 Frank Minnifield .01 .05
60 Clay Matthews .02 .10
61 Kevin Mack .01 .05
62 Tony Casillas .01 .05
63 Jay Novacek .02 .10
64 Larry Brown DB .01 .05
65 Michael Irvin .08 .25
66 Jack Del Rio .01 .05
67 Ken Willis .01 .05
68 Emmitt Smith .60 1.50
69 Alan Veingrad .01 .05
70 John Gesek .01 .05
71 Steve Beuerlein .02 .10
72 Vinson Smith RC .01 .05
73 Steve Atwater .01 .05
74 Mike Croel .01 .05
75 John Elway .50 1.25
76 Gaston Green .01 .05
77 Mike Horan .01 .05
78 Vance Johnson .01 .05
79 Karl Mecklenburg .01 .05
80 Shannon Sharpe .08 .25
81 David Treadwell .01 .05
82 Kenny Walker .01 .05
83 Greg Lewis .01 .05
84 Shawn Moore .01 .05
85 Alton Montgomery .01 .05
86 Michael Young .01 .05
87 Jerry Ball .01 .05
88 Bennie Blades .01 .05
89 Mel Gray .02 .10
90 Herman Moore .08 .25
91 Erik Kramer .02 .10
92 Willie Green .01 .05
93 George Jamison .01 .05
94 Chris Spielman .02 .10
95 Kelvin Pritchett .01 .05
96 William White .01 .05
97 Mike Utley .02 .10
98 Tony Bennett .01 .05
99 LeRoy Butler .01 .05
100 Vinnie Clark .01 .05
101 Ron Hallstrom .01 .05
102 Chris Jacke .01 .05
103 Tony Mandarich .01 .05
104 Sterling Sharpe .08 .25
105 Don Majkowski .01 .05
106 Johnny Holland .01 .05
107 Esera Tuaolo .01 .05
108 Darrell Thompson .01 .05
109 Bubba McDowell .01 .05
110 Curtis Duncan .01 .05
111 Lamar Lathon .01 .05
112 Drew Hill .01 .05
113 Bruce Matthews .01 .05
114 Bo Orlando RC .01 .05
115 Don Maggs .01 .05
116 Lorenzo White .01 .05
117 Ernest Givins .02 .10
118 Tony Jones WR .01 .05
119 Dean Steinkuhler .01 .05
120 Dean Biasucci .01 .05
121 Duane Bickett .01 .05
122 Bill Brooks .01 .05
123 Ken Clark .01 .05
124 Jessie Hester .01 .05
125 Anthony Johnson .02 .10
126 Chip Banks .01 .05
127 Mike Prior .01 .05
128 Rohn Stark .01 .05
129 Jeff Herrod .01 .05
130 Clarence Verdin .01 .05
131 Tim Manoa .01 .05
132 Brian Baldinger RC .01 .05
133 Tim Barnett .01 .05
134 J.J. Birden .01 .05
135 Deron Cherry .01 .05
136 Steve DeBerg .01 .05
137 Nick Lowery .01 .05
138 Todd McNair .01 .05
139 Christian Okoye .01 .05
140 Mark Vlasic .01 .05
141 Dan Saleaumua .01 .05
142 Neil Smith .08 .25
143 Robb Thomas .01 .05
144 Eddie Anderson .01 .05
145 Nick Bell .01 .05
146 Tim Brown .08 .25
147 Roger Craig .02 .10
148 Jeff Gossett .01 .05
149 Ethan Horton .01 .05
150 Jamie Holland .01 .05
151 Jeff Jaeger .01 .05
152 Todd Marinovich .01 .05
153 Marcus Allen .08 .25
154 Steve Smith .01 .05
155 Flipper Anderson .01 .05
156 Robert Delpino .01 .05
157 Cleveland Gary .01 .05
158 Kevin Greene .02 .10
159 Dale Hatcher .01 .05
160 Duval Love .01 .05
161 Ron Brown .01 .05
162 Jackie Slater .01 .05
163 Doug Smith .01 .05
164 Aaron Cox .01 .05
165 Larry Kelm .01 .05
166 Mark Clayton .02 .10
167 Louis Oliver .01 .05
168 Mark Higgs .01 .05
169 Aaron Craver .01 .05
170 Sammie Smith .01 .05
171 Tony Paige .01 .05
172 Jeff Cross .01 .05
173 David Griggs .01 .05
174 Richmond Webb .01 .05
175 Vestee Jackson .01 .05
176 Jim C. Jensen .01 .05
177 Anthony Carter .02 .10
178 Cris Carter .20 .50
179 Chris Doleman .01 .05
180 Rich Gannon .08 .25
181 Al Noga .01 .05
182 Randall McDaniel .02 .10
183 Todd Scott .01 .05
184 Henry Thomas .01 .05
185 Felix Wright .01 .05
186 Gary Zimmerman .01 .05
187 Herschel Walker .02 .10
188 Vincent Brown .01 .05
189 Harry Colon .01 .05
190 Irving Fryar .02 .10
191 Marv Cook .01 .05
192 Leonard Russell .02 .10
193 Hugh Millen .01 .05
194 Pat Harlow .01 .05
195 Jon Vaughn .01 .05
196 Ben Coates RC .30 .75
197 Johnny Rembert .01 .05
198 Greg McMurtry .01 .05
199 Morten Andersen .01 .05
200 Tommy Barnhardt .01 .05
201 Bobby Hebert .01 .05
202 Dalton Hilliard .01 .05
203 Sam Mills .01 .05
204 Pat Swilling .01 .05
205 Rickey Jackson .01 .05
206 Stan Brock .01 .05
207 Reginald Jones .01 .05
208 Gill Fenerty .01 .05
209 Eric Martin .01 .05
210 Matt Bahr .01 .05
211 Rodney Hampton .02 .10
212 Jeff Hostetler .02 .10
213 Pepper Johnson .01 .05
214 Leonard Marshall .01 .05
215 Doug Riesenberg .01 .05
216 Stephen Baker .01 .05
217 Mike Fox .01 .05
218 Bart Oates .01 .05
219 Everson Walls .01 .05
220 Gary Reasons .01 .05
221 Jeff Lageman .01 .05
222 Joe Kelly .01 .05
223 Mo Lewis .01 .05
224 Tony Stargell .01 .05
225 Jim Sweeney .01 .05
226 Freeman McNeil .02 .10
227 Brian Washington .01 .05
228 Johnny Hector .01 .05
229 Terance Mathis .02 .10
230 Rob Moore .02 .10
231 Brad Baxter .01 .05
232 Eric Allen .01 .05
233 Fred Barnett .02 .10
234 Jerome Brown .01 .05
235 Keith Byars .01 .05
236 William Thomas .01 .05
237 Jessie Small .01 .05
238 Robert Drummond .01 .05
239 Reggie White .08 .25
240 James Joseph .01 .05
241 Brad Goebel .01 .05
242 Clyde Simmons .01 .05
243 Rich Camarillo .01 .05
244 Ken Harvey .01 .05
245 Garth Jax .01 .05
246 Johnny Johnson .01 .05
247 Mike Jones .01 .05
248 Ernie Jones .01 .05
249 Tom Tupa .01 .05
250 Ron Wolfley .01 .05
251 Luis Sharpe .01 .05
252 Eric Swann .02 .10
253 Anthony Thompson .01 .05
254 Gary Anderson K .01 .05
255 Dermontti Dawson .02 .10
256 Jeff Graham .08 .25
257 Eric Green .01 .05
258 Louis Lipps .01 .05
259 Neil O'Donnell .02 .10
260 Rod Woodson .08 .25
261 Dwight Stone .01 .05
262 Aaron Jones .01 .05
263 Keith Willis .01 .05
264 Ernie Mills .01 .05
265 Martin Bayless .01 .05
266 Rod Bernstine .01 .05
267 John Carney .01 .05
268 John Friesz .02 .10
269 Nate Lewis .01 .05
270 Shawn Jefferson .01 .05
271 Burt Grossman .01 .05
272 Eric Moten .01 .05
273 Gary Plummer .01 .05
274 Henry Rolling .01 .05
275 Steve Hendrickson RC .01 .05
276 Michael Carter .01 .05
277 Steve Bono RC .08 .25
278 Dexter Carter .01 .05
279 Mike Cofer .01 .05
280 Charles Haley .02 .10
281 Tom Rathman .01 .05
282 Guy McIntyre .01 .05
283 John Taylor .02 .10
284 Dave Waymer .01 .05
285 Steve Wallace .01 .05
286 Jamie Williams .01 .05
287 Brian Blades .02 .10
288 Jeff Bryant .01 .05
289 Grant Feasel .01 .05
290 Jacob Green .01 .05
291 Andy Heck .01 .05
292 Kelly Stouffer .01 .05
293 John Kasay .01 .05
294 Cortez Kennedy .02 .10
295 Bryan Millard .01 .05
296 Eugene Robinson .01 .05
297 Tony Woods .01 .05
298 Jesse Anderson UER .01 .05
299 Gary Anderson RB .01 .05
300 Mark Carrier WR .02 .10
301 Reggie Cobb .01 .05
302 Robert Wilson .01 .05
303 Jesse Solomon .01 .05
304 Broderick Thomas .01 .05
305 Lawrence Dawsey .02 .10
306 Charles McRae .01 .05
307 Paul Gruber .01 .05
308 Vinny Testaverde .02 .10
309 Brian Mitchell .02 .10
310 Darrell Green .01 .05
311 Art Monk .02 .10
312 Russ Grimm .02 .10
313 Mark Rypien .01 .05
314 Bobby Wilson .01 .05
315 Wilber Marshall .01 .05
316 Gerald Riggs .01 .05
317 Chip Lohmiller .01 .05
318 Joe Jacoby .01 .05
319 Martin Mayhew .01 .05
320 Amp Lee RC .01 .05
321 Terrell Buckley RC .01 .05
322 Tommy Vardell RC .01 .05
323 Ricardo McDonald RC .01 .05
324 Joe Bowden RC .01 .05
325 Darryl Williams RC .01 .05
326 Carlos Huerta .01 .05
327 Patrick Rowe RC .01 .05
328 Siran Stacy RC .01 .05
329 Dexter McNabb RC .01 .05
330 Willie Clay RC .01 .05
331 Oliver Barnett .01 .05
332 Aundray Bruce .01 .05
333 Ken Tippins RC .01 .05
334 Jessie Tuggle .01 .05
335 Brian Jordan .02 .10
336 Andre Rison .02 .10
337 Houston Hoover .01 .05
338 Bill Fralic .01 .05
339 Pat Chaffey RC .01 .05
340 Keith Jones .01 .05
341 Jamie Dukes RC .01 .05
342 Chris Mohr .01 .05
343 John Davis .01 .05
344 Ray Bentley .01 .05
345 Scott Norwood .01 .05
346 Shane Conlan .01 .05
347 Steve Tasker .02 .10
348 Will Wolford .01 .05
349 Gary Baldinger RC .01 .05
350 Kirby Jackson .01 .05
351 Jamie Mueller .01 .05
352 Pete Metzelaars .01 .05
353 Richard Dent .02 .10
354 Ron Rivera .01 .05
355 Jim Morrissey .01 .05
356 John Roper .01 .05
357 Steve McMichael .02 .10
358 Ron Morris .01 .05
359 Darren Lewis .01 .05
360 Anthony Morgan .01 .05
361 Stan Thomas .01 .05
362 James Thornton .01 .05
363 Brad Muster .01 .05
364 Tim Krumrie .01 .05
365 Lee Johnson .01 .05
366 Eric Ball .01 .05
367 Alonzo Mitz RC .01 .05
368 David Grant .01 .05
369 Lynn James .01 .05
370 Lewis Billups .01 .05
371 Jim Breech .01 .05
372 Alfred Williams .01 .05
373 Wayne Haddix .01 .05
374 Tim McGee .01 .05
375 Michael Jackson .02 .10
376 Leroy Hoard .02 .10
377 Tony Jones T .01 .05
378 Vince Newsome .01 .05
379 Todd Philcox RC .01 .05
380 Eric Metcalf .02 .10
381 John Rienstra .01 .05
382 Matt Stover .01 .05
383 Brian Hansen .01 .05
384 Joe Morris .01 .05
385 Anthony Pleasant .01 .05
386 Mark Stepnoski .01 .05
387 Erik Williams .01 .05
388 Jimmie Jones .01 .05
389 Kevin Gogan .01 .05
390 Manny Hendrix RC .01 .05
391 Issiac Holt .01 .05
392 Ken Norton .02 .10
393 Tommie Agee .01 .05
394 Alvin Harper .02 .10
395 Alexander Wright .01 .05
396 Mike Saxon .01 .05
397 Michael Brooks .01 .05
398 Bobby Humphrey .01 .05
399 Ken Lanier .01 .05
400 Steve Sewell .01 .05
401 Robert Perryman .01 .05
402 Wymon Henderson .01 .05
403 Keith Kartz .01 .05
404 Clarence Kay .01 .05
405 Keith Traylor .01 .05
406 Doug Widell .01 .05
407 Dennis Smith .01 .05
408 Marc Spindler .01 .05
409 Lomas Brown .01 .05
410 Robert Clark .01 .05
411 Eric Andolsek .01 .05
412 Mike Farr .01 .05
413 Ray Crockett .01 .05
414 Jeff Campbell .01 .05
415 Dan Owens .01 .05
416 Jim Arnold .01 .05
417 Barry Sanders .50 1.25
418 Eddie Murray .01 .05
419 Vince Workman .01 .05
420 Ed West .01 .05
421 Charles Wilson .01 .05
422 Perry Kemp .01 .05
423 Chuck Cecil .01 .05
424 James Campen .01 .05

425 Robert Brown .01 .05
426 Brian Noble .01 .05
427 Rich Moran .01 .05
428 Vai Sikahema .01 .05
429 Allen Rice .01 .05
430 Haywood Jeffires .02 .10
431 Warren Moon .08 .25
432 Greg Montgomery .01 .05
433 Sean Jones .01 .05
434 Richard Johnson CB .01 .05
435 Al Smith .01 .05
436 Johnny Meads .01 .05
437 William Fuller .01 .05
438 Mike Munchak .02 .10
439 Ray Childress .01 .05
440 Cody Carlson .01 .05
441 Scott Radecic .01 .05
442 Quintus McDonald RC .01 .05
443 Eugene Daniel .01 .05
444 Mark Herrmann RC .01 .05
445 John Baylor RC .01 .05
446 Dave McCloughan .01 .05
447 Mark Vander Poel .01 .05
448 Randy Dixon .01 .05
449 Keith Taylor .01 .05
450 Alan Grant .01 .05
451 Tony Siragusa .01 .05
452 Rich Baldinger .01 .05
453 Derrick Thomas .08 .25
454 Bill Jones RC .01 .05
455 Troy Stradford .01 .05
456 Barry Word .01 .05
457 Tim Grunhard .01 .05
458 Chris Martin .01 .05
459 Jayice Pearson RC .01 .05
460 Dino Hackett .01 .05
461 David Lutz .01 .05
462 Albert Lewis .01 .05
463 Fred Jones RC .01 .05
464 Winston Moss .01 .05
465 Sam Graddy RC .01 .05
466 Steve Wisniewski .01 .05
467 Jay Schroeder .01 .05
468 Ronnie Lott .02 .10
469 Willie Gault .02 .10
470 Greg Townsend .01 .05
471 Max Montoya .01 .05
472 Howie Long .08 .25
473 Lionel Washington .01 .05
474 Riki Ellison .01 .05
475 Tom Newberry .01 .05
476 Damone Johnson .01 .05
477 Pat Terrell .01 .05
478 Marcus Dupree .08 .25
479 Todd Lyght .01 .05
480 Buford McGee .01 .05
481 Bern Brostek .01 .05
482 Jim Price .01 .05
483 Robert Young .01 .05
484 Tony Zendejas .01 .05
485 Robert Bailey RC .01 .05
486 Alvin Wright .01 .05
487 Pat Carter .01 .05
488 Pete Stoyanovich .01 .05
489 Reggie Roby .01 .05
490 Harry Galbreath .01 .05
491 Mike McGruder RC .01 .05
492 J.B. Brown .01 .05
493 E.J. Junior .01 .05
494 Ferrell Edmunds .01 .05
495 Scott Secules .01 .05
496 Greg Baty RC .01 .05
497 Mike Iaquaniello .01 .05
498 Keith Sims .01 .05
499 John Randle .02 .10
500 Joey Browner .01 .05
501 Steve Jordan .01 .05
502 Darrin Nelson .01 .05
503 Audray McMillian .01 .05
504 Harry Newsome .01 .05
505 Hassan Jones .01 .05
506 Ray Berry .01 .05
507 Mike Merriweather .01 .05
508 Leo Lewis .01 .05
509 Tim Irwin .01 .05
510 Kirk Lowdermilk .01 .05
511 Alfred Anderson .01 .05
512 Michael Timpson RC .01 .05
513 Jerome Henderson .01 .05
514 Andre Tippett .01 .05
515 Chris Singleton .01 .05
516 John Stephens .01 .05
517 Ronnie Lippett .01 .05
518 Bruce Armstrong .01 .05
519 Marion Hobby RC .01 .05
520 Tim Goad .01 .05
521 Mickey Washington RC .01 .05
522 Fred Smerlas .01 .05
523 Wayne Martin .01 .05
524 Frank Warren .01 .05
525 Floyd Turner .01 .05
526 Wesley Carroll .01 .05
527 Gene Atkins .01 .05
528 Vaughan Johnson .01 .05
529 Hoby Brenner .01 .05
530 Renaldo Turnbull .01 .05
531 Joel Hilgenberg .01 .05
532 Craig Heyward .02 .10
533 Vince Buck .01 .05
534 Jim Dombrowski .01 .05
535 Fred McAfee RC .01 .05
536 Phil Simms .02 .10
537 Lewis Tillman .01 .05
538 John Elliott .01 .05
539 Dave Meggett .02 .10
540 Mark Collins .01 .05
541 Ottis Anderson .02 .10
542 Bobby Abrams RC .01 .05
543 Sean Landeta .01 .05
544 Brian Williams OL .01 .05
545 Erik Howard .01 .05
546 Mark Ingram .01 .05
547 Kanavis McGhee .01 .05
548 Kyle Clifton .01 .05
549 Marvin Washington .01 .05
550 Jeff Criswell .01 .05
551 Dave Cadigan .01 .05
552 Chris Burkett .01 .05
553 Erik McMillan .01 .05
554 James Hasty .01 .05
555 Louie Aguiar RC .01 .05
556 Troy Johnson RC .01 .05
557 Troy Taylor RC .01 .05
558 Pat Kelly RC .01 .05
559 Heath Sherman .01 .05
560 Roger Ruzek .01 .05
561 Andre Waters .01 .05
562 Izel Jenkins .01 .05
563 Keith Jackson .02 .10
564 Byron Evans .01 .05
565 Wes Hopkins .01 .05
566 Rich Miano .01 .05
567 Seth Joyner .01 .05
568 Thomas Sanders .01 .05
569 David Alexander .01 .05
570 Jeff Kemp .01 .05
571 Jock Jones RC .01 .05
572 Craig Patterson RC .01 .05
573 Robert Massey .01 .05
574 Bill Lewis .01 .05
575 Freddie Joe Nunn .01 .05
576 Aeneas Williams .02 .10
577 John Jackson WR .01 .05
578 Tim McDonald .01 .05
579 Michael Zordich RC .01 .05
580 Eric Hill .01 .05
581 Lorenzo Lynch .01 .05
582 Vernice Smith RC .01 .05
583 Greg Lloyd .02 .10
584 Carnell Lake .01 .05
585 Hardy Nickerson .02 .10
586 Delton Hall .01 .05
587 Gerald Williams .01 .05
588 Bryan Hinkle .01 .05
589 Barry Foster .02 .10
590 Bubby Brister .02 .10
591 Rick Strom RC .01 .05
592 David Little .01 .05
593 Leroy Thompson .01 .05
594 Eric Bieniemy .01 .05
595 Courtney Hall .01 .05
596 George Thornton .01 .05
597 Donnie Elder .01 .05
598 Billy Ray Smith .01 .05
599 Gill Byrd .01 .05
600 Marion Butts .01 .05
601 Ronnie Harmon .01 .05
602 Anthony Shelton .01 .05
603 Mark May .01 .05
604 Craig McEwen RC .01 .05
605 Steve Young .25 .60
606 Keith Henderson .01 .05
607 Pierce Holt .01 .05
608 Roy Foster .01 .05
609 Don Griffin .01 .05
610 Harry Sydney .01 .05
611 Todd Bowles .08 .25
612 Ted Washington .01 .05
613 Johnnie Jackson .01 .05
614 Jesse Sapolu .01 .05
615 Brent Jones .02 .10
616 Travis McNeal .01 .05
617 Darrick Brilz RC .01 .05
618 Terry Wooden .01 .05
619 Tommy Kane .01 .05
620 Nesby Glasgow .01 .05
621 Dwayne Harper .01 .05
622 Rick Tuten .01 .05
623 Chris Warren .02 .10
624 John L. Williams .01 .05
625 Rufus Porter .01 .05
626 David Daniels .01 .05
627 Keith McCants .01 .05
628 Reuben Davis .01 .05
629 Mark Royals .01 .05
630 Marty Carter RC .01 .05
631 Ian Beckles .01 .05
632 Ron Hall .01 .05
633 Eugene Marve .01 .05
634 Willie Drewrey .01 .05
635 Tom McHale RC .01 .05
636 Kevin Murphy .01 .05
637 Robert Hardy RC .01 .05
638 Ricky Sanders .01 .05
639 Gary Clark .02 .10
640 Andre Collins .01 .05
641 Brad Edwards .01 .05
642 Monte Coleman .01 .05
643 Clarence Vaughn RC .01 .05
644 Fred Stokes .01 .05
645 Charles Mann .01 .05
646 Earnest Byner .01 .05
647 Jim Lachey .01 .05
648 Jeff Bostic .01 .05
649 Chris Mims RC .01 .05
650 George Williams RC .01 .05
651 Ed Cunningham RC .01 .05
652 Tony Smith WR RC .01 .05
653 Will Furrer RC .01 .05
654 Matt Elliott RC .01 .05
655 Mike Mooney RC .01 .05
656 Eddie Blake RC .01 .05
657 Leon Searcy RC .01 .05
658 Kevin Turner RC .01 .05
659 Keith Hamilton RC .02 .10
660 Alan Haller RC .01 .05

1992 Pacific Bob Griese

This nine-card standard-size set captures highlights from the career of Hall of Famer Bob Griese. These cards were randomly inserted in second series foil and jumbo packs. They were also randomly inserted in triple folder and five-card change-maker packs. Griese personally autographed 1,000 cards. These cards are individually numbered on the back. The cards are numbered on the back (10-18) continuing with the numbering of the Legends of the Game (Steve) Largent series.

COMPLETE SET (9) 2.00 5.00
COMMON GRIESE (10-18) .25 .60
AU Bob Griese AUTO 20.00 50.00

1992 Pacific Steve Largent

is nine-card standard-size set captures highlights from the career of Hall of Famer Steve Largent. The cards were randomly inserted in first series packs as well as Triple Holder and change-maker packs. Largent personally autographed 1,000 cards and these cards are individually numbered on the back. The color action photos on the fronts have white borders, with the player's name and a caption in a multicolored stripe cutting across the bottom of the picture. In a horizontal format, the backs carry another color photo and career summary.

COMPLETE SET (9) 2.00 5.00
COMMON LARGENT (1-9) .25 .60
AU Steve Largent AUTO 30.00 60.00

1992 Pacific Picks The Pros

This 25-card standard-size set features Pacific's picks for the top player at each position. The color action player photos on the fronts have either gold or silver foil borders, with the words "Pacific Picks the Pros" in corresponding foil lettering in a multicolored stripe running down the left side of the picture. The gold foil cards were randomly inserted in first series foil packs, while the silver foil cards were found in first series jumbo packs. There is no difference in value between the two versions. On a background of different shades of red and yellow, the diagonally oriented backs present career summaries.

COMPLETE SET (25) 8.00 20.00
*SILVER: .4X TO 1X GOLD
1 Mark Rypien .10 .30
2 Marv Cook .10 .30
3 Jim Lachey .10 .30
4 Darrell Green .10 .30
5 Derrick Thomas .60 1.50
6 Thurman Thomas .60 1.50
7 Kent Hull .10 .30
8 Tim McDonald .10 .30
9 Mike Croel .10 .30
10 Anthony Munoz .25 .60
11 Jerome Brown .10 .30
12 Reggie White .60 1.50
13 Gill Byrd .10 .30
14 Jessie Tuggle .10 .30
15 Randall McDaniel .10 .30
16 Sam Mills .10 .30
17 Pat Swilling .10 .30
18 Eugene Robinson .10 .30
19 Michael Irvin .60 1.50
20 Emmitt Smith 4.00 10.00
21 Jeff Gossett .10 .30
22 Jeff Jaeger .10 .30
23 William Fuller .10 .30
24 Mike Munchak .25 .60
25 Andre Rison .25 .60

1992 Pacific Prism Inserts

This ten-card standard-size set features top NFL running backs. According to Pacific, 10,000 of each card were produced. They were randomly inserted into second series foil packs and Triple Folder card packs.

COMPLETE SET (10) 5.00 12.00
1 Thurman Thomas .40 1.00
2 Gaston Green .07 .20
3 Christian Okoye .07 .20
4 Leonard Russell .15 .40
5 Mark Higgs .07 .20
6 Emmitt Smith 2.50 6.00
7 Barry Sanders 2.00 5.00
8 Rodney Hampton .15 .40
9 Earnest Byner .07 .20
10 Herschel Walker .15 .40

1992 Pacific Statistical Leaders

This 30-card standard-size set features the team statistical leaders from the 28 NFL teams, plus two cards devoted to the AFC and NFC rushing leaders. The cards were randomly inserted into both series foil packs, Triple Folder card packs, and change-maker (25 cents) packs. The whole set of these Stat Leaders was included as an insert with 1992 Pacific factory sets. The cards are checklisted alphabetically according to team name.

COMPLETE SET (30) 5.00 10.00
ONE SET PER FACTORY SET
1 Chris Miller .07 .20
2 Thurman Thomas .20 .50
3 Jim Harbaugh .20 .50
4 Jim Breech .02 .10
5 Kevin Mack .02 .10
6 Emmitt Smith 1.50 3.00
7 Gaston Green .02 .10
8 Barry Sanders 1.25 2.50
9 Tony Bennett .02 .10
10 Warren Moon .20 .50
11 Bill Brooks .02 .10
12 Christian Okoye .02 .10
13 Jay Schroeder .02 .10
14 Robert Delpino .02 .10
15 Mark Higgs .02 .10
16 John Randle .07 .20
17 Leonard Russell .07 .20
18 Pat Swilling .02 .10
19 Rodney Hampton .07 .20
20 Terance Mathis .07 .20
21 Fred Barnett .07 .20
22 Aeneas Williams .07 .20
23 Neil O'Donnell .07 .20
24 Marion Butts .02 .10
25 Steve Young .60 1.25
26 John L. Williams .02 .10
27 Reggie Cobb .02 .10
28 Mark Rypien .02 .10
29 Thurman Thomas LL .20 .50
30 Emmitt Smith LL 1.50 3.00

1993 Pacific Prototypes

These five standard-size cards were issued to preview the design of the 1993 Pacific Plus football series. Each card was packed in a cello pack with an ad card. The color action photos on the fronts are tilted slightly to the left and set on a two-color marbleized card face reflecting the team's colors. The player's name appears in script at the bottom of the picture, with the team helmet in the lower left corner. On two-toned marbelized background, the horizontal backs carry a color close-up shot, biography, statistics, and career highlights. Running across the text portion are the words "1993 Prototypes." The cards were given away at the July 1993 National Sports Collectors Convention in Chicago and used as sales samples. The production run was reportedly 5,000 sets.

COMPLETE SET (5) 6.00 15.00
1 Emmitt Smith 2.40 6.00
2 Barry Sanders 2.40 6.00
3 Derrick Thomas .60 1.50
4 Jim Everett .60 1.50
5 Steve Young 1.20 3.00

1993 Pacific

The 1993 Pacific football set consists of 440 standard-size cards. Just 5,000 cases or 99,000 of each card were reportedly produced. Randomly inserted throughout the 12-card foil packs were a 25-card Pacific Picks the Pros gold foil set and a 20-card Prism set. The production run on the insert sets was 8,000 each. The cards are checklisted according to NFC and AFC divisional alignments. The set closes with the following topical subsets: NFL Stars (393-417) and Rookies (418-440). Rookie Cards include Jerome Bettis, Drew Bledsoe, Reggie Brooks, Curtis Conway, Garrison Hearst, O.J. McDuffie, Natrone Means, Glyn Milburn, Rick Mirer, Robert Smith and Kevin Williams. Separately numbered checklist cards were also randomly inserted into packs.

COMPLETE SET (440) 10.00 20.00
1 Emmitt Smith .60 1.50
2 Troy Aikman .30 .75
3 Larry Brown DB .01 .05
4 Tony Casillas .01 .05
5 Thomas Everett .01 .05
6 Alvin Harper .02 .10
7 Michael Irvin .08 .25
8 Charles Haley .02 .10
9 Leon Lett RC .02 .10
10 Kevin Smith .02 .10
11 Robert Jones .01 .05
12 Jimmy Smith .08 .25
13 Derrick Gainer RC .01 .05
14 Lin Elliott .01 .05
15 William Thomas .01 .05
16 Clyde Simmons .01 .05
17 Seth Joyner .01 .05
18 Randall Cunningham .08 .25
19 Byron Evans .01 .05
20 Fred Barnett .02 .10
21 Calvin Williams .02 .10
22 James Joseph .01 .05
23 Heath Sherman .01 .05
24 Siran Stacy .01 .05
25 Andy Harmon .02 .10
26 Eric Allen .01 .05
27 Herschel Walker .02 .10
28 Vai Sikahema .01 .05
29 Earnest Byner .01 .05
30 Jeff Bostic .01 .05
31 Monte Coleman .01 .05
32 Ricky Ervins .01 .05
33 Darrell Green .01 .05
34 Mark Schlereth .01 .05
35 Mark Rypien .01 .05
36 Art Monk .02 .10
37 Brian Mitchell .02 .10
38 Chip Lohmiller .01 .05
39 Charles Mann .01 .05
40 Shane Collins .01 .05
41 Jim Lachey .01 .05
42 Desmond Howard .02 .10
43 Rodney Hampton .02 .10
44 Dave Brown RC .08 .25
45 Mark Collins .01 .05
46 Jarrod Bunch .01 .05
47 William Roberts .01 .05
48 Sean Landeta .01 .05
49 Lawrence Taylor .08 .25
50 Ed McCaffrey .08 .25
51 Bart Oates .01 .05
52 Pepper Johnson .01 .05
53 Eric Dorsey .01 .05
54 Erik Howard .01 .05
55 Phil Simms .02 .10
56 Derek Brown TE .01 .05
57 Johnny Bailey .01 .05
58 Rich Camarillo .01 .05
59 Larry Centers RC .08 .25
60 Chris Chandler .02 .10
61 Randal Hill .01 .05
62 Ricky Proehl .01 .05
63 Freddie Joe Nunn .01 .05
64 Robert Massey .01 .05
65 Aeneas Williams .01 .05
66 Luis Sharpe .01 .05
67 Eric Swann .02 .10
68 Timm Rosenbach .01 .05
69 Anthony Edwards RC .01 .05
70 Greg Davis .01 .05
71 Terry Allen .08 .25
72 Anthony Carter .02 .10
73 Cris Carter .08 .25
74 Roger Craig .02 .10
75 Jack Del Rio .01 .05
76 Chris Doleman .01 .05
77 Rich Gannon .08 .25
78 Hassan Jones .01 .05
79 Steve Jordan .01 .05
80 Randall McDaniel .02 .10
81 Sean Salisbury .01 .05
82 Harry Newsome .01 .05
83 Carlos Jenkins .01 .05
84 Jake Reed .08 .25
85 Edgar Bennett .08 .25
86 Tony Bennett .01 .05
87 Terrell Buckley .01 .05
88 Ty Detmer .08 .25
89 Brett Favre .75 2.00
90 Chris Jacke .01 .05
91 Sterling Sharpe .08 .25
92 James Campen .01 .05
93 Brian Noble .01 .05
94 Lester Archambeau RC .01 .05
95 Harry Sydney .01 .05
96 Corey Harris .01 .05
97 Don Majkowski .01 .05
98 Ken Ruettgers .01 .05
99 Lomas Brown .01 .05
100 Jason Hanson .01 .05
101 Robert Porcher .01 .05
102 Chris Spielman .02 .10
103 Erik Kramer .02 .10
104 Tracy Scroggins .01 .05
105 Rodney Peete .01 .05
106 Barry Sanders .50 1.25
107 Herman Moore .08 .25
108 Brett Perriman .08 .25
109 Mel Gray .02 .10
110 Dennis Gibson .01 .05
111 Bennie Blades .01 .05
112 Andre Ware .01 .05
113 Gary Anderson RB .01 .05
114 Tyji Armstrong .01 .05
115 Reggie Cobb .01 .05
116 Marty Carter .01 .05
117 Lawrence Dawsey .01 .05
118 Steve DeBerg .01 .05
119 Ron Hall .01 .05
120 Courtney Hawkins .01 .05
121 Broderick Thomas .01 .05
122 Keith McCants .01 .05
123 Bruce Reimers .01 .05
124 Darrick Brownlow .01 .05
125 Mark Wheeler .01 .05
126 Ricky Reynolds .01 .05
127 Neal Anderson .01 .05
128 Trace Armstrong .01 .05
129 Mark Carrier DB .01 .05
130 Richard Dent .02 .10
131 Wendell Davis .01 .05
132 Darren Lewis .01 .05
133 Tom Waddle .01 .05
134 Jim Harbaugh .08 .25
135 Steve McMichael .02 .10
136 William Perry .02 .10
137 Alonzo Spellman .01 .05
138 John Roper .01 .05
139 Peter Tom Willis .01 .05
140 Dante Jones .01 .05
141 Harris Barton .01 .05
142 Michael Carter .01 .05
143 Eric Davis .01 .05
144 Dana Hall .01 .05
145 Amp Lee .01 .05
146 Don Griffin .01 .05
147 Jerry Rice .40 1.00
148 Ricky Watters .08 .25
149 Steve Young .30 .75
150 Bill Romanowski .01 .05
151 Klaus Wilmsmeyer .01 .05
152 Steve Bono .02 .10
153 Tom Rathman .01 .05
154 Odessa Turner .01 .05
155 Morten Andersen .01 .05
156 Richard Cooper .01 .05
157 Toi Cook .01 .05
158 Quinn Early .02 .10
159 Vaughn Dunbar .01 .05
160 Rickey Jackson .01 .05
161 Wayne Martin .01 .05
162 Hoby Brenner .01 .05
163 Joel Hilgenberg .01 .05
164 Mike Buck .01 .05
165 Torrance Small .01 .05
166 Eric Martin .01 .05
167 Vaughan Johnson .01 .05
168 Sam Mills .01 .05
169 Steve Broussard .01 .05
170 Darion Conner .01 .05
171 Drew Hill .01 .05
172 Chris Hinton .01 .05
173 Chris Miller .02 .10
174 Tim McKyer .01 .05
175 Norm Johnson .01 .05
176 Mike Pritchard .02 .10
177 Andre Rison .02 .10
178 Deion Sanders .20 .50
179 Tony Smith RB .01 .05
180 Bruce Pickens .01 .05
181 Michael Haynes .02 .10
182 Jessie Tuggle .01 .05
183 Marc Boutte .01 .05
184 Don Bracken .01 .05
185 Bern Brostek .01 .05
186 Henry Ellard .02 .10
187 Jim Everett .02 .10
188 Sean Gilbert .02 .10
189 Cleveland Gary .01 .05
190 Todd Kinchen .01 .05
191 Pat Terrell .01 .05
192 Jackie Slater .01 .05
193 David Lang .01 .05
194 Flipper Anderson .01 .05
195 Tony Zendejas .01 .05
196 Roman Phifer .01 .05
197 Steve Christie .01 .05
198 Cornelius Bennett .02 .10
199 Phil Hansen .01 .05
200 Don Beebe .01 .05
201 Mark Kelso .01 .05
202 Bruce Smith .08 .25
203 Darryl Talley .01 .05
204 Andre Reed .02 .10
205 Mike Lodish .01 .05
206 Jim Kelly .08 .25
207 Thurman Thomas .08 .25
208 Kenneth Davis .01 .05
209 Frank Reich .02 .10
210 Kent Hull .01 .05
211 Marco Coleman .01 .05
212 Bryan Cox .01 .05
213 Jeff Cross .01 .05
214 Mark Higgs .01 .05
215 Keith Jackson .02 .10
216 Scott Miller .01 .05
217 John Offerdahl .01 .05
218 Dan Marino .60 1.50
219 Keith Sims .01 .05
220 Chuck Klingbeil .01 .05
221 Troy Vincent .01 .05
222 Mike Williams WR RC .01 .05
223 Pete Stoyanovich .01 .05
224 J.B. Brown .01 .05
225 Ashley Ambrose .01 .05
226 Jason Belser RC .01 .05
227 Jeff George .08 .25
228 Quentin Coryatt .02 .10
229 Duane Bickett .01 .05
230 Steve Emtman .01 .05
231 Anthony Johnson .02 .10
232 Rohn Stark .01 .05
233 Jessie Hester .01 .05
234 Reggie Langhorne .01 .05
235 Clarence Verdin .01 .05
236 Dean Biasucci .01 .05
237 Jack Trudeau .01 .05
238 Tony Siragusa .01 .05
239 Chris Burkett .01 .05
240 Brad Baxter .01 .05
241 Rob Moore .02 .10
242 Browning Nagle .01 .05
243 Jim Sweeney .01 .05
244 Kurt Barber .01 .05
245 Siupeli Malamala RC .01 .05
246 Mike Brim .01 .05
247 Mo Lewis .01 .05
248 Johnny Mitchell .01 .05
249 Ken Whisenhunt RC .10 .30
250 James Hasty .01 .05
251 Kyle Clifton .01 .05
252 Terance Mathis .02 .10
253 Ray Agnew .01 .05
254 Eugene Chung .01 .05
255 Marv Cook .01 .05
256 Johnny Rembert .01 .05
257 Maurice Hurst .01 .05
258 Jon Vaughn .01 .05
259 Leonard Russell .02 .10
260 Pat Harlow .01 .05
261 Andre Tippett .01 .05
262 Michael Timpson .01 .05
263 Greg McMurtry .01 .05
264 Chris Singleton .01 .05
265 Reggie Redding RC .01 .05
266 Walter Stanley .01 .05
267 Gary Anderson K .01 .05
268 Merril Hoge .01 .05
269 Barry Foster .02 .10
270 Charles Davenport .01 .05
271 Jeff Graham .02 .10
272 Adrian Cooper .01 .05
273 David Little .01 .05
274 Neil O'Donnell .08 .25
275 Rod Woodson .08 .25
276 Ernie Mills .01 .05
277 Dwight Stone .01 .05
278 Darren Perry .01 .05
279 Dermontti Dawson .02 .10
280 Carlton Haselrig .01 .05
281 Pat Coleman .01 .05
282 Ernest Givins .02 .10
283 Warren Moon .08 .25
284 Haywood Jeffires .02 .10
285 Cody Carlson .01 .05
286 Ray Childress .01 .05
287 Bruce Matthews .01 .05
288 Webster Slaughter .01 .05
289 Bo Orlando .01 .05
290 Lorenzo White .01 .05
291 Eddie Robinson .01 .05
292 Bubba McDowell .01 .05
293 Bucky Richardson .01 .05
294 Sean Jones .01 .05
295 David Brandon .01 .05
296 Shawn Collins .01 .05
297 Lawyer Tillman .01 .05
298 Bob Dahl .01 .05
299 Kevin Mack .01 .05
300 Bernie Kosar .02 .10
301 Tommy Vardell .01 .05
302 Jay Hilgenberg .01 .05
303 Michael Dean Perry .02 .10
304 Michael Jackson .02 .10
305 Eric Metcalf .02 .10
306 Rico Smith RC .01 .05
307 Stevon Moore RC .01 .05
308 Leroy Hoard .02 .10
309 Eric Ball .01 .05
310 Derrick Fenner .01 .05
311 James Francis .01 .05
312 Ricardo McDonald .01 .05
313 Tim Krumrie .01 .05
314 Carl Pickens .02 .10
315 David Klingler .01 .05
316 Donald Hollas RC .01 .05
317 Harold Green .01 .05
318 Daniel Stubbs .01 .05
319 Alfred Williams .01 .05
320 Darryl Williams .01 .05
321 Mike Arthur RC .01 .05
322 Leonard Wheeler .01 .05
323 Gill Byrd .01 .05
324 Eric Bieniemy .01 .05
325 Marion Butts .01 .05
326 John Carney .01 .05
327 Stan Humphries .02 .10
328 Ronnie Harmon .01 .05
329 Junior Seau .08 .25
330 Nate Lewis .01 .05
331 Harry Swayne .01 .05
332 Leslie O'Neal .02 .10
333 Eric Moten .01 .05
334 Blaise Winter RC .01 .05
335 Anthony Miller .02 .10
336 Gary Plummer .01 .05
337 Willie Davis .08 .25
338 J.J. Birden .01 .05
339 Tim Barnett .01 .05
340 Dave Krieg .02 .10
341 Barry Word .01 .05
342 Tracy Simien .01 .05
343 Christian Okoye .01 .05
344 Todd McNair .01 .05
345 Dan Saleaumua .01 .05
346 Derrick Thomas .08 .25
347 Harvey Williams .02 .10
348 Kimble Anders RC .08 .25
349 Tim Grunhard .01 .05
350 Tony Hargain UER RC .01 .05
351 Simon Fletcher .01 .05
352 John Elway .60 1.50
353 Mike Croel .01 .05
354 Steve Atwater .01 .05
355 Tommy Maddox .08 .25
356 Karl Mecklenburg .01 .05
357 Shane Dronett .01 .05
358 Kenny Walker .01 .05
359 Reggie Rivers RC .01 .05
360 Cedric Tillman RC .01 .05
361 Arthur Marshall RC .01 .05
362 Greg Lewis .01 .05
363 Shannon Sharpe .08 .25
364 Doug Widell .01 .05
365 Todd Marinovich .01 .05
366 Nick Bell .01 .05
367 Eric Dickerson .02 .10
368 Max Montoya .01 .05
369 Winston Moss .01 .05
370 Howie Long .08 .25
371 Willie Gault .01 .05
372 Tim Brown .08 .25
373 Steve Smith .01 .05
374 Steve Wisniewski .01 .05
375 Alexander Wright .01 .05
376 Ethan Horton .01 .05
377 Napoleon McCallum .01 .05
378 Terry McDaniel .01 .05
379 Patrick Hunter .01 .05
380 Robert Blackmon .01 .05
381 John Kasay .01 .05
382 Cortez Kennedy .02 .10
383 Andy Heck .01 .05
384 Bill Hitchcock RC .01 .05
385 Rick Mirer RC .08 .25
386 Jeff Bryant .01 .05
387 Eugene Robinson .01 .05
388 John L. Williams .01 .05
389 Chris Warren .02 .10
390 Rufus Porter .01 .05
391 Joe Tofflemire RC .01 .05
392 Dan McGwire .01 .05
393 Boomer Esiason .02 .10
394 Brad Muster .01 .05
395 James Lofton .02 .10
396 Tim McGee .01 .05
397 Steve Beuerlein .02 .10
398 Gaston Green .01 .05
399 Bill Brooks .01 .05
400 Ronnie Lott .02 .10
401 Jay Schroeder .01 .05
402 Marcus Allen .08 .25
403 Kevin Greene .02 .10
404 Kirk Lowdermilk .01 .05
405 Hugh Millen .01 .05
406 Pat Swilling .01 .05
407 Bobby Hebert .01 .05
408 Carl Banks .01 .05
409 Jeff Hostetler .02 .10
410 Leonard Marshall .01 .05
411 Ken O'Brien .01 .05
412 Joe Montana .60 1.50
413 Reggie White .08 .25
414 Gary Clark .02 .10
415 Johnny Johnson .01 .05
416 Tim McDonald .01 .05
417 Pierce Holt .01 .05
418 Gino Torretta RC .02 .10
419 Glyn Milburn RC .08 .25
420 O.J.McDuffie RC .08 .25
421 Coleman Rudolph RC .01 .05
422 Reggie Brooks RC .02 .10
423 Garrison Hearst RC .25 .60
424 Leonard Renfro RC .01 .05
425 Kevin Williams RC WR .08 .25
426 Demetrius DuBose RC .01 .05
427 Elvis Grbac RC .50 1.25
428 Lincoln Kennedy RC .01 .05
429 Carlton Gray RC .01 .05
430 Micheal Barrow RC .08 .25
431 George Teague RC .02 .10
432 Curtis Conway RC .15 .40
433 Natrone Means RC .08 .25
434 Jerome Bettis RC 2.00 5.00
435 Drew Bledsoe RC .75 2.00
436 Robert Smith RC .40 1.00
437 Deon Figures RC .01 .05
438 Qadry Ismail RC .08 .25
439 Chris Slade RC .02 .10
440 Dana Stubblefield RC .08 .25

1993 Pacific Picks the Pros Gold

ese 25 standard-size cards showcasing Pacific's picks at each position were random inserts in 1993 Pacific packs. Cards from the parallel silver version of this set were randomly inserted in packs of 1993 Pacific Triple Folders.

COMPLETE SET (25) 15.00 40.00
1 Jerry Rice 4.00 8.00
2 Sterling Sharpe 1.00 2.00
3 Richmond Webb .15 .40
4 Harris Barton .15 .40
5 Randall McDaniel .15 .40
6 Steve Wisniewski .15 .40
7 Mark Stepnoski .15 .40
8 Steve Young 3.00 6.00
9 Emmitt Smith 6.00 12.00
10 Barry Foster .30 .75
11 Nick Lowery .15 .40
12 Reggie White 1.00 2.00
13 Leslie O'Neal .30 .75
14 Cortez Kennedy .30 .75
15 Ray Childress .15 .40
16 Vaughan Johnson .15 .40
17 Wilber Marshall .15 .40
18 Junior Seau 1.00 2.00
19 Sam Mills .15 .40
20 Rod Woodson 1.00 2.00
21 Ricky Reynolds .15 .40
22 Steve Atwater .15 .40
23 Chuck Cecil .15 .40
24 Rich Camarillo .15 .40
25 Dale Carter .15 .40

1993 Pacific Silver Prism Inserts

There are three slightly different versions of this 20-card standard-size set. The difference involves the prismatic backgrounds. The standard 1993 Pacific Prism Inserts were produced with triangular prismatic backgrounds in quantities of 8,000 cards each. They were randomly inserted in regular (12-card maroon-colored) Pacific packs as well as Triple Folder packs. The circular versions of the prismatic background cards were inserted one per special (gold-colored) retail packs. The third version uses a gold triangular prismatic background. The production of these cards was reportedly limited to 1,000 each, and they were randomly inserted in 1993 Pacific Triple Folder packs. The fronts feature color player action cut-outs over borderless prismatic foil backgrounds. The player's name appears in team-colored block lettering at the bottom. The borderless back carries the same player photo, but this time with its original on-field background. The player's name appears in white cursive lettering near a lower corner. The set features 20 of the NFL's top players on a "Prism" background that makes the player contrast sharply with the background. The backs display a full-bleed color action player photo with the player's name and position in script. The cards are numbered on the back at the lower right "X of 20."

COMPLETE SET (20) 25.00 60.00
*CIRCULAR BACKGROUND: SAME PRICE
CIRCULAR:ONE PER SPEC.RET.PACK
1 Troy Aikman 2.00 5.00
2 Jerome Bettis 6.00 15.00
3 Drew Bledsoe 2.50 6.00
4 Reggie Brooks .10 .30
5 Brett Favre 5.00 12.00
6 Barry Foster .25 .60
7 Garrison Hearst .75 2.00
8 Michael Irvin .60 1.50
9 Cortez Kennedy .25 .60
10 David Klingler .10 .30
11 Dan Marino 4.00 10.00
12 Rick Mirer .30 .75
13 Joe Montana 4.00 10.00
14 Jay Novacek .10 .30
15 Jerry Rice 2.50 6.00
16 Barry Sanders 3.00 8.00
17 Sterling Sharpe .60 1.50
18 Emmitt Smith 4.00 10.00
19 Thurman Thomas .60 1.50
20 Steve Young 2.00 5.00

1994 Pacific

is set consists of 450 standard size cards featuring full-bleed color photos. The player's name and position are in gold foil at the bottom. The backs are dominated by a color with statistics at the bottom. The players are grouped alphabetically within their team subsets. The set closes with a Rookies (417-450) subset. Rookie Cards in this set include Mario Bates, Lake Dawson, Trent Dilfer, Marshall Faulk, William Floyd, Greg Hill. Charles Johnson, Errict Rhett, Darnay Scott, and Heath Shuler. A Sterling Sharpe Promo card was produced and priced at the end of our listings.

COMPLETE SET (450) 15.00 30.00
1 Troy Aikman .40 1.00
2 Charles Haley .02 .10
3 Alvin Harper .02 .10
4 Michael Irvin .08 .25
5 Jim Jeffcoat .01 .05
6 Daryl Johnston .02 .10
7 Robert Jones .01 .05
8 Brock Marion RC .08 .25
9 Russell Maryland .01 .05
10 Ken Norton .02 .10
11 Jay Novacek .02 .10
12 Emmitt Smith .60 1.50
13 Kevin Smith .01 .05
14 Tony Tolbert .01 .05
15 Kevin Williams WR .02 .10
16 Don Beebe .01 .05
17 Cornelius Bennett .02 .10
18 Bill Brooks .01 .05
19 Steve Christie .01 .05
20 Russell Copeland .01 .05
21 Kenneth Davis .01 .05
22 Kent Hull .01 .05
23 Jim Kelly .08 .25
24 Pete Metzelaars .01 .05
25 Andre Reed .02 .10
26 Frank Reich .02 .10
27 Bruce Smith .08 .25
28 Darryl Talley .01 .05
29 Steve Tasker .02 .10
30 Thurman Thomas .08 .25
31 Steve Bono .02 .10
32 Dexter Carter .01 .05
33 Kevin Fagan .01 .05
34 Dana Hall .01 .05
35 Brent Jones .02 .10
36 Amp Lee .01 .05
37 Marc Logan .01 .05
38 Tim McDonald .01 .05
39 Guy McIntyre .01 .05
40 Tom Rathman .01 .05
41 Jerry Rice .40 1.00
42 Dana Stubblefield .02 .10
43 Steve Wallace .01 .05
44 Ricky Watters .02 .10
45 Steve Young .30 .75
46 Marcus Allen .08 .25
47 Kimble Anders .02 .10
48 Tim Barnett .01 .05
49 J.J. Birden .01 .05
50 Dale Carter .01 .05
51 Jonathan Hayes .01 .05
52 Dave Krieg .02 .10
53 Albert Lewis .01 .05
54 Nick Lowery .01 .05
55 Joe Montana .75 2.00
56 Neil Smith .02 .10
57 John Stephens .01 .05
58 Derrick Thomas .08 .25
59 Harvey Williams .02 .10
60 Micheal Barrow .01 .05
61 Gary Brown .01 .05
62 Cody Carlson .01 .05
63 Ray Childress .01 .05
64 Curtis Duncan .01 .05
65 Ernest Givins .02 .10
66 Haywood Jeffires .02 .10
67 Wilber Marshall .01 .05
68 Bubba McDowell .01 .05
69 Warren Moon .08 .25
70 Mike Munchak .02 .10
71 Marcus Robertson .01 .05
72 Webster Slaughter .01 .05
73 Gary Wellman RC .01 .05
74 Lorenzo White .01 .05
75 Ray Crockett .01 .05
76 Jason Hanson .01 .05
77 Rodney Holman .01 .05
78 George Jamison .01 .05
79 Erik Kramer .02 .10
80 Ryan McNeil .01 .05
81 Derrick Moore .01 .05
82 Herman Moore .08 .25
83 Rodney Peete .01 .05
84 Brett Perriman .02 .10
85 Barry Sanders .60 1.50
86 Chris Spielman .02 .10
87 Pat Swilling .01 .05
88 Vernon Turner .01 .05
89 Andre Ware .01 .05
90 Michael Brooks .01 .05
91 Dave Brown .02 .10
92 Derek Brown TE .01 .05
93 Jarrod Bunch .01 .05
94 Chris Calloway .01 .05
95 Kent Graham .02 .10
96 Rodney Hampton .02 .10
97 Mark Jackson .01 .05
98 Ed McCaffrey .08 .25
99 Dave Meggett .01 .05
100 Aaron Pierce .01 .05
101 Mike Sherrard .01 .05
102 Phil Simms .02 .10
103 Lewis Tillman .01 .05
104 Eddie Anderson .01 .05
105 Patrick Bates .01 .05
106 Nick Bell .01 .05
107 Tim Brown .08 .25
108 Willie Gault .01 .05
109 Jeff Gossett .01 .05
110 Ethan Horton .01 .05
111 Jeff Hostetler .02 .10
112 Rocket Ismail .02 .10
113 Chester McGlockton .01 .05
114 Anthony Smith .01 .05
115 Steve Smith .01 .05
116 Greg Townsend .01 .05
117 Steve Wisniewski .01 .05
118 Alexander Wright .01 .05
119 Steve Atwater .01 .05
120 Rod Bernstine .01 .05
121 Mike Croel .01 .05
122 Shane Dronett .01 .05
123 Jason Elam .02 .10
124 John Elway .75 2.00
125 Brian Habib .01 .05
126 Rondell Jones .01 .05
127 Tommy Maddox .08 .25
128 Karl Mecklenburg .01 .05
129 Glyn Milburn .02 .10
130 Derek Russell .01 .05
131 Shannon Sharpe .02 .10
132 Dennis Smith .01 .05
133 Edgar Bennett .08 .25
134 Tony Bennett .01 .05
135 Robert Brooks .08 .25
136 Terrell Buckley .01 .05
137 LeRoy Butler .01 .05
138 Mark Clayton .01 .05
139 Ty Detmer .02 .10
140 Brett Favre .75 2.00
141 John Jurkovic RC .02 .10
142 Bryce Paup .02 .10
143 Sterling Sharpe .02 .10
144 George Teague .01 .05

145 Darrell Thompson .01 .05
146 Ed West .01 .05
147 Reggie White .08 .25
148 Terry Allen .02 .10
149 Anthony Carter .02 .10
150 Cris Carter .20 .50
151 Roger Craig .02 .10
152 Jack Del Rio .01 .05
153 Chris Doleman .01 .05
154 Scottie Graham RC .02 .10
155 Eric Guliford RC .01 .05
156 Qadry Ismail .08 .25
157 Steve Jordan .01 .05
158 Randall McDaniel .02 .10
159 Jim McMahon .02 .10
160 Audray McMillian .01 .05
161 Sean Salisbury .01 .05
162 Robert Smith .08 .25
163 Henry Thomas .01 .05
164 Gary Anderson K .01 .05
165 Deon Figures .01 .05
166 Barry Foster .01 .05
167 Jeff Graham .01 .05
168 Kevin Greene .02 .10
169 Dave Hoffman .01 .05
170 Merril Hoge .01 .05
171 Gary Jones .01 .05
172 Greg Lloyd .02 .10
173 Ernie Mills .01 .05
174 Neil O'Donnell .08 .25
175 Darren Perry .01 .05
176 Leon Searcy .01 .05
177 Leroy Thompson .01 .05
178 Willie Williams RC .01 .05
179 Rod Woodson .02 .10
180 Keith Byars .01 .05
181 Marco Coleman .01 .05
182 Bryan Cox .01 .05
183 Irving Fryar .02 .10
184 John Grimsley .01 .05
185 Mark Higgs .01 .05
186 Mark Ingram .01 .05
187 Keith Jackson .01 .05
188 Terry Kirby .08 .25
189 Dan Marino .75 2.00
190 O.J.McDuffie .08 .25
191 Scott Mitchell .02 .10
192 Pete Stoyanovich .01 .05
193 Troy Vincent .01 .05
194 Richmond Webb .01 .05
195 Brad Baxter .01 .05
196 Chris Burkett .01 .05
197 Rob Carpenter WR .01 .05
198 Boomer Esiason .02 .10
199 Johnny Johnson .01 .05
200 Jeff Lageman .01 .05
201 Mo Lewis .01 .05
202 Ronnie Lott .02 .10
203 Leonard Marshall .01 .05
204 Terance Mathis .02 .10
205 Johnny Mitchell .01 .05
206 Rob Moore .02 .10
207 Anthony Prior .01 .05
208 Blair Thomas .01 .05
209 Brian Washington .01 .05
210 Eric Bieniemy .01 .05
211 Marion Butts .01 .05
212 Gill Byrd .01 .05
213 John Carney .01 .05
214 Darren Carrington .01 .05
215 John Friesz .02 .10
216 Ronnie Harmon .01 .05
217 Stan Humphries .02 .10
218 Nate Lewis .01 .05
219 Natrone Means .08 .25
220 Anthony Miller .02 .10
221 Chris Mims .01 .05
222 Eric Moten .01 .05
223 Leslie O'Neal .01 .05
224 Junior Seau .08 .25
225 Morten Andersen .01 .05
226 Gene Atkins .01 .05
227 Derek Brown RBK .01 .05
228 Toi Cook .01 .05
229 Vaughn Dunbar .01 .05
230 Quinn Early .02 .10
231 Reggie Freeman .01 .05
232 Tyrone Hughes .02 .10
233 Rickey Jackson .01 .05
234 Eric Martin .01 .05
235 Sam Mills .01 .05
236 Brad Muster .01 .05
237 Torrance Small .01 .05
238 Irv Smith .01 .05
239 Wade Wilson .01 .05
240 Eric Allen .01 .05
241 Victor Bailey .01 .05
242 Fred Barnett .02 .10
243 Mark Bavaro .01 .05
244 Bubby Brister .02 .10
245 Randall Cunningham .08 .25
246 Antone Davis .01 .05
247 Britt Hager RC .01 .05
248 Vaughn Hebron .01 .05
249 James Joseph .01 .05
250 Seth Joyner .01 .05
251 Rich Miano .01 .05
252 Heath Sherman .01 .05
253 Clyde Simmons .01 .05
254 Herschel Walker .02 .10
255 Calvin Williams .02 .10
256 Jerry Ball .01 .05
257 Mark Carrier WR .02 .10
258 Michael Jackson .02 .10
259 Mike Johnson .01 .05
260 James Jones DT .01 .05
261 Brian Kinchen .01 .05
262 Clay Matthews .01 .05
263 Eric Metcalf .02 .10
264 Stevon Moore .01 .05
265 Michael Dean Perry .02 .10
266 Todd Philcox .01 .05
267 Anthony Pleasant .01 .05
268 Vinny Testaverde .02 .10
269 Eric Turner .01 .05
270 Tommy Vardell .01 .05
271 Neal Anderson .01 .05
272 Trace Armstrong .01 .05
273 Mark Carrier DB .01 .05
274 Bob Christian .01 .05
275 Curtis Conway .08 .25
276 Richard Dent .02 .10
277 Robert Green .01 .05
278 Jim Harbaugh .08 .25
279 Craig Heyward .02 .10
280 Terry Obee .01 .05
281 Alonzo Spellman .01 .05
282 Tom Waddle .01 .05
283 Peter Tom Willis .01 .05
284 Donnell Woolford .01 .05
285 Tim Worley .01 .05
286 Chris Zorich .01 .05
287 Steve Broussard .01 .05
288 Darion Conner .01 .05
289 Jumpy Geathers .01 .05
290 Michael Haynes .02 .10
291 Bobby Hebert .01 .05
292 Lincoln Kennedy .01 .05
293 Chris Miller .01 .05
294 David Mims RC .01 .05
295 Erric Pegram .01 .05
296 Mike Pritchard .01 .05
297 Andre Rison .02 .10
298 Deion Sanders .20 .50
299 Chuck Smith .01 .05
300 Tony Smith RB .01 .05
301 Johnny Bailey .01 .05
302 Steve Beuerlein .02 .10
303 Chuck Cecil .01 .05
304 Chris Chandler .02 .10
305 Gary Clark .02 .10
306 Rick Cunningham RC .01 .05
307 Ken Harvey .01 .05
308 Garrison Hearst .08 .25
309 Randal Hill .01 .05
310 Robert Massey .01 .05
311 Ronald Moore .01 .05
312 Ricky Proehl .01 .05
313 Eric Swann .02 .10
314 Aeneas Williams .01 .05
315 Michael Bates .01 .05
316 Brian Blades .02 .10
317 Carlton Gray .01 .05
318 Paul Green RC .01 .05
319 Patrick Hunter .01 .05
320 John Kasay .01 .05
321 Cortez Kennedy .02 .10
322 Kelvin Martin .01 .05
323 Dan McGwire .01 .05
324 Rick Mirer .08 .25
325 Eugene Robinson .01 .05
326 Rick Tuten .01 .05
327 Chris Warren .02 .10
328 John L. Williams .01 .05
329 Reggie Cobb .01 .05
330 Horace Copeland .01 .05
331 Lawrence Dawsey .01 .05
332 Santana Dotson .02 .10
333 Craig Erickson .01 .05
334 Ron Hall .01 .05
335 Courtney Hawkins .01 .05
336 Keith McCants .01 .05
337 Hardy Nickerson .02 .10
338 Mazio Royster RC .01 .05
339 Broderick Thomas .01 .05
340 Casey Weldon RC .08 .25
341 Mark Wheeler .01 .05
342 Vince Workman .01 .05
343 Flipper Anderson .01 .05
344 Jerome Bettis .20 .50
345 Richard Buchanan .01 .05
346 Shane Conlan .01 .05
347 Troy Drayton .01 .05
348 Henry Ellard .02 .10
349 Jim Everett .02 .10
350 Cleveland Gary .01 .05
351 Sean Gilbert .01 .05
352 David Lang .01 .05
353 Todd Lyght .01 .05
354 T.J. Rubley .01 .05
355 Jackie Slater .01 .05
356 Russell White .02 .10
357 Bruce Armstrong .01 .05
358 Drew Bledsoe .30 .75
359 Vincent Brisby .02 .10
360 Vincent Brown .01 .05
361 Ben Coates .02 .10
362 Marv Cook .01 .05
363 Ray Crittenden RC .01 .05
364 Corey Croom RC .01 .05
365 Pat Harlow .01 .05
366 Dion Lambert .01 .05
367 Greg McMurtry .01 .05
368 Leonard Russell .01 .05
369 Scott Secules .01 .05
370 Chris Slade .01 .05
371 Michael Timpson .01 .05
372 Kevin Turner .01 .05
373 Ashley Ambrose .01 .05
374 Dean Biasucci .01 .05
375 Duane Bickett .01 .05
376 Quentin Coryatt .01 .05
377 Rodney Culver .01 .05
378 Sean Dawkins RC .08 .25
379 Jeff George .08 .25
380 Jeff Herrod .01 .05
381 Jessie Hester .01 .05
382 Anthony Johnson .02 .10
383 Reggie Langhorne .01 .05
384 Roosevelt Potts .01 .05
385 William Schultz RC .01 .05
386 Rohn Stark .01 .05
387 Clarence Verdin .01 .05
388 Carl Banks .01 .05
389 Reggie Brooks .02 .10
390 Earnest Byner .01 .05
391 Tom Carter .01 .05
392 Cary Conklin .01 .05
393 Pat Eilers RC .01 .05
394 Ricky Ervins .01 .05
395 Rich Gannon .08 .25
396 Darrell Green .01 .05
397 Desmond Howard .02 .10
398 Chip Lohmiller .01 .05
399 Sterling Palmer RC .01 .05
400 Mark Rypien .01 .05
401 Ricky Sanders .01 .05
402 Johnny Thomas CB .01 .05
403 John Copeland .01 .05
404 Derrick Fenner .01 .05
405 Alex Gordon .01 .05
406 Harold Green .01 .05
407 Lance Gunn .01 .05
408 David Klingler .01 .05
409 Ricardo McDonald .01 .05
410 Tim McGee .01 .05
411 Reggie Rembert .01 .05
412 Patrick Robinson .01 .05
413 Jay Schroeder .01 .05
414 Erik Wilhelm .01 .05
415 Alfred Williams .01 .05
416 Darryl Williams .01 .05
417 Sam Adams RC .02 .10
418 Mario Bates RC .08 .25
419 James Bostic RC .08 .25
420 Bucky Brooks RC .01 .05
421 Jeff Burris RC .02 .10
422 Shante Carver RC .01 .05
423 Jeff Cothran RC .01 .05
424 Lake Dawson RC .02 .10
425 Trent Dilfer RC .50 1.25
426 Marshall Faulk RC 2.00 5.00
427 Cory Fleming RC .01 .05
428 William Floyd RC .08 .25
429 Glenn Foley RC .08 .25
430 Rob Fredrickson RC .02 .10
431 Charlie Garner RC .50 1.25
432 Greg Hill RC .08 .25
433 Charles Johnson RC .08 .25
434 Calvin Jones RC .01 .05
435 Jimmy Klingler RC .01 .05
436 Antonio Langham RC .02 .10
437 Kevin Lee RC .01 .05
438 Chuck Levy RC .01 .05
439 Willie McGinest RC .08 .25
440 Jamir Miller RC .02 .10
441 Johnnie Morton RC .20 .50
442 David Palmer RC .08 .25
443 Errict Rhett RC .08 .25
444 Corey Sawyer RC .02 .10
445 Darnay Scott RC .20 .50
446 Heath Shuler RC .08 .25
447 Lamar Smith RC .50 1.25
448 Dan Wilkinson RC .02 .10
449 Bernard Williams RC .02 .05
450 Bryant Young RC .15 .40
P1 Sterling Sharpe Promo .30 .75

1994 Pacific Crystalline

Randomly inserted in packs, this 20-card standard-size set features the top 20 NFL running backs. One half of the card is transparent, the other half has a color action-packed image placed in the center. That portion of the back has a small photo and 1993 highlights. Only 7,000 sets were produced.

COMPLETE SET (20) 40.00 75.00
STATED ODDS 1:7
STATED PRINT RUN 7000 SETS
1 Emmitt Smith 12.50 25.00
2 Jerome Bettis 4.00 8.00
3 Thurman Thomas 2.00 4.00
4 Erric Pegram .30 .75
5 Barry Sanders 12.50 25.00
6 Leonard Russell .30 .75
7 Rodney Hampton .75 1.50
8 Chris Warren .75 1.50
9 Reggie Brooks .75 1.50
10 Ronald Moore .30 .75
11 Gary Brown .30 .75
12 Ricky Watters .75 1.50
13 Johnny Johnson .30 .75
14 Rod Bernstine .30 .75
15 Marcus Allen 2.00 4.00
16 Leroy Thompson .30 .75
17 Marion Butts .30 .75
18 Herschel Walker .75 1.50
19 Barry Foster .30 .75
20 Roosevelt Potts .30 .75

1994 Pacific Gems of the Crown

Randomly inserted in packs, this 36-card standard-size set features a striking design that contrasts the crystal-clear photography and etched gold foil frame. Horizontal backs contain a photo and 1993 highlights. Only 7,000 sets were produced. A signed John Elway card (hand numbered of 50-cards signed) was randomly seeded (at a rate of 1:43,200) in 1995 Pacific Prisms series 2 packs. Each of these signed Elway cards includes an embossed Pacific seal of authenticity.

COMPLETE SET (36) 50.00 100.00
STATED ODDS 1:7
STATED PRINT RUN 7000 SETS
1 Troy Aikman 2.50 6.00
2 Marcus Allen .60 1.50
3 Jerome Bettis 1.25 3.00
4 Drew Bledsoe 2.00 5.00
5 Reggie Brooks .25 .60
6 Gary Brown .10 .30
7 Tim Brown .60 1.50
8 Cody Carlson .10 .30
9 John Elway 5.00 12.00
10 Boomer Esiason .25 .60
11 Brett Favre 5.00 12.00
12 Rodney Hampton .25 .60
13 Alvin Harper .25 .60
14 Jeff Hostetler .25 .60
15 Jim Kelly .60 1.50
16 Dan Marino 5.00 12.00
17 Eric Martin .10 .30
18 O.J. McDuffie .60 1.50
19 Natrone Means .60 1.50
20 Rick Mirer .60 1.50
21 Joe Montana 5.00 12.00
22 Herman Moore .60 1.50
23 Ronald Moore .10 .30
24 Neil O'Donnell .60 1.50
25 Erric Pegram .10 .30
26 Roosevelt Potts .10 .30
27 Jerry Rice 2.50 6.00
28 Barry Sanders 4.00 10.00
29 Shannon Sharpe .25 .60
30 Sterling Sharpe .25 .60
31 Emmitt Smith 4.00 10.00
32 Thurman Thomas .60 1.50
33 Herschel Walker .25 .60
34 Chris Warren .25 .60
35 Ricky Watters .25 .60
36 Steve Young 2.00 5.00
9AU John Elway AUTO/50 75.00 150.00

1994 Pacific Knights of the Gridiron

This 20-card standard-size set was randomly inserted in packs. The set features top rookies and draft picks on a gold prism background. Horizontal backs have a player photo in a picture frame to the left with highlights and the Pacific Collection logo to the right. Only 7,000 sets were produced. The set is sequenced in alphabetical order.

COMPLETE SET (20) 30.00 60.00
STATED ODDS 1:7
STATED PRINT RUN 7000 SETS
1 Mario Bates .30 .75
2 Jerome Bettis 2.50 6.00
3 Drew Bledsoe 4.00 10.00
4 Vincent Brisby .50 1.25
5 Reggie Brooks .10 .30
6 Derek Brown RBK .25 .60
7 Jeff Burris .10 .30
8 Trent Dilfer 1.50 4.00
9 Troy Drayton .25 .60
10 Marshall Faulk 6.00 15.00
11 William Floyd .30 .75
12 Rocket Ismail .50 1.25
13 Terry Kirby 1.25 3.00
14 Thomas Lewis .25 .60
15 Natrone Means 1.25 3.00
16 Rick Mirer 1.25 3.00
17 David Palmer .30 .75
18 Errict Rhett .30 .75
19 Darnay Scott .60 1.50
20 Heath Shuler .30 .75

1994 Pacific Marquee Prisms

is 36 card standard-size set was produced in both silver and gold. These cards were inserted one per marquee prism pack. Although either a silver or gold card was issued in each pack, gold cards are much more difficult to obtain. They were inserted approximately two per box. In either case, the player is superimposed over the silver or gold background. A marquee design with the player's name and position is at the bottom. Backs have a player photo to the left and a marquee with the player's name to the right. The set is sequenced in alphabetical order.

COMPLETE SET (36) 10.00 25.00
ONE SILVER OR GOLD PER MARQUEE PACK
*GOLDS: 2.5X to 6X BASIC INSERTS
GOLD STATED ODDS 1:18
1 Troy Aikman 1.00 2.00
2 Marcus Allen .20 .50
3 Jerome Bettis .40 1.00
4 Drew Bledsoe .75 1.50
5 Reggie Brooks .07 .20
6 Dave Brown .07 .20
7 Ben Coates .07 .20
8 Reggie Cobb .02 .10
9 Curtis Conway .20 .50
10 John Elway 2.00 4.00
11 Marshall Faulk 2.50 5.00
12 Brett Favre 2.00 4.00
13 Barry Foster .02 .10
14 Rodney Hampton .07 .20
15 Michael Irvin .20 .50
16 Terry Kirby .20 .50
17 Dan Marino 2.00 4.00
18 Natrone Means .20 .50
19 Rick Mirer .20 .50
20 Joe Montana 2.00 4.00
21 Warren Moon .20 .50
22 Ronald Moore .02 .10
23 David Palmer .08 .25
24 Errict Rhett .08 .25
25 Jerry Rice 1.00 2.00
26 Bucky Richardson .02 .10
27 Barry Sanders 1.50 3.00
28 Shannon Sharpe .07 .20
29 Sterling Sharpe .07 .20
30 Heath Shuler .08 .25
31 Emmitt Smith 1.50 3.00
32 Irving Spikes .02 .10
33 Thurman Thomas .20 .50
34 Chris Warren .07 .20
35 Ricky Watters .07 .20
36 Steve Young .75 1.50

1995 Pacific

This 450 card set was issued in one series and featured 12 cards per pack. Rookie Cards in this set include Jeff Blake, Kerry Collins, Joey Galloway, Steve McNair, Rashaan Salaam, Kordell Stewart, J.J Stokes, Yancey Thigpen and Michael Westbrook. Natrone Means standard sized and jumbo (7" by 9 3/4") promo cards were produced and are included below.

COMPLETE SET (450) 10.00 25.00
1 Randy Baldwin .02 .10
2 Tommy Barnhardt .02 .10
3 Tim McKyer .02 .10
4 Sam Mills .07 .20
5 Brian O'Neal .02 .10
6 Frank Reich .02 .10
7 Jack Trudeau .02 .10
8 Vernon Turner .02 .10
9 Kerry Collins RC .75 2.00
10 Shawn King .02 .10
11 Steve Beuerlein .07 .20
12 Derek Brown TE .02 .10
13 Reggie Clark .02 .10
14 Reggie Cobb .02 .10
15 Desmond Howard .07 .20
16 Jeff Lageman .02 .10
17 Kelvin Pritchett .02 .10
18 Cedric Tillman .02 .10
19 Tony Boselli RC .10 .30
20 James O. Stewart RC .50 1.25
21 Eric Davis .02 .10
22 William Floyd .07 .20
23 Elvis Grbac .10 .30
24 Brent Jones .02 .10
25 Ken Norton, Jr. .07 .20
26 Bart Oates .02 .10
27 Jerry Rice .40 1.00
28 Deion Sanders .15 .40
29 John Taylor .02 .10
30 Adam Walker RC .02 .10
31 Steve Wallace .02 .10
32 Ricky Watters .07 .20
33 Lee Woodall .02 .10
34 Bryant Young .07 .20
35 Steve Young .30 .75
36 J.J. Stokes RC .10 .30
37 Troy Aikman .40 1.00
38 Larry Allen .07 .20
39 Chris Boniol RC .02 .10
40 Lincoln Coleman .02 .10
41 Charles Haley .07 .20
42 Alvin Harper .02 .10
43 Chad Hennings .07 .20
44 Michael Irvin .10 .30
45 Daryl Johnston .07 .20
46 Leon Lett .02 .10
47 Nate Newton .07 .20
48 Jay Novacek .07 .20
49 Emmitt Smith .60 1.50
50 James Washington .02 .10
51 Kevin Williams .07 .20
52 Sherman Williams RC .02 .10
53 Barry Foster .07 .20
54 Eric Green .02 .10
55 Kevin Greene .07 .20
56 Andre Hastings .07 .20
57 Charles Johnson .07 .20
58 Greg Lloyd .07 .20
59 Ernie Mills .02 .10
60 Byron Bam Morris .02 .10
61 Neil O'Donnell .07 .20
62 Darren Perry .02 .10
63 Yancey Thigpen RC .07 .20
64 Mike Tomczak .02 .10
65 John L. Williams .02 .10
66 Rod Woodson .07 .20
67 Mark Bruener RC .07 .20
68 Kordell Stewart RC .60 1.50
69 Jeff Brohm RC .02 .10
70 Andre Coleman .02 .10
71 Reuben Davis .02 .10
72 Dennis Gibson .02 .10
73 Darrien Gordon .02 .10
74 Stan Humphries .07 .20
75 Shawn Jefferson .02 .10
76 Tony Martin .07 .20
77 Natrone Means .07 .20
78 Shannon Mitchell RC .02 .10
79 Leslie O'Neal .07 .20
80 Alfred Pupunu .02 .10
81 Stanley Richard .02 .10
82 Junior Seau .10 .30
83 Mark Seay .07 .20
84 Derrick Alexander WR .10 .30
85 Carl Banks .02 .10
86 Isaac Booth .02 .10
87 Rob Burnett .02 .10
88 Earnest Byner .02 .10
89 Steve Everitt .02 .10
90 Leroy Hoard .02 .10
91 Pepper Johnson .02 .10
92 Antonio Langham .02 .10
93 Eric Metcalf .07 .20
94 Anthony Pleasant .02 .10
95 Frank Stams .02 .10
96 Vinny Testaverde .07 .20
97 Eric Turner .02 .10
98 Mike Miller RC .02 .10
99 Craig Powell RC .02 .10
100 Gene Atkins .02 .10
101 Aubrey Beavers .02 .10
102 Tim Bowens .02 .10
103 Keith Byars .02 .10
104 Bryan Cox .02 .10
105 Aaron Craver .02 .10
106 Jeff Cross .02 .10
107 Irving Fryar .07 .20
108 Dan Marino .75 2.00
109 O.J. McDuffie .10 .30
110 Bernie Parmalee .07 .20
111 James Saxon .02 .10
112 Keith Sims .02 .10
113 Irving Spikes .07 .20
114 Pete Mitchell RC .07 .20
115 Terry Allen .07 .20
116 Cris Carter .10 .30
117 Adrian Cooper .02 .10
118 Bernard Dafney .02 .10
119 Jack Del Rio .02 .10
120 Vencie Glenn .02 .10
121 Qadry Ismail .07 .20
122 Carlos Jenkins .02 .10
123 Andrew Jordan .02 .10
124 Ed McDaniel .02 .10
125 Warren Moon .07 .20
126 David Palmer .07 .20
127 John Randle .07 .20
128 Jake Reed .07 .20
129 Derrick Alexander DE RC .02 .10
130 Chad May RC .02 .10
131 Korey Stringer RC .10 .30
132 Bruce Armstrong .02 .10
133 Drew Bledsoe .25 .60
134 Vincent Brisby .02 .10
135 Troy Brown .10 .30
136 Vincent Brown .02 .10
137 Marion Butts .02 .10
138 Ben Coates .07 .20
139 Ray Crittenden .02 .10
140 Maurice Hurst .02 .10
141 Aaron Jones .02 .10
142 Willie McGinest .07 .20
143 Marty Moore RC .10 .30
144 Mike Pitts .02 .10
145 Leroy Thompson .02 .10
146 Michael Timpson .02 .10
147 Bennie Blades .02 .10
148 Jocelyn Borgella .02 .10
149 Anthony Carter .07 .20
150 Willie Clay .02 .10
151 Mel Gray .02 .10
152 Mike Johnson .02 .10
153 Dave Krieg .02 .10
154 Robert Massey .02 .10
155 Scott Mitchell .07 .20
156 Herman Moore .10 .30
157 Johnnie Morton .07 .20
158 Barry Sanders .60 1.50
159 Chris Spielman .07 .20
160 Broderick Thomas .02 .10
161 Cory Schlesinger RC .07 .20
162 Marcus Allen .10 .30
163 Donnell Bennett .07 .20
164 J.J. Birden .02 .10
165 Matt Blundin RC .02 .10
166 Steve Bono .07 .20
167 Dale Carter .07 .20
168 Lake Dawson .07 .20
169 Ron Dickerson RC .02 .10
170 Lin Elliott .02 .10
171 Jaime Fields .02 .10
172 Greg Hill .07 .20
173 Danan Hughes .02 .10
174 Neil Smith .07 .20
175 Steve Stenstrom RC .02 .10
176 Edgar Bennett .07 .20
177 Robert Brooks .10 .30
178 Mark Brunell .25 .60
179 Doug Evans RC .10 .30
180 Brett Favre .75 2.00
181 Corey Harris .02 .10
182 LeShon Johnson .07 .20
183 Sean Jones .02 .10
184 Lenny McGill RC .02 .10
185 Terry Mickens .02 .10
186 Sterling Sharpe .07 .20
187 Joe Sims .02 .10
188 Darrell Thompson .02 .10
189 Reggie White .10 .30
190 Craig Newsome RC .02 .10
191 Tim Brown .10 .30
192 Vince Evans .02 .10
193 Rob Fredrickson .02 .10
194 Andrew Glover RC .02 .10
195 Jeff Hostetler .07 .20
196 Rocket Ismail .07 .20
197 Jeff Jaeger .02 .10
198 James Jett .07 .20
199 Chester McGlockton .07 .20
200 Don Mosebar .02 .10
201 Tom Rathman .02 .10
202 Harvey Williams .02 .10
203 Steve Wisniewski .02 .10
204 Alexander Wright .02 .10
205 Napoleon Kaufman RC .50 1.25
206 Trace Armstrong .02 .10
207 Curtis Conway .10 .30
208 Raymont Harris .02 .10
209 Erik Kramer .02 .10
210 Nate Lewis .02 .10
211 Shane Matthews RC .10 .30
212 John Thierry .02 .10
213 Lewis Tillman .02 .10
214 Tom Waddle .02 .10
215 Steve Walsh .02 .10
216 James Williams T RC .02 .10
217 Donnell Woolford .02 .10
218 Chris Zorich .02 .10
219 Rashaan Salaam RC .07 .20
220 John Booty .02 .10
221 Michael Brooks .02 .10
222 Dave Brown .07 .20
223 Chris Calloway .02 .10
224 Gary Downs .02 .10
225 Kent Graham .07 .20
226 Keith Hamilton .02 .10
227 Rodney Hampton .07 .20
228 Brian Kozlowski .02 .10
229 Thomas Lewis .07 .20
230 Dave Meggett .02 .10
231 Aaron Pierce .02 .10
232 Mike Sherrard .02 .10
233 Phillippi Sparks .02 .10
234 Tyrone Wheatley RC .50 1.25
235 Trev Alberts .02 .10
236 Aaron Bailey RC .02 .10
237 Jason Belser .02 .10
238 Tony Bennett .02 .10
239 Kerry Cash .02 .10
240 Marshall Faulk .50 1.25
241 Stephen Grant .02 .10
242 Jeff Herrod .02 .10
243 Ronald Humphrey .02 .10
244 Kirk Lowdermilk .02 .10
245 Don Majkowski .02 .10
246 Tony McCoy .02 .10
247 Floyd Turner .02 .10
248 Lamont Warren .02 .10
249 Zack Crockett RC .07 .20
250 Michael Bankston .02 .10
251 Larry Centers .07 .20
252 Gary Clark .02 .10
253 Ed Cunningham .02 .10
254 Garrison Hearst .10 .30
255 Eric Hill .02 .10
256 Terry Irving .02 .10
257 Lorenzo Lynch .02 .10
258 Jamir Miller .02 .10
259 Ronald Moore .02 .10
260 Terry Samuels .02 .10
261 Jay Schroeder .02 .10
262 Eric Swann .07 .20
263 Aeneas Williams .02 .10
264 Frank Sanders RC .10 .30
265 Morten Andersen .02 .10
266 Mario Bates .07 .20
267 Derek Brown RBK .02 .10
268 Darion Conner .02 .10
269 Quinn Early .07 .20
270 Jim Everett .02 .10
271 Michael Haynes .07 .20
272 Wayne Martin .02 .10
273 Derrell Mitchell RC .02 .10
274 Lorenzo Neal .02 .10
275 Jimmy Spencer .02 .10
276 Winfred Tubbs .02 .10
277 Renaldo Turnbull .02 .10
278 Jeff Uhlenhake .02 .10
279 Steve Atwater .02 .10
280 Keith Burns RC .02 .10
281 Butler By'Not'e RC .07 .20
282 Jeff Campbell .02 .10
283 Derrick Clark RC .02 .10
284 Shane Dronett .02 .10
285 Jason Elam .07 .20
286 John Elway .75 2.00
287 Jerry Evans .02 .10
288 Karl Mecklenburg .02 .10
289 Glyn Milburn .02 .10
290 Anthony Miller .07 .20
291 Tom Rouen .02 .10
292 Leonard Russell .02 .10
293 Shannon Sharpe .07 .20
294 Steve Russ RC .02 .10
295 Mel Agee .02 .10
296 Lester Archambeau .02 .10
297 Bert Emanuel .10 .30
298 Jeff George .07 .20
299 Craig Heyward .07 .20
300 Bobby Hebert .02 .10
301 D.J. Johnson .02 .10
302 Mike Kenn .02 .10
303 Terance Mathis .07 .20
304 Clay Matthews .07 .20
305 Erric Pegram .07 .20
306 Andre Rison .07 .20
307 Chuck Smith .02 .10
308 Jessie Tuggle .02 .10
309 Lorenzo Styles RC .02 .10
310 Cornelius Bennett .07 .20
311 Bill Brooks .02 .10
312 Jeff Burris .02 .10
313 Carwell Gardner .02 .10
314 Kent Hull .02 .10
315 Yonel Jourdain .02 .10
316 Jim Kelly .10 .30
317 Vince Marrow .02 .10
318 Pete Metzelaars .02 .10
319 Andre Reed .07 .20
320 Kurt Schulz RC .02 .10
321 Bruce Smith .10 .30
322 Darryl Talley .02 .10
323 Matt Darby .02 .10
324 Justin Armour RC .02 .10
325 Todd Collins RC .50 1.25
326 David Alexander DE .02 .10
327 Eric Allen .02 .10
328 Fred Barnett .07 .20
329 Randall Cunningham .10 .30
330 William Fuller .02 .10
331 Charlie Garner .10 .30
332 Vaughn Hebron .02 .10
333 James Joseph .02 .10
334 Bill Romanowski .02 .10
335 Ken Rose .02 .10
336 Jeff Snyder .02 .10
337 William Thomas .02 .10
338 Herschel Walker .07 .20
339 Calvin Williams .07 .20
340 Dave Barr RC .02 .10
341 Chidi Ahanotu .02 .10
342 Barney Bussey .02 .10
343 Horace Copeland .02 .10
344 Trent Dilfer .10 .30
345 Craig Erickson .02 .10
346 Paul Gruber .02 .10
347 Courtney Hawkins .02 .10
348 Lonnie Marts .02 .10
349 Martin Mayhew .02 .10
350 Hardy Nickerson .02 .10
351 Errict Rhett .07 .20
352 Lamar Thomas .02 .10
353 Charles Wilson .02 .10
354 Vince Workman .02 .10
355 Derrick Brooks RC .60 1.50
356 Warren Sapp RC .60 1.50
357 Sam Adams .02 .10
358 Michael Bates .02 .10
359 Brian Blades .07 .20
360 Carlton Gray .02 .10
361 Bill Hitchcock .02 .10
362 Cortez Kennedy .07 .20
363 Rick Mirer .07 .20
364 Eugene Robinson .02 .10
365 Michael Sinclair .02 .10
366 Steve Smith .02 .10
367 Bob Spitulski .02 .10
368 Rick Tuten .02 .10
369 Chris Warren .07 .20
370 Terrence Warren .02 .10
371 Christian Fauria RC .07 .20
372 Joey Galloway RC .60 1.50
373 Boomer Esiason .07 .20
374 Aaron Glenn .02 .10
375 Victor Green RC .02 .10
376 Johnny Johnson .02 .10
377 Mo Lewis .02 .10
378 Ronnie Lott .07 .20
379 Nick Lowery .02 .10
380 Johnny Mitchell .02 .10
381 Rob Moore .07 .20
382 Adrian Murrell .07 .20
383 Anthony Prior .02 .10
384 Brian Washington .02 .10
385 Matt Willig RC .02 .10
386 Kyle Brady RC .10 .30
387 Flipper Anderson .02 .10
388 Johnny Bailey .02 .10
389 Jerome Bettis .10 .30
390 Isaac Bruce .20 .50
391 Shane Conlan .02 .10
392 Troy Drayton .02 .10
393 D'Marco Farr .02 .10
394 Jessie Hester .02 .10
395 Todd Kinchen .02 .10
396 Ron Middleton .02 .10
397 Chris Miller .02 .10
398 Marquez Pope .02 .10
399 Robert Young .02 .10
400 Tony Zendejas .02 .10
401 Kevin Carter RC .10 .30
402 Reggie Brooks .07 .20
403 Tom Carter .02 .10
404 Andre Collins .02 .10
405 Pat Eilers .02 .10
406 Henry Ellard .07 .20
407 Ricky Ervins .02 .10
408 Gus Frerotte .07 .20
409 Ken Harvey .02 .10
410 Jim Lachey .02 .10
411 Brian Mitchell .02 .10
412 Reggie Roby .02 .10
413 Heath Shuler .07 .20
414 Tyronne Stowe .02 .10
415 Tydus Winans .02 .10
416 Cory Raymer RC .02 .10
417 Michael Westbrook RC .10 .30
418 Jeff Blake RC .30 .75
419 Steve Broussard .02 .10
420 Dave Cadigan .02 .10
421 Jeff Cothran .02 .10
422 Derrick Fenner .02 .10
423 James Francis .02 .10
424 Lee Johnson .02 .10
425 Louis Oliver .02 .10
426 Carl Pickens .07 .20
427 Jeff Query .02 .10
428 Corey Sawyer .02 .10
429 Darnay Scott .07 .20
430 Dan Wilkinson .07 .20
431 Alfred Williams .02 .10
432 Ki-Jana Carter RC .10 .30
433 David Dunn RC .02 .10
434 John Walsh RC .02 .10
435 Gary Brown .02 .10
436 Pat Carter .02 .10
437 Ray Childress .02 .10
438 Ernest Givins .02 .10
439 Haywood Jeffires .02 .10
440 Lamar Lathon .02 .10
441 Bruce Matthews .02 .10
442 Marcus Robertson .02 .10
443 Eddie Robinson .02 .10
444 Malcolm Seabron RC .02 .10
445 Webster Slaughter .02 .10
446 Al Smith .02 .10
447 Billy Joe Tolliver .02 .10
448 Lorenzo White .02 .10
449 Steve McNair RC 1.25 3.00
450 Rodney Thomas RC .07 .20
P1 Natrone Means Promo .40 1.00
P1J Natrone Means Promo .40 1.00

1995 Pacific Blue

COMPLETE BLUE SET (450) 100.00 200.00
*STARS: 3.5X TO 7X BASIC CARDS
*RCs: 2X TO 4X BASIC CARDS
STATED ODDS 9:37 RETAIL

1995 Pacific Platinum

COMPLETE SET (450) 100.00 200.00
*STARS: 3X TO 6X BASIC CARDS
*RCs: 1.5X TO 3X BASIC CARDS
STATED ODDS 9:37 HOBBY

1995 Pacific Cramer's Choice

is six card set was randomly inserted in packs at a rate of one in 720 packs and features Pacific President and CEO, Michael Cramer's, selection of the top NFL players in six different categories including top running back, top defensive player, top rookie, etc. Card fronts are die cut in the shape of a trophy with a holographic background. The bottom of the card front has a black marble background with the card title, player's name and their category. Card backs feature a small head shot of the player with commentary. Cards are numbered with a "CC" prefix.

COMPLETE SET (6) 30.00 80.00
STATED ODDS 1:720
CC1 Ki-Jana Carter 2.50 6.00
CC2 Emmitt Smith 12.50 30.00
CC3 Marshall Faulk 10.00 25.00
CC4 Jerry Rice 8.00 20.00
CC5 Deion Sanders 3.00 8.00
CC6 Steve Young 6.00 15.00

1995 Pacific Gems of the Crown

is 36 card set was randomly inserted in packs at a rate of two in 37 packs and features superstars within a holographic foil-etched design. Card fronts also contain a shot of the player against a regular background with the player's name blocked in foil at the bottom. Card backs are horizontal with a navy background and feature a shot of the player and a brief summary. Cards are numbered with a "GC" prefix.

COMPLETE SET (36) 50.00 100.00
STATED ODDS 2:37
GC1 Jim Kelly 1.25 3.00
GC2 Kerry Collins 3.00 8.00
GC3 Darnay Scott .75 2.00
GC4 Jeff Blake 1.25 3.00
GC5 Terry Allen .75 2.00
GC6 Emmitt Smith 6.00 15.00
GC7 Michael Irvin 1.25 3.00
GC8 Troy Aikman 4.00 10.00
GC9 John Elway 8.00 20.00
GC10 Dave Krieg .40 1.00
GC11 Barry Sanders 6.00 15.00
GC12 Brett Favre 8.00 20.00
GC13 Marshall Faulk 5.00 12.00
GC14 Marcus Allen 1.25 3.00
GC15 Tim Brown 1.25 3.00
GC16 Bernie Parmalee .75 2.00
GC17 Dan Marino 8.00 20.00
GC18 Cris Carter 1.25 3.00
GC19 Drew Bledsoe 2.50 6.00
GC20 Mario Bates .75 2.00
GC21 Rodney Hampton .75 2.00
GC22 Ben Coates .75 2.00
GC23 Charles Johnson .75 2.00
GC24 Byron Bam Morris .40 1.00
GC25 Stan Humphries .75 2.00
GC26 Deion Sanders 1.50 4.00
GC27 Jerry Rice 4.00 10.00
GC28 Ricky Watters .75 2.00
GC29 Steve Young 3.00 8.00
GC30 Natrone Means .75 2.00
GC31 William Floyd .75 2.00
GC32 Chris Warren .75 2.00
GC33 Rick Mirer .75 2.00
GC34 Jerome Bettis 1.25 3.00
GC35 Errict Rhett .75 2.00
GC36 Heath Shuler .75 2.00

1995 Pacific G-Force

This 10 card set was randomly inserted in packs at a ratio of one in 37 and feature the top running backs of the NFL. Card fronts have a black background with different colors shooting out from the center. The word "G-Force" is located at the top of the card and the player's name is located at the bottom. Their total rushing numbers from 1994 are also listed in four different areas on the front of the card. Card backs contain the same background with a headshot of the player and a brief commentary. Cards are numbered with a "GF" prefix.

COMPLETE SET (10) 12.50 30.00
STATED ODDS 1:37
GF1 Marcus Allen 1.25 2.50
GF2 Terry Allen .75 1.50
GF3 Emmitt Smith 6.00 12.00
GF4 Barry Sanders 6.00 12.00
GF5 Marshall Faulk 5.00 10.00
GF6 Rodney Hampton .75 1.50
GF7 Natrone Means .75 1.50
GF8 Chris Warren .75 1.50
GF9 Jerome Bettis 1.25 2.50
GF10 Errict Rhett .75 1.50

1995 Pacific Gold Crown Die Cuts

This 20 card set was randomly inserted into packs at a rate of one in 37 packs and features the top players in the NFL. Card fronts are die cut in the shape of a crown at the top and feature either holographic gold foil or flat gold foil. Card fronts also contain the player's name at the bottom of the card in the same holographic gold foil or flat gold foil. Card backs feature a shot of the player, his name and a brief commentary.

COMP.HOLOFOIL SET (20) 50.00 100.00
*FLAT GOLDS: .6X TO 1.5X BASIC INSERTS
STATED ODDS 1:37
DC1 Ki-Jana Carter 1.25 3.00
DC2 Michael Irvin 1.25 3.00
DC3 Emmitt Smith 6.00 15.00
DC4 Troy Aikman 4.00 10.00
DC5 John Elway 8.00 20.00
DC6 Barry Sanders 6.00 15.00
DC7 Marshall Faulk 5.00 12.00
DC8 Dan Marino 8.00 20.00
DC9 Ben Coates .75 2.00
DC10 Drew Bledsoe 2.50 6.00
DC11 Byron Bam Morris .40 1.00
DC12 Jerry Rice 4.00 10.00
DC13 William Floyd .75 2.00
DC14 Steve Young 3.00 8.00
DC15 Natrone Means .75 2.00
DC16 Deion Sanders 1.50 4.00
DC17 Rick Mirer .75 2.00
DC18 Chris Warren .75 2.00
DC19 Jerome Bettis 1.25 3.00
DC20 Errict Rhett .75 2.00

1995 Pacific Hometown Heroes

This 10 card set was randomly inserted in packs at a ratio of one in 37 packs and features information on where top players went to high school and where they started their football careers. Card fronts feature a full bleed photo with the player's name and the "Hometown Heroes" slogan in blue holographic foil at the bottom. There is also a flag on the left side of the card that represents the state where the player played. Card backs are horizontal with an orange background and contains two shots of the player - one literally in the state he played and another on the side of it. The also contain a brief commentary. Cards are numbered with a "HH" prefix.

COMPLETE SET (10) 20.00 40.00
STATED ODDS 1:37
HH1 Emmitt Smith 4.00 8.00
HH2 Troy Aikman 2.50 5.00
HH3 Barry Sanders 4.00 8.00
HH4 Marshall Faulk 3.00 6.00
HH5 Dan Marino 5.00 10.00
HH6 Drew Bledsoe 1.50 3.00
HH7 Natrone Means .40 1.00
HH8 Steve Young 2.00 4.00
HH9 Jerry Rice 2.50 5.00
HH10 Errict Rhett .40 1.00

1995 Pacific Rookies

This 20 card set was randomly inserted into packs at a rate of two in 37 packs and feature Pacific's choices of the top rookies of 1995. Card fronts feature the rookies in their college uniforms with their pro team's helmet in the lower right hand corner. The rookie's name is listed horizontally along the side in a prism-foil. Card backs contain a head shot of the player in his college uniform in the top left hand corner. A brief commentary on the player is listed under the shot.

COMPLETE SET (20) 20.00 40.00
STATED ODDS 2:37
1 Dave Barr .08 .25
2 Kyle Brady .30 .75
3 Mark Bruener .20 .50
4 Ki-Jana Carter .30 .75
5 Kerry Collins 2.00 5.00
6 Todd Collins .75 2.00
7 Christian Fauria .20 .50
8 Joey Galloway 1.50 4.00
9 Chris T.Jones .08 .25
10 Napoleon Kaufman 1.25 3.00
11 Chad May .08 .25
12 Steve McNair 3.00 8.00
13 Rashaan Salaam .20 .50
14 Warren Sapp 1.50 4.00
15 James O. Stewart 1.25 3.00
16 Kordell Stewart 1.50 4.00
17 J.J. Stokes .30 .75
18 Michael Westbrook .30 .75
19 Tyrone Wheatley 1.25 3.00
20 Sherman Williams .08 .25

1995 Pacific Young Warriors

This 20 card set was randomly inserted in packs at a rate of two in 37 packs and features Pacific's selection of the best second year players in the NFL. Card fronts contain a full foil gold background with the player's name in their team colors along the bottom. The set name "Young Warriors" is etched in the gold foil along the right side of the card. Card backs have an orange-brown background with an outline of the player nestled between two columns and brief statistical fact underneath it.

COMPLETE SET (20) 15.00 30.00
STATED ODDS 2:37
1 Bert Emanuel 1.50 3.00
2 Darnay Scott 1.00 2.00
3 Dan Wilkinson 1.00 2.00
4 Derrick Alexander WR 1.50 3.00
5 Willie McGinest 1.00 2.00
6 Marshall Faulk 6.00 12.00
7 Lake Dawson 1.00 2.00
8 Greg Hill 1.00 2.00
9 Tim Bowens .40 1.00
10 David Palmer 1.00 2.00
11 Aaron Glenn .40 1.00
12 Mario Bates 1.00 2.00
13 Charles Johnson 1.00 2.00
14 Byron Bam Morris .40 1.00
15 William Floyd 1.00 2.00
16 Adam Walker .40 1.00
17 Bryant Young 1.00 2.00
18 Trent Dilfer 1.50 3.00
19 Errict Rhett 1.00 2.00
20 Heath Shuler 1.00 2.00

1996 Pacific

This 450-card set was issued in one series and distributed in 12-card packs.The set features borderless color action player photos with gold foil highlights. Two parallel sets were also issued: Red Foil and Blue Foil. The scorching red foil version was inserted in retail only packs at the rate of nine in 37. The electric blue foil version was inserted at the same rate in hobby only packs. The cards are grouped alphabetically within teams and checklisted below alphabetically according to teams. Two different Chris Warren Promo cards were also produced.

COMPLETE SET (450) 20.00 40.00
1 Jeff Feagles .02 .10
2 Rob Moore .07 .20
3 Clyde Simmons .02 .10
4 Mike Buck .02 .10
5 Aeneas Williams .02 .10
6 Simeon Rice RC .40 1.00
7 Garrison Hearst .07 .20
8 Eric Swann .02 .10
9 Dave Krieg .02 .10
10 Leeland McElroy RC .07 .20
11 Oscar McBride .02 .10
12 Frank Sanders .07 .20
13 Larry Centers .07 .20
14 Seth Joyner .02 .10
15 Stevie Anderson .02 .10
16 Craig Heyward .02 .10
17 Devin Bush .02 .10
18 Eric Metcalf .02 .10
19 Jeff George .07 .20
20 Richard Huntley RC .07 .20
21 Jamal Anderson RC .20 .50
22 Bert Emanuel .07 .20
23 Terance Mathis .02 .10
24 Roman Fortin .02 .10
25 Jessie Tuggle .02 .10
26 Morten Andersen .02 .10
27 Chris Doleman .02 .10
28 D.J. Johnson .02 .10
29 Kevin Ross .02 .10
30 Michael Jackson .07 .20
31 Eric Zeier .02 .10
32 Jonathan Ogden RC .40 1.00
33 Eric Turner .02 .10
34 Andre Rison .07 .20
35 Lorenzo White .02 .10
36 Earnest Byner .02 .10
37 Derrick Alexander WR .07 .20
38 Brian Kinchen .02 .10
39 Anthony Pleasant .02 .10
40 Vinny Testaverde .07 .20
41 Pepper Johnson .02 .10
42 Frank Hartley .02 .10
43 Craig Powell .02 .10
44 Leroy Hoard .02 .10
45 Kent Hull .02 .10
46 Bryce Paup .02 .10
47 Andre Reed .07 .20
48 Darick Holmes .02 .10
49 Russell Copeland .02 .10
50 Jerry Ostroski RC .02 .10
51 Chris Green .02 .10
52 Eric Moulds RC .50 1.25
53 Justin Armour .02 .10
54 Jim Kelly .15 .40
55 Cornelius Bennett .02 .10
56 Steve Tasker .02 .10
57 Thurman Thomas .15 .40
58 Bruce Smith .07 .20
59 Todd Collins .07 .20
60 Shawn King .02 .10
61 Don Beebe .02 .10
62 [illegible] [illegible] .10
63 Tim McKyer .02 .10
64 Darion Conner .02 .10
65 Pete Metzelaars .02 .10
66 Derrick Moore .02 .10
67 Blake Brockermeyer .02 .10
68 Tim Biakabutuka RC .15 .40
69 Sam Mills .02 .10
70 Vince Workman .02 .10
71 Kerry Collins .15 .40
72 Carlton Bailey .02 .10
73 Mark Carrier WR .02 .10
74 Donnell Woolford .02 .10
75 Walt Harris RC .02 .10
76 John Thierry .02 .10
77 Al Fontenot RC .02 .10
78 Lewis Tillman .02 .10
79 Curtis Conway .15 .40
80 Chris Zorich .02 .10
81 Mark Carrier DB .02 .10
82 Bobby Engram RC .15 .40
83 Alonzo Spellman .02 .10
84 Rashaan Salaam .07 .20
85 Michael Timpson .02 .10
86 Nate Lewis .02 .10
87 James Williams T .02 .10
88 Jeff Graham .02 .10
89 Erik Kramer .02 .10
90 Willie Anderson .02 .10
91 Tony McGee .02 .10
92 Marco Battaglia .02 .10
93 Dan Wilkinson .02 .10
94 John Walsh .02 .10
95 Eric Bieniemy .02 .10
96 Ricardo McDonald .02 .10
97 Carl Pickens .07 .20
98 Kevin Sargent .02 .10
99 David Dunn .02 .10
100 Jeff Blake .15 .40
101 Harold Green .02 .10
102 James Francis .02 .10
103 John Copeland .02 .10
104 Darnay Scott .07 .20
105 Darren Woodson .07 .20
106 Jay Novacek .02 .10
107 Charles Haley .07 .20
108 Mark Tuinei .02 .10
109 Michael Irvin .15 .40
110 Troy Aikman .40 1.00
111 Chris Boniol .02 .10
112 Sherman Williams .02 .10
113 Deion Sanders .25 .60
114 Emmitt Smith .60 1.50
115 Eric Bjornson .02 .10
116 Nate Newton .02 .10
117 Larry Allen .02 .10
118 Kevin Williams .02 .10
119 Leon Lett .02 .10
120 John Mobley .02 .10
121 Anthony Miller .07 .20
122 Brian Habib .02 .10
123 Aaron Craver .02 .10
124 Glyn Milburn .02 .10
125 Shannon Sharpe .07 .20
126 Steve Atwater .02 .10
127 Jason Elam .07 .20
128 John Elway .75 2.00
129 Reggie Rivers .02 .10
130 Mike Pritchard .02 .10
131 Vance Johnson .02 .10
132 Terrell Davis .30 .75
133 Tyrone Braxton .02 .10
134 Ed McCaffrey .07 .20
135 Brett Perriman .02 .10
136 Chris Spielman .02 .10
137 Luther Elliss .02 .10
138 Johnnie Morton .07 .20
139 Zefross Moss .02 .10
140 Barry Sanders .60 1.50
141 Lomas Brown .02 .10
142 Cory Schlesinger .02 .10
143 Jason Hanson .02 .10
144 Kevin Glover .02 .10
145 Ron Rivers RC .07 .20
146 Aubrey Matthews .02 .10
147 Reggie Brown LB RC .02 .10
148 Herman Moore .07 .20
149 Scott Mitchell .07 .20
150 Brett Favre .75 2.00
151 Sean Jones .02 .10
152 LeRoy Butler .02 .10
153 Mark Chmura .07 .20
154 Derrick Mayes RC .15 .40
155 Mark Ingram .02 .10
156 Antonio Freeman .15 .40
157 Chris Darkins RC .02 .10
158 Robert Brooks .15 .40
159 William Henderson .15 .40
160 George Koonce .02 .10
161 Craig Newsome .02 .10
162 Darius Holland .02 .10
163 George Teague .02 .10
164 Edgar Bennett .07 .20
165 Reggie White .15 .40
166 Micheal Barrow .02 .10
167 Mel Gray .02 .10
168 Anthony Dorsett .02 .10
169 Roderick Lewis .02 .10
170 Henry Ford .02 .10
171 Mark Stepnoski .02 .10
172 Chris Sanders .07 .20
173 Anthony Cook .02 .10
174 Eddie Robinson .02 .10
175 Steve McNair .30 .75
176 Haywood Jeffires .02 .10
177 Eddie George RC .50 1.25
178 Marion Butts .02 .10
179 Malcolm Seabron .02 .10
180 Rodney Thomas .02 .10
181 Ken Dilger .07 .20
182 Zack Crockett .02 .10
183 Tony Bennett .02 .10
184 Quentin Coryatt .02 .10
185 Marshall Faulk .20 .50
186 Sean Dawkins .02 .10
187 Jim Harbaugh .07 .20
188 Eugene Daniel .02 .10
189 Roosevelt Potts .02 .10
190 Lamont Warren .02 .10
191 Will Wolford .02 .10
192 Tony Siragusa .02 .10
193 Aaron Bailey .02 .10
194 Trev Alberts .02 .10
195 Kevin Hardy .07 .20
196 Greg Spann .02 .10
197 Steve Beuerlein .07 .20
198 Steve Taneyhill .02 .10
199 Vaughn Dunbar .02 .10
200 Mark Brunell .25 .60
201 Bernard Carter .02 .10
202 James O. Stewart .07 .20
203 Tony Boselli .02 .10
204 Chris Doering .02 .10
205 Willie Jackson .07 .20
206 Tony Brackens RC .15 .40
207 Ernest Givins .02 .10
208 Le'Shai Maston .02 .10
209 Pete Mitchell .07 .20
210 Desmond Howard .07 .20
211 Vinnie Clark .02 .10
212 Jeff Lageman .02 .10
213 Derrick Walker .02 .10
214 Dan Saleaumua .02 .10
215 Derrick Thomas .15 .40
216 Neil Smith .07 .20
217 Willie Davis .02 .10
218 Mark Collins [illegible] .10
219 Lake Dawson .02 .10
220 Greg Hill .07 .20
221 Anthony Davis .02 .10
222 Kimble Anders .07 .20
223 Webster Slaughter .02 .10
224 Tamarick Vanover .07 .20
225 Marcus Allen .15 .40
226 Steve Bono .02 .10
227 Will Shields .02 .10
228 Karim Abdul-Jabbar RC .15 .40
229 Tim Bowens .02 .10
230 Keith Sims .02 .10
231 Terry Kirby .07 .20
232 Gene Atkins .02 .10
233 Dan Marino .75 2.00
234 Richmond Webb .02 .10
235 Gary Clark .02 .10
236 O.J. McDuffie .07 .20
237 Marco Coleman .02 .10
238 Bernie Parmalee .02 .10
239 Randal Hill .02 .10
240 Bryan Cox .02 .10
241 Irving Fryar .07 .20
242 Derrick Alexander DE .02 .10
243 Qadry Ismail .07 .20
244 Warren Moon .07 .20
245 Cris Carter .15 .40
246 Chad May .02 .10
247 Robert Smith .07 .20
248 Fuad Reveiz .02 .10
249 Orlando Thomas .02 .10
250 Chris Hinton .02 .10
251 Jack Del Rio .02 .10
252 Moe Williams RB RC .40 1.00
253 Roy Barker .02 .10
254 Jake Reed .07 .20
255 Adrian Cooper .02 .10
256 Curtis Martin .30 .75
257 Ben Coates .07 .20
258 Drew Bledsoe .25 .60
259 Maurice Hurst .02 .10
260 Troy Brown .15 .40
261 Bruce Armstrong .02 .10
262 Myron Guyton .02 .10
263 Dave Meggett .02 .10
264 Terry Glenn RC .40 1.00
265 Chris Slade .02 .10
266 Vincent Brisby .02 .10
267 Willie McGinest .02 .10
268 Vincent Brown .02 .10
269 Will Moore .02 .10
270 Jay Barker .02 .10
271 Ray Zellars .02 .10
272 Derek Brown RBK .02 .10
273 William Roaf .02 .10
274 Quinn Early .02 .10
275 Michael Haynes .02 .10
276 Rufus Porter .02 .10
277 Renaldo Turnbull .02 .10
278 Wayne Martin .02 .10
279 Tyrone Hughes .02 .10
280 Irv Smith .02 .10
281 Eric Allen .02 .10
282 Mark Fields .02 .10
283 Mario Bates .07 .20
284 Jim Everett .02 .10
285 Vince Buck .02 .10
286 Alex Molden RC .02 .10
287 Tyrone Wheatley .07 .20
288 Chris Calloway .02 .10
289 Jessie Armstead .02 .10
290 Arthur Marshall .02 .10
291 Aaron Pierce .02 .10
292 Dave Brown .02 .10
293 Rodney Hampton .07 .20
294 Jumbo Elliott .02 .10
295 Mike Sherrard .02 .10
296 Howard Cross .02 .10
297 Michael Brooks .02 .10
298 Herschel Walker .07 .20
299 Danny Kanell RC .15 .40
300 Keith Elias .02 .10
301 Bobby Houston .02 .10
302 Dexter Carter .02 .10
303 Tony Casillas .02 .10
304 Kyle Brady .02 .10
305 Glenn Foley .07 .20
306 Ronald Moore .02 .10
307 Ryan Yarborough .02 .10
308 Aaron Glenn .02 .10
309 Adrian Murrell .07 .20
310 Boomer Esiason .07 .20
311 Kyle Clifton .02 .10
312 Wayne Chrebet .25 .60
313 Erik Howard .02 .10
314 Keyshawn Johnson RC .40 1.00
315 Marvin Washington .02 .10
316 Johnny Mitchell .02 .10
317 Alex Van Dyke RC .07 .20
318 Billy Joe Hobert .07 .20
319 Andrew Glover .02 .10
320 Vince Evans .02 .10
321 Chester McGlockton .02 .10
322 Pat Swilling .02 .10
323 Rocket Ismail .02 .10
324 Eddie Anderson .02 .10
325 Rickey Dudley RC .15 .40
326 Steve Wisniewski .02 .10
327 Harvey Williams .02 .10
328 Napoleon Kaufman .15 .40
329 Tim Brown .15 .40
330 Jeff Hostetler .02 .10
331 Anthony Smith .02 .10
332 Terry McDaniel .02 .10
333 Charlie Garner .07 .20
334 Ricky Watters .07 .20
335 Brian Dawkins RC .50 1.25
336 Randall Cunningham .15 .40
337 Gary Anderson .02 .10
338 Calvin Williams .02 .10
339 Chris T. Jones .07 .20
340 Bobby Hoying RC .15 .40
341 William Fuller .02 .10
342 William Thomas .02 .10
343 Mike Mamula .02 .10
344 Fred Barnett .02 .10
345 Rodney Peete .02 .10
346 Mark McMillian .02 .10
347 Bobby Taylor .02 .10
348 Yancey Thigpen .07 .20
349 Neil O'Donnell .07 .20
350 Rod Woodson .07 .20
351 Kordell Stewart .15 .40
352 Dermontti Dawson .08 .20
353 Norm Johnson .02 .10
354 Ernie Mills .02 .10
355 Byron Bam Morris .02 .10
356 Mark Bruener .02 .10
357 Kevin Greene .07 .20
358 Greg Lloyd .07 .20
359 Andre Hastings .02 .10
360 Erric Pegram .02 .10
361 Carnell Lake .02 .10
362 Dwayne Harper .02 .10
363 Ronnie Harmon .02 .10
364 Leslie O'Neal .02 .10
365 John Carney .02 .10
366 Stan Humphries .07 .20
367 Brian Roche RC .02 .10
368 Terrell Fletcher .02 .10
369 Shaun Gayle .02 .10
370 Alfred Pupunu .02 .10
371 Shawn Jefferson .02 .10
372 Junior Seau .15 .40
373 Mark Seay .02 .10
374 Aaron Hayden .02 .10
375 Tony Martin .07 .20
376 Steve Young .30 .75
377 J.J. Stokes .15 .40
378 Jerry Rice .40 1.00
379 Derek Loville .02 .10
380 Lee Woodall .02 .10
381 Terrell Owens RC 1.00 2.50
382 Elvis Grbac .07 .20
383 Ricky Ervins .02 .10
384 Eric Davis .02 .10
385 Dana Stubblefield .07 .20
386 Gary Plummer .02 .10
387 Tim McDonald .02 .10
388 William Floyd .07 .20
389 Ken Norton Jr. .02 .10
390 Merton Hanks .02 .10
391 Bart Oates .02 .10
392 Brent Jones .02 .10
393 Steve Broussard .02 .10
394 Robert Blackmon .02 .10
395 Rick Tuten .02 .10
396 Pete Kendall .02 .10
397 John Friesz .02 .10
398 Terry Wooden .02 .10
399 Rick Mirer .07 .20
400 Chris Warren .07 .20
401 Joey Galloway .15 .40
402 Howard Ballard .02 .10
403 Jason Kyle .02 .10
404 Kevin Mawae .02 .10
405 Mack Strong .15 .40
406 Reggie Brown RBK RC .02 .10
407 Cortez Kennedy .02 .10
408 Sean Gilbert .02 .10
409 J.T. Thomas .02 .10
410 Shane Conlan .02 .10
411 Johnny Bailey .02 .10
412 Mark Rypien .02 .10
413 Leonard Russell .02 .10
414 Troy Drayton .02 .10
415 Jerome Bettis .15 .40
416 Jessie Hester .02 .10
417 Isaac Bruce .15 .40
418 Roman Phifer .02 .10
419 Todd Kinchen .02 .10
420 Alexander Wright .02 .10
421 Marcus Jones RC .02 .10
422 Horace Copeland .02 .10
423 Eric Curry .02 .10
424 Courtney Hawkins .02 .10
425 Alvin Harper .02 .10
426 Derrick Brooks .15 .40
427 Errict Rhett .07 .20
428 Trent Dilfer .15 .40
429 Hardy Nickerson .02 .10
430 Brad Culpepper .02 .10
431 Warren Sapp .02 .10
432 Reggie Roby .02 .10
433 Santana Dotson .02 .10
434 Jerry Ellison .02 .10
435 Lawrence Dawsey .02 .10
436 Heath Shuler .07 .20
437 Stanley Richard .07 .20
438 Rod Stephens .02 .10
439 Stephen Davis RC .60 1.50
440 Terry Allen .07 .20
441 Michael Westbrook .15 .40
442 Ken Harvey .02 .10
443 Coleman Bell .02 .10
444 Marvcus Patton .02 .10
445 Gus Frerotte .07 .20
446 Leslie Shepherd .02 .10
447 Tom Carter .02 .10
448 Brian Mitchell .02 .10
449 Darrell Green .02 .10
450A Tony Woods .02 .10
450B Chris Warren Promo .20 .50
CW1 Chris Warren Promo .40 1.00

1996 Pacific Blue

COMPLETE SET (450) 150.00 300.00
*STARS: 3X TO 6X BASIC CARDS
*RCs: 1.5X TO 3X BASIC CARDS
STATED ODDS 9:37

1996 Pacific Red

COMPLETE SET (450) 200.00 400.00
*STARS: 4X TO 8X BASIC CARDS
*RCs: 2X TO 4X BASIC CARDS
STATED ODDS 9:37

1996 Pacific Silver

COMPLETE SET (450) 150.00 300.00
*STARS: 3X TO 6X BASIC CARDS
*RCs: 1.5X TO 3X BASIC CARDS
RANDOM INSERTS IN SPECIAL RETAIL

1996 Pacific Bomb Squad

Randomly inserted in packs at the rate of one in 73, this 10-card set features color photos of the NFL's finest passer/receiver combinations. One player is displayed on each side for a double sided card.

COMPLETE SET (10) 40.00 100.00
STATED ODDS 1:73
1 J.Blake 2.50 6.00
C.Pickens
2 J.Elway 10.00 25.00
A.Miller
3 S.Mitchell 4.00 10.00
H.Moore
4 T.Aikman 5.00 12.00
J.Novacek
5 B.Favre 12.50 30.00
R.Brooks
6 S.McNair 4.00 10.00
C.Sanders
7 D.Marino 12.50 30.00
I.Fryar
8 D.Bledsoe 6.00 15.00
T.Glenn
9 K.Stewart 4.00 10.00
K.Stewart
10 S.Young 7.50 20.00
J.Rice

1996 Pacific Card Supials

Randomly inserted in packs at a rate of one in 37, this 36-paired-card insert set features color action player photos with gold foil highlights of some of the greatest NFL players. A smaller card was made to pair with the regular size card of the same player. The backs carry a slot for insertion of the small card which completes the color picture.

COMPLETE SET (72) 150.00 300.00
COMP.LARGE SET (36) 100.00 200.00
COMP.SMALL SET (36) 50.00 125.00
LARGE CARDS PRICED BELOW
*SMALL CARDS: .3X TO .7X LARGE
STATED ODDS 1:37
1 Garrison Hearst .75 2.00
2 Jeff George .75 2.00
3 Eric Zeier .40 1.00
4 Jim Kelly 1.50 4.00
5 Kerry Collins 1.50 4.00
6 Rashaan Salaam .75 2.00
7 Jeff Blake 1.50 4.00
8 Troy Aikman 4.00 10.00
9 Emmitt Smith 6.00 15.00
10 Terrell Davis 3.00 8.00
11 John Elway 8.00 20.00
12 Deion Sanders 2.50 6.00
13 Barry Sanders 6.00 15.00
14 Brett Favre 8.00 20.00
15 Steve McNair 3.00 8.00
16 Marshall Faulk 2.00 5.00
17 Mark Brunell 2.50 6.00
18 Tamarick Vanover .75 2.00
19 Dan Marino 0.00 20.00
20 Cris Carter 1.50 4.00
21 Keyshawn Johnson 4.00 10.00
22 Rodney Hampton .75 2.00
23 Curtis Martin 3.00 8.00
24 Drew Bledsoe 2.50 6.00
25 Mario Bates .75 2.00
26 Napoleon Kaufman 1.50 4.00
27 Ricky Watters .75 2.00
28 Kordell Stewart 1.50 4.00
29 Junior Seau 1.50 4.00
30 Steve Young 3.00 8.00
31 Jerry Rice 4.00 10.00
32 Isaac Bruce 1.50 4.00
33 Joey Galloway 1.50 4.00
34 Chris Warren .75 2.00
35 Errict Rhett .75 2.00
36 Michael Westbrook 1.50 4.00

1996 Pacific Cramer's Choice

Randomly inserted in packs at the rate of one in 721, this 10-card set features Michael Cramer's, Pacific Trading Cards President, selection of the top NFL players. Cards are die cut in the shape of a trophy with a color player image on a silver foil background. The bottom of the card has a brown marble border with gold foil printing. The backs carry a small player head shot with commentary.

COMPLETE SET (10) 60.00 150.00
STATED ODDS 1:721
CC1 Emmitt Smith 10.00 25.00
CC2 John Elway 12.50 30.00
CC3 Barry Sanders 10.00 25.00
CC4 Brett Favre 12.50 30.00
CC5 Reggie White 2.50 6.00
CC6 Dan Marino 12.50 30.00
CC7 Curtis Martin 5.00 12.00
CC8 Keyshawn Johnson 6.00 15.00
CC9 Kordell Stewart 2.50 6.00
CC10 Jerry Rice 6.00 15.00

1996 Pacific Gems of the Crown

This 36-card standard-size set features leading NFL players. The horizontal fronts have the player's photo framed by the team name on the left and his last name on the right. The horizontal backs have some textual information as well as another player photo. The cards are numbered with a "GC" prefix. Cards #1-18 were inserted approximately two every 37 Pacific Dynagon packs and cards #19-36 were random inserts in the regular 1996 Pacific issue.

COMPLETE SET (36) 125.00 250.00
COMP.SERIES 1 SET (18) 60.00 100.00
COMP.SERIES 2 SET (18) 90.00 150.00
1-18: STATED ODDS 2:37 DYNAGON
19-36: STATED ODDS 1:37 PACIFIC
GC1 Kerry Collins 1.50 4.00
GC2 Rashaan Salaam .75 2.00
GC3 Steve Young 3.00 8.00
GC4 Rodney Thomas .40 1.00
GC5 Michael Westbrook 1.50 4.00
GC6 Cris Carter 1.50 4.00
GC7 Jerry Rice 4.00 10.00
GC8 Drew Bledsoe 2.50 6.00
GC9 Steve McNair 3.00 8.00
GC10 Terrell Davis 3.00 8.00
GC11 Barry Sanders 6.00 15.00
GC12 Robert Brooks 1.50 4.00
GC13 Chris Warren .75 2.00
GC14 Marshall Faulk 2.00 5.00
GC15 John Elway 8.00 20.00
GC16 Isaac Bruce 1.50 4.00
GC17 Emmitt Smith 6.00 15.00
GC18 Thurman Thomas 1.50 4.00
GC19 Garrison Hearst .75 2.00
GC20 Jeff Blake 1.50 4.00
GC21 Troy Aikman 4.00 10.00
GC22 Deion Sanders 2.50 6.00
GC23 Brett Favre 8.00 20.00
GC24 Robert Smith .75 2.00
GC25 Mario Bates .75 2.00
GC26 Napoleon Kaufman 1.50 4.00
GC27 Kordell Stewart 1.50 4.00
GC28 Jim Kelly 1.50 4.00
GC29 Jim Harbaugh .75 2.00
GC30 Tamarick Vanover .75 2.00
GC31 Dan Marino 8.00 20.00
GC32 Warren Moon .75 2.00
GC33 Curtis Martin 3.00 8.00
GC34 Rodney Hampton .75 2.00
GC35 Ricky Watters .75 2.00
GC36 Joey Galloway 1.50 4.00

1996 Pacific Gold Crown Die Cuts

Randomly inserted in packs at the rate of one in 37, this 20-card set features color player photos with a die cut crown at the top of the card and gold foil highlights. The backs carry a small player head photo with a paragraph about the player.

COMPLETE SET (20) 60.00 150.00
GOLD STATED ODDS 1:37
1 Emmitt Smith 8.00 20.00
2 Troy Aikman 5.00 12.00
3 Barry Sanders 8.00 20.00
4 Kerry Collins 2.00 5.00
5 Jeff Blake 2.00 5.00
6 John Elway 10.00 25.00
7 Terrell Davis 4.00 10.00
8 Deion Sanders 3.00 8.00
9 Brett Favre 10.00 25.00
10 Dan Marino 10.00 25.00
11 Eddie George 2.50 6.00
12 Curtis Martin 2.50 6.00
13 Drew Bledsoe 2.50 6.00
14 Keyshawn Johnson 2.00 5.00
15 Napoleon Kaufman 1.50 4.00
16 Kordell Stewart 2.00 5.00
17 Steve Young 4.00 10.00
18 Jerry Rice 5.00 12.00
19 Joey Galloway 2.00 5.00
20 Chris Warren 1.50 4.00

1996 Pacific Platinum Crown Die Cuts

COMPLETE SET (20) 75.00 150.00
PC1 Barry Sanders 8.00 20.00
PC2 Emmitt Smith 8.00 20.00
PC3 Brett Favre 10.00 25.00
PC4 John Elway 10.00 25.00
PC5 Dan Marino 10.00 25.00
PC7 Jerry Rice 6.00 15.00
PC8 Troy Aikman 5.00 12.00
PC9 Marshall Faulk 4.00 10.00
PC9 Deion Sanders 4.00 10.00
PC10 Steve Young 5.00 12.00

1996 Pacific Power Corps

ndomly inserted in special retail packs only available at Wal-Mart stores, this 20-card set features color player photos of some of the best players of the 1995 season on a gold highlighted background. The backs carry a small triangular head photo with information as to why this player was selected for this set. Six players' cards are available in a foiling variation.

COMPLETE SET (20) 40.00 75.00
STATED ODDS 6:21 SPECIAL RETAIL
*FOIL PARAL (1/11/14/17-19): 1X to 2.5X
ONLY SIX FOIL CARDS MADE
PC1 Troy Aikman 2.50 5.00
PC2 Jeff Blake 1.00 2.00
PC3 Drew Bledsoe 1.50 3.00
PC4 Kerry Collins 1.00 2.00
PC5 Terrell Davis 2.00 4.00
PC6 John Elway 5.00 10.00
PC7 Marshall Faulk 1.25 2.50
PC8 Brett Favre 5.00 10.00
PC9 Joey Galloway 1.00 2.00
PC10 Garrison Hearst .40 1.00
PC11 Dan Marino 5.00 10.00
PC12 Curtis Martin 2.00 4.00
PC13 Steve McNair 2.00 4.00
PC14 Jerry Rice 2.50 5.00
PC15 Rashaan Salaam .40 1.00
PC16 Barry Sanders [illegible]
PC17 Emmitt Smith 4.00 8.00
PC18 Kordell Stewart 1.00 2.00
PC19 Chris Warren .40 1.00
PC20 Steve Young 2.00 4.00

1996 Pacific The Zone

ndomly inserted in packs at the rate of one in 145, this 20-card set features color photos of some of last season's most productive NFL players. The cards are die cut in the shape of a football goal post with the player's name and team name printed in gold foil on the post. The backs carry a player head photo with his playing position and city of the team.

COMPLETE SET (20) 60.00 150.00
STATED ODDS 1:145
1 Jim Kelly 1.50 4.00
2 Rashaan Salaam .75 2.00
3 Carl Pickens .75 2.00
4 Jeff Blake 1.50 4.00
5 Kerry Collins 1.50 4.00
6 Emmitt Smith 6.00 15.00
7 Troy Aikman 4.00 10.00
8 John Elway 8.00 20.00
9 Barry Sanders 6.00 15.00
10 Herman Moore .75 2.00
11 Scott Mitchell .75 2.00
12 Brett Favre 8.00 20.00
13 Robert Brooks 1.50 4.00
14 Marshall Faulk 2.00 5.00
15 Dan Marino 8.00 20.00
16 Drew Bledsoe 2.50 6.00
17 Curtis Martin 3.00 8.00
18 Steve Young 3.00 8.00
19 Jerry Rice 4.00 10.00
20 Chris Warren .75 2.00

1996 Pacific Super Bowl

is six-card set was produced with both a gold and bronze foil border. The bronze set was made available through a special wrapper redemption program at the 1996 Super Bowl Card Show in Phoenix. Collectors with five wrappers would receive one card and 30-pack wrappers were good for a complete set. The fronts feature color action player photos with a bronze foil overlay going up the sides of the card along with the Super Bowl Card Show logo. The gold foil set was available via a wrapper redemption program with 1995 Triple Folders. Collectors could receive a complete set by sending 18 Triple Folders wrappers to Pacific along with $5.95. The gold cards are basically a parallel to the bronze issue, but contain a Super Bowl XXX logo on the cardfronts.

COMP.GOLD SET (6) 4.00 10.00
*BRONZE CARDS: SAME PRICE
1 Chris Warren .40 1.00
2 Kordell Stewart .80 2.00
3 Curtis Martin .80 2.00
4 Errict Rhett .40 1.00
5 Neil O'Donnell .40 1.00
6 Barry Sanders 1.60 4.00

1997 Pacific

e 1997 Pacific set was issued in one series totalling 450 cards and distributed in 12-card packs with a suggested retail price of $2.49. The fronts feature borderless action color player photos with gold foil printing. The backs carry player information and career statistics. The cards are grouped alphabetically within teams. Four different parallels sets were released in various forms of packaging. The Platinum Blue foil parallel was the toughest to pull with, reportedly, only 67-sets produced.

COMPLETE SET (450) 15.00 30.00
1 Lomas Brown .07 .20
2 Pat Carter .07 .20
3 Larry Centers .10 .30
4 Matt Darby .07 .20
5 Marcus Dowdell .07 .20
6 Aaron Graham .07 .20
7 Kent Graham .07 .20
8 LeShon Johnson .07 .20
9 Seth Joyner .07 .20
10 Leeland McElroy .07 .20
11 Rob Moore .10 .30
12 Simeon Rice .10 .30
13 Eric Swann .07 .20
14 Aeneas Williams .07 .20
15 Morten Andersen .07 .20
16 Jamal Anderson .20 .50
17 Lester Archambeau .07 .20
18 Cornelius Bennett .07 .20
19 J.J. Birden .07 .20
20 Antone Davis .07 .20
21 Bert Emanuel .10 .30
22 Travis Hall RC .07 .20
23 Bobby Hebert .07 .20
24 Craig Heyward .07 .20
25 Terance Mathis .10 .30
26 Tim McKyer .07 .20
27 Eric Metcalf .10 .30
28 Jessie Tuggle .07 .20
29 Derrick Alexander WR .10 .30
30 Orlando Brown .07 .20
31 Rob Burnett .07 .20
32 Earnest Byner .07 .20
33 Ray Ethridge .07 .20
34 Steve Everitt .07 .20
35 Carwell Gardner .07 .20
36 Michael Jackson .10 .30
37 Jermaine Lewis .20 .50
38 Stevon Moore .07 .20
39 Byron Bam Morris .07 .20
40 Jonathan Ogden .07 .20
41 Vinny Testaverde .10 .30
42 Todd Collins .07 .20
43 Russell Copeland .07 .20
44 Quinn Early .07 .20
45 John Fina .07 .20
46 Phil Hansen .07 .20
47 Eric Moulds .20 .50
48 Bryce Paup .07 .20
49 Andre Reed .10 .30
50 Kurt Schulz .07 .20
51 Bruce Smith .10 .30
52 Chris Spielman .07 .20
53 Steve Tasker .07 .20
54 Thurman Thomas .20 .50
55 Carlton Bailey .07 .20
56 Michael Bates .07 .20
57 Blake Brockermeyer .07 .20
58 Mark Carrier WR .07 .20
59 Kerry Collins .20 .50
60 Eric Davis .07 .20
61 Kevin Greene .10 .30
62 Rocket Ismail .10 .30
63 Anthony Johnson .07 .20
64 Shawn King .07 .20
65 Greg Kragen .07 .20
66 Sam Mills .07 .20
67 Tyrone Poole .07 .20
68 Wesley Walls .10 .30
69 Mark Carrier DB .07 .20
70 Curtis Conway .10 .30
71 Bobby Engram .10 .30
72 Jim Flanigan .07 .20
73 Al Fontenot .07 .20
74 Raymont Harris .07 .20
75 Walt Harris .07 .20
76 Andy Heck .07 .20
77 Dave Krieg .07 .20
78 Rashaan Salaam .07 .20
79 Vinson Smith .07 .20
80 Alonzo Spellman .07 .20
81 Michael Timpson .07 .20
82 James Williams .07 .20
83 Ashley Ambrose .07 .20
84 Eric Bieniemy .07 .20
85 Jeff Blake .10 .30
86 Ki-Jana Carter .07 .20
87 John Copeland .07 .20
88 David Dunn .07 .20
89 Jeff Hill .07 .20
90 Ricardo McDonald .07 .20
91 Tony McGee .07 .20
92 Greg Myers RC .07 .20
93 Carl Pickens .10 .30
94 Corey Sawyer .07 .20
95 Darnay Scott .10 .30
96 Dan Wilkinson .07 .20
97 Troy Aikman .40 1.00
98 Larry Allen .07 .20
99 Eric Bjornson .07 .20
100 Ray Donaldson .07 .20
101 Michael Irvin .20 .50
102 Daryl Johnston .10 .30
103 Nate Newton .07 .20
104 Deion Sanders .20 .50
105 Jim Schwartz RC .07 .20
106 Emmitt Smith .60 1.50
107 Broderick Thomas .07 .20
108 Tony Tolbert .07 .20
109 Erik Williams .07 .20
110 Sherman Williams .07 .20
111 Darren Woodson .07 .20
112 Steve Atwater .07 .20
113 Aaron Craver .07 .20
114 Ray Crockett .07 .20
115 Terrell Davis .25 .60
116 Jason Elam .10 .30
117 John Elway .75 2.00
118 Todd Kinchen .07 .20
119 Ed McCaffrey .10 .30
120 Anthony Miller .07 .20
121 John Mobley .07 .20
122 Michael Dean Perry .07 .20
123 Reggie Rivers .07 .20
124 Shannon Sharpe .10 .30
125 Alfred Williams .07 .20
126 Reggie Brown LB .10 .30
127 Luther Elliss .07 .20
128 Kevin Glover .07 .20
129 Jason Hanson .07 .20
130 Pepper Johnson .07 .20
131 Glyn Milburn .07 .20
132 Scott Mitchell .10 .30
133 Herman Moore .10 .30
134 Johnnie Morton .10 .30
135 Brett Perriman .07 .20
136 Robert Porcher .07 .20
137 Ron Rivers .07 .20
138 Barry Sanders .60 1.50
139 Henry Thomas .07 .20
140 Don Beebe .07 .20
141 Edgar Bennett .10 .30
142 Robert Brooks .10 .30
143 LeRoy Butler .07 .20
144 Mark Chmura .10 .30
145 Brett Favre .75 2.00
146 Antonio Freeman .20 .50
147 Chris Jacke .07 .20
148 Travis Jervey .10 .30
149 Sean Jones .07 .20
150 Dorsey Levens .20 .50
151 John Michels .07 .20
152 Craig Newsome .07 .20
153 Eugene Robinson .07 .20
154 Reggie White .20 .50
155 Micheal Barrow .07 .20
156 Blaine Bishop .07 .20
157 Chris Chandler .10 .30
158 Anthony Cook .07 .20
159 Malcolm Floyd .07 .20
160 Eddie George .20 .50
161 Roderick Lewis .07 .20
162 Steve McNair .25 .60
163 John Henry Mills RC .07 .20
164 Derek Russell .07 .20
165 Chris Sanders .07 .20
166 Mark Stepnoski .07 .20
167 Frank Wycheck .07 .20
168 Robert Young .07 .20
169 Trev Alberts .07 .20
170 Aaron Bailey .07 .20
171 Tony Bennett .07 .20
172 Ray Buchanan .07 .20
173 Quentin Coryatt .07 .20
174 Eugene Daniel .07 .20
175 Sean Dawkins .07 .20
176 Ken Dilger .07 .20
177 Marshall Faulk .25 .60
178 Jim Harbaugh .10 .30
179 Marvin Harrison .20 .50
180 Paul Justin .07 .20
181 Lamont Warren .07 .20
182 Bernard Whittington .07 .20
183 Tony Boselli .07 .20
184 Tony Brackens .07 .20
185 Mark Brunell .25 .60
186 Brian DeMarco .07 .20
187 Rich Griffith .07 .20
188 Kevin Hardy .07 .20
189 Willie Jackson .07 .20
190 Jeff Lageman .07 .20
191 Keenan McCardell .10 .30
192 Natrone Means .10 .30
193 Pete Mitchell .07 .20
194 Joel Smeenge .07 .20
195 Jimmy Smith .10 .30
196 James O.Stewart .10 .30
197 Marcus Allen .20 .50
198 John Alt .07 .20
199 Kimble Anders .10 .30
200 Steve Bono .10 .30
201 Vaughn Booker RC .07 .20
202 Dale Carter .07 .20
203 Mark Collins .07 .20
204 Greg Hill .07 .20
205 Joe Horn .20 .50
206 Dan Saleaumua .07 .20
207 Will Shields .07 .20
208 Neil Smith .10 .30
209 Derrick Thomas .20 .50
210 Tamarick Vanover .10 .30
211 Karim Abdul-Jabbar .10 .30
212 Fred Barnett .07 .20
213 Tim Bowens .07 .20
214 Kirby Dar Dar RC .10 .30
215 Troy Drayton .07 .20
216 Craig Erickson .07 .20
217 Daryl Gardener .07 .20
218 Randal Hill .07 .20
219 Dan Marino .75 2.00
220 O.J. McDuffie .10 .30
221 Bernie Parmalee .07 .20
222 Stanley Pritchett .07 .20
223 Daniel Stubbs .07 .20
224 Zach Thomas .20 .50
225 Derrick Alexander DE .07 .20
226 Cris Carter .20 .50
227 Jeff Christy .07 .20
228 Qadry Ismail .10 .30
229 Brad Johnson .20 .50
230 Andrew Jordan .07 .20
231 Randall McDaniel .07 .20
232 David Palmer .07 .20
233 John Randle .10 .30
234 Jake Reed .10 .30
235 Scott Sisson .07 .20
236 Korey Stringer .07 .20
237 Darryl Talley .07 .20
238 Orlando Thomas .07 .20
239 Bruce Armstrong .07 .20
240 Drew Bledsoe .25 .60
241 Willie Clay .07 .20
242 Ben Coates .10 .30
243 Ferric Collons RC .07 .20
244 Torry Glenn .20 .50
245 Jerome Henderson .07 .20
246 Shawn Jefferson .07 .20
247 Dietrich Jells .07 .20
248 Ty Law .10 .30
249 Curtis Martin .25 .60

Card	Low	High
250 Willie McGinest	.07	.20
251 Dave Meggett	.07	.20
252 Lawyer Milloy	.10	.30
253 Chris Slade	.07	.20
254 Je'rod Cherry	.07	.20
255 Jim Everett	.07	.20
256 Mark Fields	.07	.20
257 Michael Haynes	.07	.20
258 Tyrone Hughes	.07	.20
259 Haywood Jeffires	.07	.20
260 Wayne Martin	.07	.20
261 Mark McMillian	.07	.20
262 Rufus Porter	.07	.20
263 William Roaf	.07	.20
264 Torrance Small	.07	.20
265 Renaldo Turnbull	.07	.20
266 Ray Zellars	.07	.20
267 Jessie Armstead	.07	.20
268 Chad Bratzke	.07	.20
269 Dave Brown	.07	.20
270 Chris Calloway	.07	.20
271 Howard Cross	.07	.20
272 Lawrence Dawsey	.07	.20
273 Rodney Hampton	.10	.30
274 Danny Kanell	.07	.20
275 Arthur Marshall	.07	.20
276 Aaron Pierce	.07	.20
277 Phillippi Sparks	.07	.20
278 Amani Toomer	.10	.30
279 Charles Way	.07	.20
280 Richie Anderson	.10	.30
281 Fred Baxter	.07	.20
282 Wayne Chrebet	.20	.50
283 Kyle Clifton	.07	.20
284 Jumbo Elliott	.07	.20
285 Aaron Glenn	.07	.20
286 Jeff Graham	.07	.20
287 Bobby Hamilton RC	.07	.20
288 Keyshawn Johnson	.20	.50
289 Adrian Murrell	.10	.30
290 Neil O'Donnell	.10	.30
291 Webster Slaughter	.07	.20
292 Alex Van Dyke	.07	.20
293 Marvin Washington	.07	.20
294 Joe Aska	.07	.20
295 Jerry Ball	.07	.20
296 Tim Brown	.20	.50
297 Rickey Dudley	.10	.30
298 Pat Harlow	.07	.20
299 Nolan Harrison	.07	.20
300 Billy Joe Hobert	.10	.30
301 James Jett	.10	.30
302 Napoleon Kaufman	.20	.50
303 Lincoln Kennedy	.07	.20
304 Albert Lewis	.07	.20
305 Chester McGlockton	.07	.20
306 Pat Swilling	.07	.20
307 Steve Wisniewski	.07	.20
308 Darion Conner	.07	.20
309 Ty Detmer	.10	.30
310 Jason Dunn	.07	.20
311 Irving Fryar	.10	.30
312 James Fuller	.07	.20
313 William Fuller	.07	.20
314 Charlie Garner	.10	.30
315 Bobby Hoying	.10	.30
316 Tom Hutton	.07	.20
317 Chris T. Jones	.07	.20
318 Mike Mamula	.07	.20
319 Mark Seay	.07	.20
320 Bobby Taylor	.07	.20
321 Ricky Watters	.10	.30
322 Jahine Arnold	.07	.20
323 Jerome Bettis	.20	.50
324 Chad Brown	.07	.20
325 Mark Bruener	.07	.20
326 Andre Hastings	.07	.20
327 Norm Johnson	.07	.20
328 Levon Kirkland	.07	.20
329 Carnell Lake	.07	.20
330 Greg Lloyd	.07	.20
331 Ernie Mills	.07	.20
332 Orpheus Roye RC	.07	.20
333 Kordell Stewart	.20	.50
334 Yancey Thigpen	.10	.30
335 Mike Tomczak	.07	.20
336 Rod Woodson	.10	.30
337 Tony Banks	.10	.30
338 Bern Brostek	.07	.20
339 Isaac Bruce	.20	.50
340 Ernie Conwell	.07	.20
341 Keith Crawford RC	.07	.20
342 Wayne Gandy	.07	.20
343 Harold Green	.07	.20
344 Carlos Jenkins	.07	.20
345 Jimmie Jones	.07	.20
346 Eddie Kennison	.10	.30
347 Todd Lyght	.07	.20
348 Leslie O'Neal	.07	.20
349 Lawrence Phillips	.07	.20
350 Greg Robinson	.07	.20
351 Darren Bennett	.07	.20
352 Lewis Bush	.07	.20
353 Eric Castle	.07	.20
354 Terrell Fletcher	.07	.20
355 Darrien Gordon	.07	.20
356 Kurt Gouveia	.07	.20
357 Aaron Hayden	.07	.20
358 Stan Humphries	.10	.30
359 Tony Martin	.10	.30
360 Vaughn Parker RC	.07	.20
361 Brian Roche	.07	.20
362 Leonard Russell	.07	.20
363 Junior Seau	.20	.50
364 Roy Barker	.07	.20
365 Harris Barton	.07	.20
366 Dexter Carter	.07	.20
367 Chris Doleman	.07	.20
368 Tyronne Drakeford	.07	.20
369 Elvis Grbac	.10	.30
370 Derek Loville	.07	.20
371 Tim McDonald	.07	.20
372 Ken Norton	.07	.20
373 Terrell Owens	.25	.60
374 Gary Plummer	.07	.20
375 Jerry Rice	.40	1.00
376 Dana Stubblefield	.07	.20
377 Lee Woodall	.07	.20
378 Steve Young	.25	.60
379 Robert Blackmon	.07	.20
380 Brian Blades	.07	.20
381 Carlester Crumpler	.07	.20
382 Christian Fauria	.07	.20
383 John Friesz	.07	.20
384 Joey Galloway	.10	.30
385 Derrick Graham	.07	.20
386 Cortez Kennedy	.07	.20
387 Warren Moon	.20	.50
388 Winston Moss	.07	.20
389 Mike Pritchard	.07	.20
390 Michael Sinclair	.07	.20
391 Lamar Smith	.20	.50
392 Chris Warren	.10	.30
393 Chidi Ahanotu	.07	.20
394 Mike Alstott	.20	.50
395 Reggie Brooks	.07	.20
396 Trent Dilfer	.20	.50
397 Jerry Ellison	.07	.20
398 Paul Gruber	.07	.20
399 Alvin Harper	.07	.20
400 Courtney Hawkins	.07	.20
401 Dave Moore	.07	.20
402 Errict Rhett	.07	.20
403 Warren Sapp	.10	.30
404 Nilo Silvan	.07	.20
405 Regan Upshaw	.07	.20
406 Casey Weldon	.07	.20
407 Terry Allen	.20	.50
408 Jamie Asher	.07	.20
409 Bill Brooks	.07	.20
410 Tom Carter	.07	.20
411 Henry Ellard	.07	.20
412 Gus Frerotte	.07	.20
413 Darrell Green	.10	.30
414 Ken Harvey	.07	.20
415 Tre Johnson	.07	.20
416 Brian Mitchell	.07	.20
417 Rich Owens	.07	.20
418 Heath Shuler	.07	.20
419 Michael Westbrook	.10	.30
420 Tony Woods RC	.07	.20
421 Reidel Anthony RC	.20	.50
422 Darnell Autry RC	.10	.30
423 Tiki Barber RC	1.25	3.00
424 Pat Barnes RC	.20	.50
425 Terry Battle RC	.07	.20
426 Will Blackwell RC	.10	.30
427 Peter Boulware RC	.20	.50
428 Rae Carruth RC	.07	.20
429 Troy Davis RC	.10	.30
430 Jim Druckenmiller RC	.10	.30
431 Warrick Dunn RC	.60	1.50
432 Marc Edwards RC	.07	.20
433 James Farrior RC	.20	.50
434 Yatil Green RC	.10	.30
435 Byron Hanspard RC	.10	.30
436 Ike Hilliard RC	.30	.75
437 David LaFleur RC	.07	.20
438 Kevin Lockett RC	.10	.30
439 Sam Madison RC	.20	.50
440 Brian Manning RC	.10	.30
441 Orlando Pace RC	.20	.50
442 Jake Plummer RC	1.00	2.50
443 Chad Scott RC	.10	.30
444 Sedrick Shaw RC	.10	.30
445 Antowain Smith RC	.50	1.25
446 Shawn Springs RC	.10	.30
447 Ross Verba RC	.07	.20
448 Bryant Westbrook RC	.07	.20
449 Renaldo Wynn RC	.07	.20
450 Jimmy Johnson CO	.10	.30
S1 Mark Brunell Sample	.40	1.00

1997 Pacific Copper

COMPLETE SET (450)	100.00	200.00
*STARS: 3X TO 6X BASIC CARDS		
*RCs: 1.5X TO 3X BASIC CARDS		
ONE PER HOBBY PACK		

1997 Pacific Platinum Blue

*STARS: 10X TO 25X BASIC CARDS
*RCs: 5X TO 12X BASIC CARDS
STATED ODDS 1:73
STATED PRINT RUN 67 SETS

1997 Pacific Red

COMPLETE SET (450)	150.00	300.00
*STARS: 5X TO 10X BASIC CARDS		
*RCs: 2.5X TO 5X BASIC CARDS		
REDS ONE PER SPECIAL RETAIL PACK		

1997 Pacific Silver

COMPLETE SET (450)	125.00	250.00
*STARS: 4X TO 8X BASIC CARDS		
*RCs: 2X TO 4X BASIC CARDS		
ONE PER RETAIL PACK		

1997 Pacific Big Number Die Cuts

Randomly inserted in packs at a rate of one in 37, this 20-card set features a die-cut replica of the portion of the player's jersey with his number and last name. The backs carry a color player photo and player information.

COMPLETE SET (20)	25.00	60.00
STATED ODDS 1:37		
1 Jamal Anderson	1.50	4.00
2 Kerry Collins	1.50	4.00
3 Troy Aikman	3.00	8.00
4 Emmitt Smith	5.00	12.00
5 Terrell Davis	2.00	5.00
6 John Elway	6.00	15.00
7 Barry Sanders	5.00	12.00
8 Brett Favre	6.00	15.00
9 Eddie George	1.50	4.00
10 Mark Brunell	2.00	5.00
11 Marcus Allen	1.50	4.00
12 Karim Abdul-Jabbar	1.00	2.50
13 Dan Marino	6.00	15.00
14 Drew Bledsoe	2.00	5.00
15 Curtis Martin	2.00	5.00
16 Napoleon Kaufman	1.50	4.00
17 Jerome Bettis	1.50	4.00
18 Eddie Kennison	1.00	2.50
19 Jerry Rice	3.00	8.00
20 Steve Young	2.00	5.00

1997 Pacific Mark Brunell

Pacific Trading Cards issued two Mark Brunell inserts for each of four football products of 1997: Pacific, Invincible, Crown Royale, and Revolution. Although released in separate issues, the cards carry a similar design and are numbered #1-8. Cards #1 and 2 were issued in Crown Collection, Cards #3 and 4 were included in Invincible, Cards #5 and 6 were in Crown Royale and #7 and 8 were inserted in Revolution.

COMPLETE SET (8)	12.50	30.00
COMMON CARD (1-8)	1.50	4.00
INSERTS IN VARIOUS PACIFIC PRODUCTS		

1997 Pacific Card Supials

Randomly inserted in packs at a rate of one in 37, this 36-paired card insert set features color action player photos of some of the best players in the NFL. A smaller die cut football-shaped card was made to pair with the regular size card of the same player. Packs carried a pair of one small and one large card. The backs carry a slot for insertion of the small card.

COMPLETE SET (72)	60.00	150.00
COMP.LARGE SET (36)	40.00	100.00
COMP.SMALL SET (36)	25.00	60.00
*SMALL CARDS: .3X TO .8X LARGE		
STATED ODDS 1:37		
1 Todd Collins	1.00	2.50
2 Kerry Collins	1.00	2.50
3 Wesley Walls	1.00	2.50
4 Jeff Blake	1.00	2.50
5 Troy Aikman	2.00	5.00
6 Emmitt Smith	2.50	6.00
7 Terrell Davis	1.25	3.00
8 John Elway	5.00	12.00
9 Herman Moore	1.25	3.00
10 Barry Sanders	2.50	6.00
11 Brett Favre	3.00	8.00
12 Dorsey Levens	1.25	3.00
13 Eddie George	1.25	3.00
14 Steve McNair	1.50	4.00
15 Marshall Faulk	1.25	3.00
16 Mark Brunell	1.25	3.00
17 Natrone Means	1.25	3.00
18 Marcus Allen	1.50	4.00
19 Karim Abdul-Jabbar	1.00	2.50
20 Dan Marino	5.00	12.00
21 Brad Johnson	1.25	3.00
22 Drew Bledsoe	1.25	3.00
23 Terry Glenn	1.25	3.00
24 Curtis Martin	1.50	4.00
25 Napoleon Kaufman	1.00	2.50
26 Ricky Watters	1.25	3.00
27 Jerome Bettis	1.50	4.00
28 Kordell Stewart	1.00	2.50
29 Tony Banks	1.25	3.00
30 Isaac Bruce	1.50	4.00
31 Eddie Kennison	1.00	2.50
32 Jerry Rice	3.00	8.00
33 Steve Young	2.00	5.00
34 Joey Galloway	1.25	3.00
35 Chris Warren	1.00	2.50
36 Gus Frerotte	1.00	2.50

1997 Pacific Cramer's Choice

ndomly inserted in packs at a rate of one in 721, this 10-card set features players picked by Pacific President and CEO, Michael Cramer, as the best in the NFL. The fronts display a color player cut-out on a pyramid diecut shaped background. The backs carry player information.

COMPLETE SET (10)	100.00	250.00
STATED ODDS 1:721		
1 Kevin Greene	2.50	6.00
2 Emmitt Smith	12.50	30.00
3 Terrell Davis	5.00	12.00
4 John Elway	15.00	40.00
5 Barry Sanders	12.50	30.00
6 Brett Favre	15.00	40.00
7 Eddie George	4.00	10.00
8 Mark Brunell	5.00	12.00
9 Terry Glenn	4.00	10.00
10 Jerry Rice	8.00	20.00

1997 Pacific Gold Crown Die Cuts

Randomly inserted in packs at a rate of one in 37, this 36-card set features some of the top players in the NFL. The fronts carry color player images and are die cut in the shape of a crown at the top with gold foil highlights.

COMPLETE SET (36)	50.00	120.00
STATED ODDS 1:37		
1 Larry Centers	1.00	2.50
2 Vinny Testaverde	1.00	2.50
3 Kerry Collins	1.50	4.00
4 Kevin Greene	1.00	2.50
5 Anthony Johnson	.60	1.50
6 Jeff Blake	1.00	2.50
7 Troy Aikman	3.00	8.00
8 Emmitt Smith	5.00	12.00
9 Terrell Davis	2.00	5.00
10 John Elway	6.00	15.00
11 Barry Sanders	5.00	12.00
12 Brett Favre	6.00	15.00
13 Antonio Freeman	1.50	4.00
14 Eddie George	1.50	4.00
15 Marshall Faulk	2.00	5.00
16 Mark Brunell	2.00	5.00
17 Jimmy Smith	1.00	2.50
18 Marcus Allen	1.50	4.00
19 Karim Abdul-Jabbar	1.00	2.50
20 Dan Marino	6.00	15.00
21 Brad Johnson	1.50	4.00
22 Drew Bledsoe	2.00	5.00
23 Terry Glenn	1.50	4.00
24 Curtis Martin	2.00	5.00
25 Adrian Murrell	1.00	2.50
26 Tim Brown	1.50	4.00
27 Jerome Bettis	1.50	4.00
28 Kordell Stewart	1.50	4.00
29 Tony Banks	1.00	2.50
30 Terrell Owens	2.00	5.00
31 Jerry Rice	3.00	8.00
32 Steve Young	2.00	5.00
33 Chris Warren	1.00	2.50
34 Terry Allen	1.50	4.00
35 Gus Frerotte	.60	1.50
36 Jim Druckenmiller	1.00	2.50

1997 Pacific Team Checklists

ndomly inserted in packs at a rate of one in 37, this 30-card set features color action and head photos of three of the team's best players with their team's 1997 Pacific card checklist on the back.

COMPLETE SET (30)	40.00	100.00
STATED ODDS 1:37		
1 Centers	1.00	2.50
Graham		
L.John.		
2 J.Ander	2.50	6.00
Emanl		
Andersen		
3 Testa	1.50	4.00
D.Alex WR		
Jackson		
4 T.Collins	1.00	2.50
Tasker		
B.Smith		
5 K.Collins	2.50	6.00
Walls		
Greene		
6 Salaam	1.00	2.50
R.Harris		
Conway		
7 Blake	1.00	2.50
Pickens		
Ki.Cart		
8 E.Smith	6.00	15.00
Aikman		
M.Irvin		
9 Elway	5.00	12.00
T.Davis		
Atwater		
10 B.Sand	5.00	12.00
Moore		
Mitchell		
11 Favre	7.50	20.00
R.White		
Freeman		
12 McNair	5.00	12.00
George		
C.Sand		
13 Faulk	1.50	4.00
Harbaugh		
M.Hrrsn		
14 Brunell	3.00	8.00
McCard.		
Means		
15 Allen	2.50	6.00
D.Carter		
D.Thom		
16 Marino	7.50	20.00
Jabbar		
Z.Thomas		
17 B.Johnson	2.50	6.00
C.Carter		
Reed		
18 Bledsoe	5.00	12.00
C.Martin		
Glenn		
19 Everett	1.00	2.50
W.Martin		
Zellars		
20 D.Brown	1.00	2.50
Hamp		
Toomer		
21 K.Johnson	2.50	6.00
Mrrell		
O'Donn		
22 Kaufman	2.50	6.00
T.Brown		
McGloc		
23 Watters	1.50	4.00
T.Detmer		
Fryar		
24 Bettis	3.00	8.00
K.Stewart		
Blackwell		
25 Banks	1.50	4.00
Kennison		
Bruce		
26 T.Martin	1.00	2.50
Humph		
Seau		
27 S.Young	5.00	12.00
Rice		
Owens		
28 Warren	2.50	6.00
Galloway		
Kennedy		
29 Dilfer	1.50	4.00
Rhett		
M.Alstott		
30 Frerotte	2.50	6.00
T.Allen		
Westbrook		

1997 Pacific The Zone

Randomly inserted in packs at a rate of one in 73, this 20-card set features a color player photo on a goal post die-cut card with the player's name and position at the bottom.

COMPLETE SET (20)	40.00	100.00
STATED ODDS 1:73		
1 Kerry Collins	2.00	5.00
2 Jeff Blake	1.25	3.00
3 Emmitt Smith	6.00	15.00
4 Terrell Davis	2.50	6.00
5 John Elway	8.00	20.00
6 Barry Sanders	6.00	15.00
7 Brett Favre	8.00	20.00
8 Mark Brunell	2.50	6.00
9 Karim Abdul-Jabbar	1.25	3.00
10 Dan Marino	8.00	20.00
11 Drew Bledsoe	2.50	6.00
12 Terry Glenn	2.00	5.00
13 Curtis Martin	2.50	6.00
14 Napoleon Kaufman	2.00	5.00
15 Jerome Bettis	2.00	5.00
16 Eddie Kennison	1.25	3.00
17 Tony Martin	1.25	3.00
18 Jerry Rice	4.00	10.00
19 Steve Young	2.50	6.00
20 Terry Allen	2.00	5.00

1997 Pacific Roy Firestone

This 6-card set was issued to promote Roy Firestone's involvement with Pacific Trading Cards. Each card includes Roy in a similar card design to various 1997 Pacific football products.

COMPLETE SET (6)	1.20	3.00
COMMON CARD (1-6)	.20	.50

1998 Pacific

e 1998 Pacific set was issued in one series totalling 450 cards and was distributed in ten-card packs with a suggested retail price of $2.19. The fronts feature color action player photos with silver foil highlights. The backs carry player information and career statistics.

Card	Low	High
COMPLETE SET (450)	25.00	60.00
1 Mario Bates	.15	.40
2 Lomas Brown	.08	.25
3 Larry Centers	.08	.25
4 Chris Gedney	.08	.25
5 Terry Irving	.08	.25
6 Tom Knight	.08	.25
7 Eric Metcalf	.08	.25
8 Jamir Miller	.08	.25
9 Rob Moore	.15	.40
10 Joe Nedney	.08	.25
11 Jake Plummer	.25	.60
12 Simeon Rice	.15	.40
13 Frank Sanders	.15	.40
14 Eric Swann	.08	.25
15 Aeneas Williams	.08	.25
16 Morten Andersen	.08	.25
17 Jamal Anderson	.25	.60
18 Michael Booker	.08	.25
19 Keith Brooking RC	.60	1.50
20 Ray Buchanan	.08	.25
21 Devin Bush	.08	.25
22 Chris Chandler	.15	.40
23 Tony Graziani	.08	.25
24 Harold Green	.08	.25
25 Byron Hanspard	.08	.25
26 Todd Kinchen	.08	.25
27 Tony Martin	.15	.40
28 Terance Mathis	.15	.40
29 Eugene Robinson	.08	.25
30 O.J. Santiago	.08	.25
31 Chuck Smith	.08	.25
32 Jessie Tuggle	.08	.25
33 Bob Whitfield	.08	.25
34 Peter Boulware	.08	.25
35 Jay Graham	.08	.25
36 Eric Green	.08	.25
37 Jim Harbaugh	.15	.40
38 Michael Jackson	.08	.25
39 Jermaine Lewis	.15	.40
40 Ray Lewis	.25	.60
41 Michael McCrary	.08	.25
42 Stevon Moore	.08	.25
43 Jonathan Ogden	.08	.25
44 Errict Rhett	.15	.40
45 Matt Stover	.08	.25
46 Rod Woodson	.15	.40
47 Eric Zeier	.15	.40
48 Ruben Brown	.08	.25
49 Steve Christie	.08	.25
50 Quinn Early	.08	.25
51 John Fina	.08	.25
52 Doug Flutie	.25	.60
53 Phil Hansen	.08	.25
54 Lonnie Johnson	.08	.25
55 Rob Johnson	.15	.40
56 Henry Jones	.08	.25
57 Eric Moulds	.25	.60
58 Andre Reed	.15	.40
59 Antowain Smith	.25	.60
60 Bruce Smith	.15	.40
61 Thurman Thomas	.25	.60
62 Ted Washington	.08	.25
63 Michael Bates	.08	.25
64 Tim Biakabutuka	.15	.40
65 Blake Brockermeyer	.08	.25
66 Mark Carrier	.08	.25
67 Rae Carruth	.08	.25
68 Kerry Collins	.15	.40
69 Doug Evans	.08	.25
70 William Floyd	.08	.25
71 Sean Gilbert	.08	.25
72 Rocket Ismail	.08	.25
73 John Kasay	.08	.25
74 Fred Lane	.08	.25
75 Lamar Lathon	.08	.25
76 Muhsin Muhammad	.15	.40
77 Wesley Walls	.15	.40
78 Edgar Bennett	.08	.25
79 Tom Carter	.08	.25
80 Curtis Conway	.15	.40
81 Bobby Engram	.15	.40
82 Curtis Enis RC	.30	.75
83 Jim Flanigan	.08	.25
84 Walt Harris	.08	.25
85 Jeff Jaeger	.08	.25
86 Erik Kramer	.08	.25
87 John Mangum	.08	.25
88 Glyn Milburn	.08	.25
89 Barry Minter	.08	.25
90 Chris Penn	.08	.25
91 Todd Sauerbrun	.08	.25
92 James Williams	.08	.25
93 Ashley Ambrose	.08	.25
94 Willie Anderson	.08	.25
95 Eric Bieniemy	.08	.25
96 Jeff Blake	.15	.40
97 Ki-Jana Carter	.08	.25
98 John Copeland	.08	.25
99 Corey Dillon	.25	.60
100 Tony McGee	.08	.25
101 Neil O'Donnell	.15	.40
102 Carl Pickens	.15	.40
103 Kevin Sargent	.08	.25
104 Darnay Scott	.15	.40
105 Takeo Spikes RC	.60	1.50
106 Troy Aikman	.50	1.25
107 Larry Allen	.08	.25
108 Eric Bjornson	.08	.25
109 Billy Davis	.08	.25
110 Jason Garrett RC	.50	1.25
111 Michael Irvin	.25	.60
112 Daryl Johnston	.15	.40
113 David LaFleur	.08	.25
114 Everett McIver	.08	.25
115 Ernie Mills	.08	.25
116 Nate Newton	.08	.25
117 Deion Sanders	.25	.60
118 Emmitt Smith	.75	2.00
119 Kevin Smith	.08	.25
120 Erik Williams	.08	.25
121 Steve Atwater	.08	.25
122 Tyrone Braxton	.08	.25
123 Ray Crockett	.08	.25
124 Terrell Davis	.25	.60
125 Jason Elam	.08	.25
126 John Elway	1.00	2.50
127 Willie Green	.08	.25
128 Brian Griese RC	1.25	3.00
129 Tony Jones	.08	.25
130 Ed McCaffrey	.15	.40
131 John Mobley	.08	.25
132 Tom Nalen	.08	.25
133 Marcus Nash RC	.30	.75
134 Bill Romanowski	.08	.25
135 Shannon Sharpe	.15	.40
136 Neil Smith	.15	.40
137 Rod Smith	.15	.40
138 Keith Traylor	.08	.25
139 Stephen Boyd	.08	.25
140 Mark Carrier DB	.08	.25
141 Charlie Batch RC	.60	1.50
142 Jason Hanson	.08	.25
143 Scott Mitchell	.15	.40
144 Herman Moore	.15	.40
145 Johnnie Morton	.15	.40
146 Robert Porcher	.08	.25
147 Ron Rivers	.08	.25
148 Barry Sanders	.75	2.00
149 Tracy Scroggins	.08	.25
150 David Sloan	.08	.25
151 Tommy Vardell	.08	.25
152 Kerwin Waldroup	.08	.25
153 Bryant Westbrook	.08	.25
154 Robert Brooks	.15	.40
155 Gilbert Brown	.08	.25
156 LeRoy Butler	.08	.25
157 Mark Chmura	.15	.40
158 Earl Dotson	.08	.25
159 Santana Dotson	.08	.25
160 Brett Favre	1.00	2.50
161 Antonio Freeman	.25	.60
162 Raymont Harris	.08	.25
163 William Henderson	.15	.40
164 Vonnie Holliday RC	.50	1.25
165 George Koonce	.08	.25
166 Dorsey Levens	.25	.60
167 Derrick Mayes	.15	.40
168 Craig Newsome	.08	.25
169 Ross Verba	.08	.25
170 Reggie White	.25	.60
171 Elijah Alexander	.08	.25
172 Aaron Bailey	.08	.25
173 Jason Belser	.08	.25
174 Robert Blackmon	.08	.25
175 Zack Crockett	.08	.25
176 Ken Dilger	.08	.25
177 Marshall Faulk	.30	.75
178 Tarik Glenn	.08	.25
179 Marvin Harrison	.25	.60
180 Tony Mandarich	.08	.25
181 Peyton Manning RC	8.00	20.00
182 Marcus Pollard	.08	.25
183 Lamont Warren	.08	.25
184 Tavian Banks RC	.50	1.25
185 Reggie Barlow	.08	.25
186 Tony Boselli	.08	.25
187 Tony Brackens	.08	.25
188 Mark Brunell	.25	.60
189 Kevin Hardy	.08	.25
190 Mike Hollis	.08	.25
191 Jeff Lageman	.08	.25
192 Keenan McCardell	.15	.40
193 Pete Mitchell	.08	.25
194 Bryce Paup	.08	.25
195 Leon Searcy	.08	.25
196 Jimmy Smith	.15	.40
197 James Stewart	.15	.40
198 Fred Taylor RC	1.00	2.50
199 Renaldo Wynn	.08	.25
200 Derrick Alexander WR	.15	.40
201 Kimble Anders	.15	.40
202 Donnell Bennett	.08	.25
203 Dale Carter	.08	.25
204 Anthony Davis	.08	.25
205 Rich Gannon	.25	.60
206 Tony Gonzalez	.25	.60
207 Elvis Grbac	.15	.40
208 James Hasty	.08	.25
209 Leslie O'Neal	.08	.25
210 Andre Rison	.15	.40
211 Rashaan Shehee RC	.50	1.25
212 Will Shields	.08	.25
213 Pete Stoyanovich	.08	.25
214 Derrick Thomas	.25	.60
215 Tamarick Vanover	.08	.25
216 Karim Abdul-Jabbar	.25	.60
217 Trace Armstrong	.08	.25
218 John Avery RC	.50	1.25
219 Tim Bowens	.08	.25
220 Terrell Buckley	.08	.25
221 Troy Drayton	.08	.25
222 Daryl Gardener	.08	.25
223 Damon Huard RC	1.25	3.00
224 Charles Jordan	.08	.25
225 Dan Marino	1.00	2.50
226 O.J. McDuffie	.15	.40
227 Bernie Parmalee	.08	.25
228 Stanley Pritchett	.08	.25
229 Derrick Rodgers	.08	.25
230 Lamar Thomas	.08	.25
231 Zach Thomas	.25	.60
232 Richmond Webb	.08	.25
233 Derrick Alexander DE	.08	.25
234 Jerry Ball	.08	.25
235 Cris Carter	.25	.60
236 Randall Cunningham	.25	.60
237 Charles Evans	.08	.25
238 Corey Fuller	.08	.25
239 Andrew Glover	.08	.25
240 Leroy Hoard	.08	.25
241 Brad Johnson	.25	.60
242 Ed McDaniel	.08	.25
243 Randall McDaniel	.08	.25
244 Randy Moss RC	4.00	10.00
245 John Randle	.15	.40
246 Jake Reed	.15	.40
247 Dwayne Rudd	.08	.25
248 Robert Smith	.25	.60
249 Bruce Armstrong	.08	.25
250 Drew Bledsoe	.40	1.00
251 Vincent Brisby	.08	.25
252 Tedy Bruschi	.50	1.25
253 Ben Coates	.15	.40
254 Derrick Cullors	.08	.25
255 Terry Glenn	.25	.60
256 Shawn Jefferson	.08	.25
257 Ted Johnson	.08	.25
258 Ty Law	.15	.40
259 Willie McGinest	.08	.25
260 Lawyer Milloy	.15	.40
261 Sedrick Shaw	.08	.25
262 Chris Slade	.08	.25
263 Troy Davis	.08	.25
264 Mark Fields	.08	.25
265 Andre Hastings	.08	.25
266 Billy Joe Hobert	.08	.25
267 Qadry Ismail	.15	.40
268 Tony Johnson	.08	.25
269 Sammy Knight RC	.25	.60
270 Wayne Martin	.08	.25
271 Chris Naeole	.08	.25
272 Keith Poole	.08	.25
273 William Roaf	.08	.25
274 Pio Sagapolutele	.08	.25
275 Danny Wuerffel	.15	.40
276 Ray Zellars	.08	.25
277 Jessie Armstead	.08	.25
278 Tiki Barber	.25	.60
279 Chris Calloway	.08	.25
280 Percy Ellsworth	.08	.25
281 Sam Garnes RC	.30	.75
282 Kent Graham	.08	.25
283 Ike Hilliard	.15	.40
284 Danny Kanell	.15	.40
285 Corey Miller	.08	.25
286 Phillippi Sparks	.08	.25
287 Michael Strahan	.15	.40
288 Amani Toomer	.15	.40
289 Charles Way	.08	.25
290 Tyrone Wheatley	.15	.40
291 Tito Wooten	.08	.25
292 Kyle Brady	.08	.25
293 Keith Byars	.08	.25
294 Wayne Chrebet	.25	.60
295 John Elliott	.08	.25
296 Glenn Foley	.15	.40
297 Aaron Glenn	.08	.25
298 Keyshawn Johnson	.25	.60
299 Curtis Martin	.25	.60
300 Otis Smith	.08	.25
301 Vinny Testaverde	.15	.40
302 Alex Van Dyke	.08	.25
303 Dedric Ward	.08	.25
304 Greg Biekert	.08	.25
305 Tim Brown	.25	.60
306 Rickey Dudley	.08	.25
307 Jeff George	.15	.40
308 Pat Harlow	.08	.25
309 Desmond Howard	.15	.40
310 James Jett	.15	.40
311 Napoleon Kaufman	.25	.60
312 Lincoln Kennedy	.08	.25
313 Russell Maryland	.08	.25
314 Darrell Russell	.08	.25
315 Eric Turner	.08	.25
316 Steve Wisniewski	.08	.25
317 Charles Woodson RC	1.50	4.00
318 James Darling RC	.30	.75
319 Jason Dunn	.08	.25
320 Irving Fryar	.15	.40
321 Charlie Garner	.15	.40
322 Jeff Graham	.08	.25
323 Bobby Hoying	.15	.40
324 Chad Lewis	.15	.40
325 Rodney Peete	.08	.25
326 Freddie Solomon	.08	.25
327 Duce Staley	.30	.75
328 Bobby Taylor	.08	.25
329 William Thomas	.08	.25
330 Kevin Turner	.08	.25
331 Troy Vincent	.08	.25
332 Jerome Bettis	.25	.60
333 Will Blackwell	.08	.25
334 Mark Bruener	.08	.25
335 Andre Coleman	.08	.25
336 Dermontti Dawson	.20	.50
337 Jason Gildon	.08	.25
338 Courtney Hawkins	.08	.25
339 Charles Johnson	.08	.25
340 Levon Kirkland	.08	.25
341 Carnell Lake	.08	.25
342 Tim Lester	.08	.25
343 Joel Steed	.08	.25
344 Kordell Stewart	.25	.60
345 Will Wolford	.08	.25
346 Tony Banks	.15	.40
347 Isaac Bruce	.25	.60
348 Ernie Conwell	.08	.25
349 D'Marco Farr	.08	.25
350 Wayne Gandy	.08	.25
351 Jerome Pathon RC	.60	1.50
352 Eddie Kennison	.15	.40
353 Amp Lee	.08	.25
354 Keith Lyle	.08	.25
355 Ryan McNeil	.08	.25
356 Jerald Moore	.08	.25
357 Orlando Pace	.08	.25
358 Roman Phifer	.08	.25
359 David Thompson RC	.30	.75
360 Darren Bennett	.08	.25
361 John Carney	.08	.25
362 Marco Coleman	.08	.25
363 Terrell Fletcher	.08	.25
364 William Fuller	.08	.25
365 Charlie Jones	.08	.25
366 Freddie Jones	.08	.25
367 Ryan Leaf RC	.60	1.50
368 Natrone Means	.15	.40
369 Junior Seau	.25	.60
370 Terrance Shaw	.08	.25
371 Tremayne Stephens RC	.30	.75
372 Bryan Still	.08	.25
373 Aaron Taylor	.08	.25
374 Greg Clark	.08	.25
375 Ty Detmer	.15	.40
376 Jim Druckenmiller	.08	.25
377 Marc Edwards	.08	.25
378 Merton Hanks	.08	.25
379 Garrison Hearst	.25	.60
380 Chuck Levy	.08	.25
381 Ken Norton	.08	.25
382 Terrell Owens	.25	.60
383 Marquez Pope	.08	.25
384 Jerry Rice	.50	1.25
385 Irv Smith	.08	.25
386 J.J. Stokes	.15	.40
387 Iheanyi Uwaezuoke	.08	.25
388 Bryant Young	.08	.25
389 Steve Young	.30	.75
390 Sam Adams	.08	.25
391 Chad Brown	.08	.25
392 Christian Fauria	.08	.25
393 Joey Galloway	.15	.40
394 Ahman Green RC	1.50	4.00
395 Walter Jones	.08	.25
396 Cortez Kennedy	.08	.25
397 Jon Kitna	.25	.60
398 James McKnight	.25	.60
399 Warren Moon	.25	.60
400 Mike Pritchard	.08	.25
401 Michael Sinclair	.08	.25
402 Shawn Springs	.08	.25
403 Ricky Watters	.15	.40
404 Darryl Williams	.08	.25
405 Mike Alstott	.25	.60
406 Reidel Anthony	.15	.40
407 Derrick Brooks	.25	.60
408 Brad Culpepper	.08	.25
409 Trent Dilfer	.25	.60
410 Warrick Dunn	.25	.60
411 Bert Emanuel	.15	.40
412 Jacquez Green RC	.50	1.25
413 Paul Gruber	.08	.25
414 Patrick Hape RC	.50	1.25
415 Dave Moore	.08	.25
416 Hardy Nickerson	.08	.25
417 Warren Sapp	.15	.40
418 Robb Thomas	.08	.25
419 Regan Upshaw	.08	.25
420 Karl Williams	.08	.25
421 Blaine Bishop	.08	.25
422 Anthony Cook	.08	.25
423 Willie Davis	.08	.25
424 Al Del Greco	.08	.25
425 Kevin Dyson	.25	.60
426 Henry Ford	.08	.25
427 Eddie George	.25	.60
428 Jackie Harris	.08	.25
429 Steve McNair	.25	.60
430 Chris Sanders	.08	.25
431 Mark Stepnoski	.08	.25
432 Yancey Thigpen	.08	.25
433 Barron Wortham	.08	.25
434 Frank Wycheck	.08	.25
435 Stephen Alexander RC	.50	1.25
436 Terry Allen	.25	.60
437 Jamie Asher	.08	.25
438 Bob Dahl	.08	.25
439 Stephen Davis	.08	.25
440 Cris Dishman	.08	.25
441 Gus Frerotte	.08	.25
442 Darrell Green	.15	.40
443 Trent Green	.30	.75
444 Ken Harvey	.08	.25
445 Skip Hicks RC	.50	1.25
446 Jeff Hostetler	.08	.25
447 Brian Mitchell	.08	.25
448 Leslie Shepherd	.08	.25
449 Michael Westbrook	.15	.40
450 Dan Wilkinson	.08	.25
S1 Warrick Dunn Sample	.40	1.00

1998 Pacific Platinum Blue

*STARS: 8X TO 20X BASIC CARDS
*ROOKIES: 2.5X TO 6X BASIC CARDS
STATED ODDS 1:73 HOB/RET

1998 Pacific Red

COMPLETE SET (450)	100.00	200.00
*STARS: 1.2X TO 3X BASIC CARDS		
*RC'S: .5X TO 1X BASIC CARDS		
ONE PER SPECIAL RETAIL PACK		

1998 Pacific Cramer's Choice

ndomly inserted in packs at the rate of one in 721, this 10-card set features color action images of players selected by Pacific President/CEO, Michael Cramer, printed on dual-foiled, die-cut trophy-shaped cards.

COMPLETE SET (10)	75.00	200.00
STATED ODDS 1:721		
1 Terrell Davis	5.00	12.00
2 John Elway	15.00	40.00
3 Barry Sanders	12.50	30.00
4 Brett Favre	15.00	40.00
5 Peyton Manning	30.00	80.00
6 Mark Brunell	4.00	10.00
7 Dan Marino	15.00	40.00
8 Ryan Leaf	4.00	10.00
9 Jerry Rice	8.00	20.00
10 Warrick Dunn	4.00	10.00

1998 Pacific Dynagon Turf

Randomly inserted in packs at the rate of four in 37, this 20-card set features color action images of top players silhouetted on a mirror-patterned full-foil background. A limited addition Titanium parallel set was also produced and numbered to just 99.

COMPLETE SET (20)	50.00	100.00
STATED ODDS 4:37		
*TITANIUM/99: 2.5X TO 6X BASIC INSERT		
TITANIUM STATED PRINT RUN 99		
1 Corey Dillon	1.25	3.00
2 Troy Aikman	2.50	6.00
3 Emmitt Smith	4.00	10.00
4 Terrell Davis	1.25	3.00
5 John Elway	5.00	12.00
6 Barry Sanders	4.00	10.00
7 Brett Favre	5.00	12.00
8 Peyton Manning	10.00	25.00
9 Mark Brunell	1.25	3.00
10 Dan Marino	5.00	12.00
11 Drew Bledsoe	2.00	5.00
12 Curtis Martin	1.25	3.00
13 Napoleon Kaufman	1.25	3.00
14 Jerome Bettis	1.25	3.00
15 Kordell Stewart	1.25	3.00
16 Ryan Leaf	1.00	2.50
17 Jerry Rice	2.50	6.00
18 Steve Young	1.50	4.00
19 Warrick Dunn	1.25	3.00
20 Eddie George	1.25	3.00

1998 Pacific Gold Crown Die Cuts

ndomly inserted in packs at the rate of one in 37, this 36-card set features color action player images printed on 24-pt. crown die-cut cards.

COMPLETE SET (36)	50.00	120.00
STATED ODDS 1:37		
1 Jake Plummer	1.50	4.00
2 Antowain Smith	1.00	2.50
3 Curtis Enis	.50	1.25
4 Corey Dillon	1.50	4.00
5 Troy Aikman	3.00	8.00
6 Deion Sanders	1.50	4.00
7 Emmitt Smith	5.00	12.00
8 Terrell Davis	1.50	4.00
9 John Elway	6.00	15.00
10 Barry Sanders	5.00	12.00
11 Brett Favre	6.00	15.00
12 Dorsey Levens	.50	1.25
13 Marshall Faulk	1.50	4.00
14 Peyton Manning	12.00	30.00
15 Mark Brunell	1.50	4.00
16 Fred Taylor	1.50	4.00
17 Derrick Thomas	1.50	4.00
18 Dan Marino	6.00	15.00
19 Brad Johnson	1.00	2.50
20 Robert Smith	.50	1.25
21 Drew Bledsoe	1.50	4.00
22 Glenn Foley	.50	1.25
23 Curtis Martin	1.50	4.00
24 Napoleon Kaufman	1.00	2.50
25 Charles Woodson	2.00	5.00
26 Jerome Bettis	1.50	4.00
27 Kordell Stewart	1.50	4.00
28 Ryan Leaf	.50	1.25
29 Garrison Hearst	1.00	2.50
30 Jerry Rice	3.00	8.00
31 J.J. Stokes	.50	1.25
32 Steve Young	2.00	5.00
33 Joey Galloway	1.00	2.50
34 Ricky Watters	1.00	2.50
35 Warrick Dunn	1.50	4.00
36 Eddie George	1.50	4.00

1998 Pacific Team Checklists

Randomly inserted in packs at the rate of two in 37, this 30-cards set features color action photos of top players from each of the 30 1998 NFL teams. The backs carry the pictured player's team checklist for the base set.

COMPLETE SET (30)	75.00	150.00
STATED ODDS 2:37		
1 Jake Plummer	2.00	5.00
2 Jamal Anderson	2.00	5.00

3 Eric Zeier 1.25 3.00
4 Rob Johnson 1.25 3.00
5 Fred Lane .75 2.00
6 Curtis Enis .60 1.50
7 Corey Dillon 2.00 5.00
8 Troy Aikman 4.00 10.00
9 John Elway 8.00 20.00
10 Barry Sanders 6.00 15.00
11 Brett Favre 8.00 20.00
12 Peyton Manning 15.00 30.00
13 Mark Brunell 2.00 5.00
14 Elvis Grbac 1.25 3.00
15 Dan Marino 8.00 20.00
16 Robert Smith 2.00 5.00
17 Drew Bledsoe 3.00 8.00
18 Danny Wuerffel 1.25 3.00
19 Tiki Barber 2.00 5.00
20 Curtis Martin 2.00 5.00
21 Napoleon Kaufman 2.00 5.00
22 Duce Staley 2.50 6.00
23 Kordell Stewart 2.00 5.00
24 Tony Banks 1.25 3.00
25 Ryan Leaf 1.25 3.00
26 Jerry Rice 4.00 10.00
27 Warren Moon 2.00 5.00
28 Warrick Dunn 2.00 5.00
29 Eddie George 2.00 5.00
30 Terry Allen 2.00 5.00

1998 Pacific Timelines

Randomly inserted in hobby packs only at the rate of one in 181, this 20-card hobby set features color action player photos with player information on the back.

COMPLETE SET (20) 125.00 300.00
STATED ODDS 1:181 HOBBY
1 Troy Aikman 8.00 20.00
2 Deion Sanders 4.00 10.00
3 Emmitt Smith 12.50 30.00
4 Terrell Davis 4.00 10.00
5 John Elway 15.00 40.00
6 Barry Sanders 12.50 30.00
7 Brett Favre 15.00 40.00
8 Peyton Manning 40.00 80.00
9 Mark Brunell 4.00 10.00
10 Dan Marino 15.00 40.00
11 Drew Bledsoe 6.00 15.00
12 Curtis Martin 4.00 10.00
13 Jerome Bettis 4.00 10.00
14 Kordell Stewart 4.00 10.00
15 Ryan Leaf 3.00 8.00
16 Jerry Rice 8.00 20.00
17 Steve Young 5.00 12.00
18 Ricky Watters 2.50 6.00
19 Warrick Dunn 4.00 10.00
20 Eddie George 4.00 10.00

1999 Pacific

The 1999 Pacific set was issued in one series totalling 450 cards and was distributed in 12-card packs with a suggested retail price of $2.49. The fronts feature color action player photos. The backs carry player information and career statistics.

COMPLETE SET (450) 30.00 80.00
1 Mario Bates .15 .40
2 Larry Centers .15 .40
3 Chris Gedney .15 .40
4 Kwamie Lassiter RC .25 .60
5 Johnny McWilliams .15 .40
6 Eric Metcalf .15 .40
7 Rob Moore .15 .40
8 Adrian Murrell .15 .40
9 Jake Plummer .15 .40
10 Simeon Rice .15 .40
11 Frank Sanders .15 .40
12 Andre Wadsworth .15 .40
13 Aeneas Williams .15 .40
14 M.Pittman/R.Anderson RC .25 .60
15 Morten Andersen .15 .40
16 Jamal Anderson .20 .50
17 Lester Archambeau .15 .40
18 Chris Chandler .20 .50
19 Bob Christian .15 .40
20 Steve DeBerg .15 .40
21 Tim Dwight .20 .50
22 Tony Martin .20 .50
23 Terance Mathis .15 .40
24 Eugene Robinson .20 .50
25 O.J. Santiago .15 .40
26 Chuck Smith .15 .40
27 Jessie Tuggle .15 .40
28 Jammi German .15 .40
Ken Oxendine
29 Peter Boulware .15 .40
30 Jay Graham .15 .40
31 Jim Harbaugh .20 .50
32 Priest Holmes .15 .40
33 Michael Jackson .15 .40
34 Jermaine Lewis .15 .40
35 Ray Lewis .25 .60
36 Michael McCrary .15 .40
37 Jonathan Ogden .20 .50
38 Errict Rhett .15 .40
39 James Roe RC .25 .60
40 Floyd Turner .15 .40
41 Rod Woodson .25 .60
42 Eric Zeier .15 .40
43 Wally Richardson .15 .40
Patrick Johnson
44 Ruben Brown .15 .40
45 Quinn Early .15 .40
46 Doug Flutie .25 .60
47 Sam Gash .15 .40
48 Phil Hansen .15 .40
49 Lonnie Johnson .15 .40
50 Rob Johnson .20 .50
51 Eric Moulds .15 .40
52 Andre Reed .25 .60
53 Jay Riemersma .15 .40
54 Antowain Smith .15 .40
55 Bruce Smith .20 .50
56 Thurman Thomas .20 .50
57 Ted Washington .15 .40
58 J.Linton/Kamil Loud RC .25 .60
59 Michael Bates .15 .40
60 Steve Beuerlein .20 .50
61 Tim Biakabutuka .20 .50
62 Mark Carrier WR .20 .50
63 Eric Davis .15 .40
64 William Floyd .20 .50
65 Sean Gilbert .15 .40
66 Kevin Greene .25 .60
67 Rocket Ismail .20 .50
68 Anthony Johnson .15 .40
69 Fred Lane .15 .40
70 Muhsin Muhammad .15 .40
71 Winslow Oliver .15 .40
72 Wesley Walls .20 .50
73 D.Craig RC/S.Matthews .40 1.00
74 Edgar Bennett .20 .50
75 Curtis Conway .20 .50
76 Bobby Engram .15 .40
77 Curtis Enis .15 .40
78 Ty Hallock RC .25 .60
79 Walt Harris .15 .40
80 Jeff Jaeger .15 .40
81 Erik Kramer .20 .50
82 Glyn Milburn .15 .40
83 Chris Penn .15 .40
84 Steve Stenstrom .15 .40
85 Ryan Wetnight .15 .40
86 J.Allen RC/m.Moreno .30 .75
87 Ashley Ambrose .15 .40
88 Brandon Bennett RC .25 .60
89 Eric Bieniemy .15 .40
90 Jeff Blake .20 .50
91 Corey Dillon .15 .40
92 Paul Justin .15 .40
93 Eric Kresser RC .25 .60
94 Tremain Mack .15 .40
95 Tony McGee .15 .40
96 Neil O'Donnell .20 .50
97 Carl Pickens .20 .50
98 Darnay Scott .15 .40
99 Takeo Spikes .15 .40
100 Ty Detmer .15 .40
101 Chris Gardocki .15 .40
102 Damon Gibson .15 .40
103 Antonio Langham .15 .40
104 Jerris McPhail .15 .40
105 Irv Smith .15 .40
106 Freddie Solomon .15 .40
107 S.Milanovich/F.Brock RC .25 .60
108 Troy Aikman .30 .75
109 Larry Allen .25 .60
110 Eric Bjornson .15 .40
111 Billy Davis .15 .40
112 Michael Irvin .25 .60
113 David LaFleur .15 .40
114 Ernie Mills .15 .40
115 Nate Newton .20 .50
116 Deion Sanders .20 .50
117 Emmitt Smith .40 1.00
118 Chris Warren .20 .50
119 Bubby Brister .15 .40
120 Terrell Davis .20 .50
121 Jason Elam .15 .40
122 John Elway .40 1.00
123 Willie Green .15 .40
124 Howard Griffith .15 .40
125 Vaughn Hebron .15 .40
126 Ed McCaffrey .20 .50
127 John Mobley .15 .40
128 Bill Romanowski .20 .50
129 Shannon Sharpe .20 .50
130 Neil Smith .15 .40
131 Rod Smith .20 .50
132 B.Griese/M.Nash .15 .40
133 Charlie Batch .15 .40
134 Stephen Boyd .15 .40
135 Mark Carrier DB .15 .40
136 Germane Crowell .15 .40
137 Terry Fair .15 .40
138 Jason Hanson .15 .40
139 Greg Jeffries RC .25 .60
140 Herman Moore .20 .50
141 Johnnie Morton .20 .50
142 Robert Porcher .15 .40
143 Ron Rivers .15 .40
144 Barry Sanders .40 1.00
145 Tommy Vardell .20 .50
146 Bryant Westbrook .15 .40
147 Robert Brooks .20 .50
148 LeRoy Butler .20 .50
149 Mark Chmura .15 .40
150 Tyrone Davis .15 .40
151 Brett Favre .50 1.25
152 Antonio Freeman .20 .50
153 Raymont Harris .20 .50
154 Vonnie Holliday .15 .40
155 Darick Holmes .15 .40
156 Dorsey Levens .20 .50
157 Brian Manning .15 .40
158 Derrick Mayes .15 .40
159 Roell Preston .15 .40
160 Jeff Thomason .15 .40
161 Tyrone Williams .20 .50
162 C.Bradford/M.Blair RC .30 .75
163 Aaron Bailey .15 .40
164 Ken Dilger .15 .40
165 Marshall Faulk .20 .50
166 E.G. Green .15 .40
167 Marvin Harrison .20 .50
168 Craig Heyward .20 .50
169 Peyton Manning .75 2.00
170 Jerome Pathon .15 .40
171 Marcus Pollard .15 .40
172 Torrance Small .15 .40
173 Mike Vanderjagt .15 .40
174 Lamont Warren .20 .50
175 Tavian Banks .15 .40
176 Reggie Barlow .15 .40
177 Tony Boselli .20 .50
178 Tony Brackens .15 .40
179 Mark Brunell .20 .50
180 Kevin Hardy .15 .40
181 Damon Jones .15 .40
182 Jamie Martin .15 .40
183 Keenan McCardell .20 .50
184 Pete Mitchell .15 .40
185 Bryce Paup .15 .40
186 Jimmy Smith .20 .50
187 Fred Taylor .15 .40
188 A.Whitted/C.Howard .15 .40
189 Derrick Alexander WR .15 .40
190 Kimble Anders .15 .40
191 Donnell Bennett .15 .40
192 Dale Carter .15 .40
193 Rich Gannon .20 .50
194 Tony Gonzalez .20 .50
195 Elvis Grbac .15 .40
196 Joe Horn .15 .40
197 Kevin Lockett .15 .40
198 Byron Bam Morris .15 .40
199 Andre Rison .20 .50
200 Derrick Thomas .25 .60
201 Tamarick Vanover .20 .50
202 Gregory Favors .15 .40
Rashaan Shehee
203 Karim Abdul-Jabbar .15 .40
204 Trace Armstrong .15 .40
205 John Avery .15 .40
206 Lorenzo Bromell RC .25 .60
207 Terrell Buckley .20 .50
208 Oronde Gadsden .15 .40
209 Sam Madison .15 .40
210 Dan Marino .50 1.25
211 O.J. McDuffie .20 .50
212 Ed Perry RC .25 .60
213 Jason Taylor .20 .50
214 Lamar Thomas .15 .40
215 Zach Thomas .20 .50
216 H.Lusk/Nate Jacquet RC .25 .60
217 T.Doxzon RC/D.Huard .25 .60
218 Gary Anderson .15 .40
219 Cris Carter .25 .60
220 Randall Cunningham .20 .50
221 Andrew Glover .15 .40
222 Matthew Hatchette .20 .50
223 Brad Johnson .20 .50
224 Ed McDaniel .15 .40
225 Randall McDaniel .25 .60
226 Randy Moss .20 .50
227 David Palmer .15 .40
228 John Randle .25 .60
229 Jake Reed .20 .50
230 Robert Smith .15 .40
231 Todd Steussie .15 .40
232 S.Colinet RC/K.Mays .25 .60
233 J.Fiedler RC/Bouman RC .40 1.00
234 Drew Bledsoe .20 .50
235 Troy Brown .15 .40
236 Ben Coates .20 .50
237 Derrick Cullors .15 .40
238 Robert Edwards .15 .40
239 Terry Glenn .20 .50
240 Shawn Jefferson .15 .40
241 Ty Law .25 .60
242 Lawyer Milloy .15 .40
243 Lovett Purnell RC .25 .60
244 Sedrick Shaw .15 .40
245 Tony Simmons .15 .40
246 Chris Slade .15 .40
247 R.Rutledge/Anth.Ladd RC .25 .60
248 Chris Floyd .15 .40
Harold Shaw
249 Ink Aleaga RC .25 .60
250 Cameron Cleeland .15 .40
251 Kerry Collins .15 .40
252 Troy Davis .15 .40
253 Sean Dawkins .15 .40
254 Mark Fields .15 .40
255 Andre Hastings .15 .40
256 Sammy Knight .15 .40
257 Keith Poole .15 .40
258 William Roaf .15 .40
259 Lamar Smith .15 .40
260 Danny Wuerffel .20 .50
261 J.Wilcox RC/B.Bech RC .25 .60
262 C.Bordano RC/W.Perry .25 .60
263 Jessie Armstead .20 .50
264 Tiki Barber .20 .50
265 Chad Bratzke .15 .40
266 Gary Brown .15 .40
267 Chris Calloway .15 .40
268 Howard Cross .15 .40
269 Kent Graham .15 .40
270 Ike Hilliard .15 .40
271 Danny Kanell .15 .40
272 Michael Strahan .20 .50
273 Amani Toomer .15 .40
274 Charles Way .15 .40
275 G.Comella RC/M.Cherry .25 .60
276 Kyle Brady .15 .40
277 Keith Byars .15 .40
278 Chad Cascadden .20 .50
279 Wayne Chrebet .15 .40
280 Bryan Cox .20 .50
281 Glenn Foley .15 .40
282 Aaron Glenn .15 .40
283 Keyshawn Johnson .20 .50
284 Leon Johnson .15 .40
285 Mo Lewis .15 .40
286 Curtis Martin .20 .50
287 Otis Smith .15 .40
288 Vinny Testaverde .15 .40
289 Dedric Ward .15 .40
290 Tim Brown .25 .60
291 Rickey Dudley .15 .40
292 Jeff George .15 .40
293 Desmond Howard .20 .50
294 James Jett .15 .40
295 Lance Johnstone .15 .40
296 Randy Jordan .15 .40
297 Napoleon Kaufman .15 .40
298 Lincoln Kennedy .15 .40
299 Terry Mickens .15 .40
300 Darrell Russell .15 .40
301 Harvey Williams .15 .40
302 Ch.Woodson/J.Ritchie .25 .60
303 R.Williams/J.Williams RC .25 .60
304 Koy Detmer .15 .40
305 Hugh Douglas .20 .50
306 Jason Dunn .15 .40
307 Irving Fryar .20 .50
308 Charlie Garner .20 .50
309 Jeff Graham .15 .40
310 Bobby Hoying .15 .40
311 Rodney Peete .20 .50
312 Allen Rossum .20 .50
313 Duce Staley .15 .40
314 William Thomas .15 .40
315 Kevin Turner .15 .40
316 K.Sinceno RC/C.Walker RC .25 .60
317 Jahine Arnold .15 .40
318 Jerome Bettis .25 .60
319 Will Blackwell .15 .40
320 Mark Bruener .15 .40
321 Dermontti Dawson .20 .50
322 Chris Fuamatu-Ma'afala .15 .40
323 Courtney Hawkins .15 .40
324 Richard Huntley .15 .40
325 Charles Johnson .15 .40
326 Levon Kirkland .15 .40
327 Kordell Stewart .15 .40
328 Hines Ward .20 .50
329 Dewayne Washington .15 .40
330 Tony Banks .20 .50
331 Steve Bono .15 .40
332 Isaac Bruce .25 .60
333 June Henley RC .25 .60
334 Robert Holcombe .15 .40
335 Mike Jones LB .15 .40
336 Eddie Kennison .20 .50
337 Amp Lee .15 .40
338 Jerald Moore .15 .40
339 Ricky Proehl .15 .40
340 J.T. Thomas .15 .40
341 Derrick Harris .15 .40
Az-Zahir Hakim
342 Roland Williams .15 .40
Grant Wistrom
343 Kurt Warner RC/Horne 5.00 12.00
344 Terrell Fletcher .15 .40
345 Greg Jackson .15 .40
346 Charlie Jones .15 .40
347 Freddie Jones .15 .40
348 Ryan Leaf .20 .50
349 Natrone Means .20 .50
350 Mikhael Ricks .15 .40
351 Junior Seau .20 .50
352 Bryan Still .15 .40
353 T.Stephens/Thelwell RC .25 .60
354 Greg Clark .15 .40
355 Marc Edwards .20 .50
356 Merton Hanks .15 .40
357 Garrison Hearst .15 .40
358 R.W. McQuarters .15 .40
359 Ken Norton Jr. .15 .40
360 Terrell Owens .20 .50
361 Jerry Rice .60 1.50
362 J.J. Stokes .15 .40
363 Bryant Young .20 .50
364 Steve Young .30 .75
365 Chad Brown .15 .40
366 Christian Fauria .15 .40
367 Joey Galloway .20 .50
368 Ahman Green .20 .50
369 Cortez Kennedy .20 .50
370 Jon Kitna .15 .40
371 James McKnight .15 .40
372 Mike Pritchard .15 .40
373 Michael Sinclair .15 .40
374 Shawn Springs .15 .40
375 Ricky Watters .20 .50
376 Darryl Williams .15 .40
377 R.Wilson/K.Joseph RC .40 1.00
378 Mike Alstott .15 .40
379 Reidel Anthony .15 .40
380 Derrick Brooks .25 .60
381 Trent Dilfer .15 .40
382 Warrick Dunn .15 .40
383 Bert Emanuel .20 .50
384 Jacquez Green .15 .40
385 Patrick Hape .15 .40
386 John Lynch .20 .50
387 Dave Moore .15 .40
388 Hardy Nickerson .15 .40
389 Warren Sapp .20 .50
390 Karl Williams .15 .40
391 Blaine Bishop .15 .40
392 Joe Bowden .15 .40
393 Isaac Byrd RC .25 .60
394 Willie Davis .15 .40
395 Al Del Greco .15 .40
396 Kevin Dyson .15 .40
397 Eddie George .20 .50
398 Jackie Harris .20 .50
399 Dave Krieg .20 .50
400 Steve McNair .20 .50
401 Michael Roan .15 .40
402 Yancey Thigpen .15 .40
403 Frank Wycheck .20 .50
404 Derrick Mason .15 .40
Steve Matthews
405 Stephen Alexander .15 .40
406 Terry Allen .20 .50
407 Jamie Asher .15 .40
408 Stephen Davis .15 .40
409 Darrell Green .25 .60
410 Trent Green .15 .40
411 Skip Hicks .15 .40
412 Brian Mitchell .20 .50
413 Leslie Shepherd .15 .40
414 Michael Westbrook .15 .40
415 T.Hardy/R.Abdullah RC .25 .60
416 C.Thomas RC/M.Quinn RC .30 .75
417 J.Quinn/K.Holcomb RC .40 1.00
418 B.Alford/B.Spence .15 .40
419 A.Haase RC/C.King .25 .60
420 J.Thrash RC/K.Hankton .40 1.00
421 F.Beasley/Itula Mili RC .30 .75
422 Champ Bailey RC .50 1.25
423 D'Wayne Bates RC .25 .60
424 Michael Bishop RC .40 1.00
425 David Boston RC .25 .60
426 Shawn Bryson RC .25 .60
427 Tim Couch RC .30 .75
428 Scott Covington RC .25 .60
429 Daunte Culpepper RC .40 1.00
430 Autry Denson RC .25 .60
431 Troy Edwards RC .25 .60
432 Kevin Faulk RC .25 .60
433 Joe Germaine RC .30 .75
434 Torry Holt RC .50 1.25
435 Brock Huard RC .25 .60
436 Sedrick Irvin RC .25 .60
437 Edgerrin James RC .40 1.00
438 Andy Katzenmoyer RC .30 .75
439 Shaun King RC .25 .60
440 Rob Konrad RC .25 .60
441 Donovan McNabb RC 1.50 4.00
442 Cade McNown RC .25 .60
443 Billy Miller RC .25 .60
444 Dee Miller RC .25 .60
445 Sirr Parker RC .25 .60
446 Peerless Price RC .25 .60
447 Akili Smith RC .25 .60
448 Tai Streets RC .30 .75
449 Ricky Williams RC .40 1.00
450 Amos Zereoue RC .25 .60
S1 Warrick Dunn Sample .25 .60

1999 Pacific Copper

*VETS/99: 8X TO 20X BASIC CARDS
*ROOKIES/99: 5X TO 12X BASIC RC
COPPER PRINT RUN 99 SERIAL #'d SETS
343 Kurt Warner 30.00 80.00
Tony Horne

1999 Pacific Gold

*VETS/199: 6X TO 15X BASIC CARDS
*ROOKIES/199: 4X TO 10X BASIC RC
GOLD PRINT RUN 199 SER.#'d SETS
343 Kurt Warner 25.00 60.00
Tony Horne

1999 Pacific Opening Day

*VETS/45: 12X TO 30X BASIC CARDS
*ROOKIES/45: 8X TO 20X BASIC RC
OPENING DAY PRINT RUN 45 SER.#'d SETS
343 Kurt Warner 75.00 200.00
Tony Horne

1999 Pacific Platinum Blue

ETS/75: 10X TO 25X BASIC CARDS
*ROOKIES/75: 6X TO 15X BASIC RC
PLAT.BLUE PRINT RUN 75 SER.#'d SETS
343 Kurt Warner 40.00 100.00
Tony Horne

1999 Pacific Red

ED VETS: 5X TO 12X BASIC CARDS
*RED ROOKIES: 3X TO 8X
RED STATED ODDS 4:25 SPECIAL RETAIL
343 Kurt Warner 25.00 60.00
Tony Horne

1999 Pacific Cramer's Choice

ndomly inserted in packs, this 10-card set features color action photos of players picked by Pacific President/CEO Michael Cramer printed on a die-cut pyramid-design trophy card. Only 299 serially numbered sets were produced.

COMPLETE SET (10) 75.00 200.00
STATED PRINT RUN 299 SERIAL #'d SETS
1 Jamal Anderson 6.00 15.00
2 Terrell Davis 6.00 15.00
3 John Elway 20.00 50.00
4 Barry Sanders 20.00 50.00
5 Brett Favre 20.00 50.00
6 Peyton Manning 20.00 50.00
7 Fred Taylor 6.00 15.00
8 Dan Marino 20.00 50.00
9 Randall Cunningham 6.00 15.00
10 Randy Moss 15.00 40.00

1999 Pacific Dynagon Turf

ndomly inserted in packs at the rate of two in 25, this 20-card set features color action photos of some of football's greatest stars on a silver full-foil background. A Titanium parallel version numbered of 99 was also produced of each card.

COMPLETE SET (20) 40.00 80.00
STATED ODDS 2:25
*TITANIUM/99: 3X TO 8X BASIC INSERTS
1 Jake Plummer .75 2.00
2 Jamal Anderson 1.25 3.00
3 Doug Flutie 1.25 3.00
4 Emmitt Smith 2.50 6.00
5 Terrell Davis 1.25 3.00
6 John Elway 4.00 10.00
7 Barry Sanders 4.00 10.00
8 Brett Favre 4.00 10.00
9 Peyton Manning 4.00 10.00
10 Mark Brunell 1.25 3.00
11 Fred Taylor 1.25 3.00
12 Dan Marino 4.00 10.00
13 Randall Cunningham 1.25 3.00
14 Randy Moss 3.00 8.00
15 Drew Bledsoe 1.50 4.00
16 Curtis Martin 1.25 3.00
17 Jerome Bettis 1.25 3.00
18 Jerry Rice 2.50 6.00
19 Jon Kitna 1.25 3.00
20 Eddie George 1.25 3.00

1999 Pacific Gold Crown Die Cuts

ndomly inserted in packs at the rate of one in 25, this 36-card set features color action photos of some of football's most elite players printed on dual-foiled die-cut thick 24 pt. card stock.

COMPLETE SET (36) 75.00 200.00
STATED ODDS 1:25
1 Jake Plummer 1.50 4.00
2 Jamal Anderson 2.50 6.00
3 Priest Holmes 4.00 10.00
4 Doug Flutie 2.50 6.00
5 Antowain Smith 2.50 6.00
6 Corey Dillon 2.50 6.00
7 Troy Aikman 5.00 12.00
8 Emmitt Smith 5.00 12.00
9 Terrell Davis 2.50 6.00
10 John Elway 8.00 20.00
11 Brian Griese 2.50 6.00
12 Charlie Batch 2.50 6.00
13 Barry Sanders 8.00 20.00
14 Brett Favre 8.00 20.00
15 Antonio Freeman 2.50 6.00
16 Marshall Faulk 3.00 8.00
17 Peyton Manning 8.00 20.00
18 Mark Brunell 2.50 6.00
19 Fred Taylor 2.50 6.00
20 Dan Marino 8.00 20.00
21 Randall Cunningham 2.50 6.00
22 Randy Moss 6.00 15.00
23 Drew Bledsoe 3.00 8.00
24 Keyshawn Johnson 2.50 6.00
25 Curtis Martin 2.50 6.00
26 Napoleon Kaufman 2.50 6.00
27 Jerome Bettis 2.50 6.00
28 Kordell Stewart 1.50 4.00
29 Terrell Owens 2.50 6.00
30 Jerry Rice 5.00 12.00
31 Steve Young 3.00 8.00
32 Joey Galloway 1.50 4.00
33 Jon Kitna 2.50 6.00
34 Trent Dilfer 2.50 6.00
35 Warrick Dunn 2.50 6.00
36 Eddie George 2.50 6.00

1999 Pacific Pro Bowl Die Cuts

Randomly inserted in packs at the rate of one in 49, this 20-card set features color action photos of 20 of the NFL's Pro Bowlers printed on cards with a die-cut erupting volcano design.

COMPLETE SET (20) 50.00 120.00
STATED ODDS 1:49
1 Jamal Anderson 3.00 8.00
2 Chris Chandler 2.00 5.00
3 Doug Flutie 3.00 8.00
4 Deion Sanders 3.00 8.00
5 Emmitt Smith 6.00 15.00
6 Terrell Davis 3.00 8.00
7 John Elway 10.00 25.00
8 Barry Sanders 10.00 25.00
9 Antonio Freeman 3.00 8.00
10 Marshall Faulk 4.00 10.00
11 Randall Cunningham 3.00 8.00
12 Randy Moss 8.00 20.00
13 Robert Smith 3.00 8.00
14 Ty Law 2.00 5.00
15 Keyshawn Johnson 3.00 8.00
16 Curtis Martin 3.00 8.00
17 Jerry Rice 6.00 15.00
18 Steve Young 4.00 10.00
19 Mike Alstott 3.00 8.00
20 Eddie George 3.00 8.00

1999 Pacific Record Breakers

ndomly inserted in hobby packs only, this 20-card set features color action photos of some of the NFL's top performers printed on full-foil cards. Only 199 serial-numbered sets were produced.

COMPLETE SET (20) 200.00 400.00
STATED PRINT RUN 199 SERIAL #'d SETS
1 Jake Plummer 3.00 8.00
2 Jamal Anderson 5.00 12.00
3 Doug Flutie 5.00 12.00
4 Troy Aikman 10.00 25.00
5 Emmitt Smith 10.00 25.00
6 Terrell Davis 5.00 12.00
7 John Elway 15.00 40.00
8 Barry Sanders 15.00 40.00
9 Brett Favre 15.00 40.00
10 Marshall Faulk 6.00 15.00
11 Peyton Manning 15.00 40.00
12 Mark Brunell 5.00 12.00
13 Fred Taylor 5.00 12.00
14 Dan Marino 15.00 40.00
15 Randall Cunningham 5.00 12.00
16 Randy Moss 12.50 30.00
17 Drew Bledsoe 6.00 15.00
18 Curtis Martin 5.00 12.00
19 Jerry Rice 10.00 25.00
20 Steve Young 6.00 15.00

1999 Pacific Team Checklists

ndomly inserted in packs at the rate of two in 25, this 31-card set features color photos of a top player from each of the 31 NFL teams in 1999 with a holographic silver-foiled NFL logo of his team printed on the card. The backs carry the complete main set checklist for the respective team.

COMPLETE SET (31) 25.00 60.00
STATED ODDS 2:25
1 Jake Plummer .60 1.50
2 Jamal Anderson 1.00 2.50
3 Priest Holmes 1.50 4.00
4 Doug Flutie 1.00 2.50
5 Muhsin Muhammad .60 1.50
6 Curtis Enis .40 1.00
7 Corey Dillon 1.00 2.50
8 Ty Detmer .40 1.00
9 Emmitt Smith 2.00 5.00
10 John Elway 3.00 8.00
11 Barry Sanders 3.00 8.00
12 Brett Favre 3.00 8.00
13 Peyton Manning 3.00 8.00
14 Fred Taylor 1.00 2.50
15 Andre Rison .60 1.50
16 Dan Marino 3.00 8.00
17 Randy Moss 2.50 6.00
18 Drew Bledsoe 1.25 3.00
19 Cameron Cleeland .40 1.00
20 Ike Hilliard .40 1.00
21 Curtis Martin 1.00 2.50
22 Napoleon Kaufman 1.00 2.50
23 Duce Staley 1.00 2.50
24 Jerome Bettis 1.00 2.50
25 Isaac Bruce 1.00 2.50
26 Ryan Leaf 1.00 2.50
27 Steve Young 1.25 3.00
28 Joey Galloway .60 1.50
29 Warrick Dunn 1.00 2.50
30 Eddie George 1.00 2.50
31 Michael Westbrook .60 1.50

1999 Pacific Backyard Football

is set was distributed through the Backyard Football computer software package. The NFL player cards utilize the cardfronts of the base 1999 Pacific football cards with a slightly redesigned cardback and new card number. Additionally, there are 10-unnumbered cards featuring the animated characters from the game.

COMPLETE SET (18) 4.00 10.00
1 Drew Bledsoe .40 1.00
2 Randall Cunningham .30 .75
3 John Elway .80 2.00
4 Brett Favre .80 2.00
5 Dan Marino .80 2.00
6 Jerry Rice .50 1.25
7 Barry Sanders .80 2.00
8 Steve Young .40 1.00
NNO Lisa Crocket .08 .25
NNO Angela Delvecchio .08 .25
NNO Marky Dubois .08 .25
NNO Gretchen Hasselhoff .08 .25
NNO Ricky Johnson .08 .25
NNO Achmed Khan .08 .25
NNO Maria Luna .08 .25
NNO Pablo Sanchez .08 .25
NNO Jocinda Smith .08 .25
NNO Reese Worthington .08 .25

2000 Pacific

Released as a 450-card set, 2000 Pacific consists of 400 regular cards and 50 rookie cards. Cards feature full-color action shots and silver foil highlights. 2000 Pacific was packaged in 36-pack boxes containing 12 cards each and carried a suggested retail price of $2.79.

COMPLETE SET (450) 25.00 60.00
1 Mario Bates .15 .40
2 David Boston .15 .40
3 Rob Fredrickson .15 .40
4 Terry Hardy .15 .40
5 Rob Moore .15 .40
6 Adrian Murrell .15 .40
7 Michael Pittman .15 .40
8 Jake Plummer .15 .40
9 Simeon Rice .20 .50
10 Frank Sanders .15 .40
11 Aeneas Williams .15 .40
12 M.Cody/A.McCullough .15 .40
13 D.McKinley RC/J.Makovicka .15 .40
14 Jamal Anderson .20 .50
15 Chris Calloway .15 .40
16 Chris Chandler .20 .50
17 Bob Christian .15 .40
18 Tim Dwight .20 .50
19 Jammi German .15 .40
20 Ronnie Harris .15 .40
21 Terance Mathis .15 .40
22 Ken Oxendine .15 .40
23 O.J. Santiago .15 .40
24 Bob Whitfield .15 .40
25 E.Baker/R.Kelly .15 .40
26 Justin Armour .15 .40
27 Tony Banks .15 .40
28 Peter Boulware .15 .40
29 Stoney Case .15 .40
30 Priest Holmes .15 .40
31 Qadry Ismail .15 .40
32 Patrick Johnson .15 .40
33 Michael McCrary .15 .40
34 Jonathan Ogden .20 .50
35 Errict Rhett .20 .50
36 Duane Starks .15 .40
37 Doug Flutie .20 .50
38 Rob Johnson .20 .50
39 Jonathan Linton .15 .40
40 Eric Moulds .15 .40
41 Peerless Price .20 .50
42 Andre Reed .25 .60
43 Jay Riemersma .15 .40
44 Antowain Smith .20 .50
45 Bruce Smith .20 .50
46 Thurman Thomas .20 .50
47 Kevin Williams .15 .40
48 B.Collins/S.Jackson .15 .40
49 Michael Bates .15 .40
50 Steve Beuerlein .20 .50
51 Tim Biakabutuka .20 .50
52 Antonio Edwards .15 .40
53 Donald Hayes .15 .40
54 Patrick Jeffers .15 .40
55 Anthony Johnson .15 .40
56 Jeff Lewis .15 .40
57 Eric Metcalf .15 .40
58 Muhsin Muhammad .15 .40
59 Jason Peter .15 .40
60 Wesley Walls .15 .40
61 John Allred .15 .40
62 Marty Booker .15 .40
63 Curtis Conway .20 .50
64 Bobby Engram .15 .40
65 Curtis Enis .15 .40
66 Shane Matthews .15 .40
67 Cade McNown .15 .40
68 Glyn Milburn .15 .40
69 Jim Miller .15 .40
70 Marcus Robinson .20 .50
71 Ryan Wetnight .15 .40
72 J.Allen/M.Brooks .15 .40
73 Jeff Blake .20 .50
74 Corey Dillon .15 .40
75 Rodney Heath RC .15 .40
76 Willie Jackson .15 .40
77 Tremain Mack .15 .40
78 Tony McGee .15 .40
79 Carl Pickens .20 .50
80 Darnay Scott .20 .50
81 Akili Smith .15 .40
82 Takeo Spikes .15 .40
83 Craig Yeast .15 .40
84 M.Basnight/N.Williams .15 .40
85 Karim Abdul-Jabbar .15 .40
86 Darrin Chiaverini .15 .40
87 Tim Couch .20 .50
88 Marc Edwards .15 .40
89 Kevin Johnson .15 .40
90 Terry Kirby .15 .40
91 Daylon McCutcheon .15 .40
92 Jamir Miller .15 .40
93 Leslie Shepherd .15 .40
94 Irv Smith .15 .40
95 M.Campbell/J.Dearth .15 .40
96 Z.Davis RC/D.Dunn RC .15 .40
97 M.Hill/T.Saleh RC .15 .40
98 Troy Aikman .30 .75
99 Eric Bjornson .15 .40
100 Dexter Coakley .15 .40
101 Greg Ellis .15 .40
102 Rocket Ismail .20 .50
103 David LaFleur .15 .40
104 Ernie Mills .15 .40
105 Jeff Ogden .15 .40
106 R.Neufeld RC/R.Thomas .15 .40
107 Deion Sanders .20 .50
108 Emmitt Smith .40 1.00
109 Chris Warren .15 .40
110 M.Lucky/J.Tucker .15 .40
111 Byron Chamberlain .15 .40
112 Terrell Davis .20 .50
113 Jason Elam .15 .40
114 Olandis Gary .20 .50
115 Brian Griese .15 .40
116 Ed McCaffrey .20 .50
117 Trevor Pryce .15 .40
118 Bill Romanowski .15 .40
119 Shannon Sharpe .20 .50
120 Rod Smith .20 .50
121 Al Wilson .15 .40
122 A.Cooper/C.Watson .15 .40
123 Charlie Batch .15 .40
124 Stephen Boyd .15 .40
125 Chris Claiborne .15 .40
126 Germane Crowell .15 .40
127 Terry Fair .15 .40
128 Gus Frerotte .15 .40
129 Jason Hanson .15 .40
130 Greg Hill .15 .40
131 Herman Moore .15 .40
132 Johnnie Morton .20 .50
133 Barry Sanders .40 1.00
134 David Sloan .15 .40
135 B.Olivo/C.Sauter .15 .40
136 Corey Bradford .15 .40
137 Tyrone Davis .15 .40
138 Brett Favre .50 1.25
139 Antonio Freeman .20 .50
140 Vonnie Holliday .15 .40
141 Dorsey Levens .20 .50
142 Keith McKenzie .15 .40
143 Mike McKenzie .15 .40
144 Bill Schroeder .20 .50
145 Jeff Thomason .15 .40
146 Frank Winters RC .15 .40
147 Cornelius Bennett .15 .40
148 Tony Blevins RC .15 .40
149 Chad Bratzke .15 .40
150 Ken Dilger .15 .40
151 Tarik Glenn .15 .40
152 E.G. Green .15 .40
153 Marvin Harrison .20 .50
154 Edgerrin James .20 .50
155 Peyton Manning .60 1.50
156 Jerome Pathon .15 .40
157 Marcus Pollard .15 .40
158 Terrence Wilkins .15 .40
159 I.Jones RC/P.Shields RC .15 .40
160 Reggie Barlow .15 .40
161 Aaron Beasley .15 .40
162 Tony Boselli .20 .50
163 Tony Brackens .15 .40
164 Kyle Brady .15 .40
165 Mark Brunell .20 .50
166 Jay Fiedler .20 .50
167 Kevin Hardy .15 .40
168 Carnell Lake .15 .40
169 Keenan McCardell .20 .50
170 Jonathan Quinn .15 .40
171 Jimmy Smith .20 .50
172 James Stewart .15 .40
173 Fred Taylor .20 .50
174 L.Jackson RC/S.Mack .15 .40
175 Derrick Alexander .15 .40
176 Donnell Bennett .15 .40
177 Donnie Edwards .15 .40
178 Tony Gonzalez .20 .50
179 Elvis Grbac .15 .40
180 James Hasty .15 .40
181 Joe Horn .20 .50
182 Lonnie Johnson .15 .40
183 Kevin Lockett .15 .40
184 Larry Parker .15 .40
185 Tony Richardson RC .15 .40
186 Rashaan Shehee .15 .40
187 Tamarick Vanover .15 .40
188 Trace Armstrong .15 .40
189 Oronde Gadsden .20 .50
190 Damon Huard .15 .40
191 Nate Jacquet .15 .40
192 James Johnson .15 .40
193 Rob Konrad .15 .40
194 Sam Madison .15 .40
195 Dan Marino .50 1.25
196 Tony Martin .20 .50
197 O.J. McDuffie .20 .50
198 Stanley Pritchett .15 .40
199 Tim Ruddy .15 .40
200 Patrick Surtain .15 .40
201 Zach Thomas .20 .50
202 Cris Carter .25 .60
203 Duane Clemons .15 .40
204 Carlester Crumpler .15 .40
205 Daunte Culpepper .20 .50
206 Jeff George .20 .50
207 Matthew Hatchette .15 .40
208 Leroy Hoard .15 .40
209 Randy Moss .20 .50
210 John Randle .25 .60
211 Jake Reed .20 .50
212 Robert Smith .15 .40
213 Robert Tate .15 .40
214 Terry Allen .20 .50
215 Bruce Armstrong .15 .40
216 Drew Bledsoe .20 .50
217 Ben Coates .15 .40
218 Kevin Faulk .15 .40
219 Terry Glenn .20 .50
220 Shawn Jefferson .15 .40
221 Andy Katzenmoyer .15 .40
222 Ty Law .25 .60
223 Willie McGinest .20 .50
224 Lawyer Milloy .20 .50
225 Tony Simmons .15 .40
226 M.Bishop/S.Morey RC .15 .40
227 Cameron Cleeland .15 .40
228 Troy Davis .15 .40
229 Jake Delhomme RC .20 .50
230 Andre Hastings .15 .40
231 Eddie Kennison .15 .40
232 Wilmont Perry .15 .40
233 Dino Philyaw .15 .40
234 Keith Poole .15 .40
235 William Roaf .15 .40
236 Billy Joe Tolliver .15 .40
237 Fred Weary .15 .40
238 Ricky Williams .20 .50
239 Franklin RC/M.Powell RC .15 .40
240 Jessie Armstead .15 .40
241 Tiki Barber .20 .50
242 Dan Campbell .15 .40
243 Kerry Collins .15 .40
244 Percy Ellsworth .15 .40
245 Kent Graham .15 .40
246 Ike Hilliard .15 .40
247 Cedric Jones .15 .40
248 Bashir Levingston RC .15 .40
249 Pete Mitchell .15 .40
250 Michael Strahan .20 .50
251 Amani Toomer .15 .40
252 Charles Way .15 .40
253 Andre Weathers RC .15 .40
254 Richie Anderson .15 .40
255 Wayne Chrebet .15 .40
256 Marcus Coleman .15 .40
257 Bryan Cox .15 .40
258 Jason Fabini RC .15 .40
259 Robert Farmer RC .15 .40
260 Keyshawn Johnson .20 .50
261 Ray Lucas .15 .40
262 Curtis Martin .20 .50
263 Kevin Mawae .15 .40
264 Eric Ogbogu .15 .40
265 Bernie Parmalee .15 .40
266 Vinny Testaverde .15 .40
267 Dedric Ward .15 .40
268 Eric Barton RC .15 .40
269 Tim Brown .25 .60
270 Tony Bryant .15 .40
271 Rickey Dudley .15 .40
272 Rich Gannon .20 .50
273 Bobby Hoying .15 .40
274 James Jett .15 .40
275 Napoleon Kaufman .20 .50
276 Jon Ritchie .15 .40
277 Darrell Russell .15 .40
278 Kenny Shedd .15 .40
279 Marquis Walker RC .15 .40
280 Tyrone Wheatley .15 .40
281 Charles Woodson .25 .60
282 Luther Broughton RC .15 .40
283 Al Harris RC .25 .60
284 Greg Jefferson .15 .40
285 Dietrich Jells .15 .40
286 Charles Johnson .15 .40
287 Chad Lewis .15 .40
288 Mike Mamula .15 .40
289 Donovan McNabb .20 .50
290 Doug Pederson .15 .40
291 Allen Rossum .15 .40
292 Torrance Small .15 .40
293 Duce Staley .15 .40
294 Jerome Bettis .25 .60
295 Kris Brown .15 .40
296 Mark Bruener .20 .50
297 Troy Edwards .20 .50
298 Jason Gildon .15 .40
299 Richard Huntley .15 .40
300 Bobby Shaw RC .15 .40
301 Scott Shields RC .15 .40
302 Kordell Stewart .15 .40
303 Hines Ward .20 .50
304 Amos Zereoue .15 .40
305 M.Cushing RC/J.Tuman .15 .40

306 P.Gonzalez/A.Wright RC .20 .50
307 Isaac Bruce .25 .60
308 Kevin Carter .15 .40
309 Marshall Faulk .20 .50
310 London Fletcher RC .40 1.00
311 Joe Germaine .15 .40
312 Az-Zahir Hakim .15 .40
313 Torry Holt .20 .50
314 Tony Horne .15 .40
315 Mike Jones LB .15 .40
316 Dexter McCleon .20 .50
317 Orlando Pace .15 .40
318 Ricky Proehl .15 .40
319 Kurt Warner .40 1.00
320 Roland Williams .15 .40
321 Grant Wistrom .15 .40
322 J.Hodgins RC/J.Watson .15 .40
323 Jermaine Fazande .15 .40
324 Jeff Graham .15 .40
325 Jim Harbaugh .20 .50
326 Raylee Johnson .15 .40
327 Charlie Jones .15 .40
328 Freddie Jones .15 .40
329 Natrone Means .20 .50
330 Chris Penn .15 .40
331 Mikhael Ricks .15 .40
332 Junior Seau .20 .50
333 R.Davis RC/R.Reed RC .15 .40
334 Fred Beasley .15 .40
335 Brentson Buckner .15 .40
336 Greg Clark .15 .40
337 Dave Fiore RC .15 .40
338 Charlie Garner .20 .50
339 Mark Harris RC .15 .40
340 Ramos McDonald RC .15 .40
341 Terrell Owens .20 .50
342 Jerry Rice .60 1.50
343 Lance Schulters .15 .40
344 J.J. Stokes .20 .50
345 Bryant Young .15 .40
346 Steve Young .30 .75
347 Jeff Garcia .15 .40
348 Fabien Bownes RC .15 .40
349 Chad Brown .15 .40
350 Reggie Brown .15 .40
351 Sean Dawkins .15 .40
352 Christian Fauria .15 .40
353 Ahman Green .20 .50
354 Walter Jones .20 .50
355 Cortez Kennedy .20 .50
356 Jon Kitna .15 .40
357 Derrick Mayes .15 .40
358 Charlie Rogers .15 .40
359 Shawn Springs .15 .40
360 Ricky Watters .20 .50
361 Donne Abraham .15 .40
362 Mike Alstott .15 .40
363 Reidel Anthony .15 .40
364 Ronde Barber .15 .40
365 Derrick Brooks .15 .40
366 Warrick Dunn .15 .40
367 Jacquez Green .15 .40
368 Marcus Jones .15 .40
369 Shaun King .15 .40
370 John Lynch .20 .50
371 Warren Sapp .20 .50
372 Steve White RC .15 .40
373 M.Gramatica/K.McLeod RC .15 .40
374 Blaine Bishop .15 .40
375 Al Del Greco .15 .40
376 Kevin Dyson .20 .50
377 Eddie George .20 .50
378 Jevon Kearse .15 .40
379 Derrick Mason .15 .40
380 Bruce Matthews .15 .40
381 Steve McNair .20 .50
382 Neil O'Donnell .15 .40
383 Yancey Thigpen .15 .40
384 Frank Wycheck .20 .50
385 K.Daft/L.Brown .15 .40
386 Stephen Alexander .15 .40
387 Champ Bailey .20 .50
388 Larry Centers .15 .40
389 Marco Coleman .15 .40
390 Albert Connell .15 .40
391 Stephen Davis .15 .40
392 Irving Fryar .20 .50
393 Skip Hicks .15 .40
394 Brad Johnson .20 .50
395 Michael Westbrook .15 .40
396 O.Ayanbadejo RC/L.Gordon RC .20 .50
397 D.Driver/R.Powell .30 .75
398 T.Bouman/J.Brigham RC .15 .40
399 B.Huard/S.Bonner .15 .40
400 M.Sellers/S.George RC .15 .40
401 Shaun Alexander RC .40 1.00
402 LaVar Arrington RC .50 1.25
403 Tom Brady RC 30.00 60.00
404 Demario Brown RC .25 .60
405 Plaxico Burress RC .30 .75
406 Trung Canidate RC .25 .60
407 Giovanni Carmazzi RC .25 .60
408 Kwame Cavil RC .25 .60
409 Chrys Chukwuma RC .25 .60
410 Ron Dayne RC .40 1.00
411 Reuben Droughns RC .25 .60
412 Ron Dugans RC .25 .60
413 Deon Dyer RC .25 .60
414 Danny Farmer RC .25 .60
415 Chafie Fields RC .25 .60
416 Trevor Gaylor RC .25 .60
417 Sherrod Gideon RC .25 .60
418 Joey Goodspeed RC .25 .60
419 Joe Hamilton RC .25 .60
420 Tony Hartley RC .25 .60
421 Todd Husak RC .25 .60
422 Trevor Insley RC .25 .60
423 Thomas Jones RC .30 .75
424 Marcus Knight RC .25 .60
425 Jamal Lewis RC .40 1.00
426 Anthony Lucas RC .25 .60
427 Tee Martin RC .25 .60
428 Rondell Mealey RC .25 .60
429 Sylvester Morris RC .25 .60
430 Chad Morton RC .30 .75
431 Dennis Northcutt RC .25 .60
432 Chad Pennington RC .30 .75
433 Rodnick Phillips RC .25 .60
434 Mareno Philyaw RC .25 .60
435 Jerry Porter RC .40 1.00
436 Travis Prentice RC .25 .60
437 Tim Rattay RC .30 .75
438 Chris Redman RC .25 .60
439 J.R. Redmond RC .25 .60
440 Gari Scott RC .25 .60
441 Keith Smith RC .25 .60
442 Terrelle Smith RC .25 .60
443 R.Jay Soward RC .25 .60
444 Quinton Spotwood RC .25 .60
445 Shyrone Stith RC .25 .60
446 Travis Taylor RC .25 .60
447 Troy Walters RC .25 .60
448 Peter Warrick RC .25 .60
449 Dez White RC .25 .60
450 Michael Wiley RC .25 .60

2000 Pacific Copper

-400 VETS/75: 8X TO 20X BASIC CARDS
*401-450 ROOKIES/75: 5X TO 12X RC
STATED PRINT RUN 75 SERIAL #'d SETS
403 Tom Brady 125.00 250.00

2000 Pacific Gold

ETS 1-400: 4X TO 10X BASIC CARDS
*ROOKIES 401-450: 2.5X TO 6X
RETAIL GOLD PRINT RUN 199
403 Tom Brady 125.00 200.00

2000 Pacific Platinum Blue Draft Picks

*PLAT.BLUE ROOKIES: 2X TO 5X
STATED PRINT RUN 399 SER.#'d SETS
403 Tom Brady 100.00 200.00

2000 Pacific Premiere Date

ETS 1-400: 6X TO 15X BASIC CARDS
*ROOKIES 401-450: 4X TO 10X
STATED PRINT RUN 78 SER.#'d SETS
403 Tom Brady 300.00 600.00

2000 Pacific Draft Picks 999

OOKIES/999: 1.2X TO 3X BASIC RC
STATED PRINT RUN 999 SER.#'d SETS

2000 Pacific AFC Leaders

ndomly inserted in packs at the rate of one in 37, this 10-card set features top players from the AFC on an all-foil insert card. Each card contains a full color action photo and the featured player's team logo.

COMPLETE SET (10) 7.50 20.00
STATED ODDS 1:37
1 Tim Couch .75 2.00
2 Olandis Gary .75 2.00
3 Marvin Harrison .75 2.00
4 Edgerrin James .75 2.00
5 Peyton Manning 2.50 6.00
6 Mark Brunell .75 2.00
7 Jimmy Smith .75 2.00
8 Drew Bledsoe .75 2.00
9 Keyshawn Johnson .75 2.00
10 Eddie George .75 2.00

2000 Pacific Autographs

ndomly inserted in packs, this 50-card set features authentic autographs and the "Pacific Authentic Autograph" stamp on the card front. The cards were not serial numbered but Pacific did release signing numbers on them as listed below. Some cards were issued via mail redemptions that carried an expiration date of 3/31/2001.

PACIFIC ANNC'D PRINT RUNS BELOW
51 Tim Biakabutuka/200* 6.00 15.00
70 Marcus Robinson/200* 6.00 15.00
87 Tim Couch/100* 8.00 20.00
154 Edgerrin James/50* 20.00 50.00
229 Jake Delhomme/500* 6.00 15.00
307 Isaac Bruce/100* 10.00 25.00
319 Kurt Warner/253* 15.00 40.00
344 J.J. Stokes/100* 8.00 20.00
362 Mike Alstott/100* 6.00 15.00
377 Eddie George/60* 15.00 40.00
391 Stephen Davis/100* 6.00 15.00
401 Shaun Alexander/150* 10.00 25.00
403 Tom Brady/200* 350.00 500.00
404 Demario Brown/300* 5.00 12.00
405 Plaxico Burress/300* 6.00 15.00
406 Trung Canidate/300* 5.00 12.00
407 Giovanni Carmazzi/200* 5.00 12.00
408 Kwame Cavil/300* 5.00 12.00
410 Ron Dayne/200* 8.00 20.00
411 Reuben Droughns/200* 5.00 12.00
412 Ron Dugans/400* 5.00 12.00
414 Danny Farmer/250* 5.00 12.00
415 Chafie Fields/400* 5.00 12.00
417 Sherrod Gideon/200* 5.00 12.00
419 Joe Hamilton/200* 5.00 12.00
420 Tony Hartley/200* 5.00 12.00
421 Todd Husak/300* 5.00 12.00
423 Thomas Jones/300* 6.00 15.00
424 Marcus Knight/200* 5.00 12.00
425 Jamal Lewis/100* 10.00 25.00
426 Anthony Lucas/200* 5.00 12.00
427 Tee Martin/200* 5.00 12.00
428 Rondell Mealey/200* 5.00 12.00
429 Sylvester Morris/100* 6.00 15.00
431 Dennis Northcutt/200* 5.00 12.00
432 Chad Pennington/150* 8.00 20.00
434 Mareno Philyaw/200* 5.00 12.00
435 Jerry Porter/200* 8.00 20.00
436 Travis Prentice/300* 5.00 12.00
437 Tim Rattay/200* 6.00 15.00
438 Chris Redman/150* 6.00 15.00
439 J.R. Redmond/200* 5.00 12.00
443 R.Jay Soward/400* 5.00 12.00
445 Shyrone Stith/200* 5.00 12.00
446 Travis Taylor/200* 5.00 12.00
447 Troy Walters/300* 5.00 12.00
448 Peter Warrick/288* 5.00 12.00
449 Dez White/300* 5.00 12.00
450 Michael Wiley/300* 5.00 12.00

2000 Pacific Cramer's Choice

Randomly inserted in packs at the rate of one in 721, this 10-card set is die cut and pictures the featured player against a backdrop of the "Cramer's Choice" trophy.

COMPLETE SET (10) 75.00 200.00
STATED ODDS 1:721
1 Tim Couch 5.00 12.00
2 Emmitt Smith 10.00 25.00
3 Brett Favre 12.00 30.00
4 Edgerrin James 5.00 12.00
5 Peyton Manning 15.00 40.00
6 Randy Moss 5.00 12.00
7 Marshall Faulk 5.00 12.00
8 Kurt Warner 10.00 25.00
9 Eddie George 5.00 12.00
10 Peter Warrick 4.00 10.00

2000 Pacific Finest Hour

ndomly inserted in packs at the rate of one in 73, this 20-card set features top performances by some of the NFL's finest. Full-color action photos are set against a background consisting of a clock on one side and the featured player's team logo on the other.

STATED ODDS 1:73
1 Terrell Davis 1.00 2.50
2 Barry Sanders 2.00 5.00
3 Brett Favre 2.50 6.00
4 Edgerrin James 1.00 2.50
5 Drew Bledsoe 1.00 2.50
6 Damon Huard .75 2.00
7 Randy Moss 1.00 2.50
8 Kurt Warner 2.00 5.00
9 Jerry Rice 3.00 8.00
10 Stephen Davis .75 2.00
11 Shaun Alexander 1.25 3.00
12 Peter Warrick .75 2.00
13 Chris Redman .75 2.00
14 Chad Pennington 1.00 2.50
15 Tom Brady 50.00 100.00
16 Plaxico Burress 1.00 2.50
17 Todd Husak .75 2.00
18 Jamal Lewis 1.25 3.00
19 Thomas Jones 1.00 2.50
20 Ron Dayne 1.25 3.00

2000 Pacific Game Worn Jerseys

ndomly inserted one in every five boxes, this 9-card set features swatches of game-worn jerseys.

STATED ODDS 1:5 BOXES
1 Kurt Warner 10.00 25.00
2 Fred Taylor 4.00 10.00
3 Ricky Williams 5.00 12.00
4 Ike Hilliard 4.00 10.00
5 Tim Brown 6.00 15.00
6 Brett Favre 12.00 30.00
7 Jon Kitna 4.00 10.00
8 Kordell Stewart 4.00 10.00
9 Natrone Means 5.00 12.00

2000 Pacific Gold Crown Die Cuts

Randomly inserted in packs at the rate of one in 37, this 36-card set features crown die-cut cards. Card fronts feature full-color action shots and are enhanced with silver holographic foil.

COMPLETE SET (36) 40.00 100.00
STATED ODDS 1:37
1 Jake Plummer .75 2.00
2 Cade McNown .75 2.00
3 Corey Dillon .75 2.00
4 Akili Smith .75 2.00
5 Tim Couch 1.00 2.50
6 Kevin Johnson .75 2.00
7 Olandis Gary 1.00 2.50
8 Brian Griese .75 2.00
9 Marvin Harrison 1.00 2.50
10 Edgerrin James 1.00 2.50
11 Mark Brunell 1.00 2.50
12 Fred Taylor .75 2.00
13 Damon Huard .75 2.00
14 Dan Marino 2.50 6.00
15 Randy Moss 1.00 2.50
16 Drew Bledsoe 1.00 2.50
17 Ricky Williams 1.00 2.50
18 Keyshawn Johnson 1.00 2.50
19 Donovan McNabb 1.00 2.50
20 Marshall Faulk 1.00 2.50
21 Kurt Warner 2.00 5.00
22 Jon Kitna .75 2.00
23 Jerry Rice 3.00 8.00
24 Shaun King .75 2.00
25 Eddie George 1.00 2.50
26 Steve McNair 1.00 2.50
27 Stephen Davis .75 2.00
28 Brad Johnson 1.00 2.50
29 Shaun Alexander 1.25 3.00
30 Plaxico Burress 1.00 2.50
31 Ron Dayne 1.25 3.00
32 Joe Hamilton .75 2.00
33 Thomas Jones 1.00 2.50
34 Chad Pennington 1.00 2.50
35 Chris Redman .75 2.00
36 Peter Warrick .75 2.00

2000 Pacific NFC Leaders

Randomly inserted in packs at the rate of one in 37, this 10-card set features top players from the NFC on an all-foil insert card. Each card contains a full color action photo and the featured player's team logo.

COMPLETE SET (10) 10.00 25.00
STATED ODDS 1:37
1 Marcus Robinson .75 2.00
2 Troy Aikman 1.25 3.00
3 Emmitt Smith 1.50 4.00
4 Cris Carter 1.00 2.50
5 Randy Moss .75 2.00
6 Isaac Bruce 1.00 2.50
7 Marshall Faulk .75 2.00
8 Kurt Warner 1.50 4.00
9 Stephen Davis .60 1.50
10 Brad Johnson .75 2.00

2000 Pacific Pro Bowl Die Cuts

ndomly inserted in packs at the rate of one in 37, this 20-card set features players from the 2000 Pro Bowl. Cards contain player photos set against a die-cut background of a crashing wave that is highlighted with laser etched blue foil.

COMPLETE SET (20) 20.00 50.00
STATED ODDS 1:37
1 Steve Beuerlein 1.00 2.50
2 Corey Dillon .75 2.00
3 Emmitt Smith 2.00 5.00
4 Marvin Harrison 1.00 2.50
5 Edgerrin James 1.00 2.50
6 Peyton Manning 3.00 8.00
7 Mark Brunell 1.00 2.50
8 Jimmy Smith 1.00 2.50
9 Tony Gonzalez 1.00 2.50
10 Cris Carter 1.25 3.00
11 Randy Moss 1.00 2.50
12 Rich Gannon 1.00 2.50
13 Keyshawn Johnson 1.00 2.50
14 Terry Glenn 1.00 2.50
15 Marshall Faulk 1.00 2.50
16 Kurt Warner 2.00 5.00
17 Mike Alstott .75 2.00
18 Eddie George 1.00 2.50
19 Stephen Davis .75 2.00
20 Brad Johnson 1.00 2.50

2000 Pacific Reflections

ndomly inserted in packs at the rate of on in 145, this 20-card set features a die-cut card shaped like a helmet where the player's image is "reflected" through the tinted glass face mask.

COMPLETE SET (20) 30.00 80.00
STATED ODDS 1:145
1 Cade McNown 1.00 2.50
2 Tim Couch 1.25 3.00
3 Troy Aikman 2.00 5.00
4 Emmitt Smith 2.50 6.00
5 Terrell Davis 1.25 3.00
6 Barry Sanders 2.50 6.00
7 Brett Favre 3.00 8.00
8 Marvin Harrison 1.25 3.00
9 Edgerrin James 1.25 3.00
10 Mark Brunell 1.25 3.00
11 Fred Taylor 1.00 2.50
12 Dan Marino 3.00 8.00
13 Randy Moss 1.25 3.00
14 Ricky Williams 1.25 3.00
15 Marshall Faulk 1.25 3.00
16 Kurt Warner 2.50 6.00
17 Jon Kitna 1.00 2.50
18 Shaun King 1.00 2.50
19 Eddie George 1.25 3.00
20 Stephen Davis 1.00 2.50

2001 Pacific

leased as a 530-card set, 2001 Pacific consists of 450 regular veteran cards and 80 serial numbered rookie cards. The cards feature full-color action shots and silver foil highlights. 2001 Pacific was packaged in 36-pack boxes containing 10 cards each and carried a suggested retail price of $2.99. Some rookies were issued as redemption cards which carried an expiration date of 12/31/2001.

COMP.SET w/o SP's (450) 25.00 50.00
ROOKIE QB PRINT RUN 1000
ROOKIE RB PRINT RUN 1500
ROOKIE WR PRINT RUN 1750
ROOKIE DEF/OTHER PRINT RUN 2500
1 David Boston .15 .40
2 Mac Cody .15 .40
3 Chris Gedney .15 .40
4 Chris Greisen .15 .40
5 Terry Hardy .15 .40
6 MarTay Jenkins .15 .40
7 Thomas Jones .15 .40
8 Joel Makovicka .15 .40
9 Tywan Mitchell .15 .40
10 Rob Moore .15 .40
11 Michael Pittman .20 .50
12 Jake Plummer .15 .40
13 Frank Sanders .15 .40
14 Aeneas Williams .15 .40
15 Jamal Anderson .20 .50
16 Eugene Baker .15 .40
17 Chris Chandler .20 .50
18 Tim Dwight .20 .50
19 Brian Finneran .20 .50
20 Jammi German .15 .40
21 Shawn Jefferson .15 .40
22 Doug Johnson .15 .40
23 Danny Kanell .20 .50
24 Reggie Kelly .15 .40
25 Terance Mathis .15 .40
26 Derek Rackley .15 .40
27 Ron Rivers .15 .40
28 Maurice Smith .15 .40
29 Sam Adams .15 .40
30 Obafemi Ayanbadejo .15 .40
31 Tony Banks .15 .40
32 Trent Dilfer .15 .40
33 Sam Gash .15 .40
34 Priest Holmes .15 .40
35 Qadry Ismail .15 .40
36 Pat Johnson .15 .40
37 Jamal Lewis .25 .60
38 Jermaine Lewis .15 .40
39 Ray Lewis .25 .60
40 Chris Redman .25 .60
41 Shannon Sharpe .20 .50
42 Brandon Stokley .15 .40
43 Travis Taylor .15 .40
44 Shawn Bryson .15 .40
45 Kwame Cavil .15 .40
46 Sam Cowart .15 .40
47 Doug Flutie .20 .50
48 Rob Johnson .20 .50
49 Jonathan Linton .15 .40
50 Jeremy McDaniel .15 .40
51 Sammy Morris .15 .40
52 Eric Moulds .15 .40
53 Peerless Price .15 .40
54 Jay Riemersma .15 .40
55 Antowain Smith .20 .50
56 Chris Watson .15 .40
57 Marcellus Wiley .15 .40
58 Michael Bates .15 .40
59 Steve Beuerlein .20 .50
60 Tim Biakabutuka .15 .40
61 Isaac Byrd .15 .40
62 Dameyune Craig .15 .40
63 William Floyd .15 .40
64 Karl Hankton .15 .40
65 Donald Hayes .15 .40
66 Chris Hetherington RC .15 .40
67 Brad Hoover .20 .50
68 Patrick Jeffers .15 .40
69 Muhsin Muhammad .15 .40
70 Iheanyi Uwaezuoke .15 .40
71 Wesley Walls .15 .40
72 James Allen .15 .40
73 Marlon Barnes .15 .40
74 D'Wayne Bates .15 .40
75 Marty Booker .15 .40
76 Macey Brooks .15 .40
77 Bobby Engram .15 .40
78 Curtis Enis .15 .40
79 Mark Hartsell RC .15 .40
80 Eddie Kennison .20 .50
81 Shane Matthews .15 .40
82 Cade McNown .20 .50
83 Jim Miller .20 .50
84 Marcus Robinson .20 .50
85 Brian Urlacher .30 .75
86 Dez White .20 .50
87 Brandon Bennett .15 .40
88 Steve Bush RC .15 .40
89 Corey Dillon .15 .40
90 Ron Dugans .15 .40
91 Danny Farmer .15 .40
92 Damon Griffin .15 .40
93 Clif Groce .15 .40
94 Curtis Keaton .15 .40
95 Scott Mitchell .15 .40
96 Darnay Scott .20 .50
97 Akili Smith .15 .40
98 Peter Warrick .15 .40
99 Nick Williams .15 .40
100 Craig Yeast .15 .40
101 Bobby Brown .15 .40
102 Darrin Chiaverini .15 .40
103 Tim Couch .15 .40
104 JaJuan Dawson .15 .40
105 Marc Edwards .15 .40
106 Kevin Johnson .15 .40
107 Dennis Northcutt .15 .40
108 David Patten .15 .40
109 Doug Pederson .15 .40
110 Travis Prentice .15 .40
111 Errict Rhett .20 .50
112 Aaron Shea .15 .40
113 Kevin Thompson .15 .40
114 Jamel White .15 .40
115 Spergon Wynn .15 .40
116 Troy Aikman .30 .75
117 Chris Brazzell .15 .40
118 Randall Cunningham .20 .50
119 Jackie Harris .20 .50
120 Damon Hodge .15 .40
121 Rocket Ismail .20 .50
122 David LaFleur .15 .40
123 Wane McGarity .15 .40
124 James McKnight .15 .40
125 Emmitt Smith .40 1.00
126 Clint Stoerner .20 .50
127 Jason Tucker .15 .40
128 Michael Wiley .15 .40
129 Anthony Wright .15 .40
130 Mike Anderson .15 .40
131 Dwayne Carswell .15 .40
132 Byron Chamberlain .15 .40
133 Desmond Clark .15 .40
134 Chris Cole .15 .40
135 KaRon Coleman .15 .40
136 Terrell Davis .20 .50
137 Gus Frerotte .15 .40
138 Olandis Gary .15 .40
139 Brian Griese .15 .40
140 Howard Griffith .15 .40
141 Jarious Jackson .15 .40
142 Ed McCaffrey .20 .50
143 Scottie Montgomery RC .15 .40
144 Rod Smith .20 .50
145 Charlie Batch .15 .40
146 Stoney Case .15 .40
147 Germane Crowell .15 .40
148 Larry Foster .15 .40
149 Desmond Howard .20 .50
150 Sedrick Irvin .15 .40
151 Herman Moore .15 .40
152 Johnnie Morton .20 .50
153 Robert Porcher .15 .40
154 Cory Sauter .15 .40
155 Cory Schlesinger .15 .40
156 David Sloan .15 .40
157 Brian Stablein .15 .40
158 James Stewart .15 .40
160 Corey Bradford .15 .40
160 Tyrone Davis .15 .40
161 Donald Driver .20 .50
162 Brett Favre .50 1.25
163 Bubba Franks .15 .40
164 Antonio Freeman .25 .60
165 Herbert Goodman .15 .40
166 Ahman Green .20 .50
167 Matt Hasselbeck .15 .40
168 William Henderson .15 .40
169 Charles Lee .15 .40
170 Dorsey Levens .20 .50
171 Bill Schroeder .20 .50
172 Darren Sharper .20 .50
173 Matt Snider .15 .40
174 Danny Wuerffel .20 .50
175 Ken Dilger .15 .40
176 Jim Finn .15 .40
177 Lennox Gordon .15 .40
178 E.G. Green .15 .40
179 Marvin Harrison .20 .50
180 Kelly Holcomb .20 .50
181 Trevor Insley .15 .40
182 Edgerrin James .20 .50
183 Peyton Manning .60 1.50
184 Kevin McDougal .15 .40
185 Jerome Pathon .15 .40
186 Marcus Pollard .15 .40
187 Justin Snow .15 .40
188 Terrence Wilkins .15 .40
189 Reggie Barlow .15 .40
190 Kyle Brady .15 .40
191 Mark Brunell .20 .50
192 Kevin Hardy .15 .40
193 Anthony Johnson .15 .40
194 Stacey Mack .15 .40
195 Jamie Martin .15 .40
196 Keenan McCardell .20 .50
197 Daimon Shelton .15 .40
198 Jimmy Smith .20 .50
199 R.Jay Soward .15 .40
200 Shyrone Stith .15 .40
201 Fred Taylor .15 .40
202 Alvis Whitted .15 .40
203 Jermaine Williams .15 .40
204 Derrick Alexander .15 .40
205 Kimble Anders .15 .40
206 Donnell Bennett .15 .40
207 Mike Cloud .15 .40
208 Todd Collins .15 .40
209 Tony Gonzalez .20 .50
210 Elvis Grbac .20 .50
211 Dante Hall .25 .60
212 Kevin Lockett .15 .40
213 Warren Moon .25 .60
214 Frank Moreau .15 .40
215 Sylvester Morris .15 .40
216 Larry Parker .15 .40
217 Tony Richardson .15 .40
218 Trace Armstrong .15 .40
219 Autry Denson .15 .40
220 Bert Emanuel .15 .40
221 Jay Fiedler .20 .50
222 Oronde Gadsden .15 .40
223 Damon Huard .20 .50
224 James Johnson .15 .40
225 Rob Konrad .15 .40
226 Tony Martin .20 .50
227 O.J. McDuffie .15 .40
228 Mike Quinn .15 .40
229 Lamar Smith .20 .50
230 Jason Taylor .25 .60
231 Thurman Thomas .20 .50
232 Zach Thomas .20 .50
233 Todd Douman .15 .40
234 Bubby Brister .15 .40
235 Cris Carter .25 .60
236 Daunte Culpepper .20 .50
237 John Davis RC .15 .40
238 Robert Griffith .15 .40
239 Matthew Hatchette .15 .40
240 Jim Kleinsasser .20 .50
241 Randy Moss .20 .50
242 John Randle .20 .50
243 Robert Smith .15 .40
244 Chris Walsh RC .15 .40
245 Troy Walters .15 .40
246 Moe Williams .15 .40
247 Michael Bishop .20 .50
248 Drew Bledsoe .20 .50
249 Troy Brown .15 .40
250 Tedy Bruschi .20 .50
251 Tony Carter .15 .40
252 Shockmain Davis .15 .40
253 Kevin Faulk .15 .40
254 Terry Glenn .20 .50
255 Ty Law .25 .60
256 Lawyer Milloy .15 .40
257 J.R. Redmond .15 .40
258 Harold Shaw .15 .40
259 Tony Simmons .15 .40
260 Jermaine Wiggins .15 .40
261 Jeff Blake .20 .50
262 Aaron Brooks .15 .40
263 Cam Cleeland .15 .40
264 Andrew Glover .15 .40
265 La'Roi Glover .15 .40
266 Joe Horn .15 .40
267 Kevin Houser .15 .40
268 Willie Jackson .15 .40
269 Jerald Moore .15 .40
270 Chad Morton .15 .40
271 Keith Poole .15 .40
272 Terrelle Smith .15 .40
273 Ricky Williams .20 .50
274 Robert Wilson .15 .40
275 Jessie Armstead .15 .40
276 Tiki Barber .20 .50
277 Mike Cherry .15 .40
278 Kerry Collins .15 .40
279 Greg Comella .15 .40
280 Thabiti Davis .15 .40
281 Ron Dayne .20 .50
282 Ron Dixon .15 .40
283 Ike Hilliard .15 .40
284 Joe Jurevicius .15 .40
285 Jason Sehorn .20 .50
286 Michael Strahan .20 .50
287 Amani Toomer .15 .40
288 Craig Walendy .15 .40
289 Damon Washington RC .15 .40
290 Richie Anderson .15 .40
291 Anthony Becht .15 .40
292 Wayne Chrebet .15 .40
293 Laveranues Coles .20 .50
294 Bryan Cox .20 .50
295 Marvin Jones .15 .40
296 Mo Lewis .15 .40
297 Ray Lucas .15 .40
298 Curtis Martin .20 .50
299 Bernie Parmalee .15 .40
300 Chad Pennington .15 .40
301 Jerald Sowell .15 .40
302 Dwight Stone .15 .40
303 Vinny Testaverde .15 .40
304 Dedric Ward .15 .40
305 Tim Brown .25 .60
306 Zack Crockett .15 .40
307 Scott Dreisbach .15 .40
308 Rickey Dudley .15 .40
309 David Dunn .15 .40
310 Mondriel Fulcher .15 .40
311 Rich Gannon .20 .50
312 James Jett .15 .40
313 Randy Jordan .20 .50
314 Napoleon Kaufman .15 .40
315 Rodney Peete .15 .40
316 Jerry Porter .15 .40
317 Andre Rison .20 .50
318 Tyrone Wheatley .20 .50
319 Charles Woodson .25 .60
320 Darnell Autry .15 .40
321 Na Brown .15 .40
322 Hugh Douglas .15 .40
323 Charles Johnson .15 .40
324 Chad Lewis .15 .40
325 Cecil Martin .15 .40
326 Donovan McNabb .20 .50
327 Brian Mitchell .20 .50
328 Todd Pinkston .15 .40
329 Ron Powlus .20 .50
330 Stanley Pritchett .15 .40
331 Torrance Small .15 .40
332 Duce Staley .15 .40
333 Troy Vincent .20 .50
334 Chris Warren .20 .50
335 Jerome Bettis .25 .60
336 Plaxico Burress .15 .40
337 Troy Edwards .15 .40
338 Chris Fuamatu-Ma'afala .15 .40
339 Cory Geason .15 .40
340 Kent Graham .20 .50
341 Courtney Hawkins .15 .40
342 Richard Huntley .15 .40
343 Tee Martin .20 .50
344 Bobby Shaw .15 .40
345 Kordell Stewart .15 .40
346 Hines Ward .20 .50
347 Destry Wright RC .15 .40
348 Amos Zereoue .15 .40
349 Isaac Bruce .25 .60
350 Trung Canidate .15 .40
351 Marshall Faulk .20 .50
352 London Fletcher .20 .50
353 Joe Germaine .15 .40
354 Trent Green .15 .40
355 Az-Zahir Hakim .15 .40
356 James Hodgins .15 .40
357 Robert Holcombe .15 .40
358 Torry Holt .20 .50
359 Tony Horne .15 .40
360 Ricky Proehl .15 .40
361 Chris Thomas RC .15 .40
362 Kurt Warner .40 1.00
363 Justin Watson .15 .40
364 Kenny Bynum .15 .40
365 Robert Chancey .15 .40
366 Curtis Conway .20 .50
367 Jermaine Fazande .15 .40
368 Terrell Fletcher .15 .40
369 Trevor Gaylor .15 .40
370 Jeff Graham .15 .40
371 Jim Harbaugh .20 .50
372 Rodney Harrison .15 .40
373 Ronney Jenkins .15 .40
374 Freddie Jones .15 .40
375 Reggie Jones .15 .40
376 Ryan Leaf .15 .40
377 Junior Seau .20 .50
378 Fred Beasley .15 .40
379 Greg Clark .15 .40
380 Jeff Garcia .15 .40
381 Charlie Garner .20 .50
382 Terry Jackson .15 .40
383 Brian Jennings .15 .40
384 Travis Jervey .15 .40
385 Jonas Lewis .15 .40
386 Terrell Owens .20 .50
387 Jerry Rice .50 1.25
388 Paul Smith .15 .40
389 J.J. Stokes .15 .40
390 Tai Streets .15 .40
391 Justin Swift .15 .40
392 Shaun Alexander .15 .40
393 Karsten Bailey .15 .40
394 Chad Brown .15 .40
395 Sean Dawkins .15 .40
396 Christian Fauria .15 .40
397 Brock Huard .15 .40
398 Darrell Jackson .20 .50
399 Jon Kitna .15 .40
400 Derrick Mayes .15 .40
401 Itula Mili .15 .40
402 Charlie Rogers .15 .40
403 Mack Strong .20 .50
404 Ricky Watters .20 .50
405 James Williams WR .15 .40
406 Rabih Abdullah .15 .40
407 Mike Alstott .15 .40
408 Reidel Anthony .15 .40
409 Derrick Brooks .15 .40
410 Warrick Dunn .15 .40
411 Jacquez Green .15 .40
412 Joe Hamilton .15 .40
413 Keyshawn Johnson .20 .50
414 Shaun King .15 .40
415 Charles Kirby RC .15 .40
416 Warren Sapp .20 .50
417 Aaron Stecker .15 .40
418 Todd Yoder .15 .40
419 Eric Zeier .15 .40
420 Chris Coleman .15 .40
421 Kevin Dyson .15 .40
422 Eddie George .25 .60
423 Jevon Kearse .15 .40
424 Erron Kinney .15 .40
425 Mike Leach .15 .40
426 Derrick Mason .15 .40
427 Steve McNair .20 .50
428 Lorenzo Neal .15 .40
429 Carl Pickens .20 .50
430 Chris Sanders .15 .40
431 Yancey Thigpen .15 .40
432 Rodney Thomas .15 .40
433 Frank Wycheck .15 .40
434 Stephen Alexander .15 .40
435 Champ Bailey .20 .50
436 Larry Centers .15 .40
437 Albert Connell .15 .40
438 Stephen Davis .15 .40
439 Zeron Flemister RC .15 .40
440 Irving Fryar .20 .50
441 Jeff George .20 .50
442 Skip Hicks .15 .40
443 Todd Husak .15 .40
444 Brad Johnson .20 .50
445 Adrian Murrell .20 .50
446 Deion Sanders .20 .50
447 Mike Sellers .15 .40
448 Derrius Thompson .15 .40
449 James Thrash .20 .50
450 Michael Westbrook .15 .40
451 Alex Bannister AU/1750 RC 4.00 10.00
452 Kevan Barlow AU/1500 RC 5.00 12.00
453 Drew Brees AU/1000 RC 250.00 500.00
454 Travis Henry AU/1500 RC 5.00 12.00
455 Chad Johnson AU/1750 RC 10.00 25.00
456 M.McMahon AU/1000 RC 5.00 12.00
457 B.Newcombe AU/1750 RC 5.00 12.00
458 Sage Rosenfels AU/1000 RC 5.00 12.00
459 L.Tomlinson AU/1500 RC 20.00 50.00
460 Chris Weinke AU/1000 RC 5.00 12.00
461 Tay Cody RC .75 2.00
462 Adam Archuleta RC 1.00 2.50
463 Will Allen RC 1.25 3.00
464 Moran Norris RC .75 2.00
465 Tommy Polley RC .75 2.00
466 Ennis Davis RC .75 2.00
467 Jamar Fletcher RC .75 2.00
468 Derrick Gibson RC .75 2.00
469 Sedrick Hodge RC .75 2.00
470 Willie Howard RC .75 2.00
471 Steve Hutchinson RC 2.00 5.00
472 Michael Stone RC .75 2.00
473 Vinny Sutherland/1750 RC 1.00 2.50
474 Joe Tafoya RC .75 2.00
475 Maurice Williams RC .75 2.00
476 Pork Chop Womack RC .75 2.00
477 Chad Ward RC .75 2.00
478 Scotty Anderson/1750 RC 1.00 2.50
479 Gary Baxter RC .75 2.00
480 M.Tuiasosopo/1000 RC 2.00 5.00
481 Tim Hasselbeck/1000 RC 2.00 5.00
482 Clevan Thomas RC .75 2.00
483 Marcus Stroud RC 1.00 2.50
484 John Schlecht RC .75 2.00
485 Brandon Spoon RC 1.00 2.50
486 Alex Lincoln RC .75 2.00
487 Anthony Thomas/1750 RC 1.50 4.00
488 Freddie Mitchell/1750 RC 1.00 2.50
489 Brian Allen RC .75 2.00
490 Zeke Moreno RC 1.00 2.50
491 Tony Driver RC 1.00 2.50
492 Kynan Forney RC .75 2.00
493 Reggie Wayne/1750 RC 2.00 5.00
494 Larry Casher RC .75 2.00
495 Fred Wakefield RC .75 2.00
496 Jeff Backus RC .75 2.00
497 Jarrod Cooper RC 1.00 2.50
498 Heath Evans RC 1.00 2.50
499 James Jackson/1500 RC 1.00 2.50
500 Jabari Holloway RC .75 2.00
501 Quincy Morgan/1750 RC 1.25 3.00
502 Josh Booty/1000 RC 2.00 5.00
503 Ja'Mar Toombs RC .75 2.00
504 Jason McKinley/1000 RC 1.50 4.00
505 Reggie White/1500 RC 1.00 2.50
506 Todd Heap/1750 RC 1.25 3.00
507 Rudi Johnson/1500 RC 1.50 4.00
508 Snoop Minnis/1750 RC 1.00 2.50
509 David Terrell/1750 RC 1.25 3.00
510 Torrance Marshall RC .75 2.00
511 Michael Bennett/1500 RC 1.25 3.00
512 Chris Chambers/1750 RC 1.00 2.50
513 Ben Leard/1000 RC 1.50 4.00
514 Rod Gardner/1750 RC 1.25 3.00
515 Michael Vick/1000 RC 4.00 10.00
516 Josh Heupel/1000 RC 2.50 6.00
517 Jesse Palmer/1000 RC 2.00 5.00
518 Quincy Carter/1000 RC 2.00 5.00
519 A.J. Feeley/1000 RC 2.00 5.00
520 David Rivers/1000 RC 1.50 4.00
521 Deuce McAllister/1500 RC 1.50 4.00
522 LaMont Jordan/1500 RC 1.50 4.00
523 David Allen/1500 RC 1.00 2.50
524 Correll Buckhalter/1500 RC 1.00 2.50
525 Travis Minor/1500 1.25 3.00
526 Koren Robinson/1750 RC 1.25 3.00
527 Santana Moss/1750 RC 1.50 4.00
528 Robert Ferguson/1750 RC 1.50 4.00
529 T.J.Houshmndzdh/1750 RC 1.25 3.00
530 Cedrick Wilson/1750 RC 1.25 3.00

2001 Pacific Hobby LTD

ETERANS: 6X TO 15X BASIC CARDS
STATED PRINT RUN 99 SER.#'d SETS

2001 Pacific Premiere Date

ETERANS: 12X TO 30X BASIC CARDS
STATED PRINT RUN 45 SER.#'d SETS

2001 Pacific Retail LTD

ETERANS: 4X TO 10X BASIC CARDS
STATED PRINT RUN 299 SER.#'d SETS

2001 Pacific All-Rookie Team

ndomly inserted at a rate of one in 37 packs this 10-card set featured the top rookie class of 2001. These cards show the player in action as well as a photo of his face, and they were highlighted with silver foil.

COMPLETE SET (10) 12.50 30.00
STATED ODDS 1:37
1 Kevan Barlow .60 1.50
2 Drew Brees 3.00 8.00
3 Travis Henry .60 1.50
4 Chad Johnson .75 2.00
5 Freddie Mitchell .50 1.25
6 Anthony Thomas .75 2.00
7 LaDainian Tomlinson 2.50 6.00
8 Marques Tuiasosopo .60 1.50
9 Reggie Wayne 1.00 2.50
10 Chris Weinke .60 1.50

2001 Pacific Cramer's Choice

ndomly inserted in packs this 10-card set is die cut and pictures the featured player against a backdrop of the "Cramer's Choice" trophy.

COMPLETE SET (10) 100.00 200.00
STATED PRINT RUN 99 SER.#'d SETS
1 Trent Dilfer 4.00 10.00
2 Jamal Lewis 6.00 15.00
3 Emmitt Smith 12.00 30.00
4 Brett Favre 12.00 30.00
5 Edgerrin James 5.00 12.00
6 Peyton Manning 15.00 40.00
7 Randy Moss 5.00 12.00
8 Marshall Faulk 5.00 12.00
9 Kurt Warner 10.00 25.00
10 Eddie George 6.00 15.00

2001 Pacific Game Gear

Randomly inserted into packs, this 25-card set features swatches of game-worn jerseys or swatches of game used face-masks. These cards were printed to a stated print run of 99 serial numbered sets.

STATED PRINT RUN 20-99
1 Thomas Jones J 6.00 15.00
2 Jake Plummer J 6.00 15.00
3 Rod Woodson J 10.00 25.00
4 Rob Johnson J 8.00 20.00
5 Corey Dillon J 6.00 15.00
6 Akili Smith J 6.00 15.00
7 Peter Warrick J 6.00 15.00
8 Mark Brunell J 8.00 20.00
9 Keenan McCardell J/20 15.00 40.00
10 Fred Taylor J 6.00 15.00
11 Dan Marino J 20.00 50.00
12 Trent Green J 6.00 15.00
13 Kurt Warner J 15.00 40.00
14 Jerry Rice J/20 60.00 120.00
15 Brock Huard J/20 12.00 30.00
16 Jamal Lewis F 10.00 25.00
17 Peter Warrick F 6.00 15.00
18 Mike Anderson F 6.00 15.00
19 Edgerrin James F 8.00 20.00
20 Daunte Culpepper F 8.00 20.00
21 Randy Moss F 8.00 20.00
22 Ron Dayne F 8.00 20.00
23 Marshall Faulk F 8.00 20.00
24 Kurt Warner F 15.00 40.00
25 Eddie George F 10.00 25.00

2001 Pacific Gold Crown Die Cuts

ndomly inserted in packs at the rate of one in 73 packs, this 30-card set features crown die-cut cards. Card fronts feature full-color action shots and are enhanced with gold holographic foil.

COMPLETE SET (30) 30.00 80.00
STATED ODDS 1:73
1 Jamal Lewis 1.50 4.00
2 Corey Dillon 1.00 2.50
3 Peter Warrick 1.00 2.50
4 Troy Aikman 2.00 5.00
5 Emmitt Smith 2.50 6.00
6 Mike Anderson 1.00 2.50
7 Terrell Davis 1.25 3.00
8 Brian Griese 1.00 2.50
9 Brett Favre 3.00 8.00
10 Marvin Harrison 1.25 3.00
11 Edgerrin James 1.25 3.00
12 Peyton Manning 4.00 10.00
13 Mark Brunell 1.25 3.00
14 Fred Taylor 1.00 2.50

15 Cris Carter 1.50 4.00
16 Daunte Culpepper 1.25 3.00
17 Randy Moss 1.25 3.00
18 Drew Bledsoe 1.25 3.00
19 Ricky Williams 1.25 3.00
20 Kerry Collins 1.00 2.50
21 Ron Dayne 1.25 3.00
22 Curtis Martin 1.25 3.00
23 Donovan McNabb 1.25 3.00
24 Jerome Bettis 1.50 4.00
25 Isaac Bruce 1.50 4.00
26 Marshall Faulk 1.25 3.00
27 Kurt Warner 2.50 6.00
28 Jeff Garcia 1.00 2.50
29 Jerry Rice 3.00 8.00
30 Steve McNair 1.25 3.00

2001 Pacific Impact Zone

ndomly inserted at a rate of one in 37 packs this 20-card set features 20 of the hottest players in the NFL. This set was highlighted by gold foil stamping.

COMPLETE SET (20) 12.50 30.00
STATED ODDS 1:37
1 Jamal Lewis .60 1.50
2 Corey Dillon .40 1.00
3 Peter Warrick .40 1.00
4 Emmitt Smith 1.00 2.50
5 Mike Anderson .40 1.00
6 Brian Griese .40 1.00
7 Edgerrin James .50 1.25
8 Mark Brunell .50 1.25
9 Fred Taylor .40 1.00
10 Randy Moss .50 1.25
11 Ricky Williams .50 1.25
12 Ron Dayne .50 1.25
13 Curtis Martin .50 1.25
14 Rich Gannon .50 1.25
15 Donovan McNabb .50 1.25
16 Marshall Faulk .50 1.25
17 Jerry Rice 1.25 3.00
18 Mike Alstott .40 1.00
19 Warrick Dunn .40 1.00
20 Eddie George .60 1.50

2001 Pacific Pro Bowl Die Cuts

Randomly inserted in packs at the rate of one in 37, this 20-card set features players from the 2001 Pro Bowl. Cards contain player photos set against a die-cut background of palm trees on the beach that is highlighted with gold foil stamping.

COMPLETE SET (20) 12.50 30.00
STATED ODDS 1:37
1 Eric Moulds .60 1.50
2 Corey Dillon .60 1.50
3 Marvin Harrison .75 2.00
4 Edgerrin James .75 2.00
5 Peyton Manning 2.50 6.00
6 Jimmy Smith .75 2.00
7 Tony Gonzalez .75 2.00
8 Elvis Grbac .75 2.00
9 Cris Carter 1.00 2.50
10 Daunte Culpepper .75 2.00
11 Joe Horn .60 1.50
12 Rich Gannon .75 2.00
13 Donovan McNabb .75 2.00
14 Torry Holt .75 2.00
15 Jeff Garcia .60 1.50
16 Terrell Owens .75 2.00
17 Warrick Dunn .60 1.50
18 Eddie George 1.00 2.50
19 Derrick Mason .60 1.50
20 Stephen Davis .60 1.50

2001 Pacific War Room

Randomly inserted at a rate of two in 37 packs, this 20-card set highlights some of the top draft picks from the 2001 NFL Draft. This set was highlighted by the gold foil stamping.

COMPLETE SET (20) 20.00 50.00
STATED ODDS 2:37
1 Alex Bannister .60 1.50
2 Kevan Barlow .75 2.00
3 Josh Booty .75 2.00
4 Drew Brees 4.00 10.00
5 Tim Hasselbeck .75 2.00
6 Travis Henry .75 2.00
7 James Jackson .60 1.50
8 Chad Johnson 1.00 2.50
9 Rudi Johnson 1.00 2.50
10 Mike McMahon .75 2.00
11 Snoop Minnis .60 1.50
12 Freddie Mitchell .60 1.50
13 Quincy Morgan .75 2.00
14 Bobby Newcombe .75 2.00
15 Sage Rosenfels .75 2.00
16 Anthony Thomas 1.00 2.50
17 LaDainian Tomlinson 3.00 8.00
18 Marques Tuiasosopo .75 2.00
19 Reggie Wayne 1.25 3.00
20 Chris Weinke .75 2.00

2001 Pacific Brown Royale

This 9-card die cut set was distributed at the 2001 National Sports Collector's Convention in Cleveland. Each features a Cleveland Browns player on the front and a 2001 NFL rookie on the back. The dog bone shaped cards were serial numbered of 1000.

COMPLETE SET (18) 20.00 50.00
1 S.Wynn/D.Brees 3.00 8.00
2 T.Couch/M.Tuiasosopo 2.00 5.00
3 E.Rhett/A.Thomas 5.00 12.00
4 J.White/J.Jackson 2.00 5.00
5 T.Prentice/L.Tomlinson 3.00 8.00
6 D.Northcutt/K.Robinson 2.00 5.00
7 J.Dawson/R.Gardner 2.00 5.00
8 Kev.Johnson/D.Terrell 2.50 6.00
9 Q.Morgan/S.Moss 2.00 5.00

2002 Pacific

This 500-card set includes 450 veterans and 50 rookies. Product was released in late spring/early summer 2002. Boxes contained 36 packs of 10 cards. Pack SRP was $2.99. Please note that cards 501-525 were only available in packs of 2002 Pacific Heads Update.

COMPLETE SET (500) 50.00 100.00
ROOKIE STATED ODDS ONE PER PACK
1 David Boston .15 .40
2 Arnold Jackson .15 .40
3 MarTay Jenkins .15 .40
4 Thomas Jones .15 .40
5 Kwamie Lassiter .15 .40
6 Joel Makovicka .15 .40
7 Ronald McKinnon .15 .40
8 Tywan Mitchell .15 .40
9 Michael Pittman .20 .50
10 Jake Plummer .15 .40
11 Frank Sanders .15 .40
12 Kyle Vanden Bosch .20 .50
13 Jamal Anderson .20 .50
14 Keith Brooking .15 .40
15 Chris Chandler .20 .50
16 Bob Christian .15 .40
17 Alge Crumpler .20 .50
18 Brian Finneran .15 .40
19 Shawn Jefferson .15 .40
20 Patrick Kerney .15 .40
21 Terance Mathis .15 .40
22 Maurice Smith .15 .40
23 Rodney Thomas .20 .50
24 Darrick Vaughn .15 .40
25 Michael Vick .20 .50
26 Sam Adams .15 .40
27 Terry Allen .20 .50
28 Obafemi Ayanbadejo .15 .40
29 Peter Boulware .15 .40
30 Jason Brookins .15 .40
31 Randall Cunningham .20 .50
32 Elvis Grbac .15 .40
33 Todd Heap .15 .40
34 Qadry Ismail .15 .40
35 Jamal Lewis .20 .50
36 Ray Lewis .25 .60
37 Chris Redman .15 .40
38 Shannon Sharpe .20 .50
39 Brandon Stokley .15 .40
40 Travis Taylor .15 .40
41 Moe Williams .15 .40
42 Rod Woodson .25 .60
43 Shawn Bryson .15 .40
44 Larry Centers .15 .40
45 Nate Clements .15 .40
46 London Fletcher .20 .50
47 Reggie Germany .15 .40
48 Travis Henry .15 .40
49 Jeremy McDaniel .15 .40
50 Sammy Morris .15 .40
51 Eric Moulds .15 .40
52 Peerless Price .15 .40
53 Jay Riemersma .15 .40
54 Alex Van Pelt .15 .40
55 Tim Biakabutuka .20 .50
56 Isaac Byrd .15 .40
57 Doug Evans .15 .40
58 Donald Hayes .15 .40
59 Chris Hetherington .15 .40
60 Brad Hoover .15 .40
61 Richard Huntley .15 .40
62 Patrick Jeffers .20 .50
63 Matt Lytle .15 .40
64 Dan Morgan .15 .40
65 Muhsin Muhammad .15 .40
66 Mike Rucker RC .25 .60
67 Steve Smith .25 .60
68 Wesley Walls .20 .50
69 Chris Weinke .15 .40
70 James Allen .15 .40
71 Fred Baxter .15 .40
72 Marty Booker .15 .40
73 Mike Brown .15 .40
74 Rosevelt Colvin RC .30 .75
75 Phillip Daniels .15 .40
76 Leon Johnson .15 .40
77 Shane Matthews .15 .40
78 Jim Miller .15 .40
79 Tony Parrish .15 .40
80 Marcus Robinson .20 .50
81 David Terrell .15 .40
82 Anthony Thomas .20 .50
83 Brian Urlacher .25 .60
84 Ted Washington .15 .40
85 Dez White .15 .40
86 Brandon Bennett .15 .40
87 Corey Dillon .15 .40
88 Ron Dugans .15 .40
89 Danny Farmer .15 .40
90 T.J. Houshmandzadeh .15 .40
91 Chad Johnson .15 .40
92 Curtis Keaton .15 .40
93 Jon Kitna .15 .40
94 Tony McGee .20 .50
95 Lorenzo Neal .15 .40
96 Darnay Scott .20 .50
97 Akili Smith .20 .50
98 Justin Smith .20 .50
99 Takeo Spikes .15 .40
100 Peter Warrick .15 .40
101 Tim Couch .15 .40
102 JaJuan Dawson .15 .40
103 Benjamin Gay .15 .40
104 Anthony Henry .15 .40
105 James Jackson .15 .40
106 Kevin Johnson .15 .40
107 Andre King .15 .40
108 Jamir Miller .15 .40
109 Quincy Morgan .15 .40
110 Dennis Northcutt .15 .40
111 O.J. Santiago .15 .40
112 Jamel White .15 .40
113 Quincy Carter .15 .40
114 Darrin Chiaverini .15 .40
115 Dexter Coakley .15 .40
116 Joey Galloway .20 .50
117 Troy Hambrick .15 .40
118 Rocket Ismail .20 .50
119 Dat Nguyen .15 .40
120 Ken-Yon Rambo .15 .40
121 Emmitt Smith .40 1.00
122 Reggie Swinton .15 .40
123 Robert Thomas .15 .40
124 Michael Wiley .15 .40
125 Anthony Wright .15 .40
126 Mike Anderson .15 .40
127 Dwayne Carswell .15 .40
128 Desmond Clark .15 .40
129 Chris Cole .15 .40
130 Terrell Davis .20 .50
131 Gus Frerotte .15 .40
132 Olandis Gary .20 .50
133 Brian Griese .15 .40
134 Kevin Kasper .15 .40
135 Ed McCaffrey .20 .50
136 Phil McGeoghan RC .15 .40
137 John Mobley .15 .40
138 Scottie Montgomery .15 .40
139 Deltha O'Neal .15 .40
140 Trevor Pryce .15 .40
141 Rod Smith .20 .50
142 Al Wilson .20 .50
143 Scotty Anderson .15 .40
144 Charlie Batch .15 .40
145 Aveion Cason .15 .40
146 Germane Crowell .15 .40
147 Reuben Droughns .20 .50
148 Bert Emanuel .20 .50
149 Larry Foster .15 .40
150 Az-Zahir Hakim .15 .40
151 Desmond Howard .20 .50
152 Mike McMahon .15 .40
153 Herman Moore .15 .40
154 Johnnie Morton .20 .50
155 Robert Porcher .15 .40
156 Cory Schlesinger .15 .40
157 David Sloan .15 .40
158 James Stewart .15 .40
159 Lamont Warren .15 .40
160 Donald Driver .20 .50
161 Brett Favre .50 1.25
162 Bubba Franks .15 .40
163 Antonio Freeman .25 .60
164 Kabeer Gbaja-Biamila .15 .40
165 Terry Glenn .20 .50
166 Ahman Green .20 .50
167 William Henderson .15 .40
168 Dorsey Levens .20 .50
169 David Martin .15 .40
170 Rondell Mealey .15 .40
171 Bill Schroeder .15 .40
172 Darren Sharper .15 .40
173 Avion Black .15 .40
174 Tony Boselli .20 .50
175 Corey Bradford .15 .40
176 Marcus Coleman .15 .40
177 Leomont Evans .15 .40
178 Aaron Glenn .15 .40
179 Trevor Insley .15 .40
180 Jermaine Lewis .15 .40
181 Anthony Malbrough .15 .40
182 Frank Moreau .15 .40
183 Mike Quinn .15 .40
184 Charlie Rogers .15 .40
185 Jamie Sharper .20 .50
186 Matt Snider .15 .40
187 Gary Walker .15 .40
188 Kevin Williams RC .40 1.00
189 Kailee Wong .15 .40
190 Chad Bratzke .15 .40
191 Ken Dilger .15 .40
192 Marvin Harrison .20 .50
193 Edgerrin James .20 .50
194 Kevin McDougal .15 .40
195 Rob Morris .15 .40
196 Jerome Pathon .15 .40
197 Marcus Pollard .15 .40
198 Dominic Rhodes .15 .40
199 Marcus Washington .15 .40
200 Reggie Wayne .20 .50
201 Terrence Wilkins .15 .40
202 Tony Brackens .15 .40
203 Kyle Brady .15 .40
204 Mark Brunell .20 .50
205 Donovin Darius .15 .40
206 Sean Dawkins .20 .50
207 Damon Gibson .15 .40
208 Elvis Joseph .15 .40
209 Stacey Mack .15 .40
210 Keenan McCardell .20 .50
211 Hardy Nickerson .15 .40
212 Jonathan Quinn .15 .40
213 Micah Ross RC .15 .40
214 Jimmy Smith .20 .50
215 Fred Taylor .15 .40
216 Patrick Washington .15 .40
217 Derrick Alexander .15 .40
218 Mike Cloud .15 .40
219 Donnie Edwards .15 .40
220 Tony Gonzalez .20 .50
221 Trent Green .15 .40
222 Dante Hall .15 .40
223 Priest Holmes .15 .40
224 Eddie Kennison .20 .50
225 Snoop Minnis .15 .40
226 Larry Parker .15 .40
227 Marvcus Patton .15 .40
228 Tony Richardson .15 .40
229 Mikhael Ricks .15 .40
230 Chris Chambers .15 .40
231 Jay Fiedler .20 .50
232 Oronde Gadsden .15 .40
233 Rob Konrad .15 .40
234 Sam Madison .15 .40
235 Brock Marion .15 .40
236 James McKnight .15 .40
237 Travis Minor .15 .40
238 Jeff Ogden .20 .50
239 Lamar Smith .15 .40
240 Jason Taylor .20 .50
241 Zach Thomas .20 .50
242 Dedric Ward .15 .40
243 Ricky Williams .20 .50
244 Michael Bennett .15 .40
245 Todd Bouman .15 .40
246 Cris Carter .25 .60
247 Byron Chamberlain .15 .40
248 Doug Chapman .15 .40
249 Kenny Clark RC .15 .40
250 Daunte Culpepper .20 .50
251 Nate Jacquet .15 .40
252 Jim Kleinsasser .25 .60
253 Harold Morrow .15 .40
254 Randy Moss .20 .50
255 Jake Reed .20 .50
256 Spergon Wynn .15 .40
257 Drew Bledsoe .20 .50
258 Tom Brady 1.25 3.00
259 Troy Brown .15 .40
260 Fred Coleman .15 .40
261 Marc Edwards .15 .40
262 Kevin Faulk .15 .40
263 Bobby Hamilton .15 .40
264 Ty Law .25 .60
265 Lawyer Milloy .15 .40
266 David Patten .15 .40
267 J.R. Redmond .15 .40
268 Antowain Smith .20 .50
269 Adam Vinatieri .15 .40
270 Jermaine Wiggins .15 .40
271 Aaron Brooks .15 .40
272 Cam Cleeland .15 .40
273 Charlie Clemons RC .15 .40
274 James Fenderson RC .15 .40
275 La'Roi Glover .15 .40
276 Joe Horn .15 .40
277 Willie Jackson .15 .40
278 Sammy Knight .15 .40
279 Michael Lewis RC .20 .50
280 Deuce McAllister .20 .50
281 Terrelle Smith .15 .40
282 Boo Williams .15 .40
283 Robert Wilson .15 .40
284 Tiki Barber .20 .50
285 Micheal Barrow .15 .40
286 Kerry Collins .15 .40
287 Greg Comella .15 .40
288 Thabiti Davis .15 .40
289 Ron Dayne .20 .50
290 Ron Dixon .15 .40
291 Ike Hilliard .15 .40
292 Joe Jurevicius .15 .40
293 Michael Strahan .20 .50
294 Amani Toomer .15 .40
295 Damon Washington .15 .40
296 John Abraham .20 .50
297 Richie Anderson .15 .40
298 Anthony Becht .15 .40
299 Wayne Chrebet .15 .40
300 Laveranues Coles .20 .50
301 James Farrior .15 .40
302 Marvin Jones .15 .40
303 LaMont Jordan .20 .50
304 Curtis Martin .20 .50
305 Santana Moss .20 .50
306 Chad Pennington .15 .40
307 Kevin Swayne .15 .40
308 Vinny Testaverde .15 .40
309 Craig Yeast .15 .40
310 Greg Biekert .15 .40
311 Tim Brown .25 .60
312 Zack Crockett .15 .40
313 Rich Gannon .20 .50
314 Charlie Garner .20 .50
315 Sebastian Janikowski .15 .40
316 Randy Jordan .15 .40
317 Terry Kirby .15 .40
318 Jerry Porter .15 .40
319 Jerry Rice .50 1.25
320 Jon Ritchie .15 .40
321 Tyrone Wheatley .20 .50
322 Roland Williams .15 .40
323 Charles Woodson .25 .60
324 Correll Buckhalter .15 .40
325 Brian Dawkins .25 .60
326 Hugh Douglas .15 .40
327 A.J. Feeley .15 .40
328 Chad Lewis .15 .40
329 Cecil Martin .15 .40
330 Brian Mitchell .20 .50
331 Freddie Mitchell .15 .40
332 Todd Pinkston .15 .40
333 Rod Smart RC .20 .50
334 Duce Staley .15 .40
335 James Thrash .20 .50
336 Jeremiah Trotter .15 .40
337 Troy Vincent .20 .50
338 Kendrell Bell .15 .40
339 Jerome Bettis .25 .60
340 Demetrius Brown RC .15 .40
341 Plaxico Burress .15 .40
342 Troy Edwards .15 .40
343 Chris Fuamatu-Ma'afala .15 .40
344 Jason Gildon .20 .50
345 Earl Holmes .15 .40
346 Joey Porter .20 .50
347 Chad Scott .15 .40
348 Bobby Shaw .15 .40
349 Kordell Stewart .15 .40
350 Hines Ward .20 .50
351 Amos Zereoue .15 .40
352 Adam Archuleta .15 .40
353 Dre Bly .15 .40
354 Isaac Bruce .25 .60
355 Trung Canidate .15 .40
356 Ernie Conwell .15 .40
357 Marshall Faulk .20 .50
358 Torry Holt .20 .50
359 Leonard Little .20 .50
360 Yo Murphy .15 .40
361 Ricky Proehl .20 .50
362 Kurt Warner .20 .50
363 Aeneas Williams .15 .40
364 Drew Brees .50 1.25
365 Curtis Conway .20 .50
366 Tim Dwight .15 .40
367 Terrell Fletcher .15 .40
368 Doug Flutie .20 .50
369 Jeff Graham .15 .40
370 Rodney Harrison .15 .40
371 Ronney Jenkins .15 .40
372 Raylee Johnson .15 .40
373 Freddie Jones .15 .40
374 Ryan McNeil .15 .40
375 Junior Seau .20 .50
376 LaDainian Tomlinson .25 .60
377 Marcellus Wiley .15 .40
378 Kevan Barlow .15 .40
379 Fred Beasley .15 .40
380 Zack Bronson RC .15 .40
381 Andre Carter .15 .40
382 Jeff Garcia .15 .40
383 Garrison Hearst .15 .40
384 Terry Jackson .15 .40
385 Eric Johnson .15 .40
386 Saladin McCullough RC .15 .40
387 Terrell Owens .20 .50
388 Ahmed Plummer .15 .40
389 J.J. Stokes .15 .40
390 Tai Streets .15 .40
391 Vinny Sutherland .15 .40
392 Bryant Young .15 .40
393 Shaun Alexander .15 .40
394 Chad Brown .15 .40
395 Kerwin Cook RC .15 .40
396 Trent Dilfer .15 .40
397 Bobby Engram .15 .40
398 Christian Fauria .15 .40
399 Matt Hasselbeck .15 .40
400 Darrell Jackson .20 .50
401 John Randle .20 .50
402 Koren Robinson .15 .40
403 Anthony Simmons .15 .40
404 Mack Strong .15 .40
405 Ricky Watters .20 .50
406 James Williams WR .15 .40
407 Mike Alstott .15 .40
408 Ronde Barber .15 .40
409 Derrick Brooks .15 .40
410 Jameel Cook .15 .40
411 Warrick Dunn .15 .40
412 Jacquez Green .15 .40
413 Brad Johnson .20 .50
414 Keyshawn Johnson .20 .50
415 Rob Johnson .20 .50
416 John Lynch .20 .50
417 Dave Moore .15 .40
418 Warren Sapp .20 .50
419 Aaron Stecker .15 .40
420 Karl Williams .15 .40
421 Drew Bennett .20 .50
422 Eddie Berlin .15 .40
423 Rafael Cooper RC .15 .40
424 Kevin Dyson .20 .50
425 Eddie George .20 .50
426 Mike Green .15 .40
427 Skip Hicks .15 .40
428 Jevon Kearse .15 .40
429 Erron Kinney .15 .40
430 Derrick Mason .15 .40
431 Justin McCareins .20 .50
432 Steve McNair .20 .50
433 Neil O'Donnell .20 .50
434 Frank Wycheck .15 .40
435 Reidel Anthony .15 .40
436 Jessie Armstead .15 .40
437 Champ Bailey .20 .50
438 Tony Banks .15 .40
439 Michael Bates .15 .40
440 Donnell Bennett .15 .40
441 Ki-Jana Carter .20 .50
442 Stephen Davis .15 .40
443 Zeron Flemister .15 .40
444 Rod Gardner .15 .40
445 Kevin Lockett .15 .40
446 Eric Metcalf .15 .40
447 Sage Rosenfels .20 .50
448 Fred Smoot .20 .50
449 Michael Westbrook .15 .40
450 Danny Wuerffel .20 .50
451 Jason McAddley RC .50 1.25
452 Freddie Milons RC .40 1.00
453 Bryan Thomas RC .40 1.00
454 Levi Jones RC .40 1.00
455 William Green RC .50 1.25
456 Luke Staley RC .40 1.00
457 Daniel Graham RC .50 1.25
458 David Garrard RC .50 1.25
459 Reche Caldwell RC .50 1.25
460 Andra Davis RC .40 1.00
461 Lito Sheppard RC .60 1.50
462 Chris Hope RC .60 1.50
463 Javon Walker RC .60 1.50
464 David Carr RC .40 1.00
465 Alan Harper RC .40 1.00
466 Adrian Peterson RC .50 1.25
467 Kelly Campbell RC .50 1.25
468 Ashley Lelie RC .40 1.00
469 Kurt Kittner RC .40 1.00
470 Antwaan Randle El RC .50 1.25
471 Ladell Betts RC .60 1.50
472 Josh Reed RC .50 1.25
473 Clinton Portis RC .60 1.50
474 Ron Johnson RC .50 1.25
475 Eric Crouch RC .60 1.50
476 Tracey Wistrom RC .50 1.25
477 David Neill RC .40 1.00
478 Ronald Curry RC .40 1.00
479 Lamar Gordon RC .50 1.25
480 Damien Anderson RC .40 1.00
481 Napoleon Harris RC .50 1.25
482 Zak Kustok RC .40 1.00
483 Rocky Calmus RC .50 1.25
484 Roy Williams RC .40 1.00
485 Joey Harrington RC .40 1.00
486 Maurice Morris RC .50 1.25
487 Antonio Bryant RC .60 1.50
488 Josh McCown RC .60 1.50
489 John Henderson RC .50 1.25
490 Quentin Jammer RC .60 1.50
491 Mike Williams RC .40 1.00
492 Patrick Ramsey RC .50 1.25
493 Kenyon Coleman RC .40 1.00
494 DeShaun Foster RC .60 1.50
495 Brian Poli-Dixon RC .40 1.00
496 Cliff Russell RC .40 1.00
497 Brian Westbrook RC .75 2.00
498 Andre Davis RC .40 1.00
499 Larry Tripplett RC .40 1.00
500 Lamont Thompson RC .50 1.25
501 T.J. Duckett RC .40 1.00
502 Dameon Hunter RC .40 1.00
503 Javin Hunter RC .40 1.00
504 Tellis Redmon RC .40 1.00
505 Chester Taylor RC .60 1.50
506 Randy Fasani RC .40 1.00
507 Julius Peppers RC 1.00 2.50
508 Jamin Elliott RC .40 1.00
509 Chad Hutchinson RC .40 1.00
510 Eddie Drummond RC .40 1.00
511 Craig Nall RC .50 1.25
512 Jabar Gaffney RC .40 1.00
513 Jonathan Wells RC .50 1.25
514 Shaun Hill RC .60 1.50
515 Deion Branch RC .60 1.50
516 Rohan Davey RC .60 1.50
517 J.T. O'Sullivan RC .50 1.25
518 Tim Carter RC .50 1.25
519 Daryl Jones RC .40 1.00
520 Jeremy Shockey RC .60 1.50
521 Seth Burford RC .40 1.00
522 Brandon Doman RC .40 1.00
523 Jerramy Stevens RC .60 1.50
524 Travis Stephens RC .40 1.00
525 Marquise Walker RC .40 1.00

2002 Pacific Chicago National

Available via a wrapper redemption at the Pacific booth during the 2002 Chicago National Convention, this 8-card set was serial-numbered to just 500 copies. Collectors had to open a box of 2002 Pacific football or 2001-02 Pacific hockey product to receive the set. Each card featured an NHL player and an NFL player on either side.

COMPLETE SET (8) 12.00 30.00
1 Ilya Kovalchuk / Michael Vick 2.00 5.00
2 Joe Thornton / Tom Brady 4.00 10.00
3 Eric Daze / Anthony Thomas 2.00 5.00
4 Peter Forsberg / Brian Griese 2.00 5.00
5 Mike Modano / Emmitt Smith 2.50 6.00
6 Steve Yzerman / Joey Harrington 2.00 5.00
7 Eric Lindros / Ron Dayne 1.50 4.00
8 Chris Pronger / Kurt Warner 2.00 5.00

2002 Pacific Extreme LTD

ETS 1-450: 20X TO 50X BASIC CARDS
*ROOKIES 451-500: 8X TO 20X BASIC CARDS
STATED ODDS 1:145
STATED PRINT RUN 24 SER.#'d SETS

2002 Pacific LTD

ETS 1-450: 8X TO 20X BASIC CARDS
*ROOKIES 451-500: 3X TO 8X
STATED ODDS 1:37
STATED PRINT RUN 71 SER.#'d SETS

2002 Pacific Premiere Date

ETS 1-450: 12X TO 30X BASIC CARDS
*ROOKIES 451-500: 5X TO 12X
STATED ODDS 1:37 HOBBY
STATED PRINT RUN 36 SER.#'d SETS

2002 Pacific Cramer's Choice

Inserted at a rate of 1:721 packs, this 10-card insert features Pacific's picks for the top NFL players. The cards were serial numbered of 120-sets.

STATED ODDS 1:721
STATED PRINT RUN 120 SER.#'d SETS
1 David Boston 5.00 12.00
2 Anthony Thomas 6.00 15.00
3 Emmitt Smith 12.00 30.00
4 Brett Favre 15.00 40.00
5 Priest Holmes 5.00 12.00
6 Tom Brady 40.00 100.00
7 Marshall Faulk 6.00 15.00
8 Kurt Warner 6.00 15.00
9 Terrell Owens 6.00 15.00
10 Shaun Alexander 5.00 12.00

2002 Pacific Draft Force

Inserted in packs at a rate of 1:145, this 20-card insert set showcases some of the top draft picks for 2002.

COMPLETE SET (20) 30.00 80.00
STATED ODDS 1:145
1 William Green 1.50 4.00
2 Luke Staley 1.25 3.00
3 Reche Caldwell 1.50 4.00
4 David Carr 1.25 3.00
5 Ashley Lelie 1.25 3.00
6 Kurt Kittner 1.25 3.00
7 Antwaan Randle El 1.50 4.00
8 Ladell Betts 2.00 5.00
9 Josh Reed 1.50 4.00
10 Clinton Portis 2.00 5.00
11 Eric Crouch 2.00 5.00
12 Lamar Gordon 1.50 4.00
13 Joey Harrington 1.25 3.00
14 Maurice Morris 1.50 4.00
15 Antonio Bryant 2.00 5.00
16 Josh McCown 2.00 5.00
17 Patrick Ramsey 1.50 4.00
18 DeShaun Foster 2.00 5.00
19 Brian Westbrook 2.50 6.00
20 Andre Davis 1.25 3.00

2002 Pacific Feature Attractions

Inserted in packs at a rate of 1:37, this 20-card insert set resembles that of a movie poster.

COMPLETE SET (20) 25.00 60.00
STATED ODDS 1:37
1 Michael Vick .75 2.00
2 Anthony Thomas .75 2.00
3 Emmitt Smith 1.50 4.00
4 Brett Favre 2.00 5.00
4 Brian Griese .60 1.50
6 Ahman Green .75 2.00
7 Edgerrin James .75 2.00
8 Priest Holmes .60 1.50
9 Ricky Williams .75 2.00
10 Daunte Culpepper .75 2.00
11 Tom Brady 5.00 12.00
12 Ron Dayne .75 2.00
13 Curtis Martin .75 2.00
14 Jerry Rice 2.00 5.00
15 Marshall Faulk .75 2.00
16 Torry Holt .75 2.00
17 Kurt Warner .75 2.00
18 LaDainian Tomlinson 1.00 2.50
19 Warrick Dunn .60 1.50
20 Eddie George .75 2.00

2002 Pacific Game Worn Jerseys

Inserted in packs at a rate of 2:37 hobby and 1 per retail box, this 50-card insert set features pieces of authentic game-worn jerseys.

STATED ODDS 2:37 HOBBY BOXES
STATED ODDS ONE PER RETAIL BOX
1 David Boston 2.50 6.00
2 MarTay Jenkins 2.50 6.00
3 Jake Plummer 2.50 6.00
4 Michael Vick 3.00 8.00
5 Jamal Lewis 3.00 8.00
6 Travis Henry 2.50 6.00
7 Steve Smith 4.00 10.00
8 Anthony Thomas 3.00 8.00
9 Peter Warrick 2.50 6.00
10 Quincy Carter 2.50 6.00
11 Terrell Davis 3.00 8.00
12 Mike McMahon 2.50 6.00
13 Brett Favre 8.00 20.00
14 Antonio Freeman 4.00 10.00
15 Ahman Green 3.00 8.00
16 Marvin Harrison 3.00 8.00
17 Reggie Wayne 3.00 8.00
18 Mark Brunell 3.00 8.00
19 Priest Holmes 2.50 6.00
20 Snoop Minnis 2.50 6.00
21 Chris Chambers 2.50 6.00
22 Ricky Williams 3.00 8.00
23 Daunte Culpepper 3.00 8.00
24 Randy Moss 3.00 8.00
25 Spergon Wynn 2.50 6.00
26 Drew Bledsoe 3.00 8.00
27 Tom Brady 20.00 50.00
28 Aaron Brooks 2.50 6.00
29 Jesse Palmer 2.50 6.00
30 Curtis Martin 3.00 8.00
31 Santana Moss 3.00 8.00
32 Tim Brown 4.00 10.00
33 Jerry Rice 8.00 20.00
34 Marques Tuiasosopo 2.50 6.00
35 Correll Buckhalter 2.50 6.00
36 Jerome Bettis 4.00 10.00
37 Marshall Faulk 3.00 8.00
38 Kurt Warner 3.00 8.00
39 Aeneas Williams 2.50 6.00
40 LaDainian Tomlinson 4.00 10.00
41 Kevan Barlow 2.50 6.00
42 Terrell Owens 3.00 8.00
43 Shaun Alexander 2.50 6.00
44 Trent Dilfer 2.50 6.00
45 Matt Hasselbeck 2.50 6.00
46 Warrick Dunn 2.50 6.00
47 Justin McCareins 3.00 8.00
48 Steve McNair 3.00 8.00
49 Tony Banks 2.50 6.00
50 Sage Rosenfels 3.00 8.00

2002 Pacific Pro Bowl Die Cuts

Inserted in packs at a rate of 1:37, this 20-card insert set is die-cut in the shape of Diamond Head, a famous volcano in Hawaii -- home of the Pro Bowl.

COMPLETE SET (20) 25.00 60.00
STATED ODDS 1:37
1 David Boston 1.25 3.00
2 Brian Urlacher 2.00 5.00
3 Corey Dillon 1.25 3.00
4 Ahman Green 1.50 4.00
5 Marvin Harrison 1.50 4.00
6 Priest Holmes 1.25 3.00
7 Troy Brown 1.25 3.00
8 Curtis Martin 1.50 4.00
9 Tim Brown 2.00 5.00
10 Rich Gannon 1.50 4.00
11 Kordell Stewart 1.25 3.00
12 Hines Ward 1.50 4.00
13 Marshall Faulk 1.50 4.00
14 Torry Holt 1.50 4.00
15 Kurt Warner 1.50 4.00
16 Jeff Garcia 1.25 3.00
17 Garrison Hearst 1.25 3.00
18 Terrell Owens 1.50 4.00
19 Mike Alstott 1.25 3.00
20 Keyshawn Johnson 1.50 4.00

2002 Pacific Rocket Launchers

serted in packs at a rate of 2:37, this 20-card insert set launches itself into the next century with its unique futuristic design. The featured player on each card front is also computer enhanced with a grid-like design.

COMPLETE SET (20) 12.50 30.00
STATED ODDS 2:37
1 Jake Plummer .50 1.25
2 Michael Vick .60 1.50
3 Chris Weinke .50 1.25
4 Tim Couch .50 1.25
5 Quincy Carter .50 1.25
6 Brian Griese .50 1.25
7 Mark Brunell .60 1.50
8 Daunte Culpepper .60 1.50
9 Drew Bledsoe .60 1.50
10 Tom Brady 4.00 10.00
11 Aaron Brooks .50 1.25
12 Kerry Collins .50 1.25
13 Kordell Stewart .50 1.25
14 Drew Brees 1.50 4.00
15 Jeff Garcia .50 1.25
16 Brad Johnson .60 1.50
17 Steve McNair .60 1.50
18 David Carr .50 1.25
19 Joey Harrington .50 1.25
20 Patrick Ramsey .60 1.50

2002 Pacific War Room

serted at a rate of 1:73 packs, this 10-card insert set has color action shots of each featured player along with his college stats running along the right side of the card fronts.

COMPLETE SET (10) 12.00 30.00
STATED ODDS 1:73
1 William Green 1.00 2.50
2 David Carr .75 2.00
3 Ashley Lelie .75 2.00
4 Kurt Kittner .75 2.00
5 Josh Reed 1.00 2.50
6 Clinton Portis 1.25 3.00
7 Joey Harrington .75 2.00
8 Josh McCown 1.25 3.00
9 Patrick Ramsey 1.00 2.50
10 DeShaun Foster 1.25 3.00

2002 Pacific Adrenaline

leased in September, 2002, this set features 288 cards including over 100 rookies. Boxes contained 36 packs, 10 cards per pack. There were 20 boxes per case. SRP was $2.99 per pack.

COMPLETE SET (288) 25.00 50.00
1 Damien Anderson RC .40 1.00
2 David Boston .20 .50
3 Wendell Bryant RC .40 1.00
4 Thomas Jones .20 .50
5 Jason McAddley RC .50 1.25
6 Josh McCown RC .60 1.50
7 Jake Plummer .20 .50
8 Frank Sanders .20 .50
9 Josh Scobey RC .50 1.25
10 Keith Brooking .20 .50
11 T.J. Duckett RC .40 1.00
12 Warrick Dunn .20 .50
13 Brian Finneran .20 .50
14 Kahlil Hill RC .40 1.00
15 Shawn Jefferson .20 .50
16 Kurt Kittner RC .40 1.00
17 Will Overstreet RC .40 1.00
18 Michael Vick .25 .60
19 Ron Johnson RC .50 1.25
20 Jamal Lewis .25 .60
21 Ray Lewis .30 .75
22 Chris Redman .20 .50
23 Tellis Redmon RC .40 1.00
24 Brandon Stokley .20 .50
25 Chester Taylor RC .60 1.50
26 Travis Taylor .20 .50
27 Anthony Weaver RC .40 1.00
28 Drew Bledsoe .25 .60
29 Shawn Bryson .20 .50
30 Larry Centers .20 .50
31 Ryan Denney RC .40 1.00
32 Travis Henry .20 .50
33 Richard Huntley .20 .50
34 Eric Moulds .20 .50
35 Peerless Price .20 .50
36 Josh Reed RC .50 1.25
37 Isaac Byrd .20 .50
38 Randy Fasani RC .40 1.00
39 DeShaun Foster RC .60 1.50
40 Kyle Johnson RC .40 1.00
41 Muhsin Muhammad .20 .50
42 Julius Peppers RC 1.00 2.50
43 Lamar Smith .20 .50
44 Steve Smith .30 .75
45 Chris Weinke .20 .50
46 Marty Booker .20 .50
47 Chris Chandler .25 .60
48 Eric McCoo RC .40 1.00
49 Jim Miller .20 .50
50 Adrian Peterson RC .50 1.25
51 Marcus Robinson .25 .60
52 David Terrell .20 .50
53 Anthony Thomas .25 .60
54 Brian Urlacher .30 .75
55 Corey Dillon .20 .50
56 Gus Frerotte .20 .50
57 Chad Johnson .20 .50
58 Jon Kitna .20 .50
59 Justin Smith .25 .60
60 Takeo Spikes .20 .50
61 Lamont Thompson RC .50 1.25
62 Peter Warrick .20 .50
63 Michael Westbrook .20 .50
64 Tim Couch .20 .50
65 Andre Davis RC .40 1.00
66 JaJuan Dawson .20 .50
67 William Green RC .50 1.25
68 James Jackson .20 .50
69 Kevin Johnson .20 .50
70 Jamir Miller .20 .50
71 Quincy Morgan .20 .50
72 Jamel White .20 .50
73 Antonio Bryant RC .60 1.50
74 Quincy Carter .20 .50
75 Woody Dantzler RC .50 1.25
76 Joey Galloway .25 .60
77 Ennis Haywood RC .40 1.00
78 Chad Hutchinson RC .40 1.00
79 Rocket Ismail .25 .60
80 Emmitt Smith .50 1.25
81 Roy Williams RC .40 1.00
82 Mike Anderson .20 .50
83 Terrell Davis .25 .60
84 Brian Griese .20 .50
85 Herb Haygood RC .40 1.00
86 Ashley Lelie RC .40 1.00
87 Ed McCaffrey .25 .60
88 Deltha O'Neal .20 .50
89 Clinton Portis RC .60 1.50
90 Rod Smith .25 .60
91 Scotty Anderson .20 .50
92 Eddie Drummond RC .40 1.00
93 Az-Zahir Hakim .20 .50
94 Joey Harrington RC .40 1.00
95 Mike McMahon .20 .50
96 James Mungro RC .60 1.50
97 Bill Schroeder .20 .50
98 Luke Staley RC .40 1.00
99 James Stewart .20 .50
100 Marques Anderson RC .50 1.25
101 Najeh Davenport RC .40 1.00
102 Brett Favre .60 1.50
103 Robert Ferguson .25 .60
104 Bubba Franks .20 .50
105 Terry Glenn .25 .60
106 Ahman Green .25 .60
107 Craig Nall RC .50 1.25
108 Javon Walker RC .60 1.50
109 James Allen .20 .50
110 Jarrod Baxter RC .40 1.00
111 Corey Bradford .20 .50
112 David Carr RC .40 1.00
113 Delvon Flowers RC .40 1.00
114 Jabar Gaffney RC .40 1.00
115 Jermaine Lewis .20 .50
116 Travis Prentice .20 .50
117 Jonathan Wells RC .50 1.25
118 Brian Allen RC .40 1.00
119 Chad Bratzke .20 .50
120 Marvin Harrison .25 .60
121 Qadry Ismail .20 .50
122 Edgerrin James .25 .60
123 Peyton Manning .75 2.00
124 Rob Morris .20 .50
125 Dominic Rhodes .20 .50
126 Reggie Wayne .25 .60
127 Tony Brackens .20 .50
128 Mark Brunell .25 .60
129 Donovin Darius .20 .50
130 David Garrard RC .50 1.25
131 John Henderson RC .50 1.25
132 Stacey Mack .20 .50
133 Bobby Shaw .20 .50
134 Jimmy Smith .25 .60
135 Fred Taylor .20 .50
136 Omar Easy RC .50 1.25
137 Eddie Freeman RC .40 1.00
138 Tony Gonzalez .25 .60
139 Trent Green .20 .50
140 Priest Holmes .20 .50
141 Eddie Kennison .25 .60
142 Snoop Minnis .20 .50
143 Johnnie Morton .25 .60
144 Ryan Sims RC .60 1.50
145 Chris Chambers .20 .50
146 Jay Fiedler .25 .60
147 Oronde Gadsden .20 .50
148 Leonard Henry RC .40 1.00
149 James McKnight .20 .50
150 Travis Minor .20 .50
151 Sam Simmons RC .40 1.00
152 Zach Thomas .25 .60
153 Ricky Williams .25 .60
154 Derrick Alexander .20 .50
155 Jeremy Allen RC .40 1.00
156 Atrews Bell RC .40 1.00
157 Michael Bennett .20 .50
158 Kelly Campbell RC .50 1.25
159 Byron Chamberlain .20 .50
160 Doug Chapman .20 .50
161 Daunte Culpepper .25 .60
162 Randy Moss .25 .60
163 Tom Brady 1.50 4.00
164 Deion Branch RC .60 1.50
165 Troy Brown .20 .50
166 Rohan Davey RC .60 1.50
167 Kevin Faulk .20 .50
168 Daniel Graham RC .50 1.25
169 David Patten .20 .50
170 Antowain Smith .25 .60
171 Antwoine Womack RC .40 1.00
172 Aaron Brooks .20 .50
173 Charlie Clemons .20 .50
174 Joe Horn .20 .50
175 Sammy Knight .20 .50
176 Deuce McAllister .25 .60
177 J.T. O'Sullivan RC .50 1.25
178 Jerome Pathon .20 .50
179 Donte Stallworth RC .60 1.50
180 Ricky Williams RC .50 1.25
181 Tiki Barber .25 .60
182 Tim Carter RC .50 1.25
183 Kerry Collins .20 .50
184 Ron Dayne .25 .60
185 Ike Hilliard .20 .50
186 Daryl Jones RC .40 1.00

187 Jeremy Shockey RC .60 1.50
188 Michael Strahan .25 .60
189 Amani Toomer .20 .50
190 Wayne Chrebet .20 .50
191 Laveranues Coles .25 .60
192 Alan Harper RC .40 1.00
193 LaMont Jordan .25 .60
194 Curtis Martin .25 .60
195 Chad Morton .20 .50
196 Santana Moss .25 .60
197 Vinny Testaverde .20 .50
198 Bryan Thomas RC .40 1.00
199 Tim Brown .30 .75
200 Ronald Curry RC .40 1.00
201 Rich Gannon .25 .60
202 Charlie Garner .25 .60
203 Napoleon Harris RC .50 1.25
204 Larry Ned RC .40 1.00
205 Jerry Rice .60 1.50
206 Tyrone Wheatley .25 .60
207 Charles Woodson .30 .75
208 Michael Lewis RC .50 1.25
209 Donovan McNabb .25 .60
210 Freddie Milons RC .40 1.00
211 Freddie Mitchell .20 .50
212 Todd Pinkston .20 .50
213 Lito Sheppard RC .60 1.50
214 Duce Staley .20 .50
215 James Thrash .25 .60
216 Brian Westbrook RC .75 2.00
217 Kendrell Bell .20 .50
218 Jerome Bettis .30 .75
219 Plaxico Burress .20 .50
220 Verron Haynes RC .40 1.00
221 Chris Hope RC .60 1.50
222 Lee Mays RC .40 1.00
223 Antwaan Randle El RC .50 1.25
224 Kordell Stewart .20 .50
225 Hines Ward .25 .60
226 Isaac Bruce .30 .75
227 Eric Crouch RC .60 1.50
228 Marshall Faulk .25 .60
229 Lamar Gordon RC .50 1.25
230 Torry Holt .25 .60
231 Leonard Little .25 .60
232 Robert Thomas RC .40 1.00
233 Kurt Warner .25 .60
234 Terrence Wilkins .20 .50
235 Drew Brees .60 1.50
236 Seth Burford RC .40 1.00
237 Reche Caldwell RC .50 1.25
238 Curtis Conway .25 .60
239 Doug Flutie .25 .60
240 Quentin Jammer RC .60 1.50
241 Brian Poli-Dixon RC .40 1.00
242 Junior Seau .25 .60
243 LaDainian Tomlinson .30 .75
244 Kevan Barlow .20 .50
245 Andre Carter .20 .50
246 Brandon Doman RC .40 1.00
247 Jeff Garcia .20 .50
248 Garrison Hearst .20 .50
249 Terrell Owens .25 .60
250 Derek Smith RC .50 1.25
251 J.J. Stokes .20 .50
252 Vinny Sutherland .20 .50
253 Shaun Alexander .20 .50
254 Chad Brown .20 .50
255 Trent Dilfer .20 .50
256 Bobby Engram .20 .50
257 Darrell Jackson .25 .60
258 Nakoa McElrath RC .40 1.00
259 Maurice Morris RC .50 1.25
260 Koren Robinson .20 .50
261 Jerramy Stevens RC .60 1.50
262 Mike Alstott .20 .50
263 Derrick Brooks .20 .50
264 Brad Johnson .25 .60
265 Keyshawn Johnson .25 .60
266 Keenan McCardell .25 .60
267 Michael Pittman .25 .60
268 Warren Sapp .25 .60
269 Travis Stephens RC .40 1.00
270 Marquise Walker RC .40 1.00
271 Rocky Calmus RC .50 1.25
272 Kevin Dyson .25 .60
273 Eddie George .25 .60
274 Albert Haynesworth RC .60 1.50
275 Derrick Mason .20 .50
276 Steve McNair .25 .60
277 Dicenzo Miller RC .40 1.00
278 Jake Schifino RC .40 1.00
279 Tank Williams RC .50 1.25
280 Champ Bailey .25 .60
281 Ladell Betts RC .60 1.50
282 Stephen Davis .20 .50
283 Rod Gardner .20 .50
284 Jacquez Green .20 .50
285 Shane Matthews .20 .50
286 Patrick Ramsey RC .50 1.25
287 Cliff Russell RC .40 1.00
288 Jeremiah Trotter .20 .50

2002 Pacific Adrenaline Blue

*ROOKIES: 1.5X TO 4X BASIC CARDS
STATED ODDS 2:37
STATED PRINT RUN 165 SER.#'d SETS

2002 Pacific Adrenaline Red

ETS: 1X TO 2.5X BASIC CARDS
*ROOKIES: .5X TO 1.2X
ONE PER PACK

2002 Pacific Adrenaline Driven

Inserted at a rate of 1:5, this set features cards of the NFL's top offensive players.

COMPLETE SET (27) 20.00 50.00
STATED ODDS 1:5
1 T.J. Duckett .50 1.25
2 Michael Vick .60 1.50
3 Drew Bledsoe .60 1.50
4 DeShaun Foster .75 2.00
5 Anthony Thomas .60 1.50
6 William Green .60 1.50
7 Emmitt Smith 1.25 3.00
8 Ashley Lelie .50 1.25
9 Clinton Portis .75 2.00
10 Joey Harrington .50 1.25
11 Brett Favre 1.50 4.00
12 Javon Walker .75 2.00
13 David Carr .50 1.25
14 Edgerrin James .60 1.50
15 Ricky Williams .60 1.50
16 Daunte Culpepper .60 1.50
17 Randy Moss .60 1.50
18 Tom Brady 4.00 10.00
19 Donte Stallworth .75 2.00
20 Jerry Rice 1.50 4.00
21 Antwaan Randle El .60 1.50
22 Eric Crouch .75 2.00
23 Marshall Faulk .00 1.60
24 Kurt Warner .60 1.50
25 Drew Brees 1.50 4.00
26 LaDainian Tomlinson .75 2.00
27 Patrick Ramsey .60 1.50

2002 Pacific Adrenaline Game Worn Jerseys

serted at a rate of 2:37, cards in this set feature swatches of authentic game used jerseys. There is also a Gold parallel to this set serial #'d to 25.

STATED ODDS 2:37
*GOLD/25: .75X TO 2X BASIC JSY
GOLD STATED PRINT RUN 25 SETS
1 Thomas Jones 2.00 5.00
2 Jake Plummer 2.00 5.00
3 Michael Vick 2.50 6.00
4 Chris Redman 2.00 5.00
5 Drew Bledsoe 2.50 6.00
6 Peerless Price 2.00 5.00
7 Brian Urlacher 3.00 8.00
8 Corey Dillon 2.00 5.00
9 Takeo Spikes 2.00 5.00
10 Tim Couch 2.00 5.00
11 Ken-Yon Rambo 2.00 5.00
12 Emmitt Smith 5.00 12.00
13 Mike Anderson 2.00 5.00
14 Brett Favre 6.00 15.00
15 Terry Glenn 2.50 6.00
16 Edgerrin James 2.50 6.00
17 Peyton Manning 8.00 20.00
18 Mark Brunell 2.50 6.00
19 Stacey Mack 2.00 5.00
20 Fred Taylor 2.00 5.00
21 Tony Richardson 2.00 5.00
22 Ricky Williams 2.50 6.00
23 Daunte Culpepper 2.50 6.00
24 Jim Kleinsasser 3.00 8.00
25 Randy Moss 2.50 6.00
26 Christian Fauria 2.00 5.00
27 Patrick Pass 2.00 5.00
28 Ron Dayne 2.50 6.00
29 Anthony Becht 2.00 5.00
30 LaMont Jordan 2.50 6.00
31 Curtis Martin 2.50 6.00
32 Jerry Rice 6.00 15.00
33 Jon Ritchie 2.00 5.00
34 Donovan McNabb 2.50 6.00
35 Brian Mitchell 2.50 6.00
36 Jerome Bettis 3.00 8.00
37 Mark Bruener 2.50 6.00
38 Kordell Stewart 2.00 5.00
39 Marshall Faulk 2.50 6.00
40 Kurt Warner 2.50 6.00
41 Terrence Wilkins 2.00 5.00
42 Drew Brees 6.00 15.00
43 Trevor Gaylor 2.00 5.00
44 LaDainian Tomlinson 3.00 8.00
45 Jeff Garcia 2.00 5.00
46 Terrell Owens 2.50 6.00
47 Shaun Alexander 2.00 5.00
48 Eddie George 2.50 6.00
49 Steve McNair 2.50 6.00
50 Shane Matthews 2.00 5.00

2002 Pacific Adrenaline Playmakers

Inserted at a rate of 1:5, this set features some of the NFL's top playmakers.

COMPLETE SET (18) 10.00 25.00
STATED ODDS 1:5
1 T.J. Duckett .40 1.00
2 Michael Vick .50 1.25
3 Anthony Thomas .50 1.25
4 William Green .50 1.25
5 Emmitt Smith 1.00 2.50
6 Ashley Lelie .40 1.00
7 Joey Harrington .40 1.00
8 Brett Favre 1.25 3.00
9 David Carr .40 1.00
10 Randy Moss .50 1.25
11 Tom Brady 3.00 8.00
12 Donte Stallworth .60 1.50
13 Jerry Rice 1.25 3.00
14 Donovan McNabb .50 1.25
15 Eric Crouch .60 1.50
16 Marshall Faulk .50 1.25
17 Kurt Warner .50 1.25
18 LaDainian Tomlinson .60 1.50

2002 Pacific Adrenaline Power Surge

serted at a rate of 2:37, this set features 6 players likely to surge their team to victory.

COMPLETE SET (6) 10.00 25.00
STATED ODDS 2:37
1 Michael Vick .75 2.00
2 Emmitt Smith 1.50 4.00
3 Joey Harrington .60 1.50
4 Brett Favre 2.00 5.00
5 David Carr .60 1.50
6 Tom Brady 5.00 12.00

2002 Pacific Adrenaline Rookie Report

serted at a rate of 1:7, this set focuses on twelve of the NFL's best 2002 rookies.

COMPLETE SET (12) 10.00 25.00
STATED ODDS 1:7
1 T.J. Duckett .30 .75
2 DeShaun Foster .50 1.25
3 William Green .40 1.00
4 Ashley Lelie .30 .75
5 Clinton Portis .50 1.25
6 Joey Harrington .30 .75
7 Javon Walker .50 1.25
8 David Carr .30 .75
9 Jabar Gaffney .30 .75
10 Donte Stallworth .50 1.25
11 Antwaan Randle El .40 1.00
12 Patrick Ramsey .40 1.00

2002 Pacific Adrenaline Rush

serted at a rate of 1:5, this set highlights the NFL's top runningbacks.

COMPLETE SET (18) 10.00 25.00
STATED ODDS 1:5
1 T.J. Duckett .40 1.00
2 DeShaun Foster .60 1.50
3 Anthony Thomas .50 1.25
4 Corey Dillon .40 1.00
5 William Green .50 1.25
6 Emmitt Smith 1.00 2.50
7 Terrell Davis .50 1.25
8 Clinton Portis .60 1.50
9 Ahman Green .50 1.25
10 Edgerrin James .50 1.25
11 Priest Holmes .40 1.00
12 Ricky Williams .50 1.25
13 Curtis Martin .50 1.25
14 Jerome Bettis .50 1.25
15 Marshall Faulk .50 1.25
16 LaDainian Tomlinson .60 1.50
17 Shaun Alexander .40 1.00
18 Eddie George .50 1.25

1996 Pacific Dynagon

e 1996 Dynagon Prism set was issued in one series totalling 144 cards. The set was issued in two card packs with 36 packs in a box and 20 boxes in a case. Against a gold background which includes a NFL football, the player's photo is shown. The player's name is printed on the right. The horizontal backs include another photo as well as some text. The set is sequenced in alphabetical order within alphabetical team order. Rookie Cards include Tim Biakabutuka, Eddie George, Terry Glenn, Keyshawn Johnson and Lawrence Phillips.

COMPLETE SET (144) 25.00 60.00
1 Larry Centers .30 .75
2 Garrison Hearst .30 .75
3 Dave Krieg .15 .40
4 Frank Sanders .30 .75
5 Jeff George .30 .75
6 Craig Heyward .15 .40
7 Terance Mathis .15 .40
8 Eric Metcalf .15 .40
9 Todd Collins .30 .75
10 Darick Holmes .15 .40
11 Jim Kelly .60 1.50
12 Eric Moulds RC 1.50 4.00
13 Bryce Paup .15 .40
14 Thurman Thomas .60 1.50
15 Tim Biakabutuka RC .60 1.50
16 Blake Brockermeyer .15 .40
17 Mark Carrier WR .15 .40
18 Kerry Collins .60 1.50
19 Derrick Moore .15 .40
20 Bobby Engram RC .60 1.50
21 Jeff Graham .15 .40
22 Erik Kramer .15 .40
23 Rashaan Salaam .30 .75
24 Steve Stenstrom .15 .40
25 Chris Zorich .15 .40
26 Jeff Blake .60 1.50
27 David Dunn .15 .40
28 Carl Pickens .30 .75
29 Darnay Scott .30 .75
30 Earnest Byner .15 .40
31 Leroy Hoard .15 .40
32 Keenan McCardell .60 1.50
33 Eric Zeier .15 .40
34 Troy Aikman 1.25 3.00
35 Chris Boniol .15 .40
36 Michael Irvin .60 1.50
37 Daryl Johnston .30 .75
38 Deion Sanders .75 2.00
39 Emmitt Smith 2.00 5.00
40 Stepfret Williams .15 .40
41 John Elway 2.50 6.00
42 Terrell Davis 1.00 2.50
43 Anthony Miller .30 .75
44 Shannon Sharpe .30 .75
45 Scott Mitchell .30 .75
46 Herman Moore .30 .75
47 Brett Perriman .15 .40
48 Barry Sanders 2.00 5.00
49 Cory Schlesinger .15 .40
50 Edgar Bennett .30 .75
51 Robert Brooks .60 1.50
52 Mark Chmura .30 .75
53 Brett Favre 2.50 6.00
54 Reggie White .60 1.50
55 Eddie George RC 1.50 4.00
56 Steve McNair 1.00 2.50
57 Chris Sanders .30 .75
58 Rodney Thomas .15 .40
59 Ben Bronson RC .15 .40
60 Zack Crockett .15 .40
61 Marshall Faulk .75 2.00
62 Jim Harbaugh .30 .75
63 Mark Brunell .75 2.00
64 Kevin Hardy RC .60 1.50
65 Willie Jackson .30 .75
66 Pete Mitchell .30 .75
67 James O.Stewart .30 .75
68 Marcus Allen .60 1.50
69 Steve Bono .15 .40
70 Lake Dawson .15 .40
71 Neil Smith .30 .75
72 Tamarick Vanover .30 .75
73 Irving Fryar .30 .75
74 Terry Kirby .30 .75
75 Dan Marino 2.50 6.00
76 O.J. McDuffie .30 .75
77 Bernie Parmalee .15 .40
78 Stanley Pritchett RC .30 .75
79 Cris Carter .60 1.50
80 Qadry Ismail .30 .75
81 Chad May .15 .40
82 Warren Moon .30 .75
83 Robert Smith .30 .75
84 Drew Bledsoe .75 2.00
85 Ben Coates .30 .75
86 Terry Glenn RC 1.25 3.00
87 Curtis Martin 1.00 2.50
88 Willie McGinest .15 .40
89 Mario Bates .30 .75
90 Jim Everett .15 .40
91 Wayne Martin .15 .40
92 Shane Pahukoa RC .15 .40
93 Ray Zellars .15 .40
94 Dave Brown .15 .40
95 Chris Calloway .15 .40
96 Rodney Hampton .30 .75
97 Tyrone Wheatley .30 .75
98 Wayne Chrebet .75 2.00
99 Glenn Foley .30 .75
100 Keyshawn Johnson RC 1.25 3.00
101 Adrian Murrell .30 .75
102 Alex Van Dyke RC .30 .75
103 Tim Brown .60 1.50
104 Billy Joe Hobert .30 .75
105 Rocket Ismail .15 .40
106 Napoleon Kaufman .60 1.50
107 Harvey Williams .15 .40
108 Charlie Garner .30 .75
109 Rodney Peete .15 .40
110 Ricky Watters .30 .75
111 Calvin Williams .15 .40
112 Mark Bruener .15 .40
113 Kevin Greene .30 .75
114 Ernie Mills .15 .40
115 Kordell Stewart .60 1.50
116 Yancey Thigpen .30 .75
117 Dave Barr .15 .40
118 Jerome Bettis .60 1.50
119 Isaac Bruce .60 1.50
120 Lawrence Phillips RC .60 1.50
121 J.T. Thomas .15 .40
122 Ronnie Harmon .15 .40
123 Aaron Hayden RC .15 .40
124 Stan Humphries .30 .75
125 Junior Seau .60 1.50
126 William Floyd .30 .75
127 Elvis Grbac .30 .75
128 Jerry Rice 1.25 3.00
129 J.J. Stokes .60 1.50
130 Steve Young 1.00 2.50
131 Joey Galloway .60 1.50
132 Cortez Kennedy .15 .40
133 Kevin Mawae .15 .40
134 Rick Mirer .30 .75
135 Chris Warren .30 .75
136 Trent Dilfer .60 1.50
137 Jerry Ellison .15 .40
138 Alvin Harper .15 .40
139 Errict Rhett .30 .75
140 Terry Allen .30 .75
141 Brian Mitchell .15 .40
142 Gus Frerotte .30 .75
143 Michael Westbrook .60 1.50
144 Heath Shuler .30 .75

1996 Pacific Dynagon Best Kept Secrets

sued one per pack, these 100 standard-size cards feature many lesser known players who rarely get proper recognition for their skills. The players photo is in the middle with his name in the lower right. The back features another photo as well as some text information. The cards were numbered with a "BKS" prefix.

COMPLETE SET (100) 15.00 30.00
ONE PER PACK
1 Wendall Gaines .07 .20
2 Randy Kirk .07 .20
3 Anthony Redmon .07 .20
4 Bernard Wilson .07 .20
5 Ron Davis .07 .20
6 Roell Preston .15 .40
7 Robbie Tobeck .07 .20
8 Harold Bishop .07 .20
9 Dan Footman .07 .20
10 Ernest Hunter .07 .20
11 Tony Cline .07 .20
12 Kurt Schulz .07 .20
13 Alex Van Pelt .50 1.25
14 Howard Griffith .07 .20
15 Mark Thomas .07 .20
16 Keshon Johnson DB .07 .20
17 Kevin Miniefield .07 .20
18 Steve Stenstrom .15 .40
19 Jeff Cothran .07 .20
20 Jeff Hill .07 .20
21 Alundis Brice .07 .20
22 Cory Fleming .07 .20
23 Kendell Watkins .07 .20
24 Charlie Williams .07 .20
25 Byron Chamberlain .60 1.50
26 Jerry Evans .07 .20
27 Rod Smith WR 1.25 3.00
28 Kevin Hickman .07 .20
29 Ron Rivers .15 .40
30 Henry Thomas .07 .20
31 Keith Crawford .07 .20
32 Doug Evans .15 .40
33 William Henderson .25 .60
34 John Jurkovic .07 .20
35 Blaine Bishop .07 .20
36 Kenny Davidson .07 .20
37 Erik Norgard .07 .20
38 Derwin Gray .07 .20
39 Ellis Johnson .07 .20
40 Tony McCoy .07 .20
41 Glen Sanders .07 .20
42 Bernard Whittington .07 .20
43 Travis Davis .07 .20
44 Rogerick Green .07 .20
45 Rob Johnson .25 .60
46 Curtis Marsh .07 .20
47 Matt Blundin .15 .40
48 Lin Elliott .07 .20
49 Pellom McDaniels .07 .20
50 Kirby Dar Dar .15 .40
51 Jeff Kopp .07 .20
52 Billy Milner .07 .20
53 Tuineau Alipate .07 .20
54 Jeff Brady .07 .20
55 David Dixon .07 .20
56 Mike Morris .07 .20
57 Max Lane .07 .20
58 Tim Roberts .07 .20
59 Reggie E.White .07 .20
60 Tommy Hodson .07 .20
61 Joe Johnson .15 .40
62 Gary Downs .07 .20
63 Gary Harrell .07 .20
64 Robert Harris .07 .20
65 Kenyon Rasheed .07 .20
66 Richie Anderson .25 .60
67 Matt Brock .07 .20
68 Hugh Douglas .15 .40
69 Jeff Gossett .07 .20
70 Mike Jones .07 .20
71 Mike Morton .07 .20
72 Anthony Smith .07 .20
73 Jay Fiedler 1.50 4.00
74 Frank Wainright .07 .20
75 Marc Woodard .07 .20
76 Eric Zomalt .07 .20
77 Chad Brown .07 .20
78 James Parrish .07 .20
79 Justin Strzelczyk .07 .20
80 Darryl Ashmore .07 .20
81 Gerald McBurrows .07 .20
82 Lovell Pinkney .07 .20
83 Lewis Bush .07 .20
84 Eric Castle .07 .20
85 Terrance Shaw .07 .20
86 Frank Pollack .07 .20
87 Kirk Scrafford .07 .20
88 Alfred Williams .07 .20
89 Carlton Gray .07 .20
90 James McKnight .60 1.50
91 Todd Peterson .07 .20
92 Dean Wells .07 .20
93 Curtis Buckley .07 .20
94 Thomas Everett .07 .20
95 Pete Pierson .07 .20
96 Jamie Asher .15 .40
97 William Bell .07 .20
98 Trent Green .75 2.00
99 Richard Huntley .15 .40
100 Terrell Owens 2.00 5.00

1996 Pacific Dynagon Dynamic Duos

This 24 card standard-size insert set features pairs of teammates. In a novel twist, the first half of the pair is located in hobby packs while the second half is located in retail packs. The hobby inserts are "DD1-DD12" while the retail inserts are "DD13-DD24". These cards were inserted into each type of pack at a rate of one in 37.

COMPLETE SET (24) 60.00 120.00
DD1-DD12: STATED ODDS 1:37 HOBBY
DD13-DD24: STATED ODDS 1:37 RETAIL
DD1 Troy Aikman 3.00 8.00
DD2 Jerry Rice 3.00 8.00
DD3 Brett Favre 6.00 15.00
DD4 Marshall Faulk 2.00 5.00
DD5 Carl Pickens .75 2.00
DD6 Terrell Davis 2.50 6.00
DD7 Curtis Martin 2.50 6.00
DD8 Dan Marino 6.00 15.00
DD9 Herman Moore .75 2.00
DD10 Kordell Stewart 1.50 4.00
DD11 Emmitt Smith 5.00 12.00
DD12 Trent Dilfer 1.50 4.00
DD13 Deion Sanders 2.00 5.00
DD14 Steve Young 2.50 6.00
DD15 Robert Brooks 1.50 4.00
DD16 Jim Harbaugh .75 2.00
DD17 Jeff Blake 1.50 4.00
DD18 John Elway 6.00 15.00
DD19 Drew Bledsoe 2.00 5.00
DD20 Bernie Parmalee .40 1.00
DD21 Barry Sanders 5.00 12.00
DD22 Kevin Greene .75 2.00
DD23 Sherman Williams .40 1.00
DD24 Errict Rhett .75 2.00

1996 Pacific Dynagon Kings of the NFL

is 10-card standard-size set was inserted approximately one every 361 packs. The player's name is on top with a crown and the crowning achievement printed in gold foil on the bottom. In the middle is the player photo. The back has more details about that record as well as another photo. The cards are numbered with a "K" prefix.

COMPLETE SET (10) 60.00 150.00
STATED ODDS 1:361
K1 Emmitt Smith 8.00 20.00
K2 Dan Marino 10.00 25.00
K3 Barry Sanders 8.00 20.00
K4 Curtis Martin 4.00 10.00
K5 Brett Favre 10.00 25.00
K6 Kordell Stewart 2.50 6.00
K7 Emmitt Smith 8.00 20.00
K8 Jerry Rice 5.00 12.00
K9 John Elway 10.00 25.00
K10 Dan Marino 10.00 25.00

1996 Pacific Dynagon Tandems

This 72 card standard-size set is a mini-parallel to the regular Pacific Dynagon set. Unlike the regular issue, these cards are not sequenced in the same order. They are numbered in white ink in the lower left corner and feature two base brand Dynagon cards back-to-back. The cards were inserted at the rate of 1:37 packs.

COMPLETE SET (72) 150.00 400.00
STATED ODDS 1:37
1 D.Marino / T.Aikman 12.50 30.00
2 E.Smith / R.Salaam 10.00 25.00
3 J.Kelly / J.Elway 12.50 30.00
4 S.Young / B.Favre 12.50 30.00
5 C.Martin / T.Davis 7.50 20.00
6 K.Stewart / N.Kaufman 4.00 10.00
7 B.Sanders / J.Rice 12.50 30.00
8 J.Galloway / J.J.Stokes 4.00 10.00
9 K.Collins / J.Blake 4.00 10.00
10 D.Sanders / R.White 6.00 15.00
11 H.Moore / M.Chmura 2.50 6.00
12 E.Zeier / T.Wheatley 2.50 6.00
13 E.Rhett / R.Brooks 2.50 6.00
14 T.Dilfer / S.McNair 6.00 15.00
15 M.Faulk / D.Bledsoe 6.00 15.00
16 T.Vanover / M.Westbrook 2.50 6.00
17 H.Shuler / J.Bettis 4.00 10.00
18 I.Bruce / T.Brown 4.00 10.00
19 T.Allen / C.Warren 2.50 6.00
20 B.Mitchell / A.Van Dyke 2.50 6.00
21 J.Ellison / K.Mawae 1.50 4.00
22 A.Harper / S.Pritchett 2.50 6.00
23 R.Mirer / E.Grbac 2.50 6.00
24 C.Kennedy / J.Seau 4.00 10.00
25 W.Floyd / A.Hayden 2.50 6.00
26 S.Humphries / D.Barr 2.50 6.00
27 J.T.Thomas / S.Williams 1.50 4.00
28 R.Harmon / Y.Thigpen 2.50 6.00
29 E.Mills / C.Williams 1.50 4.00
30 E.George / M.Bruener 4.00 10.00
31 K.Greene / E.Moulds 4.00 10.00
32 R.Watters / H.Williams 2.50 6.00
33 R.Peete / K.Johnson 4.00 10.00
34 C.Garner / A.Murrell 2.50 6.00
35 R.Ismail / W.Chrebet 4.00 10.00
36 B.J.Hobert / G.Foley 1.50 4.00
37 R.Hampton / B.Coates 2.50 6.00
38 C.Calloway / Q.Ismail 2.50 6.00
39 D.Brown / W.Moon 4.00 10.00
40 R.Zellars / R.Smith 2.50 6.00
41 S.Pahukoa / B.Parmalee 1.50 4.00
42 W.Martin / N.Smith 1.50 4.00
43 J.Everett / S.Bono 2.50 6.00
44 M.Bates / T.Kirby 2.50 6.00
45 W.McGinest / L.Phillips 4.00 10.00
46 C.May / M.Brunell 2.50 6.00
47 C.Carter / O.J.McDuffie 4.00 10.00
48 I.Fryar / L.Dawson 2.50 6.00
49 M.Allen / J.O.Stewart 4.00 10.00
50 W.Jackson / T.Glenn 2.50 6.00
51 P.Mitchell / K.Hardy 2.50 6.00
52 J.Harbaugh / S.Mitchell 2.50 6.00
53 Z.Crockett / R.Thomas 2.50 6.00
54 B.Bronson / C.Sanders 2.50 6.00
55 E.Bennett / T.Biakabutuka 2.50 6.00
56 B.Perriman / A.Miller 2.50 6.00
57 C.Schlesinger / D.Johnston 2.50 6.00
58 S.Sharpe / M.Irvin 4.00 10.00
59 C.Boniol / T.Thomas 4.00 10.00
60 K.McCardell / D.Scott 2.50 6.00
61 L.Hoard / C.Zorich 1.50 4.00
62 E.Byner / J.Graham 2.50 6.00
63 C.Pickens / D.Holmes 1.50 4.00
64 D.Dunn / M.Carrier WR 2.50 6.00
65 S.Stenstrom / T.Collins 2.50 6.00
66 E.Kramer / D.Moore 2.50 6.00
67 B.Engram / L.Centers 2.50 6.00
68 G.Hearst / J.George 2.50 6.00
69 D.Krieg / C.Heyward 2.50 6.00
70 F.Sanders / T.Mathis 2.50 6.00
71 G.Frerotte / E.Metcalf 2.50 6.00
72 B.Paup / B.Brockermeyer 1.50 4.00

1997 Pacific Dynagon

is 144-card set was issued in three card packs and recognizes some of the hottest players in the NFL. The fronts feature action color player images on a background of a football helmet and rays foiled in gold. The backs carry player information.

COMPLETE SET (144) 40.00 80.00
1 Larry Centers .40 1.00
2 Kent Graham .25 .60
3 Leeland McElroy .25 .60
4 Frank Sanders .40 1.00
5 Jamal Anderson .50 1.25
6 Bert Emanuel .40 1.00
7 Bobby Hebert .25 .60
8 Terance Mathis .40 1.00
9 Eric Metcalf .40 1.00
10 Derrick Alexander WR .40 1.00
11 Earnest Byner .25 .60
12 Michael Jackson .40 1.00
13 Vinny Testaverde .40 1.00
14 Quinn Early .25 .60
15 Jim Kelly .50 1.25
16 Eric Moulds .50 1.25
17 Andre Reed .40 1.00
18 Bruce Smith .40 1.00
19 Thurman Thomas .50 1.25
20 Tim Biakabutuka .40 1.00
21 Mark Carrier WR .25 .60
22 Kerry Collins .50 1.25
23 Kevin Greene .40 1.00
24 Anthony Johnson .25 .60
25 Wesley Walls .40 1.00
26 Curtis Conway .40 1.00
27 Bobby Engram .40 1.00
28 Raymont Harris .25 .60
29 Dave Krieg .25 .60
30 Rashaan Salaam .25 .60
31 Jeff Blake .40 1.00
32 Ki-Jana Carter .25 .60
33 Garrison Hearst .40 1.00
34 Carl Pickens .40 1.00
35 Darnay Scott .40 1.00
36 Troy Aikman 1.00 2.50
37 Chris Boniol .25 .60
38 Michael Irvin .50 1.25
39 Deion Sanders .50 1.25
40 Emmitt Smith 1.50 4.00
41 Herschel Walker .40 1.00
42 Terrell Davis .60 1.50
43 John Elway 2.00 5.00
44 Ed McCaffrey .40 1.00
45 Shannon Sharpe .40 1.00
46 Alfred Williams .25 .60
47 Scott Mitchell .40 1.00
48 Herman Moore .40 1.00
49 Brett Perriman .25 .60
50 Barry Sanders 1.50 4.00
51 Edgar Bennett .40 1.00
52 Robert Brooks .40 1.00
53 Mark Chmura .40 1.00
54 Brett Favre 2.00 5.00
55 Antonio Freeman .50 1.25
56 Desmond Howard .40 1.00
57 Reggie White .50 1.25
58 Chris Chandler .40 1.00
59 Eddie George .50 1.25
60 James McKeehan .25 .60
61 Steve McNair .60 1.50
62 Chris Sanders .25 .60
63 Sean Dawkins .25 .60
64 Ken Dilger .25 .60
65 Marshall Faulk .60 1.50
66 Jim Harbaugh .40 1.00
67 Marvin Harrison .50 1.25
68 Tony Boselli .25 .60
69 Mark Brunell .60 1.50
70 Keenan McCardell .40 1.00
71 Natrone Means .40 1.00
72 Jimmy Smith .40 1.00
73 Marcus Allen .50 1.25
74 Kimble Anders .40 1.00
75 Dale Carter .25 .60
76 Greg Hill .25 .60
77 Derrick Thomas .50 1.25
78 Tamarick Vanover .40 1.00
79 Karim Abdul-Jabbar .50 1.25
80 Dan Marino 2.00 5.00
81 O.J. McDuffie .40 1.00
82 Jerris McPhail .25 .60
83 Zach Thomas .50 1.25
84 Cris Carter .50 1.25
85 Brad Johnson .50 1.25
86 Jake Reed .40 1.00
87 Robert Smith .40 1.00
88 Drew Bledsoe .60 1.50
89 Ben Coates .40 1.00
90 Terry Glenn .50 1.25
91 Curtis Martin .60 1.50
92 Willie McGinest .25 .60
93 Jim Everett .25 .60
94 Michael Haynes .25 .60
95 Haywood Jeffires .25 .60
96 Ray Zellars .25 .60
97 Dave Brown .25 .60
98 Rodney Hampton .40 1.00
99 Danny Kanell .40 1.00
100 Thomas Lewis .25 .60
101 Wayne Chrebet .50 1.25
102 Keyshawn Johnson .50 1.25
103 Adrian Murrell .40 1.00
104 Neil O'Donnell .40 1.00
105 Tim Brown .50 1.25
106 Rickey Dudley .40 1.00
107 Jeff Hostetler .25 .60
108 Napoleon Kaufman .50 1.25
109 Ty Detmer .40 1.00
110 Jason Dunn .25 .60
111 Irving Fryar .40 1.00
112 Chris T. Jones .25 .60
113 Ricky Watters .40 1.00
114 Jerome Bettis .50 1.25
115 Chad Brown .25 .60
116 Kordell Stewart .50 1.25
117 Mike Tomczak .25 .60
118 Rod Woodson .40 1.00
119 Tony Banks .40 1.00
120 Isaac Bruce .50 1.25
121 Eddie Kennison .40 1.00
122 Lawrence Phillips .25 .60
123 Terrell Fletcher .25 .60
124 Stan Humphries .40 1.00
125 Tony Martin .40 1.00
126 Junior Seau .50 1.25
127 Elvis Grbac .40 1.00
128 Terrell Owens .60 1.50
129 Ted Popson RC .25 .60
130 Jerry Rice 1.00 2.50
131 Steve Young .60 1.50
132 John Friesz .25 .60
133 Joey Galloway .40 1.00
134 Michael McCrary .25 .60
135 Lamar Smith .50 1.25
136 Chris Warren .40 1.00
137 Mike Alstott .50 1.25
138 Trent Dilfer .50 1.25
139 Courtney Hawkins .25 .60
140 Errict Rhett .25 .60
141 Terry Allen .50 1.25
142 Henry Ellard .25 .60
143 Gus Frerotte .25 .60
144 Leslie Shepherd .25 .60
C Mark Brunell Sample .75 2.00

1997 Pacific Dynagon Copper

COMPLETE SET (144) 300.00 600.00
*COPPER STARS: 2X TO 5X HI COL.
STATED ODDS 2:37 HOBBY

1997 Pacific Dynagon Red

COMPLETE SET (144) 300.00 600.00
*RED CARDS: 4X TO 8X BASIC CARDS
STATED ODDS 4:21 SPECIAL RETAIL

1997 Pacific Dynagon Silver

COMPLETE SET (144) 400.00 800.00
*SILVER CARDS: 3.5X TO 7X BASIC CARDS
STATED ODDS 2:37 RETAIL

1997 Pacific Dynagon Best Kept Secrets

This 110-card bonus set was randomly inserted at the rate of one or two in every pack. The fronts feature color action player photos with gold borders in a multi-color geometric-design frame. The backs carry player information.

COMPLETE SET (110) 10.00 25.00
ONE OR TWO PER PACK
1 Mark Brunell .30 .75
2 Bob Dahl .08 .25
3 Tommy Bennett .08 .25
4 Jamal Anderson .25 .60
5 Jermaine Lewis .25 .60
6 Chris Brantley .08 .25
7 Mathew Campbell .08 .25
8 Jeff Jaeger .08 .25
9 Marco Battaglia .08 .25
10 Troy Aikman .50 1.25
11 Terrell Davis .30 .75
12 Jeff Hartings .25 .60
13 Brett Favre 1.25 2.50
14 Eddie George .25 .60
15 Elijah Alexander .08 .25
16 Bryan Barker .08 .25
17 Louie Aguiar .08 .25
18 Karim Abdul-Jabbar .25 .60
19 Greg DeLong .08 .25
20 Drew Bledsoe .30 .75
21 Jim Everett .08 .25
22 Keith Elias .08 .25
23 Richie Anderson .15 .40
24 Joe Aska .08 .25
25 Barrett Brooks .08 .25
26 Jerome Bettis .25 .60
27 Darryl Ashmore .08 .25
28 Tony Berti .08 .25
29 Frank Pollack .08 .25
30 Joey Galloway .15 .40
31 Jason Maniecki .08 .25
32 Trent Green .30 .75
33 Pat Carter .08 .25
34 Ruben Brown .08 .25
35 Kerry Collins .25 .60
36 Keith Jennings .08 .25
37 Randall Godfrey .08 .25
38 David Diaz-Infante .08 .25
39 Derek Price .08 .25
40 William Henderson .15 .40
41 James Ritchey .08 .25
42 Richard Dent .08 .25
43 Ben Coleman .08 .25
44 Shane Burton .15 .40
45 Dixon Edwards .08 .25
46 Ted Johnson .25 .60
47 Harry Boatswain .08 .25
48 Derrick Fenner .08 .25
49 Ty Detmer .15 .40
50 Corey Holliday .08 .25
51 Jerry Rice .50 1.25
52 Boomer Esiason .15 .40
53 Jeff Pahukoa .08 .25
54 Scott Otis .08 .25
55 Darick Holmes .08 .25
56 Frank Garcia C .08 .25
57 Michael Lowery .08 .25
58 Jeff Blake .15 .40
59 Dale Hellestrae .08 .25
60 John Elway 1.00 2.50
61 Barry Sanders .75 2.00
62 Dorsey Levens .25 .60
63 James Roberson .08 .25
64 Jim Harbaugh .15 .40
65 Travis Davis .08 .25
66 Marcus Allen .25 .60
67 Steve Emtman .08 .25
68 Martin Harrison .08 .25
69 Curtis Martin .30 .75
70 Anthony Newman .08 .25
71 Ron Stone .08 .25
72 Reggie Cobb .08 .25
73 Robert Jenkins .08 .25
74 Morris Unutoa .08 .25
75 Kordell Stewart .25 .60
76 Raylee Johnson .15 .40
77 Tommy Thompson .08 .25
78 Dou Innocent .08 .25
79 Jim Pyne .08 .25
80 Jim Kelly .25 .60
81 Leeland McElroy .08 .25
82 Dan Stryzinski .08 .25
83 James Roe .08 .25
84 Anthony Johnson .08 .25
85 Chris Villarrial .08 .25
86 Kerry Joseph .25 .60
87 Emmitt Smith .75 2.00
88 Jeff Lewis .08 .25
89 Kerwin Waldroup .08 .25
90 Aaron Taylor .08 .25
91 Sheddrick Wilson .08 .25
92 Chris Hetherington .15 .40
93 Bryan Schwartz .08 .25
94 Reggie Tongue .08 .25
95 Dan Marino 1.00 2.50
96 Warren Moon .25 .60
97 Pio Sagapolutele .08 .25
98 Austin Robbins .08 .25
99 Stan White .08 .25
100 Keyshawn Johnson .25 .60
101 Napoleon Kaufman .25 .60
102 Ricky Watters .15 .40
103 Jon Witman .15 .40
104 Jermaine Ross .08 .25
105 Leonard Russell .08 .25
106 Iheanyi Uwaezuoke .15 .40
107 Gino Torretta .08 .25
108 Robb Thomas .08 .25
109 Shar Pourdanesh .08 .25
110 Gabe Northern .08 .25

1997 Pacific Dynagon Careers

Randomly inserted in packs at a rate of two in 271, this set honors ten of the NFL's all-time greats and their individual achievements. Foiled in gold, the fronts feature color action player images on a football background. The backs carry information about the player's achievements.

COMPLETE SET (10) 40.00 100.00
STATED ODDS: 2:721
*HOLO.GOLDS: 1.2X TO 3X BASIC INSERTS
*SILVERS: 2X TO 4X BASIC INSERTS
*PURPLES: 2X TO 4X BASIC INSERTS
STATED PRINT RUN 30 EACH COLOR
1 Jim Kelly 2.00 5.00
2 Emmitt Smith 6.00 15.00
3 John Elway 8.00 20.00
4 Barry Sanders 6.00 15.00
5 Brett Favre 8.00 20.00
6 Reggie White 2.00 5.00
7 Dan Marino 8.00 20.00
8 Drew Bledsoe 2.50 6.00
9 Jerry Rice 4.00 10.00
10 Steve Young 2.50 6.00

1997 Pacific Dynagon Player of the Week

Randomly inserted in packs at a rate of one in 37, this 20-card set features color action player images of the weekly winners from the 1996 season, as voted on by visitors to the Pacific Trading Cards website, and a 1996 MVP, Super Bowl MVP, and Pro Bowl MVP.

COMPLETE SET (20) 30.00 80.00
STATED ODDS 1:37
1 Karim Abdul-Jabbar 1.25 3.00

Card	Low	High
2 Eddie George	1.25	3.00
3 Curtis Martin	1.50	4.00
4 Mark Brunell	1.50	4.00
5 John Elway	5.00	12.00
6 Drew Bledsoe	1.50	4.00
7 Emmitt Smith	4.00	10.00
8 Terrell Davis	1.50	4.00
9 Troy Aikman	2.50	6.00
10 Jerry Rice	2.50	6.00
11 Dan Marino	5.00	12.00
12 Barry Sanders	4.00	10.00
13 Brett Favre	5.00	12.00
14 Steve Young	1.50	4.00
15 Kerry Collins	1.25	3.00
16 Eddie Kennison	1.00	2.50
17 Terry Allen	1.25	3.00
18 Brett Favre	5.00	12.00
19 Desmond Howard	1.00	2.50
20 Mark Brunell	1.50	4.00

1997 Pacific Dynagon Royal Connections

ndomly inserted in packs at a rate of one in 73, this 30-card set features color player photos of 15 of the best quarterback-receiver combinations in the league. Each card is die-cut and can stand alone or be matched up with its companion card to form a complete pair.

Card	Low	High
COMPLETE SET (30)	100.00	200.00
STATED ODDS: 1:73		
1A Kent Graham	1.25	3.00
1B Larry Centers	2.00	5.00
2A Jim Kelly	2.50	6.00
2B Andre Reed	2.00	5.00
3A Kerry Collins	2.50	6.00
3B Wesley Walls	2.00	5.00
4A Jeff Blake	2.00	5.00
4B Carl Pickens	2.00	5.00
5A Troy Aikman	5.00	12.00
5B Michael Irvin	2.50	6.00
6A John Elway	10.00	25.00
6B Shannon Sharpe	2.00	5.00
7A Brett Favre	10.00	25.00
7B Antonio Freeman	2.50	6.00
8A Mark Brunell	2.50	6.00
8B Keenan McCardell	2.00	5.00
9A Dan Marino	10.00	25.00
9B O.J. McDuffie	2.00	5.00
10A Brad Johnson	2.50	6.00
10B Jake Reed	2.00	5.00
11A Drew Bledsoe	3.00	8.00
11B Terry Glenn	2.50	6.00
12A Ty Detmer	2.00	5.00
12B Irving Fryar	2.00	5.00
13A Kordell Stewart	2.50	6.00
13B Charles Johnson	2.00	5.00
14A Tony Banks	2.00	5.00
14B Isaac Bruce	2.50	6.00
15A Steve Young	3.00	8.00
15B Jerry Rice	5.00	12.00

1997 Pacific Dynagon Tandems

ndomly inserted at the rate of one in 37 packs, this 72-card set features the same 144 players from the main set but are matched up to form 72 "double-fronted" cards that are foiled in emerald.

Card	Low	High
COMPLETE SET (72)	50.00	120.00
STATED ODDS: 1:37		
1 J.Bettis E.George	1.50	4.00
2 J.Anderson E.Moulds	1.50	4.00
3 K.Collins K.Stewart	1.50	4.00
4 J.Blake T.Detmer	1.25	3.00
5 M.Irvin T.Brown	1.50	4.00
6 D.Sanders R.Zellars	1.50	4.00
7 E.Smith S.Young	5.00	12.00
8 T.Davis B.Sanders	5.00	12.00
9 J.Elway D.Marino	6.00	15.00
10 R.Brooks E.Kennison	1.25	3.00
11 M.Chmura S.Sharpe	1.25	3.00
12 B.Favre M.Brunell	5.00	12.00
13 A.Freeman I.Bruce	1.50	4.00
14 D.Howard N.Means	1.25	3.00
15 R.White K.Johnson	1.50	4.00
16 E.Bennett C.Sanders	.75	2.00
17 T.Glenn J.Rice	4.00	10.00
18 S.McNair K.Abdul-Jabbar	1.50	4.00
19 M.Faulk T.Vanover	2.00	5.00
20 G.Frerotte B.Johnson	1.25	3.00
21 J.Kelly T.Biakabutuka	1.50	4.00
22 L.Phillips B.Coates	.75	2.00
23 N.Kaufman T.Owens	3.00	8.00
24 E.Grbac J.Seau	1.50	4.00
25 D.Bledsoe T.Banks	1.50	4.00
26 C.Martin T.Aikman	4.00	10.00
27 C.Conway B.Perriman	1.25	3.00
28 B.Engram L.Centers	.75	2.00
29 R.Harris E.Metcalf	.75	2.00
30 D.Krieg D.Alexander	.75	2.00
31 R.Salaam L.McElroy	1.25	3.00
32 K.Jana Carter H.Moore	1.25	3.00
33 G.Hearst E.Byner	1.25	3.00
34 C.Pickens F.Sanders	1.25	3.00
35 D.Scott M.Jackson	1.25	3.00
36 C.Boniol K.Graham	.75	2.00
37 H.Walker T.Thomas	1.50	4.00
38 E.McCaffrey Q.Early	1.25	3.00
39 A.Williams M.Alstott	1.25	3.00
40 S.Mitchell M.Carrier	.75	2.00
41 B.Emanuel H.Ellard	.75	2.00
42 B.Hebert T.Dilfer	1.25	3.00
43 T.Mathis A.Reed	1.25	3.00
44 V.Testaverde C.Warren	1.25	3.00
45 B.Smith K.Greene	1.50	4.00
46 A.Johnson T.Allen	1.25	3.00
47 W.Walls E.Rhett	1.25	3.00
48 J.Friesz J.Hostetler	.75	2.00
49 J.Galloway L.Shepherd	1.25	3.00
50 M.McCrary C.Jones	.75	2.00
51 L.Smith C.Hawkins	1.25	3.00
52 R.Dudley J.Dunn	1.25	3.00
53 I.Fryar T.Martin	1.25	3.00
54 T.Popson R.Watters	1.25	3.00
55 C.Brown Z.Thomas	1.50	4.00
56 M.Tomczak S.Humphries	1.25	3.00
57 R.Woodson W.McGinest	1.25	3.00
58 T.Fletcher J.McPhail	.75	2.00
59 O.J.McDuffie C.Carter	1.50	4.00
60 J.Reed M.Allen	1.50	4.00
61 R.Smith G.Hill	1.25	3.00
62 J.Everett D.Brown	.75	2.00
63 M.Haynes J.McKeehan	.75	2.00
64 H.Jeffires S.Dawkins	.75	2.00
65 R.Hampton A.Murrell	1.25	3.00
66 D.Kanell M.Harrison	1.50	4.00
67 T.Lewis D.Carter	.75	2.00
68 W.Chrebet K.Dilger	1.50	4.00
69 N.O'Donnell C.Chandler	1.25	3.00
70 J.Harbaugh J.Smith	1.25	3.00
71 D.Thomas T.Boselli	1.50	4.00
72 K.McCardell K.Anders	1.25	3.00

2001 Pacific Dynagon

This 150-card set had 100 veterans and 50 serial numbered rookies. The rookies were either numbered to 199, 499, or 699 and were all autographed. The cards featured a holofoil design for the background, and a gold foil stamp indicating the featured player and the set name. These were issued as a hobby only set. Cards number 132, 136 and 148 were not released.

Card	Low	High
COMP.SET w/o SP's (100)	15.00	40.00
127-150 ROOKIE AU PRINT RUN 699		
1 David Boston	.25	.60
2 Thomas Jones	.25	.60
3 Jake Plummer	.25	.60
4 Jamal Anderson	.30	.75
5 Tim Dwight	.30	.75
6 Elvis Grbac	.30	.75
7 Jamal Lewis	.40	1.00
8 Ray Lewis	.40	1.00
9 Shannon Sharpe	.30	.75
10 Rob Johnson	.30	.75
11 Eric Moulds	.25	.60
12 Peerless Price	.25	.60
13 Tim Biakabutuka	.25	.60
14 Patrick Jeffers	.25	.60
15 Muhsin Muhammad	.25	.60
16 James Allen	.25	.60
17 Cade McNown	.30	.75
18 Marcus Robinson	.30	.75
19 Brian Urlacher	.50	1.25
20 Corey Dillon	.25	.60
21 Akili Smith	.25	.60
22 Peter Warrick	.25	.60
23 Tim Couch	.25	.60
24 Kevin Johnson	.25	.60
25 Randall Cunningham	.30	.75
26 Emmitt Smith	.60	1.50
27 Mike Anderson	.25	.60
28 Terrell Davis	.30	.75
29 Brian Griese	.25	.60
30 Ed McCaffrey	.30	.75
31 Rod Smith	.30	.75
32 Charlie Batch	.25	.60
33 Johnnie Morton	.30	.75
34 James Stewart	.25	.60
35 Brett Favre	.75	2.00
36 Antonio Freeman	.40	1.00
37 Ahman Green	.30	.75
38 Marvin Harrison	.30	.75
39 Edgerrin James	.30	.75
40 Peyton Manning	1.00	2.50
41 Mark Brunell	.30	.75
42 Keenan McCardell	.30	.75
43 Jimmy Smith	.30	.75
44 Fred Taylor	.25	.60
45 Derrick Alexander	.25	.60
46 Tony Gonzalez	.30	.75
47 Sylvester Morris	.25	.60
48 Jay Fiedler	.30	.75
49 Oronde Gadsden	.25	.60
50 Lamar Smith	.30	.75
51 Cris Carter	.40	1.00
52 Daunte Culpepper	.30	.75
53 Randy Moss	.30	.75
54 Drew Bledsoe	.30	.75
55 Terry Glenn	.30	.75
56 J.R. Redmond	.25	.60
57 Aaron Brooks	.25	.60
58 Joe Horn	.25	.60
59 Ricky Williams	.30	.75
60 Tiki Barber	.30	.75
61 Kerry Collins	.25	.60
62 Ron Dayne	.30	.75
63 Amani Toomer	.25	.60
64 Wayne Chrebet	.25	.60
65 Curtis Martin	.30	.75
66 Vinny Testaverde	.25	.60
67 Tim Brown	.40	1.00
68 Rich Gannon	.30	.75
69 Tyrone Wheatley	.30	.75
70 Charles Johnson	.25	.60
71 Donovan McNabb	.30	.75
72 Duce Staley	.25	.60
73 Jerome Bettis	.40	1.00
74 Plaxico Burress	.25	.60
75 Kordell Stewart	.25	.60
76 Isaac Bruce	.40	1.00
77 Marshall Faulk	.30	.75
78 Torry Holt	.30	.75
79 Kurt Warner	.60	1.50
80 Curtis Conway	.30	.75
81 Doug Flutie	.30	.75
82 Jeff Garcia	.25	.60
83 Charlie Garner	.30	.75
84 Terrell Owens	.30	.75
85 Jerry Rice	.75	2.00
86 Shaun Alexander	.25	.60
87 Matt Hasselbeck	.25	.60
88 Darrell Jackson	.30	.75
89 Mike Alstott	.25	.60
90 Warrick Dunn	.25	.60
91 Brad Johnson	.30	.75
92 Keyshawn Johnson	.30	.75
93 Shaun King	.25	.60
94 Eddie George	.40	1.00
95 Jevon Kearse	.25	.60
96 Derrick Mason	.25	.60
97 Steve McNair	.30	.75
98 Stephen Davis	.25	.60
99 Jeff George	.30	.75
100 Deion Sanders	.30	.75
101 Michael Bennett AU RC	8.00	20.00
102 Drew Brees AU RC	500.00	1000.00
103 Chris Chambers AU RC	6.00	15.00
104 LaMont Jordan AU RC	10.00	25.00
105 Deuce McAllister AU RC	10.00	25.00
106 Koren Robinson AU RC	8.00	20.00
107 David Terrell AU RC	8.00	20.00
108 LaDain Tomlinson AU RC	50.00	100.00
109 Marques Tuiasosopo AU RC	8.00	20.00
110 Michael Vick AU RC	30.00	80.00
111 Chris Weinke AU RC	8.00	20.00
112 Kevan Barlow AU RC	5.00	12.00
113 Josh Booty AU RC	5.00	12.00
114 Rod Gardner AU RC	5.00	12.00
115 Todd Heap AU RC	5.00	12.00
116 Travis Henry AU RC	5.00	12.00
117 James Jackson AU RC	4.00	10.00
118 Chad Johnson AU RC	20.00	40.00
119 Rudi Johnson AU RC	6.00	15.00
120 Ben Leard AU RC	4.00	10.00
121 Quincy Morgan AU RC	5.00	12.00
122 Snoop Minnis AU RC	4.00	10.00
123 Freddie Mitchell AU RC	4.00	10.00
124 Sage Rosenfels AU RC	5.00	12.00
125 Anthony Thomas AU RC	6.00	15.00
126 Reggie Wayne AU RC	20.00	40.00
127 Dan Alexander AU RC	4.00	10.00
128 Will Allen AU RC	5.00	12.00
129 Scotty Anderson AU RC	3.00	8.00
130 Adam Archuleta AU RC	4.00	10.00
131 Alex Bannister AU RC	3.00	8.00
133 Tay Cody AU RC	3.00	8.00
134 Tony Dixon AU RC	3.00	8.00
135 Heath Evans AU RC	4.00	10.00
137 Derrick Gibson AU RC	3.00	8.00
138 Edgerton Hartwell AU RC	3.00	8.00
139 Tim Hasselbeck AU RC	4.00	10.00
140 Jabari Holloway AU RC	3.00	8.00
141 Torrance Marshall AU RC	3.00	8.00
142 Jason McKinley AU RC	3.00	8.00
143 Mike McMahon AU RC	4.00	10.00
144 Bobby Newcombe AU RC	4.00	10.00
145 Moran Norris AU RC	3.00	8.00
146 Tommy Polley AU RC	3.00	8.00
147 Vinny Sutherland AU RC	3.00	8.00
149 Reggie White AU RC	3.00	8.00
150 Cedrick Wilson AU RC	4.00	10.00

2001 Pacific Dynagon Premiere Date

*VETERANS: 3X TO 8X BASIC CARDS
STATED PRINT RUN 135 SER.#'d SETS

2001 Pacific Dynagon Red

*VETERANS: 4X TO 10X BASIC CARDS
STATED PRINT RUN 99 SERIAL #'d SETS

2001 Pacific Dynagon Retail

Card	Low	High
COMP.SET w/o RC's (100)	12.50	25.00
*RETAIL VETS 1-100: .3X TO .8X HOB		
101-150 ROOKIE ODDS 1:4 RET		
102 Drew Brees RC	3.00	8.00
103 Chris Chambers RC	.50	1.25
104 LaMont Jordan RC	.75	2.00
105 Deuce McAllister RC	.75	2.00
106 Koren Robinson RC	.60	1.50
107 David Terrell RC	.60	1.50
108 LaDainian Tomlinson RC	2.50	6.00
109 Marques Tuiasosopo RC	.60	1.50
110 Michael Vick RC	1.25	3.00
111 Chris Weinke RC	.60	1.50
112 Kevan Barlow RC	.60	1.50
113 Josh Booty RC	.60	1.50
114 Rod Gardner RC	.60	1.50
115 Todd Heap RC	.60	1.50
116 Travis Henry RC	.60	1.50
117 James Jackson RC	.50	1.25
118 Chad Johnson RC	.75	2.00
119 Rudi Johnson RC	.75	2.00
120 Ben Leard RC	.50	1.25
121 Quincy Morgan RC	.60	1.50
122 Snoop Minnis RC	.50	1.25
123 Freddie Mitchell RC	.50	1.25
124 Sage Rosenfels RC	.60	1.50
125 Anthony Thomas RC	.75	2.00
126 Reggie Wayne RC	1.00	2.50
127 Dan Alexander RC	.60	1.50
128 Will Allen RC	.75	2.00
129 Scotty Anderson RC	.50	1.25
130 Adam Archuleta RC	.60	1.50
131 Alex Bannister RC	.50	1.25
132 Gary Baxter RC	.50	1.25
133 Tay Cody RC	.50	1.25
134 Tony Dixon RC	.50	1.25
135 Heath Evans RC	.60	1.50
136 Jamar Fletcher RC	.50	1.25
137 Derrick Gibson RC	.50	1.25
138 Edgerton Hartwell RC	.50	1.25
139 Tim Hasselbeck RC	.60	1.50
140 Jabari Holloway RC	.50	1.25
141 Torrance Marshall RC	.50	1.25
142 Jason McKinley RC	.50	1.25
143 Mike McMahon RC	.60	1.50
144 Bobby Newcombe RC	.60	1.50
145 Moran Norris RC	.50	1.25
146 Tommy Polley RC	.50	1.25
147 Vinny Sutherland RC	.50	1.25
148 Ja'Mar Toombs RC	.50	1.25
149 Reggie White RC	.50	1.25
150 Cedrick Wilson RC	.60	1.50

2001 Pacific Dynagon Retail Silver

*VETERANS: 2.5X TO 6X BASIC RETAIL
STATED PRINT RUN 199 SER.#'d SETS

2001 Pacific Dynagon Big Numbers

This 20-card set was randomly inserted in packs and was serial numbered to 799. The card design was a die-cut of the featured player's jersey and a photo of the player.

Card	Low	High
COMPLETE SET (20)	20.00	50.00
STATED PRINT RUN 799 SER.#'d SETS		
1 Cade McNown	1.25	3.00
2 Peter Warrick	1.00	2.50
3 Tim Couch	1.00	2.50
4 Mike Anderson	1.00	2.50
5 Brian Griese	1.00	2.50
6 Cris Carter	1.50	4.00
7 Mark Brunell	1.25	3.00
8 Drew Bledsoe	1.25	3.00
9 Ricky Williams	1.25	3.00
10 Ron Dayne	1.25	3.00
11 Curtis Martin	1.25	3.00
12 Rich Gannon	1.25	3.00
13 Jerome Bettis	1.50	4.00
14 Torry Holt	1.25	3.00
15 Jeff Garcia	1.00	2.50
16 Jerry Rice	3.00	8.00
17 Warrick Dunn	1.00	2.50
18 Eddie George	1.50	4.00
19 Steve McNair	1.25	3.00
20 Stephen Davis	1.00	2.50

2001 Pacific Dynagon Canton Bound

This 10-card set was inserted into packs and was serial numbered to 99. The cards featured a picture of the player's future bust for the Hall of Fame. The set contained 10 players who were on track for the Hall 5 years from their retirement.

Card	Low	High
COMPLETE SET (10)	50.00	120.00
STATED PRINT RUN 99 SER.#'d SETS		
1 Emmitt Smith	6.00	15.00
2 Brett Favre	8.00	20.00
3 Edgerrin James	3.00	8.00
4 Peyton Manning	10.00	25.00
5 Dan Marino	8.00	20.00
6 Cris Carter	4.00	10.00
7 Randy Moss	3.00	8.00
8 Marshall Faulk	3.00	8.00
9 Kurt Warner	6.00	15.00
10 Jerry Rice	8.00	20.00

2001 Pacific Dynagon Dynamic Duos

This 20-card set was randomly inserted into packs and sequentially numbered to 1499. The cards featured teammates that made a 'Dynamic Duo'. The cards were highlighted with silver-foil lettering.

Card	Low	High
COMPLETE SET (20)	20.00	50.00
STATED PRINT RUN 1499 SER.#'d SETS		
1 J.Plummer/D.Boston	.60	1.50
2 J.Lewis/P.Holmes	1.00	2.50
3 R.Johnson/E.Moulds	.60	1.50
4 C.McNown/M.Robinson	.75	2.00
5 C.Dillon/P.Warrick	.60	1.50
6 T.Couch/Kev.Johnson	.60	1.50
7 M.Anderson/T.Davis	.75	2.00
8 B.Griese/R.Smith	.75	2.00
9 B.Favre/A.Freeman	2.00	5.00
10 P.Manning/M.Harrison	2.50	6.00
11 M.Brunell/F.Taylor	.75	2.00
12 D.Culpepper/R.Moss	.75	2.00
13 D.Bledsoe/T.Glenn	.75	2.00
14 T.Barber/R.Dayne	.75	2.00
15 R.Gannon/T.Brown	1.00	2.50
16 D.McNabb/D.Staley	.75	2.00
17 K.Warner/T.Holt	1.50	4.00
18 J.Garcia/T.Owens	.75	2.00
19 M.Alstott/W.Dunn	.60	1.50
20 S.McNair/D.Mason	.75	2.00

2001 Pacific Dynagon Freshman Phenoms

This 10-card set was randomly inserted in packs and was serial numbered to 599. The set featured 10 of the top draft picks from the 2001 NFL Draft.

Card	Low	High
COMPLETE SET (10)	40.00	80.00
STATED PRINT RUN 599 SER.#'d SETS		
1 Michael Bennett	1.50	4.00
2 Drew Brees	15.00	40.00
3 Josh Heupel	2.00	5.00
4 Deuce McAllister	2.00	5.00
5 Santana Moss	2.00	5.00
6 Ken-Yon Rambo	1.25	3.00
7 Koren Robinson	1.50	4.00
8 David Terrell	1.50	4.00
9 LaDainian Tomlinson	6.00	15.00
10 Michael Vick	3.00	8.00

2001 Pacific Dynagon Game Used Footballs

This 20-card set was randomly inserted into packs at a rate of 1:82 hobby and 1:481 retail, had a stated print run of 214 serial numbered sets. The cards contained a swatch of a game used football which was cut out in the shape of a football. The card design was highlighted by gold-foil lettering.

Card	Low	High
STATED ODDS 1:82 HOB 1:481 RET		
STATED PRINT RUN 214 SER.#'d SETS		
1 Jamal Lewis	6.00	15.00
2 Peter Warrick	4.00	10.00
3 Tim Couch	4.00	10.00
4 Emmitt Smith	10.00	25.00
5 Mike Anderson	4.00	10.00
6 Terrell Davis	5.00	12.00
7 Brett Favre	12.00	30.00
8 Edgerrin James	5.00	12.00
9 Peyton Manning	15.00	40.00
10 Mark Brunell	5.00	12.00
11 Fred Taylor	4.00	10.00
12 Daunte Culpepper	5.00	12.00
13 Randy Moss	5.00	12.00
14 Drew Bledsoe	5.00	12.00
15 Ricky Williams	5.00	12.00
16 Donovan McNabb	5.00	12.00
17 Marshall Faulk	5.00	12.00
18 Kurt Warner	10.00	25.00
19 Jerry Rice	12.00	30.00
20 Eddie George	6.00	15.00

2001 Pacific Dynagon Logo Optics

ndomly inserted in packs this 20-card set features a split photo, one side is of the player and the other features the team helmet cut into the card. Each card in the set was serial numbered to 499.

Card	Low	High
COMPLETE SET (20)	15.00	40.00
STATED PRINT RUN 499 SER.#'d SETS		
1 Jamal Lewis	1.25	3.00
2 Eric Moulds	.75	2.00
3 Corey Dillon	.75	2.00
4 Emmitt Smith	2.00	5.00
5 Terrell Davis	1.00	2.50
6 Brian Griese	.75	2.00
7 Edgerrin James	1.00	2.50
8 Fred Taylor	.75	2.00
9 Lamar Smith	1.00	2.50
10 Daunte Culpepper	1.00	2.50
11 Ricky Williams	1.00	2.50
12 Curtis Martin	1.00	2.50
13 Tyrone Wheatley	1.00	2.50
14 Donovan McNabb	1.00	2.50
15 Jerome Bettis	1.25	3.00
16 Marshall Faulk	1.00	2.50
17 Jeff Garcia	.75	2.00
18 Warrick Dunn	.75	2.00
19 Eddie George	1.25	3.00
20 Stephen Davis	.75	2.00

2001 Pacific Dynagon Premiere Players

Randomly inserted into packs this 20-card set was serial numbered to 999. The set featured some of the top draft picks from the 2001 NFL Draft. These cards were highlighted with gold-foil lettering.

Card	Low	High
COMPLETE SET (20)	30.00	80.00
STATED PRINT RUN 999 SER.#'d SETS		
1 David Allen	.75	2.00
2 Kevan Barlow	1.00	2.50
3 Michael Bennett	1.00	2.50
4 Drew Brees	10.00	25.00
5 Chris Chambers	.75	2.00
6 Josh Heupel	1.25	3.00
7 James Jackson	.75	2.00
8 LaMont Jordan	1.25	3.00
9 Deuce McAllister	1.25	3.00
10 Freddie Mitchell	.75	2.00
11 Santana Moss	1.25	3.00
12 Ken-Yon Rambo	.75	2.00
13 Koren Robinson	1.00	2.50
14 David Terrell	1.00	2.50
15 Anthony Thomas	1.25	3.00
16 LaDainian Tomlinson	4.00	10.00
17 Marques Tuiasosopo	1.00	2.50
18 Michael Vick	2.00	5.00
19 Reggie Wayne	1.50	4.00
20 Chris Weinke	1.00	2.50

2001 Pacific Dynagon Top of the Class

Randomly inserted in packs at a rate of 1:1 hobby and 1:4 retail packs. The 25-card set featured the top draft picks from the 2001 NFL Draft. The set design had an action photo of the player and a shadow of his face for the background, and it was highlighted with gold-foil lettering.

Card	Low	High
COMPLETE SET (25)	15.00	40.00
STATED ODDS 1:1 HOD 1:4 RET		
1 Kevan Barlow	.50	1.25
2 Michael Bennett	.50	1.25
3 Drew Brees	2.50	6.00
4 Chris Chambers	.40	1.00
5 Rod Gardner	.50	1.25
6 Travis Henry	.50	1.25
7 Josh Heupel	.60	1.50
8 James Jackson	.40	1.00
9 Chad Johnson	.60	1.50
10 LaMont Jordan	.60	1.50
11 Deuce McAllister	.60	1.50
12 Mike McMahon	.50	1.25
13 Snoop Minnis	.40	1.00
14 Travis Minor	.50	1.25
15 Freddie Mitchell	.40	1.00
16 Santana Moss	.60	1.50
17 Ken-Yon Rambo	.40	1.00
18 Koren Robinson	.50	1.25
19 David Terrell	.50	1.25
20 Anthony Thomas	.60	1.50
21 LaDainian Tomlinson	2.00	5.00
22 Marques Tuiasosopo	.50	1.25
23 Michael Vick	1.00	2.50
24 Reggie Wayne	.75	2.00
25 Chris Weinke	.50	1.25

2002 Pacific Exclusive

Released in late-October, 2002, this 200 card set contains a good mix of veterans and rookies, along with several autographed rookie cards. Boxes contained 18 packs of 6 cards. Boxes were packed 16 per case. Each box contained an authentic bobble head doll. Also available in packs were rookie updates for 2002 Pacific, Pacific Atomic, and Pacific Heads Up.

Card	Low	High
ROOKIE AU/100-1045 ODDS 1:21		
1 David Boston	.30	.75
2 Thomas Jones	.30	.75
3 Jake Plummer	.30	.75
4 Frank Sanders	.30	.75
5 Josh Scobey RC	.60	1.50
6 Warrick Dunn	.30	.75
7 Brian Finneran	.30	.75
8 Kahlil Hill RC	.50	1.25
9 Shawn Jefferson	.30	.75
10 Kurt Kittner RC	.50	1.25
11 Michael Vick	.40	1.00
12 Ron Johnson RC	.60	1.50
13 Jamal Lewis	.40	1.00
14 Ray Lewis	.50	1.25
15 Chris Redman	.30	.75
16 Brandon Stokley	.30	.75
17 Chester Taylor RC	.75	2.00
18 Travis Taylor	.30	.75
19 Drew Bledsoe	.40	1.00
20 Travis Henry	.30	.75
21 Eric Moulds	.30	.75
22 Peerless Price	.30	.75
23 Randy Fasani RC	.50	1.25
24 Muhsin Muhammad	.30	.75
25 Lamar Smith	.30	.75
26 Steve Smith	.50	1.25
27 Chris Weinke	.30	.75
28 Marty Booker	.30	.75
29 Jim Miller	.30	.75
30 Adrian Peterson RC	.60	1.50
31 Marcus Robinson	.40	1.00
32 David Terrell	.30	.75
33 Anthony Thomas	.40	1.00
34 Brian Urlacher	.50	1.25
35 Corey Dillon	.30	.75
36 Chad Johnson	.30	.75
37 Jon Kitna	.30	.75
38 Michael Westbrook	.30	.75
39 Peter Warrick	.30	.75
40 Tim Couch	.30	.75
41 JaJuan Dawson	.30	.75
42 James Jackson	.30	.75
43 Kevin Johnson	.30	.75
44 Quincy Morgan	.30	.75
45 Quincy Carter	.30	.75
46 Joey Galloway	.40	1.00
47 Troy Hambrick	.30	.75
48 Chad Hutchinson RC	.50	1.25
49 Rocket Ismail	.40	1.00
50 Emmitt Smith	.75	2.00
51 Mike Anderson	.30	.75
52 Terrell Davis	.40	1.00
53 Brian Griese	.30	.75
54 Herb Haygood RC	.50	1.25
55 Ed McCaffrey	.40	1.00
56 Rod Smith	.40	1.00
57 Germane Crowell	.30	.75
58 Az-Zahir Hakim	.30	.75
59 Mike McMahon	.30	.75
60 Bill Schroeder	.30	.75
61 Luke Staley RC	.50	1.25
62 James Stewart	.30	.75
63 Brett Favre	1.00	2.50
64 Robert Ferguson	.40	1.00
65 Bubba Franks	.30	.75
66 Terry Glenn	.40	1.00
67 Ahman Green	.40	1.00
68 Craig Nall RC	.60	1.50
69 James Allen	.30	.75
70 Corey Bradford	.30	.75
71 Jermaine Lewis	.30	.75
72 Travis Prentice	.30	.75
73 Brian Allen RC	.50	1.25
74 Marvin Harrison	.40	1.00
75 Edgerrin James	.40	1.00
76 Peyton Manning	1.25	3.00
77 Reggie Wayne	.40	1.00
78 Mark Brunell	.40	1.00
79 Patrick Johnson	.30	.75
80 Jimmy Smith	.40	1.00
81 Fred Taylor	.30	.75
82 Tony Gonzalez	.40	1.00
83 Trent Green	.30	.75
84 Priest Holmes	.30	.75
85 Johnnie Morton	.40	1.00
86 Chris Chambers	.30	.75
87 Jay Fiedler	.40	1.00
88 Oronde Gadsden	.30	.75
89 Leonard Henry RC	.50	1.25
90 Travis Minor	.30	.75
91 Sam Simmons RC	.50	1.25
92 Ricky Williams	.40	1.00
93 Derrick Alexander	.30	.75
94 Michael Bennett	.30	.75
95 Daunte Culpepper	.40	1.00
96 Randy Moss	.40	1.00
97 Tom Brady	2.50	6.00
98 Deion Branch RC	.75	2.00
99 Troy Brown	.30	.75
100 Rohan Davey RC	.75	2.00
101 Donald Hayes	.30	.75
102 David Patten	.30	.75
103 Antowain Smith	.40	1.00
104 Antwoine Womack RC	.50	1.25
105 Aaron Brooks	.30	.75
106 Joe Horn	.30	.75
107 Deuce McAllister	.40	1.00
108 J.T. O'Sullivan RC	.60	1.50
109 Jerome Pathon	.30	.75
110 Tiki Barber	.40	1.00
111 Tim Carter RC	.60	1.50
112 Kerry Collins	.30	.75
113 Ron Dayne	.40	1.00
114 Ike Hilliard	.30	.75
115 Amani Toomer	.30	.75
116 Wayne Chrebet	.30	.75
117 Laveranues Coles	.40	1.00
118 Curtis Martin	.40	1.00
119 Santana Moss	.40	1.00
120 Vinny Testaverde	.30	.75
121 Tim Brown	.50	1.25
122 Ronald Curry RC	.50	1.25
123 Rich Gannon	.40	1.00
124 Charlie Garner	.40	1.00
125 Larry Ned RC	.50	1.25
126 Jerry Rice	1.00	2.50
127 Tyrone Wheatley	.40	1.00
128 Donovan McNabb	.40	1.00
129 Freddie Mitchell	.30	.75
130 Todd Pinkston	.30	.75
131 Duce Staley	.30	.75
132 James Thrash	.40	1.00
133 Jerome Bettis	.50	1.25
134 Plaxico Burress	.30	.75
135 Kordell Stewart	.30	.75
136 Hines Ward	.40	1.00
137 Amos Zereoue	.30	.75
138 Isaac Bruce	.50	1.25
139 Trung Canidate	.30	.75
140 Eric Crouch RC	.75	2.00
141 Marshall Faulk	.40	1.00
142 Lamar Gordon RC	.60	1.50
143 Torry Holt	.40	1.00
144 Kurt Warner	.40	1.00
145 Terrence Wilkins	.30	.75
146 Drew Brees	1.00	2.50
147 Seth Burford RC	.50	1.25
148 Reche Caldwell RC	.60	1.50
149 Curtis Conway	.40	1.00
150 Tim Dwight	.30	.75
151 Doug Flutie	.40	1.00
152 LaDainian Tomlinson	.50	1.25
153 Kevan Barlow	.30	.75
154 Brandon Doman RC	.50	1.25
155 Jeff Garcia	.30	.75
156 Garrison Hearst	.30	.75
157 Terrell Owens	.40	1.00
158 J.J. Stokes	.30	.75
159 Shaun Alexander	.30	.75
160 Trent Dilfer	.30	.75
161 Darrell Jackson	.40	1.00
162 Koren Robinson	.30	.75
163 Mike Alstott	.30	.75
164 Brad Johnson	.40	1.00
165 Keyshawn Johnson	.40	1.00
166 Keenan McCardell	.40	1.00
167 Michael Pittman	.40	1.00
168 Travis Stephens RC	.50	1.25
169 Marquise Walker RC	.50	1.25
170 Kevin Dyson	.40	1.00
171 Eddie George	.40	1.00
172 Derrick Mason	.30	.75
173 Steve McNair	.40	1.00
174 Reidel Anthony	.30	.75
175 Ladell Betts RC	.75	2.00
176 Stephen Davis	.30	.75
177 Rod Gardner	.30	.75
178 Jacquez Green	.30	.75
179 Shane Matthews	.30	.75
180 Cliff Russell RC	.50	1.25
181 Josh McCown AU/779 RC	8.00	20.00
182 T.J. Duckett RC	.50	1.25
183 Josh Reed RC	.60	1.50
184 DeShaun Foster AU/105 RC	10.00	25.00
185 Andre Davis AU/778 RC	5.00	12.00
186 William Green RC	.60	1.50
187 Antonio Bryant AU/575 RC	8.00	20.00
188 Ashley Lelie AU/100 RC	6.00	15.00
189 Clinton Portis AU/524 RC	8.00	20.00
190 Joey Harrington RC	.50	1.25
191 Javon Walker AU/519 RC	8.00	20.00
192 David Carr AU/100 RC	6.00	15.00
193 Jabar Gaffney AU/103 RC	6.00	15.00
194 Jonathan Wells AU/615 RC	6.00	15.00
195 David Garrard AU/787 RC	6.00	15.00
196 Donte Stallworth RC	.75	2.00
197 Brian Westbrook AU/930 RC	10.00	25.00
198 Ant Randle El AU/788 RC	6.00	15.00
199 Maurice Morris AU/1045 RC	6.00	15.00
200 Patrick Ramsey RC	.60	1.50

2002 Pacific Exclusive Blue

Card	Low	High
UE PRINT RUN 299 SER.#'d SETS		
5 Josh Scobey	1.50	4.00
8 Kahlil Hill	1.25	3.00
10 Kurt Kittner	1.25	3.00
12 Ron Johnson	1.50	4.00
17 Chester Taylor	2.00	5.00
23 Randy Fasani	1.25	3.00
30 Adrian Peterson	1.50	4.00
48 Chad Hutchinson	1.25	3.00
54 Herb Haygood	1.25	3.00
61 Luke Staley	1.25	3.00
68 Craig Nall	1.50	4.00
73 Brian Allen	1.25	3.00
89 Leonard Henry	1.25	3.00
91 Sam Simmons	1.25	3.00
98 Deion Branch	2.00	5.00
100 Rohan Davey	2.00	5.00
104 Antwoine Womack	1.25	3.00
108 J.T. O'Sullivan	1.50	4.00
111 Tim Carter	1.50	4.00
122 Ronald Curry	1.25	3.00
125 Larry Ned	1.25	3.00
140 Eric Crouch	2.00	5.00
142 Lamar Gordon	1.50	4.00
147 Seth Burford	1.25	3.00
148 Reche Caldwell	1.50	4.00
154 Brandon Doman	1.25	3.00
168 Travis Stephens	1.25	3.00
169 Marquise Walker	1.25	3.00
175 Ladell Betts	2.00	5.00
180 Cliff Russell	1.25	3.00
181 Josh McCown	2.00	5.00
182 T.J. Duckett	1.25	3.00
183 Josh Reed	1.50	4.00
184 DeShaun Foster	2.00	5.00
185 Andre Davis	1.25	3.00
186 William Green	1.50	4.00
187 Antonio Bryant	2.00	5.00
188 Ashley Lelie	1.25	3.00
189 Clinton Portis	2.00	5.00
190 Joey Harrington	1.25	3.00
191 Javon Walker	2.00	5.00
192 David Carr	1.25	3.00
193 Jabar Gaffney	1.25	3.00
194 Jonathan Wells	1.50	4.00
195 David Garrard	1.50	4.00
196 Donte Stallworth	2.00	5.00
197 Brian Westbrook	2.50	6.00
198 Antwaan Randle El	1.50	4.00
199 Maurice Morris	1.50	4.00
200 Patrick Ramsey	1.50	4.00

2002 Pacific Exclusive Gold

*VETS: 1.2X TO 3X BASIC CARDS
ONE GOLD PER PACK

2002 Pacific Exclusive Retail

Retail packs of Pacific Exclusive featured the same 200-cards as the hobby version except that each of the 14-Autographed Rookie Cards from hobby were replaced with unsigned versions in the retail packs. We've included only listings for those 14-replacement cards.

Card	Low	High
181 Josh McCown RC	.75	2.00
184 DeShaun Foster RC	.75	2.00
185 Andre Davis RC	.50	1.25
187 Antonio Bryant RC	.75	2.00
188 Ashley Lelie RC	.50	1.25
189 Clinton Portis RC	.75	2.00
191 Javon Walker RC	.75	2.00
192 David Carr RC	.50	1.25
193 Jabar Gaffney RC	.50	1.25
194 Jonathan Wells RC	.60	1.50
195 David Garrard RC	.60	1.50
197 Brian Westbrook RC	1.00	2.50
198 Antwaan Randle El RC	.60	1.50
199 Maurice Morris RC	.60	1.50

2002 Pacific Exclusive Advantage

Inserted at a rate of 1:6, this set highlights 20 of the NFL's top offensive players.

Card	Low	High
COMPLETE SET (20)	20.00	50.00
STATED ODDS 1:6		
1 Michael Vick	.75	2.00
2 Drew Bledsoe	.75	2.00
3 Anthony Thomas	.75	2.00
4 Corey Dillon	.60	1.50
5 Tim Couch	.60	1.50
6 Emmitt Smith	1.50	4.00
7 Brett Favre	2.00	5.00
8 Edgerrin James	.75	2.00
9 Peyton Manning	2.50	6.00
10 Ricky Williams	.75	2.00
11 Daunte Culpepper	.75	2.00
12 Randy Moss	.75	2.00
13 Tom Brady	5.00	12.00
14 Jerry Rice	2.00	5.00
15 Donovan McNabb	.75	2.00
16 Marshall Faulk	.75	2.00
17 Kurt Warner	.75	2.00
18 Drew Brees	2.00	5.00
19 LaDainian Tomlinson	1.00	2.50
20 Shaun Alexander	.60	1.50

2002 Pacific Exclusive Destined for Greatness

Inserted at a rate of 1:11, this set showcases many of the NFL's top 2002 rookies, who are destined to be amongst the NFL's greatest.

Card	Low	High
COMPLETE SET (10)	10.00	25.00
STATED ODDS 1:11		
1 T.J. Duckett	.50	1.25
2 DeShaun Foster	.75	2.00
3 William Green	.60	1.50
4 Ashley Lelie	.50	1.25
5 Clinton Portis	.75	2.00
6 Joey Harrington	.50	1.25
7 David Carr	.50	1.25
8 Donte Stallworth	.75	2.00
9 Antwaan Randle El	.60	1.50
10 Patrick Ramsey	.60	1.50

2002 Pacific Exclusive Etched in Stone

Inserted at a rate of 1:21, this set features ten players whose career numbers speak for themselves, and are etched in stone for all to see.

Card	Low	High
COMPLETE SET (10)	12.50	30.00
STATED ODDS 1:21		
1 Michael Vick	.75	2.00
2 Anthony Thomas	.75	2.00
3 Emmitt Smith	1.50	4.00
4 Brett Favre	2.00	5.00
5 Peyton Manning	2.50	6.00
6 Randy Moss	.75	2.00
7 Tom Brady	5.00	12.00
8 Jerry Rice	2.00	5.00
9 Marshall Faulk	.75	2.00
10 Kurt Warner	.75	2.00

2002 Pacific Exclusive Game Worn Jerseys

Inserted at a rate of 2:21, this set features game worn jersey cards. In addition, there is also a gold parallel version #'d to 25.

Card	Low	High
STATED ODDS 2:21		
*GOLD/25: .75X TO 2X BASIC JSY		
GOLD JSY PRINT RUN 25 SETS		
1 Frank Sanders	2.00	5.00
2 Jamal Anderson	2.50	6.00
3 Quentin McCord	2.00	5.00
4 Michael Vick	2.50	6.00
5 Jeremy McDaniel	2.00	5.00
6 Jay Riemersma	2.00	5.00
7 Charlie Rogers	2.00	5.00
8 Marcus Robinson	2.50	6.00
9 Brian Urlacher	3.00	8.00
10 Corey Dillon	2.00	5.00
11 Michael Westbrook	2.00	5.00
12 Tim Couch	2.00	5.00
13 Aaron Shea	2.00	5.00
14 Emmitt Smith	5.00	12.00
15 Kevin Kasper	2.00	5.00
16 Rob Moore	2.00	5.00
17 Brett Favre	6.00	15.00
18 Robert Ferguson	2.50	6.00
19 Ahman Green	2.50	6.00
20 Avion Black	2.00	5.00
21 Clif Groce	2.00	5.00
22 Brock Huard	2.50	6.00
23 Peyton Manning	8.00	20.00
24 Troy Walters	2.00	5.00
25 Mark Brunell	2.50	6.00
26 Bobby Shaw	2.00	5.00
27 Jimmy Smith	2.50	6.00
28 Ricky Williams	2.50	6.00
29 Daunte Culpepper	2.50	6.00
30 Randy Moss	2.50	6.00
31 Aaron Brooks	2.00	5.00
32 Terrelle Smith	2.00	5.00
33 Laveranues Coles	2.50	6.00
34 Curtis Martin	2.50	6.00
35 Rich Gannon	2.50	6.00
36 Jerry Rice	6.00	15.00
37 Donovan McNabb	2.50	6.00
38 James Thrash	2.50	6.00
39 Jerome Bettis	3.00	8.00
40 Plaxico Burress	2.00	5.00
41 Chris Fuamatu-Ma'afala	2.00	5.00
42 Marshall Faulk	2.50	6.00
43 Kurt Warner	2.50	6.00
44 Drew Brees	6.00	15.00
45 Terrell Fletcher	2.00	5.00
46 Shaun Alexander	2.00	5.00
47 Brad Johnson	2.50	6.00
48 Michael Pittman	2.50	6.00
49 Aaron Stecker	2.00	5.00
50 Erron Kinney	2.00	5.00

2002 Pacific Exclusive Great Expectations

Inserted at a rate of 1:6, this set showcases twenty players expected to make an impact in the NFL throughout their careers.

Card	Low	High
COMPLETE SET (20)	12.50	30.00
STATED ODDS 1:6		
1 Josh McCown	.60	1.50
2 T.J. Duckett	.40	1.00
3 Josh Reed	.50	1.25
4 DeShaun Foster	.60	1.50
5 Andre Davis	.40	1.00
6 William Green	.50	1.25
7 Antonio Bryant	.60	1.50
8 Ashley Lelie	.40	1.00
9 Clinton Portis	.60	1.50
10 Joey Harrington	.40	1.00
11 Javon Walker	.60	1.50
12 David Carr	.40	1.00
13 Jabar Gaffney	.40	1.00
14 Jonathan Wells	.50	1.25
15 David Garrard	.50	1.25
16 Donte Stallworth	.60	1.50
17 Brian Westbrook	.75	2.00
18 Antwaan Randle El	.50	1.25
19 Maurice Morris	.50	1.25
20 Patrick Ramsey	.50	1.25

2002 Pacific Exclusive Maximum Overdrive

Inserted at a rate of 1:6, this set features players who kick it into overdrive when they need to make a big play.

COMPLETE SET (30) 20.00 50.00
STATED ODDS 1:6
1 T.J. Duckett .40 1.00
2 Michael Vick .50 1.25
3 DeShaun Foster .60 1.50
4 Anthony Thomas .50 1.25
5 Tim Couch .40 1.00
6 Andre Davis .40 1.00
7 William Green .50 1.25
8 Antonio Bryant .60 1.50
9 Emmitt Smith 1.00 2.50
10 Ashley Lelie .40 1.00
11 Clinton Portis .60 1.50
12 Joey Harrington .40 1.00
13 Brett Favre 1.25 3.00
14 Javon Walker .60 1.50
15 David Carr .40 1.00
16 Jabbar Gaffney .40 1.00
17 Peyton Manning 1.50 4.00
18 Ricky Williams .50 1.25
19 Daunte Culpepper .50 1.25
20 Randy Moss .50 1.25
21 Tom Brady 3.00 8.00
22 Donte Stallworth .60 1.50
23 Jerry Rice 1.25 3.00
24 Donovan McNabb .50 1.25
25 Antwaan Randle El .50 1.25
26 Marshall Faulk .50 1.25
27 Kurt Warner .50 1.25
28 Drew Brees 1.25 3.00
29 LaDainian Tomlinson .60 1.50
30 Patrick Ramsey .50 1.25

1995 Pacific Gridiron

cific produced 750 hobby cases (blue foil) and 750 retail cases (red foil). Each set also had a parallel set representing 10 percent of the sets produced. Just 30 "Gold" sets were produced, with two gold cards seeded per hobby or retail case.This 100-card set measures 3 1/2" by 5". The fronts feature full-color action shots which bleed to the borders. The backs have a write-up of the player's performance in the game pictured in the front photo. The back also has an inset photo. Pacific founders Mike and Cheryl Cramer took many of the photos used in this set. Rookie Cards in this set include Jeff Blake, Ki-Jana Carter, and Steve McNair. Natrone Means appears on four different promo cards as listed below.

COMP.BLUE SET (100) 20.00 50.00
1 Natrone Means .20 .50
2 Dave Meggett .10 .30
3 Curtis Conway .20 .50
4 Sam Adams .10 .30
5 Qadry Ismail .20 .50
6 Steve Young .75 2.00
7 Errict Rhett .20 .50
8 Nate Lewis .10 .30
9 Barry Sanders 2.00 5.00
10 Sterling Sharpe .20 .50
11 Steve Beuerlein .20 .50
12 Irving Spikes .20 .50
13 Byron Bam Morris .10 .30
14 Eric Metcalf .20 .50
15 Michael Irvin .40 1.00
16 Dan Marino 2.00 5.00
17 Stan Humphries .20 .50
18 Leroy Hoard .20 .50
19 Marcus Allen .40 1.00
20 Barry Foster .20 .50
21 Ronald Moore .10 .30
22 Rodney Hampton .20 .50
23 Ben Coates .20 .50
24 Vernon Turner .10 .30
25 Shannon Sharpe .20 .50
26 Larry Centers .20 .50
27 Mack Strong RC .75 2.00
28 Reggie White .40 1.00
29 Harvey Williams .10 .30
30 Darnay Scott .20 .50
31 Drew Bledsoe 1.00 2.50
32 Marshall Faulk .75 2.00
33 Troy Aikman 1.00 2.50
34 Boomer Esiason .20 .50
35 Bobby Hebert .10 .30
36 Brian Mitchell .10 .30
37 Andre Rison .20 .50
38 Brett Favre 2.00 5.00
39 Don Majkowski .10 .30
40 Johnny Johnson .10 .30
41 Mark Carrier WR .20 .50
42 James Joseph .10 .30
43 Mario Bates .20 .50
44 Craig Heyward .20 .50
45 Henry Ellard .20 .50
46 Thurman Thomas .40 1.00
47 Jerome Bettis .40 1.00
48 Dave Brown .20 .50
49 Lorenzo White .10 .30
50 Joe Montana 2.00 5.00
51 Vinny Testaverde .20 .50
52 Lake Dawson .20 .50
53 Michael Timpson .10 .30
54 Ricky Ervins .10 .30
55 Cris Carter .40 1.00
56 Raymont Harris .10 .30
57 Andre Coleman .10 .30
58 Craig Erickson .10 .30
59 Jeff Hostetler .20 .50
60 Deion Sanders .60 1.50
61 Eric Turner .10 .30
62 Daryl Johnston .20 .50
63 Bernie Parmalee .20 .50
64 Ricky Watters .20 .50
65 David Palmer .20 .50
66 Aaron Glenn .10 .30
67 Todd Kinchen .10 .30
68 Edgar Bennett .20 .50
69 Mel Gray .10 .30
70 Randall Cunningham .40 1.00
71 Michael Haynes .20 .50
72 Chris Miller .10 .30
73 Glyn Milburn .10 .30
74 Steve McNair RC 2.50 6.00
75 Lewis Tillman .10 .30
76 Chuck Levy .10 .30
77 Carl Pickens .20 .50
78 Michael Bates .10 .30
79 Jeff Blake RC .60 1.50
80 O.J. McDuffie .40 1.00
81 Tim Brown .40 1.00
82 Haywood Jeffires .10 .30
83 Jeff Burris .10 .30
84 John Elway 2.00 5.00
85 Charles Johnson .20 .50
86 Emmitt Smith 2.00 5.00
87 William Floyd .20 .50
88 Herschel Walker .20 .50
89 Rick Mirer .20 .50
90 Roosevelt Potts .10 .30
91 Rod Woodson .20 .50
92 Greg Hill .20 .50
93 Junior Seau .40 1.00
94 Dave Krieg .10 .30
95 Jim Kelly .40 1.00
96 Warren Moon .40 1.00
97 Leroy Thompson .10 .30
98 Ki-Jana Carter RC .40 1.00
99 Herman Moore .40 1.00
100 Jerry Rice 1.00 2.50
P1 Natrone Means .40 1.00
P2 Natrone Means .40 1.00
P3 Natrone Means .40 1.00
P4 Natrone Means Promo Blue .40 1.00
P5 Natrone Means Promo .40 1.00

1995 Pacific Gridiron Copper

COMP.COPPER SET (100) 100.00 200.00
*COPPER STARS: 1.2X TO 3X BASIC CARDS
*COPPER RCs: .8X TO 2X BASIC CARDS

1995 Pacific Gridiron Gold

*GOLD STARS: 20X TO 50X BASIC CARDS
*GOLD RCs: 12X TO 30X BASIC CARDS

1995 Pacific Gridiron Platinum

COMP.PLATINUM SET (100) 100.00 200.00
*PLATINUM STARS: 1.2X TO 3X BASIC CARDS
*PLATINUM RCs: .8X TO 2X BASIC CARDS

1995 Pacific Gridiron Red

COMP.RED SET (100) 20.00 50.00
*RED CARDS: SAME PRICE AS BLUES

1996 Pacific Gridiron

The 1996 Pacific Gridiron set was issued in one series totalling 125 cards in 2-card packs with 36 packs per box and 20 boxes per case. The was a hobby version with each printed with blue foil highlights on the front and a red foil retail version. The oversized cards measure roughly 3 1/2" by 5". The set is sequenced in alphabetical order within alphabetical team order.

COMPLETE SET (125) 12.50 30.00
1 Larry Centers .15 .40
2 Garrison Hearst .15 .40
3 Dave Krieg .08 .25
4 Frank Sanders .15 .40
5 Jamal Anderson RC .40 1.00
6 J.J. Birden .08 .25
7 Eric Metcalf .08 .25
8 Jeff George .15 .40
9 Cornelius Bennett .08 .25
10 Todd Collins .15 .40
11 Darick Holmes .08 .25
12 Jim Kelly .30 .75
13 Bryce Paup .08 .25
14 Bob Christian .08 .25
15 Kerry Collins .30 .75
16 Pete Metzelaars .08 .25
17 Derrick Moore .08 .25
18 Curtis Conway .30 .75
19 Jim Flanigan .08 .25
20 Erik Kramer .08 .25
21 Rashaan Salaam .15 .40
22 Eric Bieniemy .08 .25
23 Jeff Blake .30 .75
24 Tony McGee .08 .25
25 Darnay Scott .15 .40
26 Vashone Adams RC .08 .25
27 Leroy Hoard .08 .25
28 Andre Rison .15 .40
29 Tommy Vardell .08 .25
30 Troy Aikman .75 2.00
31 Michael Irvin .30 .75
32 Daryl Johnston .15 .40
33 Deion Sanders .40 1.00
34 Emmitt Smith 1.25 3.00
35 Terrell Davis .60 1.50
36 John Elway 1.50 4.00
37 Ed McCaffrey .15 .40
38 Anthony Miller .15 .40
39 Scott Mitchell .15 .40
40 Brett Perriman .08 .25
41 Barry Sanders 1.25 3.00
42 Chris Spielman .08 .25
43 Edgar Bennett .15 .40
44 Robert Brooks .30 .75
45 Brett Favre 1.50 4.00
46 Antonio Freeman .30 .75
47 Reggie White .30 .75
48 Haywood Jeffires .08 .25
49 Steve McNair .60 1.50
50 Rodney Thomas .08 .25
51 Frank Wycheck .08 .25
52 Ashley Ambrose .08 .25
53 Mark Brunell .50 1.25
54 Ken Dilger .15 .40
55 Marshall Faulk .40 1.00
56 Jim Harbaugh .15 .40
57 Tony Boselli .08 .25
58 Pete Mitchell .15 .40
59 James O.Stewart .15 .40
60 Marcus Allen .30 .75
61 Steve Bono .08 .25
62 Lake Dawson .08 .25
63 Tamarick Vanover .15 .40
64 Bryan Cox .08 .25
65 Dan Marino 1.50 4.00
66 O.J. McDuffie .15 .40
67 Bernie Parmalee .08 .25
68 Cris Carter .30 .75
69 Rocket Ismail .08 .25
70 Warren Moon .15 .40
71 Robert Smith .15 .40
72 Drew Bledsoe .50 1.25
73 Vincent Brisby .08 .25
74 Ben Coates .15 .40
75 Curtis Martin .60 1.50
76 Mario Bates .15 .40
77 Derek Brown RBK .08 .25
78 Jim Everett .08 .25
79 Dave Brown .08 .25
80 Chris Calloway .08 .25
81 Rodney Hampton .15 .40
82 Tyrone Wheatley .15 .40
83 Kyle Brady .08 .25
84 Wayne Chrebet .40 1.00
85 Adrian Murrell .15 .40
86 Tim Brown .30 .75
87 Rob Carpenter .08 .25
88 Charlie Garner .15 .40
89 Daryl Hobbs RC .08 .25
90 Napoleon Kaufman .30 .75
91 Rodney Peete .08 .25
92 Ricky Watters .15 .40
93 Calvin Williams .08 .25
94 Kevin Greene .15 .40
95 Greg Lloyd .15 .40
96 Neil O'Donnell .15 .40
97 Erric Pegram .08 .25
98 Kordell Stewart .30 .75
99 Yancey Thigpen .15 .40
100 Rod Woodson .15 .40
101 Isaac Bruce .30 .75
102 Jerome Bettis .30 .75
103 J.T. Thomas .08 .25
104 Ronnie Harmon .08 .25
105 Aaron Hayden RC .08 .25
106 Stan Humphries .15 .40
107 Alfred Pupunu .08 .25
108 William Floyd .15 .40
109 Brent Jones .08 .25
110 Jerry Rice .75 2.00
111 J.J. Stokes .30 .75
112 John Taylor .08 .25
113 Steve Young .50 1.25
114 Harvey Williams .08 .25
115 John Friesz .08 .25
116 Joey Galloway .30 .75
117 Cortez Kennedy .08 .25
118 Rick Mirer .15 .40
119 Chris Warren .15 .40
120 Trent Dilfer .30 .75
121 Alvin Harper .08 .25
122 Errict Rhett .15 .40
123 Terry Allen .15 .40
124 Gus Frerotte .15 .40
125 Michael Westbrook .30 .75
S1 Chris Warren Sample .40 1.00

1996 Pacific Gridiron Copper

COMP.COPPER SET (125) 100.00 200.00
*COPPER STARS: 2X TO 5X BASIC CARDS
*COPPER RCs: 1.2X TO 3X BASIC CARDS
STATED ODDS 4:37 HOBBY

1996 Pacific Gridiron Gold

*GOLD STARS: 20X TO 50X BASIC CARDS
*GOLD RCs: 12X TO 30X BASIC CARDS

1996 Pacific Gridiron Platinum

COMP.PLATINUM SET (125) 100.00 200.00
*PLATINUM STARS: 2X TO 5X BASIC CARDS
*PLATINUM RCs: 1.2X TO 3X BASIC CARDS
STATED ODDS 4:37 RETAIL

1996 Pacific Gridiron Red

*RED: .4X TO 1X BLUE CARDS

1996 Pacific Gridiron Driving Force

Randomly inserted in packs at a rate of one in 73, this 10-card set turns the spotlight towards some of the NFL's top running backs. The busy fronts include the words "Driving Force" on the left and the player's name on the bottom. The back contains another photo as well as some career textual information. The cards are numbered with a "DF" prefix

COMPLETE SET (10) 15.00 40.00
STATED ODDS 1:73
DF1 Chris Warren .75 2.00
DF2 Emmitt Smith 6.00 15.00
DF3 Barry Sanders 6.00 15.00
DF4 Rashaan Salaam .75 2.00
DF5 Errict Rhett .75 2.00
DF6 Curtis Martin 3.00 8.00
DF7 Garrison Hearst .75 2.00
DF8 Marshall Faulk 2.00 5.00
DF9 Terrell Davis 3.00 8.00
DF10 Edgar Bennett .75 2.00

1996 Pacific Gridiron Gems

Randomly inserted in packs at a rate of three in four, this 50-card set contains photographs of leading NFL players. The cards are numbered with a "GG" prefix.

COMPLETE SET (50) 12.00 30.00
STATED ODDS 27:37
GG1 J.J. Birden .08 .25
GG2 Garrison Hearst .15 .40
GG3 Bryce Paup .08 .25
GG4 Kerry Collins .30 .75
GG5 Alonzo Spellman .08 .25
GG6 Chris Zorich .08 .25
GG7 Harold Green .08 .25
GG8 Lee Johnson .08 .25
GG9 Eric Zeier .15 .40
GG10 Troy Aikman .75 2.00
GG11 Deion Sanders .40 1.00
GG12 Emmitt Smith 1.25 3.00
GG13 John Elway 1.50 4.00
GG14 Mike Pritchard .08 .25
GG15 Shane Bonham .08 .25
GG16 Barry Sanders 1.25 3.00
GG17 Edgar Bennett .15 .40
GG18 Brett Favre 1.50 4.00
GG19 Reggie White .30 .75
GG20 Eddie Robinson .08 .25
GG21 Marshall Faulk .40 1.00
GG22 Brian Stablein .08 .25
GG23 Don Davey .08 .25
GG24 Neil Smith .15 .40
GG25 Derrick Thomas .30 .75
GG26 Eric Green .08 .25
GG27 Jake Reed .15 .40
GG28 Troy Brown .20 .50
GG29 Will Moore .08 .25
GG30 Wesley Walls .15 .40
GG31 Herschel Walker .15 .40
GG32 Keyshawn Johnson .50 1.25
GG33 Billy Joe Hobert .08 .25
GG34 Ricky Watters .15 .40
GG35 Ernie Mills .08 .25
GG36 Kordell Stewart .30 .75
GG37 Terrell Fletcher .08 .25
GG38 Junior Seau .30 .75
GG39 Elvis Grbac .15 .40
GG40 Gary Plummer .08 .25
GG41 Jerry Rice .75 2.00
GG42 Steve Young .50 1.25
GG43 Carlester Crumpler .08 .25
GG44 Joey Galloway .30 .75
GG45 Cortez Kennedy .08 .25
GG46 Chris Warren .15 .40
GG47 Greg Robinson .08 .25
GG48 Errict Rhett .15 .40
GG49 Terry Allen .15 .40
GG50 Stanley Richard .08 .25

1996 Pacific Gridiron Gold Crown Die Cuts

Randomly inserted in packs at a rate of one in 37, this 20-card set was available via redemption card only (with an expiration date of 12/31/1996). Each redemption card bore one player's name and card number and collectors could redeem their card for that player's Gold Crown Die Cut. We've priced the actual Die Cut prize cards below.

COMPLETE SET (20) 75.00 150.00
STATED ODDS 1:37
LISTED PRICES ARE FOR PRIZE CARDS
GC1 Barry Sanders 8.00 20.00
GC2 Ricky Watters 1.00 2.50
GC3 Troy Aikman 5.00 12.00
GC4 Deion Sanders 2.50 6.00
GC5 Kerry Collins 2.00 5.00
GC6 Dan Marino 10.00 25.00
GC7 Steve Young 3.00 8.00
GC8 Drew Bledsoe 3.00 8.00
GC9 Jerry Rice 5.00 12.00
GC10 Steve McNair 4.00 10.00
GC11 Joey Galloway 2.00 5.00
GC12 John Elway 8.00 20.00
GC13 Terrell Davis 4.00 10.00
GC14 Rashaan Salaam 1.00 2.50
GC15 Kordell Stewart 2.00 5.00
GC16 Emmitt Smith 8.00 20.00
GC17 Curtis Martin 4.00 10.00
GC18 Marshall Faulk 2.50 6.00
GC19 Brett Favre 10.00 25.00
GC20 Chris Warren 1.00 2.50

1996 Pacific Gridiron Rock Solid Rookies

Randomly inserted in packs at a rate of one in 121, this six-card set features leading 1995 rookies. Similar to other Pacific Gridiron cards, they measure 3 1/2" by 5". The cards are numbered with an "RP" prefix.

COMPLETE SET (6) 40.00 80.00
STATED ODDS 1:121
RP1 Joey Galloway 6.00 15.00
RP2 Napoleon Kaufman 6.00 15.00
RP3 Michael Westbrook 4.00 10.00
RP4 Kerry Collins 6.00 15.00
RP5 Aaron Hayden 2.50 6.00
RP6 Kordell Stewart 6.00 15.00

2002 Pacific Heads Up

This 175-card base set includes 125 veterans and 50 rookies. The rookie cards are serially numbered to 1090. The cards were distributed as both a hobby and retail product. Please note that cards 176-195 were only available in packs of 2002 Pacific Heads Update.

COMP.SET w/o SP's (125) 10.00 25.00
ROOKIE PRINT RUN 1090 SER.#'d SETS
1 David Boston .25 .60
2 Thomas Jones .25 .60
3 Jake Plummer .25 .60
4 Jamal Anderson .30 .75
5 Warrick Dunn .25 .60
6 Shawn Jefferson .25 .60
7 Michael Vick .30 .75
8 Jamal Lewis .30 .75
9 Chris Redman .25 .60
10 Brandon Stokley .25 .60
11 Travis Taylor .25 .60
12 Drew Bledsoe .30 .75
13 Travis Henry .25 .60
14 Eric Moulds .25 .60
15 Peerless Price .25 .60
16 Alex Van Pelt .25 .60
17 Muhsin Muhammad .25 .60
18 Lamar Smith .25 .60
19 Steve Smith .40 1.00
20 Chris Weinke .25 .60
21 Marty Booker .25 .60
22 Jim Miller .25 .60
23 David Terrell .25 .60
24 Anthony Thomas .30 .75
25 Corey Dillon .25 .60
26 Chad Johnson .25 .60
27 Jon Kitna .25 .60
28 Peter Warrick .25 .60
29 Tim Couch .25 .60
30 James Jackson .25 .60
31 Kevin Johnson .25 .60
32 Quincy Morgan .25 .60
33 Quincy Carter .25 .60
34 Joey Galloway .30 .75
35 Rocket Ismail .30 .75
36 Emmitt Smith .60 1.50
37 Terrell Davis .30 .75
38 Brian Griese .25 .60
39 Ed McCaffrey .30 .75
40 Rod Smith .30 .75
41 Scotty Anderson .25 .60
42 Az-Zahir Hakim .25 .60
43 Mike McMahon .25 .60
44 Bill Schroeder .25 .60
45 Brett Favre .75 2.00
46 Robert Ferguson .30 .75
47 Terry Glenn .30 .75
48 Ahman Green .30 .75
49 James Allen .25 .60
50 Corey Bradford .25 .60
51 Jermaine Lewis .25 .60
52 Marvin Harrison .30 .75
53 Edgerrin James .30 .75
54 Peyton Manning 1.00 2.50
55 Reggie Wayne .30 .75
56 Mark Brunell .30 .75
57 Keenan McCardell .30 .75
58 Jimmy Smith .30 .75
59 Fred Taylor .25 .60
60 Derrick Alexander .25 .60
61 Tony Gonzalez .30 .75
62 Trent Green .25 .60
63 Priest Holmes .25 .60
64 Chris Chambers .25 .60
65 Jay Fiedler .30 .75
66 James McKnight .25 .60
67 Ricky Williams .30 .75
68 Michael Bennett .25 .60
69 Daunte Culpepper .30 .75
70 Randy Moss .30 .75
71 Tom Brady 2.00 5.00
72 Troy Brown .25 .60
73 Antowain Smith .30 .75
74 Aaron Brooks .25 .60
75 Joe Horn .25 .60
76 Willie Jackson .25 .60
77 Deuce McAllister .30 .75
78 Tiki Barber .30 .75
79 Kerry Collins .25 .60
80 Ron Dayne .30 .75
81 Ike Hilliard .25 .60
82 Wayne Chrebet .25 .60
83 Laveranues Coles .30 .75
84 Curtis Martin .30 .75
85 Vinny Testaverde .25 .60
86 Tim Brown .40 1.00
87 Rich Gannon .30 .75
88 Charlie Garner .30 .75
89 Jerry Rice .75 2.00
90 Correll Buckhalter .25 .60
91 Donovan McNabb .30 .75
92 Duce Staley .25 .60
93 James Thrash .30 .75
94 Jerome Bettis .40 1.00
95 Plaxico Burress .25 .60
96 Kordell Stewart .25 .60
97 Hines Ward .30 .75
98 Isaac Bruce .40 1.00
99 Marshall Faulk .30 .75
100 Torry Holt .30 .75
101 Kurt Warner .30 .75
102 Drew Brees .75 2.00
103 Tim Dwight .25 .60
104 Doug Flutie .30 .75
105 LaDainian Tomlinson .40 1.00
106 Jeff Garcia .25 .60
107 Garrison Hearst .25 .60
108 Terrell Owens .30 .75
109 J.J. Stokes .25 .60
110 Shaun Alexander .25 .60
111 Trent Dilfer .25 .60
112 Darrell Jackson .30 .75
113 Koren Robinson .25 .60
114 Mike Alstott .25 .60
115 Brad Johnson .30 .75
116 Keyshawn Johnson .30 .75
117 Michael Pittman .30 .75
118 Kevin Dyson .30 .75
119 Eddie George .30 .75
120 Derrick Mason .25 .60
121 Steve McNair .30 .75
122 Reidel Anthony .25 .60
123 Stephen Davis .25 .60
124 Rod Gardner .25 .60
125 Jacquez Green .25 .60
126 Jason McAddley RC 1.25 3.00
127 Josh McCown RC 1.50 4.00
128 T.J. Duckett RC 1.00 2.50
129 Kahlil Hill RC 1.00 2.50
130 Kurt Kittner RC 1.00 2.50
131 Ron Johnson RC 1.25 3.00
132 Chester Taylor RC 1.50 4.00
133 Josh Reed RC 1.25 3.00
134 Randy Fasani RC 1.00 2.50
135 DeShaun Foster RC 1.50 4.00
136 Julius Peppers RC 2.50 6.00
137 Eric McCoo RC 1.00 2.50
138 Adrian Peterson RC 1.25 3.00
139 Andre Davis RC 1.00 2.50
140 William Green RC 1.25 3.00
141 Antonio Bryant RC 1.50 4.00
142 Roy Williams RC 1.00 2.50
143 Ashley Lelie RC 1.00 2.50
144 Clinton Portis RC 1.50 4.00
145 Joey Harrington RC 1.00 2.50
146 Luke Staley RC 1.00 2.50
147 Javon Walker RC 1.50 4.00
148 David Carr RC 1.00 2.50
149 Jabar Gaffney RC 1.00 2.50
150 Jonathan Wells RC 1.25 3.00
151 David Garrard RC 1.25 3.00
152 Leonard Henry RC 1.00 2.50
153 Major Applewhite RC 1.50 4.00
154 Deion Branch RC 1.50 4.00
155 Rohan Davey RC 1.50 4.00
156 Daniel Graham RC 1.25 3.00
157 Antwoine Womack RC 1.00 2.50
158 J.T. O'Sullivan RC 1.25 3.00
159 Donte Stallworth RC 1.50 4.00
160 Jeremy Shockey RC 1.50 4.00
161 Ronald Curry RC 1.00 2.50
162 Larry Ned RC 1.00 2.50
163 Freddie Milons RC 1.00 2.50
164 Brian Westbrook RC 2.00 5.00
165 Lee Mays RC 1.00 2.50
166 Antwaan Randle El RC 1.25 3.00
167 Eric Crouch RC 1.50 4.00
168 Lamar Gordon RC 1.25 3.00
169 Reche Caldwell RC 1.25 3.00
170 Maurice Morris RC 1.25 3.00
171 Travis Stephens RC 1.00 2.50
172 Marquise Walker RC 1.00 2.50
173 Ladell Betts RC 1.50 4.00
174 Patrick Ramsey RC 1.25 3.00
175 Cliff Russell RC 1.00 2.50
176 Dameon Hunter RC 1.00 2.50
177 Javin Hunter RC 1.00 2.50
178 Tellis Redmon RC 1.00 2.50
179 Ed Reed RC 6.00 15.00
180 Jamin Elliott RC 1.00 2.50
181 Chad Hutchinson RC 1.00 2.50
182 Eddie Drummond RC 1.00 2.50
183 Najeh Davenport RC 1.00 2.50
184 Craig Nall RC 1.25 3.00
185 Jarrod Baxter RC 1.00 2.50
186 Marc Boerigter RC 1.50 4.00
187 Kelly Campbell RC 1.25 3.00
188 Shaun Hill RC 1.50 4.00
189 Tim Carter RC 1.25 3.00
190 Daryl Jones RC 1.00 2.50
191 Phillip Buchanon RC 1.50 4.00
192 Napoleon Harris RC 1.25 3.00
193 Seth Burford RC 1.00 2.50
194 Brandon Doman RC 1.00 2.50
195 Jerramy Stevens RC 1.50 4.00

2002 Pacific Heads Up Blue

*VETS 1-125: 2X TO 5X BASIC CARDS
*ROOKIES 126-175: .5X TO 1.2X
BLUE/210 ODDS 2:19 HOB, 1:25 RET
STATED PRINT RUN 210 SER.#'d SETS

2002 Pacific Heads Up Purple

*VETS 1-125: 10X TO 25X BASIC CARDS
*ROOKIES 126-175: 2X TO 5X
PURPLE PRINT RUN 25 SER.#'d SETS

2002 Pacific Heads Up Red

*VETS 1-125: 4X TO 10X BASIC CARDS
*ROOKIES 126-175: 1X TO 2.5X
RED/65 STATED ODDS 1:19 HOB
STATED PRINT RUN 65 SER.#'d SETS

2002 Pacific Heads Up Bobble Head Dolls

Inserted at a rate of one per box, this 14-card set showcases some of the top NFL veterans and young stars. Each bobble head is made of porcelain and comes in its own separate box.

STATED ODDS 1 PER BOX
1 Jerome Bettis 6.00 15.00
2 Tom Brady 30.00 80.00
3 David Carr 4.00 10.00
4 Daunte Culpepper 5.00 12.00
5 Marshall Faulk 5.00 12.00
6 Brett Favre 12.00 30.00
7 Randy Moss 5.00 12.00
8 Jerry Rice 12.00 30.00
9 Emmitt Smith 10.00 25.00
10 Anthony Thomas 5.00 12.00
11 LaDainian Tomlinson 6.00 15.00
12 Michael Vick 5.00 12.00
13 Kurt Warner 5.00 12.00
14 Ricky Williams 5.00 12.00

2002 Pacific Heads Up Game Worn Jersey Quads

serted in hobby packs at a rate of 2:19 and retail packs at 1:97, this 50-card insert is standard sized. Each card features silver foil and a piece of game-worn jersey from four different NFL players. A Gold foil version was also produced with each serial numbered of 45.

STATED ODDS 2:19 HOB, 1:97 RET
*GOLD/45: .8X TO 2X BASIC QUAD
GOLD PRINT RUN 45 SER.#'d SETS
1 David Boston 2.50 6.00
Thomas Jones
Jake Plummer
Frank Sanders
2 Bill Gramatica 2.50 6.00
Mar Tay Jenkins
Joel Makovicka
Tywan Mitchell
3 Obafemi Ayanbadejo 2.50 6.00
Todd Heap
Chris Redman
Travis Taylor
4 Shawn Bryson 2.50 6.00
Reggie Germany
Sammy Morris
Jay Riemersma
5 Isaac Byrd 3.00 8.00
Muhsin Muhammad
Wesley Walls
Chris Weinke
6 Marty Booker 4.00 10.00
Jim Miller
David Terrell
Brian Urlacher
7 Corey Dillon 3.00 8.00
Chad Johnson
Darnay Scott
Peter Warrick
8 Curtis Keaton 3.00 8.00
Scott Mitchell
Brad St. Louis
Nick Williams
9 Tim Couch 2.50 6.00
JaJuan Dawson
Kevin Johnson
Jamel White
10 Rambo/Gall/Ism/Emmitt 6.00 15.00
11 Troy Hambrick 3.00 8.00
Michael Wiley
Darren Woodson
Anthony Wright
12 Mike Anderson 3.00 8.00
Olandis Gary
Brian Griese
Rod Smith
13 Favre/Free/Grn/Mart 8.00 20.00
14 Tyrone Davis 3.00 8.00
Robert Ferguson
Bubba Franks
William Henderson
15 Harr/James/Mann/Poll 10.00 25.00
16 Mark Brunell 3.00 8.00
Keenan McCardell
Jimmy Smith
Fred Taylor
17 Tony Gonzalez 3.00 8.00
Trent Green
Sylvester Morris
Tony Richardson
18 Jay Fiedler 3.00 8.00
Oronde Gadsden
Travis Minor
Zach Thomas
19 Michael Bennett 4.00 10.00
Cris Carter
Daunte Culpepper
Randy Moss
20 Bled/Brady/Brown/pass 20.00 50.00
21 Aaron Brooks 3.00 8.00
Joe Horn
Deuce McAllister
Robert Wilson
22 Tiki Barber 3.00 8.00
Kerry Collins
Ron Dayne
Amani Toomer
23 Jonathan Carter 3.00 8.00
Ron Dixon
Ike Hilliard
Jason Sehorn
24 Anthony Becht 3.00 8.00
Laveranues Coles
Curtis Martin
Chad Pennington
25 Brown/Crock/Rice/Woods 8.00 20.00
26 David Dunn 3.00 8.00
James Jett
Randy Jordan
Jerry Porter
27 Chad Lewis 3.00 8.00
Donovan McNabb
Brian Mitchell
Todd Pinkston
28 Bett/Burr/Stew/Ward 4.00 10.00
29 Isaac Bruce 4.00 10.00
Marshall Faulk
Torry Holt
Kurt Warner JSY
30 Brees/Flut/Seau/Tomlnsn 8.00 20.00
31 Terrell Fletcher 2.50 6.00
Trevor Gaylor
Ronney Jenkins
Fred McCrary
32 Jeff Garcia 3.00 8.00
Terrell Owens
Tim Rattay
J.J. Stokes
33 Fred Beasley 3.00 8.00
Greg Clark
Paul Smith
Cedrick Wilson
34 Shaun Alexander 3.00 8.00
Alex Bannister
Matt Hasselbeck
Darrell Jackson
35 Brock Huard 3.00 8.00
Itula Mili
Mack Strong
James Williams
36 Joe Hamilton 3.00 8.00
Brad Johnson
Rob Johnson
Shaun King
37 Mike Alstott 3.00 8.00
Keyshawn Johnson
Warren Sapp
Aaron Stecker
38 Kevin Dyson 3.00 8.00
Eddie George
Derrick Mason
Steve McNair
39 David Boston 2.50 6.00
Jake Plummer
Corey Dillon
Peter Warrick
(Game Used Pants)
40 Isaac Bruce 4.00 10.00
Marshall Faulk
Torry Holt
Kurt Warner P
41 Terry Hardy 2.50 6.00
Chris Greisen
Dennis McKinley
Brian Gilmore
42 Marcel Shipp 3.00 8.00
Jamal Anderson
Skip Hicks
Lamont Jordan
43 Rob Moore 2.50 6.00
Quentin McCord
Avion Black
Patrick Johnson
44 Elvis Grbac 3.00 8.00
KevinThompson
Tee Martin
Todd Husak
45 Aaron Shea 3.00 8.00
David Sloan
Pete Mitchell
Mark Breuner
46 Chris Hetherington 4.00 10.00
Stanley Pritchett
Frank Moreau
Jim Kleinsasser
47 Tony Simmons 2.50 6.00
Na Brown
Charles Johnson
Bobby Shaw
48 Culp/McN/Brun/Vick 3.00 8.00
49 Emmitt/Wilms/Martin/Green 6.00 15.00
50 Couch/Favre/McN/Brees 8.00 20.00

2002 Pacific Heads Up Head First

serted in both hobby (1:19) and retail (1:49) packs, this 16-card insert features current or former first-round draft picks.

STATED ODDS 1:19 HOB, 1:49 RET
1 Michael Vick 1.00 2.50
2 Brian Urlacher 1.25 3.00
3 Tim Couch .75 2.00
4 William Green 1.00 2.50
5 Emmitt Smith 2.00 5.00
6 Joey Harrington .75 2.00
7 David Carr .75 2.00
8 Edgerrin James 1.00 2.50
9 Peyton Manning 3.00 8.00
10 Ricky Williams 1.00 2.50
11 Randy Moss 1.00 2.50
12 Jerry Rice 2.50 6.00
13 Donovan McNabb 1.00 2.50
14 Marshall Faulk 1.00 2.50
15 LaDainian Tomlinson 1.25 3.00
16 Shaun Alexander .75 2.00

2002 Pacific Heads Up Inside the Numbers

Inserted in hobby packs at a rate of 2:19 and retail packs at 2:25, this 24-card insert gives an in-depth look at the stats of both rookies and veterans.

STATED ODDS 2:19 HOB, 2:25 RET
1 T.J. Duckett .60 1.50
2 Michael Vick .75 2.00
3 DeShaun Foster 1.00 2.50
4 Anthony Thomas .75 2.00
5 William Green .75 2.00
6 Emmitt Smith 1.50 4.00
7 Terrell Davis .75 2.00
8 Joey Harrington .60 1.50
9 Brett Favre 2.00 5.00
10 David Carr .60 1.50
11 Jabar Gaffney .60 1.50
12 Edgerrin James .75 2.00
13 Peyton Manning 2.50 6.00
14 Ricky Williams .75 2.00
15 Daunte Culpepper .75 2.00
16 Randy Moss .75 2.00
17 Tom Brady 5.00 12.00
18 Donte Stallworth 1.00 2.50
19 Jerry Rice 2.00 5.00
20 Donovan McNabb .75 2.00
21 Marshall Faulk .75 2.00
22 Kurt Warner .75 2.00
23 LaDainian Tomlinson 1.00 2.50
24 Patrick Ramsey .75 2.00

2002 Pacific Heads Up Prime Picks

is 10-card insert is inserted in both hobby (1:37) and retail (1:97) packs. The set spotlights 2002 NFL rookies.

STATED ODDS 1:37 HOB, 1:97 RET
1 T.J. Duckett .60 1.50
2 DeShaun Foster 1.00 2.50
3 William Green .75 2.00
4 Ashley Lelie .60 1.50
5 Joey Harrington .60 1.50
6 Javon Walker 1.00 2.50
7 David Carr .60 1.50
8 Jabar Gaffney .60 1.50
9 Donte Stallworth 1.00 2.50
10 Patrick Ramsey .75 2.00

2002 Pacific Heads Update

leased in late November 2002, this set contains 175 cards including over 70 rookies. Boxes contained 18 packs of 6 cards, and were packed 6 boxes per case. Each box also contained one bobble head doll. Retail boxes contained 24 packs of 3 cards. There were 20 boxes per retail case.

COMPLETE SET (175) 40.00 80.00
1 David Boston .25 .60
2 Wendell Bryant RC .50 1.25
3 Thomas Jones .25 .60
4 Jason McAddley RC .60 1.50
5 Josh McCown RC .75 2.00
6 Jake Plummer .25 .60
7 T.J. Duckett RC .50 1.25
8 Warrick Dunn .25 .60
9 Shawn Jefferson .25 .60
10 Kurt Kittner RC .50 1.25
11 Michael Vick .30 .75
12 Dameon Hunter RC .50 1.25
13 Javin Hunter RC .50 1.25
14 Ron Johnson RC .60 1.50
15 Jamal Lewis .30 .75
16 Ray Lewis .40 1.00
17 Chris Redman .25 .60
18 Tellis Redmon RC .50 1.25
19 Ed Reed RC 4.00 10.00
20 Chester Taylor RC .75 2.00
21 Drew Bledsoe .30 .75
22 Travis Henry .25 .60
23 Eric Moulds .25 .60
24 Josh Reed RC .60 1.50
25 Randy Fasani RC .50 1.25
26 DeShaun Foster RC .75 2.00
27 Muhsin Muhammad .25 .60
28 Julius Peppers RC 1.25 3.00
29 Lamar Smith .25 .60
30 Chris Weinke .25 .60
31 Marty Booker .25 .60
32 Jamin Elliott RC .50 1.25
33 Jim Miller .25 .60
34 Adrian Peterson RC .60 1.50
35 Anthony Thomas .30 .75
36 Brian Urlacher .40 1.00
37 Corey Dillon .25 .60
38 Gus Frerotte .25 .60
39 Peter Warrick .25 .60
40 Michael Westbrook .25 .60
41 Tim Couch .25 .60
42 Andre Davis RC .50 1.25
43 William Green RC .60 1.50
44 Kevin Johnson .25 .60
45 Quincy Morgan .25 .60
46 Antonio Bryant RC .75 2.00
47 Quincy Carter .25 .60
48 Joey Galloway .30 .75
49 Chad Hutchinson RC .50 1.25
50 Emmitt Smith .60 1.50
51 Roy Williams RC .50 1.25
52 Terrell Davis .30 .75
53 Brian Griese .25 .60
54 Ashley Lelie RC .50 1.25
55 Clinton Portis RC .75 2.00
56 Rod Smith .30 .75
57 Eddie Drummond RC .50 1.25
58 Joey Harrington RC .50 1.25
59 Mike McMahon .25 .60
60 Bill Schroeder .25 .60
61 James Stewart .25 .60
62 Najeh Davenport RC .50 1.25
63 Brett Favre .75 2.00
64 Tony Fisher RC .50 1.25
65 Terry Glenn .30 .75
66 Ahman Green .30 .75
67 Craig Nall RC .60 1.50
68 Javon Walker RC .75 2.00
69 James Allen .25 .60
70 Jarrod Baxter RC .50 1.25
71 Corey Bradford .25 .60
72 David Carr RC .50 1.25
73 Jabar Gaffney RC .50 1.25
74 Jermaine Lewis .25 .60
75 Ed Stansbury RC .50 1.25
76 Jonathan Wells RC .60 1.50
77 Dwight Freeney RC 1.00 2.50
78 Marvin Harrison .30 .75
79 Edgerrin James .30 .75
80 Peyton Manning 1.00 2.50
81 Ricky Williams RC .60 1.50
82 Mark Brunell .30 .75
83 David Garrard RC .60 1.50
84 John Henderson RC .60 1.50
85 Jimmy Smith .30 .75
86 Fred Taylor .25 .60
87 Marc Boerigter RC .75 2.00
88 Omar Easy RC .60 1.50
89 Tony Gonzalez .30 .75
90 Trent Green .25 .60
91 Priest Holmes .25 .60
92 Chris Chambers .25 .60
93 Jay Fiedler .30 .75
94 Ricky Williams .30 .75
95 Michael Bennett .25 .60
96 Kelly Campbell RC .60 1.50
97 Daunte Culpepper .30 .75
98 Shaun Hill RC .75 2.00
99 Randy Moss .30 .75
100 Tom Brady 2.00 5.00
101 Deion Branch RC .75 2.00
102 Troy Brown .25 .60
103 Rohan Davey RC .75 2.00
104 Daniel Graham RC .60 1.50
105 Antowain Smith .30 .75
106 Aaron Brooks .25 .60
107 Joe Horn .25 .60
108 Deuce McAllister .30 .75
109 J.T. O'Sullivan RC .60 1.50
110 Donte Stallworth RC .75 2.00
111 Tiki Barber .30 .75
112 Tim Carter RC .60 1.50
113 Kerry Collins .25 .60
114 Daryl Jones RC .50 1.25
115 Jeremy Shockey RC .75 2.00
116 Amani Toomer .25 .60
117 Laveranues Coles .30 .75
118 Curtis Martin .30 .75
119 Vinny Testaverde .25 .60
120 Bryan Thomas RC .50 1.25
121 Tim Brown .40 1.00
122 Phillip Buchanon RC .75 2.00
123 Rich Gannon .30 .75
124 Napoleon Harris RC .60 1.50
125 Jerry Rice .75 2.00
126 Donovan McNabb .30 .75
127 Freddie Milons RC .50 1.25
128 Lito Sheppard RC .75 2.00
129 Duce Staley .25 .60
130 James Thrash .30 .75

131 Brian Westbrook RC 1.00 2.50
132 Jerome Bettis .40 1.00
133 Verron Haynes RC .50 1.25
134 Lee Mays RC .50 1.25
135 Antwaan Randle El RC .60 1.50
136 Kordell Stewart .25 .60
137 Hines Ward .30 .75
138 Isaac Bruce .40 1.00
139 Marshall Faulk .30 .75
140 Lamar Gordon RC .60 1.50
141 Torry Holt .30 .75
142 Robert Thomas RC .50 1.25
143 Kurt Warner .30 .75
144 Drew Brees .75 2.00
145 Seth Burford RC .50 1.25
146 Reche Caldwell RC .60 1.50
147 Doug Flutie .30 .75
148 Quentin Jammer RC .75 2.00
149 LaDainian Tomlinson .40 1.00
150 Brandon Doman RC .50 1.25
151 Jeff Garcia .25 .60
152 Garrison Hearst .25 .60
153 Terrell Owens .30 .75
154 Mike Rumph RC .50 1.25
155 Shaun Alexander .25 .60
156 Trent Dilfer .25 .60
157 Darrell Jackson .30 .75
158 Maurice Morris RC .60 1.50
159 Koren Robinson .25 .60
160 Jerramy Stevens RC .75 2.00
161 Brad Johnson .30 .75
162 Keyshawn Johnson .30 .75
163 Keenan McCardell .30 .75
164 Travis Stephens RC .50 1.25
165 Marquise Walker RC .50 1.25
166 Eddie George .30 .75
167 Albert Haynesworth RC .75 2.00
168 Derrick Mason .25 .60
169 Steve McNair .30 .75
170 Ladell Betts RC .75 2.00
171 Stephen Davis .25 .60
172 Rod Gardner .25 .60
173 Shane Matthews .25 .60
174 Patrick Ramsey RC .60 1.50
175 Cliff Russell RC .50 1.25

2002 Pacific Heads Update Blue

*VETS: 2X TO 5X BASIC CARDS
*ROOKIES: 1X TO 2.5X
FOUR PER HOBBY BOX

2002 Pacific Heads Update Red

ETS: 1.2X TO 3X BASIC CARDS
*ROOKIES: .6X TO 1.5X
STATED ODDS 1:2 RETAIL

2002 Pacific Heads Update Big Numbers

serted at a rate of 1:5, this set features Pacific's die-cut technology, cut out in the shape of the players jersey number.

COMPLETE SET (20) 25.00 60.00
STATED ODDS 1:5 HOB, 1:13 RET
1 Michael Vick 1.00 2.50
2 Anthony Thomas 1.00 2.50
3 Tim Couch .75 2.00
4 William Green 1.00 2.50
5 Antonio Bryant 1.25 3.00
6 Emmitt Smith 2.00 5.00
7 Ashley Lelie .75 2.00
8 Joey Harrington .75 2.00
9 Brett Favre 2.50 6.00
10 David Carr .75 2.00
11 Peyton Manning 3.00 8.00
12 Ricky Williams 1.00 2.50
13 Daunte Culpepper 1.00 2.50
14 Randy Moss 1.00 2.50
15 Tom Brady 6.00 15.00
16 Donte Stallworth 1.25 3.00
17 Jerry Rice 2.50 6.00
18 Marshall Faulk 1.00 2.50
19 Kurt Warner 1.00 2.50
20 LaDainian Tomlinson 1.25 3.00

2002 Pacific Heads Update Bobble Head Dolls

Inserted one per box, this set is composed of porcelain bobble head dolls of some of the NFL's best and youngest players.

STATED ODDS ONE PER BOX
1 Drew Bledsoe 5.00 12.00
2 T.J. Duckett 4.00 10.00
3 Eddie George 5.00 12.00
4 Ahman Green 5.00 12.00
5 William Green 5.00 12.00
6 Joey Harrington 4.00 10.00
7 Peyton Manning 15.00 40.00

2002 Pacific Heads Update Command Performance

serted at a rate of 1:5, this set highlights some of the NFL's top offensive performers.

COMPLETE SET (20) 25.00 60.00
STATED ODDS 1:5 HOB, 1:13 RET
1 David Boston .75 2.00
2 Anthony Thomas 1.00 2.50
3 Corey Dillon .75 2.00
4 Tim Couch .75 2.00
5 Emmitt Smith 2.00 5.00
6 Brett Favre 2.50 6.00
7 Ahman Green 1.00 2.50
8 Ricky Williams 1.00 2.50
9 Daunte Culpepper 1.00 2.50
10 Randy Moss 1.00 2.50
11 Tom Brady 6.00 15.00
12 Curtis Martin 1.00 2.50
13 Jerry Rice 2.50 6.00
14 Donovan McNabb 1.00 2.50
15 Marshall Faulk 1.00 2.50
16 Kurt Warner 1.00 2.50
17 Drew Brees 2.50 6.00
18 LaDainian Tomlinson 1.25 3.00
19 Shaun Alexander .75 2.00
20 Steve McNair 1.00 2.50

2002 Pacific Heads Update Game Worn Jerseys

serted at a rate of 2:19 hobby, this set features premium game worn jersey swatches. In addition, there is also a gold parallel version #'d to 25.

JERSEY/50-450 ODDS 2:19 HOB
*GOLD/25: .8X TO 2X BASIC JSY/100-450
*GOLD/25: .6X TO 1.5X BASIC JSY/50-95
GOLD PRINT RUN 25 SER.#'d SETS
1 David Boston/215 3.00 8.00
2 Bryan Gilmore/250 3.00 8.00
3 Thomas Jones/350 3.00 8.00
4 Jake Plummer/215 3.00 8.00
5 Frank Sanders/335 3.00 8.00
6 Warrick Dunn/315 3.00 8.00
7 Michael Vick/250 4.00 10.00
8 Drew Bledsoe/160 4.00 10.00
9 Corey Dillon/350 3.00 8.00
10 Peter Warrick/410 3.00 8.00
11 Tim Couch/50 4.00 10.00
12 Jamel White/105 3.00 8.00
13 Emmitt Smith/270 8.00 20.00
14 Mike Anderson/215 3.00 8.00
15 Terrell Davis/250 4.00 10.00
16 Brian Griese/115 3.00 8.00
17 Ed McCaffrey/225 4.00 10.00
18 Brett Favre/50 12.00 30.00
19 Ahman Green/95 5.00 12.00
20 Marvin Harrison/150 4.00 10.00
21 Qadry Ismail/95 4.00 10.00
22 Peyton Manning/180 12.00 30.00
23 Mark Brunell/390 4.00 10.00
24 Jimmy Smith/200 4.00 10.00
25 Fred Taylor/425 3.00 8.00
26 Tony Gonzalez/305 4.00 10.00
27 Desmond Clark/275 3.00 8.00
28 Zach Thomas/195 4.00 10.00
29 Ricky Williams/125 4.00 10.00
30 Derrick Alexander/225 3.00 8.00
31 Cris Carter/305 5.00 12.00
32 Randy Moss/350 4.00 10.00
33 Tom Brady/85 30.00 80.00
34 Christian Fauria/255 3.00 8.00
35 Deuce McAllister/95 5.00 12.00
36 Curtis Martin/175 4.00 10.00
37 Tim Brown/375 5.00 12.00
38 Rich Gannon/165 4.00 10.00
39 Jerry Rice/255 10.00 25.00
40 Jon Ritchie/450 3.00 8.00
41 Correll Buckhalter/305 3.00 8.00
42 Donovan McNabb/315 4.00 10.00
43 Marshall Faulk/225 4.00 10.00
44 Kurt Warner/185 4.00 10.00
45 Terrence Wilkins/225 3.00 8.00
46 Shaun Alexander/400 3.00 8.00
47 Trent Dilfer/115 3.00 8.00
48 Itula Mili/185 3.00 8.00
49 Joe Jurevicius/100 3.00 8.00
50 Michael Pittman/145 4.00 10.00

2002 Pacific Heads Update Generations

Inserted at a rate of 1:5, this set highlights many of the NFL's top 2002 rookies, and pairs them with a veteran counterpart.

COMPLETE SET (20) 25.00 60.00
STATED ODDS 1:5 HOB, 1:13 RET
1 B.Favre/D.Carr 2.00 5.00
2 P.Manning/J.Harrington 2.50 6.00
3 K.Warner/P.Ramsey .75 2.00
4 E.Smith/W.Green 1.50 4.00
5 J.Bettis/T.Duckett 1.00 2.50
6 R.Moss/A.Lelie .75 2.00
7 J.Rice/D.Stallworth 2.00 5.00
8 T.Brady/J.McCown 5.00 12.00
9 A.Thomas/D.Foster 1.00 2.50
10 M.Vick/D.Garrard .75 2.00
11 M.Faulk/M.Morris .75 2.00
12 D.Culpepper/R.Davey 1.00 2.50
13 T.Couch/R.Fasani .60 1.50
14 L.Tomlinson/C.Portis 1.00 2.50
15 I.Bruce/J.Gaffney 1.00 2.50
16 M.Harrison/J.Walker 1.00 2.50
17 K.Stewart/A.Randle El .75 2.00
18 D.Boston/A.Bryant 1.00 2.50
19 T.Owens/A.Davis .75 2.00
20 R.Williams/J.Wells .75 2.00

2001 Pacific Impressions

This 216 card set was issued late in 2001. These cards all featured cards printed entirely on canvas. The set was issued in three card packs with an SRP of $5.99 per pack which were issued 16 packs to a box. Cards numbered 145-216 featured rookies and were inserted at stated odds of one in 17 and were serial numbered to 117.

COMP.SET w/o RC's (144) 40.00 80.00
ROOKIE/117 STATED ODDS 1:17
1 David Boston .30 .75
2 Thomas Jones .30 .75
3 Rob Moore .30 .75
4 Michael Pittman .40 1.00
5 Jake Plummer .30 .75
6 Jamal Anderson .40 1.00
7 Chris Chandler .40 1.00
8 Shawn Jefferson .30 .75
9 Terance Mathis .30 .75
10 Elvis Grbac .40 1.00
11 Qadry Ismail .30 .75
12 Jamal Lewis .50 1.25
13 Ray Lewis .50 1.25
14 Shannon Sharpe .40 1.00
15 Shawn Bryson .30 .75
16 Rob Johnson .40 1.00
17 Sammy Morris .30 .75
18 Eric Moulds .30 .75
19 Peerless Price .30 .75
20 Tim Biakabutuka .30 .75
21 Richard Huntley .30 .75
22 Patrick Jeffers .30 .75
23 Dameyune Craig .30 .75
24 Muhsin Muhammad .30 .75
25 James Allen .30 .75
26 Marcus Robinson .40 1.00
27 Brian Urlacher .60 1.50
28 Corey Dillon .30 .75
29 Jon Kitna .30 .75
30 Akili Smith .30 .75
31 Peter Warrick .30 .75
32 Tim Couch .30 .75
33 Kevin Johnson .30 .75
34 Dennis Northcutt .30 .75
35 JaJuan Dawson .30 .75
36 Joey Galloway .40 1.00
37 Rocket Ismail .40 1.00
38 Emmitt Smith .75 2.00
39 Mike Anderson .30 .75
40 Terrell Davis .40 1.00
41 Brian Griese .30 .75
42 Ed McCaffrey .40 1.00
43 Rod Smith .40 1.00
44 Charlie Batch .30 .75
45 Germane Crowell .30 .75
46 Herman Moore .30 .75
47 Johnnie Morton .40 1.00
48 James Stewart .30 .75
49 Brett Favre 1.00 2.50
50 Antonio Freeman .50 1.25
51 Ahman Green .40 1.00
52 Dorsey Levens .40 1.00
53 Bill Schroeder .40 1.00
54 Marvin Harrison .40 1.00
55 Edgerrin James .40 1.00
56 Peyton Manning 1.25 3.00
57 Jerome Pathon .30 .75
58 Terrence Wilkins .30 .75
59 Mark Brunell .40 1.00
60 Keenan McCardell .40 1.00
61 Jimmy Smith .40 1.00
62 Fred Taylor .30 .75
63 Derrick Alexander .30 .75
64 Tony Gonzalez .40 1.00
65 Trent Green .30 .75
66 Priest Holmes .30 .75
67 Jay Fiedler .40 1.00
68 Oronde Gadsden .30 .75
69 O.J. McDuffie .30 .75
70 Cade McNown .40 1.00
71 Lamar Smith .40 1.00
72 Zach Thomas .40 1.00
73 Cris Carter .50 1.25
74 Daunte Culpepper .40 1.00
75 Randy Moss .40 1.00
76 Travis Prentice .30 .75
77 Drew Bledsoe .40 1.00
78 Kevin Faulk .30 .75
79 Charles Johnson .30 .75
80 J.R. Redmond .30 .75
81 Jeff Blake .40 1.00
82 Aaron Brooks .30 .75
83 Albert Connell .30 .75
84 Joe Horn .30 .75
85 Ricky Williams .40 1.00
86 Tiki Barber .40 1.00
87 Kerry Collins .30 .75
88 Ron Dayne .40 1.00
89 Ike Hilliard .30 .75
90 Amani Toomer .30 .75
91 Richie Anderson .30 .75
92 Wayne Chrebet .30 .75
93 Laveranues Coles .40 1.00
94 Curtis Martin .40 1.00
95 Chad Pennington .30 .75
96 Vinny Testaverde .30 .75
97 Tim Brown .50 1.25
98 Rich Gannon .40 1.00
99 Charlie Garner .40 1.00
100 Jerry Rice 1.00 2.50
101 Tyrone Wheatley .40 1.00
102 Charles Woodson .50 1.25
103 Todd Pinkston .30 .75
104 Donovan McNabb .40 1.00
105 Duce Staley .30 .75
106 James Thrash .40 1.00
107 Jerome Bettis .50 1.25
108 Plaxico Burress .30 .75
109 Bobby Shaw .30 .75
110 Kordell Stewart .30 .75
111 Hines Ward .40 1.00
112 Isaac Bruce .50 1.25
113 Marshall Faulk .40 1.00
114 Az-Zahir Hakim .30 .75
115 Torry Holt .40 1.00
116 Kurt Warner .75 2.00
117 Curtis Conway .40 1.00
118 Tim Dwight .40 1.00
119 Doug Flutie .40 1.00
120 Jeff Graham .30 .75
121 Jeff Garcia .30 .75
122 Garrison Hearst .40 1.00
123 Terrell Owens .40 1.00
124 J.J. Stokes .30 .75
125 Tai Streets .30 .75
126 Shaun Alexander .30 .75
127 Matt Hasselbeck .30 .75
128 Darrell Jackson .40 1.00
129 Ricky Watters .40 1.00
130 Mike Alstott .30 .75
131 Warrick Dunn .30 .75
132 Jacquez Green .30 .75
133 Brad Johnson .40 1.00
134 Keyshawn Johnson .40 1.00
135 Warren Sapp .40 1.00
136 Kevin Dyson .30 .75
137 Eddie George .50 1.25
138 Jevon Kearse .30 .75
139 Derrick Mason .30 .75
140 Steve McNair .40 1.00
141 Champ Bailey .40 1.00
142 Stephen Davis .30 .75
143 Jeff George .40 1.00
144 Michael Westbrook .30 .75
145 Bobby Newcombe RC 3.00 8.00
146 Corey Brown RC 2.50 6.00
147 Quentin McCord RC 3.00 8.00
148 Vinny Sutherland RC 2.50 6.00
149 Michael Vick RC 6.00 15.00
150 Chris Barnes RC 2.50 6.00
151 Tim Hasselbeck RC 3.00 8.00
152 Todd Heap RC 3.00 8.00
153 Nate Clements RC 3.00 8.00
154 Reggie Germany RC 2.50 6.00
155 Travis Henry RC 3.00 8.00
156 Dee Brown RC 2.50 6.00
157 Dan Morgan RC 3.00 8.00
158 Steve Smith RC 8.00 20.00
159 Chris Weinke RC 3.00 8.00
160 David Terrell RC 3.00 8.00
161 Anthony Thomas RC 4.00 10.00
162 T.J. Houshmandzadeh RC 3.00 8.00
163 Chad Johnson RC 4.00 10.00
164 Rudi Johnson RC 4.00 10.00
165 James Jackson RC 2.50 6.00
166 Andre King RC 2.50 6.00
167 Quincy Morgan RC 3.00 8.00
168 Quincy Carter RC 3.00 8.00
169 Kevin Kasper RC 2.50 6.00
170 Scotty Anderson RC 2.50 6.00
171 Mike McMahon RC 3.00 8.00
172 Robert Ferguson RC 4.00 10.00
173 Jamal Reynolds RC 2.50 6.00
174 Reggie Wayne RC 5.00 12.00
175 Marcus Stroud RC 3.00 8.00
176 Derrick Blaylock RC 3.00 8.00
177 Ryan Helming RC 2.50 6.00
178 Snoop Minnis RC 2.50 6.00
179 Chris Chambers RC 2.50 6.00
180 Josh Heupel RC 4.00 10.00
181 Travis Minor RC 3.00 8.00
182 Michael Bennett RC 3.00 8.00
183 Deuce McAllister RC 4.00 10.00
184 Onome Ojo RC 2.50 6.00
185 Will Allen RC 4.00 10.00
186 Jonathan Carter RC 2.50 6.00
187 Jesse Palmer RC 3.00 8.00
188 Corey Alston RC 2.50 6.00
189 LaMont Jordan RC 4.00 10.00
190 Santana Moss RC 4.00 10.00
191 Derek Combs RC 2.50 6.00
192 Derrick Gibson RC 2.50 6.00
193 Ken-Yon Rambo RC 2.50 6.00
194 Marques Tuiasosopo RC 3.00 8.00
195 Correll Buckhalter RC 2.50 6.00
196 Freddie Mitchell RC 2.50 6.00
197 Chris Taylor RC 2.50 6.00
198 Adam Archuleta RC 3.00 8.00
199 Damione Lewis RC 3.00 8.00
200 Francis St.Paul RC 2.50 6.00
201 Milton Wynn RC 2.50 6.00
202 Drew Brees RC 50.00 100.00
203 LaDainian Tomlinson RC 12.00 30.00
204 Kevan Barlow RC 3.00 8.00
205 Andre Carter RC 3.00 8.00
206 Cedrick Wilson RC 3.00 8.00
207 Alex Bannister RC 2.50 6.00
208 Josh Booty RC 3.00 8.00
209 Heath Evans RC 3.00 8.00
210 Ken Lucas RC 3.00 8.00
211 Koren Robinson RC 3.00 8.00
212 Dan Alexander RC 3.00 8.00
213 Eddie Berlin RC 2.50 6.00
214 Rod Gardner RC 3.00 8.00
215 Damerien McCants RC 3.00 8.00
216 Sage Rosenfels RC 3.00 8.00

2001 Pacific Impressions Hobby Red Backs

*VETS 1-144: 1.5X TO 4X BASIC CARDS
*ROOKIES 145-216: .25X TO .6X
RED BACK/280 ODDS 2:4 HOBBY
STATED PRINT RUN 280 SER.#'d SETS

2001 Pacific Impressions Premiere Date

*VETS 1-144: 5X TO 12X BASIC CARDS
*ROOKIES 145-216: .8X TO 2X
PREMIERE DATE/50 ODDS 1:17 HOB
STATED PRINT RUN 50 SER.#'d SETS
202 Drew Brees 200.00 300.00

2001 Pacific Impressions Retail

COMP.SET w/o SPs (144) 30.00 60.00
*RETAIL VETS 1-144: .25X TO .6X HOBBY
RETAIL ROOKIE STATED ODDS 1:4
145 Bobby Newcombe RC .60 1.50
146 Corey Brown RC .50 1.25
147 Quentin McCord RC .60 1.50
148 Vinny Sutherland RC .50 1.25
149 Michael Vick RC 1.25 3.00
150 Chris Barnes RC .50 1.25
151 Tim Hasselbeck RC .60 1.50
152 Todd Heap RC .60 1.50
153 Nate Clements RC .60 1.50
154 Reggie Germany RC .50 1.25
155 Travis Henry RC .60 1.50
156 Dee Brown RC .50 1.25
157 Dan Morgan RC .60 1.50
158 Steve Smith RC 1.50 4.00
159 Chris Weinke RC .50 1.25
160 David Terrell RC .60 1.50
161 Anthony Thomas RC .75 2.00
162 T.J. Houshmandzadeh RC .60 1.50
163 Chad Johnson RC .75 2.00
164 Rudi Johnson RC .75 2.00
165 James Jackson RC .50 1.25
166 Andre King RC .50 1.25
167 Quincy Morgan RC .60 1.50
168 Quincy Carter RC .60 1.50
169 Kevin Kasper RC .50 1.25
170 Scotty Anderson RC .50 1.25
171 Mike McMahon RC .60 1.50
172 Robert Ferguson RC .75 2.00
173 Jamal Reynolds RC .50 1.25
174 Reggie Wayne RC 1.00 2.50
175 Marcus Stroud RC .60 1.50
176 Derrick Blaylock RC .60 1.50
177 Ryan Helming RC .50 1.25
178 Snoop Minnis RC .50 1.25
179 Chris Chambers RC .50 1.25
180 Josh Heupel RC .75 2.00
181 Travis Minor RC .60 1.50
182 Michael Bennett RC .60 1.50
183 Deuce McAllister RC .75 2.00
184 Onome Ojo RC .50 1.25
185 Will Allen RC .75 2.00
186 Jonathan Carter RC .50 1.25
187 Jesse Palmer RC .60 1.50
188 Corey Alston RC .50 1.25
189 LaMont Jordan RC .75 2.00
190 Santana Moss RC .75 2.00
191 Derek Combs RC .50 1.25
192 Derrick Gibson RC .50 1.25
193 Ken-Yon Rambo RC .50 1.25
194 Marques Tuiasosopo RC .60 1.50
195 Correll Buckhalter RC .50 1.25
196 Freddie Mitchell RC .50 1.25
197 Chris Taylor RC .50 1.25
198 Adam Archuleta RC .60 1.50
199 Damione Lewis RC .60 1.50
200 Francis St.Paul RC .50 1.25
201 Milton Wynn RC .50 1.25
202 Drew Brees RC 12.00 30.00
203 LaDainian Tomlinson RC 2.50 6.00
204 Kevan Barlow RC .60 1.50
205 Andre Carter RC .60 1.50
206 Cedrick Wilson RC .60 1.50
207 Alex Bannister RC .50 1.25
208 Josh Booty RC .60 1.50
209 Heath Evans RC .60 1.50
210 Ken Lucas RC .60 1.50
211 Koren Robinson RC .60 1.50
212 Dan Alexander RC .60 1.50
213 Eddie Berlin RC .50 1.25
214 Rod Gardner RC .60 1.50
215 Damerien McCants RC .60 1.50
216 Sage Rosenfels RC .60 1.50

2001 Pacific Impressions Shadow

*VETS 1-144: 6X TO 15X BASIC CARDS
*ROOKIES 101-216: .8X TO 2X
SHADOW/25 ODDS 1:65 HOB, 1:193 RET
STATED PRINT RUN 25 SER.#'d SETS

2001 Pacific Impressions Classic Images

Inserted in packs at stated odds of one in 65 hobby and one in 97 retail, these 10 cards feature drawings of how we will remember these players on the field.

COMPLETE SET (10) 20.00 50.00
STATED ODDS 1:65 HOB, 1:97 RET
1 Emmitt Smith 2.50 6.00
2 Terrell Davis 1.25 3.00
3 Brett Favre 3.00 8.00
4 Edgerrin James 1.25 3.00
5 Peyton Manning 4.00 10.00
6 Daunte Culpepper 1.25 3.00
7 Randy Moss 1.25 3.00
8 Jerry Rice 3.00 8.00
9 Donovan McNabb 1.25 3.00
10 Kurt Warner 2.50 6.00

2001 Pacific Impressions First Impressions

Issued at stated odds of one in 33 hobby and one in 97 retail, these 20 cards feature some of the leading rookies of 2001. Each card front has a portrait drawing as well as an action shot.

COMPLETE SET (20) 30.00 80.00
STATED ODDS 1:33 HOB, 1:97 RET
1 Michael Vick 1.50 4.00
2 Travis Henry .75 2.00
3 Chris Weinke .75 2.00
4 David Terrell .75 2.00
5 Anthony Thomas 1.00 2.50
6 Chad Johnson 1.00 2.50
7 Quincy Carter .75 2.00
8 Reggie Wayne 1.25 3.00
9 Chris Chambers .60 1.50
10 Michael Bennett .75 2.00
11 Deuce McAllister 1.00 2.50
12 Jesse Palmer .75 2.00
13 LaMont Jordan 1.00 2.50
14 Santana Moss 1.00 2.50
15 Marques Tuiasosopo .75 2.00
16 Freddie Mitchell .60 1.50
17 Drew Brees 8.00 20.00
18 LaDainian Tomlinson 3.00 8.00
19 Rod Gardner .75 2.00
20 Sage Rosenfels .75 2.00

2001 Pacific Impressions Future Foundations

Inserted in hobby packs at stated odds of one in 257, these 10 cards feature some of the most popular rookies entering the 2001 season. These cards were serial numbered to 50.

STATED ODDS 1:257 HOBBY
STATED PRINT RUN 50 SER.#'d SETS
1 Michael Vick 6.00 15.00
2 Chris Weinke 3.00 8.00
3 David Terrell 3.00 8.00
4 Michael Bennett 3.00 8.00
5 Deuce McAllister 4.00 10.00
6 Santana Moss 4.00 10.00
7 Freddie Mitchell 2.50 6.00
8 Drew Brees 40.00 80.00
9 LaDainian Tomlinson 12.00 30.00
10 Koren Robinson 3.00 8.00

2001 Pacific Impressions Lasting Impressions

sued at stated odds of one in 17 hobby and one in 25 retail, these 20 cards feature some of the leading stars of 2001. Each card front has a portrait drawing as well as an action shot.

COMPLETE SET (20) 20.00 50.00
STATED ODDS 1:17 HOB, 1:25 RET
1 Jamal Lewis 1.00 2.50
2 Peter Warrick .60 1.50
3 Emmitt Smith 1.50 4.00
4 Mike Anderson .60 1.50
5 Terrell Davis .75 2.00
6 Brian Griese .60 1.50
7 Brett Favre 2.00 5.00
8 Edgerrin James .75 2.00
9 Peyton Manning 2.50 6.00
10 Mark Brunell .75 2.00
11 Daunte Culpepper .75 2.00
12 Randy Moss .75 2.00
13 Drew Bledsoe .75 2.00
14 Ricky Williams .75 2.00
15 Ron Dayne .75 2.00
16 Jerry Rice 2.00 5.00
17 Donovan McNabb .75 2.00
18 Marshall Faulk .75 2.00
19 Kurt Warner 1.50 4.00
20 Eddie George 1.00 2.50

2001 Pacific Impressions Renderings

Issued at stated odds of two in 17 hobby and two in 25 retail, these 20 cards feature two artist drawings of leading rookies entering the 2001 season.

COMPLETE SET (20) 12.50 30.00
STATED ODDS 2:17 HOB, 2:25 RET
1 Michael Vick .60 1.50
2 Travis Henry .30 .75
3 Chris Weinke .30 .75
4 David Terrell .30 .75
5 Anthony Thomas .40 1.00
6 Chad Johnson .40 1.00
7 James Jackson .25 .60
8 Quincy Carter .30 .75
9 Reggie Wayne .50 1.25
10 Chris Chambers .25 .60
11 Michael Bennett .30 .75
12 Deuce McAllister .40 1.00
13 LaMont Jordan .40 1.00
14 Santana Moss .40 1.00
15 Marques Tuiasosopo .30 .75
16 Freddie Mitchell .25 .60
17 Drew Brees 4.00 10.00
18 LaDainian Tomlinson 1.25 3.00
19 Kevan Barlow .30 .75
20 Rod Gardner .30 .75

2001 Pacific Impressions Triple Threads

Inserted in packs at a rate of three in 17 hobby and one in 97 retail packs, these 35 cards feature three swatches of game-worn jersey on them.

STATED ODDS 3:17 HOB,1:97 RET
1 Boston/Jones/Plummer 4.00 10.00
2 Makovicka/McKinley/Mitchell 4.00 10.00
3 Anderson/Alstott/S.Davis 5.00 12.00
4 Ismail/P.Johnson/Stokley 4.00 10.00
5 Biakbtka/Hoover/Muhammad 5.00 12.00
6 Weinke/Tuiasosopo/Brees 15.00 40.00
7 Huntley/Kreider/Zereoue 12.00 30.00
8 Matthews/McNown/Miller 5.00 12.00
9 Engram/Robinson/White 5.00 12.00
10 Dugans/Farmer/Yeast 4.00 10.00
11 Bush/McGee/St. Louis 4.00 10.00
12 Dillon/Watters/George 4.00 10.00
13 Dawson/Prentice/Rhett 5.00 12.00
14 Couch/Aikman/Warner 10.00 25.00
15 Clark/Coleman/Griffith 4.00 10.00
16 Frerotte/McCaffrey/R.Smith 5.00 12.00
17 Griese/Favre/Bledsoe 12.00 30.00
18 T.Davis/Martin/Tomlinson 15.00 40.00
19 Batch/Morton/Stewart 4.00 10.00
20 Goodman/Green/Levens 5.00 12.00
21 Harris/Jmes/Manning UER 15.00 40.00
22 Dilger/Gordon/Wilkins 4.00 10.00
23 Brunell/J.Smith/Taylor 5.00 12.00
24 Fiedler/Gadsden/L.Smith 5.00 12.00
25 Carter/Culpepper/R.Moss 6.00 15.00
26 S.Davis/K.Faulk/Glenn 5.00 12.00
27 Blake/Brooks/Horn 5.00 12.00
28 Barber/Collins/Dayne 5.00 12.00
29 Chrebet/Stone/Testaverde 4.00 10.00
30 Brown/Gannon/Wheatley 6.00 15.00
31 Burress/Edwards/Hawkins 4.00 10.00
32 Carmazzi/Mirer/Rattay 4.00 10.00
33 S.Alexan/D.Jack/J.Will.WR 4.00 10.00
34 R.Brown/Rogers/Strong 5.00 12.00
35 R.Anth/J.Green/Key.Johnson 5.00 12.00

1996 Pacific Invincible

The 1996 Pacific Invincible set was issued in one series totalling 150 cards and distributed in three-card packs. The set offers a "cel" inlay in each of the 150 cards. Each card carried an "I" prefix on the card number. Jeff Blake #31 was inserted later in the production run due to the Braille embossing causing it to be short-printed versus the rest of the set. Several parallel card versions were also produced: bronze foil for hobby and silver foil for retail. There was a Platinum Blue series made which parallels both hobby and retail that was more difficult to pull. A Chris Warren Promo card was produced and modeled after the Pro Bowl insert set.

COMPLETE SET (150) 25.00 60.00
1 Larry Centers .40 1.00
2 Garrison Hearst .40 1.00
3 Seth Joyner .25 .60
4 Simeon Rice RC 2.00 5.00
5 Eric Swann .25 .60
6 Bert Emanuel .40 1.00
7 Jeff George .40 1.00
8 Craig Heyward .25 .60
9 Terance Mathis .25 .60
10 Eric Metcalf .25 .60
11 Derrick Alexander WR .40 1.00
12 Leroy Hoard .25 .60
13 Andre Rison .40 1.00
14 Tommy Vardell .25 .60
15 Eric Zeier .25 .60
16 Jim Kelly .75 2.00
17 Eric Moulds RC 2.00 5.00
18 Bryce Paup .25 .60
19 Bruce Smith .40 1.00
20 Thurman Thomas .75 2.00
21 Tim Biakabutuka RC .75 2.00
22 Blake Brockermeyer .25 .60
23 Kerry Collins .75 2.00
24 Howard Griffith .25 .60
25 Lamar Lathon .25 .60
26 Mark Carrier DB .25 .60
27 Curtis Conway .75 2.00
28 Erik Kramer .25 .60
29 Rashaan Salaam .40 1.00
30 Alonzo Spellman .25 .60
31 Jeff Blake Braille SP 2.00 5.00
32 Harold Green .25 .60
33 Carl Pickens .40 1.00
34 Darnay Scott .40 1.00
35 Dan Wilkinson .25 .60
36 Troy Aikman 1.25 3.00
37 Jay Novacek .25 .60
38 Deion Sanders 1.00 2.50
39 Emmitt Smith 2.00 5.00
40 Kevin Williams .25 .60
41 Terrell Davis 1.00 2.50
42 John Elway 2.50 6.00
43 Anthony Miller .40 1.00
44 Michael Dean Perry .25 .60
45 Shannon Sharpe .40 1.00
46 Scott Mitchell .40 1.00
47 Herman Moore .40 1.00
48 Brett Perriman .25 .60
49 Barry Sanders 2.00 5.00
50 Chris Spielman .25 .60
51 Edgar Bennett .40 1.00
52 Robert Brooks .75 2.00
53 Brett Favre 2.50 6.00
54 Derrick Mayes RC .75 2.00
55 Reggie White .75 2.00
56 Eddie George RC 2.00 5.00
57 Haywood Jeffires .25 .60
58 Steve McNair 1.00 2.50
59 Chris Sanders .40 1.00
60 Rodney Thomas .25 .60
61 Tony Bennett .25 .60
62 Quentin Coryatt .25 .60
63 Ken Dilger .40 1.00
64 Marshall Faulk 1.00 2.50
65 Jim Harbaugh .40 1.00
66 Tony Boselli .25 .60
67 Mark Brunell .75 2.00
68 Kevin Hardy RC .75 2.00
69 Desmond Howard .40 1.00
70 James O.Stewart .40 1.00
71 Marcus Allen .75 2.00
72 Steve Bono .25 .60
73 Neil Smith .40 1.00
74 Derrick Thomas .75 2.00
75 Tamarick Vanover .40 1.00
76 Karim Abdul-Jabbar RC .75 2.00
77 Irving Fryar .40 1.00
78 Eric Green .25 .60
79 Dan Marino 2.50 6.00
80 Bernie Parmalee .25 .60
81 Cris Carter .75 2.00
82 Warren Moon .40 1.00
83 Jake Reed .40 1.00
84 Robert Smith .40 1.00
85 Moe Williams RB RC 2.00 5.00
86 Drew Bledsoe 1.00 2.50
87 Ben Coates .40 1.00
88 Terry Glenn RC 1.50 4.00
89 Curtis Martin 1.00 2.50
90 Dave Meggett .25 .60
91 Mario Bates .40 1.00
92 Jim Everett .25 .60
93 Michael Haynes .25 .60
94 Torrance Small .25 .60
95 Ray Zellars .25 .60
96 Kyle Brady .25 .60
97 Wayne Chrebet .75 2.00
98 Keyshawn Johnson RC 1.50 4.00
99 Adrian Murrell .40 1.00
100 Alex Van Dyke RC .40 1.00
101 Michael Brooks .25 .60
102 Dave Brown .25 .60
103 Chris Calloway .25 .60
104 Rodney Hampton .40 1.00
105 Amani Toomer RC 1.50 4.00
106 Tyrone Wheatley .40 1.00
107 Tim Brown .75 2.00
108 Rickey Dudley RC .75 2.00
109 Billy Joe Hobert .40 1.00
110 Rocket Ismail .40 1.00
111 Napoleon Kaufman .75 2.00
112 Harvey Williams .25 .60
113 Charlie Garner .40 1.00
114 Bobby Hoying RC .75 2.00
115 Rodney Peete .25 .60
116 Ricky Watters .40 1.00
117 Greg Lloyd .40 1.00
118 Erric Pegram .25 .60
119 Kordell Stewart .75 2.00
120 Yancey Thigpen .40 1.00
121 Jon Witman RC .40 1.00
122 Aaron Hayden .25 .60
123 Stan Humphries .40 1.00
124 Tony Martin .40 1.00
125 Leslie O'Neal .25 .60
126 Junior Seau .75 2.00
127 Jerome Bettis .75 2.00
128 Isaac Bruce .75 2.00
129 Ernie Conwell RC .25 .60
130 Lawrence Phillips RC .75 2.00
131 William Floyd .40 1.00
132 Terrell Owens RC 4.00 10.00
133 Jerry Rice 1.25 3.00
134 J.J. Stokes .75 2.00
135 Steve Young 1.00 2.50
136 Brian Blades .25 .60
137 Christian Fauria .25 .60
138 Joey Galloway .75 2.00
139 Rick Mirer .40 1.00
140 Chris Warren .40 1.00
141 Horace Copeland .25 .60
142 Trent Dilfer .75 2.00
143 Alvin Harper .25 .60
144 Dave Moore .25 .60
145 Errict Rhett .40 1.00
146 Terry Allen .40 1.00
147 Gus Frerotte .40 1.00
148 Brian Mitchell .25 .60
149 Heath Shuler .40 1.00
150 Michael Westbrook .75 2.00
PCC1 Chris Warren Promo .60 1.50

1996 Pacific Invincible Bronze

COMPLETE SET (149) 150.00 300.00
*STARS: 1.5X TO 4X BASIC CARDS
*RCs: .8X TO 2X BASIC CARDS
STATED ODDS 4:25 HOBBY

1996 Pacific Invincible Platinum Blue

TARS: 2X TO 5X BASIC CARDS
*RCs: 1X TO 2.5X BASIC CARDS
STATED ODDS 1:25

1996 Pacific Invincible Silver

COMPLETE SET (149) 125.00 250.00
*STARS: 1.2X TO 3X BASIC CARDS
*RCs: .6X TO 1.5X BASIC CARDS
STATED ODDS 4:25 RETAIL

1996 Pacific Invincible Kick Starter Die Cuts

Randomly inserted in packs at a rate of one in 49, this 20-card set features color action player images on a die cut gold foil football background. The backs carry another player photo with a paragraph about the player.

COMPLETE SET (20) 40.00 100.00
STATED ODDS 1:49
KS1 Jeff Blake 2.50 6.00
KS2 Tim Brown 2.50 6.00
KS3 Kerry Collins 2.50 6.00
KS4 John Elway 8.00 20.00
KS5 Marshall Faulk 3.00 8.00
KS6 Brett Favre 8.00 20.00
KS7 Keyshawn Johnson 2.50 6.00
KS8 Dan Marino 8.00 20.00
KS9 Curtis Martin 3.00 8.00
KS10 Steve McNair 3.00 8.00
KS11 Errict Rhett 1.25 3.00
KS12 Jerry Rice 4.00 10.00
KS13 Rashaan Salaam 1.25 3.00
KS14 Barry Sanders 6.00 15.00
KS15 Deion Sanders 3.00 8.00
KS16 Emmitt Smith 6.00 15.00
KS17 Kordell Stewart 2.50 6.00
KS18 Tamarick Vanover 1.25 3.00
KS19 Chris Warren 1.25 3.00
KS20 Ricky Watters 1.25 3.00

1996 Pacific Invincible Pro Bowl

ndomly inserted in packs at a rate of one in 25, this 20-card set features color images of players who made the Pro Bowl at the end last season and are printed on a metallic football field background. The backs another player photo with a paragraph about the player.

COMPLETE SET (20) 25.00 60.00
STATED ODDS 1:25
1 Jeff Blake 2.00 5.00
2 Steve Bono .60 1.50
3 Tim Brown 2.00 5.00
4 Cris Carter 2.00 6.00
5 Ben Coates 1.00 2.50
6 Brett Favre 6.00 15.00
7 Jim Harbaugh 1.00 2.50
8 Curtis Martin 2.50 6.00
9 Warren Moon 1.00 2.50
10 Herman Moore 1.00 2.50
11 Carl Pickens 1.00 2.50
12 Jerry Rice 3.00 8.00
13 Barry Sanders 5.00 12.00
14 Shannon Sharpe 1.00 2.50
15 Emmitt Smith 5.00 12.00
16 Yancey Thigpen 1.00 2.50
17 Chris Warren 1.00 2.50
18 Ricky Watters 1.00 2.50
19 Reggie White 2.00 5.00
20 Steve Young 2.50 6.00

1996 Pacific Invincible Smash Mouth

Inserted at the rate of approximately two per pack of the 1996 Pacific Invincible regular set, this 180-card set features color player images printed to look as if they are crashing out of the card. The backs carry a small player head photo and a paragraph about the player.

COMPLETE SET (180) 10.00 20.00
TWO PER PACK
1 Marcus Dowdell .05 .15
2 Karl Dunbar .05 .15
3 Eric England .05 .15
4 Garrison Hearst .07 .20
5 Bryan Reeves .05 .15
6 Simeon Rice .15 .40
7 Jeff George .07 .20
8 Bobby Hebert .05 .15
9 Craig Heyward .05 .15
10 David Richards .05 .15
11 Elbert Shelley .05 .15
12 Lonnie Johnson .05 .15
13 Jim Kelly .15 .40
14 Corbin Lacina .05 .15
15 Bryce Paup .05 .15
16 Sam Rogers .05 .15
17 Bruce Smith .07 .20
18 Thurman Thomas .15 .40
19 Carl Banks .05 .15
20 Dan Footman .05 .15
21 Louis Riddick .05 .15
22 Matt Stover .05 .15
23 Tommy Barnhardt .05 .15
24 Kerry Collins .15 .40
25 Mark Dennis .05 .15
26 Matt Elliott .05 .15
27 Eric Guliford .05 .15
28 Lamar Lathon .05 .15
29 Joe Cain .05 .15
30 Marty Carter .05 .15
31 Robert Green .05 .15
32 Erik Kramer .05 .15
33 Todd Perry .05 .15
34 Rashaan Salaam .07 .20
35 Alonzo Spellman .05 .15
36 Jeff Blake .15 .40
37 Andre Collins .05 .15
38 Todd Kelly .05 .15
39 Carl Pickens .07 .20
40 Kevin Sargent .05 .15
41 Troy Aikman .40 1.00
42 Charles Haley .07 .20
43 Daryl Johnston .07 .20
44 Nate Newton .05 .15
45 Deion Sanders .25 .60
46 Emmitt Smith .60 1.50
47 Steve Atwater .05 .15
48 Terrell Davis .30 .75
49 John Elway .75 2.00
50 Michael Dean Perry .05 .15
51 Shannon Sharpe .07 .20
52 David Wyman .05 .15
53 Bennie Blades .05 .15
54 Kevin Glover .05 .15
55 Herman Moore .07 .20
56 Robert Porcher .05 .15
57 Barry Sanders .60 1.50
58 Henry Thomas .05 .15
59 Edgar Bennett .07 .20
60 Robert Brooks .15 .40
61 Brett Favre .75 2.00
62 Harry Galbreath .05 .15
63 Sean Jones .05 .15
64 Reggie White .15 .40
65 Blaine Bishop .05 .15
66 Chuck Cecil .05 .15
67 Cris Dishman .05 .15
68 Steve McNair .30 .75
69 Rodney Thomas .05 .15
70 Jason Belser .05 .15
71 Ray Buchanan .05 .15
72 Quentin Coryatt .05 .15
73 Marshall Faulk .20 .50
74 Jim Harbaugh .07 .20
75 Devon McDonald .05 .15
76 Tony Boselli .05 .15
77 Tony Brackens .07 .20
78 Mark Brunell .25 .60
79 Don Davey .05 .15
80 Rich Griffith .05 .15
81 Kevin Hardy .07 .20
82 Mickey Washington .05 .15
83 Louie Aguiar .05 .15
84 Dan Saleaumua .05 .15
85 Will Shields .05 .15
86 Neil Smith .05 .15
87 Derrick Thomas .07 .20
88 Tamarick Vanover .07 .20
89 Gene Atkins .05 .15
90 Bryan Cox .05 .15
91 Steve Emtman .05 .15
92 Chris Gray .05 .15
93 Dan Marino .75 2.00
94 Derrick Alexander DE .05 .15
95 Cris Carter .15 .40
96 Jeff Christy .05 .15
97 Robert Smith .07 .20
98 Korey Stringer .08 .25
99 Orlando Thomas .05 .15
100 Esera Tuaolo .05 .15
101 Drew Bledsoe .25 .60
102 Eddie Cade .05 .15
103 Mike Jones .05 .15
104 Curtis Martin .30 .75
105 Willie McGinest .05 .15
106 Chris Slade .05 .15
107 Eric Allen .05 .15
108 Mario Bates .07 .20
109 Jim Dombrowski .05 .15
110 Wayne Martin .05 .15
111 William Roaf .05 .15
112 Irv Smith .05 .15
113 Michael Brooks .05 .15
114 Stacey Dillard .05 .15
115 Rodney Hampton .07 .20
116 Doug Riesenberg .05 .15
117 Coleman Rudolph .05 .15
118 Tyrone Wheatley .07 .20
119 Kyle Brady .05 .15
120 Roger Duffy .05 .15
121 Keyshawn Johnson .30 .75
122 Gary Jones .05 .15
123 Eddie Anderson .05 .15
124 Rickey Dudley .15 .40
125 Napoleon Kaufman .15 .40
126 Greg Skrepenak .05 .15
127 Pat Swilling .05 .15
128 Steve Wisniewski .05 .15
129 William Fuller .05 .15
130 Kurt Gouveia .05 .15
131 Andy Harmon .05 .15
132 Mike Mamula .05 .15
133 Guy McIntyre .05 .15
134 Ricky Watters .07 .20
135 Kevin Greene .07 .20
136 Bill Johnson .05 .15
137 [illegible] .05 .15
138 Greg Lloyd .07 .20

139 Erric Pegram .05 .15
140 Leon Searcy .05 .15
141 Shane Conlan .05 .15
142 Troy Drayton .05 .15
143 Wayne Gandy .05 .15
144 Sean Gilbert .05 .15
145 Carlos Jenkins .05 .15
146 Lawrence Phillips .07 .20
147 Aaron Hayden .05 .15
148 Stan Humphries .07 .20
149 Leslie O'Neal .05 .15
150 Bo Orlando .05 .15
151 Junior Seau .07 .20
152 Harry Swayne .05 .15
153 Harris Barton .05 .15
154 Merton Hanks .05 .15
155 Rod Milstead .05 .15
156 Ken Norton Jr. .05 .15
157 Gary Plummer .05 .15
158 Jerry Rice .40 1.00
159 Steve Wallace .05 .15
160 Steve Young .30 .75
161 James Atkins .05 .15
162 Brian Blades .05 .15
163 Matt Joyce .05 .15
164 Cortez Kennedy .05 .15
165 Kevin Mawae .05 .15
166 Winston Moss .05 .15
167 Chris Warren .07 .20
168 Derrick Brooks .05 .15
169 Trent Dilfer .15 .40
170 Santana Dotson .05 .15
171 Alvin Harper .05 .15
172 Hardy Nickerson .05 .15
173 Errict Rhett .07 .20
174 Warren Sapp .25 .60
175 Terry Allen .07 .20
176 John Gesek .05 .15
177 Ken Harvey .05 .15
178 Tre Johnson .05 .15
179 Rod Stephens .05 .15
180 Michael Westbrook .15 .40

1996 Pacific Invincible Chris Warren

Randomly inserted in packs at the rate of one in 10, this 10-card set honors Seattle Seahawks running back Chris Warren. The fronts feature color action player photos with a simulated stone column inside border and gold marble outside border. The backs each carry different small head photos and paragraphs about his outstanding efforts and career.

COMPLETE SET (10) 1.50 4.00
COMMON CARD (CW1-CW10) .20 .50

1997 Pacific Invincible

The 1997 Pacific Invincible set was issued in one series totalling 150 cards and distributed in three-card packs. The fronts feature color player images on a gold, green, yellow stripe-design background with a "cel" inlay of the player's head. The backs carry player information. Several parallel versions were also produced: copper foil for hobby and silver foil for retail. There was a Platinum Blue series made which parallels both hobby and retail and was more difficult to pull.

COMPLETE SET (150) 40.00 100.00
1 Larry Centers .40 1.00
2 Kent Graham .25 .60
3 LeShon Johnson .25 .60
4 Leeland McElroy .25 .60
5 Jake Plummer RC 4.00 10.00
6 Frank Sanders .40 1.00
7 Morten Andersen .25 .60
8 Jamal Anderson .60 1.50
9 Bert Emanuel .40 1.00
10 Bobby Hebert .25 .60
11 Roell Preston .25 .60
12 Derrick Alexander WR .40 1.00
13 Michael Jackson .40 1.00
14 Byron Bam Morris .25 .60
15 Vinny Testaverde .40 1.00
16 Todd Collins .25 .60
17 Andre Reed .40 1.00
18 Antowain Smith RC 2.00 5.00
19 Steve Tasker .25 .60
20 Thurman Thomas .60 1.50
21 Tim Biakabutuka .40 1.00
22 Rae Carruth RC .25 .60
23 Kerry Collins .60 1.50
24 Kevin Greene .40 1.00
25 Anthony Johnson .25 .60
26 Wesley Walls .40 1.00
27 Darnell Autry RC .40 1.00
28 Curtis Conway .40 1.00
29 Raymont Harris .25 .60
30 Rashaan Salaam .25 .60
31 Jeff Blake .40 1.00
32 Ki-Jana Carter .25 .60
33 David Dunn .25 .60
34 Carl Pickens .40 1.00
35 Darnay Scott .40 1.00
36 Troy Aikman 1.25 3.00
37 Michael Irvin .60 1.50
38 Deion Sanders .60 1.50
39 Emmitt Smith 1.25 3.00
40 Herschel Walker .40 1.00
41 Kevin Williams .25 .60
42 Steve Atwater .25 .60
43 Terrell Davis .75 2.00
44 John Elway 2.50 6.00
45 Ed McCaffrey .40 1.00
46 Shannon Sharpe .40 1.00
47 Scott Mitchell .40 1.00
48 Herman Moore .40 1.00
49 Brett Perriman .25 .60
50 Barry Sanders 2.00 5.00
51 Edgar Bennett .40 1.00
52 Robert Brooks .40 1.00
53 Brett Favre 2.50 6.00
54 Antonio Freeman .60 1.50
55 Dorsey Levens .60 1.50
56 Reggie White .60 1.50
57 Eddie George .60 1.50
58 Steve McNair .75 2.00
59 Chris Sanders .40 1.00
60 Sean Dawkins .25 .60
61 Marshall Faulk .75 2.00
62 Jim Harbaugh .40 1.00
63 Marvin Harrison .60 1.50
64 Brian Stablein .25 .60
65 Mark Brunell .75 2.00
66 Keenan McCardell .40 1.00
67 Natrone Means .40 1.00
68 Pete Mitchell .25 .60
69 Jimmy Smith .40 1.00
70 Marcus Allen .60 1.50
71 Kimble Anders .40 1.00
72 Greg Hill .25 .60
73 Kevin Lockett RC .40 1.00
74 Derrick Thomas .60 1.50
75 Tamarick Vanover .40 1.00
76 Karim Abdul-Jabbar .40 1.00
77 Yatil Green RC .40 1.00
78 Randal Hill .25 .60
79 Dan Marino 2.50 6.00
80 Stanley Pritchett .25 .60
81 Irving Spikes .25 .60
82 Cris Carter .60 1.50
83 Brad Johnson .60 1.50
84 Robert Smith .40 1.00
85 Darryl Talley .25 .60
86 Drew Bledsoe .75 2.00
87 Ben Coates .40 1.00
88 Terry Glenn .60 1.50
89 Curtis Martin .75 2.00
90 Sedrick Shaw RC .40 1.00
91 Mario Bates .25 .60
92 Troy Davis RC .40 1.00
93 Jim Everett .25 .60
94 Michael Haynes .25 .60
95 Tiki Barber RC 5.00 12.00
96 Dave Brown .25 .60
97 Rodney Hampton .40 1.00
98 Ike Hilliard RC 1.25 3.00
99 Danny Kanell .25 .60
100 Wayne Chrebet .60 1.50
101 Keyshawn Johnson .60 1.50
102 Adrian Murrell .40 1.00
103 Neil O'Donnell .40 1.00
104 Alex Van Dyke .25 .60
105 Joe Aska .25 .60
106 Tim Brown .60 1.50
107 Rickey Dudley .40 1.00
108 Napoleon Kaufman .60 1.50
109 Carl Kidd RC .25 .60
110 Ty Detmer .40 1.00
111 Jason Dunn .25 .60
112 Irving Fryar .40 1.00
113 Bobby Hoying .40 1.00
114 Ricky Watters .40 1.00
115 Jerome Bettis .60 1.50
116 Charles Johnson .40 1.00
117 Greg Lloyd .25 .60
118 Kordell Stewart .60 1.50
119 Rod Woodson .40 1.00
120 Tony Banks .40 1.00
121 Isaac Bruce .60 1.50
122 Eddie Kennison .40 1.00
123 Lawrence Phillips .25 .60
124 Stan Humphries .40 1.00
125 Tony Martin .40 1.00
126 Corey Dillon RC 5.00 12.00
127 Leonard Russell .25 .60
128 Junior Seau .60 1.50
129 Jim Druckenmiller RC .40 1.00
130 Marc Edwards RC .40 1.00
131 Ken Norton Jr. .25 .60
132 Terrell Owens .75 2.00
133 Jerry Rice 1.25 3.00
134 Iheanyi Uwaezuoke .25 .60
135 Steve Young .75 2.00
136 John Friesz .25 .60
137 Joey Galloway .40 1.00
138 Warren Moon .60 1.50
139 Todd Peterson RC .25 .60
140 Chris Warren .40 1.00
141 Mike Alstott .60 1.50
142 Reidel Anthony RC .60 1.50
143 Trent Dilfer .60 1.50
144 Warrick Dunn RC 2.50 6.00
145 Errict Rhett .25 .60
146 Terry Allen .60 1.50
147 Henry Ellard .25 .60
148 Gus Frerotte .25 .60
149 Brian Mitchell .25 .60
150 Leslie Shepherd .25 .60
S1 Mark Brunell Sample 1.25 3.00

1997 Pacific Invincible Copper

COMPLETE SET (150) 250.00 600.00
*COPPER STARS: 2.5X TO 6X
*COPPER RCs: 1.2X TO 3X BASIC CARDS
STATED ODDS 2:37 HOBBY

1997 Pacific Invincible Platinum Blue

*PLAT.BLUE VETS: 3X TO 8X BASIC CARDS
*PLAT.BLUE RCs: 1X TO 2.5X BASIC CARDS
STATED ODDS 1:73

1997 Pacific Invincible Red

MPLETE SET (150) 250.00 600.00
*RED STARS: 2.5X TO 6X
*RED RCs: 1.2X TO 3X BASIC CARDS
STATED ODDS 2:37

1997 Pacific Invincible Silver

COMPLETE SET (150) 200.00 500.00
*SILVER STARS: 2X TO 5X BASIC CARDS
*SILVER RCs: 1X TO 2.5X BASIC CARDS
STATED ODDS 2:37 RETAIL

1997 Pacific Invincible Canton, OH

Randomly inserted in packs at a rate of one in 361, this 10-card set features color action player images on a pedestal with a crown in the background. Only players likely to be inducted into the Pro Football Hall of Fame in Canton are included. The backs carry player information.

COMPLETE SET (10) 40.00 100.00
STATED ODDS 1:361
1 Troy Aikman 4.00 10.00
2 Emmitt Smith 8.00 20.00
3 John Elway 8.00 20.00
4 Barry Sanders 6.00 15.00
5 Brett Favre 8.00 20.00
6 Reggie White 2.50 6.00
7 Marcus Allen 2.50 6.00
8 Dan Marino 8.00 20.00
9 Jerry Rice 5.00 12.00
10 Steve Young 3.00 8.00

1997 Pacific Invincible Moments in Time

Randomly inserted in packs at a rate of one in 73, this 20-card set features a small color action player photo on a die-cut card with a scoreboard design background. The backs carry player information.

COMPLETE SET (20) 30.00 80.00
STATED ODDS 1:73
1 Kerry Collins 1.50 4.00
2 Troy Aikman 3.00 8.00
3 Emmitt Smith 5.00 12.00
4 Terrell Davis 2.00 5.00
5 John Elway 6.00 15.00
6 Barry Sanders 5.00 12.00
7 Brett Favre 6.00 15.00
8 Reggie White 1.50 4.00
9 Eddie George 1.50 4.00
10 Mark Brunell 1.50 4.00
11 Marcus Allen 1.50 4.00
12 Karim Abdul-Jabbar 1.00 2.50
13 Dan Marino 6.00 15.00
14 Drew Bledsoe 2.00 5.00
15 Terry Glenn 1.50 4.00
16 Curtis Martin 2.00 5.00
17 Jerome Bettis 1.50 4.00
18 Eddie Kennison 1.00 2.50
19 Jerry Rice 3.00 8.00
20 Steve Young 2.00 5.00

1997 Pacific Invincible Pop Cards

Randomly inserted in packs at a rate of 2:37, this 10-card set features color action player photos. The backs carry a removable "pop card" which revealed a small 1/4 piece of another player card. The four small pieces for each player could be combined to complete a photo puzzle. All four pieces of the same player could be redeemed for a limited edition gold foil card of the featured player.

COMPLETE SET (10) 25.00 60.00
OVERALL STATED ODDS 2:37
*PUZZLE PIECES: .1X TO .3X BASIC INSERTS
*MISSING PUZZLE: .2X TO .5X BASIC INSERTS
*GOLD PRIZES: 1X TO 2.5X BASIC INSERTS
1 Kerry Collins 1.25 3.00
2 Troy Aikman 2.50 6.00
3 Emmitt Smith 3.00 8.00
4 John Elway 6.00 15.00
5 Barry Sanders 3.00 8.00
6 Brett Favre 4.00 10.00
7 Mark Brunell 1.50 4.00
8 Dan Marino 6.00 15.00
9 Drew Bledsoe 1.50 4.00
10 Jerry Rice 4.00 10.00

1997 Pacific Invincible Smash Mouth

ndomly inserted in packs, this 220-card set features oval color action player photos with the player's name printed in the bottom border. The backs carry player information.

COMPLETE SET (220) 10.00 20.00
ONE OR TWO PER PACK
1 Don Majkowski .07 .20
2 Leo Araguz .07 .20
3 John Carney .07 .20
4 Brett Favre .75 2.00
5 Cole Ford .07 .20
6 Marty Carter .07 .20
7 John Elway .75 2.00
8 Mark Brunell .25 .60
9 Rodney Peete .07 .20
10 Jeff Feagles .07 .20
11 Drew Bledsoe .25 .60
12 Kerry Collins .20 .50
13 Dan Marino .75 2.00
14 Torrian Gray .07 .20
15 Reidel Anthony .20 .50
16 Jim Druckenmiller .10 .30
17 Jim Everett .07 .20
18 Pat Barnes .20 .50
19 Ike Hilliard .20 .50
20 Barry Sanders .60 1.50
21 Terry Allen .20 .50
22 Emmitt Smith .60 1.50
23 Antowain Smith .30 .75
24 Robert Griffith .07 .20
25 Mickey Washington .07 .20
26 Napoleon Kaufman .20 .50
27 Eddie George .20 .50
28 Curtis Martin .25 .60
29 Anthony Lynn .07 .20
30 Terrell Davis .25 .60
31 Steve Broussard .07 .20
32 Ricky Watters .10 .30
33 Karim Abdul-Jabbar .20 .50
34 Thurman Thomas .20 .50
35 Ross Verba .07 .20
36 Jerome Bettis .20 .50
37 Chad Cota .07 .20
38 Antonio Langham .07 .20
39 Brett Maxie .07 .20
40 James Hasty .07 .20
41 Conrad Hamilton .07 .20
42 Chris Warren .10 .30
43 George Jones .10 .30
44 Byron Hanspard .10 .30
45 Henri Crockett .07 .20
46 Brent Alexander .07 .20
47 John Lynch .10 .30
48 Renaldo Wynn .07 .20
49 Jared Tomich .07 .20
50 James Francis .07 .20
51 Brian Williams LB .07 .20
52 Kevin Mawae .07 .20
53 Marvcus Patton .07 .20
54 Michael Barber .07 .20
55 Robert Jones .07 .20
56 Ernest Dixon .07 .20
57 Mo Lewis .07 .20
58 Peter Boulware .20 .50
59 Wayne Simmons .07 .20
60 Anthony Redmon .07 .20
61 Tim Ruddy .07 .20
62 Victor Green .07 .20
63 Kirk Lowdermilk .07 .20
64 John Jurkovic .07 .20
65 John Jackson .07 .20
66 Kevin Gogan .07 .20
67 Adam Schreiber .07 .20
68 Mike Morris .07 .20
69 Albert Connell .20 .50
70 Tony Mayberry .07 .20
71 Mark Tuinei .07 .20
72 Harry Swayne .07 .20
73 Todd Steussie .07 .20
74 Glenn Parker .07 .20
75 D'Marco Farr .07 .20
76 Ed Simmons .07 .20
77 Tarik Glenn .20 .50
78 Rick Hamilton .07 .20
79 Dave Szott .07 .20
80 Jerry Rice .40 1.00
81 Tim Brown .20 .50
82 Charlie Jones .10 .30
83 Jerry Wunsch .07 .20
84 Lonnie Johnson .07 .20
85 Reggie Johnson .07 .20
86 Willie Davis .07 .20
87 Greg Clark .07 .20
88 Deems May .07 .20
89 J.J.Birden .07 .20
90 Chuck Smith .07 .20
91 Coleman Rudolph .07 .20
92 Leon Johnson .10 .30
93 Trace Armstrong .07 .20
94 John Thierry .07 .20
95 Dean Wells .07 .20
96 Mike Jones DE .07 .20
97 Mike Lodish .07 .20
98 Tony Siragusa .07 .20
99 Daved Benefield .07 .20
100 Michael Bankston .07 .20
101 Jamal Anderson .20 .50
102 Greg Montgomery .07 .20
103 Mark Maddox .07 .20
104 Matt Elliott .07 .20
105 Joe Cain .07 .20
106 Jeff Blake .10 .30
107 Troy Aikman .40 1.00
108 Brian Habib .07 .20
109 Pete Chryplewicz .07 .20
110 Earl Dotson .07 .20
111 Joe Bowden .07 .20
112 Marshall Faulk .25 .60
113 Reggie Barlow .07 .20
114 Marcus Allen .20 .50
115 Jeff Buckey .07 .20
116 Mitch Berger .07 .20
117 Corwin Brown .07 .20
118 Troy Davis .10 .30
119 Rodney Hampton .10 .30
120 Tom Knight .07 .20
121 Michael Booker .07 .20
122 Matt Stover .07 .20
123 Mark Pike .07 .20
124 Rohn Stark .07 .20
125 Todd Sauerbrun .07 .20
126 Corey Dillon .75 2.00
127 Tyji Armstrong .07 .20
128 Vaughn Hebron .07 .20
129 Antonio London .07 .20
130 Santana Dotson .07 .20
131 Cris Dishman .07 .20
132 Stephen Grant .07 .20
133 Mike Hollis .07 .20
134 Martin Bayless .07 .20
135 Sam Madison .20 .50
136 Esera Tuaolo .07 .20
137 Hason Graham .07 .20
138 Jim Dombrowski .07 .20
139 Bernard Holsey .07 .20
140 Kyle Brady .07 .20
141 David Klingler .07 .20
142 Don Griffin .07 .20
143 Bernard Dafney .07 .20
144 Derrick Harris .07 .20
145 Charles Johnson .10 .30
146 Dedrick Dodge .07 .20
147 Antonio Edwards .07 .20
148 Jorge Diaz .07 .20
149 Marc Logan .07 .20
150 Lou D'Agostino .07 .20
151 Lance Johnstone .07 .20
152 Ray Farmer .07 .20
153 Brentson Buckner .07 .20
154 Tony Banks .10 .30
155 'Omar Ellison .07 .20
156 Derrick Deese .07 .20
157 Howard Ballard .07 .20
158 Ronde Barber .75 2.00
159 Gus Frerotte .07 .20
160 Leeland McElroy .07 .20
161 Devin Bush .07 .20
162 Eddie Sutter .07 .20
163 Sam Rogers .07 .20
164 Carl Simpson .07 .20
165 Lee Johnson .07 .20
166 Tony Casillas .07 .20
167 Randy Hilliard .07 .20
168 Ryan McNeil .07 .20
169 William Henderson .10 .30
170 Irv Eatman .07 .20
171 Derwin Gray .07 .20
172 Rob Johnson .20 .50
173 Derrick Walker .07 .20
174 Chris Singleton .07 .20
175 Chris Walsh .07 .20
176 Marty Moore .20 .50
177 Paul Green .07 .20
178 Brian Williams OL .07 .20
179 Robert Farmer .07 .20
180 Derrick Witherspoon .07 .20
181 Jim Miller .20 .50
182 James Harris DE .07 .20
183 Shannon Mitchell .07 .20
184 Steve Young .25 .60
185 Ronnie Harris .07 .20
186 Trent Dilfer .20 .50
187 Joe Patton .07 .20
188 Jake Plummer .60 1.50
189 Ron George .07 .20
190 Vinny Testaverde .10 .30
191 Ryan Wetnight .07 .20
192 Steve Tovar .07 .20
193 Godfrey Myles .07 .20
194 Rod Smith WR .20 .50
195 Zefross Moss .07 .20
196 Jerald Sowell .07 .20
197 Jason Layman .07 .20
198 Ray McElroy .07 .20
199 Tom McManus .07 .20
200 Shawn Wooden .07 .20
201 Tony Johnson .07 .20
202 James Farrior .20 .50
203 Marc Woodard .07 .20
204 Chad Scott .10 .30
205 Dwayne White .07 .20
206 Warrick Dunn .40 1.00
207 Joe Wolf .07 .20
208 Dedric Ward .10 .30
209 Bennie Thompson .07 .20
210 Bracy Walker .07 .20
211 Tracy Scroggins .07 .20
212 Derrick Mason .30 .75
213 Ed King .07 .20
214 Harry Galbreath .07 .20
215 Joel Steed .07 .20
216 Jackie Harris .07 .20
217 Craig Sauer .07 .20
218 Reinard Wilson .10 .30
219 Barron Wortham .07 .20
220 Errict Rhett .07 .20

1997 Pacific Invincible Smash Mouth X-tra

Randomly inserted in packs, this 59-card set features action color player photos with a thin gold inner border. The player's name is printed down one side of the card. The backs carry player information.

COMPLETE SET (59) 7.50 15.00
ONE OR TWO PER PACK
1 Steve Young .25 .60
2 Jeff Blake .10 .30
3 Troy Aikman .40 1.00
4 Brett Favre .75 2.00
5 Gus Frerotte .07 .20
6 Tony Banks .10 .30
7 John Elway .75 2.00
8 Mark Brunell .25 .60
9 Rodney Peete .07 .20
10 Trent Dilfer .20 .50
11 Drew Bledsoe .25 .60
12 Kerry Collins .20 .50
13 Dan Marino .75 2.00
14 Vinny Testaverde .10 .30
15 Reidel Anthony .20 .50
16 Jim Druckenmiller .10 .30
17 Jim Everett .07 .20
18 Pat Barnes .20 .50
19 Ike Hilliard .20 .50
20 Barry Sanders .60 1.50
21 Terry Allen .20 .50
22 Emmitt Smith .60 1.50
23 Antowain Smith .30 .75
24 Jake Plummer .60 1.50
25 Vaughn Hebron .07 .20
26 Napoleon Kaufman .20 .50
27 Eddie George .20 .50
28 Curtis Martin .25 .60
29 Rodney Hampton .10 .30
30 Terrell Davis .25 .60
31 Marshall Faulk .25 .60
32 Ricky Watters .10 .30
33 Karim Abdul-Jabbar .20 .50
34 Thurman Thomas .20 .50
35 Troy Davis .10 .30
36 Jerome Bettis .20 .50
37 Warrick Dunn .40 1.00
38 Leeland McElroy .07 .20
39 William Henderson .10 .30
40 Jamal Anderson .20 .50
41 Errict Rhett .07 .20
42 Chris Warren .10 .30
43 George Jones .10 .30
44 Byron Hanspard .10 .30
45 Jerald Sowell .07 .20
46 Marcus Allen .20 .50
47 Kirk Lowdermilk .07 .20
48 Brian Habib .07 .20
49 Derrick Mason .30 .75
50 Jerry Rice .40 1.00
51 Albert Connell .20 .50
52 Kyle Brady .07 .20
53 Tim Brown .20 .50
54 Charles Johnson .10 .30
55 Jackie Harris .07 .20
56 Lonnie Johnson .07 .20
57 Deems May .07 .20
58 Peter Boulware .20 .50
59 Wayne Simmons .07 .20

2001 Pacific Invincible

In July of 2001 Pacific released Invincible. The 300-card set featured 44 short printed rookies numbered to 299 and six rookie jersey cards serial numberd to 250. The base set design had a gold background with the player photo and a small clear cell with the player's head shot in the bottom left corner. The veteran player cards were serial numbered to 1000.

COMP.SET w/o SP's (250) 90.00 150.00
251-300 ROOKIE PRINT RUN 299
1 David Boston .50 1.25
2 MarTay Jenkins .50 1.25
3 Thomas Jones .50 1.25
4 Rob Moore .50 1.25
5 Michael Pittman .60 1.50
6 Jake Plummer .50 1.25
7 Frank Sanders .50 1.25
8 Jamal Anderson .60 1.50
9 Chris Chandler .60 1.50
10 Jammi German .50 1.25
11 Shawn Jefferson .50 1.25
12 Doug Johnson .50 1.25
13 Terance Mathis .50 1.25
14 Rodney Thomas .50 1.25
15 Elvis Grbac .60 1.50
16 Qadry Ismail .50 1.25
17 Jamal Lewis .75 2.00
18 Jermaine Lewis .50 1.25
19 Ray Lewis .75 2.00
20 Chris Redman .75 2.00
21 Shannon Sharpe .60 1.50
22 Travis Taylor .50 1.25
23 Shawn Bryson .50 1.25
24 Larry Centers .50 1.25
25 Rob Johnson .60 1.50
26 Jeremy McDaniel .50 1.25
27 Sammy Morris .50 1.25
28 Eric Moulds .50 1.25
29 Peerless Price .50 1.25
30 Antowain Smith .60 1.50
31 Michael Bates .50 1.25
32 Tim Biakabutuka .50 1.25
33 Isaac Byrd .50 1.25
34 Brad Hoover .60 1.50
35 Patrick Jeffers .50 1.25
36 Jeff Lewis .50 1.25
37 Muhsin Muhammad .50 1.25
38 Wesley Walls .50 1.25
39 James Allen .50 1.25
40 Marty Booker .50 1.25
41 Macey Brooks .50 1.25
42 Bobby Engram .50 1.25
43 Cade McNown .60 1.50
44 Marcus Robinson .60 1.50
45 Brian Urlacher 1.00 2.50
46 Dez White .60 1.50
47 Brandon Bennett .50 1.25
48 Corey Dillon .50 1.25
49 Danny Farmer .50 1.25
50 Jon Kitna .50 1.25
51 Darnay Scott .60 1.50
52 Akili Smith .50 1.25
53 Peter Warrick .50 1.25
54 Craig Yeast .50 1.25
55 Tim Couch .50 1.25
56 JaJuan Dawson .50 1.25
57 Curtis Enis .50 1.25
58 Kevin Johnson .50 1.25
59 Dennis Northcutt .50 1.25
60 Travis Prentice .50 1.25
61 Errict Rhett .60 1.50
62 Tony Banks .50 1.25
63 Randall Cunningham .60 1.50
64 Rocket Ismail .60 1.50
65 Wane McGarity .50 1.25
66 Carl Pickens .60 1.50
67 Emmitt Smith 1.25 3.00
68 Jason Tucker .50 1.25
69 Michael Wiley .50 1.25
70 Mike Anderson .50 1.25
71 Terrell Davis .60 1.50
72 Gus Frerotte .50 1.25
73 Olandis Gary .50 1.25
74 Brian Griese .50 1.25
75 Eddie Kennison .60 1.50
76 Ed McCaffrey .60 1.50
77 Rod Smith .60 1.50
78 Charlie Batch .50 1.25
79 Germane Crowell .50 1.25
80 Larry Foster .50 1.25
81 Desmond Howard .60 1.50
82 Herman Moore .50 1.25
83 Johnnie Morton .60 1.50
84 Robert Porcher .50 1.25
85 James Stewart .50 1.25
86 Donald Driver .60 1.50
87 Brett Favre 1.50 4.00
88 Bubba Franks .50 1.25
80 Antonio Freeman .75 2.00
90 Ahman Green .60 1.50
91 William Henderson .50 1.25
92 Dorsey Levens .60 1.50
93 Bill Schroeder .60 1.50
94 Ken Dilger .50 1.25
95 E.G. Green .50 1.25
96 Marvin Harrison .60 1.50
97 Edgerrin James .60 1.50
98 Peyton Manning 2.00 5.00
99 Jerome Pathon .50 1.25
100 Marcus Pollard .50 1.25
101 Terrence Wilkins .50 1.25
102 Kyle Brady .50 1.25
103 Mark Brunell .60 1.50
104 Stacey Mack .50 1.25
105 Keenan McCardell .60 1.50
106 Jimmy Smith .60 1.50
107 R. Jay Soward .50 1.25
108 Shyrone Stith .50 1.25
109 Fred Taylor .50 1.25
110 Derrick Alexander WR .50 1.25
111 Kimble Anders .50 1.25
112 Todd Collins .50 1.25
113 Tony Gonzalez .60 1.50
114 Trent Green .50 1.25
115 Priest Holmes .50 1.25
116 Tony Horne .50 1.25
117 Frank Moreau .50 1.25
118 Sylvester Morris .50 1.25
119 Tony Richardson .50 1.25
120 Jay Fiedler .60 1.50
121 Oronde Gadsden .50 1.25
122 James Johnson .50 1.25
123 Ray Lucas .50 1.25
124 Tony Martin .60 1.50
125 O.J. McDuffie .50 1.25
126 James McKnight .50 1.25
127 Lamar Smith .60 1.50
128 Jason Taylor .75 2.00
129 Zach Thomas .60 1.50
130 Dedric Ward .50 1.25
131 Cris Carter .75 2.00
132 Daunte Culpepper .60 1.50
133 Randy Moss .60 1.50
134 Chris Walsh RC .50 1.25
135 Troy Walters .50 1.25
136 Moe Williams .50 1.25
137 Drew Bledsoe .60 1.50
138 Troy Brown .50 1.25
139 Kevin Faulk .50 1.25
140 Terry Glenn .60 1.50
141 Ty Law .75 2.00
142 Lawyer Milloy .50 1.25
143 David Patten .50 1.25
144 J.R. Redmond .50 1.25
145 Tony Simmons .50 1.25
146 Jeff Blake .60 1.50
147 Aaron Brooks .50 1.25
148 Albert Connell .50 1.25
149 Joe Horn .50 1.25
150 Willie Jackson .50 1.25
151 Chad Morton .50 1.25
152 Keith Poole .50 1.25
153 Ricky Williams .60 1.50
154 Robert Wilson .50 1.25
155 Jessie Armstead .50 1.25
156 Tiki Barber .60 1.50
157 Kerry Collins .50 1.25
158 Ron Dayne .60 1.50
159 Ron Dixon .50 1.25
160 Ike Hilliard .50 1.25
161 Jason Sehorn .60 1.50
162 Michael Strahan .60 1.50
163 Amani Toomer .50 1.25
164 Richie Anderson .50 1.25
165 Wayne Chrebet .50 1.25
166 Laveranues Coles .60 1.50
167 Matthew Hatchette .50 1.25
168 Marvin Jones .50 1.25
169 Curtis Martin .60 1.50
170 Chad Pennington .50 1.25
171 Vinny Testaverde .50 1.25
172 Tim Brown .75 2.00
173 Zack Crockett .50 1.25
174 Rich Gannon .60 1.50
175 Charlie Garner .60 1.50
176 James Jett .50 1.25
177 Randy Jordan .60 1.50
178 Andre Rison .60 1.50
179 Tyrone Wheatley .60 1.50
180 Charles Woodson .75 2.00
181 Darnell Autry .50 1.25
182 Charles Johnson .50 1.25
183 Chad Lewis .50 1.25
184 Donovan McNabb .60 1.50
185 Todd Pinkston .50 1.25
186 Stanley Pritchett .50 1.25
187 Torrance Small .50 1.25
188 Duce Staley .50 1.25
189 James Thrash .60 1.50
190 Jerome Bettis .75 2.00
191 Plaxico Burress .50 1.25
192 Troy Edwards .50 1.25
193 Courtney Hawkins .50 1.25
194 Richard Huntley .50 1.25
195 Bobby Shaw .50 1.25
196 Kordell Stewart .50 1.25
197 Hines Ward .60 1.50
198 Isaac Bruce .75 2.00
199 Trung Canidate .50 1.25
200 Marshall Faulk .60 1.50
201 Az-Zahir Hakim .50 1.25
202 Torry Holt .60 1.50
203 Ricky Proehl .50 1.25
204 Kurt Warner 1.25 3.00
205 Aeneas Williams .50 1.25
206 Curtis Conway .60 1.50
207 Tim Dwight .60 1.50
208 Jermaine Fazande .50 1.25
209 Terrell Fletcher .50 1.25
210 Doug Flutie .60 1.50
211 Jeff Graham .50 1.25
212 Freddie Jones .50 1.25
213 Reggie Jones .50 1.25
214 Junior Seau .60 1.50
215 Fred Beasley .50 1.25
216 Jeff Garcia .50 1.25
217 Terrell Owens .60 1.50
218 Jerry Rice 1.50 4.00
219 Paul Smith .50 1.25
220 J.J. Stokes .50 1.25
221 Tai Streets .50 1.25
222 Shaun Alexander .50 1.25
223 Karsten Bailey .50 1.25
224 Matt Hasselbeck .50 1.25
225 Brock Huard .50 1.25
226 Darrell Jackson .60 1.50
227 Shawn Springs .50 1.25
228 Ricky Watters .60 1.50
229 James Williams WR .50 1.25
230 Mike Alstott .50 1.25
231 Reidel Anthony .50 1.25
232 Warrick Dunn .50 1.25
233 Jacquez Green .50 1.25
234 Brad Johnson .60 1.50
235 Keyshawn Johnson .60 1.50
236 Shaun King .50 1.25
237 Warren Sapp .60 1.50
238 Kevin Dyson .50 1.25
239 Eddie George .75 2.00
240 Jevon Kearse .50 1.25
241 Derrick Mason .50 1.25
242 Steve McNair .60 1.50
243 Chris Sanders .50 1.25
244 Frank Wycheck .50 1.25
245 Stephen Alexander .50 1.25
246 Stephen Davis .50 1.25
247 Irving Fryar .60 1.50
248 Jeff George .60 1.50
249 Kevin Lockett .50 1.25
250 Michael Westbrook .50 1.25
251 Bobby Newcombe RC 1.50 4.00
252 Alge Crumpler RC 2.00 5.00
253 Vinny Sutherland RC 1.25 3.00
254 Michael Vick RC 3.00 8.00
255 Travis Henry RC 1.50 4.00
256 Dan Morgan RC 1.50 4.00
257 Chris Weinke JSY/250 RC 4.00 10.00
258 David Terrell RC 1.50 4.00
259 A.Thomas JSY/250 RC 5.00 12.00
260 T.J. Houshmandzadeh RC 1.50 4.00
261 Chad Johnson RC 2.00 5.00
262 Rudi Johnson RC 2.00 5.00
263 James Jackson RC 1.25 3.00
264 Quincy Morgan RC 1.50 4.00
265 Scotty Anderson RC 1.25 3.00
266 Mike McMahon RC 1.50 4.00
267 Robert Ferguson RC 2.00 5.00
268 Reggie Wayne RC 3.00 8.00
269 Snoop Minnis RC 1.25 3.00
270 Chris Chambers RC 1.25 3.00
271 Josh Heupel RC 2.00 5.00
272 Travis Minor RC 1.50 4.00
273 Michael Bennett RC 1.50 4.00
274 Ben Leard RC 1.25 3.00
275 Deuce McAllister RC 2.00 5.00
276 Moran Norris RC 1.25 3.00
277 Jesse Palmer RC 1.50 4.00
278 LaMont Jordan RC 2.00 5.00
279 Santana Moss RC 2.00 5.00
280 Ken-Yon Rambo RC 1.25 3.00
281 M.Tuiasosopo JSY/250 RC 4.00 10.00
282 Correll Buckhalter RC 1.25 3.00
283 A.J. Feeley RC 1.50 4.00
284 F.Mitchell JSY/250 RC 3.00 8.00
285 Joey Getherall RC 1.25 3.00
286 Chris Taylor RC 1.25 3.00
287 Adam Archuleta RC 1.50 4.00
288 David Rivers RC 1.25 3.00
289 Drew Brees JSY/250 RC 50.00 100.00
290 L.Tomlinson JSY/250 RC 15.00 40.00
291 David Allen RC 1.25 3.00
292 Kevan Barlow RC 1.50 4.00
293 Cedrick Wilson RC 1.50 4.00
294 Alex Bannister RC 1.25 3.00
295 Josh Booty RC 1.50 4.00
296 Heath Evans RC 1.50 4.00
297 Koren Robinson RC 1.50 4.00
298 Dan Alexander RC 1.50 4.00
299 Rod Gardner RC 1.50 4.00
300 Sage Rosenfels RC 1.50 4.00

2001 Pacific Invincible Blue

*VETS 1-250: 1.2X TO 3X BASIC CARDS
*VET JSY 1-250: 2.5X TO 6X BASIC CARDS
1-250 VETERAN PRINT RUN 250
*ROOKIES: .8X TO 2X BASIC RC
*ROOKIES: .4X TO 1X BASIC JSY
251-300 ROOKIE PRINT RUN 99

2001 Pacific Invincible Premiere Date

*VETS 1-250: 2.5X TO 6X BASIC CARDS
*ROOKIES 251-300: 1X TO 2.5X BASE RC
*ROOKIES: .5X TO 1.2X BASE JSY RC
STATED PRINT RUN 55 SERIAL #'d SETS

2001 Pacific Invincible Red

ETS: .5X TO 1.2X BASIC CARDS
*VET JSY: 1.5X TO 4X BASIC CARDS
1-250 VETERAN PRINT RUN 750
*ROOKIES: .4X TO 1X BASE RC
*ROOKIES: .2X TO .5X BASE JSY RC
251-300 ROOKIE PRINT RUN 199

2001 Pacific Invincible Retail

MP.SET w/o RC's (250) 30.00 60.00
251 Bobby Newcombe RC .60 1.50
252 Alge Crumpler RC .75 2.00
253 Vinny Sutherland RC .50 1.25
254 Michael Vick RC 1.25 3.00
255 Travis Henry RC .60 1.50
256 Dan Morgan RC .60 1.50
257 Chris Weinke RC .60 1.50
258 David Terrell RC .60 1.50
259 Anthony Thomas RC .75 2.00
260 T.J. Houshmandzadeh RC .60 1.50
261 Chad Johnson RC .75 2.00
262 Rudi Johnson RC .75 2.00
263 James Jackson RC .50 1.25
264 Quincy Morgan RC .60 1.50
265 Scotty Anderson RC .50 1.25
266 Mike McMahon RC .60 1.50
267 Robert Ferguson RC .75 2.00
268 Reggie Wayne RC 1.00 2.50
269 Snoop Minnis RC .50 1.25
270 Chris Chambers RC .50 1.25
271 Josh Heupel RC .75 2.00
272 Travis Minor RC .60 1.50
273 Michael Bennett RC .60 1.50
274 Ben Leard RC .50 1.25
275 Deuce McAllister RC .75 2.00
276 Moran Norris RC .50 1.25
277 Jesse Palmer RC .60 1.50
278 LaMont Jordan RC .75 2.00
279 Santana Moss RC .75 2.00
280 Ken-Yon Rambo RC .50 1.25
281 Marques Tuiasosopo RC .60 1.50
282 Correll Buckhalter RC .50 1.25
283 A.J. Feeley RC .60 1.50
284 Freddie Mitchell RC .50 1.25
285 Joey Getherall RC .50 1.25
286 Chris Taylor RC .50 1.25
287 Adam Archuleta RC .60 1.50
288 David Rivers RC .50 1.25
289 Drew Brees RC 3.00 8.00
290 LaDainian Tomlinson RC 2.50 6.00
291 David Allen RC .50 1.25
292 Kevan Barlow RC .60 1.50
293 Cedrick Wilson RC .60 1.50
294 Alex Bannister RC .50 1.25
295 Josh Booty RC .60 1.50
296 Heath Evans RC .60 1.50
297 Koren Robinson RC .60 1.50
298 Dan Alexander RC .60 1.50
299 Rod Gardner RC .60 1.50
300 Sage Rosenfels RC .60 1.50

2001 Pacific Invincible Afterburners

Randomly inserted in packs of 2001 Pacific Invincible, this 20-card set featured the top speedsters looking forward to the 2001 NFL season. Each of these cards were serial numbered to 2000. The cardfronts were bright orange and yellow and they were highlighted with gold-foil lettering. The cardbacks contained a brief description about the featured players' skills.

COMPLETE SET (20) 15.00 40.00
STATED PRINT RUN 2000 SER.#'d SETS
1 Jamal Lewis 1.25 3.00
2 Eric Moulds .75 2.00
3 David Terrell 1.00 2.50
4 Corey Dillon .75 2.00
5 Peter Warrick .75 2.00
6 Marvin Harrison 1.00 2.50
7 Edgerrin James 1.00 2.50
8 Jimmy Smith 1.00 2.50
9 Fred Taylor .75 2.00
10 Sylvester Morris .75 2.00
11 Chris Chambers .60 1.50
12 Michael Bennett .75 2.00
13 Randy Moss 1.00 2.50
14 Santana Moss 1.00 2.50
15 Tim Brown 1.25 3.00
16 Isaac Bruce 1.25 3.00
17 Marshall Faulk 1.00 2.50
18 Torry Holt 1.00 2.50
19 LaDainian Tomlinson 3.00 8.00
20 Warrick Dunn .75 2.00

2001 Pacific Invincible Fast Forward

ndomly inserted in 2001 Pacific Invincible, this 20-card set featured the top playmakers from the 2000 NFL season. The card design had a horizontal view along with silver-foil lettering to highlight the cards.Each card was serial numbered to 1000.

COMPLETE SET (20) 30.00 80.00
STATED PRINT RUN 1000 SER.#'d SETS
1 Jamal Lewis 1.50 4.00
2 Eric Moulds 1.00 2.50
3 Emmitt Smith 2.50 6.00
4 Mike Anderson 1.00 2.50
5 Marvin Harrison 1.25 3.00
6 Jimmy Smith 1.25 3.00
7 Cris Carter 1.50 4.00
8 Daunte Culpepper 1.25 3.00
9 Randy Moss 1.25 3.00
10 Ricky Williams 1.25 3.00
11 Ron Dayne 1.25 3.00
12 Curtis Martin 1.25 3.00
13 Rich Gannon 1.25 3.00
14 Jerome Bettis 1.50 4.00
15 Isaac Bruce 1.50 4.00
16 Marshall Faulk 1.25 3.00
17 Torry Holt 1.25 3.00
18 Kurt Warner 2.50 6.00
19 Jeff Garcia 1.00 2.50
20 Jerry Rice 3.00 8.00

2001 Pacific Invincible Heat Seekers

ndomly inserted in 2001 Pacific Invincible packs, this 20-card set featured the top quarterbacks from the NFL and also a few from the 2001 rookie class. The cards were die-cut on 2 sides, and featured a flaming football with gold-foil highlights. Each card was serial numbered to 750.

COMPLETE SET (20) 30.00 80.00
STATED PRINT RUN 750 SER.#'d SETS
1 Jake Plummer 1.00 2.50
2 Michael Vick 2.50 6.00
3 Rob Johnson 1.25 3.00
4 Cade McNown 1.25 3.00
5 Akili Smith 1.00 2.50
6 Tim Couch 1.00 2.50
7 Brian Griese 1.00 2.50
8 Charlie Batch 1.00 2.50
9 Brett Favre 3.00 8.00
10 Peyton Manning 4.00 10.00
11 Mark Brunell 1.25 3.00
12 Daunte Culpepper 1.25 3.00
13 Drew Bledsoe 1.25 3.00
14 Aaron Brooks 1.00 2.50
15 Rich Gannon 1.25 3.00
16 Marques Tuiasosopo 1.25 3.00
17 Kurt Warner 2.50 6.00
18 Jeff Garcia 1.00 2.50
19 Steve McNair 1.25 3.00
20 Jeff George 1.25 3.00

2001 Pacific Invincible New Sensations

w Sensations featured 30 of the top rookies from the 2001 NFL Draft pictured in their college uniforms with a silver-foil logo of the NFL team that had drafted them. The cards also used silver-foil for the lettering, and each card was serial numbered to 1250.

COMPLETE SET (30) 20.00 50.00
STATED PRINT RUN 1250 SER.#'d SETS
1 Vinny Sutherland .40 1.00
2 Michael Vick 1.00 2.50
3 Travis Henry .50 1.25
4 Chris Weinke .50 1.25
5 David Terrell .50 1.25
6 Anthony Thomas .60 1.50
7 Chad Johnson .60 1.50
8 James Jackson .40 1.00
9 Quincy Morgan .50 1.25
10 Mike McMahon .50 1.25
11 Reggie Wayne .75 2.00
12 Snoop Minnis .40 1.00
13 Chris Chambers .40 1.00
14 Josh Heupel .60 1.50
15 Travis Minor .50 1.25
16 Michael Bennett .50 1.25
17 Deuce McAllister .60 1.50
18 LaMont Jordan .60 1.50
19 Santana Moss .60 1.50
20 Ken-Yon Rambo .40 1.00
21 Marques Tuiasosopo .50 1.25
22 Correll Buckhalter .40 1.00
23 Freddie Mitchell .40 1.00
24 Drew Brees 8.00 20.00
25 LaDainian Tomlinson 2.00 5.00
26 Kevan Barlow .50 1.25
27 Josh Booty .50 1.25
28 Koren Robinson .50 1.25
29 Rod Gardner .50 1.25
30 Sage Rosenfels .50 1.25

2001 Pacific Invincible Rookie Die Cuts

ndomly inserted in packs of 2001 Pacific Invincible, this set featured 10 of the top rookies from the 2001 NFL Draft. Each card was serial numbered to 100. The cards were die-cut on 2 sides.

COMPLETE SET (10) 30.00 80.00
STATED PRINT RUN 100 SER.#'d SETS
1 Michael Vick 4.00 10.00
2 Chris Weinke 2.00 5.00
3 David Terrell 2.00 5.00
4 Michael Bennett 2.00 5.00
5 Deuce McAllister 2.50 6.00
6 Freddie Mitchell 1.50 4.00
7 Drew Brees 25.00 50.00
8 LaDainian Tomlinson 8.00 20.00
9 Koren Robinson 2.00 5.00
10 Rod Gardner 2.00 5.00

2001 Pacific Invincible School Colors

Ramdomly inserted in packs of 2001 Pacific Invincible, this 60-card set featured some of the top stars from the NFL pictured in their alma mater's uniform.The cards are highlighted with silver-foil lettering and they were serial numbered to 2750.

COMPLETE SET (60) 30.00 80.00
STATED PRINT RUN 2750 SER.#'d SETS
1 Doug Flutie .60 1.50
2 Tim Hasselbeck .60 1.50
3 Darrell Jackson .60 1.50
4 Jesse Palmer .60 1.50
5 Emmitt Smith 1.25 3.00
6 Fred Taylor .50 1.25
7 Warrick Dunn .50 1.25
8 Snoop Minnis .50 1.25
9 Travis Minor .60 1.50
10 Peter Warrick .50 1.25
11 Chris Weinke .60 1.50
12 Terrell Davis .60 1.50
13 Olandis Gary .50 1.25
14 Randy Moss .60 1.50
15 Chad Pennington .50 1.25
16 James Jackson .50 1.25
17 Edgerrin James .60 1.50
18 Santana Moss .60 1.50
19 Reggie Wayne .75 2.00
20 Brian Griese .50 1.25
21 David Terrell .60 1.50
22 Anthony Thomas .75 2.00
23 Tyrone Wheatley .60 1.50
24 Ahman Green .60 1.50
25 Dan Alexander .60 1.50
26 Correll Buckhalter .50 1.25
27 Bobby Newcombe .60 1.50
28 Torry Holt .60 1.50
29 Koren Robinson .60 1.50
30 Jerome Bettis .75 2.00
31 Tim Brown .75 2.00
32 Joey Getherall .50 1.25
33 Jabari Holloway .50 1.25
34 David Boston .50 1.25
35 Cris Carter .75 2.00
36 Eddie George .75 2.00
37 Ken-Yon Rambo .50 1.25
38 Kevan Barlow .60 1.50
39 Curtis Martin .60 1.50
40 Mike Alstott .50 1.25
41 Drew Brees 10.00 25.00
42 Vinny Sutherland .50 1.25
43 Marvin Harrison .60 1.50
44 Kevin Johnson .50 1.25
45 Donovan McNabb .60 1.50
46 Travis Henry .60 1.50
47 Jamal Lewis .75 2.00
48 Peyton Manning 2.00 5.00
49 Troy Aikman 1.00 2.50
50 Cade McNown .60 1.50
51 Freddie Mitchell .50 1.25
52 Keyshawn Johnson .60 1.50
53 Junior Seau .60 1.50
54 Rob Johnson .60 1.50
55 Mark Brunell .60 1.50
56 Corey Dillon .50 1.25
57 Marques Tuiasosopo .60 1.50
58 Ron Dayne .60 1.50
59 Michael Bennett .60 1.50
60 Chris Chambers .40 1.00

2001 Pacific Invincible Widescreen

Randomly inserted in packs of 2001 Pacific Invincible, this 20-card set featured a widescreen format while featuring some of the top stars from the NFL. Each card was serial numbered to 2500, and they were highlighted with silver-foil lettering.

COMPLETE SET (20) 15.00 40.00
STATED PRINT RUN 2500 SER.#'d SETS
1 Corey Dillon .75 2.00
2 Peter Warrick .75 2.00
3 Tim Couch .75 2.00
4 Kevin Johnson .75 2.00
5 Brian Griese .75 2.00
6 Brett Favre 2.50 6.00
7 Peyton Manning 3.00 8.00
8 Fred Taylor .75 2.00
9 Sylvester Morris .75 2.00
10 Drew Bledsoe 1.00 2.50
11 Tyrone Wheatley 1.00 2.50
12 Donovan McNabb 1.00 2.50
13 Jerome Bettis 1.25 3.00
14 Plaxico Burress .75 2.00
15 Jeff Garcia .75 2.00
16 Terrell Owens 1.00 2.50
17 Shaun Alexander .75 2.00
18 Eddie George 1.25 3.00
19 Derrick Mason .75 2.00
20 Steve McNair 1.00 2.50

2001 Pacific Invincible XXXVI

Randomly inserted in packs of 2001 Pacific Invincible, this set featured 20 players who were expecting to make a difference in reaching Super Bowl XXXVI. Each card was die-cut on 2 sides and serial numbered to 499. The cardfronts used a gold-foil to highlight the logos and lettering.

COMPLETE SET (20) 40.00 100.00
STATED PRINT RUN 499 SER.#'d SETS
1 Jamal Lewis 1.50 4.00
2 Rob Johnson 1.25 3.00
3 Mike Anderson 1.00 2.50
4 Terrell Davis 1.25 3.00
5 Brett Favre 3.00 8.00
6 Marvin Harrison 1.25 3.00
7 Edgerrin James 1.25 3.00
8 Mark Brunell 1.25 3.00
9 Cris Carter 1.50 4.00
10 Daunte Culpepper 1.25 3.00
11 Ricky Williams 1.25 3.00
12 Ron Dayne 1.25 3.00
13 Curtis Martin 1.25 3.00
14 Rich Gannon 1.25 3.00
15 Donovan McNabb 1.25 3.00
16 Marshall Faulk 1.25 3.00
17 Kurt Warner 2.50 6.00
18 Warrick Dunn 1.00 2.50
19 Eddie George 1.50 4.00
20 Steve McNair 1.25 3.00

1996 Pacific Litho-Cel

is 100-card set was distributed in three-card packs with a mixture of "litho" cards and "cel" cards. Action player photos are featured on the front of the Litho card in limited color with a different action photo of the same player on the back in full color. The Cel version of each card was produced in 1-color and made to be combined with a Litho card to make the front photo of the player magically appear in full color. The prices below refer to the basic "litho" cards.

COMPLETE SET (100) 15.00 40.00
*CEL CARDS: .4X TO 1X LITHO
1 Kent Graham .20 .50
2 LeShon Johnson .20 .50
3 Leeland McElroy RC .30 .75
4 Frank Sanders .30 .75
5 Jamal Anderson RC .50 1.25
6 Cornelius Bennett .20 .50
7 Bobby Hebert .20 .50
8 Earnest Byner .20 .50
9 Michael Jackson .30 .75
10 Vinny Testaverde .30 .75
11 Jim Kelly .40 1.00
12 Andre Reed .30 .75
13 Bruce Smith .30 .75
14 Thurman Thomas .40 1.00
15 Kerry Collins .40 1.00
16 Lamar Lathon .20 .50
17 Kevin Greene .30 .75
18 Bobby Engram RC .40 1.00
19 Erik Kramer .20 .50
20 Rashaan Salaam .30 .75
21 Jeff Blake .40 1.00
22 Garrison Hearst .30 .75
23 Carl Pickens .30 .75
24 Darnay Scott .30 .75
25 Troy Aikman .60 1.50
26 Eric Bjornson .20 .50
27 Deion Sanders .50 1.25
28 Emmitt Smith 1.00 2.50
29 Terrell Davis .50 1.25
30 John Elway 1.25 3.00
31 Anthony Miller .30 .75
32 John Mobley .20 .50
33 Scott Mitchell .30 .75
34 Herman Moore .30 .75
35 Brett Perriman .20 .50
36 Barry Sanders 1.00 2.50
37 Edgar Bennett .30 .75
38 Robert Brooks .40 1.00
39 Brett Favre 1.25 3.00
40 Reggie White .40 1.00
41 Chris Chandler .30 .75
42 Eddie George RC 1.00 2.50
43 Steve McNair .50 1.25
44 Chris Sanders .30 .75
45 Ken Dilger .30 .75
46 Marshall Faulk .50 1.25
47 Jim Harbaugh .30 .75
48 Mark Brunell .50 1.25
49 Keenan McCardell .40 1.00
50 James O.Stewart .30 .75
51 Marcus Allen .40 1.00
52 Steve Bono .20 .50
53 Greg Hill .30 .75
54 Tamarick Vanover .30 .75
55 Karim Abdul-Jabbar RC .40 1.00
56 Dan Marino 1.25 3.00
57 Zach Thomas RC .75 2.00
58 Cris Carter .40 1.00
59 Warren Moon .30 .75
60 Robert Smith .30 .75
61 Drew Bledsoe .50 1.25
62 Terry Glenn RC .75 2.00
63 Curtis Martin .50 1.25
64 Mario Bates .30 .75
65 Jim Everett .20 .50
66 Haywood Jeffires .20 .50
67 Dave Brown .20 .50
68 Rodney Hampton .30 .75
69 Amani Toomer RC .75 2.00
70 Adrian Murrell .30 .75
71 Neil O'Donnell .30 .75
72 Alex Van Dyke RC .30 .75
73 Tim Brown .40 1.00
74 Jeff Hostetler .20 .50
75 Napoleon Kaufman .40 1.00
76 Irving Fryar .30 .75
77 Chris T. Jones .30 .75
78 Ricky Watters .30 .75
79 Jerome Bettis .40 1.00
80 Kordell Stewart .40 1.00
81 Tony Banks RC .40 1.00
82 Eddie Kennison RC .40 1.00
83 Lawrence Phillips RC .40 1.00
84 Stan Humphries .30 .75
85 Tony Martin .30 .75
86 Leonard Russell .20 .50
87 Junior Seau .40 1.00
88 Jerry Rice .60 1.50
89 J.J. Stokes .40 1.00
90 Tommy Vardell .20 .50
91 Steve Young .50 1.25
92 Joey Galloway .40 1.00
93 Rick Mirer .30 .75
94 Chris Warren .30 .75
95 Mike Alstott RC .75 2.00
96 Trent Dilfer .40 1.00
97 Nilo Silvan .20 .50
98 Terry Allen .30 .75
99 Gus Frerotte .30 .75
100 Michael Westbrook .40 1.00
P1 Chris Warren Promo .40 1.00
P2 Chris Warren Promo .40 1.00
P3 Chris Warren Promo .40 1.00
P4 Chris Warren Promo .40 1.00

1996 Pacific Litho-Cel Bronze

COMPLETE SET (100) 150.00 300.00
*VETS: 2.5X TO 6X BASIC LITHO
*ROOKIES: 1.2X TO 3X BASIC LITHO
STATED ODDS 3:25 RETAIL

1996 Pacific Litho-Cel Silver

COMPLETE SET (100) 125.00 250.00
*VETS: 2X TO 5X BASIC LITHO
*ROOKIES 1X TO 2.5X BASIC LITHO
STATED ODDS 3:25 HOBBY

1996 Pacific Litho-Cel Feature Performers

Randomly inserted in packs at a rate of one in 25, this 20-card set features top NFL player images on a gold foil background with the outline of the team's helmet imprinted on the lower half. The backs carry a paragraph about the player beside a color player photo.

COMPLETE SET (20) 40.00 100.00
STATED ODDS 1:25
FP1 Jim Kelly 2.00 5.00
FP2 Troy Aikman 3.00 8.00
FP3 Deion Sanders 2.50 6.00
FP4 Emmitt Smith 5.00 12.00
FP5 Terrell Davis 2.50 6.00
FP6 John Elway 6.00 15.00
FP7 Herman Moore 1.00 2.50
FP8 Barry Sanders 5.00 12.00
FP9 Robert Brooks 2.00 5.00
FP10 Brett Favre 6.00 15.00
FP11 Eddie George 2.50 6.00
FP12 Jim Harbaugh 1.00 2.50
FP13 Marcus Allen 2.00 5.00
FP14 Karim Abdul-Jabbar 1.00 2.50
FP15 Dan Marino 6.00 15.00
FP16 Joey Galloway 2.00 5.00
FP17 Curtis Martin 2.50 6.00
FP18 Jerome Bettis 2.00 5.00
FP19 Jerry Rice 3.00 8.00
FP20 Steve Young 2.50 6.00

1996 Pacific Litho-Cel Game Time

Randomly inserted one in every pack, this 96-card set features color player photos on the fronts with a border of different team ticket stubs. Cards #GT97-GT100 are printed with a gold foil border. The backs carry a player head photo in a stopwatch frame with a paragraph about the player.

COMPLETE SET (100) 7.50 20.00
ONLY #GT97-GT100 PRINTED IN GOLD FOIL
ONE GAME TIME PER PACK
GT1 Eddie George .25 .60
GT2 Larry Bowie .02 .10
GT3 Jarius Hayes .02 .10
GT4 Jamal Anderson .15 .40
GT5 Ernest Hunter .02 .10
GT6 Darick Holmes .02 .10
GT7 Kerry Collins .15 .40
GT8 Raymont Harris .02 .10
GT9 Jeff Blake .15 .40
GT10 Troy Aikman .40 1.00
GT11 Terrell Davis .30 .75
GT12 Kevin Glover .02 .10
GT13 Brett Favre .75 2.00
GT14 Al Del Greco .02 .10
GT15 Marshall Faulk .25 .60
GT16 Bryan Barker .02 .10
GT17 Rich Gannon .15 .40
GT18 Dwight Hollier .02 .10
GT19 Dixon Edwards .02 .10
GT20 Drew Bledsoe .25 .60
GT21 Paul Green .02 .10
GT22 Lawrence Dawsey .02 .10
GT23 Ron Carpenter DB .02 .10
GT24 Joe Aska .02 .10
GT25 Joe Panos .02 .10
GT26 Norm Johnson .02 .10
GT27 Tony Banks .15 .40
GT28 Darren Bennett .02 .10
GT29 Steve Israel .02 .10
GT30 Michael Barber .02 .10
GT31 Dexter Nottage .02 .10
GT32 Kwamie Lassiter .15 .40
GT33 Travis Hall .02 .10
GT34 Greg Montgomery .02 .10
GT35 Jim Kelly .15 .40
GT36 Matt Elliott .02 .10
GT37 Jack Jackson .02 .10
GT38 Ki-Jana Carter .07 .20
GT39 Deion Sanders .25 .60
GT40 Jason Elam .07 .20
GT41 Johnnie Morton .07 .20
GT42 Darius Holland .02 .10
GT43 Sheddrick Wilson .02 .10
GT44 Derrick Frazier .02 .10
GT45 Travis Davis .02 .10
GT46 Pellom McDaniels .02 .10
GT47 Dan Marino .75 2.00
GT48 Ben Hanks .02 .10
GT49 Tedy Bruschi 2.50 6.00
GT50 Tommy Hodson .02 .10
GT51 Amani Toomer .20 .50
GT52 Brian Hansen .02 .10
GT53 Paul Butcher .02 .10
GT54 Kevin Turner .02 .10
GT55 Darren Perry .02 .10
GT56 Mike Gruttadauria .02 .10
GT57 Charlie Jones .02 .10
GT58 Iheanyi Uwaezuoke .02 .10
GT59 Glenn Montgomery .02 .10
GT60 Mike Alstott .20 .50
GT61 Joe Patton .02 .10
GT62 Leeland McElroy .07 .20
GT63 Robbie Tobeck .02 .10
GT64 Vinny Testaverde .07 .20
GT65 Chris Spielman .02 .10
GT66 Anthony Johnson .07 .20
GT67 Todd Sauerbrun .02 .10
GT68 Jeff Hill .02 .10
GT69 Emmitt Smith .60 1.50
GT70 John Elway .75 2.00
GT71 Barry Sanders .60 1.50
GT72 Brian Williams LB .02 .10
GT73 Chris Gardocki .02 .10
GT74 Jimmy Smith .15 .40
GT75 Ricky Siglar .02 .10
GT76 Tim Ruddy .02 .10
GT77 Moe Williams .40 1.00
GT78 Willie Clay .02 .10
GT79 Henry Lusk .02 .10
GT80 Brian Williams OL .02 .10
GT81 Ronald Moore .02 .10
GT82 Trey Junkin .02 .10
GT83 James Willis .02 .10
GT84 Joel Steed .02 .10
GT85 Jamie Martin .75 2.00
GT86 Shawn Lee .02 .10
GT87 Steve Young .30 .75
GT88 Barrett Robbins .02 .10
GT89 Charles Dimry .02 .10
GT90 Darryl Pounds .02 .10
GT91 Herschel Walker .07 .20
GT92 Bill Romanowski .02 .10
GT93 David Tate .02 .10
GT94 Marrio Grier .02 .10
GT95 Rodney Young .02 .10
GT96 Lamar Smith .15 .40
GT97 Don Beebe .10 .30
GT98 Ty Detmer .25 .60
GT99 Ted Popson .10 .30
GT100 Natrone Means .25 .60

1996 Pacific Litho-Cel Litho-Proof

Randomly inserted in packs at a rate of one in 97, this 36-card set features borderless color action player photos with the words "Litho-Proof" printed down the right side. Only 360 of each card was produced with each sequentially numbered.

COMPLETE SET (36) 150.00 300.00
STATED PRINT RUN 360 SERIAL #'d SETS
STATED ODDS 1:97
*CERTIFIED CARDS: .8X TO 2X BASIC INSERTS
CERTIFIED STATED ODDS 1:481
1 Jim Kelly 5.00 12.00
2 Kerry Collins 4.00 10.00
3 Rashaan Salaam 2.50 6.00
4 Jeff Blake 3.00 8.00
5 Carl Pickens 2.50 6.00
6 Troy Aikman 6.00 15.00
7 Deion Sanders 5.00 12.00
8 Emmitt Smith 10.00 25.00
9 Terrell Davis 5.00 12.00
10 John Elway 12.00 30.00
11 Herman Moore 2.50 6.00
12 Barry Sanders 10.00 25.00
13 Robert Brooks 3.00 8.00
14 Brett Favre 12.00 30.00
15 Reggie White 4.00 10.00
16 Eddie George 4.00 10.00
17 Marshall Faulk 5.00 12.00
18 Jim Harbaugh 3.00 8.00
19 Mark Brunell 4.00 10.00
20 Marcus Allen 4.00 10.00
21 Steve Bono 2.50 6.00
22 Karim Abdul-Jabbar 2.50 6.00
23 Dan Marino 12.00 30.00
24 Warren Moon 3.00 8.00
25 Drew Bledsoe 4.00 10.00
26 Curtis Martin 5.00 12.00
27 Amani Toomer 3.00 8.00
28 Tim Brown 4.00 10.00
29 Napoleon Kaufman 2.50 6.00
30 Ricky Watters 3.00 8.00
31 Jerome Bettis 4.00 10.00
32 Kordell Stewart 3.00 8.00
33 Jerry Rice 6.00 15.00
34 Steve Young 5.00 12.00
35 Joey Galloway 3.00 8.00
36 Terry Allen 3.00 8.00

1996 Pacific Litho-Cel Moments in Time

Randomly inserted in packs at a rate of one in 49, this 20-card set features action color player photos on a die-cut card with a scoreboard designed border. The backs carry another player photo with the particular game date and a paragraph about the pictured player's great moments of that game.

COMPLETE SET (20) 75.00 200.00
STATED ODDS 1:49
MT1 Jim Kelly 3.00 8.00
MT2 Kerry Collins 3.00 8.00
MT3 Rashaan Salaam 1.50 4.00
MT4 Troy Aikman 5.00 12.00
MT5 Deion Sanders 4.00 10.00
MT6 Emmitt Smith 8.00 20.00
MT7 Terrell Davis 4.00 10.00
MT8 John Elway 10.00 25.00
MT9 Barry Sanders 8.00 20.00
MT10 Robert Brooks 3.00 8.00
MT11 Brett Favre 10.00 25.00
MT12 Marshall Faulk 4.00 10.00
MT13 Jim Harbaugh 1.50 4.00
MT14 Steve Bono 1.00 2.50
MT15 Dan Marino 10.00 25.00
MT16 Drew Bledsoe 4.00 10.00
MT17 Curtis Martin 4.00 10.00
MT18 Jerry Rice 5.00 12.00
MT19 Steve Young 4.00 10.00
MT20 Terry Allen 1.50 4.00

1998 Pacific Omega

The 1998 Pacific Omega set was issued in one series totalling 250 standard size cards and distributed in eight-card packs with a suggested retail price of $1.99. The fronts feature color action player photos etched with silver foil. The backs carry player information and career statistics.

COMPLETE SET (250) 15.00 40.00
1 Larry Centers .08 .25
2 Rob Moore .15 .40
3 Michael Pittman RC .75 1.50
4 Jake Plummer .25 .60
5 Simeon Rice .15 .40
6 Frank Sanders .15 .40
7 Eric Swann .08 .25
8 Morten Andersen .08 .25
9 Jamal Anderson .25 .60
10 Chris Chandler .15 .40
11 Harold Green .08 .25
12 Byron Hanspard .08 .25
13 Terance Mathis .15 .40
14 O.J. Santiago .08 .25
15 Peter Boulware .08 .25
16 Jay Graham .08 .25
17 Eric Green .08 .25
18 Michael Jackson .08 .25
19 Jermaine Lewis .15 .40
20 Ray Lewis .25 .60
21 Jonathan Ogden .08 .25
22 Eric Zeier .15 .40
23 Steve Christie .08 .25
24 Todd Collins .08 .25
25 Quinn Early .08 .25
26 Eric Moulds .25 .60
27 Andre Reed .15 .40
28 Antowain Smith .25 .60
29 Bruce Smith .15 .40
30 Thurman Thomas .25 .60
31 Ted Washington .08 .25
32 Michael Bates .08 .25
33 Tim Biakabutuka .15 .40
34 Mark Carrier .08 .25
35 Rae Carruth .08 .25
36 Kerry Collins .15 .40
37 Kevin Greene .15 .40
38 Fred Lane .08 .25
39 Muhsin Muhammad .15 .40
40 Wesley Walls .15 .40
41 Curtis Conway .15 .40
42 Bobby Engram .15 .40
43 Curtis Enis RC .20 .50
44 Walt Harris .08 .25
45 Erik Kramer .08 .25
46 Chris Penn .08 .25
47 Ryan Wetnight RC .08 .25
48 Jeff Blake .15 .40
49 Ki-Jana Carter .08 .25
50 John Copeland .08 .25
51 Corey Dillon .25 .60
52 Tony McGee .08 .25
53 Carl Pickens .15 .40
54 Darnay Scott .15 .40
55 Takeo Spikes RC .50 1.25
56 Troy Aikman .50 1.25
57 Eric Bjornson .08 .25
58 Greg Ellis RC .20 .50
59 Michael Irvin .25 .60
60 Daryl Johnston .15 .40
61 David LaFleur .08 .25
62 Deion Sanders .25 .60
63 Emmitt Smith .75 2.00
64 Jason Garrett RC .40 1.00
65 Nicky Sualua RC .15 .40
66 Steve Atwater .08 .25
67 Terrell Davis .25 .60
68 John Elway 1.00 2.50
69 Brian Griese RC 1.00 2.50
70 Ed McCaffrey .15 .40
71 John Mobley .08 .25
72 Marcus Nash RC .20 .50
73 Shannon Sharpe .15 .40
74 Neil Smith .15 .40
75 Rod Smith .15 .40
76 Charlie Batch RC .50 1.25
77 Germane Crowell RC .30 .75
78 Jason Hanson .08 .25
79 Scott Mitchell .15 .40
80 Herman Moore .15 .40
81 Johnnie Morton .15 .40
82 Barry Sanders .75 2.00
83 Tommy Vardell .08 .25
84 Robert Brooks .15 .40
85 Gilbert Brown .08 .25
86 LeRoy Butler .08 .25
87 Mark Chmura .15 .40
88 Brett Favre 1.00 2.50
89 Antonio Freeman .25 .60
90 William Henderson .15 .40
91 Vonnie Holliday RC .30 .75
92 Dorsey Levens .25 .60
93 Reggie White .25 .60
94 Aaron Bailey .08 .25
95 Quentin Coryatt .08 .25
96 Zack Crockett .08 .25
97 Ken Dilger .08 .25
98 Marshall Faulk .30 .75
99 E.G. Green RC .30 .75
100 Marvin Harrison .25 .60
101 Peyton Manning RC 6.00 15.00
102 Jerome Pathon RC .50 1.25
103 Tavian Banks RC .30 .75
104 Tony Boselli .08 .25
105 Tony Brackens .08 .25
106 Mark Brunell .25 .60
107 Kevin Hardy .08 .25
108 Keenan McCardell .15 .40
109 Pete Mitchell .08 .25
110 Jimmy Smith .15 .40
111 James Stewart .15 .40
112 Fred Taylor RC .75 2.00
113 Kimble Anders .15 .40
114 Dale Carter .08 .25
115 Tony Gonzalez .25 .60
116 Elvis Grbac .15 .40
117 Donnell Bennett .08 .25
118 Andre Rison .15 .40
119 Rashaan Shehee RC .30 .75
120 Derrick Thomas .25 .60
121 Tamarick Vanover .08 .25
122 Karim Abdul-Jabbar .25 .60
123 John Avery RC .30 .75
124 Troy Drayton .08 .25
125 John Dutton RC .20 .50
126 Craig Erickson .08 .25
127 Dan Marino 1.00 2.50
128 O.J. McDuffie .15 .40
129 Jerris McPhail .08 .25
130 Stanley Pritchett .08 .25
131 Larry Shannon RC .20 .50
132 Zach Thomas .25 .60
133 Cris Carter .25 .60
134 Randall Cunningham .25 .60
135 Andrew Glover .08 .25
136 Brad Johnson .25 .60
137 Randall McDaniel .08 .25
138 David Palmer .08 .25
139 John Randle .15 .40
140 Jake Reed .15 .40
141 Robert Smith .25 .60
142 Drew Bledsoe .40 1.00
143 Ben Coates .15 .40
144 Robert Edwards RC .30 .75
145 Terry Glenn .25 .60
146 Shawn Jefferson .08 .25
147 Willie McGinest .08 .25
148 Tony Simmons RC .30 .75
149 Chris Slade .08 .25
150 Troy Davis .08 .25
151 Mark Fields .08 .25
152 Andre Hastings .08 .25
153 Billy Joe Hobert .08 .25
154 William Roaf .08 .25
155 Heath Shuler .08 .25
156 Danny Wuerffel .15 .40
157 Ray Zellars .08 .25
158 Jessie Armstead .08 .25
159 Tiki Barber .25 .60
160 Chris Calloway .08 .25
161 Mike Cherry .08 .25
162 Danny Kanell .15 .40
163 Amani Toomer .15 .40
164 Charles Way .08 .25
165 Tyrone Wheatley .15 .40
166 Kyle Brady .08 .25
167 Wayne Chrebet .25 .60
168 Glenn Foley .15 .40
169 Scott Frost RC .20 .50
170 Keyshawn Johnson .25 .60
171 Leon Johnson .08 .25
172 Alex Van Dyke .08 .25
173 Dedric Ward .08 .25
174 Tim Brown .25 .60
175 Rickey Dudley .08 .25
176 Jeff George .15 .40
177 Desmond Howard .15 .40
178 James Jett .15 .40
179 Napoleon Kaufman .25 .60
180 Darrell Russell .08 .25
181 Charles Woodson RC 1.25 3.00
182 Jason Dunn .08 .25
183 Irving Fryar .15 .40
184 Charlie Garner .15 .40
185 Bobby Hoying .15 .40
186 Chris T. Jones .08 .25
187 Michael Timpson .08 .25
188 Kevin Turner .08 .25
189 Jerome Bettis .25 .60
190 Will Blackwell .08 .25
191 Mark Bruener .08 .25
192 Charles Johnson .08 .25
193 George Jones .08 .25
194 Levon Kirkland .08 .25
195 Kordell Stewart .25 .60
196 Hines Ward RC 2.50 5.00
197 Tony Banks .15 .40
198 Isaac Bruce .25 .60
199 Ernie Conwell .08 .25
200 Robert Holcombe RC .30 .75
201 Eddie Kennison .15 .40
202 Amp Lee .08 .25
203 Orlando Pace .08 .25
204 Charlie Jones .08 .25
205 Freddie Jones .08 .25
206 Ryan Leaf RC .50 1.25
207 Natrone Means .15 .40
208 Junior Seau .25 .60
209 Bryan Still .08 .25
210 Greg Clark .08 .25
211 Jim Druckenmiller .08 .25
212 Marc Edwards .08 .25
213 Garrison Hearst .25 .60
214 Terrell Owens .25 .60
215 Jerry Rice .50 1.25
216 J.J. Stokes .15 .40
217 Bryant Young .08 .25
218 Steve Young .30 .75
219 Chad Brown .08 .25
220 Joey Galloway .15 .40
221 Cortez Kennedy .08 .25
222 Jon Kitna .25 .60
223 James McKnight .25 .60
224 Warren Moon .25 .60
225 Michael Sinclair .08 .25
226 Ricky Watters .15 .40
227 Mike Alstott .25 .60
228 Reidel Anthony .15 .40
229 Derrick Brooks .25 .60
230 Trent Dilfer .25 .60
231 Warrick Dunn .25 .60
232 Dave Moore .08 .25
233 Hardy Nickerson .08 .25
234 Warren Sapp .15 .40
235 Karl Williams .08 .25
236 Willie Davis .08 .25
237 Kevin Dyson RC .50 1.25
238 Eddie George .25 .60
239 Derrick Mason .15 .40
240 Steve McNair .25 .60
241 Chris Sanders .08 .25
242 Frank Wycheck .08 .25
243 Terry Allen .25 .60
244 Jamie Asher .08 .25
245 Gus Frerotte .08 .25
246 Darrell Green .15 .40
247 Skip Hicks RC .30 .75
248 Brian Mitchell .08 .25
249 Leslie Shepherd .08 .25
250 Michael Westbrook .15 .40

1998 Pacific Omega EO Portraits

Randomly inserted in packs at a rate of one in 73, this 20-card set features color action player photos with the shadow of the player's head printed over the photos using Electro-Optical technology.

COMPLETE SET (20) 50.00 120.00
STATED ODDS 1:73
1 Jake Plummer 2.00 5.00
2 Corey Dillon 2.00 5.00
3 Troy Aikman 4.00 10.00
4 Emmitt Smith 6.00 15.00
5 Terrell Davis 2.00 5.00
6 John Elway 8.00 20.00
7 Barry Sanders 6.00 15.00
8 Brett Favre 8.00 20.00
9 Dorsey Levens 2.00 5.00
10 Peyton Manning 8.00 20.00
11 Mark Brunell 2.00 5.00
12 Dan Marino 8.00 20.00
13 Drew Bledsoe 3.00 8.00
14 Jerome Bettis 2.00 5.00
15 Kordell Stewart 2.00 5.00
16 Ryan Leaf .60 1.50
17 Jerry Rice 4.00 10.00
18 Steve Young 2.50 6.00
19 Warrick Dunn 2.00 5.00
20 Eddie George 2.00 5.00

1998 Pacific Omega Face To Face

Randomly inserted in packs at the rate of one in 145, this 10-card set features color action photos of two superstars printed on one card to look as if they are staring at each other.

COMPLETE SET (10) 125.00 250.00
STATED ODDS 1:145
1 P.Manning R.Leaf 10.00 25.00
2 B.Sanders W.Dunn 12.50 30.00
3 D.Marino J.Elway 15.00 40.00
4 J.Rice A.Freeman 7.50 20.00
5 J.Plummer D.Bledsoe 6.00 15.00
6 C.Dillon E.George 6.00 15.00
7 E.Smith T.Davis 12.50 30.00
8 S.Young M.Brunell 6.00 15.00
9 K.Stewart S.McNair 6.00 15.00
10 T.Aikman B.Favre 15.00 40.00

1998 Pacific Omega Online

Randomly inserted in packs at the rate of four in 37, this 36-card set features color action photos of top players printed on fully foiled etched design cards with his team's web site address at the bottom. The player's name is printed on a facsimile computer keyboard under his picture.

COMPLETE SET (36) 30.00 80.00
STATED ODDS 4:37
1 Jake Plummer 1.25 3.00
2 Antowain Smith .75 2.00
3 Curtis Enis .40 1.00
4 Corey Dillon 1.25 3.00
5 Troy Aikman 2.50 6.00
6 Emmitt Smith 4.00 10.00
7 Terrell Davis 1.25 3.00
8 John Elway 5.00 12.00
9 Shannon Sharpe .75 2.00
10 Herman Moore .40 1.00
11 Barry Sanders 4.00 10.00
12 Brett Favre 5.00 12.00
13 Antonio Freeman .75 2.00
14 Dorsey Levens .40 1.00
15 Peyton Manning 8.00 20.00
16 Marshall Faulk 1.50 4.00
17 Mark Brunell 1.25 3.00
18 Fred Taylor 1.25 3.00
19 Dan Marino 5.00 12.00
20 Robert Smith .40 1.00
21 Drew Bledsoe 2.00 5.00
22 Tiki Barber 1.25 3.00
23 Danny Kanell .40 1.00
24 Tim Brown 1.25 3.00
25 Napoleon Kaufman .75 2.00
26 Charles Woodson 1.50 4.00
27 Jerome Bettis 1.25 3.00
28 Kordell Stewart 1.25 3.00
29 Ryan Leaf .40 1.00
30 Jerry Rice 2.50 6.00
31 Steve Young 1.50 4.00
32 Joey Galloway .75 2.00
33 Trent Dilfer .75 2.00
34 Warrick Dunn 1.25 3.00
35 Eddie George 1.25 3.00
36 Steve McNair 1.25 3.00

1998 Pacific Omega Prisms

Randomly inserted in packs at the rate of one in 37, this 20-card set features color action player images printed on prismatic foil cards.

COMPLETE SET (20) 60.00 150.00
STATED ODDS 1:37
1 Jake Plummer 1.50 4.00
2 Corey Dillon 1.50 4.00
3 Troy Aikman 3.00 8.00
4 Emmitt Smith 5.00 12.00
5 Terrell Davis 1.50 4.00
6 John Elway 6.00 15.00
7 Barry Sanders 5.00 12.00
8 Brett Favre 6.00 15.00
9 Peyton Manning 12.00 30.00
10 Mark Brunell 1.50 4.00
11 Dan Marino 6.00 15.00
12 Drew Bledsoe 2.50 6.00
13 Napoleon Kaufman 1.50 4.00
14 Jerome Bettis 1.50 4.00
15 Kordell Stewart 1.50 4.00
16 Ryan Leaf 1.00 2.50
17 Jerry Rice 3.00 8.00
18 Steve Young 2.00 5.00
19 Warrick Dunn 1.50 4.00
20 Eddie George 1.50 4.00

1998 Pacific Omega Rising Stars

Randomly inserted in packs at a rate of 4:37, this set features young players printed with a silver foil format. A hobby only parallel set was also issued with each card featuring one of five different color foil logo treatments on the front. Each parallel was serial numbered as follows: Blue foil cards serially numbered to 100; Red foil cards serially numbered to 75; Green foil cards serially numbered to 50; Purple foil cards serially numbered to 25; and Gold foil cards serially numbered to 1.

COMPLETE SET (30) 40.00 80.00
STATED ODDS 4:37 HOBBY
*BLUE/100: 3X TO 8X SILVER
*GREEN/50: 5X TO 12X SILVER
*PURPLE/25: 8X TO 20X SILVER
*RED/75: 4X TO 10X SILVER
UNPRICED GOLD PRINT RUN 1
1 Michael Pittman .75 2.00
2 Keith Brooking .30 .75
3 Duane Starks .30 .75
4 Curtis Enis .30 .75
5 Marcus Nash .30 .75
6 Brian Griese 1.50 4.00
7 Terry Fair .30 .75
8 Germane Crowell .50 1.25
9 Charlie Batch .75 2.00
10 E.G. Green .50 1.25
11 Peyton Manning 10.00 25.00
12 Jerome Pathon .75 2.00
13 Fred Taylor 1.25 3.00
14 Tavian Banks .50 1.25
15 Rashaan Shehee .50 1.25
16 John Avery .50 1.25
17 John Dutton .30 .75
18 Robert Edwards .50 1.25
19 Tony Simmons .50 1.25
20 Joe Jurevicius .50 1.25
21 Scott Frost .30 .75
22 Charles Woodson 1.25 3.00
23 Hines Ward 3.00 8.00
24 Robert Holcombe .50 1.25
25 Az-Zahir Hakim .75 2.00
26 Ryan Leaf .75 2.00
27 Ahman Green .75 2.00
28 Kevin Dyson .75 2.00
29 Stephen Alexander .50 1.25
30 Skip Hicks .50 1.25

1999 Pacific Omega

Released as a 250-card set, the 1999 Pacific Omega football features single and dual prospect cards, and base set cards sporting three action photos of each player and are accentuated by foil highlights. Packaged in 36-pack boxes with packs contain six cards, Pacific Omega carried a suggested retail price of $1.99.

COMPLETE SET (250) 20.00 40.00
1 Mario Bates .12 .30
2 David Boston RC .20 .50
3 Rob Moore .12 .30
4 Adrian Murrell .12 .30
5 Jake Plummer .12 .30
6 Frank Sanders .12 .30
7 Aeneas Williams .12 .30
8 J.Makovicka/L.Shelton RC .20 .50
9 Jamal Anderson .15 .40
10 Ray Buchanan .12 .30
11 Chris Chandler .15 .40
12 Tim Dwight .15 .40
13 Byron Hanspard .12 .30
14 Terance Mathis .12 .30
15 O.J. Santiago .12 .30
16 D.Kanell C.Calloway .12 .30
17 Peter Boulware .12 .30
18 Priest Holmes .12 .30
19 Patrick Johnson .12 .30
20 Jermaine Lewis .12 .30
21 Ray Lewis .20 .50
22 Michael McCrary .12 .30
23 Jonathan Ogden .15 .40
24 T.Banks S.Mitchell .15 .40
25 Doug Flutie .20 .50
26 Rob Johnson .15 .40
27 Eric Moulds .12 .30
28 Andre Reed .20 .50
29 Antowain Smith .12 .30
30 Bruce Smith .15 .40
31 Kevin Williams .12 .30
32 S.Bryson/P.Price RC .20 .50
33 Steve Beuerlein .15 .40
34 Tim Biakabutuka .15 .40
35 Rae Carruth .12 .30
36 Dameyune Craig RC .30 .75
37 William Floyd .15 .40
38 Kevin Greene .20 .50
39 Muhsin Muhammad .12 .30
40 Wesley Walls .15 .40
41 Edgar Bennett .15 .40
42 Robert Chancey RC .20 .50
43 Curtis Conway .15 .40
44 Bobby Engram .12 .30
45 Curtis Enis .12 .30
46 Cade McNown RC .20 .50
47 Ryan Wetnight .12 .30
48 D.Bates/Mar.Booker RC .20 .50
49 Jeff Blake .15 .40
50 Scott Covington RC .20 .50
51 Corey Dillon .12 .30
52 James Hundon .12 .30
53 Carl Pickens .15 .40
54 Darnay Scott .12 .30
55 Akili Smith RC .20 .50
56 Craig Yeast RC .20 .50
57 Tim Couch RC .25 .60
58 Ty Detmer .12 .30
59 Marc Edwards .15 .40
60 Kevin Johnson RC .25 .60
61 Terry Kirby .12 .30
62 Sedrick Shaw .12 .30
63 Leslie Shepherd .12 .30
64 Chiaverini/McCutcheon RC .20 .50
65 Troy Aikman .25 .60
66 Michael Irvin .20 .50
67 David LaFleur .12 .30
68 Wane McGarity RC .20 .50
69 Ernie Mills .12 .30
70 Deion Sanders .15 .40
71 Emmitt Smith .30 .75
72 R.Ismail J.McKnight .15 .40
73 Bubby Brister .12 .30
74 Byron Chamberlain RC .25 .60
75 Terrell Davis .15 .40
76 Olandis Gary RC .30 .75
77 Brian Griese .12 .30
78 Ed McCaffrey .15 .40
79 Shannon Sharpe .15 .40
80 Rod Smith .15 .40
81 T.McGriff/A.Wilson RC .30 .75
82 Charlie Batch .12 .30
83 Chris Claiborne RC .20 .50
84 Germane Crowell .12 .30
85 Terry Fair .12 .30
86 Sedrick Irvin RC .20 .50
87 Herman Moore .15 .40
88 Johnnie Morton .15 .40
89 Barry Sanders .30 .75
90 Mark Chmura .12 .30
91 Brett Favre .40 1.00
92 Antonio Freeman .15 .40
93 Desmond Howard .15 .40
94 Dorsey Levens .15 .40
95 Derrick Mayes .12 .30
96 Bill Schroeder .15 .40
97 A.Brooks/D.Miller RC .25 .60
98 E.G. Green .12 .30
99 Marvin Harrison .15 .40
100 Edgerrin James RC .30 .75
101 Peyton Manning .80 1.50
102 Jerome Pathon .12 .30
103 Marcus Pollard .12 .30
104 Ken Dilger .12 .30
105 Derrick Alexander WR .12 .30
106 Reggie Barlow .12 .30
107 Tony Boselli .15 .40

108 Mark Brunell .15 .40
109 George Jones .12 .30
110 Keenan McCardell .15 .40
111 Jimmy Smith .15 .40
112 James Stewart .12 .30
113 Fred Taylor .12 .30
114 Kimble Anders .12 .30
115 Mike Cloud RC .20 .50
116 Tony Gonzalez .15 .40
117 Elvis Grbac .12 .30
118 Byron Bam Morris .12 .30
119 Andre Rison .15 .40
120 Derrick Thomas .20 .50
121 Karim Abdul-Jabbar .12 .30
122 Oronde Gadsden .12 .30
123 James Johnson RC .20 .50
124 Rob Konrad RC .20 .50
125 Dan Marino .40 1.00
126 O.J. McDuffie .15 .40
127 Lamar Thomas .12 .30
128 Zach Thomas .15 .40
129 Cris Carter .20 .50
130 Daunte Culpepper RC .30 .75
131 Randall Cunningham .15 .40
132 Matthew Hatchette .15 .40
133 Leroy Hoard .12 .30
134 David Palmer .12 .30
135 John Randle .20 .50
136 Randy Moss .15 .40
137 Robert Smith .12 .30
138 Drew Bledsoe .15 .40
139 Ben Coates .15 .40
140 Kevin Faulk RC .20 .50
141 Terry Glenn .15 .40
142 Shawn Jefferson .12 .30
143 Ty Law .20 .50
144 Tony Simmons .12 .30
145 Bishop RC/Katzenmoyer RC .25 .60
146 Cameron Cleeland .12 .30
147 Andre Hastings .12 .30
148 Billy Joe Hobert .12 .30
149 Joe Johnson .12 .30
150 Keith Poole .12 .30
151 William Roaf .12 .30
152 Billy Joe Tolliver .12 .30
153 Ricky Williams RC .30 .75
154 Tiki Barber .15 .40
155 Gary Brown .12 .30
156 Kent Graham .12 .30
157 Ike Hilliard .12 .30
158 David Patten .15 .40
159 Jason Sehorn .15 .40
160 Amani Toomer .12 .30
161 Montgomery RC/Petit.RC .20 .50
162 Wayne Chrebet .12 .30
163 Bryan Cox .15 .40
164 Aaron Glenn .12 .30
165 Keyshawn Johnson .15 .40
166 Leon Johnson .12 .30
167 Curtis Martin .15 .40
168 Vinny Testaverde .12 .30
169 Dedric Ward .12 .30
170 Tim Brown .20 .50
171 Rickey Dudley .12 .30
172 James Jett .12 .30
173 Napoleon Kaufman .12 .30
174 Jon Ritchie .12 .30
175 Darrell Russell .12 .30
176 Charles Woodson .20 .50
177 R.Gannon .15 .40
H.Shuler
178 Hugh Douglas .15 .40
179 Donovan McNabb RC 1.50 4.00
180 Allen Rossum .15 .40
181 Duce Staley .12 .30
182 Kevin Turner .12 .30
183 C.Johnson .12 .30
D.Pederson
184 B.Gardner .20 .50
C.Martin RC
185 Jerome Bettis .20 .50
186 Mark Bruener .12 .30
187 Troy Edwards RC .20 .50
188 Courtney Hawkins .12 .30
189 Levon Kirkland .12 .30
190 Kordell Stewart .12 .30
191 Hines Ward .15 .40
192 M.Johnson/A.Zereoue RC .20 .50
193 Greg Clark .12 .30
194 Terrell Fletcher .12 .30
195 Charlie Jones .12 .30
196 Cecil Collins RC .20 .50
197 Natrone Means .15 .40
198 Mikhael Ricks .12 .30
199 Junior Seau .15 .40
200 Bryan Still .12 .30
201 Ryan Thelwell RC .20 .50
202 Garrison Hearst .12 .30
203 Terry Jackson RC .20 .50
204 R.W. McQuarters .12 .30
205 Terrell Owens .15 .40
206 Jerry Rice .50 1.25
207 J.J. Stokes .12 .30
208 L.Phillips .15 .40
T.Vardell
209 Steve Young .25 .60
210 Karsten Bailey RC .20 .50
211 Chad Brown .12 .30
212 Christian Fauria .12 .30
213 Joey Galloway .15 .40
214 Ahman Green .15 .40
215 Brock Huard RC .20 .50
216 Cortez Kennedy .15 .40
217 Jon Kitna .12 .30
218 Ricky Watters .15 .40
219 Isaac Bruce .20 .50
220 Az-Zahir Hakim .12 .30
221 June Henley RC .20 .50
222 Greg Hill .12 .30
223 Torry Holt RC .40 1.00
224 Amp Lee .12 .30
225 Ricky Proehl .12 .30
226 M.Faulk .15 .40
T.Green
227 Mike Alstott .12 .30
228 Reidel Anthony .12 .30
229 Trent Dilfer .12 .30
230 Warrick Dunn .12 .30
231 Bert Emanuel .15 .40
232 Jacquez Green .12 .30
233 Warren Sapp .15 .40
234 Shaun King RC .25 .60
McFar.RC
235 Mike Archie RC .30 .75
236 Kevin Dyson .12 .30
237 Eddie George .15 .40
238 Derrick Mason .12 .30
239 Steve McNair .15 .40
240 Yancey Thigpen .12 .30
241 Frank Wycheck .15 .40
242 Jevon Kearse RC/Hall RC .25 .60
243 Stephen Alexander .12 .30
244 Champ Bailey RC .40 1.00
245 Stephen Davis .12 .30
246 Skip Hicks .12 .30
247 James Thrash RC .30 .75
248 Michael Westbrook .12 .30
249 Dan Wilkinson .15 .40
250 B.Johnson .15 .40
L.Centers

1999 Pacific Omega Copper

*COPPER STARS: 8X TO 20X BASIC CARDS
*COPPER RCs: 3X TO 8X
COPPER STATED PRINT RUN 99 SER.#'d SETS
RANDOM INSERTS IN HOBBY PACKS

1999 Pacific Omega Gold

COMPLETE SET (250) 200.00 400.00
*GOLD STARS: 4X TO 10X BASIC CARDS
*GOLD ROOKIES: 1.5X TO 4X
GOLD STATED PRINT RUN 299 SER.#'d SETS
RANDOM INSERTS IN RETAIL PACKS

1999 Pacific Omega Platinum Blue

*PLAT.BLUE STARS: 8X TO 20X BASIC CARDS
*PLAT.BLUE ROOKIES: 3X TO 8X
PLATINUM BLUE PRINT RUN 75 SER.#'d SETS
RANDOM INSERTS IN HOBBY/RETAIL

1999 Pacific Omega Premiere Date

REM.DATE STARS: 10X TO 25X BASIC CARDS
*PREMIERE DATE ROOKIES: 4X TO 10X
PREMIERE DATE PRINT RUN 60 SER.#'d SETS

1999 Pacific Omega 5-Star Attack

Randomly inserted in packs at the rate of four in 37, this 30-card set features the most dominating offensive veterans and rookies. A five-tier parallel set was released also. It features Blue, Red, Green, Purple, and Gold foil versions of the base card and moving up each consecutive tier yields a smaller print run.

COMPLETE SET (30) 25.00 60.00
STATED ODDS 4:37
*BLUE FOILS: 2.5X TO 6X BASIC INSERTS
BLUE STATED PRINT RUN 100 SER.#'d SETS
*GREEN FOILS: 4X TO 10X BASIC INSERTS
GREEN STATED PRINT RUN 50 SER.#'d SETS
*PURPLE FOILS: 6X TO 15X BASIC INSERTS
PURPLE STATED PRINT RUN 25 SER.#'d SETS
*RED FOILS: 3X TO 8X BASIC INSERTS
RED STATED PRINT RUN 75 SER.#'d SETS
1 Chris Chandler .50 1.25
2 Tim Couch .50 1.25
3 Peyton Manning 2.50 6.00
4 Dan Marino 2.50 6.00
5 Drew Bledsoe 1.00 2.50
6 Vinny Testaverde .50 1.25
7 Randall Cunningham .75 2.00
8 Doug Flutie .75 2.00
9 Charlie Batch .75 2.00
10 Mark Brunell .75 2.00
11 Steve Young 1.00 2.50
12 Jon Kitna .75 2.00
13 Jamal Anderson .75 2.00
14 Priest Holmes 1.25 3.00
15 Emmitt Smith 1.50 4.00
16 Fred Taylor .75 2.00
17 Curtis Martin .75 2.00
18 Eddie George .75 2.00
19 Ed McCaffrey .50 1.25
20 Antonio Freeman .75 2.00
21 Randy Moss 2.00 5.00
22 Keyshawn Johnson .75 2.00
23 Terrell Owens .75 2.00
24 Joey Galloway .50 1.25
25 Cade McNown .40 1.00
26 Akili Smith .40 1.00
27 Edgerrin James 2.00 5.00
28 Daunte Culpepper 2.00 5.00
29 Ricky Williams 1.00 2.50
30 Donovan McNabb 2.50 6.00

1999 Pacific Omega Draft Class

ndomly inserted in packs at the rate of one in 145, this 10-card set boasts a dual-player card, where the featured players hold in common the same draft year.

COMPLETE SET (10) 25.00 60.00
STATED ODDS 1:145
1 D.Green 5.00 12.00
D.Marino
2 J.Rice 3.00 8.00
B.Smith
3 T.Aikman 6.00 15.00
B.Sanders
4 S.Sharpe 3.00 8.00
E.Smith
5 B.Favre 5.00 12.00
H.Moore
6 D.Bledsoe 2.00 5.00
M.Brunell
7 T.Davis 2.00 5.00
C.Martin
8 W.Dunn 2.00 5.00
J.Plummer
9 P.Manning 4.00 10.00
R.Moss
10 T.Couch 2.50 6.00
R.Williams

1999 Pacific Omega EO Portraits

ndomly inserted in packs at the rate of one in 73, this 20-card set showcases cards that contain foil portraits of the featured player.

COMPLETE SET (20) 40.00 100.00
STATED ODDS 1:73
1 Jake Plummer 1.25 3.00
2 Jamal Anderson 1.25 3.00
3 Akili Smith .60 1.50
4 Tim Couch .60 1.50
5 Troy Aikman 4.00 10.00
6 Emmitt Smith 4.00 10.00
7 Terrell Davis 2.00 5.00
8 Barry Sanders 6.00 15.00
9 Brett Favre 6.00 15.00
10 Peyton Manning 6.00 15.00
11 Mark Brunell 2.00 5.00
12 Fred Taylor 1.25 3.00
13 Dan Marino 6.00 15.00
14 Randy Moss 5.00 12.00
15 Ricky Williams 2.00 5.00
16 Curtis Martin 2.00 5.00
17 Jerry Rice 4.00 10.00
18 Jon Kitna 2.00 5.00
19 Warrick Dunn 2.00 5.00
20 Eddie George 2.00 5.00

1999 Pacific Omega Gridiron Masters

ndomly inserted in packs at the rate of four in 37, this 36-card set features both rookies and veterans who have made an impact on the NFL.

COMPLETE SET (36) 20.00 50.00
STATED ODDS 4:37
1 David Boston .40 1.00
2 Jake Plummer .40 1.00
3 Jamal Anderson .60 1.50
4 Chris Chandler .40 1.00
5 Priest Holmes 1.00 2.50
6 Doug Flutie .60 1.50
7 Akili Smith .30 .75
8 Cade McNown .30 .75
9 Tim Couch .40 1.00
10 Deion Sanders .60 1.50
11 Emmitt Smith 1.25 3.00
12 Rod Smith .40 1.00
13 Charlie Batch .60 1.50
14 Herman Moore .40 1.00
15 Barry Sanders 2.00 5.00
16 Antonio Freeman .60 1.50
17 Edgerrin James 1.50 4.00
18 Mark Brunell .60 1.50
19 Fred Taylor .60 1.50
20 Randall Cunningham .60 1.50
21 Randy Moss 1.50 4.00
22 Terry Glenn .60 1.50
23 Keyshawn Johnson .60 1.50
24 Curtis Martin .60 1.50
25 Vinny Testaverde .40 1.00
26 Donovan McNabb 2.00 5.00
27 Jerome Bettis .60 1.50
28 Terrell Owens .60 1.50
29 Jerry Rice 1.25 3.00
30 Steve Young .75 2.00
31 Joey Galloway .40 1.00
32 Jon Kitna .60 1.50
33 Warrick Dunn .60 1.50
34 Shaun King .40 1.00
35 Eddie George .60 1.50
36 Steve McNair .60 1.50

1999 Pacific Omega TD 99

Randomly inserted in packs at the rate of one in 37, this 20-card set features top touchdown scorers. Featured players include Terrell Davis, Fred Taylor and Brett Favre.

COMPLETE SET (20) 25.00 50.00
STATED ODDS 1:37
1 Jamal Anderson 1.00 2.50
2 Priest Holmes 1.50 4.00
3 Doug Flutie 1.00 2.50
4 Tim Couch .60 1.50
5 Troy Aikman 2.00 5.00
6 Emmitt Smith 2.00 5.00
7 Terrell Davis 1.00 2.50
8 Herman Moore .60 1.50
9 Brett Favre 3.00 8.00
10 Antonio Freeman 1.00 2.50
11 Mark Brunell 1.00 2.50
12 Fred Taylor 1.00 2.50
13 Randall Cunningham 1.00 2.50
14 Randy Moss 2.50 6.00
15 Drew Bledsoe 1.25 3.00
16 Terrell Owens 1.00 2.50
17 Steve Young 1.25 3.00
18 Jon Kitna 1.00 2.50
19 Warrick Dunn 1.00 2.50
20 Eddie George 1.00 2.50

2000 Pacific Omega

leased in late October 2000, Pacific Omega features a 250-card base set comprised of 150 veteran cards, 75 rookie cards sequentially numbered to 500, and 25 dual player prospect cards sequentially numbered to 500. Omega was packaged in 36-pack boxes with each pack containing six cards.

COMP.SET w/o SP's (150) 7.50 20.00
1 David Boston .15 .40
2 Dave Brown .15 .40
3 Rob Moore .15 .40
4 Jake Plummer .15 .40
5 Simeon Rice .20 .50
6 Frank Sanders .15 .40
7 Jamal Anderson .20 .50
8 Chris Chandler .20 .50
9 Tim Dwight .20 .50
10 Terance Mathis .15 .40
11 Tony Banks .15 .40
12 Peter Boulware .15 .40
13 Priest Holmes .15 .40
14 Qadry Ismail .15 .40
15 Doug Flutie .20 .50
16 Rob Johnson .20 .50
17 Jonathan Linton .15 .40
18 Eric Moulds .15 .40
19 Peerless Price .20 .50
20 Antowain Smith .20 .50
21 Steve Beuerlein .20 .50
22 Tim Biakabutuka .20 .50
23 Patrick Jeffers .15 .40
24 Muhsin Muhammad .15 .40
25 Wesley Walls .15 .40
26 Bobby Engram .15 .40
27 Curtis Enis .15 .40
28 Cade McNown .15 .40
29 Marcus Robinson .20 .50
30 Willie Anderson .15 .40
31 Michael Basnight .15 .40
32 Corey Dillon .15 .40
33 Akili Smith .15 .40
34 Tim Couch .20 .50
35 Kevin Johnson .15 .40
36 Wali Rainer .15 .40
37 Troy Aikman .30 .75
38 Dexter Coakley .15 .40
39 Rocket Ismail .20 .50
40 Emmitt Smith .40 1.00
41 Chris Warren .15 .40
42 Terrell Davis .20 .50
43 Olandis Gary .20 .50
44 Brian Griese .15 .40
45 Ed McCaffrey .20 .50
46 Rod Smith .20 .50
47 Charlie Batch .15 .40
48 Germane Crowell .15 .40
49 Herman Moore .15 .40
50 Johnnie Morton .20 .50
51 Barry Sanders .40 1.00
52 Corey Bradford .15 .40
53 Brett Favre .50 1.25
54 Antonio Freeman .20 .50
55 Dorsey Levens .20 .50
56 Bill Schroeder .20 .50
57 Ken Dilger .15 .40
58 Marvin Harrison .20 .50
59 Edgerrin James .20 .50
60 Peyton Manning .60 1.50
61 Jerome Pathon .15 .40
62 Terrence Wilkins .15 .40
63 Mark Brunell .20 .50
64 Keenan McCardell .20 .50
65 Jimmy Smith .20 .50
66 Fred Taylor .15 .40
67 Derrick Alexander .15 .40
68 Donnell Bennett .15 .40
69 Tony Gonzalez .20 .50
70 Elvis Grbac .15 .40
71 Tony Richardson RC .15 .40
72 Oronde Gadsden .20 .50
73 Damon Huard .15 .40
74 James Johnson .15 .40
75 Dan Marino .50 1.25
76 Tony Martin .20 .50
77 O.J. McDuffie .20 .50
78 Cris Carter .25 .60
79 Daunte Culpepper .20 .50
80 Randy Moss .20 .50
81 Robert Smith .15 .40
82 Drew Bledsoe .20 .50
83 Kevin Faulk .15 .40
84 Terry Glenn .20 .50
85 P.J. Franklin RC .15 .40
86 Keith Poole .15 .40
87 Ricky Williams .20 .50
88 Tiki Barber .20 .50
89 Kerry Collins .15 .40
90 Ike Hilliard .15 .40
91 Amani Toomer .15 .40
92 Wayne Chrebet .15 .40
93 Ray Lucas .15 .40
94 Curtis Martin .20 .50
95 Vinny Testaverde .15 .40
96 Tim Brown .25 .60
97 Rich Gannon .20 .50
98 James Jett .20 .50
99 Napoleon Kaufman .20 .50
100 Tyrone Wheatley .15 .40
101 Charles Woodson .25 .60
102 Brian Dawkins .25 .60
103 Charles Johnson .15 .40
104 Donovan McNabb .20 .50
105 Torrance Small .15 .40
106 Duce Staley .15 .40
107 Jerome Bettis .25 .60
108 Troy Edwards .15 .40
109 Richard Huntley .15 .40
110 Kordell Stewart .15 .40
111 Hines Ward .20 .50
112 Isaac Bruce .25 .60
113 Marshall Faulk .20 .50
114 Az-Zahir Hakim .15 .40
115 Torry Holt .20 .50
116 Tony Horne .15 .40
117 Kurt Warner .40 1.00
118 Jermaine Fazande .15 .40
119 Jeff Graham .15 .40
120 Jim Harbaugh .20 .50
121 Mikhael Ricks .15 .40
122 Junior Seau .20 .50
123 Jeff Garcia .15 .40
124 Charlie Garner .20 .50
125 Terrell Owens .20 .50
126 Jerry Rice .60 1.50
127 J.J. Stokes .20 .50
128 Jon Kitna .15 .40
129 Derrick Mayes .15 .40
130 Charlie Rogers .15 .40
131 Shawn Springs .15 .40
132 Ricky Watters .20 .50
133 Mike Alstott .15 .40
134 Reidel Anthony .15 .40
135 Warrick Dunn .15 .40
136 Jacquez Green .15 .40
137 Shaun King .15 .40
138 Warren Sapp .20 .50
139 Kevin Dyson .20 .50
140 Eddie George .20 .50
141 Jevon Kearse .15 .40
142 Steve McNair .20 .50
143 Yancey Thigpen .15 .40
144 Frank Wycheck .20 .50
145 Champ Bailey .20 .50
146 Larry Centers .15 .40
147 Albert Connell .15 .40
148 Stephen Davis .15 .40
149 Brad Johnson .20 .50
150 Michael Westbrook .15 .40
151 Thomas Jones RC 2.50 6.00
152 Jay Tant RC 2.00 5.00
153 Doug Johnson RC 2.00 5.00
154 Mareno Philyaw RC 2.00 5.00
155 Jamal Lewis RC 3.00 8.00
156 Chris Redman RC 2.00 5.00
157 Travis Taylor RC 2.00 5.00
158 Kwame Cavil RC 2.00 5.00
159 Corey Moore RC 2.00 5.00
160 Deon Grant RC 2.00 5.00
161 Frank Murphy RC 2.00 5.00
162 Dez White RC 2.00 5.00
163 Ron Dugans RC 2.00 5.00
164 Tony Hartley RC 2.00 5.00
165 Curtis Keaton RC 2.00 5.00
166 Peter Warrick RC 2.00 5.00
167 Courtney Brown RC 2.50 6.00
168 JaJuan Dawson RC 2.00 5.00
169 Dennis Northcutt RC 2.00 5.00
170 Travis Prentice RC 2.00 5.00
171 Aaron Shea RC 2.50 6.00
172 Michael Wiley RC 2.00 5.00
173 Chris Cole RC 2.50 6.00
174 Jarious Jackson RC 2.50 6.00
175 Deltha O'Neal RC 2.00 5.00
176 Reuben Droughns RC 2.00 5.00
177 Bubba Franks RC 2.00 5.00
178 Anthony Lucas RC 2.00 5.00
179 Rondell Mealey RC 2.00 5.00
180 Ibn Green RC 2.00 5.00
181 Kevin McDougal RC 2.00 5.00
182 R.Jay Soward RC 2.00 5.00
183 Shyrone Stith RC 2.00 5.00
184 Dante Hall RC 2.00 5.00
185 Frank Moreau RC 2.00 5.00
186 Sylvester Morris RC 2.00 5.00
187 Deon Dyer RC 2.00 5.00
188 Ben Kelly RC 2.00 5.00
189 Quinton Spotwood RC 2.00 5.00
190 Troy Walters RC 2.00 5.00
191 Tom Brady RC 200.00 400.00
192 J.R. Redmond RC 2.00 5.00
193 David Stachelski RC 2.00 5.00
194 Marc Bulger RC 2.50 6.00
195 Sherrod Gideon RC 2.00 5.00
196 Chad Morton RC 2.50 6.00
197 Ron Dayne RC 3.00 8.00
198 Anthony Becht RC 2.00 5.00
199 Laveranues Coles RC 2.50 6.00
200 Chad Pennington RC 2.50 6.00
201 Sebastian Janikowski RC 3.00 8.00
202 Marcus Knight RC 2.00 5.00
203 Jerry Porter RC 3.00 8.00
204 Todd Pinkston RC 2.00 5.00
205 Gari Scott RC 2.00 5.00
206 Plaxico Burress RC 2.50 6.00
207 Danny Farmer RC 2.00 5.00
208 Tee Martin RC 2.00 5.00
209 Hank Poteat RC 2.00 5.00
210 Trung Canidate RC 2.00 5.00
211 Patrick Batteaux RC 2.00 5.00
212 Trevor Gaylor RC 2.00 5.00
213 Ronney Jenkins RC 2.00 5.00
214 Terrence McCaskey RC 2.00 5.00
215 JaJuan Seider RC 2.00 5.00
216 Giovanni Carmazzi RC 2.00 5.00
217 Chafie Fields RC 2.00 5.00
218 Jonas Lewis RC 2.00 5.00
219 Tim Rattay RC 2.50 6.00
220 Shaun Alexander RC 3.00 8.00
221 Darrell Jackson RC 2.00 5.00
222 James Williams RC 2.00 5.00
223 Joe Hamilton RC 2.00 5.00
224 Erron Kinney RC 2.00 5.00
225 Todd Husak RC 2.00 5.00
226 P.Burress 1.25 3.00
D.Farmer
227 R.Dayne 1.50 4.00
J.Hamilton
228 P.Warrick 1.00 2.50
R.Dugans
229 T.Jones 1.25 3.00
C.Keaton
230 S.Alexander 1.50 4.00
R.Droughns
231 T.Taylor 1.00 2.50
D.Jackson
232 G.Carmazzi 1.25 3.00
T.Rattay
233 T.Canidate 1.00 2.50
J.R.Redmond
234 Syl.Morris 1.00 2.50
R.Soward
235 T.Prentice 1.00 2.50
T.Gaylor
236 T.Pinkston 1.00 2.50
S.Gideon
237 F.Murphy 1.00 2.50
D.White
238 T.Brady/C.Redman 100.00 200.00
239 J.Lewis 1.50 4.00
Tee Martin
240 R.Mealey 1.00 2.50
S.Stith
241 M.Wiley 1.25 3.00
C.Morton
242 L.Coles 1.50 4.00
S.Janikowski
243 T.Walters 1.00 2.50
T.Husak
244 M.Bulger 1.50 4.00
J.Porter
245 M.Philyaw 1.00 2.50
D.Johnson
246 D.Northcutt 1.25 3.00
C.Brown
247 J.Jackson 1.25 3.00
C.Cole
248 J.Dawson 1.00 2.50
G.Scott
249 Q.Spotwood 1.00 2.50
C.Fields
250 C.Pennington 1.25 3.00
J.Williams

2000 Pacific Omega Copper

*COPPER VETS: 10X TO 25X BASIC CARDS

2000 Pacific Omega Gold

*GOLD VETS: 6X TO 15X BASIC CARDS
GOLD/95 ODDS 1:37 RETAIL
GOLD PRINT RUN 95 SER.#'d SETS

2000 Pacific Omega Platinum Blue

*BLUE VETS: 12X TO 30X BASIC CARDS
BLUE/51 STATED ODDS 1:145
BLUE PRINT RUN 51 SER.#'d SETS

2000 Pacific Omega Premiere Date

*PREM.DATE VETS: 6X TO 15X BASIC CARD
PREMIERE DATE PRINT RUN 92 SER.#'d SETS
PREMIERE DATE/92 ODDS 1:37 HOBBY

2000 Pacific Omega AFC Conference Contenders

ndomly inserted in packs at the rate of two in 37, this 18-card set featus top players from the AFC on a red background with gold foil highlights.

COMPLETE SET (18) 10.00 25.00
STATED ODDS 2:37
1 Jamal Lewis .75 2.00
2 Akili Smith .50 1.25
3 Peter Warrick .50 1.25
4 Tim Couch .60 1.50
5 Terrell Davis .60 1.50
6 Brian Griese .50 1.25
7 Marvin Harrison .60 1.50
8 Edgerrin James .60 1.50
9 Mark Brunell .60 1.50
10 Fred Taylor .50 1.25
11 Jimmy Smith .60 1.50
12 Curtis Martin .60 1.50
13 Tim Brown .75 2.00
14 Jerome Bettis .75 2.00
15 Plaxico Burress .60 1.50
16 Jon Kitna .50 1.25
17 Eddie George .60 1.50
18 Steve McNair .60 1.50

2000 Pacific Omega Autographs

ndomly inserted in Hobby boxes at the rate of one in four and Retail boxes at the rate of one in 10, cards in this set feaure bronze or black colored foil printing on a die-cut design. Each also features an authentic player signature below the photo on the front. Kurt Warner was issued via a mail redemption card that carried an expiration date of 6/30/2001.

STATED ODDS 1:4 HOB.BOX,1:10 RET.BOX
1 Drew Bledsoe 20.00 40.00
2 Mark Brunell 6.00 15.00
3 Stephen Davis 5.00 12.00
4 Torry Holt 6.00 15.00
5 Edgerrin James 12.00 30.00
6 Kurt Warner 25.00 60.00
7 Tyrone Wheatley 5.00 12.00

2000 Pacific Omega EO Portraits

ndomly inserted in packs at the rate of one in 73, this 20-card set feaures player action photography on the left side of the card, and a laser cut player portrait on the right.

COMPLETE SET (20) 20.00 50.00
STATED ODDS 1:73
UNPRICED PARALLEL #'d OF 1 SET
1 Jake Plummer .60 1.50
2 Peter Warrick .60 1.50
3 Tim Couch .75 2.00
4 Troy Aikman 1.25 3.00
5 Emmitt Smith 1.50 4.00
6 Terrell Davis .75 2.00
7 Brett Favre 2.00 5.00
8 Edgerrin James .75 2.00
9 Peyton Manning 2.50 6.00
10 Mark Brunell .75 2.00
11 Fred Taylor .60 1.50
12 Randy Moss .75 2.00
13 Drew Bledsoe .75 2.00
14 Ricky Williams .75 2.00
15 Ron Dayne 1.00 2.50
16 Chad Pennington .75 2.00
17 Marshall Faulk .75 2.00
18 Kurt Warner 1.50 4.00
19 Jerry Rice 2.50 6.00
20 Eddie George .75 2.00

2000 Pacific Omega Fourth and Goal

ndomly inserted Hobby packs at the rate of four in 37, this 36-card set features top Wide Receivers, Quarterbacks, Running Racks, and Rookies on a base card with three borders and colors to match each respective player's NFL team. A parallel set was produced with each card serial numbered from 10 to 100-sets.

COMPLETE SET (36) 10.00 25.00
STATED ODDS 4:37 HOBBY
*1-9 PARA/100: 2X TO 5X BASIC INSERT
1-9 PARALLEL PRINT RUN 100 SETS
*10-18 PARA/50: 2.5X TO 6X BASIC INSERT
10-18 PARALLEL PRINT RUN 50 SETS
*19-27 PARA/25: 4X TO 10X BASIC INSERT
19-27 PARALLEL PRINT RUN 25 SETS
*28-36 PARA/10: 10X TO 15X BASIC INSERT
28-36 PARALLEL PRINT RUN 10 SETS
1 Eric Moulds .40 1.00
2 Marcus Robinson .50 1.25
3 Antonio Freeman .50 1.25
4 Marvin Harrison .50 1.25
5 Jimmy Smith .50 1.25
6 Cris Carter .60 1.50
7 Randy Moss .50 1.25
8 Tim Brown .60 1.50
9 Isaac Bruce .60 1.50
10 Emmitt Smith 1.00 2.50
11 Edgerrin James .50 1.25
12 Fred Taylor .40 1.00
13 Robert Smith .40 1.00
14 Curtis Martin .50 1.25
15 Marshall Faulk .50 1.25
16 Warrick Dunn .40 1.00
17 Eddie George .50 1.25
18 Stephen Davis .40 1.00
19 Steve Beuerlein .50 1.25
20 Akili Smith .40 1.00
21 Tim Couch .50 1.25
22 Brian Griese .40 1.00
23 Mark Brunell .50 1.25
24 Daunte Culpepper .50 1.25
25 Kurt Warner 1.00 2.50
26 Jon Kitna .40 1.00
27 Shaun King .40 1.00
28 Thomas Jones .40 1.00
29 Jamal Lewis .50 1.25
30 Travis Taylor .30 .75
31 Peter Warrick .30 .75
32 Ron Dayne .50 1.25
33 Chad Pennington .40 1.00
34 Plaxico Burress .40 1.00
35 Giovanni Carmazzi .40 1.00
36 Shaun Alexander .50 1.25

2000 Pacific Omega Game Worn Jerseys

Randomly inserted in packs, this 10-card set features authentic swatches of game worn jerseys.

COMPLETE SET (10) 75.00 150.00
1 Keenan McCardell 4.00 10.00
2 Fred Taylor 3.00 8.00
3 Dan Marino 10.00 25.00
4 Wayne Chrebet 3.00 8.00
5 Jerome Bettis 10.00 25.00
6 Charles Johnson 3.00 8.00
7 Donovan McNabb 4.00 10.00
8 Kevin Turner 4.00 10.00
9 Brock Huard 3.00 8.00
10 Cortez Kennedy 10.00 25.00

2000 Pacific Omega Generations

Randomly inserted in packs at the rate of one in 145, this 20-card set pairs a star rookie with a veteran player of the same position.

STATED ODDS 1:145
1 C.McNown/D.White .75 2.00
2 T.Couch/D.Northcutt 1.00 2.50
3 T.Aikman/C.Pennington 1.50 4.00
4 E.Smith/T.Jones 2.00 5.00
5 T.Davis/J.Lewis 1.25 3.00
6 B.Favre/G.Carmazzi 2.50 6.00
7 M.Harrison/T.Taylor 1.00 2.50
8 E.James/S.Alexander 1.25 3.00
9 P.Manning/T.Martin 3.00 8.00
10 M.Brunell/R.Soward 1.00 2.50
11 C.Carter/Syl.Morris 1.25 3.00
12 R.Moss/P.Warrick 1.00 2.50
13 D.Bledsoe/T.Brady 100.00 200.00
14 J.Bettis/R.Dayne 1.25 3.00
15 M.Faulk/T.Canidate 1.00 2.50
16 K.Warner/C.Redman 2.00 5.00
17 J.Rice/P.Burress 3.00 8.00
18 W.Dunn/J.Redmond .75 2.00
19 E.George/R.Droughns 1.00 2.50
20 S.Davis/T.Prentice .75 2.00

2000 Pacific Omega NFC Conference Contenders

Randomly inserted in packs at the rate of two in 37, this 18-card set featus top players from the NFC on a blue background with gold foil highlights.

COMPLETE SET (18) 10.00 25.00
STATED ODDS 2:37
1 Thomas Jones .60 1.50
2 Cade McNown .50 1.25
3 Ron Dayne .75 2.00
4 Donovan McNabb .60 1.50
5 Emmitt Smith 1.25 3.00
6 Jake Plummer .50 1.25
7 Randy Moss .60 1.50
8 Marshall Faulk .60 1.50
9 Kurt Warner 1.25 3.00
10 Ricky Williams .60 1.50
11 Marcus Robinson .60 1.50
12 Warrick Dunn .50 1.25
13 Jerry Rice 2.00 5.00
14 Jamal Anderson .60 1.50
15 Cris Carter .75 2.00
16 Brad Johnson .60 1.50
17 Stephen Davis .50 1.25
18 Shaun King .50 1.25

2000 Pacific Omega Stellar Performers

ndomly seeded in packs at the rate of one in 37, this 20-card set feautes full color action shots set against a circular bordered background. Each card contains silver foil highlights.

COMPLETE SET (20) 10.00 25.00
STATED ODDS 1:37
1 Tim Couch .50 1.25
2 Troy Aikman .75 2.00
3 Emmitt Smith 1.00 2.50
4 Brian Griese .40 1.00
5 Brett Favre 1.25 3.00
6 Edgerrin James .50 1.25
7 Peyton Manning 1.50 4.00
8 Mark Brunell .50 1.25
9 Fred Taylor .40 1.00
10 Randy Moss .50 1.25
11 Drew Bledsoe .50 1.25
12 Isaac Bruce .60 1.50
13 Marshall Faulk .50 1.25
14 Kurt Warner 1.00 2.50
15 Jerry Rice 1.50 4.00
16 Jon Kitna .40 1.00
17 Shaun King .40 1.00
18 Eddie George .50 1.25
19 Steve McNair .50 1.25
20 Stephen Davis .40 1.00

1997 Pacific Philadelphia

e 1997 Pacific Philadelphia set was issued in one series totaling 330 cards and was distributed in eight-card packs with a suggested retail of $1.49. Each pack contained five regular series cards with either three bonus cards or two bonus and one insert card. The fronts feature color action player photos in a white border. The backs carry player information and career statistics.

COMPLETE SET (330) 25.00 50.00
1 Kevin Butler .07 .20
2 Larry Centers .10 .30
3 Kent Graham .07 .20
4 Leeland McElroy .07 .20
5 Ronald McKinnon RC .10 .30
6 Johnny McWilliams .07 .20
7 Brad Otis .07 .20
8 Frank Sanders .10 .30
9 Rob Selby .07 .20
10 Cedric Smith .07 .20
11 Joe Staysniak RC .07 .20
12 Cornelius Bennett .07 .20
13 David Brandon .07 .20
14 Tyrone Brown .07 .20
15 John Burrough .07 .20
16 Browning Nagle .07 .20
17 Dan Owens .07 .20
18 Anthony Phillips .07 .20
19 Roell Preston .07 .20
20 Darnell Walker .07 .20
21 Bob Whitfield .07 .20
22 Mike Zandofsky .07 .20
23 Vashone Adams .07 .20
24 Derrick Alexander WR .10 .30
25 Harold Bishop .07 .20
26 Jeff Blackshear .07 .20
27 Donald Brady RC .07 .20
28 Mike Frederick .07 .20
29 Tim Goad .07 .20
30 DeRon Jenkins .07 .20
31 Ray Lewis .30 .75
32 Rick Lyle .07 .20
33 Byron Bam Morris .07 .20
34 Chris Brantley .07 .20
35 Jeff Burris .07 .20
36 Todd Collins .07 .20
37 Rob Coons .07 .20
38 Corbin Lacina RC .07 .20
39 Emanuel Martin .07 .20
40 Marlo Perry .07 .20
41 Shawn Price .07 .20
42 Thomas Smith .07 .20
43 Matt Stevens RC .07 .20
44 Thurman Thomas .20 .50
45 Jay Barker .07 .20
46 Tim Biakabutuka .10 .30
47 Kerry Collins .20 .50
48 Matt Elliott .07 .20
49 Howard Griffith .07 .20
50 Anthony Johnson .07 .20
51 John Kasay .07 .20
52 Muhsin Muhammad .10 .30
53 Winslow Oliver .07 .20
54 Walter Rasby .07 .20
55 Gerald Williams .07 .20
56 Mark Butterfield .07 .20
57 Bryan Cox .07 .20
58 Mike Faulkerson .07 .20
59 Paul Grasmanis .07 .20
60 Robert Green .07 .20
61 Jack Jackson .07 .20
62 Bobby Neely .07 .20
63 Todd Perry .07 .20
64 Evan Pilgrim .07 .20
65 Octus Polk .07 .20
66 Rashaan Salaam .07 .20
67 Willie Anderson .07 .20
68 Jeff Blake .10 .30
69 Scott Brumfield .07 .20
70 Jeff Cothran .07 .20
71 Gerald Dixon .07 .20
72 Garrison Hearst .10 .30
73 James Hundon RC .20 .50
74 Brian Milne .07 .20
75 Troy Sadowski .07 .20
76 Tom Tumulty .07 .20
77 Kimo von Oelhoffen RC 1.25 3.00
78 Troy Aikman .40 1.00
79 Dale Hellestrae .07 .20
80 Roger Harper .07 .20
81 Michael Irvin .20 .50
82 John Jett .07 .20
83 Kelvin Martin .07 .20
84 Deion Sanders .20 .50
85 Darrin Smith .07 .20
86 Emmitt Smith .60 1.50
87 Herschel Walker .10 .30
88 Charlie Williams .07 .20
89 Glenn Cadrez .07 .20
90 Dwayne Carswell RC .20 .50
91 Terrell Davis .25 .60
92 David Diaz-infante .07 .20
93 John Elway .75 2.00
94 Harald Hasselback .07 .20
95 Tory James .07 .20
96 Bill Musgrave .07 .20
97 Ralph Tamm .07 .20
98 Maa Tanuvasa RC .07 .20
99 Gary Zimmerman .07 .20
100 Shane Bonham .07 .20
101 Stephen Boyd RC .07 .20
102 Jeff Hartings RC .40 1.00
103 Hessley Hempstead .07 .20
104 Scott Kowalkowski .07 .20
105 Herman Moore .10 .30
106 Barry Sanders .60 1.50
107 Tony Semple .07 .20
108 Ryan Stewart .07 .20
109 Mike Wells .07 .20
110 Richard Woodley .07 .20
111 Brett Favre .75 2.00
112 Bernardo Harris RC .10 .30
113 Keith McKenzie RC .07 .20
114 Terry Mickens .07 .20
115 Doug Pederson RC .20 .50
116 Jeff Thomason RC .07 .20
117 Adam Timmerman RC .07 .20
118 Reggie White .20 .50
119 Bruce Wilkerson .07 .20
120 Gabe Wilkins RC .07 .20
121 Tyrone Williams RC .07 .20
122 Al Del Greco .07 .20
123 Anthony Dorsett .07 .20
124 Josh Evans .07 .20
125 Eddie George .20 .50
126 Lemanski Hall RC .07 .20
127 Ronnie Harmon .07 .20
128 Steve McNair .25 .60
129 Michael Roan .07 .20
130 Marcus Robertson .07 .20
131 Jon Runyan .07 .20
132 Chris Sanders .07 .20
133 Kerwin Bell .07 .20
134 Marshall Faulk .25 .60
135 Clif Groce RC .07 .20
136 Jim Harbaugh .10 .30
137 Marvin Harrison .20 .50
138 Eric Mahlum .07 .20
139 Tony Mandarich .07 .20
140 Dedric Mathis .07 .20
141 Marcus Pollard RC .07 .20
142 Scott Slutzker .07 .20
143 Mark Stock .07 .20
144 Bucky Brooks .07 .20
145 Mark Brunell .25 .60
146 Kendricke Bullard .07 .20
147 Randy Jordan .07 .20
148 Jeff Kopp .07 .20
149 Le'Shai Maston .07 .20
150 Keenan McCardell .10 .30
151 Clyde Simmons .07 .20
152 Jimmy Smith .10 .30
153 Rich Tylski RC .07 .20
154 Dave Widell .07 .20
155 Marcus Allen .20 .50
156 Keith Cash .07 .20
157 Donnie Edwards .10 .30
158 Trezelle Jenkins .07 .20
159 Sean LaChapelle .07 .20
160 Greg Manusky RC .07 .20
161 Steve Matthews RC .07 .20
162 Pellom McDaniels RC .07 .20
163 Chris Penn .07 .20
164 Danny Villa .07 .20
165 Jerome Woods .07 .20
166 Karim Abdul-Jabbar .20 .50
167 John Bock .07 .20
168 O.J. Brigance RC .07 .20
169 Norman Hand RC .07 .20
170 Anthony Harris .07 .20
171 Larry Izzo RC .07 .20
172 Charles Jordan .07 .20
173 Dan Marino .75 2.00
174 Everett McIver .07 .20
175 Joe Nedney RC .07 .20
176 Robert Wilson RC .07 .20
177 David Dixon .07 .20
178 Charles Evans .07 .20
179 Hunter Goodwin RC .07 .20
180 Ben Hanks .07 .20
181 Warren Moon .20 .50
182 Harold Morrow RC .20 .50
183 Fernando Smith .07 .20
184 Robert Smith .10 .30
185 Sean Vanhorse .07 .20
186 Jay Walker .07 .20
187 Dewayne Washington .07 .20
188 Moe Williams .20 .50
189 Mike Bartrum RC .07 .20
190 Drew Bledsoe .25 .60
191 Troy Brown .10 .30
192 Chad Eaton RC .07 .20
193 Sam Gash .07 .20
194 Mike Gisler .07 .20
195 Curtis Martin .25 .60
196 David Richards .07 .20
197 Todd Rucci .07 .20
198 Chris Sullivan .07 .20
199 Adam Vinatieri RC 10.00 25.00
200 Doug Brien .07 .20
201 Derek Brown RBK .07 .20
202 Lee DeRamus .07 .20
203 Jim Everett .07 .20
204 Mercury Hayes .07 .20
205 Joe Johnson .07 .20
206 Henry Lusk RC .07 .20
207 Andy McCollum .07 .20
208 Alex Molden .07 .20
209 Ray Zellars .07 .20
210 Marcus Buckley .07 .20
211 Doug Coleman RC .07 .20
212 Percy Ellsworth RC .07 .20
213 Rodney Hampton .10 .30
214 Brian Saxton .07 .20
215 Jason Sehorn .10 .30
216 Stan White .07 .20
217 Corey Widmer .07 .20
218 Rodney Young .07 .20
219 Rob Zatechka .07 .20
220 Henry Bailey .07 .20
221 Chad Cascadden RC .07 .20
222 Wayne Chrebet .20 .50
223 Tyrone Davis .07 .20

224 Kwame Ellis .07 .20
225 Glenn Foley .10 .30
226 Erik Howard .07 .20
227 Gary Jones S .07 .20
228 Adrian Murrell .10 .30
229 Marc Spindler .07 .20
230 Lonnie Young .07 .20
231 Eric Zomalt .07 .20
232 Tim Brown .20 .50
233 Aundray Bruce .07 .20
234 Darren Carrington .07 .20
235 Rick Cunningham .07 .20
236 Rob Homberg .07 .20
237 Jeff Hostetler .07 .20
238 Lorenzo Lynch .07 .20
239 Barrett Robbins .07 .20
240 Dan Turk .07 .20
241 Harvey Williams .07 .20
242 Brian Dawkins .20 .50
243 Ty Detmer .10 .30
244 Troy Drake .07 .20
245 Rhett Hall .07 .20
246 Joe Panos .07 .20
247 Johnny Thomas .07 .20
248 Kevin Turner .07 .20
249 Ricky Watters .10 .30
250 Derrick Witherspoon RC .07 .20
251 Sylvester Wright .07 .20
252 Jerome Bettis .20 .50
253 Carlos Emmons RC .07 .20
254 Jason Gildon .07 .20
255 Jonathan Hayes .07 .20
256 Kevin Henry .07 .20
257 Jerry Olsavsky .07 .20
258 Erric Pegram .07 .20
259 Brendan Stai .07 .20
260 Justin Strzelczyk .07 .20
261 Mike Tomczak .07 .20
262 Tony Banks .10 .30
263 Hayward Clay .07 .20
264 Percell Gaskins .07 .20
265 Eddie Kennison .10 .30
266 Aaron Laing .07 .20
267 Keith Lyle .07 .20
268 Jamie Martin RC 1.00 2.50
269 Lawrence Phillips .07 .20
270 Zach Wiegert .07 .20
271 Toby Wright .07 .20
272 Darren Bennett .07 .20
273 Tony Berti .07 .20
274 Freddie Bradley .07 .20
275 Joe Cocozzo .07 .20
276 Andre Coleman .07 .20
277 Marco Coleman .07 .20
278 Rodney Harrison RC .40 1.00
279 David Hendrix .07 .20
280 Leonard Russell .07 .20
281 Sean Salisbury .07 .20
282 Dennis Brown .07 .20
283 Chris Dalman .07 .20
284 Brent Jones .10 .30
285 Sean Manuel .07 .20
286 Marquez Pope .07 .20
287 Jerry Rice .40 1.00
288 Kirk Scrafford .07 .20
289 Iheanyi Uwaezuoke .10 .30
290 Tommy Vardell .07 .20
291 Steve Young .25 .60
292 James Atkins .07 .20
293 T.J. Cunningham .07 .20
294 Stan Gelbaugh .07 .20
295 James Logan .07 .20
296 James McKnight RC .60 1.50
297 Rick Mirer .07 .20
298 Todd Peterson RC .07 .20
299 Fred Thomas .07 .20
300 Rick Tuten .07 .20
301 Chris Warren .10 .30
302 Donnie Abraham RC .20 .50
303 Trent Dilfer .20 .50
304 Kenneth Gant .07 .20
305 Jeff Gooch .10 .30
306 Courtney Hawkins .07 .20
307 Tyoka Jackson RC .07 .20
308 Melvin Johnson S RC .07 .20
309 Lonnie Marts .07 .20
310 Hardy Nickerson .07 .20
311 Errict Rhett .07 .20
312 Terry Allen .20 .50
313 Flipper Anderson .07 .20
314 William Bell .07 .20
315 Scott Blanton RC .07 .20
316 Leomont Evans RC .07 .20
317 Gus Frerotte .07 .20
318 Darryl Morrison .07 .20
319 Matt Turk .07 .20
320 Jeff Uhlenhake .07 .20
321 Brian Walker RC .07 .20
322 Mark Brunell LL .20 .50
323 Barry Sanders LL .30 .75
324 Isaac Bruce LL .20 .50
325 Terry Allen LL .10 .30
326 Steve Young LL .20 .50
327 Jerry Rice LL .20 .50
328 Ricky Watters LL .10 .30
329 Kevin Greene LL .07 .20
330 Brett Favre LL .40 1.00
S1 Mark Brunell Sample .75 2.00

1997 Pacific Philadelphia Gold

serted in packs at the rate of three per pack, this 200-card bonus set features borderless color player action photos with gold foil highlights. The backs carry player information. Copper (hobby), Red (special retail) and Silver (retail) parallel sets were also produced and randomly inserted at the rate of 2:37 in their respective pack types.

COMPLETE SET (200) 15.00 30.00
1 Ryan Christopherson .05 .15
2 James Dexter .05 .15
3 Boomer Esiason .08 .25
4 Jarius Hayes .05 .15
5 Eric Hill .05 .15
6 Trey Junkin .05 .15
7 Kwamie Lassiter .15 .40
8 Patrick Bates .05 .15
9 Brad Edwards .05 .15
10 Roman Fortin .05 .15
11 Harper Le Bel .05 .15
12 Lorenzo Styles .05 .15
13 Robbie Tobeck .05 .15
14 Mike Caldwell .05 .15
15 Eric Green .05 .15
16 Brian Kinchen .05 .15
17 Eric Turner .05 .15
18 Jerrol Williams .05 .15
19 Eric Zeier .08 .25
20 Darick Holmes .05 .15
21 Ken Irvin .05 .15
22 Jerry Ostroski .05 .15
23 Andre Reed .08 .25
24 Steve Tasker .05 .15
25 Thurman Thomas .15 .40
26 Steve Beuerlein .08 .25
27 Kerry Collins .15 .40
28 Eric Davis .05 .15
29 Norberto Garrido .05 .15
30 Lamar Lathon .05 .15
31 Andre Royal .05 .15
32 Tony Carter .05 .15
33 Jerry Fontenot .05 .15
34 Raymont Harris .05 .15
35 Anthony Marshall .05 .15
36 Barry Minter .05 .15
37 Steve Stenstrom .05 .15
38 Donnell Woolford .05 .15
39 Ken Blackman .05 .15
40 Jeff Blake .08 .25
41 Carl Pickens .08 .25
42 Artie Smith .05 .15
43 Ramondo Stallings .05 .15
44 Melvin Tuten .05 .15
45 Joe Walter .05 .15
46 Troy Aikman .40 1.00
47 Billy Davis .05 .15
48 Chad Hennings .05 .15
49 Emmitt Smith .60 1.50
50 George Teague .05 .15
51 Kevin Williams .05 .15
52 Terrell Davis .25 .60
53 John Elway .75 2.00
54 Tom Nalen .05 .15
55 Bill Romanowski .05 .15
56 Rod Smith WR .15 .40
57 Dan Williams .05 .15
58 Mike Compton .05 .15
59 Eric Lynch .05 .15
60 Aubrey Matthews .05 .15
61 Pete Metzelaars .05 .15
62 Herman Moore .08 .25
63 Barry Sanders .60 1.50
64 Keith Washington .05 .15
65 Edgar Bennett .08 .25
66 Brett Favre .75 2.00
67 Lamont Hollinquest .05 .15
68 Keith Jackson .05 .15
69 Derrick Mayes .08 .25
70 Andre Rison .08 .25
71 Eddie George .15 .40
72 Mel Gray .05 .15
73 Darryll Lewis .05 .15
74 John Henry Mills .05 .15
75 Rodney Thomas .05 .15
76 Gary Walker .05 .15
77 Troy Auzenne .05 .15
78 Sammie Burroughs .05 .15
79 Jim Harbaugh .08 .25
80 Tony McCoy .05 .15
81 Brian Stablein .05 .15
82 Kipp Vickers .05 .15
83 Aaron Beasley .05 .15
84 Mark Brunell .25 .60
85 Don Davey .05 .15
86 Chris Hudson .05 .15
87 Greg Huntington .05 .15
88 Ernie Logan .05 .15
89 Donnell Bennett .05 .15
90 Anthony Davis .05 .15
91 Tim Grunhard .05 .15
92 Danan Hughes .05 .15
93 Tony Richardson .08 .25
94 Tracy Simien .05 .15
95 Karim Abdul-Jabbar .15 .40
96 Dwight Hollier .05 .15
97 John Kidd .05 .15
98 Dan Marino .75 2.00
99 Jerris McPhail .05 .15
100 Irving Spikes .05 .15
101 Richmond Webb .05 .15
102 Jeff Brady .05 .15
103 Richard Brown .05 .15
104 Corey Fuller .05 .15
105 John Gerak .05 .15
106 Scottie Graham .05 .15
107 Amp Lee .05 .15
108 Drew Bledsoe .25 .60
109 Tedy Bruschi .30 .75
110 Todd Collins .05 .15
111 Bob Kratch .05 .15
112 Curtis Martin .25 .60
113 Dave Meggett .05 .15
114 Tom Tupa .05 .15
115 Eric Allen .05 .15
116 Mario Bates .05 .15
117 Clarence Jones .05 .15
118 Sean Lumpkin .05 .15
119 Doug Nussmeier .05 .15
120 Irv Smith .05 .15
121 Winfred Tubbs .05 .15
122 Willie Beamon .05 .15
123 Greg Bishop .05 .15
124 Dave Brown .05 .15
125 Gary Downs .05 .15
126 Thomas Lewis .05 .15
127 Michael Strahan .08 .25
128 Tyrone Wheatley .08 .25
129 Matt Brock .05 .15
130 Mike Chalenski .05 .15
131 Roger Duffy .05 .15
132 John Hudson .05 .15
133 Frank Reich .05 .15
134 David Williams T .05 .15
135 Greg Biekert .05 .15
136 Mike Jones LB .05 .15
137 Napoleon Kaufman .15 .40
138 Carl Kidd .05 .15
139 Terry McDaniel .05 .15
140 Mike Morton .05 .15
141 Olanda Truitt .05 .15
142 Gary Anderson K .05 .15
143 Richard Cooper .05 .15
144 Jimmie Johnson TE .05 .15
145 Joe Kelly .05 .15
146 William Thomas .05 .15
147 Ricky Watters .08 .25
148 Ed West .05 .15
149 Michael Zordich .05 .15
150 Jerome Bettis .15 .40
151 Dermontti Dawson .10 .30
152 Lethon Flowers .05 .15
153 Charles Johnson .08 .25
154 Darren Perry .05 .15
155 Kordell Stewart .15 .40
156 Will Wolford .05 .15
157 Isaac Bruce .15 .40
158 Kevin Carter .05 .15
159 Torin Dorn .05 .15
160 Leo Goeas .05 .15
161 Gerald McBurrows .05 .15
162 Chuck Osborne .05 .15
163 J.T. Thomas .05 .15
164 Dwayne Gordon .05 .15
165 Stan Humphries .08 .25
166 Shawn Lee .05 .15
167 Chris Mims .05 .15
168 John Parrella .05 .15
169 Junior Seau .15 .40
170 Bryan Still .05 .15
171 Curtis Buckley .05 .15
172 William Floyd .08 .25
173 Merton Hanks .05 .15
174 Terry Kirby .08 .25
175 Jerry Rice .40 1.00
176 J.J. Stokes .08 .25
177 Jeff Wilkins .05 .15
178 Bryant Young .08 .25
179 Sam Adams .05 .15
180 John Friesz .05 .15
181 Joey Galloway .08 .25
182 Pete Kendall .05 .15
183 Jason Kyle .05 .15
184 Darryl Williams .05 .15
185 Ronnie Williams .05 .15
186 Mike Alstott .15 .40
187 Trent Dilfer .15 .40
188 Tyrone Legette .05 .15
189 Martin Mayhew .05 .15
190 Jason Odom .05 .15
191 Warren Sapp .08 .25
192 Karl Williams .05 .15
193 Terry Allen .15 .40
194 Romeo Bandison .05 .15
195 Alcides Catanho .05 .15
196 Gus Frerotte .05 .15
197 William Gaines .05 .15
198 Ken Harvey .05 .15
199 Trevor Matich .05 .15
200 Scott Turner .05 .15
S1 Mark Brunell Sample .40 1.00

1997 Pacific Philadelphia Copper

COMPLETE SET (200) 60.00 120.00
*COPPER: 2X TO 4X GOLD
STATED ODDS 2:37 HOBBY

1997 Pacific Philadelphia Red

COMPLETE SET (200) 40.00 80.00
*REDS: 1.2X TO 2.5X GOLDS

1997 Pacific Philadelphia Silver

COMPLETE SET (200) 125.00 250.00
*SILVERS: 3.5X TO 7X GOLDS
STATED ODDS 2:37 RETAIL

1997 Pacific Philadelphia Heart of the Game

ndomly inserted in packs at a rate of one in 73, this 20-card set features borderless color action player photos on the fronts with player information on the backs.

COMPLETE SET (20) 40.00 100.00
STATED ODDS 1:73
1 Thurman Thomas 1.50 4.00
2 Kerry Collins 1.50 4.00
3 Troy Aikman 3.00 8.00
4 Emmitt Smith 5.00 12.00
5 Terrell Davis 2.00 5.00
6 John Elway 6.00 15.00
7 Barry Sanders 5.00 12.00
8 Brett Favre 6.00 15.00
9 Antonio Freeman 1.50 4.00
10 Marshall Faulk 2.00 5.00
11 Mark Brunell 2.00 5.00
12 Marcus Allen 1.50 4.00
13 Dan Marino 6.00 15.00
14 Drew Bledsoe 2.00 5.00
15 Curtis Martin 2.00 5.00
16 Napoleon Kaufman 1.50 4.00
17 Jerome Bettis 1.50 4.00
18 Isaac Bruce 1.50 4.00
19 Jerry Rice 3.00 8.00
20 Steve Young 2.00 5.00

1997 Pacific Philadelphia Milestones

Randomly inserted in packs at a rate of one in 37, this 20-card set features color action player images on a team-color helmet with a gold ribbon running from the top of the card to the bottom stating the player's accomplishment and name. The backs carry additional player information.

COMPLETE SET (20) 100.00 200.00
STATED ODDS 1:37
1 Simeon Rice 3.00 8.00
2 Thurman Thomas 3.00 8.00
3 Troy Aikman 6.00 15.00
4 Emmitt Smith 10.00 25.00
5 Terrell Davis 4.00 10.00
6 John Elway 12.50 30.00
7 Brett Favre 12.50 30.00
8 Desmond Howard 2.00 5.00
9 Reggie White 3.00 8.00
10 Mark Brunell 4.00 10.00
11 Marcus Allen 3.00 8.00
12 Karim Abdul-Jabbar 3.00 8.00
13 Dan Marino 12.50 30.00
14 Drew Bledsoe 4.00 10.00
15 Terry Glenn 3.00 8.00
16 Curtis Martin 4.00 10.00
17 Tony Banks 2.00 5.00
18 Jerry Rice 6.00 15.00
19 Steve Young 4.00 10.00
20 Terry Allen 3.00 8.00

1997 Pacific Philadelphia Photoengravings

Randomly inserted in packs at a rate of two in 37, this 36-card set with rounded corners features color action photos of players from the waist up set in a thin frame on a background with engraved-looking abstract design. The backs carry information about the player.

COMPLETE SET (36) 40.00 100.00
STATED ODDS 2:37
1 Thurman Thomas 1.25 3.00
2 Kerry Collins 1.25 3.00
3 Jeff Blake .75 2.00
4 Troy Aikman 2.50 6.00
5 Deion Sanders 1.25 3.00
6 Emmitt Smith 4.00 10.00
7 Terrell Davis 1.50 4.00
8 John Elway 5.00 12.00
9 Herman Moore .75 2.00
10 Barry Sanders 4.00 10.00
11 Brett Favre 5.00 12.00
12 Desmond Howard .75 2.00
13 Dorsey Levens 1.25 3.00
14 Eddie George 1.25 3.00
15 Marshall Faulk 1.50 4.00
16 Jim Harbaugh .75 2.00
17 Marvin Harrison 1.25 3.00
18 Mark Brunell 1.50 4.00
19 Keenan McCardell .75 2.00
20 Karim Abdul-Jabbar 1.25 3.00
21 Dan Marino 5.00 12.00
22 Brad Johnson 1.25 3.00
23 Drew Bledsoe 1.50 4.00
24 Terry Glenn 1.25 3.00
25 Curtis Martin 1.50 4.00
26 Keyshawn Johnson 1.25 3.00
27 Tim Brown 1.25 3.00
28 Napoleon Kaufman 1.25 3.00
29 Ricky Watters .75 2.00
30 Jerome Bettis 1.25 3.00
31 Kordell Stewart 1.50 4.00
32 Eddie Kennison .75 2.00
33 Jerry Rice 2.50 6.00
34 Steve Young 1.50 4.00
35 Chris Warren .75 2.00
36 Terry Allen 1.25 3.00

1993 Pacific Prisms

After debuting as an insert set in the 1992 Pacific NFL series, Pacific decided to release a 108-card (plus one checklist) set of Prism cards. The standard-size cards comprising this set were issued in one-card packs and feature on their fronts color player action cut-outs over borderless triangular prismatic foil backgrounds. Seventeen thousand of each card were produced. The cards are checklisted alphabetically according to teams. Rookie Cards include Jerome Bettis, Drew Bledsoe, Reggie Brooks, Garrison Hearst, Rick Mirer and Robert Smith. Two promo cards (Emmitt Smith and Drew Bledsoe) were produced and are listed below. They were released primarily at the Chicago National Card Collectors Convention and each looks very similar to its regular issue card. The promos however differ slightly on the backs in relation to the small player and helmet photos. The player photo is touching the helmet and the helmet photo is smaller on the promo cards. Reportedly 5,500 of each promo was produced.

COMPLETE SET (109) 15.00 40.00
1 Chris Miller .30 .75
2 Mike Pritchard .30 .75
3 Andre Rison .30 .75
4 Deion Sanders 1.00 2.50
5 Tony Smith RB .20 .50
6 Jim Kelly .60 1.50
7 Andre Reed .40 1.00
8 Thurman Thomas .60 1.50
9 Neal Anderson .20 .50
10 Jim Harbaugh .40 1.00
11 Donnell Woolford .20 .50
12 David Klingler .20 .50
13 Carl Pickens .30 .75
14 Alfred Williams .20 .50
15 Michael Jackson .30 .75
16 Bernie Kosar .30 .75
17 Tommy Vardell .20 .50
18 Troy Aikman 1.25 3.00
19 Alvin Harper .30 .75
20 Michael Irvin .60 1.50
21 Russell Maryland .20 .50
22 Emmitt Smith 2.50 6.00
23 John Elway 2.50 6.00
24 Tommy Maddox .40 1.00
25 Shannon Sharpe .60 1.50
26 Herman Moore .40 1.00
27 Rodney Peete .20 .50
28 Barry Sanders 2.00 5.00
29 Pat Swilling .20 .50
30 Terrell Buckley .20 .50
31 Brett Favre 3.00 8.00
32 Sterling Sharpe .40 1.00
33 Reggie White .60 1.50
34 Ernest Givins .30 .75
35 Haywood Jeffires .30 .75
36 Warren Moon .60 1.50
37 Lorenzo White .20 .50
38 Steve Emtman .20 .50
39 Jeff George .40 1.00
40 Reggie Langhorne .20 .50
41 Dale Carter .20 .50
42 Joe Montana 2.50 6.00
43 Derrick Thomas .60 1.50
44 Barry Word .20 .50
45 Nick Bell .20 .50
46 Eric Dickerson .30 .75
47 Jeff Jaeger .20 .50
48 Jerome Bettis RC 4.00 10.00
49 Henry Ellard .30 .75
50 Jim Everett .30 .75
51 Cleveland Gary .20 .50
52 Marco Coleman .20 .50
53 Mark Higgs .20 .50
54 Keith Jackson .30 .75
55 Dan Marino 2.50 6.00
56 Troy Vincent .20 .50
57 Terry Allen .40 1.00
58 Jack Del Rio .20 .50
59 Sean Salisbury .20 .50
60 Robert Smith RC 1.25 3.00
61 Drew Bledsoe RC 3.00 8.00
62 Marv Cook .20 .50
63 Irving Fryar .30 .75
64 Leonard Russell .30 .75
65 Andre Tippett .20 .50
66 Morten Andersen .20 .50
67 Vaughn Dunbar .20 .50
68 Eric Martin .20 .50
69 Dave Brown RC .40 1.00
70 Rodney Hampton .30 .75
71 Phil Simms .30 .75
72 Lawrence Taylor .60 1.50
73 Ronnie Lott .30 .75
74 Johnny Mitchell .20 .50
75 Rob Moore .30 .75
76 Browning Nagle .20 .50
77 Fred Barnett .30 .75
78 Randall Cunningham .60 1.50
79 Herschel Walker .30 .75
80 Gary Clark .30 .75
81 Ken Harvey .20 .50
82 Garrison Hearst RC 1.00 2.50
83 Ricky Proehl .20 .50
84 Barry Foster .30 .75
85 Ernie Mills .20 .50
86 Neil O'Donnell .60 1.50
87 Stan Humphries .30 .75
88 Leslie O'Neal .30 .75
89 Junior Seau .60 1.50
90 Amp Lee .20 .50
91 Jerry Rice 1.50 4.00
92 Ricky Watters .60 1.50
93 Steve Young 1.25 3.00
94 Cortez Kennedy .30 .75
95 Rick Mirer RC .60 1.50
96 Eugene Robinson .20 .50
97 Chris Warren .30 .75
98 John L. Williams .20 .50
99 Reggie Cobb .20 .50
100 Lawrence Dawsey .20 .50
101 Santana Dotson .30 .75
102 Courtney Hawkins .20 .50
103 Reggie Brooks RC .30 .75
104 Ricky Ervins .20 .50
105 Desmond Howard .40 1.00
106 Art Monk .40 1.00
107 Mark Rypien .20 .50
108 Ricky Sanders .20 .50
NNO Checklist Card .15 .40
P22 Emmitt Smith Promo 2.50 6.00
P61 Drew Bledsoe Promo 1.25 3.00

1994 Pacific Prisms

These 128 standard-size cards feature borderless fronts with color action player photos cut out and superimposed on a prism-patterned background. There were reportedly 16,000 of each card produced in silver foil and 1,138 of each card produced in gold foil. Each pack contained either a silver or gold Prism card. Rookie Cards include Mario Bates, Marshall Faulk, William Floyd, Greg Hill, Charles Johnson, Errict Rhett and Heath Shuler.

COMPLETE SET (128) 20.00 50.00
1 Troy Aikman UER 1.50 4.00
2 Marcus Allen .50 1.25
3 Morten Andersen .15 .40
4 Fred Barnett .30 .75
5 Mario Bates RC .50 1.25
6 Edgar Bennett .50 1.25
7 Rod Bernstine .15 .40
8 Jerome Bettis .75 2.00
9 Steve Beuerlein .30 .75
10 Brian Blades .30 .75
11 Drew Bledsoe 1.25 3.00
12 Vincent Brisby .30 .75
13 Reggie Brooks .30 .75
14 Derek Brown RBK .15 .40
15 Gary Brown .15 .40
16 Tim Brown .50 1.25
17 Marion Butts .15 .40
18 Keith Byars .15 .40
19 Cody Carlson .15 .40
20 Anthony Carter .30 .75
21 Tom Carter .15 .40
22 Gary Clark .30 .75
23 Ben Coates .30 .75
24 Reggie Cobb .15 .40
25 Curtis Conway .30 .75
26 John Copeland .15 .40
27 Randall Cunningham .50 1.25
28 Willie Davis .30 .75
29 Sean Dawkins RC .50 1.25
30 Lawrence Dawsey .15 .40
31 Richard Dent .30 .75
32 Trent Dilfer RC 1.25 3.00
33 Troy Drayton .15 .40
34 Vaughn Dunbar .15 .40
35 Henry Ellard .30 .75
36 John Elway 3.00 8.00
37 Craig Erickson .15 .40
38 Boomer Esiason .30 .75
39 Marshall Faulk RC 5.00 10.00
40 Brett Favre 3.00 8.00
41 William Floyd RC .50 1.25
42 Glenn Foley RC .50 1.25
43 Barry Foster .15 .40
44 Irving Fryar .30 .75
45 Jeff George .50 1.25
46 Scottie Graham RC .30 .75
47 Rodney Hampton .30 .75
48 Jim Harbaugh .50 1.25
49 Alvin Harper .30 .75
50 Courtney Hawkins .15 .40
51 Garrison Hearst .50 1.25
52 Vaughn Hebron .15 .40
53 Greg Hill RC .50 1.25
54 Jeff Hostetler .30 .75
55 Michael Irvin .50 1.25
56 Qadry Ismail .30 .75
57 Rocket Ismail .30 .75
58 Anthony Johnson .30 .75
59 Charles Johnson RC .50 1.25
60 Johnny Johnson .15 .40
61 Brent Jones .30 .75
62 Kyle Clifton .15 .40
63 Jim Kelly .30 .75
64 Cortez Kennedy .30 .75
65 Terry Kirby .50 1.25
66 David Klingler .15 .40
67 Erik Kramer .30 .75
68 Reggie Langhorne .15 .40
69 Chuck Levy RC .15 .40
70 Dan Marino 3.00 8.00
71 O.J.McDuffie .50 1.25
72 Natrone Means .50 1.25
73 Eric Metcalf .30 .75
74 Glyn Milburn .30 .75
75 Anthony Miller .30 .75
76 Rick Mirer .50 1.25
77 Johnny Mitchell .15 .40
78 Scott Mitchell .30 .75
79 Joe Montana 3.00 8.00
80 Warren Moon .30 .75
81 Derrick Moore .15 .40
82 Herman Moore .50 1.25
83 Rob Moore .30 .75
84 Ronald Moore .15 .40
85 Johnnie Morton RC 1.50 4.00
86 Neil O'Donnell .30 .75
87 David Palmer RC .50 1.25
88 Erric Pegram .15 .40
89 Carl Pickens .30 .75
90 Anthony Pleasant .15 .40
91 Roosevelt Potts .15 .40
92 Mike Pritchard .15 .40
93 Andre Reed .30 .75
94 Errict Rhett RC .50 1.25
95 Jerry Rice 1.50 4.00
96 Andre Rison .30 .75
97 Greg Robinson .15 .40
98 T.J.Rubley RC .15 .40
99 Leonard Russell .15 .40
100 Barry Sanders 2.50 6.00
101 Deion Sanders 1.00 2.50
102 Ricky Sanders .15 .40
103 Junior Seau .50 1.25
104 Shannon Sharpe .30 .75
105 Sterling Sharpe .30 .75
106 Heath Shuler RC .50 1.25
107 Phil Simms .30 .75
108 Webster Slaughter .15 .40
109 Bruce Smith .50 1.25
110 Emmitt Smith 3.00 8.00
111 Irv Smith .15 .40
112 Robert Smith .50 1.25
113 Vinny Testaverde .30 .75
114 Derrick Thomas .50 1.25
115 Thurman Thomas .30 .75
116 Leroy Thompson .15 .40
117 Lewis Tillman .15 .40
118 Michael Timpson .15 .40
119 Herschel Walker .30 .75
120 Chris Warren .30 .75
121 Ricky Watters .30 .75
122 Lorenzo White .15 .40
123 Reggie White .50 1.25
124 Dan Wilkinson RC .30 .75
125 Kevin Williams WR .30 .75
126 Steve Young 1.25 3.00
CL1 Checklist 1 .10 .30
CL2 Checklist 2 .10 .30
S1 Sterling Sharpe Promo .40 1.00

1994 Pacific Prisms Gold

COMPLETE SET (126) 125.00 250.00
*STARS: 1.2X TO 3X BASIC CARDS
*GOLD RCs: .8X TO 2X BASIC CARDS
ANNOUNCED PRINT RUN 1138 SETS

1994 Pacific Prisms Team Helmets

Randomly inserted in foil packs, this 30-card standard size set features a borderless front with a colored picture of a team helmet set against a silver tiled background. The team's name appears at the bottom. The back features a brief history of the team on a background consisting of a ghosted version of the team helmet. The cards are numbered on the back by "X of 30".

COMPLETE SET (30) 2.00 5.00
1 Arizona Cardinals .08 .25
2 Atlanta Falcons .08 .25
3 Buffalo Bills .08 .25
4 Carolina Panthers .10 .30
5 Chicago Bears .08 .25
6 Cincinnati Bengals .08 .25
7 Cleveland Browns .08 .25
8 Dallas Cowboys .20 .50
9 Denver Broncos .08 .25
10 Detroit Lions .08 .25
11 Green Bay Packers .20 .50
12 Houston Oilers .08 .25
13 Indianapolis Colts .08 .25
14 Jacksonville Jaguars .08 .25
15 Kansas City Chiefs .08 .25
16 Los Angeles Raiders .10 .30
17 Los Angeles Rams .08 .25
18 Miami Dolphins .20 .50
19 Minnesota Vikings .08 .25
20 New England Patriots .08 .25
21 New Orleans Saints .08 .25
22 New York Giants .08 .25
23 New York Jets .08 .25
24 Philadelphia Eagles .08 .25
25 Pittsburgh Steelers .20 .50
26 San Diego Chargers .08 .25
27 San Francisco 49ers .20 .50
28 Seattle Seahawks .08 .25
29 Tampa Bay Buccaneers .08 .25
30 Washington Redskins .20 .50

1995 Pacific Prisms

This 216 card standard-size set was issued in two-card packs including one player card and either a Super Bowl information card, a team card or a uniform card. The set was issued in two series, both containing 108 cards each. A John Elway autograph card, featuring an embossed Pacific logo, was also randomly inserted in the series 2 product. The card was hand signed and hand numbered of 50 and was from the 1994 Pacific Gems of the Crown insert set. It could be found approximately one in every 43,200 packs. We've included this card with the 1994 Pacific Gems of the Crown listings. Finally, a two card unnumbered expansion set was issued in regular packs that contain a red foil-etched background. A Natrone Means Promo card (#1) was produced in both silver and gold foil and priced below.

COMPLETE SET (216) 30.00 80.00
COMP.SERIES 1 (108) 15.00 40.00
COMP.SERIES 2 (108) 15.00 40.00
1 Chuck Levy .08 .25
2 Ronald Moore .08 .25
3 Jay Schroeder .08 .25
4 Bert Emanuel .40 1.00
5 Terance Mathis .20 .50
6 Andre Rison .20 .50
7 Bucky Brooks .08 .25
8 Jeff Burris .08 .25
9 Jim Kelly .40 1.00
10 Lewis Tillman .08 .25
11 Steve Walsh .08 .25
12 Chris Zorich .08 .25
13 Jeff Blake RC 1.00 2.50
14 Steve Broussard .08 .25
15 Jeff Cothran .08 .25
16 Earnest Byner .08 .25
17 Leroy Hoard .08 .25
18 Vinny Testaverde .20 .50
19 Troy Aikman 1.00 2.50
20 Alvin Harper .08 .25
21 Leon Lett .08 .25
22 Jay Novacek .20 .50
23 John Elway 2.00 5.00
24 Karl Mecklenburg .08 .25
25 Leonard Russell .08 .25
26 Mel Gray .08 .25
27 Dave Krieg .08 .25
28 Barry Sanders 1.50 4.00
29 Chris Spielman .20 .50
30 Robert Brooks .40 1.00
31 LeShon Johnson .20 .50
32 Sterling Sharpe .20 .50
33 Ernest Givins .08 .25
34 Billy Joe Tolliver .08 .25
35 Lorenzo White .08 .25
36 Charles Arbuckle .08 .25
37 Sean Dawkins .20 .50
38 Marshall Faulk 1.25 3.00
39 Marcus Allen .40 1.00
40 Donnell Bennett .20 .50
41 Matt Blundin RC .08 .25
42 Greg Hill .20 .50
43 Tim Brown .40 1.00
44 Billy Joe Hobert .20 .50
45 Rocket Ismail .20 .50
46 James Jett .20 .50
47 Tim Bowens .08 .25
48 Irving Fryar .20 .50
49 O.J. McDuffie .40 1.00
50 Irving Spikes .20 .50
51 Terry Allen .20 .50
52 Cris Carter .40 1.00
53 Amp Lee .08 .25
54 Drew Bledsoe .60 1.50
55 Willie McGinest .20 .50
56 Leroy Thompson .08 .25
57 Michael Timpson .08 .25
58 Michael Haynes .20 .50
59 Derrell Mitchell RC .08 .25
60 Dave Brown .20 .50
61 Thomas Lewis .20 .50
62 Dave Meggett .08 .25
63 Boomer Esiason .20 .50
64 Aaron Glenn .08 .25
65 Ronnie Lott .20 .50
66 Randall Cunningham .40 1.00
67 Charlie Garner .40 1.00
68 Herschel Walker .20 .50
69 Barry Foster .20 .50
70 Charles Johnson .20 .50
71 Jim Miller RC 1.25 3.00
72 Rod Woodson .20 .50
73 Andre Coleman .08 .25
74 Natrone Means .20 .50
75 Shannon Mitchell RC .08 .25
76 Junior Seau .40 1.00
77 Elvis Grbac .40 1.00
78 Deion Sanders .60 1.50
79 Adam Walker RC .08 .25
80 Ricky Watters .20 .50
81 Michael Bates .08 .25
82 Brian Blades .20 .50
83 Eugene Robinson .08 .25
84 Chris Warren .20 .50
85 Jerome Bettis .40 1.00
86 Troy Drayton .08 .25
87 Chris Miller .08 .25
88 Trent Dilfer .40 1.00
89 Hardy Nickerson .08 .25
90 Errict Rhett .20 .50
91 Henry Ellard .20 .50
92 Gus Frerotte .20 .50
93 Ricky Ervins .08 .25
94 Dave Barr RC .08 .25
95 Kyle Brady RC .40 1.00
96 Mark Bruener RC .20 .50
97 Ki-Jana Carter RC .40 1.00
98 Kerry Collins RC 2.00 5.00
99 Joey Galloway RC 2.00 5.00
100 Napoleon Kaufman RC 1.50 4.00
101 Steve McNair RC 4.00 10.00
102 Craig Newsome RC .08 .25
103 Rashaan Salaam RC .20 .50
104 Kordell Stewart RC 2.00 5.00
105 J.J. Stokes RC .40 1.00
106 Rodney Thomas RC .20 .50
107 Michael Westbrook RC .40 1.00
108 Tyrone Wheatley RC 1.50 4.00
109 Larry Centers .20 .50
110 Garrison Hearst .40 1.00
111 Jamir Miller .08 .25
112 Jeff George .20 .50
113 Craig Heyward .20 .50
114 Cornelius Bennett .20 .50
115 Andre Reed .20 .50
116 Randy Baldwin .08 .25
117 Tommy Barnhardt .08 .25
118 Sam Mills .20 .50
119 Brian O'Neal .08 .25
120 Frank Reich .08 .25
121 Tony Smith RB .08 .25
122 Lawyer Tillman .08 .25
123 Jack Trudeau .08 .25
124 Vernon Turner .08 .25
125 Curtis Conway .40 1.00
126 Erik Kramer .08 .25
127 Nate Lewis .08 .25
128 Carl Pickens .20 .50
129 Darnay Scott .20 .50
130 Dan Wilkinson .20 .50
131 Derrick Alexander WR .40 1.00
132 Carl Banks .08 .25
133 Michael Irvin .40 1.00
134 Emmitt Smith 1.50 4.00
135 Kevin Williams WR .20 .50
136 Glyn Milburn .08 .25
137 Anthony Miller .20 .50
138 Shannon Sharpe .20 .50
139 Scott Mitchell .20 .50
140 Herman Moore .40 1.00
141 Edgar Bennett .20 .50
142 Brett Favre 2.00 5.00
143 Reggie White .40 1.00
144 Gary Brown .08 .25
145 Haywood Jeffires .08 .25
146 Webster Slaughter .08 .25
147 Craig Erickson .08 .25
148 Paul Justin .08 .25
149 Lamont Warren .08 .25
150 Steve Beuerlein .20 .50
151 Derek Brown TE .08 .25
152 Mark Brunell .60 1.50
153 Reggie Cobb .08 .25
154 Desmond Howard .20 .50
155 Kelvin Pritchett .08 .25
156 James O. Stewart RC 1.50 4.00
157 Cedric Tillman .08 .25
158 Kimble Anders .20 .50
159 Lake Dawson .20 .50
160 Keith Byars .08 .25
161 Dan Marino 2.00 5.00
162 Bernie Parmalee .20 .50
163 Qadry Ismail .20 .50
164 Warren Moon .20 .50
165 Jake Reed .20 .50
166 Marion Butts .08 .25
167 Ben Coates .20 .50
168 Mario Bates .20 .50
169 Quinn Early .20 .50
170 Jim Everett .08 .25
171 Rodney Hampton .20 .50
172 Mike Horan .08 .25
173 Mike Sherrard .08 .25
174 Johnny Johnson .08 .25
175 Adrian Murrell .20 .50
176 Andrew Glover RC .08 .25
177 Jeff Hostetler .20 .50
178 Harvey Williams .08 .25
179 Fred Barnett .20 .50
180 Vaughn Hebron .00 .25
181 Jeff Sydner .08 .25
182 Kevin Greene .20 .50
183 Byron Bam Morris .08 .25
184 Neil O'Donnell .20 .50
185 Stan Humphries .20 .50
186 Tony Martin .20 .50
187 Mark Seay .20 .50
188 William Floyd .20 .50
189 Rickey Jackson .08 .25
190 Jerry Rice 1.00 2.50
191 Steve Young .75 2.00
192 Cortez Kennedy .20 .50
193 Rick Mirer .20 .50
194 Jessie Hester .08 .25
195 Curtis Martin UER RC 4.00 10.00
196 Horace Copeland .08 .25
197 Charles Wilson .08 .25
198 Reggie Brooks .20 .50
199 Brian Mitchell .08 .25
200 Heath Shuler .20 .50
201 Justin Armour RC .08 .25
202 Jay Barker RC .08 .25
203 Zack Crockett RC .20 .50
204 Christian Fauria RC .20 .50
205 Antonio Freeman RC 1.50 4.00
206 Chad May RC .08 .25
207 Frank Sanders RC .40 1.00
208 Steve Stenstrom RC .08 .25
209 Lorenzo Styles RC .08 .25
210 Sherman Williams RC .08 .25
211 Ray Zellars RC .20 .50
212 Eric Zeier RC .40 1.00
213 Joey Galloway .75 2.00
214 Napoleon Kaufman .60 1.50
215 Rashaan Salaam .20 .50
216 J.J. Stokes .40 1.00
NNO Steve Beuerlein EE .40 1.00
NNO Barry Foster EE .40 1.00
P1 Natrone Means Promo .40 1.00
P2 Natrone Means Promo .40 1.00

1995 Pacific Prisms Gold

MPLETE SET (216) 125.00 250.00
*STARS: 1.5X TO 3X BASIC CARDS
*RCs: 1X TO 2X BASIC CARDS
STATED ODDS 2:37

1995 Pacific Prisms Connections

This 20 card set was randomly inserted in series two hobby and retail packs at a rate of one in 73 packs. Cards 1A-10A were randomly inserted in retail packs while cards 1B-10B were inserted into hobby. Each individual card had a quarterback/receiver combination with the quarterbacks using the "A" prefix and the receivers the "B" prefix. Card fronts have either a green etched foil background or a blue holofoil background. The Blue Holofoil background is a parallel that was randomly inserted. According to Pacific, less than 200 of the sets exist. Card fronts also have the player's team across the top and the player's name across the bottom. When the "A" and the "B" cards are linked they form the "Royal Connections" logo in the middle of the card. Card backs are vertical with a photo of the player in an oval with a statistical summary underneath. Cards are numbered with a "RC" prefix.

COMPLETE GREEN SET (20) 40.00 80.00
1A-10A: STATED ODDS 1:73 SER.2 RET.
1B-10B: STATED ODDS 1:73 SER.2 HOB.
*BLUE HOLOFOILS: 2X TO 5X BASIC INSERTS
BLUE HOLO:10% OF TOTAL PRINT RUN
1A Steve Young 2.50 6.00
1B Jerry Rice 3.00 8.00
2A Dan Marino 6.00 15.00
2B Irving Fryar .60 1.50
3A Drew Bledsoe 2.00 5.00
3B Ben Coates .60 1.50
4A John Elway 6.00 15.00
4B Shannon Sharpe .60 1.50
5A Jeff Hostetler .60 1.50
5B Tim Brown 1.25 3.00
6A Warren Moon .60 1.50
6B Cris Carter 1.25 3.00
7A Neil O'Donnell .60 1.50
7B Charles Johnson .60 1.50
8A Troy Aikman 3.00 8.00
8B Michael Irvin 1.25 3.00
9A Stan Humphries .60 1.50
9B Shawn Jefferson .30 .75
10A Jim Kelly 1.25 3.00
10B Andre Reed .60 1.50

1995 Pacific Prisms Kings of the NFL

This 10 card set was randomly inserted into series 2 packs at a rate of one in 361 packs and features the leaders in ten different NFL categories. Card fronts contain a full bleed photo with a gold holographic foil design at the top, bottom and running behind the player. The top of the card signifies what the player led the NFL in and the player's name is at the bottom. Card backs contain a head shot of the player with the player's name underneath it, followed by a summary of the previous season.

COMPLETE SET (10) 60.00 150.00
SER.2 STATED ODDS 1:361
1 Emmitt Smith 8.00 20.00
2 Steve Young 4.00 10.00
3 Jerry Rice 5.00 12.00
4 Deion Sanders 3.00 8.00
5 Emmitt Smith 8.00 20.00
6 Dan Marino 10.00 25.00
7 Drew Bledsoe 3.00 8.00
8 Barry Sanders 8.00 20.00
9 Marshall Faulk 6.00 15.00
10 Marshall Faulk 6.00 15.00
Means

1995 Pacific Prisms Red Hot Rookies

is nine-card standard-size set, featuring leading prospects, was inserted one in every 73 hobby packs. The player's image is featured against a metallic red background and features the rookies in their college uniforms. The player's name is located up the left side. The backs contain a player photo and highlights.

COMPLETE SET (9) 30.00 80.00
STATED ODDS 1:73 SER.1 HOBBY
1 Ki-Jana Carter 1.25 3.00
2 Joey Galloway 6.00 15.00
3 Steve McNair 12.50 30.00
4 Tyrone Wheatley 5.00 12.00
5 Kerry Collins 6.00 15.00
6 Rashaan Salaam .60 1.50
7 Michael Westbrook 1.25 3.00
8 J.J. Stokes 1.25 3.00
9 Napoleon Kaufman 5.00 12.00

1995 Pacific Prisms Red Hot Stars

serted one in every 73 retail packs, this nine-card standard-size set features some of the NFL's best players. The player's image is featured against a red foil-etched background. The player's name is at the bottom of the card. The backs feature a player photo and highlights.

COMPLETE SET (9) 40.00 100.00
STATED ODDS 1:73 SER.1 RETAIL
1 Barry Sanders 8.00 20.00
2 Steve Young 4.00 10.00
3 Emmitt Smith 8.00 20.00
4 Drew Bledsoe 3.00 8.00
5 Natrone Means 1.00 2.50
6 Dan Marino 10.00 25.00
7 Marshall Faulk 6.00 15.00

8 Jerry Rice 5.00 12.00
9 Errict Rhett 1.00 2.50

1999 Pacific Prisms

is 150 card set was released in mid November of 1999. Notable rookies found within the set include Tim Couch, Donovan Mcnabb, and Ricky Williams. Also veteran stars such as Dan Marino and Emmitt Smith. Hobby packs carried a suggested retail price of $4.99 per pack with 5 cards per pack and the Retail only version carried a $2.99 suggested retail price per pack containing 3 cards.

COMPLETE SET (150) 30.00 80.00
1 David Boston RC .30 .75
2 Rob Moore .20 .50
3 Adrian Murrell .20 .50
4 Jake Plummer .20 .50
5 Frank Sanders .20 .50
6 Jamal Anderson .25 .60
7 Chris Chandler .25 .60
8 Tim Dwight .25 .60
9 Terance Mathis .20 .50
10 Peter Boulware .20 .50
11 Priest Holmes .20 .50
12 Pat Johnson .20 .50
13 Jermaine Lewis .20 .50
14 Doug Flutie .30 .75
15 Eric Moulds .20 .50
16 Peerless Price RC .30 .75
17 Antowain Smith .20 .50
18 Bruce Smith .25 .60
19 Steve Beuerlein .25 .60
20 Tim Biakabutuka .25 .60
21 Muhsin Muhammad .20 .50
22 Wesley Walls .25 .60
23 Edgar Bennett .25 .60
24 Curtis Conway .25 .60
25 Bobby Engram .20 .50
26 Curtis Enis .20 .50
27 Cade McNown RC .30 .75
28 Jeff Blake .25 .60
29 Scott Covington RC .30 .75
30 Corey Dillon .20 .50
31 Carl Pickens .25 .60
32 Akili Smith RC .30 .75
33 Craig Yeast RC .30 .75
34 Tim Couch RC .40 1.00
35 Ty Detmer .20 .50
36 Kevin Johnson RC .40 1.00
37 Terry Kirby .20 .50
38 Leslie Shepherd .20 .50
39 Troy Aikman .40 1.00
40 Michael Irvin .30 .75
41 Deion Sanders .25 .60
42 Emmitt Smith .50 1.25
43 Bubby Brister .20 .50
44 Terrell Davis .25 .60
45 Brian Griese .20 .50
46 Ed McCaffrey .25 .60
47 Shannon Sharpe .25 .60
48 Rod Smith .25 .60
49 Charlie Batch .20 .50
50 Germane Crowell .20 .50
51 Sedrick Irvin RC .30 .75
52 Herman Moore .25 .60
53 Johnnie Morton .25 .60
54 Barry Sanders .50 1.25
55 Mark Chmura .20 .50
56 Brett Favre .60 1.50
57 Antonio Freeman .25 .60
58 Dorsey Levens .25 .60
59 Ken Dilger .20 .50
60 Marvin Harrison .25 .60
61 Edgerrin James RC .50 1.25
62 Peyton Manning 1.00 2.50
63 Jerome Pathon .20 .50
64 Mark Brunell .25 .60
65 Keenan McCardell .25 .60
66 Jimmy Smith .25 .60
67 Fred Taylor .20 .50
68 Derrick Alexander .20 .50
69 Mike Cloud RC .30 .75
70 Tony Gonzalez .25 .60
71 Elvis Grbac .20 .50
72 Andre Rison .25 .60
73 Cecil Collins RC .30 .75
74 Oronde Gadsden .20 .50
75 James Johnson RC .30 .75
76 Dan Marino .60 1.50
77 O.J. McDuffie .25 .60
78 Lamar Thomas .20 .50
79 Cris Carter .30 .75
80 Daunte Culpepper RC .50 1.25
81 Randall Cunningham .25 .60
82 Matthew Hatchette .25 .60
83 Randy Moss .25 .60
84 John Randle .30 .75
85 Robert Smith .20 .50
86 Drew Bledsoe .25 .60
87 Ben Coates .25 .60
88 Kevin Faulk RC .30 .75
89 Terry Glenn .25 .60
90 Shawn Jefferson .20 .50
91 Cam Cleeland .20 .50
92 Billy Joe Hobert .20 .50
93 Keith Poole .20 .50
94 Ricky Williams RC .50 1.25
95 Gary Brown .20 .50
96 Kent Graham .20 .50
97 Ike Hilliard .20 .50
98 Amani Toomer .20 .50
99 Wayne Chrebet .20 .50
100 Keyshawn Johnson .25 .60
101 Curtis Martin .25 .60
102 Vinny Testaverde .20 .50
103 Tim Brown .30 .75
104 James Jett .20 .50
105 Napoleon Kaufman .20 .50
106 Charles Woodson .30 .75
107 Koy Detmer .20 .50
108 Donovan McNabb RC 2.50 6.00
109 Duce Staley .20 .50
110 Kevin Turner .20 .50
111 Jerome Bettis .30 .75
112 Mark Bruener .20 .50
113 Troy Edwards RC .30 .75
114 Levon Kirkland .20 .50
115 Kordell Stewart .20 .50
116 Amos Zereoue RC .30 .75
117 Isaac Bruce .30 .75
118 Marshall Faulk .25 .60
119 Joe Germaine RC .40 1.00
120 Trent Green .20 .50
121 Torry Holt RC .60 1.50
122 Ryan Leaf .25 .60
123 Natrone Means .25 .60
124 Mikhael Ricks .20 .50
125 Junior Seau .25 .60
126 Garrison Hearst .20 .50
127 Terrell Owens .25 .60
128 Jerry Rice .75 2.00
129 J.J. Stokes .20 .50
130 Steve Young .40 1.00
131 Chad Brown .20 .50
132 Joey Galloway .25 .60
133 Brock Huard RC .30 .75
134 Jon Kitna .20 .50
135 Ricky Watters .25 .60
136 Mike Alstott .20 .50
137 Reidel Anthony .20 .50
138 Trent Dilfer .20 .50
139 Warrick Dunn .20 .50
140 Jacquez Green .20 .50
141 Shaun King RC .30 .75
142 Darnell McDonald RC .30 .75
143 Eddie George .25 .60
144 Steve McNair .25 .60
145 Yancey Thigpen .20 .50
146 Frank Wycheck .25 .60
147 Champ Bailey RC .60 1.50
148 Albert Connell .20 .50
149 Skip Hicks .20 .50
150 Michael Westbrook .20 .50

1999 Pacific Prisms Holographic Blue

*STARS: 10X TO 25X HI COL.
*RCs: 2.5X TO 6X
STATED PRINT RUN 80 SER.#'d SETS
RANDOM INSERTS IN HOBBY/RETAIL

1999 Pacific Prisms Holographic Gold

MPLETE SET (150) 150.00 300.00
*STARS: 2X TO 5X HI COL.
*RCs: .8X TO 2X
STATED PRINT RUN 480 SERIAL #'d SETS
RANDOM INSERTS IN HOBBY/RETAIL

1999 Pacific Prisms Holographic Mirror

*STARS: 6X TO 15X HI COL.
*RCs: 2X TO 5X
STATED PRINT RUN 150 SERIAL #'d SETS
RANDOM INSERT IN HOBBY/RETAIL

1999 Pacific Prisms Holographic Purple

*STARS: 3X TO 8X HI COL.
*RCs: 1.2X TO 3X
STATED ODDS 320 SERIAL #'d SETS
RANDOM INSERTS IN HOBBY

1999 Pacific Prisms Premiere Date

*STARS: 8X TO 20X HI COL.
*RCs: 2X TO 5X
STATED PRINT RUN 61 SERIAL #'d SETS
ONE PER HOBBY BOX

1999 Pacific Prisms Dial-a-Stats

Randomly inserted in packs at a rate of 1 in 193 packs, this 10 card insert set featuring top stars and rookies and allowed collectors to "dial up" stats in a number of statistical categories.

COMPLETE SET (10) 40.00 100.00
STATED ODDS 1:193
1 Tim Couch 2.00 5.00
2 Emmitt Smith 6.00 15.00
3 Terrell Davis 3.00 8.00
4 Barry Sanders 10.00 25.00
5 Brett Favre 10.00 25.00
6 Mark Brunell 3.00 8.00
7 Dan Marino 10.00 25.00
8 Ricky Williams 3.00 8.00
9 Curtis Martin 3.00 8.00
10 Terrell Owens 3.00 8.00

1999 Pacific Prisms Ornaments

ndomly inserted in packs at a rate of 1 in 25 packs, this 20 card die-cut insert set features a card design that is intended to actually hang the cards on a Christmas tree in an ornament fashion. Rookies and stars can be found within this set set such as Ricky Williams and Troy Aikman.

COMPLETE SET (20) 75.00 150.00
STATED ODDS 1:25
1 Jake Plummer 1.50 4.00
2 Jamal Anderson 2.50 6.00
3 Cade McNown .75 2.00
4 Tim Couch 1.50 4.00
5 Troy Aikman 5.00 12.00
6 Deion Sanders 2.50 6.00
7 Emmitt Smith 5.00 12.00
8 Terrell Davis 2.50 6.00
9 Barry Sanders 8.00 20.00
10 Brett Favre 8.00 20.00
11 Peyton Manning 8.00 20.00
12 Mark Brunell 2.50 6.00
13 Fred Taylor 2.50 6.00
14 Dan Marino 8.00 20.00
15 Randy Moss 6.00 15.00
16 Drew Bledsoe 3.00 8.00
17 Terrell Owens 2.50 6.00
18 Jerry Rice 5.00 12.00
19 Steve Young 3.00 8.00
20 Jon Kitna 2.50 6.00

1999 Pacific Prisms Prospects

Randomly inserted at a rate of 1 in 97 packs this hobby only insert set of 10 players includes all of the key rookies of the 1999 class such as Ricky Williams, Cade McNown, and Daunte Culpepper.

COMPLETE SET (10) 40.00 80.00
STATED ODDS 1:97 HOBBY
1 David Boston 1.25 3.00
2 Cade McNown .60 1.50
3 Akili Smith .60 1.50
4 Tim Couch 1.25 3.00
5 Edgerrin James 4.00 10.00
6 Cecil Collins 1.00 2.50
7 Daunte Culpepper 4.00 10.00
8 Ricky Williams 2.00 5.00
9 Donovan McNabb 5.00 12.00
10 Torry Holt 3.00 8.00

1999 Pacific Prisms Sunday's Best

Randomly inserted in packs at a rate of 2 in 25 packs, this 20 card insert set done with a clear holographic foil features both top rookies such as Tim Couch and Ricky Williams as well as verteran stars such as Jerry Rice and Steve Young.

COMPLETE SET (20) 40.00 80.00
STATED ODDS 2:25
1 Jake Plummer .75 2.00
2 Akili Smith .40 1.00
3 Tim Couch .75 2.00
4 Emmitt Smith 2.50 6.00
5 Terrell Davis 1.25 3.00
6 Barry Sanders 4.00 10.00
7 Brett Favre 4.00 10.00
8 Peyton Manning 4.00 10.00
9 Mark Brunell 1.25 3.00
10 Fred Taylor 1.25 3.00
11 Dan Marino 4.00 10.00
12 Randy Moss 3.00 8.00
13 Drew Bledsoe 1.50 4.00
14 Ricky Williams 1.25 3.00
15 Curtis Martin 1.25 3.00
16 Terrell Owens 1.25 3.00
17 Jerry Rice 2.50 6.00
18 Steve Young 1.50 4.00
19 Jon Kitna 1.25 3.00
20 Eddie George 1.25 3.00

2001 Pacific Prism Atomic

This 198 card set was issued in November, 2001. The cards were issued in five card packs which came 24 packs to a box and 16 boxes to a case. The SRP on the packs were $5.99 for hobby and $2.99 for retail packs. The rookie cards were issued at stated odds of two in 25 and were serial numbered to 506.

COMP.SET w/o RC's (148) 30.00 60.00
149-198 ROOKIE/506 ODDS 2:25
ROOKIE PRINT RUN 506 SER.#'d SETS
1 David Boston .25 .60
2 Thomas Jones .25 .60
3 Rob Moore .25 .60
4 Michael Pittman .30 .75
5 Jake Plummer .25 .60
6 Jamal Anderson .30 .75
7 Chris Chandler .30 .75
8 Shawn Jefferson .25 .60
9 Terance Mathis .25 .60
10 Elvis Grbac .30 .75
11 Qadry Ismail .25 .60
12 Jamal Lewis .40 1.00
13 Ray Lewis .40 1.00
14 Shannon Sharpe .30 .75
15 Shawn Bryson .25 .60
16 Rob Johnson .30 .75
17 Sammy Morris .25 .60
18 Eric Moulds .25 .60
19 Peerless Price .25 .60
20 Tim Biakabutuka .25 .60
21 Richard Huntley .25 .60
22 Patrick Jeffers .25 .60
23 Jeff Lewis .25 .60
24 Muhsin Muhammad .25 .60
25 James Allen .25 .60
26 Cade McNown .30 .75
27 Marcus Robinson .30 .75
28 Brian Urlacher .50 1.25
29 Corey Dillon .25 .60
30 Jon Kitna .25 .60
31 Akili Smith .25 .60
32 Peter Warrick .25 .60
33 Tim Couch .25 .60
34 Kevin Johnson .25 .60
35 Dennis Northcutt .25 .60
36 Travis Prentice .25 .60
37 Tony Banks .25 .60
38 Joey Galloway .30 .75
39 Rocket Ismail .30 .75
40 Emmitt Smith .60 1.50
41 Anthony Wright .25 .60
42 Mike Anderson .25 .60
43 Terrell Davis .30 .75
44 Olandis Gary .25 .60
45 Brian Griese .25 .60
46 Ed McCaffrey .30 .75
47 Rod Smith .30 .75
48 Charlie Batch .25 .60
49 Germane Crowell .25 .60
50 Herman Moore .25 .60
51 Johnnie Morton .30 .75
52 James Stewart .25 .60
53 Brett Favre .75 2.00
54 Antonio Freeman .40 1.00
55 Ahman Green .30 .75
56 Dorsey Levens .30 .75
57 Bill Schroeder .30 .75
58 Marvin Harrison .30 .75
59 Edgerrin James .30 .75
60 Peyton Manning 1.00 2.50
61 Jerome Pathon .25 .60
62 Terrence Wilkins .25 .60
63 Mark Brunell .30 .75
64 Keenan McCardell .30 .75
65 Jimmy Smith .30 .75
66 Fred Taylor .25 .60
67 Derrick Alexander .25 .60
68 Tony Gonzalez .30 .75
69 Trent Green .25 .60
70 Priest Holmes .25 .60
71 Sylvester Morris .25 .60
72 Jay Fiedler .30 .75
73 Oronde Gadsden .25 .60
74 O.J. McDuffie .25 .60
75 Lamar Smith .30 .75
76 Zach Thomas .30 .75
77 Daunte Culpepper .30 .75
78 Cris Carter .40 1.00
79 Randy Moss .30 .75
80 Chris Walsh RC .25 .60
81 Moe Williams .25 .60
82 Drew Bledsoe .30 .75
83 Kevin Faulk .25 .60
84 Terry Glenn .30 .75
85 Charles Johnson .25 .60
86 J.R. Redmond .25 .60
87 Jeff Blake .30 .75
88 Aaron Brooks .25 .60
89 Albert Connell .25 .60
90 Joe Horn .25 .60
91 Ricky Williams .30 .75
92 Tiki Barber .30 .75
93 Kerry Collins .25 .60
94 Ron Dayne .30 .75
95 Ike Hilliard .25 .60
96 Amani Toomer .25 .60
97 Richie Anderson .25 .60
98 Wayne Chrebet .25 .60
99 Curtis Martin .30 .75
100 Chad Pennington .25 .60
101 Vinny Testaverde .25 .60
102 Tim Brown .40 1.00
103 Rich Gannon .30 .75
104 Charlie Garner .30 .75
105 Jerry Rice .75 2.00
106 Tyrone Wheatley .30 .75
107 Charles Woodson .40 1.00
108 Darnell Autry .25 .60
109 Donovan McNabb .30 .75
110 Duce Staley .25 .60
111 James Thrash .30 .75
112 Jerome Bettis .40 1.00
113 Plaxico Burress .25 .60
114 Bobby Shaw .25 .60
115 Kordell Stewart .25 .60
116 Hines Ward .30 .75
117 Isaac Bruce .40 1.00
118 Marshall Faulk .30 .75
119 Az-Zahir Hakim .25 .60
120 Torry Holt .30 .75
121 Kurt Warner .60 1.50
122 Curtis Conway .30 .75
123 Tim Dwight .30 .75
124 Doug Flutie .30 .75
125 Dave Dickenson RC .30 .75
126 Jeff Garcia .25 .60
127 Terrell Owens .30 .75
128 J.J. Stokes .25 .60
129 Tai Streets .25 .60
130 Shaun Alexander .25 .60
131 Trent Dilfer .25 .60
132 Matt Hasselbeck .25 .60
133 Darrell Jackson .30 .75
134 Ricky Watters .30 .75
135 Mike Alstott .25 .60
136 Warrick Dunn .25 .60
137 Brad Johnson .30 .75
138 Keyshawn Johnson .30 .75
139 Warren Sapp .30 .75
140 Kevin Dyson .25 .60
141 Eddie George .40 1.00
142 Jevon Kearse .25 .60
143 Derrick Mason .25 .60
144 Steve McNair .30 .75
145 Champ Bailey .30 .75
146 Stephen Davis .25 .60
147 Jeff George .30 .75
148 Michael Westbrook .25 .60
149 Quentin McCord RC 2.50 6.00
150 Vinny Sutherland RC 2.00 5.00
151 Michael Vick RC 5.00 12.00
152 Chris Barnes RC 2.00 5.00
153 Reggie Germany RC 2.00 5.00
154 Travis Henry RC 2.50 6.00
155 Dee Brown RC 2.00 5.00
156 Dan Morgan RC 2.50 6.00
157 Steve Smith RC 6.00 15.00
158 Chris Weinke RC 2.50 6.00
159 David Terrell RC 2.50 6.00
160 Anthony Thomas RC 3.00 8.00
161 Chad Johnson RC 3.00 8.00
162 Rudi Johnson RC 3.00 8.00
163 James Jackson RC 2.00 5.00
164 Andre King RC 2.00 5.00
165 Quincy Morgan RC 2.50 6.00
166 Quincy Carter RC 2.50 6.00
167 Kevin Kasper RC 2.00 5.00
168 Scotty Anderson RC 2.00 5.00
169 Mike McMahon RC 2.50 6.00
170 Robert Ferguson RC 3.00 8.00
171 Reggie Wayne RC 4.00 10.00
172 Derrick Blaylock RC 2.50 6.00
173 Snoop Minnis RC 2.00 5.00
174 Chris Chambers RC 2.00 5.00
175 Josh Heupel RC 3.00 8.00
176 Travis Minor RC 2.50 6.00
177 Michael Bennett RC 2.50 6.00
178 Deuce McAllister RC 3.00 8.00
179 Jonathan Carter RC 2.00 5.00
180 Jesse Palmer RC 2.50 6.00
181 LaMont Jordan RC 3.00 8.00
182 Santana Moss RC 3.00 8.00
183 Ken-Yon Rambo RC 2.00 5.00
184 Marques Tuiasosopo RC 2.50 6.00
185 Correll Buckhalter RC 2.00 5.00
186 Freddie Mitchell RC 2.00 5.00
187 Milton Wynn RC 2.00 5.00
188 Drew Brees RC 25.00 50.00
189 LaDainian Tomlinson RC 10.00 25.00
190 Kevan Barlow RC 2.50 6.00
191 Cedrick Wilson RC 2.50 6.00
192 Alex Bannister RC 2.00 5.00
193 Josh Booty RC 2.50 6.00
194 Koren Robinson RC 2.50 6.00
195 Eddie Berlin RC 2.00 5.00
196 Rod Gardner RC 2.50 6.00
197 Darnerien McCants RC 2.50 6.00
198 Sage Rosenfels RC 2.50 6.00
S1 Eddie George SAMPLE .50 1.25
S2 Jamal Lewis SAMPLE .75 2.00
S3 Randy Moss SAMPLE .60 1.50
S4 Emmitt Smith SAMPLE 1.00 2.50

2001 Pacific Prism Atomic Blue

*VETS 1-148: 12X TO 30X BASIC CARDS
1-148 VETERAN/29 ODDS 1:193
1-148 VETERAN PRINT RUN 29
149-198 ROOKIE/19 ODDS 1:1153
149-198 ROOKIE PRINT RUN 19

2001 Pacific Prism Atomic Gold

*VETS 1-148: 3X TO 8X BASIC CARDS
*149-196 ROOKIES: .5X TO 1.2X
GOLD/116 ODDS 2:25 HOBBY
STATED PRINT RUN 116 SER.#'d SETS
188 Drew Brees 50.00 100.00

2001 Pacific Prism Atomic Premiere Date

*VETERANS: 3X TO 8X BASIC CARDS
PREMIERE DATE/86 ODDS 1:25
STATED PRINT RUN 86 SER.#'d SETS

2001 Pacific Prism Atomic Red

ETS 1-148: 2.5X TO 6X BASIC CARDS
*ROOKIES 149-198: .4X TO 1X
RED/310 ODDS 4:25 RETAIL
STATED PRINT RUN 310 SER.#'d SETS

2001 Pacific Prism Atomic Core Players

Inserted at a rate of one in 25, these 20 cards feature players who are crucial to their team's sucsess.

COMPLETE SET (20) 15.00 40.00
STATED ODDS 1:25
1 Jamal Lewis .75 2.00
2 Peter Warrick .50 1.25
3 Tim Couch .50 1.25
4 Emmitt Smith 1.25 3.00
5 Mike Anderson .50 1.25
6 Terrell Davis .60 1.50
7 Brett Favre 1.50 4.00
8 Edgerrin James .60 1.50
9 Peyton Manning 2.00 5.00
10 Fred Taylor .50 1.25
11 Randy Moss .60 1.50
12 Ricky Williams .60 1.50
13 Ron Dayne .60 1.50
14 Jerry Rice 1.50 4.00
15 Donovan McNabb .60 1.50
16 Marshall Faulk .60 1.50
17 Kurt Warner 1.25 3.00
18 Jeff Garcia .50 1.25
19 Eddie George .75 2.00
20 Steve McNair .60 1.50

2001 Pacific Prism Atomic Energy

Issued at a rate of one in 49, these 20 cards feature some of the leading 2001 rookies.

COMPLETE SET (20) 15.00 40.00
STATED ODDS 1:49
1 Michael Vick 1.00 2.50
2 Travis Henry .50 1.25
3 Chris Weinke .50 1.25
4 David Terrell .50 1.25
5 Anthony Thomas .60 1.50
6 Quincy Carter .50 1.25
7 Reggie Wayne .75 2.00
8 Josh Heupel .60 1.50
9 Michael Bennett .50 1.25
10 Deuce McAllister .60 1.50
11 Jesse Palmer .50 1.25
12 LaMont Jordan .60 1.50
13 Santana Moss .60 1.50
14 Marques Tuiasosopo .50 1.25
15 Freddie Mitchell .40 1.00
16 Drew Brees 8.00 20.00
17 LaDainian Tomlinson 2.00 5.00
18 Koren Robinson .50 1.25
19 Rod Gardner .50 1.25
20 Sage Rosenfels .50 1.25

2001 Pacific Prism Atomic Jerseys

Issued at a rate of four in 25 hobby packs, these 100 cards feature game worn jersey swatches from various NFL players.

STATED ODDS 4:25 HOBBY
1 Mac Cody 3.00 8.00
2 MarTay Jenkins 3.00 8.00
3 Thomas Jones 3.00 8.00
4 Rob Moore 3.00 8.00
5 Chris Chandler 4.00 10.00
6 Bob Christian 3.00 8.00
7 Jamal Lewis 5.00 12.00
8 Larry Centers 3.00 8.00
9 Rob Johnson 4.00 10.00
10 Peerless Price 3.00 8.00
11 Brad Hoover 4.00 10.00
12 Muhsin Muhammad 3.00 8.00
13 Chris Weinke 4.00 10.00
14 James Allen 3.00 8.00
15 Macey Brooks 3.00 8.00
16 Bobby Engram 3.00 8.00
17 Anthony Thomas 5.00 12.00
18 Brian Urlacher 6.00 15.00
19 Corey Dillon SP 4.00 10.00
20 Bobby Brown 3.00 8.00
21 Tim Couch 3.00 8.00
22 Curtis Enis 3.00 8.00
23 Emmitt Smith 8.00 20.00
24 Anthony Wright 3.00 8.00
25 Mike Anderson SP 4.00 10.00
26 Eddie Kennison 4.00 10.00
27 James Stewart 3.00 8.00
28 Brett Favre 10.00 25.00
29 Bubba Franks 3.00 8.00
30 William Henderson 3.00 8.00
31 Marvin Harrison 4.00 10.00
32 Edgerrin James 4.00 10.00
33 Peyton Manning SP 15.00 40.00
34 Mark Brunell 4.00 10.00
35 Keenan McCardell 4.00 10.00
36 Jimmy Smith 4.00 10.00
37 R.Jay Soward 3.00 8.00
38 Fred Taylor 3.00 8.00
39 Sylvester Morris 3.00 8.00
40 Autry Denson 3.00 8.00
41 Jay Fiedler 4.00 10.00
42 James Johnson 3.00 8.00
43 Zach Thomas 4.00 10.00
44 Cris Carter 5.00 12.00
45 Daunte Culpepper 4.00 10.00
46 Randy Moss 4.00 10.00
47 Drew Bledsoe 4.00 10.00
48 Aaron Brooks 3.00 8.00
49 Joe Horn 3.00 8.00
50 Terrelle Smith 3.00 8.00
51 Tiki Barber 4.00 10.00
52 Kerry Collins 3.00 8.00
53 Greg Comella 3.00 8.00
54 Ron Dixon 3.00 8.00
55 Ike Hilliard 3.00 8.00
56 Joe Jurevicius 3.00 8.00
57 Richie Anderson 3.00 8.00
58 Laveranues Coles 4.00 10.00
59 Matthew Hatchette 3.00 8.00
60 Curtis Martin 4.00 10.00
61 Dwight Stone 3.00 8.00
62 Vinny Testaverde 3.00 8.00
63 David Dunn 3.00 8.00
64 Napoleon Kaufman 3.00 8.00
65 Jerry Porter 3.00 8.00
66 Jerry Rice 10.00 25.00
67 Andre Rison 4.00 10.00
68 Marques Tuiasosopo 4.00 10.00
69 Tyrone Wheatley 4.00 10.00
70 Charles Woodson 5.00 12.00
71 Donovan McNabb 4.00 10.00
72 Freddie Mitchell 3.00 8.00
73 Duce Staley 3.00 8.00
74 Ernie Conwell 3.00 8.00
75 Marshall Faulk 4.00 10.00
76 Az-Zahir Hakim 3.00 8.00
77 Torry Holt 4.00 10.00
78 Ricky Proehl 3.00 8.00
79 Drew Brees 30.00 60.00
80 Curtis Conway 4.00 10.00
81 Freddie Jones 3.00 8.00
82 Junior Seau 4.00 10.00
83 LaDainian Tomlinson 8.00 20.00
84 Jeff Garcia 3.00 8.00
85 Terrell Owens 4.00 10.00
86 J.J. Stokes 3.00 8.00
87 Tai Streets 3.00 8.00
88 Karsten Bailey 3.00 8.00
89 Brock Huard 3.00 8.00
90 James Williams 3.00 8.00
91 Reidel Anthony 3.00 8.00
92 Jacquez Green 3.00 8.00
93 Joe Hamilton 3.00 8.00
94 Keyshawn Johnson 4.00 10.00
95 Warren Sapp 4.00 10.00
96 Kevin Dyson 3.00 8.00
97 Jevon Kearse 3.00 8.00
98 Derrick Mason 3.00 8.00
99 Stephen Alexander 3.00 8.00
100 Kevin Lockett 3.00 8.00

2001 Pacific Prism Atomic Jersey Patches

Issued in hobby packs only at the rate of 2 in 25, this 136-card set featured patch swatches from jerseys of a variety of NFL players. Most cards from #1-100 were essentially a parallel version to the base Jersey set while cards #101-150 were produced in the Patch version only.

COMMON CARD 5.00 12.00
SEMISTARS 6.00 15.00
UNLISTED STARS 8.00 20.00
STATED ODDS 2:25 HOBBY
18 Brian Urlacher 12.00 30.00
23 Emmitt Smith 15.00 40.00
33 Peyton Manning 25.00 60.00
66 Jerry Rice 20.00 50.00
71 Donovan McNabb 8.00 20.00
125 Tom Brady 500.00 1000.00
140 Dan Kreider 25.00 50.00

2001 Pacific Prism Atomic Rookie Reaction

Issued at a rate of one in 49, these 20 cards feature some of the leading 2001 rookies.

COMPLETE SET (20) 15.00 40.00
STATED ODDS 1:49
1 Michael Vick 1.00 2.50
2 Travis Henry .50 1.25
3 Chris Weinke .50 1.25
4 David Terrell .50 1.25
5 Anthony Thomas .60 1.50
6 James Jackson .40 1.00
7 Quincy Carter .50 1.25
8 Reggie Wayne .75 2.00
9 Josh Heupel .60 1.50
10 Michael Bennett .50 1.25
11 Deuce McAllister .60 1.50
12 LaMont Jordan .60 1.50
13 Santana Moss .60 1.50
14 Marques Tuiasosopo .50 1.25
15 Freddie Mitchell .40 1.00
16 Drew Brees 2.50 6.00
17 LaDainian Tomlinson 2.00 5.00
18 Kevan Barlow .50 1.25
19 Koren Robinson .50 1.25
20 Rod Gardner .50 1.25

2001 Pacific Prism Atomic Statosphere

sued at a rate of one in 25, these 20 cards were split between hobby and retail. Cards 1-10 were issued in hobby packs while cards 11-20 were issued in retail packs.

COMPLETE SET (20) 15.00 40.00
STATED ODDS 1:25
1-10 FOUND IN HOBBY
11-20 FOUND IN RETAIL
1 Chris Weinke .60 1.50
2 Tim Couch .50 1.25
3 Brian Griese .50 1.25
4 Peyton Manning 2.00 5.00
5 Mark Brunell .60 1.50
6 Daunte Culpepper .60 1.50
7 Drew Bledsoe .60 1.50
8 Kurt Warner 1.25 3.00
9 Jeff Garcia .50 1.25
10 Steve McNair .60 1.50
11 Jamal Lewis .75 2.00
12 Peter Warrick .50 1.25
13 Emmitt Smith 1.25 3.00
14 Terrell Davis .60 1.50
15 Edgerrin James .60 1.50
16 Fred Taylor .50 1.25
17 Randy Moss .60 1.50
18 Ricky Williams .60 1.50
19 Jerry Rice 1.50 4.00
20 Marshall Faulk .60 1.50

2001 Pacific Prism Atomic Strategic Arms

Issued at a rate of one in 769, these 10 cards feature some leading NFL quarterbacks. These cards are serial numbered to 86 sets.

COMPLETE SET (10) 75.00 150.00
STATED ODDS 1:769
STATED PRINT RUN 86 SER.#'d SETS
1 Michael Vick 8.00 20.00
2 Tim Couch 3.00 8.00
3 Brian Griese 3.00 8.00
4 Brett Favre 10.00 25.00
5 Peyton Manning 12.00 30.00
6 Mark Brunell 4.00 10.00
7 Daunte Culpepper 4.00 10.00
8 Drew Bledsoe 4.00 10.00
9 Donovan McNabb 4.00 10.00
10 Kurt Warner 8.00 20.00

2001 Pacific Prism Atomic Team Nucleus

Issued at a rate of one in 25, these 10 cards feature three key players from selected NFL teams.

COMPLETE SET (10) 10.00 25.00
STATED ODDS 1:25
1 Urlacher/Thomas/Terrell 1.50 4.00
2 C.Johnson/Dillon/Warrick 1.25 3.00
3 Griese/T.Davis/Anderson 1.00 2.50
4 Wayne/James/Harrison 1.50 4.00
5 Brunell/Taylor/J.Smith 1.00 2.50
6 Culpepper/Bennett/R.Moss 1.00 2.50
7 Pennington/Jordan/S.Moss 1.25 3.00
8 Warner/Faulk/Bruce 2.00 5.00
9 Flutie/Brees/Tomlinson 5.00 12.00
10 McNair/George/Mason 1.25 3.00

2000 Pacific Prism Prospects

Released as a 200-card base set consisting of 100 veteran cards an 100 rookie cards sequentially numbered to 1000, Prism Prospects features full color player action photography set against a holofoil background which is embossed to represent a football field. A black line across the bottom of the card contains the player's name and position. Prism Prospects was packaged in six pack boxes with packs containing three cards each and carried a suggested retail price of $34.99. Each Hobby box also contained a special pack with one Beckett Grading Services graded card.

COMP.SET w/o SP's (100) 10.00 25.00
1 David Boston .15 .40
2 Jake Plummer .15 .40
3 Jamal Anderson .20 .50
4 Chris Chandler .20 .50
5 Tim Dwight .20 .50
6 Terance Mathis .15 .40
7 Tony Banks .15 .40
8 Priest Holmes .15 .40
9 Doug Flutie .20 .50
10 Rob Johnson .20 .50
11 Eric Moulds .15 .40
12 Antowain Smith .20 .50
13 Steve Beuerlein .20 .50
14 Tim Biakabutuka .20 .50
15 Muhsin Muhammad .15 .40
16 Bobby Engram .15 .40
17 Curtis Enis .15 .40
18 Cade McNown .15 .40
19 Marcus Robinson .20 .50
20 Corey Dillon .15 .40
21 Akili Smith .15 .40
22 Tim Couch .20 .50
23 Kevin Johnson .15 .40
24 Troy Aikman .30 .75
25 Joey Galloway .20 .50
26 Rocket Ismail .20 .50
27 Emmitt Smith .40 1.00
28 Terrell Davis .20 .50
29 Olandis Gary .20 .50
30 Brian Griese .15 .40
31 Charlie Batch .15 .40
32 Herman Moore .15 .40
33 Johnnie Morton .20 .50
34 Brett Favre .50 1.25
35 Antonio Freeman .20 .50
36 Dorsey Levens .20 .50
37 Marvin Harrison .20 .50
38 Edgerrin James .20 .50
39 Peyton Manning .60 1.50
40 Mark Brunell .20 .50
41 Keenan McCardell .20 .50
42 Jimmy Smith .20 .50
43 Fred Taylor .15 .40
44 Donnell Bennett .15 .40
45 Tony Gonzalez .20 .50
46 Elvis Grbac .15 .40
47 Damon Huard .15 .40
48 James Johnson .15 .40
49 Cris Carter .25 .60
50 Daunte Culpepper .20 .50
51 Randy Moss .20 .50
52 Robert Smith .15 .40
53 Drew Bledsoe .20 .50
54 Kevin Faulk .15 .40
55 Terry Glenn .20 .50
56 Jeff Blake .20 .50
57 Ricky Williams .20 .50
58 Kerry Collins .15 .40
59 Ike Hilliard .15 .40
60 Amani Toomer .15 .40
61 Wayne Chrebet .15 .40
62 Curtis Martin .20 .50
63 Vinny Testaverde .15 .40
64 Tim Brown .25 .60
65 Rich Gannon .20 .50
66 Napoleon Kaufman .20 .50
67 Tyrone Wheatley .15 .40
68 Donovan McNabb .20 .50
69 Duce Staley .15 .40
70 Jerome Bettis .25 .60
71 Troy Edwards .15 .40
72 Kordell Stewart .15 .40
73 Isaac Bruce .25 .60
74 Torry Holt .20 .50
75 Marshall Faulk .20 .50
76 Kurt Warner .40 1.00
77 Jermaine Fazande .15 .40
78 Jim Harbaugh .20 .50
79 Ryan Leaf .20 .50
80 Junior Seau .20 .50
81 Jeff Garcia .15 .40
82 J.J. Stokes .20 .50
83 Terrell Owens .20 .50
84 Jerry Rice .60 1.50
85 Jon Kitna .15 .40
86 Derrick Mayes .15 .40
87 Ricky Watters .20 .50
88 Mike Alstott .15 .40
89 Warrick Dunn .15 .40
90 Jacquez Green .15 .40
91 Shaun King .15 .40
92 Eddie George .20 .50
93 Jevon Kearse .15 .40
94 Steve McNair .20 .50
95 Carl Pickens .20 .50
96 Stephen Davis .15 .40
97 Jeff George .20 .50
98 Brad Johnson .20 .50
99 Deion Sanders .20 .50
100 Michael Westbrook .15 .40
101 Jabari Issa RC 1.50 4.00
102 Thomas Jones RC 2.00 5.00
103 Sekou Sanyika RC 1.50 4.00
104 Jay Tant RC 1.50 4.00
105 Raynoch Thompson RC 1.50 4.00
106 Doug Johnson RC 1.50 4.00
107 Mark Simoneau RC 1.50 4.00
108 Jamal Lewis RC 2.50 6.00
109 Chris Redman RC 1.50 4.00
110 Travis Taylor RC 1.50 4.00
111 Kwame Cavil RC 1.50 4.00
112 Corey Moore RC 1.50 4.00
113 Rashard Anderson RC 1.50 4.00
114 Lester Towns RC 1.50 4.00
115 Paul Edinger RC 2.50 6.00
116 Brian Urlacher RC 8.00 20.00
117 Dez White RC 1.50 4.00
118 Ron Dugans RC 1.50 4.00
119 Danny Farmer RC 1.50 4.00
120 Curtis Keaton RC 1.50 4.00
121 Peter Warrick RC 1.50 4.00
122 Courtney Brown RC 2.00 5.00
123 Lamar Chapman RC 1.50 4.00
124 JaJuan Dawson RC 1.50 4.00
125 Dennis Northcutt RC 1.50 4.00
126 Travis Prentice RC 1.50 4.00
127 Aaron Shea RC 2.00 5.00
128 Spergon Wynn RC 1.50 4.00
129 Dwayne Goodrich RC 1.50 4.00
130 Orantes Grant RC 1.50 4.00
131 Kareem Larrimore RC 1.50 4.00
132 Michael Wiley RC 1.50 4.00
133 Mike Anderson RC 1.50 4.00
134 Chris Cole RC 2.00 5.00
135 Jarious Jackson RC 2.00 5.00
136 Jerry Johnson RC 1.50 4.00
137 Kenoy Kennedy RC 1.50 4.00
138 Deltha O'Neal RC 1.50 4.00
139 Reuben Droughns RC 1.50 4.00
140 Barrett Green RC 1.50 4.00
141 Bubba Franks RC 1.50 4.00
142 Kevin McDougal RC 1.50 4.00
143 Marcus Washington RC 2.00 5.00
144 T.J. Slaughter RC 1.50 4.00
145 R.Jay Soward RC 1.50 4.00
146 Shyrone Stith RC 1.50 4.00
147 William Bartee RC 1.50 4.00
148 Dante Hall RC 1.50 4.00
149 Frank Moreau RC 1.50 4.00
150 Sylvester Morris RC 1.50 4.00
151 Deon Dyer RC 1.50 4.00
152 Ben Kelly RC 1.50 4.00
153 Tyrone Carter RC 2.00 5.00
154 Doug Chapman RC 1.50 4.00
155 Troy Walters RC 1.50 4.00
156 Tom Brady RC 200.00 300.00
157 Patrick Pass RC 1.50 4.00
158 J.R. Redmond RC 1.50 4.00
159 Marc Bulger RC 2.00 5.00
160 Darren Howard RC 1.50 4.00
161 Chad Morton RC 2.00 5.00
162 Mareno Philyaw RC 1.50 4.00
163 Terrelle Smith RC 1.50 4.00
164 Ralph Brown RC 1.50 4.00
165 Ron Dayne RC 2.50 6.00
166 Brandon Short RC 1.50 4.00
167 John Abraham RC 2.50 6.00
168 Anthony Becht RC 1.50 4.00
169 Laveranues Coles RC 2.00 5.00
170 Shaun Ellis RC 2.00 5.00
171 Chad Pennington RC 2.00 5.00
172 Sebastian Janikowski RC 4.00 10.00
173 Jerry Porter RC 2.50 6.00
174 Todd Pinkston RC 1.50 4.00
175 Gari Scott RC 1.50 4.00
176 Corey Simon RC 2.00 5.00
177 Plaxico Burress RC 2.00 5.00
178 Tee Martin RC 1.50 4.00
179 Hank Poteat RC 1.50 4.00
180 Rogers Beckett RC 1.50 4.00
181 Trevor Gaylor RC 1.50 4.00
182 Ronney Jenkins RC 1.50 4.00
183 Giovanni Carmazzi RC 1.50 4.00
184 Chafie Fields RC 1.50 4.00
185 Ahmed Plummer RC 1.50 4.00
186 Tim Rattay RC 2.00 5.00
187 Jeff Ulbrich RC 1.50 4.00
188 Shaun Alexander RC 2.50 6.00
189 Darrell Jackson RC 1.50 4.00
190 Rodnick Phillips RC 1.50 4.00
191 James Williams RC 1.50 4.00
192 Trung Canidate RC 1.50 4.00
193 Joe Hamilton RC 1.50 4.00
194 DeMario Brown RC 1.50 4.00
195 Keith Bulluck RC 2.00 5.00
196 Chris Coleman RC 1.50 4.00
197 Erron Kinney RC 1.50 4.00
198 Billy Volek RC 2.50 6.00
199 Todd Husak RC 1.50 4.00
200 Chris Samuels RC 2.50 6.00

2000 Pacific Prism Prospects Holographic Blue

OLOBLUE VETS: 5X TO 12X BASIC CARDS
HOLO.BLUE PRINT RUN 100 SER.#'d SETS

2000 Pacific Prism Prospects Holographic Mirror

OLO.MIRROR: 6X TO 15X BASIC CARDS
HOLO.MIRROR PRINT RUN 75 SER.#'d SETS

2000 Pacific Prism Prospects Premiere Date

*PREM.DATE: 3X TO 8X BASIC CARDS
PREM.DATE PRINT RUN 138 SER.#'d SETS

2000 Pacific Prism Prospects Fortified With Stars

ndomly inserted in packs at the rate of one in 97 Hobby and one in 241 retail, this 10-card set features players set on a cereal box. The cereal box name incorporates the featured player's name and a full color action photograph.

COMPLETE SET (10) 30.00 80.00
STATED ODDS 1:97 HOB, 1:241 RET
1 Jake Plummer 1.25 3.00
2 Peerless Price 1.50 4.00
3 Tim Couch 1.50 4.00
4 Brett Favre 4.00 10.00
5 Drew Bledsoe 1.50 4.00
6 Tyrone Wheatley 1.25 3.00
7 Plaxico Burress 1.50 4.00
8 Jerome Bettis 2.00 5.00
9 Jerry Rice 5.00 12.00
10 Jon Kitna 1.25 3.00

2000 Pacific Prism Prospects Game Worn Jerseys

ndomly seeded in packs, this 10-card set features a player action photo on the left side with background colors to match each player's team colors. The background is made up of a faded player photo in the tone of the background colors. A square swatch of a game worn jersey is placed on the right side of the card.

COMPLETE SET (10) 30.00 80.00
*PATCH/78-100: .6X TO 1.5X BASIC JSY
*PATCH/35: 1X TO 2.5X BASIC JSY
*PATCH/15-23: 1.2X TO 3X BASIC JSY
PATCH PRINT RUN 15-100
1 Randall Cunningham 2.50 6.00
2 Mark Brunell 2.50 6.00
3 Fred Taylor 2.00 5.00
4 Dan Marino 6.00 15.00
5 Drew Bledsoe 2.50 6.00
6 Wayne Chrebet 2.00 5.00
7 Kordell Stewart 2.00 5.00
8 Jerry Rice 8.00 20.00
9 Steve Young 4.00 10.00
10 Jon Kitna 2.00 5.00

2000 Pacific Prism Prospects MVP Candidates

ndomly inserted in packs at the rate of one in 25 Hobby and one in 49 Retail, this 10-card set features top players in action set against a blue background containing a football field and the words MVP in blue-tone print. Cards are accented with gold foil highlights.

COMPLETE SET (10) 12.50 30.00
STATED ODDS 1:25 HOB, 1:49 RET
1 Peter Warrick .60 1.50
2 Emmitt Smith 1.50 4.00
3 Brett Favre 2.00 5.00
4 Edgerrin James .75 2.00
5 Peyton Manning 2.50 6.00
6 Randy Moss .75 2.00
7 Ricky Williams .75 2.00
8 Marshall Faulk .75 2.00
9 Kurt Warner 1.50 4.00
10 Eddie George .75 2.00

2000 Pacific Prism Prospects Rookie Dial-A-Stats

ndomly inserted in packs at the rate of one in 193 Hobby and one in 481 Retail, this 10-card set features a full color player action photo on the right side with gold foil highlights. The left side of the card features a cut out box where a wheel has been attached to the card, held on by a circular fastener in the middle of the card, that can be turned to reveal player statistics through the cut out box.

COMPLETE SET (10) 12.00 30.00
STATED ODDS 1:193 HOB, 1;481 RET
1 Thomas Jones 1.00 2.50
2 Jamal Lewis 1.25 3.00
3 Chris Redman .75 2.00
4 Peter Warrick .75 2.00
5 R.Jay Soward .75 2.00
6 Ron Dayne 1.25 3.00
7 Laveranues Coles 1.00 2.50
8 Chad Pennington 1.00 2.50
9 Plaxico Burress 1.00 2.50
10 Shaun Alexander 1.25 3.00

2000 Pacific Prism Prospects ROY Candidates

ndomly inserted in packs at the rate of one in 25 Hobby and one in 49 retail, this 10-card set features the same style card stock as the MVP Candidates. Player action photography is set against a blue-tone background with a football field on the bottom and the letters ROY on the top. Cards are accented with silver foil highlights.

COMPLETE SET (10) 10.00 25.00
STATED ODDS 1:25 HOB, 1:49 RET
1 Thomas Jones .50 1.25
2 Jamal Lewis .60 1.50
3 Travis Taylor .40 1.00
4 Peter Warrick .40 1.00
5 Sylvester Morris .40 1.00
6 Doug Chapman .40 1.00
7 Ron Dayne .60 1.50
8 Chad Pennington .50 1.25
9 Plaxico Burress .50 1.25
10 Shaun Alexander .60 1.50

2000 Pacific Prism Prospects Sno-Globe Die Cuts

ndomly inserted in packs at the rate of one in 25 Hobby and one in 49 retial, this 20-card set features a circular die cut along the top of the card with a blue name box along the bottom of the card where the players name appears in holofoil. Full color action shots are set in the middle of a "snow globe" that features a stadium backdrop.

COMPLETE SET (20) 40.00 100.00
STATED ODDS 1:25 HOB, 1:49 RET
1 Cade McNown 1.25 3.00
2 Tim Couch 1.50 4.00
3 Troy Aikman 2.50 6.00
4 Emmitt Smith 3.00 8.00
5 Terrell Davis 1.50 4.00
6 Brian Griese 1.25 3.00
7 Brett Favre 4.00 10.00
8 Peyton Manning 5.00 12.00
9 Edgerrin James 1.50 4.00
10 Mark Brunell 1.50 4.00
11 Damon Huard 1.25 3.00
12 Daunte Culpepper 1.50 4.00
13 Randy Moss 1.50 4.00
14 Drew Bledsoe 1.50 4.00
15 Jon Kitna 1.25 3.00
16 Marshall Faulk 1.50 4.00
17 Kurt Warner 3.00 8.00
18 Eddie George 1.50 4.00
19 Steve McNair 1.50 4.00
20 Stephen Davis 1.25 3.00

1992 Pacific Triple Folders

e 28 cards in this set measure 3 1/2" by 5" when folded and display a glossy action color player photo on the front. The player's name and position are printed in block letters. The two panels that make up the front photo are split down the center and can be opened to reveal three separate photos on the inside. The center panel carries an action color player photo and the player's name in block letters. The left inside panel has an action player photo while the right inside panel has a posed close-up shot. The backs carry career highlights and statistics. The background and lettering are team color-coded. The players chosen represent each of the 28 NFL teams, and the cards are arranged alphabetically according to team name. Each triple folder card pack contained a bonus card from one of the following insert sets: Steve Largent subset, Bob Griese subset, team Statistical Leader subset, gold and silver foil subset, Rushing Leader Prism subset, or Checklist Card subset.

COMPLETE SET (28) 8.00 20.00
1 Chris Miller .25 .60
2 Thurman Thomas .40 1.00
3 Neal Anderson .25 .60
4 Tim McGee .10 .30
5 Kevin Mack .10 .30
6 Emmitt Smith 2.00 5.00
7 John Elway 2.00 5.00
8 Barry Sanders 2.00 5.00
9 Sterling Sharpe .40 1.00
10 Warren Moon .40 1.00
11 Bill Brooks .10 .30
12 Christian Okoye .10 .30
13 Nick Bell .10 .30
14 Robert Delpino .10 .30
15 Mark Higgs .10 .30
16 Rich Gannon .40 1.00
17 Leonard Russell .10 .30
18 Pat Swilling .25 .60
19 Rodney Hampton .25 .60
20 Rob Moore .25 .60
21 Reggie White .40 1.00
22 Johnny Johnson .10 .30
23 Neil O'Donnell .25 .60
24 Marion Butts .10 .30
25 Steve Young .80 2.00
26 John L. Williams .10 .30
27 Reggie Cobb .10 .30
28 Mark Rypien .10 .30

1993 Pacific Triple Folders

ese 30 cards measure approximately 3 1/2" by 10 1/8" when folded out and feature gray-bordered color player action shots on all of their panels, except the backs. When the front panels are closed they merge into a single color player action photo, with the player's name and position printed in team color-coded marbleized lettering down the left side and along the bottom. On a team color-coded marbleized background, the back carries the player's name, position, team, career highlights, and 1992 stats. There were reportedly only 2,500 cases of Triple Folders produced by Pacific.

COMPLETE SET (30) 10.00 25.00
1 Thurman Thomas .40 1.00
2 Carl Pickens .25 .60
3 Glyn Milburn .25 .60
4 Lorenzo White .10 .30
5 Anthony Johnson .10 .30
6 Joe Montana 2.00 5.00
7 Nick Bell .10 .30
8 Dan Marino 1.60 4.00
9 Anthony Carter .10 .30
10 Drew Bledsoe 1.20 3.00
11 Rob Moore .25 .60
12 Barry Foster .10 .30
13 Stan Humphries .25 .60
14 Cortez Kennedy .25 .60
15 Rick Mirer .25 .60
16 Deion Sanders .50 1.25
17 Curtis Conway .25 .60
18 Tommy Vardell .10 .30
19 Emmitt Smith 1.60 4.00
20 Barry Sanders 1.60 4.00
21 Brett Favre 1.60 4.00
22 Cleveland Gary .10 .30
23 Morten Andersen .10 .30
24 Marcus Buckley .10 .30
25 Rodney Hampton .25 .60
26 Herschel Walker .10 .30
27 Garrison Hoarst .40 1.00
28 Jerry Rice .80 2.00
29 Lawrence Dawsey .10 .30
30 Desmond Howard .25 .60

1993 Pacific Triple Folders Gold Prism Inserts

There are three slightly different versions of this 20-card standard-size set. The difference involves the prismatic backgrounds. The standard 1993 Pacific Prism Inserts were produced with triangular silver prismatic backgrounds and were randomly inserted in regular Pacific packs as well as Triple Folder packs. A circular version of the silver background cards was inserted one per special (gold-colored) Pacific retail packs. The third version (this set) uses a gold triangular prismatic background. The production of these cards was reportedly limited to 1000 each, and they were randomly inserted in 1993 Pacific Triple Folder packs. The fronts feature color player action cut-outs over borderless prismatic foil backgrounds. The player's name appears in team-colored block lettering at the bottom. The backs display a full-bleed color action player photo with the player's name and position in script.

COMPLETE SET (20) 80.00 200.00
*GOLD CARDS: 1.2X TO 3X PACIFIC SILVERS

1993 Pacific Triple Folders Rookies and Stars

Randomly inserted in Triple Folder packs, these 20 standard-size cards feature borderless color player action shots on their fronts. The player's name and position appears in white cursive lettering in a lower corner. On a team-colored background consisting of football icons, the back carries the player's name, position, team name and helmet, and 1992 season highlights. Card numbers 2-8, 11, 13, and 19 are rookies; the remainder are superstars.

COMPLETE SET (20) 8.00 20.00
1 Troy Aikman .80 2.00
2 Victor Bailey .10 .30
3 Jerome Bettis .60 1.50
4 Drew Bledsoe 1.20 3.00
5 Reggie Brooks .10 .30
6 Derek Brown RBK .10 .30
7 Marcus Buckley .10 .30
8 Curtis Conway .30 .75
9 Brett Favre 1.60 4.00
10 Barry Foster .10 .30
11 Garrison Hearst .40 1.00
12 Cortez Kennedy .10 .30
13 Rick Mirer .20 .50
14 Joe Montana 1.60 4.00
15 Jerry Rice .80 2.00
16 Barry Sanders 1.60 4.00
17 Sterling Sharpe .20 .50
18 Emmitt Smith 1.60 4.00
19 Robert Smith .40 1.00
20 Thurman Thomas .20 .50

1994 Pacific Triple Folders

ese 33 cards measure approximately 3 1/2" by 5" when folded and feature white-bordered color action player shots on all of their panels. When the front panels are closed, they merge into a single color action player photo with the player's first name printed on the bottom. When opened, the inside reveals another color action player photo. The player's last name is printed on the bottom with a team helmet on the left and right. On a team color-coded background, the backs carry the player's name and position and a career highlight. The set is arranged in alphabetical order by teams. In addition to a Triple Folder card, each pack included one bonus card from either the Gems of the Crown, Crown Collection Crystalline, or Knights of the Gridiron subsets. Also, randomly inserted in Triple Folder packs only were the Rookies and Stars 40-card insert. Less than 2,999 individually-numbered cases were produced.

COMPLETE SET (33) 10.00 25.00
1 Ronald Moore .30 .75
2 Erric Pegram .20 .50
3 Jim Kelly .40 1.00
4 Thurman Thomas .40 1.00
5 Curtis Conway .40 1.00
6 Vinny Testaverde .20 .50
7 Troy Aikman .80 2.00
8 Emmitt Smith 1.20 3.00
9 John Elway 1.60 4.00
10 Shannon Sharpe .30 .75
11 Barry Sanders 1.60 4.00
12 Brett Favre 1.60 4.00
13 Sterling Sharpe .30 .75
14 Gary Brown .20 .50
15 Marshall Faulk 1.20 3.00
16 Joe Montana 1.60 4.00
17 Rocket Ismail .30 .75
18 Jerome Bettis .40 1.00
19 Dan Marino 1.60 4.00
20 David Palmer .20 .50
21 Drew Bledsoe .80 2.00
22 Ben Coates .30 .75
23 Derrick Ned .20 .50
24 Rodney Hampton .30 .75
25 Boomer Esiason .30 .75
26 Barry Foster .20 .50
27 Charles Johnson .30 .75
28 Natrone Means .30 .75
29 Steve Young .60 1.50
30 Rick Mirer .30 .75
31 Chris Warren .20 .50
32 Trent Dilfer .40 1.00
33 Heath Shuler .30 .75

1994 Pacific Triple Folders Rookies and Stars

is 40-card standard-size set was randomly inserted only in Triple Folder packs. The fronts feature color action player shots with a computer generated backgound. The player's name and position in gold-foil appears on the bottom. On the same background, the backs carry a posed color action photo with the player's name, position and a career highlight. The set is arranged in team alphabetical order.

COMPLETE SET (40) 10.00 25.00
1 Ronald Moore .20 .50
2 Jeff George .20 .50
3 Jim Kelly .30 .75
4 Thurman Thomas .20 .50
5 Curtis Conway .30 .75
6 Darnay Scott .30 .75
7 Vinny Testaverde .10 .30
8 Troy Aikman .80 2.00
9 Emmitt Smith 1.20 3.00
10 John Elway 1.60 4.00
11 Shannon Sharpe .20 .50
12 Barry Sanders 1.60 4.00
13 LeShon Johnson .10 .30
14 Sterling Sharpe .20 .50
15 Gary Brown .10 .30
16 Marshall Faulk 1.60 4.00
17 Lake Dawson .20 .50
18 Greg Hill .20 .50
19 Joe Montana 1.60 4.00
20 Tim Brown .30 .75
21 Jerome Bettis .40 1.00
22 Dan Marino 1.60 4.00
23 Terry Allen .30 .75
24 David Palmer .20 .50
25 Drew Bledsoe .80 2.00
26 Ben Coates .20 .50
27 Michael Haynes .10 .30
28 Rodney Hampton .20 .50
29 Thomas Lewis .10 .30
30 Aaron Glenn .30 .75
31 Charlie Garner .20 .50
32 Charles Johnson .20 .50
33 Byron Bam Morris .10 .30
34 Natrone Means .30 .75
35 Ricky Watters .20 .50
36 Steve Young .50 1.25
37 Rick Mirer .20 .50
38 Trent Dilfer .30 .75
39 Errict Rhett .20 .50
40 Heath Shuler .30 .75

1995 Pacific Triple Folders

This 48 card set was issued late in 1995 by Pacific and is the first Triple Folder set that features cards that are standard sized when folded. When opened, the length of the cards double in size while the width remains the same as a standard card. The card fronts are full bleed horizontal game shots of the player with the player's name in the lower left hand corner. When opened, the card forms three panels. The left and right panel both feature individual player shots, while the middle shows another full bleed shot showing the completion of the play the folded shot showed. Card backs feature a field in the background with a shot of the player and a brief commentary. Packs include one insert each. In addition, a Super Bowl XXX Wrapper Redemption was offered. Collectors could get a special six-card set by sending in 18 1995 Triple Folder wrappers plus $5.95 for shipping and handling. A Natrone Means promo card was produced and priced below.

COMPLETE SET (48) 10.00 30.00
1 Garrison Hearst .20 .50
2 Kerry Collins .60 1.50
3 Jeff George .10 .30
4 Herschel Walker .07 .20
5 Lake Dawson .10 .30
6 Cris Carter .20 .50
7 Byron Bam Morris .07 .20
8 Jim Kelly .20 .50
9 Rashaan Salaam .10 .30
10 Eric Zeier .10 .30
11 Curtis Martin 1.00 2.50
12 Jerry Rice .75 2.00
13 Chris Warren .10 .30
14 Trent Dilfer .20 .50
15 Terry Allen .20 .50
16 Jeff Blake .40 1.00
17 Drew Bledsoe .75 2.00
18 Tim Brown .20 .50
19 Wayne Chrebet 1.50 4.00
20 Bernie Parmalee .07 .20
21 Stan Humphries .10 .30
22 Jerome Bettis .20 .50
23 Michael Westbrook .40 1.00
24 Charlie Garner .07 .20
25 Mario Bates .10 .30
26 Marcus Allen .20 .50
27 James O. Stewart .60 1.50
28 Ben Coates .10 .30
29 Tyrone Wheatley .40 1.00
30 Steve Young .60 1.50
31 Natrone Means .10 .30
32 Terrell Davis 2.50 6.00
33 Napoleon Kaufman .60 1.50
34 Charles Johnson .10 .30
35 Barry Sanders 1.50 4.00
36 John Elway 1.50 4.00
37 Joey Galloway .75 2.00
38 Brett Favre 1.50 4.00
39 Errict Rhett .10 .30
40 Gary Brown .07 .20
41 Reggie White .20 .50
42 Steve Bono .20 .50
43 Marshall Faulk .75 2.00
44 Dan Marino 1.50 4.00
45 Emmitt Smith 1.25 3.00
46 Troy Aikman .75 2.00
47 Ricky Watters .10 .30
48 Michael Irvin .20 .50
P1 Natrone Means Promo .40 1.00

1995 Pacific Triple Folders Big Guns

Inserted two in every 37 packs, this 12 card set features NFL quarterbacks who passed for 350 yards or more in at least one game the previous season. Card fronts contain almost a full holographic foil background with a shot of the player in the center and the player's name on the bottom in the same foil. The "Big Guns of the NFL" logo is located in the bottom right of the card. Card backs are horizontal with a football in the background and a brief commentary on the game the player threw for at least 350 yards in.

COMPLETE SET (12) 20.00 50.00
BG1 Drew Bledsoe 2.50 6.00
BG2 Dan Marino 5.00 12.00
BG3 Warren Moon 2.00 4.00
BG4 John Elway 5.00 12.00
BG5 Jeff Blake 2.00 4.00
BG6 Brett Favre 5.00 12.00
BG7 Steve Young 2.50 6.00
BG8 Boomer Esiason 1.50 2.50
BG9 Jim Everett 1.50 2.50
BG10 Jim Kelly 2.00 4.00
BG11 Jeff George 1.50 2.50
BG12 Dave Krieg 1.50 2.50

1995 Pacific Triple Folders Careers

This eight card set was randomly inserted into packs at a rate of one in 181 or four per case. Card fronts have a holographic gold foil background with the player's name etched into it. Cardbacks are horizontal with a head shot of the player and some bullet point information about the player's accomplishments. Cards are numbered with a "C" prefix.

COMPLETE SET (8) 50.00 120.00
C1 Troy Aikman 6.00 15.00
C2 Marcus Allen 4.00 10.00
C3 John Elway 10.00 25.00
C4 Dan Marino 10.00 25.00
C5 Jerry Rice 6.00 15.00
C6 Barry Sanders 10.00 25.00
C7 Emmitt Smith 7.50 20.00
C8 Steve Young 5.00 12.00

1995 Pacific Triple Folders Crystalline

This 20 card set was randomly inserted into packs at a rate of four in 37 and have an acetate design. Card fronts are clear at the top and are colored in the team's colors at the bottom. The player's name is in gold foil and the player's team name appears in clear block letters at the bottom. Card backs contain biographical information and a brief commentary. Cards are numbered with a "Cr" prefix.

COMPLETE SET (20) 15.00 40.00
CR1 Troy Aikman 1.50 4.00
CR2 Jeff Blake .50 1.25
CR3 Drew Bledsoe 1.25 3.00
CR4 Kerry Collins .75 2.00
CR5 John Elway 2.50 6.00
CR6 Marshall Faulk .75 2.00
CR7 Gus Frerotte .30 .75
CR8 Joey Galloway 1.00 2.50
CR9 Garrison Hearst .30 .75
CR10 Jeff Hostetler .30 .75
CR11 Dan Marino 2.50 6.00
CR12 Natrone Means .50 1.25
CR13 Errict Rhett .30 .75
CR14 Rashaan Salaam .60 1.50
CR15 Barry Sanders 2.50 6.00
CR16 Deion Sanders .75 2.00
CR17 Emmitt Smith 2.00 5.00
CR18 J.J. Stokes .50 1.25
CR19 Steve Young 1.25 3.00
CR20 Eric Zeier .30 .75

1995 Pacific Triple Folders Rookies and Stars

This 36 card set was randomly inserted in packs at a rate of three in four packs and features top rookies and stars from the NFL. Card fronts are a full bleed photo with gold foil checkered from the middle down to the bottom of the card. The player's name is located at the bottom of the card. Card backs feature a photo of the player and information about him. Three different parallels of this set exist: a Blue, a Raspberry and a Silver. Across the production run, the Raspberry and Silver parallels were inserted at a rate of three in 37 packs. The Blue parallel was inserted in retail packs (3:4 packs), the Raspberry in hobby packs and the Silver in retail packs.

COMPLETE GOLD SET (36) 12.50 30.00
*BLUE CARDS: SAME PRICE AS GOLD
*RASPBERRY: 1.5X TO 4X BASIC INSERTS
*SILVERS: 1.5X TO 4X BASIC INSERTS
RS1 Garrison Hearst .20 .50
RS2 Darick Holmes .10 .30
RS3 Kerry Collins .75 2.00
RS4 Rashaan Salaam .20 .50
RS5 Jeff Blake .40 1.00
RS6 Eric Zeier .20 .50
RS7 Troy Aikman .50 1.25
RS8 Eric Bjornson .10 .30
RS9 Deion Sanders .30 .75
RS10 Emmitt Smith .75 2.00
RS11 Sherman Williams .10 .30
RS12 Terrell Davis 2.00 5.00
RS13 John Elway 1.00 2.50
RS14 Barry Sanders 1.00 2.50
RS15 Steve McNair 1.00 2.50
RS16 Marshall Faulk .40 1.00
RS17 James O. Stewart .60 1.50
RS18 Steve Bono .10 .30
RS19 Tamarick Vanover .20 .50
RS20 Dan Marino 1.00 2.50
RS21 Drew Bledsoe .50 1.25
RS22 Curtis Martin .75 2.00
RS23 Tyrone Wheatley .40 1.00
RS24 Tim Brown .20 .50
RS25 Napoleon Kaufman .60 1.50
RS26 Ricky Watters .10 .30
RS27 Natrone Means .10 .30
RS28 Jerry Rice .50 1.25
RS29 J.J. Stokes .40 1.00
RS30 Steve Young .40 1.00
RS31 Joey Galloway .60 1.50
RS32 Chris Warren .10 .30
RS33 Jerome Bettis .20 .50
RS34 Errict Rhett .10 .30
RS35 Terry Allen .20 .50
RS36 Michael Westbrook .50 1.25

1995 Pacific Triple Folders Teams

serted at a rate of nine in 37 packs, this 30 card set features a different card for each NFL team, highlighting each team's three highest profile players on one card. Card fronts contain a full bleed shot of the first player with his name at the bottom. Card backs contain the same design with a different player. When opened the card forms a larger shot of the third player with the same design, except the player's name is located at the top in gold-etched foil and the team name and logo is located in a circular gold-etched design at the bottom.

COMPLETE SET (30) 20.00 40.00
1 G.Hearst/D.Krieg/R.Moore .40 1.00
2 E.Metcalf/J.George/T.Mathis .40 1.00
3 D.Holmes/J.Kelly/A.Reed .40 1.00
4 B.Favre/R.White/Bennett 2.00 5.00
5 S.McNair/Jeffires/Chandler .60 1.50
6 M.Faulk/Harbaugh/Dawkins .60 1.50
7 K.Collins/Christian/McKyer .60 1.50
8 R.Salaam/Kramer/Timpson .40 1.00
9 C.Pickens/Blake/Scott .40 1.00
10 Rison/Testaverde/Hoard .30 .75
11 E.Smith/T.Aikman/Irvin 1.50 4.00
12 T.Davis/Elway/Sh.Sharpe 3.00 8.00
13 B.Sanders/Mitchell/Moore 2.00 5.00
14 J.O.Stewart/Brunell/Howard .60 1.50
15 M.Allen/S.Bono/G.Hill .40 1.00
16 D.Marino/Parmalee/Fryar 2.00 5.00
17 R.Smith/W.Moon/C.Carter .60 1.50
18 C.Martin/D.Bledsoe/Coates 1.50 4.00
19 M.Bates/J.Everett/M.Haynes .30 .75
20 R.Hampton/D.Brown/H.Walker .30 .75
21 W.Chrebet/K.Brady/A.Murrell 1.25 3.00
22 N.Kaufman/Hostetler/T.Brown 1.00 2.50
23 R.Watters/C.Garner/M.Mamula .30 .75
24 B.Morris/M.Tomczak/C.Johnson .30 .75
25 N.Means/S.Humphries/T.Martin .40 1.00
26 J.Rice/S.Young/J.J.Stokes 1.25 3.00
27 C.Warren/Mirer/J.Galloway 1.00 2.50
28 J.Bettis/K.Carter/I.Bruce .60 1.50
29 E.Rhett/T.Dilfer/A.Harper .40 1.00
30 T.Allen/Frerotte/Westbrook .60 1.50

1932 Packers Walker's Cleaners

This set of photos was issued in early 1932 by Walker's Cleaners in the Green Bay area to commemorate the 1929-1931 3-time World Champions. Each large photo was printed in sepia tone and included a facsimile autograph of the featured player as well as the photographer's notation. Each photo also includes a strip on the left side with two holes punched in order to fit into an album that was made available to anyone who built a complete set.. The photos are often found with the two-hole section trimmed off. Lastly a small cover sheet was included with each photo that featured a photo number, sponsorship mentions, a bio of the player and information about obtaining the album. Photos with the cover sheet still attached are valued at roughly double photos without. We've listed the blank backed photos below according to the photo number on the small cover sheets.

COMPLETE SET (27) 6000.00 10000.00
1 Curly Lambeau 800.00 1200.00
2 Frank Baker 150.00 300.00
3 Russ Saunders 150.00 300.00
4 Wuert Engelmann 150.00 300.00
5 Hank Bruder 200.00 400.00
6 Waldo Don Carlos 150.00 300.00
7 Roger Grove 150.00 300.00
8 Mike Michalske 250.00 500.00
9 Milt Gantenbein 150.00 300.00
10 Lavie Dilweg 200.00 400.00
11 Verne Lewellen 200.00 400.00
12 Red Dunn 150.00 300.00
13 Johnny Blood McNally 300.00 600.00
14 Jug Earp 200.00 400.00
15 Arnie Herber 300.00 600.00
16 Dick Stahlman 150.00 300.00
17 Red Sleight 150.00 300.00
18 Rudy Comstock 150.00 300.00
19 Jim Bowdoin 150.00 300.00
20 Hurdis McCrary 150.00 300.00
21 Bo Molenda 150.00 300.00
22 Cal Hubbard 500.00 800.00
23 Paul Fitzgibbon 150.00 300.00
24 Tom Nash 150.00 300.00
25 Mule Wilson 200.00 400.00
26 Howard Woodin 150.00 300.00
27 Nate Barragar 150.00 300.00
NNO Album 200.00 400.00

1955 Packers Miller Brewing Postcards

1 Tobin Rote 20.00 40.00

1955 Packers Team Issue

This set of large (roughly 8 1/2" by 10 1/2") black and white photos was issued by the Packers around 1955. Each photo was printed on thick stock and includes the player's name and team name within a white box on the front. The photos are blankbacked. Any additions to the list below are appreciated.

1 Charlie Brackens 75.00 150.00
3 Al Carmichael 35.00 60.00
4 Howard Ferguson 35.00 60.00
5 Billy Howton 50.00 80.00
6 Gary Knafelc 35.00 60.00
10 Veryl Switzer 35.00 60.00

1959 Packers Team Issue

The Packers released this set of photos to fans in 1959. They were commonly released in a Green Bay Packers envelope with each measuring roughly 5" by 7" featuring a black and white player photo. The team name appears above the photo and the player's name, position, college, height, and weight is included below the photo. Some photos vary slightly in size and style of print type used while others have sponsor logos on the fronts as noted below. All photos, except Nitschke, feature action shots and a facsimile autograph. The photos were also printed on thin paper stock, are blankbacked, and listed below alphabetically.

COMPLETE SET (30) 400.00 700.00
1 Tom Bettis 7.50 15.00
2 Nate Borden 7.50 15.00
3 Lew Carpenter 7.50 15.00
4 Dan Currie 7.50 15.00
5 Bill Forester 7.50 15.00
6 Bob Freeman 7.50 15.00
7 Forrest Gregg 20.00 35.00
8 Hank Gremminger 7.50 15.00
9 Dave Hanner 7.50 15.00
10 Jerry Helluin 7.50 15.00
11 Paul Hornung 35.00 60.00
12 Gary Knafelc 7.50 15.00
13 Jerry Kramer 20.00 35.00
14 Vince Lombardi CO 125.00 200.00
15 Norm Masters 7.50 15.00
16 Lamar McHan 7.50 15.00
17 Max McGee 10.00 20.00
18 Don McIlhenny 7.50 15.00
19 Steve Meilinger 7.50 15.00
20 Ray Nitschke 30.00 50.00
21 Babe Parilli 10.00 20.00
22 Bill Quinlan 7.50 15.00
23 Jim Ringo 20.00 35.00
24 Al Romine 7.50 15.00
25 Bob Skoronski 10.00 20.00
26 Bart Starr 40.00 75.00
27 John Symank 7.50 15.00
28 Jim Taylor 30.00 50.00
29 Jim Temp 7.50 15.00
30 Emlen Tunnell 20.00 35.00

1961 Packers Lake to Lake

The 1961 Lake to Lake Green Bay Packers set consists of 36 unnumbered, green and white cards each measuring approximately 2 1/2" by 3 1/4". The fronts contain the card number, the player's uniform number, his position, and his height, weight, and college. The backs contain advertisements for the Packer fans to obtain Lake to Lake premiums. Card numbers 1-8 and 17-24 are the most difficult cards to obtain and cards #33-36 are also in shorter supply than #9-16 and #25-32 which are the easiest cards in the set. Lineman Ken Iman's card was issued ten years before his Rookie Card; Defensive back Herb Adderley's card was issued three years before his Rookie Card.

COMPLETE SET (36) 1800.00 3000.00
1 Jerry Kramer SP 100.00 175.00
2 Norm Masters SP 75.00 125.00
3 Willie Davis SP 100.00 175.00
4 Bill Quinlan SP 75.00 125.00
5 Jim Temp SP 75.00 125.00
6 Emlen Tunnell SP 90.00 150.00
7 Gary Knafelc SP 75.00 125.00
8 Hank Jordan SP 125.00 200.00
9 Bill Forester 4.00 8.00
10 Paul Hornung 15.00 25.00
11 Jesse Whittenton 4.00 8.00
12 Andy Cvercko 4.00 8.00
13 Jim Taylor 10.00 20.00
14 Hank Gremminger 4.00 8.00
15 Tom Moore 4.00 8.00
16 John Symank 4.00 8.00
17 Max McGee SP 90.00 150.00
18 Bart Starr SP 250.00 400.00
19 Ray Nitschke SP 150.00 250.00
20 Dave Hanner SP 75.00 125.00
21 Tom Bettis SP 75.00 125.00
22 Fuzzy Thurston SP 90.00 150.00
23 Lew Carpenter SP 75.00 125.00
24 Boyd Dowler SP 90.00 150.00
25 Ken Iman 4.00 8.00
26 Bob Skoronski 4.00 8.00
27 Forrest Gregg 6.00 12.00
28 Jim Ringo 6.00 12.00
29 Ron Kramer 4.00 8.00
30 Herb Adderley 7.50 15.00
31 Dan Currie 4.00 8.00
32 John Roach 4.00 8.00
33 Dale Hackbart SP 75.00 125.00
34 Larry Hickman SP 75.00 125.00
35 Nelson Toburen SP 75.00 125.00
36 Willie Wood SP 100.00 175.00

1965 Packers Team Issue

This set of small (5" by 7") black and white photos was issued by the Packers around 1965. Each photo was printed on thick stock, includes the player name, position, and team name below the photo and are blankbacked. Any additions to the list below are appreciated.

1 Herb Adderley 7.50 15.00
2 Lionel Aldridge 6.00 12.00
3 Jim Taylor 15.00 25.00
4 Fuzzy Thurston 7.50 15.00

1966 Packers Mobil Posters

This eight-poster set of the Green Bay Packers measures approximately 11" by 14" and features art prints suitable for framing of various game action pictures. The fronts carry a color action art piece and the backs are blank. The posters were distributed in envelopes that included the title of the artwork and the poster number. Although players are not specifically identified, we've made attempts to identify some key players. The prints are listed below according to the number and title on the envelope.

COMPLETE SET (8) 125.00 250.00
1 The Pass 30.00 60.00
2 The Block 15.00 30.00
3 The Punt 12.50 25.00
4 The Sweep 18.00 30.00
5 The Catch 15.00 30.00
6 The Tackle 12.50 25.00
7 The Touchdown 12.50 25.00
8 The Extra Point 20.00 40.00

1966 Packers Team Issue

The Green Bay Packers issued player photos over a number of years in the late 1960s. Most of the 8" by 10" photos may have even been issued across a number of years. This set was most likely released in 1966 and can be differentiated by the text included below the black and white player photo. Included (reading left to right) are the player's position (initials), his name in all caps, and full team name in all caps. Any additions to this list are appreciated.

1 Donny Anderson 7.50 15.00
2 Gale Gillingham 6.00 12.00
3 Jim Grabowski 6.00 12.00

1967 Packers Socka-Tumee Prints

These large (roughly 9' x 10 1/2") art prints feature a Packers player in contact with another NFL player in an exagerated action scene that includes a portion of the picture's frame being broken away. While the player is not specifically identified, the artwork is detailed enough to identify a specific player as noted below.

1 Jim Grabowski 25.00 50.00
2 Ray Nitschke 60.00 100.00
3 Don Chandler 25.00 50.00

1967 Packers Team Issue 5x7

These black and white player photos were released by the Green Bay Packers around 1967. Each measures approximately 5" by 7" and includes the player's name, his position (spelled out in full) and team name below the photo. They are blankbacked and unnumbered. Any additions to this list are appreciated.

COMPLETE SET (13) 100.00 175.00
1 Donny Anderson 6.00 12.00
2 Zeke Bratkowski 6.00 12.00
3 Willie Davis 7.50 15.00
4 Gale Gillingham 5.00 10.00
5 Bob Jeter 5.00 10.00
6 Hank Jordan 7.50 15.00
7 Ron Kostelnik 5.00 10.00
8 Jerry Kramer 7.50 15.00
9 Ray Nitschke 10.00 20.00
10 Dave Robinson 7.50 15.00
11 Bob Skoronski 5.00 10.00
12 Bart Starr 20.00 40.00
13 Travis Williams 5.00 10.00

1967 Packers Team Issue 8x10

e Green Bay Packers issued roughly 8" by 10" player photos over a number of years in the late 1960s. Most of the photos were issued across a number of years. This set was most likely released in 1967 and can be differentiated by the text included below the black and white player photo. Included (reading left to right) are the player's name in all caps, position spelled out in caps, and the city "GREEN BAY" in all caps. Any additions to this list are appreciated.

1 Boyd Dowler 7.50 15.00
2 Bart Starr 20.00 40.00
3 Bart Starr 20.00 40.00
4 Bart Starr 20.00 40.00

1968-69 Packers Team Issue

This team-issued set consists of black-and-white player photos with each measuring approximately 8" by 10". They were printed on thin glossy paper and likely released over a number of years. The player's name, position, and team name are printed in black in the bottom white border. Although they are very similar to the 1971-72 release, the printing used for the text is generally larger. The team name is approximately 1 3/4" to 2" long. The cardbacks are blank. The photos are unnumbered and checklisted below in alphabetical order.

COMPLETE SET (51) 250.00 500.00
1 Herb Adderley 7.50 15.00
2 Herb Adderley 7.50 15.00
3 Larry Agajanian 6.00 12.00
4 Lionel Aldridge 6.00 12.00
5 Phil Bengston CO 6.00 12.00
6 Ken Bowman 6.00 12.00
7 Dave Bradley 6.00 12.00
8 Zeke Bratkowski 7.50 15.00
9 Bob Brown 6.00 12.00
10 Lee Roy Caffey 6.00 12.00
11 Fred Carr 6.00 12.00
12 Fred Carr 6.00 12.00
13 Don Chandler 6.00 12.00
14 Carroll Dale 7.50 15.00
15 Willie Davis 7.50 15.00
16 Willie Davis 7.50 15.00
17 Boyd Dowler 7.50 15.00
18 Jim Flanigan 6.00 12.00
19 Marv Fleming 7.50 15.00
20 Forrest Gregg 7.50 15.00
21 Dave Hampton 6.00 12.00
22 Leon Harden 6.00 12.00
23 Doug Hart 6.00 12.00
24 Bill Hayhoe 6.00 12.00
25 Dick Himes 6.00 12.00
26 Don Horn 6.00 12.00
27 Bob Hyland 6.00 12.00
28 Claudis James 6.00 12.00
29 Bob Jeter 6.00 12.00
30 Ron Jones 6.00 12.00
31 Jerry Kramer 7.50 15.00
32 Vince Lombardi CO 15.00 30.00
33 Bill Lueck 6.00 12.00
34 Max McGee 7.50 15.00
35 Mike Mercer 6.00 12.00
36 Rich Moore 6.00 12.00
37 Ray Nitschke 10.00 20.00
38 Francis Peay 6.00 12.00
39 Elijah Pitts 6.00 12.00
40 Dave Robinson LB 7.50 15.00
41 John Rowser 6.00 12.00
42 Gordon Rule 6.00 12.00
43 John Spilis 6.00 12.00
44 Bart Starr 15.00 30.00
45 Bill Stevens 6.00 12.00
46 Phil Vandersea 6.00 12.00
47 Jim Weatherwax 6.00 12.00
48 Perry Williams 6.00 12.00
49 Travis Williams 6.00 12.00
50 Francis Winkler 6.00 12.00
51 Willie Wood 7.50 15.00

1969 Packers Drenks Potato Chip Pins

e 1969 Packers Drenks Potato Chip set contains 20 pins, each measuring approximately 1 1/8" in diameter. The fronts have a green and white background, with a black and white headshot in the center of the white football-shaped area. The team name at the top and player information at the bottom follow the curve of the pin. The pins are unnumbered and checklisted below in alphabetical order.

COMPLETE SET (20) 75.00 150.00
1 Herb Adderley 5.00 10.00
2 Lionel Aldridge 3.00 6.00
3 Donny Anderson 4.00 8.00
4 Ken Bowman 3.00 6.00
5 Carroll Dale 3.00 6.00
6 Willie Davis 5.00 10.00
7 Boyd Dowler 4.00 8.00
8 Marv Fleming 4.00 8.00
9 Gale Gillingham 3.00 6.00
10 Jim Grabowski 3.00 6.00
11 Forrest Gregg 5.00 10.00
12 Don Horn 3.00 6.00
13 Bob Jeter 3.00 6.00
14 Hank Jordan 5.00 10.00
15 Ray Nitschke 7.50 15.00
16 Elijah Pitts 3.00 6.00
17 Dave Robinson 4.00 8.00
18 Bart Starr 12.50 25.00
19 Travis Williams 3.00 6.00
20 Willie Wood 5.00 10.00

1969 Packers Tasco Prints

Tasco Associates produced this set of Green Bay Packers prints. The fronts feature a large color artist's rendering of the player along with the player's name and position. The backs are blank and unnumbered. The prints measure approximately 11" by 16."

COMPLETE SET (8) 175.00 300.00
1 Donny Anderson 20.00 35.00
2 Willie Davis 25.00 40.00
3 Boyd Dowler 20.00 35.00
4 Jim Grabowski 18.00 30.00
5 Hank Jordan 25.00 40.00
6 Ray Nitschke 30.00 50.00
7 Bart Starr 50.00 80.00
8 Willie Wood 25.00 40.00

1970 Packers Volpe Tumblers

1 Ray Nitschke 20.00 40.00
2 Dave Robinson 10.00 20.00
3 Carroll Dale 10.00 20.00
4 Donny Anderson 10.00 20.00
5 Willie Wood 12.50 25.00

1971-72 Packers Team Issue

is team-issued set consists of black-and-white player photos with each measuring approximately 8" by 10". They were printed on thin glossy paper. The player's name, position, and team name are printed in black in the bottom white border. Although they are very similar to the 1968-69 release, the printing used for the text is generally smaller. The team name is approximately 1 1/2" long. The cardbacks are blank. Several players have two photos in the set. Furthermore, Napper never played in the NFL, and Pittman never played for the Packers, suggesting that these photos may have been taken during training camp or preseason. The photos are unnumbered and checklisted below in alphabetical order.

COMPLETE SET (44) 150.00 300.00
1 John Brockington 6.00 12.00
2 Bob Brown DT 5.00 10.00
3 Willie Buchanon 6.00 12.00
4 Jim Carter 5.00 10.00
5 Carroll Dale 6.00 12.00
6 Dan Devine CO 6.00 12.00
GM
7 Ken Ellis 5.00 10.00
8 Len Garrett 5.00 10.00
9 Gale Gillingham 5.00 10.00
10 Leland Glass 5.00 10.00
11 Charlie Hall DB 5.00 10.00
12 Jim Hill 5.00 10.00
13 Dick Himes 5.00 10.00
14 Bob Hudson 5.00 10.00
15 Bob Hudson 5.00 10.00
16 Kevin Hunt 5.00 10.00
17 Scott Hunter 6.00 12.00
Passing action posed
18 Scott Hunter 6.00 12.00
Arm raised to pass
Thin paper stock
19 Dave Kopay 5.00 10.00
20 Bob Kroll 5.00 10.00
21 Pete Lammons 5.00 10.00
22 MacArthur Lane 6.00 12.00
23 Bill Lueck 5.00 10.00
24 Al Matthews 5.00 10.00
25 Mike McCoy DT 5.00 10.00
26 Rich McGeorge 5.00 10.00
27 Lou Michaels 6.00 12.00
28 Charlie Napper 5.00 10.00
29 Ray Nitschke 7.50 15.00
30 Charlie Pittman 5.00 10.00
31 Alden Roche 5.00 10.00
32 Malcolm Snider 5.00 10.00
33 Malcolm Snider 5.00 10.00
34 Jon Staggers 5.00 10.00
35 Jerry Tagge 5.00 10.00
36 Isaac Thomas 5.00 10.00
37 Isaac Thomas 5.00 10.00
38 Vern Vanoy 5.00 10.00
39 Ron Widby 5.00 10.00
40 Ron Widby 5.00 10.00
41 Clarence Williams 5.00 10.00
42 Perry Williams RB 5.00 10.00
43 Keith Wortman 5.00 10.00
44 Coaching Staff 7.50 15.00

1972 Packers Coke Cap Liners

This set of cap liners were issued inside the caps of bottles of Coca-Cola in the Green Bay area in 1972. Each clear plastic liner features a black and white photo of the featured player. They were to be attached to a saver sheet that could be partially or completely filled in order to be exchanged for various prizes from Coke.

COMPLETE SET (22) 50.00 100.00
1 Ken Bowman 2.50 5.00
2 John Brockington 3.00 6.00
3 Bob Brown 2.50 5.00
4 Fred Carr 2.50 5.00
5 Jim Carter 2.50 5.00
6 Carroll Dale 3.00 6.00
7 Ken Ellis 2.50 5.00
8 Gale Gillingham 2.50 5.00
9 Dave Hampton 2.50 5.00
10 Doug Hart 2.50 5.00
11 Jim Hill 2.50 5.00
12 Dick Himes 2.50 5.00
13 Scott Hunter 2.50 5.00
14 MacArthur Lane 3.00 6.00
15 Bill Lueck 2.50 5.00
16 Al Matthews 2.50 5.00
17 Rich McGeorge 2.50 5.00
18 Ray Nitschke 6.00 12.00
19 Francis Peay 2.50 5.00
20 Dave Robinson 4.00 8.00
21 Alden Roche 2.50 5.00
22 Bart Starr 10.00 20.00

1975 Packers Pizza Hut Glasses

This set of glasses was issued by Pizza Hut in the mid-1970s to honor past Green Bay Packers greats. Each glass includes Packer green and gold colored highlights with a black and white picture of the featured player.

COMPLETE SET (6) 50.00 100.00
1 Wille Davis 5.00 10.00
2 Paul Hornung 10.00 20.00
3 Jerry Kramer 5.00 10.00
4 Vince Lombardi 20.00 40.00
5 Ray Nitschke 7.50 15.00
6 Bart Starr 12.50 25.00

1975 Packers Team Issue

The Green Bay Packers issued this set of 15-photos along with a saver album sponsored by Roundy's Food Store. Each measures approximately 6" by 9". The fronts feature posed color photos of the players kneeling with their right hand resting on their helmets. Facsimile autographs are inscribed across the pictures. The backs are blank. The cards are unnumbered and checklisted below in alphabetical order.

COMPLETE SET (15) 50.00 100.00
1 John Brockington 5.00 10.00
2 Willie Buchanon 5.00 10.00
3 Fred Carr 4.00 8.00
4 Jim Carter 4.00 8.00
5 Jack Concannon 4.00 8.00
6 Bill Curry 5.00 10.00
7 John Hadl 6.00 12.00
8 Bill Lueck 4.00 8.00
9 Chester Marcol 4.00 8.00
10 Al Matthews 4.00 8.00
11 Rich McGeorge 4.00 8.00
12 Alden Roche 4.00 8.00
13 Barry Smith 4.00 8.00
14 Barty Smith 4.00 8.00
15 Clarence Williams 4.00 8.00
NNO Album 10.00 20.00

1976-77 Packers Team Issue 5x7

These photos were issued by the Packers, feature black-and-white player images, and measure approximately 5" by 7". They were printed on thin glossy paper with the player's name and position initials on the top line and the team name on the bottom line of type printed below the player's image.The photos are blankbacked, unnumbered and checklisted below in alphabetical order.

COMPLETE SET (28)	75.00	125.00
1 Bert Askson	3.00	6.00
2 John Brockington	4.00	8.00
3 Willie Buchanon	4.00	8.00
4 Mike Butler	3.00	6.00
5 Fred Carr	3.00	6.00
6 Jim Carter	3.00	6.00
7 Charlie Hall	3.00	6.00
8 Willard Harrell 1	3.00	6.00
9 Willard Harrell 2	3.00	6.00
10 Bob Hyland	3.00	6.00
11 Melvin Jackson	3.00	6.00
12 Ezra Johnson	3.00	6.00
13 Mark Koncar	3.00	6.00
14 Steve Luke	3.00	6.00
15 Chester Marcol	3.00	6.00
16 Mike McCoy DB	3.00	6.00
17 Mike Mccoy DT	3.00	6.00
18 Rich Mcgeorge	3.00	6.00
19 Steve Odom	3.00	6.00
20 Ken Payne	3.00	6.00
21 Tom Perko	3.00	6.00
22 Dave Pureifory	3.00	6.00
23 Alden Roche	3.00	6.00
24 Barty Smith 1	3.00	6.00
25 Barty Smith 2	3.00	6.00
26 Perry Smith	3.00	6.00
27 Cliff Taylor	3.00	6.00
28 Tom Toner	3.00	6.00

1976-77 Packers Team Issue 8x10

These team-issued photos feature black-and-white player images with each measuring approximately 8" by 10". They were printed on thin glossy paper with the player's name, position (initials), and team name printed in black in the bottom white border. Most feature the player in a kneeling pose with his hand on his helmet. The photos are blankbacked, unnumbered and checklisted below in alphabetical order.

COMPLETE SET (33)	125.00	250.00
1 Dave Beverly	4.00	8.00
2 Mike Butler	4.00	8.00
3 Jim Culbreath	4.00	8.00
4 Lynn Dickey	5.00	10.00
5 Derrel Gofourth	4.00	8.00
6 Johnnie Gray	4.00	8.00
7 Will Harrell	4.00	8.00
8 Dennis Havig	4.00	8.00
9 Melvin Jackson	4.00	8.00
10 Greg Koch	4.00	8.00
11 Mark Koncar	4.00	8.00
12 Larry McCarren	4.00	8.00
13 Mike McCoy DB	4.00	8.00
14 Mike McCoy DT	4.00	8.00
15 Terdell Middleton	4.00	8.00
16 Tim Moresco	4.00	8.00
17 Steve Okoniewski	4.00	8.00
18 Tom Perko	4.00	8.00
19 Terry Randolph	4.00	8.00
20 Alden Roche	4.00	8.00
21 Dave Roller	4.00	8.00
22 Barty Smith	4.00	8.00
23 Ollie Smith	4.00	8.00
24 Clifton Taylor	4.00	8.00
25 Aundra Thompson	4.00	8.00
26 Tom Toner	4.00	8.00
27 Eric Torkelson	4.00	8.00
28 Bruce Van Dyke	4.00	8.00
29 Randy Vataha	4.00	8.00
30 Steve Wagner	4.00	8.00
31 David Whitehurst	5.00	10.00
32 Clarence Williams	4.00	8.00
33 Keith Wortman	4.00	8.00

1981 Packers Team Sheets

ese 2-sheets measure roughly 8" by 10" and feature 16-small black and white player photos on the fronts. The backs are blank and unnumbered.

COMPLETE SET (2)	4.00	10.00
1 Defense	2.00	5.00
2 Offense	2.00	5.00

1983 Packers Police

is 19-card set is somewhat more difficult to find than the other Packers Police sets. Reportedly, there were just 11,000 total sets distributed. There are three different types of backs: First Wisconsin Banks, without First Wisconsin Banks, and Waukesha P.D. The hardest to get of these three is the set without First Wisconsin Banks. All cards are approximately 2 5/8" by 4 1/8". Card backs are printed in green ink on white card stock. A safety tip ("Packer Tips") is given on the back. Cards are unnumbered except for uniform number.

COMPLETE SET (19)	18.00	30.00
10 Jan Stenerud	1.25	3.00
12 Lynn Dickey	.75	2.00
24 Johnnie Gray	.40	1.00
29 Mike McCoy DB	.40	1.00
31 Gerry Ellis	.40	1.00
40 Eddie Lee Ivery	.75	2.00
52 George Cumby	.40	1.00
53 Mike Douglass	.60	1.50
54 Larry McCarren	.40	1.00
59 John Anderson	.60	1.50
63 Terry Jones	.40	1.00
64 Syd Kitson	.40	1.00
68 Greg Koch	.40	1.00
80 James Lofton	2.00	5.00
82 Paul Coffman	.75	2.00
83 John Jefferson	1.00	2.50
85 Phillip Epps	.75	2.00
90 Ezra Johnson	.40	1.00
NNO Bart Starr CO	3.00	8.00

1984 Packers Police

is 25-card set is numbered on the back. The card backs were printed in green ink. Cards were sponsored by First Wisconsin banks, the local law enforcement agency, and the Green Bay Packers. The cards measure approximately 2 5/8" by 4".

COMPLETE SET (25)	5.00	12.00
1 John Jefferson	.40	1.00
2 Forrest Gregg CO	.75	2.00
3 John Anderson	.25	.60
4 Eddie Garcia	.15	.40
5 Tim Lewis	.15	.40
6 Jessie Clark	.15	.40
7 Karl Swanke	.15	.40
8 Lynn Dickey	.40	1.00
9 Eddie Lee Ivery	.25	.60
10 Dick Modzelewski CO	.15	.40
11 Mark Murphy	.15	.40
12 David Drechsler	.15	.40
13 Mike Douglass	.15	.40
14 James Lofton	1.25	3.00
15 Bucky Scribner	.15	.40
16 Randy Scott	.15	.40
17 Mark Lee	.25	.60
18 Gerry Ellis	.15	.40
19 Terry Jones	.15	.40
20 Greg Koch	.15	.40
21 Bob Schnelker CO	.15	.40
22 George Cumby	.15	.40
23 Larry McCarren	.15	.40
24 Syd Kitson	.15	.40
25 Paul Coffman	.25	.60

1984 Packers Team Issue

These team-issued photos feature black-and-white player images with each measuring approximately 8" by 10". They were printed on thin glossy paper with the player's name, position (initials), and team name printed in black in the bottom white border. Most feature the player in a kneeling pose with his hand on his helmet. The photos are blankbacked, unnumbered and checklisted below in alphabetical order.

COMPLETE SET (9)	15.00	25.00
1 Mark Cannon	1.25	3.00
2 Al Del Greco	1.50	4.00
3 Mike Douglass	1.25	3.00
4 Ron Hallstrom	1.25	3.00
5 Estus Hood	1.25	3.00
6 Tim Lewis	1.25	3.00
7 Mike Meade	1.25	3.00
8 Mark Murphy	1.25	3.00
9 Bucky Scribner	1.25	3.00

1985 Packers Police

This 25-card set of Green Bay Packers is numbered on the back. Cards measure approximately 2 3/4" by 4". The backs contain a "1985 Packer Tip". Each player's uniform number is given on the card front.

COMPLETE SET (25)	3.00	8.00
1 Forrest Gregg CO	.60	1.50
2 Paul Coffman	.25	.60
3 Terry Jones	.15	.40
4 Ron Hallstrom	.15	.40
5 Eddie Lee Ivery	.25	.60
6 John Anderson	.15	.40
7 Tim Lewis	.15	.40
8 Bob Schnelker CO	.15	.40
9 Al Del Greco	.15	.40
10 Mark Murphy	.25	.60
11 Tim Huffman	.15	.40
12 Del Rodgers	.15	.40
13 Mark Lee	.25	.60
14 Tom Flynn	.15	.40
15 Dick Modzelewski CO	.15	.40
16 Randy Scott	.15	.40
17 Bucky Scribner	.15	.40
18 George Cumby	.15	.40
19 James Lofton	.75	2.00
20 Mike Douglass	.25	.60
21 Alphonso Carreker	.15	.40
22 Greg Koch	.15	.40
23 Gerry Ellis	.15	.40
24 Ezra Johnson	.15	.40
25 Lynn Dickey	.40	1.00

1986 Packers Police

is 25-card set of Green Bay Packers is unnumbered except for uniform number. Cards measure approximately 2 3/4" by 4" and the backs contain a "Safety Tip". The fronts features the prominent heading "1986 Packers". Card backs are written in green ink on white card stock.

COMPLETE SET (25)	3.00	8.00
10 Al Del Greco	.15	.40
12 Lynn Dickey	.40	1.00
16 Randy Wright	.40	1.00
26 Tim Lewis	.15	.40
31 Gerry Ellis	.15	.40
33 Jessie Clark	.15	.40
37 Mark Murphy	.25	.60
40 Eddie Lee Ivery	.25	.60
41 Tom Flynn	.15	.40
42 Gary Ellerson	.15	.40
55 Randy Scott	.15	.40
58 Mark Cannon	.15	.40
59 John Anderson	.15	.40
65 Ron Hallstrom	.15	.40
67 Karl Swanke	.15	.40
76 Alphonso Carreker	.15	.40
80 James Lofton	.75	2.00
82 Paul Coffman	.25	.60
85 Phillip Epps	.25	.60
90 Ezra Johnson	.15	.40
91 Brian Noble	.25	.60
93 Robert Brown	.15	.40
94 Charles Martin	.15	.40
99 John Dorsey	.15	.40
NNO Forrest Gregg CO	.50	1.25

1986 Packers Team Sheets

These 8" by 10" sheets were issued primarily to the media for use as player images for print. Each features 10-players with the player's jersey number, name, and position beneath his picture. The sheets are blankbacked and unnumbered.

COMPLETE SET (5)	12.00	30.00
1 Vince Ferragamo	3.00	8.00
Al Del Greco		
Robbie Bosco		
Randy		
2 Tom Neville	5.00	12.00
Alan Veingrad		
Dan Knight		
Ken Ruettg		
3 Walter Stanley	2.50	6.00
Mark Lewis		
Ezra Johnson		
Brian No		
4 Ken Stills	2.50	6.00
Gerry Ellis		
Jessie Clark		
Mike Moffit		
5 Miles Turpin	2.50	6.00
Randy Scott		
Burnell Dent		
Rich Mora		

1987 Packers Ace Fact Pack

This 33-card set measures approximately 2 1/4" by 3 5/8". These cards feature rounded corners and a playing card type design on the back. There were 22 player cards issued which we have checklisted alphabetically. These cards were made in West Germany (by Ace Fact Pack) for release in Great Britain to capitalize on the popularity of American Football overseas. The set contains members of the Green Bay Packers.

COMPLETE SET (33)	30.00	80.00
1 John Anderson	1.25	3.00
2 Robbie Bosco UER	1.25	3.00
3 Don Bracken	1.25	3.00
4 John Cannon	1.25	3.00
5 Alphonso Carreker	1.25	3.00
6 Kenneth Davis	2.00	5.00
7 Al Del Greco	2.00	5.00
8 Gary Ellerson	1.25	3.00
9 Gerry Ellis	1.25	3.00
10 Phillip Epps	2.00	5.00
11 Ron Hallstrom	1.25	3.00
12 Mark Lee	1.25	3.00
13 Bobby Leopold	1.25	3.00
14 Charles Martin	1.25	3.00
15 Brian Noble	1.25	3.00
16 Ken Ruettgers	2.00	5.00
17 Randy Scott	1.25	3.00
18 Walter Stanley	1.25	3.00
19 Ken Stills	1.25	3.00
20 Keith Uecker	1.25	3.00
21 Ed West	2.00	5.00
22 Randy Wright	1.25	3.00
23 Packers Helmet	1.25	3.00
24 Packers Information	1.25	3.00
25 Packers Uniform	1.25	3.00
26 Game Record Holders	1.25	3.00
27 Season Record Holders	1.25	3.00
28 Career Record Holders	1.25	3.00
29 Record 1967-86	1.25	3.00
30 1986 Team Statistics	1.25	3.00
31 All-Time Greats	1.25	3.00
32 Roll of Honour	1.25	3.00
33 Lambeau Field/	2.00	5.00

1987 Packers Police

This 22-card set of Green Bay Packers is numbered on the front in the lower right corner below the photo. Sponsors were the Employers Health Insurance Company, Arson Task Force, local law enforcement agencies, and the Green Bay Packers. Cards measure 2 3/4" by 4". The backs contain a "Safety Tip". The fronts features the prominent heading "1987 Packers". Card backs are written in green ink on white card stock. Cards 5, 6, and 20 were never issued as apparently they were scheduled to be players who were later cut and released from the team. Reportedly 35,000 sets were distributed.

COMPLETE SET (22)	3.00	8.00
1 Forrest Gregg CO	.60	1.50
2 Tiger Greene	.15	.40
3 Ron Hallstrom	.15	.40
4 Ezra Johnson	.15	.40
7 Robert Brown	.15	.40
8 Tom Neville T	.15	.40
9 Rich Moran	.15	.40
10 Ken Ruettgers	.15	.40
11 Alan Veingrad	.15	.40
12 Mark Lee	.15	.40
13 John Dorsey	.15	.40
14 Paul Ott Carruth	.15	.40
15 Randy Wright	.15	.40
16 Phillip Epps	.25	.60
17 Al Del Greco	.15	.40
18 Tim Harris	.40	1.00
19 Kenneth Davis	.40	1.00
21 John Anderson	.25	.60
22 Mark Murphy	.25	.60
23 Ken Stills	.15	.40
24 Brian Noble	.25	.60
25 Mark Cannon	.15	.40

1988 Packers Police

e 1988 Police Green Bay Packers set contains 25 cards measuring approximately 2 3/4" by 4". There are 24 player cards and one coach card. The backs have football tips and safety tips. The cards are unnumbered so they are listed below in alphabetical order.

COMPLETE SET (25)	4.00	10.00
1 John Anderson	.15	.40
2 Jerry Boyarsky	.15	.40
3 Don Bracken	.15	.40
4 Dave Brown	.15	.40
5 Mark Cannon	.15	.40
6 Alphonso Carreker	.15	.40
7 Paul Ott Carruth	.15	.40
8 Kenneth Davis	.40	1.00
9 John Dorsey	.15	.40
10 Brent Fullwood	.15	.40
11 Tiger Greene	.15	.40
12 Ron Hallstrom	.15	.40
13 Tim Harris	.40	1.00
14 Johnny Holland	.25	.60
15 Lindy Infante CO	.25	.60
16 Mark Lee	.15	.40
17 Don Majkowski	.40	1.00
18 Rich Moran	.15	.40
19 Mark Murphy	.15	.40
20 Ken Ruettgers	.25	.60
21 Walter Stanley	.25	.60
22 Keith Uecker	.15	.40
23 Ed West	.15	.40
24 Randy Wright	.15	.40
25 Max Zendejas	.15	.40

1989 Packers Police

The 1989 Police Green Bay Packers set contains 15 numbered cards measuring approximately 2 3/4" by 4". The fronts have white borders and color action photos bordered in Packers yellow; the vertically oriented backs have safety tips. These cards were printed on very thin stock. Sterling Sharpe appears in his Rookie Card year.

COMPLETE SET (15)	2.50	6.00
1 Lindy Infante CO	.25	.60
2 Don Majkowski	.40	1.00
3 Brent Fullwood	.15	.40
4 Mark Lee	.25	.60
5 Dave Brown	.15	.40
6 Mark Murphy	.25	.60
7 Johnny Holland	.25	.60
8 John Anderson	.25	.60
9 Ken Ruettgers	.25	.60
10 Sterling Sharpe	.75	2.00
11 Ed West	.15	.40
12 Walter Stanley	.25	.60
13 Brian Noble	.25	.60
14 Shawn Patterson	.15	.40
15 Tim Harris	.25	.60

1990 Packers Police

This 20-card set, which measures approximately 2 3/4" by 4", was issued by police departments in Wisconsin and featured members of the 1990 Green Bay Packers. The fronts have white borders with a "Packers '90" title on the front and the name of the subject along with their position and NFL experience. The backs of the card feature a safety tip and small ads for the sponsors of the set.

COMPLETE SET (20)	5.00	12.00
1 Lindy Infante CO	.30	.75
2 Keith Woodside	.20	.50
3 Chris Jacke	.30	.75
4 Chuck Cecil	.30	.75
5 Tony Mandarich	.20	.50
6 Brent Fullwood	.20	.50
7 Robert Brown	.20	.50
8 Scott Stephen	.20	.50
9 Anthony Dilweg	.20	.50
10 Mark Murphy	.20	.50
11 Johnny Holland	.30	.75
12 Sterling Sharpe	.75	2.00
13 Tim Harris	.30	.75
14 Ed West	.20	.50
15 Jeff Query	.20	.50
16 Mark Lee	.20	.50
17 Rich Moran	.20	.50
18 Perry Kemp	.30	.75
19 Brian Noble	.30	.75
20 Don Majkowski	.40	1.00

1990 Packers Shultz

In 1990 the Shultz Say-O-Stores of Wisconsin featured a 15-week Flashback Game. Game tickets were given out at Piggly Wiggly and Sav-U Food stores. The tickets measured approximately 2" by 3 3/8" and were printed on thin white cardboard stock. The fronts displayed a picture of a Packer in a TV set framework, while the back had the rules governing the game. There were 13 players per week, and each week the cards had a different-colored border (apparently by error, the 14th week had 14 cards). On each Wednesday, the stores displayed a poster of the winning player, and customers who had a ticket matching the player on the poster could win the dollar amount specified in the TV set. The cards are checklisted by weeks as follows: 1 (1-13), 2 (14-26), 3 (27-39), 4 (40-52), 5 (53-65), 6 (66-78), 7 (79-91), 8 (92-104), 9 (105-17), 10 (118-30), 11 (131-43), 12 (144-56), 13 (157-69), 14 (170-83), and 15 (184-96). The winning card for each week is indicated by "WIN" after the player's name.

COMPLETE SET (181)	300.00	500.00
1 Carl Bland WIN		
2 Robert Brown	1.50	3.00
3 Burnell Dent	1.50	3.00
4 Herman Fontenot	1.50	3.00
5 Brent Fullwood	1.50	3.00
6 Michael Haddix	1.50	4.00
7 Perry Kemp	1.50	3.00
8 Don Majkowski	2.00	5.00
9 Mark Murphy	1.50	3.00
10 Jeff Query	1.50	3.00
11 Sterling Sharpe	3.20	8.00
12 Ed West	1.50	3.00
13 Keith Woodside	1.50	3.00
14 Jerry Boyarsky	1.50	3.00
15 Robert Brown	1.50	3.00
16 Chuck Cecil	1.50	3.00
17 Brent Fullwood	1.50	3.00
18 Ron Hallstrom	1.50	3.00
19 Perry Kemp	1.50	3.00
20 Don Majkowski	2.00	5.00
21 Rich Moran WIN		
22 Bob Nelson	1.50	3.00
23 Brian Noble	1.50	3.00
24 Jeff Query	1.50	3.00
25 Ed West	1.50	3.00
26 Blaise Winter	1.50	3.00
27 Billy Ard	1.50	3.00
28 Dave Brown	1.50	3.00
29 Burnell Dent	1.50	3.00
30 Tiger Greene	1.50	3.00
31 Mark Lee	1.50	3.00
32 Don Majkowski	2.00	5.00
33 Rich Moran	1.50	3.00
34 Brian Noble WIN		
35 Ron Pitts	1.50	3.00
36 Ken Ruettgers	1.50	3.00
37 Keith Uecker	1.50	3.00
38 Keith Woodside	1.50	3.00
39 Vince Workman	1.50	3.00
40 Carl Bland	1.50	3.00
41 Don Bracken	1.50	3.00
42 Blair Bush	1.50	3.00
43 Michael Haddix	1.50	4.00
44 Johnny Holland	1.50	3.00
45 Chris Jacke	1.50	4.00
46 Don Majkowski	2.00	5.00
47 Perry Kemp WIN		
48 Tony Mandarich	1.50	3.00
49 Shawn Patterson	1.50	3.00
50 Sterling Sharpe	3.20	8.00
51 Scott Stephens	1.50	3.00
52 Alan Veingrad	1.50	3.00
53 Jerry Boyarsky	1.50	3.00
54 Robert Brown	1.50	3.00
55 Chuck Cecil	1.50	3.00
56 Ron Hallstrom	1.50	3.00
57 Herman Fontenot WIN		
58 Tim Harris	1.50	4.00
59 Mark Lee	1.50	3.00
60 Don Majkowski	2.00	5.00
61 Mark Murphy	1.50	3.00
62 Bob Nelson	1.50	3.00
63 Jeff Query	1.50	3.00
64 Blaise Winter	1.50	3.00
65 Vince Workman	1.50	3.00
66 Billy Ard	1.50	3.00
67 Don Bracken	1.50	3.00
68 Robert Brown WIN		
69 Brent Fullwood	1.50	3.00
70 Tiger Greene	1.50	3.00
71 Chris Jacke	1.50	4.00
72 Don Majkowski	2.00	5.00
73 Rich Moran	1.50	3.00
74 Shawn Patterson	1.50	3.00
75 Sterling Sharpe	3.20	8.00
76 Keith Uecker	1.50	3.00
77 Alan Veingrad	1.50	3.00
78 Keith Woodside	1.50	3.00
79 Carl Bland	1.50	3.00
80 Dave Brown	1.50	3.00
81 Blair Bush	1.50	3.00
82 Herman Fontenot	1.50	3.00
83 Michael Haddix	1.50	4.00
84 Tim Harris	1.50	4.00
85 Johnny Holland	1.50	3.00
86 Perry Kemp	1.50	3.00
87 Don Majkowski	2.00	5.00
88 Tony Mandarich	1.50	3.00
89 Ron Pitts	1.50	3.00
90 Vince Workman	1.50	3.00
91 Sterling Sharpe WIN		
92 Billy Ard	1.50	3.00
93 Don Bracken	1.50	3.00
94 Burnell Dent	1.50	3.00
95 Brent Fullwood	1.50	3.00
96 Ron Hallstrom	1.50	3.00
97 Tim Harris WIN		
98 Chris Jacke	1.50	4.00
99 Don Majkowski	2.00	5.00
100 Mark Murphy	1.50	3.00
101 Brian Noble	1.50	3.00
102 Scott Stephens	1.50	3.00
103 Ed West	1.50	3.00
104 Keith Woodside	1.50	3.00
105 Jerry Boyarsky	1.50	3.00
106 Robert Brown	1.50	3.00
107 Herman Fontenot	1.50	3.00
108 Michael Haddix	1.50	4.00
109 Johnny Holland	1.50	3.00
110 Mark Lee	1.50	3.00
111 Don Majkowski WIN		
112 Bob Nelson	1.50	3.00
113 Shawn Patterson	1.50	3.00
114 Jeff Query	1.50	3.00
115 Alan Veingrad	1.50	3.00
116 Blaise Winter	1.50	3.00
117 Vince Workman	1.50	3.00
118 Carl Bland	1.50	3.00
119 Dave Brown	1.50	3.00
120 Blair Bush	1.50	3.00
121 Chuck Cecil	1.50	3.00
122 Herman Fontenot	1.50	3.00
123 Tiger Greene	1.50	3.00
124 Perry Kemp	1.50	3.00
125 Don Majkowski	2.00	5.00
126 Mark Murphy WIN		
127 Brian Noble	1.50	3.00
128 Ken Ruettgers	1.50	3.00
129 Keith Uecker	1.50	3.00
130 Vince Workman	1.50	3.00
131 Jerry Boyarsky	1.50	3.00
132 Burnell Dent	1.50	3.00
133 Brent Fullwood	1.50	3.00
134 Michael Haddix	1.50	4.00
135 Tim Harris	1.50	4.00
136 Chris Jacke	1.50	4.00
137 Don Majkowski WIN		
138 Tony Mandarich	1.50	3.00
139 Rich Moran	1.50	3.00
140 Ron Pitts	1.50	3.00
141 Ken Ruettgers	1.50	3.00
142 Sterling Sharpe	3.20	8.00
143 Ed West	1.50	3.00
144 Billy Ard	1.50	3.00
145 Dave Brown WIN		
146 Tiger Greene	1.50	3.00
147 Tim Harris	1.50	4.00
148 Johnny Holland	1.50	3.00
149 Mark Lee	1.50	3.00
150 Don Majkowski	2.00	5.00
151 Bob Nelson	1.50	3.00
152 Jeff Query	1.50	3.00
153 Scott Stephens	1.50	3.00
154 Alan Veingrad	1.50	3.00
155 Blaise Winter	1.50	3.00
156 Vince Workman	1.50	3.00
157 Carl Bland	1.50	3.00
158 Robert Brown	1.50	3.00
159 Blair Bush	1.50	3.00
160 Herman Fontenot	1.50	3.00
161 Brent Fullwood	1.50	3.00
162 Chris Jacke WIN		
163 Don Majkowski	2.00	5.00
164 Mark Murphy	1.50	3.00
165 Brian Noble	1.50	3.00
166 Shawn Patterson	1.50	3.00
167 Sterling Sharpe	3.20	8.00
168 Ed West	1.50	3.00
169 Keith Woodside	1.50	3.00
170 Don Bracken	1.50	3.00
171 Dave Brown	1.50	3.00
172 Chuck Cecil	1.50	3.00
173 Burnell Dent	1.50	3.00
174 Michael Haddix	1.50	4.00
175 Tim Harris WIN		
176 Johnny Holland	1.50	3.00
177 Ron Hallstrom	1.50	3.00
178 Don Majkowski	2.00	5.00
179 Tony Mandarich	1.50	3.00
180 Rich Moran	1.50	3.00
181 Ron Pitts	1.50	3.00
182 Ken Ruettgers	1.50	3.00
183 Keith Uecker	1.50	3.00
184 Jerry Boyarsky	1.50	3.00
185 Herman Fontenot	1.50	3.00
186 Brent Fullwood	1.50	3.00
187 Ron Hallstrom WIN		
188 Tim Harris	1.50	4.00
189 Chris Jacke	1.50	4.00
190 Perry Kemp	1.50	3.00
191 Don Majkowski	2.00	5.00
192 Bob Nelson	1.50	3.00
193 Jeff Query	1.50	3.00
194 Scott Stephens	1.50	3.00
195 Alan Veingrad	1.50	3.00
196 Vince Workman	1.50	3.00

1990 Packers Super Bowl I 25th Anniversary

This 45-card standard size set was issued by Champion Cards of Owosso, Michigan and produced by Pacific Trading Cards, Inc. This set celebrated the 25th anniversary of the 1966 Green Bay Packers, the first team to win the Super Bowl. This set has a mix of color and sepia-toned photos and a mix of action and portrait shots on the front with a biography of the player on the back of the card. The only member of the 1966 Packers not featured in this set is Paul Hornung.

COMPLETE SET (45)	6.00	15.00
1 Introduction Card	.20	.50
2 Bart Starr	.80	2.00
3 Herb Adderley	.30	.75
4 Bob Skoronski	.08	.25
5 Tom Brown	.14	.35
6 Lee Roy Caffey	.14	.35
7 Ray Nitschke	.40	1.00
8 Carroll Dale	.14	.35
9 Jim Taylor	.50	1.25
10 Ken Bowman	.08	.25
11 Gale Gillingham	.14	.35
12 Jim Grabowski	.20	.50
13 Dave Robinson	.20	.50
14 Donny Anderson	.20	.50
15 Willie Wood	.30	.75
16 Zeke Bratkowski	.20	.50
17 Doug Hart	.08	.25
18 Jerry Kramer	.30	.75
19 Marv Fleming	.14	.35
20 Lionel Aldridge	.14	.35
21 Bill Red Mack UER	.08	.25
22 Ron Kostelnik	.08	.25
23 Boyd Dowler	.20	.50
24 Vince Lombardi CO	.80	2.00
25 Forrest Gregg	.30	.75
26 Max McGee Superstar	.14	.35
27 Fuzzy Thurston	.20	.50
28 Bob Brown DT	.14	.35
29 Willie Davis	.30	.75
30 Elijah Pitts	.20	.50
31 Hank Jordan	.30	.75
32 Bart Starr	.80	2.00
33 Super Bowl I	.30	.75
34 1966 Packers	.20	.50
35 Max McGee	.20	.50
36 Jim Weatherwax	.08	.25
37 Bob Long	.08	.25
38 Don Chandler	.14	.35
39 Bill Anderson	.08	.25
40 Tommy Crutcher	.14	.35
41 Dave Hathcock	.08	.25
42 Steve Wright	.08	.25
43 Phil Vandersea	.08	.25
44 Bill Curry	.20	.50
45 Bob Jeter	.14	.35

1991 Packers Police

This 20-card standard-size set was printed on white card stock. These cards feature player action shots on the fronts enclosed by yellow and green borders. A yellow banner design in the top left corner has "1991 Packers" printed in black. Player's name and position appear in gold in the top right green border. College team and years played with Packers are noted in a gold band at bottom. The backs are printed in green ink and have Packer (safety) tips based on the player's position. Sponsor names appear at the bottom of card. Only card number 1 is printed horizontally front and back.

COMPLETE SET (20)	2.80	7.00
1 Lambeau Field	.10	.30
2 Sterling Sharpe	.60	1.50
3 James Campen	.10	.30
4 Chuck Cecil	.20	.50
5 Lindy Infante CO	.20	.50
6 Keith Woodside	.10	.30
7 Perry Kemp	.10	.30
8 Johnny Holland	.20	.50
9 Don Majkowski	.20	.50
10 Tony Bennett	.40	1.00
11 LeRoy Butler	.20	.50
12 Tony Mandarich	.10	.30
13 Darrell Thompson	.20	.50
14 Matt Brock	.10	.30
15 Charles Wilson	.40	1.00
16 Brian Noble	.20	.50
17 Ed West	.10	.30
18 Chris Jacke	.10	.30
19 Blair Kiel	.20	.50
20 Mark Murphy	.10	.30

1991 Packers Super Bowl II

is 50-card Green Bay Packers set was released by Sportscards of Michigan and commemorates the 25th anniversary of the team's win in Super Bowl II. The cards are printed on thin card stock and measure the standard size (2 1/2" by 3 1/2"). The fronts feature either black and white or color player photos with dark green borders. The player's name, team logo, and "Super Bowl II" appear in a yellow stripe below the picture. The backs have biography and career highlights. The cards are numbered on the back.

COMPLETE SET (50)	4.80	12.00
1 Intro Card	.20	.50
2 Steve Wright	.08	.25
3 Jim Flanigan LB	.08	.25
4 Tom Brown	.14	.35
5 Tommy Joe Crutcher	.14	.35
6 Doug Hart	.14	.35
7 Bob Hyland	.08	.25
8 John Rowser	.08	.25
9 Bob Skoronski	.08	.25
10 Jim Weatherwax	.08	.25
11 Ben Wilson	.08	.25
12 Don Horn	.14	.35
13 Allen Brown MISS	.08	.25
14 Dick Capp	.08	.25
15 Super Bowl II Action	.20	.50
16 Ice Bowl: The Play	.60	1.50
17 Chuck Mercein	.14	.35
18 Herb Adderley	.30	.75
19 Ken Bowman	.08	.25
20 Lee Roy Caffey	.14	.35
21 Carroll Dale	.14	.35
22 Marv Fleming	.14	.35
23 Jim Grabowski	.20	.50
24 Bob Jeter	.14	.35
25 Jerry Kramer	.30	.75
26 Max McGee	.20	.50
27 Elijah Pitts	.20	.50
28 Bart Starr	.80	2.00
29 Fuzzy Thurston	.20	.50
30 Willie Wood	.30	.75
31 Lionel Aldridge	.14	.35
32 Donny Anderson	.20	.50
33 Zeke Bratkowski	.20	.50
34 Bob Brown DT	.14	.35
35 Don Chandler	.14	.35
36 Willie Davis	.30	.75
37 Boyd Dowler	.20	.50
38 Gale Gillingham	.14	.35
39 Hank Jordan	.30	.75
40 Ron Kostelnik	.08	.25
41 Vince Lombardi CO	.80	2.00
42 Bob Long	.08	.25
43 Ray Nitschke	.40	1.00
44 Dave Robinson	.20	.50
45 Bart Starr MVP	.60	1.50
46 Travis Williams	.14	.35
47 1967 Packers Team	.20	.50
48 Ice Bowl Game Summary	.08	.25
49 Ice Bowl	.08	.25
NNO Packer Pro Shop	.08	.25

1992 Packers Hall of Fame

This 110-card standard-size set features all 106 Packer Hall of Fame inductees. It was available to collectors exclusively at the Packer Hall of Fame gift shop, and yearly updates will be issued as new members are selected for induction to the Hall of Fame. The cards are printed on thin cardboard stock. The fronts display black and white or color player photos enclosed by an oval gold border on a dark green card face. The player's name, position, and jersey number are in a gold band beneath the picture. The horizontally oriented backs carry biography and career highlights. The player's name appears in green in a gold banner at the top, while the card number is printed on a small helmet at the bottom center. The initial release had no #1 card, but two #45 cards. The Lavern Dilweg card was corrected in later printings as #1.

COMPLETE SET (110)	15.00	40.00
1 Lavern Dilweg UER	.15	.40
(Back is that of card/45 card&		
2 Red Dunn	.08	.25
3 Mike Michalske	.15	.40
4 Cal Hubbard	.15	.40
5 Johnny Blood McNally	.15	.40
6 Verne Lewellen	.07	.20
7 Cub Buck	.07	.20
8 Whitey Woodin	.07	.20
9 Jug Earp	.07	.20
10 Charlie Mathys	.07	.20
11 Andrew Turnbull PRES	.07	.20
12 Curly Lambeau	.40	1.00
13 George Calhoun PUB	.07	.20
14 Boob Darling	.07	.20
15 Eddie Jankowski	.07	.20
16 Swede Johnston	.07	.20
17 George Svendsen	.07	.20
18 Bob Monnett	.07	.20
19 Joe Laws	.07	.20
20 Tiny Engebretsen	.07	.20
21 Milt Gantenbein	.07	.20
22 Hank Bruder	.07	.20
23 Clarke Hinkle	.20	.50
24 Lon Evans	.07	.20
25 Buckets Goldenberg	.07	.20
26 Nate Barrager	.07	.20
27 Arnie Herber	.15	.40
28 Lee Joannes PRES	.07	.20
29 Jerry Clifford VP	.07	.20
30 Pete Tinsley	.07	.20
31 Buford Ray	.07	.20
32 Andy Uram	.07	.20
33 Larry Craig	.07	.20
34 Charles Brock	.07	.20
35 Ted Fritsch Sr.	.08	.25
36 Lou Brock	.07	.20
37 Carl Mulleneaux	.07	.20
38 Harry Jacunski	.07	.20
39 Cecil Isbell	.15	.40
40 Bud Svendsen	.07	.20
41 Russ Letlow	.07	.20
42 Don Hutson	.50	1.25
43 Irv Comp	.07	.20
44 John Martinkovic	.07	.20
45A Bobby Dillon	.08	.25
45B Lavern Dilweg UER	.15	.40
46 Wilner Burke	.07	.20
47 Dick Wildung	.07	.20
48 Bill Howton	.15	.40
49 Tobin Rote	.15	.40
50 Jim Ringo	.20	.50
51 Deral Teteak	.07	.20
52 Bob Forte	.07	.20
53 Tony Canadeo	.20	.50
54 Al Carmichael	.07	.20
55 Bob Mann	.07	.20
56 Jack Vainisi	.07	.20
57 Ken Bowman	.07	.20
58 Bob Skoronski	.07	.20
59 Dave Hanner	.08	.25
60 Bill Forester	.08	.25
61 Fred Cone	.07	.20
62 Lionel Aldridge	.08	.25
63 Carroll Dale	.08	.25
64 Howard Ferguson	.07	.20
65 Gary Knafelc	.07	.20
66 Ron Kramer	.08	.25
67 Forrest Gregg	.20	.50
68 Phil Bengtson CO	.07	.20
69 Dan Currie	.07	.20
70 Al Schneider	.07	.20
71 Bob Jeter	.08	.25
72 Jesse Whittenton	.08	.25
73 Hank Gremminger	.07	.20
74 Ron Kostelnik	.07	.20
75 Gale Gillingham	.08	.25
76 Lee Roy Caffey	.08	.25
77 Hank Jordan	.20	.50
78 Boyd Dowler	.15	.40
79 Fred Carr	.08	.25
80 Bud Jorgensen TR	.07	.20
81 Eugene Brusky	.07	.20
82 Fred Trowbridge	.07	.20
83 Jan Stenerud	.20	.50
84 Jerry Atkinson	.07	.20
85 Larry McCarren	.07	.20
86 Fred Leicht	.07	.20
87 Max McGee	.15	.40
88 Zeke Bratkowski	.15	.40
89 Dave Robinson	.15	.40
90 Herb Adderley	.20	.50
91 Dominic Olejniczak	.08	.25
92 Jerry Kramer	.20	.50
93 Super Bowl I	.08	.25
94 Don Chandler	.07	.20
95 John Brockington	.15	.40
96 Lynn Dickey	.08	.25
97 Bart Starr	1.50	4.00
98 Willie Wood	.30	.75
99 Packer Hall of Fame	.08	.25
100 Donny Anderson	.08	.25
101 Chester Marcol	.08	.25
102 Fuzzy Thurston	.08	.25
103 Paul Hornung	.60	1.50
104 Jim Taylor	.60	1.50
105 Vince Lombardi CO	1.50	4.00
106 Willie Davis	.20	.50
107 Ray Nitschke	.30	.75
108 Elijah Pitts	.08	.25
NNO Honor Roll	.08	.25
NNO Packer Hall of Fame	.08	.25

1992 Packers Police

This 20-card set features players of the Packers. The cards were printed with a green border and color player photograph on front. Cardbacks are white with green printing. We've assigned numbers to the unnumbered issue according to alphabetical order.

COMPLETE SET (20)	10.00	25.00
1 Tony Bennett	.40	1.00
2 Matt Brock	.10	.30
3 LeRoy Butler	.10	.30
4 Vinnie Clark	.20	.50
5 Brett Favre	7.50	20.00
6 Jackie Harris	.40	1.00
7 Johnny Holland	.10	.30
8 Mike Holmgren CO	1.00	2.50
9 Chris Jacke	.10	.30
10 Sherman Lewis CO	.40	1.00
11 Don Majkowski	.20	.50
12 Tony Mandarich	.10	.30
13 Paul McJulien	.10	.30
14 Brian Noble	.20	.50
14 Bryce Paup	.40	1.00
16 Ray Rhodes CO	.40	1.00
17 Tootie Robbins	.10	.30
18 Sterling Sharpe	.60	1.50
19 Darrell Thompson	.10	.30
20 Ron Wolf GM	.20	.50

1993 Packers Archives Postcards

These 40 postcards were made by Champion Cards of Green Bay to commemorate the Packers' 75th anniversary and, except for the unnumbered title card, measure approximately 3 1/2" by 5 1/2". The white-bordered postcards are framed by team color-coded lines and feature mostly black-and-white archival photos of Packer players and teams of yesteryear. Most of the cards display the Packers' 75th anniversary logo in the lower left. The horizontal white backs carry on their left sides information about the subject depicted on the front. On the right side is a ghosted Champion Cards logo. The postcards are numbered on the back within a football icon that appears at the bottom.

COMPLETE SET (40)	12.50	25.00
1 The First Team 1919	.40	1.00
2 The 1920s	.30	.75
3 The 1930s	.30	.75
4 The 1940s	.30	.75
5 The 1950s	.30	.75
6 The 1960s	.30	.75
7 The 1970s	.30	.75
8 The 1980s	.30	.75
9 The 1990s	.30	.75
10 Curly Lambeau 1919	.40	1.00
11 Jim Ringo 1953	.40	1.00
12 Ice Bowl 1967	.40	1.00
13 Jerry Kramer 1958	.40	1.00
14 Ray Nitschke 1958	.50	1.25
15 Fuzzy Thurston 1959	.40	1.00
16 James Lofton 1978-86	.40	1.00
17 Super Bowl I Action	.40	1.00
18 Don Hutson 1935-45	.50	1.25
19 Tony Canadeo 1941-43/46-52	.40	1.00
20 Bobby Dillon 1952-59	.30	.75
21 The Quarterback	.40	1.00
22 Willie Wood 1960-71	.40	1.00
23 Dave Beverly 1975-80	.30	.75
24 James Lofton 1978	.40	1.00
25 Tim Harris 1986-90	.40	1.00
26 1929 Championship Team	.30	.75
27 1930 Championship Team	.30	.75
28 1931 Championship Team	.30	.75
29 1936 Championship Team	.30	.75
30 1939 Championship Team	.30	.75
31 1944 Championship Team	.30	.75
32 1961 Championship Team	.40	1.00
33 1962 Championship Team	.40	1.00
34 1965 Championship Team	.40	1.00
35 1966 Championship Team	.40	1.00
36 1967 Championship Team	.40	1.00
37 Old City Stadium	.30	.75
38 New City Stadium	.30	.75
39 Lambeau Field - 1992	.30	.75
NNO Title card	.40	1.00

1993 Packers Police

These 20 standard-size cards were issued to commemorate the Packers' 75th anniversary and feature on their fronts white-bordered color player photos. Two team color-coded stripes edge the pictures at the bottom. The 75th anniversary logo appears at the upper left, and the words "Celebrating 75 Years of Pro Football 1919-1993" appear below the photo. The white back carries the player's name, position, years in the NFL, alma mater, and Packers helmet at the upper left. Below are safety messages written by area grade schoolers.

COMPLETE SET (20)	6.00	15.00
1 Ron Wolf GM	.10	.30
2 Wayne Simmons	.20	.50
3 James Campen	.10	.30
4 Matt Brock	.10	.30
5 Mike Holmgren CO	.50	1.25
6 Brian Noble	.20	.50
7 Ken O'Brien	.20	.50
8 George Teague	.20	.50
9 Brett Favre	4.00	10.00
10 LeRoy Butler	.20	.50
11 Harry Galbreath	.10	.30
12 Chris Jacke	.20	.50
13 Sterling Sharpe	.40	1.00
14 Terrell Buckley	.20	.50
15 Ken Ruettgers	.20	.50
16 Johnny Holland	.20	.50
17 Edgar Bennett	.40	1.00
18 Jackie Harris	.30	.75
19 Tony Bennett	.30	.75
20 Reggie White	.60	1.50

1994 Packers Police

This 20-card standard-size set was issued courtesy of the Alma Fire Department and the Green Bay Packer Organization. The fronts display color player photos accented by team color-coded borders. The player's name and uniform number are printed in the green bar beneath the picture. On a white background in dark green print, the backs carry a student tip by Fond du Lac elementary school children and list the set's sponsors.

COMPLETE SET (20)	4.00	10.00
1 Sherman Lewis CO	.30	.75
2 Sterling Sharpe	.30	.75
3 Ken Ruettgers	.20	.50
4 Reggie White	.50	1.25
5 Edgar Bennett	.40	1.00
6 Fritz Shurmur CO	.20	.50
7 Brett Favre	1.50	4.00
8 John Jurkovic	.30	.75
9 Robert Brooks	.40	1.00
10 Reggie Cobb	.08	.25
11 Bryce Paup	.30	.75
12 Harry Galbreath	.08	.25
13 Mike Holmgren CO	.50	1.25
14 Ed West	.08	.25
15 Sean Jones	.30	.75
16 Ron Wolf GM	.08	.25
17 Chris Jacke	.20	.50
18 Wayne Simmons	.20	.50
19 LeRoy Butler	.08	.25
20 George Teague	.20	.50

1995 Packers Safety Fritsch

This 20-card set of the Green Pay Packers features color action player photos in a thin green border. The set was produced by Larry Fritsch Cards and sponsored by the local Fire Department. The backs carry a student safety tip.

COMPLETE SET (20)	3.20	8.00
1 Mike Holmgren CO	.40	1.00
2 Ron Wolf VP	.08	.25
GM		

3 Brett Favre 1.20 3.00
4 Ty Detmer .40 1.00
5 Chris Jacke .20 .50
6 Craig Hentrich .08 .25
7 Craig Newsome .08 .25
8 George Teague .20 .50
9 Edgar Bennett .30 .75
10 LeRoy Butler .08 .25
11 George Koonce .08 .25
12 John Jurkovic .20 .50
13 Aaron Taylor .08 .25
14 Ken Ruettgers .08 .25
15 Robert Brooks .40 1.00
16 Mark Chmura .50 1.25
17 Reggie White .40 1.00
18 Doug Evans .20 .50
19 Sean Jones .20 .50
20 Wayne Simmons .20 .50

1995 Packers Sentry Brett Favre

This roughly 8-5/8" by 6-3/4" card was distributed at a Green Bay Packers game during the 1995 season. The unnumbered card was included as part of a perforated sheet that contained an assortment of advertisements. The price below reflects that of the card in uncut sheet form.

1 Brett Favre .80 2.00

1996 Packers Collector's Choice ShopKo

is 90-card standard-sized set was distributed and produced by Upper Deck for ShopKo, a retailer with stores in the Wisconsin area. The cards feature a unique Collector's Choice design and card numbering and include the following subsets: Season to Remember (#GB31-GB50), Legends of the Green and Gold (#GB51-GB69), and Leaders of the Pack (#GB70-GB90).

COMPLETE SET (90) 16.00 40.00
GB1 Brett Favre 1.60 4.00
GB2 Mark Chmura .15 .40
GB3 Edgar Bennett .30 .75
GB4 Robert Brooks .30 .75
GB5 Antonio Freeman .60 1.50
GB6 Travis Jervey .15 .40
GB7 Craig Newsome .08 .25
GB8 Reggie White .30 .75
GB9 Sean Jones .08 .25
GB10 LeRoy Butler .15 .40
GB11 Chris Jacke .08 .25
GB12 Derrick Mayes .30 .75
GB13 Chris Darkins .15 .40
GB14 Keith Jackson .08 .25
GB15 Terry Mickens .08 .25
GB16 Dorsey Levens .60 1.50
GB17 Jim McMahon .15 .40
GB18 Craig Hentrich .08 .25
GB19 George Koonce .08 .25
GB20 William Henderson .08 .25
GB21 Doug Evans .15 .40
GB22 Mike Prior .08 .25
GB23 Wayne Simmons .08 .25
GB24 Darius Holland .08 .25
GB25 Gilbert Brown .30 .75
GB26 Aaron Taylor .08 .25
GB27 Frank Winters .08 .25
GB28 Ken Ruettgers .08 .25
GB29 Earl Dotson .08 .25
GB30 Eugene Robinson .08 .25
GB31 Brett Favre SR 1.00 2.50
GB32 Brett Favre SR 1.00 2.50
GB33 Brett Favre SR 1.00 2.50
GB34 Edgar Bennett SR .15 .40
GB35 Edgar Bennett SR .15 .40
GB36 Robert Brooks SR .15 .40
GB37 Robert Brooks SR .15 .40
GB38 Mark Chmura SR .15 .40
GB39 Mark Chmura SR .15 .40
GB40 LeRoy Butler SR .08 .25
GB41 LeRoy Butler SR .08 .25
GB42 Craig Newsome SR .08 .25
GB43 Craig Newsome SR .08 .25
GB44 Reggie White SR .15 .40
GB45 Reggie White SR .15 .40
GB46 Sean Jones SR .08 .25
GB47 Sean Jones SR .08 .25
GB48 Antonio Freeman SR .30 .75
GB49 Chris Jacke SR .08 .25
GB50 Offensive Line SR .08 .25
GB51 Forrest Gregg LGG .15 .40
GB52 Paul Hornung LGG .30 .75
GB53 Willie Davis LGG .15 .40
GB54 Vince Lombardi CO LGG .30 .75
GB55 Ray Nitschke LGG .15 .40
GB56 Willie Wood LGG .15 .40
GB57 Don Hutson LGG .15 .40
GB58 Don Majkowski LGG .08 .25
GB59 Bryce Paup LGG .08 .25
GB60 Sterling Sharpe LGG .08 .25
GB61 Ted Hendricks LGG .08 .25
GB62 Lynn Dickey LGG .08 .25
GB63 James Lofton LGG .08 .25
GB64 Brett Favre LGG 1.00 2.50
GB65 Edgar Bennett LGG .15 .40
GB66 Reggie White LGG .15 .40
GB67 John Jurkovic LGG .08 .25
GB68 Mike Holmgren CO LGG .15 .40
GB69 Ron Wolf LGG .08 .25
GB70 Forrest Gregg LP .15 .40
GB71 Paul Hornung LP .15 .40
GB72 Willie Davis LP .15 .40
GB73 Ray Nitschke LP .15 .40
GB74 Willie Wood LP .15 .40
GB75 Don Hutson LP .15 .40
GB76 Sterling Sharpe LP .08 .25
GB77 Don Majkowski LP .08 .25
GB78 Ted Hendricks LP .08 .25
GB79 Lynn Dickey LP .08 .25
GB80 James Lofton LP .08 .25
GB81 Brett Favre LP 1.00 2.50
GB82 Edgar Bennett LP .15 .40
GB83 Robert Brooks LP .15 .40
GB84 Mark Chmura LP .15 .40
GB85 Reggie White LP .08 .25
GB86 Sean Jones LP .08 .25
GB87 Chris Jacke LP .08 .25
GB88 LeRoy Butler LP .08 .25
GB89 Craig Newsome LP .08 .25
GB90 Checklist Card .08 .25

1996 Packers Police

e Green Bay Packers issued this set in 1996 sponsored by Citgo. The cards feature a green border with the team and year "Packers 1996" at the top of the cardfront. The cardbacks feature green text on white card stock.

COMPLETE SET (20) 3.00 8.00
1 Edgar Bennett .30 .75
2 Robert Brooks .30 .75
3 Gilbert Brown .30 .75
4 LeRoy Butler .20 .50
5 Mark Chmura .30 .75
6 Earl Dotson .08 .25
7 Doug Evans .20 .50
8 Brett Favre 1.50 4.00
9 Antonio Freeman .80 2.00
10 Craig Hentrich .08 .25
11 Chris Jacke .20 .50
12 Wayne Simmons .20 .50
13 George Koonce .08 .25
14 Craig Newsome .08 .25
15 Ken Ruettgers .08 .25
16 Keith Jackson .20 .50
17 Aaron Taylor .08 .25
18 Reggie White .40 1.00
19 Mike Holmgren .30 .75
20 Ron Wolf .08 .25

1996 Packers Sentry

This set was issued as a perforated sheet along with a group of advertisements at a 1996 Packers home game. The set was sponsored by Sentry Foods and highlights various games of the 1995 season.

COMPLETE SET (8) 2.40 6.00
1 Sept. 11, 1995 .30 .75
R.White
2 Sept. 17, 1995 .80 2.00
Favre
3 Oct. 15, 1995 .80 2.00
Favre
4 Oct. 22, 1995 .08 .25
W.Simmons
5 Nov. 12, 1995 .15 .40
E.Bennett
6 Nov. 26, 1995 .08 .25
7 Dec. 3, 1995 .30 .75
8 Team Photo .15 .40

1997 Packers Collector's Choice

per Deck released several team sets in 1997 in a blister pack wrapper. Each of the 14-cards in this set are very similar to the base Collector's Choice cards except for the card numbering on the cardback. A cover/checklist card was added featuring the team helmet.

COMPLETE SET (14) 1.60 4.00
GB1 Robert Brooks .05 .15
GB2 Antonio Freeman .08 .25
GB3 Keith Jackson .02 .10
GB4 Mark Chmura .05 .15
GB5 Brett Favre .80 2.00
GB6 Sean Jones .02 .10
GB7 Reggie White .08 .25
GB8 LeRoy Butler .02 .10
GB9 Craig Newsome .02 .10
GB10 Edgar Bennett .05 .15
GB11 William Henderson .02 .10
GB12 Dorsey Levens .08 .25
GB13 Gilbert Brown .05 .15
GB14 Packers Logo CL .40 1.00

1997 Packers Collector's Choice ShopKo

r the second straight year, a 90-card standard-sized Upper Deck set was distributed and produced for ShopKo, a retailer with stores in the Wisconsin area. The fronts of cards 1-59 feature action color player photos within a white border. The backs carry another smaller player photo with biographical information, statistics, and a "Did You Know" fact about the pictured player. The fronts of the various subset cards (#60-90) feature borderless color action player photos with player information on the backs. All cards have gold foil highlights. The cards were issued in foil pack and factory set form and feature a Collector's Choice logo. Each factory set box included one randomly inserted Road to the Super Bowl Jumbo card.

COMP.FACT.SET (91) 16.00 40.00
GB1 Robert Brooks .30 .75
GB2 Antonio Freeman .50 1.25
GB3 Keith Jackson .15 .40
GB4 Mark Chmura .15 .40
GB5 Brett Favre 1.60 4.00
GB6 Reggie White .30 .75
GB7 LeRoy Butler .08 .25
GB8 Craig Newsome .08 .25
GB9 Sean Jones .08 .25
GB10 Edgar Bennett .15 .40
GB11 William Henderson .08 .25
GB12 Dorsey Levens .50 1.25
GB13 Travis Jervey .15 .40
GB14 Jim McMahon .15 .40
GB15 Aaron Taylor .08 .25
GB16 Frank Winters .08 .25
GB17 Earl Dotson .08 .25
GB18 Adam Timmerman .08 .25
GB19 Bruce Wilkerson .08 .25
GB20 John Michels .08 .25
GB21 Don Beebe .08 .25
GB22 Andre Rison .15 .40
GB23 Desmond Howard .15 .40
GB24 Terry Mickens .08 .25
GB25 Derrick Mayes .15 .40
GB26 Chris Jacke .08 .25
GB27 Gilbert Brown .15 .40
GB28 Santana Dotson .08 .25
GB29 George Koonce .08 .25
GB30 Wayne Simmons .08 .25
GB31 Brian Williams .08 .25
GB32 Ron Cox .08 .25
GB33 Doug Evans .08 .25
GB34 Eugene Robinson .08 .25
GB35 Mike Prior .08 .25
GB36 Tyrone Williams .08 .25
GB37 Sherman Lewis .15 .40
GB38 Fritz Shurmur CO .15 .40
GB39 Gordon(Red) Batty .08 .25
GB40 Lambeau Field .15 .40
GB41 Brett Favre SR 1.00 2.50
GB42 Brett Favre SR 1.00 2.50
GB43 Edgar Bennett SR .15 .40
GB44 Edgar Bennett SR .15 .40
GB45 Antonio Freeman SR .30 .75
GB46 Antonio Freeman SR .30 .75
GB47 Dorsey Levens SR .30 .75
GB48 Andre Rison SR .15 .40
GB49 Keith Jackson SR .08 .25
GB50 Don Beebe SR .08 .25
GB51 Reggie White SR .30 .75
GB52 Packer Defense SR .15 .40
GB53 Craig Newsome SR .08 .25
GB54 Eugene Robinson SR .08 .25
GB55 Desmond Howard SR .15 .40
GB56 Robert Brooks SR .30 .75
GB57 Chris Jacke SR .08 .25
GB58 Mike Holmgren SR .15 .40
GB59 Ron Wolf SR .08 .25
GB60 Brett Favre RSB 1.00 2.50
GB61 Brett Favre RSB 1.00 2.50
GB62 Edgar Bennett RSB .15 .40
GB63 Edgar Bennett RSB .15 .40
GB64 Dorsey Levens RSB .30 .75
GB65 Dorsey Levens RSB .30 .75
GB66 Antonio Freeman RSB .30 .75
GB67 Antonio Freeman RSB .30 .75
GB68 Andre Rison RSB .15 .40
GB69 Don Beebe RSB .08 .25
GB70 Mark Chmura RSB .15 .40
GB71 Reggie White RSB .30 .75
GB72 Eugene Robinson RSB .08 .25
GB73 Desmond Howard RSB .15 .40
GB74 Desmond Howard RSB .15 .40
GB75 Craig Newsome RSB .08 .25
GB76 Tyrone Williams RSB .08 .25
GB77 Chris Jacke RSB .15 .40
GB78 Wayne Simmons RSB .08 .25
GB79 Offensive Line .08 .25
Timmerman
GB80 Brett Favre BB 1.00 2.50
GB81 Antonio Freeman BB .30 .75
GB82 Reggie White BB .30 .75
GB83 Wayne Simmons BB .08 .25
GB84 Edgar Bennett BB .15 .40
GB85 Andre Rison BB .15 .40
GB86 Dorsey Levens BB .30 .75
GB87 Chris Jacke BB .08 .25
GB88 The Secondary .08 .25
GB89 Desmond Howard BB .15 .40
GB90 Team Logo CL .08 .25

1997 Packers Playoff

is 50-card set honors the 1997 Super Bowl XXXI World Champions, the Green Bay Packers. The fronts feature borderless color action player photos with the Super Bowl logo printed at the bottom and player's name on one side. The backs carry the score of the championship game with the New England Patriots and player information on a faint background of the dome in New Orleans.

COMPLETE SET (50) 6.00 15.00
1 Super Bowl XXXI Champions .07 .20
2 Brett Favre MVP 1.60 4.00
3 Reggie White .30 .75
Minister of Defense
4 Desmond Howard MVP .15 .40
5 NFC Championship Trophy Presentation .07 .20
6 Mike Holmgren CO .15 .40
7 Brett Favre 1.60 4.00
8 Chris Jacke .07 .20
9 Craig Hentrich .07 .20
10 Craig Newsome .07 .20
11 Dorsey Levens .60 1.50
12 Doug Evans .07 .20
13 Edgar Bennett .30 .75
14 LeRoy Butler .07 .20
15 Eugene Robinson .07 .20
16 Brian Williams LB .07 .20
17 Frank Winters .07 .20
18 Ron Cox .07 .20
19 Wayne Simmons .07 .20
20 Adam Timmerman .07 .20
21 Bruce Wilkerson .07 .20
22 Santana Dotson .07 .20
23 Earl Dotson .07 .20
24 Aaron Taylor .07 .20
25 Desmond Howard .15 .40
26 Don Beebe .07 .20
27 Andre Rison .15 .40
28 Antonio Freeman .60 1.50
29 Terry Mickens .07 .20
30 Keith Jackson .15 .40
31 Mark Chmura .30 .75
32 Reggie White .30 .75
33 Gilbert Brown .15 .40
34 Sean Jones .07 .20
35 Robert Brooks .30 .75
George Koonce
36 Derrick Mayes .15 .40
Gary Brown T
37 Jim McMahon .15 .40
38 William Henderson .07 .20
39 Travis Jervey .15 .40
Roderick Mullen
40 Tyrone Williams .07 .20
41 John Michels .07 .20
42 Mike Prior .07 .20
43 Calvin Jones .07 .20
Jeff Thomason
44 Brett Favre 1.60 4.00
45 Jeff Dellenbach .07 .20
46 Bernardo Harris .07 .20
47 Darius Holland .07 .20
48 Lamont Hollinquest .07 .20
49 Lindsay Knapp .07 .20
50 Gabe Wilkins .07 .20

1997 Packers Police

The Packers, along with a host of sponsors, produced this set for the 1997 Super Bowl Championship club. The cardfronts feature a colorful design along with a color photo, while the backs were produced simply in green on white card stock.

COMPLETE SET (20) 3.00 8.00
1 Super Bowl XXXI Trophy .08 .25
2 Mike Holmgren CO .20 .50
3 Ron Wolf GM .08 .25
4 Brett Favre 1.50 4.00
5 Reggie White .40 1.00
6 LeRoy Butler .08 .25
7 Frank Winters .08 .25
8 Aaron Taylor .08 .25
9 Robert Brooks .20 .50
10 Gilbert Brown .20 .50
11 Mark Chmura .20 .50
12 Earl Dotson .08 .25
13 Santana Dotson .08 .25
14 Doug Evans .08 .25
15 Antonio Freeman .40 1.00
16 William Henderson .08 .25
17 Craig Hentrich .08 .25
18 Dorsey Levens .30 .75
19 Craig Newsome .08 .25
20 Edgar Bennett .20 .50

1997 Packers Score

is 15-card set of the Green Bay Packers was distributed in five-card packs with a suggested retail price of $1.99. The fronts feature color action player photos with white borders and the player's name and team logo printed in team color foil at the bottom. The backs carry player information and career statistics. Platinum Team parallel cards were randomly seeded in packs featuring all foil cardfronts.

COMPLETE SET (15) 3.20 8.00
*PLATINUM TEAMS: 1X TO 2X
1 Brett Favre 1.25 3.00
2 Andre Rison .15 .40
3 Robert Brooks .15 .40
4 Keith Jackson .08 .25
5 Edgar Bennett .15 .40
6 Reggie White .30 .75
7 Dorsey Levens .40 1.00
8 Antonio Freeman .40 1.00
9 Mark Chmura .15 .40
10 Wayne Simmons .08 .25
11 Eugene Robinson .08 .25
12 Brian Williams LB .08 .25
13 Doug Evans .08 .25
14 LeRoy Butler .08 .25
15 Gilbert Brown .15 .40

1997 Packers Upper Deck Legends

is oversized (roughly 3 1/2" by 5") set was produced by Upper Deck for distributiion through larger retail chains. The cards were sold in complete factory set form in a specially designed display box. Each card features a top "Legends of the Green and Gold" color photo surrounded by an antique style beige border.

COMPLETE SET (20) 8.00 20.00
GB1 Forrest Gregg .50 1.25
GB2 Paul Hornung .80 2.00
GB3 Willie Davis .50 1.25
GB4 Ray Nitschke .50 1.25
GB5 Willie Wood .50 1.25
GB6 Don Hutson .50 1.25
GB7 Don Majkowski .30 .75
GB8 Bryce Paup .30 .75
GB9 Sterling Sharpe .50 1.25
GB10 Ted Hendricks .30 .75
GB11 Lynn Dickey .30 .75
GB12 James Lofton .30 .75
GB13 Brett Favre 2.00 5.00
GB14 Edgar Bennett .80 2.00
GB15 Reggie White .80 2.00
GB16 LeRoy Butler .30 .75
GB17 John Jurkovic .30 .75
GB18 Mike Holmgren CO .50 1.25
GB19 Ron Wolf GM .30 .75
GB20 Packer Helmet CL .30 .75

1997 Packers vs. Bears Sentry

Issued at a Packers home game with the Bears in 1997, Sentry Foods sponsored this set. The cards were released as an uncut sheet of 6-cards and six different smaller ad cards. Each card includes a color photo from one historic Packers vs. Bears game with no particular players identified. We've included names of some of the top featured players below. The cards are unnumbered and listed below in chronological order.

COMPLETE SET (6) 1.60 4.00
1 Dec.16, 1973 .20 .50
Brockington
2 Sept. 7, 1980 .20 .50
Marcol
3 Nov. 5, 1989 .20 .50
St.Sharpe
4 Oct. 31, 1994 .30 .75
E.Bennett
T.Armstrong
5 Nov. 12, 1995 1.00 2.50
Favre
E.Bennett
6 Oct. 6, 1996 .30 .75
Re.White
R.Salaam

1997 Packers vs. Vikings Sentry

Issued at a game with the Vikings in 1997, Sentry Foods sponsored this set for Packers' fans. The cards were released as an uncut sheet of 9-cards and one ad-card for the Junior Power Pack kids club. Each card includes a color photo from one historic Packers vs. Vikings game with no particular players identified. We've included names of some of the top featured players below. The cards are unnumbered and listed below in chronological order.

COMPLETE SET (9) 2.40 6.00
1 Dec. 3, 1967 .40 1.00
2 Dec. 10, 1972 .40 1.00
S.Hunter
C.Eller
3 Nov. 26, 1978 .30 .75
C.Foreman
4 Nov. 11, 1979 .30 .75
5 Oct. 26, 1980 .40 1.00
L.Dickey
6 Nov. 13, 1983 .30 .75
7 Dec. 13, 1987 .30 .75
P.O.Carruth
8 Nov. 26, 1989 .30 .75
D.Majik
9 Sept. 4, 1994 .40 1.00

1998 Packers Police

With the sponsorship of local crime prevention authorities, the Packers produced this set for the 1998 team. The cardfronts feature a colorful design along with a color player photo, while the backs were produced simply in green on white card stock.

COMPLETE SET (20) 3.20 8.00
1 Ron Wolf GM .08 .25
2 Robert Brooks .20 .50
3 Gilbert Brown .08 .25
4 Mike Holmgren CO .20 .50
5 LeRoy Butler .08 .25
6 Mark Chmura .20 .50
7 Earl Dotson .08 .25
8 Santana Dotson .08 .25
9 Brett Favre 1.50 4.00
10 Antonio Freeman .40 1.00
11 Bernardo Harris .08 .25
12 William Henderson .08 .25
13 Dorsey Levens .40 1.00
14 Craig Newsome .08 .25
15 Adam Timmerman .08 .25
16 Ross Verba .08 .25
17 Reggie White .40 1.00
18 Brian Williams LB .08 .25
19 Tyrone Williams .08 .25
20 Frank Winters .08 .25

1998 Packers Upper Deck ShopKo

is 90-card set produced by Upper Deck for ShopKo, a retailer with stores in the Wisconsin area, was distributed in 10-card packs. The cards feature a partial yellow border and gold foil highlights on the cardfronts. The card numbering includes a GB prefix on the first 55-cards and the set includes the following subsets: Leaders of the Pack (P1-P15) and Tundra Titans (T1-T20). A Title Defense parallel set was also produced and randomly inserted in packs (1:4 packs ratio).

COMPLETE SET (90) 10.00 25.00
1 Brett Favre 1.20 3.00
2 Ryan Longwell .08 .25
3 Steve Bono .30 .75
4 Craig Hentrich .08 .25
5 Doug Pederson .08 .25
6 Craig Newsome .08 .25
7 Aaron Hayden .08 .25
8 Dorsey Levens .40 1.00
9 Mark Collins .08 .25
10 Roderick Mullen .08 .25
11 William Henderson .08 .25
12 Travis Jervey .15 .40
13 Doug Evans .08 .25
14 Edgar Bennett .15 .40
15 LeRoy Butler .15 .40
16 Tyrone Williams .08 .25
17 Emory Smith .08 .25
18 Mike Prior .08 .25
19 Eugene Robinson .15 .40
20 Darren Sharper .40 1.00
21 Chris Darkins .15 .40
22 Brian Williams .08 .25
23 Frank Winters .08 .25
24 George Koonce .08 .25
25 Seth Joyner .08 .25
26 Bernardo Harris .08 .25
27 Lamont Hollinquest .08 .25
28 Anthony Fogle .08 .25
29 Marco Rivera .30 .75
30 Adam Timmerman .08 .25
31 Bruce Wilkerson .08 .25
32 Jeff Dellenbach .08 .25
33 Joe Andruzzi .08 .25
34 Santana Dotson .08 .25
35 Earl Dotson .08 .25
36 Aaron Taylor .08 .25
37 John Michels .08 .25
38 Ross Verba .08 .25
39 Derrick Mayes .15 .40
40 Tyrone Davis .08 .25
41 Don Beebe .15 .40
42 Jeff Thomason .08 .25
43 Bill Schroeder .30 .75
44 Terry Mickens .08 .25
45 Antonio Freeman .50 1.25
46 Robert Brooks .15 .40
47 Mark Chmura .30 .75
48 Darius Holland .08 .25
49 Reggie White .30 .75
50 Gilbert Brown .08 .25
51 Bob Kuberski .08 .25
52 Keith McKenzie .08 .25
53 Paul Frase .08 .25
54 Gabe Wilkins .08 .25
55 Jermaine Smith .08 .25
P1 Mike Holmgren CO LP .15 .40
P2 Sherman Lewis CO LP .15 .40
P3 Fritz Shurmur CO LP .08 .25
P4 Ron Wolf GM LP .08 .25
P5 Brett Favre LP .80 2.00
P6 Reggie White LP .15 .40
P7 Dorsey Levens LP .30 .75
P8 Gilbert Brown LP .08 .25
P9 Eugene Robinson LP .08 .25
P10 Antonio Freeman LP .30 .75
P11 Mark Chmura LP .15 .40
P12 Seth Joyner LP .08 .25
P13 LeRoy Butler LP .08 .25
P14 Robert Brooks LP .15 .40
P15 Travis Jervey LP .08 .25
T1 Brett Favre TT .80 2.00
T2 Reggie White TT .15 .40
T3 Dorsey Levens TT .30 .75
T4 Antonio Freeman TT .30 .75
T5 LeRoy Butler TT .08 .25
T6 Santana Dotson TT .08 .25
T7 Frank Winters TT .08 .25
T8 Robert Brooks TT .15 .40
T9 Mark Chmura TT .15 .40
T10 Travis Jervey TT .08 .25
T11 Gilbert Brown TT .08 .25
T12 Seth Joyner TT .08 .25
T13 William Henderson TT .08 .25
T14 Derrick Mayes TT .15 .40
T15 Doug Evans TT .08 .25
T16 Ross Verba TT .08 .25
T17 Tyrone Williams TT .08 .25
T18 Gabe Wilkins TT .08 .25
T19 Eugene Robinson TT .08 .25
T20 Darren Sharper TT .25 .60

1998 Packers Upper Deck ShopKo Title Defense

COMP.TITLE DEF.SET (90) 24.00 60.00
*TITLE DEFENSE CARDS: 1.5X TO 3X

1998 Packers Upper Deck ShopKo II

This 90-card set was produced by Upper Deck for ShopKo, a retailer with stores in the Wisconsin area. It was distributed in late 1998 as a second series set to the original Upper Deck Shopko set released earlier in the year. The fronts features color action player photos with green foil highlights, and the backs carry player information. Unlike series one, the cards contain no prefixes on the card numbers. The set also contains the topical subsets: Game Dated (51-65), and Pack Comeback (66-90). The Ray Nitschke tribute card is listed at the bottom of the checklist.

COMPLETE SET (90) 8.00 20.00
1 Brett Favre 1.20 3.00
2 Ryan Longwell .08 .25
3 Doug Pederson .08 .25
4 Craig Newsome .08 .25
5 Emory Smith .08 .25
6 Aaron Hayden .08 .25
7 Dorsey Levens .40 1.00
8 Roderick Mullen .08 .25
9 Travis Jervey .15 .40
10 William Henderson .08 .25
11 LeRoy Butler .15 .40
12 Tyrone Williams .08 .25
13 Mike Prior .08 .25
14 Darren Sharper .25 .60
15 Chris Darkins .15 .40
16 Anthony Hicks .08 .25
17 Brian Williams .08 .25
18 Frank Winters .08 .25
19 George Koonce .08 .25
20 Bernardo Harris .08 .25
21 Lamont Hollinquest .08 .25
22 Seth Joyner .08 .25
23 Marco Rivera .30 .75
24 Adam Timmerman .08 .25
25 Bruce Wilkerson .08 .25
26 Jeff Dellenbach .08 .25
27 Joe Andruzzi .08 .25
28 Santana Dotson .08 .25
29 Earl Dotson .08 .25
30 John Michels .08 .25
31 Ross Verba .08 .25
32 Derrick Mayes .15 .40
33 Tyrone Davis .08 .25
34 Jeff Thomason .08 .25
35 Bill Schroeder .08 .25
36 Antonio Freeman .50 1.25
37 Robert Brooks .15 .40
38 Mark Chmura .30 .75
39 Reggie White .30 .75
40 Gilbert Brown .08 .25
41 Bob Kuberski .08 .25
42 Keith McKenzie .08 .25
43 Jermaine Smith .08 .25
44 Eric Curry .08 .25
45 Doug Widell .08 .25
46 Vaughn Booker .08 .25
47 Vonnie Holliday .08 .25
48 Glyn Milburn .08 .25
49 Antonio London .08 .25
50 Jonathan Brown .08 .25
51 Brett Favre GD .80 2.00
52 Robert Brooks GD .15 .40
53 Antonio Freeman GD .30 .75
54 Dorsey Levens GD .30 .75
55 Mark Chmura GD .15 .40
56 Reggie White GD .15 .40
57 LeRoy Butler GD .08 .25
58 Travis Jervey GD .08 .25
59 Gilbert Brown GD .08 .25
60 William Henderson GD .08 .25
61 Ryan Longwell GD .08 .25
62 Seth Joyner GD .08 .25
63 Derrick Mayes GD .08 .25
64 Ross Verba GD .08 .25
65 Santana Dotson GD .08 .25
66 Brett Favre PC .80 2.00
67 Mark Chmura PC .15 .40
68 Dorsey Levens PC .30 .75
69 Robert Brooks PC .15 .40
70 Antonio Freeman PC .30 .75
71 Derrick Mayes PC .08 .25
72 Frank Winters PC .08 .25
73 Anthony Fogle PC .08 .25
74 Emory Smith PC .08 .25
75 Mike Prior PC .08 .25
76 Adam Timmerman PC .08 .25
77 Ross Verba PC .08 .25
78 Reggie White PC .15 .40
79 Gilbert Brown PC .08 .25
80 Seth Joyner PC .08 .25
81 LeRoy Butler PC .08 .25
82 Craig Newsome PC .08 .25
83 Ryan Longwell PC .08 .25
84 Travis Jervey PC .08 .25
85 William Henderson PC .08 .25
86 Darren Sharper PC .15 .40
87 Bernardo Harris PC .08 .25
88 Bruce Wilkerson PC .08 .25
89 Earl Dotson PC .08 .25
90 John Michels PC .08 .25
RN1 Ray Nitschke .40 1.00

1998 Packers Upper Deck ShopKo II Lambeau Lineups

Randomly inserted in packs, this 30-card set features color player photos with player information carried on the backs.

COMPLETE SET (30) 4.00 10.00
LL1 Brett Favre 1.20 3.00
LL2 Dorsey Levens .40 1.00
LL3 Reggie White .30 .75
LL4 Doug Widell .08 .25
LL5 William Henderson .08 .25
LL6 Aaron Hayden .08 .25
LL7 Robert Brooks .15 .40
LL8 Antonio Freeman .40 1.00
LL9 Mark Chmura .15 .40
LL10 Derrick Mayes .08 .25
LL11 Seth Joyner .08 .25
LL12 Darren Sharper .15 .40
LL13 LeRoy Butler .08 .25
LL14 Craig Newsome .08 .25
LL15 Travis Jervey .08 .25
LL16 Bill Schroeder .08 .25
LL17 Ross Verba .08 .25
LL18 Frank Winters .08 .25
LL19 Jermaine Smith .08 .25
LL20 Jonathan Brown .08 .25
LL21 Adam Timmerman .08 .25
LL22 Santana Dotson .08 .25
LL23 Gilbert Brown .08 .25
LL24 Pat Terrell .08 .25
LL25 Lamont Hollinquest .08 .25
LL26 Tyrone Williams .08 .25
LL27 Glyn Milburn .08 .25
LL28 Roderick Mullen .08 .25
LL29 Ryan Longwell .08 .25
LL30 Sean Landeta .08 .25

1998 Packers Upper Deck ShopKo II Super Pack

Randomly inserted in packs, this 30-card set features color action player photos on the fronts with player information displayed on the backs. Each card was serial numbered to 350.

COMPLETE SET (30) 10.00 25.00
S1 Brett Favre 3.00 8.00
S2 Dorsey Levens .75 2.00
S3 Antonio Freeman 1.00 2.50
S4 Robert Brooks .50 1.25
S5 Ryan Longwell .30 .75
S6 William Henderson .50 1.25
S7 Aaron Hayden .30 .75
S8 Derrick Mayes .30 .75
S9 Frank Winters .30 .75
S10 Bill Schroeder .30 .75
S11 Ross Verba .30 .75
S12 Travis Jervey .30 .75
S13 John Michels .30 .75
S14 Adam Timmerman .30 .75
S15 Earl Dotson .30 .75
S16 Lamont Hollinquest .30 .75
S17 Santana Dotson .30 .75
S18 Reggie White 1.25 3.00
S19 Gilbert Brown .30 .75
S20 LeRoy Butler .30 .75
S21 Craig Newsome .30 .75
S22 Roderick Mullen .30 .75
S23 Mike Prior .30 .75
S24 Brian Williams .30 .75
S25 Keith McKenzie .30 .75
S26 Tyrone Williams .30 .75
S27 Jonathan Brown .30 .75
S28 Darren Sharper .75 2.00
S29 George Koonce .30 .75
S30 Mark Chmura .50 1.25

1999 Packers Police

With the sponsorship of the Town of Hull Fire Dept. and Larry Fritsch Cards, this set was produced for the 1999 Packers team. The cardfronts feature a colorful "Green Bay Packers 1999" design along with a color player photo, while the backs were produced simply in green on white card stock. Variations in the sponsor and the law enforcement region on the unnumbered cardbacks can be found.

COMPLETE SET (20) 3.20 8.00
1 Gilbert Brown .08 .25
2 LeRoy Butler .08 .25
3 Mark Chmura .15 .40
4 Earl Dotson .08 .25
5 Santana Dotson .08 .25
6 Brett Favre 1.20 3.00
7 Antonio Freeman .30 .75
8 Bernardo Harris .08 .25
9 William Henderson .08 .25
10 Vonnie Holliday .30 .75
11 George Koonce .08 .25
12 Dorsey Levens .30 .75
13 Ryan Longwell .08 .25
14 Marco Rivera .15 .40
15 Darren Sharper .20 .50
16 Ross Verba .08 .25
17 Brian Williams LB .08 .25
18 Tyrone Williams .08 .25
19 Ron Wolf GM .08 .25
20 Ray Rhodes CO .15 .40

2000 Packers Police

The Packers continued the longest running series of Police sponsored cards in 2000. Each features a color photo, year, and player name on the cardfronts along with a simple green and white cardback. Variations in the sponsor on the unnumbered cardbacks can be found.

COMPLETE SET (20) 4.00 8.00
1 Ron Wolf GM .08 .25
2 Mike Sherman CO .08 .25
3 LeRoy Butler .15 .40
4 Earl Dotson .08 .25
5 Santana Dotson .08 .25
6 Brett Favre 1.25 3.00
7 Antonio Freeman .30 .75
8 Bernardo Harris .08 .25
9 William Henderson .08 .25
10 Vonnie Holliday .15 .40
11 Dorsey Levens .30 .75
12 Russell Maryland .08 .25
13 Mike McKenzie .08 .25
14 Bill Schroeder .30 .75
15 Darren Sharper .20 .50
16 Ross Verba .08 .25
17 Mike Wahle .08 .25
18 Brian Williams LB .08 .25
19 Tyrone Williams .08 .25
20 Frank Winters .08 .25

2001 Packers 1936 Champion Series

is 33-card set was made by Champion Series to commemorate the Packers' 1936 NFL Championship. Each standard-sized card was printed in an antique orange color on the front with a simple white and maroon cardback. The cardbacks also include the card number.

COMPLETE SET (33) 8.00 12.00
1 Curly Lambeau CO 1.25 3.00
2 Red Smith CO .20 .50
3 Don Hutson .75 2.00
4 Clarke Hinkle .50 1.25
5 Arnie Herber .30 .75
6 Charles Goldenberg .30 .75
7 Johnny Blood McNally .50 1.25
8 Joe Laws .20 .50
9 Walt Kiesling .30 .75
10 Russ Letlow .20 .50
11 George Sauer .30 .75
12 Al Rose .20 .50
13 Lon Evans .20 .50
14 Bob Monnett .20 .50
15 Henry Bruder .20 .50
16 Milt Gantenbein .20 .50
17 Chester Johnston .20 .50
18 Frank Butler .20 .50
19 George Svendsen .20 .50
20 Ernie Smith .20 .50
21 Adolph Schwammel .20 .50
22 Herman Schneidman .20 .50
23 Paul Engebretsen .20 .50
24 Paul Miller .20 .50
25 Bernard Scherer .20 .50
26 Lou Gordon .20 .50
27 Harry Mattos .20 .50
28 Cal Clemens .20 .50
29 Wayland Becker .20 .50
30 Tony Paulekas .20 .50
31 Champ Seibold .20 .50
32 1936 Championship Program .20 .50
33 1936 Packers Team Photo .30 .75

2001 Packers Police

The 2001 Packers Police set features the team name "Green Bay Packers 2001" at the top of the cardfronts along with a player photo produced with a halo effect. The backs were produced simply in green on white card stock. The card number appears in the lower right hand corner. Variations in the sponsor on the cardbacks can be found.

COMPLETE SET (20) 4.00 8.00
1 Mike Sherman CO .08 .25
2 Brett Favre 1.25 3.00
3 Bill Schroeder .15 .40
4 Antonio Freeman .30 .75
5 Marco Rivera .15 .40
6 Ahman Green .30 .75
7 William Henderson .08 .25
8 Mike Flanagan .08 .25
9 Russell Maryland .08 .25
10 Santana Dotson .08 .25
11 John Thierry .08 .25
12 Vonnie Holliday .15 .40
13 Na'il Diggs .08 .25
14 Bernardo Harris .08 .25
15 Nate Wayne .08 .25
16 Tyrone Williams .08 .25
17 LeRoy Butler .15 .40
18 Darren Sharper .08 .25
19 Ryan Longwell .08 .25
20 Allen Rossum .08 .25

2002 Packers Police

The 2002 Packers Police was sponsored by the Fox River Mall, Grand Chute Police Department, and the Grand Chute Lions Club. The cardfronts feature the team name "Green Bay Packers" at the top and the year near the bottom of the card. The backs were produced simply in green on white card stock. The card number is included in the lower right hand corner. Variations in the sponsor on the cardbacks (such as Larry Fritsch Cards) can be found.

COMPLETE SET (20) 4.00 8.00
1 Ahman Green .40 1.00
2 Brett Favre 1.25 3.00
3 Bubba Franks .30 .75
4 Chad Clifton .08 .25
5 Darren Sharper .15 .40
6 Gilbert Brown .08 .25
7 Kabeer Gbaja-Biamila .30 .75
8 Tyrone Williams .08 .25
9 Mark Tauscher .08 .25
10 Mike McKenzie .08 .25
11 Mike Sherman CO .08 .25
12 Mike Wahle .08 .25
13 Na'il Diggs .08 .25
14 Nate Wayne .08 .25
15 Robert Ferguson .15 .40
16 Ryan Longwell .08 .25
17 Vonnie Holliday .15 .40
18 William Henderson .15 .40
19 Joe Johnson .08 .25
20 Terry Glenn .15 .40

2003 Packers Police

The 2003 Packers Police set was again sponsored by Larry Fritsch Cards, Inc. Another version was sponsored by Doyles Farm and distributed by the New Richmond Police Dept. The cards feature the team name "Packers 2003" along the left border of the cardfronts. The backs were produced simply with green printing on white card stock. The card numbers appear in the upper right hand corner. Variations in the sponsor on the cardbacks can be found. Reportedly, over 125,000 total sets were produced.

COMPLETE SET (20) 4.00 8.00
1 Mike Sherman CO .08 .25
2 Brett Favre 1.25 3.00
3 Ryan Longwell .08 .25
4 Ahman Green .40 1.00
5 William Henderson .15 .40
6 Mike McKenzie .08 .25
7 Darren Sharper .15 .40
8 Mike Flanagan .08 .25
9 Na'il Diggs .08 .25
10 Marco Rivera .08 .25
11 Mark Truscher .08 .25
12 Chad Clifton .08 .25
13 Donald Driver .30 .75
14 Javon Walker .30 .75
15 Bubba Franks .15 .40
16 Robert Ferguson .15 .40
17 Joe Johnson .08 .25
18 Kabeer Gbaja-Biamila .15 .40
19 Rod Walker .08 .25
20 Cletidus Hunt .08 .25

2004 Packers Police

e Packers continued their streak of issuing a Police set in 2004. This set was again sponsored by Larry Fritsch Cards, Inc. in conjunction with Stevens Point and the Town of Hull as noted on the cardbacks. Another version was sponsored by Doyles Farm and distributed by the New Richmond Police Dept. The cardfronts on this version are the same but the sponsorship information differs on the cardbacks. The cards feature the team name "Green Bay Packers 2004" along the right border of the cardfronts. The backs were produced simply with green printing on white card stock. The card numbers appear in the lower left hand corner.

COMPLETE SET (20) 4.00 8.00
1 Mike Sherman CO .08 .25
2 Brett Favre 1.25 3.00
3 Ryan Longwell .08 .25
4 Ahman Green .40 1.00
5 Al Harris .15 .40
6 Darren Sharper .15 .40
7 Najeh Davenport .15 .40
8 Hannibal Navies .08 .25
9 Nick Barnett .08 .25
10 Na'il Diggs .08 .25
11 Mark Tauscher .08 .25
12 Mike Wahle .08 .25
13 Aaron Kampman .40 1.00
14 Grady Jackson .08 .25
15 Chad Clifton .08 .25
16 Donald Driver .30 .75
17 Javon Walker .30 .75
18 Bubba Franks .15 .40
19 Robert Ferguson .15 .40
20 Kabeer Gbaja-Biamila .15 .40

2005 Packers Activa Medallions

COMPLETE SET (22) 30.00 60.00
1 Nick Barnett 1.25 3.00
2 Ahmad Carroll 1.25 3.00
3 Chad Clifton 1.25 3.00
4 Najeh Davenport 1.25 3.00
5 Nail Diggs 1.25 3.00
6 Donald Driver 1.25 3.00
7 Brett Favre 2.00 5.00
8 Robert Ferguson 1.25 3.00
9 Tony Fisher 1.25 3.00
10 Mike Flanagan 1.25 3.00
11 Bubba Franks 1.25 3.00
12 Kabeer Gbaja-Biamila 1.25 3.00
13 Ahman Green 1.50 4.00
14 Al Harris 1.25 3.00
15 William Henderson 1.25 3.00
16 Grady Jackson 1.25 3.00
17 Aaron Kampman 1.25 3.00
18 Ryan Longwell 1.25 3.00
19 Aaron Rodgers 2.50 6.00
20 Mark Tauscher 1.25 3.00
21 Javon Walker 1.25 3.00
22 Packers Logo 1.00 2.50

2005 Packers Police

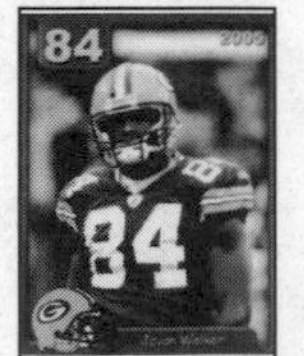

The Packers continued their long tradition by issuing a Police set again in 2005. This set was again sponsored by Larry Fritsch Cards with another version sponsored by Fox River Mall distributed by the Grand Chute Police Dept. The cardfronts on the versions are the same but the sponsorship information differs on the backs. The cards feature the team helmet below the image and the year of issue above the photo on the cardfronts. The backs were produced simply with green printing on white card stock. The card numbers appear in the lower left hand corner.

COMPLETE SET (20) 3.00 8.00
1 Mike Sherman CO .08 .25
2 Ted Thompson GM .08 .25
3 Brett Favre 1.25 3.00
4 Ryan Longwell .08 .25
5 Ahman Green .30 .75
6 Al Harris .08 .25
7 William Henderson .15 .40
8 Nick Barnett .15 .40

9 Mike Flanagan .08 .25
10 Na'il Diggs .08 .25
11 Mark Tauscher .08 .25
12 Aaron Kampman .30 .75
13 Grady Jackson .08 .25
14 Chad Clifton .08 .25
15 Donald Driver .15 .40
16 Javon Walker .30 .75
17 Bubba Franks .15 .40
18 Robert Ferguson .15 .40
19 Kabeer Gbaja-Biamila .15 .40
20 Corey Williams .15 .40

2005 Packers Topps XXL

COMPLETE SET (4) 6.00 15.00
1 Brett Favre 1.25 3.00
2 Aaron Rodgers 6.00 15.00
3 Ahman Green .50 1.25
4 Javon Walker .30 .75

2006 Packers Police

The Packers continued their tradition in football cards by issuing a Police set for 2006. This set was again sponsored by Larry Fritsch Cards as well as a variety of regional law enforcement agencies. The cardfronts on each version are the same but the sponsorship information differs on the backs. The cards feature a thin black border on the front along with the year of issue ghosted into the background. The backs were produced simply with green printing on white card stock.

COMPLETE SET (20) 3.00 8.00
1 Ted Thompson GM .30 .75
2 Mike McCarthy CO .30 .75
3 Brett Favre 1.00 2.50
4 Aaron Rodgers 1.25 3.00
5 Charles Woodson .50 1.25
6 Marquand Manuel .30 .75
7 Ahman Green .40 1.00
8 Al Harris .40 1.00
9 William Henderson .30 .75
10 Samkon Gado .30 .75
11 Nick Collins .40 1.00
12 A.J. Hawk .40 1.00
13 Nick Barnett .30 .75
14 Mark Tauscher .30 .75
15 Aaron Kampman .40 1.00
16 Chad Clifton .30 .75
17 Donald Driver .40 1.00
18 Bubba Franks .30 .75
19 Robert Ferguson .30 .75
20 Kabeer Gbaja-Biamila .30 .75

2006 Packers Topps

COMPLETE SET (12) 3.00 6.00
GB1 Aaron Rodgers 1.00 2.50
GB2 Robert Ferguson .25 .60
GB3 Sam Gado .25 .60
GB4 Donald Driver .30 .75
GB5 Nick Barnett .25 .60
GB6 A.J. Hawk .30 .75
GB7 Najeh Davenport .25 .60
GB8 Brett Favre .75 2.00
GB9 Ahman Green .30 .75
GB10 Bubba Franks .25 .60
GB11 Charles Woodson .40 1.00
GB12 Greg Jennings .40 1.00

2007 Packers Police

The Packers continued the longest running tradition in football cards by issuing a Police set for 2007. This set was again sponsored by Larry Fritsch Cards as well as a variety of regional law enforcement agencies including: Altoona Police Dept. and Campbellsport Police Dept. The cardfronts on each version are the same but the sponsorship information differs on the backs. The cards feature a green border on the front along with the year of issue and a special "25-Years" logo to celebrate the Packers Police set run. The backs were produced simply with green printing on white card stock.

COMPLETE SET (20) 4.00 10.00
1 Ted Thompson GM .25 .60
2 Mike McCarthy CO .25 .60
3 Brett Favre .75 2.00
4 Aaron Rodgers .75 2.00
5 Donald Driver .30 .75
6 Greg Jennings .25 .60
7 Chad Clifton .25 .60
8 Mark Tauscher .25 .60
9 Daryn Colledge .25 .60
10 Scott Wells .25 .60
11 Aaron Kampman .30 .75
12 Kabeer Gbaja-Biamila .25 .60
13 Cullen Jenkins .25 .60
14 Ryan Pickett .25 .60
15 Justin Harrell .25 .60
16 A.J. Hawk .25 .60
17 Nick Barnett .25 .60
18 Al Harris .25 .60
19 Charles Woodson .40 1.00
20 Nick Collins .25 .60

2007 Packers Topps

COMPLETE SET (12) 3.00 6.00
1 Donald Driver .50 1.25
2 Brett Favre 1.25 3.00
3 AJ Hawk .40 1.00
4 Brandon Jackson .40 1.00
5 Greg Jennings .40 1.00
6 Vernand Morency .50 1.25
7 Charles Woodson .60 1.50
8 Aaron Kampman .50 1.25
9 Bubba Franks .40 1.00
10 Nick Barnett .40 1.00
11 Kabeer Gbaja-Biamila .40 1.00
12 Justin Harrell .40 1.00

2008 Packers Police

e Packers continued one of the longest running traditions in football cards by issuing a Police set again for 2008. This set was sponsored by a variety of regional law enforcement agencies including: Amery Police Dept. The cardfronts on each version are the same but the sponsorship information differs on the backs. The cards feature a green border on the front along with the year of issue. The backs were produced simply with green printing on white card stock.

COMPLETE SET (20) 4.00 8.00
1 Ted Thompson GM .20 .50
2 Mike McCarthy CO .20 .50
3 Aaron Rodgers .60 1.50
4 Ryan Grant .25 .60
5 Donald Driver .25 .60
6 Donald Lee .25 .60
7 Greg Jennings .20 .50
8 Cullen Jenkins .20 .50
9 Brandon Jackson .25 .60
10 Al Harris .20 .50
11 Mark Tauscher .20 .50
12 Jason Spitz .20 .50
13 Ryan Pickett .20 .50
14 Aaron Kampman .25 .60
15 John Jolly .20 .50
16 Mason Crosby .20 .50
17 Nick Barnett .20 .50
18 Chad Clifton .20 .50
19 A.J. Hawk .20 .50
20 Charles Woodson .30 .75

2008 Packers Topps

COMPLETE SET (12) 2.50 5.00
1 Greg Jennings .40 1.00
2 Donald Driver .50 1.25
3 Ryan Grant .50 1.25
4 Donald Lee .50 1.25
5 James Jones .40 1.00
6 Al Harris .40 1.00
7 Aaron Rodgers 1.25 3.00
8 A.J. Hawk .40 1.00
9 Aaron Kampman .50 1.25
10 Nick Barnett .40 1.00
11 Brian Brohm .40 1.00
12 Jordy Nelson 1.25 3.00

2009 Packers Police

MPLETE SET (20) 4.00 8.00
1 Ted Thompson GM .20 .50
2 Mike McCarthy CO .20 .50
3 Aaron Rodgers .75 2.00
4 Donald Driver .25 .60
5 Greg Jennings .20 .50
6 Mason Crosby .20 .50
7 Ryan Grant .25 .60
8 Daryn Colledge .20 .50
9 Chad Clifton .20 .50
10 Jason Spitz .20 .50
11 Cullen Jenkins .20 .50
12 Aaron Kampman .25 .60
13 Nick Barnett .20 .50
14 A.J. Hawk .20 .50
15 Al Harris .20 .50
16 Charles Woodson .30 .75
17 Nick Collins .20 .50
18 Ryan Pickett .20 .50
19 B.J. Raji .25 .60
20 Clay Matthews .75 2.00

2010 Packers Police

COMPLETE SET (20) 4.00 8.00
1 Ted Thompson GM .20 .50
2 Mike McCarthy CO .20 .50
3 Aaron Rodgers .75 2.00
4 Donald Driver .25 .60
5 Greg Jennings .20 .50
6 Jermichael Finley .20 .50
7 Ryan Grant .25 .60
8 Mark Tauscher .20 .50
9 Chad Clifton .20 .50
10 Scott Wells .20 .50
11 Cullen Jenkins .20 .50
12 Ryan Pickett .20 .50
13 B.J. Raji .25 .60
14 Nick Barnett .20 .50
15 Brandon Chillar .20 .50
16 A.J. Hawk .20 .50
17 Clay Matthews .30 .75
18 Charles Woodson .30 .75
19 Nick Collins .20 .50
20 Mason Crosby .20 .50

2011 Packers Panini Super Bowl XLV

This set was sold exclusively at the 2011 Super Bowl Card Show in Dallas. The cards feature the Super Bowl XLV logo on the fronts and the backs are numbered.

COMPLETE SET (9) 8.00 20.00
1 Aaron Rodgers 2.00 5.00
2 John Kuhn 1.25 3.00
3 Charles Woodson 1.25 3.00
4 Donald Driver 1.00 2.50
5 Greg Jennings .75 2.00
6 James Jones .75 2.00
7 Jordy Nelson 1.00 2.50
8 Clay Matthews 1.25 3.00
9 James Starks .75 2.00

2011 Packers Police

COMPLETE SET (20) 3.00 6.00
1 Ted Thompson GM .20 .50
2 Mike McCarthy CO .20 .50
3 Aaron Rodgers .75 2.00
4 Donald Driver .25 .60
5 Greg Jennings .20 .50
6 Jermichael Finley .20 .50
7 Josh Sitton .20 .50
8 Chad Clifton .20 .50
9 Scott Wells .20 .50
10 Ryan Pickett .20 .50
11 B.J. Raji .20 .50
12 Desmond Bishop .20 .50
13 A.J. Hawk .20 .50
14 Clay Matthews .40 1.00
15 Tramon Williams .20 .50
16 Charles Woodson .30 .75
17 Nick Collins .20 .50
18 Tim Masthay .20 .50
19 Ryan Grant .20 .50
20 Mason Crosby .20 .50

2011 Packers Topps Super Bowl XLV

COMPLETE SET (27) 6.00 12.00
1 Aaron Rodgers .75 2.00
2 Greg Jennings .25 .60
3 James Jones .25 .60
4 Donald Driver .30 .75
5 Jordy Nelson .30 .75
6 James Starks .25 .60
7 Brandon Jackson .25 .60
8 John Kuhn .40 1.00
9 Andrew Quarless .25 .60
10 Jermichael Finley .25 .60
11 Charles Woodson .40 1.00
12 Clay Matthews .40 1.00
13 A.J. Hawk .25 .60
14 B.J. Raji .25 .60
15 Nick Collins .25 .60
16 Tramon Williams .25 .60
17 Desmond Bishop .25 .60
18 Sam Shields .25 .60
19 Chad Clifton .25 .60
20 Green Bay Packers .60 1.50
21 Wild Card Weekend .30 .75
22 Divisional Playoffs .60 1.50
23 NFC Championship .60 1.50
24 NFC Championship .30 .75
25 Super Bowl XLV .60 1.50
26 Super Bowl XLV .25 .60
27 Super Bowl XLV Champs .60 1.50

2012 Packers Police

COMPLETE SET (20) 3.00 6.00
1 Ted Thompson GM .20 .50
2 Mike McCarthy CO .20 .50
3 Aaron Rodgers .75 2.00
4 Greg Jennings .20 .50
5 Jordy Nelson .25 .60
6 Jermichael Finley .20 .50
7 T.J. Lang .20 .50
8 Josh Sitton .20 .50
9 John Kuhn .20 .50
10 Bryan Bulaga .20 .50
11 Ryan Pickett .20 .50
12 B.J. Raji .20 .50
13 Desmond Bishop .20 .50
14 A.J. Hawk .20 .50
15 Clay Matthews .40 1.00
16 Tramon Williams .20 .50
17 Charles Woodson .30 .75
18 Morgan Burnett .20 .50
19 Mason Crosby .20 .50
20 Tim Masthay .20 .50

2013 Packers Police

COMPLETE SET (20) 3.00 6.00
1 Ted Thompson GM .20 .50
2 Mike McCarthy CO .20 .50
3 Aaron Rodgers .75 2.00
4 James Jones .20 .50
5 Jordy Nelson .25 .60
6 Randall Cobb .25 .60
7 Jermichael Finley .20 .50
8 T.J. Lang .20 .50
9 Josh Sitton .20 .50
10 Bryan Bulaga .20 .50
11 John Kuhn .20 .50
12 Ryan Pickett .20 .50
13 B.J. Raji .20 .50
14 Brad Jones .20 .50
15 A.J. Hawk .20 .50
16 Clay Matthews .30 .75
17 Tramon Williams .20 .50
18 Morgan Burnett .20 .50
19 Sam Shields .20 .50
20 Tim Masthay .20 .50

2014 Packers Police

COMPLETE SET (20) 3.00 6.00
1 Ted Thompson GM .20 .50
2 Mike McCarthy CO .20 .50
3 Aaron Rodgers .75 2.00
4 Jordy Nelson .25 .60
5 Randall Cobb .25 .60
6 T.J. Lang .20 .50
7 Josh Sitton .20 .50
8 David Bakhtiari .20 .50
9 Eddie Lacy .20 .50
10 John Kuhn .20 .50
11 B.J. Raji .20 .50
12 Mike Daniels .20 .50
13 A.J. Hawk .20 .50
14 Clay Matthews .30 .75
15 Tramon Williams .20 .50
16 Morgan Burnett .20 .50
17 Sam Shields .30 .75
18 Julius Peppers .25 .60
19 Mason Crosby .20 .50
20 Tim Masthay .20 .50

2016 Panini

1 Drew Brees .20 .50
2 Coby Fleener .12 .30
3 DeAngelo Williams .12 .30
4 DeMeco Ryans .12 .30
5 Brandon Marshall .12 .30
6 Jay Cutler .12 .30
7 Kelvin Benjamin .15 .40
8 DeMarcus Ware .15 .40
9 Chris Long .12 .30
10 John Brown .15 .40
11 Blaine Gabbert .12 .30
12 Dwayne Allen .12 .30
13 Ryan Shazier .12 .30
14 Sam Bradford .12 .30
15 Ryan Fitzpatrick .12 .30
16 Matt Forte .12 .30
17 Ted Ginn Jr. .12 .30
18 Emmanuel Sanders .20 .50
19 Kenny Britt .12 .30
20 Patrick Peterson .12 .30
21 Mark Ingram .15 .40
22 Frank Gore .15 .40
23 J.J. Watt .20 .50
24 Malcolm Jenkins .15 .40
25 Chris Ivory .15 .40
26 Jeremy Langford .15 .40
27 Josh Norman .12 .30
28 C.J. Anderson .15 .40
29 Jared Cook .12 .30
30 Tyrann Mathieu .15 .40
31 Brandin Cooks .15 .40
32 Robert Mathis .12 .30
33 DeAndre Hopkins .15 .40
34 Matt Ryan .15 .40
35 Eric Decker .12 .30
36 Alshon Jeffery .15 .40
37 Greg Olsen .15 .40
38 Travis Benjamin .12 .30
39 Joe Flacco .15 .40
40 Philip Rivers .20 .50
41 Marques Colston .12 .30
42 Tony Romo .15 .40
43 Alfred Blue .12 .30
44 Devonta Freeman .15 .40
45 Darrelle Revis .12 .30
46 Kevin White .12 .30
47 Luke Kuechly .15 .40
48 Gary Barnidge .12 .30
49 Steve Smith .15 .40
50 Keenan Allen .15 .40
51 Willie Snead .15 .40
52 Jason Witten .15 .40
53 Brian Hoyer .12 .30
54 Julio Jones .20 .50
55 Muhammad Wilkerson .12 .30
56 Martellus Bennett .12 .30
57 Tom Brady .50 1.25
58 Duke Johnson .12 .30
59 Kamar Aiken .12 .30
60 Melvin Gordon .15 .40
61 Ben Watson .12 .30
62 Dez Bryant .20 .50
63 Cecil Shorts III .12 .30
64 Mohamed Sanu .12 .30
65 Matthew Stafford .15 .40
66 A.J. Green .20 .50
67 Julian Edelman .20 .50
68 Joe Haden .12 .30
69 Justin Forsett .15 .40
70 Antonio Gates .12 .30
71 Russell Wilson .25 .60
72 Terrance Williams .12 .30
73 Jadeveon Clowney .12 .30
74 Vic Beasley Jr. .12 .30
75 Golden Tate .12 .30
76 Andy Dalton .15 .40
77 Rob Gronkowski .20 .50
78 Donte Whitner .12 .30
79 Terrell Suggs .12 .30
80 Malcom Floyd .12 .30
81 Marshawn Lynch .15 .40
82 Darren McFadden .12 .30
83 Marcus Mariota .20 .50
84 Jacob Tamme .12 .30
85 Chris Johnson .12 .30
86 Jeremy Hill .12 .30
87 Chandler Jones .12 .30
88 Josh McCown .12 .30
89 Buck Allen .12 .30
90 Danny Woodhead .15 .40
91 Thomas Rawls .12 .30
92 Sean Lee .15 .40
93 Dorial Green-Beckham .12 .30
94 Eli Manning .15 .40
95 Ameer Abdullah .12 .30
96 Giovani Bernard .12 .30
97 Danny Amendola .15 .40
98 Jameis Winston .20 .50
99 Kirk Cousins .20 .50
100 Eric Weddle .12 .30
101 Doug Baldwin .15 .40
102 Cole Beasley .20 .50
103 Delanie Walker .12 .30
104 Odell Beckham Jr. .20 .50
105 Ezekiel Ansah .12 .30
106 Tyler Eifert .15 .40
107 LeGarrette Blount .15 .40
108 Doug Martin .15 .40
109 Matt Jones .15 .40
110 Jamaal Charles .15 .40
111 Tyler Lockett .15 .40
112 Ryan Tannehill .15 .40
113 Antonio Andrews .12 .30
114 Rashad Jennings .12 .30
115 Aaron Rodgers .40 1.00
116 Dre Kirkpatrick .12 .30
117 Amari Cooper .20 .50
118 Mike Evans .15 .40
119 DeSean Jackson .15 .40
120 Alex Smith .15 .40
121 Jimmy Graham .20 .50
122 Jarvis Landry .15 .40
123 Michael Griffin .12 .30
124 Victor Cruz .15 .40
125 Eddie Lacy .12 .30
126 Sammy Watkins .20 .50
127 Derek Carr .20 .50
128 Vincent Jackson .12 .30
129 Alfred Morris .12 .30
130 Travis Kelce .20 .50
131 Richard Sherman .20 .50
132 Lamar Miller .12 .30
133 Teddy Bridgewater .15 .40
134 Dominique Rodgers-Cromartie .12 .30
135 Jordy Nelson .15 .40
136 LeSean McCoy .20 .50
137 Latavius Murray .12 .30
138 Austin Seferian-Jenkins .12 .30
139 Jordan Reed .12 .30
140 Justin Houston .12 .30
141 Bobby Wagner .12 .30
142 Ndamukong Suh .15 .40
143 Adrian Peterson .20 .50
144 Jason Pierre-Paul .12 .30
145 Randall Cobb .15 .40
146 Tyrod Taylor .15 .40
147 Michael Crabtree .12 .30
148 Lavonte David .12 .30
149 Pierre Garcon .15 .40
150 Jeremy Maclin .12 .30
151 Ben Roethlisberger .20 .50
152 DeVante Parker .15 .40
153 Stefon Diggs .15 .40
154 Blake Bortles .12 .30
155 James Starks .12 .30
156 Mario Williams .12 .30
157 Khalil Mack .20 .50
158 Gerald McCoy .12 .30
159 Carlos Hyde .12 .30
160 Charcandrick West .12 .30
161 Antonio Brown .20 .50
162 Reshad Jones .12 .30
163 Mike Wallace .12 .30
164 Allen Robinson .15 .40
165 Ha Ha Clinton-Dix .12 .30
166 Paul Posluszny .12 .30
167 Malcolm Smith .20 .50
168 Carson Palmer .15 .40
169 Anquan Boldin .12 .30
170 Eric Berry .15 .40
171 Karlos Williams .12 .30
172 Jordan Matthews .15 .40
173 Anthony Barr .12 .30
174 Allen Hurns .12 .30
175 Clay Matthews .20 .50
176 Peyton Manning .40 1.00
177 Todd Gurley .20 .50
178 Larry Fitzgerald .15 .40
179 Torrey Smith .12 .30
180 Andrew Luck .25 .60
181 Heath Miller .12 .30
182 Zach Ertz .15 .40
183 Harrison Smith .12 .30
184 T.J. Yeldon .12 .30
185 Cam Newton .20 .50
186 Demaryius Thomas .15 .40
187 Tavon Austin .12 .30
188 David Johnson .20 .50
189 Navorro Bowman .15 .40
190 T.Y. Hilton .15 .40
191 Le'Veon Bell .15 .40
192 DeMarco Murray .15 .40
193 Calvin Johnson .20 .50
194 Julius Thomas .12 .30
195 Jonathan Stewart .12 .30
196 Von Miller .15 .40
197 Aaron Donald .20 .50
198 Michael Floyd .12 .30
199 Colin Kaepernick .15 .40
200 Andre Johnson .15 .40
201 Corey Coleman RC .40 1.00
202 Eli Apple RC .30 .75
203 Ricardo Louis RC .25 .60
204 Thomas Duarte RC .25 .60
205 Shilique Calhoun RC .25 .60
206 Sterling Shepard RC .30 .75
207 Sheldon Rankins RC .30 .75
208 Su'a Cravens RC .25 .60
209 Ezekiel Elliott RC 1.25 3.00
210 Tajae Sharpe RC .30 .75
211 Glenn Gronkowski RC .25 .60
212 Keenan Reynolds RC .30 .75
213 Hunter Henry RC .30 .75
214 Jaylon Smith RC .25 .60
215 Karl Joseph RC .25 .60
216 Jalen Ramsey RC .40 1.00
217 Emmanuel Ogbah RC .30 .75
218 Jared Goff RC 1.50 4.00
219 Darius Jackson RC .30 .75
220 Jarran Reed RC .25 .60
221 Tyler Boyd RC .30 .75
222 Will Redmond RC .40 1.00
223 Tyler Ervin RC .25 .60
224 William Jackson III RC .30 .75
225 Vernon Hargreaves III RC .40 1.00
226 Vonn Bell RC .30 .75
227 DeAndre Washington RC .25 .60
228 Wendell Smallwood RC .25 .60
229 Jeff Driskel RC .25 .60
230 Will Fuller RC .40 1.00
231 Jerell Adams RC .25 .60
232 Vernon Butler RC .25 .60
233 Chris Jones RC .25 .60
234 Jordan Howard RC .60 1.50
235 Joey Bosa RC .50 1.25
236 Jonathan Bullard RC .25 .60
237 Xavien Howard RC .30 .75
238 Jonathan Williams RC .30 .75
239 Moritz Bohringer RC .25 .60
240 Jacoby Brissett RC .30 .75
241 Josh Doctson RC .30 .75
242 Kenny Lawler RC .40 1.00
243 Rico Gathers RC .25 .60
244 Kenyan Drake RC .40 1.00
245 Kelvin Taylor RC .25 .60
246 Kendall Fuller RC .30 .75
247 Jordan Payton RC .25 .60
248 Kenneth Dixon RC .25 .60
249 Jake Rudock RC .25 .60
250 Kenny Clark RC .25 .60
251 Adolphus Washington RC .25 .60
252 Austin Johnson RC .25 .60
253 Alex Collins RC .30 .75
254 Chris Moore RC .30 .75
255 Noah Spence RC .25 .60
256 Artie Burns RC .30 .75
257 Aaron Burbridge RC .25 .60
258 A'Shawn Robinson RC .25 .60
259 Kevin Hogan RC .30 .75
260 Austin Hooper RC .25 .60
261 Kolby Listenbee RC .25 .60
262 Maliek Collins RC .25 .60
263 Laquon Treadwell RC .30 .75
264 Michael Thomas RC .50 1.25
265 Keanu Neal RC .25 .60
266 Leonard Floyd RC .30 .75
267 Kevin Dodd RC .25 .60
268 Leonte Carroo RC .25 .60
269 Brandon Doughty RC .25 .60
270 Mackensie Alexander RC .25 .60
271 Braxton Miller RC .25 .60
272 Cody Kessler RC .25 .60
273 Malcolm Mitchell RC .25 .60
274 Connor Cook RC .30 .75
275 C.J. Prosise RC .25 .60
276 Cardale Jones RC .25 .60
277 Brandon Allen RC .25 .60
278 Carson Wentz RC 2.50 6.00
279 Nate Sudfeld RC .25 .60
280 Christian Hackenberg RC .25 .60
281 Nelson Spruce RC .25 .60
282 Reggie Ragland RC .25 .60
283 Nick Vannett RC .25 .60
284 Robert Nkemdiche RC .30 .75
285 Paul Perkins RC .25 .60
286 Paxton Lynch RC .25 .60
287 Myles Jack RC .30 .75
288 Pharoh Cooper RC .25 .60
289 Dak Prescott RC 1.25 3.00
290 Rashard Higgins RC .25 .60
291 Daniel Braverman RC .25 .60
292 Trevor Davis RC .25 .60
293 Darron Lee RC .25 .60
294 Devontae Booker RC .30 .75
295 DeForest Buckner RC .25 .60
296 Demarcus Ayers RC .25 .60
297 Kamalei Correa RC .25 .60
298 Demarcus Robinson RC .25 .60
299 Shaq Lawson RC .25 .60
300 Derrick Henry RC .60 1.50

2016 Panini Blue

*VETS/99: 2.5X TO 6X BASIC CARDS
*ROOKIES/99: 1.5X TO 4X BASIC CARDS

2016 Panini Bravery Green

*VETS: 2.5X TO 6X BASIC CARDS
*ROOKIES/199: 1.2X TO 3X BASIC CARDS

2016 Panini Chainmail Armor

*VETS: 2X TO 5X BASIC CARDS
*ROOKIES/: 1.2X TO 3X BASIC CARDS
STATED VET ODDS 1:24 RETAIL
STATED ROOKIE ODDS 1:47 RETAIL

2016 Panini Chivalry

*VETS: 2.5X TO 6X BASIC CARDS
*ROOKIES/199: 1.2X TO 3X BASIC CARDS

2016 Panini Knight's Templar Foil

*VETS: 1.2X TO 3X BASIC CARDS
*ROOKIES/: .8X TO 2X BASIC CARDS
STATED VET ODDS 1:4 RETAIL
STATED ROOKIE ODDS 1:8 RETAIL

2016 Panini Red

*VETS/49: 4X TO 10X BASIC CARDS

2016 Panini Sacrifice Die Cuts

*VETS: 2.5X TO 6X BASIC CARDS
*ROOKIES/199: 1.2X TO 3X BASIC CARDS

2016 Panini Shining Armor Rainbow Foil

*VETS: 1.5X TO 4X BASIC CARDS
*ROOKIES/: 1X TO 2.5X BASIC CARDS
STATED VET ODDS 1:12 RETAIL
STATED ROOKIE ODDS 1:24 RETAIL

2016 Panini Accolades

1 Dan Marino 1.50 4.00
2 Adrian Peterson .75 2.00
3 Gale Sayers .75 2.00
4 Peyton Manning 1.50 4.00
5 Bruce Smith .60 1.50
6 Emmitt Smith 1.25 3.00
7 Brett Favre 1.50 4.00
8 Michael Strahan .60 1.50
9 Joe Montana 2.00 5.00
10 Tony Dorsett .75 2.00
11 Drew Brees .75 2.00
12 Tony Romo .60 1.50
13 DeAngelo Hall .60 1.50
14 Aaron Rodgers 1.50 4.00
15 Ted Hendricks .50 1.25
16 Jerry Rice 1.25 3.00
17 Terrell Davis .60 1.50
18 Eric Dickerson .60 1.50
19 Joe Namath 1.00 2.50
20 LaDainian Tomlinson .60 1.50

2016 Panini Autographs

1 Drew Brees
2 Coby Fleener 4.00 10.00
3 DeAngelo Williams 12.00 30.00
6 Jay Cutler 4.00 10.00
7 Kelvin Benjamin 5.00 12.00
8 DeMarcus Ware 5.00 12.00
11 Blaine Gabbert 4.00 10.00
14 Sam Bradford
26 Jeremy Langford 5.00 12.00
28 C.J. Anderson 5.00 12.00
32 Robert Mathis 4.00 10.00
34 Matt Ryan 30.00 60.00
35 Eric Decker 4.00 10.00
37 Greg Olsen 5.00 12.00
39 Joe Flacco
40 Philip Rivers
41 Marques Colston 4.00 10.00
42 Tony Romo
46 Kevin White 4.00 10.00
47 Luke Kuechly
57 Tom Brady 75.00 150.00
60 Melvin Gordon
65 Matthew Stafford
71 Russell Wilson
72 Terrance Williams 4.00 10.00
74 Vic Beasley Jr. 4.00 10.00
76 Andy Dalton 5.00 12.00
82 Darren McFadden 4.00 10.00
90 Danny Woodhead 5.00 12.00
93 Dorial Green-Beckham 4.00 10.00
94 Eli Manning
98 Jameis Winston
108 Doug Martin 5.00 12.00
109 Matt Jones 5.00 12.00
110 Jamaal Charles 5.00 12.00
111 Tyler Lockett 12.00 30.00
112 Ryan Tannehill
115 Aaron Rodgers
117 Amari Cooper 15.00 40.00
124 Victor Cruz 5.00 12.00
125 Eddie Lacy 4.00 10.00
128 Vincent Jackson 4.00 10.00
131 Richard Sherman 25.00 50.00
132 Lamar Miller 4.00 10.00
133 Teddy Bridgewater 5.00 12.00
135 Jordy Nelson 20.00 40.00
137 Latavius Murray 4.00 10.00
138 Austin Seferian-Jenkins 4.00 10.00
141 Bobby Wagner 4.00 10.00
145 Randall Cobb 5.00 12.00
148 Lavonte David 4.00 10.00
151 Ben Roethlisberger 75.00 150.00
152 DeVante Parker 5.00 12.00
153 Stefon Diggs 5.00 12.00
154 Blake Bortles 4.00 10.00
155 James Starks 4.00 10.00
165 Ha Ha Clinton-Dix 4.00 10.00
167 Malcolm Smith 6.00 15.00
168 Carson Palmer 5.00 12.00
169 Anquan Boldin 4.00 10.00
172 Jordan Matthews 5.00 12.00
176 Peyton Manning 75.00 150.00
179 Torrey Smith 4.00 10.00
180 Andrew Luck 30.00 60.00
181 Heath Miller 10.00 25.00
182 Zach Ertz 5.00 12.00
184 T.J. Yeldon 4.00 10.00
186 Demaryius Thomas 5.00 12.00
187 Tavon Austin 4.00 10.00
189 Navorro Bowman 5.00 12.00
194 Julius Thomas 4.00 10.00
198 Michael Floyd 4.00 10.00
199 Colin Kaepernick 5.00 12.00

2016 Panini Combine Champions

STATED ODDS 1:6 RETAIL
1 Travis Feeney .50 1.25
2 Josh Doctson .50 1.25
3 D.J. Foster .50 1.25
4 Jalen Ramsey .60 1.50
5 Devon Cajuste .40 1.00
6 Ricardo Louis .40 1.00
7 Darron Lee .40 1.00
8 Kolby Listenbee .40 1.00
9 Daniel Lasco .40 1.00
10 Keith Marshall .40 1.00
11 Will Fuller .60 1.50
12 Vernon Hargreaves III .60 1.50
13 Sterling Shepard .50 1.25
14 Braxton Miller .40 1.00
15 Justin Simmons .50 1.25
16 Derrick Henry 1.00 2.50
17 Tyler Ervin .40 1.00
18 Ezekiel Elliott 2.00 5.00
19 Dadi Lhomme Nicolas .50 1.25
20 Joey Bosa .75 2.00

2016 Panini Decorated

STATED ODDS 1:6 RETAIL
1 Adrian Peterson .75 2.00
2 Tony Dorsett .75 2.00
3 LaDainian Tomlinson .60 1.50
4 Marshall Faulk .60 1.50
5 Brett Favre 1.50 4.00
6 Dan Marino 1.50 4.00
7 Joe Montana 2.00 5.00
8 Odell Beckham Jr. .75 2.00
9 Aaron Rodgers 1.50 4.00
10 Barry Sanders 1.25 3.00
11 Tom Brady 2.00 5.00
12 Drew Brees .75 2.00
13 Kurt Warner .60 1.50
14 Terrell Davis .60 1.50
15 Emmitt Smith 1.25 3.00
16 Jerry Rice 1.25 3.00
17 John Elway 1.25 3.00
18 Cam Newton .75 2.00
19 Peyton Manning 1.50 4.00
20 Eric Dickerson .60 1.50

2016 Panini First Impressions Autographs

1 Kenyan Drake 5.00 12.00
2 Corey Coleman
3 Mackensie Alexander 3.00 8.00
4 Alex Collins 4.00 10.00
6 Jared Goff
7 Vernon Hargreaves III 5.00 12.00
8 Ezekiel Elliott
9 DeForest Buckner 3.00 8.00
10 Michael Thomas 6.00 15.00
11 Jonathan Williams 4.00 10.00
12 Paul Perkins 3.00 8.00
13 Jacoby Brissett 4.00 10.00
14 Jordan Howard 8.00 20.00
16 Derrick Henry
17 Hunter Henry 4.00 10.00
18 Laquon Treadwell
19 T.J. Green 5.00 12.00
20 Carson Wentz 50.00 100.00
21 Tyler Ervin 3.00 8.00
22 Joey Bosa 6.00 15.00
23 Keith Marshall 3.00 8.00
24 Kelvin Taylor
25 Cody Kessler 3.00 8.00
26 Paxton Lynch 40.00 80.00
27 Devontae Booker 4.00 10.00
28 Josh Doctson
29 Aaron Burbridge 3.00 8.00
30 Will Fuller
31 Eli Apple 4.00 10.00
32 Braxton Miller
33 Thomas Duarte 3.00 8.00
34 Pharoh Cooper 3.00 8.00
35 Jalen Ramsey 5.00 12.00
36 Connor Cook 4.00 10.00
37 De'Runnya Wilson 3.00 8.00
38 Cardale Jones
39 Braxton Addison 3.00 8.00
40 C.J. Prosise 3.00 8.00

2016 Panini Gridiron Warriors Jerseys

1 Jameis Winston/199 2.00 5.00
2 Allen Robinson/199 1.50 4.00
3 Joe Flacco/49 2.50 6.00
4 Andy Dalton/99 2.00 5.00
5 Marcus Mariota/199 2.00 5.00
6 Brandin Cooks/199 1.50 4.00
7 Philip Rivers/99 2.50 6.00
8 Davante Adams/199 1.25 3.00
9 Todd Gurley/199 2.00 5.00
10 Devonta Freeman/199 1.50 4.00
11 Jarvis Landry/199 1.50 4.00
12 Amari Cooper/199 2.00 5.00
13 Larry Fitzgerald/99 2.00 5.00
14 Blake Bortles/99 1.50 4.00
15 Odell Beckham Jr./199 2.00 5.00
16 Cordarrelle Patterson/199 1.25 3.00
17 Ryan Tannehill/99 2.00 5.00
18 Derek Carr/199 2.00 5.00
19 Donte Moncrief/199 1.50 4.00
20 Eli Manning/49 2.50 6.00

2016 Panini Heir to the Throne Autographs

1 Connor Cook
2 Demarcus Robinson 3.00 8.00
3 Josh Doctson 4.00 10.00
4 KeiVarae Russell 3.00 8.00
5 Carson Wentz 50.00 100.00
6 Andrew Billings 4.00 10.00
7 Corey Coleman
8 Glenn Gronkowski 3.00 8.00
9 Jared Goff
10 Vonn Bell 4.00 10.00
11 Ezekiel Elliott 75.00 150.00
12 Nate Sudfeld 3.00 8.00
13 Cardale Jones
14 Austin Johnson 3.00 8.00
15 Will Fuller
16 Tajae Sharpe 6.00 15.00
17 Paul Perkins 3.00 8.00
18 Jack Conklin 5.00 12.00
19 Derrick Henry
20 Nick Vannett 3.00 8.00
21 Laquon Treadwell 20.00 40.00
22 Nelson Spruce 3.00 8.00
23 Michael Thomas 6.00 15.00
24 Daniel Braverman 3.00 8.00
25 C.J. Prosise 3.00 8.00
26 A'Shawn Robinson 3.00 8.00
27 Joey Bosa
28 Vernon Butler 3.00 8.00
29 Paxton Lynch 3.00 8.00
30 Byron Marshall 3.00 8.00

2016 Panini Knight School

1 Jared Goff 2.50 6.00
2 Jalen Ramsey .60 1.50
3 Connor Cook .50 1.25
4 Vernon Hargreaves III .60 1.50
5 Derrick Henry 1.00 2.50
6 Myles Jack .50 1.25
7 Corey Coleman .60 1.50
8 Michael Thomas .75 2.00
9 Joey Bosa .75 2.00
10 Josh Doctson .50 1.25
11 Paxton Lynch .40 1.00
12 Shaq Lawson .40 1.00
13 Ezekiel Elliott 2.00 5.00
14 DeForest Buckner .40 1.00
15 Laquon Treadwell .50 1.25

2016 Panini Legends of the Shield

STATED ODDS 1:6 RETAIL
1 Mike Singletary .75 2.00
2 Larry Csonka .60 1.50
3 Roger Craig .60 1.50
4 Franco Harris .75 2.00
5 Bob Griese .75 2.00
6 Emmitt Smith 1.25 3.00
7 Rod Smith .60 1.50
8 Darrell Green .60 1.50
9 John Elway 1.25 3.00
10 Jim Kelly .75 2.00
11 Rod Woodson .60 1.50
12 Edgerrin James .60 1.50
13 Andre Reed .60 1.50
14 Marcus Allen .60 1.50
15 Eric Dickerson .60 1.50
16 Joe Montana 2.00 5.00
17 Thurman Thomas .60 1.50
18 Cris Carter .75 2.00
19 Joe Theismann .75 2.00
20 Tony Dorsett .75 2.00

2016 Panini Quest Jerseys

*PRIME/25: 1X TO 2.5X BASIC JSY/199
1 Odell Beckham Jr. 2.00 5.00
2 Devonta Freeman 1.50 4.00
3 Stefon Diggs 1.50 4.00
4 Jarvis Landry 1.50 4.00
5 Todd Gurley 2.00 5.00
6 Allen Robinson 1.50 4.00
7 Kelvin Benjamin 1.50 4.00
8 Blake Bortles 1.25 3.00
9 Marcus Mariota 2.00 5.00
10 Davante Adams 1.25 3.00
11 Sammy Watkins 2.00 5.00
12 Jameis Winston 2.00 5.00
13 Teddy Bridgewater 1.50 4.00
14 Jordan Matthews 1.50 4.00
15 Tyler Lockett 1.50 4.00
16 Amari Cooper 2.00 5.00
17 Brandin Cooks 1.50 4.00
18 Khalil Mack 2.00 5.00
19 Mike Evans 1.50 4.00
20 Derek Carr 2.00 5.00

2016 Panini Rookie Calligraphy

1 Xavien Howard 3.00 8.00
2 Jared Goff
3 Maliek Collins 2.50 6.00
4 Connor Cook 3.00 8.00
5 Austin Hooper 2.50 6.00
6 Josh Doctson 3.00 8.00
7 Trevone Boykin 2.50 6.00
8 Carson Wentz
9 Jordan Williams-Lambert 2.50 6.00
10 Corey Coleman 4.00 10.00
11 Reggie Ragland 2.50 6.00
12 Derrick Henry 6.00 15.00
13 Daryl Worley 2.50 6.00
14 Ezekiel Elliott
15 Kevin Hogan 3.00 8.00
16 Cardale Jones 2.50 6.00
17 Brandon Doughty 2.50 6.00
18 Will Fuller 4.00 10.00
19 Adolphus Washington 2.50 6.00
20 Paul Perkins 2.50 6.00
21 Yannick Ngakoue 4.00 10.00
22 Paxton Lynch 2.50 6.00
23 Su'a Cravens 2.50 6.00
24 Laquon Treadwell 3.00 8.00
25 Aaron Green 2.50 6.00
26 Michael Thomas 5.00 12.00
27 Kendall Fuller 3.00 8.00
28 C.J. Prosise 2.50 6.00
29 Emmanuel Ogbah 3.00 8.00
30 Joey Bosa 5.00 12.00

2016 Panini Royal Family

1 G.Grnkwski/R.Grnkwski 1.50 4.00
2 C.Long/K.Long 1.00 2.50
3 E.Manning/P.Manning 3.00 8.00
4 S.Sharpe/S.Sharpe 1.50 4.00
5 C.Matthews/J.Matthews 1.50 4.00

2016 Panini Squires Jerseys

*PRIME/25: .8X TO 2X BASIC JSY
1 Jared Goff 5.00 12.00
2 Carson Wentz 6.00 15.00
3 Joey Bosa 3.00 8.00
4 Ezekiel Elliott 8.00 20.00
5 Corey Coleman 2.50 6.00
6 Will Fuller 2.50 6.00
7 Josh Doctson 2.00 5.00
8 Laquon Treadwell 2.00 5.00
9 DeAndre Washington 1.50 4.00
10 Paxton Lynch 4.00 10.00
11 Christian Hackenberg 1.50 4.00
12 Cody Kessler 1.50 4.00
13 Kenyan Drake 2.50 6.00
14 Derrick Henry 4.00 10.00
15 C.J. Prosise 1.50 4.00
16 Hunter Henry 2.00 5.00
17 Michael Thomas 3.00 8.00
18 Sterling Shepard 3.00 8.00
19 Leonte Carroo 1.50 4.00
20 Braxton Miller 1.50 4.00
21 Connor Cook 2.00 5.00
22 Chris Moore 2.00 5.00
23 Moritz Bohringer 1.50 4.00
24 Ricardo Louis 1.50 4.00
25 Pharoh Cooper 1.50 4.00
26 Tyler Ervin 1.50 4.00
27 Demarcus Robinson 1.50 4.00
28 Kenneth Dixon 1.50 4.00
29 Dak Prescott 8.00 20.00
30 Devontae Booker 2.00 5.00
31 Cardale Jones 1.50 4.00
32 Trevor Davis 1.50 4.00
33 Paul Perkins 1.50 4.00
34 Jordan Howard 3.00 8.00
35 Wendell Smallwood 1.50 4.00
36 Jonathan Williams 2.00 5.00
37 Kevin Hogan 2.00 5.00
38 Alex Collins 2.00 5.00
39 Keenan Reynolds 2.00 5.00
40 Tyler Boyd 2.00 5.00

2017 Panini

1 Carlos Hyde .12 .30
2 Torrey Smith .12 .30
3 Alshon Jeffery .15 .40
4 Jordan Howard .20 .50
5 Andy Dalton .15 .40
6 A.J. Green .20 .50
7 LeSean McCoy .20 .50
8 Sammy Watkins .20 .50
9 Tyrod Taylor .15 .40
10 Trevor Siemian .12 .30
11 Von Miller .15 .40
12 Demaryius Thomas .15 .40
13 Joe Haden .12 .30
14 Joe Thomas .12 .30
15 Jamie Collins .12 .30
16 Jameis Winston .15 .40
17 Mike Evans .15 .40
18 Gerald McCoy .12 .30
19 Carson Palmer .15 .40
20 Larry Fitzgerald .15 .40
21 Patrick Peterson .12 .30
22 Philip Rivers .20 .50
23 Joey Bosa .20 .50
24 Melvin Gordon .15 .40
25 Alex Smith .15 .40
26 Travis Kelce .20 .50
27 Tyreek Hill .20 .50
28 Frank Gore .15 .40
29 Andrew Luck .25 .60
30 T.Y. Hilton .15 .40
31 Dak Prescott .20 .50
32 Ezekiel Elliott .25 .60
33 Dez Bryant .20 .50
34 Jason Witten .15 .40
35 Ryan Tannehill .15 .40
36 Jarvis Landry .15 .40
37 Jay Ajayi .15 .40
38 Carson Wentz .25 .60
39 Mike Glennon .15 .40

40 Jordan Matthews .12 .30
41 Matt Ryan .15 .40
42 Julio Jones .20 .50
43 Devonta Freeman .15 .40
44 Vic Beasley Jr. .12 .30
45 Eli Manning .15 .40
46 Odell Beckham Jr. .20 .50
47 Sterling Shepard .15 .40
48 Landon Collins .12 .30
49 Blake Bortles .12 .30
50 Allen Robinson .15 .40
51 Paul Posluszny .12 .30
52 Matt Forte .12 .30
53 Eric Decker .12 .30
54 Brandon Marshall .12 .30
55 Matthew Stafford .15 .40
56 Golden Tate III .12 .30
57 Marvin Jones Jr. .12 .30
58 Aaron Rodgers .40 1.00
59 Jordy Nelson .15 .40
60 Eddie Lacy .12 .30
61 Ha Ha Clinton-Dix .12 .30
62 Cam Newton .20 .50
63 Navorro Bowman .15 .40
64 Luke Kuechly .15 .40
65 Greg Olsen .15 .40
66 Tom Brady .50 1.25
67 Rob Gronkowski .20 .50
68 Julian Edelman .20 .50
69 Chris Hogan .12 .30
70 Derek Carr .20 .50
71 Amari Cooper .20 .50
72 Khalil Mack .20 .50
73 Jared Goff .20 .50
74 Todd Gurley II .20 .50
75 Aaron Donald .20 .50
76 Joe Flacco .15 .40
77 Mike Wallace .12 .30
78 Terrell Suggs .12 .30
79 Justin Tucker .12 .30
80 Kirk Cousins .20 .50
81 DeSean Jackson .15 .40
82 Robert Kelley .12 .30
83 Ryan Kerrigan .12 .30
84 Drew Brees .20 .50
85 Brandin Cooks .15 .40
86 Mark Ingram .15 .40
87 Russell Wilson .25 .60
88 Richard Sherman .20 .50
89 Doug Baldwin .15 .40
90 Bobby Wagner .12 .30
91 Ben Roethlisberger .20 .50
92 Antonio Brown .20 .50
93 Le'Veon Bell .15 .40
94 James Harrison .15 .40
95 Marcus Mariota .20 .50
96 DeMarco Murray .15 .40
97 Brian Orakpo .12 .30
98 Adrian Peterson .20 .50
99 Sam Bradford .12 .30
100 Danielle Hunter .12 .30
101 Mitchell Trubisky RC 1.25 3.00
102 Deshaun Watson RC 1.50 4.00
103 DeShone Kizer RC .25 .60
104 Patrick Mahomes II RC 3.00 8.00
105 Nathan Peterman RC .30 .75
106 Davis Webb RC .25 .60
107 R. Joshua Dobbs RC .30 .75
108 C.J. Beathard RC .25 .60
109 Dalvin Cook RC .60 1.50
110 Leonard Fournette RC .75 2.00
111 Christian McCaffrey RC .60 1.50
112 Joe Mixon RC .50 1.25
113 Jonathan Allen RC .30 .75
114 O.J. Howard RC .30 .75
115 Mike Williams RC .40 1.00
116 Corey Davis RC .40 1.00
117 Cooper Kupp RC .40 1.00
118 Tre'Davious White RC .25 .60
119 Kareem Hunt RC .50 1.25
120 Josh Reynolds RC .25 .60
121 Evan Engram RC .30 .75
122 Donnel Pumphrey RC .30 .75
123 James Conner RC .50 1.25
124 Wayne Gallman RC .30 .75
125 Myles Garrett RC .75 2.00
126 Jabrill Peppers RC .40 1.00
127 Teez Tabor RC .30 .75
128 Charles Harris RC .25 .60
129 Raekwon McMillan RC .25 .60
130 Reuben Foster RC .25 .60
131 Derek Barnett RC .30 .75
132 Zach Cunningham RC .30 .75
133 Adoree' Jackson RC .30 .75
134 Budda Baker RC .25 .60
135 Marcus Maye RC .25 .60
136 Jarrad Davis RC .30 .75
137 Samaje Perine RC .25 .60
138 Jehu Chesson RC .30 .75
139 Taco Charlton RC .25 .60
140 Sidney Jones RC .25 .60
141 Chris Godwin RC .30 .75
142 Marcus Williams RC .25 .60
143 Ryan Anderson RC .25 .60
144 Gareon Conley RC .25 .60
145 Takkarist McKinley RC .25 .60
146 Zay Jones RC .30 .75
147 Ryan Switzer RC .30 .75
148 Jeremy McNichols RC .25 .60
149 Kevin King RC .30 .75
150 Chidobe Awuzie RC .30 .75
151 Marlon Mack RC .40 1.00
152 DeMarcus Walker RC .25 .60
153 Brian Hill RC .25 .60
154 Justin Evans RC .25 .60
155 Dede Westbrook RC .25 .60
156 Gerald Everett RC .25 .60
157 Tyus Bowser RC .25 .60
158 JuJu Smith-Schuster RC .60 1.50
159 Malik McDowell RC .25 .60
160 Jamal Adams RC .25 .60
161 Cam Robinson RC .25 .60
162 Tim Williams RC .30 .75
163 Marlon Humphrey RC .25 .60
164 Derek Rivers RC .30 .75
165 Taywan Taylor RC .25 .60
166 Amara Darboh RC .25 .60
167 Mack Hollins RC .25 .60
168 Marshon Lattimore RC .30 .75
169 Malik Hooker RC .25 .60
170 John Ross III RC .30 .75
171 T.J. Watt RC .75 2.00
172 Chad Hansen RC .25 .60
173 Quincy Wilson RC .25 .60
174 Solomon Thomas RC .25 .60
175 Jamaal Williams RC .25 .60
176 D'Onta Foreman RC .30 .75
177 Joe Williams RC .25 .60
178 Carlos Henderson RC .25 .60
179 Ryan Ramczyk RC .25 .60
180 Garett Bolles RC .25 .60
181 David Njoku RC .30 .75
182 Haason Reddick RC .25 .60
183 Shelton Gibson RC .25 .60
184 Obi Melifonwu RC .25 .60
185 Trent Taylor RC .30 .75
186 Adam Shaheen RC .25 .60
187 Dalvin Tomlinson RC .25 .60
188 Josh Jones RC .25 .60
189 Antonio Garcia RC .25 .60
190 Chad Williams RC .25 .60
191 Tarik Cohen RC .50 1.25
192 Rodney Adams RC .25 .60
193 Isaiah McKenzie RC .25 .60
194 T.J. Logan RC .40 1.00
195 Curtis Samuel RC .30 .75
196 Alvin Kamara RC 1.00 2.50
197 Josh Malone RC .25 .60
198 ArDarius Stewart RC .25 .60
199 Kenny Golladay RC .40 1.00
200 DeAngelo Yancey RC .25 .60

2017 Panini Knight's Templar Foil

27 Tyreek Hill .75 2.00
29 Andrew Luck 1.00 2.50
31 Dak Prescott .75 2.00
32 Ezekiel Elliott 1.00 2.50
38 Carson Wentz 1.00 2.50
59 Jordy Nelson .60 1.50
67 Rob Gronkowski .75 2.00

2017 Panini Accolades

*GREEN/399: .1X TO 2X BASIC
*RED/25: 2X TO 5X BASIC
1 Dak Prescott .75 2.00
2 Calvin Johnson .75 2.00
3 Randy Moss .60 1.50
4 Howie Long .75 2.00
5 Matt Ryan .60 1.50
6 Tom Brady 2.00 5.00
7 Antonio Brown .75 2.00
8 Casey Hayward .50 1.25
9 Vic Beasley Jr. .50 1.25
10 Drew Brees .75 2.00
11 Marshawn Lynch .60 1.50
12 Matt Bryant .50 1.25
13 Brett Favre 1.50 4.00
14 Peyton Manning 1.50 4.00
15 Adrian Peterson .75 2.00
16 Rob Gronkowski .75 2.00
17 J.J. Watt .75 2.00
18 Jerry Rice 1.25 3.00
19 Ben Roethlisberger .75 2.00
20 David Johnson .75 2.00

2017 Panini Decorated

1 Cam Newton 1.00 2.50
2 J.J. Watt 1.00 2.50
3 Kurt Warner .75 2.00
4 Brett Favre 2.00 5.00
5 Thurman Thomas .75 2.00
6 LaDainian Tomlinson .75 2.00
7 Charles Woodson 1.00 2.50
8 Randy Moss .75 2.00
9 Odell Beckham Jr. 1.00 2.50
10 Matt Ryan .75 2.00
11 Von Miller .75 2.00
12 Lawrence Taylor 1.00 2.50
13 Bruce Smith .75 2.00
14 Deion Sanders .75 2.00
15 Brian Urlacher 1.00 2.50
16 Marcus Allen .75 2.00
17 Joe Theismann 1.00 2.50
18 Aaron Rodgers 2.00 5.00
19 Adrian Peterson 1.00 2.50
20 Marcus Peters .60 1.50

2017 Panini Kick Squad

1 Dan Bailey 1.25 3.00
2 Justin Tucker 1.25 3.00
3 Morten Andersen 1.25 3.00
4 Sebastian Janikowski 1.25 3.00
5 Stephen Gostkowski 1.25 3.00

2017 Panini Knight School

1 Deshaun Watson 2.00 5.00
2 Mitchell Trubisky 1.50 4.00
3 Davis Webb .30 .75
4 Patrick Mahomes II 4.00 10.00
5 Brad Kaaya .30 .75
6 Leonard Fournette 1.00 2.50
7 Dalvin Cook .75 2.00
8 Christian McCaffrey .75 2.00
9 D'Onta Foreman .40 1.00
10 Alvin Kamara 1.25 3.00
11 Mike Williams .50 1.25
12 Corey Davis .50 1.25
13 John Ross III .40 1.00
14 JuJu Smith-Schuster .75 2.00
15 Dede Westbrook .30 .75

2017 Panini Knights of the Round

1 Tom Brady 25.00 60.00
2 Matt Ryan 8.00 20.00
3 Julio Jones 10.00 25.00
4 Antonio Brown 10.00 25.00
5 Le'Veon Bell 8.00 20.00
6 Ezekiel Elliott 12.00 30.00
7 Dak Prescott 10.00 25.00
8 Odell Beckham Jr. 10.00 25.00
9 A.J. Green 10.00 25.00
10 Derek Carr 10.00 25.00
11 David Johnson 10.00 25.00
12 Cam Newton 10.00 25.00
13 Aaron Rodgers 20.00 50.00
14 Jameis Winston 8.00 20.00
15 Marcus Mariota 10.00 25.00
16 Russell Wilson 12.00 30.00
17 Drew Brees 10.00 25.00
18 Joe Flacco 8.00 20.00
19 J.J. Watt 10.00 25.00
20 Matthew Stafford 8.00 20.00
21 Randy Moss 8.00 20.00
22 Calvin Johnson 10.00 25.00
23 Howie Long 10.00 25.00
24 Dan Marino 20.00 50.00
25 Emmitt Smith 15.00 40.00
26 Peyton Manning 20.00 50.00
27 Brian Urlacher 10.00 25.00
28 Brett Favre 20.00 50.00
29 Jim Kelly 10.00 25.00
30 Terry Bradshaw 15.00 40.00

2017 Panini Legends of the Shield

1 Calvin Johnson 1.00 2.50
2 Randy Moss .75 2.00
3 Peyton Manning 2.00 5.00
4 Dan Marino 2.00 5.00
5 Emmitt Smith 1.50 4.00
6 Jerry Rice 1.50 4.00
7 Brett Favre 2.00 5.00
8 Joe Namath 1.25 3.00
9 Brian Urlacher 1.00 2.50
10 Lawrence Taylor 1.00 2.50
11 Jim Brown 1.25 3.00
12 Gale Sayers 1.00 2.50
13 Barry Sanders 1.50 4.00
14 Roger Staubach 1.25 3.00
15 Warren Sapp .75 2.00
16 Terry Bradshaw 1.50 4.00
17 Ray Lewis 1.00 2.50
18 Jerome Bettis 1.00 2.50
19 Morten Andersen .60 1.50
20 Steve Largent 1.00 2.50

2017 Panini MVP Predictor

1 Ezekiel Elliott
2 Matt Ryan 4.00 10.00
3 Tom Brady 12.00 30.00
4 J.J. Watt 5.00 12.00
5 Andrew Luck 6.00 15.00
6 Aaron Rodgers 10.00 25.00
7 Le'Veon Bell 4.00 10.00
8 David Johnson 5.00 12.00
9 Derek Carr 5.00 12.00
10 Wild Card

2017 Panini Offensive POY Predictor

1 Matt Ryan 4.00 10.00
2 Matthew Stafford 4.00 10.00
3 Ezekiel Elliott 6.00 15.00
4 Aaron Rodgers 10.00 25.00
5 Tom Brady 12.00 30.00
6 Adrian Peterson 5.00 12.00
7 Derek Carr 5.00 12.00
8 David Johnson 5.00 12.00
9 Dak Prescott 5.00 12.00
10 Wild Card

2017 Panini Offensive ROY Predictor

1 Deshaun Watson 10.00 25.00
2 Mike Williams 2.50 6.00
3 Joe Mixon 3.00 8.00
4 Leonard Fournette 5.00 12.00
5 Dalvin Cook 4.00 10.00
6 John Ross III 2.00 5.00
7 Corey Davis 2.50 6.00
8 O.J. Howard 2.00 5.00
9 Mitchell Trubisky 8.00 20.00
10 Wild Card

2017 Panini Squires Jerseys Prime

1 Mitchell Trubisky 12.00 30.00
2 Leonard Fournette 8.00 20.00
3 Corey Davis 4.00 10.00
4 Mike Williams 4.00 10.00
5 Christian McCaffrey 6.00 15.00
6 John Ross III 3.00 8.00
7 Patrick Mahomes II 30.00 80.00
8 Deshaun Watson 15.00 40.00
9 O.J. Howard 3.00 8.00
10 Evan Engram 3.00 8.00
13 Dalvin Cook 6.00 15.00
14 Joe Mixon 5.00 12.00
15 DeShone Kizer 2.50 6.00
16 JuJu Smith-Schuster 6.00 15.00
17 Alvin Kamara 10.00 25.00
18 Cooper Kupp 4.00 10.00
19 Taywan Taylor 2.50 6.00
20 ArDarius Stewart 2.50 6.00
21 Carlos Henderson 2.50 6.00
22 Chris Godwin 3.00 8.00
23 Kareem Hunt 5.00 12.00
24 Davis Webb 2.50 6.00
25 D'Onta Foreman 3.00 8.00
26 C.J. Beathard 2.50 6.00
27 James Conner 5.00 12.00
28 Amara Darboh 2.50 6.00
29 Kenny Golladay 4.00 10.00
30 Dede Westbrook 2.50 6.00
31 Samaje Perine 2.50 6.00
32 Josh Reynolds 2.50 6.00
33 Mack Hollins 2.50 6.00
34 Joe Williams 2.50 6.00
35 Jamaal Williams 2.50 6.00
36 R. Joshua Dobbs 30.00 80.00
37 Wayne Gallman 3.00 8.00
38 Marlon Mack 4.00 10.00
39 Jeremy McNichols 2.50 6.00
40 Nathan Peterman 3.00 8.00

2017 Panini The Rooks

1 Dalvin Cook 1.50 4.00
2 DeShone Kizer .60 1.50
3 Alvin Kamara 2.50 6.00
4 Corey Davis 1.00 2.50
5 Davis Webb .60 1.50
6 O.J. Howard .75 2.00
7 John Ross III .75 2.00
8 Deshaun Watson 4.00 10.00
9 David Njoku .75 2.00
10 Brad Kaaya .60 1.50
11 Myles Garrett 2.00 5.00
12 JuJu Smith-Schuster 1.50 4.00
13 Mitchell Trubisky 3.00 8.00
14 Samaje Perine .60 1.50
15 Mike Williams 1.00 2.50
16 Leonard Fournette 2.00 5.00
17 Zay Jones .75 2.00
18 Christian McCaffrey 1.50 4.00
19 Curtis Samuel .75 2.00
20 Patrick Mahomes II 8.00 20.00

2018 Panini

1 David Johnson .20 .50
2 Sam Bradford .12 .30
3 Adrian Peterson .20 .50
4 Larry Fitzgerald .15 .40
5 Mike Iupati .12 .30
6 J.J. Nelson .12 .30
7 Elijhaa Penny .12 .30
8 Chandler Jones .12 .30
9 Haason Reddick .12 .30
10 Deone Bucannon .12 .30
11 Matt Ryan .15 .40
12 Tevin Coleman .12 .30
13 Devonta Freeman .15 .40
14 Mohamed Sanu .12 .30
15 Deion Jones .12 .30
16 Julio Jones .20 .50
17 Matt Bryant .12 .30
18 Desmond Trufant .12 .30
19 Vic Beasley Jr. .12 .30
20 Austin Hooper .12 .30
21 Joe Flacco .15 .40
22 Alex Collins .12 .30
23 Terrell Suggs .12 .30
24 Justin Tucker .12 .30
25 Eric Weddle .12 .30
26 Breshad Perriman .12 .30
27 Marlon Humphrey .12 .30
28 Brandon Williams .12 .30
29 Michael Crabtree .12 .30
30 A.J. McCarron .12 .30
31 LeSean McCoy .20 .50
32 Kelvin Benjamin .15 .40
33 Tre'Davious White .12 .30
34 Zay Jones .12 .30
35 Charles Clay .12 .30
36 Kyle Williams .12 .30
37 Steve Hauschka .12 .30
38 Nathan Peterman .12 .30
39 Jordan Poyer .12 .30
40 Cam Newton .20 .50
41 Christian McCaffrey .20 .50
42 Luke Kuechly .15 .40
43 Greg Olsen .15 .40
44 Torrey Smith .12 .30
45 Julius Peppers .15 .40
46 Devin Funchess .12 .30
47 Graham Gano .12 .30
48 Curtis Samuel .12 .30
49 Mitchell Trubisky .20 .50
50 Jordan Howard .20 .50
51 Tarik Cohen .15 .40
52 Danny Trevathan .12 .30
53 Eddie Jackson .12 .30
54 Kyle Fuller .12 .30
55 Kyle Long .12 .30
56 Allen Robinson .15 .40
57 Kevin White .12 .30
58 Andy Dalton .15 .40
59 A.J. Green .20 .50
60 Joe Mixon .15 .40
61 Giovani Bernard .12 .30
62 Dre Kirkpatrick .12 .30
63 Carlos Dunlap .12 .30
64 Geno Atkins .12 .30
65 Brandon LaFell .12 .30
66 Tyler Boyd .12 .30
67 Tyrod Taylor .15 .40
68 Josh Gordon .12 .30
69 Jabrill Peppers .12 .30
70 Corey Coleman .12 .30
71 Myles Garrett .20 .50
72 Jarvis Landry .15 .40
73 Carlos Hyde .12 .30
74 Joe Schobert .12 .30
75 David Njoku .12 .30
76 Dak Prescott .20 .50
77 Ezekiel Elliott .25 .60
78 Zack Martin .12 .30
79 Allen Hurns .12 .30
80 Jason Witten .15 .40
81 Cole Beasley .15 .40
82 Ryan Switzer .12 .30
83 Terrance Williams .12 .30
84 Sean Lee .15 .40
85 Jourdan Lewis .12 .30
86 Case Keenum .15 .40
87 Von Miller .15 .40
88 C.J. Anderson .15 .40
89 Emmanuel Sanders .20 .50
90 Demaryius Thomas .15 .40
91 Chris Harris Jr. .12 .30
92 Devontae Booker .12 .30
93 Derek Wolfe .12 .30
94 Bradley Roby .12 .30
95 Andy Janovich .12 .30
96 Jake Butt .15 .40
97 Matthew Stafford .15 .40
98 Golden Tate III .12 .30
99 Marvin Jones Jr. .12 .30
100 Matt Prater .12 .30
101 Theo Riddick .12 .30
102 Darius Slay .12 .30
103 Ezekiel Ansah .12 .30
104 Kenny Golladay .12 .30
105 LeGarrette Blount .15 .40
106 Aaron Rodgers .40 1.00
107 Davante Adams .15 .40
108 Aaron Jones .15 .40
109 Clay Matthews .15 .40
110 Nick Perry .12 .30
111 Randall Cobb .15 .40
112 Ha Ha Clinton-Dix .12 .30
113 Ty Montgomery .12 .30
114 Jimmy Graham .20 .50
115 Mason Crosby .12 .30
116 Deshaun Watson .25 .60
117 Lamar Miller .12 .30
118 DeAndre Hopkins .15 .40
119 J.J. Watt .20 .50
120 Jadeveon Clowney .12 .30
121 Will Fuller V .12 .30
122 Whitney Mercilus .12 .30
123 D'Onta Foreman .12 .30
124 Andrew Luck .25 .60
125 Jacoby Brissett .12 .30
126 T.Y. Hilton .15 .40
127 Adam Vinatieri .12 .30
128 Jack Doyle .12 .30
129 Marlon Mack .12 .30
130 Malik Hooker .12 .30
131 T.J. Green .12 .30
132 Blake Bortles .12 .30
133 Leonard Fournette .20 .50
134 Jalen Ramsey .15 .40
135 Marqise Lee .12 .30
136 T.J. Yeldon .12 .30
137 Myles Jack .12 .30
138 A.J. Bouye .12 .30
139 Calais Campbell .12 .30
140 Dede Westbrook .12 .30
141 Telvin Smith .12 .30
142 Patrick Mahomes II .50 1.25
143 Travis Kelce .20 .50
144 Reggie Ragland .12 .30
145 Kareem Hunt .15 .40
146 Tyreek Hill .20 .50
147 Eric Berry .15 .40
148 Sammy Watkins .20 .50
149 Justin Houston .12 .30
150 Dee Ford .12 .30
151 Jared Goff .20 .50
152 Todd Gurley II .20 .50
153 Cooper Kupp .15 .40
154 Tavon Austin .12 .30
155 Aaron Donald .20 .50
156 Robert Woods .15 .40
157 Brandin Cooks .15 .40
158 Ndamukong Suh .15 .40
159 Marcus Peters .12 .30
160 Philip Rivers .20 .50
161 Mike Williams .12 .30
162 Melvin Gordon .15 .40
163 Joey Bosa .20 .50
164 Keenan Allen .15 .40
165 Hunter Henry .12 .30
166 Casey Hayward .12 .30
167 Melvin Ingram .12 .30
168 Travis Benjamin .12 .30
169 Antonio Gates .12 .30
170 Ryan Tannehill .15 .40
171 Danny Amendola .15 .40
172 Laremy Tunsil .12 .30
173 Kenyan Drake .12 .30
174 Kiko Alonso .12 .30
175 Kenny Stills .12 .30
176 Cameron Wake .12 .30
177 Xavien Howard .12 .30
178 DeVante Parker .15 .40
179 Kirk Cousins .20 .50
180 Adam Thielen .20 .50
181 Stefon Diggs .15 .40
182 Anthony Barr .12 .30
183 Harrison Smith .20 .50
184 Xavier Rhodes .12 .30
185 Dalvin Cook .15 .40
186 Kyle Rudolph .12 .30
187 Andrew Sendejo .12 .30
188 Latavius Murray .12 .30
189 Tom Brady .50 1.25
190 Rob Gronkowski .20 .50
191 James Harrison .15 .40
192 Dont'a Hightower .12 .30
193 Chris Hogan .12 .30
194 Devin McCourty .12 .30
195 Rex Burkhead .12 .30
196 Patrick Chung .12 .30
197 Jeremy Hill .12 .30
198 Stephon Gilmore .12 .30
199 James White .15 .40
200 Drew Brees .20 .50
201 Alvin Kamara .15 .40
202 Mark Ingram .15 .40
203 Michael Thomas .20 .50
204 Manti Te'o .12 .30
205 Cameron Jordan .12 .30
206 Cameron Meredith .12 .30
207 Ted Ginn Jr. .12 .30
208 Kenny Vaccaro .12 .30
209 Marshon Lattimore .12 .30
210 Eli Manning .15 .40
211 Odell Beckham Jr. .20 .50
212 Damon Harrison .12 .30
213 Sterling Shepard .15 .40
214 Evan Engram .12 .30
215 Landon Collins .12 .30
216 Janoris Jenkins .12 .30
217 Jonathan Stewart .12 .30
218 Olivier Vernon .12 .30
219 Teddy Bridgewater .15 .40
220 Bilal Powell .12 .30
221 Elijah McGuire .12 .30
222 Jamal Adams .15 .40
223 Jermaine Kearse .12 .30
224 Leonard Williams .12 .30
225 Austin Seferian-Jenkins .12 .30
226 Quincy Enunwa .12 .30
227 Robby Anderson .12 .30
228 Derek Carr .20 .50
229 Marshawn Lynch .15 .40
230 Amari Cooper .20 .50
231 DeAndre Washington .12 .30
232 Khalil Mack .20 .50
233 Navorro Bowman .15 .40
234 Bruce Irvin .12 .30
235 Jordy Nelson .15 .40
236 Jared Cook .12 .30
237 Carson Wentz .25 .60
238 Jay Ajayi .15 .40
239 Zach Ertz .15 .40
240 Alshon Jeffery .15 .40
241 Nick Foles .15 .40
242 Michael Bennett .12 .30
243 Ronald Darby .12 .30
244 Fletcher Cox .12 .30
245 Jason Peters .12 .30
246 Ben Roethlisberger .20 .50
247 Antonio Brown .20 .50
248 Le'Veon Bell .15 .40
249 JuJu Smith-Schuster .20 .50
250 T.J. Watt .15 .40
251 Jesse James .12 .30
252 Maurkice Pouncey .12 .30
253 Artie Burns .20 .50
254 Martavis Bryant .12 .30
255 Jimmy Garoppolo .25 .60
256 Marquise Goodwin .12 .30
257 Jerick McKinnon .12 .30
258 Reuben Foster .12 .30
259 Richard Sherman .20 .50
260 George Kittle .12 .30
261 Matt Breida .15 .40
262 DeForest Buckner .12 .30
263 Pierre Garcon .15 .40
264 Russell Wilson .25 .60
265 Cliff Avril .12 .30
266 Bobby Wagner .12 .30
267 Chris Carson .15 .40
268 Earl Thomas III .15 .40
269 Kam Chancellor .20 .50
270 Doug Baldwin .15 .40
271 Tyler Lockett .15 .40
272 Jameis Winston .15 .40
273 Adam Humphries .12 .30
274 Mike Evans .15 .40
275 O.J. Howard .12 .30
276 DeSean Jackson .15 .40
277 Vernon Hargreaves III .12 .30
278 Cameron Brate .12 .30
279 Jason Pierre-Paul .12 .30
280 Gerald McCoy .12 .30
281 Marcus Mariota .20 .50
282 Derrick Henry .20 .50
283 Eric Decker .15 .40
284 Corey Davis .15 .40
285 Delanie Walker .12 .30
286 Rishard Matthews .12 .30
287 Adoree' Jackson .12 .30
288 Dion Lewis .12 .30
289 Brian Orakpo .12 .30
290 Taywan Taylor .12 .30
291 Alex Smith .15 .40
292 Josh Norman .12 .30
293 Chris Thompson .12 .30
294 Samaje Perine .12 .30
295 Jordan Reed .12 .30
296 Jamison Crowder .12 .30
297 Josh Doctson .12 .30
298 Ryan Kerrigan .12 .30
299 Bashaud Breeland .12 .30
300 Vernon Davis .12 .30
301 Minkah Fitzpatrick RC .50 1.25
302 Denzel Ward RC .60 1.50
303 Bradley Chubb RC .40 1.00
304 Harold Landry RC .25 .60
305 Josh Rosen RC .75 2.00
306 Sam Darnold RC 1.50 4.00
307 Josh Allen RC 1.00 2.50
308 Baker Mayfield RC 2.50 6.00
309 Lamar Jackson RC 1.50 4.00
310 Mason Rudolph RC .60 1.50
311 Kurt Benkert RC .30 .75
312 Riley Ferguson RC .40 1.00
313 Saquon Barkley RC 2.00 5.00
314 Derrius Guice RC .50 1.25
315 Ronald Jones II RC .25 .60
316 Nick Chubb RC .75 2.00
317 Kerryon Johnson RC .40 1.00
318 Sony Michel RC .75 2.00
319 John Kelly RC .30 .75
320 Rashaad Penny RC .40 1.00
321 Calvin Ridley RC .60 1.50
322 Christian Kirk RC .40 1.00
323 Courtland Sutton RC .40 1.00
324 James Washington RC .50 1.25
325 Anthony Miller RC .40 1.00
326 Deontay Burnett RC .30 .75
327 Michael Gallup RC .50 1.25
328 D.J. Chark RC .30 .75
329 Dallas Goedert RC .30 .75
330 Deon Cain RC .30 .75
331 Joshua Jackson RC .50 1.25
332 Isaiah Oliver RC .25 .60
333 Arden Key RC .25 .60
334 Quadree Henderson RC .30 .75
335 Chase Edmonds RC .25 .60
336 Kyle Lauletta RC .40 1.00
337 Vita Vea RC .40 1.00
338 Roquan Smith RC .75 2.00
339 Malik Jefferson RC .30 .75
340 Rashaan Evans RC .40 1.00
341 Tremaine Edmunds RC .50 1.25
342 Ogbonnia Okoronkwo RC .40 1.00
343 Luke Falk RC .30 .75
344 Mike White RC .30 .75
345 Richie James RC .25 .60
346 Trey Quinn RC .25 .60
347 Josh Adams RC .50 1.25
348 Bo Scarbrough RC .30 .75
349 Royce Freeman RC .30 .75
350 Akrum Wadley RC .25 .60
351 Kalen Ballage RC .30 .75
352 Mark Walton RC .30 .75
353 Derwin James RC .50 1.25
354 Ronnie Harrison RC .30 .75
355 Mark Andrews RC .40 1.00
356 Mike Gesicki RC .30 .75
357 D.J. Moore RC .50 1.25
358 Marcell Ateman RC .30 .75
359 Simmie Cobbs Jr. RC .40 1.00
360 Allen Lazard RC .25 .60
361 Dante Pettis RC .40 1.00
362 Jaleel Scott RC .25 .60
363 Jordan Lasley RC .25 .60
364 Damion Ratley RC .30 .75
365 Troy Fumagalli RC .30 .75
366 Justin Watson RC .30 .75
367 Jaire Alexander RC .40 1.00
368 Boston Scott RC .30 .75
369 DaeSean Hamilton RC .30 .75
370 Dorance Armstrong Jr. RC .25 .60
371 Josh Sweat RC .30 .75
372 Dylan Cantrell RC .25 .60
373 Jordan Whitehead RC .25 .60
374 Jerome Baker RC .30 .75
375 Austin Proehl RC .25 .60
376 Connor Williams RC .50 1.25
377 Orlando Brown RC .40 1.00
378 Tanner Lee RC .30 .75
379 Kyle Allen RC .30 .75
380 Kamryn Pettway RC .40 1.00
381 Nyheim Hines RC .30 .75
382 Dalton Schultz RC .30 .75
383 Ryan Izzo RC .25 .60
384 Auden Tate RC .25 .60
385 Equanimeous St. Brown RC .40 1.00
386 J'Mon Moore RC .25 .60
387 J.T. Barrett RC .40 1.00
388 Chase Litton RC .30 .75
389 Taven Bryan RC .25 .60
390 Justin Reid RC .25 .60
391 Donte Jackson RC .40 1.00
392 Leighton Vander Esch RC .75 2.00
393 Keke Coutee RC .30 .75
394 Tre'Quan Smith RC .40 1.00
395 Korey Robertson RC .30 .75
396 Antonio Callaway RC .30 .75
397 Byron Pringle RC .30 .75
398 Braxton Berrios RC .25 .60
399 Ray-Ray McCloud RC .25 .60
400 Hayden Hurst RC .30 .75

2018 Panini Gold Knight

*VETS: 8X TO 20X BASIC CARDS
*ROOKIES: 4X TO 10X BASIC CARDS

2018 Panini Silver Knight

*VETS/50: 5X TO 12X BASIC CARDS
*ROOKIES/50: 2.5X TO 6X BASIC CARDS

2018 Panini Autographs

8 Chandler Jones/25 5.00 12.00
9 Haason Reddick
12 Tevin Coleman/25 5.00 12.00
19 Vic Beasley Jr./25 5.00 12.00
22 Alex Collins/75 3.00 8.00
24 Justin Tucker/25 5.00 12.00
25 Eric Weddle/25 5.00 12.00
27 Marlon Humphrey/99 3.00 8.00
29 Michael Crabtree
38 Nathan Peterman/50 4.00 10.00
39 Jordan Poyer/99 3.00 8.00
48 Curtis Samuel/50 4.00 10.00
49 Mitchell Trubisky/15
57 Kevin White
60 Joe Mixon/50 5.00 12.00
61 Giovani Bernard/20 6.00 15.00
65 Brandon LaFell
66 Tyler Boyd/40 4.00 10.00
70 Corey Coleman/15 6.00 15.00
78 Zack Martin/25 5.00 12.00
79 Allen Hurns
82 Ryan Switzer/99 3.00 8.00
95 Andy Janovich
96 Jake Butt/50 5.00 12.00
102 Darius Slay/50 4.00 10.00
105 LeGarrette Blount/25 6.00 15.00
108 Aaron Jones/99 4.00 10.00
113 Ty Montgomery
116 Deshaun Watson/15
123 D'Onta Foreman/50 4.00 10.00
128 Jack Doyle/99 3.00 8.00
129 Marlon Mack/50 4.00 10.00
130 Malik Hooker/99 3.00 8.00
131 T.J. Green/50 4.00 10.00
137 Myles Jack/40 4.00 10.00
140 Dede Westbrook/50 4.00 10.00
147 Eric Berry/40 5.00 12.00
154 Tavon Austin/25 5.00 12.00
155 Aaron Donald/99 5.00 12.00
157 Brandin Cooks
159 Marcus Peters/99 3.00 8.00
167 Melvin Ingram/50 4.00 10.00
174 Kiko Alonso/40 4.00 10.00
177 Xavien Howard/50 4.00 10.00
183 Harrison Smith/25 8.00 20.00
184 Xavier Rhodes/50 4.00 10.00
188 Latavius Murray
196 Patrick Chung
197 Jeremy Hill
198 Stephon Gilmore/25 5.00 12.00
201 Alvin Kamara/75 4.00 10.00
204 Manti Te'o/25 5.00 12.00
206 Cameron Meredith
209 Marshon Lattimore/50 4.00 10.00
212 Damon Harrison
213 Sterling Shepard/25
217 Jonathan Stewart/20 6.00 15.00
218 Olivier Vernon
222 Jamal Adams/99 4.00 10.00
223 Jermaine Kearse/25 5.00 12.00
229 Marshawn Lynch/15 15.00 40.00
231 DeAndre Washington/99 3.00 8.00
239 Zach Ertz/20
241 Nick Foles
242 Michael Bennett/20 6.00 15.00
244 Fletcher Cox/25 5.00 12.00
249 JuJu Smith-Schuster/25
250 T.J. Watt/50 5.00 12.00
252 Maurkice Pouncey/50 4.00 10.00
253 Artie Burns/50 6.00 15.00
257 Jerick McKinnon/25 5.00 12.00
273 Adam Humphries/30 5.00 12.00
275 O.J. Howard/75 3.00 8.00
277 Vernon Hargreaves III/99 3.00 8.00
279 Jason Pierre-Paul
284 Corey Davis/25 6.00 15.00
289 Brian Orakpo/25 5.00 12.00
290 Taywan Taylor/99 3.00 8.00
294 Samaje Perine/97 3.00 8.00
297 Josh Doctson/25 5.00 12.00
299 Bashaud Breeland/50 4.00 10.00
301 Minkah Fitzpatrick/99 6.00 15.00
302 Denzel Ward/99 8.00 20.00
303 Bradley Chubb/99 5.00 12.00
304 Harold Landry/99 3.00 8.00
305 Josh Rosen/60
306 Sam Darnold/25
307 Josh Allen/60 40.00 80.00
308 Baker Mayfield/20 75.00 150.00
310 Mason Rudolph/50 25.00 50.00
311 Kurt Benkert/99 4.00 10.00
312 Riley Ferguson/99 5.00 12.00
313 Saquon Barkley/60 100.00 200.00
314 Derrius Guice/20 12.00 30.00
315 Ronald Jones II/99 3.00 8.00
316 Nick Chubb/20 20.00 50.00
317 Kerryon Johnson/99 5.00 12.00
318 Sony Michel/99 10.00 25.00
319 John Kelly/99 4.00 10.00
321 Calvin Ridley/20
322 Christian Kirk/20
323 Courtland Sutton/99 5.00 12.00
324 James Washington/99 6.00 15.00
325 Anthony Miller/99 5.00 12.00
326 Deontay Burnett/99 4.00 10.00
327 Michael Gallup/99 6.00 15.00
328 D.J. Chark/99 4.00 10.00
329 Dallas Goedert/99 4.00 10.00
331 Joshua Jackson/99 6.00 15.00
332 Isaiah Oliver/99 3.00 8.00
333 Arden Key/99 3.00 8.00
336 Kyle Lauletta/99 5.00 12.00
337 Vita Vea/99 5.00 12.00
338 Roquan Smith/99 10.00 25.00
339 Malik Jefferson/99 4.00 10.00
340 Rashaan Evans/99 5.00 12.00
341 Tremaine Edmunds/99 6.00 15.00
343 Luke Falk/99 4.00 10.00
344 Mike White/99 4.00 10.00
345 Richie James/99 3.00 8.00
346 Trey Quinn/99 3.00 8.00
347 Josh Adams/99 6.00 15.00
348 Bo Scarbrough/99 4.00 10.00
349 Royce Freeman/99 4.00 10.00
350 Akrum Wadley/99 3.00 8.00
351 Kalen Ballage/99 4.00 10.00
352 Mark Walton/99 4.00 10.00
353 Derwin James/99 6.00 15.00
354 Ronnie Harrison/99 4.00 10.00
355 Mark Andrews/99 5.00 12.00
356 Mike Gesicki/99 4.00 10.00
357 D.J. Moore/99 6.00 15.00
358 Marcell Ateman/99 4.00 10.00
359 Simmie Cobbs Jr./99 5.00 12.00
360 Allen Lazard/90 0.00 0.00
361 Dante Pettis/99 5.00 12.00
363 Jordan Lasley/99 3.00 8.00
365 Troy Fumagalli/50 5.00 12.00
367 Jaire Alexander/99 5.00 12.00
369 DaeSean Hamilton/99 4.00 10.00
371 Josh Sweat/99 4.00 10.00
375 Austin Proehl/25 5.00 12.00
376 Connor Williams/25
378 Tanner Lee/99 4.00 10.00
379 Kyle Allen/99 4.00 10.00
381 Nyheim Hines/85 4.00 10.00
383 Ryan Izzo/99 3.00 8.00
384 Auden Tate/99 3.00 8.00
387 J.T. Barrett/50
388 Chase Litton/99 4.00 10.00
389 Taven Bryan/50 4.00 10.00
390 Justin Reid/50 4.00 10.00
392 Leighton Vander Esch/99 10.00 25.00
394 Tre'Quan Smith/99 5.00 12.00
399 Ray-Ray McCloud/99 3.00 8.00
400 Hayden Hurst/99 4.00 10.00

2018 Panini Champions of Tomorrow

*GOLD/20: 1X TO 2.5X BASIC INSERTS
1 Dalvin Cook .75 2.00
2 Ezekiel Elliott 1.25 3.00
3 Kareem Hunt .75 2.00
4 Alvin Kamara .75 2.00
5 Leonard Fournette 1.00 2.50
6 Patrick Mahomes II 2.50 6.00
7 Deshaun Watson 1.25 3.00
8 Jimmy Garoppolo 1.25 3.00
9 Christian McCaffrey 1.00 2.50
10 Jared Goff 1.00 2.50

2018 Panini Honored Swatches

*PRIME/15: .8X TO 2X BASIC JSY
1 Odell Beckham Jr. 2.50 6.00
2 Antonio Brown 2.50 6.00
3 Ezekiel Elliott 3.00 8.00
4 Le'Veon Bell 2.00 5.00
5 Aaron Rodgers 5.00 12.00
6 Drew Brees 2.50 6.00
7 Alshon Jeffery 2.00 5.00
8 A.J. Green 2.50 6.00
9 Terry Bradshaw 4.00 10.00
10 Julio Jones 2.50 6.00
11 Champ Bailey 2.00 5.00
12 Todd Gurley II 2.50 6.00
13 David Johnson 2.50 6.00
14 Michael Strahan 2.00 5.00
15 Ray Lewis 2.50 6.00
16 Warren Moon 2.50 6.00
17 Russell Wilson 3.00 8.00
18 LaDainian Tomlinson 2.00 5.00
19 Ty Law 2.50 6.00
20 Matt Ryan 2.00 5.00

2018 Panini Human Highlight Reel

*GOLD/20: 1X TO 2.5X BASIC INSERTS
1 Antonio Brown 1.00 2.50
2 Julio Jones 1.00 2.50
3 Ezekiel Elliott 1.25 3.00
4 Alvin Kamara .75 2.00
5 Odell Beckham Jr. 1.00 2.50
6 Le'Veon Bell .75 2.00
7 Stefon Diggs .75 2.00
8 Tom Brady 2.50 6.00
9 DeAndre Hopkins .75 2.00
10 Russell Wilson 1.25 3.00
11 David Johnson 1.00 2.50
12 Aaron Rodgers 2.00 5.00
13 Kareem Hunt .75 2.00
14 Cam Newton 1.00 2.50
15 Jordan Howard 1.00 2.50
16 T.Y. Hilton .75 2.00
17 Leonard Fournette 1.00 2.50
18 Todd Gurley II 1.00 2.50
19 Keenan Allen .75 2.00
20 Carson Wentz 1.25 3.00

2018 Panini Lightspeed

*GOLD/20: 1X TO 2.5X BASIC INSERTS
1 Tyreek Hill 1.00 2.50
2 Marquise Goodwin .60 1.50
3 J.J. Nelson .60 1.50
4 Ted Ginn Jr. .60 1.50
5 DeSean Jackson .75 2.00
6 Jakeem Grant .60 1.50
7 John Ross III .75 2.00
8 Brandin Cooks .75 2.00
9 Melvin Gordon .75 2.00
10 Odell Beckham Jr. 1.00 2.50
11 Antonio Brown 1.00 2.50
12 Taywan Taylor .60 1.50
13 Elijah McGuire .60 1.50
14 A.J. Green 1.00 2.50
15 Leonard Fournette 1.00 2.50
16 Nelson Agholor .60 1.50
17 Travis Benjamin .60 1.50
18 Ezekiel Elliott 1.25 3.00
19 Tavon Austin .60 1.50
20 Amari Cooper 1.00 2.50

2018 Panini Panini All Pro

*GOLD/20: 1X TO 2.5X BASIC INSERTS
1 Tom Brady 2.50 6.00
2 Todd Gurley II 1.00 2.50
3 Rob Gronkowski 1.00 2.50
4 Antonio Brown 1.00 2.50
5 DeAndre Hopkins .75 2.00
6 Calais Campbell .60 1.50
7 Aaron Donald 1.00 2.50
8 Von Miller .75 2.00
9 Jalen Ramsey .75 2.00
10 Le'Veon Bell .75 2.00
11 Travis Kelce 1.00 2.50
12 Greg Zuerlein .60 1.50
13 Julio Jones 1.00 2.50
14 Adam Thielen 1.00 2.50
15 Alvin Kamara .75 2.00

2018 Panini Quest Jumbo Rookie Memorabilia

1 Sam Darnold 6.00 15.00
2 Josh Rosen 6.00 15.00
3 Baker Mayfield 6.00 15.00
4 Josh Allen 5.00 12.00
5 Mason Rudolph 4.00 10.00
6 Saquon Barkley 12.00 30.00
7 Derrius Guice 3.00 8.00
8 Nick Chubb 5.00 12.00
9 Sony Michel 4.00 10.00
10 Ronald Jones II 1.50 4.00
11 Calvin Ridley 4.00 10.00
12 Courtland Sutton 2.50 6.00
13 Christian Kirk 2.50 6.00
14 Anthony Miller 2.50 6.00
15 D.J. Chark 2.00 5.00
16 D.J. Moore 3.00 8.00
17 Lamar Jackson 6.00 15.00
18 Mike Gesicki 2.00 5.00
19 Kyle Lauletta 2.50 6.00
20 Mike White 2.00 5.00
21 Mark Walton 2.00 5.00
22 Royce Freeman 2.00 5.00
23 Kerryon Johnson 2.50 6.00
24 Rashaad Penny 2.50 6.00
25 Kalen Ballage 2.00 5.00
26 Nyheim Hines 2.00 5.00
27 Ito Smith 2.00 5.00
28 James Washington 3.00 8.00
29 Keke Coutee 2.00 5.00
30 J'Mon Moore 1.50 4.00
31 Michael Gallup 3.00 8.00
32 Dante Pettis 2.50 6.00
33 Jaylen Samuels 2.00 5.00
34 DaeSean Hamilton 2.00 5.00
35 Tre'Quan Smith 2.50 6.00
36 Jaleel Scott 1.50 4.00
37 Marquez Valdes-Scantling 2.00 5.00

38 Daurice Fountain 2.00 5.00
39 Hayden Hurst 2.00 5.00
40 Bradley Chubb 2.50 6.00

2012 Panini Jumbo Materials Toronto Fall Expo

DW Danny Watkins 4.00 10.00
MD Marcell Dareus 4.00 10.00

2012 Panini Materials Toronto Fall Expo

8 Robert Griffin III SP
9 T.J. Graham 3.00 8.00
10 Ryan Broyles 4.00 10.00
11 Danny Watkins 3.00 8.00

2012 Panini Black

1-200/R1-R35 STATED PRINT RUN 349
1 Aaron Rodgers 3.00 8.00
2 Greg Jennings 1.25 3.00
3 Jordy Nelson 1.50 4.00
4 Joe Flacco 1.50 4.00
5 Anquan Boldin 1.25 3.00
6 Ray Rice 1.25 3.00
7 Ray Lewis 2.00 5.00
8 Andy Dalton 1.50 4.00
9 A.J. Green 2.00 5.00
10 BenJarvus Green-Ellis 1.50 4.00
11 Josh Cribbs 1.25 3.00
12 Greg Little 1.25 3.00
13 Ben Roethlisberger 2.00 5.00
14 Mike Wallace 1.25 3.00
15 Isaac Redman 2.00 5.00
16 Matt Schaub 1.25 3.00
17 Andre Johnson 1.50 4.00
18 Arian Foster 1.50 4.00
19 Reggie Wayne 1.50 4.00
20 Austin Collie 1.25 3.00
21 Donald Brown 1.25 3.00
22 Blaine Gabbert 1.25 3.00
23 Maurice Jones-Drew 1.25 3.00
24 Marcedes Lewis 1.25 3.00
25 Jake Locker 2.00 5.00
26 Kenny Britt 1.25 3.00
27 Chris Johnson 1.25 3.00
28 Ryan Fitzpatrick 1.25 3.00
29 Steve Johnson 1.50 4.00
30 Fred Jackson 1.50 4.00
31 Reggie Bush 1.25 3.00
32 Davone Bess 1.25 3.00
33 Daniel Thomas 1.25 3.00
34 Tom Brady 5.00 12.00
35 Rob Gronkowski 2.00 5.00
36 Wes Welker 1.50 4.00
37 Aaron Hernandez 1.50 4.00
38 Mark Sanchez 1.25 3.00
39 Shonn Greene 1.25 3.00
40 Tim Tebow 2.00 5.00
41 Santonio Holmes 1.25 3.00
42 Peyton Manning 4.00 10.00
43 Demaryius Thomas 2.00 5.00
44 Willis McGahee 1.25 3.00
45 Matthew Stafford 1.50 4.00
46 Calvin Johnson 2.00 5.00
47 Ndamukong Suh 1.50 4.00
48 Jay Cutler 1.25 3.00
49 Brandon Marshall 1.50 4.00
50 Matt Forte 1.25 3.00
51 Cam Newton 2.00 5.00
52 Steve Smith 1.50 4.00
53 DeAngelo Williams 1.25 3.00
54 Larry Fitzgerald 1.50 4.00
55 Kevin Kolb 1.25 3.00
56 Beanie Wells 1.25 3.00
57 Matt Ryan 1.50 4.00
58 Michael Turner 1.25 3.00
59 Roddy White 1.25 3.00
60 Christian Ponder 1.25 3.00
61 Percy Harvin 1.25 3.00
62 Adrian Peterson 2.00 5.00
63 Drew Brees 2.00 5.00
64 Marques Colston 1.25 3.00
65 Darren Sproles 1.50 4.00
66 Eli Manning 1.50 4.00
67 Ahmad Bradshaw 1.25 3.00
68 Hakeem Nicks 1.25 3.00
69 Victor Cruz 1.50 4.00
70 Carson Palmer 1.50 4.00
71 Darren McFadden 1.25 3.00
72 Darrius Heyward-Bey 1.25 3.00
73 Michael Vick 1.50 4.00
74 LeSean McCoy 2.00 5.00
75 DeSean Jackson 1.50 4.00
76 Jeremy Maclin 1.25 3.00
77 Philip Rivers 2.00 5.00
78 Antonio Gates 1.50 4.00
79 Ryan Mathews 1.50 4.00
80 Alex Smith 1.50 4.00
81 Frank Gore 1.50 4.00
82 Vernon Davis 1.25 3.00
83 Tony Romo 1.50 4.00
84 DeMarco Murray 1.50 4.00
85 Dez Bryant 2.00 5.00
86 Jason Witten 1.50 4.00
87 Marshawn Lynch 1.50 4.00
88 Golden Tate 1.25 3.00
89 Sidney Rice 1.25 3.00
90 Sam Bradford 1.25 3.00
91 Steven Jackson 1.25 3.00
92 Dallas Clark 1.25 3.00
93 Josh Freeman 1.50 4.00
94 Vincent Jackson 1.25 3.00
95 Santana Moss 1.50 4.00
96 Pierre Garcon 1.50 4.00
97 Roy Helu 1.25 3.00
98 Matt Cassel 1.25 3.00
99 Jamaal Charles 1.50 4.00
100 Dwayne Bowe 1.50 4.00
101 Adrien Robinson RC 1.50 4.00
102 Alfred Morris RC 1.50 4.00
103 Andre Branch RC 1.50 4.00
104 B.J. Coleman RC 1.50 4.00
105 B.J. Cunningham RC 1.50 4.00
106 Bobby Rainey RC 1.50 4.00
107 Bobby Wagner RC 2.50 6.00
108 Brandon Bolden RC 1.50 4.00
109 Brandon Hardin RC 2.00 5.00
110 Brandon Taylor RC 1.50 4.00
111 Bruce Irvin RC 2.00 5.00
112 Bryce Brown RC 1.50 4.00
113 Case Keenum RC 3.00 8.00
114 Casey Hayward RC 1.50 4.00
115 Chandler Harnish RC 1.50 4.00
116 Chandler Jones RC 1.50 4.00
117 Chris Polk RC 1.50 4.00
118 Chris Rainey RC 1.50 4.00
119 Cory Harkey RC 2.00 5.00
120 Coty Sensabaugh RC 2.00 5.00
121 Courtney Upshaw RC 2.00 5.00
122 Cyrus Gray RC 1.50 4.00
123 Dan Herron RC 1.50 4.00
124 Danny Coale RC 1.50 4.00
125 David DeCastro RC 1.50 4.00
126 Davin Meggett RC 1.50 4.00
127 Deangelo Peterson RC 1.50 4.00
128 Demario Davis RC 1.50 4.00
129 Derek Wolfe RC 2.00 5.00
130 Devon Still RC 2.00 5.00
131 Devon Wylie RC 1.50 4.00
132 Dont'a Hightower RC 2.50 6.00
133 Dontari Poe RC 1.50 4.00
134 Dre Kirkpatrick RC 1.50 4.00
135 Bill Bentley RC 2.00 5.00
136 Jeff Demps RC 2.00 5.00
137 Josh Gordon RC 4.00 10.00
138 Fletcher Cox RC 2.50 6.00
139 George Iloka RC 1.50 4.00
140 Gerell Robinson RC 1.50 4.00
141 Rod Streater RC 2.50 6.00
142 Harrison Smith RC 1.50 4.00
143 Jamell Fleming RC 1.50 4.00
144 James Hanna RC 1.50 4.00
145 Janoris Jenkins RC 2.00 5.00
146 Jared Crick RC 1.50 4.00
147 Jeff Fuller RC 1.50 4.00
148 Jerel Worthy RC 1.50 4.00
149 Jonathan Martin RC 1.50 4.00
150 Josh Robinson RC 2.50 6.00
151 Juron Criner RC 1.50 4.00
152 Kellen Moore RC 2.00 5.00
153 Kendall Reyes RC 1.50 4.00
154 Keshawn Martin RC 2.00 5.00
155 Kevin Zeitler RC 1.50 4.00
156 Kirk Cousins RC 6.00 15.00
157 Ladarius Green RC 1.50 4.00
158 LaVon Brazill RC 2.50 6.00
159 Lavonte David RC 2.50 6.00
160 Luke Kuechly RC 4.00 10.00
161 Marc Tyler RC 1.50 4.00
162 Mark Barron RC 1.50 4.00
163 Marquis Maze RC 1.50 4.00
164 Marvin Jones RC 1.50 4.00
165 Marvin McNutt RC 1.50 4.00
166 Matt Kalil RC 1.50 4.00
167 Melvin Ingram RC 1.50 4.00
168 Michael Brockers RC 1.50 4.00
169 Michael Smith RC 2.00 5.00
170 Mike Martin RC 2.00 5.00
171 Morris Claiborne RC 1.50 4.00
172 Mychal Kendricks RC 2.50 6.00
173 Najee Goode RC 1.50 4.00
174 Nick Perry RC 2.00 5.00
175 Olivier Vernon RC 2.50 6.00
176 Omar Bolden RC 2.00 5.00
177 Orson Charles RC 1.50 4.00
178 Quinton Coples RC 1.50 4.00
179 Rhett Ellison RC 2.00 5.00
180 Riley Reiff RC 1.50 4.00
181 Rishard Matthews RC 1.50 4.00
182 Ronnell Lewis RC 1.50 4.00
183 Ryan Lindley RC 1.50 4.00
184 Sean Spence RC 2.00 5.00
185 Shea McClellin RC 2.00 5.00
186 Stephon Gilmore RC 2.00 5.00
187 T.Y. Hilton RC 3.00 8.00
188 Tauren Poole RC 1.50 4.00
189 Tavon Wilson RC 2.00 5.00
190 Terrance Ganaway RC 2.00 5.00
191 Tim Benford RC 1.50 4.00
192 Tommy Streeter RC 1.50 4.00
193 Travis Benjamin RC 1.50 4.00
194 Trumaine Johnson RC 1.50 4.00
195 Tyrone Crawford RC 1.50 4.00
196 Vick Ballard RC 2.00 5.00
197 Vinny Curry RC 2.00 5.00
198 Vontaze Burfict RC 2.00 5.00
199 Whitney Mercilus RC 1.50 4.00
200 Zach Brown RC 1.50 4.00
R1 Andrew Luck JSY AU RC 100.00 200.00
R2 Robert Griffin III JSY AU RC 6.00 15.00
R3 Trent Richardson JSY AU RC 5.00 12.00
R4 Ryan Tannehill JSY AU RC 8.00 20.00
R5 Justin Blackmon JSY AU RC 5.00 12.00
R6 Brandon Weeden JSY AU RC 5.00 12.00
R7 Brock Osweiler JSY AU RC 5.00 12.00
R8 Michael Floyd JSY AU RC 5.00 12.00
R9 Kendall Wright JSY AU RC 5.00 12.00
R10 A.J. Jenkins JSY AU RC 5.00 12.00
R11 Doug Martin JSY AU RC 8.00 20.00
R12 Lamar Miller JSY AU RC 8.00 20.00
R13 Isaiah Pead JSY AU RC 5.00 12.00
R14 David Wilson JSY AU RC 5.00 12.00
R15 Stephen Hill JSY AU RC 5.00 12.00
R16 Mohamed Sanu JSY AU RC 8.00 20.00
R17 Bernard Pierce JSY AU RC 5.00 12.00
R18 Nick Foles JSY AU RC 40.00 80.00
R19 LaMichael James JSY AU RC 5.00 12.00
R20 Rueben Randle JSY AU RC 5.00 12.00
R21 Coby Fleener JSY AU RC 5.00 12.00
R22 Ryan Broyles JSY AU RC 5.00 12.00
R23 Dwayne Allen JSY AU RC 5.00 12.00
R24 Ronnie Hillman JSY AU RC 5.00 12.00
R25 Russell Wilson JSY AU RC 75.00 150.00
R26 Michael Egnew JSY AU RC 5.00 12.00
R27 Chris Givens JSY AU RC 5.00 12.00
R28 Joe Adams JSY AU RC 5.00 12.00
R29 Robert Turbin JSY AU RC 5.00 12.00
R30 Nick Toon JSY AU RC 5.00 12.00
R31 T.J. Graham JSY AU RC 5.00 12.00
R32 Brian Quick JSY AU RC 5.00 12.00
R33 DeVier Posey JSY AU RC 5.00 12.00
R34 Jarius Wright JSY AU RC 5.00 12.00
R35 Alshon Jeffery JSY AU RC 12.00 30.00

2012 Panini Black Gold

-100 VETS/49: .6X TO 1.5X BASIC CARDS
*101-200 ROOKIE/49: .6X TO 1.5X BASIC RC

2012 Panini Black Platinum

*1-100 VETS/25: .8X TO 2X BASIC CARDS
*101-200 ROOKIE/25: .8X TO 2X BASIC RC

2012 Panini Black Captains

1 Larry Fitzgerald 3.00 8.00
2 Matt Ryan 3.00 8.00
3 Ryan Fitzpatrick 2.50 6.00
4 Steve Smith 3.00 8.00
5 Brian Urlacher 4.00 10.00
6 Champ Bailey 3.00 8.00
7 Matthew Stafford 3.00 8.00
8 Andre Johnson 3.00 8.00
9 Blaine Gabbert 2.50 6.00
10 Matt Cassel 2.50 6.00
11 Kevin Williams 3.00 8.00
12 D'Qwell Jackson 2.50 6.00
13 Tom Brady 10.00 25.00
14 Drew Brees 5.00 12.00
15 Eli Manning 3.00 8.00
16 Darren McFadden 2.50 6.00
17 Ben Roethlisberger 6.00 15.00
18 Philip Rivers 4.00 10.00
19 Frank Gore 3.00 8.00
20 Steven Jackson 2.50 6.00
21 Josh Freeman 3.00 8.00
22 Rey Maualuga 2.50 6.00
23 London Fletcher 4.00 10.00
24 Jake Locker 4.00 10.00
25 DeMarcus Ware 4.00 10.00
26 Red Bryant 2.50 6.00

2012 Panini Black Honors

1 Tom Brady 5.00 12.00
2 Peyton Manning 4.00 10.00
3 Brett Favre 4.00 10.00
4 Ray Lewis 2.00 5.00
5 LaDainian Tomlinson 2.00 5.00
6 Barry Sanders 3.00 8.00
7 Emmitt Smith 3.00 8.00
8 Andre Johnson 1.50 4.00
9 Jerry Rice 3.00 8.00
10 Drew Brees 2.00 5.00
11 Marshall Faulk 1.50 4.00
12 Bart Starr 3.00 8.00
13 Eli Manning 1.50 4.00
14 Priest Holmes 1.25 3.00
15 Randy Moss 1.50 4.00
16 Larry Fitzgerald 1.50 4.00
17 Steve Young 2.50 6.00
18 Dan Marino 4.00 10.00
19 DeMarcus Ware 2.00 4.00
20 Ed Reed 1.50 4.00

2012 Panini Black Man 2 Man

1 D.Bryant/N.Asomugha 2.00 5.00
2 C.Bailey/D.Bowe 1.50 4.00
3 H.Nicks/M.Jenkins 1.25 3.00
4 D.McCourty/S.Holmes 1.25 3.00
5 D.Revis/W.Welker 1.50 4.00
6 A.Cromartie/S.Johnson 1.50 4.00
7 J.Maclin/T.Thomas 1.25 3.00
8 B.Grimes/S.Smith 1.50 4.00
9 A.Green/J.Haden 2.00 5.00
10 D.Hall/M.Austin 1.25 3.00
11 A.Johnson/C.Finnegan 1.50 4.00
12 J.Joseph/R.Wayne 1.50 4.00
13 M.Crabtree/P.Peterson 1.25 3.00
14 C.Johnson/C.Woodson 2.00 5.00
15 C.Gamble/R.White 1.25 3.00
16 D.Rodgers-Cromartie/S.Moss 1.50 4.00
17 C.Rogers/L.Fitzgerald 1.50 4.00
18 D.Jackson/D.Robinson 1.50 4.00
19 A.Boldin/I.Taylor 1.25 3.00
20 C.Tillman/G.Jennings 1.50 4.00
21 L.Webb/M.Wallace 1.25 3.00

2012 Panini Black Marks of Distinction

1 Eli Manning/25 30.00 80.00
2 Andre Reed/49 12.00 30.00
3 Ahmad Bradshaw/49 12.00 30.00
4 Anquan Boldin/30 8.00 20.00
5 Antonio Gates/20 12.00 30.00
6 Archie Manning/18 20.00 50.00
8 Beanie Wells/49 8.00 20.00
9 BenJarvus Green-Ellis/49 12.00 30.00
10 Brandon Jacobs/49 8.00 20.00
11 Brandon Lloyd/49 12.00 30.00
12 Brandon Pettigrew/49 8.00 20.00
13 Brian Cushing/75 8.00 20.00
14 Brian Hartline/75 8.00 20.00
15 Brian Orakpo/75 8.00 20.00
16 Eric Dickerson/25 40.00 80.00
17 Charles Woodson/21 75.00 150.00
18 Torrey Smith/49 8.00 20.00
20 Dallas Clark/44 8.00 20.00
21 Sonny Jurgensen/49 12.00 30.00
22 Darren Sproles/25 12.00 30.00
23 Darrius Heyward-Bey/75 6.00 15.00
24 David Nelson/99 6.00 15.00
25 DeAngelo Williams/34 8.00 20.00
27 Deuce McAllister/20 12.00 30.00
28 Devin Hester/49 12.00 30.00
29 Donald Driver/25 15.00 40.00
30 Doug Flutie/25 12.00 30.00
31 Frank Gore/20 12.00 30.00
32 Fred Davis/99 8.00 20.00
33 Fred Jackson/49 10.00 25.00
34 Fred Taylor/28 12.00 30.00
35 Greg Jennings/49 8.00 20.00
36 Greg Little/99 6.00 15.00
37 Greg Olsen/49 10.00 25.00
38 Heath Miller/49 12.00 30.00
39 Brandon LaFell/75 6.00 15.00
40 Jacoby Ford/99 6.00 15.00
41 James Laurinaitis/99 10.00 25.00
42 James Starks/99 6.00 15.00
43 Jared Allen/69 6.00 15.00
44 Jason Witten/25 30.00 60.00
45 Adrian Peterson/25 40.00 100.00
46 Jermaine Gresham/84 6.00 15.00
47 Jermichael Finley/88 10.00 25.00
49 Jordy Nelson/75 10.00 25.00
50 Jay Novacek/49 12.00 30.00
51 Keyshawn Johnson/20 12.00 30.00
52 Knowshon Moreno/49 8.00 20.00
53 Jon Beason/99 8.00 20.00
54 LeGarrette Blount/99 8.00 20.00
55 London Fletcher/49 12.00 30.00
56 Mario Williams/49 8.00 20.00
57 Marshawn Lynch/49 30.00 60.00
58 Cam Newton/25 50.00 100.00
59 Michael Turner/33 8.00 20.00
60 Nnamdi Asomugha/49 8.00 20.00
61 Owen Daniels/49 10.00 25.00
62 Patrick Willis/49 15.00 40.00
63 Percy Harvin/49 8.00 20.00
64 Herman Moore/99 8.00 20.00
65 Pierre Garcon/49 10.00 25.00
66 Pierre Thomas/49 8.00 20.00
67 Plaxico Burress/49 8.00 20.00
68 Vinny Testaverde/49 10.00 25.00
69 Daryle Lamonica/49 10.00 25.00
70 Rob Gronkowski/49 15.00 40.00
71 Roddy White/25 10.00 25.00
72 Matt Cassel/25 10.00 25.00
73 Roy Helu/49 8.00 20.00
74 Ryan Fitzpatrick/25 10.00 25.00
76 Matt Schaub/25 10.00 25.00
77 DeMarcus Ware/49 12.00 30.00
78 Alex Smith/25 12.00 30.00
79 Steve Johnson/49 10.00 25.00
82 Brett Favre/25 75.00 150.00
83 Vincent Jackson/49 8.00 20.00
84 Von Miller/20 12.00 30.00
85 =D1618&"/"&J1618 6.00 15.00

2012 Panini Black Materials Combos

RIME/33-49: .5X TO 1.2X BASIC COMBO
*PRIME/15-28: .6X TO 1.5X BASIC COMBO
1 B.Wells/E.James/25 6.00 15.00
3 E.Reed/R.Lewis/50 10.00 25.00
4 D.Flutie/R.Fitzpatrick/50 6.00 15.00
5 D.Williams/S.Smith/50 5.00 12.00
6 E.Smith/T.Dorsett/50 15.00 40.00
7 T.Romo/T.Aikman/50 12.00 30.00
8 C.Bailey/V.Miller/35 10.00 25.00
9 A.Rodgers/D.Jackson/50 10.00 25.00
10 A.Johnson/A.Foster/50 5.00 12.00
12 F.Taylor/M.Jones-Drew/25 6.00 15.00
13 D.Henderson/D.Bowe/50 5.00 12.00
14 J.Charles/R.Williams/50 5.00 12.00
15 A.Peterson/H.Walker/50 12.00 30.00
16 T.Brady/W.Welker/50 8.00 20.00
17 D.Brees/M.Colston/50 6.00 15.00
18 E.Manning/H.Nicks/50 5.00 12.00
19 M.Sanchez/S.Greene/50 4.00 10.00
20 D.McFadden/F.Jones/50 4.00 10.00
23 P.Rivers/R.Mathews/50 6.00 15.00
24 J.Montana/V.Davis/50 20.00 50.00
26 M.Faulk/S.Jackson/50 5.00 12.00
27 J.Elway/R.Smith/50 12.00 30.00
29 J.Freeman/K.Johnson/50 5.00 12.00
30 D.Brooks/W.Sapp/50 6.00 15.00
31 C.Johnson/E.George/50 6.00 15.00
32 D.Hester/S.Moss/50 5.00 12.00
33 K.Warner/L.Fitzgerald/50 5.00 12.00
35 J.Flacco/R.Rice/50 5.00 12.00
36 M.Forte/W.Payton/50 15.00 40.00
37 B.Urlacher/J.Cutler/50 6.00 15.00
39 J.Witten/J.Novacek/50 10.00 25.00
40 D.Bryant/M.Irvin/50 12.00 30.00
42 E.McCaffrey/E.Decker/50 8.00 20.00
43 A.Boldin/T.Suggs/50 4.00 10.00
45 D.Driver/G.Jennings/50 5.00 12.00
46 B.Favre/S.Sharpe/50 10.00 25.00
48 D.Bowe/M.Cassel/50 5.00 12.00
49 A.Bradshaw/T.Barber/50 5.00 12.00
50 M.Wallace/R.Mendenhall/50 4.00 10.00

2012 Panini Black Materials Quads

*PRIME/49: .5X TO 1.2X BASIC QUAD/75
*PRIME/28-33: .6X TO 1.5X BASIC QUAD/75
*PRIME/25: .5X TO 1.2X BASIC QUAD/25
1 Favre/Marino/Elway/Moon/75 25.00 60.00
2 Bettis/Allen/Holmes/Dorsett/75 12.00 30.00
3 Brees/Manning/Brady/Romo/75 15.00 40.00
5 Jhnsn/Brynt/Nicks/Fitzgrad/75 12.00 30.00
8 Boldin/Reed/Wallce/Polam/50 12.00 30.00
9 Rodgers/Vick/Cunng/S.Yng/75 15.00 40.00
11 Bowe/Floyd/Cassel/Rivers/75 12.00 30.00
12 Sndrs/Jhnsn/Jns-Drw/Dunn/25 15.00 40.00
13 Austin/Mthws/Grne/Welker/75 10.00 25.00
15 Driver/Warnr/Hassel/Lewis/75 12.00 30.00
16 Cutler/Freeman/Moss/Smith/75 10.00 25.00
18 McFad/Chrles/Forte/Jcksn/75 10.00 25.00

2012 Panini Black Materials Triples

*PRIME/30-49: .5X TO 1.2X BASIC TRIPLE/50
*PRIME/15: .6X TO 1.5X BASIC TRIPLE/50
*PRIME/15: .5X TO 1.2X BASIC TRIPLE/25
1 Wells/James/Plummer/50 6.00 15.00
2 Abraham/Turner/White/50 5.00 12.00
3 Boldin/Reed/Ngata/40 6.00 15.00
5 Williams/Stewart/Smith/50 6.00 15.00
6 Johnson/Hester/Gore/19 8.00 20.00
7 Manning/Wallace/Willis/50 6.00 15.00
8 Sanchez/Cassel/Polamalu/50 8.00 20.00
11 Stokley/McCaffrey/Decker/25 15.00 40.00
14 Gates/Floyd/Rivers/50 8.00 20.00
15 Ward/Farrior/Harrison/50 12.00 30.00
17 Nicks/Cutler/Peppers/50 6.00 15.00
18 Johnson/Kearse/Hasselbeck/50 5.00 12.00
20 Bowe/Charles/Cassel/50 6.00 15.00
21 Jackson/Maclin/Vick/50 6.00 15.00
22 Martin/McCourty/Brady/50 20.00 50.00
23 Flacco/Lewis/Rice/50 10.00 25.00
24 Flutie/Kelly/Fitzpatrick/50 10.00 25.00
28 Lynch/Alexander/Miller/50 6.00 15.00

2012 Panini Black NFL Equipment

Maurice Jones-Drew/20 5.00 12.00
2 Adrian Peterson/99 8.00 20.00
3 Ray Lewis/99 5.00 12.00
4 Marcedes Lewis/99 3.00 8.00
5 Greg Jennings/99 3.00 8.00
6 Terrell Suggs/99 3.00 8.00
7 Michael Turner/99 3.00 8.00
8 Steve Smith/99 4.00 10.00
9 Brian Urlacher/99 5.00 12.00
10 Devin Hester/99 4.00 10.00
11 Philip Rivers/99 5.00 12.00
12 Roddy White/99 3.00 8.00
13 Santonio Holmes/80 3.00 8.00
14 Dez Bryant/99 5.00 12.00
15 Miles Austin/25 5.00 12.00
16 Tony Romo/99 4.00 10.00
17 Donald Driver/99 4.00 10.00
18 Charles Woodson/40 8.00 20.00
19 Arian Foster/99 4.00 10.00
20 Dwayne Bowe/99 4.00 10.00
22 Michael Vick/99 4.00 10.00
23 Vernon Davis/99 3.00 8.00
24 Tom Brady/49 15.00 40.00
25 Andre Johnson/99 4.00 10.00
26 Marques Colston/99 3.00 8.00
27 Devery Henderson/99 3.00 8.00
28 Eli Manning/99 4.00 10.00
32 Jeremy Maclin/99 3.00 8.00
33 DeSean Jackson/99 4.00 10.00
34 Troy Polamalu/99 5.00 12.00
35 Rashard Mendenhall/99 3.00 8.00
36 Mike Wallace/99 3.00 8.00
37 James Harrison/60 6.00 15.00
38 Heath Miller/99 3.00 8.00
39 Ben Roethlisberger/18 8.00 20.00
40 Antonio Gates/99 4.00 10.00
42 Ryan Mathews/99 4.00 10.00
45 Frank Gore/99 4.00 10.00
46 Jamaal Charles/99 4.00 10.00
47 Steven Jackson/99 3.00 8.00
48 Chris Johnson/49 4.00 10.00
49 Santana Moss/99 4.00 10.00
51 Jake Plummer/99 3.00 8.00
52 Kurt Warner/99 4.00 10.00
54 Christian Ponder/99 3.00 8.00
55 Jim Kelly/99 5.00 12.00
56 Doug Flutie/99 4.00 10.00
57 Joe Flacco/99 4.00 10.00
58 Corey Dillon/20 5.00 12.00
59 Emmitt Smith/22 15.00 40.00
61 Roger Staubach/99 8.00 20.00
62 Brett Favre/99 10.00 25.00
63 Sterling Sharpe/99 5.00 12.00
68 Curtis Martin/99 4.00 10.00
70 Jerome Bettis/35 12.00 30.00
71 Brian Orakpo/99 4.00 10.00
72 Steve Young/99 6.00 15.00
73 Jerry Rice/99 8.00 20.00
75 Wes Welker/99 4.00 10.00

2012 Panini Black NFL Equipment Prime

*PRIME/49: .6X TO 1.5X BASIC JSY/60-99
*PRIME/49: .4X TO 1X BASIC JSY/20-25
*PRIME/15 25: .8X TO 2X BASIC JSY/80 99
29 Hakeem Nicks/49 5.00 12.00
66 Marcus Allen/49 8.00 20.00

2012 Panini Black NFL Equipment Combos

RIME/35-49: .5X TO 1.2X COMBO/50-99
*PRIME/20-28: .6X TO 1.5X COMBO/99
*PRIME/20-28: .5X TO 1.2X COMBO/49-50
*PRIME/20-28: .4X TO 1X COMBO/20-25
1 Maurice Jones-Drew/20 6.00 15.00
2 Adrian Peterson/99 10.00 25.00
3 Ray Lewis/99 6.00 15.00
4 Marcedes Lewis/50 5.00 12.00
5 Greg Jennings/99 4.00 10.00
6 Terrell Suggs/99 4.00 10.00
7 Michael Turner/99 4.00 10.00
8 Steve Smith/99 5.00 12.00
9 Brian Urlacher/99 6.00 15.00
10 Devin Hester/99 5.00 12.00
11 Philip Rivers/99 6.00 15.00
12 Roddy White/99 4.00 10.00
13 Santonio Holmes/45 5.00 12.00
14 Dez Bryant/99 6.00 15.00
16 Tony Romo/99 5.00 12.00
17 Donald Driver/50 6.00 15.00
18 Charles Woodson/99 10.00 25.00
19 Arian Foster/99 5.00 12.00
20 Dwayne Bowe/99 5.00 12.00
22 Michael Vick/99 5.00 12.00
23 Vernon Davis/99 4.00 10.00
24 Tom Brady/49 20.00 50.00
25 Andre Johnson/99 5.00 12.00
26 Marques Colston/99 4.00 10.00
27 Devery Henderson/99 4.00 10.00
28 Eli Manning/99 5.00 12.00
30 Dustin Keller/15 6.00 15.00
32 Jeremy Maclin/99 4.00 10.00
33 DeSean Jackson/99 5.00 12.00
34 Troy Polamalu/99 6.00 15.00
35 Rashard Mendenhall/99 4.00 10.00
36 Mike Wallace/99 4.00 10.00
37 James Harrison/25 12.00 30.00
38 Heath Miller/99 4.00 10.00
40 Antonio Gates/99 5.00 12.00
41 Malcom Floyd/20 6.00 15.00
42 Ryan Mathews/99 5.00 12.00
43 Patrick Willis/25 8.00 20.00
44 Michael Crabtree/20 6.00 15.00
45 Frank Gore/20 8.00 20.00
46 Jamaal Charles/99 5.00 12.00
47 Steven Jackson/99 4.00 10.00
48 Chris Johnson/99 4.00 10.00
49 Santana Moss/99 5.00 12.00
50 Edgerrin James/99 5.00 12.00
51 Jake Plummer/99 4.00 10.00
52 Kurt Warner/99 5.00 12.00
54 Christian Ponder/99 4.00 10.00
55 Jim Kelly/99 6.00 15.00
56 Doug Flutie/99 5.00 12.00
57 Joe Flacco/99 5.00 12.00
58 Corey Dillon/99 4.00 10.00
59 Emmitt Smith/99 12.00 30.00
60 Michael Irvin/49 8.00 20.00
61 Roger Staubach/99 10.00 25.00
62 Brett Favre/99 12.00 30.00
63 Sterling Sharpe/99 6.00 15.00
65 Fred Taylor/99 4.00 10.00
66 Marcus Allen/49 8.00 20.00
68 Curtis Martin/99 5.00 12.00
69 Priest Holmes/99 4.00 10.00
70 Jerome Bettis/20 20.00 50.00
71 Brian Orakpo/99 5.00 12.00
72 Steve Young/99 8.00 20.00
73 Jerry Rice/99 10.00 25.00
74 Tim Brown/15 10.00 25.00
75 Wes Welker/99 5.00 12.00

2012 Panini Black NFL Equipment Signatures

1 Antonio Gates/15 12.00 30.00
2 Darren McFadden/20
3 Jamaal Charles/20 12.00 30.00
4 Jeremy Maclin/20 10.00 25.00
6 Josh Cribbs/20 10.00 25.00
9 Steve Largent/20 15.00 40.00
10 Ray Rice/20 15.00 40.00
11 Shonn Greene/20
12 Steve Smith/20 15.00 40.00
13 Ryan Fitzpatrick/20 10.00 25.00
14 Von Miller/20 15.00 40.00
15 Cris Carter/20 30.00 60.00
16 Doug Flutie/20 12.00 30.00
20 Barry Sanders/20 60.00 120.00
21 Ronnie Lott/20 15.00 40.00
22 Ozzie Newsome/20 15.00 40.00
23 Jason Witten/20 30.00 60.00
24 Steve Bartkowski/20 12.00 30.00
25 Steve Young/20 30.00 60.00

2012 Panini Black Onyx Rookie Materials

*PRIME/49: .6X TO 1.5X BASIC JSY/299
*JUM PRIME/25: .8X TO 2X BASIC JSY/299
*JSY # PRIME/10: 1.2X TO 3X BASIC JSY/299
1 Andrew Luck 15.00 40.00
2 Robert Griffin III 2.00 5.00
3 Trent Richardson 1.50 4.00
4 Ryan Tannehill 2.50 6.00
5 Justin Blackmon 1.50 4.00
6 Brandon Weeden 1.50 4.00
7 Brock Osweiler 1.50 4.00
8 Michael Floyd 1.50 4.00
9 Kendall Wright 1.50 4.00
10 A.J. Jenkins 1.50 4.00
11 Doug Martin 2.50 6.00
12 Lamar Miller 2.50 6.00
13 Isaiah Pead 1.50 4.00
14 David Wilson 1.50 4.00
15 Stephen Hill 1.50 4.00
16 Mohamed Sanu 2.50 6.00
17 Bernard Pierce 1.50 4.00
18 Nick Foles 4.00 10.00
19 LaMichael James 1.50 4.00
20 Rueben Randle 1.50 4.00
21 Coby Fleener 1.50 4.00
22 Ryan Broyles 3.00 8.00
23 Dwayne Allen 1.50 4.00
24 Ronnie Hillman 1.50 4.00
25 Russell Wilson 12.00 30.00
26 Michael Egnew 1.50 4.00
27 Chris Givens 1.50 4.00
28 Joe Adams 1.50 4.00
29 Robert Turbin 1.50 4.00
30 Nick Toon 1.50 4.00
31 T.J. Graham 1.50 4.00
32 Brian Quick 1.50 4.00
33 DeVier Posey 1.50 4.00
34 Jarius Wright 1.50 4.00
35 Alshon Jeffery 3.00 8.00

2012 Panini Black Onyx Rookie Materials Signatures

*ONYX AU/25: .5X TO 1.2X JSY AU RC/349
1 Andrew Luck 125.00 250.00
2 Robert Griffin III 8.00 20.00
25 Russell Wilson 150.00 250.00

2012 Panini Black Rookie Signature Materials Prime Black

*PRM BLK/25: .5X TO 1.2X JSY AU RC/349
1 Andrew Luck 200.00 400.00
2 Robert Griffin III 8.00 20.00
4 Ryan Tannehill 10.00 25.00
18 Nick Foles 40.00 100.00
25 Russell Wilson 150.00 250.00

2012 Panini Black Rookie Signature Materials Prime Gold

*PRM GLD/99: .4X TO 1X JSY AU RC/349
1 Andrew Luck 100.00 200.00
25 Russell Wilson 75.00 150.00

2012 Panini Black Rookie Signature Materials Prime Platinum

*PRM PLAT/49: .5X TO 1.2X JSY AU RC/349
1 Andrew Luck 200.00 350.00
25 Russell Wilson 125.00 250.00

2012 Panini Black Rookie Signatures

*BLACK/25: .6X TO 1.5X BASIC AU/125-199
*GOLD/49-99: .5X TO 1.2X BASIC AU/125-199
*PLATINUM/49: .5X TO 1.2X BASIC AU/125-199
*PLATINUM/25: .6X TO 1.5X BASIC AU/125-199
EXCH EXPIRATION: 6/19/2014
101 Adrien Robinson/199 4.00 10.00
102 Alfred Morris/125 4.00 10.00
103 Andre Branch/199 4.00 10.00
104 B.J. Coleman/125 4.00 10.00
105 B.J. Cunningham/199 4.00 10.00
106 Bobby Rainey/199 4.00 10.00
107 Bobby Wagner/199 6.00 15.00
108 Brandon Bolden/199 4.00 10.00
109 Brandon Hardin/199 5.00 12.00
110 Brandon Taylor/199 4.00 10.00
111 Bruce Irvin/199 8.00 20.00
112 Bryce Brown/125 4.00 10.00
113 Case Keenum/199 8.00 20.00
114 Casey Hayward/199 4.00 10.00
115 Chandler Harnish/199 4.00 10.00
116 Chandler Jones/125 4.00 10.00
117 Chris Polk/199 4.00 10.00
118 Chris Rainey/125 4.00 10.00
119 Cory Harkey/199 5.00 12.00
120 Coty Sensabaugh/199 5.00 12.00
121 Courtney Upshaw/199 5.00 12.00
122 Cyrus Gray/199 4.00 10.00
123 Dan Herron/199 4.00 10.00
124 Danny Coale/199 4.00 10.00
125 David DeCastro/199 4.00 10.00
126 Davin Meggett/199 4.00 10.00
127 Deangelo Peterson/199 4.00 10.00
128 Demario Davis/199 4.00 10.00
129 Derek Wolfe/125 8.00 20.00
130 Devon Still/199 5.00 12.00
131 Devon Wylie/125 4.00 10.00
132 Dont'a Hightower/199 6.00 15.00
133 Dontari Poe/125 4.00 10.00
134 Dre Kirkpatrick/125 4.00 10.00
135 Bill Bentley/199 5.00 12.00
136 Jeff Demps/199 5.00 12.00
137 Josh Gordon/199 10.00 25.00
138 Fletcher Cox/199 6.00 15.00
139 George Iloka/199 4.00 10.00
140 Gerell Robinson/199 4.00 10.00
141 Rod Streater/125 6.00 15.00
142 Harrison Smith/199 4.00 10.00
143 Jamell Fleming/199 4.00 10.00
144 James Hanna/199 4.00 10.00
145 Janoris Jenkins/199 5.00 12.00
146 Jared Crick/125 4.00 10.00
147 Jeff Fuller/199 4.00 10.00
148 Jerel Worthy/199 4.00 10.00
149 Jonathan Martin/199 4.00 10.00
150 Josh Robinson/199 6.00 15.00
151 Juron Criner/199 4.00 10.00
152 Kellen Moore/199 5.00 12.00
153 Kendall Reyes/199 4.00 10.00
154 Keshawn Martin/125 5.00 12.00
155 Kevin Zeitler/199 4.00 10.00
156 Kirk Cousins/199 12.00 30.00
157 Ladarius Green/199 4.00 10.00
158 LaVon Brazill/199 6.00 15.00
159 Lavonte David/199 6.00 15.00
160 Luke Kuechly/199 10.00 25.00
161 Marc Tyler/199 4.00 10.00
162 Mark Barron/125 4.00 10.00
163 Marquis Maze/199 4.00 10.00
164 Marvin Jones/199 4.00 10.00
165 Marvin McNutt/199 4.00 10.00
166 Matt Kalil/125 4.00 10.00
167 Melvin Ingram/125 4.00 10.00
168 Michael Brockers/125 4.00 10.00
169 Michael Smith/125 5.00 12.00
170 Mike Martin/199 5.00 12.00
171 Morris Claiborne/199 4.00 10.00
172 Mychal Kendricks/199 6.00 15.00
173 Najee Goode/199 4.00 10.00
174 Nick Perry/125
175 Olivier Vernon/199 6.00 15.00
176 Omar Bolden/199 5.00 12.00
177 Orson Charles/199 4.00 10.00
178 Quinton Coples/199 4.00 10.00
179 Rhett Ellison/199 5.00 12.00
180 Riley Reiff/199 4.00 10.00
181 Rishard Matthews/199 4.00 10.00
182 Ronnell Lewis/199 4.00 10.00
183 Ryan Lindley/199 4.00 10.00
184 Sean Spence/199 5.00 12.00
185 Shea McClellin/125 5.00 12.00
186 Stephon Gilmore/125 5.00 12.00
187 T.Y. Hilton/125 8.00 20.00
188 Tauren Poole/199 4.00 10.00
189 Tavon Wilson/199 5.00 12.00
190 Terrance Ganaway/199 5.00 12.00
191 Tim Benford/199 4.00 10.00
192 Tommy Streeter/125 4.00 10.00
193 Travis Benjamin/199 4.00 10.00
194 Trumaine Johnson/199 4.00 10.00
195 Tyrone Crawford/199 4.00 10.00
196 Vick Ballard/199 10.00 25.00
197 Vinny Curry/199 5.00 12.00
198 Vontaze Burfict/199 5.00 12.00
199 Whitney Mercilus/199 4.00 10.00
200 Zach Brown/199 4.00 10.00

2012 Panini Black Stat Line Materials

1 Tom Brady/99 20.00 50.00
2 Wes Welker/99 6.00 15.00
3 Aaron Rodgers/50 12.00 30.00
4 Eli Manning/99 6.00 15.00
5 Adrian Peterson/99 8.00 20.00
6 Chris Johnson/50 5.00 12.00
7 Drew Brees/99 8.00 20.00
9 Philip Rivers/99 8.00 20.00
10 Ahmad Bradshaw/99 5.00 12.00
11 Miles Austin/25 6.00 15.00
12 London Fletcher/99 6.00 15.00
13 Calvin Johnson/25 10.00 25.00
14 Tony Gonzalez/15 8.00 20.00
15 Jason Witten/99 6.00 15.00
16 Ray Lewis/75 10.00 25.00
17 Andre Johnson/75 6.00 15.00
18 Reggie Wayne/50 6.00 15.00
19 Michael Vick/99 6.00 15.00
21 Larry Fitzgerald/99 6.00 15.00
22 Ray Rice/99 5.00 12.00
23 Steve Smith/99 6.00 15.00
24 Devin Hester/99 6.00 15.00
27 Arian Foster/99 6.00 15.00
28 Maurice Jones-Drew/20 6.00 15.00
29 Dwayne Bowe/99 6.00 15.00
30 Ed Reed/99 6.00 15.00

2012 Panini Black Stat Line Materials Prime

COMMON CARD/30-49 8.00 20.00
UNL.STARS/30-49 10.00 25.00
COMMON CARD/14-25 10.00 25.00
1 Tom Brady/49 25.00 60.00
2 Wes Welker/49 8.00 20.00
4 Eli Manning/49 8.00 20.00
5 Adrian Peterson/49 10.00 25.00
6 Chris Johnson/42 6.00 15.00
8 DeMarcus Ware/20 12.00 30.00
9 Philip Rivers/49 10.00 25.00
10 Ahmad Bradshaw/49 6.00 15.00
11 Miles Austin/49 6.00 15.00
12 London Fletcher/49 8.00 20.00
14 Tony Gonzalez/30 8.00 20.00
15 Jason Witten/49 8.00 20.00
16 Ray Lewis/14 15.00 40.00
19 Michael Vick/49 8.00 20.00
21 Larry Fitzgerald/49 8.00 20.00
22 Ray Rice/49 6.00 15.00
23 Steve Smith/30 8.00 20.00
24 Devin Hester/40 8.00 20.00
26 DeMarco Murray/25 10.00 25.00
27 Arian Foster/49 8.00 20.00
29 Dwayne Bowe/49 8.00 20.00

2012 Panini Black Weaponry

Ray Rice 1.25 3.00
2 A.J. Green 2.00 5.00
3 Mike Wallace 1.25 3.00
4 Andre Johnson 1.50 4.00
5 Greg Little 1.25 3.00
6 Chris Johnson 1.25 3.00
7 Steve Johnson 1.50 4.00
8 Wes Welker 1.50 4.00
9 Santonio Holmes 1.25 3.00
10 Dwayne Bowe 1.50 4.00
11 Darren McFadden 1.25 3.00
12 Reggie Wayne 1.50 4.00
13 Matt Forte 1.25 3.00
14 Calvin Johnson 2.00 5.00
15 Greg Jennings 1.25 3.00
16 Adrian Peterson 3.00 8.00
17 Roddy White 1.25 3.00
18 Maurice Jones-Drew 1.25 3.00
19 Steve Smith 1.50 4.00
20 Darren Sproles 1.50 4.00
21 Dez Bryant 2.00 5.00
22 Reggie Bush 1.25 3.00
23 Hakeem Nicks 1.25 3.00
24 Ryan Mathews 1.50 4.00
25 Vincent Jackson 1.25 3.00
26 Larry Fitzgerald 1.50 4.00
27 LeSean McCoy 2.00 5.00
28 Steven Jackson 1.25 3.00
29 Marshawn Lynch 1.50 4.00
30 Kenny Britt 1.25 3.00

2013 Panini Black

EXCH EXPIRATION: 7/22/2015
1 Adrian Peterson 2.00 5.00
2 Peyton Manning 4.00 10.00
3 Calvin Johnson 2.00 5.00
4 Tom Brady 5.00 12.00
5 J.J. Watt 1.50 4.00
6 Aaron Rodgers 3.00 8.00
7 Donte Whitner 1.25 3.00
8 Arian Foster 1.50 4.00
9 Von Miller 1.50 4.00
10 Patrick Willis 1.50 4.00
11 Drew Brees 2.00 5.00
12 DeMarcus Ware 2.00 5.00
13 Ray Rice 1.25 3.00
14 Andre Johnson 1.25 3.00
15 Robert Griffin III 1.25 3.00
16 A.J. Green 2.00 5.00
17 Matt Ryan 1.50 4.00
18 Ed Reed 1.50 4.00
19 Joe Flacco 1.50 4.00
20 Jamaal Charles 1.50 4.00
21 Reggie Wayne 1.50 4.00
22 Larry Fitzgerald 1.50 4.00
23 Andrew Luck 3.00 8.00
24 Marshawn Lynch 1.50 4.00
25 Rob Gronkowski 2.00 5.00
26 Julio Jones 2.00 5.00
27 Brandon Marshall 1.50 4.00
28 Joe Thomas 1.25 3.00
29 Justin Smith 1.25 3.00
30 Vince Wilfork 1.25 3.00
31 Clay Matthews 2.00 5.00
32 Frank Gore 1.50 4.00
33 Patrick Peterson 1.25 3.00
34 Charles Tillman 1.50 4.00
35 Dez Bryant 2.00 5.00
36 Geno Atkins 1.25 3.00
37 NaVorro Bowman 1.50 4.00
38 Vernon Davis 1.25 3.00
39 Roddy White 1.25 3.00
40 Ndamukong Suh 1.50 4.00
41 Jason Witten 1.50 4.00
42 Haloti Ngata 1.25 3.00
43 Eli Manning 1.50 4.00
44 Wes Welker 1.50 4.00
45 LeSean McCoy 2.00 5.00
46 Cam Newton 2.00 5.00
47 Tony Gonzalez 1.50 4.00
48 Duane Brown 1.25 3.00
49 Justin Houston 1.25 3.00
50 Richard Sherman 2.00 5.00
51 Russell Wilson 4.00 10.00
52 Vincent Jackson 1.25 3.00
53 Champ Bailey 1.50 4.00
54 Julius Peppers 1.50 4.00
55 Jason Pierre-Paul 1.25 3.00
56 Terrell Suggs 1.25 3.00
57 Doug Martin 1.50 4.00
58 Victor Cruz 1.50 4.00
59 Derrick Johnson 1.25 3.00
60 Jared Allen 1.25 3.00
61 Ben Roethlisberger 2.00 5.00
62 Chris Johnson 1.25 3.00
63 Stephen Tulloch 1.25 3.00
64 Alfred Morris 1.25 3.00
65 Dwayne Bowe 1.50 4.00
66 Earl Thomas 1.50 4.00
67 Darrelle Revis 1.25 3.00
68 Demaryius Thomas 1.50 4.00
69 Tim Jennings 1.25 3.00
70 Chad Greenway 1.50 4.00
71 Trent Richardson 1.25 3.00
72 Mario Williams 1.25 3.00
73 Antonio Gates 1.50 4.00
74 Robert Mathis 1.25 3.00
75 Brandon Flowers 1.25 3.00
76 Matthew Stafford 1.50 4.00
77 Joe Staley 1.25 3.00
78 Luke Kuechly 1.50 4.00
79 Dwight Freeney 1.50 4.00
80 Colin Kaepernick 1.50 4.00
81 Logan Mankins 1.25 3.00
82 Lance Briggs 1.50 4.00
83 Steve Smith 1.50 4.00
84 Charles Woodson 2.00 5.00
85 London Fletcher 1.50 4.00
86 Bernard Pollard 1.25 3.00
87 Jacoby Jones 1.25 3.00
88 Cameron Wake 1.25 3.00
89 Percy Harvin 1.25 3.00
90 Troy Polamalu 2.00 5.00
91 Gerald McCoy 1.25 3.00
92 Anquan Boldin 1.25 3.00
93 Daryl Washington 1.25 3.00
94 Max Unger 1.25 3.00
95 Dashon Goldson 1.25 3.00
96 Heath Miller 1.25 3.00
97 Maurice Jones-Drew 1.25 3.00
98 Trent Williams 1.25 3.00
99 Dennis Pitta 1.25 3.00
100 Jimmy Graham 2.00 5.00
101 Aaron Mellette RC 1.25 3.00
102 Ace Sanders RC 1.25 3.00
103 Alan Bonner RC 1.25 3.00
104 Alec Ogletree RC 1.25 3.00
105 Alex Okafor RC 1.25 3.00
106 Arthur Brown RC 1.25 3.00
107 Barkevious Mingo RC 1.25 3.00
108 Benny Cunningham RC 2.00 5.00
109 B.J. Daniels RC 2.00 5.00
110 Bjoern Werner RC 1.25 3.00
111 Blidi Wreh-Wilson RC 1.50 4.00
112 Brad Sorensen RC 1.25 3.00
113 Brice Butler RC 1.25 3.00
114 Caleb Sturgis RC 2.00 5.00
115 Chance Warmack RC 1.25 3.00
116 Cierre Wood RC 1.25 3.00
117 Chris Gragg RC 1.25 3.00
118 Chris Harper RC 1.25 3.00
119 Chris Thompson RC 1.25 3.00
120 Cobi Hamilton RC 1.25 3.00
121 Russell Shepard RC 1.25 3.00
122 Corey Fuller RC 1.25 3.00
123 Cornellius Carradine RC 1.25 3.00
124 D.J. Fluker RC 1.25 3.00
125 D.J. Hayden RC 1.25 3.00
126 D.J. Swearinger RC 1.25 3.00
127 Da'Rick Rogers RC 1.25 3.00
128 Damontre Moore RC 1.25 3.00
129 Darius Slay RC 1.25 3.00
130 Datone Jones RC 1.25 3.00
131 David Amerson RC 1.25 3.00
132 Dee Milliner RC 1.25 3.00
133 Dennis Johnson RC 1.25 3.00
134 Desmond Trufant RC 1.25 3.00
135 Dion Sims RC 1.25 3.00
136 Dustin Hopkins RC 1.25 3.00
137 Earl Wolff RC 2.00 5.00
138 Eric Fisher RC 1.25 3.00
139 Eric Reid RC 1.50 4.00
140 Ezekiel Ansah RC 1.25 3.00
141 Jamar Taylor RC 1.25 3.00
142 Jamie Collins RC 1.25 3.00
143 Jarvis Jones RC 1.25 3.00
144 Jawan Jamison RC 1.25 3.00
145 Johnathan Cyprien RC 1.25 3.00
146 Johnthan Banks RC 1.25 3.00
147 Jon Bostic RC 1.25 3.00
148 Jordan Poyer RC 1.25 3.00
149 Josh Boyce RC 1.25 3.00
150 Justin Brown RC 2.00 5.00
151 Kenjon Barner RC 1.25 3.00
152 Kenny Vaccaro RC 1.25 3.00
153 Khiry Robinson RC 2.00 5.00
154 Marlon Brown RC 2.00 5.00
155 Kevin Minter RC 1.25 3.00
156 Kiko Alonso RC 1.50 4.00
157 Latavius Murray RC 1.50 4.00
158 Ryan Griffin RC 1.25 3.00
159 Levine Toilolo RC 1.50 4.00
160 Luke Joeckel RC 1.25 3.00
161 Luke Willson RC 2.00 5.00
162 Margus Hunt RC 1.25 3.00
163 Marquess Wilson RC 2.00 5.00
164 Matt Elam RC 1.25 3.00
165 Matt Scott RC 1.25 3.00
166 Nick Moody RC 1.50 4.00
167 Michael Cox RC 1.50 4.00
168 Mike James RC 2.00 5.00
169 Mychal Rivera RC 1.25 3.00
170 Nick Kasa RC 1.25 3.00
171 Onterio McCalebb RC 1.50 4.00
172 Phillip Thomas RC 1.25 3.00
173 Ray Graham RC 1.25 3.00

174 Rex Burkhead RC 1.50 4.00
175 Robert Alford RC 1.25 3.00
176 Rodney Smith RC 1.25 3.00
177 Ryan Griffin RC 1.25 3.00
178 Ryan Spadola RC 1.50 4.00
179 Sam Montgomery RC 1.25 3.00
180 Zach Sudfeld RC 1.25 3.00
181 Sheldon Richardson RC 1.25 3.00
182 Sio Moore RC 1.25 3.00
183 Spencer Ware RC 1.25 3.00
184 Tavarres King RC 1.25 3.00
185 Theo Riddick RC 1.25 3.00
186 Travis Kelce RC 3.00 8.00
187 Tyler Bray RC 1.25 3.00
188 Tyrann Mathieu RC 2.00 5.00
189 Xavier Rhodes RC 1.25 3.00
190 Zac Dysert RC 1.25 3.00
191 Zac Stacy RC 1.25 3.00
192 Kenbrell Thompkins RC 2.00 5.00
193 C.J. Anderson RC 2.50 6.00
194 Jack Doyle RC 1.25 3.00
195 Jaron Brown RC 1.25 3.00
196 Jeff Tuel RC 1.25 3.00
197 Kawann Short RC 1.25 3.00
198 Matt McGloin RC 4.00 10.00
199 Matt Simms RC 1.50 4.00
200 Michael Ford RC 2.00 5.00
201 Aaron Dobson AU/99 RC 4.00 10.00
202 Andre Ellington AU/99 RC 8.00 20.00
203 Christine Michael AU/99 RC 8.00 20.00
204 C.Patterson AU/49 RC 5.00 12.00
205 DeAndre Hopkins AU/49 RC 12.00 30.00
206 Denard Robinson AU/99 RC 4.00 10.00
207 Dion Jordan AU/99 RC 4.00 10.00
208 Eddie Lacy AU/49 RC 5.00 12.00
209 EJ Manuel AU/49 RC 5.00 12.00
210 Gavin Escobar AU/99 RC 4.00 10.00
211 Geno Smith AU/49 RC 5.00 12.00
212 Giovani Bernard AU/49 RC 5.00 12.00
213 J.Franklin AU/99 RC 4.00 10.00
214 Jordan Reed AU/99 RC 6.00 15.00
215 Joseph Randle AU/99 RC 4.00 10.00
216 Justin Hunter AU/49 RC 5.00 12.00
217 Keenan Allen AU/49 RC 10.00 25.00
218 Kenny Stills AU/99 RC 4.00 10.00
219 Knile Davis AU/99 RC 4.00 10.00
220 Landry Jones AU/49 RC 5.00 12.00
221 Le'Veon Bell AU/99 RC 12.00 30.00
222 Manti Te'o AU/49 RC 6.00 15.00
223 Marcus Lattimore AU/99 RC EXCH 4.00 10.00
224 Markus Wheaton AU/99 RC 4.00 10.00
225 M.Goodwin AU/99 RC 4.00 10.00
226 Matt Barkley AU/49 RC 5.00 12.00
227 Mike Gillislee AU/99 RC 4.00 10.00
228 Mike Glennon AU/49 RC 5.00 12.00
229 Montee Ball AU/99 RC 4.00 10.00
230 Quinton Patton AU/99 RC 4.00 10.00
231 Robert Woods AU/99 RC 6.00 15.00
232 Ryan Nassib AU/49 RC 10.00 25.00
233 Stedman Bailey AU/99 RC 4.00 10.00
234 Stepfan Taylor AU/99 RC 4.00 10.00
235 Tavon Austin AU/99 RC 5.00 12.00
236 T.Williams AU/49 RC 5.00 12.00
237 Tyler Eifert AU/99 RC 4.00 10.00
238 Tyler Wilson AU/49 RC 5.00 12.00
239 V.McDonald AU/99 RC 5.00 12.00
240 Zach Ertz AU/99 RC 8.00 20.00

2013 Panini Black Gold

*1-100 VETS/49: .6X TO 1.5X BASIC CARDS
*101-200 ROOKIES/49: .6X TO 1.5X BASIC RC
*201-240 ROOK.AU/25: .6X TO 1.5X AU/99

2013 Panini Black Platinum

*1-100 VETS/25: .8X TO 2X BASIC CARDS
*101-200 ROOKIES/25: .8X TO 2X BASIC RC

2013 Panini Black Autographs Silver

*GOLD/25: .6X TO 1.5X BASIC AU/49-99
1 Andre Brown/99 5.00 12.00
2 Art Monk/25 25.00 50.00
3 Charles Clay/99 4.00 10.00
4 Brian Cushing/49 4.00 10.00
5 Bryce Brown/99 5.00 12.00
6 Cecil Shorts/99 4.00 10.00
7 Chris Givens/25 6.00 15.00
8 Clay Matthews/25 15.00 40.00
9 Danario Alexander/99 4.00 10.00
10 David Wilson/99 4.00 10.00
11 Chris Ivory/99 5.00 12.00
12 Donald Driver/25 8.00 20.00
13 Dwayne Allen/99 4.00 10.00
14 Frank Gifford/25
15 Golden Tate/49 8.00 20.00
16 Joe Montana/25 75.00 150.00
17 Kenny Britt/99 4.00 10.00
18 LaDainian Tomlinson/25 30.00 60.00
19 Lamar Miller/99 4.00 10.00
20 Lance Alworth/25 20.00 40.00
21 Larry Csonka/25
22 Luke Kuechly/25 25.00 50.00
23 Mark Ingram/99 5.00 12.00
24 Michael Floyd/99 4.00 10.00
25 Michael Irvin/25 15.00 40.00
26 Patrick Peterson/25 6.00 15.00
27 Randall Cobb/25 8.00 20.00
28 Richard Sherman/49 40.00 100.00
29 Robert Griffin III/25 6.00 15.00
30 Robert Housler/99 4.00 10.00
31 Robert Mathis/99 6.00 15.00
32 Robert Turbin/99 4.00 10.00
33 Trindon Holliday/99 8.00 20.00
34 Rueben Randle/99 4.00 10.00
35 Jeremy Kerley/99 4.00 10.00
36 T.Y. Hilton/99 5.00 12.00
37 Case Keenum/99 5.00 12.00
39 Kendall Wright/99 4.00 10.00
40 Nick Foles/99 12.00 30.00

2013 Panini Black Metal Captains

1 Aaron Rodgers 6.00 15.00
2 Alex Smith 5.00 12.00
3 Andre Johnson 2.50 6.00
4 Andrew Luck 12.00 30.00
5 Andy Dalton 3.00 8.00
6 Antonio Gates 3.00 8.00
7 Ben Roethlisberger 4.00 10.00
8 Calvin Johnson 4.00 10.00
9 Cam Newton 4.00 10.00
10 Cameron Wake 2.50 6.00
11 Carson Palmer 3.00 8.00
12 Champ Bailey 3.00 8.00
13 Colin Kaepernick 3.00 8.00
14 Darren McFadden 3.00 8.00
15 DeMarcus Ware 4.00 10.00
16 D'Qwell Jackson 2.50 6.00
17 Drew Brees 4.00 10.00
18 Dwayne Bowe 3.00 8.00
19 Eli Manning 3.00 8.00
20 Fred Jackson 3.00 8.00
21 Gerald McCoy 2.50 6.00
22 J.J. Watt 3.00 8.00
23 Jake Locker 3.00 8.00
24 James Laurinaitis 3.00 8.00
25 Jason Witten 3.00 8.00
26 Jay Cutler 5.00 12.00
27 Jerod Mayo 3.00 8.00
28 Julius Peppers 3.00 8.00
29 Justin Tuck 2.50 6.00
30 Larry Fitzgerald 3.00 8.00
31 London Fletcher 3.00 8.00
32 Luke Kuechly 3.00 8.00
33 Matt Ryan 3.00 8.00
34 Matt Schaub 2.50 6.00
35 Matthew Stafford 3.00 8.00
36 Maurice Jones-Drew 5.00 12.00
37 Ndamukong Suh 3.00 8.00
38 Patrick Peterson 2.50 6.00
39 Patrick Willis 3.00 8.00
40 Peyton Manning 8.00 20.00
41 Philip Rivers 4.00 10.00
42 Reggie Wayne 3.00 8.00
43 Robert Griffin III 2.50 6.00
44 Russell Wilson 8.00 20.00
45 Ryan Tannehill 3.00 8.00
46 Sam Bradford 2.50 6.00
47 Steve Smith 3.00 8.00
48 Tom Brady 8.00 20.00
49 Tony Romo 3.00 8.00
50 Vincent Jackson 2.50 6.00

2013 Panini Black Metal Rookies

1 Aaron Dobson 1.25 3.00
2 Andre Ellington 1.25 3.00
3 Christine Michael 1.25 3.00
4 Cordarrelle Patterson 1.25 3.00
5 DeAndre Hopkins 3.00 8.00
6 Denard Robinson 1.25 3.00
7 Dion Jordan 1.25 3.00
8 Eddie Lacy 1.25 3.00
9 EJ Manuel 1.25 3.00
10 Gavin Escobar 1.25 3.00
11 Geno Smith 1.25 3.00
12 Giovani Bernard 1.25 3.00
13 Johnathan Franklin 1.25 3.00
14 Jordan Reed 2.00 5.00
15 Joseph Randle 1.25 3.00
16 Justin Hunter 1.25 3.00
17 Keenan Allen 2.50 6.00
18 Kenny Stills 1.25 3.00
19 Knile Davis 1.25 3.00
20 Landry Jones 1.25 3.00
21 Le'Veon Bell 4.00 10.00
22 Manti Te'o 1.50 4.00
23 Marcus Lattimore 1.25 3.00
24 Markus Wheaton 1.25 3.00
25 Marquise Goodwin 1.25 3.00
26 Matt Barkley 1.25 3.00
27 Mike Gillislee 1.25 3.00
28 Mike Glennon 1.25 3.00
29 Montee Ball 1.25 3.00
30 Quinton Patton 1.25 3.00
31 Robert Woods 2.00 5.00
32 Ryan Nassib 1.25 3.00
33 Stedman Bailey 1.25 3.00
34 Stepfan Taylor 1.25 3.00
35 Tavon Austin 1.50 4.00
36 Terrance Williams 1.25 3.00
37 Tyler Eifert 1.25 3.00
38 Tyler Wilson 1.25 3.00
39 Vance McDonald 1.50 4.00
40 Zach Ertz 2.50 6.00
41 Aaron Mellette 1.25 3.00
42 Alec Ogletree 1.25 3.00
43 Bacarri Rambo 1.50 4.00
44 Brice Butler 1.25 3.00
45 Eric Reid 1.50 4.00
46 Jaron Brown 1.25 3.00
47 Kenbrell Thompkins 2.00 5.00
48 Kiko Alonso 1.50 4.00
49 Marlon Brown 2.00 5.00
50 Tyrann Mathieu 2.00 5.00

2013 Panini Black On-Card Autographs

EXCH EXPIRATION: 7/22/2015
1 A.J. Green 12.00 30.00
2 Aaron Rodgers EXCH 125.00 250.00
3 Adrian Peterson EXCH 75.00 135.00
4 Alfred Morris EXCH 10.00 25.00
5 Andrew Luck EXCH 100.00 200.00
7 Antonio Gates EXCH 8.00 20.00
8 C.J. Spiller 6.00 15.00
9 Cam Newton 40.00 80.00
12 Colin Kaepernick EXCH 40.00 80.00
16 Doug Martin EXCH 8.00 20.00
17 Drew Brees 40.00 100.00
22 Jamaal Charles
23 Jason Witten EXCH
26 Larry Fitzgerald EXCH
27 LeSean McCoy
32 Peyton Manning 60.00 120.00
36 Russell Wilson EXCH 60.00 120.00
37 Ryan Tannehill EXCH 20.00 40.00
39 Troy Polamalu EXCH 40.00 80.00
40 Victor Cruz EXCH 8.00 20.00

2013 Panini Black Onyx Materials

*PRIME/25: 1X TO 2.5X JSY/199-299
*PRIME/25: .8X TO 2X JSY/49-99
*JUMBO PRM/25: 1.2X TO 3X JSY/199-299
*JUMBO PRM/25: 1X TO 2.5X JSY/49-99
*JUMBO PRM/25: .8X TO 2X JSY/25
*JUMBO/49-99: .6X TO 1.5X JSY/199-299
*JUMBO/49-99: .5X TO 1.2X JSY/49-99
1 Eli Manning/299 2.50 6.00
2 Chris Johnson/199 2.00 5.00
3 Calvin Johnson/99 4.00 10.00
4 Darren McFadden/299 2.50 6.00
5 DeMarco Murray/99 3.00 8.00
6 Peyton Manning/299 12.00 30.00
7 DeSean Jackson/299 2.50 6.00
8 Marques Colston/299 2.00 5.00
9 Jamaal Charles/299 2.50 6.00
10 Frank Gore/99 3.00 8.00
11 A.J. Green/199 3.00 8.00
12 Joe Flacco/299 2.50 6.00
13 Julio Jones/299 3.00 8.00
14 Charles Tillman/299 2.50 6.00
15 Larry Fitzgerald/299 2.50 6.00
16 Malcom Floyd/299 2.00 5.00
17 Antonio Brown/99 4.00 10.00
18 Alfred Morris/99 2.50 6.00
19 Ray Rice/299 2.00 5.00
20 Ryan Mathews/299 2.50 6.00
21 Sam Bradford/299 2.00 5.00
22 Steve Johnson/299 2.50 6.00
23 Steve Smith/299 2.50 6.00
24 Robert Griffin III/299 2.00 5.00
25 Tony Romo/299 2.50 6.00
26 Andre Johnson/99 2.50 6.00
27 Brian Hartline/299 2.00 5.00
28 Drew Brees/299 3.00 8.00
29 Adrian Peterson/199 3.00 8.00
30 Colin Kaepernick/299 2.50 6.00
31 Reggie Wayne/99 3.00 8.00
32 Matthew Stafford/299 2.50 6.00
33 Matt Ryan/299 2.50 6.00
34 Sidney Rice/25 4.00 10.00
35 Cam Newton/99 4.00 10.00
36 LeSean McCoy/299 3.00 8.00
37 Hakeem Nicks/49 2.50 6.00
38 Demaryius Thomas/199 2.50 6.00
39 Vincent Jackson/9
40 Dez Bryant/99 4.00 10.00

2013 Panini Black Onyx Rookie Materials

*PRIME/25: 1X TO 2.5X BASIC JSY/299
*PRIME/25: .8X TO 2X BASIC JSY/99
*PRIME/25: .4X TO 1X BASIC JSY/10
*JUMBO/99: .6X TO 1.5X BASIC JSY/299
*JUMBO/99: .5X TO 1.2X BASIC JSY/99
*JUMBO/25: .8X TO 2X BASIC JSY/99
*JUMBO/10: 1X TO 2.5X BASIC JSY/99
1 Aaron Dobson/99 1.50 4.00
2 Andre Ellington/299 1.25 3.00
3 Christine Michael/49 1.50 4.00
4 Cordarrelle Patterson/299 1.25 3.00
5 DeAndre Hopkins/99 4.00 10.00
6 Denard Robinson/299 1.25 3.00
7 Dion Jordan/299 1.25 3.00
8 Eddie Lacy/99 1.50 4.00
9 EJ Manuel/99 1.50 4.00
10 Gavin Escobar/99 1.50 4.00
11 Geno Smith/299 1.25 3.00
12 Giovani Bernard/299 1.25 3.00
13 Johnathan Franklin/299 1.25 3.00
14 Jordan Reed/299 2.00 5.00
15 Joseph Randle/299 1.25 3.00
16 Justin Hunter/99 1.50 4.00
17 Keenan Allen/99 3.00 8.00
18 Kenny Stills/299 1.25 3.00
19 Knile Davis/99 1.50 4.00
20 Landry Jones/299 1.25 3.00
21 Le'Veon Bell/99 5.00 12.00
22 Manti Te'o/299 1.50 4.00
23 Marcus Lattimore/299 1.25 3.00
24 Markus Wheaton/299 1.25 3.00
25 Marquise Goodwin/99 1.50 4.00
26 Matt Barkley/99 1.50 4.00
27 Mike Gillislee/299 1.25 3.00
28 Mike Glennon/99 1.50 4.00
29 Montee Ball/299 1.25 3.00
30 Quinton Patton/299 1.25 3.00
31 Robert Woods/99 2.50 6.00
32 Ryan Nassib/299 1.25 3.00
33 Stedman Bailey/299 1.25 3.00
34 Stepfan Taylor/299 1.25 3.00
35 Tavon Austin/99 2.00 5.00
36 Terrance Williams/10 3.00 8.00
37 Tyler Eifert/99 1.50 4.00
38 Tyler Wilson/99 1.50 4.00
39 Vance McDonald/99 2.00 5.00
40 Zach Ertz/99 3.00 8.00

2013 Panini Black Onyx Rookie Materials Prime Signatures

*GOLD/25: .5X TO 1.2X JSY AU/99
1 Aaron Dobson 5.00 12.00
2 Andre Ellington 5.00 12.00
3 Christine Michael 10.00 25.00
4 Cordarrelle Patterson 5.00 12.00
5 DeAndre Hopkins 12.00 30.00
6 Denard Robinson 5.00 12.00
7 Dion Jordan 5.00 12.00
8 Eddie Lacy 5.00 12.00
9 EJ Manuel 5.00 12.00
10 Gavin Escobar 5.00 12.00
11 Geno Smith 5.00 12.00
12 Giovani Bernard 5.00 12.00
13 Johnathan Franklin 5.00 12.00
14 Jordan Reed 8.00 20.00
15 Joseph Randle 5.00 12.00
16 Justin Hunter 5.00 12.00
17 Keenan Allen 20.00 50.00
18 Kenny Stills 5.00 12.00
19 Knile Davis 5.00 12.00
20 Landry Jones 5.00 12.00
21 Le'Veon Bell 15.00 40.00
22 Manti Te'o 6.00 15.00
23 Marcus Lattimore 5.00 12.00
24 Markus Wheaton 5.00 12.00
25 Marquise Goodwin 5.00 12.00
26 Matt Barkley 5.00 12.00
27 Mike Gillislee 5.00 12.00
28 Mike Glennon 5.00 12.00
29 Montee Ball 5.00 12.00
30 Quinton Patton 5.00 12.00
31 Robert Woods 8.00 20.00
32 Ryan Nassib 5.00 12.00
33 Stedman Bailey 5.00 12.00
34 Stepfan Taylor 5.00 12.00
35 Tavon Austin 6.00 15.00
36 Terrance Williams 5.00 12.00
37 Tyler Eifert 5.00 12.00
38 Tyler Wilson 5.00 12.00
39 Vance McDonald 6.00 15.00
40 Zach Ertz 10.00 25.00

2013 Panini Black Rookie Signature Materials Prime

*GOLD/25: .6X TO 1.5X JSY AU/299
201 Aaron Dobson 4.00 10.00
202 Andre Ellington 4.00 10.00
203 Christine Michael 8.00 20.00
204 Cordarrelle Patterson 4.00 10.00
205 DeAndre Hopkins 10.00 25.00
206 Denard Robinson 4.00 10.00
207 Dion Jordan 4.00 10.00
208 Eddie Lacy 4.00 10.00
209 EJ Manuel 4.00 10.00
210 Gavin Escobar 4.00 10.00
211 Geno Smith 4.00 10.00
212 Giovani Bernard 4.00 10.00
213 Johnathan Franklin 4.00 10.00
214 Jordan Reed 6.00 15.00
215 Joseph Randle 4.00 10.00
216 Justin Hunter 4.00 10.00
217 Keenan Allen 15.00 40.00
218 Kenny Stills 4.00 10.00
219 Knile Davis 4.00 10.00
220 Landry Jones 4.00 10.00
221 Le'Veon Bell 12.00 30.00
222 Manti Te'o 5.00 12.00
223 Marcus Lattimore 4.00 10.00
224 Markus Wheaton 4.00 10.00
225 Marquise Goodwin 4.00 10.00
226 Matt Barkley 4.00 10.00
227 Mike Gillislee 4.00 10.00
228 Mike Glennon 4.00 10.00
229 Montee Ball 4.00 10.00
230 Quinton Patton 4.00 10.00
231 Robert Woods 6.00 15.00
232 Ryan Nassib 4.00 10.00
233 Stedman Bailey 4.00 10.00
234 Stepfan Taylor 4.00 10.00
235 Tavon Austin 5.00 12.00
236 Terrance Williams 4.00 10.00
237 Tyler Eifert 4.00 10.00
238 Tyler Wilson 4.00 10.00
239 Vance McDonald 5.00 12.00
240 Zach Ertz 8.00 20.00

2013 Panini Black Rookie Signatures

*GOLD/25: .6X TO 1.5X BASIC AU/199
*GOLD/25: .5X TO 1.2X BASIC AU/99
102 Ace Sanders/99 4.00 10.00
103 Alan Bonner/99 4.00 10.00
105 Alex Okafor/99 4.00 10.00
106 Arthur Brown/99 4.00 10.00
108 Benny Cunningham/199 5.00 12.00
109 B.J. Daniels/199 5.00 12.00
111 Blidi Wreh-Wilson/199 4.00 10.00
112 Brad Sorensen/99 4.00 10.00
113 Brice Butler/99 4.00 10.00
114 Caleb Sturgis/199 5.00 12.00
115 Chance Warmack/99 4.00 10.00
116 Cierre Wood/199 3.00 8.00
117 Chris Gragg/99 4.00 10.00
118 Chris Harper/99 4.00 10.00
119 Chris Thompson/99 4.00 10.00
120 Cobi Hamilton/199 3.00 8.00
121 Russell Shepard/199 3.00 8.00
122 Corey Fuller/199 3.00 8.00
123 Cornellius Carradine/99 4.00 10.00
124 D.J. Fluker/99 4.00 10.00
125 D.J. Hayden/99 4.00 10.00
126 D.J. Swearinger/199 3.00 8.00
127 Da'Rick Rogers/99 4.00 10.00
129 Darius Slay/99 4.00 10.00
130 Datone Jones/99 4.00 10.00
131 David Amerson/199 3.00 8.00
133 Dennis Johnson/99 4.00 10.00
134 Desmond Trufant/199 3.00 8.00
135 Dion Sims/99 4.00 10.00
136 Dustin Hopkins/99 4.00 10.00
137 Earl Wolff/199 5.00 12.00
138 Eric Fisher/99 4.00 10.00
139 Eric Reid/99 8.00 20.00
140 Ezekiel Ansah/99 4.00 10.00
141 Jamar Taylor/99 4.00 10.00
142 Jamie Collins/199 3.00 8.00
143 Jarvis Jones/99 4.00 10.00
144 Jawan Jamison/99 4.00 10.00
145 Johnathan Cyprien/99 4.00 10.00
146 Johnthan Banks/199 3.00 8.00
147 Jon Bostic/99 4.00 10.00
149 Josh Boyce/199 3.00 8.00
150 Justin Brown/99 6.00 15.00
151 Kenjon Barner/99 4.00 10.00
152 Kenny Vaccaro/99 4.00 10.00
153 Khiry Robinson/199 5.00 12.00
154 Marlon Brown/199 5.00 12.00
155 Kevin Minter/99 4.00 10.00
156 Kiko Alonso/199 4.00 10.00
157 Latavius Murray/99 12.50 25.00
158 Ryan Griffin/199 3.00 8.00
159 Levine Toilolo/199 4.00 10.00
160 Joseph Fauria/199 3.00 8.00
161 Luke Willson/199 5.00 12.00
162 Margus Hunt/199 3.00 8.00
164 Matt Elam/199 3.00 8.00
165 Matt Scott/99 4.00 10.00
166 Nick Moody/199 4.00 10.00
167 Michael Cox/199 4.00 10.00
168 Mike James/199 5.00 12.00
169 Mychal Rivera/199 3.00 8.00
170 Nick Kasa/199 3.00 8.00
171 Kerwynn Williams/199 3.00 8.00
172 Phillip Thomas/99 4.00 10.00
173 Ray Graham/199 3.00 8.00
174 Rex Burkhead/199 10.00 25.00
175 Robert Alford/99 4.00 10.00
176 Rodney Smith/199 3.00 8.00
177 Ryan Griffin/199 8.00 20.00
178 Ryan Spadola/199 4.00 10.00
179 Sam Montgomery/199 3.00 8.00
180 Zach Sudfeld/199 3.00 8.00
181 Ryan Otten/199 3.00 8.00
182 Sio Moore/199 3.00 8.00
183 Spencer Ware/199 3.00 8.00
184 Tavarres King/99 4.00 10.00
185 Theo Riddick/99 4.00 10.00
186 Travis Kelce/199 8.00 20.00
187 Tyler Bray/199 3.00 8.00
188 Tyrann Mathieu/99 6.00 15.00
189 Xavier Rhodes/99 4.00 10.00
190 Zac Dysert/99 4.00 10.00
191 Zac Stacy/199 3.00 8.00
192 Kenbrell Thompkins/199 5.00 12.00
193 C.J. Anderson/199 12.50 25.00
194 Jack Doyle/199 3.00 8.00
195 Jaron Brown/199 3.00 8.00
196 Jeff Tuel/199 3.00 8.00
197 Timothy Wright/199 4.00 10.00
198 Matt McGloin/199 10.00 25.00
199 Matt Simms/199 4.00 10.00
200 Michael Ford/199 5.00 12.00

2013 Panini Black Shadow Box Jersey Signatures

VETERAN PRINT RUN 10-25
1 Aaron Dobson/99 10.00 25.00
2 Andre Ellington/99
3 Christine Michael/99 10.00 25.00
4 Cordarrelle Patterson/49
6 DeAndre Hopkins/49
8 Denard Robinson/99 10.00 25.00
9 Dion Jordan/99 10.00 25.00
11 Eddie Lacy/49 25.00 60.00
13 EJ Manuel/49
14 Gavin Escobar/99 10.00 25.00
16 Geno Smith/49 10.00 25.00
18 Giovani Bernard/49 10.00 25.00
19 Johnathan Franklin/99 10.00 25.00
20 Jordan Reed/99 15.00 40.00
21 Joseph Randle/99 10.00 25.00
22 Justin Hunter/49 10.00 25.00
24 Keenan Allen/49 30.00 60.00
26 Kenny Stills/99 10.00 25.00
27 Knile Davis/99 10.00 25.00
28 Landry Jones/49 25.00 50.00
29 Le'Veon Bell/99 30.00 80.00
31 Manti Te'o/49 12.00 30.00
33 Marcus Lattimore/99 10.00 25.00
35 Markus Wheaton/99 10.00 25.00
36 Marquise Goodwin/99 10.00 25.00
37 Matt Barkley/49 10.00 25.00
39 Mike Gillislee/99 10.00 25.00
40 Mike Glennon/49
41 Montee Ball/99 10.00 25.00
43 Quinton Patton/99 10.00 25.00
44 Robert Woods/99 15.00 40.00
45 Ryan Nassib/49 10.00 25.00
46 Stedman Bailey/99 15.00 40.00
47 Stepfan Taylor/99 15.00 40.00
48 Tavon Austin/99 12.00 30.00
50 Terrance Williams/49 10.00 25.00
51 Tyler Eifert/99 10.00 25.00
53 Tyler Wilson/49 10.00 25.00
54 Vance McDonald/99 12.00 30.00
55 Zach Ertz/99 20.00 50.00
58 Ryan Tannehill/25
65 LeSean McCoy/25
66 Colin Kaepernick/25 75.00 125.00
69 Alfred Morris/25 10.00 25.00
72 Jamaal Charles/25
76 Jason Witten/25 EXCH
77 Andy Dalton/25 30.00 60.00
78 A.J. Green/25
81 Jerome Bettis/25
82 Marshall Faulk/25 40.00 80.00
83 Earl Campbell/25

2011 Panini Black Friday

1 Aaron Rodgers 1.25 3.00
2 Tom Brady 1.00 2.50
3 Adrian Peterson .75 2.00
4 Ray Rice .50 1.25
5 Jamaal Charles .50 1.25
6 Andre Johnson .50 1.25
7 Calvin Johnson .60 1.50

2011 Panini Black Friday Rookies

RC6 Cam Newton 6.00 12.00
RC7 Mark Ingram 2.00 5.00
RC8 Julio Jones 2.00 5.00
RC9 Andy Dalton 2.50 6.00
RC10 A.J. Green 2.00 5.00

2011 Panini Black Friday

Beanie Wells .50 1.25
CM Colt McCoy .50 1.25
DJ DeSean Jackson .60 1.50
DM Donovan McNabb .60 1.50
DW DeAngelo Williams .50 1.25
EM Eli Manning .60 1.50
JB Jahvid Best .50 1.25
JJW J.J. Watt 2.00 5.00
LB LeGarrette Blount .60 1.50
MA Miles Austin .50 1.25
MS Matt Stafford .60 1.50
PM Peyton Manning 1.50 4.00
RW Roddy White .50 1.25
SB Sam Bradford .50 1.25

2011 Panini Black Friday Autographs

40 Tim Tebow BC/25 40.00 100.00
BW Beanie Wells/25 8.00 20.00
CM Colt McCoy/20 8.00 20.00
JB Jahvid Best/22 8.00 20.00
JJW J.J. Watt/20 50.00 100.00
LB LeGarrette Blount/25 10.00 25.00
MF Marshall Faulk EA 10.00 25.00
TT Tim Tebow EIB 40.00 100.00

2011 Panini Black Friday Autograph Patches

CN Cam Newton/24* 150.00 250.00

2011 Panini Black Friday Draft Day Materials

DDBG Blaine Gabbert/25* 2.00 5.00
DDCN Cam Newton/40* 10.00 25.00
DDJJ Julio Jones/20* 6.00 15.00
DDMI Mark Ingram/25* 3.00 8.00
DDMP Mike Pouncey/25* 3.00 8.00
DDPP Patrick Peterson/20* 4.00 10.00
DDAJG A.J. Green/20* 5.00 12.00

2011 Panini Black Friday Draft Day Materials Autographs

DDCJ Cameron Jordan/25 10.00 25.00
DDMD Marcell Dareus/20 8.00 20.00
DDPA Prince Amukamara/20 8.00 20.00
DDRK Ryan Kerrigan/20 15.00 40.00
DDVM Von Miller/25 20.00 50.00

2011 Panini Black Friday Pro Bowl Materials Footballs

PBAF Arian Foster/19* 5.00 12.00
PBAP Adrian Peterson/22* 8.00 20.00
PBCJ Calvin Johnson/24* 8.00 20.00
PBCJ Chris Johnson/20* 5.00 12.00
PBDB Drew Brees/20* 8.00 20.00
PBDH DeAngelo Hall/18* 5.00 12.00
PBJC Jamaal Charles/18* 6.00 15.00
PBLF Larry Fitzgerald/21* 6.00 15.00
PBMR Matt Ryan/20* 6.00 15.00
PBMV Michael Vick/23* 6.00 15.00
PBPR Philip Rivers/19* 8.00 20.00
PBRL Ray Lewis/24* 8.00 20.00

2011 Panini Black Friday Pro Bowl Materials Jerseys

PBAF Arian Foster/23* 5.00 12.00
PBAP Adrian Peterson/45* 6.00 15.00
PBDB Drew Brees/21* 8.00 20.00
PBDB Dwayne Bowe/24* 6.00 15.00
PBJC Jamaal Charles/22* 6.00 15.00
PBLF Larry Fitzgerald/24* 6.00 15.00
PBMV Michael Vick/8*
PBRL Ray Lewis/20* 8.00 20.00
PBRW Reggie Wayne/7*
PBSJ Steven Jackson/24* 5.00 12.00

2011 Panini Black Friday Pro Bowl Materials Pylons

PBAF Arian Foster/24* 5.00 12.00
PBAP Adrian Peterson/44* 8.00 20.00
PBCJ Calvin Johnson/44* 8.00 20.00
PBCJ Chris Johnson/23* 5.00 12.00
PBDB Drew Brees/24* 8.00 20.00
PBJC Jamaal Charles/24* 6.00 15.00
PBLF Larry Fitzgerald/24* 6.00 15.00
PBMR Matt Ryan/23* 6.00 15.00
PBMV Michael Vick/24* 6.00 15.00
PBPR Philip Rivers/24* 8.00 20.00

2011 Panini Black Friday Super Bowl Materials Pylons

*FOOTBALL/24-30: .4X TO 1X PYLON
SB1 Aaron Rodgers/32* 25.00 60.00
SB2 A.J. Hawk/23* 5.00 12.00
SB3 Ben Roethlisberger/19* 15.00 40.00
SB4 Charles Woodson/24* 15.00 40.00
SB5 Clay Matthews/23* 15.00 40.00
SB6 Greg Jennings/18* 15.00 40.00
SB7 Hines Ward/19* 15.00 40.00
SB8 James Jones/21* 10.00 25.00
SB9 James Starks/21* 10.00 25.00
SB10 Jordy Nelson/18* 12.00 30.00
SB11 Mason Crosby/20* 10.00 25.00
SB12 Mike Wallace/15* 10.00 25.00
SB13 Nick Collins/18* 10.00 25.00
SB14 Rashard Mendenhall/18* 10.00 25.00
SB15 Troy Polamalu/18* 15.00 40.00

2012 Panini Black Friday

-23 CRACKED ICE/25*: 6X TO 15X BASE HI
24-50 CRACKED ICE/25: 2.5X TO 6X BASE HI
1 Peyton Manning .75 2.00
2 Cam Newton .50 1.25
3 Calvin Johnson .40 1.00
4 Eli Manning .50 1.25
5 Aaron Rodgers .75 2.00
6 Arian Foster .50 1.25
7 Jamaal Charles .40 1.00
24 Andrew Luck/599 6.00 15.00
25 Robert Griffin III/599 6.00 15.00
26 Doug Martin/599 2.00 5.00
27 Trent Richardson/599 2.50 6.00
28 Brandon Weeden/599 1.50 4.00
29 Ryan Tannehill/599 2.00 5.00
30 Michael Floyd/599 1.25 3.00
48 Russell Wilson/599 3.00 8.00
49 Justin Blackmon/599 1.00 2.50
50 Alfred Morris/599 4.00 10.00

2012 Panini Black Friday Black Holofoil

CRACKED ICE/25: 3X TO 8X BASE HI
6 Robert Griffin III 5.00 12.00
7 Cam Newton .60 1.50
8 Darren McFadden .50 1.25
9 Tim Tebow 1.00 2.50
10 Clay Matthews .50 1.25
11 Troy Polamalu .60 1.50
12 Calvin Johnson .50 1.25
13 Ray Lewis .50 1.25
14 Andrew Luck 5.00 12.00

2012 Panini Black Friday Gold Border

CRACKED ICE/25*: 4X TO 10X BASE HI
1 Robert Griffin III 3.00 8.00

2012 Panini Black Friday Happy Holidays Christmas Hats

AL Andrew Luck 30.00 60.00
TR Trent Richardson 10.00 25.00
RG3 Robert Griffin III 30.00 60.00

2012 Panini Black Friday Kings

CRACKED ICE/25: 2X TO 5X BASE HI
1 Jim Brown .60 1.50
2 Joe Namath .60 1.50
3 John Riggins .40 1.00

2012 Panini Black Friday Rookie Jumbo Materials

1 DeMarco Murray 5.00 12.00
2 Cam Newton 12.00 30.00
3 Andy Dalton 6.00 15.00
4 Jake Locker 6.00 15.00
5 Andrew Luck SP 15.00 40.00
6 Robert Griffin III SP 15.00 40.00

2012 Panini Black Friday Rookie Kings

CRACKED ICE/25: 2X TO 5X BASE HI
1 Andrew Luck 3.00 8.00
2 Morris Claiborne .75 2.00
3 Justin Blackmon .75 2.00
4 Trent Richardson 1.25 3.00
10 Russell Wilson 1.50 4.00

2012 Panini Black Friday Rookie Materials Hats

1 Robert Griffin III SP 20.00 40.00
2 Trent Richardson 5.00 12.00
3 Justin Blackmon 2.50 6.00
4 Brandon Weeden 2.50 6.00
5 Ryan Tannehill 5.00 12.00
6 Doug Martin 4.00 10.00
7 Michael Floyd 2.50 6.00
8 Kendall Wright 2.00 5.00
9 Lamar Miller 2.50 6.00
10 Brock Osweiler 2.50 6.00
11 Isaiah Pead 2.00 5.00
12 Russell Wilson 5.00 12.00
13 Alshon Jeffery 2.50 6.00

2012 Panini Black Friday Super Bowl Materials Footballs

INSERTS IN BLACK FRIDAY PACKS
1 Eli Manning 60.00 120.00
2 Ahmad Bradshaw 15.00 40.00
3 Hakeem Nicks 8.00 20.00
4 Victor Cruz 25.00 50.00
5 Tom Brady 40.00 80.00
2AU Ahmad Bradshaw AUTO 30.00 60.00

2012 Panini Black Friday Super Bowl Materials Pylons

INSERTS IN BLACK FRIDAY PACKS
1 Eli Manning 25.00 50.00
2 Ahmad Bradshaw 10.00 25.00
3 Hakeem Nicks 8.00 20.00
4 Victor Cruz 20.00 40.00
5 Mario Manningham 10.00 25.00
6 Justin Tuck SP 25.00 50.00
7 Jason Pierre-Paul 8.00 20.00
8 Chase Blackburn SP 40.00 80.00
9 Lawrence Tynes SP 10.00 25.00
10 Tom Brady 30.00 60.00
11 Wes Welker 12.00 30.00
12 Aaron Hernandez 12.00 30.00
13 Rob Gronkowski 15.00 40.00
14 Danny Woodhead SP 15.00 40.00
15 Stephen Gostkowski SP 12.00 30.00
3AU Rob Gronkowski AUTO 75.00 150.00

2012 Panini Black Friday Super Bowl MVP Materials Pylons

INSERTS IN BLACK FRIDAY PACKS
1 Eli Manning 12.00 30.00
2 Aaron Rodgers 30.00 60.00

2012 Panini Black Friday Manufactured Patch Autographs

INSERTS IN BLACK FRIDAY PACKS
AD1 Andy Dalton Pink NFL 20.00 40.00
AL Andrew Luck 150.00 250.00
BW Brandon Weeden Pink NFL 15.00 40.00
CF Coby Fleener 10.00 25.00
DH Dont'a Hightower NFL 10.00 25.00
DK Dre Kirkpatrick NFL 6.00 15.00
DS Devon Still NFL 5.00 12.00
FC Fletcher Cox NFL 5.00 12.00
IP Isaiah Pead NFL 8.00 20.00
JB1 Justin Blackmon Pink NFL 15.00 30.00
KR Kendall Reyes NFL 5.00 12.00
LD Lavonte David 6.00 15.00
MB Michael Brockers NFL 6.00 15.00
MC Morris Claiborne Pink NFL 25.00 50.00
MF Michael Floyd 10.00 25.00
MI Melvin Ingram NFL 6.00 15.00
MS Mohamed Sanu
NP Nick Perry NFL 10.00 25.00
QC Quinton Coples NFL 8.00 20.00
RGIII Robert Griffin III 100.00 200.00
SG Stephon Gilmore NFL 5.00 12.00
SM Shea McClellin NFL 6.00 15.00
TR1 Trent Richardson 15.00 40.00
WM Whitney Mercilus 6.00 15.00

2012 Panini Black Friday Thanksgiving

INSERTS IN BLACK FRIDAY PACKS
CRACKED ICE/25: 2.5X TO 6X BASIC CARDS
1 Matthew Stafford .60 1.50
2 Andre Johnson .60 1.50
3 Tony Romo .60 1.50
4 Robert Griffin III .50 1.25
5 Rob Gronkowski .75 2.00
6 Tim Tebow .75 2.00

2012 Panini Black Friday Tools of the Trade Cowboys Equipment Bags

1 Tony Romo 6.00 15.00
2 Dez Bryant 6.00 15.00

2013 Panini Black Friday

CRACKED ICE/35: 5X TO 12X BASIC CARDS
LAVA FLOW/150: 2X TO 5X BASIC CARDS
1 Colin Kaepernick FB .40 1.00
5 Tom Brady FB .50 1.25
9 Andrew Luck FB .75 2.00
13 Adrian Peterson FB .40 1.00
17 Peyton Manning FB 1.00 2.50
21 Russell Wilson FB .50 1.25
24 Aaron Rodgers FB .60 1.50
27 Eric Fisher FB .30 .75
28 Luke Joeckel FB .30 .75
33 Eddie Lacy/299 FB 2.50 6.00
34 Montee Ball/299 FB 1.00 2.50
35 Matt Barkley/299 FB .75 2.00
36 Manti Te'o/299 FB 1.00 2.50
37 Le'Veon Bell/299 FB 1.50 4.00
38 Cordarrelle Patterson/299 FB 1.50 4.00
49 Giovani Bernard/299 FB 1.25 3.00
51 EJ Manuel JSY/99 FB 2.50 6.00
52 Geno Smith JSY/99 FB 2.00 5.00
53 Tavon Austin JSY/99 FB 2.00 5.00

2013 Panini Black Friday Autographs

1 Colin Kaepernick
5 Tom Brady
9 Andrew Luck
13 Adrian Peterson
17 Peyton Manning
21 Russell Wilson
24 Aaron Rodgers
27 Eric Fisher
28 Luke Joeckel
33 Eddie Lacy
34 Montee Ball
35 Matt Barkley
36 Manti Te'o 25.00 50.00
37 Le'Veon Bell 40.00 80.00
38 Cordarrelle Patterson 8.00 20.00
49 Giovani Bernard
51 EJ Manuel
52 Geno Smith
53 Tavon Austin

2013 Panini Black Friday Collection

CRACKED ICE/35: 4X TO 10X BASIC CARDS
LAVA FLOW/150: 1.5X TO 4X BASIC CARDS
11 J.J. Watt .40 1.00
12 Wes Welker .40 1.00
13 Colin Kaepernick .50 1.25
14 Tim Tebow .40 1.00
15 Andrew Luck .60 1.50
16 Arian Foster .40 1.00
17 Robert Griffin III .40 1.00

2013 Panini Black Friday Hall of Fame Class of 2013 Autographs

1 Warren Sapp
2 Cris Carter 30.00 60.00
3 Larry Allen 30.00 60.00
4 Jonathan Ogden 30.00 60.00
5 Bill Parcells
6 Curley Culp 30.00 60.00
7 Dave Robinson

2013 Panini Black Friday Happy Holidays

DR Denard Robinson 1.50 4.00
EJM EJ Manuel 3.00 8.00
EL Eddie Lacy 4.00 10.00
GE Gavin Escobar 1.25 3.00
GM Geno Smith 2.00 5.00
MB Montee Ball 1.50 4.00
MT Manti Te'o 2.00 5.00
RGIII Robert Griffin III SP 4.00 10.00
TA Tavon Austin 1.50 4.00

2013 Panini Black Friday Jumbo Materials

AB Antonio Brown 4.00 10.00
JG Jimmy Graham 4.00 10.00
JW Jason Witten 5.00 12.00

2013 Panini Black Friday Manufactured Patch Autographs

AL Andrew Luck 75.00 125.00
KW Kendall Wright 5.00 12.00
RGIII Robert Griffin III
TB Tim Brown 10.00 25.00

2013 Panini Black Friday Pink Materials

BCA1 Cordarrelle Patterson 1.00 2.50
BCA2 DeAndre Hopkins 2.50 6.00
BCA3 Eddie Lacy 5.00 12.00
BCA4 EJ Manuel 1.00 2.50
BCA5 Geno Smith 1.00 2.50
BCA6 Giovani Bernard 1.00 2.50
BCA7 Le'Veon Bell 3.00 8.00
BCA8 Manti Te'o 1.25 3.00
BCA9 Marcus Lattimore 1.00 2.50
BCA10 Matt Barkley 1.00 2.50
BCA11 Montee Ball 1.00 2.50
BCA12 Ryan Nassib 1.00 2.50
BCA13 Robert Woods 1.50 4.00
BCA14 Tyler Eifert 1.00 2.50
BCA15 Tavon Austin 1.25 3.00
BCA16 Denard Robinson 1.00 2.50
BCA17 Chris Johnson FB SP 6.00 15.00
BCA18 Sam Bradford FB SP 6.00 15.00
BCA19 Greg Zuerlein FB SP 6.00 15.00
BCA20 Ryan Tannehill FB SP 8.00 20.00

2013 Panini Black Friday Pink Patch Autographs

AG Antonio Gates 12.00 30.00
AL Andrew Luck
BC Brandon Carr
BW Ben Watson
DM Doug Martin 12.00 30.00
RB Rex Burkhead
RT Ryan Tannehill
WR Willie Roaf

2013 Panini Black Friday Super Bowl Materials

1 Joe Flacco 4.00 10.00
2 Ray Rice 3.00 8.00
3 Anquan Boldin 3.00 8.00
4 Ed Reed 4.00 10.00
5 Haloti Ngata 3.00 8.00
6 Jacoby Jones 3.00 8.00
7 Torrey Smith 3.00 8.00
8 Bernard Pierce 3.00 8.00
9 Colin Kaepernick 4.00 10.00

2013 Panini Black Friday Super Bowl MVP

1 Joe Flacco 6.00 15.00

2013 Panini Black Friday VIP

CRACKED ICE/35: 2.5X TO 6X BASIC CARDS
LAVA FLOW/150: 1.2X TO 3X BASIC CARDS
3 Justin Hunter .75 2.00
4 Ryan Nassib .75 2.00
5 Marcus Lattimore .75 2.00
6 DeAndre Hopkins 1.25 3.00
7 Tyler Eifert .75 2.00

2014 Panini Black Friday Happy Holidays

COMPLETE SET (6) 15.00 40.00
AE Andre Ellington 3.00 8.00
BC Brandin Cooks 3.00 8.00
CH Carlos Hyde 3.00 8.00
MB Matt Barkley 3.00 8.00
TS Tom Savage 3.00 8.00
TM Tre Mason 4.00 10.00
COMPLETE SET (15)
CRACKED ICE/25: 1.2X TO 3X BASIC INSERT
1 Johnny Manziel FB 5.00 12.00
2 Blake Bortles FB 4.00 10.00
3 Mike Evans FB 3.00 8.00
4 Odell Beckham Jr. FB 6.00 15.00
5 Le'Veon Bell FB 4.00 10.00
6 Jadeveon Clowney FB 2.50 6.00
7 Teddy Bridgewater FB 4.00 10.00

2014 Panini Black Friday Manufactured Patch Autographs

AB Ahmad Bradshaw 8.00 20.00
BC Brandin Cooks 10.00 25.00
CO Chad Owens 6.00 15.00
DR Denard Robinson 8.00 20.00
JC Jadeveon Clowney 6.00 15.00
ML Marqise Lee 10.00 25.00
RR Ricky Ray 10.00 25.00
SW Sammy Watkins 12.00 30.00

2014 Panini Black Friday Pink Materials

TOWEL ICE/25: 1X TO 2.5X BASIC TOWEL
BALL ICE/25: .8X TO 2X BASIC BALL
1 Johnny Manziel 6.00 15.00
2 Sammy Watkins 5.00 12.00
3 Brandin Cooks 2.00 5.00
4 Bishop Sankey 1.25 3.00
5 Derek Carr 5.00 12.00
6 Blake Bortles 5.00 12.00
7 Teddy Bridgewater 5.00 12.00
8 Andre Williams 1.25 3.00
9 De'Anthony Thomas 1.25 3.00
10 Dri Archer 1.25 3.00
11 Jadeveon Clowney 1.50 4.00
12 Terrance West 1.25 3.00
13 Terrance Williams 2.50 6.00
14 EJ Manuel 2.50 6.00
15 Eddie Lacy 2.50 6.00
16 Keenan Allen 3.00 8.00
17 Tom Brady FB SP 12.00 30.00
18 A.J. Green FB SP 5.00 12.00
19 Andre Ellington 2.50 6.00
20 Johnny Manziel FB SP 8.00 20.00

2014 Panini Black Friday Pink Materials Cracked Ice Autographs

4 Bishop Sankey 5.00 12.00
8 Andre Williams 5.00 12.00
9 De'Anthony Thomas 5.00 12.00
10 Dri Archer 5.00 12.00
12 Terrance West 5.00 12.00
13 Terrance Williams
14 EJ Manuel
16 Keenan Allen
19 Andre Ellington 5.00 12.00

2014 Panini Black Friday Salute to Service Materials Towels

CRACKED ICE/25: 1.2X TO 3X BASIC TOWEL
1 Johnny Manziel 6.00 15.00
2 Odell Beckham Jr. 8.00 20.00
3 Blake Bortles 5.00 12.00
4 Marqise Lee 1.50 4.00
5 Teddy Bridgewater 5.00 12.00
6 Carlos Hyde 1.50 4.00
7 Kelvin Benjamin 4.00 10.00
8 Tre Mason 1.25 3.00
9 Eric Ebron 1.50 4.00
10 Donte Moncrief 1.25 3.00
11 Jimmy Garoppolo cap 10.00 25.00
12 Tom Savage 1.25 3.00
13 Mike Evans 3.00 8.00
14 Aaron Murray 1.25 3.00
15 A.J. McCarron 1.25 3.00

2014 Panini Black Friday Tools of the Trade Towels

CRACKED ICE/25: 1.2X TO 3X BASIC TOTT
1 Johnny Manziel 1.50 4.00
2 Sammy Watkins 1.50 4.00
3 Blake Bortles 1.25 3.00
4 Teddy Bridgewater 1.50 4.00
5 Jadeveon Clowney 3.00 8.00
AL Andrew Luck 5.00 12.00

2014 Panini Black Friday

*1-21 ICE VETS/25: 6X TO 15X BASIC CARDS
*22-50 ICE ROOKIE/25: 2X TO 5X BASIC CARDS/499
*JSY ICE/25: 1.2X TO 3X BASIC JSY/99
1-21 THICK STOCK/50: 1.5X TO 4X BASIC CARDS
22-50 THICK STOCK/50: .8X TO 2X BASIC CARDS
7 Andrew Luck FB .50 1.25
8 Peyton Manning FB .75 2.00
9 Calvin Johnson FB .30 .75
10 Tom Brady FB .50 1.25
11 Colin Kaepernick FB .30 .75
12 Dez Bryant FB .30 .75
13 Russell Wilson FB .40 1.00
14 Aaron Rodgers FB .60 1.50
29 Bishop Sankey FB .75 2.00
30 Derek Carr FB 2.00 5.00
31 Kelvin Benjamin FB 2.00 5.00
32 Marqise Lee FB 1.25 3.00
33 Jimmy Garoppolo FB 1.25 3.00
34 Odell Beckham Jr. FB 3.00 8.00
35 Mike Evans FB 1.25 3.00
36 Carlos Hyde FB 1.00 2.50
37 Brandin Cooks FB 1.25 3.00
38 Jadeveon Clowney FB 1.00 2.50
39 De'Anthony Thomas FB 1.00 2.50
59 Sammy Watkins FB JSY 3.00 8.00
60 Teddy Bridgewater FB JSY 4.00 10.00
61 Blake Bortles FB JSY 3.00 8.00
62 Johnny Manziel FB JSY 4.00 10.00

2014 Panini Black Friday Collection

*CRACKED ICE/25: 4X TO 10X BASIC CARDS
THICK STOCK/50: 1.2X TO 3X BASIC CARDS
9 Joe Namath FB .75 2.00
10 Richard Sherman FB .60 1.50
11 Colin Kaepernick FB .60 1.50
12 LeSean McCoy FB .50 1.25
13 Dez Bryant FB .50 1.25
14 Robert Griffin III FB .40 1.00
15 Rob Gronkowski FB .50 1.25
16 Jimmy Graham FB .40 1.00
17 Jadeveon Clowney FB .60 1.50
18 Giovani Bernard FB .50 1.25
20 Johnny Manziel FB 1.25 3.00
28 Jamaal Charles FB .40 1.00
29 Ndamukong Suh FB .40 1.00
30 Patrick Peterson FB .40 1.00

2014 Panini Black Friday Collection Autographs

ANNOUNCED PRINT RUN 25 OR LESS
9 Joe Namath FB
10 Richard Sherman FB
11 Colin Kaepernick FB
12 LeSean McCoy FB
13 Dez Bryant FB
14 Robert Griffin III FB
15 Rob Gronkowski FB
16 Jimmy Graham FB
17 Jadeveon Clowney FB
18 Giovani Bernard FB
20 Johnny Manziel FB 20.00 50.00
28 Jamaal Charles FB
29 Ndamukong Suh FB
30 Patrick Peterson FB

2014 Panini Black Friday Rookie Portraits

*CRACKED ICE/25: 3X TO 8X BASIC CARDS
THICK STOCK/50: 1X TO 2.5X BASIC CARDS
1 Johnny Manziel FB 1.25 3.00
2 Sammy Watkins FB 1.00 2.50
3 Teddy Bridgewater FB 1.25 3.00
4 Blake Bortles FB 1.25 3.00
5 A.J. McCarron FB .60 1.50
6 Aaron Murray FB .75 2.00
7 Jimmy Garoppolo FB 1.00 2.50
8 Logan Thomas FB .60 1.50
9 Khalil Mack FB .60 1.50

2014 Panini Black Friday Rookie Portraits Autographs

1 Johnny Manziel FB 20.00 50.00
2 Sammy Watkins FB 40.00 80.00
3 Teddy Bridgewater FB 40.00 80.00
4 Blake Bortles FB 30.00 60.00
5 A.J. McCarron FB 10.00 25.00
6 Aaron Murray FB 6.00 15.00
7 Jimmy Garoppolo FB 10.00 25.00
8 Logan Thomas FB 5.00 12.00
9 Khalil Mack FB 10.00 25.00

2015 Panini Black Friday

*CRACKED/25: 1X TO 2.5X BASIC CARDS
*THICK/50: .8X TO 2X BASIC CARDS
1 J.J. Watt .75 2.00
2 Aaron Rodgers 2.00 5.00
3 Marshawn Lynch .75 2.00
4 Rob Gronkowski .75 2.00
5 Odell Beckham Jr. .75 2.00
6 Jamaal Charles .75 2.00
7 Dez Bryant .75 2.00
8 Andrew Luck 1.25 3.00
35 Jameis Winston 2.00 5.00
36 Marcus Mariota 2.00 5.00
37 Amari Cooper 2.00 5.00
38 Kevin White 1.25 3.00
39 DeVante Parker 1.25 3.00
40 Melvin Gordon 1.25 3.00
41 Todd Gurley 2.00 5.00
42 T.J. Yeldon 1.25 3.00
43 Ameer Abdullah 1.25 3.00
44 Phillip Dorsett 1.25 3.00
51 Jarryd Hayne 1.25 3.00

2015 Panini Black Friday Collection

*CRACKED/25: 1X TO 2.5X BASIC CARDS
*THICK/50: .8X TO 2X BASIC CARDS
15 Tom Brady 1.25 3.00
16 Tyrann Mathieu 1.25 3.00
17 J.J. Watt 1.25 3.00
18 Eddie Lacy 1.25 3.00
19 Odell Beckham Jr. 1.25 3.00
20 Julian Edelman 1.25 3.00
21 Russell Wilson 1.25 3.00
22 Jameis Winston 1.25 3.00
JT Justin Tucker 1.25 3.00

2015 Panini Black Friday Happy Holidays Materials

*CRACKED/25: .8X TO 2X BASIC HAT
AA Ameer Abdullah 2.50 6.00
AC Amari Cooper 2.50 6.00
BP Breshad Perriman 2.50 6.00
BS Bishop Sankey 2.50 6.00
DP DeVante Parker 2.50 6.00
JW Jameis Winston 2.50 6.00
MG Melvin Gordon 2.50 6.00
MM Marcus Mariota 2.50 6.00
NA Nelson Agholor 2.50 6.00
TG Todd Gurley 2.50 6.00

2015 Panini Black Friday Manufactured Patches

*CRACKED/25: .8X TO 2X BASIC PATCH
1 Jameis Winston 2.50 6.00
2 Russell Wilson 2.50 6.00
3 Tim Tebow 2.50 6.00
4 Peyton Manning 5.00 12.00

2015 Panini Black Friday Rookie Materials Jerseys

*CRACKED/25: .8X TO 2X BASIC JSY
2 Karlos Williams 2.50 6.00

2016 Panini Black Friday

1 Teddy Bridgewater .75 2.00
2 T.Y. Hilton .75 2.00
3 Tony Romo .75 2.00
4 Tyrod Taylor .75 2.00
5 Ryan Tannehill .75 2.00
6 Robert Griffin III .75 2.00
7 Richard Sherman .75 2.00
8 NaVorro Bowman .75 2.00
9 Matt Ryan .75 2.00
10 Mark Ingram .75 2.00
11 Luke Kuechly .75 2.00
12 Lamar Miller .75 2.00
13 Kirk Cousins .75 2.00
14 Khalil Mack .75 2.00
15 Keenan Allen .75 2.00
16 Kam Chancellor .75 2.00
17 Julian Edelman .75 2.00
18 Josh Norman .75 2.00
19 Jordy Nelson .75 2.00
20 Jordan Matthews .75 2.00
21 Joe Flacco .75 2.00
22 Jay Cutler .75 2.00
23 Greg Olsen .75 2.00
24 Golden Tate III .75 2.00
25 Eric Decker .75 2.00
26 Eli Manning .75 2.00
27 Doug Martin .75 2.00
28 Devonta Freeman .75 2.00
29 Derek Carr .75 2.00
30 Demaryius Thomas .75 2.00
31 DeMarco Murray .75 2.00
32 David Johnson .75 2.00
33 Carson Palmer .75 2.00
34 Brock Osweiler .75 2.00
35 Brandon McManus .75 2.00
36 Ben Roethlisberger .75 2.00
37 Andy Dalton .75 2.00
38 Allen Robinson .75 2.00
39 Alex Smith .75 2.00
40 Aaron Donald .75 2.00
41 Barry Sanders 1.50 4.00
42 Peyton Manning 1.50 4.00
43 Bo Jackson 1.50 4.00
44 Dan Marino 1.50 4.00
45 John Elway 1.50 4.00
46 Jerry Rice 1.50 4.00
47 Troy Aikman 1.50 4.00
48 Eric Dickerson 1.50 4.00
49 Jerome Bettis 1.50 4.00
50 Brett Favre 1.50 4.00
51 Braxton Miller 1.25 3.00
52 C.J. Prosise 1.25 3.00
53 Cardale Jones 1.25 3.00
54 Carson Wentz 4.00 10.00
55 Cody Kessler 1.25 3.00
56 Corey Coleman 1.25 3.00
57 Dak Prescott 2.50 6.00
58 DeAndre Washington 1.25 3.00
59 Derrick Henry 1.25 3.00
60 Devontae Booker 1.25 3.00
61 Ezekiel Elliott 2.50 6.00
62 Jalen Ramsey 1.25 3.00
63 Jared Goff 1.25 3.00
64 Will Fuller V 1.25 3.00
65 Josh Doctson 1.25 3.00
66 Kenneth Dixon 1.25 3.00
67 Kenyan Drake 1.25 3.00
68 Laquon Treadwell 1.25 3.00
69 Michael Thomas 1.25 3.00
70 Paul Perkins 1.25 3.00
71 Paxton Lynch 1.25 3.00
72 Sterling Shepard 1.25 3.00
73 Tyler Boyd 1.25 3.00
74 Wendell Smallwood 1.25 3.00
75 Jon Dorenbos 1.25 3.00

2016 Panini Black Friday Cracked Ice

*VETS: .75X TO 2X BASIC CARDS
*ROOKIES: 1X TO 2.5X BASIC CARDS
54 Carson Wentz 25.00 50.00

2016 Panini Black Friday Thick Stock

*VETS: .6X TO 1.5X BASIC CARDS
*ROOKIES: .8X TO 2X BASIC CARDS
54 Carson Wentz 8.00 20.00

2016 Panini Black Friday Wedges

*VETS: .6X TO 1.5X BASIC CARDS
*ROOKIES: .8X TO 2X BASIC CARDS
54 Carson Wentz 8.00 20.00

2016 Panini Black Friday Happy Holidays Materials

*CRACKED/25: .8X TO 2X BASIC MEM
1 Jameis Winston 2.50 6.00
2 Devin Funchess 1.50 4.00
3 Derrick Henry 4.00 10.00
4 Kevin White 1.50 4.00
5 T.J. Yeldon 1.50 4.00
6 Derek Carr 2.50 6.00
7 Jeremy Langford 2.00 5.00
8 Marcus Mariota 2.50 6.00
9 Leonard Williams 1.50 4.00
10 Tevin Coleman 2.00 5.00
11 Thomas Rawls 1.50 4.00
12 Tyler Lockett 2.00 5.00
13 Vance McDonald 1.50 4.00
14 Paxton Lynch 1.50 4.00
15 Carson Wentz 10.00 25.00
16 Laquon Treadwell 2.00 5.00
17 Jared Goff 10.00 25.00
18 Ezekiel Elliott 6.00 15.00
19 Braxton Miller 1.50 4.00
20 Josh Doctson 2.00 5.00

2016 Panini Black Friday Panini Collection

1 Aaron Rodgers 1.50 4.00
2 Adrian Peterson 1.50 4.00
3 A.J. Green 1.50 4.00
4 Andrew Luck 1.50 4.00
5 Antonio Brown 1.50 4.00
6 Cam Newton 1.50 4.00
7 DeAndre Hopkins 1.50 4.00
8 Dez Bryant 1.50 4.00
9 Drew Brees 1.50 4.00
10 Jamaal Charles 1.50 4.00
11 Jameis Winston 1.50 4.00
12 Jarvis Landry 1.50 4.00
13 J.J. Watt 1.50 4.00
14 Julio Jones 1.50 4.00
15 Le'Veon Bell 1.50 4.00
16 Marcus Mariota 1.50 4.00
17 Ndamukong Suh 1.50 4.00
18 Odell Beckham Jr. 1.50 4.00
19 Rob Gronkowski 1.50 4.00
20 Russell Wilson 1.50 4.00
21 Todd Gurley 1.50 4.00
22 Tom Brady 1.50 4.00
23 Tyrann Mathieu 1.50 4.00
24 Von Miller 1.50 4.00
25 Santa Claus 1.50 4.00
SC Santa Claus 1.50 4.00

2016 Panini Black Friday Tools of the Trade Towels

*CRACKED/25: .8X TO 2X BASIC TOWEL
1 Jared Goff 2.50 6.00
2 Corey Coleman 2.50 6.00
3 Cardale Jones 2.50 6.00
4 Cody Kessler 2.50 6.00
5 Christian Hackenberg 2.50 6.00
6 Ezekiel Elliott 4.00 10.00
7 Sterling Shepard 2.50 6.00
8 Connor Cook 2.50 6.00
9 C.J. Prosise 2.50 6.00
10 Michael Thomas 2.50 6.00
11 Paxton Lynch 2.50 6.00
12 Joey Bosa 2.50 6.00
13 Will Fuller V 2.50 6.00
14 Devontae Booker 2.50 6.00
15 Dak Prescott 4.00 10.00

2017 Panini Black Friday Cracked Ice

*VETS: .75X TO 2X BASIC CARDS
*ROOKIES: 1X TO 2.5X BASIC CARDS
67 Deshaun Watson 8.00 20.00

2017 Panini Black Friday Decoy

*VETS: .6X TO 1.5X BASIC CARDS
*ROOKIES: .8X TO 2X BASIC CARDS

2017 Panini Black Friday Wedges

*VETS: .6X TO 1.5X BASIC CARDS
*ROOKIES: .8X TO 2X BASIC CARDS

2017 Panini Black Friday Autographs

1 Russell Wilson
2 Drew Brees
3 J.J. Watt 30.00 60.00
4 Aaron Rodgers
5 Ben Roethlisberger 50.00 100.00
6 Jordy Nelson
7 Marcus Mariota
8 Clay Matthews 10.00 25.00
9 Matthew Stafford
10 DeMarco Murray
11 Todd Gurley II
12 Eli Manning
13 Jameis Winston
14 Adrian Peterson
15 Julian Edelman
16 Cam Newton
17 Marshawn Lynch
18 Dak Prescott
19 Odell Beckham Jr.
20 Derek Carr 15.00 40.00
21 Von Miller
22 Ezekiel Elliott
23 Joe Flacco
24 Amari Cooper
25 Julio Jones 30.00 60.00
26 Carson Palmer 25.00 50.00
27 Matt Forte
28 David Johnson
29 Richard Sherman
30 Devonta Freeman
31 Andrew Luck 25.00 50.00
32 Jordan Howard 8.00 20.00
33 Tom Brady
34 Andy Dalton
35 Larry Fitzgerald
36 Carson Wentz
37 Matt Ryan
38 DeAndre Hopkins
39 Rob Gronkowski
40 Dez Bryant
41 Brett Favre
42 Emmitt Smith
43 Terry Bradshaw
44 John Elway
45 Jerry Rice
46 Peyton Manning
47 Calvin Johnson
48 Randy Moss
49 Dan Marino
50 Barry Sanders
51 Kenny Golladay 4.00 10.00
52 Dalvin Cook 20.00 40.00
53 Mitchell Trubisky
54 Curtis Samuel 8.00 20.00
55 Mike Williams
56 Alvin Kamara 25.00 50.00
57 Patrick Mahomes II
58 Kareem Hunt
59 T.J. Watt
60 O.J. Howard
61 R. Joshua Dobbs
62 Joe Mixon 4.00 10.00
63 Leonard Fournette 20.00 50.00
64 DeShone Kizer
65 Christian McCaffrey 20.00 50.00
66 D'Onta Foreman 4.00 10.00
67 Deshaun Watson 50.00 100.00
68 Myles Carrett
69 Evan Engram 4.00 10.00
70 Cooper Kupp
71 James Conner
72 Zay Jones
73 Corey Davis 4.00 10.00
74 JuJu Smith-Schuster 40.00 80.00
75 John Ross III 4.00 10.00

2017 Panini Black Friday Happy Holidays Memorabilia

*CRACKED/25: .8X TO 2X BASIC MEM
HHFCD Corey Davis 2.50 6.00
HHFDC Dalvin Cook 2.50 6.00
HHFDF D'Onta Foreman 2.50 6.00
HHFDK DeShone Kizer 2.50 6.00
HHFDW Deshaun Watson 4.00 10.00
HHFEE Evan Engram 2.50 6.00
HHFJJ JuJu Smith-Schuster 2.50 6.00
HHFJR John Ross III 2.50 6.00
HHFLB Le'Veon Bell 2.50 6.00
HHFLF Leonard Fournette 3.00 8.00
HHFMT Mitchell Trubisky 3.00 8.00
HHFMW Mike Williams 2.50 6.00
HHFNP Nathan Peterman 2.50 6.00
HHFOJ O.J. Howard 2.50 6.00
HHFPM Patrick Mahomes II 40.00 80.00

2017 Panini Black Friday Panini Collection

*CRACKED/25: .8X TO 2X BASIC INSERTS
*DECOY/50: .6X TO 1.5X BASIC INSERTS
*WEDGE/50: .6X TO 1.5X BASIC INSERTS
1 Marshawn Lynch 1.50 4.00
2 Dak Prescott 1.50 4.00
3 A.J. Green 1.50 4.00
4 Derek Carr 1.50 4.00
5 Odell Beckham Jr. 1.50 4.00
6 Aaron Rodgers 2.00 5.00
7 Tyrann Mathieu 1.50 4.00
8 Julio Jones 1.50 4.00
9 Tom Brady 2.00 5.00
10 Christian McCaffrey 1.50 4.00
11 Leonard Fournette 1.50 4.00
12 J.J. Watt 1.50 4.00
13 Mitchell Trubisky 1.50 4.00
14 Deshaun Watson 2.00 5.00
15 DeShone Kizer 1.50 4.00
16 Antonio Brown 1.50 4.00
17 Landon Collins 1.50 4.00
18 Dez Bryant 1.50 4.00
19 David Johnson 1.50 4.00
20 Von Miller 1.50 4.00
21 Mike Evans 1.50 4.00
22 Jordan Howard 1.50 4.00
23 Michael Thomas 1.50 4.00
24 Khalil Mack 1.50 4.00
25 Rob Gronkowski 1.50 4.00

2017 Panini Black Friday Patches

*CRACKED/25: .8X TO 2X BASIC PATCH
BFFAB Antonio Brown 2.50 6.00
BFFAC Amari Cooper SP 2.50 6.00
BFFAR Aaron Rodgers 4.00 10.00
BFFCN Cam Newton 2.50 6.00
BFFJJ Julio Jones 2.50 6.00
BFFMR Matt Ryan 2.50 6.00
BFFOB Odell Beckham Jr. 2.50 6.00
BFFRG Rob Gronkowski 2.50 6.00
BFFTB Tom Brady 6.00 15.00
BFFTY T.Y. Hilton SP 2.50 6.00

2017 Panini Black Friday Salute to Service Memorabilia

*CRACKED/25: .8X TO 2X BASIC MEM
SSACP Amari Cooper 2.50 6.00
SSDCK Dalvin Cook 2.50 6.00
SSDHR Derrick Henry 2.50 6.00
SSDSK DeShone Kizer 2.50 6.00
SSDWS Deshaun Watson 2.50 6.00
SSEZE Ezekiel Elliott 2.50 6.00
SSJBA Joey Bosa 2.50 6.00
SSJGF Jared Goff 2.50 6.00
SSJRH Jordan Howard 2.50 6.00
SSJSS JuJu Smith-Schuster 2.50 6.00
SSJWS Jameis Winston 2.50 6.00
SSLFN Leonard Fournette 2.50 6.00
SSMGD Melvin Gordon 2.50 6.00
SSMMO Marcus Mariota 2.50 6.00
SSMTB Mitchell Trubisky 2.50 6.00
SSMTH Michael Thomas 2.50 6.00
SSOJH O.J. Howard 2.50 6.00
SSPLY Paxton Lynch 2.50 6.00
SSPM2 Patrick Mahomes II 25.00 50.00
SSTGL Todd Gurley II 2.50 6.00

2017 Panini Black Friday Tools of the Trade Memorabilia

*CRACKED/25: .8X TO 2X BASIC JSY
TTFCD Corey Davis 3.00 8.00
TTFCM Christian McCaffrey 3.00 8.00
TTFDC Dalvin Cook 3.00 8.00
TTFDK DeShone Kizer 3.00 8.00
TTFDW Deshaun Watson 3.00 8.00
TTFEE Evan Engram 3.00 8.00
TTFJC James Conner 3.00 8.00
TTFJJ JuJu Smith-Schuster 3.00 8.00
TTFJM Joe Mixon 3.00 8.00
TTFJR John Ross III 3.00 8.00
TTFLF Leonard Fournette 3.00 8.00
TTFMT Mitchell Trubisky 3.00 8.00
TTFMW Mike Williams 3.00 8.00
TTFOJ O.J. Howard 3.00 8.00
TTFPM Patrick Mahomes II 10.00 25.00

2014 Panini Black Gold

1 Aaron Rodgers 6.00 15.00
2 Colin Kaepernick 2.50 6.00
3 Russell Wilson 5.00 12.00
4 Andrew Luck 4.00 10.00
5 Peyton Manning 8.00 20.00
6 Drew Brees 3.00 8.00
7 Tom Brady 8.00 20.00
8 Cam Newton 3.00 8.00
9 Ben Roethlisberger 3.00 8.00
10 Eli Manning 2.50 6.00
11 DeMarco Murray 2.50 6.00
12 Arian Foster 2.50 6.00
13 LeSean McCoy 3.00 8.00
14 Jamaal Charles 2.50 6.00
15 Matt Forte 2.00 5.00
16 Eddie Lacy 2.00 5.00
17 Marshawn Lynch 2.50 6.00
18 Doug Martin 2.50 6.00
19 Alfred Morris 2.00 5.00
20 Zac Stacy 2.00 5.00
21 Calvin Johnson 3.00 8.00
22 A.J. Green 3.00 8.00
23 Julio Jones 3.00 8.00
24 Dez Bryant 3.00 8.00
25 Brandon Marshall 2.00 5.00
26 Andre Johnson 2.50 6.00
27 Larry Fitzgerald 2.50 6.00
28 Demaryius Thomas 2.50 6.00
29 Randall Cobb 4.00 10.00
30 Vincent Jackson 2.00 5.00
31 Jimmy Graham 3.00 8.00
32 Rob Gronkowski 3.00 8.00
33 Antonio Gates 2.00 5.00
34 Vernon Davis 2.00 5.00
35 Jordan Cameron 2.00 5.00
36 J.J. Watt 3.00 8.00
37 Luke Kuechly 2.50 6.00
38 Terrell Suggs 2.00 5.00
39 Richard Sherman 3.00 8.00
40 Troy Polamalu 3.00 8.00
41 Robert Woods 2.50 6.00
42 Ryan Tannehill 2.50 6.00
43 Eric Decker 2.00 5.00
44 Robert Griffin III 2.00 5.00
45 Joe Flacco 2.50 6.00
46 Matt Ryan 2.50 6.00
47 Nick Foles 2.50 6.00
48 Cordarrelle Patterson 2.00 5.00
49 Nate Washington 2.00 5.00
50 Darren McFadden 2.00 5.00
51 Johnny Unitas 6.00 15.00
52 Joe Namath 5.00 12.00
53 Joe Montana 10.00 25.00
54 Dan Marino 8.00 20.00
55 John Elway 6.00 15.00
56 Brett Favre 8.00 20.00
57 Earl Campbell 4.00 10.00
58 Walter Payton 8.00 20.00
59 Eric Dickerson 3.00 8.00
60 Barry Sanders 6.00 15.00
61 Emmitt Smith 6.00 15.00
62 Jerry Rice 6.00 15.00
63 Michael Irvin 4.00 10.00
64 Dick Butkus 5.00 12.00
65 Lawrence Taylor 4.00 10.00
66 Jadeveon Clowney RC 2.00 5.00
67 Khalil Mack RC 6.00 15.00
68 Brandin Cooks RC 2.50 6.00
69 Terrance West RC 1.50 4.00
70 Ka'Deem Carey RC 1.50 4.00
71 De'Anthony Thomas RC 1.50 4.00
72 Carlos Hyde RC 2.00 5.00
73 Andre Williams RC 1.50 4.00
74 Devonta Freeman RC 2.50 6.00
75 Dri Archer RC 1.50 4.00
76 Jeremy Hill RC 2.00 5.00
77 Bishop Sankey RC 1.50 4.00
78 Tre Mason RC 1.50 4.00
79 Paul Richardson RC 2.00 5.00
80 Davante Adams RC 2.50 6.00
81 Donte Moncrief RC 1.50 4.00
82 Jarvis Landry RC 3.00 8.00
83 Cody Latimer RC 2.00 5.00
84 Marqise Lee RC 2.00 5.00
85 Odell Beckham Jr. RC 4.00 10.00
86 Jordan Matthews RC 2.50 6.00
87 Kelvin Benjamin RC 2.50 6.00
88 Mike Evans RC 4.00 10.00
89 Sammy Watkins RC 2.50 6.00
90 Allen Hurns RC 2.00 5.00
91 John Brown RC 2.50 6.00
92 Martavis Bryant RC 2.00 5.00
93 Zach Mettenberger RC 1.50 4.00
94 Aaron Murray RC 1.50 4.00
95 Derek Carr RC 10.00 25.00
96 Alfred Blue RC 1.50 4.00
97 Jerick McKinnon RC 2.00 5.00
98 Teddy Bridgewater RC 2.50 6.00
99 Blake Bortles RC 2.00 5.00
100 Johnny Manziel RC 2.50 6.00
101 D.Street/Z.Martin AU RC 10.00 25.00
102 J.Abbrederis/J.Janis AU RC 10.00 25.00
103 C.Kndjio/C.Rchrdsn AU RC 5.00 12.00
104 I.Crowell/P.Desir AU RC 5.00 12.00
105 A.Hitchens/D.Vaughan AU RC 4.00 10.00
106 R.Ross/J.Wright AU RC 5.00 12.00
107 T.Lewan/A.Andrews AU RC 4.00 10.00
108 J.Verrett/M.Grice AU RC 4.00 10.00
109 Q.Enunwa/T.Reilly AU RC 6.00 15.00
110 D.Yankey/J.McKinnon AU RC 5.00 12.00
111 A.Blue/C.Fiedorowicz AU RC 4.00 10.00
112 L.Taliaferro/T.Jernigan AU RC 8.00 20.00
114 A.Donald/M.Roberson AU RC 8.00 20.00
116 A.Hurns/A.Robinson AU RC 6.00 15.00
118 H.Clinton-Dix/C.Pryor AU RC 4.00 10.00
120 J.Amaro/A.SfrnJnkns AU RC 4.00 10.00
122 J.Brown/T.Niklas AU RC 6.00 15.00
124 C.Sims/R.Herron AU RC 4.00 10.00
125 J.Mtthws/G.Rbnsn AU RC 4.00 10.00

2014 Panini Black Gold Gold

*VETS/99: .6X TO 1.5X BASIC CARDS/199
*ROOKIES/99: .6X TO 1.5X BASIC CARDS/199
*RETIRED/49: .6X TO 1.5X BASIC CARDS/99
*ROOK AU/49: .6X TO 1.5X ROOK AU/99
85 Odell Beckham Jr. 6.00 15.00
113 James Wilder Jr. AU
Tevin Reese AU

2014 Panini Black Gold Gold Foil

*VETS/25: 1X TO 2.5X BASIC CARDS/199
*ROOKIES/25: .8X TO 2X BASIC CARDS/199
85 Odell Beckham Jr. 8.00 20.00

2014 Panini Black Gold Autographs

1 Bo Jackson/15 40.00 80.00
2 Richard Sherman/15 40.00 80.00
3 Andrew Luck/15 40.00 80.00
5 Dwayne Bowe/25 8.00 20.00
7 Jordy Nelson/75 30.00 60.00
8 Julius Thomas/99 4.00 10.00
11 Luke Kuechly/75 15.00 40.00
12 Michael Floyd/75 4.00 10.00
14 Danny Woodhead/99 15.00 30.00
15 Tim Brown/15 40.00 80.00

2014 Panini Black Gold Autographs Gold

*GOLD/25: .6X TO 1.5X AU/99
11 Luke Kuechly/25 30.00 80.00

2014 Panini Black Gold Dual Team Symbols

*SILVER/25: .6X TO 1.5X DUAL TEAM/99
1 J.Manziel/T.West 4.00 10.00
2 D.Archer/L.Bell 10.00 25.00
3 S.Watkins/E.Manuel 4.00 10.00
4 M.Evans/V.Jackson 6.00 15.00
5 J.Clowney/J.Watt 4.00 10.00
6 J.Jones/D.Carr 15.00 40.00
7 C.Hyde/F.Gore 3.00 8.00
8 S.Jackson/D.Freeman 4.00 10.00
9 D.Street/D.Bryant 4.00 10.00
10 J.McKinnon/T.Bridgewater 4.00 10.00
11 M.Colston/B.Cooks 4.00 10.00
12 M.Lynch/P.Richardson 6.00 15.00
13 A.Rodgers/D.Adams 20.00 40.00
14 T.Hilton/D.Moncrief 15.00 30.00
15 C.Newton/K.Benjamin 4.00 10.00

2014 Panini Black Gold Gold Standard

1 Johnny Unitas 50.00 100.00
2 Walter Payton 100.00 200.00
3 Dan Marino 125.00 200.00
4 Barry Sanders 50.00 100.00
5 Joe Montana 150.00 250.00
6 Lawrence Taylor 60.00 100.00
7 John Elway 40.00 100.00
8 Joe Namath 40.00 80.00
9 Calvin Johnson 40.00 80.00
10 Peyton Manning 75.00 150.00
11 Tom Brady 75.00 150.00
12 Colin Kaepernick 30.00 60.00
13 Russell Wilson 100.00 200.00
14 J.J. Watt 40.00 100.00
15 Andrew Luck
16 Drew Brees 25.00 60.00
17 Cam Newton 75.00 120.00
18 Aaron Rodgers
19 LeSean McCoy 20.00 50.00
20 Johnny Manziel 12.00 30.00
21 Blake Bortles 10.00 25.00
22 Derek Carr 50.00 100.00
23 Brandin Cooks 12.00 30.00
24 Teddy Bridgewater 50.00 100.00
25 Mike Evans 20.00 50.00

2014 Panini Black Gold Gold Strike Autographs

1 LaDainian Tomlinson/25
3 Steve Johnson/99 5.00 12.00
7 Danny Woodhead/99 15.00 30.00
8 Geno Smith/25 6.00 15.00
9 Vincent Jackson/99 4.00 10.00
10 C.J. Spiller/99 4.00 10.00
11 Nick Foles/25 8.00 20.00
12 J.J. Watt/25 75.00 125.00
13 Greg Jennings/49 5.00 12.00
14 Torrey Smith/99 4.00 10.00
15 Rob Gronkowski/49 30.00 60.00
16 Jamaal Charles/25 25.00 50.00
17 Eddie Lacy/25 6.00 15.00
18 Luke Kuechly/49 75.00 120.00
19 Ben Tate/99 4.00 10.00
20 Julius Thomas/99 4.00 10.00
21 Giovani Bernard/49 5.00 12.00
22 DeSean Jackson/49 6.00 15.00
23 Alshon Jeffery/49 6.00 15.00
24 Andre Ellington/99 4.00 10.00
25 Zac Stacy/25 6.00 15.00

2014 Panini Black Gold Gold Strike Autographs Gold

*GOLD AU/25: .6X TO 1.5X AU/99
*GOLD AU/25: .5X TO 1.2X AU/49
*GOLD AU/25: .4X TO 1X AU/25

2014 Panini Black Gold Golden Opportunity Dual Jerseys

*PRIME/49: .5X TO 1.2X JSY/149
1 J.Garoppolo/T.Brady 20.00 50.00
2 R.Woods/S.Watkins 8.00 20.00
3 A.Murray/A.Smith 3.00 8.00
4 D.Street/D.Bryant 8.00 20.00
5 S.Greene/B.Sankey 2.50 6.00
6 A.Dalton/A.McCarron 3.00 8.00
7 G.Bernard/J.Hill 3.00 8.00
8 C.Latimer/D.Thomas 3.00 8.00
10 M.Evans/V.Jackson 6.00 15.00
11 C.Hyde/F.Gore 3.00 8.00
12 B.Cooks/M.Colston 4.00 10.00
13 O.Beckham Jr./V.Cruz 6.00 15.00
14 C.Shorts III/M.Lee 3.00 8.00
15 J.Manziel/B.Favre 8.00 20.00

2014 Panini Black Gold Golden Receivers Jerseys

*PRIME/25: .6X TO 1.5X JSY/99
1 Calvin Johnson 4.00 10.00
2 Dez Bryant 8.00 20.00
3 Danny Amendola 3.00 8.00
4 Vincent Jackson 2.50 6.00
5 A.J. Green 4.00 10.00
6 Robert Woods 3.00 8.00
7 Mike Wallace 2.50 6.00
8 Demaryius Thomas 3.00 8.00
9 Dwayne Bowe 3.00 8.00
10 Jerry Rice 12.00 30.00
11 Jordan Matthews 3.00 8.00
12 Kelvin Benjamin 3.00 8.00
13 Brandin Cooks 3.00 8.00
14 Sammy Watkins 3.00 8.00
15 Mike Evans 5.00 12.00

2014 Panini Black Gold Grand Debut Autograph Jerseys

1 Johnny Manziel/25 12.00 30.00
2 Blake Bortles/25 10.00 25.00
3 Teddy Bridgewater/25 12.00 30.00
4 Carlos Hyde/99 6.00 15.00
5 Sammy Watkins/99 8.00 20.00
6 Mike Evans/99 12.00 30.00
7 Terrance West/99 5.00 12.00
8 Derek Carr/99 30.00 60.00
9 Brandin Cooks/99 8.00 20.00
10 Bishop Sankey/99 5.00 12.00

2014 Panini Black Gold Grand Debut Autograph Jerseys Prime

*PRIME/25: .6X TO 1.5X JSY AU/99
8 Derek Carr/25 150.00 250.00

2014 Panini Black Gold Massive Materials

*PRIME/49: .5X TO 1.2X JSY/99
*PRIME/25: .5X TO 1.2X JSY/49
*PRIME/25: .6X TO 1.5X JSY/99
1 Johnny Manziel/99 4.00 10.00
2 Derek Carr/99 15.00 40.00
3 Blake Bortles/99 3.00 8.00
4 Carlos Hyde/99 3.00 8.00
5 Bishop Sankey/99 2.50 6.00
6 Terrance West/99 2.50 6.00
7 Kelvin Benjamin/99 4.00 10.00
8 Sammy Watkins/99 4.00 10.00
9 Mike Evans/99 6.00 15.00
10 A.J. Green/99 4.00 10.00
11 Odell Beckham Jr./99 6.00 15.00
12 Peyton Manning/49 10.00 25.00
13 Jamaal Charles/99 8.00 20.00
14 Tony Romo/49 10.00 25.00
15 Rob Gronkowski/49 8.00 20.00

2014 Panini Black Gold Mother Lode Rookie Jerseys

*PRIME/99: .5X TO 1.2X JSY/299
1 Johnny Manziel 3.00 8.00
2 Derek Carr 6.00 15.00
3 Blake Bortles 2.50 6.00
4 Teddy Bridgewater 3.00 8.00
5 Jadeveon Clowney 2.50 6.00
6 Mike Evans 5.00 12.00
7 Sammy Watkins 3.00 8.00
8 Carlos Hyde 2.50 6.00
9 Bishop Sankey 2.00 5.00
10 Terrance West 2.00 5.00
11 Kelvin Benjamin 3.00 8.00
12 Brandin Cooks 3.00 8.00
13 Donte Moncrief 2.00 5.00
14 Khalil Mack 8.00 20.00
15 Eric Ebron 2.50 6.00
16 Austin Seferian-Jenkins 2.00 5.00
17 A.J. McCarron 2.00 5.00
18 Tom Savage 2.00 5.00
19 Jimmy Garoppolo 15.00 40.00
20 Aaron Murray 2.00 5.00
21 Devonta Freeman 3.00 8.00
22 Davante Adams 3.00 8.00
23 Jordan Matthews 3.00 8.00
24 Marqise Lee 2.50 6.00
25 Dri Archer 2.00 5.00

2014 Panini Black Gold NFL Seal of Approval

*SILVER/25: .6X TO 1.5X SEAL/149
1 Colin Kaepernick 4.00 10.00
2 Frank Gore 4.00 10.00
3 Carlos Hyde 3.00 8.00
4 Matt Forte 3.00 8.00
5 Ka'Deem Carey 2.50 6.00
6 A.J. Green 5.00 12.00
7 A.J. McCarron 2.50 6.00
8 C.J. Spiller 3.00 8.00
9 Sammy Watkins 4.00 10.00
10 Peyton Manning 15.00 30.00
11 Demaryius Thomas 4.00 10.00
12 Cody Latimer 3.00 8.00
13 Josh Gordon 3.00 8.00
14 Johnny Manziel 4.00 10.00
15 Terrance West 2.50 6.00
16 Vincent Jackson 3.00 8.00
17 Mike Evans 6.00 15.00
18 Larry Fitzgerald 4.00 10.00
19 John Brown 4.00 10.00
20 Philip Rivers 5.00 12.00
21 Antonio Gates 3.00 8.00
22 Jason Verrett 2.50 6.00
23 Jamaal Charles 5.00 12.00
24 De'Anthony Thomas 2.50 6.00
25 Andrew Luck 15.00 30.00
26 Reggie Wayne 6.00 15.00
27 Donte Moncrief 2.50 6.00
28 Tony Romo 8.00 20.00
29 Dez Bryant 10.00 25.00
30 Mike Wallace 3.00 8.00
31 Jarvis Landry 5.00 12.00
32 Nick Foles 4.00 10.00
33 Jordan Matthews 4.00 10.00
34 Matt Ryan 4.00 10.00
35 Julio Jones 5.00 12.00
36 Devonta Freeman 6.00 15.00
37 Eli Manning 4.00 10.00
38 Odell Beckham Jr. 6.00 15.00
39 Denard Robinson 3.00 8.00
40 Blake Bortles 3.00 8.00
41 Marqise Lee 3.00 8.00
42 Geno Smith 3.00 8.00
43 Eric Decker 3.00 8.00
44 Matthew Stafford 4.00 10.00
45 Calvin Johnson 5.00 12.00
46 Eric Ebron 3.00 8.00
47 Aaron Rodgers 15.00 30.00
48 Ha Ha Clinton-Dix 3.00 8.00
49 Cam Newton 5.00 12.00
50 Kelvin Benjamin 4.00 10.00
51 Tom Brady 20.00 40.00
52 Jimmy Garoppolo 6.00 15.00
53 Derek Carr 15.00 40.00
54 Maurice Jones-Drew 3.00 8.00
55 Sam Bradford 3.00 8.00
56 Tre Mason 2.50 6.00
57 Joe Flacco 4.00 10.00
58 Terrell Suggs 3.00 8.00
59 Robert Griffin III 3.00 8.00
60 Alfred Morris 3.00 8.00
61 Drew Brees 5.00 12.00
62 Jimmy Graham 5.00 12.00
63 Brandin Cooks 4.00 10.00
64 Russell Wilson 15.00 30.00
65 Marshawn Lynch 6.00 15.00
66 Ben Roethlisberger 10.00 25.00
67 Le'Veon Bell 4.00 10.00
68 Dri Archer 2.50 6.00
69 Arian Foster 4.00 10.00
70 J.J. Watt 15.00 30.00
71 Jadeveon Clowney 3.00 8.00
72 Zach Mettenberger 2.50 6.00
73 Bishop Sankey 2.50 6.00
74 Cordarrelle Patterson 3.00 8.00
75 Teddy Bridgewater 4.00 10.00

2014 Panini Black Gold Rookie Autograph Jerseys

*PRIME/49: .5X TO 1.2X JSY AU/199
*PRIME/25: .6X TO 1.5X JSY AU/199
1 Aaron Murray/199 5.00 12.00
2 A.J. McCarron/199 5.00 12.00
3 Allen Robinson/199 8.00 20.00
4 Andre Williams/199 5.00 12.00
5 Asa Watson/199 5.00 12.00
6 Austin Seferian-Jenkins/199 5.00 12.00
7 Bishop Sankey/199 5.00 12.00
8 Brandin Cooks/199 8.00 20.00
9 Carlos Hyde/199 6.00 15.00
10 Charles Sims/199 5.00 12.00
11 Cody Latimer/199 6.00 15.00
12 Connor Shaw/199 5.00 12.00
13 Davante Adams/199 20.00 40.00
14 De'Anthony Thomas/199 5.00 12.00
15 Devonta Freeman/199 8.00 20.00
16 Donte Moncrief/199 5.00 12.00
17 Dri Archer/199 5.00 12.00
18 Eric Ebron/199 8.00 20.00
19 Jadeveon Clowney/199 6.00 15.00
20 Jarvis Landry/199 10.00 25.00
21 Jeremy Hill/199 6.00 15.00
22 Jimmy Garoppolo/199 60.00 125.00
23 Jordan Matthews/199 8.00 20.00
24 Ka'Deem Carey/199 5.00 12.00
25 Kelvin Benjamin/199 8.00 20.00
26 Khalil Mack/199 25.00 60.00
27 Logan Thomas/199 5.00 12.00
28 Marqise Lee/199 6.00 15.00
29 Mike Evans/199 12.00 30.00
30 Odell Beckham Jr./199 30.00 80.00
31 Sammy Watkins/99 8.00 20.00
32 Tajh Boyd/199 5.00 12.00
33 Teddy Bridgewater/99 8.00 20.00
34 Terrance West/199 5.00 12.00
35 Tom Savage/199 5.00 12.00
36 Tre Mason/199 5.00 12.00
37 Michael Sam/199 5.00 12.00
38 Blake Bortles/99 6.00 15.00
39 Derek Carr/99
40 Johnny Manziel/99 8.00 20.00

2014 Panini Black Gold Rookie Autograph Jerseys Prime

*PRIME/49: .5X TO 1.2X JSY AU/199
*PRIME/25: .6X TO 1.5X JSY AU/199

2014 Panini Black Gold Rookie Autographs

*GOLD/25: .6X TO 1.5X AU/99
*GOLD/25: .5X TO 1.2X AU/49
*GOLD/25: .4X TO 1X AU/25
1 Johnny Manziel/25 12.00 30.00
2 Derek Carr/25 60.00 120.00
3 Blake Bortles/25 10.00 25.00
4 Teddy Bridgewater/25 12.00 30.00
5 Terrance West/99 5.00 12.00
6 Brandin Cooks/99 8.00 20.00
7 Michael Sam/99 5.00 12.00
8 Mike Evans/49 15.00 40.00
9 Bishop Sankey/99 15.00 30.00
11 Sammy Watkins/25 12.00 30.00
12 Marqise Lee/99 6.00 15.00
14 Ka'Deem Carey/99 5.00 12.00
15 Eric Ebron/99 6.00 15.00
16 Austin Seferian-Jenkins/99 5.00 12.00
17 Jimmy Garoppolo/49 25.00 50.00
19 Tom Savage/49 6.00 15.00
20 Jeremy Hill/99 6.00 15.00
21 Isaiah Crowell/99 6.00 15.00
22 Aaron Murray/99 5.00 12.00
24 Jordan Matthews/99 8.00 20.00
25 Anthony Barr/99 5.00 12.00
26 Kelvin Benjamin/99 8.00 20.00
27 Devin Street/99 5.00 12.00
28 Kevin Norwood/99 8.00 20.00
29 John Brown/99 8.00 20.00
31 Paul Richardson/99 6.00 15.00
32 Jarvis Landry/99 10.00 25.00
34 Carlos Hyde/99 6.00 15.00
35 Logan Thomas/99 5.00 12.00

2014 Panini Black Gold Rookie Team Symbols

*SILVER/25: .6X TO 1.5X TEAM/99
1 Johnny Manziel 4.00 10.00
2 Blake Bortles 3.00 8.00
3 Teddy Bridgewater 4.00 10.00
4 Derek Carr 15.00 40.00
5 Carlos Hyde 3.00 8.00
6 Bishop Sankey 2.50 6.00
7 Terrance West 2.50 6.00
8 Brandin Cooks 4.00 10.00
9 Sammy Watkins 4.00 10.00
10 Kelvin Benjamin 4.00 10.00
11 Marqise Lee 3.00 8.00
12 Mike Evans 6.00 15.00
13 Eric Ebron 3.00 8.00
14 Jadeveon Clowney 3.00 8.00
15 Jordan Matthews 4.00 10.00
16 A.J. McCarron 2.50 6.00
17 Ka'Deem Carey 2.50 6.00
18 Devonta Freeman 4.00 10.00
19 Tre Mason 2.50 6.00
20 Dri Archer 2.50 6.00
21 Calvin Pryor 2.50 6.00
22 C.J. Mosley 3.00 8.00
23 Odell Beckham Jr. 6.00 15.00
24 John Brown 4.00 10.00
25 Donte Moncrief 2.50 6.00
26 Tom Savage 2.50 6.00
27 Ha Ha Clinton-Dix 3.00 8.00
28 Zack Martin 3.00 8.00
29 Anthony Barr 2.50 6.00
30 Jeremy Hill 3.00 8.00
31 Austin Seferian-Jenkins 2.50 6.00
32 Jason Verrett 2.50 6.00
33 Andre Williams 2.50 6.00
34 Allen Hurns 3.00 8.00
35 Aaron Murray 2.50 6.00

2014 Panini Black Gold Rookie Tetrad Jerseys

*PRIME/49: .6X TO 1.5X JSY/299
1 Johnny Manziel 3.00 8.00
2 Jadeveon Clowney 2.50 6.00
3 Brandin Cooks 3.00 8.00
4 Carlos Hyde 2.50 6.00
5 Kelvin Benjamin 3.00 8.00
6 Blake Bortles 2.50 6.00
7 Sammy Watkins 6.00 15.00
8 Teddy Bridgewater 3.00 8.00
9 Derek Carr 6.00 15.00
10 Bishop Sankey 2.00 5.00

2014 Panini Black Gold Sizeable Signatures Jerseys

*PRIME/25: .6X TO 1.5X JSY AU/99
8 Andre Ellington/99 6.00 15.00
10 Giovani Bernard/99 6.00 15.00
11 Antonio Gates/49 8.00 20.00
13 Kenny Stills/99 6.00 15.00
14 Manti Te'o/99 8.00 20.00
15 Ryan Tannehill/49 10.00 25.00
16 Torrey Smith/99 6.00 15.00
17 Vincent Jackson/49 8.00 20.00
19 DeMarco Murray/49 10.00 25.00
20 Terrance Williams/99 10.00 25.00
21 Terrell Davis/25 30.00 60.00
22 Gale Sayers/25 30.00 60.00
24 Robert Mathis/99 6.00 15.00
25 Steve Largent/25 15.00 40.00

2014 Panini Black Gold Sizeable Signatures Rookie Jerseys

1 Johnny Manziel/99 10.00 25.00
2 Teddy Bridgewater/99 10.00 25.00
3 Blake Bortles/99 8.00 20.00
4 Jadeveon Clowney/149 6.00 15.00
5 Derek Carr/149 40.00 100.00
6 Sammy Watkins/149 8.00 20.00
7 Mike Evans/149 20.00 50.00
8 Eric Ebron/149 8.00 20.00
9 Jimmy Garoppolo/149 40.00 100.00
10 Marqise Lee/149 6.00 15.00
11 Tre Mason/199 5.00 12.00
12 Kelvin Benjamin/199 8.00 20.00
13 Tom Savage/199 5.00 12.00
14 Carlos Hyde/199 6.00 15.00
15 Bishop Sankey/199 5.00 12.00

16 Austin Seferian-Jenkins/199 5.00 12.00
17 Aaron Murray/199 5.00 12.00
18 Khalil Mack/199 20.00 50.00
19 Terrance West/199 5.00 12.00
20 Michael Sam/199 5.00 12.00
21 Paul Richardson/199 6.00 15.00
22 Jordan Matthews/199 8.00 20.00
23 Dri Archer/199 5.00 12.00
24 Brandin Cooks/199 8.00 20.00
25 Andre Williams/199 5.00 12.00

2014 Panini Black Gold Sizeable Signatures Rookie Jerseys Prime

2 Teddy Bridgewater/25 50.00 100.00
3 Blake Bortles/25 10.00 25.00

2014 Panini Black Gold Team Symbols

*SILVER/25: .6X TO 1.5X TEAM/149
1 Colin Kaepernick 4.00 10.00
2 Jerry Rice 12.00 30.00
3 Matt Forte 3.00 8.00
4 Walter Payton 15.00 40.00
5 A.J. Green 5.00 12.00
6 EJ Manuel 3.00 8.00
7 Peyton Manning 15.00 30.00
8 John Elway 12.00 30.00
9 Barkevious Mingo 3.00 8.00
10 Vincent Jackson 3.00 8.00
11 Larry Fitzgerald 4.00 10.00
12 Philip Rivers 5.00 12.00
13 Jamaal Charles 5.00 12.00
14 Andrew Luck 25.00 50.00
15 Reggie Wayne 6.00 15.00
16 Tony Romo 8.00 20.00
17 DeMarco Murray 4.00 10.00
18 Ryan Tannehill 4.00 10.00
19 Dan Marino 15.00 40.00
20 LeSean McCoy 5.00 12.00
21 Nick Foles 4.00 10.00
22 Matt Ryan 4.00 10.00
23 Julio Jones 5.00 12.00
24 Eli Manning 4.00 10.00
25 Victor Cruz 4.00 10.00
26 Cecil Shorts 3.00 8.00
27 Geno Smith 3.00 8.00
28 Matthew Stafford 4.00 10.00
29 Calvin Johnson 5.00 12.00
30 Aaron Rodgers 15.00 30.00
31 Brett Favre 15.00 40.00
32 Cam Newton 5.00 12.00
33 Luke Kuechly 4.00 10.00
34 Tom Brady 12.00 30.00
35 Bo Jackson 20.00 50.00
36 Sam Bradford 3.00 8.00
37 Kurt Warner 6.00 15.00
38 Joe Flacco 4.00 10.00
39 Robert Griffin III 3.00 8.00
40 Alfred Morris 3.00 8.00
41 Drew Brees 5.00 12.00
42 Jimmy Graham 5.00 12.00
43 Russell Wilson 15.00 30.00
44 Richard Sherman 5.00 12.00
45 Ben Roethlisberger 15.00 30.00
46 Terry Bradshaw 10.00 25.00
47 Arian Foster 4.00 10.00
48 J.J. Watt 15.00 30.00
49 Nate Washington 3.00 8.00
50 Cordarrelle Patterson 3.00 8.00

2014 Panini Black Gold Versus Dual Jerseys

*PRIME/25: .6X TO 1.5X JSY/99
1 P.Manning/T.Brady 30.00 60.00
2 C.Kaepernick/R.Sherman 20.00 40.00
3 B.Favre/W.Sapp 15.00 40.00
4 B.Sanders/E.Smith 20.00 50.00
5 D.Marino/J.Elway 15.00 40.00
6 J.Manziel/B.Bortles 4.00 10.00
7 K.Benjamin/M.Evans 6.00 15.00
8 R.Griffin III/A.Luck 8.00 20.00
9 G.Smith/E.Manuel 4.00 10.00
10 T.West/J.Hill 3.00 8.00
11 C.Finnegan/A.Johnson 5.00 12.00
12 M.Colston/R.White 4.00 10.00
13 T.Suggs/L.Bell 5.00 12.00
14 E.Lacy/M.Forte 4.00 10.00
15 E.Manning/P.Manning 12.00 30.00

2015 Panini Black Gold

1 Blake Bortles 2.00 5.00
2 Antonio Brown 3.00 8.00
3 C.J. Anderson 2.50 6.00
4 LeSean McCoy 3.00 8.00
5 Philip Rivers 3.00 8.00
6 DeMarco Murray 2.50 6.00
7 Colin Kaepernick 2.50 6.00
8 Tony Romo 2.50 6.00
9 Eli Manning 2.50 6.00
10 Joe Flacco 2.50 6.00
11 Carson Palmer 2.50 6.00
12 Andrew Luck 4.00 10.00
13 Jordy Nelson 2.50 6.00
14 Tom Brady 8.00 20.00
15 Jamaal Charles 2.50 6.00
16 Matt Forte 2.00 5.00
17 A.J. Green 3.00 8.00
18 Peyton Manning 6.00 15.00
19 Julio Jones 3.00 8.00
20 Nick Foles 2.50 6.00
21 Alfred Morris 2.00 5.00
22 Andre Johnson 2.50 6.00
23 Adrian Peterson 3.00 8.00
24 Brandon Marshall 2.00 5.00
25 Odell Beckham Jr. 3.00 8.00
26 Ben Roethlisberger 3.00 8.00
27 Derek Carr 3.00 8.00
28 Eddie Lacy 2.00 5.00
29 Ryan Tannehill 2.50 6.00
30 Dez Bryant 3.00 8.00
31 Kendall Wright 2.00 5.00
32 Matthew Stafford 2.50 6.00
33 Marshawn Lynch 2.50 6.00
34 Demaryius Thomas 2.50 6.00
35 Drew Brees 3.00 8.00
36 Rob Gronkowski 3.00 8.00
37 Jason Witten 2.50 6.00
38 T.Y. Hilton 2.50 6.00
39 DeSean Jackson 2.50 6.00
40 Johnny Manziel 2.50 6.00
41 Matt Ryan 2.50 6.00
42 J.J. Watt 3.00 8.00
43 Sam Bradford 2.00 5.00
44 Aaron Rodgers 6.00 15.00
45 Richard Sherman 3.00 8.00
46 Russell Wilson 4.00 10.00
47 Calvin Johnson 3.00 8.00
48 Mike Evans 2.50 6.00
49 Le'Veon Bell 2.50 6.00
50 Cam Newton 3.00 8.00
51 Dan Marino 8.00 20.00
52 John Elway 6.00 15.00
53 Jim Kelly 4.00 10.00
54 Joe Montana 10.00 25.00
55 Tim Brown 4.00 10.00
56 Brett Favre 8.00 20.00
57 Roger Staubach 5.00 12.00
58 Walter Payton 8.00 20.00
59 Marshall Faulk 3.00 8.00
60 Jerry Rice 6.00 15.00
61 Shannon Sharpe 3.00 8.00
62 Barry Sanders 6.00 15.00
63 Cris Carter 4.00 10.00
64 Jerome Bettis 4.00 10.00
65 Emmitt Smith 6.00 15.00
66 Chris Conley RC 1.50 4.00
67 Marcus Mariota RC 6.00 15.00
68 Tevin Coleman RC 2.00 5.00
69 Phillip Dorsett RC 1.50 4.00
70 Ty Montgomery RC 1.50 4.00
71 Amari Cooper RC 5.00 12.00
72 Vic Beasley Jr. RC 2.00 5.00
73 Todd Gurley RC 6.00 15.00
74 Jaelen Strong RC 2.00 5.00
75 Kevin White RC 2.00 5.00
76 Duke Johnson RC 2.50 6.00
77 Ameer Abdullah RC 2.50 6.00
78 Tyler Lockett RC 2.50 6.00
79 Leonard Williams RC 1.50 4.00
80 Garrett Grayson RC 1.50 4.00
81 Devin Funchess RC 2.50 6.00
82 Randy Gregory RC 1.50 4.00
83 Breshad Perriman RC 1.50 4.00
84 Shane Ray RC 1.50 4.00
85 David Cobb RC 1.50 4.00
86 Matt Jones RC 1.50 4.00
87 Jeremy Langford RC 1.50 4.00
88 DeVante Parker RC 2.50 6.00
89 Dorial Green-Beckham RC 1.50 4.00
90 Landon Collins RC 2.00 5.00
91 Melvin Gordon RC 4.00 10.00
92 Jamison Crowder RC 2.00 5.00
93 Justin Hardy RC 1.50 4.00
94 Jameis Winston RC 4.00 10.00
95 Sammie Coates RC 2.00 5.00
96 Trae Waynes RC 1.50 4.00
97 Nelson Agholor RC 2.00 5.00
98 T.J. Yeldon RC 1.50 4.00
99 David Johnson RC 4.00 10.00
100 Bud Dupree RC 2.00 5.00

2015 Panini Black Gold Gold Foil

*GOLD FOIL/49: .6X TO 1.5X BASIC CARDS/199

2015 Panini Black Gold White Gold

*WHT. GOLD/99: .5X TO 1.2X BASIC CARDS/199

2015 Panini Black Gold White Gold Foil

*WHT FOIL/25: .8X TO 2X BASIC CARDS/199

2015 Panini Black Gold Autograph Jerseys

AUJAB Antonio Brown/25 40.00 80.00
AUJAD Andy Dalton/49 6.00 15.00
AUJBR Ben Roethlisberger/25 75.00 125.00
AUJBS Bruce Smith/49 6.00 15.00
AUJCC Cris Carter/25 40.00 80.00
AUJCS Cecil Shorts III/49 5.00 12.00
AUJCW Cameron Wake/25 30.00 60.00
AUJDC Dwight Clark/99 8.00 20.00
AUJDT Demaryius Thomas/49 20.00 40.00
AUJEC Earl Campbell/49 20.00 40.00
AUJED Eric Dickerson/49 25.00 50.00
AUJJK Jim Kelly/25 40.00 80.00
AUJJM Johnny Manziel/25 8.00 20.00
AUJJN Joe Namath/15 90.00 150.00
AUJKA Keenan Allen/99 5.00 12.00
AUJKW Kendall Wright/99 4.00 10.00
AUJMA Marcus Allen/49 20.00 40.00
AUJRS Richard Sherman/25 40.00 80.00
AUJRW Rod Woodson/49 30.00 60.00
AUJSY Steve Young/25 30.00 60.00
AUJTA Troy Aikman/25 60.00 120.00
AUJTB1 Tim Brown/99 20.00 40.00
AUJTD Terrell Davis/49 30.00 60.00
AUJTD2 Tony Dorsett/49 30.00 60.00

2015 Panini Black Gold Autographs

*GOLD/25: .6X TO 1.5X BASIC AU/99
*GOLD/25: .5X TO 1.2X BASIC AU/49
BGAAD Aaron Dobson/99 3.00 8.00
BGAAR Andre Reed/99 10.00 25.00
BGAAS Alex Smith/25
BGACA C.J. Anderson/99 4.00 10.00
BGADB Derrick Brooks/99 8.00 20.00
BGADM Darren McFadden/99 10.00 25.00
BGADS Darren Sproles/99 4.00 10.00
BGADU Dick Butkus/15
BGAED Eric Decker/49 4.00 10.00
BGAHE Herman Edwards/99 8.00 20.00
BGAIW Ickey Woods/99 8.00 20.00
BGAJC Jay Cutler/49 20.00 40.00
BGAJN Jordy Nelson/99 20.00 40.00
BGAKS Kenny Stills/99 3.00 8.00
BGAKW Kurt Warner/25 50.00 100.00
BGAMH Micah Hyde/99 10.00 25.00
BGAMI Michael Irvin/25 50.00 100.00
BGAPH Percy Harvin/49
BGARB Robert Brooks/99 12.00 30.00
BGARW Randy White/49 20.00 40.00
BGASJ Steve Johnson/99 4.00 10.00

2015 Panini Black Gold Draft Symbols

*WHITE/49: .6X TO 1.5X BASIC INSERTS/149
DRFT1 Jameis Winston 6.00 15.00
DRFT2 Marcus Mariota 10.00 25.00
DRFT3 Amari Cooper 8.00 20.00
DRFT4 Leonard Williams 2.50 6.00
DRFT5 Kevin White 3.00 8.00
DRFT6 Vic Beasley Jr. 3.00 8.00
DRFT7 Todd Gurley 12.00 30.00
DRFT8 Trae Waynes 2.50 6.00
DRFT9 DeVante Parker 4.00 10.00
DRFT10 Melvin Gordon 6.00 15.00
DRFT11 Kevin Johnson 2.50 6.00
DRFT12 Arik Armstead 2.50 6.00
DRFT13 Nelson Agholor 3.00 8.00
DRFT14 Bud Dupree 3.00 8.00
DRFT15 Shane Ray 2.50 6.00
DRFT16 Shaq Thompson 3.00 8.00
DRFT17 Breshad Perriman 2.50 6.00
DRFT18 Byron Jones 4.00 10.00
DRFT19 Phillip Dorsett 2.50 6.00
DRFT20 Landon Collins 3.00 8.00
DRFT21 T.J. Yeldon 2.50 6.00
DRFT22 Devin Smith 2.50 6.00
DRFT23 Dorial Green-Beckham 2.50 6.00
DRFT24 Devin Funchess 4.00 10.00
DRFT25 Ameer Abdullah 4.00 10.00
DRFT26 Tyler Lockett 4.00 10.00
DRFT27 Jaelen Strong 3.00 8.00
DRFT28 Tevin Coleman 3.00 8.00
DRFT29 Garrett Grayson 2.50 6.00
DRFT30 Chris Conley 2.50 6.00
DRFT31 David Johnson 6.00 15.00
DRFT32 Sammie Coates 3.00 8.00
DRFT33 Sean Mannion 2.50 6.00
DRFT34 Ty Montgomery 2.50 6.00
DRFT35 Cameron Artis-Payne 2.50 6.00

2015 Panini Black Gold Duel Symbols

*WHT GOLD/49: .6X TO X 1.5BASIC INSERTS/149
DTS1 P.Manning/T.Brady 10.00 25.00
DTS2 D.Bryant/O.Beckham Jr. 4.00 10.00
DTS3 C.Kaepernick/R.Wilson 5.00 12.00
DTS4 A.Luck/J.Watt 5.00 12.00
DTS5 B.Roethlisberger/J.Flacco 4.00 10.00
DTS6 A.Rodgers/M.Stafford 8.00 20.00
DTS7 K.Cousins/T.Romo 4.00 10.00
DTS8 D.Carr/A.Smith 4.00 10.00
DTS9 E.Manning/S.Bradford 3.00 8.00
DTS10 D.Brees/M.Ryan 4.00 10.00
DTS11 B.Perriman/S.Coates 3.00 8.00
DTS12 D.Parker/D.Smith 4.00 10.00
DTS13 J.Nelson/K.White 3.00 8.00
DTS14 M.Gordon/A.Cooper 8.00 20.00
DTS15 J.Winston/M.Mariota 6.00 15.00

2015 Panini Black Gold Franchise Gold

*WHT GOLD/99: .5X TO 1.2X BASIC INSERTS/199
*GOLD FOIL/49: .6X TO 1.5X BASIC INSERTS/199
FB1 Prkr/Mrno/Tnnhll 8.00 20.00
FG2 Jffry/Whte/Mrshll 3.00 8.00
FB2 Smth/Irvn/Rmo 6.00 15.00
FG3 Cpr/Rce/Brwn 8.00 20.00
FB3 Fvre/Mjkwski/Rdgrs 8.00 20.00
FG4 Rthlsbrgr/Hrrs/Brdshw 5.00 12.00
FB4 Jhnsn/Wrght/Mrta 10.00 25.00
FG5 Wnstn/Jcksn/Brks 10.00 25.00
FB5 Mntna/Gre/Rce 10.00 25.00
FG6 Clstn/Brs/Wllms 4.00 10.00
FB6 Lnch/Lrgnt/Wlsn 5.00 12.00
FG7 Mnng/Tylr/Bckhm 4.00 10.00
FB7 Sndrs/Jhnsn/Stffrd 6.00 15.00
FG8 Flk/Jcksn/Grly 10.00 25.00
FB8 Lck/Mnng/Wyne 8.00 20.00

2015 Panini Black Gold Gilded Signatures

EILEF Ereck Flowers 3.00 8.00
GILBD Bud Dupree 10.00 25.00
GILCAP Cameron Artis-Payne 2.50 6.00
GILCW Clive Walford 2.50 6.00
GILDD DaVaris Daniels 2.50 6.00
GILDL Dezmin Lewis 2.50 6.00
GILDS Danny Shelton 2.50 6.00
GILEG Eddie Goldman 2.50 6.00
GILEH Eli Harold 2.50 6.00
GILEK Eric Kendricks 8.00 20.00
GILJH Josh Harper 2.50 6.00
GILJJ Jesse James 3.00 8.00
GILJN J.J. Nelson 2.50 6.00
GILJS Josh Shaw 4.00 10.00
GILKB Kenny Bell 4.00 10.00
GILLC Landon Collins 6.00 15.00
GILMA Mario Alford 2.50 6.00
GILMB Malcolm Brown 3.00 8.00
GILME Mario Edwards Jr. 2.50 6.00
GILMP MyCole Pruitt 2.50 6.00
GILNO Nick O'Leary 2.50 6.00
GILOO Owamagbe Odighizuwa 3.00 8.00
GILQR Quinten Rollins 8.00 20.00
GILSA Stephone Anthony 10.00 25.00
GILSR Shane Ray 6.00 15.00
GILST Shaq Thompson 3.00 8.00
GILTD Titus Davis 3.00 8.00
GILTK Tyler Kroft 3.00 8.00
GILTW Trae Waynes 2.50 6.00
GILVB Vic Beasley Jr. 3.00 8.00

2015 Panini Black Gold Gilded Signatures White Gold

*WHITE/49: .6X TO 1.5X BASIC AU/149
GILRG Randy Gregory 12.00 30.00

2015 Panini Black Gold Gold Prospecting Quad Materials

*WHT GOLD/99: .5X TO 1.2X BASIC JSY/199
*PRIME/49: .6X TO 1.5X BASIC JSY/199
GP4AA Ameer Abdullah 3.00 8.00
GP4AC Amari Cooper 6.00 15.00
GP4DF Devin Funchess 3.00 8.00
GP4DGB Dorial Green-Beckham 2.00 5.00
GP4DJ David Johnson 5.00 12.00
GP4DP DeVante Parker 3.00 8.00
GP4DU Duke Johnson 3.00 8.00
GP4JW Jameis Winston 8.00 20.00
GP4KW Karlos Williams 2.00 5.00
GP4MG Melvin Gordon 5.00 12.00
GP4MJ Matt Jones 2.00 5.00
GP4MM Marcus Mariota 8.00 20.00
GP4MW Maxx Williams 2.00 5.00
GP4NA Nelson Agholor 2.50 6.00
GP4SC Sammie Coates 2.50 6.00
GP4TC Tevin Coleman 2.50 6.00
GP4TG Todd Gurley 10.00 25.00
GP4TL Tyler Lockett 3.00 8.00
GP4TM Ty Montgomery 2.00 5.00
GP4TY T.J. Yeldon 2.00 5.00

2015 Panini Black Gold Gold Stars

*WHT GOLD/99: .5X TO 1.2X BASIC INSERTS/199
*GOLD/49: .6X TO 1.5X BASIC INSERTS/199
GOS1 Tom Brady 8.00 20.00
GOS2 Dez Bryant 3.00 8.00
GOS3 Peyton Manning 6.00 15.00
GOS4 Antonio Brown 3.00 8.00
GOS5 Adrian Peterson 3.00 8.00
GOS6 Aaron Rodgers 6.00 15.00
GOS7 Marshawn Lynch 2.50 6.00
GOS8 Andrew Luck 4.00 10.00
GOS9 Odell Beckham Jr. 3.00 8.00
GOS10 Calvin Johnson 3.00 8.00

2015 Panini Black Gold Golden Days

*WHT GOLD/99: .5X TO 1.2X BASIC INSERTS/199
*GOLD/49: .6X TO 1.5X BASIC INSERTS/199
*WHT FOIL/25: .8X TO 2X BASIC INSERTS/199
GDA1 Peyton Manning 6.00 15.00
GDA2 Larry Fitzgerald 2.50 6.00
GDA3 Johnny Manziel 2.50 6.00
GDA4 Amari Cooper 5.00 12.00
GDA5 Drew Brees 3.00 8.00
GDA6 Ryan Tannehill 2.50 6.00
GDA7 Dez Bryant 3.00 8.00
GDA8 Bo Jackson 5.00 12.00
GDA9 DeAndre Hopkins 2.50 6.00
GDA10 Sam Bradford 2.00 5.00
GDA11 Cam Newton 3.00 8.00
GDA12 Tom Brady 8.00 20.00
GDA13 Melvin Gordon 4.00 10.00
GDA14 Eddie Lacy 2.00 5.00
GDA15 Joe Flacco 2.50 6.00
GDA16 Jameis Winston 4.00 10.00
GDA17 Marcus Mariota 6.00 15.00
GDA18 Anquan Boldin 2.00 5.00
GDA19 LeSean McCoy 3.00 8.00
GDA20 Calvin Johnson 3.00 8.00
GDA21 T.J. Yeldon 1.50 4.00
GDA22 Barry Sanders 6.00 15.00
GDA23 Le'Veon Bell 2.50 6.00
GDA24 LaDainian Tomlinson 3.00 8.00
GDA25 Jamaal Charles 2.50 6.00
GDA26 Jimmy Graham 3.00 8.00
GDA27 Devin Smith 1.50 4.00
GDA28 Odell Beckham Jr. 3.00 8.00
GDA29 Julio Jones 3.00 8.00
GDA30 Andrew Luck 4.00 10.00
GDA31 DeSean Jackson 2.50 6.00
GDA32 Adrian Peterson 3.00 8.00
GDA33 Andy Dalton 2.50 6.00
GDA34 Todd Gurley 8.00 20.00
GDA35 Kevin White 2.00 5.00

2015 Panini Black Gold Golden Ground Game Materials

*WHT GOLD/99: .5X TO 1.2X BASIC JSY/199
*WHT GOLD/49: .5X TO 1.2X BASIC JSY/99
*PRIME/49: .6X TO 1.5X BASIC JSY
GGGAP Adrian Peterson/99 5.00 12.00
GGGBS Barry Sanders/99 8.00 20.00
GGGCH Carlos Hyde/199 2.50 6.00
GGGDF Devonta Freeman/199 3.00 8.00
GGGDJ David Johnson/199 6.00 15.00
GGGED Eric Dickerson/99 4.00 10.00
GGGES Emmitt Smith/99 8.00 20.00
GGGLT LaDainian Tomlinson/199 3.00 8.00
GGGMG Melvin Gordon/199 6.00 15.00
GGGTG Todd Gurley/199 12.00 30.00

2015 Panini Black Gold Golden Opportunity Materials

*WHT GOLD/75-99: .5X TO 1.2X BASIC JSY/149-199
*WHT GOLD/49: .5X TO 1.2X BASIC JSY/99
*PRIME/49: .6X TO 1.5X BASIC JSY/149-199
*PRIME/25: .6X TO 1.5X BASIC JSY/99
*PRIME/25: .8X TO 2X BASIC JSY/199
GOATL D.Freeman/T.Coleman/199 3.00 8.00
GOAZ C.Johnson/D.Johnson/199 6.00 15.00
GOBUF K.Williams/L.McCoy/199 4.00 10.00
GOCAR D.Funchess/K.Benjamin/199 4.00 10.00
GODET A.Abdullah/B.Sanders/99 8.00 20.00
GOGB R.Cobb/T.Montgomery/99 4.00 10.00
GOIND T.Hilton/P.Dorsett/99 4.00 10.00
GOMIA J.Landry/D.Parker/199
GONO D.Brees/G.Grayson/199 4.00 10.00
GOOAK A.Cooper/T.Brown/99 10.00 25.00
GOPHI J.Matthews/N.Agholor/199 3.00 8.00
GOPIT A.Brown/S.Coates/99 5.00 12.00
GOSEA T.Lockett/D.Baldwin/149 4.00 10.00
GOSTL M.Faulk/T.Gurley II/199 12.00 30.00
GOWAS A.Morris/M.Jones/99 3.00 8.00

2015 Panini Black Gold Grand Debut Autograph Jerseys

GDAA Ameer Abdullah/49 10.00 25.00
GDBH Brett Hundley/49 6.00 15.00
GDBP Breshad Perriman/49 6.00 15.00
GDBR Bryce Petty/49 6.00 15.00
GDBU Buck Allen/199 6.00 15.00
GDCC Chris Conley/49 6.00 15.00
GDDC David Cobb/199 4.00 10.00
GDDF Devin Funchess/49 10.00 25.00
GDDJ David Johnson/49
GDDP DeVante Parker/99 8.00 20.00
GDDU Duke Johnson/99 8.00 20.00
GDJC Jamison Crowder/199 5.00 12.00
GDJH Justin Hardy/199 4.00 10.00
GDJS Jaelen Strong/49 8.00 20.00
GDJW Jameis Winston/49 15.00 40.00
GDKW Kevin White/49
GDMD Mike Davis/49 6.00 15.00
GDMG Melvin Gordon/49 15.00 40.00
GDMJ Matt Jones/99
GDMM Marcus Mariota/49 30.00 60.00
GDNA Nelson Agholor/49
GDPD Phillip Dorsett/49 6.00 15.00
GDSC Sammie Coates/99 6.00 15.00
GDSD Stefon Diggs/99 12.00 30.00
GDTC Tevin Coleman/99 6.00 15.00
GDTG Todd Gurley/49 60.00 125.00
GDTM Ty Montgomery/99 8.00 20.00
GDTY T.J. Yeldon/99 5.00 12.00
GDVM Vince Mayle/199 5.00 12.00

2015 Panini Black Gold Grand Debut Autograph Jerseys Prime

*PRIME/49: .6X TO 1.5X BASIC JSY AU/199
*PRIME/25: .6X TO 1.5X BASIC JSY AU/99
*PRIME/25: .5X TO 1.2X BASIC JSY AU/49

2015 Panini Black Gold Massive Materials

*WHT GOLD/99: .5X TO 1.2X BASIC JSY/149-199
*WHT GOLD/49: .5X TO 1.2X BASIC JSY/99
*WHT GOLD/25: .6X TO 1.5X BASIC JSY/75-99
*PRIME/49: .6X TO 1.5X BASIC JSY/199
*PRIME/25: .6X TO 1.5X BASIC JSY/99
MSMAA Ameer Abdullah/199 4.00 10.00
MSMAC Amari Cooper/199 8.00 20.00
MSMAG A.J. Green/99 5.00 12.00
MSMBB Blake Bortles/199 2.50 6.00
MSMBC Brandin Cooks/199 3.00 8.00
MSMCH Carlos Hyde/199 2.50 6.00
MSMDC Derek Carr/199 4.00 10.00
MSMJE Julian Edelman/75 8.00 20.00
MSMJJ Julio Jones/99 5.00 12.00
MSMJM Jordan Matthews/199 3.00 8.00
MSMJW Jameis Winston/199 6.00 15.00
MSMMM Marcus Mariota/199 10.00 25.00
MSMOBJ Odell Beckham Jr./199 4.00 10.00
MSMRT Ryan Tannehill/149 3.00 8.00
MSMTL Tyler Lockett/199 4.00 10.00

2015 Panini Black Gold Metallic Marks

MMAA Ameer Abdullah 8.00 20.00
MMAC Amari Cooper 30.00 60.00
MMBA Buck Allen 6.00 15.00
MMBH Brett Hundley 5.00 12.00
MMBP Bryce Petty 5.00 12.00
MMBP Breshad Perriman 5.00 12.00
MMCC Chris Conley 5.00 12.00
MMDC David Cobb 5.00 12.00
MMDF Devin Funchess 8.00 20.00
MMDGB Dorial Green-Beckham 5.00 12.00
MMDJ David Johnson 20.00 40.00
MMDP DeVante Parker 8.00 20.00
MMDS Devin Smith 5.00 12.00
MMDU Duke Johnson 8.00 20.00
MMGG Garrett Grayson 5.00 12.00
MMJA Jay Ajayi 8.00 20.00
MMJC Jamison Crowder 6.00 15.00
MMJH Justin Hardy 5.00 12.00
MMJL Jeremy Langford 20.00 40.00
MMJS Jaelen Strong 6.00 15.00
MMJW Jameis Winston 12.00 30.00
MMKW Kevin White 6.00 15.00
MMKW Karlos Williams 5.00 12.00
MMLW Leonard Williams 5.00 12.00
MMMD Mike Davis 5.00 12.00
MMMG Melvin Gordon 12.00 30.00
MMMJ Matt Jones 5.00 12.00
MMMM Marcus Mariota 50.00 100.00
MMMW Maxx Williams 5.00 12.00
MMNA Nelson Agholor 6.00 15.00
MMPD Phillip Dorsett 5.00 12.00
MMRG Rashad Greene 5.00 12.00
MMSC Sammie Coates 6.00 15.00
MMSD Stefon Diggs 12.00 30.00
MMSM Sean Mannion 5.00 12.00
MMTC Tevin Coleman 6.00 15.00
MMTG Todd Gurley 50.00 100.00
MMTL Tyler Lockett 8.00 20.00
MMTM Ty Montgomery 5.00 12.00
MMTY T.J. Yeldon 5.00 12.00
MMVM Vince Mayle 6.00 15.00

2015 Panini Black Gold Metallic Marks White Gold

*WHITE/49: .5X TO 1.2X BASIC AU/99
*WHITE/25: .6X TO 1.5X BASIC AU/99
MMAC Amari Cooper/25 40.00 80.00

2015 Panini Black Gold Mother Lode Rookie Jerseys

*WHT GOLD/99: .5X TO 1.2X BASIC JSY/199
*PRIME/49: .6X TO 1.5X BASIC JSY/199
MLAA Ameer Abdullah 4.00 10.00
MLAC Amari Cooper 8.00 20.00
MLBP Breshad Perriman 2.50 6.00
MLDC David Cobb 2.50 6.00
MLDF Devin Funchess 4.00 10.00
MLDJ David Johnson 6.00 15.00
MLDP DeVante Parker 4.00 10.00
MLJW Jameis Winston 6.00 15.00
MLLW Leonard Williams 2.50 6.00
MLMG Melvin Gordon 6.00 15.00
MLMJ Matt Jones 2.50 6.00
MLMM Marcus Mariota 10.00 25.00
MLNA Nelson Agholor 3.00 8.00
MLPD Phillip Dorsett 2.50 6.00
MLSD Stefon Diggs 6.00 15.00
MLTC Tevin Coleman 3.00 8.00
MLTG Todd Gurley 12.00 30.00
MLTL Tyler Lockett 4.00 10.00
MLTM Ty Montgomery 2.50 6.00
MLTY T.J. Yeldon 2.50 6.00

2015 Panini Black Gold NFL Seal of Approval

*WHT/49: .6X TO 1.5X BASIC INSERTS/149
SOA1 Julio Jones 4.00 10.00
SOA2 Justin Hardy 2.00 5.00
SOA3 David Johnson 5.00 12.00
SOA4 Steve Smith 3.00 8.00
SOA5 Maxx Williams 2.00 5.00
SOA6 Karlos Williams 2.00 5.00
SOA7 Cam Newton 4.00 10.00
SOA8 Kevin White 2.50 6.00
SOA9 Andy Dalton 3.00 8.00
SOA10 Duke Johnson 3.00 8.00
SOA11 Jason Witten 3.00 8.00
SOA12 Dez Bryant 4.00 10.00
SOA13 Peyton Manning 8.00 20.00
SOA14 Matthew Stafford 3.00 8.00
SOA15 Aaron Rodgers 8.00 20.00
SOA16 Eddie Lacy 2.50 6.00
SOA17 Arian Foster 3.00 8.00
SOA18 Andrew Luck 5.00 12.00
SOA19 Phillip Dorsett 2.00 5.00
SOA20 Rashad Greene 2.00 5.00
SOA21 Jamaal Charles 3.00 8.00
SOA22 Jay Ajayi 3.00 8.00
SOA23 Adrian Peterson 4.00 10.00
SOA24 Tom Brady 10.00 25.00
SOA25 Rob Gronkowski 4.00 10.00
SOA26 Drew Brees 4.00 10.00
SOA27 Mark Ingram 3.00 8.00
SOA28 Eli Manning 3.00 8.00
SOA29 Odell Beckham Jr. 4.00 10.00
SOA30 Leonard Williams 2.00 5.00
SOA31 Devin Smith 2.00 5.00
SOA32 Derek Carr 4.00 10.00
SOA33 Amari Cooper 6.00 15.00
SOA34 DeMarco Murray 3.00 8.00
SOA35 Nelson Agholor 2.50 6.00
SOA36 Martavis Bryant 2.50 6.00
SOA37 Le'Veon Bell 3.00 8.00
SOA38 Melvin Gordon 5.00 12.00
SOA39 Colin Kaepernick 3.00 8.00
SOA40 Mike Davis 2.00 5.00
SOA41 Marshawn Lynch 3.00 8.00
SOA42 Russell Wilson 5.00 12.00
SOA43 Nick Foles 3.00 8.00
SOA44 Todd Gurley 8.00 20.00
SOA45 Mike Evans 3.00 8.00
SOA46 Jameis Winston 5.00 12.00
SOA47 Marcus Mariota 8.00 20.00
SOA48 Dorial Green-Beckham 2.00 5.00
SOA49 Matt Jones 2.00 5.00
SOA50 Pierre Garcon 3.00 8.00

2015 Panini Black Gold Quad Panini Black Gold Team Symbols

*WHTIE GOLD/49: .6X TO 1.5X BASIC INSERTS/149
QTS1 Frmn/Jns/Ryn/Clmn 5.00 12.00
QTS2 Prrmn/Smth/Alln/Flcco 4.00 10.00
QTS3 Fnchss/Nwtn/Bnjmn/Kchly 5.00 12.00
QTS4 Brnt/Wttn/Rndle/Rmo 5.00 12.00
QTS5 Wre/Sndrs/Thms/Mnng 10.00 25.00
QTS6 Abdllh/Jhnsn/Bll/Stffrd 5.00 12.00
QTS7 Rdgrs/Lcy/Nlsn/Mntgmry 10.00 25.00
QTS8 Gre/Hltn/Lck/Drstt 6.00 15.00
QTS9 LFll/Grnkwski/Brdy/Edlmn 12.00 30.00
QTS10 Mrtn/Wnstn/McCy/Evns 8.00 20.00
QTS11 Bckhm/Crz/Wllms/Mnng 5.00 12.00
QTS12 Cpr/Jcksn/Crr/Brwn 10.00 25.00
QTS13 Brwn/Rthlsbrgr/Bll/Cts 5.00 12.00
QTS14 Lnch/Lcktt/Bldwn/Wlsn 6.00 15.00
QTS15 GrnBckhm/Snky/Cbb/Mrta 12.00 30.00

2015 Panini Black Gold Rookie Autographs

RAUAA Ameer Abdullah/49 6.00 15.00
RAUBP Bryce Petty/49 4.00 10.00
RAUBP Breshad Perriman/49 4.00 10.00
RAUBU Buck Allen/99
RAUCAP Cameron Artis-Payne/99 3.00 8.00
RAUCC Chris Conley/49 4.00 10.00
RAUCW Clive Walford/99 3.00 8.00
RAUDC David Cobb/99 3.00 8.00
RAUDF Devin Funchess/49 6.00 15.00
RAUDG Deontay Greenberry/99 3.00 8.00
RAUDGB Dorial Green-Beckham/99
RAUDJ David Johnson/49 20.00 40.00
RAUDP DeVante Parker/49 6.00 15.00
RAUDS Devin Smith/99
RAUJA Jay Ajayi/99
RAUJC Jamison Crowder/99
RAUJH Justin Hardy/99 3.00 8.00
RAUJJ Jesse James/99 4.00 10.00
RAUJL Jeremy Langford/99
RAUJW Jameis Winston/49 25.00 50.00
RAUKB Kenny Bell/99 5.00 12.00
RAUKW Kevin White/49
RAULW Leonard Williams/49 4.00 10.00
RAUMD Mike Davis/49 4.00 10.00
RAUMG Melvin Gordon/49 20.00 40.00
RAUMM Marcus Mariota/49 30.00 60.00
RAUNA Nelson Agholor/49 5.00 12.00
RAUPD Phillip Dorsett/49
RAURG Rashad Greene/99 3.00 8.00
RAUSM Sean Mannion/49 4.00 10.00
RAUTG Todd Gurley/49 60.00 120.00
RAUTL Tyler Lockett/99
RAUVM Vince Mayle/99 4.00 10.00

2015 Panini Black Gold Rookie Goldmine

*WHT GOLD/99: .5X TO 1.2X BASIC INSERTS/199
*GOLD/49: .6X TO 1.5X BASIC INSERTS/199
*WHT FOIL/25: .8X TO 2X BASIC INSERTS/199
RGM1 Jameis Winston 4.00 10.00
RGM2 Marcus Mariota 6.00 15.00
RGM3 Amari Cooper 5.00 12.00
RGM4 Kevin White 2.00 5.00
RGM5 Todd Gurley 6.00 15.00
RGM6 Melvin Gordon 4.00 10.00
RGM7 DeVante Parker 2.50 6.00
RGM8 Phillip Dorsett 1.50 4.00
RGM9 Breshad Perriman 1.50 4.00
RGM10 Sammie Coates 2.00 5.00
RGM11 Nelson Agholor 2.00 5.00
RGM12 Ameer Abdullah 2.50 6.00
RGM13 T.J. Yeldon 1.50 4.00
RGM14 David Johnson 4.00 10.00
RGM15 Bryce Petty 1.50 4.00
RGM16 Devin Funchess 2.50 6.00
RGM17 Tevin Coleman 2.00 5.00
RGM18 Jaelen Strong 2.00 5.00
RGM19 Dorial Green-Beckham 1.50 4.00
RGM20 Chris Conley 1.50 4.00

2015 Panini Black Gold Shadowbox Swatches

*WHT GOLD/99: .5X TO 1.2X BASIC JSY149-199
*WHT GOLD/49: .6X TO 1.5X BASIC JSY/149-199
*WHT GOLD/25: .8X TO 2X BASIC JSY/149-199
*WHT GOLD/25: .6X TO 1.5X BASIC JSY/99
*WHT GOLD/15: 1X TO 2.5X BASIC JSY/149-199
SBSSS Steve Smith/199 3.00 8.00
SBSAB Antonio Brown/199 4.00 10.00
SBSAC Amari Cooper/199 10.00 25.00
SBSAL Andrew Luck/99
SBSAP Adrian Peterson/149 6.00 15.00
SBSBF Brett Favre/99 12.00 30.00
SBSBS Barry Sanders/99 8.00 20.00
SBSCK Colin Kaepernick/99 4.00 10.00
SBSCM Clay Matthews/149 6.00 15.00
SBSDM Dan Marino/199 8.00 20.00
SBSDW DeMarcus Ware/199 3.00 8.00
SBSJH Jeremy Hill/199 2.50 6.00
SBSJJ J.J. Watt/99 5.00 12.00
SBSJW Jameis Winston/199 10.00 25.00
SBSMM Marcus Mariota/199 10.00 25.00
SBSPM Peyton Manning/99 25.00 50.00
SBSTB Tom Brady/149 12.00 30.00
SBSTK Travis Kelce/149 4.00 10.00
SBSTW Terrance Williams/199 2.50 6.00
SBSWP Walter Payton/149 15.00 40.00

2015 Panini Black Gold Sizeable Rookie Signature Jerseys

SSRAA Ameer Abdullah/99 8.00 20.00
SSRAC Amari Cooper/49
SSRBH Brett Hundley/149 4.00 10.00
SSRBP Bryce Petty/99
SSRBR Breshad Perriman/99 5.00 12.00
SSRCC Chris Conley/99 5.00 12.00
SSRDF Devin Funchess/199 6.00 15.00
SSRDGB Dorial Green-Beckham/199 4.00 10.00
SSRDJ David Johnson/199 20.00 40.00
SSRDP DeVante Parker/149 6.00 15.00
SSRDS Devin Smith/199 4.00 10.00
SSRDU Duke Johnson/199 6.00 15.00
SSRGG Garrett Grayson/99 5.00 12.00
SSRJA Jay Ajayi/199 6.00 15.00
SSRJL Jeremy Langford/199 4.00 10.00
SSRJS Jaelen Strong/199 5.00 12.00
SSRJW Jameis Winston/99 30.00 60.00
SSRKW Kevin White/99 6.00 15.00
SSRLW Leonard Williams/149 4.00 10.00
SSRMD Mike Davis/199 4.00 10.00
SSRMG Melvin Gordon/99 12.00 30.00
SSRMJ Matt Jones/199 4.00 10.00
SSRMM Marcus Mariota/99 40.00 80.00
SSRMW Maxx Williams/199 4.00 10.00
SSRNA Nelson Agholor/99
SSRPD Phillip Dorsett/199 4.00 10.00
SSRRG Rashad Greene/199 4.00 10.00
SSRSC Sammie Coates/199 5.00 12.00
SSRSD Stefon Diggs/199 10.00 25.00
SSRSM Sean Mannion/99 5.00 12.00
SSRTC Tevin Coleman/199 5.00 12.00
SSRTG Todd Gurley/49 50.00 100.00
SSRTL Tyler Lockett/199 6.00 15.00
SSRTM Ty Montgomery/199 4.00 10.00
SSRTY T.J. Yeldon/199 4.00 10.00

2015 Panini Black Gold Sizeable Rookie Signature Jerseys Prime

*PRIME/49: .6X TO 1.5X BASIC JSY AU/149-199
*PRIME/49: .4X TO 1X BASIC JSY AU/49
*PRIME/25: .6X TO 1.5X BASIC JSY AU/99
*PRIME/25: .5X TO 1.2X BASIC JSY AU/49
*PRIME/49: .5X TO 1.2X BASIC JSY AU/99
SSRAC Amari Cooper/25 50.00 100.00

2015 Panini Black Gold Sizeable Signature Jerseys

SSAL Andrew Luck/25
SSAP Adrian Peterson/15
SSBJ Bo Jackson/49
SSDM Dan Marino/25
SSJN Jordy Nelson/70 40.00 80.00
SSJR Jerry Rice/15 100.00 200.00
SSJT Joe Theismann/49 15.00 40.00
SSLM Lamar Miller/99 4.00 10.00
SSMA Matt Forte/49 5.00 12.00
SSMC Marques Colston/49 5.00 12.00
SSMF Marshall Faulk/49
SSOBJ Odell Beckham Jr./99 25.00 50.00
SSPM Peyton Manning/25
SSPP Patrick Peterson/25
SSRC Roger Craig/99 15.00 40.00
SSRT Ryan Tannehill/99 5.00 12.00
SSSL Steve Largent/49 25.00 50.00
SSTK Travis Kelce/49 8.00 20.00
SSTR Tony Romo/25 25.00 50.00

2015 Panini Black Gold Team Symbols

*WHT GOLD/49: .6X TO 1.5X BASIC INSERTS/149
TMS1 Matt Ryan 3.00 8.00
TMS2 Tevin Coleman 2.50 6.00
TMS3 Michael Floyd 2.50 6.00
TMS4 Joe Flacco 3.00 8.00
TMS5 Breshad Perriman 2.00 5.00
TMS6 LeSean McCoy 4.00 10.00
TMS7 Jim Kelly 5.00 12.00
TMS8 Luke Kuechly 3.00 8.00
TMS9 Devin Funchess 3.00 8.00
TMS10 Walter Payton 10.00 25.00
TMS11 Brian Urlacher 5.00 12.00
TMS12 A.J. Green 4.00 10.00
TMS13 Jeremy Hill 2.50 6.00
TMS14 Travis Benjamin 2.50 6.00
TMS15 Troy Aikman 6.00 15.00
TMS16 Emmitt Smith 8.00 20.00
TMS17 Terrell Davis 4.00 10.00
TMS18 Peyton Manning 8.00 20.00
TMS19 Calvin Johnson 4.00 10.00
TMS20 Ameer Abdullah 3.00 8.00
TMS21 Aaron Rodgers 8.00 20.00
TMS22 Jordy Nelson 3.00 8.00
TMS23 J.J. Watt 4.00 10.00
TMS24 Jaelen Strong 2.50 6.00
TMS25 Andrew Luck 5.00 12.00
TMS26 Phillip Dorsett 2.00 5.00
TMS27 Blake Bortles 2.50 6.00
TMS28 T.J. Yeldon 2.00 5.00
TMS29 Jeremy Maclin 2.50 6.00
TMS30 Marcus Allen 5.00 12.00
TMS31 DeVante Parker 3.00 8.00
TMS32 Ryan Tannehill 3.00 8.00
TMS33 Teddy Bridgewater 3.00 8.00
TMS34 Adrian Peterson 4.00 10.00
TMS35 Tom Brady 10.00 25.00
TMS36 Rob Gronkowski 4.00 10.00
TMS37 Drew Brees 4.00 10.00
TMS38 Garrett Grayson 2.00 5.00
TMS39 Odell Beckham Jr. 4.00 10.00
TMS40 Lawrence Taylor 5.00 12.00
TMS41 Brandon Marshall 2.50 6.00
TMS42 Bryce Petty 2.00 5.00
TMS43 Tim Brown 5.00 12.00
TMS44 Amari Cooper 6.00 15.00
TMS45 Sam Bradford 2.50 6.00
TMS46 DeMarco Murray 3.00 8.00
TMS47 Terry Bradshaw 6.00 15.00
TMS48 Ben Roethlisberger 4.00 10.00
TMS49 Philip Rivers 4.00 10.00
TMS50 Melvin Gordon 5.00 12.00
TMS51 Jerry Rice 8.00 20.00
TMS52 Steve Young 6.00 15.00
TMS53 Russell Wilson 5.00 12.00
TMS54 Tyler Lockett 3.00 8.00
TMS55 Marshall Faulk 4.00 10.00
TMS56 Todd Gurley 8.00 20.00
TMS57 Jameis Winston 5.00 12.00
TMS58 Marcus Mariota 8.00 20.00
TMS59 John Riggins 4.00 10.00
TMS60 Alfred Morris 2.50 6.00

2015 Panini Black Gold Versus Dual Jerseys

VDJL D.Johnson/T.Lockett/199 5.00 12.00
VSAC C.Anderson/J.Charles/199 2.50 6.00
VSBB D.Bryant/O.Beckham Jr./99 4.00 10.00
VSCG A.Cooper/M.Gordon/199 5.00 12.00
VSJH D.Johnson/J.Hill/199 3.00 8.00
VSKT J.Kelly/L.Taylor/99 4.00 10.00
VSMW M.Mariota/J.Winston/199 8.00 20.00
VSNR C.Newton/M.Ryan/99 4.00 10.00
VSPC B.Perriman/S.Coates/199 2.50 6.00
VSPW D.Parker/S.Watkins/199 3.00 8.00
VSRB D.Revis/T.Brady/99 10.00 25.00
VSSB R.Staubach/T.Bradshaw/49 10.00 25.00
VSWM K.White/T.Montgomery/199 2.50 6.00
VSWW K.Williams/L.Williams/199 2.00 5.00
VSYA S.Young/T.Aikman/199 4.00 10.00

2016 Panini Black Gold

1 Tony Romo 2.50 6.00
2 Dez Bryant 3.00 8.00
3 Emmitt Smith 5.00 12.00
4 Eli Manning 2.50 6.00
5 Odell Beckham Jr. 3.00 8.00
6 Lawrence Taylor 3.00 8.00
7 Ryan Mathews 2.50 6.00
8 Randall Cunningham 2.50 6.00
9 Kirk Cousins 3.00 8.00
10 Jordan Reed 2.00 5.00
11 John Riggins 2.50 6.00
12 David Johnson 3.00 8.00
13 Larry Fitzgerald 2.50 6.00
14 Kurt Warner 2.50 6.00
15 Todd Gurley II 3.00 8.00
16 Marshall Faulk 2.50 6.00
17 Carlos Hyde 2.00 5.00
18 Joe Montana 8.00 20.00
19 Jerry Rice 5.00 12.00
20 Russell Wilson 4.00 10.00
21 Marshawn Lynch 2.50 6.00
22 Alshon Jeffery 2.50 6.00
23 Jeremy Langford 2.50 6.00
24 Walter Payton 6.00 15.00
25 Matthew Stafford 2.50 6.00
26 Barry Sanders 5.00 12.00
27 Aaron Rodgers 6.00 15.00
28 Brett Favre 6.00 15.00
29 Stefon Diggs 2.50 6.00
30 Adrian Peterson 3.00 8.00
31 Warren Moon 3.00 8.00
32 Matt Ryan 2.50 6.00
33 Julio Jones 3.00 8.00
34 Deion Sanders 2.50 6.00
35 Cam Newton 3.00 8.00
36 Luke Kuechly 2.50 6.00
37 Kevin Greene 3.00 8.00
38 Drew Brees 3.00 8.00
39 Archie Manning 2.50 6.00
40 Jameis Winston 3.00 8.00
41 Doug Martin 2.50 6.00
42 Derrick Brooks 2.00 5.00
43 Sammy Watkins 3.00 8.00
44 Jim Kelly 3.00 8.00
45 Ryan Tannehill 2.50 6.00
46 Dan Marino 6.00 15.00
47 Tom Brady 8.00 20.00
48 Rob Gronkowski 3.00 8.00
49 Curtis Martin 2.50 6.00
50 Matt Forte 2.00 5.00
51 Joe Namath 4.00 10.00
52 Demaryius Thomas 2.50 6.00
53 Peyton Manning 6.00 15.00
54 John Elway 5.00 12.00
55 Jamaal Charles 2.50 6.00
56 Marcus Allen 2.50 6.00
57 Derek Carr 3.00 8.00
58 Amari Cooper 3.00 8.00
59 Bo Jackson 4.00 10.00
60 Philip Rivers 3.00 8.00
61 LaDainian Tomlinson 2.50 6.00
62 Joe Flacco 2.50 6.00
63 Ray Lewis 3.00 8.00
64 Andy Dalton 2.50 6.00
65 A.J. Green 3.00 8.00
66 Boomer Esiason 2.50 6.00
67 Terrelle Pryor 2.00 5.00
68 Jim Brown 4.00 10.00
69 Ben Roethlisberger 3.00 8.00
70 Antonio Brown 3.00 8.00
71 Terry Bradshaw 4.00 10.00
72 Brock Osweiler 2.00 5.00
73 J.J. Watt 3.00 8.00
74 Earl Campbell 3.00 8.00
75 Andrew Luck 4.00 10.00
76 Marvin Harrison 2.50 6.00
77 Blake Bortles 2.00 5.00
78 Maurice Jones-Drew 2.00 5.00
79 Marcus Mariota 3.00 8.00
80 DeMarco Murray 2.50 6.00
81 Eddie George 2.50 6.00
82 Christian Hackenberg JSY AU RC 4.00 10.00
83 Derrick Henry JSY AU RC 10.00 25.00
84 Joey Bosa JSY AU RC 25.00 50.00
85 Laquon Treadwell JSY AU RC 5.00 12.00
86 Jared Goff JSY AU RC 40.00 80.00
87 C.J. Prosise JSY AU RC 4.00 10.00
88 Jordan Howard JSY AU RC 10.00 25.00
89 Michael Thomas JSY AU RC 8.00 20.00
90 Carson Wentz JSY AU RC 60.00 125.00
91 Paul Perkins JSY AU RC 4.00 10.00
92 Tyler Boyd JSY AU RC 5.00 12.00
93 Kenyan Drake JSY AU RC 6.00 15.00
94 Paxton Lynch JSY AU RC 25.00 50.00
95 Braxton Miller JSY AU RC 4.00 10.00
96 Jonathan Williams JSY AU RC 5.00 12.00
97 Leonte Carroo JSY AU RC 4.00 10.00
98 Chris Moore JSY AU RC 5.00 12.00
99 Cody Kessler JSY AU RC 4.00 10.00
100 Ezekiel Elliott JSY AU RC EXCH 60.00 125.00
101 Pharoh Cooper JSY AU RC 4.00 10.00
102 Wendell Smallwood JSY AU RC 4.00 10.00
103 Devontae Booker JSY AU RC 5.00 12.00
104 Corey Coleman JSY AU RC 6.00 15.00
105 Cardale Jones JSY AU RC 4.00 10.00
106 Sterling Shepard JSY AU RC 5.00 12.00
107 Keenan Reynolds JSY AU RC 5.00 12.00
108 Hunter Henry JSY AU RC 5.00 12.00
109 Tyler Ervin JSY AU RC 4.00 10.00
110 Dak Prescott JSY AU RC 40.00 80.00
111 Josh Doctson JSY AU RC EXCH 5.00 12.00
112 Alex Collins JSY AU RC 5.00 12.00
113 Ricardo Louis JSY AU RC 4.00 10.00
114 DeAndre Washington JSY AU RC 4.00 10.00
115 Malcolm Mitchell JSY AU RC 4.00 10.00
116 Trevor Davis JSY AU RC 4.00 10.00
117 Moritz Bohringer JSY AU RC 4.00 10.00
118 Demarcus Robinson JSY AU RC 4.00 10.00
119 Connor Cook JSY AU RC 5.00 12.00
120 Kenneth Dixon JSY AU RC 4.00 10.00
121 Will Fuller V JSY AU RC EXCH 6.00 15.00
122 Jacoby Brissett AU RC 4.00 10.00
123 Jakeem Grant AU RC 3.00 8.00
124 Tajae Sharpe AU RC 4.00 10.00
125 Brandon Allen AU RC 3.00 8.00
126 Tyreek Hill AU RC 40.00 80.00
128 Cody Core AU RC 3.00 8.00
129 Jalen Richard AU RC 20.00 40.00
130 Rashard Higgins AU RC 3.00 8.00
131 Jalen Ramsey AU RC 10.00 25.00

2016 Panini Black Gold Holo Gold

*VETS/25: .8X TO 2X BASIC CARDS/225

2016 Panini Black Gold Holo White Gold

*VETS/50: .6X TO 1.5X BASIC CARDS/225

2016 Panini Black Gold White Gold

*VETS/100: .5X TO 1.2X BASIC CARDS/225
*ROOK JSY AU/99: .5X TO 1.2X BASIC JSY AU/225
*ROOK AU/99: .5X TO 1.2X BASIC AU/225

2016 Panini Black Gold Autograph Jerseys

1 Marcus Mariota/25 25.00 50.00
3 Earl Campbell/25 20.00 50.00
4 Ameer Abdullah/99 4.00 10.00
5 Todd Gurley II/49 25.00 50.00
6 Emmitt Smith/25 100.00 200.00
7 Devin Funchess/99 4.00 10.00
8 Jameis Winston/25 15.00 40.00
9 Josh Gordon/49 5.00 12.00
10 DeMarcus Ware/58
11 Matt Ryan/25 25.00 50.00
12 Kirk Cousins/49 12.00 30.00
13 Andrew Luck/25 30.00 60.00
14 David Johnson/49 15.00 40.00
15 Jeremy Langford/99 5.00 12.00

2016 Panini Black Gold Franchise Gold

*WHITE/100: .5X TO 1.2X BASIC INSERTS
*HOLO WHT/50: .6X TO 1.5X BASIC INSERTS/225
*HOLO GOLD/25: .8X TO 2X BASIC INSERTS/225
*REV BLK/15: 1X TO 2.5X BASIC INSERTS
1 Rdgrs/Strr/Fvre 25.00 50.00
2 Stbch/Rmo/Akmn 5.00 12.00
3 Mnng/Jms/Hrrsn 8.00 20.00
4 Rd/Lws/Sggs 4.00 10.00
5 Bll/Brwn/Rthbrgr 4.00 10.00
6 Mrry/Hnry/Mrta 6.00 15.00
7 Elwy/Smth/Dvs 6.00 15.00
8 Thms/Rd/Klly 4.00 10.00

9 Dggs/Brdgwtr/Prtsn 4.00 10.00
10 Edlmn/Grnkwski/Brdy 10.00 25.00
11 Shrmn/Thms/Chnclr 4.00 10.00
12 Cpr/Rce/Brwn 6.00 15.00
13 Hrrs/Grne/Brdshw 5.00 12.00
14 Smth/Ellt/Drstt 12.00 30.00
15 Plmr/Jhnsn/Ftzgrld 4.00 10.00
16 Brtls/Ivry/Rbnsn 3.00 8.00
17 Mntna/Ltt/Rce 10.00 25.00
18 McMhn/Sngltry/Pytn 8.00 20.00

2016 Panini Black Gold Gilded Signatures

1 Gary Barnidge/199 2.50 6.00
2 Jermaine Kearse/199 6.00 15.00
3 Zach Ertz/99 4.00 10.00
4 Edgerrin James/49 10.00 25.00
5 Charles Haley/49
6 Greg Olsen/49
7 Doug Baldwin/49 15.00 40.00
8 Charlie Joiner/199 2.50 6.00
9 Blake Bortles/25
10 Y.A. Tittle/99 10.00 25.00
11 Devonta Freeman/49
12 John Hannah/199 2.50 6.00
13 Allen Hurns/199 2.50 6.00
14 Luke Kuechly/49 15.00 40.00
15 Drew Pearson/99 4.00 10.00
16 Charcandrick West/199 2.50 6.00
17 Brock Osweiler/49 4.00 10.00
18 Troy Brown/199 6.00 15.00
19 Josh Gordon/199 10.00 25.00
20 Matt Jones/199 3.00 8.00
21 Jerick McKinnon/49 4.00 10.00

2016 Panini Black Gold Gold Nuggets

*WHT GLD/100: .5X TO 1.2X BASIC INSERTS/225
*HOLO WHT/50: .6X TO 1.5X BASIC INSERTS/225
*HOLO GLD/25: .8X TO 2X BASIC INSERTS/225
*REV BLK/15: 1X TO 2.5X BASIC INSERTS/225
1 Kurt Warner 3.00 8.00
2 Warren Moon 3.00 8.00
3 Tom Brady 8.00 20.00
4 Antonio Brown 3.00 8.00
5 Richard Sherman 3.00 8.00
6 Tony Romo 2.50 6.00
7 Rod Smith 2.50 6.00
8 Darren Sproles 2.50 6.00
9 James Harrison 2.50 6.00
10 Shannon Sharpe 3.00 8.00
11 Julian Edelman 3.00 8.00
12 Antonio Gates 2.00 5.00
13 Brandon Marshall 2.00 5.00
14 Terrell Davis 2.50 6.00
15 Adam Vinatieri 2.50 6.00

2016 Panini Black Gold Gold Prospecting Quad Materials

*PRIME/25: .5X TO 1.2X BASIC JSY/249
*WHT GOLD/199: .4X TO 1X BASIC JSY/249
*WHT PRIME/50: .6X TO 1.5X BASIC JSY/249
1 Chris Moore 3.00 8.00
2 Jordan Howard 5.00 12.00
3 Tyler Boyd 3.00 8.00
4 Corey Coleman 4.00 10.00
5 Dak Prescott 12.00 30.00
6 Ezekiel Elliott 12.00 30.00
7 Devontae Booker 3.00 8.00
8 Paxton Lynch 2.50 6.00
9 Braxton Miller 2.50 6.00
10 Will Fuller V 4.00 10.00
11 Jared Goff 8.00 20.00
12 Kenyan Drake 4.00 10.00
13 Leonte Carroo 2.50 6.00
14 Laquon Treadwell 3.00 8.00
15 Moritz Bohringer 2.50 6.00
16 Michael Thomas 5.00 12.00
17 Paul Perkins 2.50 6.00
18 Sterling Shepard 3.00 8.00
19 Christian Hackenberg 2.50 6.00
20 Connor Cook 3.00 8.00
21 Carson Wentz 15.00 40.00
22 Joey Bosa 5.00 12.00
23 C.J. Prosise 2.50 6.00
24 Derrick Henry 6.00 15.00
25 Josh Doctson 3.00 8.00

2016 Panini Black Gold Gold Rush

*WHT GLD/100: .5X TO 1.2X BASIC INSERTS/225
*HOLO WHT/50: .6X TO 1.5X BASIC INSERTS/225
*HOLO GLD/25: .8X TO 2X BASIC INSERTS/225
*REV BLK/15: 1X TO 2.5X BASIC INSERTS/225
1 Barry Sanders 5.00 12.00
2 Todd Gurley II 3.00 8.00
3 Ezekiel Elliott 10.00 25.00
4 Curtis Martin 2.50 6.00
5 Walter Payton 6.00 15.00
6 Adrian Peterson 3.00 8.00
7 Earl Campbell 3.00 8.00
8 Jim Brown 4.00 10.00
9 Emmitt Smith 5.00 12.00
10 Derrick Henry 5.00 12.00
11 Marshall Faulk 2.50 6.00
12 LaDainian Tomlinson 2.50 6.00
13 Jerome Bettis 3.00 8.00
14 David Johnson 3.00 8.00
15 Thurman Thomas 2.50 6.00

2016 Panini Black Gold Gold Strike Autographs

1 Bo Jackson/99
2 Bill Parcells/99 30.00 60.00
3 Peyton Manning/25
4 Ickey Woods/99
5 Steve Grogan/99 6.00 15.00
6 Ozzie Newsome/99 8.00 20.00
7 Andre Reed/99 8.00 20.00
8 Roger Staubach/25
9 Derrick Brooks/99 6.00 15.00
10 Jerome Bettis/25
11 Charles Haley/99 10.00 25.00
12 Barry Sanders/30 100.00 200.00
13 Dan Marino/25 125.00 250.00
14 Randall Cunningham/99 20.00 50.00
15 Troy Aikman/25
16 Joe Montana/25
17 Don Majkowski/99 12.00 30.00
18 Michael Irvin/25 20.00 50.00
19 Thurman Thomas/99
20 Dan Hampton/99
21 Kevin Greene/91
22 Marshawn Lynch/49 20.00 50.00
23 Archie Manning/99
24 Hines Ward/99 40.00 80.00
25 Carl Eller/99
26 Tim Brown/99
27 Jim Kelly/49
28 Marshall Faulk/99 20.00 50.00
30 Willie McGinest/99 12.00 30.00
31 Joe Namath/25

2016 Panini Black Gold Golden Hands Jerseys

1 Jerry Rice/49 10.00 25.00
2 A.J. Green/99 5.00 12.00
3 Julio Jones/99 5.00 12.00
4 Corey Coleman/199 4.00 10.00
5 Cris Carter/49 6.00 15.00
6 Demaryius Thomas/99 4.00 10.00
7 Antonio Brown/99 5.00 12.00
8 Laquon Treadwell/199 3.00 8.00
9 Marvin Harrison/49 5.00 12.00
10 Amari Cooper/199 4.00 10.00
11 Odell Beckham Jr./175 4.00 10.00
12 Michael Thomas/199 5.00 12.00
13 Allen Robinson/199 3.00 8.00
14 Larry Fitzgerald/99 4.00 10.00
15 Sterling Shepard/199 3.00 8.00

2016 Panini Black Gold Golden Opportunity Materials

1 J.Goff/T.Gurley/199 15.00 40.00
2 D.Thomas/P.Lynch/99 4.00 10.00
3 A.Cooper/C.Cook/199 4.00 10.00
4 T.Romo/E.Elliott/99 15.00 40.00
5 D.Henry/M.Mariota/199 6.00 15.00
6 K.Drake/R.Tannehill/99 5.00 12.00
7 C.Prosise/R.Wilson/99 6.00 15.00
8 C.Moore/J.Flacco/99 4.00 10.00
9 C.Anderson/D.Booker/99 4.00 10.00
10 R.Mathews/W.Smallwood/99 4.00 10.00
11 D.Washington/D.Carr/125 5.00 12.00
12 J.Bosa/J.Seau/99 6.00 15.00
13 O.Beckham/S.Shepard/199 4.00 10.00
14 T.Boyd/A.Green/99 5.00 12.00
15 L.Treadwell/T.Bridgewater/99 4.00 10.00
16 H.Henry/A.Gates/99 4.00 10.00

2016 Panini Black Gold Golden Prospects Signatures

*PRIME79-99: .5X TO 1.2X BASIC AU/199
*PRIME/49: .6X TO 1.5X BASIC AU/199
*PRIME/49: .5X TO 1.2X BASIC AU/99
1 Eli Apple/199 3.00 8.00
2 William Jackson III/149 3.00 8.00
3 Robert Nkemdiche/199 3.00 8.00
5 Shaq Lawson/199 2.50 6.00
6 Darron Lee/99 3.00 8.00
8 Keanu Neal/199 2.50 6.00
9 Jake Rudock/199 6.00 15.00
10 Adam Gotsis/199 2.50 6.00
11 A'Shawn Robinson/199 2.50 6.00
12 Jaylon Smith/199 8.00 20.00
14 Myles Jack/199 3.00 8.00
15 Noah Spence/199 2.50 6.00
16 Reggie Ragland/199 2.50 6.00
17 Su'a Cravens/199 2.50 6.00
18 Vonn Bell/199 3.00 8.00
19 Austin Hooper/199 2.50 6.00
20 Nick Vannett/199 2.50 6.00

2016 Panini Black Gold Grand Debut Autograph Jerseys

1 Jared Goff/49 25.00 60.00
2 Carson Wentz/49 40.00 80.00
3 Paxton Lynch/99 3.00 8.00
4 Christian Hackenberg/99 3.00 8.00
5 Connor Cook/99 4.00 10.00
6 Cody Kessler/149 2.50 6.00
7 Dak Prescott/149 40.00 80.00
8 Cardale Jones/99 3.00 8.00
9 Jacoby Brissett/149 3.00 8.00
10 Ezekiel Elliott/49 90.00 150.00
11 Derrick Henry/49 10.00 25.00
12 Kenyan Drake/149 4.00 10.00
13 C.J. Prosise/99 3.00 8.00
14 Tyler Ervin/149 2.50 6.00
15 Devontae Booker/149 3.00 8.00
16 Paul Perkins/149 2.50 6.00
17 Wendell Smallwood/149 2.50 6.00
18 Corey Coleman/49 6.00 15.00
19 Laquon Treadwell/49 5.00 12.00
20 Josh Doctson/99 4.00 10.00
21 Will Fuller V/99 5.00 12.00
22 Sterling Shepard/99 4.00 10.00
23 Michael Thomas/99 6.00 15.00
24 Tyler Boyd/99 4.00 10.00
25 Malcolm Mitchell/149 12.00 30.00
26 Braxton Miller/149 2.50 6.00
27 Leonte Carroo/149 2.50 6.00
28 Chris Moore/149 3.00 8.00
29 Ricardo Louis/149 2.50 6.00
30 Pharoh Cooper/149 2.50 6.00
31 Trevor Davis/149 2.50 6.00

2016 Panini Black Gold HOF Symbols

1 Troy Aikman 8.00 20.00
2 Fred Biletnikoff 6.00 15.00
3 Barry Sanders 15.00 40.00
4 Cris Carter 6.00 15.00
5 Jerome Bettis 6.00 15.00
6 Marvin Harrison 5.00 12.00
7 Bart Starr 10.00 25.00
8 Emmitt Smith 10.00 25.00
9 Steve Largent 6.00 15.00
10 Terry Bradshaw 8.00 20.00
11 Jerry Rice 10.00 25.00
12 Joe Namath 8.00 20.00
13 Red Grange 8.00 20.00
14 Michael Irvin 6.00 15.00
15 John Elway 10.00 25.00
16 Reggie White 6.00 15.00
17 Walter Payton 12.00 30.00
18 Junior Seau 5.00 12.00
19 Brett Favre 12.00 30.00
20 John Riggins 5.00 12.00
21 Deion Sanders 5.00 12.00
22 Dan Marino 15.00 40.00
23 Jim Brown 8.00 20.00
24 Joe Montana 15.00 40.00

2016 Panini Black Gold Massive Materials

1 Jameis Winston/49 6.00 15.00
2 Marcus Mariota/49 6.00 15.00
3 David Johnson/49 6.00 15.00
4 Todd Gurley II/99 5.00 12.00
5 Ameer Abdullah/49 4.00 10.00
6 Tyler Lockett/65 5.00 12.00
7 Amari Cooper/49 6.00 15.00
8 Carson Wentz/199 12.00 30.00
9 Jared Goff/199 10.00 25.00
10 Ezekiel Elliott/199 12.00 30.00
11 Derrick Henry/199 6.00 15.00
12 Sterling Shepard/199 3.00 8.00
13 Chris Moore/199 3.00 8.00
14 Laquon Treadwell/199 3.00 8.00
15 Will Fuller V/199 4.00 10.00

2016 Panini Black Gold Metallic Marks

*WHITE/50: .5X TO 1.2X BASIC AU/99
1 Cardale Jones 3.00 8.00
2 Carson Wentz 60.00 125.00
3 Christian Hackenberg 3.00 8.00
4 Cody Kessler 3.00 8.00
5 Connor Cook 4.00 10.00
6 Dak Prescott 40.00 80.00
7 Jared Goff 50.00 100.00
8 Kevin Hogan 4.00 10.00
9 Paxton Lynch 3.00 8.00
10 Alex Collins 4.00 10.00
11 C.J. Prosise 3.00 8.00
12 DeAndre Washington 3.00 8.00
13 Derrick Henry 25.00 50.00
14 Devontae Booker 4.00 10.00
15 Ezekiel Elliott 60.00 125.00
16 Jonathan Williams 4.00 10.00
17 Jordan Howard 12.00 30.00
18 Keenan Reynolds 4.00 10.00
19 Kenneth Dixon 3.00 8.00
20 Kenyan Drake 5.00 12.00
21 Paul Perkins 3.00 8.00
22 Tyler Ervin 3.00 8.00
23 Wendell Smallwood 3.00 8.00
24 Hunter Henry 4.00 10.00
25 Joey Bosa 12.00 30.00
26 Braxton Miller 3.00 8.00
27 Chris Moore 4.00 10.00
28 Corey Coleman 5.00 12.00
29 Demarcus Robinson 3.00 8.00
30 Josh Doctson 4.00 10.00
31 Laquon Treadwell 4.00 10.00
32 Leonte Carroo 3.00 8.00
33 Michael Thomas 12.00 30.00
34 Moritz Bohringer 3.00 8.00
35 Pharoh Cooper 3.00 8.00
36 Ricardo Louis 3.00 8.00
37 Sterling Shepard 12.00 30.00
38 Trevor Davis 3.00 8.00
39 Tyler Boyd 4.00 10.00
40 Will Fuller V

2016 Panini Black Gold Mother Lode Rookie Triple Jerseys

1 Kenneth Dixon 2.00 5.00
2 Cardale Jones 2.00 5.00
3 Tyler Boyd 2.50 6.00
4 Cody Kessler 2.00 5.00
5 Corey Coleman 3.00 8.00
6 Dak Prescott 10.00 25.00
7 Ezekiel Elliott 15.00 40.00
8 Devontae Booker 2.50 6.00
9 Paxton Lynch 2.00 5.00
10 Tyler Ervin 2.00 5.00
11 Will Fuller V 3.00 8.00
12 Jared Goff 12.00 30.00
13 Kenyan Drake 3.00 8.00
14 Laquon Treadwell 2.50 6.00
15 Michael Thomas 4.00 10.00
16 Paul Perkins 2.00 5.00
17 Sterling Shepard 2.50 6.00
18 Christian Hackenberg 2.00 5.00
19 Connor Cook 2.50 6.00
20 DeAndre Washington 2.00 5.00
21 Carson Wentz 8.00 20.00
22 Wendell Smallwood 2.00 5.00
23 C.J. Prosise 2.00 5.00
24 Derrick Henry 5.00 12.00
25 Josh Doctson 2.50 6.00

2016 Panini Black Gold NFL Seal of Approval

*WHITE/15: .5X TO 1.2X BASIC INSERTS/25
1 Cam Newton 8.00 20.00
2 Drew Brees 8.00 20.00
3 Tom Brady 20.00 50.00
4 Marcus Mariota 8.00 20.00
5 Blake Bortles 5.00 12.00
6 Aaron Rodgers 15.00 40.00
7 Ben Roethlisberger 8.00 20.00
8 Derek Carr 8.00 20.00
9 Russell Wilson 10.00 25.00
10 Andrew Luck 10.00 25.00
11 Tony Romo 6.00 15.00
12 Adrian Peterson 8.00 20.00
13 Todd Gurley II 8.00 20.00
14 Devonta Freeman 6.00 15.00
15 Le'Veon Bell 6.00 15.00
16 Jeremy Langford 6.00 15.00
17 David Johnson 8.00 20.00
18 Julio Jones 8.00 20.00
19 Antonio Brown 8.00 20.00
20 DeAndre Hopkins 6.00 15.00
21 Odell Beckham Jr. 8.00 20.00
22 Larry Fitzgerald 6.00 15.00
23 Rob Gronkowski 8.00 20.00
24 J.J. Watt 8.00 20.00
25 Khalil Mack 8.00 20.00

2016 Panini Black Gold Rookie Gold Mine

*WHITE/100: .5X TO 1.2X BASIC INSTS/225
*HOLO WHT/50: .6X TO 1.5X BASIC INSTS/225
*HOLO/25: .8X TO 2X BASIC INSERTS/225
*REV BLK/15: 1X TO 2.5X BASIC INSTS/225
1 Jared Goff 12.00 30.00
2 Carson Wentz 20.00 50.00
3 Paxton Lynch 2.00 5.00
4 Christian Hackenberg 2.00 5.00
5 Ezekiel Elliott 10.00 25.00
6 Derrick Henry 5.00 12.00
7 Kenyan Drake 3.00 8.00
8 C.J. Prosise 2.00 5.00
9 Wendell Smallwood 2.00 5.00
10 Corey Coleman 3.00 8.00
11 Laquon Treadwell 2.50 6.00
12 Josh Doctson 2.50 6.00
13 Tyler Boyd 2.50 6.00
14 Sterling Shepard 2.50 6.00
15 Joey Bosa 4.00 10.00

2016 Panini Black Gold Rookie Tetrad Materials

1 Wntz/Gff/Lnch/Hcknbrg 20.00 50.00
2 Jns/Ksslr/Ck/Prsctt 10.00 25.00
3 Hnry/Prse/Ellt/Drke 10.00 25.00
4 Bkr/Dxn/Ervn/Prkns 2.50 6.00
5 Cllns/Wshtn/Hwrd/Smllwd 5.00 12.00
6 Clmn/Dctsn/Trdwll/Fllr 3.00 8.00
7 Shprd/Byd/Mllr/Thms 4.00 10.00
8 Bhrngr/Mre/Cro/Ls 2.50 6.00
9 Bsa/Mllr/Jns/Thms 4.00 10.00
10 Wntz/Hnry/Elltt/Gff 20.00 50.00

2016 Panini Black Gold Sizeable Signature Jerseys

1 Blake Bortles/49
2 Barry Sanders/22
3 Giovani Bernard/99 4.00 10.00
4 Warren Moon/99
5 Dan Marino/25
6 John Elway/15 150.00 250.00
7 LaDainian Tomlinson/99 20.00 50.00
8 Brett Favre/15
9 Marvin Harrison/25
10 Jerry Rice/15
11 Ben Roethlisberger/25 100.00 200.00
12 C.J. Anderson/99 5.00 12.00
13 Ray Lewis/49
14 Rod Woodson/99 25.00 50.00
15 J.J. Watt/15 40.00 100.00

2016 Panini Black Gold VS Dual Jerseys

*PRIME/49: .6X TO 1.5X BASIC JSY/199
*PRIME/49: .5X TO 1.2X BASIC JSY/99
*PRIME/25: .6X TO 1.5X BASIC JSY/99
*PRIME/49: .6X TO 1.5X BASIC JSY/199
*PRIME/49: .5X TO 1.2X BASIC JSY/80-99
*PRIME/15: .5X TO 1.2X BASIC JSY/25
1 V.Miller/C.Newton/25 8.00 20.00
2 T.Brady/P.Manning/25 20.00 50.00
3 D.Sanders/J.Rice/25 12.00 30.00
4 J.Winston/M.Mariota/80 5.00 12.00
5 J.Montana/S.Young/25 20.00 50.00
6 B.Favre/A.Rodgers/25 15.00 40.00
7 D.Johnson/T.Gurley II/99 5.00 12.00
8 D.Booker/C.Anderson/99 4.00 10.00
9 C.Wentz/J.Goff/199 15.00 40.00
10 D.Henry/E.Elliott/199 8.00 20.00
11 C.Coleman/L.Treadwell/199 4.00 10.00

2016 Panini Black Gold Collegiate

*WHITE GOLD/75: .4X TO 1X BASIC CARDS
*GOLD FOIL/49: .5X TO 1.2X BASIC CARDS
*WHITE FOIL/25: .6X TO 1.5X BASIC CARDS
1 A.J. Green/99 3.00 8.00
2 Aaron Rodgers/99 6.00 15.00
4 Adrian Peterson/75 3.00 8.00
8 Andrew Luck/99 4.00 10.00
10 Andy Dalton/99 2.50 6.00
14 Barry Sanders/99 5.00 12.00
15 Ben Roethlisberger/99 3.00 8.00
18 Bo Jackson/99 4.00 10.00
21 Calvin Johnson/99 3.00 8.00
22 Cam Newton/99 3.00 8.00
25 Charles Woodson/99 3.00 8.00
29 Dan Marino/99 6.00 15.00
30 Deion Sanders/99 2.50 6.00
31 DeMarco Murray/99 2.50 6.00
33 Derek Carr/99 3.00 8.00
35 Dez Bryant/99 3.00 8.00
36 Drew Brees/99 3.00 8.00
39 Eddie Lacy/99 2.00 5.00
41 Eli Manning/99 2.50 6.00
44 Frank Thomas/99 3.00 8.00
49 J.J. Watt/99 3.00 8.00
51 Jamaal Charles/99 2.50 6.00
53 Jason Witten/99 2.50 6.00
54 Jim McMahon/99 2.50 6.00
56 Jimmy Graham/99 3.00 8.00
57 Joe Flacco/99 2.50 6.00
58 Joe Namath/99 4.00 10.00
60 John Elway/99 5.00 12.00
62 Johnny Manziel/99 2.50 6.00
72 LeSean McCoy/99 3.00 8.00
73 Le'Veon Bell/99 2.50 6.00
79 Odell Beckham Jr./99 3.00 8.00
82 Peyton Manning/99 6.00 15.00
83 Philip Rivers/99 3.00 8.00
86 Rob Gronkowski/99 3.00 8.00
90 Russell Wilson/99 4.00 10.00
95 Tim Tebow/99 3.00 8.00
96 Tom Brady/99 8.00 20.00
99 Tony Romo/99 2.50 6.00

2016 Panini Black Gold Collegiate Gold

101 Jared Goff AU 60.00 120.00
102 Joey Bosa AU 15.00 40.00
103 Laquon Treadwell AU 10.00 25.00
104 Paxton Lynch AU
105 Connor Cook AU 10.00 25.00
106 Ezekiel Elliott AU 100.00 200.00
107 Carson Wentz AU
108 Corey Coleman AU 12.00 30.00
109 Hunter Henry AU 10.00 25.00
110 Derrick Henry AU 20.00 50.00
111 Michael Thomas AU 15.00 40.00
112 Josh Doctson AU 10.00 25.00
113 Tyler Boyd AU 10.00 25.00
114 Pharoh Cooper AU 8.00 20.00
115 Alex Collins AU 10.00 25.00
116 Christian Hackenberg AU 30.00 60.00
117 Kenneth Dixon AU 8.00 20.00
118 Sterling Shepard AU 10.00 25.00
120 Devontae Booker AU 10.00 25.00
121 Dak Prescott AU 60.00 120.00
122 Leonte Carroo AU 8.00 20.00
123 Jordan Howard AU 20.00 50.00
124 Cardale Jones AU 8.00 20.00
126 Braxton Miller AU 8.00 20.00
127 Paul Perkins AU 8.00 20.00
128 Demarcus Robinson AU 8.00 20.00
129 Kenyan Drake AU 12.00 30.00
131 Nick Vannett AU 8.00 20.00
132 Jonathan Williams AU 10.00 25.00
133 Braxton Addison AU 8.00 20.00
135 Aaron Burbridge AU 8.00 20.00
136 Austin Hooper AU 8.00 20.00
137 Keyarris Garrett AU 8.00 20.00
138 Jordan Payton AU 8.00 20.00
139 Jeff Driskel AU 8.00 20.00
140 Aaron Green AU 8.00 20.00
141 Malcolm Mitchell AU 8.00 20.00
142 Keith Marshall AU 8.00 20.00
144 Kolby Listenbee AU 8.00 20.00
145 Kevin Hogan AU 10.00 25.00
146 Tyler Ervin AU 8.00 20.00
147 Josh Ferguson AU 8.00 20.00
148 Daniel Lasco AU 8.00 20.00

2016 Panini Black Gold Collegiate Autographs

*GOLD/25: .8X TO 2X BASIC AU/199
*GOLD/25: .6X TO 1.5X BASIC AU/99
4 Wendell Smallwood/199 3.00 8.00
6 A'Shawn Robinson/99 4.00 10.00
10 Chris Moore/99 5.00 12.00
11 Demarcus Ayers/199 3.00 8.00
12 Darron Lee/99 4.00 10.00
13 Eli Apple/99 5.00 12.00
14 Emmanuel Ogbah/199 4.00 10.00
16 Keenan Reynolds/99 5.00 12.00
17 Jarran Reed/99 4.00 10.00
23 Jonathan Bullard/99 4.00 10.00
24 Ricardo Louis/99 4.00 10.00
26 Trevor Davis/99 4.00 10.00
27 Kevin Dodd/99 4.00 10.00
28 Austin Johnson/99 4.00 10.00
29 Laremy Tunsil/99 4.00 10.00
30 Kendall Fuller/99 5.00 12.00
31 Tyler Higbee/99 4.00 10.00
33 Mackensie Alexander/99 4.00 10.00
34 Vonn Bell/99 5.00 12.00
36 Jerell Adams/99 4.00 10.00
37 Joshua Perry/199 3.00 8.00
42 Reggie Ragland/99 4.00 10.00
43 Cody Core/99 4.00 10.00
46 Thomas Duarte/99 4.00 10.00
47 Sheldon Rankins/99 5.00 12.00
48 Shilique Calhoun/99 4.00 10.00
101 Jared Goff/99 25.00 60.00
102 Joey Bosa/99 8.00 20.00
103 Laquon Treadwell/99 20.00 40.00
104 Paxton Lynch/99 4.00 10.00
105 Connor Cook/99 5.00 12.00
106 Ezekiel Elliott/99 50.00 100.00
107 Carson Wentz/99 40.00 80.00
108 Corey Coleman/99 6.00 15.00
109 Hunter Henry/99 5.00 12.00
110 Derrick Henry/99 10.00 25.00
111 Michael Thomas/99 8.00 20.00
112 Josh Doctson/99 5.00 12.00
113 Tyler Boyd/99 12.00 30.00
114 Pharoh Cooper/99 4.00 10.00
115 Alex Collins/99 5.00 12.00
116 Christian Hackenberg/99 4.00 10.00
117 Kenneth Dixon/99 4.00 10.00
118 Sterling Shepard/99 5.00 12.00
120 Devontae Booker/99 5.00 12.00
121 Dak Prescott/99 30.00 60.00
122 Leonte Carroo/99 4.00 10.00
123 Jordan Howard/99 10.00 25.00
124 Cardale Jones/99 4.00 10.00
126 Braxton Miller/99 4.00 10.00
127 Paul Perkins/99 4.00 10.00
128 Demarcus Robinson/99 4.00 10.00
129 Kenyan Drake/99 6.00 15.00
131 Nick Vannett/99 4.00 10.00
132 Jonathan Williams/99 5.00 12.00
133 Bralon Addison/99 4.00 10.00
135 Aaron Burbridge/99 4.00 10.00
136 Austin Hooper/99 4.00 10.00
137 Keyarris Garrett/99 4.00 10.00
138 Jordan Payton/99 4.00 10.00
139 Jeff Driskel/99 4.00 10.00
140 Aaron Green/99 4.00 10.00
141 Malcolm Mitchell/99 4.00 10.00
142 Keith Marshall/99 4.00 10.00
144 Kolby Listenbee/99 4.00 10.00
145 Kevin Hogan/99 5.00 12.00
146 Tyler Ervin/99 4.00 10.00
147 Josh Ferguson/99 4.00 10.00
148 Daniel Lasco/99 4.00 10.00

2016 Panini Black Gold Collegiate Golden Opportunity Materials

*WHITE GOLD/99: .5X TO 1.2X BASIC JSY/199
*PRIME/25: .8X TO 2X BASIC JSY/199
2 Alex Collins 2.00 5.00
3 Austin Hooper 1.50 4.00
4 Carson Wentz 10.00 25.00
5 Christian Hackenberg 1.50 4.00
6 Cody Kessler 1.50 4.00
7 Corey Coleman 2.50 6.00
9 Derrick Henry 4.00 10.00
11 Ezekiel Elliott 8.00 20.00
12 Hunter Henry 2.00 5.00
14 Jared Goff 10.00 25.00
15 Joey Bosa 3.00 8.00
16 Josh Doctson 2.00 5.00
19 Kenyan Drake 2.50 6.00
21 Laquon Treadwell 2.00 5.00
23 Michael Thomas 3.00 8.00
24 Braxton Miller 1.50 4.00
25 Will Fuller 2.50 6.00
26 Leonte Carroo 1.50 4.00
28 Sterling Shepard 2.00 5.00
30 Tyler Boyd 2.00 5.00

2016 Panini Black Gold Collegiate Massive Materials

*WHITE GOLD/49: .6X TO 1.5X BASIC JSY/199
*PRIME/25: .8X TO 2X BASIC JSY/199
*PRIME/15: 1X TO 2.5X BASIC JSY/199
2 Austin Hooper 1.50 4.00
3 Carson Wentz 10.00 25.00
4 Jacoby Brissett 2.00 5.00
5 Corey Coleman 2.50 6.00
7 Derrick Henry 4.00 10.00
9 Ezekiel Elliott 8.00 20.00
10 Hunter Henry 2.00 5.00
12 Jared Goff 10.00 25.00
13 Joey Bosa 3.00 8.00
14 Josh Doctson 2.00 5.00
18 Laquon Treadwell 2.00 5.00
20 Michael Thomas 3.00 8.00
21 Braxton Miller 1.50 4.00
22 C.J. Prosise 1.50 4.00
25 Tyler Boyd 2.00 5.00

2016 Panini Black Gold Collegiate Rated Rookie Symbols

*WHTE GLD/99: .5X TO 1.2X BASIC INSERT/199
*BLK GLD/25: .8X TO 2X BASIC INSERTS/199
2 Alex Collins 1.25 3.00
3 Austin Hooper 1.00 2.50
5 DeForest Buckner 1.00 2.50
6 Sterling Shepard 1.25 3.00
9 Carson Wentz 10.00 25.00
11 Christian Hackenberg 1.00 2.50
12 Connor Cook 1.25 3.00
13 Corey Coleman 1.50 4.00
14 Dak Prescott 8.00 20.00
17 Derrick Henry 2.50 6.00
18 De'Runnya Wilson 1.00 2.50
19 Devontae Booker 1.25 3.00
21 Ezekiel Elliott 5.00 12.00
25 Hunter Henry 1.25 3.00
26 Daniel Lasco 1.00 2.50
29 Jared Goff 6.00 15.00
31 Joey Bosa 2.00 5.00
32 Jordan Howard 2.50 6.00
33 Josh Doctson 1.25 3.00
34 Kenneth Dixon 1.00 2.50
35 Kenny Lawler 1.50 4.00
38 Laquon Treadwell 1.25 3.00
39 Leonte Carroo 1.00 2.50
40 Tyler Boyd 1.25 3.00
42 Michael Thomas 2.00 5.00
44 Paul Perkins 1.00 2.50
45 Paxton Lynch 1.00 2.50
46 Pharoh Cooper 1.00 2.50

2016 Panini Black Gold Collegiate Shadowbox Swatches

*WHITE GLD/99: .5X TO 1.2X BASIC JSY/199
*PRIME/25: .8X TO 2X BASIC JSY/199
2 Carson Wentz 10.00 25.00
3 Jacoby Brissett 2.00 5.00
4 Corey Coleman 2.50 6.00
6 Derrick Henry 4.00 10.00
8 Ezekiel Elliott 8.00 20.00
10 Jared Goff 10.00 25.00
11 Joey Bosa 3.00 8.00
15 Laquon Treadwell 2.00 5.00
17 Michael Thomas 3.00 8.00
18 Will Fuller 2.50 6.00

2016 Panini Black Gold Collegiate Sizeable Signatures Jerseys

1 Aaron Burbridge/99 4.00 10.00
2 C.J. Prosise/25 6.00 15.00
4 Aaron Rodgers/12
5 Alex Collins/99 5.00 12.00
7 Austin Hooper/99 4.00 10.00
8 Braxton Miller/25
9 Cardale Jones/99 4.00 10.00
10 Carson Wentz/99 40.00 100.00
11 Christian Hackenberg/99 4.00 10.00
12 Connor Cook/99 5.00 12.00
13 Corey Coleman/99
14 Dak Prescott/99 60.00 125.00
17 Derrick Henry/99 10.00 25.00
19 Devontae Booker/99 5.00 12.00
20 Ezekiel Elliott/99 60.00 125.00
21 Hunter Henry/99 5.00 12.00
22 Daniel Lasco/99 4.00 10.00
23 Jared Goff/99 25.00 60.00
24 Joey Bosa/25 12.00 30.00
25 Jonathan Williams/99 5.00 12.00
26 Jordan Howard/99 10.00 25.00
27 Jordan Payton/99 4.00 10.00
28 Kolby Listenbee/99 4.00 10.00
29 Josh Doctson/99 5.00 12.00
30 DeAndre Washington/99 4.00 10.00
32 Kenneth Dixon/99 4.00 10.00
34 Kenyan Drake/99 10.00 25.00
36 Keyarris Garrett/99 4.00 10.00
38 Laquon Treadwell/99
39 Leonte Carroo/99 4.00 10.00
41 Michael Thomas/99 8.00 20.00
42 Paul Perkins/99 4.00 10.00
43 Will Fuller/25 10.00 25.00
44 Pharoh Cooper/99 4.00 10.00
47 Sterling Shepard/99 12.00 30.00

2016 Panini Black Gold Collegiate Team Symbols

*WHTE GLD/99: .5X TO 1.2X BASIC INSERTS/199
*BLK GLD/25: .8X TO 2X BASIC INSERTS/199
2 Alex Collins 1.25 3.00
3 Austin Hooper 1.00 2.50
5 DeForest Buckner 1.00 2.50
6 Sterling Shepard 1.25 3.00
9 Carson Wentz 10.00 25.00
11 Christian Hackenberg 1.00 2.50
12 Connor Cook 1.25 3.00
13 Corey Coleman 1.50 4.00
14 Dak Prescott 10.00 25.00
17 Derrick Henry 2.50 6.00
18 De'Runnya Wilson 1.00 2.50
19 Devontae Booker 1.25 3.00
21 Ezekiel Elliott 5.00 12.00
25 Hunter Henry 1.25 3.00
26 Daniel Lasco 1.00 2.50
29 Jared Goff 6.00 15.00
31 Joey Bosa 2.00 5.00
32 Jordan Howard 2.50 6.00
33 Josh Doctson 1.25 3.00
34 Kenneth Dixon 1.00 2.50
35 Kenny Lawler 1.50 4.00
38 Laquon Treadwell 1.25 3.00
39 Leonte Carroo 1.00 2.50
40 Tyler Boyd 1.25 3.00
42 Michael Thomas 2.00 5.00
44 Paul Perkins 1.00 2.50
45 Paxton Lynch 1.00 2.50
46 Pharoh Cooper 1.00 2.50

2013 Panini Building Blocks

*GOLD/25: 1.2X TO 3X BASIC INSERTS
*PURPLE/49: 1X TO 2.5X BASIC INSERTS
*RED/99: .8X TO 2X BASIC INSERTS
1 Cordarrelle Patterson .50 1.25
2 DeAndre Hopkins 1.25 3.00
3 Denard Robinson .50 1.25
4 Eddie Lacy .50 1.25
5 EJ Manuel .50 1.25
6 Gavin Escobar .50 1.25
7 Geno Smith .50 1.25
8 Giovani Bernard .50 1.25
9 Joseph Randle .50 1.25
10 Justin Hunter .50 1.25
11 Keenan Allen 1.00 2.50
12 Knile Davis .50 1.25
13 Le'Veon Bell 1.50 4.00
14 Markus Wheaton .50 1.25
15 Marquise Goodwin .50 1.25
16 Mike Gillislee .50 1.25
17 Montee Ball .50 1.25
18 Quinton Patton .50 1.25
19 Robert Woods .75 2.00
20 Stedman Bailey .50 1.25
21 Stepfan Taylor .50 1.25
22 Tavon Austin .60 1.50
23 Terrance Williams .50 1.25
24 Tyler Eifert .50 1.25
25 Tyler Wilson .50 1.25

2010 Panini Century Sports Dual Stamp Combo Dual Memorabilia Prime

STATED PRINT RUN 100 SER.#'d SETS
1 Rockne/Bryant/100 15.00 40.00

2010 Panini Century Sports Dual Stamp Memorabilia

STATED PRINT RUN 50 SER.#'d SETS
1 Jim Thorpe 100.00 150.00
Jim Thorpe/50

2010 Panini Century Sports Dual Stamp Memorabilia Prime

STATED PRINT RUN 1 SER.#'d SET
NO PRICING DUE TO SCARCITY
1 Jim Thorpe
Jim Thorpe/1

2010 Panini Century Sports Stamp Materials

STATED PRINT RUN 1-250
NO PRICING ON QTY 25 OR LESS
6A Knute Rockne/250 22c 15.00 40.00
6B Knute Rockne/250 32c 15.00 40.00

2015 Panini Clear Vision

1 Colin Kaepernick 1.00 2.50
2A Joe Montana 3.00 8.00
2B Joe Montana SP 12.00 30.00
3 Matt Forte .75 2.00
4 Alshon Jeffery 1.00 2.50
5 A.J. Green 1.25 3.00
6 Andy Dalton 1.00 2.50
7 Thurman Thomas 1.00 2.50
8 LeSean McCoy 1.25 3.00
9A Peyton Manning 2.50 6.00
9B Peyton Manning SP 10.00 25.00
10 Demaryius Thomas 1.00 2.50
11 Dwayne Bowe 1.00 2.50
12 Vincent Jackson .75 2.00
13 Gerald McCoy .75 2.00
14 Larry Fitzgerald 1.00 2.50
15 Patrick Peterson .75 2.00
16 Philip Rivers 1.25 3.00
17 Keenan Allen 1.00 2.50
18 Jamaal Charles 1.00 2.50
19 Alex Smith 1.00 2.50
20A Andrew Luck 1.50 4.00
20B Andrew Luck SP 6.00 15.00
21 T.Y. Hilton 1.00 2.50
22A Tony Romo 1.00 2.50
22B Tony Romo SP 4.00 10.00
23 Dez Bryant 1.25 3.00
24 Ryan Tannehill 1.00 2.50
25A Dan Marino 2.50 6.00
25B Dan Marino SP 10.00 25.00
26 DeMarco Murray 1.00 2.50
27 Sam Bradford .75 2.00
28 Matt Ryan 1.00 2.50
29 Julio Jones 1.25 3.00
30 Eli Manning 1.00 2.50
31A Lawrence Taylor 1.25 3.00
31B Lawrence Taylor SP 5.00 12.00
32 Denard Robinson .75 2.00
33A Joe Namath 1.50 4.00
33B Joe Namath SP 6.00 15.00
34 Eric Decker .75 2.00
35 Matthew Stafford 1.00 2.50
36A Calvin Johnson 1.25 3.00
36B Calvin Johnson SP 5.00 12.00
37A Aaron Rodgers 2.50 6.00
37B Aaron Rodgers SP 10.00 25.00
38 Eddie Lacy .75 2.00
39 Cam Newton 1.25 3.00
40A Tom Brady 3.00 8.00
40B Tom Brady SP 12.00 30.00
41 Rob Gronkowski 1.25 3.00
42A Bo Jackson 1.50 4.00
42B Bo Jackson SP 6.00 15.00
43 Nick Foles 1.00 2.50
44 Kurt Warner 1.00 2.50
45 Joe Flacco 1.00 2.50
46 Steve Smith 1.00 2.50
47 Robert Griffin III .75 2.00
48 Alfred Morris .75 2.00
49A Drew Brees 1.25 3.00
49B Drew Brees SP 5.00 12.00
50 Mark Ingram 1.00 2.50
51A Russell Wilson 1.50 4.00
51B Russell Wilson SP 6.00 15.00
52 Richard Sherman 1.25 3.00
53 Earl Thomas 1.00 2.50
54 Ben Roethlisberger 1.25 3.00
55A Le'Veon Bell 1.00 2.50
55B Le'Veon Bell SP 4.00 10.00
56A J.J. Watt 1.25 3.00
56B J.J. Watt SP 5.00 12.00
57 DeAndre Hopkins 1.00 2.50
58 Kendall Wright .75 2.00
59 Cordarrelle Patterson .75 2.00
60 Jerick McKinnon .75 2.00
61 Jeremy Hill SS .75 2.00
62 Sammy Watkins SS 1.00 2.50
63 Terrance West SS .75 2.00
64 Mike Evans SS 1.00 2.50
65 John Brown SS 1.00 2.50
66 Branden Oliver SS 1.00 2.50
67 Donte Moncrief SS 1.00 2.50
68 Zack Martin SS .75 2.00
69 Jordan Matthews SS 1.00 2.50
70 Odell Beckham Jr. SS 1.25 3.00
71 Blake Bortles SS .75 2.00
72 Davante Adams SS 1.00 2.50
73 Kelvin Benjamin SS 1.00 2.50
74 Derek Carr SS 1.25 3.00
75 Tre Mason SS 1.00 2.50
76 C.J. Mosley SS 1.25 3.00
77 Brandin Cooks SS 1.00 2.50
78 Martavis Bryant SS .75 2.00
79 Bishop Sankey SS .75 2.00
80 Teddy Bridgewater SS 1.00 2.50
81 Brett Favre RR 2.50 6.00
82 Peyton Manning RR 2.50 6.00
83 Steve Young RR 1.50 4.00
84 Marshawn Lynch RR 1.00 2.50
85 Drew Brees RR 1.25 3.00
86 Cris Carter RR 1.25 3.00
87 Kurt Warner RR 1.00 2.50
88 Deion Sanders RR 1.00 2.50
89 Marshall Faulk RR 1.00 2.50
90 Jerome Bettis RR 1.25 3.00
91 Wes Welker RR 1.00 2.50
92 Reggie Bush RR .75 2.00
93 Jay Cutler RR .75 2.00
94 John Riggins RR 1.00 2.50
95 Anquan Boldin RR .75 2.00
96 Doug Flutie RR 1.00 2.50
97 Brandon Marshall RR .75 2.00
98 Tim Tebow RR 1.00 2.50
99 Eric Dickerson RR 1.00 2.50
100 Justin Forsett RR 1.00 2.50
101A Jameis Winston RC 2.50 6.00
101B Jameis Winston SP 3.00 8.00
102A Marcus Mariota RC 4.00 10.00
102B Marcus Mariota SP 5.00 12.00
103A Amari Cooper RC 3.00 8.00
103B Amari Cooper SP 4.00 10.00
104A Kevin White RC 1.25 3.00
104B Kevin White SP 1.50 4.00
105A Melvin Gordon RC 2.50 6.00
105B Melvin Gordon SP 3.00 8.00
106A Ameer Abdullah RC 1.50 4.00
106B Ameer Abdullah SP 2.00 5.00
107A Leonard Williams RC 1.00 2.50
107B Leonard Williams SP 1.25 3.00
108A Brett Hundley RC 1.00 2.50
108B Brett Hundley SP 1.25 3.00
109A Bryce Petty RC 1.00 2.50
109B Bryce Petty SP 1.25 3.00
110A Todd Gurley RC 4.00 10.00
110B Todd Gurley SP 5.00 12.00
111A T.J. Yeldon RC 1.00 2.50
111B T.J. Yeldon SP 1.25 3.00
112A DeVante Parker RC 1.50 4.00
112B DeVante Parker SP 2.00 5.00
113A Jaelen Strong RC 1.25 3.00
113B Jaelen Strong SP 1.50 4.00
114A Sammie Coates RC 1.25 3.00
114B Sammie Coates SP 1.50 4.00
115A Jay Ajayi RC 1.50 4.00
115B Jay Ajayi SP 2.00 5.00
116A Tevin Coleman RC 1.25 3.00
116B Tevin Coleman SP 1.50 4.00
117A Phillip Dorsett RC 1.00 2.50
117B Phillip Dorsett SP 1.25 3.00
118A D.Green-Beckham RC 1.00 2.50
118B D.Green-Beckham SP 1.25 3.00
119A Duke Johnson RC 1.50 4.00
119B Duke Johnson SP 2.00 5.00
120A Devin Funchess RC 1.50 4.00
120B Devin Funchess SP 2.00 5.00
121 David Johnson RC 2.50 6.00
122 Rashad Greene RC 1.00 2.50
123 Nelson Agholor RC 1.25 3.00
124 Devin Smith RC 1.00 2.50
125 Breshad Perriman RC 1.00 2.50
126 Maxx Williams RC 1.00 2.50
127 Tyler Lockett RC 1.50 4.00
128 Garrett Grayson RC 1.00 2.50
129 Chris Conley RC 1.00 2.50
130 Sean Mannion RC 1.00 2.50
131 Ty Montgomery RC 1.00 2.50
132 Matt Jones RC 1.00 2.50
133 Jamison Crowder RC 1.25 3.00
134 Jeremy Langford RC 1.00 2.50
135 Justin Hardy RC 1.00 2.50
136 Vince Mayle RC 1.25 3.00
137 Buck Allen RC 1.25 3.00
138 Mike Davis RC 1.00 2.50
139 David Cobb RC 1.00 2.50
140 Stefon Diggs RC 2.50 6.00
141 Dante Fowler Jr. RC 1.50 4.00
142 Clive Walford RC 1.00 2.50
143 Karlos Williams RC 1.00 2.50
144 Kenny Bell RC 1.50 4.00
145 Cameron Artis-Payne RC 1.00 2.50
146 Byron Jones RC 1.50 4.00
147 Vic Beasley Jr. RC 1.25 3.00
148 Trae Waynes RC 1.00 2.50
149 Kevin Johnson RC 1.00 2.50
150 Arik Armstead RC 1.00 2.50
151 Marcus Peters RC 1.50 4.00
152 Bud Dupree RC 1.25 3.00
153 Shane Ray RC 1.00 2.50
154 Shaq Thompson RC 1.25 3.00
155 Stephone Anthony RC 1.00 2.50
156 Malcom Brown RC 1.00 2.50
157 Randy Gregory RC 1.00 2.50
158 Landon Collins RC 1.25 3.00
159 Preston Smith RC 1.25 3.00
160 Ronald Darby RC 1.00 2.50
161 Tony Lippett RC 1.00 2.50
162 Tyler Kroft RC 1.25 3.00
163 Jesse James RC 1.25 3.00
164 J.J. Nelson RC 1.00 2.50
165 Nick O'Leary RC 1.00 2.50

2015 Panini Clear Vision Blue

*BLUE/99: .6X TO 1.5X BASIC ROOKIES
*BLUE/99: .75X TO 2X BASIC VETS
*BLUE/99: .5X TO 1.2X SP ROOKIES

2015 Panini Clear Vision Clarity

CL1 Teddy Bridgewater 3.00 8.00
CL2 Bishop Sankey 2.50 6.00
CL3 J.J. Watt 6.00 15.00
CL4 Antonio Brown 6.00 15.00
CL5 Richard Sherman 4.00 10.00
CL6 Mark Ingram 3.00 8.00
CL7 DeSean Jackson 3.00 8.00
CL8 C.J. Mosley 4.00 10.00
CL9 Marshall Faulk 3.00 8.00
CL10 Derek Carr 4.00 10.00
CL11 Tom Brady 15.00 30.00
CL12 Kelvin Benjamin 3.00 8.00
CL13 Aaron Rodgers 8.00 20.00
CL14 Barry Sanders 6.00 15.00
CL15 Joe Namath 5.00 12.00
CL16 Blake Bortles 2.50 6.00
CL17 Odell Beckham Jr. 4.00 10.00
CL18 Matt Ryan 3.00 8.00
CL19 Nick Foles 3.00 8.00
CL20 Dan Marino 8.00 20.00
CL21 Tony Romo 3.00 8.00
CL22 Andrew Luck 6.00 15.00
CL23 Tamba Hali 2.50 6.00
CL24 Philip Rivers 4.00 10.00
CL25 Patrick Peterson 2.50 6.00
CL26 Mike Evans 3.00 8.00
CL27 Johnny Manziel 3.00 8.00
CL28 Peyton Manning 8.00 20.00
CL29 Sammy Watkins 3.00 8.00
CL30 Jeremy Hill 2.50 6.00
CL31 Brian Urlacher 4.00 10.00
CL32 Colin Kaepernick
CL33 Emmitt Smith 6.00 15.00
CL34 Michael Strahan 3.00 8.00
CL35 Doug Flutie 3.00 8.00
CL36 Julio Jones 4.00 10.00
CL37 Cris Carter 4.00 10.00
CL38 Jay Cutler 2.50 6.00
CL39 Matthew Stafford 3.00 8.00
CL40 Lamar Miller 2.50 6.00
CL41 DeAndre Hopkins 3.00 8.00
CL42 Russell Wilson 5.00 12.00

2015 Panini Clear Vision Red

*RED/25: 2X TO 5X BASIC VETS
*RED/25: 1.5X TO 4X BASIC ROOKIES
*RED/25: 1.2X TO 3X SP ROOKIES

2015 Panini Clear Vision Stained Glass

SG1 Brett Favre 8.00 20.00
SG2 Joe Montana 10.00 25.00
SG3 John Elway 6.00 15.00
SG4 Dan Marino 8.00 20.00
SG5 Terry Bradshaw 5.00 12.00
SG6 Roger Staubach 5.00 12.00
SG7 Steve Young 5.00 12.00

2015 Panini Clear Vision Autographs

CVSAL Andrew Luck/25 60.00 150.00
CVSBJ Bo Jackson/25 50.00 120.00
CVSBR Ben Roethlisberger/15 125.00 250.00
CVSBS Barry Sanders/15 125.00 200.00
CVSCK Colin Kaepernick/15 25.00 60.00
CVSDBE Drew Brees/25 30.00 80.00
CVSDC Derek Carr/50 20.00 50.00
CVSDH Dan Hampton/50 12.00 30.00
CVSDM DeMarco Murray/50 15.00 40.00
CVSDRB Derrick Brooks/25 25.00 60.00
CVSJB Jerome Bettis/25 50.00 120.00
CVSJJ J.J. Watt/50 30.00 80.00
CVSJM Johnny Manziel/25 20.00 50.00
CVSKW Kurt Warner/35 50.00 100.00
CVSMF Marshall Faulk/25 20.00 50.00
CVSMS Matthew Stafford/25 25.00 60.00
CVSPM Peyton Manning/15 100.00 200.00
CVSPR Philip Rivers/25 25.00 60.00
CVSRS Roger Staubach/15 50.00 120.00
CVSRSH Richard Sherman/50 30.00 80.00
CVSRW Russell Wilson/15 50.00 120.00
CVSTR Tony Romo/25 40.00 100.00

2015 Panini Clear Vision C Thru Autographs

CTAG A.J. Green/44 20.00 50.00
CTAL Andrew Luck/50 50.00 100.00
CTBP Bill Parcells/25 30.00 60.00
CTBS Barry Sanders/25
CTBS Bruce Smith/25 40.00 80.00
CTBU Brian Urlacher/25 60.00 120.00
CTDBO Derrick Brooks/50 12.00 30.00
CTDBY Dez Bryant/50 40.00 80.00
CTDC Derek Carr/50
CTEC Earl Campbell/50 30.00 60.00
CTED Eric Dickerson/50 30.00 60.00
CTEM Eli Manning/25 40.00 80.00
CTET Earl Thomas/50 15.00 40.00
CTGS Gale Sayers/50 20.00 50.00
CTJM Johnny Manziel/50 15.00 40.00
CTJN Jordy Nelson/50 15.00 40.00
CTJW Jason Witten/50 15.00 40.00
CTKB Kelvin Benjamin/50 15.00 40.00
CTKW Kurt Warner/25
CTLTA Lawrence Taylor/25 50.00 100.00
CTLTO LaDainian Tomlinson/50 30.00 60.00
CTMR Matt Ryan/25
CTOB Odell Beckham Jr./36 20.00 50.00
CTRG Rob Gronkowski/50 20.00 50.00
CTRS Richard Sherman/15 75.00 150.00
CTRWA Reggie Wayne/50 15.00 40.00
CTRWI Russell Wilson/25 50.00 100.00
CTTA Troy Aikman/25
CTTBI Teddy Bridgewater/50 30.00 60.00
CTTC Tony Dorsett/25 40.00 80.00
CTTD Terrell Davis/50 15.00 40.00

2015 Panini Clear Vision Clear Choice Jerseys Autographs

CCJAC Amari Cooper/35 40.00 80.00
CCJDG D.Green-Beckham/50 6.00 15.00
CCJDP DeVante Parker/50 10.00 25.00
CCJDP Bryce Petty/50 6.00 15.00
CCJJW Jameis Winston/25 40.00 80.00
CCJKW Kevin White/35 8.00 20.00
CCJMG Melvin Gordon/50 15.00 40.00
CCJMM Marcus Mariota/25 60.00 125.00
CCJPD Phillip Dorsett/50 6.00 15.00
CCJTG Todd Gurley/50 25.00 60.00

2015 Panini Clear Vision Clear Choice Jerseys Prime Autographs

*PRIME AU/15-25: .5X TO 1.2X JSY AU/35-50
CCJAC Amari Cooper/15 40.00 100.00
CCJTG Todd Gurley/25 60.00 120.00

2015 Panini Clear Vision Clear Cloth Jerseys

*PRIME/25: .8X TO 2X BASIC JSY/99
*PRIME/25: .6X TO 1.5X BASIC JSY/49-50
CCAJ Alshon Jeffery/99 3.00 8.00
CCAP Adrian Peterson/99 4.00 10.00
CCBB Blake Bortles/99 2.50 6.00
CCCB Cole Beasley/99 4.00 10.00
CCCK Colin Kaepernick/99 5.00 12.00
CCCS Charles Sims/99 2.50 6.00
CCDC Derek Carr/99 4.00 10.00
CCEM Eli Manning/50 4.00 10.00
CCJF Johnny Manziel/99 3.00 8.00
CCJFL Joe Flacco/49 4.00 10.00
CCJS Jonathan Stewart/49 3.00 8.00
CCKA Keenan Allen/25 5.00 12.00
CCKB Kelvin Benjamin/99 3.00 8.00
CCKW Kendall Wright/99 2.50 6.00
CCLT Lorenzo Taliaferro/49 3.00 8.00
CCOB Odell Beckham Jr./99 4.00 10.00
CCPM Peyton Manning/25 12.00 30.00
CCSW Sammy Watkins/99 3.00 8.00
CCTB Teddy Bridgewater/99 3.00 8.00
CCTH T.Y. Hilton/99 3.00 8.00

2015 Panini Clear Vision Clear History Dual Jerseys

*PRIME/49: .5X TO 1.2X BASIC JSY/99
*PRIME/15-25: .8X TO 2X BASIC JSY/99
CHBF Brett Favre 15.00 40.00
CHBS Bishop Sankey 3.00 8.00
CHCI Chris Ivory 4.00 10.00
CHCM Curtis Martin 6.00 15.00
CHCP Carson Palmer 4.00 10.00
CHDA Davante Adams 4.00 10.00
CHDC Derek Carr 10.00 25.00
CHDF Doug Flutie 6.00 15.00
CHDF Devonta Freeman 4.00 10.00
CHDJ DeSean Jackson 4.00 10.00
CHDT De'Anthony Thomas 5.00 12.00
CHED Eric Dickerson 6.00 15.00
CHEE Eric Ebron 3.00 8.00
CHJA Jared Allen 3.00 8.00
CHJE John Elway 12.00 30.00
CHJF Johnny Manziel 4.00 10.00
CHJH Jeremy Hill 3.00 8.00
CHJL Jarvis Landry 4.00 10.00
CHJMA Jordan Matthews 4.00 10.00
CHJMO Joe Montana 20.00 50.00
CHJN Joe Namath 10.00 25.00
CHJP Julius Peppers 4.00 10.00
CHKB Kelvin Benjamin 4.00 10.00
CHKM Khalil Mack 5.00 12.00
CHMA Marcus Allen 8.00 20.00
CHME Mike Evans 4.00 10.00
CHMF Marshall Faulk 6.00 15.00
CHML Marqise Lee 3.00 8.00
CHMW Mike Wallace 3.00 8.00
CHOB Odell Beckham Jr. 6.00 15.00
CHPH Percy Harvin 3.00 8.00
CHRB Reggie Bush 3.00 8.00
CHSW Sammy Watkins 4.00 10.00
CHTB Teddy Bridgewater 6.00 15.00
CHTM Tre Mason 4.00 10.00

2015 Panini Clear Vision Clear Shots

*BLUE/99: .5X TO 1.2X BASIC INSERTS
*RED/25: .8X TO 2X BASIC INSERTS
CS1 Andrew Luck 5.00 12.00
CS2 Russell Wilson 5.00 12.00
CS3 Dez Bryant 4.00 10.00
CS4 Aaron Rodgers 8.00 20.00
CS5 Peyton Manning 8.00 20.00
CS6 Tom Brady 8.00 20.00
CS7 J.J. Watt 5.00 12.00
CS8 Dan Marino 8.00 20.00
CS9 Jerry Rice 6.00 15.00
CS10 Barry Sanders 6.00 15.00
CS11 Steve Young 5.00 12.00
CS12 Odell Beckham Jr. 4.00 10.00
CS13 Calvin Johnson 4.00 10.00
CS14 Emmitt Smith 6.00 15.00
CS15 Rob Gronkowski 4.00 10.00
CS16 Cam Newton 4.00 10.00
CS17 Ben Roethlisberger 6.00 15.00
CS18 Drew Brees 4.00 10.00

2015 Panini Clear Vision Clear Winners

*BLUE/99: .5X TO 1.2X BASIC INSERTS
*RED/25: .8X TO 2X BASIC INSERTS
CW1 Joe Montana 15.00 40.00
CW2 Troy Aikman 5.00 12.00
CW3 Tom Brady 10.00 25.00
CW4 Peyton Manning 8.00 20.00
CW5 John Elway 6.00 15.00
CW6 Russell Wilson 5.00 12.00
CW7 Aaron Rodgers 8.00 20.00
CW8 Ben Roethlisberger 5.00 12.00
CW9 Brett Favre 8.00 20.00

2015 Panini Clear Vision Double Vision

*BLUE/99: .5X TO 1.2X BASIC INSERTS
*RED/25: .8X TO 2X BASIC INSERTS
DV1 O.Beckham/V.Cruz 3.00 8.00
DV2 M.Evans/V.Jackson 2.50 6.00
DV3 G.Bernard/J.Hill 2.00 5.00
DV4 J.Garoppolo/T.Brady 8.00 20.00
DV5 A.Robinson/M.Lee 2.50 6.00
DV6 D.Thomas/J.Charles 2.50 6.00
DV7 J.Nelson/R.Cobb 2.50 6.00
DV8 D.Hester/J.Jones 3.00 8.00
DV9 B.Cooks/M.Colston 2.50 6.00

2015 Panini Clear Vision Framed Fabrics

FFAB Antonio Brown/75 8.00 20.00
FFAF Arian Foster/49 5.00 12.00
FFAG Antonio Gates/99 2.50 6.00
FFAJ Alshon Jeffery/99 3.00 8.00
FFAL Andrew Luck/49 8.00 20.00
FFAP Adrian Peterson/99 4.00 10.00
FFAR Aaron Rodgers/25
FFBB Blake Bortles/99 2.50 6.00
FFBJ Bo Jackson/99 10.00 25.00
FFBS Barry Sanders/25
FFCC Cris Collinsworth/99 6.00 15.00
FFCK Colin Kaepernick/99 3.00 8.00
FFDB Drew Brees/99 4.00 10.00
FFDM Dan Marino/99 15.00 40.00
FFED Eric Dickerson/99 6.00 15.00
FFES Emmitt Smith/99 12.00 30.00
FFJE John Elway/99 12.00 30.00
FFJED Julian Edelman/49 6.00 15.00
FFJM Johnny Manziel/99 3.00 8.00
FFJN Joe Namath/99 12.00 30.00
FFJR Jerry Rice/99 12.00 30.00
FFLD Len Dawson/99 8.00 20.00
FFLF Larry Fitzgerald/49 5.00 12.00
FFLT Lawrence Taylor/99 10.00 25.00
FFMF Marshall Faulk/99 6.00 15.00
FFML Marshawn Lynch/99 3.00 8.00
FFOB Odell Beckham Jr./99 4.00 10.00
FFPG Pierre Garcon/99 3.00 8.00
FFPM Peyton Manning/99 8.00 20.00
FFPR Philip Rivers/99 4.00 10.00
FFRG Rob Gronkowski/49 6.00 15.00
FFRG3 Robert Griffin III/25
FFRW Russell Wilson/25
FFTA Troy Aikman/99 10.00 25.00
FFTB Tom Brady/25

2015 Panini Clear Vision Framed Fabrics Prime

*PRIME/49: .5X TO 1.2X BASIC JSY/75-99
*PRIME/15-25: .5X TO 1.2X BASIC JSY/49
*PRIME/15-25: .6X TO 1.5X BASIC JSY/75-99
FFML Marshawn Lynch/15 40.00 80.00

2015 Panini Clear Vision Jerseys

*PRIME/25: .6X TO 1.5X BASIC JSY/99
*PRIME/25: .5X TO 1.2X BASIC JSY/49
1 Tom Brady/25 20.00 50.00
2 Dan Marino/99 15.00 40.00
3 Jeremy Hill/99 3.00 8.00
4 Demaryius Thomas/99 4.00 10.00
5 Philip Rivers/99 5.00 12.00
6 Andrew Luck/99 6.00 15.00
7 Matt Ryan/99 4.00 10.00
8 Jerry Rice/99 12.00 30.00
9 Brett Favre/49 20.00 50.00
10 J.J. Watt/25
11 Donte Moncrief/99 4.00 10.00
12 Kam Chancellor/99 10.00 25.00
13 Odell Beckham Jr./99 5.00 12.00
14 Cam Newton/99 5.00 12.00
15 Tre Mason/99 4.00 10.00
16 C.J. Mosley/99 5.00 12.00
17 Russell Wilson/99 6.00 15.00
18 Blake Bortles/99 3.00 8.00
19 Bo Jackson/99 10.00 25.00
20 Joseph Randle/99 3.00 8.00
21 DeAndre Hopkins/99 4.00 10.00
22 Jim Kelly/99 8.00 20.00
23 Le'Veon Bell/99 4.00 10.00
24 Tony Dorsett/99 8.00 20.00
25 Jordan Matthews/99 4.00 10.00
26 Andre Williams/99 3.00 8.00
27 Davante Adams/99 4.00 10.00
28 Steve Largent/99 8.00 20.00
29 Mark Sanchez/99 3.00 8.00
30 Khalil Mack/99 5.00 12.00
31 Dontari Poe/99 3.00 8.00
32 Andre Ellington/99 3.00 8.00
33 DeSean Jackson/99 5.00 12.00
34 Terrance Williams/99 3.00 8.00
35 Matt Forte/49 4.00 10.00
36 Marques Colston/99 3.00 8.00
37 Jeremy Kerley/99 3.00 8.00
38 Kendall Wright/99 3.00 8.00
39 Teddy Bridgewater/99 4.00 10.00
40 Aaron Rodgers/25 15.00 40.00

2015 Panini Clear Vision Jumbo Jerseys

*PRIME/49: .5X TO 1.2X BASIC JSY/99
*PRIME/15-25: .6X TO 1.5X BASIC JSY/99
*PRIME/15-25: .5X TO 1.2X BASIC JSY/49
1 Tony Romo/49 5.00 12.00
2 Terrance West/99 3.00 8.00
3 Julio Jones/49 6.00 15.00
4 Jeremy Hill/99 3.00 8.00
5 Lamar Miller/99 3.00 8.00
6 Justin Houston/99 3.00 8.00
7 Johnny Manziel/99 4.00 10.00
8 Mike Evans/99 4.00 10.00
9 Demaryius Thomas/99 4.00 10.00
10 Marqise Lee/99 3.00 8.00
11 Brandin Cooks/99 4.00 10.00
12 Bishop Sankey/99 3.00 8.00
13 Michael Floyd/49 4.00 10.00
14 Chris Long/99
15 Alfred Morris/25 5.00 12.00
16 Odell Beckham Jr./99 6.00 15.00
17 Sammy Watkins/99 4.00 10.00
18 Derek Carr/99 5.00 12.00
19 Carlos Hyde/99 3.00 8.00
20 Devon Still/99 5.00 12.00
21 Tamba Hali/99 5.00 12.00
22 Zack Martin/99 3.00 8.00
23 Jay Cutler/99 3.00 8.00
24 Thurman Thomas/99 6.00 15.00
25 Matthew Stafford/40 5.00 12.00
26 Vernon Davis/49 4.00 10.00
27 Branden Oliver/49 5.00 12.00
28 Andrew Luck/25 10.00 25.00
29 Chris Ivory/49 5.00 12.00
30 Justin Hunter/99 3.00 8.00

2015 Panini Clear Vision Rookie Clear Cloth Jerseys

*PRIME/49: .5X TO 1.2X BASIC JSY/99
RCCAA Ameer Abdullah 4.00 10.00
RCCAC Amari Cooper 8.00 20.00
RCCBA Buck Allen 3.00 8.00
RCCBH Brett Hundley 2.50 6.00
RCCBP Bryce Petty 2.50 6.00
RCCBRP Breshad Perriman 2.50 6.00
RCCCC Chris Conley 2.50 6.00
RCCDC David Cobb 2.50 6.00
RCCDF Devin Funchess 4.00 10.00
RCCDGB D.Green-Beckham 2.50 6.00
RCCDJ David Johnson 6.00 15.00
RCCDP DeVante Parker 4.00 10.00
RCCDS Devin Smith 2.50 6.00
RCCDU Duke Johnson 4.00 10.00
RCCGG Garrett Grayson 2.50 6.00
RCCJA Jay Ajayi 4.00 10.00
RCCJC Jamison Crowder 3.00 8.00
RCCJH Justin Hardy 2.50 6.00
RCCJL Jeremy Langford 2.50 6.00
RCCJS Jaelen Strong 3.00 8.00
RCCJW Jameis Winston 6.00 15.00
RCCKW Kevin White 3.00 8.00
RCCLW Leonard Williams 2.50 6.00
RCCMD Mike Davis 2.50 6.00
RCCMG Melvin Gordon 6.00 15.00
RCCMJ Matt Jones 2.50 6.00
RCCMM Marcus Mariota 10.00 25.00
RCCMW Maxx Williams 2.50 6.00
RCCNA Nelson Agholor 3.00 8.00
RCCPD Phillip Dorsett 2.50 6.00
RCCRG Rashad Greene 2.50 6.00
RCCSC Sammie Coates 3.00 8.00
RCCSD Stefon Diggs 6.00 15.00
RCCSM Sean Mannion 2.50 6.00
RCCTC Tevin Coleman 3.00 8.00
RCCTG Todd Gurley 10.00 25.00
RCCTL Tyler Lockett 4.00 10.00
RCCTM Ty Montgomery 2.50 6.00
RCCTY T.J. Yeldon 2.50 6.00
RCCVM Vince Mayle 3.00 8.00

2015 Panini Clear Vision Rookie Clear Vision Autographs

RCSAC Amari Cooper/35 30.00 60.00
RCSBP Bryce Petty/50 6.00 15.00
RCSDGB D.Green-Beckham/50 6.00 15.00
RCSDP DeVante Parker/50 10.00 25.00
RCSJW Jameis Winston/25 25.00 50.00
RCSKW Kevin White/35 12.00 30.00
RCSMG Melvin Gordon/50 15.00 40.00
RCSMM Marcus Mariota/25 30.00 60.00
RCSPD Phillip Dorsett/50 6.00 15.00
RCSTG Todd Gurley/50 40.00 80.00

2015 Panini Clear Vision Rookie Vision

*BLUE/99: .5X TO 1.2X BASIC INSERTS
*RED/25: .8X TO 2X BASIC INSERTS
RV1 Jameis Winston 2.50 6.00
RV2 Marcus Mariota 4.00 10.00
RV3 Amari Cooper 3.00 8.00
RV4 Kevin White 1.25 3.00
RV5 Todd Gurley 4.00 10.00
RV6 DeVante Parker 1.50 4.00
RV7 Melvin Gordon 2.50 6.00
RV8 Nelson Agholor 1.25 3.00
RV9 Breshad Perriman 1.00 2.50
RV10 Brett Hundley 1.00 2.50
RV11 T.J. Yeldon 1.00 2.50
RV12 Bryce Petty 1.00 2.50
RV13 Garrett Grayson 1.00 2.50
RV14 Sammie Coates 1.25 3.00
RV15 D.Green-Beckham 1.00 2.50
RV16 Ameer Abdullah 1.50 4.00
RV17 Devin Funchess 1.50 4.00
RV18 Jaelen Strong 1.25 3.00

2015 Panini Clear Vision Team Vision

*BLUE/99: .5X TO 1.2X BASIC INSERTS
*RED/25: .8X TO 2X BASIC INSERTS
TV1 Frmn/Jnes/Ryn 2.50 6.00
TV2 Msly/Flcco/Sggs 2.50 6.00
TV3 Spllr/McCy/Wtkns 2.50 6.00
TV4 Nwtn/Bnjmn/Kchly 2.50 6.00
TV5 Jffry/Ctlr/Frte 2.00 5.00
TV6 Grn/Dltn/Hll 2.50 6.00
TV7 Mngo/Crwll/Mnzl 2.00 5.00
TV8 Brynt/Wttn/Rmo 2.50 6.00
TV9 Andrsn/Thms/Mnng 5.00 12.00
TV10 Jhnsn/Bll/Sttfrd 2.50 6.00
TV11 Rdgrs/Khn/Nlsn 5.00 12.00
TV12 Lck/Flner/Hltn 3.00 8.00
TV13 Rbnsn/Brtls/Rbnsn 2.00 5.00
TV14 Poe/Chrls/Klce 2.50 6.00
TV15 Grms/Lndry/Tnnhll 2.00 5.00
TV16 Jnngs/McKnn/Brdgwtr 2.00 5.00
TV17 Amndla/Grnkwski/Brdy 6.00 15.00
TV18 Brs/Ingrm/Clstn 2.50 6.00
TV19 Mnng/PrrePl/Bckhm 2.50 6.00
TV20 Mrry/Cpr/Brdfrd 2.00 5.00
TV21 Brwn/Rthlsbrgr/Bll 2.50 6.00
TV22 Wddle/Alln/Rvrs 2.50 6.00
TV23 Bldn/Hyde/Kprnck 2.00 5.00
TV24 Lynch/Shrmn/Wlsn 3.00 8.00
TV25 Fles/Astn/Msn 2.00 5.00
TV26 Mrtn/McCy/Evns 2.00 5.00
TV27 Mrrs/Jcksn/Grffn 2.00 5.00

2016 Panini Clear Vision

1A Carson Palmer 1.00 2.50
1B Carson Palmer L1 SP
2 Larry Fitzgerald 1.00 2.50
3 David Johnson 1.25 3.00
4 Devonta Freeman 1.00 2.50
5 Julio Jones 1.25 3.00
6 Joe Flacco 1.00 2.50
7A Steve Smith Sr. 1.00 2.50
7B Steve Smith Sr. L1 SP
8A LeSean McCoy 1.25 3.00
8B LeSean McCoy L2 SP
9 Sammy Watkins 1.25 3.00
10 Cam Newton 1.25 3.00
11 Luke Kuechly 1.00 2.50
12 Jay Cutler .75 2.00
13 Jeremy Langford 1.00 2.50
14 A.J. Green 1.25 3.00
15 Andy Dalton 1.00 2.50
16 Joe Haden .75 2.00
17 Duke Johnson .75 2.00
18 Dez Bryant 1.25 3.00
19 Tony Romo 1.00 2.50
20A Peyton Manning 2.50 6.00
20B Peyton Manning L2 SP
21 Demaryius Thomas 1.00 2.50
22 Von Miller 1.00 2.50
23 Matthew Stafford 1.00 2.50
24 Ameer Abdullah .75 2.00
25 Aaron Rodgers 2.50 6.00
26 Eddie Lacy .75 2.00
27 DeAndre Hopkins 1.00 2.50
28 J.J. Watt 1.25 3.00
29 Andrew Luck 1.50 4.00
30 T.Y. Hilton 1.00 2.50
31 Blake Bortles .75 2.00
32 Allen Robinson 1.00 2.50
33 Jamaal Charles 1.00 2.50
34 Travis Kelce 1.25 3.00
35 Todd Gurley 1.25 3.00
36 Aaron Donald 1.25 3.00
37 Jarvis Landry 1.00 2.50
38 Ryan Tannehill 1.00 2.50
39 Adrian Peterson 1.25 3.00
40 Teddy Bridgewater 1.00 2.50
41 Tom Brady 3.00 8.00
42 Rob Gronkowski 1.25 3.00
43 Julian Edelman 1.25 3.00
44A Drew Brees 1.25 3.00
44B Drew Brees L2 SP
45 Mark Ingram 1.00 2.50
46 Odell Beckham Jr. 1.25 3.00
47 Eli Manning 1.00 2.50
48A Brandon Marshall .75 2.00
48B Brandon Marshall L1 SP
49 Muhammad Wilkerson .75 2.00
50A Darrelle Revis .75 2.00
50B Darrelle Revis L1 SP
51 Amari Cooper 1.25 3.00
52 Derek Carr 1.25 3.00
53 Sam Bradford .75 2.00
54 Zach Ertz 1.00 2.50
55 Antonio Brown 1.25 3.00
56 Ben Roethlisberger 1.25 3.00
57 Le'Veon Bell 1.00 2.50
58 Philip Rivers 1.25 3.00
59 Keenan Allen 1.00 2.50
60 Carlos Hyde .75 2.00
61 NaVorro Bowman 1.00 2.50
62 Russell Wilson 1.50 4.00
63 Doug Baldwin 1.00 2.50
64 Richard Sherman 1.25 3.00
65 Jameis Winston 1.25 3.00
66 Mike Evans 1.00 2.50
67 Marcus Mariota 1.25 3.00
68A DeMarco Murray 1.00 2.50
68B DeMarco Murray L1 SP
69 Kirk Cousins 1.25 3.00
70A DeSean Jackson 1.00 2.50
70B DeSean Jackson L1 SP
71 Earl Campbell 1.25 3.00
72A Jerry Rice 2.00 5.00
72B Jerry Rice L1 SP
72C Jerry Rice L2 SP
73A Doug Flutie 1.00 2.50
73B Doug Flutie L1 SP
73C Doug Flutie L2 SP
74A Brett Favre 2.50 6.00
74B Brett Favre L1 SP
74C Brett Favre L2 SP
75 Joe Greene 1.25 3.00
76A Steve Young 1.50 4.00
76B Steve Young L2 SP
77 Hines Ward 1.00 2.50
78 Jim Kelly 1.25 3.00
79A Kurt Warner 1.00 2.50
79B Kurt Warner L1 SP
79C Kurt Warner L2 SP
80 Barry Sanders 2.00 5.00
81A LaDainian Tomlinson 1.00 2.50
81B LaDainian Tomlinson L2 SP
82A Cris Carter 1.25 3.00
82B Cris Carter L2 SP
83 Bo Jackson 1.50 4.00
84 Roger Staubach 1.50 4.00
85 Joe Namath 1.50 4.00
85B Joe Namath L2 SP
86A Emmitt Smith 2.00 5.00
86B Emmitt Smith L1 SP
87 Terry Bradshaw 1.50 4.00
88A Jerome Bettis 1.25 3.00
88B Jerome Bettis L2 SP
89A Tony Dorsett 1.25 3.00
89B Tony Dorsett L2 SP
90 Steve Largent 1.25 3.00
91 John Elway 2.00 5.00
92A Warren Moon 1.25 3.00
92B Warren Moon L1 SP
93 Troy Aikman 1.50 4.00
94 Dan Marino 2.50 6.00
95A Charles Haley 1.25 3.00
95B Charles Haley L1 SP
96A Joe Montana 3.00 8.00
96B Joe Montana L2 SP
97 Randall Cunningham 1.00 2.50
97B Randall Cunningham L1 SP
98A Eric Dickerson 1.00 2.50
98B Eric Dickerson L2 SP
99A Ronnie Lott 1.00 2.50
99B Ronnie Lott L1 SP
100 Rod Woodson 1.00 2.50
101 Mackensie Alexander L1 RC 1.00 2.50
102 Vernon Hargreaves III L1 RC 1.50 4.00
103 Eli Apple L1 RC 1.25 3.00
104 Moritz Bohringer L1 RC 1.00 2.50
105 Shaq Lawson L1 RC 1.00 2.50
106 Jonathan Bullard L1 RC 1.00 2.50
107 Emmanuel Ogbah L1 RC 1.25 3.00
108 Kevin Dodd L1 RC 1.00 2.50
109 Kamalei Correa L1 RC 1.00 2.50
110 Robert Nkemdiche L1 RC 1.25 3.00
111 Jarran Reed L1 RC 1.00 2.50
112 Kenny Clark L1 RC 1.00 2.50
113 Darian Thompson L1 RC 1.00 2.50
114 Reggie Ragland L1 RC 1.00 2.50
115 Cody Kessler L1 RC 1.00 2.50
116 Darron Lee L1 RC 1.00 2.50
117 Leonard Floyd L1 RC 1.25 3.00
118 Jaylon Smith L1 RC 1.00 2.50
119 Noah Spence L1 RC 1.00 2.50
120 Christian Hackenberg L1 RC 1.00 2.50
121 Dak Prescott L1 RC 5.00 12.00
122 Cardale Jones L1 RC 1.00 2.50
123 Artie Burns L1 RC 1.25 3.00
124 Brandon Doughty L1 RC 1.00 2.50
125 Kevin Hogan L1 RC 1.25 3.00
126 Kenneth Dixon L1 RC 1.00 2.50
127 Devontae Booker L1 RC 1.25 3.00
128 Jordan Howard L1 RC 2.50 6.00
129 Kenyan Drake L1 RC 1.50 4.00
130 Paul Perkins L1 RC 1.00 2.50
131 Jonathan Williams L1 RC 1.25 3.00
132 C.J. Prosise L1 RC 1.00 2.50
133 Ricardo Louis L1 RC 1.00 2.50
134 Keanu Neal L1 RC 1.00 2.50
135 Sheldon Rankins L1 RC 1.25 3.00
136 Vonn Bell L1 RC 1.25 3.00
137 Karl Joseph L1 RC 1.00 2.50
138 Vernon Butler L1 RC 1.00 2.50
139 Austin Hooper L1 RC 1.00 2.50
140 Nick Vannett L1 RC 1.00 2.50
141 Keenan Reynolds L1 RC 1.25 3.00
142 Tyler Boyd L1 RC 1.25 3.00
143 Pharoh Cooper L1 RC 1.00 2.50
144 Rashard Higgins L1 RC 1.00 2.50
145 Sterling Shepard L1 RC 1.25 3.00
146 Braxton Miller L1 RC 1.00 2.50
147 Malcolm Mitchell L1 RC 1.00 2.50
148 William Jackson III L1 RC 1.25 3.00
149 Leonte Carroo L1 RC 1.00 2.50
150 Trevor Davis L1 RC 1.00 2.50
151 Jalen Ramsey L2 RC 2.00 5.00
152 DeForest Buckner L2 RC 1.25 3.00
153 A'Shawn Robinson L2 RC 1.25 3.00
154 Chris Moore L2 RC 1.50 4.00
155 Myles Jack L2 RC 1.50 4.00
156 Paxton Lynch L2 RC 1.25 3.00
157 Connor Cook L2 RC 1.50 4.00
158 Derrick Henry L2 RC 3.00 8.00
159 Alex Collins L2 RC 1.50 4.00
160 Jacoby Brissett L2 RC 1.50 4.00
161 Hunter Henry L2 RC 1.50 4.00
162 Corey Coleman L2 RC 2.00 5.00
163 Michael Thomas L2 RC 2.50 6.00
164 Josh Doctson L2 RC 1.50 4.00
165 Will Fuller L2 RC 2.00 5.00
166 Joey Bosa L3 RC 3.00 8.00
167 Jared Goff L3 RC 20.00 50.00
168 Carson Wentz L3 RC 20.00 50.00
169 Ezekiel Elliott L3 RC 25.00 50.00
170 Laquon Treadwell L3 RC 2.00 5.00

2016 Panini Clear Vision Blue

*VETS/99: .8X TO 2X BASIC CARDS
*ROOKIES/99: .6X TO 1.5X BASIC RC/999
*ROOKIES/99: .5X TO 1.2X BASIC RC/399
*ROOKIES/99: .4X TO 1X BASIC RC/99

2016 Panini Clear Vision Bronze

*VETS/79: .8X TO 2X BASIC CARDS
*ROOKIES/79: .6X TO 1.5X BASIC RC/999
*ROOKIES/79: .5X TO 1.2X BASIC RC/399
*ROOKIES/79: .4X TO 1X BASIC RC/99

2016 Panini Clear Vision Emerald

*VETS/19: 1.5X TO 4X BASIC CARDS
*ROOKIES/19: 1.25X TO 3X BASIC RC/999
*ROOKIES/19: 1X TO 2.5X BASIC RC/399
*ROOKIES/19: .8X TO 2X BASIC RC/99
96A Joe Montana 30.00 60.00

2016 Panini Clear Vision Gold

*VETS/29: 1.2X TO 3X BASIC CARDS
*ROOKIES/29: 1X TO 2.5X BASIC RC/999
*ROOKIES/29: .8X TO 2X BASIC RC/399
*ROOKIES/29: .6X TO 1.5X BASIC RC/99

2016 Panini Clear Vision Red

*VETS/49: 1X TO 2.5X BASIC CARDS
*ROOKIES/49: .8X TO 2X BASIC RC/999
*ROOKIES/49: .6X TO 1.5X BASIC RC/399
*ROOKIES/49: .5X TO 1.2X BASIC RC/99

2016 Panini Clear Vision Autographs

*GOLD/25: .5X TO 1.2X BASIC AU/35-50
*GOLD/15: .6X TO 1.5X BASIC AU/35-50
*GOLD/15: .5X TO 1.2X BASIC AU/25
1 Warren Moon/25 25.00 60.00
2 Kirk Cousins/50 20.00 50.00
3 Patrick Peterson/50 12.00 30.00
4 Derek Carr/50 20.00 50.00
6 Paul Hornung/50 20.00 50.00
7 Len Dawson/50 20.00 50.00
9 Marcus Mariota/15 60.00 120.00
10 Clay Matthews/35 30.00 60.00
11 Gale Sayers/40 20.00 50.00
14 Danny Woodhead/45 15.00 40.00
15 Jerome Bettis/40 EXCH 40.00 80.00
17 Bruce Smith/25 20.00 50.00
18 Luke Kuechly/50 30.00 60.00
19 Richard Sherman/15 EXCH 30.00 80.00
21 Fred Biletnikoff/50 EXCH
22 Eric Dickerson/40 15.00 40.00
23 Rod Woodson/40 EXCH 15.00 40.00
24 Ozzie Newsome/50 15.00 40.00
25 Michael Strahan/25 20.00 50.00

2016 Panini Clear Vision C Thru Autographs

2 Doug Flutie/30 20.00 50.00
3 Fran Tarkenton/40 20.00 50.00
5 Joe Greene/50 40.00 890.00
7 Raymond Berry/40 15.00 40.00
9 Steve Smith Sr./40
10 Hines Ward/50 15.00 40.00
11 Jason Witten/40 EXCH 15.00 40.00
12 Jim Kelly/15 EXCH 40.00 80.00
13 Kurt Warner/15 30.00 60.00
15 Darrell Green/45 EXCH 25.00 60.00
16 Lawrence Taylor/50 EXCH 20.00 50.00
17 James Harrison/50 25.00 60.00
18 Von Miller/50 EXCH 15.00 40.00
19 Amari Cooper/40 30.00 60.00
22 LaDainian Tomlinson/35 15.00 40.00
23 Dez Bryant/32 25.00 60.00

2016 Panini Clear Vision Clear Change Dual Jerseys

1 Jameis Winston/99 4.00 10.00
2 Doug Flutie/40 4.00 10.00
3 Eric Dickerson/50 4.00 10.00
4 Derek Carr/99 4.00 10.00
5 Champ Bailey/25 5.00 12.00
6 Jerry Rice/15 15.00 40.00
7 Odell Beckham Jr./99 4.00 10.00
8 Marcus Mariota/99 4.00 10.00
9 Adrian Peterson/15
10 Devonta Freeman/99 3.00 8.00
11 LeSean McCoy/99 4.00 10.00
12 Sammy Watkins /99 4.00 10.00
13 Dan Marino/25
14 Melvin Gordon/99 3.00 8.00
15 DeSean Jackson/99 3.00 8.00
16 Joe Montana/50 30.00 60.00
17 Jarvis Landry/50 4.00 10.00
18 Peyton Manning/25 25.00 50.00
19 Eric Decker/75 2.50 6.00
20 T.J. Yeldon/99 2.50 6.00
21 Todd Gurley/99 4.00 10.00
22 Amari Cooper/99 4.00 10.00
23 Jeremy Langford/99 3.00 8.00
24 DeVante Parker/50 4.00 10.00
25 Mike Evans/75 3.00 8.00
26 Emmanuel Sanders/50 5.00 12.00
27 Karlos Williams/25 4.00 10.00
28 Carson Palmer/25 5.00 12.00
29 Ryan Mathews/99 3.00 8.00
30 Devin Funchess/99 2.50 6.00
31 Matt Jones/99 3.00 8.00
32 Darren McFadden/75 2.50 6.00
33 Kevin White/99 2.50 6.00
34 Duke Johnson/99 2.50 6.00
35 DeMarcus Ware/50 4.00 10.00

2016 Panini Clear Vision Clear Choice Jerseys Autographs

1 Paxton Lynch/99 5.00 12.00
2 Jared Goff/50 30.00 60.00
3 Carson Wentz/99 50.00 100.00
4 Christian Hackenberg/75 5.00 12.00
5 Connor Cook/75 6.00 15.00
6 Dak Prescott/99 40.00 80.00
7 Cardale Jones/50 6.00 15.00
8 Ezekiel Elliott/50 60.00 125.00
9 Derrick Henry/50 15.00 40.00
10 Alex Collins/50 8.00 20.00
11 Devontae Booker/99 6.00 15.00
12 Kenneth Dixon/99 5.00 12.00
13 Jonathan Williams/99 6.00 15.00
14 Jordan Howard/50 15.00 40.00
15 Laquon Treadwell/75 6.00 15.00
16 Corey Coleman/75 8.00 20.00
17 Michael Thomas/75 10.00 25.00
18 Josh Doctson/75 6.00 15.00
19 Will Fuller/75 8.00 20.00
20 Braxton Miller/99 5.00 12.00

2016 Panini Clear Vision Clear Choice Jerseys Prime Autographs

*PRIME/25: .6X TO 1.5X BASIC JSY AU/99
*PRIME/25: .5X TO 1.2X BASIC JSY AU/50
*PRIME/15: .8X TO 2X BASIC JSY AU/75
*PRIME/15-20: .6X TO 1.5X BASIC JSY AU/50
6 Dak Prescott/25 100.00 200.00

2016 Panini Clear Vision Clear Cloth Jerseys

1 Todd Gurley/99 4.00 10.00
2 Tyler Lockett/99 3.00 8.00
3 Kirk Cousins/90 4.00 10.00
4 Jeremy Langford/99 3.00 8.00
5 Allen Robinson/99 3.00 8.00
6 Travis Benjamin/90 2.50 6.00
7 John Elway/25 10.00 25.00
8 Blake Bortles/99 2.50 6.00
9 Marcus Allen/50 4.00 10.00
10 Jameis Winston/99 4.00 10.00
11 Marcus Mariota/99 4.00 10.00
12 Teddy Bridgewater/25 5.00 12.00
13 Jarvis Landry/99 3.00 8.00
14 Larry Fitzgerald/99 3.00 8.00
15 Clay Matthews/15 8.00 20.00
16 LeSean McCoy/76 4.00 10.00
17 Sam Bradford/50 3.00 8.00
18 Geno Atkins/99 2.50 6.00
19 Jerry Rice/50 8.00 20.00
20 Amari Cooper/99 4.00 10.00
21 Ronnie Lott/50 4.00 10.00
22 Dorial Green-Beckham/99 2.50 6.00
23 Andy Dalton/99 3.00 8.00
24 Kevin White/99 2.50 6.00
25 T.J. Yeldon/99 2.50 6.00
26 Julio Jones/50 5.00 12.00
27 Jordan Reed/50 3.00 8.00
28 Marshall Faulk/25 5.00 12.00
29 Jimmy Graham/50 5.00 12.00
30 Ozzie Newsome/50 4.00 10.00
31 Ryan Kerrigan/99 2.50 6.00
32 Devin Funchess/99 2.50 6.00
33 DeMarcus Ware/50 4.00 10.00
34 Jerome Bettis/50 5.00 12.00
35 Melvin Gordon/99 3.00 8.00
36 Ameer Abdullah/99 2.50 6.00
37 Derek Carr/50 5.00 12.00
38 Stefon Diggs/99 3.00 8.00
39 Mark Ingram/25 5.00 12.00
40 Emmanuel Sanders/99 4.00 10.00

2016 Panini Clear Vision Clear Heirs

*BLUE/99: .5X TO 1.2X BASIC INSERTS
*BRONZE/79: .5X TO 1.2X BASIC INSERTS
*RED/49: .6X TO 1.5X BASIC INSERTS
*GOLD/29: .8X TO 2X BASIC INSERTS
*EMERALD/19: 1X TO 2.5X BASIC INSERTS
1 F.Gore/C.Hyde 2.50 6.00
2 T.Rawls/M.Lynch 2.50 6.00
3 J.Charles/C.West 2.50 6.00
4 D.Hopkins/A.Johnson 2.50 6.00
5 B.Favre/A.Rodgers 6.00 15.00
6 V.Cruz/O.Beckham 3.00 8.00
7 R.White/J.Jones 3.00 8.00
8 M.Faulk/T.Gurley 3.00 8.00
9 M.Irvin/D.Bryant 3.00 8.00
10 T.Brady/J.Garoppolo 8.00 20.00
11 P.Manning/A.Luck 6.00 15.00
12 M.Forte/J.Langford 2.50 6.00
13 A.Brown/H.Ward 3.00 8.00
14 T.Brown/A.Cooper 3.00 8.00
15 J.Brown/L.Fitzgerald 2.50 6.00
16 R.Mathews/D.Murray 2.50 6.00
17 L.Miller/A.Foster 2.50 6.00
18 M.Forte/C.Ivory 2.50 6.00

2016 Panini Clear Vision Clear History

*BLUE/99: .5X TO 1.2X BASIC INSERTS
*BRONZE/79: .5X TO 1.2X BASIC INSERTS
*RED/49: .6X TO 1.5X BASIC INSERTS
*GOLD/29: .8X TO 2X BASIC INSERTS
*EMERALD/19: 1X TO 2.5X BASIC INSERTS
1 Ptrsn/Brdgwtr/Dggs 3.00 8.00
2 Brynt/Wttn/Romo 3.00 8.00
3 Rvrs/Alln/Grdn 3.00 8.00
4 Jnes/Csns/Jcksn 3.00 8.00
5 McCy/Tylr/Wtkns 3.00 8.00
6 Brtls/Rbnsn/Yldn 2.50 6.00
7 Edlmn/Grnkwski/Brdy 8.00 20.00
8 Tnnhill/Prkr/Lndry 2.50 6.00
9 Bll/Brwn/Rthlsbrgr 3.00 8.00
10 Hpkns/Wtt/Clwny 3.00 8.00
11 Mck/Crr/Cpr 3.00 8.00
12 Rwls/Wlsn/Grhm 4.00 10.00
13 Ftzgrld/Plmr/Jhnsn 3.00 8.00
14 Mthws/Hltn/Lck 4.00 10.00
15 Nwtn/Stwrt/Bnjmn 3.00 8.00
16 Evns/Wnstn/Mrtn 3.00 8.00
17 Lcy/Rdgrs/Nlsn 6.00 15.00
18 Thms/Andrsn/Mnng 6.00 15.00

2016 Panini Clear Vision Clear Rivals

*BLUE/99: .5X TO 1.2X BASIC INSERTS
*BRONZE/79: .5X TO 1.2X BASIC INSERTS
*RED/49: .6X TO 1.5X BASIC INSERTS
*GOLD/29: .8X TO 2X BASIC INSERTS
*EMERALD/19: 1X TO 2.5X BASIC INSERTS
1 J.Norman/O.Beckham 3.00 8.00
2 P.Manning/T.Brady 8.00 20.00
3 E.Smith/B.Sanders 5.00 12.00
4 T.Bradshaw/R.Staubach 4.00 10.00
5 J.Kelly/D.Marino 6.00 15.00
6 R.Wilson/C.Kaepernick 4.00 10.00
7 T.Romo/E.Manning 2.50 6.00
8 B.Favre/A.Rodgers 6.00 15.00
9 M.Irvin/J.Rice 5.00 12.00
10 B.Rthlsbrgr/T.Suggs 3.00 8.00
11 P.Rivers/J.Cutler 3.00 8.00
12 J.Haden/A.Green 3.00 8.00
13 R.Sherman/D.Revis 3.00 8.00
14 M.Strahan/B.Favre 6.00 15.00
15 J.Watt/A.Luck 4.00 10.00
16 C.Newton/V.Miller 3.00 8.00
17 S.Young/J.Montana 8.00 20.00
18 B.Urlacher/A.Peterson 3.00 8.00

2016 Panini Clear Vision Clear Shots

*BLUE/99: .5X TO 1.2X BASIC INSERTS
*BRONZE/79: .5X TO 1.2X BASIC INSERTS
*RED/49: .6X TO 1.5X BASIC INSERTS
*GOLD/29: .8X TO 2X BASIC INSERTS
*EMERALD/19: 1X TO 2.5X BASIC INSERTS
1 Julio Jones 2.50 6.00
2 Adrian Peterson 2.50 6.00
3 Andrew Luck 3.00 8.00
4 DeAndre Hopkins 2.00 5.00
5 Bo Jackson 3.00 8.00
6 Peyton Manning 5.00 12.00
7 Le'Veon Bell 2.00 5.00
8 Cris Carter 2.50 6.00
9 Joe Montana 6.00 15.00

2016 Panini Clear Vision Framed Fabrics

1 Eli Manning/50 4.00 10.00
2 Karlos Williams/99 2.50 6.00
3 Russell Wilson/15
4 Brett Favre/25 20.00 40.00
5 Jameis Winston/99 4.00 10.00
6 J.J. Watt/25 6.00 15.00
7 John Elway/50
8 A.J. Green/99 4.00 10.00
9 Todd Gurley/99 4.00 10.00
10 Cam Newton/65 5.00 12.00
11 Tom Brady/50 20.00 40.00
12 Aaron Rodgers/15
13 Jeremy Langford/99 3.00 8.00
14 Amari Cooper/99 4.00 10.00
15 Andrew Luck/50 6.00 15.00
16 Odell Beckham Jr./50 5.00 12.00
17 Mike Singletary/50 5.00 12.00
18 Peyton Manning/75 8.00 20.00
19 Cris Carter/50 5.00 12.00
20 Jason Witten/99 15.00 30.00
21 Maurice Jones-Drew/50 3.00 8.00
22 Marcus Mariota/99 4.00 10.00
23 Sammy Watkins /50 5.00 12.00
24 Allen Robinson/99 3.00 8.00
25 Drew Brees/25 6.00 15.00
26 T.Y. Hilton/99 3.00 8.00
27 Harrison Smith/75 20.00 40.00
28 Antonio Brown/75 4.00 10.00
30 Warren Moon/25 20.00 40.00
31 Dez Bryant/25 6.00 15.00
34 T.J. Yeldon/99 2.50 6.00
35 Ed Reed/70 4.00 10.00

2016 Panini Clear Vision Jerseys

1 Cam Newton/50 5.00 12.00
2 Tyler Lockett/99 3.00 8.00
3 Von Miller/90 3.00 8.00
4 Philip Rivers/25 6.00 15.00
5 Tony Dorsett/25 6.00 15.00
6 Len Dawson/25 25.00 50.00
7 Ben Roethlisberger/25 6.00 15.00
8 Ameer Abdullah/99 2.50 6.00
9 Drew Brees/50 5.00 12.00
10 Roger Staubach/25
11 Karlos Williams/99 2.50 6.00
12 Andrew Luck/99 5.00 12.00
13 Matt Jones/99 3.00 8.00
14 Devin Funchess/99 2.50 6.00
15 Earl Campbell/99
16 Joe Montana/75 15.00 40.00
17 LaDainian Tomlinson/99 3.00 8.00
18 Marvin Harrison/99 3.00 8.00
19 Jonathan Stewart/99 2.50 6.00
20 Charles Haley/20

2016 Panini Clear Vision Mega Jerseys

COMMON CARD 2.50 6.00
SEMISTARS 3.00 8.00
UNLISTED STARS 4.00 10.00
STATED PRINT RUN 99 SER.#'d SETS
1 Ameer Abdullah 2.50 6.00
2 Giovani Bernard 2.50 6.00
3 Blake Bortles 2.50 6.00
4 Derek Carr 4.00 10.00
5 Sammie Coates 2.50 6.00
6 Amari Cooper 4.00 10.00
7 Andy Dalton 3.00 8.00
8 Stefon Diggs 3.00 8.00
9 Tyler Eifert 3.00 8.00
10 Melvin Gordon 3.00 8.00
11 A.J. Green 4.00 10.00
12 Todd Gurley 4.00 10.00
13 Tamba Hali 2.50 6.00
14 Jeremy Hill 2.50 6.00
15 David Johnson 4.00 10.00
16 Matt Jones 3.00 8.00
17 Jeremy Langford 3.00 8.00
18 Tyler Lockett 3.00 8.00
19 Khalil Mack 4.00 10.00
20 Marcus Mariota 4.00 10.00
21 LeSean McCoy 4.00 10.00
22 Lamar Miller 2.50 6.00
23 Von Miller 3.00 8.00
24 Allen Robinson 3.00 8.00
25 Ryan Tannehill 3.00 8.00
26 DeMarcus Ware 3.00 8.00
27 Sammy Watkins 4.00 10.00
28 Karlos Williams 2.50 6.00
29 Jameis Winston 4.00 10.00
30 T.J. Yeldon 2.50 6.00

2016 Panini Clear Vision Rookie Clear Cloth Jerseys

*PRIME/49: .5X TO 1.2X BASIC JSY/99
1 Jared Goff 15.00 40.00
2 Carson Wentz 15.00 40.00
3 Paxton Lynch 2.50 6.00
4 Connor Cook 3.00 8.00
5 Christian Hackenberg 2.50 6.00
6 Cardale Jones 2.50 6.00
7 Dak Prescott 12.00 30.00
8 Cody Kessler 2.50 6.00
9 Derrick Henry 10.00 25.00
10 Ezekiel Elliott 12.00 30.00
11 C.J. Prosise 2.50 6.00
12 Paul Perkins 2.50 6.00
13 Jordan Howard 6.00 15.00
14 Alex Collins 3.00 8.00
15 Devontae Booker 3.00 8.00
16 Kenneth Dixon 2.50 6.00
17 Kenyan Drake 4.00 10.00
18 Kevin Hogan 3.00 8.00
19 Jonathan Williams 3.00 8.00
20 Moritz Bohringer 2.50 6.00
21 Laquon Treadwell 3.00 8.00
22 Corey Coleman 4.00 10.00
23 Josh Doctson 3.00 8.00
24 Will Fuller 4.00 10.00
25 Michael Thomas 5.00 12.00
26 Braxton Miller 2.50 6.00
27 Leonte Carroo 2.50 6.00
28 Sterling Shepard 3.00 8.00
29 DeAndre Washington 2.50 6.00
30 Pharoh Cooper 2.50 6.00
31 Tyler Ervin 2.50 6.00
32 Trevor Davis 2.50 6.00
33 Wendell Smallwood 2.50 6.00
34 Tyler Boyd 3.00 8.00
35 Demarcus Robinson 2.50 6.00
36 Hunter Henry 3.00 8.00
37 Ricardo Louis 2.50 6.00
38 Keenan Reynolds 3.00 8.00
39 Joey Bosa 5.00 12.00
40 Chris Moore 3.00 8.00

2016 Panini Clear Vision Visionary Signatures

1 Bo Jackson/15
2 Aaron Rodgers/15
3 Roger Staubach/15 50.00 100.00
5 Joe Namath/20 60.00 120.00
6 Ben Roethlisberger/20 60.00 120.00
8 Steve Largent/25 25.00 60.00
9 Tony Romo/15

2012 Panini Contenders

COMP.SET w/o RC's (100) 8.00 20.00
*UNLISTED ROOKIE SP: .5X TO 1.2X AU RC
EXCH EXPIRATION: 8/6/2014
SP RC's MISSING VITAL STATS ON BACK
1 Larry Fitzgerald .25 .60
2 Early Doucet .20 .50
3 Beanie Wells .20 .50
4 Matt Ryan .25 .60
5 Michael Turner .20 .50
6 Roddy White .20 .50
7 Joe Flacco .25 .60
8 Ray Lewis .30 .75
9 Ray Rice .20 .50
10 Torrey Smith .20 .50
11 Ryan Fitzpatrick .20 .50
12 Fred Jackson .25 .60
13 Steve Johnson .25 .60
14 Cam Newton .30 .75
15 DeAngelo Williams .20 .50
16 Steve Smith .25 .60
17 Jay Cutler .20 .50
18 Matt Forte .20 .50
19 Brandon Marshall .25 .60
20 Andy Dalton .25 .60
21 A.J. Green .30 .75
22 BenJarvus Green-Ellis .25 .60
23 Greg Little .20 .50
24 Josh Cribbs .20 .50
25 Tony Romo .25 .60
26 Miles Austin .20 .50
27 Dez Bryant .30 .75
28 DeMarco Murray .25 .60
29 Peyton Manning .75 2.00
30 Demaryius Thomas .30 .75
31 Willis McGahee .20 .50
32 Matthew Stafford .25 .60
33 Calvin Johnson .30 .75
34 Ndamukong Suh .25 .60
35 Aaron Rodgers .50 1.25
36 Greg Jennings .20 .50
37 Jordy Nelson .25 .60
38 Matt Schaub .20 .50
39 Arian Foster .25 .60
40 Andre Johnson .25 .60
41 Reggie Wayne .25 .60
42 Donnie Avery .20 .50
43 Donald Brown .20 .50
44 Blaine Gabbert .20 .50
45 Maurice Jones-Drew .20 .50
46 Laurent Robinson .20 .50

47 Matt Cassel .20 .50
48 Jamaal Charles .25 .60
49 Dwayne Bowe .25 .60
50 Reggie Bush .20 .50
51 Cameron Wake .25 .60
52 Anthony Fasano .20 .50
53 Christian Ponder .20 .50
54 Adrian Peterson .30 .75
55 Percy Harvin .20 .50
56 Tom Brady .75 2.00
57 Aaron Hernandez .25 .60
58 Rob Gronkowski .30 .75
59 Wes Welker .25 .60
60 Drew Brees .30 .75
61 Marques Colston .20 .50
62 Jimmy Graham .30 .75
63 Eli Manning .25 .60
64 Ahmad Bradshaw .20 .50
65 Victor Cruz .25 .60
66 Hakeem Nicks .20 .50
67 Mark Sanchez .20 .50
68 Tim Tebow .30 .75
69 Santonio Holmes .20 .50
70 Carson Palmer .25 .60
71 Darren McFadden .20 .50
72 Darrius Heyward-Bey .20 .50
73 Michael Vick .25 .60
74 LeSean McCoy .30 .75
75 DeSean Jackson .25 .60
76 Ben Roethlisberger .30 .75
77 Antonio Brown .30 .75
78 Mike Wallace .20 .50
79 Philip Rivers .30 .75
80 Ryan Mathews .25 .60
81 Antonio Gates .25 .60
82 Alex Smith .25 .60
83 Frank Gore .25 .60
84 Randy Moss .25 .60
85 Vernon Davis .20 .50
86A Richard Sherman RC 6.00 15.00
86B Richard Sherman AU 125.00 200.00
87 Marshawn Lynch .25 .60
88 Sidney Rice .20 .50
89 Sam Bradford .20 .50
90 Steven Jackson .20 .50
91 Danny Amendola .25 .60
92 Josh Freeman .25 .60
93 Dallas Clark .20 .50
94 Vincent Jackson .20 .50
95 Kenny Britt .20 .50
96 Jake Locker .30 .75
97 Chris Johnson .20 .50
98 Pierre Garcon .25 .60
99 London Fletcher .25 .60
100 Santana Moss .25 .60
101A A.Morris AU/456* RC 12.00 30.00
101B Alfred Morris AU SP/50* 20.00 15.00
102A Adrien Robinson AU RC 2.50 6.00
102B A.Robinson AU SP/200* 5.00 12.00
103A A.Branch AU/500* RC EX 3.00 8.00
103B A.Branch AU SP/75* EX 15.00 40.00
104A B.Coleman AU/242* RC 15.00 40.00
104B B.Coleman AU SP/50* 20.00 50.00
105A B.J. Cunningham AU RC 2.50 6.00
105B B.Cunningham AU SP/200* 5.00 12.00
106A Bobby Rainey AU RC 2.50 6.00
106B Bobby Rainey AU SP 3.00 8.00
107A B.Wagner AU/290* RC 6.00 15.00
107B B.Wagner AU SP/49* 25.00 50.00
108A Brandon Hardin AU RC 3.00 8.00
108B Brandon Hardin AU SP 4.00 10.00
109A Brandon Taylor AU RC 2.50 6.00
109B Brandon Taylor AU SP 3.00 8.00
110A Bruce Irvin AU RC 5.00 12.00
110B Bruce Irvin AU SP/200* 6.00 15.00
111A B.Brown AU/205* RC 10.00 25.00
111B B.Brown AU SP/75* 15.00 40.00
112A Case Keenum AU RC 40.00 80.00
112B Case Keenum AU SP 40.00 100.00
113A Casey Hayward AU RC 2.50 6.00
113B Casey Hayward AU SP 10.00 25.00
114A Chandler Harnish AU RC 2.50 6.00
114B Chandler Harnish AU SP 3.00 8.00
115A Chandler Jones AU RC 2.50 6.00
115B Chandler Jones AU SP 3.00 8.00
116A Chris Polk AU RC 2.50 6.00
116B Chris Polk AU SP 3.00 8.00
117A C.Rainey AU/288* RC 30.00 60.00
117B C.Rainey AU SP/50* 60.00 100.00
118A J.Gordon AU/500* RC 8.00 20.00
118B J.Gordon AU SP/100* 12.00 30.00
119A Coty Sensabaugh AU RC 2.50 6.00
119B Coty Sensabaugh AU SP 3.00 8.00
120A C.Upshaw AU/57* RC 8.00 20.00
120B C.Upshaw AU SP/200* 6.00 15.00
121A Cyrus Gray AU RC 2.50 6.00
121B Cyrus Gray AU SP/200* 5.00 12.00
122A Dan Herron AU RC 2.50 6.00
122B Dan Herron AU SP 3.00 8.00
123A Danny Coale AU RC 4.00 10.00
123B Danny Coale AU SP 5.00 12.00
124A D.DeCastro AU/259* RC 15.00 30.00
124B D.DeCastro AU SP/10*
125A Nigel Bradham AU RC 3.00 8.00
125B Nigel Bradham AU SP/200* 6.00 15.00
126A D.Peterson AU/550* RC 3.00 8.00
126B D.Peterson AU SP Rams 4.00 10.00
127A Demario Davis AU RC 2.50 6.00
127B Demario Davis AU SP 3.00 8.00
128A D.Wolfe AU/294* RC EX 12.00 30.00
128B D.Wolfe AU SP/50* EX 25.00 50.00
129A Devon Still AU/500* RC 4.00 10.00
129B Devon Still AU SP/75* 8.00 20.00
130A Devon Wylie AU RC 2.50 6.00
130B Devon Wylie AU SP/200* 5.00 12.00
131A D.Hightower AU/47* RC 50.00 120.00
131B D.Hightower AU SP/10*
132A D.Poe AU/134* RC 15.00 40.00
132B D.Poe AU SP/25* 40.00 100.00
133A Kirkpatrick AU/259* RC EX 12.00 30.00
133B Kirkpatrick AU SP/50* EX 25.00 50.00
134A Bill Bentley AU RC 3.00 8.00
134B Bill Bentley AU SP 4.00 10.00
135A J.Demps AU/99* RC wht 8.00 20.00
135B Jeff Demps AU/25* blue 12.00 30.00
136A Josh Cooper AU RC 3.00 8.00
136B Josh Cooper AU SP/200* 6.00 15.00
137A F.Cox AU/112* RC grn 8.00 20.00
137B Fletcher Cox AU/25* wht 30.00 60.00
138A G.Iloka AU/206* RC 10.00 25.00
138B G.Iloka AU SP/25* 30.00 60.00
139A Gerell Robinson AU RC 3.00 8.00
139B Gerell Robinson AU SP 4.00 10.00
140A R.Streater AU RC wht 4.00 10.00
140B Streater AU SP/200* blk 8.00 20.00
141A H.Smith AU/290* RC 12.50 25.00
141B H.Smith AU SP/25* 50.00 100.00
142A Jamell Fleming AU RC 2.50 6.00
142B Jamell Fleming AU SP 3.00 8.00
143A J.Hanna AU/227* RC 4.00 10.00
143B J.Hanna AU SP/50* 15.00 40.00
144A J.Jenkins AU/292* RC 12.00 30.00
144B J.Jenkins AU SP/50* 15.00 40.00
145A J.Crick AU RC red 2.50 6.00
145B J.Crick AU SP/75* wht 6.00 15.00
146A Jeff Fuller AU RC 2.50 6.00
146B Jeff Fuller AU SP 3.00 8.00
147A J.Worthy AU/269* RC EX 10.00 25.00
147B J.Worthy AU SP/50* EX 30.00 60.00
148A Jonathan Martin AU RC 3.00 8.00
148B Jonathan Martin AU SP 4.00 10.00
149A Josh Robinson AU RC 4.00 10.00
149B Josh Robinson AU SP 5.00 12.00
150A Juron Criner AU/500* RC 3.00 8.00
150B Juron Criner AU SP/200* 8.00 20.00
151A Kellen Moore AU/198* RC 6.00 15.00
151B Kellen Moore AU SP/50* 8.00 20.00
152A Kendall Reyes AU RC blu 2.50 6.00
152B Kendall Reyes AU SP wht 3.00 8.00
153A Keshawn Martin AU RC 3.00 8.00
153B Keshawn Martin AU SP 4.00 10.00
154A Kevin Zeitler AU RC 2.50 6.00
154B Kevin Zeitler AU SP 3.00 8.00
155A Kirk Cousins AU RC 75.00 150.00
155B K.Cousins AU SP/175* 100.00 200.00
156A Ladarius Green AU RC 8.00 20.00
156B Ladarius Green AU SP 8.00 20.00
157A L.Brazill AU/262* RC 6.00 15.00
157B L.Brazill AU SP/25* 15.00 40.00
158A Lavonte David AU RC 4.00 10.00
158B Lavonte David AU SP 5.00 12.00
159A L.Kuechly AU/235* RC blu 60.00 120.00
159B L.Kuechly AU/25* wht 100.00 200.00
160A Marc Tyler AU RC 2.50 6.00
160B Marc Tyler AU SP 3.00 8.00
161A M.Barron AU/295* RC 4.00 10.00
161B M.Barron AU SP/50* 6.00 15.00
162A J.Lane AU/276* RC 10.00 25.00
162B J.Lane AU SP/50* 25.00 50.00
163A M.Jones AU/313* RC 4.00 10.00
163B Marvin Jones AU SP/25* 10.00 25.00
164A Marvin McNutt AU RC 2.50 6.00
164B Marvin McNutt AU SP 3.00 8.00
165A Matt Kalil AU RC prpl 2.50 6.00
165B M.Kalil AU SP/100* wht 5.00 12.00
166A Melvin Ingram AU RC 2.50 6.00
166B Melvin Ingram AU SP 3.00 8.00
167A Brockers AU/38* RC EX 125.00 200.00
167B Brockers AU SP/25* EX 125.00 200.00
168A M.Smith AU/99* RC EX 30.00 60.00
168B M.Smith AU SP/25* EX 50.00 100.00
169A Mike Martin AU RC 3.00 8.00
169B Mike Martin AU SP 4.00 10.00
170A M.Claiborne AU/500* RC 3.00 8.00
170B M.Claiborne AU SP/75* 6.00 15.00
171A M.Kendricks AU/500* RC 4.00 10.00
171B M.Kendricks AU SP/99* 25.00 50.00
172A Najee Goode AU RC 2.50 6.00
172B Najee Goode AU SP 3.00 8.00
173A Nick Perry AU RC 3.00 8.00
173B Nick Perry AU SP/200* 6.00 15.00
174A Olivier Vernon AU RC 4.00 10.00
174B Olivier Vernon AU SP 5.00 12.00
175A Omar Bolden AU RC 3.00 8.00
175B Omar Bolden AU SP 4.00 10.00
176A Orson Charles AU RC 2.50 6.00
176B O.Charles AU SP/200* 5.00 12.00
177A Q.Coples AU/550* RC 3.00 8.00
177B Q.Coples AU SP/115* 5.00 12.00
178A Rhett Ellison AU RC 3.00 8.00
178B Rhett Ellison AU SP 4.00 10.00
179A Riley Reiff AU/231* RC 4.00 10.00
179B Riley Reiff AU SP/25* 10.00 25.00
180A Rishard Matthews AU RC 2.50 6.00
180B R.Matthews AU SP/200* 5.00 12.00
181A R.Lewis AU/266* RC EX 10.00 25.00
181B R.Lewis AU SP/50* EX 20.00 40.00
182A Ryan Lindley AU RC 2.50 6.00
182B Ryan Lindley AU SP 3.00 8.00
183A Sean Spence AU RC 3.00 8.00
183B Sean Spence AU SP 4.00 10.00
184A Shea McClellin AU RC 3.00 8.00
184B S.McClellin AU/100* SP 6.00 15.00
185A Stephon Gilmore AU RC 5.00 12.00
185B S.Gilmore AU SP/50* 25.00 50.00
186A T.Hilton AU/260* RC 40.00 80.00
186B T.Hilton AU SP/50* EX 60.00 100.00
187A G.Zuerlein AU/454* RC 5.00 12.00
187B G.Zuerlein AU SP/175* 8.00 20.00
188A Tavon Wilson AU RC 3.00 8.00
188B Tavon Wilson AU SP 4.00 10.00
189A T.Ganaway AU RC ball 3.00 8.00
189B T.Ganaway AU SP/200* 6.00 15.00
190A Tim Benford AU RC 2.50 6.00
190B Tim Benford AU SP 3.00 8.00
191A T.Streeter AU/238* RC EX 10.00 25.00
191B T.Streeter AU SP/50* EX 25.00 50.00
192A Travis Benjamin AU RC 2.50 6.00
192B Travis Benjamin AU SP/200* 5.00 12.00
193A Trumaine Johnson AU RC 2.50 6.00
193B Trumaine Johnson AU SP 3.00 8.00
194A Tyrone Crawford AU RC 2.50 6.00
194B Tyrone Crawford AU SP 3.00 8.00
195A V.Burfict AU RC wht 3.00 8.00
195B V.Burfict AU SP brwn 4.00 10.00
196A W.Mercilus AU/150* RC 8.00 20.00
196B W.Mercilus AU SP/25* 30.00 60.00
197A Vick Ballard AU RC 6.00 15.00
197B Vick Ballard AU SP 8.00 20.00
198A Vinny Curry AU RC 3.00 8.00
198B Vinny Curry AU SP 4.00 10.00
199A Zach Brown AU RC 2.50 6.00
199B Zach Brown AU SP 3.00 8.00
200A B.Bolden AU/202* RC EX 4.00 10.00
200B B.Bolden AU SP/50 EX 15.00 40.00
201A A.Luck AU/550* RC 400.00 800.00
201B Luck AU SP/75* bth hnd 600.00 1000.00
202A R.Griffin III AU/238* RC 20.00 50.00
202B RG III AU SP/50* pass 40.00 80.00
203A T.Rchrdson AU/550* RC 8.00 20.00
203B T.Rchrdsn AU SP/125* nke 12.00 30.00
204A R.Tannehill AU/550* RC 10.00 25.00
204B Tannehill AU SP/200* rgh 15.00 40.00
205A J.Blackmon AU/550* RC 3.00 8.00
205B J.Blackmon AU SP/125* 15.00 40.00
206A B.Weeden AU/550* RC 3.00 8.00
206B B.Weeden AU SP/125* 5.00 12.00
207A Brock Osweiler AU RC 12.00 30.00
207B Osweiler AU SP/125* orn 15.00 40.00
208A M.Floyd AU RC w/o ball 2.50 6.00
208B M.Floyd AU SP/125* 5.00 12.00
209A Kendall Wright AU RC 2.50 6.00
209B K.Wright AU SP/125* 5.00 12.00
210A A.J. Jenkins AU RC 2.50 6.00
210B A.Jenkins AU SP/200* 5.00 12.00
211A Doug Martin AU/550* RC 6.00 15.00
211B D.Martin AU SP/125* bth 12.00 30.00
212A Lamar Miller AU RC 4.00 10.00
212B Lamar Miller AU SP/125* 8.00 20.00
213A Isaiah Pead AU/500* RC 3.00 8.00
213B Isaiah Pead AU SP/200* 5.00 12.00
214A David Wilson AU RC 2.50 6.00
214B D.Wilson AU SP/200* 5.00 12.00
215A S.Hill AU RC EXCH 5.00 12.00
215B S.Hill AU SP/200* EX 12.50 25.00
216A M.Sanu AU/550* RC 5.00 12.00
216B M.Sanu AU SP/200* 8.00 20.00
217A B.Pierce AU RC EXCH 8.00 20.00
217B B.Pierce AU SP/200* EX 12.00 30.00
218A Nick Foles AU/550* RC 60.00 125.00
218B Nick Foles AU SP/200* 100.00 200.00
219A LaMichael James AU RC 5.00 12.00
219B L.James AU SP/100* 10.00 25.00
220A R.Randle AU RC 6.00 15.00
220B R.Randle AU SP/200* 10.00 25.00
221A Coby Fleener AU RC wht 2.50 6.00
221B C.Fleener AU SP/200* blu 5.00 12.00
222A Ryan Broyles AU RC 2.50 6.00
222B R.Broyles AU SP/200* 12.00 30.00
223A Dwayne Allen AU RC 2.50 6.00
223B Dwayne Allen AU SP/200* 5.00 12.00
224A Ronnie Hillman AU RC 10.00 20.00
224B R.Hillman AU SP/200* 15.00 30.00
225A R.Wilson AU/550* RC EX 200.00 400.00
225B R.Wilson AU/25* EXCH 400.00 800.00
226A Michael Egnew AU RC 2.50 6.00
226B M.Egnew AU SP/200* 5.00 12.00
227A Chris Givens AU RC 2.50 6.00
227B C.Givens AU SP/200* 5.00 12.00
228A Joe Adams AU RC wht 2.50 6.00
228B J.Adams AU SP/200* blu 5.00 12.00
229A Robert Turbin AU RC 2.50 6.00
229B R.Turbin AU SP/200* 5.00 12.00
230A Nick Toon AU RC EXCH 6.00 15.00
230B N.Toon AU SP/200* EX 10.00 25.00
231A T.J. Graham AU RC 2.50 6.00
231B T.J. Graham AU SP/200* 5.00 12.00
232A Brian Quick AU RC 2.50 6.00
232B Brian Quick AU SP/200* 5.00 12.00
233A D.Posey AU RC EXCH 2.50 6.00
233B D.Posey AU SP/200* 5.00 12.00
234A Jarius Wright AU RC 2.50 6.00
234B Jarius Wright AU SP/200* 5.00 12.00
235A A.Jeffery AU RC 15.00 40.00
235B A.Jeffery AU SP/145* 25.00 50.00
236 D.Thompson AU/550* RC 4.00 10.00
237 J.Tucker AU/275* RC 15.00 40.00
238 Damaris Johnson AU RC 2.50 6.00
239 E.Rodriguez AU/275* RC 20.00 50.00
240 Kris Adams AU/275* RC 12.00 30.00
241 D.Richrdsn AU/275* RC 12.00 30.00
242 L.Dunbar AU/275* RC EX 15.00 40.00
243 Blair Walsh AU/275* RC 12.00 30.00
244 Miles Burris AU RC 4.00 10.00
245 Josh Norman AU/550* RC 20.00 40.00

2012 Panini Contenders Cracked Ice

*1-100 VETS/20: 12X TO 30X BASIC CARDS
*ROOK/20: 1X TO 2.5X PLAYOFF AU/94-99
*ROOK/20: .6X TO 1.5X PLAYOFF AU/49
86 Richard Sherman 300.00 500.00
101 Alfred Morris AU 60.00 120.00
118 Josh Gordon AU 60.00 120.00
155 Kirk Cousins AU 200.00 300.00
201 Andrew Luck AU 1500.00 2500.00
202 Robert Griffin III AU 75.00 150.00
203 Trent Richardson AU 75.00 150.00
204 Ryan Tannehill AU 40.00 100.00
205 Justin Blackmon AU 12.00 30.00
207 Brock Osweiler AU 50.00 100.00
208 Michael Floyd AU 20.00 50.00
209 Kendall Wright AU 25.00 60.00
211 Doug Martin AU 50.00 100.00
217 Bernard Pierce AU 75.00 150.00
218 Nick Foles AU 200.00 400.00
225 Russell Wilson AU 1200.00 2000.00

2012 Panini Contenders Playoff Ticket

*1-100 VETS/99: 3X TO 8X BASIC CARDS
EXCH EXPIRATION: 8/6/2014
86 Richard Sherman 150.00 300.00
101 Alfred Morris AU 30.00 80.00
102 Adrien Robinson AU 4.00 10.00
103 Andre Branch AU 4.00 10.00
104 B.J. Coleman AU 4.00 10.00
105 B.J. Cunningham AU 4.00 10.00
106 Bobby Rainey AU 8.00 20.00
107 Bobby Wagner AU/49 30.00 60.00
108 Brandon Hardin AU 5.00 12.00
109 Brandon Taylor AU 4.00 10.00
110 Bruce Irvin AU 8.00 20.00
111 Bryce Brown AU 4.00 10.00
112 Case Keenum AU 8.00 20.00
113 Casey Hayward AU 4.00 10.00
114 Chandler Harnish AU 4.00 10.00
115 Chandler Jones AU 4.00 10.00
116 Chris Polk AU 4.00 10.00
117 Chris Rainey AU 4.00 10.00
118 Josh Gordon AU 20.00 50.00
119 Coty Sensabaugh AU 5.00 12.00
120 Courtney Upshaw AU 5.00 12.00
121 Cyrus Gray AU 8.00 20.00
122 Dan Herron AU 4.00 10.00
123 Danny Coale AU 4.00 10.00
124 David DeCastro AU 10.00 25.00
125 Nigel Bradham AU 5.00 12.00
126 Deangelo Peterson AU 4.00 10.00
127 Demario Davis AU 4.00 10.00
128 Derek Wolfe AU EXCH 5.00 12.00
129 Devon Still AU 5.00 12.00
130 Devon Wylie AU 4.00 10.00
131 Dont'a Hightower AU 12.00 30.00
132 Dontari Poe AU 4.00 10.00
133 Dre Kirkpatrick AU EXCH 4.00 10.00
134 Bill Bentley AU 5.00 12.00
135 Jeff Demps AU 5.00 12.00
136 Josh Cooper AU 5.00 12.00
137 Fletcher Cox AU 6.00 15.00
138 George Iloka AU 4.00 10.00
139 Gerell Robinson AU 4.00 10.00
140 Rod Streater AU 6.00 15.00
141 Harrison Smith AU 12.00 30.00
142 Jamell Fleming AU 4.00 10.00
143 James Hanna AU 8.00 20.00
144 Janoris Jenkins AU 5.00 12.00
145 Jared Crick AU 4.00 10.00
146 Jeff Fuller AU 4.00 10.00
147 Jerel Worthy AU EXCH 4.00 10.00
148 Jonathan Martin AU 4.00 10.00
149 Josh Robinson AU 6.00 15.00
150 Juron Criner AU 4.00 10.00
151 Kellen Moore AU 12.00 30.00
152 Kendall Reyes AU 4.00 10.00
153 Keshawn Martin AU 5.00 12.00
154 Kevin Zeitler AU 4.00 10.00
155 Kirk Cousins AU 150.00 250.00
156 Ladarius Green AU 8.00 20.00
157 LaVon Brazill AU 8.00 20.00
158 Lavonte David AU 10.00 25.00
159 Luke Kuechly AU 60.00 120.00
160 Marc Tyler AU 4.00 10.00
161 Mark Barron AU 15.00 40.00
162 Jorvorskie Lane AU 12.00 30.00
163 Marvin Jones AU 4.00 10.00
164 Marvin McNutt AU 4.00 10.00
165 Matt Kalil AU 4.00 10.00
166 Melvin Ingram AU 4.00 10.00
167 Michael Brockers AU EXCH 15.00 30.00
168 Michael Smith AU 5.00 12.00
169 Mike Martin AU 5.00 12.00
170 Morris Claiborne AU 12.00 30.00
171 Mychal Kendricks AU 6.00 15.00
172 Najee Goode AU 4.00 10.00
173 Nick Perry AU 10.00 25.00
174 Olivier Vernon AU 6.00 15.00
175 Omar Bolden AU 5.00 12.00
176 Orson Charles AU 4.00 10.00
177 Quinton Coples AU 4.00 10.00
178 Rhett Ellison AU 5.00 12.00
179 Riley Reiff AU 4.00 10.00
180 Rishard Matthews AU 4.00 10.00
181 Ronnell Lewis AU 4.00 10.00
182 Ryan Lindley AU 4.00 10.00
183 Sean Spence AU 5.00 12.00
184 Shea McClellin AU 5.00 12.00
185 Stephon Gilmore AU 5.00 12.00
186 T.Y. Hilton AU 40.00 80.00
187 Greg Zuerlein AU 8.00 20.00
188 Tavon Wilson AU 5.00 12.00
189 Terrance Ganaway AU 5.00 12.00
190 Tim Benford AU 4.00 10.00
191 Tommy Streeter AU 4.00 10.00
192 Travis Benjamin AU 4.00 10.00
193 Trumaine Johnson AU 4.00 10.00
194 Tyrone Crawford AU 4.00 10.00
195 Vontaze Burfict AU 8.00 20.00
196 Whitney Mercilus AU 4.00 10.00
197 Vick Ballard AU 12.00 30.00
198 Vinny Curry AU 5.00 12.00
199 Zach Brown AU 4.00 10.00
200 Brandon Bolden AU 15.00 40.00
201 Andrew Luck AU 500.00 1000.00
202 Robert Griffin III AU 25.00 60.00
203 Trent Richardson AU 5.00 12.00
204 Ryan Tannehill AU 15.00 40.00
205 Justin Blackmon AU 5.00 12.00
206 Brandon Weeden AU 5.00 12.00
207 Brock Osweiler AU 25.00 60.00
208 Michael Floyd AU 8.00 20.00
209 Kendall Wright AU 5.00 12.00
210 A.J. Jenkins AU 5.00 12.00
211 Doug Martin AU 8.00 20.00
212 Lamar Miller AU 30.00 60.00
213 Isaiah Pead AU 10.00 25.00
214 David Wilson AU 5.00 12.00
215 Stephen Hill AU 5.00 12.00
216 Mohamed Sanu AU 8.00 20.00
217 Bernard Pierce AU 10.00 25.00
218 Nick Foles AU 100.00 200.00
219 LaMichael James AU 5.00 12.00
220 Rueben Randle AU 10.00 25.00
221 Coby Fleener AU 5.00 12.00
222 Ryan Broyles AU 12.00 30.00
223 Dwayne Allen AU 5.00 12.00
224 Ronnie Hillman AU 20.00 40.00
225 Russell Wilson AU 400.00 650.00
226 Michael Egnew AU 5.00 12.00
227 Chris Givens AU 5.00 12.00
228 Joe Adams AU 5.00 12.00
229 Robert Turbin AU 15.00 40.00
230 Nick Toon AU EXCH 10.00 25.00
231 T.J. Graham AU 5.00 12.00
232 Brian Quick AU 5.00 12.00
233 DeVier Posey AU 5.00 12.00
234 Jarius Wright AU 5.00 12.00
235 Alshon Jeffery AU 40.00 100.00

2012 Panini Contenders Draft Class Autographs

1 F.Cox/N.Foles 60.00 125.00
2 Weeden/Richardson 8.00 20.00
3 Coby Fleener/Dwayne Allen 8.00 20.00
4 A.Jenkins/L.James 8.00 20.00
5 D.Wilson/R.Randle 8.00 20.00
6 D.Martin/M.Barron 12.00 30.00
7 L.Miller/M.Egnew 12.00 30.00
8 Turbin/Wilson EXCH 150.00 250.00
9 Quinton Coples/Stephen Hill 8.00 20.00
10 M.Claiborne/T.Crawford 8.00 20.00
11 Chris Givens/Janoris Jenkins 10.00 25.00
12 Dre Kirkpatrick/Mohamed Sanu 12.00 30.00
13 Stephon Gilmore/T.J. Graham 10.00 25.00
14 DeVier Posey/Whitney Mercilus 8.00 20.00
15 Osweiler/R.Hillman 8.00 20.00
16 M.Floyd/R.Lindley 8.00 20.00
17 C.Jones/Hightower 12.00 30.00
18 B.J. Coleman/Nick Perry 10.00 25.00
19 Kendall Reyes/Melvin Ingram 12.00 30.00
20 Ronnell Lewis/Ryan Broyles 8.00 20.00

2012 Panini Contenders Legendary Champions

LACK/50: 1X TO 2.5X BASIC INSERTS
*GOLD/100: .8X TO 2X BASIC INSERTS
1 Eli Manning .75 2.00
2 Aaron Rodgers 1.50 4.00
3 Drew Brees 1.00 2.50
4 Santonio Holmes .60 1.50
5 Peyton Manning 2.00 5.00
6 Hines Ward 1.00 2.50
7 Deion Branch .75 2.00
8 Tom Brady 2.50 6.00
9 Ray Lewis 1.00 2.50
10 Kurt Warner 1.00 2.50
11 John Elway 2.00 5.00
12 Terrell Davis 1.00 2.50
13 Steve Young 1.50 4.00
14 Emmitt Smith 2.00 5.00
15 Troy Aikman 1.50 4.00
16 Joe Montana 3.00 8.00
17 Jerry Rice 2.00 5.00
18 Phil Simms 1.00 2.50
19 Marcus Allen 1.25 3.00
20 Jim Plunkett 1.00 2.50
21 Terry Bradshaw 1.50 4.00
22 Greg Jennings .60 1.50
23 James Harrison .75 2.00
24 Dwight Freeney .60 1.50
25 Rod Smith .75 2.00

2012 Panini Contenders MVP Contenders

MPLETE SET (15) 6.00 15.00
*BLACK/50: 1.2X TO 3X BASIC INSERTS
*GOLD/100: 1X TO 2.5X BASIC INSERTS
1 Ray Rice .60 1.50
2 A.J. Green 1.00 2.50
3 Arian Foster .75 2.00
4 Tom Brady 2.50 6.00
5 Peyton Manning 2.00 5.00
6 Darren McFadden .60 1.50
7 Calvin Johnson 1.00 2.50
8 Aaron Rodgers 1.50 4.00
9 Adrian Peterson 1.00 2.50
10 Matt Ryan .75 2.00
11 Cam Newton 1.00 2.50
12 Drew Brees 1.00 2.50
13 Tony Romo .75 2.00
14 Eli Manning .75 2.00
15 LeSean McCoy 1.00 2.50

2012 Panini Contenders NFL Ink

2 Antonio Brown/25 15.00 40.00
3 Brandon Pettigrew/25 10.00 25.00
4 C.J. Spiller/25 10.00 25.00
6 Demaryius Thomas/25 15.00 40.00
7 Darren McFadden/25 10.00 25.00
9 Jonathan Stewart/25 10.00 25.00
10 DeSean Jackson/20 12.00 30.00
11 Jonathan Baldwin/49 8.00 20.00
12 Greg Little/25 10.00 25.00
13 Victor Cruz/15 25.00 50.00
14 Randall Cobb/15 12.00 30.00
15 Torrey Smith/25 10.00 25.00
16 Josh Freeman/25 12.00 30.00
19 Jordy Nelson/15 25.00 50.00

2012 Panini Contenders NFL Ink Combos

3 J.Gresham/L.Kendricks/25 8.00 20.00
5 B.Jacobs/R.Williams/25 8.00 20.00
6 J.Cribbs/R.Cobb/25 10.00 25.00
13 N.Asomugha/V.Miller/25 10.00 25.00

2012 Panini Contenders Rookie Ink

1 Andrew Luck/25* 200.00 350.00
2 Robert Griffin III/25* 25.00 60.00
3 Trent Richardson/75* 15.00 40.00
4 Ryan Tannehill/75* 25.00 50.00
5 Justin Blackmon/75* 4.00 10.00
6 Brandon Weeden/75* 4.00 10.00
7 Brock Osweiler/75* 4.00 10.00
8 Michael Floyd/75* 4.00 10.00
9 Kendall Wright/75* 4.00 10.00
10 A.J. Jenkins/75* 4.00 10.00
11 Doug Martin/75* 6.00 15.00
12 Lamar Miller/75* 15.00 30.00
13 Isaiah Pead/75* 4.00 10.00
14 David Wilson/75* 4.00 10.00
15 Stephen Hill/75* 4.00 10.00
16 Mohamed Sanu/75* 6.00 15.00
17 Bernard Pierce/75* 12.00 30.00
18 LaMichael James/75* 4.00 10.00
19 Rueben Randle/75* 4.00 10.00
20 Coby Fleener/75* 4.00 10.00
21 Ryan Broyles/75* 4.00 10.00
22 Ronnie Hillman/75* 4.00 10.00
23 Russell Wilson/75* 125.00 200.00
24 Chris Givens/75* 4.00 10.00
25 Joe Adams/75* 4.00 10.00
26 Robert Turbin/75* 4.00 10.00
27 Brian Quick/75* 4.00 10.00
28 DeVier Posey/75* 6.00 15.00
29 Jarius Wright/75* 4.00 10.00
30 Alshon Jeffery/75* 8.00 20.00

2012 Panini Contenders Rookie Stallions

LACK/50: 2X TO 5X BASIC INSERTS
*GOLD/100: 1.2X TO 3X BASIC INSERTS
1 Andrew Luck 3.00 8.00
2 Robert Griffin III .40 1.00
3 Bernard Pierce .30 .75
4 Doug Martin .50 1.25
5 Justin Blackmon .30 .75
6 Kendall Wright .30 .75
7 Mohamed Sanu .50 1.25
8 Robert Turbin .30 .75
9 Russell Wilson 2.50 6.00
10 Ryan Tannehill .50 1.25
11 Stephen Hill .30 .75
12 Trent Richardson .30 .75
13 Alfred Morris .30 .75
14 Bruce Irvin .40 1.00
15 Chandler Jones .30 .75
16 Lavonte David .50 1.25
17 Mark Barron .30 .75
18 Morris Claiborne .30 .75
19 Nick Perry .40 1.00
20 Vontaze Burfict .40 1.00
21 Shea McClellin .40 1.00
22 Mychal Kendricks .50 1.25
23 Luke Kuechly .75 2.00
24 Ronnie Hillman .30 .75
25 Alshon Jeffery .60 1.50

2012 Panini Contenders Rookie Stallions Autographs

4 Ryan Tannehill/25 12.00 30.00
5 Justin Blackmon/25 5.00 12.00
6 Michael Floyd/25 5.00 12.00
7 Kendall Wright/25 5.00 12.00
8 Robert Turbin/25 5.00 12.00
9 Doug Martin/25 8.00 20.00
10 David Wilson/25 5.00 12.00
11 Luke Kuechly/25 20.00 40.00
12 Bruce Irvin/25 6.00 15.00
13 Stephen Hill/25 5.00 12.00
14 Alshon Jeffery/25 10.00 25.00
15 Morris Claiborne/25
16 Mark Barron/25 20.00 40.00
17 Chris Givens/25 5.00 12.00
18 Lamar Miller/25 8.00 20.00
19 Janoris Jenkins/25
20 Russell Wilson/25 100.00 175.00
21 Mohamed Sanu/25 8.00 20.00
22 Chandler Jones/25 5.00 12.00
23 Rueben Randle/25 5.00 12.00
24 Fletcher Cox/25 8.00 20.00
25 =D1118&"/"&J1118 5.00 12.00

2012 Panini Contenders ROY Contenders

LACK/50: 2X TO 5X BASIC INSERTS
*GOLD/100: 1.2X TO 3X BASIC INSERTS
1 Andrew Luck 3.00 8.00
2 Brandon Weeden .30 .75
3 Doug Martin .50 1.25
4 Justin Blackmon .30 .75
5 Kendall Wright .30 .75
6 Michael Floyd .30 .75
7 Robert Griffin III .40 1.00
8 Russell Wilson 3.00 8.00
9 Ryan Tannehill .50 1.25
10 Stephen Hill .30 .75
11 Trent Richardson .30 .75
12 Alfred Morris .30 .75
13 Chandler Jones .30 .75
14 Luke Kuechly .75 2.00
15 Mark Barron .30 .75
16 Morris Claiborne .30 .75
17 Robert Turbin .30 .75
18 Alshon Jeffery .60 1.50
19 Bernard Pierce .30 .75
20 David Wilson .30 .75
21 Rueben Randle .30 .75
22 Bruce Irvin .40 1.00
23 Janoris Jenkins .40 1.00
24 Melvin Ingram .30 .75
25 Vontaze Burfict .40 1.00

2012 Panini Contenders Signs of Greatness

1 Aaron Hernandez/15 15.00 40.00
2 Antonio Brown/15 15.00 40.00
3 Andy Dalton/15 12.00 30.00
4 Brandon Pettigrew/15 10.00 25.00
6 Darren McFadden/15 15.00 40.00
7 Jimmy Graham/15 15.00 40.00
9 DeSean Jackson/15
10 Kenny Britt/15 10.00 25.00
11 Greg Olsen/15 12.00 30.00
12 Greg Little/15 10.00 25.00
13 Hakeem Nicks/15 10.00 25.00
14 Dwayne Bowe/15 12.00 30.00
15 Mario Williams/15
17 Matt Forte/15 10.00 25.00
18 Arian Foster/15 EXCH
20 Torrey Smith/15 10.00 25.00
21 Reggie Wayne/15 15.00 40.00
24 Ryan Mathews/15 12.00 30.00
26 Vernon Davis/15 10.00 25.00
28 Von Miller/15 15.00 40.00
29 Sean Lee/15 15.00 40.00
30 Larry Fitzgerald/15 EXCH 15.00 40.00

2013 Panini Contenders

COMP.SET w/o RC's (100) 6.00 15.00
CARD #B SP VARIATION MISSING STARS ON BACK LOGO
EXCH EXPIRATION: 6/26/2015
GROUP A ANNC'D PRINT RUN 50 OR LESS
GROUP B ANNC'D PRINT RUN 200 OR LESS
1 Colin Kaepernick .25 .60
2 Anquan Boldin .20 .50
3 Frank Gore .25 .60
4 NaVorro Bowman .25 .60
5 Jay Cutler .20 .50
6 Brandon Marshall .25 .60
7 Matt Forte .20 .50
8 Andy Dalton .25 .60
9 A.J. Green .30 .75
10 BenJarvus Green-Ellis .25 .60
11 Steve Johnson .25 .60
12 C.J. Spiller .20 .50
13 Mario Williams .20 .50
14 Peyton Manning .60 1.50
15 Demaryius Thomas .25 .60
16 Wes Welker .25 .60
17 Eric Decker .20 .50
18 Brandon Weeden .20 .50
19 Greg Little .20 .50
20 Trent Richardson .20 .50
21 Darrelle Revis .20 .50
22 Vincent Jackson .20 .50
23 Doug Martin .25 .60
24 Carson Palmer .25 .60
25 Larry Fitzgerald .25 .60
26 Rashard Mendenhall .20 .50
27 Philip Rivers .30 .75
28 Eddie Royal .20 .50
29 Ryan Mathews .25 .60
30 Alex Smith .25 .60
31 Dwayne Bowe .25 .60
32 Jamaal Charles .25 .60
33 Andrew Luck .50 1.25
34 Reggie Wayne .25 .60
35 T.Y. Hilton .25 .60
36 Tony Romo .25 .60
37 Dez Bryant .30 .75
38 Miles Austin .20 .50
39 DeMarco Murray .25 .60
40 Ryan Tannehill .25 .60
41 Mike Wallace .20 .50
42 Lamar Miller .20 .50
43 Michael Vick .25 .60
44 DeSean Jackson .25 .60
45 LeSean McCoy .30 .75
46 Matt Ryan .25 .60
47 Julio Jones .30 .75
48 Steven Jackson .20 .50
49 Eli Manning .25 .60
50 Victor Cruz .25 .60
51 Hakeem Nicks .20 .50
52 Chad Henne .20 .50
53 Justin Blackmon .20 .50
54 Maurice Jones-Drew .20 .50
55 Bilal Powell .20 .50
56 Stephen Hill .20 .50
57 Chris Ivory .25 .60
58 Matthew Stafford .25 .60
59 Calvin Johnson .30 .75
60 Reggie Bush .20 .50
61 Aaron Rodgers .50 1.25
62 Jordy Nelson .25 .60
63 James Jones .20 .50
64 Cam Newton .30 .75
65 Steve Smith .25 .60
66 Jonathan Stewart .20 .50
67 Tom Brady .75 2.00
68 Danny Amendola .25 .60
69 Stevan Ridley .20 .50
70 Terrelle Pryor .25 .60
71 Jacoby Ford .20 .50
72 Darren McFadden .25 .60
73 Sam Bradford .20 .50
74 Chris Givens .20 .50
75 Jared Cook .20 .50
76 Joe Flacco .25 .60
77 Torrey Smith .20 .50
78 Ray Rice .20 .50
79 Robert Griffin III .20 .50
80 Pierre Garcon .25 .60
81 Alfred Morris .20 .50
82 Drew Brees .30 .75
83 Marques Colston .20 .50
84 Mark Ingram .25 .60
85 Russell Wilson .60 1.50
86 Sidney Rice .20 .50
87 Golden Tate .20 .50
88 Marshawn Lynch .25 .60
89 Ben Roethlisberger .30 .75
90 Antonio Brown .30 .75
91 Troy Polamalu .30 .75
92 Matt Schaub .20 .50
93 Andre Johnson .20 .50
94 Arian Foster .25 .60
95 Jake Locker .25 .60
96 Kenny Britt .20 .50
97 Chris Johnson .20 .50
98 Christian Ponder .20 .50
99 Greg Jennings .20 .50
100 Adrian Peterson .30 .75
101A A.Mellette AU SP B RC 2.50 6.00
101B A.Mellette AU/200* 5.00 12.00
102A A.Sanders AU RC 2.50 6.00
102B A.Sanders AU SP B 5.00 12.00
103A Alan Bonner AU RC 2.50 6.00
103B Alan Bonner AU SP 5.00 12.00
104A A.Ogletree AU SP B RC EX 8.00 20.00
104B A.Ogletree AU/110* EXCH 20.00 40.00
105A Joseph Fauria AU RC 2.50 6.00
105B Alex Okafor AU/30* RC 20.00 40.00
106A Arthur Brown AU/30* RC 12.00 30.00
106B Timothy Wright AU RC 3.00 8.00
107A B.Mingo AU/110* RC 15.00 40.00
107B B.Mingo AU SP A 30.00 80.00
108A B.Cunningham AU RC 4.00 10.00
108B B.Cunningham AU SP 8.00 20.00
109A B.Daniels AU RC 4.00 10.00
109B B.Daniels AU SP 8.00 20.00
110A B.Werner AU/110* RC 12.00 30.00
110B B.Werner AU SP A 30.00 60.00
111A B.Sorensen AU RC 2.50 6.00
111B B.Sorensen AU SP A
112A Brice Butler AU RC 2.50 6.00
112B Brice Butler AU SP 5.00 12.00
113A B.Wilson AU RC 4.00 10.00
113B B.Wilson AU SP B 10.00 25.00
114A C.Sturgis AU RC teal 5.00 12.00
114B C.Sturgis AU SP A wht 25.00 50.00
115A Sharrif Floyd AU RC 5.00 12.00
115B C.Warmack AU/30* RC 125.00 200.00
116A C.Anderson AU RC 15.00 30.00
116B C.Anderson AU SP 20.00 40.00
117A Ryan Otten AU RC 2.50 6.00
117B C.Gragg AU/30* RC 20.00 40.00
118A Chris Harper AU RC 5.00 12.00
118B Chris Harper AU SP A 30.00 60.00
119A C.Thompson AU RC 3.00 8.00
119B C.Thompson AU SP B 12.00 30.00
120A C.Hamilton AU RC 2.50 6.00
120B C.Hamilton AU SP 5.00 12.00
121A C.Wood AU RC 3.00 8.00
121B C.Wood AU SP 6.00 15.00
122A C.Fuller AU/30* RC w/FB 40.00 80.00
122B C.Fuller AU/30* no FB 40.00 80.00
123A C.Carradine AU RC 4.00 10.00
123B C.Carradine AU SP 8.00 20.00
124A D.J. Fluker AU RC 8.00 20.00
124B D.J. Fluker AU SP A 25.00 50.00
125A D.J. Hayden AU RC 5.00 12.00
125B D.J. Hayden AU SP B 15.00 40.00
126A D.Moore AU/110* RC 10.00 25.00
126B D.Moore AU SP A 20.00 40.00
127A D.Rogers AU RC 6.00 15.00
127B D.Rogers AU SP 15.00 40.00
128A D.Slay AU/100* RC 15.00 30.00
129A D.Jones AU RC 2.50 6.00
129B D.Jones AU SP A 40.00 80.00
130A David Amerson AU RC 2.50 6.00
130B M.Davis AU SP RC 2.50 6.00
131A D.Mliner AU/110* RC EXCH 15.00 40.00
131B D.Milliner AU SP A EXCH 30.00 60.00
132A D.Johnson AU RC 2.50 6.00
132B D.Johnson AU SP B 10.00 25.00
133A D.Trufant AU/30* RC fwrd 60.00 100.00
133B D.Trufant AU/30* lft shld 60.00 100.00
134A Dion Sims AU RC 2.50 6.00
134B Dion Sims AU SP B 5.00 12.00
135A D.Swearinger AU RC 2.50 6.00
135B D.Swearinger AU SP 5.00 12.00
136A D.Hopkins AU RC 2.50 6.00
136B D.Hopkins AU SP B 10.00 25.00
137A Earl Wolff AU RC 3.00 8.00
137B Earl Wolff AU SP B 6.00 15.00
138A Eric Fisher AU RC 2.50 6.00
138B Eric Fisher AU SP A 30.00 60.00
139A Eric Reid AU RC 8.00 20.00
(red jersey)
139B Eric Reid AU SP B 15.00 40.00
(white jersey)
140A E.Ansah AU RC 8.00 20.00
140B E.Ansah AU SP A
141A Jamar Taylor AU RC 2.50 6.00
141B Jamar Taylor AU SP A 12.00 30.00
142A Jamie Collins AU RC 2.50 6.00
142B Jamie Collins AU SP A 5.00 12.00
143A J.Jones AU/110* RC 10.00 25.00
143B Jarvis Jones AU SP A 40.00 80.00
144A J.Jamison AU RC 2.50 6.00
144B J.Jamison AU SP A 20.00 40.00
145A J.Banks AU RC 2.50 6.00
145B J.Banks AU SP A 20.00 40.00
146A Jon Bostic AU RC 2.50 6.00
146B Jon Bostic AU SP 5.00 12.00
147A J.Cyprien AU RC 4.00 10.00
147B J.Cyprien AU SP A 30.00 60.00
148A J.Poyer AU/110* RC 8.00 20.00
148B Jordan Poyer AU SP A 30.00 60.00
149A J.Boyce AU/81* RC 25.00 50.00
149B Josh Boyce AU SP A 30.00 60.00
(standing pose)
150A Justin Brown AU RC 4.00 10.00
150B Justin Brown AU SP 8.00 20.00
151A K.Thompkins AU RC 4.00 10.00
151B K.Thompkins AU SP B 8.00 20.00
152A Kenjon Barner AU RC 2.50 6.00
152B K.Barner AU SP B 5.00 12.00
153A Kenny Vaccaro AU RC 4.00 10.00
153B K.Vaccaro AU SP A 8.00 20.00
154A Khiry Robinson AU RC 4.00 10.00
154B Khiry Robinson AU SP 8.00 20.00
155A Jeff Tuel AU RC 2.50 6.00
155B Jeff Tuel AU SP 5.00 12.00
156A Kevin Minter AU RC 2.50 6.00
156B Kevin Minter AU SP A 20.00 40.00
157A Kiko Alonso AU RC 3.00 8.00
157B Kiko Alonso AU SP 6.00 15.00
158A L.Murray AU RC 12.00 30.00
158B L.Murray AU SP A 30.00 60.00
159A Kawann Short AU RC 2.50 6.00
159B Kerwynn Williams AU RC 2.50 6.00
160A Levine Toilolo AU RC 3.00 8.00
160B Levine Toilolo AU SP 6.00 15.00
161A Luke Joeckel AU RC 2.50 6.00
161B C.Vernon AU SP RC 6.00 15.00
162A Luke Willson AU RC 6.00 15.00
162B Luke Willson AU SP 10.00 25.00
163A Margus Hunt AU RC 5.00 12.00
163B Margus Hunt AU SP A 20.00 40.00
164A M.Wilson AU/110* RC 20.00 50.00
164B M.Wilson AU SP A 30.00 80.00
165A Matt Elam AU/142* RC 8.00 20.00
165B Matt Elam AU SP A 20.00 40.00
166A Matt Scott AU/47* RC 40.00 80.00
166B Matt Scott AU SP A
167A Matt Simms AU RC 3.00 8.00
167B Matt Simms AU SP B 12.00 30.00
168A Michael Cox AU RC 3.00 8.00
168B Michael Cox AU SP 6.00 15.00
169A Mike James AU RC 4.00 10.00
169B Mike James AU SP A 40.00 80.00
170A Mychal Rivera AU RC 5.00 12.00
170B M.Rivera AU SP A 30.00 60.00
171A Nick Kasa AU RC 5.00 12.00
171B Nick Kasa AU SP A 30.00 80.00
172A Jasper Collins AU RC 4.00 10.00
173A Phillip Thomas AU RC 3.00 8.00
173B P.Thomas AU SP A 40.00 80.00
174A Ray Graham AU RC 2.50 6.00
174B Ray Graham AU SP 5.00 12.00
175A R.Burkhead AU RC 3.00 8.00
175B R.Burkhead AU SP A 75.00 135.00
176A Robert Alford AU RC 2.50 6.00
176B Robert Alford AU SP A 20.00 50.00
177A Rodney Smith AU RC 2.50 6.00
177B Rodney Smith AU SP A 25.00 50.00
178A R.Griffin TE AU RC 2.50 6.00
178B R.Griffin TE AU SP 5.00 12.00
179A R.Griffin QB AU RC 2.50 6.00
179B R.Griffin QB AU SP 5.00 12.00
180A S.Montgomery AU RC 2.50 6.00
180B S.Montgomery AU SP A 40.00 80.00
181A Ryan Spadola AU RC 3.00 8.00
181B Ryan Spadola AU SP 6.00 15.00
182A R.Shepard AU RC 2.50 6.00
182B R.Shepard AU SP B 8.00 20.00
183A Sio Moore AU RC 2.50 6.00
183B Sio Moore AU SP 5.00 12.00
184A Spencer Ware AU RC 2.50 6.00
184B Spencer Ware AU SP B 5.00 12.00
185A Tavarres King AU RC 4.00 10.00
185B Tavarres King AU SP A 25.00 60.00
186A Theo Riddick AU RC 2.50 6.00
186B Theo Riddick AU SP A 30.00 60.00
187A Travis Kelce AU RC 30.00 60.00
187B Travis Kelce AU SP A 50.00 100.00
188A Tyler Bray AU RC 8.00 20.00
188B Tyler Bray AU SP A 30.00 80.00
189A T.Mathieu AU/25* RC 175.00 300.00
189B Tyrann Mathieu AU/25* 175.00 300.00
190A X.Rhodes AU/130* RC 12.50 25.00
190B Xavier Rhodes AU SP A 30.00 60.00
191A Zac Dysert AU RC 2.50 6.00
(dropping back)
191B Zac Dysert AU SP A 40.00 80.00
(scrambling forward)
192A Zac Stacy AU RC 2.50 6.00
(running with football)
192B Zac Stacy AU SP 5.00 12.00
(running without football)
193A Jack Doyle AU RC 2.50 6.00
193B Jack Doyle AU SP 5.00 12.00
194A Jaron Brown AU RC 2.50 6.00
194B Jaron Brown AU SP 5.00 12.00
195A K.Webster AU RC 3.00 8.00
195B K.Webster AU SP A 20.00 40.00
196A Marlon Brown AU RC 4.00 10.00
196B Marlon Brown AU SP 8.00 20.00
197A Matt McGloin AU RC 8.00 20.00
(both hands on football)
197B Matt McGloin AU SP 20.00 40.00
(one hand on football)
198A Michael Ford AU RC 4.00 10.00
198B Michael Ford AU SP 8.00 20.00
199A Nick Moody AU RC 3.00 8.00
199B Nick Moody AU SP 6.00 15.00
200A Zach Sudfeld AU RC 2.50 6.00
200B Zach Sudfeld AU SP 20.00 40.00
201A Aaron Dobson AU RC 2.50 6.00
201B Aaron Dobson AU SP 12.00 30.00
202A A.Ellington AU RC 6.00 15.00
202B A.Ellington AU SP 10.00 25.00
203A C.Michael AU RC 2.50 6.00
203B C.Michael AU SP 5.00 12.00
204A C.Patterson AU RC 2.50 6.00
204B C.Patterson AU SP 5.00 12.00
205A D.Hopkins AU RC 15.00 30.00
205B D.Hopkins AU SP 30.00 60.00
206A D.Robinson AU RC 2.50 6.00
206B D.Robinson AU SP 5.00 12.00
207A Dion Jordan AU RC 2.50 6.00
207B Dion Jordan AU SP 5.00 12.00
208A Eddie Lacy AU RC 25.00 60.00
208B Eddie Lacy AU SP 40.00 80.00
209A EJ Manuel AU RC 2.50 6.00
209B EJ Manuel AU SP 5.00 12.00
210A Gavin Escobar AU RC 2.50 6.00
210B Gavin Escobar AU SP 6.00 15.00
211A Geno Smith AU RC 2.50 6.00
211B Geno Smith AU SP 5.00 12.00
212A G.Bernard AU RC 2.50 6.00
212B G.Bernard AU SP 5.00 12.00
213A J.Franklin AU RC 2.50 6.00
213B J.Franklin AU SP 5.00 12.00
214A Jordan Reed AU RC 10.00 25.00
214B Jordan Reed AU SP 15.00 40.00
215A Joseph Randle AU RC 2.50 6.00
215B Joseph Randle AU SP 5.00 12.00
216A Justin Hunter AU RC 6.00 15.00
216B Justin Hunter AU SP 10.00 25.00
217A Keenan Allen AU RC 12.00 30.00
217B Keenan Allen AU SP 25.00 60.00
218A Kenny Stills AU RC 8.00 20.00
218B Kenny Stills AU SP 12.00 30.00
219A Knile Davis AU RC 6.00 15.00
219B Knile Davis AU SP 10.00 25.00
220A Landry Jones AU RC 6.00 15.00
220B Landry Jones AU SP 5.00 12.00
221A Le'Veon Bell AU RC 50.00 100.00
221B Le'Veon Bell AU SP 75.00 125.00
222A Manti Te'o AU RC 3.00 8.00
222B Manti Te'o AU SP 6.00 15.00
223A M.Lattimore AU RC 2.50 6.00
223B M.Lattimore AU SP 5.00 12.00

224A M.Wheaton AU RC 2.50 6.00
224B M.Wheaton AU SP 5.00 12.00
225A M.Goodwin AU RC 2.50 6.00
225B M.Goodwin AU SP 5.00 12.00
226A Matt Barkley AU RC 6.00 15.00
226B Matt Barkley AU SP 5.00 12.00
227A Mike Gillislee AU RC 2.50 6.00
227B Mike Gillislee AU SP 5.00 12.00
228A Mike Glennon AU RC 2.50 6.00
228B Mike Glennon AU SP 5.00 12.00
229A Montee Ball AU RC 2.50 6.00
229B Montee Ball AU SP 5.00 12.00
230A Quinton Patton AU RC 2.50 6.00
230B Quinton Patton AU SP 5.00 12.00
231A Robert Woods AU RC 4.00 10.00
231B Robert Woods AU SP 8.00 20.00
232A Ryan Nassib AU RC 8.00 20.00
232B Ryan Nassib AU SP 10.00 25.00
233A S.Bailey AU RC 2.50 6.00
233B S.Bailey AU SP 5.00 12.00
234A Stepfan Taylor AU RC 2.50 6.00
234B Stepfan Taylor AU SP 5.00 12.00
235A T.Austin AU RC 3.00 8.00
235B T.Austin AU SP 6.00 15.00
236A T.Williams AU RC 6.00 15.00
236B T.Williams AU SP 10.00 25.00
237A Tyler Eifert AU RC 2.50 6.00
237B Tyler Eifert AU SP 5.00 12.00
238A Tyler Wilson AU RC 2.50 6.00
238B Tyler Wilson AU SP 5.00 12.00
239A V.McDonald AU RC 3.00 8.00
239B V.McDonald AU SP 6.00 15.00
240A Zach Ertz AU RC 5.00 12.00
240B Zach Ertz AU SP 10.00 25.00

2013 Panini Contenders Cracked Ice

*1-100 VETS/21: 12X TO 30X BASIC CARDS
*101-200 ROOK.AU/21: 1X TO 2.5X PLAY.AU/99
*201-240 ROOK.AU/21: 1X TO 2.5X PLAY.AU/99
MOST HAVE TWO CARDS OF EQUAL VALUE
192A Zac Stacy AU 10.00 25.00
204A Cordarrelle Patterson AU 12.00 30.00
208A Eddie Lacy AU 200.00 400.00
209A EJ Manuel AU 150.00 300.00
217A Keenan Allen AU 60.00 120.00
221A Le'Veon Bell AU 100.00 200.00
223A Marcus Lattimore AU 100.00 200.00
228A Mike Glennon AU 12.00 30.00
229A Montee Ball AU 12.00 30.00

2013 Panini Contenders Playoff Ticket

*1-100 VETS/99: 3X TO 8X BASIC CARDS
MOST HAVE TWO CARDS OF EQUAL VALUE
33 Andrew Luck 8.00 20.00
61 Aaron Rodgers 6.00 15.00
85 Russell Wilson 6.00 15.00
101A Aaron Mellette AU 8.00 20.00
102A Ace Sanders AU 12.00 30.00
103A Alan Bonner AU 4.00 10.00
104A Alec Ogletree AU EXCH 4.00 10.00
105A Alex Okafor AU 4.00 10.00
105B Joseph Fauria AU 6.00 15.00
106A Arthur Brown AU 10.00 25.00
106B Timothy Wright AU 5.00 12.00
107A Barkevious Mingo AU 10.00 25.00
108A Benny Cunningham AU 6.00 15.00
109A B.J. Daniels AU 6.00 15.00
110A Bjoern Werner AU 6.00 15.00
111A Brad Sorensen AU 4.00 10.00
112A Brice Butler AU 4.00 10.00
113A Blidi Wreh-Wilson AU 5.00 12.00
114A Caleb Sturgis AU 6.00 15.00
115A Chance Warmack AU 4.00 10.00
115B Sharrif Floyd AU 4.00 10.00
116A C.J. Anderson AU 25.00 50.00
117A Chris Gragg AU 4.00 10.00
117B Ryan Otten AU 4.00 10.00
118A Chris Harper AU 4.00 10.00
119A Chris Thompson AU 4.00 10.00
120A Cobi Hamilton AU 4.00 10.00
121A Cierre Wood AU 4.00 10.00
122A Corey Fuller AU 4.00 10.00
123A Cornellius Carradine AU 4.00 10.00
124A D.J. Fluker AU 4.00 10.00
125A D.J. Hayden AU 6.00 15.00
126A Damontre Moore AU 4.00 10.00
127A Da'Rick Rogers AU 10.00 25.00
128A Darius Slay AU 4.00 10.00
129A Datone Jones AU 4.00 10.00
130A David Amerson AU 4.00 10.00
130B Marcus Davis AU 4.00 10.00
131A Dee Milliner AU EXCH 4.00 10.00
132A Dennis Johnson AU 4.00 10.00
133A Desmond Trufant AU 4.00 10.00
134A Dion Sims AU 4.00 10.00
135A D.J. Swearinger AU 4.00 10.00
136A Dustin Hopkins AU 4.00 10.00
137A Earl Wolff AU 6.00 15.00
138A Eric Fisher AU 4.00 10.00
139A Eric Reid AU 12.00 30.00
140A Ezekiel Ansah AU 4.00 10.00
141A Jamar Taylor AU 4.00 10.00
142A Jamie Collins AU 4.00 10.00
143A Jarvis Jones AU 15.00 40.00
144A Jawan Jamison AU 4.00 10.00
145A Johnthan Banks AU 4.00 10.00
146A Jon Bostic AU 4.00 10.00
147A Johnathan Cyprien AU 4.00 10.00
148A Jordan Poyer AU 4.00 10.00
149A Josh Boyce AU 10.00 25.00
150A Justin Brown AU 6.00 15.00
151A Kenbrell Thompkins AU 6.00 15.00
152A Kenjon Barner AU 4.00 10.00
153A Kenny Vaccaro AU 6.00 15.00
154A Khiry Robinson AU 6.00 15.00
155A Jeff Tuel AU 4.00 10.00
156A Kevin Minter AU 4.00 10.00
157A Kiko Alonso AU 5.00 12.00
158A Latavius Murray AU 25.00 50.00
159A Kawann Short AU 4.00 10.00
159B Kerwynn Williams AU 4.00 10.00
160A Levine Toilolo AU 5.00 12.00
161A Luke Joeckel AU 4.00 10.00
161B Conner Vernon AU 4.00 10.00
162A Luke Willson AU 6.00 15.00
163A Margus Hunt AU 5.00 12.00
164A Marquess Wilson AU 6.00 15.00
165A Matt Elam AU 8.00 20.00
166A Matt Scott AU 4.00 10.00
167A Matt Simms AU 5.00 12.00
168A Michael Cox AU 5.00 12.00
169A Mike James AU 6.00 15.00
170A Mychal Rivera AU 4.00 10.00
171A Nick Kasa AU 4.00 10.00
172A Jasper Collins AU 4.00 10.00
173A Phillip Thomas AU 4.00 10.00
174A Ray Graham AU 4.00 10.00
175A Rex Burkhead AU 5.00 12.00
176A Robert Alford AU 4.00 10.00
177A Rodney Smith AU 4.00 10.00
178A Ryan Griffin TE AU 6.00 15.00
179A Ryan Griffin QB AU 4.00 10.00
180A Sam Montgomery AU 4.00 10.00
181A Ryan Spadola AU 5.00 12.00
182A Russell Shepard AU 4.00 10.00
183A Sio Moore AU 6.00 15.00
184A Spencer Ware AU 6.00 15.00
185A Tavarres King AU 4.00 10.00
186A Theo Riddick AU 8.00 20.00
187A Travis Kelce AU 50.00 100.00
188A Tyler Bray AU 4.00 10.00
189A Tyrann Mathieu AU 12.00 30.00
190A Xavier Rhodes AU 10.00 25.00
191A Zac Dysert AU 12.00 30.00
192A Zac Stacy AU 4.00 10.00
193A Jack Doyle AU 4.00 10.00
194A Jaron Brown AU 4.00 10.00
195A Kayvon Webster AU 5.00 12.00
196A Marlon Brown AU 6.00 15.00
197A Matt McGloin AU 10.00 25.00
198A Michael Ford AU 8.00 20.00
199A Nick Moody AU 5.00 12.00
200A Zach Sudfeld AU 4.00 10.00
201A Aaron Dobson AU 5.00 12.00
202A Andre Ellington AU 12.00 30.00
203A Christine Michael AU 5.00 12.00
204A Cordarrelle Patterson AU 5.00 12.00
205A DeAndre Hopkins AU 30.00 60.00
206A Denard Robinson AU 5.00 12.00
207A Dion Jordan AU 5.00 12.00
208A Eddie Lacy AU 50.00 100.00
209A EJ Manuel AU 5.00 12.00
210A Gavin Escobar AU 5.00 12.00
211A Geno Smith AU 5.00 12.00
212A Giovani Bernard AU 5.00 12.00
213A Johnathan Franklin AU 5.00 12.00
214A Jordan Reed AU 12.00 30.00
215A Joseph Randle AU 5.00 12.00
216A Justin Hunter AU 12.00 30.00
217A Keenan Allen AU 40.00 80.00
218A Kenny Stills AU 15.00 40.00
219A Knile Davis AU 15.00 40.00
220A Landry Jones AU 10.00 25.00
221A Le'Veon Bell AU 50.00 100.00
222A Manti Te'o AU 6.00 15.00
223A Marcus Lattimore AU 5.00 12.00
224A Markus Wheaton AU 5.00 12.00
225A Marquise Goodwin AU 5.00 12.00
226A Matt Barkley AU 12.00 30.00
227A Mike Gillislee AU 5.00 12.00
228A Mike Glennon AU 5.00 12.00
229A Montee Ball AU 5.00 12.00
230A Quinton Patton AU 5.00 12.00
231A Robert Woods AU 8.00 20.00
232A Ryan Nassib AU 5.00 12.00
233A Stedman Bailey AU 5.00 12.00
234A Stepfan Taylor AU 5.00 12.00
235A Tavon Austin AU 6.00 15.00
236A Terrance Williams AU 10.00 25.00
237A Tyler Eifert AU 5.00 12.00
238A Tyler Wilson AU 5.00 12.00
239A Vance McDonald AU 6.00 15.00
240A Zach Ertz AU 10.00 25.00

2013 Panini Contenders Draft Class

GOLD/99: 1X TO 2.5X BASIC INSERTS
1 Andre Ellington .30 .75
2 Christine Michael .30 .75
3 Dion Jordan .30 .75
4 Eddie Lacy .30 .75
5 Giovani Bernard .30 .75
6 Jordan Reed .50 1.25
7 Kenny Stills .30 .75
8 Le'Veon Bell 1.00 2.50
9 Markus Wheaton .30 .75
10 Marquise Goodwin .30 .75
11 Mike Gillislee .30 .75
12 Montee Ball .30 .75
13 Robert Woods .50 1.25
14 Ryan Nassib .30 .75
15 Stedman Bailey .30 .75
16 Stepfan Taylor .30 .75
17 Terrance Williams .30 .75
18 Tyler Eifert .30 .75
19 Vance McDonald .40 1.00
20 Zach Ertz .60 1.50

2013 Panini Contenders Draft Class Autographs

1 Aaron Dobson 6.00 15.00
2 Cordarrelle Patterson 6.00 15.00
3 DeAndre Hopkins 15.00 40.00
4 Denard Robinson 6.00 15.00
5 EJ Manuel 6.00 15.00
6 Gavin Escobar 6.00 15.00
8 Johnathan Franklin 6.00 15.00
9 Joseph Randle 6.00 15.00
11 Keenan Allen 30.00 60.00
12 Knile Davis 6.00 15.00
14 Manti Te'o 10.00 25.00
15 Marcus Lattimore 6.00 15.00
17 Mike Glennon 6.00 15.00
20 Tyler Wilson 6.00 15.00

2013 Panini Contenders Legendary Contenders

GOLD/99: .8X TO 2X BASIC INSERTS
1 Barry Sanders 2.00 5.00
2 Brett Favre 2.50 6.00
3 Cris Carter 1.25 3.00
4 Dan Marino 2.50 6.00
5 Deion Sanders 1.00 2.50
6 Emmitt Smith 2.00 5.00
7 Jerry Rice 2.00 5.00
8 John Elway 2.00 5.00
9 Steve Young 1.50 4.00
10 Walter Payton 2.50 6.00

2013 Panini Contenders Legendary Contenders Autographs

1 Charlie Joiner 15.00 40.00
2 Gale Sayers 15.00 40.00
3 Jim Kiick 12.00 30.00
4 Jamal Lewis 12.00 30.00
5 Joe Montana 60.00 120.00
6 LaDainian Tomlinson 30.00 60.00
7 Rocket Ismail 20.00 50.00
8 Terry Bradshaw 40.00 80.00
9 Tim Brown 20.00 50.00
10 Warren Sapp 25.00 50.00

2013 Panini Contenders MVP Contenders

GOLD/99: 1.2X TO 3X BASIC INSERTS
1 Robert Griffin III .40 1.00
2 Calvin Johnson .60 1.50
3 Tom Brady 1.50 4.00
4 Drew Brees .60 1.50
5 Peyton Manning 1.25 3.00
6 Jamaal Charles .50 1.25
7 Dez Bryant .60 1.50
8 Arian Foster .50 1.25
9 Joe Flacco .50 1.25
10 Russell Wilson 1.25 3.00

2013 Panini Contenders MVP Contenders Autographs

1 Peyton Manning/25
2 Adrian Peterson/25 50.00 100.00
6 Colin Kaepernick/25 60.00 120.00
8 LeSean McCoy/25 15.00 40.00
9 Aaron Rodgers/25 125.00 200.00

2013 Panini Contenders NFL Ink

7 Richard Sherman/25 125.00 250.00
11 Clay Matthews/25 30.00 60.00
12 Coby Fleener/25
13 Colin Kaepernick/25
16 Victor Cruz/25 10.00 25.00
20 Ryan Tannehill/25 15.00 40.00

2013 Panini Contenders Rookie Ink

1 Aaron Dobson 5.00 12.00
2 Andre Ellington 12.00 30.00
3 Christine Michael 5.00 12.00
4 Cordarrelle Patterson 5.00 12.00
5 DeAndre Hopkins 12.00 30.00
6 Denard Robinson 5.00 12.00
7 Dion Jordan 5.00 12.00
8 Eddie Lacy 60.00 100.00
9 EJ Manuel 5.00 12.00
10 Gavin Escobar 5.00 12.00
11 Geno Smith 5.00 12.00
12 Giovani Bernard 5.00 12.00
13 Johnathan Franklin 5.00 12.00
14 Jordan Reed 8.00 20.00
15 Joseph Randle 5.00 12.00
16 Justin Hunter 5.00 12.00
17 Keenan Allen 25.00 50.00
18 Kenny Stills 5.00 12.00
19 Knile Davis 5.00 12.00
20 Landry Jones 5.00 12.00
21 Le'Veon Bell 25.00 60.00
22 Manti Te'o 6.00 15.00
23 Marcus Lattimore 5.00 12.00
24 Markus Wheaton 5.00 12.00
25 Marquise Goodwin 5.00 12.00
26 Matt Barkley 5.00 12.00
27 Mike Gillislee 5.00 12.00
28 Mike Glennon 5.00 12.00
29 Montee Ball 5.00 12.00
30 Quinton Patton 10.00 25.00
31 Robert Woods 8.00 20.00
32 Ryan Nassib 5.00 12.00
33 Stedman Bailey 5.00 12.00
34 Stepfan Taylor 5.00 12.00
35 Tavon Austin 6.00 15.00
36 Terrance Williams 5.00 12.00
37 Tyler Eifert 5.00 12.00
38 Tyler Wilson 5.00 12.00
39 Vance McDonald 6.00 15.00
40 Zach Ertz 10.00 25.00

2013 Panini Contenders Round Numbers

GOLD/99: .8X TO 2X BASIC INSERTS
1 E.Fisher/L.Joeckel .50 1.25
3 D.Hopkins/T.Austin 1.25 3.00
4 D.Hayden/D.Milliner .50 1.25
5 G.Escobar/V.McDonald .60 1.50
6 A.Dobson/R.Woods .75 2.00
7 L.Bell/M.Ball 1.50 4.00
8 B.Wilson/T.Mathieu .75 2.00
9 K.Allen/T.Williams 1.00 2.50
10 M.Wheaton/S.Bailey .50 1.25
11 M.Barkley/T.Wilson .50 1.25
12 J.Franklin/Q.Patton .50 1.25
13 D.Robinson/S.Taylor .50 1.25
14 J.Randle/M.Gillislee .50 1.25
15 R.Burkhead/T.Riddick .60 1.50
16 S.Richardson/S.Lotulelei .60 1.50
17 A.Ogletree/J.Jones .50 1.25
18 K.Minter/M.Te'o .60 1.50
19 C.Michael/E.Lacy .50 1.25
20 K.Davis/M.Glennon .50 1.25

2013 Panini Contenders Round Numbers Autographs

1 S.Bailey/T.Williams
2 V.McDonald/Z.Ertz 12.00 30.00
3 C.Patterson/D.Hopkins 15.00 40.00
4 G.Bernard/L.Bell 25.00 60.00
5 E.Manuel/X.Rhodes 6.00 15.00
6 E.Lacy/M.Ball 50.00 120.00
7 Wheaton/Goodwin 6.00 15.00
8 J.Reed/K.Davis 10.00 25.00
9 D.Jordan/E.Ansah 6.00 15.00
10 J.Hunter/R.Woods 10.00 25.00
11 M.Barkley/R.Nassib
12 A.Dobson/G.Smith 6.00 15.00
13 J.Franklin/M.Lattimore 6.00 15.00
14 L.Jones/T.Wilson 6.00 15.00
15 J.Randle/S.Taylor 6.00 15.00
16 D.Robinson/K.Stills 6.00 15.00
17 C.Michael/G.Escobar 6.00 15.00
18 A.Sanders/J.Boyce 6.00 15.00
19 E.Reid/K.Vaccaro 20.00 40.00
20 T.Austin/T.Eifert 8.00 20.00

2013 Panini Contenders ROY Contenders

GOLD/99: 1X TO 2.5X BASIC INSERTS
1 Cordarrelle Patterson .30 .75
2 DeAndre Hopkins .75 2.00
3 Eddie Lacy .30 .75
4 EJ Manuel .30 .75
5 Geno Smith .30 .75
6 Giovani Bernard .30 .75
7 Keenan Allen .60 1.50
8 Le'Veon Bell 1.00 2.50
9 Mike Glennon .30 .75
10 Montee Ball .30 .75
11 Robert Woods .50 1.25
12 Terrance Williams .30 .75
13 Tavon Austin .40 1.00
14 Tyler Eifert .30 .75
15 Kenbrell Thompkins .50 1.25
16 Tyrann Mathieu .50 1.25
17 Ezekiel Ansah .30 .75
18 Kiko Alonso .40 1.00
19 Eric Reid .40 1.00
20 Andre Ellington .30 .75

2013 Panini Contenders ROY Contenders Autographs

1 Cordarrelle Patterson 6.00 15.00
2 DeAndre Hopkins 15.00 40.00
3 Eddie Lacy 6.00 15.00
4 EJ Manuel 6.00 15.00
5 Geno Smith 6.00 15.00
6 Giovani Bernard 6.00 15.00
7 Keenan Allen 30.00 60.00
8 Le'Veon Bell 30.00 60.00
9 Mike Glennon 6.00 15.00
10 Montee Ball 6.00 15.00
11 Robert Woods 10.00 25.00
12 Terrance Williams 6.00 15.00
13 Tavon Austin 8.00 20.00
14 Tyler Eifert 6.00 15.00
15 Kenbrell Thompkins
16 Tyrann Mathieu 10.00 25.00
17 Ezekiel Ansah 6.00 15.00
18 Kiko Alonso 8.00 20.00
19 Eric Reid 30.00 60.00
20 Andre Ellington 12.00 30.00

2013 Panini Contenders Touchdown Tandems

GOLD/99: X TO X BASIC INSERTS
1 A.Rodgers/J.Jones 1.25 3.00
2 E.Decker/P.Manning 1.50 4.00
3 D.Bryant/T.Romo .75 2.00
4 R.Gronkowski/T.Brady 2.00 5.00
5 B.Marshall/J.Cutler .60 1.50
6 A.Green/A.Dalton .75 2.00
7 D.Brees/M.Colston .75 2.00
8 E.Manning/V.Cruz .60 1.50
9 M.Ryan/T.Gonzalez .60 1.50
10 C.Johnson/M.Stafford .75 2.00
11 M.Wallace/R.Tannehill .60 1.50
12 J.Flacco/T.Smith .60 1.50
13 A.Gates/P.Rivers .75 2.00
14 G.Tate/R.Wilson 1.50 4.00
15 A.Luck/R.Wayne 1.25 3.00
16 B.Roethlisberger/H.Miller .75 2.00
17 A.Johnson/M.Schaub .50 1.25
18 P.Garcon/R.Griffin .60 1.50
19 C.Newton/S.Smith .75 2.00
20 C.Kaepernick/V.Davis .60 1.50

2014 Panini Contenders

COMP.SET w/o RC's (100) 6.00 15.00
101-200 A CARD# SEC LISTED ON BOTTOM
101-200 B CARD# SEAT LISTED ON BOTTOM
*UNLISTED AU VARIATION: .6X TO 1.5X AU RC
PANINI ANNC'D PRINT RUNS BELOW
AU* INSERTED IN RETAIL ONLY
1 Vernon Davis .20 .50
2 Frank Gore .25 .60
3 Colin Kaepernick .25 .60
4 Jay Cutler .20 .50
5 Matt Forte .20 .50
6 Alshon Jeffery .25 .60
7 Brandon Marshall .20 .50
8 Giovani Bernard .20 .50
9 Andy Dalton .25 .60
10 A.J. Green .30 .75
11 EJ Manuel .20 .50
12 C.J. Spiller .20 .50
13 Mike Williams .25 .60
14 Montee Ball .20 .50
15 Peyton Manning .60 1.50
16 Demaryius Thomas .25 .60
17 Julius Thomas .20 .50
18 Brian Hoyer .20 .50
19 Ben Tate .20 .50
20 Vincent Jackson .20 .50
21 Doug Martin .25 .60
22 Josh McCown .20 .50
23 Larry Fitzgerald .25 .60
24 Andre Ellington .20 .50
25 Carson Palmer .25 .60
26 Malcom Floyd .20 .50
27 Ryan Mathews .25 .60
28 Philip Rivers .30 .75
29 Dwayne Bowe .25 .60
30 Jamaal Charles .25 .60
31 Alex Smith .25 .60
32 Andrew Luck .40 1.00
33 Trent Richardson .20 .50
34 Reggie Wayne .25 .60
35 Dez Bryant .30 .75
36 DeMarco Murray .25 .60
37 Tony Romo .25 .60
38 Jason Witten .25 .60
39 Brian Hartline .20 .50
40 Ryan Tannehill .25 .60
41 Mike Wallace .20 .50
42 Nick Foles .25 .60
43 Jeremy Maclin .20 .50
44 LeSean McCoy .30 .75
45 Julio Jones .30 .75
46 Matt Ryan .25 .60
47 Roddy White .20 .50
48 Victor Cruz .25 .60
49 Eli Manning .25 .60
50 Rueben Randle .20 .50
51 Chad Henne .20 .50
52 Marcedes Lewis .20 .50
53 Cecil Shorts III .20 .50
54 Eric Decker .20 .50
55 Chris Ivory .25 .60
56 Geno Smith .20 .50
57 Reggie Bush .20 .50
58 Calvin Johnson .30 .75
59 Matthew Stafford .25 .60
60 Golden Tate .25 .60
61 Eddie Lacy .20 .50
62 Jordy Nelson .25 .60
63 Aaron Rodgers .60 1.50
64 Cam Newton .30 .75
65 Greg Olsen .25 .60
66 Luke Kuechly .25 .60
67 Tom Brady .75 2.00
68 Rob Gronkowski .30 .75
69 Stevan Ridley .20 .50
70 Danny Amendola .25 .60
71 Maurice Jones-Drew .20 .50
72 Matt Schaub .20 .50
73 Sam Bradford .20 .50
74 Tavon Austin .20 .50
75 Zac Stacy .20 .50
76 Joe Flacco .25 .60
77 Torrey Smith .20 .50
78 Steve Smith Sr. .25 .60
79 Robert Griffin III .20 .50
80 DeSean Jackson .25 .60
81 Alfred Morris .20 .50
82 Drew Brees .30 .75
83 Jimmy Graham .30 .75
84 Marques Colston .20 .50
85 Mark Ingram .25 .60
86 Richard Sherman .30 .75
87 Russell Wilson .50 1.25
88 Marshawn Lynch .25 .60
89 Le'Veon Bell .25 .60
90 Ben Roethlisberger .30 .75
91 Antonio Brown .30 .75
92 Andre Johnson .25 .60
93 Arian Foster .25 .60
94 J.J. Watt .30 .75
95 Nate Washington .20 .50
96 Jake Locker .25 .60
97 Shonn Greene .20 .50
98 Greg Jennings .20 .50
99 Cordarrelle Patterson .20 .50
100 Adrian Peterson .30 .75
101A Aaron Donald AU* RC 1.00 25.00
101B Aaron Donald AU/50* 40.00 80.00
103A Anthony Barr AU RC 4.00 10.00
103B Anthony Barr AU/25* 40.00 100.00
104A Antonio Andrews AU RC 2.00 5.00
104B Antonio Andrews AU SP 3.00 8.00
105A Arthur Lynch AU RC 2.00 5.00
105B Arthur Lynch AU/25*
107A Brandon Coleman AU* RC 2.00 5.00
107B Brandon Coleman AU/151* 6.00 15.00
108A Solomon Patton AU RC 2.50 6.00
108B Solomon Patton AU/100* 6.00 15.00
109A Bruce Ellington AU* RC 6.00 15.00
109B Bruce Ellington AU/150* 10.00 25.00
110A C.J. Fiedorowicz AU RC 2.00 5.00
110B C.J. Fiedorowicz AU/25*
112A Calvin Pryor AU RC 2.00 5.00
112B Calvin Pryor AU SP 3.00 8.00
113A Chris Borland AU RC 2.00 5.00
113B Chris Borland AU/25* 8.00 20.00
114A Chris Smith AU* RC 2.00 5.00
114B Chris Smith AU* SP 3.00 8.00
115A Cody Hoffman AU RC 2.00 5.00
115B Cody Hoffman AU SP 3.00 8.00
116A Crockett Gillmore AU/150* RC 6.00 15.00
116B Crockett Gillmore AU/25*
118A Cyrus Kouandjio AU RC 2.50 6.00
118B Cyrus Kouandjio AU SP 4.00 10.00
119A Darqueze Dennard AU RC 2.50 6.00
119B Darqueze Dennard AU/15*
120A Jay Prosch AU* RC 3.00 8.00
120B David Fales AU/150* RC 12.00 30.00
121A David Yankey AU RC 2.00 5.00
121B David Yankey AU SP 3.00 8.00
122A Dee Ford AU/151* RC 8.00 20.00
122B Dee Ford AU/5*
124A Deone Bucannon AU RC 2.00 5.00
124B Deone Bucannon AU SP 3.00 8.00
125A Devin Street AU RC 2.00 5.00
125B Devin Street AU SP 10.00 25.00
126A Dominique Easley AU RC 5.00 12.00
126B Dominique Easley AU/75* 15.00 30.00
127A Ed Reynolds AU RC 2.00 5.00
127B Ed Reynolds AU/150* 6.00 15.00
128A Garrett Gilbert AU* RC 2.00 5.00
128B Garrett Gilbert AU SP 3.00 8.00
129A Greg Robinson AU RC 2.00 5.00
129B Greg Robinson AU/150* 6.00 15.00
130A Ha Ha Clinton-Dix AU/50* RC 10.00 25.00
130B Ha Ha Clinton-Dix AU/25* 150.00 250.00
131A Henry Josey AU* RC 3.00 8.00
131B Henry Josey AU/150* 6.00 15.00
132A Isaiah Crowell AU/23* RC 50.00 100.00
132B Isaiah Crowell AU/100* 8.00 20.00
133A Christian Kirksey AU* RC 2.00 5.00
133B Jace Amaro AU/50* RC
134A Jackson Jeffcoat AU* RC 3.00 8.00
134B Jackson Jeffcoat AU SP 5.00 12.00
135B Jake Matthews AU/10* RC
136A James White AU RC
136B James White AU SP
138A Jared Abbrederis AU RC 4.00 10.00
138B Jared Abbrederis AU SP 6.00 15.00
139A Jason Verrett AU/25* RC
139B Jason Verrett AU/15* 150.00 250.00
140A Jeff Janis AU/89* RC 10.00 25.00
140B Jeff Janis AU SP 6.00 15.00
141A Jerick McKinnon AU RC 2.50 6.00
141B Jerick McKinnon AU/50* 20.00 50.00
142A Jimmie Ward AU RC 3.00 8.00
142B Jimmie Ward AU/75* 8.00 20.00
143A John Brown AU RC 3.00 8.00
143B John Brown AU/150* 10.00 25.00
144A Jordan Lynch AU RC 2.50 6.00
144B Jordan Lynch AU/200* 8.00 20.00
145B Josh Huff AU/50* RC 25.00 50.00
147A Keith Wenning AU RC 2.50 6.00
147B Keith Wenning AU/50* 40.00 80.00
148A Kevin Norwood AU RC 2.00 5.00
148B Kevin Norwood AU/150* 6.00 15.00
149A Kony Ealy AU/50* RC 40.00 80.00
149B Kony Ealy AU/10*
151A Kyle Van Noy AU RC 2.50 6.00
151B Kyle Van Noy AU/25*
152A Darrin Reaves AU RC 2.50 6.00
152B Lache Seastrunk AU/100* RC 20.00 40.00
153A Lamarcus Joyner AU/72*RC 8.00 20.00
153B Lamarcus Joyner AU/150* 10.00 25.00
154A Lorenzo Taliaferro AU RC 4.00 10.00
154B Lorenzo Taliaferro AU/150* 12.00 30.00
155A Senorise Perry AU RC 2.50 6.00
155B Senorise Perry AU/100* 6.00 15.00
156A Marcus Roberson AU RC 2.50 6.00
156B Marcus Roberson AU/75* 8.00 20.00
157A Marcus Smith AU RC 2.00 5.00
157B Marcus Smith AU/200* 6.00 15.00
158B Marion Grice AU/25* RC
159B Martavis Bryant AU RC 12.00 30.00
160A Matt Hazel AU RC 2.00 5.00
160B Matt Hazel AU SP 3.00 8.00
162A Michael Sam AU/200* RC 15.00 30.00
162B Michael Sam AU/50* 8.00 20.00
163A Mike Davis AU RC 2.00 5.00
163B Mike Davis AU/75* 4.00 10.00
164A Pierre Desir AU* RC 2.00 5.00
164B Pierre Desir AU/25* 8.00 20.00
165A Preston Brown AU RC 2.00 5.00
165B Preston Brown AU/50* 8.00 20.00
166A Quincy Enunwa AU RC 3.00 8.00
166B Quincy Enunwa AU/150* 12.00 30.00
167A Rajion Neal AU RC 2.00 5.00
167B Rajion Neal AU/50* 8.00 20.00
168A R.Hageman AU/25* RC 100.00 200.00
168B Ra'Shede Hageman AU/5*
169A Richard Rodgers AU RC 3.00 8.00
169B Richard Rodgers AU SP 5.00 12.00
170B Robert Herron AU/25* RC
171B Ryan Shazier AU RC 15.00 40.00
172A Scott Crichton AU RC 2.00 5.00
172B Scott Crichton AU/75* 8.00 20.00
173A Shaq Evans AU* RC 10.00 25.00
173B Shaq Evans AU/10*
174A Shayne Skov AU RC 2.00 5.00
174B Shayne Skov AU/150* 8.00 20.00
175A Stephon Tuitt AU RC 3.00 8.00
175B Stephon Tuitt AU/25*
176A Anthony Hitchens AU* RC 6.00 15.00
176B Anthony Hitchens AU SP 6.00 15.00
177B Taylor Lewan AU/15* RC 150.00 250.00
180A Timmy Jernigan AU/25* RC 75.00 150.00
180B Timmy Jernigan AU/25* 75.00 150.00
181A Travis Swanson AU* RC 2.00 5.00
181B Travis Swanson AU/25* 150.00 250.00
182A Trent Murphy AU RC 2.00 5.00
182B Trent Murphy AU/50* 20.00 40.00
183A Trevor Reilly AU* RC 2.00 5.00
183B Trevor Reilly AU/100* 6.00 15.00
184A Troy Niklas AU/50* RC 20.00 40.00
185A Tyler Gaffney AU RC 2.00 5.00
185B Tyler Gaffney AU/200* 6.00 15.00
186A Xavier Su'A-Filo AU* RC 2.50 6.00
186B Xavier Su'A-Filo AU SP 4.00 10.00
187A Yawin Smallwood AU/247* RC 6.00 15.00
187B Yawin Smallwood AU SP 3.00 8.00
189A Zack Martin AU RC 8.00 20.00
189B Zack Martin AU SP 12.00 30.00
190A Allen Hurns AU/125* RC 15.00 40.00
190B Allen Hurns AU/25* 30.00 60.00
192A Branden Oliver AU RC 3.00 8.00
192B Branden Oliver AU SP 5.00 12.00
193A Rashad Ross AU/249* RC 6.00 15.00
193B Rashad Ross AU SP 3.00 8.00
194A James Wright AU* RC 3.00 8.00
194B James Wright AU SP 5.00 12.00
195A Silas Redd AU RC 4.00 10.00
195B Silas Redd AU/150* 12.00 30.00
196A Isaiah Burse AU* RC 2.00 5.00
196B Isaiah Burse AU/150* 15.00 40.00
197A Taylor Gabriel AU RC 2.50 6.00
197B Taylor Gabriel AU/150* 15.00 40.00
198A Orleans Darkwa AU* RC 3.00 8.00
198B Orleans Darkwa AU/150* 10.00 25.00
199A Alfred Blue AU* RC 5.00 12.00
199B Alfred Blue AU/100* 10.00 25.00
200A Philly Brown AU RC 2.50 6.00
200B Philly Brown AU 2.50 6.00
201A A.Murray AU RC 2.50 6.00
201B A.Murray AU SP B 4.00 10.00
201C Aaron Murray AU/25* 100.00 200.00
202A A.McCarron AU RC 20.00 40.00
202B A.McCarron AU/105* 20.00 40.00
202C A.McCarron AU/25* 75.00 125.00
203A A.Robinson AU RC 6.00 15.00
203B A.Robinson AU SP B 8.00 20.00
204A A.Williams AU RC 6.00 15.00
204B A.Williams AU SP B 10.00 25.00
205A A.Watson AU RC 2.50 6.00
205B A.Watson AU SP B 4.00 10.00
206A A.Seferian-Jenkins AU RC 2.50 6.00
206B A.Seferian-Jenkins AU SP B 4.00 10.00
207A B.Cooks AU RC 4.00 10.00
207B B.Cooks AU SP B 6.00 15.00
208A C.Hyde AU RC EXCH 8.00 20.00
208B C.Hyde AU SP B EXCH 12.00 30.00
208C C.Hyde AU SP C EXCH
209A C.Sims AU RC 2.50 6.00
209B C.Sims AU SP B 4.00 10.00
210A C.Latimer AU RC 3.00 8.00
210B C.Latimer AU SP B 8.00 20.00
211A C.Shaw AU RC 2.50 6.00
211B C.Shaw AU SP B 4.00 10.00
212A D.Adams AU RC EXCH 12.00 30.00
212B D.Adams AU SP B EXCH 20.00 50.00
212C D.Adams AU SP C EXCH 75.00 125.00
213A D.Thomas AU RC 2.50 6.00
213B D.Thomas AU SP B 4.00 10.00
214A D.Carr AU RC 100.00 200.00
214B Derek Carr AU/155* 150.00 300.00
214C Derek .Carr AU/25* 400.00 600.00
215A D.Freeman AU RC 15.00 30.00
215B D.Freeman AU SP B 20.00 50.00
215C D.Freeman AU/25* 40.00 80.00
216A D.Moncrief AU RC EXCH 12.50 25.00
216B D.Moncrief AU SP B EXCH 15.00 40.00
217A D.Archer AU RC 2.50 6.00
217B D.Archer AU SP B 4.00 10.00
218A E.Ebron AU RC 3.00 8.00
218B E.Ebron AU/150* 8.00 20.00
218C Eric Ebron AU/25* 12.00 30.00
219A J.Clowney AU RC 3.00 8.00
219B J.Clowney AU/50* 12.00 30.00
219C J.Clowney AU/25* 12.00 30.00
220A J.Landry AU RC 25.00 50.00
220B J.Landry AU SP B 30.00 60.00
221A J.Garoppolo AU RC 300.00 600.00
221B J.Garoppolo AU/75* 400.00 800.00
221C J.Garoppolo AU/27* 900.00 1500.00
222A J.Matthews AU RC 8.00 20.00
222B J.Matthews AU SP B 6.00 15.00
222C J.Matthews AU/25* 40.00 80.00
223A K.Carey AU RC 2.50 6.00
223B K.Carey AU SP B 4.00 10.00
224A K.Mack AU RC EXCH 8.00 20.00
224B K.Mack AU SP EXCH 12.00 30.00
225A L.Thomas AU RC 2.50 6.00
225B L.Thomas AU/158* 6.00 15.00
226B M.Lee AU/55* 6.00 15.00
226C Marqise Lee AU/25* 30.00 60.00
227A O.Beckham Jr. AU RC 60.00 120.00
227B O.Beckham Jr. AU/206* 150.00 250.00
227C O.Beckham Jr. AU/25* 200.00 400.00
228A P.Richardson AU RC 8.00 20.00
228B P.Richardson AU SP B 12.00 30.00
229A T.Boyd AU RC 2.50 6.00
229B T.Boyd AU SP B 4.00 10.00
230A T.West AU RC 2.50 6.00
230B T.West AU SP B 4.00 10.00
231A T.Savage AU RC 5.00 12.00
231B T.Savage AU SP B 4.00 10.00
231C T.Savage AU/25*
232A J.Hill AU RC 8.00 20.00
232B J.Hill AU SP B 12.00 30.00
233A T.Mason AU RC 8.00 20.00
233B T.Mason AU SP B 12.00 30.00
234A B.Sankey AU RC 8.00 20.00
234B B.Sankey AU SP B 12.00 30.00
234C B.Sankey AU/25* 150.00 250.00
235A K.Benjamin AU RC 30.00 60.00
235B K.Benjamin AU/104* 30.00 60.00
235C K.Benjamin AU/25*
236A M.Evans AU RC 15.00 40.00
236B Mike Evans AU/154* 40.00 80.00
236C Mike Evans AU/25* 150.00 250.00
237A S.Watkins AU RC 15.00 40.00
237B S.Watkins AU/103* 30.00 60.00
237C S.Watkins AU/25* 40.00 80.00
238A B.Bortles AU RC 6.00 15.00
238B B.Bortles AU/100* 60.00 120.00
238C Blake Bortles AU/27* 150.00 300.00
239A T.Bridgewater AU RC 15.00 40.00
239B T.Bridgewater AU/103* 25.00 60.00
239C T.Bridgewater AU/25* 75.00 150.00
240A J.Manziel AU RC 12.00 30.00
240B Johnny Manziel AU/50* 25.00 60.00
240C Johnny Manziel AU/27* 40.00 80.00
241 Juwan Thompson AU* SP RC 3.00 8.00
242 Terrance Mitchell AU SP RC 3.00 8.00
243 Chandler Catanzaro AU* SP RC 2.50 6.00
244 Walter Powell AU* SP RC 2.00 5.00
245 Cody Parkey AU SP RC 2.50 6.00
248 Dustin Vaughan AU SP RC 2.00 5.00
249 E.J. Gaines AU SP RC 2.00 5.00
250 Glenn Winston AU* SP RC 2.50 6.00
251 Walt Aikens AU SP RC 2.50 6.00

2014 Panini Contenders Championship Ticket

*1-100 VETS/99: 5X TO 12X BASIC CARDS
*101-199 ROOK/99: .5X TO 1.2X PLAY.AU/199
*201-240 ROOK/49: .5X TO 1.2X PLAY.AU/99
MOST HAVE TWO CARDS OF EQUAL VALUE
188A Zach Mettenberger AU 30.00 60.00
201A Aaron Murray AU/49 6.00 15.00
214A Derek Carr AU/49 125.00 250.00
221A Jimmy Garoppolo AU/49 600.00 1000.00
227A Odell Beckham Jr. AU/49 250.00 500.00
238A Blake Bortles AU/49 60.00 120.00
239A Teddy Bridgewater AU/49 75.00 150.00

2014 Panini Contenders Cracked Ice

*1-100 VETS/22: 12X TO 30X BASIC CARDS
*101-199 ROOK.AU/22: 1X TO 2.5X PLAY.AU/199
*201-240 ROOK.AU/22: .8X TO 2X PLAY.AU/99
MOST HAVE 2-3 CARDS OF EQUAL VALUE
113A Chris Borland AU 8.00 20.00
159B Martavis Bryant AU 75.00 150.00
171A Ryan Shazier AU 50.00 120.00
171B Ryan Shazier AU 50.00 120.00
188A Zach Mettenberger AU 50.00 100.00
201A Aaron Murray AU 60.00 100.00
214A Derek Carr AU 350.00 600.00
216A Donte Moncrief AU EXCH 90.00 150.00
221A Jimmy Garoppolo AU 2500.00 4000.00
227A Odell Beckham Jr. AU 500.00 1000.00
232A Jeremy Hill AU 90.00 150.00
233A Tre Mason AU 75.00 125.00
235A Kelvin Benjamin AU 125.00 250.00
236A Mike Evans AU 150.00 250.00
237A Sammy Watkins AU 100.00 200.00
238A Blake Bortles AU 100.00 200.00
239A Teddy Bridgewater AU 75.00 150.00

2014 Panini Contenders Playoff Ticket

*1-100 VETS/199: 2.5X TO 6X BASIC CARDS
MOST HAVE TWO CARDS OF EQUAL VALUE
EXCH EXPIRATION: 7/8/2016
101A Aaron Donald AU 8.00 20.00
103A Anthony Barr AU 6.00 15.00
104A Antonio Andrews AU 3.00 8.00
105A Arthur Lynch AU 3.00 8.00
107A Brandon Coleman AU 3.00 8.00
108A Solomon Patton AU 4.00 10.00
109A Bruce Ellington AU 3.00 8.00
110A C.J. Fiedorowicz AU 3.00 8.00
112A Calvin Pryor AU 3.00 8.00
113A Chris Borland AU 3.00 8.00
114A Chris Smith AU 3.00 8.00
115A Cody Hoffman AU 3.00 8.00
116A Crockett Gillmore AU 4.00 10.00
118A Cyrus Kouandjio AU 4.00 10.00
119A Darqueze Dennard AU 4.00 10.00
120A Jay Prosch AU 5.00 12.00
120B David Fales AU 6.00 15.00
121A David Yankey AU 3.00 8.00
124A Deone Bucannon AU 3.00 8.00
125A Devin Street AU 3.00 8.00
126A Dominique Easley AU 3.00 8.00
127A Ed Reynolds AU 3.00 8.00
128A Garrett Gilbert AU 3.00 8.00
129A Greg Robinson AU 3.00 8.00
130A Ha Ha Clinton-Dix AU 4.00 10.00
131A Henry Josey AU 3.00 8.00
132A Isaiah Crowell AU 4.00 10.00
133A Christian Kirksey AU 3.00 8.00
133B Jace Amaro AU 3.00 8.00
134A Jackson Jeffcoat AU 4.00 10.00
137A James Wilder Jr. AU 4.00 10.00
138A Jared Abbrederis AU 8.00 20.00
139A Jason Verrett AU 3.00 8.00
140A Jeff Janis AU 3.00 8.00
141A Jerick McKinnon AU 4.00 10.00
142A Jimmie Ward AU 4.00 10.00
143A John Brown AU 5.00 12.00
144A Jordan Lynch AU 4.00 10.00
146A Ja'Wuan James AU 3.00 8.00
147A Keith Wenning AU 4.00 10.00
148A Kevin Norwood AU 3.00 8.00
149A Kony Ealy AU 4.00 10.00
151A Kyle Van Noy AU 4.00 10.00
152A Darrin Reaves AU 4.00 10.00
152B Lache Seastrunk AU 3.00 8.00
153A Lamarcus Joyner AU 4.00 10.00
154A Lorenzo Taliaferro AU 3.00 8.00
155A Senorise Perry AU 4.00 10.00
156A Marcus Roberson AU 4.00 10.00
157A Marcus Smith AU 3.00 8.00
158A Marion Grice AU 3.00 8.00
160A Matt Hazel AU 3.00 8.00
162A Michael Sam AU 3.00 8.00
163A Mike Davis AU 3.00 8.00
164A Pierre Desir AU 3.00 8.00
165A Preston Brown AU 3.00 8.00
166A Quincy Enunwa AU 5.00 12.00
167A Rajion Neal AU 3.00 8.00
168A Ra'Shede Hageman AU 3.00 8.00
169A Richard Rodgers AU 5.00 12.00
171A Ryan Shazier AU 20.00 50.00
172A Scott Crichton AU 3.00 8.00
173A Shaq Evans AU 3.00 8.00
174A Shayne Skov AU 3.00 8.00
175A Stephon Tuitt AU 5.00 12.00
176A Anthony Hitchens AU 3.00 8.00
180A Timmy Jernigan AU 3.00 8.00
181A Travis Swanson AU 3.00 8.00
182A Trent Murphy AU 3.00 8.00
183A Trevor Reilly AU 3.00 8.00
184A Troy Niklas AU 3.00 8.00
185A Tyler Gaffney AU 3.00 8.00
186A Xavier Su'A-Filo AU 4.00 10.00
187A Yawin Smallwood AU 3.00 8.00
188A Zach Mettenberger AU 12.00 30.00
189A Zack Martin AU 10.00 25.00
190A Allen Hurns AU 4.00 10.00
192A Branden Oliver AU 5.00 12.00
193A Rashad Ross AU 3.00 8.00
194A James Wright AU 4.00 10.00
195A Silas Redd AU 6.00 15.00
196A Isaiah Burse AU 3.00 8.00
197A Taylor Gabriel AU 4.00 10.00
198A Orleans Darkwa AU 5.00 12.00
199A Alfred Blue AU 6.00 15.00
200A Philly Brown AU 4.00 10.00
201A Aaron Murray AU/99 5.00 12.00
202A A.J. McCarron AU/99 25.00 60.00
203A Allen Robinson AU/99 20.00 50.00
204A Andre Williams AU/99 12.00 30.00
205A Asa Watson AU/99 5.00 12.00
206A Austin Seferian-Jenkins AU/99 5.00 12.00
207A Brandin Cooks AU/99 8.00 20.00
208A Carlos Hyde AU/99 20.00 50.00
209A Charles Sims AU/99 5.00 12.00
210A Cody Latimer AU/99 6.00 15.00
211A Connor Shaw AU/99 12.00 30.00
212A Davante Adams AU/99 EXCH 25.00 60.00
213A De'Anthony Thomas AU/99 5.00 12.00
214A Derek Carr AU/99 100.00 200.00
215A Devonta Freeman AU/99 30.00 80.00
216A Donte Moncrief AU/99 EXCH 25.00 60.00
217A Dri Archer AU/99 5.00 12.00
218A Eric Ebron AU/99 6.00 15.00
219A Jadeveon Clowney AU/99 6.00 15.00
220A Jarvis Landry AU/99 40.00 80.00
221A Jimmy Garoppolo AU/99 400.00 800.00
222A Jordan Matthews AU/99 8.00 20.00
223A Ka'Deem Carey AU/99 5.00 12.00
224A Khalil Mack AU/99 EXCH 15.00 40.00
225A Logan Thomas AU/99 5.00 12.00
226A Marqise Lee AU/99 6.00 15.00
227A Odell Beckham Jr. AU/99 150.00 250.00
228A Paul Richardson AU/99 10.00 25.00
229A Tajh Boyd AU/99 5.00 12.00
230A Terrance West AU/99 5.00 12.00
231A Tom Savage AU/99 5.00 12.00
232A Jeremy Hill AU/99 20.00 50.00
233A Tre Mason AU/99 12.00 30.00
234A Bishop Sankey AU/99 15.00 40.00
235A Kelvin Benjamin AU/99 40.00 80.00
236A Mike Evans AU/99 50.00 100.00
237A Sammy Watkins AU/99 25.00 60.00
238A Blake Bortles AU/99 12.00 30.00
239A Teddy Bridgewater AU/99 20.00 50.00
240A Johnny Manziel AU/99 12.00 30.00

2014 Panini Contenders Alma Mater Autographs

2 E.Manuel/K.Benjamin 10.00 25.00
4 T.Bridgewater/C.Pryor 15.00 40.00
5 A.McCarron/E.Lacy 6.00 15.00
6 B.Sankey/A.Sfrn-Jnkns 6.00 15.00
7 T.Boyd/S.Watkins 10.00 25.00
8 T.Mathieu/J.Hill 15.00 40.00
9 T.Mason/B.Jackson 50.00 100.00

2014 Panini Contenders Draft Class

*GOLD/199: .5X TO 1.2X BASIC INSERTS
*HOLOGOLD/99: .6X TO 1.5X BASIC INSERTS
RDA1 Johnny Manziel .60 1.50
RDA2 Teddy Bridgewater .60 1.50
RDA3 Blake Bortles .50 1.25
RDA4 Sammy Watkins .60 1.50
RDA5 Mike Evans 1.00 2.50
RDA6 Kelvin Benjamin .60 1.50
RDA7 Bishop Sankey .40 1.00
RDA8 Tre Mason .40 1.00
RDA9 Jeremy Hill .50 1.25
RDA10 Marqise Lee .50 1.25
RDA11 Khalil Mack 1.50 4.00
RDA12 Jordan Matthews .60 1.50
RDA13 Jadeveon Clowney .50 1.25
RDA14 Eric Ebron .50 1.25
RDA15 Dri Archer .40 1.00
RDA16 Donte Moncrief .40 1.00
RDA17 Derek Carr 2.50 6.00
RDA18 Cody Latimer .50 1.25
RDA19 Brandin Cooks .60 1.50
RDA20 Andre Williams .40 1.00

2014 Panini Contenders Draft Class Autographs

RDAAM A.J. McCarron/50* 15.00 40.00
RDAAMU Aaron Murray 3.00 8.00
RDAAW Andre Williams 3.00 8.00
RDABB Blake Bortles/50* 10.00 25.00
RDABC Brandin Cooks EXCH 5.00 12.00
RDABS Bishop Sankey 8.00 20.00
RDACL Cody Latimer 4.00 10.00
RDADA Davante Adams EXCH 10.00 25.00
RDADAR Dri Archer EXCH 3.00 8.00
RDADC Derek Carr/100* 25.00 60.00
RDADM Donte Moncrief EXCH 12.00 30.00
RDADT De'Anthony Thomas 3.00 8.00
RDAEE Eric Ebron/100* 5.00 12.00
RDAJC Jadeveon Clowney/100* 5.00 12.00
RDAJG Jimmy Garoppolo/100* 20.00 50.00
RDAJH Jeremy Hill 4.00 10.00
RDAJM Johnny Manziel/50* 15.00 40.00
RDAJO Jordan Matthews 10.00 25.00
RDAKB Kelvin Benjamin/100* 20.00 40.00
RDAKC Ka'Deem Carey 3.00 8.00
RDAKM Khalil Mack EXCH 8.00 20.00
RDALT Logan Thomas/100* 4.00 10.00
RDAME Mike Evans/100* 20.00 40.00
RDAML Marqise Lee/100* 5.00 12.00
RDAPR Paul Richardson 8.00 20.00
RDASW Sammy Watkins/50* 6.00 15.00
RDATB Teddy Bridgewater/50* 12.00 30.00
RDATM Tre Mason EXCH 10.00 25.00
RDATS Tom Savage 3.00 8.00
RDATW Terrance West 3.00 8.00

2014 Panini Contenders Legendary Contenders

*GOLD/199: .5X TO 1.2X BASIC INSERTS
*HOLOGOLD/99: .6X TO 1.5X BASIC INSERTS
1 Joe Namath 1.50 4.00
2 John Elway 2.00 5.00
3 Lawrence Taylor 3.00 8.00
4 Tony Dorsett 1.25 3.00
5 Bo Jackson 1.50 4.00
6 Jim Kelly 1.25 3.00
7 Steve Young 1.50 4.00
8 Frank Gifford 1.00 2.50
9 Joe Montana 3.00 8.00
10 Ronnie Lott 1.00 2.50

2014 Panini Contenders MVP Contenders

*GOLD/199: .5X TO 1.2X BASIC INSERTS
*HOLOGOLD/99: .6X TO 1.5X BASIC INSERTS
1 Tom Brady 1.50 4.00
2 Peyton Manning 2.50 6.00
3 DeMarco Murray .50 1.25

4 Colin Kaepernick .50 1.25
5 Cam Newton .60 1.50
6 Andrew Luck .75 2.00
7 Drew Brees .60 1.50
8 Calvin Johnson .60 1.50
9 Russell Wilson 1.00 2.50
10 LeSean McCoy .60 1.50

2014 Panini Contenders NFL Ink

NFLCS C.J. Spiller/25* 8.00 20.00
NFLDB Dwayne Bowe/25*
NFLDBR Drew Brees/15* 40.00 80.00
NFLDM DeMarcus Ware/25* 25.00 50.00
NFLEL Eddie Lacy/25* 8.00 20.00
NFLEM Eli Manning/15* 25.00 50.00
NFLGE Gavin Escobar/25* 8.00 20.00
NFLJC Jamaal Charles/25* 20.00 40.00
NFLMJ Mike James/25* 8.00 20.00
NFLMR Matt Ryan/25* 30.00 60.00
NFLMS Matthew Stafford/15* 30.00 60.00
NFLNF Nick Foles/25* 12.00 30.00
NFLRB Ronnie Brown/25* 8.00 20.00
NFLRM Ryan Mallett/15* 10.00 25.00
NFLRS Richard Sherman/15* 60.00 120.00
NFLRT Ryan Tannehill/25* 20.00 40.00
NFLRW Reggie Wayne/25* Retail 10.00 25.00
NFLTH T.Y. Hilton/25* 25.00 50.00
NFLTR Tony Romo/15* 50.00 100.00
NFLVM Von Miller/25* 12.00 30.00

2014 Panini Contenders Rookie Ink

SP ANNOUNCED PRINT RUN LESS THAN 250
1 Michael Sam 2.50 6.00
2 David Fales SP/75* Retail 20.00 40.00
3 Anthony Barr 2.50 6.00
5 Ha Ha Clinton-Dix 3.00 8.00
6 Greg Robinson Retail 2.50 6.00
7 Stephon Tuitt 4.00 10.00
8 Zack Martin 6.00 15.00
10 Ryan Shazier 4.00 10.00
11 Rajion Neal Retail 2.50 6.00
12 Lache Seastrunk SP/75* 4.00 10.00
13 Shaq Evans Retail 6.00 15.00
15 Marcus Roberson Retail 3.00 8.00
16 Devin Street 6.00 15.00
17 Dominique Easley Retail 2.50 6.00
18 Jason Verrett 2.50 6.00
20 Timmy Jernigan 2.50 6.00
22 Jeff Janis SP/100* 4.00 10.00
23 Jace Amaro SP/100* 4.00 10.00
24 Darqueze Dennard Retail 3.00 8.00
25 Aaron Donald Retail 6.00 15.00
27 C.J. Fiedorowicz 2.50 6.00
28 Chris Borland 2.50 6.00
29 Cyrus Kouandjio 3.00 8.00
30 Isaiah Crowell 3.00 8.00

2014 Panini Contenders Rookie Ink Rookie Premiere

PANINI ANNOUNCED PRINT RUNS BELOW
EXCH EXPIRATION: 7/8/2016
RRIAJM A.J. McCarron/75* 10.00 25.00
RRIAM Aaron Murray 3.00 8.00
RRIAR Allen Robinson 8.00 20.00
RRIASJ Austin Seferian-Jenkins 3.00 8.00
RRIAW Asa Watson 3.00 8.00
RRIAWI Andre Williams 3.00 8.00
RRIBB Blake Bortles/75* 5.00 12.00
RRIBC Brandin Cooks 5.00 12.00
RRIBS Bishop Sankey 8.00 20.00
RRICH Carlos Hyde 4.00 10.00
RRICL Cody Latimer 4.00 10.00
RRICS Connor Shaw 3.00 8.00
RRICSI Charles Sims/100* 4.00 10.00
RRIDA Davante Adams EXCH 12.00 30.00
RRIDAR Dri Archer 3.00 8.00
RRIDC Derek Carr/50* 30.00 60.00
RRIDF Devonta Freeman 12.00 30.00
RRIDM Donte Moncrief EXCH 8.00 20.00
RRIDT De'Anthony Thomas 3.00 8.00
RRIEE Eric Ebron/25* 5.00 12.00
RRIJC Jadeveon Clowney/75* 5.00 12.00
RRIJG Jimmy Garoppolo/87* 150.00 250.00
RRIJH Jeremy Hill 4.00 10.00
RRIJL Jarvis Landry 6.00 15.00
RRIJM Johnny Manziel/75* 6.00 15.00
RRIJO Jordan Matthews 5.00 12.00
RRIKB Kelvin Benjamin/100* 20.00 40.00
RRIKC Ka'Deem Carey/96* 6.00 15.00
RRIKM Khalil Mack EXCH 8.00 20.00
RRILT Logan Thomas/100* 4.00 10.00
RRIME Mike Evans/100* 20.00 40.00
RRIML Marqise Lee/75* 5.00 12.00
RRIOB Odell Beckham Jr. 75.00 150.00
RRIPR Paul Richardson 8.00 20.00
RRISW Sammy Watkins/75* 30.00 60.00
RRITB Teddy Bridgewater/75* 6.00 15.00
RRITJ Tajh Boyd 4.00 10.00
RRITM Tre Mason 3.00 8.00
RRITS Tom Savage 3.00 8.00
RRITW Terrance West 3.00 8.00

2014 Panini Contenders Rookie Ink Rookie Premiere Gold

*GOLD/25: .75X TO 2X BASIC AU
GOLD/25: .6X TO 1.5X BASIC AU/250
RRIME Mike Evans 50.00 100.00
RRIOB Odell Beckham Jr. 100.00 200.00

2014 Panini Contenders Rookie Ticket Buyback Autographs

56 Danny Woodhead/39 50.00 100.00

2014 Panini Contenders Rookie Ticket Jerseys

SOME HAVE TWO CARDS PRICED EQUALLY
1 Aaron Murray 1.25 3.00
2 Logan Thomas 1.25 3.00
3 Allen Robinson 2.00 5.00
4 Andre Williams 1.25 3.00
5 Asa Watson 1.50 4.00
6 Austin Seferian-Jenkins 1.25 3.00
7 Brandin Cooks 2.00 5.00
8 Carlos Hyde 1.50 4.00
9 Charles Sims 1.25 3.00
10 Cody Latimer 1.50 4.00
11 Jace Amaro SP/20*
12 Davante Adams 2.00 5.00
13 De'Anthony Thomas 1.25 3.00
14 Terrance West 1.25 3.00
15 Devonta Freeman 2.00 5.00
16 Donte Moncrief 1.25 3.00
17 Dri Archer 1.25 3.00
18 Eric Ebron 1.50 4.00
19 Tajh Boyd 1.25 3.00
20 Jarvis Landry 2.50 6.00
21A Jimmy Garoppolo 10.00 25.00
21B Jimmy Garoppolo 10.00 25.00
22A Jordan Matthews 2.00 5.00
22B Jordan Matthews 2.00 5.00
23A Ka'Deem Carey 1.25 3.00
23B Ka'Deem Carey 1.25 3.00
24A Khalil Mack 5.00 12.00
24B Khalil Mack 5.00 12.00
25A A.J. McCarron 1.25 3.00
25B A.J. McCarron 1.25 3.00
26A Marqise Lee 1.50 4.00
26B Marqise Lee 1.50 4.00
27A Odell Beckham Jr. 8.00 20.00
27B Odell Beckham Jr. 8.00 20.00
28A Paul Richardson 1.50 4.00
28B Paul Richardson 1.50 4.00
29A Jadeveon Clowney 1.50 4.00
29B Jadeveon Clowney 1.50 4.00
30A Derek Carr 3.00 8.00
30B Derek Carr 3.00 8.00
31A Tom Savage 1.25 3.00
31B Tom Savage 1.25 3.00
32A Jeremy Hill 1.50 4.00
32B Jeremy Hill 1.50 4.00
33A Tre Mason 1.25 3.00
33B Tre Mason 1.25 3.00
34A Bishop Sankey 1.25 3.00
34B Bishop Sankey 1.25 3.00
35A Kelvin Benjamin 3.00 8.00
35B Kelvin Benjamin 3.00 8.00
36A Mike Evans 3.00 8.00
36B Mike Evans 3.00 8.00
37A Sammy Watkins 4.00 10.00
37B Sammy Watkins 4.00 10.00
38A Blake Bortles 1.50 4.00
38B Blake Bortles 1.50 4.00
39A Teddy Bridgewater 3.00 8.00
39B Teddy Bridgewater 3.00 8.00
40A Johnny Manziel 2.00 5.00
40B Johnny Manziel 2.00 5.00

2014 Panini Contenders Round Numbers

*GOLD/199: .5X TO 1.2X BASIC INSERTS
*HOLOGOLD/99: .6X TO 1.5X BASIC INSERTS
1 B.Bortles/J.Manziel .75 2.00
2 J.Clowney/D.Ford .60 1.50
3 D.Carr/J.Garoppolo 4.00 10.00
4 M.Lee/A.Robinson .75 2.00
5 T.Mason/D.Archer .50 1.25
6 C.Fiedorowicz/L.Nix III .50 1.25
7 D.Moncrief/T.West .50 1.25
8 D.Freeman/A.Williams .75 2.00
9 K.Carey/D.Thomas .50 1.25
10 L.Thomas/T.Savage .50 1.25
11 A.Murray/A.McCarron .50 1.25
12 Z.Mettenberger/D.Fales .50 1.25
13 J.McKinnon/J.Brown .75 2.00
14 J.Wright/J.Janis .60 1.50
15 S.Watkins /M.Evans .75 2.00
16 C.Pryor/H.Clinton-Dix .60 1.50
17 B.Bortles/T.Bridgewater .75 2.00
18 B.Cooks/K.Benjamin .75 2.00
19 A.Sfrn-Jnkns/J.Amaro .50 1.25
20 B.Sankey/J.Hill .60 1.50

2014 Panini Contenders Round Numbers Autographs

3 D.Carr/J.Garoppolo/25 200.00 400.00
4 M.Lee/A.Robinson/25
6 C.Fiedorowicz/L.Nix III/25 6.00 15.00
8 D.Freeman/A.Williams/25 20.00 50.00
9 K.Carey/D.Thomas/25 6.00 15.00
10 L.Thomas/T.Savage/25 6.00 15.00
11 A.Murray/A.McCarron/25 20.00 50.00
13 J.Brown/J.McKinnon/25 10.00 25.00
14 J.Wright/J.Janis/25
15 S.Watkins /M.Evans/25 50.00 100.00
16 C.Pryor/H.Clinton-Dix/25 8.00 20.00
18 B.Cooks/K.Benjamin/25 40.00 80.00
19 A.Sfrn-Jnkns/J.Amaro/25 8.00 20.00
20 B.Sankey/J.Hill/25 8.00 20.00

2014 Panini Contenders ROY Contenders

*GOLD/199: .5X TO 1.2X BASIC INSERTS
*HOLOGOLD/99: .6X TO 1.5X BASIC INSERTS
ROY1 Johnny Manziel .60 1.50
ROY2 Derek Carr 2.50 6.00
ROY3 Teddy Bridgewater .60 1.50
ROY4 Blake Bortles .50 1.25
ROY5 Sammy Watkins .60 1.50
ROY6 Marqise Lee .50 1.25
ROY7 Jordan Matthews .60 1.50
ROY8 Brandin Cooks .60 1.50
ROY9 Mike Evans 1.00 2.50
ROY10 Davante Adams .60 1.50
ROY11 Kelvin Benjamin .60 1.50
ROY12 Bishop Sankey .40 1.00
ROY13 Tre Mason .40 1.00
ROY14 Jeremy Hill .50 1.25
ROY15 Andre Williams .40 1.00
ROY16 Dri Archer .40 1.00
ROY17 Terrance West .40 1.00
ROY18 Khalil Mack 1.50 4.00
ROY19 Jadeveon Clowney .50 1.25
ROY20 Eric Ebron .50 1.25

2014 Panini Contenders ROY Contenders Autographs

SP ANNOUNCED PRINT RUN LESS THAN 250
ROYAM A.J. McCarron SP/250* 10.00 25.00
ROYAMU Aaron Murray 3.00 8.00
ROYAW Andre Williams 3.00 8.00
ROYBB Blake Bortles SP/250* 5.00 12.00
ROYBC Brandin Cooks 5.00 12.00
ROYBS Bishop Sankey 8.00 20.00
ROYCL Cody Latimer 4.00 10.00
ROYDA Davante Adams EXCH 12.00 30.00
ROYDAR Dri Archer 3.00 8.00
ROYDC Derek Carr SP/250* 50.00 100.00
ROYDM Donte Moncrief EXCH 12.00 30.00
ROYDT De'Anthony Thomas 3.00 8.00
ROYEE Eric Ebron SP/250* 5.00 12.00
ROYJC Jadeveon Clowney SP/250* 5.00 12.00
ROYJG Jimmy Garoppolo SP/250* 150.00 250.00
ROYJH Jeremy Hill 10.00 25.00
ROYJM Johnny Manziel SP/250* 6.00 15.00
ROYJO Jordan Matthews 5.00 12.00
ROYKB Kelvin Benjamin SP/250* 12.00 30.00
ROYKC Ka'Deem Carey 3.00 8.00
ROYKM Khalil Mack EXCH 8.00 20.00
ROYLT Logan Thomas 3.00 8.00
ROYME Mike Evans SP/250* 25.00 50.00
ROYML Marqise Lee SP/250* 5.00 12.00
ROYPR Paul Richardson 8.00 20.00
ROYSW Sammy Watkins SP/250* 25.00 60.00
ROYTB Teddy Bridgewater SP/250* 6.00 15.00
ROYTM Tre Mason 10.00 25.00
ROYTS Tom Savage SP/250* 4.00 10.00
ROYTW Terrance West 3.00 8.00

2014 Panini Contenders Touchdown Tandems

*GOLD/199: .5X TO 1.2X BASIC INSERTS
*HOLOGOLD/99: .6X TO 1.5X BASIC INSERTS
1 T.Romo 1.50 4.00
D.Bryant
2 P.Manning 1.50 4.00
D.Thomas
3 E.Manning .60 1.50
V.Cruz
4 C.Newton .75 2.00
K.Benjamin
5 A.Smith .60 1.50
D.Bowe
6 J.Cutler .60 1.50
A.Jeffery
7 D.Carr 3.00 8.00
J.Jones
8 A.Rodgers 2.50 6.00
J.Nelson
9 R.Griffin III .60 1.50
P.Garcon
10 M.Stafford .75 2.00
C.Johnson
11 M.Eyan .75 2.00
J.Jones
12 N.Foles .75 2.00
J.Matthews
13 A.Luck 1.00 2.50
T.Hilton
14 E.Manuel .75 2.00
S.Watkins
15 P.Rivers .75 2.00
A.Gates
16 R.Wilson 1.25 3.00
P.Harvin
17 J.Flacco .60 1.50
S.Smith
18 R.Tannehill .60 1.50
M.Wallace
19 B.Bortles .60 1.50
M.Lee
20 T.Brady 2.00 5.00
D.Amendola

2015 Panini Contenders

101-241 A TEAM HELMET UPPER LEFT
101-241 B TEAM LOGO UPPER LEFT
101-241 C PLAYER IN COLLEGE JSY
*UNLISTED B AU VARIATION: .6X TO 1.5X AU RC
1 Peyton Manning .60 1.50
2 C.J. Anderson .25 .60
3 Demaryius Thomas .25 .60
4 Alex Smith .25 .60
5 Jeremy Maclin .20 .50
6 Jamaal Charles .25 .60
7 Derek Carr .30 .75
8 Latavius Murray .20 .50
9 Charles Woodson .30 .75
10 Philip Rivers .30 .75
11 Malcom Floyd .20 .50
12 Antonio Gates .20 .50
13 Carson Palmer .25 .60
14 Andre Ellington .20 .50
15 Larry Fitzgerald .25 .60
16 Colin Kaepernick .25 .60
17 Anquan Boldin .20 .50
18 Carlos Hyde .20 .50
19 Russell Wilson .40 1.00
20 Doug Baldwin .25 .60
21 Marshawn Lynch .25 .60
22 Richard Sherman .30 .75
23 Nick Foles .25 .60
24 Tavon Austin .20 .50
25 Jared Cook .20 .50
26 Arian Foster .25 .60
27 DeAndre Hopkins .25 .60
28 J.J. Watt .30 .75
29 Andrew Luck .40 1.00
30 Frank Gore .25 .60
31 T.Y. Hilton .25 .60
32 Andre Johnson .25 .60
33 Blake Bortles .20 .50
34 Marqise Lee .20 .50
35 Julius Thomas .20 .50
36 Delanie Walker .20 .50
37 Bishop Sankey .20 .50
38 Kendall Wright .20 .50
39 Matt Ryan .25 .60
40 Julio Jones .30 .75
41 Devonta Freeman .25 .60
42 Cam Newton .30 .75
43 Kelvin Benjamin .25 .60
44 Jonathan Stewart .20 .50
45 Vincent Jackson .20 .50
46 Doug Martin .25 .60
47 Mike Evans .25 .60
48 Joe Flacco .25 .60
49 Justin Forsett .25 .60
50 Steve Smith .25 .60
51 Andy Dalton .25 .60
52 Jeremy Hill .25 .60
53 A.J. Green .30 .75
54 Josh McCown .25 .60
55 Isaiah Crowell .20 .50
56 Travis Benjamin .20 .50
57 Ben Roethlisberger .30 .75
58 Le'Veon Bell .25 .60
59 Antonio Brown .30 .75
60 Jay Cutler .20 .50
61 Matt Forte .20 .50
62 Alshon Jeffery .25 .60
63 Matthew Stafford .25 .60
64 Calvin Johnson .30 .75
65 Golden Tate .20 .50
66 Aaron Rodgers .60 1.50
67 Jordy Nelson .25 .60
68 Eddie Lacy .20 .50
69 Randall Cobb .25 .60
70 Teddy Bridgewater .25 .60
71 Adrian Peterson .30 .75
72 Mike Wallace .20 .50
73 Sammy Watkins .25 .60
74 LeSean McCoy .30 .75
75 Tyrod Taylor .25 .60
76 Ryan Tannehill .25 .60
77 Ndamukong Suh .25 .60
78 Jarvis Landry .25 .60
79 Tom Brady .75 2.00
80 Julian Edelman .30 .75
81 Rob Gronkowski .30 .75
82 LeGarrette Blount .25 .60
83 Brandon Marshall .20 .50
84 Geno Smith .20 .50
85 Eric Decker .20 .50
86 Marques Colston .20 .50
87 Tony Romo .25 .60
88 Dez Bryant .30 .75
89 Drew Brees .30 .75
90 Joseph Randle .20 .50
91 Emmanuel Sanders .25 .60
92 Eli Manning .25 .60
93 Victor Cruz .25 .60
94 Odell Beckham Jr. .30 .75
95 DeMarco Murray .25 .60
96 Sam Bradford .20 .50
97 Jordan Matthews .25 .60
98 Kirk Cousins .30 .75
99 DeSean Jackson .25 .60
100 Alfred Morris .20 .50
101A Kenny Bell AU RC 3.00 8.00
101B Kenny Bell AU/100* SP B 6.00 15.00
102A Cameron Artis-Payne AU/250* RC SP A 3.00 8.00
102B Cameron Artis-Payne AU/100* SP B 12.00 30.00
103 Dante Fowler Jr. AU/170* RC SP A
104A Vic Beasley Jr. AU/250* RC SP A 4.00 10.00
104B Vic Beasley Jr. AU/124* SP A 5.00 12.00
105 Trae Waynes AU/150* RC 4.00 10.00
106 Danny Shelton AU RC 2.00 5.00
108 Arik Armstead AU RC 2.00 5.00
109A Marcus Peters AU/50* RC SP B
109B Marcus Peters AU/24* SP B
110A Bud Dupree AU/250* RC SP A 8.00 20.00
110B Bud Dupree AU/100* SP B 10.00 25.00
111A Shane Ray AU RC
111B Shane Ray AU/100* SP B
112 Shaq Thompson AU/50* RC SP B 40.00 80.00
113 Stephone Anthony AU RC 2.00 5.00
114 Landon Collins AU/100* RC SP B 25.00 50.00
115 Mario Edwards Jr. AU RC 2.00 5.00
116 Eddie Goldman AU RC 2.00 5.00
117A Jalen Collins AU RC 2.00 5.00
117B Jalen Collins AU/100* SP B
118A Benardrick McKinney AU RC 2.00 5.00
118B Benardrick McKinney AU/100* SP B 5.00 12.00
119 Eric Kendricks AU RC 2.00 5.00
120A Eric Rowe AU RC 2.00 5.00
121B Denzel Perryman AU/100* SP B
122 Ronald Darby AU/48* RC SP B 60.00 120.00
123 Senquez Golson AU RC 2.00 5.00
124 Markus Golden AU RC 2.00 5.00
125 Randy Gregory AU/50* RC SP B 50.00 100.00
126 Quinten Rollins AU RC 4.00 10.00
127A Clive Walford AU RC 2.00 5.00
127B Clive Walford AU/100* SP B
128A Owamagbe Odighizuwa AU RC 2.50 6.00
128B Owamagbe Odighizuwa AU/100* SP B
129 P.J. Williams AU RC 2.50 6.00
130A Eli Harold AU/266* RC A 10.00 25.00
130B Eli Harold AU/100* SP B 12.00 30.00
131A Tyler Kroft AU RC 2.50 6.00
131B Tyler Kroft AU/200* SP A 4.00 10.00
132A Danielle Hunter AU RC 2.50 6.00
132B Danielle Hunter AU/100* SP B
133 Carl Davis AU RC 2.50 6.00
134A Dezmin Lewis AU RC 2.00 5.00
134B Dezmin Lewis AU/100* SP B
135 Paul Dawson AU RC 2.50 6.00
136 Trey Flowers AU RC 3.00 8.00
137A Blake Bell AU RC 3.00 8.00
137B Blake Bell AU/100* SP B
138A Josh Shaw AU RC 3.00 8.00
138B Josh Shaw AU/100* SP B 6.00 15.00
139 Kwon Alexander AU RC 2.50 6.00
140 Gerald Christian AU RC 2.50 6.00
141 MyCole Pruitt AU RC 2.00 5.00
142A Davis Tull AU RC 2.00 5.00
142B Davis Tull AU/100* SP B 4.00 10.00
143A J.J. Nelson AU RC 2.00 5.00
143B J.J. Nelson AU/100* SP B 8.00 20.00
144A Jesse James AU RC 2.50 6.00
144B Jesse James AU/100* SP B 12.00 30.00
145A Nick O'Leary AU RC 2.00 5.00
145B Nick O'Leary AU/100* SP B
146A Darren Waller AU RC 2.50 6.00
146B Darren Waller AU/100* SP B
147A Josh Robinson AU RC
147B Josh Robinson AU/100* SP B 4.00 10.00
148 Ben Koyack AU/221* RC SP A 5.00 12.00
149A Marcus Murphy AU/254* RC SP A
149B Marcus Murphy AU/100* SP B
150A Deontay Greenberry AU/254* RC SP A 3.00 8.00
150B Deontay Greenberry AU/100* SP B 6.00 15.00
151 Ifo Ekpre-Olomu AU RC 2.00 5.00
152 DaVaris Daniels AU RC 2.00 5.00
153A Tre McBride AU RC 2.00 5.00
153B Tre McBride AU/100* SP B
154 Antwan Goodley AU RC 2.00 5.00
155A Titus Davis AU RC 2.50 6.00
155B Titus Davis AU/100* SP B 5.00 12.00
156 Rannell Hall AU RC 2.00 5.00
157A Mario Alford AU RC 2.00 5.00
157B Mario Alford AU/100* SP B 4.00 10.00
158 Malcom Brown AU/198* RC SP A 3.00 8.00
159 Josh Harper AU RC 2.00 5.00
160 Taylor Heinicke AU RC 3.00 8.00
161 Jeff Heuerman AU RC 2.50 6.00
162A Tony Lippett AU/100* RC SP B 15.00 40.00
162B Tony Lippett AU/100* SP B
163 Preston Smith AU RC 2.50 6.00
164 Devin Gardner AU RC 3.00 8.00
165 Bryan Bennett AU RC 2.00 5.00
166 Michael Bennett AU RC 2.00 5.00
167 Jordan Taylor AU RC 2.50 6.00
168 Da'Ron Brown AU RC 2.00 5.00
169 Michael Dyer AU RC 3.00 8.00
170A Eric Tomlinson AU RC 2.50 6.00
170B Eric Tomlinson AU/100* SP B
171 DeAndrew White AU/47* RC SP B 75.00 150.00
172A Derron Smith AU RC 2.00 5.00
172B Derron Smith AU SP 3.00 8.00
173A Cameron Erving AU RC 2.50 6.00
173B Cameron Erving AU/100* SP B 10.00 25.00
174 Andrus Peat AU RC 2.00 5.00
175 Dres Anderson AU RC 2.00 5.00
176 Cody Fajardo AU RC 2.50 6.00
177A Levi Norwood AU RC 2.00 5.00
177B Levi Norwood AU SP 3.00 8.00
178 Malcolm Brown AU RC 2.50 6.00
179 Nate Orchard AU RC 2.00 5.00
180A Shane Carden AU RC 2.00 5.00
180B Shane Carden AU SP B 4.00 10.00
181 Ereck Flowers AU RC 2.50 6.00
182 Cedric Ogbuehi AU RC 2.00 5.00
183A Nick Boyle AU/248* RC SP A 3.00 8.00
183B Nick Boyle AU/100* SP B
184A Terrence Magee
184B Terrence Magee AU/100* SP B 6.00 15.00
185 Byron Jones AU RC 6.00 15.00
186 Charcandrick West AU RC 2.50 6.00
187 Lorenzo Mauldin AU/174* RC SP A 3.00 8.00
188 Brandon Scherff AU RC 3.00 8.00
189 Hau'oli Kikaha AU RC 2.50 6.00
190 Geneo Grissom AU RC 2.00 5.00
191 Jaquiski Tartt AU RC 2.00 5.00
192 Corey Grant AU RC 3.00 8.00
193 Dreamius Smith AU RC 5.00 12.00
194A Kenny Hilliard AU RC 2.00 5.00
194B Kenny Hilliard AU/100* SP B 4.00 10.00
195 Dominique Brown AU RC 2.00 5.00
196 Kurtis Drummond AU RC 2.50 6.00
197 Kevin White AU RC 2.50 6.00
198A Doran Grant AU RC 3.00 8.00
198B Doran Grant AU/100* SP B
199A Kaelin Clay AU RC 2.00 5.00
199B Kaelin Clay AU/200* SP A
200 Jordan Phillips AU RC 2.00 5.00
201A Melvin Gordon AU RC 15.00 40.00
201B Melvin Gordon AU/50* SP B
201C Melvin Gordon AU/50* SP B
202A Ameer Abdullah AU/300* RC SP A 12.00 30.00
202B Ameer Abdullah AU/50* SP B 25.00 50.00
202C Ameer Abdullah AU/50* SP B
203A Breshad Perriman AU/92* RC SP B 40.00 80.00
203B Breshad Perriman AU/25* SP B
203C Breshad Perriman AU/25* SP B 12.00 30.00
204A Brett Hundley AU/100* RC SP B 75.00 150.00
204B Brett Hundley AU/25* SP 75.00 150.00
205A Bryce Petty AU RC B 8.00 20.00
205B Bryce Petty AU/100* SP 25.00 50.00
206A Buck Allen AU/201* RC SP A 5.00 12.00
206B Buck Allen AU/25* SP B 25.00 50.00
207A Chris Conley AU RC 2.00 5.00
207B Chris Conley AU/80* SP B
208A David Cobb AU RC 2.00 5.00
208B David Cobb AU/100* SP B 80.00 20.00
209A David Johnson AU RC 25.00 50.00
209B David Johnson AU/200* SP A 50.00 100.00
210A DeVante Parker AU RC 10.00 25.00
210B DeVante Parker/50* SP B 50.00 100.00
210C DeVante Parker AU/50* SP B
211A Devin Funchess AU/250* RC SP A 8.00 20.00
211B Devin Funchess AU/50* SP B 10.00 25.00
211C Devin Funchess AU/50* SP B 10.00 25.00
212A Devin Smith AU/201* RC SP A 6.00 15.00
212B Devin Smith AU/100* SP B 12.00 30.00
212C Devin Smith AU/50* SP B 12.00 30.00
213A Dorial Green-Beckham AU RC 2.00 5.00
213B Dorial Green-Beckham AU/50* SP B 5.00 12.00
214A Duke Johnson AU RC 5.00 12.00
214B Duke Johnson AU/50* SP B 8.00 20.00
215A Garrett Grayson AU/100* RC SP B 25.00 60.00
215B Garrett Grayson AU/50* SP B 25.00 60.00
215C Garrett Grayson AU/50* SP B 25.00 60.00
216A Jaelen Strong AU/100* RC SP B 40.00 80.00
216B Jaelen Strong AU/50* SP B 40.00 80.00
217A Jameis Winston AU RC 40.00 80.00
217B Jameis Winston AU/25* SP B 250.00 400.00
217C Jameis Winston AU/25* SP B 125.00 200.00
218A Jamison Crowder AU RC 6.00 15.00
218B Jamison Crowder AU/50* SP B 30.00 60.00
219A Jay Ajayi AU/201* RC SP A 6.00 15.00
219B Jay Ajayi AU/50* SP 8.00 20.00
220A Jeremy Langford AU RC 12.00 30.00
220B Jeremy Langford AU/100* SP B 20.00 40.00
221A Justin Hardy AU RC 2.00 5.00
221B Justin Hardy AU/250* SP A 6.00 15.00
222A Karlos Williams AU RC 2.00 5.00
222B Karlos Williams AU/250* SP A 15.00 40.00
223A Kevin White AU/200* RC SP A 4.00 10.00
223B Kevin White AU/100* SP B 5.00 12.00
223C Kevin White AU/25* SP B 8.00 20.00
224A Leonard Williams AU/201* RC SP A 3.00 8.00
224B Leonard Williams AU/150* SP A 4.00 10.00
225A Marcus Mariota AU RC 40.00 80.00
225B Marcus Mariota AU/24* SP B 150.00 300.00
225C Marcus Mariota AU/50* SP B 100.00 200.00
226A Matt Jones AU RC 8.00 20.00
226B Matt Jones AU/250* SP A 20.00 50.00
227A Maxx Williams AU RC 5.00 12.00
227B Maxx Williams AU/250* SP A 6.00 15.00
228A Amari Cooper AU RC 50.00 100.00
228B Amari Cooper AU/50* SP B 60.00 125.00
228C Amari Cooper AU/30* SP B 100.00 200.00
229A Mike Davis AU/201* RC SP A 6.00 15.00
229B Mike Davis AU/85* SP B 10.00 25.00
230A Nelson Agholor AU/200* RC SP A 6.00 15.00
230B Nelson Agholor AU/50* SP B 25.00 50.00
230C Nelson Agholor AU/50* SP 12.00 30.00
231A Phillip Dorsett AU RC SP B 6.00 15.00
231B Phillip Dorsett AU/50* SP 15.00 40.00
231C Phillip Dorsett AU/150* SP 4.00 10.00
232A Rashad Greene AU RC 2.00 5.00
232B Rashad Greene AU/50* SP B 8.00 20.00
233A Sammie Coates AU RC SP B 8.00 20.00
233B Sammie Coates AU/144* SP A 12.00 30.00
233C Sammie Coates AU/200* SP 10.00 25.00
234A Sean Mannion AU/131* RC SP A 8.00 20.00
234B Sean Mannion AU/100* SP B 10.00 25.00
235A Stefon Diggs AU RC 10.00 25.00
235B Stefon Diggs AU/200* SP A 25.00 50.00
236A T.J. Yeldon AU RC 2.00 5.00
236B T.J. Yeldon AU/50* SP B 15.00 30.00
236C T.J. Yeldon AU/50* SP B 5.00 12.00
237A Tevin Coleman AU/200* RC SP A 6.00 15.00
237B Tevin Coleman AU/50* SP B 30.00 60.00
237C Tevin Coleman AU/50* SP B
238A Todd Gurley AU RC 40.00 80.00
238B Todd Gurley AU/145* SP A 75.00 150.00
238C Todd Gurley AU/145* SP A 75.00 150.00
239A Ty Montgomery AU RC 2.00 5.00
239B Ty Montgomery AU/200* SP A
240A Tyler Lockett AU RC 3.00 8.00
240B Tyler Lockett AU/200* SP A 5.00 12.00
240C Tyler Lockett AU/50* SP B
241A Vince Mayle AU RC 2.50 6.00
241B Vince Mayle AU/50* SP
242 Gerod Holliman AU RC 3.00 8.00
243 Charles Gaines AU RC 3.00 8.00
244 Ramik Wilson AU RC 2.50 6.00
245 Lorenzo Doss AU RC 2.00 5.00
246 C.J. Uzomah AU RC 2.00 5.00
247 Casey Pierce AU RC 2.00 5.00
248 Jahwan Edwards AU RC 2.50 6.00
249 Trey Williams AU/174* RC SP A 4.00 10.00
250 Wes Saxton AU RC 2.50 6.00
251 Lucky Whitehead AU RC 5.00 12.00
252 DeAndre Smelter AU RC 2.00 5.00
253 Trevor Siemian AU RC 12.00 30.00
254 Thomas Rawls AU RC 5.00 12.00
255 Damarious Randall AU RC 2.50 6.00
256 Geremy Davis AU RC 2.50 6.00
257 Quandre Diggs AU RC 2.00 5.00
258 Jaxon Shipley AU/174** RC SP A 3.00 8.00
259 Jalston Fowler AU RC 2.50 6.00
260 Chris Harper AU RC 2.50 6.00
261 Keith Mumphery AU RC 2.00 5.00
262 Terron Ward AU RC 2.50 6.00
263 Alonzo Harris AU RC 3.00 8.00
264 Nick Marshall AU RC 3.00 8.00
265 E.J. Bibbs AU RC 2.50 6.00
266 Cameron Meredith AU RC 8.00 20.00
267 James O'Shaughnessy AU RC 2.00 5.00
268 Malcolm Johnson AU RC 2.00 5.00
269 Anthony Harris AU RC 5.00 12.00
270 La'el Collins AU RC 2.50 6.00
271 Jarryd Hayne RC/100* SP B 30.00 60.00
272 T.J. Clemmings AU RC 2.00 5.00
273 D'Joun Smith AU RC 3.00 8.00
274 Frank Clark AU RC 5.00 12.00
275 Jordan Richards AU RC 2.00 5.00
276 Austin Hill AU RC 2.00 5.00
277 Jake Ryan AU RC 5.00 12.00
278 Zack Hodges AU RC 2.00 5.00
279 Zach Zenner AU RC 10.00 25.00
280 Zach Vigil AU RC 2.50 6.00
281 Gus Johnson AU RC 3.00 8.00
282 Jake Waters AU RC 2.50 6.00
283 A.J. Cann AU RC 2.50 6.00
284 Tyrell Williams AU RC 2.50 6.00
285 Tyler Murphy AU RC 3.00 8.00
286 Jordan Hicks AU RC 6.00 15.00
287 Kamar Aiken AU RC 2.50 6.00
288 Willie Snead AU RC 8.00 20.00
289 Chip Kelly AU/148* SP A 15.00 40.00
290 Dan Quinn AU 12.00 30.00
291 Chuck Pagano AU/98* SP B 15.00 40.00
292 Bruce Arians AU/148* SP A 12.00 30.00
293 Sean Payton AU/232* SP A 15.00 40.00

2015 Panini Contenders Championship Ticket

101A Kenny Bell AU/99 6.00 15.00
101B Kenny Bell AU/25 12.00 30.00
102A Cameron Artis-Payne AU/25 8.00 20.00
102B Cameron Artis-Payne AU/25 8.00 20.00
103 Dante Fowler Jr. AU/99 6.00 15.00
104A Vic Beasley Jr. AU/99 5.00 12.00
104B Vic Beasley Jr. AU/99 5.00 12.00
105 Trae Waynes AU/49 6.00 15.00
106 Danny Shelton AU/99 4.00 10.00
108 Arik Armstead AU/99 4.00 10.00
110A Bud Dupree AU/25 10.00 25.00
110B Bud Dupree AU/25 10.00 25.00
111B Shane Ray AU/25 20.00 40.00
112 Shaq Thompson AU/99 5.00 12.00
113 Stephone Anthony AU/99 4.00 10.00
114 Landon Collins AU/49 8.00 20.00
115 Mario Edwards Jr. AU/99 4.00 10.00
116 Eddie Goldman AU/99 4.00 10.00
117 Jalen Collins AU/99 4.00 10.00
118A Benardrick McKinney AU/99 4.00 10.00
118B Benardrick McKinney AU/25 8.00 20.00
119 Eric Kendricks AU/99 4.00 10.00
120 Eric Rowe AU/99 4.00 10.00
123 Senquez Golson AU/99 4.00 10.00
124A Markus Golden AU/99 4.00 10.00
124B Markus Golden AU/99 4.00 10.00
126 Quinten Rollins AU/99 8.00 20.00
127A Clive Walford AU/99 4.00 10.00
127B Clive Walford AU/25 30.00 60.00
128A Owamagbe Odighizuwa AU/99 5.00 12.00
128B Owamagbe Odighizuwa AU/25 10.00 25.00
129 P.J. Williams AU/99 5.00 12.00
130A Eli Harold AU/25 12.00 30.00
130B Eli Harold AU/25 12.00 30.00
131A Tyler Kroft AU/99 5.00 12.00
131B Tyler Kroft AU/99 5.00 12.00
132A Danielle Hunter AU/99 5.00 12.00
132B Danielle Hunter AU/25 10.00 25.00
133 Carl Davis AU/99 5.00 12.00
134A Dezmin Lewis AU/99 4.00 10.00
134B Dezmin Lewis AU/25 8.00 20.00
135 Paul Dawson AU/99 5.00 12.00
136 Trey Flowers AU/99 6.00 15.00
137A Blake Bell AU/99 6.00 15.00
137B Blake Bell AU/25 12.00 30.00
138A Josh Shaw AU/99 6.00 15.00
138B Josh Shaw AU/25 12.00 30.00
139 Kwon Alexander AU/99 5.00 12.00
140 Gerald Christian AU/99 5.00 12.00
141 MyCole Pruitt AU/99 4.00 10.00
142A Davis Tull AU/99 4.00 10.00
142B Davis Tull AU/25 8.00 20.00
143A J.J. Nelson AU/99 4.00 10.00
143B J.J. Nelson AU/25 8.00 20.00
144A Jesse James AU/99 5.00 12.00
144B Jesse James AU/25 30.00 60.00
145A Nick O'Leary AU/99 4.00 10.00
145B Nick O'Leary AU/25 8.00 20.00
146A Darren Waller AU/99 5.00 12.00
146B Darren Waller AU/25 30.00 60.00
147A Josh Robinson AU/99 4.00 10.00
147B Josh Robinson AU/25 8.00 20.00
148 Ben Koyack AU/99 6.00 15.00
149A Marcus Murphy AU/99 4.00 10.00
149B Marcus Murphy AU/25 8.00 20.00
150A Deontay Greenberry AU/25 8.00 20.00
150B Deontay Greenberry AU/25 8.00 20.00
151 Ifo Ekpre-Olomu AU/99 4.00 10.00
152 DaVaris Daniels AU/99 4.00 10.00
153A Tre McBride AU/49 6.00 15.00
153B Tre McBride AU/25 8.00 20.00
154 Antwan Goodley AU/99 4.00 10.00
155A Titus Davis AU/99 5.00 12.00
155B Titus Davis AU/25 10.00 25.00
156 Rannell Hall AU/99 4.00 10.00
157A Mario Alford AU/99 4.00 10.00
157B Mario Alford AU/25 8.00 20.00
158 Malcom Brown AU/99 4.00 10.00
159 Josh Harper AU/49 6.00 15.00
160 Taylor Heinicke AU/99 6.00 15.00
161 Jeff Heuerman AU/99 5.00 12.00
162A Tony Lippett AU/25 8.00 20.00
162B Tony Lippett AU/25 8.00 20.00
163 Preston Smith AU/99 5.00 12.00
164 Devin Gardner AU/99 6.00 15.00
165 Bryan Bennett AU/99 4.00 10.00
166 Michael Bennett AU/99 4.00 10.00
167 Jordan Taylor AU/99 5.00 12.00
169 Michael Dyer AU/99 6.00 15.00
170A Eric Tomlinson AU/99 5.00 12.00
170B Eric Tomlinson AU/25 10.00 25.00
171 DeAndrew White AU/15 30.00 60.00
172A Derron Smith AU/99 4.00 10.00
172B Derron Smith AU/25 8.00 20.00
173A Cameron Erving AU/99 5.00 12.00
173B Cameron Erving AU/25 10.00 25.00
174 Andrus Peat AU/99 4.00 10.00
175 Dres Anderson AU/99 4.00 10.00
176 Cody Fajardo AU/99 5.00 12.00
177A Levi Norwood AU/99 4.00 10.00
177B Levi Norwood AU/99 4.00 10.00
178 Malcolm Brown AU/99 5.00 12.00
179 Nate Orchard AU/99 4.00 10.00
180A Shane Carden AU/99 4.00 10.00
180B Shane Carden AU/25 8.00 20.00
181 Ereck Flowers AU/99 5.00 12.00
182 Cedric Ogbuehi AU/99 4.00 10.00
183A Nick Boyle AU/25 8.00 20.00
183B Nick Boyle AU/25 8.00 20.00
184A Terrence Magee AU/99 6.00 15.00
184B Terrence Magee AU/25 12.00 30.00
185 Byron Jones AU/99 8.00 20.00
186 Charcandrick West AU/99 5.00 12.00
187 Lorenzo Mauldin AU/99 4.00 10.00
188 Brandon Scherff AU/99 6.00 15.00
189 Hau'oli Kikaha AU/99 5.00 12.00
190 Geneo Grissom AU/99 4.00 10.00
191 Jaquiski Tartt AU/99 4.00 10.00
192 Corey Grant AU/99 6.00 15.00
193 Dreamius Smith AU/99 10.00 25.00
194A Kenny Hilliard AU/25 8.00 20.00
194B Kenny Hilliard AU/25 8.00 20.00
195 Dominique Brown AU/99 4.00 10.00
196 Kurtis Drummond AU/99 5.00 12.00
197 Kevin White AU/99 5.00 12.00
198A Doran Grant AU/99 6.00 15.00
198B Doran Grant AU/25 12.00 30.00
199A Kaelin Clay AU/49 6.00 15.00
199B Kaelin Clay AU/49 6.00 15.00
200 Jordan Phillips AU/99 4.00 10.00
201A Melvin Gordon AU/49 25.00 50.00
201B Melvin Gordon AU/28 30.00 60.00
201C Melvin Gordon AU/28 30.00 60.00
202A Ameer Abdullah AU/25 12.00 30.00
202B Ameer Abdullah AU/25 12.00 30.00
202C Ameer Abdullah AU/49 10.00 25.00
203A Breshad Perriman AU/25 25.00 50.00
203B Breshad Perriman AU/25 25.00 50.00
203C Breshad Perriman AU/25 25.00 50.00
204A Brett Hundley AU/25 40.00 80.00
204B Brett Hundley AU/25 40.00 80.00
205A Bryce Petty AU/99 4.00 10.00
205B Bryce Petty AU/49 6.00 15.00
206A Buck Allen AU/99 5.00 12.00
206B Buck Allen AU/49 8.00 20.00
207A Chris Conley AU/99 4.00 10.00
207B Chris Conley AU/49 6.00 15.00
208A David Cobb AU/99 4.00 10.00
208B David Cobb AU/49 6.00 15.00
209A David Johnson AU/99 30.00 60.00
209B David Johnson AU/49 40.00 80.00
210A DeVante Parker AU/99 12.00 30.00
210B DeVante Parker AU/49 25.00 50.00
210C DeVante Parker AU/49 25.00 50.00
211A Devin Funchess AU/49 20.00 40.00
211B Devin Funchess AU/25 20.00 50.00
211C Devin Funchess AU/25 20.00 50.00
212A Devin Smith AU/99 4.00 10.00
212B Devin Smith AU/49 6.00 15.00
212C Devin Smith AU/49 6.00 15.00
213A Dorial Green-Beckham AU/49 20.00 40.00
213B Dorial Green-Beckham AU/25 8.00 20.00
214A Duke Johnson AU/49 10.00 25.00
214B Duke Johnson AU/25 12.00 30.00
215A Garrett Grayson AU/25 40.00 80.00
215B Garrett Grayson AU/25 40.00 80.00
216A Jaelen Strong AU/25 10.00 25.00
216B Jaelen Strong AU/25 10.00 25.00
217A Jameis Winston AU/50 150.00 300.00
217B Jameis Winston AU/25 250.00 500.00
217C Jameis Winston AU/25 250.00 500.00
218A Jamison Crowder AU/49 20.00 50.00
218B Jamison Crowder AU/49 20.00 50.00
219A Jay Ajayi AU/99 12.00 30.00
219B Jay Ajayi AU/25 30.00 60.00
220A Jeremy Langford AU/99 20.00 40.00
220B Jeremy Langford AU/49 30.00 60.00
221A Justin Hardy AU/99 4.00 10.00
221B Justin Hardy AU/49 6.00 15.00
222A Karlos Williams AU/99 10.00 25.00
222B Karlos Williams AU/49 25.00 50.00
223A Kevin White AU/49 8.00 20.00
223B Kevin White AU/25 10.00 25.00
223C Kevin White AU/25 10.00 25.00
224A Leonard Williams AU/99 4.00 10.00
224B Leonard Williams AU/49 6.00 15.00
225A Marcus Mariota AU/49 75.00 150.00
225B Marcus Mariota AU/25 100.00 200.00
225C Marcus Mariota AU/25 100.00 200.00
226A Matt Jones AU/99 15.00 30.00
226B Matt Jones AU/49 25.00 50.00
227A Maxx Williams AU/99 4.00 10.00
227B Maxx Williams AU/49 6.00 15.00
228A Amari Cooper AU/25 200.00 400.00
228B Amari Cooper AU/25 200.00 400.00
229A Mike Davis AU/99 4.00 10.00
229B Mike Davis AU/49 6.00 15.00
230A Nelson Agholor AU/25 10.00 25.00
230B Nelson Agholor AU/25 10.00 25.00
230C Nelson Agholor AU/25 10.00 25.00
231A Phillip Dorsett AU/99 15.00 30.00
231B Phillip Dorsett AU/49
231C Phillip Dorsett AU/49
232A Rashad Greene AU/99 4.00 10.00
232B Rashad Greene AU/25 8.00 20.00
233A Sammie Coates AU/99 5.00 12.00
233B Sammie Coates AU/49 8.00 20.00
233C Sammie Coates AU/49 8.00 20.00
234A Sean Mannion AU/99 4.00 10.00
234B Sean Mannion AU/49 6.00 15.00
235A Stefon Diggs AU/99 20.00 50.00
235B Stefon Diggs AU/49 30.00 80.00
236A T.J. Yeldon AU/49 6.00 15.00
236B T.J. Yeldon AU/25 8.00 20.00
236C T.J. Yeldon AU/25 8.00 20.00
237A Tevin Coleman AU/25
237B Tevin Coleman AU/25
237C Tevin Coleman AU/25
238A Todd Gurley AU/49 100.00 200.00
238B Todd Gurley AU/25 200.00 400.00
238C Todd Gurley AU/25 200.00 400.00
239A Ty Montgomery AU/99 4.00 10.00
239B Ty Montgomery AU/49 6.00 15.00
240A Tyler Lockett AU/99 25.00 50.00
240B Tyler Lockett AU/49 50.00 100.00
240C Tyler Lockett AU/49 50.00 100.00
241A Vince Mayle AU/99 5.00 12.00
241B Vince Mayle AU/49 8.00 20.00
242 Gerod Holliman AU/99 6.00 15.00
243 Charles Gaines AU/99 6.00 15.00
244 Ramik Wilson AU/99 5.00 12.00
245 Lorenzo Doss AU/99 4.00 10.00
247 Casey Pierce AU/99 4.00 10.00
248 Jahwan Edwards AU/49 8.00 20.00
249 Trey Williams AU/99 5.00 12.00
250 Wes Saxton AU/99 5.00 12.00
251 Lucky Whitehead AU/99 10.00 25.00
252 DeAndre Smelter AU/99 4.00 10.00
253 Trevor Siemian AU/99 25.00 60.00
254 Thomas Rawls AU/99 10.00 25.00
255 Damarious Randall AU/99 5.00 12.00
256 Geremy Davis AU/99 5.00 12.00
257 Quandre Diggs AU/99 4.00 10.00
258 Jaxon Shipley AU/99 4.00 10.00
259 Jalston Fowler AU/99 5.00 12.00
260 Chris Harper AU/99 5.00 12.00
261 Keith Mumphery AU/99 4.00 10.00
262 Terron Ward AU/99 5.00 12.00
263 Alonzo Harris AU/99 6.00 15.00
264 Nick Marshall AU/99 6.00 15.00
265 E.J. Bibbs AU/99 5.00 12.00
266 Cameron Meredith AU/99 6.00 15.00
267 James O'Shaughnessy AU/99 4.00 10.00
268 Malcolm Johnson AU/99 4.00 10.00
269 Anthony Harris AU/25 8.00 20.00
270 La'el Collins AU/99 5.00 12.00
271 Jarryd Hayne/23 75.00 125.00
272 T.J. Clemmings AU/99 4.00 10.00
273 D'Joun Smith AU/99 6.00 15.00
274 Frank Clark AU/99 4.00 10.00
275 Jordan Richards AU/99 4.00 10.00
276 Austin Hill AU/99 4.00 10.00
277 Jake Ryan AU/99 6.00 15.00
278 Zack Hodges AU/99 4.00 10.00
279 Zach Zenner AU/99 15.00 40.00
280 Zach Vigil AU/99 5.00 12.00
281 Gus Johnson AU/99 6.00 15.00
282 Jake Waters AU/99 5.00 12.00
283 A.J. Cann AU/99 5.00 12.00
284 Tyrell Williams AU/99 5.00 12.00
285 Tyler Murphy AU/99 6.00 15.00
286 Jordan Hicks AU/99 6.00 15.00
287 Kamar Aiken AU/99 5.00 12.00
288 Willie Snead AU/99 10.00 25.00
289 Chip Kelly AU 20.00 50.00
290 Dan Quinn AU 15.00 40.00
291 Chuck Pagano AU 20.00 50.00
292 Bruce Arians AU 15.00 40.00
293 Sean Payton AU 20.00 50.00

2015 Panini Contenders Cracked Ice

*1-100 VETS: 12X TO 30X BASIC CARDS
*101-199 ROOK: 1X TO 2.5X PLAY. AU/199
*201-240 ROOK: .8X TO 2X PLAY.AU/99
MOST HAVE TWO CARDS OF EQUAL VALUE
101-241 A TEAM HELMET UPPER LEFT
101-241 B TEAM LOGO UPPER LEFT
101-241 C PLAYER IN COLLEGE JSY
104A Vic Beasley Jr. AU 15.00 40.00
104B Vic Beasley Jr. AU 25.00 60.00
109A Marcus Peters AU
109B Marcus Peters AU
110A Bud Dupree AU 15.00 40.00
110B Bud Dupree AU 25.00 60.00
114 Landon Collins AU 12.00 40.00
144A Jesse James AU 20.00 50.00
144B Jesse James AU 30.00 80.00
201A Melvin Gordon AU 30.00 80.00
201B Melvin Gordon AU 75.00 150.00
201C Melvin Gordon AU 75.00 150.00
203B Breshad Perriman AU 20.00 50.00
203C Breshad Perriman AU 20.00 50.00
209A David Johnson AU 125.00 250.00
209B David Johnson AU 200.00 400.00
210A DeVante Parker AU 30.00 80.00
210B DeVante Parker AU 60.00 120.00
210C DeVante Parker AU 60.00 120.00
217A Jameis Winston AU 300.00 600.00
217B Jameis Winston AU 400.00 800.00
217C Jameis Winston AU 400.00 800.00
219A Jay Ajayi AU 25.00 60.00
219B Jay Ajayi AU 50.00 100.00
225A Marcus Mariota AU 150.00 300.00
225B Marcus Mariota AU 150.00 300.00
225C Marcus Mariota AU 150.00 300.00
228A Amari Cooper AU 50.00 125.00
228B Amari Cooper AU 150.00 300.00
228C Amari Cooper AU 150.00 125.00
235A Stefon Diggs AU 30.00 80.00
235B Stefon Diggs AU 50.00 100.00
237B Tevin Coleman AU 50.00 100.00
237C Tevin Coleman AU 50.00 100.00
238A Todd Gurley AU 60.00 150.00
238B Todd Gurley AU 150.00 300.00
238C Todd Gurley AU 150.00 300.00
239A Ty Montgomery AU 15.00 40.00
239B Ty Montgomery AU 25.00 60.00
240A Tyler Lockett AU 60.00 150.00
240B Tyler Lockett AU 60.00 150.00
240C Tyler Lockett AU 60.00 150.00
253 Trevor Siemian AU 50.00 120.00
254 Thomas Rawls AU 20.00 50.00
279 Zach Zenner AU 30.00 80.00
288 Willie Snead AU 12.00 30.00
289 Chip Kelly AU 20.00 50.00
291 Chuck Pagano AU 15.00 40.00
292 Bruce Arians AU 15.00 40.00
293 Sean Payton AU 20.00 50.00

2015 Panini Contenders Playoff Ticket

*1-100 VETS/199: 2.5X TO 6X BASIC CARDS
101A Kenny Bell AU/199 6.00 15.00
101B Kenny Bell AU/49 10.00 25.00
102A Cameron Artis-Payne AU/49 20.00 40.00
102B Cameron Artis-Payne AU/49 20.00 40.00
104A Vic Beasley Jr. AU/199 5.00 12.00
104B Vic Beasley Jr. AU/199 5.00 12.00
105 Trae Waynes AU/99 5.00 12.00
106 Danny Shelton AU/199 4.00 10.00
107 Kevin Johnson AU/199 4.00 10.00
108 Arik Armstead AU/199 4.00 10.00
110A Bud Dupree AU/49 15.00 30.00
110B Bud Dupree AU/49 15.00 30.00
111B Shane Ray AU/49 6.00 15.00
113 Stephone Anthony AU/199 4.00 10.00
114 Landon Collins AU/99 6.00 15.00
115 Mario Edwards Jr. AU/199 4.00 10.00
116 Eddie Goldman AU/125 5.00 12.00
117 Jalen Collins AU/199 4.00 10.00
118A Benardrick McKinney AU/125 5.00 12.00
118B Benardrick McKinney AU/49 6.00 15.00
119 Eric Kendricks AU/125 5.00 12.00
120 Eric Rowe AU/199 4.00 10.00
121 Denzel Perryman AU/125 5.00 12.00
123 Senquez Golson AU/199 4.00 10.00
124A Markus Golden AU/199 4.00 10.00
124B Markus Golden AU/199 4.00 10.00
126 Quinten Rollins AU/125 15.00 30.00
127A Clive Walford AU/199 4.00 10.00
127B Clive Walford AU/49 6.00 15.00
128A Owamagbe Odighizuwa AU/199 5.00 12.00
128B Owamagbe Odighizuwa AU/49 8.00 20.00
129 P.J. Williams AU/199 5.00 12.00
130A Eli Harold AU/49 6.00 15.00
130B Eli Harold AU/49 6.00 15.00
131A Tyler Kroft AU/125 6.00 15.00
131B Tyler Kroft AU/199 5.00 12.00

132A Danielle Hunter AU/125 6.00 15.00
132B Danielle Hunter AU/49 8.00 20.00
133 Carl Davis AU/199 5.00 12.00
134A Dezmin Lewis AU/199 4.00 10.00
134B Dezmin Lewis AU/49 6.00 15.00
135 Paul Dawson AU/199 5.00 12.00
136 Trey Flowers AU/199 6.00 15.00
137A Blake Bell AU/199 6.00 15.00
137B Blake Bell AU/49 10.00 25.00
138A Josh Shaw AU/199 6.00 15.00
138B Josh Shaw AU/49 10.00 25.00
139 Kwon Alexander AU/199 5.00 12.00
140 Gerald Christian AU/199 5.00 12.00
141 MyCole Pruitt AU/199 4.00 10.00
142A Davis Tull AU/199 4.00 10.00
142B Davis Tull AU/49 6.00 15.00
143A J.J. Nelson AU/199 4.00 10.00
143B J.J. Nelson AU/49 6.00 15.00
144A Jesse James AU/199 5.00 12.00
144B Jesse James AU/49 8.00 20.00
145A Nick O'Leary AU/199 4.00 10.00
145B Nick O'Leary AU/49 6.00 15.00
146A Darren Waller AU/199 5.00 12.00
146B Darren Waller AU/49 8.00 20.00
147A Josh Robinson AU/125
147B Josh Robinson AU/49
148 Ben Koyack AU/125 8.00 20.00
149A Marcus Murphy AU/125 5.00 12.00
149B Marcus Murphy AU/49 6.00 15.00
150A Deontay Greenberry AU/49 6.00 15.00
150B Deontay Greenberry AU/49 6.00 15.00
152 DaVaris Daniels AU/99 5.00 12.00
153A Tre McBride AU/99 5.00 12.00
153B Tre McBride AU/49 6.00 15.00
154 Antwan Goodley AU/199 4.00 10.00
155A Titus Davis AU/199 5.00 12.00
155B Titus Davis AU/49 8.00 20.00
156 Rannell Hall AU/199 4.00 10.00
157A Mario Alford AU/199 4.00 10.00
157B Mario Alford AU/49 6.00 15.00
159 Josh Harper AU/99 5.00 12.00
160 Taylor Heinicke AU/199 6.00 15.00
161 Jeff Heuerman AU/199 5.00 12.00
162A Tony Lippett AU/49 6.00 15.00
162B Tony Lippett AU/49 6.00 15.00
163 Preston Smith AU/199 5.00 12.00
164 Devin Gardner AU/199 6.00 15.00
165 Bryan Bennett AU/125 5.00 12.00
166 Michael Bennett AU/199 4.00 10.00
167 Jordan Taylor AU/199 5.00 12.00
168 Da'Ron Brown AU/199 4.00 10.00
169 Michael Dyer AU/199 6.00 15.00
170A Eric Tomlinson AU/199 5.00 12.00
170B Eric Tomlinson AU/49 8.00 20.00
171 DeAndrew White AU/25 12.00 30.00
172A Derron Smith AU/199 4.00 10.00
172B Derron Smith AU/49 6.00 15.00
173A Cameron Erving AU/199 5.00 12.00
173B Cameron Erving AU/49 8.00 20.00
174 Andrus Peat AU/125 5.00 12.00
175 Dres Anderson AU/199 4.00 10.00
176 Cody Fajardo AU/199 5.00 12.00
177A Levi Norwood AU/199 4.00 10.00
177B Levi Norwood AU/199 4.00 10.00
178 Malcolm Brown AU/199 5.00 12.00
179 Nate Orchard AU/125 5.00 12.00
180A Shane Carden AU/125 5.00 12.00
180B Shane Carden AU/49 6.00 15.00
181 Ereck Flowers AU/125 6.00 15.00
182 Cedric Ogbuehi AU/199 4.00 10.00
183A Nick Boyle AU/99 5.00 12.00
183B Nick Boyle AU/49 6.00 15.00
184A Terrence Magee AU/125 8.00 20.00
184B Terrence Magee AU/49 10.00 25.00
185 Byron Jones AU/199 6.00 15.00
186 Charcandrick West AU/199 5.00 12.00
187 Lorenzo Mauldin AU/125 5.00 12.00
188 Brandon Scherff AU/125 8.00 20.00
189 Hau'oli Kikaha AU/199 5.00 12.00
190 Geneo Grissom AU/199 4.00 10.00
191 Jaquiski Tartt AU/199 4.00 10.00
192 Corey Grant AU/199 6.00 15.00
193 Dreamius Smith AU/199 10.00 25.00
194A Kenny Hilliard AU/49 6.00 15.00
194B Kenny Hilliard AU/49 6.00 15.00
195 Dominique Brown AU/199 4.00 10.00
196 Kurtis Drummond AU/199 5.00 12.00
197 Kevin White AU/199 5.00 12.00
198A Doran Grant AU/199 6.00 15.00
198B Doran Grant AU/49 10.00 25.00
199A Kaelin Clay AU/99 5.00 12.00
199B Kaelin Clay AU/99 5.00 12.00
200 Jordan Phillips AU/199 4.00 10.00
201A Melvin Gordon AU/99 12.00 30.00
201B Melvin Gordon AU/49 15.00 40.00
201C Melvin Gordon AU/49 15.00 40.00
202A Ameer Abdullah AU/49 10.00 25.00
202B Ameer Abdullah AU/49 10.00 25.00
202C Ameer Abdullah AU/99 8.00 20.00
203A Breshad Perriman AU/49 20.00 40.00
203B Breshad Perriman AU/49 20.00 40.00
203C Breshad Perriman AU/49 20.00 40.00
204A Brett Hundley AU/30 50.00 100.00
204B Brett Hundley AU/30 50.00 100.00
205A Bryce Petty AU/199 15.00 30.00
205B Bryce Petty AU/99 20.00 40.00
206A Buck Allen AU/199 5.00 12.00
206B Buck Allen AU/99 6.00 15.00
207A Chris Conley AU/199 4.00 10.00
207B Chris Conley AU/99 5.00 12.00
208A David Cobb AU/199 4.00 10.00
208B David Cobb AU/99 5.00 12.00
209A David Johnson AU/199 30.00 60.00
209B David Johnson AU/99 50.00 100.00
210A DeVante Parker AU/199 10.00 25.00
210B DeVante Parker AU/99 15.00 40.00
210C DeVante Parker AU/99 15.00 40.00
211A Devin Funchess AU/99 8.00 20.00
211B Devin Funchess AU/49 10.00 25.00
211C Devin Funchess AU/49 10.00 25.00
212A Devin Smith AU/199 4.00 10.00
212B Devin Smith AU/99 15.00 30.00
212C Devin Smith AU/99 15.00 30.00
213A Dorial Green-Beckham AU/99 5.00 12.00
213B Dorial Green-Beckham AU/49 6.00 15.00
214A Duke Johnson AU/99 8.00 20.00
214B Duke Johnson AU/49 10.00 25.00
215A Garrett Grayson AU/30 40.00 80.00
215B Garrett Grayson AU/30 40.00 80.00
215C Garrett Grayson AU/15 50.00 100.00
216A Jaelen Strong AU/49 8.00 20.00
216B Jaelen Strong AU/49 8.00 20.00
217A Jameis Winston AU/75 150.00 300.00
217B Jameis Winston AU/30 200.00 400.00
217C Jameis Winston AU/30 200.00 400.00
218A Jamison Crowder AU/99 15.00 30.00
218B Jamison Crowder AU/99 15.00 30.00
219A Jay Ajayi AU/199 6.00 15.00
219B Jay Ajayi AU/49 10.00 25.00
220A Jeremy Langford AU/199 20.00 40.00
220B Jeremy Langford AU/99 30.00 60.00
221A Justin Hardy AU/199 4.00 10.00
221B Justin Hardy AU/99 5.00 12.00
222A Karlos Williams AU/199 4.00 10.00
222B Karlos Williams AU/99 5.00 12.00
223A Kevin White AU/99 6.00 15.00
223B Kevin White AU/30 8.00 20.00
223C Kevin White AU/30 8.00 20.00
224A Leonard Williams AU/199 4.00 10.00
224B Leonard Williams AU/99 5.00 12.00
225A Marcus Mariota AU/99 50.00 100.00
225B Marcus Mariota AU/30 75.00 150.00
225C Marcus Mariota AU/30 75.00 150.00
226A Matt Jones AU/199 EXCH 4.00 10.00
226B Matt Jones AU/99 5.00 12.00
227A Maxx Williams AU/199 4.00 10.00
227B Maxx Williams AU/99 5.00 12.00
228A Amari Cooper AU/30 EXCH 100.00 200.00
228B Amari Cooper AU/30 EXCH 100.00 200.00
228C Amari Cooper AU/15
229A Mike Davis AU/199 4.00 10.00
229B Mike Davis AU/99 5.00 12.00
230A Nelson Agholor AU/49 8.00 20.00
230B Nelson Agholor AU/49 8.00 20.00
230C Nelson Agholor AU/49 8.00 20.00
231A Phillip Dorsett AU/199 4.00 10.00
231B Phillip Dorsett AU/99 5.00 12.00
231C Phillip Dorsett AU/99 5.00 12.00
232A Rashad Greene AU/199 4.00 10.00
232B Rashad Greene AU/49 6.00 15.00
233A Sammie Coates AU/199 5.00 12.00
233B Sammie Coates AU/99 6.00 15.00
233C Sammie Coates AU/99 6.00 15.00
234A Sean Mannion AU/199 4.00 10.00
234B Sean Mannion AU/99 5.00 12.00
235A Stefon Diggs AU/199 20.00 50.00
235B Stefon Diggs AU/99 25.00 60.00
236A T.J. Yeldon AU/99 5.00 12.00
236B T.J. Yeldon AU/49 EXCH 6.00 15.00
236C T.J. Yeldon AU/49 EXCH 6.00 15.00
237A Tevin Coleman AU/49 EXCH
237B Tevin Coleman AU/49 EXCH
237C Tevin Coleman AU/49 EXCH
238A Todd Gurley AU/99 EXCH 60.00 125.00
238B Todd Gurley AU/30 EXCH 150.00 250.00
238C Todd Gurley AU/30 EXCH 150.00 250.00
239A Ty Montgomery AU/199 4.00 10.00
239B Ty Montgomery AU/99 5.00 12.00
240A Tyler Lockett AU/199 6.00 15.00
240B Tyler Lockett AU/99 8.00 20.00
240C Tyler Lockett AU/99 8.00 20.00
241A Vince Mayle AU/199 5.00 12.00
241B Vince Mayle AU/99 6.00 15.00
242 Gerod Holliman AU/199 6.00 15.00
243 Charles Gaines AU/199 6.00 15.00
245 Lorenzo Doss AU/199 4.00 10.00
247 Casey Pierce AU/199 4.00 10.00
248 Jahwan Edwards AU/99 6.00 15.00
249 Trey Williams AU/199 5.00 12.00
250 Wes Saxton AU/199 5.00 12.00
251 Lucky Whitehead AU/199 10.00 25.00
252 DeAndre Smelter AU/199 4.00 10.00
253 Trevor Siemian AU/199 25.00 60.00
254 Thomas Rawls AU/199 10.00 25.00
255 Damarious Randall AU/199 5.00 12.00
256 Geremy Davis AU/199 5.00 12.00
257 Quandre Diggs AU/199 4.00 10.00
258 Jaxon Shipley AU/199 4.00 10.00
259 Jalston Fowler AU/199 5.00 12.00
260 Chris Harper AU/199 5.00 12.00
261 Keith Mumphery AU/199 4.00 10.00
262 Terron Ward AU/199 5.00 12.00
263 Alonzo Harris AU/199 6.00 15.00
264 Nick Marshall AU/199 6.00 15.00
265 E.J. Bibbs AU/199 5.00 12.00
266 Cameron Meredith AU/199 6.00 15.00
267 James O'Shaughnessy AU/199 4.00 10.00
268 Malcolm Johnson AU/199 4.00 10.00
269 Anthony Harris AU/49 6.00 15.00
270 La'el Collins AU/199 5.00 12.00
271 Jarryd Hayne/49 20.00 50.00
272 T.J. Clemmings AU/199 4.00 10.00
273 D'Joun Smith AU/199 6.00 15.00
274 Frank Clark AU/199 4.00 10.00
275 Jordan Richards AU/199 4.00 10.00
276 Austin Hill AU/199 4.00 10.00
277 Jake Ryan AU/199 6.00 15.00
278 Zack Hodges AU/199 4.00 10.00
279 Zach Zenner AU/199 12.00 30.00
280 Zach Vigil AU/199 5.00 12.00
281 Gus Johnson AU/199 6.00 15.00
282 Jake Waters AU/199 5.00 12.00
283 A.J. Cann AU/199 5.00 12.00
284 Tyrell Williams AU/199 5.00 12.00
285 Tyler Murphy AU/199 6.00 15.00
286 Jordan Hicks AU/199 6.00 15.00
287 Kamar Aiken AU/199 5.00 12.00
288 Willie Snead AU/199 10.00 25.00
289 Chip Kelly AU 12.00 30.00
290 Dan Quinn AU 12.00 30.00
291 Chuck Pagano AU 10.00 25.00
292 Bruce Arians AU 12.00 30.00
293 Sean Payton AU 25.00 50.00

2015 Panini Contenders Draft Class Autographs

1 Amari Cooper/20 50.00 100.00
2 Ameer Abdullah/199 4.00 10.00
3 Breshad Perriman/49 4.00 10.00
4 Brett Hundley/15 20.00 40.00
5 Bryce Petty/199 2.50 6.00
6 Buck Allen/199 3.00 8.00
7 David Cobb/199 2.50 6.00
8 DeVante Parker/199 10.00 25.00
9 Devin Funchess/49 6.00 15.00
10 Devin Smith/199 2.50 6.00
11 Dorial Green-Beckham/99 3.00 8.00
12 Duke Johnson/99 5.00 12.00
13 Garrett Grayson/25 15.00 40.00
14 Jameis Winston/25 90.00 150.00
15 Jamison Crowder/199 3.00 8.00
16 Jeremy Langford/199 2.50 6.00
17 Justin Hardy/199 2.50 6.00
18 Karlos Williams/199 2.50 6.00
19 Kevin White/25 6.00 15.00
20 Leonard Williams/199 2.50 6.00
21 Marcus Mariota/25 100.00 200.00
22 Melvin Gordon/25 15.00 40.00
23 Nelson Agholor/25
24 Phillip Dorsett/199 2.50 6.00
25 Sean Mannion/199 2.50 6.00
26 Stefon Diggs/199 10.00 25.00
27 T.J. Yeldon/99 3.00 8.00
28 Tevin Coleman/49 5.00 12.00
29 Todd Gurley/25 60.00 120.00
30 Vince Mayle/199 3.00 8.00

2015 Panini Contenders Legendary Contenders

*GOLD/199: .5X TO 1.2X BASIC INSERTS
*HOLO/99: .6X TO 1.5X BASIC INSERTS
1 Barry Sanders 2.00 5.00
2 Joe Montana 3.00 8.00
3 Terry Bradshaw 1.50 4.00
4 Brett Favre 2.50 6.00
5 Thurman Thomas 1.00 2.50
6 Lawrence Taylor 1.25 3.00
7 Eric Dickerson 1.00 2.50
8 Dan Marino 2.50 6.00
9 Steve Young 1.50 4.00
10 Emmitt Smith 2.00 5.00

2015 Panini Contenders MVP Contenders

*GOLD/199: .5X TO 1.2X BASIC INSERTS
*HOLO/99: .6X TO 1.5X BASIC INSERTS
1 Aaron Rodgers 1.25 3.00
2 Andrew Luck .75 2.00
3 Tom Brady 1.50 4.00
4 Russell Wilson .75 2.00
5 J.J. Watt .60 1.50
6 Peyton Manning 1.25 3.00
7 Adrian Peterson .60 1.50
8 Matt Ryan .50 1.25
9 DeMarco Murray .50 1.25
10 Cam Newton .60 1.50

2015 Panini Contenders Pennants

*GOLD/199: .5X TO 1.2X BASIC INSERTS
*HOLO/99: .6X TO 1.5X BASIC INSERTS
1 J.J. Watt .60 1.50
2 Aaron Rodgers 1.25 3.00
3 Tom Brady 1.50 4.00
4 DeMarco Murray .50 1.25
5 Peyton Manning 1.25 3.00
6 Calvin Johnson .60 1.50
7 Andrew Luck .75 2.00
8 Antonio Brown .60 1.50
9 Marshawn Lynch .50 1.25
10 Rob Gronkowski .60 1.50
11 Richard Sherman .60 1.50
12 Jamaal Charles .50 1.25
13 Julio Jones .60 1.50
14 Dez Bryant .60 1.50
15 Le'Veon Bell .50 1.25
16 Darrelle Revis .40 1.00
17 Eddie Lacy .40 1.00
18 Demaryius Thomas .50 1.25
19 Russell Wilson .75 2.00
20 Tony Romo .50 1.25
21 Ben Roethlisberger .60 1.50
22 Drew Brees .60 1.50
23 LeSean McCoy .60 1.50
24 Odell Beckham Jr. .60 1.50
25 T.Y. Hilton .50 1.25
26 Alshon Jeffery .50 1.25
27 Derek Carr .60 1.50
28 Cam Newton .60 1.50
29 Matt Ryan .50 1.25
30 Justin Forsett .50 1.25
31 Jameis Winston .60 1.50
32 A.J. Green .60 1.50
33 Marcus Mariota 1.00 2.50
34 Philip Rivers .60 1.50
35 Matthew Stafford .50 1.25
36 Adrian Peterson .60 1.50
37 Larry Fitzgerald .50 1.25
38 Brandon Marshall .40 1.00
39 Joe Flacco .50 1.25
40 Eli Manning .50 1.25

2015 Panini Contenders Rookie Ink

RIAH Austin Hill 2.50 6.00
RIBD Bud Dupree/50 5.00 12.00
RIBJ Byron Jones 6.00 15.00
RICAP Cameron Artis-Payne/50 4.00 10.00
RICH Chris Harper 3.00 8.00
RICW Clive Walford/200 2.50 6.00
RIDB Dominique Brown 2.50 6.00
RIDG Deontay Greenberry/25 5.00 12.00
RIDL Dezmin Lewis/500 2.50 6.00
RIDR Damarious Randall 4.00 10.00
RIDS1 Danny Shelton/450 2.50 6.00
RIDS2 DeAndre Smelter/50 4.00 10.00
RIGJ Gus Johnson 4.00 10.00
RIJJ J.J. Nelson/299 2.50 6.00
RIJR Josh Robinson/50 4.00 10.00
RIJT Jordan Taylor 3.00 8.00
RIKB Kenny Bell/350 4.00 10.00
RIKH Kenny Hilliard/100 3.00 8.00
RIMM Marcus Murphy/50 4.00 10.00
RINO Nick O'Leary/350 2.50 6.00
RIOO Owamagbe Odighizuwa/350 3.00 8.00
RISC Shane Carden/50 4.00 10.00
RITD Titus Davis/500 3.00 8.00
RITH Taylor Heinicke 8.00 20.00
RITK Tyler Kroft/500 3.00 8.00
RITM Terrence Magee 4.00 10.00
RITR Tre McBride/100 3.00 8.00
RITW Trey Williams 3.00 8.00
RIVB Vic Beasley Jr./25

2015 Panini Contenders Rookie Ink Rookie Premiere

INKAA Ameer Abdullah/199 5.00 12.00
INKAC Amari Cooper/20 40.00 80.00
INKBA Buck Allen/199 4.00 10.00
INKBH Brett Hundley/15 8.00 20.00
INKBP Bryce Petty/199 3.00 8.00
INKBP Breshad Perriman/49 5.00 12.00
INKCC Chris Conley/99 4.00 10.00
INKDC David Cobb/199 3.00 8.00
INKDF Devin Funchess/49 8.00 20.00
INKDGB Dorial Green-Beckham/99 4.00 10.00
INKDJ David Johnson/199 25.00 50.00
INKDP DeVante Parker/199 15.00 30.00
INKDS Devin Smith/199 3.00 8.00
INKDU Duke Johnson/99 6.00 15.00
INKGG Garrett Grayson/25 15.00 40.00
INKJA Jay Ajayi/199 5.00 12.00
INKJC Jamison Crowder/199 4.00 10.00
INKJH Justin Hardy/199 3.00 8.00
INKJL Jeremy Langford/199 3.00 8.00
INKJS Jaelen Strong/49 6.00 15.00
INKJW Jameis Winston/25 40.00 80.00
INKKW Karlos Williams/199 3.00 8.00
INKKW Kevin White/25 8.00 20.00
INKLW Leonard Williams/199 3.00 8.00
INKMD Mike Davis/199 3.00 8.00
INKMG Melvin Gordon/25 15.00 40.00
INKMJ Matt Jones/199 EXCH 3.00 8.00
INKMM Marcus Mariota/25 40.00 80.00
INKMW Maxx Williams/199 3.00 8.00
INKNA Nelson Agholor/25 8.00 20.00
INKPD Phillip Dorsett/199 EXCH 3.00 8.00
INKRG Rashad Greene/199 3.00 8.00
INKSC Sammie Coates/199 4.00 10.00
INKSD Stefon Diggs/199 8.00 20.00
INKSM Sean Mannion/199 3.00 8.00
INKTC Tevin Coleman/49 6.00 15.00
INKTG Todd Gurley/25 75.00 150.00
INKTL Tyler Lockett/199 5.00 12.00
INKTM Ty Montgomery/199 3.00 8.00
INKTY T.J. Yeldon/99 4.00 10.00
INKVM Vince Mayle/199 4.00 10.00

2015 Panini Contenders Rookie Ink Rookie Premiere Gold

*GOLD/25: .8X TO 2X BASIC AU/199
*GOLD/25: .6X TO 1.5X BASIC AU/99
*GOLD/25: .5X TO 1.2X BASIC AU/49
*GOLD/15: .5X TO 1.2X BASIC AU/25

2015 Panini Contenders Rookie Ticket Swatches

*VARIATION JSY: .4X TO 1X BASIC JSY
1 Jameis Winston 6.00 15.00
2 Marcus Mariota 10.00 25.00
3 Amari Cooper 5.00 12.00
4 Melvin Gordon 4.00 10.00
5 Kevin White 2.00 5.00
6 DeVante Parker 2.50 6.00
7 Dorial Green-Beckham 1.50 4.00
8 Tevin Coleman 2.00 5.00
9 Justin Hardy 1.50 4.00
10 David Cobb 1.50 4.00
11 David Johnson 4.00 10.00
12 Jamison Crowder 2.00 5.00
13 Buck Allen 2.00 5.00
14 Maxx Williams 1.50 4.00
15 Leonard Williams 1.50 4.00
16 Nelson Agholor 2.00 5.00
17 Chris Conley 1.50 4.00
18 Jeremy Langford 1.50 4.00
19 Jay Ajayi 2.50 6.00
20 Jaelen Strong 2.00 5.00
21 Rashad Greene 1.50 4.00
22 Sammie Coates 2.00 5.00
23 Sean Mannion 1.50 4.00
24 Tyler Lockett 2.50 6.00
26 Todd Gurley 8.00 20.00
27 Mike Davis 1.50 4.00
28 Matt Jones 1.50 4.00
29 Phillip Dorsett 1.50 4.00
30 Stefon Diggs 4.00 10.00
31 Garrett Grayson 1.50 4.00
32 Duke Johnson 2.50 6.00
33 Breshad Perriman 1.50 4.00
34 Ameer Abdullah 2.50 6.00
35 Brett Hundley 1.50 4.00
36 Devin Smith 1.50 4.00
37 Karlos Williams 1.50 4.00
38 T.J. Yeldon 1.50 4.00
39 Devin Funchess 2.50 6.00
40 Ty Montgomery 1.50 4.00
41 Bryce Petty 1.50 4.00

2015 Panini Contenders Round Numbers

*GOLD/199: .5X TO 1.2X BASIC INSERTS
*HOLO/99: .6X TO 1.5X BASIC INSERTS
1 M.Mariota/J.Winston 1.00 2.50
2 A.Cooper/K.White .75 2.00
3 L.Williams/N.Agholor .30 .75
4 M.Gordon/T.Gurley 1.00 2.50
5 B.Perriman/D.Parker .40 1.00
6 A.Abdullah/T.Yeldon .40 1.00
7 D.Smith/D.Funchess .40 1.00
8 K.Williams/R.Greene .25 .60
9 G.Grayson/S.Mannion .25 .60
10 D.Johnson/T.Coleman .40 1.00

2015 Panini Contenders Round Numbers Autographs

3 M.Gordon/T.Gurley 25.00 60.00
4 B.Perriman/D.Parker 10.00 25.00
6 A.Abdullah/T.Yeldon 15.00 40.00
7 D.Funchess/D.Smith 10.00 25.00
8 M.Jones/S.Coates 25.00 50.00
9 D.Johnson/T.Montgomery 25.00 50.00
10 D.Johnson/T.Coleman 10.00 25.00
11 J.Strong/T.Lockett 10.00 25.00
12 C.Conley/S.Mannion 6.00 15.00
13 B.Bell/B.Petty 10.00 25.00
14 J.Hardy/M.Davis 6.00 15.00
17 D.Cobb/J.Ajayi 10.00 25.00
18 J.James/M.Pruitt 8.00 20.00
19 T.Lippett/J.Nelson 6.00 15.00
20 E.Goldman/M.Edwards 6.00 15.00

2015 Panini Contenders ROY Contenders

*GOLD/199: .5X TO 1.2X BASIC INSERTS
*HOLO/99: .6X TO 1.5X BASIC INSERTS
1 Jameis Winston .60 1.50
2 Marcus Mariota 1.00 2.50
3 Amari Cooper .75 2.00
4 Karlos Williams .25 .60
5 Tyler Lockett .40 1.00
6 Todd Gurley 1.00 2.50
7 DeVante Parker .40 1.00
8 Melvin Gordon .60 1.50
9 Nelson Agholor .30 .75
10 Phillip Dorsett .25 .60
11 Ameer Abdullah .40 1.00
12 Dorial Green-Beckham .25 .60
13 Tevin Coleman .30 .75
14 Maxx Williams .25 .60
15 T.J. Yeldon .25 .60
16 Matt Jones .25 .60
17 Jay Ajayi .40 1.00
18 Duke Johnson .40 1.00
19 David Cobb .25 .60
20 Devin Funchess .40 1.00

2015 Panini Contenders ROY Contenders Autographs

*GOLD/25: .6X TO 1.5X BASIC AU
1 Cameron Artis-Payne 3.00 8.00
2 Kwon Alexander 4.00 10.00
3 Josh Robinson 3.00 8.00
4 Stephone Anthony 3.00 8.00
5 Karlos Williams 6.00 15.00
6 Danny Shelton 3.00 8.00
7 Vic Beasley Jr. 4.00 10.00
10 Breshad Perriman 3.00 8.00

2015 Panini Contenders ROY Contenders Autographs Rookie Premiere

*GOLD/25: .8X TO 2X BASIC AU/199
*GOLD/25: .6X TO 1.5X BASIC AU
*GOLD/25: .5X TO 1.2X BASIC AU
*GOLD/15: .5X TO 1.2X BASIC AU/25
1 Jameis Winston/25 60.00 125.00
2 Marcus Mariota/25 40.00 80.00
3 Amari Cooper/20 40.00 80.00
4 Leonard Williams/199 3.00 8.00
5 Kevin White/25 8.00 20.00
6 Todd Gurley/25 50.00 100.00
7 DeVante Parker/199 5.00 12.00
8 Melvin Gordon/25 15.00 40.00
9 Nelson Agholor/25 8.00 20.00
10 Phillip Dorsett/199 3.00 8.00
11 Ameer Abdullah/199 5.00 12.00
12 Dorial Green-Beckham/99 4.00 10.00
13 Tevin Coleman/49 6.00 15.00
14 Maxx Williams/199 3.00 8.00
15 T.J. Yeldon/99 4.00 10.00
16 Bryce Petty/199 3.00 8.00
17 Jay Ajayi/199 5.00 12.00
18 Duke Johnson/99 6.00 15.00
19 David Cobb/199 3.00 8.00
20 Devin Funchess/49 8.00 20.00
21 Jaelen Strong/49 6.00 15.00
22 David Johnson/199 25.00 50.00
23 Rashad Greene/199 3.00 8.00
24 Tyler Lockett/199 5.00 12.00
25 Devin Smith/199 3.00 8.00
26 Chris Conley/99 4.00 10.00
27 Matt Jones/199 3.00 8.00
28 Jeremy Langford/199 3.00 8.00
29 Ty Montgomery/199 3.00 8.00

2015 Panini Contenders Touchdown Tandems

*GOLD/199: .5X TO 1.2X BASIC INSERTS
*HOLO/99: .6X TO 1.5X BASIC INSERTS
1 T.Brady/R.Gronkowski 2.00 5.00
2 A.Brown/B.Roethlisberger .60 1.50
3 D.Thomas/P.Manning 1.25 3.00
4 A.Rodgers/J.Nelson 1.25 3.00
5 A.Luck/T.Hilton .75 2.00
6 T.Romo/D.Bryant .60 1.50
7 E.Manning/O.Beckham .60 1.50
8 A.Jeffery/J.Cutler .50 1.25
9 C.Johnson/M.Stafford .60 1.50
10 A.Gates/P.Rivers .60 1.50

2016 Panini Contenders

B VERSIONS SEPIA VARIATION
SP CARDS ANNC'D PRINT RUN 250 OR LESS
SP A CARDS ANNC'D PRINT RUN 99 OR LESS
1 Tony Romo .25 .60
2 Jason Witten .25 .60
3 Dez Bryant .30 .75
4 Eli Manning .25 .60
5 Odell Beckham Jr. .30 .75
6 Rashad Jennings .20 .50
7 Zach Ertz .25 .60
8 Ryan Mathews .25 .60
9 Jordan Matthews .25 .60
10 Kirk Cousins .30 .75
11 Matt Jones .25 .60
12 Jordan Reed .20 .50
13 Carson Palmer .25 .60
14 David Johnson .30 .75
15 Larry Fitzgerald .25 .60
16 Robert Quinn .25 .60
17 Todd Gurley II .30 .75
18 Tavon Austin .20 .50
19 Blaine Gabbert .20 .50
20 Carlos Hyde .20 .50
21 NaVorro Bowman .25 .60
22 Russell Wilson .40 1.00
23 Thomas Rawls .20 .50
24 Doug Baldwin .25 .60
25 Richard Sherman .30 .75
26 Jay Cutler .20 .50
27 Jeremy Langford .25 .60
28 Alshon Jeffery .25 .60
29 Kevin White .20 .50
30 Matthew Stafford .25 .60
31 Marvin Jones Jr. .20 .50
32 Golden Tate III .20 .50
33 Aaron Rodgers .60 1.50
34 Bart Starr .50 1.25
35 Jordy Nelson .25 .60
36 Sam Bradford .20 .50
37 Adrian Peterson .30 .75
38 Stefon Diggs .25 .60
39 Matt Ryan .25 .60
40 Devonta Freeman .25 .60
41 Julio Jones .30 .75
42 Cam Newton .30 .75
43 Jonathan Stewart .20 .50
44 Devin Funchess .20 .50
45 Kelvin Benjamin .25 .60
46 Drew Brees .30 .75
47 Mark Ingram .25 .60
48 Brandin Cooks .25 .60
49 Jameis Winston .30 .75
50 Doug Martin .25 .60
51 Mike Evans .25 .60
52 Tyrod Taylor .25 .60
53 LeSean McCoy .30 .75
54 Sammy Watkins .30 .75
55 Ryan Tannehill .25 .60
56 Jarvis Landry .25 .60
57 DeVante Parker .25 .60
58 Tom Brady .75 2.00
59 Julian Edelman .30 .75
60 Rob Gronkowski .30 .75
61 Ryan Fitzpatrick .20 .50
62 Matt Forte .20 .50
63 Brandon Marshall .20 .50
64 Trevor Siemian .20 .50
65 C.J. Anderson .25 .60
66 Demaryius Thomas .25 .60
67 Von Miller .25 .60
68 Alex Smith .25 .60
69 Jamaal Charles .25 .60
70 Jeremy Maclin .20 .50
71 Derek Carr .30 .75
72 Amari Cooper .30 .75
73 Khalil Mack .30 .75
74 Philip Rivers .30 .75
75 Melvin Gordon .25 .60
76 Travis Benjamin .20 .50
77 Joe Flacco .25 .60
78 Mike Wallace .20 .50
79 Steve Smith Sr. .25 .60
80 Andy Dalton .25 .60
81 Jeremy Hill .20 .50
82 A.J. Green .30 .75
83 Robert Griffin III .20 .50
84 Terrelle Pryor .20 .50
85 Ben Roethlisberger .30 .75
86 Le'Veon Bell .25 .60
87 Antonio Brown .30 .75
88 Brock Osweiler .20 .50
89 Lamar Miller .20 .50
90 DeAndre Hopkins .25 .60
91 J.J. Watt .30 .75
92 Andrew Luck .40 1.00
93 Frank Gore .25 .60
94 T.Y. Hilton .25 .60
95 Blake Bortles .20 .50
96 T.J. Yeldon .20 .50
97 Allen Robinson .25 .60
98 Marcus Mariota .30 .75
99 DeMarco Murray .25 .60
100 Delanie Walker .20 .50
101 Glenn Gronkowski AU RC 2.00 5.00
102 Jalen Ramsey AU/250* RC SP 10.00 25.00
103 Kevin Dodd AU RC 2.00 5.00
104 Ronnie Stanley AU RC 2.50 6.00
105 William Jackson III AU/42* RC SP A 6.00 15.00
106 Derek Watt AU RC 3.00 8.00
107 Keanu Neal AU RC 2.00 5.00
108 Malcolm Mitchell AU RC 6.00 15.00
109 Bralon Addison AU RC 2.00 5.00
110 Jeff Driskel AU RC 2.00 5.00
111 Jake Rudock AU RC 8.00 20.00
112 Keith Marshall AU RC 2.00 5.00
113 Rashard Higgins AU RC 2.00 5.00
114 Bronson Kaufusi AU RC 2.00 5.00
115 Germain Ifedi AU RC 2.50 6.00
116 Eric Murray AU RC 2.00 5.00
117 Myles Jack AU/250* RC SP 4.00 10.00
119 Andrew Billings AU RC 2.50 6.00
120 Darian Thompson AU RC 2.00 5.00
121 Demarcus Ayers AU RC 2.00 5.00
122 Jihad Ward AU RC 2.00 5.00
123 Jonathan Bullard AU/70* RC SP A 5.00 12.00
124 Jay Lee AU RC 2.00 5.00
125 Jack Conklin AU RC 3.00 8.00
126 Cyrus Jones AU RC 2.00 5.00
127 Tyler Higbee AU RC 2.00 5.00
128 A'Shawn Robinson AU/250* RC SP 3.00 8.00
129 Charone Peake AU RC 2.00 5.00
130 Blake Martinez AU/250* RC SP 4.00 10.00
131 Jerell Adams AU/242* RC SP 3.00 8.00
132 Cody Whitehair AU RC 3.00 8.00
133 Daniel Lasco AU RC 2.00 5.00
134 DeForest Buckner AU RC 2.00 5.00
135 Nelson Spruce AU/22* RC 8.00 20.00
136 Karl Joseph AU RC EXCH 2.00 5.00
137 Josh Ferguson AU/212 RC SP 6.00 15.00
138 Tajae Sharpe AU RC 2.50 6.00
139 Artie Burns AU RC 6.00 15.00
141 Jaylon Smith AU/250* RC SP 3.00 8.00
142 Cayleb Jones AU/68* RC SP 5.00 12.00
143 Yannick Ngakoue AU RC 3.00 8.00
144 Thomas Duarte AU RC 2.00 5.00
146 Kevon Seymour AU RC 2.00 5.00
147 Jacoby Brissett AU RC 6.00 15.00
148 Eli Apple AU RC 2.50 6.00
149 Vonn Bell AU RC 2.50 6.00
150 Chase Reynolds AU/50* RC SP A
151 Sheldon Rankins AU RC 2.50 6.00
152 Roberto Aguayo AU RC 2.00 5.00
153 Xavien Howard AU RC 2.50 6.00
154 Jalin Marshall AU RC 3.00 8.00
155 Kevin Byard AU RC 2.00 5.00
156 Ryan Kelly AU RC 3.00 8.00
157 Maliek Collins AU RC 2.00 5.00
158 Aaron Green AU RC 2.00 5.00
159 Kelvin Taylor AU/100* RC SP 4.00 10.00
160 Adam Gotsis AU RC 2.00 5.00
161 Trevone Boykin AU/182* RC SP 3.00 8.00
162 Brandon Doughty AU RC 2.00 5.00
163 Cody Core AU RC 2.00 5.00
165 Peyton Barber AU RC 2.00 5.00
166 Jeremy Cash AU RC 2.50 6.00
167 Kenny Clark AU RC 2.00 5.00
168 Devon Cajuste AU/199 RC SP 3.00 8.00
169 Miles Killebrew AU RC 2.00 5.00
170 Kamalei Correa AU RC
171 Darius Jackson AU RC 2.50 6.00
172 Dan Vitale AU/250* RC SP 3.00 8.00
173 Deion Jones AU RC
174 Jordan Payton AU RC 2.00 5.00
175 Mackensie Alexander AU RC 2.00 5.00
176 Noah Spence AU RC 2.00 5.00
177 Keyarris Garrett AU/190* RC SP 3.00 8.00
178 Reggie Ragland AU/250* RC SP 3.00 8.00
179 Rico Gathers AU RC 2.00 5.00
180 Byron Marshall AU RC 2.00 5.00
181 Su'a Cravens AU RC 2.00 5.00
182 Sean Davis AU RC 2.00 5.00
183 Vernon Hargreaves III AU RC 3.00 8.00
184 Jordan Jenkins AU RC 3.00 8.00
185 Vernon Butler AU RC 2.00 5.00
186 Kolby Listenbee AU RC 2.00 5.00
187 Maurice Canady AU/168* RC 3.00 8.00
188 Kei'Varae Russell AU RC 2.00 5.00
189 Emmanuel Ogbah AU RC 2.50 6.00
190 Brandon Allen AU RC 2.00 5.00
191 Charles Tapper AU RC 2.50 6.00
192 Taylor Decker AU RC 2.50 6.00
193 Jarran Reed AU RC 2.00 5.00
194 Jason Spriggs AU RC 2.00 5.00
197 D.J. Foster AU RC 2.50 6.00
198 Anthony Zettel AU/146* RC 8.00 20.00
199 Shaq Lawson AU RC 2.00 5.00
200 Tre Madden AU RC 2.00 5.00
202 Adolphus Washington AU RC 2.00 5.00
204 Jalen Mills AU RC 2.50 6.00
205 Jayron Kearse AU/250* RC SP 3.00 8.00
206 Leonard Floyd AU/150* RC SP 15.00 40.00
207 Scooby Wright III AU RC 2.00 5.00
208 Shilique Calhoun AU RC 2.00 5.00
209 Nick Vannett AU RC 2.00 5.00
210 Nate Sudfeld AU RC 2.00 5.00
211 Kyle Carter AU/144* RC 3.00 8.00
213 Spencer Drango AU/141* RC SP 3.00 8.00
214 Austin Johnson AU RC 2.00 5.00
215 Chris Jones AU RC 2.00 5.00
217 Daryl Worley AU RC 2.00 5.00
218 Austin Hooper AU RC 2.00 5.00
219 Carl Nassib AU RC 2.00 5.00
220 D.J. White AU RC 2.00 5.00
221 Kenny Lawler AU RC 3.00 8.00
222 Kendall Fuller AU RC 2.50 6.00
223 Daniel Braverman AU RC 2.00 5.00
224 James Bradberry AU RC 2.50 6.00
225 Brandon Williams AU RC 2.00 5.00
226 Javon Hargrave AU RC 6.00 15.00
227 Vincent Valentine AU RC
228 Jordan Jenkins AU 3.00 8.00
229 Kyler Fackrell AU/205* RC SP 15.00 40.00
230 Nick Vigil AU RC 2.00 5.00
231 Justin Simmons AU RC 2.50 6.00
232 Tyreek Hill AU RC 50.00 100.00
233 Seth DeValve AU RC 2.50 6.00
234 Mike Thomas AU RC 3.00 8.00
235 Delvin Breaux AU RC 2.50 6.00
236 Dwayne Washington AU RC 2.50 6.00
237 Cole Wick AU RC 2.50 6.00
238 Temarrick Hemingway AU RC 2.00 5.00
239 Jakeem Grant AU RC 2.00 5.00
240 Roger Lewis AU RC 2.00 5.00
241 Devin Fuller AU RC 2.50 6.00
242 Robert Kelley AU RC 8.00 20.00
243 Eli Rogers AU RC
244 A.J. Derby AU RC 2.00 5.00
245 Adam Thielen AU RC 100.00 200.00
247 Tavon Young AU RC 2.00 5.00
248 Andy Janovich AU RC 2.50 6.00
249 Brandon McManus AU/250* RC SP 3.00 8.00
250 Troymaine Pope AU RC 2.50 6.00
251 Blake Martinez AU 5.00 12.00
252 Chester Rogers AU RC 2.50 6.00
254 A'Shawn Robinson AU/138* SP 3.00 8.00
256 Tanner McEvoy AU RC 2.50 6.00
257 Dadi Lhomme Nicolas AU RC 2.50 6.00
258 Jacoby Brissett AU SP A 6.00 15.00
259 Robby Anderson AU RC 2.50 6.00
260 Charone Peake AU 2.00 5.00
261 Eli Apple AU/250* SP 4.00 10.00
262 Brandon Allen AU 2.00 5.00
263 Emmanuel Ogbah AU 2.50 6.00
264 Kenneth Farrow AU RC 2.50 6.00
265 Adam Humphries AU RC 2.00 5.00
266 Kei'Varae Russell AU 2.00 5.00
267 Juston Burris AU RC 2.00 5.00
268 Austin Hooper AU/250* SP 3.00 8.00
269 Johnny Holton AU RC 2.00 5.00
270 Jaylon Smith AU 2.00 5.00
271 Tyler Matakevich AU RC 2.00 5.00
272 Erik Swoope AU RC 2.00 5.00
273 Jayron Kearse AU/250* SP
274 Joe Callahan RC 2.50 6.00
275 Damiere Byrd AU RC 2.00 5.00
276 Paul Turner AU RC 2.50 6.00
277 Cameron Brate AU RC 2.50 6.00
278 Jhurell Pressley AU RC 2.50 6.00
279 Jordan Payton AU RC 2.00 5.00
280 Sheldon Day AU RC 2.00 5.00
281 Myles Jack AU/150* RC SP 4.00 10.00
282 Nate Sudfeld AU 2.00 5.00
283 Daniel Braverman AU 2.00 5.00
284 Kevin Dodd AU 2.00 5.00
285 Noah Spence AU 2.00 5.00
286 Nick Kwiatkoski AU RC 3.00 8.00
287 Sheldon Rankins AU 2.50 6.00
288 Thomas Duarte AU 2.00 5.00
289 Nick Vannett AU 2.00 5.00
290 Su'a Cravens AU 2.00 5.00
291 David Morgan AU RC 2.00 5.00
292 Vernon Butler AU/250* SP 3.00 8.00
293 Jalen Richard AU RC 2.50 6.00
294 Tommylee Lewis RC 2.50 6.00
295 Vernon Hargreaves III AU/250* RC SP 5.00 12.00
296 Tyreek Hill AU/150* SP 40.00 80.00
297 Hue Jackson AU 8.00 20.00
299 Gus Bradley AU 2.50 6.00
300 Mike Zimmer AU/173* SP 20.00 50.00
301A Jared Goff AU/250* RC SP 300.00 600.00
301B Jared Goff AU/25* SP A 300.00 600.00
302A Carson Wentz AU/250* RC SP 250.00 500.00
302B Carson Wentz AU/25* SP A 150.00 300.00
303A Paxton Lynch AU RC 25.00 50.00
303B Paxton Lynch AU/49* SP A 30.00 60.00
304 Christian Hackenberg AU RC 4.00 10.00
305 Cody Kessler AU RC 3.00 8.00
306 Connor Cook AU/150* RC SP 12.00 30.00
307A Dak Prescott AU/250* RC SP 100.00 200.00
307B Dak Prescott AU/25* SP 100.00 200.00
308 Cardale Jones AU/250* RC SP 3.00 8.00
309 Kevin Hogan AU/43* RC SP A 20.00 40.00
310A Ezekiel Elliott AU RC 250.00 500.00
310B Ezekiel Elliott AU/25* SP A
311A Derrick Henry AU/150* RC SP 40.00 80.00
311B Derrick Henry AU/25* SP A 50.00 100.00
312A Kenyan Drake AU RC 3.00 8.00
312B Kenyan Drake AU/199* SP 5.00 12.00
313A C.J. Prosise AU/200* RC SP 8.00 20.00
313B C.J. Prosise AU/49* SP 8.00 20.00
314 Tyler Ervin AU RC 2.00 5.00
315 Kenneth Dixon AU/48* RC SP
316A Devontae Booker AU RC 2.50 6.00
316B Devontae Booker AU/99* SP 5.00 12.00
317A Paul Perkins AU RC 2.00 5.00
317B Paul Perkins AU/99* SP 4.00 10.00
318 Jordan Howard AU RC 15.00 40.00
319 Wendell Smallwood AU RC 2.00 5.00
320 Jonathan Williams AU RC 2.50 6.00
321 Alex Collins AU RC EXCH 2.50 6.00
322 Keenan Reynolds AU/100* RC SP 5.00 12.00
323A DeAndre Washington AU RC 2.00 5.00
323B DeAndre Washington AU/199* SP 3.00 8.00
324 Joey Bosa AU/200* RC SP 30.00 60.00
325A Corey Coleman AU/250* RC SP 5.00 12.00
325B Corey Coleman AU/99* SP A 6.00 15.00
326A Laquon Treadwell AU/250* RC SP 4.00 10.00
326B Laquon Treadwell AU/90* SP A 5.00 12.00
327A Josh Doctson AU RC 6.00 15.00
327B Josh Doctson AU/99* SP 6.00 15.00
328A Will Fuller V AU RC 6.00 15.00
328B Will Fuller V AU/99* SP A 6.00 15.00
329A Sterling Shepard AU RC SP A 6.00 15.00
329B Sterling Shepard AU/99* SP 15.00 40.00
330 Michael Thomas AU/250* RC SP 25.00 50.00
331A Tyler Boyd AU RC SP A 6.00 15.00
331B Tyler Boyd AU/99* SP 8.00 20.00
332 Braxton Miller AU RC 2.00 5.00
333A Leonte Carroo AU RC 2.00 5.00
333B Leonte Carroo AU/189* SP 3.00 8.00
334 Chris Moore AU RC 2.50 6.00
335 Ricardo Louis AU RC 2.00 5.00
336 Pharoh Cooper AU RC 2.00 5.00
337 Demarcus Robinson AU RC 2.00 5.00
338A Trevor Davis AU RC 2.00 5.00
338B Trevor Davis AU/199* 3.00 8.00
339A Moritz Bohringer AU RC 2.00 5.00
339B Moritz Bohringer AU 2.00 5.00
340 Hunter Henry AU RC EXCH 2.50 6.00
341 Jared Goff AU/49* SP A 300.00 600.00
342 Carson Wentz AU/49* SP 250.00 500.00
343 Paxton Lynch AU/49* SP A 25.00 50.00
344 Christian Hackenberg AU/49* SP A 5.00 12.00
345 Cody Kessler AU/99* SP 20.00 50.00
346 Connor Cook AU/25* SP A 15.00 40.00
347 Dak Prescott AU/25* SP 100.00 200.00
348 Cardale Jones AU/99* SP 10.00 25.00
349 Kevin Hogan AU/48* SP A 20.00 40.00
350 Ezekiel Elliott AU/25* SP A
351 Derrick Henry AU/25* SP 50.00 100.00
352 Kenyan Drake AU/199* SP 6.00 15.00
353 C.J. Prosise AU/25* SP 15.00 40.00
354 Tyler Ervin AU/223* SP 3.00 8.00
355 Kenneth Dixon AU/25* SP A 40.00 80.00
356 Devontae Booker AU/99* SP 6.00 15.00
357 Paul Perkins AU/99* SP A 4.00 10.00
358A Jordan Howard AU/99* SP A 30.00 60.00
359 Wendell Smallwood AU/249* SP 3.00 8.00
360 Jonathan Williams AU/249* SP 4.00 10.00
361 Alex Collins AU/199* SP EXCH 4.00 10.00
362 Keenan Reynolds AU/192* SP 4.00 10.00
363 DeAndre Washington AU/249* SP 3.00 8.00
364 Joey Bosa AU/49* SP EXCH 30.00 60.00
365 Corey Coleman AU/98* SP A 6.00 15.00
366 Laquon Treadwell AU/99* SP 5.00 12.00
367 Josh Doctson AU/96* SP 6.00 15.00
368 Will Fuller V AU/99* SP 6.00 15.00
369 Sterling Shepard AU/99* SP 15.00 40.00
370 Michael Thomas AU/49* SP 25.00 50.00
371 Tyler Boyd AU/98* SP 8.00 20.00
372 Braxton Miller AU/49* SP 5.00 12.00
373 Leonte Carroo AU/249* SP 3.00 8.00
374 Chris Moore AU/249 SP 4.00 10.00
375 Ricardo Louis AU/199* SP 3.00 8.00
376 Pharoh Cooper AU/99* SP 4.00 10.00
377 Demarcus Robinson AU/249* SP 3.00 8.00
378 Trevor Davis AU/249* SP 3.00 8.00
379 Moritz Bohringer AU 2.00 5.00
380 Hunter Henry AU/185* SP EXCH 4.00 10.00

2016 Panini Contenders Championship Ticket

*1-100 VETS: 4X TO 10X BASIC CARDS
101 Glenn Gronkowski AU/49 6.00 15.00
102 Jalen Ramsey AU/25 30.00 80.00
103 Kevin Dodd AU/25 8.00 20.00
104 Ronnie Stanley AU/99 6.00 15.00
105 William Jackson III AU/99 6.00 15.00
106 Derek Watt AU/49 10.00 25.00
107 Keanu Neal AU/49 6.00 15.00
108 Malcolm Mitchell AU/49 25.00 60.00
109 Bralon Addison AU/49 6.00 15.00
110 Jeff Driskel AU/49 6.00 15.00
111 Jake Rudock AU/49 6.00 15.00
112 Keith Marshall AU/49 6.00 15.00
113 Rashard Higgins AU/49 6.00 15.00
114 Bronson Kaufusi AU/99 5.00 12.00
115 Germain Ifedi AU/99 6.00 15.00
116 Eric Murray AU/49 6.00 15.00
117 Myles Jack AU/99 6.00 15.00
119 Andrew Billings AU/49 8.00 20.00
120 Darian Thompson AU/99 5.00 12.00
121 Demarcus Ayers AU/99 10.00 25.00
122 Jihad Ward AU/99 5.00 12.00
123 Jonathan Bullard AU/99 5.00 12.00
124 Jay Lee AU/99 5.00 12.00
125 Jack Conklin AU/99 8.00 20.00
126 Cyrus Jones AU/99 5.00 12.00
127 Tyler Higbee AU/99 5.00 12.00
128 A'Shawn Robinson AU/99 5.00 12.00
129 Charone Peake AU/49 6.00 15.00
130 Blake Martinez AU/99 6.00 15.00
131 Jerell Adams AU/25 8.00 20.00
132 Cody Whitehair AU/99 8.00 20.00
133 Daniel Lasco AU/99 5.00 12.00
134 DeForest Buckner AU/49 6.00 15.00
135 Nelson Spruce AU/25 8.00 20.00
136 Karl Joseph AU EXCH/99 5.00 12.00
137 Josh Ferguson AU/49 6.00 15.00
138 Tajae Sharpe AU/99 6.00 15.00
139 Artie Burns AU/99 25.00 60.00
141 Jaylon Smith AU/99 5.00 12.00
142 Cayleb Jones AU/25 8.00 20.00
143 Yannick Ngakoue AU/99 8.00 20.00
144 Thomas Duarte AU/99 5.00 12.00
146 Kevon Seymour AU/99 5.00 12.00
147 Jacoby Brissett AU/99 12.00 30.00
148 Eli Apple AU/99 6.00 15.00
149 Vonn Bell AU/99 6.00 15.00
150 Chase Reynolds AU/25 8.00 20.00
151 Sheldon Rankins AU/99 6.00 15.00
152 Roberto Aguayo AU/99 5.00 12.00
153 Xavien Howard AU/99 6.00 15.00
154 Jalin Marshall AU/99 8.00 20.00
155 Kevin Byard AU/99 5.00 12.00
156 Ryan Kelly AU/99 8.00 20.00
157 Maliek Collins AU/49 6.00 15.00
158 Aaron Green AU/49 6.00 15.00
159 Kelvin Taylor AU/49 6.00 15.00
160 Adam Gotsis AU/99 5.00 12.00
161 Trevone Boykin AU/25 8.00 20.00
162 Brandon Doughty AU/99 5.00 12.00
163 Cody Core AU/99 5.00 12.00
165 Peyton Barber AU/25 8.00 20.00
166 Jeremy Cash AU/99 6.00 15.00
167 Kenny Clark AU/49 6.00 15.00
168 Devon Cajuste AU/49 6.00 15.00
169 Miles Killebrew AU/99 5.00 12.00
170 Kamalei Correa AU/99
171 Darius Jackson AU/99 6.00 15.00
172 Dan Vitale AU/99 5.00 12.00
173 Deion Jones AU/99 5.00 12.00
174 Jordan Payton AU/49 6.00 15.00
175 Mackensie Alexander AU/99 5.00 12.00
176 Noah Spence AU/99 5.00 12.00
177 Keyarris Garrett AU/99 5.00 12.00
178 Reggie Ragland AU/49 6.00 15.00
179 Rico Gathers AU/49 6.00 15.00
180 Byron Marshall AU/49 6.00 15.00
181 Su'a Cravens AU/99 5.00 12.00
182 Sean Davis AU/99 12.00 30.00
183 Vernon Hargreaves III AU/49 10.00 25.00
184 Jordan Jenkins AU/99 8.00 20.00
185 Vernon Butler AU/99
186 Kolby Listenbee AU/99 5.00 12.00
187 Maurice Canady AU/25 8.00 20.00
188 Kei'Varae Russell AU/49 6.00 15.00
189 Emmanuel Ogbah AU/49 8.00 20.00
190 Brandon Allen AU/49 6.00 15.00
191 Charles Tapper AU/99 6.00 15.00
192 Taylor Decker AU/49 8.00 20.00
193 Jarran Reed AU/99 5.00 12.00
194 Jason Spriggs AU/99 5.00 12.00
195 Robert Nkemdiche AU/49 8.00 20.00
197 D.J. Foster AU/79 6.00 15.00
198 Anthony Zettel AU/25 10.00 25.00
199 Shaq Lawson AU/25
200 Tre Madden AU/49
201 T.J. Green AU/49
202 Adolphus Washington AU/99 5.00 12.00
204 Jalen Mills AU/49 8.00 20.00
205 Jayron Kearse AU/25 8.00 20.00
206 Leonard Floyd AU/25 40.00 00.00
207 Scooby Wright III AU/99 5.00 12.00
208 Shilique Calhoun AU/49 6.00 15.00
209 Nick Vannett AU/49 6.00 15.00

210 Nate Sudfeld AU/49 6.00 15.00
211 Kyle Carter AU/25 8.00 20.00
213 Spencer Drango AU/25 8.00 20.00
214 Austin Johnson AU/49 6.00 15.00
215 Chris Jones AU/49 6.00 15.00
217 Daryl Worley AU/49 6.00 15.00
218 Austin Hooper AU/99 5.00 12.00
219 Carl Nassib AU/99 5.00 12.00
220 D.J. White AU/49 6.00 15.00
221 Kenny Lawler AU/49 10.00 25.00
222 Kendall Fuller AU/49 8.00 20.00
223 Daniel Braverman AU/99 5.00 12.00
224 James Bradberry AU/49 8.00 20.00
225 Brandon Williams AU/49 6.00 15.00
226 Javon Hargrave AU/49 10.00 25.00
227 Vincent Valentine AU/49
228 Jordan Jenkins AU/49 10.00 25.00
229 Kyler Fackrell AU/49 8.00 20.00
230 Nick Vigil AU/49 6.00 15.00
231 Justin Simmons AU/49 8.00 20.00
232 Tyreek Hill AU/49 90.00 150.00
233 Seth DeValve AU/49 8.00 20.00
234 Mike Thomas AU/49 10.00 25.00
235 Delvin Breaux AU/49 8.00 20.00
236 Dwayne Washington AU/99 6.00 15.00
237 Cole Wick AU/99 6.00 15.00
238 Temarrick Hemingway AU/99 5.00 12.00
239 Jakeem Grant AU/99 5.00 12.00
240 Roger Lewis AU/99 5.00 12.00
241 Devin Fuller AU/49 8.00 20.00
242 Robert Kelley AU/49 10.00 25.00
243 Eli Rogers AU/49 8.00 20.00
244 A.J. Derby AU/49 6.00 15.00
245 Adam Thielen AU EXCH/49 150.00 300.00
247 Tavon Young AU/49 6.00 15.00
248 Andy Janovich AU/49 8.00 20.00
249 Brandon McManus AU/25 15.00 40.00
250 Troymaine Pope AU/49 8.00 20.00
251 Blake Martinez AU/25 10.00 25.00
252 Chester Rogers AU/49 8.00 20.00
254 A'Shawn Robinson AU/49 6.00 15.00
256 Tanner McEvoy AU/99 6.00 15.00
257 Dadi Lhomme Nicolas AU/49 8.00 20.00
258 Jacoby Brissett AU/25 20.00 50.00
259 Robby Anderson AU/49 8.00 20.00
260 Charone Peake AU/49 6.00 15.00
261 Eli Apple AU/25 20.00 50.00
262 Brandon Allen AU/49 6.00 15.00
263 Emmanuel Ogbah AU/49 8.00 20.00
264 Kenneth Farrow AU/49 8.00 20.00
265 Adam Humphries AU/49 6.00 15.00
266 Kei'Varae Russell AU/49 6.00 15.00
267 Juston Burris AU/49 8.00 20.00
268 Austin Hooper AU/49 6.00 15.00
269 Johnny Holton AU/99 5.00 12.00
270 Jaylon Smith AU/49 6.00 15.00
271 Tyler Matakevich AU/49 10.00 25.00
272 Erik Swoope AU/49 6.00 15.00
273 Jayron Kearse AU/49 6.00 15.00
274 Joe Callahan/49 8.00 20.00
275 Damiere Byrd AU/49 6.00 15.00
276 Paul Turner AU/25
277 Cameron Brate AU/49 8.00 20.00
278 Jhurell Pressley AU/49 8.00 20.00
279 Jordan Payton AU/49 6.00 15.00
280 Sheldon Day AU/49 6.00 15.00
281 Myles Jack AU/99 6.00 15.00
282 Nate Sudfeld AU/49 6.00 15.00
283 Daniel Braverman AU/99 5.00 12.00
284 Kevin Dodd AU/49 6.00 15.00
285 Noah Spence AU/49 6.00 15.00
286 Nick Kwiatkoski AU/49 10.00 25.00
287 Sheldon Rankins AU/25 10.00 25.00
288 Thomas Duarte AU/25 8.00 20.00
289 Nick Vannett AU/49 6.00 15.00
290 Su'a Cravens AU/49 6.00 15.00
291 David Morgan AU/99 5.00 12.00
292 Vernon Butler AU/49
293 Jalen Richard AU/49 25.00 60.00
294 Tommylee Lewis/49 8.00 20.00
295 Vernon Hargreaves III AU/25 12.00 30.00
296 Tyreek Hill AU/25 100.00 200.00
297 Hue Jackson AU 8.00 20.00
299 Gus Bradley AU 8.00 20.00
300 Mike Zimmer AU 25.00 50.00
301A Jared Goff AU/25 600.00 1000.00
301B Jared Goff AU/25 600.00 1000.00
302A Carson Wentz AU/25 300.00 500.00
302B Carson Wentz AU/25 300.00 500.00
303A Paxton Lynch AU/25 60.00 120.00
303B Paxton Lynch AU/25 60.00 120.00
304 Christian Hackenberg AU/25 8.00 20.00
305 Cody Kessler AU/25 8.00 20.00
306 Connor Cook AU/25 10.00 25.00
307A Dak Prescott AU/25 200.00 400.00
307B Dak Prescott AU/25 200.00 400.00
308 Cardale Jones AU/25 8.00 20.00
310A Ezekiel Elliott AU/25
310B Ezekiel Elliott AU/25
311A Derrick Henry AU/25 75.00 150.00
311B Derrick Henry AU/25 75.00 150.00
312A Kenyan Drake AU/99 8.00 20.00
312B Kenyan Drake AU/99 8.00 20.00
313A C.J. Prosise AU/25 8.00 20.00
313B C.J. Prosise AU/25 8.00 20.00
314 Tyler Ervin AU/99 5.00 12.00
315 Kenneth Dixon AU/25 25.00 60.00
316A Devontae Booker AU/25 10.00 25.00
316B Devontae Booker AU/25 10.00 25.00
317A Paul Perkins AU/25 8.00 20.00
317B Paul Perkins AU/99 5.00 12.00
318 Jordan Howard AU/25 150.00 250.00
319 Wendell Smallwood AU/99 5.00 12.00
320 Jonathan Williams AU/99 6.00 15.00
321 Alex Collins AU EXCH/25 10.00 25.00
322 Keenan Reynolds AU/99 6.00 15.00
323A DeAndre Washington AU/99 5.00 12.00
323B DeAndre Washington AU/99 5.00 12.00
324 Joey Bosa AU/25 EXCH 40.00 80.00
325A Corey Coleman AU/25 12.00 30.00
325B Corey Coleman AU/49 10.00 25.00
326A Laquon Treadwell AU/25 10.00 25.00
326B Laquon Treadwell AU/39 8.00 20.00
327A Josh Doctson AU/25 10.00 25.00
327B Josh Doctson AU/49 8.00 20.00
328A Will Fuller V AU/25 12.00 30.00
328B Will Fuller V AU/25 12.00 30.00
329A Sterling Shepard AU/25 40.00 100.00
329B Sterling Shepard AU/25 40.00 100.00
330 Michael Thomas AU/25
331A Tyler Boyd AU/25 25.00 50.00
331B Tyler Boyd AU/25 25.00 50.00
332 Braxton Miller AU/25 8.00 20.00
333A Leonte Carroo AU/99 5.00 12.00
333B Leonte Carroo AU/99 5.00 12.00
334 Chris Moore AU/99 6.00 15.00
335 Ricardo Louis AU/99 5.00 12.00
336 Pharoh Cooper AU/39 6.00 15.00
337 Demarcus Robinson AU/99 5.00 12.00
338A Trevor Davis AU/99 5.00 12.00
338B Trevor Davis AU/99 5.00 12.00
339A Moritz Bohringer AU/99 5.00 12.00
339B Moritz Bohringer AU/99 5.00 12.00
340 Hunter Henry AU/99 EXCH 6.00 15.00
341 Jared Goff AU/25 600.00 1000.00
342 Carson Wentz AU/25 300.00 500.00
343 Paxton Lynch AU/25 60.00 120.00
344 Christian Hackenberg AU/25 8.00 20.00
345 Cody Kessler AU/25 8.00 20.00
346 Connor Cook AU/25 10.00 25.00
347 Dak Prescott AU/25 200.00 400.00
348 Cardale Jones AU/25 8.00 20.00
350 Ezekiel Elliott AU/25
351 Derrick Henry AU/25 75.00 150.00
352 Kenyan Drake AU/99 8.00 20.00
353 C.J. Prosise AU/25 8.00 20.00
354 Tyler Ervin AU/99 5.00 12.00
355 Kenneth Dixon AU/25 25.00 60.00
356 Devontae Booker AU/25 10.00 25.00
357 Paul Perkins AU/25 8.00 20.00
358 Jordan Howard AU/49 40.00 100.00
359 Wendell Smallwood AU/99 5.00 12.00
360 Jonathan Williams AU/99 6.00 15.00
361 Alex Collins AU EXCH/49 8.00 20.00
362 Keenan Reynolds AU/49 8.00 20.00
363 DeAndre Washington AU/99 5.00 12.00
364 Joey Bosa AU/25 EXCH 40.00 80.00
365 Corey Coleman AU/25 12.00 30.00
366 Laquon Treadwell AU/25 10.00 25.00
367 Josh Doctson AU/25 10.00 25.00
368 Will Fuller V AU/25 12.00 30.00
369 Sterling Shepard AU/25 40.00 100.00
370 Michael Thomas AU/25
371 Tyler Boyd AU/25 25.00 50.00
372 Braxton Miller AU EXCH/25 8.00 20.00
373 Leonte Carroo AU/99 5.00 12.00
374 Chris Moore AU/99 6.00 15.00
375 Ricardo Louis AU/99 5.00 12.00
376 Pharoh Cooper AU/49 6.00 15.00
377 Demarcus Robinson AU/99 5.00 12.00
378 Trevor Davis AU/99 5.00 12.00
379 Moritz Bohringer AU/99 5.00 12.00
380 Hunter Henry AU/99 EXCH 6.00 15.00

2016 Panini Contenders Playoff Ticket

*1-100 VETS/199: 2.5X TO 6X BASIC CARDS
101 Glenn Gronkowski AU/99 5.00 12.00
102 Jalen Ramsey AU/49 25.00 60.00
103 Kevin Dodd AU/49 6.00 15.00
104 Ronnie Stanley AU/199 5.00 12.00
105 William Jackson III AU/199 5.00 12.00
106 Derek Watt AU/99 8.00 20.00
107 Keanu Neal AU/99 5.00 12.00
108 Malcolm Mitchell AU/99 20.00 50.00
109 Bralon Addison AU/99 5.00 12.00
110 Jeff Driskel AU/99 5.00 12.00
111 Jake Rudock AU/99 5.00 12.00
112 Keith Marshall AU/99 5.00 12.00
113 Rashard Higgins AU/99 5.00 12.00
114 Bronson Kaufusi AU/199 4.00 10.00
115 Germain Ifedi AU/199 5.00 12.00
116 Eric Murray AU/99 5.00 12.00
117 Myles Jack AU/199 5.00 12.00
119 Andrew Billings AU/99 6.00 15.00
120 Darian Thompson AU/199 4.00 10.00
121 Demarcus Ayers AU/199 8.00 20.00
122 Jihad Ward AU/199 4.00 10.00
123 Jonathan Bullard AU/199 4.00 10.00
124 Jay Lee AU/199 4.00 10.00
125 Jack Conklin AU/199 6.00 15.00
126 Cyrus Jones AU/199 4.00 10.00
127 Tyler Higbee AU/199 4.00 10.00
128 A'Shawn Robinson AU/199 4.00 10.00
129 Charone Peake AU/99 5.00 12.00
130 Blake Martinez AU/199 5.00 12.00
131 Jerell Adams AU/49 6.00 15.00
132 Cody Whitehair AU/199 6.00 15.00
133 Daniel Lasco AU/199 4.00 10.00
134 DeForest Buckner AU/99 5.00 12.00
135 Nelson Spruce AU/25 8.00 20.00
136 Karl Joseph AU EXCH/199 4.00 10.00
137 Josh Ferguson AU/99 5.00 12.00
138 Tajae Sharpe AU/199 5.00 12.00
139 Artie Burns AU/199 20.00 50.00
141 Jaylon Smith AU/199 4.00 10.00
142 Cayleb Jones AU/49 6.00 15.00
143 Yannick Ngakoue AU/199 6.00 15.00
144 Thomas Duarte AU/199 4.00 10.00
146 Kevon Seymour AU/199 4.00 10.00
147 Jacoby Brissett AU/199 10.00 25.00
148 Eli Apple AU/199 5.00 12.00
149 Vonn Bell AU/199 5.00 12.00
150 Chase Reynolds AU/49 6.00 15.00
151 Sheldon Rankins AU/199 5.00 12.00
152 Roberto Aguayo AU/199 4.00 10.00
153 Xavien Howard AU/199 5.00 12.00
154 Jalin Marshall AU/199 6.00 15.00
155 Kevin Byard AU/199 4.00 10.00
156 Ryan Kelly AU/199 6.00 15.00
157 Maliek Collins AU/99 5.00 12.00
158 Aaron Green AU/99 5.00 12.00
159 Kelvin Taylor AU/99 5.00 12.00
160 Adam Gotsis AU/199 4.00 10.00
161 Trevone Boykin AU/49 12.00 30.00
162 Brandon Doughty AU/199 4.00 10.00
163 Cody Core AU/199 4.00 10.00
165 Peyton Barber AU/99 5.00 12.00
166 Jeremy Cash AU/199 5.00 12.00
167 Kenny Clark AU/99 5.00 12.00
168 Devon Cajuste AU/99 5.00 12.00
169 Miles Killebrew AU/199 4.00 10.00
170 Kamalei Correa AU/199
171 Darius Jackson AU/199 5.00 12.00
172 Dan Vitale AU/199 4.00 10.00
173 Deion Jones AU/199 4.00 10.00
174 Jordan Payton AU/99 5.00 12.00
175 Mackensie Alexander AU/199 4.00 10.00
176 Noah Spence AU/199 4.00 10.00
177 Keyarris Garrett AU/199 4.00 10.00
178 Reggie Ragland AU/99 5.00 12.00
179 Rico Gathers AU/99 5.00 12.00
180 Byron Marshall AU/99 5.00 12.00
181 Su'a Cravens AU/199 4.00 10.00
182 Sean Davis AU/199 10.00 25.00
183 Vernon Hargreaves III AU/99 8.00 20.00
184 Jordan Jenkins AU/199 6.00 15.00
185 Vernon Butler AU/199
186 Kolby Listenbee AU/199 4.00 10.00
187 Maurice Canady AU/49 6.00 15.00
188 Kei'Varae Russell AU/99 5.00 12.00
189 Emmanuel Ogbah AU/99 6.00 15.00
190 Brandon Allen AU/99 5.00 12.00
191 Charles Tapper AU/199 5.00 12.00
192 Taylor Decker AU/99 6.00 15.00
193 Jarran Reed AU/199 4.00 10.00
194 Jason Spriggs AU/199
195 Robert Nkemdiche AU/199
197 D.J. Foster AU/99 6.00 15.00
198 Anthony Zettel AU/49 8.00 20.00
199 Shaq Lawson AU/49 6.00 15.00
200 Tre Madden AU/99
202 Adolphus Washington AU/199 4.00 10.00
204 Jalen Mills AU/99 6.00 15.00
205 Jayron Kearse AU/49 6.00 15.00
206 Leonard Floyd AU/49 25.00 60.00
207 Scooby Wright III AU/199 4.00 10.00
208 Shilique Calhoun AU/99 5.00 12.00
209 Nick Vannett AU/99 5.00 12.00
210 Nate Sudfeld AU/99 5.00 12.00
211 Kyle Carter AU/49 6.00 15.00
213 Spencer Drango AU/49 6.00 15.00
214 Austin Johnson AU/99 5.00 12.00
215 Chris Jones AU/99 5.00 12.00
217 Daryl Worley AU/122 4.00 10.00
218 Austin Hooper AU/199 4.00 10.00
219 Carl Nassib AU/199 4.00 10.00
220 D.J. White AU/99 5.00 12.00
221 Kenny Lawler AU/99 8.00 20.00
222 Kendall Fuller AU/99 6.00 15.00
223 Daniel Braverman AU/199 4.00 10.00
224 James Bradberry AU/99 6.00 15.00
225 Brandon Williams AU/99 5.00 12.00
226 Javon Hargrave AU/99 8.00 20.00
227 Vincent Valentine AU/99
228 Jordan Jenkins AU/99 8.00 20.00
229 Kyler Fackrell AU/99 6.00 15.00
230 Nick Vigil AU/99 5.00 12.00
231 Justin Simmons AU/99 6.00 15.00
232 Tyreek Hill AU/99 90.00 150.00
233 Seth DeValve AU/99 6.00 15.00
234 Mike Thomas AU/99 8.00 20.00
235 Delvin Breaux AU/99 6.00 15.00
236 Dwayne Washington AU/99 6.00 15.00
237 Cole Wick AU/99 6.00 15.00
238 Temarrick Hemingway AU/99 5.00 12.00
239 Jakeem Grant AU/99 5.00 12.00
240 Roger Lewis AU/99 5.00 12.00
241 Devin Fuller AU/99 6.00 15.00
242 Robert Kelley AU/99 8.00 20.00
243 Eli Rogers AU/99 6.00 15.00
244 A.J. Derby AU/99 5.00 12.00
245 Adam Thielen AU EXCH/99 200.00 400.00
247 Tavon Young AU/99 5.00 12.00
248 Andy Janovich AU/99 6.00 15.00
249 Brandon McManus AU/49 12.00 30.00
250 Troymaine Pope AU/99 6.00 15.00
251 Blake Martinez AU/49 8.00 20.00
252 Chester Rogers AU/99 6.00 15.00
254 A'Shawn Robinson AU/99 5.00 12.00
256 Tanner McEvoy AU/199 5.00 12.00
257 Dadi Lhomme Nicolas AU/99 6.00 15.00
258 Jacoby Brissett AU/49 15.00 40.00
259 Robby Anderson AU/99 6.00 15.00
260 Charone Peake AU/99 5.00 12.00
261 Eli Apple AU/49
262 Brandon Allen AU/99 5.00 12.00
263 Emmanuel Ogbah AU/99 6.00 15.00
264 Kenneth Farrow AU/99 6.00 15.00
265 Adam Humphries AU/99 5.00 12.00
266 Kei'Varae Russell AU/99 5.00 12.00
267 Juston Burris AU/99 5.00 12.00
268 Austin Hooper AU/99 5.00 12.00
269 Johnny Holton AU/199 4.00 10.00
270 Jaylon Smith AU/99 5.00 12.00
271 Tyler Matakevich AU/99 8.00 20.00
272 Erik Swoope AU/99 5.00 12.00
273 Jayron Kearse AU/99 5.00 12.00
274 Joe Callahan/99 6.00 15.00
275 Damiere Byrd AU/99 5.00 12.00
276 Paul Turner AU/49
277 Cameron Brate AU/99 6.00 15.00
278 Jhurell Pressley AU/99 6.00 15.00
279 Jordan Payton AU/99 5.00 12.00
280 Sheldon Day AU/99 5.00 12.00
281 Myles Jack AU/99 6.00 15.00
282 Nate Sudfeld AU/99 5.00 12.00
283 Daniel Braverman AU/199 4.00 10.00
284 Kevin Dodd AU/99 5.00 12.00
285 Noah Spence AU/99 5.00 12.00
286 Nick Kwiatkoski AU/99 8.00 20.00
287 Sheldon Rankins AU/49 8.00 20.00
288 Thomas Duarte AU/49 6.00 15.00
289 Nick Vannett AU/99 5.00 12.00
290 Su'a Cravens AU/99 5.00 12.00
291 David Morgan AU/199 4.00 10.00
292 Vernon Butler AU/99
293 Jalen Richard AU/99 15.00 40.00
294 Tommylee Lewis/99 6.00 15.00
295 Vernon Hargreaves III AU/49 10.00 25.00
296 Tyreek Hill AU/49 90.00 150.00
297 Hue Jackson AU 6.00 15.00
299 Gus Bradley AU 6.00 15.00
300 Mike Zimmer AU 20.00 40.00
301A Jared Goff AU/25 600.00 1000.00
301B Jared Goff AU/25 600.00 1000.00
302A Carson Wentz AU/25 300.00 600.00
302B Carson Wentz AU/25 300.00 600.00
303A Paxton Lynch AU/49 50.00 100.00
303B Paxton Lynch AU/39 50.00 100.00
304 Christian Hackenberg AU/49 6.00 15.00
305 Cody Kessler AU/49 6.00 15.00
306 Connor Cook AU/25 10.00 25.00
307A Dak Prescott AU/25 200.00 400.00
307B Dak Prescott AU/25 200.00 400.00
308 Cardale Jones AU/49 6.00 15.00
310A Ezekiel Elliott AU/25
310B Ezekiel Elliott AU/25
311A Derrick Henry AU/25 75.00 150.00
311B Derrick Henry AU/25 75.00 150.00
312A Kenyan Drake AU/199 6.00 15.00
312B Kenyan Drake AU/199 6.00 15.00
313A C.J. Prosise AU/25 8.00 20.00
313B C.J. Prosise AU/49 6.00 15.00
314 Tyler Ervin AU/199 4.00 10.00
315 Kenneth Dixon AU/25 25.00 60.00
316A Devontae Booker AU/49 8.00 20.00
316B Devontae Booker AU/99 6.00 15.00
317A Paul Perkins AU/49 6.00 15.00
317B Paul Perkins AU/99 5.00 12.00
318 Jordan Howard AU/49 40.00 100.00
319 Wendell Smallwood AU/199 4.00 10.00
320 Jonathan Williams AU/199 EXCH 5.00 12.00
321 Alex Collins AU EXCH/99 6.00 15.00
322 Keenan Reynolds AU/199 5.00 12.00
323A DeAndre Washington AU/199 4.00 10.00
323B DeAndre Washington AU/199 4.00 10.00
324 Joey Bosa AU/35 EXCH 30.00 60.00
325A Corey Coleman AU/99 8.00 20.00
325B Corey Coleman AU/99 8.00 20.00
326A Laquon Treadwell AU/49 8.00 20.00
326B Laquon Treadwell AU/99 6.00 15.00
327A Josh Doctson AU/99 6.00 15.00
327B Josh Doctson AU/99 6.00 15.00
328A Will Fuller V AU/99 8.00 20.00
328B Will Fuller V AU/99 8.00 20.00
329A Sterling Shepard AU/49 8.00 20.00
329B Sterling Shepard AU/99 6.00 15.00
330 Michael Thomas AU/49 40.00 80.00
331A Tyler Boyd AU/49 12.00 30.00
331B Tyler Boyd AU/99 6.00 15.00
332 Braxton Miller AU/49 6.00 15.00
333A Leonte Carroo AU/199 4.00 10.00
333B Leonte Carroo AU/199 4.00 10.00
334 Chris Moore AU/199 5.00 12.00
335 Ricardo Louis AU/199 4.00 10.00
336 Pharoh Cooper AU/99 5.00 12.00
337 Demarcus Robinson AU/199 4.00 10.00
338A Trevor Davis AU/199 4.00 10.00
338B Trevor Davis AU/199 4.00 10.00
339A Moritz Bohringer AU/199 4.00 10.00
339B Moritz Bohringer AU/199 4.00 10.00
340 Hunter Henry AU/199 EXCH 5.00 12.00
341 Jared Goff AU/25 600.00 1000.00
342 Carson Wentz AU/25 300.00 600.00
343 Paxton Lynch AU/49 50.00 100.00
344 Christian Hackenberg AU/49 6.00 15.00
345 Cody Kessler AU/49 6.00 15.00
346 Connor Cook AU/25 10.00 25.00
347 Dak Prescott AU/25 200.00 400.00
348 Cardale Jones AU/49 6.00 15.00
350 Ezekiel Elliott AU/25
351 Derrick Henry AU/25 75.00 150.00
352 Kenyan Drake AU/199 6.00 15.00
353 C.J. Prosise AU/25 8.00 20.00
354 Tyler Ervin AU/199 4.00 10.00
355 Kenneth Dixon AU/25 25.00 60.00
356 Devontae Booker AU/49 8.00 20.00
357 Paul Perkins AU/99 5.00 12.00
358A Jordan Howard AU/99 40.00 80.00
358B J.Howard UER 200.00 400.00
P.Perkins AU
359 Wendell Smallwood AU/199 4.00 10.00
360 Jonathan Williams AU/199 EXCH 5.00 12.00
361 Alex Collins AU EXCH/99 6.00 15.00
362 Keenan Reynolds AU/199 5.00 12.00
363 DeAndre Washington AU/199 4.00 10.00
364 Joey Bosa AU/25 EXCH 40.00 80.00
365 Corey Coleman AU/49 10.00 25.00
366 Laquon Treadwell AU/49 8.00 20.00
367 Josh Doctson AU/49 8.00 20.00
368 Will Fuller V AU/99 8.00 20.00
369 Sterling Shepard AU/49 8.00 20.00
370 Michael Thomas AU/25
371 Tyler Boyd AU/49 12.00 30.00
372 Braxton Miller AU EXCH/29 8.00 20.00
373 Leonte Carroo AU/199 4.00 10.00
374 Chris Moore AU/199 5.00 12.00
375 Ricardo Louis AU/199 4.00 10.00
376 Pharoh Cooper AU/149 4.00 10.00
377 Demarcus Robinson AU/199 4.00 10.00
378 Trevor Davis AU/199 4.00 10.00
379 Moritz Bohringer AU/199 4.00 10.00
380 Hunter Henry AU/199 EXCH 5.00 12.00

2016 Panini Contenders Legendary Contenders

*GOLD/199: .6X TO 1.5X BASIC INSERTS
*HOLO/99: 1.2X TO 3X BASIC INSERTS
1 Dan Marino 1.25 3.00
2 Jerry Rice 1.00 2.50
3 Ray Lewis .60 1.50
4 Rod Woodson .50 1.25
5 Roger Staubach .75 2.00
6 Eric Dickerson .50 1.25
7 Ozzie Newsome .50 1.25
8 Lawrence Taylor .60 1.50
9 Archie Manning .50 1.25
10 Kevin Greene .60 1.50
11 Brett Favre 1.25 3.00
12 Ed Reed .50 1.25
13 Warren Moon .60 1.50
14 LaDainian Tomlinson .50 1.25
15 Jerome Bettis .60 1.50
16 Peyton Manning 1.25 3.00
17 Eddie George .50 1.25
18 Fred Dryer .40 1.00
19 John Elway 1.00 2.50
20 Barry Sanders 1.00 2.50

2016 Panini Contenders Legendary Contenders Autographs

1 Dan Marino/5
2 Jerry Rice/5
3 Ray Lewis/10 EXCH
4 Rod Woodson/49 20.00 50.00
5 Roger Staubach/10
6 Eric Dickerson/25
7 Ozzie Newsome/49 15.00 40.00
8 Lawrence Taylor/25 50.00 100.00
9 Archie Manning/29
10 Kevin Greene/49 25.00 60.00
11 Brett Favre/5
12 Ed Reed/10
13 Warren Moon/15 25.00 60.00
14 LaDainian Tomlinson/10
15 Jerome Bettis/5
16 Peyton Manning/10
17 Eddie George/49 20.00 50.00
18 Fred Dryer/25 15.00 40.00
19 John Elway/5
20 Barry Sanders/10

2016 Panini Contenders MVP Contenders

1 Antonio Brown .60 1.50
2 Andrew Luck .75 2.00
3 Jameis Winston .60 1.50
4 Aaron Rodgers 1.25 3.00
5 Derek Carr .60 1.50
6 Matthew Stafford .50 1.25
7 Todd Gurley II .60 1.50
8 Drew Brees .60 1.50
9 Von Miller .50 1.25
10 Marcus Mariota .60 1.50
11 A.J. Green .60 1.50
12 Russell Wilson .75 2.00
13 Blake Bortles .40 1.00
14 David Johnson .60 1.50
15 Adrian Peterson .60 1.50
16 Eli Manning .50 1.25
17 Ben Roethlisberger .60 1.50
18 Jeremy Langford .50 1.25
19 J.J. Watt .60 1.50
20 Amari Cooper .60 1.50

2016 Panini Contenders MVP Contenders Autographs

1 Antonio Brown/25 75.00 150.00
5 Derek Carr/49 12.00 30.00
7 Todd Gurley II/15 25.00 50.00
9 Von Miller/25 25.00 50.00
11 A.J. Green/49 8.00 20.00
13 Blake Bortles/20 8.00 20.00
18 Jeremy Langford/49
19 J.J. Watt/25 25.00 50.00

2016 Panini Contenders Rookie of the Year Contenders

*GOLD/199: .5X TO 1.2X BASIC INSERTS
*HOLO/99: .6X TO 1.5X BASIC INSERTS
1 Ezekiel Elliott 1.50 4.00
2 Josh Doctson .40 1.00
3 Corey Coleman .50 1.25
4 Kenneth Dixon .30 .75
5 Will Fuller V .50 1.25
6 Laquon Treadwell .40 1.00
7 Carson Wentz 3.00 8.00
8 Sterling Shepard .40 1.00
9 Michael Thomas .60 1.50
10 Derrick Henry .75 2.00
11 Devontae Booker .40 1.00
12 Jared Goff 2.00 5.00
13 Cody Kessler .30 .75
14 Kenyan Drake .50 1.25
15 Braxton Miller .30 .75
16 Christian Hackenberg .30 .75
17 C.J. Prosise .30 .75
18 Paul Perkins .30 .75
19 Joey Bosa .60 1.50
20 Paxton Lynch .30 .75
21 Tajae Sharpe .40 1.00
22 Dak Prescott 1.50 4.00
23 Jalen Ramsey .50 1.25
24 DeForest Buckner .30 .75
25 Darron Lee .30 .75
26 Mackensie Alexander .30 .75
27 Malcolm Mitchell .30 .75
28 Eli Apple .40 1.00
29 Rashard Higgins .30 .75
30 Myles Jack .40 1.00

2016 Panini Contenders Rookie of the Year Contenders Autographs

1 Ezekiel Elliott AU
2 Josh Doctson 5.00 12.00
3 Corey Coleman 6.00 15.00
4 Kenneth Dixon 4.00 10.00
5 Will Fuller V 6.00 15.00
6 Laquon Treadwell 5.00 12.00
7 Carson Wentz 60.00 120.00
8 Sterling Shepard 5.00 12.00
9 Michael Thomas 8.00 20.00
10 Derrick Henry 10.00 25.00
11 Devontae Booker 5.00 12.00
12 Jared Goff 100.00 200.00
13 Cody Kessler 4.00 10.00
14 Kenyan Drake 6.00 15.00
15 Braxton Miller 4.00 10.00
16 Christian Hackenberg 4.00 10.00
17 C.J. Prosise 4.00 10.00
18 Paul Perkins 4.00 10.00
19 Joey Bosa EXCH 25.00 60.00
20 Paxton Lynch 4.00 10.00
22 Dak Prescott 40.00 80.00
23 Jalen Ramsey 6.00 15.00
24 DeForest Buckner 4.00 10.00
26 Mackensie Alexander 4.00 10.00
27 Malcolm Mitchell 4.00 10.00
28 Eli Apple 5.00 12.00
29 Rashard Higgins 4.00 10.00
30 Myles Jack 5.00 12.00

2016 Panini Contenders Rookie Ticket Swatches

*VARIATION: .5X TO 1.2X BASIC JSY
1 Jared Goff 5.00 12.00
2 Carson Wentz 6.00 15.00
3 Paxton Lynch 1.50 4.00
4 Christian Hackenberg 1.50 4.00
5 Cody Kessler 1.50 4.00
6 Connor Cook 2.00 5.00
7 Dak Prescott 8.00 20.00
8 Cardale Jones 1.50 4.00
9 Kevin Hogan 2.00 5.00
10 Ezekiel Elliott 8.00 20.00
11 Derrick Henry 4.00 10.00
12 Kenyan Drake 2.50 6.00
13 C.J. Prosise 1.50 4.00
14 Tyler Ervin 1.50 4.00
15 Kenneth Dixon 1.50 4.00
16 Devontae Booker 2.00 5.00
17 Paul Perkins 1.50 4.00
18 Jordan Howard 3.00 8.00
19 Wendell Smallwood 1.50 4.00
20 Jonathan Williams 2.00 5.00
21 Alex Collins 2.00 5.00
22 Keenan Reynolds 2.00 5.00
23 DeAndre Washington 1.50 4.00
24 Corey Coleman 2.50 6.00
25 Josh Doctson 2.00 5.00
26 Will Fuller V 2.50 6.00
27 Laquon Treadwell 2.00 5.00
28 Sterling Shepard 3.00 8.00
29 Michael Thomas 3.00 8.00
30 Tyler Boyd 2.00 5.00
31 Braxton Miller 1.50 4.00
32 Leonte Carroo 1.50 4.00
33 Chris Moore 2.00 5.00
34 Ricardo Louis 1.50 4.00
35 Pharoh Cooper 1.50 4.00
36 Demarcus Robinson 1.50 4.00
37 Trevor Davis 1.50 4.00
38 Moritz Bohringer 1.50 4.00
39 Hunter Henry 2.00 5.00
40 Joey Bosa 3.00 8.00

2016 Panini Contenders Round Numbers

*GOLD/199: .5X TO 1.2X BASIC INSERTS
*HOLO/99: .6X TO 1.5X BASIC INSERTS
1 C.Wentz/J.Goff 4.00 10.00
2 C.Coleman/J.Doctson .60 1.50
3 L.Treadwell/W.Fuller .60 1.50
4 K.Joseph/K.Neal .40 1.00
5 D.Buckner/J.Bosa .75 2.00
6 E.Apple/J.Ramsey .60 1.50
7 S.Shepard/T.Boyd .50 1.25
8 J.Smith/M.Jack .50 1.25
9 A.Robinson/J.Reed .40 1.00
10 B.Miller/L.Carroo .40 1.00
11 A.Hooper/N.Vannett .40 1.00
12 C.Prosise/K.Drake .60 1.50
13 C.Cook/D.Prescott 2.00 5.00
14 D.Booker/K.Dixon .50 1.25
15 M.Mitchell/P.Cooper .40 1.00
16 A.Collins/J.Williams .50 1.25
17 D.Wshngtn/W.Smllwd .40 1.00
18 J.Howard/P.Perkins 1.00 2.50
19 J.Payton/R.Higgins .40 1.00
20 K.Lstnbe/M.Bhrngr .40 1.00

2016 Panini Contenders Super Bowl MVP Autographs

2 Hines Ward 30.00 80.00

2016 Panini Contenders Touchdown Tandems

*GOLD/199: .5X TO 1.2X BASIC INSERTS
*HOLO/99: .6X TO 1.5X BASIC INSERTS
1 A.Brown/B.Rthlsbrgr .50 1.25
2 A.Green/A.Dalton .50 1.25
3 A.Luck/T.Hilton .60 1.50
4 A.Rodgers/R.Cobb 1.00 2.50
5 C.Newton/K.Benjamin .50 1.25
6 D.Bryant/T.Romo .50 1.25
7 A.Cooper/D.Carr .50 1.25
8 E.Manning/O.Beckham .50 1.25
9 D.Murray/D.Henry .75 2.00
10 R.Grnkwski/T.Brady 1.25 3.00

2017 Panini Contenders

1 Julio Jones .30 .75
2 Matt Ryan .25 .60
3 Devonta Freeman .25 .60
4 Cam Newton .30 .75
5 Kelvin Benjamin .25 .60
6 Greg Olsen .25 .60
7 Drew Brees .30 .75
8 Adrian Peterson .30 .75
9 Michael Thomas .30 .75
10 Jameis Winston .25 .60
11 DeSean Jackson .25 .60
12 Mike Evans .25 .60
13 Lamar Miller .20 .50
14 J.J. Watt .30 .75
15 DeAndre Hopkins .25 .60
16 Andrew Luck .40 1.00
17 T.Y. Hilton .25 .60
18 Adam Vinatieri .20 .50
19 Blake Bortles .20 .50
20 Jalen Ramsey .20 .50
21 Allen Hurns .20 .50
22 Marcus Mariota .30 .75
23 DeMarco Murray .25 .60
24 Delanie Walker .20 .50
25 Jordan Howard .30 .75
26 Zach Miller .20 .50
27 Mike Glennon .25 .60
28 Matthew Stafford .25 .60
29 Ameer Abdullah .20 .50
30 Marvin Jones Jr. .20 .50
31 Aaron Rodgers .60 1.50
32 Jordy Nelson .25 .60
33 Davante Adams .25 .60
34 Stefon Diggs .25 .60
35 Sam Bradford .20 .50
36 Latavius Murray .20 .50
37 Joe Flacco .25 .60
38 Buck Allen .20 .50
39 Terrell Suggs .20 .50
40 Andy Dalton .25 .60
41 A.J. Green .30 .75
42 Jeremy Hill .20 .50
43 Corey Coleman .20 .50
44 Myles Garrett RC 1.50 4.00
45 Isaiah Crowell .20 .50
46 Ben Roethlisberger .30 .75
47 Le'Veon Bell .25 .60
48 Antonio Brown .30 .75
49 Carson Palmer .25 .60
50 David Johnson .30 .75
51 Larry Fitzgerald .25 .60
52 Jared Goff .30 .75
53 Todd Gurley II .30 .75
54 Robert Woods .25 .60
55 Brian Hoyer .20 .50
56 Carlos Hyde .20 .50
57 Pierre Garcon .25 .60
58 Russell Wilson .40 1.00
59 Thomas Rawls .20 .50
60 Eddie Lacy .20 .50
61 Doug Baldwin .25 .60
62 Trevor Siemian .20 .50
63 Jamaal Charles .25 .60
64 Von Miller .25 .60
65 Demaryius Thomas .25 .60
66 Alex Smith .25 .60
67 Tyreek Hill .30 .75
68 Travis Kelce .30 .75
69 Philip Rivers .30 .75
70 Melvin Gordon .25 .60
71 Hunter Henry .20 .50
72 Derek Carr .30 .75
73 Marshawn Lynch .25 .60
74 Amari Cooper .30 .75
75 Khalil Mack .30 .75
76 Dak Prescott .30 .75
77 Ezekiel Elliott .40 1.00
78 Dez Bryant .30 .75
79 Jason Witten .25 .60
80 Eli Manning .25 .60
81 Odell Beckham Jr. .30 .75
82 Brandon Marshall .20 .50
83 Carson Wentz .40 1.00
84 LeGarrette Blount .25 .60
85 Alshon Jeffery .25 .60
86 Kirk Cousins .30 .75
87 Robert Kelley .20 .50
88 Jamison Crowder .20 .50
89 Tyrod Taylor .25 .60
90 LeSean McCoy .30 .75
91 Jordan Matthews .20 .50
92 Jay Cutler .20 .50
93 Jay Ajayi .25 .60
94 Jarvis Landry .25 .60
95 Tom Brady .75 2.00
96 Rob Gronkowski .30 .75
97 Brandin Cooks .25 .60
98 Mike Gillislee .20 .50
99 Jermaine Kearse .20 .50
100 Josh McCown .20 .50
101 Brad Kaaya AU RC 2.00 5.00
102 T.J. Watt AU RC EXCH 15.00 40.00
103 Marlon Humphrey AU RC 2.00 5.00
104 Jake Butt AU RC 2.50 6.00
105 Greg Ward Jr. AU RC 2.00 5.00
106 Khalfani Muhammad AU/150* RC SP 8.00 20.00
107 Jamal Adams AU RC 2.00 5.00
108 Donnel Pumphrey AU RC 2.50 6.00
109 Chad Kelly AU RC 25.00 50.00
110 Marshon Lattimore AU RC 10.00 25.00
111 Quincy Wilson AU RC 2.00 5.00
112 Ryan Switzer AU RC 8.00 20.00
113 Cameron Sutton AU/195* RC SP 10.00 25.00
114 David Njoku AU RC EXCH 2.50 6.00
115 Sidney Jones AU RC 2.00 5.00
116 Solomon Thomas AU RC 2.00 5.00
117 Elijah Hood AU RC 2.00 5.00
118 Adoree' Jackson AU RC EXCH 2.50 6.00
119 Matthew Dayes AU RC 2.00 5.00
120 Malik Hooker AU RC 2.00 5.00
121 Derek Barnett AU RC 8.00 20.00
122 Charles Harris AU RC 2.00 5.00
123 Corey Clement AU RC 2.50 6.00
124 Desmond King AU RC 2.50 6.00
125 Jabrill Peppers AU RC 3.00 8.00
126 Brian Hill AU RC
127 Tarik Cohen AU/103* RC SP 20.00 50.00
128 Cordrea Tankersley AU RC 6.00 15.00
129 Tre'Davious White AU RC 2.00 5.00
130 Malachi Dupre AU RC 2.00 5.00
131 Gareon Conley AU RC
132 Jonathan Allen AU/150* RC SP 4.00 10.00
133 Stacy Coley AU RC 2.00 5.00
134 Carl Lawson AU RC 2.00 5.00
135 Taco Charlton AU RC 2.00 5.00
136 Isaiah Ford AU RC 2.00 5.00
137 Jordan Willis AU RC 2.00 5.00
138 DeMarcus Walker AU RC 2.00 5.00
139 Aaron Jones AU/250* RC SP 15.00 40.00
140 Malik McDowell AU RC 2.00 5.00
141 Robert Davis AU RC 2.00 5.00
142 Josh Malone AU RC 2.00 5.00
143 Elijah Qualls AU RC 2.00 5.00
144 Caleb Brantley AU/150* RC SP
145 Raekwon McMillan AU RC 2.00 5.00
146 Zach Cunningham AU/250* RC SP
147 Jordan Leggett AU RC 2.00 5.00
148 Noah Brown AU RC
149 Jarrad Davis AU RC 2.50 6.00
150 Tim Williams AU RC 2.50 6.00
151 Jamal Agnew AU RC 2.00 5.00
152 Chad Hansen AU RC
153 Travis Rudolph AU RC
154 Artavis Scott AU RC 2.00 5.00
155 Shelton Gibson AU RC
156 Dalvin Tomlinson AU RC 2.00 5.00
157 Derek Rivers AU RC 2.50 6.00
158 Duke Riley AU RC 2.00 5.00
159 Fabian Moreau AU RC 6.00 15.00
160 Jonnu Smith AU/137* RC SP 3.00 8.00
161 Gerald Everett AU RC 2.00 5.00
162 Isaiah McKenzie AU RC 2.00 5.00
163 Tanoh Kpassagnon AU RC 2.50 6.00
164 George Kittle AU RC 6.00 15.00
165 Josh Jones AU RC 2.50 6.00
166 Rasul Douglas AU RC 2.50 6.00
167 Rodney Adams AU RC
168 Nazair Jones AU RC 2.00 5.00
169 Haason Reddick AU RC 2.00 5.00
170 Devante Mays AU RC 2.00 5.00
171 Adam Shaheen AU RC 2.00 5.00
172 Ahkello Witherspoon AU RC 2.50 6.00
173 Shaquill Griffin AU/250* RC SP 12.00 30.00
174 T.J. Logan AU RC 3.00 8.00
175 Alex Anzalone AU RC 2.50 6.00
176 John Johnson AU RC 2.50 6.00
177 Jeremy Sprinkle AU RC 3.00 8.00
178 Matt Breida AU RC 15.00 40.00
179 Chidobe Awuzie AU RC 2.50 6.00
180 Kevin King AU RC
181 Damontae Kazee AU RC 2.50 6.00
182 Dawuane Smoot AU RC
183 Daeshon Hall AU RC 2.00 5.00
184 Deatrich Wise Jr. AU RC 3.00 8.00
185 Chris Wormley AU RC 2.00 5.00
186 Jehu Chesson AU/165* RC SP 10.00 25.00
187 Chris Carson AU RC 6.00 15.00
188 Marquez White AU RC 2.00 5.00
189 Carlos Watkins AU RC 2.00 5.00
190 Marcus Maye AU RC
191 Budda Baker AU RC 2.00 5.00
192 Jaleel Johnson AU RC
193 Tyus Bowser AU RC 2.00 5.00
194 Obi Melifonwu AU RC 2.00 5.00
195 Eddie Jackson AU RC 2.50 6.00
196 Marcus Williams AU RC 2.00 5.00
197 DeAngelo Yancey AU/167* RC SP 25.00 50.00
198 Kendell Beckwith AU RC 6.00 15.00
199 Trent Taylor AU/49* RC SP A 30.00 60.00
200 Chad Williams AU RC 2.00 5.00
201 Ryan Glasgow AU RC
202 Geronimo Allison AU RC 8.00 20.00
203 Brandon Williams AU RC 2.00 5.00
204 Ross Cockrell AU RC 2.00 5.00
205 Arthur Moats AU RC 10.00 25.00
206 Garett Bolles AU RC 2.00 5.00
207 Ryan Ramczyk AU RC 2.00 5.00
208 Jerod Evans AU RC 2.50 6.00
209 KD Cannon AU RC 2.00 5.00
210 Jalen Myrick AU RC 2.00 5.00
211 Elijah McGuire AU/147* RC SP 3.00 8.00
212 Davon Godchaux AU RC 2.00 5.00
213 Ben Boulware AU RC 5.00 12.00
214 Anthony Walker Jr. AU RC 2.00 5.00
215 Tanner Vallejo AU RC 3.00 8.00
216 Sam Rogers AU RC 2.00 5.00
217 Vince Biegel AU RC 4.00 10.00
218 Cooper Rush AU RC 10.00 25.00
219 De'Veon Smith AU/250* RC 5.00 12.00
221 Justin Evans AU RC 2.00 5.00
222 Montravius Adams AU RC 2.50 6.00
223 Josh Harvey-Clemons AU RC 2.00 5.00
224 Ryan Anderson AU RC 2.00 5.00
225 Matt Milano AU RC 2.50 6.00
226 Ejuan Price AU RC 2.00 5.00
227 Jalen Reeves-Maybin AU RC 4.00 10.00
228 Eddie Vanderdoes AU RC 2.00 5.00
229 Devine Redding AU RC 2.00 5.00
230 De'Angelo Henderson AU RC 2.00 5.00
231 Montae Nicholson AU/250* RC SP
232 Aaron Ripkowski AU RC 6.00 15.00
233 Cole Hikutini AU RC 2.00 5.00
234 Kyle Sloter AU RC 2.50 6.00
235 Billy Brown AU RC 2.00 5.00
236 Michael Rector AU RC 2.00 5.00
237 Zach Pascal AU RC 2.00 5.00
238 Damore'ea Stringfellow AU RC
239 Jacob Hollister AU RC 2.00 5.00
240 Austin Carr AU RC 2.00 5.00
241 Justin Davis AU RC 3.00 8.00
242 Victor Bolden Jr. AU RC 2.00 5.00
243 Kendrick Bourne AU RC 2.50 6.00
244 Austin Ekeler AU RC 5.00 12.00
245 Taquan Mizzell AU RC 2.00 5.00
246 Tanner Gentry AU RC 2.00 5.00
247 Tion Green AU RC 10.00 25.00
248 Michael Roberts AU RC 3.00 8.00
249 Taysom Hill AU RC 8.00 20.00
250 Brad Kaaya AU 2.00 5.00
251 T.J. Watt AU/50* SP A 60.00 125.00
252 Marshon Lattimore AU 10.00 25.00
253 Jake Butt AU 2.50 6.00
254 Jamal Adams AU/150* SP 3.00 8.00
255 Donnel Pumphrey AU 2.50 6.00
256 Chad Kelly AU/250* SP 30.00 60.00
257 David Njoku AU/250* SP EXCH 4.00 10.00
258 Solomon Thomas AU 2.00 5.00
259 Adoree' Jackson AU/250* SP EXCH 4.00 10.00
260 Matthew Dayes AU 2.00 5.00
261 Malik Hooker AU 2.00 5.00
262 Corey Clement AU/250* SP 3.00 8.00
263 Jabrill Peppers AU 3.00 8.00
264 Brian Hill AU 2.00 5.00
265 Tre'Davious White AU 2.00 5.00
266 Malachi Dupre AU 2.00 5.00
267 Taco Charlton AU 2.00 5.00
268 DeMarcus Walker AU 2.00 5.00
269 Josh Malone AU 2.00 5.00
270 Raekwon McMillan AU/150* SP 3.00 8.00
271 Zach Cunningham AU/150* SP
272 Jordan Leggett AU 2.00 5.00
273 Noah Brown AU/250* SP
274 Jamal Agnew AU/100* SP A 5.00 12.00
275 Chad Hansen AU 2.00 5.00
276 Artavis Scott AU 2.00 5.00
277 Shelton Gibson AU
278 Dalvin Tomlinson AU/150* SP 3.00 8.00
279 Derek Rivers AU/150* SP 4.00 10.00
280 Jonnu Smith AU/100* SP A 5.00 12.00
281 Gerald Everett AU/250* SP 3.00 8.00
282 George Kittle AU 6.00 15.00
283 Rodney Adams AU
284 Haason Reddick AU 2.00 5.00
285 T.J. Logan AU 3.00 8.00
286 Kevin King AU
287 Isaiah Ford AU 2.00 5.00
288 Marcus Maye AU 2.00 5.00
289 Obi Melifonwu AU/250* SP 3.00 8.00
290 Chad Williams AU/54* SP A 5.00 12.00
291 Reggie Davis AU RC 6.00 15.00
292 Trey Edmunds AU RC 2.00 5.00
293 Keelan Cole AU RC 15.00 40.00
294 Elijhaa Penny AU RC
295 Josh Woodrum AU RC 2.00 5.00
296 Kasen Williams AU RC 2.50 6.00
297 Raheem Mostert AU RC 2.00 5.00
298 Bernard Reedy AU RC 2.00 5.00
299 Mack Brown AU RC 2.00 5.00
300 Kyle Shanahan AU RC EXCH 15.00 40.00
301 Mitchell Trubisky AU/212* RC SP 200.00 300.00
302 Deshaun Watson AU RC 300.00 600.00
303 Patrick Mahomes II AU/212* RC SP 500.00 1000.00
304 DeShone Kizer AU RC 10.00 25.00
305 Davis Webb AU/62* RC SP A 75.00 150.00
306 R. Joshua Dobbs AU RC 8.00 20.00
307 C.J. Beathard AU RC 8.00 20.00
308 Nathan Peterman AU RC 5.00 12.00
309 Dalvin Cook AU RC 40.00 80.00
310 Leonard Fournette AU/212* RC SP 60.00 125.00
311 Christian McCaffrey AU RC 40.00 80.00
312 Joe Mixon AU/212* RC SP 20.00 40.00
313 Alvin Kamara AU RC 75.00 150.00
314 Marlon Mack AU RC 6.00 15.00
315 Samaje Perine AU/212* RC SP 3.00 8.00
316 Wayne Gallman AU RC EXCH 2.50 6.00
317 Kareem Hunt AU RC 15.00 40.00
318 D'Onta Foreman AU RC 2.50 6.00
319 Jeremy McNichols AU RC 2.00 5.00
320 James Conner AU RC EXCH 6.00 15.00
321 Jamaal Williams AU RC EXCH 8.00 20.00
322 Joe Williams AU RC 2.00 5.00
323 O.J. Howard AU RC 8.00 20.00
324 Evan Engram AU RC 10.00 25.00
325 Mike Williams AU/212* RC SP 5.00 12.00
326 John Ross III AU RC 2.50 6.00
327 JuJu Smith-Schuster AU RC 50.00 100.00
328 Corey Davis AU RC 8.00 20.00
329 Dede Westbrook AU RC 2.00 5.00
330 Curtis Samuel AU RC 2.50 6.00
331 Amara Darboh AU RC 2.00 5.00
332 Carlos Henderson AU RC 2.00 5.00
333 Zay Jones AU/212* RC SP 12.00 30.00
334 Cooper Kupp AU RC 30.00 60.00
335 Josh Reynolds AU RC 2.00 5.00
336 ArDarius Stewart AU/162* RC SP 3.00 8.00
337 Chris Godwin AU RC 2.50 6.00
338 Taywan Taylor AU RC EXCH 2.00 5.00
339 Kenny Golladay AU RC 3.00 8.00
340 Mack Hollins AU RC 2.00 5.00
341 Mitchell Trubisky AU/50* SP A 200.00 300.00
342 Deshaun Watson AU/150* SP 300.00 600.00
343 Patrick Mahomes II AU/100* SP A 1000.00 1500.00
344 DeShone Kizer AU/250* SP 10.00 25.00
345 Davis Webb AU/50* SP A 60.00 125.00
346 R. Joshua Dobbs AU/150* SP 10.00 25.00
347 C.J. Beathard AU/50* SP A 5.00 12.00
348 Nathan Peterman AU/222* SP 5.00 12.00
349 Dalvin Cook AU/150* SP 40.00 80.00
350 Leonard Fournette AU/150* SP 60.00 125.00
351 Christian McCaffrey AU/200* SP 50.00 100.00
352 Joe Mixon AU/75* SP A 20.00 40.00
353 Alvin Kamara AU/250* SP 50.00 100.00
354 Marlon Mack AU 6.00 15.00
355 Samaje Perine AU 2.00 5.00
356 Wayne Gallman AU EXCH 2.50 6.00
357 Kareem Hunt AU 15.00 40.00
358 D'Onta Foreman AU 2.50 6.00
359 Jeremy McNichols AU 2.00 5.00
360 James Conner AU EXCH 6.00 15.00
361 Jamaal Williams AU EXCH 8.00 20.00
362 Joe Williams AU/150* SP 3.00 8.00
363 O.J. Howard AU/250* SP 8.00 20.00
364 Evan Engram AU/200* SP 15.00 40.00
365 Mike Williams AU/150* SP 10.00 25.00
366 John Ross III AU 2.50 6.00
367 JuJu Smith-Schuster AU/250* SP 60.00 125.00
368 Corey Davis AU/250* SP 8.00 20.00
369 Dede Westbrook AU 2.00 5.00
370 Curtis Samuel AU 2.50 6.00
371 Amara Darboh AU 2.00 5.00
372 Carlos Henderson AU/250* SP 3.00 8.00
373 Zay Jones AU/100* SP A 6.00 15.00
374 Cooper Kupp AU 15.00 40.00
375 Josh Reynolds AU 2.00 5.00
376 ArDarius Stewart AU/100* SP A 5.00 12.00
377 Chris Godwin AU/150* SP 4.00 10.00
378 Taywan Taylor AU EXCH 2.00 5.00
379 Kenny Golladay AU 3.00 8.00
380 Mack Hollins AU 2.00 5.00
381 Greg Olsen AU/140* SP 10.00 25.00

382 Adam Vinatieri AU/149* SP 12.00 30.00
383 Mark Ingram AU/99* SP A 10.00 25.00
384 Robert Kelley AU 2.50 6.00
385 Jason Witten AU/49* SP A EXCH
386 Matt Ryan AU/15* SP A 40.00 80.00
387 Marcus Mariota AU/15* SP A
388 Doug Baldwin AU/199* SP 8.00 20.00
389 Carson Wentz AU/15* SP A
390 Ameer Abdullah AU 2.50 6.00
391 Drew Brees AU/15* SP A EXCH 60.00 125.00
392 John Brown AU/49* SP A 6.00 15.00
393 Mike Evans AU 6.00 15.00
394 Jordan Howard AU/199* SP 5.00 12.00
395 David Johnson AU/99* SP A 8.00 20.00
396 Kirk Cousins AU/99* SP A 20.00 40.00
397 Dan Bailey AU/199* SP 8.00 20.00
398 Michael Thomas AU
399 Chris Hogan AU
400 Terrelle Pryor Sr. AU/15* SP A 2.50 6.00

2017 Panini Contenders Championship Ticket

*1-100 VETS: 4X TO 10X BASIC CARDS
101 Brad Kaaya AU/49 6.00 15.00
102 T.J. Watt AU/49 50.00 100.00
103 Marlon Humphrey AU/25
104 Jake Butt AU/49 8.00 20.00
105 Greg Ward Jr. AU/49 6.00 15.00
106 Khalfani Muhammad AU/25 8.00 20.00
107 Jamal Adams AU/25 8.00 20.00
108 Donnel Pumphrey AU/49 8.00 20.00
109 Chad Kelly AU/25 40.00 100.00
110 Marshon Lattimore AU/25 20.00 50.00
111 Quincy Wilson AU/49 6.00 15.00
112 Ryan Switzer AU/25 10.00 25.00
113 Cameron Sutton AU/25 20.00 50.00
114 David Njoku AU/49 EXCH 8.00 20.00
115 Sidney Jones AU/49 6.00 15.00
116 Solomon Thomas AU/25 8.00 20.00
117 Elijah Hood AU/49 6.00 15.00
118 Adoree' Jackson AU/25 EXCH 10.00 25.00
119 Matthew Dayes AU/49 6.00 15.00
120 Malik Hooker AU/49 6.00 15.00
121 Derek Barnett AU/25
122 Charles Harris AU/25 8.00 20.00
123 Corey Clement AU/49 6.00 25.00
124 Desmond King AU/49 8.00 20.00
125 Jabrill Peppers AU/25 12.00 30.00
126 Brian Hill AU/49 6.00 15.00
127 Tarik Cohen AU/25 50.00 100.00
128 Cordrea Tankersley AU/25
129 Tre'Davious White AU/25 8.00 20.00
130 Malachi Dupre AU/25 8.00 20.00
131 Gareon Conley AU/49
132 Jonathan Allen AU/25 10.00 25.00
133 Stacy Coley AU/49 6.00 15.00
134 Carl Lawson AU/25 8.00 20.00
135 Taco Charlton AU/49 6.00 15.00
136 Isaiah Ford AU/49 6.00 15.00
137 Jordan Willis AU/49 6.00 15.00
138 DeMarcus Walker AU/49 6.00 15.00
139 Aaron Jones AU/25 25.00 50.00
140 Malik McDowell AU/25 8.00 20.00
141 Robert Davis AU/49 6.00 15.00
142 Josh Malone AU/49 6.00 15.00
143 Elijah Qualls AU/49 6.00 15.00
144 Caleb Brantley AU/49
145 Raekwon McMillan AU/25 8.00 20.00
146 Zach Cunningham AU/25
147 Jordan Leggett AU/49 6.00 15.00
148 Noah Brown AU/49 15.00 40.00
149 Jarrad Davis AU/25 10.00 25.00
150 Tim Williams AU/25 10.00 25.00
151 Jamal Agnew AU/49 6.00 15.00
152 Chad Hansen AU/49 6.00 15.00
153 Travis Rudolph AU/49 6.00 15.00
154 Artavis Scott AU/49 6.00 15.00
155 Shelton Gibson AU/49
156 Dalvin Tomlinson AU/25 8.00 20.00
157 Derek Rivers AU/25 10.00 25.00
158 Duke Riley AU/25 8.00 20.00
159 Fabian Moreau AU/25 10.00 25.00
160 Jonnu Smith AU/25 8.00 20.00
161 Gerald Everett AU/25 8.00 20.00
162 Isaiah McKenzie AU/25 8.00 20.00
163 Tanoh Kpassagnon AU/25 10.00 25.00
164 George Kittle AU/49 12.00 30.00
165 Josh Jones AU/49 8.00 20.00
166 Rasul Douglas AU/49 8.00 20.00
167 Rodney Adams AU/25
168 Nazair Jones AU/49 6.00 15.00
169 Haason Reddick AU/25 8.00 20.00
170 Devante Mays AU/49 6.00 15.00
171 Adam Shaheen AU/25 8.00 20.00
172 Ahkello Witherspoon AU/49 8.00 20.00
173 Shaquill Griffin AU/25 30.00 60.00
174 T.J. Logan AU/25 12.00 30.00
175 Alex Anzalone AU/49 8.00 20.00
176 John Johnson AU/49 8.00 20.00
177 Jeremy Sprinkle AU/49 6.00 15.00
178 Matt Breida AU/49 30.00 60.00
179 Chidobe Awuzie AU/25 25.00 50.00
180 Kevin King AU/25
181 Damontae Kazee AU/25 10.00 25.00
182 Dawuane Smoot AU/49 6.00 15.00
183 Daeshon Hall AU/49 6.00 15.00
184 Deatrich Wise Jr. AU/49 10.00 25.00
185 Chris Wormley AU/49 6.00 15.00
186 Jehu Chesson AU/25 10.00 25.00
187 Chris Carson AU/49 25.00 50.00
188 Marquez White AU/25 8.00 20.00
189 Carlos Watkins AU/25 8.00 20.00
190 Marcus Maye AU/49 6.00 15.00
191 Budda Baker AU/49 6.00 15.00
192 Jaleel Johnson AU/49
193 Tyus Bowser AU/49 6.00 15.00
194 Obi Melifonwu AU/49 6.00 15.00
195 Eddie Jackson AU/49 8.00 20.00
196 Marcus Williams AU/25 8.00 20.00
197 DeAngelo Yancey AU/25 8.00 20.00
198 Kendell Beckwith AU/25 8.00 20.00
199 Trent Taylor AU/25 50.00 100.00
200 Chad Williams AU/25 8.00 20.00
201 Ryan Glasgow AU/49
202 Geronimo Allison AU/49 12.00 30.00
203 Brandon Williams AU/49 6.00 15.00
204 Ross Cockrell AU/49 6.00 15.00
205 Arthur Moats AU/49 15.00 40.00
206 Garett Bolles AU/49 6.00 15.00
207 Ryan Ramczyk AU/49 6.00 15.00
208 Jerod Evans AU/25 10.00 25.00
209 KD Cannon AU/49 6.00 15.00
210 Jalen Myrick AU/25 8.00 20.00
211 Elijah McGuire AU/49 6.00 15.00
212 Davon Godchaux AU/49 6.00 15.00
213 Ben Boulware AU/49 15.00 40.00
214 Anthony Walker Jr. AU/49 6.00 15.00
215 Tanner Vallejo AU/49 10.00 25.00
216 Sam Rogers AU/49 6.00 15.00
217 Vince Biegel AU/49 12.00 30.00
218 Cooper Rush AU/49 30.00 60.00
219 De'Veon Smith AU/25 20.00 50.00
221 Justin Evans AU/49 6.00 15.00
222 Montravius Adams AU/49 8.00 20.00
223 Josh Harvey-Clemons AU/49 6.00 15.00
224 Ryan Anderson AU/49 6.00 15.00
225 Matt Milano AU/49 8.00 20.00
226 Ejuan Price AU/25 8.00 20.00
227 Jalen Reeves-Maybin AU/49 12.00 30.00
228 Eddie Vanderdoes AU/25 8.00 20.00
229 Devine Redding AU/49 6.00 15.00
230 De'Angelo Henderson AU/49 6.00 15.00
231 Montae Nicholson AU/49
232 Aaron Ripkowski AU/49 10.00 25.00
233 Cole Hikutini AU/49 6.00 15.00
234 Kyle Sloter AU/49 8.00 20.00
235 Billy Brown AU/49 6.00 15.00
236 Michael Rector AU/49 6.00 15.00
237 Zach Pascal AU/49 6.00 15.00
238 Damore'ea Stringfellow AU/49
239 Jacob Hollister AU/49 6.00 15.00
240 Austin Carr AU/49 6.00 15.00
241 Justin Davis AU/49 10.00 25.00
242 Victor Bolden Jr. AU/49 6.00 15.00
243 Kendrick Bourne AU/49 8.00 20.00
244 Austin Ekeler AU/49 12.00 30.00
245 Taquan Mizzell AU/49 6.00 15.00
246 Tanner Gentry AU/49 6.00 15.00
247 Tion Green AU/49 6.00 15.00
248 Michael Roberts AU/49 10.00 25.00
249 Taysom Hill AU/49 25.00 50.00
250 Brad Kaaya AU/49 6.00 15.00
251 T.J. Watt AU/49 50.00 100.00
252 Marshon Lattimore AU/25 20.00 50.00
253 Jake Butt AU/49 8.00 20.00
254 Jamal Adams AU/25 8.00 20.00
255 Donnel Pumphrey AU/49 8.00 20.00
256 Chad Kelly AU/25 40.00 100.00
257 David Njoku AU/49 EXCH 8.00 20.00
258 Solomon Thomas AU/25 8.00 20.00
259 Adoree' Jackson AU/25 EXCH 10.00 25.00
260 Matthew Dayes AU/49 6.00 15.00
261 Malik Hooker AU/25 8.00 20.00
262 Corey Clement AU/25 8.00 30.00
263 Jabrill Peppers AU/25 12.00 30.00
264 Brian Hill AU/49 6.00 15.00
265 Tre'Davious White AU/25 8.00 20.00
266 Malachi Dupre AU/25 8.00 20.00
267 Taco Charlton AU/25 8.00 20.00
268 DeMarcus Walker AU/49 6.00 15.00
269 Josh Malone AU/25 8.00 20.00
270 Raekwon McMillan AU/25 8.00 20.00
271 Zach Cunningham AU/25
272 Jordan Leggett AU/49 6.00 15.00
273 Noah Brown AU/49 15.00 40.00
274 Jamal Agnew AU/49 6.00 15.00
275 Chad Hansen AU/49 6.00 15.00
276 Artavis Scott AU/49 6.00 15.00
277 Shelton Gibson AU/49
278 Dalvin Tomlinson AU/25 8.00 20.00
279 Derek Rivers AU/25 10.00 25.00
280 Jonnu Smith AU/25 8.00 20.00
281 Gerald Everett AU/25 8.00 20.00
282 George Kittle AU/25 15.00 40.00
283 Rodney Adams AU/25
284 Haason Reddick AU/25 8.00 20.00
285 T.J. Logan AU/25 12.00 30.00
286 Kevin King AU/25
287 Isaiah Ford AU/49 6.00 15.00
288 Marcus Maye AU/49 6.00 15.00
289 Obi Melifonwu AU/49 6.00 15.00
290 Chad Williams AU/49 6.00 15.00
291 Reggie Davis AU/49
292 Trey Edmunds AU/49 6.00 15.00
293 Keelan Cole AU/49 20.00 50.00
294 Elijhaa Penny AU/49
295 Josh Woodrum AU/49 6.00 15.00
296 Kasen Williams AU/49 8.00 20.00
297 Raheem Mostert AU/49 6.00 15.00
298 Bernard Reedy AU/49 6.00 15.00
299 Mack Brown AU/49 6.00 15.00
300 Kyle Shanahan AU/25 EXCH 50.00 10.00
305 Davis Webb AU/15 100.00 200.00
306 R. Joshua Dobbs AU/25 30.00 60.00
307 C.J. Beathard AU/15 40.00 80.00
308 Nathan Peterman AU/15 12.00 30.00
312 Joe Mixon AU/25 50.00 100.00
313 Alvin Kamara AU/15 300.00 500.00
314 Marlon Mack AU/49 10.00 25.00
315 Samaje Perine AU/15 10.00 25.00
316 Wayne Gallman AU/49 EXCH 8.00 20.00
317 Kareem Hunt AU/25 75.00 150.00
318 D'Onta Foreman AU/15 12.00 30.00
319 Jeremy McNichols AU/49 6.00 15.00
320 James Conner AU/25 20.00 50.00
321 Jamaal Williams AU/49 EXCH 30.00 60.00
322 Joe Williams AU/49 6.00 15.00
323 O.J. Howard AU/15 50.00 100.00
324 Evan Engram AU/15 50.00 100.00
329 Dede Westbrook AU/15 10.00 25.00
330 Curtis Samuel AU/15 12.00 30.00
331 Amara Darboh AU/15 30.00 60.00
332 Carlos Henderson AU/49 6.00 15.00
333 Zay Jones AU/15 12.00 30.00
334 Cooper Kupp AU/49 30.00 60.00
335 Josh Reynolds AU/49 6.00 15.00
336 ArDarius Stewart AU/25 8.00 20.00
337 Chris Godwin AU/49 8.00 20.00
338 Taywan Taylor AU/49 EXCH 6.00 15.00
339 Kenny Golladay AU/49 10.00 25.00
340 Mack Hollins AU/49 6.00 15.00
354 Marlon Mack AU/25 12.00 30.00
357 Kareem Hunt AU/15 100.00 200.00
360 James Conner AU/25 20.00 50.00
361 Jamaal Williams AU/25 EXCH 40.00 80.00
362 Joe Williams AU/25 8.00 20.00
372 Carlos Henderson AU/25 8.00 20.00
374 Cooper Kupp AU/25 40.00 80.00
375 Josh Reynolds AU/25 8.00 20.00
376 ArDarius Stewart AU/15 10.00 25.00
377 Chris Godwin AU/25 10.00 25.00
378 Taywan Taylor AU/25 EXCH 8.00 20.00
379 Kenny Golladay AU/25 12.00 30.00
380 Mack Hollins AU/25 8.00 20.00
384 Robert Kelley AU/49 6.00 15.00
390 Ameer Abdullah AU/49 6.00 15.00
392 John Brown AU/25 10.00 25.00
394 Jordan Howard AU/25 12.00 30.00
399 Chris Hogan AU/25

2017 Panini Contenders Cracked Ice

*1-100 VETS/24: 6X TO 15X BASIC CARDS
PLAYERS WITH MULT. OF EQUAL VALUE
101 Brad Kaaya AU 30.00 60.00
102 T.J. Watt AU 200.00 300.00
103 Marlon Humphrey AU 12.00 30.00
104 Jake Butt AU 15.00 40.00
105 Greg Ward Jr. AU 12.00 30.00
106 Khalfani Muhammad AU
107 Jamal Adams AU 40.00 80.00
108 Donnel Pumphrey AU 15.00 40.00
109 Chad Kelly AU 100.00 200.00
110 Marshon Lattimore AU 60.00 125.00
111 Quincy Wilson AU 12.00 30.00
112 Ryan Switzer AU 40.00 80.00
113 Cameron Sutton AU
114 David Njoku AU EXCH 15.00 40.00
115 Sidney Jones AU 12.00 30.00
116 Solomon Thomas AU 30.00 60.00
117 Elijah Hood AU 12.00 30.00
118 Adoree' Jackson AU
119 Matthew Dayes AU 12.00 30.00
120 Malik Hooker AU 40.00 80.00
121 Derek Barnett AU
122 Charles Harris AU 12.00 30.00
123 Corey Clement AU 40.00 80.00
124 Desmond King AU 15.00 40.00
125 Jabrill Peppers AU 50.00 100.00
126 Brian Hill AU 12.00 30.00
127 Tarik Cohen AU 60.00 125.00
128 Cordrea Tankersley AU
129 Tre'Davious White AU 12.00 30.00
130 Malachi Dupre AU 12.00 30.00
131 Gareon Conley AU
132 Jonathan Allen AU
133 Stacy Coley AU 40.00 80.00
134 Carl Lawson AU 12.00 30.00
135 Taco Charlton AU 12.00 30.00
136 Isaiah Ford AU 12.00 30.00
137 Jordan Willis AU 12.00 30.00
138 DeMarcus Walker AU 12.00 30.00
139 Aaron Jones AU 75.00 150.00
140 Malik McDowell AU
141 Robert Davis AU 12.00 30.00
142 Josh Malone AU 12.00 30.00
143 Elijah Qualls AU 12.00 30.00
144 Caleb Brantley AU 12.00 30.00
145 Raekwon McMillan AU
146 Zach Cunningham AU
147 Jordan Leggett AU 12.00 30.00
148 Noah Brown AU 15.00 40.00
149 Jarrad Davis AU 30.00 60.00
150 Tim Williams AU 15.00 40.00
151 Jamal Agnew AU 12.00 30.00
152 Chad Hansen AU 12.00 30.00
153 Travis Rudolph AU
154 Artavis Scott AU 12.00 30.00
155 Shelton Gibson AU
156 Dalvin Tomlinson AU 12.00 30.00
157 Derek Rivers AU 15.00 40.00
158 Duke Riley AU 12.00 30.00
159 Fabian Moreau AU 12.00 30.00
160 Jonnu Smith AU 12.00 30.00
161 Gerald Everett AU 30.00 6.00
162 Isaiah McKenzie AU 12.00 30.00
163 Tanoh Kpassagnon AU 30.00 60.00
164 George Kittle AU 40.00 80.00
165 Josh Jones AU 25.00 60.00
166 Rasul Douglas AU 15.00 40.00
167 Rodney Adams AU
168 Nazair Jones AU 30.00 60.00
169 Haason Reddick AU 12.00 30.00
170 Devante Mays AU 12.00 30.00
171 Adam Shaheen AU 12.00 30.00
172 Ahkello Witherspoon AU 15.00 40.00
173 Shaquill Griffin AU 60.00 125.00
174 T.J. Logan AU 20.00 50.00
175 Alex Anzalone AU
176 John Johnson AU 15.00 40.00
177 Jeremy Sprinkle AU 12.00 30.00
178 Matt Breida AU 50.00 100.00
179 Chidobe Awuzie AU 25.00 60.00
180 Kevin King AU
181 Damontae Kazee AU 15.00 40.00
182 Dawuane Smoot AU
183 Daeshon Hall AU 12.00 30.00
184 Deatrich Wise Jr. AU 20.00 50.00
185 Chris Wormley AU 12.00 30.00
186 Jehu Chesson AU 15.00 40.00
187 Chris Carson AU 40.00 80.00
188 Marquez White AU 12.00 30.00
189 Carlos Watkins AU 12.00 30.00
190 Marcus Maye AU 12.00 30.00
191 Budda Baker AU 12.00 30.00
192 Jaleel Johnson AU 25.00 60.00
193 Tyus Bowser AU 12.00 30.00
194 Obi Melifonwu AU 12.00 30.00
195 Eddie Jackson AU 30.00 60.00
196 Marcus Williams AU 12.00 30.00
197 DeAngelo Yancey AU 12.00 30.00
198 Kendell Beckwith AU 12.00 30.00
199 Trent Taylor AU
200 Chad Williams AU 12.00 30.00
201 Ryan Glasgow AU
202 Geronimo Allison AU 40.00 80.00
203 Brandon Williams AU 25.00 60.00
204 Ross Cockrell AU 12.00 30.00
205 Arthur Moats AU 30.00 60.00
206 Garett Bolles AU 12.00 30.00
207 Ryan Ramczyk AU
208 Jerod Evans AU 15.00 40.00
209 KD Cannon AU
210 Jalen Myrick AU 12.00 30.00
211 Elijah McGuire AU 12.00 30.00
212 Davon Godchaux AU 12.00 30.00
213 Ben Boulware AU
214 Anthony Walker Jr. AU
215 Tanner Vallejo AU 20.00 50.00
216 Sam Rogers AU
217 Vince Biegel AU 25.00 60.00
218 Cooper Rush AU 75.00 150.00
219 De'Veon Smith AU 30.00 80.00
221 Justin Evans AU 12.00 30.00
222 Montravius Adams AU 15.00 40.00
223 Josh Harvey-Clemons AU 12.00 30.00
224 Ryan Anderson AU 12.00 30.00
225 Matt Milano AU 15.00 40.00
226 Ejuan Price AU
227 Jalen Reeves-Maybin AU 25.00 60.00
228 Eddie Vanderdoes AU 12.00 30.00
229 Devine Redding AU
230 De'Angelo Henderson AU 12.00 30.00
231 Montae Nicholson AU
232 Aaron Ripkowski AU 20.00 50.00
233 Cole Hikutini AU 12.00 30.00
234 Kyle Sloter AU 15.00 40.00
235 Billy Brown AU 12.00 30.00
236 Michael Rector AU 12.00 30.00
237 Zach Pascal AU 12.00 30.00
238 Damore'ea Stringfellow AU 15.00 40.00
239 Jacob Hollister AU 12.00 30.00
240 Austin Carr AU 12.00 30.00
241 Justin Davis AU 20.00 50.00
242 Victor Bolden Jr. AU 12.00 30.00
243 Kendrick Bourne AU 15.00 40.00
244 Austin Ekeler AU 25.00 60.00
245 Taquan Mizzell AU 12.00 30.00
246 Tanner Gentry AU 12.00 30.00
247 Tion Green AU 40.00 80.00
248 Michael Roberts AU 20.00 50.00
249 Taysom Hill AU 60.00 125.00
250 Brad Kaaya AU 30.00 60.00
251 T.J. Watt AU 200.00 300.00
252 Marshon Lattimore AU 60.00 125.00
253 Jake Butt AU 15.00 40.00
254 Jamal Adams AU 40.00 80.00
255 Donnel Pumphrey AU 15.00 40.00
256 Chad Kelly AU 100.00 200.00
257 David Njoku AU EXCH 15.00 40.00
258 Solomon Thomas AU 30.00 60.00
259 Adoree' Jackson AU 15.00 40.00
260 Matthew Dayes AU 12.00 30.00
261 Malik Hooker AU 40.00 80.00
262 Corey Clement AU 40.00 80.00
263 Jabrill Peppers AU 50.00 100.00
264 Brian Hill AU 12.00 30.00
265 Tre'Davious White AU 12.00 30.00
266 Malachi Dupre AU 12.00 30.00
267 Taco Charlton AU 12.00 30.00
268 DeMarcus Walker AU 12.00 30.00
269 Josh Malone AU 12.00 30.00
270 Raekwon McMillan AU
271 Zach Cunningham AU
272 Jordan Leggett AU 12.00 30.00
273 Noah Brown AU 15.00 40.00
274 Jamal Agnew AU 12.00 30.00
275 Chad Hansen AU 12.00 30.00
276 Artavis Scott AU 12.00 30.00
277 Shelton Gibson AU
278 Dalvin Tomlinson AU 12.00 30.00
279 Derek Rivers AU 15.00 40.00
280 Jonnu Smith AU 12.00 30.00
281 Gerald Everett AU 30.00 60.00
282 George Kittle AU 40.00 80.00
283 Rodney Adams AU
284 Haason Reddick AU 12.00 30.00
285 T.J. Logan AU 20.00 50.00
286 Kevin King AU
287 Isaiah Ford AU 12.00 30.00
288 Marcus Maye AU 12.00 30.00
289 Obi Melifonwu AU 12.00 30.00
290 Chad Williams AU 12.00 30.00
291 Reggie Davis AU 12.00 30.00
292 Trey Edmunds AU 12.00 30.00
293 Keelan Cole AU 75.00 150.00
294 Elijhaa Penny AU 12.00 30.00
295 Josh Woodrum AU 12.00 30.00
296 Kasen Williams AU 15.00 40.00
297 Raheem Mostert AU 12.00 30.00
298 Bernard Reedy AU 12.00 30.00
299 Mack Brown AU 12.00 30.00
300 Kyle Shanahan AU 100.00 200.00
301 Mitchell Trubisky AU 400.00 800.00
302 Deshaun Watson AU 1200.00 1800.00
303 Patrick Mahomes II AU 4000.00 6000.00
304 DeShone Kizer AU 75.00 150.00
305 Davis Webb AU 200.00 300.00
306 R. Joshua Dobbs AU 125.00 250.00
307 C.J. Beathard AU 40.00 80.00
308 Nathan Peterman AU 40.00 80.00
309 Dalvin Cook AU 200.00 300.00
310 Leonard Fournette AU 350.00 700.00
311 Christian McCaffrey AU 200.00 400.00
312 Joe Mixon AU 150.00 300.00
313 Alvin Kamara AU 400.00 800.00
314 Marlon Mack AU 100.00 200.00
315 Samaje Perine AU 75.00 150.00
316 Wayne Gallman AU EXCH 15.00 40.00
317 Kareem Hunt AU 75.00 150.00
318 D'Onta Foreman AU 40.00 80.00
319 Jeremy McNichols AU
320 James Conner AU 50.00 100.00
321 Jamaal Williams AU EXCH 75.00 150.00
322 Joe Williams AU 12.00 30.00
323 O.J. Howard AU 60.00 125.00
324 Evan Engram AU 60.00 125.00
325 Mike Williams AU 50.00 100.00
326 John Ross III AU 50.00 100.00
327 JuJu Smith-Schuster AU 300.00 400.00
328 Corey Davis AU
329 Dede Westbrook AU 50.00 100.00
330 Curtis Samuel AU 30.00 60.00
331 Amara Darboh AU 40.00 80.00
332 Carlos Henderson AU 12.00 30.00
333 Zay Jones AU 50.00 100.00
334 Cooper Kupp AU 100.00 200.00
335 Josh Reynolds AU 50.00 100.00
336 ArDarius Stewart AU 12.00 30.00
337 Chris Godwin AU 50.00 100.00
338 Taywan Taylor AU EXCH 12.00 30.00
339 Kenny Golladay AU 60.00 125.00
340 Mack Hollins AU 40.00 80.00
341 Mitchell Trubisky AU 400.00 800.00
342 Deshaun Watson AU 1200.00 1800.00
343 Patrick Mahomes II AU 4000.00 6000.00
344 DeShone Kizer AU 75.00 150.00
345 Davis Webb AU 200.00 300.00
346 R. Joshua Dobbs AU 125.00 250.00
347 C.J. Beathard AU 40.00 80.00
348 Nathan Peterman AU 40.00 80.00
349 Dalvin Cook AU 200.00 300.00
350 Leonard Fournette AU 350.00 700.00
351 Christian McCaffrey AU 200.00 400.00
352 Joe Mixon AU 150.00 300.00
353 Alvin Kamara AU 400.00 800.00
354 Marlon Mack AU 100.00 200.00
355 Samaje Perine AU 75.00 150.00
356 Wayne Gallman AU EXCH 15.00 40.00
357 Kareem Hunt AU 40.00 80.00
358 D'Onta Foreman AU 40.00 80.00
359 Jeremy McNichols AU 12.00 30.00
360 James Conner AU 60.00 125.00
361 Jamaal Williams AU EXCH 75.00 150.00
362 Joe Williams AU 12.00 30.00
363 O.J. Howard AU 60.00 125.00
364 Evan Engram AU 60.00 125.00
365 Mike Williams AU 50.00 100.00
366 John Ross III AU 50.00 100.00
367 JuJu Smith-Schuster AU 300.00 400.00
368 Corey Davis AU
369 Dede Westbrook AU 50.00 100.00
370 Curtis Samuel AU 30.00 60.00
371 Amara Darboh AU 40.00 80.00
372 Carlos Henderson AU 12.00 30.00
373 Zay Jones AU 50.00 100.00
374 Cooper Kupp AU 100.00 200.00
375 Josh Reynolds AU 50.00 100.00
376 ArDarius Stewart AU 12.00 30.00
377 Chris Godwin AU 50.00 100.00
378 Taywan Taylor AU EXCH 12.00 30.00
379 Kenny Golladay AU 60.00 125.00
380 Mack Hollins AU 40.00 80.00
381 Greg Olsen AU 40.00 80.00
382 Adam Vinatieri AU 40.00 80.00
383 Mark Ingram AU 15.00 40.00
384 Robert Kelley AU 12.00 30.00
385 Jason Witten AU EXCH 40.00 80.00
386 Matt Ryan AU 100.00 200.00
387 Marcus Mariota AU 50.00 100.00
388 Doug Baldwin AU 50.00 100.00
389 Carson Wentz AU 150.00 250.00
390 Ameer Abdullah AU 12.00 30.00
391 Drew Brees AU 75.00 150.00
392 John Brown AU 15.00 40.00
393 Mike Evans AU 15.00 40.00
394 Jordan Howard AU 20.00 50.00
395 David Johnson AU 20.00 50.00
396 Kirk Cousins AU 30.00 60.00
397 Dan Bailey AU 30.00 60.00
398 Michael Thomas AU
399 Chris Hogan AU
400 Terrelle Pryor Sr. AU 12.00 30.00

2017 Panini Contenders Playoff Ticket

*1-100 VETS/249: 2.5X TO 6X BASIC CARDS
101 Brad Kaaya AU/99 5.00 12.00
102 T.J. Watt AU/99 40.00 80.00
103 Marlon Humphrey AU/49
104 Jake Butt AU/99 6.00 15.00
105 Greg Ward Jr. AU/99 5.00 12.00
106 Khalfani Muhammad AU/49 6.00 15.00
107 Jamal Adams AU/49 6.00 15.00
108 Donnel Pumphrey AU/99 6.00 15.00
109 Chad Kelly AU/49 30.00 60.00
110 Marshon Lattimore AU/49 15.00 40.00
111 Quincy Wilson AU/99 5.00 12.00
112 Ryan Switzer AU/49 8.00 20.00
113 Cameron Sutton AU/49 15.00 40.00
114 David Njoku AU/99 EXCH 6.00 15.00
115 Sidney Jones AU/99 5.00 12.00
116 Solomon Thomas AU/49 6.00 15.00
117 Elijah Hood AU/99 5.00 12.00
118 Adoree' Jackson AU/49 EXCH 8.00 20.00
119 Matthew Dayes AU/99 5.00 12.00
120 Malik Hooker AU/99 5.00 12.00
121 Derek Barnett AU/49
122 Charles Harris AU/49 6.00 15.00
123 Corey Clement AU/99 6.00 15.00
124 Desmond King AU/99 6.00 15.00
125 Jabrill Peppers AU/49 10.00 25.00
126 Brian Hill AU/99 5.00 12.00
127 Tarik Cohen AU/49 40.00 80.00
128 Cordrea Tankersley AU/49
129 Tre'Davious White AU/49 6.00 15.00
130 Malachi Dupre AU/49 6.00 15.00
131 Gareon Conley AU/99
132 Jonathan Allen AU/49 8.00 20.00
133 Stacy Coley AU/99 5.00 12.00
134 Carl Lawson AU/49 6.00 15.00
135 Taco Charlton AU/99 5.00 12.00
136 Isaiah Ford AU/99 5.00 12.00
137 Jordan Willis AU/99 5.00 12.00
138 DeMarcus Walker AU/99 5.00 12.00
139 Aaron Jones AU/49 20.00 40.00
140 Malik McDowell AU/49 6.00 15.00
141 Robert Davis AU/99 5.00 12.00
142 Josh Malone AU/99 5.00 12.00
143 Elijah Qualls AU/99 5.00 12.00
144 Caleb Brantley AU/99
145 Raekwon McMillan AU/49 6.00 15.00
146 Zach Cunningham AU/49
147 Jordan Leggett AU/99 5.00 12.00
148 Noah Brown AU/99 12.00 30.00
149 Jarrad Davis AU/49 8.00 20.00
150 Tim Williams AU/49 8.00 20.00
151 Jamal Agnew AU/99 5.00 12.00
152 Chad Hansen AU/99 5.00 12.00
153 Travis Rudolph AU/99 5.00 12.00
154 Artavis Scott AU/99 5.00 12.00
155 Shelton Gibson AU/99
156 Dalvin Tomlinson AU/49 6.00 15.00
157 Derek Rivers AU/49 8.00 20.00
158 Duke Riley AU/49 6.00 15.00
159 Fabian Moreau AU/49 8.00 20.00
160 Jonnu Smith AU/49 6.00 15.00
161 Gerald Everett AU/49 6.00 15.00
162 Isaiah McKenzie AU/49 6.00 15.00
163 Tanoh Kpassagnon AU/49 8.00 20.00
164 George Kittle AU/99 10.00 25.00
165 Josh Jones AU/99 6.00 15.00
166 Rasul Douglas AU/99 6.00 15.00
167 Rodney Adams AU/49
168 Nazair Jones AU/99 5.00 12.00
169 Haason Reddick AU/49 6.00 15.00
170 Devante Mays AU/99 5.00 12.00
171 Adam Shaheen AU/49 6.00 15.00
172 Ahkello Witherspoon AU/99 6.00 15.00
173 Shaquill Griffin AU/49 25.00 50.00
174 T.J. Logan AU/49 10.00 25.00
175 Alex Anzalone AU/99 6.00 15.00
176 John Johnson AU/99 6.00 15.00
177 Jeremy Sprinkle AU/99 5.00 12.00
178 Matt Breida AU/99 8.00 20.00
179 Chidobe Awuzie AU/49 15.00 40.00
180 Kevin King AU/49
181 Damontae Kazee AU/49 8.00 20.00
182 Dawuane Smoot AU/99 5.00 12.00
183 Daeshon Hall AU/99 5.00 12.00
184 Deatrich Wise Jr. AU/99 8.00 20.00
185 Chris Wormley AU/99 5.00 12.00
186 Jehu Chesson AU/49 8.00 20.00
187 Chris Carson AU/99 15.00 40.00
188 Marquez White AU/49 6.00 15.00
189 Carlos Watkins AU/49 6.00 15.00
190 Marcus Maye AU/99
191 Budda Baker AU/99 5.00 12.00
192 Jaleel Johnson AU/99
193 Tyus Bowser AU/99 5.00 12.00
194 Obi Melifonwu AU/99 5.00 12.00
195 Eddie Jackson AU/99 6.00 15.00
196 Marcus Williams AU/49 6.00 15.00
197 DeAngelo Yancey AU/49 6.00 15.00
198 Kendell Beckwith AU/49 6.00 15.00
199 Trent Taylor AU/49 30.00 60.00
200 Chad Williams AU/49 6.00 15.00
201 Ryan Glasgow AU/99
202 Geronimo Allison AU/99 6.00 15.00
203 Brandon Williams AU/99 5.00 12.00
204 Ross Cockrell AU/99 5.00 12.00
205 Arthur Moats AU/99 5.00 12.00
206 Garett Bolles AU/99 5.00 12.00
207 Ryan Ramczyk AU/99 5.00 12.00
208 Jerod Evans AU/49 8.00 20.00
209 KD Cannon AU/99 5.00 12.00
210 Jalen Myrick AU/49 6.00 15.00
211 Elijah McGuire AU/99 5.00 12.00
212 Davon Godchaux AU/99 5.00 12.00
213 Ben Boulware AU/99 12.00 30.00
214 Anthony Walker Jr. AU/99 5.00 12.00
215 Tanner Vallejo AU/99 8.00 20.00
216 Sam Rogers AU/99 5.00 12.00
217 Vince Biegel AU/99 10.00 25.00
218 Cooper Rush AU/99 25.00 50.00
219 De'Veon Smith AU/49 15.00 40.00
221 Justin Evans AU/99 5.00 12.00
222 Montravius Adams AU/99 6.00 15.00
223 Josh Harvey-Clemons AU/99 5.00 12.00
224 Ryan Anderson AU/99 5.00 12.00
225 Matt Milano AU/99 6.00 15.00
226 Ejuan Price AU/49 6.00 15.00
227 Jalen Reeves-Maybin AU/99 10.00 25.00
228 Eddie Vanderdoes AU/49 6.00 15.00
229 Devine Redding AU/99 5.00 12.00
230 De'Angelo Henderson AU/99 5.00 12.00
231 Montae Nicholson AU/99
232 Aaron Ripkowski AU/99 8.00 20.00
233 Cole Hikutini AU/99 5.00 12.00
234 Kyle Sloter AU/99 6.00 15.00
235 Billy Brown AU/99 5.00 12.00
236 Michael Rector AU/99 5.00 12.00
237 Zach Pascal AU/99 5.00 12.00
238 Damore'ea Stringfellow AU/99
239 Jacob Hollister AU/99 5.00 12.00
240 Austin Carr AU/99 5.00 12.00
241 Justin Davis AU/99 8.00 20.00
242 Victor Bolden Jr. AU/99 5.00 12.00
243 Kendrick Bourne AU/99 6.00 15.00
244 Austin Ekeler AU/99 10.00 25.00
245 Taquan Mizzell AU/99 5.00 12.00
246 Tanner Gentry AU/99 5.00 12.00
247 Tion Green AU/99 5.00 12.00
248 Michael Roberts AU/99 8.00 20.00
249 Taysom Hill AU/99 30.00 60.00
250 Brad Kaaya AU/99 5.00 12.00
251 T.J. Watt AU/99 40.00 80.00
252 Marshon Lattimore AU/49 15.00 40.00
253 Jake Butt AU/99 6.00 15.00
254 Jamal Adams AU/49 6.00 15.00
255 Donnel Pumphrey AU/99 6.00 15.00
256 Chad Kelly AU/49 30.00 60.00
257 David Njoku AU/99 EXCH 6.00 15.00
258 Solomon Thomas AU/49 6.00 15.00
259 Adoree' Jackson AU/49 EXCH 8.00 20.00
260 Matthew Dayes AU/99 5.00 12.00
261 Malik Hooker AU/49 6.00 15.00
262 Corey Clement AU/49 8.00 20.00
263 Jabrill Peppers AU/49 10.00 25.00
264 Brian Hill AU/99 5.00 12.00
265 Tre'Davious White AU/49 6.00 15.00
266 Malachi Dupre AU/49 6.00 15.00
267 Taco Charlton AU/49 6.00 15.00
268 DeMarcus Walker AU/99 5.00 12.00
269 Josh Malone AU/49 6.00 15.00
270 Raekwon McMillan AU/49 6.00 15.00
271 Zach Cunningham AU/49
272 Jordan Leggett AU/99 5.00 12.00
273 Noah Brown AU/99 12.00 30.00
274 Jamal Agnew AU/99 5.00 12.00
275 Chad Hansen AU/99 5.00 12.00
276 Artavis Scott AU/99 5.00 12.00
277 Shelton Gibson AU/99
278 Dalvin Tomlinson AU/49 6.00 15.00
279 Derek Rivers AU/49 8.00 20.00
280 Jonnu Smith AU/49 6.00 15.00
281 Gerald Everett AU/49 6.00 15.00
282 George Kittle AU/49 12.00 30.00
283 Rodney Adams AU/49
284 Haason Reddick AU/49 6.00 15.00
285 T.J. Logan AU/49 10.00 25.00
286 Kevin King AU/49
287 Isaiah Ford AU/99 5.00 12.00
288 Marcus Maye AU/99
289 Obi Melifonwu AU/99 5.00 12.00
290 Chad Williams AU/99 5.00 12.00
291 Reggie Davis AU/99 5.00 12.00
292 Trey Edmunds AU/99 5.00 12.00
293 Keelan Cole AU/99 15.00 40.00
294 Elijhaa Penny AU/99
295 Josh Woodrum AU/99 5.00 12.00
296 Kasen Williams AU/99 6.00 15.00
297 Raheem Mostert AU/99 5.00 12.00
298 Bernard Reedy AU/99 5.00 12.00
299 Mack Brown AU/99 5.00 12.00
300 Kyle Shanahan AU/49 EXCH 40.00 80.00
301 Mitchell Trubisky AU/15 300.00 600.00
302 Deshaun Watson AU/15 125.00 250.00
303 Patrick Mahomes II AU/15 2000.00 3000.00
304 DeShone Kizer AU/15 40.00 80.00
305 Davis Webb AU/25 75.00 150.00
306 R. Joshua Dobbs AU/49 25.00 50.00
307 C.J. Beathard AU/25 40.00 80.00
308 Nathan Peterman AU/25 10.00 25.00
309 Dalvin Cook AU/15 100.00 200.00
310 Leonard Fournette AU/15 40.00 80.00
311 Christian McCaffrey AU/15 75.00 150.00
312 Joe Mixon AU/49 40.00 80.00
313 Alvin Kamara AU/25 200.00 400.00
314 Marlon Mack AU/99 8.00 20.00
315 Samaje Perine AU/25 8.00 20.00
316 Wayne Gallman AU/99 EXCH 6.00 15.00
317 Kareem Hunt AU/49 40.00 80.00
318 D'Onta Foreman AU/25 10.00 25.00
319 Jeremy McNichols AU/99 5.00 12.00
320 James Conner AU/99 12.00 30.00
321 Jamaal Williams AU/99 EXCH 25.00 50.00
322 Joe Williams AU/99 5.00 12.00
323 O.J. Howard AU/25 40.00 80.00
324 Evan Engram AU/25 40.00 80.00
325 Mike Williams AU/15
326 John Ross III AU/15 12.00 30.00
327 JuJu Smith-Schuster AU/15
328 Corey Davis AU/15 15.00 40.00
329 Dede Westbrook AU/25 8.00 20.00
330 Curtis Samuel AU/25 10.00 25.00
331 Amara Darboh AU/25 8.00 20.00
332 Carlos Henderson AU/99 5.00 12.00
333 Zay Jones AU/25 10.00 25.00
334 Cooper Kupp AU/99 20.00 50.00
335 Josh Reynolds AU/99 5.00 12.00
336 ArDarius Stewart AU/99 5.00 12.00
337 Chris Godwin AU/99 6.00 15.00
338 Taywan Taylor AU/99 EXCH 5.00 12.00
339 Kenny Golladay AU/99 8.00 20.00
340 Mack Hollins AU/99 5.00 12.00
345 Davis Webb AU/15 100.00 200.00
346 R. Joshua Dobbs AU/15 40.00 80.00
347 C.J. Beathard AU/15 40.00 80.00
348 Nathan Peterman AU/15 12.00 30.00
353 Alvin Kamara AU/15 300.00 500.00
354 Marlon Mack AU/49 10.00 25.00
355 Samaje Perine AU/15 10.00 25.00
356 Wayne Gallman AU/15 EXCH 12.00 30.00
357 Kareem Hunt AU/25 75.00 150.00
359 Jeremy McNichols AU/15 10.00 25.00
360 James Conner AU/49 15.00 40.00
361 Jamaal Williams AU/49 EXCH 30.00 60.00
362 Joe Williams AU/49 6.00 15.00
363 O.J. Howard AU/15 50.00 100.00
364 Evan Engram AU/15 50.00 100.00
370 Curtis Samuel AU/49 8.00 20.00
371 Amara Darboh AU/49 6.00 15.00
372 Carlos Henderson AU/49 6.00 15.00
374 Cooper Kupp AU/49 30.00 60.00
375 Josh Reynolds AU/49 6.00 15.00
376 ArDarius Stewart AU/49 6.00 15.00
377 Chris Godwin AU/49 8.00 20.00
378 Taywan Taylor AU/49 EXCH 6.00 15.00
379 Kenny Golladay AU/49 10.00 25.00
380 Mack Hollins AU/49 6.00 15.00
384 Robert Kelley AU/99 5.00 12.00
388 Doug Baldwin AU/15 30.00 60.00
390 Ameer Abdullah AU/99 5.00 12.00
392 John Brown AU/49 8.00 20.00
394 Jordan Howard AU/49 10.00 25.00
399 Chris Hogan AU/49

2017 Panini Contenders Legendary Contenders

*EMERALD: .6X TO 1.5X BASIC INSERTS
*SILVER/199: .8X TO 2X BASIC INSERTS
*GOLD/99: 1X TO 2.5X BASIC INSERTS
*PLATINUM/25: 1.5X TO 4X BASIC INSERTS
1 Jim Kelly .60 1.50
2 Jason Taylor .40 1.00
3 Emmitt Smith 1.00 2.50
4 Michael Vick .50 1.25
5 Alan Page .40 1.00
6 Jim Otto .40 1.00
7 Brett Favre 1.25 3.00
8 Lance Alworth .50 1.25
9 Drew Pearson .50 1.25
10 Earl Campbell .60 1.50
11 Randy Moss .50 1.25
12 Calvin Johnson .60 1.50
13 Steve Young .75 2.00
14 Chris Doleman .40 1.00
15 Mark Gastineau .40 1.00

2017 Panini Contenders MVP Contenders

*EMERALD: .6X TO 1.5X BASIC INSERTS
*SILVER/199: .8X TO 2X BASIC INSERTS
*GOLD/99: 1X TO 2.5X BASIC INSERTS
*PLATINUM/25: 1.5X TO 4X BASIC INSERTS
1 Aaron Rodgers 1.25 3.00
2 Matt Ryan .50 1.25
3 Ezekiel Elliott .75 2.00
4 Mike Evans .50 1.25
5 Drew Brees .60 1.50
6 Dak Prescott .60 1.50
7 Matthew Stafford .50 1.25
8 Derek Carr .60 1.50
9 Marcus Mariota .60 1.50
10 Jameis Winston .50 1.25
11 Antonio Brown .60 1.50
12 J.J. Watt .60 1.50
13 Ben Roethlisberger .60 1.50
14 Russell Wilson .75 2.00
15 Carson Wentz .75 2.00
16 Eli Manning .50 1.25
17 LeSean McCoy .60 1.50
18 Kirk Cousins .60 1.50
19 Jordan Howard .60 1.50
20 Philip Rivers .60 1.50
21 Cam Newton .60 1.50
22 Julio Jones .60 1.50
23 Tom Brady 1.50 4.00
24 Le'Veon Bell .50 1.25
25 Odell Beckham Jr. .60 1.50

2017 Panini Contenders MVP Contenders Autographs

2 Matt Ryan/25 30.00 60.00
3 Ezekiel Elliott/25 50.00 100.00
4 Mike Evans/49 6.00 15.00
5 Drew Brees/15 50.00 100.00
6 Dak Prescott/49 EXCH 40.00 80.00
7 Matthew Stafford/15 25.00 50.00
8 Derek Carr/25
9 Marcus Mariota/25 20.00 40.00
10 Jameis Winston/15 20.00 40.00
12 J.J. Watt/25 EXCH 30.00 60.00
15 Carson Wentz/25 75.00 150.00
17 LeSean McCoy/49 10.00 25.00
18 Kirk Cousins/49 15.00 40.00
19 Jordan Howard/49 EXCH 20.00 50.00

2017 Panini Contenders NFL Ink

*GOLD/25: .8X TO 2X BASIC AU/199
1 Jonathan Stewart/99 4.00 10.00
2 Gerald McCoy/199 3.00 8.00
3 Taylor Gabriel/199 3.00 8.00
4 Jack Doyle/199 3.00 8.00
5 Marcus Peters/199
6 LeSean McCoy/25 10.00 25.00
7 Cameron Heyward/199 6.00 15.00
8 Melvin Gordon/49 6.00 15.00
9 Delanie Walker/199 3.00 8.00
10 Richard Sherman/25 25.00 50.00
11 Luke Kuechly/25 8.00 20.00
12 Hunter Henry/99 4.00 10.00
13 Aaron Donald/99 6.00 15.00
14 Derrick Henry/25 15.00 40.00
15 Randall Cobb/99 10.00 25.00
16 Cole Beasley/99
17 Sterling Shepard/99 5.00 12.00
18 Thomas Rawls/199 3.00 8.00
20 Ha Ha Clinton-Dix/49 5.00 12.00

2017 Panini Contenders Rookie of the Year Contenders

*EMERALD: .5X TO 1.2X BASIC INSERTS
*SILVER/199: .6X TO 1.5X BASIC INSERTS
*GOLD/99: .8X TO 2X BASIC INSERTS
1 Mitchell Trubisky 1.50 4.00
2 Deshaun Watson 2.00 5.00
3 Patrick Mahomes II 8.00 20.00
4 DeShone Kizer .30 .75
5 C.J. Beathard .30 .75
6 Dalvin Cook .75 2.00
7 Leonard Fournette 1.00 2.50
8 Christian McCaffrey .75 2.00
9 Joe Mixon .60 1.50
10 Alvin Kamara 1.25 3.00
11 Marlon Mack .50 1.25
12 Samaje Perine .30 .75
13 Wayne Gallman .40 1.00
14 Kareem Hunt .60 1.50
15 Tarik Cohen .60 1.50
16 Kenny Golladay .50 1.25
17 O.J. Howard .40 1.00
18 Evan Engram .40 1.00
19 Mike Williams .50 1.25
20 John Ross III .40 1.00
21 JuJu Smith-Schuster .75 2.00
22 Corey Davis .50 1.25
23 Curtis Samuel .40 1.00
24 Carlos Henderson .30 .75
25 Zay Jones .40 1.00
26 Cooper Kupp .50 1.25
27 Jabrill Peppers .50 1.25
28 David Njoku .40 1.00
29 Jamal Adams .30 .75
30 T.J. Watt 1.00 2.50

2017 Panini Contenders Rookie of the Year Contenders Platinum

*PLATINUM/25: 1.2X TO 3X BASIC INSERTS
2 Deshaun Watson 15.00 30.00
10 Alvin Kamara 25.00 50.00

2017 Panini Contenders Rookie of the Year Contenders Autographs

1 Mitchell Trubisky/25 100.00 200.00
2 Deshaun Watson/25 150.00 300.00
3 Patrick Mahomes II/25 400.00 800.00
4 DeShone Kizer/25
5 C.J. Beathard/49 5.00 12.00
6 Dalvin Cook/25 90.00 150.00
7 Leonard Fournette/25 50.00 100.00
8 Christian McCaffrey/25 50.00 100.00
9 Joe Mixon/99 12.00 30.00
10 Alvin Kamara/99 50.00 100.00
11 Marlon Mack/199 5.00 12.00
12 Samaje Perine/199 3.00 8.00
13 Wayne Gallman/199 4.00 10.00
14 Kareem Hunt/199 12.00 30.00
15 D'Onta Foreman/49 6.00 15.00
16 Jeremy McNichols/199 3.00 8.00
17 Joe Williams/199 3.00 8.00
18 O.J. Howard/25 25.00 50.00
19 Evan Engram/49 10.00 25.00
20 Mike Williams/25 10.00 25.00
21 John Ross III/49 6.00 15.00
22 JuJu Smith-Schuster/49 50.00 100.00
23 Corey Davis/49 EXCH 8.00 20.00
24 Dede Westbrook/99 4.00 10.00
25 Curtis Samuel/99 5.00 12.00
26 Carlos Henderson/199 3.00 8.00
27 Zay Jones/99 5.00 12.00
28 Cooper Kupp/199 5.00 12.00
29 Josh Reynolds/199 3.00 8.00
30 ArDarius Stewart/199 3.00 8.00
31 Jabrill Peppers/25 10.00 25.00
32 Marshon Lattimore/99 15.00 40.00
33 Adoree' Jackson/199 EXCH 4.00 10.00
34 David Njoku/49 EXCH 6.00 15.00
35 Malik Hooker/99 4.00 10.00
36 Jamal Adams/49 5.00 12.00
37 Kenny Golladay/49 8.00 20.00
38 T.J. Watt/49 15.00 40.00
39 Adam Shaheen/199 3.00 8.00
40 Gerald Everett/199 3.00 8.00

2017 Panini Contenders Rookie Roundup Autographs

1 Mitchell Trubisky/15 100.00 200.00
2 Deshaun Watson/15 100.00 200.00
3 Patrick Mahomes II/25 125.00 250.00
4 Davis Webb/99 4.00 10.00
5 R. Joshua Dobbs/99 5.00 12.00
6 C.J. Beathard/99 4.00 10.00
7 Dalvin Cook/15 20.00 50.00
8 Leonard Fournette/15 25.00 60.00
9 Christian McCaffrey/15 40.00 80.00
10 Marlon Mack/199 5.00 12.00
11 Samaje Perine/199 3.00 8.00
12 Wayne Gallman/199 4.00 10.00
13 Kareem Hunt/149 25.00 50.00
14 D'Onta Foreman/99 5.00 12.00
15 Jeremy McNichols/49 5.00 12.00
16 Jamaal Williams/99 4.00 10.00
17 Joe Williams/25 6.00 15.00
18 O.J. Howard/25 8.00 20.00
19 Mike Williams/15 12.00 30.00
20 John Ross III/15 10.00 25.00
21 JuJu Smith-Schuster/15 50.00 100.00
22 Corey Davis/15 12.00 30.00
23 Curtis Samuel/49 6.00 15.00
24 Amara Darboh/99 4.00 10.00
25 Zay Jones/49 6.00 15.00
26 Cooper Kupp/99 6.00 15.00
27 Chris Godwin/99 5.00 12.00
28 Taywan Taylor/199 3.00 8.00
29 Kenny Golladay/199 5.00 12.00
30 Mack Hollins/199 3.00 8.00
31 Brad Kaaya/25 6.00 15.00
32 Donnel Pumphrey/99 5.00 12.00
33 Marlon Humphrey/49 5.00 12.00
34 Jake Butt/199 4.00 10.00
35 Malachi Dupre/199 3.00 8.00
36 Tarik Cohen/49 10.00 25.00
37 Chad Hansen/199 3.00 8.00
38 Jabrill Peppers/49 8.00 20.00
39 T.J. Logan/99 6.00 15.00
40 Jarrad Davis/49 6.00 15.00

2017 Panini Contenders Rookie Ticket Dual Swatches

1 J.SmthSchstr/J.Dobbs 5.00 12.00
2 D.Westbrook/L.Fournette 5.00 12.00
3 C.Davis/T.Taylor 3.00 8.00
4 D.Foreman/D.Watson 8.00 20.00
5 C.McCaffrey/C.Samuel 5.00 12.00
6 J.Mixon/J.Ross 4.00 10.00
7 C.Beathard/J.Williams 2.00 5.00
8 P.Mahomes/K.Hunt 15.00 40.00
9 N.Peterman/Z.Jones 2.50 6.00
10 C.Godwin/O.Howard 2.50 6.00
11 E.Engram/W.Gallman 2.50 6.00
12 C.Kupp/J.Reynolds 3.00 8.00
13 M.Trubisky/M.Hollins 6.00 15.00
14 D.Webb/D.Kizer 2.00 5.00
15 A.Kamara/D.Cook 5.00 12.00
16 J.Conner/J.Williams 4.00 10.00
17 S.Perine/J.McNichols 2.00 5.00
18 M.Williams/K.Golladay 3.00 8.00
19 A.Darboh/A.Stewart 2.00 5.00
20 C.Henderson/M.Mack 3.00 8.00

2017 Panini Contenders Rookie Ticket Swatches

*VARIATION: .4X TO 1X BASIC JSY
1 Mitchell Trubisky 6.00 15.00
2 Deshaun Watson 8.00 20.00
3 Patrick Mahomes II 12.00 30.00
4 DeShone Kizer 2.00 5.00
5 Davis Webb 2.00 5.00
6 R. Joshua Dobbs 2.50 6.00
7 C.J. Beathard 2.00 5.00
8 Nathan Peterman 2.50 6.00
9 Dalvin Cook 4.00 10.00
10 Leonard Fournette 5.00 12.00
11 Christian McCaffrey 4.00 10.00
12 Joe Mixon 4.00 10.00
13 Alvin Kamara 6.00 15.00
14 Marlon Mack 3.00 8.00
15 Samaje Perine 2.00 5.00
16 Wayne Gallman 2.50 6.00
17 Kareem Hunt 5.00 12.00
18 D'Onta Foreman 2.50 6.00
19 David Njoku 2.50 6.00
20 James Conner 4.00 10.00
21 Jamaal Williams 2.00 5.00
22 Joe Williams 2.00 5.00
23 O.J. Howard 2.50 6.00
24 Evan Engram 2.50 6.00
25 Mike Williams 3.00 8.00
26 John Ross III 2.50 6.00
27 JuJu Smith-Schuster 4.00 10.00
28 Corey Davis 3.00 8.00
29 Dede Westbrook 2.00 5.00
30 Curtis Samuel 2.50 6.00
31 Amara Darboh 2.00 5.00
32 Carlos Henderson 2.00 5.00
33 Zay Jones 2.50 6.00
34 Cooper Kupp 3.00 8.00
35 Josh Reynolds 2.00 5.00
36 ArDarius Stewart 2.00 5.00
37 Chris Godwin 2.50 6.00
38 Taywan Taylor 2.00 5.00
39 Kenny Golladay 3.00 8.00
40 Mack Hollins 2.00 5.00

2017 Panini Contenders Round Numbers

*EMERALD: .5X TO 1.2X BASIC INSERTS
*SILVER/199: .6X TO 1.5X BASIC INSERTS
*GOLD/99: .8X TO 2X BASIC INSERTS
*PLATINUM/99: 1.2X TO 3X BASIC INSERTS
1 Mitchell Trubisky 2.50 6.00
Deshaun Watson
2 Christian McCaffrey 1.25 3.00
Leonard Fournette
3 Jabrill Peppers 1.25 3.00
T.J. Watt
4 Jamal Adams .40 1.00
Malik Hooker
5 Corey Davis .60 1.50
Mike Williams
6 Evan Engram .50 1.25
O.J. Howard
7 Dalvin Cook 1.00 2.50
Joe Mixon
8 Sidney Jones .50 1.25
Kevin King
9 Adam Shaheen .40 1.00
Gerald Everett
10 Curtis Samuel .50 1.25
Zay Jones
11 Davis Webb .40 1.00
C.J. Beathard
12 D'Onta Foreman .75 2.00
Kareem Hunt
13 Carlos Henderson .40 1.00
Taywan Taylor
14 Kenny Golladay .60 1.50
Cooper Kupp
15 Samaje Perine .50 1.25
Wayne Gallman
16 Donnel Pumphrey .75 2.00
Tarik Cohen
17 Jehu Chesson .50 1.25
Ryan Switzer
18 Brian Hill .60 1.50
T.J. Logan
19 Isaiah McKenzie .50 1.25
Trent Taylor
20 Jake Butt .50 1.25
George Kittle

2017 Panini Contenders Round Numbers Dual Autographs

1 Deshaun Watson 150.00 250.00
Mitchell Trubisky/15
2 Christian McCaffrey 30.00 80.00
Leonard Fournette/15
3 Jabrill Peppers 30.00 80.00
T.J. Watt/15
4 Jamal Adams 10.00 25.00
Malik Hooker/15
5 Mike Williams 15.00 40.00
Corey Davis/15
6 Evan Engram 12.00 30.00
O.J. Howard/15
7 Dalvin Cook 20.00 50.00
Joe Mixon/25
8 Kevin King 10.00 25.00
Sidney Jones/25
9 Gerald Everett 8.00 20.00
Adam Shaheen/25
10 Curtis Samuel 10.00 25.00
Zay Jones/25
11 Davis Webb 6.00 15.00
C.J. Beathard/49
12 D'Onta Foreman 12.00 30.00
Kareem Hunt/49
13 Carlos Henderson 6.00 15.00
Taywan Taylor/49
14 Cooper Kupp 15.00 40.00
Kenny Golladay/49
15 Samaje Perine 6.00 15.00
Wayne Gallman/99
16 Donnel Pumphrey 10.00 25.00
Tarik Cohen/99
17 Jehu Chesson 6.00 15.00
Ryan Switzer/99
18 Brian Hill 8.00 20.00
T.J. Logan/99
19 Trent Taylor 6.00 15.00
Isaiah McKenzie/99
20 George Kittle 15.00 40.00
Jake Butt/99

2017 Panini Contenders Team Quads

*EMERALD: .6X TO 1.5X BASIC INSERTS
*SILVER/199: .8X TO 2X BASIC INSERTS
*GOLD/99: 1X TO 2.5X BASIC INSERTS
*PLATINUM/25: 1.5X TO 4X BASIC INSERTS
1 Prsctt/Ellt/Wttn/Brnt 1.00 2.50
2 Dvs/Mrry/Dckr/Mrta .75 2.00
3 Rthlsbrgr/Bll/Brwn/Hrrsn .75 2.00
4 Rdgrs/Adms/Mtthws/Cbb 1.50 4.00
5 Cks/Whte/Grnkwski/Brdy 2.00 5.00
6 Jcksn/Evns/Wnstn/Hwrd .60 1.50
7 Cpr/Crr/Mck/Lnch .75 2.00
8 Jns/Ryn/Frmn/Clmn .75 2.00
9 McCffry/Bnjmn/Kchly/Nwtn 1.25 3.00
10 Brtls/Rmsy/Rbnsn/Frntte 1.50 4.00

2018 Panini Contenders

1 Alex Smith .25 .60
2 Josh Norman .20 .50
3 Jordan Reed .20 .50
4 Marcus Mariota .30 .75
5 Corey Davis .25 .60
6 Derrick Henry .30 .75
7 Jameis Winston .25 .60
8 Mike Evans .25 .60
9 Gerald McCoy .20 .50
10 Russell Wilson .40 1.00
11 Doug Baldwin .25 .60
12 Earl Thomas III .25 .60
13 Jimmy Garoppolo .40 1.00
14 Richard Sherman .30 .75
15 Marquise Goodwin .20 .50
16 Le'Veon Bell .25 .60
17 Antonio Brown .30 .75
18 JuJu Smith-Schuster .30 .75
19 Ben Roethlisberger .30 .75
20 Carson Wentz .40 1.00
21 Alshon Jeffery .25 .60
22 Jay Ajayi .25 .60
23 Derek Carr .30 .75
24 Khalil Mack .30 .75
25 Amari Cooper .30 .75
26 Jordy Nelson .25 .60
27 Robby Anderson .20 .50
28 Leonard Williams .20 .50
29 Jamal Adams .25 .60
30 Eli Manning .25 .60
31 Odell Beckham Jr. .30 .75
32 Evan Engram .20 .50
33 Drew Brees .30 .75
34 Michael Thomas .30 .75
35 Alvin Kamara .25 .60
36 Tom Brady .75 2.00
37 Rob Gronkowski .30 .75
38 Julian Edelman .30 .75
39 Kirk Cousins .30 .75
40 Adam Thielen .30 .75
41 Stefon Diggs .25 .60
42 Ryan Tannehill .25 .60
43 Kenyan Drake .20 .50
44 Kiko Alonso .20 .50
45 Jared Goff .30 .75
46 Todd Gurley II .30 .75
47 Aaron Donald .30 .75
48 Philip Rivers .30 .75
49 Melvin Gordon .25 .60
50 Joey Bosa .30 .75
51 Patrick Mahomes II .75 2.00
52 Tyreek Hill .30 .75
53 Kareem Hunt .25 .60
54 Blake Bortles .20 .50
55 Jalen Ramsey .25 .60
56 Leonard Fournette .30 .75
57 T.Y. Hilton .25 .60
58 Andrew Luck .40 1.00
59 Marlon Mack .20 .50
60 Deshaun Watson .40 1.00
61 J.J. Watt .30 .75
62 DeAndre Hopkins .25 .60
63 Aaron Rodgers .60 1.50
64 Davante Adams .25 .60
65 Jimmy Graham .30 .75
66 Matthew Stafford .25 .60
67 Marvin Jones Jr. .20 .50
68 Darius Slay .20 .50
69 Case Keenum .25 .60
70 Von Miller .25 .60
71 Demaryius Thomas .25 .60
72 Dak Prescott .30 .75
73 Ezekiel Elliott .40 1.00
74 Sean Lee .25 .60
75 Myles Garrett .30 .75
76 Jarvis Landry .25 .60
77 Carlos Hyde .20 .50
78 Andy Dalton .25 .60
79 A.J. Green .30 .75
80 Joe Mixon .25 .60
81 Mitchell Trubisky .30 .75
82 Jordan Howard .30 .75
83 Allen Robinson II .25 .60
84 Cam Newton .30 .75
85 Christian McCaffrey .30 .75
86 Luke Kuechly .25 .60
87 Zay Jones .20 .50
88 LeSean McCoy .30 .75
89 Kelvin Benjamin .25 .60
90 Joe Flacco .25 .60
91 Michael Crabtree .20 .50
92 Terrell Suggs .20 .50
93 Matt Ryan .25 .60
94 Julio Jones .30 .75
95 Devonta Freeman .25 .60
96 Chandler Jones .20 .50
97 Larry Fitzgerald .25 .60
98 David Johnson .30 .75
99 Brandin Cooks .25 .60
100 Zach Ertz .25 .60
101A Baker Mayfield AU RC 500.00 800.00
(throwing)
101B Baker Mayfield AU SP 500.00 800.00
(running)
102A Saquon Barkley AU RC 250.00 400.00
(ball in right arm)
102B Saquon Barkley AU SP 250.00 400.00
(ball in left arm)
103A Sam Darnold AU/225* RC SP1 250.00 400.00
(running right)
103B Sam Darnold AU SP 250.00 400.00
(body facing left)
104A Bradley Chubb AU/50* RC SP2 EXCH 40.00 80.00
104B Bradley Chubb AU SP EXCH 40.00 80.00
105A Josh Allen AU RC 100.00 200.00
(facing left)
105B Josh Allen AU SP 125.00 250.00
(facing right)
106A Josh Rosen AU RC 90.00 150.00
(throwing)
106B Josh Rosen AU/200* SP1 100.00 200.00
(body facing left)
107A D.J. Moore AU RC 12.00 30.00
(ball in right arm)
107B D.J. Moore AU SP 12.00 30.00
(ball in left arm)
108 Hayden Hurst AU/25* RC SP2 12.00 30.00
109A Calvin Ridley AU RC 40.00 80.00
(ball in right arm)
109B Calvin Ridley AU SP 40.00 80.00
(ball in left arm)
110A Rashaad Penny AU RC 8.00 20.00
(running right)
110B Rashaad Penny AU SP 10.00 25.00
(running left)
111A Sony Michel AU RC EXCH 30.00 60.00
111B Sony Michel AU SP EXCH 50.00 100.00
112A Lamar Jackson AU RC 150.00 300.00
(two hands on ball)
112B Lamar Jackson AU SP 150.00 300.00
(ball in right arm)
113A Nick Chubb AU RC 25.00 50.00
(ball in left arm)
113B Nick Chubb AU SP 40.00 80.00
(ball in right arm)
114A Ronald Jones II AU RC 5.00 12.00
(ball at side)
114B Ronald Jones II AU SP 5.00 12.00
(ball at stomach)
115A Courtland Sutton AU RC EXCH 3.00 8.00
115B Courtland Sutton AU SP EXCH 5.00 12.00
116A Mike Gesicki AU RC 4.00 10.00
(running)
116B Mike Gesicki AU/50* SP2 10.00 25.00
(catching)
117A Kerryon Johnson AU RC EXCH 12.00 30.00
117B Kerryon Johnson AU SP EXCH 12.00 30.00
118A Dante Pettis AU RC 10.00 25.00
(running straight)
118B Dante Pettis AU SP 10.00 25.00
(running right)
119A Christian Kirk AU/50* RC SP2 15.00 40.00
(running)
119B Christian Kirk AU SP 15.00 40.00
(catching)
120A Anthony Miller AU RC 6.00 15.00
ball in right hand)
120B Anthony Miller AU SP 6.00 15.00
(two hands on ball)
121A Derrius Guice AU RC 25.00 50.00
ball in right hand)
121B Derrius Guice AU SP 30.00 60.00
(two hands on ball)
122A James Washington AU RC 4.00 10.00
(two arms on ball)
122B James Washington AU SP 8.00 20.00
(ball in left arm)
123A D.J. Chark Jr. AU RC 2.50 6.00
(running straight)
123B D.J. Chark Jr. AU SP 2.50 6.00
(catching)
124A Royce Freeman AU RC 2.50 6.00
(two arms on ball)
124B Royce Freeman AU/250* SP1 4.00 10.00
(catching)
125A Mason Rudolph AU RC 30.00 60.00
(ball in right hand)
125B Mason Rudolph AU SP 30.00 60.00
(two hands on ball)
126A Michael Gallup AU/250* RC SP1 15.00 40.00
(running straight)
126B Michael Gallup AU SP 15.00 40.00
(body bent)
127A Tre'Quan Smith AU RC 6.00 15.00
(running left)
127B Tre'Quan Smith AU SP 15.00 40.00
(running right)
128A Keke Coutee AU RC EXCH 2.50 6.00
128B Keke Coutee AU SP EXCH 2.50 6.00
129A Nyheim Hines AU RC 2.50 6.00
(ball in left arm)
129B Nyheim Hines AU SP 2.50 6.00
(ball in right arm)
130A Kyle Lauletta AU RC EXCH 15.00 40.00
130B Kyle Lauletta AU SP EXCH 15.00 40.00
131A Mark Walton AU RC 2.50 6.00
(ball in right arm)
131B Mark Walton AU SP 4.00 10.00
(two hands on ball)
132A DaeSean Hamilton AU RC 2.50 6.00
(ball in right arm)
132B DaeSean Hamilton AU SP 4.00 10.00
(two arms on ball)
133A Ito Smith AU RC 2.50 6.00
(running)
133B Ito Smith AU SP 2.50 6.00
(catching)
134A Kalen Ballage AU RC EXCH 2.50 6.00
134B Kalen Ballage AU/150* SP1 EXCH 4.00 10.00
135 Jaleel Scott AU RC 2.00 5.00
136A J'Mon Moore AU RC 3.00 8.00
(body facing right)
136B J'Mon Moore AU/100* SP2 5.00 12.00
(body facing left)
137A Daurice Fountain AU RC 2.50 6.00
(catching)
137B Daurice Fountain AU SP 2.50 6.00
(running)
138A Jaylen Samuels AU RC 2.50 6.00
(ball in right arm)
138B Jaylen Samuels AU SP 2.50 6.00
(two hands on ball)
139A Mike White AU RC 25.00 60.00
(looking right)
139B Mike White AU SP 25.00 60.00
(looking left)
140 Marquez Valdes-Scantling AU RC 2.50 6.00
141 Justin Jones AU RC 2.00 5.00
142 Avonte Maddox AU RC 2.50 6.00
143 Kemoko Turay AU RC 2.50 6.00
144 Jordan Thomas AU RC 2.50 6.00
145 Denzel Ward AU RC 6.00 15.00
146 Roquan Smith AU RC 6.00 15.00
147 Minkah Fitzpatrick AU RC 4.00 10.00
148 Vita Vea AU RC 3.00 8.00
149 Daron Payne AU RC 5.00 12.00
151 Tremaine Edmunds AU RC 4.00 10.00
152 Derwin James AU RC EXCH 6.00 15.00
153 Jaire Alexander AU RC 3.00 8.00
154 Leighton Vander Esch AU RC 30.00 60.00
155 Rashaan Evans AU RC 3.00 8.00
156 Terrell Edmunds AU/250* RC SP1 10.00 25.00
157 Mike Hughes AU RC
158 Harold Landry AU RC 3.00 8.00
159 Joshua Jackson AU RC 4.00 10.00
160 M.J. Stewart AU RC 2.00 5.00
161 Donte Jackson AU RC 3.00 8.00
162 Duke Dawson AU RC 2.00 5.00
164 Carlton Davis AU RC 2.50 6.00
165 Tyquan Lewis AU RC 6.00 15.00
167 Chris Warren III AU RC 3.00 8.00
170 Sam Hubbard AU RC 2.50 6.00
171 Rashaan Gaulden AU RC 2.00 5.00
172 Jake Kumerow AU RC 2.50 6.00
173 Jalyn Holmes AU RC 3.00 8.00
175 Chris Herndon IV AU RC 2.00 5.00
176 Da'Shawn Hand AU RC 3.00 8.00
177 Anthony Averett AU RC 2.50 6.00
178 Armani Watts AU RC 2.00 5.00
179 Josh Sweat AU RC 2.50 6.00
180 Chase Edmonds AU RC 2.00 5.00
181 Dalton Schultz AU RC 8.00 20.00
182 Maurice Hurst AU RC 4.00 10.00
183 Shaquem Griffin AU RC 3.00 8.00
185 Jordan Lasley AU RC 2.00 5.00
186 John Kelly AU RC 2.50 6.00
187 Ray-Ray McCloud AU RC 2.00 5.00
188 Dylan Cantrell AU RC 2.00 5.00
189 Luke Falk AU RC 2.50 6.00
190 Cedrick Wilson Jr. AU RC 2.00 5.00
191 Braxton Berrios AU RC 2.00 5.00
192 Marcell Ateman AU RC 2.50 6.00
193 Bo Scarbrough AU RC 2.50 6.00
194 Gus Edwards AU/169* RC 8.00 20.00
195 Ryan Nall AU RC 4.00 10.00
196 Auden Tate AU RC 2.00 5.00
197 Trey Quinn AU RC 2.00 5.00
198 Damoun Patterson AU RC 2.00 5.00
199 Deontay Burnett AU RC 2.50 6.00
200 Josh Adams AU RC 4.00 10.00
201 Riley Ferguson AU RC 3.00 8.00
202 Simmie Cobbs Jr. AU RC 3.00 8.00
203 Dallas Goedert AU RC 2.50 6.00
204 Rasheem Green AU RC 2.00 5.00
205 Kurt Benkert AU RC 2.50 6.00
206 Danny Etling AU RC 8.00 20.00
207 Akrum Wadley AU RC 2.00 5.00
208 Chase Litton AU RC 2.50 6.00
209 Tanner Lee AU RC 2.50 6.00
210 Dorian O'Daniel AU RC 3.00 8.00
211 Cory Littleton AU RC 2.50 6.00
212 Austin Proehl AU RC 2.00 5.00
213 D.J. Reed AU RC 2.00 5.00
214 DeAndre Goolsby AU RC 2.00 5.00
215 Dorance Armstrong Jr. AU RC 2.00 5.00
216 Durham Smythe AU RC 2.00 5.00
217 Daniel Carlson AU RC 2.00 5.00
218 Javon Wims AU RC 2.00 5.00
219 Jordan Mailata AU RC 2.00 5.00
220 Nick Mullens AU RC 40.00 80.00
223 Logan Woodside AU RC 3.00 8.00
224 Malik Jefferson AU RC 2.50 6.00
225 Marcus Allen AU RC 3.00 8.00
226 Marcus Baugh AU RC 2.00 5.00
228 Micah Kiser AU RC 2.00 5.00
229 Ogbonnia Okoronkwo AU RC 3.00 8.00
230 Quenton Nelson AU RC 30.00 60.00
231 Mike McGlinchey AU RC 4.00 10.00
232 Quadree Henderson AU RC 2.50 6.00
233 Tarvarus McFadden AU RC 2.50 6.00
234 Taven Bryan AU RC 3.00 8.00
235 Trey Marshall AU RC 2.50 6.00
236 Billy Price AU RC 2.50 6.00
237 Kolton Miller AU RC 3.00 8.00
239 Harrison Phillips AU RC 2.00 5.00
241 Alex McGough AU RC 2.50 6.00
242 Jordan Wilkins AU RC 2.50 6.00
243 Richie James AU RC 2.00 5.00
245 Denzel Ward AU 6.00 15.00
246 Roquan Smith AU 6.00 15.00
247 Minkah Fitzpatrick AU 4.00 10.00
248 Vita Vea AU 5.00 12.00
249 Daron Payne AU/200* 5.00 12.00
251 Tremaine Edmunds AU 4.00 10.00
252 Derwin James AU EXCH 6.00 15.00
253 Jaire Alexander AU 3.00 8.00
254 Leighton Vander Esch AU 30.00 60.00
255 Rashaan Evans AU 3.00 8.00
256 Cam Sims AU RC 2.50 6.00
258 Harold Landry AU/50* SP2 5.00 12.00
259 Joshua Jackson AU 4.00 10.00
260 M.J. Stewart AU 2.00 5.00
261 Donte Jackson AU 3.00 8.00
262 Duke Dawson AU 3.00 8.00
264 Carlton Davis AU 2.50 6.00
267 Chris Warren III AU 3.00 8.00
269 Trenton Cannon AU RC 2.50 6.00
270 Sam Hubbard AU 2.50 6.00
271 Rashaan Gaulden AU 2.00 5.00
272 Jake Kumerow AU 2.50 6.00
273 Jalyn Holmes AU 3.00 8.00
275 Chris Herndon IV AU/200* SP1 3.00 8.00
276 Da'Shawn Hand AU 5.00 12.00
277 Anthony Averett AU 2.50 6.00
278 Armani Watts AU 2.00 5.00
279 Josh Sweat AU 2.50 6.00
280 Chase Edmonds AU 2.00 5.00
281 Dalton Schultz AU 12.00 30.00
282 Maurice Hurst AU 6.00 15.00
283 Shaquem Griffin AU 5.00 12.00
284 Russell Gage AU RC 2.50 6.00
285 Jordan Lasley AU 2.00 5.00
286 John Kelly AU 4.00 10.00
287 Ray-Ray McCloud AU 2.00 5.00
288 Dylan Cantrell AU 2.00 5.00
289 Luke Falk AU 2.50 6.00
290 Cedrick Wilson Jr. AU 3.00 8.00
291 Braxton Berrios AU/150* SP1 3.00 8.00
293 Bo Scarbrough AU 2.50 6.00
294 Gus Edwards AU/100* SP2 12.00 30.00
295 Ryan Nall AU 4.00 10.00
296 Auden Tate AU 2.00 5.00
297 Trey Quinn AU 3.00 8.00
298 Allen Lazard AU RC 8.00 20.00
299 Deontay Burnett AU 2.50 6.00
300 Josh Adams AU 4.00 10.00
301 Riley Ferguson AU 3.00 8.00
302 Simmie Cobbs Jr. AU 5.00 12.00
303 Dallas Goedert AU 4.00 10.00
304 Rasheem Green AU/250* SP1 3.00 8.00
305 Kurt Benkert AU 2.50 6.00
306 Danny Etling AU 8.00 20.00
307 Ralph Webb AU RC 2.50 6.00
308 Chase Litton AU 2.50 6.00
309 Chad Kanoff AU RC 2.00 5.00
310 Dorian O'Daniel AU 2.00 5.00
311 Cory Littleton AU 2.50 6.00
312 Riley McCarron AU RC 2.00 5.00
313 D.J. Reed AU 2.00 5.00
314 DeAndre Goolsby AU 2.00 5.00
315 Dorance Armstrong Jr. AU 2.00 5.00
316 Durham Smythe AU 2.00 5.00
317 Daniel Carlson AU 2.00 5.00
319 Darius Leonard AU RC 25.00 50.00
321 Logan Woodside AU 3.00 8.00
322 Malik Jefferson AU 2.50 6.00
323 Tim White AU RC 2.00 5.00
324 Brandon Powell AU RC 2.50 6.00
326 Rod Smith AU RC 2.50 6.00
327 Ogbonnia Okoronkwo AU 3.00 8.00
328 Adrian Colbert AU RC 2.00 5.00
329 Mike McGlinchey AU 4.00 10.00
330 Mike Boone AU RC 2.50 6.00
331 Vyncint Smith AU RC 2.00 5.00
332 Taven Bryan AU 5.00 12.00
333 Trey Marshall AU 2.50 6.00
334 Billy Price AU 2.50 6.00
335 Kolton Miller AU 3.00 8.00
337 Detrez Newsome AU RC 2.00 5.00
338 Quinton Dunbar AU RC 2.50 6.00
339 Phillip Lindsay AU RC 200.00 300.00
340 Will Dissly AU RC 2.50 6.00

2018 Panini Contenders Championship Ticket

*1-100 VETS: 4X TO 10X BASIC CARDS
51 Patrick Mahomes II 15.00 40.00
101A Baker Mayfield AU/49 800.00 1200.00
101B Baker Mayfield AU/25
102A Saquon Barkley AU/25 400.00 800.00
105A Josh Allen AU/49 200.00 300.00
105B Josh Allen AU/25 250.00 500.00
106A Josh Rosen AU/25 200.00 400.00
107A D.J. Moore AU/49 12.00 30.00
107B D.J. Moore AU/25 15.00 40.00
110A Rashaad Penny AU/25 12.00 30.00
111A Sony Michel AU/25 200.00 300.00
112A Lamar Jackson AU/49 200.00 300.00
112B Lamar Jackson AU/25 250.00 400.00
113A Nick Chubb AU/49 40.00 100.00
113B Nick Chubb AU/25 75.00 150.00
115A Courtland Sutton AU/49 EXCH 10.00 25.00
115B Courtland Sutton AU/25 EXCH 12.00 30.00
116A Mike Gesicki AU/25 10.00 25.00
117A Kerryon Johnson AU/49 EXCH 30.00 60.00
117B Kerryon Johnson AU/25 EXCH 40.00 80.00
118A Dante Pettis AU/25 40.00 80.00
120A Anthony Miller AU/49 10.00 25.00
120B Anthony Miller AU/25 12.00 30.00
121A Derrius Guice AU/15 75.00 150.00
122A James Washington AU/49 12.00 30.00
122B James Washington AU/25 15.00 40.00
123A D.J. Chark Jr. AU/49 8.00 20.00
123B D.J. Chark Jr. AU/25 10.00 25.00
124A Royce Freeman AU/49 8.00 20.00
124B Royce Freeman AU/25 10.00 25.00
125A Mason Rudolph AU/49 50.00 100.00
125B Mason Rudolph AU/25 100.00 200.00
126A Michael Gallup AU/25 15.00 40.00
127A Tre'Quan Smith AU/49 25.00 50.00
127B Tre'Quan Smith AU/25 30.00 60.00
128A Keke Coutee AU/49 EXCH 8.00 20.00
128B Keke Coutee AU/25 EXCH 10.00 25.00
129A Nyheim Hines AU/49 8.00 20.00
129B Nyheim Hines AU/25 10.00 25.00
131A Mark Walton AU/49 8.00 20.00
131B Mark Walton AU/25 10.00 25.00
132A DaeSean Hamilton AU/25 10.00 25.00
133A Ito Smith AU/49 8.00 20.00
133B Ito Smith AU/25 10.00 25.00
134A Kalen Ballage AU/49 EXCH 8.00 20.00
134B Kalen Ballage AU/25 EXCH 10.00 25.00
135A Jaleel Scott AU/49 6.00 15.00
135B Jaleel Scott AU/25 8.00 20.00
136A J'Mon Moore AU/25 8.00 20.00
137A Daurice Fountain AU/49 8.00 20.00
137B Daurice Fountain AU/25 10.00 25.00
138A Jaylen Samuels AU/49 8.00 20.00
138B Jaylen Samuels AU/25 10.00 25.00
139A Mike White AU/15 50.00 100.00
140A Marquez Valdes-Scantling AU/15 12.00 30.00
140B Marquez Valdes-Scantling AU/25 10.00 25.00
141 Justin Jones AU/49 6.00 15.00
142 Avonte Maddox AU/49 8.00 20.00
143 Kemoko Turay AU/49 8.00 20.00
144 Jordan Thomas AU/49 8.00 20.00
145 Denzel Ward AU/49 15.00 40.00
146 Roquan Smith AU/49 20.00 50.00
147 Minkah Fitzpatrick AU/49 12.00 30.00
149 Daron Payne AU/49 10.00 25.00
151 Tremaine Edmunds AU/49 EXCH 12.00 30.00
152 Derwin James AU/49 12.00 30.00
153 Jaire Alexander AU/49 10.00 25.00
154 Leighton Vander Esch AU/49 100.00 200.00
155 Rashaan Evans AU/49 10.00 25.00
156 Terrell Edmunds AU/49 20.00 50.00
157 Mike Hughes AU/49 10.00 25.00
158 Harold Landry AU/49 6.00 15.00
159 Joshua Jackson AU/49 12.00 30.00
160 M.J. Stewart AU/49 6.00 15.00
161 Donte Jackson AU/49 10.00 25.00
162 Duke Dawson AU/49 6.00 15.00
164 Carlton Davis AU/49 8.00 20.00
167 Chris Warren III AU/49 10.00 25.00
169 Trenton Cannon AU/49 8.00 20.00
170 Sam Hubbard AU/49 8.00 20.00
171 Rashaan Gaulden AU/49 6.00 15.00
172 Jake Kumerow AU/49 8.00 20.00
173 Jalyn Holmes AU/49 10.00 25.00
175 Chris Herndon IV AU/49 6.00 15.00
176 Da'Shawn Hand AU/25 8.00 20.00
177 Anthony Averett AU/49 8.00 20.00
178 Armani Watts AU/49 6.00 15.00
179 Josh Sweat AU/49 8.00 20.00
180 Chase Edmonds AU/49 6.00 15.00
181 Dalton Schultz AU/25 10.00 25.00
182 Maurice Hurst AU/49 8.00 20.00
183 Shaquem Griffin AU/49 10.00 25.00
185 Jordan Lasley AU/49 6.00 15.00
186 John Kelly AU/49 8.00 20.00
187 Ray-Ray McCloud AU/49 6.00 15.00
188 Dylan Cantrell AU/49 6.00 15.00
189 Luke Falk AU/49 8.00 20.00
190 Cedrick Wilson Jr. AU/49 6.00 15.00
191 Braxton Berrios AU/49 6.00 15.00
192 Marcell Ateman AU/49 8.00 20.00
193 Bo Scarbrough AU/49 8.00 20.00
194 Gus Edwards AU/49 15.00 40.00
195 Ryan Nall AU/49 12.00 30.00
196 Auden Tate AU/49 6.00 15.00
197 Trey Quinn AU/49 6.00 15.00
198 Damoun Patterson AU/49 6.00 15.00
199 Deontay Burnett AU/49 8.00 20.00
200 Josh Adams AU/49 12.00 30.00
201 Riley Ferguson AU/49 10.00 25.00
202 Simmie Cobbs Jr. AU/49 10.00 25.00
203 Dallas Goedert AU/49 8.00 20.00
204 Rasheem Green AU/49 6.00 15.00
205 Kurt Benkert AU/49 8.00 20.00
206 Danny Etling AU/49 25.00 50.00
207 Akrum Wadley AU/49 6.00 15.00
208 Chase Litton AU/49 8.00 20.00
209 Tanner Lee AU/49 8.00 20.00
210 Dorian O'Daniel AU/49 6.00 15.00
211 Cory Littleton AU/49 8.00 20.00
212 Austin Proehl AU/49 6.00 15.00
213 D.J. Reed AU/49 6.00 15.00
214 DeAndre Goolsby AU/49 6.00 15.00
215 Dorance Armstrong Jr. AU/49 6.00 15.00
216 Durham Smythe AU/49 6.00 15.00
217 Daniel Carlson AU/49 6.00 15.00
218 Javon Wims AU/49 6.00 15.00
219 Jordan Mailata AU/49 6.00 15.00
223 Logan Woodside AU/49 10.00 25.00
224 Malik Jefferson AU/49 8.00 20.00
225 Marcus Allen AU/49 10.00 25.00
226 Marcus Baugh AU/49 6.00 15.00
228 Micah Kiser AU/49 6.00 15.00
229 Ogbonnia Okoronkwo AU/49 10.00 25.00
230 Quenton Nelson AU/49 10.00 25.00
231 Mike McGlinchey AU/49 12.00 30.00
232 Quadree Henderson AU/49 8.00 20.00
233 Tarvarus McFadden AU/49 8.00 20.00
234 Taven Bryan AU/49 6.00 15.00
235 Trey Marshall AU/49 8.00 20.00
236 Billy Price AU/49 8.00 20.00
237 Kolton Miller AU/49 10.00 25.00
239 Harrison Phillips AU/49 6.00 15.00
240 Marquis Haynes AU/49 6.00 15.00
241 Alex McGough AU/49 8.00 20.00
242 Jordan Wilkins AU/49 8.00 20.00
243 Richie James AU/49 6.00 15.00
244 Jordan Thomas AU/49 8.00 20.00
245 Denzel Ward AU/49 15.00 40.00
246 Roquan Smith AU/49 20.00 50.00
247 Minkah Fitzpatrick AU/49 12.00 30.00
249 Daron Payne AU/49 10.00 25.00
251 Tremaine Edmunds AU/49 EXCH 12.00 30.00
252 Derwin James AU/49 12.00 30.00
253 Jaire Alexander AU/49 10.00 25.00
254 Leighton Vander Esch AU/49 100.00 200.00
255 Rashaan Evans AU/49 10.00 25.00
256 Cam Sims AU/49 8.00 20.00
257 Mike Hughes AU/49 10.00 25.00
258 Harold Landry AU/49 6.00 15.00
259 Joshua Jackson AU/49 12.00 30.00
260 M.J. Stewart AU/49 6.00 15.00
261 Donte Jackson AU/49 10.00 25.00
262 Duke Dawson AU/49 6.00 15.00
263 Isaiah Oliver AU/49 6.00 15.00
264 Carlton Davis AU/49 8.00 20.00
267 Chris Warren III AU/25 12.00 30.00
269 Trenton Cannon AU/49 8.00 20.00
270 Sam Hubbard AU/49 8.00 20.00
271 Rashaan Gaulden AU/49 6.00 15.00
272 Jake Kumerow AU/49 8.00 20.00
273 Jalyn Holmes AU/49 10.00 25.00
275 Chris Herndon IV AU/49 6.00 15.00
276 Da'Shawn Hand AU/25 8.00 20.00
277 Anthony Averett AU/49 8.00 20.00
278 Armani Watts AU/49 6.00 15.00
279 Josh Sweat AU/49 8.00 20.00
280 Chase Edmonds AU/49 6.00 15.00
281 Dalton Schultz AU/25 10.00 25.00
282 Maurice Hurst AU/49 8.00 20.00
283 Shaquem Griffin AU/49 10.00 25.00
284 Russell Gage AU/49 8.00 20.00
285 Jordan Lasley AU/49 6.00 15.00
286 John Kelly AU/49 8.00 20.00
287 Ray-Ray McCloud AU/49 6.00 15.00
288 Dylan Cantrell AU/49 6.00 15.00
289 Luke Falk AU/49 8.00 20.00
290 Cedrick Wilson Jr. AU/49 6.00 15.00
291 Braxton Berrios AU/49 6.00 15.00
292 Marcell Ateman AU/49 8.00 20.00
293 Bo Scarbrough AU/49 8.00 20.00
294 Gus Edwards AU/49 15.00 40.00
295 Ryan Nall AU/49 12.00 30.00
296 Auden Tate AU/49 6.00 15.00
297 Trey Quinn AU/49 6.00 15.00
299 Deontay Burnett AU/49 8.00 20.00
300 Josh Adams AU/49 12.00 30.00
301 Riley Ferguson AU/49 10.00 25.00
302 Simmie Cobbs Jr. AU/49 10.00 25.00
303 Dallas Goedert AU/49 8.00 20.00
304 Rasheem Green AU/49 6.00 15.00
305 Kurt Benkert AU/49 8.00 20.00
306 Danny Etling AU/49 8.00 20.00
307 Ralph Webb AU/49 8.00 20.00
308 Chase Litton AU/49 8.00 20.00
309 Chad Kanoff AU/49 6.00 15.00
310 Dorian O'Daniel AU/49 6.00 15.00
311 Cory Littleton AU/49 8.00 20.00
312 Riley McCarron AU/49 6.00 15.00
313 D.J. Reed AU/49 6.00 15.00
314 DeAndre Goolsby AU/49 6.00 15.00
315 Dorance Armstrong Jr. AU/49 6.00 15.00
316 Durham Smythe AU/49 6.00 15.00
317 Daniel Carlson AU/49 6.00 15.00
319 Darius Leonard AU/49 15.00 40.00
321 Logan Woodside AU/49 10.00 25.00
322 Malik Jefferson AU/49 8.00 20.00
323 Tim White AU/49 6.00 15.00
324 Brandon Powell AU/49 8.00 20.00
326 Rod Smith AU/49 8.00 20.00
327 Ogbonnia Okoronkwo AU/49 10.00 25.00
328 Adrian Colbert AU/49 6.00 15.00
329 Mike McGlinchey AU/49 12.00 30.00
330 Mike Boone AU/49 8.00 20.00
331 Vyncint Smith AU/49 6.00 15.00
332 Taven Bryan AU/49 6.00 15.00
333 Trey Marshall AU/49 8.00 20.00
334 Billy Price AU/49 8.00 20.00
335 Kolton Miller AU/49 10.00 25.00
337 Detrez Newsome AU/49 6.00 15.00
338 Quinton Dunbar AU/49 8.00 20.00
339 Phillip Lindsay AU/25 200.00 300.00
340 Will Dissly AU/49 8.00 20.00

2018 Panini Contenders Cracked Ice

*1-100 VETS/24: 6X TO 15X BASIC CARDS
101A Baker Mayfield AU 2000.00 3000.00
(throwing)
101B Baker Mayfield AU 2000.00 3000.00
(running)
102A Saquon Barkley AU 2000.00 3000.00
(ball in right arm)
102B Saquon Barkley AU 2000.00 3000.00
(ball in left arm)
103A Sam Darnold AU 2000.00 3000.00
(running right)
103B Sam Darnold AU 2000.00 3000.00
(body facing left)
104A Bradley Chubb AU EXCH 75.00 150.00
104B Bradley Chubb AU EXCH 75.00 150.00
105A Josh Allen AU 1800.00 2400.00
(facing left)
105B Josh Allen AU 1800.00 2400.00
(facing right)
106A Josh Rosen AU 800.00 1200.00
(throwing)
106B Josh Rosen AU 800.00 1200.00
(body facing left)
107A D.J. Moore AU 25.00 60.00
(ball in right arm)
107B D.J. Moore AU 25.00 60.00
(ball in left arm)
108A Hayden Hurst AU 25.00 50.00
(ball in left arm)
108B Hayden Hurst AU 25.00 50.00
(ball in right arm)
109A Calvin Ridley AU 150.00 300.00
(ball in right arm)
109B Calvin Ridley AU 150.00 300.00
(ball in left arm)
110A Rashaad Penny AU 100.00 200.00
(running right)
110B Rashaad Penny AU 100.00 200.00
(running left)
111A Sony Michel AU EXCH 250.00 500.00
111B Sony Michel AU EXCH 250.00 500.00
112A Lamar Jackson AU 800.00 1200.00
(two hands on ball)
112B Lamar Jackson AU 800.00 1200.00
(ball in right arm)
113A Nick Chubb AU 300.00 600.00
(ball in left arm)
113B Nick Chubb AU 300.00 600.00
(ball in right arm)
114A Ronald Jones II AU 40.00 80.00
(ball at side)
114B Ronald Jones II AU 40.00 80.00
(ball at stomach)
115A Courtland Sutton AU EXCH 50.00 100.00
115B Courtland Sutton AU EXCH 50.00 100.00
116A Mike Gesicki AU 30.00 60.00
(running)
116B Mike Gesicki AU 30.00 60.00
(catching)
117A Kerryon Johnson AU EXCH 150.00 300.00
117B Kerryon Johnson AU EXCH 150.00 300.00
118A Dante Pettis AU 100.00 200.00
(running straight)
118B Dante Pettis AU 100.00 200.00
(running right)
119A Christian Kirk AU 100.00 200.00
(running)
119B Christian Kirk AU 100.00 200.00
(catching)
120A Anthony Miller AU 100.00 200.00
ball in right hand)
120B Anthony Miller AU 100.00 200.00
(two hands on ball)
121A Derrius Guice AU 200.00 300.00
ball in right hand)
121B Derrius Guice AU 200.00 300.00
(two hands on ball)
122A James Washington AU 75.00 150.00
(two arms on ball)
122B James Washington AU 75.00 150.00
(ball in left arm)
123A D.J. Chark Jr. AU 50.00 100.00
(running straight)
123B D.J. Chark Jr. AU 50.00 100.00
(catching)
124A Royce Freeman AU 40.00 80.00
(two arms on ball)
124B Royce Freeman AU 40.00 80.00
(catching)
125A Mason Rudolph AU 400.00 800.00
(ball in right hand)
125B Mason Rudolph AU 400.00 800.00
(two hands on ball)
126A Michael Gallup AU 200.00 400.00
(running straight)
126B Michael Gallup AU 200.00 400.00
(body bent)
127A Tre'Quan Smith AU 50.00 100.00
(running left)
127B Tre'Quan Smith AU 50.00 100.00
(running right)
128A Keke Coutee AU EXCH 100.00 200.00
128B Keke Coutee AU EXCH 100.00 200.00
129A Nyheim Hines AU 25.00 50.00
(ball in left arm)
129B Nyheim Hines AU 25.00 50.00
(ball in right arm)
130A Kyle Lauletta AU EXCH 75.00 150.00
130B Kyle Lauletta AU EXCH 75.00 150.00
131A Mark Walton AU 15.00 40.00
(ball in right arm)
131B Mark Walton AU 15.00 40.00
(two hands on ball)
132A DaeSean Hamilton AU 15.00 40.00
(ball in right arm)
132B DaeSean Hamilton AU 15.00 40.00
(two arms on ball)
133A Ito Smith AU 15.00 40.00
(running)
133B Ito Smith AU SP 15.00 40.00
(catching)
134A Kalen Ballage AU EXCH 40.00 80.00
134B Kalen Ballage AU EXCH 40.00 80.00
135A Jaleel Scott AU 12.00 30.00
(left arm across body)
135B Jaleel Scott AU 12.00 30.00
(left arm at waist)
136A J'Mon Moore AU 12.00 30.00
(body facing right)
136B J'Mon Moore AU 12.00 30.00
(body facing left)
137A Daurice Fountain AU 15.00 40.00
(catching)
137B Daurice Fountain AU 15.00 40.00
(running)
138A Jaylen Samuels AU 15.00 40.00
(ball in right arm)
138B Jaylen Samuels AU 15.00 40.00
(two hands on ball)
139A Mike White AU 50.00 100.00
(looking right)
139B Mike White AU 50.00 100.00
(looking left)
140A Marquez Valdes-Scantling AU 60.00 125.00
(running left)
140B Marquez Valdes-Scantling AU 60.00 125.00
(facing straight)
141 Justin Jones AU 12.00 30.00
142 Avonte Maddox AU 15.00 40.00
143 Kemoko Turay AU 15.00 40.00
144 Jordan Thomas AU 15.00 40.00
145 Denzel Ward AU 75.00 150.00
146 Roquan Smith AU 100.00 200.00
147 Minkah Fitzpatrick AU 25.00 60.00
148 Vita Vea AU 20.00 50.00
149 Daron Payne AU 20.00 50.00
151 Tremaine Edmunds AU EXCH 25.00 60.00
152 Derwin James AU 150.00 300.00
153 Jaire Alexander AU 50.00 100.00
154 Leighton Vander Esch AU 300.00 500.00
155 Rashaan Evans AU 20.00 50.00
156 Terrell Edmunds AU 40.00 100.00
157 Mike Hughes AU 20.00 50.00
158 Harold Landry AU 12.00 30.00
159 Joshua Jackson AU 25.00 60.00
160 M.J. Stewart AU 12.00 30.00
161 Donte Jackson AU 20.00 50.00
162 Duke Dawson AU 12.00 30.00
164 Carlton Davis AU 15.00 40.00
165 Tyquan Lewis AU 15.00 40.00
167 Chris Warren III AU 20.00 50.00
169 Trenton Cannon AU 15.00 40.00
170 Sam Hubbard AU 15.00 40.00
171 Rashaan Gaulden AU 12.00 30.00
172 Jake Kumerow AU 40.00 80.00
173 Jalyn Holmes AU 20.00 50.00
175 Chris Herndon IV AU 12.00 30.00
176 Da'Shawn Hand AU 12.00 30.00
177 Anthony Averett AU 15.00 40.00
178 Armani Watts AU 12.00 30.00
179 Josh Sweat AU 15.00 40.00
180 Chase Edmonds AU 12.00 30.00
181 Dalton Schultz AU 40.00 80.00
182 Maurice Hurst AU 15.00 40.00
183 Shaquem Griffin AU 40.00 80.00
185 Jordan Lasley AU 12.00 30.00
186 John Kelly AU 15.00 40.00
187 Ray-Ray McCloud AU 12.00 30.00
188 Dylan Cantrell AU 12.00 30.00
189 Luke Falk AU 15.00 40.00
190 Cedrick Wilson Jr. AU 12.00 30.00
191 Braxton Berrios AU 12.00 30.00
192 Marcell Ateman AU 15.00 40.00
193 Bo Scarbrough AU 15.00 40.00
194 Gus Edwards AU 50.00 100.00
195 Ryan Nall AU 25.00 60.00
196 Auden Tate AU 12.00 30.00
197 Trey Quinn AU 12.00 30.00
198 Damoun Patterson AU 12.00 30.00
199 Deontay Burnett AU 15.00 40.00
200 Josh Adams AU 25.00 60.00
201 Riley Ferguson AU 20.00 50.00
202 Simmie Cobbs Jr. AU 20.00 50.00
203 Dallas Goedert AU 15.00 40.00
204 Rasheem Green AU 12.00 30.00
205 Kurt Benkert AU 15.00 40.00
206 Danny Etling AU 100.00 200.00
207 Akrum Wadley AU 12.00 30.00
208 Chase Litton AU 15.00 40.00
209 Tanner Lee AU 15.00 40.00
210 Dorian O'Daniel AU 12.00 30.00
211 Cory Littleton AU 15.00 40.00
212 Austin Proehl AU 12.00 30.00
213 D.J. Reed AU 12.00 30.00
214 DeAndre Goolsby AU 12.00 30.00
215 Dorance Armstrong Jr. AU 12.00 30.00
216 Durham Smythe AU 12.00 30.00
217 Daniel Carlson AU 12.00 30.00
218 Javon Wims AU 12.00 30.00
219 Jordan Mailata AU 12.00 30.00
223 Logan Woodside AU 20.00 50.00
224 Malik Jefferson AU 15.00 40.00
225 Marcus Allen AU 20.00 50.00
226 Marcus Baugh AU 12.00 30.00
228 Micah Kiser AU 12.00 30.00
229 Ogbonnia Okoronkwo AU 20.00 50.00
230 Quenton Nelson AU 20.00 50.00
231 Mike McGlinchey AU 25.00 60.00
232 Quadree Henderson AU 15.00 40.00
233 Tarvarus McFadden AU 15.00 40.00
234 Taven Bryan AU 12.00 30.00
235 Trey Marshall AU 15.00 40.00
236 Billy Price AU 15.00 40.00
237 Kolton Miller AU 20.00 50.00
239 Harrison Phillips AU 12.00 30.00
240 Marquis Haynes AU 12.00 30.00
241 Alex McGough AU 15.00 40.00
242 Jordan Wilkins AU 15.00 40.00
243 Richie James AU 12.00 30.00
244 Jordan Thomas AU 15.00 40.00
245 Denzel Ward AU 30.00 80.00
246 Roquan Smith AU 40.00 100.00
247 Minkah Fitzpatrick AU 25.00 60.00
249 Daron Payne AU 20.00 50.00
251 Tremaine Edmunds AU EXCH 25.00 60.00
252 Derwin James AU 25.00 60.00
253 Jaire Alexander AU 50.00 100.00
254 Leighton Vander Esch AU 300.00 500.00
255 Rashaan Evans AU 20.00 50.00
256 Cam Sims AU 15.00 40.00
257 Mike Hughes AU 20.00 50.00
258 Harold Landry AU 12.00 30.00
259 Joshua Jackson AU 25.00 60.00
260 M.J. Stewart AU 12.00 30.00
261 Donte Jackson AU 20.00 50.00
262 Duke Dawson AU 12.00 30.00
263 Isaiah Oliver AU 12.00 30.00
264 Carlton Davis AU 15.00 40.00
267 Chris Warren III AU 20.00 50.00
269 Trenton Cannon AU 15.00 40.00
270 Sam Hubbard AU 15.00 40.00
271 Rashaan Gaulden AU 12.00 30.00
272 Jake Kumerow AU 15.00 40.00
273 Jalyn Holmes AU 20.00 50.00
275 Chris Herndon IV AU 12.00 30.00
276 Da'Shawn Hand AU 12.00 30.00
277 Anthony Averett AU 15.00 40.00
278 Armani Watts AU 12.00 30.00
279 Josh Sweat AU 15.00 40.00
280 Chase Edmonds AU 12.00 30.00
281 Dalton Schultz AU 15.00 40.00
282 Maurice Hurst AU 15.00 40.00
283 Shaquem Griffin AU 20.00 50.00
284 Russell Gage AU 15.00 40.00
285 Jordan Lasley AU 12.00 30.00
286 John Kelly AU 15.00 40.00
287 Ray-Ray McCloud AU 12.00 30.00
288 Dylan Cantrell AU 12.00 30.00
289 Luke Falk AU 15.00 40.00
290 Cedrick Wilson Jr. AU 12.00 30.00
291 Braxton Berrios AU 12.00 30.00
292 Marcell Ateman AU 15.00 40.00
293 Bo Scarbrough AU 15.00 40.00
294 Gus Edwards AU 30.00 80.00
295 Ryan Nall AU 25.00 60.00
296 Auden Tate AU 12.00 30.00
297 Trey Quinn AU 12.00 30.00
299 Deontay Burnett AU 15.00 40.00
300 Josh Adams AU 25.00 60.00
301 Riley Ferguson AU 20.00 50.00
302 Simmie Cobbs Jr. AU 20.00 50.00
303 Dallas Goedert AU 15.00 40.00
304 Rasheem Green AU 12.00 30.00

305 Kurt Benkert AU 15.00 40.00
306 Danny Etling AU 15.00 40.00
307 Ralph Webb AU 15.00 40.00
308 Chase Litton AU 15.00 40.00
309 Chad Kanoff AU 12.00 30.00
310 Dorian O'Daniel AU 12.00 30.00
311 Cory Littleton AU 15.00 40.00
312 Riley McCarron AU 12.00 30.00
313 D.J. Reed AU 12.00 30.00
314 DeAndre Goolsby AU 12.00 30.00
315 Dorance Armstrong Jr. AU 12.00 30.00
316 Durham Smythe AU 12.00 30.00
317 Daniel Carlson AU 12.00 30.00
318 Javon Wims AU 12.00 30.00
319 Darius Leonard AU 30.00 80.00
321 Logan Woodside AU 20.00 50.00
322 Malik Jefferson AU 15.00 40.00
323 Tim White AU 12.00 30.00
324 Brandon Powell AU 15.00 40.00
326 Rod Smith AU 15.00 40.00
327 Ogbonnia Okoronkwo AU 20.00 50.00
328 Adrian Colbert AU 12.00 30.00
329 Mike McGlinchey AU 25.00 60.00
330 Mike Boone AU 15.00 40.00
331 Vyncint Smith AU 12.00 30.00
332 Taven Bryan AU 12.00 30.00
333 Trey Marshall AU 15.00 40.00
334 Billy Price AU 15.00 40.00
335 Kolton Miller AU 20.00 50.00
337 Detrez Newsome AU 12.00 30.00
338 Quinton Dunbar AU 15.00 40.00
339 Phillip Lindsay AU 350.00 600.00
340 Will Dissly AU 15.00 40.00

2018 Panini Contenders Playoff Ticket

*1-100 VETS/175: 2.5X TO 6X BASIC CARDS
51 Patrick Mahomes II 8.00 20.00
101A Baker Mayfield AU/99 600.00 1000.00
(throwing)
101B Baker Mayfield AU/49 800.00 1200.00
(running)
102A Saquon Barkley AU/49 250.00 400.00
(ball in right arm)
102B Saquon Barkley AU SP/25 400.00 800.00
(ball in left arm)
103A Sam Darnold AU/15 500.00 1000.00
(running right)
104A Bradley Chubb AU/15 EXCH
105A Josh Allen AU/99 125.00 250.00
(facing left)
105B Josh Allen AU/49 200.00 300.00
(facing right)
106A Josh Rosen AU/49 125.00 250.00
(throwing)
106B Josh Rosen AU SP/25 200.00 400.00
(body facing left)
107A D.J. Moore AU/99 10.00 25.00
(ball in right arm)
107B D.J. Moore AU SP/49 12.00 30.00
(ball in left arm)
108 Hayden Hurst AU/15 12.00 30.00
(ball in left arm)
109A Calvin Ridley AU/15 25.00 60.00
(ball in right arm)
110A Rashaad Penny AU/49 10.00 25.00
(running right)
110B Rashaad Penny AU/25 12.00 30.00
(running left)
111A Sony Michel AU/49 EXCH 40.00 80.00
111B Sony Michel AU/25 EXCH 200.00 300.00
112A Lamar Jackson AU/99 100.00 200.00
(two hands on ball)
112B Lamar Jackson AU/49 200.00 300.00
(ball in right arm)
113A Nick Chubb AU/99 40.00 80.00
(ball in left arm)
113B Nick Chubb AU/49 40.00 100.00
(ball in right arm)
114A Ronald Jones II AU/25 15.00 40.00
(ball at side)
115A Courtland Sutton AU/99 EXCH 8.00 20.00
115B Courtland Sutton AU/49 EXCH 10.00 25.00
116A Mike Gesicki AU/49 8.00 20.00
(running)
116B Mike Gesicki AU/15 12.00 30.00
(catching)
117A Kerryon Johnson AU/99 EXCH 12.00 30.00
117B Kerryon Johnson AU/49 SP EXCH 30.00 60.00
118A Dante Pettis AU/49 15.00 40.00
(running straight)
118B Dante Pettis AU/25 40.00 80.00
(running right)
119A Christian Kirk AU/15 15.00 40.00
(running)
120A Anthony Miller AU/99 8.00 20.00
ball in right hand)
120B Anthony Miller AU/49 10.00 25.00
(two hands on ball)
121A Derrius Guice AU/25 40.00 80.00
ball in right hand)
122A James Washington AU/99 10.00 25.00
(two arms on ball)
122B James Washington AU/49 12.00 30.00
(ball in left arm)
123A D.J. Chark Jr. AU/99 6.00 15.00
(running straight)
123B D.J. Chark Jr. AU SP/49 8.00 20.00
(catching)
124A Royce Freeman AU/99 6.00 15.00
(two arms on ball)
124B Royce Freeman AU/49 8.00 20.00
(catching)
125A Mason Rudolph AU/99 25.00 50.00
(ball in right hand)
125B Mason Rudolph AU/49 50.00 100.00
(two hands on ball)
126A Michael Gallup AU/49 15.00 40.00
(running straight)
126B Michael Gallup AU/15 20.00 50.00
(body bent)
127A Tre'Quan Smith AU/99 15.00 40.00
(running left)
127B Tre'Quan Smith AU/49 25.00 50.00
(running right)
128A Keke Coutee AU/99 EXCH 6.00 15.00
128B Keke Coutee AU/49 EXCH 8.00 20.00
129A Nyheim Hines AU/99 6.00 15.00
(ball in left arm)
129B Nyheim Hines AU/49 8.00 20.00
(ball in right arm)
130A Kyle Lauletta AU/15 EXCH 15.00 40.00
131A Mark Walton AU/99 6.00 15.00
(ball in right arm)
131B Mark Walton AU/49 8.00 20.00
(two hands on ball)
132A DaeSean Hamilton AU/49 8.00 20.00
(ball in right arm)
132B DaeSean Hamilton AU/25 10.00 25.00
(two arms on ball)
133A Ito Smith AU/99 6.00 15.00
(running)
133B Ito Smith AU SP/49 8.00 20.00
(catching)
134A Kalen Ballage AU/99 EXCH 6.00 15.00
134B Kalen Ballage AU/49 EXCH 8.00 20.00
135A Jaleel Scott AU/99 5.00 12.00
(left arm across body)
135B Jaleel Scott AU/49 6.00 15.00
(left arm at waist)
136A J'Mon Moore AU/49 8.00 15.00
(body facing right)
136B J'Mon Moore AU/25 8.00 20.00
(body facing left)
137A Daurice Fountain AU/99 6.00 15.00
(catching)
137B Daurice Fountain AU/49 8.00 20.00
(running)
138A Jaylen Samuels AU/99 6.00 15.00
(ball in right arm)
138B Jaylen Samuels AU/49 8.00 20.00
(two hands on ball)
139A Mike White AU/25 25.00 50.00
(looking right)
139B Mike White AU/15 50.00 100.00
(looking left)
140A Marquez Valdes-Scantling AU/49 8.00 20.00
(running left)
140B Marquez Valdes-Scantling AU/15 12.00 30.00
(facing straight)
141 Justin Jones AU/99 5.00 12.00
142 Avonte Maddox AU/99 6.00 15.00
143 Kemoko Turay AU/99 6.00 15.00
144 Jordan Thomas AU/99 6.00 15.00
145 Denzel Ward AU/99 12.00 30.00
146 Roquan Smith AU/99 15.00 40.00
147 Minkah Fitzpatrick AU/99 10.00 25.00
149 Daron Payne AU/99 8.00 20.00
151 Tremaine Edmunds AU/99 EXCH 10.00 25.00
152 Derwin James AU/99 10.00 25.00
153 Jaire Alexander AU/99 8.00 20.00
154 Leighton Vander Esch AU/99 50.00 100.00
155 Rashaan Evans AU/99 8.00 20.00
156 Terrell Edmunds AU/99 15.00 40.00
157 Mike Hughes AU/99 8.00 20.00
158 Harold Landry AU/99 5.00 12.00
159 Joshua Jackson AU/99 10.00 25.00
160 M.J. Stewart AU/99 5.00 12.00
161 Donte Jackson AU/99 8.00 20.00
162 Duke Dawson AU/99 5.00 12.00
163 Isaiah Oliver AU/99 5.00 12.00
164 Carlton Davis AU/99 6.00 15.00
167 Chris Warren III AU/99 8.00 20.00
169 Trenton Cannon AU/99 6.00 15.00
170 Sam Hubbard AU/99 6.00 15.00
171 Rashaan Gaulden AU/99 5.00 12.00
172 Jake Kumerow AU/99 6.00 15.00
173 Jalyn Holmes AU/99 8.00 20.00
175 Chris Herndon IV AU/99 5.00 12.00
176 Da'Shawn Hand AU/49 6.00 15.00
177 Anthony Averett AU/99 6.00 15.00
178 Armani Watts AU/99 5.00 12.00
179 Josh Sweat AU/99 6.00 15.00
180 Chase Edmonds AU/99 5.00 12.00
181 Dalton Schultz AU/49 8.00 20.00
182 Maurice Hurst AU/99 6.00 15.00
183 Shaquem Griffin AU/99 8.00 20.00
185 Jordan Lasley AU/99 5.00 12.00
186 John Kelly AU/99 6.00 15.00
187 Ray-Ray McCloud AU/99 5.00 12.00
188 Dylan Cantrell AU/99 5.00 12.00
189 Luke Falk AU/99 6.00 15.00
190 Cedrick Wilson Jr. AU/99 5.00 12.00
191 Braxton Berrios AU/99 5.00 12.00
192 Marcell Ateman AU/99 6.00 15.00
193 Bo Scarbrough AU/99 6.00 15.00
194 Gus Edwards AU/99 12.00 30.00
195 Ryan Nall AU/99 10.00 25.00
196 Auden Tate AU/99 5.00 12.00
197 Trey Quinn AU/99 5.00 12.00
198 Damoun Patterson AU/99 5.00 12.00
199 Deontay Burnett AU/99 6.00 15.00
200 Josh Adams AU/99 10.00 25.00
201 Riley Ferguson AU/99 8.00 20.00
202 Simmie Cobbs Jr. AU/99 8.00 20.00
203 Dallas Goedert AU/99 6.00 15.00
204 Rasheem Green AU/99 5.00 12.00
205 Kurt Benkert AU/99 6.00 15.00
206 Danny Etling AU/99 15.00 40.00
207 Akrum Wadley AU/99 5.00 12.00
208 Chase Litton AU/99 6.00 15.00
209 Tanner Lee AU/99 6.00 15.00
210 Dorian O'Daniel AU/99 5.00 12.00
211 Cory Littleton AU/99 6.00 15.00
212 Austin Proehl AU/99 5.00 12.00
213 D.J. Reed AU/99 5.00 12.00
214 DeAndre Goolsby AU/99 5.00 12.00
215 Dorance Armstrong Jr. AU/99 5.00 12.00
216 Durham Smythe AU/99 5.00 12.00
217 Daniel Carlson AU/99 5.00 12.00
218 Javon Wims AU/99 5.00 12.00
219 Jordan Mailata AU/99 5.00 12.00
223 Logan Woodside AU/99 8.00 20.00
224 Malik Jefferson AU/99 6.00 15.00
225 Marcus Allen AU/99 8.00 20.00
226 Marcus Baugh AU/99 5.00 12.00
228 Micah Kiser AU/99 5.00 12.00
229 Ogbonnia Okoronkwo AU/99 8.00 20.00
230 Quenton Nelson AU/99 8.00 20.00
231 Mike McGlinchey AU/99 10.00 25.00
232 Quadree Henderson AU/99 6.00 15.00
233 Tarvarus McFadden AU/99 6.00 15.00
234 Taven Bryan AU/99 5.00 12.00
235 Trey Marshall AU/99 6.00 15.00
236 Billy Price AU/99 6.00 15.00
237 Kolton Miller AU/99 8.00 20.00
239 Harrison Phillips AU/99 5.00 12.00
240 Marquis Haynes AU/99 5.00 12.00
241 Alex McGough AU/99 6.00 15.00
242 Jordan Wilkins AU/99 6.00 15.00
243 Richie James AU/99 5.00 12.00
244 Jordan Thomas AU/99 6.00 15.00
245 Denzel Ward AU/99 12.00 30.00
246 Roquan Smith AU/99 15.00 40.00
247 Minkah Fitzpatrick AU/99 10.00 25.00
249 Daron Payne AU/99 8.00 20.00
251 Tremaine Edmunds AU/99 10.00 25.00
252 Derwin James AU/99 10.00 25.00
253 Jaire Alexander AU/99 8.00 20.00
254 Leighton Vander Esch AU/99 50.00 100.00
255 Rashaan Evans AU/99 8.00 20.00
256 Cam Sims AU/99 6.00 15.00
257 Mike Hughes AU/99 8.00 20.00
258 Harold Landry AU/99 5.00 12.00
259 Joshua Jackson AU/99 10.00 25.00
260 M.J. Stewart AU/99 5.00 12.00
261 Donte Jackson AU/99 8.00 20.00
262 Duke Dawson AU/99 5.00 12.00
263 Isaiah Oliver AU/99 5.00 12.00
264 Carlton Davis AU/99 6.00 15.00
267 Chris Warren III AU/49 10.00 25.00
269 Trenton Cannon AU/99 6.00 15.00
270 Sam Hubbard AU/99 6.00 15.00
271 Rashaan Gaulden AU/99 5.00 12.00
272 Jake Kumerow AU/99 6.00 15.00
273 Jalyn Holmes AU/99 8.00 20.00
275 Chris Herndon IV AU/99 5.00 12.00
276 Da'Shawn Hand AU/49 6.00 15.00
277 Anthony Averett AU/99 6.00 15.00
278 Armani Watts AU/99 5.00 12.00
279 Josh Sweat AU/99 6.00 15.00
280 Chase Edmonds AU/99 5.00 12.00
281 Dalton Schultz AU/49 8.00 20.00
282 Maurice Hurst AU/99 6.00 15.00
283 Shaquem Griffin AU/99 8.00 20.00
284 Russell Gage AU/99 6.00 15.00
285 Jordan Lasley AU/99 5.00 12.00
286 John Kelly AU/99 6.00 15.00
287 Ray-Ray McCloud AU/99 5.00 12.00
288 Dylan Cantrell AU/99 5.00 12.00
289 Luke Falk AU/99 6.00 15.00
290 Cedrick Wilson Jr. AU/99 5.00 12.00
291 Braxton Berrios AU/99 5.00 12.00
292 Marcell Ateman AU/99 6.00 15.00
293 Bo Scarbrough AU/99 6.00 15.00
294 Gus Edwards AU/99 12.00 30.00
295 Ryan Nall AU/99 10.00 25.00
296 Auden Tate AU/99 5.00 12.00
297 Trey Quinn AU/99 5.00 12.00
299 Deontay Burnett AU/99 6.00 15.00
300 Josh Adams AU/99 10.00 25.00
301 Riley Ferguson AU/99 8.00 20.00
302 Simmie Cobbs Jr. AU/99 8.00 20.00
303 Dallas Goedert AU/99 6.00 15.00
304 Rasheem Green AU/99 5.00 12.00
305 Kurt Benkert AU/99 6.00 15.00
306 Danny Etling AU/99 6.00 15.00
307 Ralph Webb AU/99 6.00 15.00
308 Chase Litton AU/99 6.00 15.00
309 Chad Kanoff AU/99 5.00 12.00
310 Dorian O'Daniel AU/99 5.00 12.00
311 Cory Littleton AU/99 6.00 15.00
312 Riley McCarron AU/99 5.00 12.00
313 D.J. Reed AU/99 5.00 12.00
314 DeAndre Goolsby AU/99 5.00 12.00
315 Dorance Armstrong Jr. AU/99 5.00 12.00
316 Durham Smythe AU/99 5.00 12.00
317 Daniel Carlson AU/99 5.00 12.00
319 Darius Leonard AU/99 12.00 30.00
321 Logan Woodside AU/99 8.00 20.00
322 Malik Jefferson AU/99 6.00 15.00
323 Tim White AU/99 5.00 12.00
324 Brandon Powell AU/99 6.00 15.00
326 Rod Smith AU/99 6.00 15.00
327 Ogbonnia Okoronkwo AU/99 8.00 20.00
328 Adrian Colbert AU/99 5.00 12.00
329 Mike McGlinchey AU/99 10.00 25.00
330 Mike Boone AU/99 6.00 15.00
331 Vyncint Smith AU/99 5.00 12.00
332 Taven Bryan AU/99 5.00 12.00
333 Trey Marshall AU/99 6.00 15.00
334 Billy Price AU/99 6.00 15.00
335 Kolton Miller AU/99 8.00 20.00
337 Detrez Newsome AU/99 5.00 12.00
338 Quinton Dunbar AU/99 6.00 15.00
339 Phillip Lindsay AU/49 100.00 200.00
340 Will Dissly AU/99 6.00 15.00

2018 Panini Contenders Red Zone

*1-100 VETS: 2X TO 5X BASIC CARDS
101A Baker Mayfield AU 1000.00 1500.00
(throwing)
101B Baker Mayfield AU 1000.00 1500.00
(running)
102A Saquon Barkley AU 300.00 600.00
(ball in right arm)
102B Saquon Barkley AU 300.00 600.00
(ball in left arm)
103A Sam Darnold AU 300.00 600.00
(running right)
103B Sam Darnold AU 300.00 600.00
(body facing left)
104A Bradley Chubb AU EXCH 15.00 40.00
104B Bradley Chubb AU EXCH 15.00 40.00
105A Josh Allen AU
(facing left)
105B Josh Allen AU
(facing right)
106A Josh Rosen AU 125.00 250.00
(throwing)
106B Josh Rosen AU 125.00 250.00
(body facing left)
107A D.J. Moore AU
(ball in right arm)
107B D.J. Moore AU
(ball in left arm)
108A Hayden Hurst AU 6.00 15.00
(ball in left arm)
108B Hayden Hurst AU 6.00 15.00
(ball in right arm)
109A Calvin Ridley AU 50.00 100.00
(ball in right arm)
109B Calvin Ridley AU 50.00 100.00
(ball in left arm)
110A Rashaad Penny AU 40.00 80.00
(running right)
110B Rashaad Penny AU 40.00 80.00
(running left)
111A Sony Michel AU EXCH 50.00 100.00
111B Sony Michel AU EXCH 50.00 100.00
112A Lamar Jackson AU 250.00 500.00
(two hands on ball)
112B Lamar Jackson AU 250.00 500.00
(ball in right arm)
113A Nick Chubb AU 100.00 200.00
(ball in left arm)
113B Nick Chubb AU 100.00 200.00
(ball in right arm)
114A Ronald Jones II AU 10.00 25.00
(ball at side)
114B Ronald Jones II AU 10.00 25.00
(ball at stomach)
115A Courtland Sutton AU EXCH 8.00 20.00
115B Courtland Sutton AU EXCH 8.00 20.00
116A Mike Gesicki AU 6.00 15.00
(running)
116B Mike Gesicki AU 6.00 15.00
(catching)
117A Kerryon Johnson AU EXCH 25.00 50.00
117B Kerryon Johnson AU EXCH 25.00 50.00
118A Dante Pettis AU 15.00 40.00
(running straight)
118B Dante Pettis AU 15.00 40.00
(running right)
119A Christian Kirk AU 12.00 30.00
(running)
119B Christian Kirk AU 12.00 30.00
(catching)
120A Anthony Miller AU 8.00 20.00
ball in right hand)
120B Anthony Miller AU 8.00 20.00
(two hands on ball)
121A Derrius Guice AU 40.00 80.00
ball in right hand)
121B Derrius Guice AU 40.00 80.00
(two hands on ball)
122A James Washington AU 10.00 25.00
(two arms on ball)
122B James Washington AU 10.00 25.00
(ball in left arm)
123A D.J. Chark Jr. AU 6.00 15.00
(running straight)
123B D.J. Chark Jr. AU 6.00 15.00
(catching)
124A Royce Freeman AU 6.00 15.00
(two arms on ball)
124B Royce Freeman AU 6.00 15.00
(catching)
125A Mason Rudolph AU 100.00 200.00
(ball in right hand)
125B Mason Rudolph AU 100.00 200.00
(two hands on ball)
126A Michael Gallup AU 15.00 40.00
(running straight)
126B Michael Gallup AU 15.00 40.00
(body bent)
127A Tre'Quan Smith AU 50.00 100.00
(running left)
127B Tre'Quan Smith AU 50.00 100.00
(running right)
128A Keke Coutee AU EXCH 6.00 15.00
128B Keke Coutee AU EXCH 6.00 15.00
129A Nyheim Hines AU 6.00 15.00
(ball in left arm)
129B Nyheim Hines AU 6.00 15.00
(ball in right arm)
130A Kyle Lauletta AU EXCH 30.00 60.00
130B Kyle Lauletta AU EXCH 30.00 60.00
131A Mark Walton AU 6.00 15.00
(ball in right arm)
131B Mark Walton AU 6.00 15.00
(two hands on ball)
132A DaeSean Hamilton AU 6.00 15.00
(ball in right arm)
132B DaeSean Hamilton AU 6.00 15.00
(two arms on ball)
133A Ito Smith AU 6.00 15.00
(running)
133B Ito Smith AU 6.00 15.00
(catching)
134A Kalen Ballage AU EXCH 6.00 15.00
134B Kalen Ballage AU EXCH 6.00 15.00
135A Jaleel Scott AU 5.00 12.00
(left arm across body)
135B Jaleel Scott AU 5.00 12.00
(left arm at waist)
136A J'Mon Moore AU 5.00 12.00
(body facing right)
136B J'Mon Moore AU 5.00 12.00
(body facing left)
137A Daurice Fountain AU 6.00 15.00
(catching)
137B Daurice Fountain AU 6.00 15.00
(running)
138A Jaylen Samuels AU 6.00 15.00
(ball in right arm)
138B Jaylen Samuels AU 6.00 15.00
(two hands on ball)
139A Mike White AU 25.00 50.00
(looking right)
139B Mike White AU 25.00 50.00
(looking left)
140A Marquez Valdes-Scantling AU 6.00 15.00
(running left)
140B Marquez Valdes-Scantling AU 6.00 15.00
(facing straight)

2018 Panini Contenders Ticket Stub

102A Saquon Barkley AU/26 400.00 800.00
102B Saquon Barkley AU/26 400.00 800.00
104A Bradley Chubb AU/55 EXCH 25.00 50.00
104B Bradley Chubb AU/55 EXCH 25.00 50.00
105A Josh Allen AU/17 500.00 1000.00
105B Josh Allen AU/17 500.00 1000.00
108A Hayden Hurst AU/81 6.00 15.00
108B Hayden Hurst AU/81 6.00 15.00
109A Calvin Ridley AU/18 60.00 125.00
109B Calvin Ridley AU/18 60.00 125.00
110A Rashaad Penny AU/20 15.00 40.00
110B Rashaad Penny AU/20 15.00 40.00
111A Sony Michel AU/29 100.00 200.00
111B Sony Michel AU/29 100.00 200.00
113A Nick Chubb AU/31
113B Nick Chubb AU/31
114A Ronald Jones II AU/27 15.00 40.00
114B Ronald Jones II AU/27 15.00 40.00
116A Mike Gesicki AU/86 10.00 25.00
116B Mike Gesicki AU/86 10.00 25.00
117A Kerryon Johnson AU/33 EXCH 40.00 80.00
117B Kerryon Johnson AU/33 EXCH 40.00 80.00
118A Dante Pettis AU/18 50.00 100.00
118B Dante Pettis AU/18 50.00 100.00
120A Anthony Miller AU/17 40.00 80.00
120B Anthony Miller AU/17 40.00 80.00
121A Derrius Guice AU/29 40.00 80.00
121B Derrius Guice AU/29 40.00 80.00
123A D.J. Chark Jr. AU/17 12.00 30.00
123B D.J. Chark Jr. AU/17 12.00 30.00
124A Royce Freeman AU/37 8.00 20.00
124B Royce Freeman AU/37 8.00 20.00
128A Keke Coutee AU/16 EXCH 12.00 30.00
128B Keke Coutee AU/16 EXCH 12.00 30.00
129A Nyheim Hines AU/42 8.00 20.00
129B Nyheim Hines AU/42 8.00 20.00
130A Kyle Lauletta AU/17 EXCH 30.00 60.00
130B Kyle Lauletta AU/17 EXCH 30.00 60.00
131A Mark Walton AU/32 10.00 25.00
131B Mark Walton AU/32 10.00 25.00
132A DaeSean Hamilton AU/17 12.00 30.00
132B DaeSean Hamilton AU/17 12.00 30.00
133A Ito Smith AU/25 10.00 25.00
133B Ito Smith AU/25 10.00 25.00
134A Kalen Ballage AU/33 EXCH 10.00 25.00
134B Kalen Ballage AU/33 EXCH 10.00 25.00
136A J'Mon Moore AU/82 5.00 12.00
136B J'Mon Moore AU/82 5.00 12.00
138A Jaylen Samuels AU/38 8.00 20.00
138B Jaylen Samuels AU/38 8.00 20.00
140A Marquez Valdes-Scantling AU/83 6.00 15.00
140B Marquez Valdes-Scantling AU/83 6.00 15.00
141 Justin Jones AU/91 5.00 12.00
142 Avonte Maddox AU/29 10.00 25.00
143 Kemoko Turay AU/57 8.00 20.00
144 Jordan Thomas AU/83 6.00 15.00
145 Denzel Ward AU/21 25.00 60.00
146 Roquan Smith AU/58 20.00 50.00
147 Minkah Fitzpatrick AU/29 15.00 40.00
149 Daron Payne AU/95 8.00 20.00
151 Tremaine Edmunds AU/49 EXCH 12.00 30.00
152 Derwin James AU/33 15.00 40.00
153 Jaire Alexander AU/23 15.00 40.00
154 Leighton Vander Esch AU/55 100.00 200.00
155 Rashaan Evans AU/54 10.00 25.00
156 Terrell Edmunds AU/34 25.00 60.00
157 Mike Hughes AU/21 15.00 40.00
158 Harold Landry AU/58 6.00 15.00
159 Joshua Jackson AU/37 12.00 30.00
160 M.J. Stewart AU/36 6.00 15.00
161 Donte Jackson AU/26 12.00 30.00
162 Duke Dawson AU/29 8.00 20.00
164 Carlton Davis AU/33 10.00 25.00
167 Chris Warren III AU/34 12.00 30.00
169 Trenton Cannon AU/40 8.00 20.00
170 Sam Hubbard AU/94 6.00 15.00
171 Rashaan Gaulden AU/28 8.00 20.00
172 Jake Kumerow AU/16 12.00 30.00
173 Jalyn Holmes AU/92 8.00 20.00
175 Chris Herndon IV AU/89 5.00 12.00
176 Da'Shawn Hand AU/93 5.00 12.00
177 Anthony Averett AU/28 10.00 25.00
178 Armani Watts AU/25 8.00 20.00
179 Josh Sweat AU/75 6.00 15.00
180 Chase Edmonds AU/29 8.00 20.00
181 Dalton Schultz AU/86 6.00 15.00
182 Maurice Hurst AU/73 6.00 15.00
183 Shaquem Griffin AU/49 10.00 25.00
185 Jordan Lasley AU/17 10.00 25.00
186 John Kelly AU/42 8.00 20.00
188 Dylan Cantrell AU/84 5.00 12.00
190 Cedrick Wilson Jr. AU/16 10.00 25.00
192 Marcell Ateman AU/88 6.00 15.00
193 Bo Scarbrough AU/36 8.00 20.00
194 Gus Edwards AU/49 15.00 40.00
195 Ryan Nall AU/35 12.00 30.00
196 Auden Tate AU/19 10.00 25.00
198 Damoun Patterson AU/83 5.00 12.00
199 Deontay Burnett AU/88 6.00 15.00
200 Josh Adams AU/33 15.00 40.00
201 Riley Ferguson AU/99 8.00 20.00
202 Simmie Cobbs Jr. AU/15 15.00 40.00
203 Dallas Goedert AU/88 6.00 15.00
204 Rasheem Green AU/94 5.00 12.00
207 Akrum Wadley AU/38 6.00 15.00
209 Tanner Lee AU/76 6.00 15.00
210 Dorian O'Daniel AU/44 6.00 15.00
211 Cory Littleton AU/58 8.00 20.00
212 Austin Proehl AU/87 5.00 12.00
213 D.J. Reed AU/32 8.00 20.00
214 DeAndre Goolsby AU/99 5.00 12.00
215 Dorance Armstrong Jr. AU/92 5.00 12.00
216 Durham Smythe AU/46 6.00 15.00
218 Javon Wims AU/83 5.00 12.00
219 Jordan Mailata AU/68 6.00 15.00
224 Malik Jefferson AU/45 8.00 20.00
225 Marcus Allen AU/27 12.00 30.00
226 Marcus Baugh AU/83 5.00 12.00
228 Micah Kiser AU/59 6.00 15.00
229 Ogbonnia Okoronkwo AU/45 10.00 25.00
230 Quonton Nelson AU/56 10.00 25.00
231 Mike McGlinchey AU/69 12.00 30.00
233 Tarvarus McFadden AU/33 10.00 25.00
234 Taven Bryan AU/90 5.00 12.00
236 Billy Price AU/53 8.00 20.00
237 Kolton Miller AU/77 8.00 20.00
239 Harrison Phillips AU/99 5.00 12.00
240 Marquis Haynes AU/98 5.00 12.00
242 Jordan Wilkins AU/20 12.00 30.00
244 Jordan Thomas AU/83 6.00 15.00
245 Denzel Ward AU/21 25.00 60.00
246 Roquan Smith AU/58 20.00 50.00
247 Minkah Fitzpatrick AU/29 15.00 40.00
249 Daron Payne AU/95 8.00 20.00
251 Tremaine Edmunds AU/49 EXCH 12.00 30.00
252 Derwin James AU/33 15.00 40.00
253 Jaire Alexander AU/23 15.00 40.00
254 Leighton Vander Esch AU/55 100.00 200.00
255 Rashaan Evans AU/54 10.00 25.00
256 Cam Sims AU/89 6.00 15.00
257 Mike Hughes AU/21 15.00 40.00
258 Harold Landry AU/58 6.00 15.00
259 Joshua Jackson AU/37 12.00 30.00
260 M.J. Stewart AU/36 6.00 15.00
261 Donte Jackson AU/26 12.00 30.00
262 Duke Dawson AU/52 6.00 15.00
263 Isaiah Oliver AU/20 10.00 25.00
264 Carlton Davis AU/33 10.00 25.00
267 Chris Warren III AU/34 12.00 30.00
269 Trenton Cannon AU/40 8.00 20.00
270 Sam Hubbard AU/94 6.00 15.00
271 Rashaan Gaulden AU/99 5.00 12.00
272 Jake Kumerow AU/16 12.00 30.00
273 Jalyn Holmes AU/92 8.00 20.00
275 Chris Herndon IV AU/89 5.00 12.00
276 Da'Shawn Hand AU/93 5.00 12.00
277 Anthony Averett AU/28 10.00 25.00
278 Armani Watts AU/25 8.00 20.00
279 Josh Sweat AU/75 6.00 15.00
280 Chase Edmonds AU/29 8.00 20.00
281 Dalton Schultz AU/86 6.00 15.00
282 Maurice Hurst AU/73 6.00 15.00
283 Shaquem Griffin AU/49 10.00 25.00
284 Russell Gage AU/83 6.00 15.00
285 Jordan Lasley AU/17 10.00 25.00
286 John Kelly AU/42 8.00 20.00
288 Dylan Cantrell AU/84 5.00 12.00
290 Cedrick Wilson Jr. AU/16 10.00 25.00
291 Braxton Berrios AU/55 6.00 15.00
292 Marcell Ateman AU/88 6.00 15.00
293 Bo Scarbrough AU/36 8.00 20.00
294 Gus Edwards AU/49 15.00 40.00
295 Ryan Nall AU/35 12.00 30.00
296 Auden Tate AU/19 10.00 25.00
299 Deontay Burnett AU/80 6.00 15.00
300 Josh Adams AU/33 15.00 40.00
301 Riley Ferguson AU/99 8.00 20.00
302 Simmie Cobbs Jr. AU/15 15.00 40.00
303 Dallas Goedert AU/88 6.00 15.00
304 Rasheem Green AU/94 5.00 12.00
307 Ralph Webb AU/42 8.00 20.00
310 Dorian O'Daniel AU/44 6.00 15.00
311 Cory Littleton AU/58 8.00 20.00
312 Riley McCarron AU/17 10.00 25.00
313 D.J. Reed AU/40 6.00 15.00
314 DeAndre Goolsby AU/99 5.00 12.00
315 Dorance Armstrong Jr. AU/92 5.00 12.00
316 Durham Smythe AU/46 6.00 15.00
319 Darius Leonard AU/53 15.00 40.00
322 Malik Jefferson AU/45 8.00 20.00
326 Rod Smith AU/45 8.00 20.00
327 Ogbonnia Okoronkwo AU/45 10.00 25.00
328 Adrian Colbert AU/27 8.00 20.00
329 Mike McGlinchey AU/69 12.00 30.00
330 Mike Boone AU/44 8.00 20.00
331 Vyncint Smith AU/17 10.00 25.00
332 Taven Bryan AU/90 5.00 12.00
334 Billy Price AU/53 8.00 20.00
335 Kolton Miller AU/77 8.00 20.00
337 Detrez Newsome AU/38 6.00 15.00
338 Quinton Dunbar AU/23 12.00 30.00
339 Phillip Lindsay AU/30 200.00 300.00
340 Will Dissly AU/88 6.00 15.00

2018 Panini Contenders Contenders to Canton Autographs

2 LaDainian Tomlinson/20 EXCH 50.00 100.00
4 Kurt Warner/20
5 Jerome Bettis/20 30.00 60.00
6 Terrell Davis/15 40.00 80.00
8 Ray Lewis/20 75.00 150.00
10 Curtis Martin/20

2018 Panini Contenders Draft Class Autographs

1 Baker Mayfield/25 250.00 450.00
2 Saquon Barkley/49 125.00 250.00
3 Sam Darnold/25 125.00 250.00
4 Bradley Chubb/25 EXCH 15.00 40.00
5 Josh Allen/49 EXCH 60.00 125.00
6 Josh Rosen/49 40.00 80.00
7 D.J. Moore/49 10.00 25.00
8 Calvin Ridley/25 EXCH 15.00 40.00
9 Rashaad Penny/99 6.00 15.00
10 Sony Michel/49 EXCH 50.00 100.00
12 Nick Chubb/49 15.00 40.00
13 Ronald Jones II/49 5.00 12.00
14 Courtland Sutton/99 EXCH 6.00 15.00
15 Dante Pettis/99 6.00 15.00
16 Christian Kirk/25 10.00 25.00
18 Derrius Guice/25 12.00 30.00
19 Royce Freeman/25 8.00 20.00
20 Mason Rudolph/49 40.00 80.00

2018 Panini Contenders Draft Class Autographs Gold

*GOLD/18: .8X TO 2X BASIC AU/99
*GOLD/18: .6X TO 1.5X BASIC AU/49
*GOLD/18: .5X TO 1.2X BASIC AU/25
1 Baker Mayfield 600.00 1000.00
2 Saquon Barkley 200.00 400.00

2018 Panini Contenders Legendary Contenders

*EMERALD: .6X TO 1.5X BASIC INSERTS
*GOLD/49: 1.2X TO 3X BASIC INSERTS
*RUBY: .6X TO 1.5X BASIC INSERTS
*SILVER/75: 1X TO 2.5X BASIC INSERTS
1 Brett Favre 1.25 3.00
2 Emmitt Smith 1.00 2.50
3 Joe Montana 1.50 4.00
4 Charles Woodson .60 1.50
5 Jerry Rice 1.00 2.50
6 John Elway 1.00 2.50
7 Peyton Manning 1.25 3.00
8 Terry Bradshaw 1.00 2.50
9 Dan Marino 1.25 3.00
10 Barry Sanders 1.00 2.50
11 Deion Sanders .50 1.25
12 John Riggins .50 1.25
13 Dick Butkus
14 Tony Gonzalez .50 1.25
15 Lawrence Taylor .60 1.50

2018 Panini Contenders Legendary Contenders Autographs

11 Barry Sanders/25 75.00 150.00
12 Joe Namath/25 60.00 125.00
13 Deion Sanders/25 30.00 60.00
14 John Riggins/25 25.00 50.00
15 Roger Staubach/25 50.00 100.00
16 Marshall Faulk/25 25.00 50.00
17 Steve Young/25 40.00 80.00
18 Dick Butkus/25 25.00 50.00
19 Tony Gonzalez/25 15.00 40.00
20 Lawrence Taylor/25 25.00 50.00

2018 Panini Contenders MVP Contenders

*EMERALD: .6X TO 1.5X BASIC INSERTS
*GOLD/49: 1.2X TO 3X BASIC INSERTS
*RUBY: .6X TO 1.5X BASIC INSERTS
*SILVER/75: 1X TO 2.5X BASIC INSERTS
1 Aaron Rodgers 1.25 3.00
2 Russell Wilson .75 2.00
3 Drew Brees .60 1.50
4 Tom Brady 1.50 4.00
5 Antonio Brown .60 1.50
6 Matt Ryan .50 1.25
7 Matthew Stafford .50 1.25
8 Philip Rivers .60 1.50
9 Carson Wentz .75 2.00
10 Blake Bortles .40 1.00
11 David Johnson .60 1.50
12 Derek Carr .60 1.50
13 Ezekiel Elliott .75 2.00
14 Alvin Kamara .50 1.25
15 Kareem Hunt .50 1.25
16 Kirk Cousins .60 1.50
17 Jared Goff .60 1.50
18 Jimmy Garoppolo .75 2.00
19 Patrick Mahomes II 1.50 4.00
20 Deshaun Watson .75 2.00
21 Saquon Barkley 2.00 5.00
22 Todd Gurley II .60 1.50
23 Cam Newton .60 1.50
24 Khalil Mack .60 1.50
25 Andrew Luck .75 2.00

2018 Panini Contenders MVP Contenders Autographs

5 Antonio Brown/25 15.00 40.00
6 Matt Ryan/25 12.00 30.00
7 Matthew Stafford/25 12.00 30.00
8 Philip Rivers/15 30.00 60.00
9 Carson Wentz/25 50.00 100.00
11 David Johnson/25 10.00 25.00
12 Derek Carr/25 10.00 25.00
13 Ezekiel Elliott/25 50.00 100.00
15 Kareem Hunt/49 6.00 15.00
16 Kirk Cousins/15 12.00 30.00
17 Jared Goff/25 30.00 60.00
18 Jimmy Garoppolo/25 50.00 100.00
19 Patrick Mahomes II/25 200.00 400.00
20 Deshaun Watson/25 25.00 50.00

2018 Panini Contenders NFL Ink

*GOLD/25: .8X TO 2X BASIC AU/199
*GOLD/25: .6X TO 1.5X BASIC AU/99
*GOLD/25: .5X TO 1.2X BASIC AU/49
1 Philip Rivers/15 15.00 40.00
2 Joe Flacco/15
3 Marshawn Lynch/25 10.00 25.00
4 A.J. Green/25 12.00 30.00
5 Jordy Nelson/25 10.00 25.00
6 Adam Thielen/25 50.00 100.00
7 Ezekiel Elliott/15 40.00 80.00
8 T.Y. Hilton/25 10.00 25.00
9 Jimmy Garoppolo/25 50.00 100.00
10 Aaron Donald/25 15.00 40.00
11 Marvin Jones Jr./49 6.00 15.00
12 Aqib Talib/99 5.00 12.00
13 Chandler Jones/49 6.00 15.00
14 Corey Davis/49 8.00 20.00
15 Jerick McKinnon/99 5.00 12.00
16 JuJu Smith-Schuster/25 25.00 50.00
17 Vic Beasley Jr./99 5.00 12.00
18 Ty Montgomery/99 5.00 12.00
19 Taylor Gabriel/199 4.00 10.00

2018 Panini Contenders Rookie of the Year Contenders

*EMERALD: .5X TO 1.2X BASIC INSERTS
*GOLD/49: 1X TO 2.5X BASIC INSERTS
*RUBY: .5X TO 1.2X BASIC INSERTS
*SILVER/75: .8X TO 2X BASIC INSERTS
1 Baker Mayfield 3.00 8.00
2 Saquon Barkley 2.50 6.00
3 Sam Darnold 2.00 5.00
4 Bradley Chubb .50 1.25
5 Josh Allen 1.25 3.00
6 Josh Rosen 1.00 2.50
7 D.J. Moore .60 1.50
8 Calvin Ridley .75 2.00
9 Rashaad Penny .50 1.25
10 Sony Michel 1.00 2.50
11 Lamar Jackson 2.00 5.00
12 Nick Chubb 1.00 2.50
13 Ronald Jones II .60 1.50
14 Courtland Sutton .50 1.25
15 Dante Pettis .50 1.25
16 Christian Kirk .50 1.25
17 Anthony Miller .50 1.25
18 Derrius Guice .60 1.50
19 Royce Freeman .40 1.00
20 Mason Rudolph .75 2.00
21 James Washington .60 1.50
22 Michael Gallup .60 1.50
23 Keke Coutee .40 1.00
24 Nyheim Hines .40 1.00
25 Kerryon Johnson .50 1.25
26 Kyle Lauletta .50 1.25
27 Tre'Quan Smith .50 1.25
28 J'Mon Moore .30 .75
29 DaeSean Hamilton .40 1.00
30 Mike White .40 1.00

2018 Panini Contenders Rookie of the Year Contenders Autographs

1 Baker Mayfield/25 250.00 450.00
2 Saquon Barkley/49 125.00 250.00
3 Sam Darnold/25 125.00 250.00
5 Josh Allen/49 EXCH 60.00 125.00
6 Josh Rosen/49 40.00 80.00
7 D.J. Moore/49 10.00 25.00
8 Calvin Ridley/25 EXCH 15.00 40.00
9 Rashaad Penny/99 6.00 15.00
10 Sony Michel/49 EXCH 50.00 100.00
12 Nick Chubb/49 15.00 40.00
13 Ronald Jones II/25 12.00 30.00
14 Courtland Sutton/99 EXCH 6.00 15.00
15 Dante Pettis/99 6.00 15.00
16 Christian Kirk/25 10.00 25.00
17 Anthony Miller/99 6.00 15.00
18 Derrius Guice/25 12.00 30.00
19 Royce Freeman/49 6.00 15.00
20 Mason Rudolph/49 40.00 80.00
21 James Washington/99 8.00 20.00
22 Michael Gallup/25 12.00 30.00
23 Keke Coutee/99 5.00 12.00
24 Nyheim Hines/99 5.00 12.00
25 Kerryon Johnson/99 12.00 30.00
26 Kyle Lauletta/25 10.00 25.00
27 Tre'Quan Smith/99 6.00 15.00
28 J'Mon Moore/25 6.00 15.00
29 DaeSean Hamilton/25 8.00 20.00
30 Mike White/25 8.00 20.00

2018 Panini Contenders Rookie Roundup Autographs

1 Baker Mayfield/25 250.00 450.00
2 Saquon Barkley/49 125.00 250.00
3 Sam Darnold/25 125.00 250.00
5 Josh Allen/49 EXCH 60.00 125.00
6 Josh Rosen/49 40.00 80.00
7 D.J. Moore/49 10.00 25.00
8 Calvin Ridley/25 EXCH 15.00 40.00
9 Rashaad Penny/99 6.00 15.00
10 Sony Michel/49 EXCH 50.00 100.00
11 Lamar Jackson/25 75.00 150.00
12 Nick Chubb/49 15.00 40.00
13 Ronald Jones II/25 12.00 30.00
14 Courtland Sutton/99 EXCH 6.00 15.00
15 Dante Pettis/99 6.00 15.00
16 Christian Kirk/25 10.00 25.00
17 Anthony Miller/99 6.00 15.00
18 Derrius Guice/25 12.00 30.00
19 Royce Freeman/49 6.00 15.00
20 Mason Rudolph/49 40.00 80.00

2018 Panini Contenders Rookie Ticket Dual Swatches

1 B.Mayfield/N.Chubb 15.00 40.00
2 N.Chubb/S.Michel 5.00 12.00
3 B.Mayfield/L.Jackson 15.00 40.00
4 S.Darnold/J.Allen 10.00 25.00
5 J.Rosen/C.Kirk 6.00 15.00
6 B.Mayfield/S.Barkley 15.00 40.00
7 M.Rudolph/J.Washington 5.00 12.00
8 D.Moore/C.Ridley 5.00 12.00
9 H.Hurst/L.Jackson 10.00 25.00
10 B.Chubb/C.Sutton 4.00 10.00
11 J.Moore/M.Valdes-Scantling 3.00 8.00
12 D.Fountain/N.Hines 3.00 8.00
13 S.Darnold/S.Barkley 12.00 30.00
14 B.Chubb/J.Samuels 4.00 10.00
15 A.Miller/D.Pettis 4.00 10.00
16 R.Jones II/S.Darnold 10.00 25.00
17 D.Chark Jr./D.Guice 5.00 12.00
18 T.Smith/K.Coutee 4.00 10.00
19 S.Barkley/K.Lauletta 12.00 30.00
20 M.White/M.Gallup 5.00 12.00

2018 Panini Contenders Rookie Ticket Swatches

*VARIATION: .5X TO 1.2X BASIC JSY
1 Baker Mayfield 20.00 30.00
2 Saquon Barkley 15.00 25.00
3 Sam Darnold 12.00 20.00
4 Bradley Chubb 3.00 8.00
5 Josh Allen 5.00 12.00
6 Josh Rosen 5.00 12.00
7 D.J. Moore 4.00 10.00
8 Hayden Hurst 2.50 6.00
9 Calvin Ridley 4.00 10.00
10 Rashaad Penny 3.00 8.00
11 Sony Michel 4.00 10.00
12 Lamar Jackson 12.00 20.00
13 Nick Chubb 4.00 10.00
14 Ronald Jones II 4.00 10.00
15 Courtland Sutton 3.00 8.00
16 Mike Gesicki 2.50 6.00
17 Kerryon Johnson 3.00 8.00
18 Dante Pettis 3.00 8.00
19 Christian Kirk 3.00 8.00
20 Anthony Miller 3.00 8.00
21 Derrius Guice 4.00 10.00
22 James Washington 4.00 10.00
23 D.J. Chark Jr. 2.50 6.00
24 Royce Freeman 2.50 6.00
25 Mason Rudolph 4.00 10.00
26 Michael Gallup 4.00 10.00
27 Tre'Quan Smith 3.00 8.00
28 Keke Coutee 2.50 6.00
29 Nyheim Hines 2.50 6.00
30 Kyle Lauletta 3.00 8.00
31 Mark Walton 2.50 6.00
32 DaeSean Hamilton 2.50 6.00
33 Ito Smith 2.50 6.00
34 Kalen Ballage 2.50 6.00
35 Jaleel Scott 2.00 5.00
36 J'Mon Moore 2.00 5.00
37 Daurice Fountain 2.50 6.00
38 Jaylen Samuels 2.50 6.00
39 Mike White 2.50 6.00
40 Marquez Valdes-Scantling 2.50 6.00

2018 Panini Contenders Round Numbers

*EMERALD: .6X TO 1.5X BASIC INSERTS
*GOLD/49: 1.2X TO 3X BASIC INSERTS
*RUBY: .6X TO 1.5X BASIC INSERTS
*SILVER/75: 1X TO 2.5X BASIC INSERTS
1 B.Mayfield/S.Darnold 2.50 6.00
2 J.Allen/J.Rosen 1.25 3.00
3 S.Michel/S.Barkley 2.50 6.00
4 C.Ridley/D.Moore 1.00 2.50
5 R.Jones II/N.Chubb 1.25 3.00
6 D.Pettis/C.Sutton .60 1.50
7 A.Miller/C.Kirk .60 1.50
8 D.Guice/K.Johnson .75 2.00
9 D.Chark Jr./J.Washington .75 2.00
10 M.Gallup/T.Smith .75 2.00
11 M.Walton/N.Hines .50 1.25
12 K.Ballage/I.Smith .50 1.25
13 D.Hamilton/K.Coutee .50 1.25
14 J.Moore/J.Scott .40 1.00
15 M.Valdes-Scantling/D.Fountain .50 1.25
16 B.Chubb/M.Davenport .75 2.00
17 D.James/M.Fitzpatrick .75 2.00
18 J.Alexander/D.Ward 1.00 2.50
19 T.Edmunds/T.Edmunds 1.25 3.00
20 H.Hurst/L.Jackson 2.00 5.00

2018 Panini Contenders Round Numbers Dual Autographs

1 B.Mayfield/S.Darnold/25 250.00 450.00
2 J.Allen/J.Rosen/25 50.00 100.00
3 S.Michel/S.Barkley/25 200.00 400.00
4 C.Ridley/D.Moore/25 20.00 50.00
5 N.Chubb/R.Jones II/49 20.00 50.00
6 D.Pettis/C.Sutton/99 8.00 20.00
7 A.Miller/C.Kirk/25 12.00 30.00
8 K.Johnson/D.Guice/49 12.00 30.00
9 J.Washington/D.Chark Jr./99 10.00 25.00
10 M.Gallup/T.Smith/25 15.00 40.00
16 M.Davenport/B.Chubb/25 15.00 40.00
17 M.Fitzpatrick/D.James/99 25.00 50.00
18 D.Ward/J.Alexander/99 12.00 30.00
19 T.Edmunds/T.Edmunds/99 15.00 40.00

2018 Panini Contenders Sophomore Contenders Autographs

1 Mitchell Trubisky/25 40.00 80.00
2 Leonard Fournette/25 10.00 25.00
3 Corey Davis/25 8.00 20.00
4 Jamal Adams/25 8.00 20.00
5 Christian McCaffrey/25 25.00 50.00
6 Patrick Mahomes II/25 150.00 250.00
7 Marshon Lattimore/25 6.00 15.00
8 Deshaun Watson/25 50.00 100.00
9 O.J. Howard/25 6.00 15.00
10 T.J. Watt/25 15.00 40.00
11 JuJu Smith-Schuster/25 25.00 50.00
13 Kareem Hunt/25 12.00 30.00
14 Tarik Cohen/25 8.00 20.00
15 Nathan Peterman/25 6.00 15.00
18 Malik Hooker/25 6.00 15.00
19 Mike Williams/25 6.00 15.00

2018 Panini Contenders Team Quads

*EMERALD: .6X TO 1.5X BASIC INSERTS
*GOLD/49: 1.2X TO 3X BASIC INSERTS
*RUBY: .6X TO 1.5X BASIC INSERTS
*SILVER/75: 1X TO 2.5X BASIC INSERTS
1 Grnkwski/Mchl/Brdy/Edlmn 2.00 5.00
2 Rlsbrgr/SmthSchstr/Brwn/Cnnr .75 2.00
3 Hnt/Mhms/Klce/Hll 2.00 5.00
4 Cks/Dnld/Gff/Grly .75 2.00
5 Brs/Thms/Kmra/Ingrm .75 2.00
6 Lndry/Chbb/Cllwy/Myfld 5.00 12.00
7 Cpr/Crr/Nlsn/Lnch .75 2.00
8 Mnng/Brkly/Bckhm/Shprd 4.00 10.00
9 Frmn/Jns/Ryn/Rdly 1.25 3.00
10 Csns/Thln/Ck/Dggs .75 2.00

2018 Panini Contenders Veteran Ticket Autographs

*CHAMP/49: .6X TO 1.5X BASIC AU
*CHAMP/25: .8X TO 2X BASIC AU
*CHAMP/15: 1X TO 2.5X BASIC AU
*PLAYOFF/99: .5X TO 1.2X BASIC AU
*PLAYOFF/49: .6X TO 1.5X BASIC AU
*CTUD/15: .8X TO 2X BASIC AU
1 Antonio Brown EXCH 25.00 50.00
2 Russell Wilson 75.00 150.00
3 Carson Wentz
4 Rob Gronkowski EXCH

5 Richard Sherman 15.00 40.00
6 Clay Matthews 25.00 50.00
7 Adam Thielen 50.00 100.00
8 David Johnson 6.00 15.00
9 Luke Kuechly EXCH 12.00 30.00
11 Derrick Henry 6.00 15.00
12 Aaron Donald EXCH
13 Fletcher Cox 4.00 10.00
15 T.J. Watt 8.00 20.00
17 C.J. Mosley 5.00 12.00
18 Travis Kelce 10.00 25.00
19 Tyreek Hill 12.00 30.00
20 Devonta Freeman 5.00 12.00

2018 Panini Contenders Veteran Cracked Ice Autographs

1 Antonio Brown EXCH 50.00 100.00
2 Russell Wilson 200.00 400.00
3 Carson Wentz 200.00 400.00
4 Rob Gronkowski EXCH 60.00 125.00
5 Richard Sherman 60.00 125.00
6 Clay Matthews 50.00 100.00
7 Adam Thielen 125.00 250.00
8 David Johnson 20.00 50.00
9 Luke Kuechly EXCH 50.00 100.00
11 Derrick Henry 20.00 50.00
12 Aaron Donald EXCH 60.00 125.00
15 T.J. Watt 60.00 125.00
17 C.J. Mosley 15.00 40.00
18 Travis Kelce 50.00 100.00
19 Tyreek Hill 50.00 100.00
20 Devonta Freeman 15.00 40.00

2015 Panini Contenders Draft Picks

COMP.SET w/o RC's (100) 10.00 25.00
SP1 ANNC'D PRINT RUN 250 OR LESS
SP2 ANNC'D PRINT RUN 50 OR LESS
1 A.J. Green .30 .75
2 Aaron Rodgers .60 1.50
3 Adrian Peterson .30 .75
4 Alex Smith .25 .60
5 Allen Hurns .20 .50
6 Alshon Jeffery .25 .60
7 Andre Ellington .20 .50
8 Andre Johnson .25 .60
9 Andre Williams .20 .50
10 Andrew Luck .40 1.00
11 Andy Dalton .25 .60
12 Anquan Boldin .20 .50
13 Antonio Brown .30 .75
14 Antonio Gates .20 .50
15 Arian Foster .25 .60
16 Ben Roethlisberger .30 .75
17 Blake Bortles .20 .50
18 Brandon LaFell .20 .50
19 Brandon Marshall .20 .50
20 Carson Palmer .25 .60
21 C.J. Anderson .25 .60
22 Calvin Johnson .30 .75
23 Cam Newton .30 .75
24 Charles Woodson .30 .75
25 Clay Matthews .30 .75
26 Colin Kaepernick .25 .60
27 Danny Amendola .25 .60
28 Darren Sproles .25 .60
29 DeAndre Hopkins .25 .60
30 DeMarco Murray .25 .60
31 Demaryius Thomas .25 .60
32 Derek Carr .30 .75
33 DeSean Jackson .25 .60
34 Dez Bryant .30 .75
35 Drew Brees .30 .75
36 Dwayne Bowe .25 .60
37 Dwight Freeney .20 .50
38 Earl Thomas .25 .60
39 Eddie Lacy .20 .50
40 Eli Manning .25 .60
41 Frank Gore .25 .60
42 J.J. Watt .30 .75
43 Jamaal Charles .25 .60
44 Jason Witten .25 .60
45 Jay Cutler .20 .50
46 Jeremy Hill .20 .50
47 Jimmy Graham .30 .75
48 Joe Flacco .25 .60
49 Johnny Manziel .25 .60
50 Jordan Cameron .20 .50
51 Jordan Matthews .25 .60
52 Jordy Nelson .25 .60
53 Josh Gordon .20 .50
54 Julian Edelman .30 .75
55 Julio Jones .30 .75
56 Julius Peppers .25 .60
57 Julius Thomas .20 .50
58 Justin Forsett .25 .60
59 Justin Houston .20 .50
60 Kam Chancellor .30 .75
61 Keenan Allen .25 .60
62 Kelvin Benjamin .25 .60
63 Kenny Stills .20 .50
64 Khalil Mack .30 .75
65 Larry Fitzgerald .25 .60
66 LeSean McCoy .30 .75
67 Le'Veon Bell .25 .60
68 Luke Kuechly .25 .60
69 Marshawn Lynch .25 .60
70 Martavis Bryant .20 .50
71 Matt Forte .20 .50
72 Matt Ryan .25 .60
73 Matthew Stafford .25 .60
74 Mike Evans .25 .60
75 Mike Wallace .20 .50
76 Ndamukong Suh .25 .60
77 Nick Foles .25 .60
78 Odell Beckham Jr. .30 .75
79 Patrick Peterson .20 .50
80 Paul Posluszny .20 .50
81 Peyton Manning .60 1.50
82 Philip Rivers .30 .75
83 Randall Cobb .25 .60
84 Rashad Jennings .20 .50
85 Reggie Wayne .25 .60
86 Richard Sherman .30 .75
87 Rob Gronkowski .30 .75
88 Robert Griffin III .20 .50
89 Russell Wilson .40 1.00
90 Ryan Tannehill .25 .60
91 LeGarrette Blount .25 .60
92 Sammy Watkins .25 .60
93 Steve Smith .25 .60
94 Teddy Bridgewater .25 .60
95 Terrance Williams .20 .50
96 Tom Brady .75 2.00
97 Tony Romo .25 .60
98 Troy Polamalu .30 .75
99 Vincent Jackson .20 .50
100 Wes Welker .25 .60
101A Amari Cooper AU RC SP1 100.00 200.00
101B Amari Cooper AU SP2
102A Ameer Abdullah AU RC 3.00 8.00
102B Ameer Abdullah AU SP2 25.00 50.00
103A Phillip Dorsett AU RC 12.00 30.00
103B Phillip Dorsett AU SP2 20.00 50.00
104A Vince Mayle AU RC 2.50 6.00
104B Vince Mayle AU SP2 5.00 12.00
105A Eric Kendricks AU RC 2.00 5.00
105B Eric Kendricks AU SP2 12.00 30.00
106A Brett Hundley AU RC SP1 12.00 30.00
106B Brett Hundley AU SP2 4.00 10.00
107A Blake Sims AU RC 2.00 5.00
107B Blake Sims AU SP1 3.00 8.00
108A Cameron Artis-Payne AU RC 6.00 15.00
108B Cameron Artis-Payne AU SP2
109A Clive Walford AU RC 4.00 10.00
109B Clive Walford AU SP2
110A Dres Anderson AU RC 4.00 10.00
110B Dres Anderson AU SP2 8.00 20.00
111A Danny Shelton AU RC 6.00 15.00
111B Danny Shelton AU SP2 12.00 30.00
112A Dante Fowler Jr. AU RC SP1 10.00 25.00
112B Dante Fowler Jr. AU SP2
113A David Cobb AU RC 2.00 5.00
113B David Cobb AU SP2 4.00 10.00
114A DeVante Parker AU RC SP1 25.00 50.00
114B DeVante Parker AU SP2 40.00 100.00
115A Devin Funchess AU RC 5.00 12.00
115B Devin Funchess AU SP2 10.00 25.00
116A Chris Conley AU RC 6.00 15.00
116B Chris Conley AU SP2 12.00 30.00
117A Breshad Perriman AU RC 10.00 25.00
117B Breshad Perriman AU SP2 20.00 50.00
118A Duke Johnson AU RC 6.00 15.00
118B Duke Johnson AU SP2 20.00 40.00
120A Sean Mannion AU RC 6.00 15.00
120B Sean Mannion AU SP2 25.00 50.00
122A Jameis Winston AU RC SP1 150.00 250.00
122B Jameis Winston AU SP2 150.00 250.00
123A Dominique Brown AU RC SP1 3.00 8.00
123B Dominique Brown AU SP2 4.00 10.00
124A Jay Ajayi AU RC SP1 10.00 25.00
124B Jay Ajayi AU SP2
125A Matt Jones AU RC 8.00 20.00
125B Matt Jones AU SP2 15.00 40.00
126A Josh Harper AU RC 2.00 5.00
126B Josh Harper AU SP2 4.00 10.00
127A Justin Hardy AU RC 5.00 12.00
127B Justin Hardy AU SP2 10.00 25.00
128A Kevin White AU RC SP1 4.00 10.00
128B Kevin White AU SP2
129A Landon Collins AU RC 8.00 20.00
129B Landon Collins AU SP2 15.00 40.00
130A Bud Dupree AU RC 8.00 20.00
130B Bud Dupree AU SP2 15.00 40.00
131A Marcus Mariota AU RC SP1 3.00 60.00
131B Marcus Mariota AU SP2 50.00 100.00
132A Melvin Gordon III AU RC SP1 50.00 100.00
132B Melvin Gordon III AU SP2 100.00 200.00
133A Mike Davis AU RC 6.00 15.00
133B Mike Davis AU SP2 12.00 30.00
134A Jamison Crowder AU RC 5.00 12.00
134B Jamison Crowder AU SP2 10.00 25.00
135A Nick O'Leary AU RC 2.00 5.00
135B Nick O'Leary AU SP2 4.00 10.00
136A Randy Gregory AU RC SP2 40.00 80.00
136B Randy Gregory AU SP2 40.00 80.00
137A Rashad Greene AU RC 8.00 12.00
137B Rashad Greene AU SP2 15.00 40.00
138A Sammie Coates AU RC 8.00 20.00
138B Sammie Coates AU SP2 15.00 40.00
139A Shane Carden AU RC 2.00 5.00
139B Shane Carden AU SP2
141A Shaq Thompson AU RC 2.50 6.00
141B Shaq Thompson AU SP2 5.00 12.00
142A Maxx Williams AU RC 8.00 20.00
142B Maxx Williams AU SP2 20.00 40.00
143A Stefon Diggs AU RC 10.00 25.00
143B Stefon Diggs AU SP2 20.00 50.00
144A T.J. Yeldon AU RC 2.00 5.00
144B T.J. Yeldon AU SP2 30.00 80.00
145A Terrence Magee AU RC 3.00 8.00
145B Terrence Magee AU SP2 6.00 15.00
146A Todd Gurley AU RC SP1 75.00 125.00
146B Todd Gurley AU SP2 100.00 200.00
147A Marcus Peters AU RC SP1 8.00 20.00
147B Marcus Peters AU SP2 15.00 40.00
148A Ty Montgomery AU RC SP1 10.00 25.00
148B Ty Montgomery AU SP2 20.00 50.00
149A Austin Hill AU RC 2.00 5.00
149B Austin Hill AU SP2 4.00 10.00
150A Vic Beasley AU RC 2.50 6.00
150B Vic Beasley AU SP2
151 Leonard Williams AU RC 2.00 5.00
152 Andrus Peat AU RC SP2 10.00 25.00
153 Anthony Harris AU RC 2.00 5.00
154 Arik Armstead AU RC 5.00 12.00
155 Blake Bell AU RC 3.00 8.00
156 Bo Wallace AU RC SP1 3.00 8.00
157 Taylor Heinicke AU RC 3.00 8.00
158 Brandon Scherff AU RC 3.00 8.00
159 A.J. Cann AU RC 2.50 6.00
160 Da'Ron Brown AU RC 2.00 5.00
161 Bryce Petty AU RC 8.00 20.00
162 Eric Tomlinson AU RC 2.50 6.00
163 Cedric Ogbuehi AU RC 2.00 5.00
164 Charles Gaines AU RC 3.00 8.00
166 Deontay Greenberry AU RC 2.00 5.00
167 Cody Fajardo AU RC 2.50 6.00
168 Cody Prewitt AU RC 2.50 6.00
169 Connor Halliday AU RC 3.00 8.00
170 Corey Grant AU RC 3.00 8.00
171 Danielle Hunter AU RC 2.50 6.00
172 David Johnson AU RC 15.00 30.00
173 Denzel Perryman AU RC SP1 10.00 25.00
174 Ereck Flowers AU RC 2.50 6.00
175 Derron Smith AU RC 2.00 5.00
176 Devante Davis AU RC 2.50 6.00
177 Dezmin Lewis AU RC 2.00 5.00
179 Kevin White AU RC 2.50 6.00
180 Buck Allen AU RC SP1 4.00 10.00
181 Dreamius Smith AU RC 5.00 12.00
182 E.J. Bibbs AU RC 2.50 6.00
184 Bryan Bennett AU RC 2.00 5.00
185 Gary Nova AU RC 2.00 5.00
186 Eli Harold AU RC 2.00 5.00
187 Gerald Christian AU RC 2.50 6.00
188 Kaelin Clay AU RC SP1 3.00 8.00
189 Gerod Holliman AU RC 3.00 8.00
190 Hau'oli Kikaha AU RC 2.50 6.00
191 Hutson Mason AU RC 2.00 5.00
192 Ifo Ekpre-Olomu AU RC 2.00 5.00
193 Jahwan Edwards AU RC 2.50 6.00
195 Jake Waters AU RC 2.50 6.00
196 Casey Pierce AU RC 2.00 5.00
197 Jesse James AU RC 2.50 6.00
198 Nelson Agholor AU RC 2.50 6.00
199 Jaquiski Tartt AU RC 2.00 5.00
200 Jaxon Shipley AU RC 2.00 5.00
202 Cameron Erving AU RC 2.50 6.00
203 Jordan Taylor AU RC 2.50 6.00
204 Jordon James AU RC 2.50 6.00
205 Karlos Williams AU RC 2.00 5.00
206 Jordan Phillips AU RC 2.00 5.00
207 Kenny Bell AU RC 3.00 8.00
208 Kevin Johnson AU RC 2.00 5.00
209 Kevin Parks AU RC 2.00 5.00
210 Kurtis Drummond AU RC 2.50 6.00
211 La'el Collins AU RC 6.00 15.00
212 Levi Norwood AU RC 2.00 5.00
213 Lorenzo Doss AU RC 2.00 5.00
214 Lorenzo Mauldin AU RC 2.00 5.00
215 Malcolm Agnew AU RC SP1 3.00 8.00
216 Malcolm Brown AU RC 2.50 6.00
217 Malcom Brown AU RC SP1 6.00 15.00
218 Marcus Murphy AU RC 2.00 5.00
219 Trae Waynes AU RC 2.00 5.00
220 Josh Robinson AU RC 2.00 5.00
221 Mario Edwards Jr AU RC 2.00 5.00
222 Markus Golden AU RC 2.00 5.00
223 Jeremy Langford AU RC 10.00 20.00
225 Michael Dyer AU RC 3.00 8.00
226 MyCole Pruitt AU RC 2.00 5.00
227 Nate Orchard AU RC 2.00 5.00
228 Nick Boyle AU RC 2.00 5.00
229 Nick Marshall AU RC 3.00 8.00
230 P.J. Williams AU RC 2.50 6.00
231 Antwan Goodley AU RC 2.00 5.00
232 Rannell Hall AU RC 2.00 5.00
233 Geneo Grissom AU RC 2.00 5.00
234 Owamagbe Odighizuwa AU RC 2.50 6.00
235 Paul Dawson AU RC SP1 4.00 10.00
237 Senquez Golson AU RC 5.00 12.00
238 T.J. Clemmings AU RC 2.00 5.00
239 Taylor Kelly AU RC 2.50 6.00
240 Tevin Coleman AU RC SP1 4.00 10.00
241 Ramik Wilson AU RC 2.50 6.00
242 Titus Davis AU RC 2.50 6.00
243 Tony Lippett AU RC 2.00 5.00
245 Trey Flowers AU RC 3.00 8.00
247 Tyler Kroft AU RC 2.50 6.00
248 Tyler Lockett AU RC 3.00 8.00
249 Grant Hedrick AU RC 2.00 5.00
250 Kwon Alexander AU RC 2.50 6.00
251 Eric Rowe AU RC 2.00 5.00
252 Stephone Anthony AU RC 2.00 5.00
253 Darren Waller AU RC 2.50 6.00
254 Matt Miller AU RC 2.00 5.00
255 John Crockett AU RC 3.00 8.00
256 Cam Worthy AU RC 2.00 5.00
257 Laken Tomlinson AU RC 2.00 5.00
258 Steven Nelson AU RC 2.00 5.00
259 Josh Shaw AU RC 3.00 8.00
260 Durell Eskridge AU RC 2.00 5.00
261 Mario Alford AU RC 2.00 5.00
262 Dylan Thompson AU RC 2.00 5.00
263 Kenny Hilliard AU RC 2.00 5.00
264 J.J. Nelson AU RC 2.00 5.00
265 Kenny Williams AU RC 2.00 5.00
266 Dee Hart AU RC 2.00 5.00
267 Anthony Boone AU RC 2.00 5.00
268 Gus Johnson AU RC 3.00 8.00
269 Jake Fisher AU RC 2.50 6.00
270 Carl Davis AU RC 2.50 6.00
271 DeAndrew White AU RC 3.00 8.00
272 Ronald Darby AU RC 2.00 5.00
273 Trey Williams AU RC 2.50 6.00
274 Davis Tull AU RC 2.00 5.00
275 D.J. Humphries AU RC 2.00 5.00

2015 Panini Contenders Draft Picks Bowl Ticket

*1-100 VETS/99: 4X TO 10X BASIC CARDS
*101-250 ROOK/99: .8X TO 2X BASIC AU
122A Jameis Winston AU (red jsy) 200.00 300.00
128A Kevin White AU (white jsy) 5.00 12.00
131A Marcus Mariota AU (white jsy) 50.00 100.00
132A Melvin Gordon III AU (ball in left arm) 75.00 150.00
146A Todd Gurley AU (white jsy) 100.00 200.00

2015 Panini Contenders Draft Picks College Draft Ticket Blue Foil

*BLUE: .5X TO 1.2X BASIC AU
*BLUE SP1: .6X TO 1.5X BASIC AU
*BLUE SP2: .8X TO 2X BASIC AU
*BLUE SP2: .5X TO 1.2X SP1 AU
*BLUE SP2: .4X TO 1X SP2 AU
101A Amari Cooper AU (no jsy number) SP2 100.00 200.00
122A Jameis Winston AU (red jsy) SP2 150.00 250.00
131A Marcus Mariota AU (white jsy) SP2 60.00 125.00
132A Melvin Gordon III AU (ball in left arm) SP2 100.00 200.00
146A Todd Gurley AU (white jsy) SP2 100.00 200.00

2015 Panini Contenders Draft Picks College Draft Ticket Red Foil

*RED: .5X TO 1.2X BASIC AU
*RED SP1: .6X TO 1.5X BASIC AU
*RED SP2: .8X TO 2X BASIC AU
*RED SP2: .5X TO 1.2X SP1 AU
*RED SP2: .4X TO 1X SP2 AU
101A Amari Cooper AU (no jsy number) SP2 100.00 200.00
122A Jameis Winston AU (red jsy) SP2 150.00 250.00

2015 Panini Contenders Draft Picks Cracked Ice

*1-100 VETS/23: 12X TO 30X BASIC CARDS
*101-250 ROOK.AU/23: 1X TO 2.5X PLAY.AU/199
MOST HAVE 2 CARDS OF EQUAL VALUE
122B Jameis Winston AU (white jsy) 400.00 600.00
128A Kevin White AU (white jsy) 10.00 25.00
131A Marcus Mariota AU (white jsy) 150.00 300.00
132A Melvin Gordon III AU (ball in left arm) 150.00 300.00
146A Todd Gurley AU (white jsy) 200.00 300.00
161 Bryce Petty AU 50.00 100.00

2015 Panini Contenders Draft Picks Game Day Tickets

1 Amari Cooper 1.25 3.00
2 Ameer Abdullah .60 1.50
3 Antwan Goodley .40 1.00
4 Austin Hill .40 1.00
5 Benardrick McKinney .40 1.00
6 Brett Hundley .40 1.00
7 Bryce Petty .40 1.00
8 Cameron Artis-Payne .40 1.00
9 Clive Walford .40 1.00
10 Connor Halliday .60 1.50
11 Danny Shelton .40 1.00
12 Dante Fowler Jr. .60 1.50
13 David Cobb .40 1.00
14 DeVante Parker .60 1.50
15 Devin Funchess .60 1.50
16 Chris Conley .40 1.00
17 Dres Anderson .40 1.00
18 Duke Johnson .60 1.50
19 Eddie Goldman .40 1.00
20 Garrett Grayson .40 1.00
21 Jaelen Strong .50 1.25
22 Jameis Winston 1.00 2.50
23 Buck Allen .50 1.25
24 Jay Ajayi .60 1.50
25 Jeremy Langford .40 1.00
26 Josh Harper .40 1.00
27 Justin Hardy .40 1.00
28 Kevin White .50 1.25
29 Landon Collins .50 1.25
30 Leonard Williams .40 1.00
31 Marcus Mariota 1.50 4.00
32 Melvin Gordon III 1.00 2.50
33 Mike Davis .40 1.00
34 Nelson Agholor .50 1.25
35 Nick O'Leary .40 1.00
36 Randy Gregory .40 1.00
37 Rashad Greene .40 1.00
38 Sammie Coates .50 1.25
39 Shane Carden .40 1.00
40 Shane Ray .40 1.00
41 Shaq Thompson .50 1.25
42 Taylor Kelly .50 1.25
43 Stefon Diggs 1.00 2.50
44 T.J. Yeldon .40 1.00
45 Tevin Coleman .50 1.25
46 Todd Gurley 1.50 4.00
47 Trae Waynes .40 1.00
48 Ty Montgomery .40 1.00
49 Tyler Lockett .60 1.50
50 Vic Beasley .50 1.25
51 Nick Marshall .60 1.50
52 Hutson Mason .40 1.00
53 Bud Dupree .50 1.25
54 Gary Nova .40 1.00
55 Blake Sims .40 1.00
56 Bo Wallace .40 1.00
57 Taylor Heinicke .60 1.50
58 Malcolm Agnew .40 1.00
59 Breshad Perriman .40 1.00
60 Corey Grant .60 1.50
61 Cody Fajardo .50 1.25
62 Michael Dyer .60 1.50
63 David Johnson 1.00 2.50
64 Deontay Greenberry .40 1.00
65 Devante Davis .50 1.25
67 Dezmin Lewis .40 1.00
68 Dominique Brown .40 1.00
69 E.J. Bibbs .50 1.25
70 Dreamius Smith 1.00 2.50
71 Mario Alford .40 1.00
72 Jahwan Edwards .50 1.25
73 Jake Waters .50 1.25
74 Jamison Crowder .50 1.25
76 Jesse James .50 1.25
77 Jordan Taylor .50 1.25
78 Josh Robinson .40 1.00
79 Karlos Williams .40 1.00
80 Kenny Bell .60 1.50
81 Kevin Parks .40 1.00
82 Levi Norwood .40 1.00
83 Malcolm Brown .50 1.25
84 Malcom Brown .40 1.00
85 Marcus Murphy .40 1.00
86 Matt Jones .40 1.00
87 Maxx Williams .40 1.00
88 MyCole Pruitt .40 1.00
89 Nick Boyle .40 1.00
90 Phillip Dorsett .40 1.00
91 Rannell Hall .40 1.00
92 Sean Mannion .40 1.00
93 Arik Armstead .40 1.00
94 Terrence Magee .60 1.50
95 Titus Davis .50 1.25
96 Tony Lippett .40 1.00
97 J.J. Nelson .40 1.00
98 Tyler Kroft .50 1.25
99 Vince Mayle .50 1.25
100 Casey Pierce .40 1.00

2015 Panini Contenders Draft Picks Alumni Ink

ANNC'D PRINT RUN 250 OR LESS
SP ANNC'D PRINT RUN 50 OR LESS
1 Alex Smith SP 20.00 50.00
2 Allen Hurns 6.00 15.00
3 Andrew Luck SP 150.00 250.00
4 Andy Dalton SP 20.00 50.00
5 Anquan Boldin SP 8.00 20.00
6 Arian Foster SP 10.00 25.00
7 Blake Bortles SP 8.00 20.00
8 Brandin Cooks SP 20.00 40.00
9 Brandon LaFell SP 8.00 20.00
10 Carson Palmer SP 20.00 50.00
11 C.J. Anderson 8.00 20.00
12 C.J. Spiller SP 30.00 60.00
13 Charles Clay SP 8.00 20.00
14 Coby Fleener SP 15.00 30.00
15 Danny Amendola SP 10.00 25.00
16 Darren Sproles SP 10.00 25.00
17 DeAndre Hopkins SP 25.00 50.00
18 Demaryius Thomas SP 10.00 25.00
19 Derek Carr SP 30.00 60.00
20 DeSean Jackson SP 10.00 25.00
21 Drew Brees SP 125.00 250.00
22 Earl Thomas SP 10.00 25.00
23 EJ Manuel SP 8.00 20.00
24 Eli Manning SP 50.00 100.00
25 Eric Decker SP 8.00 20.00
26 Frank Gore SP 10.00 25.00
27 Giovani Bernard SP 8.00 20.00
28 J.J. Watt SP 200.00 300.00
29 Jamaal Charles SP 10.00 25.00
30 Jason Witten SP 20.00 40.00
31 Jeremy Kerley 6.00 15.00
32 Joe Flacco SP 25.00 50.00
33 Jordan Matthews SP
34 Josh Gordon SP
35 Julius Thomas SP 8.00 20.00
36 Justin Forsett 8.00 20.00
37 Justin Houston 6.00 15.00
38 LeGarrette Blount SP
39 LeSean McCoy SP 12.00 30.00
40 Luke Kuechly SP 20.00 50.00
41 Marshawn Lynch SP 30.00 80.00
42 Matt Ryan SP 20.00 40.00
43 Matthew Stafford SP
44 Odell Beckham Jr. SP 40.00 80.00
45 Patrick Peterson SP 20.00 40.00
46 Paul Posluszny SP 8.00 20.00
47 Peyton Manning SP 250.00 350.00
48 Randall Cobb SP 10.00 25.00
49 Reggie Wayne SP 12.00 30.00
50 Richard Sherman SP 60.00 100.00
51 Rob Gronkowski SP 30.00 60.00
52 Russell Wilson SP
53 Sean Lee SP 10.00 25.00
54 Tom Brady SP 250.00 350.00
55 Steve Smith SP 10.00 25.00
56 Tony Romo SP 50.00 100.00
57 Teddy Bridgewater SP 25.00 50.00
58 Terrance Williams SP 8.00 20.00
59 Vincent Jackson SP 8.00 20.00
60 Wes Welker SP 25.00 50.00

2015 Panini Contenders Draft Picks Class Reunion

1 J.Manziel/M.Evans .60 1.50
2 O.Beckham Jr./Z.Mettenberger .75 2.00
3 D.Adams/D.Carr .75 2.00
4 Z.Mettenberger/J.Landry .60 1.50
5 K.Wright/R.Griffin III .50 1.25
6 M.Ingram/A.Jeffery .60 1.50
7 C.Fleener/A.Luck 1.00 2.50
8 A.Ellington/D.Hopkins .60 1.50
9 C.Patterson/J.Hunter .50 1.25
10 M.Barkley/R.Woods .60 1.50
11 J.Jones/M.Ingram .75 2.00
12 A.Green/J.Houston .75 2.00
13 A.Dalton/J.Kerley .60 1.50
14 J.Cotchery/P.Rivers .75 2.00
15 T.Polamalu/C.Palmer .75 2.00
16 R.Wayne/S.Moss .60 1.50
17 A.Cooper/T.Yeldon 1.00 2.50
18 J.Strong/T.Kelly .40 1.00
19 N.Marshall/S.Coates .50 1.25
20 A.Goodley/B.Petty .30 .75
21 R.Greene/J.Winston .75 2.00
22 H.Mason/T.Gurley 1.25 3.00
23 B.Hundley/E.Kendricks .30 .75
24 I.Ekpre-Olomu/M.Mariota 1.25 3.00

2015 Panini Contenders Draft Picks Collegiate Connections

1 N.Foles/R.Gronkowski .75 2.00
2 P.Harvin/T.Tebow .60 1.50
3 M.Stafford/A.Green .75 2.00
4 A.Luck/C.Fleener 1.00 2.50
5 A.Dalton/J.Kerley .60 1.50
6 J.Cameron/M.Barkley .50 1.25
7 A.Rodgers/M.Lynch 1.50 4.00
8 A.McCarron/A.Cooper 1.00 2.50
9 B.Cooks/S.Mannion .60 1.50
10 D.Parker/T.Bridgewater .50 1.25
11 B.Petty/A.Goodley .30 .75
12 J.Forsett/M.Lynch .60 1.50
13 C.Woodson/T.Brady 1.25 3.00
14 A.Luck/R.Sherman 1.00 2.50
15 A.Green/J.Houston .75 2.00
16 D.Sproles/J.Nelson .60 1.50
17 J.Charles/E.Thomas .60 1.50
18 R.Tannehill/V.Miller .60 1.50
19 D.Amendola/W.Welker .60 1.50
20 S.Smith/A.Smith .60 1.50
21 M.Evans/J.Manziel .60 1.50
22 Z.Mettenberger/O.Beckham Jr. .75 2.00
23 J.Winston/K.Benjamin .75 2.00
24 D.Carr/D.Adams .75 2.00
25 R.Wilson/J.Watt 1.00 2.50

2015 Panini Contenders Draft Picks Collegiate Connections Autographs

1 N.Foles/R.Gronkowski
2 A.Green/M.Stafford 40.00 80.00
3 A.Luck/C.Fleener
4 A.Dalton/J.Kerley
5 M.Barkley/J.Cameron
6 M.Lynch/A.Rodgers 250.00 350.00
7 A.McCarron/A.Cooper 60.00 120.00
8 T.Bridgewater/D.Parker
9 J.Forsett/M.Lynch 25.00 50.00
10 C.Woodson/T.Brady
11 A.Luck/R.Sherman
12 D.Sproles/J.Nelson
13 W.Welker/D.Amendola 30.00 60.00
14 Z.Mettenberger/O.Beckham Jr. 100.00 200.00
15 R.Wilson/J.Watt

2015 Panini Contenders Draft Picks Old School Colors

1 A.J. Green .75 2.00
2 Aaron Rodgers 1.50 4.00
3 Andrew Luck 1.00 2.50
4 Andy Dalton .60 1.50
5 Anquan Boldin .50 1.25
6 Arian Foster .60 1.50
7 Carson Palmer .60 1.50
8 C.J. Anderson .60 1.50
9 Calvin Johnson .75 2.00
10 Cam Newton .75 2.00
11 Charles Woodson .75 2.00
12 Clay Matthews .75 2.00
13 Colin Kaepernick .60 1.50
14 DeMarco Murray .60 1.50
15 Demaryius Thomas .60 1.50
16 DeSean Jackson .60 1.50
17 Dez Bryant .75 2.00
18 Drew Brees .75 2.00
19 Eddie Lacy .50 1.25
20 Eli Manning .60 1.50
21 Frank Gore .60 1.50
22 J.J. Watt .75 2.00
23 Jamaal Charles .60 1.50
24 Jason Witten .60 1.50
25 Jimmy Graham .75 2.00
26 Joe Flacco .60 1.50
27 Johnny Manziel .60 1.50
28 Jordy Nelson .60 1.50
29 Julio Jones .75 2.00
30 Julius Peppers .60 1.50
31 Justin Forsett .60 1.50
32 Larry Fitzgerald .60 1.50
33 LeGarrette Blount .60 1.50
34 LeSean McCoy .75 2.00
35 Le'Veon Bell .60 1.50
36 Marshawn Lynch .60 1.50
37 Matt Forte .50 1.25
38 Matt Ryan .60 1.50
39 Matthew Stafford .60 1.50
40 Nick Foles .60 1.50
41 Odell Beckham Jr. .75 2.00
42 Peyton Manning 1.50 4.00
43 Philip Rivers .75 2.00
44 Richard Sherman .75 2.00
45 Rob Gronkowski .75 2.00
46 Russell Wilson 1.00 2.50
47 Tom Brady 2.00 5.00
48 Tony Romo .60 1.50
49 Troy Polamalu .75 2.00
50 Wes Welker .60 1.50

2015 Panini Contenders Draft Picks Old School Colors Autographs

ANNC'D PRINT RUN 50 OR LESS
1 Aaron Rodgers 150.00 250.00
2 Andrew Luck 150.00 250.00
3 Anquan Boldin
4 Arian Foster 10.00 25.00
5 Charles Woodson
6 Drew Brees 50.00 100.00
7 Eli Manning
8 Frank Gore 10.00 25.00
9 Jamaal Charles 10.00 25.00
10 Jason Witten 30.00 60.00
11 J.J. Watt
12 Joe Flacco 10.00 25.00
13 LeGarrette Blount
14 LeSean McCoy 12.00 30.00
15 Marshawn Lynch 10.00 25.00
16 Matt Ryan 20.00 40.00
17 Matthew Stafford
18 Odell Beckham Jr. 30.00 60.00
19 Peyton Manning
20 Richard Sherman 40.00 80.00
21 Rob Gronkowski 12.00 30.00
22 Russell Wilson
23 Tom Brady 250.00 350.00
24 Tony Romo 40.00 80.00
25 Wes Welker 20.00 40.00

2015 Panini Contenders Draft Picks Passing Grades

1 Marcus Mariota 2.00 5.00
2 Jameis Winston 1.25 3.00
3 Brett Hundley .50 1.25
4 Bryce Petty .50 1.25
5 Shane Carden .50 1.25
6 Cody Fajardo .60 1.50
7 Sean Mannion .50 1.25
8 Bo Wallace .50 1.25
9 Blake Sims .50 1.25
10 Jake Waters .60 1.50
11 Garrett Grayson .50 1.25
12 Taylor Heinicke .75 2.00
13 Taylor Kelly .60 1.50
14 Connor Halliday .75 2.00
15 Nick Marshall .75 2.00
16 Hutson Mason .50 1.25
17 Gary Nova .50 1.25
18 Blake Bortles .60 1.50
19 Derek Carr 1.00 2.50
20 Teddy Bridgewater .75 2.00
21 Johnny Manziel .75 2.00
22 Jimmy Garoppolo 1.25 3.00
23 Zach Mettenberger .60 1.50
24 Andrew Luck 1.25 3.00
25 Russell Wilson 1.25 3.00

2015 Panini Contenders Draft Picks Passing Grades Autographs

ANNC'D PRINT RUN 50 OR LESS
1 Marcus Mariota 40.00 80.00
2 Jameis Winston 75.00 150.00
3 Brett Hundley 5.00 12.00
4 Bryce Petty 5.00 12.00
5 Shane Carden 5.00 12.00
6 Cody Fajardo 6.00 15.00
7 Sean Mannion 5.00 12.00
8 Bo Wallace 15.00 40.00
9 Blake Sims 5.00 12.00
10 Jake Waters 6.00 15.00

2015 Panini Contenders Draft Picks Rush Week

1 Melvin Gordon III 1.00 2.50
2 Todd Gurley 1.50 4.00
3 Ameer Abdullah .60 1.50
4 Tevin Coleman .50 1.25
5 Duke Johnson .60 1.50
6 Jay Ajayi .60 1.50
7 T.J. Yeldon .40 1.00
8 Mike Davis .40 1.00
9 Buck Allen .50 1.25
10 Cameron Artis-Payne .40 1.00
11 David Cobb .40 1.00
12 Jeremy Langford .40 1.00
13 Matt Jones .40 1.00
14 Malcolm Brown .50 1.25
15 Karlos Williams .40 1.00
16 David Johnson 1.00 2.50
17 Josh Robinson .40 1.00
18 Dominique Brown .40 1.00
19 Marcus Murphy .40 1.00
20 Jahwan Edwards .50 1.25
21 Terrence Magee .60 1.50
22 Malcolm Agnew .40 1.00
23 Corey Grant .60 1.50
24 Michael Dyer .60 1.50
25 Dreamius Smith 1.00 2.50

2015 Panini Contenders Draft Picks Rush Week Autographs

ANNC'D PRINT RUN 50 OR LESS
1 Melvin Gordon III 40.00 80.00
2 Todd Gurley 30.00 60.00
3 Ameer Abdullah 30.00 60.00
4 Tevin Coleman 6.00 15.00
5 Duke Johnson 8.00 20.00
6 Jay Ajayi 8.00 20.00
7 T.J. Yeldon 5.00 12.00
8 Mike Davis
9 Buck Allen
10 Cameron Artis-Payne 10.00 25.00
11 David Cobb 5.00 12.00
12 Jeremy Langford
13 Matt Jones 20.00 40.00
14 Malcolm Brown
15 Karlos Williams 5.00 12.00

2015 Panini Contenders Draft Picks School Colors

1 Marcus Mariota 1.25 3.00
2 Jameis Winston .75 2.00
3 Brett Hundley .30 .75
4 Bryce Petty .30 .75
5 Shane Carden .30 .75
6 Cody Fajardo .40 1.00
7 Sean Mannion .30 .75
8 Bo Wallace .30 .75
9 Blake Sims .30 .75
10 Jake Waters .40 1.00
11 Melvin Gordon III .75 2.00
12 Todd Gurley 1.25 3.00
13 Ameer Abdullah .50 1.25
14 Tevin Coleman .40 1.00
15 Duke Johnson .50 1.25
16 Jay Ajayi .50 1.25
17 T.J. Yeldon .30 .75
18 Mike Davis .30 .75
19 Buck Allen .40 1.00
20 Cameron Artis-Payne .30 .75
21 David Cobb .30 .75
22 Jeremy Langford .30 .75
23 Matt Jones .30 .75
24 Malcolm Brown .40 1.00
25 Karlos Williams .30 .75
26 Amari Cooper 1.00 2.50
27 DeVante Parker .50 1.25
28 Kevin White .40 1.00
29 Chris Conley .30 .75
30 Jaelen Strong .40 1.00
31 Devin Funchess .50 1.25
32 Sammie Coates .40 1.00
33 Ty Montgomery .30 .75
34 Josh Harper .30 .75
35 Nelson Agholor .40 1.00
36 Justin Hardy .30 .75
37 Rashad Greene .30 .75
38 Tyler Lockett .50 1.25
39 Tony Lippett .30 .75
40 Vince Mayle .40 1.00
41 Dres Anderson .30 .75
42 Phillip Dorsett .30 .75
43 Austin Hill .30 .75
45 Stefon Diggs .75 2.00
46 Trae Waynes .30 .75
47 Randy Gregory .30 .75
48 Vic Beasley .40 1.00
49 Garrett Grayson .30 .75
50 Breshad Perriman .30 .75

2015 Panini Contenders Draft Picks School Colors Autographs

ANNC'D PRINT RUN 50 OR LESS
1 Marcus Mariota 40.00 80.00
2 Jameis Winston 90.00 150.00
3 Brett Hundley 5.00 12.00
4 Bryce Petty 5.00 12.00
5 Shane Carden 5.00 12.00
6 Cody Fajardo 6.00 15.00
7 Sean Mannion 5.00 12.00
8 Bo Wallace 15.00 40.00
9 Blake Sims 5.00 12.00
10 Jake Waters 6.00 15.00
11 Melvin Gordon III 30.00 80.00
12 Todd Gurley 30.00 60.00
13 Ameer Abdullah 30.00 60.00
14 Tevin Coleman 6.00 15.00
15 Duke Johnson 8.00 20.00
16 Jay Ajayi 8.00 20.00
17 T.J. Yeldon 5.00 12.00
18 Mike Davis 5.00 12.00
19 Buck Allen 6.00 15.00
20 Cameron Artis-Payne 5.00 12.00
21 David Cobb 5.00 12.00
22 Jeremy Langford 5.00 12.00
23 Matt Jones 5.00 12.00
24 Malcolm Brown 6.00 15.00
25 Karlos Williams 5.00 12.00
26 Amari Cooper 40.00 80.00
27 DeVante Parker 8.00 20.00
28 Kevin White 6.00 15.00
29 Chris Conley 5.00 12.00
31 Devin Funchess 8.00 20.00
32 Sammie Coates 6.00 15.00
33 Ty Montgomery 5.00 12.00
34 Josh Harper 5.00 12.00
35 Nelson Agholor 6.00 15.00
36 Justin Hardy 5.00 12.00
37 Rashad Greene 5.00 12.00
38 Tyler Lockett 8.00 20.00
39 Tony Lippett 5.00 12.00
40 Vince Mayle 6.00 15.00
41 Dres Anderson 5.00 12.00
42 Phillip Dorsett 5.00 12.00
43 Austin Hill 5.00 12.00
45 Stefon Diggs 20.00 50.00
46 Trae Waynes 5.00 12.00
47 Randy Gregory 10.00 25.00
48 Vic Beasley 6.00 15.00
50 Breshad Perriman 5.00 12.00

2016 Panini Contenders Draft Picks

SP1 ANNC'D PRINT RUN 200 OR LESS
SP2 ANNC'D PRINT RUN 50 OR LESS
1 A.J. Green .30 .75
2 Aaron Rodgers .60 1.50
3 Adrian Peterson .30 .75
4 Alex Smith .25 .60
5 Allen Hurns .20 .50
6 Allen Robinson .25 .60
7 Amari Cooper .30 .75
8 Andrew Luck .40 1.00
9 Andy Dalton .25 .60
10 Antonio Brown .30 .75
11 Arian Foster .25 .60
12 Ben Roethlisberger .30 .75
13 Blake Bortles .20 .50
14 Brandon Marshall .20 .50
15 C.J. Anderson .25 .60
16 Calvin Johnson .30 .75
17 Cam Newton .30 .75
18 Cameron Wake .20 .50
19 Carlos Hyde .20 .50
20 Carson Palmer .25 .60
21 Charles Woodson .30 .75
22 Chris Johnson .20 .50
23 Clay Matthews .30 .75
24 Darrelle Revis .20 .50
25 Darren Sproles .25 .60
26 DeAndre Hopkins .25 .60
27 DeMarco Murray .25 .60
28 Demaryius Thomas .25 .60
29 Derek Carr .30 .75
30 DeSean Jackson .25 .60
31 Devonta Freeman .25 .60
32 Dez Bryant .30 .75
33 Doug Martin .25 .60
34 Drew Brees .30 .75
35 Earl Thomas .25 .60
36 Eddie Lacy .20 .50
37 Eli Manning .25 .60
38 Elvis Dumervil .20 .50
39 Emmanuel Sanders .30 .75
40 Frank Gore .25 .60
41 Giovani Bernard .20 .50
42 Greg Olsen .25 .60
43 J.J. Watt .30 .75
44 Jamaal Charles .25 .60
45 Jameis Winston .30 .75
46 James Jones .20 .50
47 Jason Witten .25 .60
48 Jeremy Hill .20 .50
49 Jeremy Maclin .20 .50
50 Jimmy Graham .30 .75
51 Joe Flacco .25 .60
52 Joe Haden .20 .50
53 Jordy Nelson .25 .60
54 Julian Edelman .30 .75
55 Julio Jones .30 .75
56 Julius Thomas .20 .50
57 Justin Forsett .25 .60
58 Justin Houston .20 .50
59 Kam Chancellor .30 .75
60 Keenan Allen .25 .60
61 Khalil Mack .30 .75
62 Kirk Cousins .30 .75
63 Larry Fitzgerald .25 .60
64 Latavius Murray .20 .50
65 LeSean McCoy .30 .75
66 Le'Veon Bell .25 .60
67 Luke Kuechly .25 .60
68 Marcus Mariota .30 .75
69 Mario Williams .20 .50
70 Mark Ingram .25 .60
71 Marshawn Lynch .25 .60
72 Matt Forte .20 .50
73 Matt Ryan .25 .60
74 Matthew Stafford .25 .60
75 Melvin Gordon .25 .60
76 Mike Evans .25 .60
77 Ndamukong Suh .25 .60
78 Nick Foles .25 .60
79 Odell Beckham Jr. .30 .75
80 Patrick Peterson .20 .50
81 Peyton Manning .60 1.50
82 Philip Rivers .30 .75
83 Randall Cobb .25 .60
84 Richard Sherman .30 .75
85 Rob Gronkowski .30 .75
86 Stefon Diggs .25 .60
87 Russell Wilson .40 1.00
88 Ryan Tannehill .25 .60
89 Sam Bradford .20 .50
90 Steve Smith .25 .60
91 Teddy Bridgewater .25 .60
92 Thomas Rawls .20 .50
93 T.J. Yeldon .20 .50
94 Todd Gurley .30 .75
95 Tom Brady .75 2.00
96 Tony Romo .25 .60
97 Travis Benjamin .20 .50
98 Tyrod Taylor .25 .60
99 Von Miller .25 .60
100 Willie Snead .25 .60
101A Joey Bosa AU RC 40.00 80.00
101B Joey Bosa AU SP 75.00 150.00
102A Jared Goff AU RC 75.00 150.00
103A Connor Cook AU RC 20.00 40.00
103B Connor Cook AU SP
104A Laquon Treadwell AU RC 30.00 60.00
104B Laquon Treadwell AU SP 25.00 50.00
105A Ezekiel Elliott AU RC 200.00 300.00
105B Ezekiel Elliott AU SP 200.00 400.00
106A Michael Thomas AU RC 12.00 30.00
106B Michael Thomas AU SP 40.00 80.00
107A Josh Doctson AU RC 15.00 40.00
107B Josh Doctson AU SP 40.00 80.00
108A Derrick Henry AU RC 50.00 100.00
108B Derrick Henry AU SP 75.00 150.00
109A Cardale Jones AU RC 25.00 50.00
109B Cardale Jones AU SP 40.00 80.00
111A Corey Coleman AU RC 15.00 30.00
111B Corey Coleman AU SP
113A Hunter Henry AU RC 8.00 20.00
113B Hunter Henry AU SP 25.00 50.00
114A Demarcus Robinson AU RC 2.00 5.00
114B Demarcus Robinson AU SP 10.00 25.00
115A Alex Collins AU RC 8.00 20.00
115B Alex Collins AU SP 10.00 25.00
117A Paul Perkins AU RC 6.00 15.00
117B Paul Perkins AU SP 12.00 30.00
119A Rashard Higgins AU RC 2.00 5.00
119B Rashard Higgins AU SP 4.00 10.00
120A Pharoh Cooper AU RC 6.00 15.00
120B Pharoh Cooper AU SP 20.00 40.00
122A Devontae Booker AU RC 2.50 6.00
122B Devontae Booker AU SP
123A De'Runnya Wilson AU RC 2.00 5.00
123B De'Runnya Wilson AU SP
124A Jordan Williams AU RC 2.00 5.00
124B Jordan Williams AU SP
125A Dak Prescott AU RC 40.00 80.00
125B Dak Prescott AU SP 75.00 150.00
126A Aaron Green AU RC 2.00 5.00
126B Aaron Green AU SP 10.00 25.00
127A Carson Wentz AU RC 125.00 200.00
127B Carson Wentz AU SP 200.00 400.00
128A Nick Vannett AU RC 8.00 20.00
128B Nick Vannett AU SP 10.00 25.00
130A Leonte Carroo AU RC 4.00 10.00
130B Leonte Carroo AU SP 10.00 25.00
131A Tre Madden AU RC 2.00 5.00
131B Tre Madden AU SP 4.00 10.00
133A Brandon Doughty AU RC 2.00 5.00
133B Brandon Doughty AU SP 8.00 20.00
135A Nelson Spruce AU RC 2.00 5.00
135B Nelson Spruce AU SP 4.00 10.00
136A Kenneth Dixon AU RC 2.00 5.00
136B Kenneth Dixon AU SP 4.00 10.00
137A Kenyan Drake AU RC 8.00 20.00
137B Kenyan Drake AU SP 25.00 50.00
138A Braxton Miller AU RC 25.00 50.00
138B Braxton Miller AU SP
139A Josh Ferguson AU RC 2.00 5.00
139B Josh Ferguson AU SP 4.00 10.00
140A Cody Kessler AU RC 2.00 5.00
140B Cody Kessler AU SP
141A Devon Cajuste AU RC 2.00 5.00
141B Devon Cajuste AU SP 4.00 10.00
142A Devon Johnson AU RC 2.50 6.00
142B Devon Johnson AU SP 5.00 12.00
143A D.J. Foster AU RC 2.50 6.00
143B D.J. Foster AU SP 5.00 12.00
144A Austin Hooper AU RC 2.00 5.00
144B Austin Hooper AU SP
145A Sterling Shepard AU RC 12.00 30.00
145B Sterling Shepard AU SP 25.00 50.00

146A Mekale McKay AU RC 2.00 5.00
146B Mekale McKay AU SP
149A Paxton Lynch AU RC 75.00 125.00
149B Paxton Lynch AU SP 125.00 250.00
151 Kyle Carter AU RC 2.00 5.00
152 Bryce Williams AU RC 2.50 6.00
153 Ryan Malleck AU RC 3.00 8.00
155 Jerell Adams AU RC 2.00 5.00
156 Byron Marshall AU RC 2.00 5.00
158 Jordan Payton AU RC 2.00 5.00
160 Jonathan Williams AU RC 2.50 6.00
161 Storm Barrs-Woods AU RC 2.00 5.00
163 Kolby Listenbee AU RC 2.00 5.00
164 Cayleb Jones AU RC 2.00 5.00
167 Vernon Hargreaves III AU RC 3.00 8.00
169 DeForest Buckner AU RC 2.00 5.00
170 Kenny Clark AU RC 2.00 5.00
172 Myles Jack AU RC 8.00 20.00
173 Reggie Ragland AU RC 6.00 15.00
175 A'Shawn Robinson AU RC 2.00 5.00
176 Su'a Cravens AU RC 2.00 5.00
177 Emmanuel Ogbah AU RC 2.50 6.00
178 Darron Lee AU RC 10.00 25.00
179 Shilique Calhoun AU RC 2.00 5.00
180 Kendall Fuller AU RC 2.50 6.00
181 Adolphus Washington AU RC 2.00 5.00
183 Vonn Bell AU RC 10.00 20.00
184 Jordan Jenkins AU RC 3.00 8.00
185 Jaydon Mickens AU RC 2.00 5.00
187 Daniel Lasco AU RC 2.00 5.00
188 Daniel Braverman AU RC 2.00 5.00
189 Hunter Sharp AU RC 2.50 6.00
190 Mike Bercovici AU RC 2.00 5.00
191 Brandon Allen AU RC 6.00 15.00
192 Trevone Boykin AU RC 2.00 5.00
194 Tra Carson AU RC 2.00 5.00
195 Malcolm Mitchell AU RC 2.00 5.00
196 Steven Scheu AU RC 2.00 5.00
197 Dan Vitale AU RC 2.00 5.00
199 Jake McGee AU RC 2.50 6.00
200 Jason Spriggs AU RC 2.00 5.00
202 Shaq Lawson AU RC 2.00 5.00
203 Jeremy Cash AU RC 2.50 6.00
204 Jonathan Bullard AU RC 2.00 5.00
206 Darian Thompson AU RC 2.00 5.00
208 Joshua Perry AU RC 2.00 5.00
210 Zack Sanchez AU RC 3.00 8.00
212 Dadi Lhomme Nicolas AU RC 2.50 6.00
214 Jalen Mills AU RC 2.50 6.00
215 Will Redmond AU RC 3.00 8.00
216 Dominique Alexander AU RC 2.00 5.00
217 Adam Gotsis AU RC 2.00 5.00
218 Kevon Seymour AU RC 2.00 5.00
219 Briean Boddy-Calhoun AU RC 2.00 5.00
220 Kentrell Brothers AU RC 2.00 5.00
221 DeAndre Washington AU RC 2.00 5.00
223 Jalin Marshall AU RC 3.00 8.00
224 Maurice Canady AU RC 2.00 5.00
226 Victor Ochi AU RC 2.50 6.00
228 Eric Striker AU RC 2.50 6.00
229 Charles Tapper AU RC 2.50 6.00
232 Laremy Tunsil AU RC 2.00 5.00
233 Taylor Decker AU RC 2.50 6.00
235 Germain Ifedi AU RC 2.50 6.00
236 Jack Conklin AU RC 3.00 8.00
237 Anthony Zettel AU RC 2.50 6.00
238 Chris Jones AU RC 2.00 5.00
239 Roberto Aguayo AU RC 2.00 5.00
240 Jarran Reed AU RC 2.00 5.00
242 Glenn Gronkowski AU RC 2.00 5.00
245 Eric Murray AU RC 2.00 5.00
246 Kyler Fackrell AU RC 2.50 6.00
247 Blake Martinez AU RC 2.50 6.00
248 Karl Joseph AU RC 2.00 5.00
250 Kelvin Taylor AU RC 2.00 5.00
252 Cody Whitehair AU RC 3.00 8.00
253 Spencer Drango AU RC 2.00 5.00
254 Max Tuerk AU RC 2.00 5.00
255 Trent Matthews AU RC 2.00 5.00
256 Keenan Reynolds AU RC 2.50 6.00
258 Jack Allen AU RC 2.50 6.00
260 Cyrus Jones AU RC 2.00 5.00
261 Luther Maddy AU RC 2.00 5.00
263 Jordan Lomax AU RC 3.00 8.00
265 Jared Norris AU RC 2.00 5.00
266 Jordan Howard AU RC 12.00 30.00
267 Scooby Wright III AU RC 2.00 5.00
268 Nate Sudfeld AU RC 2.00 5.00
273 Quinshad Davis AU RC 3.00 8.00
277 Taveze Calhoun AU RC 2.00 5.00
279 Terrance Smith AU RC 3.00 8.00
280 Nile Lawrence-Stample AU RC 2.50 6.00
284 Bronson Kaufusi AU RC 2.00 5.00
285 Ken Crawley AU RC 2.50 6.00
286 Kenny Lawler AU RC 3.00 8.00
288 D.J. White AU RC 2.00 5.00
290 Carl Nassib AU RC 2.00 5.00
293 Austin Johnson AU RC 2.00 5.00
296 Jordan Canzeri AU RC 3.00 8.00
297 De'Vondre Campbell AU RC 2.50 6.00
298 Jason Fanaika AU RC 2.00 5.00
299 Marquise Williams AU RC 2.00 5.00
300 DeAndre Houston-Carson AU RC 2.00 5.00
302 Noah Spence AU RC 2.00 5.00
305 Sean Davis AU RC 2.00 5.00
307 Antonio Morrison AU RC 2.50 6.00
308 Deion Jones AU RC 2.00 5.00
310 Derek Watt AU RC 3.00 8.00
312 Mackensie Alexander AU RC 2.00 5.00
314 Dom Williams AU RC 2.00 5.00
317 Keith Marshall AU RC 4.00 10.00
323 Vernon Adams Jr. AU RC 3.00 8.00
325 Demarcus Ayers AU RC 2.00 5.00
331 Eli Apple AU RC 2.50 6.00
339 Maliek Collins AU RC 2.00 5.00
341 Marteze Waller AU RC 3.00 8.00
345 Jeff Driskel AU RC 4.00 10.00
346 Keyarris Garrett AU RC 2.00 5.00
347 Aaron Burbridge AU RC 2.00 5.00
348 Tyler Higbee AU RC 2.00 5.00

2016 Panini Contenders Draft Picks Bowl Ticket

*1-100 VETS/99: 4X TO 10X BASIC CARDS
*101-250 ROOK/99: .8X TO 2X BASIC AU
101A Joey Bosa AU 40.00 80.00
127A Carson Wentz AU 150.00 300.00
149A Paxton Lynch AU 4.00 10.00

2016 Panini Contenders Draft Picks Alumni Ink

ANNC'D PRINT RUN 50 OR LESS
CARD #50 ANNC'D PRINT RUN 200 OR LESS
1 A.J. Green 20.00 40.00
2 Alex Smith 20.00 40.00
3 Ameer Abdullah 8.00 20.00
4 Andy Dalton
5 Anquan Boldin 8.00 20.00
6 Antonio Brown 40.00 80.00
7 Arian Foster
8 Barry Sanders 90.00 150.00
9 Ben Roethlisberger 100.00 200.00
10 Blake Bortles
11 Bo Jackson
12 Brett Favre 150.00 250.00
13 C.J. Anderson
14 Carson Palmer 10.00 25.00
15 Charles Woodson
16 Clay Matthews 20.00 40.00
17 Dan Marino 125.00 250.00
18 Darrelle Revis
19 Darren Sproles
20 DeAndre Hopkins
21 Deion Sanders 75.00 150.00
22 Demaryius Thomas 10.00 25.00
23 DeSean Jackson
24 Dion Lewis
25 Doug Martin
26 Drew Brees
27 Earl Campbell
28 Eddie Lacy 40.00 80.00
29 Eli Manning
30 Emmitt Smith 90.00 150.00
31 Eric Dickerson
32 Fran Tarkenton
33 Frank Gore 10.00 25.00
34 Fred Biletnikoff 12.00 30.00
35 Gale Sayers
36 Giovani Bernard
37 Jamaal Charles 10.00 25.00
38 Jameis Winston 100.00 200.00
39 Jason Witten 50.00 100.00
40 Jeremy Maclin 8.00 20.00
41 Jerry Rice 75.00 125.00
42 Jim Kelly 25.00 50.00
43 Jim Plunkett
44 Joe Namath 150.00 250.00
45 John Elway
46 Johnny Manziel
47 Jordy Nelson 25.00 50.00
48 Kellen Winslow 10.00 25.00
49 LaDainian Tomlinson 50.00 100.00
50 Latavius Murray 6.00 15.00
51 Len Dawson
52 Marcus Allen 30.00 60.00
53 Marcus Mariota
54 Marshall Faulk 75.00 125.00
55 Matt Ryan 10.00 25.00
56 Matthew Stafford 10.00 25.00
57 Melvin Gordon 10.00 25.00
58 Michael Irvin
59 Peyton Manning
60 Philip Rivers 75.00 150.00
61 Randall Cobb 10.00 25.00
62 Richard Sherman 30.00 60.00
63 Rob Gronkowski
64 Robert Griffin III
65 Rod Woodson
66 Ronnie Lott
67 Russell Wilson 30.00 60.00
68 Ryan Tannehill
69 Sam Bradford
70 Steve Smith Sr. 40.00 80.00
71 Steve Young
72 T.J. Yeldon 8.00 20.00
73 Teddy Bridgewater
74 Tim Tebow
75 Todd Gurley II 40.00 80.00
76 Tom Brady
77 Tony Dorsett
78 Tony Romo
79 Troy Aikman 40.00 80.00
80 Wes Welker

2016 Panini Contenders Draft Picks Class Reunion

1 A.J. Green .75 2.00
2 Aaron Rodgers 1.50 4.00
3 Adrian Peterson .75 2.00
4 Amari Cooper .75 2.00
5 Andrew Luck 1.00 2.50
6 Andy Dalton .60 1.50
7 Calvin Johnson .75 2.00
8 DeAndre Hopkins .60 1.50
9 Devonta Freeman .60 1.50
10 Dez Bryant .75 2.00
11 J.J. Watt .75 2.00
12 Jameis Winston .75 2.00
13 Julio Jones .75 2.00
14 Le'Veon Bell .60 1.50
15 Marcus Mariota .75 2.00
16 Matt Ryan .60 1.50
17 Melvin Gordon .60 1.50
18 Odell Beckham Jr. .75 2.00
19 Peyton Manning 1.50 4.00
20 Philip Rivers .75 2.00
21 Richard Sherman .75 2.00
22 Rob Gronkowski .75 2.00
23 Russell Wilson 1.00 2.50
24 Todd Gurley II .75 2.00
25 Tom Brady 2.00 5.00

2016 Panini Contenders Draft Picks Collegiate Connections

1 A.Cooper/J.Jones .75 2.00
2 N.Foles/R.Gronkowski .75 2.00
3 B.Jackson/F.Thomas 1.00 2.50
4 S.Young/J.McMahon 1.00 2.50
5 A.Rodgers/M.Lynch 1.50 4.00
6 A.Brown/T.Rawls .75 2.00
7 E.Smith/T.Tebow 1.25 3.00
8 C.Johnson/D.Thomas .75 2.00
9 J.Hill/O.Beckham .75 2.00
10 G.Olsen/J.Graham .75 2.00
11 L.Bell/K.Cousins .75 2.00
12 C.Woodson/T.Brady 2.00 5.00
13 N.Suh/R.Gregory .60 1.50
14 A.Peterson/D.Murray .75 2.00
15 B.Sanders/T.Thomas 1.25 3.00
16 D.Marino/T.Dorsett 1.50 4.00
17 D.Brees/L.Dawson .75 2.00
18 J.Elway/J.Plunkett 1.25 3.00
19 R.Sherman/A.Luck 1.00 2.50
20 L.Tomlinson/A.Dalton .60 1.50
21 P.Manning/J.Witten 1.50 4.00
22 E.Campbell/R.Williams .75 2.00
23 M.Evans/J.Manziel .60 1.50
24 B.Marshall/B.Bortles .50 1.25
25 J.Watt/R.Wilson 1.00 2.50

2016 Panini Contenders Draft Picks Game Day Tickets

1 Joey Bosa .75 2.00
2 Jared Goff 2.50 6.00
3 Connor Cook .50 1.25
4 Laquon Treadwell .50 1.25
5 Ezekiel Elliott 2.00 5.00
6 Michael Thomas .75 2.00
7 Josh Doctson .50 1.25
8 Derrick Henry 1.00 2.50
9 Cardale Jones .40 1.00
10 Christian Hackenberg .40 1.00
11 Corey Coleman .60 1.50
12 Tyler Boyd .50 1.25
13 Hunter Henry .50 1.25
14 Demarcus Robinson .40 1.00
15 Alex Collins .50 1.25
16 Paxton Lynch .40 1.00
17 Paul Perkins .40 1.00
18 Jacoby Brissett .50 1.25
19 Rashard Higgins .40 1.00
20 Pharoh Cooper .40 1.00
21 Tyler Ervin .40 1.00
22 Devontae Booker .50 1.25
23 De'Runnya Wilson .40 1.00
24 Jordan Williams .40 1.00
25 Dak Prescott 2.00 5.00
26 Aaron Green .40 1.00
27 Carson Wentz 4.00 10.00
28 Nick Vannett .40 1.00
29 Mekale McKay .40 1.00
30 Leonte Carroo .40 1.00
31 Tre Madden .40 1.00
32 Sterling Shepard .50 1.25
33 Brandon Doughty .40 1.00
34 Braxton Addison .40 1.00
35 Nelson Spruce .40 1.00
36 Kenneth Dixon .40 1.00
37 Kenyan Drake .60 1.50
38 Braxton Miller .40 1.00
39 Josh Ferguson .40 1.00
40 Cody Kessler .40 1.00
41 Devon Cajuste .40 1.00
42 Devon Johnson .50 1.25
43 D.J. Foster .50 1.25

2016 Panini Contenders Draft Picks Old School Colors

1 A.J. Green .75 2.00
2 Aaron Rodgers 1.50 4.00
3 Adrian Peterson .75 2.00
4 Amari Cooper .75 2.00
5 Andrew Luck 1.00 2.50
6 Andy Dalton .60 1.50
7 Calvin Johnson .75 2.00
8 DeAndre Hopkins .60 1.50
9 Devonta Freeman .60 1.50
10 Dez Bryant .75 2.00
11 J.J. Watt .75 2.00
12 Jameis Winston .75 2.00
13 Julio Jones .75 2.00
14 Le'Veon Bell .60 1.50
15 Marcus Mariota .75 2.00
16 Matt Ryan .60 1.50
17 Melvin Gordon .60 1.50
18 Odell Beckham Jr. .75 2.00
19 Peyton Manning 1.50 4.00
20 Philip Rivers .75 2.00
21 Richard Sherman .75 2.00
22 Rob Gronkowski .75 2.00
23 Russell Wilson 1.00 2.50
24 Todd Gurley .75 2.00
25 Tom Brady 2.00 5.00

2016 Panini Contenders Draft Picks Old School Colors Autographs

ANNC'D PRINT RUN 50 OR LESS
CARD #18 ANNC'D PRINT RUN 200 OR LESS
1 Arian Foster
2 Ben Roethlisberger
3 Blake Bortles
4 Brett Favre
5 Carson Palmer
6 Charles Woodson
7 Deion Sanders
8 Drew Brees 25.00 50.00
9 Eddie Lacy
10 Eli Manning
11 Emmitt Smith 75.00 150.00
12 Frank Gore
13 Fred Biletnikoff 12.00 30.00
14 Giovani Bernard
15 Joe Namath
16 Jordy Nelson
17 Kellen Winslow
18 Latavius Murray 6.00 15.00
19 Marcus Allen 10.00 25.00
20 Matthew Stafford 10.00 25.00
21 Michael Irvin
22 Philip Rivers
23 Russell Wilson
24 Teddy Bridgewater
25 Wes Welker 10.00 25.00

2016 Panini Contenders Draft Picks Passing Grades

1 Jared Goff 2.00 5.00
2 Connor Cook .40 1.00
3 Cardale Jones .30 .75
4 Christian Hackenberg .30 .75
5 Jim Plunkett .60 1.50
6 Carson Palmer .60 1.50
7 Dak Prescott 1.50 4.00
8 Carson Wentz 3.00 8.00
9 Brandon Doughty .30 .75
10 Cody Kessler .30 .75
11 Nate Sudfeld .30 .75
12 Kevin Hogan .40 1.00
13 Jacoby Brissett .40 1.00
14 Mike Bercovici .30 .75
15 Trevone Boykin .30 .75
16 Cam Newton .75 2.00
17 Brandon Allen .30 .75
18 Paxton Lynch .30 .75
19 Sam Bradford .50 1.25
20 Tim Tebow .50 1.25

2016 Panini Contenders Draft Picks Passing Grades Autographs

1 Jared Goff 40.00 100.00
2 Connor Cook 8.00 20.00
3 Cardale Jones 6.00 15.00
6 Carson Wentz 100.00 200.00
7 Dak Prescott 150.00 250.00
8 Paxton Lynch 6.00 15.00
9 Brandon Doughty 6.00 15.00
10 Cody Kessler 6.00 15.00

2016 Panini Contenders Draft Picks Rush Week

1 Ezekiel Elliott 2.00 5.00
2 Derrick Henry 1.00 2.50
3 Paul Perkins .40 1.00
4 Devontae Booker .50 1.25
5 Aaron Green .40 1.00
6 Tre Madden .40 1.00
7 Kenneth Dixon .40 1.00
8 Kenyan Drake .60 1.50
9 Josh Ferguson .40 1.00
10 Devon Johnson .50 1.25
11 Tony Dorsett .60 1.50
12 Marcus Allen .50 1.25
13 Bo Jackson .75 2.00
14 Daniel Lasco .40 1.00
15 Alex Collins .50 1.25
16 Jonathan Williams .50 1.25
17 Ricky Williams .50 1.25
18 Barry Sanders 1.00 2.50

2016 Panini Contenders Draft Picks Rush Week Autographs

ANNC'D PRINT RUN 50 OR LESS
1 Ezekiel Elliott 150.00 250.00
2 Derrick Henry 40.00 80.00
3 Paul Perkins 6.00 15.00
4 Devontae Booker 8.00 20.00
5 Aaron Green 6.00 15.00
6 Tre Madden 6.00 15.00
7 Kenneth Dixon 6.00 15.00
8 Kenyan Drake 10.00 25.00
9 Josh Ferguson 6.00 15.00
10 Devon Johnson 8.00 20.00

2016 Panini Contenders Draft Picks School Colors

1 Joey Bosa .60 1.50
2 Jared Goff 2.00 5.00
3 Connor Cook .40 1.00
4 Laquon Treadwell .40 1.00
5 Ezekiel Elliott 1.50 4.00
6 Michael Thomas .60 1.50
7 Josh Doctson .40 1.00
8 Derrick Henry .75 2.00
9 Cardale Jones .30 .75
10 Christian Hackenberg .30 .75
11 Corey Coleman .50 1.25
12 Tyler Boyd .40 1.00
13 Hunter Henry .40 1.00
14 Demarcus Robinson .30 .75
15 Alex Collins .40 1.00
16 Dak Prescott 1.50 4.00
17 Paul Perkins .30 .75
18 Paxton Lynch .30 .75
19 Rashard Higgins .30 .75
20 Pharoh Cooper .30 .75
21 Tyler Ervin .30 .75
22 Devontae Booker .40 1.00
23 De'Runnya Wilson .30 .75
24 Jordan Williams .30 .75

2016 Panini Contenders Draft Picks School Colors Autographs

ANNC'D PRINT RUN 50 OR LESS
1 Joey Bosa 40.00 80.00
2 Jared Goff 40.00 100.00
3 Connor Cook 8.00 20.00
4 Laquon Treadwell 8.00 20.00
5 Ezekiel Elliott 100.00 200.00
6 Michael Thomas 12.00 30.00
7 Josh Doctson 8.00 20.00
8 Derrick Henry 15.00 40.00
9 Cardale Jones 20.00 40.00
11 Corey Coleman 10.00 25.00
13 Hunter Henry 8.00 20.00
14 Demarcus Robinson 6.00 15.00
15 Alex Collins 8.00 20.00
17 Paul Perkins 6.00 15.00
19 Rashard Higgins 6.00 15.00
20 Pharoh Cooper 6.00 15.00
22 Devontae Booker 8.00 20.00
23 De'Runnya Wilson 6.00 15.00
24 Jordan Williams 6.00 15.00
25 Dak Prescott 75.00 150.00
26 Aaron Green 6.00 15.00
27 Carson Wentz 100.00 200.00
28 Nick Vannett 6.00 15.00
30 Leonte Carroo 6.00 15.00
31 Tre Madden 6.00 15.00
33 Brandon Doughty 6.00 15.00
35 Nelson Spruce 6.00 15.00
36 Kenneth Dixon 6.00 15.00
37 Kenyan Drake 10.00 25.00
38 Braxton Miller 6.00 15.00
39 Josh Ferguson 6.00 15.00
40 Cody Kessler 6.00 15.00
41 Devon Cajuste 6.00 15.00
42 Devon Johnson 8.00 20.00
43 D.J. Foster 8.00 20.00
45 Sterling Shepard 8.00 20.00
46 Mekale McKay 6.00 15.00
49 Paxton Lynch 6.00 15.00

2017 Panini Contenders Draft Picks

1 A.J. Green .30 .75
2 Aaron Rodgers .60 1.50
3 Adrian Peterson .30 .75
4 Allen Robinson .25 .60
5 Alshon Jeffery .25 .60
6 Amari Cooper .30 .75
7 Andrew Luck .40 1.00
8 Andy Dalton .25 .60
9 Antonio Brown .30 .75
10 Barry Sanders .50 1.25
11 Ben Roethlisberger .30 .75
12 Billy Sims .25 .60
13 Bo Jackson .40 1.00
14 Braxton Miller .20 .50
15 Brett Favre .60 1.50
16 Brian Bosworth .25 .60
17 Cam Newton .30 .75
18 Carlos Hyde .20 .50
19 Carson Wentz .40 1.00
20 Clay Matthews .25 .60
21 Corey Coleman .20 .50
22 Dak Prescott .30 .75
23 Dan Marino .60 1.50
24 David Johnson .30 .75
25 DeAndre Hopkins .25 .60
26 DeMarco Murray .25 .60
27 Derek Carr .30 .75
28 Derrick Henry .25 .60
29 Devonta Freeman .25 .60
30 Dez Bryant .30 .75
31 Drew Brees .30 .75
32 Earl Campbell .30 .75
33 Eddie Lacy .20 .50
34 Eli Manning .25 .60
35 Emmitt Smith .50 1.25
36 Eric Dickerson .30 .75
37 Ezekiel Elliott .40 1.00
38 Fran Tarkenton .30 .75
39 Frank Gore .25 .60
40 Gale Sayers .30 .75
41 Greg Olsen .25 .60
42 Hunter Henry .20 .50
43 Isaiah Crowell .20 .50
44 J.J. Watt .30 .75
45 Jameis Winston .25 .60
46 Jared Goff .30 .75
47 Jarvis Landry .25 .60
48 Jason Witten .25 .60
49 Jerry Rice .50 1.25
50 Jim Brown .40 1.00
51 Joe Flacco .25 .60
52 Joe Namath .40 1.00
53 John Elway .50 1.25
54 Jordan Howard .30 .75
55 Josh Doctson .20 .50
56 Julio Jones .30 .75
57 Keenan Allen .25 .60
58 Khalil Mack .30 .75
59 Kirk Cousins .30 .75
60 LaDainian Tomlinson .25 .60
61 Lamar Miller .20 .50
62 Laquon Treadwell .20 .50
63 Larry Fitzgerald .25 .60
64 Lawrence Taylor .30 .75
65 LeGarrette Blount .25 .60
66 LeSean McCoy .30 .75
67 Le'Veon Bell .25 .60
68 Luke Kuechly .25 .60
69 Marcus Allen .25 .60
70 Marcus Mariota .30 .75
71 Marshall Faulk .25 .60
72 Marvin Jones Jr. .20 .50
73 Matt Forte .20 .50
74 Matt Ryan .25 .60
75 Matthew Stafford .25 .60
76 Melvin Gordon .25 .60
77 Michael Thomas .30 .75
78 Mike Evans .25 .60
79 Odell Beckham Jr. .30 .75
80 Paxton Lynch .20 .50
81 Peyton Manning .60 1.50
82 Philip Rivers .30 .75
83 Red Grange .40 1.00
84 Rob Gronkowski .30 .75
85 Roger Staubach .40 1.00
86 Russell Wilson .40 1.00
87 Sammie Coates .20 .50
88 Sterling Shepard .25 .60
89 Steve Young .40 1.00
90 T.Y. Hilton .25 .60
91 Terry Bradshaw .50 1.25
92 Thomas Rawls .20 .50
93 Tim Tebow .30 .75
94 Todd Gurley II .30 .75
95 Tom Brady .75 2.00
96 Tony Dorsett .30 .75
97 Tony Romo .25 .60
98 Trevor Siemian .20 .50
99 Troy Aikman .40 1.00
100 Von Miller .25 .60
101A Deshaun Watson AU RC SP1 100.00 200.00
101B Deshaun Watson AU SP2
101C Deshaun Watson AU SP2
101D Deshaun Watson AU SP2
102A Leonard Fournette AU RC SP1 50.00 100.00
102B Leonard Fournette AU SP2
102C Leonard Fournette AU SP2
102D Leonard Fournette AU SP2
103A Dalvin Cook AU RC SP1 EXCH 50.00 100.00
103B Dalvin Cook AU SP2 EXCH 75.00 150.00
103C Dalvin Cook AU SP2 EXCH 75.00 150.00
103D Dalvin Cook AU SP2 EXCH 75.00 150.00
104A Mitchell Trubisky AU RC SP1 75.00 150.00
104B Mitchell Trubisky AU SP2
104C Mitchell Trubisky AU SP2 100.00 200.00
104D Mitchell Trubisky AU SP2 100.00 200.00
105A JuJu Smith-Schuster AU RC SP1 10.00 25.00
105B JuJu Smith-Schuster AU SP2 30.00 60.00
105C JuJu Smith-Schuster AU SP2
105D JuJu Smith-Schuster AU SP2
106A Brad Kaaya AU RC SP1 10.00 25.00
106B Brad Kaaya AU SP2
106C Brad Kaaya AU SP2
106D Brad Kaaya AU SP2
107A Christian McCaffrey AU RC SP1 60.00 125.00
107B Christian McCaffrey AU SP2
107C Christian McCaffrey AU SP2 75.00 150.00
107D Christian McCaffrey AU SP2 75.00 150.00
108A O.J. Howard AU RC SP1 15.00 40.00
108B O.J. Howard AU SP2
108C O.J. Howard AU SP2
108D O.J. Howard AU SP2
109A Mike Williams AU RC SP1 EXCH 30.00 60.00
109B Mike Williams AU SP2 EXCH 40.00 80.00
109C Mike Williams AU SP2 EXCH 40.00 80.00
109D Mike Williams AU SP2 EXCH 40.00 80.00
111A D'Onta Foreman AU RC SP1 15.00 40.00
111B D'Onta Foreman AU SP2 30.00 60.00
111C D'Onta Foreman AU SP2
111D D'Onta Foreman AU SP2
112A Jake Butt AU RC 2.50 6.00
112B Jake Butt AU SP2
112C Jake Butt AU SP2
112D Jake Butt AU SP2
113A Chad Kelly AU RC SP1 12.00 30.00
113B Chad Kelly AU SP2 15.00 40.00
113C Chad Kelly AU SP2
113D Chad Kelly AU SP2
114A Isaiah Ford AU RC SP1 4.00 10.00
114B Isaiah Ford AU SP2
114C Isaiah Ford AU SP2
114D Isaiah Ford AU SP2
116A John Ross AU RC SP1 20.00 40.00
116B John Ross AU SP2
116C John Ross AU SP2
116D John Ross AU SP2
117A Dede Westbrook AU RC SP1 4.00 10.00
117B Dede Westbrook AU SP2
117C Dede Westbrook AU SP2
117D Dede Westbrook AU SP2
118A Samaje Perine AU RC SP1 20.00 50.00
118B Samaje Perine AU SP2
118C Samaje Perine AU SP2
118D Samaje Perine AU SP2
119A Corey Davis AU RC SP1 20.00 50.00
119B Corey Davis AU SP2
119C Corey Davis AU SP2
119D Corey Davis AU SP2 25.00 60.00
120A Amara Darboh AU RC SP1 4.00 10.00
120B Amara Darboh AU SP2
120C Amara Darboh AU SP2
120D Amara Darboh AU SP2
121A Travis Rudolph AU RC SP1 4.00 10.00
121B Travis Rudolph AU SP2 5.00 12.00
121C Travis Rudolph AU SP2
121D Travis Rudolph AU SP2
123A Jeremy McNichols AU RC SP1 4.00 10.00
123B Jeremy McNichols AU SP2
123C Jeremy McNichols AU SP2
123D Jeremy McNichols AU SP2
124A Cooper Kupp AU RC SP1 6.00 15.00
124B Cooper Kupp AU SP2
124C Cooper Kupp AU SP2
124D Cooper Kupp AU SP2
125A Artavis Scott AU RC 2.00 5.00
125B Artavis Scott AU SP2
125C Artavis Scott AU SP2
125D Artavis Scott AU SP2
126A Joe Mixon AU RC 25.00 50.00
126B Joe Mixon AU SP2 10.00 25.00
127A Jordan Leggett AU RC 2.00 5.00
127B Jordan Leggett AU SP2 5.00 12.00
128A Evan Engram AU RC 2.50 6.00
128B Evan Engram AU SP2 6.00 15.00
129A Malachi Dupre AU RC SP2
129B Malachi Dupre AU SP2
130A Donnel Pumphrey AU RC SP2 6.00 15.00
130B Donnel Pumphrey AU SP2 6.00 15.00
131A Noah Brown AU RC 2.50 6.00
131B Noah Brown AU 2.50 6.00
132A Cooper Rush AU RC 2.50 6.00
132B Cooper Rush AU SP2 6.00 15.00
133A Stacy Coley AU RC 2.00 5.00
133B Stacy Coley AU SP2 5.00 12.00
134A Jeremy Sprinkle AU RC EXCH 2.00 5.00
134B Jeremy Sprinkle AU EXCH 2.00 5.00
135A James Quick AU RC 2.50 6.00
135B James Quick AU SP2 6.00 15.00
136A Ryan Switzer AU RC 2.50 6.00
136B Ryan Switzer AU SP1 5.00 12.00
137A ArDarius Stewart AU RC 2.00 5.00
137B ArDarius Stewart AU SP1 4.00 10.00
138A Elijah Hood AU RC 2.00 5.00
138B Elijah Hood AU SP2 5.00 12.00
139A Jehu Chesson AU RC 2.50 6.00
139B Jehu Chesson AU SP1 5.00 12.00
140A C.J. Beathard AU RC 2.00 5.00
140B C.J. Beathard AU SP2
141A Corey Clement AU RC SP1 5.00 12.00
141B Corey Clement AU SP2 6.00 15.00
142A Zay Jones AU RC SP1 5.00 12.00
142B Zay Jones AU SP2 6.00 15.00
143A Chris Godwin AU RC 2.50 6.00
143B Chris Godwin AU SP1 5.00 12.00
144A Blake Jarwin AU RC 2.00 5.00
144B Blake Jarwin AU 2.00 5.00
145A Davis Webb AU RC SP1 4.00 10.00
145B Davis Webb AU SP2 5.00 12.00
146A Darreus Rogers AU RC 4.00 10.00
146B Darreus Rogers AU 4.00 10.00
147A Curtis Samuel AU RC SP1 5.00 12.00
147B Curtis Samuel AU SP2 6.00 15.00
148A Kareem Hunt AU RC 8.00 20.00
148B Kareem Hunt AU SP2 10.00 25.00
149A Carlos Henderson AU RC
149B Carlos Henderson AU SP2
150A Elijah McGuire AU RC 2.00 5.00
150B Elijah McGuire AU SP2
151 Travin Dural AU RC 2.50 6.00
152 Pharaoh Brown AU RC 3.00 8.00
153 Damore'ea Stringfellow AU RC 2.50 6.00
154 Amba Etta-Tawo AU RC 2.00 5.00
155 Marlon Mack AU RC 3.00 8.00
156 Jerod Evans AU RC 4.00 10.00
157 James Conner AU RC
158 Brian Hill AU RC SP1 4.00 10.00
159 Speedy Noil AU RC 2.00 5.00
160 R. Joshua Dobbs AU RC 20.00 50.00
161 Justin Davis AU RC 3.00 8.00
162 Fred Ross AU RC 4.00 10.00
163 Josiah Price AU RC 2.50 6.00
164 Marcus Cox AU RC 2.50 6.00
165 Josh Reynolds AU RC 2.00 5.00
166 De'Veon Smith AU RC 5.00 12.00
167 KD Cannon AU RC SP2
168 Darrell Daniels AU RC 3.00 8.00
169 Taywan Taylor AU RC 2.00 5.00
170 Gerald Everett AU RC 2.00 5.00
171 Jahad Thomas AU RC
172 Quincy Adeboyejo AU RC 2.00 5.00
173 Alvin Kamara AU RC 15.00 40.00
174 De'Angelo Henderson AU RC 2.00 5.00
175 Seth Russell AU RC 2.50 6.00
177 Jabrill Peppers AU RC SP2 8.00 20.00
178 Malik McDowell AU RC SP1 12.00 30.00
180 Jonathan Allen AU RC SP1 5.00 12.00
181 Jamal Adams AU RC 2.00 5.00
182 Cole Hikutini AU RC 2.00 5.00
183 Marlon Humphrey AU RC SP2
184 Tim Williams AU RC 2.50 6.00
185 Derek Barnett AU RC SP2 15.00 40.00
187 Desmond King AU RC 2.50 6.00
188 Jarrad Davis AU RC
189 Carl Lawson AU RC 2.00 5.00
190 Dan Feeney AU RC 3.00 8.00
191 Solomon Thomas AU RC 2.00 5.00
192 Ben Boulware AU RC 10.00 25.00
193 Cordrea Tankersley AU RC SP2 6.00 15.00
194 Zach Cunningham AU RC 2.50 6.00
195 Budda Baker AU RC 2.00 5.00
196 Quincy Wilson AU RC 2.00 5.00
197 Charles Harris AU RC 2.00 5.00
198 Malik Hooker AU RC SP2 12.00 30.00
199 Sidney Jones AU RC 2.00 5.00
200 Haason Reddick AU RC 2.00 5.00
201 Eddie Jackson AU RC 2.50 6.00
202 Marcus Williams AU RC 2.00 5.00
204 Dawuane Smoot AU RC 2.00 5.00
205 Michael Rector AU RC 2.00 5.00
206 Adoree' Jackson AU RC SP1 5.00 12.00
207 Charles Walker AU RC 2.00 5.00
208 Cameron Sutton AU RC 6.00 15.00
209 Tre'Davious White AU RC 2.00 5.00
210 Adam Shaheen AU RC 2.00 5.00
212 Freddie Stevenson AU RC 2.50 6.00
213 Sam Rogers AU RC 2.00 5.00
214 Ricky Seals-Jones AU RC 2.00 5.00
215 Trevor Knight AU RC 2.50 6.00
216 Phazahn Odom AU RC 2.00 5.00
217 Corey Smith AU RC 3.00 8.00
218 Kenny Golladay AU RC 3.00 8.00
220 Chris Carson AU RC 3.00 8.00
221 Obi Melifonwu AU RC 2.00 5.00
222 Dare Ogunbowale AU RC 3.00 8.00
223 Brady Gustafson AU RC 2.00 5.00
224 Gabe Marks AU RC 2.00 5.00
226 Mack Hollins AU RC SP1 4.00 10.00
227 Shock Linwood AU RC 2.50 6.00
228 Rushel Shell III AU RC
229 DeAngelo Yancey AU RC 2.00 5.00
230 DeShone Kizer AU RC 30.00 60.00
231 Mitch Leidner AU RC 3.00 8.00
233 Channing Stribling AU RC 2.50 6.00
234 Taco Charlton AU RC 2.00 5.00
235 Anthony Walker Jr. AU RC 2.00 5.00
236 Elijah Qualls AU RC 2.00 5.00
237 DeMarcus Walker AU RC 2.00 5.00
238 Carlos Watkins AU RC 2.00 5.00
239 Gareon Conley AU RC 2.00 5.00
241 Chris Wormley AU RC 2.00 5.00
243 Ryan Glasgow AU RC 4.00 10.00
244 Ryan Anderson AU RC 2.00 5.00
245 Josh Harvey-Clemons AU RC 2.00 5.00
246 Daeshon Hall AU RC 2.00 5.00
247 Joseph Yearby AU RC 4.00 10.00
248 Marcus Maye AU RC 2.00 5.00
249 Steven Taylor AU RC 2.50 6.00
250 Jamaal Williams AU RC 2.00 5.00
251 Bryan Cox AU RC 4.00 10.00
252 Justin Evans AU RC 2.00 5.00
253 Marquez White AU RC
254 T.J. Watt AU RC 6.00 15.00
255 Devine Redding AU RC 2.00 5.00
256 Jaleel Johnson AU RC
257 Josh Malone AU RC 2.00 5.00
258 Trent Taylor AU RC 2.50 6.00
259 Billy Brown AU RC 2.00 5.00
260 Jalen Reeves-Maybin AU RC 4.00 10.00
261 Kendell Beckwith AU RC 2.00 5.00
262 Montravius Adams AU RC 2.50 6.00
264 Vince Biegel AU RC 4.00 10.00
265 Raekwon McMillan AU RC 2.00 5.00
266 Takkarist McKinley AU RC 2.00 5.00
267 Josh Carraway AU RC 2.00 5.00
268 Jordan Willis AU RC 6.00 15.00
269 Davon Godchaux AU RC 2.00 5.00
270 Eddie Vanderdoes AU RC 2.00 5.00
271 Matt Milano AU RC 2.50 6.00
272 Ryan Ramczyk AU RC 2.00 5.00
273 Damontae Kazee AU RC 2.50 6.00
274 Ashton Lampkin AU RC 2.00 5.00
275 Keith Kelsey AU RC
276 Kevin King AU RC 2.50 6.00
277 Chidobe Awuzie AU RC 2.50 6.00
278 Deatrich Wise Jr. AU RC 3.00 8.00
279 Sefo Liufau AU RC 2.50 6.00
280 Ejuan Price AU RC
281 Montae Nicholson AU RC
282 Shelton Gibson AU RC 2.00 5.00
283 Hardy Nickerson AU RC 2.00 5.00
284 Riley Bullough AU RC 2.00 5.00
285 Des Lawrence AU RC 2.50 6.00
286 Tony Conner AU RC 2.00 5.00
287 Randall Goforth AU RC 3.00 8.00
288 Calvin Munson AU RC 2.00 5.00
289 Fabian Moreau AU RC 2.00 5.00
290 Chad Hansen AU RC 2.00 5.00
291 Zach Pascal AU RC 2.00 5.00
292 Tanner Vallejo AU RC 3.00 8.00
293 Marshon Lattimore AU RC 12.00 30.00
294 Joe Mathis AU RC 2.00 5.00
296 Tyus Bowser AU RC 2.00 5.00
297 Matthew Dayes AU RC 2.00 5.00
298 Patrick Mahomes II AU RC 150.00 300.00
299 Jalen Myrick AU RC SP1 4.00 10.00
300 Gunner Kiel AU RC 3.00 8.00

2017 Panini Contenders Draft Picks Bowl Ticket

*VETS/99: 4X TO 10X BASIC CARDS
1-100 STATED PRINT RUN 99
101-125 STATED PRINT RUN 25
126-300 STATED PRINT RUN 99
SOME AU HAVE MULT CARDS OF EQUAL VALUE
101A Deshaun Watson AU 150.00 250.00
102A Leonard Fournette AU 175.00 350.00
103A Dalvin Cook AU EXCH 75.00 150.00
104A Mitchell Trubisky AU 150.00 250.00
105A JuJu Smith-Schuster AU 20.00 50.00
106A Brad Kaaya AU 20.00 50.00
107A Christian McCaffrey AU 100.00 200.00
108A O.J. Howard AU 10.00 25.00
109A Mike Williams AU EXCH 12.00 30.00
111A D'Onta Foreman AU 30.00 60.00
112A Jake Butt AU 10.00 25.00
113A Chad Kelly AU 25.00 60.00
114A Isaiah Ford AU 8.00 20.00
116A John Ross AU 10.00 25.00
117A Dede Westbrook AU 25.00 60.00
118A Samaje Perine AU 40.00 80.00
119A Corey Davis AU 40.00 80.00
120A Amara Darboh AU 8.00 20.00
121A Travis Rudolph AU 8.00 20.00
123A Jeremy McNichols AU 8.00 20.00
124A Cooper Kupp AU 12.00 30.00
125A Artavis Scott AU 8.00 20.00
126A Joe Mixon AU 10.00 25.00
127A Jordan Leggett AU 5.00 12.00
128A Evan Engram AU 10.00 25.00
129A Malachi Dupre AU 5.00 12.00
130A Donnel Pumphrey AU 6.00 15.00
131A Noah Brown AU 6.00 15.00
132A Cooper Rush AU 6.00 15.00
133A Stacy Coley AU 5.00 12.00
134A Jeremy Sprinkle AU EXCH
135A James Quick AU
136A Ryan Switzer AU 6.00 15.00
137A ArDarius Stewart AU 5.00 12.00
138A Elijah Hood AU 5.00 12.00
139A Jehu Chesson AU
140A C.J. Beathard AU 5.00 12.00
141A Corey Clement AU 10.00 25.00
142A Zay Jones AU 12.00 30.00
143A Chris Godwin AU 6.00 15.00
144A Blake Jarwin AU 5.00 12.00
145A Davis Webb AU 25.00 50.00
146A Darreus Rogers AU 10.00 25.00
147A Curtis Samuel AU 6.00 15.00
148A Kareem Hunt AU 10.00 25.00
149A Carlos Henderson AU 5.00 12.00
150A Elijah McGuire AU 5.00 12.00
151 Travin Dural AU 6.00 15.00
152 Pharaoh Brown AU 10.00 25.00
153 Damore'ea Stringfellow AU 6.00 15.00
154 Amba Etta-Tawo AU 5.00 12.00
155 Marlon Mack AU 8.00 20.00
156 Jerod Evans AU 6.00 15.00
157 James Conner AU 15.00 40.00
158 Brian Hill AU 5.00 12.00
159 Speedy Noil AU 5.00 12.00
160 R. Joshua Dobbs AU 20.00 40.00
161 Justin Davis AU 8.00 20.00
162 Fred Ross AU 5.00 12.00
163 Josiah Price AU 6.00 15.00
164 Marcus Cox AU 6.00 15.00
165 Josh Reynolds AU 5.00 12.00
166 De'Veon Smith AU 12.00 30.00
167 KD Cannon AU 5.00 12.00
168 Darrell Daniels AU 8.00 20.00
169 Taywan Taylor AU 5.00 12.00
170 Gerald Everett AU 5.00 12.00
171 Jahad Thomas AU 5.00 12.00
172 Quincy Adeboyejo AU 5.00 12.00
173 Alvin Kamara AU 30.00 60.00
174 De'Angelo Henderson AU 5.00 12.00
175 Seth Russell AU 6.00 15.00
177 Jabrill Peppers AU 8.00 20.00
178 Malik McDowell AU EXCH 5.00 12.00
180 Jonathan Allen AU 20.00 50.00
181 Jamal Adams AU 5.00 12.00
182 Cole Hikutini AU 5.00 12.00
183 Marlon Humphrey AU 15.00 40.00
184 Tim Williams AU 6.00 15.00
185 Derek Barnett AU 25.00 50.00
187 Desmond King AU 6.00 15.00
188 Jarrad Davis AU 6.00 15.00
189 Carl Lawson AU 5.00 12.00
190 Dan Feeney AU 8.00 20.00
191 Solomon Thomas AU 5.00 12.00
192 Ben Boulware AU
193 Cordrea Tankersley AU 12.00 30.00
194 Zach Cunningham AU 6.00 15.00
195 Budda Baker AU 5.00 12.00
196 Quincy Wilson AU 5.00 12.00
197 Charles Harris AU 5.00 12.00
198 Malik Hooker AU 25.00 50.00
199 Sidney Jones AU 5.00 12.00
200 Haason Reddick AU 5.00 12.00
201 Eddie Jackson AU 6.00 15.00
202 Marcus Williams AU 5.00 12.00
204 Dawuane Smoot AU 5.00 12.00
205 Michael Rector AU 5.00 12.00
206 Adoree' Jackson AU 30.00 60.00
207 Charles Walker AU 5.00 12.00
208 Cameron Sutton AU 5.00 12.00
209 Tre'Davious White AU 5.00 12.00
210 Adam Shaheen AU 5.00 12.00
212 Freddie Stevenson AU 6.00 15.00
213 Sam Rogers AU 5.00 12.00
214 Ricky Seals-Jones AU 5.00 12.00
215 Trevor Knight AU 6.00 15.00
216 Phazahn Odom AU 5.00 12.00
217 Corey Smith AU 8.00 20.00
218 Kenny Golladay AU 8.00 20.00
220 Chris Carson AU 8.00 20.00
221 Obi Melifonwu AU 5.00 12.00
222 Dare Ogunbowale AU 8.00 20.00
223 Brady Gustafson AU 5.00 12.00
224 Gabe Marks AU 5.00 12.00
226 Mack Hollins AU 5.00 12.00
227 Shock Linwood AU 6.00 15.00
228 Rushel Shell III AU 5.00 12.00
229 DeAngelo Yancey AU 5.00 12.00
230 DeShone Kizer AU 30.00 60.00
231 Mitch Leidner AU
233 Channing Stribling AU
234 Taco Charlton AU 5.00 12.00
235 Anthony Walker Jr. AU
236 Elijah Qualls AU
237 DeMarcus Walker AU 5.00 12.00
238 Carlos Watkins AU 5.00 12.00
239 Gareon Conley AU 5.00 12.00
241 Chris Wormley AU 5.00 12.00
243 Ryan Glasgow AU
244 Ryan Anderson AU 5.00 12.00
245 Josh Harvey-Clemons AU
246 Daeshon Hall AU 5.00 12.00
247 Joseph Yearby AU
248 Marcus Maye AU
249 Steven Taylor AU
250 Jamaal Williams AU 5.00 12.00
251 Bryan Cox AU 10.00 25.00
252 Justin Evans AU 5.00 12.00
253 Marquez White AU
254 T.J. Watt AU 15.00 40.00
255 Devine Redding AU
256 Jaleel Johnson AU
257 Josh Malone AU 5.00 12.00
258 Trent Taylor AU
259 Billy Brown AU 5.00 12.00
260 Jalen Reeves-Maybin AU
261 Kendell Beckwith AU
262 Montravius Adams AU
264 Vince Biegel AU
265 Raekwon McMillan AU 5.00 12.00
266 Takkarist McKinley AU 10.00 25.00
267 Josh Carraway AU
268 Jordan Willis AU 5.00 12.00
269 Davon Godchaux AU 5.00 12.00
270 Eddie Vanderdoes AU
271 Matt Milano AU
272 Ryan Ramczyk AU 5.00 12.00
273 Damontae Kazee AU
274 Ashton Lampkin AU
275 Keith Kelsey AU 5.00 12.00
276 Kevin King AU
277 Chidobe Awuzie AU 6.00 15.00
278 Deatrich Wise Jr. AU
279 Sefo Liufau AU 6.00 15.00
280 Ejuan Price AU
281 Montae Nicholson AU
282 Shelton Gibson AU
283 Hardy Nickerson AU
284 Riley Bullough AU
285 Des Lawrence AU
286 Tony Conner AU
287 Randall Goforth AU
288 Calvin Munson AU
289 Fabian Moreau AU 5.00 12.00
290 Chad Hansen AU 5.00 12.00
291 Zach Pascal AU
292 Tanner Vallejo AU
293 Marshon Lattimore AU 30.00 60.00
294 Joe Mathis AU
296 Tyus Bowser AU 5.00 12.00
297 Matthew Dayes AU 5.00 12.00
298 Patrick Mahomes II AU 200.00 400.00
299 Jalen Myrick AU 5.00 12.00
300 Gunner Kiel AU 8.00 20.00

2017 Panini Contenders Draft Picks Cracked Ice

*VETS/23: 8X TO 20X BASIC CARDS
*101-250 ROOK.AU/23: 1.5X TO 4X RC AU
*101-250 ROOK.AU/23: .8X TO 2X SP1 AU
*101-250 ROOK.AU/23: .6X TO 1.5X SP2 AU
SOME HAVE MULT. CARDS OF EQUAL VALUE
101A Deshaun Watson AU 250.00 500.00
white JSY
103A Dalvin Cook AU 125.00 250.00
white jsy running left EXCH

107A Christian McCaffrey AU 100.00 200.00
red jsy ball in right arm
113A Chad Kelly AU 60.00 125.00
white jsy two hands on ball
298 Patrick Mahomes II AU 1000.00 1500.00

2018 Panini Contenders Draft Picks

1 A.J. Green .30 .75
2 Aaron Rodgers .60 1.50
3 Adam Thielen .30 .75
4 Adrian Peterson .30 .75
5 Amari Cooper .30 .75
6 Andrew Luck .40 1.00
7 Antonio Brown .30 .75
8 Barry Sanders .50 1.25
9 Barry Switzer .25 .60
10 Billy Cannon .20 .50
11 Billy Sims .25 .60
12 Bo Jackson .40 1.00
13 Brett Favre .60 1.50
14 Brian Bosworth .25 .60
15 Cam Newton .30 .75
16 Carson Wentz .40 1.00
17 Charles White .20 .50
18 Charles Woodson .30 .75
19 Christian McCaffrey .30 .75
20 Clay Helton .20 .50
21 Clay Matthews .25 .60
22 Colt McCoy .20 .50
23 Corey Davis .25 .60
24 Dak Prescott .30 .75
25 Dalvin Cook .25 .60
26 Dan Marino .60 1.50
27 David Johnson .30 .75
28 DeAndre Hopkins .25 .60
29 Dede Westbrook .20 .50
30 Deion Sanders .25 .60
31 Derek Carr .30 .75
32 Derrick Henry .30 .75
33 Deshaun Watson .40 1.00
34 Dez Bryant .30 .75
35 Dick Butkus .40 1.00
36 D'Onta Foreman .20 .50
37 Drew Brees .30 .75
38 Earl Campbell .30 .75
39 Ed Reed .25 .60
40 Emmitt Smith .50 1.25
41 Eric Dickerson .30 .75
42 Ezekiel Elliott .40 1.00
43 George Rogers .25 .60
44 J.J. Watt .30 .75
45 Jabrill Peppers .20 .50
46 Jameis Winston .25 .60
47 Jason Witten .25 .60
48 Jeremy Shockey .20 .50
49 Jerry Rice .50 1.25
50 Herschel Walker .30 .75
51 Alvin Kamara .25 .60
52 Joe Namath .40 1.00
53 John Elway .50 1.25
54 John Hannah .20 .50
55 Johnny Rodgers .25 .60
56 Jordan Howard .30 .75
57 Julio Jones .30 .75
58 Kareem Hunt .25 .60
59 Khalil Mack .30 .75
60 LaDainian Tomlinson .25 .60
61 Larry Fitzgerald .25 .60
62 Leonard Fournette .30 .75
63 Le'Veon Bell .25 .60
64 Mack Brown .20 .50
65 Major Applewhite .30 .75
66 Marcus Allen .30 .75
67 Marcus Dupree .25 .60
68 Marcus Mariota .30 .75
69 Matt Ryan .25 .60
70 Matthew Stafford .25 .60
71 Michael Irvin .30 .75
72 Michael Thomas .30 .75
73 Mike Rozier .25 .60
74 Mitchell Trubisky .30 .75
75 Ndamukong Suh .25 .60
76 Nick Saban .30 .75
77 Odell Beckham Jr. .30 .75
78 Ozzie Newsome .25 .60
79 Patrick Mahomes II .75 2.00
80 Peyton Manning .60 1.50
81 Randy Moss .25 .60
82 Ray Lewis .30 .75
83 Red Grange .40 1.00
84 Ricky Williams .25 .60
85 Roger Staubach .40 1.00
86 Ron Dayne .20 .50
87 Russell Wilson .40 1.00
88 Shaun Alexander .20 .50
89 Steve Spurrier .25 .60
90 Ted Hendricks .20 .50
91 Terry Bradshaw .50 1.25
92 Tim Tebow .30 .75
93 Todd Gurley II .30 .75
94 Tom Brady .75 2.00
95 Tony Dorsett .30 .75
96 Trevor Siemian .20 .50
97 Troy Aikman .40 1.00
98 Tyreek Hill .30 .75
99 Vince Young .20 .50
100 Von Miller .25 .60
101A Sam Darnold AU RC VER 1 SP2 90.00 150.00
101B Sam Darnold AU VER 2 SP2 90.00 150.00
101C Sam Darnold AU VER 3 SP2 90.00 150.00
101D Sam Darnold AU VER 4 SP2 90.00 150.00
102A Josh Rosen AU RC VER 1 SP2 100.00 200.00
102B Josh Rosen AU VER 2 SP2 100.00 200.00
102C Josh Rosen AU VER 3 SP2 100.00 200.00
102D Josh Rosen AU VER 4 SP2 100.00 200.00
103A Josh Allen AU RC VER 1 SP2 90.00 150.00
103B Josh Allen AU VER 2 SP2 90.00 150.00
103C Josh Allen AU VER 3 SP2 90.00 150.00
103D Josh Allen AU VER 4 SP2 90.00 150.00
105A Saquon Barkley AU RC VER 1 SP2 250.00 350.00
105B Saquon Barkley AU VER 2 SP2 250.00 350.00
105C Saquon Barkley AU VER 3 SP2 250.00 350.00
105D Saquon Barkley AU VER 4 SP2 250.00 350.00
106A Derrius Guice AU RC VER 1 SP2 15.00 40.00
106B Derrius Guice AU VER 2 SP2 15.00 40.00
106C Derrius Guice AU VER 3 SP2 15.00 40.00
106D Derrius Guice AU VER 4 SP2 15.00 40.00
107A Courtland Sutton AU RC VER 1 SP1 6.00 15.00
107B Courtland Sutton AU VER 2 SP2 8.00 20.00
107C Courtland Sutton AU VER 3 SP2 8.00 20.00
107D Courtland Sutton AU VER 4 SP2 8.00 20.00
108A James Washington AU RC VER 1 SP1 8.00 20.00
108B James Washington AU VER 2 SP2 10.00 25.00
108C James Washington AU VER 3 SP2 10.00 25.00
108D James Washington AU VER 4 SP2 10.00 25.00
109A Christian Kirk AU RC VER 1 SP1 6.00 15.00
109B Christian Kirk AU VER 2 SP2 8.00 20.00
109C Christian Kirk AU VER 3 SP2 8.00 20.00
109D Christian Kirk AU VER 4 SP2 8.00 20.00
110A Calvin Ridley AU RC VER 1 SP2 25.00 50.00
110B Calvin Ridley AU VER 2 SP2 20.00 50.00
110C Calvin Ridley AU VER 3 SP2 20.00 50.00
110D Calvin Ridley AU VER 4 SP2 20.00 50.00
111A Mason Rudolph AU RC VER 1 SP2 25.00 50.00
111B Mason Rudolph AU VER 2 SP2 25.00 50.00
111C Mason Rudolph AU VER 3 SP2 25.00 50.00
111D Mason Rudolph AU VER 4 SP2 25.00 50.00
112A Nick Chubb AU RC VER 1 SP1 12.00 30.00
112B Nick Chubb AU VER 2 SP2 15.00 40.00
112C Nick Chubb AU VER 3 SP2 15.00 40.00
112D Nick Chubb AU VER 4 SP2 15.00 40.00
113A Ronald Jones II AU RC VER 1 SP1 4.00 10.00
113B Ronald Jones II AU VER 2 SP2 5.00 12.00
113C Ronald Jones II AU VER 3 SP2 5.00 12.00
113D Ronald Jones II AU VER 4 SP2 5.00 12.00
114A Deon Cain AU RC VER 1 SP1 EXCH 5.00 12.00
114B Deon Cain AU VER 2 SP2 EXCH 6.00 15.00
114C Deon Cain AU VER 3 SP2 EXCH 6.00 15.00
114D Deon Cain AU VER 4 SP2 EXCH 6.00 15.00
115A Dante Pettis AU RC VER 1 SP1 EXCH 6.00 15.00
115B Dante Pettis AU VER 2 SP2 EXCH 8.00 20.00
115C Dante Pettis AU VER 3 SP2 EXCH 8.00 20.00
115D Dante Pettis AU VER 4 SP2 EXCH 8.00 20.00
116A Kerryon Johnson AU 6.00 15.00
RC VER 1 SP1 EXCH
116B Kerryon Johnson AU VER 2 SP2 EXCH 8.00 20.00
116C Kerryon Johnson AU VER 3 SP2 EXCH 8.00 20.00
116D Kerryon Johnson AU VER 4 SP2 EXCH 8.00 20.00
117A Anthony Miller AU RC VER 1 SP1 6.00 15.00
117B Anthony Miller AU VER 2 SP2 8.00 20.00
117C Anthony Miller AU VER 3 SP2 8.00 20.00
117D Anthony Miller AU VER 4 SP2 8.00 20.00
118A Luke Falk AU RC VER 1 SP1 25.00 50.00
118B Luke Falk AU VER 2 SP2
118C Luke Falk AU VER 3 SP2
118D Luke Falk AU VER 4 SP2
119A Bo Scarbrough AU RC VER 1 SP1 EXCH 5.00 12.00
119B Bo Scarbrough AU VER 2 SP2 EXCH 6.00 15.00
119C Bo Scarbrough AU VER 3 SP2 EXCH 6.00 15.00
119D Bo Scarbrough AU VER 4 SP2 EXCH 6.00 15.00
120A Deontay Burnett AU RC VER 1 SP1 5.00 12.00
120B Deontay Burnett AU VER 2 SP2 6.00 15.00
120C Deontay Burnett AU VER 3 SP2 6.00 15.00
120D Deontay Burnett AU VER 4 SP2 6.00 15.00
121A Simmie Cobbs Jr. AU 6.00 15.00
RC VER 1 SP1 EXCH
121B Simmie Cobbs Jr. AU VER 2 SP2 EXCH 8.00 20.00
121C Simmie Cobbs Jr. AU VER 3 SP2 EXCH 8.00 20.00
121D Simmie Cobbs Jr. AU VER 4 SP2 EXCH 8.00 20.00
122A Royce Freeman AU RC VER 1 SP1 5.00 12.00
122B Royce Freeman AU VER 2 SP2 6.00 15.00
122C Royce Freeman AU VER 3 SP2 6.00 15.00
122D Royce Freeman AU VER 4 SP2 6.00 15.00
123A D.J. Chark AU RC VER 1 SP1 5.00 12.00
123B D.J. Chark AU VER 2 SP2 6.00 15.00
123C D.J. Chark AU VER 3 SP2 6.00 15.00
123D D.J. Chark AU VER 4 SP2 6.00 15.00
124A Baker Mayfield AU RC VER 1 SP2 150.00 250.00
124B Baker Mayfield AU VER 2 SP2 150.00 250.00
124C Baker Mayfield AU VER 3 SP2 150.00 250.00
124D Baker Mayfield AU VER 4 SP2 150.00 250.00
125A Nyheim Hines AU RC VER 1 SP1 5.00 12.00
125B Nyheim Hines AU VER 2 SP2 6.00 15.00
125C Nyheim Hines AU VER 3 SP2 6.00 15.00
125D Nyheim Hines AU VER 4 SP2 6.00 15.00
126A John Kelly AU RC AU VER 1 SP1 2.50 6.00
126B John Kelly AU VER 2 SP2 6.00 15.00
126C John Kelly AU VER 3 SP2 6.00 15.00
126D John Kelly AU VER 4 SP2 6.00 15.00
127A Mark Walton AU RC VER 1 SP1
127B Mark Walton AU VER 2 SP2
127C Mark Walton AU VER 3 SP2
127D Mark Walton AU VER 4 SP2
128 Trey Quinn AU RC 2.00 5.00
130 Cam Serigne AU RC
133 Richie James AU RC 2.00 5.00
134A Allen Lazard AU RC VER 1 SP1 4.00 10.00
134B Allen Lazard AU VER 2 SP2 5.00 12.00
134C Allen Lazard AU VER 3 SP2 5.00 12.00
135A Jaylen Samuels AU RC VER 1 2.50 6.00
135B Jaylen Samuels AU VER 2 2.50 6.00
135C Jaylen Samuels AU VER 3 2.50 6.00
136 Phillip Lindsay AU RC 12.00 30.00
137 Trevon Young AU RC 2.50 6.00
138 Ogbonnia Okoronkwo AU RC SP2 8.00 20.00
139 Andrew Brown AU RC 2.00 5.00
140A Rashaad Penny AU RC VER 1 SP1 6.00 15.00
140B Rashaad Penny AU VER 2 SP2
141A Sony Michel AU RC 25.00 50.00
RED JSY
141B Sony Michel AU SP2 30.00 60.00
WHITE JSY
142A Kalen Ballage AU RC VER 1 SP1 5.00 12.00
142B Kalen Ballage AU VER 2 SP2 6.00 15.00
143A Michael Gallup AU RC VER 1 SP1 8.00 20.00
143B Michael Gallup AU VER 2 SP2 10.00 25.00
144A Akrum Wadley AU RC VER 1 SP1 4.00 10.00
144B Akrum Wadley AU VER 2 SP2
145A Kamryn Pettway AU RC VER 1 SP1 6.00 15.00
145B Kamryn Pettway AU VER 2 SP2 8.00 20.00
146 Dorian O'Daniel AU RC
147A Justin Jackson AU RC SP1 5.00 12.00
WHITE JSY
147B Justin Jackson AU SP2 6.00 15.00
PURPLE JSY
148 Marcell Ateman AU RC SP1 5.00 12.00
150 Bryce Bobo AU RC SP1
151A J.T. Barrett AU RC SP2 8.00 20.00
TWO HANDS ON BALL
151B J.T. Barrett AU SP2 8.00 20.00
THROWING
152 Devonte Boyd AU RC 2.00 5.00
153A Josh Adams AU RC VER 1 SP2
153B Josh Adams AU VER 2 SP2
154A Mark Andrews AU RC 3.00 8.00
FACING RIGHT
154B Mark Andrews AU SP2 8.00 20.00
FACING LEFT
155A Robert Foster AU RC VER 1 SP2
155B Robert Foster AU VER 2 SP2
156 Jake Wieneke AU RC 2.50 6.00
157A Jester Weah AU RC VER 1 SP2
157B Jester Weah AU VER 2 SP2
158A Cedrick Wilson Jr. AU RC VER 1 SP2
158B Cedrick Wilson Jr. AU VER 2 SP2
159A Quadree Henderson AU RC 2.50 6.00
WHITE JSY
159B Quadree Henderson AU SP2
PURPLE JSY
160 J'Mon Moore AU RC 2.00 5.00
161 Janarion Grant AU RC 2.00 5.00
162 Kyle Allen AU RC SP2
164 Dallas Goedert AU RC 2.50 6.00
165 Mike Gesicki AU RC 2.50 6.00
166 DeAndre Goolsby AU RC 2.00 5.00
167 Dalton Schultz AU RC 2.50 6.00
168 Troy Fumagalli AU RC 2.50 6.00
171 Chukwuma Okorafor AU RC 2.00 5.00
172 Bradley Chubb AU RC SP2 25.00 50.00
173 Maurice Hurst AU RC SP1 5.00 12.00
174 Harold Landry AU RC SP2 5.00 12.00
175 Arden Key AU RC SP2 5.00 12.00
176 Sam Hubbard AU RC SP1 5.00 12.00
177 Roquan Smith AU RC SP1 12.00 30.00
178 Daron Payne AU RC SP1 6.00 15.00
179 Tarvarus McFadden AU RC SP1 5.00 12.00
180 Minkah Fitzpatrick AU RC SP1 8.00 20.00
181 Derwin James AU RC SP1 8.00 20.00
183 Connor Williams AU RC 4.00 10.00
184 DaeSean Hamilton AU RC SP1 5.00 12.00
185A D.J. Moore AU RC VER 1 4.00 10.00
185B D.J. Moore AU VER 2 SP2 10.00 25.00
187 Ray-Ray McCloud AU RC
188 Ronnie Harrison AU RC SP1 5.00 12.00
189 Hayden Hurst AU RC 2.50 6.00
190 Matt Linehan AU RC SP2
191 Kurt Benkert AU RC SP2 6.00 15.00
192 Kenny Hill AU RC
193 Dalyn Dawkins AU RC
194 Javon Wims AU RC SP1 4.00 10.00
195 Christopher Herndon IV AU RC
196 Ian Thomas AU RC SP1 4.00 10.00
197 Dimitri Flowers AU RC
198 Lavon Coleman AU RC
199 Chase Edmonds AU RC
200 Riley Ferguson AU RC SP2 12.00 30.00
201 Chase Litton AU RC 2.50 6.00
202 Marcus Baugh AU RC
203 Khalid Hill AU RC
204 Darren Carrington II AU RC 2.50 6.00
205 Austin Proehl AU RC
206 Max Browne AU RC
207 David Wells AU RC 2.00 5.00
208 Adam Breneman AU RC 2.50 6.00
210 Da'Shawn Hand AU RC 2.00 5.00
211 Vita Vea AU RC SP1 6.00 15.00
212 Denzel Ward AU RC SP1 10.00 25.00
213 Tyquan Lewis AU RC
214 Josh Sweat AU RC SP1
215 Orlando Brown AU RC SP2
216 Malik Jefferson AU RC SP1
217 Derrick Nnadi AU RC 2.00 5.00
218 Brandon Facyson AU RC
219 Quin Blanding AU RC 2.00 5.00
221 Jerome Baker AU RC SP1 12.00 30.00
222 Tremaine Edmunds AU RC SP1 8.00 20.00
223 Jaire Alexander AU RC 3.00 8.00
224 Anthony Averett AU RC 2.50 6.00
225 Armani Watts AU RC
227 Logan Woodside AU RC
228 Christian LaCouture AU RC
229 Keishawn Bierria AU RC 8.00 20.00
232 M.J. Stewart AU RC
233 Tony Brown AU RC
234 Dorance Armstrong Jr. AU RC 2.00 5.00
235 Trenton Thompson AU RC SP1 4.00 10.00
237 Jalyn Holmes AU RC SP1 6.00 15.00
238 Azeem Victor AU RC
239 Rashaan Evans AU RC 3.00 8.00
240 Mike McCray AU RC
241 Fred Warner AU RC
242 Duke Dawson AU RC SP1 4.00 10.00
243 Lowell Lotulelei AU RC SP2
244 Kyzir White AU RC 3.00 8.00
245 Damon Webb AU RC
246 Harrison Phillips AU RC 2.00 5.00
247 Isaiah Oliver AU RC SP2 5.00 12.00
249 Tanner Lee AU RC SP1
250 Terrell Edmunds AU RC 6.00 15.00
252 Trey Marshall AU RC
253 Folorunso Fatukasi AU RC
254 Matthew Thomas AU RC 2.50 6.00
255 Duke Ejiofor AU RC 2.00 5.00
256 Jordan Whitehead AU RC 2.00 5.00
258 Josey Jewell AU RC 2.50 6.00
259 Deatrick Nichols AU RC
260 Godwin Igwebuike AU RC
261 Rasheem Green AU RC 2.00 5.00
262 Marcus Allen AU RC 3.00 8.00
263 Micah Kiser AU RC 2.00 5.00
264 Tre Flowers AU RC
265 D.J. Reed AU RC SP1
268 Auden Tate AU RC SP1 4.00 10.00
269 Jaleel Scott AU RC 2.00 5.00
270 Steve Ishmael AU RC
271 Billy Price AU RC 2.50 6.00
272 Carlton Davis AU RC SP1 5.00 12.00
275 Martinas Rankin AU RC 2.00 5.00
276 Tegray Scales AU RC 2.00 5.00
278 Austin Allen AU RC 2.50 6.00
280 Mike White AU RC 2.50 6.00
281 Keke Coutee AU RC 2.50 6.00
282 Braxton Berrios AU RC
283 Tre'Quan Smith AU RC 3.00 8.00
284 Korey Robertson AU RC 2.50 6.00
285 Byron Pringle AU RC 2.50 6.00
286 Marcus Davenport AU RC 4.00 10.00
287 Taven Bryan AU RC 2.00 5.00
288 Jordan Wilkins AU RC
289 Tyler Conklin AU RC 2.00 5.00
290 Daurice Fountain AU RC 2.50 6.00
291 Ito Smith AU RC 2.50 6.00
293 Justin Reid AU RC 2.00 5.00
294 Mike Hughes AU RC 3.00 8.00
295 Roc Thomas AU RC 2.50 6.00
296 Nic Shimonek AU RC 3.00 8.00
297 Donte Jackson AU RC 3.00 8.00
298 Kyle Lauletta AU RC 3.00 8.00
299 Leighton Vander Esch AU RC 6.00 15.00
300 Ka'Raun White AU RC

2018 Panini Contenders Draft Picks Bowl Ticket

*VETS: 4X TO 10X BASIC CARDS
101A Sam Darnold AU 125.00 250.00
101B Sam Darnold AU 125.00 250.00
101C Sam Darnold AU 125.00 250.00
101D Sam Darnold AU 125.00 250.00
102A Josh Rosen AU 100.00 200.00
102B Josh Rosen AU 100.00 200.00
102C Josh Rosen AU 100.00 200.00
102D Josh Rosen AU 100.00 200.00
103A Josh Allen AU 100.00 200.00
103B Josh Allen AU 100.00 200.00
103C Josh Allen AU 100.00 200.00
103D Josh Allen AU 100.00 200.00
105A Saquon Barkley AU 300.00 500.00
105B Saquon Barkley AU 300.00 500.00
105C Saquon Barkley AU 300.00 500.00
105D Saquon Barkley AU 300.00 500.00
106A Derrius Guice AU 30.00 60.00
106B Derrius Guice AU 30.00 60.00
106C Derrius Guice AU 30.00 60.00
106D Derrius Guice AU 30.00 60.00
107A Courtland Sutton AU 12.00 30.00
107B Courtland Sutton AU 12.00 30.00
107C Courtland Sutton AU 12.00 30.00
107D Courtland Sutton AU 12.00 30.00
108A James Washington AU 15.00 40.00
108B James Washington AU 15.00 40.00
108C James Washington AU 15.00 40.00
108D James Washington AU 15.00 40.00
109A Christian Kirk AU 12.00 30.00
109B Christian Kirk AU 12.00 30.00
109C Christian Kirk AU 12.00 30.00
109D Christian Kirk AU 12.00 30.00
110A Calvin Ridley AU 20.00 50.00
110B Calvin Ridley AU 20.00 50.00
110C Calvin Ridley AU 20.00 50.00
110D Calvin Ridley AU 20.00 50.00
111A Mason Rudolph AU 50.00 100.00
111B Mason Rudolph AU 50.00 100.00
111C Mason Rudolph AU 50.00 100.00
111D Mason Rudolph AU 50.00 100.00
112A Nick Chubb AU 25.00 60.00
112B Nick Chubb AU 25.00 60.00
112C Nick Chubb AU 25.00 60.00
112D Nick Chubb AU 25.00 60.00
113A Ronald Jones II AU 8.00 20.00
113B Ronald Jones II AU 8.00 20.00
113C Ronald Jones II AU 8.00 20.00
113D Ronald Jones II AU 8.00 20.00
114A Deon Cain AU EXCH 10.00 25.00
114B Deon Cain AU EXCH 10.00 25.00
114C Deon Cain AU EXCH 10.00 25.00
114D Deon Cain AU EXCH 10.00 25.00
115B Dante Pettis AU EXCH 12.00 30.00
115A Dante Pettis AU EXCH 12.00 30.00
115C Dante Pettis AU EXCH 12.00 30.00
115D Dante Pettis AU EXCH 12.00 30.00
116A Kerryon Johnson AU EXCH 12.00 30.00
116B Kerryon Johnson AU EXCH 12.00 30.00
116C Kerryon Johnson AU EXCH 12.00 30.00
116D Kerryon Johnson AU EXCH 12.00 30.00
117A Anthony Miller AU 12.00 30.00
117B Anthony Miller AU 12.00 30.00
117C Anthony Miller AU 12.00 30.00
117D Anthony Miller AU 12.00 30.00
118A Luke Falk AU 40.00 100.00
118B Luke Falk AU 40.00 100.00
118C Luke Falk AU 40.00 100.00
118D Luke Falk AU 40.00 100.00
119A Bo Scarbrough AU EXCH 10.00 25.00
119B Bo Scarbrough AU EXCH 10.00 25.00
119C Bo Scarbrough AU EXCH 10.00 25.00
119D Bo Scarbrough AU EXCH 10.00 25.00
120A Deontay Burnett AU 10.00 25.00
120B Deontay Burnett AU 10.00 25.00
120C Deontay Burnett AU 10.00 25.00
120D Deontay Burnett AU 10.00 25.00
121A Simmie Cobbs Jr. AU EXCH 12.00 30.00
121B Simmie Cobbs Jr. AU EXCH 12.00 30.00
121C Simmie Cobbs Jr. AU EXCH 12.00 30.00
121D Simmie Cobbs Jr. AU EXCH 12.00 30.00
122A Royce Freeman AU 10.00 25.00
122B Royce Freeman AU 10.00 25.00
122C Royce Freeman AU 10.00 25.00
122D Royce Freeman AU 10.00 25.00
123A DJ Chark AU 10.00 25.00
123B DJ Chark AU 10.00 25.00
123C DJ Chark AU 10.00 25.00
123D DJ Chark AU 10.00 25.00
124A Baker Mayfield AU 175.00 350.00
124B Baker Mayfield AU 175.00 350.00
124C Baker Mayfield AU 175.00 350.00
124D Baker Mayfield AU 175.00 350.00
125A Nyheim Hines AU 10.00 25.00
125B Nyheim Hines AU 10.00 25.00
125C Nyheim Hines AU 10.00 25.00
125D Nyheim Hines AU 10.00 25.00
126A John Kelly AU 6.00 15.00
126B John Kelly AU 10.00 25.00
127A Mark Walton AU 6.00 15.00
127B Mark Walton AU 10.00 25.00
128 Trey Quinn AU 5.00 12.00
130 Cam Serigne AU
133 Richie James AU 5.00 12.00
134A Allen Lazard AU 5.00 12.00
134B Allen Lazard AU 8.00 20.00
135A Jaylen Samuels AU 6.00 15.00
135B Jaylen Samuels AU 6.00 15.00
136 Phillip Lindsay AU 30.00 80.00
137 Trevon Young AU 6.00 15.00
138 Ogbonnia Okoronkwo AU 8.00 20.00
139 Andrew Brown AU 5.00 12.00
140A Rashaad Penny AU 8.00 20.00
140B Rashaad Penny AU 8.00 20.00
141A Sony Michel AU 30.00 60.00
141B Sony Michel AU 30.00 60.00
142A Kalen Ballage AU 6.00 15.00
142B Kalen Ballage AU 6.00 15.00
143A Michael Gallup AU 10.00 25.00
143B Michael Gallup AU 10.00 25.00
144A Akrum Wadley AU 5.00 12.00
144B Akrum Wadley AU 5.00 12.00
145A Kamryn Pettway AU 8.00 20.00
145B Kamryn Pettway AU 8.00 20.00
146 Dorian O'Daniel AU 5.00 12.00
147A Justin Jackson AU 6.00 15.00
147B Justin Jackson AU 6.00 15.00
148 Marcell Ateman AU 6.00 15.00
150 Bryce Bobo AU
151A J.T. Barrett AU 8.00 20.00
151B J.T. Barrett AU 12.00 30.00
152 Devonte Boyd AU 8.00 20.00
153A Josh Adams AU 15.00 40.00
153B Josh Adams AU 15.00 40.00
154A Mark Andrews AU 12.00 30.00
154B Mark Andrews AU 12.00 30.00
155A Robert Foster AU
155B Robert Foster AU
156 Jake Wieneke AU 10.00 25.00
157A Jester Weah AU
157B Jester Weah AU
158A Cedrick Wilson Jr. AU 8.00 20.00
158B Cedrick Wilson Jr. AU 8.00 20.00
159A Quadree Henderson AU 10.00 25.00
159B Quadree Henderson AU 10.00 25.00
160 J'Mon Moore AU 5.00 12.00
161 Janarion Grant AU 5.00 12.00
162 Kyle Allen AU
164 Dallas Goedert AU 6.00 15.00
165 Mike Gesicki AU 6.00 15.00
166 DeAndre Goolsby AU 5.00 12.00
167 Dalton Schultz AU 6.00 15.00
168 Troy Fumagalli AU 6.00 15.00
171 Chukwuma Okorafor AU 5.00 12.00
172 Bradley Chubb AU 25.00 50.00
173 Maurice Hurst AU 6.00 15.00
174 Harold Landry AU 5.00 12.00
175 Arden Key AU 5.00 12.00
176 Sam Hubbard AU 6.00 15.00
177 Roquan Smith AU 15.00 40.00
178 Daron Payne AU 8.00 20.00
179 Tarvarus McFadden AU 6.00 15.00
180 Minkah Fitzpatrick AU 10.00 25.00
181 Derwin James AU 10.00 25.00
183 Connor Williams AU 10.00 25.00
184 DaeSean Hamilton AU 6.00 15.00
185A D.J. Moore AU 10.00 25.00
185B D.J. Moore AU 15.00 40.00
187 Ray-Ray McCloud AU
188 Ronnie Harrison AU 6.00 15.00
189 Hayden Hurst AU 6.00 15.00
190 Matt Linehan AU
191 Kurt Benkert AU 6.00 15.00
192 Kenny Hill AU
193 Dalyn Dawkins AU
194 Javon Wims AU 5.00 12.00
195 Christopher Herndon IV AU
196 Ian Thomas AU 5.00 12.00
197 Dimitri Flowers AU
198 Lavon Coleman AU
199 Chase Edmonds AU
200 Riley Ferguson AU 12.00 30.00
201 Chase Litton AU 6.00 15.00
202 Marcus Baugh AU
203 Khalid Hill AU
204 Darren Carrington II AU 6.00 15.00
205 Austin Proehl AU
206 Max Browne AU
207 David Wells AU 5.00 12.00
208 Adam Breneman AU 6.00 15.00
210 Da'Shawn Hand AU 5.00 12.00
211 Vita Vea AU 8.00 20.00
212 Denzel Ward AU 12.00 30.00
213 Tyquan Lewis AU
214 Josh Sweat AU
216 Malik Jefferson AU 6.00 15.00
217 Derrick Nnadi AU 5.00 12.00
218 Brandon Facyson AU
219 Quin Blanding AU 5.00 12.00
221 Jerome Baker AU 15.00 40.00
222 Tremaine Edmunds AU 10.00 25.00
223 Jaire Alexander AU 8.00 20.00
224 Anthony Averett AU 6.00 15.00
225 Armani Watts AU
227 Logan Woodside AU
228 Christian LaCouture AU
229 Keishawn Bierria AU
232 M.J. Stewart AU
233 Tony Brown AU
234 Dorance Armstrong Jr. AU 5.00 12.00
235 Trenton Thompson AU 5.00 12.00
237 Jalyn Holmes AU 8.00 20.00
238 Azeem Victor AU
239 Rashaan Evans AU 8.00 20.00
240 Mike McCray AU
241 Fred Warner AU
242 Duke Dawson AU 5.00 12.00
243 Lowell Lotulelei AU
244 Kyzir White AU 8.00 20.00
245 Damon Webb AU
246 Harrison Phillips AU 5.00 12.00
247 Isaiah Oliver AU 5.00 12.00
249 Tanner Lee AU
250 Terrell Edmunds AU 15.00 40.00
252 Trey Marshall AU
253 Folorunso Fatukasi AU
254 Matthew Thomas AU 6.00 15.00
255 Duke Ejiofor AU 5.00 12.00
256 Jordan Whitehead AU 5.00 12.00
258 Josey Jewell AU 6.00 15.00
259 Deatrick Nichols AU
260 Godwin Igwebuike AU
261 Rasheem Green AU 5.00 12.00
262 Marcus Allen AU 8.00 20.00
263 Micah Kiser AU 5.00 12.00
264 Tre Flowers AU
265 D.J. Reed AU
268 Auden Tate AU 5.00 12.00
269 Jaleel Scott AU 5.00 12.00
270 Steve Ishmael AU
271 Billy Price AU 6.00 15.00
272 Carlton Davis AU 6.00 15.00
275 Martinas Rankin AU 5.00 12.00
276 Tegray Scales AU 5.00 12.00
278 Austin Allen AU 6.00 15.00
280 Mike White AU 6.00 15.00
281 Keke Coutee AU 6.00 15.00
282 Braxton Berrios AU
283 Tre'Quan Smith AU 8.00 20.00
284 Korey Robertson AU 6.00 15.00
285 Byron Pringle AU 6.00 15.00
286 Marcus Davenport AU 10.00 25.00
287 Taven Bryan AU 5.00 12.00
288 Jordan Wilkins AU
289 Tyler Conklin AU 5.00 12.00
290 Daurice Fountain AU 6.00 15.00
291 Ito Smith AU 6.00 15.00
293 Justin Reid AU 5.00 12.00
294 Mike Hughes AU 8.00 20.00
295 Roc Thomas AU 6.00 15.00
296 Nic Shimonek AU 8.00 20.00
297 Donte Jackson AU 8.00 20.00
298 Kyle Lauletta AU 8.00 20.00
299 Leighton Vander Esch AU 15.00 40.00
300 Ka'Raun White AU

2018 Panini Contenders Draft Picks Building Blocks Ticket

*VETS/15: 8X TO 20X BASIC CARDS

2018 Panini Contenders Draft Picks College Playoff Ticket

*PLAY/15: .8X TO 2X BOWL AU/99
*PLAY/15: .5X TO 1.2X BOWL AU/25
101A Sam Darnold AU 200.00 350.00
101B Sam Darnold AU 200.00 350.00
101C Sam Darnold AU 200.00 350.00
101D Sam Darnold AU 200.00 350.00
102A Josh Rosen AU 125.00 250.00
102B Josh Rosen AU 125.00 250.00
102C Josh Rosen AU 125.00 250.00
102D Josh Rosen AU 125.00 250.00
103A Josh Allen AU 125.00 250.00
103B Josh Allen AU 125.00 250.00
103C Josh Allen AU 125.00 250.00
103D Josh Allen AU 125.00 250.00
105A Saquon Barkley AU 250.00 450.00
105B Saquon Barkley AU 250.00 450.00
105C Saquon Barkley AU 250.00 450.00
105D Saquon Barkley AU 250.00 450.00
111A Mason Rudolph AU 75.00 150.00
111B Mason Rudolph AU 75.00 150.00
111C Mason Rudolph AU 75.00 150.00
111D Mason Rudolph AU 75.00 150.00
124A Baker Mayfield AU 200.00 400.00
124B Baker Mayfield AU 200.00 400.00
124C Baker Mayfield AU 200.00 400.00
124D Baker Mayfield AU 200.00 400.00
141A Sony Michel AU 60.00 125.00
141B Sony Michel AU 60.00 125.00

2018 Panini Contenders Draft Picks Cracked Ice

*VETS: 12X TO 30X BASIC CARDS
*CRACKED/23: 1X TO 2.5X BOWL AU/99
*CRACKED/23: .6X TO 1.5X BOWL AU/25
101A Sam Darnold AU 350.00 600.00
101B Sam Darnold AU 350.00 600.00
101C Sam Darnold AU 350.00 600.00
101D Sam Darnold AU 350.00 600.00
102A Josh Rosen AU 200.00 400.00
102B Josh Rosen AU 200.00 400.00
102C Josh Rosen AU 200.00 400.00
102D Josh Rosen AU 200.00 400.00
103A Josh Allen AU 200.00 400.00
103B Josh Allen AU 200.00 400.00
103C Josh Allen AU 200.00 400.00
103D Josh Allen AU 200.00 400.00
105A Saquon Barkley AU 600.00 1000.00
105B Saquon Barkley AU 600.00 1000.00
105C Saquon Barkley AU 600.00 1000.00
105D Saquon Barkley AU 600.00 1000.00
111A Mason Rudolph AU 125.00 250.00
111B Mason Rudolph AU 125.00 250.00
111C Mason Rudolph AU 125.00 250.00
111D Mason Rudolph AU 125.00 250.00
124A Baker Mayfield AU 300.00 600.00
124B Baker Mayfield AU 300.00 600.00
124C Baker Mayfield AU 300.00 600.00
124D Baker Mayfield AU 300.00 600.00
136 Phillip Lindsay AU 300.00 500.00
140A Rashaad Penny AU 20.00 50.00
140B Rashaad Penny AU 20.00 50.00
141A Sony Michel AU 100.00 200.00
141B Sony Michel AU 100.00 200.00
172 Bradley Chubb AU 75.00 150.00

2018 Panini Contenders Draft Picks Diamond Ticket

*VETS/49: 5X TO 12X BASIC CARDS

2018 Panini Contenders Draft Picks Collegiate Connections

*CRACKED/23: 2X TO 5X BASIC INSERTS
1 R.Jones II/S.Darnold 3.00 8.00
2 D.Chark/D.Guice 1.00 2.50
3 J.Washington/M.Rudolph 1.25 3.00
4 B.Scarbrough/D.Henry .75 2.00
5 J.Samuels/N.Hines .60 1.50
6 N.Chubb/S.Michel 1.50 4.00
7 A.Kamara/J.Kelly .60 1.50
8 B.Mayfield/M.Andrews 5.00 12.00
9 K.Pettway/K.Johnson .75 2.00
10 D.Burnett/J.Smith-Schuster .75 2.00
11 D.Cain/D.Watson 1.00 2.50
13 J.Mora Jr./J.Rosen 1.50 4.00
14 C.Ridley/N.Saban 1.25 3.00
15 M.Gesicki/S.Barkley 4.00 10.00
16 M.Evans/C.Kirk .75 2.00
17 J.Howard/S.Cobbs Jr. .75 2.00
18 M.Mariota/R.Freeman .75 2.00
19 C.Sutton/C.Beasley .75 2.00
20 A.Miller/R.Ferguson .75 2.00

2018 Panini Contenders Draft Picks Collegiate Connections Signatures

1 R.Jones II/S.Darnold
2 D.Chark/D.Guice
3 J.Washington/M.Rudolph
4 B.Scarbrough/D.Henry
5 J.Samuels/N.Hines
6 N.Chubb/S.Michel
7 A.Kamara/J.Kelly
8 B.Mayfield/M.Andrews 100.00 200.00
9 K.Pettway/K.Johnson
10 D.Burnett/J.Smith-Schuster
11 D.Cain/D.Watson
13 J.Mora Jr./J.Rosen
15 M.Gesicki/S.Barkley 125.00 250.00
16 M.Evans/C.Kirk
17 J.Howard/S.Cobbs Jr. 10.00 25.00
20 A.Miller/R.Ferguson

2018 Panini Contenders Draft Picks Game Day Tickets

1 Sam Darnold 2.50 6.00
2 Josh Rosen 1.25 3.00
3 Josh Allen 1.50 4.00
4 Lamar Jackson 2.50 6.00
5 Saquon Barkley 3.00 8.00
6 Derrius Guice .75 2.00
7 Courtland Sutton .60 1.50
8 James Washington .75 2.00
9 Christian Kirk .60 1.50
10 Calvin Ridley 1.00 2.50
11 Mason Rudolph 1.00 2.50
12 Nick Chubb 1.25 3.00
13 Ronald Jones II .40 1.00
14 Deon Cain .50 1.25
15 Dante Pettis .60 1.50
16 Sony Michel 1.25 3.00
17 Kalen Ballage .50 1.25
18 Luke Falk .50 1.25
19 Bo Scarbrough .50 1.25
20 Michael Gallup .75 2.00
21 Simmie Cobbs Jr. .60 1.50
22 Royce Freeman .50 1.25
23 DJ Chark .50 1.25
24 Baker Mayfield 4.00 10.00
25 Akrum Wadley .40 1.00
26 John Kelly .50 1.25
27 Mark Walton .50 1.25
28 Nyheim Hines .50 1.25
29 Kerryon Johnson .60 1.50
30 Kamryn Pettway .60 1.50
31 Deontay Burnett .50 1.25
32 D.J. Moore .75 2.00
33 Anthony Miller .60 1.50
34 Allen Lazard .40 1.00
35 Jaylen Samuels .50 1.25
36 Mike White .50 1.25
37 J'Mon Moore .40 1.00
38 Mark Andrews .60 1.50
39 Marcell Ateman .50 1.25
40 Rashaad Penny .60 1.50

2018 Panini Contenders Draft Picks Game Day Tickets Cracked Ice

2 Josh Rosen 40.00 80.00
5 Saquon Barkley 50.00 100.00
24 Baker Mayfield 40.00 80.00

2018 Panini Contenders Draft Picks Old School Colors

*CRACKED/23: 2X TO 5X BASIC INSERTS
1 Aaron Rodgers 1.50 4.00
2 Antonio Brown .75 2.00
3 Barry Sanders 1.25 3.00
4 Bo Jackson 1.00 2.50
5 Brett Favre 1.50 4.00
6 Dak Prescott .75 2.00
7 Dan Marino 1.50 4.00
8 Deshaun Watson 1.00 2.50
9 Emmitt Smith 1.25 3.00
10 Ezekiel Elliott 1.00 2.50
11 Jerry Rice 1.25 3.00
12 Herschel Walker .75 2.00
13 Joe Namath 1.00 2.50
14 John Elway 1.25 3.00
15 Leonard Fournette .75 2.00
16 Odell Beckham Jr. .75 2.00
17 Peyton Manning 1.50 4.00
18 Red Grange 1.00 2.50
19 Tim Tebow .75 2.00
20 Tom Brady 2.00 5.00

2018 Panini Contenders Draft Picks School Colors

1 Sam Darnold 2.50 6.00
2 Josh Rosen 1.25 3.00
3 Josh Allen 1.50 4.00
4 Lamar Jackson 2.50 6.00
5 Saquon Barkley 3.00 8.00
6 Derrius Guice .75 2.00
7 Courtland Sutton .60 1.50
8 James Washington .75 2.00
9 Christian Kirk .60 1.50
10 Calvin Ridley 1.00 2.50
11 Mason Rudolph 1.00 2.50
12 Nick Chubb 1.25 3.00
13 Ronald Jones II .40 1.00
14 Deon Cain .50 1.25
15 Dante Pettis .60 1.50
16 Baker Mayfield 4.00 10.00
17 DJ Chark .50 1.25
18 Luke Falk .50 1.25
19 Bo Scarbrough .50 1.25
20 Simmie Cobbs Jr. .60 1.50

2018 Panini Contenders Draft Picks School Colors Cracked Ice

*CRACKED/23: 2X TO 5X BASIC INSERTS
2 Josh Rosen 30.00 80.00
5 Saquon Barkley 40.00 100.00
16 Baker Mayfield 30.00 80.00

2018 Panini Contenders Draft Picks School Colors Signatures

1 Sam Darnold 60.00 125.00
2 Josh Rosen 40.00 80.00
3 Josh Allen 40.00 80.00
5 Saquon Barkley 100.00 200.00
6 Derrius Guice 8.00 20.00
7 Courtland Sutton 6.00 15.00
8 James Washington 15.00 40.00
9 Christian Kirk 6.00 15.00
10 Calvin Ridley 10.00 25.00
11 Mason Rudolph 15.00 40.00
12 Nick Chubb 12.00 30.00
13 Ronald Jones II
14 Deon Cain 5.00 12.00
15 Dante Pettis 6.00 15.00
16 Baker Mayfield 150.00 250.00
17 DJ Chark 12.00 30.00
18 Luke Falk 5.00 12.00
19 Bo Scarbrough
20 Simmie Cobbs Jr. 6.00 15.00

2018 Panini Contenders Draft Picks School Colors Signatures Cracked Ice

*CRACKED/23: .8X TO 2X BASIC AU
1 Sam Darnold 125.00 250.00
2 Josh Rosen 100.00 200.00
3 Josh Allen 100.00 200.00
16 Baker Mayfield 300.00 500.00

2018 Panini Contenders Draft Picks Season Ticket Signatures

1 Eddie George
2 Vinny Testaverde 12.00 30.00
3 Jason White
4 Joe Washington 4.00 10.00
5 Jordan Shipley 4.00 10.00
6 Marcus Dupree
8 Mack Brown 8.00 20.00
9 Troy Smith 15.00 40.00
10 Jim Harbaugh 40.00 80.00
11 Major Applewhite
12 Steve Spurrier
13 Denard Robinson
14 Danny Wuerffel
16 Charles White 4.00 10.00
17 Colt McCoy
18 Gary Beban 4.00 10.00
19 George Rogers 5.00 12.00
20 Joe Bellino 4.00 10.00
21 John Brodie
22 Johnny Rodgers 5.00 12.00
23 Mike Rozier 10.00 25.00
24 Ron Dayne 4.00 10.00
25 Peyton Manning
26 Jim Plunkett
28 Cris Carter
29 Rob Gronkowski
30 Jeremy Shockey
31 Terry Baker 10.00 25.00
32 Bo Jackson 40.00 80.00
33 John Elway 50.00 100.00
34 Dan Marino

2018 Panini Contenders Draft Picks Season Ticket Signatures Bowl

*BOWL/99: .3X TO .8X BASIC AU
*BOWL/25: .5X TO 1.2X BASIC AU

2018 Panini Contenders Draft Picks Season Ticket Signatures Cracked Ice

*CRACKED/23: .8X TO 2X BASIC AU
1 Eddie George 100.00 200.00
14 Danny Wuerffel 75.00 150.00
25 Peyton Manning 200.00 350.00

2019 Panini Contenders Draft Picks

CARD A HAS NO BLACK BAR ON BACK
CARD B HAS 1 BLACK BAR ON BACK
CARD C HAS 2 BLACK BARS ON BACK
CARD D HAS 3 BLACK BARS ON BACK
1 A.J. Green .30 .75
2 Aaron Rodgers .60 1.50
3 Adam Thielen .30 .75
4 Adrian Peterson .30 .75
5 Alvin Kamara .25 .60
6 Amari Cooper .30 .75
7 Andrew Luck .40 1.00
8 Anthony Miller .25 .60
9 Antonio Brown .30 .75
10 Antonio Callaway .20 .50
11 Austin Ekeler .20 .50
12 Baker Mayfield .50 1.25
13 Barry Sanders .50 1.25
14 Ben Roethlisberger .25 .60
15 Bo Jackson .40 1.00
16 Bradley Chubb .25 .60
17 Brandin Cooks .25 .60
18 Brett Favre .60 1.50
19 Calvin Ridley .25 .60
20 Cam Newton .30 .75
21 Carson Wentz .40 1.00
22 Christian Kirk .20 .50
23 Christian McCaffrey .30 .75
24 Courtland Sutton .25 .60
25 Dak Prescott .30 .75
26 Dan Marino .60 1.50
27 Darius Leonard .25 .60
28 David Johnson .30 .75
29 DeAndre Hopkins .25 .60
30 Derek Carr .30 .75
31 Derrick Henry .30 .75
32 Derrius Guice .25 .60
33 Deshaun Watson .40 1.00
34 D.J. Moore .25 .60
35 Drew Brees .30 .75
36 Earl Campbell .30 .75
37 Emmitt Smith .50 1.25
38 Eric Dickerson .30 .75
39 Ezekiel Elliott .40 1.00
40 Golden Tate III .25 .60
41 Herschel Walker .30 .75
42 Ito Smith .20 .50
43 J.J. Watt .30 .75
44 James Conner .30 .75
45 Jared Goff .30 .75
46 Jerry Rice .50 1.25
47 Joe Mixon .25 .60
48 Joe Namath .40 1.00
49 John Elway .50 1.25
50 Jordan Howard .30 .75
51 Jordan Wilkins .25 .60
52 Josh Adams .25 .60
53 Josh Allen .30 .75
54 Josh Rosen .30 .75
55 JuJu Smith-Schuster .30 .75
56 Julio Jones .30 .75
57 Travis Kelce .30 .75
58 Keenan Allen .25 .60
59 Kerryon Johnson .25 .60
60 Khalil Mack .30 .75
61 Lamar Jackson .30 .75
62 Leonard Fournette .30 .75
63 Le'Veon Bell .25 .60
64 Marcus Allen .30 .75
65 Marcus Mariota .30 .75
66 Mark Andrews .20 .50
67 Marquez Valdes-Scantling .25 .60
68 Matt Breida .20 .50
69 Matt Ryan .30 .75
70 Melvin Cordon III .25 .00
71 Michael Gallup .30 .75
72 Michael Irvin .40 1.00
73 Michael Thomas .30 .75
74 Mitchell Trubisky .30 .75
75 Nick Chubb .30 .75
76 Nick Mullens .25 .60
77 Nyheim Hines .25 .60
78 Odell Beckham Jr. .30 .75
79 Patrick Mahomes II .75 2.00
80 Peyton Manning .60 1.50
81 Philip Rivers .30 .75
82 Phillip Lindsay .30 .75
83 Rashaad Penny .20 .50
84 Ray Lewis .30 .75
85 Red Grange .40 1.00
86 Roger Staubach .40 1.00
87 Royce Freeman .20 .50
88 Russell Wilson .40 1.00
89 Sam Darnold .30 .75
90 Saquon Barkley .40 1.00
91 Sony Michel .30 .75
92 Stefon Diggs .25 .60
93 Terry Bradshaw .50 1.25
94 Tim Tebow .30 .75
95 Todd Gurley II .30 .75
96 Tom Brady .75 2.00
97 Tony Dorsett .30 .75
98 Tre'Quan Smith .20 .50
99 Troy Aikman .40 1.00
100 Tyreek Hill .30 .75
101A Kyler Murray AU VER 1 SP1 200.00 400.00
101B Kyler Murray AU VER 2 SP2
101C Kyler Murray AU VER 3 SP2
101D Kyler Murray AU VER 4 SP2
102A Marquise Brown AU VER 1 SP1 12.00 30.00
102B Marquise Brown AU VER 2 SP2 15.00 40.00
102C Marquise Brown AU VER 3 SP2 15.00 40.00
102D Marquise Brown AU VER 4 SP2 15.00 40.00
103A Bryce Love AU VER 1 SP1 6.00 15.00
103B Bryce Love AU VER 2 SP2 8.00 20.00
103C Bryce Love AU VER 3 SP2 8.00 20.00
103D Bryce Love AU VER 4 SP2 8.00 20.00
104A Will Grier AU VER 1 SP1 12.00 30.00
104B Will Grier AU VER 2 SP2 15.00 40.00
104C Will Grier AU VER 3 SP2 15.00 40.00
104D Will Grier AU VER 4 SP2 15.00 40.00
105A A.J. Brown AU VER 1 SP1 EXCH 10.00 25.00
105B A.J. Brown AU VER 2 SP2 EXCH 12.00 30.00
105C A.J. Brown AU VER 3 SP2 EXCH 12.00 30.00
105D A.J. Brown AU VER 4 SP2 EXCH 12.00 30.00
106A Damien Harris AU VER 1 SP1 10.00 25.00
106B Damien Harris AU VER 2 SP2 12.00 30.00
106C Damien Harris AU VER 3 SP2 12.00 30.00
106D Damien Harris AU VER 4 SP2 12.00 30.00
107A Ryan Finley AU VER 1 SP1 8.00 20.00
107B Ryan Finley AU VER 2 SP2 10.00 25.00
107C Ryan Finley AU VER 3 SP2 10.00 25.00
107D Ryan Finley AU VER 4 SP2 10.00 25.00
108A N'Keal Harry AU VER 1 SP1 EXCH 25.00 50.00
108B N'Keal Harry AU VER 2 SP2 EXCH 25.00 60.00
108C N'Keal Harry AU VER 3 SP2 EXCH 25.00 60.00
108D N'Keal Harry AU VER 4 SP2 EXCH 25.00 60.00
109A Rodney Anderson AU VER 1 SP1 5.00 12.00
109B Rodney Anderson AU VER 2 SP2 6.00 15.00
109C Rodney Anderson AU VER 3 SP2 6.00 15.00
109D Rodney Anderson AU VER 4 SP2 6.00 15.00

110A Drew Lock AU VER 1 SP1 EXCH 20.00 50.00
110B Drew Lock AU VER 2 SP2 EXCH 25.00 60.00
110C Drew Lock AU VER 3 SP2 EXCH 25.00 60.00
110D Drew Lock AU VER 4 SP2 EXCH 25.00 60.00
111A JJ Arcega-Whiteside AU VER 1 SP1 6.00 15.00
111B JJ Arcega-Whiteside AU VER 2 SP2 8.00 20.00
111C JJ Arcega-Whiteside AU VER 3 SP2 8.00 20.00
111D JJ Arcega-Whiteside AU VER 4 SP2 8.00 20.00
112A Justice Hill AU VER 1 SP1 6.00 15.00
112B Justice Hill AU VER 2 SP2
112C Justice Hill AU VER 3 SP2
112D Justice Hill AU VER 4 SP2
113A Dwayne Haskins AU VER 1 SP1
113B Dwayne Haskins AU VER 2 SP2
113C Dwayne Haskins AU VER 3 SP2
113D Dwayne Haskins AU VER 4 SP2
114A Kelvin Harmon AU VER 1 SP1
114B Kelvin Harmon AU VER 2 SP2
114C Kelvin Harmon AU VER 3 SP2
114D Kelvin Harmon AU VER 4 SP2
115A Trayveon Williams AU VER 1 SP1 5.00 12.00
115B Trayveon Williams AU VER 2 SP2 6.00 15.00
115C Trayveon Williams AU VER 3 SP2 6.00 15.00
115D Trayveon Williams AU VER 4 SP2 6.00 15.00
116A Daniel Jones AU VER 1 SP1
116B Daniel Jones AU VER 2 SP2
116C Daniel Jones AU VER 3 SP2
116D Daniel Jones AU VER 4 SP2
117A D.K. Metcalf AU VER 1 SP1 12.00 30.00
117B D.K. Metcalf AU VER 2 SP2 15.00 40.00
117C D.K. Metcalf AU VER 3 SP2 15.00 40.00
117D D.K. Metcalf AU VER 4 SP2 15.00 40.00
118A David Montgomery AU VER 1 SP1 15.00 40.00
118B David Montgomery AU VER 2 SP2 20.00 50.00
118C David Montgomery AU VER 3 SP2 20.00 50.00
118D David Montgomery AU VER 4 SP2 20.00 50.00
119A Lil'Jordan Humphrey AU VER 1 SP1
119B Lil'Jordan Humphrey AU VER 2 SP2
119C Lil'Jordan Humphrey AU VER 3 SP2
119D Lil'Jordan Humphrey AU VER 4 SP2
120A Parris Campbell AU VER 1 SP1 10.00 25.00
120B Parris Campbell AU VER 2 SP2 12.00 30.00
120C Parris Campbell AU VER 3 SP2 12.00 30.00
120D Parris Campbell AU VER 4 SP2 12.00 30.00
121A Benny Snell Jr. AU VER 1 SP1 12.00 30.00
121B Benny Snell Jr. AU VER 2 SP2 15.00 40.00
121C Benny Snell Jr. AU VER 3 SP2 15.00 40.00
122A Josh Jacobs AU VER 1 SP1 20.00 50.00
122B Josh Jacobs AU VER 2 SP2 25.00 60.00
122C Josh Jacobs AU VER 3 SP2 25.00 60.00
122D Josh Jacobs AU VER 4 SP2 25.00 60.00
123A Hakeem Butler AU VER 1 SP1 8.00 20.00
123B Hakeem Butler AU VER 2 SP2 10.00 25.00
123C Hakeem Butler AU VER 3 SP2 10.00 25.00
123D Hakeem Butler AU VER 4 SP2 10.00 25.00
124A Darrell Henderson AU VER 1 SP1 10.00 25.00
124B Darrell Henderson AU VER 2 SP2 12.00 30.00
124D Darrell Henderson AU VER 4 SP2 12.00 30.00
125A Riley Ridley AU VER 1 SP1 6.00 15.00
125B Riley Ridley AU VER 2 SP2 8.00 20.00
125C Riley Ridley AU VER 3 SP2 8.00 20.00
125D Riley Ridley AU VER 4 SP2 8.00 20.00
126A Anthony Johnson AU VER 1 SP1 5.00 12.00
126B Anthony Johnson AU VER 2 SP2 6.00 15.00
127A Jarrett Stidham AU VER 1 SP1 20.00 50.00
127B Jarrett Stidham AU VER 2 SP2 25.00 60.00
128 L.J. Scott AU 3.00 8.00
129A Noah Fant AU VER 1 SP1 8.00 20.00
129B Noah Fant AU VER 2 SP2 10.00 25.00
130A Clayton Thorson AU VER 1 SP1 6.00 15.00
130B Clayton Thorson AU VER 2 SP2 8.00 20.00
131A Deebo Samuel AU VER 1 SP1 10.00 25.00
131B Deebo Samuel AU VER 2 SP2 12.00 30.00
132A Myles Gaskin AU VER 1 SP1 8.00 20.00
132B Myles Gaskin AU VER 2 SP2 10.00 25.00
133A Devin Singletary AU VER 1 SP1 5.00 12.00
133B Devin Singletary AU VER 2 SP2 6.00 15.00
134A Brett Rypien AU VER 1 SP1 5.00 12.00
134B Brett Rypien AU VER 2 SP2 6.00 15.00
135A David Sills V AU VER 1 SP1 12.00 30.00
135B David Sills V AU VER 2 SP2 15.00 40.00
136A Karan Higdon AU VER 1 SP1 5.00 12.00
136B Karan Higdon AU VER 2 SP2 6.00 15.00
137A Tyree Jackson AU VER 1 SP1 10.00 25.00
137B Tyree Jackson AU VER 2 SP2 12.00 30.00
138A Irv Smith Jr. AU VER 1 SP1 8.00 20.00
138B Irv Smith Jr. AU VER 2 SP2 10.00 25.00
139A Mike Weber AU VER 1 SP1 6.00 15.00
139B Mike Weber AU VER 2 SP2 8.00 20.00
140A Trace McSorley AU VER 1 SP1 10.00 25.00
140B Trace McSorley AU VER 2 SP2 12.00 30.00
141A Emanuel Hall AU VER 1 SP1 4.00 10.00
141B Emanuel Hall AU VER 2 SP2 5.00 12.00
142 Jalin Moore Jr. AU 2.00 5.00
144 Alex Barnes AU 2.50 6.00
145 Darwin Thompson AU 3.00 8.00
146 Jordan Ta'amu AU 5.00 12.00
147 Alex Wesley AU 3.00 8.00
148 Travis Fulgham AU 2.00 5.00
149 Andy Isabella AU 3.00 8.00
150 Nick Bosa AU 30.00 60.00
151 Gardner Minshew II AU 3.00 8.00
152 Dax Raymond AU 2.00 5.00
153 DaMarkus Lodge AU 2.00 5.00
154 Keelan Doss AU 2.50 6.00
155 Kaden Smith AU 2.00 5.00
156 Dexter Williams AU 2.50 6.00
157 David Long Jr. AU 2.50 6.00
158 Antoine Wesley AU 2.00 5.00
159 Anthony Ratliff-Williams AU 4.00 10.00
160 Jazz Ferguson AU 2.00 5.00
161 Ty Johnson AU 8.00 20.00
162 Josh Oliver AU 2.00 5.00
163 Caleb Wilson AU 2.00 5.00
164 Terry Godwin II AU 2.50 6.00
165 Gary Jennings Jr. AU 3.00 8.00
166 Darrin Hall AU 2.50 6.00
167 Tommy Sweeney AU 2.00 5.00
168 Jacques Patrick AU 2.00 5.00
169 Jordan Scarlett AU 2.00 5.00
170 Stanley Morgan Jr. AU 3.00 8.00
171 Jalen Hurd AU 2.50 6.00
172 T.J. Hockenson AU 5.00 12.00
173 Keenen Brown AU 2.00 5.00
174 Zach Gentry AU 2.00 5.00
175 Qadree Ollison AU 2.50 6.00
176 Miles Sanders AU 10.00 25.00
177 Greedy Williams AU 6.00 15.00
178 Deandre Baker AU 5.00 12.00
179 Zach Allen AU 3.00 8.00
180 Christian Wilkins AU 15.00 40.00
181 Te'Von Coney AU 6.00 15.00
182 Josh Allen AU 15.00 40.00
183 Montez Sweat AU 6.00 15.00
184 T.J. Edwards AU 2.00 5.00
185 D'Andre Walker AU 2.00 5.00
186 Johnathan Abram AU 2.00 5.00
187 Amani Oruwariye AU 2.50 6.00
188 Jerry Tillery AU 2.50 6.00
189 Jaylon Ferguson AU 2.00 5.00
190 Ben Burr-Kirven AU 6.00 15.00
191 Oshane Ximines AU 2.00 5.00
192 Jalen Jelks AU 6.00 15.00
193 Marvell Tell III AU 4.00 10.00
194 Jaquan Johnson AU 4.00 10.00
196 Austin Bryant AU 4.00 10.00
197 Lukas Denis AU 2.50 6.00
198 Kendall Joseph AU 4.00 10.00
199 Chase Winovich AU 6.00 15.00
200 Ryan Connelly AU 2.50 6.00
201 Gerald Willis III AU 4.00 10.00
202 Elijah Holyfield AU 3.00 8.00
203 Cameron Smith AU 2.50 6.00
204 Demarcus Christmas AU 2.50 6.00
205 C.J. Conrad AU 2.00 5.00
206 Blace Brown AU 2.00 5.00
207 Terry Beckner Jr. AU 2.00 5.00
208 Christian Miller AU 4.00 10.00
209 Isaiah Buggs AU 5.00 12.00
210 Daniel Wise AU 2.50 6.00
211 Vosean Joseph AU 2.50 6.00
212 Tyler Petite AU 3.00 8.00
213 Porter Gustin AU 3.00 8.00
214 Carl Granderson AU 3.00 8.00
215 Germaine Pratt AU 2.50 6.00
216 Ed Oliver AU 3.00 8.00
217 Deionte Thompson AU 2.50 6.00
218 Devin White AU 6.00 15.00
220 Taylor Rapp AU 2.00 5.00
221 Julian Love AU 2.50 6.00
222 Clelin Ferrell AU 3.00 8.00
223 Dexter Lawrence AU 3.00 8.00
225 Trayvon Mullen Jr. AU 3.00 8.00
226 Rashan Gary AU 4.00 10.00
227 Mack Wilson AU 2.50 6.00
228 Charles Omenihu AU 2.00 5.00
229 Jamel Dean AU 4.00 10.00
230 Jeffery Simmons AU 2.00 5.00
231 Brian Burns AU 2.50 6.00
232 Dre'Mont Jones AU 2.50 6.00
233 Tre Lamar AU 3.00 8.00
234 Chris Johnson AU 2.00 5.00
235 Tyree Kinnel AU 5.00 12.00
236 Ugo Amadi AU 2.50 6.00
237 Byron Murphy AU 2.00 5.00
238 Joe Jackson AU 2.50 6.00
240 Chauncey Gardner-Johnson AU 2.00 5.00
241 Taiwan Deal AU 2.50 6.00
242 Micky Crum AU 2.00 5.00
243 Terry McLaurin AU 2.50 6.00
244 Dillon Mitchell AU 2.50 6.00
246 Kris Boyd AU 2.50 6.00
247 Iman Marshall AU 2.50 6.00
248 Penny Hart AU 2.50 6.00
249 Derrick Baity Jr. AU 2.50 6.00
250 Marquise Copeland AU 2.50 6.00
251 Otaro Alaka AU 3.00 8.00
252 Jace Sternberger AU 2.50 6.00
253 Saivion Smith AU 2.50 6.00
254 Chase Hansen AU 3.00 8.00
256 Khalil Hodge AU 2.50 6.00
257 Greg Gaines AU 2.50 6.00
258 Andrew Wingard AU 3.00 8.00
259 Juan Thornhill AU 2.00 5.00
260 Easton Stick AU 3.00 8.00
261 D'Cota Dixon AU 2.50 6.00
263 Hunter Renfrow AU 4.00 10.00
264 Kyle Shurmur AU 4.00 10.00
265 Matt Sokol AU 3.00 8.00
266 KaVontae Turpin AU 3.00 8.00
267 Felton Davis III AU 5.00 12.00
268 Nyqwan Murray AU 3.00 8.00
269 Justice Hansen AU 2.50 6.00
271 Jaylen Smith AU 2.00 5.00
272 Eric Dungey AU 8.00 20.00
273 Alize Mack AU 3.00 8.00
274 Drew Sample AU 2.00 5.00
275 Foster Moreau AU 2.00 5.00
276 Travis Homer AU 2.00 5.00
277 Nick Brossette AU 2.50 6.00
278 Mecole Hardman Jr. AU 5.00 12.00
279 Jake Browning AU 5.00 12.00
281 Taylor Cornelius AU 4.00 10.00
282 Darius Slayton AU 3.00 8.00
283 Jordan Brailford AU 3.00 8.00
284 Ryquell Armstead AU 2.00 5.00
285 Tony Pollard AU 5.00 12.00
286 Brent Stockstill AU 3.00 8.00
288 Ben Banogu AU 4.00 10.00
289 Miles Boykin AU 2.50 6.00
290 Cody Thompson AU 2.00 5.00
291 Travon McMillian AU 3.00 8.00
292 David Long AU 2.50 6.00
293 Tyre Brady AU 2.00 5.00
294 Preston Williams AU 2.00 5.00
295 David Blough AU 2.50 6.00
296 Patrick Laird AU 4.00 10.00
298 Johnnie Dixon AU 2.50 6.00
299 Mike Edwards AU 4.00 10.00
300 Darnell Savage Jr. AU 3.00 8.00
301 Alexander Mattison AU 4.00 10.00
302 Jakobi Meyers AU 2.00 5.00
303 James Williams AU 2.00 5.00
304 Greg Dortch AU 2.50 6.00
305 Nasir Adderley AU 2.50 6.00
306 KeeSean Johnson AU 2.00 5.00
307 Bruce Anderson AU 2.50 6.00
308 Rock Ya-Sin AU 2.50 6.00
309 Lonnie Johnson Jr. AU 5.00 12.00
310 Isaac Nauta AU 2.50 6.00

2019 Panini Contenders Draft Picks Bowl Ticket

*PLAYOFF/99: 4X TO 10X BASIC CARDS
101A Kyler Murray AU VER 1 200.00 400.00
101B Kyler Murray AU VER 2 200.00 400.00
101C Kyler Murray AU VER 3 200.00 400.00
101D Kyler Murray AU VER 4 200.00 400.00
102A Marquise Brown AU VER 1 25.00 60.00
102B Marquise Brown AU VER 2 25.00 60.00
102C Marquise Brown AU VER 3 25.00 60.00
102D Marquise Brown AU VER 4 25.00 60.00
103A Bryce Love AU VER 1 12.00 30.00
103B Bryce Love AU VER 2 12.00 30.00
103C Bryce Love AU VER 3 12.00 30.00
103D Bryce Love AU VER 4 12.00 30.00
104A Will Grier AU VER 1 25.00 60.00
104B Will Grier AU VER 2 25.00 60.00
104C Will Grier AU VER 3 25.00 60.00
104D Will Grier AU VER 4 25.00 60.00
105A A.J. Brown AU VER 1 EXCH 20.00 50.00
105B A.J. Brown AU VER 2 EXCH 20.00 50.00
105C A.J. Brown AU VER 3 EXCH 20.00 50.00
105D A.J. Brown AU VER 4 EXCH 20.00 50.00
106A Damien Harris AU VER 1 20.00 50.00
106B Damien Harris AU VER 2 20.00 50.00
106C Damien Harris AU VER 3 20.00 50.00
106D Damien Harris AU VER 4 20.00 50.00
107A Ryan Finley AU VER 1 15.00 40.00
107B Ryan Finley AU VER 2 15.00 40.00
107C Ryan Finley AU VER 3 15.00 40.00
107D Ryan Finley AU VER 4 15.00 40.00
108A N'Keal Harry AU VER 1 EXCH 40.00 100.00
108B N'Keal Harry AU VER 2 EXCH 50.00 100.00
108C N'Keal Harry AU VER 3 EXCH 50.00 100.00
108D N'Keal Harry AU VER 4 EXCH 50.00 100.00
109A Rodney Anderson AU VER 1 10.00 25.00
109B Rodney Anderson AU VER 2 10.00 25.00
109C Rodney Anderson AU VER 3 10.00 25.00
109D Rodney Anderson AU VER 4 10.00 25.00
110A Drew Lock AU VER 1 EXCH 40.00 100.00
110B Drew Lock AU VER 2 EXCH 40.00 100.00
110C Drew Lock AU VER 3 EXCH 40.00 100.00
110D Drew Lock AU VER 4 EXCH 40.00 100.00
111A JJ Arcega-Whiteside AU VER 1 12.00 30.00
111B JJ Arcega-Whiteside AU VER 2 12.00 30.00
111C JJ Arcega-Whiteside AU VER 3 12.00 30.00
111D JJ Arcega-Whiteside AU VER 4 12.00 30.00
112A Justice Hill AU VER 1 12.00 30.00
112B Justice Hill AU VER 2 12.00 30.00
112C Justice Hill AU VER 3 12.00 30.00
112D Justice Hill AU VER 4 12.00 30.00
113A Dwayne Haskins AU VER 1 100.00 200.00
113B Dwayne Haskins AU VER 2 100.00 200.00
113C Dwayne Haskins AU VER 3 100.00 200.00
113D Dwayne Haskins AU VER 4 100.00 200.00
114A Kelvin Harmon AU VER 1 12.00 30.00
114B Kelvin Harmon AU VER 2 12.00 30.00
114C Kelvin Harmon AU VER 3 12.00 30.00
114D Kelvin Harmon AU VER 4 12.00 30.00
115A Trayveon Williams AU VER 1 10.00 25.00
115B Trayveon Williams AU VER 2 10.00 25.00
115C Trayveon Williams AU VER 3 10.00 25.00
115D Trayveon Williams AU VER 4 10.00 25.00
116A Daniel Jones AU VER 1 75.00 150.00
116B Daniel Jones AU VER 2 75.00 150.00
116C Daniel Jones AU VER 3 75.00 150.00
116D Daniel Jones AU VER 4 75.00 150.00
117A D.K. Metcalf AU VER 1 25.00 60.00
117B D.K. Metcalf AU VER 2 25.00 60.00
117C D.K. Metcalf AU VER 3 25.00 60.00
117D D.K. Metcalf AU VER 4 25.00 60.00
118A David Montgomery AU VER 1 30.00 80.00
118B David Montgomery AU VER 2 30.00 80.00
118C David Montgomery AU VER 3 30.00 80.00
118D David Montgomery AU VER 4 30.00 80.00
119A Lil'Jordan Humphrey AU VER 1 10.00 25.00
119B Lil'Jordan Humphrey AU VER 2 10.00 25.00
119C Lil'Jordan Humphrey AU VER 3 10.00 25.00
119D Lil'Jordan Humphrey AU VER 4 10.00 25.00
120A Parris Campbell AU VER 1 20.00 50.00
120B Parris Campbell AU VER 2 20.00 50.00
120C Parris Campbell AU VER 3 20.00 50.00
120D Parris Campbell AU VER 4 20.00 50.00
121A Benny Snell Jr. AU VER 1 25.00 60.00
121B Benny Snell Jr. AU VER 2 25.00 60.00
121C Benny Snell Jr. AU VER 3 25.00 60.00
122A Josh Jacobs AU VER 1 40.00 100.00
122B Josh Jacobs AU VER 2 40.00 100.00
122C Josh Jacobs AU VER 3 40.00 100.00
122D Josh Jacobs AU VER 4 40.00 100.00
123A Hakeem Butler AU VER 1 15.00 40.00
123B Hakeem Butler AU VER 2 15.00 40.00
123C Hakeem Butler AU VER 3 15.00 40.00
123D Hakeem Butler AU VER 4 15.00 40.00
124A Darrell Henderson AU VER 1 20.00 50.00
124B Darrell Henderson AU VER 2 20.00 50.00
124D Darrell Henderson AU VER 4 20.00 50.00
125A Riley Ridley AU VER 1 12.00 30.00
125B Riley Ridley AU VER 2 12.00 30.00
125C Riley Ridley AU VER 3 12.00 30.00
125D Riley Ridley AU VER 4 12.00 30.00
126A Anthony Johnson AU VER 1 6.00 15.00
126B Anthony Johnson AU VER 2 6.00 15.00
127A Jarrett Stidham AU VER 1 25.00 50.00
127B Jarrett Stidham AU VER 2 25.00 50.00
128 L.J. Scott AU 8.00 20.00
129A Noah Fant AU VER 1 SP1 10.00 25.00
129B Noah Fant AU VER 2 SP2 10.00 25.00
130A Clayton Thorson AU VER 1 SP1 8.00 20.00
130B Clayton Thorson AU VER 2 SP2 8.00 20.00
131A Deebo Samuel AU VER 1 SP1 12.00 30.00
131B Deebo Samuel AU VER 2 SP2 12.00 30.00
132A Myles Gaskin AU VER 1 SP1 10.00 25.00
132B Myles Gaskin AU VER 2 SP2 10.00 25.00
133A Devin Singletary AU VER 1 SP1 6.00 15.00
133B Devin Singletary AU VER 2 SP2 6.00 15.00
134B Brett Rypien AU VER 2 SP2 6.00 15.00
135A David Sills V AU VER 1 SP1 15.00 40.00
135B David Sills V AU VER 2 SP2 15.00 40.00
136A Karan Higdon AU VER 1 SP1 6.00 15.00
136B Karan Higdon AU VER 2 SP2 6.00 15.00
137A Tyree Jackson AU VER 1 SP1 12.00 30.00
137B Tyree Jackson AU VER 2 SP2 12.00 30.00
138A Irv Smith Jr. AU VER 1 SP1 10.00 25.00
138B Irv Smith Jr. AU VER 2 SP2 10.00 25.00
139A Mike Weber AU VER 1 SP1 8.00 20.00
139B Mike Weber AU VER 2 SP2 8.00 20.00
140A Trace McSorley AU VER 1 SP1 12.00 30.00
140B Trace McSorley AU VER 2 SP2 12.00 30.00
141A Emanuel Hall AU VER 1 SP1 5.00 12.00
141B Emanuel Hall AU VER 2 SP2 5.00 12.00
142 Jalin Moore Jr. AU 5.00 12.00
144 Alex Barnes AU 6.00 15.00
145 Darwin Thompson AU 8.00 20.00
146 Jordan Ta'amu AU 12.00 30.00
147 Alex Wesley AU 8.00 20.00
148 Travis Fulgham AU 5.00 12.00
149 Andy Isabella AU 8.00 20.00
150 Nick Bosa AU 15.00 40.00
151 Gardner Minshew II AU 8.00 20.00
152 Dax Raymond AU 5.00 12.00
153 DaMarkus Lodge AU 5.00 12.00
154 Keelan Doss AU 6.00 15.00
155 Kaden Smith AU 5.00 12.00
156 Dexter Williams AU 6.00 15.00
157 David Long Jr. AU 6.00 15.00
158 Antoine Wesley AU 5.00 12.00
159 Anthony Ratliff-Williams AU 10.00 25.00
160 Jazz Ferguson AU 5.00 12.00
161 Ty Johnson AU 20.00 50.00
162 Josh Oliver AU 5.00 12.00
163 Caleb Wilson AU 5.00 12.00
164 Terry Godwin II AU 6.00 15.00
165 Gary Jennings Jr. AU 8.00 20.00
166 Darrin Hall AU 6.00 15.00
167 Tommy Sweeney AU 5.00 12.00
168 Jacques Patrick AU 5.00 12.00
169 Jordan Scarlett AU 5.00 12.00
170 Stanley Morgan Jr. AU 8.00 20.00
171 Jalen Hurd AU 6.00 15.00
172 T.J. Hockenson AU 12.00 30.00
173 Keenen Brown AU 5.00 12.00
174 Zach Gentry AU 5.00 12.00
175 Qadree Ollison AU 6.00 15.00
176 Miles Sanders AU 25.00 50.00
177 Greedy Williams AU 15.00 40.00
178 Deandre Baker AU 12.00 30.00
179 Zach Allen AU 8.00 20.00
180 Christian Wilkins AU
181 Te'Von Coney AU 15.00 40.00
182 Josh Allen AU
183 Montez Sweat AU 15.00 40.00
184 T.J. Edwards AU 5.00 12.00
185 D'Andre Walker AU 5.00 12.00
186 Johnathan Abram AU 5.00 12.00
187 Amani Oruwariye AU 6.00 15.00
188 Jerry Tillery AU 6.00 15.00
189 Jaylon Ferguson AU 5.00 12.00
190 Ben Burr-Kirven AU 6.00 15.00
191 Oshane Ximines AU 5.00 12.00
192 Jalen Jelks AU 6.00 15.00
193 Marvell Tell III AU 10.00 25.00
194 Jaquan Johnson AU 10.00 25.00
196 Austin Bryant AU 10.00 25.00
197 Lukas Denis AU 6.00 15.00
198 Kendall Joseph AU 10.00 25.00
199 Chase Winovich AU 15.00 40.00
200 Ryan Connelly AU 6.00 15.00
201 Gerald Willis III AU 10.00 25.00
202 Elijah Holyfield AU 8.00 20.00
203 Cameron Smith AU 6.00 15.00
204 Demarcus Christmas AU 6.00 15.00
205 C.J. Conrad AU 5.00 12.00
206 Blace Brown AU 5.00 12.00
207 Terry Beckner Jr. AU 5.00 12.00
208 Christian Miller AU 10.00 25.00
209 Isaiah Buggs AU 12.00 30.00
210 Daniel Wise AU 6.00 15.00
211 Vosean Joseph AU 6.00 15.00
212 Tyler Petite AU 8.00 20.00
213 Porter Gustin AU 8.00 20.00
214 Carl Granderson AU 8.00 20.00
215 Germaine Pratt AU 6.00 15.00
216 Ed Oliver AU 8.00 20.00
217 Deionte Thompson AU 6.00 15.00
218 Devin White AU 15.00 40.00
220 Taylor Rapp AU 5.00 12.00
221 Julian Love AU 6.00 15.00
222 Clelin Ferrell AU 8.00 20.00
223 Dexter Lawrence AU 8.00 20.00
225 Trayvon Mullen Jr. AU 8.00 20.00
226 Rashan Gary AU 10.00 25.00
227 Mack Wilson AU 6.00 15.00
228 Charles Omenihu AU 5.00 12.00
229 Jamel Dean AU 10.00 25.00
230 Jeffery Simmons AU 5.00 12.00
231 Brian Burns AU 6.00 15.00
232 Dre'Mont Jones AU 6.00 15.00
233 Tre Lamar AU 8.00 20.00
234 Chris Johnson AU 5.00 12.00
235 Tyree Kinnel AU 12.00 30.00
236 Ugo Amadi AU 6.00 15.00
237 Byron Murphy AU 5.00 12.00
238 Joe Jackson AU 6.00 15.00
240 Chauncey Gardner-Johnson AU 5.00 12.00
241 Taiwan Deal AU 6.00 15.00
242 Micky Crum AU 5.00 12.00
243 Terry McLaurin AU 6.00 15.00
244 Dillon Mitchell AU 6.00 15.00
246 Kris Boyd AU 6.00 15.00
247 Iman Marshall AU 6.00 15.00
248 Penny Hart AU 6.00 15.00
249 Derrick Baity Jr. AU 6.00 15.00
250 Marquise Copeland AU 6.00 15.00
251 Otaro Alaka AU 8.00 20.00
252 Jace Sternberger AU 6.00 15.00
253 Salvion Smith AU 6.00 15.00
254 Chase Hansen AU 8.00 20.00
256 Khalil Hodge AU 6.00 15.00
257 Greg Gaines AU 6.00 15.00
258 Andrew Wingard AU 8.00 20.00
259 Juan Thornhill AU 5.00 12.00
260 Easton Stick AU 8.00 20.00
261 D'Cota Dixon AU 6.00 15.00
262 Emmanuel Butler AU 8.00 20.00
263 Hunter Renfrow AU 10.00 25.00
264 Kyle Shurmur AU 10.00 25.00
265 Matt Sokol AU 8.00 20.00
266 KaVontae Turpin AU 8.00 20.00
267 Felton Davis III AU 12.00 30.00
268 Nyqwan Murray AU 8.00 20.00
269 Justice Hansen AU 6.00 15.00
270 Blessuan Austin AU 6.00 15.00
271 Jaylen Smith AU 5.00 12.00
272 Eric Dungey AU 20.00 50.00
273 Alize Mack AU 8.00 20.00
274 Drew Sample AU 5.00 12.00
275 Foster Moreau AU 5.00 12.00
276 Travis Homer AU 5.00 12.00
277 Nick Brossette AU 6.00 15.00
278 Mecole Hardman Jr. AU 12.00 30.00
279 Jake Browning AU 12.00 30.00
281 Taylor Cornelius AU 10.00 25.00
282 Darius Slayton AU 8.00 20.00
283 Jordan Brailford AU 8.00 20.00
284 Ryquell Armstead AU 5.00 12.00
285 Tony Pollard AU 12.00 30.00
286 Brent Stockstill AU 8.00 20.00
288 Ben Banogu AU 10.00 25.00
289 Miles Boykin AU 6.00 15.00
290 Cody Thompson AU 5.00 12.00
291 Travon McMillian AU 8.00 20.00
292 David Long AU 6.00 15.00
293 Tyre Brady AU 5.00 12.00
294 Preston Williams AU 5.00 12.00
295 David Blough AU 6.00 15.00
296 Patrick Laird AU 10.00 25.00
297 Justin Layne AU 10.00 25.00
298 Johnnie Dixon AU 6.00 15.00
299 Mike Edwards AU 10.00 25.00
300 Darnell Savage Jr. AU 8.00 20.00
301 Alexander Mattison AU 10.00 25.00
302 Jakobi Meyers AU 5.00 12.00
303 James Williams AU 5.00 12.00
304 Greg Dortch AU 6.00 15.00
305 Nasir Adderley AU 6.00 15.00
306 KeeSean Johnson AU 5.00 12.00
307 Bruce Anderson AU 6.00 15.00
308 Rock Ya-Sin AU 6.00 15.00
309 Lonnie Johnson Jr. AU 12.00 30.00
310 Isaac Nauta AU 6.00 15.00

2019 Panini Contenders Draft Picks College Playoff Ticket

*PLAYOFF/18: 2X TO 5X BOWL AU/99
101A Kyler Murray AU VER 1 250.00 400.00
113A Dwayne Haskins AU VER 1 125.00 250.00
116A Daniel Jones AU VER 1 100.00 200.00

2019 Panini Contenders Draft Picks Cracked Ice

*VETS/23: 12X TO 30X BASIC CARDS
*CRACKED/23: 1X TO 2.5X BOWL AU/99
*CRACKED/23: .6X TO 1.5X BOWL AU/25
101A Kyler Murray AU VER 1 400.00 600.00
101B Kyler Murray AU VER 2 400.00 600.00
101C Kyler Murray AU VER 3 400.00 600.00
101D Kyler Murray AU VER 4 400.00 600.00
113A Dwayne Haskins AU VER 1 150.00 300.00
113B Dwayne Haskins AU VER 2 150.00 300.00
113C Dwayne Haskins AU VER 3 150.00 300.00
113D Dwayne Haskins AU VER 4 150.00 300.00
116A Daniel Jones AU VER 1 150.00 300.00
116B Daniel Jones AU VER 2 150.00 300.00
116C Daniel Jones AU VER 3 150.00 300.00
116D Daniel Jones AU VER 4 150.00 300.00

2019 Panini Contenders Draft Picks Diamond Ticket

*VETS/15: 8X TO 20X BASIC CARDS
*DIAMOND/15: .6X TO 1.5X BASIC AU/25
*DIAMOND/15: .8X TO 2X BASIC AU/99
101A Kyler Murray AU VER 1 250.00 400.00
113A Dwayne Haskins AU VER 1 125.00 250.00
116A Daniel Jones AU VER 1 100.00 200.00

2019 Panini Contenders Draft Picks Collegiate Connections

*CRACKED/23: 2X TO 5X BASIC INSERTS
*DIAMOND/15: 2X TO 5X BASIC INSERTS
1 D.Harris/I.Smith Jr. 1.25 3.00
2 H.Butler/D.Montgomery 2.00 5.00
3 E.Hall/D.Lock 2.50 6.00
4 R.Finley/K.Harmon 1.00 2.50
5 P.Campbell/D.Haskins 2.50 6.00
6 J.Bosa/N.Bosa 1.50 4.00
7 M.Brown/R.Anderson 1.50 4.00
8 B.Mayfield/L.Riley 1.25 3.00
9 D.Metcalf/A.Brown 1.50 4.00
10 A.Brown/J.Ta'amu 1.25 3.00
11 D.Metcalf/J.Ta'amu 1.50 4.00
12 B.Love/ArcgaWhtsde .75 2.00
13 P.Hornung/T.Brown .75 2.00
14 G.Jennings Jr./W.Grier 1.50 4.00
15 D.Slayton/J.Stidham 1.50 4.00
16 B.Cannon/L.Fournette .75 2.00
17 D.Henderson/T.Pollard 1.25 3.00
18 D.Sanders/B.Bowden .60 1.50
19 E.Campbell/R.Williams .75 2.00
20 D.Harris/J.Jacobs 2.50 6.00

2019 Panini Contenders Draft Picks Contenders Optic

101 Kyler Murray 200.00 300.00
102 Marquise Brown 25.00 50.00
103 Bryce Love 8.00 20.00
104 Will Grier 50.00 100.00
105 A.J. Brown EXCH 12.00 30.00
106 Damien Harris 12.00 30.00
107 Ryan Finley 10.00 25.00
108 N'Keal Harry EXCH 50.00 100.00
109 Rodney Anderson 6.00 15.00
110 Drew Lock EXCH 50.00 100.00
111 JJ Arcega-Whiteside 10.00 25.00
112 Justice Hill 8.00 20.00
113 Dwayne Haskins 100.00 200.00
114 Kelvin Harmon 8.00 20.00
115 Trayveon Williams 6.00 15.00
116 Daniel Jones 60.00 125.00
117 D.K. Metcalf 30.00 60.00
118 David Montgomery 20.00 50.00
119 Lil'Jordan Humphrey
120 Parris Campbell 12.00 30.00
121 Benny Snell Jr. 15.00 40.00
122 Josh Jacobs 60.00 125.00
123 Hakeem Butler 10.00 25.00
124 Darrell Henderson 12.00 30.00
125 Riley Ridley 8.00 20.00

2019 Panini Contenders Draft Picks Contenders Optic Hyper

*HYPER/20: .6X TO 1.5X BASIC AU
101 Kyler Murray 250.00 400.00
113 Dwayne Haskins 250.00 400.00

2019 Panini Contenders Draft Picks Contenders Optic Mojo

*MOJO/15: .6X TO 1.5X BASIC AU
101 Kyler Murray 250.00 400.00
113 Dwayne Haskins 250.00 400.00

2019 Panini Contenders Draft Picks Draft Class

*CRACKED/23: 2X TO 5X BASIC INSERTS
*DIAMOND/15: 2.5X TO 6X BASIC INSERTS
1 Kyler Murray 4.00 10.00
2 Marquise Brown 1.25 3.00
3 Bryce Love .60 1.50
4 Will Grier 1.25 3.00
5 A.J. Brown 1.00 2.50
6 Damien Harris 1.00 2.50
7 Ryan Finley .75 2.00
8 N'Keal Harry 1.25 3.00
9 Rodney Anderson .50 1.25
10 Drew Lock 2.00 5.00
11 JJ Arcega-Whiteside .60 1.50
12 Justice Hill .60 1.50
13 Dwayne Haskins 2.00 5.00
14 Kelvin Harmon .60 1.50
15 Trayveon Williams .50 1.25
16 Daniel Jones 2.00 5.00
17 D.K. Metcalf 1.25 3.00
18 David Montgomery 1.50 4.00
19 Josh Jacobs 2.00 5.00
20 Parris Campbell 1.00 2.50

2019 Panini Contenders Draft Picks Game Day Ticket Signatures

1 Kyler Murray 125.00 250.00
2 Marquise Brown EXCH 12.00 30.00
3 Bryce Love 6.00 15.00
4 Will Grier 50.00 100.00
5 A.J. Brown 10.00 25.00
6 Damien Harris 10.00 25.00
7 Ryan Finley 8.00 20.00
8 N'Keal Harry 12.00 30.00
9 Rodney Anderson 5.00 12.00
10 Drew Lock 20.00 50.00
11 JJ Arcega-Whiteside 6.00 15.00
12 Justice Hill 6.00 15.00
13 Dwayne Haskins 50.00 100.00
14 Kelvin Harmon 6.00 15.00
15 Trayveon Williams 5.00 12.00
16 Daniel Jones 30.00 60.00
17 Anthony Johnson 5.00 12.00
18 David Montgomery 15.00 40.00
19 Jarrett Stidham 12.00 30.00
20 Parris Campbell 10.00 25.00
21 Benny Snell Jr. 12.00 30.00
22 Darrell Henderson 10.00 25.00
23 Hakeem Butler 10.00 25.00
24 Josh Jacobs 20.00 50.00
25 D.K. Metcalf 12.00 30.00

2019 Panini Contenders Draft Picks Game Day Ticket Signatures Bowl

*BOWL/25: .6X TO 1.5X BASIC AU
1 Kyler Murray/25 200.00 300.00

2019 Panini Contenders Draft Picks Game Day Ticket Signatures Cracked Ice

*CRACKED/23: .8X TO 2X BASIC AU
1 Kyler Murray 250.00 400.00

2019 Panini Contenders Draft Picks Game Day Ticket Signatures Playoff

*PLAYOFF/18: .8X TO 2X BASIC AU
1 Kyler Murray 200.00 400.00

2019 Panini Contenders Draft Picks Legacy

*CRACKED/23: 2X TO 5X BASIC INSERTS
*DIAMOND/15: 2X TO 5X BASIC INSERTS
1 J.Watt/T.Watt .75 2.00
2 J.Bosa/N.Bosa 1.50 4.00
3 B.Sanders/T.Thomas 1.25 3.00
4 T.Tebow/E.Smith 1.25 3.00
5 E.Campbell/R.Williams .75 2.00
6 C.Newton/B.Jackson 1.00 2.50
7 A.Rodgers/J.Goff 1.50 4.00
8 T.Brady/C.Woodson 2.00 5.00
9 D.Marino/T.Dorsett 1.50 4.00
10 A.Manning/E.Manning .60 1.50
11 P.Manning/J.Witten 1.50 4.00
12 C.Ridley/J.Jones .75 2.00
13 B.Cannon/L.Fournette .75 2.00
14 A.Peterson/M.Dupree .75 2.00
15 M.Faulk/R.Penny .60 1.50
16 R.Lewis/E.Reed .75 2.00
17 E.George/E.Elliott 1.00 2.50
18 F.Tarkenton/H.Walker .75 2.00
19 C.Palmer/M.Allen .75 2.00
20 B.Love/C.McCaffrey .75 2.00

2019 Panini Contenders Draft Picks School Colors Signatures

1 Kyler Murray 125.00 250.00
2 Marquise Brown EXCH 12.00 30.00
3 Bryce Love 6.00 15.00
4 Will Grier 50.00 100.00
5 A.J. Brown 10.00 25.00
6 Damien Harris 10.00 25.00
7 Ryan Finley 8.00 20.00
8 N'Keal Harry 12.00 30.00
9 Rodney Anderson 5.00 12.00
10 Drew Lock 20.00 50.00
11 JJ Arcega-Whiteside 6.00 15.00
12 Justice Hill 6.00 15.00
13 Dwayne Haskins 50.00 100.00
14 Kelvin Harmon 6.00 15.00
15 Trayveon Williams 5.00 12.00
16 Daniel Jones 30.00 60.00
17 Josh Jacobs 20.00 50.00
18 David Montgomery 15.00 40.00
19 D.K. Metcalf 12.00 30.00
20 Parris Campbell 10.00 25.00

2017 Panini Contenders Optic

1 Julio Jones 1.50 4.00
2 Matt Ryan 1.25 3.00
3 Devonta Freeman 1.25 3.00
4 Cam Newton 1.50 4.00
5 Kelvin Benjamin 1.25 3.00
6 Greg Olsen 1.25 3.00
7 Drew Brees 1.50 4.00
8 Adrian Peterson 1.50 4.00
9 Michael Thomas 1.50 4.00
10 Jameis Winston 1.25 3.00
11 DeSean Jackson 1.25 3.00
12 Mike Evans 1.25 3.00
13 Lamar Miller 1.00 2.50
14 J.J. Watt 1.50 4.00
15 DeAndre Hopkins 1.25 3.00
16 Andrew Luck 2.00 5.00
17 T.Y. Hilton 1.25 3.00
18 Blake Bortles 1.00 2.50
19 Jalen Ramsey 1.00 2.50
20 Allen Hurns 1.00 2.50
21 Marcus Mariota 1.50 4.00
22 DeMarco Murray 1.25 3.00
23 Delanie Walker 1.00 2.50
24 Jordan Howard 1.50 4.00
25 Leonard Floyd 1.00 2.50
26 Matthew Stafford 1.25 3.00
27 Ameer Abdullah 1.00 2.50
28 Marvin Jones Jr. 1.00 2.50
29 Aaron Rodgers 3.00 8.00
30 Jordy Nelson 1.25 3.00
31 Davante Adams 1.25 3.00
32 Stefon Diggs 1.25 3.00
33 Sam Bradford 1.00 2.50
34 Joe Flacco 1.25 3.00
35 Buck Allen 1.00 2.50
36 Terrell Suggs 1.00 2.50
37 Andy Dalton 1.25 3.00
38 A.J. Green 1.50 4.00
39 Duke Johnson 1.00 2.50
40 Isaiah Crowell 1.00 2.50
41 Ben Roethlisberger 1.50 4.00
42 Le'Veon Bell 1.25 3.00
43 Antonio Brown 1.50 4.00
44 Carson Palmer 1.25 3.00
45 David Johnson 1.50 4.00
46 Larry Fitzgerald 1.25 3.00
47 Jared Goff 1.50 4.00
48 Todd Gurley II 1.50 4.00
49 Robert Woods 1.25 3.00
50 Jimmy Garoppolo 10.00 25.00
51 Carlos Hyde 1.00 2.50
52 Pierre Garcon 1.25 3.00
53 Russell Wilson 2.00 5.00
54 Thomas Rawls 1.00 2.50
55 Doug Baldwin 1.25 3.00
56 Trevor Siemian 1.00 2.50
57 Von Miller 1.25 3.00
58 Demaryius Thomas 1.25 3.00
59 Alex Smith 1.25 3.00
60 Tyreek Hill 1.50 4.00
61 Travis Kelce 1.50 4.00
62 Philip Rivers 1.50 4.00
63 Melvin Gordon 1.25 3.00
64 Hunter Henry 1.00 2.50
65 Derek Carr 1.50 4.00
66 Marshawn Lynch 1.25 3.00
67 Amari Cooper 1.50 4.00
68 Khalil Mack 1.50 4.00
69 Dak Prescott 1.50 4.00
70 Ezekiel Elliott 2.00 5.00
71 Dez Bryant 1.50 4.00
72 Jason Witten 1.25 3.00
73 Eli Manning 1.25 3.00
74 Odell Beckham Jr. 1.50 4.00
75 Brandon Marshall 1.00 2.50
76 Carson Wentz 2.00 5.00
77 Alshon Jeffery 1.25 3.00
78 Kirk Cousins 1.50 4.00
79 Robert Kelley 1.00 2.50
80 Jamison Crowder 1.00 2.50
81 Tyrod Taylor 1.25 3.00
82 LeSean McCoy 1.50 4.00
83 Jay Cutler 1.00 2.50
84 Jay Ajayi 1.25 3.00
85 Jarvis Landry 1.25 3.00
86 Tom Brady 4.00 10.00
87 Rob Gronkowski 1.50 4.00
88 Brandin Cooks 1.25 3.00
89 Jermaine Kearse 1.00 2.50
90 Josh McCown 1.00 2.50
91 Myles Garrett RC 4.00 10.00
92 Tarik Cohen RC 2.50 6.00
93 Reuben Foster RC 1.25 3.00
94 Cooper Rush RC 1.50 4.00
95 Takkarist McKinley RC 1.25 3.00
96 Garett Bolles RC 1.25 3.00
97 Cam Robinson RC 1.25 3.00
98 Jehu Chesson RC 1.50 4.00
99 Aaron Jones RC 3.00 8.00
100 Zach Cunningham RC 1.50 4.00
101 Mitchell Trubisky AU RC 100.00 200.00
102 Deshaun Watson AU RC 15.00 300.00
103 Patrick Mahomes II AU RC 800.00 1200.00
104 DeShone Kizer AU RC EXCH 12.00 30.00
105 Davis Webb AU RC 15.00 40.00
106 R. Joshua Dobbs AU RC 12.00 30.00
107 C.J. Beathard AU RC EXCH 5.00 12.00
108 Nathan Peterman AU RC 6.00 15.00
109 Dalvin Cook AU RC 20.00 40.00
110 Leonard Fournette AU RC 30.00 60.00
111 Christian McCaffrey AU RC 30.00 60.00
112 Joe Mixon AU RC 12.00 30.00
113 Alvin Kamara AU RC 30.00 60.00
114 Marlon Mack AU RC 8.00 20.00
115 Samaje Perine AU RC 5.00 12.00
116 Wayne Gallman AU RC 6.00 15.00
117 Kareem Hunt AU RC 12.00 30.00
118 D'Onta Foreman AU RC 6.00 15.00
119 Jeremy McNichols AU RC 5.00 12.00
120 James Conner AU RC 20.00 50.00
121 Jamaal Williams AU RC 5.00 12.00
122 Joe Williams AU RC 5.00 12.00
123 O.J. Howard AU RC 6.00 15.00
124 Evan Engram AU RC EXCH 6.00 15.00
125 Mike Williams AU RC 8.00 20.00
126 John Ross III AU RC 6.00 15.00
127 JuJu Smith-Schuster AU RC 30.00 60.00
128 Corey Davis AU RC 8.00 20.00
129 Dede Westbrook AU RC 5.00 12.00
130 Curtis Samuel AU RC 6.00 15.00
131 Amara Darboh AU RC 5.00 12.00
132 Carlos Henderson AU RC 5.00 12.00
134 Cooper Kupp AU RC 8.00 20.00
135 Josh Reynolds AU RC EXCH 5.00 12.00
136 ArDarius Stewart AU RC 5.00 12.00
137 Chris Godwin AU RC 6.00 15.00
138 Taywan Taylor AU RC 5.00 12.00
139 Kenny Golladay AU RC 8.00 20.00
140 Mack Hollins AU RC 5.00 12.00
141 Brad Kaaya AU RC 5.00 12.00
142 T.J. Watt AU RC 15.00 40.00
144 Jake Butt AU RC 6.00 15.00
145 Greg Ward Jr. AU RC 5.00 12.00
146 Jamal Adams AU RC 5.00 12.00
147 Donnel Pumphrey AU RC 6.00 15.00
148 Chad Kelly AU RC 15.00 40.00
149 Marshon Lattimore AU RC EXCH 6.00 15.00
150 Quincy Wilson AU RC 5.00 12.00
151 Ryan Switzer AU RC 6.00 15.00
152 Cameron Sutton AU RC 5.00 12.00
153 David Njoku AU RC EXCH 6.00 15.00
154 Sidney Jones AU RC 5.00 12.00
155 Solomon Thomas AU RC 5.00 12.00
156 Gareon Conley AU RC 5.00 12.00
157 Adoree' Jackson AU RC EXCH 6.00 15.00
158 Matthew Dayes AU RC 5.00 12.00
159 Malik Hooker AU RC EXCH 5.00 12.00
160 Derek Barnett AU RC EXCH 6.00 15.00
161 Charles Harris AU RC 5.00 12.00
162 Corey Clement AU RC 6.00 15.00
163 Desmond King AU RC 6.00 15.00
164 Jabrill Peppers AU RC 8.00 20.00
165 Brian Hill AU RC 5.00 12.00
167 Tre'Davious White AU RC 5.00 12.00
168 Jonathan Allen AU RC 6.00 15.00
169 Stacy Coley AU RC 5.00 12.00
170 Carl Lawson AU RC 5.00 12.00
171 Taco Charlton AU RC 5.00 12.00
172 Haason Reddick AU RC 5.00 12.00
173 Isaiah McKenzie AU RC 5.00 12.00
174 Robert Davis AU RC 5.00 12.00
175 Josh Malone AU RC 5.00 12.00
176 Elijah Qualls AU RC 5.00 12.00
177 Jarrad Davis AU RC EXCH 6.00 15.00
178 Jordan Leggett AU RC 5.00 12.00
179 Tim Williams AU RC 6.00 15.00
180 Chad Hansen AU RC 5.00 12.00
181 Artavis Scott AU RC 5.00 12.00
182 Shelton Gibson AU RC 5.00 12.00
183 Duke Riley AU RC 5.00 12.00
184 Gerald Everett AU RC 5.00 12.00
185 Tanoh Kpassagnon AU RC 6.00 15.00
186 George Kittle AU RC 5.00 12.00
187 Adam Shaheen AU RC 5.00 12.00
188 Jeremy Sprinkle AU RC 5.00 12.00
189 Matt Breida AU RC 12.00 30.00
190 Damontae Kazee AU RC 6.00 15.00
191 Dawuane Smoot AU RC 5.00 12.00
193 Deatrich Wise Jr. AU RC 8.00 20.00
194 Chris Wormley AU RC 5.00 12.00
195 Chris Carson AU RC 8.00 20.00
197 Marcus Maye AU RC 5.00 12.00
198 Tyus Bowser AU RC 5.00 12.00
199 Marcus Williams AU RC 5.00 12.00
200 Trent Taylor AU RC 40.00 80.00

2017 Panini Contenders Optic Blue

*VETS: .8X TO 2X BASIC CARDS
*ROOKIES: .6X TO 1.5X BASIC CARDS
*ROOK AU/25: X TO X BASIC AU
101 Mitchell Trubisky AU 200.00 400.00
102 Deshaun Watson AU 1200.00 1500.00
103 Patrick Mahomes II AU 2000.00 3000.00
111 Christian McCaffrey AU 125.00 250.00
127 JuJu Smith-Schuster AU 75.00 150.00

2017 Panini Contenders Optic Red

*VETS: .6X TO 1.5X BASIC CARDS
*ROOKIES: .5X TO 1.2X BASIC CARDS
*ROOK AU/75: X TO X BASIC AU
*ROOK AU/50: X TO X BASIC AU
*ROOK AU/25: X TO X BASIC AU
*ROOK AU/15: X TO X BASIC AU
101 Mitchell Trubisky AU/75 150.00 250.00
102 Deshaun Watson AU/75 250.00 500.00
103 Patrick Mahomes II AU/75 1700.00 2200.00
111 Christian McCaffrey AU/75 75.00 150.00
127 JuJu Smith-Schuster AU/75 50.00 100.00
200 Trent Taylor AU/15 60.00 125.00

2017 Panini Contenders Optic '00 Contenders Tribute Autographs

2 Brian Urlacher 100.00 200.00

2017 Panini Contenders Optic '01 Contenders Tribute Autographs

1 Drew Brees/15 250.00 400.00
2 LaDainian Tomlinson/25 90.00 150.00
3 Michael Vick/25

2017 Panini Contenders Optic '98 Contenders Tribute Autographs

2 Randy Moss/15
3 Hines Ward/25 50.00 100.00

2017 Panini Contenders Optic '99 Contenders Tribute Autographs

1 Edgerrin James 40.00 80.00
2 Ricky Williams 50.00 100.00

2017 Panini Contenders Optic All Pro Contenders

*RED/49: .5X TO 1.2X BASIC INSERTS/99
*BLUE/25: .6X TO 1.5X BASIC INSERTS/99
1 Matt Ryan 2.00 5.00
2 Ezekiel Elliott 3.00 8.00
3 Greg Olsen 2.00 5.00
4 Fletcher Cox 1.50 4.00
5 Tyreek Hill 2.50 6.00
6 Landon Collins 1.50 4.00
7 Mike Evans 2.00 5.00
8 Dont'a Hightower 1.50 4.00
9 Luke Kuechly 2.00 5.00
10 Aaron Donald 2.50 6.00
11 Ha Ha Clinton-Dix 1.50 4.00
12 Gerald McCoy 1.50 4.00
13 Geno Atkins 1.50 4.00
14 Travis Kelce 2.50 6.00
15 Aqib Talib 1.50 4.00
16 Joe Thomas 1.50 4.00
17 Jordy Nelson 2.00 5.00
18 Devonta Freeman 2.00 5.00
19 Marshawn Lynch 2.00 5.00
20 Earl Thomas III 2.00 5.00

2017 Panini Contenders Optic All Pro Contenders Autographs

1 Matt Ryan/15 40.00 80.00
2 Ezekiel Elliott 50.00 100.00
3 Greg Olsen 8.00 20.00
4 Fletcher Cox 6.00 15.00
5 Tyreek Hill 10.00 25.00
6 Landon Collins 6.00 15.00
7 Mike Evans 8.00 20.00
8 Dont'a Hightower 30.00 60.00
9 Luke Kuechly 15.00 40.00
10 Aaron Donald 15.00 40.00
11 Ha Ha Clinton-Dix 6.00 15.00
12 Gerald McCoy EXCH 6.00 15.00
13 Geno Atkins 6.00 15.00
14 Travis Kelce 10.00 25.00
15 Aqib Talib 6.00 15.00
16 Joe Thomas EXCH 30.00 60.00
17 Jordy Nelson 8.00 20.00
18 Devonta Freeman 8.00 20.00
19 Marshawn Lynch 40.00 80.00
20 Earl Thomas III 12.00 30.00

2017 Panini Contenders Optic Defensive Player of the Year Contenders

*RED/49: .5X TO 1.2X BASIC INSERTS/99
*BLUE/25: .6X TO 1.5X BASIC INSERTS/99
1 Vic Beasley Jr. 1.50 4.00
2 Richard Sherman 2.50 6.00
3 Earl Thomas III 2.00 5.00
4 Dont'a Hightower 1.50 4.00
5 Marcus Peters 1.50 4.00
6 Landon Collins 1.50 4.00
7 Ha Ha Clinton-Dix 1.50 4.00
8 Stephon Gilmore 1.50 4.00
9 Luke Kuechly 2.00 5.00
10 J.J. Watt 2.50 6.00
11 Gerald McCoy 1.50 4.00
12 Aaron Donald 2.50 6.00
13 Geno Atkins 1.50 4.00
14 Xavier Rhodes 1.50 4.00
15 Terrell Suggs 1.50 4.00
16 Von Miller 2.00 5.00
17 Fletcher Cox 1.50 4.00
18 Joey Bosa 2.50 6.00
19 Eric Weddle 1.50 4.00
20 Joe Haden 1.50 4.00

2017 Panini Contenders Optic Defensive Player of the Year Contenders Autographs

1 Vic Beasley Jr./25
2 Richard Sherman/25
3 Earl Thomas III/25 EXCH 12.00 30.00
4 Dont'a Hightower/25 30.00 60.00
5 Marcus Peters/25
6 Landon Collins/25 6.00 15.00
7 Ha Ha Clinton-Dix/25 6.00 15.00
8 Stephon Gilmore/25 15.00 40.00
9 Luke Kuechly/20 20.00 50.00
10 J.J. Watt/15
11 Gerald McCoy/25 EXCH 6.00 15.00
12 Aaron Donald/25 15.00 40.00
13 Geno Atkins/25 6.00 15.00
15 Terrell Suggs/25 12.00 30.00
17 Fletcher Cox/25 6.00 15.00
19 Eric Weddle/25 12.00 30.00

2017 Panini Contenders Optic Hall of Fame Contenders Autographs

1 Torry Holt
2 Brian Dawkins 100.00 200.00
3 Randy Moss
4 Sterling Sharpe 12.00 30.00
5 Hines Ward 25.00 50.00

6 Ray Lewis 75.00 150.00
7 Edgerrin James 8.00 20.00
8 Fred Taylor 8.00 20.00
9 Brian Urlacher
10 Ty Law

2017 Panini Contenders Optic Legendary Contenders
*RED/25: .5X TO 1.2X BASIC INSERTS/49
1 Jim Kelly 3.00 8.00
2 Jason Taylor 2.00 5.00
3 Emmitt Smith 5.00 12.00
4 Michael Vick 2.50 6.00
5 Alan Page 2.00 5.00
6 Jim Otto 2.00 5.00
7 Brett Favre 6.00 15.00
8 Lance Alworth 2.50 6.00
9 Drew Pearson 2.50 6.00
10 Earl Campbell 3.00 8.00
11 Randy Moss 2.50 6.00
12 Calvin Johnson 3.00 8.00
13 Steve Young 4.00 10.00
14 Chris Doleman 2.00 5.00
15 Mark Gastineau 2.00 5.00

2017 Panini Contenders Optic MVP Contenders
*RED/25: .6X TO 1.5X BASIC INSERTS/99
1 Aaron Rodgers 5.00 12.00
2 Matt Ryan 2.00 5.00
3 Ezekiel Elliott 3.00 8.00
4 Mike Evans 2.00 5.00
5 Drew Brees 2.50 6.00
6 Dak Prescott 2.50 6.00
7 Matthew Stafford 2.00 5.00
8 Derek Carr 2.50 6.00
9 Marcus Mariota 2.50 6.00
10 Jameis Winston 2.00 5.00
11 Tom Brady 6.00 15.00
12 J.J. Watt 2.50 6.00
13 Ben Roethlisberger 2.50 6.00
14 Russell Wilson 3.00 8.00
15 Carson Wentz 3.00 8.00
16 Alex Smith 2.00 5.00
17 LeSean McCoy 2.50 6.00
18 Rob Gronkowski 2.50 6.00
19 Jordan Howard 2.50 6.00
20 Todd Gurley II 2.50 6.00
21 Devonta Freeman 2.00 5.00
22 Melvin Gordon 2.00 5.00
23 Antonio Brown 2.50 6.00
24 Jordy Nelson 2.00 5.00
25 Luke Kuechly 2.00 5.00

2017 Panini Contenders Optic MVP Contenders Autographs
2 Matt Ryan/15 40.00 80.00
3 Ezekiel Elliott/25 50.00 100.00
4 Mike Evans/25 8.00 20.00
5 Drew Brees/15 50.00 100.00
6 Dak Prescott/25 EXCH 40.00 80.00
7 Matthew Stafford/15 15.00 40.00
8 Derek Carr/25 30.00 60.00
9 Marcus Mariota/15 40.00 80.00
10 Jameis Winston/15 EXCH 30.00 80.00
12 J.J. Watt/15
15 Carson Wentz/15 125.00 250.00
16 Alex Smith/15 10.00 25.00
17 LeSean McCoy/25 10.00 25.00
18 Rob Gronkowski/15 EXCH 60.00 125.00
19 Jordan Howard/25
20 Todd Gurley II/15 40.00 80.00
21 Devonta Freeman/25 8.00 20.00
22 Melvin Gordon/25 8.00 20.00
23 Antonio Brown/15 40.00 80.00
24 Jordy Nelson/25 8.00 20.00
25 Luke Kuechly/25 15.00 40.00

2017 Panini Contenders Optic Rookie of the Year Contenders
*RED/49: .5X TO 1.2X BASIC INSERTS/99
*BLUE/25: .6X TO 1.5X BASIC INSERTS/99
1 Mitchell Trubisky 5.00 12.00
2 Deshaun Watson 6.00 15.00
3 Patrick Mahomes II 12.00 30.00
4 DeShone Kizer 1.00 2.50
5 C.J. Beathard 1.00 2.50
6 Dalvin Cook 2.50 6.00
7 Leonard Fournette 3.00 8.00
8 Christian McCaffrey 2.50 6.00
9 Joe Mixon 2.00 5.00
10 Alvin Kamara 4.00 10.00
11 Marlon Mack 1.50 4.00
12 Samaje Perine 1.00 2.50
13 Wayne Gallman 1.25 3.00
14 Kareem Hunt 2.00 5.00
15 D'Onta Foreman 1.25 3.00
16 Kenny Golladay 1.50 4.00
17 Joe Williams 1.00 2.50
18 O.J. Howard 1.25 3.00
19 Evan Engram 1.25 3.00
20 Mike Williams 1.50 4.00
21 John Ross III 1.25 3.00
22 JuJu Smith-Schuster 2.50 6.00
23 Corey Davis 1.50 4.00
24 Dede Westbrook 1.00 2.50
25 Curtis Samuel 1.25 3.00
26 Carlos Henderson 1.00 2.50
27 Zay Jones 1.25 3.00
28 Cooper Kupp 1.50 4.00
29 Josh Reynolds 1.00 2.50
30 ArDarius Stewart 1.00 2.50

2017 Panini Contenders Optic Rookie of the Year Contenders Autographs
1 Mitchell Trubisky 90.00 150.00
2 Deshaun Watson 250.00 350.00
3 Patrick Mahomes II 150.00 300.00
4 DeShone Kizer EXCH 30.00 60.00
5 C.J. Beathard 6.00 15.00
6 Dalvin Cook 40.00 80.00
7 Leonard Fournette 50.00 100.00
8 Christian McCaffrey
9 Joe Mixon 12.00 30.00
10 Alvin Kamara
11 Marlon Mack 10.00 25.00
12 Samaje Perine 6.00 15.00
13 Wayne Gallman 8.00 20.00
14 Kareem Hunt 15.00 40.00
15 D'Onta Foreman 8.00 20.00
16 Kenny Golladay 10.00 25.00
18 O.J. Howard 15.00 40.00
19 Evan Engram
20 Mike Williams 10.00 25.00
21 John Ross III
22 JuJu Smith-Schuster
23 Corey Davis 10.00 25.00
24 Dede Westbrook 6.00 15.00
25 Curtis Samuel 8.00 20.00
26 Carlos Henderson 6.00 15.00
27 Zay Jones 8.00 20.00
28 Cooper Kupp 10.00 25.00
29 Josh Reynolds 6.00 15.00
30 ArDarius Stewart 6.00 15.00

2017 Panini Contenders Optic Round Numbers
*RED/49: .5X TO 1.2X BASIC INSERTS/75
*BLUE/25: .6X TO 1.5X BASIC INSERTS/75
1 D.Watson/M.Trubisky 6.00 15.00
2 L.Fournette/C.McCaffrey 3.00 8.00
3 T.Watt/J.Peppers 3.00 8.00
4 J.Adams/M.Hooker 1.00 2.50
5 M.Williams/C.Davis 1.50 4.00
6 O.Howard/E.Engram 1.25 3.00
7 D.Cook/J.Mixon 2.50 6.00
8 K.King/S.Jones 1.25 3.00
9 O.Everett/A.Shaheen 1.00 2.50
10 C.Samuel/Z.Jones 1.25 3.00
11 D.Webb/C.Beathard 1.00 2.50
12 D.Foreman/K.Hunt 2.00 5.00
13 C.Henderson/T.Taylor 1.00 2.50
14 C.Kupp/K.Golladay 1.50 4.00
15 W.Gallman/S.Perine 1.25 3.00
16 D.Pumphrey/T.Cohen 2.00 5.00
17 J.Chesson/R.Switzer 1.25 3.00
18 B.Hill/T.Logan 1.50 4.00
19 I.McKenzie/T.Taylor 1.25 3.00
20 G.Kittle/J.Butt 1.25 3.00
21 D.Barnett/S.Thomas 1.25 3.00
22 A.Jackson/M.Lattimore 1.25 3.00
23 D.Westbrook/J.Reynolds 1.00 2.50
24 A.Stewart/C.Godwin 1.25 3.00
25 J.Williams/J.Williams 1.00 2.50
26 J.Conner/A.Kamara 4.00 10.00
27 T.Charlton/J.Allen 1.25 3.00
28 D.Mays/C.Carson 1.50 4.00
29 A.Darboh/C.Henderson 1.00 2.50
30 J.Leggett/J.Sprinkle 1.00 2.50

2017 Panini Contenders Optic Super Bowl Contenders
*RED/49: .5X TO 1.2X BASIC INSERTS/99
*BLUE/25: .6X TO 1.5X BASIC INSERTS/99
1 Devonta Freeman 2.00 5.00
2 Matt Ryan 2.00 5.00
3 Brandin Cooks 2.00 5.00
4 Tom Brady 6.00 15.00
5 Ben Roethlisberger 2.50 6.00
6 Marcus Mariota 2.50 6.00
7 Alex Smith 2.00 5.00
8 Derek Carr 2.50 6.00
9 Aaron Rodgers 5.00 12.00
10 Demaryius Thomas 2.00 5.00
11 Dak Prescott 2.50 6.00
12 Drew Brees 2.50 6.00
13 Carson Wentz 3.00 8.00
14 Matthew Stafford 2.00 5.00
15 Stefon Diggs 2.00 5.00
16 Greg Olsen 2.00 5.00
17 Jameis Winston 2.00 5.00
18 Richard Sherman 2.50 6.00
19 DeMarco Murray 2.00 5.00
20 Tyreek Hill 2.50 6.00

2018 Panini Contenders Optic
1 Alex Smith 1.25 3.00
2 Josh Norman 1.00 2.50
3 Jordan Reed 1.00 2.50
4 Marcus Mariota 1.50 4.00
5 Corey Davis 1.25 3.00
6 Derrick Henry 1.50 4.00
7 Jameis Winston 1.25 3.00
8 Mike Evans 1.25 3.00
9 Gerald McCoy 1.00 2.50
10 Russell Wilson 2.00 5.00
11 Doug Baldwin 1.25 3.00
12 Earl Thomas III 1.25 3.00
13 Jimmy Garoppolo 2.00 5.00
14 Richard Sherman 1.50 4.00
15 Marquise Goodwin 1.00 2.50
16 James Conner 1.50 4.00
17 Antonio Brown 1.50 4.00
18 JuJu Smith-Schuster 1.50 4.00
19 Ben Roethlisberger 1.50 4.00
20 Carson Wentz 2.00 5.00
21 Alshon Jeffery 1.25 3.00
22 Jay Ajayi 1.25 3.00
23 Derek Carr 1.50 4.00
24 Khalil Mack 1.50 4.00
25 Amari Cooper 1.50 4.00
26 Jordy Nelson 1.25 3.00
27 Robby Anderson 1.00 2.50
28 Jamal Adams 1.25 3.00
29 Eli Manning 1.25 3.00
30 Odell Beckham Jr. 1.50 4.00
31 Drew Brees 1.50 4.00
32 Michael Thomas 1.50 4.00
33 Alvin Kamara 1.25 3.00
34 Tom Brady 4.00 10.00
35 Rob Gronkowski 1.50 4.00
36 Julian Edelman 1.50 4.00
37 Kirk Cousins 1.50 4.00
38 Adam Thielen 1.50 4.00
39 Stefon Diggs 1.25 3.00
40 Ryan Tannehill 1.25 3.00
41 Kenyan Drake 1.00 2.50
42 Jared Goff 1.50 4.00
43 Todd Gurley II 1.50 4.00
44 Aaron Donald 1.50 4.00
45 Philip Rivers 1.50 4.00
46 Melvin Gordon III 1.25 3.00
47 Joey Bosa 1.50 4.00
48 Patrick Mahomes II 8.00 20.00
49 Tyreek Hill 1.50 4.00
50 Kareem Hunt 1.25 3.00
51 Blake Bortles 1.00 2.50
52 Jalen Ramsey 1.25 3.00
53 Leonard Fournette 1.50 4.00
54 T.Y. Hilton 1.25 3.00
55 Andrew Luck 2.00 5.00
56 Deshaun Watson 2.00 5.00
57 J.J. Watt 1.50 4.00
58 DeAndre Hopkins 1.25 3.00
59 Aaron Rodgers 3.00 8.00
60 Davante Adams 1.25 3.00
61 Jimmy Graham 1.50 4.00
62 Matthew Stafford 1.25 3.00
63 Marvin Jones Jr. 1.00 2.50
64 Case Keenum 1.25 3.00
65 Von Miller 1.25 3.00
66 Dak Prescott 1.50 4.00
67 Ezekiel Elliott 2.00 5.00
68 Sean Lee 1.25 3.00
69 Jarvis Landry 1.25 3.00
70 Andy Dalton 1.25 3.00
71 A.J. Green 1.50 4.00
72 Mitchell Trubisky 1.50 4.00
73 Jordan Howard 1.50 4.00
74 Allen Robinson II 1.25 3.00
75 Cam Newton 1.50 4.00
76 Christian McCaffrey 1.50 4.00
77 Luke Kuechly 1.25 3.00
78 LeSean McCoy 1.50 4.00
79 Kelvin Benjamin 1.25 3.00
80 Joe Flacco 1.25 3.00
81 Michael Crabtree 1.00 2.50
82 Terrell Suggs 1.00 2.50
83 Matt Ryan 1.25 3.00
84 Julio Jones 1.50 4.00
85 Devonta Freeman 1.25 3.00
86 Larry Fitzgerald 1.25 3.00
87 David Johnson 1.50 4.00
88 Brandin Cooks 1.25 3.00
89 Zach Ertz 1.25 3.00
90 Josh Gordon 1.00 2.50
91 Equanimeous St. Brown 1.50 4.00
92 Antonio Callaway 1.25 3.00
93 Jessie Bates 1.50 4.00
94 Genard Avery RC 1.00 2.50
95 Ja'whaun Bentley RC 1.00 2.50
96 Donte Jackson 1.50 4.00
97 Mike Boone 1.25 3.00
98 Robert Foster 1.00 2.50
99 Kenny Young 1.00 2.50
100 Ian Thomas 1.00 2.50
101 Baker Mayfield AU RC 400.00 800.00
102 Saquon Barkley AU RC EXCH 100.00 200.00
103 Sam Darnold AU RC 100.00 200.00
104 Bradley Chubb AU RC 8.00 20.00
105 Josh Allen AU RC 100.00 200.00
106 Josh Rosen AU RC 50.00 100.00
107 D.J. Moore AU RC 10.00 25.00
109 Calvin Ridley AU RC 12.00 30.00
110 Rashaad Penny AU RC 8.00 20.00
111 Sony Michel AU RC EXCH 15.00 40.00
112 Lamar Jackson AU RC 75.00 150.00
113 Nick Chubb AU RC 15.00 40.00
114 Ronald Jones II AU RC 10.00 25.00
115 Courtland Sutton AU RC 8.00 20.00
116 Mike Gesicki AU RC 6.00 15.00
117 Kerryon Johnson AU RC 8.00 20.00
118 Dante Pettis AU RC 8.00 20.00
119 Christian Kirk AU RC 8.00 20.00
120 Anthony Miller AU RC 8.00 20.00
121 Derrius Guice AU RC EXCH 10.00 25.00
122 James Washington AU RC 10.00 25.00
123 D.J. Chark Jr. AU RC 6.00 15.00
124 Royce Freeman AU RC 6.00 15.00
125 Mason Rudolph AU RC 12.00 30.00
126 Michael Gallup AU RC 10.00 25.00
127 Tre'Quan Smith AU RC 8.00 20.00
128 Keke Coutee AU RC 6.00 15.00
129 Nyheim Hines AU RC 6.00 15.00
130 Kyle Lauletta AU RC 8.00 20.00
131 Mark Walton AU RC 6.00 15.00
132 DaeSean Hamilton AU RC 6.00 15.00
133 Ito Smith AU RC 6.00 15.00
134 Kalen Ballage AU RC 6.00 15.00
135 Jaleel Scott AU RC 5.00 12.00
137 Daurice Fountain AU RC 6.00 15.00
138 Jaylen Samuels AU RC 6.00 15.00
139 Mike White AU RC 6.00 15.00
140 Marquez Valdes-Scantling AU RC 6.00 15.00
141 Avonte Maddox AU RC 6.00 15.00
142 Jordan Thomas AU RC 6.00 15.00
143 Denzel Ward AU RC 12.00 30.00
144 Roquan Smith AU RC 15.00 40.00
145 Minkah Fitzpatrick AU RC 10.00 25.00
146 Nick Mullens AU RC 15.00 40.00
147 Marcus Davenport AU RC 10.00 25.00
148 Tremaine Edmunds AU RC 10.00 25.00
149 Derwin James AU RC 10.00 25.00
150 Jaire Alexander AU RC 8.00 20.00
151 Leighton Vander Esch AU RC 15.00 40.00
152 Rashaan Evans AU RC 8.00 20.00
153 Mike Hughes AU RC 8.00 20.00
154 Harold Landry AU RC 5.00 12.00
155 Joshua Jackson AU RC 10.00 25.00
156 Isaiah Oliver AU RC 5.00 12.00
157 Carlton Davis AU RC 6.00 15.00
158 Lorenzo Carter AU RC 5.00 12.00
159 Trenton Cannon AU RC 6.00 15.00
161 Josh Sweat AU RC 6.00 15.00
162 Chase Edmonds AU RC 5.00 12.00
164 Shaquem Griffin AU RC 8.00 20.00
165 Jordan Lasley AU RC 5.00 12.00
166 John Kelly AU RC 6.00 15.00
167 Dylan Cantrell AU RC 5.00 12.00
168 Luke Falk AU RC 6.00 15.00
169 Braxton Berrios AU RC 5.00 12.00
170 Marcell Ateman AU RC 6.00 15.00
171 Bo Scarbrough AU RC 6.00 15.00
172 Trey Quinn AU RC 5.00 12.00
173 Deontay Burnett AU RC 6.00 15.00
174 Riley Ferguson AU RC 8.00 20.00
175 Dallas Goedert AU RC 6.00 15.00
176 Kurt Benkert AU RC 6.00 15.00
177 Danny Etling AU RC 6.00 15.00
178 Tanner Lee AU RC 6.00 15.00
179 D.J. Reed AU RC 5.00 12.00
181 Tyler Conklin AU RC 5.00 12.00
182 Malik Jefferson AU RC 6.00 15.00
183 Mark Andrews AU RC 8.00 20.00
184 Micah Kiser AU RC 5.00 12.00
185 Ogbonnia Okoronkwo AU RC 8.00 20.00
189 Ronnie Harrison AU RC 6.00 15.00
190 Kyzir White AU RC 8.00 20.00
191 Boston Scott AU RC 6.00 15.00
192 Damion Ratley AU RC 6.00 15.00
193 Alex McGough AU RC 6.00 15.00
194 Josey Jewell AU RC 6.00 15.00
195 Chad Thomas AU RC 5.00 12.00
196 Justin Watson AU RC 6.00 15.00
197 Deon Cain AU RC 6.00 15.00
198 Darius Leonard AU RC 12.00 30.00
199 Will Dissly AU RC 6.00 15.00
200 Phillip Lindsay AU RC 30.00 60.00

2018 Panini Contenders Optic Blue
*VETS: .8X TO 2X BASIC CARDS
*ROOK/25: 1X TO 2.5X BASIC RC AU
*ROOK/15: 1.2X TO 3X BASIC RC AU
101 Baker Mayfield AU/15 1800.00 2200.00
102 Saquon Barkley AU/15 EXCH 600.00 1000.00
103 Sam Darnold AU/15 600.00 1000.00
105 Josh Allen AU/15 200.00 400.00
112 Lamar Jackson AU/15 200.00 400.00

2018 Panini Contenders Optic Orange
*VETS/49: 1X TO 2.5X BASIC CARDS
*ROOK/49: .8X TO 2X BASIC RC AU
*ROOK/25: 1X TO 2.5X BASIC RC AU
101 Baker Mayfield AU/25 900.00 1500.00
102 Saquon Barkley AU/25 EXCH 400.00 800.00
103 Sam Darnold AU/25 500.00 800.00
105 Josh Allen AU/25 175.00 350.00
112 Lamar Jackson AU/25 150.00 300.00

2018 Panini Contenders Optic Purple
*ROOK/75-99: .6X TO 1.5X BASIC RC AU
*ROOK/49: .8X TO 2X BASIC RC AU
101 Baker Mayfield AU/49 600.00 1000.00
102 Saquon Barkley AU/49 EXCH 200.00 400.00
103 Sam Darnold AU/49 150.00 300.00
105 Josh Allen AU/49 150.00 300.00
112 Lamar Jackson AU/49 100.00 200.00

2018 Panini Contenders Optic Red
*VETS/199: .6X TO 1.5X BASIC CARDS
*ROOK/149-199: .5X TO 1.2X BASIC RC AU
*ROOK/99-125: .6X TO 1.5X BASIC RC AU
*ROOK/60: .8X TO 2X BASIC RC AU
101 Baker Mayfield AU/99 500.00 900.00
102 Saquon Barkley AU/99 EXCH 125.00 250.00
103 Sam Darnold AU/99 125.00 250.00
105 Josh Allen AU/99 125.00 250.00
112 Lamar Jackson AU/60 100.00 200.00

2018 Panini Contenders Optic Class Acts
*BLUE/25: .8X TO 2X BASIC INSERTS/175
*ORANGE/49: .6X TO 1.5X BASIC INSERTS/175
*PURPLE/99: .5X TO 1.2X BASIC INSERTS/175
1 Saquon Barkley 6.00 15.00
2 Patrick Mahomes II 8.00 20.00
3 Ezekiel Elliott 1.50 4.00
4 DeAndre Hopkins 1.00 2.50
5 Andrew Luck 1.50 4.00
6 Cam Newton 1.25 3.00
7 Rob Gronkowski 1.25 3.00
8 Aaron Rodgers 2.50 6.00
9 Ben Roethlisberger 1.25 3.00
10 Tom Brady 3.00 8.00
11 Brian Urlacher 1.25 3.00
12 Peyton Manning 2.50 6.00
13 Ray Lewis 1.25 3.00
14 Terrell Davis 1.00 2.50
15 Michael Strahan 1.00 2.50
16 Troy Aikman 1.50 4.00
17 Barry Sanders 2.00 5.00
18 Jerry Rice 2.00 5.00
19 Dan Marino 2.50 6.00
20 Joe Namath 1.50 4.00

2018 Panini Contenders Optic Legendary Contenders
2018 Panini Contenders Optic Class Acts
2018 Panini Contenders Optic Class Acts
2018 Panini Contenders Optic Class Acts
1 Brett Favre 2.50 6.00
2 Emmitt Smith 2.00 5.00
3 Troy Aikman 1.50 4.00
4 Charles Woodson 1.25 3.00
5 Jerry Rice 2.00 5.00
6 John Elway 2.00 5.00
7 Peyton Manning 2.50 6.00
8 Terry Bradshaw 2.00 5.00
9 Dan Marino 2.50 6.00
10 Barry Sanders 2.00 5.00
11 Deion Sanders 1.00 2.50
12 John Riggins 1.00 2.50
13 Dick Butkus 1.50 4.00
14 Tony Gonzalez 1.00 2.50
15 Lawrence Taylor 1.25 3.00

2018 Panini Contenders Optic MVP Contenders
*BLUE/25: .8X TO 2X BASIC INSERTS/175
*ORANGE/49: .6X TO 1.5X BASIC INSERTS/175
*PURPLE/99: .5X TO 1.2X BASIC INSERTS/175
1 Aaron Rodgers 2.50 6.00
2 Drew Brees 1.25 3.00
3 Tom Brady 3.00 8.00
4 Matt Ryan 1.00 2.50
5 Carson Wentz 1.50 4.00
6 Patrick Mahomes II 3.00 8.00
7 Ezekiel Elliott 1.50 4.00
8 Alvin Kamara 1.00 2.50
9 Todd Gurley II 1.25 3.00
10 Cam Newton 1.25 3.00

2018 Panini Contenders Optic Round Numbers
*BLUE/25: .8X TO 2X BASIC INSERTS/175
*ORANGE/49: .6X TO 1.5X BASIC INSERTS/175
*PURPLE/99: .5X TO 1.2X BASIC INSERTS/175
1 B.Mayfield/S.Darnold 5.00 12.00
2 J.Allen/J.Rosen 2.50 6.00
3 S.Michel/S.Barkley 4.00 10.00
4 C.Ridley/D.Moore 2.00 5.00
5 R.Jones II/N.Chubb 2.50 6.00
6 D.Pettis/C.Sutton 1.25 3.00
7 A.Miller/C.Kirk 1.25 3.00
8 D.Guice/K.Johnson 1.50 4.00
9 D.Chark Jr./J.Washington 1.50 4.00
10 M.Gallup/T.Smith 1.50 4.00
11 M.Walton/N.Hines 1.00 2.50
12 K.Coutee/D.Hamilton 1.00 2.50
13 B.Chubb/M.Davenport 1.50 4.00
14 D.James/M.Fitzpatrick 1.50 4.00
15 J.Alexander/D.Ward 2.00 5.00

2018 Panini Contenders Optic Triple Threat
*BLUE/25: .8X TO 2X BASIC INSERTS/175
*ORANGE/49: .6X TO 1.5X BASIC INSERTS/175
*PURPLE/99: .5X TO 1.2X BASIC INSERTS/175
1 Nwtn/Olsn/McCffry 1.25 3.00
2 Cks/Gff/Grly 1.25 3.00
3 Rdgrs/Adms/Grhm 2.50 6.00
4 Trvthn/Mck/Smth 2.50 6.00
5 Hnt/Hll/Mhms 3.00 8.00
6 Frmn/Jns/Ryn 1.25 3.00
7 Grnkwski/Grdn/Brdy 3.00 8.00
8 Ck/Csns/Dggs 1.25 3.00
9 Hpkns/Wtsn/Mllr 1.50 4.00
10 Mnng/Bckhm/Brkly 4.00 10.00
11 Cpr/Prsctt/Elltt 1.50 4.00
12 Ptts/Grpplo/Brda 1.50 4.00
13 Ptrsn/Smth/Rd 1.25 3.00
14 Wntz/Ajyi/Ertz 1.50 4.00
15 Cmpbll/Rmsy/Jck 1.00 2.50
16 Brs/Kmra/Thms 1.25 3.00
17 Lck/Ebrn/Hltn 1.50 4.00
18 Chbb/Mllr/Mrshll 1.25 3.00
19 Alln/Grdn/Rvrs 1.25 3.00
20 Glldy/Jns/Stffrd 1.00 2.50

2018 Panini Contenders Optic Xs and Os
*BLUE/25: .8X TO 2X BASIC INSERTS/175
*ORANGE/49: .6X TO 1.5X BASIC INSERTS/175
*PURPLE/99: .5X TO 1.2X BASIC INSERTS/175
1 B.Mayfield/D.Ward 5.00 12.00
2 C.Wentz/F.Cox 1.50 4.00
3 K.Mack/J.Howard 1.25 3.00
4 C.Newton/L.Kuechly 1.25 3.00
5 A.Brown/T.Watt 1.25 3.00
6 T.Brady/T.Flowers 3.00 8.00
7 J.Houston/P.Mahomes II 3.00 8.00
8 J.Ramsey/L.Fournette 1.25 3.00
9 M.Gordon III/M.Ingram 1.00 2.50
10 T.Gurley II/A.Donald 1.25 3.00
11 D.Hopkins/J.Watt 1.25 3.00
12 D.Trufant/J.Jones 1.25 3.00
13 H.Smith/A.Thielen 1.25 3.00
14 A.Kamara/M.Lattimore 1.00 2.50
15 D.Slay/K.Johnson 1.25 3.00
16 W.Jackson III/A.Green 1.25 3.00
17 L.Collins/S.Barkley 4.00 10.00
18 D.Prescott/D.Lawrence 1.25 3.00
19 D.Hopkins/T.Mathieu 1.00 2.50
20 M.Fitzpatrick/K.Ballage 1.50 4.00

2013 Panini Cornerstones
*GOLD/25: 1.2X TO 3X BASIC INSERTS
*PURPLE/49: 1X TO 2.5X BASIC INSERTS
*RED/99: .8X TO 2X BASIC INSERTS
1 Robert Griffin III .75 2.00
2 Andrew Luck 2.00 5.00
3 C.J. Spiller .75 2.00
4 Ryan Tannehill 1.00 2.50
5 Tom Brady 3.00 8.00
6 Ray Rice .75 2.00
7 A.J. Green 1.25 3.00
8 Trent Richardson .75 2.00
9 Colin Kaepernick 1.00 2.50
10 Arian Foster 1.00 2.50
11 Justin Blackmon .75 2.00
12 Demaryius Thomas 1.00 2.50
13 Jamaal Charles 1.00 2.50
14 Darren McFadden 1.00 2.50
15 Tony Romo 1.00 2.50
16 Eli Manning 1.00 2.50
17 LeSean McCoy 1.25 3.00
18 Russell Wilson 2.50 6.00
19 Calvin Johnson 1.25 3.00
20 Aaron Rodgers 2.00 5.00
21 Adrian Peterson 1.25 3.00
22 Julio Jones 1.25 3.00
23 Cam Newton 1.25 3.00
24 Drew Brees 1.25 3.00
25 Doug Martin 1.00 2.50

2013 Panini Crusade
RANDOM INSERTS IN ROOKIES AND STARS
*GOLD/25: 1.2X TO 3X BASIC INSERTS
*PURPLE/49: 1X TO 2.5X BASIC INSERTS
*RED/99: .8X TO 2X BASIC INSERTS
1 Aaron Rodgers 3.00 8.00
2 Adrian Peterson 2.00 5.00
3 Russell Wilson 4.00 10.00
4 Andrew Luck 3.00 8.00
5 Arian Foster 1.50 4.00
6 Calvin Johnson 2.00 5.00
7 Peyton Manning 4.00 10.00
8 Colin Kaepernick 1.50 4.00
9 Robert Griffin III 1.25 3.00
10 Tom Brady 5.00 12.00

2018 Panini Elements
1 Larry Fitzgerald 3.00 8.00
2 David Johnson 4.00 10.00
3 Matt Ryan 3.00 8.00
4 Julio Jones 4.00 10.00
5 Joe Flacco 3.00 8.00
6 Justin Tucker 2.50 6.00
7 LeSean McCoy 4.00 10.00
8 Cam Newton 4.00 10.00
9 Luke Kuechly 3.00 8.00
10 Jordan Howard 4.00 10.00
11 Mitchell Trubisky 4.00 10.00
12 A.J. Green 4.00 10.00
13 Andy Dalton 3.00 8.00
14 Josh Gordon 2.50 6.00
15 Tyrod Taylor 3.00 8.00
16 Ezekiel Elliott 5.00 12.00
17 Dak Prescott 4.00 10.00
18 Von Miller 3.00 8.00
19 Matthew Stafford 3.00 8.00
20 Aaron Rodgers 8.00 20.00
21 Deshaun Watson 5.00 12.00
22 J.J. Watt 4.00 10.00
23 Andrew Luck 5.00 12.00
24 Leonard Fournette 4.00 10.00
25 Kareem Hunt 3.00 8.00
26 Philip Rivers 4.00 10.00
27 Joey Bosa 4.00 10.00
28 Todd Gurley II 4.00 10.00
29 Jared Goff 4.00 10.00
30 Kenyan Drake 2.50 6.00
31 Adam Thielen 4.00 10.00
32 Rob Gronkowski 4.00 10.00
33 Tom Brady 10.00 25.00
34 Drew Brees 4.00 10.00
35 Alvin Kamara 3.00 8.00
36 Odell Beckham Jr. 4.00 10.00
37 Eli Manning 3.00 8.00
38 Jamal Adams 3.00 8.00
39 Derek Carr 4.00 10.00
40 Khalil Mack 4.00 10.00
41 Carson Wentz 5.00 12.00
42 Antonio Brown 4.00 10.00
43 Le'Veon Bell 3.00 8.00
44 Ben Roethlisberger 4.00 10.00
45 Jimmy Garoppolo 5.00 12.00
46 Russell Wilson 5.00 12.00
47 Jameis Winston 3.00 8.00
48 Marcus Mariota 4.00 10.00
49 Josh Norman 2.50 6.00
50 Clay Matthews 3.00 8.00
51 Christian McCaffrey 4.00 10.00
52 Alshon Jeffery 3.00 8.00
53 Joe Montana 12.00 30.00
54 Emmitt Smith 8.00 20.00
55 Peyton Manning 10.00 25.00
56 Brett Favre 10.00 25.00
57 Jerry Rice 8.00 20.00
58 Dan Marino 10.00 25.00
59 Deion Sanders 4.00 10.00
60 Charles Woodson 5.00 12.00
61 Randy Moss 4.00 10.00
62 John Elway 8.00 20.00
63 Barry Sanders 8.00 20.00
64 Lawrence Taylor 5.00 12.00
65 Ray Lewis 5.00 12.00
66 Tony Gonzalez 4.00 10.00
67 Jerome Bettis 5.00 12.00
68 Kurt Warner 4.00 10.00
69 Bo Jackson 6.00 15.00
70 Brian Urlacher 5.00 12.00
71 Troy Aikman 6.00 15.00
72 Brian Dawkins 5.00 12.00
73 Josh Rosen AU/99 RC 50.00 100.00
74 Sam Darnold AU/99 RC 60.00 125.00
75 Josh Allen AU/99 RC 25.00 60.00
76 Baker Mayfield AU/99 RC 60.00 125.00
77 Mason Rudolph AU/99 RC 15.00 40.00
78 Lamar Jackson AU/49 RC 90.00 150.00
79 Hayden Hurst AU/199 RC 6.00 15.00
80 Kyle Lauletta AU/199 RC 8.00 20.00
81 Saquon Barkley AU/99 RC 175.00 300.00
82 Derrius Guice AU/99 RC 12.00 30.00
83 Ronald Jones II AU/199 RC 5.00 12.00
84 Nick Chubb AU/199 RC 15.00 40.00
85 Kerryon Johnson AU/199 RC 8.00 20.00
86 Rashaad Penny AU/199 RC 8.00 20.00
87 Royce Freeman AU/199 RC 6.00 15.00
88 Sony Michel AU/199 RC 15.00 40.00
89 Mike Gesicki AU/199 RC 6.00 15.00
90 Mike White AU/199 RC 6.00 15.00
91 Keke Coutee AU/199 RC 6.00 15.00
92 Calvin Ridley AU/99 RC 15.00 40.00
93 Courtland Sutton AU/199 RC 8.00 20.00
94 Anthony Miller AU/199 RC 8.00 20.00
95 Christian Kirk AU/199 RC 8.00 20.00
96 Michael Gallup AU/199 RC 10.00 25.00
97 James Washington AU/199 RC 10.00 25.00
98 Mark Walton AU/199 RC 6.00 15.00
99 Dante Pettis AU/199 RC 8.00 20.00
100 Ito Smith AU/199 RC 6.00 15.00
101 DaeSean Hamilton AU/199 RC 6.00 15.00
102 Tre'Quan Smith AU/199 RC 8.00 20.00
103 Jaleel Scott AU/199 RC 5.00 12.00
104 D.J. Chark AU/199 RC 6.00 15.00
105 Nyheim Hines AU/199 RC 6.00 15.00
106 J'Mon Moore AU/199 RC 5.00 12.00
107 Daurice Fountain AU/199 RC 6.00 15.00
108 Bradley Chubb AU/199 RC 8.00 20.00
109 Kalen Ballage AU/199 RC 6.00 15.00
110 D.J. Moore AU/199 RC 10.00 25.00
111 Jaylen Samuels AU/199 RC 6.00 15.00
112 Marquez Valdes-Scantling AU/199 RC 6.00 15.00

2018 Panini Elements Copper
*COPPER/25: .6X TO 1.5X BASIC CARDS/75
*COPPER/25: .5X TO 1.2X BASIC CARDS/50

2018 Panini Elements Gold
*GOLD AU/50: .6X TO 1.5X BASIC AU/199
*GOLD AU/25: .6X TO 1.5X BASIC AU/99
*GOLD AU/25: .5X TO 1.2X BASIC AU/49
74 Sam Darnold AU/25 150.00 300.00
75 Josh Allen AU/25 75.00 150.00
78 Lamar Jackson AU/25 100.00 200.00

2018 Panini Elements Mettle Moments
*COPPER/25: .5X TO 1.2X BASIC INSERTS/50
1 Johnny Unitas 8.00 20.00
2 Tom Brady 12.00 30.00
3 Eli Manning 4.00 10.00
4 Peyton Manning 10.00 25.00
5 Ray Lewis 5.00 12.00
6 John Elway 8.00 20.00
7 Richard Sherman 5.00 12.00
8 John Riggins 4.00 10.00
9 Aaron Rodgers 10.00 25.00
10 James Harrison 4.00 10.00
11 Terry Bradshaw 8.00 20.00
12 Von Miller 4.00 10.00
13 Adam Vinatieri 3.00 8.00
14 Stefon Diggs 4.00 10.00
15 Brett Favre 10.00 25.00
16 Adrian Peterson 5.00 12.00
17 Emmitt Smith 8.00 20.00
18 Larry Fitzgerald 4.00 10.00
19 Marshawn Lynch 4.00 10.00
20 Antonio Brown 5.00 12.00

2018 Panini Elements Neon Signatures Tier 1 Orange
*BLUE/50: .5X TO 1.2X BASIC AU/74-113
*BLUE/25: .6X TO 1.5X BASIC AU/74-113
*BLUE/25: .5X TO 1.2X BASIC AU/35-55
2 Aeneas Williams/113 6.00 15.00
4 Antonio Freeman/74 8.00 20.00
5 Brian Urlacher/18
8 David Johnson/35 15.00 40.00
9 Derrick Brooks/88 6.00 15.00
12 Jadeveon Clowney/90 6.00 15.00
13 Jared Goff/51 15.00 40.00
14 Jay Ajayi/30 12.00 30.00
15 Keenan Allen/23
16 Kelvin Benjamin/21 15.00 40.00
18 Lawrence Taylor/18 25.00 60.00
20 Melvin Gordon/16 15.00 40.00
21 Mike Williams/55 8.00 20.00
22 Patrick Peterson/15
23 Wes Welker/19 15.00 40.00

2018 Panini Elements Neon Signatures Tier 2 Orange
*BLUE/50: .5X TO 1.2X BASIC AU/88-94
1 Carson Wentz/94 50.00 100.00
2 Dak Prescott/50 30.00 60.00
3 Ezekiel Elliott/88 40.00 80.00
5 Jason Witten/35 25.00 50.00

2018 Panini Elements Neon Signatures Tier 3 Orange
13 Fred Taylor/17 12.00 30.00
25 Rod Woodson/44 12.00 30.00

2018 Panini Elements Radioactive Rookie Materials
*GOLD/99: .4X TO 1X BASIC JSY/99-125
*GOLD/49: .5X TO 1.2X BASIC JSY/99-125
1 Sam Darnold/99 10.00 25.00
2 Josh Rosen/99 10.00 25.00
3 Baker Mayfield/99 10.00 25.00
4 Josh Allen/99 8.00 20.00
5 Mason Rudolph/99 6.00 15.00
6 Saquon Barkley/99 12.00 30.00
7 Nick Chubb/99 6.00 15.00
8 Sony Michel/99 6.00 15.00
9 Derrius Guice/99 5.00 12.00
10 Bradley Chubb/99 4.00 10.00
11 D.J. Moore/125 5.00 12.00
12 Hayden Hurst/125 3.00 8.00
13 Calvin Ridley/125 6.00 15.00
14 Rashaad Penny/125 4.00 10.00
15 Lamar Jackson/125 10.00 25.00
16 Ronald Jones II/125 2.50 6.00
17 Courtland Sutton/125 4.00 10.00
18 Mike Gesicki/125 3.00 8.00
19 Kerryon Johnson/125 4.00 10.00
20 Dante Pettis/125 4.00 10.00
21 Christian Kirk/125 4.00 10.00
22 Anthony Miller/125 4.00 10.00
23 James Washington/125 5.00 12.00
24 D.J. Chark/125 3.00 8.00
25 Royce Freeman/125 3.00 8.00
26 J'Mon Moore/125 2.50 6.00
27 Michael Gallup/125 5.00 12.00
28 Tre'Quan Smith/125 4.00 10.00
29 Keke Coutee/125 3.00 8.00
30 Nyheim Hines/125 3.00 8.00
31 Kyle Lauletta/125 4.00 10.00
32 Mark Walton/125 3.00 8.00
33 DaeSean Hamilton/125 3.00 8.00
34 Ito Smith/125 3.00 8.00
35 Kalen Ballage/125 3.00 8.00
36 Jaleel Scott/125 2.50 6.00
37 Daurice Fountain/125 3.00 8.00
38 Jaylen Samuels/125 3.00 8.00
39 Mike White/125 3.00 8.00
40 Marquez Valdes-Scantling/125 3.00 8.00

2018 Panini Elements Rookie Titanium Autographs Copper
1 Josh Rosen/99 20.00 50.00
2 Sam Darnold/99 50.00 100.00
3 Josh Allen/99 25.00 60.00
4 Baker Mayfield/99 90.00 150.00
5 Mason Rudolph/99 15.00 40.00
6 Lamar Jackson/49 75.00 150.00
7 Hayden Hurst/299 5.00 12.00
8 Kyle Lauletta/350 6.00 15.00
9 Saquon Barkley/99 75.00 150.00
10 Derrius Guice/99 12.00 30.00
11 Ronald Jones II/350 4.00 10.00
12 Nick Chubb/299 12.00 30.00
13 Kerryon Johnson/350 6.00 15.00
14 Rashaad Penny/350 6.00 15.00
15 Royce Freeman/350 5.00 12.00
16 Sony Michel/299 12.00 30.00
17 Mike Gesicki/350 5.00 12.00
18 Mike White/350 5.00 12.00
19 Keke Coutee/350 5.00 12.00
20 Calvin Ridley/99 15.00 40.00
21 Courtland Sutton/99 10.00 25.00
22 Anthony Miller/350 6.00 15.00
23 Christian Kirk/99 10.00 25.00
24 Michael Gallup/350 8.00 20.00
25 James Washington/350 8.00 20.00
26 Mark Walton/350 5.00 12.00
27 Dante Pettis/350 6.00 15.00
28 Ito Smith/350 5.00 12.00
29 DaeSean Hamilton/350 5.00 12.00
30 Tre'Quan Smith/350 6.00 15.00
31 Jaleel Scott/350 4.00 10.00
32 D.J. Chark/350 5.00 12.00
33 Nyheim Hines/350 5.00 12.00
34 J'Mon Moore/350 4.00 10.00
35 Daurice Fountain/350 5.00 12.00
36 Bradley Chubb/350 6.00 15.00
37 Kalen Ballage/350 5.00 12.00
38 D.J. Moore/350 8.00 20.00
39 Jaylen Samuels/350 5.00 12.00
40 Marquez Valdes-Scantling/350 5.00 12.00

2018 Panini Elements Rookie Titanium Autographs Silver
*GOLD/125: .6X TO 1.5X BASIC AU/299-350
*GOLD/25: .6X TO 1.5X BASIC AU/99
*GOLD/25: .5X TO 1.2X BASIC AU/49
*GOLD/24: .8X TO 2X BASIC AU/99
4 Baker Mayfield/25 125.00 250.00
6 Lamar Jackson/25 100.00 200.00
9 Saquon Barkley/25 100.00 200.00

2018 Panini Elements Signatures Steel
*GOLD/25: .8X TO 2X BASIC AU/150-199
*GOLD/25: .6X TO 1.5X BASIC AU/99
*GOLD/25: .5X TO 1.2X BASIC AU/50
*GOLD/25: .4X TO 1X BASIC AU/25-30
1 Harrison Smith/150
2 J.J. Watt/15
3 Zach Thomas/25
10 Greg Olsen/50 10.00 25.00
13 Morten Andersen/199 5.00 12.00
14 Jameis Winston/15
15 Marcus Mariota/15
19 Troy Brown/99 8.00 20.00
20 Deshaun Watson/25 50.00 100.00
22 Jerome Bettis/15 40.00 80.00
23 Kenyan Drake/25 10.00 25.00
24 Matthew Stafford/15 50.00 100.00
25 Mitchell Trubisky/15
26 Rob Gronkowski/15 30.00 60.00
27 Tony Gonzalez/15
28 Bo Jackson/15
29 Leonard Fournette/15 20.00 50.00
30 Earl Campbell/15
31 Derek Carr/15 50.00 100.00
32 Richard Sherman/15
33 Clay Matthews/25
34 LaDainian Tomlinson/15 40.00 80.00
35 Dan Bailey/99 10.00 25.00
36 Neil Smith/199 5.00 12.00
37 Demaryius Thomas/15 15.00 40.00
38 Jason Taylor/25 EXCH 12.00 30.00
39 Lawrence Taylor/25 20.00 50.00
41 Christian Okoye/25
42 Fran Tarkenton/25
43 Raymond Berry/15
44 Ryan Shazier/99 6.00 15.00
45 David Johnson/25 20.00 50.00
46 Fred Taylor/25 10.00 25.00
47 Terrell Suggs/25 EXCH 20.00 50.00
48 Mike Singletary/25 15.00 40.00
49 Steve Largent/25 15.00 40.00
50 Luke Kuechly/25
51 Geno Atkins/199 5.00 12.00
52 James Lofton/25
54 Devonta Freeman/25
55 Doug Baldwin/25
56 Michael Vick/25 EXCH 12.00 30.00
58 Brian Dawkins/25 75.00 150.00
59 Jim Plunkett/25 12.00 30.00
60 Christian McCaffrey/25 15.00 40.00
61 Ricky Williams/25 12.00 30.00
62 Don Maynard/25
63 Bob Lilly/30 12.00 30.00
64 Andre Reed/30 12.00 30.00
66 Ed McCaffrey/30 12.00 30.00
67 John Lynch/30 12.00 30.00
68 Mike Alstott/30 30.00 60.00
69 Priest Holmes/30
70 Randy White/30
71 Roger Craig/25
72 Walt Garrison/50 10.00 25.00
73 Torry Holt/30 12.00 30.00
74 Travis Kelce/25 25.00 50.00
76 Sterling Sharpe/99 12.00 30.00
77 Drew Pearson/99 EXCH 8.00 20.00
78 Jeremy Shockey/99 6.00 15.00
79 Jordan Howard/99 10.00 25.00
80 Michael Bennett/99 6.00 15.00
81 Stefon Diggs/99 15.00 40.00
82 Brett Keisel/150 8.00 20.00
83 Charles Haley/150 8.00 20.00
84 Jack Youngblood/150 EXCH 5.00 12.00
85 JuJu Smith-Schuster/150 8.00 20.00
86 Mark Gastineau/150 5.00 12.00
87 Tyreek Hill/150 EXCH 8.00 20.00
88 Jim Zorn/199 5.00 12.00
89 Chris Hogan/199 5.00 12.00
90 Ickey Woods/199 5.00 12.00
91 Alvin Kamara/199 12.00 30.00
92 Kiko Alonso/199 5.00 12.00
93 Melvin Ingram/199 5.00 12.00
94 Kareem Hunt/199 6.00 15.00
95 Justin Houston/199 5.00 12.00
96 Rishard Matthews/199 5.00 12.00
97 Carl Eller/199 5.00 12.00
98 Jermaine Kearse/199 5.00 12.00
99 LeGarrette Blount/199 6.00 15.00
100 Jamison Crowder/199 5.00 12.00

2018 Panini Elements Xenon Rookie Jumbo Materials
*GOLD/50: .5X TO 1.2X BASIC JSY/99-125
1 Sam Darnold/99 10.00 25.00
2 Josh Rosen/99 10.00 25.00
3 Baker Mayfield/99 10.00 25.00
4 Josh Allen/99 8.00 20.00
5 Mason Rudolph/99 6.00 15.00
6 Saquon Barkley/99 12.00 30.00
7 Nick Chubb/99 6.00 15.00
8 Sony Michel/99 6.00 15.00
9 Derrius Guice/99 5.00 12.00
10 Bradley Chubb/99 4.00 10.00
11 D.J. Moore/125 5.00 12.00
12 Hayden Hurst/125 3.00 8.00
13 Calvin Ridley/125 6.00 15.00
14 Rashaad Penny/125 4.00 10.00
15 Lamar Jackson/125 10.00 25.00
16 Ronald Jones II/125 2.50 6.00
17 Courtland Sutton/125 4.00 10.00
18 Mike Gesicki/125 3.00 8.00
19 Kerryon Johnson/125 4.00 10.00
20 Dante Pettis/125 4.00 10.00
21 Christian Kirk/125 4.00 10.00
22 Anthony Miller/125 4.00 10.00
23 James Washington/125 5.00 12.00
24 D.J. Chark/125 3.00 8.00
25 Royce Freeman/125 3.00 8.00
26 J'Mon Moore/125 2.50 6.00
27 Michael Gallup/125 5.00 12.00
28 Tre'Quan Smith/125 4.00 10.00
29 Keke Coutee/125 3.00 8.00
30 Nyheim Hines/125 3.00 8.00
31 Kyle Lauletta/125 4.00 10.00
32 Mark Walton/125 3.00 8.00
33 DaeSean Hamilton/125 3.00 8.00
34 Ito Smith/125 3.00 8.00
35 Kalen Ballage/125 3.00 8.00
36 Jaleel Scott/125 2.50 6.00
37 Daurice Fountain/125 3.00 8.00
38 Jaylen Samuels/125 3.00 8.00
39 Mike White/125 3.00 8.00
40 Marquez Valdes-Scantling/125 3.00 8.00

2019 Panini Elements
1 Tom Brady 10.00 25.00
2 Josh Rosen 4.00 10.00
3 David Johnson 4.00 10.00
4 Larry Fitzgerald 3.00 8.00
5 Jimmy Garoppolo 4.00 10.00
6 Richard Sherman 3.00 8.00
7 Russell Wilson 5.00 12.00
8 Chris Carson 3.00 8.00
9 Doug Baldwin 3.00 8.00
10 Jared Goff 4.00 10.00
11 Todd Gurley II 4.00 10.00
12 Aaron Donald 4.00 10.00
13 Jameis Winston 3.00 8.00
14 Mike Evans 3.00 8.00
15 Gerald McCoy 2.50 6.00
16 Cam Newton 4.00 10.00
17 Luke Kuechly 3.00 8.00
18 Christian McCaffrey 4.00 10.00
19 Drew Brees 4.00 10.00
20 Alvin Kamara 3.00 8.00
21 Michael Thomas 4.00 10.00
22 Matthew Stafford 3.00 8.00
23 Kerryon Johnson 3.00 8.00
24 Darius Slay 2.50 6.00
25 Kirk Cousins 4.00 10.00
26 Adam Thielen 4.00 10.00
27 Harrison Smith 2.50 6.00
28 Khalil Mack 4.00 10.00
29 Mitchell Trubisky 4.00 10.00
30 Tarik Cohen 3.00 8.00
31 Eli Manning 3.00 8.00
32 Saquon Barkley 5.00 12.00
33 Odell Beckham Jr. 4.00 10.00
34 Adrian Peterson 4.00 10.00
35 Jordan Reed 2.50 6.00
36 Tom Brady 10.00 25.00
37 Carson Wentz 5.00 12.00
38 Tom Brady 10.00 25.00
39 Tom Brady 10.00 25.00
40 Leighton Vander Esch 3.00 8.00
41 Dak Prescott 4.00 10.00
42 Tom Brady 10.00 25.00
43 Matt Ryan 4.00 10.00
44 Julio Jones 4.00 10.00
45 Devonta Freeman 3.00 8.00
46 Tom Brady 10.00 25.00
47 Antonio Brown 4.00 10.00
48 Chris Warren III
49 Tom Brady 10.00 25.00
50 Phillip Lindsay 4.00 10.00
51 Tom Brady 10.00 25.00
52 Tom Brady 10.00 25.00
53 Tom Brady 10.00 25.00
54 Keenan Allen 3.00 8.00
55 Patrick Mahomes II 15.00 40.00
56 Tyreek Hill 4.00 10.00
57 Travis Kelce 4.00 10.00
58 Leonard Fournette 4.00 10.00
59 Jalen Ramsey 3.00 8.00
60 Telvin Smith 2.50 6.00
61 Marcus Mariota 4.00 10.00
62 Derrick Henry 4.00 10.00
63 Harold Landry 2.50 6.00
64 Andrew Luck 5.00 12.00
65 T.Y. Hilton 3.00 8.00
66 Darius Leonard 3.00 8.00
67 Deshaun Watson 5.00 12.00
68 DeAndre Hopkins 3.00 8.00

69 J.J. Watt 4.00 10.00
70 Andy Dalton 3.00 8.00
71 Joe Mixon 3.00 8.00
72 A.J. Green 4.00 10.00
73 Baker Mayfield 6.00 15.00
74 Nick Chubb 4.00 10.00
75 Myles Garrett 2.50 6.00
76 Ben Roethlisberger 3.00 8.00
77 James Conner 4.00 10.00
78 JuJu Smith-Schuster 4.00 10.00
79 Lamar Jackson 4.00 10.00
80 Justin Tucker 2.50 6.00
81 Gus Edwards 2.50 6.00
82 Sam Darnold 4.00 10.00
83 Jamal Adams 3.00 8.00
84 Robby Anderson 2.50 6.00
85 Josh Allen 4.00 10.00
86 Robert Foster 2.50 6.00
87 Tremaine Edmunds 3.00 8.00
88 Kenyan Drake 2.50 6.00
89 DeVante Parker 3.00 8.00
90 Minkah Fitzpatrick 2.50 6.00
91 Sony Michel 4.00 10.00
92 Julian Edelman 4.00 10.00
93 Davante Adams 3.00 8.00
94 Aaron Rodgers 8.00 20.00
95 Aaron Jones 3.00 8.00
96 Joe Montana 10.00 25.00
97 Case Keenum 3.00 8.00
98 Fletcher Cox 2.50 6.00
99 Josh Adams 3.00 8.00
100 Ezekiel Elliott 5.00 12.00
101 Derek Carr 4.00 10.00
102 Joe Flacco 3.00 8.00
103 Von Miller 3.00 8.00
104 Philip Rivers 4.00 10.00
105 Melvin Gordon III 3.00 8.00
106 Emmitt Smith 6.00 15.00
107 Alejandro Villanueva 3.00 8.00
108 Ray Lewis 4.00 10.00
109 Joe Montana 10.00 25.00
110 John Elway 6.00 15.00
111 Randall Cunningham 3.00 8.00
112 Lawrence Taylor 4.00 10.00
113 Brett Favre 8.00 20.00
114 Peyton Manning 8.00 20.00
115 Terry Bradshaw 6.00 15.00
116 Barry Sanders 6.00 15.00
117 Jerry Rice 6.00 15.00
118 Dan Marino 8.00 20.00
119 Le'Veon Bell 3.00 8.00
120 Nick Foles 3.00 8.00
121 Kyler Murray/75 RC 25.00 60.00
122 Nick Bosa/50 RC 10.00 25.00
123 Daniel Jones/75 RC 12.00 30.00
124 T.J. Hockenson/50 RC 8.00 20.00
125 Dwayne Haskins/75 RC 12.00 30.00
126 Noah Fant/50 RC 6.00 15.00
127 Josh Jacobs/75 RC 12.00 30.00
128 Marquise Brown/50 RC 10.00 25.00
129 N'Keal Harry/75 RC 8.00 20.00
130 Drew Lock/75 RC 12.00 30.00
131 Will Grier/75 RC 8.00 20.00
132 Damien Harris/75 RC 6.00 15.00
133 Darrell Henderson/50 RC 8.00 20.00
134 David Montgomery/50 RC 12.00 30.00
135 D.K. Metcalf/75 RC 8.00 20.00
136 A.J. Brown/50 RC 8.00 20.00
137 Parris Campbell/50 RC 8.00 20.00
138 Deebo Samuel/50 RC 8.00 20.00
139 Miles Sanders/50 RC 8.00 20.00
140 J.J. Arcega-Whiteside/50 RC 5.00 12.00
141 Irv Smith Jr./50 RC 6.00 15.00
142 Mecole Hardman Jr./75 RC 6.00 15.00
143 Andy Isabella/50 RC 5.00 12.00
144 Diontae Johnson/50 RC 4.00 10.00
145 Hunter Renfrow/75 RC 5.00 12.00
146 Miles Boykin/50 RC 4.00 10.00
147 Alexander Mattison/50 RC 6.00 15.00
148 Terry McLaurin/50 RC 4.00 10.00
149 Bryce Love/50 RC 5.00 12.00
150 Justice Hill/50 RC 5.00 12.00
151 Gary Jennings Jr./50 RC 5.00 12.00
152 Benny Snell Jr./50 RC 10.00 25.00
153 Riley Ridley/50 RC 5.00 12.00
154 Tony Pollard/50 RC 8.00 20.00
155 Devin Singletary/50 RC 4.00 10.00
156 Ryan Finley/75 RC 5.00 12.00
157 Jarrett Stidham/75 RC 8.00 20.00
158 Hakeem Butler/50 RC 6.00 15.00
159 Darius Slayton/50 RC 5.00 12.00
160 Easton Stick/75 RC 4.00 10.00
161 Kyler Murray AU/75 100.00 200.00
162 Nick Bosa AU/99 20.00 50.00
163 Daniel Jones AU/75 30.00 80.00
164 T.J. Hockenson AU/125 15.00 40.00
165 Dwayne Haskins AU/75 50.00 100.00
166 Noah Fant AU/125 12.00 30.00
167 Josh Jacobs AU/99 30.00 80.00
168 Marquise Brown AU/99 20.00 50.00
169 N'Keal Harry AU/99 20.00 50.00
170 Drew Lock AU/75 30.00 80.00
171 Will Grier AU/99 20.00 50.00
172 Damien Harris AU/99 15.00 40.00
173 Darrell Henderson AU/150 12.00 30.00
174 David Montgomery AU/125 25.00 60.00
175 D.K. Metcalf AU/99 20.00 50.00
176 A.J. Brown AU/99 15.00 40.00
177 Parris Campbell AU/99 15.00 40.00
178 Deebo Samuel AU/99 15.00 40.00
179 Miles Sanders AU/150 12.00 30.00
180 J.J. Arcega-Whiteside AU/99 10.00 25.00
181 Irv Smith Jr. AU/150 10.00 25.00
182 Mecole Hardman Jr. AU/99 15.00 40.00
183 Andy Isabella AU/150 8.00 20.00
184 Miles Boykin AU/150 6.00 15.00
185 Alexander Mattison AU/150 10.00 25.00
186 Diontae Johnson AU/150 6.00 15.00
187 Hunter Renfrow AU/199 10.00 25.00
188 Devin Singletary AU/199 6.00 15.00
189 Ryan Finley AU/99 12.00 30.00
190 Jarrett Stidham AU/125 20.00 50.00
191 Hakeem Butler AU/150 10.00 25.00
192 Bryce Love AU/99 10.00 25.00
193 Justice Hill AU/150 8.00 20.00
194 Gary Jennings Jr. AU/199 8.00 20.00
195 Benny Snell Jr. AU/150 15.00 40.00
196 Riley Ridley AU/150 8.00 20.00
197 Tony Pollard AU/150 12.00 30.00
198 Terry McLaurin AU/99 8.00 20.00
199 Easton Stick AU/150 8.00 20.00
200 Darius Slayton AU/199 8.00 20.00

2019 Panini Elements Elements of Success Materials

*GOLD/49: .5X TO 1.2X BASIC JSY/99
1 Kyler Murray 15.00 40.00
2 Nick Bosa 6.00 15.00
3 Daniel Jones 8.00 20.00
4 T.J. Hockenson 6.00 15.00
5 Dwayne Haskins 8.00 20.00
6 Noah Fant 5.00 12.00
7 Josh Jacobs 8.00 20.00
8 Marquise Brown 6.00 15.00
9 N'Keal Harry 6.00 15.00
10 Drew Lock 8.00 20.00
11 Will Grier 6.00 15.00
12 Damien Harris 6.00 15.00
13 Darrell Henderson 6.00 15.00
14 David Montgomery 6.00 15.00
15 D.K. Metcalf 6.00 15.00
16 A.J. Brown 6.00 15.00
17 Parris Campbell 6.00 15.00
18 Deebo Samuel 6.00 15.00
19 Miles Sanders 6.00 15.00
20 J.J. Arcega-Whiteside 4.00 10.00
21 Irv Smith Jr. 5.00 12.00
22 Mecole Hardman Jr. 6.00 15.00
23 Andy Isabella 4.00 10.00
24 Diontae Johnson 3.00 8.00
25 Hunter Renfrow 5.00 12.00
26 Miles Boykin 3.00 8.00
27 Alexander Mattison 5.00 12.00
28 Terry McLaurin 3.00 8.00
29 Bryce Love 4.00 10.00
30 Justice Hill 4.00 10.00
31 Gary Jennings Jr. 4.00 10.00
32 Benny Snell Jr. 6.00 15.00
33 Riley Ridley 4.00 10.00
34 Tony Pollard 6.00 15.00
35 Devin Singletary 3.00 8.00
36 Ryan Finley 5.00 12.00
37 Jarrett Stidham 6.00 15.00
38 Hakeem Butler 5.00 12.00
39 Darius Slayton 4.00 10.00
40 Easton Stick 4.00 10.00

2019 Panini Elements Mettle Moments Signatures

1 Michael Vick/25
5 J.J. Watt/15 EXCH 40.00 80.00
6 Mark Brunell/35 10.00 25.00
8 DeAndre Hopkins/25 EXCH 12.00 30.00
12 Derrick Henry/15
13 Kenyan Drake/35 8.00 20.00
14 Nick Mullens/49
15 Patrick Mahomes II/25 125.00 250.00
17 Ezekiel Elliott/15 EXCH 50.00 100.00
20 Alejandro Villanueva/35 10.00 25.00
21 Lamar Jackson/25
22 Tyreek Hill/25 EXCH 15.00 40.00
23 Amari Cooper/25 15.00 40.00
25 Adam Thielen/25 40.00 80.00
26 George Kittle/35 30.00 60.00
28 Mitchell Trubisky/15 40.00 80.00
29 Corey Davis/35 10.00 25.00

2019 Panini Elements Neon Signs Tier 1 Blue

*ORANGE/75-125: .3X TO .8X BLUE AU/50
*ORANGE/75: .25X TO .6X BLUE AU/25
*ORANGE/35-65: .3X TO .8X BLUE AU/25
*ORANGE/25: .3X TO .8X BLUE AU/15
5 Phillip Lindsay/50 25.00 60.00
6 Peyton Barber/50 8.00 20.00
7 Derrick Johnson/50 8.00 20.00
8 Billy White Shoes Johnson/50 8.00 20.00
9 Aaron Jones/25 12.00 30.00
10 Geno Atkins/50 8.00 20.00
11 Bill Bates/50 15.00 40.00
15 Eddie George/15
16 Chris Carson/25 12.00 30.00
17 Tiki Barber/15
18 Tarik Cohen/50 10.00 25.00
19 Mohamed Sanu/50 8.00 20.00
20 Kenyan Drake/50 8.00 20.00
21 Tyler Boyd/50 8.00 20.00
23 Joe Thomas/25 30.00 80.00
25 Justin Tucker/25 10.00 25.00
26 Jayon Brown/25 10.00 25.00
28 Ronde Barber/15 12.00 30.00
29 Walter Jones/50 8.00 20.00
31 Sony Michel/25 25.00 60.00
32 Robert Smith/25 15.00 40.00
33 James Lofton/50 8.00 20.00
34 Dallas Clark/25 10.00 25.00
36 Derrick Brooks/15
37 Marlon Mack/25 10.00 25.00
38 Mike Alstott/15 30.00 60.00
39 Keith Byars/35 8.00 20.00
41 Aeneas Williams/15 12.00 30.00
42 Rashaad Penny/25 10.00 25.00
43 James Washington/25 12.00 30.00
44 Kerryon Johnson/15 15.00 40.00
45 T.J. Watt/15 25.00 60.00
46 Darius Leonard/25 12.00 30.00
47 Leighton Vander Esch/25 20.00 50.00
49 Christian Okoye/15 12.00 30.00
50 Randall McDaniel/25 12.00 30.00

2019 Panini Elements Neon Signs Tier 2 Blue

1 Chris Doleman/15 12.00 30.00
2 Joe Theismann/15 15.00 40.00
3 Jim Otto/15 12.00 30.00
4 Mason Crosby/25 10.00 25.00
5 Taysom Hill/15
8 Dante Hall/25 10.00 25.00
9 Isaac Bruce/15 20.00 50.00

2019 Panini Elements Radioactive Rookie Materials

1 Kyler Murray/149 12.00 30.00
2 Nick Bosa/149 5.00 12.00
3 Daniel Jones/149 6.00 15.00
4 T.J. Hockenson/149 5.00 12.00
5 Dwayne Haskins/149 6.00 15.00
6 Noah Fant/149 4.00 10.00
7 Josh Jacobs/149 6.00 15.00
8 Marquise Brown/149 5.00 12.00
9 N'Keal Harry/149 5.00 12.00
10 Drew Lock/149 6.00 15.00
11 Will Grier/149 5.00 12.00
12 Damien Harris/149 5.00 12.00
13 Darrell Henderson/149 5.00 12.00
14 David Montgomery/149 5.00 12.00
15 D.K. Metcalf/149 5.00 12.00
16 A.J. Brown/149 5.00 12.00
17 Parris Campbell/149 5.00 12.00
18 Deebo Samuel/149 5.00 12.00
19 Miles Sanders/149 5.00 12.00
20 J.J. Arcega-Whiteside/149 3.00 8.00
21 Irv Smith Jr./149 4.00 10.00
22 Mecole Hardman Jr./149 5.00 12.00
23 Andy Isabella/149 3.00 8.00
24 Diontae Johnson/149 2.50 6.00
25 Hunter Renfrow/149 4.00 10.00
26 Miles Boykin/149 2.50 6.00
27 Alexander Mattison/149 4.00 10.00
28 Terry McLaurin/149 2.50 6.00
29 Bryce Love/149 3.00 8.00
30 Justice Hill/149 3.00 8.00
31 Gary Jennings Jr./99 4.00 10.00
32 Benny Snell Jr./149 5.00 12.00
33 Riley Ridley/99 4.00 10.00
34 Tony Pollard/149 5.00 12.00
35 Devin Singletary/149 2.50 6.00
36 Ryan Finley/149 4.00 10.00
37 Jarrett Stidham/149 5.00 12.00
38 Hakeem Butler/149 4.00 10.00
39 Darius Slayton/149 3.00 8.00
40 Easton Stick/149 3.00 8.00

2019 Panini Elements Rookie Neon Signs Orange

1 Kyler Murray/50 125.00 250.00
2 Nick Bosa/75 20.00 50.00
3 Daniel Jones/50 40.00 100.00
4 T.J. Hockenson/125 15.00 40.00
5 Dwayne Haskins/50 50.00 100.00
6 Noah Fant/125 12.00 30.00
7 Josh Jacobs/75 30.00 80.00
8 Marquise Brown/75 20.00 50.00
9 N'Keal Harry/99 20.00 50.00
10 D.K. Metcalf/75 20.00 50.00
11 A.J. Brown/75 15.00 40.00
12 Damien Harris/99 15.00 40.00
13 Ryan Finley/99 12.00 30.00
14 Deebo Samuel/99 15.00 40.00
15 Mecole Hardman Jr./99 15.00 40.00
16 Bryce Love/99 10.00 25.00
17 Parris Campbell/125 15.00 40.00
18 David Montgomery/150 20.00 50.00
19 Justice Hill/100 8.00 20.00
20 J.J. Arcega-Whiteside/150 8.00 20.00
21 Darrell Henderson/150 12.00 30.00
22 Hakeem Butler/199 10.00 25.00
23 Diontae Johnson/150 6.00 15.00
24 Miles Sanders/150 12.00 30.00
25 Easton Stick/199 8.00 20.00
26 Terry McLaurin/150 6.00 15.00
27 Riley Ridley/150 8.00 20.00
28 Miles Boykin/150 6.00 15.00
29 Irv Smith Jr./150 10.00 25.00
30 Tony Pollard/199 12.00 30.00
31 Benny Snell Jr./199 15.00 40.00
32 Alexander Mattison/199 10.00 25.00
33 Andy Isabella/199 8.00 20.00
34 Devin Singletary/199 6.00 15.00
35 Gary Jennings Jr./199 8.00 20.00
36 Hunter Renfrow/199 10.00 25.00
37 Darius Slayton/199 8.00 20.00
38 Drew Lock/50 40.00 100.00
39 Will Grier/75 20.00 50.00
40 Jarrett Stidham/125 20.00 50.00

2019 Panini Elements Rookie Neon Signs Blue

*BLUE/75-99: .5X TO 1.2X BASIC AU/150-199
*BLUE/75-99: .4X TO 1X BASIC AU/75-125
*BLUE/35-50: .5X TO 1.2X BASIC AU/75-125
*BLUE/35-50: .4X TO 1X BASIC AU/50
1 Kyler Murray/35 125.00 250.00

2019 Panini Elements Rookie Neon Signs Purple

*PURPLE/25: .8X TO 2X BASIC AU/150-199
*PURPLE/25: .6X TO 1.5X BASIC AU/75-125
*PURPLE/15: .8X TO 2X BASIC AU/75-125
*PURPLE/15: .6X TO 1.5X BASIC AU/50
5 Dwayne Haskins/15 100.00 200.00

2019 Panini Elements Rookie Neon Signs Red

*RED/35-50: .6X TO 1.5X BASIC AU/150-199
*RED/35-50: .5X TO 1.2X BASIC AU/75-125
*RED/25: .6X TO 1.5X BASIC AU/75-125
*RED/25: .5X TO 1.2X BASIC AU/50
*RED/15: .6X TO 1.5X BASIC AU/50
5 Dwayne Haskins/25 75.00 150.00

2019 Panini Elements Signatures Steel

1 Andrew Luck/15 25.00 60.00
2 Drew Brees/15 EXCH
3 Carson Wentz/15 75.00 150.00
4 Jared Goff/15
5 Marcus Mariota/15
6 Baker Mayfield/15 EXCH
7 Deshaun Watson/15
8 Ezekiel Elliott/15 EXCH 50.00 100.00
9 Kirk Cousins/15
10 Mitchell Trubisky/15 40.00 80.00
12 Jim McMahon/25 15.00 40.00
13 Warren Moon/25 15.00 40.00
14 DeAndre Hopkins/25 EXCH 12.00 30.00
15 Patrick Mahomes II/25 125.00 250.00
16 Lamar Jackson/25
17 Adam Thielen/25 40.00 80.00
18 David Johnson/25
19 Devin Hester/25 25.00 50.00
20 Archie Manning/25
21 Steve Largent/25
22 Len Dawson/25 12.00 30.00
23 Christian McCaffrey/50 12.00 30.00
24 Davante Adams/50
25 Brian Westbrook/50 15.00 40.00
26 Travis Kelce/75 EXCH 12.00 30.00
27 Tyreek Hill/75 EXCH 10.00 25.00
28 Calvin Ridley/75 8.00 20.00
29 Rod Woodson/75 12.00 30.00
30 Leighton Vander Esch/149 10.00 25.00
31 Greg Olsen/75 8.00 20.00
32 Harrison Smith/99 12.00 30.00
33 Mel Renfro/99 6.00 15.00
36 Cooper Kupp/99
37 T.J. Watt/99 12.00 30.00
38 Dante Hall/99 6.00 15.00
39 Kyle Rudolph/125
40 Daryl Johnston/125 12.00 30.00
41 Alex Collins/125 6.00 15.00
43 Bill Romanowski/125 8.00 20.00
44 Chris Spielman/149 10.00 25.00
45 Andre Rison/149 6.00 15.00
46 Alejandro Villanueva/149 6.00 15.00
47 Aqib Talib/149
48 Calais Campbell/149
49 Corey Davis/149 6.00 15.00
51 Mark Gastineau/149 5.00 12.00
52 Joe Thomas/149 15.00 40.00
53 Trent Dilfer/149 5.00 12.00
54 Randall McDaniel/149 6.00 15.00
55 Justin Tucker/149 5.00 12.00
56 Nick Chubb/149 8.00 20.00
57 Tyler Boyd/149 5.00 12.00
59 Thomas Hollywood Henderson/149 5.00 12.00
60 Kerryon Johnson/199 6.00 15.00
61 Myles Jack/199
62 Phillip Lindsay/199 15.00 40.00
63 Paul Hornung/149
64 Larry Brown/149 6.00 15.00
65 Mark Schlereth/149 5.00 12.00
66 Vance Johnson/199 5.00 12.00
67 Pepper Johnson/199 5.00 12.00
68 Aaron Rodgers/15 100.00 200.00
69 Ben Roethlisberger/15 EXCH 100.00 200.00
70 Russell Wilson/15 EXCH 75.00 150.00

2019 Panini Elements Transitions Materials

*GOLD/15: .6X TO 1.5X BASIC JSY/50
1 A.Smith/P.Mahomes II 10.00 25.00
2 D.Prescott/T.Romo 4.00 10.00
3 K.Cousins/T.Bridgewater 4.00 10.00
4 A.Rodgers/B.Favre 8.00 20.00
5 A.Luck/P.Manning 8.00 20.00
6 J.Jones/C.Ridley 4.00 10.00
7 B.Chubb/V.Miller 3.00 8.00
8 A.Brown/J.Smith-Schuster 4.00 10.00
9 L.Jackson/J.Flacco 4.00 10.00
10 D.Brees/P.Rivers 4.00 10.00

2016 Panini Encased

1 Antonio Brown 2.00 5.00
2 Peyton Manning 4.00 10.00
3 Adrian Peterson 2.00 5.00
4 Marcus Mariota 2.00 5.00
5 Tyrod Taylor 1.50 4.00
6 Mark Ingram 1.50 4.00
7 Matt Forte 1.25 3.00
8 Jeremy Maclin 1.25 3.00
9 DeSean Jackson 1.50 4.00
10 Todd Gurley II 2.00 5.00
11 LeGarrette Blount 1.50 4.00
12 Michael Irvin 2.00 5.00
13 Brock Osweiler 1.25 3.00
14 DeMarco Murray 1.50 4.00
15 LeSean McCoy 2.00 5.00
16 Brandin Cooks 1.50 4.00
17 Darrelle Revis 1.25 3.00
18 Derek Carr 2.00 5.00
19 Joe Flacco 1.50 4.00
20 Kenny Britt 1.25 3.00
21 Alshon Jeffery 1.50 4.00
22 Dan Marino 4.00 10.00
23 Lamar Miller 1.25 3.00
24 Delanie Walker 1.25 3.00
25 Sammy Watkins 2.00 5.00
26 Jameis Winston 2.00 5.00
27 Tony Romo 1.50 4.00
28 Latavius Murray 1.25 3.00
29 Terrance West 1.25 3.00
30 Carlos Hyde 1.25 3.00
31 Jeremy Langford 1.50 4.00
32 Joe Namath 2.50 6.00
33 DeAndre Hopkins 1.50 4.00
34 Matt Ryan 1.50 4.00
35 Ryan Tannehill 1.50 4.00
36 Doug Martin 1.50 4.00
37 Dez Bryant 2.00 5.00
38 Amari Cooper 2.00 5.00
39 Andy Dalton 1.50 4.00
40 Vance McDonald 1.25 3.00
41 Matthew Stafford 1.50 4.00
42 Barry Sanders 3.00 8.00
43 Andrew Luck 2.50 6.00
44 Devonta Freeman 1.50 4.00
45 Jay Ajayi 1.50 4.00
46 Mike Evans 1.50 4.00
47 Jason Witten 1.50 4.00
48 Philip Rivers 2.00 5.00
49 A.J. Green 2.00 5.00
50 Russell Wilson 2.50 6.00
51 Ameer Abdullah 1.25 3.00
52 John Riggins 1.50 4.00
53 Frank Gore 1.50 4.00
54 Julio Jones 2.00 5.00
55 Jarvis Landry 1.50 4.00
56 Trevor Siemian 1.25 3.00
57 Eli Manning 1.50 4.00
58 Keenan Allen 1.50 4.00
59 Jeremy Hill 1.25 3.00
60 Doug Baldwin 1.50 4.00
61 Aaron Rodgers 4.00 10.00
62 Steve Young 2.50 6.00
63 T.Y. Hilton 1.50 4.00
64 Cam Newton 2.00 5.00
65 Tom Brady 5.00 12.00
66 Demaryius Thomas 1.50 4.00
67 Odell Beckham Jr. 2.00 5.00
68 Antonio Gates 1.25 3.00
69 Isaiah Crowell 1.25 3.00
70 Richard Sherman 2.00 5.00
71 Eddie Lacy 1.25 3.00
72 Marvin Harrison 1.50 4.00
73 Blake Bortles 1.25 3.00
74 Jonathan Stewart 1.25 3.00
75 Julian Edelman 2.00 5.00
76 Von Miller 1.50 4.00
77 Sam Bradford 1.25 3.00
78 Carson Palmer 1.50 4.00
79 Terrelle Pryor 1.25 3.00
80 Terry Bradshaw 2.50 6.00
81 Jordy Nelson 1.50 4.00
82 Marshall Faulk 1.50 4.00
83 Allen Hurns 1.25 3.00
84 Kelvin Benjamin 1.50 4.00
85 Rob Gronkowski 2.00 5.00
86 Alex Smith 1.50 4.00
87 Ryan Mathews 1.50 4.00
88 David Johnson 2.00 5.00
89 Ben Roethlisberger 2.00 5.00
90 Brett Favre 4.00 10.00
91 Stefon Diggs 1.50 4.00
92 Brian Urlacher 2.00 5.00
93 Allen Robinson 1.50 4.00
94 Drew Brees 2.00 5.00
95 Brandon Marshall 1.25 3.00
96 Jamaal Charles 1.50 4.00
97 Kirk Cousins 2.00 5.00
98 Larry Fitzgerald 1.50 4.00
99 Le'Veon Bell 1.50 4.00
100 Jerry Rice 3.00 8.00
101 Alex Collins AU/75 5.00 12.00
102 Braxton Miller AU/75 4.00 10.00
103 C.J. Prosise AU/75 4.00 10.00
104 Cardale Jones AU/49 5.00 12.00
105 Carson Wentz AU/25 60.00 125.00
106 Chris Moore AU/75 5.00 12.00
107 Christian Hackenberg AU/49 5.00 12.00
108 Cody Kessler AU/75 4.00 10.00
109 Connor Cook AU/25 8.00 20.00
110 Corey Coleman AU/49 8.00 20.00
111 Dak Prescott AU/75 50.00 100.00
112 Demarcus Robinson AU/75 4.00 10.00
113 Derrick Henry AU/25 40.00 80.00
114 Devontae Booker AU/75 5.00 12.00
115 Ezekiel Elliott AU/49 75.00 150.00
116 Hunter Henry AU/75 5.00 12.00
117 DeAndre Washington AU/75 4.00 10.00
118 Jared Goff AU/25 40.00 100.00
119 Joey Bosa AU/75 8.00 20.00
120 Jonathan Williams AU/75 5.00 12.00
121 Jordan Howard AU/75 25.00 50.00
122 Josh Doctson AU/49 6.00 15.00
123 Keenan Reynolds AU/75 5.00 12.00
124 Kenneth Dixon AU/75 4.00 10.00
125 Kenyan Drake AU/75 6.00 15.00
126 Jacoby Brissett AU/75 5.00 12.00
127 Laquon Treadwell AU/49 6.00 15.00
128 Leonte Carroo AU/75 4.00 10.00
129 Moritz Bohringer AU/75 4.00 10.00
130 Michael Thomas AU/49 10.00 25.00
131 Paul Perkins AU/75 4.00 10.00
132 Paxton Lynch AU/25 6.00 15.00
133 Pharoh Cooper AU/75 4.00 10.00
134 Ricardo Louis AU/75 4.00 10.00
135 Sterling Shepard AU/75 5.00 12.00
136 Trevor Davis AU/75 4.00 10.00
137 Tyler Boyd AU/75 5.00 12.00
138 Tyler Ervin AU/75 4.00 10.00
139 Wendell Smallwood AU/75 4.00 10.00
140 Will Fuller V AU/49 8.00 20.00

2016 Panini Encased Pro Bowl Dual Materials

*SAPPHIRE/25: .5X TO 1.2X BASIC JSY/49
1 C.Matthews/J.Houston 4.00 10.00
2 D.Whitner/V.Miller 3.00 8.00
3 T.Frederick/T.Smith 2.50 6.00
4 J.Watt/M.Dareus 5.00 12.00
5 J.Forsett/M.Ingram 3.00 8.00
6 R.Kalil/J.Thomas 6.00 15.00
7 A.Green/A.Brown 8.00 20.00
8 D.Freeney/D.Ware 3.00 8.00
9 J.Haden/P.Peterson 2.50 6.00
10 D.Martin/J.Charles 3.00 8.00
11 A.Morris/C.Anderson 3.00 8.00
12 R.Cobb/J.Kuhn 8.00 20.00
13 D.Poe/S.Richardson 2.50 6.00
14 T.Hilton/O.Beckham 4.00 10.00
15 A.Luck/D.Brees 5.00 12.00
16 M.Lynch/R.Mathews 3.00 8.00
17 A.Vinatieri/P.McAfee 15.00 40.00
18 R.White/S.Smith 3.00 8.00
19 D.Ware/M.Williams 3.00 8.00
20 N.Mangold/T.Smith 2.50 6.00
21 K.Chancellor/B.Browner 8.00 20.00
22 T.Romo/M.Stafford 3.00 8.00
23 C.Mosley/J.Forsett 3.00 8.00
24 M.Pouncey/M.Pouncey 2.50 6.00
25 D.Murray/J.Charles 3.00 8.00

2016 Panini Encased Pro Bowl Jumbo Materials

*SAPPHIRE/25: .5X TO 1.2X BASIC JSY/49
*SAPPHIRE/15: .5X TO 1.2X BASIC JSY/25
1 Travis Kelce/49 4.00 10.00
2 Doug Martin/49 3.00 8.00
3 Charles Woodson/49 20.00 50.00
4 Richard Sherman/49 4.00 10.00
5 Tyler Lockett/49 3.00 8.00
6 Derek Carr/49 10.00 25.00
7 DeAndre Hopkins/25 4.00 10.00
8 Russell Wilson/25 6.00 15.00
9 Julio Jones/25 5.00 12.00
10 Teddy Bridgewater/49 3.00 8.00
11 Khalil Mack/49 8.00 20.00
12 Devonta Freeman/49 3.00 8.00
13 Marcus Peters/25 3.00 8.00
14 Amari Cooper/49 4.00 10.00
15 Jarvis Landry/49 3.00 8.00
16 Eli Manning/25 4.00 10.00
17 A.J. Green/25 5.00 12.00
18 Jameis Winston/25 5.00 12.00
19 T.Y. Hilton/49 3.00 8.00
20 Adrian Peterson/25 5.00 12.00
21 Clay Matthews/25 5.00 12.00
22 Todd Gurley II/25 5.00 12.00
23 Tyrod Taylor/49 3.00 8.00
24 Odell Beckham Jr./25 5.00 12.00
25 Allen Robinson/49 3.00 8.00

2016 Panini Encased Reserve Signatures

1 Travis Kelce/35 10.00 25.00
5 Kendall Wright/35 4.00 10.00
6 Geno Atkins/35 12.00 30.00
7 Mike Evans/35 5.00 12.00
13 John Brown/35 5.00 12.00
14 Allen Hurns/35 4.00 10.00
15 Lamar Miller/35 4.00 10.00
16 Bob Lilly/35 12.00 30.00
17 Ozzie Newsome/35 5.00 12.00
18 Danny Woodhead/35 5.00 12.00
19 Roger Craig/35 12.00 30.00
20 Edgerrin James/35 EXCH 20.00 40.00
21 Tyrod Taylor/35 5.00 12.00
22 James Starks/35 4.00 10.00
23 Jordan Matthews/35 5.00 12.00
25 Lenny Moore/35 4.00 10.00
27 Paul Warfield/35 5.00 12.00
28 Derrick Brooks/35 8.00 20.00
31 Walt Garrison/35 8.00 20.00
33 Stefon Diggs/35 5.00 12.00
35 Mario Manningham/35 4.00 10.00
38 Devonta Freeman/35 5.00 12.00
39 Ron Jaworski/35 5.00 12.00
41 Willie McGinest/35 8.00 20.00
42 Jeremy Hill/35 EXCH 4.00 10.00
46 C.J. Anderson/35 5.00 12.00
48 Drew Pearson/35 10.00 25.00
50 Greg Olsen/35 8.00 20.00
RSZET Zach Ertz/35 12.00 30.00
53 Kelvin Benjamin/35 EXCH 5.00 12.00
56 Charles Haley/35 8.00 20.00
58 Ed "Too Tall" Jones/35 10.00 25.00
60 Heath Miller/35 10.00 25.00

2016 Panini Encased Rookie Cap Patch Autographs

RCPAAC Alex Collins/75 6.00 15.00
RCPABM Braxton Miller/75 5.00 12.00
RCPACC Corey Coleman/49 10.00 25.00
RCPACC2 Connor Cook/25 10.00 25.00
RCPACH Christian Hackenberg/49 6.00 15.00
RCPACJ C.J. Prosise/75 5.00 12.00
RCPACJ2 Cardale Jones/49 6.00 15.00
RCPACK Cody Kessler/75 5.00 12.00
RCPACM Chris Moore/75 6.00 15.00
RCPACW Carson Wentz/25 100.00 200.00
RCPADB Devontae Booker/75 6.00 15.00
RCPADH Derrick Henry/25 60.00 125.00
RCPADP Dak Prescott/75 60.00 125.00
RCPADR Demarcus Robinson/75 5.00 12.00
RCPADW DeAndre Washington/75 5.00 12.00
RCPAEE Ezekiel Elliott/49 125.00 250.00
RCPAHH Hunter Henry/75 6.00 15.00
RCPAJB Joey Bosa/75 EXCH 30.00 60.00
RCPAJD Josh Doctson/49 8.00 20.00
RCPAJG Jared Goff/25 60.00 125.00
RCPAJH Jordan Howard/75 40.00 80.00
RCPAJW Jonathan Williams/75 6.00 15.00
RCPAKD2 Kenneth Dixon/60 12.00 30.00
RCPAKD Kenyan Drake/75 8.00 20.00
RCPAKH Kevin Hogan/75 6.00 15.00
RCPAKR Keenan Reynolds/75 6.00 15.00
RCPALC Leonte Carroo/75 5.00 12.00
RCPALT Laquon Treadwell/49 8.00 20.00
RCPAMB Moritz Bohringer/75 5.00 12.00
RCPAMT Michael Thomas/49 12.00 30.00
RCPAPC Pharoh Cooper/75 5.00 12.00
RCPAPL Paxton Lynch/25 8.00 20.00
RCPAPP Paul Perkins/75 5.00 12.00
RCPARL Ricardo Louis/75 5.00 12.00
RCPASS Sterling Shepard/75 40.00 80.00
RCPATB Tyler Boyd/75 6.00 15.00
RCPATD Trevor Davis/75 5.00 12.00
RCPATE Tyler Ervin/75 5.00 12.00
RCPAWF Will Fuller V/49 10.00 25.00
RCPAWS Wendell Smallwood/75 5.00 12.00

2016 Panini Encased Rookie Dual Memorabilia

*SAPPHIRE/25: .5X TO 1.2X BASIC JSY/49
1 Hunter Henry 2.50 6.00
2 Cardale Jones 2.00 5.00
3 Kenneth Dixon 2.00 5.00
4 Connor Cook 2.50 6.00
5 Jordan Howard 4.00 10.00
6 Derrick Henry 5.00 12.00
7 Braxton Miller 2.00 5.00
8 Tyler Boyd 2.50 6.00
9 Trevor Davis 2.00 5.00
10 Will Fuller V 3.00 8.00
11 Leonte Carroo 2.00 5.00
12 Corey Coleman 3.00 8.00
13 Pharoh Cooper 2.00 5.00
14 Ezekiel Elliott 10.00 25.00
15 Sterling Shepard 4.00 10.00
16 Jared Goff 6.00 15.00
17 Joey Bosa 4.00 10.00
18 C.J. Prosise 2.00 5.00
19 Keenan Reynolds 2.50 6.00
20 Josh Doctson 2.50 6.00
21 Dak Prescott 10.00 25.00
22 Laquon Treadwell 2.50 6.00
23 Alex Collins 2.50 6.00
24 Paxton Lynch 2.00 5.00
25 Cody Kessler 2.00 5.00
26 Carson Wentz 12.00 25.00
27 Paul Perkins 2.00 5.00
28 Christian Hackenberg 2.00 5.00
29 Devontae Booker 2.50 6.00
30 Michael Thomas 4.00 10.00

2016 Panini Encased Rookie Dual Swatch Signatures

RDSSBM Braxton Miller/75 5.00 12.00
RDSSCC Corey Coleman/49 10.00 25.00
RDSSCC2 Connor Cook/25 10.00 25.00
RDSSCH Christian Hackenberg/49 6.00 15.00
RDSSCJ C.J. Prosise/75 5.00 12.00
RDSSCJ2 Cardale Jones/49 6.00 15.00
RDSSCW Carson Wentz/25 100.00 200.00
RDSSDH Derrick Henry/25 50.00 100.00
RDSSDP Dak Prescott/75
RDSSEE Ezekiel Elliott/49 125.00 250.00
RDSSHH Hunter Henry/75 6.00 15.00
RDSSJB Joey Bosa/75 10.00 25.00
RDSSJD Josh Doctson/49 8.00 20.00
RDSSJG Jared Goff/25 50.00 125.00
RDSSLT Laquon Treadwell/49 8.00 20.00
RDSSMT Michael Thomas/49 12.00 30.00
RDSSPL Paxton Lynch/25 8.00 20.00
RDSSSS Sterling Shepard/75 6.00 15.00
RDSSTB Tyler Boyd/75 6.00 15.00
RDSSWF Will Fuller V/49 10.00 25.00

2016 Panini Encased Rookie Notable Signatures

4 Hunter Henry/75 5.00 12.00
5 Leonte Carroo/75 4.00 10.00
6 Chris Moore/75 5.00 12.00
7 Kenyan Drake/75 6.00 15.00
8 DeAndre Washington/75 4.00 10.00
9 Christian Hackenberg/49 5.00 12.00
10 Pharoh Cooper/75 4.00 10.00
12 C.J. Prosise/75 4.00 10.00
13 Paul Perkins/75 4.00 10.00
16 Moritz Bohringer/75 4.00 10.00
17 Tyler Ervin/75 4.00 10.00
18 Wendell Smallwood/75 4.00 10.00
19 Braxton Miller/75 4.00 10.00
22 Alex Collins/75 5.00 12.00
24 Ricardo Louis/75 4.00 10.00
25 Demarcus Robinson/75 4.00 10.00
26 Jonathan Williams/75 5.00 12.00
27 Keenan Reynolds/75 5.00 12.00
30 Kenneth Dixon/75 4.00 10.00
32 Connor Cook/25 8.00 20.00
34 Cardale Jones/49 5.00 12.00
37 Malcolm Mitchell/75 4.00 10.00
38 Trevor Davis/75 4.00 10.00
RNICC Corey Coleman/49 8.00 20.00
RNICK Cody Kessler/75 4.00 10.00
RNICW Carson Wentz/25 60.00 125.00
RNIDB Devontae Booker/75 5.00 12.00
RNIDH Derrick Henry/25 40.00 80.00
RNIDP Dak Prescott/75 50.00 100.00
RNIEE Ezekiel Elliott/49 125.00 250.00
RNIJB Joey Bosa/75 EXCH 8.00 20.00
RNIJD Josh Doctson/49 6.00 15.00
RNIJG Jared Goff/25 40.00 100.00
RNIJH Jordan Howard/75 25.00 50.00
RNILT Laquon Treadwell/49 EXCH 6.00 15.00
RNIMT Michael Thomas/49 10.00 25.00
RNIPL Paxton Lynch/25 6.00 15.00
RNISS Sterling Shepard/75 5.00 12.00
RNITB Tyler Boyd/75 5.00 12.00
RNIWF Will Fuller V/49 8.00 20.00

2016 Panini Encased Rookie Quad Memorabilia

*SAPPHIRE/25: .5X TO 1.2X BASIC JSY/49
1 Paul Perkins 2.00 5.00
2 Corey Coleman 3.00 8.00
3 Will Fuller V 3.00 8.00
4 Dak Prescott 10.00 25.00
5 Carson Wentz 12.00 25.00
6 Jared Goff 6.00 15.00
7 Tyler Boyd 2.50 6.00
8 Paxton Lynch 2.00 5.00
9 C.J. Prosise 2.00 5.00
10 Christian Hackenberg 2.00 5.00
11 Derrick Henry 5.00 12.00
12 Joey Bosa 4.00 10.00
13 Sterling Shepard 4.00 10.00
14 Connor Cook 2.50 6.00
15 Michael Thomas 4.00 10.00
16 Josh Doctson 2.50 6.00
17 Ezekiel Elliott 10.00 25.00
18 Cardale Jones 2.00 5.00
19 Laquon Treadwell 2.50 6.00
20 Braxton Miller 2.00 5.00

2016 Panini Encased Rookie Triple Memorabilia

*SAPPHIRE/25: .5X TO 1.2X BASIC JSY/49
1 Jared Goff 6.00 15.00
2 Chris Moore 2.50 6.00
3 Josh Doctson 2.50 6.00
4 Paxton Lynch 2.00 5.00
5 Cardale Jones 2.00 5.00
6 Christian Hackenberg 2.00 5.00
7 Braxton Miller 2.00 5.00
8 Devontae Booker 2.50 6.00
9 Corey Coleman 3.00 8.00
10 Demarcus Robinson 2.00 5.00
11 Joey Bosa 4.00 10.00
12 Jacoby Brissett 2.50 6.00
13 Dak Prescott 10.00 25.00
14 Connor Cook 2.50 6.00
15 Carson Wentz 12.00 25.00
16 Michael Thomas 4.00 10.00
17 Tyler Boyd 2.50 6.00
18 Jonathan Williams 2.50 6.00
19 Ezekiel Elliott 10.00 25.00
20 Ricardo Louis 2.00 5.00
21 C.J. Prosise 2.00 5.00
22 Malcolm Mitchell 2.00 5.00
23 Laquon Treadwell 2.50 6.00
24 Paul Perkins 2.00 5.00
25 Derrick Henry 5.00 12.00
26 Wendell Smallwood 2.00 5.00
27 Will Fuller V 3.00 8.00
28 Tyler Ervin 2.00 5.00
29 Sterling Shepard 4.00 10.00
30 Kenyan Drake 3.00 8.00

2016 Panini Encased Scripted Signatures

6 Jacoby Brissett/75 5.00 12.00
7 Chris Moore/75 5.00 12.00
8 Cardale Jones/49 5.00 12.00
9 Paul Perkins/75 4.00 10.00
11 Christian Hackenberg/49 5.00 12.00
14 C.J. Prosise/75 4.00 10.00
18 Jonathan Williams/75 5.00 12.00
19 Connor Cook/25 8.00 20.00
21 Alex Collins/75 5.00 12.00
23 Pharoh Cooper/75 4.00 10.00
26 Kenneth Dixon/75 4.00 10.00
28 Hunter Henry/75 5.00 12.00
29 Leonte Carroo/75 4.00 10.00
31 Kenyan Drake/75 6.00 15.00
32 Malcolm Mitchell/75 4.00 10.00
33 Ricardo Louis/75 4.00 10.00
34 Demarcus Robinson/75 4.00 10.00
35 Braxton Miller/75 4.00 10.00
36 Keenan Reynolds/75 5.00 12.00
37 Tajae Sharpe/75 5.00 12.00
38 Trevor Davis/75 4.00 10.00
39 Wendell Smallwood/75 4.00 10.00
40 Tyler Ervin/75 4.00 10.00
SSCCM Corey Coleman/49 8.00 20.00
SSCK Cody Kessler/75 4.00 10.00
SSCWZ Carson Wentz/25 60.00 125.00
SSDB Devontae Booker/75 5.00 12.00
SSDP Dak Prescott/75 50.00 100.00
SSEEL Ezekiel Elliott/49 75.00 150.00
SSHR Derrick Henry/25 40.00 80.00
SSJB Joey Bosa/75 8.00 20.00
SSJD Josh Doctson/49 6.00 15.00
SSJGF Jared Goff/25 40.00 100.00
SSJHW Jordan Howard/75 25.00 50.00
SSLT Laquon Treadwell/49 6.00 15.00
SSMTH Michael Thomas/49 10.00 25.00
SSPL Paxton Lynch/25 6.00 15.00
SSSSP Sterling Shepard/75 5.00 12.00
SSTB Tyler Boyd/75 5.00 12.00
SSWF Will Fuller V/49 8.00 20.00

2016 Panini Encased Substantial Rookie Swatches

*SAPPHIRE/25: .5X TO 1.2X BASIC JSY/49
1 Sterling Shepard 5.00 10.00
2 Dak Prescott 10.00 25.00
3 Connor Cook 2.50 6.00
4 Ezekiel Elliott 10.00 25.00
5 Derrick Henry 8.00 12.00
6 Carson Wentz 10.00 25.00
7 Pharoh Cooper 2.00 5.00
8 Jonathan Williams 2.50 6.00
9 Trevor Davis 2.00 5.00
10 Joey Bosa 6.00 10.00
11 Kenneth Dixon 2.00 5.00
12 Braxton Miller 2.00 5.00
13 Chris Moore 2.50 6.00
14 Devontae Booker 2.50 6.00
15 Laquon Treadwell 2.50 6.00
16 Cody Kessler 2.00 5.00
17 Tyler Ervin 2.00 5.00
18 Tyler Boyd 2.50 6.00
19 Cardale Jones 2.00 5.00
20 Ricardo Louis 2.00 5.00
21 Josh Doctson 2.50 6.00
22 Alex Collins 2.50 6.00
23 Christian Hackenberg 2.00 5.00
24 Jared Goff 10.00 15.00
25 Jacoby Brissett 2.50 6.00
26 Michael Thomas 5.00 10.00
27 Wendell Smallwood 2.00 5.00
28 C.J. Prosise 2.00 5.00
29 Keenan Reynolds 2.50 6.00
30 Demarcus Robinson 2.00 5.00
31 Hunter Henry 2.50 6.00
32 Leonte Carroo 2.00 5.00
33 Will Fuller V 3.00 8.00
34 Corey Coleman 3.00 8.00
35 Malcolm Mitchell 2.00 5.00
36 Jordan Howard 6.00 10.00
37 Paxton Lynch 2.00 5.00
38 Paul Perkins 2.00 5.00
39 Kenyan Drake 3.00 8.00

2016 Panini Encased Vaulted Veterans Material Signatures

3 Devonta Freeman/25 8.00 20.00
8 Jeremy Langford/49 6.00 15.00
10 Josh Gordon/49 5.00 12.00
11 C.J. Anderson/25 8.00 20.00
13 Geno Atkins/49 10.00 25.00
16 T.J. Yeldon/49 5.00 12.00
17 Jay Ajayi/49 6.00 15.00
19 Allen Hurns/49 5.00 12.00
22 Matt Jones/49 6.00 15.00
27 Jeremy Hill/25 EXCH 6.00 15.00
28 Jordan Matthews/25 8.00 20.00
30 Kelvin Benjamin/25 8.00 20.00

2017 Panini Encased

1 Jeremy Maclin 1.25 3.00
2 Doug Baldwin 1.50 4.00
3 Melvin Gordon 1.50 4.00
4 Cam Newton 2.00 5.00
5 Sammy Watkins 2.00 5.00
6 Jay Cutler 1.25 3.00
7 Jordan Matthews 1.25 3.00
8 Julio Jones 2.00 5.00
9 Emmanuel Sanders 2.00 5.00
10 Frank Gore 1.50 4.00
11 Allen Hurns 1.25 3.00
12 David Johnson 2.00 5.00
13 Khalil Mack 2.00 5.00
14 Carlos Hyde 1.25 3.00
15 Robby Anderson 1.25 3.00
16 Jared Goff 2.00 5.00
17 Eddie Lacy 1.25 3.00
18 Demaryius Thomas 1.50 4.00
19 Kirk Cousins 2.00 5.00
20 Adrian Peterson 2.00 5.00
21 T.Y. Hilton 1.50 4.00
22 Von Miller 1.50 4.00
23 Ezekiel Elliott 2.50 6.00
24 Travis Kelce 2.00 5.00
25 Dez Bryant 2.00 5.00
26 DeAndre Hopkins 1.50 4.00
27 LeSean McCoy 2.00 5.00
28 Marcus Mariota 2.00 5.00
29 Dak Prescott 2.00 5.00
30 C.J. Anderson 1.50 4.00
31 Isaiah Crowell 1.25 3.00
32 Clay Matthews 1.50 4.00
33 Antonio Gates 1.25 3.00
34 Antonio Brown 2.00 5.00
35 Todd Gurley II 2.00 5.00
36 Mike Wallace 1.25 3.00
37 Eric Decker 1.25 3.00
38 Matt Ryan 1.50 4.00
39 Pierre Garcon 1.50 4.00
40 Randall Cobb 1.50 4.00
41 Tarik Cohen 2.50 6.00
42 Russell Wilson 2.50 6.00
43 Allen Robinson 1.50 4.00
44 Carson Palmer 1.50 4.00
45 Marshawn Lynch 1.50 4.00
46 Lamar Miller 1.25 3.00
47 Jonathan Stewart 1.25 3.00
48 Corey Coleman 1.25 3.00
49 Tom Brady 5.00 12.00
50 Drew Brees 2.00 5.00
51 Odell Beckham Jr. 2.00 5.00
52 Amari Cooper 2.00 5.00
53 Aaron Rodgers 4.00 10.00
54 Brandon Marshall 1.25 3.00
55 Jameis Winston 1.50 4.00
56 Josh Doctson 1.25 3.00
57 Jay Ajayi 1.50 4.00
58 Alex Smith 1.50 4.00
59 DeSean Jackson 1.50 4.00
60 Rob Gronkowski 2.00 5.00
61 Stefon Diggs 1.50 4.00
62 Tyreek Hill 2.00 5.00
63 Jordy Nelson 1.50 4.00
64 Latavius Murray 1.25 3.00
65 Matt Forte 1.25 3.00
66 Jimmy Graham 2.00 5.00
67 Golden Tate III 1.25 3.00
68 LeGarrette Blount 1.50 4.00
69 Jimmy Garoppolo 2.50 6.00
70 Mike Evans 1.50 4.00
71 T.J. Watt RC 4.00 10.00
72 Jeremy Hill 1.25 3.00
73 Jarvis Landry 1.50 4.00
74 Devonta Freeman 1.50 4.00
75 Matthew Stafford 1.50 4.00
76 Adam Thielen 2.00 5.00
77 Brandin Cooks 1.50 4.00
78 DeMarco Murray 1.50 4.00
79 Joe Flacco 1.50 4.00
80 Eli Manning 1.50 4.00
81 Chris Hogan 1.25 3.00
82 Greg Olsen 1.50 4.00
83 Jordan Howard 2.00 5.00
84 Ben Roethlisberger 2.00 5.00
85 Michael Thomas 2.00 5.00
86 Myles Garrett RC 4.00 10.00
87 Tyrod Taylor 1.50 4.00
88 A.J. Green 2.00 5.00
89 Blake Bortles 1.25 3.00
90 Larry Fitzgerald 1.50 4.00
91 Jason Witten 1.50 4.00
92 Andrew Luck 2.50 6.00
93 Andy Dalton 1.50 4.00
94 Carson Wentz 2.50 6.00
95 Derek Carr 2.00 5.00
96 Ameer Abdullah 1.25 3.00
97 Robert Kelley 1.25 3.00
98 Le'Veon Bell 1.50 4.00
99 Philip Rivers 2.00 5.00
100 J.J. Watt 2.00 5.00

2017 Panini Encased Century Collection Materials

*SAPPHIRE/25: .5X TO 1.2X BASIC JSY/49
1 Dan Marino 10.00 25.00
2 Howie Long 5.00 12.00
3 Hines Ward 4.00 10.00
4 Troy Aikman 6.00 15.00
5 Terrell Davis 4.00 10.00
6 Jerome Bettis 5.00 12.00
7 Priest Holmes 3.00 8.00
8 Heath Miller 3.00 8.00
9 Marshall Faulk 4.00 10.00
10 Charles Woodson 5.00 12.00
11 Steve Young 6.00 15.00
12 Joe Namath 12.00 30.00
13 Jim Plunkett 4.00 10.00
14 Lance Alworth 4.00 10.00
15 Kurt Warner 4.00 10.00

16 Fran Tarkenton 5.00 12.00
17 Bo Jackson 6.00 15.00
18 Andre Reed 4.00 10.00
20 Jim Kelly 5.00 12.00
21 Joe Montana 12.00 30.00
22 John Riggins 4.00 10.00
23 Marcus Allen 4.00 10.00
24 Joe Theismann 5.00 12.00
25 Mark Brunell 4.00 10.00

2017 Panini Encased First Hand Materials

*SAPPHIRE/25: .5X TO 1.2X BASIC JSY/49
1 JuJu Smith-Schuster 5.00 12.00
2 Mitchell Trubisky 8.00 20.00
3 D'Onta Foreman 3.00 8.00
4 Mike Williams 4.00 10.00
5 Ezekiel Elliott 5.00 12.00
6 Patrick Mahomes II 15.00 40.00
7 Cooper Kupp 4.00 10.00
8 Evan Engram 3.00 8.00
9 Jordan Howard 4.00 10.00
10 Dalvin Cook 5.00 12.00
11 Alvin Kamara 10.00 25.00
12 Leonard Fournette 8.00 20.00
13 C.J. Beathard 2.50 6.00
14 Christian McCaffrey 6.00 15.00
15 Michael Thomas 4.00 10.00
16 Deshaun Watson 10.00 25.00
17 Jordy Nelson 3.00 8.00
18 Zay Jones 3.00 8.00
19 David Johnson 4.00 10.00
20 Joe Mixon 5.00 12.00
21 Davis Webb 2.50 6.00
22 Corey Davis 4.00 10.00
23 Dak Prescott 4.00 10.00
24 John Ross III 3.00 8.00
25 Jared Goff 4.00 10.00
26 O.J. Howard 3.00 8.00
27 Kareem Hunt 5.00 12.00
28 Curtis Samuel 3.00 8.00
29 Carson Wentz 5.00 12.00
30 DeShone Kizer 2.50 6.00

2017 Panini Encased Legendary Swatch Signatures

1 Ronnie Lott/25 12.00 30.00
3 Thurman Thomas/25 12.00 30.00
9 Joe Theismann/25 15.00 40.00
11 Fred Taylor/25 12.00 30.00
13 Fran Tarkenton/25 15.00 40.00

2017 Panini Encased Reserve Signatures

2 Ron Jaworski/49 5.00 12.00
7 Archie Manning/25 12.00 30.00
8 Eddie Lacy/49 4.00 10.00
10 Andre Reed/49 5.00 12.00
12 Chad Pennington/49 4.00 10.00
14 Ryan Shazier/49 EXCH 10.00 25.00
15 Demaryius Thomas/25 6.00 15.00
16 Eric Berry/49 8.00 20.00
17 DeSean Jackson/25 6.00 15.00
18 Rodney Harrison/49 12.00 30.00
20 Randy White/49 5.00 12.00
22 Chris Spielman/49 5.00 12.00
24 Steve Atwater/49 10.00 25.00
25 Jamaal Charles/25 6.00 15.00
26 Mike Vrabel/49 10.00 25.00
27 Luke Kuechly/25 6.00 15.00
28 Greg Olsen/49 5.00 12.00
30 Cole Deasley/49 EXCH 15.00 40.00
33 Jason Taylor/25 20.00 50.00
34 Muhammad Wilkerson/49 EXCH 4.00 10.00
35 Torry Holt/25 6.00 15.00
37 Dan Reeves/25 12.00 30.00
38 Rich Gannon/49 8.00 20.00
40 Jevon Kearse/49 4.00 10.00
42 Mark Schlereth/49 8.00 20.00
44 Mark Brunell/49 5.00 12.00
45 Fred Taylor/25 6.00 15.00
46 Christian Okoye/49 4.00 10.00
47 Earl Thomas III/25 6.00 15.00
48 Alan Page/49 4.00 10.00
50 Carlos Hyde/49 4.00 10.00
52 Vic Beasley Jr./49 4.00 10.00
54 Landon Collins/49 4.00 10.00
55 David Johnson/25 12.00 30.00
56 Louis Lipps/49 4.00 10.00
57 Adam Vinatieri/49 12.00 30.00
58 Danny Woodhead/49 5.00 12.00
60 Kevin Mawae/49 4.00 10.00

2017 Panini Encased Rookie Cap Patch Autographs

101 Mitchell Trubisky/25 100.00 200.00
102 Leonard Fournette/25 125.00 250.00
103 Corey Davis/49 EXCH 10.00 25.00
104 Mike Williams/49 10.00 25.00
105 Christian McCaffrey/49 75.00 150.00
106 John Ross/49 8.00 20.00
107 Patrick Mahomes II/25 800.00 1400.00
108 Deshaun Watson/25 500.00 800.00
109 O.J. Howard/75 30.00 60.00
110 Evan Engram/75 6.00 15.00
111 Zay Jones/75 6.00 15.00
112 Curtis Samuel/49 8.00 20.00
113 Dalvin Cook/49 60.00 125.00
114 Joe Mixon/75 30.00 60.00
115 DeShone Kizer/25 50.00 100.00
116 Juju Smith-Schuster/49 40.00 80.00
117 Alvin Kamara/75 90.00 150.00
118 Cooper Kupp/75 25.00 50.00
119 Taywan Taylor/75 5.00 12.00
120 ArDarius Stewart/75 5.00 12.00
121 Carlos Henderson/75 5.00 12.00
122 Chris Godwin/75 10.00 25.00
123 Kareem Hunt/75 20.00 50.00
124 Davis Webb/75 5.00 12.00
125 D'Onta Foreman/49 8.00 20.00
126 Kenny Golladay/75 8.00 20.00
127 C.J. Beathard/75 5.00 12.00
128 James Conner/75 12.00 30.00
129 Amara Darboh/75 5.00 12.00
130 Dede Westbrook/49 6.00 15.00
131 Samaje Perine/75 5.00 12.00
132 Josh Reynolds/75 5.00 12.00
133 Mack Hollins/75 EXCH 12.00 30.00
134 Joe Williams/75 5.00 12.00
135 Jamaal Williams/75 EXCH 15.00 40.00
136 R. Joshua Dobbs/75 6.00 15.00
137 Wayne Gallman/75 6.00 15.00
138 Marlon Mack/75 8.00 20.00
139 Jeremy McNichols/75 5.00 12.00
140 Nathan Peterman/49 8.00 20.00

2017 Panini Encased Rookie Dual Swatch Signatures

RDSAK Alvin Kamara/75 50.00 100.00
RDSCD Corey Davis/49 EXCH 10.00 25.00
RDSCK Cooper Kupp/75 12.00 30.00
RDSCM Christian McCaffrey/49 15.00 40.00
RDSCS Curtis Samuel/49 8.00 20.00
RDSDC Dalvin Cook/49 30.00 80.00
RDSDF D'Onta Foreman/49 15.00 40.00
RDSDK DeShone Kizer/25 8.00 20.00
RDSDS Deshaun Watson/25 50.00 125.00
RDSEE Evan Engram/75 6.00 15.00
RDSJJ Juju Smith-Schuster/49 30.00 60.00
RDSJS John Ross/49 8.00 20.00
RDSJX Joe Mixon/75 10.00 25.00
RDSLF Leonard Fournette/25 25.00 60.00
RDSMT Mitchell Trubisky/25 60.00 125.00
RDSMW Mike Williams/49 10.00 25.00
RDSOJ O.J. Howard/75 6.00 15.00
RDSPM Patrick Mahomes II/25 800.00 1400.00
RDSTT Taywan Taylor/75 5.00 12.00
RDSZJ Zay Jones/75 EXCH 6.00 15.00

2017 Panini Encased Rookie Endorsements

REAKM Alvin Kamara/75 50.00 100.00
RECDV Corey Davis/49 EXCH 8.00 20.00
RECJB C.J. Beathard/75 10.00 25.00
RECKP Cooper Kupp/75 15.00 40.00
RECMF Christian McCaffrey/49 12.00 30.00
REDCK Dalvin Cook/49 30.00 60.00
REDFM D'Onta Foreman/49 6.00 15.00
REDKZ DeShone Kizer/25 6.00 15.00
REDWB Davis Webb/75 4.00 10.00
REDWS Deshaun Watson/25 100.00 200.00
REEEG Evan Engram/75 5.00 12.00
REJCN James Conner/75 8.00 20.00
REJJS JuJu Smith-Schuster/49 25.00 50.00
REJMX Joe Mixon/75 8.00 20.00
REJRS John Ross III/49 6.00 15.00
REKGD Kenny Golladay/75 6.00 15.00
REKHT Kareem Hunt/75 20.00 50.00
RELFN Leonard Fournette/25 40.00 80.00
REMTB Mitchell Trubisky/25 50.00 100.00
REMWS Mike Williams/49 8.00 20.00
REOJH O.J. Howard/75 5.00 12.00
REPM2 Patrick Mahomes II/25 400.00 800.00
RERJD R. Joshua Dobbs/75 5.00 12.00
RERSW Ryan Switzer/75 5.00 12.00
RESPR Samaje Perine/75 4.00 10.00

2017 Panini Encased Rookie Notable Signatures

RNAKM Alvin Kamara/75 50.00 100.00
RNCDV Corey Davis/49 8.00 20.00
RNCJB C.J. Beathard/75 10.00 25.00
RNCKP Cooper Kupp/75 15.00 40.00
RNCMF Christian McCaffrey/49 12.00 30.00
RNDCK Dalvin Cook/49 30.00 60.00
RNDFM D'Onta Foreman/49 6.00 15.00
RNDKZ DeShone Kizer/25 6.00 15.00
RNDWB Davis Webb/75 4.00 10.00
RNDWS Deshaun Watson/25 100.00 200.00
RNEEG Evan Engram/75 5.00 12.00
RNJCN James Conner/75 8.00 20.00
RNJJS Juju Smith-Schuster/49 25.00 50.00
RNJMX Joe Mixon/75 8.00 20.00
RNJRS John Ross/49 6.00 15.00
RNKGD Kenny Golladay/75 6.00 15.00
RNKHT Kareem Hunt/75 20.00 50.00
RNLFN Leonard Fournette/25 40.00 80.00
RNMTB Mitchell Trubisky/25 50.00 100.00
RNMWS Mike Williams/49 8.00 20.00
RNOJH O.J. Howard/75 5.00 12.00
RNPM2 Patrick Mahomes II/25 400.00 800.00
RNRJD R. Joshua Dobbs/75 5.00 12.00
RNSPR Samaje Perine/75 4.00 10.00

2017 Panini Encased Rookie Quad Memorabilia

*SAPPHIRE/25: .5X TO 1.2X BASIC JSY/49
1 Joe Mixon 6.00 15.00
2 Christian McCaffrey 8.00 20.00
3 O.J. Howard 4.00 10.00
4 Deshaun Watson 12.00 30.00
5 DeShone Kizer 3.00 8.00
6 Patrick Mahomes II 15.00 40.00
7 Leonard Fournette 10.00 25.00
8 Mike Williams 5.00 12.00
9 R. Joshua Dobbs 4.00 10.00
10 John Ross III 4.00 10.00
11 Dalvin Cook 6.00 15.00
12 Mitchell Trubisky 10.00 25.00
13 Kareem Hunt 6.00 15.00
14 C.J. Beathard 3.00 8.00
15 Zay Jones 4.00 10.00
16 Corey Davis 5.00 12.00
17 Alvin Kamara 12.00 30.00
18 Evan Engram 4.00 10.00
19 Davis Webb 3.00 8.00
20 D'Onta Foreman 4.00 10.00

2017 Panini Encased Rookie Triple Memorabilia

*SAPPHIRE/25: .5X TO 1.2X BASIC JSY/49
1 DeShone Kizer 3.00 8.00
2 Zay Jones 4.00 10.00
3 Leonard Fournette 10.00 25.00
4 Alvin Kamara 12.00 30.00
5 Nathan Peterman 4.00 10.00
6 R. Joshua Dobbs 4.00 10.00
7 Davis Webb 3.00 8.00
8 James Conner 6.00 15.00
9 Cooper Kupp 5.00 12.00
10 Joe Mixon 6.00 15.00
11 Dalvin Cook 6.00 15.00
12 O.J. Howard 4.00 10.00
13 Curtis Samuel 4.00 10.00
14 Deshaun Watson 12.00 30.00
15 C.J. Beathard 3.00 8.00
16 Amara Darboh 3.00 8.00
17 Dede Westbrook 3.00 8.00
18 Kenny Golladay 5.00 12.00
19 Patrick Mahomes II 15.00 40.00
20 Corey Davis 5.00 12.00
21 Mike Williams 5.00 12.00
22 Taywan Taylor 3.00 8.00
23 Evan Engram 4.00 10.00
24 John Ross III 4.00 10.00
25 D'Onta Foreman 4.00 10.00
26 Wayne Gallman 4.00 10.00
27 Kareem Hunt 6.00 15.00
28 JuJu Smith-Schuster 6.00 15.00
29 Christian McCaffrey 8.00 20.00
30 Mitchell Trubisky 10.00 25.00

2017 Panini Encased Scripted Signatures

SSAKM Alvin Kamara/75 50.00 100.00
SSCDV Corey Davis/49 EXCH 8.00 20.00
SSCJB C.J. Beathard 10.00 25.00
SSCKP Cooper Kupp/75 15.00 40.00
SSCMF Christian McCaffrey/49 12.00 30.00
SSDCK Dalvin Cook/49 30.00 60.00
SSDFM D'Onta Foreman/49 6.00 15.00
SSDKZ DeShone Kizer/25 6.00 15.00
SSDWB Davis Webb/75 4.00 10.00
SSDWS Deshaun Watson/25 100.00 200.00
SSEEG Evan Engram/75 5.00 12.00
SSJCN James Conner/75 8.00 20.00
SSJJS Juju Smith-Schuster/49 25.00 50.00
SSJMX Joe Mixon/75 8.00 20.00
SSJRS John Ross/49 6.00 15.00
SSKGD Kenny Golladay/75 6.00 15.00
SSKHT Kareem Hunt/75 20.00 50.00
SSLFN Leonard Fournette/25 40.00 80.00
SSMTB Mitchell Trubisky/25 50.00 100.00
SSMWS Mike Williams/49 8.00 20.00
SSOJH O.J. Howard/75 5.00 12.00
SSPM2 Patrick Mahomes II/25 400.00 800.00
SSRJD R. Joshua Dobbs/75 5.00 12.00
SSSPR Samaje Perine/75 4.00 10.00

2017 Panini Encased Substantial Swatches

*SAPPHIRE/25: .5X TO 1.2X BASIC JSY/49
1 Marcus Mariota/49 5.00 12.00
2 Marshawn Lynch/49 4.00 10.00
3 Jason Witten/49 4.00 10.00
4 David Johnson/49 5.00 12.00
5 Russell Wilson/49 6.00 15.00
6 James Harrison/49 4.00 10.00
7 Antonio Brown/49 5.00 12.00
8 Jarvis Landry/49 4.00 10.00
9 Dak Prescott/49 5.00 12.00
10 Jordan Howard/49 5.00 12.00
11 Richard Sherman/49 5.00 12.00
12 Travis Kelce/49 5.00 12.00
13 Tom Brady/25 30.00 60.00
14 Carson Wentz/49 12.00 30.00
15 Jameis Winston/49 4.00 10.00
16 Chris Harris Jr./49 3.00 8.00
17 Aaron Rodgers/49 15.00 40.00
18 LeSean McCoy/49 5.00 12.00
19 Ryan Tannehill/49 4.00 10.00
20 Matt Ryan/49 4.00 10.00
21 Jared Goff/49 5.00 12.00
22 Ezekiel Elliott/49 10.00 25.00
23 J.J. Watt/25 6.00 15.00
24 Michael Thomas/49 5.00 12.00
25 Blake Bortles/49 3.00 8.00
26 Devonta Freeman/49 4.00 10.00
27 Derek Carr/49 5.00 12.00
28 DeMarco Murray/49 4.00 10.00
29 Derrick Henry/49 4.00 10.00
30 Amari Cooper/49 5.00 12.00

2017 Panini Encased Timeless Material Signatures

2 Michael Vick/25 25.00 50.00
4 Priest Holmes/25 10.00 25.00
6 Len Dawson/25 15.00 40.00
7 LaDainian Tomlinson/25 12.00 30.00
10 Mark Brunell/25 12.00 30.00
12 Heath Miller/25 10.00 25.00
14 Andre Reed/25 12.00 30.00

2018 Panini Encased

1 LeSean McCoy 2.00 5.00
2 Kelvin Benjamin 1.50 4.00
3 Tre'Davious White 1.25 3.00
4 Ryan Tannehill 1.50 4.00
5 Kenyan Drake 1.25 3.00
6 Kiko Alonso 1.25 3.00
7 Tom Brady 8.00 20.00
8 Rob Gronkowski 2.00 5.00
9 Julian Edelman 2.00 5.00
10 Jermaine Kearse 1.25 3.00
11 Leonard Williams 1.25 3.00
12 Isaiah Crowell 1.25 3.00
13 Joe Flacco 1.50 4.00
14 Michael Crabtree 1.25 3.00
15 Alex Collins 1.25 3.00
16 Andy Dalton 1.50 4.00
17 A.J. Green 2.00 5.00
18 Joe Mixon 1.50 4.00
19 Josh Gordon 1.25 3.00
20 Jarvis Landry 1.50 4.00
21 Jimmy Garoppolo 2.50 6.00
22 Carlos Hyde 1.25 3.00
23 Ben Roethlisberger 2.00 5.00
24 Le'Veon Bell 1.50 4.00
25 Antonio Brown 2.00 5.00
26 JuJu Smith-Schuster 2.00 5.00
27 Deshaun Watson 2.50 6.00
28 DeAndre Hopkins 1.50 4.00
29 J.J. Watt 2.00 5.00
30 Andrew Luck 2.50 6.00
31 T.Y. Hilton 1.50 4.00
32 Marlon Mack 1.25 3.00
33 Blake Bortles 1.25 3.00
34 Leonard Fournette 2.00 5.00
35 Jalen Ramsey 1.50 4.00
36 Marcus Mariota 2.00 5.00
37 Derrick Henry 2.00 5.00
38 Corey Davis 1.50 4.00
39 Case Keenum 1.50 4.00
40 Von Miller 1.50 4.00
41 Demaryius Thomas 1.50 4.00
42 Patrick Mahomes II 12.00 30.00
43 Kareem Hunt 1.50 4.00
44 Tyreek Hill 2.00 5.00
45 Travis Kelce 2.00 5.00
46 Philip Rivers 2.00 5.00
47 Melvin Gordon III 1.50 4.00
48 Keenan Allen 1.50 4.00
49 Derek Carr 2.00 5.00
50 Amari Cooper 2.00 5.00
51 Marshawn Lynch 1.50 4.00
52 Khalil Mack 2.00 5.00
53 Dak Prescott 2.00 5.00
54 Ezekiel Elliott 2.50 6.00
55 DeMarcus Lawrence 1.25 3.00
56 Eli Manning 1.50 4.00
57 Odell Beckham Jr. 2.00 5.00
58 Sterling Shepard 1.50 4.00
59 Carson Wentz 2.50 6.00
60 Jay Ajayi 1.50 4.00
61 Alshon Jeffery 1.50 4.00
62 Alex Smith 1.50 4.00
63 Jordan Reed 1.25 3.00
64 Josh Norman 1.25 3.00
65 Mitchell Trubisky 2.00 5.00
66 Jordan Howard 2.00 5.00
67 Allen Robinson II 1.50 4.00
68 Matthew Stafford 1.50 4.00
69 Marvin Jones Jr. 1.25 3.00
70 LeGarrette Blount 1.50 4.00
71 Aaron Rodgers 4.00 10.00
72 Davante Adams 1.50 4.00
73 Jimmy Graham 2.00 5.00
74 Clay Matthews 1.50 4.00
75 Kirk Cousins 2.00 5.00
76 Adam Thielen 2.00 5.00
77 Dalvin Cook 1.50 4.00
78 Richard Sherman 2.00 5.00
79 Matt Ryan 1.50 4.00
80 Devonta Freeman 1.50 4.00
81 Julio Jones 2.00 5.00
82 Cam Newton 2.00 5.00
83 Greg Olsen 1.50 4.00
84 Luke Kuechly 1.50 4.00
85 Drew Brees 2.00 5.00
86 Alvin Kamara 1.50 4.00
87 Michael Thomas 2.00 5.00
88 Jameis Winston 1.50 4.00
89 Mike Evans 1.50 4.00
90 Gerald McCoy 1.25 3.00
91 David Johnson 2.00 5.00
92 Larry Fitzgerald 1.50 4.00
93 Chandler Jones 1.25 3.00
94 Jared Goff 2.00 5.00
95 Todd Gurley II 2.00 5.00
96 Brandin Cooks 1.50 4.00
97 Russell Wilson 2.50 6.00
98 Doug Baldwin 1.50 4.00
99 Earl Thomas III 1.50 4.00
100 Marquise Goodwin 1.25 3.00
101 Baker Mayfield HAT AU/25 RC 300.00 500.00
102 Saquon Barkley HAT AU/25 RC EXCH 250.00 400.00
103 Sam Darnold HAT AU/25 RC 150.00 300.00
104 Bradley Chubb HAT AU/50 RC 10.00 25.00
105 Josh Allen HAT AU/25 RC 100.00 200.00
106 Josh Rosen HAT AU/25 RC 75.00 150.00
107 D.J. Moore HAT AU/50 RC 20.00 50.00
108 Hayden Hurst HAT AU/50 RC 8.00 20.00
109 Calvin Ridley HAT AU/25 RC 40.00 80.00
110 Rashaad Penny HAT AU/50 RC 10.00 25.00
111 Sony Michel HAT AU/25 RC EXCH 75.00 150.00
112 Lamar Jackson HAT AU/25 RC 125.00 250.00
113 Nick Chubb HAT AU/25 RC 75.00 150.00
114 Ronald Jones II HAT AU/50 RC 6.00 15.00
115 Courtland Sutton HAT AU/50 RC 15.00 40.00
116 Mike Gesicki HAT AU/50 RC 8.00 20.00
117 Kerryon Johnson HAT AU/50 RC 60.00 125.00
118 Dante Pettis HAT AU/50 RC 10.00 25.00
119 Christian Kirk HAT AU/25 RC 12.00 30.00
120 Anthony Miller HAT AU/50 RC 10.00 25.00
121 Derrius Guice HAT AU/25 RC 15.00 40.00
122 James Washington HAT AU/50 RC 12.00 30.00
123 D.J. Chark Jr. HAT AU/50 RC 8.00 20.00
124 Royce Freeman HAT AU/50 RC 15.00 40.00
125 Mason Rudolph HAT AU/25 RC 50.00 100.00
126 Michael Gallup HAT AU/50 RC 25.00 50.00
127 Tre'Quan Smith HAT AU/50 RC 10.00 25.00
128 Keke Coutee HAT AU/50 RC 8.00 20.00
129 Nyheim Hines HAT AU/50 RC 8.00 20.00
130 Kyle Lauletta HAT AU/50 RC 10.00 25.00
131 Mark Walton HAT AU/50 RC 8.00 20.00
132 DaeSean Hamilton HAT AU/50 RC 8.00 20.00
133 Ito Smith HAT AU/50 RC 8.00 20.00
134 Kalen Ballage HAT AU/50 RC 8.00 20.00
135 Jaleel Scott HAT AU/50 RC 6.00 15.00
136 J'Mon Moore HAT AU/50 RC 6.00 15.00
137 Daurice Fountain HAT AU/50 RC 8.00 20.00
138 Jaylen Samuels HAT AU/50 RC 8.00 20.00
139 Mike White HAT AU/50 RC 8.00 20.00
140 Marquez Valdes-Scantling HAT AU/50 RC 8.00 20.00

2018 Panini Encased Sapphire

*VETS/25: .5X TO 1.2X BASIC CARDS/50
*ROOK/25: .5X TO 1.2X BASIC CARDS/50

2018 Panini Encased Autographs

5 Kenyan Drake/20 6.00 15.00
10 Jermaine Kearse/20 6.00 15.00
12 Isaiah Crowell/20
15 Alex Collins/20 6.00 15.00
18 Joe Mixon/20 EXCH 8.00 20.00
22 Carlos Hyde/20 6.00 15.00
26 JuJu Smith-Schuster/20 EXCH 25.00 60.00
31 T.Y. Hilton/20 8.00 20.00
43 Kareem Hunt/20
44 Tyreek Hill/20 EXCH 20.00 50.00
45 Travis Kelce/20 EXCH 10.00 25.00
47 Melvin Gordon III/20 8.00 20.00
48 Keenan Allen/20
54 Ezekiel Elliott/20
66 Jordan Howard/20 10.00 25.00
67 Allen Robinson II/20 8.00 20.00
69 Marvin Jones Jr./20 6.00 15.00
70 LeGarrette Blount/20
76 Adam Thielen/20 40.00 80.00
77 Dalvin Cook/20
80 Devonta Freeman/20 8.00 20.00
83 Greg Olsen/20 8.00 20.00
84 Luke Kuechly/20
89 Mike Evans/20 8.00 20.00
90 Gerald McCoy/20 6.00 15.00
91 David Johnson/20 10.00 25.00
93 Chandler Jones/20 6.00 15.00
96 Brandin Cooks/20
98 Doug Baldwin/20
99 Earl Thomas III/20

2018 Panini Encased Century Collection Materials

*SAPPHIRE/25: .5X TO 1.2X BASIC JSY/50
1 Bruce Smith 4.00 10.00
2 Ricky Williams 4.00 10.00
3 Michael Strahan 4.00 10.00
4 John Randle 4.00 10.00
5 Peyton Manning 10.00 25.00
6 Terry Bradshaw 8.00 20.00
7 Jim Kelly 5.00 12.00
8 Dan Marino 10.00 25.00
9 Rod Woodson 5.00 12.00
10 Steve Young 6.00 15.00
11 Warren Moon 5.00 12.00
12 John Elway 8.00 20.00
13 Cris Carter 5.00 12.00
14 Hines Ward 4.00 10.00
15 Brian Dawkins 5.00 12.00
16 Tony Gonzalez 4.00 10.00
17 Darren Woodson 4.00 10.00
18 Ozzie Newsome 4.00 10.00
19 Barry Sanders 8.00 20.00
20 Ray Lewis 5.00 12.00
21 Mike Singletary 5.00 12.00
22 Michael Vick 4.00 10.00
23 Lawrence Taylor 5.00 12.00
24 Brett Favre 10.00 25.00
25 Mark Brunell 3.00 8.00

2018 Panini Encased Future Wave Materials

*SAPPHIRE/25: .5X TO 1.2X BASIC JSY/50
1 Alvin Kamara 4.00 10.00
2 Mitchell Trubisky 5.00 12.00
3 Kareem Hunt 4.00 10.00
4 Patrick Mahomes II 25.00 50.00
5 Tyreek Hill 5.00 12.00
6 Christian McCaffrey 5.00 12.00
7 Dak Prescott 5.00 12.00
8 Evan Engram 3.00 8.00
9 JuJu Smith-Schuster 5.00 12.00
10 Carson Wentz 6.00 15.00
11 Jared Goff 5.00 12.00
12 Joey Bosa 5.00 12.00
13 Joe Mixon 4.00 10.00
14 Deshaun Watson 6.00 15.00
15 Chad Williams 3.00 8.00
16 Marlon Mack 3.00 8.00
17 Derrick Henry 5.00 12.00
18 O.J. Howard 3.00 8.00
19 Dalvin Cook 4.00 10.00
20 Kenyan Drake 3.00 8.00
21 Leonard Fournette 5.00 12.00
22 Corey Davis 4.00 10.00
23 T.J. Watt 4.00 10.00
24 Will Fuller V 3.00 8.00
25 Michael Thomas 5.00 12.00
26 Mike Williams 3.00 8.00
27 Jordan Howard 5.00 12.00
28 David Njoku 3.00 8.00
29 Myles Jack 3.00 8.00
30 Cooper Kupp 4.00 10.00

2018 Panini Encased Pro Bowl Jumbo Jerseys

1 Kareem Hunt 5.00 12.00
2 Russell Wilson 8.00 20.00
3 Jalen Ramsey 5.00 12.00
4 Jared Goff 6.00 15.00
5 Todd Gurley II 6.00 15.00
6 Kyle Juszczyk 4.00 10.00
7 Drew Brees 6.00 15.00
8 Harrison Smith 6.00 15.00
9 Adam Thielen 6.00 15.00
10 A.J. Bouye 4.00 10.00
11 Terrell Suggs 4.00 10.00
12 Tyreek Hill 6.00 15.00
13 Alvin Kamara 5.00 12.00
14 Kevin Byard 4.00 10.00
15 Thomas Davis 4.00 10.00
16 Doug Baldwin 5.00 12.00
17 Marshon Lattimore 4.00 10.00
18 Travis Frederick 4.00 10.00
19 Davante Adams 5.00 12.00
20 T.Y. Hilton 5.00 12.00
21 Keenan Allen 5.00 12.00
22 Gerald McCoy 4.00 10.00
23 Yannick Ngakoue 4.00 10.00
24 Mike Daniels 4.00 10.00
25 Xavier Rhodes 4.00 10.00

2018 Panini Encased Reserve Signatures

*SAPPHIRE/25: .5X TO 1.2X BASIC AU/50
RSAD Aaron Donald/25 EXCH 8.00 20.00
RSAR Allen Robinson II/25 6.00 15.00
RSBL Bob Lilly/25
RSBS Bruce Smith/25 25.00 50.00
RSCA Carlos Hyde/50 4.00 10.00
RSCH Charles Haley/50 6.00 15.00
RSCJ C.J. Mosley/50 5.00 12.00
RSDB Deion Branch/25
RSDD Donald Driver/25
RSDF Devonta Freeman/25 6.00 15.00
RSDP Drew Pearson/25
RSDW Danny White/25
RSFC Fletcher Cox/50 10.00 25.00
RSFU Devin Funchess/25 5.00 12.00
RSGA Geno Atkins/50 4.00 10.00
RSGM Gerald McCoy/50 4.00 10.00
RSGO Greg Olsen/25
RSHC Harry Carson/50 4.00 10.00
RSHE Ted Hendricks/25 10.00 25.00
RSHW Hines Ward/25 12.00 30.00
RSIB Isaac Bruce/50 12.00 30.00
RSJH Jordan Howard/25 8.00 20.00
RSJJ JuJu Smith-Schuster/25 EXCH 25.00 50.00
RSJK Jermaine Kearse/50 4.00 10.00
RSJM Jerick McKinnon/50 4.00 10.00
RSJS Jeremy Shockey/50 10.00 25.00
RSJT Justin Tucker/50 15.00 40.00
RSKA Ken Anderson/50 12.00 30.00
RSLB LeRoy Butler/50 EXCH 15.00 40.00
RSLD Len Dawson/50 10.00 25.00
RSLM Lamar Miller/25 5.00 12.00
RSLT Lawrence Taylor/25 15.00 40.00
RSME Mike Evans/25 6.00 15.00
RSMG Mark Gastineau/50 4.00 10.00
RSMI Melvin Ingram/50 EXCH 4.00 10.00
RSMJ Marvin Jones Jr./25 5.00 12.00
RSML Marshon Lattimore/50 4.00 10.00
RSMO Warren Moon/25 30.00 60.00
RSMX Joe Mixon/50 EXCH 5.00 12.00
RSOJ O.J. Howard/50 4.00 10.00
RSON Ozzie Newsome/50 8.00 20.00
RSPM Patrick Mahomes II/25
RSRH Rodney Harrison/25 6.00 15.00
RSSH Sterling Sharpe/25
RSSL Steve Largent/25 25.00 50.00
RSTD Trent Dilfer/50 4.00 10.00
RSTG Tony Gonzalez/25 EXCH 6.00 15.00
RSTH Tyreek Hill/25 EXCH 15.00 40.00
RSTI Tim Brown/25 25.00 50.00
RSTJ T.J. Watt/50
RSTK Travis Kelce/25 EXCH 8.00 20.00
RSTR Tom Rathman/50 4.00 10.00
RSTT Thurman Thomas/25
RSVT Vinny Testaverde/50 4.00 10.00
RSWM Willis McGahee/50 4.00 10.00
RSBRU Tedy Bruschi/25 15.00 40.00

2018 Panini Encased Rookie Dual Swatch Signatures

*SAPPHIRE/25: .5X TO 1.2X BASIC JSY AU/50
RDSAM Anthony Miller/50 12.00 30.00
RDSBC Bradley Chubb/50 12.00 30.00
RDSBM Baker Mayfield/25 200.00 350.00
RDSCK Christian Kirk/25 15.00 40.00
RDSCR Calvin Ridley/25 25.00 60.00
RDSCS Courtland Sutton/50 12.00 30.00
RDSDG Derrius Guice/25 20.00 50.00
RDSDM D.J. Moore/50 15.00 40.00
RDSDP Dante Pettis/50 12.00 30.00
RDSJA Josh Allen/25
RDSJR Josh Rosen/25
RDSJW James Washington/50 15.00 40.00
RDSKJ Kerryon Johnson/50 12.00 30.00
RDSLJ Lamar Jackson/25
RDSNC Nick Chubb/25
RDSRJ Ronald Jones II/50 8.00 20.00
RDSRP Rashaad Penny/50 12.00 30.00
RDSSB Saquon Barkley/25 EXCH 150.00 300.00
RDSSD Sam Darnold/25 100.00 200.00
RDSSM Sony Michel/25 EXCH

2018 Panini Encased Rookie Endorsements

*SAPPHIRE/25: .5X TO 1.2X BASIC AU/50
REAM Anthony Miller/50 8.00 20.00
REBC Bradley Chubb/50 8.00 20.00
REBM Baker Mayfield/25 250.00 500.00
RECK Christian Kirk/25 20.00 40.00
RECR Calvin Ridley/25 15.00 40.00
RECS Courtland Sutton/50 8.00 20.00
REDC D.J. Chark Jr./50 6.00 15.00
REDF Daurice Fountain/50 6.00 15.00
REDG Derrius Guice/25 12.00 30.00
REDH DaeSean Hamilton/50 6.00 15.00
REDM D.J. Moore/50 10.00 25.00
REDP Dante Pettis/50 8.00 20.00
REGE Mike Gesicki/50 6.00 15.00
REHH Hayden Hurst/50 6.00 15.00
REIS Ito Smith/50 6.00 15.00
REJA Josh Allen/25 75.00 150.00
REJM J'Mon Moore/50 EXCH 5.00 12.00
REJR Josh Rosen/25 20.00 50.00
REJS Jaylen Samuels/50 6.00 15.00
REJW James Washington/50 10.00 25.00
REKB Kalen Ballage/50 6.00 15.00
REKC Keke Coutee/50 6.00 15.00
REKJ Kerryon Johnson/50 15.00 40.00
REKL Kyle Lauletta/50 8.00 20.00
REMG Michael Gallup/50 10.00 25.00
REMR Mason Rudolph/25 15.00 40.00
REMW Mike White/50 6.00 15.00
RENC Nick Chubb/25 40.00 80.00
RENH Nyheim Hines/50 6.00 15.00
RERF Royce Freeman/50 6.00 15.00
RERJ Ronald Jones II/50 5.00 12.00
RERP Rashaad Penny/50 8.00 20.00
RESB Saquon Barkley/25 EXCH 50.00 125.00
RESC Jaleel Scott/50 5.00 12.00
RESD Sam Darnold/25 75.00 150.00
RESM Sony Michel/25 50.00 100.00
RETS Tre'Quan Smith/50 8.00 20.00
REWA Mark Walton/50 6.00 15.00
REMVS Marquez Valdes-Scantling/50 6.00 15.00

2018 Panini Encased Rookie Quad Memorabilia

*SAPPHIRE/25: .6X TO 1.5X BASIC JSY/75
1 Baker Mayfield 25.00 60.00
2 Saquon Barkley 12.00 30.00
3 Sam Darnold 12.00 30.00
4 Bradley Chubb 4.00 10.00
5 Josh Allen 6.00 15.00
6 Josh Rosen 6.00 15.00
7 D.J. Moore 5.00 12.00
8 Hayden Hurst 3.00 8.00
9 Calvin Ridley 5.00 12.00
10 Rashaad Penny 4.00 10.00
11 Sony Michel 5.00 12.00
12 Lamar Jackson 12.00 30.00
13 Nick Chubb 5.00 12.00
14 Ronald Jones II 5.00 12.00
15 Derrius Guice 5.00 12.00
16 D.J. Chark Jr. 3.00 8.00
17 Kerryon Johnson 4.00 10.00
18 Dante Pettis 4.00 10.00
19 Christian Kirk 4.00 10.00
20 Anthony Miller 4.00 10.00

2018 Panini Encased Rookie Triple Memorabilia

*SAPPHIRE/25: .6X TO 1.5X BASIC JSY/75
1 Baker Mayfield 25.00 60.00
2 Saquon Barkley 12.00 30.00
3 Sam Darnold 12.00 30.00
4 Bradley Chubb 4.00 10.00
5 Josh Allen 6.00 15.00
6 Josh Rosen 6.00 15.00
7 D.J. Moore 5.00 12.00
8 Hayden Hurst 3.00 8.00
9 Calvin Ridley 5.00 12.00
10 Rashaad Penny 4.00 10.00
11 Sony Michel 5.00 12.00
12 Lamar Jackson 12.00 30.00
13 Nick Chubb 5.00 12.00
14 Ronald Jones II 5.00 12.00
15 Courtland Sutton 4.00 10.00
16 Mike Gesicki 3.00 8.00
17 Kerryon Johnson 4.00 10.00
18 Dante Pettis 4.00 10.00
19 Christian Kirk 4.00 10.00
20 Anthony Miller 4.00 10.00
21 Derrius Guice 5.00 12.00
22 James Washington 5.00 12.00
23 D.J. Chark Jr. 3.00 8.00
24 Royce Freeman 3.00 8.00
25 Mason Rudolph 5.00 12.00
26 Michael Gallup 5.00 12.00
27 Tre'Quan Smith 4.00 10.00
28 Keke Coutee 3.00 8.00
29 Nyheim Hines 3.00 8.00
30 Kyle Lauletta 4.00 10.00

2018 Panini Encased Substantial Rookie Swatches

*SAPPHIRE/25: .5X TO 1.2X BASIC JSY/50
1 Baker Mayfield 30.00 80.00
2 Saquon Barkley 15.00 40.00
3 Sam Darnold 15.00 40.00
4 Bradley Chubb 5.00 12.00
5 Josh Allen 8.00 20.00
6 Josh Rosen 8.00 20.00
7 D.J. Moore 6.00 15.00
8 Hayden Hurst 4.00 10.00
9 Calvin Ridley 6.00 15.00
10 Rashaad Penny 5.00 12.00
11 Sony Michel 6.00 15.00
12 Lamar Jackson 15.00 40.00
13 Nick Chubb 6.00 15.00
14 Ronald Jones II 6.00 15.00
15 Courtland Sutton 5.00 12.00
16 Mike Gesicki 4.00 10.00
17 Kerryon Johnson 5.00 12.00
18 Dante Pettis 5.00 12.00
19 Christian Kirk 5.00 12.00
20 Anthony Miller 5.00 12.00
21 Derrius Guice 6.00 15.00
22 James Washington 6.00 15.00
23 D.J. Chark Jr. 4.00 10.00
24 Royce Freeman 4.00 10.00
25 Mason Rudolph 6.00 15.00
26 Michael Gallup 6.00 15.00
27 Tre'Quan Smith 5.00 12.00
28 Keke Coutee 4.00 10.00
29 Nyheim Hines 4.00 10.00
30 Kyle Lauletta 5.00 12.00
31 Mark Walton 4.00 10.00
32 DaeSean Hamilton 4.00 10.00
33 Ito Smith 4.00 10.00
34 Kalen Ballage 4.00 10.00
35 Shaquem Griffin 5.00 12.00
36 J'Mon Moore 3.00 8.00
37 Daurice Fountain 4.00 10.00
38 Jaylen Samuels 4.00 10.00
39 Mike White 4.00 10.00
40 Marquez Valdes-Scantling 4.00 10.00

2018 Panini Encased Vaulted Veteran Material Signatures

VVAB Antonio Brown/15
VVAD Aaron Donald/25 EXCH 15.00 40.00
VVAT Adam Thielen/25
VVCD Corey Davis/50 10.00 25.00
VVCJ C.J. Mosley/50 10.00 25.00
VVDC Derek Carr/15 20.00 50.00
VVDF Devonta Freeman/25 12.00 30.00
VVDH Derrick Henry/25 15.00 40.00
VVDJ David Johnson/25 15.00 40.00
VVFU Devin Funchess/25 10.00 25.00
VVGA Geno Atkins/50 8.00 20.00
VVJH Jordan Howard/25 15.00 40.00
VVKD Kenyan Drake/50 8.00 20.00
VVLK Luke Kuechly/25 12.00 30.00
VVME Mike Evans/25
VVMG Melvin Gordon III/25 12.00 30.00
VVPM Patrick Mahomes II/25 300.00 500.00
VVSD Stefon Diggs/25
VVTK Travis Kelce/25
VVTY T.Y. Hilton/25
VVWF Will Fuller V/50

2012 Panini Father's Day

RANDOM INSERTS IN FATHER'S DAY PACKS
CRACKED ICE/25: 5X TO 12X BASE HI
15 Eli Manning .40 1.00
16 Aaron Rodgers .75 2.00
17 Tom Brady .60 1.50
18 Cam Newton .60 1.50
19 Calvin Johnson .40 1.00
20 Maurice Jones-Drew .30 .75
21 Arian Foster .40 1.00
22 Andy Dalton .40 1.00

2012 Panini Father's Day 9/11 Tribute Footballs

RANDOM INSERTS IN FATHERS DAY PACKS
AG Antonio Gates 4.00 10.00
AP Adrian Peterson 6.00 15.00
MT Mike Tolbert 4.00 10.00
MTA Mike Tolbert AU
PH Percy Harvin 4.00 10.00
PR Philip Rivers 5.00 12.00
PRA Philip Rivers AU
RM Ryan Mathews 4.00 10.00

2012 Panini Father's Day Draft Day Jumbo Patch

RANDOM INSERTS IN FATHERS DAY PACKS
1 Blaine Gabbert 6.00 15.00
2 Mark Ingram 8.00 20.00
3 A.J. Green 8.00 20.00

2012 Panini Father's Day Elements

RANDOM INSERTS IN FATHERS DAY PACKS
CRACKED ICE/25: 5X TO 12X BASE HI
1 Tom Brady .60 1.50
2 Brian Urlacher .40 1.00

2012 Panini Father's Day Elite Series

RANDOM INSERTS IN FATHERS DAY PACKS
CRACKED ICE/25: 5X TO 12X BASE HI
1 Peyton Manning .75 2.00
2 Tim Tebow .75 2.00

2012 Panini Father's Day Legends

RANDOM INSERTS IN FATHERS DAY PACKS
CRACKED ICE/25: 5X TO 12X BASE HI
5 John Elway .60 1.50
6 Joe Montana .75 2.00
7 Troy Aikman .50 1.25

2012 Panini Father's Day Manufactured Patch Autographs

RANDOM INSERTS IN FATHERS DAY PACKS
AD Andy Dalton 15.00 40.00
(Bengals logo swatch)
AL Andrew Luck 175.00 300.00
(NFL shield swatch)
CN Cam Newton 125.00 200.00
(rookie debut swatch)
JB Justin Blackmon 30.00 60.00
(NFL shield swatch)
TR Trent Richardson 40.00 100.00
(NFL shield swatch)
VM Von Miller 15.00 40.00
(Broncos logo swatch)

2012 Panini Father's Day Pro Bowl Jerseys

RANDOM INSERTS IN FATHERS DAY PACKS
1 Adrian Peterson 10.00 25.00
2 Larry Fitzgerald 5.00 12.00
3 Alex Mack 5.00 12.00
4 Billy Cundiff 4.00 10.00
5 Brian Waters 5.00 12.00
6 Carl Nicks 5.00 12.00
7 David Akers 5.00 12.00
8 Eric Weems 5.00 12.00
9 Jahri Evans 5.00 12.00
10 Jay Ratliff 6.00 15.00
11 Jeff Saturday 5.00 12.00
12 Mat McBriar 6.00 15.00
13 Montell Owens 5.00 12.00
14 Ovie Mughelli 5.00 12.00
15 Vonta Leach 5.00 12.00
AD Andy Dalton 8.00 20.00
PP Patrick Peterson 6.00 15.00
VM Von Miller 8.00 20.00
AJG A.J. Green 8.00 20.00

2012 Panini Father's Day Rookie of the Year Jerseys

RANDOM INSERTS IN FATHERS DAY PACKS
1 Cam Newton 25.00 50.00
2 Von Miller 8.00 20.00

2012 Panini Father's Day Rookies

STATED PRINT RUN 499 SER.#'d SETS
1 Andrew Luck 12.00 30.00
2 Robert Griffin III 12.00 30.00
3 Ryan Tannehill 2.50 6.00
4 Justin Blackmon 2.50 6.00
5 Trent Richardson 3.00 8.00
6 Michael Floyd 2.50 6.00

2012 Panini Father's Day Rookies Cracked Ice

CRACKED ICE/25: 2.5X TO 6X BASE HI
ANNOUNCED PRINT RUN 25
1 Andrew Luck 125.00 200.00
2 Robert Griffin III 40.00 100.00

2012 Panini Father's Day Season Highlights

RANDOM INSERTS IN FATHERS DAY PACKS
CRACKED ICE/25: 5X TO 12X BASE HI
4 Eli Manning .40 1.00
5 Aaron Rodgers .75 2.00
6 Cam Newton .60 1.50
7 Drew Brees .40 1.00
8 Peyton Manning .60 1.50
9 Tim Tebow .60 1.50
8AU Peyton Manning AU

2012 Panini Father's Day Thick Portraits

RANDOM INSERTS IN FATHERS DAY PACKS
ANNOUNCED PRINT RUN 50
1 Andrew Luck 15.00 30.00
2 Robert Griffin III 10.00 25.00
4 Peyton Manning 6.00 15.00
5 Tim Tebow 5.00 12.00

2013 Panini Father's Day

CRACKED ICE/25: 4X TO 10X BASIC CARDS
LAVA FLOW/25: 4X TO 10X BASIC CARDS
7 Andrew Luck .75 2.00
8 Robert Griffin III .60 1.50
9 Adrian Peterson .50 1.25
11 Colin Kaepernick .40 1.00
12 Peyton Manning 1.25 3.00
23 Geno Smith .75 2.00
24 Matt Barkley .50 1.25
25 Eddie Lacy 1.25 3.00
26 Manti Te'o .50 1.25
27 EJ Manuel 1.00 2.50
28 Tyrann Mathieu .50 1.25

2013 Panini Father's Day Absolute Heroes Materials

LAVA FLOW/25: 1X TO 2.5X BASIC JSY
1 Marshall Faulk Colts 2.50 6.00
2 Marshall Faulk Rams 2.50 6.00

2013 Panini Father's Day Draft Day Materials

LAVA FLOW/25: .8X TO 2X BASIC JSY
1 Eric Fisher 1.50 4.00
2 Ezekiel Ansah 1.50 4.00
3 Lane Johnson 2.00 5.00
4 Luke Joeckel 1.50 4.00

2013 Panini Father's Day Elite

CRACKED ICE/25: 3X TO 8X BASIC CARDS
LAVA FLOW/25: 3X TO 8X BASIC CARDS
1 Andrew Luck 1.50 4.00

2013 Panini Father's Day NFL Rookie Materials

LAVA FLOW/25: .8X TO 2X BASIC JSY
KW Kendall Wright 1.50 4.00
RT Ryan Tannehill 2.00 5.00

2013 Panini Father's Day Pro Bowl Materials

LAVA FLOW/25: 1.2X TO 3X BASIC JSY
PBAD Andy Dalton 2.50 6.00
PBAG Antonio Gates 2.50 6.00
PBAJC A.J. Green 3.00 8.00
PBAR Aaron Rodgers 5.00 12.00
PBBM Brandon Marshall 2.50 6.00
PBCM Clay Matthews 3.00 8.00
PBCN Cam Newton 3.00 8.00
PBDB Drew Brees 3.00 8.00
PBGJ Greg Jennings 2.00 5.00
PBMJD Maurice Jones-Drew 2.00 5.00
PBPP Patrick Peterson 2.00 5.00
PBRW Russell Wilson
PBSJ Sebastian Janikowski 2.00 5.00
PBSS Steve Smith 2.50 6.00
PBVM Von Miller 2.50 6.00
PMPW Patrick Willis 2.50 6.00

2013 Panini Father's Day Pro Bowl Materials Jumbo

LAVA FLOW/25: 1.5X TO 4X BASIC JSY
AB Antonio Brown 2.00 5.00
JG Jimmy Graham 2.00 5.00

2013 Panini Father's Day Rookie Debut Materials

LAVA FLOW/25: .8X TO 2X BASIC JSY
AK A.J. Klein 1.50 4.00
BT Bruce Taylor 2.00 5.00
DC Duron Carter 1.50 4.00
DG Dwayne Gratz 1.50 4.00
DJ Datone Jones 1.50 4.00
EB Emory Blake 1.50 4.00
GB Giovani Bernard 1.50 4.00
MM Miguel Maysonet 1.50 4.00
OJ Orhian Johnson 1.50 4.00
RN Ryan Nassib 1.50 4.00
SW Sylvester Williams 1.50 4.00
TM Tyrann Mathieu 2.50 6.00

2013 Panini Father's Day Rookie Debut Materials Autographs

AK A.J. Klein 3.00 8.00
EB Emory Blake 3.00 8.00
MM Miguel Maysonet 3.00 8.00
SW Sylvester Williams 3.00 8.00

2013 Panini Father's Day Rookie Debut Materials Lava Flow Autographs

AK A.J. Klein 5.00 12.00
BT Bruce Taylor 6.00 15.00
DC Duron Carter 5.00 12.00
DG Dwayne Gratz 5.00 12.00
DJ Datone Jones 5.00 12.00
EB Emory Blake 5.00 12.00
GB Giovani Bernard 5.00 12.00
MM Miguel Maysonet 5.00 12.00
OJ Orhian Johnson 5.00 12.00
RN Ryan Nassib 5.00 12.00
SW Sylvester Williams 5.00 12.00
TM Tyrann Mathieu 8.00 20.00

2013 Panini Father's Day Rookie of the Year Materials

LAVA FLOW/25: 1.5X TO 4X BASIC JSY
ROYRGIII Robert Griffin III 5.00 12.00

2013 Panini Father's Day Salute to Service Materials Footballs

LAVA FLOW/25: .8X TO 2X BASIC FB

1 Ryan Tannehill 3.00 8.00
2 Kendall Wright 2.50 6.00
3 Chris Johnson 2.50 6.00

2013 Panini Father's Day Studio

CRACKED ICE/25: 3X TO 8X BASIC CARDS
LAVA FLOW/25: 3X TO 8X BASIC CARDS
22 Robert Griffin III .75 2.00
23 Andrew Luck 1.25 3.00
24 Geno Smith .75 2.00

2013 Panini Father's Day Super Bowl Materials

1 Aaron Rodgers Pylon 25.00 50.00
2 Jordy Nelson Pylon 15.00 40.00
3 Greg Jennings Pylon 12.00 30.00
4 James Jones Pylon 12.00 30.00
5 Donald Driver Pylon 12.00 30.00
6 Clay Matthews Pylon 15.00 40.00
7 A.J. Hawk Pylon 12.00 30.00
8 Charles Woodson Pylon 12.00 30.00
9 James Starks Pylon 12.00 30.00
10 Nick Collins Pylon 12.00 30.00
11 Mason Crosby Pylon 12.00 30.00
12 Ben Roethlisberger Pylon 12.00 30.00
13 Rashard Mendenhall Pylon 8.00 20.00
14 Mike Wallace Pylon 10.00 25.00
15 Troy Polamalu Pylon 10.00 25.00
16 Aaron Rodgers FB
17 Greg Jennings FB
18 Jordy Nelson FB
19 Clay Matthews FB
20 Troy Polamalu FB

2013 Panini Father's Day Super Bowl Materials Autographs

1 Aaron Rodgers Pylon
2 Jordy Nelson Pylon
3 Greg Jennings Pylon
4 James Jones Pylon
5 Donald Driver Pylon
6 Clay Matthews Pylon
7 A.J. Hawk Pylon 60.00 100.00
8 Charles Woodson Pylon
9 James Starks Pylon
10 Nick Collins Pylon
11 Mason Crosby Pylon 50.00 80.00
12 Ben Roethlisberger
13 Rashard Mendenhall
14 Mike Wallace Pylon 25.00 50.00
15 Troy Polamalu Pylon
16 Aaron Rodgers FB
17 Greg Jennings FB
18 Jordy Nelson FB
19 Clay Matthews FB
20 Troy Polamalu FB

2013 Panini Father's Day Team Pinnacle

CRACKED ICE/25: 3X TO 8X BASIC CARDS
LAVA FLOW/25: 3X TO 8X BASIC CARDS
4 Peyton Manning/Tom Brady 2.00 5.00
5 Adrian Peterson/Calvin Johnson 1.00 2.50
6 Robert Griffin III/Andrew Luck 1.50 4.00
7 Joe Flacco/Colin Kaepernick 1.00 2.50
13 Geno Smith/Matt Barkley .75 2.00

2013 Panini Father's Day Tim Tebow Collection Materials

COMMON TEBOW JSY 4.00 10.00
LAVA FLOW/25: .8X TO 2X BASIC JSY

2013 Panini Father's Day Tools of the Trade Materials

LAVA FLOW25: .8X TO 2X BASIC JSY
3 Jason Witten 4.00 10.00
GS Geno Smith 2.00 5.00
MB Matt Barkley 2.00 5.00
MF Marshall Faulk 5.00 12.00
TA Tavon Austin 2.50 6.00

2014 Panini Father's Day

COMPLETE SET (55) 20.00 50.00
*1-24 THICK STOCK: 1X TO 2.5X BASIC CARDS
*25-55 THICK STOCK: .5X TO 1.2X BASIC CARDS
*1-24 ICE VETS/25: 5X TO 12X BASIC CARDS
*25-55 ICE ROOKIE/25: 2X TO 5X BASIC CARDS/499
7 Andrew Luck FB .50 1.25
8 Peyton Manning FB .75 2.00
9 Tom Brady FB .50 1.25
10 Russell Wilson FB .40 1.00
11 Jamaal Charles FB .30 .75
12 Aaron Rodgers FB .60 1.50
47 Teddy Bridgewater FB 2.00 5.00
48 Johnny Manziel FB 2.00 5.00
49 Jimmy Garoppolo FB 1.25 3.00
50 Blake Bortles FB 1.50 4.00
51 Sammy Watkins FB 1.25 3.00
52 Mike Evans FB 1.25 3.00
53 Jadeveon Clowney FB 1.00 2.50
54 Greg Robinson FB .40 1.00
55 Jake Matthews FB .50 1.25

2014 Panini Father's Day Elements

COMPLETE SET (12) 5.00 12.00
*CRACKED ICE/25: 4X TO 10X BASIC CARDS
*THICK STOCK: 1.2X TO 3X BASIC CARDS
1 Calvin Johnson FB .75 2.00
2 LeSean McCoy FB .60 1.50
3 Cordarrelle Patterson FB .75 2.00
4 LeGarrette Blount FB .60 1.50
5 Drew Brees FB .75 2.00
6 Richard Sherman FB 1.00 2.50
7 Demaryius Thomas FB .60 1.50

2014 Panini Father's Day Elite

1 Johnny Manziel FB 2.00 5.00

2014 Panini Father's Day Legends

COMPLETE SET (10)
6 Barry Sanders FB .75 2.00
7 Dan Marino FB 1.00 2.50

2014 Panini Father's Day Rookie Clover Jerseys

1 EJ Manuel 3.00 8.00
2 Geno Smith 2.50 6.00
3 Marcus Lattimore 2.00 5.00

2014 Panini Father's Day Rookie Jerseys

1 Tajh Boyd FB 2.00 5.00
2 Aaron Murray FB 2.50 6.00
3 Lache Seastrunk FB 1.50 4.00
4 Chris Smith FB 1.50 4.00
5 Ricardo Allen FB 1.50 4.00
6 Ross Cockrell FB 1.50 4.00
7 Walter Powell FB 1.50 4.00
8 John Urschel FB 1.50 4.00
9 Mike Jones FB 1.50 4.00
10 Tajh Boyd FB 2.00 5.00
11 Aaron Murray FB 2.50 6.00
CB Bradley Roby FB 1.50 4.00
CP Cordarrelle Patterson FB 2.50 6.00
DH DeAndre Hopkins FB 2.00 5.00
EE Eric Ebron FB 2.50 6.00
EM EJ Manuel FB 2.50 6.00
HC Ha Ha Clinton-Dix FB 2.50 6.00
JM Johnny Manziel FB 5.00 12.00
KF Kyle Fuller FB 2.00 5.00
KM Khalil Mack FB 2.00 5.00
SM Sammy Watkins FB 3.00 8.00
JMA Jake Matthews FB 2.00 5.00

2014 Panini Father's Day Rookies

COMPLETE SET (20) 10.00 25.00
*CRACKED ICE/25: 3X TO 8X BASIC CARDS
*THICK STOCK: 1X TO 2.5X BASIC CARDS
R1 Tavon Austin FB 1.00 2.50
R2 Le'Veon Bell FB 2.00 5.00
R3 EJ Manuel FB 1.50 4.00
R4 Denard Robinson FB 1.00 2.50
R5 Geno Smith FB 1.50 4.00
R6 Cordarrelle Patterson FB 1.25 3.00

2014 Panini Father's Day Salute to Service Memorabilia

1 EJ Manuel 3.00 8.00
2 Kendall Wright 2.00 5.00
3 Geno Smith 2.50 6.00
4 Sheldon Richardson 2.00 5.00
5 Josh Gordon 2.00 5.00
6 Giovani Bernard 2.50 6.00

2014 Panini Father's Day Who Do You Collect Jerseys

AL1 Andrew Luck 5.00 12.00
Back to Pass
AL2 Andrew Luck 5.00 12.00
Smiling
AL3 Andrew Luck 5.00 12.00
Two Hands on Ball
AL4 Andrew Luck 5.00 12.00
Arms Up

2015 Panini Father's Day

1A Tom Brady 2.00 5.00
1B Tom Brady college 2.00 5.00
2 Dez Bryant .75 2.00
3 Russell Wilson .75 2.00
4A Aaron Rodgers 2.00 5.00
4B Aaron Rodgers college 2.00 5.00
5A J.J. Watt .75 2.00
5B J.J. Watt college .75 2.00
6 Teddy Bridgewater .60 1.50
7A Odell Beckham Jr. .75 2.00
7B Odell Beckham Jr. college .75 2.00
8A Andrew Luck 1.25 3.00
8B Andrew Luck college 1.25 3.00
25A Marcus Mariota 2.00 5.00
25B Marcus Mariota college 2.00 5.00
26 Melvin Gordon III 1.25 3.00
27A Jameis Winston 2.00 5.00
27B Jameis Winston college 2.00 5.00
28A Amari Cooper 2.00 5.00
28B Amari Cooper college 2.00 5.00
29 Kevin White 1.25 3.00
30 Leonard Williams 1.25 3.00
31A Todd Gurley 2.00 5.00
31B Todd Gurley college 2.00 5.00
32 Bryce Petty 1.00 2.50
33 Brett Hundley 1.00 2.50
34A Randy Gregory 1.00 2.50
34B Randy Gregory college 1.00 2.50
35 DeVante Parker 1.25 3.00
36 Dante Fowler Jr. 1.00 2.50

2015 Panini Father's Day Elements

1 Eddie Lacy 1.00 2.50
2 Richard Sherman 1.00 2.50
3 Julian Edelman 1.00 2.50
4 Demaryius Thomas 1.00 2.50
5 Luke Kuechly 1.00 2.50
6 Le'Veon Bell 1.00 2.50
7 Calvin Johnson 1.00 2.50
8 Matt Forte 1.00 2.50

2015 Panini Father's Day Game Dated Memorabilia

*CRACKED/25: .6X TO 1.5X BASIC JSY
*RINGS/25: .6X TO 1.5X BASIC JSY
1 DeMarco Murray 3.00 8.00
2 Knowshon Moreno 2.50 6.00
3 Justin Houston 2.50 6.00
4 Alex Smith 3.00 8.00
5 A.J. Green 4.00 10.00
6 Aaron Rodgers 12.00 30.00
7 Jordy Nelson 3.00 8.00
8 Randall Cobb 3.00 8.00
9 Sammy Watkins 3.00 8.00
10 Denard Robinson 2.50 6.00
11 Blake Bortles 2.50 6.00
12 Peyton Manning 12.00 30.00
13 Joe Flacco 3.00 8.00
14 Justin Forsett 3.00 8.00
15 Elvis Dumervil 2.50 6.00
16 Cameron Wake 2.50 6.00
17 Ryan Tannehill 3.00 8.00
18 Teddy Bridgewater 3.00 8.00
19 Eric Decker 2.50 6.00
20 Challenge Flag 4.00 10.00

2015 Panini Father's Day Road to Super Bowl Memorabilia

*CRACKED/25: X TO X BASIC JSY
1 Tom Brady 30.00 60.00
2 Shane Vereen 6.00 15.00
3 Rob Gronkowski 8.00 20.00
4 Julian Edelman 8.00 20.00
5 Danny Amendola 6.00 15.00
6 Jamie Collins 5.00 12.00
7 Vince Wilfork 5.00 12.00
8 Rob Ninkovich 5.00 12.00
9 Darrelle Revis 5.00 12.00
10 Dont'a Hightower 5.00 12.00
11 Devin McCourty 5.00 12.00
12 Chandler Jones 5.00 12.00
13 Malcolm Butler 8.00 20.00
14 Stephen Gostkowski 6.00 15.00
15 Tom Brady 30.00 60.00

2015 Panini Father's Day Rookie Class Jerseys

*CRACKED/25: .6X TO 1.5X BASIC JSY
1 Sammie Coates 2.50 6.00
2 Jamison Crowder 2.50 6.00
3 Stefon Diggs 5.00 12.00
4 Dominique Brown 2.00 5.00
5 Dorial Green-Beckham 2.00 5.00
6 Gerald Christian 2.50 6.00
7 Christion Jones 2.00 5.00
8 Kurtis Drummond 2.50 6.00
9 Devin Gardner 3.00 8.00
10 Mario Alford 2.00 5.00
11 Grady Jarrett 2.50 6.00
12 Ameer Abdullah 3.00 8.00
13 Tevin Coleman 2.50 6.00
14 Cameron Artis-Payne 2.00 5.00
15 Jay Ajayi 3.00 8.00
AP Andrus Peat 2.00 5.00
BS Brandon Scherff 3.00 8.00
DS Danny Shelton 2.00 5.00
TW Trae Waynes 2.00 5.00
VB Vic Beasley 2.50 6.00

2015 Panini Father's Day Sketch

*THICK: 2X TO 5X BASIC CARDS
*CRACKED/25: 2X TO 5X BASIC CARDS
6 Odell Beckham Jr. 1.00 2.50
7 DeMarco Murray 1.00 2.50
8 Marshawn Lynch 1.00 2.50
9 Antonio Brown 1.00 2.50
10 Rob Gronkowski 1.00 2.50
14 Marcus Mariota 1.25 3.00
15 Jameis Winston 1.25 3.00

2014 Panini Flawless

1 A.J. Green 40.00 100.00
2 Aaron Rodgers 250.00 400.00
3 Adrian Peterson 60.00 120.00
4 Alex Smith 30.00 80.00
5 Alfred Morris 25.00 60.00
6 Tre Mason RC 20.00 50.00
7 Andre Johnson 30.00 80.00
8 Andrew Luck 300.00 500.00
9 Andy Dalton 30.00 80.00
10 Anquan Boldin 25.00 60.00
11 Dri Archer RC 20.00 50.00
12 Antonio Gates 25.00 60.00
13 Arian Foster 30.00 80.00
14 Barry Sanders 400.00 600.00
15 Bart Starr 60.00 120.00
16 Ben Roethlisberger 75.00 150.00
17 Bo Jackson 60.00 120.00
18 Brandon Marshall 25.00 60.00
19 Brett Favre 75.00 150.00
20 C.J. Spiller 25.00 60.00
21 Calvin Johnson 75.00 150.00
22 Cam Newton 100.00 200.00
23 Charles Woodson 40.00 100.00
24 Jake Locker 30.00 80.00
25 Paul Hornung 40.00 100.00
26 Colin Kaepernick 125.00 250.00
27 Cordarrelle Patterson 60.00 120.00
28 Dan Marino 100.00 200.00
29 Dez Bryant 40.00 100.00
30 Doug Martin 30.00 80.00
31 Drew Brees 100.00 200.00
32 Derek Carr RC 100.00 200.00
33 Earl Campbell 40.00 100.00
34 Eddie Lacy 25.00 60.00
35 EJ Manuel 25.00 60.00
36 Eli Manning 60.00 120.00
37 Emmitt Smith 150.00 250.00
38 Eric Dickerson 50.00 120.00
39 Franco Harris 40.00 100.00
40 Frank Gifford 30.00 80.00
41 Gale Sayers 40.00 100.00
42 Tajh Boyd RC 20.00 50.00
43 Jeremy Hill RC 40.00 100.00
44 J.J. Watt 40.00 100.00
45 Jamaal Charles 30.00 80.00
46 Jason Witten 30.00 80.00
47 Jay Cutler 25.00 60.00
48 Jerry Rice 125.00 250.00
49 Jim Brown 60.00 120.00
50 Jimmy Graham 40.00 100.00
51 Joe Flacco 60.00 120.00
52 Joe Montana 250.00 400.00
53 Joe Namath 40.00 100.00
54 John Elway 125.00 250.00
55 John Riggins 30.00 80.00
56 Terrance West RC 20.00 50.00
57 Julio Jones 40.00 100.00
58 Allen Robinson 40.00 100.00
59 Keenan Allen 30.00 80.00
60 Kellen Winslow 30.00 80.00
61 Kurt Warner 75.00 150.00
62 LaDainian Tomlinson 60.00 120.00
63 Logan Thomas RC 20.00 50.00
64 Larry Fitzgerald 30.00 80.00
65 Len Dawson 100.00 200.00
66 LeSean McCoy 40.00 100.00
67 Le'Veon Bell 30.00 80.00
68 Marcus Allen 60.00 120.00
69 Marshall Faulk 60.00 120.00
70 Marshawn Lynch 60.00 120.00
71 Matt Forte 25.00 60.00
72 Matt Ryan 40.00 100.00
73 Matthew Stafford 60.00 120.00
74 Michael Irvin 40.00 100.00
75 Charles Sims 25.00 60.00
76 Nick Foles 30.00 80.00
77 Steve Young 75.00 150.00
78 Peyton Manning 600.00 800.00
79 Philip Rivers 40.00 100.00
80 Cody Latimer 30.00 80.00
81 Jarvis Landry RC 40.00 100.00
82 Red Grange 60.00 120.00
83 Reggie Wayne 30.00 80.00
84 Richard Sherman 60.00 120.00
85 Rob Gronkowski 40.00 100.00
86 Robert Griffin III 25.00 60.00
87 Roger Staubach 75.00 150.00
88 Russell Wilson 200.00 400.00
89 Ryan Tannehill 60.00 120.00
90 Sam Bradford 25.00 60.00
91 Terrell Davis 60.00 120.00
92 Terry Bradshaw 75.00 150.00
93 Tom Brady 300.00 500.00
94 Tony Dorsett 40.00 100.00
95 Tony Romo 30.00 80.00
96 Troy Aikman 150.00 300.00
97 Troy Polamalu 40.00 100.00
98 Victor Cruz 30.00 80.00
99 Vincent Jackson 25.00 60.00
100 Wes Welker 30.00 80.00
101 Jadeveon Clowney RC 25.00 60.00
102 Blake Bortles RC 25.00 60.00
103 Sammy Watkins RC 125.00 250.00
104 Mike Evans RC 75.00 150.00
105 Eric Ebron RC 25.00 60.00
106 Odell Beckham Jr. RC 175.00 300.00
107 Brandin Cooks RC 30.00 80.00
108 Johnny Manziel RC 50.00 100.00
109 Kelvin Benjamin RC 30.00 80.00
110 Teddy Bridgewater RC 100.00 200.00
111 Marqise Lee RC 40.00 100.00
112 Jordan Matthews RC 30.00 80.00
113 Paul Richardson RC 25.00 60.00
114 Bishop Sankey RC 60.00 120.00
115 Davante Adams RC 60.00 125.00
116 Carlos Hyde RC 25.00 60.00
117 Jimmy Garoppolo RC 200.00 400.00
118 Tom Savage RC 20.00 50.00
119 Aaron Murray RC 20.00 50.00
120 A.J. McCarron RC 20.00 50.00

2014 Panini Flawless All Pro Ink

*RUNY/15: .5X TO 1.2X BASIC AU/25
1 Andrew Luck 200.00 300.00
2 Antonio Gates 12.00 30.00
4 Nick Foles 15.00 40.00
5 Eli Manning 60.00 120.00
6 J.J. Watt 75.00 125.00
7 Jamaal Charles 15.00 40.00
10 Russell Wilson 75.00 150.00

2014 Panini Flawless Autographs

*BLUE/20: .4X TO 1X BASIC AU/25
*RUBY/15: .5X TO 1.2X BASIC AU/25
*PINK/14: .5X TO 1.2X BASIC AU/25
1 Aaron Dobson 12.00 30.00
2 Alfred Morris 12.00 30.00
3 Alshon Jeffery 15.00 40.00
4 Andre Ellington 12.00 30.00
5 Andrew Luck 125.00 250.00
6 Antonio Brown 40.00 80.00
7 Ben Roethlisberger 50.00 100.00
9 C.J. Spiller 12.00 30.00
10 Cecil Shorts 12.00 30.00
11 Colin Kaepernick 40.00 100.00
12 Cordarrelle Patterson 12.00 30.00
13 Danny Amendola 15.00 40.00
14 DeAndre Hopkins 15.00 40.00
15 DeMarco Murray 15.00 40.00
16 Demaryius Thomas 15.00 40.00
17 DeSean Jackson 15.00 40.00
19 Dwayne Bowe 15.00 40.00
20 Eddie Lacy 12.00 30.00
21 Frank Gore 15.00 40.00
22 Geno Smith 12.00 30.00
23 Giovani Bernard 12.00 30.00
24 Greg Jennings 12.00 30.00
25 Jamaal Charles 15.00 40.00
26 Jason Witten 15.00 40.00
27 Jordan Cameron 12.00 30.00
28 Jordan Reed 12.00 30.00
29 Jordy Nelson 25.00 60.00
30 Josh Gordon 12.00 30.00
32 Julius Thomas 12.00 30.00
33 Justin Blackmon 12.00 30.00
34 Keenan Allen 15.00 40.00
35 Kenbrell Thompkins 12.00 30.00
36 Kenny Stills 12.00 30.00
37 Kiko Alonso 12.00 30.00
39 Luke Kuechly 25.00 60.00
40 Marlon Brown 12.00 30.00
42 Michael Floyd 12.00 30.00
43 Mike Glennon 15.00 40.00
44 Montee Ball 12.00 30.00
45 Nick Foles 15.00 40.00
46 Randall Cobb 20.00 50.00
47 Richard Sherman 60.00 125.00
48 Robert Woods 15.00 40.00
49 Russell Wilson 75.00 150.00
50 Sean Lee 15.00 40.00
51 Steve Johnson 15.00 40.00
62 Terrance Williams 12.00 30.00
53 Timothy Wright 12.00 30.00
54 Zac Stacy 12.00 30.00
55 Zach Ertz 15.00 40.00

2014 Panini Flawless Benchmarks Ruby

3 Dan Marino 150.00 300.00
5 Peyton Manning 150.00 300.00

2014 Panini Flawless Greats Autographs Ruby

9 Tom Brady 500.00 900.00

2014 Panini Flawless Greats Dual Patch Autographs

2 Antonio Gates/25 40.00 100.00
3 Barry Sanders/25 300.00 400.00
5 Drew Brees/25 125.00 250.00
7 Peyton Manning/25 300.00 500.00
8 Bo Jackson/25 150.00 250.00
14 Carl Eller/13
16 Curtis Martin/25 50.00 125.00
17 Dan Marino/25 250.00 400.00
20 Earl Campbell/25 60.00 150.00
21 Emmitt Smith/25 300.00 400.00
22 Eric Dickerson/25 60.00 120.00
26 Jackie Slater/25 40.00 100.00
29 Jerome Bettis/24 75.00 150.00
30 Jerry Rice/25 200.00 300.00
32 Jim Kelly/25 60.00 150.00
34 Joe Namath/25 150.00 250.00
36 Randy White/25 50.00 125.00
38 Larry Csonka/25 75.00 150.00
39 Fran Tarkenton/25 60.00 150.00
41 Marshall Faulk/25 50.00 120.00
47 Paul Warfield/25 40.00 100.00
50 Rod Woodson/25 50.00 125.00
51 Roger Staubach/25 100.00 200.00
52 Ronnie Lott/25 50.00 120.00
53 Steve Largent/25 60.00 150.00
55 Terrell Davis/25 25.00 60.00
57 Thurman Thomas/25 50.00 125.00
58 Warren Moon/14

2014 Panini Flawless Greats Patches Autographs

2 Antonio Gates 20.00 50.00
3 Barry Sanders 250.00 400.00
7 Peyton Manning 300.00 500.00
8 Brett Favre 200.00 400.00
9 Bruce Smith 30.00 80.00
12 Curtis Martin 60.00 120.00
13 Dan Marino 150.00 300.00
14 Earl Campbell 40.00 100.00
15 Emmitt Smith 200.00 300.00
16 Eric Dickerson 30.00 80.00
17 Gale Sayers 60.00 120.00
18 Jan Stenerud 25.00 60.00
19 Jerome Bettis 75.00 150.00
20 Jerry Rice 200.00 300.00
21 Jim Kelly 40.00 100.00
22 Joe Montana 150.00 300.00
24 Fran Tarkenton 40.00 100.00
25 Larry Csonka 40.00 100.00
26 Marshall Faulk 75.00 150.00
30 Paul Warfield 30.00 80.00
32 Lawrence Taylor 75.00 150.00
33 Rod Woodson 30.00 80.00
34 Roger Staubach 100.00 200.00
35 Ronnie Lott 30.00 80.00
37 Randy White 30.00 80.00
38 Terrell Davis 40.00 100.00
39 Thurman Thomas 30.00 80.00

2014 Panini Flawless Greats Patches Autographs Ruby

3 Barry Sanders 300.00 500.00
7 Peyton Manning 400.00 600.00
8 Brett Favre 250.00 500.00
13 Dan Marino 200.00 400.00
40 Warren Moon 75.00 150.00

2014 Panini Flawless Hall of Fame Autographs

*RUBY/15: .5X TO 1.2X BASIC AU/25
2 Fran Tarkenton 20.00 50.00
3 Franco Harris 20.00 50.00
4 Frank Gifford 15.00 40.00
5 John Riggins 15.00 40.00
6 Kellen Winslow 15.00 40.00
7 Lance Alworth
7 Lance Alworth
8 Len Dawson 20.00 50.00
9 Michael Irvin 20.00 50.00

2014 Panini Flawless Inscriptions

*BLUE/20: .4X TO 1X BASIC AU/25
*RUBY/15: .5X TO 1.2X BASIC AU/25
*PINK/14: .5X TO 1.2X BASIC AU/25
1 Aaron Dobson 12.00 30.00
2 Alfred Morris 12.00 30.00
3 Alshon Jeffery 15.00 40.00
4 Andre Ellington 12.00 30.00
5 Antonio Brown 40.00 80.00
6 Cecil Shorts 12.00 30.00
7 Cordarrelle Patterson 12.00 30.00
8 Danny Amendola 15.00 40.00
9 DeAndre Hopkins 15.00 40.00
10 Demaryius Thomas 15.00 40.00
11 Doug Martin 15.00 40.00
12 Eddie Lacy 12.00 30.00
13 Eric Decker 12.00 30.00
14 Giovani Bernard 12.00 30.00
15 J.J. Watt 100.00 200.00
16 Jordan Cameron 12.00 30.00
17 Jordan Reed 12.00 30.00
18 Jordy Nelson 40.00 80.00
19 Josh Gordon 12.00 30.00
20 Julius Thomas 12.00 30.00
21 Keenan Allen 12.00 30.00
22 Kenbrell Thompkins 12.00 30.00
23 Kenny Stills 12.00 30.00
24 Kiko Alonso 12.00 30.00
25 Knile Davis 12.00 30.00
27 Luke Kuechly 20.00 50.00
28 Manti Te'o 15.00 40.00
29 Michael Floyd 12.00 30.00
30 Mike Glennon 15.00 40.00
31 Montee Ball 12.00 30.00
32 Nick Foles 15.00 40.00
33 Randall Cobb 20.00 50.00
34 Reggie Wayne 15.00 40.00
35 Rob Gronkowski 40.00 80.00
36 Robert Woods 15.00 40.00
37 Sean Lee 15.00 40.00
38 Tavon Austin 12.00 30.00
39 Terrance Williams 12.00 30.00
40 Timothy Wright 12.00 30.00
42 Victor Cruz 15.00 40.00
43 Vincent Jackson 12.00 30.00
44 Zac Stacy 12.00 30.00
45 Zach Ertz 15.00 40.00

2014 Panini Flawless Memorable Marks

*RUBY/15: .5X TO 1.2X BASIC AU/25
1 Alshon Jeffery 15.00 40.00
2 Cam Newton 50.00 100.00
3 Colin Kaepernick 60.00 120.00
4 Cordarrelle Patterson 12.00 30.00
5 Eddie Lacy 12.00 30.00
6 J.J. Watt 75.00 125.00
8 Josh Gordon 12.00 30.00
9 Kiko Alonso 12.00 30.00
10 LeSean McCoy 20.00 50.00

2014 Panini Flawless Patches

*RUBY/15: .5X TO 1.2X BASIC PATCH/20-25
*RUBY/15: .4X TO 1X BASIC PATCH/15
1 A.J. Green/25 20.00 50.00
2 Adrian Peterson/25 20.00 50.00
3 Alex Smith/25 15.00 40.00
4 Alfred Morris/25 12.00 30.00
5 Andrew Luck/25 25.00 60.00
6 Andy Dalton/25 15.00 40.00
7 Antonio Gates/25 12.00 30.00
8 Eddie Lacy/25 12.00 30.00
9 Tom Brady/25 75.00 150.00
10 C.J. Spiller/25 12.00 30.00
11 Calvin Johnson/25 20.00 50.00
12 Cam Newton/25 20.00 50.00
13 Ronnie Lott/20 15.00 40.00
14 Julius Peppers/25 15.00 40.00
15 DeMarco Murray/25 15.00 40.00
16 Cordarrelle Patterson/25 12.00 30.00
18 Ozzie Newsome/25 15.00 40.00
19 Dez Bryant/25 20.00 50.00
20 Demaryius Thomas/25 15.00 40.00
21 Dwayne Bowe/25 15.00 40.00
22 EJ Manuel/25 12.00 30.00
23 Eli Manning/25 15.00 40.00
24 Emmitt Smith/25 30.00 80.00
25 Fred Jackson/25 15.00 40.00
26 Giovani Bernard/25 12.00 30.00
27 Jamaal Charles/25 15.00 40.00
28 Dan Marino/25 60.00 120.00
29 Lester Hayes/15 20.00 50.00
30 Jimmy Graham/25 20.00 50.00
31 Joe Flacco/25 15.00 40.00
32 Jordan Cameron/25 12.00 30.00
33 Alshon Jeffery/25 15.00 40.00
34 Josh Gordon/25 12.00 30.00
35 Julio Jones/25 20.00 50.00
36 Matt Forte/25 12.00 30.00
37 Joe Namath/25 25.00 60.00
38 Wes Welker/25 15.00 40.00
39 Colin Kaepernick/25 15.00 40.00
40 Keenan Allen/25 15.00 40.00
41 Ken Anderson/15 20.00 50.00
42 Larry Fitzgerald/25 15.00 40.00
43 LeSean McCoy/25 20.00 50.00
44 Marques Colston/25 12.00 30.00
45 Marshawn Lynch/25 15.00 40.00
46 Matt Ryan/25 15.00 40.00
47 Matthew Stafford/25 15.00 40.00
49 Mike Wallace/25 12.00 30.00
50 Montee Ball/25 12.00 30.00
51 Patrick Peterson/25 12.00 30.00
52 Peyton Manning/25 100.00 200.00
53 Philip Rivers/25 20.00 50.00
54 Ray Rice/25 12.00 30.00
55 Reggie Bush/25 12.00 30.00
56 Richard Sherman/25 50.00 100.00
57 Robert Griffin III/25 12.00 30.00
58 Roddy White/25 12.00 30.00
59 Russell Wilson/25 30.00 80.00
60 Ryan Mathews/25 15.00 40.00
61 Ryan Tannehill/25 15.00 40.00
63 Terrell Suggs/25 12.00 30.00
64 Tony Romo/25 15.00 40.00
65 Torrey Smith/25 12.00 30.00
66 Von Miller/25 15.00 40.00

2014 Panini Flawless Patches Autographs

1 A.J. Green 30.00 80.00
4 Alfred Morris 20.00 50.00
7 Andy Dalton 25.00 60.00
8 Anquan Boldin 20.00 50.00
9 Antonio Brown 30.00 80.00
10 Antonio Gates
12 Bo Jackson 100.00 200.00
15 C.J. Spiller 20.00 50.00
17 Cam Newton 30.00 80.00
18 Cameron Wake 20.00 50.00
19 Cecil Shorts 20.00 50.00
20 Champ Bailey 25.00 60.00
21 James Laurinaitis 25.00 60.00
22 Colin Kaepernick 75.00 150.00
23 Cordarrelle Patterson 20.00 50.00
25 Danny Woodhead 25.00 60.00
26 Darren Sproles 25.00 60.00
27 DeAndre Hopkins 25.00 60.00
28 DeMarco Murray 25.00 60.00
29 Demaryius Thomas 25.00 60.00
30 DeSean Jackson 25.00 60.00
32 Doug Martin 25.00 60.00
34 Dwayne Bowe 25.00 60.00
35 Earl Thomas 60.00 125.00
36 Eddie Lacy 20.00 50.00
37 EJ Manuel 20.00 50.00
38 Eli Manning 25.00 60.00
39 Eric Decker 20.00 50.00
40 Frank Gore 25.00 60.00
41 Fred Jackson 25.00 60.00
42 Geno Smith 25.00 60.00
43 Giovani Bernard 20.00 50.00
44 Greg Jennings 20.00 50.00
45 Jamaal Charles 25.00 60.00
47 Jason Witten 25.00 60.00
49 Joe Flacco 30.00 80.00
50 Jordan Cameron 20.00 50.00
51 Jordan Reed 20.00 50.00
52 Josh Gordon 20.00 50.00
55 Justin Blackmon 20.00 50.00
57 Keenan Allen 25.00 60.00
59 Kenny Stills 20.00 50.00
60 Kiko Alonso 20.00 50.00
61 Knile Davis 20.00 50.00
62 Knowshon Moreno 20.00 50.00
64 LeSean McCoy 30.00 80.00
66 Manti Te'o 25.00 60.00
67 Marshawn Lynch 100.00 200.00
69 Matt Ryan 40.00 100.00
72 Michael Floyd 20.00 50.00
74 Montee Ball 20.00 50.00
75 Nick Foles 25.00 60.00
76 Peyton Manning 300.00 600.00
80 Richard Sherman 100.00 200.00
83 Robert Mathis 20.00 50.00
84 Robert Woods 25.00 60.00
85 Russell Wilson 150.00 250.00
87 Ryan Tannehill 75.00 150.00
88 Steve Johnson 25.00 60.00
89 Steve Smith 25.00 60.00
91 Tavon Austin 20.00 50.00
92 Tom Brady 600.00 1000.00
94 Tony Romo 100.00 200.00
95 Torrey Smith 20.00 50.00
97 Victor Cruz 30.00 80.00
98 Vincent Jackson 20.00 50.00
99 Wes Welker 25.00 60.00
100 Zac Stacy 20.00 50.00

2014 Panini Flawless Rookie Autographs

*BLUE/20: .4X TO 1X BASIC AU/25
*RUBY/15: .5X TO 1.2X BASIC AU/25
*PINK/14: .5X TO 1.2X BASIC AU/25
1 Jadeveon Clowney 12.00 30.00
2 Blake Bortles 12.00 30.00
3 Sammy Watkins 15.00 40.00
4 Mike Evans 30.00 60.00
5 Eric Ebron 12.00 30.00
6 Odell Beckham Jr. 75.00 150.00
7 Brandin Cooks 15.00 40.00
8 Johnny Manziel 15.00 40.00
9 Kelvin Benjamin 15.00 40.00
10 Teddy Bridgewater 30.00 60.00
11 Marqise Lee 12.00 30.00
12 Jordan Matthews 15.00 40.00
13 Paul Richardson 12.00 30.00
14 Bishop Sankey 10.00 25.00
15 Davante Adams 15.00 40.00
17 Jimmy Garoppolo 200.00 300.00
18 Tom Savage 12.00 30.00
19 Aaron Murray 10.00 25.00
20 A.J. McCarron 10.00 25.00

2014 Panini Flawless Rookie Flawless Signatures

*AUTO/25: .4X TO 1X ROOKIE AU/25
*BLUE/20: .4X TO 1X BASIC AU/25
*RUBY/15: .5X TO 1.2X BASIC AU/25
*PINK/14: .5X TO 1.2X BASIC AU/25
17 Jimmy Garoppolo 200.00 300.00

2014 Panini Flawless Rookie Inscriptions

*INSCRIPTIONS/25: .4X TO 1X BASIC AU/25
*BLUE/20: .4X TO 1X BASIC AU/25
*RUBY/15: .5X TO 1.2X BASIC AU/25
*PINK/14: .5X TO 1.2X BASIC AU/25

2014 Panini Flawless Rookie Patches

*RUBY/15: .5X TO 1.2X BASIC PATCH/25
1 Jadeveon Clowney 8.00 20.00
2 Blake Bortles 8.00 20.00
3 Sammy Watkins 10.00 25.00
4 Mike Evans 15.00 40.00
5 Eric Ebron 8.00 20.00
6 Odell Beckham Jr. 40.00 80.00
7 Brandin Cooks 10.00 25.00
8 Johnny Manziel 10.00 25.00
9 Kelvin Benjamin 10.00 25.00
10 Teddy Bridgewater 15.00 40.00
11 Marqise Lee 8.00 20.00
12 Jordan Matthews 10.00 25.00
13 Paul Richardson 8.00 20.00
14 Bishop Sankey 6.00 15.00
15 Davante Adams 10.00 25.00
16 Carlos Hyde 8.00 20.00
17 Jimmy Garoppolo 25.00 60.00
18 Tom Savage 6.00 15.00
19 Aaron Murray 6.00 15.00
20 A.J. McCarron 6.00 15.00
21 Tre Mason 6.00 15.00
22 Cody Latimer 8.00 20.00
23 Andre Williams 6.00 15.00
24 Jarvis Landry 15.00 40.00
25 Derek Carr 40.00 100.00
26 Logan Thomas 6.00 15.00
27 Donte Moncrief 6.00 15.00
28 Tajh Boyd 6.00 15.00
29 Devonta Freeman 20.00 50.00
30 Charles Sims 6.00 15.00
31 Dri Archer 6.00 15.00
32 Terrance West 6.00 15.00
33 Khalil Mack 25.00 60.00
34 Ka'Deem Carey 6.00 15.00

2014 Panini Flawless Rookie Patches Autographs

1 Jadeveon Clowney 15.00 40.00
2 Blake Bortles 15.00 40.00
3 Sammy Watkins 75.00 150.00
4 Mike Evans 75.00 150.00
5 Eric Ebron 15.00 40.00
6 Odell Beckham Jr. 150.00 300.00
7 Brandin Cooks 20.00 50.00
8 Johnny Manziel 20.00 50.00
9 Kelvin Benjamin 20.00 50.00
10 Teddy Bridgewater 100.00 200.00
11 Marqise Lee 15.00 40.00
12 Jordan Matthews 20.00 50.00
13 Paul Richardson 15.00 40.00
14 Bishop Sankey 12.00 30.00
15 Davante Adams 20.00 50.00
17 Jimmy Garoppolo 1200.00 1800.00
18 Tom Savage 12.00 30.00
19 Aaron Murray 12.00 30.00
20 A.J. McCarron 12.00 30.00

2014 Panini Flawless Rookie Patches Autographs Ruby

6 Odell Beckham Jr. 175.00 350.00
10 Teddy Bridgewater 125.00 250.00
17 Jimmy Garoppolo 1500.00 2000.00

2014 Panini Flawless Team Panini Autographs

*RUBY/15: .5X TO 1.2X BASIC AU/25
1 Aaron Dobson 12.00 30.00
2 Alfred Morris 12.00 30.00
3 Alshon Jeffery 15.00 40.00
4 Andre Ellington 12.00 30.00
5 Antonio Brown 40.00 80.00
6 Arian Foster 15.00 40.00
7 C.J. Spiller 12.00 30.00
8 Cecil Shorts 12.00 30.00
9 Cordarrelle Patterson 12.00 30.00
10 Danny Amendola 15.00 40.00
11 DeAndre Hopkins 15.00 40.00
12 DeMarco Murray 15.00 40.00
13 Demaryius Thomas 15.00 40.00
14 DeSean Jackson 15.00 40.00
15 Doug Martin 15.00 40.00
16 Eddie Lacy 12.00 30.00
17 Eric Decker 12.00 30.00
18 Giovani Bernard 12.00 30.00
19 Jordan Cameron 12.00 30.00
20 Jordan Reed 12.00 30.00
21 Jordy Nelson 40.00 80.00
22 Josh Gordon 12.00 30.00
24 Julius Thomas 12.00 30.00
25 Keenan Allen 15.00 40.00
26 Kenbrell Thompkins 12.00 30.00
27 Kenny Stills 12.00 30.00
28 Knile Davis 12.00 30.00
29 Knowshon Moreno 12.00 30.00
31 Luke Kuechly 25.00 40.00
32 Manti Te'o 15.00 40.00
34 Michael Floyd 12.00 30.00
35 Mike Glennon 15.00 40.00
36 Montee Ball 12.00 30.00
37 Nick Foles 15.00 40.00
38 Percy Harvin 12.00 30.00
39 Randall Cobb 20.00 50.00
41 Richard Sherman 90.00 150.00
42 Rob Gronkowski 30.00 60.00
43 Robert Woods 15.00 40.00
44 Sean Lee 15.00 40.00
45 Steve Johnson 15.00 40.00
46 Tavon Austin 12.00 30.00
47 Terrance Williams 12.00 30.00
48 Timothy Wright 12.00 30.00
50 Zach Ertz 15.00 40.00

2014 Panini Flawless Transitions Autographs

*RUBY: .5X TO 1.2X BASIC AU/25
1 Anquan Boldin 25.00 60.00
2 Brett Favre 100.00 200.00
3 Curtis Martin 15.00 40.00
4 Deion Sanders 40.00 80.00
5 Wes Welker 20.00 50.00

2015 Panini Flawless

1 Johnny Unitas 40.00 100.00
2 Charles Woodson 25.00 60.00
3 Tom Brady 100.00 200.00
4 Antonio Brown 25.00 60.00
5 DeMarco Murray 20.00 50.00
6 Adrian Peterson 25.00 60.00
7 Cris Collinsworth 20.00 50.00
8 J.J. Watt 25.00 60.00
9 Jay Cutler 15.00 40.00
10 Steve Largent 25.00 60.00
11 Emmitt Smith 50.00 100.00
12 Michael Strahan 20.00 50.00
13 Andy Dalton 20.00 50.00
14 Joe Namath 30.00 80.00
15 Nick Foles 20.00 50.00
16 Fred Biletnikoff 25.00 60.00
17 Terry Bradshaw 30.00 80.00
18 Bob Griese 25.00 60.00
19 Randy White 20.00 50.00
20 Brian Urlacher 25.00 60.00
21 Thurman Thomas 20.00 50.00
22 Aaron Rodgers 60.00 120.00
23 Andrew Luck 60.00 120.00
24 Jerry Rice 50.00 100.00
25 Ben Roethlisberger 25.00 60.00
26 Michael Irvin 25.00 60.00
27 Larry Csonka 20.00 50.00
28 Rob Gronkowski 25.00 60.00
29 Johnny Manziel 20.00 50.00
30 Steve Young 30.00 80.00
31 Peyton Manning 60.00 120.00
32 Joe Theismann 25.00 60.00
33 Rod Woodson 20.00 50.00
34 Jim Plunkett 20.00 50.00
35 Colin Kaepernick 20.00 50.00
36 Larry Fitzgerald 20.00 50.00
37 Kurt Warner 20.00 50.00
38 Ronnie Lott 20.00 50.00
39 Richard Sherman 25.00 60.00
40 Mike Ditka 25.00 60.00
41 Calvin Johnson 25.00 60.00
42 Sam Bradford 15.00 40.00
43 Julio Jones 25.00 60.00
44 Matthew Stafford 20.00 50.00
45 Darrelle Revis 15.00 40.00
46 Tony Romo 20.00 50.00
47 Clay Matthews 25.00 60.00
48 Paul Hornung 25.00 60.00
49 Dan Marino 40.00 100.00
50 Eric Dickerson 20.00 50.00
51 Troy Aikman 30.00 80.00
52 T.Y. Hilton 20.00 50.00
53 Mike Evans 20.00 50.00
54 Derek Carr 25.00 60.00
55 Bo Jackson 30.00 80.00
56 Gale Sayers 25.00 60.00
57 Eli Manning 20.00 50.00
58 Eddie Lacy 15.00 40.00
59 Carson Palmer 20.00 50.00
60 Brett Favre 75.00 125.00
61 Jim Kelly 25.00 60.00
62 Andre Johnson 20.00 50.00
63 Brandon Marshall 15.00 40.00
64 Carlos Hyde 15.00 40.00
65 Red Grange 30.00 80.00
66 Arian Foster 20.00 50.00
67 Dez Bryant 25.00 60.00
68 Alfred Morris 15.00 40.00
69 LeSean McCoy 25.00 60.00
70 Ryan Tannehill 20.00 50.00
71 Hines Ward 20.00 50.00
72 Cris Carter 25.00 60.00
73 Tavon Austin 15.00 40.00
74 A.J. Green 25.00 60.00
75 Shannon Sharpe 20.00 50.00
76 Antonio Gates 15.00 40.00
77 Russell Wilson 50.00 100.00
78 Roger Staubach 30.00 80.00
79 Earl Campbell 25.00 60.00
80 Matt Ryan 20.00 50.00
81 Clyde "Bulldog" Turner 20.00 50.00
82 Tim Tebow 20.00 50.00
83 John Riggins 20.00 50.00
84 Odell Beckham Jr. 25.00 60.00
85 Tim Brown 25.00 60.00
86 John Elway 40.00 80.00
87 Joe Flacco 20.00 50.00
88 Le'Veon Bell 20.00 50.00
89 Matt Forte 15.00 40.00
90 Paul Warfield 20.00 50.00
91 Marshall Faulk 20.00 50.00
92 Jerome Bettis 25.00 60.00
93 Philip Rivers 25.00 60.00
94 Deion Sanders 20.00 50.00
95 Warren Moon 25.00 60.00
96 Bruce Smith 20.00 50.00
97 John Stallworth 20.00 50.00
98 Franco Harris 25.00 60.00
99 LaDainian Tomlinson 20.00 50.00
100 Walter Payton 60.00 120.00
101 Cam Newton 25.00 60.00
102 Ron Jaworski 20.00 50.00
103 Joe Montana 100.00 200.00
104 Marshawn Lynch 20.00 50.00
105 Arnie Herber 25.00 60.00
106 Terrell Davis 20.00 50.00
107 Marcus Allen 25.00 60.00
108 Fran Tarkenton 25.00 60.00
109 Andre Reed 20.00 50.00
110 Demaryius Thomas 20.00 50.00
111 Bart Starr 40.00 100.00
112 Marcus Allen 25.00 60.00
113 Barry Sanders 40.00 100.00
114 Jamaal Charles 20.00 50.00
115 Ted Hendricks 15.00 40.00
116 Teddy Bridgewater 20.00 50.00
117 Drew Brees 25.00 60.00
118 Lawrence Taylor 25.00 60.00
119 Kurt Warner 20.00 50.00
120 Blake Bortles 15.00 40.00
121 Jameis Winston RC 100.00 200.00
122 Marcus Mariota RC 40.00 80.00
123 Melvin Gordon RC 30.00 80.00
124 Todd Gurley II RC 150.00 300.00
125 Amari Cooper RC 50.00 100.00
126 David Johnson RC 30.00 80.00
127 Nelson Agholor RC 15.00 40.00
128 Rashad Greene RC 12.00 30.00
129 Ameer Abdullah RC 20.00 50.00
130 Karlos Williams RC 12.00 30.00
131 Tyler Lockett RC 20.00 50.00
132 Tevin Coleman RC 15.00 40.00
133 Breshad Perriman RC 12.00 30.00
134 Kevin White RC 15.00 40.00
135 DeVante Parker RC 20.00 50.00
136 Duke Johnson RC 20.00 50.00
137 T.J. Yeldon RC 12.00 30.00
138 Matt Jones RC 12.00 30.00
139 Phillip Dorsett RC 12.00 30.00
140 Ty Montgomery RC 12.00 30.00

2015 Panini Flawless Ruby

*RUBY/15: .5X TO 1.2X BASIC CARDS/25
121 Jameis Winston 125.00 250.00
125 Amari Cooper 75.00 150.00

2015 Panini Flawless Autographs Ruby

*BASIC AU/25: .3X TO .8X RUBY/15
*BLUE/20: .3X TO .8X RUBY AU/25
SAB Antonio Brown
SAF Antonio Freeman 25.00 60.00
SAJ Alshon Jeffery 20.00 50.00
SAR Andre Reed 20.00 50.00
SCA C.J. Anderson 20.00 50.00
SCJ Charlie Joiner 15.00 40.00
SDC Dwight Clark 20.00 50.00
SDC Derek Carr 40.00 80.00
SDH Dan Hampton 15.00 40.00
SDM Don Majkowski 20.00 50.00
SDT Demaryius Thomas 20.00 50.00
SED Eric Decker 15.00 40.00
SES Emmanuel Sanders 20.00 50.00

SGO Greg Olsen 20.00 50.00
SHE Herman Edwards 15.00 40.00
SHM Heath Miller 15.00 40.00
SJC Jamaal Charles 20.00 50.00
SJC Jay Cutler 15.00 40.00
SJS Jackie Smith 15.00 40.00
SLK Luke Kuechly 20.00 50.00
SLM Lamar Miller 15.00 40.00
SMC Marques Colston 15.00 40.00
SMQ Mike Quick 15.00 40.00
SMS Mike Singletary 25.00 60.00
SNF Nick Foles 20.00 50.00
SPH Paul Hornung 25.00 60.00
SPW Paul Warfield 20.00 50.00
SRC Roger Craig 20.00 50.00
SRT Ryan Tannehill 20.00 50.00
SRW Russell Wilson
SVJ Vincent Jackson 15.00 40.00

2015 Panini Flawless Dual Patches
1 Andy Dalton 10.00 25.00
2 Walter Payton 50.00 100.00
3 Mike Singletary 12.00 30.00
4 Tom Brady 30.00 80.00
5 Peyton Manning 25.00 60.00
6 Peyton Manning 25.00 60.00
7 Tony Romo 10.00 25.00
8 Dez Bryant 12.00 30.00
9 Aaron Rodgers 25.00 60.00
10 Adrian Peterson 12.00 30.00
11 LeSean McCoy 12.00 30.00
12 Jerry Rice 20.00 50.00
15 Brett Favre 25.00 60.00
16 Steve Largent 12.00 30.00
19 Larry Fitzgerald 10.00 25.00

2015 Panini Flawless Greats Autographs Ruby
*BASIC AU/25: .3X TO .8X RUBY/15
*BLUE/20: .4X TO 1X RUBY/15
GABF Brett Favre 100.00 200.00
GABL Bob Lilly 20.00 50.00
GAFH Franco Harris 25.00 60.00
GAJG Joe Greene 25.00 60.00
GAJL James Lofton 15.00 40.00
GATH Ted Hendricks 15.00 40.00
GAWM Warren Moon 25.00 60.00

2015 Panini Flawless Greats Dual Patches Autographs Ruby
1 Dan Marino 150.00 300.00
2 Fred Taylor 20.00 50.00
3 Jim McMahon 40.00 100.00
4 Joe Montana 150.00 300.00
5 Joe Namath 125.00 250.00
6 John Riggins 50.00 125.00
7 LaDainian Tomlinson 60.00 125.00
8 Larry Csonka 40.00 100.00
9 Len Dawson 30.00 80.00
10 Marcus Allen 50.00 125.00
11 Marshall Faulk 50.00 125.00
12 Michael Strahan 50.00 125.00
15 Ricky Williams 25.00 60.00
16 Troy Aikman 125.00 250.00
17 Wilbert Montgomery 20.00 50.00
19 Darrelle Revis 20.00 50.00
20 Peyton Manning 175.00 350.00
28 Bob Griese 30.00 80.00
30 Brian Urlacher 30.00 80.00
33 Devin Hester 25.00 60.00
35 Eric Dickerson 60.00 125.00
39 Roger Craig 25.00 60.00
59 Earl Campbell 30.00 80.00

2015 Panini Flawless Greats Dual Patches Autographs
*BASIC AU/25: .3X TO .8X RUBY/15
2 Fred Taylor 15.00 40.00
3 Jim McMahon 40.00 80.00
4 Joe Montana 125.00 250.00
5 Joe Namath 100.00 200.00
6 John Riggins 50.00 100.00
8 Larry Csonka 40.00 80.00
10 Marcus Allen 50.00 100.00
11 Marshall Faulk 50.00 100.00
12 Michael Strahan 50.00 100.00
14 Ricky Williams 20.00 50.00
15 Ricky Williams 20.00 50.00
17 Wilbert Montgomery 15.00 40.00
20 Peyton Manning 150.00 300.00
33 Devin Hester 20.00 50.00

2015 Panini Flawless Greats Dual Patches Autographs Blue
*BLUE/20: .4X TO 1X RUBY/15
4 Joe Montana 150.00 300.00
5 Joe Namath 125.00 250.00
20 Peyton Manning 175.00 350.00

2015 Panini Flawless Greats Patches Autographs Ruby
GPAAP Adrian Peterson 50.00 125.00
GPABF Brett Favre 200.00 300.00
GPABG Bob Griese 30.00 80.00
GPABU Brian Urlacher 50.00 125.00
GPACM Curtis Martin 25.00 60.00
GPADH Devin Hester 25.00 60.00
GPADM Dan Marino 150.00 300.00
GPADR Darrelle Revis 20.00 50.00
GPAED Eric Dickerson 25.00 60.00
GPAFT Fred Taylor 20.00 50.00
GPAJT Joe Theismann 30.00 80.00
GPAJW Jason Witten 25.00 60.00
GPALT LaDainian Tomlinson 60.00 125.00
GPAMS Michael Strahan 50.00 125.00
GPAMS Mike Singletary 30.00 80.00
GPAPM Peyton Manning 175.00 350.00
GPARC Roger Craig 25.00 60.00
GPARS Roger Staubach 150.00 250.00
GPASY Steve Young 75.00 150.00
GPATB Tom Brady 600.00 1000.00
GPATD Tony Dorsett 30.00 80.00
GPAWM Wilbert Montgomery 20.00 50.00

2015 Panini Flawless Greats Patches Autographs
*BASIC AU/25: .3X TO .8X RUBY/15
GPAPM Peyton Manning 150.00 300.00

2015 Panini Flawless Greats Patches Autographs Blue
*BLUE/20: .4X TO 1X RUBY/15

2015 Panini Flawless Hall of Fame Autographs Ruby
*BASIC AU/25: .3X TO .8X RUBY/15
*BLUE/20: .4X TO 1X RUBY/15
HOFAR Andre Reed 20.00 50.00
HOFAW Aeneas Williams 15.00 40.00
HOFBL Bob Lilly 20.00 50.00
HOFCC Cris Carter 25.00 60.00
HOFES Emmitt Smith 150.00 250.00
HOFJB Jerome Bettis 50.00 100.00
HOFMA Marcus Allen 25.00 60.00
HOFMD Mike Ditka 25.00 60.00
HOFTB Tim Brown 25.00 60.00

2015 Panini Flawless Inscriptions Ruby
*BASIC AU/25: .3X TO .8X RUBY/15
*BLUE/20: .3X TO .8X RUBY/15
IAJ Alshon Jeffery 20.00 50.00
IAW Aeneas Williams 15.00 40.00
IBJ Bo Jackson 30.00 80.00
ICJ Charlie Joiner 15.00 40.00
ICM Curtis Martin 20.00 50.00
IDB Dez Bryant 40.00 80.00
IDB Drew Brees 50.00 125.00
IDC Dwight Clark 20.00 50.00
IDH Dan Hampton 15.00 40.00
IDM Don Majkowski 20.00 50.00
IEJ Edgerrin James 20.00 50.00
IFH Franco Harris 25.00 60.00
IHC Harold Carmichael 15.00 40.00
IHE Herman Edwards 15.00 40.00
IJB Jerome Bettis 40.00 100.00
IJL James Lofton 15.00 40.00
IJS Jackie Smith 15.00 40.00
IMC Mark Chmura 15.00 40.00
IMQ Mike Quick 15.00 40.00
IMS Mike Singletary 25.00 60.00
IPW Paul Warfield 20.00 50.00
IRB Robert Brooks 20.00 50.00
IRC Roger Craig 20.00 50.00
ITD Trent Dilfer 15.00 40.00

2015 Panini Flawless Memorable Marks Ruby
*BASIC AU/25: .3X TO .8X RUBY/15
*BLUE/20: .3X TO .8X RUBY/15
MMAL Andrew Luck 75.00 150.00
MMBO Bo Jackson 50.00 100.00
MMCJ Charlie Joiner 15.00 40.00
MMDB Dick Butkus 30.00 80.00
MMJT Joe Theismann 25.00 60.00
MMKW Kurt Warner 20.00 50.00
MMTB Tim Brown 25.00 60.00
MMTB Tom Brady 350.00 600.00
MMWS Warren Sapp 20.00 50.00

2015 Panini Flawless Patches
PAD Andy Dalton 10.00 25.00
PAG A.J. Green 12.00 30.00
PAG Antonio Gates 8.00 20.00
PAP Adrian Peterson 12.00 30.00
PAS Alex Smith 10.00 25.00
PBB Blake Bortles 8.00 20.00
PBK Brett Keisel 8.00 20.00
PCA C.J. Anderson 10.00 25.00
PCB Champ Bailey 10.00 25.00
PCL Chris Long 8.00 20.00
PCP Clinton Portis 8.00 20.00
PDB Derrick Brooks 8.00 20.00
PDB Dez Bryant 12.00 30.00
PDM Darren McFadden 8.00 20.00
PDM Don Majkowski 10.00 25.00
PDM DeMarco Murray 10.00 25.00
PDT Demaryius Thomas 10.00 25.00
PDW DeMarcus Ware 10.00 25.00
PEB Eric Berry 10.00 25.00
PES Emmanuel Sanders 10.00 25.00
PJA Jared Allen 8.00 20.00
PJC Jamaal Charles 10.00 25.00
PJH Joe Haden 8.00 20.00
PJH Jeremy Hill 8.00 20.00
PJJ Julio Jones 12.00 30.00
PJL Jarvis Landry 10.00 25.00
PJL James Laurinaitis 10.00 25.00
PJM Johnny Manziel 10.00 25.00
PJM Jordan Matthews 10.00 25.00
PJP Julius Peppers 10.00 25.00
PJS Jonathan Stewart 8.00 20.00
PKB Kelvin Benjamin 10.00 25.00
PKC Kirk Cousins 12.00 30.00
PLF Larry Fitzgerald 10.00 25.00
PLM Lamar Miller 8.00 20.00
PLM LeSean McCoy 12.00 30.00
PMB Martellus Bennett 8.00 20.00
PMF Matt Forte 8.00 20.00
PMT Manti Te'o 10.00 25.00
PPH Percy Harvin 8.00 20.00
PPP Paul Posluszny 8.00 20.00
PRT Ryan Tannehill 10.00 25.00
PSS Steve Smith Sr. 10.00 25.00
PSW Sammy Watkins 10.00 25.00
PTE Tyler Eifert 10.00 25.00
PTR Tony Romo 10.00 25.00
PTT Tyrod Taylor 10.00 25.00
PVD Vernon Davis 8.00 20.00
PVM Von Miller 10.00 25.00
PWP Walter Payton

2015 Panini Flawless Progressions Signatures
*BLUE/20: .5X TO 1.2X BASIC AU/25
*RUBY/15: .5X TO 1.2X BASIC AU/25
FPSAA Ameer Abdullah 15.00 40.00
FPSAC Amari Cooper 30.00 80.00
FPSBA Buck Allen 12.00 30.00
FPSBH Brett Hundley 10.00 25.00
FPSBP Bryce Petty 10.00 25.00
FPSBP Breshad Perriman 10.00 25.00
FPSCC Chris Conley 10.00 25.00
FPSDC David Cobb 10.00 25.00
FPSDF Devin Funchess 15.00 40.00
FPSDG Dorial Green-Beckham 10.00 25.00
FPSDJ Duke Johnson 15.00 40.00
FPSDJ David Johnson 25.00 60.00
FPSDP DeVante Parker 15.00 40.00
FPSDS Devin Smith 10.00 25.00
FPSGG Garrett Grayson 10.00 25.00
FPSJA Jay Ajayi 15.00 40.00
FPSJC Jamison Crowder 12.00 30.00
FPSJH Justin Hardy 10.00 25.00
FPSJL Jeremy Langford 10.00 25.00
FPSJS Jaelen Strong 12.00 30.00
FPSJW Jameis Winston 25.00 60.00
FPSKW Kevin White 12.00 30.00
FPSKW Karlos Williams 10.00 25.00
FPSLW Leonard Williams 10.00 25.00
FPSMD Mike Davis 10.00 25.00
FPSMG Melvin Gordon 25.00 60.00
FPSMJ Matt Jones 10.00 25.00
FPSMM Marcus Mariota 40.00 80.00
FPSMW Maxx Williams 10.00 25.00
FPSNA Nelson Agholor 12.00 30.00
FPSPD Phillip Dorsett 10.00 25.00
FPSRG Rashad Greene 10.00 25.00
FPSSC Sammie Coates 12.00 30.00
FPSSD Stefon Diggs 25.00 60.00
FPSSM Sean Mannion 10.00 25.00
FPSTC Tevin Coleman 12.00 30.00
FPSTG Todd Gurley II 40.00 100.00
FPSTL Tyler Lockett 15.00 40.00
FPSTM Ty Montgomery 10.00 25.00
FPSTY T.J. Yeldon 10.00 25.00

2015 Panini Flawless Rookie Autographs
RABH Brett Hundley 10.00 25.00
RABP Breshad Perriman 10.00 25.00
RACC Chris Conley 10.00 25.00
RADC David Cobb 10.00 25.00
RADF Devin Funchess 15.00 40.00
RADG Dorial Green-Beckham 10.00 25.00
RADJ Duke Johnson 15.00 40.00
RADS Devin Smith 10.00 25.00
RAJA Jay Ajayi 15.00 40.00
RAJS Jaelen Strong 12.00 30.00
RAJW Jameis Winston 25.00 60.00
RAMG Melvin Gordon 25.00 60.00
RAMJ Matt Jones 10.00 25.00
RAMM Marcus Mariota 40.00 80.00
RASC Sammie Coates 12.00 30.00
RATC Tevin Coleman 12.00 30.00
RATL Tyler Lockett 15.00 40.00

2015 Panini Flawless Rookie Autographs Blue
*BLUE/20: .4X TO 1X BASIC AU/25

2015 Panini Flawless Rookie Autographs Ruby
*RUBY/15: .5X TO 1.2X BASIC AU/25

2015 Panini Flawless Rookie Inscriptions
RIAA Ameer Abdullah 15.00 40.00
RIDC David Cobb 10.00 25.00
RIDG Dorial Green-Beckham 10.00 25.00
RIDJ David Johnson 25.00 60.00
RIDP DeVante Parker 15.00 40.00
RIDS Devin Smith 10.00 25.00
RIJA Jay Ajayi 15.00 40.00
RIJS Jaelen Strong 12.00 30.00
RIJW Jameis Winston 25.00 60.00
RIKW Kevin White 12.00 30.00
RIMG Melvin Gordon 25.00 60.00
RIMJ Matt Jones 10.00 25.00
RIMM Marcus Mariota 40.00 80.00
RINA Nelson Agholor 12.00 30.00
RITC Tevin Coleman 12.00 30.00
RITM Ty Montgomery 10.00 25.00
RITY T.J. Yeldon 10.00 25.00

2015 Panini Flawless Rookie Inscriptions Blue
*BLUE/20: .4X TO 1X BASIC AU/25

2015 Panini Flawless Rookie Inscriptions Ruby
*RUBY/15: .5X TO 1.2X BASIC AU/25

2015 Panini Flawless Rookie NFL Collegiate Dual Patches
*BLUE/20: .4X TO 1X BASIC JSY/25
*RUBY/15: .5X TO 1.2X BASIC JSY/25
1 Jameis Winston 20.00 50.00
2 Marcus Mariota 25.00 60.00
3 Melvin Gordon 20.00 50.00
4 Todd Gurley 40.00 80.00
5 Sammie Coates 10.00 25.00
6 Amari Cooper 25.00 60.00
7 Ameer Abdullah 12.00 30.00
8 Buck Allen 10.00 25.00
9 Brett Hundley 8.00 20.00
10 DeVante Parker 12.00 30.00
11 Duke Johnson 12.00 30.00
12 Jaelen Strong 10.00 25.00
13 Jamison Crowder 10.00 25.00
14 Matt Jones 8.00 20.00
15 Maxx Williams 8.00 20.00
16 Breshad Perriman 8.00 20.00
17 Nelson Agholor 10.00 25.00
18 Phillip Dorsett 8.00 20.00
19 Tyler Lockett 12.00 30.00
20 Rashad Greene 8.00 20.00
21 T.J. Yeldon 8.00 20.00
22 Tevin Coleman 10.00 25.00
24 Leonard Williams 8.00 20.00
25 Garrett Grayson 8.00 20.00
26 Mike Davis 8.00 20.00
27 Devin Funchess 12.00 30.00
28 Jeremy Langford 8.00 20.00
29 Kevin White 10.00 25.00
30 Bryce Petty 8.00 20.00

2015 Panini Flawless Rookie Patches
RPAA Ameer Abdullah 12.00 30.00
RPAC Amari Cooper 30.00 80.00
RPBA Buck Allen 10.00 25.00
RPBP Breshad Perriman 8.00 20.00
RPBP Bryce Petty 8.00 20.00
RPDF Devin Funchess 12.00 30.00
RPDJ Duke Johnson 12.00 30.00
RPDJ David Johnson 20.00 50.00
RPDP DeVante Parker 12.00 30.00
RPJC Jamison Crowder 10.00 25.00
RPJL Jeremy Langford 8.00 20.00
RPJS Jaelen Strong 10.00 25.00
RPJW Jameis Winston 20.00 50.00
RPKW Kevin White
RPKW Karlos Williams 8.00 20.00
RPLW Leonard Williams 8.00 20.00
RPMD Mike Davis 8.00 20.00
RPMG Melvin Gordon 20.00 50.00
RPMJ Matt Jones 8.00 20.00
RPMM Marcus Mariota 25.00 60.00
RPMW Maxx Williams 8.00 20.00
RPNA Nelson Agholor 10.00 25.00
RPPD Phillip Dorsett 8.00 20.00
RPRG Rashad Greene 8.00 20.00
RPSC Sammie Coates 10.00 25.00
RPTC Tevin Coleman 10.00 25.00
RPTG Todd Gurley 30.00 80.00
RPTL Tyler Lockett
RPTM Ty Montgomery 8.00 20.00
RPTY T.J. Yeldon 8.00 20.00

2015 Panini Flawless Rookie Patches Autographs
RPAAA Ameer Abdullah 12.00 30.00
RPAAC Amari Cooper 75.00 150.00
RPABH Brett Hundley 8.00 20.00
RPADC David Cobb 8.00 20.00
RPADJ David Johnson 60.00 125.00
RPADP DeVante Parker 12.00 30.00
RPADS Devin Smith 8.00 20.00
RPAJA Jay Ajayi 12.00 30.00
RPAJW Jameis Winston 175.00 350.00
RPAKW Kevin White 10.00 25.00
RPAMG Melvin Gordon 20.00 50.00
RPAMJ Matt Jones 8.00 20.00
RPAMM Marcus Mariota 50.00 100.00
RPANA Nelson Agholor 10.00 25.00
RPAPD Phillip Dorsett 8.00 20.00
RPATC Tevin Coleman 10.00 25.00
RPATG Todd Gurley 100.00 200.00
RPATL Tyler Lockett 12.00 30.00
RPATM Ty Montgomery 8.00 20.00
RPATY T.J. Yeldon 8.00 20.00

2015 Panini Flawless Rookie Patches Autographs Blue
*BLUE/20: X TO X BASIC JSY AU/25
RPAJW Jameis Winston 250.00 400.00
RPAMM Marcus Mariota 50.00 125.00

2015 Panini Flawless Rookie Patches Autographs Ruby
RPAJW Jameis Winston 250.00 400.00
RPAMM Marcus Mariota 50.00 125.00

2015 Panini Flawless Rookie Signatures
RFSAA Ameer Abdullah 15.00 40.00
RFSBH Brett Hundley 10.00 25.00
RFSBP Breshad Perriman 10.00 25.00
RFSDF Devin Funchess 15.00 40.00
RFSDG Dorial Green-Beckham 10.00 25.00
RFSDJ Duke Johnson 15.00 40.00
RFSDP DeVante Parker 15.00 40.00
RFSJS Jaelen Strong 12.00 30.00
RFSJW Jameis Winston 25.00 60.00
RFSKW Kevin White 12.00 30.00
RFSMG Melvin Gordon 25.00 60.00
RFSMM Marcus Mariota
RFSNA Nelson Agholor 12.00 30.00
RFSSC Sammie Coates 12.00 30.00
RFSTY T.J. Yeldon 10.00 25.00

2015 Panini Flawless Rookie Signatures Blue
*BLUE/20: .4X TO 1X BASIC AU/25

2015 Panini Flawless Rookie Signatures Ruby
*RUBY/15: .5X TO 1.2X BASIC AU/25
RFSJW Jameis Winston 30.00 80.00

2015 Panini Flawless Team Panini Autographs Ruby
TPAAL Andrew Luck 100.00 200.00
TPACA C.J. Anderson 20.00 50.00
TPADB Dez Bryant 50.00 100.00
TPADC Dwight Clark 20.00 50.00
TPADC Derek Carr 25.00 60.00
TPADH Dan Hampton 15.00 40.00
TPADT Demaryius Thomas 20.00 50.00
TPAEL Eddie Lacy 15.00 40.00
TPAES Emmanuel Sanders 20.00 50.00
TPAGO Greg Olsen 20.00 50.00
TPAHW Hines Ward 20.00 50.00
TPAJH Jack Ham 30.00 80.00
TPAJH James Harrison 60.00 120.00
TPAJW Jason Witten 40.00 80.00
TPAJW Jameis Winston 30.00 80.00
TPALK Luke Kuechly 40.00 80.00
TPALM Lamar Miller 15.00 40.00
TPAME Mike Evans 20.00 50.00
TPAMG Melvin Gordon 30.00 80.00
TPAMM Marcus Mariota 60.00 150.00
TPAMR Matt Ryan 20.00 50.00
TPAMS Matthew Stafford 20.00 50.00
TPANF Nick Foles 20.00 50.00
TPARS Richard Sherman 50.00 100.00
TPART Ryan Tannehill 20.00 50.00
TPARW Ricky Williams 20.00 50.00
TPASJ Steve Johnson 20.00 50.00
TPATK Travis Kelce 25.00 60.00
TPATS Torrey Smith 15.00 40.00

2015 Panini Flawless Team Panini Autographs
*BASIC AU/25: .3X TO .8X RUBY/15
31 Matt Forte

2015 Panini Flawless Team Panini Autographs Blue
TPAAL Andrew Luck 90.00 150.00
TPAJW Jameis Winston 25.00 60.00

2015 Panini Flawless Teammates Patches
1 A.Green/A.Dalton 20.00 50.00
2 L.McCoy/S.Watkins 20.00 50.00
3 D.Thomas/E.Sanders 15.00 40.00
4 D.Bryant/T.Romo 20.00 50.00
5 R.Tannehill/J.Landry 15.00 40.00
6 B.Bortles/A.Robinson 15.00 40.00
7 M.Stafford/C.Johnson 20.00 50.00
8 A.Ellington/L.Fitzgerald 15.00 40.00
9 B.Urlacher/C.Tillman 20.00 50.00
10 J.Nelson/R.Cobb 15.00 40.00
12 E.Berry/J.Charles 15.00 40.00
13 J.Edelman/R.Gronkowski 50.00 100.00
16 K.Chancellor/E.Thomas 20.00 50.00
18 L.McCoy/D.Jackson 20.00 50.00
19 J.Jones/R.White 20.00 50.00
20 D.Ware/P.Manning 50.00 100.00

2015 Panini Flawless Victors Autographs Ruby
*BASIC AU/25: .3X TO .8X RUBY/15
*BLUE/20: .4X TO 1X RUBY/15
FVADA Danny Amendola 20.00 50.00
FVADC Dwight Clark 20.00 50.00
FVAEM Eli Manning 20.00 50.00
FVARS Richard Sherman 50.00 125.00
FVASY Steve Young 50.00 125.00
FVATA Troy Aikman 50.00 125.00
FVATB Tom Brady 400.00 800.00

2016 Panini Flawless
*RUBY/15: .4X TO 1X BASIC CARDS
1 Carson Palmer 15.00 40.00
2 David Johnson 20.00 50.00
3 Larry Fitzgerald 15.00 40.00
4 Matt Ryan 15.00 40.00
5 Julio Jones 20.00 50.00
6 Joe Flacco 15.00 40.00
7 Steve Smith 15.00 40.00
8 LeSean McCoy 20.00 50.00
9 Sammy Watkins 20.00 50.00
10 Cam Newton 20.00 50.00
11 Kelvin Benjamin 15.00 40.00
12 Luke Kuechly 15.00 40.00
13 Jonathan Stewart 12.00 30.00
14 Alshon Jeffery 15.00 40.00
15 Davante Adams 12.00 30.00
16 Andy Dalton 15.00 40.00
17 A.J. Green 20.00 50.00
18 Isaiah Crowell 12.00 30.00
19 Terrelle Pryor 12.00 30.00
20 Tony Romo 15.00 40.00
21 Jason Witten 15.00 40.00
22 Dez Bryant 20.00 50.00
23 Demaryius Thomas 15.00 40.00
24 Von Miller 15.00 40.00
25 Matthew Stafford 15.00 40.00
26 Golden Tate III 12.00 30.00
27 Zach Zenner 12.00 30.00
28 Aaron Rodgers 40.00 100.00
29 Jordy Nelson 15.00 40.00
30 Clay Matthews 20.00 50.00
31 Lamar Miller 12.00 30.00
32 DeAndre Hopkins 15.00 40.00
33 J.J. Watt 20.00 50.00
34 Andrew Luck 25.00 60.00
35 T.Y. Hilton 15.00 40.00
36 Blake Bortles 12.00 30.00
37 Allen Robinson 15.00 40.00
38 Chris Ivory 15.00 40.00
39 Spencer Ware 12.00 30.00
40 Jeremy Maclin 12.00 30.00
41 Todd Gurley II 20.00 50.00
42 Ryan Tannehill 15.00 40.00
43 Jarvis Landry 15.00 40.00
44 Adrian Peterson 20.00 50.00
45 Stefon Diggs 15.00 40.00
46 Tom Brady 175.00 350.00
47 Rob Gronkowski 20.00 50.00
48 Julian Edelman 20.00 50.00
49 Drew Brees 20.00 50.00
50 Mark Ingram 15.00 40.00
51 Brandin Cooks 15.00 40.00
52 Eli Manning 15.00 40.00
53 Odell Beckham Jr. 40.00 100.00
54 Jay Ajayi 15.00 40.00
55 Matt Forte 12.00 30.00
56 Brandon Marshall 12.00 30.00
57 Derek Carr 20.00 50.00
58 Amari Cooper 20.00 50.00
59 Khalil Mack 20.00 50.00
60 Jordan Matthews 15.00 40.00
61 Zach Ertz 15.00 40.00
62 Ben Roethlisberger 20.00 50.00
63 Le'Veon Bell 15.00 40.00
64 Antonio Brown 20.00 50.00
65 Philip Rivers 20.00 50.00
66 Melvin Gordon 15.00 40.00
67 Tyrell Williams 12.00 30.00
68 Carlos Hyde 12.00 30.00
69 Navorro Bowman 15.00 40.00
70 Russell Wilson 90.00 150.00
71 Richard Sherman 20.00 50.00
72 Tyler Lockett 15.00 40.00
73 Jameis Winston 20.00 50.00
74 Michael Bennett 12.00 30.00
75 Mike Evans 15.00 40.00
76 Marcus Mariota 20.00 50.00
77 DeMarco Murray 15.00 40.00
78 Kirk Cousins 20.00 50.00
79 Jordan Reed 12.00 30.00
80 Jamison Crowder 12.00 30.00
81 Jared Goff RC 125.00 250.00
82 Carson Wentz RC 250.00 400.00
83 Paxton Lynch RC 12.00 30.00
84 Dak Prescott RC 125.00 250.00
85 Cody Kessler RC 12.00 30.00
86 Tyreek Hill RC 40.00 100.00
87 Ezekiel Elliott RC 150.00 300.00
88 Derrick Henry RC 30.00 80.00
89 Devontae Booker RC 15.00 40.00
90 Jordan Howard RC 30.00 80.00
91 Corey Coleman RC 20.00 50.00
92 Laquon Treadwell RC 15.00 40.00
93 Will Fuller V RC 20.00 50.00
94 Sterling Shepard RC 15.00 40.00
95 Michael Thomas RC 25.00 60.00
96 Tyler Boyd RC 15.00 40.00
97 Josh Doctson RC 15.00 40.00
98 Malcolm Mitchell RC 12.00 30.00
99 Joey Bosa RC 25.00 60.00
100 Hunter Henry RC 15.00 40.00
101 Ed Reed 15.00 40.00
102 Ray Lewis 20.00 50.00
103 Jim Kelly 20.00 50.00
104 Jim Thorpe 25.00 60.00
105 Walter Payton 40.00 100.00
106 Red Grange 25.00 60.00
107 Jim Brown 25.00 60.00
108 Troy Aikman 25.00 60.00
109 Emmitt Smith 30.00 80.00
110 John Elway 40.00 100.00
111 Barry Sanders 30.00 80.00
112 Calvin Johnson 20.00 50.00
113 Brett Favre 40.00 100.00
114 Earl Campbell 20.00 50.00
115 Peyton Manning 40.00 100.00
116 Marvin Harrison 15.00 40.00
117 Bo Jackson 25.00 60.00
118 Dan Marino 40.00 100.00
119 Randy Moss 15.00 40.00
120 Tedy Bruschi 15.00 40.00
121 Lawrence Taylor 20.00 50.00
122 Joe Namath 25.00 60.00
123 Dick Butkus 25.00 60.00
124 Reggie White 20.00 50.00
125 Terry Bradshaw 40.00 100.00
126 Jack Lambert 12.00 30.00
127 Jerome Bettis 20.00 50.00
128 Junior Seau 15.00 40.00
129 LaDainian Tomlinson 15.00 40.00
130 Joe Montana 100.00 200.00
131 Jerry Rice 30.00 80.00
132 Steve Young 40.00 80.00
133 Kurt Warner 15.00 40.00
134 John Riggins 15.00 40.00
135 Derrick Thomas 20.00 50.00
136 Bart Starr CM 40.00 100.00
137 Johnny Unitas CM 30.00 80.00
138 Tom Brady CM 175.00 350.00
139 Peyton Manning CM 40.00 100.00
140 Russell Wilson CM 90.00 150.00
141 Drew Brees CM 20.00 50.00
142 Aaron Rodgers CM 40.00 100.00
143 Emmitt Smith CM 30.00 80.00
144 Ben Roethlisberger CM 20.00 50.00
145 Adam Vinatieri CM 15.00 40.00

2016 Panini Flawless Benchmarks
*RUBY/15: .5X TO 1.2X BASIC AU/25
*SILVER15-20: .5X TO 1.2X BASIC AU/25
1 LaDainian Tomlinson/20
2 Eric Dickerson/15
9 Marshall Faulk/15 20.00 50.00
12 Adam Vinatieri/25 15.00 40.00
17 Len Dawson/20 25.00 60.00
19 Jason Witten/25 40.00 80.00

2016 Panini Flawless Dual Diamond Memorabilia
*RUBY/15: .5X TO 1.2X BASIC JSY/25
*RUBY/15: .4X TO 1X BASIC JSY/15-20
*SILVER/15: .5X TO 1.2X BASIC JSY/25
*SILVER/15: .4X TO 1X BASIC JSY/15-20
1 L.Bell/J.Bettis/25 20.00 50.00
2 C.Wentz/R.Cunningham/25 20.00 50.00
5 C.Carter/L.Treadwell/15 12.00 30.00
6 C.Cook/D.Carr/20 12.00 30.00
7 C.Jones/T.Taylor/20 10.00 25.00
9 C.Coleman/G.Barnidge/15 10.00 25.00
11 D.Henry/E.George/15 20.00 50.00
12 A.Collins/M.Lynch/15 10.00 25.00
13 D.Booker/T.Davis/20 10.00 25.00
14 J.Howard/J.Langford/15 10.00 25.00
15 D.Washington/M.Allen/15 10.00 25.00
16 T.Rawls/C.Prosise/20 8.00 20.00
17 J.Seau/J.Bosa/15 15.00 40.00
19 D.Hopkins/W.Fuller V/15 12.00 30.00
20 S.Shepard/O.Beckham Jr./20 12.00 30.00
21 B.Cooks/M.Thomas/20 12.00 30.00
22 T.Boyd/A.Green/15 12.00 30.00
23 A.Boldin/C.Moore/15 10.00 25.00
24 D.Adams/T.Davis/15 8.00 20.00
25 H.Henry/A.Gates/15 10.00 25.00

2016 Panini Flawless Dual Patch Autographs
*RUBY/15: .5X TO 1.2X BASIC JSY AU/25
*SILVER/20: .5X TO 1.2X BASIC JSY AU/25
5 Kurt Warner/20 60.00 125.00
20 Eric Berry/25
22 Trevor Siemian/25
27 Sterling Sharpe/25 40.00 80.00
28 Von Miller/25 40.00 80.00
29 Tyler Eifert/25 20.00 50.00

2016 Panini Flawless Flawless Finishes Autographs
*RUBY/15: .5X TO 1.2X BASIC AU/25
*SILVER/15-20: .5X TO 1.2X BASIC AU/25
*SILVER/15-20: .4X TO 1X BASIC AU/20
1 Franco Harris/25 20.00 50.00
2 Herman Edwards/20 20.00 50.00
4 Dwight Clark/25 15.00 40.00
6 Adam Vinatieri/25 15.00 40.00

2016 Panini Flawless Flawless Signatures
*RUBY/15: .5X TO 1.2X BASIC AU/25
*RUBY/15: .4X TO 1X BASIC AU/15
*SILVER/15-20: .5X TO 1.2X BASIC AU/25
*SILVER/15-20: .4X TO 1X BASIC AU/15-20
7 Derek Carr/25 30.00 60.00
15 David Johnson/25 20.00 50.00
19 Le'Veon Bell/15 30.00 80.00
24 Jordy Nelson/25 15.00 40.00
26 Sammy Watkins/20 25.00 60.00
27 Marvin Jones Jr./25 12.00 30.00
28 Adam Vinatieri/25 15.00 40.00
29 Richard Sherman/15 25.00 60.00

2016 Panini Flawless Greats Dual Patch Autographs
*RUBY/15: .5X TO 1.2X BASIC JSY AU/25
*SILVER/15-20: .5X TO 1.2X BASIC JSY AU/25
*SILVER/15-20: .4X TO 1X BASIC JSY AU/20
2 Eddie George/15 60.00 125.00
3 LaDainian Tomlinson/15
4 Marcus Allen/25 20.00 50.00
13 Tony Dorsett/15 60.00 125.00
14 Howie Long/15 50.00 100.00
18 Eric Dickerson/15 60.00 125.00
19 Hines Ward/25 20.00 50.00
24 Clinton Portis/25

2016 Panini Flawless Hall of Fame Autographs
*RUBY/15: .5X TO 1.2X BASIC AU/25
*SILVER/15-20: .5X TO 1.2X BASIC AU/25
*SILVER/15-20: .4X TO 1X BASIC AU/15-20
3 Chris Doleman/25 12.00 30.00
5 Jack Lambert/15 40.00 80.00
6 Thurman Thomas/15 20.00 50.00
7 Charles Haley/20 25.00 60.00
8 Lawrence Taylor/25 20.00 50.00
11 Ozzie Newsome/15 20.00 50.00
16 Bruce Smith/20 20.00 50.00

2016 Panini Flawless Memorable Marks
*RUBY/15: .5X TO 1.2X BASIC AU/25
*SILVER/15-20: .5X TO 1.2X BASIC AU/25
*SILVER/15-20: .4X TO 1X BASIC AU/25
8 Terrell Davis/20 20.00 50.00
9 Ed Reed/15 40.00 80.00
10 Rod Woodson/25 15.00 40.00
12 Bruce Smith/20 20.00 50.00
14 Randy Moss/15 150.00 300.00
15 Kurt Warner/20 20.00 50.00
20 LaDainian Tomlinson/20

2016 Panini Flawless Momentous Patch Autographs
*RUBY/15: .5X TO 1.2X BASIC JSY AU/25
*RUBY/15: .4X TO 1X BASIC JSY AU/15
*SILVER/15-20: .5X TO 1.2X BASIC JSY AU/25
*SILVER/15-20: .4X TO 1X BASIC JSY AU/15
2 Laquon Treadwell/15 20.00 50.00
5 Dak Prescott/25 75.00 150.00
8 Sterling Shepard/25 15.00 40.00
14 Tyler Boyd/25 15.00 40.00
16 Adam Vinatieri/25 15.00 40.00
18 Devontae Booker/25 15.00 40.00
21 Corey Coleman/15 25.00 60.00
23 Doug Baldwin/15 20.00 50.00
25 Allen Robinson/25 15.00 40.00
27 Braxton Miller/25 12.00 30.00
29 Michael Thomas/25 25.00 60.00
30 DeAngelo Williams/15 15.00 40.00

2016 Panini Flawless Now and Then Signatures
*RUBY/15: .5X TO 1.2X BASIC AU/25
*RUBY/15: .4X TO 1X BASIC AU/20
*SILVER/15-20: .5X TO 1.2X BASIC AU/25
*SILVER/15-20: .4X TO 1X BASIC AU/15-20
5 Carlos Hyde/20 15.00 40.00
10 LaDainian Tomlinson/15
11 Steve Largent/20 25.00 60.00
12 Hines Ward/15 50.00 100.00
13 Lawrence Taylor/15 25.00 60.00
15 Jimmy Johnson/25 20.00 50.00
16 Ameer Abdullah/25 12.00 30.00
17 David Johnson/25 20.00 50.00
18 Maurice Jones-Drew/15 15.00 40.00
19 Doug Flutie/25 15.00 40.00
20 Allen Robinson/25 15.00 40.00

2016 Panini Flawless Patch Autographs
*RUBY/15: .5X TO 1.2X BASIC JSY AU/25
*RUBY/15: .4X TO 1X BASIC JSY AU/20
*SILVER/15-20: .5X TO 1.2X BASIC JSY AU/25
*SILVER/15-20: .4X TO 1X BASIC JSY AU/15-20
3 Allen Hurns/25 15.00 40.00
4 Allen Robinson/15 25.00 60.00
11 Brandin Cooks/15 25.00 60.00
31 Eric Berry/20
31 Eric Berry/20
46 Joe Flacco/20 25.00 60.00
47 John Kuhn/20 20.00 50.00
55 Luke Kuechly/15 25.00 60.00
58 Matt Jones/15 25.00 60.00
63 Rod Woodson/15 25.00 60.00
67 Stefon Diggs/15 25.00 60.00
73 Tyler Eifert/15 25.00 60.00

2016 Panini Flawless Patches
*RUBY/15: .4X TO 1X BASIC JSY/20
1 Bobby Layne/15 10.00 25.00
2 Von Miller/20 10.00 25.00
3 Antonio Brown/20 15.00 40.00
4 A.J. Green/20 12.00 30.00
5 Ray Lewis/20 15.00 40.00
6 Ed Reed/20 10.00 25.00
7 Joe Flacco/15 10.00 25.00
8 Walter Payton/20 50.00 100.00
9 Brian Urlacher/20 12.00 30.00
10 Barry Sanders/20 50.00 100.00
13 Adrian Peterson/20 12.00 30.00
15 Julio Jones/20 20.00 50.00
16 Cam Newton/20 12.00 30.00
17 Drew Brees/20 12.00 30.00
18 Jameis Winston/20 12.00 30.00
20 Andrew Luck/20 15.00 40.00
21 Devonta Freeman/20 10.00 25.00
22 Davante Adams/20 8.00 20.00
23 Blake Bortles/20 8.00 20.00
24 Eddie George/20 15.00 40.00
25 Marcus Mariota/20 12.00 30.00
27 Dez Bryant/20 12.00 30.00
28 Jason Witten/20 10.00 25.00
29 Tony Romo/20 10.00 25.00
30 Eli Manning/20 10.00 25.00
31 Khalil Mack/20 12.00 30.00
32 Odell Beckham Jr./20 12.00 30.00
33 John Riggins/20 10.00 25.00
34 Jay Ajayi/20 10.00 25.00
35 David Johnson/20 12.00 30.00
36 Larry Fitzgerald/20 10.00 25.00
37 Todd Gurley II/20 12.00 30.00
39 Randy Moss/15 20.00 50.00
41 Steve Young/20 15.00 40.00
42 Russell Wilson/20 15.00 40.00
43 Marshawn Lynch/20 10.00 25.00
44 John Elway/15 20.00 50.00
46 Amari Cooper/20 12.00 30.00
47 Tyler Lockett/20 10.00 25.00
48 Dan Marino/15 25.00 60.00
49 Rob Gronkowski/15 12.00 30.00
50 Junior Seau/15 10.00 25.00

2016 Panini Flawless Rookie Autographs
*RUBY/15: .5X TO 1.2X BASIC AU/25
*RUBY/15: .4X TO 1X BASIC AU/20
*SILVER/20: .5X TO 1.2X BASIC AU/25
*SILVER/15-20: .4X TO 1X BASIC AU/20
1 Jared Goff/15 60.00 125.00
2 Carson Wentz/15 200.00 400.00
3 Paxton Lynch/15 12.00 30.00
4 Dak Prescott/25 60.00 125.00
5 Connor Cook/20 12.00 30.00
6 Christian Hackenberg/20 10.00 25.00
7 Ezekiel Elliott/15 150.00 250.00
9 C.J. Prosise/20 10.00 25.00
10 Devontae Booker/25 10.00 25.00
11 Kenneth Dixon/20 10.00 25.00
12 Paul Perkins/20 10.00 25.00
13 DeAndre Washington/25 8.00 20.00
14 Kenyan Drake/25 12.00 30.00
15 Tyler Ervin/25 8.00 20.00
16 Corey Coleman/25 12.00 30.00
17 Laquon Treadwell/25 10.00 25.00
18 Josh Doctson/25 10.00 25.00
19 Will Fuller V/25 12.00 30.00
20 Sterling Shepard/25 10.00 25.00
21 Michael Thomas/25 15.00 40.00
22 Tyler Boyd/25 10.00 25.00
23 Braxton Miller/25 8.00 20.00
25 Joey Bosa/25 15.00 40.00

2016 Panini Flawless Rookie Flawless Signatures
*RUBY/15: .5X TO 1.2X BASIC AU/25
*RUBY/15: .4X TO 1X BASIC AU/20
*SILVER/20: .5X TO 1.2X BASIC AU/25
*SILVER/15-20: .4X TO 1X BASIC AU/20
1 Ezekiel Elliott/15 150.00 300.00
2 Sterling Shepard/20 12.00 30.00
3 Michael Thomas/20 20.00 50.00
5 Devontae Booker/20 12.00 30.00
6 Corey Coleman/20 15.00 40.00
7 Carson Wentz/15 200.00 400.00
8 Laquon Treadwell/20 12.00 30.00
9 Jared Goff/15 60.00 125.00
10 Kenneth Dixon/20 10.00 25.00
11 DeAndre Washington/25 8.00 20.00
12 Tyler Boyd/25 10.00 25.00
13 Paxton Lynch/20 12.00 30.00
14 Dak Prescott/25 60.00 125.00
15 Alex Collins/25 10.00 25.00
16 Paul Perkins/25 8.00 20.00
17 Will Fuller V/25 12.00 30.00
18 Connor Cook/20 12.00 30.00
19 Cody Kessler/25 8.00 20.00
20 Josh Doctson/25 10.00 25.00
21 Braxton Miller/25 8.00 20.00
22 Cardale Jones/25 8.00 20.00
23 Jordan Howard/25 20.00 50.00
24 Malcolm Mitchell/25 8.00 20.00
25 Tajae Sharpe/25 10.00 25.00

2016 Panini Flawless Rookie Now and Then Signatures
*RUBY/15: .5X TO 1.2X BASIC AU/25
*RUBY/15: .4X TO 1X BASIC AU/20
*SILVER/20: .5X TO 1.2X BASIC AU/25
*SILVER/15-20: .4X TO 1X BASIC AU/20
1 Derrick Henry/20 25.00 60.00
2 Corey Coleman/20 15.00 40.00
3 Joey Bosa/25 15.00 40.00
4 Devontae Booker/25 10.00 25.00
5 Sterling Shepard/25 10.00 25.00
6 Josh Doctson/20 12.00 30.00
7 Connor Cook/20 12.00 30.00
8 Paxton Lynch/20 12.00 30.00
9 Michael Thomas/20 20.00 50.00
10 Dak Prescott/20 75.00 150.00
11 Laquon Treadwell/20 12.00 30.00
12 Carson Wentz/15 200.00 400.00
13 Tyler Boyd/20 12.00 30.00
14 Malcolm Mitchell/25 8.00 20.00
15 Braxton Miller/25 8.00 20.00
16 Jared Goff/15 60.00 125.00
17 Tajae Sharpe/25 10.00 25.00
18 Chris Moore/25 10.00 25.00
19 Cody Kessler/25 8.00 20.00
20 Christian Hackenberg
21 Ezekiel Elliott/20 150.00 300.00
22 Alex Collins/25 10.00 25.00
23 Cardale Jones/20 10.00 25.00
24 Kenyan Drake/25 12.00 30.00
25 Jonathan Williams/25 10.00 25.00

2016 Panini Flawless Rookie Patch Autographs
1 Jared Goff/20 100.00 200.00
2 Carson Wentz/20 300.00 500.00
3 Paxton Lynch/20 25.00 50.00
4 Christian Hackenberg/25 12.00 30.00
5 Connor Cook/25 15.00 40.00
6 Dak Prescott/25 75.00 150.00
7 Ezekiel Elliott/25 300.00 600.00
8 Derrick Henry/20 75.00 150.00
9 Devontae Booker/25 15.00 40.00
10 Paul Perkins/20 15.00 40.00
11 DeAndre Washington/25 12.00 30.00
12 Corey Coleman/25 20.00 50.00
13 Josh Doctson/25 15.00 40.00
14 Will Fuller V/25 20.00 50.00
15 Laquon Treadwell/25 15.00 40.00
16 Sterling Shepard/25 15.00 40.00
17 Michael Thomas/25 50.00 100.00
18 Tyler Boyd/25 15.00 40.00
19 Braxton Miller/25 12.00 30.00
20 Tajae Sharpe/25 15.00 40.00
21 Malcolm Mitchell/25 12.00 30.00
22 Cody Kessler/25 12.00 30.00
23 Joey Bosa/25 25.00 60.00
24 Hunter Henry/25 15.00 40.00
25 Jordan Howard/25 75.00 150.00

2016 Panini Flawless Rookie Patch Autographs Ruby
*RUBY/15: .5X TO 1.2X BASIC JSY AU/25

2016 Panini Flawless Rookie Patch Autographs Silver
*SILVER/15-20: .5X TO 1.2X BASIC JSY AU/25
6 Dak Prescott/15 100.00 200.00
7 Ezekiel Elliott/15 200.00 400.00

2016 Panini Flawless Rookie Patches
*RUBY/15: .5X TO 1.2X BASIC JSY/25
*SILVER/20: .5X TO 1.2X BASIC JSY/25
1 Chris Moore 6.00 15.00
2 Kenneth Dixon 5.00 12.00
3 Cardale Jones 5.00 12.00
4 Jordan Howard 10.00 25.00
5 Tyler Boyd 6.00 15.00
6 Cody Kessler 5.00 12.00
7 Corey Coleman 8.00 20.00
8 Dak Prescott 25.00 60.00
9 Ezekiel Elliott 25.00 60.00
10 Devontae Booker 6.00 15.00
11 Paxton Lynch 12.00 30.00
12 Braxton Miller 5.00 12.00
13 Will Fuller V 8.00 20.00
14 Jared Goff 15.00 40.00
15 Tyreek Hill 20.00 50.00
16 Leonte Carroo 5.00 12.00
17 Laquon Treadwell 6.00 15.00
18 Jacoby Brissett 6.00 15.00
19 Malcolm Mitchell 5.00 12.00
20 Michael Thomas 10.00 25.00
21 Paul Perkins 5.00 12.00
22 Sterling Shepard 10.00 25.00
23 Christian Hackenberg 5.00 12.00
24 Connor Cook 6.00 15.00
25 Carson Wentz 30.00 60.00
26 Wendell Smallwood 5.00 12.00
27 Joey Bosa 10.00 25.00
28 C.J. Prosise 5.00 12.00
29 Derrick Henry 12.00 30.00
30 Josh Doctson 6.00 15.00

2016 Panini Flawless Rookie Progression Signatures
*RUBY/15: .5X TO 1.2X BASIC AU/25
*RUBY/15: .4X TO 1X BASIC AU/20
*SILVER/15-20: .5X TO 1.2X BASIC AU/25
*SILVER/15-20: .4X TO 1X BASIC AU/20
1 Sterling Shepard/25 10.00 25.00
2 Michael Thomas/20 20.00 50.00
3 Corey Coleman/20 15.00 40.00
4 Laquon Treadwell/20 12.00 30.00
5 Tyler Boyd/25 10.00 25.00
7 Will Fuller V/20 15.00 40.00
8 Chris Moore/25 10.00 25.00
9 Josh Doctson/20 12.00 30.00
10 Trevor Davis/25 8.00 20.00
11 Pharoh Cooper/25 8.00 20.00
12 Demarcus Robinson/25 8.00 20.00
13 Ezekiel Elliott/20 150.00 300.00
14 Derrick Henry/15 25.00 60.00
15 Devontae Booker/20 12.00 30.00
16 C.J. Prosise/20 10.00 25.00
17 Paul Perkins/20 10.00 25.00
18 Kenyan Drake/20 15.00 40.00
19 Jordan Howard/20 25.00 60.00
20 Alex Collins/25 10.00 25.00
21 DeAndre Washington/25 8.00 20.00
22 Dak Prescott/25 60.00 125.00
23 Jared Goff/20 60.00 125.00
24 Carson Wentz/20 200.00 400.00
25 Paxton Lynch/15 25.00 60.00

2016 Panini Flawless Star Swatch Signatures
*RUBY/15: .5X TO 1.2X BASIC JSY AU/25
*SILVER/15-20: .5X TO 1.2X BASIC JSY AU/25
1 Allen Robinson/25 20.00 50.00
2 Golden Tate III/25 15.00 40.00

3 C.J. Anderson/15
3 C.J. Anderson/15
7 Todd Gurley II/25 25.00 60.00
8 David Johnson/25 25.00 60.00
9 Ryan Fitzpatrick/25 15.00 40.00
10 Mike Evans/25 20.00 50.00
14 Blake Bortles/15 20.00 50.00
15 Jamaal Charles/25 20.00 50.00

2016 Panini Flawless Triple Patches

*RUBY/15: .4X TO 1X BASIC JSY/20
1 Elltt/Prsctt/Brnt/20 40.00 100.00
2 Mnng/Bckhm/Shprd/20 12.00 30.00
4 Prsctt/Gff/Wntz/20 60.00 125.00
5 Gff/Cpr/Grly II/20 20.00 50.00
6 Wlsn/Rwls/Lcktt/15 15.00 40.00
8 Mrta/Hnry/Shrpe/20 15.00 40.00
9 Rbnsn/Brtls/Hrns/15 10.00 25.00
13 Nwtn/Bnjmn/Fnchss/20 12.00 30.00
16 Thms/Fllr/Shprd/20 12.00 30.00
17 Grn/Dltn/Byd/15 12.00 30.00

2017 Panini Flawless

1 Larry Fitzgerald 15.00 40.00
2 David Johnson 20.00 50.00
3 Carson Palmer 15.00 40.00
4 Matt Ryan 15.00 40.00
5 Julio Jones 20.00 50.00
6 Devonta Freeman 15.00 40.00
7 Joe Flacco 15.00 40.00
8 Alex Collins 12.00 30.00
9 Tyrod Taylor 15.00 40.00
10 LeSean McCoy 20.00 50.00
11 Nathan Peterman RC 8.00 20.00
12 Cam Newton 20.00 50.00
13 Kelvin Benjamin 15.00 40.00
14 Curtis Samuel RC 8.00 20.00
15 Tarik Cohen RC 12.00 30.00
16 Jordan Howard 20.00 50.00
17 Adam Shaheen 12.00 30.00
18 Andy Dalton 15.00 40.00
19 A.J. Green 20.00 50.00
20 David Njoku RC 8.00 20.00
21 Jabrill Peppers RC 10.00 25.00
22 Myles Garrett RC 20.00 50.00
23 Dak Prescott 20.00 50.00
24 Ezekiel Elliott 25.00 60.00
25 Jason Witten 15.00 40.00
26 Ryan Switzer RC 8.00 20.00
27 Brock Osweiler 12.00 30.00
28 C.J. Anderson 15.00 40.00
29 Von Miller 15.00 40.00
30 Matthew Stafford 15.00 40.00
31 Golden Tate III 12.00 30.00
32 Aaron Rodgers 40.00 100.00
33 Jimmy Garoppolo 100.00 200.00
34 Davante Adams 15.00 40.00
35 Jordy Nelson 15.00 40.00
36 D'Onta Foreman 15.00 40.00
37 DeAndre Hopkins 15.00 40.00
38 J.J. Watt 20.00 50.00
39 Andrew Luck 25.00 60.00
40 T.Y. Hilton 15.00 40.00
41 Marlon Mack RC 10.00 25.00
42 Blake Bortles 12.00 30.00
43 Dede Westbrook RC 6.00 15.00
44 Jalen Ramsey 12.00 30.00
45 Alex Smith 15.00 40.00
46 Tyreek Hill 20.00 50.00
47 Travis Kelce 20.00 50.00
48 Jared Goff 20.00 50.00
49 Todd Gurley II 20.00 50.00
50 Cooper Kupp RC 10.00 25.00
51 Philip Rivers 20.00 50.00
52 Melvin Gordon 15.00 40.00
53 Keenan Allen 15.00 40.00
54 Jay Ajayi 15.00 40.00
55 Jarvis Landry 15.00 40.00
56 Case Keenum 15.00 40.00
57 Adam Thielen 20.00 50.00
58 Tom Brady 100.00 200.00
59 Rob Gronkowski 20.00 50.00
60 Brandin Cooks 15.00 40.00
61 Drew Brees 20.00 50.00
62 Adrian Peterson 20.00 50.00
63 Michael Thomas 20.00 50.00
64 Eli Manning 15.00 40.00
65 Davis Webb RC 6.00 15.00
66 Sterling Shepard 15.00 40.00
67 Odell Beckham Jr. 20.00 50.00
68 Jermaine Kearse 12.00 30.00
69 ArDarius Stewart RC 6.00 15.00
70 Jamal Adams RC 6.00 15.00
71 Derek Carr 20.00 50.00
72 Marshawn Lynch 15.00 40.00
73 Amari Cooper 20.00 50.00
74 Khalil Mack 20.00 50.00
75 Carson Wentz 50.00 100.00
76 Alshon Jeffery 15.00 40.00
77 Mack Hollins RC 6.00 15.00
78 Ben Roethlisberger 20.00 50.00
79 R. Joshua Dobbs RC 8.00 20.00
80 Le'Veon Bell 15.00 40.00
81 JuJu Smith-Schuster RC 15.00 40.00
82 Antonio Brown 20.00 50.00
83 T.J. Watt RC 20.00 50.00
84 Carlos Hyde 12.00 30.00
85 C.J. Beathard RC 6.00 15.00
86 Joe Williams RC 6.00 15.00
87 Russell Wilson 25.00 60.00
88 Chris Carson 20.00 50.00
89 Doug Baldwin 15.00 40.00
90 Amara Darboh RC 6.00 15.00
91 Jameis Winston 15.00 40.00
92 Mike Evans 15.00 40.00
93 Chris Godwin RC 8.00 20.00
94 Marcus Mariota 20.00 50.00
95 DeMarco Murray 15.00 40.00
96 Derrick Henry 15.00 40.00
97 Taywan Taylor 12.00 30.00
98 Kirk Cousins 20.00 50.00
99 Aaron Jones RC 15.00 40.00
100 Josh Norman 12.00 30.00
101 Otto Graham 15.00 40.00
102 Walter Payton 40.00 100.00
103 Jim Taylor 15.00 40.00
104 Art Shell 20.00 50.00
105 Reggie White 20.00 50.00
106 Johnny Unitas 30.00 80.00
107 Red Grange 25.00 60.00
108 Jerry Rice 30.00 80.00
109 Drew Bledsoe 15.00 40.00
110 Lawrence Taylor 20.00 50.00
111 Joe Montana 50.00 125.00
112 Peyton Manning 40.00 100.00
113 Barry Sanders 30.00 80.00
114 Brett Favre 40.00 100.00
115 John Elway 30.00 80.00
116 Dan Marino 40.00 100.00
117 Emmitt Smith 30.00 80.00
118 Brian Dawkins 12.00 30.00
119 Lance Alworth 15.00 40.00
120 Terry Bradshaw 30.00 80.00
121 Tony Gonzalez 15.00 40.00
122 Randy Moss 15.00 40.00
123 Bo Jackson 25.00 60.00
124 Jerome Bettis 20.00 50.00
125 Zach Thomas 15.00 40.00
126 Charles Woodson 20.00 50.00
127 Michael Vick 15.00 40.00
128 Chris Spielman 15.00 40.00
129 Jason Taylor 12.00 30.00
130 Ty Law 20.00 50.00
131 Mitchell Trubisky AU RC 150.00 300.00
132 Patrick Mahomes II AU RC 800.00 1400.00
133 Deshaun Watson AU RC 200.00 400.00
134 DeShone Kizer AU RC 8.00 20.00
135 Alvin Kamara AU RC 60.00 125.00
136 Leonard Fournette AU RC 75.00 150.00
137 Dalvin Cook AU RC 50.00 100.00
138 Christian McCaffrey AU RC 50.00 100.00
139 Joe Mixon AU RC 15.00 40.00
140 Kareem Hunt AU RC 25.00 50.00
141 James Conner AU RC 15.00 40.00
142 Jamaal Williams AU RC 8.00 20.00
143 Samaje Perine AU RC 8.00 20.00
144 O.J. Howard AU RC 10.00 25.00
145 Evan Engram AU RC 10.00 25.00
146 Mike Williams AU RC 15.00 40.00
147 Corey Davis AU RC 12.00 30.00
148 John Ross III AU RC 10.00 25.00
149 Zay Jones AU RC 10.00 25.00
150 Kenny Golladay AU RC 12.00 30.00

2017 Panini Flawless Sapphire

*VETS/15: .4X TO 1X BASIC CARDS
*ROOKIES/15: .4X TO 1X BASIC CARDS
*ROOK JSY AU/15: .4X TO 1X BASIC CARDS
132 Patrick Mahomes II AU 800.00 1400.00

2017 Panini Flawless 1st Round Gems Autographs

*RUBY/15: .5X TO 1.2X BASIC AU/25
*SILVER/20: .5X TO 1.2X BASIC AU/25
3 Ed Too Tall Jones/25 12.00 30.00
6 Lawrence Taylor/25 20.00 50.00
10 Rod Woodson/25 15.00 40.00
11 Tim Brown/25 20.00 50.00
20 LaDainian Tomlinson/25 15.00 40.00

2017 Panini Flawless All Pro Ink

*RUBY/15: .5X TO 1.2X BASIC AU/25
*SILVER/20: .5X TO 1.2X BASIC AU/25
4 Lawrence Taylor/15 25.00 60.00
7 Bob Lilly/15 20.00 50.00
10 Randy White/15 20.00 50.00
12 Jack Ham/15 40.00 80.00
14 James Harrison/15 30.00 60.00
15 Alan Page/25 12.00 30.00
18 Rod Woodson/25 15.00 40.00
22 Larry Allen/25 20.00 50.00
24 Zach Thomas/25 40.00 80.00
25 Brian Dawkins/25 50.00 100.00
26 Ted Hendricks/15 15.00 40.00

2017 Panini Flawless Distinguished Patch Autographs

4 Troy Aikman/15 75.00 150.00
6 Dan Marino/15 150.00 250.00
7 Jim Kelly/15 30.00 80.00
10 Mike Alstott/20 40.00 100.00
11 Roger Craig/25 20.00 50.00
12 Barry Sanders/15 200.00 350.00
14 Marcus Allen/25 20.00 50.00
15 LaDainian Tomlinson/20 100.00 200.00
16 Earl Campbell/15 50.00 100.00
17 Joe Theismann/25 25.00 60.00
19 Jerome Bettis/15 60.00 125.00
20 John Riggins/15 25.00 60.00
22 Jerry Rice/15 100.00 200.00
24 Tony Dorsett/15 50.00 100.00
25 Andre Reed/25 20.00 50.00

2017 Panini Flawless Dual Patch Autographs

*RUBY/15: .5X TO 1.2X BASIC JSY AU/25
*SILVER/15-20: .5X TO 1.2X BASIC JSY AU/25
*SILVER/15-20: X TO X BASIC JSY AU
1 Brett Keisel/25 15.00 40.00
2 Edgerrin James/15 25.00 60.00
3 Clinton Portis/15 20.00 50.00
4 Steve Largent/15 30.00 80.00
6 Bob Lilly/25 20.00 50.00
8 Adam Vinatieri/15 20.00 50.00
10 Tedy Bruschi/20 50.00 100.00
12 Tevin Coleman/25 20.00 50.00
14 Latavius Murray/25 15.00 40.00
15 Melvin Gordon/25 20.00 50.00
16 Roger Craig/25 20.00 50.00
20 Tyler Lockett/25 20.00 50.00
21 Greg Olsen/15 25.00 60.00
22 Robert Kelley/15 20.00 50.00
23 C.J. Anderson/15 25.00 60.00
24 Priest Holmes/15 20.00 50.00

2017 Panini Flawless Flawless Penmanship

*RUBY/15: .5X TO 1.2X BASIC AU/25
*SILVER/20: .5X TO 1.2X BASIC AU/25
6 Warren Moon/25 20.00 50.00
17 Bob Griese/25 20.00 50.00
19 Dak Prescott/25 40.00 80.00
23 Thurman Thomas/25 15.00 40.00
25 Jim Kelly/25 20.00 50.00

2017 Panini Flawless Flawless Rookie Signatures

*RUBY/15: .5X TO 1.2X BASIC AU/25
*RUBY/15: .4X TO 1X BASIC AU/20
*SILVER/15-20: .5X TO 1.2X BASIC AU/25
*SILVER/15-20: .4X TO 1X BASIC AU/20
1 Mitchell Trubisky/20 100.00 200.00
2 Deshaun Watson/20 150.00 250.00
3 DeShone Kizer/20 8.00 20.00
4 Patrick Mahomes II/20 500.00 1000.00
5 Nathan Peterman/20 10.00 25.00
6 Dalvin Cook/20 40.00 80.00
7 Leonard Fournette/20 60.00 125.00
8 Christian McCaffrey/20 50.00 100.00
9 Kareem Hunt/25 15.00 40.00
10 Joe Mixon/20 15.00 40.00
11 Samaje Perine/25 6.00 15.00
12 James Conner/20 15.00 40.00
13 Alvin Kamara/20 90.00 150.00
14 C.J. Beathard/20 8.00 20.00
15 O.J. Howard/20 10.00 25.00
16 Evan Engram/20 10.00 25.00
17 Dede Westbrook/25 6.00 15.00
18 Carlos Henderson/25 6.00 15.00
19 Corey Davis/20 12.00 30.00
20 JuJu Smith-Schuster/25 30.00 60.00
21 Curtis Samuel/25 8.00 20.00
22 Taywan Taylor/25 6.00 15.00
23 Zay Jones/20 10.00 25.00
24 Kenny Golladay/20 12.00 30.00
25 T.J. Watt/25 30.00 60.00

2017 Panini Flawless Flawless Signatures

*RUBY/15: .5X TO 1.2X BASIC AU/25
*SILVER/15-20: .5X TO 1.2X BASIC AU/25
*SILVER/15-20: .4X TO 1X BASIC AU/15
1 Ricky Williams/15 40.00 80.00
2 Brett Keisel/25 12.00 30.00
4 Stefon Diggs/25 15.00 40.00
6 Priest Holmes/15 15.00 40.00
8 Dan Bailey/25 12.00 30.00
9 Ed McCaffrey/15 15.00 40.00
10 Brian Bosworth/15 20.00 50.00
13 Mike Alstott/15 15.00 40.00
16 Carlos Hyde/25 12.00 30.00
25 Tyler Lockett/15 20.00 50.00
26 Sterling Shepard/15 20.00 50.00
27 Adam Vinatieri/25 12.00 30.00

2017 Panini Flawless Hall of Fame Autographs

*RUBY/15: .5X TO 1.2X BASIC AU/25
*SILVER/20: .5X TO 1.2X BASIC AU/25
1 Morten Andersen/25 12.00 30.00
8 Andre Reed/25 15.00 40.00
13 Rod Woodson/25 15.00 40.00

2017 Panini Flawless Patch Autographs

*RUBY/15: .5X TO 1.2X BASIC JSY AU/25
*SILVER/20: .5X TO 1.2X BASIC JSY AU/25
*SILVER/15: X TO X BASIC JSY AU/15-20
1 Brett Keisel/25 15.00 40.00
27 Terrelle Pryor Sr./20 20.00 50.00
29 Latavius Murray/25 15.00 40.00
30 Carlos Hyde/20 20.00 50.00
40 Tyler Lockett/25 20.00 50.00
41 Greg Olsen/25 20.00 50.00
45 James Harrison/15 100.00 200.00
46 Jim Plunkett/15 25.00 60.00
40 Stefon Diggs/25 20.00 50.00
51 Priest Holmes/20 20.00 50.00
53 Andre Reed/20 25.00 60.00
61 Tyreek Hill/20 30.00 80.00
70 Ricky Williams/15 50.00 100.00
72 Sterling Shepard/20 25.00 60.00
73 Jordan Howard/20 30.00 80.00

2017 Panini Flawless Patches

*RUBY/15: .5X TO 1.2X BASIC JSY/25
*SILVER/15: .5X TO 1.2X BASIC JSY/25
*SILVER/15: .4X TO 1X BASIC JSY/15
1 Allen Hurns/25 6.00 15.00
2 Amari Cooper/15 12.00 30.00
3 Andy Dalton/25 8.00 20.00
4 Antonio Brown/15 12.00 30.00
5 Brett Keisel/15 8.00 20.00
6 Carson Wentz/15 15.00 40.00
7 Chris Thompson/25 6.00 15.00
8 Curtis Martin/15 10.00 25.00
9 Dak Prescott/25 10.00 25.00
10 David Johnson/15 12.00 30.00
11 DeAndre Hopkins/15 10.00 25.00
12 Doug Baldwin/25 8.00 20.00
13 Ed Reed/15 10.00 25.00
14 Edgerrin James/15 10.00 25.00
15 Eric Berry/15 10.00 25.00
16 Ezekiel Elliott/25 12.00 30.00
17 Howie Long/15 12.00 30.00
18 Hunter Henry/25 6.00 15.00
19 Jadeveon Clowney/25 6.00 15.00
20 Jameis Winston/15 10.00 25.00
21 Jared Goff/25 10.00 25.00
22 Jarvis Landry/25 8.00 20.00
23 Jerome Bettis/15 20.00 40.00
24 Terrell Davis/15 10.00 25.00
25 Ronnie Lott/25 8.00 20.00
26 Joe Namath/15 15.00 40.00
27 Joey Bosa/25 10.00 25.00
28 Jordan Howard/25 10.00 25.00
29 Khalil Mack/25 10.00 25.00
30 Lawrence Taylor/15 25.00 50.00
31 LeSean McCoy/25 10.00 25.00
32 Marcus Mariota/25 10.00 25.00
33 John Riggins/15 10.00 25.00
34 Mark Ingram/25 8.00 20.00
35 Matt Forte/15 8.00 20.00
36 Michael Thomas/25 10.00 25.00
37 Michael Vick/15 10.00 25.00
39 Odell Beckham Jr./15 12.00 30.00
41 Ricky Williams/15 10.00 25.00
42 Russell Wilson/15 15.00 40.00
44 Terry Bradshaw/15 20.00 50.00
45 Todd Gurley II/25 10.00 25.00
46 Tony Gonzalez/15 10.00 25.00
47 Tony Romo/25 8.00 20.00
48 Tyrod Taylor/15 10.00 25.00
49 Walter Payton/15 40.00 80.00
50 Will Fuller V/25 6.00 15.00

2017 Panini Flawless Premium Ink

*RUBY/15: .5X TO 1.2X BASIC AU/25
*SILVER/15-20: .5X TO 1.2X BASIC AU/25
*SILVER/15-20: .4X TO 1X BASIC AU/15-20
4 Kirk Cousins/15 25.00 60.00
7 Jordy Nelson/15 20.00 50.00
9 Jordan Howard/25 20.00 50.00
15 Terrelle Pryor Sr./25 12.00 30.00
20 Doug Baldwin/25 15.00 40.00
21 Michael Bennett/25 12.00 30.00
22 C.J. Anderson/25 15.00 40.00
23 Tyreek Hill/25 20.00 50.00
24 Melvin Gordon/20 20.00 50.00
25 Joey Bosa/20 25.00 60.00
28 Ben Roethlisberger/15 90.00 150.00
35 Cooper Kupp/25 10.00 25.00
36 Christian McCaffrey/25 40.00 80.00
37 O.J. Howard/25 8.00 20.00
38 Kenny Golladay/25 10.00 25.00
39 Leonard Fournette/25 50.00 100.00
40 Dalvin Cook/25 30.00 60.00

2017 Panini Flawless Rookie Autographs

*RUBY/15: .5X TO 1.2X BASIC AU/25
*RUBY/15: .4X TO 1X BASIC AU/20
*SILVER/15-20: .5X TO 1.2X BASIC AU/25
*SILVER/15-20: X TO X BASIC AU/20
1 Mitchell Trubisky/20 100.00 200.00
2 Deshaun Watson/20 150.00 250.00
3 DeShone Kizer/20 8.00 20.00
4 Patrick Mahomes II/20 500.00 1000.00
5 Dalvin Cook/20 40.00 80.00
6 Leonard Fournette/20 60.00 125.00
7 Christian McCaffrey/20 50.00 100.00
8 Alvin Kamara/20 90.00 150.00
9 Kareem Hunt/25 15.00 40.00
10 D'Onta Foreman/20 10.00 25.00
11 Samaje Perine/25 6.00 15.00
12 Wayne Gallman/20 10.00 25.00
13 Jamaal Williams/25 6.00 15.00
14 Taywan Taylor/25 6.00 15.00
15 O.J. Howard/20 10.00 25.00
16 Evan Engram/25 8.00 20.00
17 Mike Williams/20 12.00 30.00
18 John Ross III/20 10.00 25.00
19 Corey Davis/20 12.00 30.00
20 JuJu Smith-Schuster/20 40.00 80.00
21 Curtis Samuel/20 10.00 25.00
22 Mack Hollins/20 8.00 20.00
23 Cooper Kupp/20 12.00 30.00
24 Zay Jones/20 10.00 25.00
25 Kenny Golladay/20 12.00 30.00

2017 Panini Flawless Rookie Patch Autographs

1 Mitchell Trubisky 100.00 200.00
2 Deshaun Watson 150.00 300.00
3 DeShone Kizer 12.00 30.00
4 Patrick Mahomes II 900.00 1400.00
5 Nathan Peterman 15.00 40.00
6 R. Joshua Dobbs 15.00 40.00
7 C.J. Beathard 12.00 30.00
8 T.J. Watt 40.00 100.00
9 Dalvin Cook 50.00 100.00
10 Leonard Fournette 50.00 100.00
11 Christian McCaffrey 40.00 80.00
12 Joe Mixon 25.00 60.00
13 Alvin Kamara 100.00 200.00
14 Kareem Hunt 25.00 60.00
16 James Conner 25.00 60.00
17 Jamaal Williams 12.00 30.00
18 Joe Williams 12.00 30.00
19 O.J. Howard 15.00 40.00
20 Mike Williams 20.00 50.00
21 John Ross III 15.00 40.00
22 Corey Davis 20.00 50.00
23 Cooper Kupp 20.00 50.00
24 Zay Jones 15.00 40.00
25 Kenny Golladay 20.00 50.00

2017 Panini Flawless Rookie Patch Autographs Ruby

*RUBY/15: .5X TO 1.2X BASIC JSY AU/25
2 Deshaun Watson 400.00 800.00
4 Patrick Mahomes II 600.00 1000.00

2017 Panini Flawless Rookie Patch Autographs Silver

*SILVER/20: .5X TO 1.2X BASIC JSY AU
2 Deshaun Watson 400.00 800.00
4 Patrick Mahomes II 600.00 1000.00

2017 Panini Flawless Rookie Patches

*SILVER/20: .5X TO 1.2X BASIC JSY/25
*RUBY/15: .5X TO 1.2X BASIC JSY/25
1 Alvin Kamara 20.00 50.00
2 Chris Godwin 8.00 20.00
3 Christian McCaffrey 12.00 30.00
4 C.J. Beathard 6.00 15.00
5 Cooper Kupp 10.00 25.00
6 Corey Davis 10.00 25.00
7 Curtis Samuel 8.00 20.00
8 Dalvin Cook 12.00 30.00
9 David Njoku 8.00 20.00
10 Deshaun Watson 25.00 60.00
11 DeShone Kizer 6.00 15.00
12 D'Onta Foreman 8.00 20.00
13 Evan Engram 8.00 20.00
14 Jabrill Peppers 10.00 25.00
15 James Conner 12.00 30.00
16 Joe Mixon 12.00 30.00
17 John Ross III 8.00 20.00
18 JuJu Smith-Schuster 12.00 30.00
19 Kareem Hunt 12.00 30.00
20 Kenny Golladay 10.00 25.00
21 Leonard Fournette 15.00 40.00
22 Matt Breida 10.00 25.00
23 Mike Williams 10.00 25.00
24 Mitchell Trubisky 20.00 50.00
25 O.J. Howard 8.00 20.00
26 Patrick Mahomes II 60.00 125.00
27 R. Joshua Dobbs 8.00 20.00
28 Ryan Switzer 8.00 20.00
29 T.J. Watt 12.00 30.00
30 Zay Jones 8.00 20.00

2017 Panini Flawless Star Swatch Signatures

*RUBY/15: .5X TO 1.2X BASIC JSY AU/25
*SILVER/20: .5X TO 1.2X BASIC JSY AU/25
*SILVER/15: .4X TO 1X BASIC JSY AU/20
1 Dak Prescott/15 30.00 80.00
3 Carson Wentz/15 150.00 250.00
4 Tyreek Hill/15 30.00 80.00
5 Sterling Shepard/15 25.00 60.00
6 Jordan Howard/15 30.00 80.00
11 Adam Vinatieri/15 20.00 50.00
12 Jordy Nelson/15 25.00 60.00
16 Terrelle Pryor Sr./20 20.00 50.00
19 Latavius Murray/25 15.00 40.00
20 Carlos Hyde/20 20.00 50.00
25 Derek Carr/15 50.00 100.00

2018 Panini Flawless Distinguished Patch Autographs

*RUDY/15: .5X TO 1.2X BASIC JSY AU/25
*SILVER/20: .5X TO 1.2X BASIC JSY AU/25
2 Barry Sanders/15
3 Jerome Bettis/15 30.00 80.00
4 Steve Young/15 75.00 150.00
5 Steven Jackson/25 20.00 50.00
7 Brian Urlacher/15
11 John Elway/15 200.00 300.00
13 Dan Marino/15 200.00 300.00
16 Drew Bledsoe/25 60.00 125.00
18 John Randle/25 40.00 80.00
19 John Riggins/15 25.00 60.00
20 Michael Vick/25 20.00 50.00
21 Marcus Allen/25 25.00 60.00
22 Ty Law/20 30.00 80.00
23 Keyshawn Johnson/20 25.00 60.00
24 Joe Namath/15 75.00 150.00

2018 Panini Flawless Dual Diamond Memorabilia

*SILVER/15: .4X TO 1X BASIC JSY/20
1 C.Kirk/J.Rosen 15.00 40.00
2 N.Chubb/B.Mayfield 50.00 125.00
3 B.Chubb/R.Freeman 12.00 30.00
4 K.Lauletta/S.Barkley 40.00 100.00
6 J.Namath/S.Darnold 30.00 80.00
7 J.Kelly/J.Allen 20.00 50.00
8 J.Jones/C.Ridley 15.00 40.00
9 S.Michel/J.White 15.00 40.00
11 J.Goff/T.Gurley II 12.00 30.00
12 B.Sanders/S.Barkley 40.00 100.00
13 A.Jeffery/C.Wentz 15.00 40.00
14 P.Mahomes II/T.Hill 20.00 50.00
15 K.Cousins/A.Thielen 12.00 30.00
16 A.Kamara/D.Brees 12.00 30.00
17 D.Adams/A.Rodgers 15.00 40.00
18 K.Johnson/M.Stafford 12.00 30.00
19 D.Hopkins/D.Watson 15.00 40.00
20 A.Miller/M.Trubisky 12.00 30.00

2018 Panini Flawless Dual Patch Autographs

1 Aaron Rodgers
2 Rob Gronkowski
3 Derek Carr 30.00 80.00
4 Drew Brees
5 Jason Taylor 25.00 60.00
6 Kirk Cousins 50.00 100.00
7 Cris Carter
9 Carson Wentz
10 Ben Roethlisberger
11 Jared Goff 100.00 200.00
12 Patrick Mahomes II 250.00 500.00
13 Dan Marino 200.00 300.00
14 Danny White 20.00 50.00
15 Devin Hester 25.00 60.00
16 Ricky Williams 25.00 60.00
17 Steve Largent
20 Chris Thompson 20.00 50.00
21 Corey Davis 25.00 60.00
22 DeAndre Hopkins 25.00 60.00
23 Andrew Luck 125.00 250.00
24 JuJu Smith-Schuster
25 Matthew Stafford
26 Matt Ryan
27 Peyton Barber
28 Ryan Kerrigan 20.00 50.00
29 Russell Wilson

2018 Panini Flawless Flawless Rookie Signatures

1 Shaquem Griffin/25 10.00 25.00
2 Roquan Smith/25 20.00 50.00
3 Denzel Ward/25 15.00 40.00
4 Minkah Fitzpatrick/25 12.00 30.00
5 Anthony Miller/15 12.00 30.00
6 Baker Mayfield/25
7 Bradley Chubb/15 12.00 30.00
8 Calvin Ridley/15 20.00 50.00
9 Christian Kirk/15 12.00 30.00
10 Courtland Sutton/15 12.00 30.00
11 D.J. Moore /15 15.00 40.00
12 Ito Smith/25 8.00 20.00
13 James Washington/15 15.00 40.00
14 Jaylen Samuels/25 8.00 20.00
15 Josh Allen/15
16 Josh Rosen/25 40.00 80.00
17 Lamar Jackson/25 75.00 150.00
18 Nick Mullens/25 20.00 50.00
19 Michael Gallup/15 15.00 40.00
20 Nyheim Hines/25 8.00 20.00
21 Royce Freeman/15 10.00 25.00
22 Sam Darnold/25 125.00 250.00
23 Saquon Barkley/25 150.00 300.00
24 Sony Michel/15 25.00 60.00
25 Tre'Quan Smith/25 10.00 25.00

2018 Panini Flawless Flawless Rookie Signatures Ruby

*RUBY/15: .5X TO 1.2X BASIC AU/25
23 Saquon Barkley/15 200.00 400.00

2018 Panini Flawless Flawless Rookie Signatures Silver

*SILVER/20: .5X TO 1.2X BASIC AU/25
23 Saquon Barkley/20 200.00 400.00

2018 Panini Flawless Greats Autographs

*SILVER/15: .4X TO 1X BASIC AU/20
4 Bill Romanowski/20 20.00 50.00
7 Bob Lilly/20 20.00 50.00
13 Chris Spielman/20 15.00 40.00
14 Christian Okoye/20 15.00 40.00
17 Dallas Clark/20 15.00 40.00
19 Dante Hall/20 15.00 40.00
20 Daryl Johnston/20 20.00 50.00
26 Isaac Bruce/20 25.00 60.00
27 Jack Youngblood/20 15.00 40.00
31 Jim Plunkett/20 20.00 50.00
38 Mike Alstott/20 15.00 40.00
39 Reggie Wayne/20 20.00 50.00
41 Randy White/20 20.00 50.00
42 Robert Smith/20 15.00 40.00
47 Tom Rathman/20 15.00 40.00
50 Zach Thomas/20 20.00 50.00

2018 Panini Flawless Hall of Fame Autographs

1 Brian Dawkins/20 25.00 60.00
6 Jason Taylor/20 20.00 50.00
7 LaDainian Tomlinson/20 20.00 50.00
11 Tim Brown/20 25.00 60.00
12 Charles Haley/20 25.00 60.00
18 Rod Woodson/20 25.00 60.00

2018 Panini Flawless Rookie Patches

*SILVER/20: .5X TO 1.2X BASIC JSY/25
*RUBY/15: .5X TO 1.2X BASIC JSY/25
1 Saquon Barkley 40.00 80.00
2 Josh Allen 15.00 40.00
3 Baker Mayfield 40.00 80.00
4 Sam Darnold 25.00 60.00
5 Lamar Jackson 25.00 60.00
6 Mason Rudolph 12.00 30.00
7 Josh Rosen 12.00 30.00
8 Michael Gallup 12.00 30.00
9 Calvin Ridley 12.00 30.00
10 Christian Kirk 10.00 25.00
11 James Washington 12.00 30.00
12 Bradley Chubb 10.00 25.00
13 Kerryon Johnson 10.00 25.00
14 D.J. Moore 12.00 30.00
15 Sony Michel 12.00 30.00
16 Nick Chubb 12.00 30.00
17 Rashaad Penny 10.00 25.00
18 Courtland Sutton 10.00 25.00
19 Derrius Guice 12.00 30.00
20 Royce Freeman 8.00 20.00
21 Dante Pettis 10.00 25.00
22 Marquez Valdes-Scantling 8.00 20.00
23 Mike White 8.00 20.00
24 Kyle Lauletta 10.00 25.00
25 Anthony Miller 10.00 25.00
26 Shaquem Griffin 10.00 25.00
27 Tre'Quan Smith 10.00 25.00
28 Nyheim Hines 8.00 20.00
29 Ronald Jones II 12.00 30.00
30 Keke Coutee 8.00 20.00

2018 Panini Flawless Star Swatch Signatures

*RUBY/15: .5X TO 1.2X BASIC JSY AU/25
*SILVER/20: .5X TO 1.2X BASIC JSY AU/25
1 A.J. Green/25 25.00 60.00
2 Aaron Donald/25 25.00 60.00
3 J.J. Watt/15 60.00 125.00
4 Andrew Luck/15 125.00 250.00
8 Christian McCaffrey/25 25.00 60.00
9 Cooper Kupp/25 20.00 50.00
13 Derek Carr/25 25.00 60.00
15 Jared Goff/15 100.00 200.00
16 Jay Ajayi/25 20.00 50.00
21 Rob Gronkowski/15 60.00 125.00
24 T.J. Watt/25 20.00 50.00

2018 Panini Flawless Collegiate

1 Aaron Rodgers 25.00 60.00
2 Adrian Peterson 12.00 30.00
3 Andrew Luck 15.00 40.00
5 Anthony Miller 12.00 30.00
6 Baker Mayfield 80.00 200.00
7 Barry Sanders 20.00 50.00
10 Billy Sims 10.00 25.00
11 Bo Jackson 15.00 40.00
12 Bradley Chubb 12.00 30.00
13 Brett Favre 25.00 60.00
14 Brian Bosworth 10.00 25.00
15 Calvin Ridley 20.00 50.00
17 Chris Spielman 8.00 20.00
18 Christian Kirk 12.00 30.00
20 Christian McCaffrey 12.00 30.00
21 Clay Matthews 10.00 25.00
23 Courtland Sutton 12.00 30.00
24 Cris Carter 12.00 30.00
25 Dak Prescott 12.00 30.00
26 Dan Marino 25.00 60.00
28 Denzel Ward 20.00 50.00
29 Derrius Guice 15.00 40.00
30 Derwin James 15.00 40.00
31 D.J. Chark Jr. 10.00 25.00
32 D.J. Moore 15.00 40.00
34 Ed Reed 10.00 25.00
35 Eddie George 10.00 25.00
36 Ezekiel Elliott 25.00 50.00
37 Fran Tarkenton 12.00 30.00
38 Frank Gore 10.00 25.00
40 Herschel Walker 12.00 30.00
41 James Washington 15.00 40.00
44 Jim Plunkett 10.00 25.00
46 Joe Namath 15.00 40.00
47 John Elway 20.00 50.00
49 Josh Allen 30.00 80.00
51 Josh Rosen 25.00 60.00
52 Julio Jones 12.00 30.00
60 Lamar Jackson 50.00 125.00
64 Marcus Allen 12.00 30.00
66 Mason Rudolph 20.00 50.00
67 Michael Irvin 12.00 30.00
72 Nick Chubb 25.00 60.00
73 Nick Saban 100.00 200.00
74 Nyheim Hines 10.00 25.00
76 Peyton Manning 40.00 80.00
77 Rashaad Penny 12.00 30.00
78 Ray Lewis 25.00 50.00
80 Ronald Jones II 8.00 20.00
81 Ronnie Lott 10.00 25.00
82 Roquan Smith 25.00 60.00
84 Russell Wilson 15.00 40.00
85 Sam Bradford 8.00 20.00
86 Sam Darnold 50.00 125.00
87 Saquon Barkley 75.00 150.00
89 Sony Michel 25.00 60.00
91 Terrell Davis 10.00 25.00
93 Tim Tebow 12.00 30.00
94 Todd Gurley II 12.00 30.00
95 Tom Brady 100.00 200.00
97 Tremaine Edmunds 15.00 40.00
101 Josh Rosen JSY AU RC 50.00 100.00
102 Sam Darnold JSY AU RC 60.00 125.00
103 Josh Allen JSY AU RC 40.00 80.00
105 Baker Mayfield JSY AU RC 100.00 200.00
106 Saquon Barkley JSY AU RC 200.00 400.00
107 Derrius Guice JSY AU RC 12.00 30.00
108 D.J. Moore JSY AU RC 12.00 30.00
109 Hayden Hurst JSY AU RC 8.00 20.00
110 Nick Chubb JSY AU RC 30.00 60.00
111 Mason Rudolph JSY AU RC 15.00 40.00
112 Ronald Jones II JSY AU RC 6.00 15.00
113 Christian Kirk JSY AU RC 10.00 25.00
114 Calvin Ridley JSY AU RC 60.00 125.00
115 James Washington JSY AU RC 12.00 30.00
116 Courtland Sutton JSY AU RC 10.00 25.00
117 Deon Cain JSY AU RC 8.00 20.00
118 Simmie Cobbs Jr. JSY AU RC 10.00 25.00
119 Dante Pettis JSY AU RC 10.00 25.00
120 D.J. Chark Jr. JSY AU RC 8.00 20.00
121 Allen Lazard JSY AU RC 6.00 15.00
122 Anthony Miller JSY AU RC 10.00 25.00
123 Luke Falk JSY AU RC 8.00 20.00
124 Rashaad Penny JSY AU RC 10.00 25.00
126 Nyheim Hines JSY AU RC 8.00 20.00
127 Deontay Burnett JSY AU RC 8.00 20.00
128 Michael Gallup JSY AU RC 12.00 30.00
129 Josh Adams JSY AU RC 12.00 30.00
130 Kerryon Johnson JSY AU RC 10.00 25.00
131 Trey Quinn JSY AU RC 6.00 15.00
132 Sony Michel JSY AU RC 20.00 50.00
133 Auden Tate JSY AU RC 6.00 15.00
134 Royce Freeman JSY AU RC 8.00 20.00
135 John Kelly JSY AU RC 8.00 20.00
136 Bo Scarbrough JSY AU RC 8.00 20.00
137 J.T. Barrett JSY AU RC 10.00 25.00
138 Marcell Ateman JSY AU RC 8.00 20.00
139 Akrum Wadley JSY AU RC 6.00 15.00
141 Mark Andrews JSY AU RC 10.00 25.00
142 Jaylen Samuels JSY AU RC 8.00 20.00
143 Kalen Ballage JSY AU RC 8.00 20.00
144 Kamryn Pettway JSY AU RC 10.00 25.00
145 J'Mon Moore JSY AU RC 6.00 15.00
147 Robert Foster JSY AU RC 6.00 15.00
148 Kurt Benkert JSY AU RC 8.00 20.00
149 Riley Ferguson JSY AU RC 10.00 25.00
150 Deon Cain JSY AU RC 8.00 20.00
151 Nick Chubb JSY AU RC 30.00 60.00
152 Sony Michel JSY AU RC 20.00 50.00
153 D.J. Chark Jr. JSY AU RC 8.00 20.00
154 Derrius Guice JSY AU RC 12.00 30.00
155 Nyheim Hines JSY AU RC 8.00 20.00
156 DaeSean Hamilton JSY AU RC 8.00 20.00
157 Nic Shimonek JSY AU RC 10.00 25.00
158 John Kelly JSY AU RC 8.00 20.00
159 Christian Kirk JSY AU RC 10.00 25.00
160 Mason Rudolph JSY AU RC 15.00 40.00
161 James Washington JSY AU RC 12.00 30.00
162 Josh Rosen JSY AU RC 50.00 100.00
163 Sam Darnold JSY AU RC 60.00 125.00
164 Saquon Barkley JSY AU RC 200.00 400.00
165 Baker Mayfield JSY AU RC 100.00 200.00
167 Chase Litton JSY AU RC 8.00 20.00
168 Mike White JSY AU RC 8.00 20.00
170 Josh Allen JSY AU RC 40.00 80.00

2016 Panini Gala

1 Andrew Luck 5.00 12.00
2 Tom Brady
3 Todd Gurley 4.00 10.00
4 Joe Flacco 3.00 8.00
5 DeMarco Murray 3.00 8.00
6 A.J. Green 4.00 10.00
7 Matt Ryan 3.00 8.00
8 Allen Robinson 3.00 8.00
9 Tyrod Taylor 3.00 8.00
10 Aaron Rodgers 8.00 20.00
11 Demaryius Thomas 3.00 8.00
12 Ryan Tannehill 3.00 8.00
13 Larry Fitzgerald 3.00 8.00
14 Isaiah Crowell 2.50 6.00
15 Derek Carr 4.00 10.00
16 Russell Wilson 5.00 12.00
17 Ryan Fitzpatrick 2.50 6.00
18 Jason Witten 3.00 8.00
19 Matthew Stafford 3.00 8.00
20 Ben Roethlisberger 4.00 10.00
21 Colin Kaepernick 3.00 8.00
22 Travis Kelce 4.00 10.00
23 Steve Smith Sr. 3.00 8.00
24 Kirk Cousins 4.00 10.00
25 J.J. Watt 4.00 10.00
26 Danny Woodhead 3.00 8.00
27 Adrian Peterson 4.00 10.00
28 Andy Dalton 3.00 8.00
29 Eddie Lacy 2.50 6.00
30 T.Y. Hilton 3.00 8.00
31 Devonta Freeman 3.00 8.00
32 Travis Benjamin 2.50 6.00
33 Peyton Manning 8.00 20.00
34 Odell Beckham Jr. 4.00 10.00
35 Julian Edelman 4.00 10.00
36 Drew Brees 4.00 10.00
37 Brandon Marshall 2.50 6.00
38 Sam Bradford 2.50 6.00
39 Alex Smith 3.00 8.00
40 Alshon Jeffery 3.00 8.00
41 Lamar Miller 2.50 6.00
42 DeSean Jackson 3.00 8.00
43 Blake Bortles 2.50 6.00
44 Jonathan Stewart 2.50 6.00
45 Sammy Watkins 4.00 10.00
46 Jameis Winston 4.00 10.00
47 Antonio Brown 4.00 10.00
48 Kendall Wright 2.50 6.00
49 Tony Romo 3.00 8.00
50 Thomas Rawls 2.50 6.00
51 Tyler Eifert 3.00 8.00
52 Amari Cooper 4.00 10.00
53 Teddy Bridgewater 3.00 8.00
54 DeAndre Hopkins 3.00 8.00
55 Jordy Nelson 3.00 8.00
56 Emmanuel Sanders 4.00 10.00
57 Golden Tate 2.50 6.00
58 Jarvis Landry 3.00 8.00
59 Julio Jones 4.00 10.00
60 Philip Rivers 4.00 10.00
61 Brandin Cooks 3.00 8.00
62 Rob Gronkowski 4.00 10.00
63 Jay Cutler 2.50 6.00
64 Latavius Murray 2.50 6.00
65 Carson Palmer 3.00 8.00
66 Le'Veon Bell 3.00 8.00
67 Mike Evans 3.00 8.00
68 Allen Hurns 2.50 6.00
69 Jordan Reed 2.50 6.00
70 Eric Decker 2.50 6.00
71 Stefon Diggs 3.00 8.00
72 Dez Bryant 4.00 10.00
73 Cam Newton 4.00 10.00
74 LeSean McCoy 4.00 10.00
75 Eli Manning 3.00 8.00
76 Tavon Austin 2.50 6.00
77 Jeremy Maclin 2.50 6.00
78 Torrey Smith 2.50 6.00
79 Marcus Mariota 4.00 10.00
80 Luke Kuechly 3.00 8.00
81 Rashad Jennings 2.50 6.00
82 Jeremy Hill 2.50 6.00
83 Darren McFadden 2.50 6.00
84 Matt Forte 2.50 6.00
85 Jamaal Charles 3.00 8.00
86 David Johnson 4.00 10.00
87 Delanie Walker 2.50 6.00
88 Doug Martin 3.00 8.00
89 Kamar Aiken 2.50 6.00
90 Jordan Matthews 3.00 8.00
91 T.J. Yeldon 2.50 6.00
92 Randall Cobb 3.00 8.00
93 Gary Barnidge 2.50 6.00
94 C.J. Anderson 3.00 8.00
95 Jimmy Graham 4.00 10.00
96 Mark Ingram 3.00 8.00
97 Khalil Mack 4.00 10.00
98 Eric Ebron 2.50 6.00
99 Frank Gore 3.00 8.00
100 Steve Johnson 3.00 8.00
101 Steve Young
102 Brett Favre
103 Michael Irvin 4.00 10.00
104 Fran Tarkenton 10.00 25.00
105 Jerry Rice
106 Jerome Bettis 4.00 10.00
107 Cris Carter 4.00 10.00
108 Lawrence Taylor 4.00 10.00
109 Dan Marino
110 Bo Jackson
111 Tim Brown 4.00 10.00
112 Warren Moon 4.00 10.00
113 John Elway 6.00 15.00
114 Emmitt Smith
115 Steve Largent 4.00 10.00
116 Joe Montana
117 Eric Dickerson 3.00 8.00
118 Bruce Smith 3.00 8.00
119 Roger Staubach 10.00 25.00
120 Barry Sanders
121 Terry Bradshaw 5.00 12.00
122 Andre Reed 3.00 8.00
123 Brian Urlacher 4.00 10.00
124 Curtis Martin 3.00 8.00
125 Franco Harris 4.00 10.00
126 Derrick Brooks 2.50 6.00
127 John Riggins 3.00 8.00
128 Ronnie Lott 3.00 8.00
129 Shannon Sharpe 4.00 10.00
130 James Lofton 3.00 8.00
131 Joe Namath 25.00 50.00
132 Marshall Faulk 3.00 8.00
133 Jim Kelly 4.00 10.00
134 Mike Ditka 4.00 10.00
135 LaDainian Tomlinson 3.00 8.00
136 Dan Fouts 3.00 8.00
137 Tony Dorsett 4.00 10.00
138 Ozzie Newsome 3.00 8.00
139 Rod Woodson 3.00 8.00
140 Troy Aikman 5.00 12.00
141 Marcus Allen 3.00 8.00
142 Charlie Joiner 2.50 6.00
143 Michael Strahan 3.00 8.00
144 Hines Ward 3.00 8.00
145 Thurman Thomas 3.00 8.00

2016 Panini Gala Action Autographs

*JADE/25: .5X TO 1.2X BASIC AU/49
1 DeVante Parker/49 5.00 12.00
3 Jeremy Maclin/25 5.00 12.00
5 A.J. Green/25 12.00 30.00
7 C.J. Anderson/49 5.00 12.00
9 Chris Conley/49 4.00 10.00
10 Jeremy Langford/49 5.00 12.00
11 Giovani Bernard/25 5.00 12.00
13 Duke Johnson/49 4.00 10.00
14 Devonta Freeman/49 5.00 12.00
15 Matt Jones/49 5.00 12.00
16 Emmanuel Sanders/49 6.00 15.00
18 Zach Ertz/49 5.00 12.00
19 T.J. Yeldon/49 4.00 10.00
20 Jordy Nelson/25 15.00 40.00
21 Devin Funchess/49 4.00 10.00
23 James Starks/49 4.00 10.00
24 Torrey Smith/25 5.00 12.00
26 DeAndre Hopkins/25 15.00 40.00
27 David Johnson/49 10.00 25.00
28 Maxx Williams/25 6.00 15.00
29 John Brown/49 5.00 12.00
30 Dorial Green-Beckham/49 4.00 10.00

2016 Panini Gala Cinematic Rookie Signatures

1 Aaron Burbridge 3.00 8.00
2 Alex Collins 4.00 10.00
3 Artie Burns 30.00 60.00
4 Brandon Allen 3.00 8.00
5 C.J. Prosise 3.00 8.00
6 Cardale Jones 3.00 8.00
7 Carson Wentz 50.00 100.00
8 Charone Peake 3.00 8.00
9 Chris Jones 3.00 8.00
10 Chris Moore 4.00 10.00
11 Christian Hackenberg 3.00 8.00
12 Corey Coleman 5.00 12.00
13 Dak Prescott 30.00 60.00
14 Daniel Lasco 3.00 8.00
15 Darron Lee 3.00 8.00
16 Derrick Henry 8.00 20.00
17 Ezekiel Elliott 50.00 100.00
18 Hunter Henry 4.00 10.00
19 Jacoby Brissett 4.00 10.00
20 Jalen Ramsey 5.00 12.00
21 Jared Goff 25.00 50.00
22 Joey Bosa 6.00 15.00
23 Jonathan Williams 4.00 10.00
24 Josh Doctson 4.00 10.00
25 Karl Joseph 3.00 8.00
26 Keanu Neal 3.00 8.00
27 Keenan Reynolds 4.00 10.00
28 Kenneth Dixon 3.00 8.00
29 Kenyan Drake 5.00 12.00
30 Laquon Treadwell 25.00 50.00
32 Mackensie Alexander 3.00 8.00
33 Michael Thomas 6.00 15.00
34 Moritz Bohringer 3.00 8.00
35 Myles Jack 4.00 10.00
36 Nate Sudfeld 3.00 8.00
37 Nick Vannett 3.00 8.00
38 Paxton Lynch 3.00 8.00
39 Pharoh Cooper 3.00 8.00
40 Reggie Ragland 3.00 8.00
41 Ronnie Stanley 4.00 10.00
42 Sheldon Rankins 4.00 10.00
43 Sterling Shepard 4.00 10.00
44 T.J. Green 5.00 12.00
45 Taylor Decker 4.00 10.00
46 Trevor Davis 3.00 8.00
47 Tyler Boyd 12.00 30.00
48 Tyler Ervin 3.00 8.00
49 Tyler Higbee 3.00 8.00
50 Will Fuller 5.00 12.00

2016 Panini Gala Cinematic Rookie Signatures Jade

*JADE/25: .6X TO 1.5X BASIC AU/99
7 Carson Wentz 75.00 150.00

2016 Panini Gala Cinematic Signatures

*JADE/25: .6X TO 1.5X BASIC AU/99
*JADE/25: .5X TO 1.2X BASIC AU/49
1 David Johnson/99 12.00 25.00
3 DeAndre Hopkins/25 10.00 25.00
5 Mike Evans/25 10.00 25.00
6 Devin Funchess/99 3.00 8.00
7 Matt Jones/99 4.00 10.00
8 A.J. Green/25 15.00 40.00
9 Ameer Abdullah/49 4.00 10.00
12 Tyrod Taylor/25 6.00 15.00
13 James Starks/49 4.00 10.00
14 Allen Robinson/99 4.00 10.00
15 Travis Kelce/49 6.00 15.00
17 Greg Olsen/49 5.00 12.00
19 Derek Carr/25 25.00 50.00
21 Chris Conley/49 4.00 10.00
22 Jeremy Langford/99 4.00 10.00
23 Eric Decker/25 15.00 40.00
24 Keenan Allen/99 4.00 10.00
26 Steve Smith Sr./25 10.00 25.00
27 Brandin Cooks/25 6.00 15.00
28 Doug Martin/25 6.00 15.00
29 Sammy Watkins/25 8.00 20.00
30 Allen Hurns/25 5.00 12.00
31 Lamar Miller/49 4.00 10.00

32 John Brown/99 4.00 10.00
33 Dez Bryant/25
34 Blake Bortles/25 12.00 30.00
36 Ryan Tannehill/25 6.00 15.00
37 David Cobb/99 3.00 8.00
38 Gary Barnidge/49 4.00 10.00
39 Jordan Matthews/25 6.00 15.00
41 Brock Osweiler/49 4.00 10.00
42 Thomas Rawls/99 12.00 30.00
43 Tyler Eifert/99 4.00 10.00
45 Jordy Nelson/25
46 Devonta Freeman/49 5.00 12.00
47 Marcus Mariota/25
48 Kirk Cousins/25 30.00 60.00
49 Demaryius Thomas/25 6.00 15.00

2016 Panini Gala Coming Attractions Jerseys

*JADE/25: .5X TO 1.2X BASIC JSY/49
1 Braxton Miller 2.50 6.00
2 C.J. Prosise 2.50 6.00
3 Carson Wentz 25.00 50.00
4 Christian Hackenberg 2.50 6.00
5 Connor Cook 3.00 8.00
6 Corey Coleman 4.00 10.00
7 Dak Prescott 12.00 30.00
8 Derrick Henry 6.00 15.00
9 Devontae Booker 3.00 8.00
10 Ezekiel Elliott 12.00 30.00
11 Jared Goff 8.00 20.00
12 Josh Doctson 3.00 8.00
13 Kenyan Drake 4.00 10.00
14 Laquon Treadwell 3.00 8.00
15 Michael Thomas 5.00 12.00
16 Paul Perkins 2.50 6.00
17 Paxton Lynch 2.50 6.00
18 Sterling Shepard 3.00 8.00
19 Tyler Boyd 3.00 8.00
20 Will Fuller 4.00 10.00

2016 Panini Gala Double Feature Jerseys

*JADE/25: .5X TO 1.2X BASIC JSY/49
1 J.Winston/M.Evans/49 4.00 10.00
2 D.Bryant/T.Romo/49 4.00 10.00
3 D.Moncrief/T.Hilton/49 3.00 8.00
4 A.Hurns/A.Robinson/49 3.00 8.00
5 J.Graham/R.Wilson/25 6.00 15.00
6 A.Ptrsn/T.Brdgwtr/49 4.00 10.00
7 E.Manning/O.Bckhm/49 4.00 10.00
8 J.Jones/M.Ryan/49 4.00 10.00
9 A.Gates/P.Rivers/49 4.00 10.00
10 J.Cutler/J.Langford/49 3.00 8.00
11 E.Lacy/R.Cobb/49 3.00 8.00
12 D.Ware/V.Miller/49 3.00 8.00
13 R.Grnkwski/T.Brady/25 12.00 30.00
14 J.Landry/R.Tannehill/49 3.00 8.00
15 M.Mariota/D.Walker/49 4.00 10.00
16 B.Cooks/D.Brees/49 4.00 10.00
17 A.Cooper/D.Carr/49 4.00 10.00
18 T.Taylor/S.WatkinsÂ♦49 3.00 8.00
19 C.Kprnck/C.Hyde/49 3.00 8.00
20 A.Green/A.Dalton/49 4.00 10.00

2016 Panini Gala Main Attractions Jerseys

*JADE/25: .5X TO 1.2X BASIC JSY/49
*JADE/25: .4X TO 1X BASIC JSY/25
1 Odell Beckham Jr./49 4.00 10.00
2 Jameis Winston/49 4.00 10.00
3 Rob Gronkowski/49 4.00 10.00
4 A.J. Green/49 4.00 10.00
5 Teddy Bridgewater/49 3.00 8.00
6 Amari Cooper/49 4.00 10.00
7 Brett Favre/25
8 Brian Urlacher/49 4.00 10.00
9 Jerry Rice/25
10 Devonta Freeman/49 3.00 8.00
11 Philip Rivers/49 4.00 10.00
12 Jarvis Landry/49 3.00 8.00
13 Russell Wilson/25 6.00 15.00
14 Adrian Peterson/25 5.00 12.00
15 Todd Gurley/49 4.00 10.00
16 Andy Dalton/49 3.00 8.00
17 Cris Carter/49 4.00 10.00
18 Davante Adams/49 2.50 6.00
19 LaDainian Tomlinson/25 4.00 10.00
20 Donte Moncrief/49 3.00 8.00
21 Randall Cobb/49 3.00 8.00
22 Marcus Mariota/49 4.00 10.00
23 Ryan Tannehill/49 3.00 8.00
24 Allen Hurns/49 2.50 6.00
25 Andrew Luck/25
26 Antonio Gates/49 2.50 6.00
27 Demaryius Thomas/25 4.00 10.00
28 Mark Ingram/49 3.00 8.00
29 DeMarcus Ware/49 3.00 8.00
30 Antonio Brown/49 10.00 25.00
31 Tony Romo/49 3.00 8.00
32 Mike Evans/49 3.00 8.00
33 Sammy Watkins/49 4.00 10.00
34 Allen Robinson/49 3.00 8.00
35 Barry Sanders/25
36 Blake Bortles/49 2.50 6.00
37 Eli Manning/49 3.00 8.00
38 Derek Carr/49 4.00 10.00
39 Brandon Marshall/49 2.50 6.00
40 Cam Newton/25 5.00 12.00

2016 Panini Gala Silver Screen Rookie Signatures

1 A'Shawn Robinson 4.00 10.00
2 Austin Hooper 4.00 10.00
3 Brandon Doughty 4.00 10.00
4 Braxton Miller 4.00 10.00
5 C.J. Prosise 4.00 10.00
6 Cardale Jones 4.00 10.00
7 Carson Wentz 50.00 100.00
8 Cody Kessler 4.00 10.00
9 Connor Cook 5.00 12.00
10 Corey Coleman 6.00 15.00
11 Dak Prescott 30.00 60.00
12 DeAndre Washington 4.00 10.00
13 DeForest Buckner 4.00 10.00
14 Demarcus Robinson 4.00 10.00
15 Derrick Henry 10.00 25.00
16 Devontae Booker 5.00 12.00
17 Ezekiel Elliott 60.00 125.00
18 Jack Conklin 6.00 15.00
20 Jared Goff 30.00 60.00
21 Jarran Reed 4.00 10.00
22 Jeff Driskel 4.00 10.00
23 Jordan Howard 10.00 25.00
24 Josh Doctson 5.00 12.00
25 Kelvin Taylor 4.00 10.00
26 Kenyan Drake 6.00 15.00
27 Kevin Dodd 4.00 10.00
28 Kevin Hogan 5.00 12.00
29 Kolby Listenbee 4.00 10.00
30 Laquon Treadwell 10.00 25.00
31 Laremy Tunsil 4.00 10.00
32 Leonte Carroo 4.00 10.00
33 Malcolm Mitchell 4.00 10.00
34 Paul Perkins 4.00 10.00
35 Paxton Lynch 4.00 10.00
36 Rashard Higgins 4.00 10.00
37 Ricardo Louis 4.00 10.00
38 Robert Nkemdiche 10.00 25.00
39 Ryan Kelly 6.00 15.00
42 Sterling Shepard 30.00 60.00
43 Su'a Cravens 4.00 10.00
44 Tyler Boyd 5.00 12.00
45 Vernon Hargreaves III 6.00 15.00
46 Vonn Bell 5.00 12.00
47 Wendell Smallwood 4.00 10.00
48 Will Fuller 6.00 15.00
49 William Jackson III 5.00 12.00
50 Kenny Lawler 6.00 15.00

2016 Panini Gala Silver Screen Rookie Signatures Jade

*JADE/25: .6X TO 1.5X BASIC AU/99
17 Ezekiel Elliott 75.00 150.00

2016 Panini Gala Silver Screen Signatures

*JADE/25: .6X TO 1.5X BASIC AU/99
*JADE/25: .5X TO 1.2X BASIC AU/49
1 Charlie Joiner/25 5.00 12.00
4 Andy Dalton/25
5 Dorial Green-Beckham/99 3.00 8.00
6 James White/99 4.00 10.00
7 Jason Witten/25 25.00 50.00
8 Don Majkowski/99 20.00 40.00
10 Brandin Cooks/49 5.00 12.00
11 Ty Montgomery/99 4.00 10.00
13 DeSean Jackson/25 6.00 15.00
14 Ricky Williams/49 5.00 12.00
15 Travis Kelce/25 8.00 20.00
17 Brock Osweiler/25 5.00 12.00
18 Karlos Williams/99 3.00 8.00
19 Charles Haley/99 5.00 12.00
20 Torrey Smith/25 5.00 12.00
21 Dan Hampton/25 5.00 12.00
22 Zach Ertz/49 5.00 12.00
23 Golden Tate/49 4.00 10.00
24 Luke Kuechly/25
25 Jamison Crowder/99 3.00 8.00
28 T.J. Yeldon/99 3.00 8.00
30 C.J. Anderson/49 5.00 12.00
32 Chris Conley/99 3.00 8.00
33 Jeremy Hill/25
35 Walt Garrison/99 15.00 30.00
36 Julius Thomas/49 4.00 10.00
37 Marcus Peters/99 15.00 30.00
38 Ozzie Newsome/99 4.00 10.00
39 Ed Too Tall Jones/99 15.00 30.00
40 Jeremy Langford/99 4.00 10.00
41 Thomas Rawls/99 10.00 25.00
42 Emmanuel Sanders/49 6.00 15.00
43 Giovani Bernard/25 5.00 12.00
44 Allen Hurns/99 3.00 8.00
45 Justin Forsett/99 4.00 10.00
48 Steve Grogan/99 3.00 8.00
49 Carl Eller/49 8.00 20.00

2016 Panini Gala Starring Role Signatures

1 Jordan Matthews/25 10.00 25.00
2 Antonio Brown/25 30.00 60.00
3 DeMarcus Ware/25 10.00 25.00
4 David Johnson/25 12.00 30.00
5 Tyler Eifert/25 10.00 25.00
6 Ryan Tannehill/25 10.00 25.00
8 Allen Robinson/25 10.00 25.00
9 Greg Olsen/25
10 Sammy Watkins/25 12.00 30.00
11 Mike Evans/25 10.00 25.00
15 Julius Thomas/25 8.00 20.00
16 DeSean Jackson/25 10.00 25.00
17 Jameis Winston/25 25.00 50.00
18 Steve Smith Sr./25 10.00 25.00
19 Travis Kelce/25 15.00 40.00
21 Keenan Allen/25 10.00 25.00
22 Ameer Abdullah/25 8.00 20.00
23 Derek Carr/25
25 Lamar Miller/25 8.00 20.00
27 Demaryius Thomas/25 10.00 25.00
29 Doug Martin/25 10.00 25.00
30 Luke Kuechly/25 30.00 60.00
34 Alex Smith/25 10.00 25.00
36 Brandin Cooks/25 10.00 25.00
39 Kelvin Benjamin/25 10.00 25.00
40 Andy Dalton/25 10.00 25.00

2016 Panini Gala Studio Swatches

*JADE/25: .5X TO 1.2X BASIC JSY/49
1 Blake Bortles 2.50 6.00
2 Odell Beckham Jr. 4.00 10.00
3 Jameis Winston 4.00 10.00
4 Sammy Watkins 4.00 10.00
5 Marcus Mariota 4.00 10.00
6 Mike Evans 3.00 8.00
7 Derek Carr 4.00 10.00
8 Todd Gurley 4.00 10.00
9 Amari Cooper 4.00 10.00
10 Stefon Diggs 3.00 8.00

2016 Panini Gala Vintage Materials

*JADE/25: .5X TO 1.2X BASIC JSY/49
1 Jim Kelly 5.00 12.00
2 Roger Staubach 6.00 15.00
3 John Elway 12.00 30.00
4 Barry Sanders
5 Joe Montana 15.00 40.00
6 Marcus Allen 4.00 10.00
7 Curtis Martin 4.00 10.00
8 Jerome Bettis 8.00 20.00
9 Jerry Rice 12.00 30.00
10 Brett Favre 12.00 30.00

2012 Panini Golden Age

COMP.SET w/o SP's (146) 15.00 40.00
SP ANNCD PRINT RUN OF 92 PER
22 John Heisman .20 .50
33 Red Grange .60 1.50
33SP Red Grange SP 10.00 25.00
92 Joe Namath .75 2.00

2012 Panini Golden Age Mini Broadleaf Blue Ink

*MINI BLUE: 2.5X TO 6X BASIC

2012 Panini Golden Age Mini Broadleaf Brown Ink

*MINI BROWN: .6X TO 1.5X BASIC
APPX.ODDS ONE PER PACK

2012 Panini Golden Age Mini Crofts Candy Blue Ink

*MINI BLUE: 1.5X TO 4X BASIC

2012 Panini Golden Age Mini Crofts Candy Red Ink

*MINI RED: 1.5X TO 4X BASIC
APPX.ODDS 1:8 HOBBY

2012 Panini Golden Age Mini Ty Cobb Tobacco

*MINI COBB: 2.5X TO 6X BASIC

2012 Panini Golden Age Batter-Up

APPX.ODDS 1:12 HOBBY
8 Red Grange 1.50 4.00

2012 Panini Golden Age Ferguson Bakery Pennants Blue

ISSUED AS BOX TOPPERS
14 Red Grange 6.00 15.00
19 Joe Namath 8.00 20.00

2012 Panini Golden Age Ferguson Bakery Pennants Yellow

ISSUED AS BOX TOPPERS
14 Red Grange 6.00 15.00
19 Joe Namath 8.00 20.00

2012 Panini Golden Age Headlines

MPLETE SET (15) 12.50 30.00
APPX.ODDS 1:12 HOBBY
14 Joe Namath 4.00 10.00

2012 Panini Golden Age Newark Evening World Supplement

APPX.ODDS 1:24 HOBBY
6 Red Grange 3.00 8.00

2013 Panini Golden Age

14 Fielding Yost .20 .50
18 Knute Rockne .75 2.00
34A Jim Thorpe .60 1.50
34B Jim Thorpe SP 15.00 40.00
44 Doak Walker .50 1.25
46 Red Grange .60 1.50
100 Fred Biletnikoff .30 .75
103 Carl Eller .20 .50
105 Bob Griese .50 1.25
106A Jim Kiick .20 .50
106B Jim Kiick SP 10.00 25.00
107 Don Maynard .30 .75
115A Earl Campbell .50 1.25
115B Earl Campbell SP 10.00 25.00
116 Lem Barney .20 .50
117 Bo Schembechler .30 .75
131 Barry Switzer .30 .75

2013 Panini Golden Age White

*WHITE: 3X TO 8X BASIC
NO WHITE SP PRICING AVAILABLE

2013 Panini Golden Age Bread For Energy

6 Jim Kiick .40 1.00

2013 Panini Golden Age Delong Gum

COMPLETE SET (30) 40.00 80.00
10 Bo Schembechler .75 2.00
11 Jim Kiick 1.25 3.00
19 Earl Campbell 1.25 3.00

2013 Panini Golden Age Exhibits

1 Jim Thorpe 6.00 15.00
39 Lem Barney 4.00 10.00

2013 Panini Golden Age Headlines

COMPLETE SET (15) 8.00 20.00
2 Red Grange 2.00 5.00
7 Bob Griese 1.50 4.00
15 Earl Campbell 1.50 4.00

2013 Panini Golden Age Historic Signatures

EXCHANGE DEADLINE 12/26/2014
BS Barry Switzer 20.00 50.00
CE Carl Eller 6.00 15.00
EC Earl Campbell
FB Fred Biletnikoff 6.00 15.00
JK Jim Kiick 5.00 12.00
LB Lem Barney 8.00 20.00

2013 Panini Golden Age Mini American Caramel Blue Back

*MINI BLUE: 1.2X TO 3X BASIC

2013 Panini Golden Age Mini American Caramel Red Back

*MINI RED: 2X TO 5X BASIC

2013 Panini Golden Age Mini Carolina Brights Green Back

*MINI GREEN: .75X TO 2X BASIC

2013 Panini Golden Age Mini Carolina Brights Purple Back

*MINI PURPLE: 2X TO 5X BASIC

2013 Panini Golden Age Mini Nadja Caramels Back

*MINI NADJA: 2X TO 5X BASIC

2013 Panini Golden Age Museum Age Memorabilia

11 Knute Rockne 10.00 25.00

2013 Panini Golden Age Playing Cards

COMPLETE SET (53) 50.00 100.00
15 Red Grange 1.50 4.00
35 Bo Schembechler 1.25 3.00
40 Barry Switzer .50 1.25

2013 Panini Golden Age Tip Top Bread Labels

COMPLETE SET (10) 10.00 25.00
8 Red Grange 2.00 5.00

2014 Panini Golden Age

COMP.SET w/o SP's (150) 12.00 30.00
51 Tom Harmon .25 .60
58 Ernie Nevers .25 .60
61 Elroy Hirsch .25 .60
70 Clyde Bulldog Turner .25 .60
150 Terry Bradshaw .40 1.00

2014 Panini Golden Age Mini Croft's Swiss Milk Cocoa

*MINI CROFTS: 2.5X TO 6X BASIC

2014 Panini Golden Age Mini Hindu Brown Back

*MINI HINDU BROWN: 2X TO 5X BASIC

2014 Panini Golden Age Mini Hindu Red Back

*MINI HINDU RED: 2.5X TO 6X BASIC

2014 Panini Golden Age Mini Mono Brand Blue Back

*MINI MONO BLUE: 1.5X TO 4X BASIC

2014 Panini Golden Age Mini Mono Brand Green Back

*MINI MONO GREEN: 1.5X TO 4X BASIC

2014 Panini Golden Age Mini Smith's Mello Mint

*MINI MELLO: 5X TO 12X BASIC

2014 Panini Golden Age White

*WHITE: 2.5X TO 6X BASIC

2014 Panini Golden Age Box Bottoms Black Back

*RED BACK: .4X TO 1X BLK BACK
*BLANK BACK: .6X TO 1.5X BLK BACK
3 Red Grange 2.50 6.00
6 Clyde Bulldog Turner 1.50 4.00
9 Ernie Nevers 1.50 4.00

2014 Panini Golden Age Fan Craze

COMPLETE SET (8) 6.00 15.00
3 Tom Harmon .75 2.00

2014 Panini Golden Age First Fifty

*1ST FIFTY: 3X TO 8X BASIC
STATED PRINT RUN 50 SER.#'d SETS

2014 Panini Golden Age Headlines

COMPLETE SET (9) 10.00 25.00
4 1958 NFL Championship Game 1.25 3.00
8 Monday Night Football 1.25 3.00

2011 Panini Gold Standard

1-250 STATED PRINT RUN 299
251-286 ROOK.JSY AU PRINT RUN 325-525
1 Tom Brady 5.00 12.00
2 Peyton Manning 4.00 10.00
3 Adrian Peterson 2.00 5.00
4 Troy Polamalu 3.00 8.00
5 Andre Johnson 1.50 4.00
6 Darrelle Revis 1.25 3.00
7 Drew Brees 2.00 5.00
8 Aaron Rodgers 4.00 10.00
9 Chris Johnson 1.25 3.00
10 Larry Fitzgerald 1.50 4.00
11 Charles Woodson 2.00 5.00
12 Nnamdi Asomugha 1.25 3.00
13 Clay Matthews 2.00 5.00
14 Michael Vick 1.50 4.00
15 Antonio Gates 1.25 3.00
16 Patrick Willis 1.50 4.00
17 Roddy White 1.25 3.00
18 Arian Foster 1.25 3.00
19 Philip Rivers 2.00 5.00
20 Calvin Johnson 2.00 5.00
21 DeSean Jackson 1.50 4.00
22 Maurice Jones-Drew 1.25 3.00
23 Reggie Wayne 1.50 4.00
24 Devin Hester 1.50 4.00
25 Jamaal Charles 1.50 4.00
26 Jason Witten 1.50 4.00
27 Steven Jackson 1.25 3.00
28 Ben Roethlisberger 2.50 6.00
29 Michael Turner 1.25 3.00
30 Dwayne Bowe 1.50 4.00
31 Tony Gonzalez 1.50 4.00
32 Champ Bailey 1.50 4.00
33 Brian Urlacher 2.00 5.00
34 Wes Welker 1.50 4.00
35 Ndamukong Suh 1.50 4.00
36 Matt Ryan 1.50 4.00
37 Marques Colston 1.25 3.00
38 Asante Samuel 1.25 3.00
39 Ray Rice 1.25 3.00
40 Brandon Lloyd 1.25 3.00
41 Brandon Marshall 1.50 4.00
42 Jerod Mayo 1.25 3.00
43 Miles Austin 1.25 3.00
44 Tony Romo 1.50 4.00
45 Greg Jennings 1.25 3.00
46 Santonio Holmes 1.25 3.00
47 Dallas Clark 1.25 3.00
48 Jared Allen 1.25 3.00
49 Mike Williams 1.50 4.00
50 Josh Freeman 1.50 4.00
51 Vernon Davis 1.25 3.00
52 Joe Flacco 1.50 4.00
53 Frank Gore 1.50 4.00
54 Darren McFadden 1.25 3.00
55 Donovan McNabb 1.50 4.00
56 Ahmad Bradshaw 1.25 3.00
57 Anquan Boldin 1.25 3.00
58 Braylon Edwards 1.25 3.00
59 Carson Palmer 1.50 4.00
60 Chad Henne 1.50 4.00
61 Chris Cooley 1.25 3.00
62 Colt McCoy 1.25 3.00
63 Marcedes Lewis 1.25 3.00
64 DeAngelo Williams 1.25 3.00
65 Dez Bryant 2.00 5.00
66 Donald Driver 1.50 4.00
67 Eli Manning 1.50 4.00
68 Felix Jones 1.25 3.00
69 Greg Olsen 1.50 4.00
70 Hakeem Nicks 1.25 3.00
71 Heath Miller 1.25 3.00
72 Hines Ward 1.50 4.00
73 Jahvid Best 1.25 3.00
74 Jay Cutler 1.25 3.00
75 Jeremy Maclin 1.25 3.00
76 Jonathan Stewart 1.25 3.00
77 Knowshon Moreno 1.25 3.00
78 LaDainian Tomlinson 2.00 5.00
79 Lee Evans 1.50 4.00
80 LeSean McCoy 2.00 5.00
81 Malcom Floyd 1.25 3.00
82 Mark Sanchez 1.25 3.00
83 Matt Cassel 1.25 3.00
84 Matt Forte 1.25 3.00
85 Matt Schaub 1.25 3.00
86 Matthew Stafford 1.50 4.00
87 Michael Crabtree 1.25 3.00
88 Mike Wallace 1.25 3.00
89 Percy Harvin 1.25 3.00
90 Peyton Hillis 1.25 3.00
91 Kenny Britt 1.25 3.00
92 Rashard Mendenhall 1.25 3.00
93 Ray Lewis 2.00 5.00
94 Reggie Bush 1.25 3.00
95 Ryan Mathews 1.50 4.00
96 Sam Bradford 1.25 3.00
97 Sidney Rice 1.25 3.00
98 Steve Smith 1.50 4.00
99 Tim Tebow 2.00 5.00
100 Tony Moeaki 1.25 3.00
101 Jerry Rice 4.00 10.00
102 Jim Brown 3.00 8.00
103 Joe Montana 6.00 15.00
104 Walter Payton 5.00 12.00
105 Dick Butkus 3.00 8.00
106 Barry Sanders 4.00 10.00
107 Brett Favre 6.00 15.00
108 Dan Marino 5.00 12.00
109 John Elway 4.00 10.00
110 Emmitt Smith 4.00 10.00
111 Joe Greene 2.50 6.00
112 Ronnie Lott 2.00 5.00
113 Deacon Jones 2.00 5.00
114 Gale Sayers 2.50 6.00
115 Deion Sanders 2.00 5.00
116 Raymond Berry 2.00 5.00
117 Roger Staubach 3.00 8.00
118 Bart Starr 4.00 10.00
119 Eric Dickerson 2.00 5.00
120 Forrest Gregg 1.50 4.00
121 Marshall Faulk 2.00 5.00
122 Paul Warfield 2.00 5.00
123 Marcus Allen 2.50 6.00
124 Fran Tarkenton 2.50 6.00
125 Michael Irvin 2.50 6.00
126 Lenny Moore 1.50 4.00
127 Joe Namath 3.00 8.00
128 Bo Jackson 3.00 8.00
129 Bob Griese 2.50 6.00
130 Franco Harris 2.50 6.00
131 Jim Kelly 2.50 6.00
132 Jim Taylor 2.00 5.00
133 Len Dawson 2.50 6.00
134 Paul Hornung 2.50 6.00
135 Richard Dent 1.50 4.00
136 Sonny Jurgensen 2.00 5.00
137 Tommy McDonald 2.00 5.00
138 Y.A. Tittle 2.50 6.00
139 Alan Page 1.50 4.00
140 Bob Lilly 2.00 5.00
141 Charlie Joiner 1.50 4.00
142 Chuck Bednarik 2.00 5.00
143 Don Maynard 2.00 5.00
144 Earl Campbell 2.50 6.00
145 Frank Gifford 2.00 5.00
146 Brett Favre 6.00 15.00
147 Dan Fouts 2.00 5.00
148 Warren Moon 2.50 6.00
149 Terrell Davis 2.00 5.00
150 Troy Aikman 3.00 8.00
151 Aaron Williams RC 1.50 4.00
152 Adrian Clayborn RC 1.50 4.00
153 Ahmad Black RC 2.00 5.00
154 Akeem Ayers RC 1.50 4.00
155 Aldon Smith RC 1.50 4.00
156 Aldrick Robinson RC 2.00 5.00
157 Allen Bradford RC 1.50 4.00
158 Anthony Allen RC 1.50 4.00
159 Anthony Castonzo RC 1.50 4.00
160 Anthony Sherman RC 1.50 4.00
161 Baron Batch RC 2.00 5.00
162 Brandon Harris RC 1.50 4.00
163 Brooks Reed RC 2.00 5.00
164 Bruce Carter RC 1.50 4.00
165 Cameron Heyward RC 2.00 5.00
166 Cameron Jordan RC 2.00 5.00
167 Cecil Shorts RC 1.50 4.00
168 Charles Clay RC 1.50 4.00
169 Chris Culliver RC 1.50 4.00
170 Corey Liuget RC 1.50 4.00
171 D.J. Williams RC 1.50 4.00
172 Daniel Hardy RC 2.00 5.00
173 Danny Watkins RC 1.50 4.00
174 Da'Quan Bowers RC 1.50 4.00
175 Da'Rel Scott RC 1.50 4.00
176 David Ausberry RC 1.50 4.00
177 DeMarco Sampson RC 1.50 4.00
178 DeMarcus Van Dyke RC 2.00 5.00
179 Denarius Moore RC 1.50 4.00
180 Derek Sherrod RC 1.50 4.00
181 Dion Lewis RC 2.00 5.00
182 Dwayne Harris RC 1.50 4.00
183 Evan Royster RC 1.50 4.00
184 Gabe Carimi RC 2.00 5.00
185 Greg Jones RC 2.00 5.00
186 Greg McElroy RC 2.50 6.00
187 Greg Salas RC 1.50 4.00
188 J.J. Watt RC 12.50 25.00
189 Jabaal Sheard RC 1.50 4.00
190 Jacquizz Rodgers RC 1.50 4.00
191 Jaiquawn Jarrett RC 1.50 4.00
192 James Carpenter RC 2.00 5.00
193 Jarvis Jenkins RC 1.50 4.00
194 Jay Finley RC 2.00 5.00
195 Jeremy Kerley RC 2.50 6.00
196 Jimmy Smith RC 1.50 4.00
197 Johnny Patrick RC 2.00 5.00
198 Johnny White RC 1.50 4.00
199 Jonas Mouton RC 2.00 5.00
200 Jordan Cameron RC 2.00 5.00
201 Julius Thomas RC 2.00 5.00
202 Justin Houston RC 2.00 5.00
203 Kealoha Pilares RC 1.50 4.00
204 Kelvin Sheppard RC 1.50 4.00
205 Kris Durham RC 1.50 4.00
206 Lance Kendricks RC 1.50 4.00
207 Lee Smith RC 2.00 5.00
208 Luke Stocker RC 1.50 4.00
209 Terrelle Pryor RC 2.50 6.00
210 Marcus Gilchrist RC 1.50 4.00
211 Martez Wilson RC 1.50 4.00
212 Marvin Austin RC 1.50 4.00
213 Mason Foster RC 1.50 4.00
214 Mike Pouncey RC 2.50 6.00
215 Muhammad Wilkerson RC 1.50 4.00
216 Nate Irving RC 2.00 5.00
217 Nate Solder RC 1.50 4.00
218 Nathan Enderle RC 1.50 4.00
219 Nick Fairley RC 1.50 4.00
220 Niles Paul RC 1.50 4.00
221 Owen Marecic RC 1.50 4.00
222 Patrick Peterson RC 3.00 8.00
223 Phil Taylor RC 1.50 4.00
224 Prince Amukamara RC 1.50 4.00
225 Quinton Carter RC 1.50 4.00
226 Rahim Moore RC 1.50 4.00
227 Ras-I Dowling RC 1.50 4.00
228 Richard Gordon RC 1.50 4.00
229 Ricky Stanzi RC 1.50 4.00
230 Robert Housler RC 1.50 4.00
231 Robert Quinn RC 1.50 4.00
232 Ronald Johnson RC 1.50 4.00
233 Roy Helu RC 1.50 4.00
234 Ryan Kerrigan RC 2.00 5.00
235 Ryan Taylor RC 2.00 5.00
236 Ryan Whalen RC 1.50 4.00
237 Scotty McKnight RC 1.50 4.00
238 Shane Bannon RC 1.50 4.00
239 Doug Baldwin RC 12.50 25.00
240 Shaun Chapas RC 1.50 4.00
241 Stanley Havili RC 1.50 4.00
242 Stephen Burton RC 1.50 4.00
243 Stephen Paea RC 1.50 4.00
244 T.J. Yates RC 1.50 4.00
245 Tandon Doss RC 1.50 4.00
246 Terrell McClain RC 2.00 5.00
247 Tyler Sash RC 1.50 4.00
248 Tyrod Taylor RC 3.00 8.00
249 Tyron Smith RC 2.00 5.00
250 Virgil Green RC 1.50 4.00
251 C.Newton JSY AU/325 RC 60.00 120.00
252 V.Miller JSY AU/525 RC 12.00 30.00
253 Marcell Dareus JSY AU/525* RC 5.00 12.00
254 A.J. Green JSY AU/325 RC 25.00 60.00
255 Julio Jones JSY AU/525 RC 40.00 80.00
256 Jake Locker JSY AU/325 RC 6.00 15.00
257 B.Gabbert JSY AU/325 RC 6.00 15.00
258 C.Ponder JSY AU/325 RC 6.00 15.00
259 J.Baldwin JSY AU/525 RC 5.00 12.00
260 Mark Ingram JSY AU/325 RC 10.00 25.00
261 A.Dalton JSY AU/525 RC 15.00 40.00
262 Kaepernick JSY AU/525 RC 8.00 20.00
263 R.Williams JSY AU/525 RC 5.00 12.00
264 K.Rudolph JSY AU/499 RC 5.00 12.00
265 T.Young JSY AU/499 RC 5.00 12.00
266 S.Vereen JSY AU/525 RC 6.00 15.00
267 M.Leshoure JSY AU/525 RC 10.00 25.00
268 Torrey Smith JSY AU/525 RC 5.00 12.00
269 Greg Little JSY AU/525 RC 6.00 15.00
270 D.Thomas JSY AU/525 RC 5.00 12.00
271 R.Cobb JSY AU/525 RC 8.00 20.00
272 D.Murray JSY AU/525 RC 10.00 25.00
273 Stevan Ridley JSY AU/525 RC 5.00 12.00
274 Ryan Mallett JSY AU/525 RC 6.00 15.00
275 Austin Pettis JSY AU/525 RC 5.00 12.00
276 L.Hankerson JSY AU/525 RC 5.00 12.00
277 V.Brown JSY AU/525 RC 5.00 12.00
278 J.Jernigan JSY AU/525 RC 5.00 12.00
279 Alex Green JSY AU/525 RC 5.00 12.00
280 Clyde Gates JSY AU/525 RC 8.00 20.00
281 K.Hunter JSY AU/525 RC 10.00 25.00
282 Delone Carter JSY AU/525 RC 5.00 12.00
283 Taiwan Jones JSY AU/525 RC 5.00 12.00
284 B.Powell JSY AU/499 RC 6.00 15.00
285 J.Harper JSY AU/525 RC 5.00 12.00
286 J.Todman JSY AU/525 RC 5.00 12.00

2011 Panini Gold Standard Black Gold

UNPRICED BLACK GOLD PRINT RUN 10

2011 Panini Gold Standard Platinum Gold

*1-100 VETS/25: 1X TO 2.5X BASIC CARDS
*101-150 LEGEND/25: 1X TO 2.5X BASIC CARDS
*151-250 ROOKIE/25: 1X TO 2.5X BASIC CARDS

2011 Panini Gold Standard Autographs Silver

UNPRICED VET/LEG AU PRINT RUN 1-5
151-250 ROOKIE AU PRINT RUN 299-499
*GOLD ROOKIE/25: .8X TO 2X SILVER AU/499
*GOLD ROOKIE/25: .6X TO 1.5X SILVER AU/299
151 Aaron Williams/499 3.00 8.00
152 Adrian Clayborn/499 3.00 8.00
153 Ahmad Black/499 4.00 10.00
154 Akeem Ayers/499 3.00 8.00
156 Aldrick Robinson/499 5.00 12.00
157 Allen Bradford/499 3.00 8.00
158 Anthony Allen/499 3.00 8.00
159 Anthony Castonzo/499 3.00 8.00
162 Brandon Harris/499 3.00 8.00
165 Cameron Heyward/499 4.00 10.00
166 Cameron Jordan/499 4.00 10.00
167 Cecil Shorts/499 3.00 8.00
170 Corey Liuget/499 3.00 8.00
171 D.J. Williams/499 3.00 8.00
174 Da'Quan Bowers/499 3.00 8.00
175 Da'Rel Scott/499 3.00 8.00
179 Denarius Moore/499 12.00 30.00
181 Dion Lewis/499 4.00 10.00
182 Dwayne Harris/499 3.00 8.00
183 Evan Royster/499 3.00 8.00
185 Greg Jones/499 4.00 10.00
186 Greg McElroy/499 5.00 12.00
187 Greg Salas/499 3.00 8.00
188 J.J. Watt/499 50.00 100.00
190 Jacquizz Rodgers/499 3.00 8.00
195 Jeremy Kerley/499 5.00 12.00
196 Jimmy Smith/499 3.00 8.00
198 Johnny White/499 3.00 8.00
200 Jordan Cameron/499 4.00 10.00
201 Julius Thomas/499 4.00 10.00
202 Justin Houston/499 4.00 10.00
203 Kealoha Pilares/499 3.00 8.00
205 Kris Durham/499 3.00 8.00
206 Lance Kendricks/499 3.00 8.00
208 Luke Stocker/499 3.00 8.00
209 Terrelle Pryor/299 6.00 15.00
211 Martez Wilson/499 3.00 8.00
220 Niles Paul/499 3.00 8.00
223 Phil Taylor/499 3.00 8.00
224 Prince Amukamara/499 3.00 8.00
225 Quinton Carter/499 3.00 8.00
226 Rahim Moore/499 3.00 8.00
229 Ricky Stanzi/499 3.00 8.00
232 Ronald Johnson/499 3.00 8.00
233 Roy Helu/499 3.00 8.00
234 Ryan Kerrigan/499 4.00 10.00
236 Ryan Whalen/499 3.00 8.00
237 Scotty McKnight/499 3.00 8.00
241 Stanley Havili/499 3.00 8.00
242 Stephen Burton/499 3.00 8.00
243 Stephen Paea/499 3.00 8.00
244 T.J. Yates/499 3.00 8.00
245 Tandon Doss/499 3.00 8.00
247 Tyler Sash/499 3.00 8.00
248 Tyrod Taylor/499 6.00 15.00
249 Tyron Smith/499 4.00 10.00

2011 Panini Gold Standard Gold Leaf Rookies

STATED PRINT RUN 299 SER.#'d SETS
UNPRICED 14K PRINT RUN 6-10
UNPRICED AUTO PRINT RUN 5
1 Cam Newton 5.00 12.00
2 Von Miller 1.50 4.00
3 Marcell Dareus 1.00 2.50
4 A.J. Green 2.50 6.00
5 Julio Jones 3.00 8.00
6 Jake Locker 1.00 2.50
7 Blaine Gabbert 1.00 2.50
8 Christian Ponder 1.00 2.50
9 Jonathan Baldwin 1.00 2.50
10 Mark Ingram 1.50 4.00
11 Andy Dalton 2.00 5.00
12 Colin Kaepernick 1.50 4.00
13 Ryan Williams 1.00 2.50
14 Kyle Rudolph 1.00 2.50
15 Titus Young 1.00 2.50
16 Shane Vereen 1.25 3.00
17 Mikel Leshoure 1.00 2.50
18 Torrey Smith 1.00 2.50
19 Greg Little 1.25 3.00
20 Daniel Thomas 1.00 2.50
21 Randall Cobb 1.50 4.00
22 DeMarco Murray 2.00 5.00
23 Stevan Ridley 1.00 2.50
24 Ryan Mallett 1.00 2.50
25 Austin Pettis 1.00 2.50
26 Leonard Hankerson 1.00 2.50
27 Vincent Brown 1.00 2.50
28 Jerrel Jernigan 1.00 2.50
29 Alex Green 1.00 2.50
30 Clyde Gates 1.00 2.50
31 Kendall Hunter 1.00 2.50
32 Delone Carter 1.00 2.50
33 Taiwan Jones 1.00 2.50
34 Bilal Powell 1.25 3.00
35 Jamie Harper 1.00 2.50
36 Jordan Todman 1.00 2.50

2011 Panini Gold Standard Gold Leaf Rookies Materials

STATED PRINT RUN 299 SER.#'d SETS
*PRIME/25: .8X TO 2X BASIC JSY/299
1 Cam Newton 8.00 20.00
2 Von Miller 2.50 6.00
3 Marcell Dareus 1.50 4.00
4 A.J. Green 4.00 10.00
5 Julio Jones 5.00 12.00
6 Jake Locker 1.50 4.00
7 Blaine Gabbert 1.50 4.00
8 Christian Ponder 1.50 4.00
9 Jonathan Baldwin 1.50 4.00
10 Mark Ingram 2.50 6.00
11 Andy Dalton 3.00 8.00
12 Colin Kaepernick 2.50 6.00
13 Ryan Williams 1.50 4.00
14 Kyle Rudolph 1.50 4.00
15 Titus Young 1.50 4.00
16 Shane Vereen 2.00 5.00
17 Mikel Leshoure 1.50 4.00
18 Torrey Smith 1.50 4.00
19 Greg Little 2.00 5.00
20 Daniel Thomas 1.50 4.00
21 Randall Cobb 2.50 6.00
22 DeMarco Murray 3.00 8.00
23 Stevan Ridley 1.50 4.00
24 Ryan Mallett 1.50 4.00
25 Austin Pettis 1.50 4.00
26 Leonard Hankerson 1.50 4.00
27 Vincent Brown 1.50 4.00
28 Jerrel Jernigan 1.50 4.00
29 Alex Green 3.00 8.00
30 Clyde Gates 1.50 4.00
31 Kendall Hunter 1.50 4.00
32 Delone Carter 1.50 4.00
33 Taiwan Jones 1.50 4.00
34 Bilal Powell 2.00 5.00
35 Jamie Harper 1.50 4.00
36 Jordan Todman 1.50 4.00

2011 Panini Gold Standard Gold Leaf Rookies Materials Autographs

STATED PRINT RUN 50 SER.#'d SETS
1 Cam Newton 75.00 150.00
2 Von Miller 12.00 30.00
4 A.J. Green 30.00 80.00
5 Julio Jones 25.00 60.00
6 Jake Locker 5.00 12.00
7 Blaine Gabbert 5.00 12.00
8 Christian Ponder 5.00 12.00
9 Jonathan Baldwin 5.00 12.00
10 Mark Ingram 8.00 20.00
11 Andy Dalton 10.00 25.00
12 Colin Kaepernick 8.00 20.00
13 Ryan Williams 5.00 12.00
14 Kyle Rudolph 5.00 12.00
15 Titus Young 5.00 12.00
16 Shane Vereen 6.00 15.00
17 Mikel Leshoure 5.00 12.00
18 Torrey Smith 5.00 12.00
19 Greg Little
20 Daniel Thomas 5.00 12.00
21 Randall Cobb 8.00 20.00
22 DeMarco Murray 10.00 25.00
24 Ryan Mallett 5.00 12.00
26 Leonard Hankerson 5.00 12.00
27 Vincent Brown 5.00 12.00
28 Jerrel Jernigan 5.00 12.00
29 Alex Green 5.00 12.00
33 Taiwan Jones 5.00 12.00
34 Bilal Powell 6.00 15.00
35 Jamie Harper 5.00 12.00
36 Jordan Todman 5.00 12.00

2011 Panini Gold Standard Gold Leaf Rookies Materials Autographs Prime

*PRIME/25: .6X TO 1.5X JSY AU/50
PRIME PRINT RUN 25 SER.#'d SETS
1 Cam Newton/25 100.00 250.00
3 Marcell Dareus/25 8.00 20.00
12 Colin Kaepernick/25 12.00 30.00
30 Clyde Gates/25 8.00 20.00

2011 Panini Gold Standard Gold Leaf Stars

STATED PRINT RUN 299 SER.#'d SETS
1 Tom Brady 4.00 10.00
2 Philip Rivers 1.50 4.00
3 Aaron Rodgers 2.50 6.00
4 Michael Vick 1.25 3.00
5 Ben Roethlisberger 1.50 4.00
6 Chris Johnson 1.00 2.50
7 Joe Flacco 1.25 3.00
8 Matt Cassel 1.00 2.50
9 Adrian Peterson 1.50 4.00
10 Peyton Manning 3.00 8.00
11 Matt Ryan 1.25 3.00
12 Brandon Lloyd 1.00 2.50
13 Drew Brees 1.50 4.00
14 Dwayne Bowe 1.25 3.00
15 David Garrard 1.00 2.50
16 Roddy White 1.00 2.50
17 Jay Cutler 1.00 2.50
18 Andre Johnson 1.25 3.00
19 Eli Manning 1.25 3.00
20 Reggie Wayne 1.25 3.00
21 Arian Foster 1.00 2.50
22 Larry Fitzgerald 1.25 3.00
23 Maurice Jones-Drew 1.00 2.50
24 Greg Jennings 1.00 2.50
25 Matt Schaub 1.00 2.50

2011 Panini Gold Standard Gold Leaf Stars Materials

STATED PRINT RUN 49-99
*PRIME/25: .6X TO 1.5X BASIC JSY/49-99
1 Tom Brady/99 12.00 30.00
2 Philip Rivers/49 5.00 12.00
3 Aaron Rodgers/49 10.00 25.00
4 Michael Vick/99 4.00 10.00
6 Chris Johnson/49 3.00 8.00
7 Joe Flacco/49 4.00 10.00
8 Matt Cassel/99 3.00 8.00
9 Adrian Peterson/49 5.00 12.00
10 Peyton Manning/99 10.00 25.00
11 Matt Ryan/99 4.00 10.00
12 Brandon Lloyd/99 3.00 8.00
13 Drew Brees/49 5.00 12.00
14 Dwayne Bowe/49 4.00 10.00
15 David Garrard/49 3.00 8.00
16 Roddy White/49 3.00 8.00
17 Jay Cutler/99 3.00 8.00
18 Andre Johnson/49 4.00 10.00
19 Eli Manning/99 4.00 10.00
20 Reggie Wayne/49 4.00 10.00
22 Larry Fitzgerald/99 4.00 10.00
23 Maurice Jones-Drew/99 3.00 8.00
25 Matt Schaub/99 3.00 8.00

2011 Panini Gold Standard Gold Reserve Materials

STATED PRINT RUN 99-299
*PRIME/18-25: .8X TO 2X BASIC JSY
*PRIME/18-25: .6X TO 1.5X BASIC JSY
1 Sam Bradford/299 2.50 6.00
2 Percy Harvin/150 2.50 6.00
3 Josh Freeman/99 4.00 10.00
5 Tim Tebow/99 12.00 30.00
6 Colt McCoy/99 3.00 8.00
7 Darrelle Revis/299 2.50 6.00
8 Dez Bryant/99 5.00 12.00
9 Malcom Floyd/299 2.50 6.00
10 Hakeem Nicks/299 2.50 6.00
11 Jerod Mayo/99 4.00 10.00
13 Jeremy Maclin/299 2.50 6.00
14 Vernon Davis/299 2.50 6.00
15 Darren McFadden/299 2.50 6.00
16 Patrick Willis/299 3.00 8.00
17 Mark Sanchez/299 2.50 6.00
18 Michael Crabtree/99 3.00 8.00
19 DeSean Jackson/299 3.00 8.00
20 Matthew Stafford/299 3.00 8.00

2011 Panini Gold Standard Gold Reserve Materials Autographs

STATED PRINT RUN 10-25
UNPRICED PRIME AU PRINT RUN 5-10
3 Josh Freeman/25 15.00 40.00
6 Colt McCoy/25 12.00 30.00
7 Darrelle Revis/25 12.00 30.00
9 Malcom Floyd/25 12.00 30.00
10 Hakeem Nicks/25 12.00 30.00
14 Vernon Davis/25 12.00 30.00
16 Patrick Willis/25 20.00 50.00
18 Michael Crabtree/25 12.00 30.00
19 DeSean Jackson/25 15.00 40.00
20 Matthew Stafford/25 30.00 80.00

2011 Panini Gold Standard Gold Rush

STATED PRINT RUN 299 SER.#'d SETS
1 Arian Foster 1.00 2.50
2 Jamaal Charles 1.25 3.00
3 Michael Turner 1.00 2.50
4 Maurice Jones-Drew 1.00 2.50
5 Rashard Mendenhall 1.00 2.50
6 Adrian Peterson 1.50 4.00
7 Chris Johnson 1.00 2.50
8 Steven Jackson 1.00 2.50
9 Ahmad Bradshaw 1.00 2.50
10 Ray Rice 1.00 2.50
11 Peyton Hillis 1.00 2.50
12 Darren McFadden 1.00 2.50
13 Cedric Benson 1.00 2.50
14 LeSean McCoy 1.50 4.00
15 BenJarvus Green-Ellis 1.00 2.50
16 Matt Forte 1.00 2.50
17 LaDainian Tomlinson 1.50 4.00
18 Frank Gore 1.25 3.00
19 Felix Jones 1.00 2.50
20 Knowshon Moreno 1.00 2.50
21 LeGarrette Blount 1.25 3.00
22 DeAngelo Williams 1.00 2.50
23 Ryan Torain 1.00 2.50
24 Ryan Mathews 1.25 3.00
25 Michael Vick 1.25 3.00

2011 Panini Gold Standard Gold Rush Materials

STATED PRINT RUN 49-99
*PRIME/20-25: .8X TO 2X BASIC JSY/49-99
1 Arian Foster/49 4.00 10.00
2 Jamaal Charles/49 3.00 8.00
3 Michael Turner/99 2.50 6.00
4 Maurice Jones-Drew/99 2.50 6.00
5 Rashard Mendenhall/49 2.50 6.00
6 Adrian Peterson/49 4.00 10.00
7 Chris Johnson/49 2.50 6.00
8 Steven Jackson/99 2.50 6.00
9 Ahmad Bradshaw/49 2.50 6.00
10 Ray Rice/99 2.50 6.00
11 Peyton Hillis/99 2.50 6.00
12 Darren McFadden/99 2.50 6.00
13 Cedric Benson/99 2.50 6.00
14 LeSean McCoy/99 2.50 6.00
15 BenJarvus Green-Ellis/99 5.00 12.00
16 Matt Forte/99 2.50 6.00
17 LaDainian Tomlinson/49 4.00 10.00
18 Frank Gore/99 3.00 8.00
19 Felix Jones/99 2.50 6.00

20 Knowshon Moreno/99 2.50 6.00
22 DeAngelo Williams/99 2.50 6.00
23 Ryan Torain/99 2.50 6.00
24 Ryan Mathews/49 3.00 8.00
25 Michael Vick/99 3.00 8.00

2011 Panini Gold Standard Golden Age

STATED PRINT RUN 299 SER.#'d SETS
1 Jim Brown 2.50 6.00
2 Deacon Jones 1.50 4.00
3 Gale Sayers 2.00 5.00
4 Raymond Berry 1.50 4.00
5 Bart Starr 3.00 8.00
6 Forrest Gregg 1.25 3.00
7 Paul Warfield 1.50 4.00
8 Fran Tarkenton 2.00 5.00
9 Lenny Moore 1.25 3.00
10 Joe Namath 2.50 6.00
11 Bob Griese 2.00 5.00
12 Walter Payton 4.00 10.00
13 Dick Butkus 2.50 6.00
14 Joe Greene 2.00 5.00
15 Franco Harris 2.00 5.00
16 Jim Taylor 1.50 4.00
17 Len Dawson 2.00 5.00
18 Sid Luckman 1.50 4.00
19 Sammy Baugh 2.00 5.00
20 Don Maynard 1.50 4.00
21 Chuck Bednarik 1.50 4.00
22 Jim Thorpe 2.50 6.00
23 Frank Gifford 1.50 4.00
24 Red Grange 3.00 6.00
25 Dutch Clark 1.50 4.00

2011 Panini Gold Standard Golden Age Materials

STATED PRINT RUN 25-99
*PRIME/25: .8X TO 2X BASIC JSY/99
*PRIME/25: .6X TO 1.5X BASIC JSY/25
1 Jim Brown/25 10.00 25.00
2 Deacon Jones/25 6.00 15.00
3 Gale Sayers/99 6.00 15.00
4 Raymond Berry/99 5.00 12.00
5 Bart Starr/99 10.00 25.00
6 Forrest Gregg/99 6.00 15.00
7 Paul Warfield/99 5.00 12.00
8 Fran Tarkenton/99 6.00 15.00
9 Lenny Moore/99 4.00 10.00
10 Joe Namath/5
11 Bob Griese/99 6.00 15.00
12 Walter Payton/99 12.00 30.00
13 Dick Butkus/99 8.00 20.00
14 Joe Greene/99 6.00 15.00
15 Franco Harris/99 6.00 15.00
17 Len Dawson/25 8.00 20.00
18 Sid Luckman/30 8.00 20.00
19 Sammy Baugh/25 8.00 20.00
20 Don Maynard/99 5.00 12.00
22 Jim Thorpe/25 60.00 120.00

2011 Panini Gold Standard Golden Anniversary

STATED PRINT RUN 299 SER.#'d SETS
1 Tom Brady 4.00 10.00
2 Wes Welker 1.25 3.00
3 BenJarvus Green-Ellis 1.00 2.50
4 Jerod Mayo 1.00 2.50
5 Curtis Martin 1.25 3.00
6 Adrian Peterson 1.50 4.00
7 Brett Favre 4.00 10.00
8 Jared Allen 1.00 2.50
9 Percy Harvin 1.00 2.50
10 Fran Tarkenton 2.00 5.00
11 Antonio Gates 1.00 2.50
12 Philip Rivers 1.50 4.00
13 Vincent Jackson 1.00 2.50
14 Ryan Mathews 1.25 3.00
15 Dan Fouts 1.50 4.00
16 Darrelle Revis 1.00 2.50
17 Joe Namath 2.50 6.00
18 Mark Sanchez 1.00 2.50
19 Santonio Holmes 1.00 2.50
20 Braylon Edwards 1.00 2.50
21 Charles Woodson 1.50 4.00
22 Darren McFadden 1.00 2.50
23 Nnamdi Asomugha 1.00 2.50
24 Jerry Rice 3.00 8.00
25 Rolando McClain 1.00 2.50
26 Dwayne Bowe 1.25 3.00
27 Jamaal Charles 1.25 3.00
28 Len Dawson 2.00 5.00
29 Priest Holmes 1.25 3.00
30 Matt Cassel 1.00 2.50
31 Earl Campbell 2.00 5.00
32 Warren Moon 2.00 5.00
33 Chris Johnson 1.00 2.50
34 Eddie George 1.50 4.00
35 Kenny Britt 1.00 2.50
36 Brandon Lloyd 1.00 2.50
37 John Elway 3.00 8.00
38 Knowshon Moreno 1.00 2.50
39 Terrell Davis 1.50 4.00
40 Tim Tebow 1.50 4.00
41 C.J. Spiller 1.00 2.50
42 Jim Kelly 2.00 5.00
43 Lee Evans 1.25 3.00
44 Thurman Thomas 1.50 4.00
45 Bruce Smith 1.50 4.00
46 Troy Aikman 2.50 6.00
47 Emmitt Smith 3.00 8.00
48 Miles Austin 1.00 2.50
49 Tony Romo 1.25 3.00
50 Dez Bryant 1.50 4.00

2011 Panini Gold Standard Golden Anniversary Materials

STATED PRINT RUN 25-99
*PRIME/20-25: .6X TO 1.5X BASIC JSY/49-99
*PRIME/25: .5X TO 1.2X BASIC JSY/25
1 Tom Brady/99 12.00 30.00
2 Wes Welker/99 4.00 10.00
3 BenJarvus Green-Ellis/99 6.00 15.00
4 Jerod Mayo/49 3.00 8.00
5 Curtis Martin/10
6 Adrian Peterson/49 5.00 12.00
7 Brett Favre/99 12.00 30.00
8 Jared Allen/49 5.00 12.00
9 Percy Harvin/99 3.00 8.00
10 Fran Tarkenton/99 6.00 15.00
11 Antonio Gates/99 3.00 8.00
12 Philip Rivers/99 6.00 15.00
14 Ryan Mathews/49 4.00 10.00
15 Dan Fouts/99 5.00 12.00
16 Darrelle Revis/99 3.00 8.00
17 Joe Namath/25 12.00 30.00
18 Mark Sanchez/99 3.00 8.00
19 Santonio Holmes/99 3.00 8.00
20 Braylon Edwards/99 3.00 8.00
22 Darren McFadden/99 3.00 8.00
23 Nnamdi Asomugha/49 5.00 12.00
24 Jerry Rice/99 10.00 25.00
26 Dwayne Bowe/49 4.00 10.00
27 Jamaal Charles/49 4.00 10.00
28 Len Dawson/99 6.00 15.00
29 Priest Holmes/99 4.00 10.00
30 Matt Cassel/99 3.00 8.00
31 Earl Campbell/25 8.00 20.00
32 Warren Moon/99 6.00 15.00
33 Chris Johnson/49 3.00 8.00
34 Eddie George/99 5.00 12.00
35 Kenny Britt/99 3.00 8.00
36 Brandon Lloyd/99 3.00 8.00
37 John Elway/99 10.00 25.00
38 Knowshon Moreno/99 3.00 8.00
39 Terrell Davis/25 6.00 15.00
40 Tim Tebow/49 5.00 12.00
41 C.J. Spiller/49 3.00 8.00
42 Jim Kelly/99 6.00 15.00
43 Lee Evans/49 4.00 10.00
44 Thurman Thomas/99 5.00 12.00
45 Bruce Smith/99 5.00 12.00
46 Troy Aikman/99 8.00 20.00
47 Emmitt Smith/99 10.00 25.00
48 Miles Austin/99 3.00 8.00
49 Tony Romo/99 4.00 10.00
50 Dez Bryant/49 5.00 12.00

2011 Panini Gold Standard Golden Anniversary 1961 Autographs

AUTO STATED PRINT RUN 3-99
4 Boyd Dowler/99 10.00 25.00

2011 Panini Gold Standard Golden Anniversary 1961 Materials

STATED PRINT RUN 25-50
*PRIME/25: .6X TO 1.5X BASIC JSY/50
*PRIME/25: .5X TO 1.2X BASIC JSY/20-25
1 Paul Hornung/25 8.00 20.00
2 Y.A. Tittle/50 6.00 15.00
3 Bart Starr/25 12.00 30.00
6 Fran Tarkenton/25 8.00 20.00
7 Jim Brown/20 10.00 25.00
8 Tommy McDonald/25 6.00 15.00
10 Hugh McElhenny/50

2011 Panini Gold Standard Golden Anniversary 1961 Materials Autographs

JERSEY AUTO PRINT RUN 10-25
UNPRICED PRIME AU PRINT RUN 1-10
3 Bart Starr/15 100.00 200.00
6 Fran Tarkenton/15 30.00 60.00
10 Hugh McElhenny/25 20.00 50.00

2011 Panini Gold Standard Gridiron Gold Materials

STATED PRINT RUN 30-299
*PRIME/25: .8X TO 2X BASIC JSY/299
*PRIME/25: .6X TO 1.5X BASIC JSY/55-99
*PRIME/25: .5X TO 1.2X BASIC JSY/30
1 Calvin Johnson/299 5.00 12.00
2 Antonio Gates/299 2.50 6.00
3 Tony Romo/299 3.00 8.00
4 DeMarcus Ware/299 4.00 10.00
5 Miles Austin/299 2.50 6.00
6 Tom Brady/99 12.00 30.00
7 Marques Colston/299 2.50 6.00
8 Philip Rivers/299 4.00 10.00
9 Jason Witten/299 3.00 8.00
10 Charles Woodson/30 12.00 30.00
11 Clay Matthews/99 6.00 15.00
12 Brian Urlacher/299 5.00 12.00
13 Adrian Peterson/99 5.00 12.00
14 Troy Polamalu/299 8.00 20.00
16 Drew Brees/99 5.00 12.00
17 Jared Allen/99 5.00 12.00
18 Chris Johnson/99 3.00 8.00
19 Hines Ward/55 6.00 15.00
20 Peyton Manning/299 8.00 20.00

2011 Panini Gold Standard Gridiron Gold Materials Autographs

JERSEY AUTO PRINT RUN 5-20
19 Hines Ward/20 50.00 100.00

2011 Panini Gold Standard Hall of Gold Materials

STATED PRINT RUN 25-299
*PRIME/25: .8X TO 2X JSY/140-299
*PRIME/25: .6X TO 1.5X JSY/50-99
*PRIME/25: .5X TO 1.2X JSY/25-35
1 Emmitt Smith/299 8.00 20.00
2 Marshall Faulk/25 6.00 15.00
3 Deion Sanders/140 6.00 15.00
4 Jerry Rice/55 12.00 30.00
5 Richard Dent/299 4.00 10.00
6 Joe Montana/299 12.00 30.00
7 Barry Sanders/35 12.00 30.00
8 Dan Marino/299 8.00 20.00
9 John Elway/299 8.00 20.00
11 Michael Irvin/220 5.00 12.00
12 Jim Kelly/299 5.00 12.00
13 Roger Staubach/99 8.00 20.00
14 Sonny Jurgensen/50 5.00 12.00
15 Y.A. Tittle/50 6.00 15.00
16 Joe Namath/25 10.00 25.00
17 Jim Brown/25 10.00 25.00
18 Warren Moon/299 5.00 12.00
19 Thurman Thomas/150 4.00 10.00
20 Troy Aikman/299 6.00 15.00

2011 Panini Gold Standard Hall of Gold Materials Autographs

STATED PRINT RUN 3-25
3 Deion Sanders/25 40.00 80.00
7 Barry Sanders/25 60.00 120.00
8 Dan Marino/25 75.00 150.00
10 Eric Dickerson/25 25.00 50.00

2017 Panini Gold Standard

1 Julio Jones 1.50 4.00
2 Emmanuel Sanders 1.50 4.00
3 Ty Montgomery 1.00 2.50
4 Jamie Collins 1.00 2.50
5 Khalil Mack 1.50 4.00
6 Jordan Howard 1.50 4.00
7 Blake Bortles 1.00 2.50
8 Derrick Henry 1.25 3.00
9 Philip Rivers 1.50 4.00
10 Kenny Britt 1.00 2.50
11 Alex Smith 1.25 3.00
12 Jordan Matthews 1.00 2.50
13 Matt Forte 1.00 2.50
14 Larry Fitzgerald 1.25 3.00
15 Rob Gronkowski 1.50 4.00
16 Marcus Mariota 1.50 4.00
17 Devonta Freeman 1.25 3.00
18 A.J. Green 1.50 4.00
19 Chandler Jones 1.00 2.50
20 Mark Ingram 1.25 3.00
21 Andrew Luck 2.00 5.00
22 LeGarrette Blount 1.25 3.00
23 Chris Ivory 1.25 3.00
24 Jeremy Hill 1.00 2.50
25 Antonio Brown 1.50 4.00
26 Sammy Watkins 1.50 4.00
27 Doug Baldwin 1.25 3.00
28 Mike Evans 1.25 3.00
29 Le'Veon Bell 1.25 3.00
30 Richard Sherman 1.50 4.00
31 Eli Manning 1.25 3.00
32 Tyrod Taylor 1.25 3.00
33 Terrelle Pryor Sr. 1.00 2.50
34 Cody Kessler 1.00 2.50
35 Lamar Miller 1.00 2.50
36 Doug Martin 1.25 3.00
37 Jonathan Stewart 1.00 2.50
38 Carlos Hyde 1.00 2.50
39 Marvin Jones Jr. 1.00 2.50
40 Ryan Mathews 1.25 3.00
41 Pierre Garcon 1.25 3.00
42 Eric Berry 1.25 3.00
43 Landon Collins 1.00 2.50
44 Tavon Austin 1.00 2.50
45 Jordy Nelson 1.25 3.00
46 Josh McCown 1.00 2.50
47 Ryan Tannehill 1.25 3.00
48 Jared Goff 1.50 4.00
49 Von Miller 1.25 3.00
50 Brandin Cooks 1.25 3.00
51 Todd Gurley II 1.50 4.00
52 Lorenzo Alexander 1.00 2.50
53 Travis Kelce 1.50 4.00
54 Robert Kelley 1.00 2.50
55 J.J. Watt 1.50 4.00
56 Kelvin Benjamin 1.25 3.00
57 Julian Edelman 1.50 4.00
58 Michael Thomas 1.50 4.00
59 Clay Matthews 1.25 3.00
60 Adam Vinatieri 1.00 2.50
61 Jay Ajayi 1.25 3.00
62 Mike Wallace 1.00 2.50
63 Vance McDonald 1.00 2.50
64 Jarvis Landry 1.25 3.00
65 Delanie Walker 1.00 2.50
66 Cameron Meredith 1.00 2.50
67 Kirk Cousins 1.50 4.00
68 Tyreek Hill 1.50 4.00
69 Matthew Stafford 1.25 3.00
70 Jimmy Graham 1.50 4.00
71 Derek Carr 1.50 4.00
72 Antonio Gates 1.00 2.50
73 Brandon LaFell 1.00 2.50
74 DeSean Jackson 1.25 3.00
75 Eric Ebron 1.00 2.50
76 Joe Flacco 1.25 3.00
77 Demaryius Thomas 1.25 3.00
78 Trevor Siemian 1.00 2.50
79 Isaiah Crowell 1.00 2.50
80 Melvin Gordon 1.25 3.00
81 Alshon Jeffery 1.25 3.00
82 T.Y. Hilton 1.25 3.00
83 Sam Bradford 1.00 2.50
84 Adam Thielen 1.50 4.00
85 DeAndre Hopkins 1.25 3.00
86 Colin Kaepernick 1.25 3.00
87 Dez Bryant 1.50 4.00
88 Golden Tate III 1.00 2.50
89 Cameron Wake 1.00 2.50
90 T.J. Yeldon 1.00 2.50
91 Darren Sproles 1.25 3.00
92 Jeremy Kerley 1.00 2.50
93 Davante Adams 1.25 3.00
94 Cameron Brate 1.00 2.50
95 Greg Olsen 1.25 3.00
96 Amari Cooper 1.50 4.00
97 Sterling Shepard 1.25 3.00
98 LeSean McCoy 1.50 4.00
99 Joey Bosa 1.50 4.00
100 Carson Wentz 2.00 5.00
101 Terrell Suggs 1.00 2.50
102 Andy Dalton 1.25 3.00
103A Jameis Winston Buccaneers 1.25 3.00
104 Allen Robinson 1.25 3.00
105 Will Fuller V 1.00 2.50
106 Frank Gore 1.25 3.00
107 Vic Beasley Jr. 1.00 2.50
108 James Harrison 1.25 3.00
109 Terrance West 1.00 2.50
110 Carson Palmer 1.25 3.00
111 Eric Decker 1.00 2.50
112 Matt Ryan 1.25 3.00
113 Michael Crabtree 1.00 2.50
114 Stefon Diggs 1.25 3.00
115 Jason Witten 1.25 3.00
116B DeMarco Murray Eagles 1.25 3.00
116C DeMarco Murray Cowboys 1.25 3.00
117B Brandon Marshall Broncos 1.00 2.50
117F Brandon Marshall Bears 1.00 2.50
118A Tom Brady 4.00 10.00
119B Aaron Rodgers 3.00 8.00
120A Ezekiel Elliott 2.00 5.00
121A Cam Newton 1.50 4.00
122 Adrian Peterson 1.50 4.00
123A Drew Brees 1.50 4.00
124A Ben Roethlisberger 1.50 4.00
125A David Johnson 1.50 4.00
126A Dak Prescott 1.50 4.00
127A Russell Wilson 2.00 5.00
128A Odell Beckham Jr. 1.50 4.00
129A Joe Montana 4.00 10.00
130A Brett Favre Packers 3.00 8.00
131A Emmitt Smith 2.50 6.00
132A Warren Moon Oilers 1.50 4.00
133A Kevin Greene Rams 1.25 3.00
133C Kevin Greene Panthers 1.25 3.00
133D Kevin Greene Steelers 1.25 3.00
134A Jerry Rice 49ers 2.50 6.00
134B Jerry Rice Raiders 2.50 6.00
135A Peyton Manning 3.00 8.00
136A Eric Dickerson Rams 1.50 4.00
136C Eric Dickerson Colts 1.50 4.00
137A Dan Marino 3.00 8.00
138A Barry Sanders 2.50 6.00
139A Deion Sanders Cowboys 1.25 3.00
139E Deion Sanders Falcons 1.25 3.00
140A Mike Ditka Bears 1.50 4.00
140D Mike Ditka Cowboys 1.50 4.00
141 Haason Reddick RC 1.50 4.00
142 Khalfani Muhammad RC 1.50 4.00
143 Jarrad Davis RC 2.00 5.00
144 Jake Elliott RC 3.00 8.00
145 Jonnu Smith RC 1.50 4.00
146 Donnel Pumphrey RC 2.00 5.00
147 Charles Harris RC 1.50 4.00
148 Trent Taylor RC 2.00 5.00
149 Adoree' Jackson RC 2.00 5.00
150 Brad Kaaya RC 1.50 4.00
151 Marshon Lattimore RC 2.00 5.00
152 Elijah Hood RC 1.50 4.00
153 Marlon Humphrey RC 1.50 4.00
154 Garett Bolles RC 1.50 4.00
155 Tarik Cohen RC 3.00 8.00
156 Shelton Gibson RC 1.50 4.00
157 Jamal Adams RC 1.50 4.00
158 T.J. Logan RC 2.50 6.00
159 Reuben Foster RC 1.50 4.00
160 Stacy Coley RC 1.50 4.00
161 Solomon Thomas RC 1.50 4.00
162 Malachi Dupre RC 1.50 4.00
163 Michael Roberts RC 2.50 6.00
164 Ryan Ramczyk RC 1.50 4.00
165 Ryan Switzer RC 2.00 5.00
166 Rodney Adams RC 1.50 4.00
167 T.J. Watt RC 5.00 12.00
168 Aaron Jones RC 4.00 10.00
169 Taco Charlton RC 1.50 4.00
170 David Moore RC 1.50 4.00
171 Myles Garrett RC 5.00 12.00
172 Chris Carson RC 2.50 6.00
173 Gerald Everett RC 1.50 4.00
174 Kevin King RC 2.00 5.00
175 Jehu Chesson RC 2.00 5.00
176 Josh Malone RC 1.50 4.00
177 Malik Hooker RC 1.50 4.00
178 Elijah McGuire RC 1.50 4.00
179 Jonathan Allen RC 2.00 5.00
180 Isaiah Ford RC 1.50 4.00
181 Tre'Davious White RC 1.50 4.00
182 Matthew Dayes RC 1.50 4.00
183 Adam Shaheen RC 1.50 4.00
184 Teez Tabor RC 2.00 5.00
185 Chad Hansen RC 1.50 4.00
186 Isaiah McKenzie RC 1.50 4.00
187 Derek Barnett RC 2.00 5.00
188 De'Angelo Henderson RC 1.50 4.00
189 Gareon Conley RC 1.50 4.00
190 Devante Mays RC 1.50 4.00
191 Jabrill Peppers RC 2.50 6.00
192 Chad Kelly RC 1.50 4.00
193 Chad Williams RC 1.50 4.00
194 Raekwon McMillan RC 1.50 4.00
195 Brian Hill RC 1.50 4.00
196 DeAngelo Yancey RC 1.50 4.00
197 David Njoku RC 2.00 5.00
198 Robert Davis RC 1.50 4.00
199 Takkarist McKinley RC 1.50 4.00
200 Noah Brown RC 2.00 5.00
201 Mitchell Trubisky JSY AU/49 RC 60.00 125.00
202 Leonard Fournette JSY AU/49 RC 40.00 80.00
203 Corey Davis JSY AU/75 RC 25.00 50.00
204 Mike Williams JSY AU/49 RC 6.00 15.00
205 Christian McCaffrey JSY AU/49 RC 50.00 100.00
206 John Ross JSY AU/75 RC 4.00 10.00
207 Patrick Mahomes II JSY AU/49 RC 200.00 400.00
208 Deshaun Watson JSY AU/49 RC 75.00 150.00
209 O.J. Howard JSY AU/99 RC 10.00 25.00
210 Evan Engram JSY AU/99 RC 4.00 10.00
211 Alvin Kamara JSY AU/99 RC 12.00 30.00
212 Amara Darboh JSY AU/99 RC 3.00 8.00
213 ArDarius Stewart JSY AU/99 RC 3.00 8.00
214 Carlos Henderson JSY AU/99 RC 3.00 8.00
215 Cooper Kupp JSY AU/99 RC 5.00 12.00
216 Curtis Samuel JSY AU/75 RC 4.00 10.00
217 Dalvin Cook JSY AU/49 RC 40.00 80.00
218 Davis Webb JSY AU/99 RC 3.00 8.00
219 DeShone Kizer JSY AU/49 RC 25.00 50.00
220 D'Onta Foreman JSY AU/75 RC 4.00 10.00
221 Joe Mixon JSY AU/99 RC 6.00 15.00
222 JuJu Smith-Schuster JSY AU/75 RC 8.00 20.00
223 C.J. Beathard JSY AU/99 RC 3.00 8.00
224 Chris Godwin JSY AU/99 RC 4.00 10.00
225 James Conner JSY AU/99 RC 10.00 25.00
226 Kareem Hunt JSY AU/99 RC 8.00 20.00
227 Taywan Taylor JSY AU/99 RC 3.00 8.00
228 Zay Jones JSY AU/99 RC 4.00 10.00
229 Dede Westbrook JSY AU/75 RC 3.00 8.00
230 Kenny Golladay JSY AU/99 RC 5.00 12.00
231 Samaje Perine JSY AU/99 RC 12.00 30.00
232 Josh Reynolds JSY AU/99 RC 3.00 8.00
233 Mack Hollins JSY AU/99 RC 3.00 8.00
234 Joe Williams JSY AU/99 RC 3.00 8.00
235 Nathan Peterman JSY AU/99 RC 4.00 10.00
236 Jeremy McNichols JSY AU/99 RC 3.00 8.00
237 Jamaal Williams JSY AU/99 RC 10.00 25.00
238 R. Joshua Dobbs JSY AU/99 RC 15.00 40.00
239 Wayne Gallman JSY AU/99 RC 4.00 10.00
240 Marlon Mack JSY AU/99 RC 5.00 12.00
241 Mitchell Trubisky JSY AU/49 60.00 125.00
242 Leonard Fournette JSY AU/49 40.00 80.00
243 Corey Davis JSY AU/49 6.00 15.00
244 Mike Williams JSY AU/49 6.00 15.00
245 Christian McCaffrey JSY AU/49 50.00 100.00
246 John Ross JSY AU/49 5.00 12.00
247 Patrick Mahomes II JSY AU/49 200.00 400.00
248 Deshaun Watson JSY AU/49 75.00 150.00
249 O.J. Howard JSY AU/75 10.00 25.00
250 Evan Engram JSY AU/75 4.00 10.00
251 Alvin Kamara JSY AU/75 12.00 30.00
252 Amara Darboh JSY AU/75 3.00 8.00
253 ArDarius Stewart JSY AU/75 3.00 8.00
254 Carlos Henderson JSY AU/75 3.00 8.00
255 Cooper Kupp JSY AU/75 5.00 12.00
256 Curtis Samuel JSY AU/49 5.00 12.00
257 Dalvin Cook JSY AU/49 40.00 80.00
258 Davis Webb JSY AU/75 3.00 8.00
259 DeShone Kizer JSY AU/49 25.00 50.00
260 D'Onta Foreman JSY AU/49 5.00 12.00
261 Joe Mixon JSY AU/75 6.00 15.00
262 JuJu Smith-Schuster JSY AU/49 10.00 25.00
263 C.J. Beathard JSY AU/75 3.00 8.00
264 Chris Godwin JSY AU/75 4.00 10.00
265 James Conner JSY AU/75 10.00 25.00
266 Kareem Hunt JSY AU/75 8.00 20.00
267 Taywan Taylor JSY AU/75 3.00 8.00
268 Zay Jones JSY AU/75 4.00 10.00
269 Dede Westbrook JSY AU/49 4.00 10.00
270 Kenny Golladay JSY AU/75 5.00 12.00
271 Mitchell Trubisky JSY AU/49 60.00 125.00
272 Leonard Fournette JSY AU/49 40.00 80.00
273 Corey Davis JSY AU/49 6.00 15.00
274 Mike Williams JSY AU/49 6.00 15.00
275 Christian McCaffrey JSY AU/49 50.00 100.00
276 John Ross JSY AU/49 5.00 12.00
277 Patrick Mahomes II JSY AU/49 200.00 400.00
278 Deshaun Watson JSY AU/49 75.00 150.00
279 O.J. Howard JSY AU/75 10.00 25.00
280 Evan Engram JSY AU/75 4.00 10.00
281 Alvin Kamara JSY AU/75 12.00 30.00
282 Amara Darboh JSY AU/75 3.00 8.00
283 ArDarius Stewart JSY AU/75 3.00 8.00
284 Carlos Henderson JSY AU/75 3.00 8.00
285 Cooper Kupp JSY AU/75 5.00 12.00
286 Curtis Samuel JSY AU/49 5.00 12.00
287 Dalvin Cook JSY AU/49 40.00 80.00
288 Davis Webb JSY AU/75 3.00 8.00
289 DeShone Kizer JSY AU/49 25.00 50.00
290 D'Onta Foreman JSY AU/49 5.00 12.00
291 Joe Mixon JSY AU/75 6.00 15.00
292 JuJu Smith-Schuster JSY AU/49 10.00 25.00
293 C.J. Beathard JSY AU/75 3.00 8.00
294 Chris Godwin JSY AU/75 4.00 10.00
295 James Conner JSY AU/75 10.00 25.00
296 Kareem Hunt JSY AU/75 8.00 20.00
297 Taywan Taylor JSY AU/75 3.00 8.00
298 Zay Jones JSY AU/75 4.00 10.00
299 Dede Westbrook JSY AU/49 4.00 10.00
300 Kenny Golladay JSY AU/75 5.00 12.00
301 Mitchell Trubisky JSY AU/49 60.00 125.00
302 Leonard Fournette JSY AU/49 40.00 80.00
303 Corey Davis JSY AU/49 6.00 15.00
304 Mike Williams JSY AU/49 6.00 15.00
305 Christian McCaffrey JSY AU/49 50.00 100.00
306 John Ross JSY AU/49 5.00 12.00
307 Patrick Mahomes II JSY AU/49 200.00 400.00
308 Deshaun Watson JSY AU/49 75.00 150.00
309 O.J. Howard JSY AU/49 12.00 30.00
310 Evan Engram JSY AU/49 5.00 12.00
311 Alvin Kamara JSY AU/49 15.00 40.00
312 Amara Darboh JSY AU/49 4.00 10.00
313 ArDarius Stewart JSY AU/49 4.00 10.00
314 Carlos Henderson JSY AU/49 4.00 10.00
315 Cooper Kupp JSY AU/49 6.00 15.00
316 Curtis Samuel JSY AU/49 5.00 12.00
317 Dalvin Cook JSY AU/49 40.00 80.00
318 Davis Webb JSY AU/49 4.00 10.00
319 DeShone Kizer JSY AU/49 25.00 50.00
320 D'Onta Foreman JSY AU/49 5.00 12.00
321 Joe Mixon JSY AU/49 8.00 20.00
322 JuJu Smith-Schuster JSY AU/49 10.00 25.00
323 C.J. Beathard JSY AU/49 4.00 10.00
324 Chris Godwin JSY AU/49 5.00 12.00
325 James Conner JSY AU/49 12.00 30.00
326 Kareem Hunt JSY AU/49 12.00 30.00
327 Taywan Taylor JSY AU/49 4.00 10.00
328 Zay Jones JSY AU/49 5.00 12.00
329 Dede Westbrook JSY AU/49 4.00 10.00
330 Kenny Golladay JSY AU/49 6.00 15.00
331 Samaje Perine JSY AU/99 12.00 30.00
332 Josh Reynolds JSY AU/99 3.00 8.00
333 Mack Hollins JSY AU/99 3.00 8.00
334 Joe Williams JSY AU/99 3.00 8.00
335 Nathan Peterman JSY AU/99 4.00 10.00
336 Jeremy McNichols JSY AU/99 10.00 25.00
337 Jamaal Williams JSY AU/99 10.00 25.00
338 R. Joshua Dobbs JSY AU/99 15.00 40.00
339 Wayne Gallman JSY AU/99 4.00 10.00
340 Marlon Mack JSY AU/99 5.00 12.00

2017 Panini Gold Standard Platinum

*VETS/49: .5X TO 1.2X BASIC CARDS/79
*ROOK/49: .5X TO 1.2X BASIC CARDS/79

2017 Panini Gold Standard Rookie Jersey Autographs Prime

*PRIME/25: .6X TO 1.5X BASIC JSY AU/75-99
*PRIME/25: .5X TO 1.2X BASIC JSY AU/49
201 Mitchell Trubisky 100.00 200.00
205 Christian McCaffrey 100.00 200.00
207 Patrick Mahomes II 250.00 500.00
208 Deshaun Watson 150.00 250.00

2017 Panini Gold Standard Gold Gear

*PRIME: .5X TO 1.2X BASIC JSY
1 Cam Newton/25 5.00 12.00
2 Jerome Bettis/25 8.00 20.00
3 Joe Haden/49 2.50 6.00
4 Steve Young/25 10.00 25.00
5 Demaryius Thomas/49 3.00 8.00
6 Mike Evans/49 3.00 8.00
7 T.Y. Hilton/49 3.00 8.00
8 Adrian Peterson/25 5.00 12.00
9 Julio Jones/25 5.00 12.00
10 Joe Namath/25 15.00 40.00
11 Giovani Bernard/99 2.00 5.00
12 Rod Woodson/25 4.00 10.00
13 Tyron Smith/99 2.00 5.00
14 Jerry Rice/25 8.00 20.00
15 Eric Ebron/99 2.00 5.00
16 Kendall Wright/99 2.00 5.00
17 Josh Gordon/49 2.50 6.00
19 Joe Flacco/25 4.00 10.00
20 Derek Carr/49 4.00 10.00
21 Andy Dalton/49 3.00 8.00
22 Keenan Allen/49 3.00 8.00
23 John Elway/25 8.00 20.00
24 Tyler Lockett/99 2.50 6.00
25 Brett Favre/25 10.00 25.00
26 Sterling Shepard/99 2.50 6.00
27 Jay Ajayi/99 2.50 6.00
28 Odell Beckham Jr./49 4.00 10.00
29 Jim Kelly/25 5.00 12.00
30 Jordan Matthews/99 2.00 5.00

2017 Panini Gold Standard Gold Jacket Signatures

*PLATINUM/49: .5X TO 1.2X BASIC AU/83-99
*PLATINUM/25: .6X TO 1.5X BASIC AU/87
*PLATINUM/25: .5X TO 1.2X BASIC AU/64
1 Hugh McElhenny/99 4.00 10.00
3 Dan Hampton/83 3.00 8.00
5 Elvin Bethea/99 3.00 8.00
7 Y.A. Tittle/99 5.00 12.00
9 Fred Dean/99 3.00 8.00
11 Willie Roaf/99 3.00 8.00
13 Dermontti Dawson/87 8.00 20.00
15 Floyd Little/99 10.00 25.00
17 Dave Wilcox/64 4.00 10.00
19 Jimmy Johnson/99 8.00 20.00
20 Charley Trippi/99 3.00 8.00

2017 Panini Gold Standard Gold Rush Materials

*PRIME: .5X TO 1.2X BASIC JSY
1 Mark Ingram/49 3.00 8.00
2 LeSean McCoy/49 4.00 10.00
3 John Riggins/25 4.00 10.00
4 Ty Montgomery/99 2.00 5.00
5 James White/99 2.50 6.00
6 Todd Gurley II/99 3.00 8.00
7 Doug Martin/49 3.00 8.00
8 Thomas Rawls/49 2.50 6.00
9 Jerome Bettis/49 6.00 15.00
10 Jordan Howard/99 3.00 8.00
11 Eddie Lacy/49 2.50 6.00
12 Jeremy Hill/99 2.00 5.00
13 Tony Dorsett/25 5.00 12.00
14 Jay Ajayi/99 2.50 6.00
15 Carlos Hyde/99 2.00 5.00
16 Melvin Gordon/99 2.50 6.00
17 Franco Harris/49 4.00 10.00
18 Ezekiel Elliott/99 4.00 10.00
19 Le'Veon Bell/49 3.00 8.00
20 David Johnson/99 3.00 8.00

2017 Panini Gold Standard Gold Scripts

*PLATINUM/49: .5X TO 1.2X BASIC AU/99
*PLATINUM/25: .5X TO 1.2X BASIC AU/49
1 John Brown/49 5.00 12.00
3 Neil Smith/99 3.00 8.00
5 Dick LeBeau/25 5.00 12.00
7 David Carr/25 5.00 12.00
9 Steve Tasker/25 5.00 12.00
11 Charles Sims/99 3.00 8.00
13 Desmond Trufant/99 3.00 8.00
14 Ricky Williams/25 10.00 25.00
15 Kevin Mawae/25 5.00 12.00
17 Eric Weddle/25 5.00 12.00
19 Eric Berry/49 5.00 12.00
21 Mohamed Sanu/99 3.00 8.00
23 John Kuhn/99 3.00 8.00
24 Dwight Clark/25 6.00 15.00
25 Willie McGinest/25 5.00 12.00
27 Joe Haden/25 5.00 12.00
29 Ahmad Rashad/49 5.00 12.00
31 Ernest Givins/99 3.00 8.00
33 Travis Benjamin/99 3.00 8.00
34 Torry Holt/25 6.00 15.00
35 Allen Hurns/25 5.00 12.00
37 Mark Gastineau/25 5.00 12.00
39 Dermontti Dawson/49 5.00 12.00

2017 Panini Gold Standard Gold Strike Material Autographs

2 Steve Atwater/25 8.00 20.00
4 Jerick McKinnon/49 5.00 12.00
6 Gilbert Brown/99 4.00 10.00
8 Sterling Sharpe/25 8.00 20.00
10 Chris Ivory/25 8.00 20.00
12 Willie Roaf/25 6.00 15.00
14 Jim Zorn/99 4.00 10.00
16 Byron Jones/99 4.00 10.00
18 Kabeer Gbaja-Biamila/25 6.00 15.00
20 Derrick Brooks/25 6.00 15.00
22 Mike Vrabel/49 5.00 12.00
24 Jermaine Kearse/99 4.00 10.00
26 Henry Ellard/99 4.00 10.00
27 Don Maynard/25 8.00 20.00
28 Ray Guy/25 15.00 40.00
30 Haloti Ngata/25 6.00 15.00
32 Delanie Walker/49 5.00 12.00
34 Carlos Hyde/99 4.00 10.00
36 Morten Andersen/99 4.00 10.00
37 Paul Hornung/25 10.00 25.00
38 Chris Spielman/25 8.00 20.00
40 Mark Brunell/25 8.00 20.00

2017 Panini Gold Standard Golden Jumbo Threads

*PRIME: .5X TO 1.2X BASIC JSY
1 Josh Doctson/99 2.00 5.00
2 Brandin Cooks/75 2.50 6.00
3 Tony Romo/25 4.00 10.00
4 David Johnson/75 3.00 8.00
5 Tyrod Taylor/49 3.00 8.00
6 Ameer Abdullah/75 2.00 5.00
7 Paxton Lynch/99 2.00 5.00
8 Paul Perkins/99 2.00 5.00
9 Michael Thomas/99 3.00 8.00
10 LeSean McCoy/49 4.00 10.00
11 Jeremy Hill/75 2.00 5.00
12 Amari Cooper/75 3.00 8.00
13 Jordan Reed/49 2.50 6.00
14 Sammy Watkins/49 4.00 10.00
15 Devonta Freeman/75 2.50 6.00
16 Jadeveon Clowney/75 2.00 5.00
17 Ty Montgomery/75 2.00 5.00
18 DeAndre Washington/99 2.00 5.00
19 Leonard Williams/75 2.00 5.00
20 Corey Coleman/99 2.00 5.00
21 Devontae Booker/99 2.00 5.00
22 Joey Bosa/99 3.00 8.00
23 Von Miller/49 3.00 8.00
24 Jordan Howard/99 3.00 8.00
25 Kelvin Benjamin/75 2.50 6.00
26 T.J. Yeldon/75 2.00 5.00
27 Donte Moncrief/75 2.50 6.00
28 Hunter Henry/99 2.50 6.00
29 Wendell Smallwood/99 2.00 5.00
30 Davante Adams/75 2.50 6.00
31 DeAndre Hopkins/75 2.50 6.00
32 Doug Martin/49 3.00 8.00
33 Will Fuller V/99 2.00 5.00
34 Cody Kessler/99 2.00 5.00
35 Tyler Boyd/99 2.00 5.00
36 Kenyan Drake/99 2.00 5.00
37 Jared Goff/99 3.00 8.00
38 C.J. Prosise/99 2.00 5.00
39 Carlos Hyde/75 2.00 5.00
40 Andrew Luck/25 6.00 15.00
41 Blake Bortles/75 2.00 5.00
42 Tevin Coleman/75 2.50 6.00
43 Colin Kaepernick/75 2.50 6.00
44 Dak Prescott/99 3.00 8.00
45 Ezekiel Elliott/99 4.00 10.00
46 Malcolm Mitchell/49 3.00 8.00
47 Laquon Treadwell/99 2.00 5.00
48 Derrick Henry/99 2.50 6.00
49 Jameis Winston/75 2.50 6.00
50 Ryan Tannehill/49 3.00 8.00

2017 Panini Gold Standard Golden Rookies Autographs

*PLATINUM/49: .6X TO 1.5X BASIC AU/149
1 Jonathan Allen 4.00 10.00
2 Carlos Watkins 3.00 8.00
3 Kendell Beckwith 3.00 8.00
4 Corey Clement 4.00 10.00
5 Raekwon McMillan 3.00 8.00
6 Chad Hansen 3.00 8.00
7 Haason Reddick 3.00 8.00
8 Shelton Gibson 3.00 8.00
9 Solomon Thomas 3.00 8.00
10 Elijah Hood 3.00 8.00
11 Jabrill Peppers 5.00 12.00
12 Davon Godchaux 3.00 8.00
13 Kevin King 4.00 10.00
14 Travis Rudolph 3.00 8.00
15 Sidney Jones 3.00 8.00
16 Jake Butt 4.00 10.00
17 Jarrad Davis 4.00 10.00
18 Aaron Jones 8.00 20.00
19 Marshon Lattimore 4.00 10.00
20 Matthew Dayes 3.00 8.00
21 Gerald Everett 3.00 8.00
22 Elijah Qualls 3.00 8.00
23 Obi Melifonwu 3.00 8.00
24 Marlon Humphrey 3.00 8.00
25 Tim Williams 4.00 10.00
26 Jordan Leggett 3.00 8.00
27 Charles Harris 3.00 8.00
28 Brad Kaaya 3.00 8.00
29 Malik Hooker 3.00 8.00
30 Chad Kelly 15.00 40.00
31 Dalvin Tomlinson 3.00 8.00
32 Artavis Scott 3.00 8.00
33 DeMarcus Walker 3.00 8.00
34 Josh Malone 3.00 8.00
35 Zach Cunningham 4.00 10.00
36 Brian Hill 3.00 8.00
37 Tre'Davious White 3.00 8.00
38 Stacy Coley 3.00 8.00
39 Adoree' Jackson 4.00 10.00
41 Jordan Willis 3.00 8.00
42 KD Cannon 3.00 8.00
43 Cameron Sutton 3.00 8.00
44 Derek Barnett 10.00 25.00
45 Ryan Switzer 4.00 10.00
46 Donnel Pumphrey 4.00 10.00
47 T.J. Watt 25.00 50.00
48 Isaiah Ford 3.00 8.00
49 Jamal Adams 3.00 8.00
50 Carl Lawson 3.00 8.00

2017 Panini Gold Standard Gridiron Gold Materials

*PRIME: .5X TO 1.2X BASIC JSY
1 Le'Veon Bell/49 3.00 8.00
2 Paxton Lynch/99 2.00 5.00
3 Blake Bortles/99 2.00 5.00
4 Dak Prescott/99 3.00 8.00
5 Stefon Diggs/99 2.50 6.00
6 Derrick Henry/99 2.50 6.00
7 Todd Gurley II/99 3.00 8.00
8 Ezekiel Elliott/99 4.00 10.00
9 Jacoby Brissett/49 2.50 6.00
10 Jordan Howard/99 3.00 8.00
11 Russell Wilson/25 6.00 15.00
12 Tony Romo/25 4.00 10.00
13 Brandin Cooks/49 3.00 8.00
14 Davante Adams/99 2.50 6.00
15 Sterling Shepard/99 2.50 6.00
16 Devonta Freeman/49 3.00 8.00
17 Marcus Mariota/99 3.00 8.00
18 Jameis Winston/99 2.50 6.00
19 Tyler Eifert/99 2.50 6.00
20 Josh Doctson/99 2.00 5.00
21 Amari Cooper/49 4.00 10.00
22 Tyler Boyd/99 2.00 5.00
23 Corey Coleman/99 2.00 5.00
24 DeAndre Washington/99 2.00 5.00
25 Carson Wentz/99 4.00 10.00
26 Devontae Booker/99 2.00 5.00
27 Jeremy Langford/99 2.50 6.00
28 Jared Goff/99 3.00 8.00
29 Eddie Lacy/49 2.50 6.00
30 Michael Thomas/99 3.00 8.00

2017 Panini Gold Standard Newly Minted Memorabilia Duals

*PRIME/25: .8X TO 2X BASIC JSY/149
1 C.Davis/T.Taylor 5.00 12.00
2 D.Westbrook/L.Fournette 10.00 25.00
3 J.Conner/J.Smith-Schuster 4.00 10.00
4 K.Hunt/P.Mahomes 4.00 10.00
5 J.Reynolds/C.Kupp 3.00 8.00
7 D.Webb/E.Engram 2.50 6.00
8 J.Mixon/J.Ross 4.00 10.00
9 J.Mixon/S.Perine 4.00 10.00
10 D.Foreman/D.Watson 10.00 25.00

2017 Panini Gold Standard Newly Minted Memorabilia Triples

1 Rss/Dvs/Wllms 6.00 15.00
2 Wtsn/Wllms/Gllmn 12.00 30.00
3 Frmn/Rynlds/Mhms 30.00 80.00
4 Wstbrk/Mxn/Prne 5.00 12.00
5 Kmra/Rynlds/Dbbs 5.00 12.00
6 Rss/Mxn/Wllms 5.00 12.00
7 Trbsky/Mhms/Wtsn 12.00 30.00
8 Wbb/Engrm/Gllmn 3.00 8.00
9 McCffry/Ck/Frntte 12.00 30.00
10 SmthSchstr/Cnnr/Dbbs 5.00 12.00

2017 Panini Gold Standard White Gold Materials

*PRIME: .5X TO 1.2X BASIC JSY
1 James White/99 2.50 6.00
2 Matt Ryan/25 4.00 10.00
3 Khalil Mack/99 3.00 8.00
4 Alshon Jeffery/99 2.50 6.00
5 Terry Bradshaw/25
6 Tony Dorsett/25 5.00 12.00
7 Dwight Clark/49 3.00 8.00
8 DeMarcus Ware/49 3.00 8.00
9 Tajae Sharpe/49 2.50 6.00
10 Allen Robinson/99 2.50 6.00
11 Drew Brees/25 5.00 12.00
12 Ed Reed/25 4.00 10.00
13 Zach Ertz/99 2.50 6.00
14 Geno Atkins/99 2.00 5.00
15 Melvin Gordon/99 2.50 6.00
16 Travis Frederick/99 2.00 5.00
17 Joe Montana/25 15.00 40.00
18 Paul Hornung/25 5.00 12.00
19 Carson Wentz/99 4.00 10.00
20 Jarvis Landry/99 2.50 6.00
21 Eli Manning/25 4.00 10.00
22 Luke Kuechly/49 3.00 8.00
23 Franco Harris/25 5.00 12.00
24 Ozzie Newsome/25 4.00 10.00
25 Philip Rivers/25 5.00 12.00
26 Peyton Manning/25 10.00 25.00
27 Earl Thomas III/49 3.00 8.00
28 Aaron Rodgers/25 10.00 25.00
29 John Riggins/25 4.00 10.00
30 Cordarrelle Patterson/99 2.00 5.00

2018 Panini Gold Standard

1 Tom Brady 4.00 10.00
2 Julian Edelman 1.50 4.00
3 Rob Gronkowski 1.50 4.00
4 James White 1.25 3.00
5 LeSean McCoy 1.50 4.00
6 Kelvin Benjamin 1.25 3.00
7 Charles Clay 1.00 2.50
8 Ryan Tannehill 1.25 3.00
9 Kenyan Drake 1.00 2.50
10 DeVante Parker 1.25 3.00
11 Cameron Wake 1.00 2.50
12 Reshad Jones 1.00 2.50
13 Josh McCown 1.00 2.50
14 Darron Lee 1.00 2.50
15 Jermaine Kearse 1.00 2.50
16 Jamal Adams 1.25 3.00
17 Joe Flacco 1.25 3.00
18 Alex Collins 1.00 2.50
19 Terrell Suggs 1.00 2.50
20 Eric Weddle 1.00 2.50
21 A.J. Green 1.50 4.00
22 Andy Dalton 1.25 3.00
23 Joe Mixon 1.25 3.00
24 Vontaze Burfict 1.00 2.50
25 Josh Gordon 1.00 2.50
26 Tyrod Taylor 1.25 3.00
27 Jarvis Landry 1.25 3.00
28 Carlos Hyde 1.00 2.50
29 Myles Garrett 1.50 4.00
30 Antonio Brown 1.50 4.00
31 T.J. Watt 1.25 3.00
32 JuJu Smith-Schuster 1.50 4.00
33 Le'Veon Bell 1.25 3.00
34 Ben Roethlisberger 1.50 4.00
35 Alejandro Villanueva 1.25 3.00
36 DeAndre Hopkins 1.25 3.00
37 Deshaun Watson 2.00 5.00
38 D'Onta Foreman 1.00 2.50
39 J.J. Watt 1.50 4.00
40 T.Y. Hilton 1.25 3.00
41 Andrew Luck 2.00 5.00
42 Adam Vinatieri 1.00 2.50
43 Jack Doyle 1.00 2.50
44 Marqise Lee 1.00 2.50
45 Leonard Fournette 1.50 4.00
46 Jalen Ramsey 1.25 3.00
47 Blake Bortles 1.00 2.50
48 Marcus Mariota 1.50 4.00
49 Derrick Henry 1.50 4.00
50 Delanie Walker 1.00 2.50
51 Corey Davis 1.25 3.00
52 Case Keenum 1.25 3.00
53 Von Miller 1.25 3.00
54 Demaryius Thomas 1.25 3.00
55 Brandon Marshall 1.00 2.50
56 Emmanuel Sanders 1.50 4.00
57 Sammy Watkins 1.50 4.00
58 Tyreek Hill 1.50 4.00
59 Kareem Hunt 1.25 3.00
60 Travis Kelce 1.50 4.00
61 Patrick Mahomes II 4.00 10.00
62 Keenan Allen 1.25 3.00
63 Philip Rivers 1.50 4.00
64 Melvin Gordon 1.25 3.00
65 Casey Hayward 1.00 2.50
66 Derek Carr 1.50 4.00
67 Khalil Mack 1.50 4.00
68 Amari Cooper 1.50 4.00
69 Marshawn Lynch 1.25 3.00
70 Dak Prescott 1.50 4.00
71 Cole Beasley 1.25 3.00
72 Ezekiel Elliott 2.00 5.00
73 DeMarcus Lawrence 1.00 2.50
74 Jason Witten 1.25 3.00
75 Odell Beckham Jr. 1.50 4.00
76 Evan Engram 1.00 2.50
77 Eli Manning 1.25 3.00
78 Damon Harrison 1.00 2.50
79 Landon Collins 1.00 2.50
80 Alshon Jeffery 1.25 3.00
81 Carson Wentz 2.00 5.00
82 Jake Elliott 1.25 3.00
83 Jay Ajayi 1.25 3.00
84 Jason Kelce 1.00 2.50
85 Alex Smith 1.25 3.00
86 Chris Thompson 1.00 2.50
87 Jamison Crowder 1.00 2.50
88 Josh Norman 1.00 2.50
89 Dustin Hopkins 1.00 2.50
90 Matthew Stafford 1.25 3.00
91 Marvin Jones Jr. 1.00 2.50
92 Golden Tate III 1.00 2.50
93 Ezekiel Ansah 1.00 2.50
94 Davante Adams 1.25 3.00
95 Jimmy Graham 1.50 4.00
96 Aaron Rodgers 3.00 8.00
97 Aaron Jones 1.25 3.00
98 Kirk Cousins 1.50 4.00
99 Adam Thielen 1.50 4.00
100 Stefon Diggs 1.25 3.00
101 Dalvin Cook 1.25 3.00
102 Harrison Smith 1.50 4.00
103 Julio Jones 1.50 4.00
104 Devonta Freeman 1.25 3.00
105 Matt Ryan 1.25 3.00
106 Deion Jones 1.00 2.50
107 Cam Newton 1.50 4.00
108 Devin Funchess 1.00 2.50
109 Greg Olsen 1.25 3.00
110 Christian McCaffrey 1.50 4.00
111 Drew Brees 1.50 4.00
112 Mark Ingram 1.25 3.00
113 Alvin Kamara 1.25 3.00
114 Michael Thomas 1.50 4.00
115 Jameis Winston 1.25 3.00
116 Cameron Brate 1.00 2.50
117 Mike Evans 1.25 3.00
118 DeSean Jackson 1.25 3.00
119 Sam Bradford 1.00 2.50
120 Larry Fitzgerald 1.25 3.00
121 David Johnson 1.50 4.00
122 Patrick Peterson 1.00 2.50
123 Chandler Jones 1.00 2.50
124 Jared Goff 1.50 4.00
125 Todd Gurley II 1.50 4.00
126 Cooper Kupp 1.25 3.00
127 Robert Woods 1.25 3.00
128 Aaron Donald 1.50 4.00
129 Jimmy Garoppolo 2.00 5.00
130 Jerick McKinnon 1.00 2.50
131 Marquise Goodwin 1.00 2.50
132 Richard Sherman 1.50 4.00

133 Doug Baldwin 1.25 3.00
134 Russell Wilson 2.00 5.00
135 Earl Thomas 1.25 3.00
136 Tyler Lockett 1.25 3.00
137 Jordan Howard 1.50 4.00
138 Danny Trevathan 1.00 2.50
139 Mitchell Trubisky 1.50 4.00
140 Allen Robinson 1.25 3.00
141 Denzel Ward RC 4.00 10.00
142 Quenton Nelson RC 2.50 6.00
143 Roquan Smith RC 5.00 12.00
144 Mike McGlinchey RC 3.00 8.00
145 Minkah Fitzpatrick RC 3.00 8.00
146 Vita Vea RC 2.50 6.00
147 Daron Payne RC 2.50 6.00
148 Marcus Davenport RC 3.00 8.00
149 Kolton Miller RC 2.50 6.00
150 Tremaine Edmunds RC 3.00 8.00
151 Derwin James RC 3.00 8.00
152 Jaire Alexander RC 2.50 6.00
153 Leighton Vander Esch RC 5.00 12.00
154 Frank Ragnow RC 2.00 5.00
155 Billy Price RC 2.00 5.00
156 Rashaan Evans RC 2.50 6.00
157 Isaiah Wynn RC 1.50 4.00
158 Terrell Edmunds RC 5.00 12.00
159 Taven Bryan RC 1.50 4.00
160 Mike Hughes RC 2.50 6.00
161 Austin Corbett RC 2.50 6.00
162 Darius Leonard RC 4.00 10.00
163 Harold Landry RC 1.50 4.00
164 Joshua Jackson RC 3.00 8.00
165 Breeland Speaks RC 2.00 5.00
166 Uchenna Nwosu RC 2.50 6.00
167 Dallas Goedert RC 2.00 5.00
168 Jessie Bates RC 2.50 6.00
169 Duke Dawson RC 1.50 4.00
170 Lorenzo Carter RC 1.50 4.00
171 Fred Warner RC 1.50 4.00
172 Malik Jefferson RC 2.00 5.00
173 Mark Andrews RC 2.50 6.00
174 Arden Key RC 1.50 4.00
175 Antonio Callaway RC 2.00 5.00
176 Shaquem Griffin RC 2.50 6.00
177 John Kelly RC 2.00 5.00
178 Equanimeous St. Brown RC 2.50 6.00
179 Luke Falk RC 2.00 5.00
180 Maurice Hurst RC 2.00 5.00
181 Tanner Lee RC 2.00 5.00
182 Danny Etling RC 2.00 5.00
183 Alex McGough RC 2.00 5.00
184 Logan Woodside RC 2.50 6.00
185 Chase Edmonds RC 1.50 4.00
186 Jordan Wilkins RC 2.00 5.00
187 Bo Scarbrough RC 2.00 5.00
188 Justin Watson RC 2.00 5.00
189 Jordan Lasley RC 1.50 4.00
190 Damion Ratley RC 2.00 5.00
191 Russell Gage RC 2.00 5.00
192 Cedrick Wilson Jr. RC 1.50 4.00
193 Braxton Berrios RC 1.50 4.00
194 Marcell Ateman RC 2.00 5.00
195 David Williams RC 2.00 5.00
196 Kemoko Turay RC 2.00 5.00
197 M.J. Stewart RC 1.50 4.00
198 Donte Jackson RC 2.50 6.00
199 Tyquan Lewis RC 2.00 5.00
200 Orlando Brown RC 2.50 6.00
201 Baker Mayfield JSY AU/99 RC 100.00 200.00
202 Sam Darnold JSY AU/99 RC 40.00 80.00
203 Saquon Barkley JSY AU/99 RC 100.00 200.00
204 Josh Rosen JSY AU/99 RC 12.00 30.00
205 Josh Allen JSY AU/99 RC 25.00 60.00
206 Lamar Jackson JSY AU/99 RC 50.00 100.00
207 Calvin Ridley JSY AU/99 RC 20.00 50.00
208 Derrius Guice JSY AU/99 RC 12.00 30.00
209 Sony Michel JSY AU/99 RC 25.00 50.00
210 Mason Rudolph JSY AU/99 RC 15.00 40.00
211 Nick Chubb JSY AU/99 RC 12.00 30.00
212 Christian Kirk JSY AU/99 RC 6.00 15.00
213 Courtland Sutton JSY AU/99 RC 6.00 15.00
214 D.J. Moore JSY AU/99 RC 10.00 25.00
215 Rashaad Penny JSY AU/99 RC 6.00 15.00
216 Dante Pettis JSY AU/99 RC 6.00 15.00
217 James Washington JSY AU/99 RC 8.00 20.00
218 Ronald Jones II JSY AU/99 RC 4.00 10.00
219 Anthony Miller JSY AU/99 RC 6.00 15.00
220 Kerryon Johnson JSY AU/99 RC 10.00 25.00
221 Bradley Chubb JSY AU/99 RC 6.00 15.00
222 Kyle Lauletta JSY AU/99 RC 6.00 15.00
223 Royce Freeman JSY AU/99 RC 5.00 12.00
224 Mike Gesicki JSY AU/99 RC 5.00 12.00
225 Hayden Hurst JSY AU/99 RC 8.00 20.00
226 Nyheim Hines JSY AU/99 RC 5.00 12.00
227 Michael Gallup JSY AU/99 RC 15.00 40.00
228 D.J. Chark JSY AU/99 RC EXCH 5.00 12.00
229 Mike White JSY AU/99 RC 5.00 12.00
230 J'Mon Moore JSY AU/99 RC 4.00 10.00
231 Kalen Ballage JSY AU/99 RC 5.00 12.00
232 Ito Smith JSY AU/99 RC 5.00 12.00
233 Keke Coutee JSY AU/99 RC 5.00 12.00
234 DaeSean Hamilton JSY AU/99 RC 5.00 12.00
235 Jaleel Scott JSY AU/99 RC 4.00 10.00
236 Mark Walton JSY AU/99 RC 5.00 12.00
237 Jaylen Samuels JSY AU/99 RC 5.00 12.00
238 Daurice Fountain JSY AU/99 RC 5.00 12.00
239 Tre'Quan Smith JSY AU/99 RC 6.00 15.00
240 Marquez Valdes-Scantling JSY AU/99 RC 5.00 12.00
241 Baker Mayfield JSY AU/75 50.00 100.00
242 Sam Darnold JSY AU/75 40.00 80.00
243 Saquon Barkley JSY AU/75 100.00 200.00
244 Josh Rosen JSY AU/75 12.00 30.00
245 Josh Allen JSY AU/75 25.00 60.00
246 Calvin Ridley JSY AU/75 20.00 50.00
247 Derrius Guice JSY AU/75 12.00 30.00
248 Sony Michel JSY AU/75 25.00 50.00
249 Mason Rudolph JSY AU/75 15.00 40.00
250 Nick Chubb JSY AU/75 12.00 30.00
251 Christian Kirk JSY AU/75 6.00 15.00
252 Courtland Sutton JSY AU/75 6.00 15.00
253 D.J. Moore JSY AU/75 10.00 25.00
254 Rashaad Penny JSY AU/75 6.00 15.00
255 Dante Pettis JSY AU/75 6.00 15.00
256 James Washington JSY AU/75 8.00 20.00
257 Ronald Jones II JSY AU/75 4.00 10.00
258 Anthony Miller JSY AU/75 6.00 15.00
259 Kerryon Johnson JSY AU/75 10.00 25.00
260 Bradley Chubb JSY AU/75 6.00 15.00
261 Kalen Ballage JSY AU/75 5.00 12.00
262 Ito Smith JSY AU/75 5.00 12.00
263 Keke Coutee JSY AU/75 5.00 12.00
264 DaeSean Hamilton JSY AU/75 5.00 12.00
265 Jaleel Scott JSY AU/75 4.00 10.00
266 Mark Walton JSY AU/75 5.00 12.00
267 Jaylen Samuels JSY AU/75 5.00 12.00
268 Daurice Fountain JSY AU/75 5.00 12.00
269 Tre'Quan Smith JSY AU/75 6.00 15.00
270 Marquez Valdes-Scantling JSY AU/75 5.00 12.00
271 Baker Mayfield JSY AU/49 60.00 125.00
272 Sam Darnold JSY AU/49 50.00 100.00
273 Saquon Barkley JSY AU/49 150.00 250.00
274 Josh Rosen JSY AU/49 15.00 40.00
275 Josh Allen JSY AU/49 30.00 80.00
277 Calvin Ridley JSY AU/75 20.00 50.00
278 Derrius Guice JSY AU/75 12.00 30.00
279 Sony Michel JSY AU/75 25.00 50.00
280 Mason Rudolph JSY AU/75 15.00 40.00
281 Nick Chubb JSY AU/75 12.00 30.00
282 Christian Kirk JSY AU/75 6.00 15.00
283 Courtland Sutton JSY AU/75 6.00 15.00
284 D.J. Moore JSY AU/75 10.00 25.00
285 Rashaad Penny JSY AU/75 6.00 15.00
286 Dante Pettis JSY AU/75 6.00 15.00
287 James Washington JSY AU/75 8.00 20.00
288 Ronald Jones II JSY AU/75 4.00 10.00
289 Anthony Miller JSY AU/75 6.00 15.00
290 Kerryon Johnson JSY AU/75 10.00 25.00
291 Bradley Chubb JSY AU/75 6.00 15.00
292 Kyle Lauletta JSY AU/75 6.00 15.00
293 Royce Freeman JSY AU/75 5.00 12.00
294 Mike Gesicki JSY AU/75 5.00 12.00
295 Hayden Hurst JSY AU/75 8.00 20.00
296 Nyheim Hines JSY AU/75 5.00 12.00
297 Michael Gallup JSY AU/75 15.00 40.00
298 D.J. Chark JSY AU/75 EXCH 5.00 12.00
299 Mike White JSY AU/75 5.00 12.00
300 J'Mon Moore JSY AU/75 4.00 10.00
301 Baker Mayfield JSY AU/49 60.00 125.00
302 Sam Darnold JSY AU/49 50.00 100.00
303 Saquon Barkley JSY AU/49 150.00 250.00
304 Josh Rosen JSY AU/49 15.00 40.00
305 Josh Allen JSY AU/49 30.00 80.00
307 Calvin Ridley JSY AU/49 25.00 60.00
308 Derrius Guice JSY AU/75 12.00 30.00
309 Sony Michel JSY AU/75 25.00 50.00
310 Mason Rudolph JSY AU/75 15.00 40.00
311 Nick Chubb JSY AU/75 12.00 30.00
312 Christian Kirk JSY AU/75 6.00 15.00
313 Courtland Sutton JSY AU/75 6.00 15.00
314 D.J. Moore JSY AU/75 10.00 25.00
315 Rashaad Penny JSY AU/75 6.00 15.00
316 Dante Pettis JSY AU/99 5.00 12.00
317 James Washington JSY AU/99 8.00 20.00
318 Ronald Jones II JSY AU/99 4.00 10.00
319 Anthony Miller JSY AU/99 6.00 15.00
320 Kerryon Johnson JSY AU/99 10.00 25.00
321 Bradley Chubb JSY AU/99 6.00 15.00
322 Kyle Lauletta JSY AU/99 6.00 15.00
323 Royce Freeman JSY AU/99 5.00 12.00
324 Mike Gesicki JSY AU/99 5.00 12.00
325 Hayden Hurst JSY AU/99 8.00 20.00
326 Nyheim Hines JSY AU/99 5.00 12.00
327 Michael Gallup JSY AU/99 15.00 40.00
328 D.J. Chark JSY AU/99 EXCH 5.00 12.00
329 Mike White JSY AU/99 5.00 12.00
330 J'Mon Moore JSY AU/99 4.00 10.00
331 Kalen Ballage JSY AU/99 5.00 12.00
332 Ito Smith JSY AU/99 5.00 12.00
333 Keke Coutee JSY AU/99 5.00 12.00
334 DaeSean Hamilton JSY AU/99 5.00 12.00
335 Jaleel Scott JSY AU/99 4.00 10.00
336 Mark Walton JSY AU/99 5.00 12.00
337 Jaylen Samuels JSY AU/99 5.00 12.00
338 Daurice Fountain JSY AU/99 5.00 12.00
339 Tre'Quan Smith JSY AU/99 6.00 15.00
340 Marquez Valdes-Scantling JSY AU/99 5.00 12.00

2018 Panini Gold Standard Platinum

*VETS/49: .5X TO 1.2X BASIC CARDS/99
*ROOK/49: .5X TO 1.2X BASIC CARDS/99

2018 Panini Gold Standard Rookie Jersey Autographs Prime

*PRIME/49: .5X TO 1.2X BASIC JSY AU/75-99
*PRIME/25: .6X TO 1.5X BASIC JSY AU/75-99
*PRIME/25: .5X TO 1.2X BASIC JSY AU/49
203 Saquon Barkley/25 250.00 400.00
206 Lamar Jackson/25 200.00 300.00
243 Saquon Barkley/25 250.00 400.00
273 Saquon Barkley/25 250.00 400.00
276 Lamar Jackson/25 200.00 300.00
303 Saquon Barkley/25 250.00 400.00
306 Lamar Jackson/25 200.00 300.00

2018 Panini Gold Standard Rose Gold

*VETS/25: .6X TO 1.5X BASIC CARDS/99
*ROOK/25: .6X TO 1.5X BASIC CARDS/99

2018 Panini Gold Standard Gold Gear

*PRIME/49: .5X TO 1.2X BASIC JSY/125
1 Cris Carter 3.00 8.00
2 Tim Brown 3.00 8.00
3 Fred Taylor 2.00 5.00
4 Terrell Suggs 2.00 5.00
5 Mike Evans 2.50 6.00
6 Joe Flacco 2.50 6.00
7 T.J. Watt 2.50 6.00
8 Clay Matthews 2.50 6.00
9 Derek Carr 3.00 8.00
10 Jabrill Peppers 2.00 5.00
11 Golden Tate III 2.00 5.00
12 Jason Witten 2.50 6.00
13 David Njoku 2.00 5.00
14 Matthew Stafford 2.50 6.00
15 Russell Wilson 4.00 10.00
16 Marcus Mariota 3.00 8.00
17 Tyler Lockett 2.50 6.00
18 Jameis Winston 2.50 6.00
19 Matt Ryan 2.50 6.00
20 Doug Baldwin 2.50 6.00
21 LaDainian Tomlinson 2.50 6.00
22 Marshawn Lynch 2.50 6.00
23 Michael Irvin 3.00 8.00
24 Jim Kelly 3.00 8.00
25 Shane Ray 2.00 5.00
26 Travis Kelce 3.00 8.00
27 Earl Thomas III 2.50 6.00
28 Luke Kuechly 2.50 6.00
29 Jack Doyle 2.00 5.00
30 DeSean Jackson 2.50 6.00

2018 Panini Gold Standard Gold Jacket Signatures

*PLATINUM/49: .5X TO 1.2X BASIC AU/99
*PLATINUM/25: .5X TO 1.2X BASIC AU/49
3 Morten Andersen/99 3.00 8.00
6 Ray Guy/99 3.00 8.00
7 Andre Reed/99 4.00 10.00
10 Paul Hornung/49 10.00 25.00
12 Charles Haley/49 6.00 15.00
13 Larry Allen/25 8.00 20.00
14 Dick LeBeau/99 3.00 8.00
16 Bruce Matthews/99 3.00 8.00
17 Rayfield Wright/49 4.00 10.00
19 Marv Levy/25 12.00 30.00

2018 Panini Gold Standard Gold Rush Materials

*PRIME/49: .5X TO 1.2X BASIC JSY/125
1 Latavius Murray 2.00 5.00
2 Aaron Jones 2.50 6.00
3 Barry Sanders 5.00 12.00
4 Tony Dorsett 3.00 8.00
5 Roger Craig 2.50 6.00
6 Clinton Portis 2.00 5.00
7 Marshawn Lynch 2.50 6.00
8 Ezekiel Elliott 4.00 10.00
9 Alvin Kamara 2.50 6.00
10 Todd Gurley II 3.00 8.00
11 Leonard Fournette 3.00 8.00
12 Kareem Hunt 2.50 6.00
13 Dalvin Cook 2.50 6.00
14 Jordan Howard 3.00 8.00
15 Devontae Booker 2.00 5.00
16 Derrick Henry 3.00 8.00
17 Melvin Gordon 2.50 6.00
18 Devonta Freeman 2.50 6.00
19 D'Onta Foreman 2.00 5.00
20 David Johnson 3.00 8.00

2018 Panini Gold Standard Gold Strike Autographs

*PLATINUM/49: .5X TO 1.2X BASIC AU/75-99
*PLATINUM/25: .6X TO 1.5X BASIC AU/75-99
*PLATINUM/15-22: .8X TO 2X BASIC AU/75-99
*PLATINUM/25: .5X TO 1.2X BASIC AU/49
1 Justin Tucker/49 10.00 25.00
2 Alvin Kamara/99 8.00 20.00
3 Vance Johnson/99 3.00 8.00
4 Everson Walls/99 3.00 8.00
6 Brent Jones/49 10.00 25.00
7 Chris Hogan/99 3.00 8.00
8 Michael Vick/25 10.00 25.00
9 Zay Jones/99 3.00 8.00
10 Corey Clement/75 3.00 8.00
11 Jaelen Strong/49 4.00 10.00
12 Michael Thomas/49
13 Kellen Winslow/75 4.00 10.00
14 O.J. Howard/99 3.00 8.00
15 Ron Yary/49 4.00 10.00
16 Ryan Switzer/99 3.00 8.00
18 Joe Mixon/99 4.00 10.00
19 Aaron Jones/49 5.00 12.00
20 Ricky Williams/25 6.00 15.00
21 Jerick McKinnon/49 8.00 20.00
22 Michael Bennett/25 5.00 12.00
23 Alex Collins/99 3.00 8.00
24 John Kuhn/99 3.00 8.00
25 Jeff Garcia/49 4.00 10.00
26 Jehu Chesson/99 3.00 8.00
27 Geno Atkins/99 3.00 8.00
28 Larry Allen/49 6.00 15.00
30 Christian Okoye/99 3.00 8.00
31 Ahmad Rashad/99 4.00 10.00
32 Jermaine Kearse/99 3.00 8.00
33 DeAndre Washington/99 3.00 8.00
34 Kenyan Drake/24 6.00 15.00
36 Andre Reed/99 4.00 10.00
37 Kenny Golladay/99 3.00 8.00
38 Ezekiel Elliott/25 40.00 80.00
39 Tom Rathman/99 3.00 8.00
40 Chris Long/49 12.00 30.00
44 Keenan Allen/25 6.00 15.00
47 David Johnson/25 8.00 20.00
48 Ozzie Newsome/49 5.00 12.00
49 Willis McGahee/99 3.00 8.00
50 Brett Keisel/25 5.00 12.00
52 Mack Hollins/99 3.00 8.00
53 Trent Dilfer/49 4.00 10.00
54 Rich Gannon/25 6.00 15.00
55 Brian Dawkins/25 50.00 100.00
56 Kareem Hunt/25 12.00 30.00

2018 Panini Gold Standard Golden Age Autographs

*PLATINUM/25: .6X TO 1.5X BASIC AU/99
*PLATINUM/25: .5X TO 1.2X BASIC AU/49
3 Charlie Joiner/99 3.00 8.00
6 Carl Eller/49 4.00 10.00
11 Jack Ham/25 12.00 30.00
12 Jimmy Johnson/20
14 Ray Guy/99 3.00 8.00
17 Jack Youngblood/49 4.00 10.00
18 John Hannah/75
21 Kellen Winslow/99 4.00 10.00
23 Ozzie Newsome/25 6.00 15.00
24 Paul Warfield/25 6.00 15.00

2018 Panini Gold Standard Golden Jumbo Threads

*PRIME/49: .5X TO 1.2X BASIC JSY/125
*PRIME/26-29: .6X TO 1.5X BASIC JSY/125
1 Shaun Alexander/125 2.00 5.00
2 Geno Atkins/125 2.00 5.00
4 DeVante Parker/125 2.50 6.00
5 Telvin Smith/125 2.00 5.00
6 Andy Dalton/125 2.50 6.00
7 Tyler Eifert/125 2.50 6.00
8 Jarvis Landry/125 2.50 6.00
9 Zay Jones/125 2.00 5.00
10 Marqise Lee/125 2.00 5.00
11 A.J. Green/125 3.00 8.00
12 Dez Bryant/125 3.00 8.00
13 Emmanuel Sanders/125 3.00 8.00
14 Tyrod Taylor/125 2.50 6.00
15 Tyron Smith/125 2.00 5.00
16 Dak Prescott/125 3.00 8.00
17 Trent Williams/125 2.00 5.00
18 LaVar Arrington/114 2.00 5.00
20 Richie Incognito/125 2.00 5.00
21 Tedy Bruschi/125 3.00 8.00
22 Keenan Allen/125 2.50 6.00
23 Jimmy Garoppolo/125 6.00 15.00
24 Aqib Talib/125 2.00 5.00
25 Matthew Stafford/125 2.50 6.00
26 Blake Bortles/125 2.00 5.00
27 Hines Ward/125 2.50 6.00
28 DeAndre Hopkins/125 2.50 6.00
29 Tony Romo/125 2.50 6.00
30 Cole Beasley/125 2.50 6.00
31 Terrance Williams/125 2.00 5.00
35 Melvin Gordon/125 2.50 6.00
37 Jordan Poyer/125 2.00 5.00
38 Zack Martin/125 2.00 5.00
39 Ryan Tannehill/125 2.50 6.00
40 Giovani Bernard/125 2.00 5.00
41 Jordan Matthews/125 2.00 5.00
42 Reshad Jones/125 2.00 5.00
43 Darqueze Dennard/125 2.00 5.00
44 Jerry Hughes/125 2.00 5.00
45 Adam Jones/125 2.00 5.00
46 Jourdan Lewis/125 2.00 5.00
47 Cameron Wake/125 2.00 5.00
48 Marquise Goodwin/125 2.00 5.00
49 Michael Vick/125 2.50 6.00
50 Kiko Alonso/125 2.00 5.00

2018 Panini Gold Standard Golden Rookies Autographs

*PLATINUM/49: .6X TO 1.5X BASIC AU/149
*PLATINUM/49: .5X TO 1.2X BASIC AU/99
1 Antonio Callaway/149 8.00 20.00
2 Arden Key/149 4.00 10.00
3 Auden Tate/149 4.00 10.00
4 Austin Proehl/149 4.00 10.00
5 Bo Scarbrough/149 5.00 12.00
6 Braxton Berrios/149 4.00 10.00
7 Chase Edmonds/149 4.00 10.00
8 Carlton Davis/149 5.00 12.00
9 Cedrick Wilson Jr./149 4.00 10.00
10 Richie James/149 4.00 10.00
11 Dallas Goedert/149 5.00 12.00
12 Dalton Schultz/149 5.00 12.00
13 Marcell Ateman/149 5.00 12.00
14 John Kelly/149 5.00 12.00
15 Daron Payne/149 6.00 15.00
16 Denzel Ward/149 10.00 25.00
17 Chase Litton/149 5.00 12.00
18 Derrick Nnadi/149 4.00 10.00
19 Derwin James/149 8.00 20.00
20 Donte Jackson/149 6.00 15.00
21 Duke Dawson/149 4.00 10.00
22 Fred Warner/149 4.00 10.00
23 Harold Landry/149 4.00 10.00
24 Ray-Ray McCloud/149 4.00 10.00
25 Isaiah Oliver/149 4.00 10.00
26 Jaire Alexander/149 6.00 15.00
27 Jalyn Holmes/149 6.00 15.00
28 Jerome Baker/149 5.00 12.00
29 Dylan Cantrell/149 4.00 10.00
30 Luke Falk/149 5.00 12.00
31 Jordan Lasley/149 4.00 10.00
32 Joshua Jackson/149 8.00 20.00
33 Justin Reid/149 4.00 10.00
34 Ian Thomas/149 4.00 10.00
35 Leighton Vander Esch/149 12.00 30.00
36 Lorenzo Carter/149 4.00 10.00
37 M.J. Stewart/149 4.00 10.00
38 Malik Jefferson/149 5.00 12.00
39 Marcus Davenport/149 8.00 20.00
40 Mark Andrews/149 6.00 15.00
41 Mike Hughes/149 6.00 15.00
42 Minkah Fitzpatrick/149 10.00 25.00
43 Dorance Armstrong Jr./149 4.00 10.00
44 Maurice Hurst/149 5.00 12.00
45 Rashaan Evans/149 6.00 15.00
46 Tanner Lee/149 5.00 12.00
47 Rasheem Green/149 4.00 10.00
48 Ronnie Harrison/149 5.00 12.00
49 Roquan Smith/149 12.00 30.00
50 Sam Hubbard/149 5.00 12.00
51 Shaquem Griffin/149 10.00 25.00
52 Justin Jackson/149 5.00 12.00
53 Taven Bryan/99 5.00 12.00
54 Terrell Edmunds/149 12.00 30.00
55 Trey Quinn/149 4.00 10.00
56 Tremaine Edmunds/149 8.00 20.00
57 Tyler Conklin/149 4.00 10.00
58 Tyquan Lewis/149 5.00 12.00
59 Harrison Phillips/149 4.00 10.00
60 Vita Vea/149 6.00 15.00

2018 Panini Gold Standard Good as Gold Autograph Materials

*PRIME/49: .5X TO 1.2X BASIC JSY AU/99-125
*PRIME/25-34: .6X TO 1.5X BASIC JSY AU/99-125
*PRIME/25: .5X TO 1.2X BASIC JSY AU/49
2 Carson Wentz/25 60.00 125.00
3 Tyreek Hill/25 10.00 25.00
4 Antonio Brown/25 40.00 80.00
5 Marlon Mack/125 4.00 10.00
6 Willis McGahee/125 4.00 10.00
10 Kenyan Drake/125 4.00 10.00
11 Kiko Alonso/125 4.00 10.00
12 Aaron Jones/125 5.00 12.00
13 T.J. Watt/125 8.00 20.00
14 Jabrill Peppers/125 8.00 20.00
15 Corey Davis/99 5.00 12.00
16 Jamal Adams/125 5.00 12.00
17 Shaq Lawson/125 4.00 10.00
19 Chris Thompson/25 6.00 15.00
21 Brett Keisel/99 8.00 20.00
22 Cooper Kupp/99
23 Andre Reed/49 6.00 15.00
25 Alvin Kamara/125 8.00 20.00
26 Jordan Howard/49 8.00 20.00
27 Brian Dawkins/25 40.00 80.00
30 Eric Berry/125 10.00 25.00
32 Samaje Perine/125 4.00 10.00
33 Wayne Gallman/125 4.00 10.00
36 Joe Mixon/125 5.00 12.00
37 Marshon Lattimore/125 4.00 10.00
38 Thurman Thomas/25 8.00 20.00
39 D'Onta Foreman/125 4.00 10.00
40 Patrick Mahomes II/25

2018 Panini Gold Standard Gridiron Gold Materials

*PRIME/49: .5X TO 1.2X BASIC JSY/125
1 Joe Flacco 2.50 6.00
2 Rod Woodson 3.00 8.00
3 Greg Olsen 2.50 6.00
4 Luke Kuechly 2.50 6.00
5 Tony Romo 2.50 6.00
6 T.J. Watt 2.50 6.00
7 Jerry Rice 5.00 12.00
8 Steve Young 4.00 10.00
9 Hines Ward 2.50 6.00
10 Brian Dawkins 3.00 8.00
11 Clinton Portis 2.00 5.00
12 Terrell Suggs 2.00 5.00
13 Fred Taylor 2.00 5.00
14 Michael Irvin 3.00 8.00
15 Roger Craig 2.50 6.00
16 Clay Matthews 2.50 6.00
17 Marshawn Lynch 2.50 6.00
18 James Harrison 2.50 6.00
19 Tony Dorsett 3.00 8.00
20 Jason Witten 2.50 6.00
21 Marcus Allen 3.00 8.00
22 Charles Woodson 8.00 20.00
23 Len Dawson 3.00 8.00
24 LaDainian Tomlinson 2.50 6.00
25 Bo Jackson 8.00 20.00
26 Edgerrin James 2.50 6.00
27 Howie Long 3.00 8.00
28 Joe Namath 8.00 20.00
29 Earl Campbell 3.00 8.00
30 Jerome Bettis 3.00 8.00

2018 Panini Gold Standard Newly Minted Memorabilia

*PRIME/49: .6X TO 1.5X BASIC JSY/199
1 Baker Mayfield 6.00 15.00
2 Sam Darnold 6.00 15.00
3 Saquon Barkley 8.00 20.00
4 Josh Rosen 6.00 15.00
5 Josh Allen 5.00 12.00
6 Lamar Jackson 6.00 15.00
7 Calvin Ridley 3.00 8.00
8 Derrius Guice 3.00 8.00
9 Sony Michel 3.00 8.00
10 Mason Rudolph 4.00 10.00
11 Nick Chubb 4.00 10.00
12 Christian Kirk 2.50 6.00
13 Courtland Sutton 2.50 6.00
14 D.J. Moore 3.00 8.00
15 Rashaad Penny 2.50 6.00
16 Dante Pettis 2.50 6.00
17 James Washington 3.00 8.00
18 Ronald Jones II 3.00 8.00
19 Anthony Miller 2.50 6.00
20 Kerryon Johnson 2.50 6.00
21 Bradley Chubb 2.50 6.00
22 Kyle Lauletta 2.50 6.00
23 Royce Freeman 2.00 5.00
24 Mike Gesicki 2.00 5.00
25 Hayden Hurst 2.00 5.00
26 Nyheim Hines 2.00 5.00
27 Michael Gallup 3.00 8.00
28 D.J. Chark 2.00 5.00
29 Mike White 2.00 5.00
30 Mark Walton 2.00 5.00
31 J'Mon Moore 1.50 4.00
32 Kalen Ballage 2.00 5.00
33 Ito Smith 2.00 5.00
34 Jaylen Samuels 2.00 5.00
35 Keke Coutee 2.00 5.00
36 DaeSean Hamilton 2.00 5.00
37 Jaleel Scott 1.50 4.00
38 Daurice Fountain 2.00 5.00
39 Tre'Quan Smith 2.50 6.00
40 Marquez Valdes-Scantling 2.00 5.00

2018 Panini Gold Standard Newly Minted Memorabilia Duals

*PRIME/49: .6X TO 1.5X BASIC JSY/199
1 C.Kirk/J.Rosen 8.00 20.00
2 C.Ridley/I.Smith 5.00 12.00
3 H.Hurst/L.Jackson 8.00 20.00
4 B.Mayfield/N.Chubb 8.00 20.00
5 M.Gallup/M.White 4.00 10.00
6 B.Chubb/C.Sutton 3.00 8.00
7 J.Moore/M.VldsScntlng 2.50 6.00
8 D.Fountain/N.Hines 2.50 6.00
9 K.Lauletta/S.Barkley 10.00 25.00
10 J.Washington/M.Rudolph 5.00 12.00

2018 Panini Gold Standard Newly Minted Memorabilia Triples

*PRIME/49: .6X TO 1.5X BASIC JSY/199
1 Hrst/Sctt/Jcksn 8.00 20.00
2 Chbb/Sttn/Frmn 3.00 8.00
3 Wshngtn/Smls/Rdlph 5.00 12.00
4 Chbb/Smls/Hns 3.00 8.00
5 Hmltn/Gscki/Brkly 10.00 25.00
6 Myfld/Alln/Drnld 8.00 20.00
7 Chbb/Pnny/Mchl 6.00 15.00
8 Rdly/Ptts/Mre 5.00 12.00
9 Rdly/Mre/Smth 5.00 12.00
10 Myfld/Mre/Brkly 10.00 25.00

2018 Panini Gold Standard White Gold Materials

*PRIME/49: .5X TO 1.2X BASIC JSY/125
1 Aaron Rodgers 12.00 30.00
2 Odell Beckham Jr. 3.00 8.00
3 Ezekiel Elliott 4.00 10.00
4 Carson Wentz 6.00 15.00
5 Jared Goff 3.00 8.00
6 Dak Prescott 3.00 8.00
7 Antonio Brown 3.00 8.00
8 Rob Gronkowski 3.00 8.00
9 Harrison Smith 3.00 8.00
10 Russell Wilson 4.00 10.00
11 Derek Carr 3.00 8.00
12 JuJu Smith-Schuster 3.00 8.00
13 Todd Gurley II 3.00 8.00
14 Deshaun Watson 4.00 10.00
15 Matthew Stafford 2.50 6.00

2019 Panini Gold Standard

1 Patrick Mahomes II 4.00 10.00
2 Sammy Watkins 1.50 4.00
3 Travis Kelce 1.50 4.00
4 Alex Smith 1.25 3.00
5 Adrian Peterson 1.50 4.00
6 Derrius Guice 1.25 3.00
7 Marcus Mariota 1.50 4.00
8 Corey Davis 1.25 3.00
9 Derrick Henry 1.50 4.00
10 Jameis Winston 1.25 3.00
11 Mike Evans 1.25 3.00
12 Gerald McCoy 1.00 2.50
13 Russell Wilson 2.00 5.00
14 Doug Baldwin 1.25 3.00
15 Tyler Lockett 1.25 3.00
16 Jimmy Garoppolo 1.50 4.00
17 Nick Mullens 1.25 3.00
18 Richard Sherman 1.25 3.00
19 Ben Roethlisberger 1.25 3.00
20 James Conner 1.50 4.00
21 T.J. Watt 1.25 3.00
22 Carson Wentz 2.00 5.00
23 Alshon Jeffery 1.25 3.00
24 Nick Foles 1.25 3.00
25 Derek Carr 1.50 4.00
26 Marshawn Lynch 1.25 3.00
27 JuJu Smith-Schuster 1.50 4.00
28 Sam Darnold 1.50 4.00
29 Jamal Adams 1.25 3.00
30 Robby Anderson 1.00 2.50
31 Odell Beckham Jr. 1.50 4.00
32 Eli Manning 1.25 3.00
33 Saquon Barkley 2.00 5.00
34 Drew Brees 1.50 4.00
35 Alvin Kamara 1.25 3.00
36 Michael Thomas 1.50 4.00
37 Tom Brady 4.00 10.00
38 Sony Michel 1.50 4.00
39 Rob Gronkowski 1.50 4.00
40 Kirk Cousins 1.50 4.00
41 Adam Thielen 1.50 4.00
42 Stefon Diggs 1.25 3.00
43 Kenyan Drake 1.00 2.50
44 George Kittle 1.00 2.50
45 Kiko Alonso 1.00 2.50
46 Jared Goff 1.50 4.00
47 Todd Gurley II 1.50 4.00
48 Aaron Donald 1.50 4.00
49 Brandin Cooks 1.25 3.00
50 Philip Rivers 1.50 4.00
51 Joey Bosa 1.25 3.00
52 Melvin Gordon III 1.25 3.00
53 Keenan Allen 1.25 3.00
54 Leonard Fournette 1.50 4.00
55 Jalen Ramsey 1.25 3.00
56 Andrew Luck 2.00 5.00
57 Darius Leonard 1.25 3.00
58 T.Y. Hilton 1.25 3.00
59 Deshaun Watson 2.00 5.00
60 J.J. Watt 1.50 4.00
61 DeAndre Hopkins 1.25 3.00
62 Aaron Rodgers 3.00 8.00
63 Davante Adams 1.25 3.00
64 Blake Martinez 1.00 2.50
65 Matthew Stafford 1.25 3.00
66 Golden Tate III 1.25 3.00
67 Kerryon Johnson 1.25 3.00
68 Von Miller 1.25 3.00
69 Bradley Chubb 1.25 3.00
70 Phillip Lindsay 1.50 4.00
71 Dak Prescott 1.50 4.00
72 Ezekiel Elliott 2.00 5.00
73 Leighton Vander Esch 1.25 3.00
74 Amari Cooper 1.50 4.00
75 Baker Mayfield 2.50 6.00
76 Myles Garrett 1.00 2.50
77 Nick Chubb 1.50 4.00
78 Jarvis Landry 1.25 3.00
79 Andy Dalton 1.25 3.00
80 Joe Mixon 1.25 3.00
81 A.J. Green 1.50 4.00
82 Khalil Mack 1.50 4.00
83 Mitchell Trubisky 1.50 4.00
84 Tarik Cohen 1.25 3.00
85 Cam Newton 1.50 4.00
86 Christian McCaffrey 1.50 4.00
87 Luke Kuechly 1.25 3.00
88 Josh Allen 1.50 4.00
89 LeSean McCoy 1.50 4.00
90 Zay Jones 1.00 2.50
91 Lamar Jackson 1.50 4.00
92 Le'Veon Bell 1.25 3.00
93 Terrell Suggs 1.00 2.50
94 Matt Ryan 1.50 4.00
95 Calvin Ridley 1.25 3.00
96 Julio Jones 1.50 4.00
97 Josh Rosen 1.50 4.00
98 Larry Fitzgerald 1.25 3.00
99 David Johnson 1.50 4.00
100 Antonio Brown 1.50 4.00
101 Julian Edelman 1.50 4.00
102 Nick Foles 1.25 3.00
103 Tom Brady 4.00 10.00
104 Von Miller 1.25 3.00
105 Tom Brady 4.00 10.00
106 Malcolm Smith 1.00 2.50
107 Joe Flacco 1.25 3.00
108 Eli Manning 1.25 3.00
109 Aaron Rodgers 3.00 8.00
110 Drew Brees 1.50 4.00
111 Eli Manning 1.25 3.00
112 Peyton Manning 3.00 8.00
113 Hines Ward 1.50 4.00
114 Deion Branch 1.00 2.50
115 Tom Brady 4.00 10.00
116 Ray Lewis 1.50 4.00
117 Kurt Warner 1.25 3.00
118 John Elway 2.50 6.00
119 Terrell Davis 1.25 3.00
120 Pat McAfee 1.25 3.00
121 Brett Favre 3.00 8.00
122 Brian Urlacher 1.50 4.00
123 Jerry Rice 2.50 6.00
124 Roger Staubach 2.00 5.00
125 Joe Montana 4.00 10.00
126 Joe Thomas 1.00 2.50
127 Curtis Martin 1.25 3.00
128 Troy Aikman 2.00 5.00
129 Michael Irvin 2.00 5.00
130 Mike Alstott 1.00 2.50
131 Barry Sanders 2.50 6.00
132 Jerome Bettis 1.50 4.00
133 Brian Dawkins 1.50 4.00
134 Ed Reed 1.25 3.00
135 Lawrence Taylor 1.50 4.00
136 Deion Sanders 1.25 3.00
137 Dan Marino 3.00 8.00
138 Tony Gonzalez 1.25 3.00
139 Mike Golic 1.00 2.50
140 Randy Moss 1.25 3.00
141 Quinnen Williams RC 1.50 4.00
142 Clelin Ferrell RC 2.50 6.00
143 Devin White RC 5.00 12.00
144 Josh Allen RC 6.00 15.00
145 Ed Oliver RC 2.50 6.00
146 Devin Bush II RC 6.00 15.00
147 Jonah Williams RC 4.00 10.00
148 Rashan Gary RC 3.00 8.00
149 Christian Wilkins RC 6.00 15.00
150 Brian Burns RC 2.00 5.00
151 Dexter Lawrence RC 2.50 6.00
152 Jeffery Simmons RC 1.50 4.00
153 Darnell Savage Jr. RC 2.50 6.00
154 Montez Sweat RC 5.00 12.00
155 Johnathan Abram RC 1.50 4.00
156 Jerry Tillery RC 2.00 5.00
157 L.J. Collier RC 1.50 4.00
158 Deandre Baker RC 4.00 10.00
159 Byron Murphy RC 1.50 4.00
160 Rock Ya-Sin RC 2.00 5.00
161 Sean Murphy-Bunting RC 2.00 5.00
162 Trayvon Mullen Jr. RC 2.50 6.00
163 Jahlani Tavai RC 2.00 5.00
164 Joejuan Williams RC 2.00 5.00
165 Greedy Williams RC 5.00 12.00
166 Marquise Blair RC 2.00 5.00
167 Ben Banogu RC 3.00 8.00
168 Drew Sample RC 1.50 4.00
169 Jalen Hurd RC 2.00 5.00
170 Trysten Hill RC 2.50 6.00
171 Nasir Adderley RC 2.00 5.00
172 Taylor Rapp RC 1.50 4.00
173 Juan Thornhill RC 1.50 4.00
174 Zach Allen RC 2.50 6.00
175 Josh Oliver RC 1.50 4.00
176 Jace Sternberger RC 2.00 5.00
177 Chase Winovich RC 5.00 12.00
178 Kahale Warring RC 2.00 5.00
179 Julian Love RC 2.00 5.00
180 Trevon Wesco RC 2.50 6.00
181 Foster Moreau RC 1.50 4.00
182 Ryquell Armstead RC 1.50 4.00
183 Zach Gentry RC 1.50 4.00
184 Qadree Ollison RC 2.00 5.00
185 Clayton Thorson RC 2.50 6.00
186 KeeSean Johnson RC 1.50 4.00
187 Kaden Smith RC 1.50 4.00
188 Gardner Minshew II RC 2.50 6.00
189 Trayveon Williams RC 2.00 5.00
190 Isaac Nauta RC 2.00 5.00
191 Dexter Williams RC 2.00 5.00
192 Trace McSorley RC 4.00 10.00
193 Travis Homer RC 1.50 4.00
194 Rodney Anderson RC 2.00 5.00
195 Mike Weber RC 2.50 6.00
196 Dakota Allen RC 2.50 6.00
197 Kelvin Harmon RC 2.50 6.00
198 John Ursua RC 1.50 4.00
199 Mitch Wishnowsky RC 1.50 4.00
200 Matt Gay RC 1.50 4.00
201 Dwayne Haskins JSY AU RC 50.00 100.00
202 Kyler Murray JSY AU RC 100.00 200.00
203 Drew Lock JSY AU RC 30.00 60.00
204 Daniel Jones JSY AU RC 40.00 80.00
205 Will Grier JSY AU RC 15.00 40.00
206 Ryan Finley JSY AU RC 8.00 20.00
207 Jarrett Stidham JSY AU RC 15.00 40.00
208 Josh Jacobs JSY AU RC 20.00 50.00
209 Damien Harris JSY AU RC 10.00 25.00
210 Darrell Henderson JSY AU RC 10.00 25.00
211 David Montgomery JSY AU RC 15.00 40.00
212 Marquise Brown JSY AU RC 12.00 30.00
213 D.K. Metcalf JSY AU RC 20.00 50.00
214 A.J. Brown JSY AU RC 10.00 25.00
215 Parris Campbell JSY AU RC 10.00 25.00
217 Deebo Samuel JSY AU RC 10.00 25.00
218 Nick Bosa JSY AU RC 15.00 40.00
219 N'Keal Harry JSY AU RC 20.00 50.00
220 Noah Fant JSY AU RC 8.00 20.00
221 T.J. Hockenson JSY AU RC 10.00 25.00
222 Easton Stick JSY AU RC 6.00 15.00
223 Diontae Johnson JSY AU RC 5.00 12.00
224 Hunter Renfrow JSY AU RC 8.00 20.00
225 Miles Sanders JSY AU RC 12.00 30.00
226 Bryce Love JSY AU RC 6.00 15.00
227 Justice Hill JSY AU RC 6.00 15.00
228 Benny Snell Jr. JSY AU RC 12.00 30.00
229 Devin Singletary JSY AU RC 12.00 30.00
230 Darius Slayton JSY AU RC 6.00 15.00
231 JJ Arcega-Whiteside JSY AU RC 6.00 15.00
232 Alexander Mattison JSY AU RC 8.00 20.00
233 Gary Jennings Jr. JSY AU RC 6.00 15.00
234 Mecole Hardman Jr. JSY AU RC 10.00 25.00
235 Tony Pollard JSY AU RC 10.00 25.00
236 Riley Ridley JSY AU RC 6.00 15.00
237 Terry McLaurin JSY AU RC 5.00 12.00
238 Andy Isabella JSY AU RC 6.00 15.00
239 Miles Boykin JSY AU RC 5.00 12.00
240 Irv Smith Jr. JSY AU RC 8.00 20.00
241 Dwayne Haskins JSY AU 50.00 100.00
242 Kyler Murray JSY AU 100.00 200.00
243 Drew Lock JSY AU 30.00 60.00
244 Daniel Jones JSY AU 40.00 80.00
245 Will Grier JSY AU 15.00 40.00
246 Ryan Finley JSY AU 8.00 20.00
247 Jarrett Stidham JSY AU 15.00 40.00
248 Josh Jacobs JSY AU 20.00 50.00
249 Damien Harris JSY AU 10.00 25.00
250 Darrell Henderson JSY AU 10.00 25.00
251 David Montgomery JSY AU 15.00 40.00
252 Marquise Brown JSY AU 12.00 30.00
253 D.K. Metcalf JSY AU 20.00 50.00
254 A.J. Brown JSY AU 10.00 25.00
255 Parris Campbell JSY AU 10.00 25.00
256 Hakeem Butler JSY AU 8.00 20.00
257 Deebo Samuel JSY AU 10.00 25.00
258 Nick Bosa JSY AU 15.00 40.00
259 N'Keal Harry JSY AU 20.00 50.00
260 Noah Fant JSY AU 8.00 20.00
261 T.J. Hockenson JSY AU 10.00 25.00
262 Diontae Johnson JSY AU 5.00 12.00
263 Miles Sanders JSY AU 12.00 30.00
264 Justice Hill JSY AU 6.00 15.00
265 Devin Singletary JSY AU 12.00 30.00
266 JJ Arcega-Whiteside JSY AU 6.00 15.00
267 Gary Jennings Jr. JSY AU 6.00 15.00
268 Tony Pollard JSY AU 10.00 25.00
269 Mecole Hardman Jr. JSY AU 10.00 25.00
270 Miles Boykin JSY AU 5.00 12.00
271 Dwayne Haskins JSY AU /49 60.00 125.00
272 Kyler Murray JSY AU /49 125.00 250.00
273 Drew Lock JSY AU /49 40.00 80.00
274 Daniel Jones JSY AU /49 50.00 100.00
275 Will Grier JSY AU /75 15.00 40.00
276 Ryan Finley JSY AU /75 8.00 20.00
277 Jarrett Stidham JSY AU /75 15.00 40.00
278 Josh Jacobs JSY AU /75 20.00 50.00
279 Damien Harris JSY AU /75 10.00 25.00
280 Darrell Henderson JSY AU /75 10.00 25.00
281 David Montgomery JSY AU /75 15.00 40.00
282 Marquise Brown JSY AU /75 12.00 30.00
283 D.K. Metcalf JSY AU /75 20.00 50.00
284 A.J. Brown JSY AU /75 10.00 25.00
285 Parris Campbell JSY AU /75 10.00 25.00
286 Deebo Samuel JSY AU /75 10.00 25.00
287 Nick Bosa JSY AU /75 15.00 40.00
288 N'Keal Harry JSY AU /75 20.00 50.00
289 Noah Fant JSY AU /75 8.00 20.00
290 T.J. Hockenson JSY AU /75 10.00 25.00
291 Easton Stick JSY AU /75 6.00 15.00
292 Hunter Renfrow JSY AU /75 8.00 20.00
293 Bryce Love JSY AU /75 6.00 15.00
294 Benny Snell Jr. JSY AU /75 12.00 30.00
295 Darius Slayton JSY AU /75 6.00 15.00
296 Alexander Mattison JSY AU /75 8.00 20.00
297 Mecole Hardman Jr. JSY AU /75 10.00 25.00
298 Riley Ridley JSY AU /75 6.00 15.00
299 Andy Isabella JSY AU /75 6.00 15.00
300 Irv Smith Jr. JSY AU /75 8.00 20.00
301 Dwayne Haskins JSY AU /49 60.00 125.00
302 Kyler Murray JSY AU /49 125.00 250.00
303 Drew Lock JSY AU /49 40.00 80.00
304 Daniel Jones JSY AU /49 50.00 100.00
305 Will Grier JSY AU /99 15.00 40.00
306 Ryan Finley JSY AU /99 8.00 20.00
307 Jarrett Stidham JSY AU /99 15.00 40.00
308 Josh Jacobs JSY AU /99 20.00 50.00
309 Damien Harris JSY AU /99 10.00 25.00
310 Darrell Henderson JSY AU /99 10.00 25.00
311 David Montgomery JSY AU /99 15.00 40.00
312 Marquise Brown JSY AU /99 12.00 30.00
313 D.K. Metcalf JSY AU /99 20.00 50.00
314 A.J. Brown JSY AU /99 10.00 25.00
315 Parris Campbell JSY AU /99 10.00 25.00
317 Deebo Samuel JSY AU /99 10.00 25.00
318 Nick Bosa JSY AU /99 15.00 40.00
319 N'Keal Harry JSY AU /99 20.00 50.00
320 Noah Fant JSY AU /99 8.00 20.00
321 T.J. Hockenson JSY AU /99 10.00 25.00
322 Easton Stick JSY AU /99 6.00 15.00
323 Diontae Johnson JSY AU /99 5.00 12.00
324 Hunter Renfrow JSY AU /99 8.00 20.00
325 Miles Sanders JSY AU /99 12.00 30.00
326 Bryce Love JSY AU /99 6.00 15.00
327 Justice Hill JSY AU /99 6.00 15.00
328 Benny Snell Jr. JSY AU /99 12.00 30.00
329 Devin Singletary JSY AU /99 12.00 30.00
330 Darius Slayton JSY AU /99 6.00 15.00
331 JJ Aega-Whiteside JSY AU /99 6.00 15.00
332 Alexander Mattison JSY AU /99 8.00 20.00
333 Gary Jennings Jr. JSY AU /99 6.00 15.00
334 Mecole Hardman Jr. JSY AU /99 10.00 25.00
335 Tony Pollard JSY AU /99 10.00 25.00
336 Riley Ridley JSY AU /99 6.00 15.00
337 Terry McLaurin JSY AU /99 5.00 12.00
338 Andy Isabella JSY AU /99 6.00 15.00
339 Miles Boykin JSY AU /99 5.00 12.00
340 Irv Smith Jr. JSY AU /99 8.00 20.00

2019 Panini Gold Standard Platinum

*VETS/75: .4X TO 1X BASIC CARDS/99
*ROOK/49: .5X TO 1.2X BASIC CARDS/99

2019 Panini Gold Standard Rookie Jersey Autographs Prime

*PRIME/49: .5X TO 1.2X BASIC JSY AU/75-99
*PRIME/25: .5X TO 1.2X BASIC JSY AU/49
202 Kyler Murray 125.00 250.00
242 Kyler Murray 125.00 250.00
272 Kyler Murray 150.00 300.00

2019 Panini Gold Standard Rose Gold

*VETS/25: .6X TO 1.5X BASIC CARDS/99
*ROOKIES/25: .6X TO 1.5X BASIC CARDS/99

2019 Panini Gold Standard Gold Gear

*PRIME/49: .5X TO 1.2X BASIC JSY AU/99-199
*PRIME/25: .6X TO 1.5X BASIC JSY AU/99-199
*PRIME/15: .8X TO 2X BASIC JSY AU/99-199
1 Brian Westbrook 2.00 5.00
2 Jared Goff 3.00 8.00
3 Greg Olsen 2.50 6.00
4 Carson Wentz 4.00 10.00
5 Josh Allen 3.00 8.00
6 Mohamed Sanu 2.00 5.00
7 Calvin Ridley 2.50 6.00
8 Kyle Long 2.00 5.00
9 Kerryon Johnson 2.50 6.00
10 Travis Kelce 3.00 8.00
11 Jordan Howard 3.00 8.00
12 James Conner 3.00 8.00
13 Delanie Walker 2.00 5.00
14 D.J. Moore 2.50 6.00
15 James White 2.50 6.00
16 Deshaun Watson 4.00 10.00
17 Christian McCaffrey 3.00 8.00
18 Joe Mixon 2.50 6.00
19 Nick Chubb 3.00 8.00
20 Michael Gallup 3.00 8.00
21 Bradley Chubb 2.50 6.00
22 Kenny Golladay 2.00 5.00
23 Davante Adams 2.50 6.00
24 Leonard Fournette 3.00 8.00
25 Joey Bosa 2.50 6.00
26 Cooper Kupp 2.50 6.00
27 Matt Ryan 3.00 8.00
28 Dalvin Cook 2.50 6.00
29 Sony Michel 3.00 8.00
30 Sterling Shepard 2.50 6.00
31 Sam Darnold 3.00 8.00
32 Marshawn Lynch 2.50 6.00
33 Richard Sherman 2.50 6.00
34 O.J. Howard 2.00 5.00
35 Marcus Mariota 3.00 8.00
36 Ryan Kerrigan 2.00 5.00
37 Jordan Reed 2.00 5.00
38 David Johnson 3.00 8.00
39 Alejandro Villanueva 2.50 6.00
40 James Harrison 2.50 6.00

2019 Panini Gold Standard Gold Rush Jerseys

*PRIME/49: .5X TO 1.2X BASIC INSERTS/99-199
*PRIME/25: .6X TO 1.5X BASIC INSERTS/99-199
*PRIME/25: .5X TO 1.2X BASIC INSERTS/50
*PRIME/20: .8X TO 2X BASIC INSERTS/99-199
1 A.J. Green/199 3.00 8.00
2 Minkah Fitzpatrick/199 2.00 5.00
3 Larry Fitzgerald/99 2.50 6.00
4 Julio Jones/199 3.00 8.00
5 LeSean McCoy/199 3.00 8.00
6 Mitchell Trubisky/199 3.00 8.00
7 Jarvis Landry/99 2.50 6.00
8 DeMarcus Lawrence/50 2.50 6.00
9 Andrew Luck/199 4.00 10.00
10 Patrick Mahomes II/199 8.00 20.00
11 Calvin Johnson/199 2.50 6.00
12 Steven Jackson/199 2.00 5.00
13 Tremaine Edmunds/199 2.50 6.00
14 Aaron Jones/199 2.50 6.00
15 Zach Thomas/199 2.00 5.00
16 Emmanuel Sanders/199 3.00 8.00
17 Brandon McManus/199 2.00 5.00
18 Luke Kuechly/199 2.50 6.00
19 Tyler Eifert/199 2.50 6.00
20 Trent Williams/199 2.00 5.00
21 Tony Romo/199 2.50 6.00
22 Aaron Donald/199 3.00 8.00
23 T.J. Watt/199 2.50 6.00
24 Stefon Diggs/199 2.50 6.00
25 Saquon Barkley/199 4.00 10.00
26 Russell Wilson/199 4.00 10.00
27 Rob Gronkowski/199 3.00 8.00
28 Philip Rivers/199 3.00 8.00
29 Tiki Barber/100 2.00 5.00
30 Mike Williams/199 2.00 5.00
31 Michael Thomas/199 3.00 8.00
32 Melvin Gordon III/199 2.50 6.00
33 Kiko Alonso/199 2.00 5.00
34 Kenyan Drake/199 2.00 5.00
35 Keenan Allen/199 2.50 6.00
36 David Njoku/199 2.00 5.00
37 Isaac Bruce/199 3.00 8.00
38 Hines Ward/199 3.00 8.00
39 Harrison Smith/199 2.00 5.00
40 Geno Atkins/199 2.00 5.00

2019 Panini Gold Standard Golden Debut Autographs

*PLATINUM/25: .6X TO 1.5X BASIC AU/99
CDADH Dwayne Haskins/25 75.00 150.00
CDAKM Kyler Murray/25 125.00 250.00
CDADL Drew Lock/25 30.00 80.00
CDADJ Daniel Jones/25 30.00 80.00
CDAMB Marquise Brown/99 12.00 30.00
CDADM D.K. Metcalf/99 12.00 30.00
CDANH N'Keal Harry/99 25.00 50.00
CDAJJ Josh Jacobs/99 20.00 50.00
CDATH T.J. Hockenson/99 10.00 25.00
CDANB Nick Bosa/99 12.00 30.00

2019 Panini Gold Standard Golden Pairs Jerseys

*PRIME/49: .5X TO 1.2X BASIC JSY/149
*PRIME/25: .6X TO 1.5X BASIC JSY/149
1 C.Ridley/J.Jones 4.00 10.00
2 N.Chubb/B.Mayfield 6.00 15.00
3 D.Prescott#[E.Elliott 5.00 12.00
4 T.Davis/J.Elway 6.00 15.00
5 R.Lewis/T.Suggs 4.00 10.00
6 C.Johnson/M.Stafford 3.00 8.00
7 J.Clowney/J.Watt 4.00 10.00
8 J.Rice/S.Young 5.00 12.00
9 D.Brees/M.Thomas 4.00 10.00
10 K.Cousins/S.Diggs 4.00 10.00
11 M.Gordon/P.Rivers 4.00 10.00
12 P.Mahomes/T.Kelce 15.00 40.00
13 M.Irvin/T.Aikman 10.00 25.00
14 P.Manning/E.James 12.00 30.00
15 D.Hopkins/D.Watson 5.00 12.00
16 A.Kamara/M.Ingram 3.00 8.00
17 S.Jackson/I.Bruce 4.00 10.00
18 J.Taylor/Z.Thomas 2.50 6.00
19 D.Henry/M.Mariota 4.00 10.00
20 D.Hampton/M.Singletary 3.00 8.00

2019 Panini Gold Standard Golden Rookies Autographs

1 Clayton Thorson 5.00 12.00
2 Trayveon Williams 4.00 10.00
3 Darnell Savage Jr. 5.00 12.00
4 Jerry Tillery 4.00 10.00
5 Dexter Williams 4.00 10.00
6 Myles Gaskin 6.00 15.00
7 Mike Weber 5.00 12.00
8 Ryquell Armstead 3.00 8.00
9 L.J. Collier 3.00 8.00
10 Jordan Scarlett 3.00 8.00
11 Qadree Ollison 4.00 10.00
12 Nasir Adderley 4.00 10.00
13 Taylor Rapp 3.00 8.00
14 Josh Oliver 3.00 8.00
15 Dillon Mitchell 4.00 10.00
16 Chase Winovich 10.00 25.00
17 Oshane Ximines 3.00 8.00
18 Dre Greenlaw 3.00 8.00
19 Gardner Minshew II 5.00 12.00
20 Josh Allen 12.00 30.00
21 Travis Homer 3.00 8.00
22 Greedy Williams 10.00 25.00
23 Deandre Baker 8.00 20.00
24 Julian Love 4.00 10.00
25 Trayvon Mullen Jr. 5.00 12.00
26 Byron Murphy 3.00 8.00
27 Rashan Gary 6.00 15.00
28 Clelin Ferrell 5.00 12.00
29 Jaylon Ferguson 3.00 8.00
30 Kelvin Harmon 5.00 12.00
31 Zach Allen 5.00 12.00
32 Brian Burns 4.00 10.00
34 Ed Oliver 5.00 12.00
35 Dexter Lawrence 5.00 12.00
36 Christian Wilkins 12.00 30.00
37 Jeffery Simmons 3.00 8.00
38 Devin White 10.00 25.00
39 Devin Bush II 12.00 30.00
40 Deionte Thompson 4.00 10.00
41 Johnathan Abram 3.00 8.00
42 Caleb Wilson 3.00 8.00
43 Brett Rypien 4.00 10.00
44 Trace McSorley 8.00 20.00
45 Rodney Anderson 4.00 10.00
46 KeeSean Johnson 3.00 8.00
48 Travis Fulgham 3.00 8.00
49 Tyree Jackson 8.00 20.00
50 Rock Ya-Sin 4.00 10.00

2019 Panini Gold Standard Good as Gold Jersey Autographs

*PRIME/49: .5X TO 1.2X BASIC JSY AU/99-149
*PRIME/25: .6X TO 1.5X BASIC JSY AU/99-149
*PRIME/25: .5X TO 1.2X BASIC JSY AU/49
1 Geno Atkins/149 4.00 10.00
2 Devin Hester/49 6.00 15.00
3 Phillip Lindsay/149 15.00 40.00
4 Earl Campbell/49 8.00 20.00
5 Tim Brown/49 10.00 25.00
6 Tarik Cohen/149 5.00 12.00
7 Rob Gronkowski/25 25.00 50.00
8 Jordan Reed/49 5.00 12.00
9 Andre Reed/49 6.00 15.00
10 Roger Craig/49 6.00 15.00
11 Zach Thomas/49 25.00 50.00
12 Brian Westbrook/49 10.00 25.00
13 Mark Duper/149 4.00 10.00
14 Dick Butkus/25 15.00 40.00
15 Ickey Woods/25 6.00 15.00
16 Steve Largent/49 6.00 15.00
17 Rod Woodson/49 6.00 15.00
18 Davante Adams/49 EXCH 10.00 25.00
19 T.J. Watt/149 EXCH 8.00 20.00
20 Edgerrin James/49 6.00 15.00
21 Kenyan Drake/149 4.00 10.00
22 Travis Kelce/49 EXCH 15.00 40.00
23 Vance Johnson/149 4.00 10.00
25 Chris Spielman/49 10.00 25.00
27 DeAndre Hopkins/49 12.00 30.00
28 Steven Jackson/49 5.00 12.00
29 Greg Olsen/49 6.00 15.00
30 Bill Romanowski/99 5.00 12.00
31 Danny White/99 5.00 12.00
32 Jason Witten/49 30.00 60.00
33 Hines Ward/49 12.00 30.00
34 Alshon Jeffery/49 10.00 25.00
35 John Lynch/49 5.00 12.00
36 Eric Weddle/99 4.00 10.00
37 Deshaun Watson/25 30.00 60.00
38 Patrick Mahomes II/49 125.00 250.00
39 Mitchell Trubisky/25 40.00 80.00

2019 Panini Gold Standard Hall of Gold Threads

*PRIME/49: .5X TO 1.2X BASIC JSY/149
1 Tony Gonzalez 2.50 6.00
2 Tony Dorsett 3.00 8.00
3 Terrell Davis 2.50 6.00
4 Steve Young 4.00 10.00
5 Steve Largent 2.50 6.00
6 Ozzie Newsome 2.50 6.00
7 Mike Singletary 2.50 6.00
8 Michael Strahan 3.00 8.00
9 Michael Irvin 4.00 10.00
10 Marshall Faulk 2.50 6.00
11 Marcus Allen 3.00 8.00
12 Lawrence Taylor 3.00 8.00
13 Kurt Warner 2.50 6.00
14 John Riggins 2.50 6.00
15 John Elway 5.00 12.00
16 Joe Theismann 2.50 6.00
17 Jerry Rice 5.00 12.00
18 Jerome Bettis 3.00 8.00
19 Howie Long 2.50 6.00
20 Dick Butkus 4.00 10.00

2019 Panini Gold Standard Mother Lode Materials

*PRIME/49: .5X TO 1.2X BASIC JSY/149
1 JuJu Smith-Schuster 4.00 10.00
2 Calvin Ridley 3.00 8.00
3 Baker Mayfield 40.00 100.00
4 Lamar Jackson 4.00 10.00
5 Saquon Barkley 5.00 12.00
6 Josh Allen 4.00 10.00
7 Deshaun Watson 5.00 12.00
8 Mitchell Trubisky 4.00 10.00
9 Sam Darnold 4.00 10.00
10 Sony Michel 4.00 10.00
11 Nick Chubb 4.00 10.00
12 James Conner 4.00 10.00
13 Christian McCaffrey 4.00 10.00
14 Michael Gallup 4.00 10.00
15 Michael Thomas 4.00 10.00
16 Dalvin Cook 3.00 8.00
17 Joey Bosa 3.00 8.00
18 Cooper Kupp 3.00 8.00
19 Patrick Mahomes II 40.00 100.00
20 Anthony Miller 3.00 8.00

2019 Panini Gold Standard Newly Minted Memorabilia

*PRIME/49: .6X TO 1.5X BASIC JSY/199
1 Dwayne Haskins 5.00 12.00
2 Kyler Murray 10.00 25.00
3 Drew Lock 5.00 12.00
4 Daniel Jones 5.00 12.00
5 Will Grier 4.00 10.00
6 Ryan Finley 3.00 8.00
7 Jarrett Stidham 4.00 10.00
8 Josh Jacobs 5.00 12.00
9 Damien Harris 4.00 10.00
10 Darrell Henderson 4.00 10.00
11 David Montgomery 4.00 10.00
12 Marquise Brown 4.00 10.00
13 D.K. Metcalf 4.00 10.00
14 A.J. Brown 4.00 10.00
15 Parris Campbell 4.00 10.00
16 Hakeem Butler 3.00 8.00
17 Deebo Samuel 4.00 10.00
18 Nick Bosa 4.00 10.00
19 N'Keal Harry 4.00 10.00
20 Noah Fant 3.00 8.00
21 T.J. Hockenson 4.00 10.00
22 Easton Stick 2.50 6.00
23 Diontae Johnson 2.00 5.00
24 Hunter Renfrow 3.00 8.00
25 Miles Sanders 4.00 10.00
26 Bryce Love 2.50 6.00
27 Justice Hill 2.50 6.00
28 Benny Snell Jr. 4.00 10.00
29 Devin Singletary 2.00 5.00
30 Darius Slayton 2.50 6.00
31 JJ Arcega-Whiteside 2.50 6.00
32 Alexander Mattison 3.00 8.00
33 Gary Jennings Jr. 2.50 6.00
34 Mecole Hardman Jr. 4.00 10.00
35 Tony Pollard 4.00 10.00
36 Riley Ridley 2.50 6.00
37 Terry McLaurin 2.00 5.00
38 Andy Isabella 2.50 6.00
39 Miles Boykin 2.00 5.00
40 Irv Smith Jr. 3.00 8.00

2019 Panini Gold Standard Newly Minted Memorabilia Duals

*PRIME/49: .6X TO 1.5X BASIC JSY/199
1 R.Ridley/M.Hardman 5.00 12.00
2 K.Murray/M.Brown 12.00 30.00
3 H.Butler/K.Murray 12.00 30.00
4 N.Fant/D.Lock 6.00 15.00
5 J.Stidham/N.Harry 5.00 12.00
6 B.Love/D.Haskins 6.00 15.00
7 D.Slayton/D.Jones 6.00 15.00
8 D.Metcalf/G.Jennings 5.00 12.00
9 D.Haskins/K.Murray 12.00 30.00
10 N.Fant/T.Hockenson 5.00 12.00

2019 Panini Gold Standard White Gold Materials

*PRIME/49: .5X TO 1.2X BASIC JSY/149
*PRIME/25: .6X TO 1.5X BASIC JSY/149
1 Ryan Kerrigan 2.00 5.00
2 Adrian Peterson 3.00 8.00
3 Ben Roethlisberger 2.50 6.00
4 Brett Keisel 2.00 5.00
5 Clay Matthews 2.50 6.00
6 Devin Hester 2.50 6.00
7 Harrison Smith 2.00 5.00
8 J.J. Watt 3.00 8.00
9 Jason Witten 2.50 6.00
10 Joe Theismann 2.50 6.00
11 John Elway 5.00 12.00
12 Travis Kelce 3.00 8.00
13 Thurman Thomas 2.50 6.00
14 Steve Largent 2.50 6.00
15 Sammy Watkins 3.00 8.00
16 Russell Wilson 4.00 10.00
17 Mike Singletary 2.50 6.00
18 Michael Vick 2.50 6.00
19 Marshawn Lynch 2.50 6.00
20 Marquise Goodwin 2.00 5.00

2010 Panini Gridiron Gear

COMP.SET w/o RC's (150) 8.00 20.00
251-285 ROOK.JSY AU PRINT RUN 164-326
1 Chris Wells .20 .50
2 Larry Fitzgerald .25 .60
3 Steve Breaston .20 .50
4 Tim Hightower .20 .50
5 Curtis Lofton .20 .50
6 Matt Ryan .25 .60
7 Michael Turner .20 .50
8 Roddy White .20 .50
9 Anquan Boldin .20 .50
10 Joe Flacco .25 .60
11 Ray Lewis .30 .75
12 Ray Rice .20 .50
13 T.J. Houshmandzadeh .20 .50
14 Willis McGahee .20 .50
15 Lee Evans .25 .60
16 Marshawn Lynch .25 .60
17 Roscoe Parrish .20 .50
18 Ryan Fitzpatrick .20 .50
19 DeAngelo Williams .20 .50
20 Dwayne Jarrett .20 .50
21 Jonathan Stewart .20 .50
22 Steve Smith .25 .60
23 Brian Urlacher .30 .75
24 Devin Aromashodu .20 .50
25 Devin Hester .25 .60
26 Jay Cutler .20 .50
27 Julius Peppers .25 .60
28 Matt Forte .20 .50
29 Carson Palmer .25 .60
30 Cedric Benson .20 .50
31 Chad Ochocinco .20 .50
32 Terrell Owens .25 .60
33 Benjamin Watson .20 .50
34 Jerome Harrison .20 .50
35 Josh Cribbs .20 .50
36 Mohamed Massaquoi .25 .60
37 DeMarcus Ware .25 .60
38 Felix Jones .20 .50
39 Jason Witten .25 .60
40 Miles Austin .20 .50
41 Tony Romo .25 .60
42 Brandon Lloyd .20 .50
43 Eddie Royal .20 .50
44 Knowshon Moreno .20 .50
45 Kyle Orton .20 .50
46 Brandon Pettigrew .20 .50
47 Calvin Johnson .30 .75
48 Matthew Stafford .25 .60
49 Nate Burleson .20 .50
50 Aaron Rodgers .60 1.50
51 Clay Matthews .30 .75
52 Donald Driver .25 .60
53 Greg Jennings .20 .50
54 Jermichael Finley .20 .50
55 Andre Johnson .25 .60
56 Arian Foster .25 .60
57 Kevin Walter .25 .60
58 Matt Schaub .20 .50
59 Owen Daniels .20 .50
60 Austin Collie .20 .50
61 Dallas Clark .20 .50
62 Joseph Addai .20 .50
63 Peyton Manning .75 2.00
64 Reggie Wayne .25 .60
65 David Garrard .20 .50
66 Marcedes Lewis .20 .50
67 Maurice Jones-Drew .20 .50
68 Mike Sims-Walker .20 .50
69 Chris Chambers .20 .50
70 Dwayne Bowe .25 .60
71 Jamaal Charles .25 .60
72 Matt Cassel .20 .50
73 Thomas Jones .20 .50
74 Anthony Fasano .20 .50
75 Brandon Marshall .25 .60
76 Brian Hartline .25 .60
77 Chad Henne .25 .60
78 Ronnie Brown .20 .50
79 Adrian Peterson .30 .75
80 Bernard Berrian .20 .50
81 Brett Favre .60 1.50
82 Percy Harvin .20 .50
83 Sidney Rice .20 .50
84 Visanthe Shiancoe .25 .60
85 Brandon Meriweather .20 .50
86 Fred Taylor .20 .50
87 Randy Moss .25 .60
88 Tom Brady .75 2.00
89 Wes Welker .25 .60
90 Devery Henderson .20 .50
91 Drew Brees .30 .75
92 Marques Colston .20 .50
93 Pierre Thomas .20 .50
94 Reggie Bush .20 .50
95 Robert Meachem .20 .50
96 Ahmad Bradshaw .20 .50
97 Brandon Jacobs .20 .50
98 Eli Manning .25 .60
99 Hakeem Nicks .20 .50
100 Steve Smith USC .20 .50
101 Braylon Edwards .20 .50
102 Darrelle Revis .20 .50
103 LaDainian Tomlinson .30 .75
104 Mark Sanchez .20 .50
105 Shonn Greene .20 .50
106 Darren McFadden .20 .50
107 Darrius Heyward-Bey .25 .60
108 Bruce Gradkowski .20 .50
109 Louis Murphy .20 .50
110 Zach Miller .20 .50
111 DeSean Jackson .25 .60
112 Jeremy Maclin .20 .50
113 Kevin Kolb .20 .50
114 LeSean McCoy .30 .75
115 Michael Vick UER .25 .60
116 Ben Roethlisberger .30 .75
117 Heath Miller .20 .50
118 Hines Ward .25 .60
119 Mike Wallace .20 .50
120 Rashard Mendenhall .20 .50
121 Troy Polamalu .30 .75
122 Antonio Gates .25 .60
123 Darren Sproles .25 .60
124 Malcom Floyd .20 .50
125 Philip Rivers .30 .75
126 Frank Gore .25 .60
127 Michael Crabtree .20 .50
128 Patrick Willis .25 .60
129 Vernon Davis .20 .50
130 John Carlson .20 .50
131 Leon Washington .20 .50
132 Matt Hasselbeck .20 .50
133 Mike Williams USC .20 .50
134 Danny Amendola .30 .75
135 James Laurinaitis .25 .60
136 Mark Clayton .20 .50
137 Steven Jackson .20 .50
138 Cadillac Williams .20 .50
139 Josh Freeman .25 .60
140 Kellen Winslow Jr. .20 .50
141 Reggie Brown .20 .50
142 Bo Scaife .20 .50
143 Chris Johnson .20 .50
144 Justin Gage .20 .50
145 Nate Washington .20 .50
146 Vince Young .20 .50
147 Chris Cooley .20 .50
148 Clinton Portis .20 .50
149 Donovan McNabb .25 .60
150 Santana Moss .25 .60
151 Aaron Hernandez RC .75 2.00
152 Andrew Quarless RC .75 2.00
153 Anthony Dixon RC .75 2.00
154 Anthony McCoy RC .75 2.00
155 Antonio Brown RC 6.00 15.00
156 Blair White RC .75 2.00
157 Brandon Banks RC 4.00 10.00
158 Brandon Graham RC 1.00 2.50
159 Brandon Spikes RC .75 2.00
160 Brian Price RC .75 2.00
161 Brody Eldridge RC 1.25 3.00
162 Bryan Bulaga RC .75 2.00
163 Carlos Dunlap RC .75 2.00
164 Carlton Mitchell RC .75 2.00
165 Chris Cook RC .75 2.00
166 Chris Gronkowski RC 1.25 3.00
167 Chris Ivory RC 2.00 5.00
168 Chris McGaha RC .75 2.00
169 Clay Harbor RC .75 2.00
170 Corey Wootton RC .75 2.00
171 Dan LeFevour RC .75 2.00
172 Dan Williams RC .75 2.00
173 Danario Alexander RC .75 2.00
174 Daryl Washington RC .75 2.00
175 David Gettis RC .75 2.00
176 David Nelson RC 1.25 3.00
177 David Reed RC .75 2.00
178 Deji Karim RC 1.00 2.50
179 Dennis Pitta RC .75 2.00
180 Derrick Morgan RC .75 2.00
181 Devin McCourty RC 1.00 2.50
182 Dezmon Briscoe RC .75 2.00
183 Dominique Curry RC 1.00 2.50
184 Dominique Franks RC .75 2.00
185 Donald Jones RC 1.25 3.00
186 Dorin Dickerson RC .75 2.00
187 Duke Calhoun RC 1.00 2.50
188 Earl Thomas RC 2.00 5.00
189 Ed Dickson RC .75 2.00
190 Ed Wang RC 1.25 3.00
191 Everson Griffen RC .75 2.00
192 Fendi Onobun RC 1.00 2.50
193 Garrett Graham RC .75 2.00
194 Jacoby Ford RC .75 2.00
195 Jared Odrick RC 1.00 2.50
196 Jason Pierre-Paul RC 1.25 3.00
197 Jason Worilds RC .75 2.00
198 Javier Arenas RC .75 2.00
199 Jeff Cumberland RC 1.00 2.50
200 Jeremy Horne RC 1.00 2.50
201 Jeremy Williams RC .75 2.00
202 Jerry Hughes RC .75 2.00
203 Jim Dray RC 1.00 2.50
204 Jimmy Graham RC 2.00 5.00
205 Joe Haden RC 1.25 3.00
206 Joe Webb RC .75 2.00
207 John Conner RC .75 2.00
208 John Skelton RC 1.00 2.50
209 Joique Bell RC .75 2.00
210 Kareem Jackson RC .75 2.00
211 Keiland Williams RC 1.00 2.50
212 Keith Toston RC 1.25 3.00
213 Kerry Meier RC 1.00 2.50
214 Koa Misi RC 1.00 2.50
215 Kyle Williams RC 1.25 3.00
216 Kyle Wilson RC .75 2.00
217 LeGarrette Blount RC 1.50 4.00
218 Lamarr Houston RC 1.00 2.50
219 Logan Paulsen RC 1.00 2.50
220 Marc Mariani RC 1.25 3.00
221 Marlon Moore RC 1.25 3.00
222 Max Hall RC 1.25 3.00
223 Max Komar RC 1.25 3.00
224 Michael Hoomanawanui RC 1.25 3.00
225 Michael Palmer RC 1.00 2.50
226 Mickey Shuler RC 1.25 3.00
227 Morgan Burnett RC 1.00 2.50
228 Nate Allen RC 1.25 3.00
229 Nate Byham RC .75 2.00
230 NaVorro Bowman RC 1.50 4.00
231 Patrick Robinson RC 1.00 2.50
232 Perrish Cox RC 1.00 2.50
233 Preston Parker RC 1.00 2.50
234 Ricky Sapp RC .75 2.00
235 Riley Cooper RC .75 2.00
236 Roberto Wallace RC 1.00 2.50
237 Russell Okung RC .75 2.00
238 Rusty Smith RC 1.25 3.00
239 Sean Lee RC 1.50 4.00
240 Sean Weatherspoon RC .75 2.00
241 Sergio Kindle RC .75 2.00
242 Stephen Williams RC 1.25 3.00
243 T.J. Ward RC 1.25 3.00
244 Taylor Mays RC .75 2.00
245 Thaddeus Lewis RC 1.00 2.50
246 Tony Moeaki RC 1.00 2.50
247 Tony Pike RC .75 2.00
248 Trent Williams RC 1.00 2.50
249 Tyson Alualu RC .75 2.00
250 Victor Cruz RC 1.50 4.00
251 S.Bradford JSY AU/244 RC 6.00 15.00
252 N.Suh JSY AU/196 RC 10.00 25.00
253 Gerald McCoy JSY AU/209 RC 5.00 12.00
254 Eric Berry JSY AU/199 RC 8.00 20.00
255 R.McClain JSY AU/197 RC 5.00 12.00
256 C.J. Spiller JSY AU/228 RC 5.00 12.00
257 R.Mathews JSY AU/263 RC 5.00 12.00
258 J.Gresham JSY AU/167 RC 5.00 12.00
259 D.Thomas JSY AU/173 RC 12.00 30.00
260 Dez Bryant JSY AU/293 RC 30.00 60.00
261 Tim Tebow JSY AU/259 RC 20.00 50.00
262 Jahvid Best JSY AU/204 RC 5.00 12.00
263 D.McCluster JSY AU/185 RC 6.00 15.00
264 A.Benn JSY AU/186 RC 5.00 12.00
265 Gronkowski JSY AU/164 RC 40.00 80.00
266 J.Clausen JSY AU/223 RC 5.00 12.00
267 Toby Gerhart JSY AU/171 RC 5.00 12.00
268 Ben Tate JSY AU/205 RC 6.00 15.00
269 M.Hardesty JSY AU/186 RC 5.00 12.00
270 Golden Tate JSY AU/326 RC 6.00 15.00
271 D.Williams JSY AU/206 RC 5.00 12.00
272 B.LaFell JSY AU/188 RC 8.00 20.00
273 E.Sanders JSY AU/182 RC 8.00 20.00
274 J.Shipley JSY AU/177 RC 5.00 12.00
275 Colt McCoy JSY AU/255 RC 6.00 15.00
276 Eric Decker JSY AU/167 RC 6.00 15.00
277 A.Roberts JSY AU/207 RC 6.00 15.00
278 A.Edwards JSY AU/183 RC 6.00 15.00
279 Taylor Price JSY AU/184 RC 5.00 12.00
280 M.Gilyard JSY AU/173 RC 5.00 12.00
281 M.Williams JSY AU/170 RC 10.00 25.00
282 M.Easley JSY AU/178 RC 5.00 12.00
283 Joe McKnight JSY AU/167 RC 5.00 12.00
284 Mike Kafka JSY AU/169 RC 6.00 15.00
285 J.Dwyer JSY AU/269 RC 5.00 12.00

2010 Panini Gridiron Gear Gold O's

*VETS: 2.5X TO 6X BASIC CARDS
*ROOKIES: .8X TO 2X BASIC CARDS
STATED PRINT RUN 100 SER.#'d SETS

2010 Panini Gridiron Gear Gold X's

*VETS: 2.5X TO 6X BASIC CARDS
*ROOKIES: .8X TO 2X BASIC CARDS
STATED PRINT RUN 100 SER.#'d SETS

2010 Panini Gridiron Gear Platinum O's

*VETS: 5X TO 12X BASIC CARDS
*ROOKIES: 1.5X TO 4X BASIC CARDS
STATED PRINT RUN 25 SER.#'d SETS

2010 Panini Gridiron Gear Platinum X's

*VETS: 5X TO 12X BASIC CARDS
*ROOKIES: 1.5X TO 4X BASIC CARDS
STATED PRINT RUN 25 SER.#'d SETS

2010 Panini Gridiron Gear Silver O's

*VETS: 2X TO 5X BASIC CARDS
*ROOKIES: .6X TO 1.5X BASIC CARDS
STATED PRINT RUN 250 SER.#'d SETS

2010 Panini Gridiron Gear Silver X's

*VETS: 2X TO 5X BASIC CARDS
*ROOKIES: .6X TO 1.5X BASIC CARDS
STATED PRINT RUN 250 SER.#'d SETS

2010 Panini Gridiron Gear Autographs Gold X's

STATED PRINT RUN 99-299
EXCH EXPIRATION: 6/1/2012
151 Aaron Hernandez/299 3.00 8.00
153 Anthony Dixon/199 3.00 8.00
154 Anthony McCoy/199 3.00 8.00
155 Antonio Brown/199 30.00 80.00
156 Blair White/99 4.00 10.00
157 Brandon Banks/99 15.00 30.00
158 Brandon Graham/199 4.00 10.00
159 Brandon Spikes/299 3.00 8.00
162 Bryan Bulaga/299 3.00 8.00
164 Carlton Mitchell/99 4.00 10.00
167 Chris Ivory/99 10.00 25.00
168 Chris McGaha/99 4.00 10.00
170 Corey Wootton/299 3.00 8.00
171 Dan LeFevour/99 4.00 10.00
173 Danario Alexander/299 3.00 8.00
175 David Gettis/99 4.00 10.00
176 David Nelson/99 6.00 15.00
177 David Reed/99 4.00 10.00
178 Deji Karim/99 5.00 12.00
179 Dennis Pitta/99 4.00 10.00
180 Derrick Morgan/299 3.00 8.00
181 Devin McCourty/299 4.00 10.00
183 Dominique Curry/99 5.00 12.00
184 Dominique Franks/299 3.00 8.00
185 Donald Jones/99 6.00 15.00
188 Earl Thomas/299 8.00 20.00
189 Ed Dickson/299 3.00 8.00
190 Ed Wang/99 6.00 15.00
191 Everson Griffen/299 3.00 8.00
192 Fendi Onobun/99 5.00 12.00
193 Garrett Graham/299 3.00 8.00
194 Jacoby Ford/299 3.00 8.00
196 Jason Pierre-Paul/299 5.00 12.00
197 Jason Worilds/299 3.00 8.00
198 Javier Arenas/99 4.00 10.00
201 Jeremy Williams/99 4.00 10.00
202 Jerry Hughes/299 3.00 8.00
204 Jimmy Graham/299 10.00 25.00
205 Joe Haden/299 5.00 12.00
206 Joe Webb/99 4.00 10.00
207 John Conner/99 4.00 10.00
208 John Skelton/299 4.00 10.00
209 Joique Bell/99 4.00 10.00
211 Keiland Williams/99 5.00 12.00
213 Kerry Meier/99 5.00 12.00
214 Koa Misi/99 5.00 12.00
217 LeGarrette Blount/99 8.00 20.00
218 Lamarr Houston/99 5.00 12.00
220 Marc Mariani/99 6.00 15.00
221 Marlon Moore/99 6.00 15.00
222 Max Hall/99 6.00 15.00
223 Max Komar/99 6.00 15.00
224 Michael Hoomanawanui/99 6.00 15.00
225 Michael Palmer/99 5.00 12.00
226 Mickey Shuler/99 6.00 15.00
227 Morgan Burnett/299 4.00 10.00
228 Nate Allen/299 5.00 12.00
231 Patrick Robinson/299 4.00 10.00
232 Perrish Cox/299 4.00 10.00
233 Preston Parker/99 5.00 12.00
234 Ricky Sapp/299 3.00 8.00
235 Riley Cooper/99 4.00 10.00
238 Rusty Smith/99 6.00 15.00
239 Sean Lee/299 6.00 15.00
240 Sean Weatherspoon/299 3.00 8.00
241 Sergio Kindle/299 3.00 8.00
242 Stephen Williams/99 6.00 15.00
243 T.J. Ward/99 6.00 15.00
244 Taylor Mays/299 3.00 8.00
245 Thaddeus Lewis/99 5.00 12.00
246 Tony Moeaki/99 10.00 25.00
247 Tony Pike/99 4.00 10.00
249 Tyson Alualu/99 4.00 10.00
250 Victor Cruz/99 8.00 20.00

2010 Panini Gridiron Gear Autographs Platinum O's

1-149 UNPRICED PLAT.PRINT RUN 1
COMMON ROOKIE 6.00 15.00
ROOKIE SEMISTARS 8.00 20.00
ROOKIE UNL.STARS 10.00 25.00
151-250 ROOKIE PLAT.PRINT RUN 25
EXCH EXPIRATION: 6/1/2012
151 Aaron Hernandez/25 6.00 15.00
152 Andrew Quarless/25 6.00 15.00
155 Antonio Brown/25 60.00 120.00
157 Brandon Banks/25 12.00 30.00
159 Brandon Spikes/25 6.00 15.00
167 Chris Ivory/25 15.00 40.00
169 Clay Harbor/25 6.00 15.00
176 David Nelson/25 10.00 25.00
181 Devin McCourty/25 8.00 20.00
187 Duke Calhoun/25 8.00 20.00
194 Jacoby Ford/25 6.00 15.00
196 Jason Pierre-Paul/25 10.00 25.00
211 Keiland Williams/25 8.00 20.00
217 LeGarrette Blount/25
220 Marc Mariani/25 10.00 25.00
222 Max Hall/25 10.00 25.00
223 Max Komar/25 10.00 25.00
226 Mickey Shuler/25 10.00 25.00
246 Tony Moeaki/25 15.00 40.00
248 Trent Williams/25 EXCH 8.00 20.00
250 Victor Cruz/25 12.00 30.00

2010 Panini Gridiron Gear Crash Course

*GOLD/100: .6X TO 1.5X BASIC INSERTS
*PLATINUM/25: .8X TO 2X BASIC INSERTS
*SILVER/250: .5X TO 1.2X BASIC INSERTS
1 R.Lewis/D.Keller 1.00 2.50
2 D.Revis/R.Moss .75 2.00
3 P.Manning/M.Williams 2.50 6.00
4 E.Manning/D.Ware .75 2.00
5 A.Rodgers/J.Allen 1.25 3.00
6 C.Ochocinco/T.Polamalu 1.00 2.50
7 L.Fitzgerald/P.Willis .75 2.00
8 T.Brady/J.Taylor 2.50 6.00
9 J.Witten/A.Ross .75 2.00
10 B.Orakpo/L.McCoy 1.00 2.50

2010 Panini Gridiron Gear Crash Course Jerseys

STATED PRINT RUN 100-250
*PRIME/25: .8X TO 2X BASIC JSY
1 R.Lewis/D.Keller/250 5.00 12.00
2 D.Revis/R.Moss/250 3.00 8.00
3 P.Manning/M.Williams/250 10.00 25.00
4 E.Manning/D.Ware/250 3.00 8.00
5 A.Rodgers/J.Allen/100 6.00 15.00
6 C.Ochocinco/T.Polamalu/100 6.00 15.00
7 L.Fitzgerald/P.Willis/100 4.00 10.00
9 J.Witten/A.Ross/250 3.00 8.00
10 B.Orakpo/L.McCoy/250 4.00 10.00

2010 Panini Gridiron Gear Gamebreakers

*GOLD/100: .6X TO 1.5X BASIC INSERTS
*SILVER/250: .5X TO 1.2X BASIC INSERTS
*PLATINUM/25: .8X TO 2X BASIC INSERTS
1 Larry Fitzgerald .75 2.00
2 Dallas Clark .60 1.50
3 Arian Foster .75 2.00
4 Adrian Peterson 1.00 2.50
5 Visanthe Shiancoe .75 2.00
6 Chris Johnson .60 1.50
7 Reggie Wayne .75 2.00
8 Brent Celek .60 1.50
9 Peyton Manning 2.50 6.00
10 DeAngelo Williams .60 1.50
11 Darren McFadden .60 1.50
12 Aaron Rodgers 2.00 5.00
13 Miles Austin .60 1.50
14 Maurice Jones-Drew .60 1.50
15 Jamaal Charles .75 2.00
16 Ronnie Brown .60 1.50
17 Matt Forte .60 1.50
18 Drew Brees 1.00 2.50
19 Calvin Johnson 1.00 2.50
20 Ray Lewis 1.00 2.50
21 Wes Welker .75 2.00
22 DeSean Jackson .75 2.00
23 Percy Harvin .60 1.50
24 Michael Crabtree .60 1.50
25 Vernon Davis .60 1.50
26 Devery Henderson .60 1.50
27 Devin Hester .75 2.00
28 Vince Young .60 1.50
29 Frank Gore .75 2.00
30 Rashard Mendenhall .60 1.50

2010 Panini Gridiron Gear Gamebreakers Jerseys

STATED PRINT RUN 10-250
1 Larry Fitzgerald/100 3.00 8.00
4 Adrian Peterson/250 4.00 10.00
5 Visanthe Shiancoe/250 3.00 8.00
6 Chris Johnson/75 2.50 6.00
8 Brent Celek/250 2.50 6.00
9 Peyton Manning/250 10.00 25.00
11 Darren McFadden/250 2.50 6.00
12 Aaron Rodgers/100 6.00 15.00
14 Maurice Jones-Drew/250 2.50 6.00
15 Jamaal Charles/250 3.00 8.00
17 Matt Forte/250 2.50 6.00
18 Drew Brees/145 4.00 10.00
19 Calvin Johnson/180 4.00 10.00
20 Ray Lewis/150 5.00 12.00
22 DeSean Jackson/250 3.00 8.00
24 Michael Crabtree/35 3.00 8.00
25 Vernon Davis/100 2.50 6.00
27 Devin Hester/175 3.00 8.00
28 Vince Young/250 2.50 6.00
29 Frank Gore/35 4.00 10.00

2010 Panini Gridiron Gear Gamebreakers Jerseys Combos

STATED PRINT RUN 12-100
1 Larry Fitzgerald/100 3.00 8.00
2 Dallas Clark/44 3.00 8.00
4 Adrian Peterson/100 4.00 10.00
5 Visanthe Shiancoe/100 3.00 8.00
6 Chris Johnson/100 2.50 6.00
8 Brent Celek/100 2.50 6.00
9 Peyton Manning/100 10.00 25.00
10 DeAngelo Williams/15 4.00 10.00
11 Darren McFadden/100 2.50 6.00
13 Miles Austin/20 4.00 10.00
14 Maurice Jones-Drew/100 2.50 6.00
15 Jamaal Charles/100 3.00 8.00
17 Matt Forte/100 2.50 6.00
18 Drew Brees/100 4.00 10.00
19 Calvin Johnson/100 4.00 10.00
20 Ray Lewis/100 5.00 12.00
22 DeSean Jackson/100 3.00 8.00
25 Vernon Davis/50 3.00 8.00
27 Devin Hester/100 3.00 8.00
28 Vince Young/100 2.50 6.00

2010 Panini Gridiron Gear Gamebreakers Jerseys Prime

PRIME STATED PRINT RUN 11-50
4 Adrian Peterson/50 6.00 15.00
5 Visanthe Shiancoe/50 5.00 12.00
6 Chris Johnson/50 4.00 10.00
8 Brent Celek/50 4.00 10.00
9 Peyton Manning/50 15.00 40.00
11 Darren McFadden/50 4.00 10.00
14 Maurice Jones-Drew/50 4.00 10.00
15 Jamaal Charles/50 5.00 12.00
16 Ronnie Brown/50 4.00 10.00
17 Matt Forte/50 4.00 10.00
19 Calvin Johnson/50 6.00 15.00
20 Ray Lewis/25 10.00 25.00
21 Wes Welker/50 5.00 12.00
22 DeSean Jackson/50 5.00 12.00
23 Percy Harvin/50 4.00 10.00
25 Vernon Davis/50 4.00 10.00
26 Devery Henderson/50 4.00 10.00
27 Devin Hester/50 5.00 12.00
30 Rashard Mendenhall/50 4.00 10.00

2010 Panini Gridiron Gear Gamebreakers Jerseys Combos Prime

COMBO PRIME PRINT RUN 5-25
4 Adrian Peterson/25 8.00 20.00
5 Visanthe Shiancoe/25 6.00 15.00
6 Chris Johnson/25 5.00 12.00
8 Brent Celek/25 5.00 12.00
9 Peyton Manning/25 20.00 50.00
11 Darren McFadden/25 5.00 12.00
13 Miles Austin/15 5.00 12.00
14 Maurice Jones-Drew/25 5.00 12.00
15 Jamaal Charles/25 6.00 15.00
16 Ronnie Brown/25 5.00 12.00
17 Matt Forte/25 5.00 12.00
19 Calvin Johnson/25 8.00 20.00
20 Ray Lewis/25 10.00 25.00
21 Wes Welker/25 6.00 15.00
22 DeSean Jackson/25 6.00 15.00
23 Percy Harvin/25 5.00 12.00
25 Vernon Davis/25 5.00 12.00
26 Devery Henderson/25 5.00 12.00
27 Devin Hester/25 6.00 15.00
30 Rashard Mendenhall/25 5.00 12.00

2010 Panini Gridiron Gear Jerseys O's

STATED PRINT RUN 30-199
2 Larry Fitzgerald/199 3.00 8.00
11 Ray Lewis/30 6.00 15.00
14 Willis McGahee/199 2.50 6.00
15 Lee Evans/65 3.00 8.00
23 Brian Urlacher/100 4.00 10.00
26 Jay Cutler/199 2.50 6.00
28 Matt Forte/199 2.50 6.00
29 Carson Palmer/199 3.00 8.00
30 Cedric Benson/199 2.50 6.00
37 DeMarcus Ware/199 3.00 8.00
38 Felix Jones/199 2.50 6.00
41 Tony Romo/199 3.00 8.00
44 Knowshon Moreno/130 2.50 6.00
45 Kyle Orton/100 2.50 6.00
50 Aaron Rodgers/100 5.00 12.00
58 Matt Schaub/100 2.50 6.00
62 Joseph Addai/199 2.50 6.00
63 Peyton Manning/199 10.00 25.00
65 David Garrard/30 3.00 8.00
67 Maurice Jones-Drew/199 2.50 6.00
68 Mike Sims-Walker/50 3.00 8.00
70 Dwayne Bowe/199 3.00 8.00
71 Jamaal Charles/199 3.00 8.00
72 Matt Cassel/199 2.50 6.00
79 Adrian Peterson/199 4.00 10.00
80 Bernard Berrian/199 2.50 6.00
81 Brett Favre/199 8.00 20.00
83 Sidney Rice/199 2.50 6.00
86 Fred Taylor/100 2.50 6.00
88 Tom Brady/199 10.00 25.00
92 Marques Colston/199 2.50 6.00
95 Robert Meachem/125 2.50 6.00
97 Brandon Jacobs/199 2.50 6.00
101 Braylon Edwards/199 2.50 6.00
102 Darrelle Revis/55 3.00 8.00
106 Darren McFadden/199 2.50 6.00
109 Louis Murphy/199 2.50 6.00
111 DeSean Jackson/199 3.00 8.00
113 Kevin Kolb/199 2.50 6.00
117 Heath Miller/199 2.50 6.00
122 Antonio Gates/199 3.00 8.00
123 Darren Sproles/150 3.00 8.00
125 Philip Rivers/199 4.00 10.00
128 Patrick Willis/199 3.00 8.00
129 Vernon Davis/199 2.50 6.00
142 Bo Scaife/199 2.50 6.00
143 Chris Johnson/100 2.50 6.00
146 Vince Young/199 2.50 6.00
148 Clinton Portis/70 2.50 6.00

2010 Panini Gridiron Gear Jerseys Prime

STATED PRINT RUN 1-50
2 Larry Fitzgerald/30 5.00 12.00
6 Matt Ryan/40 5.00 12.00
8 Roddy White/50 4.00 10.00
11 Ray Lewis/50 8.00 20.00
14 Willis McGahee/30 4.00 10.00
15 Lee Evans/50 5.00 12.00
21 Jonathan Stewart/50 4.00 10.00
23 Brian Urlacher/50 6.00 15.00
25 Devin Hester/50 5.00 12.00
26 Jay Cutler/50 4.00 10.00
28 Matt Forte/50 4.00 10.00
29 Carson Palmer/50 5.00 12.00
30 Cedric Benson/50 4.00 10.00
31 Chad Ochocinco/50 4.00 10.00
37 DeMarcus Ware/50 5.00 12.00
38 Felix Jones/50 4.00 10.00
39 Jason Witten/50 5.00 12.00
41 Tony Romo/50 5.00 12.00
43 Eddie Royal/50 4.00 10.00
44 Knowshon Moreno/50 4.00 10.00
47 Calvin Johnson/50 6.00 15.00
52 Donald Driver/50 5.00 12.00
62 Joseph Addai/50 4.00 10.00
63 Peyton Manning/50 15.00 40.00
65 David Garrard/50 4.00 10.00
67 Maurice Jones-Drew/50 4.00 10.00
68 Mike Sims-Walker/50 4.00 10.00
70 Dwayne Bowe/50 5.00 12.00
71 Jamaal Charles/50 5.00 12.00
72 Matt Cassel/50 4.00 10.00
78 Ronnie Brown/50 4.00 10.00
79 Adrian Peterson/50 6.00 15.00
80 Bernard Berrian/50 4.00 10.00
81 Brett Favre/25 20.00 50.00
83 Sidney Rice/50 4.00 10.00
84 Visanthe Shiancoe/50 5.00 12.00
87 Randy Moss/25 6.00 15.00
88 Tom Brady/50 15.00 40.00
89 Wes Welker/50 5.00 12.00
92 Marques Colston/50 4.00 10.00
95 Robert Meachem/45 4.00 10.00
97 Brandon Jacobs/50 4.00 10.00
101 Braylon Edwards/50 4.00 10.00
102 Darrelle Revis/50 4.00 10.00
104 Mark Sanchez/25 5.00 12.00
106 Darren McFadden/50 4.00 10.00
109 Louis Murphy/50 4.00 10.00
111 DeSean Jackson/50 5.00 12.00
113 Kevin Kolb/50 4.00 10.00
114 LeSean McCoy/50 6.00 15.00
117 Heath Miller/50 4.00 10.00
120 Rashard Mendenhall/40 4.00 10.00
122 Antonio Gates/50 5.00 12.00
123 Darren Sproles/50 5.00 12.00
125 Philip Rivers/50 6.00 15.00
128 Patrick Willis/50 5.00 12.00
129 Vernon Davis/50 4.00 10.00
137 Steven Jackson/50 4.00 10.00
138 Cadillac Williams/50 4.00 10.00
142 Bo Scaife/50 4.00 10.00
143 Chris Johnson/50 4.00 10.00
147 Chris Cooley/50 4.00 10.00
148 Clinton Portis/50 4.00 10.00
150 Santana Moss/50 5.00 12.00

2010 Panini Gridiron Gear NFL Gridiron Signatures

STATED PRINT RUN 14-30
1 Aaron Rodgers/15 150.00 250.00
2 Reggie Wayne/14 15.00 40.00
3 Felix Jones/15 12.00 30.00
4 Donald Driver/15 20.00 50.00
5 Calvin Johnson/15 20.00 50.00
6 Fran Tarkenton/15 20.00 50.00
7 Rashard Mendenhall/15 12.00 30.00
8 Brandon Jacobs/15 12.00 30.00
9 Barry Sanders/15 75.00 135.00
10 Thurman Thomas/15 20.00 50.00
11 Jim Kelly/15 20.00 50.00
12 Cadillac Williams/15 12.00 30.00
13 LeSean McCoy/15 20.00 50.00
14 Michael Turner/15 12.00 30.00
15 Darren Sproles/30 10.00 25.00
16 Chris Cooley/15 20.00 50.00
17 Kevin Kolb/15 12.00 30.00
18 Maurice Jones-Drew/15 12.00 30.00
19 Ryan Grant/15 15.00 40.00
20 Tony Gonzalez/15 15.00 40.00
23 Junior Seau/15 40.00 80.00

2010 Panini Gridiron Gear NFL Nation

*GOLD/100: .6X TO 1.5X BASIC INSERTS
*PLATINUM/25: .8X TO 2X BASIC INSERTS
*SILVER/250: .5X TO 1.2X BASIC INSERTS
1 Steve Smith .75 2.00
2 Donald Driver .75 2.00
3 Kyle Orton .60 1.50
4 Cadillac Williams .60 1.50
5 Ray Rice .60 1.50
6 Matt Schaub .60 1.50
7 Brian Urlacher 1.00 2.50
8 Chad Ochocinco .60 1.50
9 Shonn Greene .60 1.50
10 Andre Johnson .75 2.00
11 Jay Cutler .60 1.50
12 Michael Turner .60 1.50
13 Eli Manning .75 2.00
14 Dwayne Bowe .75 2.00
15 Antonio Gates .75 2.00
16 Pierre Thomas .60 1.50
17 Matt Ryan .75 2.00
18 Jason Witten .75 2.00
19 Brett Favre 2.00 5.00
20 Tony Gonzalez .75 2.00
21 LaDainian Tomlinson 1.00 2.50
22 Knowshon Moreno .60 1.50
23 Patrick Willis .75 2.00
24 Donovan McNabb .75 2.00
25 Ben Roethlisberger 1.00 2.50
26 Lee Evans .75 2.00
27 Steven Jackson .60 1.50
28 LeSean McCoy 1.00 2.50
29 Reggie Bush .60 1.50
30 Matthew Stafford .75 2.00

2010 Panini Gridiron Gear NFL Nation Jerseys

STATED PRINT RUN 15-250
3 Kyle Orton/245 2.50 6.00
6 Matt Schaub/230 2.50 6.00
7 Brian Urlacher/85 4.00 10.00
11 Jay Cutler/250 2.50 6.00
14 Dwayne Bowe/250 3.00 8.00
15 Antonio Gates/250 3.00 8.00
17 Matt Ryan/35 4.00 10.00
19 Brett Favre/250 10.00 25.00
22 Knowshon Moreno/80 2.50 6.00
23 Patrick Willis/100 3.00 8.00
26 Lee Evans/100 3.00 8.00
28 LeSean McCoy/15 6.00 15.00
30 Matthew Stafford/85 3.00 8.00

2010 Panini Gridiron Gear NFL Nation Jerseys Combos

STATED PRINT RUN 50-100
3 Kyle Orton/100 2.50 6.00
6 Matt Schaub/100 2.50 6.00
7 Brian Urlacher/100 4.00 10.00
11 Jay Cutler/100 2.50 6.00
14 Dwayne Bowe/100 3.00 8.00
15 Antonio Gates/100 3.00 8.00
17 Matt Ryan/100 3.00 8.00
19 Brett Favre/100 8.00 20.00
22 Knowshon Moreno/100 2.50 6.00
23 Patrick Willis/100 3.00 8.00
26 Lee Evans/100 3.00 8.00
28 LeSean McCoy/50 5.00 12.00

2010 Panini Gridiron Gear NFL Nation Jerseys Combos Prime

STATED PRINT RUN 10-25
2 Donald Driver/25 6.00 15.00

Card	Low	High
4 Cadillac Williams/25	5.00	12.00
7 Brian Urlacher/25	8.00	20.00
8 Chad Ochocinco/25	5.00	12.00
11 Jay Cutler/25	5.00	12.00
14 Dwayne Bowe/25	6.00	15.00
15 Antonio Gates/25	6.00	15.00
18 Jason Witten/25	6.00	15.00
22 Knowshon Moreno/25	5.00	12.00
23 Patrick Willis/25	6.00	15.00
26 Lee Evans/25	6.00	15.00
27 Steven Jackson/25	5.00	12.00
28 LeSean McCoy/25	8.00	20.00

2010 Panini Gridiron Gear NFL Nation Jerseys Prime

PRIME STATED PRINT RUN 10-50

Card	Low	High
2 Donald Driver/50	5.00	12.00
4 Cadillac Williams/50	4.00	10.00
7 Brian Urlacher/50	6.00	15.00
8 Chad Ochocinco/50	4.00	10.00
11 Jay Cutler/50	4.00	10.00
14 Dwayne Bowe/50	5.00	12.00
15 Antonio Gates/50	5.00	12.00
18 Jason Witten/50	5.00	12.00
19 Brett Favre/20	30.00	60.00
22 Knowshon Moreno/50	4.00	10.00
23 Patrick Willis/50	5.00	12.00
26 Lee Evans/50	5.00	12.00
27 Steven Jackson/50	4.00	10.00
28 LeSean McCoy/50	6.00	15.00

2010 Panini Gridiron Gear NFL Nation Jerseys Autographs

JERSEY AUTO PRINT RUN 5-15
EXCH EXPIRATION: 6/1/2012

Card	Low	High
1 Steve Smith/15	12.00	30.00
2 Donald Driver/15		
3 Kyle Orton/15	10.00	25.00
6 Matt Schaub/15	10.00	25.00
12 Michael Turner/15	10.00	25.00
17 Matt Ryan/15	20.00	50.00
20 Tony Gonzalez/15	15.00	40.00
28 LeSean McCoy/15	15.00	40.00

2010 Panini Gridiron Gear NFL Pro Gridiron Signatures

STATED PRINT RUN 10-50
EXCH EXPIRATION: 6/1/2012

Card	Low	High
1 Jim Brown/25	40.00	80.00
2 Joe Namath/25	40.00	100.00
3 Floyd Little/25	15.00	40.00
4 John Randle/25	25.00	50.00
5 Michael Strahan/25	15.00	40.00
6 Rickey Jackson/25	15.00	40.00
9 Don Maynard/25	12.00	30.00
13 Jim Otto/50	12.00	30.00
14 Joe Klecko/50	12.00	30.00
15 Jimmy Orr/50	10.00	25.00
20 William Perry/50	12.00	30.00
21 Bernard Berrian/25		
23 Pierre Garcon/25	15.00	40.00
24 Chris Wells/25	12.00	30.00
25 Austin Collie/25	15.00	40.00
26 Daryle Lamonica/50	12.00	30.00
27 Ed McCaffrey/25	15.00	40.00
28 Bill Bates/50	12.00	30.00
29 Charley Taylor/50	12.00	30.00
30 Keyshawn Johnson/25	15.00	40.00
31 L.C. Greenwood/25	15.00	40.00
32 Leroy Kelly/50	12.00	30.00
33 Lydell Mitchell/50	10.00	25.00
34 Willie Lanier/25	12.00	30.00
35 Pete Retzlaff/50		
36 Rod Smith/25	15.00	40.00
37 Russ Grimm/50	15.00	40.00
39 Todd Christensen/50	10.00	25.00
41 Craig James/25	15.00	40.00
42 Heath Miller/25	12.00	30.00
43 Roddy White/25	12.00	30.00
45 Cedric Benson/25		
46 Darren Sproles/25	15.00	40.00
48 Josh Cribbs/25	15.00	40.00
49 Jeremy Maclin/25	12.00	30.00
50 Ryan Grant/25	15.00	40.00

2010 Panini Gridiron Gear Plates and Patches

STATED PRINT RUN 50 SER.#'d SETS

Card	Low	High
1 Hines Ward	6.00	15.00
2 Carson Palmer	6.00	15.00
3 Randy Moss	6.00	15.00
4 Adrian Peterson	8.00	20.00
5 Troy Polamalu	12.00	30.00
6 Maurice Jones-Drew	5.00	12.00
7 Clinton Portis	5.00	12.00
8 Mark Sanchez	5.00	12.00
9 Chris Cooley	5.00	12.00
10 Brett Favre	25.00	60.00
11 Tony Romo	6.00	15.00
12 Chris Johnson	5.00	12.00
13 Philip Rivers	8.00	20.00
14 Sidney Rice	8.00	20.00
15 Vernon Davis	5.00	12.00

2010 Panini Gridiron Gear Rookie Gridiron Gems Jerseys Prime

STATED PRINT RUN 50 SER.#'d SETS
*BASE JSY/25: .4X TO 1X PRIME/50
*COMBO/25: .5X TO 1.2X PRIME/50
*COMBO PRIME/50: .5X TO 1.2X PRM/50
*JUMBO/25: .5X TO 1.2X PRIME/50
*JUMBO PRIME/10: 1X TO 2.5X PRM/50
*RETAIL/50: .4X TO 1X PRIME/50
*TRIO/50: .5X TO 1.2X PRIME/50
*TRIO PRIME/50: .6X TO 1.5X PRIME/50

Card	Low	High
251 Sam Bradford	2.00	5.00
252 Ndamukong Suh	3.00	8.00
253 Gerald McCoy	1.50	4.00
254 Eric Berry	2.50	6.00
255 Rolando McClain	1.50	4.00
256 C.J. Spiller	1.50	4.00
257 Ryan Mathews	1.50	4.00
258 Jermaine Gresham	1.50	4.00
259 Demaryius Thomas	4.00	10.00
260 Dez Bryant	5.00	12.00
261 Tim Tebow	5.00	12.00
262 Jahvid Best	1.50	4.00
263 Dexter McCluster	2.00	5.00
264 Arrelious Benn	1.50	4.00
265 Rob Gronkowski	5.00	12.00
266 Jimmy Clausen	1.50	4.00
267 Toby Gerhart	1.50	4.00
268 Ben Tate	1.50	4.00
269 Montario Hardesty	1.50	4.00
270 Golden Tate	2.00	5.00
271 Damian Williams	2.00	5.00
272 Brandon LaFell	2.50	6.00
273 Emmanuel Sanders	2.50	6.00
274 Jordan Shipley	1.50	4.00
275 Colt McCoy	2.00	5.00
276 Eric Decker	2.00	5.00
277 Andre Roberts	2.00	5.00
278 Armanti Edwards	2.00	5.00
279 Taylor Price	1.50	4.00
280 Mardy Gilyard	1.50	4.00
281 Mike Williams	1.50	4.00
282 Marcus Easley	1.50	4.00
283 Joe McKnight	1.50	4.00
284 Mike Kafka	2.00	5.00
285 Jonathan Dwyer	1.50	4.00

2010 Panini Gridiron Gear Rookie Gridiron Gems Jerseys Trios Autographs Prime

*TRIO AU/20: .6X TO 1.5X BASIC JSY AU
TRIO AUTO STATED PRINT RUN 20
*CMB PRIME AU/15: .6X TO 1.5X BASIC JSY AU
*PRIME AU/10: .6X TO 1.5X BASIC JSY AU
EXCH EXPIRATION: 6/1/2012

Card	Low	High
251 Sam Bradford	10.00	25.00
261 Tim Tebow	40.00	100.00

2010 Panini Gridiron Gear Rookie Orientation

*GOLD/100: .6X TO 1.5X BASIC INSERTS
*PLATINUM/25: .8X TO 2X BASIC INSERTS
*SILVER/250: .5X TO 1.2X BASIC INSERTS

Card	Low	High
1 Demaryius Thomas	1.25	3.00
2 Jordan Shipley	.50	1.25
3 Sam Bradford	.60	1.50
4 Jonathan Dwyer	.50	1.25
5 Eric Berry	.75	2.00
6 Montario Hardesty	.50	1.25
7 Arrelious Benn	.50	1.25
8 Joe McKnight	.50	1.25
9 Colt McCoy	.60	1.50
10 Rolando McClain	.50	1.25
11 Dexter McCluster	.60	1.50
12 Jermaine Gresham	.50	1.25
13 Eric Decker	.60	1.50
14 Ndamukong Suh	1.00	2.50
15 Mike Kafka	.60	1.50
16 Andre Roberts	.60	1.50
17 Rob Gronkowski	1.50	4.00
18 Dez Bryant	1.25	3.00
19 Gerald McCoy	.50	1.25
20 Taylor Price	.50	1.25
21 Jahvid Best	.50	1.25
22 Armanti Edwards	.60	1.50
23 C.J. Spiller	.50	1.25
24 Brandon LaFell	.75	2.00
25 Mardy Gilyard	.50	1.25
26 Tim Tebow	1.50	4.00
27 Ben Tate	.50	1.25
28 Golden Tate	.60	1.50
29 Emmanuel Sanders	.75	2.00
30 Jimmy Clausen	.50	1.25
31 Ryan Mathews	.50	1.25
32 Toby Gerhart	.50	1.25
33 Damian Williams	.50	1.25
34 Mike Williams	.50	1.25
35 Marcus Easley	.50	1.25

2010 Panini Gridiron Gear Rookie Orientation Jerseys

STATED PRINT RUN 299 SER.#'d SETS
*PRIME/25: 1X TO 2.5X BASIC JSY/299

Card	Low	High
1 Demaryius Thomas/299	4.00	10.00
2 Jordan Shipley/299	1.50	4.00
3 Sam Bradford/299	2.00	5.00
4 Jonathan Dwyer/299	1.50	4.00
5 Eric Berry/299	2.50	6.00
6 Montario Hardesty/299	1.50	4.00
7 Arrelious Benn/299	1.50	4.00
8 Joe McKnight/299	1.50	4.00
9 Colt McCoy/299	2.00	5.00
10 Rolando McClain/299	2.00	5.00
11 Dexter McCluster/299	2.50	6.00
12 Jermaine Gresham/299	2.00	5.00
13 Eric Decker/299	2.50	6.00
14 Ndamukong Suh/299	4.00	10.00
15 Mike Kafka/299	2.50	6.00
16 Andre Roberts/299	2.50	6.00
17 Rob Gronkowski/299	6.00	15.00
18 Dez Bryant/299	5.00	12.00
19 Gerald McCoy/299	2.00	5.00
20 Taylor Price/299	2.00	5.00
21 Jahvid Best/299	2.00	5.00
22 Armanti Edwards/299	2.50	6.00
23 C.J. Spiller/299	2.00	5.00
24 Brandon LaFell/299	3.00	8.00
25 Mardy Gilyard/299	2.00	5.00
26 Tim Tebow/299	6.00	15.00
27 Ben Tate/299	2.00	5.00
28 Golden Tate/299	2.50	6.00
29 Emmanuel Sanders/299	3.00	8.00
30 Jimmy Clausen/299	2.00	5.00
31 Ryan Mathews/100	2.00	5.00
32 Toby Gerhart/299	2.00	5.00
33 Damian Williams/299	2.00	5.00
34 Mike Williams/299	2.00	5.00
35 Marcus Easley/299	2.00	5.00

2010 Panini Gridiron Gear Rookie Orientation Jerseys Autographs

STATED PRINT RUN 50 SER.#'d SETS
*PRIME/15: .6X TO 1.5X BASIC JSY AU/50
EXCH EXPIRATION: 6/1/2012

Card	Low	High
1 Demaryius Thomas	10.00	25.00
2 Jordan Shipley	4.00	10.00
3 Sam Bradford	5.00	12.00
4 Jonathan Dwyer	4.00	10.00
5 Eric Berry	6.00	15.00
6 Montario Hardesty	4.00	10.00
7 Arrelious Benn	4.00	10.00
8 Joe McKnight	4.00	10.00
9 Colt McCoy	5.00	12.00
10 Rolando McClain	4.00	10.00
12 Jermaine Gresham	4.00	10.00
13 Eric Decker	5.00	12.00
15 Mike Kafka	5.00	12.00
16 Andre Roberts	5.00	12.00
17 Rob Gronkowski	25.00	50.00
18 Dez Bryant	30.00	60.00
20 Taylor Price	4.00	10.00
21 Jahvid Best	4.00	10.00
22 Armanti Edwards	5.00	12.00
23 C.J. Spiller	4.00	10.00
24 Brandon LaFell	6.00	15.00
25 Mardy Gilyard	4.00	10.00
26 Tim Tebow	30.00	80.00
27 Ben Tate	4.00	10.00
28 Golden Tate	5.00	12.00
29 Emmanuel Sanders	6.00	15.00
30 Jimmy Clausen	4.00	10.00
31 Ryan Mathews	4.00	10.00
32 Toby Gerhart	4.00	10.00
33 Damian Williams	4.00	10.00
34 Mike Williams	4.00	10.00
35 Marcus Easley	4.00	10.00

2010 Panini Gridiron Gear Rookie Orientation Materials Quad

STATED PRINT RUN 150 SER.#'d SETS
*PRIME/25: .8X TO 2X BASIC QUAD/150

Card	Low	High
1 Bradford/Suh/McCoy/Berry	3.00	8.00
2 Brdfrd/Tebow/Clausn/McCoy	5.00	12.00
3 Spiller/Mathews/Best/Gerhart	1.50	4.00
4 Thoms/Bryant/McClstr/Benn	4.00	10.00
5 Tate/Williams/LaFell/Sanders	2.50	6.00
6 Shiply/Deckr/Robrts/Edwrds	2.00	5.00
7 Price/Gilyard/Williams/Easley	1.50	4.00
8 Hrdsty/McKnght/Grshm/Grnkw	5.00	12.00
9 Brdfrd/Tebw/Spiller/Mathws	5.00	12.00
10 Suh/McCoy/Berry/McClain	3.00	8.00

2010 Panini Gridiron Gear Rookie Orientation Materials Triple

STATED PRINT RUN 250 SER.#'d SETS
*PRIME/25: .8X TO 2X BASIC TRIPLE/250

Card	Low	High
1 Clausen/LaFell/Edwards	2.50	6.00
2 McCoy/Benn/Williams	1.50	4.00
3 Thomas/Tebow/Decker	12.00	30.00
4 Spiller/Mathews/Best	1.50	4.00
5 Bradford/McCoy/Gresham	2.00	5.00
6 Gerhart/Tate/Hardesty	1.50	4.00
7 Benn/Tate/Williams	2.00	5.00
8 Suh/Berry/McClain	3.00	8.00
9 Thomas/Bryant/McCluster	6.00	15.00
10 Bradford/Tebow/Clausen	5.00	12.00

2011 Panini Gridiron Gear

Card	Low	High
COMP.SET w/o RC's (150)	8.00	20.00
ROOKIE JSY AU PRINT RUN 197-317		
1 Deion Branch	.20	.50
2 Devin McCourty	.20	.50
3 Jerod Mayo	.20	.50
4 Tom Brady	.75	2.00
5 Wes Welker	.25	.60
6 Darrelle Revis	.20	.50
7 Dustin Keller	.25	.60
8 LaDainian Tomlinson	.30	.75
9 Mark Sanchez	.20	.50
10 Shonn Greene	.20	.50
11 Brandon Marshall	.25	.60
12 Chad Henne	.25	.60
13 Davone Bess	.20	.50
14 Karlos Dansby	.20	.50
15 Fred Jackson	.20	.50
16 Ryan Fitzpatrick	.20	.50
17 Steve Johnson	.20	.50
18 Lee Evans	.25	.60
19 Ben Roethlisberger	.30	.75
20 Hines Ward	.25	.60
21 Lawrence Timmons	.20	.50
22 Mike Wallace	.20	.50
23 Rashard Mendenhall	.20	.50
24 Anquan Boldin	.20	.50
25 Ed Reed	.25	.60
26 Joe Flacco	.25	.60
27 Ray Lewis	.30	.75
28 Ray Rice	.20	.50
29 Colt McCoy	.20	.50
30 Mohamed Massaquoi	.20	.50
31 Peyton Hillis	.20	.50
32 T.J. Ward	.20	.50
33 Cedric Benson	.20	.50
34 Dhani Jones	.20	.50
35 Jermaine Gresham	.20	.50
36 Jordan Shipley	.20	.50
37 Antoine Bethea	.20	.50
38 Dallas Clark	.20	.50
39 Peyton Manning	.60	1.50
40 Pierre Garcon	.25	.60
41 Reggie Wayne	.25	.60
42 Paul Posluszny	.20	.50
43 Marcedes Lewis	.20	.50
44 Maurice Jones-Drew	.20	.50
45 Mike Thomas	.25	.60
46 Andre Johnson	.25	.60
47 Arian Foster	.20	.50
48 Kevin Walter	.20	.50
49 Matt Schaub	.20	.50
50 Chris Hope	.20	.50
51 Chris Johnson	.20	.50
52 Nate Washington	.20	.50
53 Derrick Johnson	.20	.50
54 Dwayne Bowe	.25	.60
55 Jamaal Charles	.25	.60
56 Matt Cassel	.20	.50
57 Thomas Jones	.20	.50
58 Antonio Gates	.20	.50
59 Mike Tolbert	.20	.50
60 Philip Rivers	.30	.75
61 Ryan Mathews	.25	.60
62 Vincent Jackson	.20	.50
63 Darren McFadden	.20	.50
64 Darrius Heyward-Bey	.20	.50
65 Jason Campbell	.20	.50
66 Tyvon Branch	.20	.50
67 Brandon Lloyd	.20	.50
68 Champ Bailey	.25	.60
69 D.J. Williams	.20	.50
70 Knowshon Moreno	.20	.50
71 Tim Tebow	.30	.75
72 DeSean Jackson	.25	.60
73 Jeremy Maclin	.20	.50
74 Kevin Kolb	.20	.50
75 LeSean McCoy	.30	.75
76 Michael Vick	.25	.60
77 Brandon Jacobs	.20	.50
78 Eli Manning	.25	.60
79 Hakeem Nicks	.20	.50
80 Mario Manningham	.20	.50
81 DeMarcus Ware	.25	.60
82 Dez Bryant	.30	.75
83 Felix Jones	.20	.50
84 Miles Austin	.20	.50
85 Tony Romo	.25	.60
86 DeAngelo Hall	.20	.50
87 Donovan McNabb	.25	.60
88 London Fletcher	.25	.60
89 Ryan Torain	.20	.50
90 Brian Urlacher	.30	.75
91 Jay Cutler	.20	.50
92 Johnny Knox	.20	.50
93 Matt Forte	.20	.50
94 Aaron Rodgers	.50	1.25
95 A.J. Hawk	.20	.50
96 Charles Woodson	.30	.75
97 Greg Jennings	.20	.50
98 Jermichael Finley	.20	.50
99 Calvin Johnson	.30	.75
100 Jahvid Best	.20	.50
101 Matthew Stafford	.25	.60
102 Ndamukong Suh	.25	.60
103 Adrian Peterson	.30	.75
104 Chad Greenway	.25	.60
105 Percy Harvin	.20	.50
106 Visanthe Shiancoe	.25	.60
107 Curtis Lofton	.20	.50
108 Matt Ryan	.25	.60
109 Michael Turner	.20	.50
110 Roddy White	.20	.50
111 Tony Gonzalez	.25	.60
112 Drew Brees	.30	.75
113 Jonathan Vilma	.20	.50
114 Marques Colston	.20	.50
115 Pierre Thomas	.20	.50
116 Reggie Bush	.20	.50
117 Josh Freeman	.25	.60
118 Kellen Winslow Jr.	.20	.50
119 LeGarrette Blount	.25	.60
120 Mike Williams	.25	.60
121 Ronde Barber	.20	.50
122 DeAngelo Williams	.20	.50
123 Jonathan Stewart	.20	.50
124 Steve Smith	.25	.60
125 Marshawn Lynch	.25	.60
126 Matt Hasselbeck	.20	.50
127 Mike Williams USC	.20	.50
128 Brandon Gibson	.20	.50
129 Danny Amendola	.25	.60
130 James Laurinaitis	.20	.50
131 Sam Bradford	.20	.50
132 Steven Jackson	.20	.50
133 Alex Smith QB	.25	.60
134 Frank Gore	.25	.60
135 Michael Crabtree	.20	.50
136 Patrick Willis	.25	.60
137 Vernon Davis	.20	.50
138 Beanie Wells	.20	.50
139 Larry Fitzgerald	.25	.60
140 Paris Lenon	.20	.50
141 Ahmad Bradshaw	.20	.50
142 Ronnie Brown	.25	.60
143 Santonio Holmes	.20	.50
144 Sidney Rice	.20	.50
145 Santana Moss	.25	.60
146 Asante Samuel	.20	.50
147 Nnamdi Asomugha	.20	.50
148 Brandon Meriweather	.20	.50
149 Jared Allen	.20	.50
150 Jared Cook	.20	.50
151 Aaron Williams RC	.75	2.00
152 Adrian Clayborn RC	.75	2.00
153 Ahmad Black RC	1.00	2.50
154 Akeem Ayers RC	.75	2.00
155 Aldon Smith RC	.75	2.00
156 Aldrick Robinson RC	1.00	2.50
157 Allen Bradford RC	.75	2.00
158 Anthony Allen RC	.75	2.00
159 Anthony Castonzo RC	.75	2.00
160 Brandon Harris RC	.75	2.00
161 Cameron Heyward RC	1.00	2.50
162 Cameron Jordan RC	1.00	2.50
163 Cecil Shorts RC	.75	2.00
164 Corey Liuget RC	.75	2.00
165 D.J. Williams RC	.75	2.00
166 Da'Quan Bowers RC	.75	2.00
167 Da'Rel Scott RC	.75	2.00
168 Denarius Moore RC	.75	2.00
169 Dion Lewis RC	1.00	2.50
170 Dwayne Harris RC	.75	2.00
171 Evan Royster RC	.75	2.00
172 Greg Jones RC	1.00	2.50
173 Greg McElroy RC	1.25	3.00
174 Greg Salas RC	.75	2.00
175 J.J. Watt RC	4.00	10.00
176 Jacquizz Rodgers RC	.75	2.00
177 Jeremy Kerley RC	1.25	3.00
178 Jimmy Smith RC	.75	2.00
179 Johnny White RC	.75	2.00
180 Jordan Cameron RC	1.00	2.50
181 Julius Thomas RC	1.00	2.50
182 Justin Houston RC	1.00	2.50
183 Kealoha Pilares RC	.75	2.00
184 Kris Durham RC	.75	2.00
185 Lance Kendricks RC	.75	2.00
186 Luke Stocker RC	.75	2.00
187 Marcus Cannon RC	.75	2.00
188 Martez Wilson RC	.75	2.00
189 Nathan Enderle RC	.75	2.00
190 Nick Fairley RC	.75	2.00
191 Niles Paul RC	.75	2.00
192 Owen Marecic RC	.75	2.00
193 Patrick Peterson RC	1.50	4.00
194 Phil Taylor RC	.75	2.00
195 Prince Amukamara RC	.75	2.00
196 Quinton Carter RC	.75	2.00
197 Rahim Moore RC	.75	2.00
198 Ricky Stanzi RC	.75	2.00
199 Robert Housler RC	.75	2.00
200 Robert Quinn RC	.75	2.00
201 Ronald Johnson RC	.75	2.00
202 Roy Helu RC	.75	2.00
203 Ryan Kerrigan RC	1.00	2.50
204 Ryan Whalen RC	.75	2.00
205 Scotty McKnight RC	.75	2.00
206 Shane Bannon RC	.75	2.00
207 Stanley Havili RC	.75	2.00
208 Stephen Burton RC	.75	2.00
209 Stephen Paea RC	.75	2.00
210 T.J. Yates RC	.75	2.00
211 Tandon Doss RC	.75	2.00
212 Tyler Sash RC	.75	2.00
213 Tyrod Taylor RC	1.50	4.00
214 Tyron Smith RC	1.00	2.50
215 Baron Batch RC	1.00	2.50
216 Damien Berry RC	1.00	2.50
217 Derrick Locke RC	1.00	2.50
218 Jay Finley RC	1.00	2.50
219 John Clay RC	1.25	3.00
220 Terrelle Pryor RC	1.25	3.00
221 Pat Devlin RC	1.25	3.00
222 Darvin Adams RC	.75	2.00
223 David Ausberry RC	.75	2.00
224 DeAndre Brown RC	1.25	3.00
225 DeMarco Sampson RC	.75	2.00
226 Mark Dell RC	1.00	2.50
227 O.J. Murdock RC	1.00	2.50
228 Brooks Reed RC	1.00	2.50
229 Bruce Carter RC	.75	2.00
230 Jabaal Sheard RC	.75	2.00
231 Jaiquawn Jarrett RC	.75	2.00
232 Jarvis Jenkins RC	.75	2.00
233 Jonas Mouton RC	1.00	2.50
234 Marcus Gilchrist RC	.75	2.00
235 Marvin Austin RC	.75	2.00
236 Muhammad Wilkerson RC	.75	2.00
237 Ras-I Dowling RC	.75	2.00
238 Akeem Dent RC	1.00	2.50
239 Dontay Moch RC	.75	2.00
240 Mason Foster RC	.75	2.00
241 Kelvin Sheppard RC	.75	2.00
242 Darryl Gamble RC	.75	2.00
243 Chris Matthews RC	8.00	20.00
244 Courtney Smith RC	.75	2.00
245 Dane Sanzenbacher RC	.75	2.00
246 Jock Sanders RC	1.00	2.50
247 Lestar Jean RC	.75	2.00
248 Marcus Harris RC	.75	2.00
249 Terrence Toliver RC	1.00	2.50
250 Tori Gurley RC	1.00	2.50
R1 Von Miller JSY AU/299 RC	12.00	30.00
R2 V.Brown JSY AU/299 RC	5.00	12.00
R3 T.Smith JSY AU/303 RC	5.00	12.00
R4 Titus Young JSY AU/287 RC	5.00	12.00
R5 T.Jones JSY AU/304 RC	5.00	12.00
R6 S.Ridley JSY AU/303 RC	5.00	12.00
R7 S.Vereen JSY AU/317 RC	6.00	15.00
R8 R.Williams JSY AU/202 RC	5.00	12.00
R9 Ryan Mallett JSY AU/197 RC	5.00	12.00
R10 R. Cobb JSY AU/304 RC	8.00	20.00
R11 M.Leshoure JSY AU/199 RC	5.00	12.00
R12 Mark Ingram JSY AU/201 RC	8.00	20.00
R13 M.Dareus JSY AU/300 RC	5.00	12.00
R14 L.Hankerson JSY AU/304 RC	5.00	12.00
R15 K.Rudolph JSY AU/299 RC	5.00	12.00
R16 K.Hunter JSY AU/304 RC	5.00	12.00
R17 Julio Jones JSY AU/204 RC	25.00	50.00
R18 J.Todman JSY AU/309 RC	5.00	12.00
R19 J.Baldwin JSY AU/302 RC	5.00	12.00
R20 J.Jernigan JSY AU/298 RC	5.00	12.00
R21 J.Harper JSY AU/304 RC	5.00	12.00
R22 J.Locker JSY AU/204 RC	5.00	12.00
R23 Greg Little JSY AU/300 RC	6.00	15.00
R24 D.Murray JSY AU/304 RC	10.00	25.00
R25 D.Carter JSY AU/304 RC	5.00	12.00
R26 D.Thomas JSY AU/300 RC	5.00	12.00
R27 Kaepernick JSY AU/205 RC	8.00	20.00
R28 Clyde Gates JSY AU/305 RC	5.00	12.00
R29 C.Ponder JSY AU/210 RC	5.00	12.00
R30 C.Newton JSY AU/204 RC	40.00	100.00
R31 B.Gabbert JSY AU/204 RC	5.00	12.00
R32 Bilal Powell JSY AU/303 RC	6.00	15.00
R33 Austin Pettis JSY AU/299 RC	5.00	12.00
R34 Andy Dalton JSY AU/204 RC	15.00	40.00
R35 Alex Green JSY AU/304 RC	5.00	12.00
R36 A.J. Green JSY AU/199 RC	20.00	50.00

2011 Panini Gridiron Gear Gold O's

*1-150 VETS/100: 2.5X TO 6X BASIC CARDS
*151-250 ROOKIE/100: .6X TO 1.5X BASIC RC

2011 Panini Gridiron Gear Gold X's

*1-150 VETS/100: 2.5X TO 6X BASIC CARDS
*151-250 ROOKIE/100: .6X TO 1.5X BASIC RC

2011 Panini Gridiron Gear Platinum O's

*1-150 VETS/25: 5X TO 12X BASIC CARDS
*151-250 ROOKIE/25: 1.2X TO 3X BASIC RC

2011 Panini Gridiron Gear Platinum X's

*1-150 VETS/25: 5X TO 12X BASIC CARDS
*151-250 ROOKIE/25: 1.2X TO 3X BASIC RC

2011 Panini Gridiron Gear Silver O's

*1-150 VETS/250: 2X TO 5X BASIC CARDS
*151-250 ROOKIE/250: .5X TO 1.2X BASIC RC

2011 Panini Gridiron Gear Silver X's

*1-150 VETS/250: 2X TO 5X BASIC CARDS
*151-250 ROOKIE/250: .5X TO 1.2X BASIC RC

2011 Panini Gridiron Gear Autographs Gold

UNPRICED VETERAN PRINT RUN 5
ROOKIE STATED PRINT RUN 290-299
*PLATINUM/25: .6X TO 1.5X GOLD/290-299

Card	Low	High
151 Aaron Williams/299	3.00	8.00
152 Adrian Clayborn/299	3.00	8.00
153 Ahmad Black/299	4.00	10.00
154 Akeem Ayers/299	3.00	8.00
155 Aldon Smith/299 EXCH	3.00	8.00
156 Aldrick Robinson/299	4.00	10.00
157 Allen Bradford/299	3.00	8.00
158 Anthony Allen/299	3.00	8.00
159 Anthony Castonzo/299	3.00	8.00
160 Brandon Harris/299	3.00	8.00
161 Cameron Heyward/299	4.00	10.00
162 Cameron Jordan/299	4.00	10.00
163 Cecil Shorts/299	3.00	8.00
164 Corey Liuget/299	3.00	8.00
165 D.J. Williams/299	3.00	8.00
166 Da'Quan Bowers/299	3.00	8.00
167 Da'Rel Scott/299	3.00	8.00
168 Denarius Moore/299	10.00	25.00
169 Dion Lewis/299	4.00	10.00
170 Dwayne Harris/299	3.00	8.00
171 Evan Royster/299	3.00	8.00
172 Greg Jones/299	4.00	10.00
173 Greg McElroy/299	5.00	12.00
174 Greg Salas/299	3.00	8.00
175 J.J. Watt/299	40.00	80.00
176 Jacquizz Rodgers/299	3.00	8.00
177 Jeremy Kerley/290	5.00	12.00
178 Jimmy Smith/299	3.00	8.00
179 Johnny White/299	3.00	8.00
180 Jordan Cameron/299	4.00	10.00
181 Julius Thomas/299	4.00	10.00
182 Justin Houston/299	4.00	10.00
183 Kealoha Pilares/299	3.00	8.00
184 Kris Durham/299 EXCH	3.00	8.00
185 Lance Kendricks/299	3.00	8.00
186 Luke Stocker/299	3.00	8.00
187 Marcus Cannon/299	3.00	8.00
188 Martez Wilson/299	3.00	8.00
191 Niles Paul/299	3.00	8.00
194 Phil Taylor/299	3.00	8.00
195 Prince Amukamara/299	3.00	8.00
196 Quinton Carter/299	3.00	8.00
197 Rahim Moore/299	3.00	8.00
198 Ricky Stanzi/299	3.00	8.00
201 Ronald Johnson/299	3.00	8.00
202 Roy Helu/299	3.00	8.00
203 Ryan Kerrigan/299	4.00	10.00
204 Ryan Whalen/299	3.00	8.00
205 Scotty McKnight/299	3.00	8.00
207 Stanley Havili/299	3.00	8.00
209 Stephen Paea/299	3.00	8.00
210 T.J. Yates/299	3.00	8.00
212 Tyler Sash/299	3.00	8.00
213 Tyrod Taylor/299	6.00	15.00
214 Tyron Smith/299	4.00	10.00
220 Terrelle Pryor/299	5.00	12.00

2011 Panini Gridiron Gear Crash Course

RANDOM INSERTS IN PACKS
*GOLD/100: .6X TO 1.5X BASIC INSERTS
*PLATINUM/25: 1X TO 2.5X BASIC INSERTS
*SILVER/250: .5X TO 1.2X BASIC INSERTS

Card	Low	High
1 J.Beason/M.Turner	.60	1.50
2 P.Willis/S. Jackson	.75	2.00
3 C.Finnegan/A.Foster	.60	1.50
4 R.Lewis/R.Mendenhall	1.00	2.50
5 T.Suggs/C.Benson	.60	1.50
6 D.Freeney/C.Johnson	.60	1.50
7 J.Harrison/R.Rice	.75	2.00
8 D.Ryans/M.Jones-Drew	.60	1.50
9 B.Urlacher/A.Peterson	1.00	2.50
10 D.Ware/A.Bradshaw	.75	2.00

2011 Panini Gridiron Gear Crash Course Jerseys

STATED PRINT RUN 10-250
*PRIME/25: .8X TO 2X BASIC JSY/100-250
*PRIME/25: .6X TO 1.5X BASIC JSY/50
*PRIME/25: .5X TO 1.2X BASIC JSY/25

Card	Low	High
1 J.Beason/M.Turner		
2 P.Willis/S. Jackson	3.00	8.00
3 C.Finnegan/A.Foster	3.00	8.00
4 R.Lewis/R.Mendenhall	8.00	20.00
5 T.Suggs/C.Benson	2.50	6.00
6 D.Freeney/C.Johnson	2.50	6.00
7 J.Harrison/R.Rice	5.00	12.00
8 D.Ryans/M.Jones-Drew	3.00	8.00
9 B.Urlacher/A.Peterson	6.00	15.00
10 D.Ware/A.Bradshaw	4.00	10.00

2011 Panini Gridiron Gear Gamebreakers

*GOLD/100: .6X TO 1.5X BASIC INSERTS
*PLATINUM/25: 1X TO 2.5X BASIC INSERTS
*SILVER/250: .5X TO 1.2X BASIC INSERTS

Card	Low	High
1 Arian Foster	.60	1.50
2 Dwayne Bowe	.75	2.00
3 BenJarvus Green-Ellis	.60	1.50
4 Adrian Peterson	1.00	2.50
5 Peyton Hillis	.60	1.50
6 Rashard Mendenhall	.60	1.50
7 Greg Jennings	.60	1.50
8 Calvin Johnson	1.00	2.50
9 Chris Johnson	.60	1.50
10 Michael Turner	.60	1.50
11 Hakeem Nicks	.60	1.50
12 Mike Tolbert	.60	1.50
13 Brandon Lloyd	.60	1.50
14 Mike Williams	.75	2.00
15 Mike Wallace	.60	1.50
16 Rob Gronkowski	1.00	2.50
17 Roddy White	.60	1.50
18 Steve Johnson	.60	1.50
19 Antonio Gates	.60	1.50
20 Marcedes Lewis	.60	1.50
21 Darren McFadden	.60	1.50
22 Jeremy Maclin	.60	1.50
23 Kenny Britt	.60	1.50
24 LeSean McCoy	1.00	2.50
25 Mario Manningham	.60	1.50
26 Matt Forte	.60	1.50
27 Michael Vick	.75	2.00
28 Brandon Jacobs	.60	1.50
29 Jason Witten	.75	2.00
30 Austin Collie	.60	1.50

2011 Panini Gridiron Gear Gamebreakers Jerseys

STATED PRINT RUN 25-250
*PRIME/50: .6X TO 1.5X BASIC JSY/99-250
*PRIME/50: .5X TO 1.2X BASIC JSY/50

Card	Low	High
1 Arian Foster/250	2.50	6.00
2 Dwayne Bowe/250	3.00	8.00
4 Adrian Peterson/25	6.00	15.00
5 Peyton Hillis/100	2.50	6.00
6 Rashard Mendenhall/250	2.50	6.00
9 Chris Johnson/250	2.50	6.00
10 Michael Turner/250	2.50	6.00
11 Hakeem Nicks/250	2.50	6.00
13 Brandon Lloyd/250	2.50	6.00
15 Mike Wallace/250	4.00	10.00
17 Roddy White/50	3.00	8.00
18 Steve Johnson/100	4.00	10.00
19 Antonio Gates/250	2.50	6.00
20 Marcedes Lewis/99	2.50	6.00
21 Darren McFadden/250	2.50	6.00
22 Jeremy Maclin/250	2.50	6.00
23 Kenny Britt/250	2.50	6.00
24 LeSean McCoy/250	4.00	10.00
26 Matt Forte/100	2.50	6.00
27 Michael Vick/250	3.00	8.00
28 Brandon Jacobs/250	2.50	6.00
29 Jason Witten/250	4.00	10.00

2011 Panini Gridiron Gear Gamebreakers Jerseys Autographs

STATED PRINT RUN 5-15

Card	Low	High
3 BenJarvus Green-Ellis/15	30.00	60.00
23 Kenny Britt/15		
29 Jason Witten/15	25.00	50.00

2011 Panini Gridiron Gear Gamebreakers Jerseys Combos

STATED PRINT RUN 25-100
*PRIME/25: .8X TO 2X BASIC JSY/100
*PRIME/25: .6X TO 1.5X BASIC JSY/50

Card	Low	High
1 Arian Foster/100	3.00	8.00
2 Dwayne Bowe/100	4.00	10.00
3 BenJarvus Green-Ellis/100	3.00	8.00
4 Adrian Peterson/25	8.00	20.00
5 Peyton Hillis/50	4.00	10.00
6 Rashard Mendenhall/100	3.00	8.00
8 Calvin Johnson/100	5.00	12.00
9 Chris Johnson/100	3.00	8.00
10 Michael Turner/100	3.00	8.00
11 Hakeem Nicks/100	3.00	8.00
13 Brandon Lloyd/100	3.00	8.00
15 Mike Wallace/100	3.00	8.00
17 Roddy White/50	4.00	10.00
18 Steve Johnson/50	4.00	10.00
19 Antonio Gates/100	3.00	8.00
20 Marcedes Lewis/50	4.00	10.00
21 Darren McFadden/100	3.00	8.00
22 Jeremy Maclin/100	3.00	8.00
23 Kenny Britt/100	3.00	8.00
24 LeSean McCoy/100	5.00	12.00
26 Matt Forte/100	3.00	8.00
27 Michael Vick/100	4.00	10.00
28 Brandon Jacobs/100	3.00	8.00
29 Jason Witten/100	5.00	12.00

2011 Panini Gridiron Gear Jerseys O's

STATED PRINT RUN 25-299

Card	Low	High
4 Tom Brady/49	12.00	30.00
5 Wes Welker/49	4.00	10.00
6 Darrelle Revis/49	3.00	8.00
8 LaDainian Tomlinson/299	4.00	10.00
9 Mark Sanchez/49	3.00	8.00
10 Shonn Greene/49	3.00	8.00
11 Brandon Marshall/49	4.00	10.00
12 Chad Henne/49	4.00	10.00
15 Fred Jackson/49	3.00	8.00
16 Ryan Fitzpatrick/49	3.00	8.00
17 Steve Johnson/49	3.00	8.00
19 Ben Roethlisberger/49	5.00	12.00
22 Mike Wallace/49	3.00	8.00
23 Rashard Mendenhall/49	3.00	8.00
24 Anquan Boldin/49	3.00	8.00
26 Joe Flacco/299	3.00	8.00
27 Ray Lewis/49	5.00	12.00
28 Ray Rice/49	3.00	8.00
29 Colt McCoy/49	3.00	8.00
33 Cedric Benson/49	3.00	8.00
35 Jermaine Gresham/49	3.00	8.00
36 Jordan Shipley/49	3.00	8.00
38 Dallas Clark/49	3.00	8.00
39 Peyton Manning/249	8.00	20.00
41 Reggie Wayne/299	3.00	8.00
43 Marcedes Lewis/49	3.00	8.00
44 Maurice Jones-Drew/25	4.00	10.00
45 Mike Thomas/49	4.00	10.00
46 Andre Johnson/299	3.00	8.00
47 Arian Foster/299	2.50	6.00
49 Matt Schaub/49	3.00	8.00
51 Chris Johnson/49	3.00	8.00
54 Dwayne Bowe/49	4.00	10.00
55 Jamaal Charles/49	4.00	10.00
56 Matt Cassel/49	3.00	8.00
58 Antonio Gates/49	3.00	8.00
60 Philip Rivers/49	5.00	12.00
61 Ryan Mathews/49	4.00	10.00
63 Darren McFadden/49	3.00	8.00
65 Jason Campbell/49	3.00	8.00
67 Brandon Lloyd/49	3.00	8.00
70 Knowshon Moreno/49	3.00	8.00
71 Tim Tebow/49	5.00	12.00
72 DeSean Jackson/49	4.00	10.00
73 Jeremy Maclin/49	3.00	8.00
75 LeSean McCoy/299	4.00	10.00
76 Michael Vick/49	4.00	10.00
77 Brandon Jacobs/299	2.50	6.00
78 Eli Manning/49	4.00	10.00
79 Hakeem Nicks/299	2.50	6.00
81 DeMarcus Ware/49	5.00	12.00
82 Dez Bryant/249	4.00	10.00
83 Felix Jones/49	3.00	8.00
84 Miles Austin/49	5.00	12.00
85 Tony Romo/49	4.00	10.00
86 DeAngelo Hall/49	3.00	8.00
88 London Fletcher/49	4.00	10.00
89 Ryan Torain/49	3.00	8.00
90 Brian Urlacher/49	5.00	12.00
91 Jay Cutler/49	3.00	8.00
92 Johnny Knox/49	3.00	8.00
93 Matt Forte/99	2.50	6.00
94 Aaron Rodgers/25	15.00	40.00
95 A.J. Hawk/299	2.50	6.00
99 Calvin Johnson/49	5.00	12.00
100 Jahvid Best/49	3.00	8.00
101 Matthew Stafford/49	4.00	10.00
102 Ndamukong Suh/49	4.00	10.00
103 Adrian Peterson/25	6.00	15.00
104 Chad Greenway/49	4.00	10.00
105 Percy Harvin/49	3.00	8.00
106 Visanthe Shiancoe/49	4.00	10.00
108 Matt Ryan/49	4.00	10.00
109 Michael Turner/49	3.00	8.00
110 Roddy White/49	3.00	8.00
111 Tony Gonzalez/49	4.00	10.00
114 Marques Colston/49	3.00	8.00
115 Pierre Thomas /49	3.00	8.00
118 Kellen Winslow Jr./49	3.00	8.00
122 DeAngelo Williams/136	2.50	6.00
123 Jonathan Stewart/249	2.50	6.00
124 Steve Smith/49	4.00	10.00
129 Danny Amendola/49	4.00	10.00
131 Sam Bradford/49	3.00	8.00
132 Steven Jackson/49	3.00	8.00
134 Frank Gore/299	3.00	8.00
135 Michael Crabtree/99	2.50	6.00
136 Patrick Willis/49	4.00	10.00
137 Vernon Davis/49	3.00	8.00
138 Beanie Wells/49	3.00	8.00
141 Ahmad Bradshaw/299	2.50	6.00
143 Santonio Holmes/49	3.00	8.00
145 Santana Moss/49	4.00	10.00
149 Jared Allen/49	5.00	12.00

2011 Panini Gridiron Gear Jerseys Prime

STATED PRINT RUN 2-50

Card	Low	High
4 Tom Brady/50	15.00	40.00
5 Wes Welker/50	5.00	12.00
6 Darrelle Revis/50	4.00	10.00
7 Dustin Keller/50	5.00	12.00
8 LaDainian Tomlinson/50	6.00	15.00
10 Shonn Greene/50	4.00	10.00
11 Brandon Marshall/50	5.00	12.00
12 Chad Henne/50	5.00	12.00
15 Fred Jackson/25	5.00	12.00
16 Ryan Fitzpatrick/50	4.00	10.00
17 Steve Johnson/50	4.00	10.00
22 Mike Wallace/50	4.00	10.00
24 Anquan Boldin/50	4.00	10.00
25 Ed Reed/50	5.00	12.00
26 Joe Flacco/50	5.00	12.00
27 Ray Lewis/50	6.00	15.00
28 Ray Rice/50	4.00	10.00
29 Colt McCoy/50	4.00	10.00
33 Cedric Benson/50	4.00	10.00
35 Jermaine Gresham/50	4.00	10.00
36 Jordan Shipley/50	4.00	10.00
38 Dallas Clark/50	4.00	10.00
39 Peyton Manning/50	12.00	30.00
40 Pierre Garcon/50	5.00	12.00
43 Marcedes Lewis/50	4.00	10.00
44 Maurice Jones-Drew/50	4.00	10.00
45 Mike Thomas/50	5.00	12.00
46 Andre Johnson/50	5.00	12.00
49 Matt Schaub/50	4.00	10.00
51 Chris Johnson/50	4.00	10.00
52 Nate Washington/50	4.00	10.00
54 Dwayne Bowe/50	5.00	12.00
55 Jamaal Charles/50	5.00	12.00
56 Matt Cassel/50	4.00	10.00
58 Antonio Gates/50	4.00	10.00
60 Philip Rivers/50	6.00	15.00
61 Ryan Mathews/50	5.00	12.00
62 Vincent Jackson/50	4.00	10.00
63 Darren McFadden/50	4.00	10.00
65 Jason Campbell/39	4.00	10.00
67 Brandon Lloyd/50	4.00	10.00
70 Knowshon Moreno/50	4.00	10.00
71 Tim Tebow/50	6.00	15.00
72 DeSean Jackson/50	5.00	12.00
73 Jeremy Maclin/50	4.00	10.00
78 Eli Manning/50	5.00	12.00
79 Hakeem Nicks/50	4.00	10.00
81 DeMarcus Ware/50	5.00	12.00
82 Dez Bryant/50	6.00	15.00
83 Felix Jones/50	4.00	10.00
84 Miles Austin/50	6.00	15.00
85 Tony Romo/50	5.00	12.00
86 DeAngelo Hall/50	4.00	10.00
88 London Fletcher/50	5.00	12.00
89 Ryan Torain/50	4.00	10.00
90 Brian Urlacher/50	6.00	15.00
91 Jay Cutler/50	4.00	10.00
92 Johnny Knox/50	4.00	10.00
93 Matt Forte/50	4.00	10.00
95 A.J. Hawk/50	4.00	10.00
99 Calvin Johnson/50	6.00	15.00
101 Matthew Stafford/50	5.00	12.00
102 Ndamukong Suh/50	5.00	12.00
104 Chad Greenway/50	5.00	12.00
105 Percy Harvin/50	4.00	10.00
106 Visanthe Shiancoe/50	5.00	12.00
108 Matt Ryan/50	5.00	12.00
109 Michael Turner/50	4.00	10.00
110 Roddy White/50	4.00	10.00
111 Tony Gonzalez/50	5.00	12.00
114 Marques Colston/50	4.00	10.00
118 Kellen Winslow Jr./50	4.00	10.00
122 DeAngelo Williams/50	4.00	10.00
123 Jonathan Stewart/50	4.00	10.00
124 Steve Smith/50	5.00	12.00
129 Danny Amendola/50	5.00	12.00
130 James Laurinaitis/50	4.00	10.00
131 Sam Bradford/50	4.00	10.00
132 Steven Jackson/50	4.00	10.00
133 Alex Smith QB/50	5.00	12.00
135 Michael Crabtree/17	5.00	12.00
136 Patrick Willis/50	5.00	12.00
137 Vernon Davis/50	4.00	10.00
138 Beanie Wells/50	4.00	10.00
141 Ahmad Bradshaw/25	5.00	12.00
143 Santonio Holmes/50	4.00	10.00
145 Santana Moss/50	5.00	12.00
146 Asante Samuel/50	4.00	10.00
149 Jared Allen/50	6.00	15.00

2011 Panini Gridiron Gear NFL Gridiron Signatures

STATED PRINT RUN 5-25

Card	Low	High
3 Troy Polamalu/20	90.00	150.00
19 Aaron Rodgers/21	200.00	300.00
20 Ben Roethlisberger/20	60.00	120.00
21 Calvin Johnson/25 EXCH		
22 Drew Brees/25	50.00	100.00
23 Dwayne Bowe/25 EXCH		
24 Larry Fitzgerald/25	20.00	50.00

2011 Panini Gridiron Gear NFL Nation

*GOLD/100: .6X TO 1.5X BASIC INSERTS
*PLATINUM/25: 1X TO 2.5X BASIC INSERTS
*SILVER/250: .5X TO 1.2X BASIC INSERTS

Card	Low	High
1 Adrian Peterson	1.00	2.50
2 Braylon Edwards	.60	1.50
3 Patrick Willis	.75	2.00
4 DeMarcus Ware	.75	2.00
5 Darren McFadden	.60	1.50
6 Maurice Jones-Drew	.60	1.50
7 Drew Brees	1.00	2.50
8 Bob Sanders	.60	1.50
9 Hines Ward	.75	2.00
10 Roy Williams	.60	1.50
11 Santana Moss	.75	2.00
12 Jonathan Vilma	.60	1.50
13 Shawne Merriman	.60	1.50
14 T.J. Houshmandzadeh	.60	1.50
15 Steven Jackson	.60	1.50
16 Devin Hester	.75	2.00
17 Reggie Wayne	.75	2.00
18 Vince Young	.60	1.50
19 Antonio Gates	.60	1.50
20 Mario Williams	.60	1.50
21 Reggie Bush	.60	1.50
22 Carson Palmer	.75	2.00
23 Willis McGahee	.60	1.50
24 Dwight Freeney	.60	1.50
25 Ben Roethlisberger	1.00	2.50
26 Tony Gonzalez	.75	2.00
27 Larry Fitzgerald	.75	2.00
28 Michael Vick	.75	2.00
29 Chad Ochocinco	.60	1.50
30 Ed Reed	.75	2.00

2011 Panini Gridiron Gear NFL Nation Jerseys

STATED PRINT RUN 25-250

Card	Low	High
1 Adrian Peterson/25	6.00	15.00
3 Patrick Willis/250	3.00	8.00
4 DeMarcus Ware/250	4.00	10.00
5 Darren McFadden/250	2.50	6.00
6 Maurice Jones-Drew/100	2.50	6.00
7 Drew Brees/250	4.00	10.00
9 Hines Ward/250	4.00	10.00
11 Santana Moss/250	3.00	8.00
15 Steven Jackson/250	2.50	6.00
16 Devin Hester/250	3.00	8.00
17 Reggie Wayne/250	3.00	8.00
19 Antonio Gates/250	2.50	6.00
22 Carson Palmer/250	3.00	8.00
24 Dwight Freeney/250	2.50	6.00
26 Tony Gonzalez/250	3.00	8.00

27 Larry Fitzgerald/250 3.00 8.00
28 Michael Vick/250 3.00 8.00
30 Ed Reed/225 3.00 8.00

2011 Panini Gridiron Gear NFL Nation Jerseys Prime

*PRIME/50: .6X TO 1.5X BASIC JSY/100-250
PRIME STATED PRINT RUN 5-50
25 Ben Roethlisberger/25 10.00 25.00

2011 Panini Gridiron Gear NFL Nation Jerseys Autographs

JSY AU PRINT RUN 5-15
11 Santana Moss/15 12.00 30.00

2011 Panini Gridiron Gear NFL Nation Jerseys Combos

STATED PRINT RUN 25-100
*PRIME/25: .8X TO 2X BASIC COMBO
1 Adrian Peterson/25 6.00 15.00
3 Patrick Willis/100 4.00 10.00
4 DeMarcus Ware/100 5.00 12.00
5 Darren McFadden/100 3.00 8.00
6 Maurice Jones-Drew/100 3.00 8.00
9 Hines Ward/75 5.00 12.00
11 Santana Moss/100 4.00 10.00
15 Steven Jackson/100 3.00 8.00
16 Devin Hester/100 4.00 10.00
17 Reggie Wayne/100 4.00 10.00
19 Antonio Gates/100 3.00 8.00
22 Carson Palmer/100 4.00 10.00
24 Dwight Freeney/100 3.00 8.00
25 Ben Roethlisberger/100 5.00 12.00
26 Tony Gonzalez/100 4.00 10.00
27 Larry Fitzgerald/100 4.00 10.00
28 Michael Vick/100 4.00 10.00
30 Ed Reed/100 4.00 10.00

2011 Panini Gridiron Gear NFL Pro Gridiron Signatures

STATED PRINT RUN 10-30
1 Alan Page/30 10.00 25.00
3 Bo Jackson/15 50.00 100.00
6 Danny White/15 15.00 40.00
7 Ed Too Tall Jones/30 10.00 25.00
9 Forrest Gregg/30
10 Franco Harris/15 30.00 60.00
12 Jim McMahon/15 20.00 50.00
13 Jim Plunkett/30 15.00 40.00
14 Joe Greene/30 15.00 40.00
15 Lenny Moore /30 10.00 25.00
16 Marcus Allen/15 20.00 50.00
17 Mark Duper/30 10.00 25.00
18 Michael Irvin/30 25.00 50.00
19 Paul Hornung/30 15.00 40.00
20 Paul Warfield/30 12.00 30.00
21 Priest Holmes/30 10.00 25.00
22 Randall Cunningham/15 20.00 50.00
23 Raymond Berry/30 12.00 30.00
24 Steve Bartkowski/30
25 Alex Karras/30 12.00 30.00
26 Billy Howton/30 10.00 25.00
27 Bobby Bell/30 10.00 25.00
28 Boyd Dowler/30 15.00 40.00
29 Cliff Harris/30 12.00 30.00
30 Don Perkins/30 12.00 30.00
31 Dub Jones/30 12.00 30.00
32 Frank Gifford/25 15.00 40.00
33 Fred Williamson/30 12.00 30.00
34 Harlon Hill/30 10.00 25.00
35 Keyshawn Johnson/30
36 Lee Roy Selmon/30 12.00 30.00
37 Leroy Kelly/30 12.00 30.00
38 Lydell Mitchell/30 10.00 25.00
39 Mike Curtis/30 10.00 25.00
40 Ozzie Newsome/30 12.00 30.00
41 Paul Krause/30 12.00 30.00
42 Rick Casares/30 12.00 30.00
43 Ron Mix/30 10.00 25.00
44 Russ Grimm/30 12.00 30.00
45 Sterling Sharpe/30 15.00 40.00
46 Willie Brown/30 10.00 25.00
47 Charley Taylor/30 10.00 25.00
48 Deacon Jones/30 15.00 40.00
49 James Lofton/30 15.00 40.00
50 Michael Strahan/25 15.00 40.00

2011 Panini Gridiron Gear Plates and Patches

STATED PRINT RUN 10-100
UNPRICED AUTO PRINT RUN 1-10
1 Eli Manning/100 6.00 15.00
3 Antonio Gates/100 5.00 12.00
4 Chris Cooley/100 5.00 12.00
5 Colt McCoy/100 5.00 12.00
6 DeAngelo Williams/50 5.00 12.00
7 DeSean Jackson/100 6.00 15.00
8 Heath Miller/100 5.00 12.00
9 Jamaal Charles/100 6.00 15.00
10 James Laurinaitis/50 5.00 12.00
11 Marques Colston/50 5.00 12.00
12 Miles Austin/100 8.00 20.00
13 Roddy White/100 5.00 12.00
14 Santana Moss/100 6.00 15.00
15 Vernon Davis/100 5.00 12.00

2011 Panini Gridiron Gear Rookie Gridiron Gems Jerseys Retail

STATED PRINT RUN 99 SER.#'d SETS
*HOBBY JSY/25: .5X TO 1.2X RETAIL/99
*JUMBO/25: .6X TO 1.5X RETAIL JSY/99
*JUM.PRIME/10: 1.2X TO 3X RET.JSY/99
*PRIME/50: .5X TO 1.2X RETAIL JSY/99
*COMBO/25: .6X TO 1.5X RETAIL JSY/99
*CMB.PRIME/50: .8X TO 2X RETAIL/99
*TRIO/50: .6X TO 1.5X RETAIL JSY/99
*TRIO PRIME/50: 1X TO 2.5X RETAIL/99
1 Von Miller 2.00 5.00
2 Vincent Brown 1.25 3.00
3 Torrey Smith 1.25 3.00
4 Titus Young 1.25 3.00
5 Taiwan Jones 1.25 3.00
6 Stevan Ridley 1.25 3.00
7 Shane Vereen 1.50 4.00
8 Ryan Williams 1.25 3.00
9 Ryan Mallett 1.25 3.00
10 Randall Cobb 2.00 5.00
11 Mikel Leshoure 1.25 3.00
12 Mark Ingram 2.00 5.00
13 Marcell Dareus 1.25 3.00
14 Leonard Hankerson 1.25 3.00
15 Kyle Rudolph 1.25 3.00
16 Kendall Hunter 1.25 3.00
17 Julio Jones 4.00 10.00
18 Jordan Todman 1.25 3.00
19 Jonathan Baldwin 1.25 3.00
20 Jerrel Jernigan 1.25 3.00
21 Jamie Harper 1.25 3.00
22 Jake Locker 1.25 3.00
23 Greg Little 1.50 4.00
24 DeMarco Murray 2.50 6.00
25 Delone Carter 1.25 3.00
26 Daniel Thomas 1.25 3.00
27 Colin Kaepernick 2.00 5.00
28 Clyde Gates 1.25 3.00
29 Christian Ponder 1.25 3.00
30 Cam Newton 6.00 15.00
31 Blaine Gabbert 1.25 3.00
32 Bilal Powell 1.50 4.00
33 Austin Pettis 1.25 3.00
34 Andy Dalton 2.50 6.00
35 Alex Green 1.25 3.00
36 A.J. Green 3.00 8.00

2011 Panini Gridiron Gear Rookie Gridiron Gems Jerseys Trios Autographs Prime

*TRIO PRIME/20: .6X TO 1.5X BASE JSY AU RC
TRIO PRINT RUN 20 SER.#'d SETS
*COMBO PRIME/15: .4X TO 1X TRIO AU/20

2011 Panini Gridiron Gear Rookie Orientation

*GOLD/100: .6X TO 1.5X BASIC INSERTS
*PLATINUM/25: 1X TO 2.5X BASIC INSERTS
*SILVER/250: .5X TO 1.2X BASIC INSERTS
1 A.J. Green 1.25 3.00
2 Austin Pettis .50 1.25
3 Clyde Gates .50 1.25
4 Greg Little .60 1.50
5 Jerrel Jernigan .50 1.25
6 Jonathan Baldwin .50 1.25
7 Julio Jones 1.50 4.00
8 Leonard Hankerson .50 1.25
9 Randall Cobb .75 2.00
10 Titus Young .50 1.25
11 Torrey Smith .50 1.25
12 Vincent Brown .50 1.25
13 Bilal Powell .60 1.50
14 Daniel Thomas .50 1.25
15 Delone Carter .50 1.25
16 DeMarco Murray 1.00 2.50
17 Jamie Harper .50 1.25
18 Alex Green .50 1.25
19 Jordan Todman .50 1.25
20 Ryan Williams .50 1.25
21 Shane Vereen .60 1.50
22 Stevan Ridley .50 1.25
23 Taiwan Jones .50 1.25
24 Mark Ingram .75 2.00
25 Mikel Leshoure .50 1.25
26 Kendall Hunter .50 1.25
27 Kyle Rudolph .50 1.25
28 Andy Dalton 1.00 2.50
29 Blaine Gabbert .50 1.25
30 Cam Newton 2.50 6.00
31 Christian Ponder .50 1.25
32 Colin Kaepernick .75 2.00
33 Jake Locker .50 1.25
34 Ryan Mallett .50 1.25
35 Marcell Dareus .50 1.25
36 Von Miller .75 2.00

2011 Panini Gridiron Gear Rookie Orientation Jerseys

STATED PRINT RUN 299 SER.#'d SETS
*PRIME/25: 1X TO 2.5X BASIC JSY/299
1 A.J. Green 3.00 8.00
2 Austin Pettis 1.25 3.00
3 Clyde Gates 1.25 3.00
4 Greg Little 1.50 4.00
5 Jerrel Jernigan 1.25 3.00
6 Jonathan Baldwin 1.25 3.00
7 Julio Jones 4.00 10.00
8 Leonard Hankerson 1.25 3.00
9 Randall Cobb 2.00 5.00
10 Titus Young 1.25 3.00
11 Torrey Smith 1.25 3.00
12 Vincent Brown 1.25 3.00
13 Bilal Powell 1.50 4.00
14 Daniel Thomas 1.25 3.00
15 Delone Carter 1.25 3.00
16 DeMarco Murray 2.50 6.00
17 Jamie Harper 1.25 3.00
18 Alex Green 1.25 3.00
19 Jordan Todman 1.25 3.00
20 Ryan Williams 1.25 3.00
21 Shane Vereen 1.50 4.00
22 Stevan Ridley 1.25 3.00
23 Taiwan Jones 1.25 3.00
24 Mark Ingram 2.00 5.00
25 Mikel Leshoure 1.25 3.00
26 Kendall Hunter 1.25 3.00
27 Kyle Rudolph 1.25 3.00
28 Andy Dalton 2.50 6.00
29 Blaine Gabbert 1.25 3.00
30 Cam Newton 6.00 15.00
31 Christian Ponder 1.25 3.00
32 Colin Kaepernick 2.00 5.00
33 Jake Locker 1.25 3.00
34 Ryan Mallett 1.25 3.00
35 Marcell Dareus 1.25 3.00
36 Von Miller 2.00 5.00

2011 Panini Gridiron Gear Rookie Orientation Jerseys Autographs

STATED PRINT RUN 50 SER.#'d SETS
*PRIME/15: .6X TO 1.5X JSY AU/50
1 A.J. Green 15.00 40.00
2 Austin Pettis 4.00 10.00
3 Clyde Gates 4.00 10.00
4 Greg Little 5.00 12.00
5 Jerrel Jernigan 4.00 10.00
6 Jonathan Baldwin 4.00 10.00
7 Julio Jones 15.00 40.00
8 Leonard Hankerson 4.00 10.00
9 Randall Cobb 6.00 15.00
10 Titus Young 4.00 10.00
11 Torrey Smith 4.00 10.00
12 Vincent Brown 4.00 10.00
13 Bilal Powell 5.00 12.00
14 Daniel Thomas 4.00 10.00
15 Delone Carter 4.00 10.00
16 DeMarco Murray 8.00 20.00
17 Jamie Harper EXCH 4.00 10.00
18 Alex Green 4.00 10.00
19 Jordan Todman 4.00 10.00
20 Ryan Williams EXCH 4.00 10.00
21 Shane Vereen 5.00 12.00
22 Stevan Ridley 4.00 10.00
23 Taiwan Jones 4.00 10.00
24 Mark Ingram 6.00 15.00
25 Mikel Leshoure 4.00 10.00
26 Kendall Hunter 4.00 10.00
27 Kyle Rudolph 4.00 10.00
28 Andy Dalton 8.00 20.00
29 Blaine Gabbert 4.00 10.00
30 Cam Newton 40.00 100.00
31 Christian Ponder 4.00 10.00
32 Colin Kaepernick 6.00 15.00
33 Jake Locker 4.00 10.00
34 Ryan Mallett 4.00 10.00
35 Marcell Dareus EXCH
36 Von Miller 10.00 25.00

2011 Panini Gridiron Gear Rookie Orientation Materials Quad

STATED PRINT RUN 150 SER.#'d SETS
*PRIME/25: .8X TO 2X BASIC QUAD/150
1 Newton/Miller/Dareus/Green 10.00 25.00
2 Locker/Gabbert/Ponder/Dalton 3.00 8.00
3 Green/Jones/Baldwin/Young 5.00 12.00
4 Ingram/Williams/Vereen/Thomas 2.50 6.00
5 Ponder/Rudolph/Green/Cobb 2.50 6.00
6 Smith/Little/Pettis/Hankerson 4.00 10.00
7 Murray/Ridley/Carter/Jones 3.00 8.00
8 Hunter/Powell/Harper/Todman 3.00 8.00

2011 Panini Gridiron Gear Rookie Orientation Materials Triple

STATED PRINT RUN 250 SER.#'d SETS
*PRIME/25: .8X TO 2X BASIC TRIO/250
1 Newton/Green/Ingram 8.00 20.00
2 Jones/Locker/Williams 5.00 12.00
3 Gabbert/Baldwin/Vereen 2.00 5.00
4 Ponder/Young/Leshoure 1.50 4.00
5 Dalton/Kaepernick/Mallett 3.00 8.00
6 Thomas/Ridley/Powell 2.00 5.00
7 Murray/Hankerson/Jernigan 3.00 8.00
8 Pettis/Little/Smith 2.00 5.00

2010 Panini Hall of Fame

This 8-card set, featuring members of the 2010 Pro Football Hall of Fame class, was created by Panini and issued at the induction ceremony in Canton in August 2010.
COMPLETE SET (8) 5.00 12.00
1 Emmitt Smith 1.50 4.00
2 Jerry Rice 1.50 4.00
3 Russ Grimm .60 1.50
4 Rickey Jackson .60 1.50
5 Floyd Little .60 1.50
6 John Randle .60 1.50
7 Dick LeBeau .60 1.50
NNO Cover Card .40 1.00

2011 Panini Hall of Fame Class of 2011

1 Marshall Faulk 2.00 5.00
2 Richard Dent 1.50 4.00
3 Chris Hanburger 1.25 3.00
4 Les Richter 1.25 3.00
5 Ed Sabol 1.25 3.00
6 Deion Sanders 2.00 5.00
7 Shannon Sharpe 1.50 4.00
8 Cover Card 1.00 2.00

2012 Panini Hall of Fame Class of 2012 Enshrinement National VIP

COMPLETE SET (7) 5.00 12.00
ISSUED TO VIP ATTENDEES
1 Curtis Martin 1.00 2.50
2 Dermontti Dawson .75 2.00
3 Chris Doleman .75 2.00
4 Cortez Kennedy .75 2.00
5 Willie Roaf .75 2.00
6 Jack Butler .75 2.00
NNO Cover Card .20 .50

2012 Panini Hall of Fame Class of 2012 Black Friday Autographs

1 Curtis Martin 75.00 125.00
2 Dermontti Dawson 60.00 100.00
3 Chris Doleman 40.00 80.00
4 Cortez Kennedy 40.00 80.00
5 Willie Roaf 60.00 100.00
6 Jack Butler 60.00 100.00

2013 Panini Hall of Fame Class of 2013 Enshrinement

COMPLETE SET (8) 7.50 15.00
1 Warren Sapp 1.00 2.50
2 Cris Carter 1.25 3.00
3 Larry Allen 1.00 2.50
4 Jonathan Ogden 1.00 2.50
5 Bill Parcells 1.00 2.50
6 Curley Culp .75 2.00
7 Dave Robinson .75 2.00
8 Cover Card .40 1.00

2014 Panini Hall of Fame Class of 2014 Enshrinement

AR Andre Reed 1.00 2.50
AW Aeneas Williams .75 2.00
CH Claude Humphrey .75 2.00
DB Derrick Brooks 1.00 2.50
MS Michael Strahan 1.00 2.50
RG Ray Guy .75 2.00
WJ Walter Jones .75 2.00
CC Coupon Cover Card .40 1.00
CL Checklist Card .40 1.00

2016 Panini Honors

1 David Johnson 2.50 6.00
2 Larry Fitzgerald 2.00 5.00
3 Matt Ryan 2.00 5.00
4 Julio Jones 2.50 6.00
5 Joe Flacco 2.00 5.00
6 Steve Smith Sr. 2.00 5.00
7 Tyrod Taylor 2.00 5.00
8 LeSean McCoy 2.50 6.00
9 Cam Newton 2.50 6.00
10 Kelvin Benjamin 2.00 5.00
11 Luke Kuechly 2.00 5.00
12 Jay Cutler 1.50 4.00
13 Alshon Jeffery 2.00 5.00
14 Andy Dalton 2.00 5.00
15 A.J. Green 2.50 6.00
16 Isaiah Crowell 1.50 4.00
17 Terrelle Pryor 1.50 4.00
18 Dez Bryant 2.50 6.00
19 Jason Witten 2.00 5.00
20 Tony Romo 2.00 5.00
21 Trevor Siemian 1.50 4.00
22 Demaryius Thomas 2.00 5.00
23 Von Miller 2.00 5.00
24 Matthew Stafford 2.00 5.00
25 Marvin Jones Jr. 1.50 4.00
26 Aaron Rodgers 5.00 12.00
27 Davante Adams 1.50 4.00
28 Jordy Nelson 2.00 5.00
29 Lamar Miller 1.50 4.00
30 DeAndre Hopkins 2.00 5.00
31 J.J. Watt 2.50 6.00
32 Andrew Luck 3.00 8.00
33 T.Y. Hilton 2.00 5.00
34 Blake Bortles 1.50 4.00
35 Allen Robinson 2.00 5.00
36 Travis Kelce 2.50 6.00
37 Alex Smith 2.00 5.00
38 Spencer Ware 1.50 4.00
39 Todd Gurley II 2.50 6.00
40 Aaron Donald 2.50 6.00
41 Ryan Tannehill 2.00 5.00
42 Jarvis Landry 2.00 5.00
43 Jay Ajayi 2.00 5.00
44 Sam Bradford 1.50 4.00
45 Adrian Peterson 2.50 6.00
46 Stefon Diggs 2.00 5.00
47 Tom Brady 6.00 15.00
48 Rob Gronkowski 2.50 6.00
49 LeGarrette Blount 2.00 5.00
50 Drew Brees 2.50 6.00
51 Brandin Cooks 2.00 5.00
52 Eli Manning 2.00 5.00
53 Odell Beckham Jr. 2.50 6.00
54 Matt Forte 1.50 4.00
55 Brandon Marshall 1.50 4.00
56 Derek Carr 2.50 6.00
57 Amari Cooper 2.50 6.00
58 Ryan Mathews 2.00 5.00
59 Jordan Matthews 2.00 5.00
60 Ben Roethlisberger 2.50 6.00
61 Le'Veon Bell 2.00 5.00
62 Antonio Brown 2.50 6.00
63 Philip Rivers 2.50 6.00
64 Melvin Gordon 2.00 5.00
65 Navorro Bowman 2.00 5.00
66 Carlos Hyde 1.50 4.00
67 Russell Wilson 3.00 8.00
68 Thomas Rawls 1.50 4.00
69 Tyler Lockett 2.00 5.00
70 Jameis Winston 2.50 6.00
71 Mike Evans 2.00 5.00
72 Marcus Mariota 2.50 6.00
73 DeMarco Murray 2.00 5.00
74 Kirk Cousins 2.50 6.00
75 Jordan Reed 1.50 4.00
76 Jared Goff AU RC 25.00 60.00
77 Carson Wentz AU RC 75.00 150.00
78 Dak Prescott AU RC 40.00 80.00
79 Paxton Lynch AU RC 4.00 10.00
80 Cody Kessler AU RC 4.00 10.00
81 Jacoby Brissett AU RC 5.00 12.00
82 Ezekiel Elliott AU RC 75.00 150.00
83 Derrick Henry AU RC 10.00 25.00
84 Kenneth Dixon AU RC 4.00 10.00
85 Devontae Booker AU RC 5.00 12.00
86 DeAndre Washington AU RC 4.00 10.00
87 Jordan Howard AU RC 15.00 40.00
88 Corey Coleman AU RC 6.00 15.00
89 Tajae Sharpe AU RC 5.00 12.00
90 Braxton Miller AU RC 4.00 10.00
91 Laquon Treadwell AU RC 5.00 12.00
92 Will Fuller V AU RC 6.00 15.00
93 Sterling Shepard AU RC 5.00 12.00
94 Tyler Boyd AU RC 5.00 12.00
95 Michael Thomas AU RC 8.00 20.00
96 Josh Doctson AU RC 5.00 12.00
97 Hunter Henry AU RC 5.00 12.00
98 Jalen Ramsey AU RC 6.00 15.00
99 Tyreek Hill AU RC 15.00 40.00
100 Joey Bosa AU RC 8.00 20.00

2016 Panini Honors Gold

*VETS/15: .8X TO 2X BASIC CARDS/99
*ROOK/50: .5X TO 1.2X BASIC RC AU/99
*ROOK/25: .9X TO 1.5X BASIC RC AU/99
77 Carson Wentz AU 100.00 200.00

2016 Panini Honors Green

*ROOK/25: .6X TO 1.5X BASIC RC AU/99
*ROOK/15: .8X TO 2X BASIC RC AU/99
77 Carson Wentz AU 125.00 250.00

2016 Panini Honors Red

77 Carson Wentz AU 75.00 150.00
78 Dak Prescott AU 30.00 80.00

2018 Panini Honors

*BLUE/25: .6X TO 1.5X BASIC CARDS/99
*GOLD/75: .4X TO 1X BASIC CARDS/99
1 Tom Brady 6.00 15.00
2 Dan Marino 5.00 12.00
3 Jim Kelly 2.50 6.00
4 Joe Namath 3.00 8.00
5 Ben Roethlisberger 2.50 6.00
6 Ray Lewis 2.50 6.00
7 Joe Mixon 2.00 5.00
8 Myles Garrett 2.50 6.00
9 Deshaun Watson 3.00 8.00
10 Andrew Luck 3.00 8.00
11 Marcus Mariota 2.50 6.00
12 Leonard Fournette 2.50 6.00
13 Patrick Mahomes II 6.00 15.00
14 Philip Rivers 2.50 6.00
15 Case Keenum 2.00 5.00
16 Derek Carr 2.50 6.00
17 Ezekiel Elliott 3.00 8.00
18 Alex Smith 2.00 5.00
19 Carson Wentz 3.00 8.00
20 Eli Manning 2.00 5.00
21 Mitchell Trubisky 2.50 6.00
22 Adam Thielen 2.50 6.00
23 Aaron Rodgers 5.00 12.00
24 Matthew Stafford 2.00 5.00
25 Drew Brees 2.50 6.00
26 Christian McCaffrey 2.50 6.00
27 Michael Vick 2.00 5.00
28 Mike Evans 2.00 5.00
29 Jared Goff 2.50 6.00
30 Russell Wilson 3.00 8.00
31 David Johnson 2.50 6.00
32 Jimmy Garoppolo 3.00 8.00

2018 Panini Honors Signatures

13 Patrick Mahomes II/35 150.00 300.00
15 Case Keenum/35
26 Christian McCaffrey/49 25.00 50.00
31 David Johnson/20 10.00 25.00

2014 Panini Hot Rookies

1 Carson Palmer .25 .60
2 Larry Fitzgerald .25 .60
3 Michael Floyd .20 .50
4 Andre Ellington .20 .50
5 Tyrann Mathieu .25 .60
6 Robert Housler .20 .50
7 Patrick Peterson .20 .50
8 Matt Ryan .25 .60
9 Julio Jones .30 .75
10 Roddy White .20 .50
11 Harry Douglas .20 .50
12 Steven Jackson .20 .50
13 Jacquizz Rodgers .20 .50
14 Levine Toilolo .20 .50
15 Joe Flacco .25 .60
16 Torrey Smith .20 .50
17 Marlon Brown .20 .50
18 Ray Rice .20 .50
19 Bernard Pierce .20 .50
20 Dennis Pitta .20 .50
21 Steve Smith .25 .60
22 Terrell Suggs .20 .50
23 EJ Manuel .20 .50
24 Steve Johnson .25 .60
25 Robert Woods .25 .60
26 C.J. Spiller .20 .50
27 Fred Jackson .25 .60
28 Mario Williams .20 .50
29 Kiko Alonso .20 .50
30 Cam Newton .30 .75
31 Greg Hardy .20 .50
32 Jerricho Cotchery .20 .50
33 DeAngelo Williams .20 .50
34 Jonathan Stewart .20 .50
35 Greg Olsen .25 .60
36 Luke Kuechly .25 .60
37 Jay Cutler .20 .50
38 Tim Jennings .20 .50
39 Brandon Marshall .20 .50
40 Alshon Jeffery .25 .60
41 Matt Forte .20 .50
42 Lance Briggs .25 .60
43 Martellus Bennett .20 .50
44 Andy Dalton .25 .60
45 A.J. Green .30 .75
46 Marvin Jones .20 .50
47 Giovani Bernard .20 .50
48 BenJarvus Green-Ellis .25 .60
49 Jermaine Gresham .20 .50
50 Tyler Eifert .25 .60
51 Geno Atkins .20 .50
52 Brian Hoyer .20 .50
53 Josh Gordon .20 .50
54 Ben Tate .20 .50
55 Jordan Cameron .20 .50
56 Joe Haden .20 .50
57 Barkevious Mingo .20 .50
58 Tony Romo .25 .60
59 Dez Bryant .30 .75
60 Terrance Williams .20 .50
61 DeMarco Murray .25 .60
62 Lance Dunbar .20 .50
63 Jason Witten .25 .60
64 Sean Lee .25 .60
65 Morris Claiborne .20 .50
66 Peyton Manning .60 1.50
67 Demaryius Thomas .25 .60
68 Wes Welker .25 .60
69 Montee Ball .20 .50
70 DeMarcus Ware .25 .60
71 Julius Thomas .20 .50
72 Von Miller .25 .60
73 Matthew Stafford .25 .60
74 Calvin Johnson .30 .75
75 Kris Durham .20 .50
76 Reggie Bush .20 .50
77 Golden Tate .25 .60
78 Brandon Pettigrew .20 .50
79 Nick Fairley .20 .50
80 Aaron Rodgers .60 1.50
81 Jordy Nelson .25 .60
82 Randall Cobb .25 .60
83 Andrew Quarless .20 .50
84 Julius Peppers .25 .60
85 Eddie Lacy .20 .50
86 Clay Matthews .30 .75
87 Case Keenum .25 .60
88 Andre Johnson .25 .60
89 DeAndre Hopkins .25 .60
90 Arian Foster .25 .60
91 Dennis Johnson .20 .50
92 Garrett Graham .20 .50
93 J.J. Watt .30 .75
94 Andrew Luck .40 1.00
95 Reggie Wayne .25 .60
96 T.Y. Hilton .25 .60
97 Hakeem Nicks .20 .50
98 Trent Richardson .20 .50
99 Vick Ballard .20 .50
100 Vontae Davis .20 .50
101 Chad Henne .20 .50
102 Justin Blackmon .20 .50
103 Cecil Shorts .20 .50
104 Ace Sanders .20 .50
105 Toby Gerhart .20 .50
106 Marcedes Lewis .20 .50
107 Alex Smith .25 .60
108 Dwayne Bowe .25 .60
109 Derrick Johnson .20 .50
110 Jamaal Charles .25 .60
111 Knile Davis .20 .50
112 Eric Berry .25 .60
113 Justin Houston .20 .50
114 Ryan Tannehill .25 .60
115 Mike Wallace .20 .50
116 Brian Hartline .20 .50
117 Lamar Miller .20 .50
118 Daniel Thomas .20 .50
119 Charles Clay .20 .50
120 Cameron Wake .20 .50
121 Matt Cassel .20 .50
122 Cordarrelle Patterson .20 .50
123 Greg Jennings .20 .50
124 Adrian Peterson .30 .75
125 Xavier Rhodes .20 .50
126 Kyle Rudolph .20 .50
127 Captain Munnerlyn .20 .50
128 Tom Brady .75 2.00
129 Danny Amendola .25 .60
130 Kenbrell Thompkins .20 .50
131 Julian Edelman .30 .75
132 Stevan Ridley .20 .50
133 Darrelle Revis .20 .50
134 Rob Gronkowski .30 .75
135 Drew Brees .30 .75
136 Marques Colston .20 .50
137 Kenny Stills .20 .50
138 Khiry Robinson .25 .60
139 Jairus Byrd .20 .50
140 Pierre Thomas .20 .50
141 Mark Ingram .25 .60
142 Jimmy Graham .30 .75
143 Eli Manning .25 .60
144 Victor Cruz .25 .60
145 Rueben Randle .20 .50
146 Rashad Jennings .20 .50
147 David Wilson .20 .50
148 Prince Amukamara .20 .50
149 Jason Pierre-Paul .20 .50
150 Geno Smith .20 .50
151 Jeremy Kerley .20 .50
152 Eric Decker .20 .50
153 Chris Ivory .25 .60
154 Michael Vick .25 .60
155 Sheldon Richardson .20 .50
156 Justin Tuck .20 .50
157 Matt McGloin .25 .60
158 Andre Holmes RC .30 .75
159 Denarius Moore .20 .50
160 Darren McFadden .20 .50
161 James Jones .20 .50
162 Matt Schaub .20 .50
163 Nick Foles .25 .60
164 Arrelious Benn .20 .50
165 Jeremy Maclin .20 .50
166 Riley Cooper .25 .60
167 LeSean McCoy .30 .75
168 Bryce Brown .20 .50
169 Brent Celek .20 .50
170 Darren Sproles .25 .60
171 Ben Roethlisberger .30 .75
172 Antonio Brown .30 .75
173 Maurkice Pouncey .20 .50
174 Le'Veon Bell .25 .60
175 Heath Miller .20 .50
176 Troy Polamalu .30 .75
177 Philip Rivers .30 .75
178 Keenan Allen .25 .60
179 Eddie Royal .20 .50
180 Ryan Mathews .25 .60
181 Danny Woodhead .25 .60
182 Antonio Gates .20 .50
183 Manti Te'o .25 .60
184 Eric Weddle .20 .50
185 Colin Kaepernick .25 .60
186 Anquan Boldin .20 .50
187 Michael Crabtree .20 .50
188 Frank Gore .25 .60
189 Kendall Hunter .20 .50
190 Vernon Davis .20 .50
191 Aldon Smith .20 .50
192 Patrick Willis .25 .60
193 Russell Wilson .50 1.25
194 Doug Baldwin .25 .60
195 Percy Harvin .20 .50
196 Bruce Irvin .20 .50
197 Marshawn Lynch .25 .60
198 Zach Miller .20 .50
199 Richard Sherman .30 .75
200 Kam Chancellor .30 .75
201 Malcolm Smith .30 .75
202 Sam Bradford .20 .50
203 Tavon Austin .20 .50
204 Chris Givens .20 .50
205 Zac Stacy .20 .50
206 Daryl Richardson .20 .50
207 Jared Cook .20 .50
208 James Laurinaitis .25 .60
209 Mike Glennon .25 .60
210 Josh McCown .20 .50
211 Vincent Jackson .20 .50
212 Doug Martin .25 .60
213 Mike James .20 .50
214 Timothy Wright .20 .50
215 Lavonte David .20 .50
216 Jake Locker .25 .60
217 Dexter McCluster .25 .60
218 Kendall Wright .20 .50
219 Justin Hunter .20 .50
220 Nate Washington .20 .50
221 Chris Johnson .20 .50
222 Shonn Greene .20 .50
223 Delanie Walker .20 .50
224 Robert Griffin III .20 .50
225 Pierre Garcon .25 .60
226 Santana Moss .25 .60
227 Alfred Morris .20 .50
228 Andre Roberts .20 .50
229 Jordan Reed .20 .50
230 Brian Orakpo .20 .50
231 Peyton Manning H100 .60 1.50
232 Adrian Peterson H100 .30 .75
233 Drew Brees H100 .30 .75
234 Calvin Johnson H100 .30 .75
235 Tom Brady H100 .75 2.00
236 Aaron Rodgers H100 .60 1.50
237 LeSean McCoy H100 .30 .75
238 Jamaal Charles H100 .25 .60
239 A.J. Green H100 .30 .75
240 Brandon Marshall H100 .20 .50
241 Arian Foster H100 .25 .60
242 Dez Bryant H100 .30 .75
243 Jimmy Graham H100 .30 .75
244 Larry Fitzgerald H100 .25 .60
245 Tony Romo H100 .25 .60
246 Marshawn Lynch H100 .25 .60
247 Andrew Luck H100 .40 1.00
248 Andre Johnson H100 .25 .60
249 Russell Wilson H100 .50 1.25
250 Demaryius Thomas H100 .25 .60
251 Matthew Stafford H100 .25 .60
252 Julio Jones H100 .30 .75
253 Wes Welker H100 .25 .60
254 Cam Newton H100 .30 .75
255 J.J. Watt H100 .30 .75
256 Josh Gordon H100 .20 .50
257 Geno Atkins H100 .20 .50
258 Philip Rivers H100 .30 .75
259 Jordy Nelson H100 .25 .60
260 Alshon Jeffery H100 .25 .60
261 Matt Forte H100 .20 .50
262 Richard Sherman H100 .30 .75
263 Luke Kuechly H100 .25 .60
264 Von Miller H100 .25 .60
265 Rob Gronkowski H100 .30 .75
266 Colin Kaepernick H100 .25 .60
267 Patrick Peterson H100 .20 .50
268 Antonio Brown H100 .30 .75
269 Joe Haden H100 .20 .50
270 Percy Harvin H100 .20 .50
271 Earl Thomas H100 .25 .60
272 Vontaze Burfict H100 .20 .50
273 Reggie Wayne H100 .25 .60
274 Robert Mathis H100 .20 .50
275 Julius Thomas H100 .20 .50
276 Clay Matthews H100 .30 .75
277 Frank Gore H100 .25 .60
278 Robert Quinn H100 .25 .60
279 Vernon Davis H100 .20 .50
280 Vincent Jackson H100 .20 .50
281 Alfred Morris H100 .20 .50
282 DeSean Jackson H100 .25 .60
283 Mario Williams H100 .20 .50
284 NaVorro Bowman H100 .25 .60
285 Cameron Jordan H100 .20 .50
286 Reggie Bush H100 .20 .50
287 Victor Cruz H100 .25 .60
288 Eric Berry H100 .25 .60
289 Charles Tillman H100 .25 .60
290 Paul Posluszny H100 .20 .50
291 Anquan Boldin H100 .20 .50
292 Jordan Cameron H100 .20 .50
293 Ndamukong Suh H100 .25 .60
294 Joe Flacco H100 .25 .60
295 Lavonte David H100 .20 .50
296 Greg Hardy H100 .20 .50
297 Ben Roethlisberger H100 .30 .75
298 Derrick Johnson H100 .20 .50
299 Chris Johnson H100 .20 .50
300 Tamba Hali H100 .20 .50
301 Eric Decker H100 .20 .50
302 Nate Solder H100 .30 .75
303 Tyron Smith H100 .20 .50
304 Torrey Smith H100 .20 .50
305 Matt Ryan H100 .25 .60
306 Aldon Smith H100 .20 .50
307 Eli Manning H100 .25 .60
308 Doug Martin H100 .25 .60
309 Jay Cutler H100 .20 .50
310 Ray Rice H100 .20 .50
311 Justin Houston H100 .20 .50
312 Jason Witten H100 .25 .60
313 Jared Allen H100 .20 .50
314 Darrelle Revis H100 .20 .50
315 Dwayne Bowe H100 .25 .60
316 Tim Jennings H100 .20 .50
317 Matt Prater H100 .30 .75
318 Roddy White H100 .20 .50
319 Brian Orakpo H100 .20 .50
320 Cameron Wake H100 .20 .50
321 Pierre Garcon H100 .25 .60
322 Jason Pierre-Paul H100 .20 .50
323 Terrell Suggs H100 .20 .50
324 Keenan Allen H100 .25 .60
325 Robert Griffin III H100 .20 .50
326 Kiko Alonso H100 .20 .50
327 Demarco Murray H100 .25 .60
328 Devin McCourty H100 .20 .50
329 DeMarcus Ware H100 .25 .60
330 T.J. Ward H100 .20 .50
331 A.J. McCarron RC .30 .75
332 Aaron Donald RC .75 2.00
333 Aaron Murray RC .30 .75
334 Ahmad Dixon RC .30 .75
335 Allen Robinson RC .50 1.25
336 Andre Williams RC .30 .75
337 Anthony Barr RC .30 .75
338 Austin Seferian-Jenkins RC .30 .75
339 Bishop Sankey RC .30 .75
340 Blake Bortles RC .40 1.00
341 Bradley Roby RC .30 .75
342 Brandin Cooks RC .50 1.25
343 Brandon Coleman RC .30 .75
344 Brett Smith RC .30 .75
345 Bruce Ellington RC .30 .75
346 C.J. Fiedorowicz RC .30 .75
347 C.J. Mosley RC .40 1.00
348 Calvin Pryor RC .30 .75
349 Carlos Hyde RC .40 1.00
350 Charles Sims RC .30 .75
351 Chris Borland RC .30 .75
352 Chris Smith RC .30 .75
353 Cody Latimer RC .40 1.00
354 Connor Shaw RC .30 .75
355 Cyril Richardson RC .30 .75
356 Cyrus Kouandjio RC .40 1.00
357 Darqueze Dennard RC .40 1.00
358 Davante Adams RC .50 1.25
359 David Fales RC .30 .75
360 David Yankey RC .30 .75
361 De'Anthony Thomas RC .30 .75
362 Dee Ford RC .30 .75
363 Deone Bucannon RC .30 .75
364 Derek Carr RC 2.00 5.00
365 Devonta Freeman RC .50 1.25
366 Donte Moncrief RC .30 .75
367 Dri Archer RC .30 .75
368 Ed Reynolds RC .30 .75
369 Eric Ebron RC .40 1.00
370 Greg Robinson RC .30 .75
371 Ha Ha Clinton-Dix RC .40 1.00
372 Jace Amaro RC .30 .75
373 Jackson Jeffcoat RC .40 1.00
374 Jadeveon Clowney RC .40 1.00
375 Jake Matthews RC .30 .75
376 Jalen Saunders RC .30 .75
377 James White RC .60 1.50
378 James Wilder Jr. RC .40 1.00
379 Jared Abbrederis RC .30 .75
380 Jarvis Landry RC .60 1.50
381 Jason Verrett RC .30 .75
382 Jeff Janis RC .30 .75
383 Jeremy Hill RC .40 1.00
384 Jerick McKinnon RC .40 1.00
385 Tom Savage RC .30 .75
386 Jimmy Garoppolo RC 2.50 6.00
387 Johnny Manziel RC .50 1.25
388 Jordan Matthews RC .50 1.25
389 Josh Huff RC .40 1.00
390 Ka'Deem Carey RC .30 .75
391 Kelvin Benjamin RC .50 1.25
392 Kevin Norwood RC .30 .75
393 Khalil Mack RC 1.25 3.00
394 Kony Ealy RC .40 1.00
395 Kyle Fuller RC .30 .75
396 Kyle Van Noy RC .40 1.00
397 L'Damian Washington RC .40 1.00
398 Lache Seastrunk RC .30 .75
399 Lamarcus Joyner RC .40 1.00
400 Logan Thomas RC .30 .75
401 Louis Nix III RC .30 .75
402 Marcus Roberson RC .40 1.00
403 Marcus Smith RC .30 .75
404 Marion Grice RC .30 .75
405 Marqise Lee RC .40 1.00
406 Martavis Bryant RC .40 1.00
407 Michael Campanaro RC .30 .75
408 Michael Sam RC .30 .75
409 Mike Davis RC .30 .75
410 Mike Evans RC .75 2.00
411 Odell Beckham Jr. RC .75 2.00
412 Paul Richardson RC .40 1.00
413 Isaiah Crowell RC .40 1.00
414 Ra'Shede Hageman RC .30 .75
415 Robert Herron RC .30 .75
416 Ryan Grant RC .30 .75
417 Ryan Shazier RC .50 1.25
418 Sammy Watkins RC .50 1.25
419 Scott Crichton RC .30 .75
420 Shaq Evans RC .30 .75
421 Shayne Skov RC .30 .75
422 Stephon Tuitt RC .50 1.25
423 Storm Johnson RC .30 .75
424 Tajh Boyd RC .30 .75
425 Taylor Lewan RC .30 .75
426 Teddy Bridgewater RC .50 1.25
427 Telvin Smith RC .30 .75
428 Terrance West RC .30 .75
429 Tevin Reese RC .30 .75
430 Timmy Jernigan RC .30 .75
431 TJ Jones RC .50 1.25
432 Travis Swanson RC .30 .75
433 Tre Mason RC .30 .75
434 Trent Murphy RC .30 .75
435 Trevor Reilly RC .30 .75
436 Troy Niklas RC .30 .75
437 Xavier Su'A-Filo RC .40 1.00
438 Yawin Smallwood RC .30 .75
439 Zach Mettenberger RC .30 .75
440 Zack Martin RC .40 1.00

2014 Panini Hot Rookies Artist's Proof

*1-330 VETS/35: 4X TO 10X BASIC CARDS
*331-440 ROOKIES/35: 2X TO 5X BASIC RC

2014 Panini Hot Rookies Gold Zone

*1-330 VETS/50: 2.5X TO 6X BASIC CARDS
*331-440 ROOKIES/50: 1.5X TO 4X BASIC RC

2014 Panini Hot Rookies Prizm Red

*ROOKIES/149: .8X TO 2X BASIC RC

2014 Panini Hot Rookies Prizm Red Power

*ROOKIES/25: 2.5X TO 6X BASIC RC

2014 Panini Hot Rookies Red Zone

*1-330 VETS/20: 6X TO 15X BASIC CARDS
*331-440 ROOKIES/20: 3X TO 8X BASIC RC

2014 Panini Hot Rookies Scorecard

*1-330 VETS/99: 2X TO 5X BASIC CARDS
*331-440 ROOKIES/99: 1.2X TO 3X BASIC RC

2014 Panini Hot Rookies Showcase

*1-330 VETS/79: 2X TO 5X BASIC CARDS
*331-440 ROOKIES/79: 1.2X TO 3X BASIC RC

2014 Panini Hot Rookies Air Mail

*GOLD/50: .8X TO 2X BASIC INSERTS
*RED/20: 2X TO 5X BASIC INSERTS
AM1 Peyton Manning 3.00 8.00
AM2 Tom Brady 2.50 6.00
AM3 Josh Gordon .60 1.50
AM4 Pierre Garcon .75 2.00
AM5 Andrew Luck 1.25 3.00
AM6 Brandon Marshall .60 1.50
AM7 Jordy Nelson .75 2.00
AM8 Colin Kaepernick .75 2.00
AM9 Russell Wilson 1.50 4.00
AM10 DeSean Jackson .75 2.00

2014 Panini Hot Rookies All-Time Franchise Players

*GOLD/50: .8X TO 2X BASIC INSERTS
*RED/20: 2X TO 5X BASIC INSERTS
1 Dan Marino 2.50 6.00
2 John Elway 2.00 5.00
3 Jerry Rice 2.00 5.00
4 Barry Sanders 2.00 5.00
5 Emmitt Smith 2.00 5.00
6 Brett Favre 2.50 6.00

2014 Panini Hot Rookies Brothers In Arms

*GOLD/50: .8X TO 2X BASIC INSERTS
*RED/20: 1.5X TO 4X BASIC INSERTS
BA1 L.Fitzgerald/P.Fanaika .60 1.50
BA2 J.Jones/R.White .75 2.00
BA3 Ray Rice .50 1.25
BA4 Fred Jackson .60 1.50
BA5 Newton/Tolbert/Chandler .75 2.00
BA6 Marshall/Jeffery/Mills .60 1.50
BA7 Sanu/G.Bernard/Eifert .60 1.50
BA8 G.Barnidge/B.Winn .50 1.25
BA9 J.Witten/M.Austin .60 1.50
BA10 D.Thomas/O.Franklin .60 1.50
BA11 C.Johnson/B.Pettigrew .75 2.00
BA12 N.Perry/C.Matthews .75 2.00
BA13 Garrett Graham .50 1.25
BA14 T.Hilton/G.Cherilus .60 1.50
BA15 Mike Brown .50 1.25
BA16 Dwayne Bowe .60 1.50
BA17 C.Clay/B.Hartline .50 1.25
BA18 Cassel/Kalil/Patterson .50 1.25
BA19 Thompkins/Hoomanawanui .50 1.25
BA20 Graham/Watson/Sproles .75 2.00
BA21 R.Barden/C.Snee .50 1.25
BA22 G.Smith/Hill/Colon .50 1.25
BA23 Brice Butler .50 1.25
BA24 LeSean McCoy .75 2.00
BA25 B.Roethlisberger/C.Hubbard .75 2.00
BA26 Royal/K.Allen/Brown .60 1.50
BA27 Colin Kaepernick .60 1.50
BA28 Doug Baldwin .60 1.50
BA29 Cory Harkey .50 1.25
BA30 M.Williams/D.Martin .60 1.50
BA31 Kendall Wright .50 1.25
BA32 P.Garcon/L.Hankerson .60 1.50

2014 Panini Hot Rookies Franchise

*GOLD/50: .8X TO 2X BASIC INSERTS
*RED/20: 2X TO 5X BASIC INSERTS
F1 Aaron Rodgers 2.00 5.00
F2 Adrian Peterson 1.00 2.50
F3 A.J. Green 1.00 2.50
F4 Arian Foster .75 2.00
F5 Matt Forte .60 1.50
F6 Calvin Johnson 1.00 2.50
F7 Cam Newton 1.00 2.50
F8 C.J. Spiller .60 1.50
F9 Colin Kaepernick .75 2.00
F10 Drew Brees 1.00 2.50
F11 Jamaal Charles .75 2.00
F12 Joe Flacco .75 2.00
F13 Julio Jones 1.00 2.50
F14 Larry Fitzgerald .75 2.00
F15 LeSean McCoy 1.00 2.50
F16 Andrew Luck 1.25 3.00
F17 Peyton Manning 2.00 5.00
F18 Philip Rivers 1.00 2.50
F19 Robert Griffin III .60 1.50
F20 Russell Wilson 1.50 4.00
F21 Tom Brady 2.50 6.00
F22 Tony Romo .75 2.00

2014 Panini Hot Rookies Hot Rookies

*ARTIST PROOF/35: 1.5X TO 4X BASIC INSERTS
*GOLD ZONE/50: 1.2X TO 3X BASIC INSERTS
*RED ZONE/20: 2X TO 5X BASIC INSERTS
*SHOWCASE/99: .8X TO 2X BASIC INSERTS
PRIZM RED/149: .6X TO 1.5X BASIC INSERTS
*RED POWER/25: 1.5X TO 4X BASIC INSERTS
HR1 Johnny Manziel .75 2.00
HR2 Teddy Bridgewater .75 2.00

HR3 Blake Bortles .60 1.50
HR4 Sammy Watkins .75 2.00
HR5 Mike Evans 1.25 3.00
HR6 Marqise Lee .60 1.50
HR7 Odell Beckham Jr. 1.25 3.00
HR8 Brandin Cooks .75 2.00
HR9 Kelvin Benjamin .75 2.00
HR10 Derek Carr 3.00 8.00
HR11 Jimmy Garoppolo 4.00 10.00
HR12 A.J. McCarron .50 1.25
HR13 Carlos Hyde .60 1.50
HR14 Ka'Deem Carey .50 1.25
HR15 Bishop Sankey .50 1.25
HR16 Allen Robinson .75 2.00
HR17 Davante Adams .75 2.00
HR18 Jordan Matthews .75 2.00
HR19 Paul Richardson .60 1.50
HR20 Eric Ebron .60 1.50
HR21 Charles Sims .50 1.25
HR22 Darqueze Dennard .60 1.50
HR23 Andre Williams .50 1.25
HR24 Terrance West .50 1.25
HR25 Devonta Freeman .75 2.00
HR26 Zach Mettenberger .50 1.25
HR27 Aaron Murray .50 1.25
HR28 Tom Savage .50 1.25
HR29 Jadeveon Clowney .60 1.50
HR30 Jace Amaro .50 1.25
HR31 Austin Seferian-Jenkins .50 1.25
HR32 Jarvis Landry 1.00 2.50
HR33 Donte Moncrief .50 1.25
HR34 Martavis Bryant .60 1.50
HR35 Bruce Ellington .50 1.25
HR36 Cody Latimer .60 1.50
HR37 Dri Archer .50 1.25
HR38 Jerick McKinnon .60 1.50
HR39 Jeremy Hill .60 1.50
HR40 Tre Mason .50 1.25
HR41 Troy Niklas .50 1.25
HR42 De'Anthony Thomas .50 1.25
HR43 Josh Huff .60 1.50
HR44 Logan Thomas .50 1.25
HR45 Anthony Barr .50 1.25
HR46 Ha Ha Clinton-Dix .60 1.50
HR47 John Brown .75 2.00
HR48 Kony Ealy .60 1.50
HR49 C.J. Mosley .60 1.50
HR50 Khalil Mack 2.00 5.00

2014 Panini Hot Rookies Hot Rookies Prizm Red Jerseys

HRAM A.J. McCarron/50 2.50 6.00
HRAR Allen Robinson/50 4.00 10.00
HRAW Andre Williams/50 2.50 6.00
HRBB Blake Bortles/50 3.00 8.00
HRBC Brandin Cooks/50 4.00 10.00
HRBS Bishop Sankey/50 2.50 6.00
HRCH Carlos Hyde/50 3.00 8.00
HRCL Cody Latimer/50 3.00 8.00
HRCS Charles Sims/50 2.50 6.00
HRDA Dri Archer/50 2.50 6.00
HRDA Davante Adams/50 4.00 10.00
HRDC Derek Carr/50 8.00 20.00
HRDF Devonta Freeman/50 4.00 10.00
HRDM Donte Moncrief/50 2.50 6.00
HRDT De'Anthony Thomas/50 2.50 6.00
HREE Eric Ebron/50 3.00 8.00
HRJA Jace Amaro/50 3.00 8.00
HRJC Jadeveon Clowney/50 3.00 8.00
HRJG Jimmy Garoppolo/50 20.00 50.00
HRJH Jeremy Hill/50 3.00 8.00
HRJL Jarvis Landry/50 5.00 12.00
HRJM Johnny Manziel/50 4.00 10.00
HRKB Kelvin Benjamin/50 4.00 10.00
HRKC Ka'Deem Carey/50 2.50 6.00
HRKM Khalil Mack/50 12.00 30.00
HRLT Logan Thomas/50 2.50 6.00
HRME Mike Evans/50 6.00 15.00
HRML Marqise Lee/50 3.00 8.00
HROB Odell Beckham Jr./50 20.00 40.00
HRPR Paul Richardson/50 3.00 8.00
HRSW Sammy Watkins/50 4.00 10.00
HRTB Teddy Bridgewater/50 4.00 10.00
HRTS Tom Savage/50 2.50 6.00
HRTW Terrance West/50 2.50 6.00
THTM Tre Mason/50 2.50 6.00
HRAMU Aaron Murray/50 2.50 6.00
HRASJ Austin Seferian-Jenkins/50 2.50 6.00
JRJMA Jordan Matthews/50 4.00 10.00

2014 Panini Hot Rookies Hot Rookies Autographs

HRAB Anthony Barr/99 5.00 12.00
HRAJ Austin Seferian-Jenkins/99 5.00 12.00
HRAM Aaron Murray/99 5.00 12.00
HRAM A.J. McCarron/75 5.00 12.00
HRAR Allen Robinson/99 8.00 20.00
HRAW Andre Williams/99 5.00 12.00
HRBB Blake Bortles/50 8.00 20.00
HRBC Brandin Cooks/99 8.00 20.00
HRBE Bruce Ellington/99 5.00 12.00
HRBS Bishop Sankey/99 5.00 12.00
HRCH Carlos Hyde/75 6.00 15.00
HRCL Cody Latimer/99 6.00 15.00
HRCS Charles Sims/99 5.00 12.00
HRDA Dri Archer/99 5.00 12.00
HRDC Derek Carr/75 30.00 80.00
HRDD Darqueze Dennard/99 6.00 15.00
HRDF Devonta Freeman/99 8.00 20.00
HRDM Donte Moncrief/99 5.00 12.00
HRDT De'Anthony Thomas/99 5.00 12.00
HREE Eric Ebron/99 6.00 15.00
HRHC Ha Ha Clinton-Dix/99 6.00 15.00
HRJA Jace Amaro/99 5.00 12.00
HRJC Jadeveon Clowney/75 6.00 15.00
HRJG Jimmy Garoppolo/99 50.00 100.00
HRJHU Josh Huff/99 6.00 15.00
HRJH Jeremy Hill/99 6.00 15.00
HRJMC Jerick McKinnon/99 6.00 15.00
HRJM Johnny Manziel/50 10.00 25.00
HRKB Kelvin Benjamin/99 8.00 20.00
HRKC Ka'Deem Carey/99 5.00 12.00
HRKE Kony Ealy/99 6.00 15.00
HRKM Khalil Mack/99 20.00 50.00
HRLT Logan Thomas/99 5.00 12.00
HRME Mike Evans/50 15.00 40.00
HRML Marqise Lee/75 6.00 15.00
HRME Odell Beckham Jr./99 50.00 100.00
HRPR Paul Richardson/99 10.00 25.00
HRSW Sammy Watkins/75 30.00 60.00
HRTB Teddy Bridgewater/50 10.00 25.00
HRTM Tre Mason/99 5.00 12.00
HRTN Troy Niklas/99 5.00 12.00
HRTS Tom Savage/99 5.00 12.00
HRTW Terrance West/99 5.00 12.00

2014 Panini Hot Rookies Hot Rookies Autographs Showcase

*SHOWCASE/25: .5X TO 1.2X BASIC AU/50-99
HRJM Johnny Manziel 10.00 25.00

2014 Panini Hot Rookies Inscriptions

IAA Tennessee Titans 2.50 6.00
IAB Houston Texans 2.50 6.00
IAB Philadelphia Eagles 2.50 6.00
IAD New England Patriots 2.50 6.00
IAE Arizona Cardinals 2.50 6.00
IAG Green Bay Packers 2.50 6.00
IAH Cleveland Browns 2.50 6.00
IAR New York Giants 2.50 6.00
IBC St. Louis Rams 3.00 8.00
IBR Baltimore Ravens 2.50 6.00
IBB Oakland Raiders 2.50 6.00
IBQ St. Louis Rams 2.50 6.00
ICC Miami Dolphins 2.50 6.00
ICG St. Louis Rams 2.50 6.00
ICG Buffalo Bills 2.50 8.00
ICH Green Bay Packers 2.50 6.00
ICH Buffalo Bills 25.00 60.00
ICH Cincinnati Bengals 2.50 6.00
ICI New York Jets 3.00 8.00
ICK Houston Texans 3.00 8.00
ICP Philadelphia Eagles 2.50 6.00
ICR Pittsburgh Steelers 2.50 6.00
ICS Miami Dolphins 2.50 6.00
ICU Baltimore Ravens 2.50 6.00
ICV Oakland Raiders 2.50 6.00
ICW Tennessee Titans 2.50 6.00
IDA Indianapolis Colts 2.50 6.00
IDD Pittsburgh Steelers 2.50 6.00
IDH Dallas Cowboys 2.50 6.00
IDJ Miami Dolphins 2.50 6.00
IDJ Houston Texans 2.50 6.00
IDL Cleveland Browns 2.50 6.00
IDP Baltimore Ravens 2.50 6.00
IDR Indianapolis Colts 2.50 6.00
IDW Tennessee Titans 2.50 6.00
IDW New England Patriots 2.50 6.00
IEP Tampa Bay Buccaneers 2.50 6.00
IER San Francisco 49ers 4.00 10.00
IEW Philadelphia Eagles 2.50 6.00
IFG San Francisco 49ers 4.00 10.00
IFJ Pittsburgh Steelers 2.50 6.00
IGB Cincinnati Bengals 2.50 6.00
IGC Minnesota Vikings 2.50 6.00
IGM Cincinnati Bengals 3.00 8.00
IIP St. Louis Rams 2.50 6.00
IJB Chicago Bears 2.50 6.00
IJB Green Bay Packers 2.50 6.00
IJB Pittsburgh Steelers 2.50 6.00
IJB Arizona Cardinals 2.50 6.00
IJC Cleveland Browns
IJH Dallas Cowboys 2.50 6.00
IJJ St. Louis Rams 2.50 6.00
IJK New York Jets 2.50 6.00
IJR Dallas Cowboys 2.50 6.00
IJS Baltimore Ravens 2.50 6.00
IJT Jacksonville Jaguars 2.50 6.00
IJT Baltimore Ravens 2.50 6.00
IKB Carolina Panthers 2.50 6.00
IKC Washington Redskins 10.00 25.00
IKD Kansas City Chiefs 2.50 6.00
IKM Houston Texans 2.50 6.00
IKM Arizona Cardinals 2.50 6.00
IKS Carolina Panthers 2.50 6.00
IKW San Diego Chargers 2.50 6.00
IKW Tennessee Titans 2.50 6.00
ILW Seattle Seahawks 3.00 8.00
IMB Baltimore Ravens 2.50 6.00
IMC New York Giants 2.50 6.00
IME Miami Dolphins 2.50 6.00
IMF Arizona Cardinals 2.50 6.00
IMS New York Jets 2.50 6.00
IMS Seattle Seahawks 30.00 60.00
IMW Pittsburgh Steelers 2.50 6.00
INW Tennessee Titans 2.50 6.00
IPA New York Giants 2.50 6.00
IPT Washington Redskins 2.50 6.00
IRB Cincinnati Bengals 3.00 8.00
IRB San Diego Chargers 2.50 6.00
IRH Arizona Cardinals 2.50 6.00
IRM Denver Broncos 2.50 6.00
IRN New York Giants
IRR New York Giants
IRT Seattle Seahawks 2.50 6.00
IRT Miami Dolphins
ITG Arizona Cardinals 2.50 6.00
ITH New York Giants 2.50 6.00
ITM Arizona Cardinals
ITW Dallas Cowboys 2.50 6.00
ITW Tampa Bay Buccaneers 2.50 6.00

2014 Panini Hot Rookies Rookie Signatures

331 A.J. McCarron 2.50 6.00
332 Aaron Donald 6.00 15.00
333 Aaron Murray 2.50 6.00
334 Ahmad Dixon 2.50 6.00
335 Allen Robinson 4.00 10.00
336 Andre Williams 2.50 6.00
337 Anthony Barr 2.50 6.00
338 Austin Seferian-Jenkins 2.50 6.00
339 Bishop Sankey 2.50 6.00
340 Blake Bortles 3.00 8.00
341 Bradley Roby 2.50 6.00
342 Brandin Cooks 4.00 10.00
343 Brandon Coleman 2.50 6.00
344 Brett Smith 2.50 6.00
345 Bruce Ellington 2.50 6.00
346 C.J. Fiedorowicz 2.50 6.00
348 Calvin Pryor 2.50 6.00
349 Carlos Hyde 3.00 8.00
350 Charles Sims 2.50 6.00
351 Chris Borland 2.50 6.00
352 Chris Smith 2.50 6.00
353 Cody Latimer 3.00 8.00
354 Connor Shaw 2.50 6.00
357 Darqueze Dennard 3.00 8.00
359 David Fales 2.50 6.00
360 David Yankey 2.50 6.00
361 De'Anthony Thomas 2.50 6.00
362 Dee Ford 2.50 6.00
363 Deone Bucannon 2.50 6.00
364 Derek Carr 15.00 40.00
365 Devonta Freeman 4.00 10.00
366 Donte Moncrief 2.50 6.00
367 Dri Archer 2.50 6.00
368 Ed Reynolds 2.50 6.00
369 Eric Ebron 3.00 8.00
370 Greg Robinson 2.50 6.00
371 Ha Ha Clinton-Dix 3.00 8.00
372 Jace Amaro 2.50 6.00
374 Jadeveon Clowney 3.00 8.00
375 Jake Matthews 2.50 6.00
378 James Wilder Jr. 3.00 8.00
379 Jared Abbrederis 2.50 6.00
380 Jarvis Landry 5.00 12.00
381 Jason Verrett 2.50 6.00
382 Jeff Janis 2.50 6.00
383 Jeremy Hill 3.00 8.00
384 Jerick McKinnon 3.00 8.00
385 Tom Savage 2.50 6.00
386 Jimmy Garoppolo 30.00 60.00
387 Johnny Manziel 4.00 10.00
389 Josh Huff 3.00 8.00
390 Ka'Deem Carey 2.50 6.00
391 Kelvin Benjamin 4.00 10.00
392 Kevin Norwood 2.50 6.00
393 Khalil Mack 10.00 25.00
394 Kony Ealy 3.00 8.00
395 Kyle Fuller 2.50 6.00
396 Kyle Van Noy 3.00 8.00
397 L'Damian Washington 3.00 8.00
398 Lache Seastrunk 2.50 6.00
399 Lamarcus Joyner 3.00 8.00
400 Logan Thomas 2.50 6.00
401 Louis Nix III 2.50 6.00
402 Marcus Roberson 3.00 8.00
403 Marcus Smith 2.50 6.00
404 Marion Grice 2.50 6.00
405 Marqise Lee 3.00 8.00
407 Michael Campanaro 2.50 6.00
408 Michael Sam 2.50 6.00
409 Mike Davis 2.50 6.00
410 Mike Evans 6.00 15.00
411 Odell Beckham Jr. 25.00 50.00
412 Paul Richardson 3.00 8.00
413 Isaiah Crowell 3.00 8.00
414 Ra'Shede Hageman 2.50 6.00
415 Robert Herron 2.50 6.00
417 Ryan Shazier 4.00 10.00
418 Sammy Watkins 4.00 10.00
419 Scott Crichton 2.50 6.00
420 Shaq Evans 2.50 6.00
421 Shayne Skov 2.50 6.00
424 Tajh Boyd 2.50 6.00
425 Taylor Lewan 2.50 6.00
426 Teddy Bridgewater 4.00 10.00
427 Telvin Smith 2.50 6.00
428 Terrance West 2.50 6.00
429 Tevin Reese 2.50 6.00
430 Timmy Jernigan 2.50 6.00
432 Travis Swanson 2.50 6.00
433 Tre Mason 2.50 6.00
434 Trent Murphy 2.50 6.00
435 Trevor Reilly 2.50 6.00
436 Troy Niklas 2.50 6.00
438 Yawin Smallwood 2.50 6.00
440 Zack Martin 5.00 12.00

2014 Panini Hot Rookies Rookie Signatures Black

*BLACK/15: 1X TO 2.5X BASIC AU
386 Jimmy Garoppolo 75.00 150.00

2014 Panini Hot Rookies Rookie Signatures Blue

*BLUE/75-99: .6X TO 1.5X BASIC AU
*BLUE/49: .8X TO 2X BASIC AU
386 Jimmy Garoppolo/75 50.00 100.00

2014 Panini Hot Rookies Rookie Signatures Purple

*PURPLE/50: .8X TO 2X BASIC AU
*PURPLE/25: 1X TO 2.5X BASIC AU
386 Jimmy Garoppolo/25 75.00 150.00

2014 Panini Hot Rookies Rookie Signatures Red

*RED/75: .6X TO 1.5X BASIC AU
*RED/35-50: .8X TO 2X BASIC AU
386 Jimmy Garoppolo/50 60.00 125.00

2014 Panini Hot Rookies Score Franchise Fabrics Autographs

*PRIME/49: .5X TO 1.2X BASIC JSY AU
*PRIME/25: .6X TO 1.5X BASIC JSY AU
FFBO Brock Osweiler 6.00 15.00
FFDM Doug Martin 6.00 15.00
FFDP1 Dontari Poe 5.00 12.00
FFDP2 DeVier Posey 5.00 12.00
FFDW Delanie Walker 5.00 12.00
FFFG Frank Gore 8.00 20.00
FFJC Jordan Cameron 5.00 12.00
FFJK Jeremy Kerley 5.00 12.00
FFKW Kendall Wright 5.00 12.00
FFMB Mark Barron 5.00 12.00
FFMF Michael Floyd SP 5.00 12.00
FFMR Matt Ryan SP 12.00 30.00
FFSM Shea McClellin 6.00 15.00
FFVC Victor Cruz 6.00 15.00

2014 Panini Hot Rookies Score Future Franchise Fabrics Autographs

*PRIME/25: .8X TO 2X BASIC INSERTS
FFFCG Chris Gragg 3.00 8.00
FFFCH Chris Hogan 25.00 60.00
FFFDJ Dion Jordan 3.00 8.00
FFFGE Gavin Escobar 3.00 8.00
FFFJF Johnathan Franklin SP 3.00 8.00
FFFJH Justin Hunter 3.00 8.00
FFFJR Joseph Randle 3.00 8.00
FFFKD Knile Davis 5.00 12.00
FFFKS Kenny Stills SP 3.00 8.00
FFFMB Montee Ball SP 3.00 8.00
FFFMW Markus Wheaton 3.00 8.00
FFFST Stepfan Taylor 3.00 8.00
FFFTA Tavon Austin 6.00 15.00
FFFTE Tyler Eifert 4.00 10.00
FFFZS Zac Stacy SP 8.00 20.00

2017 Panini Illusions

1 D.Prescott/T.Romo 1.00 2.50
2 E.Smith/E.Elliott 1.50 4.00
3 J.Witten/J.Novacek .75 2.00
4 D.Bryant/M.Irvin 1.00 2.50
5 E.Manning/P.Simms .75 2.00
6 V.Cruz/O.Beckham Jr. 1.00 2.50
7 L.Taylor/J.Pierre-Paul 1.00 2.50
8 C.Wentz/R.Jaworski 1.25 3.00
9 L.McCoy/L.Blount 1.00 2.50
10 A.Jeffery/D.Jackson .75 2.00
11 J.Theismann/K.Cousins 1.00 2.50
12 J.Riggins/R.Kelley .75 2.00
13 B.Smith/R.Kerrigan .75 2.00
14 C.Palmer/K.Warner .75 2.00
15 C.Johnson/D.Johnson 1.00 2.50
16 L.Fitzgerald/A.Boldin .75 2.00
17 J.Goff/K.Warner 1.00 2.50
18 T.Gurley II/M.Faulk 1.00 2.50
19 S.Watkins/T.Holt 1.00 2.50
20 B.Hoyer/S.Young 1.25 3.00
21 C.Hyde/R.Craig .75 2.00
22 R.Lott/N.Bowman .75 2.00
23 J.Rice/P.Garcon 1.50 4.00
24 J.Zorn/R.Wilson 1.25 3.00
25 M.Lynch/T.Rawls .75 2.00
26 D.Baldwin/S.Largent 1.00 2.50
27 J.McMahon/M.Glennon .75 2.00
28 J.Howard/G.Sayers 1.00 2.50
29 L.Floyd/M.Singletary 1.00 2.50
30 B.Layne/M.Stafford .75 2.00
31 A.Abdullah/B.Sanders 1.50 4.00
32 C.Johnson/M.Jones Jr. 1.00 2.50
33 B.Favre/A.Rodgers 2.00 5.00
34 S.Sharpe/D.Adams .75 2.00
35 D.Howard/J.Nelson .75 2.00
36 J.Kuhn/A.Ripkowski 1.00 2.50
37 S.Bradford/R.Gannon .60 1.50
38 A.Peterson/L.Murray 1.00 2.50
39 R.Moss/S.Diggs .75 2.00
40 M.Ryan/M.Vick .75 2.00
41 A.Rison/J.Jones 1.00 2.50
42 D.Sanders/K.Neal .75 2.00
43 C.Newton/J.Peppers 1.00 2.50
44 K.Benjamin/S.Smith .75 2.00
45 K.Greene/L.Kuechly .75 2.00
46 A.Manning/D.Brees 1.00 2.50
47 R.Williams/A.Peterson 1.00 2.50
48 M.Thomas/B.Cooks 1.00 2.50
49 J.Winston/D.Williams .75 2.00
50 M.Evans/V.Jackson .75 2.00
51 G.McCoy/W.Sapp .75 2.00
52 J.Kelly/T.Taylor 1.00 2.50
53 T.Thomas/L.McCoy 1.00 2.50
54 A.Reed/J.Matthews .75 2.00
55 D.Marino/J.Cutler 2.00 5.00
56 J.Ajayi/L.Csonka .75 2.00
57 J.Taylor/N.Suh .75 2.00
58 S.Grogan/T.Brady 2.50 6.00
59 B.Cooks/T.Brown .75 2.00
60 D.Amendola/D.Branch .75 2.00
61 T.Law/P.Chung 1.00 2.50
62 J.McCown/J.Namath 1.25 3.00
63 C.Martin/M.Forte .75 2.00
64 J.Elway/T.Siemian 1.50 4.00
65 T.Davis/J.Charles .75 2.00
66 R.Smith/D.Thomas .75 2.00
67 V.Miller/S.Atwater .75 2.00
68 J.Montana/A.Smith 2.50 6.00
69 D.Johnson/M.Vrabel .60 1.50
70 J.Houston/N.Smith .60 1.50
71 P.Rivers/D.Fouts 1.00 2.50
72 M.Gordon/L.Tomlinson .75 2.00
73 K.Allen/L.Alworth .75 2.00
74 A.Gates/H.Henry .60 1.50
75 D.Carr/J.Plunkett 1.00 2.50
76 B.Jackson/M.Lynch 1.25 3.00
77 A.Cooper/T.Brown 1.00 2.50
78 K.Mack/H.Long 1.00 2.50
79 S.Smith/J.Maclin .75 2.00
80 D.Woodhead/P.Holmes .75 2.00
81 R.Lewis/T.Suggs 1.00 2.50
82 A.Dalton/K.Anderson .75 2.00
83 I.Woods/J.Hill .60 1.50
84 J.Collins/P.Johnson .60 1.50
85 J.Brown/I.Crowell 1.25 3.00
86 O.Newsome/C.Coleman .75 2.00
87 B.Roethlisberger/T.Bradshaw 1.50 4.00
88 L.Bell/J.Bettis 1.00 2.50
89 A.Brown/H.Ward 1.00 2.50
90 J.Harrison/J.Greene 1.00 2.50
91 J.Watt/M.Williams 1.00 2.50
92 B.Cushing/J.Clowney .60 1.50
93 A.Luck/P.Manning 2.00 5.00
94 F.Gore/E.James .75 2.00
95 T.Hilton/R.Wayne .75 2.00
96 B.Bortles/M.Brunell .75 2.00
97 F.Taylor/C.Ivory .75 2.00
98 M.Mariota/W.Moon 1.00 2.50
99 D.Murray/E.George .75 2.00
100 J.Kearse/J.Casey .60 1.50
101 Mitchell Trubisky JSY AU RC 30.00 60.00
102 Leonard Fournette JSY AU RC 12.00 30.00
103 Corey Davis JSY AU RC EXCH 6.00 15.00
104 Mike Williams JSY AU RC 6.00 15.00
105 Christian McCaffrey JSY AU RC 10.00 25.00
106 John Ross III JSY AU RC 5.00 12.00
107 Patrick Mahomes II JSY AU RC 200.00 400.00
108 Deshaun Watson JSY AU RC 50.00 100.00
109 O.J. Howard JSY AU RC 5.00 12.00
110 Evan Engram JSY AU RC 5.00 12.00
111 Zay Jones JSY AU RC 5.00 12.00
112 Curtis Samuel JSY AU RC 5.00 12.00
113 Dalvin Cook JSY AU RC 15.00 40.00
114 Joe Mixon JSY AU RC EXCH 8.00 20.00
115 DeShone Kizer JSY AU RC 4.00 10.00
116 JuJu Smith-Schuster JSY AU RC 15.00 40.00
117 Alvin Kamara JSY AU RC 15.00 40.00
118 Cooper Kupp JSY AU RC 6.00 15.00
119 Taywan Taylor JSY AU RC 4.00 10.00
120 ArDarius Stewart JSY AU RC 4.00 10.00
121 Carlos Henderson JSY AU RC 4.00 10.00
122 Chris Godwin JSY AU RC 5.00 12.00
123 Kareem Hunt JSY AU RC EXCH 8.00 20.00
124 Davis Webb JSY AU RC 4.00 10.00
125 D'Onta Foreman JSY AU RC 5.00 12.00
126 Kenny Golladay JSY AU RC 6.00 15.00
127 C.J. Beathard JSY AU RC 4.00 10.00
128 James Conner JSY AU RC 8.00 20.00
129 Amara Darboh JSY AU RC 4.00 10.00
130 Dede Westbrook JSY AU RC 4.00 10.00
131 Samaje Perine JSY AU RC 4.00 10.00
132 Josh Reynolds JSY AU RC 4.00 10.00
133 Mack Hollins JSY AU RC 4.00 10.00
134 Joe Williams JSY AU RC 4.00 10.00
135 Jamaal Williams JSY AU RC 4.00 10.00
136 R. Joshua Dobbs JSY AU RC 5.00 12.00
137 Wayne Gallman JSY AU RC 5.00 12.00
138 Marlon Mack JSY AU RC 6.00 15.00
139 Jeremy McNichols JSY AU RC 4.00 10.00
140 Nathan Peterman JSY AU RC 5.00 12.00
141 Brad Kaaya AU/150 RC 2.50 6.00
142 Chad Kelly AU/150 RC 2.50 6.00
143 Corey Clement AU/150 RC 3.00 8.00
144 Donnel Pumphrey AU/150 RC 3.00 8.00
145 Elijah Hood AU/150 RC 2.50 6.00
146 Tarik Cohen AU/150 RC 5.00 12.00
147 T.J. Logan AU/150 RC 4.00 10.00
148 Devante Mays AU/250 RC 2.00 5.00
149 Marlon Humphrey AU/150 RC 2.50 6.00
150 Marshon Lattimore AU/150 RC 3.00 8.00
151 Quincy Wilson AU/150 RC 2.50 6.00
152 Adoree' Jackson AU/150 RC 3.00 8.00
153 Sidney Jones AU/250 RC 2.00 5.00
154 Tre'Davious White AU/250 RC 2.00 5.00
155 Cameron Sutton AU/150 RC 2.50 6.00
156 Gareon Conley AU/150 RC 2.50 6.00
157 Carl Lawson AU/250 RC 2.00 5.00
158 Kevin King AU/250 RC 2.50 6.00
159 Ahkello Witherspoon AU/250 RC 2.50 6.00
160 Jonathan Allen AU/150 RC 3.00 8.00
161 Derek Barnett AU/150 RC
162 Charles Harris AU/150 RC 2.50 6.00
163 Taco Charlton AU/150 RC 2.50 6.00
164 Solomon Thomas AU/150 RC 2.50 6.00
165 Derek Rivers AU/250 RC 2.50 6.00
166 Malik McDowell AU/250 RC 2.00 5.00
167 Raekwon McMillan AU/250 RC 2.00 5.00
168 Zach Cunningham AU/250 RC 2.50 6.00
169 Jarrad Davis AU/250 RC 2.50 6.00
170 Jabrill Peppers AU/150 RC 4.00 10.00
171 T.J. Watt AU/150 RC 8.00 20.00
172 Tyus Bowser AU/250 RC 2.00 5.00
173 Haason Reddick AU/250 RC 2.00 5.00
174 Budda Baker AU/250 RC 2.00 5.00
175 Marcus Maye AU/250 RC 2.00 5.00
176 Jamal Adams AU/150 RC 2.50 6.00
177 Malik Hooker AU/150 RC 2.50 6.00
178 Obi Melifonwu AU/250 RC 2.00 5.00
179 Jake Butt AU/150 RC 3.00 8.00
180 David Njoku AU/150 RC 3.00 8.00
181 Jonnu Smith AU/250 RC 2.00 5.00
182 Adam Shaheen AU/250 RC 2.00 5.00
183 Gerald Everett AU/250 RC 2.00 5.00
184 Malachi Dupre AU/150 RC 2.50 6.00
185 Noah Brown AU/150 RC 3.00 8.00
186 Ryan Switzer AU/150 RC 3.00 8.00
187 Shelton Gibson AU/150 RC 2.50 6.00
188 Josh Malone AU/150 RC 2.50 6.00
189 Chad Hansen AU/250 RC 2.00 5.00
190 Chad Williams AU/150 RC 2.50 6.00

2017 Panini Illusions Clear Shots

CS1 Vic Beasley Jr. .75 2.00
CS2 Von Miller 1.00 2.50
CS3 Cliff Avril .75 2.00
CS4 Ryan Kerrigan .75 2.00
CS5 Chandler Jones .75 2.00
CS6 Khalil Mack 1.25 3.00
CS7 Brian Orakpo .75 2.00
CS8 Joey Bosa 1.25 3.00
CS9 Sean Lee 1.00 2.50
CS10 Julius Peppers 1.00 2.50
CS11 Joe Greene 1.25 3.00
CS12 Lawrence Taylor 1.25 3.00
CS13 Rodney Harrison .75 2.00
CS14 Mike Singletary 1.25 3.00
CS15 Bruce Smith 1.00 2.50
CS6 Brian Urlacher 1.25 3.00
CS17 Ronnie Lott 1.00 2.50
CS18 Kam Chancellor 1.25 3.00
CS19 Steve Atwater 1.00 2.50
CS20 Ray Lewis 1.25 3.00

2017 Panini Illusions Elusive Ink

*BLUE/25: .6X TO 1.5X BASIC AU/75-100
*BLUE/25: .5X TO 1.2X BASIC AU/50
*BLUE/25: .4X TO 1X BASIC AU/25-30
*BLUE/25: .3X TO .8X BASIC AU/20
1 Jim Otto/30 6.00 15.00
3 Carl Banks/100 4.00 10.00
4 Kyle Juszczyk/100 4.00 10.00
5 Ross Cockrell/100 4.00 10.00
6 Aqib Talib/30 12.00 30.00
7 Ken Anderson/30 12.00 30.00
8 Geronimo Allison/100 12.00 30.00
9 Dan Reeves/30 8.00 20.00
10 Desmond Howard/30 8.00 20.00
11 Doug Williams/30 8.00 20.00
12 Chuck Foreman/30 6.00 15.00
13 Ahmad Rashad/30 8.00 20.00
14 Tom Mack/30
15 Louis Lipps/75 4.00 10.00
16 Rickey Jackson/30 6.00 15.00
17 Larry Brown/20 8.00 20.00
18 Andre Rison/30 8.00 20.00
19 Ron Yary/30 6.00 15.00
20 Mel Renfro/30 6.00 15.00
21 Rayfield Wright/30 8.00 20.00
23 Jurrell Casey/100 4.00 10.00
24 Zach Thomas/50 15.00 40.00
25 John Randle/25 12.00 30.00
26 Larry Allen/50 8.00 20.00
27 John Lynch/50 6.00 15.00
28 Pepper Johnson/100 4.00 10.00
29 Fred Dryer/30 6.00 15.00
30 LaVar Arrington/50

2017 Panini Illusions First Impressions Memorabilia

*BLUE/100: .5X TO 1.2X BASIC JSY
*RED/50: .6X TO 1.5X BASIC JSY
*GREEN/25: .8X TO 2X BASIC JSY
1 Mitchell Trubisky 6.00 15.00
2 Leonard Fournette 8.00 20.00
3 Corey Davis 3.00 8.00
4 Mike Williams 3.00 8.00
5 Christian McCaffrey 6.00 15.00
6 John Ross III 2.50 6.00
7 Patrick Mahomes II 15.00 40.00
8 Deshaun Watson 10.00 25.00
9 O.J. Howard 2.50 6.00
10 Evan Engram 2.50 6.00
11 Zay Jones 2.50 6.00
12 Curtis Samuel 2.50 6.00
13 Dalvin Cook 4.00 10.00
14 Joe Mixon 4.00 10.00
15 DeShone Kizer 2.00 5.00
16 JuJu Smith-Schuster 4.00 10.00
17 Alvin Kamara 6.00 15.00
18 Cooper Kupp 3.00 8.00
19 Taywan Taylor 2.00 5.00
20 ArDarius Stewart 2.00 5.00
21 Carlos Henderson 2.00 5.00
22 Chris Godwin 2.50 6.00
23 Kareem Hunt 4.00 10.00
24 Davis Webb 2.00 5.00
25 D'Onta Foreman 2.50 6.00
26 Kenny Golladay 3.00 8.00
27 C.J. Beathard 2.00 5.00
28 James Conner 4.00 10.00
29 Amara Darboh 2.00 5.00
30 Dede Westbrook 2.00 5.00
31 Samaje Perine 2.00 5.00
32 Josh Reynolds 2.00 5.00
33 Mack Hollins 2.00 5.00
34 Joe Williams 2.00 5.00
35 Jamaal Williams 2.00 5.00
36 R. Joshua Dobbs 2.50 6.00
37 Wayne Gallman 2.50 6.00
38 Marlon Mack 3.00 8.00
39 Jeremy McNichols 2.00 5.00
40 Nathan Peterman 2.50 6.00

2017 Panini Illusions Illusionists

1 David Johnson 1.25 3.00
2 Ezekiel Elliott 1.50 4.00
3 LeSean McCoy 1.25 3.00
4 Jordy Nelson 1.00 2.50
5 Devonta Freeman 1.00 2.50
6 Mike Evans 1.00 2.50
7 Davante Adams 1.00 2.50
8 Antonio Brown 1.25 3.00
9 DeMarco Murray 1.00 2.50
10 Tyreek Hill 1.25 3.00
11 Odell Beckham Jr. 1.25 3.00
12 Tom Brady 3.00 8.00
13 Le'Veon Bell 1.00 2.50
14 Julio Jones 1.25 3.00
15 Jordan Howard 1.25 3.00
16 Aaron Rodgers 2.50 6.00
17 Jay Ajayi 1.00 2.50
18 Drew Brees 1.25 3.00
19 Amari Cooper 1.25 3.00
20 Russell Wilson 1.50 4.00

2017 Panini Illusions Legacies Dual Memorabilia

*BLUE/15: .8X TO 2X BASIC JSY/100
*BLUE/15: .6X TO 1.5X BASIC JSY/50
*BLUE/15: .5X TO 1.2X BASIC JSY/25
1 D.Prescott/T.Aikman/50 8.00 20.00
2 J.Theismann/K.Cousins/50 6.00 15.00
3 A.Boldin/L.Fitzgerald/50 5.00 12.00
4 J.Kelly/T.Taylor/50 6.00 15.00
5 D.Marino/R.Tannehill/25 15.00 40.00
6 D.Webb/E.Manning/100 4.00 10.00
7 B.Roethlisberger/T.Bradshaw/50 10.00 25.00
8 D.Murray/E.George/25 6.00 15.00
9 A.Kamara/R.Williams/50 12.00 30.00
10 J.Riggins/S.Perine/100 4.00 10.00
11 L.Tomlinson/M.Gordon/100 4.00 10.00
12 J.Conner/J.Bettis/50 8.00 20.00
13 A.Smith/J.Montana/25 20.00 50.00
14 A.Gates/M.Williams/25 8.00 20.00
15 E.James/M.Mack/25 8.00 20.00
16 D.Carr/J.Plunkett/100 5.00 12.00
17 K.Hunt/P.Holmes/50 8.00 20.00
18 J.Elway/P.Lynch/25 12.00 30.00
19 J.Goff/K.Warner/25 8.00 20.00
20 E.Smith/E.Elliott/25 12.00 30.00

2017 Panini Illusions Legacies Triple Memorabilia

*BLUE/15: .8X TO 2X BASIC JSY/100
*BLUE/15: .6X TO 1.5X BASIC JSY/50
*BLUE/15: .5X TO 1.2X BASIC JSY/25
1 Brdshw/Brdy/Mntna/25 75.00 150.00
2 Fvre/Mrno/Elwy/25 40.00 80.00
3 Klly/Yng/Mnng/25 20.00 50.00
4 Rthlsbrgr/Brs/Rdgrs/25 20.00 50.00
5 Akmn/Nmth/Wrnr/25 12.00 30.00
6 Nwtn/Wlsn/Prsctt/25 12.00 30.00
7 Lck/Flcco/Ryn/25 12.00 30.00
8 Crr/Wnstn/Mrta/100 6.00 15.00
9 Sndrs/Smth/Thms/25 15.00 40.00
10 Tmlnsn/Flk/Alln/25 8.00 20.00
11 Cmpbll/Btts/Ptrsn/25 10.00 25.00
12 Jhnsn/Elltt/Bll/100 8.00 20.00
13 Hwrd/Ajyi/Grly/100 6.00 15.00
14 McCffry/Ck/Frntte/100 10.00 25.00
15 Rd/Rce/Mss/25 15.00 40.00
16 Wrd/Lrgnt/Brwn/25 10.00 25.00
17 Brwn/Ftzgrld/Bldwn/50 8.00 20.00
18 Jns/Cpr/Bckhm/100 6.00 15.00
19 Dvs/Rss/Wllms/100 6.00 15.00
20 Mck/Mllr/Bsa/50 8.00 20.00

2017 Panini Illusions Living Legends

1 Ben Roethlisberger 1.25 3.00
2 Jason Witten 1.00 2.50
3 Eli Manning 1.00 2.50
4 Larry Fitzgerald 1.00 2.50
5 Navorro Bowman 1.00 2.50
6 Richard Sherman 1.25 3.00
7 Haloti Ngata .75 2.00
8 Aaron Rodgers 2.50 6.00
9 Julius Peppers 1.00 2.50
10 Drew Brees 1.25 3.00
11 Tom Brady 3.00 8.00
12 Von Miller 1.00 2.50
13 Eric Berry 1.00 2.50
14 Antonio Gates .75 2.00
15 Sebastian Janikowski .75 2.00
16 Terrell Suggs .75 2.00
17 Joe Thomas .75 2.00
18 James Harrison 1.00 2.50
19 Adam Vinatieri .75 2.00
20 J.J. Watt 1.25 3.00

2017 Panini Illusions Matching Numbers

1 C.Newton/W.Moon 1.50 4.00
2 D.Hampton/J.Watt 1.50 4.00
3 J.Winston/R.Wilson 2.00 5.00
4 B.Favre/D.Carr 3.00 8.00
5 J.Rice/S.Largent 2.50 6.00
6 E.Campbell/T.Thomas 1.50 4.00
7 B.Roethlisberger/J.Elway 2.50 6.00
8 S.Young/M.Mariota 2.00 5.00
9 F.Harris/M.Allen 1.50 4.00
10 T.Bradshaw/R.Staubach 2.50 6.00
11 C.Wentz/L.Fitzgerald 2.00 5.00
12 A.Rodgers/T.Brady 4.00 10.00
13 D.Marino/K.Warner 3.00 8.00
14 E.Elliott/D.Sanders 2.00 5.00
15 J.Harrison/M.Strahan 1.25 3.00
16 J.Montana/L.Dawson 4.00 10.00
17 O.Beckham Jr./D.Maynard 1.50 4.00
18 A.Green/P.Manning 3.00 8.00
19 A.Peterson/M.Faulk 1.50 4.00
20 B.Sanders/E.Reed 2.50 6.00

2017 Panini Illusions Mirror Dual Signatures

*BLUE/15-20: .5X TO 1.2X BASIC AU/25
5 C.Beasley/R.Switzer/25 8.00 20.00
6 R.Kelley/S.Perine/25 5.00 12.00
7 L.Murray/D.Cook/25
8 R.Matthews/C.Davis/25 8.00 20.00
11 T.Coleman/B.Hill/25 6.00 15.00
12 C.Samuel/G.Olsen/25 6.00 15.00
13 L.Miller/D.Foreman/25 6.00 15.00
14 O.Howard/C.Brate/25
15 K.Hunt/S.Ware/25
16 J.Howard/T.Cohen/25
17 P.Perkins/W.Gallman/25 6.00 15.00
18 C.Hyde/J.Williams/25 5.00 12.00
19 C.Godwin/M.Evans/25 6.00 15.00
20 T.Holt/J.Reynolds/25 6.00 15.00
21 M.Hollins/S.Gibson/25 5.00 12.00
22 J.Chesson/T.Hill/25 8.00 20.00
23 A.Stewart/C.Hansen/25 5.00 12.00
24 D.Walker/J.Smith/25 5.00 12.00
25 M.McDowell/M.Bennett/25 10.00 25.00
26 R.Shazier/T.Watt/25 15.00 40.00
27 J.Haden/J.Peppers/15 10.00 25.00
28 J.Jones/H.Clinton-Dix/25 6.00 15.00
29 B.Cooks/T.Brown/25
30 T.Lockett/A.Darboh/25 6.00 15.00

2017 Panini Illusions Mystique

1 Myles Garrett 2.00 5.00
2 Mitchell Trubisky 3.00 8.00
3 Leonard Fournette 2.00 5.00
4 Corey Davis 1.00 2.50
5 Jamal Adams .60 1.50
6 Mike Williams 1.00 2.50
7 Christian McCaffrey 1.50 4.00
8 John Ross III .75 2.00
9 Patrick Mahomes II 25.00 50.00
10 Marshon Lattimore .75 2.00
11 Deshaun Watson 4.00 10.00
12 O.J. Howard .75 2.00
13 Evan Engram .75 2.00
14 Gareon Conley .60 1.50
15 Jabrill Peppers 1.00 2.50
16 David Njoku .75 2.00
17 T.J. Watt 2.00 5.00
18 Zay Jones .75 2.00
19 Curtis Samuel .75 2.00
20 Dalvin Cook 1.50 4.00

2017 Panini Illusions Rookie Dual Signs

1 M.Humphrey/T.Williams/50 6.00 15.00
2 N.Peterman/Z.Jones/20 10.00 25.00
3 C.McCaffrey/C.Samuel/20 20.00 50.00
4 M.Trubisky/A.Shaheen/20 40.00 100.00
5 J.Mixon/J.Ross III/20 15.00 40.00
6 J.Peppers/D.Njoku/20 12.00 30.00
7 N.Brown/R.Switzer/100 5.00 12.00
8 C.Henderson/J.Butt/25 8.00 20.00
9 M.Hooker/Q.Wilson/25 6.00 15.00
10 D.Westbrook/L.Fournette/20 30.00 60.00
11 J.Chesson/K.Hunt/25
12 C.Kupp/J.Reynolds/25 10.00 25.00
13 A.Kamara/M.Lattimore/25 50.00 100.00
14 E.Engram/W.Gallman/25 8.00 20.00
15 J.Adams/M.Maye/25
16 C.Sutton/T.Watt/25
17 J.Williams/C.Beathard/20 8.00 20.00
18 C.Godwin/O.Howard/20 10.00 25.00
19 A.Jackson/C.Davis/20 12.00 30.00
20 J.Allen/S.Perine/20 10.00 25.00

2017 Panini Illusions Rookie Endorsements

*BLUE/50: .6X TO 1.5X BASIC AU/150
*BLUE/50: .4X TO 1X BASIC AU/50
*RED/25: .8X TO 2X BASIC AU/150
*RED/25: .5X TO 1.2X BASIC AU/50
1 Jeremy McNichols/50 4.00 10.00
2 T.J. Logan/50 6.00 15.00
3 Donnel Pumphrey/50 5.00 12.00
4 Tarik Cohen/50 12.00 30.00
5 Ryan Switzer/50 5.00 12.00
6 Josh Malone/50 4.00 10.00
7 Davis Webb/50 4.00 10.00
8 Solomon Thomas/50 4.00 10.00
9 Tim Williams/50 5.00 12.00
10 Taywan Taylor/50 4.00 10.00
11 Chad Williams/50 4.00 10.00
12 Samaje Perine/50 4.00 10.00
13 Marshon Lattimore/50 5.00 12.00
14 Zay Jones/50 5.00 12.00
15 David Njoku/50 5.00 12.00
16 Jamal Adams/50 4.00 10.00
17 T.J. Watt/50 20.00 50.00
18 Jabrill Peppers/50 6.00 15.00
19 Christian McCaffrey/50
20 O.J. Howard/50 5.00 12.00
21 Matthew Dayes/150 2.50 6.00
22 Khalfani Muhammad/150 2.50 6.00
23 Brian Hill/150 2.50 6.00
24 Shelton Gibson/150 2.50 6.00
25 Trent Taylor/150 3.00 8.00
26 Elijah Hood/150 2.50 6.00
27 Deatrich Wise Jr./150 4.00 10.00
28 Eddie Jackson/150 3.00 8.00
29 Jehu Chesson/150 3.00 8.00
30 Chad Hansen/150 2.50 6.00
31 Cordrea Tankersley/150 3.00 8.00
32 Cameron Sutton/150 2.50 6.00
33 Fabian Moreau/150 2.50 6.00
34 Jordan Willis/150 2.50 6.00
35 Montravius Adams/150 3.00 8.00
36 Jonnu Smith/150 2.50 6.00
37 Sidney Jones/150 2.50 6.00
38 Marlon Humphrey/150 2.50 6.00
39 Marcus Maye/150 2.50 6.00
40 Ryan Anderson/150 2.50 6.00

2017 Panini Illusions Rookie Idols Dual Memorabilia

*BLUE/25: .6X TO 1.5X BASIC JSY/100
*BLUE/25: .5X TO 1.2X BASIC JSY/50
*BLUE/25: .4X TO 1X BASIC JSY/25
1 D.Watson/T.Brady/25 30.00 60.00
2 B.Favre/P.Mahomes II/25 15.00 40.00
3 N.Peterman/B.Roethlisberger/25 8.00 20.00
4 E.Manning/D.Webb/25 6.00 15.00
5 D.Cook/M.Faulk/25 10.00 25.00
6 A.Peterson/L.Fournette/25 15.00 40.00
7 A.Kamara/M.Vick/25 12.00 30.00
8 S.Perine/M.Lynch/25 6.00 15.00
9 M.Allen/W.Gallman/25 6.00 15.00
10 B.Sanders/K.Hunt/25 12.00 30.00
11 E.Berry/J.Conner/100 6.00 15.00
12 G.Olsen/O.Howard/100 4.00 10.00
13 M.Williams/C.Johnson/25 8.00 20.00
14 C.Davis/R.Moss/25 8.00 20.00
15 D.Jackson/J.Ross/100 4.00 10.00
16 A.Darboh/L.Fitzgerald/100 4.00 10.00
17 C.Kupp/L.Fitzgerald/100 5.00 12.00
18 A.Stewart/J.Jones/100 5.00 12.00
19 K.Golladay/M.Forte/50 6.00 15.00
20 D.Njoku/J.Graham/50 6.00 15.00

2017 Panini Illusions Rookie Reflection Dual Patch Autographs

*BLUE/15: .6X TO 1.5X BASIC JSY AU/50
*BLUE/15: .5X TO 1.2X BASIC JSY AU/25
*BLUE/15: .4X TO 1X BASIC JSY AU/20
1 D.Foreman/D.Watson/20 50.00 100.00
2 K.Hunt/P.Mahomes II/20 150.00 300.00
3 N.Peterman/Z.Jones/25 8.00 20.00
4 D.Webb/E.Engram/25 15.00 40.00
5 C.Beathard/J.Williams/25 6.00 15.00
6 D.Westbrook/L.Fournette/20 30.00 60.00
7 C.Davis/T.Taylor/25 10.00 25.00
8 J.Reynolds/C.Kupp/25 10.00 25.00
9 C.Godwin/O.Howard/25 8.00 20.00
10 J.Smith-Schuster/R.Dobbs/25 15.00 40.00
11 J.Mixon/J.Ross III/20 15.00 40.00
12 C.McCaffrey/C.Samuel/20 20.00 50.00
13 M.Hollins/M.Trubisky/20
14 A.Kamara/D.Cook/25 40.00 80.00
15 S.Perine/W.Gallman/25 8.00 20.00
16 J.Conner/J.Williams/50 10.00 25.00
17 J.McNichols/M.Mack/50 8.00 20.00
18 A.Darboh/K.Golladay/50 8.00 20.00
19 D.Kizer/M.Williams/20 30.00 60.00
20 A.Stewart/C.Henderson/50 5.00 12.00

2017 Panini Illusions Rookie Reflection Dual Patches

*BLUE/25: .6X TO 1.5X BASIC JSY/100
1 P.Mahomes II/M.Trubisky 30.00 60.00
2 D.Kizer/D.Watson 15.00 40.00
3 D.Webb/C.Beathard 3.00 8.00
4 N.Peterman/R.Dobbs 4.00 10.00
5 E.Engram/O.Howard 4.00 10.00
6 D.Foreman/L.Fournette 12.00 30.00
7 C.McCaffrey/J.Mixon 10.00 25.00
8 A.Kamara/D.Cook 10.00 25.00
9 K.Hunt/M.Mack 8.00 20.00
10 S.Perine/W.Gallman 4.00 10.00
11 J.McNichols/J.Williams 3.00 8.00
12 J.Conner/J.Williams 6.00 15.00
13 C.Davis/M.Williams 5.00 12.00
14 D.Westbrook/J.Smith-Schuster 6.00 15.00
15 C.Samuel/J.Ross III 4.00 10.00
16 T.Taylor/Z.Jones 4.00 10.00
17 C.Henderson/C.Kupp 5.00 12.00
18 A.Darboh/K.Golladay 5.00 12.00
19 A.Stewart/C.Godwin 4.00 10.00
20 J.Reynolds/M.Hollins 3.00 8.00

2017 Panini Illusions Spotlight Memorabilia

*BLUE/100: .5X TO 1.2X BASIC JSY
*RED/25: .8X TO 2X BASIC JSY
1 Tom Brady 8.00 20.00
2 Drew Brees 3.00 8.00
3 Dak Prescott 3.00 8.00
4 Marcus Mariota 3.00 8.00
5 Russell Wilson 4.00 10.00
6 Matt Ryan 2.50 6.00
7 Aaron Rodgers 6.00 15.00
8 Andrew Luck 4.00 10.00
9 Derek Carr 3.00 8.00
10 Jameis Winston 2.50 6.00
11 Ezekiel Elliott 4.00 10.00
12 DeMarco Murray 2.50 6.00
13 Jordan Howard 3.00 8.00
14 David Johnson 3.00 8.00
15 Le'Veon Bell 2.50 6.00
16 Julio Jones 3.00 8.00
17 Kelvin Benjamin 2.50 6.00
18 Davante Adams 2.50 6.00
19 Michael Thomas 3.00 8.00
20 Antonio Brown 3.00 8.00

2017 Panini Illusions Veteran Signs

*BLUE/50: .6X TO 1.5X BASIC AU/125-150
*BLUE/25: .8X TO 2X BASIC AU/125-150
*BLUE/25: .6X TO 1.5X BASIC AU/75
*BLUE/25: .5X TO 1.2X BASIC AU/50
*BLUE/15: .4X TO 1X BASIC AU/20
*RED/25: .8X TO 2X BASIC AU/125-150
*RED/15: 1X TO 2.5X BASIC AU/125-150
1 Jameis Winston/20
2 Ezekiel Elliott/20 40.00 80.00
3 James White/150 4.00 10.00
4 Melvin Gordon/50 6.00 15.00
5 Tyreek Hill/125 5.00 12.00
6 Dak Prescott/20 50.00 100.00
7 Carlos Hyde/150 3.00 8.00
8 Marcus Mariota/20 25.00 50.00
9 Sterling Shepard/150 4.00 10.00
10 Cameron Heyward/150 3.00 8.00
11 Fletcher Cox/150 3.00 8.00
12 Devonta Freeman/50 6.00 15.00
13 Jack Doyle/150 3.00 8.00
14 Terrelle Pryor/150 3.00 8.00
15 Dont'a Hightower/150 8.00 20.00
16 Jordan Howard/50 8.00 20.00
17 Kyle Rudolph/150 3.00 8.00
18 Spencer Ware/150 3.00 8.00
19 DeMarco Murray/50 6.00 15.00
20 Pierre Garcon/150 4.00 10.00
21 Hunter Henry/150 3.00 8.00
22 Jay Ajayi/150 4.00 10.00
24 Jason Taylor/20 15.00 40.00
25 Adam Thielen/150 40.00 80.00
26 Robert Kelley/150 3.00 8.00
27 Chris Hogan/150 12.00 30.00
29 Ha Ha Clinton-Dix/75 4.00 10.00
30 Aaron Donald/150 5.00 12.00

2018 Panini Illusions

1 A.Miller/W.Gault 1.00 2.50
2 B.Mayfield/V.Testaverde 6.00 15.00
3 B.Chubb/V.Miller 1.00 2.50
4 C.Ridley/J.Jones 1.50 4.00
5 C.Kirk/L.Fitzgerald 1.00 2.50
6 C.Sutton/D.Thomas 1.00 2.50
7 D.Moore/K.Benjamin 1.25 3.00
8 D.Chark Jr./M.Lee .75 2.00
9 D.Hamilton/R.Smith .75 2.00
10 D.Pettis/J.Rice 1.50 4.00
11 D.Fountain/R.Wayne .75 2.00
12 C.Portis/D.Guice 1.25 3.00
13 H.Hurst/S.Sharpe .75 2.00
14 I.Smith/W.Dunn .75 2.00
15 J.Scott/T.Smith .60 1.50
16 A.Brown/J.Washington 1.25 3.00
17 J.Samuels/J.Bettis 1.00 2.50
18 D.Driver/J.Moore .75 2.00
19 J.Kelly/J.Allen 2.50 6.00
20 J.Rosen/K.Warner 2.00 5.00
21 K.Ballage/R.Williams .75 2.00
22 D.Hopkins/K.Coutee .75 2.00
23 B.Sanders/K.Johnson 1.50 4.00
24 E.Manning/K.Lauletta 1.00 2.50
25 L.Jackson/T.Dilfer 4.00 10.00
26 J.Hill/M.Walton .75 2.00
27 M.Valdes-Scantling/S.Sharpe .75 2.00
28 M.Rudolph/T.Bradshaw 1.50 4.00
29 M.Gallup/M.Irvin 1.25 3.00
30 J.Thomas/M.Gesicki .75 2.00
31 D.White/M.White .75 2.00
32 I.Crowell/N.Chubb 2.00 5.00
33 E.James/N.Hines .75 2.00
34 R.Penny/S.Alexander 1.00 2.50
35 R.Jones II/W.Dunn .60 1.50
36 R.Freeman/T.Davis .75 2.00
37 J.Namath/S.Darnold 4.00 10.00
38 O.Anderson/S.Barkley 5.00 12.00
39 C.Martin/S.Michel 2.00 5.00

40 B.Cooks/T.Smith 1.00 2.50
41 J.Harbaugh/M.Trubisky 1.00 2.50
42 F.Taylor/L.Fournette 1.00 2.50
43 C.Davis/R.Moss .75 2.00
44 C.McCaffrey/J.Stewart 1.00 2.50
45 J.Montana/P.Mahomes II 2.50 6.00
46 D.Watson/M.Schaub 1.25 3.00
47 E.Engram/J.Shockey .60 1.50
48 A.Peterson/D.Cook 1.00 2.50
49 H.Ward/J.Smith-Schuster 1.00 2.50
50 A.Kamara/R.Williams .75 2.00
51 C.Kupp/I.Bruce 1.00 2.50
52 K.Hunt/P.Holmes .75 2.00
53 C.Joiner/M.Williams .60 1.50
54 J.Williams/J.Taylor .75 2.00
55 J.Ajayi/R.Watters .75 2.00
56 A.Smith/J.Theismann 1.00 2.50
57 K.Warner/S.Bradford .75 2.00
58 D.Henry/E.George 1.00 2.50
59 M.Ditka/T.Burton 1.00 2.50
60 M.Crabtree/M.Wallace .60 1.50
61 J.Garcia/T.Taylor .75 2.00
62 J.Landry/P.Warfield .75 2.00
63 A.Hurns/D.Pearson .75 2.00
64 C.Keenum/J.Elway 1.50 4.00
65 G.Olsen/W.Walls .75 2.00
66 A.Rison/T.Hill 1.00 2.50
67 B.Cooks/T.Holt .75 2.00
68 A.Donald/J.Youngblood 1.00 2.50
69 F.Gore/R.Williams .75 2.00
70 F.Tarkenton/K.Cousins 1.00 2.50
71 J.Nelson/T.Brown 1.00 2.50
72 J.McKinnon/R.Craig .75 2.00
73 J.Plunkett/T.Brady 2.50 6.00
74 M.Allen/M.Lynch 1.00 2.50
75 A.Luck/B.Jones 1.25 3.00
76 B.Roethlisberger/T.Bradshaw 1.50 4.00
77 A.Rodgers/D.Majkowski 2.00 5.00
78 J.Garoppolo/J.Montana 2.50 6.00
79 C.Wentz/M.Vick 1.25 3.00
80 T.Gonzalez/T.Kelce 1.00 2.50
81 D.Prescott/T.Aikman 1.25 3.00
82 E.Elliott/H.Walker 1.25 3.00
83 J.Ham/T.Watt .75 2.00
84 I.Woods/J.Mixon .75 2.00
85 H.Smith/P.Krause 1.00 2.50
86 D.Sanders/R.Sherman 1.00 2.50
87 A.Collins/P.Holmes .60 1.50
88 J.Gordon/T.Pryor .60 1.50
89 L.Bell/R.Bleier .75 2.00
90 A.Thielen/C.Carter 1.00 2.50
91 L.McCoy/W.McGahee 1.00 2.50
92 D.Brees/P.Rivers 1.00 2.50
93 R.Wilson/W.Moon 1.25 3.00
94 J.Winston/S.Young 1.25 3.00
95 A.Hooper/T.Gonzalez .75 2.00
96 C.Bailey/J.Norman .75 2.00
97 D.Carr/R.Gannon 1.00 2.50
98 A.Vinatieri/S.Gostkowski .60 1.50
99 B.Dawkins/M.Jenkins 1.00 2.50
100 D.Lawrence/E.Jones .60 1.50
101 Anthony Miller JSY AU/449 RC 4.00 10.00
102 Baker Mayfield JSY AU/175 RC 60.00 125.00
103 Bradley Chubb JSY AU/99 RC 6.00 15.00
104 Calvin Ridley JSY AU/99 RC 10.00 25.00
105 Christian Kirk JSY AU/99 RC 6.00 15.00
106 Courtland Sutton JSY AU/299 RC 4.00 10.00
107 D.J. Moore JSY AU/225 RC 5.00 12.00
108 D.J. Chark Jr. JSY AU/399 RC EXCH 3.00 8.00
109 DaeSean Hamilton JSY AU/399 RC 3.00 8.00
110 Dante Pettis JSY AU/299 RC 4.00 10.00
111 Daurice Fountain JSY AU/499 RC 3.00 8.00
112 Derrius Guice JSY AU/99 RC EXCH 8.00 20.00
114 Ito Smith JSY AU/499 RC 3.00 8.00
115 Jaleel Scott JSY AU/499 RC EXCH 2.50 6.00
116 James Washington JSY AU/399 RC 5.00 12.00
117 Jaylen Samuels JSY AU/499 RC 3.00 8.00
118 J'Mon Moore JSY AU/499 RC 2.50 6.00
119 Josh Allen JSY AU/199 RC 12.00 30.00
120 Josh Rosen JSY AU/199 RC 10.00 25.00
121 Kalen Ballage JSY AU/449 RC 3.00 8.00
123 Kerryon Johnson JSY AU/399 RC 4.00 10.00
124 Kyle Lauletta JSY AU/99 RC 6.00 15.00
125 Lamar Jackson JSY AU/75 RC 40.00 80.00
126 Mark Walton JSY AU/499 RC EXCH 3.00 8.00
127 Marquez Valdes-Scantling JSY AU/499 RC 3.00 8.00
128 Mason Rudolph JSY AU/325 RC 6.00 15.00
129 Michael Gallup JSY AU/149 RC 6.00 15.00
130 Mike Gesicki JSY AU/149 RC 4.00 10.00
131 Mike White JSY AU/99 RC 5.00 12.00
132 Nick Chubb JSY AU/325 RC 8.00 20.00
133 Nyheim Hines JSY AU/499 RC 3.00 8.00
134 Rashaad Penny JSY AU/299 RC EXCH 4.00 10.00
135 Ronald Jones II JSY AU/399 RC 2.50 6.00
136 Royce Freeman JSY AU/349 RC 3.00 8.00
137 Sam Darnold JSY AU/99 RC 40.00 80.00
138 Saquon Barkley JSY AU/225 RC 60.00 125.00
139 Sony Michel JSY AU/225 RC 12.00 30.00
140 Tre'Quan Smith JSY AU/499 RC 4.00 10.00
141 Chase Edmonds AU/199 RC 2.00 5.00
142 Isaiah Oliver AU/199 RC 2.00 5.00
143 Jordan Lasley AU/199 RC 2.00 5.00
144 Mark Andrews AU/199 RC 3.00 8.00
145 Austin Proehl AU/199 RC 2.00 5.00
146 Ray-Ray McCloud AU/199 RC 2.00 5.00
147 Tremaine Edmunds AU/199 RC 4.00 10.00
148 Russell Gage AU/199 RC 2.50 6.00
149 Dylan Cantrell AU/199 RC 2.00 5.00
150 Justin Jackson AU/199 RC 2.50 6.00
151 Roquan Smith AU/175 RC 6.00 15.00
152 Auden Tate AU/199 RC
153 Antonio Callaway AU/199 RC
154 Denzel Ward AU/175 RC 6.00 15.00
155 Bo Scarbrough AU/199 RC 2.50 6.00
156 Cedrick Wilson Jr. AU/199 RC 2.00 5.00
157 Dalton Schultz AU/199 RC 2.50 6.00
158 Leighton Vander Esch AU/199 RC 8.00 20.00
159 Jaire Alexander AU/199 RC 3.00 8.00
160 Joshua Jackson AU/199 RC 4.00 10.00
161 Justin Reid AU/199 RC 2.00 5.00
162 Tyquan Lewis AU/199 RC 2.50 6.00
163 Tanner Lee AU/199 RC 2.50 6.00
164 Ronnie Harrison AU/199 RC 2.50 6.00
165 Chase Litton AU/199 RC 2.50 6.00
166 Derwin James AU/199 RC 4.00 10.00
167 Minkah Fitzpatrick AU/175 RC 4.00 10.00
168 Mike Hughes AU/199 RC 3.00 8.00
169 Tyler Conklin AU/199 RC 2.00 5.00
170 Braxton Berrios AU/199 RC 2.00 5.00
171 Duke Dawson AU/199 RC 2.00 5.00
172 Marcus Davenport AU/199 RC 4.00 10.00
173 Lorenzo Carter AU/199 RC 2.00 5.00
174 Arden Key AU/199 RC 2.00 5.00
175 Maurice Hurst AU/199 RC 2.50 6.00
176 Ian Thomas AU/199 RC
177 Dallas Goedert AU/199 RC 2.50 6.00
178 Terrell Edmunds AU/175 RC 6.00 15.00
179 John Kelly AU/199 RC 2.50 6.00
180 Richie James AU/199 RC 2.00 5.00
181 Fred Warner AU/199 RC 2.00 5.00
182 Rasheem Green AU/199 RC 2.00 5.00
183 Shaquem Griffin AU/199 RC 10.00 25.00
184 Kurt Benkert AU/199 RC 2.50 6.00
185 Carlton Davis AU/199 RC 2.50 6.00
186 Vita Vea AU/199 RC 3.00 8.00
187 Harold Landry AU/199 RC 2.00 5.00
188 Rashaan Evans AU/199 RC 3.00 8.00
189 Luke Falk AU/175 RC 2.50 6.00
190 Trey Quinn AU/199 RC 2.00 5.00

2018 Panini Illusions Black

*BLACK/25: 1.5X TO 4X BASIC CARDS

2018 Panini Illusions Blue

*VETS/249: .6X TO 1.5X BASIC CARDS
*ROOK JSY AU/75-100: .6X TO 1.5X BASIC JSY AU/325-499
*ROOK JSY AU/75-100: .5X TO 1.2X BASIC JSY AU/149-225
*ROOK JSY AU/75-100: .4X TO 1X BASIC JSY AU/99
*ROOK JSY AU/50: .5X TO 1.2X BASIC JSY AU/75
*ROOK AU/100: .5X TO 1.2X BASIC AU/175-199

2018 Panini Illusions Gold

*VETS/499: .5X TO 1.2X BASIC CARDS

2018 Panini Illusions Green

*VETS: 1X TO 2.5X BASIC CARDS
*ROOK JSY AU/25: 1X TO 2.5X BASIC JSY AU/325-499
*ROOK JSY AU/25: .8X TO 2X BASIC JSY AU/149-225
*ROOK JSY AU/25: .6X TO 1.5X BASIC JSY AU/75-99
*ROOK AU/25: .8X TO 2X BASIC AU/175-199

2018 Panini Illusions Pink

*PINK/75: 1X TO 2.5X BASIC CARDS

2018 Panini Illusions Red

*VETS: .8X TO 2X BASIC CARDS
*ROOK JSY AU/50: .8X TO 2X BASIC JSY AU/325-499
*ROOK JSY AU/50: .6X TO 1.5X BASIC JSY AU/149-225
*ROOK JSY AU/35-50: .5X TO 1.2X BASIC JSY AU/75-99
*ROOK AU/50: .6X TO 1.5X BASIC AU/175-1199

2018 Panini Illusions Clear Shots

*GOLD/299: .5X TO 1.2X BASIC INSERTS
*BLUE/149: .6X TO 1.5X BASIC INSERTS
*RED/99: .6X TO 1.5X BASIC INSERTS
*BLACK/25: 1X TO 2.5X BASIC INSERTS
1 Aaron Donald 1.25 3.00
2 Bobby Wagner .75 2.00
3 Luke Kuechly 1.00 2.50
4 C.J. Mosley 1.00 2.50
5 Reuben Foster .75 2.00
6 Von Miller 1.00 2.50
7 Justin Houston .75 2.00
8 Chandler Jones .75 2.00
9 Jadeveon Clowney .75 2.00
10 Eric Berry 1.00 2.50
11 T.J. Watt 1.00 2.50
12 Earl Thomas III 1.00 2.50
13 Ryan Kerrigan .75 2.00
14 Terrell Suggs .75 2.00
15 Calais Campbell .75 2.00
16 Joey Bosa 1.25 3.00
17 DeMarcus Lawrence .75 2.00
18 Khalil Mack 1.25 3.00
19 Myles Garrett 1.25 3.00
20 Bud Dupree .75 2.00

2018 Panini Illusions First Impressions Memorabilia

*BLUE/100: .5X TO 1.2X BASIC JSY/299-499
*BLUE/100: .4X TO 1X BASIC JSY/100
*RED/50: .6X TO 1.5X BASIC JSY/299-499
*RED/50: .5X TO 1.2X BASIC JSY/149-199
*GREEN/25: .8X TO 2X BASIC JSY/299-499
*GREEN/25: .6X TO 1.5X BASIC JSY/149-199
1 Anthony Miller/199 4.00 10.00
2 Baker Mayfield/149 15.00 25.00
3 Bradley Chubb/199 4.00 10.00
4 Calvin Ridley/199 8.00 12.00
5 Christian Kirk/499 3.00 8.00
6 Courtland Sutton/499 3.00 8.00
7 D.J. Moore/199 5.00 12.00
8 D.J. Chark Jr./499 2.50 6.00
9 DaeSean Hamilton/499 2.50 6.00
10 Dante Pettis/499 3.00 8.00
11 Daurice Fountain/499 2.50 6.00
12 Derrius Guice/199 5.00 12.00
13 Hayden Hurst/499 2.50 6.00
14 Ito Smith/499 2.50 6.00
15 Jaleel Scott/499 2.00 5.00
16 James Washington/499 4.00 10.00
17 Jaylen Samuels/499 2.50 6.00
18 J'Mon Moore/499 2.00 5.00
19 Josh Allen/199 12.00 20.00
20 Josh Rosen/149 12.00 20.00
21 Kalen Ballage/499 2.50 6.00
22 Keke Coutee/499 2.50 6.00
23 Kerryon Johnson/499 3.00 8.00
24 Kyle Lauletta/499 3.00 8.00
25 Lamar Jackson/149 15.00 25.00
26 Mark Walton/499 2.50 6.00
27 Marquez Valdes-Scantling/499 2.50 6.00
28 Mason Rudolph/199 6.00 15.00
29 Michael Gallup/199 5.00 12.00
30 Mike Gesicki/499 2.50 6.00
31 Mike White/499 2.50 6.00
32 Nick Chubb/199 8.00 20.00
33 Nyheim Hines/499 2.50 6.00
34 Rashaad Penny/199 4.00 10.00
35 Ronald Jones II/499 2.00 5.00
36 Royce Freeman/499 2.50 6.00
37 Sam Darnold/149 15.00 25.00
38 Saquon Barkley/149 20.00 30.00
39 Sony Michel/299 6.00 12.00
40 Tre'Quan Smith/499 3.00 8.00

2018 Panini Illusions Illusionists

*GOLD/299: .5X TO 1.2X BASIC INSERTS
*BLUE/149: .6X TO 1.5X BASIC INSERTS
*RED/99: .6X TO 1.5X BASIC INSERTS
*BLACK/25: 1X TO 2.5X BASIC INSERTS
1 Saquon Barkley 6.00 15.00
2 Baker Mayfield 8.00 20.00
3 Patrick Mahomes II 3.00 8.00
4 Brett Favre 2.50 6.00
5 Jerry Rice 2.00 5.00
6 Steve Young 1.50 4.00
7 Derek Carr 1.25 3.00
8 Randy Moss 1.00 2.50
9 Alvin Kamara 1.00 2.50
10 Lamar Jackson 5.00 12.00
11 Calvin Ridley 2.00 5.00
12 D.J. Moore 1.50 4.00
13 Royce Freeman 1.00 2.50
14 Tyreek Hill 1.25 3.00
15 Deshaun Watson 1.50 4.00
16 Michael Vick 1.00 2.50
17 Harrison Smith 1.25 3.00
18 Devin Hester 1.00 2.50
19 Barry Sanders 2.00 5.00
20 Bo Jackson 1.50 4.00

2018 Panini Illusions Illusionists Autographs Holo Silver

9 Alvin Kamara/25 12.00 30.00
12 D.J. Moore/75 10.00 25.00
13 Royce Freeman/99 4.00 10.00
17 Harrison Smith/75 8.00 20.00

2018 Panini Illusions Legacies Dual Memorabilia

*BLUE/15: .8X TO 2X BASIC JSY/100
*BLUE/15: .6X TO 1.5X BASIC JSY/50
*BLUE/15: .5X TO 1.2X BASIC JSY/25
1 J.Namath/S.Darnold/50 12.00 30.00
2 J.Kelly/J.Allen/100 8.00 20.00
3 J.Rosen/K.Warner/25 12.00 30.00
4 J.Watt/T.Watt/25 6.00 15.00
5 J.Montana/P.Mahomes II/50 8.00 20.00
6 D.Guice/J.Riggins/50 6.00 15.00
7 M.Lynch/R.Penny/50 5.00 12.00
8 B.Chubb/V.Miller/25 6.00 15.00
9 B.Roethlisberger/M.Rudolph/25 10.00 25.00
10 E.James/N.Hines/100 3.00 8.00
11 R.Freeman/T.Davis/50 4.00 10.00
12 M.Thomas/T.Smith/50 5.00 12.00
13 E.Manning/K.Lauletta/25 6.00 15.00
14 A.Brown/H.Ward/25 6.00 15.00
15 T.Gonzalez/T.Kelce/50 5.00 12.00
16 E.Dickerson/T.Gurley II/25 6.00 15.00
17 A.Peterson/D.Cook/25 6.00 15.00
18 C.Carter/S.Diggs/100 4.00 10.00
19 J.Flacco/L.Jackson/100 10.00 25.00
20 E.Manning/O.Beckham Jr./25 6.00 15.00

2018 Panini Illusions Legacies Triple Memorabilia

*BLUE/15: .6X TO 1.5X BASIC JSY/50
1 Prsctt/Rmo/Akmn 8.00 20.00
2 Andrsn/Bkr/Dvs 5.00 12.00
3 Mrry/Hnry/Cmpbll 6.00 15.00
4 Jms/Gre/Hns 5.00 12.00
5 Chris/Hnt/Alln 6.00 15.00
6 Jcksn/Alln/Lnch 8.00 20.00
7 Ajyi/Blige/Wllms 5.00 12.00
8 Prts/Gce/Rggns 8.00 20.00
9 Rdgrs/Brdshw/Akmn 12.00 30.00
10 Cmpbll/Lwrnce/Mllr 5.00 12.00
11 Brwn/Jns/Alln 6.00 15.00
12 Hnt/Bll/Grly 6.00 15.00
13 Hnt/Mhms/Hll 15.00 40.00
14 Elltt/Frntte/Brkly 15.00 40.00
15 Mre/SmthSchstr/Thms 8.00 20.00
16 Myfld/Wntz/Wtsn 15.00 40.00
17 Hrst/Hnry/Hwrd 5.00 12.00
18 Rd/Klly/Thms 6.00 15.00
19 Gts/Wttn/Gnzlz 5.00 12.00
20 Mntna/Stbch/Brdy 15.00 40.00

2018 Panini Illusions Living Legends

*GOLD/299: .5X TO 1.2X BASIC INSERTS
*BLUE/149: .6X TO 1.5X BASIC INSERTS
*RED/99: .6X TO 1.5X BASIC INSERTS
*BLACK/25: 1X TO 2.5X BASIC INSERTS
1 Drew Brees 1.25 3.00
2 Aaron Rodgers 2.50 6.00
3 Philip Rivers 1.25 3.00
4 Antonio Brown 1.25 3.00
5 Tom Brady 3.00 8.00
6 Rob Gronkowski 1.25 3.00
7 Antonio Gates .75 2.00
8 Terrell Suggs .75 2.00
9 Eli Manning 1.00 2.50
10 Ben Roethlisberger 1.25 3.00
11 Stephen Gostkowski .75 2.00
12 Matthew Stafford 1.00 2.50
13 A.J. Green 1.25 3.00
14 Clay Matthews 1.00 2.50
15 Matt Ryan 1.00 2.50
16 Russell Wilson 1.50 4.00
17 Eric Berry 1.00 2.50
18 Luke Kuechly 1.00 2.50
19 LeSean McCoy 1.25 3.00
20 J.J. Watt 1.25 3.00

2018 Panini Illusions Matching Numbers

*GOLD/299: .5X TO 1.2X BASIC INSERTS
*BLUE/149: .6X TO 1.5X BASIC INSERTS
*RED/99: .6X TO 1.5X BASIC INSERTS
*BLACK/25: 1X TO 2.5X BASIC INSERTS
1 D.Fouts/S.Darnold 5.00 12.00
2 A.Green/C.Ridley 2.00 5.00
3 J.Allen/P.Rivers 3.00 8.00
4 J.Rosen/R.Wilson 2.50 6.00
5 C.Kirk/O.Beckham Jr. 1.25 3.00
6 A.Callaway/J.Jones 1.25 3.00
7 D.Johnson/N.Chubb 2.50 6.00
8 T.Bradshaw/T.Brady 3.00 8.00
9 A.Rodgers/R.Staubach 2.50 6.00
10 A.Thielen/L.Alworth 1.25 3.00
11 F.Tarkenton/J.Garoppolo 1.50 4.00
12 L.Bell/S.Barkley 6.00 15.00
13 E.Elliott/L.Tomlinson 1.50 4.00
14 E.George/K.Hunt 1.00 2.50
15 D.Cook/K.Johnson 1.25 3.00
16 T.Davis/T.Gurley II 1.25 3.00
17 B.Chubb/T.Suggs 1.25 3.00
18 J.Watt/J.Taylor 1.25 3.00
19 B.Dawkins/E.Reed 1.25 3.00
20 E.Thomas III/E.Berry 1.00 2.50

2018 Panini Illusions Mirror Dual Signatures

1 S.Griffin/S.Griffin/25 75.00 150.00
2 J.Jeffcoat/L.Lett/15
6 B.Jones/T.Rathman/20 10.00 25.00
7 J.Mixon/M.Walton/20 12.00 30.00
9 A.Jones/T.Montgomery/20
11 C.Keenum/C.Sutton/20 15.00 40.00
12 J.Washington/J.Smith-Schuster/15 20.00 50.00
13 D.Fountain/T.Hilton/15 12.00 30.00

2018 Panini Illusions Mystique

*GOLD/299: .5X TO 1.2X BASIC INSERTS
*BLUE/149: .6X TO 1.5X BASIC INSERTS
*RED/99: .6X TO 1.5X BASIC INSERTS
*BLACK/25: 1X TO 2.5X BASIC INSERTS
1 Sam Darnold 5.00 12.00
2 Josh Allen 3.00 8.00
3 Josh Rosen 2.50 6.00
4 Rashaad Penny 1.25 3.00
5 Ezekiel Elliott 1.50 4.00
6 Travis Kelce 1.25 3.00
7 Jimmy Garoppolo 1.50 4.00
8 Michael Thomas 1.25 3.00
9 Kareem Hunt 1.00 2.50
10 Derrius Guice 1.50 4.00
11 Courtland Sutton 1.25 3.00
12 Sony Michel 2.50 6.00
13 Joe Mixon 1.00 2.50
14 JuJu Smith-Schuster 1.25 3.00
15 Julio Jones 1.25 3.00
16 Marshawn Lynch 1.00 2.50
17 Dak Prescott 1.25 3.00
18 Le'Veon Bell 1.00 2.50
19 Tarik Cohen 1.00 2.50
20 Adam Thielen 1.25 3.00

2018 Panini Illusions Mystique Autographs Holo Silver

4 Rashaad Penny/75 5.00 12.00
5 Ezekiel Elliott/25 50.00 100.00
6 Travis Kelce/25 15.00 40.00
7 Jimmy Garoppolo/25 10.00 25.00
9 Kareem Hunt/99 15.00 40.00
10 Derrius Guice/25 10.00 25.00
11 Courtland Sutton/75 5.00 12.00
12 Sony Michel/25 15.00 40.00
13 Joe Mixon/15 8.00 20.00
14 JuJu Smith-Schuster/25 8.00 20.00
19 Tarik Cohen/75 4.00 10.00
20 Adam Thielen/25 30.00 60.00

2018 Panini Illusions Rookie Dual Signs

*BLUE/15: .5X TO 1.2X BASIC AU/25
3 J.Scott/J.Lasley 8.00 20.00
4 A.Proehl/R.McCloud 8.00 20.00
5 J.Akins/K.Coutee 10.00 25.00
6 M.Jefferson/S.Hubbard 10.00 25.00
8 L.Vander Esch/M.Gallup 25.00 60.00
10 J.Alexander/J.Jackson 15.00 40.00
11 R.Harrison/T.Bryan 10.00 25.00
12 A.Watts/D.Nnadi 8.00 20.00
13 D.James/K.White 15.00 40.00
14 J.Baker/M.Fitzpatrick 15.00 40.00
15 J.Holmes/M.Hughes 12.00 30.00
17 M.Davenport/T.Smith 15.00 40.00
18 A.Key/M.Hurst 10.00 25.00
20 H.Landry/R.Evans 12.00 30.00

2018 Panini Illusions Rookie Endorsements

1 Baker Mayfield/25 100.00 200.00
2 Josh Allen/25 40.00 80.00
4 Saquon Barkley/35 90.00 150.00
5 Derrius Guice/25 10.00 25.00
6 Rashaad Penny/25 8.00 20.00
7 D.J. Moore/100 6.00 15.00
8 Calvin Ridley/50 10.00 25.00
9 D.J. Chark Jr./100 4.00 10.00
11 Bradley Chubb/35 6.00 15.00
12 Josh Rosen/25 50.00 100.00
13 Sam Darnold/35 40.00 80.00
14 Mason Rudolph/75 8.00 20.00
15 Mark Walton/150 3.00 8.00
16 Royce Freeman/150 3.00 8.00
17 Sony Michel/50 12.00 30.00
18 Courtland Sutton/100 5.00 12.00
19 Michael Gallup/150 5.00 12.00
20 Christian Kirk/85 5.00 12.00
21 Mike Gesicki/100 4.00 10.00
22 Mike White/100 4.00 10.00
23 Kyle Lauletta/75 6.00 15.00
24 Nick Chubb/85 10.00 25.00
25 Daurice Fountain/150 3.00 8.00
26 Marquez Valdes-Scantling/150 3.00 8.00
27 Jaleel Scott/150 2.50 6.00
28 Tre'Quan Smith/150 4.00 10.00
29 DaeSean Hamilton/150 3.00 8.00
30 Jaylen Samuels/150 3.00 8.00
31 Dante Pettis/100 5.00 12.00
32 J'Mon Moore/150 2.50 6.00
33 Keke Coutee/150 3.00 8.00
34 James Washington/100 6.00 15.00
35 Ito Smith/150 3.00 8.00
36 Nyheim Hines/150 3.00 8.00
37 Kalen Ballage/150 3.00 8.00
38 Kerryon Johnson/100 5.00 12.00
39 Anthony Miller/100 5.00 12.00
40 Ronald Jones II/100 3.00 8.00

2018 Panini Illusions Rookie Endorsements Blue

*BLUE/50: .6X TO 1.5X BASIC AU/150
*BLUE/50: .5X TO 1.2X BASIC AU/75-100
*BLUE/25: .5X TO 1.2X BASIC AU/35-50
*BLUE/15: .6X TO 1.5X BASIC AU/35-50
*BLUE/15: .5X TO 1.2X BASIC AU/25
4 Saquon Barkley/25 100.00 200.00

2018 Panini Illusions Rookie Endorsements Green Variation

*GRN VAR/25: .8X TO 2X BASIC AU/150
*GRN VAR/25: .6X TO 1.5X BASIC AU/75-100
*GRN VAR/15: 1X TO 2.5X BASIC AU/150
*GRN VAR/15: .8X TO 2X BASIC AU/75-100
*GRN VAR/15: .6X TO 1.5X BASIC AU/35-50
*GRN VAR/15: .5X TO 1.2X BASIC AU/25

2018 Panini Illusions Rookie Endorsements Red

*RED/25: .8X TO 2X BASIC AU/150
*RED/25: .6X TO 1.5X BASIC AU/75-100
*RED/25: .5X TO 1.2X BASIC AU/35-50
*RED/25: .4X TO 1X BASIC AU/25
*RED/15: .6X TO 1.5X BASIC AU/35-50
4 Saquon Barkley/25 100.00 200.00

2018 Panini Illusions Rookie Endorsements Red Variation

*RED VAR/35-49: .6X TO 1.5X BASIC AU/150
*RED VAR/35-49: .5X TO 1.2X BASIC AU/75-150
*RED VAR/35-49: .4X TO 1X BASIC AU/35-50
*RED VAR/35-49: .3X TO .8X BASIC AU/25
*RED VAR/25-30: .5X TO 1.2X BASIC AU/35-50
*RED VAR/25-30: .4X TO 1X BASIC AU/25
3 Lamar Jackson/30
4 Saquon Barkley/25 100.00 200.00

2018 Panini Illusions Rookie Idols Dual Memorabilia

*BLUE/25: .6X TO 1.5X BASIC JSY/100
*BLUE/25: .5X TO 1.2X BASIC JSY/50
*BLUE/25: .4X TO 1X BASIC JSY/25
1 B.Sanders/K.Johnson/50 8.00 20.00
2 B.Mayfield/B.Favre/50 12.00 30.00
4 J.Rosen/P.Manning/25 12.00 30.00
5 C.Ridley/J.Jones/50 8.00 20.00
6 C.Kirk/L.Fitzgerald/25 6.00 15.00
7 D.Freeman/I.Smith/50 4.00 10.00
8 C.Sutton/D.Thomas/50 5.00 12.00
9 A.Brown/J.Washington/25 8.00 20.00
10 R.Jones II/W.Dunn/25 4.00 10.00
11 D.Hopkins/K.Coutee/100 3.00 8.00
13 D.Adams/J.Moore/25 5.00 12.00
14 C.Newton/D.Moore/25 8.00 20.00
15 J.Samuels/J.Bettis/25 6.00 15.00
16 C.Martin/S.Michel/25 10.00 25.00
17 K.Ballage/R.Williams/100 3.00 8.00
18 D.Hamilton/E.Sanders/25 6.00 15.00
19 J.Washington/M.Irvin/100 5.00 12.00
20 D.Bryant/M.Gallup/100 5.00 12.00

2018 Panini Illusions Rookie Reflection Dual Patch Autographs Blue

*PATCH/49: .3X TO .8X BLUE JSY AU/25
1 Baker Mayfield Nick Chubb/15 100.00 200.00
2 Daurice Fountain Nyheim Hines/25 12.00 30.00
3 DaeSean Hamilton Royce Freeman/25 12.00 30.00
4 Bradley Chubb Courtland Sutton/25 15.00 40.00
5 J'Mon Moore Marquez Valdes-Scantling/25 15.00 40.00
6 Christian Kirk Josh Rosen/15 40.00 100.00
7 Calvin Ridley Ito Smith/15
8 Courtland Sutton Royce Freeman/25 15.00 40.00
9 Kalen Ballage Mike Gesicki/25 12.00 30.00
10 Kyle Lauletta Saquon Barkley/15 75.00 150.00
11 James Washington Mason Rudolph/20 40.00 80.00
12 Michael Gallup Mike White/25 20.00 50.00
13 Ronald Jones II Sam Darnold/15 75.00 150.00
14 Derrius Guice D.J. Chark Jr./25 EXCH 20.00 50.00
15 D.J. Moore Tre'Quan Smith/25 20.00 50.00
16 Jaylen Samuels Mark Walton/25 EXCH 12.00 30.00
17 Kerryon Johnson Sony Michel/20 40.00 100.00
18 Jaleel Scott Keke Coutee/25 EXCH 12.00 30.00
19 Anthony Miller Josh Allen/15 40.00 80.00
20 Dante Pettis Rashaad Penny/20 EXCH 20.00 50.00

2018 Panini Illusions Rookie Reflection Dual Patches

*BLUE/25: .6X TO 1.5X BASIC JSY/100
1 B.Mayfield/N.Chubb 10.00 25.00
2 D.Fountain/N.Hines 3.00 8.00
3 D.Hamilton/R.Freeman 3.00 8.00
4 B.Chubb/C.Sutton 4.00 10.00
5 J.Moore/M.Valdes-Scantling 3.00 8.00
6 C.Kirk/J.Rosen 8.00 20.00
7 C.Ridley/I.Smith 6.00 15.00
8 H.Hurst/L.Jackson 10.00 25.00
9 K.Ballage/M.Gesicki 3.00 8.00
10 K.Lauletta/S.Barkley 12.00 30.00
11 J.Washington/M.Rudolph 6.00 15.00
12 D.Guice/D.Chark Jr. 5.00 12.00
13 R.Jones II/S.Darnold 10.00 25.00
14 D.Pettis/R.Penny 4.00 10.00
15 D.Moore/T.Smith 5.00 12.00
16 J.Samuels/M.Walton 3.00 8.00
17 K.Johnson/S.Michel 6.00 15.00
18 J.Scott/K.Coutee 3.00 8.00
19 A.Miller/J.Allen 8.00 20.00
20 M.Gallup/M.White 5.00 12.00

2018 Panini Illusions Spotlight Memorabilia

*BLUE/100: .6X TO 1.5X BASIC JSY/399
*BLUE/100: .5X TO 1.2X BASIC JSY/199
*RED/25: 1X TO 2.5X BASIC JSY/399
*RED/25: .8X TO 2X BASIC JSY/199
1 Patrick Mahomes II/199 8.00 20.00
2 DeSean Jackson/399 2.00 5.00
3 Leonard Fournette/399 2.50 6.00
4 Dak Prescott/199 3.00 8.00
5 Deshaun Watson/199 4.00 10.00
6 Rob Gronkowski/399 2.50 6.00
7 Mike Evans/399 2.00 5.00
8 David Johnson/399 2.50 6.00
9 Michael Thomas/399 2.50 6.00
10 Odell Beckham Jr./199 3.00 8.00
11 Matt Ryan/399 2.00 5.00
12 Kareem Hunt/399 2.00 5.00
13 Mitchell Trubisky/199 3.00 8.00
14 Adam Thielen/399 2.50 6.00
15 Will Fuller V/399 1.50 4.00
16 Joey Bosa/399 2.50 6.00
17 Alvin Kamara/199 2.50 6.00
18 JuJu Smith-Schuster/199 3.00 8.00
19 Matthew Stafford/399 2.00 5.00
20 Carson Wentz/199 4.00 10.00

2018 Panini Illusions Veteran Signs

*BLUE/50: .5X TO 1.2X BASIC AU/75-99
*BLUE/25: .5X TO 1.2X BASIC AU/35-50
*RED/25: .6X TO 1.5X BASIC AU/75-99
*RED/15: .6X TO 1.5X BASIC AU/35-50
1 Tyreek Hill/25 10.00 25.00
2 Fletcher Cox/50 4.00 10.00
3 Adam Thielen/15 50.00 100.00
4 Ty Montgomery/75 3.00 8.00
5 Patrick Mahomes II/15 100.00 200.00
6 Ezekiel Elliott/15 40.00 80.00
7 Hunter Henry/35 4.00 10.00
9 Aaron Donald/25 8.00 20.00
11 Christian McCaffrey/25 15.00 40.00
12 Vincent Jackson/25 6.00 15.00
13 Marqise Lee/25 5.00 12.00
16 James White/99 4.00 10.00
17 Kareem Hunt/99 8.00 20.00
18 Jake Elliott/99 12.00 30.00
20 Derrick Johnson/35 4.00 10.00
21 Corey Davis/50 5.00 12.00
22 Kenyan Drake/75 3.00 8.00
23 Xavier Rhodes/99 3.00 8.00
24 Chris Long/50 12.00 30.00
25 Marvin Jones Jr./35 4.00 10.00
26 JuJu Smith-Schuster/50 10.00 25.00
27 Melvin Ingram/99 3.00 8.00
30 Jamal Adams/99 4.00 10.00
31 D'Onta Foreman/75 3.00 8.00
32 Marlon Humphrey/99 3.00 8.00
33 T.Y. Hilton/15 8.00 20.00
35 Pierre Garcon/50 5.00 12.00
36 Tarik Cohen/75 4.00 10.00
37 Sterling Shepard/99 4.00 10.00
38 Taywan Taylor/99 3.00 8.00
39 Alex Smith/15

2016 Panini Impeccable

1 Larry Fitzgerald 2.50 6.00
2 Kurt Warner 2.50 6.00
3 David Johnson 3.00 8.00
4 A.J. Green 3.00 8.00
5 Andy Dalton 2.50 6.00
6 Boomer Esiason 2.50 6.00
7 John Elway 5.00 12.00
8 Von Miller 2.50 6.00
9 Demaryius Thomas 2.50 6.00
10 Jameis Winston 3.00 8.00
11 Mike Evans 2.50 6.00
12 Derrick Brooks 2.00 5.00
13 Sammy Watkins 3.00 8.00
14 Thurman Thomas 2.50 6.00
15 Tyrod Taylor 2.50 6.00
16 Jim Kelly 3.00 8.00
17 Philip Rivers 3.00 8.00
18 Keenan Allen 2.50 6.00
19 LaDainian Tomlinson 2.50 6.00
20 Jeremy Langford 2.50 6.00
21 Kevin White 2.00 5.00
22 Gale Sayers 3.00 8.00
23 Jamaal Charles 2.50 6.00
24 Jeremy Maclin 2.00 5.00
25 Len Dawson 3.00 8.00
26 Paul Warfield 2.50 6.00
27 Ozzie Newsome 2.50 6.00
28 Duke Johnson 2.00 5.00
29 Andrew Luck 4.00 10.00
30 Peyton Manning 6.00 15.00
31 Johnny Unitas 5.00 12.00
32 Tony Romo 2.50 6.00
33 Dez Bryant 3.00 8.00
34 Emmitt Smith 5.00 12.00
35 Troy Aikman 4.00 10.00
36 Devonta Freeman 2.50 6.00
37 Julio Jones 3.00 8.00
38 Matt Ryan 2.50 6.00
39 Eli Manning 2.50 6.00
40 Odell Beckham Jr. 3.00 8.00
41 Michael Strahan 2.50 6.00
42 DeAndre Hopkins 2.50 6.00
43 J.J. Watt 3.00 8.00
44 Earl Campbell 3.00 8.00
45 Blake Bortles 2.00 5.00
46 Allen Robinson 2.50 6.00
47 Maurice Jones-Drew 2.00 5.00
48 Joe Namath 4.00 10.00
49 Brandon Marshall 2.00 5.00
50 Darrelle Revis 2.00 5.00
51 Matthew Stafford 2.50 6.00
52 Ameer Abdullah 2.00 5.00
53 Barry Sanders 5.00 12.00
54 Ryan Tannehill 2.50 6.00
55 Jarvis Landry 2.50 6.00
56 Dan Marino 6.00 15.00
57 Aaron Rodgers 6.00 15.00
58 Jordy Nelson 2.50 6.00
59 Brett Favre 6.00 15.00
60 Kevin Greene 3.00 8.00
61 Cam Newton 3.00 8.00
62 Jonathan Stewart 2.00 5.00
63 Tom Brady 8.00 20.00
64 Rob Gronkowski 3.00 8.00
65 Deion Branch 2.00 5.00
66 Ryan Mathews 2.50 6.00
67 Jordan Matthews 2.50 6.00
68 Randall Cunningham 2.50 6.00
69 Derek Carr 3.00 8.00
70 Amari Cooper 3.00 8.00
71 Bo Jackson 4.00 10.00
72 Todd Gurley 3.00 8.00
73 Marshall Faulk 2.50 6.00
74 Tavon Austin 2.00 5.00
75 Joe Flacco 2.50 6.00
76 Steve Smith Sr. 2.50 6.00
77 Ray Lewis 3.00 8.00
78 Drew Brees 3.00 8.00
79 Brandin Cooks 2.50 6.00
80 Archie Manning 2.50 6.00
81 Steve Young 4.00 10.00
82 Carlos Hyde 2.00 5.00
83 Jerry Rice 5.00 12.00
84 Joe Montana 8.00 20.00
85 Russell Wilson 4.00 10.00
86 Thomas Rawls 2.00 5.00
87 Steve Largent 3.00 8.00
88 Hines Ward 2.50 6.00
89 Ben Roethlisberger 3.00 8.00
90 Antonio Brown 3.00 8.00
91 Jerome Bettis 3.00 8.00
92 Marcus Mariota 3.00 8.00
93 Eddie George 2.50 6.00
94 DeMarco Murray 2.50 6.00
95 Teddy Bridgewater 2.50 6.00
96 Adrian Peterson 3.00 8.00
97 Warren Moon 3.00 8.00
98 Kirk Cousins 3.00 8.00
99 Matt Jones 2.50 6.00
100 John Riggins 2.50 6.00
101 Jalen Ramsey AU RC 5.00 12.00
102 Tajae Sharpe AU RC 4.00 10.00
103 Jacoby Brissett AU RC 4.00 10.00
104 Moritz Bohringer AU RC 3.00 8.00
105 Reggie Ragland AU RC 3.00 8.00
106 Rashard Higgins AU RC 3.00 8.00
107 DeForest Buckner AU RC 3.00 8.00
108 Kolby Listenbee AU RC 3.00 8.00
109 Aaron Burbridge AU RC 3.00 8.00
110 Myles Jack AU RC 4.00 10.00
111 Jerell Adams AU RC 3.00 8.00
112 Kelvin Taylor AU RC 3.00 8.00
113 Eli Apple AU RC 4.00 10.00
114 Nate Sudfeld AU RC 3.00 8.00
115 Jake Rudock AU RC 3.00 8.00
116 Noah Spence AU RC 3.00 8.00
117 Sean Davis AU RC 8.00 20.00
119 Jordan Payton AU RC 3.00 8.00
120 Kamalei Correa AU RC 3.00 8.00
121 Jeff Driskel AU RC 3.00 8.00
122 Vernon Hargreaves III AU RC 5.00 12.00
123 Brandon Doughty AU RC 3.00 8.00
124 Daniel Lasco AU RC 3.00 8.00
125 Karl Joseph AU RC 3.00 8.00
126 Thomas Duarte AU RC 3.00 8.00
127 Demarcus Ayers AU RC 3.00 8.00
128 Sheldon Rankins AU RC 4.00 10.00
129 Kenny Lawler AU RC 5.00 12.00
130 Daniel Braverman AU RC 3.00 8.00
131 Keanu Neal AU RC 3.00 8.00
132 Nick Vannett AU RC 3.00 8.00
133 Kenny Clark AU RC 3.00 8.00
134 Keith Marshall AU RC 3.00 8.00
135 Charone Peake AU RC 3.00 8.00
136 Jaylon Smith AU RC 12.00 30.00
137 Mackensie Alexander AU RC 3.00 8.00
139 Kevin Dodd AU RC 3.00 8.00
140 Jarran Reed AU RC 3.00 8.00
141 A'Shawn Robinson AU RC 3.00 8.00
142 Robert Nkemdiche AU RC 4.00 10.00
143 Adam Gotsis AU RC 3.00 8.00
144 Emmanuel Ogbah AU RC 4.00 10.00
145 Austin Johnson AU RC 3.00 8.00
146 Vernon Butler AU RC 3.00 8.00
148 Austin Hooper AU RC 3.00 8.00
149 Su'a Cravens AU RC 6.00 15.00
150 Vonn Bell AU RC 4.00 10.00
151 J.Goff HEL PAT AU RC 75.00 150.00
152 C.Wentz HEL PAT AU RC 200.00 400.00
153 J.Bosa HEL PAT AU RC 20.00 50.00
154 E.Elliott HEL PAT AU RC 200.00 400.00
155 C.Coleman HEL PAT AU RC 15.00 40.00
156 W.Fuller HEL PAT AU RC 15.00 40.00
157 J.Doctson HEL PAT AU RC 12.00 30.00
158 L.Treadwell HEL PAT AU RC 12.00 30.00
159 P.Lynch HEL PAT AU RC 10.00 25.00
160 H.Henry HEL PAT AU RC 10.00 25.00
161 S.Shepard HEL PAT AU RC 12.00 30.00
162 D.Henry HEL PAT AU RC 25.00 60.00
163 M.Thomas HEL PAT AU RC 20.00 50.00
164 C.Hackenberg HEL PAT AU RC 10.00 25.00
165 T.Boyd HEL PAT AU RC 12.00 30.00
166 K.Drake HEL PAT AU RC 15.00 40.00
167 T.Davis HEL PAT AU RC 10.00 25.00
168 B.Miller HEL PAT AU RC 10.00 25.00
169 L.Carroo HEL PAT AU RC 10.00 25.00
170 C.Prosise HEL PAT AU RC 10.00 25.00
171 D.Washington HEL PAT AU RC 10.00 25.00
172 C.Kessler HEL PAT AU RC 10.00 25.00
173 D.Robinson HEL PAT AU RC 10.00 25.00
174 C.Cook HEL PAT AU RC 12.00 30.00
175 C.Moore HEL PAT AU RC 12.00 30.00
176 M.Bohringer HEL PAT AU RC 10.00 25.00
177 R.Louis HEL PAT AU RC 10.00 25.00
178 P.Cooper HEL PAT AU RC 10.00 25.00
179 T.Ervin HEL PAT AU RC 10.00 25.00
180 K.Dixon HEL PAT AU RC 10.00 25.00
181 D.Prescott HEL PAT AU RC 100.00 200.00
182 D.Booker HEL PAT AU RC 12.00 30.00
183 C.Jones HEL PAT AU RC 10.00 25.00
184 P.Perkins HEL PAT AU RC 10.00 25.00
185 J.Howard HEL PAT AU RC 25.00 60.00
186 W.Smallwood HEL PAT AU RC 10.00 25.00
187 J.Williams HEL PAT AU RC 10.00 25.00
188 K.Hogan HEL PAT AU RC 12.00 30.00
189 A.Collins HEL PAT AU RC 12.00 30.00
190 K.Reynolds HEL PAT AU RC 12.00 30.00

2016 Panini Impeccable Elegance Rookie Helmet and Nameplate Autographs

*NAME/15: .8X TO 2X BASIC RC JSY AU/75
152 Carson Wentz 400.00 800.00
181 Dak Prescott 200.00 400.00

2016 Panini Impeccable Silver

*VETS/25: .6X TO 1.5X BASIC CARDS/75
*ROOK/25: .6X TO 1.5X BASIC RC AU/99

2016 Panini Impeccable Elegance Retired Patch Autographs

4 Joe Namath/15 100.00 200.00
5 Warrick Dunn/50
6 Marcus Allen/30 12.00 30.00
8 Marvin Harrison/15 20.00 50.00
9 Ray Lewis/50 150.00 300.00
10 Champ Bailey/50 12.00 30.00

2016 Panini Impeccable Elegance Veteran Patch Autographs

*GOLD/25: .6X TO 1.5X BASIC JSY AU/75-99
*GOLD/25: .5X TO 1.2X BASIC JSY AU/55
*GOLD/25: .4X TO 1X BASIC JSY AU/25-30
*GOLD/25: .3X TO .8X BASIC JSY AU/15
*GOLD/15: .5X TO 1.2X BASIC JSY AU/25
*GOLD/15: .4X TO 1X BASIC JSY AU/15
1 A.J. Green/75 25.00 50.00
4 Allen Robinson/99 6.00 15.00
7 Antonio Gates/75 5.00 12.00
9 Blake Bortles/20 8.00 20.00
10 Duke Johnson/99 5.00 12.00
11 Luke Kuechly/25 40.00 80.00
12 Emmanuel Sanders/15 15.00 40.00
13 Ameer Abdullah/99 5.00 12.00
14 David Johnson/99 20.00 50.00
16 DeMarcus Ware/99 15.00 40.00
17 Derek Carr/85 30.00 60.00
18 Dez Bryant/25 40.00 80.00
21 Antonio Brown/15 40.00 80.00
22 Eric Decker/25 8.00 20.00
23 Jamaal Charles/25 10.00 25.00
24 Jameis Winston/15 40.00 80.00
25 Jarvis Landry/99 6.00 15.00
27 Jeremy Langford/99 6.00 15.00
28 Kirk Cousins/99 15.00 40.00
29 Marcus Mariota/25 40.00 80.00
30 Matt Ryan/15
33 Philip Rivers/15 30.00 60.00
34 Andy Dalton/15 12.00 30.00
35 Teddy Bridgewater/15 12.00 30.00
37 Clay Matthews/20 30.00 60.00
38 Ryan Tannehill/30 10.00 25.00
39 Sammy Watkins/99 8.00 20.00
40 Stefon Diggs/99 10.00 25.00
41 T.J. Yeldon/99 5.00 12.00
43 Todd Gurley/99 30.00 60.00
46 Travis Kelce/99 8.00 20.00
47 Tyler Eifert/99 6.00 15.00
49 Tyrod Taylor/55 8.00 20.00
50 Von Miller/25 40.00 80.00

2016 Panini Impeccable Impeccable Stats Autographs

3 Ameer Abdullah/36 6.00 15.00
4 David Johnson/55 25.00 50.00
5 Duke Johnson/39 6.00 15.00
6 Jeremy Langford/83 6.00 15.00
7 Devin Funchess/31 6.00 15.00
10 Karlos Williams/47 6.00 15.00
15 Stefon Diggs/40 8.00 20.00

2016 Panini Impeccable Indelible Ink

3 Andre Reed/15 20.00 50.00
4 Rod Woodson/15 25.00 50.00
7 Travis Kelce/50 10.00 25.00
9 Rocky Bleier/15 75.00 150.00
12 Mike Evans/25 15.00 40.00
14 Brock Osweiler/50 6.00 15.00
15 Doug Baldwin/25 40.00 80.00
19 Randall Cunningham/25 25.00 50.00
22 Carl Eller/15 10.00 25.00
24 Ickey Woods/21 8.00 20.00
26 Troy Brown/50 12.00 30.00
27 Dan Hampton/17 10.00 25.00
30 Allen Robinson/50 8.00 20.00
39 Devonta Freeman/50 8.00 20.00
40 John Brown/50 8.00 20.00
42 Ozzie Newsome/30 15.00 40.00
47 Carlos Hyde/50 6.00 15.00
48 Ron Jaworski/20 10.00 25.00
49 Thomas Rawls/50 6.00 15.00

2017 Panini Impeccable

1 Jordan Matthews 2.00 5.00
2 Tyrod Taylor 2.50 6.00
3 Eli Manning 2.50 6.00
4 DeSean Jackson 2.50 6.00
5 Melvin Gordon 2.50 6.00
6 Julian Edelman 3.00 8.00
7 Andrew Luck 4.00 10.00
8 Jeremy Langford 2.50 6.00
9 Dez Bryant 3.00 8.00
10 C.J. Anderson 2.50 6.00
11 Alshon Jeffery 2.50 6.00
12 LeSean McCoy 3.00 8.00
13 Odell Beckham Jr. 3.00 8.00
14 Carson Palmer 2.50 6.00
15 Joey Bosa 3.00 8.00
16 Carlos Hyde 2.00 5.00
17 Frank Gore 2.50 6.00
18 Andy Dalton 2.50 6.00
19 Ryan Tannehill 2.50 6.00
20 Demaryius Thomas 2.50 6.00
21 Matt Ryan 3.00 8.00
22 Sammy Watkins 3.00 8.00
23 Brandon Marshall 2.00 5.00
24 David Johnson 3.00 8.00
25 Alex Smith 2.50 6.00
26 Pierre Garcon 2.50 6.00
27 T.Y. Hilton 2.50 6.00
28 Jeremy Hill 2.00 5.00
29 Jay Ajayi 2.50 6.00
30 Isaiah Crowell 2.00 5.00
31 Devonta Freeman 2.50 6.00
32 Jameis Winston 3.00 8.00
33 Blake Bortles 2.00 5.00
34 Larry Fitzgerald 2.50 6.00
35 Jeremy Maclin 2.00 5.00
36 Mike Glennon 2.50 6.00
37 Dak Prescott 3.00 8.00
38 A.J. Green 3.00 8.00
39 Jarvis Landry 2.50 6.00
40 Corey Coleman 2.00 5.00
41 Julio Jones 3.00 8.00
42 Doug Martin 2.50 6.00
43 Allen Robinson 2.50 6.00
44 Philip Rivers 3.00 8.00
45 Tyreek Hill 3.00 8.00
46 Jordan Howard 3.00 8.00
47 Ezekiel Elliott 4.00 10.00
48 Von Miller 2.50 6.00
49 Carson Wentz 4.00 10.00
50 Myles Garrett RC 6.00 15.00
51 Le'Veon Bell 2.50 6.00
52 Cam Newton 3.00 8.00
53 Marcus Mariota 3.00 8.00
54 Rob Gronkowski 3.00 8.00
55 Stefon Diggs 3.00 8.00
56 Todd Gurley II 3.00 8.00
57 Kirk Cousins 3.00 8.00
58 Allen Hurns 2.00 5.00
59 Michael Thomas 3.00 8.00
60 Golden Tate III 2.00 5.00
61 Antonio Brown 3.00 8.00
62 Jonathan Stewart 2.00 5.00
63 DeMarco Murray 2.50 6.00
64 Derek Carr 3.00 8.00
65 Adrian Peterson 3.00 8.00
66 Tavon Austin 2.00 5.00
67 Jordan Reed 2.00 5.00
68 Khalil Mack 3.00 8.00
69 Russell Wilson 4.00 10.00
70 Marvin Jones Jr. 2.00 5.00
71 Lamar Miller 2.00 5.00
72 Kelvin Benjamin 2.50 6.00
73 Quincy Enunwa 2.00 5.00
74 Marshawn Lynch 2.50 6.00
75 LeGarrette Blount 2.50 6.00
76 Joe Flacco 2.50 6.00
77 Terrelle Pryor Sr. 2.00 5.00
78 Matt Forte 2.00 5.00
79 Eddie Lacy 2.00 5.00
80 Aaron Rodgers 6.00 15.00
81 DeAndre Hopkins 2.50 6.00
82 Tom Brady 8.00 20.00
83 Sam Bradford 2.00 5.00
84 Amari Cooper 3.00 8.00
85 Jason Witten 2.50 6.00
86 Travis Kelce 3.00 8.00
87 Drew Brees 3.00 8.00
88 Eric Decker 2.00 5.00
89 Richard Sherman 3.00 8.00
90 Jordy Nelson 2.50 6.00
91 J.J. Watt 3.00 8.00
92 Brandin Cooks 2.50 6.00
93 Latavius Murray 2.00 5.00
94 Jared Goff 3.00 8.00
95 Jamaal Charles 2.50 6.00
96 Mike Wallace 2.00 5.00
97 Mark Ingram 2.50 6.00
98 Matthew Stafford 2.50 6.00
99 Ben Roethlisberger 3.00 8.00
100 Randall Cobb 2.50 6.00
101 Mitchell Trubisky HEL PAT/75 RC 100.00 200.00
102 Leonard Fournette HEL PAT/75 RC 50.00 100.00
103 Corey Davis HEL PAT/75 RC 15.00 40.00
104 Mike Williams HEL PAT/75 RC 15.00 40.00
105 Christian McCaffrey HEL PAT/75 RC 60.00 125.00
106 John Ross III HEL PAT/75 RC 12.00 30.00
107 Patrick Mahomes II HEL PAT/75 RC 400.00 800.00
108 Deshaun Watson HEL PAT/75 RC 150.00 300.00
109 O.J. Howard HEL PAT/61 RC 12.00 30.00
110 Evan Engram HEL PAT/75 RC 12.00 30.00
111 Zay Jones HEL PAT/75 RC 12.00 30.00
112 Curtis Samuel HEL PAT/75 RC 12.00 30.00
113 Dalvin Cook HEL PAT/75 RC 50.00 100.00
114 Joe Mixon HEL PAT/75 RC 20.00 50.00
115 DeShone Kizer HEL PAT/75 RC EXCH 10.00 25.00
116 JuJu Smith-Schuster HEL PAT/75 RC 25.00 60.00
117 Alvin Kamara HEL PAT/75 RC 40.00 100.00

118 Cooper Kupp HEL PAT/75 RC 15.00 40.00
119 Taywan Taylor HEL PAT/75 RC 10.00 25.00
120 ArDarius Stewart HEL PAT/75 RC 10.00 25.00
121 Carlos Henderson HEL PAT/75 RC 10.00 25.00
122 Chris Godwin HEL PAT/75 RC 12.00 30.00
123 Kareem Hunt HEL PAT/75 RC 25.00 60.00
124 Davis Webb HEL PAT/75 RC 10.00 25.00
125 D'Onta Foreman HEL PAT/75 RC 12.00 30.00
126 Kenny Golladay HEL PAT/75 RC 15.00 40.00
127 C.J. Beathard HEL PAT/75 RC 10.00 25.00
128 James Conner HEL PAT/75 RC 20.00 50.00
129 Amara Darboh HEL PAT/75 RC 10.00 25.00
130 Dede Westbrook HEL PAT/75 RC 10.00 25.00
131 Samaje Perine HEL PAT/75 RC 10.00 25.00
132 Josh Reynolds HEL PAT/75 RC 10.00 25.00
133 Mack Hollins HEL PAT/74 RC 10.00 25.00
134 Joe Williams HEL PAT/72 RC 10.00 25.00
135 Jamaal Williams HEL PAT/75 RC 10.00 25.00
136 R. Joshua Dobbs HEL PAT/75 RC 12.00 30.00
137 Wayne Gallman HEL PAT/75 RC 12.00 30.00
138 Marlon Mack HEL PAT/75 RC 15.00 40.00
139 Jeremy McNichols HEL PAT/75 RC 10.00 25.00
140 Nathan Peterman HEL PAT/75 RC 12.00 30.00
141 Sidney Jones AU RC 3.00 8.00
142 Elijah Hood AU RC 3.00 8.00
143 Kevin King AU RC 4.00 10.00
144 Jabrill Peppers AU RC 5.00 12.00
145 Jonnu Smith AU RC 3.00 8.00
146 Adam Shaheen AU RC 3.00 8.00
147 Malik Hooker AU RC 3.00 8.00
149 Noah Brown AU RC 4.00 10.00
150 Charles Harris AU RC 3.00 8.00
151 Solomon Thomas AU RC 3.00 8.00
152 Elijah Qualls AU RC 3.00 8.00
153 Tarik Cohen AU RC 15.00 40.00
154 Jake Butt AU RC 4.00 10.00
155 Jordan Leggett AU RC 3.00 8.00
156 Adoree' Jackson AU RC 4.00 10.00
157 Malik McDowell AU RC 3.00 8.00
158 Cameron Sutton AU RC 3.00 8.00
159 Quincy Wilson AU RC 3.00 8.00
160 DeMarcus Walker AU RC 3.00 8.00
161 Stacy Coley AU RC 3.00 8.00
162 Gareon Conley AU RC 3.00 8.00
163 Tim Williams AU RC 4.00 10.00
164 Jamal Adams AU RC 3.00 8.00
165 Jordan Willis AU RC 3.00 8.00
166 Brad Kaaya AU RC 3.00 8.00
167 Marlon Humphrey AU RC 3.00 8.00
168 Chad Hansen AU RC 3.00 8.00
169 Raekwon McMillan AU RC 3.00 8.00
170 Derek Barnett AU RC 4.00 10.00
171 T.J. Watt AU RC 25.00 50.00
172 Gerald Everett AU RC 3.00 8.00
173 Tre'Davious White AU RC 3.00 8.00
174 Jarrad Davis AU RC 4.00 10.00
175 Josh Malone AU RC 3.00 8.00
176 Brian Hill AU RC 3.00 8.00
177 Marshon Lattimore AU RC 4.00 10.00
178 Chad Kelly AU RC 30.00 60.00
179 Ryan Switzer AU RC 4.00 10.00
180 Desmond King AU RC 4.00 10.00
181 Taco Charlton AU RC 3.00 8.00
182 Isaiah Ford AU RC 3.00 8.00
183 Zach Cunningham AU RC 4.00 10.00
184 Jonathan Allen AU RC 4.00 10.00
185 Malachi Dupre AU RC 3.00 8.00
187 Matthew Dayes AU RC 3.00 8.00
189 Shelton Gibson AU RC 3.00 8.00
190 Donnel Pumphrey AU RC 4.00 10.00

2017 Panini Impeccable Elegance Rookie Helmet and Glove Autographs

*HEL GLOVE/15: .8X TO 2X HEL JSY AU/75
107 Patrick Mahomes II 900.00 1500.00
108 Deshaun Watson 300.00 600.00

2017 Panini Impeccable Elegance Rookie Helmet and Nameplate Autographs

*HEL NAME/25: .6X TO 1.5X HEL JSY AU/75
107 Patrick Mahomes II 800.00 1200.00
108 Deshaun Watson 300.00 600.00

2017 Panini Impeccable Gold

*GOLD/25: .6X TO 1.5X BASIC RC AU/75

2017 Panini Impeccable Silver

*VETS: .6X TO 1.5X BASIC CARDS/75
*ROOK AU/49: .5X TO 1.2X BASIC AU/49

2017 Panini Impeccable Elegance Retired Patch Autographs

2 Phil Simms/25 12.00 30.00
4 Jerome Bettis/25 50.00 100.00
8 Sterling Sharpe/25 25.00 50.00
10 Jeff Garcia/25 10.00 25.00
12 Franco Harris/25 EXCH 15.00 40.00
20 Thurman Thomas/25 12.00 30.00

2017 Panini Impeccable Elegance Veteran Patch Autographs

*SILVER/25: .5X TO 1.2X BASIC JSY AU/49
3 Geno Atkins/49 8.00 20.00
5 Lamar Miller/49 8.00 20.00
8 Allen Robinson/49 10.00 25.00
12 Terrell Suggs/25 EXCH 30.00 60.00
13 Jarvis Landry/49 10.00 25.00
19 Brandin Cooks/49 10.00 25.00
23 Keenan Allen/49 EXCH 10.00 25.00
24 DeMarco Murray/25 EXCH 12.00 30.00
29 Cole Beasley/49 20.00 50.00
31 Emmanuel Sanders/49 12.00 30.00
35 Stefon Diggs/49 10.00 25.00
37 Tyreek Hill/49 30.00 60.00
38 C.J. Anderson/49 10.00 25.00
39 Dak Prescott/25 EXCH 60.00 125.00

2017 Panini Impeccable Impeccable Seasons Autographs

2 Carl Eller/15 20.00 40.00
7 Tim Brown/16 20.00 40.00
9 Brett Favre/16 150.00 250.00
10 Andre Reed/15 15.00 40.00
11 Bruce Smith/15 25.00 50.00
17 Dan Marino/17 150.00 250.00
18 Ray Lewis/17 60.00 125.00
19 Jerry Rice/16 100.00 200.00

2017 Panini Impeccable Impeccable Stats Autographs

2 Steve Grogan/75 5.00 12.00
5 Rod Woodson/71 12.00 30.00
6 Jarvis Landry/94 6.00 15.00
7 Ricky Williams/66 6.00 15.00
8 Willie McGinest/86 5.00 12.00
10 Emmanuel Sanders/79 8.00 20.00
11 Roger Staubach/11
12 Torry Holt/74 6.00 15.00
14 Devonta Freeman/73 6.00 15.00
16 Kellen Winslow/89 6.00 15.00
17 Charlie Joiner/65 5.00 12.00
18 Priest Holmes/72 5.00 12.00
19 Randy Moss/23 100.00 200.00
21 Drew Brees/11
22 Roger Craig/73 6.00 15.00
24 Jim Plunkett/72 6.00 15.00
25 Keenan Allen/67 6.00 15.00
26 Andre Reed/87 6.00 15.00
28 Edgerrin James/80 6.00 15.00
30 Joe Theismann/77 10.00 25.00

2017 Panini Impeccable Impeccable Victory Autographs

*SILVER/25: .5X TO 1.2X BASIC AU/49
1 C.J. Anderson/49 8.00 20.00
2 Willie McGinest/49 6.00 15.00
7 Jeff Garcia/49 6.00 15.00
10 Dan Hampton/49 6.00 15.00

12 Troy Brown/49 6.00 15.00
13 Brett Keisel/49 25.00 50.00
14 Jeff Saturday/49 6.00 15.00
16 Mark Brunell/49 8.00 20.00
18 Rob Ninkovich/49 EXCH 6.00 15.00
21 Charles Haley/49 10.00 25.00
23 Dak Prescott/25
26 Jordy Nelson/25 30.00 60.00
27 Roger Craig/49 8.00 20.00
28 Mike Singletary/25 25.00 50.00
29 Doug Williams/25
32 Don Maynard/49
33 Hines Ward/25 25.00 50.00
36 Randall Cobb/25 10.00 25.00
37 Darren Woodson/49 12.00 30.00
41 Doug Flutie/49 8.00 20.00
42 Rod Woodson/49 25.00 50.00

2017 Panini Impeccable Indelible Ink

*SILVER/25: .5X TO 1.2X BASIC AU/49
1 Ron Jaworski/49 8.00 20.00
3 Kordell Stewart/49 6.00 15.00
5 Ickey Woods/49 6.00 15.00
6 DeMarco Murray/25 10.00 25.00
9 Jarvis Landry/49 8.00 20.00
11 Jevon Kearse/49 6.00 15.00
13 Y.A. Tittle/49 10.00 25.00
15 Gary Barnidge/49 6.00 15.00
16 Steve Largent/25 12.00 30.00
17 Rodney Harrison/49 EXCH 6.00 15.00
19 Sterling Sharpe/49 8.00 20.00
21 Chad Pennington/49
23 Charlie Joiner/49 6.00 15.00
24 Marcus Allen/25 10.00 25.00
25 John Hannah/49 6.00 15.00
26 Eddie Lacy/49 6.00 15.00
27 Champ Bailey/49 8.00 20.00
29 Travis Kelce/49 10.00 25.00
31 Mark Schlereth/49 6.00 15.00
33 Cole Beasley/49 10.00 25.00
35 Steve Grogan/49 6.00 15.00
36 Ricky Williams/49 8.00 20.00
37 Priest Holmes/49 15.00 40.00
41 Carl Eller/49 6.00 15.00
43 Stefon Diggs/49 8.00 20.00
44 Jason Taylor/25 50.00 100.00
45 Geno Atkins/49 6.00 15.00
47 Torry Holt/49 8.00 20.00
49 Ozzie Newsome/49 8.00 20.00

2017 Panini Impeccable Silver NFL Shields

1 Steve Young 75.00 150.00
2 Cam Newton 30.00 80.00
3 Tom Brady 400.00 800.00
4 Julio Jones 30.00 80.00
5 Joe Montana 100.00 200.00
6 Dan Marino 100.00 200.00
7 Aaron Rodgers 100.00 200.00
8 Jim Brown 75.00 150.00
9 Andrew Luck 60.00 125.00
10 Carson Wentz 75.00 150.00
11 Jerry Rice 75.00 150.00
12 John Elway 100.00 200.00
13 John Riggins 25.00 60.00
14 Peyton Manning 75.00 150.00
15 Russell Wilson 125.00 250.00
16 Joe Namath 60.00 125.00
17 Ezekiel Elliott 100.00 200.00
18 Deion Sanders 75.00 150.00
19 Walter Payton 100.00 200.00
20 Randy Moss 75.00 150.00
21 LaDainian Tomlinson 60.00 125.00
22 Ed Reed 50.00 100.00
23 Brett Favre 100.00 200.00
24 Eric Dickerson 30.00 80.00
25 J.J. Watt 75.00 150.00
26 Drew Brees 125.00 250.00
27 Barry Sanders 100.00 200.00
28 Ray Lewis 50.00 100.00
29 Von Miller 60.00 125.00
30 Adrian Peterson 30.00 80.00
31 Michael Vick 50.00 100.00
32 Troy Aikman 75.00 150.00
33 Odell Beckham Jr. 50.00 100.00
34 Howie Long 50.00 100.00
35 Dak Prescott 75.00 150.00
36 Christian McCaffrey 60.00 125.00
37 Deshaun Watson 150.00 300.00
38 Mitchell Trubisky 100.00 200.00
39 Leonard Fournette 100.00 200.00
40 Dalvin Cook 75.00 150.00

2018 Panini Impeccable

1 Joe Namath 4.00 10.00
2 Devonta Freeman 2.50 6.00
3 Eli Manning 2.50 6.00
4 Melvin Gordon 2.50 6.00
5 LeSean McCoy 3.00 8.00
6 Tony Gonzalez 2.50 6.00
7 Eddie George 2.50 6.00
8 Keenan Allen 2.50 6.00
9 Ed Reed 2.50 6.00
10 Drew Brees 3.00 8.00
11 Charles Woodson 3.00 8.00
12 Joe Montana 8.00 20.00
13 A.J. Green 3.00 8.00
14 Adam Thielen 3.00 8.00
15 Jimmy Garoppolo 4.00 10.00
16 Derek Carr 3.00 8.00
17 Davante Adams 2.50 6.00
18 Aaron Rodgers 6.00 15.00
19 Leonard Fournette 3.00 8.00
20 Ezekiel Elliott 4.00 10.00
21 Marquise Goodwin 2.00 5.00
22 Antonio Brown 3.00 8.00
23 David Johnson 3.00 8.00
24 Kelvin Benjamin 2.50 6.00
25 John Elway 5.00 12.00
26 Marshawn Lynch 2.50 6.00
27 Tom Brady 8.00 20.00
28 Carson Wentz 4.00 10.00
29 Derrick Henry 3.00 8.00
30 Blake Bortles 2.00 5.00
31 Aaron Donald 3.00 8.00
32 Philip Rivers 3.00 8.00
33 Shaun Alexander 2.00 5.00
34 Jamal Adams 2.50 6.00
35 Le'Veon Bell 2.50 6.00
36 Brian Urlacher 3.00 8.00
37 Tyrod Taylor 2.50 6.00
38 Kirk Cousins 3.00 8.00
39 Cam Newton 3.00 8.00
40 Jimmy Graham 3.00 8.00
41 Alvin Kamara 2.50 6.00
42 Ben Roethlisberger 3.00 8.00
43 Rob Gronkowski 3.00 8.00
44 Case Keenum 2.50 6.00
45 DeAndre Hopkins 2.50 6.00
46 Ryan Tannehill 2.50 6.00
47 Eric Dickerson 3.00 8.00
48 Evan Engram 2.00 5.00
49 Matt Ryan 2.50 6.00
50 Dak Prescott 3.00 8.00
51 Andy Dalton 2.50 6.00
52 Odell Beckham Jr. 3.00 8.00
53 D'Onta Foreman 2.00 5.00
54 Jordan Howard 3.00 8.00
55 Doug Baldwin 2.50 6.00
56 Travis Kelce 3.00 8.00
57 Bruce Smith 2.50 6.00
58 Marvin Jones Jr. 2.00 5.00
59 Kareem Hunt 2.50 6.00
60 Kenyan Drake 2.00 5.00
61 Zach Ertz 2.50 6.00
62 Chandler Jones 2.00 5.00
63 Patrick Mahomes II 8.00 20.00
64 Allen Robinson 2.50 6.00
65 Josh Gordon 2.00 5.00
66 Jarvis Landry 2.50 6.00
67 Jay Ajayi 2.50 6.00
68 Joe Flacco 2.50 6.00
69 JuJu Smith-Schuster 3.00 8.00
70 Emmitt Smith 5.00 12.00
71 Alex Smith 2.50 6.00
72 Julio Jones 3.00 8.00
73 Julius Peppers 2.50 6.00
74 Michael Thomas 3.00 8.00
75 Mitchell Trubisky 3.00 8.00
76 Marcus Mariota 3.00 8.00
77 Barry Sanders 5.00 12.00
78 Julian Edelman 3.00 8.00
79 Mike Evans 2.50 6.00
80 Brett Favre 6.00 15.00
81 Jameis Winston 2.50 6.00
82 Von Miller 2.50 6.00
83 Chris Thompson 2.00 5.00
84 Larry Fitzgerald 2.50 6.00
85 Jared Goff 3.00 8.00
86 Khalil Mack 3.00 8.00
87 Russell Wilson 4.00 10.00
88 Randy Moss 2.50 6.00
89 Deshaun Watson 4.00 10.00
90 Todd Gurley II 3.00 8.00
91 Andrew Luck 4.00 10.00
92 Joe Mixon 2.50 6.00
93 Emmanuel Sanders 3.00 8.00
94 Eric Weddle 2.00 5.00
95 Dan Marino 6.00 15.00
96 Christian McCaffrey 3.00 8.00
97 Jermaine Kearse 2.00 5.00
98 Matthew Stafford 2.50 6.00
99 Peyton Manning 6.00 15.00
100 T.Y. Hilton 2.50 6.00
101 Anthony Miller HEL PAT AU RC 15.00 40.00
102 Baker Mayfield HEL PAT AU RC 150.00 300.00
103 Bradley Chubb HEL PAT AU RC EXCH 15.00 40.00
104 Calvin Ridley HEL PAT AU RC 25.00 60.00
105 Christian Kirk HEL PAT AU RC 15.00 40.00
106 Courtland Sutton HEL PAT AU RC 15.00 40.00
107 D.J. Moore HEL PAT AU RC EXCH 20.00 50.00
108 DaeSean Hamilton HEL PAT AU RC 12.00 30.00
109 Dante Pettis HEL PAT AU RC 15.00 40.00
110 Daurice Fountain HEL PAT AU RC 12.00 30.00
111 Derrius Guice HEL PAT AU RC 20.00 50.00
112 D.J. Chark Jr. HEL PAT AU RC 12.00 30.00
113 Hayden Hurst HEL PAT AU RC 12.00 30.00
114 Ito Smith HEL PAT AU RC 12.00 30.00
115 Jaleel Scott HEL PAT AU RC 10.00 25.00
116 James Washington HEL PAT AU RC 20.00 50.00
117 Jaylen Samuels HEL PAT AU RC 12.00 30.00
118 J'Mon Moore HEL PAT AU RC 10.00 25.00
119 Josh Allen HEL PAT AU RC 75.00 150.00
120 Josh Rosen HEL PAT AU RC 60.00 125.00
121 Kalen Ballage HEL PAT AU RC 12.00 30.00
122 Keke Coutee HEL PAT AU RC 12.00 30.00
123 Kerryon Johnson HEL PAT AU RC EXCH 30.00 60.00
124 Kyle Lauletta HEL PAT AU RC 15.00 40.00
125 Lamar Jackson HEL PAT AU RC 75.00 150.00
126 Mark Walton HEL PAT AU RC 12.00 30.00
127 Marquez Valdes-Scantling HEL PAT AU RC 12.00 30.00
128 Mason Rudolph HEL PAT AU RC 25.00 60.00
129 Michael Gallup HEL PAT AU RC 20.00 50.00
130 Mike Gesicki HEL PAT AU RC 12.00 30.00
131 Mike White HEL PAT AU RC 12.00 30.00
132 Nick Chubb HEL PAT AU RC 40.00 80.00
133 Nyheim Hines HEL PAT AU RC 12.00 30.00
134 Rashaad Penny HEL PAT AU RC EXCH 15.00 40.00
135 Ronald Jones II HEL PAT AU RC 10.00 25.00
136 Royce Freeman HEL PAT AU RC 12.00 30.00
137 Sam Darnold HEL PAT AU RC 125.00 250.00
138 Saquon Barkley HEL PAT AU RC EXCH 150.00 300.00
139 Sony Michel HEL PAT AU RC 30.00 80.00
140 Tre'Quan Smith HEL PAT AU RC 15.00 40.00
141 Marcell Ateman AU RC 4.00 10.00
142 Bo Scarbrough AU RC 4.00 10.00
143 Denzel Ward AU RC 8.00 20.00
144 Shaquem Griffin AU RC 8.00 20.00
145 Minkah Fitzpatrick AU RC 6.00 15.00
146 Terrell Edmunds AU RC 10.00 25.00
147 Roquan Smith AU RC 10.00 25.00
148 Dallas Goedert AU RC 4.00 10.00
149 Derwin James AU RC 10.00 25.00
150 Simmie Cobbs Jr. AU RC 5.00 12.00
151 Arden Key AU RC 3.00 8.00
153 Carlton Davis AU RC 4.00 10.00
154 Cedrick Wilson Jr. AU RC 3.00 8.00
155 Jaire Alexander AU RC 5.00 12.00
156 John Kelly AU RC 4.00 10.00
157 Jordan Lasley AU RC 3.00 8.00
158 Josh Adams AU RC 6.00 15.00
159 Joshua Jackson AU RC 6.00 15.00
160 Leighton Vander Esch AU RC 10.00 25.00
161 Malik Jefferson AU RC 4.00 10.00
162 Marcus Davenport AU RC 6.00 15.00
163 Mark Andrews AU RC 5.00 12.00
164 Mike Hughes AU RC 5.00 12.00
165 Rashaan Evans AU RC 5.00 12.00
166 Ronnie Harrison AU RC 4.00 10.00
167 Tremaine Edmunds AU RC 6.00 15.00
168 Daron Payne AU RC 5.00 12.00
169 Ian Thomas AU RC 3.00 8.00
170 Justin Jackson AU RC 4.00 10.00
171 Maurice Hurst AU RC 4.00 10.00
173 Vita Vea AU RC 5.00 12.00
175 Dorance Armstrong Jr. AU RC 3.00 8.00
176 Duke Dawson AU RC 3.00 8.00
177 Lorenzo Carter AU RC 3.00 8.00
178 Quenton Nelson AU RC 5.00 12.00
179 Trey Quinn AU RC 3.00 8.00
181 Austin Proehl AU RC 3.00 8.00
182 Dalton Schultz AU RC 4.00 10.00
183 Dylan Cantrell AU RC 3.00 8.00
184 Braxton Berrios AU RC 3.00 8.00
185 Chase Edmonds AU RC 3.00 8.00
186 Ray-Ray McCloud AU RC 3.00 8.00
187 Lavon Coleman AU RC 4.00 10.00
188 Logan Woodside AU RC 5.00 12.00
189 Roc Thomas AU RC 4.00 10.00
190 Jordan Wilkins AU RC 4.00 10.00

2018 Panini Impeccable Elegance Rookie Helmet and Glove Autographs

*GLOVE AU/15: .8X TO 2X BASIC JSY AU/75
119 Josh Allen 125.00 250.00
137 Sam Darnold 200.00 400.00
138 Saquon Barkley EXCH 350.00 500.00

2018 Panini Impeccable Elegance Rookie Helmet and Nameplate Autographs

*NAME/25: .6X TO 1.5X BASIC JSY AU/75
102 Baker Mayfield 200.00 350.00
119 Josh Allen 100.00 200.00
138 Saquon Barkley EXCH 250.00 400.00

2018 Panini Impeccable Red

*RED/49: .5X TO 1.2X BASIC AU/75

2018 Panini Impeccable Silver

*VETS/25: .6X TO 1.5X BASIC CARDS/75
*ROOK AU/25: .6X TO 1.5X BASIC AU/75

2018 Panini Impeccable Elegance Retired Patch Autographs

*SILVER/25: .6X TO 1.5X BASIC JSY AU/75
*SILVER/25: .5X TO 1.2X BASIC JSY AU/49
1 Tony Gonzalez/25 15.00 40.00
2 Tedy Bruschi/49 15.00 40.00
3 Rod Woodson/49 12.00 30.00
4 Clinton Portis/49 8.00 20.00
6 Vance Johnson/75 6.00 15.00
7 Paul Hornung/75 10.00 25.00
8 Thurman Thomas/25 12.00 30.00
9 Bob Lilly/25 12.00 30.00
10 Heath Miller/25 15.00 40.00
11 Andre Reed/25 12.00 30.00
13 Barry Sanders/15 100.00 200.00
14 Ozzie Newsome/49 10.00 25.00
16 Tim Brown/25 15.00 40.00
17 Bo Jackson/25 EXCH 50.00 100.00
19 Steve Largent/25 EXCH 15.00 40.00
20 Michael Vick/49 30.00 60.00

2018 Panini Impeccable Elegance Veteran Patch Autographs

*SILVER/25: .6X TO 1.5X BASIC JSY AU/75
*SILVER/25: .5X TO 1.2X BASIC JSY AU/39-49
1 Derek Carr/25 EXCH 15.00 40.00
7 Luke Kuechly/39 EXCH
8 Travis Kelce/49 12.00 30.00
10 Clay Matthews/25 EXCH 12.00 30.00
13 Tyler Lockett/75 8.00 20.00
14 Melvin Gordon/49 EXCH 10.00 25.00
16 Mike Evans/49 EXCH 10.00 25.00
17 Eric Berry/75 15.00 40.00
18 T.J. Watt/75 8.00 20.00
19 Emmanuel Sanders/75 10.00 25.00
20 Jordan Howard/75 10.00 25.00
21 Zach Ertz/75 8.00 20.00
22 Kareem Hunt/75
23 Corey Davis/75 8.00 20.00
24 Davis Webb/75 6.00 15.00
25 JuJu Smith-Schuster/75 15.00 40.00
26 Greg Olsen/75 8.00 20.00
27 Aaron Donald/15 20.00 50.00
30 Carson Wentz/15 60.00 125.00
33 T.Y. Hilton/25
34 C.J. Mosley/49 10.00 25.00
36 Samaje Perine/75 6.00 15.00
37 Ty Montgomery/75 6.00 15.00
38 Chris Thompson/75 6.00 15.00
39 Cooper Kupp/75 8.00 20.00

2018 Panini Impeccable Extravagance Patch Autographs

*SILVER/25: .5X TO 1.2X BASIC JSY AU/49
1 Aaron Rodgers/15 250.00 400.00
2 Joe Namath/15 90.00 150.00
4 Philip Rivers/15 40.00 80.00
6 Ray Lewis/15 75.00 150.00
7 Brian Dawkins/49 40.00 80.00
8 Thurman Thomas/25 12.00 30.00
9 Tim Brown/25 15.00 40.00
10 Ricky Williams/49 25.00 50.00
12 Bob Lilly/49 10.00 25.00
13 Rob Gronkowski/15 40.00 80.00
15 Jim Kelly/15

2018 Panini Impeccable Impeccable Draft Picks Autographs

8 Jack Youngblood/20 25.00 50.00

2018 Panini Impeccable Indelible Ink

*SILVER/25: .5X TO 1.2X BASIC AU/49
*SILVER/15: .5X TO 1.2X BASIC AU/25
IIAL Andrew Luck/25 30.00 60.00
IIAT Adam Thielen/25 60.00 125.00
IIAV Adam Vinatieri/49 10.00 25.00
IIBD Brian Dawkins/49 30.00 60.00
IIBG Bob Griese/25 15.00 40.00
IICH Carlos Hyde/49 6.00 15.00
IICH Chirs Hogan/49
IICO Christian Okoye/49 6.00 15.00
IICW Carson Wentz/25 60.00 125.00
IIDB1 Doug Baldwin/49 8.00 20.00
IIDB2 Deion Branch/49 6.00 15.00
IIDB3 Dick Butkus/25
IIDC Dallas Clark/49 6.00 15.00
IIDJ David Johnson/49 10.00 25.00
IIEE Ezekiel Elliott/49 40.00 80.00
IIET Earl Thomas III/49 8.00 20.00
IIFT Fran Tarkenton/49 10.00 25.00
IIFT Fred Taylor/25 8.00 20.00
IIHW Hines Ward/25 30.00 60.00
IIJG Jared Goff/25 EXCH 40.00 100.00
IIJH Jack Ham/49 15.00 40.00
IIJN Jordy Nelson/25 10.00 25.00
IIJP Jim Plunkett/49 8.00 20.00
IIJU JuJu Smith-Schuster/49 12.00 30.00
IIKC Kirk Cousins/25 40.00 80.00
IILA LaVar Arrington/49 6.00 15.00
IIMB Mark Brunell/49 6.00 15.00
IIME Mike Evans/49 EXCH 8.00 20.00
IIMG Melvin Gordon/49 EXCH
IIMS Matthew Stafford/25
IIMV Michael Vick/49 25.00 50.00
IINS Neil Smith/49 12.00 30.00
IIPM Patrick Mahomes II/49 150.00 300.00
IIRG Rich Gannon/49 8.00 20.00
IIRW Randy White/49 8.00 20.00
IITD Tony Dorsett/25
IITL Ty Law/49 15.00 40.00
IITT Thurman Thomas/49 8.00 20.00

2018 Panini Impeccable Jerseys

*SILVER/25: .6X TO 1.5X BASIC JSY/75
*SILVER/25: .5X TO 1.2X BASIC JSY/50
1 Aaron Rodgers/50 10.00 25.00
2 Patrick Mahomes II/50 12.00 30.00
3 Deshaun Watson/50 6.00 15.00
4 Ezekiel Elliott/25 8.00 20.00
5 Carson Wentz/50 6.00 15.00
6 Dak Prescott/75 4.00 10.00
7 Rob Gronkowski/50 5.00 12.00
8 Cris Carter/25 6.00 15.00
9 Emmanuel Sanders/50 5.00 12.00
10 Mike Evans/75 3.00 8.00
11 Joe Flacco/75 3.00 8.00
12 Clay Matthews/75 3.00 8.00
13 Marshawn Lynch/50 4.00 10.00
14 Mitchell Trubisky/50 5.00 12.00
15 Kareem Hunt/75 3.00 8.00
16 Golden Tate III/75 2.50 6.00
17 Jameis Winston/50 4.00 10.00
18 Derrick Henry/50 5.00 12.00
19 Matthew Stafford/75 3.00 8.00
20 Antonio Gates/75 2.50 6.00

2018 Panini Impeccable Masterstrokes

6 Jerome Bettis/15
12 Hines Ward/25 50.00 100.00
13 Warren Moon/25 60.00 125.00
18 Roger Craig/49 8.00 20.00
19 Earl Campbell/25 50.00 100.00
20 Rich Gannon/49 8.00 20.00

2018 Panini Impeccable Silver 49ers

1 Joe Montana 100.00 200.00
2 Jerry Rice 75.00 150.00
3 Steve Young 75.00 150.00
4 Ricky Watters 25.00 60.00
5 Roger Craig 50.00 100.00

2018 Panini Impeccable Silver Broncos

1 John Elway 100.00 200.00
2 Terrell Davis 60.00 125.00
3 Shannon Sharpe 50.00 100.00
4 Peyton Manning 75.00 150.00
5 Champ Bailey 50.00 100.00

2018 Panini Impeccable Silver Hall of Famers

1 Randy Moss 75.00 150.00
2 Brian Urlacher 30.00 80.00
3 Brian Dawkins 75.00 150.00
4 Cris Carter 100.00 200.00
5 Emmitt Smith 125.00 250.00
6 Jack Lambert 125.00 250.00
7 Terry Bradshaw 100.00 200.00
8 Dan Fouts 50.00 100.00
9 Deion Sanders 100.00 200.00
10 Shannon Sharpe 50.00 100.00
11 Rod Woodson 75.00 150.00
12 John Riggins 25.00 60.00
13 Bill Parcells 50.00 100.00
14 Curtis Martin 50.00 100.00
15 Howie Long 50.00 100.00
16 Brett Favre 100.00 200.00
17 John Randle 50.00 100.00
18 Eric Dickerson 30.00 80.00
19 Jack Ham 25.00 60.00
20 Steve Largent 75.00 150.00

2018 Panini Impeccable Silver NFL Shields

1 Saquon Barkley 350.00 600.00
2 Baker Mayfield 350.00 600.00
3 Sam Darnold 125.00 250.00
4 Josh Allen 80.00 200.00
5 Josh Rosen 60.00 150.00
6 Lamar Jackson 125.00 250.00
7 Sony Michel 125.00 250.00
8 Bradley Chubb 30.00 80.00
9 D.J. Moore 40.00 100.00
10 Rashaad Penny 30.00 80.00
11 Calvin Ridley 75.00 150.00
12 Tom Brady 300.00 600.00
13 John Randle 50.00 100.00
14 Tony Gonzalez 50.00 100.00
15 Ty Law 30.00 80.00
16 Warren Sapp 25.00 60.00
17 Cris Carter 100.00 200.00
18 Randy Moss 75.00 150.00
19 Jimmy Garoppolo 75.00 150.00
20 Patrick Mahomes II 300.00 600.00
21 Aaron Rodgers 100.00 200.00
22 Joe Montana 100.00 200.00
23 Deion Sanders 100.00 200.00
24 Alvin Kamara 75.00 150.00
25 Brian Dawkins 75.00 150.00
26 Derek Carr 30.00 80.00
27 Le'Veon Bell 100.00 200.00
28 Kareem Hunt 60.00 125.00
29 Adam Thielen 100.00 200.00
30 Russell Wilson 100.00 200.00
31 Ben Roethlisberger 125.00 250.00
32 Antonio Brown 125.00 250.00
33 Matt Ryan 25.00 60.00
34 Lawrence Taylor 60.00 125.00
35 Julio Jones 30.00 80.00
36 Odell Beckham Jr. 50.00 100.00
37 Todd Gurley II 60.00 125.00
38 Carson Wentz 75.00 150.00
39 Dan Marino 100.00 200.00
40 Roger Staubach 75.00 150.00

2016 Panini Infinity

1 Tyrod Taylor 1.00 2.50
2 LeSean McCoy 1.25 3.00
3 Sammy Watkins 1.25 3.00
4 Ryan Tannehill 1.00 2.50
5 Jarvis Landry 1.00 2.50
6 Ndamukong Suh 1.00 2.50
7 Tom Brady 3.00 8.00
8 Rob Gronkowski 1.25 3.00
9 Julian Edelman 1.25 3.00
10 Matt Forte .75 2.00
11 Brandon Marshall .75 2.00
12 Eric Decker .75 2.00
13 Joe Flacco 1.00 2.50
14 Steve Smith 1.00 2.50
15 Justin Forsett 1.00 2.50
16 Andy Dalton 1.00 2.50
17 Jeremy Hill .75 2.00
18 A.J. Green 1.25 3.00
19 Duke Johnson .75 2.00
20 Gary Barnidge .75 2.00
21 Ben Roethlisberger 1.25 3.00
22 Le'Veon Bell 1.00 2.50
23 Antonio Brown 1.25 3.00
24 Brock Osweiler .75 2.00
25 Lamar Miller .75 2.00
26 DeAndre Hopkins 1.00 2.50
27 J.J. Watt 1.25 3.00
28 Andrew Luck 1.50 4.00
29 T.Y. Hilton 1.00 2.50
30 Blake Bortles .75 2.00
31 Allen Robinson 1.00 2.50
32 T.J. Yeldon .75 2.00
33 Marcus Mariota 1.25 3.00
34 DeMarco Murray 1.00 2.50
35 C.J. Anderson 1.00 2.50
36 Demaryius Thomas 1.00 2.50
37 Von Miller 1.00 2.50
38 Alex Smith 1.00 2.50
39 Jamaal Charles 1.00 2.50
40 Jeremy Maclin .75 2.00
41 Derek Carr 1.25 3.00
42 Latavius Murray .75 2.00
43 Amari Cooper 1.25 3.00
44 Philip Rivers 1.25 3.00
45 Melvin Gordon 1.00 2.50
46 Antonio Gates .75 2.00
47 Tony Romo 1.00 2.50
48 Dez Bryant 1.25 3.00
49 Jason Witten 1.00 2.50
50 Eli Manning 1.00 2.50
51 Odell Beckham Jr. 1.25 3.00
52 Sam Bradford .75 2.00
53 Jordan Matthews 1.00 2.50
54 Kirk Cousins 1.25 3.00
55 Matt Jones 1.00 2.50
56 Jordan Reed .75 2.00
57 Jay Cutler .75 2.00
58 Jeremy Langford 1.00 2.50
59 Alshon Jeffery 1.00 2.50
60 Matthew Stafford 1.00 2.50
61 Ameer Abdullah .75 2.00
62 Golden Tate III .75 2.00
63 Aaron Rodgers 2.50 6.00
64 Eddie Lacy .75 2.00
65 Clay Matthews 1.25 3.00
66 Teddy Bridgewater 1.00 2.50
67 Adrian Peterson 1.25 3.00
68 Stefon Diggs 1.00 2.50
69 Matt Ryan 1.00 2.50
70 Devonta Freeman 1.00 2.50
71 Julio Jones 1.25 3.00
72 Cam Newton 1.25 3.00
73 Kelvin Benjamin 1.00 2.50
74 Luke Kuechly 1.00 2.50
75 Drew Brees 1.25 3.00
76 Mark Ingram 1.00 2.50
77 Brandin Cooks 1.00 2.50
78 Jameis Winston 1.25 3.00
79 Doug Martin 1.00 2.50
80 Mike Evans 1.00 2.50
81 Carson Palmer 1.00 2.50
82 David Johnson 1.25 3.00
83 Larry Fitzgerald 1.00 2.50
84 Todd Gurley 1.25 3.00
85 Tavon Austin .75 2.00
86 Colin Kaepernick 1.00 2.50
87 Carlos Hyde .75 2.00
88 Russell Wilson 1.50 4.00
89 Thomas Rawls .75 2.00
90 Doug Baldwin 1.00 2.50
91 Jim Kelly 1.25 3.00
92 Thurman Thomas 1.00 2.50
93 Dan Marino 2.50 6.00
94 Curtis Martin 1.00 2.50
95 Joe Namath 1.50 4.00
96 Roger Staubach 1.50 4.00
97 Tony Dorsett 1.25 3.00
98 Y.A. Tittle 1.25 3.00
99 Lawrence Taylor 1.25 3.00
100 Randall Cunningham 1.00 2.50
101 Darrell Green 1.00 2.50
102 Ickey Woods .75 2.00
103 Ozzie Newsome 1.00 2.50
104 Terry Bradshaw 1.50 4.00
105 Franco Harris 1.25 3.00
106 Joe Greene 1.25 3.00
107 Gale Sayers 1.25 3.00
108 Brian Urlacher 1.25 3.00
109 Barry Sanders 2.00 5.00
110 Brett Favre 2.50 6.00
111 James Lofton 1.00 2.50
112 Fran Tarkenton 1.25 3.00
113 Cris Carter 1.25 3.00
114 Peyton Manning 2.50 6.00
115 Marvin Harrison 1.00 2.50
116 Fred Taylor .75 2.00
117 Warren Moon 1.25 3.00
118 Earl Campbell 1.25 3.00
119 Derrick Brooks .75 2.00
120 John Elway 2.00 5.00
121 Rod Smith 1.00 2.50
122 Len Dawson 1.25 3.00
123 Marcus Allen 1.00 2.50
124 Tim Brown 1.25 3.00
125 Charles Woodson 1.25 3.00
126 LaDainian Tomlinson 1.00 2.50
127 Kellen Winslow 1.00 2.50
128 Kurt Warner 1.00 2.50
129 Aeneas Williams .75 2.00
130 Eric Dickerson 1.00 2.50
131 Marshall Faulk 1.00 2.50
132 Joe Montana 3.00 8.00
133 Jerry Rice 2.00 5.00
134 Roger Craig 1.00 2.50
135 Steve Largent 1.25 3.00
136 Jalen Ramsey RC 1.50 4.00
137 DeForest Buckner RC 1.00 2.50
138 Leonard Floyd RC 1.25 3.00
139 Eli Apple RC 1.25 3.00
140 Vernon Hargreaves III RC 1.50 4.00
141 Sheldon Rankins RC 1.25 3.00
142 Karl Joseph RC 1.00 2.50
143 Keanu Neal RC 1.00 2.50
144 Shaq Lawson RC 1.00 2.50
145 Darron Lee RC 1.00 2.50
146 William Jackson III RC 1.25 3.00
147 Artie Burns RC 1.25 3.00
148 Kenny Clark RC 1.00 2.50
149 Robert Nkemdiche RC 1.25 3.00
150 Vernon Butler RC 1.00 2.50
151 Kevin Dodd RC 1.00 2.50
152 Jaylon Smith RC 1.00 2.50
153 Myles Jack RC 1.25 3.00
154 Chris Jones RC 1.00 2.50
155 Xavien Howard RC 1.25 3.00
156 Noah Spence RC 1.00 2.50
157 Reggie Ragland RC 1.00 2.50
158 A'Shawn Robinson RC 1.00 2.50
159 Jarran Reed RC 1.00 2.50
160 T.J. Green RC 1.50 4.00
161 Vonn Bell RC 1.25 3.00
162 Roberto Aguayo RC 1.00 2.50
163 Austin Hooper RC 1.00 2.50
164 Nick Vannett RC 1.00 2.50
165 Jacoby Brissett RC 1.25 3.00
166 Tyler Higbee RC 1.00 2.50
167 Tajae Sharpe RC 1.25 3.00
168 Jordan Payton RC 1.00 2.50
169 Nate Sudfeld RC 1.00 2.50
170 Jakeem Grant RC 1.00 2.50
171 Kolby Listenbee RC 1.00 2.50
172 Derek Watt RC 1.50 4.00
173 Cody Core RC 1.00 2.50
174 Mike Thomas RC 1.50 4.00
175 Kelvin Taylor RC 1.00 2.50
176 Aaron Burbridge RC 1.00 2.50
177 Brandon Doughty RC 1.00 2.50
178 Devin Lucien RC 1.25 3.00
179 Daniel Braverman RC 1.00 2.50
180 Daniel Lasco RC 1.00 2.50
181 Jared Goff AU RC 40.00 80.00
182 Carson Wentz AU RC 75.00 150.00
183 Joey Bosa AU RC 6.00 15.00
184 Ezekiel Elliott AU RC 60.00 125.00
185 Corey Coleman AU RC 5.00 12.00
186 Will Fuller AU RC 5.00 12.00
187 Josh Doctson AU RC 4.00 10.00
188 Laquon Treadwell AU RC 4.00 10.00
189 Paxton Lynch AU RC 3.00 8.00
190 Hunter Henry AU RC 4.00 10.00
191 Sterling Shepard AU RC 4.00 10.00
192 Derrick Henry AU RC 8.00 20.00
193 Michael Thomas AU RC 6.00 15.00
194 Christian Hackenberg AU RC 3.00 8.00
195 Kenyan Drake AU RC 5.00 12.00
196 Braxton Miller AU RC 3.00 8.00
197 Leonte Carroo AU RC 3.00 8.00
198 C.J. Prosise AU RC 3.00 8.00
199 DeAndre Washington AU RC 3.00 8.00
200 Cody Kessler AU RC 10.00 25.00
201 Tyler Boyd AU RC 8.00 20.00
202 Connor Cook AU RC 4.00 10.00
203 Chris Moore AU RC 4.00 10.00
204 Ricardo Louis AU RC 3.00 8.00
205 Pharoh Cooper AU RC 3.00 8.00
206 Tyler Ervin AU RC 3.00 8.00
207 Demarcus Robinson AU RC 3.00 8.00
208 Kenneth Dixon AU RC 3.00 8.00
209 Dak Prescott AU RC 40.00 80.00
210 Devontae Booker AU RC 4.00 10.00
211 Cardale Jones AU RC 3.00 8.00
212 Paul Perkins AU RC 3.00 8.00
213 Jordan Howard AU RC 8.00 20.00
214 Wendell Smallwood AU RC 3.00 8.00
215 Jonathan Williams AU RC 4.00 10.00
216 Kevin Hogan AU RC 4.00 10.00
217 Trevor Davis AU RC 3.00 8.00
218 Alex Collins AU RC 4.00 10.00
219 Keenan Reynolds AU RC 4.00 10.00
220 Moritz Bohringer AU RC 3.00 8.00

2016 Panini Infinity Common

*VETS/88: .6X TO 1.5X BASIC CARDS
*ROOKIES/88: .5X TO 1.2X BASIC CARDS

2016 Panini Infinity Eternal Gr8ts

1 Archie Manning 1.50 4.00
2 Jerry Rice 3.00 8.00
3 Marshall Faulk 1.50 4.00
4 Marvin Harrison 1.50 4.00
5 Michael Irvin 2.00 5.00
6 Peyton Manning 4.00 10.00
7 Steve Young 2.50 6.00
8 Troy Aikman 2.50 6.00

2016 Panini Infinity Exalted Autographs

1 Boomer Esiason/188 4.00 10.00
2 John Hannah/149 3.00 8.00
3 Lawrence Taylor/49 12.00 30.00
4 Brian Bosworth/88 5.00 12.00
5 Larry Csonka/49 15.00 40.00
6 Reggie Wayne/88 5.00 12.00
7 Champ Bailey/188 4.00 10.00
8 Y.A. Tittle/288 5.00 12.00
9 Ricky Williams/49 6.00 15.00
10 Roger Staubach/49 40.00 80.00
11 Drew Pearson/188 4.00 10.00
12 Floyd Little/88 4.00 10.00
13 Tim Brown/88 10.00 25.00
15 Curtis Martin/15 10.00 25.00
16 Kurt Warner/25 15.00 40.00
17 Eric Dickerson/25 12.00 30.00
18 Shannon Sharpe/25 10.00 25.00
20 Joe Theismann/40 8.00 20.00

2016 Panini Infinity Infinite Ink

1 Allen Hurns/288 3.00 8.00
2 Jerrell Freeman/388 3.00 8.00
3 Deone Bucannon/388 3.00 8.00
4 Marvin Jones/388 6.00 15.00
5 Thomas Rawls/188 EXCH 8.00 12.00
6 Dorial Green-Beckham/188 3.00 8.00
7 Ty Montgomery/388 4.00 10.00
8 Charcandrick West/88 4.00 10.00
9 John Brown/188 4.00 10.00
10 Jared Abbrederis/188 3.00 8.00
11 C.J. Anderson/288 4.00 10.00
12 Karlos Williams/288 3.00 8.00
13 Gary Barnidge/288 6.00 15.00
14 Mike Davis/388 3.00 8.00
15 T.J. Yeldon/288 3.00 8.00
16 Jamison Crowder/388 3.00 8.00
17 James Starks/288 3.00 8.00
18 Tyler Eifert/288 4.00 10.00
19 Justin Hardy/388 3.00 8.00
20 David Cobb/88 4.00 10.00

2016 Panini Infinity Infinite Materials

1 A.J. Green/88 3.00 8.00
2 Adrian Peterson/88 3.00 8.00
3 Allen Hurns/88 2.00 5.00
4 Amari Cooper/88 3.00 8.00
5 Ameer Abdullah/88 2.00 5.00
6 Andrew Luck/88 4.00 10.00
7 Blake Bortles/88 2.00 5.00
8 Brandin Cooks/88 2.50 6.00
9 C.J. Anderson/88 2.50 6.00
10 Cam Newton/88 3.00 8.00
11 Cole Beasley/88 3.00 8.00
12 David Johnson/88 3.00 8.00
13 Derek Carr/88 3.00 8.00
14 Devonta Freeman/88 2.50 6.00
15 Jameis Winston/88 3.00 8.00
16 Jarvis Landry/88 2.50 6.00
17 Jeremy Hill/88 2.00 5.00
18 Jeremy Langford/88 2.50 6.00
19 Jordan Reed/88 2.00 5.00
20 Julio Jones/88 3.00 8.00
21 Karlos Williams/88 2.00 5.00
22 Le'Veon Bell/88 2.50 6.00
23 Marcus Mariota/18 6.00 15.00
24 Mike Evans/18 5.00 12.00
25 Odell Beckham Jr./88 3.00 8.00
26 Russell Wilson/88 4.00 10.00
27 Sammy Watkins/88 3.00 8.00
28 T.Y. Hilton/88 2.50 6.00
29 Todd Gurley/88 3.00 8.00
30 Tyler Lockett/88 2.50 6.00

2016 Panini Infinity Infinite Potential

1 Carson Wentz 15.00 40.00
2 Corey Coleman 2.50 6.00
3 Derrick Henry 4.00 10.00
4 Devontae Booker 2.00 5.00
5 Ezekiel Elliott 8.00 20.00
6 Jared Goff 10.00 25.00
7 Joey Bosa 3.00 8.00
8 Laquon Treadwell 2.00 5.00
9 Paxton Lynch 1.50 4.00
10 Will Fuller 2.50 6.00

2016 Panini Infinity Infinitude

1 Adrian Peterson 2.00 5.00
2 Ben Roethlisberger 2.00 5.00
3 Clay Matthews 2.00 5.00
4 Dez Bryant 2.00 5.00
5 Drew Brees 2.00 5.00
6 Khalil Mack 2.00 5.00
7 Kirk Cousins 2.00 5.00
8 Philip Rivers 2.00 5.00
9 Richard Sherman 2.00 5.00
10 Rob Gronkowski 2.00 5.00

2016 Panini Infinity Locker Room Legend Autographs

3 Peyton Manning/18 150.00 250.00

2016 Panini Infinity Myriad Marks

1 Blake Bortles/49 5.00 12.00
2 Marcus Peters/188 EXCH 6.00 15.00
3 Teddy Bridgewater/188 12.00 30.00
4 Latavius Murray/25 6.00 15.00
5 Devonta Freeman/88 5.00 12.00
6 Marcus Mariota/25 25.00 50.00
7 Matt Ryan/25 15.00 40.00
10 Richard Sherman/49 25.00 50.00
11 Tony Romo/88 20.00 40.00
12 Kelvin Benjamin/88 EXCH 5.00 12.00
13 Emmanuel Sanders/188 EXCH 5.00 12.00
14 Matt Jones/288 4.00 10.00
15 Robert Mathis/15 8.00 20.00
16 Matthew Stafford/25 12.00 30.00
17 Jordy Nelson/88 10.00 25.00
18 Todd Gurley/88 20.00 50.00
19 Andrew Luck/25 40.00 80.00
20 Jameis Winston/25 15.00 40.00

2016 Panini Infinity No Limits

1 Amari Cooper 2.00 5.00
2 Blake Bortles 1.25 3.00
3 DeAndre Hopkins 1.50 4.00
4 Derek Carr 2.00 5.00
5 Jameis Winston 2.00 5.00
6 Jeremy Langford 1.50 4.00
7 Le'Veon Bell 1.50 4.00
8 Marcus Mariota 2.00 5.00
9 Odell Beckham Jr. 2.00 5.00
10 Teddy Bridgewater 1.50 4.00

2016 Panini Infinity Retired Numbers Jerseys

1 Barry Sanders 12.00 30.00
2 Brett Favre 10.00 25.00
3 Cris Carter 5.00 12.00
4 Curtis Martin 4.00 10.00
5 Dan Fouts 4.00 10.00
6 Dan Marino 20.00 40.00
7 Earl Campbell 5.00 12.00
8 Eric Dickerson 4.00 10.00
9 Fran Tarkenton 5.00 12.00
10 Gale Sayers 5.00 12.00
11 Jerry Rice 10.00 25.00
12 Jim Kelly 5.00 12.00
13 Joe Montana 12.00 30.00
14 Joe Namath 20.00 40.00
15 John Elway 8.00 20.00
16 LaDainian Tomlinson 4.00 10.00
17 Lawrence Taylor 5.00 12.00
18 Len Dawson 5.00 12.00
19 Marshall Faulk 4.00 10.00
20 Emmitt Smith 8.00 20.00
21 Peyton Manning 25.00 50.00
22 Michael Strahan 4.00 10.00
23 Steve Largent 5.00 12.00
24 Steve Young 6.00 15.00
25 Warren Moon 5.00 12.00

2016 Panini Infinity Rookie Autographs

1 Jalen Ramsey/388 4.00 10.00
2 DeForest Buckner/388 2.50 6.00
3 William Jackson III/488 3.00 8.00
4 Eli Apple/288 3.00 8.00
5 Vernon Hargreaves III/488 4.00 10.00
6 Artie Burns/388 12.00 30.00
7 Jerell Adams/488 2.50 6.00
8 Keanu Neal/488 2.50 6.00
9 Brandon Allen/488 2.50 6.00
10 Tyler Higbee/488 2.50 6.00
11 Daniel Lasco/488 2.50 6.00
12 Kenny Clark/388 2.50 6.00
13 Robert Nkemdiche/388 3.00 8.00
14 Vernon Butler/388 2.50 6.00
15 Jacoby Brissett/488 3.00 8.00

16 Jaylon Smith/488 2.50 6.00
17 Myles Jack/388 3.00 8.00
18 Chris Jones/388 2.50 6.00
19 Xavien Howard/488 3.00 8.00
20 Daniel Braverman/388 2.50 6.00
21 Reggie Ragland/349 2.50 6.00
22 Jeff Driskel/488 2.50 6.00
23 Rashard Higgins/388 2.50 6.00
24 A'Shawn Robinson/488 2.50 6.00
25 Austin Hooper/388 2.50 6.00
26 Tajae Sharpe/388 3.00 8.00
27 Su'a Cravens/488 2.50 6.00
28 Mackensie Alexander/388 2.50 6.00
29 Nick Vannett/488 2.50 6.00
30 Vonn Bell/388 3.00 8.00

2016 Panini Infinity Rookie Infinite Jerseys

1 Joey Bosa 4.00 10.00
2 Alex Collins 2.50 6.00
3 Braxton Miller 2.00 5.00
4 C.J. Prosise 2.00 5.00
5 Cardale Jones 2.00 5.00
6 Carson Wentz 12.00 30.00
7 Chris Moore 2.50 6.00
8 Christian Hackenberg 2.00 5.00
9 Cody Kessler 2.00 5.00
10 Connor Cook 2.50 6.00
11 Corey Coleman 3.00 8.00
12 Dak Prescott 6.00 15.00
13 Demarcus Robinson 2.00 5.00
14 Derrick Henry 5.00 12.00
15 Devontae Booker 2.50 6.00
16 Ezekiel Elliott 6.00 15.00
17 Hunter Henry 2.50 6.00
18 DeAndre Washington 2.00 5.00
19 Jared Goff 8.00 20.00
20 Jonathan Williams 2.50 6.00
21 Jordan Howard 4.00 10.00
22 Josh Doctson 2.50 6.00
23 Keenan Reynolds 2.50 6.00
24 Kenneth Dixon 2.00 5.00
25 Kenyan Drake 3.00 8.00
26 Kevin Hogan 2.50 6.00
27 Laquon Treadwell 2.50 6.00
28 Leonte Carroo 2.00 5.00
30 Michael Thomas 4.00 10.00
31 Paul Perkins 2.00 5.00
32 Paxton Lynch 2.00 5.00
33 Pharoh Cooper 2.00 5.00
34 Ricardo Louis 2.00 5.00
35 Sterling Shepard 2.50 6.00
36 Trevor Davis 2.00 5.00
37 Tyler Boyd 2.50 6.00
38 Tyler Ervin 2.00 5.00
39 Wendell Smallwood 2.00 5.00
40 Will Fuller 3.00 8.00
41 Moritz Bohringer 2.00 5.00

2016 Panini Infinity Rookie Jerseys

1 Jared Goff 10.00 25.00
2 Carson Wentz 15.00 40.00
3 Joey Bosa 3.00 8.00
4 Ezekiel Elliott 8.00 20.00
5 Corey Coleman 2.50 6.00
6 Will Fuller 2.50 6.00
7 Josh Doctson 2.00 5.00
8 Laquon Treadwell 2.00 5.00
9 Paxton Lynch 1.50 4.00
10 Hunter Henry 2.00 5.00
11 Sterling Shepard 2.00 5.00
12 Derrick Henry 6.00 15.00
13 Michael Thomas 3.00 8.00
14 Christian Hackenberg 1.50 4.00
15 Kenyan Drake 2.50 6.00
16 Braxton Miller 1.50 4.00
17 Leonte Carroo 1.50 4.00
18 C.J. Prosise 1.50 4.00
19 DeAndre Washington 1.50 4.00
20 Cody Kessler 1.50 4.00
21 Tyler Boyd 2.00 5.00
22 Connor Cook 2.00 5.00
23 Chris Moore 2.00 5.00
24 Ricardo Louis 1.50 4.00
25 Pharoh Cooper 1.50 4.00
26 Tyler Ervin 1.50 4.00
27 Demarcus Robinson 1.50 4.00
28 Kenneth Dixon 1.50 4.00
29 Dak Prescott 8.00 20.00
30 Devontae Booker 2.00 5.00
31 Cardale Jones 1.50 4.00
32 Paul Perkins 1.50 4.00
33 Jordan Howard 4.00 10.00
34 Wendell Smallwood 1.50 4.00
35 Jonathan Williams 2.00 5.00
36 Kevin Hogan 2.00 5.00
37 Trevor Davis 1.50 4.00
38 Alex Collins 2.00 5.00
39 Keenan Reynolds 2.00 5.00
40 Moritz Bohringer 1.50 4.00

2016 Panini Infinity Rookie Jerseys Combo

1 K.Dixon/C.Moore 2.50 6.00
2 C.Jones/J.Williams 2.50 6.00
3 C.Kessler/C.Coleman 3.00 8.00
4 D.Prescott/E.Elliott 12.00 30.00
5 D.Booker/P.Lynch 2.50 6.00
6 B.Miller/W.Fuller V 3.00 8.00
7 D.Robinson/K.Hogan 2.50 6.00
8 J.Goff/P.Cooper 6.00 15.00
9 K.Drake/L.Carroo 3.00 8.00
10 L.Treadwell/M.Bohringer 2.50 6.00
11 P.Perkins/S.Shepard 2.50 6.00
12 C.Wentz/W.Smallwood 12.00 30.00
13 J.Bosa/H.Henry 4.00 10.00
14 A.Collins/C.Prosise 2.50 6.00
15 C.Wentz/J.Goff 12.00 30.00
16 D.Henry/E.Elliott 6.00 15.00
17 W.Fuller V/C.Coleman 3.00 8.00
18 J.Doctson/L.Treadwell 2.50 6.00
19 C.Cook/D.Washington 2.50 6.00
20 T.Boyd/T.Davis 2.50 6.00

2016 Panini Infinity Rookie Jerseys Dual

1 Joey Bosa 4.00 10.00
2 Alex Collins 2.50 6.00
3 Braxton Miller 2.00 5.00
4 C.J. Prosise 2.00 5.00
5 Cardale Jones 2.00 5.00
6 Carson Wentz 20.00 50.00
7 Chris Moore 2.50 6.00
8 Christian Hackenberg 2.00 5.00
9 Cody Kessler 2.00 5.00
10 Connor Cook 2.50 6.00
11 Corey Coleman 3.00 8.00
12 Dak Prescott 10.00 25.00
13 Demarcus Robinson 2.00 5.00
14 Derrick Henry 8.00 20.00
15 Devontae Booker 2.50 6.00
16 Ezekiel Elliott 10.00 25.00
17 Hunter Henry 2.50 6.00
18 DeAndre Washington 2.00 5.00
19 Jared Goff 12.00 30.00
20 Jonathan Williams 2.50 6.00
21 Jordan Howard 5.00 12.00
22 Josh Doctson 2.50 6.00
23 Keenan Reynolds 2.50 6.00
24 Kenneth Dixon 2.00 5.00
25 Kenyan Drake 3.00 8.00
26 Kevin Hogan 2.50 6.00
27 Laquon Treadwell 2.50 6.00
28 Leonte Carroo 2.00 5.00
30 Michael Thomas 4.00 10.00
31 Paul Perkins 2.00 5.00
32 Paxton Lynch 2.00 5.00
33 Pharoh Cooper 2.00 5.00
34 Ricardo Louis 2.00 5.00
35 Sterling Shepard 2.50 6.00
36 Trevor Davis 2.00 5.00
37 Tyler Boyd 2.50 6.00
38 Tyler Ervin 2.00 5.00
39 Wendell Smallwood 2.00 5.00
40 Will Fuller 3.00 8.00
41 Moritz Bohringer 2.00 5.00

2016 Panini Infinity Rookie Jerseys Quads

1 Wntz/Prsctt/Gff/Lnch 30.00 80.00
2 Mllr/Bsa/Thms/Jns 6.00 15.00
3 Hnry/Prsse/Ellt/Drke 15.00 40.00
4 Hlr/Clmn/Dctsn/Trdwll 5.00 12.00
5 Bkr/Dxn/Prkns/Ervn 4.00 10.00

2016 Panini Infinity Rookie Jerseys Trios

1 Bsa/Wntz/Gff 25.00 60.00
2 Lnch/Wntz/Gff 25.00 60.00
3 Bkr/Hnry/Drke 8.00 20.00
4 Dctsn/Fllr/Clmn 4.00 10.00
5 Mllr/Elltt/Jns 12.00 30.00
6 Clmn/Dctsn/Shprd 4.00 10.00
7 Hcknbrg/Ksslr/Prsctt 12.00 30.00
8 Prsse/Ervn/Prkns 2.50 6.00
9 Bhrngr/Trdwll/Dvs 3.00 8.00
10 Ksslr/Clmn/Louis 4.00 10.00

2016 Panini Infinity Rookie Jersyes Sixes

1 Wtz/Prctt/Gff/Hckbg/Kslr/Lnch 30.00 80.00
2 Prse/Hry/Eltt/Bkr/Dxn/Dke 15.00 40.00
3 Tdwl/Fllr/Clmn/Dcsn/Tms/Shpd 6.00 15.00

2016 Panini Infinity Seasoned Pros Swatches

1 A.J. Hawk 2.00 5.00
2 Alex Smith 2.50 6.00
3 Andy Dalton 2.50 6.00
4 Antonio Brown 3.00 8.00
5 Antonio Gates 2.00 5.00
6 Ben Roethlisberger 6.00 15.00
7 Clay Matthews 3.00 8.00
8 DeMarcus Ware 2.50 6.00
9 Demaryius Thomas 2.50 6.00
10 Derrick Johnson 2.00 5.00
11 DeSean Jackson 2.50 6.00
12 Dez Bryant 3.00 8.00
13 Dontari Poe 2.00 5.00
14 Drew Brees 3.00 8.00
15 Eli Manning 2.50 6.00
16 Emmanuel Sanders 3.00 8.00
17 Eric Berry 2.50 6.00
18 Eric Ebron 2.00 5.00
19 J.J. Watt 3.00 8.00
20 Jamaal Charles 2.50 6.00
21 Jason Witten 2.50 6.00
22 Jay Cutler 2.00 5.00
23 Joe Flacco 2.50 6.00
24 Joe Haden 2.00 5.00
25 Jonathan Stewart 2.00 5.00
26 Jordan Cameron 2.00 5.00
27 Julius Peppers 2.50 6.00
28 Larry Fitzgerald 2.50 6.00
29 LeSean McCoy 3.00 8.00
30 Mark Ingram 2.50 6.00
31 Matt Ryan 2.50 6.00
32 Matthew Stafford 2.50 6.00
33 Paul Posluszny 2.00 5.00
34 Philip Rivers 3.00 8.00
35 Reggie Nelson 2.00 5.00
36 Sam Bradford 2.00 5.00
37 Tom Brady 8.00 20.00
38 Tony Romo 2.50 6.00
39 Tyler Eifert 2.50 6.00
40 Von Miller 2.50 6.00

2016 Panini Infinity Team8s Materials

1 Hns/Btls/Rbsn/Tms/Lee/Pszy/Ydn/Rbn 5.00 12.00
2 Hns/Chrh/Brnt/Rmo/Bsly/MFdn/Sck/Wms 6.00 15.00
3 Cmn/Jns/Tnhl/Wke/Prkr/Ldry/Ajyi/Stlls 5.00 12.00
4 Smth/Jhn/Chls/Mcln/Hli/Bry/Hstn/Klce 6.00 15.00
5 Rby/Adsn/Hrs/Sdrs/Hlmn/Wre/Thms/Mlr 6.00 15.00

2016 Panini Instant

1 Cam Newton/140* 2.00 5.00
2 Dak Prescott/112* 6.00 15.00
3 Ezekiel Elliott/120* 6.00 15.00
4 Antonio Brown/112* 2.00 5.00
5 Todd Gurley/69* 2.50 6.00
6 Tom Brady SB LI 5.00 12.00
7 Cam Newton/65* 2.50 6.00
8 Trevor Siemian/62* 1.50 4.00
9 Carson Wentz/230* 12.00 30.00
10 A.J. Green/65* 2.50 6.00
11 Aaron Rodgers/61* 5.00 12.00
12 Brandin Cooks/65* 2.00 5.00
13 Will Fuller/69* 2.50 6.00
14 Jameis Winston/66* 2.50 6.00
15 Drew Brees/66* 2.50 6.00
16 Spencer Ware/62* 1.50 4.00
17 Alex Smith/62* 2.00 5.00
18 DeMarco Murray/62* 2.00 5.00
19 Derek Carr/63* 2.50 6.00
20 Sterling Shepard/69* 2.00 5.00
21 Ezekiel Elliott/139* 6.00 15.00
22 Stephen Gostkowski SB LI 2.00 5.00
23 Matthew Stafford/62* 2.00 5.00
24 Larry Fitzgerald/63* 2.00 5.00
25 Jimmy Garoppolo/62* 3.00 8.00
26 B.Rthlsbrgr 2.50 6.00
A.Brown
27 Carlos Hyde/62* 1.50 4.00
28 Carson Wentz/110* 12.00 30.00
29 Drew Brees/63* 2.50 6.00
30 Ryan Shazier/66* 1.50 4.00
31 DeAngelo Williams/62* 1.50 4.00
32 Matt Forte/64* 1.50 4.00
33 Bruce Smith/64* 2.00 5.00
34 Corey Coleman ERR 2.50 6.00
numbered out of 64
35 LeGarrette Blount/62* 2.00 5.00
36 Kelvin Benjamin/64* 2.00 5.00
37 J.J. Watt/64* 2.50 6.00
38 Dak Prescott/64* 8.00 20.00
39 Julio Jones/64* 2.50 6.00
40 Philip Rivers/64* 2.50 6.00
41 M.Brockers/A.Donald 2.50 6.00
42 Jordy Nelson/64* 2.00 5.00
43 Stefon Diggs/64* 2.00 5.00
44 Drew Brees/64* 2.50 6.00
45 Eli Manning 2.00 5.00
46 Carson Wentz/310* 12.00 30.00
47 Corey Coleman/64* 2.50 6.00
48 Matt Ryan/64* 2.00 5.00
49 Von Miller/64* 2.00 5.00
50 Cam Newton/64* 2.50 6.00
51 Jacoby Brissett/85* 1.50 4.00
52 Aaron Rodgers/64* 5.00 12.00
53 LeSean McCoy/64* 2.50 6.00
54 Marvin Jones/64* 1.50 4.00
55 Minnesota Vikings 1.50 4.00
Everson Griffen/64*
56 Odell Beckham Jr./66* 2.50 6.00
57 Terrelle Pryor/65* 1.50 4.00
58 Carson Wentz/384* 12.00 30.00
59 Kansas City Chiefs 1.50 4.00
Marcus Peters/62*
60 Trevone Boykin 1.25 3.00
61 T.Y. Hilton/64* 2.00 5.00
62 Dak Prescott/100* 6.00 15.00
63 Ezekiel Elliott/156* 6.00 15.00
64 Dak Prescott 6.00 15.00
Ezekiel Elliott/154*
65 Tevin Coleman 2.00 5.00
Devnota Freeman/52*
66 Carson Wentz/319* 12.00 30.00
67 Trevor Siemian/88* 1.25 3.00
68 Derrick Johnson/52* 1.50 4.00
69 Jameis Winston/57* 2.50 6.00
70 Andy Dalton 2.50 6.00
A.J. Green
71 Blake Bortles/51* 1.50 4.00
72 Matt Ryan 2.50 6.00
Julio Jones/53*
73 Jordan Howard/142* 3.00 8.00
74 Tanner McEvoy/73* 2.00 5.00
75 Derek Carr 2.50 6.00
Michael Crabtree/53*
76 Will Fuller/62* 2.50 6.00
77 Russell Wilson/58* 3.00 8.00
78 Jordan Reed/52* 1.50 4.00
79 Paxton Lynch/154* 1.25 3.00
80 David Johnson/57* 2.50 6.00
81 Dak Prescott/113* 6.00 15.00
82 Ben Roethlisberger/73* 2.50 6.00
83 Le'Veon Bell/63* 2.00 5.00
84 Sam Bradford/75* 1.25 3.00
85 Ezekiel Elliott/135* 6.00 15.00
86 Julio Jones/53* 2.50 6.00
87 Aqib Talib/83* 1.25 3.00
88 Ben Roethlisberger/81* 2.00 5.00
89 Larry Fitzgerald/58* 2.00 5.00
90 David Johnson/53* 2.50 6.00
91 Tom Brady/81* 5.00 12.00
92 Adam Thielen/166* 25.00 50.00
93 Jordan Howard/66* 4.00 10.00
94 Ben Roethlisberger/58* 2.50 6.00
95 Marcus Mariota/53* 2.50 6.00
96 Paxton Lynch/69* 1.50 4.00
97 Ezekiel Elliott/174* 6.00 15.00
98 Cole Beasley 2.00 5.00
99 Dak Prescott/199* 6.00 15.00
100 Joey Bosa/72* 3.00 8.00
101 Amari Cooper/52* 2.50 6.00
102 Hunter Henry/56* 2.00 5.00
103 Greg Olsen/56* 2.00 5.00
104 Mike Evans/51* 2.00 5.00
105 Frank Gore/51* 2.00 5.00
106 Ezekiel Elliott/134* 6.00 15.00
107 Tom Brady/80* 5.00 12.00
108 Vic Beasley Jr./52* 1.50 4.00
109 Sammie Coates/52* 1.50 4.00
110 Hunter Henry/54* 2.00 5.00
111 LeSean McCoy/86* 2.00 5.00
112 Golden Tate/51* 1.25 3.00
113 Cam Newton/53* 2.50 6.00
114 Case Keenum 2.00 5.00
Kenny Britt/51*
115 Jay Ajayi/53* 2.00 5.00
116 Wendell Smallwood/75* 1.25 3.00
117 Rob Gronkowski/63* 2.50 6.00
118 Brandin Cooks/52* 2.00 5.00
119 Michael Thomas/58* 3.00 8.00
120 Odell Beckham Jr./57* 2.50 6.00
121 Marcus Mariota/51* 2.50 6.00
122 Spencer Ware 2.00 5.00
Jamaal Charles/52*
123 Dak Prescott/160* 6.00 15.00
124 Ezekiel Elliott/159* 6.00 15.00
125 Alex Collins/62* 2.00 5.00
126 Brett Favre/79* 4.00 10.00
127 Lamar Miller/51* 1.50 4.00
128 David Johnson/53* 2.50 6.00
129 Tom Brady M/73* 6.00 15.00
130 Eli Manning M/53* 2.00 5.00
131 Dak Prescott RB/155* 6.00 15.00
132 Dak Prescott 6.00 15.00
Ezekiel Elliott/282*
133 Drew Brees/58* 2.50 6.00
134 David Irving/79* 1.25 3.00
135 Odell Beckham Jr./57* 2.50 6.00
136 Aaron Rodgers 4.00 10.00
137 Davante Adams 1.25 3.00
138 Randall Cobb 2.00 5.00
Ty Montgomery/52*
139 A.J. Green 1.50 4.00
140 Kevin Hogan/58* 2.00 5.00
141 Jeremy Hill/52* 1.50 4.00
142 Tyreek Hill/107* 5.00 12.00
143 Carson Wentz/153* 12.00 30.00
144 Andrew Luck/61* 3.00 8.00
145 T.Y. Hilton/51* 2.00 5.00
146 Julio Jones/57* 2.50 6.00
147 Mike Evans 2.50 6.00
Jameis Winston/51*
148 Peyton Barber 1.25 3.00
149 Tom Brady 5.00 12.00
Rob Gronkowski/76*
150 Antonio Brown/55* 2.50 6.00
151 Devontae Booker/70* 2.00 5.00
152 Adam Vinatieri RB 2.00 5.00
153 Michael Thomas/59* 3.00 8.00
154 Jay Ajayi/79* 1.50 4.00
155 Joey Bosa/60* 3.00 8.00
156 Melvin Gordon/53* 2.00 5.00
157 Carson Wentz 12.00 30.00
Dak Prescott/198*
158 Derrick Henry/82* 3.00 8.00
159 Kirk Cousins/54* 2.50 6.00
160 Robert Kelley 2.00 5.00
161 Tom Brady/86* 5.00 12.00
162 Jonathan Williams/58* 2.00 5.00
163 Jonathan Stewart/51* 1.50 4.00
164 Derek Carr/74* 2.50 6.00
165 Amari Cooper 2.50 6.00
166 Devontae Booker/74* 2.00 5.00
167 Aaron Rodgers 5.00 12.00
168 Geronimo Allison 1.50 4.00
Trevor Davis/67*
169 Ezekiel Elliott/134* 6.00 15.00
170 Dez Bryant/62* 2.50 6.00
171 Dak Prescott/154* 6.00 15.00
172 Jordan Howard 3.00 8.00
173 Rob Gronkowski M/68* 2.50 6.00
174 Jason Witten 1.50 4.00
175 Dak Prescott/113* 6.00 15.00
176 Derek Carr/51* 2.50 6.00
177 Khalil Mack/56* 2.50 6.00
178 Tom Brady/78* 5.00 12.00
179 Mike Evans 1.50 4.00
180 Cameron Brate/52* 2.00 5.00
181 Julio Jones 2.00 5.00
182 Carson Wentz/83* 12.00 30.00
183 Mike Wallace 1.25 3.00
184 Eli Rogers 1.50 4.00
185 Jason Witten 2.00 5.00
186 Dak Prescott/68* 8.00 20.00
187 Ezekiel Elliott/85* 6.00 15.00
188 Jay Ajayi/54* 2.00 5.00
189 Kenyan Drake/54* 2.50 6.00
190 Mark Ingram 1.50 4.00
Tim Hightower
191 Michael Thomas/53* 3.00 8.00
192 Marcus Mariota/63* 2.50 6.00
193 Latavius Murray 1.25 3.00
194 Jimmy Graham/59* 2.50 6.00
195 Ezekiel Elliott/78* 6.00 15.00
196 Melvin Gordon/62* 2.00 5.00
197 Thomas Davis/57* 1.50 4.00
198 Russell Wilson/63* 3.00 8.00
199 Joe Flacco/52* 2.00 5.00
200 Marcus Mariota/66* 2.50 6.00
201 DeMarco Murray/51* 2.00 5.00
202 Tojoe Chorpe/51* 2.00 5.00
203 Jordan Taylor/66* 1.50 4.00
204 Justin Simmons 2.00 5.00
Will Parks/66*
205 Ezekiel Elliott/218* 6.00 15.00
206 David Johnson/53* 2.50 6.00
207 Dak Prescott/199* 6.00 15.00
208 Ezekiel Elliott/212* 6.00 15.00
209 Dez Bryant/52* 2.50 6.00
210 Le'Veon Bell 1.50 4.00
211 Ezekiel Elliott/242* 6.00 15.00
212 LeGarrette Blount/62* 2.00 5.00
213 Russell Wilson 2.50 6.00
Doug Baldwin/75*
214 C.J. Prosise/74* 1.50 4.00
215 Sterling Shepard/61* 2.00 5.00
216 Philip Rivers 2.00 5.00
217 Ezekiel Elliott 6.00 15.00
218 Ezekiel Elliott/150* 6.00 15.00
219 Marcus Mariota/62* 2.50 6.00
220 Eric Berry/52* 2.00 5.00
221 Antonio Brown 2.00 5.00
222 Cam Newton/53* 2.50 6.00
223 Le'Veon Bell/55* 2.00 5.00
224 James Harrison 1.50 4.00
225 Ezekiel Elliott/253* 6.00 15.00
226 Dak Prescott/286* 6.00 15.00
227 Xavier Rhodes 1.50 4.00
Cordarrelle Patterson/53*
228 Jared Goff/94* 8.00 20.00
229 C.J. Prosise/58* 1.50 4.00
230 Doug Baldwin 3.00 8.00
Russell Wilson/60*
231 Ezekiel Elliott/286* 6.00 15.00
232 Peyton Manning/72* 5.00 12.00
233 Tom Brady/83* 5.00 12.00
234 Malcolm Mitchell/57* 1.50 4.00
235 Robert Kelley/78* 2.00 5.00
236 Kirk Cousins 2.00 5.00
237 Ezekiel Elliott 6.00 15.00
Dak Prescott/523*
238 Steve Smith 1.50 4.00
239 Dak Prescott/236* 6.00 15.00
240 David Johnson/52* 2.50 6.00
241 Landon Collins/51* 1.50 4.00
242 Le'Veon Bell 1.50 4.00
243 Kirk Cousins/60* 2.50 6.00
244 Dak Prescott/234* 6.00 15.00
245 Ezekiel Elliott/222* 6.00 15.00
246 Le'Veon Bell 1.50 4.00
247 LeSean McCoy/63* 2.50 6.00
248 Derrick Henry/51* 4.00 10.00
249 Odell Beckham Jr./56* 2.50 6.00
250 Colin Kaepernick 1.50 4.00
251 Jared Goff/86* 8.00 20.00
252 Willie Snead 1.50 4.00
Tim Hightower
253 Michael Thomas/63* 3.00 8.00
254 Jameis Winston 2.50 6.00
Mike Evans/63*
255 Tom Brady/67* 6.00 15.00
256 Malcolm Mitchell/62* 1.50 4.00
257 Khalil Mack 2.00 5.00
258 Tyreek Hill 5.00 12.00
259 Dak Prescott 6.00 15.00
Ezekiel Elliott/386*
260 Larry Fitzgerald M 1.50 4.00
261 Tom Brady M/68* 6.00 15.00
262 Ezekiel Elliott/224* 6.00 15.00
263 Drew Brees/54* 2.50 6.00
264 Jason Pierre-Paul 1.25 3.00
265 Antonio Brown/53* 2.50 6.00
266 Ezekiel Elliott/154* 6.00 15.00
267 Dak Prescott/192* 6.00 15.00
268 Devontae Booker 1.50 4.00
269 Carson Wentz/66* 15.00 40.00
270 Jordan Howard 3.00 8.00
271 LeGarrette Blount 1.50 4.00
272 Sterling Shepard 1.50 4.00
273 Thomas Rawls 1.25 3.00
274 Tyler Lockett 1.50 4.00
275 Andrew Luck 2.50 6.00
276 Dak Prescott 6.00 15.00
Ezekiel Elliott/305*
277 Larry Fitzgerald M 1.50 4.00
278 Julius Peppers M 1.50 4.00
279 Tom Brady RB/92* 5.00 12.00
280 Dak Prescott PLAY/479* 6.00 15.00
281 Ezekiel Elliott PLAY/479* 6.00 15.00
282 Dez Bryant PLAY/479* 2.00 5.00
283 Cole Beasley PLAY/479* 2.00 5.00
284 Terrance Williams PLAY/479* 1.25 3.00
285 Jason Witten PLAY/479* 1.50 4.00
286 Tyron Smith PLAY/479* 1.25 3.00
287 Ronald Leary PLAY/479* 1.25 3.00
288 Travis Frederick PLAY/479* 1.25 3.00
289 Zack Martin PLAY/479* 1.25 3.00
290 Doug Free PLAY/479* 1.25 3.00
291 Tyrone Crawford PLAY/479* 1.25 3.00
292 Maliek Collins PLAY/479* 1.25 3.00
293 Terrell McClain PLAY/479* 1.25 3.00
294 Jack Crawford PLAY/479* 1.25 3.00
295 Damien Wilson PLAY/479* 1.25 3.00
296 Anthony Hitchens PLAY 1.25 3.00
297 Sean Lee PLAY/479* 1.50 4.00
298 Brandon Carr PLAY/479* 1.25 3.00
299 Morris Claiborne PLAY/479* 1.25 3.00
300 Orlando Scandrick PLAY/479* 1.25 3.00
301 Barry Church PLAY/479* 1.25 3.00
302 Byron Jones PLAY/479* 1.25 3.00
303 Lucky Whitehead PLAY/479* 1.25 3.00
304 Dan Bailey PLAY/479* 1.25 3.00
305 Jordan Howard 3.00 8.00
306 Joe Flacco 1.50 4.00
307 Eric Berry 1.50 4.00
308 David Johnson 2.00 5.00
309 Tyreek Hill/69* 6.00 15.00
310 Le'Veon Bell/64* 2.00 5.00
311 Matthew Stafford 1.50 4.00
312 Robert Kelley/95* 2.00 5.00
313 Carson Wentz 12.00 30.00
314 DeSean Jackson 1.50 4.00
315 Carlos Hyde 1.25 3.00
316 Jared Goff 8.00 20.00
317 Dak Prescott/190* 6.00 15.00
318 Ezekiel Elliott/210* 6.00 15.00
319 Eli Manning 2.50 6.00
Odell Beckham Jr./57*
320 Chris Hogan/83* 1.25 3.00
321 Tom Brady/77* 5.00 12.00
322 Tyreek Hill/74* 6.00 15.00
323 Tom Brady/69* 6.00 15.00
324 Vic Beasley Jr. 1.25 3.00
325 Le'Veon Bell/61* 2.00 5.00
326 Russell Wilson PLAY/64* 3.00 8.00
327 Thomas Rawls PLAY/64* 1.50 4.00
328 C.J. Prosise PLAY/64* 1.50 4.00
329 Doug Baldwin PLAY/64* 2.00 5.00
330 Tyler Lockett PLAY/64* 2.00 5.00
331 Jermaine Kearse PLAY/64* 1.50 4.00
332 Jimmy Graham PLAY/64* 2.50 6.00
333 George Fant PLAY/64* 1.50 4.00
334 Mark Glowinski PLAY/64* 1.50 4.00
335 Justin Britt PLAY/64* 1.50 4.00
336 Germain Ifedi PLAY/64* 2.00 5.00
337 Bradley Sowell PLAY/64* 1.50 4.00
338 Michael Bennett PLAY/64* 1.50 4.00
339 Frank Clark PLAY/64* 1.50 4.00
340 Tony McDaniel PLAY/64* 1.50 4.00
341 Cliff Avril PLAY/64* 1.50 4.00
342 Mike Morgan PLAY/64* 1.50 4.00
343 Cassius Marsh PLAY/64* 1.50 4.00
344 Bobby Wagner PLAY/64* 1.50 4.00
345 K.J. Wright PLAY/64* 1.50 4.00
346 Richard Sherman PLAY/64* 2.50 6.00
347 DeShawn Shead PLAY/64* 1.50 4.00
348 Kam Chancellor PLAY/64* 2.50 6.00
349 Earl Thomas PLAY/64* 2.00 5.00
34a Corey Coleman/104* 2.00 5.00
350 Steven Hauschka PLAY/64* 1.50 4.00
351 Matt Moore 1.25 3.00
352 Kenneth Dixon 1.25 3.00
353 Ty Montgomery/52* 2.00 5.00
354 Jordan Howard 3.00 8.00
355 Ezekiel Elliott/455* 6.00 15.00
356 Eli Rogers/83* 1.50 4.00
357 Tom Savage 1.25 3.00
358 Tyreek Hill/69* 6.00 15.00
359 Derrick Henry 3.00 8.00
360 Devonta Freeman 1.50 4.00
361 Tom Brady/79* 5.00 12.00
362 LeGarrette Blount 1.50 4.00
363 Dak Prescott/230* 6.00 15.00
364 Ezekiel Elliott/262* 6.00 15.00
365 Tom Brady PLAY/122* 5.00 12.00
366 LeGarrette Blount PLAY/122* 1.50 4.00
367 James White PLAY/122* 1.50 4.00
368 Julian Edelman PLAY/122* 2.00 5.00
369 Chris Hogan PLAY/122* 1.25 3.00
370 Malcolm Mitchell PLAY/122* 1.25 3.00
371 Rob Gronkowski PLAY/122* 2.00 5.00
372 Martellus Bennett PLAY/122* 1.25 3.00
373 Nate Solder PLAY/122* 1.25 3.00
374 Joe Thuney PLAY/122* 1.25 3.00
375 David Andrews PLAY/122* 1.25 3.00
376 Shaq Mason PLAY/122* 1.25 3.00
377 Marcus Cannon PLAY/122* 1.25 3.00
378 Chris Long PLAY/122* 1.25 3.00
379 Alan Branch PLAY/122* 1.25 3.00
380 Malcolm Brown PLAY/122* 1.25 3.00
381 Trey Flowers PLAY/122* 1.25 3.00
382 Elendon Roberts PLAY/122* 1.25 3.00
383 Dont'a Hightower PLAY/122* 1.25 3.00
384 Rob Ninkovich PLAY/122* 1.25 3.00
385 Logan Ryan PLAY/122* 1.25 3.00
386 Malcolm Butler PLAY/122* 2.00 5.00
387 Patrick Chung PLAY/122* 1.25 3.00
388 Devin McCourty PLAY/122* 1.25 3.00
389 Stephen Gostkowski PLAY/122* 1.50 4.00
390 Derek Carr PLAY 2.00 5.00
391 Latavius Murray PLAY 1.25 3.00
392 Jalen Richard PLAY 1.50 4.00
393 Jamize Olawale PLAY 1.25 3.00
394 Amari Cooper PLAY 2.00 5.00
395 Michael Crabtree PLAY 1.25 3.00
396 Seth Roberts PLAY 1.50 4.00
397 Donald Penn PLAY 1.25 3.00
398 Kelechi Osemele PLAY 1.25 3.00
399 Rodney Hudson PLAY 1.25 3.00
400 Gabe Jackson PLAY 1.25 3.00
401 Austin Howard PLAY 1.25 3.00
402 Jihad Ward PLAY 1.25 3.00
403 Stacy McGee PLAY 1.25 3.00
404 Dan Williams PLAY 1.25 3.00
405 Khalil Mack PLAY 2.00 5.00
406 Bruce Irvin PLAY 1.25 3.00
407 Perry Riley PLAY 1.25 3.00
408 Malcolm Smith PLAY 2.00 5.00
409 David Amerson PLAY 1.25 3.00
410 Sean Smith PLAY 1.25 3.00
411 Reggie Nelson PLAY 1.25 3.00
412 Karl Joseph PLAY 1.25 3.00
413 Marquette King PLAY 1.25 3.00
414 Sebastian Janikowski PLAY 1.25 3.00
415 Cam Newton 2.00 5.00
416 Ezekiel Elliott/237* 6.00 15.00
417 Drew Brees 2.00 5.00
418 David Irving/95* 1.25 3.00
419 Brandin Cooks 1.50 4.00
420 Dak Prescott 6.00 15.00
Ezekiel Elliott/385*
421 Jay Ajayi 1.50 4.00
422 Adam Thielen/137* 25.00 50.00
423 Tom Brady/150* 5.00 12.00
424 Ezekiel Elliott/580* 6.00 15.00
425 Antonio Brown/93* 2.00 5.00
426 Tyreek Hill/106* 5.00 12.00
427 Dontari Poe/70* 1.50 4.00
428 Dak Prescott/392* 6.00 15.00
429 Dak Prescott/202* 6.00 15.00
430 Ezekiel Elliott/250* 6.00 15.00
431 Dez Bryant/80* 2.00 5.00
432 Dak Prescott/156* 6.00 15.00
433 Matthew Slater SB LI 1.50 4.00
434 Jalen Ramsey 2.00 5.00
435 David Johnson 2.00 5.00
436 Ryan Tannehill PLAY 1.50 4.00
437 Matt Moore PLAY 1.25 3.00
438 Jay Ajayi PLAY 1.50 4.00
439 Kenyan Drake PLAY 2.00 5.00
440 Jarvis Landry PLAY 1.50 4.00
441 DeVante Parker PLAY 1.50 4.00
442 Kenny Stills PLAY 1.25 3.00
443 Dion Sims PLAY 1.25 3.00
444 Branden Albert PLAY 1.25 3.00
445 Laremy Tunsil PLAY 1.25 3.00
446 Mike Pouncey PLAY 1.25 3.00
447 Jermon Bushrod PLAY 1.25 3.00
448 Ju' Wuan James PLAY 1.25 3.00
449 Cameron Wake PLAY 1.25 3.00
450 Ndamukong Suh PLAY 1.50 4.00
451 Jordan Phillips PLAY 1.25 3.00
452 Mario Williams PLAY 1.25 3.00
453 Donald Butler PLAY 1.25 3.00
454 Kiko Alonso PLAY 1.25 3.00
455 Jelani Jenkins PLAY 1.25 3.00
456 Byron Maxwell PLAY 1.25 3.00
457 Xavien Howard PLAY 1.50 4.00
458 Isa-Abdul Quddus PLAY 1.25 3.00
459 Michael Thomas PLAY 2.50 6.00
460 Andrew Franks PLAY 1.25 3.00
461 Matt Ryan PLAY/66* 2.00 5.00
462 Devonta Freeman PLAY/66* 2.00 5.00
463 Tevin Coleman PLAY/66* 2.00 5.00
464 Patrick Di' Marco PLAY/66* 1.50 4.00
465 Julio Jones PLAY/66* 2.50 6.00
466 Mohamed Sanu PLAY/66* 1.50 4.00
467 Taylor Gabriel PLAY/66* 1.50 4.00
468 Austin Hooper PLAY/66* 1.50 4.00
469 Jake Matthews PLAY/66* 1.50 4.00
470 Andy LeVitre PLAY/66* 1.50 4.00
471 Alex Mack PLAY/66* 1.50 4.00
472 Chris Chester PLAY/66* 1.50 4.00
473 Ryan Schreader PLAY/66* 1.50 4.00
474 Brooks Reed PLAY/66* 1.50 4.00
475 Jonathan Babineaux PLAY/66* 1.50 4.00
476 Grady Jarrett PLAY/66* 1.50 4.00
477 Tyson Jackson PLAY/66* 1.50 4.00
478 Vic Beasley Jr. PLAY/66* 1.50 4.00
479 Deion Jones PLAY/66* 1.50 4.00
480 De' Vondre Campbell PLAY/66* 2.00 5.00
481 Robert Alford PLAY/66* 1.50 4.00
482 Jalen Collins PLAY/66* 1.50 4.00
483 Ricardo Allen PLAY/66* 1.50 4.00
484 Keanu Neal PLAY/66* 1.50 4.00
485 Matt Bryant PLAY/66* 1.50 4.00
486 Eli Manning PLAY/63* 2.00 5.00
487 Rashad Jennings PLAY/63* 1.50 4.00
488 Paul Perkins PLAY/63* 1.50 4.00
489 Odell Beckham Jr. PLAY/63* 2.50 6.00
490 Sterling Shepard PLAY/63* 2.00 5.00
491 Victor Cruz PLAY/63* 2.00 5.00
492 Will Tye PLAY/63* 1.50 4.00
493 Ereck Flowers PLAY/63* 1.50 4.00
494 Justin Pugh PLAY/63* 1.50 4.00
495 Weston Richburg PLAY/63* 1.50 4.00
496 John Jerry PLAY/63* 1.50 4.00
497 Bobby Hart PLAY/63* 1.50 4.00
498 Jason Pierre-Paul PLAY/63* 1.50 4.00
499 Damon Harrison PLAY/63* 1.50 4.00
500 Johnathan Hankins PLAY/63* 1.50 4.00
501 Olivier Vernon PLAY/63* 1.50 4.00
502 Devon Kennard PLAY/63* 1.50 4.00
503 Kelvin Sheppard PLAY/63* 1.50 4.00
504 Jonathan Casillas PLAY/63* 1.50 4.00
505 Dominique Rodgers-Cromartie PLAY/63* 1.50 4.00
506 Landon Collins PLAY/63* 1.50 4.00
507 Andrew Adams PLAY/63* 1.50 4.00
508 Janoris Jenkins PLAY/63* 1.50 4.00
509 Dwayne Harris PLAY/63* 1.50 4.00
510 Robbie Gould PLAY/63* 1.50 4.00
511 Ben Roethlisberger PLAY/112* 2.00 5.00
512 Le' Veon Bell PLAY/112* 1.50 4.00
513 DeAngelo Williams PLAY/112* 1.25 3.00
514 Antonio Brown PLAY/112* 2.00 5.00
515 Eli Rogers PLAY/112* 1.50 4.00
516 Sammie Coates PLAY/112* 1.25 3.00
517 Ladarius Green PLAY/112* 1.25 3.00
518 Jesse James PLAY/112* 1.25 3.00
519 Alejandro Villanueva PLAY 1.25 3.00
520 Ramon Foster PLAY/112* 1.25 3.00
521 Maurkice Pouncey PLAY/112* 1.25 3.00
522 David DeCastro PLAY/112* 1.25 3.00
523 Marcus Gilbert PLAY/112* 1.25 3.00
524 Ricardo Mathews PLAY/112* 1.25 3.00
525 Javon Hargrave PLAY/112* 1.25 3.00
526 Stephon Tuitt PLAY/112* 1.25 3.00
527 Bud Dupree PLAY/112* 1.25 3.00
528 Ryan Shazier PLAY/112* 1.25 3.00
529 Lawrence Timmons PLAY/112* 1.50 4.00
530 James Harrison PLAY/112* 1.50 4.00
531 Artie Burns PLAY/112* 1.50 4.00
532 Mike Mitchell PLAY/112* 1.25 3.00
533 Sean Davis PLAY/112* 1.25 3.00
534 Ross Cockrell PLAY/112* 1.25 3.00
535 Chris Boswell PLAY/112* 1.25 3.00
536 Tom Savage PLAY/62* 1.50 4.00
537 Brock Osweiler PLAY/62* 1.50 4.00
538 Lamar Miller PLAY/62* 1.50 4.00
539 Alfred Blue PLAY 1.50 4.00
540 DeAndre Hopkins PLAY/62* 2.00 5.00
541 Will Fuller V PLAY/62* 2.50 6.00
542 C.J. Fiedorowicz PLAY/62* 2.00 5.00
543 Duane Brown PLAY/62* 1.50 4.00
544 Xavier Su'a-Filo PLAY/62* 1.50 4.00
545 Greg Mancz PLAY/62* 1.50 4.00
546 Jeff Allen PLAY/62* 1.50 4.00
547 Chris Clark PLAY/62* 1.50 4.00
548 J.J. Watt PLAY/62* 2.50 6.00
549 Vince Wilfork PLAY/62* 1.50 4.00
550 Jadeveon Clowney PLAY/62* 1.50 4.00
551 Whitney Mercilus PLAY/62* 1.50 4.00
552 Brian Cushing PLAY/62* 1.50 4.00
553 Benardrick McKinney PLAY/62* 1.50 4.00
554 John Simon PLAY/62* 1.50 4.00
555 Kareem Jackson PLAY/62* 1.50 4.00
556 Johnathan Joseph PLAY/62* 1.50 4.00
557 Quintin Demps PLAY/62* 1.50 4.00
558 Shaq Mason SB LI 1.50 4.00
559 Logan Ryan SB LI 1.50 4.00
560 Nick Novak PLAY/62* 1.50 4.00
561 Rob Ninkovich SB LI 1.25 3.00
562 Jamaal Charles PLAY/115* 1.50 4.00
563 Spencer Ware PLAY/115* 1.25 3.00
564 Jeremy Maclin PLAY/115* 1.25 3.00
565 Chris Conley PLAY/115* 1.25 3.00
566 Tyreek Hill PLAY/115* 5.00 12.00
567 Travis Kelce PLAY/115* 2.00 5.00
568 Demetrius Harris PLAY/115* 1.25 3.00
569 Laurent Duvernay-Tardif PLAY/115* 1.25 3.00
570 Eric Fisher PLAY/115* 1.25 3.00
571 Zach Fulton PLAY/115* 1.25 3.00
572 Mitch Morse PLAY/115* 1.25 3.00
573 Rakeem Nunez-Noches PLAY/115* 1.25 3.00
574 Mitchell Schwartz PLAY/115* 1.25 3.00
575 Dontari Poe PLAY/115* 1.25 3.00
576 Chris Jones PLAY/115* 1.25 3.00
577 Justin Houston PLAY/115* 1.25 3.00
578 Derrick Johnson PLAY/115* 1.25 3.00
579 Ramik Wilson PLAY/115* 1.25 3.00
580 Dee Ford PLAY/115* 1.25 3.00
581 Marcus Peters PLAY/115* 1.25 3.00
582 Phillip Gaines PLAY/115* 1.25 3.00
583 Eric Berry PLAY/115* 1.50 4.00
584 Ron Parker PLAY/115* 1.25 3.00
585 Cairo Santos PLAY/115* 1.25 3.00
586 Dak Prescott PLAY/220* 6.00 15.00
587 Ezekiel Elliott PLAY/220* 6.00 15.00
588 Dez Bryant PLAY/220* 2.00 5.00
589 Cole Beasley PLAY/220* 2.00 5.00
590 Terrance Williams PLAY/220* 1.25 3.00
591 Sean Lee PLAY/220* 1.50 4.00
592 Benson Mayowa PLAY/220* 1.25 3.00
593 David Irving PLAY/220* 1.25 3.00
594 Brandon Carr PLAY/220* 1.25 3.00
595 Morris Claiborne PLAY/220* 1.25 3.00
596 Byron Jones PLAY/220* 1.25 3.00
597 Dan Bailey PLAY/220* 1.25 3.00
598 Tom Brady/59* 6.00 15.00
599 Julian Edelman/54* 2.50 6.00
600 Michael Floyd/78* 1.25 3.00
601 Tony Romo/79* 1.50 4.00
602 Carson Wentz/73* 15.00 40.00
603 Jordan Howard/57* 4.00 10.00
604 Devontae Booker/54* 2.00 5.00
605 Tyreek Hill/134* 5.00 12.00
606 Paul Perkins/67* 1.50 4.00
607 Tom Brady/75* 5.00 12.00
608 Drew Brees/54* 2.50 6.00
609 Ezekiel Elliott/329* 6.00 15.00
610 T.Y. Hilton 1.50 4.00
611 Michael Thomas 2.50 6.00
612 Matt Ryan 1.50 4.00
613 Brent Grimes 1.25 3.00
614 Aaron Rodgers/54* 5.00 12.00
615 Ezekiel Elliott 6.00 15.00
Dak Prescott/1251*
616 Dak Prescott 6.00 15.00
Tom Brady/305*
617 Matthew Stafford PLAY 1.50 4.00
618 Theo Riddick PLAY 1.25 3.00
619 Dwayne Washington PLAY 1.50 4.00
620 Zach Zenner PLAY 1.25 3.00
621 Golden Tate III PLAY 1.25 3.00
622 Marvin Jones Jr. PLAY 1.25 3.00
623 Anquan Boldin PLAY 1.25 3.00
624 Eric Ebron PLAY 1.25 3.00
625 Taylor Decker PLAY 1.50 4.00
626 Graham Glasgow PLAY 1.25 3.00
627 Travis Swanson PLAY 1.25 3.00
628 Larry Warford PLAY 1.25 3.00
629 Riley Reiff PLAY 1.25 3.00
630 Devin Taylor PLAY 1.25 3.00
631 Tyrunn Walker PLAY 1.25 3.00
632 Haloti Ngata PLAY 1.25 3.00
633 Ezekiel Ansah PLAY 1.25 3.00
634 DeAndre Levy PLAY 1.25 3.00
635 Tahir Whitehead PLAY 1.25 3.00
636 Josh Bynes PLAY 1.25 3.00
637 Darius Slay PLAY 1.25 3.00
638 Nevin Lawson PLAY 1.25 3.00
639 Tavon Wilson PLAY 1.25 3.00
640 Glover Quin PLAY 1.25 3.00
641 Matt Prater PLAY 1.25 3.00
642 Aaron Rodgers PLAY 4.00 10.00
643 Eddie Lacy PLAY/79* 1.25 3.00
644 Ty Montgomery PLAY/79* 1.50 4.00
645 Jordy Nelson PLAY/79* 1.50 4.00
646 Davante Adams PLAY/79* 1.25 3.00
647 Randall Cobb PLAY/79* 1.50 4.00
648 Jared Cook PLAY/79* 1.25 3.00
649 David Bakhtiari PLAY/79* 1.25 3.00
650 Lane Taylor PLAY/79* 1.25 3.00
651 J.C. Tretter PLAY/79* 1.25 3.00
652 T.J. Lang PLAY/79* 1.25 3.00
653 Bryan Bulaga PLAY/79* 1.25 3.00
654 Kenny Clark PLAY/79* 1.25 3.00
655 Letroy Guion PLAY/79* 1.25 3.00
656 Mike Daniels PLAY/79* 1.25 3.00
657 Julius Peppers PLAY/79* 1.50 4.00
658 Nick Perry PLAY/79* 1.25 3.00
659 Jake Ryan PLAY/79* 1.25 3.00
660 Blake Martinez PLAY/79* 1.50 4.00
661 Clay Matthews PLAY/79* 2.00 5.00
662 Damarious Randall PLAY/79* 1.25 3.00
663 Quinten Rollins PLAY/79* 1.50 4.00
664 Morgan Burnett PLAY/79* 1.25 3.00
665 Ha Ha Clinton-Dix PLAY/79* 1.25 3.00
666 Mason Crosby PLAY/79* 1.25 3.00
667 Alex Smith PLAY 1.50 4.00
668 Spencer Ware PLAY 1.25 3.00
669 Charcandrick West PLAY 1.25 3.00
670 Jeremy Maclin PLAY 1.25 3.00
671 Chris Conley PLAY 1.25 3.00
672 Tyreek Hill PLAY 5.00 12.00
673 Travis Kelce PLAY 2.00 5.00
674 Dontari Poe PLAY 1.25 3.00
675 Chris Jones PLAY 1.25 3.00
676 Justin Houston PLAY 1.25 3.00
677 Marcus Peters PLAY 1.25 3.00
678 Eric Berry PLAY 1.50 4.00
679 Matt Ryan ALL PRO/107* 1.50 4.00
680 Ezekiel Elliott ALL PRO/107* 6.00 15.00
681 David Johnson ALL PRO/107* 2.00 5.00
682 Antonio Brown ALL PRO/107* 2.00 5.00
683 Julio Jones ALL PRO/107* 2.00 5.00
684 Travis Kelce ALL PRO/107* 2.00 5.00
685 Tyron Smith ALL PRO/107* 1.25 3.00
686 Kelechi Osemele ALL PRO/107* 1.25 3.00
687 Travis Frederick ALL PRO/107* 1.25 3.00
688 Zack Martin ALL PRO/107* 1.25 3.00
689 Jack Conklin ALL PRO/107* 2.00 5.00
690 Khalil Mack ALL PRO/107* 2.00 5.00
691 Aaron Donald ALL PRO 2.00 5.00
692 Damon Harrison ALL PRO/107* 1.25 3.00
693 Vic Beasley ALL PRO/107* 1.25 3.00
694 Von Miller ALL PRO/107* 1.50 4.00
695 Bobby Wagner ALL PRO/107* 1.25 3.00
696 Sean Lee ALL PRO/107* 1.50 4.00
697 Aqib Talib ALL PRO/107* 1.25 3.00
698 Marcus Peters ALL PRO/107* 1.25 3.00
699 Chris Harris ALL PRO/107* 1.25 3.00
700 Landon Collins ALL PRO/107* 1.25 3.00
701 Eric Berry ALL PRO/107* 1.50 4.00
702 Justin Tucker ALL PRO/107* 1.25 3.00
703 Johnny Hekker ALL PRO/107* 1.25 3.00
704 Cordarrelle Patterson ALL PRO/107* 1.25 3.00
705 Tyreek Hill ALL PRO/107* 5.00 12.00
706 Matthew Slater ALL PRO/107* 1.25 3.00
707 Doug Baldwin 1.50 4.00
708 Thomas Rawls 1.25 3.00
709 Antonio Brown 2.00 5.00
710 Le' Veon Bell 1.50 4.00
711 Aaron Rodgers 5.00 12.00
712 Randall Cobb 4.00 10.00
Aaron Rodgers
713 Brock Osweiler PLAY 1.25 3.00
714 Lamar Miller PLAY 1.25 3.00
715 DeAndre Hopkins PLAY 1.50 4.00
716 Will Fuller PLAY 2.00 5.00
717 C.J. Fiedorowicz PLAY 1.50 4.00
718 Jadeveon Clowney PLAY 1.25 3.00
719 Whitney Mercilus PLAY 1.25 3.00
720 Benardrick McKinney PLAY 1.25 3.00
721 Brian Cushing PLAY 1.25 3.00
722 A.J. Bouye PLAY 1.25 3.00
723 Andre Hal PLAY 1.25 3.00
724 Johnathan Joseph PLAY 1.25 3.00
725 Russell Wilson PLAY 2.50 6.00
726 Thomas Rawls PLAY 1.25 3.00
727 Alex Collins PLAY 1.50 4.00
728 Doug Baldwin PLAY 1.50 4.00
729 Paul Richardson PLAY 1.25 3.00
730 Jimmy Graham PLAY 2.00 5.00
731 Cliff Avril PLAY 1.25 3.00
732 Michael Bennett PLAY 1.25 3.00
733 Bobby Wagner PLAY 1.25 3.00
734 K.J. Wright PLAY 1.25 3.00
735 Richard Sherman PLAY 2.00 5.00
736 Kam Chancellor PLAY 2.00 5.00
737 Ben Roethlisberger PLAY 2.00 5.00
738 Le' Veon Bell PLAY 1.50 4.00
739 Antonio Brown PLAY 2.00 5.00
740 Eli Rogers PLAY 1.50 4.00
741 Demarcus Ayers PLAY 1.25 3.00
742 Lawrence Timmons PLAY 1.50 4.00
743 James Harrison PLAY 1.50 4.00
744 Ryan Shazier PLAY 1.25 3.00
745 Bud Dupree PLAY 1.25 3.00
746 Ross Cockrell PLAY 1.25 3.00
747 Artie Burns PLAY 1.50 4.00
748 Sean Davis PLAY 1.25 3.00
749 Aaron Rodgers PLAY 4.00 10.00
750 Ty Montgomery PLAY 1.50 4.00
751 Christine Michael PLAY 1.25 3.00
752 Jordy Nelson PLAY 1.50 4.00
753 Randall Cobb PLAY 1.50 4.00
754 Davante Adams PLAY 1.25 3.00
755 Jared Cook PLAY 1.25 3.00
756 Jake Ryan PLAY 1.25 3.00
757 Julius Peppers PLAY 1.50 4.00
758 Clay Matthews PLAY 1.50 4.00
759 Damarious Randall PLAY 1.25 3.00
760 Mason Crosby PLAY 1.25 3.00
761 TBA
762 Aaron Rodgers 6.00 15.00
Dak Prescott/169*
763 Matt Ryan 1.50 4.00
764 Julio Jones 2.00 5.00
765 Tom Brady 5.00 12.00
766 Dion Lewis 1.25 3.00
767 Ezekiel Elliott/193* 6.00 15.00
768 Dak Prescott/212* 6.00 15.00
769 Aaron Rodgers 5.00 12.00
770 Mason Crosby 1.25 3.00
771 Le' Veon Bell 1.50 4.00
772 Chris Boswell 1.25 3.00
773 Matt Ryan PLAY 1.50 4.00
774 Devonta Freeman PLAY 1.50 4.00
775 Tevin Coleman PLAY 1.50 4.00
776 Julio Jones PLAY 2.00 5.00
777 Mohamed Sanu PLAY 1.25 3.00
778 Taylor Gabriel PLAY 1.25 3.00
779 Levine Toilolo PLAY 1.25 3.00
780 Vic Beasley Jr. PLAY 1.25 3.00
781 Brooks Reed PLAY 1.25 3.00
782 Deion Jones PLAY 1.25 3.00
783 Jonathan Babineaux PLAY 1.25 3.00
784 Keanu Neal PLAY 1.25 3.00
785 Tom Brady PLAY/70* 5.00 12.00
786 LeGarrette Blount PLAY/70* 2.00 5.00
787 Dion Lewis PLAY/70* 1.50 4.00
788 James White PLAY/70* 2.00 5.00
789 Julian Edelman PLAY/70* 2.50 6.00
790 Chris Hogan PLAY/70* 1.50 4.00
791 Martellus Bennett PLAY/70* 1.50 4.00
792 Dont'a Hightower PLAY/70* 1.50 4.00
793 Rob Ninkovich PLAY/70* 1.50 4.00
794 Logan Ryan PLAY/70* 1.50 4.00
795 Malcolm Butler PLAY/70* 2.50 6.00
796 Devin McCourty PLAY/70* 1.50 4.00
797 Aaron Rodgers PLAY/73* 5.00 12.00
798 Ty Montgomery PLAY/73* 2.00 5.00
799 Christine Michael PLAY/73* 1.50 4.00
800 Davante Adams PLAY/73* 1.50 4.00
801 Randall Cobb PLAY/73* 2.00 5.00
802 Geronimo Allison PLAY/73* 1.50 4.00
803 Richard Rodgers PLAY/73* 2.00 5.00
804 Jared Cook PLAY/73* 1.50 4.00
805 Julius Peppers PLAY/73* 2.00 5.00
806 Clay Matthews PLAY/73* 2.50 6.00
807 Nick Perry PLAY/73* 1.50 4.00
808 Micah Hyde PLAY/73* 1.50 4.00
809 Ben Roethlisberger PLAY 2.00 5.00
810 Le' Veon Bell PLAY 1.50 4.00
811 Antonio Brown PLAY 2.00 5.00
812 Eli Rogers PLAY 1.50 4.00
813 Jesse James PLAY 1.25 3.00
814 James Harrison PLAY 1.50 4.00
815 Ryan Shazier PLAY 1.25 3.00
816 Bud Dupree PLAY 1.25 3.00

817 Lawrence Timmons PLAY 1.50 4.00
818 Ross Cockrell PLAY 1.25 3.00
819 Artie Burns PLAY 1.50 4.00
820 Sean Davis PLAY 1.25 3.00
821 Matt Ryan/53* 2.00 5.00
822 Julio Jones 2.00 5.00
823 Tom Brady 5.00 12.00
824 Chris Hogan/84* 1.25 3.00
825 Julian Edelman 2.00 5.00
826 Tom Brady 5.00 12.00
Matt Ryan/135*
827 Matt Ryan SB LI 1.50 4.00
828 Devonta Freeman SB LI 1.50 4.00
829 Tevin Coleman SB LI 1.50 4.00
830 Julio Jones SB LI 2.00 5.00
831 Mohamed Sanu SB LI 1.25 3.00
832 Taylor Gabriel SB LI 1.25 3.00
833 Austin Hooper SB LI 1.25 3.00
834 Jake Matthews SB LI 1.25 3.00
835 Andy LeVitre SB LI 1.25 3.00
836 Alex Mack SB LI 1.25 3.00
837 Chris Chester SB LI 1.25 3.00
838 Ryan Schraeder SB LI 1.25 3.00
839 Brooks Reed SB LI 1.25 3.00
840 Jonathan Babineaux SB LI 1.25 3.00
841 Grady Jarrett SB LI 1.25 3.00
842 Tyler Jackson SB LI 1.25 3.00
843 Vic Beasley SB LI 1.25 3.00
844 Deion Jones SB LI 1.25 3.00
845 De' Vondre Campbell SB LI 1.50 4.00
846 Robert Alford SB LI 1.25 3.00
847 Jalen Collins SB LI 1.25 3.00
848 Ricardo Allen SB LI 1.25 3.00
849 Keanu Neal SB LI 1.25 3.00
850 Matt Bryant SB LI 1.25 3.00
851 Tom Brady SB LI 5.00 12.00
852 LeGarrette Blount SB LI 1.50 4.00
853 Dion Lewis SB LI 1.25 3.00
854 Julian Edelman SB LI 2.00 5.00
855 Chris Hogan SB LI 1.25 3.00
856 Malcolm Mitchell SB LI 1.25 3.00
857 Martellus Bennett SB LI 1.25 3.00
858 Nate Solder SB LI 1.25 3.00
859 Joe Thuney SB LI 1.25 3.00
860 David Andrews SB LI 1.25 3.00
861 Shaq Mason SB LI 1.25 3.00
862 Marcus Cannon SB LI 1.25 3.00
863 Chris Long SB LI 1.25 3.00
864 Nate Solder SB LI 1.25 3.00
865 Malcolm Brown SB LI 1.25 3.00
866 Trey Flowers SB LI 1.25 3.00
867 Shea McClellin SB LI 1.25 3.00
868 Dont'a Hightower SB LI 1.25 3.00
869 Rob Ninkovich SB LI 1.25 3.00
870 Logan Ryan SB LI 1.25 3.00
871 Malcolm Butler SB LI 2.00 5.00
872 Patrick Chung SB LI 1.25 3.00
873 Devin McCourty SB LI 1.25 3.00
874 Stephen Gostkowski SB LI 1.50 4.00
875 Dak Prescott PRO 6.00 15.00
876 Ezekiel Elliott PRO 6.00 15.00
877 Lorenzo Alexander 2.00 5.00
Travis Kelce
PRO MVP
878 Tom Brady 5.00 12.00
879 Matt Ryan MVP 1.50 4.00
880 Khalil Mack DPOY 2.00 5.00
881 Dak Prescott 6.00 15.00
882 Joey Bosa 2.50 6.00
883 Jordy Nelson 1.50 4.00
884 Eli Manning 1.50 4.00
Larry Fitzgerald
885 LaDainian Tomlinson 1.50 4.00
886 Terrell Davis 1.50 4.00
887 Kurt Warner 1.50 4.00
888 Morten Anderson 1.25 3.00
889 New England Patriots Logo SB LI
890 Tom Brady SB LI 5.00 12.00
891 LeGarrette Blount SB LI 1.50 4.00
892 James White SB LI 1.50 4.00
893 Dion Lewis SB LI 1.25 3.00
894 Julian Edelman SB LI 2.00 5.00
895 Chris Hogan SB LI 1.25 3.00
896 Danny Amendola SB LI 1.50 4.00
897 Malcolm Mitchell SB LI 1.25 3.00
898 Matthew Slater SB LI 1.25 3.00
899 Martellus Bennett SB LI 1.25 3.00
900 Rob Gronkowski SB LI 2.00 5.00
901 Nate Solder SB LI 1.25 3.00
902 Joe Thuney SB LI 1.25 3.00
903 David Andrews SB LI 1.25 3.00
904 Shaq Mason SB LI 1.25 3.00
905 Marcus Cannon SB LI 1.25 3.00
906 Chris Long SB LI 1.25 3.00
907 Alan Branch SB LI 1.25 3.00
908 Malcolm Brown SB LI 1.25 3.00
909 Trey Flowers SB LI 1.25 3.00
910 Shea McClellin SB LI 1.25 3.00
911 Dont'a Hightower SB LI 1.25 3.00
912 Rob Ninkovich SB LI 1.25 3.00
913 Logan Ryan SB LI 1.25 3.00
914 Malcolm Butler SB LI 2.00 5.00
915 Patrick Chung SB LI 1.25 3.00
916 Devin McCourty SB LI 1.25 3.00
917 Eric Rowe SB LI 1.25 3.00
918 Duron Harmon SB LI 1.25 3.00
919 Barkevious Mingo SB LI 1.25 3.00
920 Elandon Roberts SB LI 1.25 3.00
921 Jabaal Sheard SB LI 1.25 3.00
922 Kyle Van Noy SB LI 1.25 3.00
923 Ryan Allen SB LI 1.25 3.00
924 Stephen Gostkowski SB LI 1.50 4.00
925 Julio Jones 2.00 5.00
926 James White 1.50 4.00
927 Tom Brady 5.00 12.00
928 Tom Brady 5.00 12.00
Passing Yards
929 Tom Brady 5.00 12.00
Super Bowl MVPs
930 Tom Brady 5.00 12.00
Most Super Bowl Wins QB
931 Tom Brady 5.00 12.00
Largest Comeback
932 Tom Brady 5.00 12.00
Most Completions

2016 Panini Instant Blue
*BLUE/25: .6X TO 1.5X BASIC CARDS/75-1251
*BLUE/25: .5X TO 1.2X BASIC CARDS/51-74

2016 Panini Instant Orange
*ORANGE/50: .5X TO 1.2X BASIC CARDS/75-1251
*ORANGE/25: .4X TO 1X BASIC CARDS/51-74

2016 Panini Instant Black Friday Rookies
1 Dak Prescott 3.00 8.00
2 Ezekiel Elliott 3.00 8.00
3 Jard Goff 4.00 10.00
4 Paxton Lynch 1.25 3.00
5 Devontae Booker 1.50 4.00
6 Derrick Henry 3.00 8.00
7 Carson Wentz 4.00 10.00
8 Sterling Shepard 1.50 4.00
9 Michael Thomas 2.50 6.00
10 Corey Coleman 2.00 5.00

2016 Panini Instant Leonard Fournette
LF1 Leonard Fournette 3.00 8.00

2016 Panini Instant Rookie Happy Holidays Santa Hats
CH Christian Hackenberg 10.00
CJ Cardale Jones 10.00
DP Dak Prescott 12.00
EE Ezekiel Elliott 12.00
KD Kenyan Drake 10.00
LC Leonte Carroo 10.00
MT Michael Thomas 10.00
PL Paxton Lynch 10.00
SS Sterling Shepard 10.00
TB Tyler Boyd 10.00

2016 Panini Instant Tools of the Trade
EE Ezekiel Elliott 5.00 12.00
DP Dak Prescott 5.00 12.00
Dropback
DP Dak Prescott 5.00 12.00
Sideline Hat

2016 Panini Kickoff
1 Aaron Rodgers .60 1.50
2 Cam Newton .30 .75
3 Andrew Luck .40 1.00
4 Blake Bortles .20 .50
5 Tom Brady .75 2.00
6 Drew Brees .30 .75
7 Philip Rivers .30 .75
8 Russell Wilson .40 1.00
9 Jameis Winston .30 .75
10 Marcus Mariota .30 .75
11 LeSean McCoy .30 .75
12 Todd Gurley II .30 .75
13 Adrian Peterson .30 .75
14 Le'Veon Bell .25 .60
15 Rob Gronkowski .30 .75
16 Jason Witten .25 .60
17 Larry Fitzgerald .25 .60
18 Julio Jones .30 .75
19 Alshon Jeffery .25 .60
20 A.J. Green .30 .75
21 Dez Bryant .30 .75
22 Jarvis Landry .25 .60
23 Odell Beckham Jr. .30 .75
24 Brandon Marshall .20 .50
25 Antonio Brown .30 .75
26 DeAndre Hopkins .25 .60
27 Demaryius Thomas .25 .60
28 Marshal Yanda .20 .50
29 Joe Thomas .20 .50
30 Eric Berry .25 .60
31 Josh Norman .20 .50
32 Von Miller .25 .60
33 Ezekiel Ansah .20 .50
34 J.J. Watt .30 .75
35 Khalil Mack .30 .75
36 Fletcher Cox .20 .50
37 NaVorro Bowman .25 .60
38 Stephen Gostkowski .25 .60
39 Brandon McManus .20 .50
40 Johnny Hekker .20 .50
41 Robert Nkemdiche .75 2.00
42 Keanu Neal .60 1.50
43 Ronnie Stanley .75 2.00
44 Kenneth Dixon .60 1.50
45 Cardale Jones .60 1.50
46 Vernon Butler .60 1.50
47 Leonard Floyd .75 2.00
48 Tyler Boyd .75 2.00
49 Corey Coleman 1.00 2.50
50 Cody Kessler .60 1.50
51 Ezekiel Elliott 3.00 8.00
52 Dak Prescott 3.00 8.00
53 Jaylon Smith .60 1.50
54 Paxton Lynch .60 1.50
55 Devontae Booker .75 2.00
56 Andy Janovich .75 2.00
57 A'Shawn Robinson .60 1.50
58 Kenny Clark .60 1.50
59 Will Fuller V 1.00 2.50
60 Braxton Miller .60 1.50
61 Ryan Kelly 1.00 2.50
62 Jalan Ramsey 1.00 2.50
63 Myles Jack .75 2.00
64 Demarcus Robinson .60 1.50
65 Jared Goff 4.00 10.00
66 Pharoh Cooper .60 1.50
67 Kenyan Drake 1.00 2.50
68 Laquon Treadwell .75 2.00
69 Moritz Bohringer .60 1.50
70 Jacoby Brissett .75 2.00
71 Malcolm Mitchell .60 1.50
72 Michael Thomas 1.25 3.00
73 Sterling Shepard .75 2.00
74 Eli Apple .75 2.00
75 Christian Hackenberg .60 1.50
76 DeAndre Washington .60 1.50
77 Marquette King 3.00 8.00
78 Connor Cook .75 2.00
79 Carson Wentz 6.00 15.00
80 Wendell Smallwood .60 1.50
81 Artie Burns .75 2.00
82 Joey Bosa 1.25 3.00
83 Hunter Henry .75 2.00
84 C.J. Prosise .60 1.50
85 Alex Collins .75 2.00
86 DeForest Buckner .60 1.50
87 Vernon Hargreaves III 1.00 2.50
88 Roberto Aguayo .60 1.50
89 Derrick Henry 1.50 4.00
90 Josh Doctson .75 2.00

2016 Panini Kickoff Thick Stock
*VETS: 2X TO 5X BASIC CARDS
*ROOKIES: .6X TO 1.5X BASIC CARDS

2016 Panini Kickoff Football Inserts
*WEDGES/50: 1.2X TO 3X BASIC INSERTS
*THICK/50: 1.2X TO 3X BASIC INSERTS
*CRACKED/25: 2X TO 5X BASIC INSERTS
1 Ray Hamilton .30 .75
2 J.J. Watt .50 1.25
3 Clay Matthews .50 1.25
4 Jordy Nelson .40 1.00
5 Antonio Brown .50 1.25
6 Ezekiel Ansah .30 .75
7 Stephen Gostkowski .40 1.00
8 Austin Davis .40 1.00
9 Logan Mankins .30 .75
10 Jared Abbrederis .30 .75

2016 Panini Kickoff Game Date Memorabilia
*GALAACTIC/25: .6X TO 1.5X BASIC MEM
1 Aaron Rodgers 6.00 15.00
2 Marcus Mariota 3.00 8.00
3 Teddy Bridgewater 2.50 6.00
4 Kamar Aiken 2.00 5.00
5 Ndamukong Suh 2.50 6.00
6 Ryan Tannehill 2.50 6.00
7 Jarvis Landry 2.50 6.00
8 Tyrod Taylor 2.50 6.00
9 Jeremy Hill 2.00 5.00
10 Sammy Watkins 3.00 8.00
11 Preston Brown 2.00 5.00
12 Blake Bortles 2.00 5.00
13 Joe Thomas 2.00 5.00
14 Ryan Tannehill 2.50 6.00
15 Challenge Flag 3.00 8.00

2016 Panini Kickoff Memorabilia
*GALACTIC/25: .6X TO 1.5X BASIC MEM
1 Braxton Miller 1.50 4.00
2 C.J. Prosise 1.50 4.00
3 Cardale Jones 1.50 4.00
4 Carson Wentz 6.00 15.00
5 Kevin Hogan 2.00 5.00
6 Cody Kessler 1.50 4.00
7 Corey Coleman 2.50 6.00
8 Keenan Reynolds 2.00 5.00
9 Derrick Henry 4.00 10.00
10 Devontae Booker 2.00 5.00
11 Ezekiel Elliott 8.00 20.00
12 Hunter Henry 2.00 5.00
13 Dak Prescott 8.00 20.00
14 Josh Doctson 2.00 5.00
15 Kenyan Drake 2.50 6.00
16 Laquon Treadwell 2.00 5.00
17 Michael Thomas 3.00 8.00
18 Paul Perkins 1.50 4.00
19 Paxton Lynch SP 4.00 10.00
20 Jordan Howard 3.00 8.00
21 Sterling Shepard 3.00 8.00
22 Tyler Boyd 2.00 5.00
23 Wendell Smallwood 1.50 4.00
24 Will Fuller V 3.00 8.00
25 Kenneth Dixon 1.50 4.00

2016 Panini Kickoff Pink Wristbands
*GALACTIC/25: .6X TO 1.5X BASIC MEM
1 Jared Goff 10.00 25.00
2 Kenyan Drake 2.50 6.00
3 Josh Doctson 2.00 5.00
4 Derrick Henry 4.00 10.00
5 Carson Wentz 15.00 40.00
6 Paxton Lynch 1.50 4.00
7 Joey Bosa 3.00 8.00
8 Corey Coleman 2.50 6.00
9 Ezekiel Elliott 8.00 20.00
10 Sterling Shepard 2.00 5.00
11 Amari Cooper 2.50 6.00
12 Marcus Mariota 2.50 6.00
13 Jameis Winston 2.50 6.00
14 Mike Evans 2.00 5.00
15 Devonta Freeman 2.00 5.00
16 Khalil Mack 2.50 6.00
17 Todd Gurley II SP 3.00 8.00
18 Allen Robinson 2.00 5.00
19 Jordan Reed 1.50 4.00
20 Odell Beckham Jr. 2.50 6.00
21 Andy Dalton 2.00 5.00
22 Vontaze Burfict 1.50 4.00
23 Jarvis Landry 2.00 5.00
24 Sammy Watkins 2.50 6.00
25 Tyrod Taylor 2.00 5.00
26 Kevin White 1.50 4.00
27 Jay Ajayi 2.00 5.00
28 Matt Jones 2.00 5.00
29 David Johnson 2.50 6.00
30 Laquon Treadwell 2.00 5.00
31 Kelvin Benjamin 2.00 5.00
32 Blake Bortles 1.50 4.00
33 Ameer Abdullah SP 2.00 5.00
34 Teddy Bridgewater SP 2.50 6.00
35 DeVante Parker SP 2.50 6.00

2017 Panini Kickoff
*CRACKED/25: .2X TO 5X BASIC CARDS
1 Tom Brady .60 1.50
2 Von Miller .20 .50
3 Julio Jones .25 .60
4 Antonio Brown .25 .60
5 Khalil Mack .25 .60
6 Aaron Rodgers .50 1.25
7 Ezekiel Elliott .30 .75
8 Odell Beckham Jr. .25 .60
9 Le'Veon Bell .20 .50
10 Matt Ryan .20 .50
11 Derek Carr .25 .60
12 David Johnson .25 .60
13 Eric Berry .20 .50
14 Dak Prescott .25 .60
15 Aaron Donald .25 .60
16 Drew Brees .25 .60
17 A.J. Green .25 .60
18 Tyrnn Smith .15 .40
19 Patrick Peterson .15 .40
20 Luke Kuechly .20 .50
21 Richard Sherman .25 .60
22 Ben Roethlisberger .25 .60
23 Rob Gronkowski .25 .60
24 Russell Wilson .30 .75
25 Joe Thomas .15 .40
26 Travis Kelce .25 .60
27 LeSean McCoy .25 .60
28 Landon Collins .15 .40
29 Mike Evans .20 .50
30 Earl Thomas III .20 .50
31 Matthew Stafford .20 .50
32 Marcus Peters .15 .40
33 DeMarco Murray .20 .50
34 Kam Chancellor .25 .60
35 J.J. Watt .25 .60
36 Tyreek Hill .25 .60
37 Aqib Talib .15 .40
38 Fletcher Cox .15 .40
39 Bobby Wagner .15 .40
40 Vic Beasley Jr. .15 .40
41 Devonta Freeman .20 .50
42 Jarvis Landry .20 .50
43 Marshal Yanda .15 .40
44 Cam Newton .25 .60
45 Larry Fitzgerald .20 .50
46 Michael Bennett .15 .40
47 Trent Williams .15 .40
48 Jordy Nelson .20 .50
49 Jadeveon Clowney .15 .40
50 Marcus Mariota .25 .60
51 Andrew Luck .30 .75
52 Gerald McCoy .15 .40
53 Amari Cooper .25 .60
54 Janoris Jenkins .15 .40
55 Ndamukong Suh .20 .50
56 Cliff Avril .15 .40
57 Jameis Winston .20 .50
58 Zack Martin .15 .40
59 Josh Norman .15 .40
60 Dez Bryant .25 .60
61 T.Y. Hilton .20 .50
62 Cameron Wake .15 .40
63 Chris Harris .15 .40
64 Casey Hayward .15 .40
65 Jordan Reed .15 .40
66 Xavier Rhodes .15 .40
67 Greg Olsen .20 .50
68 Geno Atkins .15 .40
69 Jay Ajayi .20 .50
70 Kirk Cousins .25 .60
71 Julian Edelman .25 .60
72 Taylor Lewan .15 .40
73 Philip Rivers .25 .60
74 Harrison Smith .15 .40
75 Delanie Walker .15 .40
76 Justin Houston .15 .40
77 Ha Ha Clinton-Dix .15 .40
78 Brian Orakpo .15 .40
79 Sean Lee .20 .50
80 LeGarrette Blount .20 .50
81 Alex Smith .20 .50
82 Clay Matthews .20 .50
83 Calais Campbell .15 .40
84 Mike Daniels .15 .40
85 Chandler Jones .15 .40
86 Jurrell Casey .15 .40
87 Travis Frederick .15 .40
88 Doug Baldwin .20 .50
89 Thomas Davis .15 .40
90 Malcolm Jenkins .20 .50
91 Lorenzo Alexander .15 .40
92 Everson Griffen .15 .40
93 Brandon Graham .15 .40
94 Dont'a Hightower .15 .40
95 Kelechi Osemele .15 .40
96 Damon Harrison .15 .40
97 David DeCastro .15 .40
98 Adrian Peterson .25 .60
99 Malcolm Butler .25 .60
100 Joey Bosa .25 .60

2017 Panini Kickoff Memorabilia
*CRACKED/25: 1X TO 2.5X BASIC MEM
AA Ameer Abdullah 1.50 4.00
AC Amari Cooper 2.50 6.00
AR Allen Robinson 2.00 5.00
CP C.J. Prosise 1.50 4.00
DF Devonta Freeman 2.00 5.00
DP Dak Prescott 2.50 6.00
EE Ezekiel Elliott 3.00 8.00
JA Jay Ajayi 2.00 5.00
JB Joey Bosa 2.50 6.00
JH Jordan Howard 2.50 6.00
JW Jameis Winston 2.00 5.00
KM Khalil Mack 2.50 6.00
MM Marcus Mariota 2.50 6.00
MT Michael Thomas 2.50 6.00
SD Stefon Diggs 2.00 5.00
SS Sterling Shepard 2.00 5.00
SW Sammy Watkins 2.50 6.00
TE Tyler Eifert 2.00 5.00
TL Tyler Lockett 2.00 5.00
TM Ty Montgomery 1.50 4.00

2017 Panini Kickoff National Champions
*CRACKED/25: 2X TO 5X BASIC INSERTS
1 Deshaun Watson 1.25 3.00
2 Mike Williams .30 .75
3 Ben Boulware .50 1.25
4 Wayne Gallman .25 .60
5 Carlos Watkins .20 .50
6 Jordan Leggett .20 .50
7 Mike Williams .30 .75
8 Deshaun Watson 1.25 3.00
9 Deshaun Watson 1.25 3.00

2017 Panini Kickoff Pro Bowl Memorabilia
*CRACKED/25: 2X TO 5X BASIC MEM
1 Dak Prescott 2.50 6.00
2 Ezekiel Elliott 3.00 8.00
3 Jordan Howard 2.50 6.00
4 Andy Dalton 2.00 5.00
5 Alex Smith 2.00 5.00
6 Philip Rivers 2.50 6.00
7 Jay Ajayi 2.00 5.00
8 DeMarco Murray 2.00 5.00
9 T.Y. Hilton 2.00 5.00
10 Kirk Cousins 2.50 6.00
11 Drew Brees 2.50 6.00
12 Doug Baldwin 2.00 5.00
13 Delanie Walker 1.50 4.00
14 Odell Beckham Jr. 2.50 6.00
15 Kyle Juszczyk 1.50 4.00
16 Dez Bryant 2.50 6.00
17 Demaryius Thomas 2.00 5.00
18 Richard Sherman 2.50 6.00
19 Von Miller 2.00 5.00
20 Britton Colquitt 1.50 4.00
21 Johnny Hekker 1.50 4.00
22 Matt Prater 1.50 4.00
23 Justin Tucker 1.50 4.00
MVP1 Lorenzo Alexander 1.50 4.00
MVP2 Travis Kelce 2.50 6.00

2017 Panini Kickoff Road to the Super Bowl Game Used Balls
*CRACKED/25: 2X TO 5X BASIC BALL
1 Tom Brady 30.00 60.00
2 Chris Hogan 3.00 8.00
3 Malcolm Mitchell 4.00 10.00
4 Tom Brady 30.00 60.00
5 Stephen Gostkowski 3.00 8.00
6 Dion Lewis 3.00 8.00
7 Tom Brady 30.00 60.00
8 LeGarrette Blount 4.00 10.00
9 James White 4.00 10.00
10 Julian Edelman 5.00 12.00

2019 Panini Legacy
1 David Johnson .30 .75
2 Larry Fitzgerald .25 .60
3 Josh Rosen .30 .75
4 Matt Ryan .30 .75
5 Devonta Freeman .25 .60
6 Julio Jones .30 .75
7 Christian Kirk .20 .50
8 Lamar Jackson .30 .75
9 Justin Tucker .20 .50
10 Terrell Suggs .20 .50
11 LeSean McCoy .30 .75
12 Tremaine Edmunds .25 .60
13 Josh Allen .30 .75
14 Cam Newton .30 .75
15 Christian McCaffrey .30 .75
16 Luke Kuechly .25 .60
17 Mitchell Trubisky .30 .75
18 Tarik Cohen .25 .60
19 Khalil Mack .30 .75
20 Kyle Long .20 .50
21 Andy Dalton .25 .60
22 A.J. Green .30 .75
23 Joe Mixon .25 .60
24 D.J. Moore .25 .60
25 Nick Chubb .30 .75
26 Baker Mayfield .50 1.25
27 Dak Prescott .30 .75
28 Ezekiel Elliott .40 1.00
29 Amari Cooper .30 .75
30 Leighton Vander Esch .25 .60
31 Joe Flacco .25 .60
32 Von Miller .25 .60
33 Phillip Lindsay .30 .75
34 Matthew Stafford .25 .60
35 Sony Michel .30 .75
36 Darius Slay .20 .50
37 Aaron Rodgers .60 1.50
38 Davante Adams .25 .60
39 Aaron Jones .25 .60
40 Jamaal Williams .20 .50
41 Deshaun Watson .40 1.00
42 Jordan Thomas .20 .50
43 DeAndre Hopkins .25 .60
44 J.J. Watt .30 .75
45 Andrew Luck .40 1.00
46 Marlon Mack .20 .50
47 T.Y. Hilton .25 .60
48 Nick Foles .25 .60
49 Leonard Fournette .30 .75
50 Jalen Ramsey .25 .60
51 Patrick Mahomes II .75 2.00
52 Spencer Ware .20 .50
53 Travis Kelce .30 .75
54 Tyreek Hill .30 .75
55 Philip Rivers .30 .75
56 Melvin Gordon III .25 .60
57 Keenan Allen .25 .60
58 Jared Goff .30 .75
59 Todd Gurley II .30 .75
60 Marcus Peters .20 .50
61 Aqib Talib .20 .50
62 Kenyan Drake .20 .50
63 Kenny Stills .20 .50
64 Kirk Cousins .30 .75
65 Dalvin Cook .25 .60
66 Adam Thielen .30 .75
67 Dont'a Hightower .20 .50
68 Tom Brady .75 2.00
69 Rob Gronkowski .30 .75
70 James White .25 .60
71 Drew Brees .30 .75
72 Alvin Kamara .25 .60
73 Michael Thomas .30 .75
74 Eli Manning .25 .60
75 Odell Beckham Jr. .30 .75
76 Saquon Barkley .40 1.00
77 Jamal Adams .25 .60
78 Sam Darnold .30 .75
79 Derek Carr .30 .75
80 Marshawn Lynch .25 .60
81 Carson Wentz .40 1.00
82 Alshon Jeffery .25 .60
83 Michael Bennett .20 .50
84 Ben Roethlisberger .25 .60
85 James Conner .30 .75
86 Antonio Brown .30 .75
87 JuJu Smith-Schuster .30 .75
88 Jimmy Garoppolo .30 .75
89 George Kittle .20 .50
90 Russell Wilson .40 1.00
91 Doug Baldwin .25 .60
92 Chris Carson .25 .60
93 Jameis Winston .25 .60
94 Mike Evans .25 .60
95 Adam Humphries .20 .50
96 Marcus Mariota .30 .75
97 Derrick Henry .30 .75
98 Matt Breida .20 .50
99 Alex Smith .25 .60
100 Adrian Peterson .30 .75
101 Earl Campbell .30 .75
102 Ed Reed .25 .60
103 Joe Montana .75 2.00
104 Jerry Kramer .20 .50
105 Dick Butkus .40 1.00
106 John Taylor .20 .50
107 Charlie Joiner .20 .50
108 Keith Brooking .20 .50
109 Troy Aikman .40 1.00
110 John Elway .50 1.25
111 Barry Sanders .50 1.25
112 Brett Favre .60 1.50
113 Warren Moon .30 .75
114 Greg Lloyd .25 .60
115 Leslie O'Neal .20 .50
116 Eric Metcalf .20 .50
117 Neal Anderson .20 .50
118 Joe Namath .40 1.00
119 Dan Marino .60 1.50
120 Brian Dawkins .30 .75
121 Bart Scott .20 .50
122 Eric Dickerson .30 .75
123 LeRoy Butler .20 .50
124 Tony Siragusa .20 .50
125 Kellen Winslow .25 .60
126 Wesley Walls .20 .50
127 Ozzie Newsome .25 .60
128 Emmitt Smith .50 1.25
129 Peyton Manning .60 1.50
130 Terry Bradshaw .50 1.25
131 Billy Joe DuPree .20 .50
132 Walt Garrison .25 .60
133 Robert Smith .20 .50
134 Rodney Hampton .20 .50
135 Sterling Sharpe .25 .60
136 Thomas Hollywood Henderson .20 .50
137 Ickey Woods .20 .50
138 Andre Reed .25 .60
139 Mark Gastineau .20 .50
140 Roger Craig .25 .60
141 A.J. Brown RC 1.00 2.50
142 Alex Barnes RC .50 1.25
143 Benny Snell Jr. RC 1.25 3.00
144 Travis Homer RC .40 1.00
145 Bryce Love RC .60 1.50
146 Caleb Wilson RC .40 1.00
147 Byron Murphy RC .40 1.00
148 Clelin Ferrell RC .60 1.50
149 D.K. Metcalf RC 1.25 3.00
150 Damien Harris RC 1.00 2.50
151 Daniel Jones RC 2.00 5.00
152 Darrell Henderson RC 1.00 2.50
153 David Montgomery RC 1.50 4.00
154 David Sills V RC 1.25 3.00
155 Deandre Baker RC 1.00 2.50
156 Deebo Samuel RC 1.00 2.50
157 Deionte Thompson RC .50 1.25
158 Devin Bush II RC 1.50 4.00
159 Devin Singletary RC .50 1.25
160 Devin White RC 1.25 3.00
161 Dexter Lawrence RC .60 1.50
162 Tyree Jackson RC 1.00 2.50
163 Drew Lock RC 2.00 5.00
164 Dwayne Haskins RC 2.00 5.00
165 Ed Oliver RC .60 1.50
166 Gardner Minshew II RC .60 1.50
167 Gary Jennings Jr. RC .60 1.50
168 Greedy Williams RC 1.25 3.00
169 Hakeem Butler RC .75 2.00
170 Irv Smith Jr. RC .75 2.00
171 Jachai Polite RC .50 1.25
172 Jarrett Stidham RC 1.25 3.00
173 Jaylon Ferguson RC .40 1.00
174 Jeffery Simmons RC .40 1.00
175 J.J. Arcega-Whiteside RC .60 1.50
176 Johnathan Abram RC .40 1.00
177 Josh Allen RC 1.50 4.00
178 Josh Jacobs RC 2.00 5.00
179 Julian Love RC .50 1.25
180 Justice Hill RC .60 1.50
181 Kelvin Harmon RC .60 1.50
182 Kyler Murray RC 4.00 10.00
183 Lil'Jordan Humphrey RC .50 1.25
184 Mack Wilson RC .50 1.25
185 Marquise Brown RC 1.25 3.00
186 Myles Gaskin RC .75 2.00
187 N'Keal Harry RC 1.25 3.00
188 Nick Bosa RC 1.25 3.00
189 Noah Fant RC .75 2.00
190 Parris Campbell RC 1.00 2.50
191 Preston Williams RC .40 1.00
192 Andy Isabella RC .60 1.50
193 Rashan Gary RC .75 2.00
194 Riley Ridley RC .60 1.50
195 Ryan Finley RC .75 2.00
196 Terry McLaurin RC .50 1.25
197 Trayvon Mullen Jr. RC .60 1.50
198 Will Grier RC 1.25 3.00
199 T.J. Hockenson RC 1.00 2.50
200 Montez Sweat RC 1.25 3.00

2019 Panini Legacy Blue
*VETS/50: 2.5X TO 6X BASIC CARDS
*ROOKIES/50: 1.2X TO 3X BASIC CARDS

2019 Panini Legacy Indigo
*VETS/25: 3X TO 8X BASIC CARDS
*ROOKIES/25: 1.5X TO 4X BASIC CARDS

2019 Panini Legacy Orange
*VETS/199: 1.5X TO 4X BASIC CARDS
*ROOK/199: .8X TO 2X BASIC CARDS

2019 Panini Legacy Premium Edition
*VETS: 1X TO 2.5X BASIC CARDS
*ROOKIES: .6X TO 1.5X BASIC CARDS

2019 Panini Legacy Premium Edition Bronze
*VETS/35: 2.5X TO 6X BASIC CARDS
*ROOKIES/35: 1.2X TO 3X BASIC CARDS

2019 Panini Legacy Premium Edition Gold
*VETS/25: 3X TO 8X BASIC CARDS
*ROOKIES/25: 1.5X TO 4X BASIC CARDS

2019 Panini Legacy Premium Edition Ruby
*VETS/100: 2X TO 5X BASIC CARDS
*ROOK/100: 1X TO 2.5X BASIC CARDS

2019 Panini Legacy Premium Edition Sapphire
*VETS/50: 2.5X TO 6X BASIC CARDS
*ROOKIES/50: 1.2X TO 3X BASIC CARDS

2019 Panini Legacy Premium Edition Silver
*VETS: 1.5X TO 4X BASIC CARDS
*ROOKIES: .8X TO 2X BASIC CARDS

2019 Panini Legacy Red
*VETS/299: 1.5X TO 4X BASIC CARDS
*ROOK/299: .8X TO 2X BASIC CARDS

2019 Panini Legacy Yellow
*VETS/165: 1.5X TO 4X BASIC CARDS
*ROOK/165: .8X TO 2X BASIC CARDS

2019 Panini Legacy Fan Favorites
*GREEN/100: .6X TO 1.5X BASIC INSERTS
*BLUE/50: .8X TO 2X BASIC INSERTS
*INDIGO/25: 1X TO 2.5X BASIC INSERTS
1 Alejandro Villanueva .60 1.50
2 Leighton Vander Esch .60 1.50
3 Eli Manning .60 1.50
4 Tarik Cohen .60 1.50
5 Darius Leonard .60 1.50
6 Phillip Lindsay .75 2.00
7 George Kittle .50 1.25
8 Jamal Adams .60 1.50
9 Marshawn Lynch .60 1.50
10 Derwin James .60 1.50

2019 Panini Legacy For the Ages
*GREEN/100: .6X TO 1.5X BASIC INSERTS
*BLUE/50: .8X TO 2X BASIC INSERTS
*INDIGO/25: 1X TO 2.5X BASIC INSERTS
1 Drew Brees .75 2.00
2 Saquon Barkley 1.00 2.50
3 Tyreek Hill .75 2.00
4 Mitchell Trubisky .75 2.00
5 Ezekiel Elliott 1.00 2.50
6 DeAndre Hopkins .60 1.50
7 Patrick Mahomes II 2.00 5.00
8 Odell Beckham Jr. .75 2.00
9 Kenyan Drake .50 1.25
10 Baker Mayfield 1.25 3.00
11 Kyle Rudolph .50 1.25
12 Cole Beasley .75 2.00
13 Aaron Rodgers
14 Vance McDonald .50 1.25
15 A.J. Green .75 2.00
16 Ryan Fitzpatrick .50 1.25
17 Derrick Henry .75 2.00
18 Nick Foles .60 1.50
19 Amari Cooper .75 2.00
20 Khalil Mack .75 2.00

2019 Panini Legacy Futures Dual Patch Autographs
1 Dwayne Haskins/15 150.00 300.00
2 Daniel Jones/15 150.00 300.00
3 Drew Lock/15 60.00 125.00
4 Damien Harris/15 25.00 60.00
5 Marquise Brown/15
6 T.J. Hockenson/50 15.00 40.00
7 A.J. Brown/15 30.00 80.00
8 D.K. Metcalf/15 30.00 80.00
9 Josh Jacobs/15
10 Parris Campbell/15
11 Ryan Finley/25 15.00 40.00
12 Darrell Henderson/15 25.00 60.00
13 Tyree Jackson/50 15.00 40.00
14 Anthony Johnson/50 8.00 20.00
15 Bryce Love/15 15.00 40.00
16 Noah Fant/25 15.00 40.00
17 Rodney Anderson/25 10.00 25.00
18 Trayveon Williams/25 10.00 25.00
19 Hakeem Butler/50 12.00 30.00
20 J.J. Arcega-Whiteside/50 10.00 25.00
21 Kelvin Harmon/50 10.00 25.00
22 Deebo Samuel/15 25.00 60.00
23 Gardner Minshew II/50
24 Jarrett Stidham/35 30.00 60.00
25 Dexter Williams/35 8.00 20.00
26 Karan Higdon/35 8.00 20.00
27 Miles Sanders/35
28 Dillon Mitchell/50 8.00 20.00
29 Justice Hill/35 15.00 40.00
30 Myles Gaskin/40 12.00 30.00
31 Antoine Wesley/40 6.00 15.00
32 Lil'Jordan Humphrey/40 6.00 15.00
33 Emanuel Hall/40
34 Riley Ridley/40
35 Stanley Morgan Jr./40 10.00 25.00

2019 Panini Legacy Futures Ink Combos
1 D.Haskins/K.Murray 200.00 400.00
2 J.Allen/N.Bosa
3 D.Jones/D.Lock
4 W.Grier/R.Finley 20.00 50.00
5 D.Harris/J.Jacobs 25.00 60.00
6 M.Brown/D.Metcalf 15.00 40.00
7 A.Brown/N.Harry 15.00 40.00
8 P.Campbell/A.Johnson 12.00 30.00
9 D.Montgomery/D.Henderson 20.00 50.00
10 G.Williams/D.Baker 15.00 40.00
11 E.Holyfield/R.Ridley 8.00 20.00
12 B.Love/R.Anderson 8.00 20.00
13 A.Barnes/T.Williams 5.00 12.00
14 I.Smith Jr./N.Fant 10.00 25.00
15 D.Thompson/M.Wilson 5.00 12.00
16 K.Harmon/R.Finley 8.00 20.00
17 D.Samuel/H.Butler 12.00 30.00
18 J.Arcega-Whiteside/K.Harmon 6.00 15.00
19 D.Bush II/K.Higdon
20 A.Brown/D.Metcalf 12.00 30.00
21 M.Brown/R.Anderson
22 L.Humphrey/A.Wesley 6.00 15.00
23 J.Stidham/G.Minshew II 15.00 40.00
24 D.Williams/M.Sanders 12.00 30.00
25 J.Hill/E.Holyfield 8.00 20.00

2019 Panini Legacy Futures Patch Autographs
1 Dwayne Haskins 50.00 100.00
2 Kyler Murray 125.00 250.00
3 Daniel Jones 50.00 100.00
4 Drew Lock 20.00 50.00
5 Will Grier 12.00 30.00
6 Damien Harris 10.00 25.00
7 Marquise Brown 12.00 30.00
8 T.J. Hockenson 10.00 25.00
9 A.J. Brown 15.00 40.00
10 D.K. Metcalf 15.00 40.00
11 Josh Jacobs 20.00 50.00
12 Parris Campbell 10.00 25.00
13 Ryan Finley 8.00 20.00
14 Darrell Henderson 12.00 30.00
15 Tyree Jackson 10.00 25.00
16 Anthony Johnson 5.00 12.00
17 Bryce Love 6.00 15.00
18 Noah Fant 8.00 20.00
19 Rodney Anderson 5.00 12.00
20 Trayveon Williams 5.00 12.00
21 Irv Smith Jr. 8.00 20.00
22 Hakeem Butler 8.00 20.00
23 J.J. Arcega-Whiteside 6.00 15.00
24 Kelvin Harmon 6.00 15.00
25 Deebo Samuel 10.00 25.00
26 Gardner Minshew II 6.00 15.00
27 Jarrett Stidham 12.00 30.00
28 Dexter Williams 5.00 12.00
29 Karan Higdon 5.00 12.00
30 Miles Sanders 10.00 25.00
31 Terry McLaurin 5.00 12.00
32 Justice Hill 10.00 25.00
33 Myles Gaskin 8.00 20.00
34 Dillon Mitchell 5.00 12.00
35 Antoine Wesley 4.00 10.00
36 Lil'Jordan Humphrey 5.00 12.00
37 David Sills V 12.00 30.00
38 Emanuel Hall 8.00 20.00
39 Riley Ridley 15.00 40.00
40 Stanley Morgan Jr 6.00 15.00

2019 Panini Legacy Lasting Legacies
*GREEN/100: .6X TO 1.5X BASIC INSERTS
*BLUE/50: .8X TO 2X BASIC INSERTS
*INDIGO/25: 1X TO 2.5X BASIC INSERTS
1 Joe Namath 1.00 2.50
2 Darrell Green .50 1.25
3 Tom Brady 2.00 5.00
4 Ray Lewis .75 2.00
5 Dan Marino 1.50 4.00
6 Dick Butkus 1.00 2.50
7 Barry Sanders 1.25 3.00
8 Jim Brown 1.00 2.50
9 Jack Ham .60 1.50
10 Emmitt Smith 1.25 3.00
11 Lawrence Taylor .75 2.00
12 Larry Fitzgerald .60 1.50
13 Alan Page .50 1.25
14 Terry Bradshaw 1.25 3.00
15 Bruce Smith .60 1.50
16 Michael Irvin 1.00 2.50
17 Anthony Munoz .50 1.25
18 Aaron Rodgers 1.50 4.00
19 Drew Brees .75 2.00
20 Ed Reed .60 1.50

2019 Panini Legacy Premium Penmanship
1 David Johnson
3 Josh Rosen
4 Matt Ryan
5 Devonta Freeman 3.00 8.00
7 Christian Kirk 2.50 6.00
8 Lamar Jackson
9 Justin Tucker 8.00 20.00
12 Tremaine Edmunds 3.00 8.00
13 Josh Allen
15 Christian McCaffrey
18 Tarik Cohen 6.00 15.00
20 Kyle Long 5.00 12.00
21 Andy Dalton
22 A.J. Green
24 D.J. Moore 3.00 8.00
25 Nick Chubb 8.00 20.00
28 Ezekiel Elliott
29 Amari Cooper
31 Case Keenum
33 Phillip Lindsay 12.00 30.00
35 Sony Michel
36 Darius Slay 2.50 6.00
37 Aaron Rodgers 8.00 20.00
39 Aaron Jones 3.00 8.00
40 Jamaal Williams 2.50 6.00
42 Jordan Thomas 2.50 6.00
43 DeAndre Hopkins
44 J.J. Watt
45 Andrew Luck
46 Marlon Mack 6.00 15.00
47 T.Y. Hilton
48 Nick Foles
51 Patrick Mahomes II 90.00 150.00
52 Spencer Ware 2.50 6.00
60 Marcus Peters 2.50 6.00
61 Aqib Talib 2.50 6.00
67 Dont'a Hightower 2.50 6.00
77 Jamal Adams 3.00 8.00
82 Alshon Jeffery
83 Michael Bennett 2.50 6.00
85 James Conner
92 Chris Carson 3.00 8.00
95 Adam Humphries 2.50 6.00
97 Derrick Henry
98 Matt Breida 2.50 6.00
100 Adrian Peterson
101 Earl Campbell
102 Ed Reed 3.00 8.00
103 Joe Montana
104 Jerry Kramer 12.00 30.00
105 Dick Butkus
106 John Taylor 2.50 6.00
107 Charlie Joiner 2.50 6.00
108 Keith Brooking 2.50 6.00
110 John Elway
111 Barry Sanders
112 Brett Favre
113 Warren Moon
114 Greg Lloyd 10.00 25.00
115 Leslie O'Neal 2.50 6.00
116 Eric Metcalf 2.50 6.00
117 Neal Anderson 2.50 6.00
118 Joe Namath
119 Dan Marino
120 Brian Dawkins
121 Bart Scott 2.50 6.00
122 Eric Dickerson
123 LeRoy Butler 12.00 30.00
124 Tony Siragusa 2.50 6.00
125 Kellen Winslow 3.00 8.00
126 Wesley Walls 2.50 6.00
127 Ozzie Newsome
128 Emmitt Smith
129 Peyton Manning
130 Terry Bradshaw
131 Billy Joe DuPree 2.50 6.00
132 Walt Garrison 3.00 8.00
133 Robert Smith 2.50 6.00
134 Rodney Hampton 2.50 6.00
135 Sterling Sharpe 3.00 8.00
136 Thomas Hollywood Henderson 6.00 15.00
137 Ickey Woods 2.50 6.00
138 Andre Reed 3.00 8.00
139 Mark Gastineau 2.50 6.00
140 Roger Craig 3.00 8.00
141 A.J. Brown 6.00 15.00
142 Alex Barnes 3.00 8.00
143 Benny Snell Jr. 10.00 25.00
144 Travis Homer 2.50 6.00
145 Bryce Love 4.00 10.00
146 Caleb Wilson 2.50 6.00
147 Byron Murphy 2.50 6.00
148 Clelin Ferrell 4.00 10.00
149 D.K. Metcalf 8.00 20.00
150 Damien Harris 10.00 25.00
151 Daniel Jones 15.00 40.00
152 Darrell Henderson 6.00 15.00
154 David Sills V 8.00 20.00
155 Deandre Baker 6.00 15.00
156 Deebo Samuel 6.00 15.00
157 Deionte Thompson 3.00 8.00
159 Devin Singletary 3.00 8.00
160 Devin White 8.00 20.00
161 Dexter Lawrence 4.00 10.00
162 Tyree Jackson 6.00 15.00
163 Drew Lock 12.00 30.00
164 Dwayne Haskins 50.00 100.00
165 Ed Oliver 4.00 10.00
166 Gardner Minshew II 4.00 10.00
167 Gary Jennings Jr. 4.00 10.00
168 Greedy Williams 8.00 20.00
169 Hakeem Butler 5.00 12.00
170 Irv Smith Jr. 5.00 12.00
172 Jarrett Stidham 8.00 20.00
173 Jaylon Ferguson 2.50 6.00
174 Jeffery Simmons 2.50 6.00
175 J.J. Arcega-Whiteside 4.00 10.00
176 Johnathan Abram 2.50 6.00
177 Josh Allen
178 Josh Jacobs 12.00 30.00
179 Julian Love 3.00 8.00
180 Justice Hill 4.00 10.00
181 Kelvin Harmon 6.00 15.00
182 Kyler Murray 100.00 200.00
183 Lil'Jordan Humphrey 3.00 8.00
184 Mack Wilson 3.00 8.00
185 Marquise Brown 12.00 30.00
186 Myles Gaskin 5.00 12.00
187 N'Keal Harry 12.00 30.00

188 Nick Bosa 8.00 20.00
189 Noah Fant 5.00 12.00
190 Parris Campbell 6.00 15.00
191 Preston Williams 2.50 6.00
192 Andy Isabella 4.00 10.00
193 Rashan Gary 5.00 12.00
194 Riley Ridley 4.00 10.00
195 Ryan Finley 5.00 12.00
196 Terry McLaurin 3.00 8.00
197 Trayvon Mullen Jr. 4.00 10.00
198 Will Grier 8.00 20.00
199 T.J. Hockenson 6.00 15.00
200 Montez Sweat 8.00 20.00

2019 Panini Legacy Record Book

*GREEN/100: .8X TO 2X BASIC INSERTS
*BLUE/50: 1X TO 2.5X BASIC INSERTS
*INDIGO/25: 1.2X TO 3X BASIC INSERTS
1 Drew Brees .60 1.50
2 Peyton Manning 1.25 3.00
3 Emmitt Smith 1.00 2.50
4 Jerry Rice 1.00 2.50
5 Adam Vinatieri .40 1.00
6 Paul Krause .40 1.00
7 Zach Thomas .40 1.00
8 Joe Montana 1.50 4.00
9 Larry Fitzgerald .50 1.25
10 Stephen Gostkowski .40 1.00
11 Zach Ertz .50 1.25
12 Steve Young .75 2.00
13 Devin Hester .50 1.25
14 Bruce Smith .50 1.25
15 Jason Witten .50 1.25
16 Morten Andersen .40 1.00
17 Tom Brady 1.50 4.00
18 LaDainian Tomlinson .50 1.25
19 Brett Favre 1.25 3.00
20 Nick Chubb .60 1.50
21 JuJu Smith-Schuster .60 1.50
22 Terrell Suggs .40 1.00
23 Paul Hornung .60 1.50
24 Marshall Faulk .50 1.25
25 Ed Reed .50 1.25
26 Randy Moss .50 1.25
27 Saquon Barkley .75 2.00
28 Rod Woodson .50 1.25
29 Odell Beckham Jr. .60 1.50
30 Warren Moon .60 1.50

2019 Panini Legacy Timeless Talents

*GREEN/100: .6X TO 1.5X BASIC INSERTS
*BLUE/50: .8X TO 2X BASIC INSERTS
*INDIGO/25: 1X TO 2.5X BASIC INSERTS
1 Kurt Warner .60 1.50
2 Bo Jackson 1.00 2.50
3 Jim Kelly .75 2.00
4 Mike Ditka .60 1.50
5 Dan Fouts .60 1.50
6 Terrell Davis .60 1.50
7 Ray Lewis .75 2.00
8 Paul Hornung .75 2.00
9 Edgerrin James .60 1.50
10 Curley Culp .60 1.50
11 Howie Long .60 1.50
12 Jason Taylor .60 1.50
13 Chris Doleman .50 1.25
14 Roger Craig .60 1.50
15 Charles Haley .75 2.00
16 Tim Brown .60 1.50
17 Deion Sanders .60 1.50
18 Jack Youngblood .50 1.25
19 Earl Campbell .75 2.00
20 Thurman Thomas .60 1.50

2018 Panini Luminance

1 Jimmy Garoppolo .75 2.00
2 Carlos Hyde .40 1.00
3 Marquise Goodwin .40 1.00
4 Mitchell Trubisky .60 1.50
5 Jordan Howard .60 1.50
6 Tarik Cohen .50 1.25
7 Andy Dalton .50 1.25
8 Joe Mixon .50 1.25
9 A.J. Green .60 1.50
10 Tyrod Taylor .50 1.25
11 LeSean McCoy .60 1.50
12 Kelvin Benjamin .50 1.25
13 Demaryius Thomas .50 1.25
14 Emmanuel Sanders .60 1.50
15 Von Miller .50 1.25
16 Marshawn Lynch .50 1.25
17 Jabrill Peppers .40 1.00
18 Josh Gordon .40 1.00
19 Jameis Winston .50 1.25
20 Mike Evans .50 1.25
21 Kwon Alexander .40 1.00
22 Sam Bradford .40 1.00
23 Larry Fitzgerald .50 1.25
24 David Johnson .60 1.50
25 Philip Rivers .60 1.50
26 Melvin Gordon .50 1.25
27 Keenan Allen .50 1.25
28 Alex Smith .50 1.25
29 Kareem Hunt .50 1.25
30 Tyreek Hill .60 1.50
31 Travis Kelce .60 1.50
32 T.Y. Hilton .50 1.25
33 Andrew Luck .75 2.00
34 Malik Hooker .40 1.00
35 Dak Prescott .60 1.50
36 Ezekiel Elliott .75 2.00
37 Jason Witten .50 1.25
38 Ryan Tannehill .50 1.25
39 Kenyan Drake .40 1.00
40 Jarvis Landry .50 1.25
41 Carson Wentz .75 2.00
42 Jay Ajayi .50 1.25
43 Zach Ertz .50 1.25
44 Matt Ryan .50 1.25
45 Devonta Freeman .50 1.25
46 Julio Jones .60 1.50
47 Eli Manning .50 1.25
48 Evan Engram .40 1.00
49 Odell Beckham Jr. .60 1.50
50 Blake Bortles .40 1.00
51 Leonard Fournette .60 1.50
52 Allen Robinson .50 1.25
53 Josh McCown .40 1.00
54 Teddy Bridgewater .50 1.25
55 Jamal Adams .50 1.25
56 Matthew Stafford .50 1.25
57 Marvin Jones Jr. .40 1.00
58 Ezekiel Ansah .40 1.00
59 Aaron Rodgers 1.25 3.00
60 Davante Adams .50 1.25
61 Jimmy Graham .60 1.50
62 Cam Newton .60 1.50
63 Devin Funchess .40 1.00
64 Christian McCaffrey .60 1.50
65 Tom Brady 1.50 4.00
66 Rob Gronkowski .60 1.50
67 Julian Edelman .60 1.50
68 Derek Carr .60 1.50
69 Amari Cooper .60 1.50
70 Khalil Mack .60 1.50
71 Jared Goff .60 1.50
72 Todd Gurley II .60 1.50
73 Cooper Kupp .50 1.25
74 Aaron Donald .60 1.50
75 Joe Flacco .50 1.25
76 Alex Collins .40 1.00
77 Eric Weddle .40 1.00
78 Kirk Cousins .60 1.50
79 Chris Thompson .40 1.00
80 Jamison Crowder .40 1.00
81 Drew Brees .60 1.50
82 Alvin Kamara [illegible]
83 Michael Thomas .60 1.50
84 Russell Wilson .75 2.00
85 Doug Baldwin .50 1.25
86 Earl Thomas III .50 1.25
87 Ben Roethlisberger .60 1.50
88 Le'Veon Bell .50 1.25
89 Antonio Brown .60 1.50
90 JuJu Smith-Schuster .60 1.50
91 Patrick Mahomes II 1.50 4.00
92 Deshaun Watson .75 2.00
93 D'Onta Foreman .40 1.00
94 DeAndre Hopkins .50 1.25
95 Marcus Mariota .60 1.50
96 Derrick Henry .60 1.50
97 Delanie Walker .40 1.00
98 Case Keenum .50 1.25
99 Dalvin Cook .50 1.25
100 Adam Thielen .60 1.50
101 Akrum Wadley RC .50 1.25
102 Allen Lazard RC .50 1.25
103 Anthony Miller RC .75 2.00
104 Arden Key RC .50 1.25
105 Auden Tate RC .50 1.25
106 Austin Allen RC .60 1.50
107 Baker Mayfield RC 5.00 12.00
108 Billy Price RC .60 1.50
109 Bo Scarbrough RC .60 1.50
110 Bradley Chubb RC .75 2.00
111 Kyle Lauletta RC .75 2.00
112 Calvin Ridley RC 1.25 3.00
113 Carlton Davis RC .60 1.50
114 Cedrick Wilson Jr. RC .50 1.25
115 Christian Kirk RC .75 2.00
116 Shaquem Griffin RC .75 2.00
117 Leighton Vander Esch RC 1.50 4.00
118 Courtland Sutton RC .75 2.00
119 D.J. Chark RC .60 1.50
120 D.J. Moore RC 1.00 2.50
121 DaeSean Hamilton RC .60 1.50
122 Dallas Goedert RC .60 1.50
123 Dalton Schultz RC .60 1.50
124 Jaire Alexander RC .75 2.00
125 Dante Pettis RC .75 2.00
126 Daron Payne RC .75 2.00
127 Darren Carrington II RC .60 1.50
128 DeAndre Goolsby RC .50 1.25
129 Denzel Ward RC 1.25 3.00
130 Deon Cain RC .60 1.50
131 Deontay Burnett RC .60 1.50
132 Derrius Guice RC 1.00 2.50
133 Derwin James RC 1.00 2.50
134 Dorance Armstrong Jr. RC .50 1.25
135 Duke Dawson RC .50 1.25
136 Equanimeous St. Brown RC .75 2.00
137 Harold Landry RC .50 1.25
138 Hayden Hurst RC .60 1.50
139 J.T. Barrett RC .75 2.00
140 James Washington RC 1.00 2.50
141 Dylan Cantrell RC .50 1.25
142 Jaylen Samuels RC .60 1.50
143 Jerome Baker RC .60 1.50
144 Jester Weah RC .50 1.25
145 J'Mon Moore RC .50 1.25
146 John Kelly RC .60 1.50
147 Jordan Lasley RC .50 1.25
148 Josh Adams RC 1.00 2.50
149 Josh Allen RC 2.00 5.00
150 Josh Rosen RC 1.50 4.00
151 Joshua Jackson RC 1.00 2.50
152 Justin Jackson RC .60 1.50
153 Kalen Ballage RC .60 1.50
154 Kamryn Pettway RC .75 2.00
155 Taven Bryan RC .50 1.25
156 Kerryon Johnson RC .75 2.00
157 Kurt Benkert RC .60 1.50
158 Marquis Haynes RC .50 1.25
159 Lamar Jackson RC 3.00 8.00
160 Lavon Coleman RC .60 1.50
161 Logan Woodside RC .75 2.00
162 Luke Falk RC .60 1.50
163 Malik Jefferson RC .60 1.50
164 Marcell Ateman RC .60 1.50
165 Marquez Valdes-Scantling RC .60 1.50
166 Marcus Baugh RC .50 1.25
167 Mark Andrews RC .75 2.00
168 Mark Walton RC .60 1.50
169 Mason Rudolph RC 1.25 3.00
170 Maurice Hurst RC .60 1.50
171 Max Browne RC .60 1.50
172 Michael Gallup RC 1.00 2.50
173 Mike Gesicki RC .60 1.50
174 Minkah Fitzpatrick RC 1.00 2.50
175 Nick Chubb RC 1.50 4.00
176 Nyheim Hines RC .60 1.50
177 Ogbonnia Okoronkwo RC .75 2.00
178 Orlando Brown RC .75 2.00
179 Tre'Quan Smith RC .75 2.00
180 Rashaad Penny RC .75 2.00
181 Ray-Ray McCloud RC .50 1.25
182 Riley Ferguson RC .75 2.00
183 Robert Foster RC .50 1.25
184 Ronald Jones II RC .50 1.25
185 Ronnie Harrison RC .60 1.50
186 Roquan Smith RC 1.50 4.00
187 Royce Freeman RC .60 1.50
188 Ryan Izzo RC .50 1.25
189 Sam Darnold RC 3.00 8.00
190 Sam Hubbard RC .60 1.50
191 Saquon Barkley RC 4.00 10.00
192 Simmie Cobbs Jr. RC .75 2.00
193 Sony Michel RC 1.50 4.00
194 Tanner Lee RC .60 1.50
195 Tarvarus McFadden RC .60 1.50
196 Tremaine Edmunds RC 1.00 2.50
197 Trey Marshall RC .60 1.50
198 Trey Quinn RC .50 1.25
199 Troy Fumagalli RC .60 1.50
200 Kyzir White RC .75 2.00

2018 Panini Luminance Blue

*VETS/99: 1X TO 2.5X BASIC CARDS
*ROOK/99: .8X TO 2X BASIC CARDS

2018 Panini Luminance Gold

*VETS: .6X TO 1.5X BASIC CARDS
*ROOKIES: .5X TO 1.5X BASIC CARDS

2018 Panini Luminance Orange

*VETS/225: .8X TO 2X BASIC CARDS
*ROOK/225: .6X TO 1.5X BASIC CARDS
INSERTED IN 2018 PRESTIGE RETAIL

2018 Panini Luminance Platinum Blue

*VETS/25: 1.5X TO 4X BASIC CARDS
*ROOK/25: 1.2X TO 3X BASIC CARDS
1 Jimmy Garoppolo 12.00 30.00
191 Saquon Barkley 15.00 40.00

2018 Panini Luminance Draft Day Signatures Silver

3 Anthony Miller 8.00 20.00
4 Jaleel Scott 5.00 12.00
5 Baker Mayfield 100.00 200.00
7 Calvin Ridley 12.00 30.00
9 Christian Kirk 8.00 20.00
10 Courtland Sutton 8.00 20.00
11 DaeSean Hamilton 6.00 15.00
13 Dante Pettis 8.00 20.00
16 Derrius Guice 10.00 25.00
17 Bradley Chubb 8.00 20.00
18 D.J. Chark 6.00 15.00
19 D.J. Moore 25.00 50.00
20 Hayden Hurst 6.00 15.00
21 James Washington 10.00 25.00
22 J'Mon Moore 5.00 12.00
26 Josh Allen 40.00 80.00
27 Josh Rosen 50.00 100.00
28 Tre'Quan Smith 8.00 20.00
29 Kalen Ballage 6.00 15.00
30 Kerryon Johnson 8.00 20.00
32 Kyle Lauletta 8.00 20.00
33 Lamar Jackson 100.00 200.00
36 Mark Walton 6.00 15.00
37 Mason Rudolph 12.00 30.00
38 Michael Gallup 10.00 25.00
39 Mike White 12.00 30.00
40 Nick Chubb 15.00 40.00
41 Nyheim Hines 6.00 15.00
42 Rashaad Penny 8.00 20.00
43 Ronald Jones II 5.00 12.00
44 Royce Freeman 6.00 15.00
45 Sam Darnold 50.00 100.00
46 Saquon Barkley 100.00 200.00
48 Sony Michel 30.00 60.00
51 Mike Gesicki 6.00 15.00
52 Ito Smith 6.00 15.00
53 Keke Coutee 6.00 15.00
54 Jaylen Samuels 6.00 15.00
55 Marquez Valdes-Scantling 6.00 15.00
56 Daurice Fountain 6.00 15.00

2018 Panini Luminance Draft Day Signatures Gold

*GOLD: .8X TO 2X SILVER AU
33 Lamar Jackson 200.00 300.00
46 Saquon Barkley 150.00 300.00

2018 Panini Luminance Dynamic

1 Tom Brady 2.50 6.00
2 Ezekiel Elliott 1.25 3.00
3 Aaron Rodgers 2.00 5.00
4 Le'Veon Bell .75 2.00
5 Antonio Brown 1.00 2.50
6 Julio Jones 1.00 2.50
7 Kareem Hunt .75 2.00
8 Carson Wentz 1.25 3.00
9 Todd Gurley II 1.00 2.50
10 DeAndre Hopkins .75 2.00
11 Josh Rosen 2.00 5.00
12 Sam Darnold 4.00 10.00
13 Josh Allen 2.50 6.00
14 Baker Mayfield 6.00 15.00
15 Saquon Barkley 5.00 12.00
16 Derrius Guice 1.25 3.00
17 Calvin Ridley 1.50 4.00
18 Courtland Sutton 1.00 2.50
19 Christian Kirk 1.00 2.50
20 Lamar Jackson 4.00 10.00

2018 Panini Luminance Flash

1 Cam Newton 1.00 2.50
2 Dak Prescott 1.00 2.50
3 Marcus Mariota 1.00 2.50
4 Jameis Winston .75 2.00
5 Russell Wilson 1.25 3.00
6 Kareem Hunt .75 2.00
7 Todd Gurley II 1.00 2.50
8 Le'Veon Bell .75 2.00
9 LeSean McCoy 1.00 2.50
10 Jordan Howard 1.00 2.50
11 Leonard Fournette 1.00 2.50
12 Ezekiel Elliott 1.25 3.00
13 Alvin Kamara .75 2.00
14 Tyreek Hill 1.00 2.50
15 Josh Gordon .60 1.50
16 Adam Thielen 1.00 2.50
17 DeAndre Hopkins .75 2.00
18 Keenan Allen .75 2.00
19 Antonio Brown 1.00 2.50
20 Julio Jones 1.00 2.50

2018 Panini Luminance Ink

*GOLD/49: .5X TO 1.2X BASIC AU/75
1 Archie Manning/25 12.00 30.00
2 Len Dawson/25 15.00 40.00
3 Brett Favre/10
4 Peyton Manning/10
5 Warrick Dunn/25 10.00 25.00
6 Ezekiel Elliott/25
7 Paul Hornung/75 10.00 25.00
8 Randy Moss/10
9 Michael Thomas/75 10.00 25.00
10 Eric Berry/75 12.00 30.00

2018 Panini Luminance Jumbo Jerseys

*GOLD/49: .8X TO 2X BASIC JSY
*GOLD/21: 1.2X TO 3X BASIC JSY
*PLATINUM/25: 1X TO 2.5X BASIC JSY
1 Alvin Kamara 2.50 6.00
2 Christian McCaffrey 3.00 8.00
3 Cooper Kupp 2.50 6.00
4 Dalvin Cook 2.50 6.00
5 Deshaun Watson 4.00 10.00
6 D'Onta Foreman 2.00 5.00
7 Evan Engram 2.00 5.00
8 Joe Mixon 2.50 6.00
9 JuJu Smith-Schuster 3.00 8.00
10 Kareem Hunt 2.50 6.00
11 Leonard Fournette 3.00 8.00
12 Patrick Mahomes II 8.00 20.00
13 Matt Ryan 2.50 6.00
14 Luke Kuechly 2.50 6.00
15 Golden Tate III 2.00 5.00
16 Aaron Jones 2.50 6.00
17 Blake Bortles 2.00 5.00
18 Derek Carr 3.00 8.00
19 Earl Thomas III 2.50 6.00
20 Mike Evans 2.50 6.00
21 Stefon Diggs 2.50 6.00
22 Jared Goff 3.00 8.00
23 Jameis Winston 2.50 6.00
24 Marcus Mariota 3.00 8.00
25 Derrick Henry 3.00 8.00

2018 Panini Luminance Portrait

1 Tom Brady 2.50 6.00
2 Matthew Stafford .75 2.00
3 Drew Brees 1.00 2.50
4 Ben Roethlisberger 1.00 2.50
5 Carson Wentz 1.25 3.00
6 Dak Prescott 1.00 2.50
7 Ezekiel Elliott 1.25 3.00
8 Todd Gurley II 1.00 2.50
9 LeSean McCoy 1.00 2.50
10 Alvin Kamara .75 2.00
11 Leonard Fournette 1.00 2.50
12 Antonio Brown 1.00 2.50
13 Julio Jones 1.00 2.50
14 Keenan Allen .75 2.00
15 DeAndre Hopkins .75 2.00
16 Adam Thielen 1.00 2.50
17 Chandler Jones .60 1.50
18 Eric Weddle .60 1.50
19 J.J. Watt 1.00 2.50
20 Aaron Donald 1.00 2.50

2018 Panini Luminance Rookie Ink

1 Akrum Wadley/249 4.00 10.00
2 Allen Lazard/249 4.00 10.00
3 Anthony Miller/225 6.00 15.00
4 Arden Key/249 4.00 10.00
5 Auden Tate/249 4.00 10.00
6 Austin Allen/299 5.00 12.00
7 Baker Mayfield/125 60.00 125.00
8 Billy Price/299 5.00 12.00
9 Bo Scarbrough/225 5.00 12.00
10 Bradley Chubb/225 6.00 15.00
11 Kyle Lauletta/249 6.00 15.00
12 Calvin Ridley/199 10.00 25.00
13 Carlton Davis/249 5.00 12.00
14 Cedrick Wilson Jr./249 4.00 10.00
15 Christian Kirk/199 6.00 15.00
16 Shaquem Griffin/249 25.00 50.00
17 Leighton Vander Esch/249 12.00 30.00
18 Courtland Sutton/225 6.00 15.00
19 D.J. Chark/249 [illegible]
20 D.J. Moore/225 8.00 20.00
21 DaeSean Hamilton/249 5.00 12.00
22 Dallas Goedert/225 5.00 12.00
23 Dalton Schultz/299 5.00 12.00
24 Jaire Alexander/249 6.00 15.00
25 Dante Pettis/225 6.00 15.00
26 Daron Payne/249 6.00 15.00
27 Darren Carrington II/249 5.00 12.00
28 DeAndre Goolsby/299 4.00 10.00
29 Denzel Ward/249 10.00 25.00
31 Deontay Burnett/225 5.00 12.00
32 Derrius Guice/199 8.00 20.00
33 Derwin James/249 8.00 20.00
34 Dorance Armstrong Jr./249 4.00 10.00
35 Duke Dawson/249 4.00 10.00
36 Donte Jackson/249 6.00 15.00
37 Harold Landry/249 4.00 10.00
38 Hayden Hurst/299 5.00 12.00
39 J.T. Barrett/225 6.00 15.00
40 James Washington/225 8.00 20.00
41 Dylan Cantrell/299 4.00 10.00
42 Jaylen Samuels/299 5.00 12.00
43 Jerome Baker/249 5.00 12.00
44 Jester Weah/249 4.00 10.00
45 J'Mon Moore/249 4.00 10.00
46 John Kelly/249 5.00 12.00
47 Jordan Lasley/249 4.00 10.00
48 Josh Adams/249 8.00 20.00
49 Josh Allen/125 20.00 50.00
50 Josh Rosen/125 30.00 60.00
51 Joshua Jackson/249 8.00 20.00
52 Justin Jackson/249 5.00 12.00
53 Kalen Ballage/249 5.00 12.00
54 Kamryn Pettway/249 6.00 15.00
56 Kerryon Johnson/225 6.00 15.00
57 Kurt Benkert/225 5.00 12.00
58 Marquis Haynes/299 4.00 10.00
60 Lavon Coleman/299 5.00 12.00
61 Logan Woodside/299 6.00 15.00
62 Luke Falk/225 5.00 12.00
63 Malik Jefferson/249 5.00 12.00
64 Marcell Ateman/249 5.00 12.00
65 Marcus Allen/299 6.00 15.00
66 Marcus Baugh/299 4.00 10.00
67 Mark Andrews/249 6.00 15.00
68 Mark Walton/249 5.00 12.00
69 Mason Rudolph/199 10.00 25.00
70 Maurice Hurst/249 5.00 12.00
71 Max Browne/299 5.00 12.00
72 Michael Gallup/249 8.00 20.00
73 Mike Gesicki/249 5.00 12.00
74 Minkah Fitzpatrick/225 8.00 20.00
75 Nick Chubb/225 12.00 30.00
76 Nyheim Hines/249 5.00 12.00
77 Ogbonnia Okoronkwo/249 6.00 15.00
78 Orlando Brown/249 6.00 15.00
79 Tre'Quan Smith/249 6.00 15.00
80 Rashaad Penny/249 6.00 15.00
81 Ray-Ray McCloud/299 4.00 10.00
82 Riley Ferguson/249 6.00 15.00
83 Robert Foster/299 4.00 10.00
84 Ronald Jones II/225 4.00 10.00
85 Ronnie Harrison/249 5.00 12.00
86 Roquan Smith/249 12.00 30.00
87 Royce Freeman/225 5.00 12.00
88 Ryan Izzo/299 4.00 10.00
89 Sam Darnold/125 40.00 80.00
90 Sam Hubbard/249 5.00 12.00
91 Saquon Barkley/125 75.00 150.00
92 Simmie Cobbs Jr./225 6.00 15.00
93 Sony Michel/225 12.00 30.00
94 Tanner Lee/249 5.00 12.00
95 Tarvarus McFadden/249 5.00 12.00
96 Tremaine Edmunds/249 8.00 20.00
97 Trey Marshall/299 5.00 12.00
98 Trey Quinn/249 4.00 10.00
99 Troy Fumagalli/249 5.00 12.00
100 Kyzir White/249 6.00 15.00

2018 Panini Luminance Rookie Ink Platinum Blue

7 Baker Mayfield 100.00 200.00
91 Saquon Barkley 200.00 350.00

2018 Panini Luminance Spotlight Signatures

*GOLD/25: .6X TO 1.5X BASIC AU/125
*GOLD/25: .5X TO 1.2X BASIC AU/49
1 Deshaun Watson/15
2 Jared Goff/15
3 Michael Vick/25 8.00 20.00
4 Carson Wentz/15
5 Jordan Howard/49 8.00 20.00
6 Pierre Garcon/49 6.00 15.00
7 Xavier Rhodes/125 4.00 10.00
8 Alex Collins/125 4.00 10.00
9 Aaron Jones/125 5.00 12.00
11 Geno Atkins/125 4.00 10.00
12 Jimmy Garoppolo/25 150.00 250.00
13 Charlie Joiner/125 4.00 10.00
14 D'Onta Foreman/125 4.00 10.00
15 Ed McCaffrey/49 6.00 15.00
16 Priest Holmes/49 5.00 12.00
17 Chris Hogan/125 4.00 10.00
18 Josh Gordon/49 5.00 12.00
19 Vance Johnson/125 4.00 10.00
20 Tarik Cohen/125 5.00 12.00
21 Jeremy Shockey/49 5.00 12.00
22 Hunter Henry/49 5.00 12.00
23 Ameer Abdullah/49 5.00 12.00
24 Tyreek Hill/49 8.00 20.00
25 Adam Thielen/49 20.00 50.00

2018 Panini Luminance Vintage Materials

*GOLD/49: .8X TO 2X BASIC JSY
*PLATINUM/25: 1X TO 2.5X BASIC JSY
1 Thurman Thomas 2.50 6.00
2 Mike Singletary 3.00 8.00
3 Bob Lilly 2.50 6.00
4 Michael Irvin 3.00 8.00
5 Earl Campbell 3.00 8.00
6 Fran Tarkenton 3.00 8.00
7 Lawrence Taylor 3.00 8.00
8 Fred Taylor 2.00 5.00
9 Lance Alworth 2.50 6.00
10 Ronnie Lott 2.50 6.00
11 Joe Theismann 3.00 8.00
12 Terrell Davis 2.50 6.00
13 Len Dawson 3.00 8.00
14 Joe Namath 4.00 10.00
15 Andre Reed 2.50 6.00

2018 Panini Luminance Vintage Performers

1 Lawrence Taylor 1.00 2.50
2 Jerry Rice 1.50 4.00
3 Dick Butkus 1.25 3.00
4 Barry Sanders 1.50 4.00
5 Joe Greene 1.00 2.50
6 John Elway 1.50 4.00
7 Dan Marino 2.00 5.00
8 Ronnie Lott .75 2.00
9 Terry Bradshaw 1.50 4.00
10 Roger Staubach 1.25 3.00
11 Brett Favre 2.00 5.00
12 Randy Moss .75 2.00
13 Deion Sanders .75 2.00
14 Emmitt Smith 1.50 4.00
15 Ray Lewis 1.00 2.50
16 Bo Jackson 1.25 3.00
17 Bruce Smith .75 2.00
18 Marcus Allen 1.00 2.50
19 Steve Largent [illegible]
20 Cris Carter 1.00 2.50

2019 Panini Luminance

1 Patrick Mahomes II 1.50 4.00
2 Tyreek Hill .60 1.50
3 Travis Kelce .60 1.50
4 Tom Brady 1.50 4.00
5 Rob Gronkowski .60 1.50
6 Sony Michel .60 1.50
7 Deshaun Watson .75 2.00
8 J.J. Watt .60 1.50
9 DeAndre Hopkins .50 1.25
10 Lamar Jackson .60 1.50
11 Eric Weddle .40 1.00
12 Justin Tucker .40 1.00
13 Philip Rivers .60 1.50
14 Joey Bosa .50 1.25
15 Keenan Allen .50 1.25
16 Melvin Gordon III .50 1.25
17 Andrew Luck .75 2.00
18 T.Y. Hilton .50 1.25
19 Darius Leonard .50 1.25
20 Ben Roethlisberger .50 1.25
21 JuJu Smith-Schuster .60 1.50
22 James Conner .60 1.50
23 Antonio Brown .60 1.50
24 Marcus Mariota .60 1.50
25 Derrick Henry .60 1.50
26 Corey Davis .50 1.25
27 Baker Mayfield 1.00 2.50
28 Nick Chubb .60 1.50
29 Myles Garrett .40 1.00
30 Kenyan Drake .40 1.00
31 Le'Veon Bell .50 1.25
32 Minkah Fitzpatrick .40 1.00
33 Von Miller .50 1.25
34 Bradley Chubb .50 1.25
35 Phillip Lindsay .60 1.50
36 A.J. Green .60 1.50
37 Joe Mixon .50 1.25
38 Andy Dalton .50 1.25
39 Josh Allen .60 1.50
40 Zay Jones .40 1.00
41 Tremaine Edmunds .50 1.25
42 Jalen Ramsey .50 1.25
43 Leonard Fournette .60 1.50
44 Dede Westbrook .40 1.00
45 Sam Darnold .60 1.50
46 Jamal Adams .50 1.25
47 Robby Anderson .40 1.00
48 Derek Carr .60 1.50
49 Jared Cook .40 1.00
50 DeMarcus Lawrence .40 1.00
51 Drew Brees .60 1.50
52 Alvin Kamara .50 1.25
53 Marshon Lattimore .40 1.00
54 Michael Thomas .60 1.50
55 Jared Goff .60 1.50
56 Todd Gurley II .60 1.50
57 Aaron Donald .60 1.50
58 Mitchell Trubisky .60 1.50
59 Tarik Cohen .50 1.25
60 Khalil Mack .60 1.50
61 Dak Prescott .60 1.50
62 Ezekiel Elliott .75 2.00
63 Amari Cooper .60 1.50
64 Russell Wilson .75 2.00
65 Tyler Lockett .50 1.25
66 Chris Carson .50 1.25
67 Nick Foles .50 1.25
68 Zach Ertz .50 1.25
69 Alshon Jeffery .50 1.25
70 Kirk Cousins .60 1.50
71 Adam Thielen .60 1.50
72 Stefon Diggs .50 1.25
73 Matt Ryan .60 1.50
74 Calvin Ridley .50 1.25
75 Julio Jones .60 1.50
76 Alex Smith .50 1.25
77 Adrian Peterson .60 1.50
78 Jordan Reed .40 1.00
79 Cam Newton .60 1.50
80 Luke Kuechly .50 1.25
81 Christian McCaffrey .60 1.50
82 Aaron Rodgers 1.25 3.00
83 Aaron Jones .50 1.25
84 Davante Adams .50 1.25
85 Matthew Stafford .50 1.25
86 Kerryon Johnson .50 1.25
87 Kenny Golladay .40 1.00
88 Saquon Barkley .75 2.00
89 Odell Beckham Jr. .60 1.50
90 Landon Collins .40 1.00
91 Jameis Winston .50 1.25
92 Mike Evans .50 1.25
93 Gerald McCoy .40 1.00
94 Jimmy Garoppolo .60 1.50
95 Nick Mullens .50 1.25
96 George Kittle .40 1.00
97 Matt Breida .40 1.00
98 Larry Fitzgerald .50 1.25
99 Josh Rosen .60 1.50
100 David Johnson .60 1.50
101 Greedy Williams RC 1.50 4.00
102 Deandre Baker RC 1.25 3.00
103 Julian Love RC .60 1.50
104 Trayvon Mullen Jr. RC .75 2.00
105 Byron Murphy RC .50 1.25
106 Chauncey Gardner-Johnson RC .50 1.25
107 Nick Bosa RC 1.50 4.00
108 Rashan Gary RC 1.00 2.50
109 Clelin Ferrell RC .75 2.00
110 Jaylon Ferguson RC .50 1.25
111 Jachai Polite RC .60 1.50
112 Zach Allen RC .75 2.00
113 Brian Burns RC .60 1.50
114 Montez Sweat RC 1.50 4.00
115 Austin Bryant RC 1.00 2.50
116 Quinnen Williams RC .50 1.25
117 Ed Oliver RC .75 2.00
118 Dexter Lawrence RC .75 2.00
119 Christian Wilkins RC 2.00 5.00
120 Jeffery Simmons RC .50 1.25
121 Dre'Mont Jones RC .60 1.50
122 Devin White RC 1.50 4.00
123 Devin Bush II RC 2.00 5.00
124 Darnell Savage Jr. RC .75 2.00
125 Mack Wilson RC .60 1.50
126 Germaine Pratt RC .60 1.50
127 D'Andre Walker RC .50 1.25
128 Tony Pollard RC 1.25 3.00
129 Josh Allen RC 2.00 5.00
130 Dwayne Haskins RC 2.50 6.00
131 Kyler Murray RC 5.00 12.00
132 Daniel Jones RC 2.50 6.00
133 Drew Lock RC 2.50 6.00
134 Will Grier RC 1.50 4.00
135 Ryan Finley RC 1.00 2.50
136 Gardner Minshew II RC .75 2.00
137 Jarrett Stidham RC 1.50 4.00
138 Brett Rypien RC .60 1.50
139 Trace McSorley RC 1.25 3.00
140 Tyree Jackson RC 1.25 3.00
141 Jalen Hurd RC .60 1.50
142 Jake Browning RC 1.25 3.00
143 David Blough RC .60 1.50
144 Clayton Thorson RC .75 2.00
145 Damien Harris RC 1.25 3.00
146 Josh Jacobs RC 2.50 6.00
147 Bryce Love RC .75 2.00
148 Darrell Henderson RC 1.25 3.00
149 David Montgomery RC 2.00 5.00
150 Rodney Anderson RC .60 1.50
151 Trayveon Williams RC .60 1.50
152 Alex Barnes RC .60 1.50
153 Dexter Williams RC .60 1.50
154 Karan Higdon RC .60 1.50
155 Miles Sanders RC 1.25 3.00
156 Elijah Holyfield RC .75 2.00
157 Justice Hill RC .75 2.00
158 Myles Gaskin RC 1.00 2.50
159 Benny Snell Jr. RC 1.50 4.00
160 Devin Singletary RC .60 1.50
161 L.J. Scott RC .75 2.00
162 Travis Homer RC .50 1.25
163 Patrick Laird RC 1.00 2.50
164 Darwin Thompson RC .75 2.00
165 Easton Stick RC .75 2.00
166 Deionte Thompson RC .60 1.50
167 Johnathan Abram RC .50 1.25
168 Noah Fant RC 1.00 2.50
169 Irv Smith Jr. RC 1.00 2.50
170 Caleb Wilson RC .50 1.25
171 T.J. Hockenson RC 1.25 3.00
172 Marquise Brown RC 1.50 4.00
173 N'Keal Harry RC 1.50 4.00
174 A.J. Brown RC 1.25 3.00
175 D.K. Metcalf RC 1.50 4.00
176 Parris Campbell RC 1.25 3.00
177 Anthony Johnson RC .60 1.50
178 Hakeem Butler RC 1.00 2.50
179 J.J. Arcega-Whiteside RC .75 2.00
180 Kelvin Harmon RC .75 2.00
181 Deebo Samuel RC 1.25 3.00
182 Diontae Johnson RC .60 1.50
183 Lil'Jordan Humphrey RC .60 1.50
184 Preston Williams RC .50 1.25
185 Gary Jennings Jr. RC .75 2.00
186 David Sills V RC 1.50 4.00
187 Emanuel Hall RC .50 1.25
188 Riley Ridley RC .75 2.00
189 Stanley Morgan Jr. RC .75 2.00
190 Dillon Mitchell RC .60 1.50
191 Keelan Doss RC .60 1.50
192 Terry Godwin II RC .60 1.50
193 Hunter Renfrow RC 1.00 2.50
194 Qadree Ollison RC .60 1.50
195 Mecole Hardman Jr. RC 1.25 3.00
196 Darius Slayton RC .75 2.00
197 Tyre Brady RC .50 1.25
198 Anthony Ratliff-Williams RC 1.00 2.50
199 Greg Dortch RC .60 1.50
200 Miles Boykin RC .60 1.50

2019 Panini Luminance Blue

*VETS/99: 1X TO 2.5X BASIC CARDS
*ROOK/99: .8X TO 2X BASIC CARDS

2019 Panini Luminance Gold

*VETS/225: .8X TO 2X BASIC CARDS
*ROOK/225: .6X TO 1.5X BASIC CARDS

2019 Panini Luminance Green

*VETS/49: 1.2X TO 3X BASIC CARDS
*ROOK/99: 1X TO 2.5X BASIC CARDS

2019 Panini Luminance Orange

*VETS/25: 1.5X TO 4X BASIC CARDS
*ROOK/25: 1.2X TO 3X BASIC CARDS

2019 Panini Luminance Bright Beginnings Materials

*GOLD/49: .5X TO 1.2X BASIC JSY/99
*RED/25: .6X TO 1.5X BASIC JSY/25
1 Baker Mayfield 10.00 25.00
2 Saquon Barkley 10.00 25.00
3 Lamar Jackson 6.00 15.00
4 Tarik Cohen 3.00 8.00
5 Nick Chubb 4.00 10.00
6 Sony Michel 4.00 10.00
7 Deshaun Watson 5.00 12.00
8 Alvin Kamara 3.00 8.00
9 Patrick Mahomes II 10.00 25.00
10 JuJu Smith-Schuster 4.00 10.00
11 Calvin Ridley 3.00 8.00
12 Dante Pettis 3.00 8.00
13 Sam Darnold 4.00 10.00
14 James Conner 4.00 10.00
15 Mike Williams 2.50 6.00
16 Kerryon Johnson 3.00 8.00
17 Michael Gallup 4.00 10.00
18 Anthony Miller 3.00 8.00
19 Josh Allen 4.00 10.00
20 Josh Rosen 4.00 10.00

2019 Panini Luminance Draft Day Signatures Silver

1 Nick Bosa 15.00 40.00
2 Dwayne Haskins 60.00 125.00
3 Kyler Murray 125.00 250.00
4 Drew Lock 25.00 60.00
5 Daniel Jones 25.00 60.00
6 Will Grier 15.00 40.00
7 Ryan Finley 10.00 25.00
8 Jarrett Stidham 15.00 40.00
9 Easton Stick 8.00 20.00
10 Mecole Hardman Jr. 20.00 50.00
12 Josh Jacobs 25.00 60.00
13 Damien Harris 12.00 30.00
14 Darrell Henderson 12.00 30.00
15 David Montgomery 20.00 50.00
17 Miles Sanders 25.00 50.00
18 Bryce Love 8.00 20.00
19 Justice Hill 8.00 20.00
20 Benny Snell Jr. 15.00 40.00
21 Devin Singletary 6.00 15.00
24 Hunter Renfrow 10.00 25.00
25 Tony Pollard 12.00 30.00
26 Marquise Brown 15.00 40.00
27 D.K. Metcalf 15.00 40.00
28 A.J. Brown 12.00 30.00
29 Parris Campbell 12.00 30.00
30 Hakeem Butler 10.00 25.00
31 Deebo Samuel 12.00 30.00
32 N'Keal Harry 15.00 40.00
33 Darius Slayton 8.00 20.00
34 J.J. Arcega-Whiteside 8.00 20.00
35 Alexander Mattison 10.00 25.00
37 Diontae Johnson 6.00 15.00
38 Riley Ridley 8.00 20.00
39 Noah Fant 10.00 25.00
40 Irv Smith Jr. 10.00 25.00
44 T.J. Hockenson 12.00 30.00
45 Gary Jennings Jr. 8.00 20.00
48 Terry McLaurin 6.00 15.00
49 Andy Isabella 8.00 20.00
50 Miles Boykin 6.00 15.00

2019 Panini Luminance Dynamic

*ORANGE/100: .6X TO 1.5X BASIC INSERTS
1 Patrick Mahomes II 2.50 6.00
2 Tom Brady 2.50 6.00
3 Drew Brees 1.00 2.50
4 Aaron Rodgers 2.00 5.00
5 Andrew Luck 1.25 3.00
6 Saquon Barkley 1.25 3.00
7 Philip Rivers 1.00 2.50
8 Russell Wilson 1.25 3.00
9 Ezekiel Elliott 1.25 3.00
10 Adam Thielen 1.00 2.50

2019 Panini Luminance Dynamic Rookies

*ORANGE/100: .6X TO 1.5X BASIC INSERTS
1 Dwayne Haskins 3.00 8.00
2 Daniel Jones 3.00 8.00
3 Drew Lock 3.00 8.00
4 Will Grier 2.00 5.00
5 Damien Harris 1.50 4.00
6 Bryce Love 1.00 2.50
7 Kyler Murray 6.00 15.00
8 Marquise Brown 2.00 5.00
9 Parris Campbell 1.50 4.00
10 N'Keal Harry 2.00 5.00

2019 Panini Luminance Flash

*ORANGE/100: .6X TO 1.5X BASIC INSERTS
1 Baker Mayfield 1.50 4.00
2 Lamar Jackson 1.00 2.50
3 Russell Wilson 1.25 3.00
4 Mitchell Trubisky 1.00 2.50
5 Dak Prescott 1.00 2.50
6 Deshaun Watson 1.25 3.00
7 Patrick Mahomes II 2.50 6.00
8 Adrian Peterson 1.00 2.50
9 James Conner 1.00 2.50
10 Saquon Barkley 1.25 3.00
11 Alvin Kamara .75 2.00
12 Sony Michel 1.00 2.50
13 Todd Gurley II 1.00 2.50
14 JuJu Smith-Schuster 1.00 2.50
15 Julio Jones 1.00 2.50
16 Jarvis Landry .75 2.00
17 Larry Fitzgerald .75 2.00
18 A.J. Green 1.00 2.50
19 Amari Cooper 1.00 2.50
20 DeAndre Hopkins .75 2.00

2019 Panini Luminance Illuminated Ink

*BLUE/75: .5X TO 1.2X BASIC AU/199
*BLUE/35-49: .5X TO 1.2X BASIC AU/99
*BLUE/25: .6X TO 1.5X BASIC AU/75-99
*BLUE/15: .6X TO 1.5X BASIC AU/49
*GOLD/75-99: .5X TO 1.2X BASIC AU/199
*GOLD/75-99: .4X TO 1X BASIC AU/75-99
*GOLD/49: .6X TO 1.5X BASIC AU/75-99
*GOLD/25: .5X TO 1.2X BASIC AU/49
*ORANGE/25: .8X TO 2X BASIC AU/199
*ORANGE/25: .6X TO 1.5X BASIC AU/75-99
*ORANGE/25: .5X TO 1.2X BASIC AU/49
*ORANGE/15: .6X TO 1.5X BASIC AU/49
1 Mark Clayton/49 5.00 12.00
3 Vance Johnson/99 4.00 10.00
4 Tyler Boyd/49 5.00 12.00
5 Raghib Rocket Ismail/49 5.00 12.00
6 Kerryon Johnson/199 4.00 10.00
7 Steve Atwater/49 12.00 30.00
8 Jamison Crowder/75 4.00 10.00
9 James Lofton/99 10.00 25.00
10 Marquise Goodwin/75 4.00 10.00
11 Aqib Talib/49 5.00 12.00
12 Jordan Reed/49 5.00 12.00
13 Larry Johnson/49 5.00 12.00
14 Phillip Lindsay/199 6.00 15.00
15 Aaron Jones/99 5.00 12.00
16 Tony Siragusa/75 4.00 10.00
17 Andre Rison/99 5.00 12.00
18 Marcus Peters/99 4.00 10.00
19 Nick Chubb/49 8.00 20.00
20 Ickey Woods/99 4.00 10.00
21 Landon Collins/49 5.00 12.00
22 Willie Gault/49 5.00 12.00
23 Brandon Graham/199 3.00 8.00
24 Chris Godwin/99 4.00 10.00
25 Ronde Barber/99 8.00 20.00
26 Aaron Ripkowski/199 3.00 8.00
27 D.J. Moore /199 4.00 10.00
28 C.J. Mosley/49 6.00 15.00
29 Lenny Moore /75 4.00 10.00
30 Yannick Ngakoue/199 3.00 8.00

2019 Panini Luminance Jersey Autographs

*GOLD/49: .5X TO 1.2X BASIC JSY AU/99
*GOLD/25: .5X TO 1.2X BASIC JSY AU/49
*RED/25: .6X TO 1.5X BASIC JSY AU
1 Patrick Mahomes II/25 200.00 300.00
2 Baker Mayfield/25 EXCH 200.00 300.00
3 Corey Davis/49 8.00 20.00
4 Edgerrin James/25 12.00 30.00
5 Barry Sanders/10
6 Marlon Mack/99 5.00 12.00
7 Harrison Smith/49 12.00 30.00
8 DeAndre Hopkins/25
9 Ezekiel Elliott/25
10 Steve Young/10
11 Tony Gonzalez/15
12 Steven Jackson/25 8.00 20.00
13 Eric Weddle/49 6.00 15.00
14 Mitchell Trubisky/25 15.00 40.00
15 Alshon Jeffery/25 10.00 25.00
16 Hines Ward/25
17 Earl Campbell/25
18 Melvin Gordon III/49
20 Christian McCaffrey/25

2019 Panini Luminance Jumbo Jerseys

*ORANGE/49: .6X TO 1.5X BASIC JSY
*RED/25: .8X TO 2X BASIC JSY
1 Marcus Mariota 3.00 8.00
2 Allen Hurns 2.00 5.00
3 Antonio Brown 3.00 8.00
4 Ben Roethlisberger 2.50 6.00
5 Deshaun Watson 4.00 10.00
6 Baker Mayfield 8.00 20.00
7 Mitchell Trubisky 3.00 8.00
8 Joe Mixon 2.50 6.00
9 Tarik Cohen 2.50 6.00
10 Lamar Jackson 5.00 12.00
11 Jameis Winston 2.50 6.00
12 Christian McCaffrey 3.00 8.00
13 Dak Prescott 3.00 8.00
14 Kerryon Johnson 2.50 6.00
15 Leonard Fournette 3.00 8.00
16 Mike Williams 2.00 5.00
17 Cooper Kupp 2.50 6.00
18 Dalvin Cook 2.50 6.00
19 James White 2.50 6.00
20 Alvin Kamara 2.50 6.00

2019 Panini Luminance Lightspeed

*ORANGE/100: .6X TO 1.5X BASIC INSERTS
1 Cam Newton 1.00 2.50
2 Tyreek Hill 1.00 2.50
3 Tarik Cohen .75 2.00
4 Lamar Jackson 1.00 2.50
5 Deshaun Watson 1.25 3.00
6 Calvin Ridley .75 2.00
7 Odell Beckham Jr. 1.00 2.50
8 Julio Jones 1.00 2.50
9 Antonio Brown 1.00 2.50
10 Russell Wilson 1.25 3.00
11 Larry Fitzgerald .75 2.00
12 Julian Edelman 1.00 2.50
13 DeAndre Hopkins .75 2.00
14 Michael Thomas 1.00 2.50
15 JuJu Smith-Schuster 1.00 2.50
16 Amari Cooper 1.00 2.50
17 Alvin Kamara .75 2.00
18 Todd Gurley II 1.00 2.50
19 David Johnson 1.00 2.50
20 Saquon Barkley 1.25 3.00

2019 Panini Luminance Luminary

*ORANGE/100: .6X TO 1.5X BASIC INSERTS
1 Dwayne Haskins 3.00 8.00
2 Daniel Jones 3.00 8.00
3 Will Grier 2.00 5.00
4 Drew Lock 3.00 8.00
5 Ryan Finley 1.25 3.00
6 Jarrett Stidham 2.00 5.00
7 Marquise Brown 2.00 5.00
8 N'Keal Harry 2.00 5.00
9 Bryce Love 1.00 2.50
10 Parris Campbell 1.50 4.00
11 Noah Fant 1.25 3.00
12 Nick Bosa 2.00 5.00
13 Devin White 2.00 5.00
14 Kyler Murray 6.00 15.00
15 A.J. Brown [illegible]
16 Damien Harris 1.50 4.00

17 Darrell Henderson 1.50 4.00
18 David Montgomery 2.50 6.00
19 Rodney Anderson .75 2.00
20 Dexter Williams .75 2.00

2019 Panini Luminance Rookie Ink

1 Greedy Williams/349 12.00 30.00
2 Deandre Baker/349 10.00 25.00
3 Julian Love/349 5.00 12.00
4 Trayvon Mullen Jr./349 6.00 15.00
5 Byron Murphy/349 4.00 10.00
6 Nick Bosa/199 12.00 30.00
7 Rashan Gary/349 8.00 20.00
8 Clelin Ferrell/349 6.00 15.00
9 Jaylon Ferguson/349 4.00 10.00
10 Miles Boykin/349 5.00 12.00
11 Zach Allen/349 6.00 15.00
12 Brian Burns/349 5.00 12.00
13 Montez Sweat/349 12.00 30.00
14 Travis Homer/349 4.00 10.00
15 Ed Oliver/349 6.00 15.00
16 Dexter Lawrence/349 6.00 15.00
17 Christian Wilkins/349 15.00 40.00
18 Jeffery Simmons/349 4.00 10.00
20 Devin White/349 12.00 30.00
22 Mack Wilson/349 5.00 12.00
23 Dwayne Haskins/99 40.00 80.00
24 Kyler Murray/99 75.00 150.00
25 Daniel Jones/99
26 Drew Lock/99 25.00 60.00
27 Will Grier/199 12.00 30.00
28 Ryan Finley/299 8.00 20.00
29 Gardner Minshew II/349 6.00 15.00
30 Jarrett Stidham/349 12.00 30.00
31 Damien Harris/199 10.00 25.00
32 Josh Jacobs/199 20.00 50.00
33 Bryce Love/299 6.00 15.00
34 Darrell Henderson/349 10.00 25.00
35 David Montgomery/349 15.00 40.00
36 Rodney Anderson/349 5.00 12.00
37 Trayveon Williams/349 5.00 12.00
38 Alex Barnes/349 5.00 12.00
39 Dexter Williams/349 5.00 12.00
40 Karan Higdon/349 5.00 12.00
41 Miles Sanders/349 10.00 25.00
42 Elijah Holyfield/349 6.00 15.00
43 Justice Hill/349 6.00 15.00
44 Myles Gaskin/349 8.00 20.00
45 Benny Snell Jr./349 12.00 30.00
46 Devin Singletary/349 5.00 12.00
47 Deionte Thompson/349 5.00 12.00
48 Johnathan Abram/349 4.00 10.00
49 Noah Fant/349 8.00 20.00
50 Irv Smith Jr./349 8.00 20.00
51 Caleb Wilson/349 4.00 10.00
52 T.J. Hockenson/349 10.00 25.00
53 Marquise Brown/199 12.00 30.00
54 N'Keal Harry/199 12.00 30.00
55 A.J. Brown/199 10.00 25.00
56 D.K. Metcalf/199 12.00 30.00
57 Parris Campbell/349 10.00 25.00
58 Anthony Johnson/349 5.00 12.00
59 Hakeem Butler/349 8.00 20.00
60 J.J. Arcega-Whiteside/349 6.00 15.00
61 Kelvin Harmon/349 6.00 15.00
62 Deebo Samuel/349 10.00 25.00
63 Antoine Wesley/349 4.00 10.00
64 Lil'Jordan Humphrey/349 5.00 12.00
65 Preston Williams/349 4.00 10.00
66 Gary Jennings Jr./349 6.00 15.00
67 David Sills V/349 12.00 30.00
68 Emanuel Hall/349 4.00 10.00
69 Riley Ridley/349 6.00 15.00
70 Stanley Morgan Jr./349 6.00 15.00

2019 Panini Luminance Rookie Ink Blue

*BLUE/75-99: .5X TO 1.2X BASIC AU/199-349
*BLUE/49: .5X TO 1.2X BASIC AU/99

2019 Panini Luminance Rookie Ink Gold

*GOLD/75-149: .5X TO 1.2X BASIC AU/199-349
*GOLD/75-149: .4X TO 1X BASIC AU/99

2019 Panini Luminance Rookie Ink Orange

*ORANGE/25: .8X TO 2X BASIC AU/199-349
*ORANGE/25: .6X TO 1.5X BASIC AU/99
23 Dwayne Haskins 100.00 200.00

2019 Panini Luminance Vintage Materials

*GOLD/49: .6X TO 1.5X BASIC JSY
*GOLD/25: 86X TO 2X BASIC JSY
*RED/25: .8X TO 2X BASIC JSY
1 Kurt Warner 2.50 6.00
2 John Lynch 2.00 5.00
3 Barry Sanders 5.00 12.00
4 Ray Lewis 3.00 8.00
5 Michael Strahan 3.00 8.00
6 Peyton Manning 6.00 15.00
7 Dan Marino 6.00 15.00
8 John Elway 5.00 12.00
9 Steve Young 4.00 10.00
10 Len Dawson 2.50 6.00

2015 Panini Luxe Autographs

*SILVER/49: .5X TO 1.2X BASIC AU/99
*SILVER/25: .6X TO 1.5X BASIC AU/99
*GOLD/25: .6X TO 1.5X BASIC AU/99
*GOLD/15: .8X TO 2X BASIC AU/99
2 Kenny Stills/99 5.00 12.00
4 Robert Brooks/25 30.00 60.00
5 Emmanuel Sanders/99 6.00 15.00
6 Lance Briggs/25 10.00 25.00
7 Eddie Lacy/25 8.00 20.00
9 Zach Ertz/99 6.00 15.00
14 C.J. Anderson/25 10.00 25.00
17 Jan Stenerud/25 8.00 20.00
19 Wilbert Montgomery/25 12.00 30.00
22 Greg Olsen/25 20.00 40.00
23 Kendall Wright/99 5.00 12.00
25 Joique Bell/99 5.00 12.00
26 Julius Thomas/99 5.00 12.00
27 Travis Kelce/99 10.00 25.00
28 Torrey Smith/25 8.00 20.00
30 Aeneas Williams/99 5.00 12.00
32 Gary Fencik/99 5.00 12.00
34 Don Majkowski/99 6.00 15.00
35 Fred Biletnikoff/99 8.00 20.00
36 Harold Carmichael/99 5.00 12.00
39 Charles Haley/99 8.00 20.00

2015 Panini Luxe Die Cut Autographs

*SILVER: .5X TO 1.2X BASIC AU
3 Cris Carter/15
11 Knile Davis/99 5.00 12.00
13 Aaron Dobson/28 8.00 20.00
14 Brandin Cooks/49 8.00 20.00
16 Coby Fleener/49 6.00 15.00
18 Charlie Joiner/49 6.00 15.00
19 Mike Quick/49 6.00 15.00
20 Trent Dilfer/49 6.00 15.00
25 Reggie Bush/25 8.00 20.00
33 Danny Amendola/25 10.00 25.00
35 Joique Bell/25 8.00 20.00
36 Eric Decker/25 8.00 20.00

2015 Panini Luxe Die Cut Rookie Autographs

*SILVER/49: .5X TO 1.2X BASIC AU/99
1 Jameis Winston/25 50.00 100.00
2 Marcus Mariota/25 50.00 100.00
3 Amari Cooper/25 40.00 80.00
4 Kevin White/25
5 Melvin Gordon/25 10.00 25.00
6 Todd Gurley/25 50.00 100.00
7 Ameer Abdullah/25 6.00 15.00
8 T.J. Yeldon/25
9 Bryce Petty/25 4.00 10.00
10 Brett Hundley/25 4.00 10.00
12 Dorial Green-Beckham/25 4.00 10.00
14 Nelson Agholor/25 5.00 12.00
15 Devin Funchess/25 6.00 15.00
16 Tevin Coleman/99 3.00 8.00
17 Sammie Coates/25 5.00 12.00
18 Ty Montgomery/49 3.00 8.00
19 Buck Allen/99 3.00 8.00
20 Jay Ajayi/99 4.00 10.00

2015 Panini Luxe Memorabilia Autographs

*SILIVER/49: .5X TO 1.2X BASIC JSY AU/99
*SILIVER/25: .5X TO 1.2X BASIC JSY AU/49
1 Alex Smith/49 10.00 25.00
2 Alshon Jeffery/49 10.00 25.00
3 Antonio Brown/25 50.00 100.00
4 Darren Sproles/25 25.00 50.00
5 Devin Hester/49 10.00 25.00
7 Richard Sherman/25 40.00 80.00
8 Ryan Tannehill/25 12.00 30.00
9 Marques Colston/49 8.00 20.00
10 C.J. Anderson/25 12.00 30.00
11 Tony Romo/25 40.00 80.00
12 Darrelle Revis/25 30.00 60.00
13 Dez Bryant/25 40.00 80.00
14 Derek Carr/99 30.00 60.00
15 Jordan Matthews/99 8.00 20.00
16 Mike Evans/99 8.00 20.00
17 Matt Forte/99 6.00 15.00
18 Andrew Luck/25 100.00 200.00
19 Lamar Miller/99 6.00 15.00

2015 Panini Luxe Memorabilia Die Cuts Prime Red

*BLUE/22-25: X TO X BASIC JSY/49
1 A.J. Green/49 5.00 12.00
2 Andy Dalton/49 4.00 10.00
3 Jeremy Hill/49 3.00 8.00
4 EJ Manuel/49 3.00 8.00
5 Sammy Watkins/49 4.00 10.00
6 Fred Jackson/49 4.00 10.00
7 Peyton Manning/49 25.00 60.00
8 Demaryius Thomas/49 4.00 10.00
9 Jamaal Charles/49 4.00 10.00
10 Alex Smith/49 4.00 10.00
11 Tony Romo/30 8.00 20.00
12 Dez Bryant/49 5.00 12.00
13 Cole Beasley/49 12.00 30.00
14 Jarvis Landry/49 4.00 10.00
15 Lamar Miller/49 3.00 8.00
16 Blake Bortles/49 3.00 8.00
17 Allen Robinson/49 4.00 10.00
18 Allen Hurns/49 3.00 8.00
19 Julian Edelman/49 12.00 30.00
20 Jimmy Garoppolo/49 6.00 15.00
21 Steve Smith/49 4.00 10.00
22 Joe Flacco/49 4.00 10.00
23 Johnny Manziel/49 4.00 10.00
24 Le'Veon Bell/49 4.00 10.00
25 Antonio Brown/49 5.00 12.00
26 Jadeveon Clowney/49 3.00 8.00
28 T.Y. Hilton/49 4.00 10.00
29 Kendall Wright/49 3.00 8.00
30 Derek Carr/49 5.00 12.00
31 Keenan Allen/49 4.00 10.00
32 Eli Manning/49 4.00 10.00
33 Odell Beckham Jr./49 5.00 12.00
34 Jordan Matthews/49 4.00 10.00
35 DeSean Jackson/49 4.00 10.00
36 Alfred Morris/49 3.00 8.00
37 Matt Forte/49 3.00 8.00
38 Alshon Jeffery/49 4.00 10.00
39 Joique Bell/49 3.00 8.00
41 Teddy Bridgewater/49 4.00 10.00
42 Cordarrelle Patterson/49 3.00 8.00
43 Matt Ryan/49 4.00 10.00
44 Julio Jones/49 5.00 12.00
45 Cam Newton/49 5.00 12.00
46 Jonathan Stewart/49 3.00 8.00
47 Drew Brees/15 8.00 20.00
48 Mark Ingram/49 4.00 10.00
49 Brandin Cooks/49 4.00 10.00
50 Mike Evans/49 4.00 10.00
51 Larry Fitzgerald/49 4.00 10.00
52 Andre Ellington/49 3.00 8.00
53 Chris Long/49 3.00 8.00
54 James Laurinaitis/49 4.00 10.00
55 Colin Kaepernick/15 6.00 15.00
56 Carlos Hyde/49 3.00 8.00
57 Marshawn Lynch/25 12.00 30.00
58 Russell Wilson/49 12.00 30.00
60 Jameis Winston/49 5.00 12.00
61 Marcus Mariota/49 8.00 20.00
62 Amari Cooper/49 6.00 15.00
63 Kevin White/49 2.50 6.00
64 Melvin Gordon/49 5.00 12.00
65 Todd Gurley/49 10.00 25.00
66 Ameer Abdullah/49 3.00 8.00
67 T.J. Yeldon/49 2.00 5.00
68 Bryce Petty/49 2.00 5.00
69 Brett Hundley/49 2.00 5.00
70 DeVante Parker/49 3.00 8.00
71 Jaelen Strong/49 2.50 6.00
72 Dorial Green-Beckham/49 2.00 5.00
73 Devin Smith/49 2.00 5.00
74 Phillip Dorsett/49 2.00 5.00
75 Nelson Agholor/49 2.50 6.00
76 Breshad Perriman/49 2.00 5.00
77 Devin Funchess/49 3.00 8.00
78 Maxx Williams/49 2.00 5.00
79 Tyler Lockett/49 3.00 8.00
80 Tevin Coleman/49 2.50 6.00
81 Garrett Grayson/49 2.00 5.00
82 Chris Conley/49 2.00 5.00
83 Duke Johnson/49 3.00 8.00
84 David Johnson/49 5.00 12.00
85 David Cobb/49 2.00 5.00
86 Sammie Coates/49 2.50 6.00
87 Sean Mannion/49 2.00 5.00
88 Ty Montgomery/49 2.00 5.00
89 Jamison Crowder/49 2.50 6.00
90 Jeremy Langford/49 2.00 5.00
91 Justin Hardy/49 2.00 5.00
92 Vince Mayle/49 2.50 6.00
93 Buck Allen/49 2.50 6.00
94 Rashad Greene/49 2.00 5.00
95 Stefon Diggs/49 5.00 12.00
96 Jay Ajayi/49 3.00 8.00
97 Leonard Williams/49 2.00 5.00
98 Mike Davis/49 2.00 5.00
99 Matt Jones/49 2.00 5.00
100 Karlos Williams/49 2.00 5.00

2015 Panini Luxe Memorabilia Prime

1 A.J. Green/25 5.00 12.00
2 Andy Dalton/25 4.00 10.00
3 Jeremy Hill/25 3.00 8.00
4 Tyler Eifert/25 4.00 10.00
5 Sammy Watkins/25 4.00 10.00
6 LeSean McCoy/25 5.00 12.00
7 Percy Harvin/25 3.00 8.00
8 Tyrod Taylor/25 4.00 10.00
9 Charles Clay/25 3.00 8.00
10 Peyton Manning/25 20.00 50.00
11 Emmanuel Sanders/25 4.00 10.00
12 Demaryius Thomas/25 4.00 10.00
13 C.J. Anderson/25 4.00 10.00
14 DeMarcus Ware/25 10.00 25.00
15 Von Miller/25 10.00 25.00
17 Dez Bryant/25 5.00 12.00
18 Darren McFadden/25 3.00 8.00
19 Terrance Williams/25 3.00 8.00
20 Cole Beasley/25 8.00 20.00
21 Greg Hardy/25 3.00 8.00
22 Jarvis Landry/25 4.00 10.00
23 Ryan Tannehill/25 4.00 10.00
24 Lamar Miller/25 3.00 8.00
25 Kenny Stills/25 3.00 8.00
26 Greg Jennings/25 3.00 8.00
27 Blake Bortles/25 3.00 8.00
28 Denard Robinson/25 3.00 8.00
29 Julius Thomas/25 3.00 8.00
30 Allen Robinson/25 4.00 10.00
31 T.J. Yeldon/25 3.00 8.00
32 Paul Posluszny/25 3.00 8.00
33 Matthew Stafford/25 8.00 20.00
34 Calvin Johnson/25 8.00 20.00
37 Alex Smith/25 4.00 10.00
38 Jamaal Charles/25 4.00 10.00
39 Eric Berry/25 4.00 10.00
40 Travis Kelce/25 5.00 12.00
41 Joe Montana/25 30.00 60.00
42 Julian Edelman/25 10.00 25.00
44 Jimmy Garoppolo/25 6.00 15.00
45 Rob Gronkowski/25 12.00 30.00
47 Justin Hunter/25 3.00 8.00
48 Kendall Wright/18 4.00 10.00
49 Devonta Freeman/25 4.00 10.00
50 Julio Jones/25 5.00 12.00
51 Roddy White/25 3.00 8.00
52 Jonathan Stewart/25 3.00 8.00
53 Kelvin Benjamin/25 4.00 10.00
54 Martellus Bennett/25 3.00 8.00
55 Matt Forte/25 3.00 8.00
56 Doug Flutie/25 4.00 10.00
57 Mike Singletary/25 5.00 12.00
58 Barkevious Mingo/25 3.00 8.00
59 Joe Haden/25 3.00 8.00
60 Johnny Manziel/25 4.00 10.00
61 Travis Benjamin/25 3.00 8.00
62 Davante Adams/25 4.00 10.00
64 Julius Peppers/25 10.00 25.00
65 Randall Cobb/25 4.00 10.00
66 Brian Cushing/25 3.00 8.00
69 T.Y. Hilton/25 4.00 10.00
70 Marcus Allen/25 5.00 12.00
71 James Laurinaitis/25 4.00 10.00
72 Tre Mason/25 4.00 10.00
74 Teddy Bridgewater/25 4.00 10.00
75 Brandin Cooks/25 4.00 10.00
76 Mark Ingram/25 4.00 10.00
77 Odell Beckham Jr./25 5.00 12.00
78 Victor Cruz/17 5.00 12.00
79 Curtis Martin/25 4.00 10.00
80 Darrelle Revis/25 3.00 8.00
81 Jordan Matthews/25 4.00 10.00
82 Zach Ertz/24 4.00 10.00
83 Antonio Brown/25 15.00 40.00
84 Brett Keisel/25 30.00 60.00
87 Le'Veon Bell/25 4.00 10.00
88 Antonio Gates/25 3.00 8.00
89 Keenan Allen/25 4.00 10.00
90 Carlos Hyde/25 3.00 8.00
91 Colin Kaepernick/25 4.00 10.00
92 Jerry Rice/25 12.00 30.00
93 Earl Thomas/25 4.00 10.00
94 Kam Chancellor/25 12.00 30.00
95 Marshawn Lynch/25 4.00 10.00
96 Russell Wilson/25 12.00 30.00
97 Mike Evans/25 4.00 10.00
99 Alfred Morris/25 3.00 8.00
100 Kirk Cousins/25 5.00 12.00

2015 Panini Luxe Rookie Autographs

*SILVER/49: .5X TO 1.2X BASIC AU/99
*SILVER/25: .5X TO 1.2X BASIC AU/49
*SILVER/15: .6X TO 1.5X BASIC AU/49
1 Jameis Winston/25 30.00 60.00
2 Marcus Mariota/25 40.00 80.00
3 Amari Cooper/25 30.00 60.00
4 Kevin White/25 6.00 15.00
5 Melvin Gordon/25 12.00 30.00
6 Todd Gurley/25 50.00 100.00
7 Ameer Abdullah/25 8.00 20.00
8 T.J. Yeldon/25 5.00 12.00
9 Bryce Petty/25 5.00 12.00
10 Brett Hundley/25 5.00 12.00
12 Jaelen Strong/99 4.00 10.00
13 Dorial Green-Beckham/25 5.00 12.00
14 Devin Smith/49 4.00 10.00
15 Phillip Dorsett/99 3.00 8.00
16 Nelson Agholor/25 6.00 15.00
17 Breshad Perriman/50 4.00 10.00
18 Devin Funchess/25 8.00 20.00
19 Maxx Williams/75 3.00 8.00
20 Tyler Lockett/49 6.00 15.00
21 Tevin Coleman/99 4.00 10.00
22 Garrett Grayson/49 4.00 10.00
23 Chris Conley/75 3.00 8.00
24 Duke Johnson/49 6.00 15.00
25 David Johnson/75 15.00 40.00
26 David Cobb/99 3.00 8.00
27 Sammie Coates/25 6.00 15.00
28 Sean Mannion/75 3.00 8.00
29 Ty Montgomery/49 4.00 10.00
30 Jamison Crowder/99 4.00 10.00
31 Jeremy Langford/99 3.00 8.00
32 Justin Hardy/99 3.00 8.00
33 Vince Mayle/99 4.00 10.00
34 Buck Allen/99 4.00 10.00
35 Rashad Greene/49 4.00 10.00
36 Stefon Diggs/49 10.00 25.00
37 Jay Ajayi/99 5.00 12.00
38 Leonard Williams/75 3.00 8.00
39 Mike Davis/99 3.00 8.00
40 Matt Jones/99 3.00 8.00

2015 Panini Luxe Rookie Memorabilia Autographs

1 Jaelen Strong 5.00 12.00
2 Dorial Green-Beckham 4.00 10.00
3 Devin Smith 4.00 10.00
4 Phillip Dorsett
5 Nelson Agholor 5.00 12.00
6 Breshad Perriman 4.00 10.00
7 Devin Funchess 6.00 15.00
8 Maxx Williams 8.00 20.00
9 Tyler Lockett 6.00 15.00
10 Jameis Winston 60.00 120.00
11 Marcus Mariota 25.00 50.00
12 Amari Cooper 15.00 40.00
13 Kevin White 5.00 12.00
14 Melvin Gordon 10.00 25.00
15 Todd Gurley II 40.00 80.00
16 Ameer Abdullah 6.00 15.00
17 T.J. Yeldon 4.00 10.00
18 Bryce Petty 4.00 10.00
19 Brett Hundley 10.00 25.00
20 DeVante Parker 6.00 15.00
21 Ty Montgomery 4.00 10.00
22 Jamison Crowder 5.00 12.00
23 Jeremy Langford 4.00 10.00
24 Justin Hardy 4.00 10.00
25 Vince Mayle 5.00 12.00
26 Buck Allen 5.00 12.00
27 Rashad Greene 4.00 10.00
28 Stefon Diggs 10.00 25.00
29 Jay Ajayi 6.00 15.00
30 Leonard Williams 4.00 10.00
31 Mike Davis 4.00 10.00
32 Matt Jones
33 Tevin Coleman 5.00 12.00
34 Garrett Grayson 4.00 10.00
35 Chris Conley 4.00 10.00
36 Duke Johnson 6.00 15.00
37 David Johnson 20.00 40.00
38 David Cobb 4.00 10.00
39 Sammie Coates 5.00 12.00
40 Sean Mannion 4.00 10.00

2015 Panini Luxe Rookie Memorabilia Autographs Prime Gold

*GOLD/25: .6X TO 1.5X BASIC JSY AU/99

2015 Panini Luxe Rookie Memorabilia Autographs Silver

*SILVER/49: .5X TO 1.2X BASIC JSY AU/99
10 Jameis Winston 75.00 150.00

2010 Panini Madden 11

1 Drew Brees AU/50 40.00 80.00

2011 Panini Madden 12 Marshall Faulk Autographs

One of these four cards was inserted into each EA Sports Madden 12 Hall of Fame edition video game released in 2011. Each card is hand signed and measures larger than standard size.
COMMON FAULK AU 20.00 40.00

2017 Panini Majestic

1 David Johnson 3.00 8.00
2 Larry Fitzgerald 2.50 6.00
3 Carson Palmer 2.50 6.00
4 Matt Ryan 2.50 6.00
5 Devonta Freeman 2.50 6.00
6 Julio Jones 3.00 8.00
7 Joe Flacco 2.50 6.00
8 Terrell Suggs 2.00 5.00
9 Steve Smith Sr. 2.50 6.00
10 Tyrod Taylor 2.50 6.00
11 LeSean McCoy 3.00 8.00
12 Sammy Watkins 3.00 8.00
13 Cam Newton 3.00 8.00
14 Kelvin Benjamin 2.50 6.00
15 Greg Olsen 2.50 6.00
16 Leonard Floyd 2.00 5.00
17 Jordan Howard 3.00 8.00
18 Alshon Jeffery 2.50 6.00
19 Andy Dalton 2.50 6.00
20 Jeremy Hill 2.00 5.00
21 A.J. Green 3.00 8.00
22 Cody Kessler 2.00 5.00
23 Corey Coleman 2.00 5.00
24 Terrelle Pryor Sr. 2.00 5.00
25 Dak Prescott 3.00 8.00
26 Ezekiel Elliott 4.00 10.00
27 Dez Bryant 3.00 8.00
28 Cole Beasley 3.00 8.00
29 Trevor Siemian 2.00 5.00
30 Von Miller 2.50 6.00
31 Demaryius Thomas 2.50 6.00
32 Paxton Lynch 2.00 5.00
33 Matthew Stafford 2.50 6.00
34 Marvin Jones Jr. 2.00 5.00
35 Theo Riddick 2.00 5.00
36 Aaron Rodgers 6.00 15.00
37 Clay Matthews 2.50 6.00
38 Jordy Nelson 2.50 6.00
39 Davante Adams 2.50 6.00
40 Jadeveon Clowney 2.00 5.00
41 Lamar Miller 2.00 5.00
42 DeAndre Hopkins 2.50 6.00
43 J.J. Watt 3.00 8.00
44 Andrew Luck 4.00 10.00
45 Frank Gore 2.50 6.00
46 T.Y. Hilton 2.50 6.00
47 Blake Bortles 2.00 5.00
48 Allen Robinson 2.50 6.00
49 Jalen Ramsey 2.00 5.00
50 Alex Smith 2.50 6.00
51 Jeremy Maclin 2.00 5.00
52 Tyreek Hill 3.00 8.00
53 Ryan Tannehill 2.50 6.00
54 Jay Ajayi 2.50 6.00
55 Jarvis Landry 2.50 6.00
56 Sam Bradford 2.00 5.00
57 Randy Moss 2.50 6.00
58 Stefon Diggs 2.50 6.00
59 Tom Brady 8.00 20.00
60 Rob Gronkowski 3.00 8.00
61 Julian Edelman 3.00 8.00
62 Drew Brees 3.00 8.00
63 Michael Thomas 3.00 8.00
64 Brandin Cooks 2.50 6.00
65 Eli Manning 2.50 6.00
66 Sterling Shepard 2.50 6.00
67 Odell Beckham Jr. 3.00 8.00
68 Matt Forte 2.00 5.00
69 Eric Decker 2.00 5.00
70 Brandon Marshall 2.00 5.00
71 Derek Carr 3.00 8.00
72 Michael Crabtree 2.00 5.00
73 Amari Cooper 3.00 8.00
74 Carson Wentz 4.00 10.00
75 Zach Ertz 2.50 6.00
76 Jordan Matthews 2.00 5.00
77 Ben Roethlisberger 3.00 8.00
78 Le'Veon Bell 2.50 6.00
79 Antonio Brown 3.00 8.00
80 James Harrison 2.50 6.00
81 Philip Rivers 3.00 8.00
82 Melvin Gordon 2.50 6.00
83 Joey Bosa 3.00 8.00
84 Carlos Hyde 2.00 5.00
85 Navorro Bowman 2.50 6.00
86 Russell Wilson 4.00 10.00
87 Doug Baldwin 2.50 6.00
88 Thomas Rawls 2.00 5.00
89 Jared Goff 3.00 8.00
90 Todd Gurley II 3.00 8.00
91 Aaron Donald 3.00 8.00
92 Jameis Winston 2.50 6.00
93 Mike Evans 2.50 6.00
94 Cameron Brate 2.00 5.00
95 Marcus Mariota 3.00 8.00
96 DeMarco Murray 2.50 6.00
97 Derrick Henry 2.50 6.00
98 Kirk Cousins 3.00 8.00
99 Robert Kelley 2.00 5.00
100 Jordan Reed 2.00 5.00
101 Mitchell Trubisky JSY AU/25 RC 100.00 200.00
102 Deshaun Watson JSY AU/25 RC 100.00 200.00
103 DeShone Kizer JSY AU/25 RC 8.00 20.00
104 Patrick Mahomes II JSY AU/49 RC 175.00 300.00
105 Brad Kaaya JSY AU/49 RC 6.00 15.00
106 Davis Webb JSY AU/199 RC 4.00 10.00
107 Jerod Evans JSY AU/199 RC 5.00 12.00
108 Chad Kelly JSY AU/199 RC 10.00 25.00
109 R. Joshua Dobbs JSY AU/199 RC 5.00 12.00
110 Ryan Switzer JSY AU/199 RC 5.00 12.00
111 Alvin Kamara JSY AU/199 RC 15.00 40.00
112 Dalvin Cook JSY AU/25 RC 50.00 100.00
113 Leonard Fournette JSY AU/25 RC 100.00 200.00
114 Christian McCaffrey JSY AU/25 RC 60.00 125.00
115 Joe Mixon JSY AU/199 RC 15.00 40.00
116 Samaje Perine JSY AU/199 RC 20.00 50.00
117 Wayne Gallman JSY AU/199 RC 5.00 12.00
118 Kareem Hunt JSY AU/199 RC 12.00 30.00
119 D'Onta Foreman JSY AU/99 RC 20.00 50.00
120 Jeremy McNichols JSY AU/199 RC 4.00 10.00
121 Corey Clement JSY AU/199 RC 5.00 12.00
122 James Conner JSY AU/199 RC 12.00 30.00
123 Donnel Pumphrey JSY AU/199 RC 20.00 50.00
124 Zay Jones JSY AU/199 RC 5.00 12.00
125 Elijah Hood JSY AU/199 RC 4.00 10.00
126 Mike Williams JSY AU/25 RC
127 Corey Davis JSY AU/99 RC 8.00 20.00
128 John Ross JSY AU/99 RC 6.00 15.00
129 Curtis Samuel JSY AU/199 RC 5.00 12.00
130 Dede Westbrook JSY AU/99 RC 25.00 50.00
131 Evan Engram JSY AU/199 RC 5.00 12.00
132 JuJu Smith-Schuster JSY AU/99 RC 20.00 40.00
133 ArDarius Stewart JSY AU/199 RC 4.00 10.00
134 Cooper Kupp JSY AU/199 RC 6.00 15.00
135 Malachi Dupre JSY AU/199 RC 4.00 10.00
136 Isaiah Ford JSY AU/199 RC 4.00 10.00
137 Amara Darboh JSY AU/199 RC 4.00 10.00
138 Chris Godwin JSY AU/199 RC 5.00 12.00
139 Noah Brown JSY AU/199 RC 5.00 12.00
140 O.J. Howard JSY AU/199 RC 5.00 12.00
141 Josh Malone AU/25 RC 4.00 10.00
142 Cooper Rush AU/25 RC 5.00 12.00
143 Brian Hill AU/25 RC 4.00 10.00
144 Jake Butt AU/25 RC 5.00 12.00
145 Bucky Hodges AU/25 RC 4.00 10.00
146 Jordan Leggett AU/49 RC 3.00 8.00
147 Carlos Henderson AU/49 RC 3.00 8.00
148 Elijah McGuire AU/49 RC 3.00 8.00
149 C.J. Beathard AU/49 RC 3.00 8.00
150 Artavis Scott AU/49 RC 3.00 8.00
151 Travis Rudolph AU/49 RC 3.00 8.00
152 Stacy Coley AU/49 RC 3.00 8.00
153 Quincy Wilson AU/25 RC 4.00 10.00
154 Jonathan Allen AU/25 RC 15.00 40.00
155 Solomon Thomas AU/25 RC 10.00 25.00
156 Malik Hooker AU/25 RC 25.00 50.00
157 Jamal Adams AU/25 RC 4.00 10.00
158 T.J. Watt AU/25 RC 30.00 60.00
159 Marshon Lattimore AU/25 RC 5.00 12.00
160 Jabrill Peppers AU/25 RC 30.00 60.00

2017 Panini Majestic Gold

*VETS/25: .6X TO 1.5X BASIC CARDS/99
*ROOK JSY AU/25: .8X TO 2X BASIC JSY AU/199
*ROOK JSY AU/15: 1X TO 2.5X BASIC JSY AU/199
*ROOK AU/25: .5X TO 1.2X BASIC AU/49

2017 Panini Majestic Astonishing Arms Autographs

*GOLD/49: .5X TO 1.2X BASIC AU/99
*GOLD/49: .4X TO 1X BASIC AU/49
*GOLD/25: .5X TO 1.2X BASIC AU/49
*GOLD/20: .5X TO 1.2X BASIC AU/25
*RED/25: .6X TO 1.5X BASIC AU/99
*RED/25: .5X TO 1.2X BASIC AU/49
*RED/20: .6X TO 1.5X BASIC AU/49
*RED/15: .5X TO 1.2X BASIC AU/25
1 Kurt Warner/15 30.00 60.00
2 Jim Kelly/15 20.00 50.00
4 Jim McMahon/25 20.00 50.00
5 Roger Staubach/15
6 Troy Aikman/15
7 John Elway/15 60.00 100.00
8 Brett Favre/15 EXCH 75.00 150.00
9 Don Majkowski/49 10.00 25.00
10 Warren Moon/15 20.00 50.00
11 Peyton Manning/15 100.00 200.00
12 Mark Brunell/99 8.00 20.00
13 Bob Griese/99 10.00 25.00
14 Dan Marino/15
15 Rich Gannon/49 8.00 20.00
16 Fran Tarkenton/25
17 Archie Manning/25 30.00 60.00
18 Y.A. Tittle/49 12.00 30.00
19 Joe Namath/15
21 Dan Fouts/15 30.00 60.00
22 Joe Montana/15 100.00 200.00
23 Steve Young/15 40.00 80.00
24 Jim Zorn/99 6.00 15.00
25 Joe Theismann/49 12.00 30.00

2017 Panini Majestic Black and Blue Dual Autographs

*RED/49: .5X TO 1.2X BASIC AU/99
1 J.Allen/S.Thomas/99 8.00 20.00
2 J.Adams/M.Hooker/99 6.00 15.00
3 D.Barnett/T.Charlton/99 20.00 50.00
4 M.Humphrey/Q.Wilson/99 6.00 15.00
5 Z.Cunningham/M.McDowell/99 8.00 20.00

2017 Panini Majestic Distinguished Defenders Autographs

*GOLD/49: .5X TO 1.2X BASIC AU/99
*GOLD/25: .6X TO 1.5X BASIC AU/99
*GOLD/25: .5X TO 1.2X BASIC AU/49
*GOLD/15: .5X TO 1.2X BASIC AU/25
*RED/25: .6X TO 1.5X BASIC AU/99
*RED/20: .8X TO 2X BASIC AU/99
*RED/20: .6X TO 1.5X BASIC AU/49
1 Deion Sanders/15 15.00 40.00
2 Ed Reed/15 50.00 100.00
3 Ray Lewis/15 50.00 100.00
4 Bruce Smith/15 15.00 40.00
5 Brian Urlacher/15 30.00 60.00
6 Dan Hampton/49 8.00 20.00
8 Bob Lilly/99 8.00 20.00
9 Randy White/49 10.00 25.00
10 Steve Atwater/99 8.00 20.00
13 Neil Smith/99 6.00 15.00
15 Carl Eller/49 8.00 20.00
16 Tedy Bruschi/25 15.00 40.00
18 Lawrence Taylor/15
19 Ted Hendricks/15
20 Howie Long/15 20.00 50.00
21 Rod Woodson/25 12.00 30.00
22 Jack Lambert/15 EXCH 12.00 30.00
23 Ronnie Lott/15 EXCH 30.00 60.00

2017 Panini Majestic Exalted Triple Materials

*GOLD/20: .6X TO 1.5X BASIC JSY/50
1 Joey Bosa 5.00 12.00
2 Ezekiel Elliott 6.00 15.00
3 Dak Prescott 5.00 12.00
4 Amari Cooper 5.00 12.00
5 Jerry Rice 8.00 20.00
6 Terrell Davis 4.00 10.00
7 Marshall Faulk 4.00 10.00
8 Tom Brady 40.00 80.00
9 Jerome Bettis 15.00 40.00
10 Brett Favre 10.00 25.00

2017 Panini Majestic Icons Materials

*GOLD/15-20: .6X TO 1.5X BASIC JSY/50
1 Barry Sanders 8.00 20.00
2 Dan Marino 10.00 25.00
3 Dwight Clark 4.00 10.00
4 Franco Harris 5.00 12.00
5 Brett Favre 10.00 25.00
6 Jerry Rice 8.00 20.00
7 Jim Kelly 5.00 12.00
8 John Elway 10.00 25.00
9 John Riggins 4.00 10.00
10 Mike Singletary 5.00 12.00
11 Paul Hornung 5.00 12.00
12 Ray Lewis 5.00 12.00
13 Sterling Sharpe 4.00 10.00
14 Terry Bradshaw 15.00 40.00
15 Tony Dorsett 5.00 12.00

2017 Panini Majestic New Blood Triple Autographs

8 Jarrad Davis 15.00 40.00
Raekwon McMillan
T.J. Watt/99
9 Jabrill Peppers 20.00 50.00
Tim Williams
Zach Cunningham/25

2017 Panini Majestic Proteges Materials

*GOLD/75: .5X TO 1.2X BASIC JSY/149
*GOLD/49: .6X TO 1.5X BASIC JSY/149
*GOLD/49: .5X TO 1.2X BASIC JSY/99
*GOLD/25: .6X TO 1.5X BASIC JSY/99
1 Carson Wentz/99 5.00 12.00
2 Cody Kessler/149 2.00 5.00
3 Connor Cook/149 2.00 5.00
4 Corey Coleman/149 2.00 5.00
5 Dak Prescott/99 4.00 10.00
6 Derrick Henry/99 3.00 8.00
7 Devontae Booker/149 2.00 5.00
8 Ezekiel Elliott/99 5.00 12.00
9 Hunter Henry/149 2.00 5.00
10 Jacoby Brissett/149 2.00 5.00
11 Jalen Ramsey/99 2.50 6.00
12 Jared Goff/149 3.00 8.00
13 Joey Bosa/149 3.00 8.00
14 Jordan Howard/149 3.00 8.00
15 Josh Doctson/149 2.00 5.00
16 Laquon Treadwell/149 2.00 5.00
17 Malcolm Mitchell/99 3.00 8.00
18 Michael Thomas/99 4.00 10.00
19 Paul Perkins/99 2.50 6.00
20 Paxton Lynch/99 2.50 6.00
21 Sterling Shepard/99 3.00 8.00
22 Tajae Sharpe/99 2.50 6.00
23 Tyler Boyd/99 2.50 6.00
24 Tyreek Hill/99 4.00 10.00
25 Will Fuller V/99 2.50 6.00

2017 Panini Majestic Regal Runners Autographs

*GOLD/49: .5X TO 1.2X BASIC AU/99
*GOLD/25: .5X TO 1.2X BASIC AU/25
*GOLD/15-20: .5X TO 1.2X BASIC AU/25
*GOLD/15: .4X TO 1X BASIC AU/20
*RED/25: .6X TO 1.5X BASIC AU/99
*RED/25: .5X TO 1.2X BASIC AU/49
*RED/15-20: .8X TO 2X BASIC AU/99
*RED/15-20: .6X TO 1.5X BASIC AU/49
*RED/15-20: .5X TO 1.2X BASIC AU/25
1 Thurman Thomas/99 12.00 30.00
2 Fred Taylor/25 EXCH 12.00 30.00
3 Jim Brown/15
5 Tony Dorsett/15
6 Emmitt Smith/15 75.00 150.00
8 Terrell Davis/25 12.00 30.00
9 Barry Sanders/15 90.00 150.00
11 Edgerrin James/15 15.00 40.00
12 Priest Holmes/49 15.00 40.00
13 Eric Dickerson/25 30.00 60.00
14 Larry Csonka/25 12.00 30.00
15 Ricky Williams/49 10.00 25.00
16 Curtis Martin/15 15.00 40.00
17 Bo Jackson/15 60.00 125.00
18 Marcus Allen/25 12.00 30.00
19 Jerome Bettis/15 30.00 60.00
21 LaDainian Tomlinson/49 15.00 40.00
22 Marshawn Lynch/15
23 Marshall Faulk/15 25.00 60.00
24 Eddie George/25 12.00 30.00
25 John Riggins/15 15.00 40.00

2017 Panini Majestic Showstoppers Materials

*GOLD/50: .5X TO 1.2X BASIC JSY/75
*GOLD/25: .6X TO 1.5X BASIC JSY/75
1 Dak Prescott 4.00 10.00
2 Ezekiel Elliott 5.00 12.00
3 Jordan Howard 4.00 10.00
4 Amari Cooper 4.00 10.00
5 Derek Carr 4.00 10.00
6 Mike Evans 3.00 8.00
7 Julio Jones 4.00 10.00
8 LeSean McCoy 4.00 10.00
9 Antonio Brown 10.00 25.00
10 Odell Beckham Jr. 4.00 10.00
11 Drew Brees 4.00 10.00
12 Von Miller 3.00 8.00
13 A.J. Green 4.00 10.00
14 Andrew Luck 5.00 12.00
15 Allen Robinson 3.00 8.00
16 Russell Wilson 8.00 20.00
17 Jameis Winston 3.00 8.00
18 Marcus Mariota 4.00 10.00
19 Kirk Cousins 4.00 10.00
20 Le'Veon Bell 3.00 8.00

2017 Panini Majestic Team Pedigree Autographs

*GOLD/49: .5X TO 1.2X BASIC AU/99
*GOLD/49: .4X TO 1X BASIC AU/55
*GOLD/25: .5X TO 1.2X BASIC AU/49
*GOLD/15: .8X TO 2X BASIC AU/99
*RED/25: .6X TO 1.5X BASIC AU/99
*RED/25: .5X TO 1.2X BASIC AU/49
3 Cole Beasley/99 20.00 40.00
5 Dan Bailey/99 6.00 15.00
11 Jay Novacek/99 8.00 20.00
13 Darren Woodson/15
14 Charles Haley/49 12.00 30.00
15 Russell Maryland/99 6.00 15.00
16 Drew Pearson/15 15.00 40.00
17 Ed Too Tall Jones/99 6.00 15.00
19 Dan Reeves/15 15.00 40.00
21 Bill Bates/49 8.00 20.00
24 Bob Lilly/15 15.00 40.00
27 Le'Veon Bell/15 15.00 40.00
29 Dermontti Dawson/99 8.00 20.00
31 Maurkice Pouncey/99 15.00 40.00
32 David DeCastro/99 6.00 15.00
33 Cameron Heyward/99 6.00 15.00
34 James Harrison/15 30.00 60.00
35 Ryan Shazier/99 6.00 15.00
39 Sammie Coates/25 10.00 25.00
44 Rocky Bleier/15 15.00 40.00
46 Kordell Stewart/99 6.00 15.00
47 Brett Keisel/55 15.00 40.00
50 Louis Lipps/99 6.00 15.00
51 Jimmy Garoppolo/15
52 Jacoby Brissett/99 6.00 15.00
53 LeGarrette Blount/15
54 James White/99 8.00 20.00
56 Malcolm Mitchell/99 8.00 20.00
57 Rob Ninkovich/99 6.00 15.00
59 Steve Grogan/99 6.00 15.00
60 Deion Branch/15
61 Mike Vrabel/99 6.00 15.00
62 Willie McGinest/99 6.00 15.00
63 Rodney Harrison/15
69 Troy Brown/99 6.00 15.00
70 John Hannah/99 6.00 15.00
73 Trevor Davis/99 6.00 15.00
77 Mason Crosby/99 6.00 15.00
79 Paul Hornung/25 15.00 40.00
81 Sterling Sharpe/15 15.00 40.00
82 Antonio Freeman/15 15.00 40.00
84 Trevor Siemian/15 12.00 30.00
85 C.J. Anderson/15 15.00 40.00
86 Devontae Booker/99 6.00 15.00
87 Andy Janovich/99 6.00 15.00
92 Brandon McManus/99 6.00 15.00
95 Steve Atwater/25 12.00 30.00
97 Ed McCaffrey/15
98 Champ Bailey/15 15.00 40.00
100 Mark Schlereth/15 12.00 30.00

2017 Panini Majestic Team Signs Dual Autographs

*GOLD/49: .5X TO 1.2X BASIC AU/99
1 O.Howard/T.Williams 5.00 12.00
2 C.Robinson/J.Allen 5.00 12.00
3 C.Lawson/M.Adams 5.00 12.00
5 A.Scott/M.Williams
6 J.Leggett/C.Tankersley 5.00 12.00
7 C.Samuel/N.Brown 5.00 12.00
8 D.Cook/T.Rudolph 15.00 40.00
10 T.White/J.Adams 4.00 10.00
11 B.Kaaya/S.Coley 15.00 40.00
12 A.Darboh/J.Butt 5.00 12.00
13 J.Peppers/T.Charlton 6.00 15.00
15 M.Hooker/M.Lattimore 15.00 40.00
16 D.Westbrook/S.Perine
17 C.Kelly/E.Engram 12.00 30.00
18 C.McCaffrey/S.Thomas 50.00 100.00
19 J.Malone/A.Kamara 15.00 40.00
20 T.Watt/C.Clement 12.00 30.00

2017 Panini Majestic Unsung Warriors Materials

*GOLD/75: .5X TO 1.2X BASIC JSY/125-149
*GOLD/35-50: .6X TO 1.5X BASIC JSY/125-149
*RED/25: .8X TO 2X BASIC JSY/125-149
1 Tevin Coleman/149 2.50 6.00
2 Stephon Gilmore/125 2.00 5.00
3 Kelvin Benjamin/125 2.50 6.00
4 Jordan Howard/149 3.00 8.00
5 Alshon Jeffery/149 2.50 6.00
6 Jeremy Hill/125 2.00 5.00
7 Cole Beasley/149 8.00 20.00
8 Chris Harris/125 2.00 5.00
9 Ameer Abdullah/125 2.00 5.00
10 Ty Montgomery/149 2.00 5.00
11 Jadeveon Clowney/125 2.00 5.00
12 T.Y. Hilton/125 2.50 6.00
13 Mark Brunell/125 2.50 6.00
14 Tyreek Hill/149 3.00 8.00
15 Dion Jordan/125 2.00 5.00
16 Teddy Bridgewater/149 2.50 6.00
17 Jimmy Garoppolo/125 4.00 10.00
18 Brandin Cooks/149 2.50 6.00
19 Mark Ingram/125 2.50 6.00
20 Sterling Shepard/149 2.50 6.00
21 Ryan Shazier/125 2.00 5.00
22 Clive Walford/125 2.00 5.00
23 Jordan Matthews/125 2.00 5.00
24 Zach Ertz/125 2.50 6.00
25 Melvin Gordon/149 2.50 6.00
26 Carlos Hyde/149 2.00 5.00
27 Earl Thomas III/125 2.50 6.00
28 Derrick Henry/125 2.50 6.00
29 Jamison Crowder/125 2.00 5.00
30 Jordan Reed/125 2.00 5.00

2017 Panini Majestic Wondrous Receivers Autographs

*GOLD/49: .5X TO 1.2X BASIC AU/99
*GOLD/25: .5X TO 1.2X BASIC AU/49
*GOLD/15: .6X TO 1.5X BASIC AU/49
*GOLD/15: .4X TO 1X BASIC AU/15
*GOLD/25: .6X TO 1.5X BASIC AU/99
*GOLD/15-20: .6X TO 1.5X BASIC AU/49
1 Raymond Berry/49 10.00 25.00
2 Andre Reed/49 10.00 25.00
3 Paul Warfield/49 10.00 25.00
4 Ozzie Newsome/25 12.00 30.00
5 Michael Irvin/15 20.00 50.00
6 Drew Pearson/49 10.00 25.00
7 Ed McCaffrey/99 12.00 30.00
8 Rod Smith/99 8.00 20.00
9 Calvin Johnson/15 100.00 200.00
10 James Lofton/49 10.00 25.00
11 Sterling Sharpe/99 8.00 20.00
13 Reggie Wayne/25 12.00 30.00
14 Tony Gonzalez/25 25.00 50.00
15 Randy Moss/15
16 Troy Brown/49 8.00 20.00
17 Don Maynard/49 10.00 25.00
18 Fred Biletnikoff/15 20.00 50.00
19 Tim Brown/25 15.00 40.00
20 Hines Ward/25 25.00 60.00
22 Charlie Joiner/49 8.00 20.00
23 Jerry Rice/15 90.00 150.00
24 Steve Largent/49 12.00 30.00
25 Torry Holt/49 10.00 25.00

2018 Panini Majestic

1 Carson Palmer 2.50 6.00
2 Larry Fitzgerald 2.50 6.00
3 David Johnson 3.00 8.00
4 Matt Ryan 2.50 6.00
5 Devonta Freeman 2.50 6.00
6 Julio Jones 3.00 8.00
7 Vic Beasley Jr. 2.00 5.00
8 Joe Flacco 2.50 6.00
9 Terrell Suggs 2.00 5.00
10 Justin Tucker 2.00 5.00
11 Tyrod Taylor 2.50 6.00
12 LeSean McCoy 3.00 8.00
13 Jordan Matthews 2.00 5.00
14 Cam Newton 3.00 8.00
15 Christian McCaffrey 3.00 8.00
16 Luke Kuechly 2.50 6.00
17 Mitchell Trubisky 3.00 8.00
18 Jordan Howard 3.00 8.00
19 Tarik Cohen 2.50 6.00
20 Andy Dalton 2.50 6.00
21 A.J. Green 3.00 8.00
22 Joe Mixon 2.50 6.00
23 DeShone Kizer 2.50 6.00
24 Myles Garrett 3.00 8.00
25 David Njoku 2.00 5.00
26 Dak Prescott 3.00 8.00
27 Ezekiel Elliott 4.00 10.00
28 Jason Witten 2.50 6.00
29 Dez Bryant 3.00 8.00
30 Trevor Siemian 2.00 5.00
31 Von Miller 2.50 6.00
32 Emmanuel Sanders 3.00 8.00
33 Matthew Stafford 2.50 6.00
34 Golden Tate III 2.00 5.00
35 Kenny Golladay 2.00 5.00
36 Aaron Rodgers 6.00 15.00
37 Jordy Nelson 2.50 6.00
38 Clay Matthews 2.50 6.00
39 J.J. Watt 3.00 8.00
40 Deshaun Watson 4.00 10.00
41 DeAndre Hopkins 2.50 6.00
42 Andrew Luck 4.00 10.00
43 T.Y. Hilton 2.50 6.00
44 Frank Gore 2.50 6.00
45 Blake Bortles 2.00 5.00
46 Leonard Fournette 3.00 8.00
47 Allen Robinson 2.50 6.00
48 Tyreek Hill 3.00 8.00
49 Alex Smith 2.50 6.00
50 Kareem Hunt 2.50 6.00
51 Eric Berry 2.50 6.00
52 Travis Kelce 3.00 8.00
53 Joey Bosa 3.00 8.00
54 Philip Rivers 3.00 8.00
55 Melvin Gordon 2.50 6.00
56 Jared Goff 3.00 8.00
57 Sammy Watkins 3.00 8.00
58 Todd Gurley II 3.00 8.00
59 Aaron Donald 3.00 8.00
60 Jarvis Landry 2.50 6.00
61 DeVante Parker 2.50 6.00
62 Ryan Tannehill 2.50 6.00
63 Stefon Diggs 2.50 6.00
64 Dalvin Cook 2.50 6.00
65 Case Keenum 2.50 6.00
66 Tom Brady 8.00 20.00
67 Rob Gronkowski 3.00 8.00
68 Brandin Cooks 2.50 6.00
69 Danny Amendola 2.50 6.00
70 Drew Brees 3.00 8.00
71 Michael Thomas 3.00 8.00
72 Mark Ingram 2.50 6.00
73 Eli Manning 2.50 6.00
74 Odell Beckham Jr. 3.00 8.00
75 Sterling Shepard 2.50 6.00

76 Robby Anderson 2.00 5.00
77 Matt Forte 2.00 5.00
78 Josh McCown 2.00 5.00
79 Derek Carr 3.00 8.00
80 Michael Crabtree 2.00 5.00
81 Amari Cooper 3.00 8.00
82 Khalil Mack 3.00 8.00
83 Carson Wentz 4.00 10.00
84 Alshon Jeffery 2.50 6.00
85 Ben Roethlisberger 3.00 8.00
86 Le'Veon Bell 2.50 6.00
87 Antonio Brown 3.00 8.00
88 Carlos Hyde 2.00 5.00
89 Pierre Garcon 2.50 6.00
90 Jimmy Garoppolo 8.00 20.00
91 Russell Wilson 4.00 -10.00
92 Doug Baldwin 2.50 6.00
93 Richard Sherman 3.00 8.00
94 Jameis Winston 2.50 6.00
95 Mike Evans 2.50 6.00
96 Gerald McCoy 2.00 5.00
97 Marcus Mariota 3.00 8.00
98 DeMarco Murray 2.50 6.00
99 Patrick Mahomes II 8.00 20.00
100 Josh Norman 2.00 5.00
101 Josh Rosen JSY AU/25 RC 100.00 200.00
102 Sam Darnold JSY AU/25 RC 150.00 250.00
103 Josh Allen JSY AU/25 RC 100.00 200.00
104 Baker Mayfield JSY AU/25 RC 200.00 300.00
105 Mason Rudolph JSY AU/49 RC 50.00 100.00
107 Luke Falk JSY AU/99 RC 6.00 15.00
108 Kurt Benkert JSY AU/99 RC 6.00 15.00
109 Saquon Barkley JSY AU/25 RC 200.00 400.00
110 Derrius Guice JSY AU/49 RC 12.00 30.00
111 Ronald Jones II JSY AU/99 RC 5.00 12.00
112 Nick Chubb JSY AU/99 RC 25.00 50.00
113 Kerryon Johnson JSY AU/99 RC 15.00 40.00
114 Rashaad Penny JSY AU/199 RC EXCH 6.00 15.00
115 Royce Freeman JSY AU/99 RC 6.00 15.00
116 Sony Michel JSY AU/49 RC 20.00 50.00
117 Bo Scarbrough JSY AU/199 RC 5.00 12.00
118 John Kelly JSY AU/199 RC 5.00 12.00
119 Akrum Wadley JSY AU/199 RC 4.00 10.00
120 Calvin Ridley JSY AU/49 RC 15.00 40.00
121 Courtland Sutton JSY AU/49 RC 10.00 25.00
122 Anthony Miller JSY AU/199 RC 6.00 15.00
123 Christian Kirk JSY AU/49 RC 10.00 25.00
124 Michael Gallup JSY AU/199 RC 8.00 20.00
125 James Washington JSY AU/99 RC 10.00 25.00
126 Deon Cain JSY AU/199 RC
127 Dante Pettis JSY AU/199 RC 6.00 15.00
128 Deontay Burnett JSY AU/199 RC 5.00 12.00
129 Mark Andrews JSY AU/199 RC 6.00 15.00
131 Auden Tate JSY AU/199 RC 4.00 10.00
132 DJ Chark JSY AU/199 RC 5.00 12.00
133 Nyheim Hines JSY AU/199 RC 5.00 12.00
134 Allen Lazard JSY AU/199 RC 4.00 10.00
135 Simmie Cobbs Jr. JSY AU/199 RC 6.00 15.00
138 D.J. Moore JSY AU/99 RC 10.00 25.00
139 Justin Jackson JSY AU/199 RC 5.00 12.00
140 Josh Adams JSY AU/199 RC 8.00 20.00

2018 Panini Majestic Gold

*VETS/50: .5X TO 1.2X BASIC CARDS/75
*ROOK/49: .6X TO 1.5X BASIC JSY AU/199
*ROOK/49: .5X TO 1.2X BASIC JSY AU/99
*ROOK/25: .5X TO 1.2X BASIC JSY AU/49

2018 Panini Majestic Holo Silver

*VETS/25: .6X TO 1.5X BASIC CARDS/75

2018 Panini Majestic Astoniching Arms Jerseys

1 Aaron Rodgers 12.00 30.00
2 Kirk Cousins 6.00 15.00
3 Matthew Stafford 5.00 12.00
4 Jim Kelly 6.00 15.00
5 Michael Vick 5.00 12.00
6 Deshaun Watson 8.00 20.00
7 Mitchell Trubisky 6.00 15.00
8 Carson Wentz 8.00 20.00
9 Marcus Mariota 6.00 15.00
10 Jared Goff 6.00 15.00
11 Fran Tarkenton 6.00 15.00
12 Matt Ryan 5.00 12.00
13 Joe Theismann 6.00 15.00
14 Troy Aikman 8.00 20.00
15 Kurt Warner 5.00 12.00
16 Tony Romo 5.00 12.00
17 Jameis Winston 5.00 12.00
18 Len Dawson 6.00 15.00
19 Blake Bortles 4.00 10.00
20 Russell Wilson 8.00 20.00
21 Patrick Mahomes II 15.00 40.00
22 Andrew Luck 8.00 20.00
23 Andy Dalton 5.00 12.00
24 Brett Favre 12.00 30.00
25 Trevor Siemian 4.00 10.00

2018 Panini Majestic Distinguished Defenders Jerseys

*GOLD/25: .5X TO 1.2X BASIC JSY/49
1 Lawrence Taylor 5.00 12.00
2 Joey Bosa 5.00 12.00
3 Luke Kuechly 4.00 10.00
4 Ndamukong Suh 4.00 10.00
5 Richard Sherman 5.00 12.00
6 Howie Long 5.00 12.00
7 Aqib Talib 3.00 8.00
8 Brett Keisel 3.00 8.00
9 Cameron Wake 3.00 8.00
10 Champ Bailey 4.00 10.00
11 Clay Matthews 4.00 10.00
12 Jadeveon Clowney 3.00 8.00
13 T.J. Watt 4.00 10.00
14 Jabrill Peppers 3.00 8.00
15 Khalil Mack 5.00 12.00
16 Kiko Alonso 3.00 8.00
17 LaVar Arrington 3.00 8.00
18 Leonard Williams 3.00 8.00
19 Ray Lewis 5.00 12.00
20 Chris Harris Jr. 3.00 8.00

2018 Panini Majestic Icons Materials

*GOLD/25: .5X TO 1.2X BASIC JSY/49
1 Steve Young 6.00 15.00
2 LaDainian Tomlinson 4.00 10.00
3 Earl Campbell 5.00 12.00
4 Fran Tarkenton 5.00 12.00
5 Heath Miller 3.00 8.00
6 Michael Vick 4.00 10.00
7 Jerome Bettis 5.00 12.00
8 Jim Kelly 5.00 12.00
9 Joe Theismann 5.00 12.00
10 Kurt Warner 4.00 10.00
11 Brett Favre 12.00 30.00
12 Dan Marino 12.00 30.00
13 Tony Romo 4.00 10.00
14 John Elway 10.00 25.00
15 John Riggins 4.00 10.00

2018 Panini Majestic Imposing Autographs

*GOLD/49: .5X TO 1.2X BASIC AU/99
*GOLD/25: .5X TO 1.2X BASIC AU/49
*SILVER/25: .6X TO 1.5X BASIC AU/99
2 John Lynch/49 EXCH 10.00 25.00
3 Brian Urlacher/15
7 Joe Greene/15
8 Richard Sherman/15
9 Bruce Smith/15
10 Howie Long/15 20.00 50.00
11 Charles Haley/99 10.00 25.00
12 Warren Sapp/25 12.00 30.00
13 Jason Taylor/25 12.00 30.00
14 Lawrence Taylor/15 20.00 50.00
15 Mike Singletary/25 15.00 40.00
16 Melvin Ingram/99 6.00 15.00
17 Terrell Suggs/25 25.00 60.00
18 Luke Kuechly/25 EXCH 12.00 30.00
19 Tedy Bruschi/25 EXCH 15.00 40.00
20 Jack Ham/49 10.00 25.00
21 Clay Matthews/15 15.00 40.00
22 Rod Woodson/25 15.00 40.00
24 Geno Atkins/99 6.00 15.00
25 Bob Lilly/49 10.00 25.00

2018 Panini Majestic Magnificent Autographs

*GOLD/25: .5X TO 1.2X BASIC AU/49
4 Deshaun Watson/15 60.00 125.00
12 Warren Moon/25 15.00 40.00
14 Jameis Winston/15
15 Marcus Marlota/15
16 Carson Wentz/15
17 Matt Ryan/15
18 Matthew Stafford/15 25.00 60.00
19 Steve Young/15 25.00 60.00
21 Derek Carr/15
22 Michael Vick/25 30.00 60.00
24 Len Dawson/25 15.00 40.00
25 Ken Anderson/49 8.00 20.00

2018 Panini Majestic Majestic Autographs Tier 1

1 Hunter Henry/49 8.00 20.00
3 Lenny Moore/49 8.00 20.00
4 Nelson Agholor/49 8.00 20.00
5 Kevin Mawae/49 8.00 20.00
7 Ron Jaworski/49 10.00 25.00
8 Michael Bennett/49 8.00 20.00
10 Charlie Joiner/99 6.00 15.00
11 Melvin Ingram/99 6.00 15.00
12 Ed Too Tall Jones/49 8.00 20.00
13 Jordan Howard/49 EXCH 12.00 30.00
14 Vinny Testaverde/49 8.00 20.00
15 Ottis Anderson/99 6.00 15.00
17 Zach Ertz/49 15.00 40.00
18 Ryan Shazier/49 8.00 20.00
19 Eric Weddle/49 8.00 20.00
20 Stephon Gilmore/49 8.00 20.00
21 Cameron Heyward/99 6.00 15.00
22 Brett Keisel/49 8.00 20.00
23 Adam Thielen/99 20.00 50.00
24 Henry Ellard/99 6.00 15.00
25 Dexter Manley/99 6.00 15.00
27 Tom Matte/99 6.00 15.00
28 Rishard Matthews/99 6.00 15.00
31 Geno Atkins/99 6.00 15.00
32 Darius Slay/99 6.00 15.00
33 Carl Eller/99 6.00 15.00
34 Neil Smith/99 6.00 15.00
35 Jim Zorn/99 6.00 15.00
37 Christian Okoye/99 6.00 15.00
38 Andre Reed/99 8.00 20.00
40 Ameer Abdullah/99 6.00 15.00

2018 Panini Majestic Majestic Autographs Tier 2

1 Landon Collins/20 12.00 30.00
2 DeSean Jackson/25
3 Len Dawson/25 15.00 40.00
5 T.Y. Hilton/25 12.00 30.00
6 Doug Martin/25 12.00 30.00
7 Golden Tate III/25 10.00 25.00
8 Mark Ingram/25 12.00 30.00
9 Ty Law/49 12.00 30.00
10 Edgerrin James/25 12.00 30.00
11 Clinton Portis/25 10.00 25.00
12 Heath Miller/25 10.00 25.00
13 Doug Flutie/25
14 Ricky Williams/25 12.00 30.00
15 Greg Olsen/25 12.00 30.00
17 Ed McCaffrey/25 12.00 30.00
18 Jack Ham/25 12.00 30.00
19 James Lofton/25 10.00 25.00
20 Jonathan Stewart/25 10.00 25.00
21 Paul Hornung/25
22 Zach Thomas/25 30.00 60.00
23 Torry Holt/25 12.00 30.00
24 Sterling Sharpe/25 12.00 30.00
25 Jeremy Shockey/25
26 Jevon Kearse/25 10.00 25.00
27 Michael Thomas/25 15.00 40.00
28 Roman Gabriel/25 10.00 25.00
29 Christian McCaffrey/25 15.00 40.00
30 Tyreek Hill/49 12.00 30.00

2018 Panini Majestic Majestic Material Autographs

1 Andre Reed/25 15.00 40.00
3 Brett Keisel/25 12.00 30.00
5 Carlos Hyde/25 12.00 30.00
6 Danny Woodhead/25 15.00 40.00
7 Doug Baldwin/25 15.00 40.00
9 Edgerrin James/15 20.00 50.00
10 Fran Tarkenton/15 25.00 60.00
11 Golden Tate III/15 15.00 40.00
12 Greg Olsen/25 15.00 40.00
13 Heath Miller/25 12.00 30.00
17 Jim Plunkett/25 15.00 40.00
18 Joe Theismann/15
19 Jordy Nelson/15 20.00 50.00
22 Lawrence Taylor/15
23 Luke Kuechly/25 EXCH 15.00 40.00
24 Michael Vick/25 15.00 40.00
25 Priest Holmes/25 12.00 30.00
27 Terrelle Pryor Sr./25 12.00 30.00
28 Thomas Rawls/25 12.00 30.00
29 Thurman Thomas/25 15.00 40.00
30 Bob Lilly/25 15.00 40.00
31 Travis Kelce/25 20.00 50.00
34 Hunter Henry/25 12.00 30.00
35 Jordan Howard/25 20.00 50.00
36 Darren Woodson/25 15.00 40.00
37 Mike Singletary/25 20.00 50.00
39 Clinton Portis/25 12.00 30.00
40 Geno Atkins/25 12.00 30.00

2018 Panini Majestic Majestic Rookie Autographs

*GOLD/99: .5X TO 1.2X BASIC AU/199-299
*SILVER/25: .8X TO 2X BASIC AU/199-299
141 Mike White/299 4.00 10.00
142 Harold Landry/299 3.00 8.00
143 Dallas Goedert/299 4.00 10.00
144 Mike Gesicki/199 4.00 10.00
145 Minkah Fitzpatrick/199 6.00 15.00
146 Bradley Chubb/199 5.00 12.00
147 Roquan Smith/199 10.00 25.00
148 Arden Key/299 3.00 8.00
149 Riley Ferguson/299 5.00 12.00
150 Joshua Jackson/299 6.00 15.00
151 Denzel Ward/299 8.00 20.00
152 Derwin James/299 6.00 15.00
153 Vita Vea/299 5.00 12.00
154 Marcell Ateman/299 4.00 10.00
155 Jordan Lasley/299 3.00 8.00
156 Maurice Hurst/299 4.00 10.00
157 Tremaine Edmunds/299 6.00 15.00
158 DaeSean Hamilton/299 4.00 10.00
159 Malik Jefferson/299 4.00 10.00
160 Rashaan Evans/299 5.00 12.00

2018 Panini Majestic Marvelous Autographs

*SILVER/25: .6X TO 1.5X BASIC AU/99
*GOLD/49: .5X TO 1.2X BASIC AU/99
*GOLD/25: .5X TO 1.2X BASIC AU/49
3 Antonio Brown/15
6 A.J. Green/25 15.00 40.00
7 Demaryius Thomas/15 15.00 40.00
8 Hines Ward/15 15.00 40.00
9 Jordy Nelson/15
10 Raymond Berry/25 12.00 30.00
13 James Lofton/25 10.00 25.00
14 Doug Baldwin/25 12.00 30.00
15 Mike Evans/25 EXCH 12.00 30.00
16 Don Maynard/25 12.00 30.00
17 Drew Pearson/49 10.00 25.00
18 Tyreek Hill/99 10.00 25.00
19 Stefon Diggs/99 8.00 20.00
21 Andre Reed/49 10.00 25.00
22 Ed McCaffrey/25 12.00 30.00
23 Torry Holt/49 10.00 25.00
25 Sterling Sharpe/49 10.00 25.00

2018 Panini Majestic New Blood Triple Autographs

5 Derrius Guice 60.00 125.00
Kerryon Johnson
Nick Chubb/25
6 Ftzptrck/Jms/Hrrsn/25 20.00 50.00
7 Evns/Smth/Edmnds/25 30.00 80.00
8 Chbb/Dvnprt/Hrst/25 20.00 50.00
9 Gdrt/Andrws/Gscki/25 15.00 40.00
10 Lsly/Wshngtn/Gllp/25 20.00 50.00

2018 Panini Majestic Regal Runners Jerseys

*GOLD/25: ..5X TO 1.2X BASIC JSY/49
1 LaDainian Tomlinson 4.00 10.00
2 Edgerrin James 4.00 10.00
3 Bo Jackson 6.00 15.00
4 DeMarco Murray 4.00 10.00
5 C.J. Anderson 4.00 10.00
6 Kenyan Drake 3.00 8.00
7 Thomas Rawls 3.00 8.00
8 Earl Campbell 5.00 12.00
9 Thurman Thomas 4.00 10.00
10 Carlos Hyde 3.00 8.00
11 Latavius Murray 3.00 8.00
12 Melvin Gordon 4.00 10.00
13 Eddie Lacy 3.00 8.00
14 Jordan Howard 5.00 12.00
15 Alvin Kamara 4.00 10.00
16 Ameer Abdullah 3.00 8.00
17 Christian McCaffrey 5.00 12.00
18 Clinton Portis 3.00 8.00
19 Derrick Henry 5.00 12.00
20 Devonta Freeman 4.00 10.00
21 Doug Martin 4.00 10.00
22 Terrell Davis 4.00 10.00
23 John Riggins 4.00 10.00
24 Kareem Hunt 4.00 10.00
25 Leonard Fournette 5.00 12.00

2018 Panini Majestic Royal Autographs

*GOLD/25: .5X TO 1.2X BASIC AU/49
4 Christian McCaffrey/49 12.00 30.00
5 Marshall Faulk/15
6 Jerome Bettis/15
7 Dalvin Cook/49 EXCH 15.00 40.00
8 Tony Dorsett/15
9 Jordan Howard/49 EXCH 12.00 30.00
10 Terrell Davis/15
11 Earl Campbell/15
12 Bo Jackson/15 60.00 125.00
13 LaDainian Tomlinson/15 EXCH 15.00 40.00
14 Eric Dickerson/15 20.00 50.00
15 Marcus Allen/25 15.00 40.00
16 LeSean McCoy/25 25.00 50.00
17 Ricky Williams/25 12.00 30.00
18 Thurman Thomas/25 12.00 30.00
19 David Johnson/25 15.00 40.00
21 Alvin Kamara/49 EXCH 25.00 50.00
23 Devonta Freeman/25 EXCH 12.00 30.00
24 Kareem Hunt/49 EXCH 10.00 25.00
25 Ezekiel Elliott/15

2018 Panini Majestic Showstoppers Materials

*GOLD/25: .5X TO 1.2X BASIC JSY/49
1 Richard Sherman 5.00 12.00
2 Ty Law 5.00 12.00
3 Earl Thomas III 4.00 10.00
4 Joey Bosa 5.00 12.00
5 Jadeveon Clowney 3.00 8.00
6 Khalil Mack 5.00 12.00
7 Anthony Barr 3.00 8.00
8 Gerald McCoy 3.00 8.00
9 Luke Kuechly 4.00 10.00
10 Lawrence Taylor 5.00 12.00
11 Howie Long 5.00 12.00
12 Aqib Talib 3.00 8.00
13 Bobby Wagner 3.00 8.00
14 Brian Urlacher 5.00 12.00
15 Bruce Smith 4.00 10.00
16 Carlos Dunlap 3.00 8.00
17 Geno Atkins 3.00 8.00
18 Kam Chancellor 5.00 12.00
19 Leonard Williams 3.00 8.00
20 Sean Lee 4.00 10.00

2018 Panini Majestic Team Signs Triple Autographs

1 Nick Chubb 75.00 150.00
Roquan Smith
Sony Michel/25
2 Minkah Fitzpatrick 20.00 50.00
Ronnie Harrison
Rashaan Evans/25
3 Derrius Guice 20.00 50.00
Arden Key
DJ Chark/25
4 James Washington 25.00 60.00
Marcell Ateman
Mason Rudolph/25
6 Quin Blanding 10.00 25.00
Andrew Brown
Micah Kiser/25
7 Damon Webb 25.00 60.00
Denzel Ward
Tyquan Lewis/25
8 Derwin James 20.00 50.00
Auden Tate
Ryan Izzo/25
10 Bo Scarbrough 25.00 60.00
Calvin Ridley
Robert Foster/25

2018 Panini Majestic Unsung Warriors Materials

*GOLD/25: .5X TO 1.2X BASIC JSY/49
*GOLD/25: .4X TO 1X BASIC JSY/25
*GOLD/20: .6X TO 1.5X BASIC JSY/49
1 Kyle Long/49 3.00 8.00
2 Gerald McCoy/49 3.00 8.00
3 Danny Woodhead/49 4.00 10.00
4 Greg Olsen/49 4.00 10.00
5 Antonio Gates/49 3.00 8.00
6 Dan Bailey/49 3.00 8.00
7 Chris Harris Jr./49 3.00 8.00
8 Matt Paradis/49 3.00 8.00
9 Danny Amendola/49 4.00 10.00
10 Derek Wolfe/49 3.00 8.00
11 Jason Witten/49 4.00 10.00
13 Joe Thomas/49 3.00 8.00
14 John Kuhn/25 4.00 10.00
15 Julian Edelman/25 6.00 15.00
17 Brent Grimes/49 3.00 8.00
18 Cameron Wake/49 3.00 8.00
19 Maurkice Pouncey/49 3.00 8.00
20 Richie Incognito/49 3.00 8.00
21 Sean Lee/49 4.00 10.00
22 Vontaze Burfict/49 3.00 8.00
23 Zack Martin/49 3.00 8.00
24 Travis Frederick/49 3.00 8.00
25 Reshad Jones/49 3.00 8.00
26 Aaron Donald/49 5.00 12.00
27 Adam Jones/49 3.00 8.00
28 Johnny Hekker/49 3.00 8.00
29 Laremy Tunsil/49 3.00 8.00
30 Mason Crosby/49 3.00 8.00

2018 Panini Majestic Wondrous Wide Outs Jerseys

*GOLD/49: .5X TO 1.2X BASIC JSY/99
1 Jordy Nelson 3.00 8.00
2 Terrelle Pryor Sr. 2.50 6.00
3 Doug Baldwin 3.00 8.00
4 Malcolm Mitchell 2.50 6.00
5 Golden Tate III 2.50 6.00
6 Hines Ward 3.00 8.00
7 Tyler Lockett 3.00 8.00
8 Andre Reed 3.00 8.00
9 Tyreek Hill 4.00 10.00
10 Cooper Kupp 3.00 8.00
11 DeAndre Hopkins 3.00 8.00
12 JuJu Smith-Schuster 4.00 10.00
13 Sterling Shepard 3.00 8.00
14 Jarvis Landry 3.00 8.00
15 Josh Doctson 2.50 6.00
16 Demaryius Thomas 3.00 8.00
17 Keenan Allen 3.00 8.00
18 Tim Brown 4.00 10.00
19 Stefon Diggs 3.00 8.00
20 Michael Thomas 4.00 10.00

2011 Panini National Convention Patch Autographs

CN Cam Newton 12.00 30.00

2012 Panini National Convention

1-20 CRACKED ICE/25: 5X TO 12X BASE HI
21-40 CRACKED ICE/25: 1.5X TO 4X BASE HI
*HOLO 1-20: 1X TO 2.5X BASIC CARDS
*HOLO 21-40: .6X TO 1.5X BASIC CARDS
*1-20 HOLO LAVA: 2X TO 5X BASE HI
*21-40 HOLO LAVA: 1X TO 2.5X BASE HI
UNPRICED PLATE ANNCD PRINT RUN 5 SETS
1 Peyton Manning .60 1.50
2 Adrian Peterson .50 1.25
3 Tom Brady .60 1.50
4 Tim Tebow .60 1.50
5 Aaron Rodgers .75 2.00
17 Bo Jackson .40 1.00
19 Curtis Martin HOF .40 1.00
21 Andrew Luck/499 5.00 12.00
22 Robert Griffin III/499 3.00 8.00
23 Trent Richardson/499 2.00 5.00
24 Justin Blackmon/499 2.50 6.00
25 Ryan Tannehill/499 2.00 5.00
26 Michael Floyd/499 2.00 5.00

2012 Panini National Convention Draft Day Materials

1 Andrew Luck 20.00 50.00
2 Trent Richardson 2.00 5.00
3 Matt Kalil 2.00 5.00
4 Morris Claiborne 2.00 5.00
5 Justin Blackmon 2.00 5.00
6 Mark Barron 2.00 5.00
7 Ryan Tannehill 3.00 8.00
8 Stephon Gilmore 2.50 6.00
9 Michael Floyd 2.00 5.00
10 Kendall Wright 2.00 5.00
11 Ryan Kerrigan 5.00 12.00
12 Patrick Peterson 5.00 12.00

2012 Panini National Convention Art Collection

CRACKED ICE/25: 4X TO 10X BASIC CARDS
1 Andrew Luck 2.50 6.00
2 Robert Griffin III .30 .75
3 Trent Richardson .25 .60

2012 Panini National Convention Rookie Manufactured Patch Autographs

*CRACKED ICE: X TO X BASE HI
AL Andrew Luck 150.00 250.00
BW Brandon Weeden 6.00 15.00
CU Courtney Upshaw 8.00 20.00
DM Davin Meggett 6.00 15.00
DP Dontari Poe 6.00 15.00
JR Josh Robinson 10.00 25.00
KB Kelvin Beachum 8.00 20.00
KW Kendall Wright 6.00 15.00
MK Matt Kalil 6.00 15.00
RGIII Robert Griffin III 30.00 80.00

2012 Panini National Convention Team Colors Baltimore

CRACKED ICE/25: 4X TO 10X BASE HI
4 Ray Lewis .75 2.00
5 Courtney Upshaw .75 2.00

2012 Panini National Convention Team Colors Washington

CRACKED ICE/25: 4X TO 10X BASE HI
2 Robert Griffin III 1.50 4.00

2012 Panini National Convention Tools of the Trade Towels

1 Andrew Luck 20.00 50.00
2 Robert Griffin III 3.00 8.00
3 Doug Martin 4.00 10.00
4 Michael Floyd 2.50 6.00
5 Ryan Tannehill 4.00 10.00
6 Trent Richardson 2.50 6.00

2012 Panini National Convention Kings VIP

COMPLETE SET (6) 12.00 30.00
1 Robert Griffin III 2.50 6.00
2 Andrew Luck 4.00 10.00

2013 Panini National Convention

1-24 CRACKED ICE/25: 4X TO 10X BASIC CARDS
25-47 CRACKED ICE/25: 2X TO 5X BASIC CARDS
*1-24 LAVA FLOW/99: 2.5X TO 6X BASIC CARDS
*25-47 LAVA FLOW/99: 1.2X TO 3X BASIC CARDS
13 Colin Kaepernick .60 1.50
14 Andrew Luck 1.00 2.50
15 Tom Brady .75 2.00
16 Aaron Rodgers .75 2.00
17 Adrian Peterson .60 1.50
18 Robert Griffin III .60 1.50
25 Eddie Lacy 3.00 8.00
26 EJ Manuel 2.00 5.00
27 Geno Smith 1.50 4.00
28 Giovani Bernard 2.00 5.00
29 Manti Te'o 1.50 4.00
30 Marcus Lattimore 1.00 2.50
31 Tavon Austin 2.00 5.00
32 Cordarrelle Patterson 1.50 4.00

2013 Panini National Convention VIP

COMPLETE SET (6) 3.00 8.00
1 EJ Manuel 1.25 3.00
4 Geno Smith .60 1.50

2013 Panini National Convention Draft Day Materials

LJ Luke Joeckel 2.00 5.00
SM Shea McClellin 2.50 6.00
FB1 Tavon Austin 2.50 6.00
FB2 Barkevious Mingo 2.00 5.00
FB3 Eric Reid 2.50 6.00
FB4 EJ Manuel 2.00 5.00
FB5 Cordarrelle Patterson 2.00 5.00

2013 Panini National Convention Kings

CRACKED ICE/25: 2.5X TO 6X BASIC CARDS
*LAVA FLOW: 1.5X TO 4X BASIC CARDS
R3 Tyler Eifert .50 1.25
R4 DeAndre Hopkins .60 1.50

2013 Panini National Convention RC

CRACKED ICE/25: 2X TO 5X BASIC CARDS
*LAVA FLOW/99: 1.2X TO 3X BASIC CARDS
RC1 EJ Manuel 2.00 5.00
RC2 Geno Smith 1.25 3.00
RC4 Rex Burkhead .75 2.00

2013 Panini National Convention Rookie Materials Glove

1 Aaron Dobson 2.50 6.00
2 Andre Ellington 2.50 6.00
3 Christine Michael 2.50 6.00
4 DeAndre Hopkins 6.00 15.00
5 Denard Robinson 2.50 6.00
6 Dion Jordan 2.50 6.00
7 EJ Manuel 2.50 6.00
8 Eddie Lacy 2.50 6.00
9 Gavin Escobar 2.50 6.00
10 Geno Smith 2.50 6.00
11 Giovani Bernard 2.50 6.00
12 Johnathan Franklin 2.50 6.00
13 Jordan Reed 4.00 10.00
14 Joseph Randle 2.50 6.00
15 Justin Hunter 2.50 6.00
16 Keenan Allen 5.00 12.00
18 Knile Davis 2.50 6.00
19 Landry Jones 2.50 6.00
20 Le'Veon Bell 8.00 20.00
22 Marcus Lattimore 2.50 6.00
23 Markus Wheaton 2.50 6.00
24 Marquise Goodwin 2.50 6.00
25 Mike Gillislee 2.50 6.00
26 Mike Glennon 2.50 6.00
27 Montee Ball 2.50 6.00
28 Quinton Patton 2.50 6.00
29 Robert Woods 4.00 10.00
30 Ryan Nassib 2.50 6.00
31 Stedman Bailey 2.50 6.00
32 Stepfan Taylor 2.50 6.00
33 Tavon Austin 3.00 8.00
34 Terrance Williams 2.50 6.00
35 Tyler Eifert 2.50 6.00
36 Tyler Wilson 2.50 6.00
37 Zach Ertz 5.00 12.00
TM Tyrann Mathieu 4.00 10.00

2013 Panini National Convention Team Colors

COMPLETE SET (10) 4.00 10.00
CRACKED ICE/25: 5X TO 12X BASIC CARDS
LAVA FLOW/99: 2.5X TO 6X BASIC CARDS
3 Red Grange .75 2.00
4 Jay Cutler .50 1.25
5 Brandon Marshall .40 1.00
6 Kyle Long .30 .75

2013 Panini National Convention Tools of the Trade Towels

1 Aaron Dobson 4.00 10.00
2 Cordarrelle Patterson 4.00 10.00
3 Denard Robinson 4.00 10.00
5 Gavin Escobar 4.00 10.00
6 Geno Smith 4.00 10.00
7 Giovani Bernard 4.00 10.00
8 Landry Jones 4.00 10.00
9 Manti Te'o 5.00 12.00
10 Marcus Lattimore 4.00 10.00
11 Montee Ball 4.00 10.00
12 Ryan Nassib 4.00 10.00
13 Tavon Austin 5.00 12.00
TRO Tony Romo 8.00 20.00

2014 Panini National Convention

*1-21 CRACKED ICE VETS/25: 4X TO 10X
*22-50 CRACKED ICE ROOKIE/25: 2X TO 5X
*THICK STOCK: .6X TO 1.5X BASIC CARDS
8 Russell Wilson FB .60 1.50
9 Eddie Lacy FB .40 1.00
10 Andrew Luck FB .75 2.00
11 Tom Brady FB .75 2.00
12 Peyton Manning FB 1.00 2.50
13 Calvin Johnson FB .40 1.00
14 Adrian Peterson FB .50 1.25
31 Jimmy Garoppolo JSY/99 FB 4.00 10.00
41 Aaron Murray FB 1.00 2.50
42 Bishop Sankey FB 1.00 2.50
43 Brandin Cooks FB 1.00 2.50
44 Derek Carr FB 2.00 5.00
45 Tre Mason FB 1.25 3.00
46 Kelvin Benjamin FB 1.25 3.00
47 Logan Thomas FB 1.00 2.50
48 Marqise Lee FB .75 2.00
49 Tom Savage FB .75 2.00
50 Jeremy Hill FB .75 2.00
51 Sammy Watkins JSY/99 FB 4.00 10.00
52 Johnny Manziel JSY/99 FB 6.00 15.00
53 Jadeveon Clowney JSY/99 FB 4.00 10.00
54 Blake Bortles JSY/99 FB 5.00 12.00
55 Teddy Bridgewater JSY/99 FB 5.00 12.00
56 Mike Evans JSY/99 FB 3.00 8.00
57 Odell Beckham Jr. JSY/99 FB 3.00 8.00
58 Eric Ebron JSY/99 FB 3.00 8.00
59 A.J. McCarron JSY/99 FB 4.00 10.00

2014 Panini National Convention City of Cleveland

*THICK STOCK: .6X TO 1.5X BASIC CARDS
*CRACKED ICE/25: 3X TO 8X BASIC CARDS
1 Johnny Manziel FB 1.50 4.00
2 Justin Gilbert FB .40 1.00
3 Joe Haden FB .40 1.00
4 John Hughes FB .40 1.00

2014 Panini National Convention Legends

*CRACKED ICE/25: 5X TO 12X BASIC CARDS
*THICK STOCK: .6X TO 1.5X BASIC CARDS
4 Jim Brown FB .40 1.00
5 Jerry Rice FB .50 1.25
6 Emmitt Smith FB .50 1.25
7 John Elway FB .50 1.25

2014 Panini National Convention Rookie Materials

*CRACKED ICE: .8X TO 2X BASIC INSERTS
CS Connor Shaw 2.00 5.00
DF Devonta Freeman 3.00 8.00
JM Jordan Matthews 3.00 8.00
LT Logan Thomas 2.00 5.00
ME Mike Evans 5.00 12.00
TB Teddy Bridgewater 3.00 8.00
TBO Tajh Boyd 2.00 5.00

2014 Panini National Convention Rookie Materials Glove

*CRACKED ICE: .8X TO 2X BASIC INSERTS
AM A.J. McCarron 2.50 6.00
AR Allen Robinson 4.00 10.00
ASJ Austin Seferian-Jenkins 2.50 6.00
AW Andre Williams 2.50 6.00
BB Blake Bortles 3.00 8.00
BC Brandin Cooks 4.00 10.00
BS Bishop Sankey 2.50 6.00
CH Carlos Hyde 3.00 8.00
CS Charles Sims 2.50 6.00
DA Dri Archer 2.50 6.00
DA Davante Adams 4.00 10.00
DL Cody Latimer 3.00 8.00
DM Donte Moncrief 2.50 6.00
DT De'Anthony Thomas 2.50 6.00
EE Eric Ebron 3.00 8.00
JC Jadaveon Clowney 3.00 8.00
JG Jimmy Garoppolo 20.00 50.00
JH Jeremy Hill 3.00 8.00
JL Jarvis Landry 5.00 12.00
KB Kelvin Benjamin 4.00 10.00
KC Ka'Deem Carey 2.50 6.00
KM Khalil Mack 10.00 25.00
ME Mike Evans 6.00 15.00
ML Marqise Lee 3.00 8.00
OB Odell Beckham Jr. 6.00 15.00
SW Sammy Watkins 4.00 10.00
TB Teddy Bridgewater 4.00 10.00
TM Tre Mason 2.50 6.00
TW Terrance West 2.50 6.00

2014 Panini National Convention Tools of the Trade Towels

BB Blake Bortles 3.00 8.00
JG Jimmy Garoppolo 20.00 50.00
JM Johnny Manziel 4.00 10.00
MA Mike Adams 2.50 6.00
ML Marqise Lee 3.00 8.00
OB Odell Beckham Jr. 6.00 15.00
SW Sammy Watkins 4.00 10.00
TB Teddy Bridgowator 4.00 10.00

2014 Panini National Convention VIP

PRIZM BLUE VETS/25: 2.5X TO 6X BASIC CARDS
PRIZM BLUE ROOKIES/25: 1.2X TO 3X
25 Robert Griffin III FB .75 2.00
26 Eddie Lacy FB .75 2.00
27 Montee Ball FB .75 2.00
28 Torrey Smith FB .60 1.50
29 Geno Smith FB .60 1.50
30 Keenan Allen FB .75 2.00
31 Russell Wilson FB 1.00 2.50
33 Mark Ingram FB .60 1.50
36 Tavon Austin FB .60 1.50
37 Cam Newton FB .75 2.00
38 Terrance Williams FB .60 1.50
40 Michael Floyd FB .60 1.50
41 Le'Veon Bell FB .75 2.00
42 Andrew Luck FB 1.25 3.00
44 Sammy Watkins FB 3.00 8.00
45 Johnny Manziel FB 5.00 12.00
46 Cordarrelle Patterson FB 3.00 8.00
52 Landry Jones FB 2.00 5.00
53 Giovani Bernard FB .60 1.50
54 Marcus Lattimore FB .60 1.50
55 Justin Hunter FB .60 1.50
56 Robert Woods FB .60 1.50
63 Adrian Peterson FB .75 2.00
64 Tom Brady FB 1.25 3.00
65 Calvin Johnson FB .75 2.00
66 Aaron Rodgers FB 1.00 2.50
67 Peyton Manning FB 1.50 4.00
69 Drew Brees FB .75 2.00
76 EJ Manuel FB .60 1.50
77 A.J. Green FB .60 1.50
78 Bishop Sankey FB 2.00 5.00
79 Blake Bortles FB 3.00 8.00
80 Carlos Hyde FB 1.50 4.00
81 Derek Carr FB 3.00 8.00
82 Eric Ebron FB 1.25 3.00
83 Jadeveon Clowney FB 1.50 4.00
84 Jimmy Garoppolo FB 1.50 4.00
85 Kelvin Benjamin FB 1.25 3.00
86 Kendall Wright FB 1.00 2.50
87 Marqise Lee FB .75 2.00
88 Mike Evans FB 2.00 5.00
89 Odell Beckham Jr. FB 1.50 4.00
90 Teddy Bridgewater FB 3.00 8.00
91 Tre Mason FB 2.50 6.00

2014 Panini National Convention VIP Rookies

COMPLETE SET (6) 6.00 15.00
1 Johnny Manziel FB 2.50 6.00
2 Blake Bortles FB 2.50 6.00

2014 Panini National Convention

*CRACKED ICE/25: 2.5X TO 6X BASIC CARDS
*THICK STOCK: .6X TO 1.5X BASIC CARDS
1 Johnny Manziel .40 1.00
2 Odell Beckham Jr. .60 1.50
3 A.J. McCarron .25 .60
4 Tre Mason .25 .60
5 Tajh Boyd .25 .60
6 Jeremy Hill .30 .75
7 Terrance West .25 .60
8 Mike Evans .60 1.50
9 Khalil Mack 1.00 2.50
10 Bishop Sankey .25 .60
11 Sammy Watkins .40 1.00
12 Teddy Bridgewater .40 1.00
13 Blake Bortles .30 .75
14 Allen Robinson .40 1.00
15 Brandin Cooks .40 1.00
16 Eric Ebron .30 .75
17 Carlos Hyde .30 .75
18 Kelvin Benjamin .40 1.00
19 Devonta Freeman .40 1.00
20 Logan Thomas .25 .60

2015 Panini National Convention

15 Tom Brady .75 2.00
16A Russell Wilson .75 2.00
16B Russell Wilson .75 2.00
College BB photo
17A Aaron Rodgers .75 2.00
17B Aaron Rodgers .75 2.00
College photo
18 Odell Beckham Jr. .60 1.50
19 Andrew Luck .60 1.50
20 Dez Bryant .50 1.25
21 Peyton Manning 1.00 2.50
22 Brett Hundley 1.50 4.00
23 Jeremy Langford 1.25 3.00
24 Devin Funchess 1.50 4.00
25 Devin Smith 1.50 4.00
26 Tyler Lockett 2.00 5.00
27 Tevin Coleman 1.50 4.00
28 Leonard Williams 1.25 3.00
51A Amari Cooper JSY/99 FB 8.00 20.00
51B Amari Cooper 2.50 6.00
College photo
52 Breshad Perriman JSY/99 FB 3.00 8.00
53 DeVante Parker JSY/99 FB 6.00 15.00
54A Jameis Winston JSY/99 FB 10.00 25.00
54B Jameis Winston 3.00 8.00
College BB photo
55A Kevin White JSY/99 FB 6.00 15.00
55B Kevin White 1.50 4.00
College photo
56A Marcus Mariota JSY/99 FB 10.00 25.00
56B Marcus Mariota 4.00 10.00
College photo
57 Melvin Gordon III JSY/99 FB 8.00 20.00
58 Nelson Agholor JSY/99 FB 4.00 10.00
59 Phillip Dorsett JSY/99 FB 3.00 8.00
60A Todd Gurley JSY/99 FB 6.00 15.00
60B Todd Gurley 2.00 5.00
College photo
61 T.J. Yeldon JSY/99 FB 3.00 8.00
62A Sean Mannion JSY/99 FB 5.00 12.00
62B Sean Mannion 1.25 3.00
College photo
63 Garrett Grayson JSY/99 FB 3.00 8.00
64 Bryce Petty JSY/99 FB 5.00 12.00
65A Ameer Abdullah JSY/99 FB 6.00 15.00
65B Ameer Abdullah 1.50 4.00
College photo

2015 Panini National Convention College Legends

*CRACKED ICE/25: 5X TO 12X BASIC CARDS
*THICK STOCK: .6X TO 1.5X BASIC CARDS
7 Johnny Manziel .40 1.00
8 Robert Griffin .40 1.00
9 Cam Newton .40 1.00
10 Carson Palmer .30 .75
11 Mark Ingram .30 .75
12 Tim Tebow .40 1.00

2015 Panini National Convention Manufactured Patch Autographs

AC Amari Cooper FB
BH Brett Hundley FB
DG Dorial Green-Beckham FB
LW Leonard Williams FB
MW Maxx Williams FB
TG Todd Gurley FB
JLD Jeremy Langford FB
JLY Jarvis Landry FB

2015 Panini National Convention Memorabilia

OB Odell Beckham Jr. 4.00 10.00

2015 Panini National Convention Rookie Jerseys

*CRACKED ICE/25: .6X TO 1.5X BASIC JSY
1FB Dante Fowler Jr. 5.00 12.00
2FB Leonard Williams 5.00 12.00
3FB Kevin Johnson 4.00 10.00
4FB Cameron Erving 4.00 10.00
5FB Cedric Ogbuehi 4.00 10.00
6FB Bud Dupree 5.00 12.00
7FB D.J. Humphreys 4.00 10.00
8FB Laken Tomlinson 4.00 10.00
9FB Kevin White 6.00 15.00

2015 Panini National Convention Rookie Gloves

*CRACKED ICE/25: .6X TO 1.5X BASIC INSERTS
AA Ameer Abdullah 3.00 8.00
AC Amari Cooper 6.00 15.00
BH Brett Hundley 2.00 5.00
BPE Bryce Petty 2.00 5.00
BPR Breshad Perriman 2.00 5.00
DF Devin Funchess 3.00 8.00
DG Dorial Green-Beckham 2.00 5.00
DJ Duke Johnson 3.00 8.00
DP Devante Parker 3.00 8.00
DS Devin Smith 2.00 5.00
GG Garrett Grayson 2.00 5.00
JA Jay Ajayi 3.00 8.00
JS Jaelen Strong 2.50 6.00
JW Jameis Winston 5.00 12.00
KW Kevin White 2.50 6.00
LW Leonard Williams 2.00 5.00
MG Melvin Gordon III 5.00 12.00
MM Marcus Mariota 8.00 20.00
MW Maxx Williams 2.00 5.00
NA Nelson Agholor 2.50 6.00
PD Phillip Dorsett 2.00 5.00
SC Sammie Coates 2.50 6.00
SM Sean Mannion 2.00 5.00
TC Tevin Coleman 2.50 6.00
TG Todd Gurley 8.00 20.00
TL Tyler Lockett 3.00 8.00
TY T.J. Yeldon 2.00 5.00

2015 Panini National Convention Team Colors

COMPLETE SET (10) 3.00 8.00
*CRACKED ICE/25: 4X TO 10X BASIC CARDS
FB1 Matt Forte .30 .75
FB2 Jay Cutler .30 .75
FB3 Alshon Jeffery .30 .75
FB4 Robbie Gould .40 1.00
FB5 Dick Butkus .50 1.25

2015 Panini National Convention Tools of the Trade Jerseys

*CRACKED ICE/25: 1X TO 2.5X BASIC JSY
7 Teddy Bridgewater 3.00 8.00
8 Odell Beckham Jr. 4.00 10.00
9 Jimmy Garoppolo 3.00 8.00

2015 Panini National Convention Tools of the Trade Towels

*CRACKED ICE/25: .8X TO 2X BASIC INSERTS
AA Ameer Abdullah 2.50 6.00
AC Amari Cooper 5.00 12.00
BPE Bryce Petty 1.50 4.00
BPR Breshad Perriman 1.50 4.00
DF Devin Funchess 2.50 6.00
DP Devante Parker 2.50 6.00
GG Garrett Grayson 1.50 4.00
JW Jameis Winston 4.00 10.00
KW Kevin White 2.00 5.00
MG Melvin Gordon III 4.00 10.00
MM Marcus Mariota 6.00 15.00
NA Nelson Agholor 2.00 5.00
PD Phillip Dorsett 1.50 4.00
TG Todd Gurley 6.00 15.00
TY T.J. Yeldon 1.50 4.00

2015 Panini National Convention VIP

COMPLETE SET (6) 3.00 8.00
*CRACKED ICE/25: 5X TO 12X BASIC CARDS
3 Jameis Winston FB .75 2.00
4 Marcus Mariota FB 1.25 3.00

2012 Panini National Treasures

STATED PRINT RUN 99 SER.#'d SETS
EXCH EXPIRATION: 10/10/2014
1 Aaron Rodgers 8.00 20.00
2 Greg Jennings 2.00 5.00
3 Jordy Nelson 2.50 6.00
4 Colin Kaepernick 2.50 6.00
5 Frank Gore 2.50 6.00
6 Vernon Davis 2.00 5.00
7 Darren Sproles 2.50 6.00
8 Drew Brees 3.00 8.00
9 Jimmy Graham 3.00 8.00
10 Marques Colston 2.00 5.00
11 Ahmad Bradshaw 2.00 5.00
12 Eli Manning 2.50 6.00
13 Hakeem Nicks 2.00 5.00
14 Victor Cruz 2.50 6.00
15 Julio Jones 3.00 8.00
16 Michael Turner 2.00 5.00
17 Matt Ryan 2.50 6.00
18 Roddy White 2.00 5.00
19 Tony Gonzalez 2.50 6.00
20 Calvin Johnson 3.00 8.00
21 Matthew Stafford 2.50 6.00
22 Mikel Leshoure 2.00 5.00
23 Brandon Marshall 2.50 6.00
24 Jay Cutler 2.00 5.00
25 Matt Forte 2.00 5.00
26 Andre Roberts 2.50 6.00
27 Kevin Kolb 2.00 5.00
28 Larry Fitzgerald 2.50 6.00
29 DeSean Jackson 2.50 6.00
30 Jeremy Maclin 2.00 5.00
31 LeSean McCoy 3.00 8.00
32 Michael Vick 2.50 6.00
33 DeMarco Murray 2.50 6.00
34 Dez Bryant 3.00 8.00
35 Jason Witten 2.50 6.00
36 Tony Romo 2.50 6.00
37 Golden Tate 2.00 5.00
38 Marshawn Lynch 2.50 6.00
39 Sidney Rice 2.00 5.00
40 Cam Newton 3.00 8.00
41 DeAngelo Williams 2.00 5.00
42 Steve Smith 2.50 6.00
43 Fred Davis 2.00 5.00
44 Pierre Garcon 2.50 6.00
45 Josh Freeman 2.50 6.00
46 Mike Williams 2.50 6.00
47 Vincent Jackson 2.00 5.00
48 Sam Bradford 2.00 5.00
49 Steven Jackson 2.00 5.00
50 Aaron Hernandez 2.50 6.00
51 Brandon Lloyd 2.00 5.00
52 Rob Gronkowski 3.00 8.00
53 Stevan Ridley 2.00 5.00
54 Tom Brady 8.00 20.00
55 Wes Walker 2.50 6.00
56 Joe Flacco 2.50 6.00
57 Ray Rice 2.00 5.00
58 Torrey Smith 2.00 5.00
59 Andre Johnson 2.50 6.00
60 Arian Foster 2.50 6.00

61 Matt Schaub 2.00 5.00
62 Demaryius Thomas 3.00 8.00
63 Eric Decker 2.00 5.00
64 Peyton Manning 6.00 15.00
65 Willis McGahee 2.00 5.00
66 Antonio Brown 3.00 8.00
67 Ben Roethlisberger 3.00 8.00
68 Mike Wallace 2.00 5.00
69 Rashard Mendenhall 2.00 5.00
70 A.J. Green 3.00 8.00
71 Andy Dalton 2.50 6.00
72 BenJarvus Green-Ellis 2.50 6.00
73 Chris Johnson 2.00 5.00
74 Jake Locker 3.00 8.00
75 Kenny Britt 2.00 5.00
76 Mark Sanchez 2.00 5.00
77 Santonio Holmes 2.00 5.00
78 Shonn Greene 2.00 5.00
79 Tim Tebow 3.00 8.00
80 Antonio Gates 2.50 6.00
81 Malcom Floyd 2.00 5.00
82 Philip Rivers 3.00 8.00
83 Ryan Mathews 2.50 6.00
84 Carson Palmer 2.50 6.00
85 Darren McFadden 2.00 5.00
86 Dwayne Bowe 2.50 6.00
87 Jamaal Charles 2.50 6.00
88 Matt Cassel 2.00 5.00
89 Brian Hartline 2.50 6.00
90 Reggie Bush 2.00 5.00
91 C.J. Spiller 2.00 5.00
92 Fred Jackson 2.50 6.00
93 Ryan Fitzpatrick 2.00 5.00
94 Steve Johnson 2.50 6.00
95 Blaine Gabbert 2.00 5.00
96 Maurice Jones-Drew 2.00 5.00
97 Greg Little 2.00 5.00
98 Mohamed Massaquoi 2.00 5.00
99 Donald Brown 2.00 5.00
100 Reggie Wayne 2.50 6.00
101 Alan Page 2.00 5.00
102 Amani Toomer 2.00 5.00
103 Andre Reed 2.50 6.00
104 Andre Rison 2.50 6.00
105 Barry Sanders 5.00 12.00
106 Bart Starr 5.00 12.00
107 Bernie Kosar 2.50 6.00
108 Billy Howton 2.00 5.00
109 Bo Jackson 4.00 10.00
110 Bob Griese 3.00 8.00
111 Boomer Esiason 2.50 6.00
112 Brent Jones 2.00 5.00
113 Brett Favre 6.00 15.00
114 Bruce Smith 2.50 6.00
115 Craig James 2.00 5.00
116 Cris Carter 3.00 8.00
117 Curtis Martin 2.50 6.00
118 Dan Fouts 2.50 6.00
119 Dan Marino 6.00 15.00
120 Danny White 2.50 6.00
121 Darrell Green 2.50 6.00
122 Daryle Lamonica 2.00 5.00
123 Dave Casper 2.00 5.00
124 Dick Butkus 4.00 10.00
125 Don Maynard 2.50 6.00
126 Doug Flutie 2.50 6.00
127 Doug Williams 2.50 6.00
128 Drew Bledsoe 2.50 6.00
129 Dwight Clark 2.50 6.00
130 Emmitt Smith 5.00 12.00
131 Eric Dickerson 2.50 6.00
132 Floyd Little 2.00 5.00
133 Forrest Gregg 2.00 5.00
134 Fran Tarkenton 3.00 8.00
135 Franco Harris 3.00 8.00
136 Fred Taylor 2.00 5.00
137 Fred Williamson 2.00 5.00
138 Gary Collins 2.00 5.00
139 Harlon Hill 2.00 5.00
140 Herman Moore 2.00 5.00
141 Howie Long 3.00 8.00
142 Isaac Bruce 3.00 8.00
143 Jack Lambert 3.00 8.00
144 Jay Novacek 2.50 6.00
145 Jerome Bettis 3.00 8.00
146 Jerry Rice 5.00 12.00
147 Jim Brown 4.00 10.00
148 Jim Kelly 3.00 8.00
149 Jim McMahon 2.50 6.00
150 Jim Plunkett 2.50 6.00
151 Jimmy Orr 2.00 5.00
152 Joe Greene 3.00 8.00
153 Joe Namath 5.00 12.00
154 John Elway 5.00 12.00
155 John Fuqua 2.50 6.00
156 John Randle 2.50 6.00
157 John Riggins 2.50 6.00
158 Keith Jackson 2.00 5.00
159 Kellen Winslow 2.50 6.00
160 Kurt Warner 2.50 6.00
161 Lance Alworth 2.50 6.00
162 Lawrence Taylor 2.50 6.00
163 Len Dawson 3.00 8.00
164 Lenny Moore 2.00 5.00
165 Leroy Kelly 2.50 6.00
166 Marcus Allen 3.00 8.00
167 Mark Carrier S 2.00 5.00
168 Mark Duper 2.00 5.00
169 Marshall Faulk 2.50 6.00
170 Marvin Harrison 2.50 6.00
171 Michael Irvin 3.00 8.00
172 Robert Newhouse 2.00 5.00
173 Ozzie Newsome 2.50 6.00
174 Paul Krause 2.00 5.00
175 Phil Simms 2.50 6.00
176 Priest Holmes 2.00 5.00
177 Rocket Ismail 2.50 6.00
178 Randall Cunningham 2.50 6.00
179 Raymond Berry 2.50 6.00
180 Richard Dent 2.50 6.00
181 Rickey Jackson 2.00 5.00
182 Rod Smith 2.00 5.00
183 Rod Woodson 2.50 6.00
184 Ronnie Lott 2.50 6.00
185 Sam Huff 2.50 6.00
186 Shannon Sharpe 2.50 6.00
187 Shaun Alexander 2.00 5.00
188 Sterling Sharpe 2.50 6.00
189 Steve Largent 3.00 8.00
190 Steve Young 4.00 10.00
191 Terrell Davis 2.50 6.00
192 Tiki Barber 2.50 6.00
193 Tim Brown 3.00 8.00
194 Tony Dorsett 3.00 8.00
195 Warren Moon 3.00 8.00
196 Warrick Dunn 2.00 5.00
197 Wayne Chrebet 2.00 5.00
198 Willie Davis 2.00 5.00
199 Willie Lanier 2.00 5.00
200 John Brodie 2.50 6.00
201 Adrien Robinson AU RC 5.00 12.00
202 Alfred Morris AU RC 5.00 12.00
203 Andre Branch AU RC 5.00 12.00
204 Greg Zuerlein AU RC 8.00 20.00
205 B.J. Cunningham AU RC 5.00 12.00
206 Bill Bentley AU RC 6.00 15.00
207 Blair Walsh AU RC 12.00 30.00
208 Bobby Rainey AU RC 15.00 30.00
209 Bobby Wagner AU RC 12.00 30.00
210 Brandon Bolden AU RC 10.00 25.00
211 Brandon Hardin AU RC 6.00 15.00
212 Brandon Taylor AU RC 5.00 12.00
213 Bruce Irvin AU RC 6.00 15.00
214 Bryce Brown AU RC 5.00 12.00
215 Casey Hayward AU RC 5.00 12.00
216 Chandler Harnish AU RC 5.00 12.00
217 Chandler Jones AU RC 5.00 12.00
218 Chris Polk AU RC 5.00 12.00
219 Dan Herron AU RC
220 Coty Sensabaugh AU RC 6.00 15.00
221 Courtney Upshaw AU RC 6.00 15.00
222 Cyrus Gray AU RC 5.00 12.00
223 Damaris Johnson AU RC 5.00 12.00
224 Daryl Richardson AU RC 20.00 40.00
225 David DeCastro AU RC 5.00 12.00
226 Deangelo Peterson AU RC 5.00 12.00
227 Demario Davis AU RC 5.00 12.00
228 Deonte Thompson AU RC 6.00 15.00
229 Derek Wolfe AU RC
230 Devon Still AU RC 6.00 15.00
231 Devon Wylie AU RC 5.00 12.00
232 Dont'a Hightower AU RC 8.00 20.00
233 Dontari Poe AU RC 5.00 12.00
234 Dre Kirkpatrick AU RC
235 Evan Rodriguez AU RC 6.00 15.00
236 Fletcher Cox AU RC 8.00 20.00
237 George Iloka AU RC 5.00 12.00
238 Harrison Smith AU RC 15.00 30.00
239 Jamell Fleming AU RC 5.00 12.00
240 James Hanna AU RC 5.00 12.00
241 Janoris Jenkins AU RC 6.00 15.00
242 Jared Crick AU RC 5.00 12.00
243 Jeff Demps AU RC 6.00 15.00
244 Jerel Worthy AU RC
245 Jonathan Martin AU RC 5.00 12.00
246 Jorvorskie Lane AU RC
247 Josh Cooper AU RC 6.00 15.00
248 Josh Gordon AU RC 20.00 50.00
249 Josh Norman AU RC 25.00 50.00
250 Josh Robinson AU RC 8.00 20.00
251 Juron Criner AU RC 5.00 12.00
252 Justin Tucker AU RC
253 Kellen Moore AU RC 6.00 15.00
254 Kendall Reyes AU RC 5.00 12.00
255 Keshawn Martin AU RC 6.00 15.00
256 Kevin Zeitler AU RC 5.00 12.00
257 Kirk Cousins AU RC 100.00 200.00
258 Kris Adams AU RC 8.00 20.00
259 Ladarius Green AU RC 12.00 30.00
260 Lance Dunbar AU RC 8.00 20.00
261 Lavonte David AU RC 8.00 20.00
262 Luke Kuechly AU RC 60.00 120.00
263 Mark Barron AU RC 5.00 12.00
264 Marvin Jones AU RC 10.00 25.00
265 Matt Kalil AU RC 5.00 12.00
266 Melvin Ingram AU RC 5.00 12.00
267 Michael Brockers AU RC
268 Michael Smith AU RC
269 Mike Martin AU RC 6.00 15.00
270 Miles Burris AU RC
271 Morris Claiborne AU RC 5.00 12.00
272 Mychal Kendricks AU RC 8.00 20.00
273 Najee Goode AU RC 5.00 12.00
274 Nick Perry AU RC 6.00 15.00
275 Nigel Bradham AU RC 6.00 15.00
276 Olivier Vernon AU RC 8.00 20.00
277 Omar Bolden AU RC 6.00 15.00
278 Orson Charles AU RC 5.00 12.00
279 Quinton Coples AU RC 5.00 12.00
280 Rhett Ellison AU RC 6.00 15.00
281 Riley Reiff AU RC 5.00 12.00
282 Rishard Matthews AU RC 5.00 12.00
283 Rod Streater AU RC
284 Ronnell Lewis AU RC 5.00 12.00
285 Ryan Lindley AU RC 5.00 12.00
286 Sean Spence AU RC 6.00 15.00
287 Shea McClellin AU RC 8.00 20.00
288 Stephon Gilmore AU RC 6.00 15.00
289 T.Y. Hilton AU RC 20.00 50.00
290 Tavon Wilson AU RC 6.00 15.00
291 Terrance Ganaway AU RC 6.00 15.00
292 Tommy Streeter AU RC
293 Travis Benjamin AU RC 5.00 12.00
294 Trumaine Johnson AU RC 5.00 12.00
295 Tyrone Crawford AU RC 5.00 12.00
296 Vick Ballard AU RC 6.00 15.00
297 Vinny Curry AU RC 6.00 15.00
298 Vontaze Burfict AU RC 6.00 15.00
299 Whitney Mercilus AU RC 5.00 12.00
300 Zach Brown AU RC
301 A.Luck JSY AU RC 1300.00 2000.00
302 R.Griffin III JSY AU RC 15.00 40.00
303 T.Richardson JSY AU RC 12.00 30.00
304 R.Tannehill JSY AU RC 50.00 100.00
305 J.Blackmon JSY AU RC 12.00 30.00
306 B.Weeden JSY AU RC 12.00 30.00
307 B.Osweiler JSY AU RC 25.00 60.00
308 M.Floyd JSY AU RC 12.00 30.00
309 K.Wright JSY AU RC 12.00 30.00
310 A.J. Jenkins JSY AU RC 12.00 30.00
311 Doug Martin JSY AU RC 40.00 80.00
312 Lamar Miller JSY AU RC 20.00 50.00
313 Isaiah Pead JSY AU RC 12.00 30.00
314 David Wilson JSY AU RC 12.00 30.00
315 Stephen Hill JSY AU RC 12.00 30.00
316 M.Sanu JSY AU RC 12.00 30.00
317 B.Pierce JSY AU RC 15.00 40.00
318 Nick Foles JSY AU RC 60.00 125.00
319 L.James JSY AU RC 12.00 30.00
320 R.Randle JSY AU RC 15.00 40.00
321 Coby Fleener JSY AU RC 12.00 30.00
322 Ryan Broyles JSY AU RC 12.00 30.00
323 Dwayne Allen JSY AU RC 12.00 30.00
324 Ronnie Hillman JSY AU RC 20.00 50.00
325 R.Wilson JSY AU RC EXCH 700.00 1200.00
326 M.Egnew JSY AU RC 12.00 30.00
327 Chris Givens JSY AU RC 12.00 30.00
328 Joe Adams JSY AU RC 12.00 30.00
329 Robert Turbin JSY AU RC 12.00 30.00
330 Nick Toon JSY AU RC 12.00 30.00
331 T.J. Graham JSY AU RC 12.00 30.00
332 Brian Quick JSY AU RC 12.00 30.00
333 DeVier Posey JSY AU RC 12.00 30.00
334 Jarius Wright JSY AU RC 12.00 30.00
335 Alshon Jeffery JSY AU RC 50.00 100.00

2012 Panini National Treasures Century Silver

*SILVER/25: .8X TO 2X BASIC CARDS

2012 Panini National Treasures Century Black Signature

1-200 VET/RETIRED PRINT RUN 1-25
*201-300 ROOKIE/25: .6X TO 1.5X AU RC/99
201-300 ROOKIE PRINT RUN 25
4 Colin Kaepernick/20 10.00 25.00
5 Frank Gore/25 12.00 30.00
22 Mikel Leshoure/25 8.00 20.00
26 Andre Roberts/25 10.00 25.00
50 Aaron Hernandez/25 12.00 30.00
51 Brandon Lloyd/25 8.00 20.00
62 Demaryius Thomas/25 12.00 30.00
63 Eric Decker/25 12.00 30.00
66 Antonio Brown/25 12.00 30.00
69 Rashard Mendenhall/25 8.00 20.00
72 BenJarvus Green-Ellis/15 10.00 25.00
75 Kenny Britt/25 8.00 20.00
95 Blaine Gabbert/25 8.00 20.00
99 Donald Brown/25 8.00 20.00
102 Amani Toomer/25 10.00 25.00
104 Andre Rison/25 15.00 40.00
107 Bernie Kosar/25 12.00 30.00
108 Billy Howton/25 10.00 25.00
111 Boomer Esiason/15 12.00 30.00
118 Dan Fouts/20 40.00 80.00
120 Danny White/25 15.00 40.00
121 Darrell Green/25 25.00 60.00
122 Daryle Lamonica/25 10.00 25.00
123 Dave Casper/25 10.00 25.00
129 Dwight Clark/25 12.00 30.00
132 Floyd Little/15 10.00 25.00
139 Harlon Hill/25 10.00 25.00
140 Herman Moore/25 10.00 25.00
142 Isaac Bruce/25 15.00 40.00
151 Jimmy Orr/15 10.00 25.00
155 John Fuqua/25 12.00 30.00
158 Keith Jackson/25 10.00 25.00
164 Lenny Moore/15 10.00 25.00
167 Mark Carrier S/25 10.00 25.00
196 Warrick Dunn/25 12.00 30.00
202 Alfred Morris/25 8.00 20.00
257 Kirk Cousins/25 150.00 300.00

2012 Panini National Treasures Century Gold Signature

1-200 VET/RETIRED PRINT RUN 5-49
*201-300 ROOKIE/49: .5X TO 1.2X AU RC/99
201-300 ROOKIE PRINT RUN 49
2 Greg Jennings/15 8.00 20.00
4 Colin Kaepernick/40 6.00 15.00
5 Frank Gore/49 10.00 25.00
8 Drew Brees/25 40.00 80.00
11 Ahmad Bradshaw/25 8.00 20.00
22 Mikel Leshoure/49 5.00 12.00
26 Andre Roberts/49 6.00 15.00
27 Kevin Kolb/25 8.00 20.00
29 DeSean Jackson/25 10.00 25.00
30 Jeremy Maclin/25 8.00 20.00
38 Marshawn Lynch/25 25.00 50.00
40 Cam Newton/25 40.00 80.00
42 Steve Smith/25 12.00 30.00
46 Mike Williams/20 10.00 25.00
50 Aaron Hernandez/49 8.00 20.00
51 Brandon Lloyd/49 5.00 12.00
62 Demaryius Thomas/49 12.00 30.00
63 Eric Decker/49 8.00 20.00
66 Antonio Brown/49 20.00 40.00
67 Ben Roethlisberger/25 40.00 80.00
68 Mike Wallace/25 8.00 20.00
69 Rashard Mendenhall/49 5.00 12.00
71 Andy Dalton/25 15.00 40.00
72 BenJarvus Green-Ellis/25 8.00 20.00
75 Kenny Britt/49 5.00 12.00
77 Santonio Holmes/25 8.00 20.00
87 Jamaal Charles/25 10.00 25.00
91 C.J. Spiller/15 12.00 30.00
95 Blaine Gabbert/49 5.00 12.00
96 Maurice Jones-Drew/25 8.00 20.00
97 Greg Little/20 8.00 20.00
99 Donald Brown/49 5.00 12.00
100 Reggie Wayne/25 10.00 25.00
101 Alan Page/19 10.00 25.00
102 Amani Toomer/49 8.00 20.00
103 Andre Reed/25 10.00 25.00
104 Andre Rison/49 10.00 25.00
105 Barry Sanders/25 75.00 125.00
107 Bernie Kosar/49 8.00 20.00
108 Billy Howton/49 6.00 15.00
110 Bob Griese/25 15.00 40.00
111 Boomer Esiason/25 12.00 30.00
113 Brett Favre/25 100.00 175.00
114 Bruce Smith/25 15.00 40.00
116 Cris Carter/25 15.00 40.00
119 Dan Marino/25 75.00 150.00
120 Danny White/49 12.00 30.00
121 Darrell Green/49 20.00 40.00
122 Daryle Lamonica/49 8.00 20.00
123 Dave Casper/49 8.00 20.00
124 Dick Butkus/25 25.00 50.00
125 Don Maynard/25 10.00 30.00
127 Doug Williams/25 12.00 30.00
128 Drew Bledsoe/25 25.00 60.00
129 Dwight Clark/49 8.00 20.00
132 Floyd Little/25 10.00 25.00
133 Forrest Gregg/25 12.00 30.00
134 Fran Tarkenton/25
135 Franco Harris/25 15.00 40.00
136 Fred Taylor/25 10.00 25.00
137 Fred Williamson/25 10.00 25.00
139 Harlon Hill/49 8.00 20.00
140 Herman Moore/49 6.00 15.00
141 Howie Long/25 15.00 40.00
142 Isaac Bruce/49 10.00 25.00
143 Jack Lambert/20 40.00 80.00
144 Jay Novacek/25 12.00 30.00
145 Jerome Bettis/25 50.00 100.00
149 Jim McMahon/25 15.00 40.00
150 Jim Plunkett/25 12.00 30.00
151 Jimmy Orr/25 10.00 25.00
152 Joe Greene/25 15.00 40.00
155 John Fuqua/49 10.00 25.00
158 Keith Jackson/49 6.00 15.00
159 Kellen Winslow/15 15.00 40.00
161 Lance Alworth/25 25.00 50.00
163 Len Dawson/25 15.00 40.00
164 Lenny Moore/25 10.00 25.00
165 Leroy Kelly/15 12.00 30.00
167 Mark Carrier S/49 6.00 15.00
172 Robert Newhouse/25 15.00 40.00
173 Ozzie Newsome/25 12.00 30.00
174 Paul Krause/25 10.00 25.00
175 Phil Simms/25 15.00 40.00
176 Priest Holmes/25 15.00 40.00
179 Raymond Berry/25 12.00 30.00
180 Richard Dent/25 12.00 30.00
182 Rod Smith/25 15.00 40.00
187 Shaun Alexander/25 10.00 25.00
189 Steve Largent/25 15.00 40.00
193 Tim Brown/25 25.00 50.00
194 Tony Dorsett/25 15.00 40.00
195 Warren Moon/25 15.00 40.00
196 Warrick Dunn/49 6.00 15.00
199 Willie Lanier/25 10.00 25.00
257 Kirk Cousins/49 125.00 250.00

2012 Panini National Treasures Century Material

*PRIME/49: .5X TO 1.2X BASIC JSY
*PRIME/25: .6X TO 1.5X BASIC JSY
1 Matt Ryan/99 4.00 10.00
2 Joe Flacco/99 4.00 10.00
3 Ryan Fitzpatrick/99 3.00 8.00
4 Jay Cutler/49 3.00 8.00
5 Andy Dalton/99 4.00 10.00
6 Tony Romo/99 4.00 10.00
8 Matt Cassel/99 3.00 8.00
9 Christian Ponder/99 3.00 8.00
10 Tom Brady/99 12.00 30.00
11 Drew Brees/99 5.00 12.00
12 Eli Manning/99 4.00 10.00
13 Mark Sanchez/99 3.00 8.00
14 Carson Palmer/49 4.00 10.00
15 Michael Vick/99 4.00 10.00
16 Philip Rivers/99 5.00 12.00
17 Michael Turner/99 3.00 8.00
18 Ray Rice/99 3.00 8.00
19 C.J. Spiller/75 3.00 8.00
20 Fred Jackson/99 4.00 10.00
21 DeAngelo Williams/99 3.00 8.00
22 Jonathan Stewart/99 3.00 8.00
23 Matt Forte/99 3.00 8.00
24 Knowshon Moreno/99 3.00 8.00
25 Willis McGahee/49 3.00 8.00
26 Arian Foster/49 4.00 10.00
27 Maurice Jones-Drew/20 5.00 12.00
28 Jamaal Charles/99 4.00 10.00
29 Reggie Bush/99 3.00 8.00
30 Adrian Peterson/99 5.00 12.00
31 Darren Sproles/10
32 Ahmad Bradshaw/99 3.00 8.00
33 Shonn Greene/99 3.00 8.00
34 Darren McFadden/99 3.00 8.00
35 LeSean McCoy/99 5.00 12.00
36 Ryan Mathews/49 4.00 10.00
38 Chris Johnson/49 3.00 8.00
39 Roddy White/25 5.00 12.00
40 Anquan Boldin/99 3.00 8.00
41 Torrey Smith/99 3.00 8.00
42 Steve Johnson/99 4.00 10.00
43 Steve Smith/49 4.00 10.00
44 Devin Hester/49 4.00 10.00
45 A.J. Green/49 5.00 12.00
47 Dez Bryant/49 5.00 12.00
48 Miles Austin/99 3.00 8.00
49 Demaryius Thomas/99 5.00 12.00
50 Eric Decker/49 3.00 8.00
51 Brandon Stokley/99 3.00 8.00
52 Andre Johnson/49 4.00 10.00
53 Kevin Walter/49 3.00 8.00
54 Dwayne Bowe/99 4.00 10.00
55 Jonathan Baldwin/99 3.00 8.00
56 Brian Hartline/49 4.00 10.00
57 Davone Bess/49 3.00 8.00
58 Percy Harvin/49 3.00 8.00
59 Wes Welker/99 4.00 10.00
60 Marques Colston/99 3.00 8.00
61 Darrius Heyward-Bey/49 3.00 8.00
62 Denarius Moore/99 3.00 8.00
63 Jacoby Ford/99 3.00 8.00
64 DeSean Jackson/99 4.00 10.00
65 Jeremy Maclin/49 3.00 8.00
66 Mike Wallace/49 3.00 8.00
67 Michael Crabtree/99 3.00 8.00
68 Sidney Rice/49 3.00 8.00
69 Santana Moss/49 4.00 10.00
70 Tony Gonzalez/49 4.00 10.00
71 Jermaine Gresham/99 3.00 8.00
72 Jason Witten/99 4.00 10.00
73 Marcedes Lewis/99 3.00 8.00
74 Anthony Fasano/99 3.00 8.00
75 Kyle Rudolph/99 3.00 8.00
76 Jimmy Graham/49 5.00 12.00
77 Dustin Keller/99 3.00 8.00
78 Antonio Gates/49 4.00 10.00
79 Vernon Davis/99 3.00 8.00
80 Fred Davis/49 3.00 8.00
81 Ray Lewis/99 6.00 15.00
82 Terrell Suggs/99 3.00 8.00
84 Brian Urlacher/49 5.00 12.00
85 Lance Briggs/99 4.00 10.00
86 Sean Lee/25 8.00 20.00
87 Elvis Dumervil/49 3.00 8.00
88 Von Miller/49 4.00 10.00
89 AJ Hawk/1
90 Karlos Dansby/99 3.00 8.00
91 Brian Orakpo/99 4.00 10.00
92 London Fletcher/99 5.00 12.00
93 Champ Bailey/49 4.00 10.00
94 Darrelle Revis/49 3.00 8.00
95 DeAngelo Hall/99 3.00 8.00
96 Ed Reed/49 4.00 10.00
97 Troy Polamalu/49 5.00 12.00
98 Julius Peppers/49 5.00 12.00
99 Jared Allen/49 3.00 8.00
100 Haloti Ngata/99 3.00 8.00

2012 Panini National Treasures Century Material Signature

5 Fred Jackson/15 12.00 30.00
7 Matt Forte/25 10.00 25.00
8 Joe Flacco/25 25.00 50.00
10 Anquan Boldin/25 15.00 40.00
12 Andy Dalton/25 12.00 30.00
13 Jermaine Gresham/25 10.00 25.00
14 Knowshon Moreno/25 10.00 25.00
15 Demaryius Thomas/25 15.00 40.00
16 Von Miller/25 15.00 40.00
17 Champ Bailey/25 12.00 30.00
18 Daniel Thomas/25 10.00 25.00
21 Matt Cassel/25 10.00 25.00
22 Jamaal Charles/25 15.00 40.00
24 Tony Moeaki/25 10.00 25.00
27 Felix Jones/25 10.00 25.00
28 Percy Harvin/25 10.00 25.00
30 Jared Allen/25 25.00 50.00
33 London Fletcher/25 12.00 30.00
34 Brian Orakpo/25 12.00 30.00
36 Sam Bradford/25 10.00 25.00
37 James Laurinaitis/25 10.00 25.00
39 Jonathan Stewart/25 10.00 25.00
41 Matt Ryan/25 25.00 50.00
45 Mike Wallace/25 10.00 25.00
48 Antonio Gates/15 12.00 30.00
51 Denarius Moore/25 10.00 25.00
52 Dustin Keller/25 10.00 25.00
55 DeSean Jackson/25 12.00 30.00
57 Ahmad Bradshaw/25 10.00 25.00
62 Drew Brees/25 50.00 100.00
65 Beanie Wells/25 10.00 25.00
70 Sean Lee/25 15.00 40.00
71 Tony Romo/25 25.00 50.00
72 Kevin Walter/25 10.00 25.00
73 Kyle Rudolph/25 10.00 25.00
74 Christian Ponder/25 10.00 25.00
78 Jeremy Maclin/25 10.00 25.00

2012 Panini National Treasures Colossal Materials

*PRIME/25: .6X TO 1.5X BASIC JSY/49
1 Vernon Davis/49 3.00 8.00
2 Lance Briggs/25 6.00 15.00
3 Julius Peppers/25 8.00 20.00
4 Fred Jackson/25 6.00 15.00
5 Steve Johnson/49 4.00 10.00
6 Elvis Dumervil/25 5.00 12.00
7 Eric Decker/25 5.00 12.00
8 Beanie Wells/49 3.00 8.00
10 Philip Rivers/49 5.00 12.00
11 Jamaal Charles/25 6.00 15.00
12 Tony Moeaki/25 5.00 12.00
13 Dez Bryant/25 8.00 20.00
15 DeSean Jackson/20 6.00 15.00
16 Michael Vick/25 6.00 15.00
18 Marcedes Lewis/25 5.00 12.00
20 Darrelle Revis/25 5.00 12.00
21 Dustin Keller/49 3.00 8.00
23 Richard Seymour/49 3.00 8.00
24 Steven Jackson/49 3.00 8.00
25 Ed Reed/25 6.00 15.00
26 Ray Lewis/25 10.00 25.00
27 DeAngelo Hall/49 3.00 8.00
29 Marques Colston/25 5.00 12.00
30 Kenny Britt/25 5.00 12.00

2012 Panini National Treasures Colossal Materials Pro Bowl

*PRIME/49: .6X TO 1.5X BASIC JSY
1 Andy Dalton 5.00 12.00
2 Von Miller 5.00 12.00
3 A.J. Green 6.00 15.00
4 Patrick Peterson 6.00 15.00
5 Philip Rivers 6.00 15.00
6 Maurice Jones-Drew 4.00 10.00
7 Ryan Mathews 5.00 12.00
8 Roddy White 4.00 10.00
9 Marshawn Lynch 8.00 20.00
10 Steve Smith 5.00 12.00
11 Charles Woodson 8.00 20.00
12 B.J. Raji 4.00 10.00
13 DeMarcus Ware 6.00 15.00
14 Jermaine Gresham 4.00 10.00
15 Dwight Freeney 4.00 10.00
16 Tony Gonzalez 5.00 12.00
17 Michael Robinson 4.00 10.00
18 Sebastian Janikowski 5.00 12.00
19 Joe Thomas 6.00 15.00
20 Vonta Leach 4.00 10.00
21 Tamba Hali 4.00 10.00
22 Elvis Dumervil 4.00 10.00
23 London Fletcher 6.00 15.00
24 Jay Ratliff 5.00 12.00
25 Charles Tillman 6.00 15.00
26 Antonio Smith 4.00 10.00
27 Eric Weddle 4.00 10.00
28 D'Brickashaw Ferguson 4.00 10.00
29 Scott Wells 4.00 10.00
30 Brandon Browner 4.00 10.00
31 Kam Chancellor 15.00 40.00
32 Corey Graham 4.00 10.00
33 Ryan Kalil 4.00 10.00
34 Marshal Yanda 6.00 15.00
35 Paul Soliai 4.00 10.00
36 Andy Lee 4.00 10.00
37 Montell Owens 4.00 10.00
38 Brandon Moore 4.00 10.00

2012 Panini National Treasures Colossal Materials Signature

2 Devin Hester/25 12.00 30.00
4 Jermaine Gresham/25 10.00 25.00
5 Andy Dalton/25 12.00 30.00
13 Brian Hartline/25 12.00 30.00
17 Ahmad Bradshaw/25 10.00 25.00
21 Jonathan Stewart/25 10.00 25.00
23 Denarius Moore/25 10.00 25.00
24 Sam Bradford/25 25.00 50.00
25 Joe Flacco/25 25.00 50.00
29 Drew Brees/25 50.00 100.00

2012 Panini National Treasures Franchise Favorites Materials

*PRIME/49: .6X TO 1.5X BASIC JSY
*PRIME/25: .8X TO 2X BASIC JSY
1 Larry Fitzgerald/99 4.00 10.00
2 Beanie Wells/99 3.00 8.00
4 Michael Turner/49 3.00 8.00
6 Ray Lewis/49 6.00 15.00
7 Anquan Boldin/49 3.00 8.00
8 Ed Reed/25 6.00 15.00
9 Joe Flacco/99 4.00 10.00
10 Jonathan Stewart/25 5.00 12.00
12 Lance Briggs/25 6.00 15.00
13 Devin Hester/49 4.00 10.00
14 Brian Urlacher/25 8.00 20.00
15 Julius Peppers/49 5.00 12.00
16 Jermaine Gresham/49 3.00 8.00
17 Andy Dalton/99 4.00 10.00
19 Jason Witten/25 6.00 15.00
20 Tony Romo/99 4.00 10.00
22 Demaryius Thomas/49 5.00 12.00
23 Von Miller/49 4.00 10.00
24 Eric Decker/49 3.00 8.00
25 Champ Bailey/25 6.00 15.00
26 Kevin Walter/20 5.00 12.00
30 Marcedes Lewis/25 5.00 12.00
31 Jonathan Baldwin/99 3.00 8.00
32 Tony Moeaki/25 5.00 12.00
33 Eric Berry/99 4.00 10.00
34 Jamaal Charles/25 6.00 15.00
35 Brian Hartline/49 4.00 10.00
36 Davone Bess/49 3.00 8.00
37 Christian Ponder/99 3.00 8.00
38 Adrian Peterson/99 5.00 12.00
39 Jared Allen/49 5.00 12.00
41 Drew Brees/99 5.00 12.00
42 Marques Colston/25 5.00 12.00
44 Ahmad Bradshaw/99 3.00 8.00
45 Osi Umenyiora/99 3.00 8.00
46 Eli Manning/99 4.00 10.00
47 Darrelle Revis/49 3.00 8.00
48 Dustin Keller/99 3.00 8.00
49 Mark Sanchez/99 3.00 8.00
50 Darrius Heyward-Bey/49 3.00 8.00
52 Richard Seymour/99 3.00 8.00
53 Denarius Moore/99 3.00 8.00
54 Michael Vick/25 6.00 15.00
55 DeSean Jackson/20 6.00 15.00
57 Ryan Mathews/25 6.00 15.00
58 Philip Rivers/49 5.00 12.00
60 Vernon Davis/49 3.00 8.00
61 Michael Crabtree/25 5.00 12.00
62 Sidney Rice/25 5.00 12.00
63 Steven Jackson/99 3.00 8.00
64 Sam Bradford/99 3.00 8.00
65 James Laurinaitis/49 3.00 8.00
66 Fred Davis/25 5.00 12.00
67 London Fletcher/25 8.00 20.00
68 DeAngelo Hall/99 3.00 8.00
69 Brian Orakpo/25 6.00 15.00
70 Santana Moss/25 6.00 15.00

2012 Panini National Treasures Franchise Favorites Signatures

1 Kevin Kolb/25 8.00 20.00
2 Steve Bartkowski/49 8.00 20.00
3 Andre Reed/25 12.00 30.00
4 Jon Beason/33 6.00 15.00
5 Jim McMahon/25 15.00 40.00
7 Josh Cribbs/49 5.00 12.00
10 Herman Moore/40 8.00 20.00
11 James Lofton/49 8.00 20.00
12 J.J. Watt/99 50.00 100.00
13 Robert Mathis/99 10.00 25.00
14 Marcedes Lewis/25 8.00 20.00
15 Len Dawson/25 15.00 40.00
18 Drew Bledsoe/25 40.00 80.00
19 Mark Ingram/25 10.00 25.00
20 Jason Pierre-Paul/49 8.00 20.00
21 Don Maynard/25 12.00 30.00
22 Howie Long/25 15.00 40.00
23 Jeremy Maclin/25 8.00 20.00
24 Heath Miller/99 8.00 20.00
25 Kellen Winslow/25 12.00 30.00
26 Patrick Willis/49 10.00 25.00
27 Steve Largent/25 15.00 40.00
28 Isaac Bruce/49 10.00 25.00
29 Josh Freeman/25 10.00 25.00
30 Santana Moss/25 10.00 25.00

2012 Panini National Treasures Gladiators

*GOLD/15: .5X TO 1.2X BASIC INSERTS
1 Alshon Jeffery 8.00 20.00
2 Andrew Luck 75.00 135.00
3 Brandon Weeden 10.00 25.00
4 Brian Quick 4.00 10.00
5 Brock Osweiler 4.00 10.00
6 Chris Givens 8.00 20.00
7 Coby Fleener 4.00 10.00
8 Doug Martin 6.00 15.00
9 Dwayne Allen 4.00 10.00
10 Joe Adams 4.00 10.00
11 Justin Blackmon 4.00 10.00
12 Kendall Wright 4.00 10.00
13 DeVier Posey 4.00 10.00
14 Nick Foles 10.00 25.00
15 Robert Griffin III 5.00 12.00
16 Robert Turbin 4.00 10.00
17 Rueben Randle 4.00 10.00
18 Russell Wilson 75.00 150.00
19 Ryan Tannehill 8.00 20.00
20 Stephen Hill 4.00 10.00
21 T.J. Graham 4.00 10.00
22 Trent Richardson 4.00 10.00

2012 Panini National Treasures Legend Century Materials

1 Amani Toomer/20 5.00 12.00
2 Barry Sanders/99 8.00 20.00
3 Bart Starr/99 8.00 20.00
4 Bernie Kosar/25 6.00 15.00
5 Bob Griese/99 5.00 12.00
6 Bobby Mitchell/99 4.00 10.00
7 Boomer Esiason/99 4.00 10.00
8 Brett Favre/99 10.00 25.00
9 Bryant Young/99 3.00 8.00
10 Chuck Howley/99 3.00 8.00
11 Cris Collinsworth/99 4.00 10.00
12 Curtis Martin/25 6.00 15.00
13 Dan Fouts/99 4.00 10.00
14 Dan Marino/99 10.00 25.00
15 Daryle Lamonica/99 3.00 8.00
17 Deion Sanders/99 6.00 15.00
18 Doug Flutie/99 4.00 10.00
20 Drew Bledsoe/99 4.00 10.00
21 Ed Too Tall Jones/99 3.00 8.00
22 Eddie George/99 4.00 10.00
23 Emmitt Smith/99 8.00 20.00
24 Eric Dickerson/99 4.00 10.00
25 Forrest Gregg/99 5.00 12.00
26 Fran Tarkenton/55 6.00 15.00
27 Fred Biletnikoff/99 5.00 12.00
28 Fred Dryer/99 3.00 8.00
29 George Blanda/99 6.00 15.00
30 Hugh McElhenny/99 4.00 10.00
31 Irving Fryar/99 3.00 8.00
32 Jake Plummer/99 3.00 8.00
33 Jay Novacek/99 4.00 10.00
34 Jerome Bettis/25 12.00 30.00
35 Jerry Rice/99 8.00 20.00
36 Jim Brown/99 8.00 20.00
37 Jim Kelly/99 5.00 12.00
38 Jim McMahon/99 4.00 10.00
39 Jim Otto/99 3.00 8.00
40 Jim Plunkett/99 4.00 10.00
42 Joe Montana/99 12.00 30.00
43 Joe Namath/99 8.00 20.00
44 John Brodie/99 6.00 15.00
45 John Elway/99 8.00 20.00
46 John Fuqua/99 4.00 10.00
47 John Hadl/99 4.00 10.00
48 John Riggins/20 6.00 15.00
49 Junior Seau/99 4.00 10.00
50 Keith Jackson/50 3.00 8.00
51 Ken Stabler/75 5.00 12.00
52 Kurt Warner/99 6.00 15.00
53 L.C. Greenwood/35 8.00 20.00
55 Lee Roy Selmon/99 5.00 12.00
56 Marcus Allen/99 5.00 12.00
57 Mark Duper/25 5.00 12.00
58 Marshall Faulk/99 4.00 10.00
59 Mike Ditka/99 6.00 15.00
61 Paul Hornung/99 5.00 12.00
62 Phil Simms/20 6.00 15.00
63 Jerry Rice/40 12.00 30.00
65 Randall Cunningham/99 4.00 10.00
66 Randall Cunningham/99 4.00 10.00
67 Randy White/15 6.00 15.00
68 Raymond Berry/99 4.00 10.00
70 Roger Staubach/99 8.00 20.00
71 Ronnie Lott/99 4.00 10.00
72 Ronnie Lott/99 6.00 15.00
73 Ronnie Lott/99 4.00 10.00
75 Emmitt Smith/25 12.00 30.00
77 Art Monk/50 5.00 12.00
81 Steve Bartkowski/50 4.00 10.00
82 Steve Largent/25 8.00 20.00
83 Steve McNair/99 5.00 12.00
84 Steve McNair/99 4.00 10.00
85 Steve Young/99 6.00 15.00
86 Ted Hendricks/99 3.00 8.00
88 Terry Bradshaw/99 8.00 20.00
89 Thurman Thomas/99 4.00 10.00
90 Tony Dorsett/99 5.00 12.00
91 Tony Dorsett/20 6.00 15.00
92 Troy Aikman/99 6.00 15.00
93 Walter Payton/99 15.00 40.00
94 Warren Moon/99 5.00 12.00
98 Willie Brown/25 5.00 12.00
99 Joe Perry/99 4.00 10.00

2012 Panini National Treasures Legend Century Materials Prime

1 Amani Toomer/49 5.00 12.00
2 Barry Sanders/49 12.00 30.00
4 Bernie Kosar/49 6.00 15.00
6 Bobby Mitchell/49 6.00 15.00
7 Boomer Esiason/49 6.00 15.00
9 Bryant Young/20 6.00 15.00
11 Cris Collinsworth/49 6.00 15.00
12 Curtis Martin/49 6.00 15.00
19 Doug Williams/21 8.00 20.00
21 Ed Too Tall Jones/30 6.00 15.00
22 Eddie George/49 6.00 15.00
23 Emmitt Smith/49 12.00 30.00
29 George Blanda/49 10.00 25.00
32 Jake Plummer/49 5.00 12.00
35 Jerry Rice/49 12.00 30.00
43 Joe Namath/49 12.00 30.00
44 John Brodie/49 10.00 25.00
45 John Elway/49 12.00 30.00
50 Keith Jackson/49 5.00 12.00
52 Kurt Warner/49 10.00 25.00
55 Lee Roy Selmon/49 8.00 20.00
58 Marshall Faulk/49 6.00 15.00
60 Ozzie Newsome/49 6.00 15.00
64 Rocket Ismail/40 6.00 15.00
66 Randall Cunningham/17 8.00 20.00
71 Ronnie Lott/49 6.00 15.00
72 Ronnie Lott/49 10.00 25.00
73 Ronnie Lott/49 6.00 15.00
74 Sam Huff/40 6.00 15.00
75 Emmitt Smith/49 12.00 30.00
76 Joe Montana/49 20.00 50.00
78 Curtis Martin/49 6.00 15.00
79 Franco Harris/35 10.00 25.00
80 Sterling Sharpe/49 6.00 15.00
83 Steve McNair/49 8.00 20.00
84 Steve McNair/23 8.00 20.00
86 Ted Hendricks/49 5.00 12.00
89 Thurman Thomas/49 6.00 15.00
91 Tony Dorsett/49 6.00 15.00
93 Walter Payton/40 25.00 60.00
96 Warrick Dunn/49 5.00 12.00
97 Wayne Chrebet/49 5.00 12.00
99 Joe Perry/49 6.00 15.00

2012 Panini National Treasures Legend Century Materials Signature

1 Amani Toomer/25 12.00 30.00
3 Art Monk/25 20.00 50.00
4 Barry Sanders/15 90.00 150.00
5 Bart Starr/25 75.00 150.00
6 Bernie Kosar/25 15.00 40.00
7 Bill Bates/25 15.00 40.00
9 Bob Griese/25 30.00 60.00
11 Boomer Esiason/25 15.00 40.00
16 Charley Taylor/20 12.00 30.00
17 Chuck Foreman/25 12.00 30.00
20 Cris Carter/20 30.00 60.00
25 Dan Fouts/25 15.00 40.00
26 Dan Marino/25 100.00 175.00
27 Darrell Green/25 25.00 50.00
28 Daryle Lamonica/25 12.00 30.00
29 Deion Sanders/15 30.00 60.00
32 Dick Butkus/25 30.00 60.00
33 Don Maynard/25 12.00 30.00
35 Doug Flutie/15 15.00 40.00
37 Drew Bledsoe Bill/25 40.00 80.00
38 Drew Bledsoe Pats/25 40.00 80.00
39 Earl Campbell/25 20.00 50.00
42 Eddie George/25 25.00 60.00
48 Forrest Gregg/25 15.00 40.00
49 Fran Tarkenton/25 20.00 50.00
50 Franco Harris/15 30.00 60.00
51 Fred Biletnikoff/25 20.00 50.00
52 Fred Dryer/25 12.00 30.00
55 Howie Long/25 20.00 50.00
56 Hugh McElhenny/15 15.00 40.00
58 Jake Plummer/25 12.00 30.00
60 Jay Novacek/25 30.00 60.00
61 Jerry Rice 49er/20 90.00 150.00
62 Jerry Rice Raidr/20 75.00 150.00
64 Jim Kelly/25 20.00 50.00
66 Jim Otto/23 12.00 30.00
67 Jim Plunkett/25 15.00 40.00
70 Joe Montana/15 125.00 200.00
71 Joe Namath/25 50.00 100.00
73 John Fuqua/25 15.00 40.00
75 John Riggins/15 20.00 50.00
76 Keith Jackson/25 15.00 40.00
78 Larry Csonka/25 30.00 60.00
80 Marcus Allen/25 20.00 50.00
81 Mark Duper/20 12.00 30.00
82 Marshall Faulk/25 15.00 40.00
84 Paul Hornung/25 20.00 50.00
85 Phil Simms/17 15.00 40.00
87 Randall Cunningham Eagl/24 15.00 40.00
88 Randall Cunningham Vike/25 15.00 40.00
90 Raymond Berry/25 12.00 30.00
95 Steve Bartkowski/16 15.00 40.00
96 Steve Largent/25 15.00 40.00
97 Steve Young/25 50.00 80.00
98 Ted Hendricks/25 12.00 30.00
100 Warren Moon/25 20.00 50.00

2012 Panini National Treasures Legend Century Materials Signature Prime

3 Art Monk/15 50.00 100.00
6 Bernie Kosar/15 20.00 50.00
10 Bobby Mitchell/15 20.00 50.00
11 Boomer Esiason/15 20.00 50.00
20 Cris Carter/15
21 Cris Collinsworth/15 20.00 50.00
44 Emmitt Smith/15 125.00 200.00
53 Fred Taylor/15 15.00 40.00
58 Jake Plummer/15 15.00 40.00
61 Jerry Rice/15 60.00 120.00
69 Joe Greene/15 25.00 60.00
71 Joe Namath/15 50.00 100.00
76 Keith Jackson/15 20.00 50.00
77 Kurt Warner/15 40.00 80.00
78 Larry Csonka/15
82 Marshall Faulk/15 20.00 50.00
83 Mike Ditka/15
93 Shannon Sharpe/15 20.00 50.00
98 Ted Hendricks/15 15.00 40.00

2012 Panini National Treasures NFL Gear Combos

*PRIME/49: .5X TO 1.2X BASIC JSY/75
*TRIPLE/49: .4X TO 1X COMBO/75
*TRIP.PRIME/25: .6X TO 1.5X COMBO/75
*QUAD/25: .5X TO 1.2X COMBO/75
*QUAD PRIME/15: .6X TO 1.5X CMB/75
1 Brian Quick 2.00 5.00
2 Doug Martin 3.00 8.00
3 David Wilson 2.00 5.00
4 LaMichael James 2.00 5.00
5 Coby Fleener 2.00 5.00
6 Jarius Wright 2.00 5.00
7 Russell Wilson 25.00 60.00
8 Chris Givens 2.00 5.00
9 Mohamed Sanu 3.00 8.00
10 Michael Floyd 2.00 5.00
11 Robert Griffin III 2.50 6.00
12 Justin Blackmon 2.00 5.00
13 Dwayne Allen 2.00 5.00
14 DeVier Posey 2.00 5.00
15 Joe Adams 2.00 5.00
16 A.J. Jenkins 2.00 5.00
17 Stephen Hill 2.00 5.00
18 Ryan Broyles 2.00 5.00
19 Nick Foles 5.00 12.00
20 Nick Toon 2.00 5.00
21 Alshon Jeffery 4.00 10.00
22 Ryan Tannehill 3.00 8.00
23 Lamar Miller 3.00 8.00
24 Andrew Luck 20.00 50.00
25 Isaiah Pead 2.00 5.00
26 Rueben Randle 2.00 5.00
27 Brandon Weeden 2.00 5.00
28 Kendall Wright 2.00 5.00
29 Bernard Pierce 2.00 5.00
30 Michael Egnew 2.00 5.00
31 T.J. Graham 2.00 5.00
32 Trent Richardson 2.00 5.00
33 Brock Osweiler 2.00 5.00
34 Ronnie Hillman 2.00 5.00
35 Robert Turbin 2.00 5.00

2012 Panini National Treasures NFL Gear Combos Signatures

*PRIME/15: .8X TO 2X COMBO/49
*TRIPLE/25: .5X TO 1.2X COMBO/49
EXCH EXPIRATION: 10/10/2014
1 Brian Quick 8.00 20.00
2 Doug Martin 8.00 20.00
3 David Wilson 5.00 12.00
4 LaMichael James 5.00 12.00
5 Coby Fleener 5.00 12.00
6 Jarius Wright 5.00 12.00
7 Russell Wilson 150.00 250.00
8 Chris Givens 5.00 12.00
9 Mohamed Sanu 10.00 25.00
10 Michael Floyd 8.00 20.00
11 Robert Griffin III 6.00 15.00
12 Justin Blackmon 5.00 12.00
13 Dwayne Allen 5.00 12.00
14 DeVier Posey 5.00 12.00
15 Joe Adams 5.00 12.00
16 A.J. Jenkins 5.00 12.00
17 Stephen Hill 5.00 12.00
18 Ryan Broyles 5.00 12.00
19 Nick Foles 40.00 80.00
20 Nick Toon 8.00 20.00
21 Alshon Jeffery 10.00 25.00
22 Ryan Tannehill 12.00 30.00
23 Lamar Miller 8.00 20.00
24 Andrew Luck 100.00 200.00
25 Isaiah Pead 5.00 12.00
26 Rueben Randle 5.00 12.00
27 Brandon Weeden 5.00 12.00
28 Kendall Wright 5.00 12.00
29 Bernard Pierce 5.00 12.00
30 Michael Egnew 5.00 12.00
31 T.J. Graham 5.00 12.00
32 Trent Richardson 5.00 12.00
33 Brock Osweiler 5.00 12.00
34 Ronnie Hillman 5.00 12.00
35 Robert Turbin 5.00 12.00

2012 Panini National Treasures NFL Gear Dual Player Materials

*PRIME/49: .8X TO 2X BASIC JSY/75
1 A.Luck/R.Griffin III 10.00 25.00
2 B.Weeden/T.Richardson 2.00 5.00
3 J.Blackmon/M.Floyd 2.00 5.00
4 N.Foles/R.Wilson 10.00 25.00
5 B.Osweiler/R.Hillman 2.00 5.00
6 A.Jeffery/R.Broyles 4.00 10.00
7 K.Wright/M.Floyd 2.00 5.00
8 N.Toon/R.Wilson 10.00 25.00
9 B.Quick/S.Hill 2.00 5.00
10 C.Fleener/D.Allen 2.00 5.00
11 K.Wright/R.Griffin III 2.50 6.00
12 R.Turbin/R.Hillman 2.00 5.00
13 B.Weeden/J.Blackmon 2.00 5.00
14 C.Givens/I.Pead 2.00 5.00
15 L.Miller/R.Tannehill 3.00 8.00
16 A.Luck/C.Fleener 12.00 30.00
17 D.Martin/T.Richardson 3.00 8.00
18 R.Turbin/R.Wilson 12.00 30.00
19 R.Griffin III/R.Broyles 2.50 6.00
20 D.Wilson/R.Randle 2.00 5.00

2012 Panini National Treasures NFL Gear Quad Signatures

*QUAD/15: .6X TO 1.5X COMBO/49
7 Russell Wilson EXCH 200.00 350.00
11 Robert Griffin III 10.00 25.00
24 Andrew Luck 400.00 700.00

2012 Panini National Treasures NFL Greatest Signatures

1 Barry Sanders/25 125.00 250.00
2 Bart Starr/25 100.00 175.00
3 Bernie Kosar/25 30.00 80.00
4 Bo Jackson/25 60.00 120.00

6 Brett Favre/25 200.00 350.00
7 Cris Carter/25 60.00 120.00
8 Dan Fouts/25 25.00 60.00
9 Dan Marino/25 150.00 300.00
10 Deion Sanders/25 75.00 135.00
11 Dick Butkus/25 75.00 150.00
12 Earl Campbell/25 30.00 80.00
13 Ed McCaffrey/25 20.00 50.00
14 Eddie George/25 75.00 150.00
16 Eric Dickerson/25 75.00 150.00
17 Fran Tarkenton/25 30.00 80.00
18 Franco Harris/25 30.00 80.00
19 Gale Sayers/25 30.00 80.00
20 Jerome Bettis/25 90.00 150.00
21 Jerry Rice/25 150.00 300.00
23 Jim Kelly/25 30.00 80.00
24 Joe Montana/25 150.00 300.00
25 John Elway/25 100.00 200.00
27 L.C. Greenwood/25 20.00 50.00
28 Marcus Allen/25 50.00 100.00
29 Marshall Faulk/25 60.00 120.00
30 Marvin Harrison/25 25.00 60.00
31 Michael Irvin/25 40.00 100.00
33 Phil Simms/25 30.00 80.00
34 Rocket Ismail/25 20.00 50.00
35 Rod Woodson/25 90.00 150.00
36 Roger Staubach/25 100.00 200.00
37 Ron Jaworski/25 60.00 120.00
38 Ronnie Lott/25 60.00 120.00
39 Steve Young/25 60.00 120.00
40 Terry Bradshaw/25 75.00 150.00
42 Tom Rathman/25 20.00 50.00
43 Tony Dorsett/25 30.00 80.00
45 Warren Moon/25 40.00 100.00
46 Dwight Clark/50 20.00 50.00

2012 Panini National Treasures NFL Signatures

EXCH EXPIRATION: 10/10/2014
1 James Starks/25 8.00 20.00
2 Ronde Barber/25 12.00 30.00
4 Jared Cook/25 8.00 20.00
6 Santonio Holmes/25 8.00 20.00
7 Donald Driver/25 25.00 50.00
9 Victor Cruz/25 10.00 25.00
10 BenJarvus Green-Ellis/25 10.00 25.00
11 Jason Witten/25 25.00 50.00
13 Jermichael Finley/25 8.00 20.00
14 Greg Little/25 8.00 20.00
15 Brent Celek/25 8.00 20.00
16 Ted Hendricks/25 10.00 25.00
17 Andre Rison/25 15.00 40.00
18 Rod Smith/25 12.00 30.00
19 Shaun Alexander/25 10.00 25.00
21 Warren Sapp/25 15.00 40.00
22 Warrick Dunn/25 10.00 25.00
23 Ken Stabler/25 15.00 40.00
24 Bruce Smith/25 15.00 40.00

2012 Panini National Treasures Prime Pairings

2 R.Newhouse/T.Dorsett/20 40.00 80.00
8 Willms/Crrer/Krse/Wdsn/25 30.00 60.00
9 Bell/Lmbrt/Sngltry/Lnier/15 60.00 120.00
10 D.Hester/J.Cribbs/25 15.00 40.00
11 Rdgrs/Ryn/Trnr/White/15 50.00 100.00
12 Spill/Jcksn/Will/Fitzpk/25 15.00 40.00
13 Cshng/Wltr/Schb/Dnls/25 30.00 60.00
15 Sprls/Brees/Ingrm/Thm/25 90.00 150.00
16 Ware/Allen/Pierre-Paul/25 40.00 80.00
18 Boldin/Flacco/Smith/25 25.00 60.00
19 Nwtn/Will/Olsn/Stwat/25 75.00 125.00
20 D.Thomas/P.Manning/25 150.00 225.00
21 Jhns/Chrls/Bldwn/Cssl/25 30.00 60.00
22 N.Bowman/P.Willis/25 40.00 80.00
23 C.Bailey/C.Woodson/25 60.00 120.00
31 J.Cutler/J.McMahon/15 50.00 100.00
41 Ware/Gore/Miller/White/15 40.00 80.00
44 B.Romanowski/R.Smith/15 75.00 135.00
46 Bethea/Asomugha/Barber/25 12.00 30.00

2012 Panini National Treasures Rookie Colossal Jersey Number Signatures

*PRIME/25: .6X TO 1.5X BASIC JSY AU/50
1 Brock Osweiler 6.00 15.00
2 Andrew Luck 150.00 300.00
3 Chris Givens 6.00 15.00
4 Alshon Jeffery 12.00 30.00
5 Dwayne Allen 6.00 15.00
6 Ryan Tannehill 20.00 50.00
7 Doug Martin 10.00 25.00
8 Rueben Randle 12.00 30.00
9 T.J. Graham 6.00 15.00
10 Michael Floyd 6.00 15.00
11 Brian Quick 6.00 15.00
12 Ronnie Hillman 6.00 15.00
13 A.J. Jenkins 6.00 15.00
14 Trent Richardson 6.00 15.00
15 Robert Turbin 6.00 15.00
16 Stephen Hill 6.00 15.00
17 Nick Foles 40.00 80.00
18 Robert Griffin III 8.00 20.00
19 DeVier Posey 6.00 15.00
20 Russell Wilson 200.00 300.00
21 Ryan Broyles 6.00 15.00
22 Kendall Wright 6.00 15.00
23 Justin Blackmon 6.00 15.00
24 Mohamed Sanu 12.00 30.00
25 Coby Fleener 6.00 15.00
26 Nick Toon 6.00 15.00
27 Jarius Wright 6.00 15.00
28 David Wilson 6.00 15.00
29 LaMichael James 6.00 15.00
30 Lamar Miller 10.00 25.00
31 Bernard Pierce 6.00 15.00
32 Brandon Weeden 10.00 25.00
33 Joe Adams 6.00 15.00
34 Isaiah Pead 6.00 15.00
35 Michael Egnew 6.00 15.00

2012 Panini National Treasures Rookie Jumbo Prime Booklet Signatures

1 Isaiah Pead 12.00 30.00
2 Rueben Randle 25.00 60.00
3 Brandon Weeden 12.00 30.00
4 Kendall Wright 12.00 30.00
5 Bernard Pierce 12.00 30.00
6 Michael Egnew 12.00 30.00
7 T.J. Graham 12.00 30.00
8 Trent Richardson 12.00 30.00
9 Brock Osweiler 12.00 30.00
10 Ronnie Hillman 12.00 30.00
11 Robert Turbin 12.00 30.00
12 Dwayne Allen 12.00 30.00
13 DeVier Posey 12.00 30.00
14 Joe Adams 12.00 30.00
15 A.J. Jenkins 12.00 30.00
16 Stephen Hill 12.00 30.00
17 Ryan Broyles 12.00 30.00
18 Nick Foles 100.00 200.00
19 Nick Toon 12.00 30.00
20 Alshon Jeffery 50.00 100.00
21 Ryan Tannehill 40.00 80.00
22 Lamar Miller 20.00 50.00
23 Andrew Luck 500.00 1000.00
25 Robert Griffin III 15.00 40.00
26 Michael Floyd 12.00 30.00
27 Mohamed Sanu 15.00 40.00
28 Chris Givens 12.00 30.00
29 Russell Wilson 250.00 600.00
30 Jarius Wright 12.00 30.00
31 Coby Fleener 12.00 30.00
32 Brian Quick 20.00 50.00
33 Doug Martin 20.00 50.00
34 David Wilson 12.00 30.00
35 LaMichael James 12.00 30.00

2012 Panini National Treasures Rookie Signature Material Black

*BLACK/25: .6X TO 1.5X JSY AU RC/99
301 Andrew Luck 2500.00 4500.00
325 Russell Wilson 1200.00 2000.00

2012 Panini National Treasures Rookie Signature Material Gold

*GOLD/49: .5X TO 1.2X JSY AU RC/99
301 Andrew Luck 1200.00 2500.00
325 Russell Wilson 800.00 1200.00

2012 Panini National Treasures Souvenir Cuts

2 Andy Robustelli/34 15.00 40.00
5 Bert Bell/90 15.00 40.00
6 Bill Dudley/19 25.00 50.00
11 Bob Waterfield/46 25.00 50.00
17 Otto Graham/33 25.00 50.00
21 Ken Strong/16 40.00 80.00
22 Joe Perry/25 20.00 40.00

2012 Panini National Treasures Souvenir Material Cuts

6 Otto Graham/25 40.00 80.00
7 Joe Perry/25 15.00 40.00

2012 Panini National Treasures Super Bowl Champion Signatures

1 Robert Newhouse/25 15.00 40.00
2 Bob Griese/25 20.00 50.00
3 Deion Sanders/19 50.00 100.00
4 Dwight Clark/25 15.00 40.00
5 Ed McCaffrey/25 15.00 40.00
6 Jack Lambert/25 50.00 100.00
7 Jay Novacek/25 40.00 80.00
8 Jerry Rice/15 100.00 200.00
9 Jim Plunkett/25 15.00 40.00
13 L.C. Greenwood/25 12.00 30.00
14 Larry Little/25 12.00 30.00
16 Paul Warfield/25 15.00 40.00
17 Phil Simms/25 15.00 40.00
18 Richard Dent/25 15.00 40.00
20 Russ Grimm/25 12.00 30.00
21 Shannon Sharpe/25 15.00 40.00
22 Ted Hendricks/25 12.00 30.00
23 Terrell Davis/20 20.00 50.00
25 Eli Manning/25 50.00 100.00

2012 Panini National Treasures Timeline Materials Custom Names

*PRIME/15-25: .6X TO 1.5X BASIC JSY/49
*PRIME/15: .5X TO 1.2X BASIC JSY/25
*TEAM NAME/40-49: .4X TO 1X NAME/49
*TEAM NAME/25: .5X TO 1.2X NAME/49
*TEAM NAME/15-30: .4X TO 1X NAME/15-25
*TN PRIME/15-25: .6X TO 1.5X BASIC JSY/49
*TN PRIME/15: .5X TO 1.2X BASIC JSY/25
2 Barry Sanders/49 15.00 40.00
3 Bart Starr/49 12.00 30.00
4 Bernie Kosar/49 8.00 20.00
5 Bo Jackson/49 10.00 25.00
6 Bob Lilly/49 6.00 15.00
7 Boomer Esiason/49 6.00 15.00
8 Cris Collinsworth/49 6.00 15.00
9 Chuck Howley/49 5.00 12.00
10 Curtis Martin/49 6.00 15.00
11 D.D. Lewis/15 8.00 20.00
12 Dan Fouts/49 6.00 15.00
13 Dan Marino/49 15.00 40.00
14 Warren Moon/49 8.00 20.00
18 Don Maynard/49 6.00 15.00
19 Amani Toomer/49 5.00 12.00
20 Ed Too Tall Jones/49 6.00 15.00
21 John Fuqua/49 6.00 15.00
22 Emmitt Smith/22 15.00 40.00
23 Eric Dickerson/49 6.00 15.00
25 Franco Harris/49 12.00 30.00
26 Fred Biletnikoff/49 8.00 20.00
27 Gale Sayers/25 10.00 25.00
28 George Blanda/49 10.00 25.00
29 Hank Stram/49 8.00 20.00
30 Keith Jackson/49 5.00 12.00
31 Walter Payton/49 20.00 50.00
32 Jay Novacek/49 8.00 20.00
33 Jerry Rice/25 15.00 40.00
34 Jim Kelly/49 12.00 30.00
35 Jim McMahon/49 10.00 25.00
36 Jim Plunkett/49 8.00 20.00
38 Joe Greene/15 15.00 40.00
39 Joe Montana/49 20.00 50.00
40 John Elway/49 12.00 30.00

2012 Panini National Treasures Timeline Materials Signature Custom Names

*TEAM NAME/15: .4X TO 1X BASIC AU/15
1 Joe Namath/15 75.00 135.00
3 Adrian Peterson/15 100.00 175.00
6 Terry Bradshaw/15 75.00 135.00
7 Steve Largent/15 25.00 50.00
9 DeSean Jackson/15 12.00 30.00
11 Doug Williams/15 25.00 50.00
12 Eli Manning/15 60.00 120.00
13 Eric Dickerson/15 25.00 50.00
19 Josh Freeman/15 12.00 30.00

2012 Panini National Treasures Virtuoso Signatures

EXCH EXPIRATION: 10/10/2014
1 Aaron Rodgers/25 EXCH 175.00 300.00
2 Adrian Peterson/25 175.00 350.00
3 Alex Smith/25 25.00 50.00
4 Anquan Boldin/25 12.00 30.00
5 Arian Foster/25 EXCH 25.00 60.00
6 Ben Roethlisberger/25 50.00 100.00
7 Cam Newton/25 40.00 80.00
8 Maurice Jones-Drew/25 12.00 30.00
9 Charles Woodson/25 60.00 120.00
10 Drew Brees/25 60.00 120.00
11 Eli Manning/25 50.00 100.00
12 Frank Gore/25 15.00 40.00
13 Greg Jennings/25 12.00 30.00
14 Hakeem Nicks/25 12.00 30.00
15 Jamaal Charles/25 15.00 40.00
16 Jay Cutler/25 30.00 60.00
17 Joe Flacco/25 40.00 80.00
18 Larry Fitzgerald/25 EXCH 30.00 60.00
19 LeSean McCoy/25 20.00 50.00
20 Marques Colston/25 12.00 30.00
21 Mark Sanchez/25 EXCH 12.00 30.00
22 Marshawn Lynch/25 40.00 80.00
23 Matt Forte/25 12.00 30.00
24 Matt Ryan/25 40.00 80.00
25 Matt Schaub/25 12.00 30.00
26 Matthew Stafford/25 30.00 60.00
27 Victor Cruz/50 10.00 25.00
28 Michael Vick/25 15.00 40.00
29 Mike Wallace/25 EXCH 12.00 30.00
30 Peyton Manning/25 200.00 350.00
31 Philip Rivers/25 EXCH 40.00 80.00
32 Ray Rice/25 12.00 30.00
33 Reggie Wayne/25 20.00 50.00
34 Rob Gronkowski/25 40.00 80.00
35 Roddy White/25 12.00 30.00
36 Sam Bradford/25 EXCH 30.00 60.00
37 Steve Smith/25 15.00 40.00
38 Tim Tebow/25 30.00 80.00
39 Tom Brady/25 250.00 400.00
40 Tony Romo/25 40.00 80.00
41 Troy Polamalu/25 EXCH 75.00 150.00
42 Antonio Brown/50 15.00 40.00
43 Antonio Gates/50 12.00 30.00
44 Beanie Wells/50 EXCH 8.00 20.00
45 Brandon Lloyd/50 8.00 20.00
46 Darren McFadden/25 12.00 30.00
47 Darren Sproles/50 10.00 25.00
48 DeMarco Murray/50 10.00 25.00
49 DeMarcus Ware/50 25.00 50.00
50 DeSean Jackson/50 12.00 30.00
51 Dez Bryant/50 20.00 50.00
52 Dwayne Bowe/50 EXCH 10.00 25.00
53 Michael Turner/50 EXCH 10.00 25.00

2013 Panini National Treasures

1-100 VETERAN PRINT RUN 99
151-340 ROOKIE PRINT RUN 99
1 Larry Fitzgerald 2.50 6.00
2 Michael Floyd 2.00 5.00
3 Patrick Peterson 2.00 5.00
4 Julio Jones 3.00 8.00
5 Matt Ryan 2.50 6.00
6 Tony Gonzalez 2.50 6.00
7 Joe Flacco 2.50 6.00
8 Ray Rice 2.00 5.00
9 Torrey Smith 2.00 5.00
10 C.J. Spiller 2.00 5.00
11 Fred Jackson 2.50 6.00
12 Steve Johnson 2.50 6.00
13 Cam Newton 3.00 8.00
14 Luke Kuechly 2.50 6.00
15 Steve Smith 2.50 6.00
16 Brandon Marshall 2.50 6.00
17 Jay Cutler 2.00 5.00
18 Matt Forte 2.00 5.00
19 A.J. Green 3.00 8.00
20 Andy Dalton 2.50 6.00
21 BenJarvus Green-Ellis 2.50 6.00
22 Brandon Weeden 2.00 5.00
23 Jordan Cameron 2.00 5.00
24 Josh Gordon 2.00 5.00
25 DeMarco Murray 2.50 6.00
26 Dez Bryant 3.00 8.00
27 Jason Witten 2.50 6.00
28 Tony Romo 2.50 6.00
29 Demaryius Thomas 2.50 6.00
30 Eric Decker 2.00 5.00
31 Julius Thomas 2.00 5.00
32 Knowshon Moreno 2.00 5.00
33 Peyton Manning 6.00 15.00
34 Wes Welker 2.50 6.00
35 Calvin Johnson 3.00 8.00
36 Matthew Stafford 2.50 6.00
37 Reggie Bush 2.00 5.00
38 Aaron Rodgers 5.00 12.00
39 Clay Matthews 3.00 8.00
40 Randall Cobb 2.50 6.00
41 Andre Johnson 2.00 5.00
42 Arian Foster 2.50 6.00
43 J.J. Watt 2.50 6.00
44 Andrew Luck 5.00 12.00
45 Reggie Wayne 2.50 6.00
46 T.Y. Hilton 2.50 6.00
47 Trent Richardson 2.00 5.00
48 Cecil Shorts III 2.00 5.00
49 Justin Blackmon 2.00 5.00
50 Maurice Jones-Drew 2.00 5.00
51 Alex Smith 2.50 6.00
52 Dwayne Bowe 2.50 6.00
53 Jamaal Charles 2.50 6.00
54 Lamar Miller 2.00 5.00
55 Mike Wallace 2.00 5.00
56 Ryan Tannehill 2.50 6.00
57 Adrian Peterson 3.00 8.00
58 Greg Jennings 2.00 5.00
59 Kyle Rudolph 2.00 5.00
60 Danny Amendola 2.50 6.00
61 Julian Edelman 3.00 8.00
62 Tom Brady 8.00 20.00
63 Drew Brees 3.00 8.00
64 Jimmy Graham 3.00 8.00
65 Marques Colston 2.00 5.00
66 David Wilson 2.00 5.00
67 Eli Manning 2.50 6.00
68 Victor Cruz 2.50 6.00
69 Bilal Powell 2.00 5.00
70 Jeremy Kerley 2.00 5.00
71 Santonio Holmes 2.00 5.00
72 Darren McFadden 2.50 6.00
73 Denarius Moore 2.00 5.00
74 Terrelle Pryor 2.50 6.00
75 DeSean Jackson 2.50 6.00
76 LeSean McCoy 3.00 8.00
77 Nick Foles 2.50 6.00
78 Antonio Brown 3.00 8.00
79 Ben Roethlisberger 3.00 8.00
80 Troy Polamalu 3.00 8.00
81 Antonio Gates 2.50 6.00
82 Danny Woodhead 6.00 15.00
83 Philip Rivers 3.00 8.00
84 Anquan Boldin 2.00 5.00
85 Colin Kaepernick 2.50 6.00
86 Frank Gore 2.50 6.00
87 Vernon Davis 2.00 5.00
88 Marshawn Lynch 2.50 6.00
89 Richard Sherman 3.00 8.00
90 Russell Wilson 6.00 15.00
91 Chris Givens 2.00 5.00
92 Sam Bradford 2.00 5.00
93 Doug Martin 2.50 6.00
94 Vincent Jackson 2.00 5.00
95 Chris Johnson 2.00 5.00
96 Jake Locker 2.50 6.00
97 Kendall Wright 2.00 5.00
98 Alfred Morris 2.00 5.00
99 Pierre Garcon 2.50 6.00
100 Robert Griffin III 2.00 5.00
101 Clyde Bulldog Turner 3.00 8.00
102 Dutch Clark 3.00 8.00
103 Jim Thorpe 5.00 12.00
104 Red Grange 5.00 12.00
105 Walter Payton 15.00 30.00
106 Art Monk 4.00 10.00
107 Barry Sanders 6.00 15.00
108 Bart Starr 6.00 15.00
109 Bo Jackson 5.00 12.00
110 Bob Griese 4.00 10.00
111 Bob Lilly 3.00 8.00
112 Brett Favre 8.00 20.00
113 Chuck Bednarik 3.00 8.00
114 Dan Fouts 3.00 8.00
115 Dan Marino 8.00 20.00
116 Dave Casper 2.50 6.00
117 Deion Sanders 3.00 8.00
118 Earl Campbell 4.00 10.00
119 Emmitt Smith 8.00 20.00
120 Eric Dickerson 3.00 8.00
121 Fran Tarkenton 4.00 10.00
122 Franco Harris 4.00 10.00
123 Frank Gifford 3.00 8.00
124 Gale Sayers 4.00 10.00
125 Jack Ham 3.00 8.00
126 Jerry Rice 6.00 15.00
127 Jim Brown 5.00 12.00
128 Joe Montana 10.00 25.00
129 Joe Namath 5.00 12.00
130 John Elway 6.00 15.00
131 John Riggins 3.00 8.00
132 Kellen Winslow 3.00 8.00
133 Lance Alworth 3.00 8.00
134 Larry Csonka 4.00 10.00
135 Len Dawson 4.00 10.00
136 Marcus Allen 4.00 10.00
137 Marshall Faulk 3.00 8.00
138 Michael Irvin 4.00 10.00
139 Mike Singletary 4.00 10.00
140 Paul Hornung 4.00 10.00
141 Raymond Berry 3.00 8.00
142 Roger Staubach 5.00 12.00
143 Ronnie Lott 3.00 8.00
144 Sonny Jurgensen 3.00 8.00
145 Steve Largent 4.00 10.00
146 Steve Young 5.00 12.00
147 Ted Hendricks 2.50 6.00
148 Terry Bradshaw 5.00 12.00
149 Tony Dorsett 4.00 10.00
150 Troy Aikman 5.00 12.00
151 Akeem Spence RC 2.50 6.00
152 Andy Mulumba RC 6.00 15.00
153 Armonty Bryant RC 3.00 8.00
154 Bacarri Rambo RC 3.00 8.00
155 Bennie Logan RC 3.00 8.00
156 Chris Jones RC 12.00 30.00
157 Chris Banjo RC 6.00 15.00
158 Corey Lemonier RC 6.00 15.00
159 Darius Johnson RC 3.00 8.00
160 Devin Taylor RC 4.00 10.00
161 Dwayne Gratz RC 2.50 6.00
162 Glenn Foster RC 3.00 8.00
163 J.J. Wilcox RC 20.00 40.00
164 Jahleel Addae RC 2.50 6.00
165 Jeff Heath RC 5.00 12.00
166 Jelani Jenkins RC 3.00 8.00
167 Joe Vellano RC 3.00 8.00
168 John Jenkins RC 2.50 6.00
169 Johnathan Hankins RC 2.50 6.00
170 Jonathan Cooper RC 2.50 6.00
171 Joplo Bartu RC 3.00 8.00
172 Josh Evans RC 2.50 6.00
173 Justin Pugh RC 2.50 6.00
174 Kawann Short RC 2.50 6.00
175 Kyle Juszczyk RC 2.50 6.00
176 Kyle Long RC 6.00 15.00
177 Lane Johnson RC 3.00 8.00
178 Leon McFadden RC 3.00 8.00
179 Logan Ryan RC 3.00 8.00
180 Marcus Cooper RC 3.00 8.00
181 MarQueis Gray RC 2.50 6.00
182 Melvin White RC 3.00 8.00
183 Micah Hyde RC 12.50 25.00
184 Michael Buchanan RC 4.00 10.00
185 Mike Catapano RC 8.00 20.00
186 Myles White RC 5.00 12.00
187 Nickell Robey RC 3.00 8.00
188 Paul Worrilow RC 3.00 8.00
189 Robert Lester RC 2.50 6.00
190 Shamarko Thomas RC 8.00 20.00
191 Sheldon Richardson RC 2.50 6.00
192 Skye Dawson RC 3.00 8.00
193 Star Lotulelei RC 3.00 8.00
194 Sylvester Williams RC 2.50 6.00
195 T.J. McDonald RC 2.50 6.00
196 Tommy Bohanon RC 3.00 8.00
197 Tony Jefferson RC 4.00 10.00
198 Travis Frederick RC 6.00 15.00
199 Vince Williams RC 6.00 15.00
200 Zach Line RC 2.50 6.00
201 Aaron Dobson JSY AU RC 15.00 40.00
202 Andre Ellington JSY AU RC 25.00 60.00
203 C.Michael JSY AU RC 15.00 40.00
204 C.Patterson JSY AU RC 12.00 30.00
205 D.Hopkins JSY AU RC 40.00 80.00
206 Denard Robinson JSY AU RC 12.00 30.00
207 Dion Jordan JSY AU RC 12.00 30.00
208 Eddie Lacy JSY AU RC 60.00 125.00
209 EJ Manuel JSY AU RC 12.00 30.00
210 Gavin Escobar JSY AU RC 15.00 40.00
211 Geno Smith JSY AU RC 12.00 30.00
212 G.Bernard JSY AU RC 12.00 30.00
213 J.Franklin JSY AU RC 12.00 30.00
214 J.Reed JSY AU RC EXCH 15.00 40.00
215 Joseph Randle JSY AU RC 12.00 30.00
216 Justin Hunter JSY AU RC 12.00 30.00
217 Keenan Allen JSY AU RC 25.00 60.00
218 Kenny Stills JSY AU RC 12.00 30.00
219 Knile Davis JSY AU RC 12.00 30.00
220 Landry Jones JSY AU RC 12.00 30.00
221 Le'Veon Bell JSY AU RC 125.00 250.00
222 Manti Te'o JSY AU RC 15.00 40.00
223 M.Lattimore JSY AU RC 12.00 30.00
224 Markus Wheaton JSY AU RC 12.00 30.00
225 M.Goodwin JSY AU RC 15.00 40.00
226 Matt Barkley JSY AU RC 12.00 30.00
227 Mike Gillislee JSY AU RC 12.00 30.00
228 Mike Glennon JSY AU RC 12.00 30.00
229 Montee Ball JSY AU RC 12.00 30.00
230 Quinton Patton JSY AU RC 12.00 30.00
231 Robert Woods JSY AU RC 20.00 50.00
232 Ryan Nassib JSY AU RC 12.00 30.00
233 Stedman Bailey JSY AU RC 12.00 30.00
234 Stepfan Taylor JSY AU RC 12.00 30.00
235 Tavon Austin JSY AU RC 15.00 40.00
236 T.Williams JSY AU RC 25.00 50.00
237 Tyler Eifert JSY AU RC 25.00 50.00
238 Tyler Wilson JSY AU RC 12.00 30.00
239 V.McDonald JSY AU RC 12.00 30.00
240 Zach Ertz JSY AU RC 15.00 40.00
242 Ace Sanders AU RC 4.00 10.00
243 Alan Bonner AU RC 4.00 10.00
246 Arthur Brown AU RC 4.00 10.00
248 Benny Cunningham AU RC 6.00 15.00
249 B.J. Daniels AU RC 6.00 15.00
251 Brad Sorensen AU RC 6.00 15.00
252 Brice Butler AU RC 8.00 20.00
253 Blidi Wreh-Wilson AU RC 5.00 12.00
254 C.J. Anderson AU RC 20.00 50.00
255 Caleb Sturgis AU RC 6.00 15.00
256 Chance Warmack AU RC 4.00 10.00
257 Chris Gragg AU RC 4.00 10.00
258 Chris Harper AU RC 4.00 10.00
259 Chris Thompson AU RC 4.00 10.00
260 Cierre Wood AU RC 4.00 10.00
261 Cobi Hamilton AU RC 4.00 10.00
262 Corey Fuller AU RC 4.00 10.00
263 Cornellius Carradine AU RC 4.00 10.00
264 D.J. Hayden AU RC 4.00 10.00
266 Da'Rick Rogers AU RC 4.00 10.00
267 Darius Slay AU RC 4.00 10.00
268 Datone Jones AU RC 4.00 10.00
269 David Amerson AU RC 4.00 10.00
271 Dennis Johnson AU RC 4.00 10.00
272 Desmond Trufant AU RC 4.00 10.00
273 Dion Sims AU RC 4.00 10.00
274 D.J. Swearinger AU RC 4.00 10.00
275 D.J. Fluker AU RC 4.00 10.00
276 Dustin Hopkins AU RC 4.00 10.00
277 Earl Wolff AU RC 5.00 12.00
278 Eric Fisher AU RC 4.00 10.00
279 Eric Reid AU RC 5.00 12.00
280 Ezekiel Ansah AU RC 4.00 10.00
281 Jack Doyle AU RC 4.00 10.00
282 Jamar Taylor AU RC 4.00 10.00
283 Jamie Collins AU RC 4.00 10.00
284 Jaron Brown AU RC 4.00 10.00
285 Jarvis Jones AU RC 4.00 10.00
286 Jawan Jamison AU RC 4.00 10.00
287 Jeff Tuel AU RC 4.00 10.00
288 Johnthan Banks AU RC 4.00 10.00
289 Jon Bostic AU RC 4.00 10.00
290 Johnathan Cyprien AU RC 4.00 10.00
291 Jordan Poyer AU RC 4.00 10.00
292 Josh Boyce AU RC 4.00 10.00
293 Justin Brown AU RC 6.00 15.00
294 K.Thompkins AU RC 8.00 20.00
295 Kenjon Barner AU RC 4.00 10.00
296 Kenny Vaccaro AU RC 8.00 20.00
297 Kerwynn Williams AU RC 4.00 10.00
298 Kevin Minter AU RC 4.00 10.00
299 Khiry Robinson AU RC 6.00 15.00
300 Kiko Alonso AU RC 5.00 12.00
301 Latavius Murray AU RC 15.00 40.00
302 Levine Toilolo AU RC 5.00 12.00
304 Luke Willson AU RC 8.00 20.00
305 Margus Hunt AU RC 4.00 10.00
306 Marlon Brown AU RC 6.00 15.00
308 Matt Elam AU RC 4.00 10.00
309 Matt McGloin AU RC 15.00 40.00
310 Matt Scott AU RC 4.00 10.00
311 Matt Simms AU RC 5.00 12.00
312 Michael Cox AU RC 5.00 12.00
313 Michael Ford AU RC 6.00 15.00
314 Mike James AU RC 6.00 15.00
315 Mychal Rivera AU RC 4.00 10.00
316 Nick Kasa AU RC 4.00 10.00
317 Nick Moody AU RC 5.00 12.00
318 Kayvon Webster AU RC 5.00 12.00
319 Phillip Thomas AU RC 4.00 10.00
320 Ray Graham AU RC 4.00 10.00
321 Rex Burkhead AU RC 6.00 15.00
322 Robert Alford AU RC 4.00 10.00
323 Rodney Smith AU RC 4.00 10.00
324 Russell Shepard AU RC 4.00 10.00
325 Ryan Griffin AU RC 4.00 10.00
326 Ryan Griffin AU RC 4.00 10.00
327 Ryan Spadola AU RC 5.00 12.00
328 Sam Montgomery AU RC 4.00 10.00
329 Sharrif Floyd AU RC 4.00 10.00
330 Sio Moore AU RC 4.00 10.00
331 Spencer Ware AU RC 10.00 25.00
332 Tavarres King AU RC 4.00 10.00
333 Theo Riddick AU RC 4.00 10.00
334 Travis Kelce AU RC 30.00 60.00
335 Tyler Bray AU RC 4.00 10.00
336 Tyrann Mathieu AU RC 6.00 15.00
337 Xavier Rhodes AU RC 4.00 10.00
338 Zac Dysert AU RC 10.00 25.00
339 Zac Stacy AU RC 4.00 10.00
340 Zach Sudfeld AU RC 4.00 10.00

2013 Panini National Treasures Century Black

*242-340 AU/25: .6X TO 1.5X BASIC AU RC
254 C.J. Anderson AU 40.00 80.00
301 Latavius Murray AU 40.00 80.00

2013 Panini National Treasures Century Gold

*242-340 AU/49: .5X TO 1.2X BASIC AU RC
254 C.J. Anderson AU 30.00 60.00

2013 Panini National Treasures Century Silver

*1-100 VET/25: .6X TO 1.5X BASIC VET/99
*101-150 RET/25: .5X TO 1.2X BASIC RET/50
*151-200 ROOK/25: .6X TO 1.5X RC/99

2013 Panini National Treasures '12 HOF Autographs

1 Chris Doleman 30.00 80.00
2 Cortez Kennedy 30.00 80.00
3 Curtis Martin 30.00 80.00
4 Dermontti Dawson 25.00 60.00
5 Jack Butler 50.00 120.00
6 Willie Roaf 25.00 60.00

2013 Panini National Treasures '13 HOF Autographs

1 Bill Parcells 40.00 80.00
2 Dave Robinson 30.00 60.00
3 Larry Allen 25.00 60.00
4 Jonathan Ogden 40.00 80.00
5 Cris Carter 40.00 100.00
6 Curley Culp 30.00 60.00
7 Warren Sapp 30.00 60.00

2013 Panini National Treasures Century Materials Silver

*GOLD/15-25: .5X TO 1.2X BASIC JSY/49
*GOLD/15: .4X TO 1X BASIC JSY/25
1 Larry Fitzgerald/49 4.00 10.00
2 Michael Floyd/49 3.00 8.00
3 Matt Ryan/49 4.00 10.00
4 Elvis Dumervil/49 3.00 8.00
5 Haloti Ngata/49 3.00 8.00
6 Jacoby Jones/49 3.00 8.00
7 Joe Flacco/49 4.00 10.00
8 Ray Rice/49 3.00 8.00
9 Terrell Suggs/49 3.00 8.00
10 Torrey Smith/49 3.00 8.00
11 C.J. Spiller/49 3.00 8.00
12 Fred Jackson/49 4.00 10.00
13 Mario Williams/49 3.00 8.00
14 Scott Chandler/49 3.00 8.00
15 Steve Johnson/49 4.00 10.00
17 Cam Newton/49 5.00 12.00
19 Gale Sayers/49 6.00 15.00
20 Mike Singletary/49 6.00 15.00
21 Walter Payton/49 15.00 40.00
22 A.J. Green/49 5.00 12.00
23 Andy Dalton/49 4.00 10.00
24 BenJarvus Green-Ellis/49 4.00 10.00
25 Geno Atkins/49 4.00 10.00
26 Jermaine Gresham/49 4.00 10.00
27 Vontaze Burfict/49 5.00 12.00
28 Brandon Weeden/49 3.00 8.00
29 D'Qwell Jackson/49 3.00 8.00
30 Jim Brown/49 8.00 20.00
31 Joe Haden/49 3.00 8.00
32 Jordan Cameron/49 3.00 8.00
33 Josh Gordon/49 6.00 15.00
34 Travis Benjamin/49 3.00 8.00
35 Deion Sanders/49 8.00 20.00
36 Dez Bryant/49 6.00 15.00
37 Tony Dorsett/49 6.00 15.00
38 Tony Romo/49 4.00 10.00
39 Troy Aikman/49 6.00 15.00
40 Champ Bailey/49 4.00 10.00
41 Demaryius Thomas/49 4.00 10.00
42 Eric Decker/49 3.00 8.00
43 John Elway/49 8.00 20.00
44 Knowshon Moreno/49 3.00 8.00
45 Peyton Manning/49 10.00 25.00
46 Von Miller/49 4.00 10.00
47 Wes Welker/49 4.00 10.00
48 Barry Sanders/49 8.00 20.00
49 Calvin Johnson/25 10.00 25.00
51 Matthew Stafford/49 4.00 10.00
52 Brett Favre/25 12.00 30.00
53 Arian Foster/25 5.00 12.00
54 Andrew Luck/49 8.00 20.00
55 T.Y. Hilton/49 4.00 10.00
56 Justin Blackmon/49 3.00 8.00
57 Maurice Jones-Drew/49 3.00 8.00
58 Alex Smith/49 4.00 10.00
59 Derrick Johnson/49 3.00 8.00
60 Dwayne Bowe/49 4.00 10.00
61 Jamaal Charles/49 4.00 10.00
62 Justin Houston/49 3.00 8.00
63 Marcus Allen/49 6.00 15.00
64 Bob Griese/49 6.00 15.00
65 Brian Hartline/49 3.00 8.00
66 Cameron Wake/49 3.00 8.00
67 Dan Marino/49 10.00 25.00
68 Daniel Thomas/49 3.00 8.00
69 Lamar Miller/49 3.00 8.00
70 Mike Wallace/49 3.00 8.00
71 Reshad Jones/49 3.00 8.00
72 Ryan Tannehill/49 4.00 10.00
73 Adrian Peterson/49 5.00 12.00
74 Tom Brady/49 10.00 25.00
75 Drew Brees/49 5.00 12.00
77 Eli Manning/49 4.00 10.00
78 Rueben Randle/49 3.00 8.00
79 Jeremy Kerley/49 3.00 8.00
80 Joe Namath/49 8.00 20.00
81 Ted Hendricks/49 4.00 10.00
82 LeSean McCoy/49 5.00 12.00
83 Antonio Brown/49 5.00 12.00
84 Bobby Layne/25 6.00 15.00
85 Antonio Gates/49 4.00 10.00
86 Philip Rivers/49 5.00 12.00
87 Colin Kaepernick/49 4.00 10.00
88 Frank Gore/49 4.00 10.00
89 Jerry Rice/49 8.00 20.00
90 Joe Montana/49 12.00 30.00
91 Ronnie Lott/49 4.00 10.00
92 Steve Young/49 8.00 20.00
93 Kam Chancellor/49 12.00 30.00
94 Russell Wilson/49 10.00 25.00
95 Chris Givens/49 3.00 8.00
96 Doug Martin/49 4.00 10.00
97 Chris Johnson/49 3.00 8.00
98 Jake Locker/49 4.00 10.00
99 Kendall Wright/49 3.00 8.00
100 Nate Washington/49 3.00 8.00

2013 Panini National Treasures Century Signature Materials Gold

2 Michael Floyd/15 10.00 25.00
5 Courtney Upshaw/25 10.00 25.00
6 Jamal Lewis/25 15.00 40.00
9 Torrey Smith/25
10 C.J. Spiller/25
11 Fred Jackson/25
12 Mario Williams/25 15.00 40.00
19 Matt Forte/25
20 A.J. Green/25
21 Andy Dalton/25 12.00 30.00
24 Jordan Cameron/25 10.00 25.00
25 Josh Gordon/25
28 DeMarcus Ware/25
29 Dez Bryant/25 25.00 50.00
30 Jason Witten/25
33 Demaryius Thomas/25
34 Eric Decker/25
35 Julius Thomas/15
37 Rahim Moore/25 10.00 25.00
41 Matthew Stafford/15
47 Andrew Luck/25 100.00 200.00
49 T.Y. Hilton/25
52 Alex Smith/15
53 Dontari Poe/25 10.00 25.00
54 Eric Berry/25
55 Dwayne Bowe/25
56 Jamaal Charles/25 15.00 40.00
58 Lamar Miller/25 10.00 25.00
59 Mike Wallace/25
65 Jimmy Graham/25
69 Rueben Randle/25 15.00 40.00
70 Victor Cruz/25 12.00 30.00
73 Harry Douglas/25 10.00 25.00
75 Darren McFadden/25
76 Terrelle Pryor/15
77 LeSean McCoy/15
80 Antonio Gates/25
82 Malcom Floyd/25
88 Sidney Rice/25 10.00 25.00
89 Zach Miller/25 20.00 50.00
90 Chris Givens/25 10.00 25.00
95 Akeem Ayers/25 10.00 25.00
96 Shonn Greene/25 10.00 25.00
97 Nate Washington/25 10.00 25.00
98 Kendall Wright/25 12.00 30.00
99 Alfred Morris/25

2013 Panini National Treasures Century Signature Materials Silver

16 Steve Smith/20 12.00 30.00
24 Jordan Cameron/49 6.00 15.00
25 Josh Gordon/49
26 Chuck Howley/49
35 Julius Thomas/49
37 Rahim Moore/49 6.00 15.00
38 Trindon Holliday/49 8.00 20.00
49 T.Y. Hilton/49
53 Dontari Poe/49 6.00 15.00
69 Rueben Randle/40 6.00 15.00
70 Victor Cruz/49 15.00 40.00
71 Jeremy Kerley/25 8.00 20.00
73 Harry Douglas/49 6.00 15.00
76 Terrelle Pryor/25
78 Jerome Bettis/49 40.00 80.00
81 Junior Seau/25 40.00 80.00
90 Chris Givens/49 6.00 15.00
95 Akeem Ayers/49 6.00 15.00
96 Shonn Greene/49 6.00 15.00
97 Nate Washington/49 8.00 20.00
98 Kendall Wright/49 6.00 15.00
99 Alfred Morris/49 6.00 15.00

2013 Panini National Treasures Century Signatures Gold

*SILVER/49: .25X TO .6X GOLD AU/25
2 Michael Floyd 5.00 12.00
4 Jamal Lewis
7 Dennis Pitta 6.00 15.00
8 Torrey Smith
9 C.J. Spiller
10 Fred Jackson
11 Chris Hogan 100.00 200.00
15 Brandon Marshall
17 Matt Forte
19 Andy Dalton 10.00 25.00
20 Jordan Cameron 5.00 12.00
21 Josh Gordon
23 DeMarcus Ware 8.00 20.00
24 Dez Bryant 25.00 50.00
25 Jason Witten
28 Demaryius Thomas
29 Von Miller
30 Eric Decker
31 Julius Thomas
33 Trindon Holliday 8.00 20.00
40 Jordy Nelson
41 Jarrett Boykin 15.00 40.00
46 T.Y. Hilton
49 Dwayne Bowe
50 Jamaal Charles 8.00 20.00
51 Charles Clay
52 Lamar Miller 5.00 12.00
53 Mike Wallace
58 Danny Amendola
60 Jimmy Graham
64 Andre Brown 6.00 15.00
65 Rueben Randle 6.00 15.00
66 Victor Cruz 8.00 20.00
67 Chris Ivory 8.00 20.00
68 Jeremy Kerley 5.00 12.00
75 Terrelle Pryor
76 LeSean McCoy
86 Richard Sherman 100.00 200.00
91 Chris Givens 5.00 12.00
94 Doug Martin 6.00 15.00
95 Vincent Jackson
96 Delanie Walker 5.00 12.00
97 Kendall Wright 5.00 12.00
98 Alfred Morris
99 Kirk Cousins

2013 Panini National Treasures Colossal Materials

*PRIME/25: .6X TO 1.5X BASIC JSY/49
1 A.J. Green 5.00 12.00
2 Alex Smith 4.00 10.00
3 Alfred Morris 3.00 8.00
4 Andrew Luck 8.00 20.00
5 Andy Dalton 4.00 10.00
6 Antonio Gates 4.00 10.00
7 Brian Hartline 3.00 8.00
8 C.J. Spiller 3.00 8.00
9 Chris Johnson 3.00 8.00
10 Colin Kaepernick 4.00 10.00
11 Demaryius Thomas 4.00 10.00
12 D'Qwell Jackson 3.00 8.00
13 Dwayne Bowe 4.00 10.00
14 Fred Jackson 4.00 10.00
15 Geno Atkins 3.00 8.00
16 Jake Locker 4.00 10.00
17 Jamaal Charles 4.00 10.00
18 Joe Flacco 4.00 10.00
19 Josh Gordon 3.00 8.00
20 Julio Jones 5.00 12.00
21 Justin Houston 3.00 8.00
22 Kendall Wright 3.00 8.00
23 Knowshon Moreno 3.00 8.00
24 Lamar Miller 3.00 8.00
25 Larry Fitzgerald 4.00 10.00
26 Mike Wallace 3.00 8.00
27 Nate Washington 3.00 8.00
28 Peyton Manning 25.00 60.00
29 Ray Rice 3.00 8.00
30 Russell Wilson 10.00 25.00
31 Robert Griffin III 3.00 8.00
32 Ryan Mathews 5.00 12.00
33 Ryan Tannehill 4.00 10.00
34 Steve Johnson 4.00 10.00
35 Wes Welker 4.00 10.00
36 Jordan Cameron 3.00 8.00

2013 Panini National Treasures Colossal Materials Signature Jersey Numbers

1 Adrian Peterson/25 75.00 150.00
2 Alfred Morris/25 EXCH 12.00 30.00
3 Andrew Luck/25 100.00 200.00
4 Andy Dalton/25 15.00 40.00
5 Antonio Gates/25 EXCH 15.00 40.00
7 Bo Jackson/25 75.00 135.00
8 Brandon Marshall/25
9 C.J. Spiller/25 20.00 50.00
10 Cam Newton/25 125.00 250.00
13 Colin Kaepernick/25 75.00 135.00
14 Dan Marino/25 100.00 200.00
16 Demaryius Thomas/25
18 Doug Martin/25 15.00 40.00
19 Drew Brees/25 50.00 100.00
20 Dwayne Bowe/25 EXCH 15.00 40.00
21 Earl Campbell/25 25.00 60.00
22 Eli Manning/25 50.00 100.00
24 Jamaal Charles/25 20.00 50.00
25 Jerry Rice/25 100.00 200.00
27 Joe Flacco/25
28 Joe Montana/25 125.00 250.00
29 Joe Namath/25 90.00 150.00
30 John Elway/25 100.00 200.00
32 LeSean McCoy/25 25.00 60.00
33 Matt Ryan/25 25.00 60.00
34 Matt Schaub/25 12.00 30.00
35 Matthew Stafford/25 25.00 60.00
36 Peyton Manning/25 175.00 300.00
37 Philip Rivers/25
40 Torrey Smith/25

2013 Panini National Treasures Colossal Pro Bowl Materials

*PRIME/25: .8X TO 2X BASIC JSY/99
*PB/99: .4X TO 1X COLOSSAL PB/99
*PB PRM/18-25: .8X TO 2X COLOS.PB/99
1 Lorenzo Alexander 3.00 8.00
2 Zane Beadles 3.00 8.00
3 Duane Brown 3.00 8.00
4 Jamaal Charles 4.00 10.00
5 Josh Cribbs 3.00 8.00
6 Owen Daniels 3.00 8.00
7 Jerome Felton 3.00 8.00
8 London Fletcher 4.00 10.00
9 Tim Jennings 3.00 8.00
10 Derrick Johnson 3.00 8.00
11 Julio Jones 5.00 12.00
12 Ryan Kerrigan 3.00 8.00
13 Doug Martin 4.00 10.00
14 Robert Mathis 3.00 8.00
15 Gerald McCoy 3.00 8.00
16 William Moore 3.00 8.00
17 Thomas Morstead 3.00 8.00
18 Chris Myers 3.00 8.00
19 Russell Okung 3.00 8.00
20 Patrick Peterson 3.00 8.00
21 Kyle Rudolph 3.00 8.00
22 Jeff Saturday 3.00 8.00
23 Matt Schaub 3.00 8.00
24 Josh Sitton 3.00 8.00
25 Chris Snee 4.00 10.00
26 Anthony Spencer 3.00 8.00
27 C.J. Spiller 3.00 8.00
28 Ndamukong Suh 4.00 10.00
29 Joe Thomas 3.00 8.00
30 J.J. Watt 8.00 20.00
31 Russell Wilson 10.00 25.00

2013 Panini National Treasures Hall of Fame 50th Anniversary Materials

*PRIME/25: .6X TO 1.5X BASIC JSY/50
1 Arnie Weinmeister/50 10.00 25.00
2 Barry Sanders/50 12.00 30.00
3 Bob Griese/50 8.00 20.00
4 Bob Lilly/50 6.00 15.00
5 Bobby Layne/50 8.00 20.00
6 Bobby Mitchell/50 6.00 15.00
7 Carl Eller/50 5.00 12.00
8 Chuck Bednarik/50 6.00 15.00
10 Curtis Martin/50 6.00 15.00
11 Dan Marino/50 15.00 40.00
12 Deion Sanders/50 10.00 25.00
14 Eric Dickerson/50 6.00 15.00
15 Fred Biletnikoff/50 8.00 20.00
16 Gale Sayers/50 8.00 20.00
18 Jerry Rice/50 12.00 30.00
19 Jim Brown/50 10.00 25.00
20 Jim Kelly/50 8.00 20.00
22 Joe Montana/50 15.00 40.00
23 Joe Namath/50 12.00 30.00
24 John Elway/50 12.00 30.00
25 Johnny Unitas/50 15.00 40.00
26 Len Dawson/50 8.00 20.00
27 Marcus Allen/50 8.00 20.00
28 Marshall Faulk/50 6.00 15.00
29 Mike Singletary/50 8.00 20.00
30 Paul Warfield/50 6.00 15.00
31 Raymond Berry/50 6.00 15.00
33 Roger Staubach/50 10.00 25.00
34 Ronnie Lott/50 6.00 15.00
35 Steve Largent/50 8.00 20.00
36 Steve Young/50 10.00 25.00
37 Ted Hendricks/50 6.00 15.00
38 Terry Bradshaw/50 10.00 25.00
39 Thurman Thomas/50 6.00 15.00
40 Tony Dorsett/50 8.00 20.00
41 Troy Aikman/50 10.00 25.00
42 Walter Payton/50 15.00 40.00

2013 Panini National Treasures Hall of Fame 50th Anniversary Signature Materials

EXCH EXPIRATION: 9/26/2015
*PRIME/15-25: .6X TO 1.5X JSY AU/50
1 Barry Sanders/50 90.00 150.00
2 Bart Starr/50 75.00 125.00
3 Bob Griese/50 20.00 50.00
4 Bob Lilly/50 15.00 40.00
5 Bobby Mitchell/50 15.00 40.00
7 Carl Eller/50 EXCH 15.00 40.00
8 Chuck Bednarik/50 15.00 40.00
10 Curtis Martin/50 25.00 60.00
11 Dan Fouts/25 50.00 120.00
13 Dan Marino/50 100.00 200.00
14 Deion Sanders/50 40.00 100.00
15 Earl Campbell/50 20.00 50.00
17 Eric Dickerson/50 20.00 50.00
18 Forrest Gregg/50 15.00 40.00
20 Fred Biletnikoff/50 20.00 50.00
21 Gale Sayers/50 30.00 60.00
22 Howie Long/25 30.00 80.00
23 Jackie Slater/50 15.00 40.00
24 Jackie Smith/50 12.00 30.00
25 Jan Stenerud/50 12.00 30.00
26 Jerry Rice/50 90.00 150.00
27 Jim Brown/50 40.00 80.00
28 Jim Kelly/50 30.00 60.00
29 Jim Otto/25 20.00 50.00

30 Joe Greene/25 25.00 60.00
31 Joe Montana/50 50.00 100.00
32 Joe Namath/50
33 John Elway/50 75.00 150.00
35 Larry Csonka/50 20.00 50.00
36 Len Dawson/50 20.00 50.00
37 Marcus Allen/50 20.00 50.00
38 Marshall Faulk/50 20.00 50.00
39 Mike Ditka/50 40.00 80.00
40 Mike Singletary/50 20.00 50.00
41 Ozzie Newsome/50 15.00 40.00
42 Paul Hornung/50 20.00 50.00
43 Paul Warfield/50 15.00 40.00
44 Randall McDaniel/50 20.00 50.00
45 Randy White/25 20.00 50.00
46 Raymond Berry/50 15.00 40.00
47 Rod Woodson/50 40.00 80.00
48 Roger Staubach/50 40.00 100.00
49 Ronnie Lott/50 20.00 50.00
51 Steve Largent/50 20.00 50.00
52 Steve Young/50 40.00 80.00
53 Ted Hendricks/50 12.00 30.00
54 Terry Bradshaw/50 40.00 80.00
55 Thurman Thomas/50 15.00 40.00
56 Tony Dorsett/50 25.00 60.00
57 Troy Aikman/50 40.00 80.00
58 Warren Moon/50 20.00 50.00

2013 Panini National Treasures Jumbo Prime Booklet Signatures

2 Alfred Morris/15 20.00 50.00
3 Andrew Luck/20 150.00 250.00
4 Andy Dalton/25 15.00 40.00
5 Antonio Gates/25 20.00 50.00
6 C.J. Spiller/25
7 Cam Newton/25 40.00 100.00
8 Colin Kaepernick/25 50.00 100.00
9 Demaryius Thomas/25
10 Doug Martin/25 40.00 80.00
12 Dwayne Bowe/25 15.00 40.00
13 Eric Decker/25
14 Jamaal Charles/25 20.00 50.00
17 Lamar Miller/25
18 LeSean McCoy/25 20.00 50.00
22 Peyton Manning/25 150.00 300.00
23 Philip Rivers/25
27 Ryan Tannehill/25 25.00 60.00
30 Torrey Smith/25
32 Von Miller/25

2013 Panini National Treasures NFL Gear Combos

*PRIME/25: .6X TO 1.5X BASIC JSY/99
*QUAD/99: .4X TO 1X BASIC JSY/99
*QUAD PRM/25: .6X TO 1.5X BASIC JSY/99
*TRIPLE/99: .4X TO 1X BASIC JSY/99
*TRIPLE PRM/25: .6X TO 1.5X BASIC JSY/99
1 Aaron Dobson 2.00 5.00
2 Andre Ellington 2.00 5.00
3 Christine Michael 2.00 5.00
4 Cordarrelle Patterson 2.00 5.00
5 DeAndre Hopkins 5.00 12.00
6 Denard Robinson 2.00 5.00
7 Dion Jordan 2.00 5.00
8 Eddie Lacy 2.00 5.00
9 EJ Manuel 2.00 5.00
10 Gavin Escobar 2.00 5.00
11 Geno Smith 2.00 5.00
12 Giovani Bernard 2.00 5.00
13 Johnathan Franklin 2.00 5.00
14 Jordan Reed 3.00 8.00
15 Joseph Randle 2.00 5.00
16 Justin Hunter 2.00 5.00
17 Keenan Allen 4.00 10.00
18 Kenny Stills 2.00 5.00
19 Knile Davis 2.00 5.00
20 Landry Jones 2.00 5.00
21 Le'Veon Bell 6.00 15.00
22 Manti Te'o 2.50 6.00
23 Marcus Lattimore 2.00 5.00
24 Markus Wheaton 2.00 5.00
25 Marquise Goodwin 2.00 5.00
26 Matt Barkley 2.00 5.00
27 Mike Gillislee 2.00 5.00
28 Mike Glennon 2.00 5.00
29 Montee Ball 2.00 5.00
30 Quinton Patton 2.00 5.00
31 Robert Woods 3.00 8.00
32 Ryan Nassib 2.00 5.00
33 Stedman Bailey 2.00 5.00
34 Stepfan Taylor 2.00 5.00
35 Tavon Austin 2.50 6.00
36 Terrance Williams 5.00 12.00
37 Tyler Eifert 2.00 5.00
38 Tyler Wilson 2.00 5.00
39 Vance McDonald 2.50 6.00
40 Zach Ertz 4.00 10.00

2013 Panini National Treasures NFL Gear Dual Player Materials

*PRIME/25: .6X TO 1.5X DUAL/97-99
1 A.Ellington/S.Taylor/99 2.00 5.00
2 M.Goodwin/R.Woods/99 3.00 8.00
3 G.Bernard/T.Eifert/99 2.00 5.00
4 G.Escobar/T.Williams/99 2.00 5.00
5 E.Lacy/J.Franklin/99 2.00 5.00
6 D.Jordan/M.Gillislee/99 2.00 5.00
7 M.Barkley/Z.Ertz/99 4.00 10.00
8 L.Bell/M.Wheaton/99 6.00 15.00
9 K.Allen/M.Te'o/99 5.00 12.00
10 Q.Patton/V.McDonald/99 2.50 6.00
11 S.Bailey/T.Austin/99 2.50 6.00
12 A.Ellington/T.Mathieu/99 3.00 8.00
13 E.Manuel/R.Woods/99 3.00 8.00
16 D.Jordan/E.Ansah/99 2.00 5.00
18 D.Hopkins/T.Austin/99 5.00 12.00
19 E.Manuel/G.Smith/99 2.00 5.00
20 K.Davis/T.Kelce/99 5.00 12.00
21 E.Manuel/K.Alonso/99 2.50 6.00
22 S.Floyd/X.Rhodes/99 4.00 10.00
23 K.Stills/K.Vaccaro/99 2.00 5.00
24 D.Milliner/S.Richardson/99 2.00 5.00
25 C.Warmack/J.Hunter/97 2.00 5.00
26 C.Thompson/J.Reed/99 3.00 8.00
27 C.Patterson/J.Hunter/99 2.00 5.00
28 G.Bernard/L.Bell/99 6.00 15.00
29 E.Lacy/M.Ball/99 2.00 5.00
30 M.Barkley/M.Glennon/99 2.00 5.00

2013 Panini National Treasures Notable Nicknames

3 Andy Dalton/25 60.00 120.00
10 Darren McFadden/25
12 Doug Martin/25
15 Frank Gore/25
29 Manti Te'o/25 20.00 50.00
30 Tyrann Mathieu/25
31 Bill Parcells/25
40 Gale Sayers/25 90.00 150.00
42 Jack Ham/25 75.00 135.00
58 Sonny Jurgensen/25 20.00 40.00

2013 Panini National Treasures Prime Pairings

1 A.Brown/B.Brown/25 12.00 30.00
3 A.Rodgers/C.Matthews/25 200.00 300.00
11 B.Powell/C.Ivory/25 10.00 25.00
12 B.Brown/L.McCoy/25 15.00 40.00
15 M.Floyd/R.Housler/25 10.00 25.00
16 H.Douglas/M.Ryan/25 15.00 40.00
17 D.Trufant/R.Alford/25 10.00 25.00
19 C.Munnerlyn/L.Kuechly/25 12.00 30.00
20 G.Graham/O.Daniels/25 10.00 25.00
21 E.Berry/S.Smith/25 15.00 40.00
22 K.Misi/O.Vernon/23 8.00 20.00
23 K.Robinson/P.Thomas/25 12.00 30.00
25 B.Butler/M.Rivera/25 10.00 25.00
26 A.Gates/K.Winslow/25

27 K.Wright/N.Washington/25 10.00 25.00
28 A.Ayers/D.Morgan/25 10.00 25.00
32 Haden/Taylor/Ward/25 12.00 30.00
33 Landry/Angerer/Davis/25 10.00 25.00
34 Cyprien/Posluszny/Alualu/24 10.00 25.00
35 Clay/Miller/Tannehill/25 12.00 30.00
36 Dbsn/Edlmn/Thmpkns/25 15.00 40.00
37 McCourty/Hightower/Mayo/20 15.00 40.00
38 Nicks/Randle/Cruz/25 20.00 50.00
39 Brown/Jacobs/Wilson/25 12.00 30.00
40 Kerley/Winslow/Hill/15 15.00 40.00
41 Cox/Kendricks/Allen/20 10.00 25.00
42 Wgnr/Mbne/Shrmn/20 60.00 120.00
43 Clayborn/Bowers/Barron/25 12.00 30.00
45 Wlms/Alnso/Wlms/Brdhm/25 10.00 25.00
47 Wttn/Bstc/McClln/Pa/25 20.00 50.00
48 Grn/Dltn/Jns/Efrt/20 50.00 100.00
50 Brdfrd/Bsn/Rvrs/Hrzlch/19 15.00 40.00
51 Rys/Englsh/Glchrst/Ingrm/24
53 Mnl/Smth/Brkly/Glnnn/25
55 Hpkns/Rd/Alln/Wllms/25
56 Rd/Wrght/Efrt/Ertz/25 15.00 40.00
57 Ogltre/Mngo/Alnso/Mre/25
58 Pttrsn/Stlls/Gdwn/Astn/25 10.00 25.00

2013 Panini National Treasures Rookie Colossal Jersey Number Signatures

*PRIME/25: .6X TO 1.5X JSY NUM/99
1 Aaron Dobson 6.00 15.00
2 Andre Ellington 12.00 30.00
3 Christine Michael 15.00 40.00
4 Cordarrelle Patterson 6.00 15.00
5 DeAndre Hopkins 15.00 40.00
6 Denard Robinson 6.00 15.00
7 Dion Jordan 6.00 15.00
8 Eddie Lacy 6.00 15.00
9 EJ Manuel 6.00 15.00
10 Gavin Escobar 6.00 15.00
11 Geno Smith 6.00 15.00
12 Giovani Bernard 6.00 15.00
13 Johnathan Franklin 6.00 15.00
14 Jordan Reed 12.00 30.00
15 Joseph Randle 6.00 15.00
16 Justin Hunter 6.00 15.00
17 Keenan Allen 12.00 30.00
18 Kenny Stills 6.00 15.00
19 Knile Davis 6.00 15.00
20 Landry Jones 6.00 15.00
21 Le'Veon Bell 30.00 80.00
22 Manti Te'o 8.00 20.00
23 Marcus Lattimore 6.00 15.00
24 Markus Wheaton 8.00 20.00
25 Marquise Goodwin 8.00 20.00
26 Matt Barkley 6.00 15.00
27 Mike Gillislee 6.00 15.00
28 Mike Glennon 6.00 15.00
29 Montee Ball 8.00 20.00
30 Quinton Patton 6.00 15.00
31 Robert Woods 10.00 25.00
32 Ryan Nassib 6.00 15.00
33 Stedman Bailey 6.00 15.00
34 Stepfan Taylor 6.00 15.00
35 Tavon Austin 8.00 20.00
36 Terrance Williams 6.00 15.00
37 Tyler Eifert 6.00 15.00
38 Tyler Wilson 6.00 15.00
39 Vance McDonald 8.00 20.00
40 Zach Ertz 12.00 30.00

2013 Panini National Treasures Rookie Jumbo Prime Booklet Signatures

1 Aaron Dobson 0.00 20.00
2 Andre Ellington 8.00 20.00
3 Christine Michael 20.00 50.00
4 Cordarrelle Patterson 8.00 20.00
5 DeAndre Hopkins 20.00 50.00
6 Denard Robinson 8.00 20.00
7 Dion Jordan 8.00 20.00
8 Eddie Lacy 8.00 20.00
9 EJ Manuel 8.00 20.00
10 Gavin Escobar 8.00 20.00
11 Geno Smith 8.00 20.00
12 Giovani Bernard 8.00 20.00
13 Johnathan Franklin 8.00 20.00
14 Jordan Reed 12.00 30.00
15 Joseph Randle 8.00 20.00
16 Justin Hunter 8.00 20.00
17 Keenan Allen 15.00 40.00
18 Kenny Stills 8.00 20.00
19 Knile Davis 15.00 40.00
20 Landry Jones 8.00 20.00
21 Le'Veon Bell 25.00 60.00
22 Manti Te'o 10.00 25.00
23 Marcus Lattimore 8.00 20.00
24 Markus Wheaton 8.00 20.00
25 Marquise Goodwin 8.00 20.00
26 Matt Barkley 8.00 20.00
27 Mike Gillislee 8.00 20.00
28 Mike Glennon 8.00 20.00
29 Montee Ball 8.00 20.00
30 Quinton Patton 8.00 20.00
31 Robert Woods 12.00 30.00
32 Ryan Nassib 8.00 20.00
33 Stedman Bailey 8.00 20.00
34 Stepfan Taylor 8.00 20.00
35 Tavon Austin 10.00 25.00
36 Terrance Williams 8.00 20.00
37 Tyler Eifert 8.00 20.00
38 Tyler Wilson 8.00 20.00
39 Vance McDonald 10.00 25.00
40 Zach Ertz 15.00 40.00

2013 Panini National Treasures Rookie NFL Gear Dual Materials Signatures

*DUAL GEAR/99: .3X TO .8X JSY NUM/99
*PRIME/25: .5X TO 1.2X JSY NUM/99
*TRIO GEAR/25: .4X TO 1X JSY NUM/99
*QUAD GEAR/25: .4X TO 1X JSY NUM/99

2013 Panini National Treasures Rookie Signature Materials Black

*NO AU/25: .6X TO 1.5X SILVER/99
*201-240 GLD/25: .6X TO 1.5X JSY AU RC/99
*256-341 GLD/15-25: .6X TO 1.5X SLV/49-99
204 Cordarrelle Patterson 15.00 40.00
208 Eddie Lacy 150.00 300.00
217 Keenan Allen 175.00 300.00
271 Zac Stacy/25 10.00 25.00

2013 Panini National Treasures Rookie Signature Materials Gold

208 Eddie Lacy/49 150.00 300.00
217 Keenan Allen/49 50.00 100.00
271 Zac Stacy/49 8.00 20.00

2013 Panini National Treasures Rookie Signature Materials Silver

164 Jahleel Addae/99 No AU 2.50 6.00
170 Jonathan Cooper/99 No AU 2.50 6.00
177 Lane Johnson/99 No AU 3.00 8.00
191 Sheldon Richardson/99 No AU 2.50 6.00
256 Chance Warmack/99 6.00 15.00
257 Chris Gragg/99 6.00 15.00
259 Chris Thompson/99 6.00 15.00
269 David Amerson/99 6.00 15.00
270 Dee Milliner/49 6.00 15.00
271 Zac Stacy/99 6.00 15.00
273 Dion Sims/99 6.00 15.00
275 D.J. Fluker/99 6.00 15.00
278 Eric Fisher/99 6.00 15.00
279 Eric Reid/99 15.00 40.00
280 Ezekiel Ansah/99 6.00 15.00
296 Kenny Vaccaro/99 6.00 15.00
300 Kiko Alonso/99 8.00 20.00
303 Luke Joeckel/99 0.00 15.00
305 Margus Hunt/99 6.00 15.00
308 Matt Elam/99 6.00 15.00
318 Kayvon Webster/99 8.00 20.00
329 Sharrif Floyd/99 6.00 15.00
334 Travis Kelce/99 30.00 60.00
336 Tyrann Mathieu/99 10.00 25.00
337 Xavier Rhodes/99 6.00 15.00
341 Nico Johnson/99 8.00 20.00

2013 Panini National Treasures Team Quads Materials

*PRIME/25: .6X TO 1.5X QUAD/40-99
*PRIME/25: .5X TO 1.2X QUAD/25
1 Ellngtn/Rbrts/Ftzgrld/Flyd/99 6.00 15.00
2 Jns/Ryn/White/Grzlz/99 8.00 20.00
3 Jns/Flcco/Rce/Smth/99 8.00 20.00
4 Spllr/Mnl/Jcksn/Alnso/99 3.00 8.00
5 Gdwn/Wds/Chndlr/Jhnsn/99 4.00 10.00
6 Nwtn/Wllms/Olsn/Smth/99 8.00 20.00
7 Jffry/Mrshll/Ctlr/Frte/99 15.00 40.00
8 Grn/Dltn/Ells/Grshm/99 8.00 20.00
9 Grn/Brnrd/Grshm/Efrt/99 4.00 10.00
10 Wdn/Cmrn/Grdn/Bnjmn/99 5.00 12.00
11 Mrry/Brynt/Wttn/Rmo/49 12.00 30.00
12 Thms/Mrno/Mnnng/Wlkr/99 15.00 40.00
13 Thms/Dckr/Thms/Wlkr/99 12.00 30.00
16 Jhnsn/Fstr/Hpkns/Schb/25 8.00 20.00
17 Lck/Flnr/Brwn/Hltn/99 10.00 25.00
18 Rbnsn/Blckmn/Jckl/Drw/99 6.00 15.00
19 Smth/McClstr/Bwe/Chrls/99 6.00 15.00
20 Jhnsn/Pe/Brry/Hstn/99 6.00 15.00
21 Hrtlne/Mllr/Wlce/Tnnhll/99 6.00 15.00
22 Ptrsn/Grnwy/Alln/Rdlph/49 8.00 20.00
24 Sprls/Brs/Grhm/Clstn/49 10.00 25.00
25 Jcbs/Wlsn/Mnnng/Ncks/49 10.00 25.00
26 Smth/Krly/Hlms/Hll/99 2.50 6.00
27 McFddn/Mre/Frd/Pryr/99 6.00 15.00
28 Jcksn/Mcln/McCy/Vck/99 8.00 20.00
30 Gts/Wdhd/Rvrs/Mthws/99 8.00 20.00
31 Gts/Ryl/Alln/Brwn/99 6.00 15.00
32 Kprnck/Gre/Wlls/Dvs/99 6.00 15.00
33 Tte/Wlsn/Rce/Mllr/40 12.00 30.00
34 Brwr/Thms/Chcllr/Shrmn/99 40.00 80.00
35 Gvns/Pd/Lrnts/Brdfrd/99 5.00 12.00
37 Jhnsn/Lckr/Wrght/Wshngtn/99 6.00 15.00
38 Mrrs/Hnkrsn/Grcn/Grffn/99 6.00 15.00

2013 Panini National Treasures Timeline Materials Custom Names Prime

*PRIME/25: .5X TO 1.2X BASIC JSY/25
*TEAM PRIME/15-25: .4X TO 1X NAME PRM
23 Josh Gordon/25 8.00 20.00

2013 Panini National Treasures Timeline Materials Signature Custom Names

*TEAM NAME/20-25: .4X TO 1X NAME/20-25
1 A.J. Green/25 20.00 50.00
5 Alfred Morris/25 10.00 25.00
6 Andy Dalton/25 12.00 30.00
7 Antonio Gates/25 12.00 30.00
11 C.J. Spiller/25 10.00 25.00
13 Darren McFadden/25 12.00 30.00
14 Demaryius Thomas/20 12.00 30.00
16 Dion Jordan/25 10.00 25.00
18 Dwayne Bowe/25 10.00 25.00
19 EJ Manuel/25 20.00 50.00
21 Eric Berry/25 12.00 30.00
23 Frank Gore/25 15.00 40.00
25 Giovani Bernard/25 6.00 15.00
26 Haloti Ngata/25 10.00 25.00
27 Jamaal Charles/25 15.00 40.00
30 Jordan Cameron/25 10.00 25.00
31 Kendall Wright/25 10.00 25.00
33 Julius Thomas/25 10.00 25.00
34 Kiko Alonso/25 8.00 20.00
35 Lamar Miller/25 10.00 25.00
37 LeSean McCoy/25 15.00 40.00
38 Matt Elam/25 10.00 25.00
44 Robert Woods/25 15.00 40.00
45 Ryan Tannehill/25 12.00 30.00
49 Tyler Eifert/25 6.00 15.00

2013 Panini National Treasures Timeline Materials Signature Custom Names Prime

*TEAM NAME/20-25: .4X TO 1X NAME/20-25
1 A.J. Green/25 20.00 50.00
5 Alfred Morris/25 12.00 30.00
6 Andy Dalton/25 15.00 40.00
7 Antonio Gates/25 15.00 40.00
11 C.J. Spiller/25 12.00 30.00
13 Darren McFadden/25 15.00 40.00
15 Dez Bryant/25 20.00 50.00
16 Dion Jordan/25 12.00 30.00
18 Dwayne Bowe/25 12.00 30.00
19 EJ Manuel/25 25.00 60.00
21 Eric Berry/25 15.00 40.00
22 Eric Decker/25 12.00 30.00
24 Fred Jackson/25 15.00 40.00
25 Giovani Bernard/25 8.00 20.00
26 Haloti Ngata/25 12.00 30.00
27 Jamaal Charles/25 20.00 50.00
30 Jordan Cameron/25 12.00 30.00
31 Kendall Wright/25 12.00 30.00
32 Josh Gordon/25 EXCH 30.00 60.00
33 Julius Thomas/25 12.00 30.00
34 Kiko Alonso/25 10.00 25.00
35 Lamar Miller/25 12.00 30.00
38 Matt Elam/25 12.00 30.00
44 Robert Woods/25 12.00 30.00
49 Tyler Eifert/25 12.00 30.00

2014 Panini National Treasures

EXCH EXPIRATION 10/8/2016
1 Julius Thomas 2.00 5.00
2 Shane Vereen 2.50 6.00
3 Antonio Brown 3.00 8.00
4 Carson Palmer 2.50 6.00
5 J.J. Watt 3.00 8.00
6 Jay Cutler 2.00 5.00
7 Kyle Orton 2.00 5.00
8 Kendall Wright 2.00 5.00
9 Tony Romo 2.50 6.00
10 Luke Kuechly 2.50 6.00
11 Andrew Hawkins 2.00 5.00
12 Alex Smith 2.50 6.00
13 Matthew Stafford 2.50 6.00
14 Andre Ellington 2.00 5.00
15 Justin Houston 2.00 5.00
16 Matt Forte 2.00 5.00
17 Ryan Tannehill 2.50 6.00
18 Delanie Walker 2.00 5.00
19 DeMarco Murray 2.50 6.00
20 Matt Ryan 2.50 6.00
21 Andy Dalton 2.50 6.00
22 Jamaal Charles 2.50 6.00
23 Reggie Bush 2.00 5.00
24 Larry Fitzgerald 2.50 6.00
25 Greg Olsen 2.50 6.00
26 Brandon Marshall 2.00 5.00
27 Lamar Miller 2.00 5.00
28 Denard Robinson 2.00 5.00
29 Dez Bryant 3.00 8.00
30 Steven Jackson 2.00 5.00
31 Giovani Bernard 2.00 5.00
32 Dwayne Bowe 2.50 6.00
33 Calvin Johnson 3.00 8.00
34 Russell Wilson 5.00 12.00
35 Elvis Dumervil 2.00 5.00
36 Andrew Luck 4.00 10.00
37 Mike Wallace 2.00 5.00
38 Toby Gerhart 2.00 5.00
39 Eli Manning 2.50 6.00
40 Julio Jones 3.00 8.00
41 A.J. Green 3.00 8.00
42 Philip Rivers 3.00 8.00
43 Aaron Rodgers 10.00 25.00
44 Marshawn Lynch 2.50 6.00
45 Brian Hoyer 2.00 5.00
46 Reggie Wayne 2.50 6.00
47 Michael Vick 2.50 6.00
48 Cecil Shorts 2.00 5.00
49 Rashad Jennings 2.00 5.00
50 Doug Martin 2.50 6.00
51 Joe Flacco 2.50 6.00
52 Ryan Mathews 2.50 6.00
53 Eddie Lacy 2.00 5.00
54 Richard Sherman 6.00 15.00
55 Tom Brady 8.00 20.00
56 T.Y. Hilton 2.50 6.00
57 Chris Ivory 2.50 6.00
58 Drew Brees 3.00 8.00
59 Victor Cruz 2.50 6.00
60 Bobby Rainey 2.00 5.00
61 Justin Forsett 2.50 6.00
62 Antonio Gates 2.00 5.00
63 Jordy Nelson 2.50 6.00
64 Colin Kaepernick 2.50 6.00
65 Rob Gronkowski 3.00 8.00
66 Arian Foster 2.50 6.00
67 Percy Harvin 2.00 5.00
68 Mark Ingram 2.50 6.00
69 Robert Griffin III 2.00 5.00
70 Vincent Jackson 2.00 5.00
71 Steve Smith 2.50 6.00
72 Darren McFadden 2.00 5.00
73 Cole Beasley RC 20.00 50.00
74 Frank Gore 2.50 6.00
75 Julian Edelman 3.00 8.00
76 Andre Johnson 2.50 6.00
77 Nick Foles 2.50 6.00
78 Jimmy Graham 3.00 8.00
79 Alfred Morris 2.00 5.00
80 Peyton Manning 10.00 25.00
81 Ben Roethlisberger 8.00 20.00
82 Maurice Jones-Drew 2.00 5.00
83 Matt Asiata 3.00 8.00
84 Michael Crabtree 2.00 5.00
85 C.J. Spiller 2.00 5.00
86 DeAndre Hopkins 2.50 6.00
87 LeSean McCoy 3.00 8.00
88 Cam Newton 3.00 8.00
89 DeSean Jackson 2.50 6.00
90 Demaryius Thomas 2.50 6.00
91 Le'Veon Bell 2.50 6.00
92 James Jones 2.00 5.00
93 Cordarrelle Patterson 2.00 5.00
94 Austin Davis 2.50 6.00
95 Fred Jackson 2.50 6.00
96 Kenny Britt 2.00 5.00
97 Shonn Greene 2.00 5.00
98 Jared Cook 2.00 5.00
99 Jeremy Maclin 2.00 5.00
100 Von Miller 2.50 6.00
101 Warren Moon 4.00 10.00
102 Joe Namath 10.00 25.00
103 Bob Lilly 3.00 8.00
104 Larry Csonka 4.00 10.00
105 Curtis Martin 3.00 8.00
106 Michael Strahan 3.00 8.00
107 Emmitt Smith 6.00 15.00
108 Rod Woodson 3.00 8.00
109 Gale Sayers 4.00 10.00
110 Steve Young 5.00 12.00
111 Troy Aikman 5.00 12.00
112 John Elway 6.00 15.00
113 Brett Favre 8.00 20.00
114 Lawrence Taylor 4.00 10.00
115 Dan Marino 8.00 20.00
116 Paul Hornung 4.00 10.00
117 Eric Dickerson 3.00 8.00
118 Roger Staubach 5.00 12.00
119 Jerome Bettis 4.00 10.00
120 Terrell Davis 1.50 4.00
121 Terry Bradshaw 5.00 12.00
122 John Randle 3.00 8.00
123 Bruce Smith 3.00 8.00
124 Len Dawson 4.00 10.00
125 Fred Taylor 2.50 6.00
126 Paul Warfield 3.00 8.00
127 Ronnie Lott 3.00 8.00
128 Fran Tarkenton 4.00 10.00
129 Jerry Rice 6.00 15.00
130 Thurman Thomas 3.00 8.00
131 Barry Sanders 8.00 20.00
132 Kurt Warner 3.00 8.00
133 Carl Eller 2.50 6.00
134 Marshall Faulk 3.00 8.00
135 Deion Sanders 3.00 8.00
136 Franco Harris 4.00 10.00
137 Randy White 3.00 8.00
138 Mike Quick 2.50 6.00
139 Jim Kelly 4.00 10.00
140 Tim Brown 4.00 10.00
141 LaDainian Tomlinson 3.00 8.00
142 Bo Jackson 5.00 12.00
143 Warren Sapp 3.00 8.00
144 Michael Irvin 4.00 10.00
145 Earl Campbell 4.00 10.00
146 Raymond Berry 3.00 8.00
147 Fred Biletnikoff 3.00 8.00
148 Steve Largent 4.00 10.00
149 Joe Montana 12.00 30.00
150 Tony Dorsett 4.00 10.00
151 Warren Moon 4.00 10.00
152 Kellen Winslow 3.00 8.00
153 Curtis Martin 3.00 8.00
154 Emmitt Smith 6.00 15.00
155 Rod Woodson 3.00 8.00
156 Mike Ditka 4.00 10.00
157 Brett Favre 8.00 20.00
158 Eric Dickerson 3.00 8.00
159 Jerome Bettis 4.00 10.00
160 Tony Dorsett 4.00 10.00
161 Brett Favre 8.00 20.00
162 Steve Young 5.00 12.00
163 Paul Warfield 3.00 8.00
164 Ronnie Lott 3.00 8.00
165 Fran Tarkenton 4.00 10.00
166 Jerry Rice 6.00 15.00
167 LaDainian Tomlinson 3.00 8.00
168 Kurt Warner 3.00 8.00
169 Marshall Faulk 3.00 8.00
170 Deion Sanders 3.00 8.00
171 Forrest Gregg 2.50 6.00
172 John Riggins 3.00 8.00
173 Bart Starr 12.00 30.00
174 Frank Gifford 3.00 8.00
175 Joe Montana 12.00 30.00
176 Johnny Unitas 6.00 15.00
177 Walter Payton 8.00 20.00
178 Brett Favre 8.00 20.00
179 Deion Sanders 3.00 8.00
180 Warren Moon 4.00 10.00
181 Justin Gilbert RC 2.50 6.00
182 Walt Aikens RC 3.00 8.00
183 T.J. Carrie RC 3.00 8.00
184 Christian Kirksey RC 2.50 6.00
185 Cody Parkey RC 3.00 8.00
186 Avery Williamson RC 4.00 10.00
187 James White RC 5.00 12.00
188 Philly Brown RC 3.00 8.00
189 Ray Agnew RC 2.50 6.00
190 Storm Johnson RC 2.50 6.00
191 Bashaud Breeland RC 2.50 6.00
192 Trey Watts RC 2.50 6.00
193 Ryan Hewitt RC 2.50 6.00
194 Ego Ferguson RC 2.50 6.00
195 Gator Hoskins RC 3.00 8.00
196 Trey Burton RC 2.50 6.00
197 Chandler Catanzaro RC 3.00 8.00
198 Corey Washington RC 4.00 10.00
199 Solomon Patton RC 3.00 8.00
200 Ryan Grant RC 2.50 6.00
201 Isaiah Crowell AU RC 5.00 12.00
202 Terrance Mitchell AU RC 6.00 15.00
203 Aaron Donald AU RC 40.00 80.00
204 Jerick McKinnon AU RC 5.00 12.00
205 Marcus Roberson AU RC 5.00 12.00
206 Rashad Ross AU RC 4.00 10.00
207 Aaron Lynch AU RC 8.00 20.00
208 Jimmie Ward AU RC 5.00 12.00
209 Kevin Norwood AU RC 4.00 10.00
210 Chris Borland AU RC 4.00 10.00
211 Marion Grice AU RC 4.00 10.00
212 Richard Rodgers AU RC 6.00 15.00
213 Branden Oliver AU RC 6.00 15.00
214 Crockett Gillmore AU RC 5.00 12.00
215 Dustin Vaughan AU RC 4.00 10.00
216 Robert Herron AU RC 4.00 10.00
217 Jake Matthews AU RC 4.00 10.00
218 Trent Murphy AU RC 4.00 10.00
219 Albert Wilson AU RC 5.00 12.00
220 John Brown AU RC 6.00 15.00
221 Martavis Bryant AU RC 10.00 25.00
222 E.J. Gaines AU RC 4.00 10.00
223 Trevor Reilly AU RC 4.00 10.00
224 Alfred Blue AU RC 4.00 10.00
225 Kony Ealy AU RC 5.00 12.00
226 Troy Niklas AU RC 4.00 10.00
228 Darrin Reaves AU RC 5.00 12.00
229 Glenn Winston AU RC 5.00 12.00
230 Silas Redd AU RC 5.00 12.00
231 Jason Verrett AU RC 4.00 10.00
232 Josh Huff AU RC 5.00 12.00
234 Kyle Van Noy AU RC 5.00 12.00
235 Greg Robinson AU RC 4.00 10.00
236 Taylor Gabriel AU RC 5.00 12.00
237 Jay Prosch AU RC 6.00 15.00
239 Juwan Thompson AU RC 6.00 15.00
240 C.J. Fiedorowicz AU RC 4.00 10.00
241 Lamarcus Joyner AU RC 5.00 12.00
242 Ha Ha Clinton-Dix AU RC 5.00 12.00
243 Jeff Janis AU RC 4.00 10.00
244 Taylor Lewan AU RC 4.00 10.00
245 Zach Mettenberger AU RC 15.00 40.00
246 Deone Bucannon AU RC 4.00 10.00
247 Isaiah Burse AU RC 4.00 10.00
249 Calvin Pryor AU RC 4.00 10.00
250 Pierre Desir AU RC 4.00 10.00
251 D.Dennard JSY AU RC 10.00 25.00
252 James Wright JSY AU RC 15.00 40.00
253 Preston Brown JSY AU RC 12.00 30.00
256 Devin Street JSY AU RC 12.00 30.00
257 Zack Martin JSY AU RC 15.00 40.00
258 A.Hitchens JSY AU RC 12.00 30.00
260 Matt Hazel JSY AU RC 12.00 30.00
262 Allen Hurns JSY AU RC 15.00 40.00
263 Chris Smith JSY AU RC 12.00 30.00
265 Anthony Barr JSY AU RC 12.00 30.00
266 D.Easley JSY AU RC 12.00 30.00
267 L.Taliaferro JSY AU RC 12.00 30.00
268 Keith Wenning JSY AU RC 15.00 40.00
270 M.Campanaro JSY AU RC 12.00 30.00
271 Ryan Shazier JSY AU RC 20.00 50.00
272 Carlos Hyde JSY AU RC 15.00 40.00
273 Malcolm Butler RC 25.00 60.00
274 J.Garoppolo JSY AU RC 2000.00 3000.00
275 Kelvin Benjamin JSY AU RC 20.00 50.00
276 T.Bridgewater JSY AU RC 100.00 200.00
277 Michael Sam JSY AU RC 12.00 30.00
278 Charles Sims JSY AU RC 12.00 30.00
279 Eric Ebron JSY AU RC 15.00 40.00
280 Bishop Sankey JSY AU RC 12.00 30.00
281 Cody Latimer JSY AU RC 15.00 40.00
282 Andre Williams JSY AU RC 12.00 30.00
285 Sammy Watkins JSY AU RC 20.00 50.00
286 Blake Bortles JSY AU RC 15.00 40.00
288 Ka'Deem Carey JSY AU RC 12.00 30.00
289 Seferian-Jenkins JSY AU RC 12.00 30.00
290 Jeremy Hill JSY AU RC 15.00 40.00
291 Allen Robinson JSY AU RC 20.00 50.00
292 Terrance West JSY AU RC 12.00 30.00
293 Donte Moncrief JSY AU RC 12.00 30.00
294 Tom Savage JSY AU RC 12.00 30.00
295 Brandin Cooks JSY AU RC 20.00 50.00
296 Derek Carr JSY AU RC 400.00 800.00
297 J.Clowney JSY AU RC 15.00 40.00
299 Jace Amaro JSY AU/35 RC 12.00 30.00
301 Davante Adams JSY AU RC 25.00 80.00
302 Tajh Boyd JSY AU RC 12.00 30.00
303 Mike Evans JSY AU RC 100.00 200.00
304 A.J. McCarron JSY AU RC 12.00 30.00
305 J.Matthews JSY AU RC 20.00 50.00
306 J.Manziel JSY AU RC 20.00 50.00
307 Asa Watson JSY AU RC 12.00 30.00
308 Tre Mason JSY AU RC 40.00 100.00
309 Jarvis Landry 15.00 40.00
310 Dri Archer JSY AU RC 12.00 30.00
311 O.Beckham JSY AU RC 300.00 500.00
312 Aaron Murray JSY AU RC 40.00 80.00
313 Marqise Lee JSY AU RC 15.00 40.00

2014 Panini National Treasures Century Numbers

*VETS/74-99: .4X TO 1X BASIC CARDS/99
*VETS/32-59: .5X TO 1.2X BASIC CARDS/99
*VETS/15-30: .6X TO 1.5X BASIC CARDS/99
*RETIRED/74-99: .4X TO 1X BASIC CARDS/99
*RETIRED/32-58: .5X TO 1.2X BASIC CARDS/99
*RETIRED/15-30: .6X TO 1.5X BASIC CARDS/99
*ROOKIES/70-98: .4X TO 1X BASIC CARDS/99
*ROOKIES/32-59: .5X TO 1.2X BASIC CARDS/99
*ROOKIES/15-28: .6X TO 1.5X BASIC CARDS/99
149 Joe Montana/16 50.00 100.00
175 Joe Montana/19 50.00 100.00

2014 Panini National Treasures Century Silver

*VETS/25: .6X TO 1.5X BASIC CARDS/99
*RETIRED: .6X TO 1.5X BASIC CARDS/99
*ROOKIES/99: .6X TO 1.5X BASIC ROOKIE/99
*ROOK. AU/99: .6X TO 1.5X BASIC ROOKIE/99
*ROOK. JSY AU/99: .6X TO 1.5X BASIC ROOKIE/99
290 Jeremy Hill JSY AU 40.00 100.00
296 Derek Carr JSY AU 1000.00 1500.00
303 Mike Evans JSY AU 100.00 200.00
305 Jordan Matthews JSY AU 125.00 250.00
308 Tre Mason JSY AU 75.00 150.00
311 O.Beckham Jr. JSY AU EXCH 400.00 600.00
312 Aaron Murray JSY AU 60.00 120.00

2014 Panini National Treasures Colossal Materials

*PRIME/50: .5X TO 1.2X BASIC JSY/75-99
*PRIME/25: .4X TO 1X BASIC JSY/15-35
*PRIME/25: .5X TO 1.2X BASIC JSY/49-60
*PRIME/25: .6X TO 1.5X BASIC JSY/75-99
1 A.J. Green/75 5.00 12.00
2 Derrick Johnson/99 3.00 8.00
3 Steve Largent/15 8.00 20.00
4 Philip Rivers/35 8.00 20.00
5 Roddy White/35 5.00 12.00
8 Joe Flacco/35 6.00 15.00
9 Peyton Manning/99 10.00 25.00
10 Bruce Smith/99 4.00 10.00
11 Andy Dalton/75 4.00 10.00
12 Lamar Miller/75 3.00 8.00
13 Jay Cutler/99 3.00 8.00
14 Von Miller/99 4.00 10.00
18 Montee Ball/99 3.00 8.00
19 Michael Strahan/35 6.00 15.00
20 Wes Welker/75 4.00 10.00
21 Deion Sanders/25 12.00 30.00
24 Mike Wallace/49 4.00 10.00
25 Pierre Thomas/35 5.00 12.00
26 C.J. Spiller/25 5.00 12.00
28 Ryan Tannehill/99 4.00 10.00
29 Demaryius Thomas/75 4.00 10.00
30 Rod Woodson/35 6.00 15.00
31 Matthew Stafford/60 5.00 12.00
32 Mario Williams/99 3.00 8.00
33 Ryan Mathews/35 6.00 15.00
34 Tony Romo/60 5.00 12.00
35 Malcom Floyd/99 3.00 8.00
36 DeMarco Murray/35 6.00 15.00
37 Dwayne Bowe/99 4.00 10.00
39 Julius Thomas/99 3.00 8.00
40 Darren McFadden/75 3.00 8.00
41 Joe Montana/99 20.00 50.00

2014 Panini National Treasures Colossal Pro Bowl Materials Prime

*PRO JSY/18-35: .6X TO 1.5X PRIME JSY/50
*PRO JSY/39-69: .4X TO 1X PRIME JSY/41-50
*PRO JSY/70-99: .3X TO .8X PRIME JSY/41-50
1 Dez Bryant/50 15.00 40.00
2 Antonio Brown/50 10.00 25.00
3 Eddie Lacy/50 4.00 10.00
4 J.J. Watt/50 20.00 50.00
5 A.J. Green/47 6.00 15.00
6 LeSean McCoy/50 6.00 15.00
7 Matt Forte/50 4.00 10.00
8 Alex Smith/17 6.00 15.00
9 Larry Fitzgerald/17 6.00 15.00
10 Cordarrelle Patterson/50 4.00 10.00
11 Ndamukong Suh/50 5.00 12.00
12 Mike Tolbert/50 4.00 10.00
13 Gerald McCoy/50 4.00 10.00
14 Paul Posluszny/41 8.00 20.00
15 Darrelle Revis/50 4.00 10.00
16 Brian Orakpo/50 4.00 10.00
17 Patrick Peterson/41 4.00 10.00
18 Cameron Wake/43 4.00 10.00
19 Vontaze Burfict/50 4.00 10.00
20 Dexter McCluster/50 5.00 12.00
21 Eric Reid/50 5.00 12.00
22 Logan Mankins/50 4.00 10.00
23 Matthew Slater/50 4.00 10.00
24 Tim Jennings/50 4.00 10.00
25 T.J. Ward/49 4.00 10.00
26 Dontari Poe/50 4.00 10.00
27 Derrick Johnson/50 4.00 10.00
28 Eric Weddle/50 4.00 10.00
29 Tyron Smith/50 10.00 25.00
30 John Abraham/50 4.00 10.00
31 Jahri Evans/50 4.00 10.00
32 Alex Mack/50 4.00 10.00
33 Duane Brown/50 4.00 10.00
34 Joe Thomas/50 10.00 25.00
36 Nick Mangold/50 4.00 10.00
37 Ryan Kalil/50 4.00 10.00

2014 Panini National Treasures Colossal Signature Materials Jersey Number

3 Geno Smith/49 10.00 25.00
6 Jordy Nelson/99 20.00 50.00
7 Antonio Gates/99 12.00 30.00
10 Nick Foles/99 10.00 25.00
14 Tony Romo/25 30.00 60.00
15 Alshon Jeffery/99 10.00 25.00
16 Kendall Wright/99 8.00 20.00
17 C.J. Spiller/99 8.00 20.00
18 Matt Ryan/25 15.00 40.00
19 Danny Amendola/99 10.00 25.00
20 Paul Posluszny/99 8.00 20.00
21 Eli Manning/25 40.00 80.00
22 Ryan Tannehill/99 15.00 40.00
26 Knowshon Moreno/99 10.00 25.00
28 Michael Floyd/99 8.00 20.00
30 Peyton Manning/18 200.00 350.00
31 Frank Gore/99 15.00 40.00
32 Steve Smith/99 15.00 40.00
35 Andy Dalton/99 10.00 25.00
38 Montee Ball/99 8.00 20.00
40 Reggie Bush/25 12.00 30.00
CJSCK Colin Kaepernick/25

2014 Panini National Treasures Colossal Signature Materials Jersey Number Prime

*PRIME/15-25: .6X TO 1.5X JSY AU/99
*PRIME/15-25: .4X TO 1X JSY AU/25
5 A.J. Green/25 20.00 50.00
25 Andrew Luck/15 200.00 350.00

2014 Panini National Treasures Green Bay Greats Memorabilia

1 A.J. Hawk/99 5.00 12.00
4 Brett Favre/99 15.00 40.00
7 Davante Adams/99 8.00 20.00
10 Forrest Gregg/99 5.00 12.00
11 Ha Ha Clinton-Dix/99 8.00 20.00
12 James Jones/99 5.00 12.00
13 John Kuhn/99 15.00 40.00
14 Jordy Nelson/99 10.00 25.00
15 Julius Peppers/99 10.00 25.00
16 Mason Crosby/99 8.00 20.00
17 Morgan Burnett/99 5.00 12.00
19 B.J. Raji/99 5.00 12.00
20 Datone Jones/99 5.00 12.00
21 Tramon Williams/99 8.00 20.00
22 Randall Cobb/99 6.00 15.00
23 Aaron Rodgers/99 15.00 40.00

2014 Panini National Treasures Green Bay Greats Signatures

1 Richard Rodgers/99 12.00 30.00
3 Ahman Green/49 20.00 50.00
4 B.J. Raji/99 12.00 30.00
7 Jan Stenerud/25 20.00 50.00
8 Micah Hyde/99 20.00 50.00
9 Donald Driver/25 30.00 80.00
10 Eddie Lacy/49 15.00 40.00
12 Ha Ha Clinton-Dix/99 6.00 15.00
15 Jordy Nelson/49 30.00 60.00
16 Paul Hornung/49 25.00 60.00
17 Randall Cobb/49 20.00 50.00
18 Antonio Freeman/99 15.00 40.00
20 James Lofton/25 30.00 80.00
22 Davante Adams/99 8.00 20.00
23 Don Majkowski/99 20.00 50.00
24 Mark Chmura/99 20.00 50.00
25 Robert Brooks/99 15.00 40.00

2014 Panini National Treasures Materials

*SILVER/35-60: .5X TO 1.2X BASIC JSY/75-99
*SILVER/15-25: .5X TO 1.2X BASIC JSY/35-60
*SILVER/15-25: .5X TO 1.2X BASIC JSY/35
1 Arian Foster/49 5.00 12.00
2 Jonathan Stewart/99 3.00 8.00
3 Kelvin Benjamin/99 3.00 8.00
4 A.J. Green/75 5.00 12.00
5 Cam Newton/49 6.00 15.00
6 Champ Bailey/99 4.00 10.00
7 Philip Rivers/35 6.00 15.00
8 Demaryius Thomas/49 5.00 12.00
9 Santana Moss/75 4.00 10.00
11 Vernon Davis/35 4.00 10.00
12 Julio Jones/35 6.00 15.00
13 Mike Evans/99 5.00 12.00
14 Alfred Morris/35 4.00 10.00
15 Marshawn Lynch/35 5.00 12.00
16 C.J. Spiller/49 4.00 10.00
17 Pierre Thomas/75 3.00 8.00
18 Dez Bryant/49 6.00 15.00
19 Steve Largent/49 8.00 20.00
20 Jay Cutler/99 3.00 8.00
21 Von Miller/99 4.00 10.00
22 Julius Thomas/99 3.00 8.00
23 Odell Beckham Jr./99 5.00 12.00
24 Andy Dalton/99 4.00 10.00
25 Martellus Bennett/99 3.00 8.00
26 Curtis Martin/35 6.00 15.00
27 Matthew Stafford/49 5.00 12.00
28 Dwayne Bowe/99 4.00 10.00
29 Steve Smith/35 5.00 12.00
30 Jerry Rice/35 15.00 40.00
31 Walter Payton/49 15.00 40.00
32 LaDainian Tomlinson/35 10.00 25.00
33 Tre Mason/99 2.00 5.00
34 Antonio Brown/35 6.00 15.00
35 Matt Ryan/35 5.00 12.00
36 Dan Marino/35 15.00 40.00
37 Roddy White/60 4.00 10.00
38 Dwight Clark/49 5.00 12.00
39 Steve Young/49 10.00 25.00
41 Wes Welker/75 4.00 10.00
42 Lamar Miller/99 3.00 8.00
43 Jeremy Hill/99 2.50 6.00
44 Antonio Gates/35 4.00 10.00
45 Mohamed Sanu/99 3.00 8.00
46 Brett Favre/25
48 Earl Campbell/35 8.00 20.00
49 Steven Jackson/60 4.00 10.00
50 Joe Flacco/60 5.00 12.00
51 Blake Bortles/99 2.50 6.00
52 Larry Csonka/35 8.00 20.00
53 Storm Johnson/49 4.00 10.00
54 Barry Sanders/35 12.00 30.00
55 Montee Ball/99 3.00 8.00
56 Darren McFadden/75 3.00 8.00
57 Roger Staubach/35 10.00 25.00
58 Eli Manning/35 5.00 12.00
59 Toby Gerhart/99 3.00 8.00
60 Joe Namath/49
61 Johnny Manziel/99 3.00 8.00
62 Len Dawson/49 12.00 30.00
63 Andre Williams/99 2.00 5.00
64 Thurman Thomas/49 6.00 15.00
65 Owen Daniels/99 3.00 8.00
66 DeAngelo Hall/99 3.00 8.00
67 Ronnie Lott/49 6.00 15.00
68 Emmanuel Sanders/99 4.00 10.00
71 Teddy Bridgewater/99 3.00 8.00
72 Malcom Floyd/75 3.00 8.00
73 Brandin Cooks/99 3.00 8.00
75 Paul Posluszny/99 3.00 8.00
76 Deion Sanders/49 6.00 15.00
77 Ryan Mathews/60 5.00 12.00
78 Eric Dickerson/35 6.00 15.00
79 Tony Dorsett/49 8.00 20.00
80 John Elway/49 12.00 30.00
81 Derek Carr/99 12.00 30.00
82 Mike Wallace/99 3.00 8.00
83 Jadeveon Clowney/99 2.50 6.00
84 Brian Hartline/99 3.00 8.00
85 Paul Warfield/35 6.00 15.00
86 DeMarco Murray/60 5.00 12.00
87 Ryan Tannehill/99 4.00 10.00
88 Fred Jackson/99 4.00 10.00
89 Tony Romo/75 4.00 10.00
90 John Riggins/49 6.00 15.00
91 Sammy Watkins/99 3.00 8.00
92 Mario Williams/99 3.00 8.00
93 Khalil Mack/99 8.00 20.00
94 Cecil Shorts/99 3.00 8.00
95 Peyton Manning/99 15.00 40.00
96 DeMarcus Ware/99 4.00 10.00
97 Sam Bradford/99 3.00 8.00
99 Torrey Smith/99 3.00 8.00
100 Johnny Unitas/99 20.00 40.00

2014 Panini National Treasures Monsters of the Midway Memorabilia

1 Bulldog Turner/34 10.00 25.00
2 Dan Hampton/99 5.00 12.00
3 Doug Flutie/99 6.00 15.00
4 Gale Sayers/99 8.00 20.00
5 Jay Cutler/99 5.00 12.00
6 Jared Allen/99 5.00 12.00
7 Lance Briggs/99 6.00 15.00
8 Matt Forte/99 5.00 12.00
9 Kyle Orton/99 5.00 12.00
11 Walter Payton/99 15.00 40.00
13 Robbie Gould/99 5.00 12.00
15 Martellus Bennett/99 5.00 12.00
17 Ka'Deem Carey/99 5.00 12.00
19 Brian Urlacher/99 8.00 20.00
20 Brandon Marshall/99 5.00 12.00
21 Alshon Jeffery/99 6.00 15.00
23 Julius Peppers/99 6.00 15.00

2014 Panini National Treasures Monsters of the Midway Signatures

2 Alshon Jeffery/49 20.00 50.00
3 Jay Cutler/25
4 Dan Hampton/49 15.00 40.00
8 Mike Ditka/15
11 Dick Butkus/25 75.00 150.00
12 Brian Urlacher/49 40.00 80.00
13 Doug Flutie/25
14 Jon Bostic/53 12.00 30.00
15 Ka'Deem Carey/99 12.00 30.00
16 Kyle Fuller/99
17 Lance Briggs/99 15.00 40.00
18 Devin Hester/25 25.00 60.00
19 Richard Dent/25 25.00 60.00
24 Gary Fencik/99 15.00 40.00

2014 Panini National Treasures Notable Nicknames

1 Johnny Manziel 20.00 50.00
2 Ben Roethlisberger 150.00 300.00
4 Joe Namath 150.00 250.00
5 Drew Brees
6 Jerome Bettis
8 Eli Manning 100.00 200.00
9 Jerry Rice 300.00 500.00
11 J.J. Watt 75.00 150.00
12 Joe Montana 400.00 600.00
14 Gale Sayers 20.00 50.00
16 LaDainian Tomlinson 75.00 150.00
17 Matt Ryan 75.00 150.00
18 Deion Sanders 50.00 100.00
19 Michael Irvin 75.00 150.00
20 Andy Dalton 15.00 40.00
21 Peyton Manning 150.00 300.00
22 Terrell Davis 25.00 60.00
23 Tom Brady 400.00 800.00
24 Earl Campbell
25 Teddy Bridgewater 60.00 125.00
26 Kelvin Benjamin 20.00 50.00
27 Carlos Hyde 15.00 40.00
28 Manti Te'o 15.00 40.00
29 Roger Staubach 200.00 400.00
31 Len Dawson 50.00 100.00
33 John Riggins
34 John Riggins
35 Derek Carr 125.00 250.00
36 Drew Brees
41 Ryan Tannehill 15.00 40.00
44 Cam Newton
45 Richard Sherman 100.00 200.00
47 Russell Wilson 100.00 200.00
48 Cam Newton
51 Tony Romo 100.00 200.00
52 Jason Witten 75.00 150.00
54 John Elway 100.00 200.00
55 Brett Favre 125.00 250.00
56 Frank Gore 15.00 40.00
57 Jim Kelly 40.00 80.00
58 Randy White 75.00 150.00
59 Fran Tarkenton 20.00 50.00
NNRG Rob Gronkowski 125.00 250.00

2014 Panini National Treasures Pen Pals Duals

1 J.Manziel/T.West 30.00 60.00
2 J.Clowney/K.Mack 12.00 30.00
3 D.Adams/D.Carr

2014 Panini National Treasures Pen Pals Quads
1 Wllms/Amro/Bckhm/Byd 50.00 100.00
2 Thms/Byd/Brdgwtr/Svge
3 Mncrf/Mtthws/Evns/Bckhm
4 Amro/Lndry/Grpplo/Wtkns 40.00 100.00

2014 Panini National Treasures Pen Pals Triple
1 Brtls/Mnzl/Brdgwtr 50.00 100.00
2 Rbnsn/Bells/Lee 30.00 60.00
3 SfrnJnkns/Sms/Evns 25.00 50.00
4 Lndry/Hll/Bckhm 90.00 150.00

2014 Panini National Treasures Prime Pairings Autographs
1 A.Ellington/C.Palmer/25 8.00 20.00
2 C.Spiller/F.Jackson/25 8.00 20.00
5 J.Cameron/J.Gordon/25 6.00 15.00
11 A.Foster/D.Hopkins/15 25.00 50.00
13 A.Hurns/B.Bortles/15 10.00 25.00
19 D.Sproles/L.McCoy/25 10.00 25.00
29 J.Matthews/N.Foles/25 10.00 25.00
31 A.Brown/M.Bryant/25 50.00 100.00
32 J.Nelson/R.Cobb/25 40.00 80.00
35 B.Cooks/K.Stills/25 10.00 25.00

2014 Panini National Treasures Prime Signings
5 Jim Kelly/15 30.00 60.00
7 A.J. Green/25
9 Blake Bortles/20 8.00 20.00
11 Derek Carr/25
16 Tony Dorsett/15
17 Andrew Luck/15
18 LaDainian Tomlinson/20 25.00 50.00
19 Bob Lilly/25
22 Rob Gronkowski/25 40.00 80.00
23 Frank Gifford/15
24 Teddy Bridgewater/20 50.00 100.00
30 Paul Hornung/25 20.00 50.00
31 Drew Brees/15
36 Warren Moon/20

2014 Panini National Treasures Pro Bowl Materials
*PRIME/25: .6X TO 1.5X PRO JSY/89-99
1 Bob Lilly/99 4.00 10.00
2 Dan Marino/99 10.00 25.00
3 Derrick Johnson/99 3.00 8.00
4 Jay Cutler/99 3.00 8.00
5 Josh Cribbs/99 3.00 8.00
6 Julio Jones/99 5.00 12.00
7 Kurt Warner/99 4.00 10.00
8 Kyle Rudolph/99 3.00 8.00
9 Larry Fitzgerald/99 4.00 10.00
10 LeSean McCoy/99 5.00 12.00
11 Cortland Finnegan/68 4.00 10.00
12 Lorenzo Alexander/99 3.00 8.00
13 Matt Schaub/99 3.00 8.00
14 Michael Irvin/55 6.00 15.00
15 Ndamukong Suh/71 5.00 12.00
16 Owen Daniels/99 3.00 8.00
17 Patrick Peterson/89 3.00 8.00
18 Peyton Manning/69 12.00 30.00
19 Davin Joseph/99 4.00 10.00
20 Robert Mathis/99 3.00 8.00
21 Ronnie Brown/99 3.00 8.00
22 Russell Wilson/26
23 Terrell Suggs/99 3.00 8.00
24 Tim Jennings/99 3.00 8.00
25 Von Miller/65 5.00 12.00
26 Nick Mangold/99 3.00 8.00
27 Joe Thomas/99 3.00 8.00
28 Duane Brown/99 3.00 8.00
29 Kevin Williams/99 3.00 8.00
30 Brandon Fields/99 3.00 8.00
31 Johnny Hekker/99 3.00 8.00

2014 Panini National Treasures Rookie Colossal Signature Materials Jersey Number
1 Jace Amaro 6.00 15.00
2 Davante Adams 10.00 25.00
3 Asa Watson 6.00 15.00
5 Tom Savage 6.00 15.00
6 Derek Carr 100.00 200.00
7 Tajh Boyd 6.00 15.00
8 A.J. McCarron 6.00 15.00
9 Dri Archer 6.00 15.00
10 Aaron Murray 6.00 15.00
12 Cody Latimer 8.00 20.00
14 Austin Seferian-Jenkins 6.00 15.00
15 Jimmy Garoppolo 125.00 250.00
16 Teddy Bridgewater 10.00 25.00
17 Andre Williams 6.00 15.00
19 Jeremy Hill 8.00 20.00
20 Terrance West 8.00 20.00
21 Mike Evans 15.00 40.00
22 Jordan Matthews 10.00 25.00
23 Odell Beckham Jr. EXCH 75.00 150.00
27 Johnny Manziel 10.00 25.00
28 Tre Mason 6.00 15.00
29 Brandin Cooks 10.00 25.00
30 Jadeveon Clowney 8.00 20.00
32 Sammy Watkins 10.00 25.00
34 Donte Moncrief 6.00 15.00
35 Charles Sims 6.00 15.00
36 Bishop Sankey 6.00 15.00
37 Blake Bortles 8.00 20.00
38 Ka'Deem Carey 6.00 15.00
39 Kelvin Benjamin 10.00 25.00
40 Michael Sam 8.00 20.00

2014 Panini National Treasures Rookie Colossal Signature Materials Jersey Number Prime
*PRIME/25: .6X TO 1.5X JSY AU/99
15 Jimmy Garoppolo 200.00 300.00
16 Teddy Bridgewater 15.00 40.00

2014 Panini National Treasures Rookie Jumbo Prime Booklet Signatures
1 Michael Sam/99 6.00 15.00
3 Jadeveon Clowney/99 10.00 25.00
4 Asa Watson/99 8.00 20.00
5 Eric Ebron/99 10.00 25.00
6 Austin Seferian-Jenkins/99 8.00 20.00
8 Jarvis Landry/99 EXCH 15.00 40.00
9 Cody Latimer/99 10.00 25.00
10 Allen Robinson/99 EXCH 12.00 30.00
11 Davante Adams/99 12.00 30.00
12 Odell Beckham Jr./99 EXCH 100.00 200.00
14 Donte Moncrief/99 8.00 20.00
15 Mike Evans/99 20.00 50.00
16 Marqise Lee/99 10.00 25.00
17 Kelvin Benjamin/99 12.00 30.00
18 Sammy Watkins/99 12.00 30.00
19 Brandin Cooks/99 12.00 30.00
20 Jordan Matthews/99 12.00 30.00
21 Charles Sims/99 15.00 40.00
22 Ka'Deem Carey/99 8.00 20.00
23 Devonta Freeman/99 12.00 30.00
24 Tre Mason/99 8.00 20.00
25 Bishop Sankey/99 8.00 20.00
26 Jeremy Hill/99 10.00 25.00
28 Dri Archer/99 8.00 20.00
29 Andre Williams/99 8.00 20.00
30 Terrance West/99 15.00 40.00
31 Tajh Boyd/99 8.00 20.00
32 Aaron Murray/99 8.00 20.00
33 Jimmy Garoppolo/99 100.00 200.00
35 Tom Savage/99 8.00 20.00
36 A.J. McCarron/99 8.00 20.00
37 Teddy Bridgewater/99 12.00 30.00
38 Blake Bortles/99 10.00 25.00
39 Derek Carr/99 100.00 200.00
40 Johnny Manziel/99 12.00 30.00

2014 Panini National Treasures Rookie Jumbo Prime Booklet Signatures Vertical
2 Jadeveon Clowney 10.00 25.00
3 Eric Ebron EXCH 10.00 25.00
4 Austin Seferian-Jenkins 8.00 20.00
5 Jarvis Landry EXCH 15.00 40.00
6 Cody Latimer 10.00 25.00
7 Allen Robinson EXCH 12.00 30.00
8 Davante Adams 12.00 30.00
10 Donte Moncrief 8.00 20.00
11 Mike Evans 20.00 50.00
12 Marqise Lee 10.00 25.00
13 Kelvin Benjamin 12.00 30.00
14 Sammy Watkins 12.00 30.00
15 Brandin Cooks 12.00 30.00
16 Jordan Matthews 12.00 30.00
17 Ka'Deem Carey 8.00 20.00
18 Devonta Freeman 12.00 30.00
19 Tre Mason 8.00 20.00
20 Bishop Sankey 8.00 20.00
21 Jeremy Hill 10.00 25.00
22 Dri Archer 8.00 20.00
23 Andre Williams 8.00 20.00
24 Terrance West 15.00 40.00
25 Aaron Murray 8.00 20.00
26 Jimmy Garoppolo 100.00 200.00
27 Tom Savage 8.00 20.00
28 A.J. McCarron 8.00 20.00
29 Teddy Bridgewater 12.00 30.00
30 Blake Bortles 10.00 25.00
31 Derek Carr 100.00 200.00
32 Johnny Manziel 12.00 30.00

2014 Panini National Treasures Rookie NFL Gear Combo Player Materials
1 B.Roby/C.Hyde 2.50 6.00
2 J.White/J.Garoppolo 15.00 40.00
3 D.Carr/J.Manziel 6.00 15.00
4 J.Clowney/T.Savage 2.50 6.00
5 D.Carr/T.Bridgewater 6.00 15.00
6 A.McCarron/J.Hill 2.50 6.00
7 D.Adams/D.Carr 6.00 15.00
8 C.Sims/M.Evans 5.00 12.00
9 D.Street/T.Savage 2.00 5.00
10 A.Williams/O.Beckham Jr. 10.00 25.00
11 B.Bortles/J.Manziel 3.00 8.00
12 D.Carr/K.Mack 6.00 15.00
13 B.Bortles/T.Bridgewater 3.00 8.00
14 B.Sankey/J.Hill 2.50 6.00
15 K.Benjamin/S.Watkins 6.00 15.00
16 B.Roby/C.Latimer 2.50 6.00
17 J.Landry/O.Beckham Jr. 10.00 25.00
18 A.Murray/D.Thomas 2.00 5.00
19 A.Seferian-Jenkins/B.Sankey 2.00 5.00
20 A.Hurns/M.Lee 2.50 6.00
21 J.Manziel/T.Bridgewater 6.00 15.00
22 C.Mosley/L.Taliaferro 2.50 6.00
23 B.Bortles/D.Carr 5.00 12.00
24 D.Freeman/K.Benjamin 6.00 15.00
25 O.Beckham Jr./S.Watkins 10.00 25.00
26 J.Manziel/T.West 6.00 15.00
27 J.Manziel/M.Evans 5.00 12.00
28 D.Street/Z.Martin 2.50 6.00
29 J.Landry/J.Hill 4.00 10.00
30 B.Bortles/S.Johnson 2.50 6.00

2014 Panini National Treasures Rookie NFL Gear Dual Materials
*PRIME/15-25: .6X TO 1.5X DUAL JSY/99
*PRIME/15-25: .5X TO 1.2X DUAL JSY/49
*PRIME/15-25: .4X TO 1X DUAL JSY/20
RGSAH Allen Hurns/49 3.00 8.00
RGSAM Aaron Murray/99 2.00 5.00
RGSAMC A.J. McCarron/99 2.00 5.00
RGSAR Allen Robinson/99 3.00 8.00
RGSAS Austin Seferian-Jenkins/99 2.00 5.00
RGSAW Andre Williams/99 2.00 5.00
RGSBB Blake Bortles/99 2.50 6.00
RGSBC Brandin Cooks/99 3.00 8.00
RGSBR Bradley Roby/99 2.00 5.00
RGSBS Bishop Sankey/99 2.00 5.00
RGSCH Carlos Hyde/99 2.50 6.00
RGSCL Cody Latimer/99 2.50 6.00
RGSCM C.J. Mosley/99 2.50 6.00
RGSCS Charles Sims/99 2.00 5.00
RGSDC Derek Carr/99 6.00 15.00
RGSDM Donte Moncrief/99 3.00 8.00
RGSDS Devin Street/20 3.00 8.00
RGSDT De'Anthony Thomas/99 2.00 5.00
RGSDV Davante Adams/99 3.00 8.00
RGSEE Eric Ebron/99 2.50 6.00
RGSJC Jadeveon Clowney/99 2.50 6.00
RGSJG Jimmy Garoppolo/99 15.00 40.00
RGSJH Jeremy Hill/99 2.50 6.00
RGSJL Jarvis Landry/99 4.00 10.00
RGSJM Johnny Manziel/99 3.00 8.00
RGSJMA Jordan Matthews/99 3.00 8.00
RGSJW James White/99 4.00 10.00
RGSKB Kelvin Benjamin/99
RGSKC Ka'Deem Carey/99 2.00 5.00
RGSKM Khalil Mack/99 8.00 20.00
RGSLT Lorenzo Taliaferro/99 2.00 5.00
RGSLTH Logan Thomas/99 2.00 5.00
RGSME Mike Evans/99 5.00 12.00
RGSML Marqise Lee/99 2.50 6.00
RGSOB Odell Beckham Jr./99 5.00 12.00
RGSSJ Storm Johnson/99 2.00 5.00
RGSSW Sammy Watkins/99 3.00 8.00
RGSTB Teddy Bridgewater/99 3.00 8.00
RGSTS Tom Savage/99 2.00 5.00
RGSTW Terrance West/99 2.00 5.00

2014 Panini National Treasures Rookie NFL Gear Dual Materials Signatures
1 Tajh Boyd/99 5.00 12.00
2 Blake Bortles/99 6.00 15.00
3 Johnny Manziel/99 8.00 20.00
4 Jeremy Hill/99 6.00 15.00
5 Dri Archer/99 5.00 12.00
6 Jimmy Garoppolo/99 75.00 150.00
7 Tom Savage/99 5.00 12.00
8 Charles Sims/99 5.00 12.00
10 Andre Williams/99 5.00 12.00
11 Mike Evans/99 12.00 30.00
13 Asa Watson/99 5.00 12.00
15 Odell Beckham Jr./99 EXCH 50.00 100.00
16 Kelvin Benjamin/99 8.00 20.00
17 Brandin Cooks/99 8.00 20.00
19 Jace Amaro/49 8.00 20.00
21 A.J. McCarron/99 5.00 12.00
22 Ka'Deem Carey/99 5.00 12.00
23 Tre Mason/99 5.00 12.00
24 Terrance West/99 5.00 12.00
25 Aaron Murray/99 5.00 12.00
27 Derek Carr/99 75.00 150.00
28 Bishop Sankey/99 5.00 12.00
31 Jordan Matthews/99 8.00 20.00
32 Austin Seferian-Jenkins/99 5.00 12.00
34 Donte Moncrief/99 5.00 12.00
35 Marqise Lee/99 6.00 15.00
36 Michael Sam/99 5.00 12.00
37 Jadeveon Clowney/99 6.00 15.00
38 Cody Latimer/99 6.00 15.00
39 Davante Adams/99 8.00 20.00
40 Sammy Watkins/99 8.00 20.00

2014 Panini National Treacuroc Rookie NFL Gear Dual Materials Signatures Prime
*PRIME/49: .5X TO 1.2X DUAL JSY AU/99
6 Jimmy Garoppolo/49 150.00 300.00
15 Odell Beckham Jr./49 100.00 200.00
26 Teddy Bridgewater/49 50.00 100.00

2014 Panini National Treasures Rookie NFL Gear Quad Materials
*PRIME/25: .6X TO 1.5X QUAD JSY/99
*PRIME/15: .4X TO 1X QUAD JSY/25
RGSAH Allen Hurns/25 4.00 10.00
RGSAM Aaron Murray/99 2.00 5.00
RGSAMC A.J. McCarron/99 2.00 5.00
RGSAR Allen Robinson/99 3.00 8.00
RGSAS Austin Seferian-Jenkins/99 2.00 5.00
RGSAW Andre Williams/99 2.00 5.00
RGSBB Blake Bortles/99
RGSBC Brandin Cooks/99 3.00 8.00
RGSBR Bradley Roby/99 2.00 5.00
RGSBS Bishop Sankey/99 2.00 5.00
RGSCH Carlos Hyde/99 2.50 6.00
RGSCL Cody Latimer/99 2.50 6.00
RGSCM C.J. Mosley/99 2.50 6.00
RGSCS Charles Sims/99 2.00 5.00
RGSDC Derek Carr/99
RGSDM Donte Moncrief/99 2.00 5.00
RGSDT De'Anthony Thomas/99 2.00 5.00
RGSDV Davante Adams/99 3.00 8.00
RGSEE Eric Ebron/99 2.50 6.00
RGSJC Jadeveon Clowney/99 2.50 6.00
RGSJG Jimmy Garoppolo/99 15.00 40.00
RGSJH Jeremy Hill/99 2.50 6.00
RGSJL Jarvis Landry/99 4.00 10.00
RGSJM Johnny Manziel/99
RGSJMA Jordan Matthews/99 3.00 8.00
RGSKB Kelvin Benjamin/99
RGSKC Ka'Deem Carey/99 2.00 5.00
RGSKM Khalil Mack/99 8.00 20.00
RGSLT Lorenzo Taliaferro/99 2.00 5.00
RGSLTH Logan Thomas/99 2.00 5.00
RGSME Mike Evans/99 5.00 12.00
RGSML Marqise Lee/99 2.50 6.00
RGSOB Odell Beckham Jr./99 5.00 12.00
RGSSJ Storm Johnson/99 2.00 5.00
RGSSW Sammy Watkins/99 3.00 8.00
RGSTB Teddy Bridgewater/99 3.00 8.00
RGSTS Tom Savage/99 2.00 5.00
RGSTW Terrance West/99 2.00 5.00

2014 Panini National Treasures Rookie NFL Gear Triple Materials
*PRIME/25: .6X TO 1.5X TRIPLE JSY/99
RGSAH Allen Hurns/35 2.50 6.00
RGSAM Aaron Murray/99 2.00 5.00
RGSAMC A.J. McCarron/99 2.00 5.00
RGSAR Allen Robinson/99 3.00 8.00
RGSAS Austin Seferian-Jenkins/99 2.00 5.00
RGSAW Andre Williams/99 2.00 5.00
RGSBB Blake Bortles/99 2.50 6.00
RGSBC Brandin Cooks/99 3.00 8.00
RGSBR Bradley Roby/99 2.00 5.00
RGSBS Bishop Sankey/99 2.00 5.00
RGSCH Carlos Hyde/99 2.50 6.00
RGSCL Cody Latimer/99 2.50 6.00
RGSCM C.J. Mosley/99 2.50 6.00
RGSCS Charles Sims/99 2.00 5.00
RGSDC Derek Carr/99
RGSDM Donte Moncrief/99 2.00 5.00
RGSDS Devin Street/15
RGSDT De'Anthony Thomas/99 2.00 5.00
RGSDV Davante Adams/99 3.00 8.00
RGSEE Eric Ebron/99 2.50 6.00
RGSJC Jadeveon Clowney/99 2.50 6.00
RGSJG Jimmy Garoppolo/99 15.00 40.00
RGSJH Jeremy Hill/99 2.50 6.00
RGSJL Jarvis Landry/99 4.00 10.00
RGSJM Johnny Manziel/99
RGSJMA Jordan Matthews/99 3.00 8.00
RGSKB Kelvin Benjamin/99 3.00 8.00
RGSKC Ka'Deem Carey/99 2.00 5.00
RGSKM Khalil Mack/99 8.00 20.00
RGSLT Lorenzo Taliaferro/99 2.00 5.00
RGSLTH Logan Thomas/99 2.00 5.00
RGSME Mike Evans/99 5.00 12.00
RGSML Marqise Lee/99 2.50 6.00
RGSOB Odell Beckham Jr./99 5.00 12.00
RGSSJ Storm Johnson/99 2.00 5.00
RGSSW Sammy Watkins/99 3.00 8.00
RGSTB Teddy Bridgewater/99
RGSTS Tom Savage/99 2.00 5.00
RGSTW Terrance West/99 2.00 5.00

2014 Panini National Treasures Signature Materials
1 LaDainian Tomlinson/25 20.00 50.00
2 Charles Sims/49 5.00 12.00
3 Paul Warfield/35 12.00 30.00
4 Devonta Freeman/49 25.00 50.00
5 Tom Savage/35 5.00 12.00
6 Jadeveon Clowney/35 6.00 15.00
9 Johnny Manziel/15 10.00 25.00
10 Antonio Gates/25 8.00 20.00
11 Larry Csonka/15 25.00 50.00
12 Carlos Hyde/49 6.00 15.00
14 Donte Moncrief/49 5.00 12.00
15 Tony Dorsett/15 25.00 50.00
18 Aaron Murray/49 5.00 12.00
19 Jordan Cameron/49 6.00 15.00
20 Austin Seferian-Jenkins/49 5.00 12.00
21 LeSean McCoy/25 12.00 30.00
22 Cody Latimer/49 6.00 15.00
23 Rob Gronkowski/35 25.00 60.00
24 Dri Archer/49 5.00 12.00
25 Tony Romo/15 30.00 60.00
26 James Laurinaitis/49 8.00 20.00
27 Julius Thomas/49 6.00 15.00
29 Jordan Matthews/49 8.00 20.00
31 Logan Thomas/49 5.00 12.00
36 Jarvis Landry/49 10.00 25.00
39 Josh Gordon/35 6.00 15.00
40 Bishop Sankey/49 5.00 12.00
41 Marqise Lee/35 6.00 15.00
42 Danny Woodhead/35 8.00 20.00
43 Sammy Watkins/25 10.00 25.00
45 Tre Mason/49 5.00 12.00
46 Jeremy Hill/49 6.00 15.00
48 A.J. McCarron/35 20.00 40.00
49 Justin Houston/49 10.00 25.00
50 Blake Bortles/15 8.00 20.00
51 Marshawn Lynch/25 40.00 100.00
52 Davante Adams/49 8.00 20.00
53 Steve Smith/15 10.00 25.00
55 Victor Cruz/25 10.00 25.00
57 Alex Smith/25 10.00 25.00
58 Allen Hurns/49 6.00 15.00
59 Ka'Deem Carey/49 5.00 12.00
60 Brandin Cooks/49 8.00 20.00
61 Matt Ryan/15
62 De'Anthony Thomas/49 5.00 12.00
63 Teddy Bridgewater/25
64 Eric Ebron/49 6.00 15.00
65 Von Miller/25 10.00 25.00
66 Jimmy Garoppolo/35 150.00 300.00
67 Danny Amendola/35 8.00 20.00
68 Allen Robinson/49 8.00 20.00
69 Kelvin Benjamin/35 8.00 20.00
71 Mike Evans/35 12.00 30.00
72 DeMarcus Ware/25 10.00 25.00
73 Terrance West/49 5.00 12.00
78 Andre Williams/49 5.00 12.00
80 C.J. Spiller/35 6.00 15.00
81 Odell Beckham Jr./49 60.00 120.00
82 Demaryius Thomas/25 12.00 30.00
83 Thurman Thomas/25 12.00 30.00
84 Fred Jackson/35 8.00 20.00
85 EJ Manuel/15 8.00 20.00
87 Cameron Wake/49 6.00 15.00
88 Andy Dalton/25 10.00 25.00
90 Carson Palmer/25 10.00 25.00
92 DeSean Jackson/25 10.00 25.00
94 Giovani Bernard/35 6.00 15.00
95 Robert Woods/49 8.00 20.00
97 Jordy Nelson/35 20.00 50.00
98 Antonio Brown/35 40.00 80.00
99 Knowshon Moreno/35 6.00 15.00
100 Champ Bailey/35 10.00 25.00

2014 Panini National Treasures Signature Materials Silver
*SILVER/15-25: .5X TO 1.2X JSY AU/35-49
*SILVER/15-25: .4X TO 1X JSY AU/15-25
81 Odell Beckham Jr./25 75.00 150.00

2014 Panini National Treasures Signatures
2 Rod Woodson/25 30.00 60.00
3 Jackie Smith/35 10.00 25.00
5 Julius Thomas/49 5.00 12.00
6 A.J. Green/25 10.00 25.00
7 Marqise Lee/35 5.00 12.00
9 Paul Posluszny/49 6.00 15.00
10 Danny Woodhead/35 10.00 25.00
13 James Laurinaitis/49 6.00 15.00
14 Tony Dorsett/15 30.00 60.00
15 Justin Houston/49 5.00 12.00
16 Ahman Green/49 8.00 20.00
17 Marshawn Lynch/25 30.00 60.00
18 Blake Bortles/25 6.00 15.00
19 Paul Warfield/35 8.00 20.00
20 Darren Sproles/35 6.00 15.00
22 Ronnie Lott/15 20.00 40.00
23 Jan Stenerud/49 6.00 15.00
24 Tre Mason/49 4.00 10.00
26 Alshon Jeffery/35 6.00 15.00
28 Bob Lilly/35 12.00 30.00
30 Daunte Culpepper/49 8.00 20.00
32 Sammy Watkins/25 8.00 20.00
36 Andre Ellington/49 5.00 12.00
37 Matthew Stafford/15
38 Brandon LaFell/49 5.00 12.00
41 Frank Gore/15 15.00 40.00
42 Sean Lee/49 12.00 30.00
43 Jimmy Garoppolo/35 125.00 250.00
44 Victor Cruz/25
46 Andrew Luck/15 100.00 200.00
47 Michael Floyd/35 5.00 12.00
49 Raymond Berry/15 10.00 25.00
51 Fred Jackson/35 6.00 15.00
52 Johnny Manziel/15 20.00 50.00
54 Vincent Jackson/35 5.00 12.00
55 LaDainian Tomlinson/25 75.00 150.00
56 Andy Dalton/15 8.00 20.00
58 C.J. Spiller/35 5.00 12.00
59 Reggie Bush/15 6.00 15.00
60 DeSean Jackson/35 6.00 15.00
61 Gale Sayers/15 30.00 60.00
62 Kelvin Benjamin/35 25.00 60.00
64 Warren Moon/25 12.00 30.00
66 Anquan Boldin/15 6.00 15.00
67 Mike Evans/35 10.00 25.00
68 Carl Eller/35 10.00 25.00
69 Reggie Wayne/15 8.00 20.00
70 Dick Butkus/15 40.00 80.00
71 Giovani Bernard/35 5.00 12.00
72 Steve Largent/15 12.00 30.00
73 Warren Sapp/15 15.00 40.00
74 Allen Hurns/49 5.00 12.00
75 Lawrence Taylor/15 30.00 60.00
76 Antonio Brown/35 10.00 25.00
77 Nick Foles/25 8.00 20.00
78 Champ Bailey/35 10.00 25.00
79 Richard Sherman/15 100.00 200.00
80 Doug Martin/35 6.00 15.00
82 Teddy Bridgewater/25 50.00 100.00
83 Jordan Matthews/49 6.00 15.00
84 LeSean McCoy/15 10.00 25.00
85 Len Dawson/15 25.00 50.00
86 Arian Foster/15 8.00 20.00
87 Derek Carr/35 30.00 80.00
89 Rob Gronkowski/35 30.00 60.00
91 Jackie Slater/35 6.00 15.00
92 Tim Brown/15 20.00 40.00
93 Josh Gordon/35 5.00 12.00
94 Bishop Sankey/49 4.00 10.00
95 Luke Kuechly/35 30.00 60.00
97 Paul Hornung/35 10.00 25.00

2014 Panini National Treasures Team Quads
*PRIME/25: .5X TO 1.2X QUAD JSY/49
1 Fitzgerald/Floyd/Peterson/Mathieu/49 6.00 15.00
2 Jones/Flacco/Smith Sr./Smith/49 6.00 15.00
3 Spiller/Jackson/Woods/Watkins/49 4.00 10.00
4 Newton/Williams/Stewart/Benjamin/49 6.00 15.00
6 Green/Dalton/Bernard/Sanu/49 8.00 20.00
7 Murray/Bryant/Witten/Romo/49 12.00 30.00
8 Thomas/Thomas/Ball/Manning/49 15.00 40.00
9 Hurns/Robinson/Bortles/Lee/49 4.00 10.00
10 Landry/Miller/Wallace/Tannehill/49 6.00 15.00
11 Cooks/Graham/Stills/Colston/49 4.00 10.00
12 Williams/Manning/Beckham Jr./Randle/49 15.00 40.00
13 Gates/Allen/Rivers/Mathews/49 8.00 20.00
14 Kaepernick/Gore/Crabtree/Davis/49 6.00 15.00
15 Seferian-Jenkins/Sims/Evans/Jackson/49 6.00 15.00
16 Walker/Wright/Washington/Greene/49 5.00 12.00
17 Morris/Reed/Garcon/Griffin III/49 6.00 15.00
18 Clark/Rice/Montana/Lott/49 50.00 100.00
19 Marino/Csonka/Warfield/Tannehill/49 25.00 50.00
20 Smith/White/Staubach/Dorsett/49 10.00 25.00
21 Green/McCarron/Dalton/Hill/49 8.00 20.00
22 Jackson/Orton/Watkins/Chandler/49 4.00 10.00
23 Ware/Sanders/Manning/Miller/49
24 Thomas/Sanders/Thomas/Welker/49 6.00 15.00
25 Smith/Thomas/Charles/Davis/49 6.00 15.00
26 Beasley/Bryant/Williams/Romo/49 12.00 30.00
27 Hartline/Clay/Landry/Wallace/49 5.00 12.00
28 Amendola/Edelman/Gronkowski/Vereen/49 8.00 20.00
29 Brown/Roethlisberger/Miller/Bell/49 8.00 20.00
30 Harris/Bettis/Woodson/Bradshaw/40 15.00 40.00
31 McFadden/Carr/Mack/Jones-Drew/49 8.00 20.00
32 Jackson/Woodson/Rice/Lott/49 12.00 30.00
33 Romanowski/Elway/Davis/Dorsett/49 12.00 30.00
34 Hampton/Butkus/Allen/Briggs/35 10.00 25.00
35 Hampton/Allen/Peppers/Payton/40 15.00 40.00
36 Rodgers/Favre/Jones/Nelson/25 50.00 100.00
37 Manning/Taylor/Strahan/Cruz/25 12.00 30.00
38 Luck/Clark/Moncrief/Manning/25 20.00 50.00
39 Manziel/Cameron/Gordon/West/49 8.00 20.00
40 Patterson/Tarkenton/Bridgewater/Moon/25 5.00 12.00

2014 Panini National Treasures Team Trios
*PRIME/25: .5X TO 1.2X TRIO JSY/99
*PRIME/25: .6X TO 1.5X TRIO JSY/49
1 Cutler/Bennett/Forte/99 4.00 10.00
2 Smith/Bowe/Charles/99 5.00 12.00
3 Rice/Montana/Lott/49 20.00 50.00
4 Berry/Houston/Hali/99 5.00 12.00
5 Spiller/Jackson/Watkins/49 10.00 25.00
6 Moreno/Wallace/Tannehill/99 5.00 12.00
7 Murray/Bryant/Romo/99 12.00 30.00
8 Morris/Griffin III/Moss/49 6.00 15.00
9 Green/Dalton/Bernard/99 6.00 15.00
10 Flacco/Smith Sr./Smith/99 5.00 12.00
11 Hurns/Robinson/Bortles/99 3.00 8.00
12 Walker/Wright/Washington/99 4.00 10.00
13 Thomas/Thomas/Manning/99 12.00 30.00
14 Gates/Woodhead/Rivers/49 8.00 20.00

2014 Panini National Treasures Timeline Materials Names
*PRIME/15-25: .5X TO 1.2X NAMES JSY/50
*PRIME/50: .4X TO 1X NAMES JSY/50
*PRIME/15-25: .4X TO 1X NAMES JSY/15-25
*TEAMS/15-25: .5X TO 1.2X NAMES JSY/50
*TEAMS/50: .4X TO 1X NAMES JSY/50
*TEAMS/15-25: .4X TO 1X NAMES JSY/15-25
1 Walter Payton/25
2 Colin Kaepernick/25
3 Odell Beckham Jr./50 12.00 30.00
4 Carlos Hyde/50 3.00 8.00
5 Jadeveon Clowney/50 3.00 8.00
6 Allen Robinson/50 4.00 10.00
7 Andre Williams/50 2.50 6.00
8 Bishop Sankey/50 2.50 6.00
9 Blake Bortles/50 3.00 8.00
10 Brandin Cooks/50 4.00 10.00
11 Davante Adams/50 4.00 10.00
12 De'Anthony Thomas/50 2.50 6.00
13 Derek Carr/50 8.00 20.00
14 Logan Thomas/50 2.50 6.00
15 Jarvis Landry/50 5.00 12.00
16 Jeremy Hill/50 3.00 8.00
17 Jimmy Garoppolo/50 20.00 50.00
18 Johnny Manziel/50 4.00 10.00
19 Jordan Matthews/50 4.00 10.00
20 Kelvin Benjamin/50 4.00 10.00
21 Khalil Mack/50 10.00 25.00
22 Marqise Lee/50 3.00 8.00
23 Mike Evans/50 6.00 15.00
24 Sammy Watkins/50 4.00 10.00
25 Teddy Bridgewater/50 4.00 10.00
26 Terrance West/50 2.50 6.00
27 Tre Mason/50 2.50 6.00
28 A.J. Green/25 10.00 25.00
31 Torrey Smith/15 6.00 15.00
32 C.J. Spiller/25 6.00 15.00
33 Fred Jackson/25 8.00 20.00
34 Antonio Brown/50 8.00 20.00
35 Andy Dalton/50 6.00 15.00
36 DeMarco Murray/25 6.00 15.00
39 Wes Welker/25 8.00 20.00
40 Cecil Shorts/25 6.00 15.00
42 Eric Berry/50 6.00 15.00
44 Mike Wallace/15 6.00 15.00
45 Ryan Tannehill/15 8.00 20.00
46 Dan Marino/25 15.00 40.00
48 Johnny Unitas/25 40.00 80.00

2014 Panini National Treasures Timeline Materials Signatures Names
*PRIME/15-25: .4X TO 1X JSY AU/15-25
2 Mike Evans/15 15.00 40.00
3 Sammy Watkins/15 10.00 25.00
4 Kelvin Benjamin/15
5 Teddy Bridgewater/15 10.00 25.00
6 Derek Carr/15 40.00 80.00
10 Austin Seferian-Jenkins/25 6.00 15.00
11 Josh Gordon/15 8.00 20.00
12 Tre Mason/25 6.00 15.00
13 Patrick Peterson/25 6.00 15.00
14 Lorenzo Taliaferro/25 6.00 15.00
15 Bishop Sankey/25 6.00 15.00
16 Doug Martin/15 10.00 25.00
17 Rob Gronkowski/15 25.00 50.00
18 Giovani Bernard/15 8.00 20.00
20 Arian Foster/15
25 Jarvis Landry/25 12.00 30.00
26 Brandin Cooks/25 10.00 25.00
29 Steve Smith/15 25.00 50.00
30 Percy Harvin/15 12.00 30.00
32 Fran Tarkenton/15 30.00 60.00
33 Torrey Smith/15 8.00 20.00
35 Cecil Shorts/25 8.00 20.00
38 Antonio Gates/15 8.00 20.00
39 Davante Adams/25 10.00 25.00
40 Terrance West/25 6.00 15.00
41 Odell Beckham Jr./25 40.00 100.00
42 Vincent Jackson/15 8.00 20.00
44 Ryan Tannehill/15 25.00 50.00
46 Andy Dalton/15 10.00 25.00
48 Eric Ebron/15 8.00 20.00
49 Jordan Matthews/25 10.00 25.00
50 Donte Moncrief/25 6.00 15.00

2014 Panini National Treasures Timeline Materials Signatures Names Prime
*PRIME/15-25: .4X TO 1X JSY AU/15-25
41 Odell Beckham Jr./25 40.00 100.00

2014 Panini National Treasures Timeline Materials Signatures Team Nicknames
2 Mike Evans/15 15.00 40.00
3 Sammy Watkins/15 10.00 25.00
4 Kelvin Benjamin/15
5 Teddy Bridgewater/15 10.00 25.00
6 Derek Carr/15 40.00 80.00
10 Austin Seferian-Jenkins/25 6.00 15.00
11 Josh Gordon/15 8.00 20.00
12 Tre Mason/25 6.00 15.00
13 Patrick Peterson/25 6.00 15.00
14 Lorenzo Taliaferro/25 6.00 15.00
15 Bishop Sankey/25 6.00 15.00
16 Doug Martin/15 10.00 25.00
17 Rob Gronkowski/15 25.00 50.00
18 Giovani Bernard/15 8.00 20.00
20 Arian Foster/15
25 Jarvis Landry/25 12.00 30.00
26 Brandin Cooks/25 10.00 25.00
29 Steve Smith/15 25.00 50.00
30 Percy Harvin/15 12.00 30.00
32 Fran Tarkenton/15 30.00 60.00
33 Torrey Smith/15 8.00 20.00
35 Cecil Shorts/25 8.00 20.00
38 Antonio Gates/15 8.00 20.00
39 Davante Adams/25 10.00 25.00
40 Terrance West/25 6.00 15.00
41 Odell Beckham Jr./25 40.00 100.00
42 Vincent Jackson/15 8.00 20.00
44 Ryan Tannehill/15 25.00 50.00
46 Andy Dalton/15 10.00 25.00
48 Eric Ebron/15 8.00 20.00
49 Jordan Matthews/25 10.00 25.00
50 Donte Moncrief/25 6.00 15.00

2015 Panini National Treasures
1 LeSean McCoy 3.00 8.00
2 Jay Cutler 2.00 5.00
3 T.Y. Hilton 2.50 6.00
4 Teddy Bridgewater 2.50 6.00
5 A.J. Green 3.00 8.00
6 DeSean Jackson 2.50 6.00
7 Antonio Brown 3.00 8.00
8 Philip Rivers 3.00 8.00
9 Doug Martin 2.50 6.00
10 Ryan Tannehill 2.50 6.00
11 Calvin Johnson 3.00 8.00
12 Tom Brady 8.00 20.00
13 Bo Jackson 5.00 12.00
14 Odell Beckham Jr. 3.00 8.00
15 Arian Foster 2.50 6.00
16 Sam Bradford 2.00 5.00
17 Jimmy Graham 3.00 8.00
18 Peyton Manning 6.00 15.00
19 Brandon Marshall 2.00 5.00
20 Blake Bortles 2.00 5.00
21 Deion Sanders 3.00 8.00
22 Johnny Manziel 2.50 6.00
23 Emmitt Smith 6.00 15.00
24 Kelvin Benjamin 2.50 6.00
25 Steve Smith 2.50 6.00
26 Eddie Lacy 2.00 5.00
27 Colin Kaepernick 2.50 6.00
28 Lawrence Taylor 4.00 10.00
29 Matt Ryan 2.50 6.00
30 Jamaal Charles 2.50 6.00
31 Drew Brees 3.00 8.00
32 LaDainian Tomlinson 3.00 8.00
33 Ben Roethlisberger 3.00 8.00
34 Roger Staubach 5.00 12.00
35 Jim Kelly 4.00 10.00
36 Eric Dickerson 3.00 8.00
37 C.J. Anderson 2.50 6.00
38 Joe Montana 10.00 25.00
39 Andy Dalton 2.50 6.00
40 Keenan Allen 2.50 6.00
41 DeMarco Murray 2.50 6.00
42 Marcus Allen 4.00 10.00
43 Tim Brown 4.00 10.00
44 Mike Evans 2.50 6.00
45 Rob Gronkowski 3.00 8.00
46 Barry Sanders 6.00 15.00
47 Andrew Luck 4.00 10.00
48 Alfred Morris 2.00 5.00
49 Larry Fitzgerald 2.50 6.00
50 James Lofton 2.00 5.00
51 Kendall Wright 2.00 5.00
52 Eli Manning 2.50 6.00
53 Jordy Nelson 2.50 6.00
54 Ndamukong Suh 2.50 6.00
55 Adrian Peterson 3.00 8.00
56 Julius Thomas 2.00 5.00
57 Matt Forte 2.00 5.00
58 Russell Wilson 4.00 10.00
59 Dez Bryant 3.00 8.00
60 DeAndre Hopkins 2.50 6.00
61 Cam Newton 3.00 8.00
62 Alex Smith 2.50 6.00
63 Julio Jones 3.00 8.00
64 Andre Johnson 2.50 6.00
65 Mark Ingram 2.50 6.00
66 Derek Carr 3.00 8.00
67 Kirk Cousins 3.00 8.00
68 Torrey Smith 2.00 5.00
69 Eric Decker 2.00 5.00
70 Matthew Stafford 2.50 6.00
71 Demaryius Thomas 2.50 6.00
72 Nick Foles 2.50 6.00
73 Jeremy Hill 2.00 5.00
74 Brett Favre 8.00 20.00
75 Carson Palmer 2.50 6.00
76 Sammy Watkins 2.50 6.00
77 Derrick Brooks 2.50 6.00
78 Le'Veon Bell 2.50 6.00
79 Jordan Matthews 2.50 6.00
80 John Riggins 3.00 8.00
81 Fran Tarkenton 4.00 10.00
82 Joe Flacco 2.50 6.00
83 Victor Cruz 2.50 6.00
84 Jerome Bettis 4.00 10.00
85 Jeremy Maclin 2.00 5.00
86 Richard Sherman 3.00 8.00
87 Julian Edelman 3.00 8.00
88 Walter Payton 8.00 20.00
89 Tony Romo 2.50 6.00
90 Dan Marino 8.00 20.00
91 Shannon Sharpe 3.00 8.00
92 J.J. Watt 3.00 8.00
93 John Elway 6.00 15.00
94 Aaron Rodgers 6.00 15.00
95 Jerry Rice 6.00 15.00
96 Joe Namath 5.00 12.00
97 Alshon Jeffery 2.50 6.00
98 Marshawn Lynch 2.50 6.00
99 Marshall Faulk 3.00 8.00
100 Luke Kuechly 2.50 6.00
101 Mike Davis JSY AU RC 12.00 30.00
102 Jeremy Langford JSY AU RC 15.00 40.00
103 Kevin White JSY AU RC 75.00 150.00
104 Karlos Williams JSY AU RC 12.00 30.00
105 Duke Johnson JSY AU RC 20.00 50.00
107 Jameis Winston JSY AU RC 250.00 500.00
108 David Johnson JSY AU RC 50.00 100.00
109 Melvin Gordon JSY AU RC 30.00 80.00
110 Chris Conley JSY AU RC 12.00 30.00
111 Phillip Dorsett JSY AU RC 12.00 30.00
112 DeVante Parker JSY AU RC 60.00 120.00
113 Jay Ajayi JSY AU RC 20.00 50.00
114 Nelson Agholor JSY AU RC 15.00 40.00
115 Justin Hardy JSY AU RC 12.00 30.00
116 Tevin Coleman JSY AU RC 15.00 40.00
117 Rashad Greene JSY AU RC 12.00 30.00
118 T.J. Yeldon JSY AU RC 12.00 30.00
119 Bryce Petty JSY AU RC 12.00 30.00
120 Devin Smith JSY AU RC 12.00 30.00
121 Leonard Williams JSY AU RC 12.00 30.00
122 Ameer Abdullah JSY AU RC 20.00 50.00
123 Brett Hundley JSY AU RC 50.00 100.00
124 Ty Montgomery JSY AU RC 12.00 30.00
125 Devin Funchess JSY AU RC 20.00 50.00
126 Amari Cooper JSY AU RC 150.00 300.00
127 Sean Mannion JSY AU RC 12.00 30.00
128 Todd Gurley JSY AU RC 125.00 250.00
129 Breshad Perriman JSY AU RC 12.00 30.00
131 Maxx Williams JSY AU RC 12.00 30.00
132 Jamison Crowder JSY AU RC 15.00 40.00
133 Matt Jones JSY AU RC 12.00 30.00
134 Garrett Grayson JSY AU RC 12.00 30.00
135 Tyler Lockett JSY AU RC 15.00 40.00
136 Sammie Coates JSY AU RC 15.00 40.00
137 Jaelen Strong JSY AU RC 15.00 40.00
138 David Cobb JSY AU RC 12.00 30.00
139 Dorial Green-Beckham JSY AU RC 15.00 40.00
140 Marcus Mariota JSY AU RC 200.00 400.00
141 Stefon Diggs JSY AU RC 30.00 80.00
142 Marcus Murphy AU/99 RC 4.00 10.00
144 Kwon Alexander AU/99 RC 5.00 12.00
145 Ben Koyack AU/99 RC 6.00 15.00
146 Benardrick McKinney AU/99 RC 4.00 10.00
147 Quinten Rollins AU/99 RC 8.00 20.00
149 Cameron Artis-Payne AU/99 RC 4.00 10.00
150 Clive Walford AU/99 RC 4.00 10.00
151 Danielle Hunter AU/99 RC 5.00 12.00
152 Danny Shelton AU/99 RC 4.00 10.00
154 Darren Waller AU/99 RC 5.00 12.00
155 Tyler Kroft AU/99 RC 5.00 12.00
156 DeAndrew White AU/99 RC 6.00 15.00
158 Lucky Whitehead AU/49 RC 12.00 30.00
159 Derron Smith AU/99 RC 4.00 10.00
160 Dezmin Lewis AU/99 RC 4.00 10.00
161 Thomas Rawls AU/99 RC 10.00 25.00
163 Eli Harold AU/99 RC 4.00 10.00
164 Ereck Flowers AU/99 RC 5.00 12.00
165 Eric Kendricks AU/99 RC 4.00 10.00
166 Geremy Davis AU/99 RC 5.00 12.00
168 Jesse James AU/99 RC 5.00 12.00
169 J.J. Nelson AU/99 RC 4.00 10.00
170 Frank Clark AU/99 RC 10.00 25.00
172 Josh Shaw AU/99 RC 6.00 15.00
173 Kenny Bell AU/99 RC 6.00 15.00
175 Landon Collins AU/99 RC 5.00 12.00
177 Marcus Peters AU/99 RC 20.00 40.00
178 Mario Alford AU/49 RC 5.00 12.00
179 Mario Edwards Jr. AU/99 RC 4.00 10.00
180 MyCole Pruitt AU/99 RC 4.00 10.00
182 Owamagbe Odighizuwa AU/99 RC 5.00 12.00
183 Charcandrick West AU/99 RC 5.00 12.00
184 Randy Gregory AU/99 RC 4.00 10.00
185 Rannell Hall AU/99 RC 4.00 10.00
187 Cameron Meredith AU/99 RC 6.00 15.00
188 Shane Ray AU/99 RC 4.00 10.00
189 Shaq Thompson AU/99 RC 5.00 12.00
190 Stephone Anthony AU/99 RC 4.00 10.00
191 Taylor Heinicke AU/99 RC 6.00 15.00
192 Terrence Magee AU/99 RC 6.00 15.00
193 Titus Davis AU/99 RC 5.00 12.00
194 Tony Lippett AU/99 RC 4.00 10.00
195 Trae Waynes AU/99 RC 4.00 10.00
196 Tre McBride AU/99 RC 4.00 10.00
197 Trey Williams AU/99 RC 5.00 12.00
198 Vic Beasley Jr. AU/99 RC 5.00 12.00
200 Blake Bell AU/99 RC 6.00 15.00

2015 Panini National Treasures Gold
*VETS: .5X TO 1.2X BASIC CARDS/99
*ROOK AU: .5X TO 1.2X BASIC
161 Thomas Rawls AU/49 12.00 30.00

2015 Panini National Treasures Holo Silver
*VETS/25: .6X TO 1.5X BASIC CARDS/99
140 Marcus Mariota JSY AU 250.00 500.00

2015 Panini National Treasures America's Team Memorabilia
*PRIME/25: .6X TO 1.5X BASIC JSY/99
*PRIME/25: .5X TO 1.2X BASIC JSY/49
ATAH Anthony Hitchens/99 5.00 12.00
ATBC Barry Church/99 6.00 15.00
ATBC Brandon Carr/99 5.00 12.00
ATBJ Byron Jones/99 8.00 20.00
ATCB Cole Beasley/99 8.00 20.00
ATCH Charles Haley/49 10.00 25.00
ATDL DeMarcus Lawrence/99 5.00 12.00
ATDM DeMarco Murray/49
ATDM Don Meredith/49 20.00 40.00
ATDS Deion Sanders/49 8.00 20.00
ATDS Devin Street/99 5.00 12.00
ATDW DeMarcus Ware/49 8.00 20.00
ATES Emmitt Smith/49 15.00 40.00
ATGE Gavin Escobar/99 5.00 12.00
ATJW Jason Witten/49 8.00 20.00
ATMD Mike Ditka/49 10.00 25.00
ATMI Michael Irvin/25 20.00 40.00
ATRS Roger Staubach/25 15.00 40.00
ATSL Sean Lee/25 10.00 25.00
ATTA Troy Aikman/49 12.00 30.00
ATTD Tony Dorsett/49 20.00 40.00
ATTL Tom Landry/49 25.00 50.00
ATTR Tony Romo/49 8.00 20.00
ATTW Terrance Williams/99 5.00 12.00
ATZM Zack Martin/99 5.00 12.00

2015 Panini National Treasures America's Team Signatures
ATSBJ Byron Jones/49 25.00 60.00
ATSBL Bob Lilly/49 20.00 50.00
ATSCH Charles Haley/49 25.00 60.00
ATSDM Darren McFadden/25 20.00 50.00
ATSDS Devin Street/49 15.00 40.00
ATSGE Gavin Escobar/49 15.00 40.00
ATSJW Jason Witten/25 50.00 100.00
ATSLC La'el Collins/49 20.00 50.00
ATSMD Mike Ditka/25 30.00 80.00
ATSRG Randy Gregory/49 20.00 50.00
ATSRS Roger Staubach/15 75.00 150.00
ATSRW Randy White/25 25.00 60.00
ATSTD Tony Dorsett/15 60.00 120.00
ATSTW Terrance Williams/25 20.00 50.00
ATSZM Zack Martin/49 15.00 40.00

2015 Panini National Treasures Century Materials
*PRIME/49: .5X TO 1.2X BASIC JSY/75-99
*SILVER/25: .6X TO 1.5X BASIC JSY/75-99
*SILVER/15: .6X TO 1.5X BASIC JSY/35-49
*PRIME/25: .5X TO 1.2X BASIC JSY/35-49
*PRIME/15: .6X TO 1.5X BASIC JSY/35
*PRIME/15: .5X TO 1.2X BASIC JSY/25
*PRIME/25: .6X TO 1.5X BASIC JSY/75-99
CMAA Ameer Abdullah/99 3.00 8.00
CMAB Antonio Brown/49 6.00 15.00
CMAC Amari Cooper/99 6.00 15.00
CMAC Antonio Cromartie/75 3.00 8.00
CMAE Andre Ellington/49 4.00 10.00
CMAG Antonio Gates/35 4.00 10.00
CMAG A.J. Green/49 6.00 15.00
CMAH A.J. Hawk/75 3.00 8.00
CMAT Aqib Talib/99 3.00 8.00
CMBB Blake Bortles/99 3.00 8.00
CMBF Brett Favre/35 12.00 30.00
CMBI Bruce Irvin/49 4.00 10.00
CMCC Charles Clay/99 3.00 8.00
CMCH Chris Harris/99 3.00 8.00
CMCH Charles Haley/49 6.00 15.00
CMCJ Calvin Johnson/49 6.00 15.00
CMCK Colin Kaepernick/25 6.00 15.00
CMCM Curtis Martin/49 5.00 12.00
CMCM Clay Matthews/25 8.00 20.00
CMCP Carson Palmer/49 5.00 12.00
CMDB Dez Bryant/35 6.00 15.00
CMDB Derrick Brooks/75 3.00 8.00
CMDF Devonta Freeman/99 4.00 10.00
CMDG Dorial Green-Beckham/99 2.00 5.00
CMDJ Derrick Johnson/99 3.00 8.00
CMDJ Duke Johnson/99 3.00 8.00
CMDJ David Johnson/99 5.00 12.00
CMDJ D'Qwell Jackson/49 4.00 10.00
CMDM Don Majkowski/99 4.00 10.00
CMDP DeVante Parker/99 3.00 8.00
CMDT Demaryius Thomas/49 5.00 12.00
CMEC Earl Campbell/49 6.00 15.00
CMED Elvis Dumervil/99 3.00 8.00
CMEJ Edgerrin James/35 5.00 12.00
CMET Earl Thomas/49 5.00 12.00
CMGS Gale Sayers/25 8.00 20.00
CMGT Golden Tate/35 4.00 10.00
CMJE Julian Edelman/49 6.00 15.00
CMJE John Elway/49 10.00 25.00
CMJF Joe Flacco/49 5.00 12.00
CMJG Jimmy Graham/49 6.00 15.00
CMJH Justin Houston/49 4.00 10.00
CMJH Joe Haden/99 3.00 8.00
CMJJ Julio Jones/49 6.00 15.00
CMJK Jim Kelly/49 6.00 15.00
CMJL James Laurinaitis/99 4.00 10.00
CMJL Jeremy Langford/99 2.00 5.00
CMJM Jim McMahon/99 4.00 10.00
CMJM Joe Montana/49 15.00 40.00
CMJN Joe Namath/49 8.00 20.00
CMJP Julius Peppers/25 6.00 15.00
CMJR John Riggins/49 5.00 12.00
CMJS Josh Sitton/99 3.00 8.00
CMJS Joe Staley/99 3.00 8.00
CMJS Jonathan Stewart/49 4.00 10.00
CMJT Julius Thomas/99 3.00 8.00
CMJU Johnny Unitas/99 12.00 30.00
CMJW Jameis Winston/99 8.00 20.00
CMKW Kyle Williams/99 3.00 8.00
CMKW Karlos Williams/99 3.00 8.00
CMLC Larry Csonka/35 5.00 12.00
CMLF Larry Fitzgerald/49 5.00 12.00
CMLM Lamar Miller/75 3.00 8.00
CMMB Martellus Bennett/75 3.00 8.00
CMMG Melvin Gordon/99 5.00 12.00
CMMI Mark Ingram/49 5.00 12.00
CMMJ Matt Jones/99 2.00 5.00
CMML Marshawn Lynch/49 5.00 12.00
CMMM Marcus Mariota/99 8.00 20.00
CMMR Matt Ryan/49 5.00 12.00
CMMS Matthew Stafford/49 5.00 12.00
CMMS Mike Singletary/49 6.00 15.00
CMNA Nelson Agholor/99 2.50 6.00
CMNB Navorro Bowman/35 5.00 12.00
CMPD Phillip Dorsett/99 2.00 5.00
CMPG Pierre Garcon/49 5.00 12.00
CMPM Peyton Manning/49 12.00 30.00
CMPP Paul Posluszny/99 3.00 8.00
CMRC Roger Craig/49 5.00 12.00
CMRJ Reshad Jones/99 3.00 8.00
CMRQ Robert Quinn/49 5.00 12.00
CMRT Ryan Tannehill/49 5.00 12.00
CMRW Roddy White/49 4.00 10.00
CMSD Stefon Diggs/99 5.00 12.00
CMSL Steve Largent/35 6.00 15.00
CMTB Tom Brady/49 15.00 40.00
CMTC Tevin Coleman/99 2.50 6.00
CMTD Tony Dorsett/75 5.00 12.00
CMTE Tyler Eifert/99 4.00 10.00
CMTG Todd Gurley/99 10.00 25.00
CMTL Tyler Lockett/99 3.00 8.00
CMTL Tom Landry/99 20.00 40.00
CMTM Ty Montgomery/99 2.00 5.00
CMTR Tony Romo/49 5.00 12.00
CMTS Terrell Suggs/49 4.00 10.00

CMTT Tyrod Taylor/99 4.00 10.00
CMTW Trent Williams/99 3.00 8.00
CMTY T.J. Yeldon/99 2.00 5.00
CMVM Von Miller/99 4.00 10.00
CMWP Walter Payton/34 20.00 50.00

2015 Panini National Treasures Colossal Materials

*PRIME/25: .6X TO 1.5X BASIC JSY/99
*PRIME/25: .5X TO 1.2X BASIC JSY/49
*PRIME/15: .5X TO 1.2X BASIC JSY/25
CMKC Kam Chancellor/25 15.00 30.00
CMAB Antonio Brown/25 8.00 20.00
CMAE Andre Ellington/49 4.00 10.00
CMAG A.J. Green/25 8.00 20.00
CMAG Antonio Gates/25 5.00 12.00
CMAH Allen Hurns/99 3.00 8.00
CMAP Adrian Peterson/25 8.00 20.00
CMBB Blake Bortles/99 3.00 8.00
CMCA C.J. Anderson/99 4.00 10.00
CMCH Charles Haley/49 6.00 15.00
CMCJ Calvin Johnson/25 8.00 20.00
CMCK Colin Kaepernick/25 6.00 15.00
CMCM Clay Matthews/25 8.00 20.00
CMDB Dez Bryant/25 8.00 20.00
CMDB Derrick Brooks/49 4.00 10.00
CMDR Darrelle Revis/49 4.00 10.00
CMEL Eddie Lacy/25 5.00 12.00
CMIC Isaiah Crowell/49 4.00 10.00
CMJC Jamaal Charles/25 6.00 15.00
CMJE Julian Edelman/25 8.00 20.00
CMJH Jeremy Hill/99 3.00 8.00
CMJJ Julio Jones/25 8.00 20.00
CMJL Jarvis Landry/99 4.00 10.00
CMJM Joe Montana/25 25.00 50.00
CMJR John Riggins/49 5.00 12.00
CMLC Larry Csonka/25 6.00 15.00
CMLF Larry Fitzgerald/25 6.00 15.00
CMLM LeSean McCoy/49 6.00 15.00
CMMA Marcus Allen/25 8.00 20.00
CMMF Matt Forte/25 5.00 12.00
CMML Marshawn Lynch/25 6.00 15.00
CMMS Mike Singletary/25 8.00 20.00
CMMS Matthew Stafford/25 6.00 15.00
CMPM Peyton Manning/49 12.00 30.00
CMRC Randall Cobb/25 6.00 15.00
CMRG Rob Gronkowski/25 8.00 20.00
CMRT Ryan Tannehill/49 5.00 12.00
CMSW Sammy Watkins/99 4.00 10.00
CMTK Travis Kelce/25 8.00 20.00
CMTR Tony Romo/25 6.00 15.00

2015 Panini National Treasures Colossal Pro Bowl Materials

*PRIME/25: .6X TO 1.5X BASIC JSY/99
*PRIME/25: .5X TO 1.2X BASIC JSY/35-49
*PRIME/15: .5X TO 1.2X BASIC JSY/25
CPMAD Andy Dalton/49 5.00 12.00
CPMAT Aqib Talib/25 5.00 12.00
CPMDS Darren Sproles/35 5.00 12.00
CPMES Emmanuel Sanders/25 6.00 15.00
CPMJF Justin Forsett/49 5.00 12.00
CPMJK John Kuhn/99 10.00 25.00
CPMJN Jordy Nelson/25 6.00 15.00
CPMJW Jason Witten/49 15.00 40.00
CPMJW J.J. Watt/49 12.00 30.00
CPMLK Luke Kuechly/49 12.00 30.00
CPMLT Lawrence Timmons/49 8.00 20.00
CPMMD Marcell Dareus/49 4.00 10.00
CPMMI Mark Ingram/49 5.00 12.00
CPMMP Maurkice Pouncey/99 10.00 25.00
CPMMS Matthew Stafford/49 5.00 12.00
CPMNM Nick Mangold/99 3.00 8.00
CPMOB Odell Beckham Jr./25 15.00 30.00
CPMRC Randall Cobb/25 6.00 15.00
CPMSR Sheldon Richardson/99 3.00 8.00
CPMSS Sam Shields/49 8.00 20.00
CPMTH Tamba Hali/49 4.00 10.00
CPMTH T.Y. Hilton/49 5.00 12.00
CPMTR Tony Romo/49 5.00 12.00
CPMTS Tyron Smith/99 3.00 8.00
CPMTW T.J. Ward/99 3.00 8.00
CPMVM Von Miller/15 8.00 20.00
CPMZM Zack Martin/99 3.00 8.00

2015 Panini National Treasures Colossal Signature Materials

*PRIME/25: .4X TO 1X BASIC JSY AU/25
*PRIME/25: .5X TO 1.2X BASIC JSY AU/49
*PRIME/15: .5X TO 1.2X BASIC JSY AU/25
COSAD Andy Dalton/15 20.00 50.00
COSAG A.J. Green/15
COSDB Derrick Brooks/25 12.00 30.00
COSDB Dez Bryant/15 25.00 60.00
COSDC Derek Carr/25 20.00 50.00
COSDJ DeSean Jackson/25 15.00 40.00
COSED Eric Dickerson/25 15.00 40.00
COSEM EJ Manuel/25 12.00 30.00
COSGB Giovani Bernard/25 12.00 30.00
COSJG Jimmy Garoppolo/25 125.00 250.00
COSJN Jordy Nelson/15 40.00 80.00
COSLM Lamar Miller/49 10.00 25.00
COSMF Michael Floyd/49 10.00 25.00
COSML Marqise Lee/25 12.00 30.00
COSMR Matt Ryan/15 20.00 50.00
COSPR Philip Rivers/15 25.00 60.00
COSRG Robert Griffin III/15 15.00 40.00
COSSW Sammy Watkins/25 15.00 40.00
COSTB Teddy Bridgewater/25 15.00 40.00
COSTR Tony Romo/15 20.00 50.00
COSVM Von Miller/49 40.00 80.00
COSWW Wes Welker/25 15.00 40.00

2015 Panini National Treasures Draft Treasures Signature Materials Booklet

1 D.Fowler Jr./B.Bortles/25 12.00 30.00
2 K.White/O.Beckham Jr./25 50.00 100.00
3 J.Clowney/K.Johnson/25 8.00 20.00
4 J.Manziel/D.Shelton/25 10.00 25.00
5 J.Matthews/V.Beasley Jr./15 12.00 30.00
6 G.Robinson/T.Gurley/25 30.00 80.00
7 D.Parker/S.Watkins/25 12.00 30.00
8 K.Mack/S.Ray/15 40.00 80.00
9 R.Shazier/B.Dupree/25 8.00 20.00
10 B.Cooks/A.Peat/25 10.00 25.00
11 C.Ogbuehi/M.Evans/25 10.00 25.00
12 T.Lewan/B.Scherff/25 12.00 30.00
13 C.Mosley/B.Perriman/25 12.00 30.00
14 L.Tomlinson/E.Ebron/25 8.00 20.00
15 T.Waynes/T.Bridgewater/25 25.00 50.00
16 C.Pryor/L.Williams/25 8.00 20.00
17 J.Verrett/M.Gordon/25 20.00 50.00
18 S.Ray/H.Clinton-Dix/15 10.00 25.00
19 B.Jones/K.Fuller/25 12.00 30.00

2015 Panini National Treasures Dual Signatures

1 M.Evans/J.Winston/25 60.00 120.00
2 C.Conley/T.Kelce/49 15.00 40.00
3 A.Brown/S.Coates/49 15.00 40.00
5 T.Gurley/M.Faulk/25 75.00 150.00
6 L.Tomlinson/M.Gordon/25 30.00 80.00
8 D.Funchess/K.Benjamin/49 15.00 40.00
12 G.Grayson/D.Brees/20 30.00 60.00
17 T.Aikman/T.Romo/20 50.00 100.00
19 A.Abdullah/B.Sanders/25
20 D.Brooks/T.Dilfer/25 12.00 30.00
21 D.Carr/D.Carr/49 15.00 40.00
22 F.Tarkenton/T.Bridgewater/25 30.00 80.00
23 T.Montgomery/J.Nelson/49 12.00 30.00
24 L.Miller/J.Ajayi/15 20.00 50.00

2015 Panini National Treasures Friends and Foes Quad Materials

*PRIME/25: .6X TO 1.5X BASIC JSY/99
*PRIME/25: .5X TO 1.2X BASIC JSY/49
1 J.Winston/R.Greene/99 8.00 20.00
2 A.Cooper/T.Yeldon/99 6.00 15.00
3 T.Gurley/C.Conley/99 10.00 25.00
4 D.Cobb/M.Williams/99 2.00 5.00
5 D.Johnson/P.Dorsett/99 3.00 8.00
6 D.Freeman/K.Williams/99 2.50 6.00
7 K.Benjamin/J.Winston/99 8.00 20.00
8 D.Parker/T.Bridgewater/99 3.00 8.00
9 B.Bortles/B.Perriman/99 2.00 5.00
10 C.Hyde/D.Smith/99 2.00 5.00
11 B.Cooks/S.Mannion/99 2.50 6.00
12 D.Carr/D.Adams/99 3.00 8.00
13 D.Thomas/M.Mariota/99 8.00 20.00
14 M.Lee/N.Agholor/99 2.50 6.00
15 D.Hopkins/S.Watkins/49 6.00 15.00
16 E.Lacy/T.Yeldon/49 6.00 15.00
17 J.Manziel/M.Evans/99 2.50 6.00
18 P.Dorsett/A.Hurns/99 2.00 5.00
19 J.Landry/O.Beckham Jr./99
20 S.Watkins/K.Williams/99 2.50 6.00
21 C.Latimer/T.Coleman/99 2.50 6.00
22 N.Agholor/L.Williams/99 2.50 6.00
23 M.Lee/R.Woods/99 2.50 6.00
24 J.Hill/J.Landry/99 2.50 6.00
25 S.Coates/T.Mason/99 2.50 6.00
26 D.Freeman/J.Winston/99 8.00 20.00
27 C.Sims/K.White/99 2.50 6.00
28 O.Beckham Jr./J.Hill/99 3.00 8.00
29 A.Seferian-Jenkins/B.Sankey/99 2.00 5.00
30 A.Luck/R.Sherman/49 10.00 25.00

2015 Panini National Treasures Greatest Treasures Materials

GTJR Jerry Rice 12.00 30.00
GTLT Lawrence Taylor 8.00 20.00
GTMD Mike Ditka 15.00 30.00
GTTB Tom Brady 20.00 50.00
GTWP Walter Payton 50.00 100.00

2015 Panini National Treasures Jumbo Material Signatures Booklet Prime

3 Derrick Brooks/25 40.00 80.00
9 Dez Bryant/25 60.00 120.00
10 Andy Dalton/25 30.00 60.00
13 Antonio Brown/25 50.00 100.00

2015 Panini National Treasures Material Signatures Prime

*PRIME/25: .4X TO 1X BASIC JSY AU/25
*PRIME/15: .6X TO 1.5X BASIC JSY AU/49
*PRIME/15: .5X TO 1.2X BASIC JSY AU/25

2015 Panini National Treasures National History Materials Booklet

*PRIME/25: .5X TO 1.2X BASIC JSY/49
*PRIME/15: .2X TO 1.5X BASIC JSY/49
NHBAA Ameer Abdullah 6.00 15.00
NHBAC Amari Cooper 12.00 30.00
NHBDF Devonta Freeman 5.00 12.00
NHBDM Donte Moncrief 5.00 12.00
NHBJH Jeremy Hill 4.00 10.00
NHBJL Jarvis Landry 5.00 12.00
NHBJW Jameis Winston
NHBME Mike Evans 5.00 12.00
NHBMG Melvin Gordon 10.00 25.00
NHBMJ Matt Jones 4.00 10.00
NHBMM Marcus Mariota 30.00 60.00
NHBNA Nelson Agholor 5.00 12.00
NHBOB Odell Beckham Jr. 6.00 15.00
NHBTG Todd Gurley 20.00 50.00
NHBTL Tyler Lockett 6.00 15.00
NHBTM Ty Montgomery 4.00 10.00

2015 Panini National Treasures NFL Gear Combo Materials

1 D.Ware/V.Miller/99 2.50 6.00
2 L.McCoy/S.Watkins/49 4.00 10.00
3 B.Urlacher/M.Singletary/49 4.00 10.00
4 E.Thomas/K.Chancellor/49 4.00 10.00
5 E.Manning/P.Manning/25 10.00 25.00
6 C.Johnson/M.Stafford/25 5.00 12.00
7 J.Hill/G.Bernard/75 2.00 5.00
8 C.Wake/N.Suh/49 3.00 8.00
9 A.Gates/P.Rivers/25 5.00 12.00
10 D.Brooks/W.Dunn/49 2.50 6.00
11 B.Jackson/M.Allen/25 6.00 15.00
12 R.Williams/M.Ingram/49 3.00 8.00
13 J.Matthews/N.Agholor/99 2.50 6.00
14 L.Tomlinson/M.Gordon/25 8.00 20.00
15 M.Davis/C.Hydo/99 2.00 5.00
16 M.Faulk/T.Gurley/25 12.00 30.00
17 S.Smith/B.Perriman/25 4.00 10.00
18 D.Freeman/T.Coleman/99 2.50 6.00
19 D.Funchess/K.Benjamin/99 3.00 8.00
20 A.Ellington/D.Johnson/49 6.00 15.00
21 D.Parker/J.Landry/99 3.00 8.00
22 J.Langford/M.Forte/25 3.00 8.00
23 I.Crowell/D.Johnson/49 4.00 10.00
24 D.Adams/T.Montgomery/99 2.50 6.00
25 A.Brown/S.Coates/49 4.00 10.00
26 A.Cooper/D.Carr/99 5.00 12.00
27 J.Hardy/J.Jones/25 5.00 12.00
28 C.Portis/M.Jones/49 2.50 6.00
29 B.Sanders/A.Abdullah/25 8.00 20.00
30 R.Cobb/D.Cobb/25 4.00 10.00

2015 Panini National Treasures NFL Gear Quad Materials

*PRIME/25: .6X TO 1.5X BASIC JSY/99
*PRIME/25: .5X TO 1.2X BASIC JSY/49
*PRIME/15: .5X TO 1.2X BASIC JSY/25
1 Andrsn/Thms/Sndrs/Mnng/25 12.00 30.00
2 Cly/Hrvn/Wtkns/Tylr/49 4.00 10.00
3 Lndry/Stlls/Mthws/Tnnhll/25 5.00 12.00
4 Brtls/Thms/Hrns/Rbnsn/49 4.00 10.00
5 Jns/Grn/Dltn/Efrt/49 5.00 12.00
6 Ebrn/Stffrd/Jhnsn/Tte/25 6.00 15.00
7 Brynt/Wttn/Rmo/Wllms/25 12.00 30.00
8 Ryn/Frmn/Jns/Whte/25 6.00 15.00
9 Smth/Dckrsn/Sndrs/Pytn/25 40.00 80.00
10 Fvre/Mrno/Mnng/Brdy/25 40.00 80.00
11 Poe/Hstn/Brry/Hli/99 3.00 8.00
12 Lck/Drstt/Mncrf/Hltn/49 6.00 15.00
13 Crtr/Trkntn/Dggs/Brdgwtr/25 30.00 60.00
14 Mnng/Bckhm/Rndle/Crz/25 12.00 30.00
15 Crmrte/Rvs/Wllms/Rchrdsn/49 3.00 8.00
16 GrnBckhm/Hntr/Wrght/Mrta/99 8.00 20.00
17 SfnJkns/Sms/Wstn/Evns/99 6.00 15.00
18 Nwtn/Brs/Ryn/Wnstn/49 10.00 25.00
19 Smth/Crr/Mnng/Rvrs/25 12.00 30.00
20 Lcy/Ptrsn/Abdllh/Frte/25 6.00 15.00

2015 Panini National Treasures NFL Gear Triple Materials

*PRIME/25: .6X TO 1.5X BASIC JSY/99
*PRIME/25: .5X TO 1.2X BASIC JSY/49
1 GrnBckhm/Bckhm/Grn/99 3.00 8.00
2 Chrch/Wnstn/Hll/99 6.00 15.00
4 Drs/Wllms/Glmre/99 2.00 5.00
5 Tlb/Hrrs/Wrd/99 2.00 5.00
6 Dnlp/Atkns/Mlga/99 2.00 5.00
7 Crr/Lee/McCln/45 3.00 8.00
8 Hli/Cnly/Dvs/99 2.00 5.00
9 Csnka/Grse/Wrfld/25 5.00 12.00
10 Edlmn/Grnkwski/Brdy/25 12.00 30.00
11 Lcy/Nlsn/Cbb/25 4.00 10.00
12 Gts/Wttn/Dvs/25 4.00 10.00
13 Grhm/Wlsn/Lcktt/49 5.00 12.00
14 Ctlr/Jffry/Whte/49 3.00 8.00
15 Plmr/Jhnsn/Ftzgrld/49 6.00 15.00
16 Csns/Jns/Grcn/99 3.00 8.00
17 Lck/Mrta/Brtls/25 12.00 30.00
18 Bckhm/Jcksn/Brynt/25 5.00 12.00
19 Hyde/Lynch/Grly/49 5.00 12.00
20 Grly/Brwn/Jns/25 5.00 12.00

2015 Panini National Treasures Personalized Treasures

PERAL Andrew Luck/15 100.00 200.00
PERCH Charles Haley/25 40.00 80.00
PERGS Gale Sayers/25
PERIW Ickey Woods/25 12.00 30.00
PERJB Jerome Bettis/25 90.00 150.00
PERJR John Riggins/49 40.00 80.00
PERRW Randy White/25 15.00 40.00
PERTB Tim Brown/25
PERTD Trent Dilfer/25 12.00 30.00
PERTD Tony Dorsett/15 25.00 60.00

2015 Panini National Treasures Rookie Colossal Signature Materials

RCOAA Ameer Abdullah/99 8.00 20.00
RCOBH Brett Hundley/49 6.00 15.00
RCOBP Bryce Petty/49 EXCH 6.00 15.00
RCOBP Breshad Perriman/99 5.00 12.00
RCOCC Chris Conley/49 6.00 15.00
RCODC David Cobb/99 5.00 12.00
RCODF Devin Funchess/99 8.00 20.00
RCODG Dorial Green-Beckham/99 5.00 12.00
RCODJ Duke Johnson/99 8.00 20.00
RCODJ David Johnson/99 EXCH 25.00 50.00
RCODP DeVante Parker/99 8.00 20.00
RCOJA Jay Ajayi/99 8.00 20.00
RCOJC Jamison Crowder/99 6.00 15.00
RCOJH Justin Hardy/99 5.00 12.00
RCOJL Jeremy Langford/99 5.00 12.00
RCOJW Jameis Winston/49 75.00 150.00
RCOKW Karlos Williams/99 5.00 12.00
RCOKW Kevin White/49 8.00 20.00
RCOLW Leonard Williams/99 5.00 12.00
RCOMD Mike Davis/99 5.00 12.00
RCOMG Melvin Gordon/99 12.00 30.00
RCOMJ Matt Jones/99 5.00 12.00
RCOMM Marcus Mariota/49 40.00 80.00
RCOMW Maxx Williams/99 5.00 12.00
RCONA Nelson Agholor/99 6.00 15.00
RCOPD Phillip Dorsett/99 5.00 12.00
RCORG Rashad Greene/99 5.00 12.00
RCOSD Stefon Diggs/99 12.00 30.00
RCOTG Todd Gurley/25 75.00 150.00
RCOTL Tyler Lockett/99 8.00 20.00
RCOTM Ty Montgomery/99 5.00 12.00
RCOTY T.J. Yeldon/99 5.00 12.00

2015 Panini National Treasures Rookie Colossal Signature Materials Prime

*PRIME/25: .6X TO 1.5X BASIC JSY AU/99
*PRIME/25: .5X TO 1.2X BASIC JSY AU/49
*PRIME/15: .8X TO 2X BASIC JSY AU/99
*PRIME/15: .6X TO 1.5X BASIC JSY AU/49
RCOJW Jameis Winston/15 200.00 400.00
RCOMM Marcus Mariota/15 50.00 100.00

2015 Panini National Treasures Rookie Dual Materials

*GOLD/49: .5X TO 1.2X BASIC JSY/99
*SILVER/25: .6X TO 1.5X BASIC JSY/99
RDMAA Ameer Abdullah 3.00 8.00
RDMAC Amari Cooper 6.00 15.00
RDMBA Buck Allen 2.50 6.00
RDMBH Brett Hundley 2.00 5.00
RDMBP Breshad Perriman 2.00 5.00
RDMBP Bryce Petty 2.00 5.00
RDMCC Chris Conley 2.00 5.00
RDMDC David Cobb 2.00 5.00
RDMDF Devin Funchess 3.00 8.00
RDMDG Dorial Green-Beckham 2.00 5.00
RDMDJ Duke Johnson 3.00 8.00
RDMDJ David Johnson 5.00 12.00
RDMDP DeVante Parker 3.00 8.00
RDMDS Devin Smith 2.00 5.00
RDMGG Garrett Grayson 2.00 5.00
RDMJA Jay Ajayi 3.00 8.00
RDMJC Jamison Crowder 2.50 6.00
RDMJH Justin Hardy 2.00 5.00
RDMJL Jeremy Langford 2.00 5.00
RDMJS Jaelen Strong 2.50 6.00
RDMJW Jameis Winston 8.00 20.00
RDMKW Karlos Williams 2.00 5.00
RDMKW Kevin White 2.50 6.00
RDMLW Leonard Williams 2.00 5.00
RDMMD Mike Davis 2.00 5.00
RDMMG Melvin Gordon 5.00 12.00
RDMMJ Matt Jones 2.00 5.00
RDMMM Marcus Mariota 8.00 20.00
RDMMW Maxx Williams 2.00 5.00
RDMNA Nelson Agholor 2.50 6.00
RDMPD Phillip Dorsett 2.00 5.00
RDMRG Rashad Greene 2.00 5.00
RDMSC Sammie Coates 2.50 6.00
RDMSD Stefon Diggs 5.00 12.00
RDMSM Sean Mannion 2.00 5.00
RDMTC Tevin Coleman 2.50 6.00
RDMTG Todd Gurley 10.00 25.00
RDMTL Tyler Lockett 3.00 8.00
RDMTM Ty Montgomery 2.00 5.00
RDMTY T.J. Yeldon 2.00 5.00

2015 Panini National Treasures Rookie Jumbo Prime Booklet Signatures

3 Kevin White 12.00 30.00
4 Karlos Williams 10.00 25.00
5 Duke Johnson 15.00 40.00
7 Jameis Winston 150.00 300.00
9 Melvin Gordon 40.00 80.00
11 Phillip Dorsett 15.00 40.00
12 DeVante Parker
13 Nelson Agholor 12.00 30.00
17 T.J. Yeldon 10.00 25.00
20 Ameer Abdullah 15.00 40.00
21 Brett Hundley 10.00 25.00
23 Devin Funchess 15.00 40.00
26 Todd Gurley 125.00 250.00
27 Breshad Perriman 10.00 25.00
36 Dorial Green-Beckham 40.00 80.00
37 Marcus Mariota 40.00 80.00
39 David Cobb 10.00 25.00
40 Jay Ajayi 15.00 40.00

2015 Panini National Treasures Rookie Jumbo Prime Booklet Signatures Vertical

1 Mike Davis/99 6.00 15.00
2 Jeremy Langford/99 15.00 40.00
3 Kevin White/49 10.00 25.00
4 Karlos Williams/99 6.00 15.00
5 Duke Johnson/99 10.00 25.00
7 Jameis Winston/49 100.00 200.00
8 David Johnson/99 40.00 80.00
9 Melvin Gordon/49 20.00 50.00
10 Chris Conley/25
11 Phillip Dorsett/99 6.00 15.00
12 DeVante Parker/49 12.00 30.00
13 Nelson Agholor/49 10.00 25.00
14 Justin Hardy/99 6.00 15.00
16 Rashad Greene/99 6.00 15.00
17 T.J. Yeldon/99 6.00 15.00
18 Bryce Petty/25
20 Ameer Abdullah/49 20.00 50.00
21 Brett Hundley/49 20.00 50.00
22 Ty Montgomery/49 8.00 20.00
23 Devin Funchess/99 10.00 25.00
24 Amari Cooper/15 100.00 200.00
26 Todd Gurley/25
27 Breshad Perriman/99 6.00 15.00
29 Maxx Williams/99 6.00 15.00
30 Jamison Crowder/99 8.00 20.00
31 Matt Jones/99 6.00 15.00
32 Leonard Williams/99 6.00 15.00
33 Tyler Lockett/99 10.00 25.00
36 Dorial Green-Beckham/99 6.00 15.00
37 Marcus Mariota/49 30.00 60.00
38 Stefon Diggs/99 15.00 40.00

2015 Panini National Treasures Rookie Material Signatures

*PRIME/15-25: .5X TO 1.2X BASIC JSY AU/49-99
2 Paul Dawson/99 6.00 15.00
3 Tyler Kroft/99 6.00 15.00
7 Randy Gregory/99 5.00 12.00
8 Byron Jones/99 8.00 20.00
9 Lucky Whitehead/49 15.00 40.00

2015 Panini National Treasures Rookie NFL Gear Combo Materials

*PRIME/25: .6X TO 1.5X BASIC JSY/99
1 K.White/J.Langford 2.50 6.00
2 D.Parker/J.Ajayi 3.00 8.00
3 T.Coleman/J.Hardy 2.50 6.00
4 T.Yeldon/R.Greene 6.00 15.00
5 B.Petty/D.Smith 2.00 5.00
6 B.Hundley/T.Montgomery 2.00 5.00
7 T.Gurley/S.Mannion 10.00 25.00
8 B.Perriman/M.Williams 2.00 5.00
9 J.Crowder/M.Jones 2.50 6.00
10 D.Green-Beckham/M.Mariota 8.00 20.00
11 D.Cobb/M.Mariota 8.00 20.00
12 J.Winston/M.Mariota 8.00 20.00
13 M.Gordon/T.Gurley 10.00 25.00
14 A.Cooper/K.White 6.00 15.00
15 T.Yeldon/A.Abdullah 6.00 15.00
16 G.Grayson/S.Mannion 2.00 5.00
17 A.Abdullah/T.Gurley 10.00 25.00
18 G.Grayson/J.Winston 8.00 20.00
19 B.Petty/M.Mariota 8.00 20.00
20 M.Jones/T.Coleman 2.50 6.00
21 D.Johnson/D.Johnson 5.00 12.00
22 T.Lockett/T.Montgomery 3.00 8.00
23 D.Funchess/J.Hardy 3.00 8.00
24 A.Cooper/M.Gordon 6.00 15.00
25 D.Parker/D.Smith 3.00 8.00
26 S.Coates/B.Perriman 2.50 6.00
27 D.Green-Beckham/P.Dorsett 2.00 5.00
28 J.Crowder/N.Agholor 2.50 6.00
29 T.Coleman/G.Grayson 2.50 6.00
30 D.Johnson/T.Lockett 5.00 12.00

2015 Panini National Treasures Rookie NFL Gear Dual Materials Signatures

*PRIME/49: .5X TO 1.2X BASIC JSY AU/99
*PRIME/25: .5X TO 1.2X BASIC JSY AU/49
*PRIME/15: .5X TO 1.2X BASIC JSY AU/25
1 Stefon Diggs/99 12.00 30.00
2 Marcus Mariota/25 30.00 80.00
3 Dorial Green-Beckham/99 5.00 12.00
4 David Cobb/99 5.00 12.00
7 Tyler Lockett/99 8.00 20.00
9 Matt Jones/99 5.00 12.00
10 Jamison Crowder/99 6.00 15.00
13 Breshad Perriman/99 5.00 12.00
14 Todd Gurley/25 50.00 100.00
17 Devin Funchess/99 8.00 20.00
18 Ty Montgomery/99 5.00 12.00
19 Brett Hundley/49 6.00 15.00
20 Ameer Abdullah/99 8.00 20.00
22 Bryce Petty/49 6.00 15.00
23 T.J. Yeldon/99 5.00 12.00
24 Rashad Greene/99 5.00 12.00
26 Justin Hardy/99 5.00 12.00
27 Nelson Agholor/49 8.00 20.00
28 Jay Ajayi/99 8.00 20.00
29 DeVante Parker/99 8.00 20.00
30 Phillip Dorsett/99 5.00 12.00
31 Chris Conley/49 6.00 15.00
32 Melvin Gordon/99 12.00 30.00
33 David Johnson/99 25.00 50.00
34 Jameis Winston/25 50.00 100.00
36 Duke Johnson/99 8.00 20.00
37 Karlos Williams/99 5.00 12.00
38 Kevin White/49 8.00 20.00
39 Jeremy Langford/99 5.00 12.00
40 Mike Davis/99 5.00 12.00

2015 Panini National Treasures Rookie Signature Materials Silver

*SILVER/25: .6X TO 1.5X BASIC JSY AU/99
*SILVER/25: .5X TO 1.2X BASIC JSY AU/49
*SILVER/15: .5X TO 1.2X BASIC JSY AU/25
RMSRTG Todd Gurley/15 100.00 200.00

2015 Panini National Treasures Rookie Signatures

RSRAA Ameer Abdullah/49 6.00 15.00
RSRBH Brett Hundley/25 20.00 40.00
RSRBP Breshad Perriman/99 3.00 8.00
RSRDC David Cobb/99 3.00 8.00
RSRDF Devin Funchess/99 5.00 12.00
RSRDG Dorial Green-Beckham/49 4.00 10.00
RSRDJ Duke Johnson/99 5.00 12.00
RSRDJ David Johnson/99 20.00 40.00
RSRDP DeVante Parker/49 15.00 30.00
RSRJA Jay Ajayi/99 5.00 12.00
RSRJC Jamison Crowder/49 5.00 12.00
RSRJH Justin Hardy/99 3.00 8.00
RSRJL Jeremy Langford/99 10.00 25.00
RSRJW Jameis Winston/25 90.00 150.00
RSRKW Karlos Williams/99 3.00 8.00
RSRLW Leonard Williams/99 3.00 8.00
RSRMD Mike Davis/99 3.00 8.00
RSRMG Melvin Gordon/25 12.00 30.00
RSRMJ Matt Jones/99 10.00 25.00
RSRMM Marcus Mariota/25 40.00 100.00
RSRNA Nelson Agholor/49 5.00 12.00
RSRPD Phillip Dorsett/99 3.00 8.00
RSRRG Rashad Greene/99 3.00 8.00
RSRSD Stefon Diggs/99 12.00 30.00
RSRTG Todd Gurley/25 50.00 100.00
RSRTL Tyler Lockett/99 10.00 25.00
RSRTM Ty Montgomery/49 4.00 10.00
RSRTY T.J. Yeldon/49 4.00 10.00

2015 Panini National Treasures Rookie Signatures Dual

RDSAB S.Anthony/V.Beasley Jr./49 6.00 15.00
RDSAC N.Agholor/J.Crowder/25 8.00 20.00
RDSAD M.Alford/P.Dawson/49 6.00 15.00
RDSAG A.Abdullah/R.Gregory/49
RDSAL A.Abdullah/J.Langford/49 20.00 40.00
RDSAW J.Ajayi/K.Williams/49 8.00 20.00
RDSBD B.Bell/M.Davis/49 8.00 20.00
RDSBF M.Brown/T.Flowers/49 8.00 20.00
RDSCA S.Coates/C.Artis-Payne/49 6.00 15.00
RDSCG L.Collins/R.Gregory/49 6.00 15.00
RDSCJ J.Crowder/M.Jones/49 6.00 15.00
RDSCM D.Cobb/M.Mariota/25 40.00 100.00
RDSCO L.Collins/O.Odighizuwa/49 6.00 15.00
RDSCS L.Collins/B.Scherff/49 8.00 20.00
RDSCW D.Cobb/M.Williams/49 5.00 12.00
RDSDJ B.Dupree/J.James/49 25.00 50.00
RDSDM S.Diggs/T.Montgomery/49
RDSDP S.Diggs/M.Pruitt/49
RDSFA D.Funchess/C.Artis-Payne/49
RDSGM D.Green-Beckham/M.Mariota/25
RDSGW M.Gordon/T.Waynes/25 15.00 40.00
RDSGY R.Greene/T.Yeldon/49 5.00 12.00
RDSLJ T.Lockett/D.Johnson/49 15.00 40.00
RDSLW J.Langford/K.White/25 25.00 60.00
RDSPL D.Parker/T.Lippett/49
RDSPW B.Perriman/M.Williams/25 6.00 15.00
RDSWA P.Williams/S.Anthony/49 6.00 15.00
RDSWA D.White/D.Anderson/49 8.00 20.00
RDSWB J.Winston/K.Bell/25
RDSWJ C.Walford/D.Johnson/49 8.00 20.00

2015 Panini National Treasures Rookie Signatures Dual Red

*RED: .5X TO 1.2X BASIC AU

2015 Panini National Treasures Signatures

*SILVER/25: .6X TO 1.5X BASIC AU/99
*SILVER/15: .6X TO 1.5X BASIC AU/49
*SILVER/15: .5X TO 1.2X BASIC AU/25
SIGAB Anthony Barr/99 4.00 10.00
SIGAD Aaron Donald/99 6.00 15.00
SIGAF Antonio Freeman/49 8.00 20.00
SIGAF Arian Foster/25 8.00 20.00
SIGAL Andrew Luck/25 75.00 150.00
SIGAR Andre Reed/25 8.00 20.00
SIGAS Austin Seferian-Jenkins/99 4.00 10.00
SIGAW Aeneas Williams/49 5.00 12.00
SIGBF Brett Favre/25 75.00 150.00
SIGBF Bubba Franks/49 5.00 12.00
SIGBJ Bo Jackson/25 40.00 80.00
SIGBM Barkevious Mingo/49 5.00 12.00
SIGBR Ben Roethlisberger/25 50.00 100.00
SIGBS Barry Sanders/25 75.00 150.00
SIGCA C.J. Anderson/49 6.00 15.00
SIGCB Champ Bailey/25 15.00 30.00
SIGCC Cris Carter/25 30.00 60.00
SIGCF Coby Fleener/49 5.00 12.00
SIGCG Crockett Gillmore/99 4.00 10.00
SIGCJ Charlie Joiner/49 5.00 12.00
SIGCK Colin Kaepernick/25 15.00 40.00
SIGCP Carson Palmer/25 20.00 40.00
SIGCP Clinton Portis/25 15.00 30.00
SIGDB Drew Brees/25 30.00 60.00
SIGDB Derrick Brooks/49 5.00 12.00
SIGDC Dallas Clark/49 5.00 12.00
SIGDC Derek Carr/25 30.00 60.00
SIGDC Dwight Clark/25 8.00 20.00
SIGDD Donald Driver/25 20.00 40.00
SIGDH Dan Hampton/49 8.00 20.00
SIGDM Don Majkowski/25 15.00 30.00
SIGDS Devin Street/49 5.00 12.00
SIGDS Deion Sanders/25 40.00 80.00
SIGDW Danny Woodhead/49 6.00 15.00
SIGEE Eric Ebron/49 5.00 12.00
SIGEL Eddie Lacy/25 15.00 30.00
SIGEM Eli Manning/25 40.00 80.00
SIGFT Fred Taylor/25 6.00 15.00
SIGGF Gary Fencik/49 5.00 12.00
SIGHC Harold Carmichael/49 5.00 12.00
SIGIC Isaiah Crowell/99 4.00 10.00
SIGIW Ickey Woods/49 5.00 12.00
SIGJB John Brown/99 5.00 12.00
SIGJB Jerome Bettis/25 50.00 100.00
SIGJB Joique Bell/49 5.00 12.00
SIGJD James Develin/99 6.00 15.00
SIGJE John Elway/25 50.00 100.00
SIGJH John Hannah/99 4.00 10.00
SIGJH Justin Hunter/49 5.00 12.00
SIGJJ Jackson Jeffcoat/99 4.00 10.00
SIGJL James Lofton/49 5.00 12.00
SIGJN Jordy Nelson/25 12.00 30.00
SIGJS Jan Stenerud/49 5.00 12.00
SIGJT Joe Theismann/25 15.00 30.00
SIGJV Jason Verrett/49 5.00 12.00
SIGKS Kenny Stills/49 5.00 12.00
SIGKW Kurt Warner/25 30.00 60.00
SIGKW Kellen Winslow/49 10.00 25.00
SIGLC Larry Csonka/25 20.00 40.00
SIGLK Luke Kuechly/25 15.00 40.00
SIGLM Latavius Murray/99 4.00 10.00
SIGLT Lorenzo Taliaferro/99 4.00 10.00
SIGMC Mark Chmura/49 5.00 12.00
SIGME Mike Evans/49 15.00 30.00
SIGMF Michael Floyd/25 6.00 15.00
SIGML Marqise Lee/49 5.00 12.00
SIGMQ Mike Quick/49 5.00 12.00
SIGMS Matthew Stafford/25 15.00 30.00
SIGMS Mike Singletary/49 8.00 20.00
SIGMT Manti Te'o/49 6.00 15.00
SIGNF Nick Foles/25 8.00 20.00
SIGPR Philip Rivers/25 15.00 30.00
SIGRB Robert Brooks/25 8.00 20.00
SIGRC Roger Craig/49 6.00 15.00
SIGRC Randall Cobb/25 8.00 20.00
SIGRG Rob Gronkowski/49 25.00 50.00
SIGRL Ronnie Lott/25 30.00 60.00
SIGRM Robert Mathis/49 5.00 12.00
SIGRT Ryan Tannehill/25 8.00 20.00
SIGRW Russell Wilson/25 50.00 100.00
SIGRW Ricky Williams/25 15.00 30.00
SIGSB Sam Bradford/25 6.00 15.00
SIGSC Scott Chandler/99 4.00 10.00
SIGSG Steve Grogan/25 6.00 15.00
SIGTB Tim Brown/25 25.00 50.00
SIGTB Troy Brown/49 5.00 12.00
SIGTD Trent Dilfer/49 5.00 12.00
SIGTE Tyler Eifert/99 5.00 12.00
SIGTK Travis Kelce/99 6.00 15.00
SIGTR Tony Romo/25 25.00 50.00
SIGWM Willie McGinest/49 8.00 20.00

2015 Panini National Treasures Steel Curtain Memorabilia

*PRIME/25: .6X TO 1.5X BASIC JSY/99
*PRIME/25: .5X TO 1.2X BASIC JSY/49
SCAB Antonio Brown/49 10.00 25.00
SCAB Antonio Brown/25 12.00 30.00
SCBD Bud Dupree/99 6.00 15.00
SCBD Bud Dupree/25 10.00 25.00
SCBR Ben Roethlisberger/25 20.00 40.00
SCBR Ben Roethlisberger/49 10.00 25.00
SCDA Dri Archer/99 5.00 12.00
SCJB Jerome Bettis/15 25.00 50.00
SCJB Jerome Bettis/25 20.00 40.00
SCJG Joe Greene/15 15.00 40.00
SCJG Joe Greene/25 25.00 50.00
SCJS John Stallworth/25 20.00 40.00
SCLB Le'Veon Bell/49 8.00 20.00
SCLB Le'Veon Bell/25 10.00 25.00
SCMW Markus Wheaton/99 5.00 12.00
SCMW Mike Wallace/49 6.00 15.00
SCRS Ryan Shazier/99 5.00 12.00
SCRS Ryan Shazier/25 8.00 20.00
SCRW Rod Woodson/25 10.00 25.00
SCRW Rod Woodson/49 8.00 20.00
SCSC Sammie Coates/99 6.00 15.00
SCSC Sammie Coates/25 10.00 25.00
SCTB Terry Bradshaw/25 15.00 40.00

2015 Panini National Treasures Steel Curtain Signatures

SCAB Antonio Brown/25 50.00 100.00
SCBD Bud Dupree/49 20.00 50.00
SCDD Dermontti Dawson/49 15.00 40.00
SCDW DeAngelo Williams/25 20.00 50.00
SCHM Heath Miller/49 15.00 40.00
SCHW Hines Ward/49 40.00 80.00
SCJB Jerome Bettis/25 75.00 150.00
SCJG Joe Greene/15 75.00 150.00
SCJH Jack Ham/25 25.00 60.00
SCJH James Harrison/49 40.00 80.00
SCJJ Jesse James/49 20.00 50.00
SCMB Martavis Bryant/49 15.00 40.00
SCPB Plaxico Burress/49 15.00 40.00
SCRW Rod Woodson/25 25.00 60.00
SCSC Sammie Coates/49 20.00 50.00

2015 Panini National Treasures Treasured Defenders Materials

TDECH Charles Haley/49 6.00 15.00
TDECM Clay Matthews/25 8.00 20.00
TDEDB Derrick Brooks/75 3.00 8.00
TDEDR Darrelle Revis/75 3.00 8.00
TDEJH Justin Houston/25 5.00 12.00
TDEKC Kam Chancellor/25 8.00 20.00
TDEKM Khalil Mack/99 5.00 12.00
TDELT Lawrence Taylor/25 8.00 20.00
TDELW Leonard Williams/99 3.00 8.00
TDEMS Mike Singletary/40 6.00 15.00

2015 Panini National Treasures Treasured Quarterbacks Materials

*PRIME: .5X TO 1.2X BASIC JSY
TQBAD Andy Dalton/49 5.00 12.00
TQBAL Andrew Luck/49 8.00 20.00
TQBBB Blake Bortles/99 3.00 8.00
TQBBF Brett Favre/25 15.00 40.00
TQBBH Brett Hundley/99 3.00 8.00
TQBBP Bryce Petty/99 3.00 8.00
TQBCN Cam Newton/25 8.00 20.00
TQBDC Derek Carr/99 5.00 12.00
TQBDM Dan Marino/25 15.00 40.00
TQBEM Eli Manning/25 6.00 15.00
TQBGG Garrett Grayson/99 3.00 8.00
TQBJE John Elway/25 12.00 30.00
TQBJM Joe Montana/25 30.00 60.00
TQBJM Johnny Manziel/99 4.00 10.00
TQBJN Joe Namath/25 10.00 25.00
TQBJW Jameis Winston/99 10.00 25.00
TQBMM Marcus Mariota/99 8.00 20.00
TQBMR Matt Ryan/25 6.00 15.00
TQBMS Matthew Stafford/25 6.00 15.00
TQBPM Peyton Manning/25 15.00 40.00
TQBPR Philip Rivers/25 8.00 20.00
TQBSM Sean Mannion/99 3.00 8.00
TQBTB Teddy Bridgewater/99 4.00 10.00
TQBTB Tom Brady/15 30.00 60.00
TQBTT Tyrod Taylor/49 5.00 12.00

2015 Panini National Treasures Treasured Receivers Materials

TWRAB Antonio Brown/25 8.00 20.00
TWRAC Amari Cooper/99 6.00 15.00
TWRAG A.J. Green/49 6.00 15.00
TWRAJ Alshon Jeffery/25 6.00 15.00
TWRAR Allen Robinson/99 4.00 10.00
TWRBC Brandin Cooks/99 4.00 10.00
TWRBP Breshad Perriman/99 3.00 8.00
TWRCC Chris Conley/99 3.00 8.00
TWRCC Cris Carter/25 8.00 20.00
TWRDB Dez Bryant/25 8.00 20.00
TWRDF Devin Funchess/99 5.00 12.00
TWRDG Dorial Green-Beckham/99 3.00 8.00
TWRDM Donte Moncrief/99 4.00 10.00
TWRDP DeVante Parker/99 5.00 12.00
TWRDT Demaryius Thomas/49 5.00 12.00
TWRDT De'Anthony Thomas/99 3.00 8.00
TWRFB Fred Biletnikoff/25 12.00 30.00
TWRJC Jamison Crowder/99 4.00 10.00
TWRJJ Julio Jones/25 8.00 20.00
TWRJL Jarvis Landry/99 4.00 10.00
TWRJM Jordan Matthews/99 4.00 10.00
TWRJR Jerry Rice/25 12.00 30.00
TWRJS Jaelen Strong/99 4.00 10.00
TWRKW Kevin White/99 2.50 6.00
TWRME Mike Evans/99 4.00 10.00
TWRNA Nelson Agholor/99 4.00 10.00
TWROB Odell Beckham Jr./99 5.00 12.00
TWRPD Phillip Dorsett/99 3.00 8.00
TWRRG Rashad Greene/99 3.00 8.00
TWRSC Sammie Coates/99 4.00 10.00
TWRSD Stefon Diggs/99 8.00 20.00
TWRSW Sammy Watkins/49 5.00 12.00
TWRTB Tim Brown/25 8.00 20.00
TWRTL Tyler Lockett/99 5.00 12.00
TWRTM Ty Montgomery/99 3.00 8.00

2015 Panini National Treasures Treasured Running Backs Materials

TRBAA Ameer Abdullah/99 4.00 10.00
TRBAP Adrian Peterson/25 8.00 20.00
TRBBA Buck Allen/99 3.00 8.00
TRBBS Barry Sanders/25 20.00 40.00
TRBCA C.J. Anderson/49 5.00 12.00
TRBCH Carlos Hyde/99 3.00 8.00
TRBCS Charles Sims/99 3.00 8.00
TRBDF Devonta Freeman/99 4.00 10.00
TRBDJ David Johnson/99 6.00 15.00
TRBDJ Duke Johnson/99 5.00 12.00
TRBED Eric Dickerson/25 6.00 15.00
TRBEL Eddie Lacy/25 5.00 12.00
TRBES Emmitt Smith/25
TRBJH Jeremy Hill/99 3.00 8.00
TRBJL Jeremy Langford/99 2.50 6.00
TRBKW Karlos Williams/99 2.50 6.00
TRBLM LeSean McCoy/49 6.00 15.00
TRBLT LaDainian Tomlinson/25 6.00 15.00
TRBMG Melvin Gordon/99 6.00 15.00
TRBMJ Matt Jones/99 2.50 6.00
TRBML Marshawn Lynch/25 6.00 15.00
TRBTG Todd Gurley/99 10.00 25.00
TRBTY T.J. Yeldon/99 2.50 6.00
TRBWP Walter Payton/25 30.00 60.00

2015 Panini National Treasures Tremendous Treasures Materials Horizontal

TTRAA Ameer Abdullah 5.00 12.00
TTRAC Amari Cooper 10.00 25.00
TTRDF Devin Funchess 5.00 12.00
TTRDG Dorial Green-Beckham 3.00 8.00
TTRDJ David Johnson 8.00 20.00
TTRDP DeVante Parker 5.00 12.00
TTRJW Jameis Winston 12.00 30.00
TTRKW Kevin White 4.00 10.00
TTRKW Karlos Williams 3.00 8.00
TTRMG Melvin Gordon 8.00 20.00
TTRMJ Matt Jones 3.00 8.00
TTRMM Marcus Mariota 12.00 30.00
TTRNA Nelson Agholor 4.00 10.00
TTRPD Phillip Dorsett 3.00 8.00
TTRSD Stefon Diggs 8.00 20.00
TTRTC Tevin Coleman 4.00 10.00
TTRTG Todd Gurley 15.00 40.00
TTRTL Tyler Lockett 5.00 12.00
TTRTM Ty Montgomery 3.00 8.00
TTRTY T.J. Yeldon 3.00 8.00

2016 Panini National Treasures

1 Carson Palmer 2.50 6.00
2 David Johnson 3.00 8.00
3 Larry Fitzgerald 2.50 6.00
4 Matt Ryan 2.50 6.00
5 Devonta Freeman 2.50 6.00
6 Julio Jones 3.00 8.00
7 Joe Flacco 2.50 6.00
8 Terrance West 2.00 5.00
9 Steve Smith 2.50 6.00
10 Tyrod Taylor 2.50 6.00
11 LeSean McCoy 3.00 8.00
12 Sammy Watkins 3.00 8.00
13 Cam Newton 3.00 8.00
14 Jonathan Stewart 2.00 5.00
15 Kelvin Benjamin 2.50 6.00
16 Jay Cutler 2.00 5.00
17 Jeremy Langford 2.50 6.00
18 Alshon Jeffery 2.50 6.00
19 Andy Dalton 2.50 6.00
20 Johnny Unitas 5.00 12.00
21 Jeremy Hill 2.00 5.00
22 A.J. Green 3.00 8.00
23 Terrelle Pryor 2.00 5.00
24 Isaiah Crowell 2.00 5.00
25 Gary Barnidge 2.00 5.00
26 Tony Romo 2.50 6.00
27 Cole Beasley 3.00 8.00
28 Dez Bryant 3.00 8.00
29 Trevor Siemian 2.00 5.00
30 C.J. Anderson 2.50 6.00
31 Demaryius Thomas 2.50 6.00
32 Von Miller 2.50 6.00
33 Matthew Stafford 2.50 6.00
34 Marvin Jones Jr. 2.00 5.00
35 Golden Tate III 2.00 5.00
36 Aaron Rodgers 6.00 15.00
37 Eddie Lacy 2.00 5.00
38 Jordy Nelson 2.50 6.00
39 Brock Osweiler 2.00 5.00
40 Lamar Miller 2.00 5.00
41 DeAndre Hopkins 2.50 6.00
42 J.J. Watt 3.00 8.00
43 Andrew Luck 4.00 10.00
44 Frank Gore 2.50 6.00
45 T.Y. Hilton 2.50 6.00
46 Blake Bortles 2.00 5.00
47 Chris Ivory 2.50 6.00
48 Allen Robinson 2.50 6.00
49 Alex Smith 2.50 6.00
50 Jamaal Charles 2.50 6.00
51 Jeremy Maclin 2.00 5.00
52 Case Keenum 2.50 6.00
53 Todd Gurley II 3.00 8.00
54 Tavon Austin 2.00 5.00
55 Aaron Donald 3.00 8.00
56 Ryan Tannehill 2.50 6.00
57 Jay Ajayi 2.50 6.00
58 Jarvis Landry 2.50 6.00
59 Sam Bradford 2.00 5.00
60 Adrian Peterson 3.00 8.00
61 Stefon Diggs 2.50 6.00
62 Tom Brady 8.00 20.00
63 Rob Gronkowski 3.00 8.00
64 Julian Edelman 3.00 8.00
65 Drew Brees 3.00 8.00
66 Mark Ingram 2.50 6.00
67 Brandin Cooks 2.50 6.00
68 Eli Manning 2.50 6.00
69 Rashad Jennings 2.00 5.00
70 Odell Beckham Jr. 3.00 8.00
71 Ryan Fitzpatrick 2.00 5.00
72 Matt Forte 2.00 5.00
73 Brandon Marshall 2.00 5.00
74 Derek Carr 3.00 8.00
75 Marquette King 2.00 5.00
76 Amari Cooper 3.00 8.00
77 Khalil Mack 3.00 8.00
78 Alejandro Villanueva RC 20.00 50.00
79 Ryan Mathews 2.50 6.00
80 Jordan Matthews 2.50 6.00
81 Ben Roethlisberger 3.00 8.00
82 Le'Veon Bell 2.50 6.00
83 Antonio Brown 3.00 8.00
84 Philip Rivers 3.00 8.00
85 Melvin Gordon 2.50 6.00
86 Keenan Allen 2.50 6.00
87 Colin Kaepernick 2.50 6.00
88 Carlos Hyde 2.00 5.00
89 Russell Wilson 4.00 10.00
90 Jimmy Graham 3.00 8.00
91 Doug Baldwin 2.50 6.00
92 Jameis Winston 3.00 8.00
93 Doug Martin 2.50 6.00
94 Mike Evans 2.50 6.00
95 Marcus Mariota 3.00 8.00
96 DeMarco Murray 2.50 6.00
97 Delanie Walker 2.00 5.00
98 Kirk Cousins 3.00 8.00
99 DeSean Jackson 2.50 6.00
100 Jordan Reed 2.00 5.00
101 Jared Goff JSY AU RC 800.00 1200.00
102 Carson Wentz JSY AU RC 1200.00 2000.00
103 Joey Bosa JSY AU RC EXCH 50.00 100.00
104 Ezekiel Elliott JSY AU RC 300.00 500.00
105 Corey Coleman JSY AU RC 20.00 50.00
106 Will Fuller V JSY AU RC 20.00 50.00
107 Josh Doctson JSY AU RC 30.00 60.00
108 Laquon Treadwell JSY AU RC 15.00 40.00
109 Paxton Lynch JSY AU RC 12.00 30.00
110 Hunter Henry JSY AU RC EXCH 15.00 40.00
111 Sterling Shepard JSY AU RC 15.00 40.00
112 Derrick Henry JSY AU RC 30.00 80.00
113 Michael Thomas JSY AU RC 60.00 125.00
114 Christian Hackenberg JSY AU RC 12.00 30.00
115 Kenyan Drake JSY AU RC 20.00 50.00
116 Braxton Miller JSY AU RC 12.00 30.00
117 Leonte Carroo JSY AU RC 12.00 30.00
118 C.J. Prosise JSY AU RC 12.00 30.00
119 Jacoby Brissett JSY AU RC 40.00 80.00
120 Cody Kessler JSY AU RC 40.00 80.00
121 Tyler Boyd JSY AU RC 15.00 40.00
122 Connor Cook JSY AU RC 15.00 40.00
123 Chris Moore JSY AU RC 15.00 40.00
124 Malcolm Mitchell JSY AU RC 30.00 60.00
125 Ricardo Louis JSY AU RC 12.00 30.00
126 Pharoh Cooper JSY AU RC 12.00 30.00
127 Tyler Ervin JSY AU RC 12.00 30.00
128 Demarcus Robinson JSY AU RC 12.00 30.00
129 Kenneth Dixon JSY AU RC 12.00 30.00
130 Dak Prescott JSY AU RC 200.00 400.00
131 Devontae Booker JSY AU RC 15.00 40.00
132 Cardale Jones JSY AU RC 30.00 60.00
133 DeAndre Washington JSY AU RC 12.00 30.00
134 Paul Perkins JSY AU RC 12.00 30.00
135 Jordan Howard JSY AU RC 100.00 200.00
136 Wendell Smallwood JSY AU RC 12.00 30.00
137 Jonathan Williams JSY AU RC 15.00 40.00
138 Trevor Davis JSY AU RC 12.00 30.00
139 Alex Collins JSY AU RC 15.00 40.00
140 Keenan Reynolds JSY AU RC 15.00 40.00
141 Moritz Bohringer JSY AU RC 12.00 30.00
142 Jalen Ramsey AU/99 RC 6.00 15.00
143 Eli Apple AU/99 RC 5.00 12.00
144 Vernon Hargreaves III AU/49 RC 8.00 20.00
145 Artie Burns AU/99 RC 20.00 40.00
148 Tajae Sharpe AU/99 RC 5.00 12.00
149 Charone Peake AU/25 RC 6.00 15.00
150 Jaylon Smith AU/99 RC 4.00 10.00
151 Mackensie Alexander AU/99 RC 4.00 10.00
152 Aaron Burbridge AU/49 RC 5.00 12.00
153 Robert Nkemdiche AU/49 RC 6.00 15.00
156 Austin Hooper AU/99 RC 4.00 10.00
157 Jordan Payton AU/99 RC 4.00 10.00
158 Tyler Higbee AU/99 RC 4.00 10.00
159 Cody Core AU/99 RC 4.00 10.00
162 Blake Martinez AU/49 RC 6.00 15.00
163 Nate Sudfeld AU/49 RC 5.00 12.00
164 Noah Spence AU/49 RC 5.00 12.00
165 Jeff Driskel AU/99 RC 4.00 10.00
166 Kenny Lawler AU/99 RC 6.00 15.00
168 Joshua Perry AU/49 RC 5.00 12.00
169 Su'a Cravens AU/99 RC 4.00 10.00
171 Jalin Marshall AU/99 RC 6.00 15.00
172 Myles Jack AU/99 RC 5.00 12.00
173 Brandon Allen AU/99 RC 4.00 10.00
174 Roberto Aguayo AU/99 RC 4.00 10.00
175 Cyrus Jones AU/99 RC 4.00 10.00
176 Nick Vannett AU/49 RC 5.00 12.00
177 Brandon Doughty AU/49 RC 5.00 12.00
178 Keith Marshall AU/99 RC 4.00 10.00
179 Xavien Howard AU/99 RC 5.00 12.00
180 Darron Lee AU/49 RC 5.00 12.00
181 Jarran Reed AU/49 RC 5.00 12.00
182 Vonn Bell AU/99 RC 5.00 12.00
185 Kyler Fackrell AU/49 RC 6.00 15.00
186 Tyreek Hill AU/49 RC 20.00 50.00
187 Kelvin Taylor AU/49 RC 5.00 12.00
188 KeiVarae Russell AU/99 RC 4.00 10.00
189 Derek Watt AU/99 RC 6.00 15.00
192 Robert Kelley AU/99 RC 6.00 15.00
193 Kendall Fuller AU/49 RC 6.00 15.00
194 William Jackson III AU/49 RC 6.00 15.00
195 Germain Ifedi AU/49 RC 6.00 15.00
196 Keanu Neal AU/49 RC 5.00 12.00
197 Rashard Higgins AU/99 RC 4.00 10.00
198 Charles Tapper AU/49 RC 6.00 15.00
199 Kevin Dodd AU/99 RC 4.00 10.00
200 Thomas Duarte AU/99 RC 4.00 10.00
201 Emmanuel Ogbah AU/99 RC 5.00 12.00

2016 Panini National Treasures Holo Silver

*VETS/25: .6X TO 1.5X BASIC CARDS/99
*ROOK JSY AU/25: .6X TO 1.5X BASIC JSY AU/99

*ROOK AU/25: .6X TO 1.5X BASIC AU/99
101 Jared Goff JSY AU 1400.00 2500.00
102 Carson Wentz JSY AU 800.00 1200.00
104 Ezekiel Elliott JSY AU 700.00 1500.00
109 Paxton Lynch JSY AU 250.00 500.00
112 Derrick Henry JSY AU 200.00 300.00
113 Michael Thomas JSY AU 150.00 300.00
130 Dak Prescott JSY AU EXCH 400.00 800.00

2016 Panini National Treasures All Decade Memorabilia

*GOLD/49: .5X TO 1.2X BASIC JSY/75-99
*GOLD/49: .4X TO 1X BASIC JSY/49
*GOLD/25: .6X TO 1.5X BASIC JSY/99
*GOLD/25: .5X TO 1.2X BASIC JSY/49
*GOLD/20: .8X TO 2X BASIC JSY/99
*GOLD/15: .5X TO 1.2X BASIC JSY/25
*SILVER/25: .6X TO 1.5X BASIC JSY/75-99
*SILVER/25: .5X TO 1.2X BASIC JSY/49
*SILVER/15: .8X TO 2X BASIC JSY/99
1 Tom Brady/25 20.00 50.00
2 Ray Lewis/49 6.00 15.00
3 DeMarcus Ware/75 4.00 10.00
4 Brian Urlacher/49 6.00 15.00
5 Ed Reed/49 5.00 12.00
6 Brett Favre/25 15.00 40.00
7 Barry Sanders/49 10.00 25.00
8 Emmitt Smith/49 10.00 25.00
9 Jerry Rice/49 10.00 25.00
10 Reggie White/49 15.00 40.00
11 Junior Seau/49 5.00 12.00
12 Ronnie Lott/49 5.00 12.00
13 Joe Montana/49 15.00 40.00
14 Peyton Manning/49 12.00 30.00
15 John Riggins/99 4.00 10.00
16 Lee Roy Selmon/99 3.00 8.00
17 Randy White/25 6.00 15.00
18 Mike Singletary/49 6.00 15.00
19 Roger Staubach/49 8.00 20.00
20 Earl Campbell/49 6.00 15.00
21 Paul Warfield/49 5.00 12.00
22 Bob Lilly/49 5.00 12.00
24 Steve Largent/99 5.00 12.00
25 Gale Sayers/25 8.00 20.00
27 Raymond Berry/99 4.00 10.00
28 Terrell Davis/99 15.00 40.00
30 Terry Bradshaw/49 8.00 20.00
31 Antonio Gates/99 3.00 8.00
32 Jamal Lewis/49 5.00 12.00
33 Rod Woodson/99 8.00 20.00
34 Ozzie Newsome/99 4.00 10.00
35 Howie Long/49 6.00 15.00
36 Edgerrin James/99 4.00 10.00
37 LaDainian Tomlinson/49 10.00 25.00
38 Derrick Brooks/99 3.00 8.00
39 Dwight Freeney/99 3.00 8.00
40 Champ Bailey/99 4.00 10.00

2016 Panini National Treasures All Decade Signatures

2 Raymond Berry/49 6.00 15.00
3 Lenny Moore/49 5.00 12.00
4 Jack Ham/25 15.00 40.00
5 Paul Hornung/49 12.00 30.00
7 Bob Lilly/49 6.00 15.00
8 Drew Pearson/49 10.00 25.00
9 Paul Warfield/25 8.00 20.00
10 Rayfield Wright/49 15.00 40.00
11 John Hannah/49 5.00 12.00
14 Earl Campbell/25 15.00 40.00
15 Franco Harris/25 25.00 50.00
16 Carl Eller/49 5.00 12.00
17 Joe Greene/25 25.00 50.00
18 Jack Lambert/25 50.00 100.00
19 Ted Hendricks/25 6.00 15.00
21 Steve Largent/25 10.00 25.00
22 James Lofton/49 10.00 25.00
23 Kellen Winslow/49 6.00 15.00
24 Ozzie Newsome/49 6.00 15.00
26 Dan Fouts/25 20.00 50.00
27 Eric Dickerson/25 15.00 40.00
28 John Riggins/25 15.00 40.00
29 Bruce Smith/25 8.00 20.00
30 Randy White/49 12.00 30.00
31 Dan Hampton/49 5.00 12.00
32 Mike Singletary/25 12.00 30.00
33 Lawrence Taylor/25 25.00 50.00
34 Ronnie Lott/25 25.00 50.00
35 Cris Carter/25 25.00 50.00
36 Tim Brown/25 10.00 25.00
37 Michael Irvin/25 25.00 50.00
43 Terrell Davis/25 25.00 50.00
44 Thurman Thomas/25 8.00 20.00
45 Warren Sapp/25 12.00 30.00
46 Rod Woodson/49 25.00 50.00
48 Aeneas Williams/49 5.00 12.00
51 LaDainian Tomlinson/25 30.00 60.00
52 Edgerrin James/25 8.00 20.00
53 Jamal Lewis/25 15.00 40.00
54 Michael Strahan/25 15.00 40.00
55 Howie Long/49 20.00 40.00
56 Derrick Brooks/49 12.00 30.00
57 Brian Urlacher/25 30.00 60.00
58 DeMarcus Ware/25 8.00 20.00
60 Ed Reed/25 30.00 60.00

2016 Panini National Treasures Collegiate Treasures Autographs

1 Blake Bortles/25 6.00 15.00
2 Corey Coleman/25 10.00 25.00
3 Ezekiel Elliott/25 100.00 200.00
4 Derrick Henry/25
5 Laquon Treadwell/25 8.00 20.00
6 Sterling Shepard/25 8.00 20.00
7 Jared Goff/25 40.00 80.00
8 Paxton Lynch/25 6.00 15.00
9 Carson Wentz/25 50.00 100.00
11 LaDainian Tomlinson/25
12 Deion Sanders/25
16 Eddie Lacy/25 6.00 15.00
17 Dez Bryant/25
18 A.J. Green/25 10.00 25.00
20 Charles Woodson/25 60.00 125.00

2016 Panini National Treasures Colossal Materials

*PRIME/25: .6X TO 1.5X BASICJSY/99
*PRIME/25: .5X TO 1.2X BASIC JSY/49
*PRIME/20: .6X TO 1.5X BASIC JSY/49
1 Brandon Marshall/25 5.00 12.00
2 Marshall Faulk/49 5.00 12.00
3 A.J. Green/49 6.00 15.00
4 Curtis Martin/49 5.00 12.00
6 Arian Foster/99 4.00 10.00
7 Earl Campbell/49 12.00 30.00
8 Blake Bortles/49 4.00 10.00
9 Tyrod Taylor/49 5.00 12.00
10 Brandin Cooks/49 5.00 12.00
11 Justin Houston/99 3.00 8.00
12 Adrian Peterson/49 6.00 15.00
13 Drew Brees/25 8.00 20.00
14 DeSean Jackson/49 5.00 12.00
15 C.J. Anderson/49 5.00 12.00
16 Antonio Gates/99 3.00 8.00
18 Jarvis Landry/99 4.00 10.00
19 Hines Ward/25 6.00 15.00
20 Melvin Gordon/99 4.00 10.00
21 DeMarcus Ware/99 4.00 10.00
22 Ed Reed/49 5.00 12.00
23 Brian Urlacher/49 6.00 15.00
24 Sammy Watkins/99 5.00 12.00
25 Alfred Morris/49 4.00 10.00
26 Jordan Reed/99 3.00 8.00
27 Amari Cooper/99 5.00 12.00
28 Rob Gronkowski/25 8.00 20.00
29 Geno Atkins/99 3.00 8.00
30 Edgerrin James/40 5.00 12.00
31 Eric Berry/49 5.00 12.00
32 Tony Romo/49 5.00 12.00
33 Terrance Williams/99 3.00 8.00
34 Bobby Wagner/49 4.00 10.00
35 Philip Rivers/49 6.00 15.00
36 Stephon Gilmore/99 3.00 8.00
37 Jameis Winston/99 5.00 12.00
38 Le'Veon Bell/49 5.00 12.00
39 Allen Hurns/99 3.00 8.00

2016 Panini National Treasures Colossal Pro Bowl Materials

*PRIME/25: .6X TO 1.5X BASIC JSY/75-99
*PRIME/15-20: .8X TO 2X BASIC JSY/75-99
1 Tyrod Taylor/99 4.00 10.00
2 DeAndre Hopkins/99 4.00 10.00
3 Doug Martin/99 4.00 10.00
4 Adam Vinatieri/99 6.00 15.00
5 Julio Jones/99 5.00 12.00
6 DeMarcus Ware/99 4.00 10.00
7 Richard Sherman/99 5.00 12.00
8 Patrick Peterson/99 3.00 8.00
9 Teddy Bridgewater/99 4.00 10.00
10 Amari Cooper/75 5.00 12.00
11 Jarvis Landry/99 4.00 10.00
12 Derek Carr/99 5.00 12.00
13 Eli Manning/99 4.00 10.00
14 Andrew Luck/99 6.00 15.00
15 Khalil Mack/75 5.00 12.00
16 Jamaal Charles/99 4.00 10.00
17 Russell Wilson/99 6.00 15.00
18 A.J. Green/99 5.00 12.00
19 Todd Gurley II/99 5.00 12.00
20 Charles Woodson/99 12.00 30.00
21 Travis Kelce/99 5.00 12.00
22 Devonta Freeman/99 4.00 10.00
23 Jameis Winston/99 5.00 12.00
24 C.J. Anderson/99 4.00 10.00
25 Odell Beckham Jr./99 5.00 12.00
26 Matt Ryan/99 4.00 10.00
27 T.Y. Hilton/99 4.00 10.00
28 Allen Robinson/99 4.00 10.00
29 Tyler Lockett/49 5.00 12.00
30 Clay Matthews/99 5.00 12.00

2016 Panini National Treasures Colossal Signature Materials

*PRIME/25: .5X TO 1.2X BASIC JSY AU/49
1 Tyrod Taylor/25 10.00 25.00
2 Ryan Tannehill/49 8.00 20.00
4 Tyler Eifert/49 8.00 20.00
6 A.J. Green/25 12.00 30.00
8 DeAndre Hopkins/25 10.00 25.00
10 Allen Robinson/49 8.00 20.00
11 Marcus Mariota/25 60.00 100.00
12 Demaryius Thomas/25 10.00 25.00
13 Jamaal Charles/25 15.00 40.00
14 Derek Carr/25 40.00 80.00
15 Keenan Allen/49 8.00 20.00
17 Eli Manning/25 50.00 100.00
18 Ameer Abdullah/49 6.00 15.00
19 Jeremy Langford/49 8.00 20.00
20 Geno Atkins/49 6.00 15.00
23 Matt Ryan/25 30.00 60.00
24 Kelvin Benjamin/49 8.00 20.00
26 Jameis Winston/25 40.00 80.00
27 David Johnson/49 20.00 50.00
28 Todd Gurley II/25 25.00 50.00
29 John Riggins/25 10.00 25.00

2016 Panini National Treasures Dual Signatures

1 T.Taylor/S.Watkins/25
2 J.Flacco/S.Smith/25 12.00 30.00
3 A.Green/A.Dalton/25 25.00 50.00
5 D.Hopkins/W.Fuller V/25
6 A.Robinson/B.Bortles/25
7 A.Smith/J.Maclin/25 12.00 30.00
8 P.Rivers/K.Allen/25
10 M.Jones Jr./M.Stafford/25 25.00 50.00
11 K.Cousins/D.Jackson/25 25.00 50.00
13 L.Treadwell/S.Diggs/25 12.00 30.00
14 B.Cooks/D.Brees/25 40.00 80.00
15 J.Winston/M.Evans/25 30.00 60.00
18 L.Moore/R.Berry/25
20 M.Allen/B.Jackson/25
21 J.Nelson/R.Cobb/25 30.00 60.00
23 E.Manning/P.Simms/25 75.00 150.00
24 D.Fouts/P.Rivers/25

2016 Panini National Treasures Friends and Foes Quad Materials

*PRIME/25: .6X TO 1.5X BASIC JSY/99
1 J.Bosa/E.Elliott 20.00 30.00
2 K.White/W.Smallwood 2.00 5.00
3 A.Cooper/D.Henry 8.00 12.00
4 A.Collins/H.Henry 2.50 6.00
5 D.Henry/K.Drake 8.00 12.00
6 M.Mitchell/T.Gurley II 3.00 8.00
7 B.Miller/J.Bosa 6.00 10.00
8 P.Cooper/M.Davis 2.00 5.00
9 C.Jones/M.Thomas 5.00 10.00
10 B.Allen/C.Kessler 2.00 5.00
11 E.Elliott/M.Thomas 20.00 30.00
12 D.Smith/E.Elliott 20.00 30.00
13 A.Cooper/K.Drake 3.00 8.00
14 C.Coleman/B.Petty 3.00 8.00
15 A.Collins/J.Williams 2.50 6.00
16 J.Howard/T.Coleman 6.00 10.00
17 B.Miller/E.Elliott 20.00 30.00
18 T.Yeldon/D.Henry 8.00 12.00
19 C.Jones/E.Elliott 20.00 30.00
20 C.Kessler/L.Williams 2.00 5.00
21 J.Bosa/M.Thomas 6.00 10.00
22 D.Smith/J.Bosa 6.00 10.00
23 J.Williams/H.Henry 2.50 6.00
24 J.Goff/T.Davis 10.00 15.00
25 C.Jones/B.Miller 2.00 5.00
26 C.Cook/J.Langford 2.50 6.00
27 B.Miller/M.Thomas 5.00 10.00
28 B.Hundley/P.Perkins 2.00 5.00
29 C.Jones/J.Bosa 6.00 10.00
30 C.Kessler/N.Agholor 2.00 5.00

2016 Panini National Treasures Material Signatures

1 Jim Kelly/25 25.00 50.00
5 Andy Dalton/25 10.00 25.00
8 Randall Cobb/25 10.00 25.00
9 Blake Bortles/25 8.00 20.00
12 Stefon Diggs/49 8.00 20.00
13 Philip Rivers/25 12.00 30.00
14 Dez Bryant/25 15.00 40.00
17 Matt Jones/49 8.00 20.00
18 Brian Urlacher/25 30.00 60.00
19 Barry Sanders/25
20 Eddie Lacy/25 8.00 20.00
21 Randall Cunningham/25 25.00 50.00
23 Brandin Cooks/49 8.00 20.00
25 Kurt Warner/25 30.00 60.00
26 Marshall Faulk/25 25.00 50.00
28 Marshawn Lynch/25 30.00 60.00
29 Antonio Gates/25 8.00 20.00
31 Sammy Watkins/49 10.00 25.00
32 Ryan Tannehill/49 8.00 20.00
33 Eric Decker/49 6.00 15.00
34 Matt Forte/25 8.00 20.00
35 Eddie George/25 10.00 25.00
36 Jeremy Hill/49 6.00 15.00
38 Mike Ditka/25 25.00 50.00
39 Andrew Luck/25 50.00 100.00
40 T.J. Yeldon/49 6.00 15.00
41 Demaryius Thomas/25 10.00 25.00
43 Alex Smith/49 8.00 20.00
44 Todd Gurley II/25
45 Ameer Abdullah/49 6.00 15.00
47 Jeremy Langford/99 6.00 15.00
48 DeAndre Hopkins/25
49 Jordy Nelson/25 25.00 50.00
50 Ben Roethlisberger/25 60.00 125.00
51 Matt Ryan/25
52 Geno Atkins/99 5.00 12.00
53 Mike Evans/49 8.00 20.00
54 David Johnson/49 20.00 40.00
55 Doug Baldwin/49 12.00 30.00

2016 Panini National Treasures National History Materials

*PRIME/25: .5X TO 1.2X BASIC JSY/49
1 Sterling Shepard 3.00 8.00
2 Connor Cook 3.00 8.00
3 Paul Perkins 2.50 6.00
4 Corey Coleman 4.00 10.00
5 Christian Hackenberg 2.50 6.00
6 Jared Goff 15.00 40.00
7 Joey Bosa 5.00 12.00
8 Derrick Henry 6.00 15.00
9 Cody Kessler 2.50 6.00
10 Ezekiel Elliott 12.00 30.00
11 Dak Prescott 12.00 30.00
12 Cardale Jones 2.50 6.00
13 Kenneth Dixon 2.50 6.00
14 Michael Thomas 5.00 12.00
15 Josh Doctson 3.00 8.00
16 Carson Wentz 25.00 60.00

2016 Panini National Treasures NFL Gear Combo Materials

*PRIME/25: .5X TO 1.5X BASIC JSY/99
*PRIME/25: .5X TO 1.2X BASIC JSY/49
1 S.Watkins/T.Taylor/99 5.00 12.00
2 A.Green/T.Boyd/99 5.00 12.00
3 D.Booker/C.Anderson/99 4.00 10.00
4 J.Ajayi/J.Landry/99 4.00 10.00
5 M.Williams/N.Suh/99 4.00 10.00
6 R.Bush/L.McCoy/99 5.00 12.00
7 E.Decker/B.Marshall/49 4.00 10.00
8 T.Brady/R.Gronkowski/25 20.00 50.00
9 E.Reed/R.Lewis/49 8.00 20.00
10 D.Williams/L.Bell/99 10.00 25.00
11 A.Robinson/B.Bortles/99 4.00 10.00
12 D.Henry/M.Mariota/99 6.00 15.00
13 J.Goff/T.Gurley II/99 8.00 20.00
14 O.Beckham Jr./S.Shepard/99 6.00 15.00
15 L.Treadwell/S.Diggs/99 4.00 10.00
16 C.Conley/D.Robinson/99 3.00 8.00
17 J.Howard/J.Langford/99 6.00 15.00
18 J.Brissett/J.Garoppolo/99 6.00 15.00
19 D.Hopkins/W.Fuller V/99 5.00 12.00
21 J.Rice/J.Montana/25 20.00 50.00
22 D.Marino/R.Tannehill/49 12.00 30.00
23 T.Gurley II/E.Dickerson/49 6.00 15.00
24 A.Cooper/P.Cooper/99 5.00 12.00
25 C.Wentz/D.Prescott/99 15.00 40.00
26 D.Henry/E.George/99 6.00 15.00
27 A.Rodgers/C.Newton/25 15.00 40.00
28 A.Dalton/R.Wilson/49 8.00 20.00

2016 Panini National Treasures NFL Gear Quad Materials

*PRIME/25: .6X TO 1.5X BASIC JSY/99
*PRIME/25: .5X TO 1.2X BASIC JSY/99
1 Tylr/McCy/Bsh/Wtkns/99 6.00 15.00
2 Tlb/Wre/Hrrs/Mllr/99 5.00 12.00
3 Prsctt/Brynt/Rmo/Ellt/99 15.00 40.00
4 Lndry/Ajyi/Prkr/Tnnhill/99 5.00 12.00
5 Atkns/Jns/Dnlp/Brfct/99 4.00 10.00
6 Prrmn/Mre/Alln/Dxn/99 5.00 12.00
7 Mllr/Hpkns/Strng/Fllr/99 5.00 12.00
8 Nlsn/Adms/Cbb/Dvs/25 8.00 20.00
9 Brwn/Ptrsn/Nwtn/Gnkski/25 10.00 25.00
10 Dnld/Wtt/Mck/Atkns/99 6.00 15.00
11 Mrshll/Edlmn/Lndry/Wtkns/99 6.00 15.00
12 Prsctt/Csns/Wntz/Mnng/99 15.00 40.00
13 Jns/Bnjmn/Cks/Evns/99 6.00 15.00
14 Prsctt/Gff/Lnch/Wntz/99 15.00 40.00
15 Clmn/Dctsn/Trdwll/Fllr/99 6.00 15.00
16 Mrno/Elwy/Mnng/Brdy/25 25.00 60.00
17 Sndrs/Lws/Ptrsn/Dckrsn/49 12.00 30.00
18 Crtr/Hrsn/Brwn/Rce/49 12.00 30.00
19 Sndrs/Mrtn/Smth/Pytn/25 20.00 50.00
20 Fvre/Mrno/Brs/Mnng/25 20.00 50.00

2016 Panini National Treasures NFL Gear Triple Materials

*PRIME/25: .6X TO 1.5X BASIC JSY/99
*PRIME/25: .5X TO 1.2X BASIC JSY/49
1 Smth/Elltt/Drstt/49 25.00 60.00
2 Thms/Smn/Sndrs/99 6.00 15.00
3 Tnhll/Prkr/Lndry/99 5.00 12.00
4 Mtthws/Aghlr/Wntz/99 8.00 20.00
5 Dctsn/Jcksn/Crwdr/99 5.00 12.00
6 Snd/Cks/Thms/45 10.00 25.00
7 Bckhm/Shprd/Crz/25 10.00 25.00
8 Ptrsn/Mrtn/Grly/49 8.00 20.00
9 Hpkns/Brwn/Jns/49 8.00 20.00
10 Mrshll/Rbnsn/Bldwn/49 6.00 15.00
11 Ptrsn/Frmn/Hll/49 8.00 20.00
12 Thms/Brry/Mthu/49 6.00 15.00
13 Lcktt/Abdllh/Pttrsn/99 5.00 12.00
14 Brtls/Crr/Plmr/99 6.00 15.00
15 Brs/Rvrs/Brdy/25 25.00 60.00
16 Hpkns/Hltn/Rbnsn/99 5.00 12.00
17 Andrsn/Chrls/Grdn/99 5.00 12.00
18 Hnry/Bkr/Ellt/99 12.00 30.00
19 Alln/Hstn/Strhn/25 8.00 20.00
20 Smth/Tmlnsn/Alln/25 15.00 40.00

2016 Panini National Treasures Peerless Signatures

1 Tyrod Taylor/25 8.00 20.00
2 A.J. Green/25 10.00 25.00
4 DeAndre Hopkins/25 8.00 20.00
5 Andrew Luck/25 50.00 100.00
6 Marcus Mariota/25 40.00 80.00
7 Dez Bryant/25 EXCH 2.00 50.00
10 Marvin Harrison/25 EXCH 30.00 60.00
12 Jameis Winston/25 25.00 50.00
13 David Johnson/25 15.00 40.00
14 Todd Gurley II/25 25.00 50.00

2016 Panini National Treasures Rookie Colossal Signature Materials Prime

*PRIME/25: .6X TO 1.5X BASIC JSY AU/99
*PRIME/25: .5X TO 1.2X BASIC JSY AU/49
4 Ezekiel Elliott/25 150.00 300.00

2016 Panini National Treasures Rookie Dual Materials

*GOLD/49: .5X TO 1.2X BASIC JSY/99
*SILVER: .6X TO 1.5X BASIC JSY/99
1 Michael Thomas 4.00 10.00
2 Connor Cook 2.50 6.00
3 Pharoh Cooper 2.00 5.00
4 Demarcus Robinson 2.00 5.00
5 Tyler Boyd 2.50 6.00
6 Hunter Henry 2.50 6.00
7 Jordan Howard 4.00 10.00
8 Alex Collins 2.50 6.00
9 Kenyan Drake 3.00 8.00
10 Carson Wentz 20.00 50.00
11 Moritz Bohringer 2.00 5.00
12 Corey Coleman 3.00 8.00
13 Ricardo Louis 2.00 5.00
14 Derrick Henry 5.00 12.00
15 Tyler Ervin 2.00 5.00
16 Jared Goff 6.00 15.00
17 Josh Doctson 2.50 6.00
18 Braxton Miller 2.00 5.00
20 Chris Moore 2.50 6.00
21 Paul Perkins 2.00 5.00
22 Dak Prescott 10.00 25.00
23 Sterling Shepard 4.00 10.00
24 Devontae Booker 2.50 6.00
25 Wendell Smallwood 2.00 5.00
26 Joey Bosa 4.00 10.00
27 Keenan Reynolds 2.50 6.00
28 C.J. Prosise 2.00 5.00
29 Laquon Treadwell 2.50 6.00
30 Christian Hackenberg 2.00 5.00
31 Paxton Lynch 5.00 12.00
32 DeAndre Washington 2.00 5.00
33 Trevor Davis 2.00 5.00
34 Ezekiel Elliott 10.00 25.00
35 Will Fuller V 3.00 8.00
36 Jonathan Williams 2.50 6.00
37 Kenneth Dixon 2.00 5.00
38 Cardale Jones 2.00 5.00
39 Leonte Carroo 2.00 5.00
40 Cody Kessler 2.00 5.00

2016 Panini National Treasures Rookie Jumbo Materials Booklet Signatures Prime

1 Jared Goff 75.00 150.00
2 Carson Wentz 125.00 250.00
3 Paxton Lynch 10.00 25.00
4 Christian Hackenberg 10.00 25.00
5 Jacoby Brissett 12.00 30.00
6 Cody Kessler 10.00 25.00
7 Connor Cook 12.00 30.00
8 Dak Prescott 60.00 125.00
9 Cardale Jones 10.00 25.00
10 Tyler Boyd 12.00 30.00
11 Ezekiel Elliott 60.00 125.00
12 Derrick Henry 25.00 60.00
13 Kenyan Drake 15.00 40.00
14 Devontae Booker 12.00 30.00
15 Kenneth Dixon 10.00 25.00
16 Corey Coleman 15.00 40.00
17 Will Fuller V 15.00 40.00
18 Josh Doctson 12.00 30.00
19 Laquon Treadwell 12.00 30.00
20 Sterling Shepard 12.00 30.00

2016 Panini National Treasures Rookie Jumbo Materials Booklet Signatures Vertical Prime

1 Jared Goff/25 60.00 150.00
2 Carson Wentz/25 100.00 200.00
3 Joey Bosa/49 EXCH
4 Ezekiel Elliott/49 200.00 400.00
5 Corey Coleman/49 12.00 30.00
6 Will Fuller V/49 12.00 30.00
7 Josh Doctson/49 10.00 25.00
8 Laquon Treadwell/49 10.00 25.00
9 Paxton Lynch/49 8.00 20.00
10 Hunter Henry/99 8.00 20.00
11 Sterling Shepard/99 8.00 20.00
12 Derrick Henry/49 20.00 50.00
13 Michael Thomas/49 15.00 40.00
14 Christian Hackenberg/49 8.00 20.00
15 Kenyan Drake/99 10.00 25.00
16 Braxton Miller/99 6.00 15.00
17 Leonte Carroo/99 6.00 15.00
18 C.J. Prosise/49 8.00 20.00
19 Cody Kessler/99 6.00 15.00
20 Tyler Boyd/99 8.00 20.00
21 Connor Cook/49 10.00 25.00
22 Chris Moore/99 8.00 20.00
23 Ricardo Louis/99 6.00 15.00
24 Pharoh Cooper/99 6.00 15.00
25 Tyler Ervin/99 6.00 15.00
26 Demarcus Robinson/99 6.00 15.00
27 Kenneth Dixon/99 6.00 15.00
28 Dak Prescott/99 EXCH 100.00 200.00
29 Devontae Booker/99 8.00 20.00
30 Cardale Jones/99 6.00 15.00
31 DeAndre Washington/99 6.00 15.00
32 Paul Perkins/99 6.00 15.00
33 Jordan Howard/99 15.00 40.00
34 Wendell Smallwood/99 6.00 15.00
35 Jonathan Williams/99 8.00 20.00
36 Trevor Davis/99 6.00 15.00
37 Alex Collins/99 8.00 20.00
38 Keenan Reynolds/99 8.00 20.00
39 Moritz Bohringer/99 6.00 15.00

2016 Panini National Treasures Rookie NFL Gear Combo Materials

*PRIME/25: .6X TO 1.5X BASIC JSY AU/99
1 E.Elliott/M.Thomas 15.00 40.00
2 P.Perkins/S.Shepard 4.00 10.00
3 C.Prosise/W.Fuller V 3.00 8.00
4 H.Henry/J.Bosa 4.00 10.00
5 C.Wentz/P.Lynch 10.00 25.00
6 K.Dixon/C.Moore 2.50 6.00
7 D.Prescott/P.Lynch 15.00 40.00
8 E.Elliott/D.Prescott 10.00 25.00
9 D.Henry/K.Drake 5.00 12.00
10 J.Brissett/M.Mitchell 2.50 6.00
11 J.Goff/T.Davis 6.00 15.00
12 D.Washington/C.Cook 2.50 6.00
13 J.Doctson/S.Shepard 4.00 10.00
14 C.Prosise/A.Collins 2.50 6.00
15 D.Prescott/J.Goff 15.00 40.00
16 C.Jones/J.Williams 2.50 6.00
17 D.Henry/E.Elliott 15.00 40.00
18 D.Booker/P.Lynch 5.00 12.00
19 J.Bosa/E.Elliott 15.00 40.00
20 P.Cooper/J.Goff 6.00 15.00
21 A.Collins/H.Henry 2.50 6.00
22 C.Wentz/W.Smallwood 10.00 25.00
23 C.Hackenberg/C.Cook 2.50 6.00
24 C.Wentz/J.Goff 10.00 25.00
25 C.Wentz/D.Prescott 15.00 40.00
26 C.Kessler/C.Coleman 3.00 8.00
27 C.Coleman/L.Treadwell 3.00 8.00
28 B.Miller/W.Fuller V 3.00 8.00
29 C.Jones/B.Miller 2.00 5.00
30 K.Drake/L.Carroo 3.00 8.00

2016 Panini National Treasures Rookie NFL Gear Dual Material Signatures

1 Jared Goff/25 125.00 250.00
2 Carson Wentz/49 75.00 150.00
3 Joey Bosa/49 EXCH 12.00 30.00
4 Ezekiel Elliott/49 75.00 150.00
5 Corey Coleman/49 10.00 25.00
6 Will Fuller V/49 10.00 25.00
7 Josh Doctson/49 8.00 20.00
8 Laquon Treadwell/49 8.00 20.00
9 Paxton Lynch/49 6.00 15.00
10 Hunter Henry/99 6.00 15.00
11 Sterling Shepard/99 6.00 15.00
12 Derrick Henry/49 15.00 40.00
13 Michael Thomas/49 12.00 30.00
14 Christian Hackenberg/49 6.00 15.00
15 Kenyan Drake/99 8.00 20.00
16 Braxton Miller/99 5.00 12.00
17 Leonte Carroo/99 5.00 12.00
18 C.J. Prosise/49 6.00 15.00
19 Jacoby Brissett/99 6.00 15.00
20 Cody Kessler/99 5.00 12.00
21 Tyler Boyd/99 6.00 15.00
22 Connor Cook/49 8.00 20.00
23 Chris Moore/99 6.00 15.00
24 Malcolm Mitchell/99 5.00 12.00
25 Ricardo Louis/99 5.00 12.00
26 Pharoh Cooper/99 5.00 12.00
27 Tyler Ervin/99 5.00 12.00
28 Demarcus Robinson/99 5.00 12.00
29 Kenneth Dixon/99 5.00 12.00
30 Dak Prescott/99 EXCH 50.00 100.00
31 Devontae Booker/99 6.00 15.00
32 Cardale Jones/99 5.00 12.00
33 DeAndre Washington/99 5.00 12.00
34 Paul Perkins/99 5.00 12.00
35 Jordan Howard/99 12.00 30.00
36 Wendell Smallwood/99 5.00 12.00
37 Jonathan Williams/99 6.00 15.00
38 Trevor Davis/99 5.00 12.00
39 Alex Collins/99 6.00 15.00
40 Keenan Reynolds/99 6.00 15.00
41 Moritz Bohringer/99 5.00 12.00

2016 Panini National Treasures Rookie NFL Gear Dual Material Signatures Prime

*PRIME: .5X TO 1.2X BASIC JSY AU
2 Carson Wentz/25 100.00 200.00
4 Ezekiel Elliott/25 200.00 300.00

2016 Panini National Treasures Rookie Photo Shoot Material Signatures

1 Jared Goff/49 100.00 200.00
2 Carson Wentz/49 75.00 150.00
3 Joey Bosa/49 EXCH 12.00 30.00
4 Ezekiel Elliott/49 150.00 250.00
5 Corey Coleman/49 10.00 25.00
6 Will Fuller V/49 10.00 25.00
7 Josh Doctson/49 8.00 20.00
8 Laquon Treadwell/49 8.00 20.00
9 Paxton Lynch/49 6.00 15.00
10 Hunter Henry/99 6.00 15.00
11 Sterling Shepard/99 6.00 15.00
12 Derrick Henry/49 15.00 40.00
13 Michael Thomas/49 12.00 30.00
14 Christian Hackenberg/49 6.00 15.00
15 Kenyan Drake/99 8.00 20.00
16 Braxton Miller/99 5.00 12.00
17 Leonte Carroo/99 5.00 12.00
18 C.J. Prosise/49 6.00 15.00
19 Cody Kessler/99 5.00 12.00
20 Tyler Boyd/99 6.00 15.00
21 Connor Cook/49 8.00 20.00
22 Chris Moore/99 6.00 15.00
23 Ricardo Louis/99 5.00 12.00
24 Pharoh Cooper/99 5.00 12.00
25 Tyler Ervin/99 5.00 12.00
26 Demarcus Robinson/99 5.00 12.00
27 Kenneth Dixon/99 5.00 12.00
28 Dak Prescott/99 EXCH 50.00 100.00
29 Devontae Booker/99 6.00 15.00
30 Cardale Jones/99 5.00 12.00
31 DeAndre Washington/99 5.00 12.00
32 Paul Perkins/99 5.00 12.00
33 Jordan Howard/99 12.00 30.00
34 Wendell Smallwood/99 5.00 12.00
35 Jonathan Williams/99 6.00 15.00
36 Trevor Davis/99 5.00 12.00
37 Alex Collins/99 6.00 15.00
38 Keenan Reynolds/99 6.00 15.00
39 Moritz Bohringer/99 5.00 12.00

2016 Panini National Treasures Rookie Photo Shoot Material Signatures Silver

*SILVER/25: .6X TO 1.5X BASIC JSY AU/99
*SILVER/25: .5X TO 1.2X BASIC JSY AU/49
4 Ezekiel Elliott 300.00 500.00

2016 Panini National Treasures Rookie Quad Materials Booklet

*PRIME/25: .5X TO 1.2X BASIC JSY/49
1 Wntz/Prscott/Gff/Lnch 40.00 100.00
2 Clmn/Dctsn/Trdwll/Fllr 6.00 15.00
3 Wntz/Ellt/Gff/Bsa 40.00 100.00

2016 Panini National Treasures Rookie Signatures

*GOLD/25: .6X TO 1.5X BASIC AU/99
*GOLD/25: .5X TO 1.2X BASIC AU/49
1 Jared Goff/25 40.00 100.00
2 Carson Wentz/25
3 Joey Bosa/49 10.00 25.00
4 Ezekiel Elliott/25 100.00 200.00
5 Corey Coleman/99 6.00 15.00
6 Will Fuller V/49 8.00 20.00
7 Josh Doctson/49 6.00 15.00
8 Laquon Treadwell/49 6.00 15.00
9 Paxton Lynch/49 5.00 12.00
10 Sterling Shepard/99 15.00 40.00
11 Derrick Henry/49 12.00 30.00
12 Michael Thomas/49 10.00 25.00
13 Christian Hackenberg/49 5.00 12.00
14 Tyler Boyd/99 5.00 12.00
15 Kenyan Drake/99 6.00 15.00
16 Braxton Miller/99 4.00 10.00
17 C.J. Prosise/49 5.00 12.00
18 Connor Cook/49 6.00 15.00
19 Cody Kessler/99 4.00 10.00
20 Pharoh Cooper/99 4.00 10.00

2016 Panini National Treasures Rookie Signatures Dual Holo Silver

*SILVER/25: .5X TO 1.2X BASIC AU/49

2016 Panini National Treasures Signatures

*GOLD: .5X TO 1.2X BASIC AU
1 Tyrod Taylor/49 6.00 15.00
2 Sammy Watkins/49 8.00 20.00
3 Jim Kelly/25 15.00 40.00
4 Thurman Thomas/25 8.00 20.00
5 Andre Reed/25 8.00 20.00
6 Ryan Tannehill/49 6.00 15.00
7 Latavius Murray/99 4.00 10.00
10 John Hannah/99 4.00 10.00
11 Eric Decker/49 5.00 12.00
12 Matt Forte/25 6.00 15.00
13 Darrelle Revis/25
15 Joe Flacco/25 12.00 30.00
16 Steve Smith/25 8.00 20.00
17 Ray Lewis/25 50.00 100.00
18 Ed Reed/25 8.00 20.00
19 Andy Dalton/49 6.00 15.00
20 Jeremy Hill/49 5.00 12.00
21 Giovani Bernard/49 5.00 12.00
22 A.J. Green/49 8.00 20.00
28 Luke Kuechly/25 8.00 20.00
29 Jerome Bettis/20 30.00 60.00
30 Franco Harris/25 25.00 50.00
32 James Harrison/25 30.00 60.00
33 Bo Jackson/49 40.00 80.00
34 Lamar Miller/99 4.00 10.00
35 DeAndre Hopkins/25 8.00 20.00
37 Andrew Luck/25 50.00 100.00
38 Frank Gore/25 8.00 20.00
41 Edgerrin James/49 6.00 15.00
42 Reggie Wayne/25 8.00 20.00
43 Blake Bortles/25 12.00 30.00
44 T.J. Yeldon/99 4.00 10.00
45 Allen Robinson/49 6.00 15.00
46 Marcus Mariota/25 30.00 60.00
47 Earl Campbell/25 25.00 50.00
48 Warren Moon/25 20.00 50.00
50 Demaryius Thomas/25 8.00 20.00
51 Trevor Siemian/49 5.00 12.00
53 Jamaal Charles/25 12.00 30.00
54 Jeremy Maclin/49 5.00 12.00
55 Derek Carr/25 40.00 80.00
57 Marcus Allen/25 60.00 125.00
58 Fred Biletnikoff/25 10.00 25.00
59 Philip Rivers/25 20.00 40.00
60 Melvin Gordon/49 6.00 15.00
61 Antonio Gates/25 6.00 15.00
62 Keenan Allen/49 6.00 15.00
64 Dez Bryant/25 25.00 50.00
67 Lawrence Taylor/25 25.00 50.00
68 Jordan Matthews/49 6.00 15.00
69 Darren Sproles/49 6.00 15.00
70 Kirk Cousins/25 20.00 40.00
71 Jay Cutler/25 6.00 15.00
72 Jeremy Langford/99 5.00 12.00
73 Brian Urlacher/25 25.00 50.00
74 Matthew Stafford/25 30.00 60.00
75 Ameer Abdullah/99 8.00 20.00
77 Eddie Lacy/49 5.00 12.00
78 Jordy Nelson/49 6.00 15.00
79 Clay Matthews/25 25.00 50.00
80 Tony Dorsett/25 30.00 60.00
83 Matt Ryan/25 30.00 60.00
84 Devonta Freeman/49 6.00 15.00
85 Ottis Anderson/99 4.00 10.00
86 Kelvin Benjamin/49 6.00 15.00
88 Brandin Cooks/49 6.00 15.00
89 Jameis Winston/25 30.00 60.00
90 Doug Martin/49 6.00 15.00
91 Mike Evans/49 6.00 15.00
92 David Johnson/49
93 Julius Thomas/99 4.00 10.00
94 Todd Gurley II/25 EXCH
95 Marshall Faulk/25 30.00 60.00
96 Ronnie Lott/49 30.00 60.00
97 Roger Craig/49 6.00 15.00
100 Doug Baldwin/49 6.00 15.00

2016 Panini National Treasures Treasure Chest Materials

1 Cowboys 100.00 200.00
2 Rookies 75.00 150.00

2016 Panini National Treasures Treasure Chest Materials Prime

1 Alfred Morris 250.00 500.00
Anthony Hitchens
Brandon Carr
Byron Jones
Cole Beasley
Dan Bailey
Ezekiel Elliott
Gavin Escobar
Jason Witten
Lucky Whitehead
Morris Claiborne
Terrance Williams
Tony Romo
Tyrone Crawford
Barry Church
Dak Prescott
Darren McFadden
DeMarcus Lawrence
Dez Bryant
Maliek Collins
Orlando Scandrick
Travis Frederick
Tyron Smith
Zack Martin
2 Braxton Miller 100.00 200.00
Cardale Jones
Chris Moore
Christian Hackenberg
Corey Coleman
Jacoby Brissett
Josh Doctson
Laquon Treadwell
Malcolm Mitchell
Michael Thomas
Paxton Lynch
Pharoh Cooper
Ricardo Louis
Will Fuller V
Carson Wentz
Cody Kessler
Connor Cook
Dak Prescott
Demarcus Robinson
Jared Goff
Leonte Carroo
Sterling Shepard
Trevor Davis
Tyler Boy

2016 Panini National Treasures Tremendous Treasures Materials

TTRAC Alex Collins/99 4.00 10.00
TTRAR Allen Robinson/49 5.00 12.00
TTRBC Brian Cushing/15 6.00 15.00
TTRBC Brent Celek/49 4.00 10.00
TTRBC Brandin Cooks/25 6.00 15.00
TTRBM Braxton Miller/99 3.00 8.00
TTRCB Cole Beasley/49 15.00 40.00
TTRCC Corey Coleman/99 5.00 12.00
TTRCC Connor Cook/99 4.00 10.00
TTRCD Carlos Dunlap/99 3.00 8.00
TTRCH Carlos Hyde/99 3.00 8.00
TTRCH Christian Hackenberg/99 3.00 8.00
TTRCJ Cardale Jones/99 3.00 8.00
TTRCK Cody Kessler/99 3.00 8.00
TTRCM Chris Moore/99 4.00 10.00
TTRCP C.J. Prosise/99 3.00 8.00
TTRCW Carson Wentz/99 15.00 40.00
TTRDB Devontae Booker/99 4.00 10.00
TTRDB Dez Bryant/25 8.00 20.00
TTRDF Devonta Freeman/99 4.00 10.00
TTRDF Devin Funchess/99 3.00 8.00
TTRDH Derrick Henry/99 8.00 20.00
TTRDJ David Johnson/49 6.00 15.00
TTRDM Devin McCourty/25 50.00 100.00
TTRDP Dak Prescott/99 15.00 40.00
TTRDR Demarcus Robinson/99 3.00 8.00
TTRDT Demaryius Thomas/49 5.00 12.00
TTRDW DeAndre Washington/99 3.00 8.00
TTREE Ezekiel Elliott/99 15.00 40.00
TTRHH Hunter Henry/99 4.00 10.00
TTRIC Isaiah Crowell/25 5.00 12.00
TTRJB Joey Bosa/99 6.00 15.00
TTRJB Jacoby Brissett/75 4.00 10.00
TTRJD Josh Doctson/99 4.00 10.00
TTRJG Jared Goff/99 10.00 25.00
TTRJH Jordan Howard/99 6.00 15.00
TTRJL Jeremy Langford/99 4.00 10.00
TTRJS Junior Seau/25 6.00 15.00
TTRJW Jonathan Williams/99 4.00 10.00
TTRKB Kelvin Benjamin/99 4.00 10.00
TTRKD Kenneth Dixon/99 3.00 8.00
TTRKD Kenyan Drake/99 5.00 12.00
TTRKM Khalil Mack/49 6.00 15.00
TTRKR Keenan Reynolds/99 4.00 10.00
TTRLC Leonte Carroo/99 3.00 8.00
TTRLT Laquon Treadwell/99 4.00 10.00
TTRMB Moritz Bohringer/99 3.00 8.00
TTRMD Marcell Dareus/99 3.00 8.00
TTRMM Marcus Mariota/99 5.00 12.00
TTRMM Malcolm Mitchell/99 3.00 8.00
TTRMT Michael Thomas/99 6.00 15.00
TTRPC Pharoh Cooper/99 3.00 8.00
TTRPL Paxton Lynch/99 3.00 8.00
TTRPP Paul Perkins/99 3.00 8.00
TTRRJ Reshad Jones/99 3.00 8.00
TTRRL Ricardo Louis/99 3.00 8.00
TTRRT Ryan Tannehill/49 5.00 12.00
TTRSS Sterling Shepard/99 4.00 10.00
TTRSW Sammy Watkins/99 5.00 12.00
TTRTB Tyler Boyd/99 4.00 10.00
TTRTD Trevor Davis/99 3.00 8.00
TTRTE Tyler Eifert/99 4.00 10.00
TTRTE Tyler Ervin/99 3.00 8.00
TTRTG Todd Gurley II/99 5.00 12.00
TTRTL Tyler Lockett/99 4.00 10.00
TTRTS Trevor Siemian/25 5.00 12.00
TTRVB Vontaze Burfict/99 3.00 8.00
TTRWF Will Fuller V/99 5.00 12.00
TTRWS Wendell Smallwood/99 3.00 8.00

2016 Panini National Treasures Tremendous Treasures Materials Horizontal

TTRBM Braxton Miller/99 3.00 8.00
TTRCC Corey Coleman/99 5.00 12.00
TTRCH Paxton Lynch/99 3.00 8.00
TTRCP C.J. Prosise/99 3.00 8.00
TTRDB Devontae Booker/99 4.00 10.00
TTRDH Derrick Henry/99 8.00 20.00
TTRDP Dak Prescott/99 15.00 40.00
TTRDR Carson Wentz/99 30.00 80.00
TTREE Ezekiel Elliott/99 15.00 40.00
TTRJB Jacoby Brissett/25 6.00 15.00
TTRJD Josh Doctson/99 4.00 10.00
TTRJG Jared Goff/99 10.00 25.00
TTRKD Kenyan Drake/99 5.00 12.00
TTRLT Laquon Treadwell/99 4.00 10.00
TTRMM Malcolm Mitchell/49 4.00 10.00
TTRMT Michael Thomas/99 6.00 15.00
TTRSS Sterling Shepard/99 4.00 10.00
TTRTB Tyler Boyd/99 4.00 10.00
TTRTD Trevor Davis/99 3.00 8.00
TTRWF Will Fuller V/99 5.00 12.00

2017 Panini National Treasures

1 A.J. Green 3.00 8.00
2 Aaron Donald 3.00 8.00
3 Aaron Rodgers 6.00 15.00
4 Adam Thielen 3.00 8.00
5 Adrian Peterson 3.00 8.00
6 Alex Smith 2.50 6.00
7 Allen Hurns 2.00 5.00
8 Alshon Jeffery 2.50 6.00
9 Amari Cooper 3.00 8.00
10 Ameer Abdullah 2.00 5.00
11 Andrew Luck 4.00 10.00
12 Andy Dalton 2.50 6.00
13 Antonio Brown 3.00 8.00
14 Barry Sanders 5.00 12.00
15 Ben Roethlisberger 3.00 8.00
16 Bilal Powell 2.00 5.00
17 Blake Bortles 2.00 5.00
18 Brandin Cooks 2.50 6.00
19 Michael Thomas 3.00 8.00
20 Cam Newton 3.00 8.00
21 Carlos Hyde 2.00 5.00
22 Carson Palmer 2.50 6.00
23 Carson Wentz 4.00 10.00
24 Chris Harris Jr. 2.00 5.00
25 Corey Coleman 2.00 5.00
26 Dak Prescott 3.00 8.00
27 Dan Marino 6.00 15.00
28 Terrance West 2.00 5.00
29 David Johnson 3.00 8.00
30 DeAndre Hopkins 2.50 6.00
31 DeMarco Murray 2.50 6.00
32 Demaryius Thomas 2.50 6.00
33 Derek Carr 3.00 8.00
34 DeSean Jackson 2.50 6.00
35 Devonta Freeman 2.50 6.00
36 Dez Bryant 3.00 8.00
37 Doug Martin 2.50 6.00
38 Drew Brees 3.00 8.00
39 Eli Manning 2.50 6.00
40 Eric Decker 2.00 5.00
41 Ezekiel Elliott 4.00 10.00
42 Frank Gore 2.50 6.00
43 Golden Tate III 2.00 5.00
44 Isaiah Crowell 2.00 5.00
45 J.J. Watt 3.00 8.00
46 Jameis Winston 2.50 6.00
47 Jared Goff 3.00 8.00
48 Jarvis Landry 2.50 6.00
49 Jay Ajayi 2.50 6.00
50 Jay Cutler 2.00 5.00
51 Jeremy Maclin 2.00 5.00
52 Jimmy Graham 3.00 8.00
53 Joe Flacco 2.50 6.00
54 Joe Montana 8.00 20.00
55 Joe Namath 4.00 10.00
56 Joey Bosa 3.00 8.00
57 Jordan Howard 3.00 8.00
58 Jordan Matthews 2.00 5.00
59 Jordy Nelson 2.50 6.00
60 Josh McCown 2.00 5.00
61 Julio Jones 3.00 8.00
62 Kelvin Benjamin 2.50 6.00
63 Jimmy Garoppolo 30.00 60.00
64 Kendall Wright 2.00 5.00
65 Khalil Mack 3.00 8.00
66 Kirk Cousins 3.00 8.00
67 Lamar Miller 2.00 5.00
68 Larry Fitzgerald 2.50 6.00
69 LeSean McCoy 3.00 8.00
70 Le'Veon Bell 2.50 6.00
71 Luke Kuechly 2.50 6.00
72 Marcus Mariota 3.00 8.00
73 Marshawn Lynch 2.50 6.00
74 Matt Ryan 2.50 6.00
75 Matthew Stafford 2.50 6.00
76 Melvin Gordon 2.50 6.00
77 Mike Evans 2.50 6.00
78 Odell Beckham Jr. 3.00 8.00
79 Philip Rivers 3.00 8.00
80 Pierre Garcon 2.50 6.00
81 Richard Sherman 3.00 8.00
82 Rob Gronkowski 3.00 8.00
83 Russell Wilson 4.00 10.00
84 Sam Bradford 2.00 5.00
85 Sterling Shepard 2.50 6.00
86 T.Y. Hilton 2.50 6.00
87 Terrelle Pryor 2.00 5.00
88 Todd Gurley II 3.00 8.00
89 Tom Brady 8.00 20.00
90 Torrey Smith 2.00 5.00
91 Travis Kelce 3.00 8.00
92 Myles Garrett 6.00 15.00
93 Ty Montgomery 2.00 5.00
94 Tyler Eifert 2.50 6.00
95 Tyreek Hill 3.00 8.00
96 Tyrod Taylor 2.50 6.00
97 Von Miller 2.50 6.00
98 Walter Payton 6.00 15.00
99 Willie Snead 2.50 6.00
100 Xavier Rhodes 2.00 5.00
101 Chad Williams AU RC 4.00 10.00
102 Brad Kaaya AU RC 4.00 10.00
103 Raekwon McMillan AU RC 4.00 10.00
104 Isaiah Ford AU RC 4.00 10.00
105 Jamal Adams AU RC 4.00 10.00
107 Malachi Dupre AU RC 4.00 10.00
108 Adoree' Jackson AU RC 5.00 12.00
109 Chad Kelly AU RC 40.00 80.00
110 Derek Barnett AU RC 5.00 12.00
111 Elijah Hood AU RC 4.00 10.00
113 Marshon Lattimore AU RC 5.00 12.00
115 Haason Reddick AU RC 4.00 10.00
118 Chad Hansen AU RC 4.00 10.00
119 Greg Ward Jr. AU RC 4.00 10.00
120 Desmond King AU RC 5.00 12.00
121 Tarik Cohen AU RC 12.00 30.00
122 Donnel Pumphrey AU RC 5.00 12.00
123 Brian Hill AU RC 4.00 10.00
124 Gareon Conley AU RC 4.00 10.00
126 Jake Butt AU RC 5.00 12.00
127 Jarrad Davis AU RC 5.00 12.00
128 Cameron Sutton AU RC 4.00 10.00
129 Matthew Dayes AU RC 4.00 10.00
130 Budda Baker AU RC 4.00 10.00
131 Marcus Williams AU RC 4.00 10.00
132 Shelton Gibson AU RC 4.00 10.00
133 Sidney Jones AU RC 4.00 10.00
134 Stacy Coley AU RC 4.00 10.00
135 Duke Riley AU RC 4.00 10.00
136 Travis Rudolph AU RC 4.00 10.00
137 Aaron Jones AU RC 10.00 25.00
138 Isaiah McKenzie AU RC 4.00 10.00
140 Kendell Beckwith AU RC 4.00 10.00
141 Tanoh Kpassagnon AU RC 5.00 12.00
142 Fabian Moreau AU RC 4.00 10.00
143 Khalfani Muhammad AU RC 4.00 10.00
144 Nazair Jones AU RC 4.00 10.00
145 Shaquill Griffin AU RC 12.00 30.00
146 Eddie Vanderdoes AU RC 4.00 10.00
147 Solomon Thomas AU RC 4.00 10.00
148 Jordan Leggett AU RC 4.00 10.00

149 Justin Evans AU RC 4.00 10.00
150 Malik McDowell AU RC 4.00 10.00
151 Robert Davis AU RC 4.00 10.00
152 Ryan Anderson AU RC 4.00 10.00
153 Eddie Jackson AU RC 5.00 12.00
154 T.J. Logan AU RC 6.00 15.00
155 Chris Carson AU RC 12.00 30.00
156 Vince Biegel AU RC 8.00 20.00
158 De'Veon Smith AU RC 10.00 25.00
159 Dawuane Smoot AU RC 4.00 10.00
160 George Kittle AU RC 6.00 15.00
161 Patrick Mahomes II JSY AU RC 5000.00 8000.00
162 Jeremy McNichols JSY AU RC 12.00 30.00
163 Corey Davis JSY AU RC 20.00 50.00
164 Kenny Golladay JSY AU RC 20.00 50.00
165 Dede Westbrook JSY AU RC 12.00 30.00
166 Josh Reynolds JSY AU RC 12.00 30.00
167 C.J. Beathard JSY AU RC 12.00 30.00
168 Evan Engram JSY AU RC 15.00 40.00
169 Deshaun Watson JSY AU RC 800.00 1500.00
170 ArDarius Stewart JSY AU RC 12.00 30.00
171 Mike Williams JSY AU RC 20.00 50.00
172 Joe Williams JSY AU RC 12.00 30.00
173 John Ross III JSY AU RC 15.00 40.00
174 Taywan Taylor JSY AU RC 12.00 30.00
175 D'Onta Foreman JSY AU RC 15.00 40.00
176 Mack Hollins JSY AU RC 12.00 30.00
177 O.J. Howard JSY AU RC 15.00 40.00
178 Samaje Perine JSY AU RC 12.00 30.00
179 Mitchell Trubisky JSY AU RC 800.00 1200.00
180 Carlos Henderson JSY AU RC 12.00 30.00
181 Christian McCaffrey JSY AU RC 75.00 150.00
182 Kareem Hunt JSY AU RC 25.00 60.00
183 JuJu Smith-Schuster JSY AU RC EXCH 75.00 150.00
184 Jamaal Williams JSY AU RC 12.00 30.00
185 Nathan Peterman JSY AU RC 15.00 40.00
186 R. Joshua Dobbs JSY AU RC 15.00 40.00
187 Zay Jones JSY AU RC EXCH 15.00 40.00
188 Amara Darboh JSY AU RC 12.00 30.00
189 Leonard Fournette JSY AU RC 125.00 250.00
190 Chris Godwin JSY AU RC 15.00 40.00
191 Dalvin Cook JSY AU RC 100.00 200.00
192 Wayne Gallman JSY AU RC 15.00 40.00
193 Curtis Samuel JSY AU RC 15.00 40.00
194 Joe Mixon JSY AU RC 25.00 60.00
195 Alvin Kamara JSY AU RC 100.00 200.00
196 Marlon Mack JSY AU RC 20.00 50.00
197 Davis Webb JSY AU RC 75.00 150.00
198 Cooper Kupp JSY AU RC 50.00 100.00
199 DeShone Kizer JSY AU RC 30.00 60.00
200 James Conner JSY AU RC 25.00 60.00
201 Ryan Switzer JSY AU RC 15.00 40.00
203 T.J. Watt JSY AU RC
204 Charles Harris JSY AU RC 12.00 30.00
205 Noah Brown JSY AU RC 15.00 40.00
206 DeMarcus Walker JSY AU RC 12.00 30.00
207 Jabrill Peppers JSY AU RC 20.00 50.00
208 Josh Malone JSY AU RC 12.00 30.00
209 Tre'Davious White JSY AU RC 12.00 30.00
210 Matt Breida JSY AU RC 20.00 50.00
212 Chidobe Awuzie JSY AU RC 15.00 40.00

2017 Panini National Treasures Holo Silver

109 Chad Kelly AU 100.00 200.00
161 Patrick Mahomes II JSY AU 5000.00 9000.00
169 Deshaun Watson JSY AU 2000.00 3000.00
179 Mitchell Trubisky JSY AU 800.00 1200.00
181 Christian McCaffrey JSY AU 125.00 250.00
182 Kareem Hunt JSY AU 40.00 100.00
189 Leonard Fournette JSY AU 100.00 200.00
191 Dalvin Cook JSY AU 150.00 300.00
195 Alvin Kamara JSY AU 125.00 250.00

2017 Panini National Treasures Purple

*VETS/75: .4X TO 1X BASIC CARDS/99

2017 Panini National Treasures Century Materials

*PRIME/49: .5X TO 1.2X BASIC JSY/99
*PRIME/25: .6X TO 1.5X BASIC JSY/99
*PRIME/25: .5X TO 1.2X BASIC JSY/49
*PRIME/15: .6X TO 1.5X BASIC JSY/49
*SILVER/25: .6X TO 1.5X BASIC JSY/99
*SILVER/25: .5X TO 1.2X BASIC JSY/49
*SILVER/15: .8X TO 2X BASIC JSY/99
*SILVER/15: .6X TO 1.5X BASIC JSY/49
1 Bart Starr/25 25.00 60.00
2 Carlos Hyde/99 3.00 8.00
3 Adam Vinatieri/99 3.00 8.00
4 Derrick Henry/99 4.00 10.00
5 Dan Bailey/99 3.00 8.00
6 LeSean McCoy/99 5.00 12.00
7 Joe Flacco/99 4.00 10.00
8 Peyton Manning/49 12.00 30.00
9 Walter Payton/49 12.00 30.00
10 Marshawn Lynch/99 4.00 10.00
11 Lance Alworth/99 4.00 10.00
12 Todd Gurley II/99 5.00 12.00
13 Tom Landry/15 12.00 30.00
14 Jordan Howard/99 5.00 12.00
15 Drew Brees/99 5.00 12.00
16 James Harrison/99 4.00 10.00
17 Joe Montana/49 15.00 40.00
18 Philip Rivers/99 5.00 12.00
19 Doug Baldwin/99 4.00 10.00
20 Terrell Suggs/49 4.00 10.00
21 Lawrence Taylor/99 5.00 12.00
22 Melvin Gordon/99 4.00 10.00
23 Allen Robinson/99 4.00 10.00
24 Corey Coleman/99 3.00 8.00
25 Chris Harris Jr./49 4.00 10.00
26 Von Miller/99 4.00 10.00
27 Johnny Unitas/25 12.00 30.00
28 Jim Thorpe/25 50.00 100.00
29 Fran Tarkenton/99 5.00 12.00
30 Antonio Gates/99 3.00 8.00
31 Matt Ryan/99 4.00 10.00
32 David Johnson/99 5.00 12.00
33 Andrew Luck/99 6.00 15.00
34 Sterling Shepard/99 4.00 10.00
35 Dak Prescott/99 5.00 12.00
36 Cole Beasley/99 5.00 12.00
37 Joe Namath/49 8.00 20.00
38 Rich Gannon/99 3.00 8.00
39 Golden Tate III/99 3.00 8.00
40 Bobby Layne/25 12.00 30.00
41 Matthew Stafford/99 4.00 10.00
42 Jay Ajayi/99 4.00 10.00
43 Barry Sanders/49 10.00 25.00
44 Michael Thomas/99 5.00 12.00
45 Ezekiel Elliott/99 6.00 15.00
46 Kiko Alonso/99 3.00 8.00
47 John Elway/49 10.00 25.00
48 Russell Wilson/99 6.00 15.00
49 Greg Olsen/99 4.00 10.00
50 Jordy Nelson/99 4.00 10.00
51 Mike Ditka/99 5.00 12.00
52 Derek Carr/99 5.00 12.00
53 Blake Bortles/99 3.00 8.00
54 C.J. Anderson/99 4.00 10.00
55 Ed Reed/99 4.00 10.00
56 Jay Cutler/99 3.00 8.00
57 Len Dawson/99 5.00 12.00
58 Steve Young/49 8.00 20.00
59 Heath Miller/99 3.00 8.00
60 Charles Woodson/99 5.00 12.00
61 Priest Holmes/99 3.00 8.00
62 Amari Cooper/99 5.00 12.00
63 Brett Favre/49 12.00 30.00
64 Tyreek Hill/99 5.00 12.00
65 Jarvis Landry/99 4.00 10.00
66 Julius Thomas/99 3.00 8.00
67 Marcus Mariota/99 5.00 12.00
68 Tom Brady/10 30.00 60.00
69 Jameis Winston/99 4.00 10.00
70 Jim Kelly/99 5.00 12.00
71 Tony Romo/99 4.00 10.00
72 Jared Goff/99 5.00 12.00
73 Curtis Martin/99 4.00 10.00
74 A.J. Green/99 5.00 12.00
75 Jeremy Hill/99 3.00 8.00
76 DeMarco Murray/99 4.00 10.00
77 Michael Vick/99 4.00 10.00
78 Tony Dorsett/99 5.00 12.00
79 Joe Theismann/99 5.00 12.00
80 Frank Gore/99 4.00 10.00
81 Troy Aikman/99 6.00 15.00
82 Carson Wentz/99 6.00 15.00
83 Demaryius Thomas/99 4.00 10.00
84 Tyler Eifert/99 4.00 10.00
85 Andy Dalton/99 4.00 10.00
86 Cameron Wake/99 3.00 8.00
87 Mark Brunell/99 4.00 10.00
88 Vance Johnson/99 3.00 8.00
89 John Riggins/99 4.00 10.00
90 Chris Hogan/99 3.00 8.00
91 Aaron Rodgers/49 12.00 30.00
92 Paxton Lynch/99 3.00 8.00
93 Dez Bryant/99 5.00 12.00
94 Tyrod Taylor/99 4.00 10.00
95 Jerry Rice/49 10.00 25.00
96 Danny Woodhead/99 4.00 10.00
97 Ndamukong Suh/99 4.00 10.00
98 Vontaze Burfict/99 3.00 8.00
99 Kurt Warner/99 4.00 10.00
100 Richard Sherman/99 5.00 12.00

2017 Panini National Treasures Colossal Material Signatures

1 Dan Marino/25 75.00 150.00
2 Eddie Lacy/49 10.00 25.00
3 Drew Brees/25 60.00 125.00
4 Andre Reed/49 12.00 30.00
5 Matt Ryan/25 30.00 60.00
6 Kirk Cousins/49 15.00 40.00
8 Jordy Nelson/25 15.00 40.00
9 Brett Favre/25 100.00 200.00
10 Joe Theismann/25 20.00 50.00
11 Joe Namath/25 50.00 100.00
12 Don Maynard/49 12.00 30.00
14 Priest Holmes/49 10.00 25.00
15 Philip Rivers/25 20.00 50.00
17 Bo Jackson/25
19 Terry Bradshaw/25 50.00 100.00
20 Fran Tarkenton/25 20.00 50.00
21 Eli Manning/25 30.00 60.00
22 Danny Woodhead/49 12.00 30.00
23 Jameis Winston/25 15.00 40.00
24 Carlos Hyde/49 10.00 25.00
25 Jim Kelly/25 20.00 50.00
26 Ezekiel Elliott/25 50.00 100.00
27 Eric Dickerson/25 20.00 50.00
28 David Johnson/25 20.00 50.00
29 Jerry Rice/25 100.00 200.00
30 Doug Baldwin/25 15.00 40.00

2017 Panini National Treasures Colossal Materials

*PRIME/25: .6X TO 1.5X BASIC JSY/99
*PRIME/25: .5X TO 1.2X BASIC JSY/49
*PRIME/15: .8X TO 2X BASIC JSY/99
*PRIME/15: .6X TO 1.5X BASIC JSY/49
1 Michael Vick/99 4.00 10.00
2 Carson Wentz/99 6.00 15.00
3 Jim Kelly/99 5.00 12.00
4 Earl Thomas III/99 4.00 10.00
5 Barry Sanders/49 10.00 25.00
6 Howie Long/99 5.00 12.00
7 Jarvis Landry/99 4.00 10.00
8 Stefon Diggs/99 4.00 10.00
9 Carlos Hyde/99 3.00 8.00
10 Aaron Rodgers/49 12.00 30.00
11 Earl Campbell/49 6.00 15.00
12 Marcus Mariota/99 5.00 12.00
13 Luke Kuechly/99 4.00 10.00
14 Jerome Bettis/49 6.00 15.00
15 Richard Sherman/99 5.00 12.00
16 Blake Bortles/99 3.00 8.00
17 Danny Woodhead/99 4.00 10.00
18 Jameis Winston/99 4.00 10.00
19 Jordy Nelson/99 4.00 10.00
20 Ezekiel Elliott/99 6.00 15.00
21 Russell Wilson/99 6.00 15.00
22 Derrick Henry/99 4.00 10.00
23 Steve Largent/99 5.00 12.00
24 Dak Prescott/99 5.00 12.00
25 Tyreek Hill/99 5.00 12.00
27 Doug Martin/99 4.00 10.00
28 Derek Carr/99 5.00 12.00
29 James Harrison/99 4.00 10.00
30 Darren Woodson/99 4.00 10.00
31 Marcus Allen/49 5.00 12.00
32 Charles Woodson/99 5.00 12.00
33 Tony Dorsett/99 5.00 12.00
34 Terrelle Pryor/99 3.00 8.00
35 Matthew Stafford/99 4.00 10.00
36 Marshawn Lynch/99 4.00 10.00
37 Golden Tate III/99 3.00 8.00
38 LaDainian Tomlinson/99 4.00 10.00

2017 Panini National Treasures Colossal Pro Bowl Materials

*PRIME/25: .6X TO 1.5X BASIC JSY/99
*PRIME/25: .5X TO 1.2X BASIC JSY/49
*PRIME/15: .8X TO 2X BASIC JSY/99
*PRIME/15: .6X TO 1.5X BASIC JSY/49
1 Andy Dalton/49 5.00 12.00
2 Alex Smith/99 4.00 10.00
3 Philip Rivers/99 5.00 12.00
4 Kirk Cousins/49 6.00 15.00
5 Drew Brees/99 5.00 12.00
6 Dak Prescott/99 5.00 12.00
7 DeMarco Murray/99 4.00 10.00
8 Jay Ajayi/99 4.00 10.00
9 Patrick Peterson/99 3.00 8.00
10 Jordan Howard/49 6.00 15.00
11 Ezekiel Elliott/99 6.00 15.00
12 T.Y. Hilton/49 5.00 12.00
13 Demaryius Thomas/49 5.00 12.00
14 Travis Kelce/49 6.00 15.00
15 Delanie Walker/49 4.00 10.00
16 Tyreek Hill/99 5.00 12.00
17 Emmanuel Sanders/99 5.00 12.00
18 Odell Beckham Jr./75 5.00 12.00
19 Doug Baldwin/49 5.00 12.00
20 Dez Bryant/99 5.00 12.00
21 Jimmy Graham/49 6.00 15.00
22 Greg Olsen/99 4.00 10.00
23 Michael Bennett/99 3.00 8.00
24 Harrison Smith/49 15.00 40.00
25 Bobby Wagner/49 6.00 15.00
26 Sean Lee/49 5.00 12.00
27 Richard Sherman/99 5.00 12.00
28 Ryan Shazier/49 4.00 10.00
29 Von Miller/99 4.00 10.00
30 Justin Tucker/49 4.00 10.00
31 Cliff Avril/99 3.00 8.00
32 Kyle Juszczyk/49 4.00 10.00

2017 Panini National Treasures Dual Signatures

7 P.Rivers/A.Gates/25 30.00 60.00
8 M.Allen/T.Brown/25 40.00 80.00
11 F.Tarkenton/C.Eller/49 25.00 50.00
12 J.Taylor/P.Hornung/25 75.00 150.00
17 A.Smith/T.Hill/25 15.00 40.00

2017 Panini National Treasures Franchise Treasures Materials

*PRIME/25: .6X TO 1.5X BASIC JSY/99
*PRIME/25: .5X TO 1.2X BASIC JSY/49
*PRIME/15-16: .8X TO 2X BASIC JSY/99
*PRIME/15: .6X TO 1.5X BASIC JSY/49
1 Len Dawson/99 5.00 12.00
2 Antonio Brown/99 5.00 12.00
3 Cam Newton/99 5.00 12.00
4 Walter Payton/49 12.00 30.00
5 Eli Manning/99 4.00 10.00
6 Von Miller/99 4.00 10.00
7 Joe Namath/49 8.00 20.00
8 Bobby Layne/25 6.00 15.00
9 Steve Young/99 6.00 15.00
10 Dave Wilcox/99 3.00 8.00
11 Joe Flacco/99 4.00 10.00
12 Barry Sanders/49 10.00 25.00
13 Tony Dorsett/99 5.00 12.00
14 Marcus Allen/99 4.00 10.00
15 Jerry Rice/49 10.00 25.00
16 Johnny Unitas/49 10.00 25.00
17 John Elway/99 8.00 20.00
18 Tom Brady/49 40.00 80.00
19 Matt Ryan/99 4.00 10.00
20 Matthew Stafford/99 4.00 10.00
21 Troy Aikman/99 6.00 15.00
22 Brett Favre/49 12.00 30.00
23 Earl Campbell/99 5.00 12.00
24 Tom Landry/25 10.00 25.00
25 Joe Montana/49 15.00 40.00
27 Russell Wilson/99 6.00 15.00
28 Aaron Rodgers/49 12.00 30.00
29 Marshall Faulk/99 4.00 10.00
30 Andrew Luck/99 6.00 15.00

2017 Panini National Treasures Material Signatures

*PRIME/25: .6X TO 1.5X BASIC JSY AU/99
*PRIME/25: .5X TO 1.2X BASIC JSY AU/49
*PRIME/25: .4X TO 1X BASIC JSY AU/34
1 John Riggins/25 15.00 40.00
2 Zach Ertz/49 12.00 30.00
3 Tony Dorsett/25 20.00 50.00
4 T.J. Watt/99 25.00 60.00
5 Phil Simms/25 15.00 40.00
6 Mark Brunell/49 12.00 30.00
7 Heath Miller/49 10.00 25.00
8 Dwight Clark/34 15.00 40.00
9 Aaron Rodgers/25 150.00 300.00
10 Joe Namath/25 50.00 100.00
11 Kurt Warner/25 15.00 40.00
12 Hunter Henry/49 10.00 25.00
13 Ed Reed/25 40.00 80.00
14 Tyreek Hill/25 20.00 50.00
15 Lawrence Taylor/25 20.00 50.00
16 Jordan Howard/49 15.00 40.00
17 Greg Olsen/49 12.00 30.00
18 Emmanuel Sanders/49 15.00 40.00
19 Russell Wilson/25 25.00 60.00
20 Michael Thomas/49 15.00 40.00
21 Jameis Winston/25 15.00 40.00
22 Will Fuller V/49 10.00 25.00
23 Derek Carr/25 20.00 50.00
24 Ha Ha Clinton-Dix/49 10.00 25.00
25 Vance Johnson/49 10.00 25.00
27 Corey Coleman/49 10.00 25.00
28 Joe Montana/25 75.00 150.00
29 Paul Hornung/49 15.00 40.00

2017 Panini National Treasures Material Treasures Signatures

*PRIME/25: .5X TO 1.2X BASIC JSY AU/49
1 Matthew Stafford/25 15.00 40.00
2 LaDainian Tomlinson/25 30.00 60.00
3 Joe Montana/25 75.00 150.00
4 Fred Taylor/25 15.00 40.00
5 Peyton Manning/25 100.00 200.00
6 Jim Plunkett/49 12.00 30.00
7 John Riggins/25 15.00 40.00
8 J.J. Watt/25 40.00 80.00
9 Marcus Mariota/25 20.00 50.00
10 Tyreek Hill/49 15.00 40.00
11 Marshall Faulk/25 15.00 40.00
12 Hines Ward/25 15.00 40.00
13 Aaron Rodgers/25 150.00 300.00
15 Ben Roethlisberger/25
16 Michael Vick/49 25.00 50.00
17 Kurt Warner/25 15.00 40.00
18 Tyler Lockett/49 12.00 30.00
19 Jerome Bettis/25 30.00 60.00
20 Mark Brunell/49 12.00 30.00
21 Richard Sherman/25 20.00 50.00
23 John Elway/25 50.00 100.00
25 Tony Romo/25
26 Rich Gannon/49 10.00 25.00
27 Mike Ditka/25 30.00 60.00
29 Tony Dorsett/25 20.00 50.00

2017 Panini National Treasures NFL Gear Combo Materials

*PRIME/25: .6X TO 1.5X BASIC JSY/99
*PRIME/25: .5X TO 1.2X BASIC JSY/49
*PRIME/15-20: .8X TO 2X BASIC JSY/99
*PRIME/15: .5X TO 1.2X BASIC JSY/25
1 A.Luck/T.Hilton/99 6.00 15.00
2 D.Prescott/D.Bryant/99 5.00 12.00
3 J.Winston/M.Evans/49 5.00 12.00
4 A.Talib/C.Harris Jr./25 5.00 12.00
5 D.Thomas/E.Sanders/99 5.00 12.00
6 N.Suh/C.Wake/99 4.00 10.00
7 G.Atkins/V.Burfict/49 4.00 10.00
8 M.Stafford/G.Tate III/99 4.00 10.00
9 D.Carr/A.Cooper/99 5.00 12.00
10 J.Landry/K.Stills/99 4.00 10.00
11 R.Wilson/D.Baldwin/99 6.00 15.00
12 D.Bryant/C.Beasley/99 5.00 12.00
13 M.Mariota/D.Murray/99 5.00 12.00
14 C.Anderson/J.Charles/99 4.00 10.00
15 J.Watt/T.Watt/49 12.00 30.00
16 K.Alonso/L.Timmons/99 4.00 10.00
17 A.Dalton/A.Green/99 5.00 12.00
18 J.Cutler/J.Landry/99 4.00 10.00
19 C.Wentz/N.Agholor/99 6.00 15.00
20 D.Prescott/E.Elliott/99 6.00 15.00

2017 Panini National Treasures Peerless Signatures

3 Rod Woodson/25 12.00 30.00
5 Curtis Martin/25 50.00 100.00
9 Ed Reed/25 25.00 50.00
12 Bruce Smith/25 15.00 40.00
14 Tim Brown/25 25.00 60.00

2017 Panini National Treasures Personalized Treasures Signatures

4 Randy White/25 15.00 40.00
5 Ozzie Newsome/25
6 Mike Alstott/25 25.00 50.00

2017 Panini National Treasures Rookie Colossal Material Signatures Prime

7 Patrick Mahomes II 400.00 600.00
25 Mitchell Trubisky 125.00 250.00

2017 Panini National Treasures Rookie Dual Materials

*SILVER/25: .6X TO 1.5X BASIC JSY/99
*RED/80-88: .4X TO 1X BASIC JSY/99
*RED/41: .5X TO 1.2X BASIC JSY/99
*RED/25-33: .6X TO 1.5X BASIC JSY/99
*RED/15-22: .8X TO 2X BASIC JSY/99
1 Dede Westbrook 2.00 5.00
2 Leonard Fournette 6.00 15.00
3 Deshaun Watson 8.00 20.00
4 Curtis Samuel 2.50 6.00
5 John Ross III 2.50 6.00
6 Davis Webb 2.00 5.00
7 O.J. Howard 2.50 6.00
8 Christian McCaffrey 4.00 10.00
9 Patrick Mahomes II 30.00 60.00
10 Nathan Peterman 2.50 6.00
11 Josh Reynolds 2.00 5.00
12 Chris Godwin 2.50 6.00
13 ArDarius Stewart 2.00 5.00
14 Joe Mixon 4.00 10.00
15 Taywan Taylor 2.00 5.00
16 Cooper Kupp 3.00 8.00
17 Samaje Perine 2.00 5.00
18 Kareem Hunt 4.00 10.00
19 Ryan Switzer 2.50 6.00
20 R. Joshua Dobbs 2.50 6.00
21 C.J. Beathard 2.00 5.00
22 Dalvin Cook 4.00 10.00
23 Mike Williams 3.00 8.00
24 Alvin Kamara 8.00 20.00
25 D'Onta Foreman 2.50 6.00
26 DeShone Kizer 2.00 5.00
27 Mitchell Trubisky 6.00 15.00
28 JuJu Smith-Schuster 4.00 10.00
29 Corey Davis 4.00 10.00
30 Zay Jones 2.50 6.00
31 Evan Engram 2.50 6.00
32 Wayne Gallman 2.50 6.00
33 Joe Williams 2.00 5.00
34 Marlon Mack 3.00 8.00
35 Mack Hollins 2.00 5.00
36 James Conner 4.00 10.00
37 Carlos Henderson 2.00 5.00
38 Jamaal Williams 2.00 5.00
39 Kenny Golladay 3.00 8.00
40 Amara Darboh 2.00 5.00

2017 Panini National Treasures Rookie Dual Signatures

2 T.White/Z.Jones/99 6.00 15.00
3 C.McCaffrey/C.Samuel/25 20.00 50.00
4 J.Ross III/J.Mixon/49 12.00 30.00
8 G.Everett/C.Kupp/99 8.00 20.00
9 C.Harris/R.McMillan/99 5.00 12.00
10 J.Adams/M.Maye/99 5.00 12.00
11 G.Conley/O.Melifonwu/99 5.00 12.00
13 T.Watt/J.Smith-Schuster/49 40.00 80.00
15 M.Breida/C.Beathard/99 8.00 20.00
16 H.Reddick/J.Davis/99 6.00 15.00
21 C.Davis/M.Williams/25 12.00 30.00
22 M.Humphrey/J.Allen/49 8.00 20.00
23 D.Webb/C.Hansen/99 5.00 12.00
27 M.Hollins/R.Switzer/99 6.00 15.00
29 A.Jackson/J.Smith-Schuster/49
32 C.McCaffrey/D.Cook/49 15.00 40.00
36 R.Dobbs/J.Conner/99 10.00 25.00
37 J.Mixon/S.Perine/99 10.00 25.00
38 J.Conner/N.Peterman/49 12.00 30.00
39 A.Kamara/R.Dobbs/99 20.00 50.00
40 M.Williams/W.Gallman/25 12.00 30.00

2017 Panini National Treasures Rookie NFL Gear Combo Materials

*PRIME/25: .6X TO 1.5X BASIC JSY/99
1 D.Watson/D.Foreman 8.00 20.00
2 J.Mixon/S.Perine 4.00 10.00
3 E.Engram/D.Webb 2.50 6.00
4 M.Trubisky/D.Watson 8.00 20.00
5 J.Conner/R.Dobbs 4.00 10.00
6 L.Fournette/D.Cook 6.00 15.00
7 K.Hunt/D.Cook 6.00 15.00
8 M.Williams/D.Watson 8.00 20.00
9 Z.Jones/N.Peterman 2.50 6.00
10 M.Hollins/R.Switzer 2.50 6.00
11 L.Fournette/D.Westbrook 6.00 15.00
12 J.Conner/N.Peterman 4.00 10.00
13 D.Webb/W.Gallman 2.50 6.00
14 P.Mahomes II/D.Watson 30.00 60.00
15 J.Smith-Schuster/R.Dobbs 4.00 10.00
16 C.Davis/M.Williams 4.00 10.00
17 T.Watt/R.Dobbs 4.00 10.00
18 D.Watson/W.Gallman 8.00 20.00
19 C.McCaffrey/C.Samuel 4.00 10.00
20 M.Trubisky/R.Switzer 6.00 15.00
21 P.Mahomes II/K.Hunt 30.00 60.00
22 A.Kamara/R.Dobbs 8.00 20.00
23 E.Engram/W.Gallman 2.50 6.00
24 L.Fournette/C.McCaffrey 6.00 15.00
25 C.Beathard/J.Williams 2.00 5.00
26 M.Williams/J.Ross III 3.00 8.00
27 C.Davis/T.Taylor 4.00 10.00
28 M.Williams/W.Gallman 3.00 8.00
29 J.Ross III/J.Mixon 4.00 10.00
30 J.Mixon/D.Westbrook 4.00 10.00
31 C.Kupp/J.Reynolds 3.00 8.00
32 M.Trubisky/P.Mahomes II 30.00 60.00
33 J.Smith-Schuster/J.Conner 4.00 10.00
34 C.McCaffrey/D.Cook 4.00 10.00
35 O.Howard/C.Godwin 2.50 6.00
36 R.Switzer/J.Ross III 2.50 6.00
37 O.Howard/A.Stewart 2.50 6.00
38 M.Trubisky/M.Hollins 6.00 15.00
39 D.Njoku/D.Kizer 2.50 6.00
40 D.Westbrook/S.Perine 2.00 5.00

2017 Panini National Treasures Rookie NFL Gear Quad Materials

*PRIME/25: .6X TO 1.5X BASIC JSY/99
1 Dvs/Hwrd/Wllms/Rss 5.00 12.00
2 Frntte/Dvs/Tylr/Wstbrk 8.00 20.00
3 SmthSchstr/Stwrt/Kpp/Tylr 5.00 12.00
4 Swtzr/Engrm/Prne/Hllns 3.00 8.00
5 Wstbrk/Hllns/Rynlds/Swtzr 3.00 8.00
6 Trbsky/Wllms/Ck/Glldy 8.00 20.00
7 Wbb/Dbbs/Ptrmn/Bthrd 3.00 8.00
8 Rss/Kzr/Njku/Mxn 5.00 12.00
9 Hnt/Prne/Cnnr/Frmn 8.00 20.00
10 McCffry/Hwrd/Gdwn/Sml 5.00 12.00
11 Engrm/Sml/Njku/Jns 3.00 8.00
12 Kpp/Rynlds/Bthrd/Wllms 4.00 10.00
13 Hndrsn/Drbh/Gdwn/Glldy 4.00 10.00
14 Wtsn/Mck/Frntte/Dvs 10.00 25.00
15 Trbsky/Frntte/Wtsn/Mhms 30.00 60.00
16 Trbsky/Mhms/Wtsn/Kzr 30.00 60.00
17 McCffry/Kmra/Ck/Mxn 10.00 25.00
18 Wtsn/Frmn/Frntte/Wstbrk 10.00 25.00
19 Wllms/Mck/Gllmn/Wllms 4.00 10.00
20 Wtsn/Tylr/Dvs/Frmn 10.00 25.00

2017 Panini National Treasures Rookie NFL Gear Trio Materials

*PRIME/25: .6X TO 1.5X BASIC JSY/99
1 Frntte/Ck/McCffry 8.00 20.00
2 Engrm/Wbb/Gllmn 3.00 8.00
3 Dvs/Rss/Wllms 5.00 12.00
4 Hnt/McCffry/Ck 8.00 20.00
5 Mhms/Frmn/Mxn 30.00 60.00
6 Trbsky/Swtzr/Hllns 8.00 20.00
7 Frntte/Engrm/Hwrd 8.00 20.00
8 Dvs/Hnt/Glldy 8.00 20.00
9 Trbsky/Dvs/Frntte 8.00 20.00
10 Trbsky/Mhms/Wtsn 30.00 60.00
11 Mxn/Frmn/Kmra 10.00 25.00
12 SmthSchstr/Dbbs/Cnnr 5.00 12.00
13 Jns/SmthSchstr/Sml 5.00 12.00
14 Wllms/Gllmn/Wtsn 10.00 25.00
15 Sml/Drbh/Gdwn 3.00 8.00
16 Mxn/Prne/Wstbrk 5.00 12.00
17 Trbsky/Wtsn/Wllms 10.00 25.00
18 Hwrd/Engrm/Njku 3.00 8.00
19 Wllms/McCffry/Rss 5.00 12.00
20 Kzr/Wbb/Bthrd 2.50 6.00

2017 Panini National Treasures Rookie NFL Gear Triple Material Signatures

1 Dede Westbrook/99 6.00 15.00
2 Alvin Kamara/99 60.00 125.00
3 Deshaun Watson/99 125.00 250.00
4 Zay Jones/99 8.00 20.00
5 DeShone Kizer/99 6.00 15.00
6 Samaje Perine/99 6.00 15.00
7 Christian McCaffrey/99 25.00 60.00
8 Joe Williams/99 6.00 15.00
9 John Ross III/99 8.00 20.00
10 Taywan Taylor/99 6.00 15.00
11 D'Onta Foreman/99 8.00 20.00
12 C.J. Beathard/99 6.00 15.00
13 Mitchell Trubisky/99 50.00 100.00
14 Davis Webb/99 6.00 15.00
15 Patrick Mahomes II/99 300.00 600.00
16 James Conner/99 12.00 30.00
17 Dalvin Cook/99 30.00 60.00
18 Kareem Hunt/99 20.00 50.00
19 JuJu Smith-Schuster/99 EXCH 25.00 50.00
20 Joe Mixon/49 12.00 30.00
21 Nathan Peterman/99 8.00 20.00
22 O.J. Howard/99 8.00 20.00
23 Leonard Fournette/99 30.00 60.00
24 Evan Engram/99 15.00 40.00
25 Mike Williams/99 10.00 25.00
26 Ryan Switzer/99 8.00 20.00
27 Corey Davis/99 10.00 25.00
28 Wayne Gallman/99 8.00 20.00
29 Curtis Samuel/99 8.00 20.00
30 R. Joshua Dobbs/99 8.00 20.00

2017 Panini National Treasures Rookie NFL Gear Triple Material Signatures Prime

*PRIME/25: .6X TO 1.5X BASIC JSY AU/99
3 Deshaun Watson 175.00 350.00

2017 Panini National Treasures Rookie Quad Materials Booklet

*PRIME/25: .5X TO 1.2X BASIC JSY/49
1 Trbsky/Kzr/Mhms/Wtsn
2 Frntte/Hnt/Ck/McCffry 25.00 50.00
3 Dvs/Rss/Wllms/Kpp 20.00 40.00

2017 Panini National Treasures Rookie Signatures

1 Deshaun Watson 90.00 150.00
2 Mitchell Trubisky 50.00 100.00
3 Leonard Fournette 50.00 100.00
4 DeShone Kizer 4.00 10.00
5 Patrick Mahomes II 300.00 600.00
6 Mike Williams 6.00 15.00
7 Christian McCaffrey 25.00 50.00
8 Dalvin Cook 25.00 50.00
9 Corey Davis 6.00 15.00
10 John Ross III 5.00 12.00
11 JuJu Smith-Schuster 30.00 60.00
12 Curtis Samuel 5.00 12.00
13 Dede Westbrook 4.00 10.00
14 D'Onta Foreman 5.00 12.00
15 Nathan Peterman 5.00 12.00
16 Alvin Kamara 30.00 60.00
17 C.J. Beathard 4.00 10.00
18 O.J. Howard 5.00 12.00
19 Zay Jones 5.00 12.00
20 Evan Engram 5.00 12.00

2017 Panini National Treasures Rookie Signatures Gold

*GOLD/25: .6X TO 1.5X BASIC AU/99
1 Deshaun Watson 150.00 250.00
5 Patrick Mahomes II 400.00 800.00

2017 Panini National Treasures Rookie Tremendous Treasures Materials

*PRIME/25: .6X TO 1.5X BASIC JSY/99
1 Christian McCaffrey 4.00 10.00
2 Patrick Mahomes II 25.00 50.00
3 Nathan Peterman 2.50 6.00
4 Dede Westbrook 2.00 5.00
5 Leonard Fournette 6.00 15.00
6 Deshaun Watson 8.00 20.00
7 Curtis Samuel 2.50 6.00
8 John Ross III 2.50 6.00
9 Davis Webb 2.00 5.00
10 O.J. Howard 2.50 6.00
11 Kareem Hunt 4.00 10.00
12 David Njoku 2.50 6.00
13 R. Joshua Dobbs 2.50 6.00
14 Josh Reynolds 2.00 5.00
15 Chris Godwin 2.50 6.00
16 ArDarius Stewart 2.00 5.00
17 Joe Mixon 4.00 10.00
18 Taywan Taylor 2.00 5.00
19 Cooper Kupp 3.00 8.00
20 Samaje Perine 2.00 5.00
21 JuJu Smith-Schuster 4.00 10.00
22 Corey Davis 3.00 8.00
23 Zay Jones 2.50 6.00
24 C.J. Beathard 2.00 5.00
25 Dalvin Cook 4.00 10.00
26 Mike Williams 3.00 8.00
27 Alvin Kamara 8.00 20.00
28 D'Onta Foreman 2.50 6.00
29 DeShone Kizer 2.00 5.00
30 Mitchell Trubisky 6.00 15.00
31 Jamaal Williams 2.00 5.00
32 Kenny Golladay 3.00 8.00
33 Amara Darboh 2.00 5.00
34 Evan Engram 2.50 6.00
35 Wayne Gallman 2.50 6.00
36 Joe Williams 2.00 5.00
37 Marlon Mack 3.00 8.00
38 Mack Hollins 2.00 5.00
39 James Conner 4.00 10.00
40 Carlos Henderson 2.00 5.00

2017 Panini National Treasures Signatures

*GOLD/25: .5X TO 1.2X BASIC AU/41-49
*SILVER/15: .6X TO 1.5X BASIC AU/49
*SILVER/15: .5X TO 1.2X BASIC AU/25
2 Jack Ham/25 12.00 30.00
3 Bill Cowher/25 50.00 100.00
7 Adam Thielen/49 40.00 80.00
8 Maurkice Pouncey/49 10.00 25.00
10 Aqib Talib/49 10.00 25.00
11 Tarik Cohen/49 10.00 25.00
12 Dan Bailey/25 12.00 30.00
13 Dick Anderson/49 5.00 12.00
15 Ken Anderson/49 10.00 25.00
17 Jerrell Freeman/49 5.00 12.00
18 Tony Casillas/49 5.00 12.00
19 Jim Otto/49 5.00 12.00
20 Brian Cushing/49 5.00 12.00
27 Hunter Henry/49 5.00 12.00
28 Gilbert Brown/49 5.00 12.00
30 C.J. Mosley/49 6.00 15.00
32 Vic Beasley Jr./49 5.00 12.00
33 Mark Moseley/49 5.00 12.00
35 Roman Gabriel/49 5.00 12.00
37 Kyle Juszczyk/49 25.00 50.00
38 Morten Andersen/49 5.00 12.00
39 Christian Okoye/49 5.00 12.00
40 Jack Youngblood/49 5.00 12.00
42 Kiko Alonso/49 5.00 12.00
47 Brian Mitchell/49 5.00 12.00
48 Neil Smith/49 5.00 12.00
50 Michael Bennett/49 10.00 25.00
53 Jim Taylor/25 30.00 60.00
55 Joe Greene/25 25.00 50.00
57 Cameron Heyward/49 5.00 12.00
58 Ryan Shazier/49 5.00 12.00
59 Lenny Moore /49 5.00 12.00
60 Terrelle Pryor/49 5.00 12.00
67 Charley Taylor/49 5.00 12.00
68 Andre Rison/49 6.00 15.00
70 Edgerrin James/25 8.00 20.00
71 Jason Taylor/25 6.00 15.00
73 Ty Law/25 15.00 40.00
75 Michael Vick/25 15.00 40.00
77 John Kuhn/49 5.00 12.00
79 Franco Harris/25 25.00 50.00
80 Clinton Portis/25 6.00 15.00
87 Louis Lipps/49 5.00 12.00
88 Rickey Jackson/43 5.00 12.00
90 Jonathan Stewart/49 5.00 12.00
91 Adam Vinatieri/49 10.00 25.00
93 Ed McCaffrey/49 10.00 25.00
95 Bill Parcells/49 8.00 20.00
97 Mario Manningham/49 5.00 12.00
98 Ron Yary/41 5.00 12.00
99 Brian Bosworth/25 12.00 30.00
100 Charles Haley/49 8.00 20.00

2017 Panini National Treasures Synced Signatures

2 M.Ryan/M.Vick/25 60.00 125.00
3 W.Sapp/A.Page/25 15.00 40.00
4 A.Page/C.Eller/25 25.00 50.00
6 R.Lott/C.Haley/25 20.00 50.00
8 F.Taylor/M.Brunell/25 15.00 40.00
10 R.Harrison/T.Law/25 50.00 100.00
12 M.Mariota/D.Murray/25 20.00 50.00
13 B.Jackson/M.Allen/25 50.00 100.00
14 B.Lilly/R.White/25 15.00 40.00
16 M.Singletary/D.Hampton/25 20.00 50.00
17 A.Smith/K.Hunt/25 30.00 60.00
18 R.Gannon/T.Brown/25 20.00 50.00
20 J.Lambert/J.Ham/25 100.00 200.00

2017 Panini National Treasures Treasured Patches

1 Jay Ajayi 10.00 25.00
2 Jason Witten 10.00 25.00
3 Andy Dalton 10.00 25.00
4 Jeremy Hill 8.00 20.00
5 Tyrod Taylor 10.00 25.00
6 Jared Goff 12.00 30.00
7 Mike Evans 10.00 25.00
8 Sterling Shepard 10.00 25.00
9 Ezekiel Elliott 15.00 40.00
10 Joey Bosa 12.00 30.00
11 Ndamukong Suh 10.00 25.00
12 Derek Carr 12.00 30.00
13 A.J. Green 12.00 30.00
14 Carson Wentz 15.00 40.00
15 LeSean McCoy 12.00 30.00
16 Jordan Howard 12.00 30.00
17 Dak Prescott 12.00 30.00
18 Michael Thomas 12.00 30.00
19 Dez Bryant 12.00 30.00
20 Corey Coleman 8.00 20.00
21 Jarvis Landry 10.00 25.00
22 Devonta Freeman 10.00 25.00

2017 Panini National Treasures Tremendous Treasures Materials

*PRIME/25: .5X TO 1.2X BASIC JSY/49
*PRIME/20: .6X TO 1.5X BASIC JSY/49
1 Dez Bryant 6.00 15.00
2 Doug Martin 5.00 12.00
3 Jarvis Landry 5.00 12.00
4 Don Maynard 5.00 12.00
5 David Johnson 6.00 15.00
6 Latavius Murray 4.00 10.00
7 Carson Wentz 8.00 20.00
8 Barry Sanders 10.00 25.00
9 Joey Bosa 6.00 15.00
10 Terry Bradshaw 10.00 25.00
11 Ndamukong Suh 5.00 12.00
12 Russell Wilson 8.00 20.00
13 Khalil Mack 6.00 15.00
14 Michael Vick 5.00 12.00
15 Jay Ajayi 5.00 12.00
16 Carlos Hyde 4.00 10.00
17 Dak Prescott 6.00 15.00
18 Tony Dorsett 6.00 15.00
19 Derrick Henry 5.00 12.00
20 Brett Keisel 6.00 15.00
21 DeVante Parker 5.00 12.00
22 Jeremy Hill 4.00 10.00
23 Jadeveon Clowney 4.00 10.00
24 Derek Carr 6.00 15.00
25 Amari Cooper 6.00 15.00
26 Marcus Allen 5.00 12.00
27 Michael Thomas 6.00 15.00
28 Mike Singletary 6.00 15.00
29 Hunter Henry 4.00 10.00
30 Edgerrin James 5.00 12.00
31 Kiko Alonso 4.00 10.00
32 Devonta Freeman 5.00 12.00
33 Allen Robinson 5.00 12.00
34 Sterling Shepard 5.00 12.00
35 Jameis Winston 5.00 12.00
36 Joe Namath 8.00 20.00
37 Jared Goff 6.00 15.00
38 Lamar Miller 4.00 10.00
39 A.J. Green 6.00 15.00
40 Clinton Portis 4.00 10.00
41 Julius Thomas 4.00 10.00
42 Kelvin Benjamin 5.00 12.00
43 Todd Gurley II 6.00 15.00
44 Earl Campbell 6.00 15.00
45 Marcus Mariota 6.00 15.00
46 Thurman Thomas 5.00 12.00
47 Corey Coleman 4.00 10.00
48 Mike Evans 5.00 12.00
49 LeSean McCoy 6.00 15.00
50 Steve Largent 6.00 15.00
51 Cole Beasley 6.00 15.00
52 Davante Adams 5.00 12.00
53 Ty Montgomery 4.00 10.00
54 Andy Dalton 5.00 12.00
55 Ezekiel Elliott 8.00 20.00
56 Charles Woodson 6.00 15.00
57 Jordan Howard 6.00 15.00
58 Kirk Cousins 6.00 15.00
59 Tyrod Taylor 5.00 12.00
60 Len Dawson 6.00 15.00

2018 Panini National Treasures

1 Johnny Unitas 5.00 12.00
2 Terrell Suggs 2.00 5.00
3 Ray Lewis 3.00 8.00
4 Kurt Warner 2.50 6.00
5 Larry Fitzgerald 2.50 6.00
6 David Johnson 3.00 8.00
7 Matt Ryan 2.50 6.00
8 Julio Jones 3.00 8.00
9 Vic Beasley Jr. 2.00 5.00
10 Jim Kelly 3.00 8.00
11 LeSean McCoy 3.00 8.00
12 George Kittle 2.00 5.00
13 Cam Newton 3.00 8.00
14 Christian McCaffrey 3.00 8.00
15 Luke Kuechly 2.50 6.00
16 Mitchell Trubisky 3.00 8.00
17 Brian Urlacher 3.00 8.00
18 Jordan Howard 3.00 8.00
19 A.J. Green 3.00 8.00
20 Andy Dalton 2.50 6.00
21 Myles Garrett 3.00 8.00
22 Jarvis Landry 2.50 6.00
23 Carlos Hyde 2.00 5.00
24 Dak Prescott 3.00 8.00
25 Ezekiel Elliott 4.00 10.00
26 Emmitt Smith 5.00 12.00
27 Von Miller 2.50 6.00
28 John Elway 5.00 12.00
29 Demaryius Thomas 2.50 6.00
30 Barry Sanders 5.00 12.00
31 Matthew Stafford 2.50 6.00
32 Golden Tate III 2.00 5.00
33 Bart Starr 5.00 12.00
34 Aaron Rodgers 6.00 15.00
35 Clay Matthews 2.50 6.00
36 Deshaun Watson 4.00 10.00
37 DeAndre Hopkins 2.50 6.00
38 J.J. Watt 3.00 8.00
39 Andrew Luck 4.00 10.00
40 Peyton Manning 6.00 15.00
41 T.Y. Hilton 2.50 6.00
42 Stefon Diggs 2.50 6.00
43 Jalen Ramsey 2.50 6.00
44 Leonard Fournette 3.00 8.00
45 Patrick Mahomes II 8.00 20.00
46 Case Keenum 2.50 6.00
47 Tony Gonzalez 2.50 6.00
48 Joey Bosa 3.00 8.00
49 Philip Rivers 3.00 8.00
50 Melvin Gordon III 2.50 6.00
51 Todd Gurley II 3.00 8.00
52 Jared Goff 3.00 8.00
53 Aaron Donald 3.00 8.00
54 Ryan Tannehill 2.50 6.00
55 Kenyan Drake 2.00 5.00
56 Dan Marino 6.00 15.00
57 Adrian Peterson 3.00 8.00
58 Kirk Cousins 3.00 8.00
59 Adam Thielen 3.00 8.00
60 Tom Brady 8.00 20.00
61 Rob Gronkowski 3.00 8.00
62 Drew Bledsoe 2.50 6.00
63 Drew Brees 3.00 8.00
64 Michael Thomas 3.00 8.00
65 Alvin Kamara 2.50 6.00
66 Odell Beckham Jr. 3.00 8.00
67 Eli Manning 2.50 6.00
68 Lawrence Taylor 3.00 8.00
69 Jamal Adams 2.50 6.00
70 Joe Namath 4.00 10.00
71 Curtis Martin 2.50 6.00
72 Derek Carr 3.00 8.00
73 Khalil Mack 3.00 8.00
74 Howie Long 3.00 8.00
75 Marshawn Lynch 2.50 6.00
76 Carson Wentz 4.00 10.00
77 Alshon Jeffery 2.50 6.00
78 Reggie White 3.00 8.00
79 Matt Breida 2.50 6.00
80 Ben Roethlisberger 3.00 8.00
81 Antonio Brown 3.00 8.00
82 T.J. Watt 2.50 6.00
83 Terry Bradshaw 5.00 12.00
84 Jimmy Garoppolo 4.00 10.00
85 Joe Montana 8.00 20.00
86 Russell Wilson 4.00 10.00
87 Doug Baldwin 2.50 6.00
88 Steve Largent 3.00 8.00
89 Jameis Winston 2.50 6.00
90 Mike Evans 2.50 6.00
91 James Conner 3.00 8.00
92 Mike Alstott 2.00 5.00
93 Marcus Mariota 3.00 8.00
94 Derrick Henry 3.00 8.00
95 Eddie George 2.50 6.00
96 Alex Smith 2.50 6.00
97 Tyreek Hill 3.00 8.00
98 Josh Norman 2.00 5.00
99 John Riggins 2.50 6.00
100 Anthony Munoz 2.50 6.00
102 Quenton Nelson AU/75 RC 25.00 50.00
104 Cory Littleton AU/75 RC 5.00 12.00
105 Nick Mullens AU/75 RC 25.00 50.00
106 Daron Payne AU/75 RC 6.00 15.00
108 Ray-Ray McCloud AU/75 RC 4.00 10.00
109 Will Dissly AU/75 RC 5.00 12.00
110 Trenton Cannon AU/75 RC 5.00 12.00
111 Javon Wims AU/75 RC 4.00 10.00
112 Trey Quinn AU/75 RC 4.00 10.00
113 Terrell Edmunds AU/25 RC 12.00 30.00
114 Mike Hughes AU/75 RC 6.00 15.00
115 Harold Landry AU/75 RC 4.00 10.00
116 Joshua Jackson AU/75 RC 8.00 20.00
117 Dallas Goedert AU/75 RC 5.00 12.00
118 Mark Andrews AU/75 RC 6.00 15.00
119 M.J. Stewart AU/75 RC 4.00 10.00
120 Donte Jackson AU/75 RC 6.00 15.00
121 Isaiah Oliver AU/75 RC 4.00 10.00
122 Carlton Davis AU/75 RC 5.00 12.00
123 Lorenzo Carter AU/75 RC 4.00 10.00
124 Chad Thomas AU/75 RC 4.00 10.00
125 Sam Hubbard AU/75 RC 5.00 12.00
126 Malik Jefferson AU/75 RC 5.00 12.00
128 Justin Jones AU/75 RC 4.00 10.00
131 Ronnie Harrison AU/75 RC 5.00 12.00
132 Harrison Phillips AU/75 RC 4.00 10.00
133 Jordan Akins AU/75 RC 4.00 10.00
134 Jalyn Holmes AU/75 RC 6.00 15.00
135 Chris Herndon IV AU/49 RC 5.00 12.00
137 Jordan Whitehead AU/75 RC 4.00 10.00
138 Durham Smythe AU/75 RC 4.00 10.00
139 Armani Watts AU/75 RC 4.00 10.00
140 Josh Sweat AU/75 RC 5.00 12.00
141 Dalton Schultz AU/75 RC 5.00 12.00
143 Connor Williams AU/75 RC 8.00 20.00
144 D.J. Reed AU/75 RC 4.00 10.00
145 Justin Watson AU/75 RC 5.00 12.00
147 Darius Leonard AU/75 RC 30.00 60.00
148 Tyler Conklin AU/75 RC 4.00 10.00
149 Ian Thomas AU/75 RC 4.00 10.00
150 Jordan Lasley AU/75 RC 4.00 10.00
151 Jordan Wilkins AU/75 RC 5.00 12.00
152 John Kelly AU/75 RC 5.00 12.00
153 Deon Cain AU/75 RC 5.00 12.00
154 Mike McGlinchey AU/75 RC 8.00 20.00
155 Russell Gage AU/75 RC 5.00 12.00
156 Luke Falk AU/75 RC 5.00 12.00
157 Fred Warner AU/75 RC 4.00 10.00
158 Danny Etling AU/75 RC 5.00 12.00
159 Alex McGough AU/75 RC 5.00 12.00
160 Marcell Ateman AU/75 RC 5.00 12.00
161 Baker Mayfield JSY AU RC 4000.00 6000.00
162 Sam Darnold JSY AU RC 1700.00 2200.00
163 Josh Allen JSY AU RC 800.00 1200.00
164 Josh Rosen JSY AU RC 400.00 800.00
165 Lamar Jackson JSY AU RC 400.00 800.00
166 Mason Rudolph JSY AU RC 200.00 400.00
167 Kyle Lauletta JSY AU RC 20.00 50.00
168 Mike White JSY AU RC 40.00 80.00
169 Saquon Barkley JSY AU RC 1000.00 1500.00
170 Rashaad Penny JSY AU RC 60.00 125.00
171 Sony Michel JSY AU RC EXCH 40.00 100.00
172 Nick Chubb JSY AU RC 200.00 400.00
173 Ronald Jones II JSY AU RC 25.00 60.00
174 Kerryon Johnson JSY AU RC 50.00 100.00
175 Derrius Guice JSY AU RC EXCH 60.00 125.00
176 Royce Freeman JSY AU RC 15.00 40.00
177 Nyheim Hines JSY AU RC 15.00 40.00
178 Mark Walton JSY AU RC 15.00 40.00
179 Ito Smith JSY AU RC 15.00 40.00
180 Kalen Ballage JSY AU RC 15.00 40.00
181 Jaylen Samuels JSY AU RC 15.00 40.00
182 Hayden Hurst JSY AU RC 15.00 40.00
183 Mike Gesicki JSY AU RC 15.00 40.00
184 D.J. Moore JSY AU RC 40.00 80.00
185 Calvin Ridley JSY AU RC 60.00 125.00
186 Courtland Sutton JSY AU RC 50.00 100.00
187 Dante Pettis JSY AU RC 50.00 100.00
188 Christian Kirk JSY AU RC 30.00 60.00
189 Anthony Miller JSY AU RC 50.00 100.00
190 James Washington JSY AU RC 25.00 60.00
191 D.J. Chark Jr. JSY AU RC 15.00 40.00
192 Michael Gallup JSY AU RC 25.00 60.00
193 Tre'Quan Smith JSY AU RC 20.00 50.00
194 Keke Coutee JSY AU RC 15.00 40.00
195 DaeSean Hamilton JSY AU RC 15.00 40.00
196 Jaleel Scott JSY AU RC 12.00 30.00
197 J'Mon Moore JSY AU RC 12.00 30.00
198 Daurice Fountain JSY AU RC 15.00 40.00
199 Marquez Valdes-Scantling JSY AU RC 15.00 40.00
200 Bradley Chubb JSY AU RC 40.00 80.00
201 Shaquem Griffin JSY AU RC 20.00 50.00
202 Phillip Lindsay JSY AU RC 50.00 125.00
203 Minkah Fitzpatrick JSY AU RC 25.00 60.00
204 Denzel Ward JSY AU RC 30.00 80.00
205 Derwin James JSY AU RC 25.00 60.00

206 Roquan Smith JSY AU RC 40.00 100.00
207 Leighton Vander Esch JSY AU RC EXCH 75.00 150.00
208 Jaire Alexander JSY AU RC 20.00 50.00
209 Tremaine Edmunds JSY AU RC 25.00 60.00
210 Rashaan Evans JSY AU RC 20.00 50.00

2018 Panini National Treasures Gold

*VETS/35: .5X TO 1.2X BASIC CARDS
*ROOK AU/49: .5X TO 1.2X BASIC RC AU/75
*ROOK AU/25. .5X TO 1.2X BASIC RC AU/49

2018 Panini National Treasures Holo Silver

*VETS/25: .6X TO 1.5X BASIC CARDS/99
*ROOK AU/25: .6X TO 1.5X BASIC RC AU/75
*ROOK AU/15: .6X TO 1.5X BASIC RC AU/49
*ROOK JSY AU/25: .6X TO 1.5X BASIC RC JSY AU/99
161 Baker Mayfield JSY AU/25 6000.00 8000.00
163 Josh Allen JSY AU/25 900.00 1500.00
164 Josh Rosen JSY AU/25 700.00 1200.00
165 Lamar Jackson JSY AU/25 700.00 1200.00
169 Saquon Barkley JSY AU/25 1600.00 2000.00

2018 Panini National Treasures Purple

*VETS/50: .5X TO 1.2X BASIC CARDS/99

2018 Panini National Treasures Rookie Patch Autographs Midnight

*ROOK JSY AU/20: .8X TO 2X BASIC RC JSY AU/99
161 Baker Mayfield 6500.00 10000.00
162 Sam Darnold 4000.00 6000.00
163 Josh Allen 2000.00 3000.00
164 Josh Rosen 1000.00 1400.00
165 Lamar Jackson 800.00 1500.00
169 Saquon Barkley 1800.00 2200.00

2018 Panini National Treasures Rookie Patch Autographs Stars and Stripes

*ROOK JSY AU/15: .8X TO 2X BASIC RC JSY AU/99
161 Baker Mayfield 6500.00 10000.00
162 Sam Darnold 4000.00 6000.00
163 Josh Allen 2000.00 3000.00
164 Josh Rosen 1000.00 1400.00
165 Lamar Jackson 800.00 1500.00
169 Saquon Barkley 1800.00 2200.00

2018 Panini National Treasures All Pro Signatures

2 Rob Gronkowski/25 50.00 100.00
3 Antonio Brown/25 25.00 50.00
4 Adam Thielen/25 40.00 80.00
5 Travis Kelce/25 EXCH 10.00 25.00
6 Calais Campbell/25 6.00 15.00
7 Aaron Donald/25 EXCH 15.00 40.00
8 Fletcher Cox/25 6.00 15.00
10 Luke Kuechly/25 8.00 20.00
12 Kevin Byard/25 6.00 15.00
13 Harrison Smith/25 EXCH 30.00 60.00
14 Darius Slay/25 6.00 15.00
15 Justin Tucker/25 12.00 30.00
16 Ezekiel Elliott/25 50.00 100.00
17 David Johnson/25 10.00 25.00
18 Landon Collins/25 6.00 15.00
19 Ha Ha Clinton-Dix/25 6.00 15.00
20 Tyreek Hill/25 EXCH 10.00 25.00

2018 Panini National Treasures Century Materials

*SILVER/25: .6X TO 1.5X BASIC JSY/75-99
*SILVER/15: .8X TO 2X BASIC JSY/75-99
*PRIME/35-49: .5X TO 1.2X BASIC JSY/75-99
1 Carson Palmer/99 4.00 10.00
2 David Johnson/99 5.00 12.00
3 Larry Fitzgerald/99 4.00 10.00
4 Julio Jones/99 5.00 12.00
5 Matt Ryan/99 4.00 10.00
6 Tony Gonzalez/75 4.00 10.00
7 Joe Flacco/99 4.00 10.00
8 Terrell Suggs/99 3.00 8.00
9 Ray Lewis/99 5.00 12.00
10 Jim Kelly/99 5.00 12.00
11 Thurman Thomas/99 4.00 10.00
12 Andre Reed/99 4.00 10.00
13 Cam Newton/75 5.00 12.00
14 Greg Olsen/99 4.00 10.00
15 Luke Kuechly/99 4.00 10.00
16 Mitchell Trubisky/99 5.00 12.00
17 Jordan Howard/99 5.00 12.00
18 Walter Payton/99 10.00 25.00
19 Joe Mixon/99 4.00 10.00
20 Andy Dalton/99 4.00 10.00
21 Carson Palmer/99 4.00 10.00
22 Jabrill Peppers/99 3.00 8.00
23 Ozzie Newsome/99 4.00 10.00
24 David Njoku/99 3.00 8.00
25 Roger Staubach/99 6.00 15.00
26 Jason Witten/99 4.00 10.00
27 Zack Martin/99 3.00 8.00
28 Dak Prescott/99 5.00 12.00
29 DeMarcus Lawrence/99 3.00 8.00
30 Brandon McManus/99 3.00 8.00
31 Jarvis Landry/99 4.00 10.00
33 John Elway/99 8.00 20.00
34 Barry Sanders/99 8.00 20.00
35 Matthew Stafford/99 4.00 10.00
36 Case Keenum/99 4.00 10.00
37 Charles Woodson/99 5.00 12.00
38 Davante Adams/99 4.00 10.00
39 Bart Starr/25 12.00 30.00
40 Deshaun Watson/99 6.00 15.00
41 D'Onta Foreman/99 3.00 8.00
42 DeAndre Hopkins/99 4.00 10.00
43 Andrew Luck/99 6.00 15.00
44 T.Y. Hilton/99 4.00 10.00
45 Marlon Mack/99 3.00 8.00
46 Blake Bortles/99 3.00 8.00
47 Leonard Fournette/99 5.00 12.00
48 Jalen Ramsey/99 4.00 10.00
49 Patrick Mahomes II/99 12.00 30.00
50 Tyreek Hill/99 5.00 12.00
51 Tony Gonzalez/99 4.00 10.00
52 Joey Bosa/99 5.00 12.00
53 Philip Rivers/99 5.00 12.00
54 Keenan Allen/99 4.00 10.00
55 Jared Goff/99 5.00 12.00
56 Aaron Donald/99 5.00 12.00
57 Cooper Kupp/99 4.00 10.00
58 Cameron Wake/99 3.00 8.00
59 Dan Marino/99 10.00 25.00
60 Kenyan Drake/99 3.00 8.00
61 Kiko Alonso/99 3.00 8.00
62 Stefon Diggs/99 4.00 10.00
63 Adrian Peterson/99 5.00 12.00
64 Kirk Cousins/99 5.00 12.00
65 John Randle/99 4.00 10.00
66 Rob Gronkowski/99 5.00 12.00
67 Drew Bledsoe/99 4.00 10.00
68 James White/99 4.00 10.00
69 Alvin Kamara/99 4.00 10.00
70 Michael Thomas/99 5.00 12.00
71 Ricky Williams/99 4.00 10.00
72 Eli Manning/99 4.00 10.00
73 Odell Beckham Jr./99 5.00 12.00
74 Lawrence Taylor/99 5.00 12.00
75 Joe Namath/99 6.00 15.00
76 Tim Tebow/49 6.00 15.00
77 Khalil Mack/99 5.00 12.00
78 Derek Carr/99 5.00 12.00
79 Marshawn Lynch/99 4.00 10.00
80 Howie Long/99 5.00 12.00
81 Carson Wentz/99 6.00 15.00
82 Alshon Jeffery/99 4.00 10.00
83 Brian Dawkins/99 5.00 12.00
84 Fletcher Cox/99 3.00 8.00
85 JuJu Smith-Schuster/99 5.00 12.00
86 Terry Bradshaw/99 8.00 20.00
87 Heath Miller/99 3.00 8.00
88 Jerry Rice/75 8.00 20.00
89 Joe Montana/99 12.00 30.00
90 Steve Young/99 6.00 15.00
91 Russell Wilson/99 6.00 15.00
92 Doug Baldwin/99 4.00 10.00
93 Mike Evans/99 4.00 10.00
94 Jameis Winston/99 4.00 10.00
95 James Conner/99 5.00 12.00
96 Marcus Mariota/99 5.00 12.00
97 Derrick Henry/99 5.00 12.00
98 Corey Davis/99 4.00 10.00

2018 Panini National Treasures Colossal Material Signatures

*PRIME/25: .5X TO 1.2X BASIC JSY AU/49
1 Tyreek Hill/49 EXCH 15.00 40.00
2 Aaron Donald/25 20.00 50.00
3 Bruce Smith/25 15.00 40.00
4 Clay Matthews/25 EXCH 30.00 60.00
5 Eric Dickerson/25 20.00 50.00
6 Adam Thielen/49 40.00 80.00
7 Michael Strahan/25 EXCH 15.00 40.00
8 John Randle/25 15.00 40.00
10 David Johnson/25 20.00 50.00
12 Matthew Stafford/25 30.00 60.00
13 Deshaun Watson/25
14 Dak Prescott/25 20.00 50.00
16 Steve Young/25
17 Earl Campbell/25 20.00 50.00
18 Patrick Mahomes II/25 150.00 300.00
19 John Riggins/25 15.00 40.00
20 Barry Sanders/25 EXCH 100.00 200.00
21 Ed Reed/25 30.00 60.00
22 LaDainian Tomlinson/25 EXCH 30.00 60.00
23 Jay Ajayi/49 12.00 30.00
24 Ray Lewis/25 40.00 80.00
25 Dan Marino/25 60.00 125.00
26 Marshall Faulk/25 15.00 40.00
27 Christian McCaffrey/25 20.00 50.00
29 Luke Kuechly/49 25.00 50.00
30 Tim Brown/49 15.00 40.00

2018 Panini National Treasures Colossal Materials

*PRIME/25: .6X TO 1.5X BASIC JSY/99
*PRIME/25: .5X TO 1.2X BASIC JSY/49
1 Marshall Faulk/99 4.00 10.00
2 Ray Lewis/99 5.00 12.00
3 Tyreek Hill/99 5.00 12.00
4 Patrick Mahomes II/99 12.00 30.00
5 Archie Manning/99 4.00 10.00
6 Adam Thielen/99 5.00 12.00
7 Michael Strahan/99 4.00 10.00
8 John Randle/99 4.00 10.00
9 Peyton Manning/99 10.00 25.00
10 David Johnson/99 5.00 12.00
11 Derrick Henry/99 5.00 12.00
12 Dan Marino/99 10.00 25.00
13 Rod Woodson/99 5.00 12.00
14 JuJu Smith-Schuster/99 5.00 12.00
15 Jordan Howard/99 5.00 12.00
16 Deshaun Watson/99 6.00 15.00
17 Alvin Kamara/99 4.00 10.00
18 Leonard Fournette/99 5.00 12.00
19 Dalvin Cook/99 4.00 10.00
20 Christian McCaffrey/99 5.00 12.00
21 Devonta Freeman/99 4.00 10.00
22 Terrell Suggs/99 3.00 8.00
23 LeSean McCoy/99 5.00 12.00
24 Joe Mixon/99 4.00 10.00
25 David Njoku/99 3.00 8.00
26 Jason Witten/99 4.00 10.00
27 Von Miller/49 5.00 12.00
28 James Conner/99 5.00 12.00
29 Aaron Rodgers/99 10.00 25.00
30 Andrew Luck/49 8.00 20.00
31 Joey Bosa/99 5.00 12.00
32 Jared Goff/99 5.00 12.00
33 Ryan Tannehill/49 5.00 12.00
34 Rob Gronkowski/99 5.00 12.00
35 Derek Carr/99 5.00 12.00
36 Carson Wentz/99 6.00 15.00
37 Hines Ward/99 4.00 10.00
38 Marquise Goodwin/99 3.00 8.00
39 Russell Wilson/99 6.00 15.00
40 Jameis Winston/99 4.00 10.00

2018 Panini National Treasures Colossal Pro Bowl Materials

*PRIME/25: .6X TO 1.5X BASIC JSY/99
1 Chandler Jones/99 3.00 8.00
2 Chris Boswell/99 3.00 8.00
3 Earl Thomas III/99 4.00 10.00
4 Eric Weddle/99 3.00 8.00
5 Geno Atkins/99 3.00 8.00
6 Graham Gano/99 3.00 8.00
7 Jarvis Landry/49 5.00 12.00
8 Jurrell Casey/99 3.00 8.00
9 Kyle Rudolph/99 3.00 8.00
10 Maurkice Pouncey/99 3.00 8.00
11 Roosevelt Nix/99 3.00 8.00
12 Melvin Ingram/99 3.00 8.00
13 Ryan Kerrigan/99 3.00 8.00
14 Taylor Lewan/99 3.00 8.00
15 Todd Gurley II/49 6.00 15.00
16 Tyreek Hill/49 6.00 15.00
17 Jack Doyle/99 3.00 8.00
18 Aqib Talib/99 3.00 8.00
19 C.J. Mosley/99 4.00 10.00
20 Darius Slay/99 3.00 8.00
21 Jalen Ramsey/99 4.00 10.00
22 Jared Goff/49 6.00 15.00
23 Pharoh Cooper/99 3.00 8.00
24 Drew Brees/49 6.00 15.00
25 Harrison Smith/99 5.00 12.00
26 Adam Thielen/49 6.00 15.00
27 A.J. Bouye/99 3.00 8.00
28 Budda Baker/99 3.00 8.00
29 Malik Jackson/99 3.00 8.00
30 Russell Wilson/99 6.00 15.00

2018 Panini National Treasures Franchise Treasures Materials

*PRIME/25: .6X TO 1.5X BASIC JSY/99
*PRIME/15: .8X TO 2X BASIC JSY/99
1 Peyton Manning 10.00 25.00
2 Terry Bradshaw 8.00 20.00
3 Reggie White 5.00 12.00
4 Adrian Peterson 5.00 12.00
5 Antonio Gates 3.00 8.00
6 Bo Jackson 6.00 15.00
7 Brett Favre 10.00 25.00
8 Brian Urlacher 5.00 12.00
9 Chris Doleman 3.00 8.00
10 Michael Irvin 5.00 12.00
11 Cris Carter 5.00 12.00
12 Dan Marino 10.00 25.00
13 Drew Brees 5.00 12.00
14 Aaron Rodgers 10.00 25.00
15 Ben Roethlisberger 5.00 12.00
16 Earl Campbell 5.00 12.00
17 Ed Reed 4.00 10.00
18 Eli Manning 4.00 10.00
19 Franco Harris 5.00 12.00
20 Jerry Rice 8.00 20.00
21 Jim McMahon 3.00 8.00
22 Joe Theismann 5.00 12.00
23 John Elway 0.00 20.00
24 LaDainian Tomlinson 4.00 10.00
25 Larry Fitzgerald 4.00 10.00
26 Lawrence Taylor 5.00 12.00
27 Mark Brunell 3.00 8.00
28 Marshall Faulk 4.00 10.00
29 Nick Foles 4.00 10.00
30 Ray Lewis 5.00 12.00

2018 Panini National Treasures Material Signatures

*PRIME/25: .5X TO 1.2X BASIC JSY AU/49
1 Matt Ryan/25
2 Mike Williams/25 12.00 30.00
3 Sammy Watkins/25 20.00 50.00
4 Hines Ward/25 15.00 40.00
5 Patrick Mahomes II/25 150.00 300.00
6 Ozzie Newsome/49 12.00 30.00
7 Philip Rivers/25 20.00 50.00
8 Marcus Allen/25 20.00 50.00
9 Harrison Smith/49 15.00 40.00
10 Jim Kelly/25 20.00 50.00
11 Steve Largent/49 EXCH 15.00 40.00
12 Tedy Bruschi/49 15.00 40.00
13 Terrell Davis/25 15.00 40.00
14 Robert Woods/49 12.00 30.00
15 Terrell Suggs/49 10.00 25.00
16 Tony Dorsett/25 20.00 50.00
17 Marquise Goodwin/49 10.00 25.00
18 Champ Bailey/25
19 Tony Romo/25 30.00 60.00
20 Fran Tarkenton/25 20.00 50.00
21 Marshawn Lynch/25 30.00 60.00
22 Warren Moon/25 20.00 50.00
23 Willie McGinest/49 10.00 25.00
25 Derrick Henry/25 20.00 50.00
26 Zack Martin/49 10.00 25.00
27 Blake Bortles/25 12.00 30.00
28 Drew Bledsoe/25 50.00 100.00
29 Dan Fouts/25 50.00 100.00
30 Ty Law/25 20.00 50.00

2018 Panini National Treasures Material Treasures Signatures

*PRIME/25: .5X TO 1.2X BASIC JSY AU/49
1 Terry Bradshaw/25 EXCH
3 Carson Wentz/25 EXCH 75.00 150.00
4 Cris Carter/25 20.00 50.00
5 Isaac Bruce/25 20.00 50.00
6 Dan Fouts/25 50.00 100.00
7 Rob Gronkowski/25 40.00 80.00
8 JuJu Smith-Schuster/25 EXCH 50.00 100.00
9 Mike Singletary/25 20.00 50.00
12 Thurman Thomas/49 12.00 30.00
14 Michael Vick/25 EXCH 15.00 40.00
15 Calais Campbell/49 10.00 25.00
18 Brian Dawkins/25 30.00 60.00
19 Howie Long/25 EXCH 20.00 50.00
20 Rod Woodson/49 15.00 40.00
21 Ezekiel Elliott/25
22 Ray Lewis/25 40.00 80.00
23 Kurt Warner/25 EXCH
24 Alejandro Villanueva/49 12.00 30.00
26 Drew Brees/25 EXCH 100.00 200.00
28 Mitchell Trubisky/25 EXCH 30.00 60.00
29 Jerome Bettis/25 40.00 80.00

2018 Panini National Treasures NFL Gear Combo Materials

*PRIME/25: .6X TO 1.5X BASIC JSY/99
1 D.Johnson/L.Fitzgerald 5.00 12.00
2 J.Jones/M.Ryan 5.00 12.00
3 J.Flacco/T.Suggs 4.00 10.00
4 C.Newton/C.McCaffrey 5.00 12.00
5 J.Howard/M.Trubisky 5.00 12.00
6 J.Mixon/A.Dalton 4.00 10.00
7 D.Prescott/E.Elliott 6.00 15.00
8 B.Chubb/V.Miller 5.00 12.00
9 A.Rodgers/D.Adams 10.00 25.00
10 P.Lindsay/T.Davis 8.00 20.00
11 P.Mahomes/T.Hill 12.00 30.00
12 K.Allen/J.Bosa 5.00 12.00
13 C.Kupp/J.Goff 5.00 12.00
14 K.Drake/R.Tannehill 4.00 10.00
15 S.Diggs/A.Thielen 5.00 12.00
16 A.Kamara/M.Thomas 5.00 12.00
17 M.Lynch/D.Carr 5.00 12.00
18 J.Winston/M.Evans 4.00 10.00
19 M.Mariota/D.Henry 5.00 12.00
20 D.Baldwin/R.Wilson 6.00 15.00

2018 Panini National Treasures Notable Nicknames

1 Torry Holt 12.00 30.00
2 Marshawn Lynch
3 Adrian Peterson EXCH 100.00 200.00
4 Joe Namath 100.00 200.00
5 Mike Alstott
6 Jevon Kearse 25.00 50.00
8 Brian Dawkins
9 Mike Singletary 15.00 40.00
10 DeAndre Hopkins 25.00 50.00

2018 Panini National Treasures Personalized Treasures Signatures

1 Rob Gronkowski/25 75.00 150.00
2 Marcus Mariota/25 75.00 150.00
3 Mitchell Trubisky/25 50.00 100.00
4 Devin Hester/25 25.00 50.00
5 Kirk Cousins/25 50.00 100.00
8 Terrell Davis/25 30.00 60.00

2018 Panini National Treasures Prime Pairings

1 Howie Long 8.00 20.00
Chris Long/25
2 James Lofton 5.00 12.00
Lynn Dickey/49
3 Jim Kelly 8.00 20.00
Andre Reed/25
4 Jim Zorn 6.00 15.00
Steve Largent/49
7 Derek Carr 8.00 20.00
Rich Gannon/25
11 Bob Griese 6.00 15.00
Paul Warfield/25
12 Fred Biletnikoff 8.00 20.00
Daryle Lamonica/25
15 Chris Doleman 6.00 15.00
John Randle/25
17 Randy White 6.00 15.00
Ed "Too Tall" Jones/25
19 Jordan Howard 8.00 20.00
Mitchell Trubisky/25
20 Jim Taylor 8.00 20.00
Paul Hornung/25

2018 Panini National Treasures Rookie Colossal Material Signatures

1 Baker Mayfield/99 200.00 400.00
2 Sam Darnold/49 125.00 250.00
3 Josh Allen/99 50.00 100.00
4 Josh Rosen/99 25.00 50.00
5 Lamar Jackson/25 125.00 250.00
6 Mason Rudolph/99 15.00 40.00
7 Kyle Lauletta/99 8.00 20.00
8 Mike White/99 6.00 15.00
9 Saquon Barkley/99 75.00 150.00
10 Rashaad Penny/99 8.00 20.00
11 Sony Michel/99 EXCH 15.00 40.00
12 Nick Chubb/99 15.00 40.00
13 Ronald Jones II/99 10.00 25.00
14 Kerryon Johnson/99 8.00 20.00
15 Derrius Guice/25 EXCH 15.00 40.00
16 Royce Freeman/99 6.00 15.00
17 Nyheim Hines/99 6.00 15.00
18 Mark Walton/99 6.00 15.00
19 Ito Smith/99 6.00 15.00
20 Kalen Ballage/99 6.00 15.00
21 Jaylen Samuels/99 6.00 15.00
22 Hayden Hurst/49 8.00 20.00
23 Mike Gesicki/99 6.00 15.00
24 D.J. Moore/99 10.00 25.00
25 Calvin Ridley/99 12.00 30.00
26 Courtland Sutton/99 8.00 20.00
27 Dante Pettis/99 8.00 20.00
28 Christian Kirk/49 10.00 25.00
29 Anthony Miller/99 8.00 20.00
30 James Washington/99 10.00 25.00
31 D.J. Chark Jr./99 6.00 15.00
32 Michael Gallup/99 10.00 25.00
33 Tre'Quan Smith/99 8.00 20.00
34 Keke Coutee/99 6.00 15.00
35 DaeSean Hamilton/99 6.00 15.00
36 Jaleel Scott/99 5.00 12.00
37 J'Mon Moore/99 5.00 12.00
38 Daurice Fountain/99 6.00 15.00
39 Marquez Valdes-Scantling/99 6.00 15.00
40 Bradley Chubb/49 10.00 25.00

2018 Panini National Treasures Rookie Colossal Material Signatures Prime

*PRIME/25: .6X TO 1.5X BASIC JSY AU/99
*PRIME/25: .5X TO 1.2X BASIC JSY AU/49
1 Baker Mayfield/25 250.00 500.00
9 Saquon Barkley/25 150.00 300.00

2018 Panini National Treasures Rookie Dual Materials

*GOLD/49: .5X TO 1.2X BASIC JSY/99
*SILVER/25: .6X TO 1.5X BASIC JSY/99
*RED/81-86: .4X TO 1X BASIC JSY/99
*RED/38-55: .5X TO 1.2X BASIC JSY/99
*RED/25-33: .6X TO 1.5X BASIC JSY/99
*RED/16-24: .8X TO 2X BASIC JSY/99
1 Baker Mayfield 12.00 30.00
2 Sam Darnold 8.00 20.00
3 Josh Allen 5.00 12.00
4 Josh Rosen 4.00 10.00
5 Lamar Jackson 8.00 20.00
6 Mason Rudolph 4.00 10.00
7 Kyle Lauletta 3.00 8.00
8 Mike White 2.50 6.00
9 Saquon Barkley 10.00 25.00
10 Rashaad Penny 3.00 8.00
11 Sony Michel 4.00 10.00
12 Nick Chubb 4.00 10.00
13 Ronald Jones II 4.00 10.00
14 Kerryon Johnson 3.00 8.00
15 Derrius Guice 4.00 10.00
16 Royce Freeman 2.50 6.00
17 Nyheim Hines 2.50 6.00
18 Mark Walton 2.50 6.00
19 Ito Smith 2.50 6.00
20 Kalen Ballage 2.50 6.00
21 Jaylen Samuels 2.50 6.00
22 Hayden Hurst 2.50 6.00
23 Mike Gesicki 2.50 6.00
24 D.J. Moore 4.00 10.00
25 Calvin Ridley 4.00 10.00
26 Courtland Sutton 3.00 8.00
27 Dante Pettis 3.00 8.00
28 Christian Kirk 3.00 8.00
29 Anthony Miller 3.00 8.00
30 James Washington 4.00 10.00
31 D.J. Chark Jr. 2.50 6.00
32 Michael Gallup 4.00 10.00
33 Tre'Quan Smith 3.00 8.00
34 Keke Coutee 2.50 6.00
35 DaeSean Hamilton 2.50 6.00
36 Jaleel Scott 2.00 5.00
37 J'Mon Moore 2.00 5.00
38 Daurice Fountain 2.50 6.00
39 Marquez Valdes-Scantling 2.50 6.00
40 Bradley Chubb 3.00 8.00

2018 Panini National Treasures Rookie Dual Signatures

1 R.Smith/A.Miller/99 20.00 50.00
3 J.Allen/T.Edmunds/25
4 H.Hurst/L.Jackson/25 60.00 150.00
6 C.Sutton/B.Chubb/99 10.00 25.00
7 N.Chubb/S.Michel/49 50.00 100.00
10 R.Penny/S.Griffin/99 10.00 25.00
11 C.Ridley/D.Moore/49 20.00 50.00
12 J.Rosen/J.Allen/25 40.00 100.00
13 L.VnEch/M.Gallup/99 50.00 100.00
14 D.James/M.Fitzpatrick/99 40.00 80.00
16 S.Darnold/R.Jones/25 60.00 150.00
17 M.Fitzpatrick/M.Gesicki/99
18 D.Leonard/Q.Nelson/99 50.00 100.00
19 J.Washington/M.Rudolph/99 15.00 40.00
24 J.Moore/J.Alexander/99 10.00 25.00
25 K.Ballage/M.Gesicki/99 8.00 20.00
27 K.Lauletta/S.Barkley/25 80.00 200.00
28 D.Pettis/N.Mullens/99 20.00 50.00
29 H.Landry/R.Evans/99 10.00 25.00
30 D.Payne/D.Guice/49 15.00 40.00

2018 Panini National Treasures Rookie Gloves Signatures

1 Baker Mayfield/25 300.00 600.00
2 Saquon Barkley/25 150.00 300.00
3 Sam Darnold/25 150.00 250.00
4 Bradley Chubb/25 12.00 30.00
5 Josh Allen/25 75.00 150.00
6 Josh Rosen/25 30.00 80.00
7 D.J. Moore/25 15.00 40.00
8 Calvin Ridley/25 20.00 50.00
9 Rashaad Penny/25 12.00 30.00
10 Sony Michel/25 EXCH 25.00 60.00
12 Nick Chubb/25 25.00 60.00
13 Ronald Jones II/25 15.00 40.00
14 Courtland Sutton/25 12.00 30.00
15 Kerryon Johnson/25 12.00 30.00
16 Dante Pettis/25 12.00 30.00
17 Anthony Miller/25 12.00 30.00
18 Derrius Guice/25 EXCH 15.00 40.00
19 James Washington/25 15.00 40.00
20 D.J. Chark Jr./25 10.00 25.00
22 Mason Rudolph/25 25.00 60.00
23 Michael Gallup/25 15.00 40.00
24 Tre'Quan Smith/25 12.00 30.00
25 Keke Coutee/25 10.00 25.00
26 Nyheim Hines/25 10.00 25.00
27 DaeSean Hamilton/25 10.00 25.00
28 Ito Smith/25 10.00 25.00
29 J'Mon Moore/25 8.00 20.00
30 Jaylen Samuels/25 10.00 25.00

2018 Panini National Treasures Rookie Jumbo Prime Signatures Booklet

*VERT/99: .4X TO 1X BASIC JSY AU/99
*VERT/99: .3X TO .8X BASIC JSY AU/49
*VERT/49: .5X TO 1.2X BASIC JSY AU/99
*VERT/49: .4X TO 1X BASIC JSY AU/49
1 Baker Mayfield/99 250.00 500.00
2 Saquon Barkley/99 150.00 300.00
3 Sam Darnold/49 100.00 200.00
4 Bradley Chubb/49 15.00 40.00
5 Josh Allen/99 60.00 125.00
6 Josh Rosen/99 40.00 80.00
7 D.J. Moore/99 15.00 40.00
8 Hayden Hurst/49 12.00 30.00
9 Calvin Ridley/99 20.00 50.00
10 Rashaad Penny/99 12.00 30.00
11 Sony Michel/99 EXCH 40.00 80.00
12 Lamar Jackson/49 100.00 200.00
13 Nick Chubb/99 25.00 60.00
14 Ronald Jones II/99 15.00 40.00
15 Courtland Sutton/99 12.00 30.00
16 Mike Gesicki/99 10.00 25.00
17 Kerryon Johnson/99 30.00 60.00
18 Dante Pettis/99 12.00 30.00
19 Anthony Miller/99 12.00 30.00
20 James Washington/99 15.00 40.00
21 D.J. Chark Jr./99 10.00 25.00
22 Royce Freeman/99 10.00 25.00
23 Mason Rudolph/99 40.00 80.00
24 Michael Gallup/99 15.00 40.00
25 Tre'Quan Smith/99 12.00 30.00
26 Keke Coutee/99 10.00 25.00
27 Nyheim Hines/99 10.00 25.00
28 Kyle Lauletta/99 12.00 30.00
29 Mark Walton/99 10.00 25.00
30 DaeSean Hamilton/99 10.00 25.00
31 J'Mon Moore/99 8.00 20.00
32 Mike White/99 10.00 25.00
33 Jaylen Samuels/99 15.00 40.00
34 Daurice Fountain/99 10.00 25.00
35 Kalen Ballage/99 10.00 25.00
36 Derrius Guice/99 EXCH 40.00 80.00

2018 Panini National Treasures Rookie Material Signatures RPS

1 Baker Mayfield/99 200.00 400.00
2 Sam Darnold/49 125.00 250.00
3 Josh Allen/99 50.00 100.00
4 Josh Rosen/99 25.00 50.00
5 Lamar Jackson/25 125.00 250.00
6 Mason Rudolph/99 15.00 40.00
7 Kyle Lauletta/99 8.00 20.00
8 Mike White/99 6.00 15.00
9 Saquon Barkley/99 75.00 150.00
10 Rashaad Penny/99 8.00 20.00
11 Sony Michel/99 EXCH 15.00 40.00
12 Nick Chubb/99 15.00 40.00
13 Ronald Jones II/99 10.00 25.00
14 Kerryon Johnson/99 8.00 20.00
15 Derrius Guice/25 EXCH 15.00 40.00
17 Nyheim Hines/99 6.00 15.00
18 Mark Walton/99 6.00 15.00
19 Ito Smith/99 6.00 15.00
20 Kalen Ballage/99 6.00 15.00
21 Jaylen Samuels/99 6.00 15.00
22 Hayden Hurst/49 8.00 20.00
23 Mike Gesicki/99 6.00 15.00
24 D.J. Moore/99 10.00 25.00
25 Calvin Ridley/99 12.00 30.00
26 Courtland Sutton/99 8.00 20.00
27 Dante Pettis/99 8.00 20.00
28 Christian Kirk/49 10.00 25.00
29 Anthony Miller/99 8.00 20.00
30 James Washington/99 10.00 25.00
31 D.J. Chark Jr./99 6.00 15.00
32 Michael Gallup/99 10.00 25.00
33 Tre'Quan Smith/99 8.00 20.00
34 Keke Coutee/99 6.00 15.00
35 DaeSean Hamilton/99 6.00 15.00
36 Jaleel Scott/99 5.00 12.00
37 J'Mon Moore/99 5.00 12.00
38 Daurice Fountain/99 6.00 15.00
39 Marquez Valdes-Scantling/99 6.00 15.00
40 Bradley Chubb/49 10.00 25.00

2018 Panini National Treasures Rookie Material Signatures RPS Green Numbers

*GREEN/82-86: .4X TO 1X BASIC JSY AU/99
*GREEN/38-55: .5X TO 1.2X BASIC JSY AU/99
*GREEN/38-55: .4X TO 1X BASIC JSY AU/49
*GREEN/25-33: .6X TO 1.5X BASIC JSY AU/99
*GREEN/25-33: .4X TO 1X BASIC JSY AU/25
*GREEN/16-24: .8X TO 2X BASIC JSY AU/99
3 Josh Allen/17 200.00 400.00
9 Saquon Barkley/26 150.00 300.00

2018 Panini National Treasures Rookie Material Signatures RPS Holo Silver

*SILVER/25: .6X TO 1.5X BASIC JSY AU/99
*SILVER/25: .5X TO 1.2X BASIC JSY AU/49
1 Baker Mayfield/25 250.00 500.00
9 Saquon Barkley/25 150.00 300.00

2018 Panini National Treasures Rookie NFL Gear Combo Materials

*PRIME/25: .6X TO 1.5X BASIC JSY/99
1 A.Miller/C.Kirk 3.00 8.00
2 N.Chubb/B.Mayfield 12.00 30.00
3 B.Chubb/C.Sutton 3.00 8.00
4 C.Ridley/D.Moore 4.00 10.00
5 C.Kirk/J.Rosen 4.00 10.00
6 C.Sutton/D.Hamilton 3.00 8.00
7 D.Hamilton/R.Freeman 2.50 6.00
8 A.Miller/D.Pettis 3.00 8.00
9 N.Hines/D.Fountain 2.50 6.00
10 D.Guice/D.Chark 4.00 10.00
11 D.Chark/D.Moore 4.00 10.00
12 M.Gesicki/H.Hurst 2.50 6.00
13 C.Ridley/I.Smith 4.00 10.00
14 J.Scott/L.Jackson 8.00 20.00
15 J.Washington/M.Rudolph 4.00 10.00
16 J.Samuels/M.Rudolph 4.00 10.00
17 J.Moore/M.VldsSctlng 2.50 6.00
18 J.Allen/J.Rosen 5.00 12.00
19 C.Kirk/J.Rosen 4.00 10.00
20 K.Ballage/M.Gesicki 2.50 6.00
21 S.Barkley/K.Lauletta 10.00 25.00
22 S.Barkley/S.Darnold 10.00 25.00
23 S.Barkley/B.Mayfield 20.00 50.00
24 B.Mayfield/L.Jackson 12.00 30.00
25 I.Smith/M.Walton 2.50 6.00
26 M.Gallup/M.White 4.00 10.00
27 N.Chubb/S.Michel 4.00 10.00
28 R.Penny/S.Michel 4.00 10.00
29 J.Allen/S.Darnold 8.00 20.00
30 J.Scott/K.Coutee 2.50 6.00
31 R.Jones/S.Darnold 8.00 20.00
32 K.Johnson/R.Jones 4.00 10.00
33 D.Guice/K.Johnson 4.00 10.00
34 M.Gallup/T.Smith 4.00 10.00
35 K.Lauletta/M.White 3.00 8.00
36 L.Jackson/H.Hurst 8.00 20.00
37 B.Chubb/N.Hines 3.00 8.00
38 A.Miller/J.Moore 3.00 8.00
39 J.Rosen/S.Darnold 8.00 20.00
40 R.Penny/S.Barkley 10.00 25.00

2018 Panini National Treasures Rookie NFL Gear Signature Combos Prime

*PRIME/25: .6X TO 1.5X BASIC JSY AU/99
*PRIME/25: .5X TO 1.2X BASIC JSY AU/49

2018 Panini National Treasures Rookie NFL Gear Signature Trios

1 Baker Mayfield/99 200.00 400.00
2 Saquon Barkley/99 100.00 200.00
3 Sam Darnold/49 75.00 150.00
4 Bradley Chubb/25 15.00 40.00
5 Josh Allen/99 40.00 80.00
6 Josh Rosen/99 30.00 60.00
7 D.J. Moore/49 15.00 40.00
8 Calvin Ridley/49 20.00 50.00
9 Rashaad Penny/49 12.00 30.00
10 Sony Michel/99 EXCH 20.00 50.00
11 Lamar Jackson/25 75.00 150.00
12 Nick Chubb/99 20.00 50.00
13 Ronald Jones II/99 12.00 30.00
14 Courtland Sutton/49 12.00 30.00
15 Kerryon Johnson/99 10.00 25.00
16 Dante Pettis/49 12.00 30.00
17 Anthony Miller/99 10.00 25.00
18 Derrius Guice/25
19 James Washington/99 12.00 30.00
20 D.J. Chark Jr./99 8.00 20.00
22 Mason Rudolph/49 40.00 80.00
23 Michael Gallup/25 20.00 50.00
24 Tre'Quan Smith/99 10.00 25.00
25 Keke Coutee/99 8.00 20.00
26 Nyheim Hines/99 8.00 20.00
27 DaeSean Hamilton/99 8.00 20.00
28 Ito Smith/99 8.00 20.00
29 J'Mon Moore/99 6.00 15.00
30 Jaylen Samuels/99 8.00 20.00

2018 Panini National Treasures Rookie NFL Gear Signature Trios Prime

*PRIME/25: .6X TO 1.5X BASIC JSY AU/99
*PRIME/25: .5X TO 1.2X BASIC JSY AU/49
2 Saquon Barkley/25 125.00 250.00
3 Sam Darnold/25 100.00 200.00

2018 Panini National Treasures Rookie Signatures

1 Baker Mayfield/99 300.00 600.00
2 Saquon Barkley/99 75.00 150.00
3 Sam Darnold/25 150.00 300.00
4 Josh Allen/99 50.00 100.00
5 Josh Rosen/99 30.00 60.00
6 D.J. Moore/99 8.00 20.00
8 Sony Michel/99 EXCH 12.00 30.00
9 Nick Chubb/99 12.00 30.00
10 Ronald Jones II/99 8.00 20.00
11 Courtland Sutton/99 6.00 15.00
12 Kerryon Johnson/99 6.00 15.00
13 Dante Pettis/99 6.00 15.00
14 Anthony Miller/99 6.00 15.00
15 Derrius Guice/25 12.00 30.00
16 James Washington/99 8.00 20.00
17 Royce Freeman/99 5.00 12.00
18 Mason Rudolph/99 10.00 25.00
19 Michael Gallup/25 12.00 30.00
20 J'Mon Moore/99 4.00 10.00

2018 Panini National Treasures Rookie Signatures Gold

*GOLD/25: .6X TO 1.5X BASIC AU/99
1 Baker Mayfield/25 700.00 1200.00

2018 Panini National Treasures Signatures

1 Aaron Donald/25
2 Aaron Jones/99 8.00 20.00
3 John Lynch/49 10.00 25.00
4 Brett Keisel/49 5.00 12.00
5 Calais Campbell/25 6.00 15.00
6 Charles Haley/49 8.00 20.00
7 Chris Doleman/35 5.00 12.00
8 Chris Long/49 10.00 25.00
9 Christian McCaffrey/25 25.00 50.00
10 Danny White/25 15.00 40.00
11 Delanie Walker/49 5.00 12.00
12 Don Maynard/25 8.00 20.00
13 Doug Williams/25 12.00 30.00
14 Drew Bledsoe/25 15.00 40.00
15 Drew Pearson/35 6.00 15.00
16 Emmitt Thomas/25 6.00 15.00
17 Eric Metcalf/25 12.00 30.00
18 Everson Griffen/25 12.00 30.00
19 Geno Atkins/49 5.00 12.00
20 Gilbert Brown/49 5.00 12.00
21 LaVar Arrington/49 10.00 25.00
22 Ha Ha Clinton-Dix/49 5.00 12.00
23 Harry Carson/25 6.00 15.00
24 Ben Roethlisberger/25 50.00 100.00
25 Troy Aikman/25 EXCH 40.00 80.00
26 Jevon Kearse/25 12.00 30.00
29 Josh Gordon/49 12.00 30.00
31 Kevin Byard/99 4.00 10.00
33 Kyle Rudolph/49 5.00 12.00
34 Landon Collins/49 5.00 12.00
35 Larry Johnson/99 4.00 10.00
36 Leon Lett/49 10.00 25.00
37 Linval Joseph/49 10.00 25.00
38 Luke Kuechly/25 12.00 30.00
39 Marquise Goodwin/49 5.00 12.00
40 Melvin Gordon III/25 12.00 30.00
41 Mike Ditka/25 25.00 50.00
42 Morten Andersen/49 5.00 12.00
43 Neil Smith/99 4.00 10.00
44 Nelson Agholor/49 5.00 12.00
46 Randy White/49 6.00 15.00
47 Ricky Williams/99 5.00 12.00
48 Robert Woods/49 6.00 15.00
49 Randy Moss/25 8.00 20.00
50 Ronnie Brown/49 5.00 12.00
51 Jason Taylor/49 12.00 30.00
53 Stephen Gostkowski/49 10.00 25.00
54 Tarik Cohen/49 10.00 25.00
55 Travis Frederick/99 4.00 10.00
56 Willie Gault/49 5.00 12.00
57 Dont'a Hightower/35 10.00 25.00
58 Jake Elliott/99 5.00 12.00
60 Justin Tucker/49 5.00 12.00
61 Lawrence Taylor/49 15.00 40.00
62 Dan Bailey/49 5.00 12.00
63 Randall Cunningham/49 15.00 40.00
64 Plaxico Burress/49 5.00 12.00
66 Alex Collins/49 5.00 12.00
67 Dick Butkus/25 30.00 60.00
68 Bob Griese/25 15.00 40.00
69 Bob Lilly/25 8.00 20.00
70 Pat McAfee/25 40.00 80.00
71 Keyshawn Johnson/25 8.00 20.00
73 Dan Hampton/49 6.00 15.00
74 Darius Slay/49 5.00 12.00
75 Roger Staubach/15 50.00 100.00
76 Daryle Lamonica/49 5.00 12.00
77 DeSean Jackson/25 8.00 20.00
78 Devin Hester/25 15.00 40.00
81 Adrian Peterson/15 60.00 125.00
82 Fred Taylor/25 12.00 30.00
84 James Conner/25 12.00 30.00
85 Jim Plunkett/25 8.00 20.00
86 Herman Edwards/25 6.00 15.00
87 Isaac Bruce/25 10.00 25.00
88 Jack Ham/25 12.00 30.00
89 Jamal Adams/25 8.00 20.00
90 James Harrison/25 8.00 20.00
91 Jerry Kramer/49 15.00 40.00
93 Jimmy Garoppolo/25 40.00 80.00
94 Jimmy Johnson/25 25.00 50.00
95 Joe Theismann/25 EXCH 15.00 40.00
96 Kenyan Drake/49 5.00 12.00
97 Jack Youngblood/99 4.00 10.00
98 Kevin Mawae/49 5.00 12.00
100 Jim Taylor/49 30.00 60.00

2018 Panini National Treasures Treasured Patches Booklet

1 Dak Prescott/25 10.00 25.00
5 Jarvis Landry/25 8.00 20.00
6 Kirk Cousins/25 10.00 25.00
7 Antonio Brown/25 10.00 25.00
8 Drew Brees/15 12.00 30.00
9 Matthew Stafford/25 8.00 20.00
10 A.J. Green/25 10.00 25.00
11 Alejandro Villanueva/25 8.00 20.00
12 Patrick Mahomes II/25 50.00 100.00
13 Rob Gronkowski/25 10.00 25.00
14 Tyreek Hill/25 10.00 25.00
15 Alvin Kamara/25 8.00 20.00
16 Mitchell Trubisky/25 10.00 25.00
17 Jared Goff/25 10.00 25.00
18 Carson Wentz/25 12.00 30.00
19 Ryan Tannehill/25 8.00 20.00
20 Christian McCaffrey/25 10.00 25.00
21 Von Miller/25 8.00 20.00
22 DeAndre Hopkins/25 8.00 20.00
23 Andrew Luck/15 15.00 40.00
24 Ezekiel Elliott/25 12.00 30.00

2018 Panini National Treasures Treasures of the Hall Booklet

1 John Riggins 8.00 20.00
2 Joe Montana 25.00 60.00
3 Troy Aikman 12.00 30.00
4 Ray Lewis 10.00 25.00
5 Brian Dawkins 10.00 25.00
6 LaDainian Tomlinson 8.00 20.00
7 Kurt Warner 8.00 20.00
8 Brett Favre 20.00 50.00
9 Jerome Bettis 10.00 25.00
10 Walter Payton 20.00 50.00
11 Jerry Rice 15.00 40.00
12 Emmitt Smith 15.00 40.00
13 Barry Sanders 15.00 40.00
14 John Elway 15.00 40.00

2018 Panini National Treasures Tremendous Treasures

*PRIME/25: .5X TO 1.2X BASIC JSY/49
*PRIME/15: .6X TO 1.5X BASIC JSY/49
1 Patrick Peterson 4.00 10.00
2 Devonta Freeman 5.00 12.00
3 Michael Vick 5.00 12.00
4 Ed Reed 5.00 12.00
5 Johnny Unitas/25 12.00 30.00
6 Bruce Smith 5.00 12.00
8 Micah Hyde 4.00 10.00
9 Tre'Davious White 4.00 10.00
10 Christian McCaffrey 6.00 15.00
11 Mike Singletary 6.00 15.00
12 Allen Robinson II 5.00 12.00
14 Geno Atkins 4.00 10.00
15 Jim Brown/25 10.00 25.00
16 Tony Romo 5.00 12.00
17 Emmitt Smith 10.00 25.00
18 Ezekiel Elliott 8.00 20.00
19 Terrell Davis 5.00 12.00
20 Von Miller 5.00 12.00
21 Clay Matthews 5.00 12.00
22 Aaron Rodgers 12.00 30.00
23 Brett Favre 12.00 30.00
24 Jadeveon Clowney 4.00 10.00
25 Will Fuller V 4.00 10.00
26 Adam Vinatieri 4.00 10.00
27 T.Y. Hilton 5.00 12.00
28 Peyton Manning 12.00 30.00
29 Mark Brunell 4.00 10.00
30 Maurice Jones-Drew 4.00 10.00
31 Ahmad Rashad 5.00 12.00
32 Travis Kelce 6.00 15.00
33 LaDainian Tomlinson 5.00 12.00
34 Lance Alworth 5.00 12.00
35 Melvin Gordon III 5.00 12.00
36 Marshall Faulk 5.00 12.00
37 Pharoh Cooper 4.00 10.00
38 Ryan Tannehill 5.00 12.00
39 Cameron Wake 4.00 10.00
40 Harrison Smith 6.00 15.00
41 Adam Thielen 6.00 15.00
42 Dalvin Cook 5.00 12.00
43 Fran Tarkenton 6.00 15.00
44 Tedy Bruschi 6.00 15.00
45 Willie McGinest 4.00 10.00
46 Drew Brees 6.00 15.00
47 Sterling Shepard 5.00 12.00
48 Evan Engram 4.00 10.00
49 Robby Anderson 4.00 10.00
50 Danny Amendola 5.00 12.00
51 Ben Roethlisberger 6.00 15.00
52 Antonio Brown 6.00 15.00
53 Matt Breida 5.00 12.00
54 Roger Craig 5.00 12.00
55 Steve Largent 6.00 15.00
56 DeSean Jackson 5.00 12.00
57 O.J. Howard 4.00 10.00
58 Clinton Portis 4.00 10.00
59 John Riggins 5.00 12.00
60 Jordan Reed 4.00 10.00

2018 Panini National Treasures Tremendous Treasures Rookies

1 Baker Mayfield 12.00 30.00
2 Sam Darnold 8.00 20.00
3 Josh Allen 5.00 12.00
4 Josh Rosen 4.00 10.00
5 Lamar Jackson 8.00 20.00
6 Mason Rudolph 4.00 10.00
7 Kyle Lauletta 3.00 8.00
8 Mike White 2.50 6.00
9 Saquon Barkley 10.00 25.00
10 Rashaad Penny 3.00 8.00
11 Sony Michel 4.00 10.00
12 Nick Chubb 4.00 10.00
13 Ronald Jones II 4.00 10.00
14 Kerryon Johnson 3.00 8.00
15 Derrius Guice 4.00 10.00
16 Royce Freeman 2.50 6.00
17 Nyheim Hines 2.50 6.00
18 Mark Walton 2.50 6.00
19 Ito Smith 2.50 6.00
20 Kalen Ballage 2.50 6.00
21 Jaylen Samuels 2.50 6.00
22 Hayden Hurst 2.50 6.00
23 Mike Gesicki 2.50 6.00
24 D.J. Moore 4.00 10.00
25 Calvin Ridley 4.00 10.00
26 Courtland Sutton 3.00 8.00
27 Dante Pettis 3.00 8.00
28 Christian Kirk 3.00 8.00
29 Anthony Miller 3.00 8.00
30 James Washington 4.00 10.00
31 D.J. Chark Jr. 2.50 6.00
32 Michael Gallup 4.00 10.00
33 Tre'Quan Smith 3.00 8.00
34 Keke Coutee 2.50 6.00
35 DaeSean Hamilton 2.50 6.00
36 Jaleel Scott 2.00 5.00
37 J'Mon Moore 2.00 5.00
38 Daurice Fountain 2.50 6.00
39 Marquez Valdes-Scantling 2.50 6.00
40 Bradley Chubb 3.00 8.00

2016 Panini National Treasures Collegiate

1 A.J. Green 3.00 8.00
2 Aaron Rodgers 6.00 15.00
3 Adrian Peterson 3.00 8.00
4 Allen Hurns 2.00 5.00
5 Allen Robinson 2.50 6.00
6 Alshon Jeffery 2.50 6.00
7 Amari Cooper 3.00 8.00
8 Andrew Luck 4.00 10.00
9 Andy Dalton 2.50 6.00
10 Antonio Brown 3.00 8.00
11 Barry Sanders 5.00 12.00
12 Ben Roethlisberger 3.00 8.00
13 Blake Bortles 2.00 5.00
14 Bo Jackson 4.00 10.00
15 Bobby Layne 2.50 6.00
16 Brandin Cooks 2.50 6.00
17 Brandon Marshall 2.00 5.00
18 Brett Favre 6.00 15.00
19 C.J. Anderson 2.50 6.00
20 Cam Newton 3.00 8.00
21 Dan Marino 6.00 15.00
22 David Johnson 3.00 8.00
23 DeAndre Hopkins 2.50 6.00
24 Deion Sanders 2.50 6.00
25 DeMarco Murray 2.50 6.00
26 Demaryius Thomas 2.50 6.00
27 Derek Carr 3.00 8.00
28 DeVante Parker 2.50 6.00
29 Devonta Freeman 2.50 6.00
30 Dez Bryant 3.00 8.00
31 Dion Lewis 2.00 5.00
32 Doak Walker 3.00 8.00
33 Doug Baldwin 2.50 6.00
34 Doug Martin 2.50 6.00
35 Drew Brees 3.00 8.00
36 Duke Johnson 2.00 5.00
37 Earl Campbell 3.00 8.00
38 Eddie Lacy 2.00 5.00
39 Eli Manning 2.50 6.00
40 Elroy Hirsch 2.50 6.00
41 Emmanuel Sanders 3.00 8.00

42 Emmitt Smith 5.00 12.00
43 Ernie Davis 2.50 6.00
44 Gale Sayers 3.00 8.00
45 George Halas 3.00 8.00
46 Greg Olsen 2.50 6.00
47 Hank Stram 2.50 6.00
48 J.J. Watt 3.00 8.00
49 Jamaal Charles 2.50 6.00
50 Jameis Winston 3.00 8.00
51 Jarvis Landry 2.50 6.00
52 Jason Witten 2.50 6.00
53 Jeremy Hill 2.00 5.00
54 Jeremy Langford 2.50 6.00
55 Jeremy Maclin 2.00 5.00
56 Jerry Rice 5.00 12.00
57 Jimmy Graham 3.00 8.00
58 Joe Namath 4.00 10.00
59 John Brown 2.50 6.00
60 John Elway 5.00 12.00
61 Jonathan Stewart 2.00 5.00
62 Jordan Matthews 2.50 6.00
63 Jordan Reed 2.00 5.00
64 Jordy Nelson 2.50 6.00
65 Julian Edelman 3.00 8.00
66 Julio Jones 3.00 8.00
67 Justin Forsett 2.50 6.00
68 Karlos Williams 2.00 5.00
69 Keenan Allen 2.50 6.00
70 Kelvin Benjamin 2.50 6.00
71 Knute Rockne 3.00 8.00
72 Lamar Miller 2.00 5.00
73 Larry Fitzgerald 2.50 6.00
74 Latavius Murray 2.00 5.00
75 Le'Veon Bell 2.50 6.00
76 LeSean McCoy 3.00 8.00
77 Luke Kuechly 2.50 6.00
78 Marcus Allen 2.50 6.00
79 Marcus Mariota 3.00 8.00
80 Mark Ingram 2.50 6.00
81 Martavis Bryant 2.00 5.00
82 Matt Forte 2.00 5.00
83 Matt Jones 2.50 6.00
84 Matt Ryan 2.50 6.00
85 Melvin Gordon 2.50 6.00
86 Michael Irvin 3.00 8.00
87 Mike Evans 2.50 6.00
88 Norm Van Brocklin 2.50 6.00
89 Odell Beckham Jr. 3.00 8.00
90 Otto Graham 2.50 6.00
91 Peyton Manning 6.00 15.00
92 Philip Rivers 3.00 8.00
93 Red Grange 4.00 10.00
94 Rob Gronkowski 3.00 8.00
95 Russell Wilson 4.00 10.00
96 T.J. Yeldon 2.00 5.00
97 Thomas Rawls 2.00 5.00
98 Todd Gurley II 3.00 8.00
99 Tom Brady 8.00 20.00
100 Tony Romo 2.50 6.00
101 Jalen Ramsey AU RC 6.00 15.00
102 Eli Apple AU RC 5.00 12.00
103 Vernon Hargreaves III AU RC 6.00 15.00
104 Karl Joseph AU RC 4.00 10.00
105 Nick Vannett AU RC 4.00 10.00
106 Tyler Ervin AU RC 4.00 10.00
107 Jerell Adams AU RC 4.00 10.00
108 Cody Core AU RC 4.00 10.00
109 Keith Marshall AU RC 4.00 10.00
110 Jeff Driskel AU RC 4.00 10.00
111 Cody Kessler JSY AU RC 8.00 20.00
112 DeAndre Washington JSY AU RC 8.00 20.00
113 Kevin Hogan JSY AU RC 10.00 25.00
114 Chris Moore JSY AU RC 10.00 25.00
115 Demarcus Robinson JSY AU RC 8.00 20.00
116 Keenan Reynolds JSY AU RC 10.00 25.00
117 Ricardo Louis JSY AU RC 8.00 20.00
118 Trevor Davis JSY AU RC 8.00 20.00
119 Wendell Smallwood JSY AU RC 8.00 20.00
120 Tyler Boyd JSY AU RC 10.00 25.00
123 Tajae Sharpe JSY AU RC 10.00 25.00
124 Nate Sudfeld JSY AU RC 8.00 20.00
125 Brandon Allen JSY AU RC 8.00 20.00
127 Brandon Doughty JSY AU RC 8.00 20.00
128 Charone Peake JSY AU RC 8.00 20.00
129 Daniel Braverman JSY AU RC 8.00 20.00
130 DeForest Buckner JSY AU RC 8.00 20.00
132 Su'a Cravens JSY AU RC 8.00 20.00
133 Scooby Wright III JSY AU RC 8.00 20.00
134 Vernon Adams Jr. JSY AU RC 12.00 30.00
135 Trevone Boykin JSY AU RC 8.00 20.00
138 Aaron Green JSY AU RC 8.00 20.00
139 Tre Madden JSY AU RC 8.00 20.00
140 Marteze Waller JSY AU RC 12.00 30.00
142 Jalin Marshall JSY AU RC 12.00 30.00
143 Cayleb Jones JSY AU RC 8.00 20.00
144 D.J. Foster JSY AU RC 10.00 25.00
145 Jaydon Mickens JSY AU RC 8.00 20.00
146 De'Runnya Wilson JSY AU RC 8.00 20.00
147 Devon Cajuste JSY AU RC 8.00 20.00
148 Bralon Addison JSY AU RC 8.00 20.00
150 Nelson Spruce JSY AU RC 8.00 20.00
151 Andre Ellington JSY 6.00 15.00
152 Andre Johnson JSY 8.00 20.00
153 Artie Burns JSY
154 Austin Seferian-Jenkins JSY 6.00 15.00
155 Bobby Layne JSY 8.00 20.00
156 Bralon Addison JSY 6.00 15.00
157 Brandin Cooks JSY 8.00 20.00
158 Brandon Allen JSY 6.00 15.00
159 Brandon Browner JSY 6.00 15.00
160 Braxton Miller JSY 4.00 10.00
161 Calais Campbell JSY 6.00 15.00
162 Buck Allen JSY 6.00 15.00
163 Cardale Jones JSY 4.00 10.00
164 Carlos Hyde JSY 6.00 15.00
165 Carson Palmer JSY 8.00 20.00
166 Cayleb Jones JSY 4.00 10.00
167 Chandler Jones JSY 6.00 15.00
168 Coby Fleener JSY 6.00 15.00
169 Cody Kessler JSY 4.00 10.00
170 D.J. Foster JSY 5.00 12.00
171 Daniel Lasco JSY 4.00 10.00
172 Darren McFadden JSY 6.00 15.00
173 De'Anthony Thomas JSY 6.00 15.00
174 DeAndre Hopkins JSY 8.00 20.00
175 DeForest Buckner JSY 4.00 10.00
176 Denard Robinson JSY 6.00 15.00
177 DeSean Jackson JSY 8.00 20.00
178 Duke Johnson JSY 6.00 15.00
179 Eddie Lacy JSY 6.00 15.00
180 Elroy Hirsch JSY 8.00 20.00
181 Emmanuel Sanders JSY 10.00 25.00
182 Ernie Davis JSY
183 Ezekiel Elliott JSY 20.00 50.00
184 Fitzgerald Toussaint JSY 6.00 15.00
185 Greg Olsen JSY 8.00 20.00
186 Hunter Henry JSY 5.00 12.00
187 Jared Goff JSY
188 Jimmy Graham JSY 10.00 25.00
189 Jim Thorpe JSY
190 Joe Flacco JSY 8.00 20.00
191 Joey Bosa JSY
192 Jonathan Stewart JSY 6.00 15.00
193 Jordan Cameron JSY 6.00 15.00
194 Josh Huff JSY 6.00 15.00
195 Julio Jones JSY 10.00 25.00
196 Ka'Deem Carey JSY 6.00 15.00
197 Karlos Williams JSY 6.00 15.00
198 Keenan Allen JSY 8.00 20.00
199 Kelvin Benjamin JSY 8.00 20.00
200 Kenny Lawler JSY 6.00 15.00
201 Joey Bosa JSY AU RC 15.00 40.00
202 Jared Goff JSY AU RC 50.00 125.00
203 Laquon Treadwell JSY AU RC 10.00 25.00
204 Carson Wentz JSY AU RC 80.00 200.00
205 Ezekiel Elliott JSY AU RC 100.00 200.00
206 Will Fuller V JSY AU RC 12.00 30.00
207 Corey Coleman JSY AU RC 12.00 30.00
208 Connor Cook JSY AU RC 10.00 25.00
209 Hunter Henry JSY AU RC 10.00 25.00
210 Michael Thomas JSY AU RC 15.00 40.00
211 Josh Doctson JSY AU RC 10.00 25.00
212 Derrick Henry JSY AU RC 20.00 50.00
214 Austin Hooper JSY AU RC 8.00 20.00
215 Pharoh Cooper JSY AU RC 8.00 20.00
216 Alex Collins JSY AU RC 10.00 25.00
217 Rashard Higgins JSY AU RC 8.00 20.00
218 Kenneth Dixon JSY AU RC 8.00 20.00
219 Christian Hackenberg JSY AU RC 8.00 20.00
220 Sterling Shepard JSY AU RC 10.00 25.00
221 Devontae Booker JSY AU RC 10.00 25.00
222 Braxton Miller JSY AU RC 8.00 20.00
223 Jordan Howard JSY AU RC 20.00 50.00
224 Kenny Lawler JSY AU RC 12.00 30.00
225 Kenyan Drake JSY AU RC 12.00 30.00
226 Leonte Carroo JSY AU RC 8.00 20.00
227 Daniel Lasco JSY AU RC 8.00 20.00
228 Paul Perkins JSY AU RC 8.00 20.00
229 C.J. Prosise JSY AU RC 8.00 20.00
230 Aaron Burbridge JSY AU RC 8.00 20.00
231 Dak Prescott JSY AU RC 40.00 80.00
232 Jonathan Williams JSY AU RC 10.00 25.00
233 Keyarris Garrett JSY AU RC 8.00 20.00
234 Kelvin Taylor JSY AU RC 8.00 20.00
235 Malcolm Mitchell JSY AU RC 15.00 40.00
236 Jordan Payton JSY AU RC 8.00 20.00
237 Cardale Jones JSY AU RC 8.00 20.00
238 Jacoby Brissett JSY AU RC 10.00 25.00
239 Josh Ferguson JSY AU RC 8.00 20.00
240 Kolby Listenbee JSY AU RC 8.00 20.00
241 Kenyan Drake JSY 6.00 15.00
242 Knile Davis JSY 6.00 15.00
243 Knute Rockne JSY 30.00 60.00
244 LeGarrette Blount JSY 8.00 20.00
245 LeSean McCoy JSY 10.00 25.00
246 Le'Veon Bell JSY 8.00 20.00
247 Marcus Allen JSY 8.00 20.00
248 Markus Wheaton JSY 6.00 15.00
249 Matt Forte JSY 6.00 15.00
250 Myles Jack JSY 5.00 12.00
251 Nick Foles JSY 8.00 20.00
252 Paul Perkins JSY 4.00 10.00
253 Phillip Dorsett JSY 6.00 15.00
254 Philly Brown JSY 6.00 15.00
255 Rob Gronkowski JSY 10.00 25.00
256 Robert Woods JSY 8.00 20.00
257 Rod Woodson JSY 8.00 20.00
258 Ronnie Hillman JSY 6.00 15.00
259 Ryan Shazier JSY 6.00 15.00
260 Sebastian Janikowski JSY 6.00 15.00
261 Stefon Diggs JSY 8.00 20.00
262 T.J. Yeldon JSY 6.00 15.00
263 Tavon Austin JSY 6.00 15.00
264 Thomas Rawls JSY 6.00 15.00
265 Travis Benjamin JSY 6.00 15.00
266 Tyrod Taylor JSY 8.00 20.00
267 Vontaze Burfict JSY 4.00 10.00
269 Tre Madden JSY 6.00 15.00

2016 Panini National Treasures Collegiate Colossal Signature Materials

*ROOKIES/99: .4X TO 1X BASIC JSY AU RC/99

2016 Panini National Treasures Collegiate Silver

*VETS: .6X TO 1.5X BASIC CARDS
*ROOK JSY AU/25: .6X TO 1.5X BASIC JSY AU/99
205 Ezekiel Elliott JSY AU 400.00 800.00

2016 Panini National Treasures Collegiate Combo Materials Booklet

1 Alex Collins 5.00 12.00
2 Braxton Miller 4.00 10.00
3 Brandon Allen 4.00 10.00
4 Cardale Jones 4.00 10.00
5 Carson Wentz
6 Chris Moore 5.00 12.00
7 Christian Hackenberg 4.00 10.00
8 Cody Kessler 4.00 10.00
9 Connor Cook 5.00 12.00
10 Corey Coleman 6.00 15.00
11 Dak Prescott 20.00 50.00
12 DeAndre Washington 4.00 10.00
13 Derrick Henry 10.00 25.00
14 Devontae Booker 5.00 12.00
15 Ezekiel Elliott 20.00 50.00
16 Huntor Henry 5.00 12.00
17 Wendell Smallwood 4.00 10.00
18 Jared Goff 12.00 30.00
19 Joey Bosa 8.00 20.00
20 Jonathan Williams 5.00 12.00
21 Jordan Howard 10.00 25.00
22 Josh Doctson 5.00 12.00
23 Keenan Reynolds 5.00 12.00
24 Tyler Boyd 5.00 12.00
25 Kenyan Drake 6.00 15.00
26 Kevin Hogan 5.00 12.00
27 Laquon Treadwell 5.00 12.00
28 Leonte Carroo 4.00 10.00
29 Sterling Shepard 5.00 12.00
30 Michael Thomas 8.00 20.00
31 Paul Perkins 4.00 10.00
32 Trevor Davis 4.00 10.00
33 Pharoh Cooper 4.00 10.00
34 Ricardo Louis 4.00 10.00

2016 Panini National Treasures Collegiate Combo Materials Signatures Booklet

1 Alex Collins/99 10.00 25.00
2 Braxton Miller/99 8.00 20.00
3 Brandon Allen/99 8.00 20.00
4 Cardale Jones/99 8.00 20.00
5 Carson Wentz/99 50.00 100.00
6 Chris Moore/99 10.00 25.00
7 Christian Hackenberg/99 8.00 20.00
8 Cody Kessler/99 8.00 20.00
9 Connor Cook/99 10.00 25.00
10 Corey Coleman/99 12.00 30.00
11 Dak Prescott/99 40.00 80.00
12 DeAndre Washington/99 8.00 20.00
13 Derrick Henry/99 20.00 50.00
14 Devontae Booker/99 10.00 25.00
15 Ezekiel Elliott/99 100.00 200.00
16 Hunter Henry/99 10.00 25.00
17 Wendell Smallwood/99 8.00 20.00
18 Jared Goff/49 30.00 125.00
19 Joey Bosa/99 15.00 40.00
20 Jonathan Williams/99 10.00 25.00
21 Jordan Howard/99 20.00 50.00
22 Josh Doctson/99 10.00 25.00
23 Keenan Reynolds/99 10.00 25.00
24 Tyler Boyd/99 10.00 25.00
25 Kenyan Drake/99 12.00 30.00
26 Kevin Hogan/99 10.00 25.00
27 Laquon Treadwell/99 10.00 25.00
28 Leonte Carroo/99 8.00 20.00
29 Sterling Shepard/99 10.00 25.00
30 Michael Thomas/99 15.00 40.00
31 Paul Perkins/99 8.00 20.00
32 Trevor Davis/99 8.00 20.00
33 Pharoh Cooper/99 8.00 20.00
34 Ricardo Louis/99 8.00 20.00

2016 Panini National Treasures Collegiate Die Cut Signatures

1 Joey Bosa 10.00 25.00
2 Jared Goff 30.00 80.00
3 Laquon Treadwell 6.00 15.00
4 Carson Wentz 50.00 125.00
5 Ezekiel Elliott 150.00 250.00
6 Paxton Lynch 5.00 12.00
7 Corey Coleman 8.00 20.00
8 Connor Cook 6.00 15.00
9 Hunter Henry 6.00 15.00
10 Michael Thomas 10.00 25.00
11 Josh Doctson 6.00 15.00
12 Derrick Henry 12.00 30.00
13 Tyler Boyd 6.00 15.00
15 Pharoh Cooper 5.00 12.00
16 Alex Collins 6.00 15.00
17 Rashard Higgins 5.00 12.00
18 Kenneth Dixon 5.00 12.00
19 Christian Hackenberg 5.00 12.00
20 Sterling Shepard 6.00 15.00
21 Devontae Booker 6.00 15.00
22 Braxton Miller 5.00 12.00
23 Jordan Howard 12.00 30.00
24 Kenny Lawler 8.00 20.00
25 Kenyan Drake 8.00 20.00
26 Leonte Carroo 5.00 12.00
27 Nick Vannett 5.00 12.00
28 Paul Perkins 5.00 12.00
29 Jordan Payton 5.00 12.00
30 Aaron Burbridge 5.00 12.00
31 Dak Prescott 30.00 60.00
32 Jonathan Williams 6.00 15.00
33 Keyarris Garrett 5.00 12.00
34 Kelvin Taylor 5.00 12.00
35 Malcolm Mitchell 5.00 12.00
36 Kolby Listenbee 5.00 12.00
37 Cardale Jones 5.00 12.00
38 Daniel Lasco 5.00 12.00
39 Josh Ferguson 5.00 12.00
40 Keith Marshall 5.00 12.00

2016 Panini National Treasures Collegiate Dual Team Materials

1 K.Drake/D.Henry/99 8.00 20.00
2 D.Robinson/K.Taylor/99 3.00 8.00
3 J.Howard/N.Sudfeld/99 8.00 20.00
5 D.Bush/A.Burns/15 8.00 20.00
6 A.Burbridge/C.Cook/99 4.00 10.00
7 D.Wilson/D.Prescott/99 15.00 40.00
8 P.Perkins/J.Payton/99 3.00 8.00
9 E.Elliott/D.Prescott/99 15.00 40.00
11 D.Robinson/K.Hogan/99 4.00 10.00
12 J.Goff/P.Cooper/99 10.00 25.00
13 J.Brissett/M.Mitchell/99 4.00 10.00
14 D.Lasco/M.Thomas/99 6.00 15.00
15 P.Perkins/S.Shepard/99 4.00 10.00
17 C.Cook/D.Washington/99 4.00 10.00
18 C.Wentz/W.Smallwood/99 20.00 50.00
19 H.Henry/J.Bosa/99 6.00 15.00
20 J.Doctson/N.Sudfeld/99 4.00 10.00
21 M.Mariota/B.Marshall/25 8.00 20.00
22 B.Petty/C.Coleman/99 5.00 12.00
23 W.Smallwood/K.White/99 3.00 8.00
24 K.Benjamin/R.Greene/25 6.00 15.00
25 D.Freeman/K.Williams/25 6.00 15.00
26 J.Jones/A.Cooper/25 8.00 20.00
27 A.Rodgers/J.Goff/25 30.00 80.00
28 G.Olsen/J.Graham/25 8.00 20.00
29 J.Bellino/R.Staubach/99 6.00 15.00
30 C.Hcknbrg/A.Robinson/99 4.00 10.00
31 J.Winston/J.Goff/99 10.00 25.00
32 C.Wentz/M.Mariota/99 20.00 50.00
33 E.Elliott/T.Gurley/99 15.00 40.00
34 A.Cooper/D.Carr/99 5.00 12.00
35 D.Hopkins/B.Osweiler/25 6.00 15.00
36 J.Winston/M.Evans/99 5.00 12.00
37 T.Bridgewater/S.Diggs/99 4.00 10.00
38 T.Gurley/J.Goff/99 10.00 25.00
39 A.Rodgers/E.Lacy/25 15.00 40.00
52 S.Shepard/B.Hield/99 4.00 10.00

2016 Panini National Treasures Collegiate Material Signatures

1 Cody Kessler/99 5.00 12.00
2 DeAndre Washington/99 5.00 12.00
3 Kevin Hogan/99 6.00 15.00
4 Chris Moore/99 6.00 15.00
5 Demarcus Robinson/99 5.00 12.00
6 Keenan Reynolds/99 6.00 15.00
7 Ricardo Louis/99 5.00 12.00
8 Trevor Davis/99 5.00 12.00
9 Wendell Smallwood/99 5.00 12.00
10 D.J. Foster/99 6.00 15.00
11 Cayleb Jones/99 5.00 12.00
12 Tre Madden/99 5.00 12.00
14 Aaron Rodgers/25
16 Allen Hurns/25 8.00 20.00
18 Ameer Abdullah/25 8.00 20.00
19 Andrew Luck/25 50.00 100.00
22 Brett Hundley/25 8.00 20.00
23 Brock Osweiler/25 8.00 20.00
24 Champ Bailey/25 10.00 25.00
25 Clive Walford/99 5.00 12.00
27 Damarious Randall/99 5.00 12.00
28 Dan Marino/25 75.00 150.00
29 De'Anthony Thomas/49 6.00 15.00
30 Derek Carr/25 30.00 60.00
31 Devin Funchess/25 8.00 20.00
32 Devin Hester/25 10.00 25.00
33 Devin Smith/49 6.00 15.00
34 Doug Baldwin/25 10.00 25.00
35 Doug Flutie/25 10.00 25.00
36 EJ Manuel/25 8.00 20.00
37 Eli Harold/99 5.00 12.00
38 Eric Dickerson/25 25.00 50.00
39 Eric Kendricks/99 5.00 12.00
40 Frank Clark/99 5.00 12.00
41 Frank Gore/25 10.00 25.00
44 Keshawn Martin/25 8.00 20.00
45 Lance Kendricks/25 8.00 20.00
46 Lawrence Taylor/25
47 Malcolm Brown/99 5.00 12.00
48 Devonta Freeman/25 10.00 25.00
49 Marcus Smith/99 5.00 12.00
50 Mario Edwards Jr./99 5.00 12.00
51 Marqise Lee/25 8.00 20.00
52 Marshall Faulk/15
53 Matt Barkley/25 8.00 20.00
55 Micah Hyde/99 5.00 12.00
56 Nelson Agholor/25 8.00 20.00
58 Reggie Wayne/25 10.00 25.00
59 Richard Sherman/25 20.00 40.00
60 Roger Staubach/25 60.00 125.00
61 Troy Aikman/17 50.00 100.00
62 Xavier Rhodes/25 8.00 20.00
63 Gale Sayers/25
64 Christian Kirksey/99 5.00 12.00
65 Terron Ward/99 5.00 12.00
66 Marcus Mariota/25 40.00 80.00

2016 Panini National Treasures Collegiate Rookie Silhouettes Materials

2 Jared Goff 15.00 40.00
3 Carson Wentz 25.00 60.00
4 Joey Bosa 5.00 12.00
5 Ezekiel Elliott 12.00 30.00
6 Derrick Henry 6.00 15.00

2016 Panini National Treasures Collegiate Signatures

1 Tyler Ervin/99 4.00 10.00
2 Jeff Driskel/99 4.00 10.00
3 A.J. Green/25 20.00 40.00
5 Andy Dalton/25 8.00 20.00
6 Antonio Brown/25 30.00 60.00
7 Archie Manning/25 15.00 40.00
8 Barry Sanders/15
11 Blake Bortles/25 6.00 15.00
13 Bob Lilly/25 12.00 30.00
15 Curtis Martin/25 12.00 30.00
18 Earl Campbell/25 15.00 40.00
19 Edgerrin James/25 20.00 40.00
21 Emmitt Smith/5
23 Frank Thomas/25 30.00 80.00
24 Fred Biletnikoff/25 10.00 25.00
25 Fred Taylor/25 12.00 30.00
30 Joe Greene/25
32 Jordan Matthews/25 8.00 20.00
33 Justin Forsett/25 8.00 20.00
34 Kirk Cousins/25 25.00 50.00
36 Latavius Murray/25 6.00 15.00
37 Lawrence Taylor/25 25.00 50.00
38 Luke Kuechly/25 10.00 25.00
39 Marshawn Lynch/25 15.00 40.00
40 Matt Jones/99 5.00 12.00
45 Paxton Lynch/25
48 Ray Lewis/25
49 Reggie Wayne/25 8.00 20.00
50 Ricky Williams/25 25.00 50.00
51 Teddy Bridgewater/25 8.00 20.00
52 Terrell Davis/25 8.00 20.00
56 Y.A. Tittle/99 8.00 20.00
57 Bob Griese/25 15.00 40.00
58 Boomer Esiason/25 8.00 20.00
60 Dan Fouts/25 20.00 50.00
63 Jim Kiick/99 4.00 10.00

2016 Panini National Treasures Collegiate Team Quad Materials

1 Lsco/Dvs/Gff/Lwlr 12.00 30.00
2 Mllr/Ellt/Bsa/Thms 25.00 60.00
3 Grn/Dctsn/Lstnbee/Bykn 5.00 12.00
4 Wshngtn/Clmn/Dctsn/Shprd 8.00 20.00
5 Brbrdge/Ck/Ellt/Hwrd 25.00 60.00
6 Prsctt/Ellt/Trdwll/Cpr 25.00 60.00
7 Hnry/Dctsn/Clmn/Hnry 10.00 25.00
8 Hpr/Gff/Crvns/Bcknr 12.00 30.00
9 Pytn/Ls/Clmn/Hggns 6.00 15.00
11 Cpr/Yldn/Hnry/Drke 10.00 25.00
12 Clmn/Ltmr/Hwrd/Sdfld 8.00 20.00
13 Hpr/Cjste/Hgn/Mntgmry 5.00 12.00
14 Alln/Ksslr/Wllms/Aghlr 4.00 10.00
15 Pyne/Ls/Cts/Msn 4.00 10.00
16 Mrry/Cnly/Mtchll/Grly 6.00 15.00
17 Shw/Clwny/Dvs/Cpr 4.00 10.00
18 Frmn/Wllms/Wnstn/Bnjmn 6.00 15.00
19 Cllns/Alln/Hnry/Wllms 5.00 12.00
20 Wntz/Wnstn/Mrta/Gff 15.00 40.00
21 Hnry/Ellt/Grdn/Grly 25.00 60.00

2016 Panini National Treasures Collegiate Team Trio Materials

2 Hgn/Hpr/Cjste/99 5.00 12.00
3 Ksslr/Crvns/Mddn/99 4.00 10.00
4 Mre/Rynlds/Dxo/99 5.00 12.00
5 Jns/Lstnbe/Wllms/99 5.00 12.00
6 Brvrmn/Bsh/Hwrd/99 10.00 25.00
7 Drke/Dghty/Crroo/99 6.00 15.00
8 Hnry/Wnstn/Mrta/99 10.00 25.00
9 Smth/Ellt/Jns/99 40.00 60.00
10 Rbnsn/Tylr/Jns/99 5.00 12.00
11 Brbrdge/Ck/Lngfrd/99 5.00 12.00
12 Pytn/Prkns/Hndly/99 4.00 10.00
13 Elwy/Lck/Shrmn/25
14 Hgn/Lck/Elwy/25

2017 Panini National Treasures Collegiate

1 Aaron Rodgers 6.00 15.00
2 Andrew Luck 4.00 10.00
3 Barry Sanders 5.00 12.00
4 Bo Jackson 4.00 10.00
5 Brett Favre 6.00 15.00
6 Carson Wentz 4.00 10.00
7 Dak Prescott 3.00 8.00
8 Dan Marino 6.00 15.00
9 Derrick Henry 2.50 6.00
10 Emmitt Smith 5.00 12.00
11 Ezekiel Elliott 4.00 10.00
12 Jared Goff 3.00 8.00
13 Jerry Rice 5.00 12.00
14 Jim Thorpe 4.00 10.00
15 Joe Namath 4.00 10.00
16 Joey Bosa 3.00 8.00
17 John Elway 5.00 12.00
18 Marcus Mariota 3.00 8.00
19 Odell Beckham Jr. 3.00 8.00
20 Paxton Lynch 2.00 5.00
21 Peyton Manning 6.00 15.00
22 Red Grange 4.00 10.00
23 Russell Wilson 4.00 10.00
24 Tim Tebow 3.00 8.00
25 Tom Brady 8.00 20.00
28 Amari Cooper JSY/25 5.00 12.00
29 Andrew Luck JSY/25 6.00 15.00
30 Dan Marino JSY/25 10.00 25.00
31 Derek Carr JSY/25 5.00 12.00
32 Eric Dickerson JSY/25 5.00 12.00
33 Gale Sayers JSY/25 5.00 12.00
34 Ezekiel Elliott JSY/25 6.00 15.00
35 Jared Goff JSY/25 5.00 12.00
36 Joey Bosa JSY/25 5.00 12.00
37 John Hannah JSY/25 3.00 8.00
38 John Elway JSY/25 8.00 20.00
39 Julio Jones JSY/25 5.00 12.00
40 Le'Veon Bell JSY/25 4.00 10.00
41 Marcus Allen JSY/25 4.00 10.00
42 Marcus Mariota JSY/25 5.00 12.00
43 Marshall Faulk JSY/25 4.00 10.00
45 Rob Gronkowski JSY/25 5.00 12.00
46 Rod Woodson JSY/25 4.00 10.00
47 Roger Staubach JSY/25 6.00 15.00
48 Thurman Thomas JSY/25 4.00 10.00
49 Terry Bradshaw JSY/25 8.00 20.00
50 Troy Aikman JSY/25 6.00 15.00
94 Micah Hyde JSY AU/49 10.00 25.00
101 Dalvin Cook JSY AU/99 40.00 80.00
102 Mike Williams JSY AU/99 8.00 20.00
103 Leonard Fournette JSY AU/99 60.00 125.00
104 Mitchell Trubisky JSY AU/99 60.00 125.00
105 Deshaun Watson JSY AU/99 60.00 125.00
106 Corey Davis JSY AU/99 8.00 20.00
107 John Ross III JSY AU/99 6.00 15.00
108 Christian McCaffrey JSY AU/49 40.00 80.00
109 JuJu Smith-Schuster JSY AU/99 12.00 30.00
110 DeShone Kizer JSY AU/99 5.00 12.00
111 Dede Westbrook JSY AU/99 5.00 12.00
112 Cooper Kupp JSY AU/99 8.00 20.00
113 Curtis Samuel JSY AU/99 6.00 15.00
114 D'Onta Foreman JSY AU/99 6.00 15.00
115 Amara Darboh JSY AU/99 5.00 12.00
116 Isaiah Ford JSY AU/99 5.00 12.00
117 Zay Jones JSY AU/99 6.00 15.00
118 Malachi Dupre JSY AU/99 5.00 12.00
119 Patrick Mahomes II JSY AU/99 400.00 800.00
120 Samaje Perine JSY AU/99 5.00 12.00
121 Chris Godwin JSY AU/99 6.00 15.00
122 Joe Mixon JSY AU/99 10.00 25.00
124 Artavis Scott JSY AU/99 5.00 12.00
125 Wayne Gallman JSY AU/99 6.00 15.00
126 Kareem Hunt JSY AU/99 60.00 125.00
127 Stacy Coley JSY AU/99 5.00 12.00
128 Jeremy McNichols JSY AU/99 5.00 12.00
129 Corey Clement JSY AU/99 6.00 15.00
130 Ryan Switzer JSY AU/99 6.00 15.00
131 James Conner JSY AU/99 10.00 25.00
132 Chad Kelly JSY AU/99 50.00 100.00
133 O.J. Howard JSY AU/99 6.00 15.00
135 Evan Engram JSY AU/99 6.00 15.00
137 Alvin Kamara JSY AU/99 20.00 50.00
138 Brad Kaaya JSY AU/99 5.00 12.00
139 Davis Webb JSY AU/99 5.00 12.00
140 Donnel Pumphrey JSY AU/99 6.00 15.00
144 Deshaun Watson SL JSY/99 12.00 30.00
145 Mike Williams SL JSY/99 5.00 12.00
146 Wayne Gallman SL JSY/99 4.00 10.00
164 Adoree' Jackson AU/99 5.00 12.00
165 Carlos Henderson AU/99 4.00 10.00
166 Taywan Taylor AU/99 4.00 10.00
167 Marlon Mack AU/99 6.00 15.00
168 Kenny Golladay AU/99 6.00 15.00
169 Brian Hill AU/99 4.00 10.00
170 Matthew Dayes AU/99 4.00 10.00
171 Josh Malone AU/99 4.00 10.00
172 Malik Hooker AU/99 4.00 10.00
173 Marshon Lattimore AU/99 5.00 12.00

2017 Panini National Treasures Collegiate Silver

*VETS/25: .6X TO 1.5X BASIC CARDS/99
*JSY AU/25: .6X TO 1.5X BASIC CARDS/99
104 Mitchell Trubisky JSY AU/25 100.00 200.00

2017 Panini National Treasures Collegiate Combo Material Signatures Booklet

1 Dalvin Cook/30 30.00 80.00
2 Mike Williams/30 20.00 50.00
3 Leonard Fournette/30 90.00 150.00
4 Mitchell Trubisky/30 60.00 150.00
5 Deshaun Watson/30 90.00 150.00
6 Corey Davis/70 12.00 30.00
7 John Ross III/70 10.00 25.00
8 Christian McCaffrey/49 40.00 100.00
9 JuJu Smith-Schuster/70 20.00 50.00
10 DeShone Kizer/30 12.00 30.00
11 Dede Westbrook/75 8.00 20.00
12 Cooper Kupp/75 12.00 30.00
13 Curtis Samuel/75 10.00 25.00
14 D'Onta Foreman/75 10.00 25.00
15 Amara Darboh/25 12.00 30.00
16 Carlos Henderson/75 8.00 20.00
17 Zay Jones/70 10.00 25.00
18 Marlon Mack/25 20.00 50.00
19 Patrick Mahomes II/25 250.00 500.00
20 Samaje Perine/65 8.00 20.00
21 Chris Godwin/70 10.00 25.00
22 Joe Mixon/75 15.00 40.00
23 Davis Webb/30 12.00 30.00
24 Joe Williams/25 12.00 30.00
25 Wayne Gallman/25 15.00 40.00
26 Kareem Hunt/75 30.00 80.00
27 R. Joshua Dobbs/25 15.00 40.00
28 Jeremy McNichols/25 12.00 30.00
29 Jamaal Williams/25 30.00 60.00
30 Mack Hollins/25 12.00 30.00
31 James Conner/70 15.00 40.00
32 C.J. Beathard/70 8.00 20.00
33 O.J. Howard/65 10.00 25.00
34 Evan Engram/70 10.00 25.00
35 Alvin Kamara/70 30.00 80.00
36 Nathan Peterman/25 15.00 40.00

2017 Panini National Treasures Collegiate Dual Signatures

4 C.Beathard/G.Kittle 60.00 125.00
5 D.King/M.Hyde 50.00 100.00

2017 Panini National Treasures Collegiate Notable Nicknames

1 Peyton Manning 200.00 350.00
2 Adrian Peterson 40.00 80.00
5 Brett Favre 75.00 150.00
6 John Elway 75.00 80.00
7 Jameis Winston 40.00 80.00
9 Mitchell Trubisky 75.00 150.00
10 Samaje Perine 25.00 50.00

2017 Panini National Treasures Collegiate Silhouette Signatures

3 Carson Wentz/25 50.00 100.00
4 Dak Prescott/25 25.00 60.00
6 Derrick Henry/25 20.00 50.00
7 Ezekiel Elliott/25 50.00 100.00
8 Jared Goff/25 25.00 60.00
10 Micah Hyde/25 15.00 40.00

2017 Panini National Treasures Collegiate Silhouettes

*SILHOUETTE/99: .4X TO 1X BASIC JSY AU/99
*SILHOUETTE/49: .5X TO 1.2X BASIC JSY AU/99
*SILHOUETTE/25: .6X TO 1.5X BASIC JSY AU/99
3 Carson Wentz/25 10.00 25.00
4 Dak Prescott/25 8.00 20.00
6 Derrick Henry/25 6.00 15.00
7 Ezekiel Elliott/25 10.00 25.00

2017 Panini National Treasures Collegiate Silhouettes Prime

*SIL PRIME/25: .6X TO 1.5X BASIC JSY AU

2017 Panini National Treasures Collegiate Team Materials Combo

1 D.Prescott/E.Elliott/99 6.00 15.00
2 A.Kamara/R.Dobbs/99 6.00 15.00
3 C.Beathard/D.King/49 8.00 20.00
4 A.Stewart/O.Howard/99 6.00 15.00
5 C.Samuel/N.Brown/99 4.00 10.00
6 C.Hansen/D.Webb/99 3.00 8.00
7 D.Cook/T.Rudolph/99 8.00 20.00
8 C.Kelly/E.Engram/99 4.00 10.00
9 J.Conner/N.Peterman/99 6.00 15.00
10 D.King/M.Hyde/49 5.00 12.00

2017 Panini National Treasures Collegiate Team Materials Quad

1 Wtsn/Gllmn/Lggtt/Wllms 10.00 25.00
2 Hnry/Drke/Hwrd/Stwrt 4.00 10.00
3 Smth/Ellt/Thms/Jns 6.00 15.00
4 Frmn/Grne/Wnstn/Bnjmn 4.00 10.00
5 Mrta/Grdn/Cpr/Bykn 5.00 12.00
6 Drbh/Pprs/Btt/Chssn 5.00 12.00
7 Bckhm/Frntte/Dpre/Drl 10.00 25.00
8 Brwn/Sml/Ellt/Bsa 6.00 15.00
9 Mxn/Wstbrk/Prne/Shprd 6.00 15.00
10 Wtsn/Kzr/Trbsky/Mhms 10.00 25.00

2018 Panini National Treasures Collegiate

1 Aaron Rodgers 6.00 15.00
2 Barry Sanders 5.00 12.00
3 Brett Favre 6.00 15.00
4 Brian Bosworth 2.50 6.00
5 Calvin Johnson 3.00 8.00
6 Charles Woodson 3.00 8.00
7 Clay Matthews 2.50 6.00
8 Dak Prescott 3.00 8.00
9 Dan Marino 6.00 15.00
10 Earl Dutch Clark 2.50 6.00
11 Emmitt Smith 5.00 12.00
12 Ezekiel Elliott 4.00 10.00
13 Herschel Walker 3.00 8.00
14 J.J. Watt 3.00 8.00
15 Jerry Rice 5.00 12.00
16 Joe Namath 4.00 10.00
17 John Elway 5.00 12.00
18 LaDainian Tomlinson 2.50 6.00
19 Leonard Fournette 3.00 8.00
20 Nick Foles 2.50 6.00
21 Odell Beckham Jr. 3.00 8.00
22 Peyton Manning 6.00 15.00
23 Red Grange 4.00 10.00
24 Tim Tebow 3.00 8.00
25 Tom Brady 8.00 20.00
26 Amari Cooper JSY/99 5.00 12.00
27 Corey Clement JSY/99 3.00 8.00
28 Dan Marino JSY/49 12.00 30.00
29 Derek Carr JSY/49 6.00 15.00
30 Deshaun Watson JSY/99 6.00 15.00
31 Eric Dickerson JSY/99 5.00 12.00
32 Ezekiel Elliott JSY/99 6.00 15.00
33 Herschel Walker JSY/99 5.00 12.00
35 Joey Bosa JSY/99 5.00 12.00
36 John Elway JSY/49 10.00 25.00
37 John Hannah JSY/99 3.00 8.00
38 Julio Jones JSY/99 5.00 12.00
39 Kareem Hunt JSY/99 4.00 10.00
40 Le'Veon Bell JSY/99 4.00 10.00
41 Leonard Fournette JSY/99 5.00 12.00
42 Marcus Allen JSY/99 5.00 12.00
43 Marcus Mariota JSY/99 5.00 12.00
44 Marshall Faulk JSY/99 4.00 10.00
45 Nick Foles JSY/49 5.00 12.00
46 Patrick Mahomes II JSY/99 12.00 30.00
47 Ricky Williams JSY/99 4.00 10.00
48 Rob Gronkowski JSY/25 8.00 20.00
49 Roger Staubach JSY/49 8.00 20.00
50 Troy Aikman JSY/49 8.00 20.00
51 Ahman Green AU/25 8.00 20.00
53 Billy Cannon AU/49 5.00 12.00
54 Charles White AU/31 6.00 15.00
55 Chris Spielman AU/49 10.00 25.00
58 Earl Campbell AU/25 10.00 25.00
61 Greg Pruitt AU/99 6.00 15.00
63 Joe Washington AU/99 4.00 10.00
66 Marcus Dupree AU/99 10.00 25.00
68 Michael Vick AU/25
72 Ron Dayne AU/49
75 Troy Smith AU/99 12.00 30.00
77 Alvin Kamara JSY AU/49 25.00 50.00
89 Joe Bellino JSY AU/25 10.00 25.00
97 Ricky Williams JSY AU/25
100 Vinny Testaverde JSY AU/49 8.00 20.00
101 Josh Rosen JSY AU/99 RC 40.00 80.00
102 Sam Darnold JSY AU/99 RC 125.00 250.00
103 Josh Allen JSY AU/99 RC 75.00 150.00
105 Baker Mayfield JSY AU/99 RC 250.00 500.00
106 Saquon Barkley JSY AU/49 RC 125.00 250.00
107 Derrius Guice JSY AU/99 RC 10.00 25.00
108 D.J. Moore JSY AU/99 RC 10.00 25.00
109 Hayden Hurst JSY AU/99 RC 6.00 15.00
110 Nick Chubb JSY AU/99 RC 15.00 40.00
111 Mason Rudolph JSY AU/99 RC 12.00 30.00
112 Ronald Jones II JSY AU/99 RC 5.00 12.00
113 Christian Kirk JSY AU/99 RC 8.00 20.00
114 Calvin Ridley JSY AU/99 RC 12.00 30.00
115 James Washington JSY AU/99 RC 10.00 25.00
116 Courtland Sutton JSY AU/99 RC 8.00 20.00
117 Deon Cain JSY AU/99 RC 6.00 15.00
118 Simmie Cobbs Jr. JSY AU/99 RC 8.00 20.00
119 Dante Pettis JSY AU/99 RC 8.00 20.00
120 D.J. Chark JSY AU/99 RC 6.00 15.00
121 Allen Lazard JSY AU/99 RC 5.00 12.00
122 Anthony Miller JSY AU/99 RC 8.00 20.00
123 Luke Falk JSY AU/99 RC 6.00 15.00
124 Rashaad Penny JSY AU/99 RC 8.00 20.00
126 Nyheim Hines JSY AU/99 RC 6.00 15.00
127 Deontay Burnett JSY AU/99 RC 6.00 15.00
128 Michael Gallup JSY AU/99 RC 15.00 40.00
129 Josh Adams JSY AU/99 RC 10.00 25.00
130 Kerryon Johnson JSY AU/99 RC 8.00 20.00
131 Trey Quinn JSY AU/99 RC 5.00 12.00
132 Sony Michel JSY AU/99 RC 15.00 40.00
133 Auden Tate JSY AU/99 RC 5.00 12.00
134 Royce Freeman JSY AU/99 RC 6.00 15.00
135 John Kelly JSY AU/99 RC 6.00 15.00
136 Bo Scarbrough JSY AU/99 RC 6.00 15.00
137 J.T. Barrett JSY AU/99 RC 12.00 30.00
138 Marcell Ateman JSY AU/99 RC 6.00 15.00
139 Akrum Wadley JSY AU/99 RC 5.00 12.00
140 Justin Jackson JSY AU/99 RC 6.00 15.00
141 Mark Andrews JSY AU/99 RC 8.00 20.00
142 Jaylen Samuels JSY AU/99 RC 6.00 15.00
143 Kalen Ballage JSY AU/99 RC 6.00 15.00
144 Kamryn Pettway JSY AU/99 RC 8.00 20.00
145 J'Mon Moore JSY AU/99 RC 5.00 12.00
146 DaeSean Hamilton JSY AU/49 RC 8.00 20.00
147 Nic Shimonek JSY AU/99 RC 8.00 20.00
148 Kurt Benkert JSY AU/99 RC 6.00 15.00
149 Chase Litton JSY AU/99 RC 6.00 15.00
151 Tre'Quan Smith AU/99 RC 8.00 20.00
152 Cedrick Wilson Jr. AU/99 RC 5.00 12.00
153 Kyle Lauletta AU/99 RC 8.00 20.00
154 Jaleel Scott AU/99 RC 5.00 12.00
155 Keke Coutee AU/99 RC 6.00 15.00
156 Marquez Valdes-Scantling AU/99 RC 6.00 15.00
157 Javon Wims AU/99 RC 12.00 30.00
158 Jake Wieneke AU/99 RC 6.00 15.00
159 Daurice Fountain AU/99 RC 6.00 15.00
160 Ito Smith AU/99 RC 6.00 15.00
161 Dylan Cantrell AU/99 RC 5.00 12.00
162 Dallas Goedert AU/99 RC 6.00 15.00
163 Denzel Ward AU/99 RC 12.00 30.00

2018 Panini National Treasures Collegiate Red

*RED/25: .6X TO 1.5X BASIC CARDS/99

2018 Panini National Treasures Collegiate Silver

*VETS/49: .5X TO 1.2X BASIC CARDS/99
*VET JSY/25: .6X TO 1.5X BASIC CARDS/99
*VET JSY/25: .5X TO 1.2X BASIC CARDS/49
*VET AU/25: .6X TO 1.5X BASIC CARDS/99
*VET AU/25: .5X TO 1.2X BASIC CARDS/49
*VET AU/20: .5X TO 1.2X BASIC CARDS/31
*VET JSY AU/25: .5X TO 1.2X BASIC CARDS/49
*RC JSY AU/25: .6X TO 1.5X BASIC CARDS/99
*RC JSY AU/25: .5X TO 1.2X BASIC CARDS/49
101 Josh Rosen JSY AU/25 100.00 200.00
102 Sam Darnold JSY AU/25 150.00 300.00

2018 Panini National Treasures Collegiate College Silhouette Signatures

101 Josh Rosen/49 20.00 50.00
102 Sam Darnold/49 40.00 100.00
103 Josh Allen/49 40.00 80.00
105 Baker Mayfield/49 100.00 200.00
106 Saquon Barkley/25 100.00 200.00
107 Derrius Guice/99 10.00 25.00
108 D.J. Moore/99 10.00 25.00
109 Mike White/99 6.00 15.00
110 Nick Chubb/99 15.00 40.00
111 Mason Rudolph/99 12.00 30.00
112 Ronald Jones II/99 5.00 12.00
113 Christian Kirk/99 8.00 20.00
114 Calvin Ridley/49 15.00 40.00
115 James Washington/99 10.00 25.00
116 Courtland Sutton/99 8.00 20.00
117 Deon Cain/49 8.00 20.00
118 Simmie Cobbs Jr./99 8.00 20.00
119 Dante Pettis/99 8.00 20.00
120 D.J. Chark/99 6.00 15.00
121 Allen Lazard/99 5.00 12.00
122 Anthony Miller/99 8.00 20.00
123 Luke Falk/99 6.00 15.00
124 Rashaad Penny/99 8.00 20.00
126 Nyheim Hines/99 6.00 15.00
127 Deontay Burnett/99 6.00 15.00
128 Michael Gallup/49 12.00 30.00
129 Josh Adams/49 12.00 30.00
130 Kerryon Johnson/99 8.00 20.00
131 Trey Quinn/99 5.00 12.00
132 Sony Michel/99 15.00 40.00
133 Auden Tate/99 5.00 12.00
134 Royce Freeman/99 6.00 15.00
135 John Kelly/99 6.00 15.00
136 Bo Scarbrough/99 6.00 15.00
137 J.T. Barrett/99 8.00 20.00
138 Marcell Ateman/99 6.00 15.00
139 Akrum Wadley/99 5.00 12.00
140 Justin Jackson/99 6.00 15.00
141 Mark Andrews/99 8.00 20.00
142 Jaylen Samuels/99 6.00 15.00
143 Kalen Ballage/99 6.00 15.00
144 Kamryn Pettway/99 8.00 20.00
145 J'Mon Moore/49 6.00 15.00
147 Robert Foster/99 5.00 12.00
148 Kurt Benkert/49 8.00 20.00
149 Riley Ferguson/25 12.00 30.00

2018 Panini National Treasures Collegiate College Silhouette Signatures Prime

*PRIME/25: .6X TO 1.5X BASIC JSY AU/99
*PRIME/25: .5X TO 1.2X BASIC JSY AU/49

2018 Panini National Treasures Collegiate Combo Material Signatures Booklet

1 Calvin Ridley/62 15.00 40.00
2 Christian Kirk/65 8.00 20.00
3 Courtland Sutton/76 8.00 20.00
4 Derrius Guice/48 12.00 30.00
5 James Washington/87 10.00 25.00
6 Josh Allen/49 40.00 80.00
7 Josh Rosen/49 20.00 50.00
9 Sam Darnold/36 40.00 100.00
10 Saquon Barkley/49 75.00 150.00
11 Baker Mayfield/46 100.00 200.00
12 D.J. Chark/99 6.00 15.00
13 Dante Pettis/99 8.00 20.00
14 Deon Cain/99 6.00 15.00
15 Mason Rudolph/99 12.00 30.00
16 Nick Chubb/31 25.00 60.00
17 Simmie Cobbs Jr./99 8.00 20.00
18 Allen Lazard/99 5.00 12.00
19 Anthony Miller/99 8.00 20.00
20 Deontay Burnett/99 6.00 15.00
21 Josh Adams/99 10.00 25.00
22 Luke Falk/59 8.00 20.00
23 Mark Walton/99 6.00 15.00
24 Michael Gallup/99 10.00 25.00
25 Nyheim Hines/99 6.00 15.00
26 Ronald Jones II/85 5.00 12.00
27 John Kelly/99 6.00 15.00
28 Kerryon Johnson/57 10.00 25.00
29 Bo Scarbrough/99 6.00 15.00
30 Jaylen Samuels/99 6.00 15.00
31 Mark Andrews/99 8.00 20.00
32 Sony Michel/42 20.00 50.00
33 J'Mon Moore/99 5.00 12.00
34 Rashaad Penny/99 8.00 20.00
35 D.J. Moore/72 10.00 25.00
36 DaeSean Hamilton/77 6.00 15.00

2018 Panini National Treasures Collegiate Combo Team Materials

1 K.Pettway/K.Johnson 5.00 12.00
2 N.Chubb/S.Michel 8.00 20.00
3 D.Guice/D.Chark 6.00 15.00
4 J.Samuels/N.Hines 4.00 10.00
5 B.Mayfield/M.Andrews 12.00 30.00
6 J.Washington/M.Rudolph 8.00 20.00
7 D.Hamilton/S.Barkley 15.00 40.00
8 C.Sutton/T.Quinn 5.00 12.00
9 A.Miller/R.Ferguson 5.00 12.00
10 R.Jones II/S.Darnold 12.00 30.00

2018 Panini National Treasures Collegiate Dual Signatures

3 C.McCoy/M.Applewhite/25 25.00 50.00

2018 Panini National Treasures Collegiate Notable Nicknames

1 Josh Rosen 40.00 80.00
2 Kamryn Pettway 10.00 25.00
3 Lamar Jackson 75.00 150.00
4 Ronald Jones II 6.00 15.00
5 D.J. Chark 8.00 20.00
6 Nyheim Hines 8.00 20.00
7 Sony Michel 40.00 80.00
8 Royce Freeman 8.00 20.00
9 Akrum Wadley 6.00 15.00
10 Justin Jackson 8.00 20.00

2018 Panini National Treasures Collegiate Rookie Silhouette Signatures

164 Lamar Jackson 30.00 80.00
167 Mark Walton 6.00 15.00
168 Bradley Chubb 8.00 20.00
170 Tre'Quan Smith 8.00 20.00
171 Shaquem Griffin 8.00 20.00
172 Keke Coutee 6.00 15.00
173 Ito Smith 6.00 15.00
175 Kyle Lauletta 8.00 20.00
176 Mike Gesicki 6.00 15.00
177 Marquez Valdes-Scantling 6.00 15.00

2018 Panini National Treasures Collegiate Rookie Silhouettes

*PRIME/25: .6X TO 1.5X BASIC JSY/99
1 Nick Chubb 10.00 25.00
2 Sony Michel 8.00 20.00
3 Calvin Ridley 8.00 20.00
4 J.T. Barrett 5.00 12.00
5 Royce Freeman 4.00 10.00
6 Deon Cain 4.00 10.00

2018 Panini National Treasures Collegiate Team Logos Autographs

1 Josh Rosen
2 Sam Darnold
3 Josh Allen 40.00 80.00
4 Lamar Jackson 75.00 150.00
5 Baker Mayfield 75.00 150.00
6 Saquon Barkley
7 Derrius Guice
8 D.J. Moore 15.00 40.00
9 Mike White 8.00 20.00
10 Nick Chubb
11 Mason Rudolph
12 Ronald Jones II 6.00 15.00
13 Christian Kirk 10.00 25.00
14 Calvin Ridley
15 James Washington
16 Courtland Sutton
17 Deon Cain 8.00 20.00
18 Simmie Cobbs Jr. 10.00 25.00
19 Dante Pettis 10.00 25.00
20 D.J. Chark 8.00 20.00
21 Allen Lazard 6.00 15.00
22 Anthony Miller
23 Luke Falk 8.00 20.00
24 Rashaad Penny 10.00 25.00
25 Mark Walton 8.00 20.00
26 Nyheim Hines 8.00 20.00
27 Deontay Burnett 8.00 20.00
28 Michael Gallup
29 Kerryon Johnson 50.00 100.00
30 Trey Quinn 6.00 15.00
31 Sony Michel 20.00 50.00
32 Auden Tate 6.00 15.00
33 Royce Freeman 8.00 20.00
34 John Kelly
35 Bo Scarbrough
36 J.T. Barrett
37 Marcell Ateman 8.00 20.00
38 Akrum Wadley 25.00 50.00
39 Justin Jackson 8.00 20.00
40 Mark Andrews 10.00 25.00

2018 Panini National Treasures Collegiate Team Quads

1 Stwrt/Scrbrgh/Rdly/Hwrd 6.00 15.00
2 Cn/Wtsn/Wllms/Gllmn 6.00 15.00
3 Myfld/Wstbrk/Mxn/Prne 15.00 40.00
4 Brntt/SmthSchstr/Jns/Drnld 12.00 30.00
5 Myfld/Wstbrk/Wtsn/Jcksn 15.00 40.00
6 Myfld/McCffry/Hnry/Wtsn 15.00 40.00
7 Cpr/Brtt/Mrta/Grdn 5.00 12.00
8 Myfld/Hnry/Jcksn/Mrta 15.00 40.00
9 Jns/Ellt/Mrta/Frmn 6.00 15.00
10 Hnry/Wtsn/Hwrd/Gllmn 6.00 15.00
11 Scrbrgh/Wtsn/Wllms/Hwrd 6.00 15.00
12 Scrbrgh/Rdly/Chbb/Mchl 6.00 15.00

2018 Panini National Treasures Collegiate Team Trios
1 Scrbrgh/Rdly/Fstr 6.00 15.00
2 Wshngtn/Atmn/Rdlph 6.00 15.00
3 Brntt/Jns/Drnld 10.00 25.00
4 Gdwn/Hmltn/Brkly 12.00 30.00
5 Sml/Elolt/Brtt 6.00 15.00
6 Kmra/Klly/Dbbs 4.00 10.00

2018 Panini Obsidian
1 Jimmy Garoppolo 1.50 4.00
2 Tom Brady 3.00 8.00
3 Antonio Brown 1.25 3.00
4 Carson Wentz 1.50 4.00
5 Julio Jones 1.25 3.00
6 Le'Veon Bell 1.00 2.50
7 Todd Gurley II 1.25 3.00
8 Aaron Donald 1.25 3.00
9 Drew Brees 1.25 3.00
10 Von Miller 1.00 2.50
11 Aaron Rodgers 2.50 6.00
12 Russell Wilson 1.50 4.00
13 Luke Kuechly 1.00 2.50
14 DeAndre Hopkins 1.00 2.50
15 Jalen Ramsey 1.00 2.50
16 Rob Gronkowski 1.25 3.00
17 Khalil Mack 1.25 3.00
18 Ben Roethlisberger 1.25 3.00
19 Alvin Kamara 1.00 2.50
20 A.J. Green 1.25 3.00
21 Travis Kelce 1.25 3.00
22 Terrell Suggs .75 2.00
23 Cam Newton 1.25 3.00
24 Larry Fitzgerald 1.00 2.50
25 Matt Ryan 1.00 2.50
26 LeSean McCoy 1.25 3.00
27 Matthew Stafford 1.00 2.50
28 Kareem Hunt 1.00 2.50
29 Adam Thielen 1.25 3.00
30 Joey Bosa 1.25 3.00
31 Jared Goff 1.25 3.00
32 Tyreek Hill 1.25 3.00
33 Keenan Allen 1.00 2.50
34 Earl Thomas III 1.00 2.50
35 Harrison Smith 1.25 3.00
36 Deshaun Watson 1.50 4.00
37 Case Keenum 1.00 2.50
38 Ezekiel Elliott 1.50 4.00
39 Joe Flacco 1.00 2.50
40 Philip Rivers 1.25 3.00
41 Leonard Fournette 1.25 3.00
42 Derek Carr 1.25 3.00
43 Stefon Diggs 1.00 2.50
44 Richard Sherman 1.25 3.00
45 Devonta Freeman 1.00 2.50
46 Odell Beckham Jr. 1.25 3.00
47 Marcus Peters .75 2.00
48 Michael Thomas 1.25 3.00
49 Marshon Lattimore .75 2.00
50 J.J. Watt 1.25 3.00
51 Kirk Cousins 1.25 3.00
52 Doug Baldwin 1.00 2.50
53 Ha Ha Clinton-Dix .75 2.00
54 Alex Smith 1.00 2.50
55 Marcus Mariota 1.25 3.00
56 Jameis Winston 1.00 2.50
57 Andrew Luck 1.50 4.00
58 Tyrod Taylor 1.00 2.50
59 Carlos Hyde .75 2.00
60 Frank Gore 1.00 2.50
61 Danny Amendola 1.00 2.50
62 Isaiah Crowell .75 2.00
63 Derrick Henry 1.25 3.00
64 Corey Davis 1.00 2.50
65 Ryan Tannehill 1.00 2.50
66 Zach Ertz 1.00 2.50
67 Fletcher Cox .75 2.00
68 Nick Foles 1.00 2.50
69 Marshawn Lynch 1.00 2.50
70 Julian Edelman 1.25 3.00
71 Blake Bortles .75 2.00
72 Patrick Mahomes II 3.00 8.00
73 Mitchell Trubisky 1.25 3.00
74 Christian McCaffrey 1.25 3.00
75 JuJu Smith-Schuster 1.25 3.00
76 D'Onta Foreman .75 2.00
77 Marvin Jones Jr. .75 2.00
78 Davante Adams 1.00 2.50
79 Jordy Nelson 1.00 2.50
80 Dak Prescott 1.25 3.00
81 Jaylon Smith .75 2.00
82 Joe Mixon 1.00 2.50
83 Andy Dalton 1.00 2.50
84 Sam Bradford .75 2.00
85 David Johnson 1.25 3.00
86 Melvin Gordon 1.00 2.50
87 Dalvin Cook 1.00 2.50
88 Jordan Howard 1.25 3.00
89 Mike Evans 1.00 2.50
90 Eli Manning 1.00 2.50
91 Brett Favre 2.50 6.00
92 Jerry Rice 2.00 5.00
93 Randy Moss 1.00 2.50
94 Peyton Manning 2.50 6.00
95 Emmitt Smith 2.00 5.00
96 Barry Sanders 2.00 5.00
97 Terry Bradshaw 2.00 5.00
98 Joe Namath 1.50 4.00
99 Lawrence Taylor 1.25 3.00
100 Joe Montana 3.00 8.00
101 Saquon Barkley RC 15.00 40.00
102 Lamar Jackson RC 8.00 20.00
103 Baker Mayfield RC 15.00 40.00
104 Josh Allen RC 5.00 12.00
105 Sam Darnold RC 8.00 20.00
106 Josh Rosen RC 4.00 10.00
107 Calvin Ridley RC 3.00 8.00
108 Nick Chubb RC 4.00 10.00
109 Derrius Guice RC 2.50 6.00
110 Sony Michel RC 4.00 10.00
111 Mason Rudolph RC 3.00 8.00
112 D.J. Moore RC 2.50 6.00
113 Christian Kirk RC 2.00 5.00
114 Rashaad Penny RC 2.00 5.00
115 Bradley Chubb RC 2.00 5.00
116 Anthony Miller RC 2.00 5.00
117 Kerryon Johnson RC 2.00 5.00
118 Ronald Jones II RC 1.25 3.00
119 James Washington RC 2.50 6.00
120 Dante Pettis RC 2.00 5.00
121 Courtland Sutton RC 2.00 5.00
122 Royce Freeman RC 1.50 4.00
123 Mike White RC 1.50 4.00
124 Kalen Ballage RC 1.50 4.00
125 Keke Coutee RC 1.50 4.00
126 Mark Walton RC 1.50 4.00
127 Michael Gallup RC 2.50 6.00
128 Nyheim Hines RC 1.50 4.00
129 Hayden Hurst RC 1.50 4.00
130 Mike Gesicki RC 1.50 4.00
131 Kyle Lauletta RC 2.00 5.00
132 Jaleel Scott RC 1.25 3.00
133 Ito Smith RC 1.50 4.00
134 DaeSean Hamilton RC 1.50 4.00
135 D.J. Chark Jr. RC 1.50 4.00
136 J'Mon Moore RC 1.25 3.00
137 Jaylen Samuels RC 1.50 4.00
138 Cam Sims RC 1.50 4.00
139 Tre'Quan Smith RC 2.00 5.00
140 Marquez Valdes-Scantling RC 1.50 4.00
141 Denzel Ward RC 3.00 8.00
142 Quenton Nelson RC 2.00 5.00
143 Roquan Smith RC 4.00 10.00
144 Minkah Fitzpatrick RC 2.50 6.00
145 Fred Warner RC 1.25 3.00
146 Daron Payne RC 2.00 5.00
147 Marcus Davenport RC 2.50 6.00
148 Tremaine Edmunds RC 2.50 6.00
149 Derwin James RC 2.50 6.00
150 Jaire Alexander RC 2.00 5.00
151 Leighton Vander Esch RC 10.00 25.00
152 Rashaan Evans RC 2.00 5.00
153 Terrell Edmunds RC 4.00 10.00
154 Mike Hughes RC 2.00 5.00
155 Harold Landry RC 1.25 3.00
156 Joshua Jackson RC 2.50 6.00
157 Dallas Goedert RC 1.50 4.00
158 M.J. Stewart RC 1.25 3.00
159 Ronnie Harrison RC 1.50 4.00
160 Will Dissly RC 1.50 4.00
161 Isaiah Oliver RC 1.25 3.00
162 Carlton Davis RC 1.50 4.00
163 Javon Wims RC 1.25 3.00
164 Malik Jefferson RC 1.50 4.00
165 Antonio Callaway RC 1.50 4.00
166 Chase Edmonds RC 1.25 3.00
167 Dalton Schultz RC 1.50 4.00
168 John Kelly RC 1.50 4.00
169 Mike Boone RC 1.50 4.00
170 Rasheem Green RC 1.25 3.00
171 Russell Gage RC 1.50 4.00
172 Boston Scott RC 1.50 4.00
173 Alex McGough RC 1.50 4.00
174 Justin Watson RC 1.50 4.00
175 Danny Etling RC 1.50 4.00
176 Damion Ratley RC 1.50 4.00
177 Richie James RC 1.25 3.00
178 Derrick Nnadi RC 1.25 3.00
179 Sam Hubbard RC 1.50 4.00
180 Shaquem Griffin RC 2.00 5.00
181 Jerome Baker RC 1.50 4.00
182 Bo Scarbrough RC 1.50 4.00
183 Maurice Hurst RC 1.50 4.00
184 Troy Fumagalli RC 1.50 4.00
185 Chris Warren III RC 2.00 5.00
186 Chad Thomas RC 1.25 3.00
187 Lorenzo Carter RC 1.25 3.00
188 Jordan Akins RC 1.25 3.00
189 Mike McGlinchey RC 2.50 6.00
190 Durham Smythe RC 1.25 3.00
191 Arden Key RC 1.25 3.00
192 Auden Tate RC 1.25 3.00
193 Breeland Speaks RC 1.50 4.00
194 Chris Board RC 1.25 3.00
195 Mark Andrews RC 2.00 5.00
196 Jordan Wilkins RC 1.50 4.00
197 Jordan Lasley RC 1.25 3.00
198 Phillip Lindsay RC 5.00 12.00
199 Ian Thomas RC 1.25 3.00
200 Tanner Lee RC 1.50 4.00

2018 Panini Obsidian Electric Etch Green
*VETS: .6X TO 1.5X BASIC CARDS
*ROOKIES: .6X TO 1.5X BASIC CARDS
101 Saquon Barkley 30.00 80.00

2018 Panini Obsidian Electric Etch Orange
*VETS: .5X TO 1.2X BASIC CARDS
*ROOKIES: .5X TO 1.2X BASIC CARDS
101 Saquon Barkley 25.00 60.00

2018 Panini Obsidian Electric Etch Purple
*VETS: .4X TO 1X BASIC CARDS
*ROOKIES: .4X TO 1X BASIC CARDS
101 Saquon Barkley 20.00 50.00

2018 Panini Obsidian Atomic Materials
*GREEN/25: .6X TO 1.5X BASIC JSY/100
1 Aaron Donald 4.00 10.00
2 Adam Thielen 4.00 10.00
3 David Johnson 4.00 10.00
4 Ben Roethlisberger 4.00 10.00
5 Harrison Smith 4.00 10.00
6 Christian McCaffrey 4.00 10.00
7 Dak Prescott 4.00 10.00
8 Rob Gronkowski 4.00 10.00
9 Terrell Suggs 2.50 6.00
10 Mike Evans 3.00 8.00
11 Joe Flacco 3.00 8.00
12 Antonio Brown 4.00 10.00
13 Leonard Fournette 4.00 10.00
14 T.J. Watt 3.00 8.00
15 Clay Matthews 3.00 8.00
16 Patrick Mahomes II 10.00 25.00
17 JuJu Smith-Schuster 4.00 10.00
18 Mitchell Trubisky 4.00 10.00
19 Marshawn Lynch 3.00 8.00
20 Derek Carr 4.00 10.00
21 Lamar Miller 2.50 6.00
22 Andy Dalton 3.00 8.00
23 Golden Tate III 2.50 6.00
24 Jason Witten 3.00 8.00
25 Aaron Rodgers 8.00 20.00
26 LaDainian Tomlinson 3.00 8.00
27 Bo Jackson 5.00 12.00
28 Matthew Stafford 3.00 8.00
29 Peyton Manning 8.00 20.00
30 Earl Thomas III 3.00 8.00
31 Kareem Hunt 3.00 8.00
32 Cooper Kupp 3.00 8.00
33 Jared Goff 4.00 10.00
34 Carson Wentz 5.00 12.00
35 Robby Anderson 2.50 6.00
36 Deshaun Watson 5.00 12.00
37 Ezekiel Elliott 5.00 12.00
38 Alvin Kamara 3.00 8.00
39 Jimmy Garoppolo 5.00 12.00
40 Marcus Mariota 4.00 10.00
41 Derrick Henry 4.00 10.00
42 Stefon Diggs 3.00 8.00
43 Luke Kuechly 3.00 8.00
44 Earl Campbell 4.00 10.00
45 Jerome Bettis 4.00 10.00
46 Blake Bortles 2.50 6.00
47 Tony Romo 3.00 8.00
48 John Riggins 3.00 8.00
49 Kurt Warner 3.00 8.00
50 Matt Ryan 3.00 8.00
51 Doug Baldwin 3.00 8.00
52 Dalvin Cook 3.00 8.00
53 Mike Williams 2.50 6.00
54 Keenan Allen 3.00 8.00
55 Amari Cooper 4.00 10.00
56 DeAndre Hopkins 3.00 8.00
57 Julio Jones 4.00 10.00
58 Drew Brees 4.00 10.00
60 Heath Miller 2.50 6.00

2018 Panini Obsidian Aurora Autographs
COMMON CARD/75-100 3.00 8.00
SEMISTARS/75-100 4.00 10.00
UNLISTED STARS/75-100 5.00 12.00
COMMON CARD/48-50 4.00 10.00
SEMISTARS/48-50 5.00 12.00
UNLISTED STARS/48-50 6.00 15.00
COMMON CARD/25 6.00 15.00
UNLISTED STARS/25 8.00 20.00
1 Michael Vick/25
2 Jason Taylor/20 15.00 40.00
3 Ha Ha Clinton-Dix/100 3.00 8.00
4 Tarik Cohen/100 6.00 15.00
5 Christian Okoye/100 3.00 8.00
6 Robert Smith/100 15.00 40.00
7 Roger Craig/50 5.00 12.00
8 Tyreek Hill/50 10.00 25.00
9 Justin Houston/100 3.00 8.00
11 Rishard Matthews/100 3.00 8.00
12 Doug Baldwin/25 6.00 15.00
13 Dick LeBeau/48 8.00 20.00
14 Jeremy Shockey/50 4.00 10.00
15 Stefon Diggs/50 12.00 30.00
16 James Lofton/50 8.00 20.00
17 Antonio Brown/15 40.00 80.00
19 Marcus Mariota/15 40.00 80.00
20 Mike Ditka/20 15.00 40.00
21 Linval Joseph/100 15.00 40.00
22 Patrick Chung/100 8.00 20.00
23 Geno Atkins/100 3.00 8.00
24 Gilbert Brown/100 3.00 8.00
25 Michael Bennett/75 10.00 25.00
26 Jamal Adams/100 4.00 10.00
27 Peyton Barber/100 3.00 8.00
28 Pat McAfee/100 40.00 80.00
29 Travis Kelce/75 6.00 15.00
30 Derrick Johnson/100 3.00 8.00
31 Brian Orakpo/100 3.00 8.00
32 Justin Tucker/100 3.00 8.00
33 Kendall Fuller/100 3.00 8.00
34 Pierre Garcon/100 4.00 10.00
35 Charles Haley/100 5.00 12.00
36 Dallas Clark/50 8.00 20.00
37 Devin Hester/20 15.00 40.00
38 Clay Matthews/20
39 Dermontti Dawson/100 4.00 10.00
40 Pepper Johnson/100 3.00 8.00
41 Gerald McCoy/100 3.00 8.00
42 Preston Smith/100 3.00 8.00
43 Philip Rivers/20 30.00 60.00
44 Damarious Randall/100 3.00 8.00
45 Desmond Howard/20 12.00 30.00
46 Ron Jaworski/100 4.00 10.00
47 Reggie Wayne/20 12.00 30.00
48 Tony Gonzalez/20 25.00 50.00
49 Torrey Smith/75 3.00 8.00
50 Ozzie Newsome/100 4.00 10.00
51 Emmanuel Sanders/75 5.00 12.00
53 Ahman Green/50 8.00 20.00
54 Richard Sherman/20 12.00 30.00
55 Jack Ham/75 10.00 25.00
56 Ed Too Tall Jones/100 6.00 15.00
57 Cliff Harris/100 3.00 8.00
58 Archie Manning/20 8.00 20.00
59 Len Dawson/25 8.00 20.00
60 Lawrence Taylor/20 15.00 40.00

2018 Panini Obsidian Aurora Autographs Electric Etch Green
28 Pat McAfee/25 50.00 125.00

2018 Panini Obsidian Cutting Edge Materials
*GREEN/25: .5X TO 1.2X BASIC JSY/50
*ORANGE/35: .4X TO 1X BASIC JSY/50
1 Ricky Williams 4.00 10.00
2 Adam Thielen 5.00 12.00
3 Marcus Mariota 5.00 12.00
4 Jared Goff 5.00 12.00
5 Derek Carr 5.00 12.00
6 Mike Williams 3.00 8.00
7 Will Fuller V 3.00 8.00
8 LeSean McCoy 5.00 12.00
9 Rob Gronkowski 5.00 12.00
10 JuJu Smith-Schuster 5.00 12.00
11 Josh Rosen 12.00 20.00
12 Josh Allen 12.00 20.00
13 Mason Rudolph 8.00 20.00
14 Calvin Ridley 10.00 15.00
15 Nick Chubb 10.00 25.00
16 Lamar Jackson 20.00 30.00
17 Sony Michel 10.00 15.00
19 Dak Prescott 5.00 12.00
20 Travis Kelce 5.00 12.00

2018 Panini Obsidian Galaxy Gear Materials
*GREEN/25: .6X TO 1.5X BASIC JSY/100
*ORANGE/50: .6X TO 1.5X BASIC JSY/100
1 Patrick Mahomes II 10.00 25.00
2 Ezekiel Elliott 5.00 12.00
3 Antonio Brown 4.00 10.00
4 Corey Davis 3.00 8.00
5 Sterling Shepard 3.00 8.00
6 Kareem Hunt 3.00 8.00
7 Jameis Winston 3.00 8.00
8 Derrick Henry 4.00 10.00
9 Joe Mixon 3.00 8.00
10 D'Onta Foreman 2.50 6.00
11 Leonard Fournette 4.00 10.00
12 Aaron Jones 3.00 8.00
13 Joe Flacco 3.00 8.00
14 Ryan Tannehill 3.00 8.00
15 Eric Berry 3.00 8.00
16 Cooper Kupp 3.00 8.00
17 Russell Wilson 5.00 12.00
18 Michael Thomas 4.00 10.00
19 Christian McCaffrey 4.00 10.00
20 Devonta Freeman 3.00 8.00
21 Matthew Stafford 3.00 8.00
22 Eli Manning 3.00 8.00
23 Marshawn Lynch 3.00 8.00
24 Demaryius Thomas 3.00 8.00
25 Saquon Barkley 20.00 30.00
26 D.J. Moore 5.00 12.00
27 Baker Mayfield 15.00 25.00
28 Ronald Jones II 2.50 6.00
29 Rashaad Penny 4.00 10.00
30 Sam Darnold 15.00 25.00

2018 Panini Obsidian Lightning Strike Autographs
1 Case Keenum/35 5.00 12.00
5 Marcus Peters/96 6.00 15.00
6 Neil Smith/79 3.00 8.00
7 Ricky Williams/35 8.00 20.00
8 Aqib Talib/100 6.00 15.00
10 Dont'a Hightower/100 3.00 8.00
11 Marshon Lattimore/100 3.00 8.00
12 Cameron Jordan/100 3.00 8.00
13 Morten Andersen/100 3.00 8.00
14 Jake Elliott/100 4.00 10.00
15 Carlos Hyde/35 4.00 10.00
16 John Lynch/35 10.00 25.00
17 Plaxico Burress/100 3.00 8.00
18 Brian Dawkins/20 15.00 40.00
19 Ed McCaffrey/35 8.00 20.00
21 Ken Anderson/100 6.00 15.00
22 Drew Pearson/55 5.00 12.00
23 Trent Dilfer/100 3.00 8.00
24 Kareem Hunt/100 4.00 10.00
26 Christian McCaffrey/25 12.00 30.00
27 Tom Rathman/100 3.00 8.00
28 Geno Atkins/100 3.00 8.00
29 Merton Hanks/75 3.00 8.00
30 Danny White/25 5.00 12.00
31 Dante Hall/50 4.00 10.00
32 Josh Gordon/35 20.00 50.00
34 Calais Campbell/100 3.00 8.00
35 Kiko Alonso/65 4.00 10.00
36 Bruce Smith/20 8.00 20.00
37 Adam Vinatieri/25 10.00 25.00
38 Fran Tarkenton/25 25.00 50.00
40 Delanie Walker/100 3.00 8.00

2018 Panini Obsidian Lightning Strike Autographs Electric Etch Green
*GREEN/25: .6X TO 1.5X BASIC AU/75-100
*GREEN/25: .5X TO 1.2X BASIC AU/35-65
*GREEN/15: .6X TO 1.5X BASIC AU/35-50
*GREEN/15: .5X TO 1.2X BASIC AU/25
*GREEN/15: .4X TO 1X BASIC AU/20

2018 Panini Obsidian Matrix Material Autographs Electric Etch Green
*GREEN/25: .6X TO 1.5X BASIC AU/75-100
*GREEN/15: .8X TO 2X BASIC AU/75-100
*GREEN/15: .6X TO 1.5X BASIC AU/35-50
*GREEN/15: .5X TO 1.2X BASIC AU/25
6 Patrick Mahomes II/15 125.00 250.00

2018 Panini Obsidian Matrix Material Autographs Electric Etch Orange
*ORANGE/35-50: .5X TO 1.2X BASIC AU/75-100
*ORANGE/35-50: .4X TO 1X BASIC AU/35
*ORANGE/25: .5X TO 1.2X BASIC AU/35-50
*ORNAGE/20: .8X TO 2X BASIC AU/75-100
*ORNAGE/20: .5X TO 1.2X BASIC AU/25
6 Patrick Mahomes II/20 125.00 250.00

2018 Panini Obsidian Rookie Autographs Electric Etch Green
*GREEN/25: .6X TO 1.5X BASIC AU/75-100
*GREEN/15: .8X TO 2X BASIC AU/75-100
*GREEN/15: .6X TO 1.5X BASIC AU/35
1 Saquon Barkley/15 200.00 300.00
3 Baker Mayfield/15 150.00 300.00
98 Phillip Lindsay/25 100.00 200.00

2018 Panini Obsidian Rookie Autographs Electric Etch Orange
*ORNAGE/35-50: .5X TO 1.2X BASIC AU/75-100
*ORANGE/25: .6X TO 1.5X BASIC AU/75-100
*ORANGE/25: .5X TO 1.2X BASIC AU/35
1 Saquon Barkley/35 150.00 250.00
3 Baker Mayfield/25 100.00 200.00
98 Phillip Lindsay/50 75.00 150.00

2018 Panini Obsidian Rookie Eruption Materials
*GREEN/25: .6X TO 1.5X BASIC JSY/100
*ORANGE/50: .5X TO 1.2X BASIC JSY/100
1 Sam Darnold 15.00 25.00
2 Baker Mayfield 15.00 25.00
3 D.J. Moore 5.00 12.00
4 Jaleel Scott 2.50 6.00
5 Kalen Ballage 3.00 8.00
6 Keke Coutee 3.00 8.00
7 James Washington 5.00 12.00
8 Ronald Jones II 2.50 6.00
9 Kerryon Johnson 4.00 10.00
10 Derrius Guice 5.00 12.00
11 Bradley Chubb 4.00 10.00
12 Royce Freeman 3.00 8.00
13 Kyle Lauletta 4.00 10.00
14 Mike Gesicki 3.00 8.00
15 Hayden Hurst 3.00 8.00
16 Nyheim Hines 3.00 8.00
17 Michael Gallup 5.00 12.00
18 Lamar Jackson 15.00 25.00
19 Saquon Barkley 20.00 30.00
20 Anthony Miller 4.00 10.00
21 Dante Pettis 4.00 10.00
22 Courtland Sutton 4.00 10.00
23 Christian Kirk 4.00 10.00
24 Mason Rudolph 6.00 15.00
25 Nick Chubb 8.00 20.00
26 Sony Michel 8.00 12.00
27 Rashaad Penny 4.00 10.00
28 Mike White 3.00 8.00
29 Mark Walton 3.00 8.00
30 Marquez Valdes-Scantling 3.00 8.00
31 Tre'Quan Smith 4.00 10.00
32 Daurice Fountain 3.00 8.00
33 Jaylen Samuels 3.00 8.00
34 J'Mon Moore 2.50 6.00
35 D.J. Chark Jr. 3.00 8.00
36 DaeSean Hamilton 3.00 8.00
37 Ito Smith 3.00 8.00
38 Josh Rosen 10.00 15.00
39 Josh Allen 10.00 15.00
40 Calvin Ridley 8.00 12.00

2018 Panini Obsidian Rookie Jersey Autographs
1 Saquon Barkley/100 75.00 150.00
2 Lamar Jackson/75 40.00 80.00
3 Rashaad Penny/100 6.00 15.00
4 D.J. Moore/100 8.00 20.00
5 Baker Mayfield/75 100.00 200.00
6 Sam Darnold/75 50.00 100.00
7 Josh Rosen/100 12.00 30.00
8 Josh Allen/100 EXCH 25.00 50.00
9 Calvin Ridley/100 10.00 25.00
10 Derrius Guice/100 EXCH 8.00 20.00
11 Sony Michel/100 12.00 30.00
12 Nick Chubb/100 15.00 40.00
13 Mason Rudolph/100 10.00 25.00
14 Christian Kirk/100 6.00 15.00
15 Courtland Sutton/100 6.00 15.00
16 Dante Pettis/100 EXCH 6.00 15.00
17 James Washington/100 8.00 20.00
18 Ronald Jones II/100 4.00 10.00
19 Kerryon Johnson/100 EXCH 10.00 25.00
20 Anthony Miller/100 6.00 15.00
21 Bradley Chubb/100 EXCH 6.00 15.00
22 Royce Freeman/100 5.00 12.00
23 Kyle Lauletta/100 6.00 15.00
24 Mike Gesicki/100 5.00 12.00
26 Nyheim Hines/100 5.00 12.00
27 Michael Gallup/100 8.00 20.00
28 Mike White/100 5.00 12.00
29 Mark Walton/100 5.00 12.00
30 Keke Coutee/100
31 Kalen Ballage/100 5.00 12.00
32 Jaleel Scott/100 4.00 10.00
33 Ito Smith/100 5.00 12.00
34 DaeSean Hamilton/100 5.00 12.00
35 D.J. Chark Jr./100 5.00 12.00
36 J'Mon Moore/100 4.00 10.00
37 Jaylen Samuels/100 5.00 12.00
38 Daurice Fountain/100 5.00 12.00
39 Tre'Quan Smith/100 6.00 15.00
40 Marquez Valdes-Scantling/100 5.00 12.00

2018 Panini Obsidian Rookie Jersey Autographs Electric Etch Green
*GREEN/25: .6X TO 1.5X BASIC JSY AU/75-100
1 Saquon Barkley 250.00 350.00
5 Baker Mayfield 150.00 300.00

2018 Panini Obsidian Rookie Jersey Autographs Electric Etch Orange
*ORANGE/50: .5X TO 1.2X BASIC JSY AU/75-100
1 Saquon Barkley 100.00 200.00
5 Baker Mayfield 125.00 250.00

2018 Panini Obsidian Rookie Jersey Ink
1 Saquon Barkley/100 75.00 150.00
2 Lamar Jackson/75 40.00 80.00
3 Rashaad Penny/100 6.00 15.00
4 D.J. Moore/100 8.00 20.00
5 Baker Mayfield/75 100.00 200.00
6 Sam Darnold/75 50.00 100.00
7 Josh Rosen/100 12.00 30.00
8 Josh Allen/100 EXCH 25.00 50.00
9 Calvin Ridley/75 10.00 25.00
10 Derrius Guice/100 EXCH 8.00 20.00
11 Sony Michel/100 12.00 30.00
12 Nick Chubb/100 15.00 40.00
13 Mason Rudolph/100 10.00 25.00
14 Christian Kirk/100 6.00 15.00
15 Courtland Sutton/100 6.00 15.00
16 Dante Pettis/100 EXCH 6.00 15.00
17 James Washington/100 8.00 20.00
18 Ronald Jones II/100 4.00 10.00
19 Kerryon Johnson/100 EXCH 10.00 25.00
20 Anthony Miller/100 6.00 15.00
21 Bradley Chubb/100 EXCH 6.00 15.00
22 Royce Freeman/100 5.00 12.00
23 Kyle Lauletta/100 6.00 15.00
24 Kalen Ballage/100 5.00 12.00
26 Nyheim Hines/100 5.00 12.00
27 Michael Gallup/100 8.00 20.00
28 Mike White/100 5.00 12.00
29 Mark Walton/100 5.00 12.00
30 Keke Coutee/100

2018 Panini Obsidian Rookie Jersey Ink Electric Etch Green
*GREEN/25: .6X TO 1.5X BASIC JSY AU/75-100
1 Saquon Barkley 250.00 350.00
5 Baker Mayfield 150.00 300.00

2018 Panini Obsidian Rookie Jersey Ink Electric Etch Orange
*ORANGE/35-50: .5X TO 1.2X BASIC JSY AU/75-100
1 Saquon Barkley/50 100.00 200.00
5 Baker Mayfield/35 125.00 250.00

2018 Panini Obsidian Vitreous
*ORANGE/50: .5X TO 1.2X BASIC INSERTS/100
*GREEN/25: .6X TO 1.5X BASIC INSERTS/100
1 Saquon Barkley 12.00 30.00
2 Baker Mayfield 15.00 40.00
3 Sam Darnold 10.00 25.00
4 Lamar Jackson 10.00 25.00
5 Josh Rosen 5.00 12.00
6 Josh Allen 6.00 15.00
7 Shaquem Griffin 2.50 6.00
8 Calvin Ridley 4.00 10.00
9 Sony Michel 5.00 12.00
10 Mason Rudolph 4.00 10.00

2018 Panini Obsidian Volcanic Materials
*GREEN/25: .5X TO 1.2X BASIC JSY/50
1 Calvin Ridley 10.00 15.00
2 Josh Allen 12.00 20.00
3 Josh Rosen 12.00 20.00
4 Sam Darnold 20.00 30.00
5 Baker Mayfield 20.00 30.00
6 D.J. Moore 6.00 15.00
7 Rashaad Penny 5.00 12.00
8 Lamar Jackson 20.00 30.00
9 Saquon Barkley 25.00 40.00
10 Derrius Guice 6.00 15.00
11 Dante Pettis 5.00 12.00
12 Courtland Sutton 5.00 12.00
13 Christian Kirk 5.00 12.00
14 Mason Rudolph 8.00 20.00
15 Nick Chubb 10.00 25.00
16 Sony Michel 10.00 15.00
17 James Washington 6.00 15.00
18 Ronald Jones II 3.00 8.00
19 Kerryon Johnson 5.00 12.00
20 Anthony Miller 5.00 12.00
21 Bradley Chubb 5.00 12.00
22 Royce Freeman 4.00 10.00
23 Kyle Lauletta 5.00 12.00
24 Mike Gesicki 4.00 10.00
25 Hayden Hurst 4.00 10.00
26 Nyheim Hines 4.00 10.00
27 Michael Gallup 6.00 15.00
28 Mike White 4.00 10.00
29 Mark Walton 4.00 10.00
30 Marquez Valdes-Scantling 4.00 10.00
31 Tre'Quan Smith 5.00 12.00
32 Daurice Fountain 4.00 10.00
33 Jaylen Samuels 4.00 10.00
34 J'Mon Moore 3.00 8.00
35 D.J. Chark Jr. 4.00 10.00
36 DaeSean Hamilton 4.00 10.00
37 Ito Smith 4.00 10.00
38 Jaleel Scott 3.00 8.00
39 Kalen Ballage 4.00 10.00
40 Keke Coutee 4.00 10.00

2018 Panini One
1 Josh Allen JSY AU/199 RC 40.00 80.00
2 Baker Mayfield JSY AU/199 RC 150.00 300.00
3 Nick Chubb JSY AU/199 RC 20.00 50.00
4 Sony Michel JSY AU/199 RC EXCH 20.00 50.00
5 Saquon Barkley JSY AU/199 RC EXCH 100.00 200.00
6 Rashaad Penny JSY AU/199 RC 10.00 25.00
7 D.J. Moore JSY AU/199 RC 12.00 30.00
8 Courtland Sutton JSY AU/199 RC 10.00 25.00
9 Ronald Jones II JSY AU/199 RC 6.00 15.00
10 James Washington JSY AU/199 RC 12.00 30.00
11 Josh Rosen JSY AU/199 RC 20.00 50.00
12 Kerryon Johnson JSY AU/199 RC 25.00 50.00
13 Anthony Miller JSY AU/199 RC 10.00 25.00
14 Mason Rudolph JSY AU/199 RC 25.00 50.00
15 Calvin Ridley JSY AU/199 RC 15.00 40.00
16 Lamar Jackson JSY AU/49 RC 60.00 150.00
17 Sam Darnold JSY AU/199 RC 50.00 100.00
18 Derrius Guice JSY AU/149 RC 12.00 30.00
19 Christian Kirk JSY AU/199 RC 10.00 25.00
20 Bradley Chubb JSY AU/199 RC 10.00 25.00
21 Kyle Lauletta JSY AU/199 RC 10.00 25.00
22 Michael Gallup JSY AU/199 RC 12.00 30.00
23 Jaylen Samuels JSY AU/199 RC 8.00 20.00
24 Royce Freeman JSY AU/199 RC 8.00 20.00
25 Dante Pettis JSY AU/199 RC 10.00 25.00
26 Nyheim Hines JSY AU/199 RC 8.00 20.00
30 D.J. Chark Jr. JSY AU/199 RC 8.00 20.00
51 Josh Allen JSY AU/125 40.00 80.00
52 Baker Mayfield JSY AU/125 125.00 250.00
53 Nick Chubb JSY AU/199 20.00 50.00
54 Sony Michel JSY AU/199 EXCH 20.00 50.00
55 Saquon Barkley JSY AU/125 EXCH 100.00 200.00
56 Rashaad Penny JSY AU/199 10.00 25.00
57 D.J. Moore JSY AU/199 12.00 30.00
58 Courtland Sutton JSY AU/199 10.00 25.00
59 Ronald Jones II JSY AU/99 8.00 20.00
60 Marquez Valdes-Scantling JSY AU/199 8.00 20.00
61 Josh Rosen JSY AU/125 20.00 50.00
62 Kerryon Johnson JSY AU/199 25.00 50.00
63 Anthony Miller JSY AU/199 10.00 25.00
64 Mason Rudolph JSY AU/199 25.00 50.00
65 Calvin Ridley JSY AU/99 20.00 50.00
66 Lamar Jackson JSY AU/49 60.00 150.00
67 Sam Darnold JSY AU/125 60.00 125.00
68 Derrius Guice JSY AU/125 12.00 30.00
69 D.J. Chark Jr. JSY AU/199 8.00 20.00
70 Bradley Chubb JSY AU/199 10.00 25.00
71 Josh Allen AU/49 40.00 80.00
72 Baker Mayfield AU/49 250.00 500.00
73 Nick Chubb AU/49 20.00 50.00
74 Sony Michel AU/99 EXCH 15.00 40.00
75 Saquon Barkley AU/49 EXCH 100.00 200.00
76 Shaquem Griffin AU/99 12.00 30.00
77 D.J. Moore AU/49 12.00 30.00
78 Roquan Smith AU/99 25.00 50.00
79 Kerryon Johnson AU/99 15.00 40.00
80 James Washington AU/75 10.00 25.00
81 Josh Rosen AU/49 20.00 50.00
82 Phillip Lindsay AU/99 50.00 100.00
83 Deon Cain AU/99 6.00 15.00
84 Mason Rudolph AU/49 25.00 50.00
85 Calvin Ridley AU/49 15.00 40.00
86 Royce Freeman AU/99 6.00 15.00
87 Sam Darnold AU/49 50.00 100.00
88 Derrius Guice AU/49 12.00 30.00
89 Tre'Quan Smith AU/99 10.00 25.00
90 Michael Gallup AU/99 10.00 25.00

2018 Panini One Blue
*BLUE/75-99: .5X TO 1.2X BASIC JSY AU/125-199
*BLUE/75-99: .4X TO 1X BASIC JSY AU/99
*BLUE/35: .4X TO 1X BASIC JSY AU/49
*BLUE/35-49: .5X TO 1.2X BASIC AU/75-99
*BLUE/35-49: .4X TO 1X BASIC JSY AU/35
2 Baker Mayfield JSY AU/99 175.00 350.00
5 Saquon Barkley JSY AU/99 EXCH 100.00 200.00
31 Josh Allen JSY AU/49 50.00 125.00
32 Baker Mayfield JSY AU/49 250.00 500.00
33 Nick Chubb JSY AU/99 25.00 60.00
34 Sony Michel JSY AU/99 EXCH 25.00 60.00
35 Saquon Barkley JSY AU/49 EXCH 150.00 250.00
36 Rashaad Penny JSY AU/99 12.00 30.00
37 D.J. Moore JSY AU/99 15.00 40.00
38 Courtland Sutton JSY AU/99 12.00 30.00
39 Anthony Miller JSY AU/99 12.00 30.00
40 James Washington JSY AU/99 15.00 40.00
41 Josh Rosen JSY AU/49 30.00 80.00
42 Keke Coutee JSY AU/99 10.00 25.00
43 Tre'Quan Smith JSY AU/99 15.00 40.00
44 Mason Rudolph JSY AU/99 25.00 60.00
45 Calvin Ridley JSY AU/49 25.00 60.00
46 Lamar Jackson JSY AU/49 60.00 150.00
47 Sam Darnold JSY AU/49 60.00 150.00
48 Derrius Guice JSY AU/49 20.00 50.00
49 Christian Kirk JSY AU/99 12.00 30.00
50 Royce Freeman JSY AU/99 10.00 25.00
51 Josh Allen JSY AU/75 40.00 100.00
52 Baker Mayfield JSY AU/75 150.00 300.00
55 Saquon Barkley JSY AU/99 EXCH 100.00 200.00
72 Baker Mayfield AU/35 250.00 500.00
75 Saquon Barkley AU/35 EXCH 100.00 200.00

2018 Panini One Bronze
*BRONZE/49: .6X TO 1.5X BASIC JSY AU/125-199
*BRONZE/49: .5X TO 1.2X BASIC JSY AU/99
*BRONZE/25: .5X TO 1.2X BASIC JSY AU/49
*BRONZE/25: .6X TO 1.5X BASIC AU/75-99
*BRONZE/25: .5X TO 1.2X BASIC AU/49
*BRNZ(31-50)/49: .5X TO 1.2X BLUE JSY AU/99
*BRNZ(31-50)/25: .5X TO 1.2X BLUE JSY AU/49
2 Baker Mayfield JSY AU/49 250.00 500.00
5 Saquon Barkley JSY AU/49 EXCH 150.00 250.00
32 Baker Mayfield JSY AU/25 300.00 600.00
35 Saquon Barkley JSY AU/25 EXCH 200.00 400.00
52 Baker Mayfield JSY AU/49 250.00 500.00
55 Saquon Barkley JSY AU/49 EXCH 150.00 250.00
72 Baker Mayfield AU/25 300.00 600.00
75 Saquon Barkley AU/25 EXCH 100.00 200.00
95 Brett Favre JSY AU/15 150.00 250.00
96 Dan Fouts JSY AU/25 50.00 100.00
98 Earl Campbell JSY AU/25 40.00 80.00
100 Kurt Warner JSY AU/15 100.00 200.00
101 Jerome Bettis JSY AU/25 50.00 100.00
102 Derek Carr JSY AU/25 30.00 80.00
103 John Riggins JSY AU/15
105 Howie Long JSY AU/35 40.00 80.00
108 Edgerrin James JSY AU/49 25.00 50.00
109 Tedy Bruschi JSY AU/49 25.00 60.00
110 Antonio Brown JSY AU/15 75.00 150.00
115 Tony Dorsett JSY AU/25 60.00 125.00
116 Ben Roethlisberger JSY AU/15
117 Terrell Davis JSY AU/25 100.00 200.00
118 Brian Dawkins JSY AU/35 50.00 100.00
119 Ed Reed JSY AU/25 50.00 100.00
120 Drew Brees JSY AU/15 200.00 400.00
122 Deshaun Watson JSY AU/25 50.00 100.00
123 Adam Thielen JSY AU/49 50.00 100.00
124 Ezekiel Elliott JSY AU/20
125 Isaac Bruce JSY AU/49 25.00 50.00
126 JuJu Smith-Schuster JSY AU/49 30.00 60.00
127 Luke Kuechly JSY AU/35
128 Heath Miller JSY AU/49
129 Patrick Mahomes II JSY AU/49 200.00 400.00
130 Barry Sanders JSY AU/15 150.00 300.00
131 Jordan Howard JSY AU/49
134 Hines Ward JSY AU/49 25.00 50.00
135 Steve Largent JSY AU/49 15.00 40.00
137 Earl Thomas III JSY AU/49
138 Tyreek Hill JSY AU/49
139 Jason Witten JSY AU/35
140 Dalvin Cook JSY AU/49
141 Keenan Allen JSY AU/49
142 Davante Adams JSY AU/49
143 Marcus Mariota JSY AU/15 60.00 125.00
144 LaDainian Tomlinson JSY AU/35 40.00 80.00
145 Andre Reed JSY AU/49 12.00 30.00
146 Cris Carter JSY AU/15 60.00 125.00
147 Rod Woodson JSY AU/49 15.00 40.00
149 Peyton Manning JSY AU/15 150.00 250.00
150 Clay Matthews JSY AU/25 15.00 40.00
152 Ray Lewis JSY AU/15
153 Christian McCaffrey JSY AU/49 50.00 100.00
154 Jared Goff JSY AU/25 50.00 100.00
155 Len Dawson JSY AU/49 20.00 50.00
156 Warren Moon JSY AU/35 40.00 80.00
157 Harrison Smith JSY AU/49 30.00 60.00
158 Melvin Gordon III JSY AU/49 30.00 60.00
159 Archie Manning JSY AU/49 40.00 80.00
160 Leonard Fournette JSY AU/25 20.00 50.00
161 LaDainian Tomlinson JSY AU/35 30.00 80.00
163 Michael Vick JSY AU/49 25.00 50.00
168 Lawrence Taylor JSY AU/35 50.00 100.00
169 Mitchell Trubisky JSY AU/25 100.00 200.00

2018 Panini One Patch Autographs Variation Bronze
*VAR BRZ/25: .5X TO 1.2X BASIC BRONZE/49
*VAR BRZ/25: .4X TO 1X BASIC BRONZE/25

2018 Panini One Patch Autographs Variation Red
*VAR RED/15: .6X TO 1.5X BASIC JSY AU/49

2018 Panini One Red
*RED/25: .8X TO 2X BASIC JSY AU/125-199
*RED/25: .6X TO 1.5X BASIC JSY AU/99
*RED/15: .6X TO 1.5X BASIC JSY AU/49
*RED/15: .8X TO 2X BASIC AU75-99
*RED/15: .6X TO 1.5X BASIC AU/49
*RED(31-50)/25: .6X TO 1.5X BLUE JSY AU/99
*RED(31-50)/15: .6X TO 1.5X BLUE JSY AU/49
*RED(91-189)/25: .5X TO 1.2X BRZ JSY AU/35-49
*RED(91-189)/15: .6X TO 1.5X BRZ JSY AU/35-49
*RED(91-189)/5: .5X TO 1.2X BRZ JSY AU/25
2 Baker Mayfield JSY AU/25 300.00 600.00
5 Saquon Barkley JSY AU/25 EXCH 200.00 400.00
32 Baker Mayfield JSY AU/15 300.00 600.00
35 Saquon Barkley JSY AU/15 EXCH 200.00 400.00
52 Baker Mayfield JSY AU/25 300.00 600.00
55 Saquon Barkley JSY AU/25 EXCH 200.00 400.00
72 Baker Mayfield AU/15 300.00 600.00
75 Saquon Barkley AU/15 EXCH 150.00 250.00

2016 Panini Origins
1 Amari Cooper 1.50 4.00
2 Joe Flacco 1.25 3.00
3 Kenny Britt 1.00 2.50
4 Eddie Lacy 1.00 2.50
5 J.J. Watt 1.50 4.00
6 Tom Brady 4.00 10.00
7 Cam Newton 1.50 4.00
8 Jarvis Landry 1.25 3.00
9 Doug Martin 1.25 3.00
10 Jason Pierre-Paul 1.00 2.50
11 Philip Rivers 1.50 4.00
12 Justin Forsett 1.25 3.00
13 Todd Gurley 1.50 4.00
14 Jordy Nelson 1.25 3.00
15 Andrew Luck 2.00 5.00
16 Julian Edelman 1.50 4.00
17 Jonathan Stewart 1.00 2.50
18 Ndamukong Suh 1.25 3.00
19 Mike Evans 1.25 3.00
20 Tony Romo 1.25 3.00
21 Melvin Gordon 1.25 3.00
22 Steve Smith Sr. 1.25 3.00
23 Wes Welker 1.25 3.00
24 Matthew Stafford 1.25 3.00
25 Frank Gore 1.25 3.00
26 Rob Gronkowski 1.50 4.00
27 Greg Olsen 1.25 3.00
28 Kirk Cousins 1.50 4.00
29 Demaryius Thomas 1.25 3.00
30 Darren McFadden 1.00 2.50
31 Antonio Gates 1.00 2.50
32 Gary Barnidge 1.00 2.50
33 Colin Kaepernick 1.25 3.00
34 Ameer Abdullah 1.00 2.50
35 T.Y. Hilton 1.25 3.00
36 Brandon Marshall 1.00 2.50
37 Matt Ryan 1.25 3.00
38 Jordan Reed 1.00 2.50
39 Peyton Manning 3.00 8.00
40 Dez Bryant 1.50 4.00
41 Carson Palmer 1.25 3.00
42 Travis Benjamin 1.00 2.50
43 Carlos Hyde 1.00 2.50
44 Calvin Johnson 1.50 4.00
45 Blake Bortles 1.00 2.50
46 Darrelle Revis 1.00 2.50
47 Devonta Freeman 1.25 3.00
48 Matt Jones 1.25 3.00
49 Von Miller 1.25 3.00
50 Andy Dalton 1.25 3.00
51 Chris Johnson 1.00 2.50
52 Robert Griffin III 1.00 2.50
53 Torrey Smith 1.00 2.50
54 Jay Cutler 1.00 2.50
55 Allen Robinson 1.25 3.00
56 Matt Forte 1.00 2.50
57 Julio Jones 1.50 4.00
58 Sam Bradford 1.00 2.50
59 Alex Smith 1.25 3.00
60 Jeremy Hill 1.00 2.50
61 Larry Fitzgerald 1.25 3.00
62 Teddy Bridgewater 1.25 3.00
63 Ryan Fitzpatrick 1.00 2.50
64 Jeremy Langford 1.25 3.00
65 Allen Hurns 1.00 2.50
66 Tyrod Taylor 1.25 3.00
67 Drew Brees 1.50 4.00
68 Jordan Matthews 1.25 3.00
69 Jamaal Charles 1.25 3.00
70 A.J. Green 1.50 4.00
71 Russell Wilson 2.00 5.00
72 Adrian Peterson 1.50 4.00
73 John Brown 1.25 3.00
74 Alshon Jeffery 1.25 3.00
75 Marcus Mariota 1.50 4.00
76 LeSean McCoy 1.50 4.00
77 Mark Ingram 1.25 3.00
78 Zach Ertz 1.25 3.00
79 Jeremy Maclin 1.00 2.50
80 Ben Roethlisberger 1.50 4.00
81 Marshawn Lynch 1.25 3.00
82 Stefon Diggs 1.25 3.00
83 Ted Ginn Jr. 1.00 2.50
84 DeAndre Hopkins 1.25 3.00
85 DeMarco Murray 1.25 3.00
86 Sammy Watkins 1.50 4.00
87 Brandin Cooks 1.25 3.00
88 Eli Manning 1.25 3.00
89 Derek Carr 1.50 4.00
90 Le'Veon Bell 1.25 3.00
91 Doug Baldwin 1.25 3.00
92 Aaron Rodgers 3.00 8.00
93 Randall Cobb 1.25 3.00
94 Lamar Miller 1.00 2.50
95 Delanie Walker 1.00 2.50
96 Ryan Tannehill 1.25 3.00
97 Jameis Winston 1.50 4.00
98 Odell Beckham Jr. 1.50 4.00
99 Latavius Murray 1.00 2.50
100 Antonio Brown 1.50 4.00
101 Jared Goff AU RC 40.00 80.00
102 Carson Wentz AU RC 30.00 80.00
103 Joey Bosa AU RC 5.00 12.00
104 Ezekiel Elliott AU RC 50.00 100.00
105 Corey Coleman AU RC 4.00 10.00
106 Will Fuller AU RC 4.00 10.00
107 Josh Doctson AU RC 3.00 8.00
108 Laquon Treadwell AU RC 3.00 8.00
109 Paxton Lynch AU RC 25.00 60.00
110 Hunter Henry AU RC 3.00 8.00
111 Sterling Shepard AU RC 3.00 8.00
112 Derrick Henry AU RC 6.00 15.00
113 Michael Thomas AU RC 5.00 12.00
114 Christian Hackenberg AU RC 2.50 6.00
115 Kenyan Drake AU RC 4.00 10.00
116 Braxton Miller AU RC 2.50 6.00
117 Leonte Carroo AU RC 2.50 6.00
118 C.J. Prosise AU RC 2.50 6.00
119 Jacoby Brissett AU RC 3.00 8.00
120 Cody Kessler AU RC 2.50 6.00
121 Tyler Boyd AU RC 3.00 8.00
122 Connor Cook AU RC 3.00 8.00
123 Chris Moore AU RC 3.00 8.00
124 Malcolm Mitchell AU RC 2.50 6.00
125 Ricardo Louis AU RC 2.50 6.00
126 Pharoh Cooper AU RC 2.50 6.00
127 Tyler Ervin AU RC 2.50 6.00
128 Demarcus Robinson AU RC 2.50 6.00
129 Kenneth Dixon AU RC 2.50 6.00
130 Dak Prescott AU RC 30.00 60.00
131 Devontae Booker AU RC 3.00 8.00
132 Cardale Jones AU RC 2.50 6.00
133 Trevor Davis AU RC 2.50 6.00
134 Keenan Reynolds AU RC 3.00 8.00
135 Paul Perkins AU RC 2.50 6.00
136 Jordan Howard AU RC 8.00 20.00
137 Wendell Smallwood AU RC 2.50 6.00
138 Jonathan Williams AU RC 3.00 8.00
139 Kevin Hogan AU RC 3.00 8.00
140 Alex Collins AU RC 3.00 8.00

2016 Panini Origins Blue
*VETS/140: .6X TO 1.5X BASIC CARDS
*ROOK AU/49: .8X TO 2X BASIC CARDS
*ROOK AU/25: 1X TO 2.5X BASIC CARDS
101 Jared Goff/25 AU 75.00 150.00
102 Carson Wentz/25 AU 100.00 200.00
104 Ezekiel Elliott/25 AU 100.00 200.00
130 Dak Prescott/49 AU 40.00 100.00

2016 Panini Origins Red
*VETS: .5X TO 1.2X BASIC CARDS
*ROOK AU/99: .6X TO 1.5X BASIC RC AU
*ROOK AU/49: .8X TO 2X BASIC RC AU
101 Jared Goff/49 AU 60.00 125.00
102 Carson Wentz/49 AU 75.00 150.00
104 Ezekiel Elliott/49 AU 75.00 150.00
130 Dak Prescott/99 AU 50.00 125.00

2016 Panini Origins Turquoise
*VETS/60: 1X TO 2.5X BASIC CARDS
*ROOK AU/25: 1X TO 2.5X BASIC RC AU
*ROOK AU/15: 1.2X TO 3X BASIC RC AU
101 Jared Goff/15 AU 100.00 200.00
102 Carson Wentz/15 AU 100.00 200.00
104 Ezekiel Elliott/15 AU 150.00 300.00
130 Dak Prescott/25 AU 100.00 200.00

2016 Panini Origins Elemental Jerseys
1 A.J. Green 5.00 12.00
2 Allen Robinson 4.00 10.00
3 Andy Dalton 4.00 10.00
4 Blake Bortles 3.00 8.00
5 Brandon Marshall 3.00 8.00
6 Cam Newton 5.00 12.00
7 DeMarcus Ware 4.00 10.00
8 DeVante Parker 4.00 10.00
9 Drew Brees 5.00 12.00
10 Eli Manning 4.00 10.00
11 Eric Decker 3.00 8.00
12 Jarvis Landry 4.00 10.00
13 Jimmy Graham 5.00 12.00
14 Jordan Reed 3.00 8.00
15 Julius Thomas 3.00 8.00
16 Kelvin Benjamin 4.00 10.00
17 Kirk Cousins 5.00 12.00
18 Marcell Dareus 3.00 8.00
19 Mark Ingram 4.00 10.00
20 Matt Ryan 4.00 10.00
21 Paul Posluszny 3.00 8.00
22 Russell Wilson 6.00 15.00
23 Ryan Tannehill 4.00 10.00
24 T.Y. Hilton 4.00 10.00
25 Geno Atkins 3.00 8.00

2016 Panini Origins First Hand Gloves
1 Allen Robinson 5.00 12.00
2 Amari Cooper 10.00 25.00
3 Ameer Abdullah 4.00 10.00
4 Blake Bortles 4.00 10.00
5 Brandin Cooks 5.00 12.00
6 Davante Adams 4.00 10.00
7 David Johnson 6.00 15.00
8 Derek Carr 8.00 20.00
9 Devonta Freeman 5.00 12.00
10 Dorial Green-Beckham 4.00 10.00
11 Jameis Winston 10.00 25.00
12 Jarvis Landry 5.00 12.00
13 Jeremy Hill 4.00 10.00
14 Kelvin Benjamin 5.00 12.00
15 Kevin White 4.00 10.00
16 Marcus Mariota 10.00 25.00
17 Melvin Gordon 5.00 12.00
18 Mike Evans 5.00 12.00
19 Odell Beckham Jr. 12.00 30.00
20 Sammy Watkins 6.00 15.00
21 Stefon Diggs 5.00 12.00
22 T.J. Yeldon 4.00 10.00
23 Teddy Bridgewater 5.00 12.00
24 Todd Gurley 10.00 25.00
25 Tyler Lockett 8.00 20.00
26 A.J. McCarron 4.00 10.00
27 Carlos Hyde 4.00 10.00
28 DeVante Parker 5.00 12.00
29 Devin Funchess 4.00 10.00
30 Donte Moncrief 5.00 12.00
31 Duke Johnson 4.00 10.00
32 Jadeveon Clowney 4.00 10.00
33 Jamison Crowder 4.00 10.00
34 Austin Seferian-Jenkins 4.00 10.00
35 Jeremy Langford 5.00 12.00
36 Jordan Matthews 5.00 12.00
37 Khalil Mack 10.00 25.00
38 Matt Jones 5.00 12.00
39 Nelson Agholor 4.00 10.00
40 Phillip Dorsett 4.00 10.00

2016 Panini Origins Influential Jerseys
1 Allen Hurns 3.00 8.00
2 Andrew Luck 6.00 15.00
3 Ben Roethlisberger 10.00 25.00
4 Brandin Cooks 4.00 10.00
5 C.J. Anderson 4.00 10.00
6 Darren McFadden 3.00 8.00
7 DeSean Jackson 4.00 10.00
8 Dez Bryant 5.00 12.00
9 Earl Thomas III 4.00 10.00
10 Emmanuel Sanders 5.00 12.00
11 J.J. Watt 5.00 12.00
12 Jeremy Hill 3.00 8.00
13 Jonathan Stewart 3.00 8.00
14 Julio Jones 5.00 12.00
15 Keenan Allen 4.00 10.00
16 Kendall Wright 3.00 8.00
17 LeSean McCoy 5.00 12.00
18 Marcus Mariota 5.00 12.00
19 Marshawn Lynch 10.00 25.00
20 Melvin Gordon 4.00 10.00
21 Philip Rivers 5.00 12.00
22 Ryan Mathews 4.00 10.00
23 Sammy Watkins 5.00 12.00
24 Tony Romo 4.00 10.00
25 Von Miller 4.00 10.00

2016 Panini Origins Origins of Greatness Jerseys
1 Ozzie Newsome
2 Marshall Faulk
3 Tim Tebow
4 Brett Favre 12.00 30.00
5 Cris Carter 8.00 20.00
6 Barry Sanders 10.00 25.00
7 LaDainian Tomlinson 5.00 12.00
8 Brian Urlacher 6.00 15.00
9 Derrick Brooks 4.00 10.00
10 Marcus Allen 5.00 12.00

2016 Panini Origins Rookie Autographs Silver Ink
3 Joey Bosa/49 10.00 25.00
5 Corey Coleman/49 8.00 20.00
6 Will Fuller/49 8.00 20.00
7 Josh Doctson/49 6.00 15.00
8 Laquon Treadwell/49 6.00 15.00
10 Hunter Henry/99 5.00 12.00
11 Sterling Shepard/49 6.00 15.00
13 Michael Thomas/49 10.00 25.00
14 Christian Hackenberg/49 5.00 12.00
15 Kenyan Drake/99 6.00 15.00
16 Braxton Miller/49 5.00 12.00
17 Leonte Carroo/99 4.00 10.00
18 C.J. Prosise/49 5.00 12.00
19 Jacoby Brissett/99 5.00 12.00
20 Cody Kessler/49 5.00 12.00
21 Tyler Boyd/49 6.00 15.00
23 Chris Moore/99 5.00 12.00
24 Malcolm Mitchell/99 10.00 25.00
25 Ricardo Louis/99 4.00 10.00
26 Pharoh Cooper/48 5.00 12.00
27 Tyler Ervin/99 4.00 10.00
28 Demarcus Robinson/99 4.00 10.00
29 Kenneth Dixon/99 4.00 10.00
30 Dak Prescott/99 60.00 125.00
31 Devontae Booker/99 5.00 12.00
32 Cardale Jones/49 5.00 12.00
33 Trevor Davis/99 4.00 10.00
34 Keenan Reynolds/99 5.00 12.00
35 Paul Perkins/49 5.00 12.00
36 Jordan Howard/49 12.00 30.00
37 Wendell Smallwood/99 4.00 10.00
38 Jonathan Williams/99 5.00 12.00
39 Kevin Hogan/99 5.00 12.00
40 Alex Collins/49 6.00 15.00

2016 Panini Origins Rookie Jumbo Jerseys
RJJAC Alex Collins 2.50 6.00
RJJBM Braxton Miller 2.00 5.00
RJJCC Corey Coleman 3.00 8.00
RJJCH Christian Hackenberg 2.00 5.00
RJJCJ Cardale Jones 2.00 5.00
RJJCK Cody Kessler 2.00 5.00
RJJCP C.J. Prosise 2.00 5.00
RJJCW Carson Wentz 20.00 50.00
RJJDB Devontae Booker 2.50 6.00
RJJDH Derrick Henry 5.00 12.00
RJJDP Dak Prescott 10.00 25.00
RJJDW DeAndre Washington 2.00 5.00
RJJEE Ezekiel Elliott 10.00 25.00
RJJHH Hunter Henry 2.50 6.00
RJJJB Joey Bosa 4.00 10.00
RJJJD Josh Doctson 2.50 6.00
RJJJG Jared Goff 12.00 30.00
RJJJH Jordan Howard 5.00 12.00
RJJJW Jonathan Williams 2.50 6.00
RJJKD Kenyan Drake 3.00 8.00
RJJKH Kevin Hogan 2.50 6.00
RJJKR Keenan Reynolds 2.50 6.00
RJJLC Leonte Carroo 2.00 5.00
RJJLT Laquon Treadwell 3.00 8.00
RJJMT Michael Thomas 4.00 10.00
RJJPL Paxton Lynch 2.00 5.00
RJJPP Paul Perkins 2.00 5.00
RJJSS Sterling Shepard 2.50 6.00
RJJWF Will Fuller 3.00 8.00
RJJWS Wendell Smallwood 2.00 5.00

2016 Panini Origins Rookie Jumbo Patch Autographs
RJPAAC Alex Collins 5.00 12.00
RJPABM Braxton Miller 4.00 10.00
RJPACC Corey Coleman 6.00 15.00
RJPACC Connor Cook 5.00 12.00
RJPACH Christian Hackenberg 4.00 10.00
RJPACJ Cardale Jones 4.00 10.00
RJPACK Cody Kessler 4.00 10.00
RJPACM Chris Moore 5.00 12.00
RJPACP C.J. Prosise 4.00 10.00
RJPACW Carson Wentz 60.00 125.00
RJPADB Devontae Booker 10.00 25.00
RJPADH Derrick Henry 40.00 80.00
RJPADP Dak Prescott 40.00 80.00
RJPADR Demarcus Robinson 4.00 10.00
RJPADW DeAndre Washington 4.00 10.00
RJPAEE Ezekiel Elliott 50.00 100.00
RJPAHH Hunter Henry 5.00 12.00
RJPAJB Joey Bosa 8.00 20.00
RJPAJD Josh Doctson 5.00 12.00
RJPAJG Jared Goff 60.00 125.00
RJPAJH Jordan Howard 10.00 25.00
RJPAJW Jonathan Williams 5.00 12.00
RJPAKD Kenyan Drake 6.00 15.00
RJPAKH Kevin Hogan 5.00 12.00
RJPAKR Kenneth Dixon 4.00 10.00
RJPAKR Keenan Reynolds 5.00 12.00
RJPALC Leonte Carroo 4.00 10.00
RJPALT Laquon Treadwell 15.00 40.00
RJPAMB Moritz Bohringer 4.00 10.00
RJPAMT Michael Thomas 8.00 20.00
RJPAPC Pharoh Cooper 4.00 10.00
RJPAPL Paxton Lynch 40.00 80.00
RJPAPP Paul Perkins 4.00 10.00
RJPARL Ricardo Louis 4.00 10.00
RJPASS Sterling Shepard 20.00 40.00
RJPATB Tyler Boyd 12.00 30.00
RJPATD Trevor Davis 4.00 10.00
RJPATE Tyler Ervin 4.00 10.00
RJPAWF Will Fuller 6.00 15.00
RJPAWS Wendell Smallwood 4.00 10.00

2016 Panini Origins Rookie Jumbo Patch Autographs Blue
*BLUE/49: .6X TO 1.5X BASIC JSY AU

2016 Panini Origins Rookie Jumbo Patch Autographs Red
*RED/49: .5X TO 1.2X BASIC JSY AU
RJPAEE Ezekiel Elliott 75.00 150.00

2016 Panini Origins Rookie Jumbo Patch Autographs Turquoise
*TURQUOISE/25: .8X TO 2X BASIC JSY AU
RJPAEE Ezekiel Elliott 125.00 250.00

2016 Panini Origins Rookie Patch Autographs
1 Jared Goff 100.00 200.00
2 Carson Wentz 60.00 150.00
3 Joey Bosa 12.00 30.00
4 Ezekiel Elliott 150.00 250.00
5 Corey Coleman 10.00 25.00
6 Will Fuller 10.00 25.00
7 Josh Doctson 8.00 20.00
8 Laquon Treadwell 8.00 20.00
9 Paxton Lynch 6.00 15.00
10 Sterling Shepard 8.00 20.00
11 Derrick Henry 15.00 40.00
12 Michael Thomas 12.00 30.00
13 Christian Hackenberg 6.00 15.00
14 Kenyan Drake 10.00 25.00
15 Braxton Miller 6.00 15.00
16 C.J. Prosise 6.00 15.00

2016 Panini Origins Rookie Patches
*RED/99: .4X TO 1X BASIC JSY
*BLUE/49: .5X TO 1.2X BASIC JSY/125
*TURQUOISE/25: .6X TO 1.5X BASIC JSY/125
1 Jared Goff 12.00 30.00
2 Carson Wentz 20.00 50.00
3 Joey Bosa 4.00 10.00
4 Ezekiel Elliott 10.00 25.00
5 Corey Coleman 3.00 8.00
6 Will Fuller 3.00 8.00
7 Josh Doctson 2.50 6.00
8 Laquon Treadwell 2.50 6.00
9 Paxton Lynch 2.00 5.00
10 Hunter Henry 2.50 6.00
11 Sterling Shepard 2.50 6.00
12 Derrick Henry 5.00 12.00
13 Michael Thomas 4.00 10.00
14 Christian Hackenberg 2.00 5.00
15 Kenyan Drake 3.00 8.00
16 Braxton Miller 2.00 5.00
17 Leonte Carroo 2.00 5.00
18 C.J. Prosise 2.00 5.00
19 Cardale Jones 2.00 5.00
20 Cody Kessler 2.00 5.00
21 Tyler Boyd 2.50 6.00
22 Connor Cook 2.50 6.00
23 Chris Moore 2.50 6.00
24 Moritz Bohringer 2.00 5.00
25 Ricardo Louis 2.00 5.00
26 Pharoh Cooper 2.00 5.00
27 Tyler Ervin 2.00 5.00
28 Kenneth Dixon 2.00 5.00
29 Dak Prescott 10.00 25.00
30 Paul Perkins 2.00 5.00

2016 Panini Origins Rushing Stars Autographs
RSSCP C.J. Prosise 6.00 15.00
RSSEE Ezekiel Elliott 125.00 250.00
RSSEH Derrick Henry 15.00 40.00
RSSKD Kenyan Drake 10.00 25.00
RSSTE Tyler Ervin

2017 Panini Origins
1 Tom Brady 4.00 10.00
2 Cam Newton 1.50 4.00
3 J.J. Watt 1.50 4.00
4 Antonio Brown 1.50 4.00
5 Aaron Rodgers 3.00 8.00
6 Adrian Peterson 1.50 4.00
7 Luke Kuechly 1.25 3.00
8 Julio Jones 1.50 4.00
9 Rob Gronkowski 1.50 4.00
10 Odell Beckham Jr. 1.50 4.00
11 Josh Norman 1.00 2.50
12 Carson Palmer 1.25 3.00
13 Mike Glennon 1.25 3.00
14 Von Miller 1.25 3.00
15 Ezekiel Elliott 2.00 5.00
16 Dak Prescott 1.50 4.00
17 Dez Bryant 1.50 4.00
18 Jason Witten 1.25 3.00
19 Derek Carr 1.50 4.00
20 Amari Cooper 1.50 4.00
21 Khalil Mack 1.50 4.00
22 Russell Wilson 2.00 5.00
23 Doug Baldwin 1.25 3.00
24 DeAndre Hopkins 1.25 3.00
25 Ben Roethlisberger 1.50 4.00
26 James Harrison 1.25 3.00
27 Todd Gurley II 1.50 4.00
28 Jared Goff 1.50 4.00
29 Carson Wentz 2.00 5.00
30 Larry Fitzgerald 1.25 3.00
31 Matt Ryan 1.25 3.00
32 Vic Beasley Jr. 1.00 2.50
33 Drew Brees 1.50 4.00
34 Mark Ingram 1.25 3.00
35 Blake Bortles 1.00 2.50
36 Allen Robinson 1.25 3.00
37 Andy Dalton 1.25 3.00
38 Greg Olsen 1.25 3.00
39 Kelvin Benjamin 1.25 3.00
40 Ryan Tannehill 1.25 3.00
41 Jarvis Landry 1.25 3.00
42 Le'Veon Bell 1.25 3.00
43 Tyler Eifert 1.25 3.00
44 Kirk Cousins 1.50 4.00
45 Jordan Reed 1.00 2.50
46 Robert Kelley 1.00 2.50
47 Philip Rivers 1.50 4.00
48 Antonio Gates 1.00 2.50
49 Keenan Allen 1.25 3.00
50 Eli Manning 1.25 3.00
51 Devonta Freeman 1.25 3.00
52 Eric Berry 1.25 3.00
53 Clay Matthews 1.25 3.00
54 Jordy Nelson 1.25 3.00
55 Navorro Bowman 1.25 3.00
56 Leonard Floyd 1.00 2.50
57 LeSean McCoy 1.50 4.00
58 Tyrod Taylor 1.25 3.00
59 Alex Smith 1.25 3.00
60 Matt Forte 1.00 2.50
61 Andrew Luck 2.00 5.00
62 T.Y. Hilton 1.25 3.00
63 Joey Bosa 1.50 4.00
64 Sammy Watkins 1.50 4.00
65 Kam Chancellor 1.50 4.00
66 Carlos Hyde 1.00 2.50
67 Jordan Matthews 1.00 2.50
68 Alshon Jeffery 1.25 3.00
69 Sheldon Richardson 1.00 2.50
70 Leonard Williams 1.00 2.50
71 Julian Edelman 1.50 4.00
72 Jay Ajayi 1.25 3.00
73 Aaron Donald 1.50 4.00
74 Tyreek Hill 1.50 4.00
75 Travis Kelce 1.50 4.00
76 Frank Gore 1.25 3.00
77 Trevor Siemian 1.00 2.50
78 Devontae Booker 1.00 2.50
79 Demaryius Thomas 1.25 3.00
80 David Johnson 1.50 4.00
81 Jordan Howard 1.50 4.00
82 A.J. Green 1.50 4.00
83 Jadeveon Clowney 1.00 2.50
84 Allen Hurns 1.00 2.50
85 Paul Perkins 1.00 2.50
86 Brandon Marshall 1.00 2.50
87 Patrick Peterson 1.00 2.50
88 Joe Flacco 1.25 3.00
89 Mike Wallace 1.00 2.50
90 Terrell Suggs 1.00 2.50
91 Corey Coleman 1.00 2.50
92 Isaiah Crowell 1.00 2.50
93 Marcus Mariota 1.50 4.00
94 DeMarco Murray 1.25 3.00
95 Jameis Winston 1.25 3.00
96 Mike Evans 1.25 3.00
97 Matthew Stafford 1.25 3.00
98 Golden Tate III 1.00 2.50
99 Rishard Matthews 1.00 2.50
100 Gerald McCoy 1.00 2.50
101 Deshaun Watson JSY AU RC 60.00 125.00
102 Mitchell Trubisky JSY AU RC 40.00 100.00
103 DeShone Kizer JSY AU RC 4.00 10.00
104 Patrick Mahomes II JSY AU RC 150.00 300.00
105 Nathan Peterman JSY AU RC 8.00 20.00
106 Davis Webb JSY AU RC 4.00 10.00
107 C.J. Beathard JSY AU RC 4.00 10.00
108 R. Joshua Dobbs JSY AU RC 5.00 12.00
109 Leonard Fournette JSY AU RC 30.00 60.00
110 Dalvin Cook JSY AU RC 15.00 40.00
111 Christian McCaffrey JSY AU RC 25.00 60.00
112 D'Onta Foreman JSY AU RC 5.00 12.00
113 Alvin Kamara JSY AU RC 15.00 40.00
114 Samaje Perine JSY AU RC 4.00 10.00
115 Wayne Gallman JSY AU RC 5.00 12.00
116 Kareem Hunt JSY AU RC 15.00 40.00
117 Kenny Golladay JSY AU RC 6.00 15.00
118 James Conner JSY AU RC 20.00 40.00
119 Joe Mixon JSY AU RC 8.00 20.00
120 Evan Engram JSY AU RC 5.00 12.00
121 O.J. Howard JSY AU RC 5.00 12.00
122 Mike Williams JSY AU RC 6.00 15.00
123 Corey Davis JSY AU RC 6.00 15.00
124 John Ross III JSY AU RC 5.00 12.00
125 JuJu Smith-Schuster JSY AU RC 10.00 25.00
126 Zay Jones JSY AU RC 5.00 12.00
127 Curtis Samuel JSY AU RC 5.00 12.00
128 Dede Westbrook JSY AU RC 4.00 10.00
129 Carlos Henderson JSY AU RC 4.00 10.00
130 Chris Godwin JSY AU RC 5.00 12.00
131 Mack Hollins JSY AU RC 4.00 10.00
132 Cooper Kupp JSY AU RC 6.00 15.00
133 Amara Darboh JSY AU RC 4.00 10.00
134 Marlon Mack JSY AU RC 6.00 15.00
135 ArDarius Stewart JSY AU RC 4.00 10.00
136 Joe Williams JSY AU RC 4.00 10.00
137 Jamaal Williams JSY AU RC 4.00 10.00
138 Taywan Taylor JSY AU RC 4.00 10.00
139 Jeremy McNichols JSY AU RC 4.00 10.00
140 Josh Reynolds JSY AU RC 4.00 10.00

2017 Panini Origins Blue
101 Deshaun Watson JSY AU 75.00 150.00
104 Patrick Mahomes II JSY AU 250.00 400.00

2017 Panini Origins Orange
*VETS/150: .6X TO 1.5X BASIC CARDS

2017 Panini Origins Red
*VETS/299: .5X TO 1.2X BASIC CARDS
*ROOK/99: .5X TO 1.2X BASIC JSY AU
101 Deshaun Watson JSY AU 75.00 150.00
104 Patrick Mahomes II JSY AU 200.00 400.00

2017 Panini Origins Turquoise
*VETS: 1.2X TO 3X BASIC CARDS
*ROOKIES: 1.2X TO 3X BASIC JSY AU
101 Deshaun Watson JSY AU 100.00 200.00
104 Patrick Mahomes II JSY AU 300.00 500.00

2017 Panini Origins Rookie Autographs Silver Ink
1 Mitchell Trubisky/49 75.00 150.00
2 Leonard Fournette/49 40.00 80.00
3 Corey Davis/99 6.00 15.00
4 Mike Williams/49 15.00 40.00
5 Christian McCaffrey/49 50.00 100.00
6 John Ross III/99 5.00 12.00
7 Patrick Mahomes II/49 200.00 400.00
8 Deshaun Watson/49 75.00 150.00
9 O.J. Howard/99 5.00 12.00
10 Evan Engram/99 5.00 12.00
11 Zay Jones/99 5.00 12.00
12 Curtis Samuel/99 5.00 12.00
13 Dalvin Cook/49 50.00 100.00
14 Joe Mixon/99 8.00 20.00
15 DeShone Kizer/49 5.00 12.00
16 JuJu Smith-Schuster/99 10.00 25.00
17 Alvin Kamara/99 15.00 40.00
18 Cooper Kupp/99 6.00 15.00
19 Taywan Taylor/99 4.00 10.00
20 ArDarius Stewart/99 4.00 10.00
21 Carlos Henderson/99 4.00 10.00
22 Chris Godwin/99 5.00 12.00
23 Kareem Hunt/99 30.00 60.00
24 Davis Webb/99 4.00 10.00
25 D'Onta Foreman/99 5.00 12.00
26 Kenny Golladay/99 6.00 15.00
27 C.J. Beathard/99 4.00 10.00
28 James Conner/99 15.00 40.00
29 Amara Darboh/99 4.00 10.00
30 Dede Westbrook/99 4.00 10.00
31 Samaje Perine/99 4.00 10.00
32 Josh Reynolds/99 4.00 10.00
33 Mack Hollins/99 4.00 10.00
34 Joe Williams/99 4.00 10.00
35 Jeremy McNichols/99 4.00 10.00
36 Jamaal Williams/99 4.00 10.00
37 R. Joshua Dobbs/99 5.00 12.00
38 Wayne Gallman/99 5.00 12.00
39 Nathan Peterman/99 5.00 12.00
40 Marlon Mack/99 6.00 15.00

2017 Panini Origins Rookie Autographs Gold Ink
*GOLD/25: .6X TO 1.5X BASIC AU/99
*GOLD/25: .5X TO 1.2X BASIC AU/49
1 Mitchell Trubisky 125.00 250.00
2 Leonard Fournette 40.00 100.00
5 Christian McCaffrey 50.00 125.00
7 Patrick Mahomes II 250.00 500.00
8 Deshaun Watson 100.00 200.00

2017 Panini Origins Rookie Jumbo Jerseys
*RED/99: .5X TO 1.2X BASIC JSY/199
*ORANGE/75: .5X TO 1.2X BASIC JSY
*BLUE/49: .6X TO 1.5X BASIC JSY/199
*TURQUOISE/25: .8X TO 2X BASIC JSY/199
*PATCH/175: .5X TO 1.2X BASIC JSY/199
*RED PATCH/99: .6X TO 1.5X BASIC JSY/199
*ORANGE PATCH/75: .6X TO 1.5X BASIC JSY/199
*BLUE PATCH/49: .8X TO 2X BASIC JSY/199
*TURQ PATCH/25: 1X TO 2.5X BASIC JSY/199
1 Mitchell Trubisky 6.00 15.00
2 Leonard Fournette 6.00 15.00
3 Corey Davis 3.00 8.00
4 Mike Williams 3.00 8.00
5 Christian McCaffrey 6.00 15.00
6 John Ross III 5.00 12.00
7 Patrick Mahomes II 25.00 50.00
8 Deshaun Watson 10.00 25.00
9 O.J. Howard 5.00 12.00
10 Evan Engram 2.50 6.00
11 Dalvin Cook 6.00 15.00
12 Joe Mixon 5.00 12.00
13 DeShone Kizer 2.00 5.00
14 JuJu Smith-Schuster 5.00 12.00
15 Alvin Kamara 5.00 12.00
16 Cooper Kupp 3.00 8.00
17 Taywan Taylor 2.00 5.00
18 ArDarius Stewart 2.00 5.00
19 Carlos Henderson 2.00 5.00
20 Chris Godwin 2.50 6.00
21 Kareem Hunt 4.00 10.00
22 Davis Webb 2.00 5.00
23 D'Onta Foreman 2.50 6.00
24 C.J. Beathard 2.00 5.00
25 James Conner 4.00 10.00
26 Amara Darboh 2.00 5.00
27 Kenny Golladay 3.00 8.00
28 Dede Westbrook 2.00 5.00
29 Samaje Perine 2.00 5.00
30 R. Joshua Dobbs 2.50 6.00

2017 Panini Origins Rookie Patch Autographs
1 Mitchell Trubisky 100.00 200.00
2 Patrick Mahomes II 250.00 500.00
3 Deshaun Watson 100.00 200.00
4 DeShone Kizer 8.00 20.00
5 Davis Webb 8.00 20.00
6 Leonard Fournette 60.00 125.00
7 Christian McCaffrey 50.00 100.00
8 Dalvin Cook 50.00 100.00
9 Joe Mixon 15.00 40.00
10 Alvin Kamara 50.00 100.00
11 Corey Davis 12.00 30.00
12 Mike Williams 12.00 30.00
13 John Ross III 10.00 25.00
14 Zay Jones 10.00 25.00
15 Curtis Samuel 10.00 25.00
16 JuJu Smith-Schuster 20.00 50.00

2017 Panini Origins Rookie Signatures
1 Deshaun Watson 50.00 100.00
2 Mitchell Trubisky 60.00 125.00
3 DeShone Kizer 3.00 8.00
4 Patrick Mahomes II 100.00 200.00
5 Davis Webb 3.00 8.00
6 C.J. Beathard 3.00 8.00
7 R. Joshua Dobbs 4.00 10.00
8 Nathan Peterman 12.00 30.00
9 Leonard Fournette 30.00 60.00
10 Dalvin Cook 15.00 40.00
11 Christian McCaffrey 60.00 125.00
12 D'Onta Foreman 4.00 10.00
13 Alvin Kamara 12.00 30.00
14 Samaje Perine 3.00 8.00
15 Marlon Mack 5.00 12.00
16 Kareem Hunt 20.00 50.00
17 Wayne Gallman 4.00 10.00
18 James Conner 6.00 15.00
19 Joe Mixon 12.00 30.00
20 Mack Hollins 3.00 8.00
21 O.J. Howard 4.00 10.00
22 Mike Williams 5.00 12.00
23 Corey Davis 5.00 12.00
24 John Ross III 4.00 10.00
25 JuJu Smith-Schuster 15.00 40.00
26 Zay Jones 4.00 10.00
27 Curtis Samuel 4.00 10.00
28 Dede Westbrook 3.00 8.00
29 Carlos Henderson 3.00 8.00
30 Chris Godwin 4.00 10.00
31 Kenny Golladay 5.00 12.00
32 Cooper Kupp 5.00 12.00
33 Amara Darboh 3.00 8.00
34 Jeremy McNichols 3.00 8.00
35 ArDarius Stewart 3.00 8.00
36 Joe Williams 3.00 8.00
37 Josh Reynolds 3.00 8.00
38 Taywan Taylor 3.00 8.00
39 Evan Engram 4.00 10.00
40 Jamaal Williams 3.00 8.00

2017 Panini Origins Rookie Signatures Blue
*BLUE/49: .6X TO 1.5X BASIC AU
*BLUE/25: .8X TO 2X BASIC AU
2 Mitchell Trubisky/25 100.00 200.00
11 Christian McCaffrey/25 150.00 250.00

2017 Panini Origins Rookie Signatures Red
*RED/99: .5X TO 1.2X BASIC AU
*RED/49: .6X TO 1.5X BASIC AU
1 Deshaun Watson/49 75.00 150.00
2 Mitchell Trubisky/49 75.00 150.00
4 Patrick Mahomes II/49 200.00 300.00
11 Christian McCaffrey/49 100.00 200.00

2017 Panini Origins Rookie Signatures Turquoise
*TURQUOISE/25: .8X TO 2X BASIC AU

2018 Panini Origins
1 Alex Smith 1.25 3.00
2 Josh Norman 1.00 2.50
3 Samaje Perine 1.00 2.50
4 Kirk Cousins 1.50 4.00
5 Adam Thielen 1.50 4.00
6 Stefon Diggs 1.25 3.00
7 Tyrod Taylor 1.25 3.00
8 Jarvis Landry 1.25 3.00
9 Josh Gordon 1.00 2.50
10 Aaron Rodgers 3.00 8.00
11 Jimmy Graham 1.50 4.00
12 Clay Matthews 1.25 3.00
13 Patrick Mahomes II 4.00 10.00
14 Kareem Hunt 1.25 3.00
15 Travis Kelce 1.50 4.00
16 Tyreek Hill 1.50 4.00
17 Mitchell Trubisky 1.50 4.00
18 Allen Robinson 1.25 3.00
19 Jordan Howard 1.50 4.00
20 Case Keenum 1.25 3.00
21 Demaryius Thomas 1.25 3.00
22 Von Miller 1.25 3.00
23 Derek Carr 1.50 4.00
24 Jordy Nelson 1.25 3.00
25 Khalil Mack 1.50 4.00
26 Chandler Jones 1.00 2.50
27 Larry Fitzgerald 1.25 3.00
28 David Johnson 1.50 4.00
29 Richard Sherman 1.50 4.00
30 Jimmy Garoppolo 2.00 5.00
31 Jerick McKinnon 1.00 2.50
32 Leonard Williams 1.00 2.50
33 Jamal Adams 1.25 3.00
34 Robby Anderson 1.00 2.50
35 Joe Flacco 1.25 3.00
36 C.J. Mosley 1.25 3.00
37 Terrell Suggs 1.00 2.50
38 Darius Slay 1.00 2.50
39 Matthew Stafford 1.25 3.00
40 Marvin Jones Jr. 1.00 2.50
41 Matt Ryan 1.25 3.00
42 Julio Jones 1.50 4.00
43 Devonta Freeman 1.25 3.00
44 Cam Newton 1.50 4.00
45 Christian McCaffrey 1.50 4.00
46 Luke Kuechly 1.25 3.00
47 Andy Dalton 1.25 3.00
48 A.J. Green 1.50 4.00
49 Joe Mixon 1.25 3.00
50 Dak Prescott 1.50 4.00
51 Ezekiel Elliott 2.00 5.00
52 Jason Witten 1.25 3.00
53 Deshaun Watson 2.00 5.00
54 Jadeveon Clowney 1.00 2.50
55 DeAndre Hopkins 1.25 3.00
56 Andrew Luck 2.00 5.00
57 Marlon Mack 1.00 2.50
58 T.Y. Hilton 1.25 3.00
59 Blake Bortles 1.00 2.50
60 Leonard Fournette 1.50 4.00
61 Jalen Ramsey 1.25 3.00
62 Ben Roethlisberger 1.50 4.00
63 Le'Veon Bell 1.25 3.00
64 Antonio Brown 1.50 4.00
65 T.J. Watt 1.25 3.00
66 Philip Rivers 1.50 4.00
67 Joey Bosa 1.50 4.00
68 Melvin Gordon 1.25 3.00
69 Jared Goff 1.50 4.00
70 Todd Gurley II 1.50 4.00
71 Aaron Donald 1.50 4.00
72 Ryan Tannehill 1.25 3.00
73 Kenyan Drake 1.00 2.50
74 Cameron Wake 1.00 2.50
75 Tom Brady 4.00 10.00
76 Rob Gronkowski 1.50 4.00
77 Julian Edelman 1.50 4.00
78 Drew Brees 1.50 4.00
79 Michael Thomas 1.50 4.00
80 Alvin Kamara 1.25 3.00
81 Eli Manning 1.25 3.00
82 Odell Beckham Jr. 1.50 4.00
83 Dalvin Cook 1.25 3.00
84 Landon Collins 1.00 2.50
85 Carson Wentz 2.00 5.00
86 Alshon Jeffery 1.25 3.00
87 Jay Ajayi 1.25 3.00
88 Russell Wilson 2.00 5.00
89 Doug Baldwin 1.25 3.00
90 Earl Thomas III 1.25 3.00
91 Jameis Winston 1.25 3.00
92 Mike Evans 1.25 3.00
93 Gerald McCoy 1.00 2.50
94 Marcus Mariota 1.50 4.00
95 Derrick Henry 1.50 4.00
96 Delanie Walker 1.00 2.50
97 LeSean McCoy 1.50 4.00
98 A.J. McCarron 1.00 2.50
99 Kelvin Benjamin 1.25 3.00
100 Chris Hogan 1.00 2.50
101 Josh Rosen JSY AU RC 40.00 80.00
102 Sam Darnold JSY AU RC 60.00 125.00
103 Saquon Barkley JSY AU RC 90.00 150.00
104 Josh Allen JSY AU RC 40.00 80.00
105 Baker Mayfield JSY AU RC 60.00 125.00
106 Calvin Ridley JSY AU RC 10.00 25.00
107 Hayden Hurst JSY AU RC 5.00 12.00
108 Courtland Sutton JSY AU RC 6.00 15.00
109 Sony Michel JSY AU RC 12.00 30.00
110 Derrius Guice JSY AU RC 8.00 20.00
111 Christian Kirk JSY AU RC 6.00 15.00
112 Ronald Jones II JSY AU RC 8.00 20.00
113 D.J. Moore JSY AU RC 8.00 20.00
114 James Washington JSY AU RC 8.00 20.00
115 D.J. Chark JSY AU RC EXCH 5.00 12.00
116 Mason Rudolph JSY AU RC 10.00 25.00
117 Kalen Ballage JSY AU RC 5.00 12.00
118 Lamar Jackson JSY AU RC 50.00 100.00
119 Mike Gesicki JSY AU RC 5.00 12.00
120 Nyheim Hines JSY AU RC 5.00 12.00
121 Keke Coutee JSY AU RC 5.00 12.00
122 Kerryon Johnson JSY AU RC 10.00 25.00
123 Kyle Lauletta JSY AU RC 6.00 15.00
124 Mark Walton JSY AU RC 5.00 12.00
125 Tre'Quan Smith JSY AU RC 6.00 15.00
126 Michael Gallup JSY AU RC 8.00 20.00
127 Rashaad Penny JSY AU RC 6.00 15.00
128 DaeSean Hamilton JSY AU RC 5.00 12.00
129 Jaleel Scott JSY AU RC 4.00 10.00
130 Nick Chubb JSY AU RC 12.00 30.00
131 Ito Smith JSY AU RC 5.00 12.00
132 J'Mon Moore JSY AU RC 4.00 10.00
133 Daurice Fountain JSY AU RC 5.00 12.00
134 Anthony Miller JSY AU RC 6.00 15.00
135 Jaylen Samuels JSY AU RC 5.00 12.00
136 Marquez Valdes-Scantling JSY AU RC 5.00 12.00
137 Bradley Chubb JSY AU RC 6.00 15.00
138 Royce Freeman JSY AU RC 5.00 12.00
139 Mike White JSY AU RC 5.00 12.00
140 Dante Pettis JSY AU RC 6.00 15.00

2018 Panini Origins Blue
*VETS/99: 1X TO 2.5X BASIC CARDS
*ROOK/49: .6X TO 1.5X BASIC JSY AU
103 Saquon Barkley JSY AU 125.00 250.00
105 Baker Mayfield JSY AU 100.00 200.00

2018 Panini Origins Orange
*VETS/175: .8X TO 2X BASIC CARDS

2018 Panini Origins Red
*VETS/299: .6X TO 1.5X BASIC CARDS
*ROOK/75-99: .5X TO 1.2X BASIC JSY AU
*ROOK/25: .8X TO 2X BASIC JSY AU
103 Saquon Barkley JSY AU 100.00 200.00
105 Baker Mayfield JSY AU 75.00 150.00

2018 Panini Origins Turquoise
*VETS/25: 1.2X TO 3X BASIC CARDS
*ROOK/25: .8X TO 2X BASIC JSY AU
103 Saquon Barkley JSY AU 200.00 300.00
105 Baker Mayfield JSY AU 125.00 250.00

2018 Panini Origins Hometown Roots Jerseys
1 David Johnson 6.00 15.00
2 Matt Ryan 5.00 12.00
3 Joe Flacco 5.00 12.00
4 LeSean McCoy 6.00 15.00
5 Luke Kuechly 5.00 12.00
6 Jordan Howard 6.00 15.00
7 Andy Dalton 5.00 12.00
8 Von Miller 5.00 12.00
9 Matthew Stafford 5.00 12.00
10 Jarvis Landry 5.00 12.00
11 T.Y. Hilton 5.00 12.00
12 Blake Bortles 4.00 10.00
13 Tyreek Hill 6.00 15.00
14 Todd Gurley II 6.00 15.00
15 Kenyan Drake 4.00 10.00
16 Rob Gronkowski 6.00 15.00
17 Leonard Williams 4.00 10.00
18 Jamal Adams 5.00 12.00
19 Derek Carr 6.00 15.00
20 Le'Veon Bell 5.00 12.00
21 Richard Sherman 6.00 15.00
22 Jameis Winston 5.00 12.00
23 Harrison Smith 6.00 15.00
24 Jordan Reed 4.00 10.00
25 Allen Robinson 5.00 12.00
26 Mike Evans 5.00 12.00
27 DeSean Jackson 5.00 12.00
28 Russell Wilson 8.00 20.00
30 Melvin Gordon 5.00 12.00
31 Keenan Allen 5.00 12.00
32 Travis Kelce 6.00 15.00
33 Michael Thomas 6.00 15.00
34 A.J. Green 6.00 15.00
35 Heath Miller 4.00 10.00
36 John Elway 10.00 25.00
37 Jerry Rice 10.00 25.00
38 Thurman Thomas 5.00 12.00
39 Michael Irvin 6.00 15.00
40 Dan Marino 12.00 30.00

2018 Panini Origins Origins of Greatness Jerseys
1 E.Elliott/E.Smith 25.00 50.00
2 K.Hunt/P.Holmes 6.00 15.00
3 Todd Gurley II/Marshall Faulk 8.00 20.00
4 R.Williams/K.Drake 6.00 15.00
5 S.Diggs/C.Carter 8.00 20.00
6 M.Ingram/A.Kamara 6.00 15.00
7 M.Forte/J.Howard 8.00 20.00
8 E.Engram/J.Shockey 5.00 12.00
9 A.Brown/H.Ward 8.00 20.00
10 J.Bettis/L.Bell 8.00 20.00
11 L.McCoy/T.Thomas 8.00 20.00
12 W.Moon/M.Mariota 8.00 20.00
13 J.McMahon/M.Trubisky 8.00 20.00
14 C.Portis/S.Perine 5.00 12.00
15 F.Taylor/L.Fournette 8.00 20.00
16 D.Prescott/T.Aikman 10.00 25.00
17 L.Tomlinson/M.Gordon 6.00 15.00
18 A.Gates/H.Henry 5.00 12.00
19 T.Gonzalez/T.Kelce 8.00 20.00
20 D.Cook/A.Peterson 8.00 20.00

2018 Panini Origins Passing Stars Autographs
1 Baker Mayfield 125.00 250.00
2 Sam Darnold 40.00 100.00
3 Josh Allen 40.00 100.00
4 Josh Rosen 20.00 50.00

2018 Panini Origins Receiving Stars Signatures
1 D.J. Moore 12.00 30.00
2 Calvin Ridley 15.00 40.00
3 Courtland Sutton 10.00 25.00

2018 Panini Origins Rookie Signatures
1 Josh Rosen 10.00 25.00
2 Sam Darnold 60.00 125.00
3 Saquon Barkley 100.00 200.00
4 Josh Allen 25.00 50.00
5 Baker Mayfield 75.00 150.00
6 Calvin Ridley 8.00 20.00
7 Ito Smith 4.00 10.00
8 Courtland Sutton 5.00 12.00
9 Sony Michel 10.00 25.00
10 Derrius Guice 6.00 15.00
11 Christian Kirk 5.00 12.00
12 Ronald Jones II 3.00 8.00
13 D.J. Moore 6.00 15.00
14 James Washington 6.00 15.00
15 D.J. Chark 4.00 10.00
16 Mason Rudolph 8.00 20.00
17 Hayden Hurst 4.00 10.00
18 Lamar Jackson 40.00 80.00
19 Mike Gesicki 4.00 10.00
20 Kalen Ballage 4.00 10.00
21 Marquez Valdes-Scantling 4.00 10.00
22 Kerryon Johnson 8.00 20.00
23 Kyle Lauletta 5.00 12.00
24 Keke Coutee 4.00 10.00
25 Nyheim Hines 4.00 10.00
26 Michael Gallup 6.00 15.00
27 Rashaad Penny 5.00 12.00
28 DaeSean Hamilton 4.00 10.00
29 Tre'Quan Smith 5.00 12.00
30 Nick Chubb 10.00 25.00
31 Jaylen Samuels 4.00 10.00
32 Jaleel Scott 3.00 8.00
33 Daurice Fountain 4.00 10.00
34 Anthony Miller 5.00 12.00
35 J'Mon Moore 3.00 8.00
36 Mark Walton 4.00 10.00
37 Bradley Chubb 5.00 12.00
38 Royce Freeman 4.00 10.00
39 Mike White 4.00 10.00
40 Dante Pettis 5.00 12.00

2018 Panini Origins Rookie Signatures Blue
*BLUE/49: .6X TO 1.5X BASIC AU
*BLUE/25: .8X TO 2X BASIC AU
2 Sam Darnold/25 150.00 250.00
3 Saquon Barkley/25 200.00 300.00
5 Baker Mayfield/25 125.00 250.00

2018 Panini Origins Rookie Signatures Red
*RED/99: .5X TO 1.2X BASIC AU
*RED/49: .6X TO 1.5X BASIC AU
*RED/25: .8X TO 2X BASIC AU
2 Sam Darnold/49 100.00 200.00
3 Saquon Barkley/49 150.00 250.00
5 Baker Mayfield/49 100.00 200.00
18 Lamar Jackson/25 125.00 250.00

2018 Panini Origins Rookie Signatures Turquoise
*TURQ/25: .8X TO 2X BASIC AU

2018 Panini Origins Rookie Autographs Bronze Ink
1 Josh Rosen 15.00 40.00
2 Sam Darnold 30.00 80.00
3 Saquon Barkley 100.00 200.00
4 Josh Allen 40.00 80.00
5 Baker Mayfield 100.00 200.00
6 Calvin Ridley 12.00 30.00
7 Hayden Hurst 5.00 12.00
8 Courtland Sutton 8.00 20.00
9 Sony Michel 15.00 40.00
10 Derrius Guice 10.00 25.00
11 Christian Kirk 8.00 20.00
12 Ronald Jones II 4.00 10.00
13 D.J. Moore 8.00 20.00
14 James Washington 8.00 20.00
15 D.J. Chark 5.00 12.00
16 Mason Rudolph 12.00 30.00
17 Kalen Ballage 5.00 12.00
18 Lamar Jackson 50.00 100.00
19 Mike Gesicki 5.00 12.00
20 Nyheim Hines 5.00 12.00
21 Keke Coutee 5.00 12.00
22 Kerryon Johnson 10.00 25.00
23 Kyle Lauletta 6.00 15.00
24 Mark Walton 5.00 12.00
25 Tre'Quan Smith 6.00 15.00
26 Michael Gallup 8.00 20.00
27 Rashaad Penny 6.00 15.00
28 DaeSean Hamilton 5.00 12.00
29 Jaleel Scott 4.00 10.00
30 Nick Chubb 12.00 30.00
31 Ito Smith 5.00 12.00
32 J'Mon Moore 4.00 10.00
33 Daurice Fountain 5.00 12.00
34 Anthony Miller 6.00 15.00
35 Jaylen Samuels 5.00 12.00
36 Marquez Valdes-Scantling 5.00 12.00
37 Bradley Chubb
38 Royce Freeman 5.00 12.00
39 Mike White 5.00 12.00
40 Dante Pettis 6.00 15.00

2018 Panini Origins Rookie Autographs Silver Ink
*SILVER/25: .6X TO 1.5X BASIC AU/99
*SILVER/25: .5X TO 1.2X BASIC AU/49
5 Baker Mayfield 125.00 250.00

2018 Panini Origins Rookie Jumbo Jerseys
*RED/99: .5X TO 1.2X BASIC JSY
*ORANGE/75: .5X TO 1.2X BASIC JSY
*BLUE/49: .6X TO 1.5X BASIC JSY
*TURQUOISE/25: .8X TO 2X BASIC JSY
*PATCH/175: .5X TO 1.2X BASIC JSY
*RED PATCH/99: .6X TO 1.5X BASIC JSY
*ORANGE PATCH/75: .6X TO 1.5X BASIC JSY
*BLUE PATCH/49: .8X TO 2X BASIC JSY
*TURQ PATCH/25: 1X TO 2.5X BASIC JSY
1 Josh Rosen 8.00 20.00
2 Sam Darnold 8.00 20.00
3 Saquon Barkley 8.00 20.00
4 Josh Allen 6.00 15.00
5 Baker Mayfield 8.00 20.00
6 Calvin Ridley 5.00 12.00
7 Courtland Sutton 3.00 8.00
8 Sony Michel 5.00 12.00
9 Derrius Guice 4.00 10.00
10 Christian Kirk 3.00 8.00
11 Ronald Jones II 2.00 5.00
12 D.J. Moore 4.00 10.00
13 James Washington 4.00 10.00
14 D.J. Chark 2.50 6.00
15 Mason Rudolph 5.00 12.00
16 Kalen Ballage 2.50 6.00
17 Lamar Jackson 8.00 20.00
18 Mike Gesicki 2.50 6.00
19 Nyheim Hines 2.50 6.00
20 Keke Coutee 2.50 6.00
21 Kerryon Johnson 3.00 8.00
22 Kyle Lauletta 3.00 8.00
23 Mark Walton 2.50 6.00
24 Michael Gallup 4.00 10.00
25 Rashaad Penny 3.00 8.00
26 Nick Chubb 6.00 15.00
27 Anthony Miller 3.00 8.00
28 Bradley Chubb 3.00 8.00
29 Royce Freeman 2.50 6.00
30 Mike White 2.50 6.00

2018 Panini Origins Rookie Patch Autographs
1 Sam Darnold 75.00 150.00
2 Saquon Barkley 200.00 400.00
3 Josh Rosen 40.00 80.00
4 Josh Allen 75.00 150.00
5 Baker Mayfield 150.00 300.00
6 Calvin Ridley 40.00 80.00
7 Courtland Sutton 12.00 30.00
8 Sony Michel 40.00 80.00
9 Derrius Guice 25.00 50.00
10 Christian Kirk 12.00 30.00
11 Nick Chubb 30.00 60.00
13 Mason Rudolph 20.00 50.00
14 Anthony Miller 12.00 30.00
15 James Washington 15.00 40.00
16 Rashaad Penny 12.00 30.00

2018 Panini Origins Rushing Stars Signatures
1 Saquon Barkley 150.00 300.00
2 Rashaad Penny 10.00 25.00
3 Sony Michel 20.00 50.00

2017 Panini Pantheon
1 Ezekiel Elliott 10.00 25.00
2 Dak Prescott 8.00 20.00
3 Emmitt Smith 25.00 50.00
4 Troy Aikman 10.00 25.00
5 Eli Manning 6.00 15.00
6 Odell Beckham Jr. 8.00 20.00
7 Lawrence Taylor 8.00 20.00
8 Carson Wentz 10.00 25.00
9 Jordan Matthews 5.00 12.00
10 Reggie White 8.00 20.00
11 Kirk Cousins 8.00 20.00
12 Jordan Reed 5.00 12.00
13 Champ Bailey 6.00 15.00
14 David Johnson 8.00 20.00
15 Larry Fitzgerald 6.00 15.00
16 Kurt Warner 6.00 15.00
17 Jared Goff 8.00 20.00
18 Todd Gurley II 8.00 20.00
19 Jerome Bettis 8.00 20.00
20 Carlos Hyde 5.00 12.00
21 Joe Montana 20.00 50.00
22 Jerry Rice 15.00 40.00
23 Steve Young 10.00 25.00
24 Russell Wilson 10.00 25.00
25 Richard Sherman 8.00 20.00
26 Steve Largent 8.00 20.00
27 Jordan Howard 8.00 20.00
28 Brian Urlacher 8.00 20.00
29 Walter Payton 15.00 40.00
30 Matthew Stafford 6.00 15.00
31 Barry Sanders 12.00 30.00
32 Calvin Johnson 8.00 20.00
33 Aaron Rodgers 25.00 50.00
34 Jordy Nelson 6.00 15.00
35 Brett Favre 15.00 40.00
36 Adrian Peterson 8.00 20.00
37 Stefon Diggs 6.00 15.00
38 Randy Moss 6.00 15.00
39 Matt Ryan 6.00 15.00
40 Julio Jones 8.00 20.00
41 Deion Sanders 6.00 15.00
42 Cam Newton 8.00 20.00
43 Kelvin Benjamin 6.00 15.00
44 Luke Kuechly 6.00 15.00
45 Drew Brees 8.00 20.00
46 Michael Thomas 8.00 20.00
47 Archie Manning 6.00 15.00
48 Jameis Winston 6.00 15.00
49 Mike Evans 6.00 15.00
50 Derrick Brooks 5.00 12.00
51 Lamar Miller 5.00 12.00
52 J.J. Watt 8.00 20.00
53 Warren Moon 8.00 20.00
54 Andrew Luck 10.00 25.00
55 Peyton Manning 15.00 40.00
56 Marvin Harrison 6.00 15.00
57 Blake Bortles 5.00 12.00
58 Allen Robinson 6.00 15.00
59 Fred Taylor 6.00 15.00
60 Marcus Mariota 8.00 20.00
61 DeMarco Murray 6.00 15.00
62 Eddie George 6.00 15.00
63 Joe Flacco 6.00 15.00
64 Kenneth Dixon 5.00 12.00
65 Ray Lewis 8.00 20.00
66 Andy Dalton 6.00 15.00
67 A.J. Green 8.00 20.00
68 Boomer Esiason 6.00 15.00
69 Corey Coleman 5.00 12.00
70 Cody Kessler 5.00 12.00
71 Jim Brown 10.00 25.00
72 Ben Roethlisberger 8.00 20.00
73 Le'Veon Bell 6.00 15.00
74 Antonio Brown 8.00 20.00
75 Joe Greene 8.00 20.00

76 Trevor Siemian 5.00 12.00
77 Von Miller 6.00 15.00
78 John Elway 15.00 40.00
79 Alex Smith 6.00 15.00
80 Jeremy Maclin 5.00 12.00
81 Len Dawson 8.00 20.00
82 Derek Carr 8.00 20.00
83 Amari Cooper 8.00 20.00
84 Howie Long 8.00 20.00
85 Tim Brown 8.00 20.00
86 Philip Rivers 8.00 20.00
87 Melvin Gordon 6.00 15.00
88 Dan Fouts 6.00 15.00
89 Tyrod Taylor 6.00 15.00
90 LeSean McCoy 8.00 20.00
91 Jim Kelly 8.00 20.00
92 Ryan Tannehill 6.00 15.00
93 Jay Ajayi 6.00 15.00
94 Dan Marino 15.00 40.00
95 Tom Brady 40.00 80.00
96 Rob Gronkowski 8.00 20.00
97 Tedy Bruschi 8.00 20.00
98 Matt Forte 5.00 12.00
99 Eric Decker 5.00 12.00
100 Joe Namath 10.00 25.00
101 Mitchell Trubisky JSY AU/49 RC 40.00 80.00
102 Patrick Mahomes II JSY AU/49 RC 200.00 400.00
103 Deshaun Watson JSY AU/49 RC
104 DeShone Kizer JSY AU/49 RC 5.00 12.00
105 Davis Webb JSY AU/99 RC 4.00 10.00
106 C.J. Beathard JSY AU/99 RC 4.00 10.00
107 R. Joshua Dobbs JSY AU/149 RC 4.00 10.00
108 Nathan Peterman JSY AU/49 RC 6.00 15.00
109 Leonard Fournette JSY AU/49 RC 40.00 80.00
110 Christian McCaffrey JSY AU/49 RC 30.00 60.00
111 Dalvin Cook JSY AU/49 RC 12.00 30.00
112 Joe Mixon JSY AU/149 RC 6.00 15.00
113 Alvin Kamara JSY AU/99 RC 15.00 40.00
114 Kareem Hunt JSY AU/149 RC 15.00 40.00
115 D'Onta Foreman JSY AU/49 RC 6.00 15.00
116 James Conner JSY AU/149 RC 6.00 15.00
117 Samaje Perine JSY AU/99 RC 4.00 10.00
118 Joe Williams JSY AU/149 RC 3.00 8.00
119 Wayne Gallman JSY AU/99 RC 5.00 12.00
120 Marlon Mack JSY AU/149 RC 5.00 12.00
121 Jamaal Williams JSY AU/149 RC 3.00 8.00
122 Jeremy McNichols JSY AU/149 RC 3.00 8.00
123 Corey Davis JSY AU/49 RC 8.00 20.00
124 Mike Williams JSY AU/49 RC 8.00 20.00
125 John Ross III JSY AU/49 RC 6.00 15.00
126 Zay Jones JSY AU/99 RC 5.00 12.00
127 Curtis Samuel JSY AU/49 RC 6.00 15.00
128 JuJu Smith-Schuster JSY AU/49 RC 12.00 30.00
129 Cooper Kupp JSY AU/99 RC 6.00 15.00
130 Taywan Taylor JSY AU/149 RC 3.00 8.00
131 ArDarius Stewart JSY AU/149 RC 3.00 8.00
132 Carlos Henderson JSY AU/149 RC 3.00 8.00
133 Chris Godwin JSY AU/149 RC 4.00 10.00
134 Kenny Golladay JSY AU/149 RC 5.00 12.00
135 Amara Darboh JSY AU/99 RC 4.00 10.00
136 Dede Westbrook JSY AU/49 RC 5.00 12.00
137 Josh Reynolds JSY AU/149 RC 3.00 8.00
138 Mack Hollins JSY AU/149 RC 3.00 8.00
139 O.J. Howard JSY AU/99 RC 5.00 12.00
140 Evan Engram JSY AU/99 RC 5.00 12.00

2017 Panini Pantheon Gold

*ROOK JSY AU/99: .5X TO 1.2X BASIC JSY AU/149
*ROOK JSY AU/49: .6X TO 1.5X BASIC JSY AU/149
*ROOK JSY AU/25: .5X TO 1.2X BASIC JSY AU/49
*ROOK JSY AU/49: .5X TO 1.2X BASIC JSY AU/99
101 Mitchell Trubisky JSY AU/25 60.00 125.00
109 Leonard Fournette JSY AU/25 50.00 100.00

2017 Panini Pantheon Arena Acclaimed Materials

1 Deshaun Watson/49 15.00 40.00
2 Mitchell Trubisky/49 10.00 25.00
3 Patrick Mahomes II/49 40.00 100.00
4 Davis Webb/75 2.50 6.00
5 Leonard Fournette/49 15.00 40.00
6 Dalvin Cook/75 6.00 15.00
7 Christian McCaffrey/49 10.00 25.00
8 D'Onta Foreman/75 3.00 8.00
9 Samaje Perine/75 2.50 6.00
10 Alvin Kamara/99 10.00 25.00
11 Joe Mixon/99 5.00 12.00
12 O.J. Howard/75 3.00 8.00
13 Mike Williams/49 5.00 12.00
14 John Ross III/99 3.00 8.00
15 Corey Davis/49 5.00 12.00
16 JuJu Smith-Schuster/99 6.00 15.00
17 Chris Godwin/99 3.00 8.00
18 Curtis Samuel/99 3.00 8.00
19 Amara Darboh/99 2.50 6.00

2017 Panini Pantheon Gladiators Materials

1 Jim Kelly/99 4.00 10.00
2 Walter Payton/25 12.00 30.00
4 John Elway/99 6.00 15.00
5 Barry Sanders/99 6.00 15.00
7 Brett Favre/25 12.00 30.00
9 Reggie White/15 8.00 20.00
10 Peyton Manning/15 15.00 40.00
11 Johnny Unitas/99 6.00 15.00
12 Raymond Berry/15 6.00 15.00
13 Len Dawson/49 5.00 12.00
14 Marshall Faulk/25 5.00 12.00
15 Eric Dickerson/25 6.00 15.00
16 Dan Marino/25 12.00 30.00
17 Larry Csonka/25 5.00 12.00
18 Lawrence Taylor/15 8.00 20.00
19 Joe Namath/49 6.00 15.00
22 Junior Seau/99 4.00 10.00
23 Steve Young/99 5.00 12.00
24 Jerry Rice/99 6.00 15.00
25 Steve Largent/25 6.00 15.00

2017 Panini Pantheon Honored and Privileged Materials

*BRONZE/25: .6X TO 1.5X BASIC JSY/99
*GOLD/49: .5X TO 1.2X BASIC JSY/99
*GOLD/25: .6X TO 1.5X BASIC JSY/99
*GOLD/15: .8X TO 2X BASIC JSY/99
*GOLD/15: .6X TO 1.5X BASIC JSY/49
*GOLD/15: .5X TO 1.2X BASIC JSY/25
1 Matt Ryan/25 5.00 12.00
2 Matt Ryan/99 3.00 8.00
3 Ezekiel Elliott/99 5.00 12.00
4 Dak Prescott/99 4.00 10.00
5 Matt Ryan/99 3.00 8.00
6 Derek Carr/49 5.00 12.00
7 Joey Bosa/99 4.00 10.00
8 Le'Veon Bell/49 4.00 10.00
9 Khalil Mack/15 8.00 20.00
10 Jordy Nelson/25 5.00 12.00
11 Eli Manning/49 4.00 10.00
12 Larry Fitzgerald/49 4.00 10.00
13 Jameis Winston/99 3.00 8.00
14 Carson Palmer/49 4.00 10.00
15 Adrian Peterson/15 8.00 20.00
16 Todd Gurley II/99 4.00 10.00
17 Cam Newton/25 6.00 15.00
18 Drew Brees/25 6.00 15.00
20 Antonio Brown/25 6.00 15.00
22 Antonio Brown/25 6.00 15.00
23 Eric Berry/15 6.00 15.00
24 Cam Newton/25 6.00 15.00
25 Vincent Jackson/25 4.00 10.00

2017 Panini Pantheon Legendary Monuments

4 Mrtn/Smth/Pytn/Sndrs/15 25.00 60.00
5 Tmlnsn/Alln/Pytn/Smth/15 25.00 60.00
7 Mss/Smth/Brwn/Rce/15 20.00 50.00
8 Smth/Rce/Flk/Pytn/15 75.00 150.00
9 Wdsn/Rd/Wdsn/Ltt/15 12.00 30.00
10 Smth/Strhn/Whte/Ppprs/15 12.00 30.00
18 Prsctt/Wnstn/Crr/Mrta/99 6.00 15.00
19 Jhnsn/Elltt/Ajyi/Bll/99 8.00 20.00
20 Jns/Grn/Brwn/Bckham/99 6.00 15.00

2017 Panini Pantheon Script 1000

5 Lamar Miller/25 6.00 15.00
6 Jordan Howard/99 6.00 15.00
8 LeGarrette Blount/25 8.00 20.00
11 Mike Evans/49 6.00 15.00
12 Brandin Cooks/25 15.00 40.00
18 Travis Kelce/25 EXCH 10.00 25.00
20 Michael Thomas/49 8.00 20.00

2017 Panini Pantheon Script 10000

4 LaDainian Tomlinson/49 EXCH 6.00 15.00
7 Frank Gore/49 10.00 25.00
13 Tim Brown/15 12.00 30.00
14 Steve Smith Sr./49 6.00 15.00

2017 Panini Pantheon Scripts Materials

*GOLD/25: .6X TO 1.5X BASIC JSY AU/99
*GOLD/15-20: .8X TO 2X BASIC JSY AU/99
*GOLD/15-20: .5X TO 1.2X BASIC JSY AU/25
2 Malcolm Mitchell/99 6.00 15.00
3 Paxton Lynch/25 8.00 20.00
4 Dak Prescott/25 EXCH
5 Stefon Diggs/99 6.00 15.00
7 Jordan Howard/99 8.00 20.00
8 Joey Bosa/99 8.00 20.00
9 Corey Coleman/99 5.00 12.00
10 Sterling Shepard/99 6.00 15.00
11 Michael Thomas/99 8.00 20.00
12 Will Fuller V/99 5.00 12.00
14 Adam Vinatieri/49 8.00 20.00
15 Geno Atkins/99 5.00 12.00
16 Allen Robinson/49 8.00 20.00
17 Sammy Watkins/25 12.00 30.00
22 Brandin Cooks/25 10.00 25.00
23 Paul Warfield/99 6.00 15.00
24 Brett Keisel/99 5.00 12.00
26 Carlos Hyde/25 8.00 20.00
27 Clay Matthews/25 EXCH 15.00 40.00
28 Cole Beasley/99 12.00 30.00
30 David Johnson/25
31 Derek Carr/25
32 Devonta Freeman/49 8.00 20.00
33 Sammie Coates/99 5.00 12.00
34 Ed Too Tall Jones/99 5.00 12.00
37 Ozzie Newsome/99 6.00 15.00
45 James White/99 6.00 15.00
48 Rich Gannon/99 5.00 12.00
49 Ryan Shazier/99 5.00 12.00
50 Travis Kelce/99 EXCH 8.00 20.00

2017 Panini Pantheon Sympaiktis Dual Materials

*BRONZE/15: .8X TO 2X BASIC JSY/99
*BRONZE/15: .6X TO 1.5X BASIC JSY/49
*BRONZE/15: .5X TO 1.2X BASIC JSY/25
1 R.Grnkwski/T.Brady/25 15.00 40.00
2 E.Elliott/D.Prescott/99 8.00 20.00
3 E.Manning/O.Beckham/49 5.00 12.00
4 R.Sherman/R.Wilson/25 8.00 20.00
5 D.Henry/M.Mariota/99 4.00 10.00
6 M.Thomas/D.Brees/49 5.00 12.00
7 A.Cooper/D.Carr/99 4.00 10.00
8 D.Johnson/L.Fitzgerald/99 4.00 10.00
9 D.Hopkins/W.Fuller/99 3.00 8.00
10 J.Goff/T.Gurley/99 4.00 10.00
11 A.Rodgers/J.Nelson/25 12.00 30.00
12 J.Jones/M.Ryan/25 6.00 15.00
13 P.Rivers/M.Gordon/25 6.00 15.00
14 J.Winston/M.Evans/99 3.00 8.00
15 A.Green/T.Boyd/99 4.00 10.00
16 A.Peterson/S.Diggs/25 6.00 15.00
17 V.Miller/T.Siemian/49 4.00 10.00
18 A.Luck/T.Hilton/25 8.00 20.00
19 J.Crowder/K.Cousins/49 5.00 12.00
20 C.Newton/K.Benjamin/99 4.00 10.00
21 C.Coleman/C.Kessler/25 4.00 10.00
22 B.Bortles/A.Robinson/25 5.00 12.00
23 C.Wentz/W.Smallwood/49 6.00 15.00
24 J.Ajayi/R.Tannehill/25 5.00 12.00
25 L.Bell/A.Brown/25 6.00 15.00

2013 Panini Pen Pals

19-58 ANNOUNCED PRINT RUN 50 OR LESS
1 G.Bernard/T.Eifert 5.00 12.00
2 E.Lacy/J.Franklin 5.00 12.00
3 M.Barkley/Z.Ertz 10.00 25.00
4 K.Allen/M.Te'o 10.00 25.00
5 S.Bailey/T.Austin 6.00 15.00
6 M.Te'o/T.Eifert 8.00 20.00
7 A.Ellington/S.Taylor 5.00 12.00
8 C.Patterson/J.Hunter 5.00 12.00
9 Mnul/Gdwin/Woods 12.00 30.00
10 Escbr/Rndle/Wllms 12.00 30.00
11 Jnes/Bell/Whetn 25.00 60.00
12 Lttmre/Pttn/McDnld 12.00 30.00
13 Smth/Baly/Astn 10.00 25.00
14 Escbr/Efrt/McDnld/Ertz 20.00 50.00
15 Mul/Sth/Jns/Bky/Gln/Nsb 30.00 80.00
16 Ptn/Hps/Htr/Aln/Wds/Atn 20.00 50.00
17 Lcy/Brd/Rne/Bll/Lte/Bal 40.00 80.00
18 Hs/Ml/Sh/Bd/Bl/An/Et/Ez 30.00 80.00
19 Aaron Dobson 5.00 12.00
20 Andre Ellington 5.00 12.00
21 Christine Michael 8.00 20.00
22 Cordarrelle Patterson 5.00 12.00
23 DeAndre Hopkins EXCH 12.00 30.00
24 Denard Robinson 5.00 12.00
25 Dion Jordan
26 Eddie Lacy 25.00 60.00
27 EJ Manuel
28 Gavin Escobar 5.00 12.00
29 Geno Smith 5.00 12.00
30 Giovani Bernard 5.00 12.00
31 Johnathan Franklin 5.00 12.00
32 Jordan Reed
33 Joseph Randle
34 Justin Hunter 5.00 12.00
35 Keenan Allen 10.00 25.00
36 Kenny Stills 5.00 12.00
37 Knile Davis 5.00 12.00
38 Landry Jones 5.00 12.00
39 Le'Veon Bell
40 Manti Te'o 6.00 15.00
41 Marcus Lattimore 5.00 12.00
42 Markus Wheaton 5.00 12.00
43 Marquise Goodwin 5.00 12.00
44 Matt Barkley 5.00 12.00
45 Mike Gillislee 5.00 12.00
46 Mike Glennon
47 Montee Ball 5.00 12.00
48 Quinton Patton 5.00 12.00
49 Robert Woods 8.00 20.00
50 Ryan Nassib 5.00 12.00
51 Stedman Bailey
52 Stepfan Taylor 5.00 12.00
53 Tavon Austin 6.00 15.00
54 Terrance Williams 5.00 12.00
55 Tyler Eifert
56 Tyler Wilson 5.00 12.00
57 Vance McDonald 6.00 15.00
58 Zach Ertz 6.00 15.00

2011 Panini Pepsi Rookie of the Week

1 Randall Cobb .75 2.00
2 Denarius Moore .50 1.25
3 Stefen Wisniewski .75 2.00
4 Cam Newton 2.50 6.00
5 Aldon Smith .50 1.25
6 Aldon Smith .50 1.25
7 DeMarco Murray 1.00 2.50
8 Marcell Dareus .50 1.25
9 Andy Dalton 1.00 2.50
10 Denarius Moore .50 1.25
11 Torrey Smith .50 1.25
12 Andy Dalton 1.00 2.50
13 Colin McCarthy .60 1.50
14 T.J. Yates .50 1.25
15 Cam Newton 2.50 6.00
16 Cam Newton 2.50 6.00
17 Sterling Moore 1.50 4.00
18 Cam Newton 2.50 6.00

2012 Panini Pepsi Rookie of the Week

RANDOM INSERTS IN CONTENDERS RETAIL
1 Robert Griffin III .60 1.50
2 Trent Richardson .50 1.25
3 Andrew Luck 5.00 12.00
4 Robert Griffin III .60 1.50
5 Andrew Luck 5.00 12.00
6 Robert Griffin III .60 1.50
7 Alfred Morris .50 1.25
8 Andrew Luck 5.00 12.00
9 Doug Martin .75 2.00
10 Russell Wilson 4.00 10.00
11 Robert Griffin III .60 1.50
12 Robert Griffin III .60 1.50
13 Robert Griffin III .60 1.50
14 Alfred Morris .50 1.25
15 Kirk Cousins 2.00 5.00
16 Robert Griffin III .60 1.50
17 Alfred Morris .50 1.25
ROY1 Robert Griffin III 6.00 15.00
ROY2 Andrew Luck 50.00 125.00
ROY3 Doug Martin 8.00 20.00
ROY4 Russell Wilson 40.00 100.00
ROY5 Alfred Morris 5.00 12.00

2016 Panini Phoenix

1 Carson Palmer .60 1.50
2 David Johnson .75 2.00
3 Larry Fitzgerald .60 1.50
4 John Brown .60 1.50
5 Matt Ryan .60 1.50
6 Devonta Freeman .60 1.50
7 Julio Jones .75 2.00
8 Joe Flacco .60 1.50
9 Justin Forsett .60 1.50
10 Steve Smith Sr. .60 1.50
11 Tyrod Taylor .60 1.50
12 LeSean McCoy .75 2.00
13 Sammy Watkins .75 2.00
14 Cam Newton .75 2.00
15 Jonathan Stewart .50 1.25
16 Kelvin Benjamin .60 1.50
17 Luke Kuechly .60 1.50
18 Jay Cutler .50 1.25
19 Jeremy Langford .60 1.50
20 Alshon Jeffery .60 1.50
21 Andy Dalton .60 1.50
22 Jeremy Hill .50 1.25
23 Tyler Eifert .60 1.50
24 A.J. Green .75 2.00
25 Robert Griffin III .50 1.25
26 Duke Johnson .50 1.25
27 Tony Romo .60 1.50
28 Jason Witten .60 1.50
29 Dez Bryant .75 2.00
30 Sean Lee .60 1.50
31 Mark Sanchez .50 1.25
32 Emmanuel Sanders .75 2.00
33 Demaryius Thomas .60 1.50
34 Von Miller .60 1.50
35 DeMarcus Ware .60 1.50
36 Matthew Stafford .60 1.50
37 Ameer Abdullah .50 1.25
38 Golden Tate III .50 1.25
39 Aaron Rodgers 1.50 4.00
40 Eddie Lacy .50 1.25
41 Jordy Nelson .60 1.50
42 Clay Matthews .75 2.00
43 Brock Osweiler .50 1.25
44 DeAndre Hopkins .60 1.50
45 J.J. Watt .75 2.00
46 Andrew Luck 1.00 2.50
47 T.Y. Hilton .60 1.50
48 Blake Bortles .50 1.25
49 Allen Robinson .60 1.50
50 Chris Ivory .60 1.50
51 Alex Smith .60 1.50
52 Jamaal Charles .60 1.50
53 Jeremy Maclin .50 1.25
54 Ryan Tannehill .60 1.50
55 Jarvis Landry .60 1.50
56 Teddy Bridgewater .60 1.50
57 Adrian Peterson .75 2.00
58 Stefon Diggs .60 1.50
59 Tom Brady 2.00 5.00
60 Rob Gronkowski .75 2.00
61 Julian Edelman .75 2.00
62 Drew Brees .75 2.00
63 Mark Ingram .60 1.50
64 Brandin Cooks .60 1.50
65 Eli Manning .60 1.50
66 Odell Beckham Jr. .75 2.00
67 Matt Forte .50 1.25
68 Brandon Marshall .50 1.25
69 Eric Decker .50 1.25
70 Derek Carr .75 2.00
71 Latavius Murray .50 1.25
72 Amari Cooper .75 2.00
73 Khalil Mack .75 2.00
74 Sam Bradford .50 1.25
75 Jordan Matthews .60 1.50
76 Ben Roethlisberger .75 2.00
77 Le'Veon Bell .60 1.50
78 Antonio Brown .75 2.00
79 Philip Rivers .75 2.00
80 Danny Woodhead .60 1.50
81 Keenan Allen .60 1.50
82 Colin Kaepernick .60 1.50
83 Carlos Hyde .50 1.25
84 Navorro Bowman .60 1.50
85 Russell Wilson 1.00 2.50
86 Thomas Rawls .50 1.25
87 Doug Baldwin .60 1.50
88 Earl Thomas III .60 1.50
89 Todd Gurley .75 2.00
90 Tavon Austin .50 1.25
91 Aaron Donald .75 2.00
92 Jameis Winston .75 2.00
93 Doug Martin .60 1.50
94 Mike Evans .60 1.50
95 Marcus Mariota .75 2.00
96 DeMarco Murray .60 1.50
97 Kendall Wright .50 1.25
98 Kirk Cousins .75 2.00
99 Matt Jones .60 1.50
100 Jordan Reed .50 1.25
101 Jackie Smith .50 1.25
102 Ray Lewis .75 2.00
103 Jim Kelly .75 2.00
104 Thurman Thomas .60 1.50
105 Dan Hampton .50 1.25
106 Mike Singletary .75 2.00
107 Cris Collinsworth .60 1.50
108 Troy Aikman 1.00 2.50
109 Emmitt Smith 1.25 3.00
110 Michael Irvin .75 2.00
111 John Elway 1.25 3.00
112 Barry Sanders 1.25 3.00
113 Brett Favre 1.50 4.00
114 Peyton Manning 1.50 4.00
115 Marvin Harrison .60 1.50
116 Edgerrin James .60 1.50
117 Dan Marino 1.50 4.00
118 Curtis Martin .60 1.50
119 Phil Simms .60 1.50
120 Joe Namath 1.00 2.50
121 Don Maynard .60 1.50
122 Bo Jackson 1.00 2.50
123 Marcus Allen .60 1.50
124 Tim Brown .75 2.00
125 Terry Bradshaw 1.00 2.50
126 Franco Harris .75 2.00
127 John Stallworth .60 1.50
128 LaDainian Tomlinson .60 1.50
129 Dan Fouts .60 1.50
130 Kellen Winslow .60 1.50
131 Roger Craig .60 1.50
132 Steve Young 1.00 2.50
133 Jerry Rice 1.25 3.00
134 Ronnie Lott .60 1.50
135 Steve Largent .75 2.00
136 Warren Sapp .60 1.50
137 Earl Campbell .75 2.00
138 Fran Tarkenton .75 2.00
139 Paul Hornung .75 2.00
140 Y.A. Tittle .75 2.00
141 Len Dawson .75 2.00
142 James Lofton .60 1.50
143 Marshall Faulk .60 1.50
144 Kurt Warner .60 1.50
145 Gale Sayers .75 2.00
146 Jerome Bettis .75 2.00
147 Larry Csonka .60 1.50
148 Cris Carter .75 2.00
149 Raymond Berry .60 1.50
150 Michael Strahan .60 1.50
151 Jalen Ramsey RC 1.00 2.50
152 DeForest Buckner RC .60 1.50
153 Leonard Floyd RC .75 2.00
154 Eli Apple RC .75 2.00
155 Vernon Hargreaves III RC 1.00 2.50
156 Sheldon Rankins RC .75 2.00
157 Karl Joseph RC .60 1.50
158 Keanu Neal RC .60 1.50
159 Shaq Lawson RC .60 1.50
160 Darron Lee RC .60 1.50
161 William Jackson III RC .75 2.00
162 Artie Burns RC .75 2.00
163 Kenny Clark RC .60 1.50
164 Robert Nkemdiche RC .75 2.00
165 Vernon Butler RC .60 1.50
166 Emmanuel Ogbah RC .75 2.00
167 Kevin Dodd RC .60 1.50
168 Jaylon Smith RC .60 1.50
169 Myles Jack RC .75 2.00
170 Chris Jones RC .60 1.50
171 Xavien Howard RC .75 2.00
172 Noah Spence RC .60 1.50
173 Reggie Ragland RC .60 1.50
174 A'Shawn Robinson RC .60 1.50
175 Jarran Reed RC .60 1.50
176 Deion Jones RC .60 1.50
177 Su'a Cravens RC .60 1.50
178 Mackensie Alexander RC .60 1.50
179 T.J. Green RC 1.00 2.50
180 Sean Davis RC .60 1.50
181 Roberto Aguayo RC .60 1.50
182 Cyrus Jones RC .60 1.50
183 Vonn Bell RC .75 2.00
184 James Bradberry RC .75 2.00
185 Adam Gotsis RC .60 1.50
186 Austin Hooper RC .60 1.50
187 Jacoby Brissett RC .75 2.00
188 Nick Vannett RC .60 1.50
189 Charles Tapper RC .75 2.00
190 Tyler Higbee RC .60 1.50
191 Tajae Sharpe RC .75 2.00
192 Jordan Payton RC .60 1.50
193 Tyreek Hill RC 2.50 6.00
194 Nate Sudfeld RC .60 1.50
195 Kolby Listenbee RC .60 1.50
196 Jeff Driskel RC .60 1.50
197 Kelvin Taylor RC .60 1.50
198 Daniel Braverman RC .60 1.50
199 Charone Peake RC .60 1.50
200 Kenny Lawler RC 1.00 2.50
201 Alex Collins JSY AU/249 RC 4.00 10.00
202 Braxton Miller JSY AU/249 RC 3.00 8.00
203 C.J. Prosise JSY AU/249 RC 3.00 8.00
204 Cardale Jones JSY AU/99 RC 5.00 12.00
205 Carson Wentz JSY AU/49 RC 60.00 125.00
206 Chris Moore JSY AU/249 RC 4.00 10.00
207 Christian Hackenberg JSY AU/99 RC 5.00 12.00
208 Cody Kessler JSY AU/249 RC 3.00 8.00
209 Connor Cook JSY AU/49 RC 8.00 20.00
210 Corey Coleman JSY AU/99 RC 8.00 20.00
211 Dak Prescott JSY AU/249 RC 30.00 60.00
212 DeAndre Washington JSY AU/249 RC 3.00 8.00
213 Demarcus Robinson JSY AU/249 RC 3.00 8.00
214 Derrick Henry JSY AU/49 RC 15.00 40.00
215 Devontae Booker JSY AU/249 RC 4.00 10.00
216 Ezekiel Elliott JSY AU/49 RC 75.00 150.00
217 Hunter Henry JSY AU/249 RC 4.00 10.00
218 Jared Goff JSY AU/49 RC 40.00 100.00
219 Joey Bosa JSY AU/249 RC 6.00 15.00
220 Jonathan Williams JSY AU/249 RC 4.00 10.00
221 Jordan Howard JSY AU/249 RC 8.00 20.00
222 Josh Doctson JSY AU/99 RC 6.00 15.00
223 Keenan Reynolds JSY AU/249 RC 4.00 10.00
224 Kenneth Dixon JSY AU/249 RC 3.00 8.00
225 Kenyan Drake JSY AU/249 RC 5.00 12.00
226 Kevin Hogan JSY AU/249 RC 4.00 10.00
227 Laquon Treadwell JSY AU/99 RC 6.00 15.00
228 Leonte Carroo JSY AU/249 RC 3.00 8.00
229 Michael Thomas JSY AU/99 RC 10.00 25.00
230 Moritz Bohringer JSY AU/249 RC 3.00 8.00
231 Paul Perkins JSY AU/249 RC 3.00 8.00
232 Paxton Lynch JSY AU/49 RC 6.00 15.00
233 Pharoh Cooper JSY AU/249 RC 3.00 8.00
234 Ricardo Louis JSY AU/249 RC 3.00 8.00
235 Sterling Shepard JSY AU/249 RC 4.00 10.00
236 Trevor Davis JSY AU/249 RC 3.00 8.00
237 Tyler Boyd JSY AU/249 RC 4.00 10.00
238 Tyler Ervin JSY AU/249 RC 3.00 8.00
239 Wendell Smallwood JSY AU/249 RC 3.00 8.00
240 Will Fuller JSY AU/99 RC 8.00 20.00

2016 Panini Phoenix Adrenaline Rush

*ORANGE/299: .6X TO 1.5X BASIC INSERTS
*RED/349: .6X TO 1.5X BASIC INSERTS
*YELLOW/99: 1X TO 4X BASIC INSERTS
ARAP Adrian Peterson 1.00 2.50
ARBJ Bo Jackson 1.25 3.00
ARBS Barry Sanders 1.50 4.00
ARCJ Chris Johnson .60 1.50
ARCM Curtis Martin .75 2.00
ARDF Devonta Freeman .75 2.00
ARDH Derrick Henry 1.50 4.00
ARDM Doug Martin .75 2.00
AREC Earl Campbell 1.00 2.50
ARED Eric Dickerson .75 2.00
AREE Ezekiel Elliott 3.00 8.00
AREG Eddie George .75 2.00
AREJ Edgerrin James .75 2.00
ARES Emmitt Smith 1.50 4.00
ARFO Matt Forte .60 1.50
ARJB Jerome Bettis 1.00 2.50
ARJC Jamaal Charles .75 2.00
ARJR John Riggins .75 2.00
ARLB Le'Veon Bell .75 2.00
ARLM Latavius Murray .60 1.50
ARLS LeSean McCoy 1.00 2.50
ARLT LaDainian Tomlinson .75 2.00
ARMA Marcus Allen .75 2.00
ARMF Marshall Faulk .75 2.00
ARMI Mark Ingram .75 2.00
ARRW Ricky Williams .75 2.00
ARTD Tony Dorsett 1.00 2.50
ARTG Todd Gurley 1.00 2.50
ARTR Thomas Rawls .60 1.50
ARTT Thurman Thomas .75 2.00

2016 Panini Phoenix Dual Patch Autographs

1 K.Reynolds/K.Dixon 8.00 20.00
2 C.Jones/J.Williams 8.00 20.00
3 C.Kessler/C.Coleman
4 D.Prescott/E.Elliott 200.00 400.00
5 D.Booker/P.Lynch 8.00 20.00
6 B.Miller/W.Fuller 10.00 25.00
7 D.Robinson/K.Hogan 8.00 20.00
8 J.Goff/P.Cooper 40.00 100.00
9 K.Drake/L.Carroo 10.00 25.00
10 L.Treadwell/M.Bohringer 8.00 20.00
11 P.Perkins/S.Shepard 8.00 20.00
12 C.Wentz/W.Smallwood
13 H.Henry/J.Bosa 12.00 30.00
14 A.Collins/C.Prosise 8.00 20.00
15 D.Henry/K.Drake 15.00 40.00
16 C.Jones/D.Prescott
17 C.Hcknbrg/C.Cook 8.00 20.00
18 D.Booker/E.Elliott 100.00 200.00
19 C.Wentz/J.Goff 100.00 200.00
20 C.Coleman/J.Doctson 10.00 25.00

2016 Panini Phoenix Hot Rookie Material Signatures Football

HRSJG Jared Goff/49 40.00 100.00
HRSCW Carson Wentz/49 60.00 150.00
HRSPL Paxton Lynch/49 6.00 15.00
HRSDP Dak Prescott/199 20.00 50.00
HRSCH Christian Hackenberg/99 5.00 12.00
HRSCK Cody Kessler/199 4.00 10.00
HRSBM Braxton Miller/199 4.00 10.00
HRSCC Corey Coleman/99 8.00 20.00
HRSJD Josh Doctson/99 6.00 15.00
HRSLT Laquon Treadwell/99 6.00 15.00
HRSMT Michael Thomas/99 10.00 25.00
HRSSS Sterling Shepard/199 5.00 12.00
HRSWF Will Fuller/99 8.00 20.00
HRSTB Tyler Boyd/199 5.00 12.00
HRSEE Ezekiel Elliott/49 100.00 200.00
HRSKD Kenyan Drake/199 6.00 15.00
HRSDB Devontae Booker/199 5.00 12.00
HRSAC Alex Collins/199 5.00 12.00
HRSDI Kenneth Dixon/199 4.00 10.00
HRSHH Hunter Henry/199 5.00 12.00

2016 Panini Phoenix Resurgence

COMMON CARD .75 2.00
SEMISTARS 1.00 2.50
UNLISTED STARS 1.50 4.00
*ORANGE/299: .6X TO 1.5X BASIC INSERTS
*RED/349: .6X TO 1.5X BASIC INSERTS
*YELLOW/99: 1X TO 4X BASIC INSERTS
RESDF Doug Flutie .75 2.00
RESDB Drew Brees 1.00 2.50
RESEB Eric Berry .75 2.00
RESMS Matthew Stafford .75 2.00
RESMV Michael Vick .75 2.00
RESPM Peyton Manning 2.00 5.00
RESPR Philip Rivers 1.00 2.50
RESRG Rob Gronkowski 1.00 2.50
RESSS Steve Smith Sr. .75 2.00
RESTB Tom Brady 2.50 6.00

2016 Panini Phoenix Retired Signatures

1 Archie Manning/20
2 Lance Briggs/20 8.00 20.00
5 Earl Campbell/20 15.00 40.00
6 Edgerrin James/20
8 Tim Brown/20
10 Ozzie Newsome/20 8.00 20.00
11 Kellen Winslow/20 8.00 20.00
14 Boomer Esiason/20 8.00 20.00
15 Jamal Lewis/20 8.00 20.00
16 Y.A. Tittle/20 15.00 40.00
17 Steve Grogan/20 6.00 15.00
20 Champ Bailey/20 8.00 20.00

2016 Panini Phoenix Rookie Jumbo Patch Autographs

1 Alex Collins/199 4.00 10.00
2 Braxton Miller/199 3.00 8.00
3 C.J. Prosise/199 3.00 8.00
4 Cardale Jones/99 4.00 10.00
5 Carson Wentz/49 50.00 125.00
6 Chris Moore/199 4.00 10.00
7 Christian Hackenberg/99 4.00 10.00
8 Cody Kessler/199 3.00 8.00
9 Connor Cook/49 6.00 15.00
10 Corey Coleman/99 6.00 15.00
11 Dak Prescott/199 25.00 50.00
12 DeAndre Washington/199 3.00 8.00
13 Demarcus Robinson/199 3.00 8.00
14 Derrick Henry/49 12.00 30.00
15 Devontae Booker/199 4.00 10.00
16 Ezekiel Elliott/49 75.00 150.00
17 Hunter Henry/199 4.00 10.00
18 Jared Goff/49 30.00 80.00
19 Joey Bosa/199 6.00 15.00
20 Jonathan Williams/199 4.00 10.00
21 Jordan Howard/199 8.00 20.00
22 Josh Doctson/99 5.00 12.00
23 Keenan Reynolds/199 4.00 10.00
24 Kenneth Dixon/199 3.00 8.00
25 Kenyan Drake/199 5.00 12.00
26 Kevin Hogan/199 4.00 10.00
27 Laquon Treadwell/99 5.00 12.00
28 Leonte Carroo/199 3.00 8.00
29 Michael Thomas/99 8.00 20.00
30 Moritz Bohringer/199 3.00 8.00
31 Paul Perkins/199 3.00 8.00
32 Paxton Lynch/49 5.00 12.00
33 Pharoh Cooper/199 3.00 8.00
34 Ricardo Louis/199 3.00 8.00
35 Sterling Shepard/199 4.00 10.00
36 Trevor Davis/199 3.00 8.00
37 Tyler Boyd/199 4.00 10.00
38 Tyler Ervin/199 3.00 8.00
39 Wendell Smallwood/199 3.00 8.00
40 Will Fuller/99 6.00 15.00

2016 Panini Phoenix Rookie Jumbo Patch Autographs Yellow Prime

*YELLOW/25: .8X TO 2X BASIC JSY AU/199
*YELLOW/25: .6X TO 1.5X BASIC JSY AU/99

2016 Panini Phoenix Rookie Rising

COMMON CARD .60 1.50
UNLISTED STARS 1.00 2.50
*ORANGE/299: .6X TO 1.5X BASIC INSERTS
*RED/349: .6X TO 1.5X BASIC INSERTS
*YELLOW/99: 1X TO 4X BASIC INSERTS
RRAC Alex Collins .75 2.00
RRAH Austin Hooper .60 1.50
RRBM Braxton Miller .60 1.50
RRCC Corey Coleman 1.00 2.50
RRCH Christian Hackenberg .60 1.50
RRCO Connor Cook .75 2.00
RRCW Carson Wentz 6.00 15.00
RRDB Devontae Booker .75 2.00
RRDF DeForest Buckner .60 1.50
RRDH Derrick Henry 1.50 4.00
RREE Ezekiel Elliott 3.00 8.00
RRHH Hunter Henry .75 2.00
RRJB Joey Bosa 1.25 3.00
RRJD Josh Doctson .75 2.00
RRJG Jared Goff 4.00 10.00
RRJR Jalen Ramsey 1.00 2.50
RRKD Kenneth Dixon .60 1.50
RRLC Leonte Carroo .60 1.50
RRLT Laquon Treadwell .75 2.00
RRMJ Myles Jack .75 2.00
RRMT Michael Thomas 1.25 3.00
RRPL Paxton Lynch .60 1.50
RRVH Vernon Hargreaves III 1.00 2.50
RRSS Sterling Shepard .75 2.00
RRWF Will Fuller 1.00 2.50

2016 Panini Phoenix Streaking Success

COMMON CARD 1.50 4.00
UNLISTED STARS 3.00 8.00
*ORANGE/299: .6X TO 1.5X BASIC INSERTS
*RED/349: .6X TO 1.5X BASIC INSERTS
*YELLOW/99: 1X TO 4X BASIC INSERTS
SSAW Andrew Whitworth 2.00 5.00
SSDF Brett Favre 4.00 10.00
SSBS Barry Sanders 3.00 8.00
SSCW Charles Woodson 2.00 5.00
SSDB Drew Brees 2.00 5.00
SSES Emmitt Smith 3.00 8.00
SSJH Jack Ham 1.50 4.00
SSJR Jerry Rice 3.00 8.00
SSLD LaDainian Tomlinson 1.50 4.00
SSLT Lawrence Taylor 2.00 5.00
SSMI Michael Irvin 2.00 5.00
SSPM Peyton Manning 4.00 10.00
SSSG Stephen Gostkowski 1.50 4.00
SSTB Tom Brady 5.00 12.00
SSTR Tony Romo 1.50 4.00

2016 Panini Phoenix Veteran Jerseys

COMMON CARD 4.00 10.00
SEMISTARS 5.00 12.00
UNLISTED STARS 6.00 15.00
1 Larry Fitzgerald 4.00 10.00
2 Matt Ryan 4.00 10.00
3 Joe Flacco 4.00 10.00
4 Cam Newton 5.00 12.00
5 A.J. Green 5.00 12.00
6 Jason Witten 4.00 10.00
7 Tony Romo 4.00 10.00
8 DeMarcus Ware 4.00 10.00
9 Matthew Stafford 4.00 10.00
10 Aaron Rodgers 10.00 25.00
11 Jamaal Charles 4.00 10.00
12 Adrian Peterson 5.00 12.00
13 Tom Brady 12.00 30.00
14 Drew Brees 5.00 12.00
15 Eli Manning 4.00 10.00
16 Darrelle Revis 3.00 8.00
17 Ben Roethlisberger 5.00 12.00
18 Philip Rivers 5.00 12.00
19 Jimmy Graham 5.00 12.00
20 Doug Martin 4.00 10.00

2016 Panini Phoenix Watchmen

COMMON CARD 1.25 3.00
UNLISTED STARS 2.00 5.00
*ORANGE/299: .6X TO 1.5X BASIC INSERTS
*RED/349: .6X TO 1.5X BASIC INSERTS
*YELLOW/99: 1X TO 4X BASIC INSERTS
WMAT Aqib Talib 1.25 3.00
WMCH Chris Harris 1.25 3.00
WMDA David Amerson 1.25 3.00
WMDR Darrelle Revis 1.25 3.00
WMDT Desmond Trufant 1.25 3.00
WMEB Eric Berry 1.50 4.00
WMET Earl Thomas III 1.50 4.00
WMHS Harrison Smith 1.25 3.00
WMJH Joe Haden 1.25 3.00
WMJN Josh Norman 1.25 3.00
WMMA Mike Adams 1.25 3.00
WMMB Malcolm Butler 2.00 5.00
WMPP Patrick Peterson 1.25 3.00
WMRD Ronald Darby 1.25 3.00
WMRJ Reshad Jones 1.25 3.00
WMRN Reggie Nelson 1.25 3.00
WMRS Richard Sherman 2.00 5.00
WMTJ Trumaine Johnson 1.25 3.00
WMTM Tyrann Mathieu 1.50 4.00
WMVD Vontae Davis 1.25 3.00

2017 Panini Phoenix

1 Joe Flacco .60 1.50
2 Terrell Suggs .50 1.25
3 Andy Dalton .60 1.50
4 A.J. Green .75 2.00
5 J.J. Watt .75 2.00
6 DeAndre Hopkins .60 1.50
7 Isaiah Crowell .50 1.25
8 Corey Coleman .50 1.25
9 Le'Veon Bell .60 1.50
10 Ben Roethlisberger .75 2.00
11 Antonio Brown .75 2.00
12 Andrew Luck 1.00 2.50
13 T.Y. Hilton .60 1.50
14 Blake Bortles .50 1.25
15 Allen Robinson .50 1.25
16 Marcus Mariota .75 2.00
17 DeMarco Murray .60 1.50
18 Tyrod Taylor .60 1.50
19 LeSean McCoy .60 1.50
20 Ryan Tannehill .60 1.50
21 Jay Ajayi .60 1.50
22 Tom Brady 2.00 5.00
23 Rob Gronkowski .75 2.00
24 Matt Forte .50 1.25
25 Quincy Enunwa .50 1.25
26 Von Miller .60 1.50
27 Demaryius Thomas .60 1.50
28 Travis Kelce .75 2.00
29 Tyreek Hill .75 2.00
30 Philip Rivers .75 2.00
31 Joey Bosa .75 2.00
32 Derek Carr .75 2.00
33 Amari Cooper .75 2.00
34 Mike Glennon .60 1.50
35 Jordan Howard .75 2.00
36 Matthew Stafford .60 1.50
37 Marvin Jones Jr. .50 1.25
38 Aaron Rodgers 1.50 4.00
39 Jordy Nelson .60 1.50
40 Sam Bradford .50 1.25
41 Stefon Diggs .60 1.50
42 Matt Ryan .60 1.50
43 Julio Jones .75 2.00
44 Cam Newton .75 2.00
45 Luke Kuechly .60 1.50
46 Drew Brees .75 2.00
47 Adrian Peterson .75 2.00
48 Mike Evans .60 1.50
49 Jameis Winston .60 1.50
50 Dak Prescott .75 2.00
51 Ezekiel Elliott 1.00 2.50
52 Eli Manning .60 1.50
53 Odell Beckham Jr. .75 2.00
54 Carson Wentz 1.00 2.50
55 Alshon Jeffery .60 1.50
56 Josh Norman .50 1.25
57 Kirk Cousins .60 1.50
58 Larry Fitzgerald .60 1.50
59 Carson Palmer .60 1.50
60 Todd Gurley II .75 2.00
61 Aaron Donald .75 2.00
62 Carlos Hyde .50 1.25
63 Jeremy Kerley .50 1.25
64 Russell Wilson 1.00 2.50
65 Doug Baldwin .60 1.50
66 Jim Zorn .50 1.25
67 Steve Young 1.00 2.50
68 Kurt Warner .60 1.50
69 Emmitt Smith 1.25 3.00
70 John Riggins .60 1.50
71 Randall Cunningham .60 1.50
72 Michael Strahan .60 1.50
73 Roger Staubach 1.00 2.50
74 Warren Sapp .50 1.25
75 Morten Andersen .50 1.25
76 Kevin Greene .60 1.50
77 Michael Vick .60 1.50
78 Fran Tarkenton .75 2.00
79 Brett Favre 1.50 4.00
80 Calvin Johnson .75 2.00
81 Brian Urlacher .75 2.00
82 Ray Lewis .75 2.00
83 Ken Anderson .50 1.25
84 Ozzie Newsome .60 1.50
85 Franco Harris .75 2.00
86 Warren Moon .75 2.00
87 Peyton Manning 1.50 4.00
88 Mark Brunell .60 1.50
89 Jason Taylor .50 1.25
90 Jim Kelly .75 2.00
91 Dan Marino 1.50 4.00
92 Curtis Martin .60 1.50
93 Lawrence Taylor .75 2.00
94 Terrell Davis .60 1.50
95 Ty Law .75 2.00
96 LaDainian Tomlinson .60 1.50
97 Bo Jackson 1.00 2.50
98 Troy Aikman 1.00 2.50
99 Tim Brown .75 2.00
100 Tony Dorsett .75 2.00
101 Deshaun Watson RC 4.00 10.00
102 Mitchell Trubisky RC 3.00 8.00
103 DeShone Kizer RC .60 1.50
104 Patrick Mahomes II RC 15.00 40.00
105 Nathan Peterman RC .75 2.00
106 Davis Webb RC .60 1.50
107 C.J. Beathard RC .60 1.50
108 R. Joshua Dobbs RC .75 2.00
109 Leonard Fournette RC 2.00 5.00
110 Dalvin Cook RC 1.50 4.00
111 Christian McCaffrey RC 1.50 4.00
112 D'Onta Foreman RC .75 2.00
113 Alvin Kamara RC 2.50 6.00
114 Samaje Perine RC .60 1.50
115 Wayne Gallman RC .75 2.00
116 Kareem Hunt RC 1.25 3.00
117 Kenny Golladay RC 1.00 2.50
118 James Conner RC 1.25 3.00
119 Joe Mixon RC 1.25 3.00
120 Evan Engram RC .75 2.00
121 O.J. Howard RC .75 2.00
122 Mike Williams RC 1.00 2.50
123 Josh Reynolds RC .60 1.50
124 John Ross III RC .60 1.50
125 JuJu Smith-Schuster RC 1.50 4.00
126 Zay Jones RC .75 2.00
127 Corey Davis RC 1.00 2.50
128 Curtis Samuel RC .75 2.00
129 Dede Westbrook RC .60 1.50
130 Carlos Henderson RC .60 1.50
131 Chris Godwin RC .75 2.00
132 Mack Hollins RC .60 1.50
133 Cooper Kupp RC 1.00 2.50
134 Amara Darboh RC .60 1.50
135 Marlon Mack RC 1.00 2.50
136 ArDarius Stewart RC .60 1.50
137 Joe Williams RC .60 1.50
138 Jamaal Williams RC .60 1.50
139 Taywan Taylor RC .60 1.50
140 Jeremy McNichols RC .60 1.50
141 Myles Garrett RC 2.00 5.00
142 Solomon Thomas RC .60 1.50
143 Jamal Adams RC .60 1.50
144 Marshon Lattimore RC .75 2.00
145 Haason Reddick RC .60 1.50
146 Derek Barnett RC .75 2.00
147 Malik Hooker RC .60 1.50
148 Marlon Humphrey RC .60 1.50
149 Jonathan Allen RC .75 2.00
150 Adoree' Jackson RC .75 2.00
151 Jarrad Davis RC .75 2.00
152 Charles Harris RC .60 1.50
153 Gareon Conley RC .60 1.50
154 Jabrill Peppers RC 1.00 2.50
155 Taco Charlton RC .60 1.50
156 David Njoku RC .75 2.00
157 Reuben Foster RC .60 1.50
158 Kevin King RC .75 2.00
159 Malik McDowell RC .60 1.50
160 Budda Baker RC .60 1.50
161 Marcus Maye RC .60 1.50
162 Marcus Williams RC .60 1.50
163 Sidney Jones RC .60 1.50
164 Gerald Everett RC .60 1.50
165 Adam Shaheen RC .60 1.50
166 Quincy Wilson RC .60 1.50
167 Tyus Bowser RC .60 1.50
168 Ryan Anderson RC .60 1.50
169 DeMarcus Walker RC .60 1.50
170 Teez Tabor RC .75 2.00
171 Obi Melifonwu RC .60 1.50
172 Zach Cunningham RC .75 2.00
173 Josh Jones RC .75 2.00
174 Ahkello Witherspoon RC .75 2.00
175 Dawuane Smoot RC .60 1.50
176 Jordan Willis RC .60 1.50
177 Chris Wormley RC .60 1.50
178 Duke Riley RC .60 1.50
179 Alex Anzalone RC .75 2.00
180 Daeshon Hall RC .60 1.50
181 Tim Williams RC .75 2.00
182 Chad Williams RC .60 1.50
183 Fabian Moreau RC .60 1.50
184 Derek Rivers RC .75 2.00
185 Shaquill Griffin RC .75 2.00
186 John Johnson RC .75 2.00
187 Jourdan Lewis RC .60 1.50
188 Montravius Adams RC .60 1.50
189 Cameron Sutton RC .75 2.00
190 Delano Hill RC .75 2.00
191 Michael Roberts RC 1.00 2.50
192 Rasul Douglas RC .60 1.50
193 Jonnu Smith RC .75 2.00
194 Brendan Langley RC .60 1.50
195 George Kittle RC .60 1.50
196 Trey Hendrickson RC .75 2.00
197 Kendell Beckwith RC .60 1.50
198 Jehu Chesson RC .75 2.00
199 Eddie Jackson RC .75 2.00
200 Ryan Switzer RC .75 2.00

2017 Panini Phoenix Green

*VETS: 2X TO 5X BASIC CARDS
*ROOKIES: 1.5X TO 4X BASIC CARDS
104 Patrick Mahomes II 100.00 200.00

2017 Panini Phoenix Orange

*VETS: 1.2X TO 3X BASIC CARDS
*ROOKIES: 1X TO 2.5X BASIC CARDS
104 Patrick Mahomes II 60.00 125.00

2017 Panini Phoenix Pink

*VETS: .8X TO 2X BASIC CARDS
*ROOKIES: .6X TO 1.5X BASIC CARDS
104 Patrick Mahomes II 40.00 80.00

2017 Panini Phoenix Purple

*VETS: 1X TO 2.5X BASIC CARDS
*ROOKIES: .8X TO 2X BASIC CARDS
104 Patrick Mahomes II 40.00 100.00

2017 Panini Phoenix Red

*VETS: .8X TO 2X BASIC CARDS
*ROOKIES: .6X TO 1.5X BASIC CARDS
104 Patrick Mahomes II 30.00 80.00

2017 Panini Phoenix Yellow

104 Patrick Mahomes II 75.00 150.00

2017 Panini Phoenix Adrenaline Rush

*ORANGE/49: .8X TO 2X BASIC INSERTS
*RED/299: .6X TO 1.5X BASIC INSERTS
*YELLOW/25: 1.5X TO 4X BASIC INSERTS
*PURPLE/76: 1.2X TO 3X BASIC INSERTS
*PINK/199: .6X TO 1.5X BASIC INSERTS
1 Barry Sanders 1.50 4.00
2 Emmitt Smith 1.50 4.00
3 Eric Dickerson 1.00 2.50
4 Adrian Peterson 1.00 2.50
5 LaDainian Tomlinson .75 2.00

6 Ezekiel Elliott 1.25 3.00
7 Earl Campbell 1.00 2.50
8 Jerome Bettis 1.00 2.50
9 Bo Jackson 1.25 3.00
10 Marcus Allen .75 2.00
11 Le'Veon Bell .75 2.00
12 David Johnson 1.00 2.50
13 LeSean McCoy 1.00 2.50
14 Jordan Howard 1.00 2.50
15 Melvin Gordon .75 2.00
16 Devonta Freeman .75 2.00
17 Gale Sayers 1.00 2.50
18 Marshawn Lynch .75 2.00
19 John Riggins .75 2.00
20 Priest Holmes .60 1.50

2017 Panini Phoenix Dual Patch Autographs

2 C.Beathard/J.Williams 6.00 15.00
3 C.Davis/M.Williams 10.00 25.00
4 C.Davis/T.Taylor 10.00 25.00
9 E.Engram/O.Howard 8.00 20.00
15 C.Kupp/J.Reynolds 10.00 25.00
16 J.Conner/N.Peterman 12.00 30.00

2017 Panini Phoenix Hot Rookie Materials Signatures Football

*GLOVE p/r: 99: .4X TO 1X BASIC p/r 99-299
*GLOVE p/r: 25: .6X TO 1.5X BASIC p/r 99-299
*GLOVE p/r: 25: .5X TO 1.2X BASIC p/r 49
*GLOVE p/r: 15: .4X TO 1X BASIC p/r 25
1 Zay Jones/299 5.00 12.00
2 Christian McCaffrey/49 12.00 30.00
3 Mitchell Trubisky/25 30.00 80.00
4 Carlos Henderson/299 4.00 10.00
5 John Ross III/49 6.00 15.00
6 DeShone Kizer/25 6.00 15.00
7 Deshaun Watson/25 40.00 100.00
8 D'Onta Foreman/299 5.00 12.00
9 Leonard Fournette/25 20.00 50.00
10 Patrick Mahomes II/25 200.00 400.00
11 Mike Williams/49 8.00 20.00
12 Dalvin Cook/49 12.00 30.00
13 Alvin Kamara/299 15.00 40.00
14 Davis Webb/199 4.00 10.00
15 JuJu Smith-Schuster/99 10.00 25.00
16 C.J. Beathard/299 4.00 10.00
17 Amara Darboh/299 4.00 10.00
18 O.J. Howard/299 5.00 12.00
19 Corey Davis/99 6.00 15.00
20 Samaje Perine/299 4.00 10.00

2017 Panini Phoenix Legacy

1 Terry Bradshaw 1.50 4.00
2 Tom Brady 2.50 6.00
3 Dan Marino 2.00 5.00
4 Troy Aikman 1.25 3.00
5 Steve Young 1.25 3.00
6 Peyton Manning 2.00 5.00
7 Eli Manning .75 2.00
8 Brett Favre 2.00 5.00
9 Joe Theismann 1.00 2.50
10 Barry Sanders 1.50 4.00

2017 Panini Phoenix Power Surge

1 Kam Chancellor 1.00 2.50
2 Patrick Peterson .60 1.50
3 J.J. Watt 1.00 2.50
4 Willie McGinest .60 1.50
5 Ed Reed .75 2.00
6 Bruce Smith .75 2.00
7 Joe Greene 1.00 2.50
8 Mike Singletary 1.00 2.50
9 Ray Lewis 1.00 2.50
10 Lawrence Taylor 1.00 2.50
11 Luke Kuechly .75 2.00
12 Richard Sherman 1.00 2.50
13 Tyrann Mathieu .75 2.00
14 Eric Berry .75 2.00
15 Harrison Smith .60 1.50
16 Earl Thomas III .75 2.00
17 Khalil Mack 1.00 2.50
18 Von Miller .75 2.00
19 Ndamukong Suh .75 2.00
20 Vic Beasley Jr. .60 1.50
21 Sean Lee .75 2.00
22 Landon Collins .60 1.50
23 Michael Strahan .75 2.00
24 Brian Urlacher 1.00 2.50
25 Deion Sanders .75 2.00
26 Rod Woodson .75 2.00
27 Ronnie Lott .75 2.00
28 Terrell Suggs .60 1.50
29 Derrick Brooks .60 1.50
30 Charles Woodson 1.00 2.50

2017 Panini Phoenix Retired Patches

2 Lance Alworth/20 12.00 30.00
3 Randy Moss/20 12.00 30.00
8 Mark Brunell/20 12.00 30.00
10 Ricky Williams/20 12.00 30.00
11 Priest Holmes/20 10.00 25.00
12 Terrell Davis/20 12.00 30.00
13 John Riggins/20 12.00 30.00
14 Ray Lewis/20 15.00 40.00
16 Heath Miller/20 10.00 25.00
17 Bo Jackson/20 20.00 50.00
18 Kurt Warner/20 12.00 30.00

2017 Panini Phoenix Rookie Jersey Autographs

1 Nathan Peterman/299 4.00 10.00
2 Zay Jones/299 4.00 10.00
3 Christian McCaffrey/99 15.00 40.00
4 Curtis Samuel/299 4.00 10.00
5 Mitchell Trubisky/75 30.00 80.00
6 Joe Mixon/99 10.00 25.00
7 John Ross III/299 4.00 10.00
8 DeShone Kizer/75 6.00 15.00
9 Carlos Henderson/299 3.00 8.00
10 Kenny Golladay/149 6.00 15.00
11 Jamaal Williams/149 4.00 10.00
12 Deshaun Watson/75 40.00 100.00
13 D'Onta Foreman/299 4.00 10.00
14 Marlon Mack/99 8.00 20.00
15 Dede Westbrook/299 3.00 8.00
16 Leonard Fournette/75 20.00 50.00
17 Kareem Hunt/299 6.00 15.00
18 Patrick Mahomes II/75 200.00 400.00
19 Mike Williams/99 8.00 20.00
20 Cooper Kupp/99 8.00 20.00
21 Josh Reynolds/99 5.00 12.00
22 Dalvin Cook/99 12.00 30.00
23 Alvin Kamara/299 12.00 30.00
24 Davis Webb/299 3.00 8.00
25 Evan Engram/299 4.00 10.00
26 Wayne Gallman/299 4.00 10.00
27 ArDarius Stewart/99 5.00 12.00
28 Mack Hollins/299 3.00 8.00
29 James Conner/99 10.00 25.00
30 JuJu Smith-Schuster/299 8.00 20.00
31 R. Joshua Dobbs/99 6.00 15.00
32 C.J. Beathard/299 3.00 8.00
33 Joe Williams/99 5.00 12.00
34 Amara Darboh/299 3.00 8.00
35 Chris Godwin/149 5.00 12.00
36 Jeremy McNichols/299 3.00 8.00
37 O.J. Howard/299 4.00 10.00
38 Corey Davis/299 5.00 12.00
39 Taywan Taylor/299 3.00 8.00
40 Samaje Perine/299 3.00 8.00

2017 Panini Phoenix Rookie Jerseys

1 Deshaun Watson 12.00 30.00
2 Mitchell Trubisky 8.00 20.00
3 DeShone Kizer 2.50 6.00
4 Patrick Mahomes II 20.00 50.00
5 Nathan Peterman 3.00 8.00
6 Davis Webb 2.50 6.00
7 C.J. Beathard 2.50 6.00
8 R. Joshua Dobbs 3.00 8.00
9 Leonard Fournette 10.00 25.00
10 Dalvin Cook 5.00 12.00
11 Christian McCaffrey 8.00 20.00
12 D'Onta Foreman 3.00 8.00
13 Alvin Kamara 6.00 15.00
14 Samaje Perine 2.50 6.00
15 Wayne Gallman 3.00 8.00
16 Kareem Hunt 6.00 15.00
17 Kenny Golladay 4.00 10.00
18 James Conner 5.00 12.00
19 Joe Mixon 5.00 12.00
20 Evan Engram 3.00 8.00
21 O.J. Howard 3.00 8.00
22 Mike Williams 4.00 10.00
23 Josh Reynolds 2.50 6.00
24 John Ross III 3.00 8.00
25 JuJu Smith-Schuster 6.00 15.00
26 Zay Jones 3.00 8.00
27 Corey Davis 4.00 10.00
28 Curtis Samuel 3.00 8.00
29 Dede Westbrook 2.50 6.00
30 Carlos Henderson 2.50 6.00
31 Chris Godwin 3.00 8.00
32 Mack Hollins 2.50 6.00
33 Cooper Kupp 4.00 10.00
34 Amara Darboh 2.50 6.00
35 Marlon Mack 4.00 10.00
36 ArDarius Stewart 2.50 6.00
37 Joe Williams 2.50 6.00
38 Jamaal Williams 2.50 6.00
39 Taywan Taylor 2.50 6.00
40 Jeremy McNichols 2.50 6.00

2017 Panini Phoenix Rookie Jumbo Jerseys

1 Deshaun Watson 12.00 30.00
2 Mitchell Trubisky 8.00 20.00
3 DeShone Kizer 2.50 6.00
4 Patrick Mahomes II 20.00 50.00
5 Nathan Peterman 3.00 8.00
6 Davis Webb 2.50 6.00
7 C.J. Beathard 2.50 6.00
8 R. Joshua Dobbs 3.00 8.00
9 Leonard Fournette 10.00 25.00
10 Dalvin Cook 5.00 12.00
11 Christian McCaffrey 12.00 20.00
12 D'Onta Foreman 3.00 8.00
13 Alvin Kamara 10.00 15.00
14 Samaje Perine 2.50 6.00
15 Wayne Gallman 3.00 8.00
16 Kareem Hunt 5.00 12.00
17 Kenny Golladay 4.00 10.00
18 James Conner 5.00 12.00
19 Joe Mixon 5.00 12.00
20 Evan Engram 3.00 8.00
21 O.J. Howard 3.00 8.00
22 Mike Williams 4.00 10.00
23 Josh Reynolds 2.50 6.00
24 John Ross III 3.00 8.00
25 JuJu Smith-Schuster 6.00 15.00
26 Zay Jones 3.00 8.00
27 Corey Davis 4.00 10.00
28 Curtis Samuel 3.00 8.00
29 Dede Westbrook 2.50 6.00
30 Carlos Henderson 2.50 6.00
31 Chris Godwin 3.00 8.00
32 Mack Hollins 2.50 6.00
33 Cooper Kupp 4.00 10.00
34 Amara Darboh 2.50 6.00
35 Marlon Mack 4.00 10.00
36 ArDarius Stewart 2.50 6.00
37 Joe Williams 2.50 6.00
38 Jamaal Williams 2.50 6.00
39 Taywan Taylor 2.50 6.00
40 Jeremy McNichols 2.50 6.00

2017 Panini Phoenix Rookie Jumbo Patch Autographs

1 Nathan Peterman/149 6.00 15.00
2 Zay Jones/149 6.00 15.00
3 Christian McCaffrey/149 12.00 30.00
4 Curtis Samuel/149 6.00 15.00
5 Mitchell Trubisky/49 50.00 100.00
6 Joe Mixon/75 12.00 30.00
7 John Ross III/149 6.00 15.00
8 DeShone Kizer/49 8.00 20.00
9 Carlos Henderson/149 5.00 12.00
10 Kenny Golladay/49 12.00 30.00
11 Jamaal Williams/49 8.00 20.00
12 Deshaun Watson/49 75.00 150.00
13 D'Onta Foreman/149 6.00 15.00
14 Marlon Mack/49 12.00 30.00
15 Dede Westbrook/149 5.00 12.00
16 Leonard Fournette/49 30.00 80.00
17 Kareem Hunt/149 10.00 25.00
18 Patrick Mahomes II/49 150.00 300.00
19 Mike Williams/99 10.00 25.00
20 Cooper Kupp/99 10.00 25.00
21 Josh Reynolds/49 8.00 20.00
22 Dalvin Cook/149 12.00 30.00
23 Alvin Kamara/149 20.00 50.00
24 Davis Webb/149 5.00 12.00
25 Evan Engram/149 6.00 15.00
26 Wayne Gallman/149 6.00 15.00
27 ArDarius Stewart/99 6.00 15.00
28 Mack Hollins/149 5.00 12.00
29 James Conner/49 15.00 40.00
30 JuJu Smith-Schuster/149 12.00 30.00
31 R. Joshua Dobbs/49 10.00 25.00
32 C.J. Beathard/149 5.00 12.00
33 Joe Williams/49 8.00 20.00
34 Amara Darboh/149 5.00 12.00
35 Chris Godwin/49 10.00 25.00
36 Jeremy McNichols/149 5.00 12.00
37 O.J. Howard/149 6.00 15.00
38 Corey Davis/149 8.00 20.00
39 Taywan Taylor/149 5.00 12.00
40 Samaje Perine/149 5.00 12.00

2017 Panini Phoenix Rookie Rising

1 Myles Garrett 1.00 2.50
2 Jabrill Peppers .50 1.25
3 Deshaun Watson 2.00 5.00
4 Mitchell Trubisky 1.50 4.00
5 DeShone Kizer .30 .75
6 Leonard Fournette 1.00 2.50
7 Ryan Switzer .40 1.00
8 David Njoku .40 1.00
9 Dalvin Cook .75 2.00
10 Christian McCaffrey .75 2.00
11 Jamal Adams .30 .75
12 D'Onta Foreman .40 1.00
13 Dede Westbrook .30 .75
14 R. Joshua Dobbs .40 1.00
15 Patrick Mahomes II 12.00 30.00
16 Davis Webb .30 .75
17 C.J. Beathard .30 .75
18 James Conner .60 1.50
19 Joe Mixon .60 1.50
20 O.J. Howard .40 1.00
21 Mike Williams .50 1.25
22 Zay Jones .40 1.00
23 Evan Engram .40 1.00
24 Wayne Gallman .40 1.00
25 Kareem Hunt .60 1.50
26 John Ross III .40 1.00
27 JuJu Smith-Schuster .75 2.00
28 Chris Godwin .40 1.00
29 Samaje Perine .30 .75
30 Corey Davis .50 1.25

2017 Panini Phoenix Triumphant

1 Tom Brady 4.00 10.00
2 Tom Brady 4.00 10.00
3 Tom Brady 4.00 10.00
4 Tom Brady 4.00 10.00
5 Tom Brady 4.00 10.00
6 Tom Brady 4.00 10.00
7 Tom Brady 4.00 10.00
8 Tom Brady 4.00 10.00
9 Tom Brady 4.00 10.00
10 Tom Brady 4.00 10.00

2017 Panini Phoenix Veteran Jersey Autographs

1 Luke Kuechly/30 8.00 20.00
2 C.J. Anderson/30 8.00 20.00
4 Thomas Rawls/30 6.00 15.00
5 Devonta Freeman/20 8.00 20.00
7 Emmanuel Sanders/30 10.00 25.00
8 Chris Hogan/30 6.00 15.00
11 Allen Robinson/30 8.00 20.00
13 Joey Bosa/30 10.00 25.00
14 Terrelle Pryor Sr./30 6.00 15.00
15 A.J. Green/20 10.00 25.00
16 Earl Thomas III/20 8.00 20.00
17 DeMarco Murray/20 8.00 20.00
18 Carlos Hyde/30 6.00 15.00
19 Michael Thomas/30 10.00 25.00
20 Tyler Lockett/30 8.00 20.00
22 Frank Gore/20 8.00 20.00
23 Robert Kelley/30 6.00 15.00
24 Melvin Gordon/20 8.00 20.00
25 Richard Sherman/20 10.00 25.00
26 Isaiah Crowell/30 6.00 15.00
28 Mark Ingram/20 8.00 20.00
29 Quincy Enunwa/30 6.00 15.00
30 Jason Witten/20 8.00 20.00

2017 Panini Phoenix Veteran Jerseys

1 Derek Carr/25 6.00 15.00
2 Cam Newton/49 5.00 12.00
3 Russell Wilson/49 6.00 15.00
4 David Johnson/49 5.00 12.00
5 Le'Veon Bell/49 4.00 10.00
6 Tom Brady/25 15.00 40.00
7 Drew Brees/25 6.00 15.00
8 Jameis Winston/49 4.00 10.00
9 Luke Kuechly/49 4.00 10.00
10 Matthew Stafford/49 4.00 10.00
11 Odell Beckham Jr./49 5.00 12.00
12 Philip Rivers/49 5.00 12.00
13 Rob Gronkowski/49 5.00 12.00
14 Von Miller/49 4.00 10.00
15 Antonio Brown/25 6.00 15.00
16 J.J. Watt/25 6.00 15.00
17 Amari Cooper/49 5.00 12.00
18 Matt Ryan/49 4.00 10.00
19 Kelvin Benjamin/49 4.00 10.00
20 Todd Gurley II/49 5.00 12.00

2018 Panini Phoenix

1 Sam Bradford .50 1.25
2 David Johnson .75 2.00
3 Larry Fitzgerald .60 1.50
4 Matt Ryan .60 1.50
5 Devonta Freeman .60 1.50
6 Julio Jones .75 2.00
7 Joe Flacco .60 1.50
8 Terrell Suggs .50 1.25
9 Alex Collins .50 1.25
10 A.J. McCarron .50 1.25
11 LeSean McCoy .75 2.00
12 Zay Jones .50 1.25
13 Cam Newton .75 2.00
14 Christian McCaffrey .75 2.00
15 Luke Kuechly .60 1.50
16 Mitchell Trubisky .75 2.00
17 Jordan Howard .75 2.00
18 Tarik Cohen .60 1.50
19 Andy Dalton .60 1.50
20 A.J. Green .75 2.00
21 Joe Mixon .60 1.50
22 Tyrod Taylor .60 1.50
23 Josh Gordon .50 1.25
24 Jarvis Landry .60 1.50
25 Dak Prescott .75 2.00
26 Ezekiel Elliott 1.00 2.50
27 Allen Hurns .50 1.25
28 Cole Beasley .60 1.50
29 Case Keenum .60 1.50
30 Von Miller .60 1.50
31 Demaryius Thomas .60 1.50
32 Matthew Stafford .60 1.50
33 LeGarrette Blount .60 1.50
34 Golden Tate III .50 1.25
35 Aaron Rodgers 1.50 4.00
36 Jimmy Graham .75 2.00
37 Davante Adams .60 1.50
38 Clay Matthews .60 1.50
39 Deshaun Watson 1.00 2.50
40 DeAndre Hopkins .60 1.50
41 J.J. Watt .75 2.00
42 Andrew Luck 1.00 2.50
43 Marlon Mack .50 1.25
44 T.Y. Hilton .60 1.50
45 Blake Bortles .50 1.25
46 Leonard Fournette .75 2.00
47 Jalen Ramsey .60 1.50
48 Patrick Mahomes II 2.00 5.00
49 Kareem Hunt .60 1.50
50 Tyreek Hill .75 2.00
51 Jared Goff .75 2.00
52 Todd Gurley II .75 2.00
53 Aaron Donald .75 2.00
54 Philip Rivers .75 2.00
55 Melvin Gordon .60 1.50
56 Keenan Allen .60 1.50
57 Ryan Tannehill .60 1.50
58 Frank Gore .60 1.50
59 DeVante Parker .60 1.50
60 Kirk Cousins .75 2.00
61 Dalvin Cook .60 1.50
62 Stefon Diggs .60 1.50
63 Tom Brady 2.00 5.00
64 Rob Gronkowski .75 2.00
65 Rex Burkhead .50 1.25
66 Julian Edelman .75 2.00
67 Drew Brees .75 2.00
68 Alvin Kamara .60 1.50
69 Michael Thomas .75 2.00
70 Eli Manning .60 1.50
71 Odell Beckham Jr. .75 2.00
72 Evan Engram .50 1.25
73 Josh McCown .50 1.25
74 Robby Anderson .50 1.25
75 Bilal Powell .50 1.25
76 Derek Carr .75 2.00
77 Marshawn Lynch .60 1.50
78 Khalil Mack .75 2.00
79 Carson Wentz 1.00 2.50
80 Jay Ajayi .60 1.50
81 Alshon Jeffery .60 1.50
82 Ben Roethlisberger .75 2.00
83 Le'Veon Bell .60 1.50
84 Antonio Brown .75 2.00
85 T.J. Watt .60 1.50
86 Jimmy Garoppolo 1.00 2.50
87 Jerick McKinnon .50 1.25
88 Marquise Goodwin .50 1.25
89 Russell Wilson 1.00 2.50
90 Doug Baldwin .60 1.50
91 Bobby Wagner .50 1.25
92 Jameis Winston .60 1.50
93 Mike Evans .60 1.50
94 DeSean Jackson .60 1.50
95 Marcus Mariota .75 2.00
96 Derrick Henry .75 2.00
97 Rishard Matthews .50 1.25
98 Alex Smith .60 1.50
99 Jordan Reed .50 1.25
100 Josh Norman .60 1.25
101 Josh Rosen RC 2.00 5.00
102 Saquon Barkley RC 5.00 12.00
103 Sam Darnold RC 4.00 10.00
104 Bradley Chubb RC 1.00 2.50
105 Josh Allen RC 2.50 6.00
106 Baker Mayfield RC 6.00 15.00
107 D.J. Moore RC 1.25 3.00
108 Hayden Hurst RC .75 2.00
109 Calvin Ridley RC 1.50 4.00
110 Rashaad Penny RC 1.00 2.50
111 Sony Michel RC 2.00 5.00
112 Lamar Jackson RC 4.00 10.00
113 Nick Chubb RC 2.00 5.00
114 Ronald Jones II RC .60 1.50
115 Courtland Sutton RC 1.00 2.50
116 Mike Gesicki RC .75 2.00
117 Kerryon Johnson RC 1.00 2.50
118 Dante Pettis RC 1.00 2.50
119 Christian Kirk RC 1.00 2.50
120 Anthony Miller RC 1.00 2.50
121 Derrius Guice RC 1.25 3.00
122 James Washington RC 1.25 3.00
123 D.J. Chark Jr. RC .75 2.00
124 Royce Freeman RC .75 2.00
125 Mason Rudolph RC 1.50 4.00
126 Michael Gallup RC 1.25 3.00
127 Tre'Quan Smith RC 1.00 2.50
128 Keke Coutee RC .75 2.00
129 Nyheim Hines RC .75 2.00
130 Kyle Lauletta RC 1.00 2.50
131 Mark Walton RC .75 2.00
132 DaeSean Hamilton RC .75 2.00
133 Ito Smith RC .75 2.00
134 Kalen Ballage RC .75 2.00
135 Jaleel Scott RC .60 1.50
136 J'Mon Moore RC .60 1.50
137 Daurice Fountain RC .75 2.00
138 Jaylen Samuels RC .75 2.00
139 Mike White RC .75 2.00
140 Marquez Valdes-Scantling RC .75 2.00
141 Denzel Ward RC 1.50 4.00
142 Roquan Smith RC 2.00 5.00
143 Minkah Fitzpatrick RC 1.25 3.00
144 Vita Vea RC 1.00 2.50
145 Daron Payne RC 1.00 2.50
146 Marcus Davenport RC 1.25 3.00
147 Tremaine Edmunds RC 1.25 3.00
148 Derwin James RC 1.25 3.00
149 Jaire Alexander RC 1.00 2.50
150 Leighton Vander Esch RC 2.00 5.00
151 Rashaan Evans RC 1.00 2.50
152 Terrell Edmunds RC 2.00 5.00
153 Mike Hughes RC 1.00 2.50
154 Harold Landry RC .60 1.50
155 Joshua Jackson RC 1.25 3.00
156 M.J. Stewart RC .60 1.50
157 Donte Jackson RC 1.00 2.50
158 Duke Dawson RC .60 1.50
159 Isaiah Oliver RC .60 1.50
160 Carlton Davis RC .75 2.00
161 Tyquan Lewis RC .75 2.00
162 Lorenzo Carter RC .60 1.50
163 Justin Reid RC .60 1.50
164 Jerome Baker RC .75 2.00
165 Derrick Nnadi RC .60 1.50
166 Richie James RC .60 1.50
167 Justin Watson RC .75 2.00
168 Ronnie Harrison RC .75 2.00
169 Jalyn Holmes RC 1.00 2.50
170 John Kelly RC .75 2.00
171 Christopher Herndon IV RC .60 1.50
172 Da'Shawn Hand RC .60 1.50
173 Connor Williams RC 1.25 3.00
174 Armani Watts RC .60 1.50
175 Josh Sweat RC .75 2.00
176 Chase Edmonds RC .60 1.50
177 Dalton Schultz RC .75 2.00
178 Javon Wims RC .60 1.50
179 Shaquem Griffin RC 1.00 2.50
180 Troy Fumagalli RC .75 2.00
181 Jordan Lasley RC .60 1.50
182 Antonio Callaway RC .75 2.00
183 Ray-Ray McCloud RC .60 1.50
184 Dylan Cantrell RC .60 1.50
185 Luke Falk RC .75 2.00
186 Cedrick Wilson Jr. RC .60 1.50
187 Braxton Berrios RC .60 1.50
188 Marcell Ateman RC .75 2.00
189 Bo Scarbrough RC .75 2.00
190 Ryan Izzo RC .60 1.50
191 Justin Jackson RC .75 2.00
192 Auden Tate RC .60 1.50
193 Trey Quinn RC .60 1.50
194 Allen Lazard RC .60 1.50
195 Deontay Burnett RC .75 2.00
196 Josh Adams RC 1.25 3.00
197 Kurt Benkert RC .75 2.00
198 Simmie Cobbs Jr. RC 1.00 2.50
199 Dallas Goedert RC .75 2.00
200 Rasheem Green RC .60 1.50

2018 Panini Phoenix Color Burst

*VETS: .5X TO 1.2X BASIC CARDS
*ROOKIES: .6X TO 1.5X BASIC CARDS

2018 Panini Phoenix Green

*VETS: 2X TO 5X BASIC CARDS
*ROOKIES: 1.5X TO 4X BASIC CARDS

2018 Panini Phoenix Orange

*VETS: 1.2X TO 3X BASIC CARDS
*ROOKIES: 1X TO 2.5X BASIC CARDS

2018 Panini Phoenix Pink

*VETS: .8X TO 2X BASIC CARDS
*ROOKIES: .6X TO 1.5X BASIC CARDS

2018 Panini Phoenix Purple

*VETS: 1X TO 2.5X BASIC CARDS
*ROOKIES: .8X TO 2X BASIC CARDS

2018 Panini Phoenix Red

*VETS: .8X TO 2X BASIC CARDS
*ROOKIES: .6X TO 1.5X BASIC CARDS

2018 Panini Phoenix Yellow

*VETS: 1.2X TO 3X BASIC CARDS
*ROOKIES: 1X TO 2.5X BASIC CARDS

2018 Panini Phoenix Adrenaline Rush

*BURST: .5X TO 1.2X BASIC INSERTS
*RED/299: .6X TO 1.5X BASIC INSERTS
*PINK/199: .8X TO 2X BASIC INSERTS
*PURPLE/75: 1.2X TO 3X BASIC INSERTS
*ORNAGE/49: 1.5X TO 4X BASIC INSERTS
*YELLOW/25: 2X TO 5X BASIC INSERTS
1 Le'Veon Bell .75 2.00
2 Ezekiel Elliott 1.25 3.00
3 Antonio Brown 1.00 2.50
4 Julio Jones 1.00 2.50
5 Todd Gurley II 1.00 2.50
6 Alvin Kamara .75 2.00
7 A.J. Green 1.00 2.50
8 Dalvin Cook .75 2.00
9 Michael Thomas 1.00 2.50
10 Keenan Allen .75 2.00
11 Odell Beckham Jr. 1.00 2.50
12 Mike Evans .75 2.00
13 Jordy Nelson .75 2.00
14 Tyreek Hill 1.00 2.50
15 T.Y. Hilton .75 2.00
16 DeAndre Hopkins .75 2.00
17 David Johnson 1.00 2.50
18 Leonard Fournette 1.00 2.50
19 LeSean McCoy 1.00 2.50
20 Jordan Howard 1.00 2.50

2018 Panini Phoenix Agility

*BURST: .5X TO 1.2X BASIC INSERTS
*RED/299: .6X TO 1.5X BASIC INSERTS
*PINK/199: .8X TO 2X BASIC INSERTS
*PURPLE/75: 1.2X TO 3X BASIC INSERTS
*ORANGE/49: 1.5X TO 4X BASIC INSERTS
*YELLOW/25: 2X TO 5X BASIC INSERTS
1 Le'Veon Bell .75 2.00
2 Tyreek Hill 1.00 2.50
3 Ezekiel Elliott 1.25 3.00
4 Marquise Goodwin .60 1.50
5 J.J. Nelson .60 1.50
6 Ted Ginn Jr. .60 1.50
7 DeSean Jackson .75 2.00
8 Brandin Cooks .75 2.00
9 Odell Beckham Jr. 1.00 2.50
10 Julio Jones 1.00 2.50

2018 Panini Phoenix Most Valuable

*BURST: .5X TO 1.2X BASIC INSERTS
*RED/299: .6X TO 1.5X BASIC INSERTS
*PINK/199: .8X TO 2X BASIC INSERTS
*PURPLE/75: 1.2X TO 3X BASIC INSERTS
*ORANGE/49: 1.5X TO 4X BASIC INSERTS
*YELLOW/25: 2X TO 5X BASIC INSERTS
1 Tom Brady 2.50 6.00
2 Nick Foles .75 2.00
3 Von Miller .75 2.00
4 Eli Manning .75 2.00
5 Aaron Rodgers 2.00 5.00
6 Matt Ryan .75 2.00
7 Cam Newton 1.00 2.50
8 Peyton Manning 2.00 5.00
9 Terry Bradshaw 1.50 4.00
10 Joe Montana 2.50 6.00

2018 Panini Phoenix QB Vision

*BURST: .5X TO 1.2X BASIC INSERTS
*RED/299: .6X TO 1.5X BASIC INSERTS
*PINK/199: .8X TO 2X BASIC INSERTS
*PURPLE/75: 1.2X TO 3X BASIC INSERTS
*ORANGE/49: 1.5X TO 4X BASIC INSERTS
*YELLOW/25: 2X TO 5X BASIC INSERTS
1 Tom Brady 2.50 6.00
2 Carson Wentz 1.25 3.00
3 Dak Prescott 1.00 2.50
4 Matt Ryan .75 2.00
5 Ben Roethlisberger 1.00 2.50
6 Matthew Stafford .75 2.00
7 Drew Brees 1.00 2.50
8 Russell Wilson 1.25 3.00
9 Philip Rivers 1.00 2.50
10 Blake Bortles .60 1.50
11 Marcus Mariota 1.00 2.50
12 Kirk Cousins 1.00 2.50
13 Jared Goff 1.00 2.50
14 Jameis Winston .75 2.00
15 Cam Newton 1.00 2.50
16 Derek Carr 1.00 2.50
17 Eli Manning .75 2.00
18 Joe Flacco .75 2.00
19 Andy Dalton .75 2.00
20 Andrew Luck 1.25 3.00
21 Baker Mayfield 6.00 15.00
22 Mitchell Trubisky 1.00 2.50
23 Deshaun Watson 1.25 3.00
24 Case Keenum .75 2.00
25 Patrick Mahomes II 2.50 6.00
26 Josh McCown .60 1.50
27 Jimmy Garoppolo 1.25 3.00
28 Aaron Rodgers 2.00 5.00
29 Ryan Tannehill .75 2.00
30 Sam Bradford .60 1.50

2018 Panini Phoenix Retired Patches

2 Ed Reed/25 5.00 12.00
3 Jim Kelly/25 6.00 15.00
4 Michael Strahan/25 5.00 12.00
7 Tony Dorsett/25 6.00 15.00
8 John Elway/25 10.00 25.00
9 Barry Sanders/25 10.00 25.00
10 Warren Moon/25 6.00 15.00
13 Marshall Faulk/25 5.00 12.00
15 Fran Tarkenton/25 6.00 15.00
16 Dan Marino/25 12.00 30.00
17 Brian Dawkins/25 6.00 15.00
18 Hines Ward/25 5.00 12.00
19 LaDainian Tomlinson/25 5.00 12.00

2018 Panini Phoenix Retired Signatures

2 Jerry Kramer/50 40.00 80.00
3 Billy Joe DuPree/149 3.00 8.00
5 Tom Mack/99 3.00 8.00
6 Steve McMichael/99 3.00 8.00
7 Willis McGahee/50 4.00 10.00
8 Bill Bates/50 4.00 10.00
9 Jevon Kearse/50 4.00 10.00
10 Plaxico Burress/99 3.00 8.00
11 Mike Wagner/85 3.00 8.00
12 Vince Ferragamo/50 12.00 30.00
13 Larry Little/75
14 Brian Mitchell/99 3.00 8.00
15 Ron Jaworski/149 4.00 10.00
16 Christian Okoye/99 3.00 8.00
17 Ted Johnson/99 3.00 8.00
18 Mike Vrabel/99 4.00 10.00
19 Larry Johnson/99

2018 Panini Phoenix Rising Rookie Material Signatures Football

*GLOVE/99: .5X TO 1.2X FOOT AU/199
*GLOVE/99: .4X TO 1X FOOT AU/125
*GLOVE/49: .5X TO 1.2X FOOT AU/99
*GLOVE/15: .5X TO 1.2X FOOT AU/25
*HEL AU/25: .8X TO 2X BASIC GLOVE AU/199
1 Baker Mayfield/20
2 Sam Darnold/15 50.00 125.00
3 Josh Rosen/20 20.00 50.00
4 Saquon Barkley/20 125.00 250.00
5 Josh Allen/20 25.00 60.00
6 Mason Rudolph/99 8.00 20.00
7 Derrius Guice/20 EXCH 12.00 30.00
8 Nick Chubb/125 10.00 25.00
9 Sony Michel/125 10.00 25.00
10 Calvin Ridley/20 15.00 40.00
11 Christian Kirk/20 10.00 25.00
12 Anthony Miller/199 4.00 10.00
13 Ronald Jones II/199 2.50 6.00
14 Courtland Sutton/199 4.00 10.00
15 Lamar Jackson/25 30.00 80.00
16 D.J. Moore/199 5.00 12.00
17 Jaleel Scott/199 2.50 6.00
18 James Washington/199 5.00 12.00
19 Tre'Quan Smith/199 4.00 10.00
20 Daurice Fountain/199 3.00 8.00

2018 Panini Phoenix Rookie Jersey Autographs

1 Sam Darnold/50 40.00 80.00
2 Josh Rosen/125 10.00 25.00
3 Baker Mayfield/80 100.00 200.00
4 Josh Allen/125 25.00 50.00
5 Mason Rudolph/199 6.00 15.00
6 Saquon Barkley/99 75.00 150.00
7 Derrius Guice/149 EXCH 6.00 15.00
8 Nick Chubb/299 10.00 25.00
9 Ronald Jones II/299 2.50 6.00
10 Sony Michel/299 15.00 40.00
11 Calvin Ridley/50 10.00 25.00
12 Courtland Sutton/299 4.00 10.00
13 Christian Kirk/50 6.00 15.00
14 Anthony Miller/299 4.00 10.00
15 D.J. Chark Jr./160 EXCH 3.00 8.00
16 D.J. Moore/299 5.00 12.00
17 Lamar Jackson/50 40.00 80.00
18 Rashaad Penny/199
19 Bradley Chubb/149 5.00 12.00
20 Kerryon Johnson/249 4.00 10.00
21 Dante Pettis/299 4.00 10.00
22 James Washington/249 5.00 12.00
23 Royce Freeman/160 3.00 8.00
24 Michael Gallup/160 5.00 12.00
25 Tre'Quan Smith/299 4.00 10.00
26 Keke Coutee/299 3.00 8.00
27 Nyheim Hines/299 3.00 8.00
28 Kyle Lauletta/199 4.00 10.00
29 Mark Walton/249 3.00 8.00
30 Kalen Ballage/160 3.00 8.00
31 Jaleel Scott/299 2.50 6.00
32 J'Mon Moore/299 2.50 6.00
33 Daurice Fountain/299 3.00 8.00
34 Jaylen Samuels/299 3.00 8.00
35 Mike White/160 3.00 8.00
36 Marquez Valdes-Scantling/199 3.00 8.00
37 Mike Gesicki/199 3.00 8.00
38 DaeSean Hamilton/299 3.00 8.00
39 Hayden Hurst/160
40 Ito Smith/299 3.00 8.00

2018 Panini Phoenix Rookie Jersey Autographs Green Prime

*GREEN/25: .8X TO 2X BASIC JSY AU/160-299
*GREEN/25: .6X TO 1.5X BASIC JSY AU/80-149
*GREEN/25: .5X TO 1.2X BASIC JSY AU/50
*GREEN/15: .6X TO 1.5X BASIC JSY AU/50
6 Saquon Barkley/25 100.00 200.00

2018 Panini Phoenix Rookie Jersey Autographs Orange

*ORANGE/149-199: .4X TO 1X BASIC JSY AU/160-299
*ORANGE/149-199: .4X TO 1X BASIC JSY AU/160-299
*ORANGE/75-125: .5X TO 1.2X BASIC JSY AU/160-299
*ORANGE/75-125: .4X TO 1X BASIC JSY AU/80-149
3 Baker Mayfield/75 100.00 200.00

2018 Panini Phoenix Rookie Jersey Autographs Yellow Prime

*YELLOW/75: .5X TO 1.2X BASIC JSY AU/160-299
*YELLOW/75: .4X TO 1X BASIC JSY AU/80-149
*YELLOW/35-50: .5X TO 1.2X BASIC JSY AU/80-149
*YELLOW/35-50: .4X TO 1X BASIC JSY AU/50
3 Baker Mayfield/50 125.00 250.00

2018 Panini Phoenix Rookie Jerseys

*PURPLE/75: .4X TO 1X BASIC JSY/100
*YELLOW/25: .6X TO 1.5X BASIC JSY/100
1 Sam Darnold 10.00 25.00
2 Josh Rosen 8.00 20.00
3 Baker Mayfield 10.00 25.00
4 Josh Allen 8.00 20.00
5 Mason Rudolph 6.00 15.00
6 Saquon Barkley 12.00 30.00
7 Derrius Guice 5.00 12.00
8 Nick Chubb 8.00 20.00
9 Ronald Jones II 2.50 6.00
10 Sony Michel 6.00 15.00
11 Calvin Ridley 6.00 15.00
12 Courtland Sutton 4.00 10.00
13 Christian Kirk 4.00 10.00
14 Anthony Miller 4.00 10.00
15 D.J. Chark Jr. 3.00 8.00
16 D.J. Moore 5.00 12.00
17 Lamar Jackson 10.00 25.00
18 Rashaad Penny 4.00 10.00
19 Bradley Chubb 4.00 10.00
20 Kerryon Johnson 4.00 10.00
21 Dante Pettis 4.00 10.00
22 James Washington 5.00 12.00
23 Royce Freeman 3.00 8.00
24 Michael Gallup 5.00 12.00
25 Tre'Quan Smith 4.00 10.00
26 Keke Coutee 3.00 8.00
27 Nyheim Hines 3.00 8.00
28 Kyle Lauletta 4.00 10.00
29 Mark Walton 3.00 8.00
30 Kalen Ballage 3.00 8.00
31 Jaleel Scott 2.50 6.00
32 J'Mon Moore 2.50 6.00
33 Daurice Fountain 3.00 8.00
34 Jaylen Samuels 3.00 8.00
35 Mike White 3.00 8.00
36 Marquez Valdes-Scantling 3.00 8.00
37 Mike Gesicki 3.00 8.00
38 DaeSean Hamilton 3.00 8.00
39 Hayden Hurst 3.00 8.00
40 Ito Smith 3.00 8.00

2018 Panini Phoenix Rookie Jumbo Jersey Autographs

1 Sam Darnold/40 40.00 80.00
2 Josh Rosen/100 10.00 25.00
3 Baker Mayfield/70 50.00 100.00
4 Josh Allen/100 12.00 30.00
5 Mason Rudolph/149 8.00 20.00
6 Saquon Barkley/75 60.00 125.00
7 Derrius Guice/75 EXCH 6.00 15.00
8 Nick Chubb/149 10.00 25.00
9 Ronald Jones II/149 3.00 8.00
10 Sony Michel/100 10.00 25.00
11 Calvin Ridley/40 10.00 25.00
12 Courtland Sutton/149 5.00 12.00
13 Christian Kirk/40 6.00 15.00
14 Anthony Miller/149 5.00 12.00
15 D.J. Chark Jr./99 EXCH 4.00 10.00
16 D.J. Moore/149 6.00 15.00
17 Lamar Jackson/50 25.00 60.00
19 Bradley Chubb/99 5.00 12.00
20 Kerryon Johnson/149 5.00 12.00
21 Dante Pettis/149 5.00 12.00
22 James Washington/149 6.00 15.00
23 Royce Freeman/149 4.00 10.00
24 Michael Gallup/149 6.00 15.00
25 Tre'Quan Smith/149 5.00 12.00
26 Keke Coutee/149 4.00 10.00
27 Nyheim Hines/149 4.00 10.00
28 Kyle Lauletta/125 5.00 12.00
29 Mark Walton/149 4.00 10.00
31 Jaleel Scott/149 3.00 8.00
32 J'Mon Moore/149 3.00 8.00
33 Daurice Fountain/149 4.00 10.00
34 Jaylen Samuels/149 4.00 10.00
35 Mike White/149 4.00 10.00
36 Marquez Valdes-Scantling/125 4.00 10.00
37 Mike Gesicki/125 4.00 10.00
38 DaeSean Hamilton/149 4.00 10.00
40 Ito Smith/149 4.00 10.00

2018 Panini Phoenix Rookie Jumbo Jersey Autographs Green Prime

*GREEN/25: .6X TO 1.5X BASIC JSY AU/70-149

2018 Panini Phoenix Rookie Jumbo Jersey Autographs Orange

*ORANGE/75-99: .4X TO 1X BASIC JSY AU/70-149
*ORANGE/35-65: .5X TO 1.2X BASIC JSY AU/70-149
*ORANGE/35-65: .4X TO 1X BASIC JSY AU/40
*ORANGE/25-30: .5X TO 1.2X BASIC JSY AU/40-50
3 Baker Mayfield/65 75.00 150.00
6 Saquon Barkley/65 75.00 150.00

2018 Panini Phoenix Rookie Jumbo Jersey Autographs Yellow Prime

3 Baker Mayfield/50 75.00 150.00
6 Saquon Barkley/50 75.00 150.00

2018 Panini Phoenix Rookie Jumbo Jerseys

*PURPLE/75: .4X TO 1X BASIC JSY/100
*YELLOW/25: .6X TO 1.5X BASIC JSY/100
1 Sam Darnold 10.00 25.00
2 Josh Rosen 8.00 20.00
3 Baker Mayfield 10.00 25.00
4 Josh Allen 8.00 20.00
5 Mason Rudolph 6.00 15.00
6 Saquon Barkley 12.00 30.00
7 Derrius Guice 5.00 12.00
8 Nick Chubb 8.00 20.00
9 Ronald Jones II 2.50 6.00
10 Sony Michel 6.00 15.00
11 Calvin Ridley 6.00 15.00
12 Courtland Sutton 4.00 10.00
13 Christian Kirk 4.00 10.00
14 Anthony Miller 4.00 10.00
15 D.J. Chark Jr. 3.00 8.00
16 D.J. Moore 5.00 12.00
17 Lamar Jackson 10.00 25.00
18 Rashaad Penny 4.00 10.00
19 Bradley Chubb 4.00 10.00
20 Kerryon Johnson 4.00 10.00
21 Dante Pettis 4.00 10.00
22 James Washington 5.00 12.00
23 Royce Freeman 3.00 8.00
24 Michael Gallup 5.00 12.00
25 Tre'Quan Smith 4.00 10.00
26 Keke Coutee 3.00 8.00
27 Nyheim Hines 3.00 8.00
28 Kyle Lauletta 4.00 10.00
29 Mark Walton 3.00 8.00
30 Kalen Ballage 3.00 8.00
31 Jaleel Scott 2.50 6.00
32 J'Mon Moore 2.50 6.00
33 Daurice Fountain 3.00 8.00
34 Jaylen Samuels 3.00 8.00
35 Mike White 3.00 8.00
36 Marquez Valdes-Scantling 3.00 8.00
37 Mike Gesicki 3.00 8.00
38 DaeSean Hamilton 3.00 8.00
39 Hayden Hurst 3.00 8.00
40 Ito Smith 3.00 8.00

2018 Panini Phoenix Unmatched

*BURST: .5X TO 1.2X BASIC INSERTS
*RED/299: .6X TO 1.5X BASIC INSERTS
*PINK/199: .8X TO 2X BASIC INSERTS
*PURPLE/75: 1.2X TO 3X BASIC INSERTS
*ORANGE/49: 1.5X TO 4X BASIC INSERTS
*YELLOW/25: 2X TO 5X BASIC INSERTS
1 Tom Brady 2.50 6.00
2 Terry Bradshaw 1.50 4.00
3 Ezekiel Elliott 1.25 3.00
4 Eric Dickerson 1.00 2.50
5 Odell Beckham Jr. 1.00 2.50
6 Calvin Johnson 1.00 2.50
7 Cris Carter 1.00 2.50
8 Julio Jones 1.00 2.50
9 Le'Veon Bell .75 2.00
10 Emmitt Smith 1.50 4.00
11 Dan Marino 2.00 5.00
12 Carson Wentz 1.25 3.00
13 Joe Montana 2.50 6.00
14 Drew Brees 1.00 2.50
15 Aaron Rodgers 2.00 5.00
16 Joe Namath 1.25 3.00
17 Travis Kelce 1.00 2.50
18 Tony Gonzalez .75 2.00
19 Brett Favre 2.00 5.00
20 Matt Ryan .75 2.00
21 Todd Gurley II 1.00 2.50
22 Barry Sanders 1.50 4.00
23 Randy Moss .75 2.00
24 A.J. Green 1.00 2.50
25 Jim Brown 1.25 3.00
26 Peyton Manning 2.00 5.00
27 David Johnson 1.00 2.50
28 Jerome Bettis 1.00 2.50
29 Jerry Rice 1.50 4.00
30 Larry Fitzgerald .75 2.00

2018 Panini Phoenix Veteran Materials

*PURPLE/75: .4X TO 1X BASIC JSY/100
*YELLOW/25: .6X TO 1.5X BASIC JSY/100
1 Matt Ryan/100 3.00 8.00
2 Alvin Kamara/100 3.00 8.00
3 Ezekiel Elliott/25 8.00 20.00
4 Julio Jones/100 4.00 10.00
5 Odell Beckham Jr./100 4.00 10.00
6 Drew Brees/100 4.00 10.00
7 Aaron Rodgers/100 8.00 20.00
8 Dak Prescott/100 4.00 10.00
9 A.J. Green/50 5.00 12.00
10 Antonio Brown/100 4.00 10.00
11 Keenan Allen/100 3.00 8.00
12 Todd Gurley II/100 4.00 10.00
14 Von Miller/100 3.00 8.00
16 Khalil Mack/100 4.00 10.00
17 Tyreek Hill/100 4.00 10.00
18 Ben Roethlisberger/100 4.00 10.00
19 Matthew Stafford/100 3.00 8.00
20 Deshaun Watson/100 5.00 12.00

2010 Panini Plates and Patches

101-200 ROOKIE AU PRINT RUN 99-849
201-235 ROOK.JSY AU PRINT RUN 199-699
EXCH EXPIRATION: 7/26/2012
1 Larry Fitzgerald 1.25 3.00
2 Steve Breaston 1.00 2.50
3 Tim Hightower 1.00 2.50
4 Matt Ryan 1.25 3.00
5 Michael Turner 1.00 2.50
6 Roddy White 1.00 2.50
7 Anquan Boldin 1.00 2.50
8 Joe Flacco 1.25 3.00
9 Ray Rice 1.00 2.50
10 Lee Evans 1.25 3.00
11 Marshawn Lynch 1.25 3.00
12 Ryan Fitzpatrick 1.00 2.50
13 DeAngelo Williams 1.00 2.50
14 Jonathan Stewart 1.00 2.50
15 Steve Smith 1.25 3.00
16 Jay Cutler 1.00 2.50
17 Johnny Knox 1.00 2.50
18 Matt Forte 1.00 2.50
19 Carson Palmer 1.25 3.00
20 Cedric Benson 1.00 2.50
21 Chad Ochocinco 1.00 2.50
22 Ben Watson 1.00 2.50
23 Josh Cribbs 1.00 2.50
24 Peyton Hillis 1.25 3.00
25 Jason Witten 1.25 3.00
26 Marion Barber 1.25 3.00
27 Tony Romo 1.25 3.00
28 Eddie Royal 1.00 2.50
29 Knowshon Moreno 1.00 2.50
30 Kyle Orton 1.00 2.50
31 Calvin Johnson 1.50 4.00
32 Matthew Stafford 1.25 3.00
33 Nate Burleson 1.00 2.50
34 Aaron Rodgers 3.00 8.00
35 Brandon Jackson 1.00 2.50
36 Donald Driver 1.25 3.00
37 Andre Johnson 1.25 3.00
38 Arian Foster 1.25 3.00
39 Matt Schaub 1.00 2.50
40 Dallas Clark 1.00 2.50
41 Peyton Manning 4.00 10.00
42 Reggie Wayne 1.25 3.00
43 David Garrard 1.00 2.50
44 Maurice Jones-Drew 1.00 2.50
45 Mike Sims-Walker 1.00 2.50
46 Dwayne Bowe 1.25 3.00
47 Jamaal Charles 1.25 3.00
48 Matt Cassel 1.00 2.50
49 Brandon Marshall 1.25 3.00
50 Chad Henne 1.25 3.00
51 Ronnie Brown 1.00 2.50
52 Adrian Peterson 1.50 4.00
53 Brett Favre 3.00 8.00
54 Percy Harvin 1.00 2.50
55 Visanthe Shiancoe 1.25 3.00
56 BenJarvus Green-Ellis 1.50 4.00
57 Randy Moss 1.25 3.00
58 Tom Brady 4.00 10.00
59 Wes Welker 1.25 3.00
60 Drew Brees 1.50 4.00
61 Marques Colston 1.00 2.50
62 Reggie Bush 1.00 2.60

63 Ahmad Bradshaw 1.00 2.50
64 Eli Manning 1.25 3.00
65 Hakeem Nicks 1.00 2.50
66 Braylon Edwards 1.00 2.50
67 Mark Sanchez 1.00 2.50
68 Shonn Greene 1.00 2.50
69 Bruce Gradkowski 1.00 2.50
70 Darren McFadden 1.00 2.50
71 Darrius Heyward-Bey 1.25 3.00
72 DeSean Jackson 1.25 3.00
73 Jeremy Maclin 1.00 2.50
74 LeSean McCoy 1.50 4.00
75 Michael Vick 1.25 3.00
76 Ben Roethlisberger 1.50 4.00
77 Mike Wallace 1.00 2.50
78 Rashard Mendenhall 1.00 2.50
79 Troy Polamalu 1.50 4.00
80 Antonio Gates 1.25 3.00
81 Malcom Floyd 1.00 2.50
82 Philip Rivers 1.50 4.00
83 Frank Gore 1.25 3.00
84 Michael Crabtree 1.00 2.50
85 Vernon Davis 1.00 2.50
86 John Carlson 1.00 2.50
87 Leon Washington 1.00 2.50
88 Matt Hasselbeck 1.00 2.50
89 Danny Amendola 1.50 4.00
90 Mark Clayton 1.00 2.50
91 Steven Jackson 1.00 2.50
92 Cadillac Williams 1.00 2.50
93 Josh Freeman 1.25 3.00
94 Kellen Winslow Jr. 1.00 2.50
95 Chris Johnson 1.00 2.50
96 Nate Washington 1.00 2.50
97 Vince Young 1.00 2.50
98 Chris Cooley 1.00 2.50
99 Donovan McNabb 1.25 3.00
100 Santana Moss 1.25 3.00
101 Aaron Hernandez AU/549 RC 10.00 25.00
102 Andrew Quarless AU/249 RC 3.00 8.00
103 Anthony Dixon AU/449 RC 3.00 8.00
104 Anthony McCoy AU/449 RC 3.00 8.00
105 Antonio Brown AU/449 RC 30.00 60.00
106 Blair White AU/99 RC 4.00 10.00
107 Brandon Banks AU/249 RC 6.00 15.00
108 Brandon Graham AU/449 RC 4.00 10.00
109 Brandon Spikes AU/649 RC 3.00 8.00
110 Brody Eldridge AU/249 RC 5.00 12.00
111 Bryan Bulaga AU/449 RC 3.00 8.00
112 Carlos Dunlap AU/99 RC 4.00 10.00
113 Carlton Mitchell AU/199 RC 4.00 10.00
114 Chris Cook AU/849 RC 3.00 8.00
115 Chris Ivory AU/249 RC 8.00 20.00
116 Chris McGaha AU/449 RC 3.00 8.00
117 Clay Harbor AU/249 RC 3.00 8.00
118 Corey Wootton AU/449 RC 3.00 8.00
119 Dan LeFevour AU/299 RC 3.00 8.00
120 Dan Williams AU/99 RC 4.00 10.00
121 D.Washington AU/99 RC 4.00 10.00
122 David Gettis AU/449 RC 3.00 8.00
123 David Nelson AU/249 RC 7.50 15.00
124 David Reed AU/249 RC 3.00 8.00
125 Deji Karim AU/249 RC 4.00 10.00
126 Dennis Pitta AU/249 RC 6.00 15.00
127 Derrick Morgan AU/649 RC 3.00 8.00
128 Devin McCourty AU/549 RC 6.00 15.00
129 D.Briscoe AU/99 RC EXCH 4.00 10.00
130 Dominique Curry AU/249 RC 4.00 10.00
131 Dominique Franks AU/449 RC 3.00 8.00
132 Donald Jones AU/249 RC 7.50 15.00
133 Dorin Dickerson AU/249 RC 3.00 8.00
134 Duke Calhoun AU/99 RC 5.00 12.00
135 Earl Thomas AU/449 RC 8.00 20.00
136 Ed Dickson AU/449 RC 3.00 8.00
137 Ed Wang AU/249 RC 5.00 12.00
138 Everson Griffen AU/449 RC 3.00 8.00
139 Fendi Onobun AU/249 RC 4.00 10.00
140 Garrett Graham AU/449 RC 3.00 8.00
141 Jacoby Ford AU/449 RC 3.00 8.00
142 James Starks AU/449 RC 4.00 10.00
143 Jared Odrick AU/249 RC 4.00 10.00
144 Jarrett Brown AU/268 RC 3.00 8.00
145 J.Pierre-Paul AU/449 RC 5.00 12.00
146 Jason Worilds AU/449 RC 3.00 8.00
147 Javier Arenas AU/249 RC 3.00 8.00
148 Jeremy Horne AU/99 RC 5.00 12.00
149 Jeremy Williams AU/349 RC 3.00 8.00
150 Jerry Hughes AU/549 RC 3.00 8.00
151 Jim Dray AU/249 RC 4.00 10.00
152 Jimmy Graham AU/649 RC 8.00 20.00
153 Joe Haden AU/449 RC 5.00 12.00
154 Joe Webb AU/249 RC 8.00 20.00
155 John Conner AU/249 RC 3.00 8.00
156 John Skelton AU/649 RC 4.00 10.00
157 Joique Bell AU/99 RC 4.00 10.00
158 Kareem Jackson AU/99 RC 4.00 10.00
159 Keiland Williams AU/249 RC 4.00 10.00
160 Keith Toston AU/249 RC 5.00 12.00
161 Kerry Meier AU/249 RC 4.00 10.00
162 Koa Misi AU/249 RC 4.00 10.00
163 Kyle Williams AU/99 RC 6.00 15.00
164 Kyle Wilson AU/449 RC 3.00 8.00
165 Lamarr Houston AU/249 RC 4.00 10.00
166 LeGarrette Blount AU/449 RC 6.00 15.00
167 Lonyae Miller AU/199 RC 5.00 12.00
168 Marc Mariani AU/249 RC 5.00 12.00
169 Marlon Moore AU/249 RC 5.00 12.00
170 Max Hall AU/249 RC 5.00 12.00
171 Max Komar AU/99 RC 5.00 12.00
172 M.Hoomanawanui AU/249 RC 5.00 12.00
173 Mickey Shuler AU/249 RC 5.00 12.00
174 Morgan Burnett AU/449 RC 4.00 10.00
175 Nate Allen AU/99 RC 6.00 15.00
176 NaVorro Bowman AU/99 RC 8.00 20.00
177 Patrick Robinson AU/449 RC 4.00 10.00
178 Perrish Cox AU/449 RC 4.00 10.00
179 Preston Parker AU/249 RC 4.00 10.00
180 Ricky Sapp AU/549 RC 3.00 8.00
181 Riley Cooper AU/449 RC 3.00 8.00
182 Roberto Wallace AU/249 RC 4.00 10.00
183 Russell Okung AU/249 RC 3.00 8.00
184 Rusty Smith AU/249 RC 5.00 12.00
185 Michael Palmer AU/449 RC 4.00 10.00
186 Sean Lee AU/549 RC 8.00 20.00
187 Sean Weatherspoon AU/649 RC 3.00 8.00
188 Chris Gronkowski AU/449 RC 5.00 12.00
189 Seyi Ajirotutu AU/199 RC 4.00 10.00
190 Shay Hodge AU/449 RC 3.00 8.00
191 Stephen Williams AU/249 RC 5.00 12.00
192 T.J. Ward AU/249 RC 5.00 12.00
193 Taylor Mays AU/649 RC 3.00 8.00
194 T.Lewis AU/249 RC UER 6.00 15.00
195 Tony Moeaki AU/249 RC 4.00 10.00
196 Tony Pike AU/449 RC 3.00 8.00
197 Trent Williams AU/99 RC 5.00 12.00
198 Tyson Alualu AU/249 RC 3.00 8.00
199 Victor Cruz AU/249 RC 6.00 15.00
200 Zac Robinson AU/549 RC 4.00 10.00
201 Andre Roberts JSY AU/499 RC 6.00 15.00
202 A.Edwards JSY AU/699 RC 6.00 15.00
203 Arrelious Benn JSY AU/699 RC 5.00 12.00
204 Ben Tate JSY AU/699 RC 5.00 12.00
205 Brandon LaFell JSY AU/599 RC 8.00 20.00
206 C.J. Spiller JSY AU/399 RC 5.00 12.00
207 Colt McCoy JSY AU/399 RC 6.00 15.00
208 Damian Williams JSY AU/699 RC 5.00 12.00
209 D.Thomas JSY AU/699 RC 12.00 30.00
210 McCluster JSY AU/599 RC 6.00 15.00
211 Dez Bryant JSY AU/599 RC 25.00 60.00
212 E.Sanders JSY AU/699 RC 8.00 20.00
213 Eric Derry JSY AU/099 RC 8.00 20.00
214 Eric Decker JSY AU/699 RC 6.00 15.00
215 Gerald McCoy JSY AU/199 RC 6.00 15.00
216 Golden Tate JSY AU/599 RC 6.00 15.00
217 Jahvid Best JSY AU/699 RC 5.00 12.00
218 J.Gresham JSY AU/699 RC 6.00 15.00
219 Jimmy Clausen JSY AU/499 RC 5.00 12.00
220 Joe McKnight JSY AU/699 RC 6.00 15.00
221 J.Dwyer JSY AU/699 RC 5.00 12.00
222 Jordan Shipley JSY AU/699 RC 5.00 12.00
223 Marcus Easley JSY AU/699 RC 5.00 12.00
224 Mardy Gilyard JSY AU/699 RC 5.00 12.00
225 Mike Kafka JSY AU/699 RC 6.00 15.00
226 Mike Williams JSY AU/899 RC 5.00 12.00
227 M.Hardesty JSY AU/699 RC 5.00 12.00
228 N.Suh JSY AU/199 RC 12.00 30.00
229 Gronkowski JSY AU/699 RC 40.00 80.00
230 R.McClain JSY AU/699 RC 5.00 12.00
231 R.Mathews JSY AU/699 RC 5.00 12.00
232 S.Bradford JSY AU/399 RC 6.00 15.00
233 Taylor Price JSY AU/699 RC 5.00 12.00
234 Tim Tebow JSY AU/499 RC 25.00 50.00
235 Toby Gerhart JSY AU/699 RC 5.00 12.00

2010 Panini Plates and Patches Gold

*VETS 1-100: 1.2X TO 3X BASIC CARDS
*ROOKIES 101-200: .6X TO 1.5X SILVER/100
GOLD PRINT RUN 50 SER.#'d SETS

2010 Panini Plates and Patches Rookie Prime Signatures Nameplate

*NP/25: .6X TO 1.5X BASE JSY AU/399-699
*NP/25: .5X TO 1.2X BASE JSY AU/199
NAMEPLATE PRINT RUN 25
EXCH EXPIRATION: 7/26/2012
232 Sam Bradford 10.00 25.00
234 Tim Tebow 60.00 150.00

2010 Panini Plates and Patches Silver

*VETS 1-100: .8X TO 2X BASIC CARDS
SILVER PRINT RUN 100 SER.#'d SETS
101 Aaron Hernandez 2.00 5.00
102 Andrew Quarless 2.00 5.00
103 Anthony Dixon 2.00 5.00
104 Anthony McCoy 2.00 5.00
105 Antonio Brown 15.00 40.00
106 Blair White 2.00 5.00
107 Brandon Banks 4.00 10.00
108 Brandon Graham 2.50 6.00
109 Brandon Spikes 2.00 5.00
110 Brody Eldridge 3.00 8.00
111 Bryan Bulaga 2.00 5.00
112 Carlos Dunlap 2.00 5.00
113 Carlton Mitchell 2.00 5.00
114 Chris Cook 2.00 5.00
115 Chris Ivory 5.00 12.00
116 Chris McGaha 2.00 5.00
117 Clay Harbor 2.00 5.00
118 Corey Wootton 2.00 5.00
119 Dan LeFevour 2.00 5.00
120 Dan Williams 2.00 5.00
121 Daryl Washington 2.00 5.00
122 David Gettis 2.00 5.00
123 David Nelson 3.00 8.00
124 David Reed 2.00 5.00
125 Deji Karim 2.50 6.00
126 Dennis Pitta 2.00 5.00
127 Derrick Morgan 2.00 5.00
128 Devin McCourty 2.50 6.00
129 Dezmon Briscoe 2.00 5.00
130 Dominique Curry 2.50 6.00
131 Dominique Franks 2.00 5.00
132 Donald Jones 3.00 8.00
133 Dorin Dickerson 2.00 5.00
134 Duke Calhoun 2.50 6.00
135 Earl Thomas 3.00 8.00
136 Ed Dickson 2.00 5.00
137 Ed Wang 3.00 8.00
138 Everson Griffen 2.00 5.00
139 Fendi Onobun 2.50 6.00
140 Garrett Graham 2.00 5.00
141 Jacoby Ford 2.00 5.00
142 James Starks 2.50 6.00
143 Jared Odrick 2.50 6.00
144 Jarrett Brown 2.00 5.00
145 Jason Pierre-Paul 3.00 8.00
146 Jason Worilds 2.00 5.00
147 Javier Arenas 2.00 5.00
148 Jeremy Horne 2.50 6.00
149 Jeremy Williams 2.00 5.00
150 Jerry Hughes 2.00 5.00
151 Jim Dray 2.50 6.00
152 Jimmy Graham 5.00 12.00
153 Joe Haden 3.00 8.00
154 Joe Webb 2.00 5.00
155 John Conner 2.00 5.00
156 John Skelton 2.50 6.00
157 Joique Bell 2.00 5.00
158 Kareem Jackson 2.00 5.00
159 Keiland Williams 2.50 6.00
160 Keith Toston 3.00 8.00
161 Kerry Meier 2.50 6.00
162 Koa Misi 2.50 6.00
163 Kyle Williams 3.00 8.00
164 Kyle Wilson 2.00 5.00
165 Lamarr Houston 2.50 6.00
166 LeGarrette Blount 4.00 10.00
167 Lonyae Miller 2.50 6.00
168 Marc Mariani 3.00 8.00
169 Marlon Moore 3.00 8.00
170 Max Hall 3.00 8.00
171 Max Komar 3.00 8.00
172 Michael Hoomanawanui 3.00 8.00
173 Mickey Shuler 3.00 8.00
174 Morgan Burnett 2.50 6.00
175 Nate Allen 3.00 8.00
176 NaVorro Bowman 4.00 10.00
177 Patrick Robinson 2.50 6.00
178 Perrish Cox 2.50 6.00
179 Preston Parker 2.50 6.00
180 Ricky Sapp 2.00 5.00
181 Riley Cooper 2.00 5.00
182 Roberto Wallace 2.50 6.00
183 Russell Okung 2.00 5.00
184 Rusty Smith 3.00 8.00
185 Michael Palmer 2.50 6.00
186 Sean Lee 4.00 10.00
187 Sean Weatherspoon 2.00 5.00
188 Chris Gronkowski 3.00 8.00
189 Seyi Ajirotutu 2.00 5.00
190 Shay Hodge 2.00 5.00
191 Stephen Williams 3.00 8.00
192 T.J. Ward 3.00 8.00
193 Taylor Mays 2.00 5.00
194 Thaddeus Lewis 2.50 6.00
195 Tony Moeaki 2.50 6.00
196 Tony Pike 2.00 5.00
197 Trent Williams 2.50 6.00
198 Tyson Alualu 2.00 5.00
199 Victor Cruz 4.00 10.00
200 Zac Robinson 2.50 6.00

2010 Panini Plates and Patches City Limits

STATED PRINT RUN 299 SER.#'d SETS
1 DeMarcus Ware 1.50 4.00
2 Aaron Rodgers 4.00 10.00
3 Matt Ryan 1.50 4.00
4 Carson Palmer 1.50 4.00
5 Vernon Davis 1.25 3.00
6 Mark Sanchez 1.25 3.00
7 Brett Favre 4.00 10.00
8 Adrian Peterson 2.00 5.00
9 Maurice Jones-Drew 1.25 3.00
10 Drew Brees 2.00 5.00
11 Peyton Manning 5.00 12.00
12 Steve Smith 1.50 4.00
13 Ray Lewis 2.00 5.00
14 Eli Manning 1.50 4.00
15 Troy Polamalu 2.00 5.00
16 Chris Johnson 1.25 3.00
17 Larry Fitzgerald 1.50 4.00
18 Andre Johnson 1.50 4.00
19 Philip Rivers 2.00 5.00
20 Tom Brady 5.00 12.00
21 Chad Henne 1.50 4.00
22 Brian Urlacher 2.00 5.00
23 Chris Cooley 1.25 3.00
24 Kyle Orton 1.25 3.00
25 Steven Jackson 1.25 3.00

2010 Panini Plates and Patches City Limits Autographs

AUTO STATED PRINT RUN 1-15
1 DeMarcus Ware/15 25.00 50.00
14 Eli Manning/15 40.00 80.00

2010 Panini Plates and Patches City Limits Autograph Materials Prime

PRIME AU PRINT RUN 1-15
1 DeMarcus Ware/15 20.00 40.00

2010 Panini Plates and Patches City Limits Materials

STATED PRINT RUN 95-299
*PRIME/50: .6X TO 1.5X BASIC JSY
*PRIME/25: .8X TO 2X BASIC JSY
1 DeMarcus Ware/200 3.00 8.00
2 Aaron Rodgers/100 8.00 20.00
4 Carson Palmer/299 3.00 8.00
5 Vernon Davis/200 2.50 6.00
7 Brett Favre/299 8.00 20.00
8 Adrian Peterson/200 4.00 10.00
9 Maurice Jones-Drew/200 2.50 6.00
11 Peyton Manning/200 10.00 25.00
13 Ray Lewis/155 4.00 10.00
16 Chris Johnson/190 2.50 6.00
17 Larry Fitzgerald/145 3.00 8.00
18 Andre Johnson/299 3.00 8.00
19 Philip Rivers/200 4.00 10.00
20 Tom Brady/200 10.00 25.00
22 Brian Urlacher/105 4.00 10.00
23 Chris Cooley/200 4.00 10.00
24 Kyle Orton/95 4.00 10.00

2010 Panini Plates and Patches Gridiron Cut Autographs

STATED PRINT RUN 1-100
1 Red Badgro/18 20.00 50.00
2 Sammy Baugh/63 30.00 80.00
3 Bert Bell/6
4 Paul Brown/100 30.00 80.00
5 Roosevelt Brown/36 15.00 40.00
6 Tony Canadeo/37 30.00 80.00
7 Dutch Clark/9
8 George Connor/23 15.00 40.00
9 Lou Creekmur/66 20.00 50.00
10 Ernie Davis/1
11 Bill Dudley/100 15.00 40.00
12 Weeb Ewbank/100 15.00 40.00
13 Tom Fears/9
14 Ray Flaherty/3
15 Otto Graham/15 30.00 80.00
16 Red Grange/3
17 Lou Groza/69 20.00 50.00
18 George Halas/15 100.00 200.00
19 Mel Hein/16 25.00 60.00
20 Bill George/3
21 Elroy Hirsch/23 20.00 50.00
22 Lamar Hunt/6
23 Don Hutson/21 75.00 150.00
24 Vic Janowicz/19 30.00 80.00
25 Stan Jones/39 20.00 50.00
26 Tom Landry/8
27 Dick Lane/27 25.00 60.00
28 Dante Lavelli/58 15.00 40.00
31 Wellington Mara/6
32 Ollie Matson/26 20.00 50.00
33 George McAfee/61 15.00 40.00
34 Marion Motley/67 15.00 40.00
35 Jim Parker/12
36 Walter Payton/75 125.00 250.00
37 Pete Pihos/56 15.00 40.00
38 Andy Robustelli/52 15.00 40.00
39 Art Rooney/11
40 Kyle Rote/80 12.00 30.00
41 Tobin Rote/31 15.00 40.00
42 Hank Soar/33 20.00 50.00
43 Hank Stram/27 15.00 40.00
44 Ken Strong/18 30.00 80.00
45 Jim Thorpe/1
46 Bulldog Turner/6
47 Johnny Unitas/36 175.00 300.00
48 Gene Upshaw/10
49 Doak Walker/3

2010 Panini Plates and Patches Honors

STATED PRINT RUN 299 SER.#'d SETS
1 DeAngelo Williams 1.25 3.00
2 Wes Welker 1.50 4.00
3 Calvin Johnson 2.00 5.00
4 Devin Hester 1.50 4.00
5 Marques Colston 1.25 3.00
6 Randy Moss 1.50 4.00
7 Josh Cribbs 1.25 3.00
8 Dallas Clark 1.25 3.00
9 Ray Rice 1.25 3.00
10 DeSean Jackson 1.50 4.00
11 Austin Collie 1.25 3.00
12 Donald Driver 1.50 4.00
13 Reggie Wayne 1.50 4.00
14 Jay Cutler 1.25 3.00
15 Pierre Thomas 1.25 3.00
16 Chad Ochocinco 1.25 3.00
17 Matt Schaub 1.25 3.00
18 Tony Romo 1.50 4.00
19 Rashard Mendenhall 1.25 3.00
20 Antonio Gates 1.50 4.00
21 Percy Harvin 1.25 3.00
22 Tony Gonzalez 1.50 4.00
23 Frank Gore 1.50 4.00
24 Miles Austin 1.25 3.00
25 Hines Ward 1.50 4.00

2010 Panini Plates and Patches Honors Autographs

STATED PRINT RUN 5-25
11 Austin Collie/25 10.00 25.00
22 Tony Gonzalez/25 20.00 50.00
23 Frank Gore/15 15.00 40.00

2010 Panini Plates and Patches Honors Materials

STATED PRINT RUN 100-299
5 Marques Colston/175 2.50 6.00
6 Randy Moss/175 3.00 8.00
10 DeSean Jackson/175 3.00 8.00
13 Reggie Wayne/100 3.00 8.00
14 Jay Cutler/299 2.50 6.00
18 Tony Romo/175 3.00 8.00
20 Antonio Gates/299 3.00 8.00

2010 Panini Plates and Patches Honors Materials Prime

PRIME STATED PRINT RUN 20-50
2 Wes Welker 5.00 12.00
4 Devin Hester 5.00 12.00
5 Marques Colston 4.00 10.00
10 DeSean Jackson 5.00 12.00
12 Donald Driver 6.00 15.00
13 Reggie Wayne/20 5.00 12.00
14 Jay Cutler 4.00 10.00
16 Chad Ochocinco 4.00 10.00
18 Tony Romo 5.00 12.00
20 Antonio Gates 5.00 12.00

2010 Panini Plates and Patches Jerseys

STATED PRINT RUN 20-299
6 Roddy White/120 2.50 6.00
10 Lee Evans/100 3.00 8.00
16 Jay Cutler/299 2.50 6.00
17 Johnny Knox/299 2.50 6.00
18 Matt Forte/299 2.50 6.00
19 Carson Palmer/299 3.00 8.00
20 Cedric Benson/299 2.50 6.00
26 Marion Barber/299 3.00 8.00
27 Tony Romo/299 3.00 8.00
31 Calvin Johnson/299 4.00 10.00
34 Aaron Rodgers/200 8.00 20.00
37 Andre Johnson/299 3.00 8.00
41 Peyton Manning/299 10.00 25.00
43 David Garrard/100 2.50 6.00
44 Maurice Jones-Drew/210 2.50 6.00
45 Mike Sims-Walker/100 2.50 6.00
46 Dwayne Bowe/299 3.00 8.00
47 Jamaal Charles/270 3.00 8.00
48 Matt Cassel/299 2.50 6.00
52 Adrian Peterson/299 4.00 10.00
53 Brett Favre/299 8.00 20.00
57 Randy Moss/299 3.00 8.00
58 Tom Brady/155 10.00 25.00
61 Marques Colston/299 2.50 6.00
63 Ahmad Bradshaw/270 2.50 6.00
67 Mark Sanchez/20 6.00 15.00
70 Darren McFadden/299 2.50 6.00
72 DeSean Jackson/245 3.00 8.00
76 Ben Roethlisberger/299 4.00 10.00
80 Antonio Gates/299 3.00 8.00
82 Philip Rivers/270 4.00 10.00
85 Vernon Davis/105 2.50 6.00
88 Matt Hasselbeck/95 2.50 6.00
97 Vince Young/299 2.50 6.00
98 Chris Cooley/150 4.00 10.00
99 Donovan McNabb/299 3.00 8.00
100 Santana Moss/120 3.00 8.00

2010 Panini Plates and Patches Jerseys Prime

PRIME PRINT RUN 4-50
10 Lee Evans/15 6.00 15.00
16 Jay Cutler/50 4.00 10.00
17 Johnny Knox/40 4.00 10.00
18 Matt Forte/50 4.00 10.00
19 Carson Palmer/50 5.00 12.00
20 Cedric Benson/50 4.00 10.00
21 Chad Ochocinco/50 4.00 10.00
25 Jason Witten/50 5.00 12.00
26 Marion Barber/50 5.00 12.00
27 Tony Romo/50 5.00 12.00
31 Calvin Johnson/50 6.00 15.00
34 Aaron Rodgers/45 12.00 30.00
36 Donald Driver/50 6.00 15.00
41 Peyton Manning/50 15.00 40.00
46 Dwayne Bowe/20 6.00 15.00
55 Visanthe Shiancoe/50 5.00 12.00
58 Tom Brady/20 20.00 50.00
59 Wes Welker/50 5.00 12.00
61 Marques Colston/20 5.00 12.00
63 Ahmad Bradshaw/15 5.00 12.00
76 Ben Roethlisberger/25 8.00 20.00
80 Antonio Gates/45 5.00 12.00
85 Vernon Davis/50 4.00 10.00
91 Steven Jackson/35 4.00 10.00
95 Chris Johnson/20 5.00 12.00
98 Chris Cooley/25 8.00 20.00
100 Santana Moss/50 5.00 12.00

2010 Panini Plates and Patches Jerseys Prime Jersey Number

PRIME JSY # PRINT RUN 1-50
6 Roddy White/50 4.00 10.00
10 Lee Evans/50 5.00 12.00
13 DeAngelo Williams/25 5.00 12.00
14 Jonathan Stewart/35 4.00 10.00
16 Jay Cutler/50 4.00 10.00
18 Matt Forte/50 4.00 10.00
19 Carson Palmer/50 5.00 12.00
20 Cedric Benson/50 4.00 10.00
21 Chad Ochocinco/50 4.00 10.00
25 Jason Witten/50 5.00 12.00
26 Marion Barber/50 5.00 12.00
27 Tony Romo/50 5.00 12.00
29 Knowshon Moreno/50 4.00 10.00
31 Calvin Johnson/50 6.00 15.00
34 Aaron Rodgers/50 10.00 25.00
36 Donald Driver/50 6.00 15.00
37 Andre Johnson/50 5.00 12.00
39 Matt Schaub/25 5.00 12.00
40 Dallas Clark/25 5.00 12.00
41 Peyton Manning/50 15.00 40.00
42 Reggie Wayne/25 6.00 15.00
43 David Garrard/25 5.00 12.00
44 Maurice Jones-Drew/50 4.00 10.00
46 Dwayne Bowe/50 5.00 12.00
47 Jamaal Charles/50 5.00 12.00
48 Matt Cassel/50 4.00 10.00
52 Adrian Peterson/50 6.00 15.00
55 Visanthe Shiancoe/35 5.00 12.00
58 Tom Brady/50 15.00 40.00
59 Wes Welker/50 5.00 12.00
61 Marques Colston/50 4.00 10.00
63 Ahmad Bradshaw/45 4.00 10.00
70 Darren McFadden/35 4.00 10.00
72 DeSean Jackson/50 5.00 12.00
80 Antonio Gates/50 5.00 12.00
82 Philip Rivers/50 6.00 15.00
85 Vernon Davis/50 4.00 10.00
88 Matt Hasselbeck/25 5.00 12.00
92 Cadillac Williams/50 4.00 10.00
95 Chris Johnson/50 4.00 10.00
98 Chris Cooley/50 6.00 15.00
100 Santana Moss/50 5.00 12.00

2010 Panini Plates and Patches Jerseys Prime Nameplate

STATED PRINT RUN 1-25
6 Roddy White/25 5.00 12.00
10 Lee Evans/15 6.00 15.00
13 DeAngelo Williams/15 5.00 12.00
16 Jay Cutler/25 5.00 12.00
18 Matt Forte/25 5.00 12.00
19 Carson Palmer/25 6.00 15.00
20 Cedric Benson/25 5.00 12.00
21 Chad Ochocinco/25 5.00 12.00
25 Jason Witten/25 6.00 15.00
26 Marion Barber/25 6.00 15.00
27 Tony Romo/25 6.00 15.00
29 Knowshon Moreno/25 5.00 12.00
31 Calvin Johnson/25 8.00 20.00
34 Aaron Rodgers/25 15.00 40.00
36 Donald Driver/25 8.00 20.00
41 Peyton Manning/25 20.00 50.00
42 Reggie Wayne/15 6.00 15.00
43 David Garrard/25 5.00 12.00
44 Maurice Jones-Drew/25 5.00 12.00
46 Dwayne Bowe/25 6.00 16.00
47 Jamaal Charles/25 6.00 15.00
48 Matt Cassel/25 5.00 12.00
52 Adrian Peterson/25 8.00 20.00
55 Visanthe Shiancoe/25 6.00 15.00
58 Tom Brady/25 20.00 50.00
59 Wes Welker/25 6.00 15.00
61 Marques Colston/25 5.00 12.00
67 Mark Sanchez/15 5.00 12.00
70 Darren McFadden/25 5.00 12.00
72 DeSean Jackson/25 6.00 15.00
74 LeSean McCoy/25 8.00 20.00
80 Antonio Gates/25 6.00 15.00
82 Philip Rivers/25 8.00 20.00
85 Vernon Davis/25 5.00 12.00
88 Matt Hasselbeck/15 5.00 12.00
91 Steven Jackson/25 5.00 12.00
92 Cadillac Williams/25 5.00 12.00
95 Chris Johnson/25 5.00 12.00
98 Chris Cooley/25 8.00 20.00
100 Santana Moss/25 6.00 15.00

2010 Panini Plates and Patches NFL Equipment

STATED PRINT RUN 20-150
*COMBO/50-100: .5X TO 1.2X BASIC JSY
1 Willis McGahee/150 2.50 6.00
2 Darren McFadden/150 2.50 6.00
5 Braylon Edwards/125 2.50 6.00
10 David Garrard/130 2.50 6.00
11 Greg Jennings/150 2.50 6.00
12 Ben Roethlisberger/140 4.00 10.00
13 Knowshon Moreno/80 2.50 6.00
14 Vince Young/150 2.50 6.00
15 Marion Barber/150 3.00 8.00
16 Darren Sproles/130 3.00 8.00
19 Visanthe Shiancoe/20 5.00 12.00
20 Jared Allen/150 2.50 6.00
22 Matt Forte/150 2.50 6.00
23 Heath Miller/150 2.50 6.00
24 Patrick Willis/130 3.00 8.00

2010 Panini Plates and Patches NFL Equipment Prime

STATED PRINT RUN 5-50
2 Darren McFadden/15 5.00 12.00
3 Jason Witten/50 5.00 12.00
11 Greg Jennings/25 5.00 12.00
12 Ben Roethlisberger/15 8.00 20.00
13 Knowshon Moreno/35 4.00 10.00
15 Marion Barber/50 5.00 12.00
16 Darren Sproles/50 5.00 12.00
19 Visanthe Shiancoe/5
20 Jared Allen/25 5.00 12.00
21 Ronnie Brown/10
22 Matt Forte/50 4.00 10.00
23 Heath Miller/50 4.00 10.00
24 Patrick Willis/50 5.00 12.00

2010 Panini Plates and Patches NFL Equipment Combos Prime

STATED PRINT RUN 1-25
3 Jason Witten/25 6.00 15.00
9 LeSean McCoy/25 8.00 20.00
10 David Garrard/25 5.00 12.00
11 Greg Jennings/25 5.00 12.00
13 Knowshon Moreno/25 5.00 12.00
15 Marion Barber/25 6.00 15.00
16 Darren Sproles/25 6.00 15.00
20 Jared Allen/25 5.00 12.00
22 Matt Forte/25 5.00 12.00
23 Heath Miller/25 5.00 12.00
24 Patrick Willis/25 6.00 15.00

2010 Panini Plates and Patches Rookie Autographed Jumbo Materials Prime

STATED PRINT RUN 25 SER.#'d SETS
*JUMBO AU/10: .5X TO 1.2X PRIME AU/25
EXCH EXPIRATION: 7/26/2012
1 Jahvid Best 8.00 20.00
2 Golden Tate 10.00 25.00
3 Gerald McCoy 8.00 20.00
4 Eric Decker 10.00 25.00
5 Eric Berry 12.00 30.00
6 Emmanuel Sanders 12.00 30.00
7 Dez Bryant 40.00 80.00
9 Demaryius Thomas 20.00 50.00
10 Damian Williams 8.00 20.00
11 Colt McCoy 10.00 25.00
12 C.J. Spiller 8.00 20.00
13 Brandon LaFell 12.00 30.00
14 Ben Tate 8.00 20.00
15 Arrelious Benn 8.00 20.00
16 Armanti Edwards 10.00 25.00
17 Andre Roberts 10.00 25.00
18 Toby Gerhart 8.00 20.00
19 Tim Tebow 40.00 80.00
20 Taylor Price 8.00 20.00
21 Sam Bradford 10.00 25.00
22 Ryan Mathews 8.00 20.00
23 Rolando McClain 8.00 20.00
24 Rob Gronkowski 40.00 80.00
25 Ndamukong Suh 15.00 40.00
26 Montario Hardesty 8.00 20.00
27 Mike Williams 8.00 20.00
28 Mike Kafka 10.00 25.00
29 Mardy Gilyard 8.00 20.00
30 Marcus Easley 8.00 20.00
31 Jordan Shipley 8.00 20.00
32 Jonathan Dwyer 8.00 20.00
33 Joe McKnight 8.00 20.00
34 Jimmy Clausen 8.00 20.00
35 Jermaine Gresham 8.00 20.00

2010 Panini Plates and Patches Rookie Blitz

STATED PRINT RUN 299 SER.#'d SETS
1 Demaryius Thomas 2.50 6.00
2 C.J. Spiller 1.00 2.50
3 Jordan Shipley 1.00 2.50
4 Eric Decker 1.25 3.00
5 Andre Roberts 1.25 3.00
6 Toby Gerhart 1.00 2.50
7 Ndamukong Suh 2.00 5.00
8 Sam Bradford 1.25 3.00
9 Arrelious Benn 1.00 2.50
10 Eric Berry 1.50 4.00
11 Jahvid Best 1.00 2.50
12 Rolando McClain 1.00 2.50
13 Tim Tebow 3.00 8.00
14 Dexter McCluster 1.25 3.00
15 Golden Tate 1.25 3.00
16 Jonathan Dwyer 1.00 2.50
17 Mike Williams 1.00 2.50
18 Ryan Mathews 1.00 2.50
19 Rob Gronkowski 3.00 8.00
20 Taylor Price 1.00 2.50
21 Armanti Edwards 1.25 3.00
22 Jimmy Clausen 1.00 2.50
23 Jermaine Gresham 1.00 2.50
24 Brandon LaFell 1.50 4.00
25 Colt McCoy 1.25 3.00
26 Mardy Gilyard 1.00 2.50
27 Dez Bryant 2.50 6.00
28 Damian Williams 1.00 2.50
29 Gerald McCoy 1.00 2.50
30 Emmanuel Sanders 1.50 4.00

2010 Panini Plates and Patches Rookie Blitz Autograph Materials

JSY AUTO PRINT RUN 25
*PRIME/15-25: .5X TO 1.2X JSY AU/25
*AUTO/10: .4X TO 1X JSY AU/25
EXCH EXPIRATION: 7/26/2012
1 Demaryius Thomas 15.00 40.00
2 C.J. Spiller 6.00 15.00
3 Jordan Shipley 6.00 15.00
4 Eric Decker 8.00 20.00
5 Andre Roberts 8.00 20.00
6 Toby Gerhart 6.00 15.00
7 Ndamukong Suh 12.00 30.00
8 Sam Bradford 8.00 20.00
9 Arrelious Benn 6.00 15.00
10 Eric Berry 10.00 25.00
11 Jahvid Best 6.00 15.00
12 Rolando McClain 6.00 15.00
13 Tim Tebow 40.00 80.00
15 Golden Tate 8.00 20.00
16 Jonathan Dwyer 6.00 15.00
17 Mike Williams 6.00 15.00
18 Ryan Mathews 6.00 15.00
19 Rob Gronkowski 30.00 60.00
20 Taylor Price 6.00 15.00
21 Armanti Edwards 8.00 20.00
22 Jimmy Clausen 6.00 15.00
23 Jermaine Gresham 6.00 15.00
24 Brandon LaFell 10.00 25.00
25 Colt McCoy 8.00 20.00
26 Mardy Gilyard 6.00 15.00
27 Dez Bryant 40.00 80.00
28 Damian Williams 6.00 15.00
29 Gerald McCoy 6.00 15.00
30 Emmanuel Sanders 10.00 25.00

2010 Panini Plates and Patches Rookie Blitz Materials

STATED PRINT RUN 299 SER.#'d SETS
1 Demaryius Thomas 4.00 10.00
2 C.J. Spiller 1.50 4.00
3 Jordan Shipley 1.50 4.00
4 Eric Decker 2.00 5.00
5 Andre Roberts 2.00 5.00
6 Toby Gerhart 1.50 4.00
7 Ndamukong Suh 3.00 8.00
8 Sam Bradford 2.00 5.00
9 Arrelious Benn 1.50 4.00
10 Eric Berry 2.50 6.00
11 Jahvid Best 1.50 4.00
12 Rolando McClain 1.50 4.00
13 Tim Tebow 5.00 12.00
14 Dexter McCluster 2.00 5.00
15 Golden Tate 2.00 5.00
16 Jonathan Dwyer 1.50 4.00
17 Mike Williams 1.50 4.00
18 Ryan Mathews 1.50 4.00
19 Rob Gronkowski 5.00 12.00
20 Taylor Price 1.50 4.00
21 Armanti Edwards 2.00 5.00
22 Jimmy Clausen 1.50 4.00
23 Jermaine Gresham 1.50 4.00
24 Brandon LaFell 2.50 6.00
25 Colt McCoy 2.00 5.00
26 Mardy Gilyard 1.50 4.00
27 Dez Bryant 4.00 10.00
28 Damian Williams 1.50 4.00
29 Gerald McCoy 1.50 4.00
30 Emmanuel Sanders 2.50 6.00

2010 Panini Plates and Patches Rookie Jumbo Materials

STATED PRINT RUN 50 SER.#'d SETS
*PRIME/15: .8X TO 2X BASIC JSY/50
1 Jahvid Best 2.50 6.00
2 Golden Tate 3.00 8.00
3 Gerald McCoy 2.50 6.00
4 Eric Decker 3.00 8.00
5 Eric Berry 4.00 10.00
6 Emmanuel Sanders 4.00 10.00
7 Dez Bryant 6.00 15.00
8 Dexter McCluster 3.00 8.00
9 Demaryius Thomas 6.00 15.00
10 Damian Williams 2.50 6.00
11 Colt McCoy 3.00 8.00
12 C.J. Spiller 2.50 6.00
13 Brandon LaFell 4.00 10.00
14 Ben Tate 2.50 6.00
15 Arrelious Benn 2.50 6.00
16 Armanti Edwards 3.00 8.00
17 Andre Roberts 3.00 8.00
18 Toby Gerhart 2.50 6.00
19 Tim Tebow 8.00 20.00
20 Taylor Price 2.50 6.00
21 Sam Bradford 3.00 8.00
22 Ryan Mathews 2.50 6.00
23 Rolando McClain 2.50 6.00
24 Rob Gronkowski 8.00 20.00
25 Ndamukong Suh 5.00 12.00
26 Montario Hardesty 2.50 6.00
27 Mike Williams 2.50 6.00
28 Mike Kafka 3.00 8.00
29 Mardy Gilyard 2.50 6.00
30 Marcus Easley 2.50 6.00
31 Jordan Shipley 2.50 6.00
32 Jonathan Dwyer 2.50 6.00
33 Joe McKnight 2.50 6.00
34 Jimmy Clausen 2.50 6.00
35 Jermaine Gresham 2.50 6.00

2010 Panini Plates and Patches Signatures Gold

1-100 UNPRICED VET PRINT RUN 5
*GOLD/25: .8X TO 2X BASIC AU/249-849
*GOLD/25: .6X TO 1.5X BASIC AU/99-199
EXCH EXPIRATION: 7/26/2012

2010 Panini Plates and Patches Signatures Silver

*SLVR/50: .5X TO 1.2X BASE AU/249-849
*SLVR/50: .4X TO 1X BASE AU/99-199
SILVER PRINT RUN 50 SER.#'d SETS
EXCH EXPIRATION: 7/26/2012

2010 Panini Plates and Patches Team Supreme Materials

STATED PRINT RUN 2-50
1 Wes Welker/50 5.00 12.00
2 LeSean McCoy/50 6.00 15.00
3 Chad Ochocinco/50 4.00 10.00
4 Cedric Benson/50 4.00 10.00
5 Terrell Suggs/45 4.00 10.00
6 DeSean Jackson/50 5.00 12.00
7 Brandon Jacobs/50 4.00 10.00
8 Devery Henderson/50 4.00 10.00
9 Greg Jennings/40 4.00 10.00
10 Felix Jones/50 4.00 10.00
11 Reggie Wayne/50 5.00 12.00
12 Bo Scaife/35 4.00 10.00
13 Dwayne Bowe/50 5.00 12.00
14 Matthew Stafford/19 6.00 15.00
15 Darrelle Revis/7
16 Sidney Rice/50 4.00 10.00
17 Bernard Berrian/50 4.00 10.00
18 Brian Orakpo/45 4.00 10.00
19 Eddie Royal/23 5.00 12.00
20 Heath Miller/2
21 Will Smith/45 4.00 10.00
22 Calvin Johnson/50 6.00 15.00
23 Shonn Greene/50 4.00 10.00
24 Louis Murphy/50 4.00 10.00
25 Frank Gore/50 5.00 12.00
26 Adrian Peterson/50 6.00 15.00
27 Matt Cassel/45 4.00 10.00
28 Brent Celek/50 4.00 10.00
29 Darren McFadden/50 4.00 10.00
30 Lee Evans/50 5.00 12.00
31 Cadillac Williams/50 4.00 10.00
33 Vernon Davis/50 4.00 10.00
34 Marshawn Lynch/30 5.00 12.00
35 Jamaal Charles/50 5.00 12.00
36 Santana Moss/50 5.00 12.00
37 Dustin Keller/13
38 Steve Slaton/50 4.00 10.00
39 Mark Sanchez/20 5.00 12.00
40 Greg Olsen/50 5.00 12.00
41 Tom Brady/50 12.00 30.00
42 Clinton Portis/50 4.00 10.00
43 Maurice Jones-Drew/50 4.00 10.00
44 Joseph Addai/50 4.00 10.00
45 Roddy White/50 4.00 10.00
46 Tony Romo/50 5.00 12.00
47 Kevin Kolb/50 4.00 10.00
48 Darren Sproles/50 5.00 12.00
50 Brian Urlacher/45 6.00 15.00

2011 Panini Plates and Patches

1-100 VETERAN PRINT RUN 299
100-200 ROOKIE AU PRINT RUN 49-405
201-235 ROOK.JSY AU PRINT RUN 299-499
EXCH EXPIRATION: 8/1/2013
1 Joe Flacco 1.25 3.00
2 Matt Ryan 1.25 3.00
3 Josh Freeman 1.25 3.00
4 Kevin Kolb 1.00 2.50
5 Donovan McNabb 1.25 3.00
6 Jay Cutler 1.00 2.50
7 Michael Vick 1.25 3.00
8 Matt Schaub 1.00 2.50
9 Drew Brees 1.50 4.00
10 Eli Manning 1.25 3.00
11 Larry Fitzgerald 1.25 3.00
12 Tom Brady 4.00 10.00
13 Steve Johnson 1.00 2.50
14 Ryan Fitzpatrick 1.00 2.50
15 Matt Cassel 1.00 2.50
16 Chad Henne 1.25 3.00
17 Philip Rivers 1.50 4.00
18 Peyton Manning 3.00 8.00
19 Brandon Marshall 1.25 3.00
20 Darren McFadden 1.00 2.50
21 Frank Gore 1.25 3.00
22 Matt Forte 1.00 2.50
23 Arian Foster 1.00 2.50
24 Nnamdi Asomugha 1.00 2.50
25 Jamaal Charles 1.25 3.00
26 Beanie Wells 1.00 2.50
27 Ray Rice 1.00 2.50
28 Adrian Peterson 1.50 4.00
29 Joseph Addai 1.00 2.50
30 Ben Roethlisberger 1.50 4.00
31 Montario Hardesty 1.25 3.00
32 Maurice Jones-Drew 1.00 2.50
33 Michael Turner 1.00 2.50
34 Rashard Mendenhall 1.00 2.50
35 Tarvaris Jackson 1.00 2.50
36 Sam Bradford 1.00 2.50
37 Matt Hasselbeck 1.00 2.50
38 Jason Campbell 1.00 2.50
39 Steven Jackson 1.00 2.50
40 Peyton Hillis 1.00 2.50
41 Kyle Orton 1.00 2.50
42 BenJarvus Green-Ellis 1.00 2.50
43 Troy Polamalu 1.50 4.00
44 Ahmad Bradshaw 1.00 2.50
45 Mark Sanchez 1.00 2.50
46 Matthew Stafford 1.25 3.00
47 Tony Romo 1.25 3.00
48 Santonio Holmes 1.00 2.50
49 Mike Sims-Walker 1.25 3.00
50 DeSean Jackson 1.25 3.00
51 Alex Smith 1.25 3.00
52 Jordan Shipley 1.00 2.50
53 Aaron Rodgers 3.00 8.00
54 Colt McCoy 1.00 2.50
55 Terrell Suggs 1.00 2.50
56 Marques Colston 1.00 2.50
57 Percy Harvin 1.00 2.50
58 Rex Grossman 1.00 2.50
59 Nate Burleson 1.00 2.50
60 Johnny Knox 1.00 2.50
61 Plaxico Burress 1.00 2.50
62 Mike Wallace 1.00 2.50
63 Sidney Rice 1.00 2.50
64 Kenny Britt 1.00 2.50
65 Mike Williams 1.25 3.00
66 Reggie Bush 1.00 2.50
67 Fred Jackson 1.00 2.50
68 Shonn Greene 1.00 2.50
69 Rashad Jennings 1.00 2.50
70 Ryan Mathews 1.25 3.00
71 Marshawn Lynch 1.25 3.00
72 LeSean McCoy 1.50 4.00
73 Knowshon Moreno 1.00 2.50
74 Felix Jones 1.00 2.50
75 Jonathan Stewart 1.00 2.50
76 Chris Johnson 1.00 2.50
77 Michael Bush 1.00 2.50
78 Cedric Benson 1.00 2.50
79 DeAngelo Williams 1.00 2.50
80 Andre Johnson 1.25 3.00
81 Calvin Johnson 1.50 4.00
82 Dwayne Bowe 1.25 3.00
83 Wes Welker 1.25 3.00
84 Roddy White 1.00 2.50
85 Chad Ochocinco 1.00 2.50
86 Tim Hightower 1.00 2.50
87 Reggie Wayne 1.25 3.00
88 Dez Bryant 1.50 4.00
89 Steve Smith 1.25 3.00
90 Darren Sproles 1.25 3.00
91 Kellen Winslow Jr. 1.00 2.50
92 Vincent Jackson 1.00 2.50
93 Bo Scaife 1.00 2.50
94 Brandon Lloyd 1.00 2.50
95 Greg Jennings 1.00 2.50
96 Vernon Davis 1.00 2.50
97 Hakeem Nicks 1.00 2.50
98 Jermichael Finley 1.00 2.50
99 Marcedes Lewis 1.00 2.50
100 Santana Moss 1.25 3.00
101 Terrelle Pryor AU/299 RC 5.00 12.00
102 A.Williams AU/49 RC 5.00 12.00
103 Adrian Clayborn AU/49 RC 5.00 12.00
104 Ahmad Black AU/49 RC 6.00 15.00
105 Akeem Ayers AU/360 RC 3.00 8.00
106 Aldon Smith AU/49 RC EXCH
107 Aldrick Robinson AU/199 RC 5.00 12.00
108 Alex Henery AU/199 RC 15.00 30.00
109 Allen Bradford AU/273 RC 3.00 8.00
110 Anthony Allen AU/49 RC 5.00 12.00
111 A.Castonzo AU/405 RC 3.00 8.00
112 A.Sherman AU/199 RC 4.00 10.00
113 Brandon Harris AU/49 RC 5.00 12.00
114 Cameron Heyward AU/49 RC 6.00 15.00
115 Cameron Jordan AU/150 RC 5.00 12.00
116 Casey Matthews AU/199 RC 4.00 10.00
117 Cecil Shorts AU/49 RC 5.00 12.00
118 Charles Clay AU/49 RC 5.00 12.00
119 Corey Liuget AU/150 RC 4.00 10.00
120 D.J. Williams AU/183 RC 4.00 10.00
121 D.Bowers AU/150 RC 4.00 10.00
122 Da'Rel Scott AU/199 RC 4.00 10.00
123 D.Sanzenbacher AU/199 RC 8.00 20.00
124 D.Evans AU/49 RC EXCH 6.00 15.00
125 D.Ausberry AU/49 RC 5.00 12.00
126 D.Sampson AU/49 RC 5.00 12.00
127 Denarius Moore AU/405 RC 8.00 20.00
128 Dion Lewis AU/49 RC 6.00 15.00
129 Dwayne Harris AU/405 RC 3.00 8.00
130 Evan Royster AU/49 RC 5.00 12.00
131 Greg Jones AU/150 RC 5.00 12.00
132 G.McElroy AU/49 RC 8.00 20.00
133 Greg Salas AU/150 RC 4.00 10.00
134 J.J. Watt AU/150 RC 30.00 60.00
135 Jacquizz Rodgers AU/150 RC 4.00 10.00
136 Jamar Newsome AU/49 RC 5.00 12.00
137 J.Kerley AU/49 RC 8.00 20.00
138 Jimmy Smith AU/49 RC 5.00 12.00
139 Joe Lefeged AU/199 RC 5.00 12.00
140 J.White AU/49 RC 5.00 12.00
141 Jordan Cameron AU/199 RC 5.00 12.00
142 Josh Portis AU/49 RC EXCH 8.00 20.00
143 J.Thomas AU/49 RC 6.00 15.00
144 Justin Houston AU/405 RC 4.00 10.00
145 Kealoha Pilares AU/49 RC 5.00 12.00
146 Kris Durham AU/199 RC 4.00 10.00
147 Kyle Adams AU/199 RC 4.00 10.00
148 Lance Kendricks AU/405 RC 3.00 8.00

149 Lee Smith AU/199 RC 6.00 15.00
150 Luke Stocker AU/150 RC 4.00 10.00
151 Marcus Cannon AU/199 RC 4.00 10.00
152 Marcus Gilchrist AU/49 RC 5.00 12.00
153 Martez Wilson AU/99 RC 4.00 10.00
154 Mason Foster AU/199 RC 4.00 10.00
155 Dan Bailey AU/199 RC 8.00 20.00
156 N.Enderle AU/49 RC 5.00 12.00
157 Niles Paul AU/49 RC 5.00 12.00
158 O.Marecic AU/49 RC EXCH 5.00 12.00
159 Phil Taylor AU/405 RC 3.00 8.00
160 P.Amukamara AU/50 RC 5.00 12.00
161 Quinton Carter AU/199 RC 4.00 10.00
162 Rahim Moore AU/405 RC 3.00 8.00
163 Richard Gordon AU/99 RC 4.00 10.00
164 Ricky Stanzi AU/150 RC 4.00 10.00
165 Robert Housler AU/199 RC 4.00 10.00
166 Ronald Johnson AU/150 RC 4.00 10.00
167 Roy Helu AU/150 RC 4.00 10.00
168 Ryan Kerrigan AU/150 RC 5.00 12.00
169 Ryan Taylor AU/199 RC 5.00 12.00
170 Ryan Whalen AU/405 RC 3.00 8.00
171 A.Hawkins AU/49 RC EXCH 5.00 12.00
172 Shane Bannon AU/99 RC 6.00 15.00
173 Stanley Havili AU/199 RC 4.00 10.00
174 S.Burton AU/49 RC 5.00 12.00
175 Stephen Paea AU/150 RC 4.00 10.00
176 T.J. Yates AU/49 RC 5.00 12.00
177 Tandon Doss AU/150 RC 4.00 10.00
178 Tyler Sash AU/49 RC 5.00 12.00
179 Tyrod Taylor AU/199 RC 8.00 20.00
180 Tyron Smith AU/49 RC 15.00 30.00
181 Virgil Green AU/199 RC 4.00 10.00
182 W.Saunders AU/49 RC EXCH 20.00 40.00
183 Zack Pianalto AU/199 RC 5.00 12.00
184 Ar.Smith AU/49 RC EXCH 6.00 15.00
185 Colin Cochart AU/99 RC 6.00 15.00
186 Doug Baldwin AU/199 RC 10.00 25.00
187 L.Williams AU/49 RC EXCH 6.00 15.00
188 Phillip Tanner AU/99 RC 10.00 25.00
189 Brian Rolle AU/49 RC 8.00 20.00
190 Bruce Miller AU/199 RC 8.00 20.00
191 Buster Skrine AU/199 RC 5.00 12.00
192 Chimdi Chekwa AU/199 RC 5.00 12.00
193 Chris Harris AU/199 RC 5.00 12.00
194 Chris White AU/199 RC 5.00 12.00
195 Henry Hynoski AU/199 RC 10.00 25.00
196 J.Williams AU/49 RC EXCH 8.00 20.00
197 K.J. Wright AU/199 RC 8.00 20.00
199 Robert Quinn AU/199 RC 4.00 10.00
200 Patrick Peterson AU/199 RC 8.00 20.00
201 Cam Newton JSY AU/299 RC 60.00 120.00
202 V.Miller JSY AU/499 RC 12.00 30.00
203 M.Dareus JSY AU/499 RC EX
204 A.J. Green JSY AU/299 RC 20.00 50.00
205 J.Jones JSY AU/299 RC EXCH 30.00 60.00
206 Jake Locker JSY AU/299 RC 12.00 30.00
207 B.Gabbert JSY AU/299 RC 5.00 12.00
208 C.Ponder JSY AU/299 RC 5.00 12.00
209 Baldwin JSY AU/499 RC 5.00 12.00
210 Mark Ingram JSY AU/299 RC 8.00 20.00
211 Andy Dalton JSY AU/499 RC 10.00 25.00
212 C.Kaepernick JSY AU/499 RC 8.00 20.00
213 R.Williams JSY AU/499 RC 5.00 12.00
214 K.Rudolph JSY AU/499 RC EX 5.00 12.00
215 Titus Young JSY AU/499 RC 5.00 12.00
216 Shane Vereen JSY AU/499 RC 6.00 15.00
217 M.Leshoure JSY AU/499 RC 10.00 25.00
218 Torrey Smith JSY AU/499 RC 5.00 12.00
219 Greg Little JSY AU/499 RC 6.00 15.00
220 D.Thomas JSY AU/499 RC 5.00 12.00
221 R.Cobb JSY AU/499 RC 8.00 20.00
222 D.Murray JSY AU/499 RC 10.00 25.00
223 S.Ridley JSY AU/499 RC 5.00 12.00
224 Ryan Mallett JSY AU/299 RC 5.00 12.00
225 Austin Pettis JSY AU/499 RC 5.00 12.00
226 Hankerson JSY AU/499 RC 5.00 12.00
227 Vincent Brown JSY AU/499 RC 5.00 12.00
228 Jerrel Jernigan JSY AU/499 RC 5.00 12.00
229 Alex Green JSY AU/499 RC 5.00 12.00
230 Clyde Gates JSY AU/499 RC 5.00 12.00
231 K.Hunter JSY AU/499 RC 10.00 25.00
232 Delone Carter JSY AU/499 RC 5.00 12.00
233 Taiwan Jones JSY AU/499 RC 5.00 12.00
234 Bilal Powell JSY AU/499 RC 6.00 15.00
235 Jamie Harper JSY AU/499 RC 6.00 15.00
236 Jordan Todman JSY AU/499 RC 5.00 12.00

2011 Panini Plates and Patches Gold

*1-100 VETS/50: 1.2X TO 3X BASIC CARDS
*101-200 ROOKIES/50: .6X TO 1.5X SILVER/100

2011 Panini Plates and Patches Rookie Autographed Jumbo Materials

BASE JUMBO AUTO PRINT RUN 10
*PRIME/25: .4X TO 1X JUMBO AU/10
1 A.J. Green 50.00 100.00
2 Alex Green 20.00 50.00
4 Austin Pettis 10.00 25.00
6 Blaine Gabbert 10.00 25.00
7 Cam Newton 125.00 250.00
8 Christian Ponder 10.00 25.00
9 Clyde Gates 10.00 25.00
10 Colin Kaepernick 15.00 40.00
12 Delone Carter 10.00 25.00
14 Greg Little 12.00 30.00
15 Jake Locker 10.00 25.00
16 Jamie Harper 10.00 25.00
17 Jerrel Jernigan 10.00 25.00
18 Jonathan Baldwin 10.00 25.00
19 Jordan Todman 10.00 25.00
20 Julio Jones 50.00 100.00
21 Kendall Hunter 25.00 50.00
22 Kyle Rudolph 10.00 25.00
23 Leonard Hankerson 10.00 25.00
25 Mark Ingram 15.00 40.00
26 Mikel Leshoure 10.00 25.00
27 Randall Cobb 15.00 40.00
28 Ryan Mallett 10.00 25.00
30 Shane Vereen 12.00 30.00
32 Taiwan Jones 10.00 25.00
33 Titus Young 10.00 25.00
34 Torrey Smith 10.00 25.00
35 Vincent Brown 10.00 25.00
36 Von Miller 25.00 60.00

2011 Panini Plates and Patches Silver

*1-100 VETS/100: .8X TO 2X BASIC CARDS
COMMON ROOKIE (101-200) 2.00 5.00
ROOKIE SEMISTARS 2.50 6.00
ROOKIE UNL.STARS 3.00 8.00
STATED PRINT RUN 100 SER.#'d SETS
101 Terrelle Pryor 3.00 8.00
106 Aldon Smith 2.00 5.00
127 Denarius Moore 2.00 5.00
134 J.J. Watt 10.00 25.00
164 Ricky Stanzi 2.00 5.00
167 Roy Helu 2.00 5.00
169 Ryan Taylor 2.50 6.00
171 Andrew Hawkins 2.00 5.00
176 T.J. Yates 2.00 5.00
179 Tyrod Taylor 4.00 10.00
180 Tyron Smith 2.50 6.00
186 Doug Baldwin 5.00 12.00
195 Henry Hynoski 3.00 8.00
196 Jacquian Williams 3.00 8.00
198 Nick Fairley 2.00 5.00
200 Patrick Peterson 4.00 10.00

2011 Panini Plates and Patches City Limits

STATED PRINT RUN 249 SER.#'d SETS
1 Larry Fitzgerald 1.50 4.00
2 Michael Turner 1.25 3.00
3 Joe Flacco 1.50 4.00
4 DeAngelo Williams 1.25 3.00
5 Julius Peppers 1.50 4.00
6 Peyton Hillis 1.25 3.00
7 Miles Austin 1.25 3.00
8 Brandon Lloyd 1.25 3.00
9 Jahvid Best 1.25 3.00
10 Donald Driver 1.50 4.00
11 Matt Schaub 1.25 3.00
12 Peyton Manning 4.00 10.00
13 Maurice Jones-Drew 1.25 3.00
14 Tony Moeaki 1.25 3.00
15 Percy Harvin 1.25 3.00
16 Danny Woodhead 3.00 8.00
17 Devery Henderson 1.25 3.00
18 Ahmad Bradshaw 1.25 3.00
19 Jeremy Maclin 1.25 3.00
20 Heath Miller 1.25 3.00
21 Philip Rivers 2.00 5.00
22 Patrick Willis 1.50 4.00
23 Steven Jackson 1.25 3.00
24 Mike Williams 1.50 4.00
25 Santana Moss 1.50 4.00

2011 Panini Plates and Patches City Limits Autograph Materials Prime

STATED PRINT RUN 1-15
7 Miles Austin/15 30.00 60.00
9 Jahvid Best/15

2011 Panini Plates and Patches City Limits Autographs

STATED PRINT RUN 5-15
7 Miles Austin/15 15.00 40.00
9 Jahvid Best/15 10.00 25.00
10 Donald Driver/15 30.00 60.00
14 Tony Moeaki/15 10.00 25.00
20 Heath Miller/15

2011 Panini Plates and Patches City Limits Materials

STATED PRINT RUN 10-299
*PRIME/50: .8X TO 2X BASIC JSY/299
*PRIME/25: 1X TO 2.5X BASIC JSY/99
*PRIME/25: .8X TO 2X BASIC JSY/49
*PRIME/25: .6X TO 1.5X BASIC JSY/25
1 Larry Fitzgerald/10
2 Michael Turner/49 3.00 8.00
3 Joe Flacco/299 3.00 8.00
4 DeAngelo Williams/99 2.50 6.00
5 Julius Peppers/299 4.00 10.00
6 Peyton Hillis/99 4.00 10.00
7 Miles Austin/299 2.50 6.00
8 Brandon Lloyd/25 4.00 10.00
9 Jahvid Best/99 2.50 6.00
11 Matt Schaub/99 2.50 6.00
13 Maurice Jones-Drew/99 2.50 6.00
15 Percy Harvin/50 3.00 8.00
17 Devery Henderson/299 2.50 6.00
18 Ahmad Bradshaw/99 2.50 6.00
19 Jeremy Maclin/25 4.00 10.00
20 Heath Miller/15 4.00 10.00
21 Philip Rivers/99 4.00 10.00
22 Patrick Willis/99 3.00 8.00
23 Steven Jackson/99 2.50 6.00
25 Santana Moss/31 4.00 10.00

2011 Panini Plates and Patches Gridiron Cut Autographs

STATED PRINT RUN 1-50
1 Sammy Baugh/10
2 Otto Graham/49 25.00 60.00
3 Bob Waterfield/10
4 Bobby Layne/1
5 Norm Van Brocklin/1
6 Jim Finks/1
7 Charley Conerly/5
8 Joe Perry/49 25.00 50.00
9 Ernie Nevers/1
10 Clark Shaughnessy/1
11 Doc Blanchard/2
12 Tuffy Leemans/1
13 Red Grange/1
14 Bill Dudley/49 20.00 40.00
15 Ken Strong/5
16 Arnie Herber/1
17 Les Horvath/4
18 Tony Canadeo/20 30.00 60.00
19 Glenn Davis/10
20 Dick Hoak/1
21 Kyle Rote/1
22 Don Hutson/1
23 Bob Hayes/1
24 Red Cochran/15 30.00 60.00
25 John Mackey/15
26 Frank Gatski/15 25.00 50.00
27 Alex Wojciechowicz/10
28 Ray Beck/30 20.00 40.00
29 Frank Kinard/1
30 Ed Healey/4
31 Turk Edwards/1
32 Lou Groza/16 20.00 40.00
33 Emlen Tunnell/4
34 Dick Lynch/20 20.00 40.00
35 George Connor/25 20.00 40.00
36 Bill Forester/20 25.00 50.00
37 Bob Pellegrini/25 25.00 50.00
38 Ernie Holmes/15 30.00 60.00
39 Stan Jones/6
40 Henry Jordan/5
41 Andy Robustelli/49 20.00 40.00
42 Wayne Millner/1
43 Morris Badgro/23 20.00 40.00
44 Hank Stram/25 25.00 50.00
45 Weeb Ewbank/49 20.00 40.00
46 Bert Bell/16 20.00 40.00
47 Wellington Mara/1
48 Art Rooney/1
49 Pete Rozelle/1
50 Joe Foss/1

2011 Panini Plates and Patches Honors

STATED PRINT RUN 249 SER.#'d SETS
1 Drew Brees 2.00 5.00
2 Peyton Manning 4.00 10.00
3 Tom Brady 5.00 12.00
4 Michael Vick 1.50 4.00
5 Ed Reed 1.50 4.00
6 James Harrison 1.50 4.00
7 Charles Woodson 2.00 5.00
8 Troy Polamalu 2.00 5.00
9 Chris Johnson 1.25 3.00
10 Carson Palmer 1.50 4.00
11 Adrian Peterson 2.00 5.00
12 Larry Fitzgerald 1.50 4.00
13 Matt Schaub 1.25 3.00
14 DeAngelo Hall 1.25 3.00
15 Patrick Willis 1.50 4.00
16 Jerod Mayo 1.25 3.00
17 Brian Cushing 1.25 3.00
18 Ben Roethlisberger 2.00 5.00
19 Matt Ryan 1.50 4.00
20 Percy Harvin 1.25 3.00
21 Sam Bradford 1.25 3.00
22 Deion Branch 1.25 3.00
23 Hines Ward 1.50 4.00
24 Eli Manning 1.50 4.00
25 Aaron Rodgers 3.00 8.00

2011 Panini Plates and Patches Honors Autographs

STATED PRINT RUN 5-25
7 Charles Woodson/25 100.00 200.00
14 DeAngelo Hall/25 12.00 30.00
16 Jerod Mayo/25 12.00 30.00
17 Brian Cushing/25 10.00 25.00
23 Hines Ward/25 40.00 80.00

2011 Panini Plates and Patches Honors Materials

STATED PRINT RUN 10-299
*PRIME/50: .8X TO 2X BASIC JSY/199-299
*PRIME/25: 1X TO 2.5X BASIC JSY/99-299
1 Drew Brees/99 4.00 10.00
2 Peyton Manning/89 8.00 20.00
3 Tom Brady/99 10.00 25.00
4 Michael Vick/10
5 Ed Reed/99 3.00 8.00
6 James Harrison/199 3.00 8.00
7 Charles Woodson/49 15.00 30.00
9 Chris Johnson/299 2.50 6.00
10 Carson Palmer/299 3.00 8.00
12 Larry Fitzgerald/10
13 Matt Schaub/99 2.50 6.00
14 DeAngelo Hall/199 2.50 6.00
15 Patrick Willis/99 4.00 10.00
18 Ben Roethlisberger/25 6.00 15.00
19 Matt Ryan/99 3.00 8.00
20 Percy Harvin/50 3.00 8.00
21 Sam Bradford/199 2.50 6.00
23 Hines Ward/99 4.00 10.00
24 Eli Manning/199 3.00 8.00
25 Aaron Rodgers/49 12.00 30.00

2011 Panini Plates and Patches Jerseys

STATED PRINT RUN 7-299
1 Joe Flacco/299 3.00 8.00
2 Matt Ryan/99 3.00 8.00
3 Josh Freeman/7
6 Jay Cutler/299 2.50 6.00
8 Matt Schaub/99 2.50 6.00
9 Drew Brees/99 4.00 10.00
10 Eli Manning/199 3.00 8.00
11 Larry Fitzgerald/25 5.00 12.00
12 Tom Brady/99 10.00 25.00
13 Steve Johnson/82 4.00 10.00
14 Ryan Fitzpatrick/199 2.50 6.00
15 Matt Cassel/299 2.50 6.00
16 Chad Henne/99 3.00 8.00
17 Philip Rivers/99 4.00 10.00
19 Brandon Marshall/199 3.00 8.00
20 Darren McFadden/299 2.50 6.00
21 Frank Gore/199 3.00 8.00
22 Matt Forte/99 2.50 6.00
23 Arian Foster/99 2.50 6.00
25 Jamaal Charles/299 3.00 8.00
26 Beanie Wells/99 2.50 6.00
27 Ray Rice/199 4.00 10.00
29 Joseph Addai/299 2.50 6.00
30 Ben Roethlisberger/25 6.00 15.00
32 Maurice Jones-Drew/99 2.50 6.00
33 Michael Turner/49 3.00 8.00
34 Rashard Mendenhall/99 2.50 6.00
36 Sam Bradford/199 2.50 6.00
38 Jason Campbell/199 2.50 6.00
39 Steven Jackson/99 2.50 6.00
40 Peyton Hillis/99 4.00 10.00
41 Kyle Orton/199 2.50 6.00
42 BenJarvus Green-Ellis/49 8.00 20.00
44 Ahmad Bradshaw/99 2.50 6.00
45 Mark Sanchez/299 2.50 6.00
46 Matthew Stafford/99 3.00 8.00
47 Tony Romo/299 3.00 8.00
48 Santonio Holmes/94 2.50 6.00
52 Jordan Shipley/99 2.50 6.00
53 Aaron Rodgers/49 12.00 30.00
54 Colt McCoy/299 2.50 6.00
55 Terrell Suggs/299 2.50 6.00
56 Marques Colston/99 2.50 6.00
57 Percy Harvin/32 3.00 8.00
60 Johnny Knox/99 2.50 6.00
62 Mike Wallace/99 2.50 6.00
64 Kenny Britt/299 2.50 6.00
68 Shonn Greene/299 2.50 6.00
73 Knowshon Moreno/299 2.50 6.00
74 Felix Jones/299 2.50 6.00
75 Jonathan Stewart/99 2.50 6.00
76 Chris Johnson/299 2.50 6.00
79 DeAngelo Williams/99 2.50 6.00
80 Andre Johnson/99 3.00 8.00
83 Wes Welker/99 3.00 8.00
87 Reggie Wayne/99 3.00 8.00
88 Dez Bryant/199 4.00 10.00
89 Steve Smith/99 3.00 8.00
92 Vincent Jackson/99 2.50 6.00
94 Brandon Lloyd/25 4.00 10.00
96 Vernon Davis/199 2.50 6.00
97 Hakeem Nicks/199 2.50 6.00

2011 Panini Plates and Patches Jerseys Prime

STATED PRINT RUN 1-50
14 Ryan Fitzpatrick/50 4.00 10.00
15 Matt Cassel/25 5.00 12.00
17 Philip Rivers/25 8.00 20.00
19 Brandon Marshall/25 6.00 15.00
20 Darren McFadden/50 4.00 10.00
25 Jamaal Charles/50 5.00 12.00
26 Beanie Wells/25 5.00 12.00
29 Joseph Addai/25 5.00 12.00
32 Maurice Jones-Drew/25 5.00 12.00
33 Michael Turner/25 5.00 12.00
38 Jason Campbell/25 5.00 12.00
47 Tony Romo/25 6.00 15.00
54 Colt McCoy/50 4.00 10.00
56 Marques Colston/50 4.00 10.00
60 Johnny Knox/25 5.00 12.00
64 Kenny Britt/25 5.00 12.00
68 Shonn Greene/25 5.00 12.00
70 Ryan Mathews/50 5.00 12.00
73 Knowshon Moreno/25 5.00 12.00
74 Felix Jones/50 4.00 10.00
75 Jonathan Stewart/25 5.00 12.00
76 Chris Johnson/50 4.00 10.00
81 Calvin Johnson/50 6.00 15.00
83 Wes Welker/50 5.00 12.00
84 Roddy White/50 4.00 10.00
88 Dez Bryant/25 8.00 20.00
97 Hakeem Nicks/25 5.00 12.00

2011 Panini Plates and Patches Jerseys Prime Jersey Number

STATED PRINT RUN 1-50
14 Ryan Fitzpatrick/50 4.00 10.00
15 Matt Cassel/25 5.00 12.00
17 Philip Rivers/25 8.00 20.00
19 Brandon Marshall/25 6.00 15.00
20 Darren McFadden/50 4.00 10.00
25 Jamaal Charles/50 5.00 12.00
26 Beanie Wells/25 5.00 12.00
32 Maurice Jones-Drew/25 5.00 12.00
33 Michael Turner/25 5.00 12.00
38 Jason Campbell/25 5.00 12.00
47 Tony Romo/25 6.00 15.00
55 Terrell Suggs/25 5.00 12.00
56 Marques Colston/50 4.00 10.00
60 Johnny Knox/25 5.00 12.00
68 Shonn Greene/25 5.00 12.00
70 Ryan Mathews/50 5.00 12.00
73 Knowshon Moreno/25 5.00 12.00
74 Felix Jones/50 4.00 10.00
75 Jonathan Stewart/25 5.00 12.00
76 Chris Johnson/50 4.00 10.00
81 Calvin Johnson/50 6.00 15.00
83 Wes Welker/50 5.00 12.00
84 Roddy White/50 4.00 10.00
88 Dez Bryant/25 8.00 20.00
97 Hakeem Nicks/25 5.00 12.00

2011 Panini Plates and Patches Jerseys Prime Nameplate

STATED PRINT RUN 1-25
19 Brandon Marshall/25 6.00 15.00
20 Darren McFadden/25 5.00 12.00
25 Jamaal Charles/25 6.00 15.00
32 Maurice Jones-Drew/25 5.00 12.00
33 Michael Turner/25 5.00 12.00
45 Mark Sanchez/25 5.00 12.00
55 Terrell Suggs/25 5.00 12.00
56 Marques Colston/25 5.00 12.00
60 Johnny Knox/25 5.00 12.00
68 Shonn Greene/25 5.00 12.00
70 Ryan Mathews/25 6.00 15.00
73 Knowshon Moreno/25 5.00 12.00
76 Chris Johnson/25 5.00 12.00
81 Calvin Johnson/25 8.00 20.00
83 Wes Welker/25 6.00 15.00
84 Roddy White/25 5.00 12.00
88 Dez Bryant/25 8.00 20.00

2011 Panini Plates and Patches NFL Equipment

STATED PRINT RUN 20-150
*PRIME/50: .5X TO 1.2X BASIC JSY/150
*PRIME/50: .3X TO .8X BASIC JSY/25
*PRIME/25: .6X TO 1.5X BASIC JSY/150
*PRIME/25: .5X TO 1.2X BASIC JSY/50
*PRIME/25: .4X TO 1X BASIC JSY/25
*COMOBS/50: .5X TO 1.2X BASIC JSY/99-150
*COMOBS/25: .6X TO 1.5X BASIC JSY/150
*CMBO PRIME/25: .8X TO 2X BASIC JSY/150
*CMBO PRIME/25: .5X TO 1.2X BASIC JSY/25
1 Anquan Boldin/25 5.00 12.00
2 Cedric Benson/50 4.00 10.00
3 Chris Cooley/150 5.00 12.00
4 DeMarcus Ware/150 5.00 12.00
5 Devin Hester/150 4.00 10.00
6 Dexter McCluster/99 3.00 8.00
7 Eddie Royal/150 3.00 8.00
8 Jacoby Ford/150 4.00 10.00
9 Jared Allen/150 5.00 12.00
10 Jason Campbell/150 3.00 8.00
11 Jay Cutler/150 3.00 8.00
12 Jermaine Gresham/20 5.00 12.00
13 Joe Flacco/150 4.00 10.00
14 Johnny Knox/50 4.00 10.00
15 Jon Beason/150 3.00 8.00
16 Knowshon Moreno/150 3.00 8.00
17 London Fletcher/150 4.00 10.00
18 Marcedes Lewis/48 4.00 10.00
19 Matt Cassel/150 3.00 8.00
20 Matt Forte/50 4.00 10.00
21 Ryan Mathews/25 6.00 15.00
22 Steve Johnson/99 5.00 12.00
23 Tim Tebow/150 5.00 12.00
24 Tony Gonzalez/150 4.00 10.00
25 Tony Romo/150 4.00 10.00

2011 Panini Plates and Patches Rookie Blitz

STATED PRINT RUN 249 SER.#'d SETS
1 Ryan Mallett 1.00 2.50
2 Shane Vereen 1.25 3.00
3 Stevan Ridley 1.00 2.50
4 A.J. Green 2.50 6.00
5 Andy Dalton 2.00 5.00
6 Clyde Gates 1.00 2.50
7 Daniel Thomas 1.00 2.50
8 Jake Locker 1.00 2.50
9 Jamie Harper 1.00 2.50
10 Jordan Todman 1.00 2.50
11 Vincent Brown 1.00 2.50
12 Bilal Powell 1.25 3.00
13 Blaine Gabbert 1.00 2.50
14 Delone Carter 1.00 2.50
15 Greg Little 1.25 3.00
16 Jonathan Baldwin 1.00 2.50
17 Taiwan Jones 1.00 2.50
18 Torrey Smith 1.00 2.50
19 Marcell Dareus 1.00 2.50
20 Von Miller 1.50 4.00
21 Alex Green 1.00 2.50
22 Randall Cobb 1.50 4.00
23 Christian Ponder 1.00 2.50
24 Kyle Rudolph 1.00 2.50
25 Colin Kaepernick 1.50 4.00
26 Kendall Hunter 1.00 2.50
27 Mikel Leshoure 1.00 2.50
28 Titus Young 1.00 2.50
29 Austin Pettis 1.00 2.50
30 Cam Newton 5.00 12.00
31 DeMarco Murray 2.00 5.00
32 Julio Jones 3.00 8.00
33 Leonard Hankerson 1.00 2.50
34 Mark Ingram 1.50 4.00
35 Ryan Williams 1.00 2.50
36 Jerrel Jernigan 1.00 2.50

2011 Panini Plates and Patches Rookie Blitz Autograph Materials Prime

PRIME PRINT RUN 25 SER.#'d SETS
*JERSEY AU/25: .3X TO .8X PRIME AU/25
1 Ryan Mallett 8.00 20.00
2 Shane Vereen 10.00 25.00
4 A.J. Green 30.00 80.00
6 Clyde Gates 8.00 20.00
8 Jake Locker 8.00 20.00
10 Jordan Todman 8.00 20.00
11 Vincent Brown 8.00 20.00
13 Blaine Gabbert 8.00 20.00
14 Delone Carter 8.00 20.00
16 Jonathan Baldwin 8.00 20.00
17 Taiwan Jones 8.00 20.00
18 Torrey Smith 8.00 20.00
20 Von Miller 20.00 50.00
21 Alex Green 15.00 40.00
22 Randall Cobb 12.00 30.00
23 Christian Ponder 8.00 20.00
25 Colin Kaepernick 10.00 25.00
26 Kendall Hunter 15.00 40.00
27 Mikel Leshoure 8.00 20.00
28 Titus Young 8.00 20.00
29 Austin Pettis 8.00 20.00
30 Cam Newton 75.00 150.00
33 Leonard Hankerson 8.00 20.00
34 Mark Ingram 12.00 30.00
35 Ryan Williams 10.00 25.00
36 Jerrel Jernigan 8.00 20.00

2011 Panini Plates and Patches Rookie Blitz Materials

STATED PRINT RUN 99-299
1 Ryan Mallett/299 1.50 4.00
2 Shane Vereen/299 2.00 5.00
3 Stevan Ridley/299 1.50 4.00
4 A.J. Green/299 4.00 10.00
5 Andy Dalton/299 3.00 8.00
6 Clyde Gates/299 1.50 4.00
7 Daniel Thomas/299 1.50 4.00
8 Jake Locker/299 1.50 4.00
9 Jamie Harper/299 1.50 4.00
10 Jordan Todman/299 2.00 5.00
11 Vincent Brown/299 1.50 4.00
12 Bilal Powell/299 2.00 5.00
13 Blaine Gabbert/299 1.50 4.00
14 Delone Carter/299 1.50 4.00
15 Greg Little/299 2.00 5.00
16 Jonathan Baldwin/299 1.50 4.00
17 Taiwan Jones/299 1.50 4.00
18 Torrey Smith/299 1.50 4.00
19 Marcell Dareus/299 1.50 4.00
20 Von Miller/299 2.50 6.00
21 Alex Green/299 1.50 4.00
22 Randall Cobb/299 2.50 6.00
23 Christian Ponder/99 1.50 4.00
25 Colin Kaepernick/299 2.50 6.00
26 Kendall Hunter/299 1.50 4.00
27 Mikel Leshoure/299 1.50 4.00
28 Titus Young/299 1.50 4.00
29 Austin Pettis/299 1.50 4.00
30 Cam Newton/299 8.00 20.00
31 DeMarco Murray/299 3.00 8.00
32 Julio Jones/299 5.00 12.00
33 Leonard Hankerson/299 1.50 4.00
34 Mark Ingram/299 2.50 6.00
35 Ryan Williams/299 1.50 4.00
36 Jerrel Jernigan/299 1.50 4.00

2011 Panini Plates and Patches Rookie Jumbo Materials

STATED PRINT RUN 25-50
*PRIME/15: .8X TO 2X BASIC JUMBO/50
*PRIME/15: .6X TO 1.5X BASIC JUMBO/25
1 A.J. Green/50 6.00 15.00
2 Alex Green/50 2.50 6.00
3 Andy Dalton/50 5.00 12.00
4 Austin Pettis/50 2.50 6.00
5 Bilal Powell/50 3.00 8.00
6 Blaine Gabbert/50 2.50 6.00
7 Cam Newton/50 12.00 30.00
8 Christian Ponder/25 3.00 8.00
9 Clyde Gates/50 2.50 6.00
10 Colin Kaepernick/50 4.00 10.00
11 Daniel Thomas/50 2.50 6.00
12 Delone Carter/50 2.50 6.00
13 DeMarco Murray/50 5.00 12.00
14 Greg Little/50 3.00 8.00
15 Jake Locker/50 2.50 6.00
16 Jamie Harper/50 2.50 6.00
17 Jerrel Jernigan/50 2.50 6.00
18 Jonathan Baldwin/50 2.50 6.00
19 Jordan Todman/50 2.50 6.00
20 Julio Jones/50 8.00 20.00
21 Kendall Hunter/50 2.50 6.00
23 Leonard Hankerson/50 2.50 6.00
24 Marcell Dareus/50 2.50 6.00
25 Mark Ingram/50 4.00 10.00
27 Randall Cobb/50 4.00 10.00
28 Ryan Mallett/50 2.50 6.00
29 Ryan Williams/50 2.50 6.00
30 Shane Vereen/50 3.00 8.00
31 Stevan Ridley/50 2.50 6.00
32 Taiwan Jones/50 2.50 6.00
33 Titus Young/50 2.50 6.00
34 Torrey Smith/50 2.50 6.00
35 Vincent Brown/50 2.50 6.00
36 Von Miller/50 4.00 10.00

2011 Panini Plates and Patches Rookie Prime Signatures Nameplate

*PLATE AU/25: .6X TO 1.5X BASE JSY AU/499
*PLATE AU/25: .5X TO 1.2X BASE JSY AU/299
STATED PRINT RUN 25 SER.#'d SETS
EXCH EXPIRATION: 8/1/2013
201 Cam Newton 100.00 200.00
212 Colin Kaepernick 10.00 25.00

2011 Panini Plates and Patches Signatures Gold

1-100 UNPRICED VET PRINT RUN 5-10
*GOLD/25: .6X TO 1.5X AU RC/273-405
*GOLD/25: .5X TO 1.2X AU RC/99-199
*GOLD/25: .4X TO 1X AU RC/49-50
101-200 ROOKIE PRINT RUN 25
134 J.J. Watt/25 75.00 135.00
200 Patrick Peterson/25 10.00 25.00

2011 Panini Plates and Patches Signatures Silver

1-100 VETERAN PRINT RUN 10-25
*SILVER/50-100: .5X TO 1.2X AU RC/273-405
*SILVER/50-100: .4X TO 1X AU RC/99-199
*SILVER/50-100: .3X TO .8X AU RC/49-50
101-200 ROOKIE PRINT RUN 50-100
31 Montario Hardesty/25 5.00 12.00
85 Chad Ochocinco/25 6.00 15.00
93 Bo Scaife/25 4.00 10.00
195 Henry Hynoski/50 15.00 40.00
200 Patrick Peterson/50 8.00 20.00

2011 Panini Plates and Patches Team Supreme Materials

STATED PRINT RUN 4-50
1 Michael Turner/50 5.00 12.00
2 Roddy White/50 5.00 12.00
3 Terrell Suggs/50 5.00 12.00
4 Anquan Boldin/25 6.00 15.00
5 Ed Reed/35 8.00 20.00
6 Steve Johnson/15 10.00 25.00
7 Jon Beason/25 6.00 15.00
8 DeAngelo Williams/4
9 Brian Urlacher/50 8.00 20.00
10 Jermaine Gresham/20 6.00 15.00
11 Jordan Shipley/25 6.00 15.00
12 Felix Jones/50 5.00 12.00
13 Miles Austin/50 5.00 12.00
14 Brandon Lloyd/25 6.00 15.00
15 Calvin Johnson/50 8.00 20.00
16 Maurice Jones-Drew/50 5.00 12.00
17 Marcedes Lewis/6
18 Jamaal Charles/50 6.00 15.00
19 Tamba Hali/50 5.00 12.00
20 Dexter McCluster/50 5.00 12.00
21 Brandon Marshall/50 6.00 15.00
22 Bernard Berrian/50 5.00 12.00
23 Jared Allen/25 10.00 25.00
24 Wes Welker/50 6.00 15.00
25 Hakeem Nicks/25 6.00 15.00
26 Darrelle Revis/20 6.00 15.00
27 Santonio Holmes/25 6.00 15.00
28 Jason Campbell/25 6.00 15.00
29 Brent Celek/50 5.00 12.00
30 DeSean Jackson/50 6.00 15.00
31 Jeremy Maclin/50 5.00 12.00
32 James Harrison/25 8.00 20.00
33 Antonio Gates/50 5.00 12.00
34 Malcom Floyd/50 5.00 12.00
35 Patrick Willis/18 8.00 20.00
36 Earnest Graham/50 5.00 12.00
37 Chris Johnson/50 5.00 12.00
38 Cortland Finnegan/25 6.00 15.00
39 Kenny Britt/25 6.00 15.00
40 Chris Cooley/50 8.00 20.00
41 Ryan Torain/50 6.00 15.00
42 Santana Moss/50 6.00 15.00

2016 Panini Plates and Patches

*BLUE/50: .5X TO 1.2X BASIC CARDS/99
1 Carson Palmer 1.50 4.00
2 Larry Fitzgerald 1.50 4.00
3 David Johnson 2.00 5.00
4 Matt Ryan 1.50 4.00
5 Julio Jones 2.00 5.00
6 Devonta Freeman 1.50 4.00
7 Joe Flacco 1.50 4.00
8 Steve Smith Sr. 1.50 4.00
9 Mike Wallace 1.25 3.00
10 Tyrod Taylor 1.50 4.00
11 LeSean McCoy 2.00 5.00
12 Sammy Watkins 2.00 5.00
13 Cam Newton 2.00 5.00
14 Kelvin Benjamin 1.50 4.00
15 Greg Olsen 1.50 4.00
16 Luke Kuechly 1.50 4.00
17 Jay Cutler 1.25 3.00
18 Jeremy Langford 1.50 4.00
19 Alshon Jeffery 1.50 4.00
20 Andy Dalton 1.50 4.00
21 Jeremy Hill 1.25 3.00
22 A.J. Green 2.00 5.00
23 Gary Barnidge 1.25 3.00
24 Isaiah Crowell 1.25 3.00
25 Terrelle Pryor 1.25 3.00
26 Tony Romo 1.50 4.00
27 Dez Bryant 2.00 5.00
28 Jason Witten 1.50 4.00
29 Trevor Siemian 1.25 3.00
30 C.J. Anderson 1.50 4.00
31 Demaryius Thomas 1.50 4.00
32 Von Miller 1.50 4.00
33 Matthew Stafford 1.50 4.00
34 Golden Tate III 1.25 3.00
35 Marvin Jones Jr. 1.25 3.00
36 Aaron Rodgers 4.00 10.00
37 Eddie Lacy 1.25 3.00
38 Jordy Nelson 1.50 4.00
39 Clay Matthews 2.00 5.00
40 Brock Osweiler 1.25 3.00
41 DeAndre Hopkins 1.50 4.00
42 Lamar Miller 1.25 3.00
43 Andrew Luck 2.50 6.00
44 T.Y. Hilton 1.50 4.00
45 Frank Gore 1.50 4.00
46 Blake Bortles 1.25 3.00
47 Allen Robinson 1.50 4.00
48 T.J. Yeldon 1.25 3.00
49 Alex Smith 1.50 4.00
50 Jamaal Charles 1.50 4.00
51 Jeremy Maclin 1.25 3.00
52 Case Keenum 1.50 4.00
53 Todd Gurley II 2.00 5.00
54 Tavon Austin 1.25 3.00
55 Ryan Tannehill 1.50 4.00
56 Jarvis Landry 1.50 4.00
57 Jay Ajayi 1.50 4.00
58 Sam Bradford 1.25 3.00
59 Adrian Peterson 2.00 5.00
60 Stefon Diggs 1.50 4.00
61 Tom Brady 5.00 12.00
62 Rob Gronkowski 2.00 5.00
63 Julian Edelman 2.00 5.00
64 LeGarrette Blount 1.50 4.00
65 Drew Brees 2.00 5.00
66 Brandin Cooks 1.50 4.00
67 Mark Ingram 1.50 4.00
68 Eli Manning 1.50 4.00
69 Odell Beckham Jr. 2.00 5.00
70 Victor Cruz 1.50 4.00
71 Ryan Fitzpatrick 1.25 3.00
72 Matt Forte 1.25 3.00
73 Brandon Marshall 1.25 3.00
74 Derek Carr 2.00 5.00
75 Amari Cooper 2.00 5.00
76 Latavius Murray 1.25 3.00
77 Ryan Mathews 1.50 4.00
78 Jordan Matthews 1.50 4.00
79 Zach Ertz 1.50 4.00
80 Ben Roethlisberger 2.00 5.00
81 Antonio Brown 2.00 5.00
82 Le'Veon Bell 1.50 4.00
83 Philip Rivers 2.00 5.00
84 Melvin Gordon 1.50 4.00
85 Travis Benjamin 1.25 3.00
86 Russell Wilson 2.50 6.00
87 Doug Baldwin 1.50 4.00
88 Jimmy Graham 2.00 5.00
89 Colin Kaepernick 1.50 4.00
90 Carlos Hyde 1.25 3.00
91 Torrey Smith 1.25 3.00
92 Jameis Winston 2.00 5.00
93 Doug Martin 1.50 4.00
94 Mike Evans 1.50 4.00
95 Marcus Mariota 2.00 5.00
96 DeMarco Murray 1.50 4.00
97 Delanie Walker 1.25 3.00
98 Kirk Cousins 2.00 5.00
99 DeSean Jackson 1.50 4.00
100 Jordan Reed 1.25 3.00
101 Brett Favre RET 5.00 12.00
102 Kevin Greene RET 2.50 6.00
103 Marvin Harrison RET 2.00 5.00
104 Jerome Bettis RET 2.50 6.00
105 Tim Brown RET 2.50 6.00
106 Charles Haley RET 2.50 6.00
107 Junior Seau RET 2.00 5.00
108 Derrick Brooks RET 1.50 4.00
109 Andre Reed RET 2.00 5.00
110 Michael Strahan RET 2.00 5.00
111 Kurt Warner RET 2.00 5.00
112 Cris Carter RET 2.50 6.00
113 Warren Sapp RET 2.00 5.00
114 Curtis Martin RET 2.00 5.00
115 Marshall Faulk RET 2.00 5.00
116 Deion Sanders RET 2.00 5.00
117 Shannon Sharpe RET 2.50 6.00
118 Jerry Rice RET 4.00 10.00
119 Emmitt Smith RET 4.00 10.00
120 Bruce Smith RET 2.00 5.00
121 Rod Woodson RET 2.00 5.00
122 Darrell Green RET 2.00 5.00
123 Michael Irvin RET 2.50 6.00
124 Thurman Thomas RET 2.00 5.00
125 Troy Aikman RET 3.00 8.00
126 Warren Moon RET 2.50 6.00
127 Dan Marino RET 5.00 12.00
128 Steve Young RET 3.00 8.00
129 John Elway RET 4.00 10.00
130 Barry Sanders RET 4.00 10.00
131 Marcus Allen RET 2.00 5.00
132 Jim Kelly RET 2.50 6.00
133 Howie Long RET 2.50 6.00
134 Ronnie Lott RET 2.00 5.00
135 Eric Dickerson RET 2.00 5.00
136 Ozzie Newsome RET 2.00 5.00
137 Lawrence Taylor RET 2.50 6.00
138 Mike Singletary RET 2.50 6.00
139 Steve Largent RET 2.50 6.00
140 Tony Dorsett RET 2.50 6.00
141 Dan Fouts RET 2.00 5.00
142 John Riggins RET 2.00 5.00
143 Earl Campbell RET 2.50 6.00
144 Franco Harris RET 2.50 6.00
145 Ray Lewis RET 2.50 6.00
146 Terry Bradshaw RET 3.00 8.00
147 Larry Csonka RET 2.00 5.00
148 Fran Tarkenton RET 2.50 6.00
149 Roger Staubach RET 3.00 8.00
150 Joe Namath RET 3.00 8.00
151 Carson Wentz RC 10.00 25.00
152 DeAndre Washington RC 1.00 2.50
153 Hunter Henry RC 1.25 3.00
154 Dak Prescott RC 5.00 12.00
155 Laquon Treadwell RC 1.25 3.00
156 Eli Apple RC 1.25 3.00
157 Paxton Lynch RC 1.00 2.50
158 Jacoby Brissett RC 1.25 3.00
159 Joey Bosa RC 2.00 5.00
160 Austin Hooper RC 1.00 2.50
161 Wendell Smallwood RC 1.00 2.50
162 Pharoh Cooper RC 1.00 2.50
163 Myles Jack RC 1.25 3.00
164 Kenneth Dixon RC 1.00 2.50
165 C.J. Prosise RC 1.00 2.50
166 Devontae Booker RC 1.25 3.00
167 Malcolm Mitchell RC 1.00 2.50
168 Chris Moore RC 1.25 3.00
169 Cardale Jones RC 1.00 2.50
170 Leonte Carroo RC 1.00 2.50
171 Trevor Davis RC 1.00 2.50
172 Tyler Ervin RC 1.00 2.50
173 Michael Thomas RC 2.00 5.00
174 Jonathan Williams RC 1.25 3.00
175 Kenyan Drake RC 1.50 4.00
176 Alex Collins RC 1.25 3.00
177 Ezekiel Elliott RC 5.00 12.00
178 Paul Perkins RC 1.00 2.50
179 Tajae Sharpe RC 1.25 3.00
180 Jordan Howard RC 2.50 6.00
181 Leonard Floyd RC 1.25 3.00
182 Will Fuller V RC 1.50 4.00
183 Sterling Shepard RC 1.25 3.00
184 Tyler Boyd RC 1.25 3.00
185 Karl Joseph RC 1.00 2.50
186 Jalen Ramsey RC 1.50 4.00
187 Derrick Henry RC 2.50 6.00
188 Corey Coleman RC 1.50 4.00
189 Christian Hackenberg RC 1.00 2.50
190 Josh Doctson RC 1.25 3.00
191 Braxton Miller RC 1.00 2.50
192 Keenan Reynolds RC 1.25 3.00
193 Cody Kessler RC 1.00 2.50
194 Moritz Bohringer RC 1.00 2.50
195 Rashard Higgins RC 1.00 2.50
196 Tyreek Hill RC 4.00 10.00
197 Connor Cook RC 1.25 3.00
198 Ricardo Louis RC 1.00 2.50
199 DeForest Buckner RC 1.00 2.50
200 Jared Goff RC 6.00 15.00

2016 Panini Plates and Patches Canton Calligraphy

*BLUE/25: .5X TO 1.2X BASIC AU/50
2 Marvin Harrison/25 12.00 30.00
3 Kevin Greene/25 20.00 50.00
4 Derrick Brooks/50 8.00 20.00
5 Bruce Smith/50 10.00 25.00
6 Fran Tarkenton/50 12.00 30.00
10 Jerome Bettis/25 30.00 60.00
11 Charles Haley/50 12.00 30.00
12 James Lofton/50 10.00 25.00
13 Lawrence Taylor/25 25.00 50.00
14 Andre Reed/50 10.00 25.00
16 Joe Greene/25 15.00 40.00
17 Steve Young/25 40.00 80.00
18 Rod Woodson/50 10.00 25.00
19 Barry Sanders/25 75.00 150.00
20 Steve Largent/25 15.00 40.00

2016 Panini Plates and Patches Double Coverage Patches

*BLUE/25: .5X TO 1.2X BASIC PATCH/50
1 C.Wentz/D.Prescott 30.00 80.00
2 C.Wentz/J.Goff 20.00 50.00
3 D.Prescott/E.Elliott 15.00 40.00
4 D.Henry/E.Elliott 10.00 25.00
5 P.Perkins/S.Shepard 4.00 10.00
6 J.Goff/P.Cooper 10.00 25.00
7 B.Miller/W.Fuller 5.00 12.00
8 D.Booker/P.Lynch 4.00 10.00
9 J.Goff/T.Davis 10.00 25.00
10 C.Kessler/C.Coleman 5.00 12.00
11 L.Carroo/K.Drake 5.00 12.00
12 J.Brissett/M.Mitchell 4.00 10.00
13 C.Moore/K.Dixon 4.00 10.00
14 A.Collins/C.Prosise 4.00 10.00
15 D.Henry/T.Sharpe 8.00 20.00
16 W.Smallwood/C.Wentz 20.00 50.00

2016 Panini Plates and Patches Full Coverage Patches

*BLUE/25: .5X TO 1.2X BASIC PATCH/50
1 Alex Collins 4.00 10.00
2 Braxton Miller 3.00 8.00
3 C.J. Prosise 3.00 8.00
4 Cardale Jones 3.00 8.00
5 Carson Wentz 20.00 50.00
6 Chris Moore 4.00 10.00
7 Christian Hackenberg 3.00 8.00
8 Cody Kessler 3.00 8.00
9 Connor Cook 4.00 10.00
10 Corey Coleman 5.00 12.00
11 Dak Prescott 15.00 40.00
12 DeAndre Washington 3.00 8.00
13 Demarcus Robinson 3.00 8.00
14 Derrick Henry 8.00 20.00
15 Devontae Booker 4.00 10.00
16 Ezekiel Elliott 15.00 40.00
17 Hunter Henry 4.00 10.00
18 Jacoby Brissett 4.00 10.00
19 Jared Goff 10.00 25.00
20 Joey Bosa 6.00 15.00
21 Jonathan Williams 4.00 10.00
22 Jordan Howard 8.00 20.00
23 Josh Doctson 4.00 10.00
24 Keenan Reynolds 4.00 10.00
25 Kenneth Dixon 3.00 8.00
26 Kenyan Drake 5.00 12.00
27 Laquon Treadwell 4.00 10.00
28 Leonte Carroo 3.00 8.00
29 Malcolm Mitchell 3.00 8.00
30 Michael Thomas 6.00 15.00
31 Moritz Bohringer 3.00 8.00
32 Paul Perkins 3.00 8.00
33 Paxton Lynch 3.00 8.00
34 Pharoh Cooper 3.00 8.00
35 Ricardo Louis 3.00 8.00
36 Sterling Shepard 4.00 10.00
37 Tajae Sharpe 4.00 10.00
38 Trevor Davis 3.00 8.00
39 Tyler Boyd 4.00 10.00
40 Tyler Ervin 3.00 8.00
41 Wendell Smallwood 3.00 8.00
42 Will Fuller V 5.00 12.00

2016 Panini Plates and Patches Game Changers Autographs

*BLUE/50: .5X TO 1.2X BASIC AU/99
*GREEN/25: .6X TO 1.5X BASIC AU/99
2 Eric Dickerson/25
3 Dwight Clark/99 8.00 20.00
6 Antonio Brown/25 25.00 60.00
7 Franco Harris/25 25.00 50.00
8 Raymond Berry/25 12.00 30.00
9 Marshawn Lynch/25 12.00 30.00

2016 Panini Plates and Patches Pivotal Marks

*BLUE/50: .5X TO 1.2X BASIC AU/99
*BLUE/25: .5X TO 1.2X BASIC AU/50
2 Demaryius Thomas/25 12.00 30.00
3 Marcus Allen/25 12.00 30.00
4 Drew Brees/25 30.00 60.00
5 John Riggins/25 12.00 30.00
6 Eli Manning/25 30.00 60.00
7 Terrell Davis/25 12.00 30.00
8 Hines Ward/25 12.00 30.00
9 Andrew Luck/25 50.00 100.00
10 Deion Branch/99 6.00 15.00
11 Dwight Clark/50 10.00 25.00
12 Ray Lewis/25 50.00 100.00
13 Kurt Warner/25 30.00 60.00
14 Roger Staubach/25 40.00 80.00
15 Mario Manningham/99 6.00 15.00
17 Richard Sherman/25 20.00 40.00
18 James Harrison/25 30.00 60.00
19 Von Miller/25 12.00 30.00
20 Clay Matthews/25 15.00 40.00

2016 Panini Plates and Patches Rookie Patch Autographs

1 Carson Wentz/50 50.00 125.00
2 Dak Prescott/99 30.00 60.00
3 Cody Kessler/99 4.00 10.00
4 DeAndre Washington/99 4.00 10.00
5 Derrick Henry/50 12.00 30.00
6 Jonathan Williams/99 5.00 12.00
7 Jacoby Brissett/99 5.00 12.00
8 Jared Goff/50 40.00 80.00
9 Wendell Smallwood/99 4.00 10.00
10 Sterling Shepard/99 5.00 12.00

11 Tyler Boyd/99 5.00 12.00
12 Jordan Howard/99 10.00 25.00
13 Joey Bosa/99 8.00 20.00
14 Tyler Ervin/99 4.00 10.00
15 Hunter Henry/99 5.00 12.00
16 Michael Thomas/99 8.00 20.00
17 Cardale Jones/99 4.00 10.00
18 Ezekiel Elliott/50 60.00 125.00
19 Connor Cook/99 5.00 12.00
20 Devontae Booker/99 5.00 12.00
21 Paxton Lynch/50 5.00 12.00
22 Christian Hackenberg/99 4.00 10.00
23 Kenneth Dixon/99 4.00 10.00
24 Corey Coleman/99 6.00 15.00
25 Chris Moore/99 5.00 12.00
26 Kenyan Drake/99 6.00 15.00
27 Trevor Davis/99 4.00 10.00
28 Will Fuller V/99 6.00 15.00
29 Malcolm Mitchell/99 4.00 10.00
30 Braxton Miller/99 4.00 10.00
31 Alex Collins/99 5.00 12.00
32 Josh Doctson/99 5.00 12.00
33 Ricardo Louis/99 4.00 10.00
34 Leonte Carroo/99 4.00 10.00
35 Demarcus Robinson/99 4.00 10.00
36 Laquon Treadwell/99 5.00 12.00
37 Pharoh Cooper/99 4.00 10.00
38 C.J. Prosise/99 4.00 10.00
39 Paul Perkins/99 4.00 10.00
40 Keenan Reynolds/99 5.00 12.00
41 Moritz Bohringer/99 4.00 10.00
42 Tajae Sharpe/99 5.00 12.00

2016 Panini Plates and Patches Rookie Patch Autographs Blue

*BLUE/50: .5X TO 1.2X BASIC PATCH AU/99
*BLUE/25: .5X TO 1.2X BASIC PATCH AU/50
2 Dak Prescott/50 30.00 80.00

2016 Panini Plates and Patches Rookie Patch Autographs Green

*GREEN/25: .6X TO 1.5X BASIC PATCH AU/99
2 Dak Prescott/25 40.00 100.00

2016 Panini Plates and Patches Rookie Patches

*BLUE/50: .5X TO 1.2X BASIC PATCH/75
*GREEN/25: .6X TO 1.5X BASIC PATCH/75
1 Alex Collins 3.00 8.00
2 Braxton Miller 2.50 6.00
3 C.J. Prosise 2.50 6.00
4 Cardale Jones 2.50 6.00
5 Carson Wentz 10.00 25.00
6 Chris Moore 3.00 8.00
7 Christian Hackenberg 2.50 6.00
8 Cody Kessler 2.50 6.00
9 Connor Cook 3.00 8.00
10 Corey Coleman 4.00 10.00
11 Dak Prescott 12.00 30.00
12 DeAndre Washington 2.50 6.00
13 Demarcus Robinson 2.50 6.00
14 Derrick Henry 56.00 15.00
15 Devontae Booker 3.00 8.00
16 Ezekiel Elliott 12.00 30.00
17 Hunter Henry 3.00 8.00
18 Jared Goff 8.00 20.00
19 Joey Bosa 5.00 12.00
20 Jonathan Williams 3.00 8.00
21 Jordan Howard 5.00 12.00
22 Josh Doctson 3.00 8.00
23 Keenan Reynolds 3.00 8.00
24 Kenneth Dixon 2.50 6.00
25 Kenyan Drake 4.00 10.00
26 Laquon Treadwell 3.00 8.00
27 Leonte Carroo 2.50 6.00
28 Michael Thomas 5.00 12.00
29 Moritz Bohringer 2.50 6.00
30 Paul Perkins 2.50 6.00
31 Paxton Lynch 2.50 6.00
32 Pharoh Cooper 2.50 6.00
33 Ricardo Louis 2.50 6.00
34 Sterling Shepard 5.00 12.00
35 Tajae Sharpe 3.00 8.00
36 Trevor Davis 2.50 6.00
37 Tyler Boyd 3.00 8.00
38 Tyler Ervin 2.50 6.00
39 Wendell Smallwood 2.50 6.00
40 Will Fuller V 4.00 10.00

2016 Panini Plates and Patches Rookie Quad Patches

*BLUE/25: .5X TO 1.2X BASIC PATCH/50
1 Alex Collins 4.00 10.00
2 Braxton Miller 3.00 8.00
3 C.J. Prosise 3.00 8.00
4 Cardale Jones 3.00 8.00
5 Carson Wentz 12.00 30.00
6 Chris Moore 4.00 10.00
7 Christian Hackenberg 3.00 8.00
8 Cody Kessler 3.00 8.00
9 Connor Cook 4.00 10.00
10 Corey Coleman 5.00 12.00
11 Dak Prescott 15.00 40.00
12 DeAndre Washington 3.00 8.00
13 Demarcus Robinson 3.00 8.00
14 Derrick Henry 8.00 20.00
15 Devontae Booker 4.00 10.00
16 Ezekiel Elliott 15.00 40.00
17 Hunter Henry 4.00 10.00
18 Jared Goff 10.00 25.00
19 Joey Bosa 6.00 15.00
20 Jonathan Williams 4.00 10.00
21 Jordan Howard 6.00 15.00
22 Josh Doctson 4.00 10.00
23 Keenan Reynolds 4.00 10.00
24 Kenneth Dixon 3.00 8.00
25 Kenyan Drake 5.00 12.00
26 Laquon Treadwell 4.00 10.00
27 Leonte Carroo 3.00 8.00
28 Michael Thomas 6.00 15.00
29 Moritz Bohringer 3.00 8.00
30 Paul Perkins 3.00 8.00
31 Paxton Lynch 3.00 8.00
32 Pharoh Cooper 3.00 8.00
33 Ricardo Louis 3.00 8.00
34 Sterling Shepard 6.00 15.00
35 Tajae Sharpe 4.00 10.00
36 Trevor Davis 3.00 8.00
37 Tyler Boyd 4.00 10.00
38 Tyler Ervin 3.00 8.00
39 Wendell Smallwood 3.00 8.00
40 Will Fuller V 5.00 12.00

2016 Panini Plates and Patches Signal Callers Autographs

3 Ben Roethlisberger/25
4 Andrew Luck/25 50.00 100.00
5 Eli Manning/25
6 Drew Brees/25 50.00 100.00
8 Carson Wentz/25 60.00 150.00
9 Dak Prescott/25 50.00 100.00
10 Cody Kessler/50 6.00 15.00

2016 Panini Plates and Patches Upper Echelon Autographs

1 Trevor Siemian/50 8.00 20.00
2 DeAngelo Williams/50 8.00 20.00
3 Tyrod Taylor/99 8.00 20.00
4 Devonta Freeman/50 10.00 25.00
5 Roger Craig/99 8.00 20.00
6 Randy White/50 10.00 25.00
7 Jordan Matthews/99 8.00 20.00
8 Dez Bryant/25 15.00 40.00
9 Latavius Murray/99 6.00 15.00
11 Marvin Jones Jr./50 8.00 20.00
12 Doug Baldwin/25 12.00 30.00
13 Stefon Diggs/99 8.00 20.00
14 Ickey Woods/99 6.00 15.00
15 J.J. Watt/25 25.00 50.00
16 Lamar Miller/50 8.00 20.00
17 Eddie Lacy/99 6.00 15.00
18 Dan Hampton/99 6.00 15.00
19 Kelvin Benjamin/99 8.00 20.00
20 Greg Olsen/99 8.00 20.00
21 Carson Wentz/50
22 Dak Prescott/99 30.00 60.00
23 Derrick Henry/50 15.00 40.00
24 Jacoby Drissett/99 6.00 15.00
25 Jared Goff/50 40.00 100.00
26 Wendell Smallwood/99 5.00 12.00
27 Sterling Shepard/99 6.00 15.00
28 Tyler Boyd/99 6.00 15.00
29 Jordan Howard/99 12.00 30.00
30 Michael Thomas/50 12.00 30.00
31 Ezekiel Elliott/50 75.00 150.00
32 Devontae Booker/99 6.00 15.00
33 Tajae Sharpe/50 8.00 20.00
34 Kenneth Dixon/99 5.00 12.00
35 Corey Coleman/50 10.00 25.00
36 Kenyan Drake/99 8.00 20.00
37 Will Fuller V/99 8.00 20.00
38 Malcolm Mitchell/99 5.00 12.00
39 Josh Doctson/50 8.00 20.00
40 Jalen Ramsey/99 8.00 20.00

2016 Panini Plates and Patches Upper Echelon Autographs Blue

*BLUE/50: .5X TO 1.2X BASIC AU/99
*BLUE/25: .5X TO 1.2X BASIC AU/50
22 Dak Prescott/50 30.00 80.00
31 Ezekiel Elliott/25 100.00 200.00

2017 Panini Plates and Patches

1 Aaron Donald 2.00 5.00
2 Aaron Rodgers 4.00 10.00
3 Adam Thielen 2.00 5.00
4 Adrian Peterson 2.00 5.00
5 A.J. Green 2.00 5.00
6 Alex Smith 1.50 4.00
7 Allen Robinson 1.50 4.00
8 Alshon Jeffery 1.50 4.00
9 Amari Cooper 2.00 5.00
10 Ameer Abdullah 1.25 3.00
11 Andrew Luck 2.50 6.00
12 Andy Dalton 1.50 4.00
13 Antonio Brown 2.00 5.00
14 Ben Roethlisberger 2.00 5.00
15 Blake Bortles 1.25 3.00
16 Brandin Cooks 1.50 4.00
17 Jimmy Garoppolo 8.00 20.00
18 Isaiah Crowell 1.25 3.00
19 Jermaine Kearse 1.25 3.00
20 Cam Newton 2.00 5.00
21 Carlos Hyde 1.25 3.00
22 Carson Palmer 1.50 4.00
23 Carson Wentz 2.50 6.00
24 C.J. Anderson 1.50 4.00
25 Clay Matthews 1.50 4.00
26 Dak Prescott 2.00 5.00
27 Jeremy Maclin 1.25 3.00
28 Zach Ertz 1.50 4.00
29 David Johnson 2.00 5.00
30 DeMarco Murray 1.50 4.00
31 Demaryius Thomas 1.50 4.00
32 Derek Carr 2.00 5.00
33 Devonta Freeman 1.50 4.00
34 Dez Bryant 2.00 5.00
35 Doug Baldwin 1.50 4.00
36 Drew Brees 2.00 5.00
37 Duke Johnson 1.25 3.00
38 Eddie Lacy 1.25 3.00
39 Eli Manning 1.50 4.00
40 Ezekiel Elliott 2.50 6.00
41 Frank Gore 1.50 4.00
42 Gerald McCoy 1.25 3.00
43 Golden Tate III 1.25 3.00
44 Greg Olsen 1.50 4.00
45 Jadeveon Clowney 1.25 3.00
46 Jalen Ramsey 1.25 3.00
47 Jamie Collins 1.25 3.00
48 Jameis Winston 1.50 4.00
49 Jarvis Landry 1.50 4.00
50 Jason Witten 1.50 4.00
51 Jay Ajayi 1.50 4.00
52 Jay Cutler 1.25 3.00
53 Jeremy Hill 1.25 3.00
54 J.J. Watt 2.00 5.00
55 Joe Flacco 1.50 4.00
56 Joey Bosa 2.00 5.00
57 Jordan Howard 2.00 5.00
58 Jordan Matthews 1.25 3.00
59 Jordy Nelson 1.50 4.00
60 Julio Jones 2.00 5.00
61 Kelvin Benjamin 1.50 4.00
62 Zach Miller 1.25 3.00
63 Khalil Mack 2.00 5.00
64 Kirk Cousins 2.00 5.00
65 Lamar Miller 1.25 3.00
66 Larry Fitzgerald 1.50 4.00
67 Latavius Murray 1.25 3.00
68 Leonard Floyd 1.25 3.00
69 Leonard Williams 1.25 3.00
70 LeSean McCoy 2.00 5.00
71 Le'Veon Bell 1.50 4.00
72 Luke Kuechly 1.50 4.00
73 Marcus Mariota 2.00 5.00
74 Mark Ingram 1.50 4.00
75 Marshawn Lynch 1.50 4.00
76 Matt Forte 1.25 3.00
77 Matt Ryan 1.50 4.00
78 Matthew Stafford 1.50 4.00
79 Melvin Gordon 1.50 4.00
80 Mike Evans 1.50 4.00
81 Elvis Dumervil 1.25 3.00
82 Odell Beckham Jr. 2.00 5.00
83 Brandon Marshall 1.25 3.00
84 Philip Rivers 2.00 5.00
85 Richard Sherman 2.00 5.00
86 Rishard Matthews 1.25 3.00
87 Robert Kelley 1.25 3.00
88 Rob Gronkowski 2.00 5.00
89 Russell Wilson 2.50 6.00
90 Stefon Diggs 1.50 4.00
91 Sammy Watkins 2.00 5.00
92 Terrelle Pryor Sr. 1.25 3.00
93 Terrell Suggs 1.25 3.00
94 Todd Gurley II 2.00 5.00
95 Tom Brady 5.00 12.00
96 Travis Kelce 2.00 5.00
97 Jared Goff 2.00 5.00
98 T.Y. Hilton 1.50 4.00
99 Tyreek Hill 2.00 5.00
100 Tyrod Taylor 1.50 4.00
101 Emmitt Smith RET 4.00 10.00
102 Archie Manning RET 2.00 5.00
103 Barry Sanders RET 4.00 10.00
104 Brett Favre RET 5.00 12.00
105 Brian Urlacher RET 2.50 6.00
106 Bruce Smith RET 2.00 5.00
107 Calvin Johnson RET 2.50 6.00
108 Carl Eller RET 1.50 4.00
109 Champ Bailey RET 2.00 5.00
110 Charles Haley RET 2.50 6.00
111 Charles Woodson RET 2.50 6.00
112 Clinton Portis RET 1.50 4.00
113 Curtis Martin RET 2.00 5.00
114 Dan Fouts RET 2.00 5.00
115 Dan Hampton RET 1.50 4.00
116 Dan Marino RET 5.00 12.00
117 Deion Sanders RET 2.00 5.00
118 Derrick Brooks RET 1.50 4.00
119 Don Maynard RET 2.00 5.00
120 Doug Williams RET 2.00 5.00
121 Earl Campbell RET 2.50 6.00
122 Ed Reed RET 2.00 5.00
123 Eddie George RET 2.00 5.00
124 Edgerrin James RET 2.00 5.00
125 Fran Tarkenton RET 2.50 6.00
126 Franco Harris RET 2.50 6.00
127 Fred Biletnikoff RET 2.50 6.00
128 Fred Taylor RET 2.00 5.00
129 Heath Miller RET 1.50 4.00
130 Hines Ward RET 2.00 5.00
131 Howie Long RET 2.50 6.00
132 Ickey Woods RET 1.50 4.00
133 Jason Taylor RET 1.50 4.00
134 Jerome Bettis RET 2.50 6.00
135 Jevon Kearse RET 1.50 4.00
136 Jerry Rice RET 4.00 10.00
137 Jim Kelly RET 2.50 6.00
138 Jim Zorn RET 1.50 4.00
139 Joe Theismann RET 2.50 6.00
140 John Riggins RET 2.00 5.00
141 Ken Anderson RET 1.50 4.00
142 Jeremy Shockey RET 1.50 4.00
143 Kevin Greene RET 2.00 5.00
144 Kurt Warner RET 2.00 5.00
145 LaDainian Tomlinson RET 2.00 5.00
146 Lance Alworth RET 2.00 5.00
147 Lawrence Taylor RET 2.50 6.00
148 Len Dawson RET 2.50 6.00
149 Marcus Allen RET 2.00 5.00
150 Mark Brunell RET 2.00 5.00
151 Mark Gastineau RET 1.50 4.00
152 Michael Irvin RET 2.50 6.00
153 Michael Strahan RET 2.00 5.00
154 Michael Vick RET 2.00 5.00
155 Mike Singletary RET 2.50 6.00
156 Morten Andersen RET 1.50 4.00
157 Otto Graham RET 2.00 5.00
158 Paul Warfield RET 2.00 5.00
159 Peyton Manning RET 5.00 12.00
160 Phil Simms RET 2.00 5.00
161 Priest Holmes RET 1.50 4.00
162 Randall Cunningham RET 2.00 5.00
163 Randy Moss RET 2.00 5.00
164 Ray Lewis RET 2.50 6.00
165 Ricky Williams RET 2.00 5.00
166 Roger Craig RET 2.00 5.00
167 Roger Staubach RET 3.00 8.00
168 Ron Jaworski RET 2.00 5.00
169 Steve Largent RET 2.50 6.00
170 Steve Smith Sr. RET 2.00 5.00
171 Steve Young RET 3.00 8.00
172 Terrell Davis RET 2.00 5.00
173 Terry Bradshaw RET 4.00 10.00
174 Thurman Thomas RET 2.00 5.00
175 Tim Brown RET 2.50 6.00
176 Tony Dorsett RET 2.50 6.00
177 Torry Holt RET 2.00 5.00
178 Warren Moon RET 2.50 6.00
179 Warren Sapp RET 2.00 5.00
180 Ty Law RET 2.50 6.00
181 Myles Garrett RC 3.00 8.00
182 Reuben Foster RC 1.00 2.50
183 Jabrill Peppers RC 1.50 4.00
184 Solomon Thomas RC 1.00 2.50
185 Chidobe Awuzie RC 1.25 3.00
186 Jamal Adams RC 1.00 2.50
187 Taco Charlton RC 1.00 2.50
188 T.J. Watt RC 3.00 8.00
189 Jamal Agnew RC 1.00 2.50
190 Marshon Lattimore RC 1.25 3.00
191 Gerald Everett RC 1.00 2.50
192 Adam Shaheen RC 1.00 2.50
193 Cooper Rush RC 1.25 3.00
194 Eddie Jackson RC 1.25 3.00
195 Haason Reddick RC 1.00 2.50
196 Aaron Jones RC 2.50 6.00
197 Tarik Cohen RC 2.00 5.00
198 Eddie Vanderdoes RC 1.00 2.50
199 Chris Carson RC 1.50 4.00
200 Matt Breida RC 1.50 4.00
201 Zay Jones JSY AU/99 RC 5.00 12.00
202 Nathan Peterman JSY AU/99 RC 5.00 12.00
203 Christian McCaffrey JSY AU/50 RC 30.00 60.00
204 Curtis Samuel JSY AU/99 RC 5.00 12.00
205 Mitchell Trubisky JSY AU/50 RC 50.00 100.00
206 John Ross III JSY AU/99 RC 5.00 12.00
207 Joe Mixon JSY AU/99 RC 8.00 20.00
208 DeShone Kizer JSY AU/50 RC 5.00 12.00
209 Carlos Henderson JSY AU/99 RC 4.00 10.00
210 Kenny Golladay JSY AU/99 RC 6.00 15.00
211 Jamaal Williams JSY AU/99 RC 4.00 10.00
212 Deshaun Watson JSY AU/50 RC 100.00 200.00
213 D'Onta Foreman JSY AU/99 RC 5.00 12.00
214 Marlon Mack JSY AU/99 RC 6.00 15.00
215 Leonard Fournette JSY AU/50 RC
216 Dede Westbrook JSY AU/99 RC 4.00 10.00
217 Patrick Mahomes II JSY AU/50 RC 150.00 300.00
218 Kareem Hunt JSY AU/99 RC 8.00 20.00
219 Mike Williams JSY AU/50 RC 8.00 20.00
220 Cooper Kupp JSY AU/99 RC 6.00 15.00
221 Josh Reynolds JSY AU/50 RC 5.00 12.00
222 Dalvin Cook JSY AU/50 RC
223 Alvin Kamara JSY AU/99 RC 40.00 80.00
224 Evan Engram JSY AU/99 RC 5.00 12.00
225 Davis Webb JSY AU/99 RC 4.00 10.00
226 Wayne Gallman JSY AU/99 RC 5.00 12.00
227 ArDarius Stewart JSY AU/99 RC 4.00 10.00
228 Mack Hollins JSY AU/99 RC 4.00 10.00
229 JuJu Smith-Schuster JSY AU/99 RC 15.00 40.00
230 James Conner JSY AU/99 RC 8.00 20.00
231 R. Joshua Dobbs JSY AU/99 RC 5.00 12.00
232 C.J. Beathard JSY AU/99 RC 4.00 10.00
233 Joe Williams JSY AU/99 RC 4.00 10.00
234 Amara Darboh JSY AU/99 RC 4.00 10.00
235 O.J. Howard JSY AU/99 RC 5.00 12.00
236 David Njoku JSY AU/99 RC 5.00 12.00
237 Ryan Switzer JSY AU/99 RC 5.00 12.00
238 Corey Davis JSY AU/99 RC 6.00 15.00
239 Taywan Taylor JSY AU/99 RC 4.00 10.00
240 Samaje Perine JSY AU/99 RC 4.00 10.00

2017 Panini Plates and Patches Blue

*BLUE/50: .5X TO 1.2X BASIC CARDS/99
*BLUE RET/50: .5X TO 1.2X BASIC CARDS/75
*BLUE ROOK/50: .5X TO 1.2X BASIC CARDS/75
*ROOK JSY AU/50: .5X TO 1.2X BASIC JSY AU/99
*ROOK JSY AU/25: .5X TO 1.2X BASIC JSY AU/50

2017 Panini Plates and Patches Green

*GREEN VET/25: .6X TO 1.5X BASIC CARDS/99
*GREEN RET/50: .6X TO 1.5X BASIC CARDS/75
*GREEN ROOK/50: .6X TO 1.5X BASIC CARDS/75
*ROOK JSY AU/25: .6X TO 1.5X BASIC JSY AU/99
223 Alvin Kamara JSY AU/25 100.00 200.00

2017 Panini Plates and Patches Canton Calligraphy

*BLUE/49: .5X TO 1.2X BASIC AU/99
*BLUE/25: .5X TO 1.2X BASIC AU/49-50
*BLUE/20: .6X TO 1.5X BASIC AU/50
*GREEN/25: .6X TO 1.5X BASIC AU/99
1 LaDainian Tomlinson/25
2 Jason Taylor/25 10.00 25.00
3 Terrell Davis/25 EXCH 12.00 30.00
4 Morten Andersen/99 6.00 15.00
6 Tim Brown/25
7 Michael Strahan/25
8 Bob Lilly/50 10.00 25.00
10 Chris Doleman/50 8.00 20.00
11 Warren Sapp/25
12 Kellen Winslow/50 10.00 25.00
13 Marshall Faulk/15
15 Dick LeBeau/49 8.00 20.00
16 Floyd Little/99 6.00 15.00
17 Alan Page/49 8.00 20.00
18 Thurman Thomas/25 12.00 30.00
20 Warren Moon/25 15.00 40.00
21 Carl Eller/99 6.00 15.00
22 Marcus Allen/25 12.00 30.00
24 Charlie Joiner/99 6.00 15.00
26 Jack Youngblood/99 6.00 15.00
27 Howie Long/25
28 Eric Dickerson/25 15.00 40.00
30 Dan Fouts/25

2017 Panini Plates and Patches Double Coverage Patches

*BLUE/25: .5X TO 1.2X BASIC JSY/50
1 D.Freeman/M.Ryan 5.00 12.00
2 K.Golladay/M.Stafford 6.00 15.00
3 A.Darboh/D.Baldwin 5.00 12.00
4 C.Anderson/P.Lynch 5.00 12.00
5 R.Kelley/S.Perine 4.00 10.00
6 A.Kamara/M.Thomas 15.00 40.00
7 C.McCaffrey/G.Olsen 10.00 25.00
8 J.Goff/K.Warner 6.00 15.00
9 D.Cook/S.Diggs 8.00 20.00
10 J.Howard/M.Trubisky 12.00 30.00
11 J.Winston/O.Howard 5.00 12.00
12 K.Hunt/P.Mahomes 10.00 25.00
13 J.Conner/J.SmthSchstr 8.00 20.00
14 C.Kupp/J.Goff 6.00 15.00
15 D.Kizer/D.Johnson 4.00 10.00
16 J.Hill/J.Mixon 8.00 20.00
17 H.Henry/M.Williams 6.00 15.00
18 B.Bortles/L.Fournette 12.00 30.00
19 C.Davis/M.Mariota 8.00 20.00
20 F.Gore/M.Mack 6.00 15.00

2017 Panini Plates and Patches Full Coverage Patches

*BLUE/25: .5X TO 1.2X BASIC JSY/50
1 Alvin Kamara 12.00 30.00
2 Amara Darboh 3.00 8.00
3 ArDarius Stewart 3.00 8.00
4 C.J. Beathard 3.00 8.00
5 Carlos Henderson 3.00 8.00
6 Chris Godwin 4.00 10.00
7 Christian McCaffrey 8.00 20.00
8 Cooper Kupp 5.00 12.00
9 Corey Davis 5.00 12.00
10 Curtis Samuel 4.00 10.00
11 Dalvin Cook 6.00 15.00
12 Davis Webb 3.00 8.00
13 Dede Westbrook 3.00 8.00
14 Deshaun Watson 12.00 30.00
15 DeShone Kizer 3.00 8.00
16 D'Onta Foreman 4.00 10.00
17 Evan Engram 4.00 10.00
18 Jamaal Williams 3.00 8.00
19 James Conner 6.00 15.00
20 Ryan Switzer 4.00 10.00
21 Joe Mixon 6.00 15.00
22 Jabrill Peppers 5.00 12.00
23 John Ross III 4.00 10.00
24 Josh Reynolds 3.00 8.00
25 JuJu Smith-Schuster 6.00 15.00
26 Kareem Hunt 6.00 15.00
27 Kenny Golladay 5.00 12.00
28 Leonard Fournette 10.00 25.00
29 Mack Hollins 3.00 8.00
30 Marlon Mack 5.00 12.00
31 Mike Williams 5.00 12.00
32 Mitchell Trubisky 10.00 25.00
33 Nathan Peterman 4.00 10.00
34 O.J. Howard 4.00 10.00
35 Patrick Mahomes II 10.00 25.00
36 R. Joshua Dobbs 4.00 10.00
37 Samaje Perine 3.00 8.00
38 Taywan Taylor 3.00 8.00
39 Wayne Gallman 4.00 10.00
40 Zay Jones 4.00 10.00

2017 Panini Plates and Patches Gridiron Gear Patches

*BLUE/25: .5X TO 1.2X BASIC AU/50
*BLUE/20: .6X TO 1.5X BASIC AU/20
*BLUE/15: .5X TO 1.2X BASIC AU/25
1 Jerome Bettis/50 5.00 12.00
2 Hines Ward/50 4.00 10.00
3 Kurt Warner/50 4.00 10.00
4 Troy Aikman/25 8.00 20.00
5 Barry Sanders/25 10.00 25.00
6 Brett Favre/50 10.00 25.00
7 Dan Marino/50 10.00 25.00
8 Fran Tarkenton/50 5.00 12.00
9 Franco Harris/50 5.00 12.00
10 Ed Reed/25 5.00 12.00
11 Joe Theismann/50 5.00 12.00
13 Bo Jackson/25 8.00 20.00
14 Thurman Thomas/50 4.00 10.00
15 Tony Romo/50 4.00 10.00
16 Peyton Manning/25 12.00 30.00
17 Phil Simms/50 4.00 10.00
18 Priest Holmes/50 3.00 8.00
19 Rich Gannon/50 3.00 8.00
20 Terrell Davis/50 4.00 10.00

2017 Panini Plates and Patches Gridiron Gear Patches Autographs

14 Thurman Thomas/25 15.00 40.00
17 Phil Simms/25 15.00 40.00
18 Priest Holmes/25 12.00 30.00
19 Rich Gannon/25 12.00 30.00

2017 Panini Plates and Patches Marquee Marks

*BLUE/25: .5X TO 1.2X BASIC AU/50
8 Ray Lewis/25 40.00 80.00
9 Derek Carr/15 20.00 50.00
10 J.J. Watt/25
12 Edgerrin James/50 10.00 25.00
13 Andre Reed/25 12.00 30.00
14 Dak Prescott/25 EXCH 15.00 40.00
15 David Johnson/25
16 Carlos Hyde/50 8.00 20.00
17 Earl Campbell/25
19 Kirk Cousins/50 12.00 30.00
20 Luke Kuechly/50 10.00 25.00

2017 Panini Plates and Patches Plates and Patches

*BLUE/25: .5X TO 1.2X BASIC JSY/50
*BLUE/15: .5X TO 1.2X BASIC JSY/25
1 Matt Ryan/25 5.00 12.00
2 Doug Baldwin/50 4.00 10.00
3 Jameis Winston/50 4.00 10.00
5 Tyreek Hill/25 6.00 15.00
6 Tevin Coleman/25 5.00 12.00
7 James White/35 4.00 10.00
8 Paul Perkins/50 3.00 8.00
9 Jay Ajayi/50 4.00 10.00
10 Carson Wentz/50 6.00 15.00
11 Jared Goff/50 5.00 12.00
12 Blake Bortles/50 3.00 8.00
13 Danny Woodhead/25 5.00 12.00
14 Amari Cooper/50 5.00 12.00
15 Ameer Abdullah/50 3.00 8.00
16 Joey Bosa/50 5.00 12.00
17 Dak Prescott/50 5.00 12.00
18 Derrick Henry/50 4.00 10.00
19 Jarvis Landry/50 4.00 10.00
20 Melvin Gordon/50 4.00 10.00

2017 Panini Plates and Patches Plates and Patches Autographs

5 Tyreek Hill/25
7 James White/25 15.00 40.00
8 Paul Perkins/25 12.00 30.00
13 Danny Woodhead/25 15.00 40.00
17 Dak Prescott/25 20.00 50.00
20 Melvin Gordon/25 15.00 40.00

2017 Panini Plates and Patches Playmakers Autographs

*BLUE/50: .5X TO 1.2X BASIC AU/99
*BLUE/25: .5X TO 1.2X BASIC AU/50
1 Terrell Suggs/25 EXCH 25.00 50.00
2 Sterling Sharpe/50
3 Jordy Nelson/25 12.00 30.00
6 Ricky Williams/50 10.00 25.00
7 Lawrence Taylor/25
9 Todd Gurley II/25 15.00 40.00
10 Gerald McCoy/99 6.00 15.00
12 Landon Collins/50 8.00 20.00
13 Tyreek Hill/50 12.00 30.00
15 Aqib Talib/50 8.00 20.00
17 Earl Thomas III/25 12.00 30.00
18 Rod Woodson/50
19 Torry Holt/50 EXCH 10.00 25.00
20 Doug Baldwin/50 10.00 25.00

2017 Panini Plates and Patches Rookie Quad Patches

*BLUE/50: .5X TO 1.2X BASIC JSY/75
1 Alvin Kamara 10.00 25.00
2 Amara Darboh 2.50 6.00
3 ArDarius Stewart 2.50 6.00
4 C.J. Beathard 2.50 6.00
5 Carlos Henderson 2.50 6.00
6 David Njoku 3.00 8.00
7 Christian McCaffrey 6.00 15.00
8 Cooper Kupp 4.00 10.00
9 Corey Davis 4.00 10.00
10 Curtis Samuel 3.00 8.00
11 Dalvin Cook 5.00 12.00
12 Davis Webb 2.50 6.00
13 Dede Westbrook 2.50 6.00
14 Deshaun Watson 10.00 25.00
15 DeShone Kizer 2.50 6.00
16 D'Onta Foreman 3.00 8.00
17 Evan Engram 3.00 8.00
18 Jamaal Williams 2.50 6.00
19 James Conner 5.00 12.00
20 Ryan Switzer 3.00 8.00
21 Joe Mixon 5.00 12.00
22 Joe Williams 2.50 6.00
23 John Ross III 3.00 8.00
24 Josh Reynolds 2.50 6.00
25 JuJu Smith-Schuster 5.00 12.00
26 Kareem Hunt 6.00 15.00
27 Kenny Golladay 4.00 10.00
28 Leonard Fournette 8.00 20.00
29 Mack Hollins 2.50 6.00
30 Marlon Mack 4.00 10.00
31 Mike Williams 4.00 10.00
32 Mitchell Trubisky 8.00 20.00
33 Nathan Peterman 3.00 8.00
34 O.J. Howard 3.00 8.00
35 Patrick Mahomes II 25.00 60.00
36 R. Joshua Dobbs 3.00 8.00
37 Samaje Perine 2.50 6.00
38 Taywan Taylor 2.50 6.00
39 Wayne Gallman 3.00 8.00
40 Zay Jones 3.00 8.00

2017 Panini Plates and Patches Signal Callers Autographs

1 Matt Ryan/15 30.00 60.00
2 Derek Carr/15 20.00 50.00
3 Marcus Mariota/15 20.00 50.00
4 Jameis Winston/15
5 Matthew Stafford/15 15.00 40.00
10 Kirk Cousins/15 20.00 50.00

2017 Panini Plates and Patches Team Supreme Patches

*BLUE/25: .5X TO 1.2X BASIC JSY/50
1 Andy Dalton 4.00 10.00
2 Blake Bortles 3.00 8.00
3 Michael Thomas 5.00 12.00
4 Corey Coleman 3.00 8.00
5 David Johnson 5.00 12.00
6 DeAndre Hopkins 4.00 10.00
7 Devonta Freeman 4.00 10.00
8 Doug Martin 4.00 10.00
9 Frank Gore 4.00 10.00
10 Hunter Henry 3.00 8.00
11 Jadeveon Clowney 3.00 8.00
12 Jameis Winston 4.00 10.00
13 Earl Thomas III 4.00 10.00
14 Jordan Howard 5.00 12.00
15 Jimmy Garoppolo 6.00 15.00
16 Jordan Reed 3.00 8.00
17 Keenan Allen 4.00 10.00
18 Leonard Williams 3.00 8.00
19 Melvin Gordon 4.00 10.00
20 Tevin Coleman 4.00 10.00

2017 Panini Plates and Patches Team Supreme Patches Autographs

3 Michael Thomas/25
4 Corey Coleman/25 12.00 30.00
10 Hunter Henry/25 12.00 30.00
13 Earl Thomas III/20 20.00 50.00
14 Jordan Howard/25
15 Jimmy Garoppolo/25
17 Keenan Allen/25
19 Melvin Gordon/25
20 Tevin Coleman/25

2017 Panini Plates and Patches Upper Echelon Autographs

1 Zay Jones/99 EXCH 6.00 15.00
2 Nathan Peterman/99 6.00 15.00
3 Christian McCaffrey/50 15.00 40.00
4 Mitchell Trubisky/25
5 John Ross III/99 6.00 15.00
6 DeShone Kizer/25
8 D'Onta Foreman/99 6.00 15.00
9 Leonard Fournette/25
10 Dede Westbrook/99 5.00 12.00
11 Patrick Mahomes II/25 200.00 300.00
12 Kareem Hunt/99 10.00 25.00
13 Alvin Kamara/99 20.00 50.00
14 Evan Engram/99 6.00 15.00
15 C.J. Beathard/99 5.00 12.00
16 Amara Darboh/99 5.00 12.00
17 O.J. Howard/99 6.00 15.00
18 Corey Davis/50 10.00 25.00
19 Taywan Taylor/99 5.00 12.00
20 Samaje Perine/99 5.00 12.00

2018 Panini Plates and Patches

1 Sammy Watkins 2.00 5.00
2 David Johnson 2.00 5.00
3 Patrick Peterson 1.25 3.00
4 Jermaine Gresham 1.25 3.00
5 Larry Fitzgerald 1.50 4.00
6 Matt Ryan 1.50 4.00
7 Julio Jones 2.00 5.00
8 Devonta Freeman 1.50 4.00
9 Tevin Coleman 1.25 3.00
10 Mohamed Sanu 1.25 3.00
11 Vic Beasley Jr. 1.25 3.00
12 Desmond Trufant 1.25 3.00
13 Austin Hooper 1.25 3.00
14 Joe Flacco 1.50 4.00
15 Terrell Suggs 1.25 3.00
16 Alex Collins 1.25 3.00
17 Michael Crabtree 1.25 3.00
18 Willie Snead 1.50 4.00
19 Golden Tate III 1.25 3.00
20 LeSean McCoy 2.00 5.00
21 Kelvin Benjamin 1.50 4.00
22 Zay Jones 1.25 3.00
23 Charles Clay 1.25 3.00
24 Cam Newton 2.00 5.00
25 Christian McCaffrey 2.00 5.00
26 Greg Olsen 1.50 4.00
27 Devin Funchess 1.25 3.00
28 Luke Kuechly 1.50 4.00
29 Mitchell Trubisky 2.00 5.00
30 Jordan Howard 2.00 5.00
31 Allen Robinson II 1.50 4.00
32 Tarik Cohen 1.50 4.00
33 Taylor Gabriel 1.25 3.00
34 Khalil Mack 2.00 5.00
35 Roquan Smith 4.00 10.00
36 Trey Burton 1.25 3.00
37 Andy Dalton 1.50 4.00
38 A.J. Green 2.00 5.00
39 Joe Mixon 1.50 4.00
40 John Ross III 1.50 4.00
41 Geno Atkins 1.25 3.00
42 Tyrod Taylor 1.50 4.00
43 Carlos Hyde 1.25 3.00
44 Jarvis Landry 1.50 4.00
45 David Njoku 1.25 3.00
46 Myles Garrett 2.00 5.00
47 Dak Prescott 2.00 5.00
48 Ezekiel Elliott 2.50 6.00
49 Allen Hurns 1.25 3.00
50 Sean Lee 1.50 4.00
51 DeMarcus Lawrence 1.25 3.00
52 Zack Martin 1.25 3.00
53 Cole Beasley 1.50 4.00
54 Jaylon Smith 1.25 3.00
55 Case Keenum 1.50 4.00
56 Phillip Lindsay 5.00 12.00
57 Todd Davis 1.25 3.00
58 Emmanuel Sanders 2.00 5.00
59 Von Miller 1.50 4.00
60 Matthew Stafford 1.50 4.00
61 Kenny Golladay 1.25 3.00
62 Marvin Jones Jr. 1.25 3.00
63 Theo Riddick 1.25 3.00
64 Ezekiel Ansah 1.25 3.00
65 Aaron Rodgers 4.00 10.00
66 Jamaal Williams 1.25 3.00
67 Clay Matthews 1.50 4.00
68 Davante Adams 1.50 4.00
69 Randall Cobb 1.50 4.00
70 Jimmy Graham 2.00 5.00
71 Geronimo Allison 1.25 3.00
72 Aaron Jones 1.50 4.00
73 Deshaun Watson 2.50 6.00
74 Lamar Miller 1.25 3.00
75 DeAndre Hopkins 1.50 4.00
76 Will Fuller V 1.25 3.00
77 J.J. Watt 2.00 5.00
78 Andrew Luck 2.50 6.00
79 Jordan Wilkins 1.50 4.00
80 Marlon Mack 1.25 3.00
81 T.Y. Hilton 1.50 4.00
82 Jack Doyle 1.25 3.00
83 Blake Bortles 1.25 3.00
84 Leonard Fournette 2.00 5.00
85 Keelan Cole 1.25 3.00
86 Jalen Ramsey 1.50 4.00
87 Calais Campbell 1.25 3.00
88 Patrick Mahomes II 8.00 20.00
89 Kareem Hunt 1.50 4.00
90 Tyreek Hill 2.00 5.00
91 Travis Kelce 2.00 5.00
92 Eric Berry 1.50 4.00
93 Jared Goff 2.00 5.00
94 Todd Gurley II 2.00 5.00
95 Brandin Cooks 1.50 4.00
96 Aaron Donald 2.00 5.00
97 Ndamukong Suh 1.50 4.00
98 Cooper Kupp 1.50 4.00
99 Marcus Peters 1.25 3.00
100 Robert Woods 1.50 4.00
101 Philip Rivers 2.00 5.00
102 Melvin Gordon III 1.50 4.00
103 Keenan Allen 1.50 4.00
104 Derwin James 2.50 6.00
105 Mike Williams 1.25 3.00
106 Casey Hayward 1.25 3.00
107 Hunter Henry 1.25 3.00
108 Joey Bosa 2.00 5.00
109 Ryan Tannehill 1.50 4.00
110 Kenyan Drake 1.25 3.00
111 Kenny Stills 1.25 3.00
112 Cameron Wake 1.25 3.00
113 Minkah Fitzpatrick 2.50 6.00
114 Kirk Cousins 2.00 5.00
115 Dalvin Cook 1.50 4.00
116 Stefon Diggs 1.50 4.00
117 Adam Thielen 2.00 5.00
118 Anthony Barr 1.25 3.00
119 Harrison Smith 2.00 5.00
120 Kyle Rudolph 1.25 3.00
121 Xavier Rhodes 1.25 3.00
122 Tom Brady 5.00 12.00
123 James White 1.50 4.00
124 Julian Edelman 2.00 5.00
125 Rob Gronkowski 2.00 5.00
126 Chris Hogan 1.25 3.00
127 Rex Burkhead 1.25 3.00
128 Devin McCourty 1.25 3.00
129 Stephen Gostkowski 1.25 3.00
130 Drew Brees 2.00 5.00
131 Alvin Kamara 1.50 4.00
132 Michael Thomas 2.00 5.00
133 Mark Ingram II 1.50 4.00
134 Ted Ginn Jr. 1.25 3.00
135 Marcus Davenport 2.50 6.00
136 Cameron Jordan 1.25 3.00
137 Marshon Lattimore 1.25 3.00
138 Eli Manning 1.50 4.00
139 Odell Beckham Jr. 2.00 5.00
140 Evan Engram 1.25 3.00
141 Sterling Shepard 1.50 4.00
142 Jonathan Stewart 1.25 3.00
143 Janoris Jenkins 1.25 3.00
144 Landon Collins 1.25 3.00
145 Olivier Vernon 1.25 3.00
146 Josh McCown 1.25 3.00
147 Isaiah Crowell 1.25 3.00
148 Robby Anderson 1.25 3.00
149 Quincy Enunwa 1.25 3.00
150 Leonard Williams 1.25 3.00
151 Derek Carr 2.00 5.00
152 Marshawn Lynch 1.50 4.00
153 Amari Cooper 2.00 5.00
154 Jordy Nelson 1.50 4.00
155 Jared Cook 1.25 3.00
156 Carson Wentz 2.50 6.00
157 Jay Ajayi 1.50 4.00
158 Alshon Jeffery 1.50 4.00
159 Dallas Goedert 1.50 4.00
160 Nelson Agholor 1.25 3.00
161 Darren Sproles 1.25 3.00
162 Chris Long 1.25 3.00
163 Jason Peters 1.25 3.00
164 Ben Roethlisberger 2.00 5.00
165 Le'Veon Bell 1.50 4.00
166 JuJu Smith-Schuster 2.00 5.00
167 Antonio Brown 2.00 5.00
168 T.J. Watt 1.50 4.00
169 James Conner 2.00 5.00
170 Jesse James 1.25 3.00
171 Terrell Edmunds 4.00 10.00
172 Jimmy Garoppolo 2.50 6.00
173 Richard Sherman 2.00 5.00
174 Marquise Goodwin 1.25 3.00
175 Pierre Garcon 1.50 4.00
176 Nick Mullens 4.00 10.00
177 Russell Wilson 2.50 6.00
178 Chris Carson 1.50 4.00
179 Doug Baldwin 1.50 4.00
180 Shaquem Griffin 2.00 5.00
181 Tyler Lockett 1.50 4.00
182 Will Dissly 1.50 4.00
183 Bobby Wagner 1.25 3.00
184 Earl Thomas III 1.50 4.00
185 Ryan Fitzpatrick 1.25 3.00
186 Mike Evans 1.50 4.00
187 O.J. Howard 1.25 3.00
188 Peyton Barber 1.25 3.00
189 DeSean Jackson 1.50 4.00
190 Marcus Mariota 2.00 5.00
191 Derrick Henry 2.00 5.00
192 Malcolm Butler 2.00 5.00
193 Corey Davis 1.50 4.00
194 Dion Lewis 1.25 3.00
195 Alex Smith 1.50 4.00
196 Jordan Reed 1.25 3.00
197 Jamison Crowder 1.25 3.00
198 Josh Norman 1.25 3.00
199 Adrian Peterson 2.00 5.00
200 Ryan Kerrigan 1.25 3.00
201 Anthony Miller JSY AU RC 6.00 15.00
202 Calvin Ridley JSY AU RC 10.00 25.00
203 Christian Kirk JSY AU RC
204 Courtland Sutton JSY AU RC 6.00 15.00
205 DaeSean Hamilton JSY AU RC 5.00 12.00
206 Dante Pettis JSY AU RC 6.00 15.00
207 Daurice Fountain JSY AU RC 5.00 12.00
208 D.J. Chark Jr. JSY AU RC 5.00 12.00
209 D.J. Moore JSY AU RC 8.00 20.00
210 Jaleel Scott JSY AU RC 4.00 10.00
211 James Washington JSY AU RC 8.00 20.00
212 J'Mon Moore JSY AU RC 4.00 10.00
213 Keke Coutee JSY AU RC 5.00 12.00
214 Marquez Valdes-Scantling JSY AU RC 5.00 12.00
215 Michael Gallup JSY AU RC 8.00 20.00
216 Tre'Quan Smith JSY AU RC
217 Hayden Hurst JSY AU RC 5.00 12.00
218 Jaylen Samuels JSY AU RC 5.00 12.00
219 Mike Gesicki JSY AU RC 5.00 12.00
220 Derrius Guice JSY AU RC 8.00 20.00
221 Ito Smith JSY AU RC 5.00 12.00
222 Kalen Ballage JSY AU RC 5.00 12.00
223 Kerryon Johnson JSY AU RC 6.00 15.00
225 Nick Chubb JSY AU RC 12.00 30.00
226 Nyheim Hines JSY AU RC 5.00 12.00
227 Rashaad Penny JSY AU RC 6.00 15.00
228 Ronald Jones II JSY AU RC 4.00 10.00
229 Royce Freeman JSY AU RC 5.00 12.00
230 Saquon Barkley JSY AU RC EXCH 60.00 125.00
231 Sony Michel JSY AU RC 15.00 40.00
232 Baker Mayfield JSY AU RC 125.00 250.00
233 Josh Allen JSY AU RC 30.00 60.00
234 Josh Rosen JSY AU RC 12.00 30.00
235 Kyle Lauletta JSY AU RC 6.00 15.00
236 Lamar Jackson JSY AU RC 50.00 100.00
237 Mason Rudolph JSY AU RC 10.00 25.00
238 Mike White JSY AU RC 5.00 12.00
239 Sam Darnold JSY AU RC 25.00 60.00
240 Bradley Chubb JSY AU RC 6.00 15.00

2018 Panini Plates and Patches Blue

*VETS/50: .5X TO 1.2X BASIC CARDS
*ROOK/50: .5X TO 1.2X BASIC JSY AU
232 Baker Mayfield JSY AU 150.00 300.00

2018 Panini Plates and Patches Green

*VETS/20: .8X TO 2X BASIC CARDS/99
*ROOK/25: .6X TO 1.5X BASIC JSY AU/99

2018 Panini Plates and Patches Purple

*VETS/30: .6X TO 1.5X BASIC CARDS/99

2018 Panini Plates and Patches All Hall Autographs

*BLUE/50: .4X TO 1X BASIC AU/40-65
*BLUE/30: .5X TO 1.2X BASIC AU/40-65
*BLUE/20: .6X TO 1.5X BASIC AU/40-65
*PURPLE/25: .5X TO 1.2X BASIC AU/40-65
*PURPLE/15-20: .6X TO 1.5X BASIC AU/40-65
1 Jack Youngblood/65 6.00 15.00
2 Don Maynard/50
4 Morten Andersen/65 6.00 15.00
5 Rod Woodson/40 10.00 25.00
6 Randy White/50 8.00 20.00
7 Rayfield Wright/65 6.00 15.00
8 Brett Favre/15
10 Troy Aikman/15

2018 Panini Plates and Patches Double Coverage Patches

*BLUE/45: .5X TO 1.2X BASIC JSY/85
*BLUE/25-30: .6X TO 1.5X BASIC JSY/85
*BLUE/25-30: .5X TO 1.2X BASIC JSY/60
*PURPLE/20: .8X TO 2X BASIC JSY/85
*PURPLE/20: .6X TO 1.5X BASIC JSY/60
1 S.Diggs/D.Cook/85 4.00 10.00
2 D.Prescott/M.Gallup/85 6.00 15.00
3 H.Hurst/J.Scott/85 4.00 10.00
4 M.Trubisky/A.Miller/85 5.00 12.00
5 J.Goff/T.Gurley II/30 8.00 20.00
6 S.Barkley/K.Lauletta/85 15.00 40.00
7 D.Watson/W.Fuller V/85 6.00 15.00
8 C.McCaffrey/D.Moore/85 6.00 15.00
9 M.Walton/J.Mixon/85 4.00 10.00
10 J.Smith-Schuster/M.Rudolph/60 8.00 20.00
11 K.Hunt/P.Mahomes II/85 12.00 30.00
12 K.Golladay/K.Johnson/85 5.00 12.00
13 K.Drake/M.Gesicki/85 4.00 10.00
14 B.Mayfield/N.Chubb/85 20.00 50.00
15 D.Johnson/J.Rosen/85 8.00 20.00
16 J.Winston/M.Evans/85 4.00 10.00
17 M.Thomas/T.Smith/85 5.00 12.00
18 B.Chubb/R.Freeman/65 6.00 15.00
19 Z.Ertz/C.Wentz/85 6.00 15.00
20 D.Chark Jr./L.Fournette/85 5.00 12.00
21 C.Ridley/D.Freeman/18 12.00 30.00
22 R.Penny/D.Baldwin/85 5.00 12.00
23 N.Hines/M.Mack/85 4.00 10.00
24 M.Gordon III/M.Williams/85 4.00 10.00
25 T.Taylor/D.Henry/85 5.00 12.00

2018 Panini Plates and Patches Full Coverage Patches

*BLUE/45: .5X TO 1.2X BASIC JSY/75-85
*BLUE/45: .4X TO 1X BASIC JSY/35-60
*BLUE/20: .8X TO 2X BASIC JSY/75-85
*PURPLE/15-20: .8X TO 2X BASIC JSY/75-85
*PURPLE/15-20: .6X TO 1.5X BASIC JSY/35-60
*PURPLE/15-20: .5X TO 1.2X BASIC JSY/25-30
1 Joey Bosa/85 4.00 10.00
2 Michael Thomas/85 4.00 10.00
3 Tyler Lockett/85 3.00 8.00
4 Devonta Freeman/30 5.00 12.00
5 Tyreek Hill/85 4.00 10.00
6 Zach Ertz/60 4.00 10.00
7 Jadeveon Clowney/75 2.50 6.00
8 Dak Prescott/85 4.00 10.00
9 Derrick Henry/85 4.00 10.00
10 Jared Goff/85 4.00 10.00
11 Josh Doctson/85 2.50 6.00
12 Carson Wentz/75 5.00 12.00
13 Jordan Howard/85 4.00 10.00
14 Alvin Kamara/85 3.00 8.00
15 Davante Adams/85 3.00 8.00
16 Cooper Kupp/85 3.00 8.00
17 Baker Mayfield/85 15.00 40.00
18 David Johnson/25 6.00 15.00
19 Will Fuller V/85 2.50 6.00
20 Ezekiel Elliott/85 5.00 12.00
21 Sam Darnold/85 10.00 25.00
22 Melvin Gordon III/85 3.00 8.00
23 Deshaun Watson/85 5.00 12.00
24 Saquon Barkley/85 12.00 30.00
25 Amari Cooper/85 4.00 10.00
26 Josh Rosen/35 8.00 20.00
27 D.J. Moore/85
28 Dalvin Cook/85 3.00 8.00
29 Josh Allen/85 6.00 15.00
30 Kareem Hunt/80 3.00 8.00

2018 Panini Plates and Patches Gridiron Gear Patches

*BLUE/45-50: .5X TO 1.2X BASIC JSY/85-99
*BLUE/25: .6X TO 1.5X BASIC JSY/85-99
*PURPLE/20: .8X TO 2X BASIC JSY/85-99
1 Deshaun Watson/99 5.00 12.00

2 Carson Wentz/99 5.00 12.00
3 Dalvin Cook/99 3.00 8.00
4 JuJu Smith-Schuster/99 4.00 10.00
5 Melvin Gordon III/99 3.00 8.00
6 Amari Cooper/99 4.00 10.00
7 Jared Goff/99 4.00 10.00
8 Stefon Diggs/99 3.00 8.00
9 Todd Gurley II/25 6.00 15.00
10 Kareem Hunt/99 3.00 8.00
11 Alvin Kamara/85 3.00 8.00
12 Davante Adams/85 3.00 8.00
13 Will Fuller V/99 2.50 6.00
14 Dak Prescott/85 4.00 10.00
15 Jordan Howard/85 4.00 10.00
16 Rob Gronkowski/85 4.00 10.00
17 Tyreek Hill/85 4.00 10.00
18 Marcus Mariota/85 4.00 10.00
19 Adam Thielen/85 4.00 10.00
20 Ezekiel Elliott/85 5.00 12.00
22 Christian McCaffrey/85 4.00 10.00
23 Michael Thomas/99 4.00 10.00
24 Mike Evans/85 3.00 8.00
25 Patrick Mahomes II/85 15.00 40.00

2018 Panini Plates and Patches Leaps and Bounds Autographs

*BLUE/50: .5X TO 1.2X BASIC AU/99
*GREEN/20: .8X TO 2X BASIC AU/99
*GREEN/20: .5X TO 1.2X BASIC AU/25
*PURPLE/30: .6X TO 1.5X BASIC AU/99
*PURPLE/15-20: .5X TO 1.2X BASIC AU/25
1 Ezekiel Elliott/15
3 Tyreek Hill/25 EXCH 25.00 50.00
4 Duke Johnson Jr./99 5.00 12.00
5 Melvin Gordon III/25 10.00 25.00
6 David Johnson/25 12.00 30.00
7 Tevin Coleman/99 5.00 12.00
8 Aaron Rodgers/15
11 Kareem Hunt/99 6.00 15.00
12 Mike Alstott/99 5.00 12.00
13 Michael Vick/25 10.00 25.00
14 Rob Gronkowski/15 EXCH 15.00 40.00

2018 Panini Plates and Patches Marquee Marks

*BLUE/50: .5X TO 1.2X BASIC AU/75
*BLUE/40: .4X TO 1X BASIC AU/50-60
*BLUE/30: .5X TO 1.2X BASIC AU/50-60
*BLUE/15: .5X TO 1.2X BASIC AU/25
*GREEN/15-20: .8X TO 2X BASIC AU/75
*GREEN/15-20: .6X TO 1.5X BASIC AU/50-60
*PURPLE/25-30: .6X TO 1.5X BASIC AU/75
*PURPLE/25-30: .5X TO 1.2X BASIC AU/50-60
*PURPLE/20: .6X TO 1.5X BASIC AU/50-60
1 David Johnson/25 12.00 30.00
2 Adam Thielen/25
5 T.Y. Hilton/15 12.00 30.00
6 JuJu Smith-Schuster/50 10.00 25.00
9 Chris Carson/60 8.00 20.00
10 Marvin Jones Jr./75 5.00 12.00
11 Aaron Rodgers/15
13 Patrick Mahomes II/20 150.00 300.00
15 Chris Thompson/75 5.00 12.00

2018 Panini Plates and Patches Playmakers Autographs

*BLUE/49-50: .5X TO 1.2X BASIC AU/75-99
*BLUE/35-40: .4X TO 1X BASIC AU/49-65
*GREEN/15-20: .8X TO 2X BASIC AU/75-99
*PURPLE/25-30: .6X TO 1.5X BASIC AU /75-99
*PURPLE/25-30: .5X TO 1.2X BASIC AU /49-65
1 Patrick Chung/99 10.00 25.00
2 Dede Westbrook/99 5.00 12.00
5 JuJu Smith-Schuster/49 10.00 25.00
6 Devin Funchess/65 6.00 15.00
8 Calais Campbell/99 5.00 12.00
9 Nelson Agholor/65 6.00 15.00
10 Carlos Hyde/75 5.00 12.00
11 Jay Ajayi/65 8.00 20.00
13 Jake Elliott/99 6.00 15.00
14 James White/75 6.00 15.00
15 Landon Collins/99 5.00 12.00
17 Greg Olsen/65 8.00 20.00
18 Corey Davis/75 6.00 15.00
19 Christian McCaffrey/49
20 Denzel Ward/75 12.00 30.00

2018 Panini Plates and Patches Signal Callers Autographs

*BLUE/50: .5X TO 1.2X BASIC AU/99
*BLUE/25: .5X TO 1.2X BASIC AU/35
*GREEN/20: .8X TO 2X BASIC AU/99
*GREEN/20: .6X TO 1.5X BASIC AU/35-50
*PURPLE/30: .6X TO 1.5X BASIC AU/99
*PURPLE/30: .5X TO 1.2X BASIC AU/35-50
*PURPLE/15: .6X TO 1.5X BASIC AU/35
*PURPLE/15: .5X TO 1.2X BASIC AU/25
*PURPLE/15: .4X TO 1X BASIC AU/20
1 Dak Prescott/15
3 Matthew Stafford/15
4 Patrick Mahomes II/25 125.00 250.00
5 Deshaun Watson/15
7 Kirk Cousins/15 15.00 40.00
9 Carson Wentz/15
10 Sam Darnold/20 75.00 150.00
11 Michael Vick/35 8.00 20.00
12 Ken Anderson/99 5.00 12.00
13 Case Keenum/50 8.00 20.00
14 Lamar Jackson/25
15 Trent Dilfer/99 5.00 12.00
16 Josh Rosen/25
17 Josh Allen/25 30.00 80.00
18 Baker Mayfield/25
20 Jared Goff/20

2018 Panini Plates and Patches Supreme Swatches

*BLUE/50: .5X TO 1.2X BASIC JSY/75-99
*BLUE/50: .4X TO 1X BASIC JSY/55
1 Nick Chubb/99 5.00 12.00
2 Lamar Jackson/99 10.00 25.00
3 Baker Mayfield/99 15.00 40.00
4 Josh Rosen/55 8.00 20.00
5 Josh Allen/99 6.00 15.00
6 Saquon Barkley/55 15.00 40.00
7 Sam Darnold/99 10.00 25.00
8 Sony Michel/99 5.00 12.00
11 Nyheim Hines/99 3.00 8.00
12 J'Mon Moore/99 2.50 6.00
13 Courtland Sutton/75 4.00 10.00
14 Kalen Ballage/99 3.00 8.00
15 Anthony Miller/55 5.00 12.00
16 Leonard Fournette/99 4.00 10.00
17 Mike Williams/99 2.50 6.00
19 James White/55 4.00 10.00
20 Calais Campbell/55 3.00 8.00

2018 Panini Plates and Patches Talented Trios Patches

*BLUE/40-50: .5X TO 1.2X BASIC JSY/99
*BLUE/40-50: .4X TO 1X BASIC JSY/50-65
*BLUE/25: .6X TO 1.5X BASIC JSY/99
*PURPLE/20: .8X TO 2X BASIC JSY/99
*PURPLE/20: .6X TO 1.5X BASIC JSY/50-65
1 Frmn/Rdly/Clmn/65 10.00 25.00
2 Prsctt/Elltt/Gllp/50 8.00 20.00
3 Kpp/Gff/Grly/50 6.00 15.00
4 Thln/Dggs/Ck/50 6.00 15.00
5 Abdllh/Glldy/Jhnsn/50 6.00 15.00
6 Mllr/Hwrd/Trbsky/50 6.00 15.00
7 Mre/McCffry/Fnchss/99 6.00 15.00
8 Jcksn/Hrst/Sctt/50 15.00 40.00
9 Sttn/Chbb/Frmn/99 5.00 12.00
10 Jhnsn/Krk/Rsn/99 10.00 25.00
11 Ptrmn/Jns/Alln/99 10.00 25.00
12 Jhnsn/Chbb/Myfld/99 20.00 50.00
13 Wsngtn/Cnnr/SthShstr/99 6.00 15.00
14 Litta/Shprd/Brkly/99 15.00 40.00
15 Chrk/Frntte/Lee/99 5.00 12.00
16 Mre/VldsSntlng/Adms/99 4.00 10.00
17 Drke/Gscki/Tnnhll/99 4.00 10.00
18 Clwny/Wtsn/Fllr/99 6.00 15.00
19 Hnt/Mhms/Hll/99 12.00 30.00
20 Bsa/Grdn/Wllms/99 5.00 12.00

2018 Panini Plates and Patches Trio Patches

*BLUE/35: .5X TO 1.2X BASIC JSY/75-99
*BLUE/35: .4X TO 1X BASIC JSY/55
1 James Washington/75 6.00 15.00
2 Mason Rudolph/55 8.00 20.00
3 Baker Mayfield/75 20.00 50.00
4 Saquon Barkley/55 20.00 50.00
5 Ronald Jones II/75 3.00 8.00
6 DaeSean Hamilton/55 5.00 12.00
7 Daurice Fountain/99 4.00 10.00
8 Lamar Jackson/75 12.00 30.00
9 Tre'Quan Smith/99 5.00 12.00
10 D.J. Moore/55 8.00 20.00
11 Sony Michel/55 8.00 20.00
12 Nick Chubb/99 6.00 15.00
13 Dante Pettis/55 6.00 15.00
14 Keke Coutee/55 5.00 12.00
15 Kalen Ballage/99 4.00 10.00
16 Anthony Miller/55 6.00 15.00
17 Royce Freeman/55 5.00 12.00
18 Sam Darnold/55 15.00 40.00
19 Kerryon Johnson/99 5.00 12.00
20 Mike Gesicki/99 4.00 10.00
21 Delanie Walker/55 4.00 10.00
22 Blake Bortles/55 4.00 10.00
23 Deshaun Watson/55 8.00 20.00
24 Curtis Samuel/55 4.00 10.00
25 Chris Thompson/55 4.00 10.00
26 Russell Wilson/55 8.00 20.00
27 Corey Davis/65 5.00 12.00
28 Patrick Mahomes II/55 15.00 40.00
29 Leonard Fournette/55 6.00 15.00
30 Laquon Treadwell/75 3.00 8.00
31 Melvin Gordon III/55 5.00 12.00
32 Dede Westbrook/75 3.00 8.00
33 Carson Wentz/55 8.00 20.00
34 Jared Goff/55 6.00 15.00
35 JuJu Smith-Schuster/55 6.00 15.00
36 Jason Witten/55 5.00 12.00
37 Terry Bradshaw/55 10.00 25.00
38 Rob Gronkowski/55 6.00 15.00
39 Kareem Hunt/55 5.00 12.00
40 Drew Brees/55 6.00 15.00

2018 Panini Plates and Patches Upper Echelon Autographs

*BLUE/35-50: .5X TO 1.2X BASIC AU/75-99
*BLUE/35-50: .4X TO 1X BASIC AU/35-65
*BLUE/25: .5X TO 1.2X BASIC AU/35-65
*GREEN/15-20: .8X TO 2X BASIC AU/75-99
*GREEN/15-20: .6X TO 1.5X BASIC AU/35-65
*PURPLE/25-30: .6X TO 1.5X BASIC AU/75-99
*PURPLE/25-30: .5X TO 1.2X BASIC AU/35-65
*PURPLE/15-20: .6X TO 1.5X BASIC AU/35-65
*PURPLE/15-20: .4X TO 1X BASIC AU/20
1 Aaron Donald/75 8.00 20.00
2 Eric Berry/65 8.00 20.00
3 Ray Lewis/15
4 Ed Reed/15
5 Sean Lee/75
6 Ty Montgomery/99 5.00 12.00
7 Willis McGahee/99 5.00 12.00
8 Merton Hanks/75 5.00 12.00
9 Brian Dawkins/20
11 Sterling Sharpe/35
13 Ha Ha Clinton-Dix/49 6.00 15.00
14 Isaac Bruce/35 10.00 25.00
15 Jay Ajayi/35 8.00 20.00
16 Devonta Freeman/20 12.00 30.00
17 Clinton Portis/20
19 Jerome Bettis/15 15.00 40.00
20 Kenny Golladay/99 5.00 12.00

2011 Panini Playbook

1-50 VETERAN AU PRINT RUN 5-99
51-100 ROOKIE AU PRINT RUN 199-299
101-136 ROOK.JSY AU PRINT RUN 99-399
EXCH EXPIRATION: 10/4/2013
1 Philip Rivers AU/10
2 Tom Brady AU/5 EXCH
3 Anquan Boldin AU/99 6.00 15.00
4 Antonio Gates AU/15 12.00 30.00
5 Braylon Edwards AU/99 6.00 15.00
6 C.J. Spiller AU/99 6.00 15.00
7 Chris Cooley AU/99 6.00 15.00
8 Donald Driver AU/99 15.00 40.00
9 Donovan McNabb AU/99 8.00 20.00
10 Eli Manning AU/34 50.00 80.00
11 Greg Jennings AU/53 6.00 15.00
12 Greg Olsen AU/99 8.00 20.00
13 Heath Miller AU/99 10.00 25.00
14 Hines Ward AU/35 30.00 60.00
15 Jay Cutler AU/71 15.00 30.00
16 Jimmy Graham AU/99 10.00 25.00
17 Josh Freeman AU/46 10.00 25.00
18 Kevin Walter AU/99 6.00 15.00
19 LaDainian Tomlinson AU/61 20.00 40.00
20 Larry Fitzgerald AU/38 15.00 40.00
21 Lee Evans AU/99 10.00 25.00
22 Malcom Floyd AU/99 6.00 15.00
23 Michael Crabtree AU/99 6.00 15.00
24 Mike Tolbert AU/99 6.00 15.00
25 Mike Wallace AU/48 8.00 20.00
26 Peyton Manning AU/18 50.00 100.00
27 Pierre Thomas AU/99 6.00 15.00
28 Santana Moss AU/50 10.00 25.00
29 Shonn Greene AU/35 8.00 20.00
30 Steve Johnson AU/94 10.00 25.00
31 Tony Moeaki AU/99 6.00 15.00
32 Troy Polamalu AU/25 40.00 80.00
33 Aaron Rodgers AU/12
34 Arian Foster AU/33 20.00 40.00
35 Ben Roethlisberger AU/30 50.00 100.00
36 Chad Ochocinco AU/99 6.00 15.00
37 Drew Brees AU/27 30.00 60.00
38 Jermaine Gresham AU/73 6.00 15.00
39 Jonathan Stewart AU/25 12.00 30.00
40 Sidney Rice AU/49 8.00 20.00
41 Tim Tebow AU/25 30.00 80.00
42 Dez Bryant AU/9
43 Jason Witten AU/38 12.00 30.00
44 LeSean McCoy AU/34 12.00 30.00
45 Matthew Stafford AU/20
46 Miles Austin AU/13
47 Reggie Wayne AU/25 15.00 40.00
48 Ryan Grant AU/72 10.00 25.00
49 Santonio Holmes AU/25 12.00 30.00
50 Vernon Davis AU/10
51 A.Williams AU/299 RC 3.00 8.00
52 A.Clayborn AU/299 RC 3.00 8.00
53 A.Ayers AU/299 RC EXCH 3.00 8.00
54 A.Smith AU/299 RC EXCH 3.00 8.00
55 Allen Bradford AU/299 RC 3.00 8.00
56 Brandon Harris AU/299 RC 3.00 8.00
57 C.Heyward AU/199 RC 4.00 10.00
58 Cameron Jordan AU/299 RC 4.00 10.00
59 Cecil Shorts AU/299 RC 3.00 8.00
60 Corey Liuget AU/299 RC 3.00 8.00
61 D.J. Williams AU/299 RC 3.00 8.00
62 D.Bowers AU/299 RC 3.00 8.00
63 Da'Rel Scott AU/299 RC 3.00 8.00
64 Denarius Moore AU/299 RC 8.00 20.00
65 Dion Lewis AU/299 RC 4.00 10.00
66 Greg Jones AU/299 RC 4.00 10.00
67 Greg Salas AU/299 RC 8.00 20.00
68 J.J. Watt AU/299 RC 50.00 100.00
69 J.Rodgers AU/299 RC 3.00 8.00
70 Jeremy Kerley AU/299 RC 5.00 12.00
71 J.Smith AU/299 RC 3.00 8.00
72 Johnny White AU/299 RC 3.00 8.00
73 Julius Thomas AU/299 RC 4.00 10.00
74 Justin Houston AU/299 RC 4.00 10.00
75 Kris Durham AU/299 RC 3.00 8.00
76 L.Kendricks AU/299 RC 3.00 8.00
77 Luke Stocker AU/299 RC 3.00 8.00
78 N.Enderle AU/299 RC EXCH 3.00 8.00
79 Niles Paul AU/299 RC 3.00 8.00
80 Phil Taylor AU/299 RC 3.00 8.00
81 P.Amukamara AU/299 RC 3.00 8.00
82 Rahim Moore AU/299 RC 3.00 8.00
83 Ricky Stanzi AU/299 RC 3.00 8.00
84 Roy Helu AU/299 RC 3.00 8.00
85 Ryan Kerrigan AU/299 RC 6.00 15.00
86 T.J. Yates AU/299 RC 3.00 8.00
87 Tandon Doss AU/299 RC 3.00 8.00
88 Terrelle Pryor AU/299 RC 6.00 15.00
89 T.Taylor AU/299 RC 6.00 15.00
90 Joe Lefeged AU/299 RC 4.00 10.00
91 J.Williams AU/299 RC EXCH 5.00 12.00
92 K.J. Wright AU/299 RC 5.00 12.00
93 Mason Foster AU/299 RC 3.00 8.00
94 Casey Matthews AU/299 RC 3.00 8.00
95 Anthony Allen AU/299 RC 3.00 8.00
96 Armond Smith AU/299 RC 4.00 10.00
97 D.Sanzenbacher AU/299 RC 6.00 15.00
98 Doug Baldwin AU/299 RC 15.00 30.00
99 LaQuan Williams AU/299 RC 4.00 10.00
100 Mark Herzlich AU/299 RC 3.00 8.00
101 A.J. Green JSY AU/299 RC 30.00 80.00
102 Alex Green JSY AU/399 RC 8.00 20.00
103 Andy Dalton JSY AU/399 RC 15.00 40.00
104 Austin Pettis JSY AU/399 RC 8.00 20.00
105 Bilal Powell JSY AU/99 RC 15.00 40.00
106 B.Gabbert JSY AU/299 RC 8.00 20.00
107 C.Newton JSY AU/299 RC 75.00 150.00
108 C.Ponder JSY AU/299 RC 8.00 20.00
109 Clyde Gates JSY AU/399 RC 8.00 20.00
110 C.Kaepernick JSY AU/399 RC 12.00 30.00
111 Daniel Thomas JSY AU/399 RC 8.00 20.00
112 D.Carter JSY AU/399 RC 8.00 20.00
113 D.Murray JSY AU/99 RC 20.00 50.00
114 G.Little JSY AU/399 RC 12.00 30.00
115 Jake Locker JSY AU/299 RC 8.00 20.00
116 J.Harper JSY AU/399 RC 8.00 20.00
117 Jerrel Jernigan JSY AU/399 RC 8.00 20.00
118 J.Baldwin JSY AU/399 RC 8.00 20.00
119 Jordan Todman JSY AU/399 RC 8.00 20.00
120 J.Jones JSY AU/399 RC 40.00 80.00
121 Kendall Hunter JSY AU/399 RC 8.00 20.00
122 K.Rudolph JSY AU/99 RC EXCH 15.00 40.00
123 Hankerson JSY AU/399 RC 8.00 20.00
124 M.Dareus JSY AU/399 RC 10.00 25.00
125 Mark Ingram JSY AU/299 RC 12.00 30.00
126 M.Leshoure JSY AU/399 RC 8.00 20.00
127 Randall Cobb JSY AU/99 RC 20.00 50.00
128 Ryan Mallett JSY AU/299 RC 8.00 20.00
129 Ryan Williams JSY AU/399 RC 8.00 20.00
130 Shane Vereen JSY AU/399 RC 12.00 30.00
131 Stevan Ridley JSY AU/399 RC 8.00 20.00
132 Taiwan Jones JSY AU/399 RC 10.00 25.00
133 Titus Young JSY AU/399 RC 8.00 20.00
134 Torrey Smith JSY AU/399 RC 12.00 30.00
135 V.Brown JSY AU/399 RC 10.00 25.00
136 Von Miller JSY AU/349 RC 20.00 50.00

2011 Panini Playbook Gold

*VETS/15-25: .5X TO 1.2X BASIC CARDS
1-50 VETERAN PRINT RUN 1-25
*51-100 ROOKIE AU/49: .6X TO 1.5X
*101-136 ROOK.JSY AU/49: .5X TO 1.2X
51-136 ROOKIE PRINT RUN 49
EXCH EXPIRATION: 10/4/2013
101 A.J. Green JSY AU/49 30.00 80.00
107 Cam Newton JSY AU/49 125.00 250.00
120 Julio Jones JSY AU/49 EXCH 60.00 120.00

2011 Panini Playbook Platinum

*51-100 ROOKIE AU/25: .6X TO 1.5X
*101-136 ROOK.JSY AU/25: .6X TO 1.5X
STATED PRINT RUN 25 SER.#'d SETS
101 A.J. Green JSY AU 75.00 150.00
107 Cam Newton JSY AU 200.00 400.00
115 Jake Locker JSY AU 15.00 40.00
120 Julio Jones JSY AU EXCH 75.00 150.00

2011 Panini Playbook Accolades Signatures

STATED PRINT RUN 4-49
1 Charles Woodson/25 100.00 200.00
2 Arrelious Benn/49 5.00 12.00
3 Ronnie Brown/49 6.00 15.00
4 Danny White/49 12.00 30.00
5 Jim McMahon/49 12.00 30.00
6 Randall Cunningham/49 15.00 40.00
7 Paul Warfield/49 10.00 25.00
8 Andre Reed/49 10.00 25.00
9 Boomer Esiason/49 10.00 25.00
10 Junior Seau/49 30.00 60.00
11 Frank Gifford/49 15.00 40.00
12 Paul Hornung/49
13 Jerome Bettis/49 40.00 80.00
14 Priest Holmes/49 8.00 20.00
15 Doug Flutie/49 10.00 25.00
16 Steve Largent/40 12.00 30.00
17 Keyshawn Johnson/49 8.00 20.00
18 Curtis Martin/49 20.00 40.00
19 Joe Montana/25 90.00 150.00
20 Cris Carter/49 15.00 40.00
21 Mark Duper/49
22 Brett Favre/10
23 Bernie Kosar/49 15.00 40.00
24 Marcus Allen/49 12.00 30.00
25 Mark Carrier/49 10.00 25.00
26 Michael Irvin/45 20.00 40.00
27 Jim Plunkett/49 8.00 20.00
28 Bo Jackson/49 30.00 60.00
29 Ed Too Tall Jones/49 10.00 25.00
30 Joe Greene/49 20.00 40.00
31 Phil Simms/49 12.00 30.00
32 Ronnie Lott/49 12.00 30.00
33 Rod Woodson/49 25.00 50.00
34 Fran Tarkenton/49 12.00 30.00
35 Ben Tate/49
36 Eric Dickerson/49 15.00 40.00
37 Thurman Thomas/49 10.00 25.00
38 John Elway/35 60.00 120.00
39 Sterling Sharpe/49 10.00 25.00
40 Harlon Hill/49 8.00 20.00
41 Archie Manning/49 15.00 40.00
42 Daryle Lamonica/49 10.00 25.00
43 Deion Sanders/49 30.00 60.00
44 Jim Otto/49 10.00 25.00
45 Rayfield Wright/49 10.00 25.00
46 Chad Henne/49
47 Montario Hardesty/49 6.00 15.00
48 Dick Butkus/49 30.00 60.00
49 Jack Lambert/49 30.00 60.00
50 Lenny Moore/49 8.00 20.00
51 Richard Dent/49 10.00 25.00
52 Barry Sanders/25 75.00 135.00
53 Michael Strahan/40 12.00 30.00
54 Bob Griese/49 12.00 30.00
55 John Riggins/49 12.00 30.00
56 Alan Page/45 8.00 20.00
57 James Lofton/49 12.00 30.00
58 Warren Sapp/30 10.00 25.00
59 Bo Scaife/49 6.00 15.00
60 Brian Hartline/49 6.00 15.00
61 Warren Moon/30 25.00 50.00
62 Matt Moore/49 6.00 15.00
63 Danny Amendola/49 6.00 15.00
64 Felix Jones/49 5.00 12.00
65 Clay Matthews/49 25.00 50.00
66 Deacon Jones/33 10.00 25.00
67 Bill Bates/49 15.00 40.00
68 Ed McCaffrey/49 12.00 30.00
69 Terrell Davis/30 25.00 50.00
70 Bernard Berrian/49 5.00 12.00
71 Brian Cushing/49 5.00 12.00
72 Jared Allen/49 15.00 40.00
73 Emmitt Smith/40 75.00 135.00
74 Jim Kelly/12
75 Len Dawson/26 15.00 40.00
76 Knowshon Moreno/25 10.00 25.00
77 Matt Schaub/15 10.00 25.00
78 Peyton Hillis/10
79 Raymond Berry/40 10.00 25.00
80 Jimmy Graham/49 8.00 20.00
81 Wayne Chrebet/15
82 Eddie George/10
83 Matt Ryan/15 15.00 40.00
84 Tony Romo/15
85 Willie Brown/49 8.00 20.00
86 Mark Sanchez/10
87 Sam Bradford/10
88 Jamaal Charles/4
89 Joe Namath/35 50.00 120.00
90 DeAngelo Williams/18 6.00 15.00
91 London Fletcher/34 12.00 30.00
92 Tiki Barber/10
93 Bobby Bell/49 8.00 20.00
94 John Brodie/49 12.00 30.00
95 Floyd Little/25 12.00 30.00
96 Boyd Dowler/49 8.00 20.00
97 Alex Karras/49 10.00 25.00
98 Ace Parker/49 12.00 30.00
99 Leroy Kelly/49 12.00 30.00
100 Sonny Jurgensen/45 12.00 30.00

2011 Panini Playbook Chronicles Signatures

AUTO STATED PRINT RUN 1-15
25 Jimmy Orr/15 60.00 120.00
Lenny Moore
Mike Curtis
Raymond Berry

2011 Panini Playbook Grass Roots Materials

STATED PRINT RUN 2-99
*PRIME/19-25: .8X TO 2X BASIC JSY/79-99
*PRIME/19-25: .6X TO 1.5X BASIC JSY/30-49
*PRIME/25: .5X TO 1.2X BASIC JSY/28
1 Doug Williams/49 5.00 12.00
2 Miles Austin/49 4.00 10.00
3 Nate Washington/49 4.00 10.00
4 Ray Rice/49 4.00 10.00
5 Mario Manningham/49 4.00 10.00
6 Robert Meachem/49 4.00 10.00
7 Shonn Greene/49 4.00 10.00
8 Tamba Hali/49 4.00 10.00
9 Tony Gonzalez/49 5.00 12.00
10 Junior Seau/49 5.00 12.00
11 Ryan Torain/49 4.00 10.00
12 Tony Romo/49 5.00 12.00
13 Matt Hasselbeck/49 4.00 10.00
14 Joe Flacco/49 5.00 12.00
15 Hakeem Nicks/49 4.00 10.00
16 Marques Colston/49 4.00 10.00
17 Mark Sanchez/99 3.00 8.00
18 Priest Holmes/49 4.00 10.00
20 Antonio Gates/49 4.00 10.00
21 London Fletcher/49 5.00 12.00
22 Dez Bryant/49 6.00 15.00
23 Eddie George/49 5.00 12.00
24 Ed Reed/49 5.00 12.00
25 Eli Manning/40 5.00 12.00
26 Drew Brees/49 6.00 15.00
27 Darrelle Revis/49 4.00 10.00
28 Matt Cassel/49 4.00 10.00
29 Matt Ryan/49 5.00 12.00
30 Vincent Jackson/49 4.00 10.00
31 John Riggins/99 6.00 15.00
32 Matthew Stafford/49 5.00 12.00
33 Marc Mariani/49 5.00 12.00
34 Anquan Boldin/49 4.00 10.00
35 Brandon Jacobs/49 4.00 10.00
36 Devery Henderson/99 3.00 8.00
37 Lee Roy Selmon/49 6.00 15.00
38 Steve Young/49 8.00 20.00
39 Mark Duper/49 4.00 10.00
40 Malcom Floyd/49 4.00 10.00
41 DeAngelo Hall/30 4.00 10.00
42 Felix Jones/49 4.00 10.00
43 Chris Johnson/49 4.00 10.00
44 Marshall Faulk/49 5.00 12.00
45 Ahmad Bradshaw/49 4.00 10.00
46 Devin Hester/49 5.00 12.00
47 Earnest Graham/49 4.00 10.00
48 Patrick Willis/49 5.00 12.00
49 Dan Marino/99 10.00 25.00
50 Ryan Mathews/28 6.00 15.00
51 Santana Moss/49 5.00 12.00
52 Don Meredith/49 6.00 15.00
53 Chad Greenway/49 5.00 12.00
54 Danny Amendola/49 5.00 12.00
55 Joe Greene/49 6.00 15.00
56 Brian Urlacher/49 6.00 15.00
57 Keyshawn Johnson/49 5.00 12.00
58 Frank Gore/99 4.00 10.00
59 Brandon Marshall/49 5.00 12.00
60 Art Monk/49 6.00 15.00
61 LaRon Landry/49 4.00 10.00
62 Bob Lilly/49 5.00 12.00
63 Visanthe Shiancoe/49 5.00 12.00
64 Wes Welker/49 5.00 12.00
65 Maurice Jones-Drew/49 4.00 10.00
66 Jim McMahon/49 6.00 15.00
67 Calvin Johnson/49 6.00 15.00
68 Jon Beason/49 4.00 10.00
69 Anthony Fasano/49 4.00 10.00
70 Raymond Berry/49 5.00 12.00
71 Deion Sanders/49 8.00 20.00
72 Darren McFadden/49 4.00 10.00
73 Cris Carter/49 8.00 20.00
74 Tom Brady/99 12.00 30.00
75 Andre Johnson/99 4.00 10.00
76 Dick Butkus/49 8.00 20.00
77 Jahvid Best/99 3.00 8.00
78 DeAngelo Williams/49 4.00 10.00
79 Aaron Rodgers/99 12.00 30.00
80 Brent Celek/99 3.00 8.00
81 Chris Cooley/49
82 Terrell Davis/79 4.00 10.00
83 Alan Page/49 4.00 10.00
84 Cedric Benson/49 4.00 10.00
85 Jim Kelly/49 6.00 15.00
86 Boomer Esiason/49 5.00 12.00
87 Boomer Esiason/49 5.00 12.00
88 Tony Dorsett/49 6.00 15.00
89 Tony Dorsett/49 6.00 15.00
90 Brian Orakpo/49 5.00 12.00
91 Doug Flutie/99 4.00 10.00
92 Doug Flutie/49 5.00 12.00
93 Ronnie Lott/49 6.00 15.00
94 Ronnie Lott/49 6.00 15.00
96 Randy Moss/49 5.00 12.00
97 Curtis Martin/49 5.00 12.00
99 Randall Cunningham/49 6.00 15.00
100 Randall Cunningham/99 5.00 12.00

2011 Panini Playbook Limited Edition Materials

STATED PRINT RUN 49 SER.#'d SETS
*PRIME/15-25: .6X TO 1.5X BASIC JSY/49
1 Steve Bartkowski 5.00 12.00
2 Boomer Esiason 5.00 12.00
3 Bernie Kosar 5.00 12.00
4 Danny White 5.00 12.00
5 John Elway 10.00 25.00
6 Troy Aikman 8.00 20.00
7 Warren Moon 6.00 15.00
8 Bob Griese 6.00 15.00
9 Fran Tarkenton 6.00 15.00
10 Jim Plunkett 5.00 12.00
11 Philip Rivers 6.00 15.00
12 Sam Bradford 4.00 10.00
13 Jay Cutler 4.00 10.00
14 Bart Starr 10.00 25.00
15 Matt Schaub 4.00 10.00
16 Aaron Rodgers 12.00 30.00
17 Joe Namath 12.00 30.00
18 C.J. Spiller 4.00 10.00
19 Thurman Thomas 5.00 12.00
20 Gale Sayers 6.00 15.00
21 Jamaal Charles 5.00 12.00
22 Marcus Allen 6.00 15.00
23 Pierre Thomas 4.00 10.00
24 LaDainian Tomlinson 6.00 15.00
25 Franco Harris 8.00 20.00
26 Emmitt Smith 12.00 30.00
28 Steven Jackson 4.00 10.00
29 Lenny Moore 8.00 20.00
30 Johnny Knox 4.00 10.00
31 Larry Fitzgerald 5.00 12.00
32 Jacoby Ford 5.00 12.00
33 Steve Largent 6.00 15.00
34 Kenny Britt 4.00 10.00
35 Cris Collinsworth 5.00 12.00
36 Josh Cribbs 4.00 10.00
37 Paul Warfield 5.00 12.00
38 Eddie Royal 4.00 10.00
39 Brian Hartline 5.00 12.00
40 Plaxico Burress 4.00 10.00
41 Jason Witten 5.00 12.00
42 Dallas Clark 4.00 10.00
43 Terrell Suggs 4.00 10.00
44 Ray Lewis 10.00 25.00
45 Dick Lane 4.00 10.00
46 Michael Strahan 5.00 12.00
47 Howie Long 6.00 15.00
48 Haloti Ngata 4.00 10.00
49 Ndamukong Suh 8.00 20.00
50 John Randle 5.00 12.00

2011 Panini Playbook Mammoth Materials

STATED PRINT RUN 25-99
*PRIME/15-25: 1X TO 2.5X JSY/62-99
*PRIME/15-25: .8X TO 2X JSY/40-50
*PRIME/15-25: .6X TO 1.5X JSY/25
1 Calvin Johnson/42 8.00 20.00
2 Ed Reed/99 5.00 12.00
3 Robert Meachem/99 4.00 10.00
4 Jon Beason/49 5.00 12.00
5 Hakeem Nicks/99 4.00 10.00
6 Brian Urlacher/99 6.00 15.00
7 Plaxico Burress/99 4.00 10.00
8 Haloti Ngata /99 4.00 10.00
9 Miles Austin/99 4.00 10.00
10 Tamba Hali/99 6.00 15.00
11 Eddie Royal/99 4.00 10.00
12 Ray Lewis/99 6.00 15.00
13 Anthony Fasano/99 4.00 10.00
14 DeMarcus Ware/41 6.00 15.00
15 Devery Henderson/99 4.00 10.00
16 Visanthe Shiancoe/49 6.00 15.00
17 Anquan Boldin/99 4.00 10.00
18 Brian Orakpo/99 5.00 12.00
19 Ahmad Bradshaw/99 4.00 10.00
20 LaDainian Tomlinson/99 6.00 15.00
21 Drew Brees/99 6.00 15.00
22 Ryan Mathews/25 8.00 20.00
23 Joe Flacco/99 5.00 12.00
24 Devin Hester/99 5.00 12.00
25 Brandon Jacobs/99 4.00 10.00
26 Frank Gore/99 5.00 12.00
27 Marc Mariani/49 6.00 15.00
28 Marques Colston/99 4.00 10.00
29 Matt Hasselbeck/99 4.00 10.00
30 Ray Rice/99 4.00 10.00
31 Tim Tebow/50 8.00 20.00
32 DeAngelo Hall/40 5.00 12.00
33 Eli Manning/99 5.00 12.00
34 Mike Thomas/62 5.00 12.00
35 Tony Gonzalez/99 5.00 12.00
36 Chad Greenway/10
37 Vincent Jackson/49 5.00 12.00
38 Pierre Thomas/99 4.00 10.00
39 Josh Cribbs/49 5.00 12.00
40 LaRon Landry/25 6.00 15.00
41 Dallas Clark/99 4.00 10.00
42 Shonn Greene/99 4.00 10.00
43 Steven Jackson/10
44 Darren McFadden/73 4.00 10.00
45 Tom Brady/99 15.00 40.00
46 Matt Schaub/99 4.00 10.00
47 Ndamukong Suh/46 6.00 15.00
48 Jay Cutler/99 4.00 10.00
49 Santana Moss/25 8.00 20.00
50 Chris Johnson/99 4.00 10.00

2011 Panini Playbook Material Playbook

STATED PRINT RUN 5-49
*PRIME/14-25: .5X TO 1.2X BASIC INSERTS
2 Ware/Allen/Harrison/Hali/49 15.00 40.00
3 Six Def Backs/49 15.00 40.00
4 Ptr/Mc/Trn/Rce/Jhn/Bw/Hlm/49 25.00 60.00
5 Fletcher/Laurinaitis/Willis 15.00 40.00
Lewis/Matthews/Urlacher/Greenway/49
6 Fv/Mn/Sm/Pyt/Snd/Rc/Ow/49 75.00 150.00
7 Brs/Brdy/Rdgrs/Eli/Stf/Rvr/49 40.00 100.00
8 Mc/Pt/Rc/Fst/Mn/Tn/Gr/JD/49 25.00 60.00
9 Gonzalez/Ward/Gates/Fitzgerald 15.00 40.00
Wayne/Ochocinco/47
10 Smith/Jones/Strahan/Long/34 15.00 40.00
11 Page/Gregg/Greene/White/Sapp 15.00 40.00
Olsen/Karras/49
12 Kosar/Griese/Esiason/Flutie 15.00 40.00
Williams/McMahon/49
13 Mered/Staub/Whte/Aik/49 50.00 100.00
14 Grs/Stb/Mnt/Will/Aikmn/49 25.00 60.00
15 Brown/Davis/Faulk/Tomlinson/49 15.00 40.00
16 Tittle/Starr/Brodie/Stblr/49 20.00 50.00
17 Trk/Brad/Andr/Theis/49 20.00 50.00
18 Mrn/Alln/Esn/Thmas/49 30.00 80.00
19 Yng/Smith/Favre/Brdy/49 40.00 80.00
20 Cut/Hs/Knx/Bb/Frt/Br/Ur/49 25.00 60.00
21 Jhnsn/Selmon/Sapp/Alstott/49 15.00 40.00
22 Buchanan/Dawson/Holmes 15.00 40.00
Charles/Hali/Bowe/49
23 Gre/Brdie/Wllis/Yng/Lott/49 20.00 50.00
24 Kosar/Davis/Brown/Groza/Graham/Newsome/20
25 Seven Packers Greats/29 40.00 80.00
26 Six NY Jet Greats/49 15.00 40.00
27 Six Raider Greats/49 40.00 80.00
28 Brdfrd/Jcksn/Laur/Amndla/49 15.00 40.00
29 Rdg/Hwk/Mth/Jng/Wdsn/49 40.00 80.00
30 Bo/Aik/Jhn/Vck/Eli/Brd/49 30.00 80.00
32 Star 2005 Rookies/49 20.00 50.00
33 Eli/Fz/Rvr/Wn/Jck/Vl/Ev/20 20.00 50.00
34 Palmer/Johnson/Newman 15.00 40.00
Suggs/Polamalu/McGahee/Clark/Asomugha/49

2011 Panini Playbook Materials Prime

STATED PRINT RUN 1-49
1 Philip Rivers/25 10.00 25.00
3 Anquan Boldin/49 5.00 12.00
4 Antonio Gates/49 5.00 12.00
6 C.J. Spiller/42 5.00 12.00
7 Chris Cooley/49 5.00 12.00
10 Eli Manning/25 8.00 20.00
19 LaDainian Tomlinson/49 8.00 20.00
20 Larry Fitzgerald/25 8.00 20.00
22 Malcom Floyd/49 5.00 12.00
27 Pierre Thomas/49 5.00 12.00
28 Santana Moss/49 6.00 15.00
42 Dez Bryant/49 8.00 20.00
45 Matthew Stafford/14 8.00 20.00
46 Miles Austin/49 5.00 12.00

2012 Panini Playbook

EXCH EXPIRATION: 10/3/2014
1 Kevin Kolb AU/49 8.00 20.00
2 Larry Fitzgerald AU/38 15.00 40.00
3 Michael Turner AU/49 8.00 20.00
4 Matt Ryan AU/49 20.00 40.00
5 Roddy White AU/49 8.00 20.00
6 Joe Flacco AU/49 20.00 40.00
7 Torrey Smith AU/49 8.00 20.00
8 Ray Rice AU/49 8.00 20.00
9 C.J. Spiller AU/25 12.00 30.00
10 Fred Jackson AU/49 10.00 25.00
11 Ryan Fitzpatrick AU/49 8.00 20.00
12 Cam Newton AU/20 30.00 60.00
13 DeAngelo Williams AU/20 12.00 30.00
14 Steve Smith AU/49 10.00 25.00
15 Jay Cutler AU/49 8.00 20.00
16 Matt Forte AU/49 8.00 20.00
18 A.J. Green AU/49 12.00 30.00
19 Andy Dalton AU/20 15.00 40.00
20 Greg Little AU/49 8.00 20.00
21 Josh Cribbs AU/49
22 Tony Romo AU/49 20.00 50.00
23 Jason Witten AU/49 20.00 40.00
24 DeMarcus Ware AU/20 20.00 50.00
25 Peyton Manning AU/49 100.00 200.00
26 Von Miller AU/49 10.00 25.00
27 Matthew Stafford AU/49 20.00 40.00
28 Mikel Leshoure AU/49 8.00 20.00
29 Aaron Rodgers AU/49 EXCH 125.00 200.00
30 Greg Jennings AU/49 8.00 20.00
31 Charles Woodson AU/15 60.00 100.00
32 Arian Foster AU/49 15.00 30.00
33 Matt Schaub AU/49 8.00 20.00
34 Reggie Wayne AU/49 10.00 25.00
35 Antoine Bethea AU/49 8.00 20.00
36 Blaine Gabbert AU/49 8.00 20.00
37 Marcedes Lewis AU/49 8.00 20.00
38 Jamaal Charles AU/49 10.00 25.00
39 Matt Cassel AU/49 8.00 20.00
41 Reggie Bush AU/49 12.00 30.00
42 Adrian Peterson AU/25 50.00 100.00
43 Christian Ponder AU/49 8.00 20.00
44 Percy Harvin AU/49 8.00 20.00
45 Brandon Lloyd AU/49 8.00 20.00
46 Rob Gronkowski AU/49 EXCH 25.00 60.00
47 Tom Brady AU/49 150.00 250.00
48 Darren Sproles AU/49 10.00 25.00
49 Drew Brees AU/20 40.00 80.00
50 Ahmad Bradshaw AU/25 12.00 30.00
52 Jason Pierre-Paul AU/49 8.00 20.00
53 Santonio Holmes AU/49 8.00 20.00
54 Shonn Greene AU/49 8.00 20.00
55 Darren McFadden AU/49 8.00 20.00
57 Denarius Moore AU/49 8.00 20.00
58 LeSean McCoy AU/49 12.00 30.00
59 Michael Vick AU/49 12.00 30.00
60 Nnamdi Asomugha AU/49 8.00 20.00
61 Antonio Brown AU/25 25.00 60.00
62 Ben Roethlisberger AU/20 40.00 80.00
63 Heath Miller AU/49 8.00 20.00
64 Philip Rivers AU/49
65 Ryan Mathews AU/49
66 Colin Kaepernick AU/20 15.00 40.00
67 Patrick Willis AU/49 12.00 30.00
68 Marshawn Lynch AU/49 25.00 50.00
69 Josh Freeman AU/49 10.00 25.00
70 Vincent Jackson AU/49 8.00 20.00
71 Jake Locker AU/49 12.00 30.00
72 Jared Cook AU/49 8.00 20.00
73 Fred Davis AU/20 12.00 30.00
74 Pierre Garcon AU/49 EXCH 12.00 30.00
75 Santana Moss AU/49 10.00 25.00
76 Adrien Robinson AU/140 RC 3.00 8.00
77 Alfred Morris AU/140 RC 3.00 8.00
78 Andre Branch AU/140 RC 3.00 8.00
79 Greg Zuerlein AU/140 RC 5.00 12.00
80 B.J. Cunningham AU/140 RC 3.00 8.00
81 Bill Bentley AU/140 RC 4.00 10.00
82 Blair Walsh AU/140 RC 10.00 25.00
83 Bobby Rainey AU/140 RC 6.00 15.00
84 Bobby Wagner AU/140 RC 5.00 12.00
85 Brandon Bolden AU/140 RC 3.00 8.00
86 Brandon Hardin AU/140 RC 4.00 10.00
87 Brandon Taylor AU/140 RC 3.00 8.00
88 Bruce Irvin AU/140 RC 4.00 10.00
89 Bryce Brown AU/140 RC 3.00 8.00
90 Cascy Hayward AU/140 RC 3.00 8.00
91 Chandler Harnish AU/140 RC 3.00 8.00
92 Chandler Jones AU/140 RC 3.00 8.00
93 Chris Polk AU/140 RC 3.00 8.00
94 Chris Rainey AU/140 RC 3.00 8.00
95 Coty Sensabaugh AU/140 RC 4.00 10.00
96 Courtney Upshaw AU/140 RC 4.00 10.00
97 Cyrus Gray AU/140 RC 3.00 8.00
98 Damaris Johnson AU/140 RC 3.00 8.00
99 Daryl Richardson AU/140 RC 10.00 25.00
100 David DeCastro AU/140 RC 3.00 8.00
101 Deangelo Peterson AU/140 RC 3.00 8.00
102 Demario Davis AU/140 RC 3.00 8.00
103 Deonte Thompson AU/140 RC 4.00 10.00
104 Derek Wolfe AU/140 RC EXCH 4.00 10.00
105 Devon Still AU/140 RC 4.00 10.00
106 Devon Wylie AU/140 RC 3.00 8.00
107 D.Hightower AU/140 RC 5.00 12.00
108 Dontari Poe AU/140 RC 3.00 8.00
109 Dre Kirkpatrick AU/140 RC 3.00 8.00
110 Evan Rodriguez AU/140 RC 4.00 10.00
111 Fletcher Cox AU/140 RC 5.00 12.00
112 George Iloka AU/140 RC 3.00 8.00
113 Harrison Smith AU/140 RC 6.00 15.00
114 Jamell Fleming AU/140 RC 3.00 8.00
115 James Hanna AU/140 RC 3.00 8.00
116 Janoris Jenkins AU/140 RC 4.00 10.00
117 Jared Crick AU/140 RC 3.00 8.00
118 Jeff Demps AU/140 RC 4.00 10.00
119 Jerel Worthy AU/140 RC 3.00 8.00
120 Jonathan Martin AU/140 RC 3.00 8.00
121 Jorvorskie Lane AU/140 RC 4.00 10.00
122 Josh Cooper AU/140 RC 4.00 10.00
123 Josh Gordon AU/140 RC 8.00 20.00
124 Josh Norman AU/140 RC 4.00 10.00
125 Josh Robinson AU/140 RC 5.00 12.00
126 Juron Criner AU/140 RC 3.00 8.00
127 Justin Tucker AU/140 RC 10.00 25.00
128 Kellen Moore AU/140 RC 4.00 10.00
129 Kendall Reyes AU/140 RC 3.00 8.00
130 Keshawn Martin AU/140 RC 4.00 10.00
131 Kevin Zeitler AU/140 RC 3.00 8.00
132 Kirk Cousins AU/140 RC 20.00 50.00
133 Kris Adams AU/140 RC 5.00 12.00
134 Ladarius Green AU/140 RC 3.00 8.00
135 Lance Dunbar AU/140 RC 5.00 12.00
136 Lavonte David AU/140 RC 5.00 12.00
137 Luke Kuechly AU/140 RC 15.00 40.00
138 Mark Barron AU/140 RC 3.00 8.00
139 Marvin Jones AU/140 RC 3.00 8.00
140 Matt Kalil AU/140 RC 6.00 15.00
141 Melvin Ingram AU/140 RC 3.00 8.00
142 M.Brockers AU/140 RC 3.00 8.00
143 Michael Smith AU/140 RC 4.00 10.00
144 Mike Martin AU/140 RC 4.00 10.00
145 Miles Burris AU/140 RC 5.00 12.00
146 M.Claiborne AU/125 RC 3.00 8.00
147 Mychal Kendricks AU/140 RC 5.00 12.00
148 Najee Goode AU/140 RC 3.00 8.00
149 Nick Perry AU/140 RC 4.00 10.00
150 Nigel Bradham AU/140 RC 4.00 10.00
151 Olivier Vernon AU/140 RC 5.00 12.00
152 Omar Bolden AU/140 RC 4.00 10.00
153 Orson Charles AU/140 RC 3.00 8.00
154 Quinton Coples AU/140 RC 3.00 8.00
155 Rhett Ellison AU/140 RC 4.00 10.00
156 Riley Reiff AU/140 RC 3.00 8.00
157 Rishard Matthews AU/140 RC 3.00 8.00
158 Rod Streater AU/140 RC 5.00 12.00
159 Ronnell Lewis AU/140 RC 4.00 10.00
160 Ryan Lindley AU/140 RC 3.00 8.00
161 Sean Spence AU/140 RC 4.00 10.00
162 Shea McClellin AU/140 RC 4.00 10.00
163 Stephon Gilmore AU/140 RC 4.00 10.00
164 T.Y. Hilton AU/140 RC 6.00 15.00
165 Tavon Wilson AU/140 RC 4.00 10.00
166 Terrance Ganaway AU/140 RC 4.00 10.00
167 Tommy Streeter AU/140 RC 3.00 8.00
168 Travis Benjamin AU/140 RC 3.00 8.00
169 Trumaine Johnson AU/140 RC 3.00 8.00
170 Tyrone Crawford AU/140 RC 3.00 8.00
171 Vick Ballard AU/140 RC 4.00 10.00
172 Vinny Curry AU/140 RC 4.00 10.00
173 Vontaze Burfict AU/140 RC 4.00 10.00
174 Whitney Mercilus AU/140 RC 3.00 8.00
175 Zach Brown AU/140 RC 3.00 8.00
176 A.J. Jenkins JSY AU RC 8.00 20.00
177 Alshon Jeffery JSY AU RC 30.00 60.00
178 Andrew Luck JSY AU RC 75.00 150.00
179 Bernard Pierce JSY AU RC 20.00 40.00
180 B.Weeden JSY AU RC 8.00 20.00
181 Brian Quick JSY AU RC 8.00 20.00
182 Brock Osweiler JSY AU RC 8.00 20.00
183 Chris Givens JSY AU RC 8.00 20.00
184 Coby Fleener JSY AU RC 8.00 20.00
185 David Wilson JSY AU RC 8.00 20.00
186 DeVier Posey JSY AU RC 8.00 20.00
187 Doug Martin JSY AU RC 12.00 30.00
188 Dwayne Allen JSY AU RC 8.00 20.00
189 Isaiah Pead JSY AU RC 8.00 20.00
190 Jarius Wright JSY AU RC 8.00 20.00
191 Joe Adams JSY AU RC 8.00 20.00
192 J.Blackmon JSY AU RC 8.00 20.00
193 Kendall Wright JSY AU RC 8.00 20.00
194 Lamar Miller JSY AU RC 12.00 30.00
195 L.James JSY AU RC 8.00 20.00
196 Michael Egnew JSY AU RC 8.00 20.00
197 Michael Floyd JSY AU RC 8.00 20.00
198 Mohamed Sanu JSY AU RC 12.00 30.00
199 Nick Foles JSY AU RC 30.00 60.00
200 Nick Toon JSY AU RC 8.00 20.00
201 Robert Griffin III JSY AU RC 10.00 25.00
202 Robert Turbin JSY AU RC 8.00 20.00
203 Ronnie Hillman JSY AU RC 8.00 20.00
204 R.Randle JSY AU RC 8.00 20.00
205 R.Wilson JSY AU RC EXCH 75.00 150.00
206 Ryan Broyles JSY AU RC 8.00 20.00
207 R.Tannehill JSY AU RC 12.00 30.00
208 Stephen Hill JSY AU RC 8.00 20.00
209 T.J. Graham JSY AU RC 8.00 20.00
210 T.Richardson JSY AU RC 8.00 20.00

2012 Panini Playbook Gold

*GOLD AU/49: .5X TO 1.2X AU RC
*GOLD JSY AU/49: .5X TO 1.2X JSY AU RC
178 Andrew Luck JSY AU 100.00 200.00
205 Russell Wilson JSY AU 125.00 250.00

2012 Panini Playbook Platinum

*VETS/25: .5X TO 1.2X BASIC AU/38-49
*ROOKIE JSY AU/25: .6X TO 1.5X JSY AU RC
*ROOKIE AU/25: .6X TO 1.5X AU RC
178 Andrew Luck JSY AU/25 100.00 200.00
205 R.Wilson JSY AU/25 125.00 250.00

2012 Panini Playbook Accolades Signatures

1 Paul Hornung/49 12.00 30.00
2 Frank Gifford/49 25.00 50.00
3 Greg Jennings/49 5.00 12.00
4 Jason Witten/49 20.00 40.00
5 Paul Warfield/49 10.00 25.00
6 Bill Bates/49 8.00 20.00
7 Reggie Wayne/49 12.00 30.00
8 Santana Moss/49 8.00 20.00
9 Junior Seau/49 30.00 60.00
10 Drew Bledsoe/20 40.00 80.00
11 Mario Williams/49 6.00 15.00
12 Reggie Bush/49
13 Shaun Alexander/49 8.00 20.00
14 Joe Namath/49 30.00 60.00
15 Eli Manning/49 25.00 50.00
16 Antonio Gates/5
17 Chris Cooley/49 10.00 25.00
18 Fred Taylor/25 8.00 20.00
19 Andre Rison/49 12.00 30.00
20 Bruce Smith/49 20.00 40.00
21 Donald Driver/49 20.00 40.00
22 Michael Turner/49
23 Howie Long/49 20.00 40.00
24 Terrell Davis/49 12.00 30.00
25 Dan Fouts/20 30.00 60.00

2012 Panini Playbook Fabled Fabrics

1 Amani Toomer/99 4.00 10.00
3 Barry Sanders/25 15.00 40.00
4 Bernie Kosar/25 8.00 20.00
5 Bobby Mitchell/49 6.00 15.00
6 Boomer Esiason/49 5.00 12.00
7 Bryant Young/99 4.00 10.00
8 Cris Collinsworth/99 5.00 12.00
10 Dan Fouts/25 8.00 20.00
11 Dan Marino/25 15.00 40.00
12 Doug Flutie/25 8.00 20.00
14 Emmitt Smith/25 15.00 40.00
15 George Blanda/49 6.00 15.00
17 Jerry Rice/25 15.00 40.00
18 Jim Kelly/49 8.00 20.00
20 Joe Namath/99 10.00 25.00
21 John Elway/49 12.00 30.00
24 Kurt Warner/49 10.00 25.00
25 LaDainian Tomlinson/49 6.00 15.00
26 Marcus Allen/25 8.00 20.00
27 Marshall Faulk/49 6.00 15.00
28 Mike Ditka/49 8.00 20.00
31 Randy White/20 8.00 20.00
32 Ronnie Lott/99 5.00 12.00
35 Steve McNair/99 5.00 12.00
36 Ted Hendricks/49 5.00 12.00
38 Thurman Thomas/99 4.00 10.00
40 Troy Aikman/49 8.00 20.00
41 Walter Payton/25 25.00 60.00
45 Ed Too Tall Jones/49 5.00 12.00
46 Randall Cunningham/99 5.00 12.00
47 Lee Roy Selmon/99 6.00 15.00
50 Raymond Berry/99 5.00 12.00
52 Curtis Martin/20 8.00 20.00
53 John Brodie/99 6.00 15.00
56 Bob Lilly/25 8.00 20.00
58 Chuck Howley/49 5.00 12.00
59 Kerry Collins/49 5.00 12.00
61 Don Meredith/99 8.00 20.00
63 Eric Moulds/25 6.00 15.00

2012 Panini Playbook Fabled Fabrics Prime

1 Amani Toomer/25 8.00 20.00
5 Bobby Mitchell/25 10.00 25.00
6 Boomer Esiason/25 8.00 20.00
8 Cris Collinsworth/25 10.00 25.00
20 Joe Namath/25 20.00 40.00
25 LaDainian Tomlinson/25 10.00 25.00
28 Mike Ditka/20
32 Ronnie Lott/25 15.00 40.00
35 Steve McNair/25 10.00 25.00
38 Thurman Thomas/25 8.00 20.00
39 Tony Dorsett/25 12.00 30.00
43 Wayne Chrebet/25 8.00 20.00
47 Lee Roy Selmon/25 12.00 30.00
51 Keyshawn Johnson/25 10.00 25.00
53 John Brodie/20 12.00 30.00
57 Torry Holt/15 10.00 25.00
59 Kerry Collins/25 8.00 20.00
60 Jamal Lewis/25 8.00 20.00

61 Don Meredith/25 15.00 40.00
65 Joe Montana/25 30.00 80.00

2012 Panini Playbook Mammoth Materials

*PRIME/49: .6X TO 1.5X BASIC JSY/34-75
*PRIME/25: .8X TO 2X BASIC JSY/34-75
1 A.J. Jenkins/75 2.00 5.00
2 Alshon Jeffery/75 4.00 10.00
3 Andrew Luck/75 15.00 40.00
4 Bernard Pierce/75 4.00 10.00
5 Brandon Weeden/75 2.00 5.00
6 Brian Quick/75 2.00 5.00
7 Brock Osweiler/75 2.00 5.00
8 Chris Givens/75 2.00 5.00
9 Coby Fleener/75 2.00 5.00
10 David Wilson/75 2.00 5.00
11 DeVier Posey/75 2.00 5.00
12 Doug Martin/75 3.00 8.00
13 Dwayne Allen/75 2.00 5.00
14 Isaiah Pead/75 2.00 5.00
15 Jarius Wright/75 2.00 5.00
16 Joe Adams/75 2.00 5.00
17 Justin Blackmon/75 2.00 5.00
18 Kendall Wright/75 2.00 5.00
19 Lamar Miller/75 3.00 8.00
20 LaMichael James/75 2.00 5.00
21 Michael Egnew/75 2.00 5.00
22 Michael Floyd/75 2.00 5.00
23 Mohamed Sanu/75 3.00 8.00
24 Nick Foles/75 5.00 12.00
25 Nick Toon/34 2.00 5.00
26 Robert Griffin III/75 2.50 6.00
27 Robert Turbin/75 2.00 5.00
28 Ronnie Hillman/75 2.00 5.00
29 Rueben Randle/75 2.00 5.00
30 Russell Wilson/75 12.00 30.00
31 Ryan Broyles/75 2.00 5.00
32 Ryan Tannehill/75 3.00 8.00
33 Stephen Hill/75 2.00 5.00
34 T.J. Graham/75 2.00 5.00
35 Trent Richardson/75 2.00 5.00

2012 Panini Playbook Material Playbook

*PRIME/47-49: .6X TO 1.5X BASIC JSY/99
*PRIME/25: .8X TO 2X BASIC JSY/99
*PRIME/25: .6X TO 1.5X BASIC JSY/49
1 Bradshaw/Manning/Nicks Umenyiora/Brady/Welker/49 15.00 40.00
2 Sn/Pl/Fl/Gg/Aln/Brd/Tbw/99 25.00 50.00
3 Spiller/McFadden/Sproles Charles/McCoy/25 12.00 30.00
5 Url/Hst/Bn/Ct/Knx/Pp/Brg/99 25.00 50.00
6 Ponder/Flacco/Sanchez/Ryan/Rivers/99 12.00 30.00
7 Revis/Keller/Sanchez/Greene/99 10.00 25.00
8 Ptr/Fst/Frt/J-D/Rc/Mthw/49 25.00 50.00
9 Decker/Maclin/Harvin/Welker/99 12.00 30.00
10 Rc/Elw/Wrn/Mn/Eli/Lws/49 30.00 60.00
11 Scott/Dumervil/Dansby/Fletcher McClain/Lee/Hali/Suggs/99 10.00 25.00
12 Allen/Taylor/White/Miller/49 25.00 50.00
13 Jackson/Bryant/Fitzgerald/Austin White/49 12.00 30.00
14 Fasano/Gates/Davis/Gresham Graham/Lewis/Gonzalez/Davis/99 12.00 30.00
15 Joe Namath/49 40.00 80.00
18 Darren McFadden/49 15.00 40.00
19 Smith/Irvin/Aikman/49 25.00 80.00
20 Tim Tebow/49 25.00 60.00
21 Adrian Peterson/25 20.00 50.00
24 Palmer/Davis/Seau/Allen Sanchez/Cassel/Bush/99 12.00 30.00
25 Sprls/Brees/Grhm/Clstn/25 40.00 80.00
26 Boldin/Wells/Johnson Plummer/Fitzgerald/25 12.00 30.00
27 Greene/M.Blount/80 30.00 60.00
28 Tony Romo/99 15.00 40.00
29 Pl/Bld/Eli/El/Vk/Brd/Aik/99 30.00 60.00
30 Mnk/Mrt/Cm/Sm/Rc/Flk/49 25.00 60.00
31 Brs/Eli/Ryn/Brdy/Romo/99 20.00 50.00
32 Orakpo/Lewis/Merriman Polamalu/Miller/49 15.00 40.00
34 Johnson/Jackson/Jones Wallace/Smith/Smith USC/Smith/49 12.00 30.00
35 Maurice Jones-Drew/25
36 Morris Claiborne/49 12.00 30.00

2012 Panini Playbook Rookie Playbook Materials Die Cut

*PRIME/49: .6X TO 1.5X BASIC JSY/199
*PRIME/25: .8X TO 2X BASIC JSY/199
1 Andrew Luck/199 30.00 60.00
2 Brandon Weeden/199 4.00 10.00
3 Brock Osweiler/199 4.00 10.00
4 Nick Foles/199 10.00 25.00
5 Robert Griffin III/45 6.00 15.00
6 Russell Wilson/199 25.00 50.00
7 Ryan Tannehill/199 6.00 15.00
8 Bernard Pierce/199 4.00 10.00
9 David Wilson/199 4.00 10.00
10 Doug Martin/199 6.00 15.00
11 Isaiah Pead/199 4.00 10.00
12 Lamar Miller/199 6.00 15.00
13 LaMichael James/199 4.00 10.00
15 Ronnie Hillman/199 4.00 10.00
16 Trent Richardson/199 4.00 10.00
17 A.J. Jenkins/199 4.00 10.00
18 Alshon Jeffery/199 8.00 20.00
19 Brian Quick/199 4.00 10.00
20 Chris Givens/199 4.00 10.00
21 DeVier Posey/199 4.00 10.00
22 Jarius Wright/199 8.00 20.00
23 Joe Adams/199 4.00 10.00
24 Justin Blackmon/199 4.00 10.00
25 Kendall Wright/199 4.00 10.00
26 Michael Floyd/199 4.00 10.00
27 Mohamed Sanu/199 8.00 20.00
28 Nick Toon/17 6.00 15.00
29 Rueben Randle/199 4.00 10.00
30 Ryan Broyles/199 4.00 10.00
31 Stephen Hill/199 4.00 10.00
32 T.J. Graham/199 4.00 10.00
33 Coby Fleener/199 4.00 10.00
34 Dwayne Allen/199 4.00 10.00
35 Michael Egnew/199 4.00 10.00

2012 Panini Playbook Rookie Playbook Materials Die Cut Autographs

*DIE CUT VARIATION: .4X TO 1X BASIC DC
1 Andrew Luck/99 75.00 150.00
2 Brandon Weeden/99 6.00 15.00
3 Brock Osweiler/99 6.00 15.00
4 Nick Foles/99 30.00 80.00
5 Robert Griffin III/45 8.00 20.00
6 Russell Wilson/99 50.00 100.00
7 Ryan Tannehill/99 10.00 25.00
8 Bernard Pierce/99 10.00 25.00
9 David Wilson/99 6.00 15.00
10 Doug Martin/99 10.00 25.00
11 Isaiah Pead/99 10.00 25.00
12 Lamar Miller/99 10.00 25.00
13 LaMichael James/99 6.00 15.00
14 Robert Turbin/50 6.00 15.00
15 Ronnie Hillman/99 6.00 15.00
16 Trent Richardson/99 6.00 15.00
17 A.J. Jenkins/99 6.00 15.00
18 Alshon Jeffery/99 12.00 30.00
19 Brian Quick/99 12.00 30.00
20 Chris Givens/99 6.00 16.00
21 DeVier Posey/99 6.00 15.00
22 Jarius Wright/99 6.00 15.00
23 Joe Adams/99 6.00 15.00
24 Justin Blackmon/99 6.00 15.00
25 Kendall Wright/99 6.00 15.00
26 Michael Floyd/99 6.00 15.00
27 Mohamed Sanu/99 10.00 25.00
28 Nick Toon/99 10.00 25.00
29 Rueben Randle/99 6.00 15.00
30 Ryan Broyles/99 12.00 30.00
31 Stephen Hill/99 6.00 15.00
32 T.J. Graham/99 10.00 25.00
33 Coby Fleener/99 6.00 15.00
34 Dwayne Allen/99 6.00 15.00
35 Michael Egnew/99 6.00 15.00

2013 Panini Playbook

*1-100 VETS/81-88: .25X TO .6X BLUE AU/25
*1-100 VETS/32-59: .3X TO .8X BLUE AU/25
*1-100 VETS/20-29: .4X TO 1X BLUE AU/25
*1-100 VETS/15-18: .5X TO 1.2X BLUE AU/25
1-100 VETERAN PRINT RUN 4-88
101-200 ROOKIE PRINT RUN 49-299
CARDS FEATURE RED FOIL ON FRONT
101 Aaron Dobson AU/49 RC 3.00 8.00
102 Aaron Mellette AU/99 RC 3.00 8.00
103 Ace Sanders AU/99 RC 3.00 8.00
105 Alex Okafor AU/99 RC 3.00 8.00
106 Andre Ellington AU/49 RC 3.00 8.00
107 Arthur Brown AU/99 RC 3.00 8.00
108 Barkevious Mingo AU/99 RC 3.00 8.00
109 Bjoern Werner AU/99 RC 3.00 8.00
110 Brad Sorensen AU/299 RC 2.50 6.00
111 Chris Gragg AU/99 RC 3.00 8.00
112 Chris Harper AU/99 RC 3.00 8.00
113 Chris Thompson AU/299 RC 2.50 6.00
114 Christine Michael AU/49 RC 3.00 8.00
115 Blidi Wreh-Wilson AU/299 RC 3.00 8.00
116 Conner Vernon AU/99 RC 3.00 8.00
117 C.Patterson AU/49 RC 3.00 8.00
118 Corey Fuller AU/99 RC 3.00 8.00
119 D.J. Hayden AU/299 RC 2.50 6.00
120 Damontre Moore AU/99 RC 3.00 8.00
121 Da'Rick Rogers AU/199 RC 2.50 6.00
122 Darius Slay AU/99 RC 3.00 8.00
124 Cornellius Carradine AU/299 RC 2.50 6.00
125 DeAndre Hopkins AU/49 RC 8.00 20.00
129 Desmond Trufant AU/299 RC 2.50 6.00
130 Dion Jordan AU/49 RC 3.00 8.00
132 Eddie Lacy AU/49 RC 3.00 8.00
133 EJ Manuel AU/49 RC 3.00 8.00
134 D.J. Fluker AU/299 RC 2.50 6.00
138 Geno Smith AU/49 RC 3.00 8.00
139 Giovani Bernard AU/49 RC 3.00 8.00
140 Jamar Taylor AU/299 RC 2.50 6.00
142 Jasper Collins AU/99 RC 3.00 8.00
143 Dustin Hopkins AU/299 RC 2.50 6.00
144 Johnathan Cyprien AU/99 RC 3.00 8.00
145 Johnathan Franklin AU/49 RC 3.00 8.00
146 Johnthan Banks AU/299 RC 2.50 6.00
147 Jordan Poyer AU/99 RC 3.00 8.00
148 Jordan Reed AU/49 RC 5.00 12.00
149 Joseph Randle AU/49 RC 3.00 8.00
150 Josh Boyce AU/99 RC 3.00 8.00
152 Keenan Allen AU/49 RC 6.00 15.00
153 Kenjon Barner AU/299 RC 2.50 6.00
154 Kenny Stills AU/49 RC 3.00 8.00
158 Landry Jones AU/49 RC 3.00 8.00
159 Le'Veon Bell AU/49 RC 10.00 25.00
160 Kerwynn Williams AU/299 RC 2.50 6.00
161 Manti Te'o AU/49 RC 4.00 10.00
162 Marcus Davis AU/299 RC 2.50 6.00
163 Marcus Lattimore AU/49 RC 3.00 8.00
164 Margus Hunt AU/299 RC 2.50 6.00
165 Markus Wheaton AU/49 RC 3.00 8.00
166 Marquess Wilson AU/299 RC 4.00 10.00
167 Marquise Goodwin AU/49 RC 3.00 8.00
168 Matt Barkley AU/49 RC 3.00 8.00
169 Matt Elam AU/299 RC 2.50 6.00
170 Matt Scott AU/99 RC 3.00 8.00
172 Mike Glennon AU/49 RC 3.00 8.00
173 Montee Ball AU/49 RC 3.00 8.00
176 Phillip Thomas AU/99 RC 3.00 8.00
177 Quinton Patton AU/49 RC 3.00 8.00
178 Rex Burkhead AU/299 RC 3.00 8.00
180 Rodney Smith AU/299 RC 2.50 6.00
181 Ryan Nassib AU/49 RC 3.00 8.00
182 Mychal Rivera AU/299 RC 2.50 6.00
183 Ryan Swope AU/299 RC 2.50 6.00
184 Sam Montgomery AU/99 RC 3.00 8.00
185 Robert Alford AU/299 RC 2.50 6.00
187 Stepfan Taylor AU/49 RC 3.00 8.00
188 Tavarres King AU/299 RC 2.50 6.00
189 Tavon Austin AU/49 RC 4.00 10.00
190 Terrance Williams AU/49 RC 3.00 8.00
191 Theo Riddick AU/299 RC 2.50 6.00
193 Tyler Bray AU/299 RC 2.50 6.00
194 Tyler Eifert AU/49 RC 3.00 8.00
195 Tyler Wilson AU/49 RC 3.00 8.00
196 Tyrann Mathieu AU/99 RC 5.00 12.00
197 Vance McDonald AU/49 RC 4.00 10.00
198 Xavier Rhodes AU/299 RC 2.50 6.00
199 Zac Dysert AU/199 RC 2.50 6.00
200 Zach Ertz AU/49 RC 6.00 15.00

2013 Panini Playbook Blue

*101-200 ROOKIES/99: .5X TO 1.2X AU RC/299
*101-200 ROOKIES/49: .5X TO 1.2X AU RC/199
*101-200 ROOKIES/25: .6X TO 1.5X AU RC/49-99
EXCH EXPIRATION: 4/2/2015
1 Colin Kaepernick AU/25 10.00 25.00
2 Michael Crabtree AU/25 8.00 20.00
4 Frank Gore AU/25 12.00 30.00
5 Patrick Willis AU/25 12.00 30.00
6 Jay Cutler AU/25 15.00 40.00
8 Terry Bradshaw AU/25 50.00 100.00
10 Charles Woodson AU/25 40.00 80.00
12 Kevin Kolb AU/25 8.00 20.00
15 LaDainian Tomlinson AU/25 30.00 60.00
16 Demaryius Thomas AU/25 10.00 25.00
17 Peyton Manning AU/25 125.00 200.00
18 Bryce Brown AU/25 10.00 25.00
19 Von Miller AU/25 10.00 25.00
20 Brandon Weeden AU/25 8.00 20.00
21 Clay Matthews AU/25 25.00 50.00
22 Sean Lee AU/25 12.00 30.00
23 Josh Freeman AU/25 10.00 25.00
24 Doug Martin AU/25 10.00 25.00
26 Rashard Mendenhall AU/25 8.00 20.00
27 Patrick Peterson AU/25 12.00 30.00
28 Ryan Mathews AU/25 10.00 25.00
30 Jared Allen AU/25 8.00 20.00
32 Dexter McCluster AU/25 10.00 25.00
33 Vincent Brown AU/25 8.00 20.00
34 Andrew Luck AU/25 EXCH 40.00 80.00
36 T.Y. Hilton AU/25 10.00 25.00
37 Michael Floyd AU/25 8.00 20.00
40 Lamar Miller AU/25 8.00 20.00
41 Ryan Tannehill AU/25 15.00 40.00
43 Michael Vick AU/25 10.00 25.00
45 Jeremy Maclin AU/25 8.00 20.00
47 Michael Irvin AU/25 25.00 50.00
48 Joe Montana AU/25 75.00 150.00
49 Hakeem Nicks AU/25 8.00 20.00
51 David Wilson AU/25 8.00 20.00
52 Cecil Shorts III AU/25 8.00 20.00
53 Justin Blackmon AU/25 8.00 20.00
54 Maurice Jones-Drew AU/25 8.00 20.00
55 Marcedes Lewis AU/25 8.00 20.00
56 Jeremy Kerley AU/25 8.00 20.00
57 Dustin Keller AU/25 8.00 20.00
58 Matthew Stafford AU/25 12.00 30.00
59 Larry Csonka AU/25 15.00 40.00
60 Ryan Broyles AU/25 10.00 25.00
61 Randall Cobb AU/25 10.00 25.00
62 Rueben Randle AU/25 8.00 20.00
63 Art Monk AU/25 25.00 50.00
66 Alex Smith AU/25 25.00 50.00
67 Greg Olsen AU/25 10.00 25.00
69 LaMichael James AU/25 8.00 20.00
70 Matt Flynn AU/25 8.00 20.00
71 Luke Kuechly AU/25 15.00 40.00
72 Darren McFadden AU/25 10.00 25.00
74 Chris Givens AU/25 8.00 20.00
75 Daryl Richardson AU/25 8.00 20.00
76 Jared Cook AU/25 8.00 20.00
80 Robert Griffin III AU/25 8.00 20.00
83 Mark Ingram AU/25 10.00 25.00
86 Golden Tate AU/25 8.00 20.00
87 Sidney Rice AU/25 8.00 20.00
88 Richard Sherman AU/25 75.00 135.00
90 Mike Wallace AU/25 8.00 20.00
93 Owen Daniels AU/25 8.00 20.00
94 J.J. Watt AU/25 30.00 60.00
95 Kenny Britt AU/25 8.00 20.00
96 Deion Sanders AU/25 30.00 60.00
97 Danario Alexander AU/25 8.00 20.00
99 Kyle Rudolph AU/25 8.00 20.00
100 Adrian Peterson AU/25 50.00 100.00
179 Robert Woods AU/25 12.00 30.00

2013 Panini Playbook Gold

1-100 UNPRICED VETERAN PRINT RUN 10
*ROOKIES/25: .6X TO 1.5X AU RC/199-299
101-200 ROOKIE PRINT RUN 10-20

2013 Panini Playbook Coaches Signatures

EXCH EXPIRATION: 4/2/2015
1 Bill Parcells/25 EXCH 125.00 200.00
2 Mike Ditka/25 EXCH
3 Don Shula/25 EXCH 125.00 200.00
4 Marv Levy/25 EXCH
5 Joe Gibbs/25 EXCH 60.00 120.00

2013 Panini Playbook Down and Dirty Jerseys

*PRIME/25: .5X TO 1.2X BASIC JSY/32
1 Jamaal Charles 15.00 40.00
2 LeSean McCoy
3 Robert Griffin III 12.00 30.00
4 Ryan Mathews 15.00 40.00
5 Darren Sproles 15.00 40.00
6 Santonio Holmes 12.00 30.00
7 Adrian Peterson 25.00 60.00
8 Julio Jones 20.00 50.00
9 Fred Jackson 15.00 40.00
10 Jonathan Stewart 12.00 30.00
11 BenJarvus Green-Ellis 15.00 40.00
12 Justin Blackmon 12.00 30.00
13 Ray Rice 12.00 30.00
14 Alfred Morris 12.00 30.00
15 Ryan Tannehill 15.00 40.00
16 Trent Richardson 12.00 30.00

2013 Panini Playbook Jerseys Gold

1 Andrew Luck/25 25.00 60.00
2 Robert Griffin III/25 10.00 25.00
3 Russell Wilson/25 20.00 50.00
4 Colin Kaepernick/25 12.00 30.00
5 Doug Martin/25 12.00 30.00
6 Alfred Morris/25 10.00 25.00
7 Adrian Peterson/25 30.00 80.00
8 Cam Newton/25 25.00 50.00
9 Peyton Manning/15 75.00 150.00
10 Arian Foster/25
11 Joe Flacco/20
12 Darren McFadden/25 12.00 30.00
13 Eli Manning/25 12.00 30.00
14 A.J. Green/25
15 Matt Ryan/25 12.00 30.00
16 Tony Romo/25 12.00 30.00

2013 Panini Playbook Jerseys Signatures Platinum

EXCH EXPIRATION: 4/2/2015
1 Andrew Luck/25 60.00 125.00
3 Russell Wilson/25 EXCH
4 Colin Kaepernick/25 EXCH 60.00 120.00
5 Doug Martin/25 EXCH 15.00 40.00
6 Alfred Morris/25 EXCH
7 Adrian Peterson/25 EXCH
8 Cam Newton/18 EXCH
9 Peyton Manning/25
10 Arian Foster/25 EXCH 20.00 50.00
11 Joe Flacco/25 EXCH
12 Darren McFadden/25 EXCH
13 Eli Manning/25 75.00 150.00
14 A.J. Green/25 15.00 40.00
15 Matt Ryan/25 EXCH
16 Tony Romo/25 EXCH

2013 Panini Playbook Mammoth Materials

1 Matt Ryan 6.00 15.00
2 Torrey Smith 5.00 12.00
3 C.J. Spiller 5.00 12.00
4 DeAngelo Williams 5.00 12.00
5 Andy Dalton 6.00 15.00
6 Dez Bryant 8.00 20.00
7 Von Miller 6.00 15.00
8 Matt Schaub 5.00 12.00
9 Reggie Wayne 6.00 15.00
10 Dexter McCluster 6.00 15.00

2013 Panini Playbook Offense/Defense

1 A.J. Green 1.25 3.00
2 Aaron Rodgers 2.00 5.00
3 Adrian Peterson 1.25 3.00
4 Alfred Morris .75 2.00
5 Andre Johnson .75 2.00
6 Andrew Luck 2.00 5.00
7 Andy Dalton 1.00 2.50
8 Arian Foster 1.00 2.50
9 Ben Roethlisberger 1.25 3.00
10 Brandon Marshall 1.00 2.50
11 C.J. Spiller .75 2.00
12 Calvin Johnson 1.25 3.00
13 Cam Newton 1.25 3.00
14 Chris Johnson .75 2.00
15 Clay Matthews 1.25 3.00
16 Colin Kaepernick 1.00 2.50
17 Darren McFadden 1.00 2.50
18 DeMarco Murray 1.00 2.50
19 Dez Bryant 1.25 3.00
20 Doug Martin 1.00 2.50
21 Drew Brees 1.25 3.00
22 Eli Manning 1.00 2.50
23 J.J. Watt 1.00 2.50
24 Jamaal Charles 1.00 2.50
25 Jason Witten 1.00 2.50
26 Jay Cutler .75 2.00
27 Jimmy Graham 1.25 3.00
28 Joe Flacco 1.00 2.50
29 Julio Jones 1.25 3.00
30 Larry Fitzgerald 1.00 2.50
31 LeSean McCoy 1.25 3.00
32 Marques Colston .75 2.00
33 Matt Forte .75 2.00
34 Matt Schaub .75 2.00
35 Matthew Stafford 1.00 2.50
36 Maurice Jones-Drew .75 2.00
37 Percy Harvin .75 2.00
38 Peyton Manning 2.50 6.00
39 Philip Rivers 1.25 3.00
40 Ray Rice .75 2.00
41 Robert Griffin III .75 2.00
42 Russell Wilson 2.50 6.00
43 Ryan Tannehill 1.00 2.50
44 Tom Brady 3.00 8.00
45 Tony Gonzalez 1.00 2.50
46 Tony Romo 1.00 2.50
47 Trent Richardson .75 2.00
48 Troy Polamalu 1.25 3.00
49 Victor Cruz 1.00 2.50
50 Wes Welker 1.00 2.50

2013 Panini Playbook Rookie Jerseys Silver

*GOLD/25: .8X TO 2X SILVER JSY/199
201 Aaron Dobson 2.50 6.00
202 Andre Ellington 2.50 6.00
203 Christine Michael 2.50 6.00
204 Cordarrelle Patterson 2.50 6.00
205 DeAndre Hopkins 6.00 15.00
206 Denard Robinson 2.50 6.00
207 Dion Jordan 2.50 6.00
208 Eddie Lacy 2.50 6.00
209 EJ Manuel 2.50 6.00
210 Gavin Escobar 2.50 6.00
211 Geno Smith 2.50 6.00
212 Giovani Bernard 2.50 6.00
213 Johnathan Franklin 2.50 6.00
214 Jordan Reed 4.00 10.00
215 Joseph Randle 2.50 6.00
216 Justin Hunter 2.50 6.00
217 Keenan Allen 5.00 12.00
218 Kenny Stills 2.50 6.00
219 Knile Davis 2.50 6.00
220 Landry Jones 2.50 6.00
221 Le'Veon Bell 8.00 20.00
222 Manti Te'o 3.00 8.00
223 Marcus Lattimore 2.50 6.00
224 Markus Wheaton 2.50 6.00
225 Marquise Goodwin 2.50 6.00
226 Matt Barkley 2.50 6.00
227 Mike Gillislee 2.50 6.00
228 Mike Glennon 2.50 6.00
229 Montee Ball 2.50 6.00
230 Quinton Patton 2.50 6.00
231 Robert Woods 4.00 10.00
232 Ryan Nassib 2.50 6.00
233 Stedman Bailey 2.50 6.00
234 Stepfan Taylor 2.50 6.00
235 Tavon Austin 3.00 8.00
236 Terrance Williams 2.50 6.00
237 Tyler Eifert 2.50 6.00
238 Tyler Wilson 2.50 6.00
239 Vance McDonald 3.00 8.00
240 Zach Ertz 5.00 12.00

2013 Panini Playbook Rookie Jerseys Signatures Silver

*GOLD/37-99: .5X TO 1.2X SLVR/199-299
*PLATINUM/47-49: .5X TO 1.2X SLVR/199-299
*PLATINUM/25: .6X TO 1.5X SLVR/199-299
*PLAYS/25: .6X TO 1.5X SLVR/199-299
*TEAM/39-65: .5X TO 1.2X SLVR/199-299
*TEAM/25-34: .6X TO 1.5X SLVR/199-299
201 Aaron Dobson/243 5.00 12.00
202 Andre Ellington/271 10.00 25.00
203 Christine Michael/244 5.00 12.00
204 Cordarrelle Patterson/269 5.00 12.00
205 DeAndre Hopkins/271 10.00 25.00
206 Denard Robinson/199 5.00 12.00
207 Dion Jordan/271 5.00 12.00
208 Eddie Lacy/297 5.00 12.00
209 EJ Manuel/299 5.00 12.00
210 Gavin Escobar/271 5.00 12.00
211 Geno Smith/271 5.00 12.00
212 Giovani Bernard/271 5.00 12.00
213 Johnathan Franklin/271 5.00 12.00
214 Jordan Reed/271 12.00 30.00
215 Joseph Randle/271 5.00 12.00
216 Justin Hunter/271 5.00 12.00
217 Keenan Allen/299 12.00 30.00
218 Kenny Stills/271 5.00 12.00
219 Knile Davis/271 5.00 12.00
220 Landry Jones/271 5.00 12.00
221 Le'Veon Bell/260 15.00 40.00
222 Manti Te'o/271 6.00 15.00
223 Marcus Lattimore/271 5.00 12.00
224 Markus Wheaton/271 5.00 12.00
225 Marquise Goodwin/271 5.00 12.00
226 Matt Barkley/271 5.00 12.00
227 Mike Gillislee/271 5.00 12.00
228 Mike Glennon/199 EXCH 5.00 12.00
229 Montee Ball/271 5.00 12.00
230 Quinton Patton/199 5.00 12.00
231 Robert Woods/299 8.00 20.00
232 Ryan Nassib/271 5.00 12.00
233 Stedman Bailey/299 5.00 12.00
234 Stepfan Taylor/299 5.00 12.00
235 Tavon Austin/271 6.00 15.00
236 Terrance Williams/271 5.00 12.00
237 Tyler Eifert/199 EXCH 5.00 12.00
238 Tyler Wilson/199 5.00 12.00
239 Vance McDonald/271 6.00 15.00
240 Zach Ertz/299 10.00 25.00

2013 Panini Playbook Rookie Mammoth Materials

*PRIME/25: .8X TO 2X BASIC JSY/99
1 Aaron Dobson 2.00 5.00
2 Andre Ellington 2.00 5.00
3 Christine Michael 2.00 5.00
4 Cordarrelle Patterson 2.00 5.00
5 DeAndre Hopkins 5.00 12.00
6 Denard Robinson 2.00 5.00
7 Dion Jordan 2.00 5.00
8 Eddie Lacy 2.00 5.00
9 EJ Manuel 2.00 5.00
10 Gavin Escobar 2.00 5.00
11 Geno Smith 2.00 5.00
12 Giovani Bernard 2.00 5.00
13 Johnathan Franklin 2.00 5.00
14 Jordan Reed 3.00 8.00
15 Joseph Randle 2.00 5.00
16 Justin Hunter 2.00 5.00
17 Keenan Allen 4.00 10.00
18 Kenny Stills 2.00 5.00
19 Knile Davis 2.00 5.00
20 Landry Jones 2.00 5.00
21 Le'Veon Bell 6.00 15.00
22 Manti Te'o 2.50 6.00
23 Marcus Lattimore 2.00 5.00
24 Markus Wheaton 2.00 5.00
25 Marquise Goodwin 2.00 5.00
26 Matt Barkley 2.00 5.00
27 Mike Gillislee 2.00 5.00
28 Mike Glennon 2.00 5.00
29 Montee Ball 2.00 5.00
30 Quinton Patton 2.00 5.00
31 Robert Woods 3.00 8.00
32 Ryan Nassib 2.00 5.00
33 Stedman Bailey 2.00 5.00
34 Stepfan Taylor 2.00 5.00
35 Tavon Austin 2.50 6.00
36 Terrance Williams 2.00 5.00
37 Tyler Eifert 2.00 5.00
38 Tyler Wilson 2.00 5.00
39 Vance McDonald 2.50 6.00
40 Zach Ertz 4.00 10.00

2014 Panini Playbook

2 Giovani Bernard JSY AU/25 8.00 20.00
4 Alfred Morris JSY AU/75 6.00 15.00
5 Andrew Luck JSY AU/15 75.00 150.00
8 Antonio Gates JSY AU/25
9 Arian Foster JSY AU/15 12.00 30.00
14 C.J. Spiller JSY AU/35 8.00 20.00
15 Cam Newton JSY AU/15 75.00 150.00
18 Nick Foles JSY AU/75 8.00 20.00
20 Mike Glennon JSY AU/25 10.00 25.00
22 DeMarcus Ware JSY AU/25 12.00 30.00
25 Doug Martin JSY AU/25 10.00 25.00
26 Drew Brees JSY AU/15 30.00 60.00
27 Dwayne Bowe JSY AU/25 10.00 25.00
28 Eli Manning JSY AU/15 30.00 60.00
32 Gavin Escobar JSY AU/75 6.00 15.00
33 DeAndre Hopkins JSY AU/25
42 Josh Gordon JSY AU/25 8.00 20.00
43 Julius Thomas JSY AU/75 10.00 25.00
47 LeSean McCoy JSY AU/15 15.00 40.00
50 Matt Ryan JSY AU/15 12.00 30.00
51 Matthew Stafford JSY AU/15 12.00 30.00
53 Michael Floyd JSY AU/25 8.00 20.00
55 Percy Harvin JSY AU/25 8.00 20.00
56 Peyton Manning JSY AU/13
62 Richard Sherman JSY AU/25 75.00 135.00
64 Ryan Tannehill JSY AU/15 12.00 30.00
67 T.Y. Hilton JSY AU/25 10.00 25.00
69 Torrey Smith JSY AU/50 6.00 15.00
70 Victor Cruz JSY AU/25 10.00 25.00
71 Vincent Jackson JSY AU/25 8.00 20.00
73 Tony Romo JSY AU/15 40.00 80.00
74 Eddie Lacy JSY AU/25 8.00 20.00
76 Antonio Andrews AU/99 RC 3.00 8.00
77 Jake Matthews AU/99 RC 3.00 8.00
78 Anthony Barr AU/99 RC 3.00 8.00
79 Marcus Roberson AU/99 RC 4.00 10.00
80 Aaron Donald AU/99 RC 8.00 20.00
81 Kyle Fuller AU/99 RC 3.00 8.00
82 Ryan Shazier AU/99 RC 5.00 12.00
83 Zack Martin AU/99 RC 8.00 20.00
84 Tevin Reese AU/99 RC 3.00 8.00
85 Calvin Pryor AU/99 RC 3.00 8.00
86 Jace Amaro AU/99 RC 3.00 8.00
87 Ha Ha Clinton-Dix AU/99 RC 4.00 10.00
88 Dee Ford AU/99 RC 3.00 8.00
89 Darquéze Dennard AU/99 RC 4.00 10.00
90 Jason Verrett AU/99 RC 3.00 8.00
91 Marcus Smith AU/99 RC 3.00 8.00
92 Dominique Easley AU/99 RC 3.00 8.00
93 Jimmie Ward AU/99 RC 4.00 10.00
94 Xavier Su'A-Filo AU/99 RC 4.00 10.00
95 Yawin Smallwood AU/99 RC 3.00 8.00
96 Ra'Shede Hageman AU/99 RC 3.00 8.00
97 Kyle Van Noy AU/99 RC 4.00 10.00
98 Lamarcus Joyner AU/99 RC 4.00 10.00
99 Trent Murphy AU/99 RC 3.00 8.00
100 Timmy Jernigan AU/99 RC 3.00 8.00
101 Troy Niklas AU/99 RC 3.00 8.00
102 Kony Ealy AU/99 RC 4.00 10.00
103 Travis Swanson AU/99 RC 3.00 8.00
104 Chris Borland AU/99 RC 3.00 8.00
105 Louis Nix III AU/99 RC 3.00 8.00
106 Josh Huff AU/99 RC 4.00 10.00
107 John Brown AU/99 RC 8.00 20.00
108 Jerick McKinnon AU/99 RC 4.00 10.00
109 Brandon Coleman AU/99 RC 3.00 8.00
110 Cody Hoffman AU/99 RC 3.00 8.00
111 Bruce Ellington AU/87 RC 3.00 8.00
112 Shaq Evans AU/99 RC 3.00 8.00
113 Martavis Bryant AU/99 RC 4.00 10.00
114 Kevin Norwood AU/99 RC 3.00 8.00
115 Isaiah Crowell AU/99 RC 4.00 10.00
116 Telvin Smith AU/99 RC 3.00 8.00
117 David Yankey AU/99 RC 3.00 8.00
118 Devin Street AU/99 RC 3.00 8.00
119 Chris Smith AU/99 RC 3.00 8.00
120 Ed Reynolds AU/99 RC 3.00 8.00
121 Jared Abbrederis AU/99 RC 6.00 15.00
122 Rajion Neal AU/99 RC 3.00 8.00
123 David Fales AU/99 RC 3.00 8.00
124 Lache Seastrunk AU/99 RC 3.00 8.00
125 Matt Hazel AU/99 RC 3.00 8.00
126 Marion Grice AU/99 RC 3.00 8.00
127 Tyler Gaffney AU/99 RC 3.00 8.00
128 Michael Campanaro AU/99 RC 3.00 8.00
129 Trevor Reilly AU/99 RC 3.00 8.00
130 Jeff Janis AU/99 RC 5.00 12.00
131 Shayne Skov AU/99 RC 3.00 8.00
132 Mike Davis AU/99 RC 3.00 8.00
133 L'Damian Washington AU/99 RC 4.00 10.00
134 James Wilder Jr. AU/99 RC 4.00 10.00
135 Brett Smith AU/99 RC 3.00 8.00
136 Khalil Mack JSY AU RC 15.00 30.00
137 Mike Evans JSY AU RC 10.00 25.00
138 Eric Ebron JSY AU RC 5.00 12.00
139 Odell Beckham Jr. JSY AU RC 40.00 80.00
140 Brandin Cooks JSY AU RC 6.00 15.00
141 Kelvin Benjamin JSY AU RC 6.00 15.00
142 Teddy Bridgewater JSY AU RC 6.00 15.00
143 Austin Seferian-Jenkins JSY AU RC 4.00 10.00
144 Marqise Lee JSY AU RC 5.00 12.00
145 Jordan Matthews JSY AU RC 6.00 15.00
146 Paul Richardson JSY AU RC 8.00 20.00
147 Connor Shaw JSY AU RC 4.00 10.00
148 Davante Adams JSY AU RC 12.00 30.00
149 Bishop Sankey JSY AU RC 4.00 10.00
150 Jeremy Hill JSY AU RC 5.00 12.00
151 Cody Latimer JSY AU RC 5.00 12.00
152 Carlos Hyde JSY AU RC 5.00 12.00
153 Allen Robinson JSY AU RC 6.00 15.00
154 Jimmy Garoppolo JSY AU RC 50.00 100.00
155 Jarvis Landry JSY AU RC 8.00 20.00
156 Charles Sims JSY AU RC 4.00 10.00
157 Tre Mason JSY AU RC 10.00 25.00
158 Donte Moncrief JSY AU RC 4.00 10.00
159 Terrance West JSY AU RC 4.00 10.00
160 Dri Archer JSY AU RC 4.00 10.00
161 Devonta Freeman JSY AU RC 12.00 30.00
162 Andre Williams JSY AU RC 4.00 10.00
163 Ka'Deem Carey JSY AU RC 8.00 20.00
164 Logan Thomas JSY AU RC 4.00 10.00
165 De'Anthony Thomas JSY AU RC 4.00 10.00
166 Tom Savage JSY AU RC 4.00 10.00
167 Aaron Murray JSY AU RC 4.00 10.00
168 A.J. McCarron JSY AU RC 4.00 10.00
169 Derek Carr JSY AU RC 40.00 80.00
170 Tajh Boyd JSY AU RC 4.00 10.00
171 Asa Watson JSY AU RC 4.00 10.00

2014 Panini Playbook Blue

*ROOKIE AU/25: .6X TO 1.5X BASIC AU/87-99

2014 Panini Playbook Gold

*VET.JSY AU/25: .5X TO 1.2X JSY AU/50-75
*VET.JSY AU/15: .5X TO 1.2X JSY AU/25-35
*ROOK.JSY AU/99: .5X TO 1.2X JSY AU/299
171 Asa Watson JSY AU 5.00 12.00
173 Blake Bortles JSY AU 6.00 15.00
174 Sammy Watkins JSY AU 8.00 20.00
175 Johnny Manziel JSY AU 8.00 20.00

2014 Panini Playbook Green

*ROOK.JSY AU/25: 1X TO 2.5X JSY AU/299
173 Blake Bortles JSY AU 10.00 25.00
174 Sammy Watkins JSY AU 12.00 30.00

2014 Panini Playbook Platinum

*ROOK.JSY AU/49: .6X TO 1.5X JSY AU/299

2014 Panini Playbook Armory Jerseys

1 Keenan Allen 20.00 50.00
2 Richard Sherman 60.00 120.00
3 Peyton Manning 60.00 120.00
4 Eddie Lacy 12.00 30.00
5 Le'Veon Bell 15.00 40.00
6 DeAndre Hopkins 15.00 40.00
7 EJ Manuel 12.00 30.00
8 Geno Smith 15.00 40.00
9 Giovani Bernard 12.00 30.00
10 Johnny Manziel 15.00 40.00
11 Teddy Bridgewater 30.00 60.00
12 Sammy Watkins 15.00 40.00
13 Jadeveon Clowney 12.00 30.00
14 Blake Bortles 12.00 30.00
15 Mike Evans 25.00 60.00
16 Odell Beckham Jr. 60.00 120.00
17 A.J. McCarron 10.00 25.00
18 Bishop Sankey 10.00 25.00
19 Kelvin Benjamin 30.00 80.00
20 Tony Romo 15.00 40.00
21 Derek Carr 40.00 100.00
22 Jarvis Landry 25.00 60.00
23 Tre Mason 10.00 25.00
24 De'Anthony Thomas 10.00 25.00

2014 Panini Playbook Combo Materials

1 J.Clowney/T.Savage 5.00 12.00
2 A.Robinson/C.Latimer 6.00 15.00
3 J.Landry/O.Beckham Jr. 50.00 100.00
4 A.McCarron/J.Hill 5.00 12.00
5 A.Seferian-Jenkins/B.Sankey 4.00 10.00
6 L.Thomas/T.Savage 4.00 10.00
7 J.Clowney/K.Mack 15.00 40.00
8 J.Manziel/M.Evans 10.00 25.00
9 J.Amaro/T.Boyd 4.00 10.00
10 A.Luck/R.Griffin III 12.00 30.00
11 C.Kaepernick/R.Wilson 15.00 40.00
12 D.Adams/D.Carr 12.00 30.00
13 C.Shaw/J.Manziel 6.00 15.00
14 A.Watson/J.Garoppolo 30.00 80.00
15 A.Seferian-Jenkins/F.Ebron 5.00 12.00
16 M.Lee/P.Richardson 5.00 12.00
17 A.Peterson/J.Charles 10.00 25.00
18 C.Hyde/T.Mason 5.00 12.00
19 K.Benjamin/S.Watkins 6.00 15.00
20 D.Brees/K.Stills 10.00 25.00
21 A.Robinson/M.Lee 6.00 15.00
22 D.Freeman/K.Benjamin 12.00 30.00
23 B.Bortles/T.Bridgewater 6.00 15.00
24 B.Bortles/M.Lee 5.00 12.00

2014 Panini Playbook Down and Dirty Jerseys

1 DeMarco Murray/25 12.00 30.00
2 Montee Ball/25 10.00 25.00
3 Larry Fitzgerald/25 12.00 30.00
4 Brian Hartline/25 10.00 25.00
5 Jermaine Gresham/25 10.00 25.00
6 Giovani Bernard/25 10.00 25.00
7 Von Miller/25 12.00 30.00
8 Shonn Greene/25 10.00 25.00
10 Dez Bryant/25 20.00 50.00
11 Vernon Davis/25 10.00 25.00
12 Marshawn Lynch/25 12.00 30.00
13 Justin Hunter/25 10.00 25.00
14 Doug Martin/25 12.00 30.00
15 Eric Berry/25 15.00 40.00
16 Paul Posluszny/25 10.00 25.00

2014 Panini Playbook Game of Inches Jerseys

1 Colin Kaepernick 15.00 40.00
2 Darren McFadden 12.00 30.00
3 Calvin Johnson 20.00 50.00
4 Cam Newton 20.00 50.00
5 Wes Welker 15.00 40.00
7 Russell Wilson 25.00 60.00
8 Anquan Boldin 12.00 30.00
9 Adrian Peterson 20.00 50.00
10 Doug Martin 15.00 40.00
11 Robert Griffin III 12.00 30.00
12 Jamaal Charles 15.00 40.00

2014 Panini Playbook Jerseys

*GOLD ROOK/25: .8X TO 2X JSY/199
2 Colin Kaepernick/25 10.00 25.00
4 Peyton Manning/25 50.00 100.00
5 A.J. Green/25 12.00 30.00
6 Cam Newton/25 12.00 30.00
7 C.J. Spiller/25 8.00 20.00
8 Ryan Tannehill/25 10.00 25.00
9 Jordan Cameron/25 8.00 20.00
11 DeAndre Hopkins/25 10.00 25.00
12 Jamaal Charles/25 10.00 25.00
13 Keenan Allen/25 10.00 25.00
14 Tony Romo/25 10.00 25.00
15 Eli Manning/25 10.00 25.00
16 LeSean McCoy/25 12.00 30.00
17 Alfred Morris/25 8.00 20.00
18 Matt Forte/25 8.00 20.00
19 Matthew Stafford/25 10.00 25.00
22 Matt Ryan/25 10.00 25.00
23 Michael Floyd/25 8.00 20.00
25 Jimmy Graham/25 12.00 30.00
26 Doug Martin/25 10.00 25.00
27 Larry Fitzgerald/25 10.00 25.00
28 Tavon Austin/25 8.00 20.00
29 Anquan Boldin/25 8.00 20.00
30 Richard Sherman/25 15.00 40.00
136 Khalil Mack/199 10.00 25.00
137 Mike Evans/199 6.00 15.00
138 Eric Ebron/199 3.00 8.00
139 Odell Beckham Jr./199 6.00 15.00
140 Brandin Cooks/199 4.00 10.00
141 Kelvin Benjamin/199 4.00 10.00
142 Teddy Bridgewater/199 4.00 10.00
143 Austin Seferian-Jenkins/199 2.50 6.00
144 Marqise Lee/199 3.00 8.00
145 Jordan Matthews/199 4.00 10.00
146 Paul Richardson/199 3.00 8.00
147 Connor Shaw/199 2.50 6.00
148 Davante Adams/199 4.00 10.00
149 Bishop Sankey/199 2.50 6.00
150 Jeremy Hill/199 3.00 8.00
151 Cody Latimer/199 3.00 8.00
152 Carlos Hyde/199 3.00 8.00
153 Allen Robinson/199 4.00 10.00
154 Jimmy Garoppolo/199 20.00 50.00
155 Jarvis Landry/199 5.00 12.00
156 Charles Sims/199 2.50 6.00
157 Tre Mason/199 2.50 6.00
158 Donte Moncrief/199 2.50 6.00
159 Terrance West/199 2.50 6.00
160 Dri Archer/199 2.50 6.00
161 Devonta Freeman/199 4.00 10.00
162 Andre Williams/199 2.50 6.00
163 Ka'Deem Carey/199 2.50 6.00
164 Logan Thomas/199 2.50 6.00
165 De'Anthony Thomas/199 2.50 6.00
166 Tom Savage/199 2.50 6.00
167 Aaron Murray/199 2.50 6.00
168 A.J. McCarron/199 2.50 6.00
169 Derek Carr/199 8.00 20.00
170 Tajh Boyd/199 2.50 6.00
171 Asa Watson/199 2.50 6.00
172 Jadeveon Clowney/199 3.00 8.00
173 Blake Bortles/199 3.00 8.00
174 Sammy Watkins/199 4.00 10.00
175 Johnny Manziel/199 4.00 10.00

2014 Panini Playbook Jerseys Signatures Gold

7 C.J. Spiller/15 8.00 20.00
8 Ryan Tannehill/15 15.00 40.00
10 Deion Sanders/15 40.00 80.00
11 DeAndre Hopkins/25 8.00 20.00
16 LeSean McCoy/15 15.00 40.00
17 Alfred Morris/25 6.00 15.00
23 Michael Floyd/15 8.00 20.00
26 Doug Martin/15 10.00 25.00
28 Tavon Austin/25 6.00 15.00
32 Julius Thomas/21 15.00 40.00

2014 Panini Playbook Nicknames Jerseys

1 Calvin Johnson 15.00 40.00
2 Joe Namath 90.00 150.00
3 Peyton Manning 40.00 80.00
4 Adrian Peterson 12.00 30.00
5 Johnny Manziel 8.00 20.00
6 Deion Sanders 12.00 30.00
7 Darren McFadden 8.00 20.00
8 Richard Sherman 15.00 40.00
9 Matt Ryan 10.00 25.00
10 Drew Brees 15.00 40.00

2014 Panini Playbook QB Audibles Signatures

7 Logan Thomas/21 8.00 20.00

2014 Panini Playbook Rookie First Round Edition Materials

*FIRST RND/99: .4X TO 1X Xs&Os/99
*PRIME/25: 1X TO 2.5X BASIC JSY/99

2014 Panini Playbook Rookie First Round Edition Signatures

*FIRST ROUND/75: .4X TO 1X X's AND O's
6 Jake Matthews/16 6.00 15.00
8 Anthony Barr/17 6.00 15.00
12 Ha Ha Clinton-Dix/17

2014 Panini Playbook Rookie Signatures Premiere Team Photo

*TEAM/17-25: .25X TO .6X GREEN JSY AU/25

2014 Panini Playbook Rookie X's and O's Materials

*PRIME/25: .8X TO 2X BASIC JSY/99
1 Khalil Mack 4.00 10.00
2 Mike Evans 4.00 10.00
3 Eric Ebron 2.00 5.00
4 Odell Beckham Jr. 4.00 10.00
5 Brandin Cooks 2.50 6.00
6 Kelvin Benjamin 2.50 6.00
7 Teddy Bridgewater 2.50 6.00
8 Austin Seferian-Jenkins 1.50 4.00
9 Marqise Lee 2.00 5.00
10 Jordan Matthews 2.50 6.00
11 Paul Richardson 2.00 5.00
12 Connor Shaw 1.50 4.00
13 Davante Adams 2.50 6.00
14 Bishop Sankey 1.50 4.00
15 Jeremy Hill 2.00 5.00
16 Cody Latimer 2.00 5.00
17 Carlos Hyde 2.00 5.00
18 Allen Robinson 2.50 6.00
19 Jimmy Garoppolo 12.00 30.00
20 Jarvis Landry 3.00 8.00
21 Charles Sims 1.50 4.00
22 Tre Mason 1.50 4.00
23 Donte Moncrief 1.50 4.00
24 Terrance West 1.50 4.00
25 Dri Archer 1.50 4.00
26 Devonta Freeman 2.50 6.00
27 Andre Williams 1.50 4.00
28 Ka'Deem Carey 1.50 4.00
29 Logan Thomas 1.50 4.00
30 De'Anthony Thomas 1.50 4.00
31 Tom Savage 1.50 4.00
32 Aaron Murray 1.50 4.00
33 A.J. McCarron 1.50 4.00
34 Derek Carr 5.00 12.00
35 Tajh Boyd 1.50 4.00
36 Asa Watson 1.50 4.00
37 Jadeveon Clowney 2.00 5.00
38 Blake Bortles 2.00 5.00
39 Sammy Watkins 2.50 6.00
40 Johnny Manziel 2.50 6.00

2014 Panini Playbook Rookie X's and O's Signatures

1 Khalil Mack/75 10.00 25.00
2 Mike Evans/75 15.00 40.00
4 Odell Beckham Jr./75 50.00 100.00
5 Brandin Cooks/75 6.00 15.00
6 Ryan Shazier/75 6.00 15.00
7 Teddy Bridgewater/75 6.00 15.00
8 Austin Seferian-Jenkins/75 4.00 10.00
9 Asa Watson/75 4.00 10.00
10 Jordan Matthews/75 6.00 15.00
11 Paul Richardson/75 8.00 20.00
12 Kevin Norwood/75 4.00 10.00
13 Davante Adams/75 6.00 15.00
14 Kyle Fuller/15 6.00 15.00
15 Jeremy Hill/75 5.00 12.00
16 Cody Latimer/75 5.00 12.00
17 Carlos Hyde/75 5.00 12.00
18 Allen Robinson/75 6.00 15.00
19 Bishop Sankey/75 4.00 10.00
20 Jarvis Landry/75 10.00 25.00
21 Charles Sims/75 4.00 10.00
22 Tre Mason/75 4.00 10.00
23 Donte Moncrief/75 4.00 10.00
24 Terrance West/75 4.00 10.00
25 Dri Archer/75 4.00 10.00
26 Devonta Freeman/75 6.00 15.00
27 Andre Williams/75 4.00 10.00
28 Ka'Deem Carey/75 4.00 10.00
30 De'Anthony Thomas/75 4.00 10.00
31 Jeff Janis/16 6.00 15.00
32 Aaron Murray/75 4.00 10.00
34 Connor Shaw/75 4.00 10.00
35 Tajh Boyd/75 4.00 10.00
36 Zack Martin/16 12.00 30.00
38 Blake Bortles/75 5.00 12.00
39 Sammy Watkins/75 6.00 15.00
40 Johnny Manziel/75 6.00 15.00

2014 Panini Playbook Signature Plays

1-32 UNPRICED VET AU PRINT RUN 1-5
*ROOK/25: .25X TO .6X GREEN JSY AU/25
139 Odell Beckham Jr./25 100.00 175.00
175 Johnny Manziel/25 12.00 30.00

2014 Panini Playbook Triple Threats Jerseys

1 Bldn/Kprnck/Dvs/25 8.00 20.00
2 Mrry/Brynt/Rmo/25 10.00 25.00
3 Thms/Smth/Shrmn/25 12.00 30.00
4 Mrrs/Grcn/GrffnIII/25 8.00 20.00
5 Jhnsn/Stffrd/Bsh/25 12.00 30.00
6 Nwtn/Wllms/Bnjmn/25 6.00 15.00
7 Mcln/McCy/Fles/25 10.00 25.00
8 Brs/Grhm/Stlls/25 10.00 25.00
9 Mnnng/Rndle/Crz/25 8.00 20.00
10 Rdgrs/Jnes/Ryn/25 10.00 25.00
11 Mrtn/Glnnn/Jcksn/25 8.00 20.00
12 Brwn/Bll/Plmlu/25 10.00 25.00
13 Tllmn/Ctler/Frte/25 8.00 20.00
14 Brs/Mnnng/Brdy/25 25.00 60.00
16 Jhnsn/Brry/Hstn/25 10.00 25.00
17 Lck/Wyne/Mths/25 12.00 30.00
18 Alln/Rvrs/Mthws/25 10.00 25.00
19 Thms/Thms/Mnnng/25 20.00 50.00
20 Hdn/Cmrn/Grdn/25 6.00 15.00
21 Ptrsn/Pttrsn/Jnnngs/25 10.00 25.00
22 Ivry/Smth/Rchrdsn/25 8.00 20.00
23 Brdfrd/Astn/Stcy/25 6.00 15.00
24 Ltmr/Bll/Hllmn/25 8.00 20.00
25 Rd/Csns/Hnkrsn/25 10.00 25.00
26 Smth/Chrls/Dvs/25 10.00 25.00
27 Plmr/Ftzgrld/Flyd/25 8.00 20.00
28 Jhnsn/Fster/Hpkns/25 8.00 20.00
29 Spllr/Mnl/Wds/25 8.00 20.00
30 Jhnsn/Poe/Hali/25 6.00 15.00
31 Hntr/Wrght/Grne/25 6.00 15.00
32 Grn/Dltn/Brnrd/25 10.00 25.00
33 Hrtlne/Wllce/Tnnhll/25 8.00 20.00
34 Lnch/Hrvin/Wlsn/25 15.00 40.00
35 Prce/Flcco/Smth/25 8.00 20.00
37 Edlmn/Rdly/Brdy/25 20.00 50.00
38 Upshw/Elm/Sggs/25 6.00 15.00
39 McFddn/Mre/Schb/25 6.00 15.00
40 Lng/Lrnts/Qnn/25 8.00 20.00

2014 Panini Playbook X's and O's Materials

*PRIME/25: .6X TO 1.5X BASIC JSY/99
*PRIME/25: .5X TO 1.2X BASIC JSY/44
1 Malcolm Smith/99 5.00 12.00
2 Kam Chancellor/99 5.00 12.00
3 Barkevious Mingo/99 3.00 8.00
4 Geno Atkins/99 3.00 8.00
5 Giovani Bernard/99 3.00 8.00
6 Brian Cushing/99 3.00 8.00
7 Jordan Cameron/99 3.00 8.00
8 Reggie Bush/99 3.00 8.00
9 Vontaze Burfict/99 3.00 8.00
10 Robert Griffin III/99 3.00 8.00
11 Von Miller/99 4.00 10.00
12 DeMarco Murray/99 4.00 10.00
13 Cam Newton/99 5.00 12.00
14 Greg Olsen/44 5.00 12.00
15 EJ Manuel/99 3.00 8.00
16 Joe Flacco/99 4.00 10.00
17 Jacoby Jones/99 3.00 8.00

18 Arian Foster/99 4.00 10.00
19 Wes Welker/99 4.00 10.00

2015 Panini Playbook

1 A.Luck/T.Hilton 3.00 8.00
2 A.Foster/J.Watt 2.50 6.00
3 B.Sankey/K.Wright 1.50 4.00
4 B.Bortles/P.Posluszny 1.50 4.00
5 C.Newton/L.Kuechly 2.50 6.00
6 J.Jones/M.Ryan 2.50 6.00
7 D.Brees/M.Ingram 2.50 6.00
8 G.McCoy/M.Evans 2.00 5.00
9 P.Manning/V.Miller 5.00 12.00
10 P.Rivers/K.Allen 2.50 6.00
11 J.Tuck/D.Carr 2.50 6.00
12 J.Charles/J.Houston 2.00 5.00
13 M.Lynch/R.Wilson 3.00 8.00
14 C.Hyde/C.Kaepernick 2.00 5.00
15 L.Fitzgerald/A.Ellington 2.00 5.00
16 J.Laurinaitis/N.Foles 2.00 5.00
17 N.Suh/R.Tannehill 2.00 5.00
18 B.Marshall/D.Revis 1.50 4.00
19 L.McCoy/S.Watkins 2.50 6.00
20 R.Gronkowski/T.Brady 6.00 15.00
21 S.Bradford/D.Murray 2.00 5.00
22 A.Morris/R.Griffin III 1.50 4.00
23 T.Romo/D.Bryant 2.50 6.00
24 E.Manning/O.Beckham Jr. 2.50 6.00
25 A.Green/J.Hill 2.50 6.00
26 B.Roethlisberger/L.Bell 2.50 6.00
27 D.Bowe/I.Crowell 2.00 5.00
28 J.Flacco/S.Smith 2.00 5.00
29 T.Bridgewater/A.Peterson 2.50 6.00
30 C.Johnson/M.Stafford 2.50 6.00
31 A.Jeffery/M.Forte 2.00 5.00
32 A.Rodgers/J.Nelson 5.00 12.00
33 D.Clark/J.Montana 6.00 15.00
34 R.Staubach/T.Aikman 3.00 8.00
35 T.Davis/J.Elway 4.00 10.00
36 S.Young/J.Rice 4.00 10.00
37 T.Thomas/J.Kelly 2.50 6.00
38 B.Jackson/T.Brown 3.00 8.00
39 K.Warner/M.Faulk 2.00 5.00
40 L.Taylor/M.Strahan 2.50 6.00
41 T.Bradshaw/F.Harris 6.00 15.00
42 B.Favre/D.Majkowski 5.00 12.00
43 B.Urlacher/D.Hampton 2.50 6.00
44 D.Marino/L.Csonka 5.00 12.00
45 E.Smith/T.Dorsett 4.00 10.00
46 J.Bettis/R.Woodson 2.50 6.00
47 E.Campbell/W.Moon 2.50 6.00
48 D.Sanders/R.Sherman 2.50 6.00
49 J.Montana/T.Brady 8.00 20.00
50 J.Elway/P.Manning 5.00 12.00
51 Marcus Mariota JSY RC 5.00 12.00
52 David Cobb JSY RC 1.25 3.00
53 Dorial Green-Beckham JSY RC 1.25 3.00
54 Jaelen Strong JSY RC 1.50 4.00
55 Phillip Dorsett JSY RC 1.25 3.00
56 T.J. Yeldon JSY RC 1.25 3.00
57 Rashad Greene JSY RC 1.25 3.00
58 Justin Hardy JSY RC 1.25 3.00
59 Tevin Coleman JSY RC 1.50 4.00
60 Devin Funchess JSY RC 2.00 5.00
61 Garrett Grayson JSY RC 1.25 3.00
62 Jameis Winston JSY RC 3.00 8.00
63 Chris Conley JSY RC 1.25 3.00
64 Amari Cooper JSY RC 4.00 10.00
65 Melvin Gordon JSY RC 3.00 8.00
66 David Johnson JSY RC 3.00 8.00
67 Mike Davis JSY RC 1.25 3.00
68 Tyler Lockett JSY RC 6.00 15.00
69 Sean Mannion JSY RC 1.25 3.00
70 Todd Gurley JSY RC 10.00 25.00
71 DeVante Parker JSY RC 2.00 5.00
72 Jay Ajayi JSY RC 2.00 5.00
73 Bryce Petty JSY RC 1.25 3.00
74 Devin Smith JSY RC 1.25 3.00
75 Leonard Williams JSY RC 1.25 3.00
76 Nelson Agholor JSY RC 1.50 4.00
77 Jamison Crowder JSY RC 1.50 4.00
78 Matt Jones JSY RC 1.25 3.00
79 Breshad Perriman JSY RC 1.25 3.00
80 Buck Allen JSY RC 1.50 4.00
81 Maxx Williams JSY RC 1.25 3.00
82 Duke Johnson JSY RC 2.00 5.00
83 Vince Mayle JSY RC 1.50 4.00
84 Sammie Coates JSY RC 1.50 4.00
85 Jeremy Langford JSY RC 1.25 3.00
86 Kevin White JSY RC 1.50 4.00
87 Ameer Abdullah JSY RC 2.00 5.00
88 Brett Hundley JSY RC 6.00 15.00
89 Ty Montgomery JSY RC 1.25 3.00
90 Stefon Diggs JSY RC 3.00 8.00
91 Karlos Williams JSY RC 1.25 3.00

2015 Panini Playbook Gold

*VETS/199: .5X TO 1.2X BASIC CARDS/299
*ROOKIES/25: .8X TO 2X BASIC JSY/199

2015 Panini Playbook Green

*VETS/25: 1.2X TO 3X BASIC CARDS/299

2015 Panini Playbook Activ8 Materials

1 Prkr/Wnstn/White/Mrta Cpr/Wllms/Grdn/Grly 10.00 25.00

2015 Panini Playbook Armory Jerseys

1 Jameis Winston/25 12.00 30.00
2 Marcus Mariota/25 50.00 100.00
3 Julio Jones/25 20.00 50.00
4 Amari Cooper/25 15.00 40.00
5 Todd Gurley/25 20.00 50.00
6 Kevin White/25 6.00 15.00
8 Melvin Gordon/25 12.00 30.00
9 Andrew Luck/25 25.00 60.00
10 Odell Beckham Jr./25 20.00 50.00
12 Cam Newton/15 40.00 100.00

2015 Panini Playbook Down and Dirty Jerseys

1 Julian Edelman 15.00 40.00
2 Dee Ford 10.00 25.00
3 Lamar Miller 10.00 25.00
4 Jeremy Hill 10.00 25.00
5 A.J. Green 15.00 40.00
6 Sammy Watkins 12.00 30.00
7 Emmanuel Sanders 12.00 30.00
8 Bradley Roby 10.00 25.00
9 Blake Bortles 10.00 25.00
10 Tamba Hali 10.00 25.00
11 Orlando Scandrick 10.00 25.00
12 Jarvis Landry 12.00 30.00

2015 Panini Playbook Draft Edition Memorabilia

1 Dante Fowler Jr. 2.00 5.00
2 Brandon Scherff 2.00 5.00
3 Leonard Williams 1.25 3.00
4 Kevin White 1.50 4.00
5 Vic Beasley Jr. 1.50 4.00
6 Todd Gurley 5.00 12.00
7 Trae Waynes 1.25 3.00
8 Danny Shelton 1.25 3.00
9 DeVante Parker 2.00 5.00
10 Melvin Gordon 3.00 8.00
11 Kevin Johnson 1.25 3.00
12 Bud Dupree 1.50 4.00
13 Shane Ray 1.25 3.00
14 Breshad Perriman 1.25 3.00
15 Byron Jones 6.00 15.00
16 Blake Bortles 1.50 4.00
17 Teddy Bridgewater 2.00 5.00
18 Johnny Manziel 2.00 5.00
19 Odell Beckham Jr. 2.50 6.00
20 Jadeveon Clowney 1.50 4.00
21 Sammy Watkins 2.00 5.00
22 Khalil Mack 2.50 6.00
23 Mike Evans 2.00 5.00
24 Ryan Shazier 1.50 4.00
25 Ha Ha Clinton-Dix 1.50 4.00

2015 Panini Playbook Face 2 Face Materials

*PRIME/25: .5X TO 1.2X DUAL JSY/49
1 J.Winston/M.Mariota/49 12.00 30.00
2 K.White/A.Cooper/49 10.00 25.00
3 M.Gordon/T.Gurley/49 12.00 30.00
5 B.Carr/O.Beckham Jr./49 6.00 15.00
6 B.Perriman/S.Coates/49 4.00 10.00
7 D.Revis/S.Watkins/49 6.00 15.00
8 T.Hali/K.Mack/49 8.00 20.00
9 C.Wake/F.Jackson/15 8.00 20.00
10 J.Strong/P.Dorsett/49 4.00 10.00
11 J.Crowder/N.Agholor/49 4.00 10.00
12 S.Young/T.Aikman/25 12.00 30.00

2015 Panini Playbook Game of Inches Jerseys

1 Dez Bryant/25 20.00 50.00
2 Marshawn Lynch/25 15.00 40.00
3 Odell Beckham Jr./25 20.00 50.00
4 Danny Amendola/20 15.00 40.00
5 Joseph Randle/25 12.00 30.00
6 Denard Robinson/25 12.00 30.00
7 Mohamed Sanu/25 12.00 30.00
8 Cam Newton/25 20.00 50.00
9 Nate Washington/25 12.00 30.00
10 Andrew Luck/25 25.00 60.00
11 Montee Ball/25 12.00 30.00
12 Johnny Manziel/25 15.00 40.00

2015 Panini Playbook Hot Routes Jerseys

*PRIME/50: .6X TO 1.5X BASIC JSY/199
*PRIME/25: .5X TO 1.2X BASIC JSY/49
*PRIME/25: .6X TO 1.5X BASIC JSY/99
1 Odell Beckham Jr./199 2.50 6.00
2 Antonio Brown/99 3.00 8.00
3 Dez Bryant/25 8.00 20.00
4 Mike Evans/199 2.00 5.00
5 A.J. Green/49 4.00 10.00
6 DeVante Parker/199 2.00 5.00
7 Amari Cooper/199 4.00 10.00
8 Sammy Watkins/199 2.00 5.00
9 Jerry Rice/199 4.00 10.00
10 Alshon Jeffery/199 2.00 5.00
11 Phillip Dorsett/199 1.25 3.00
12 Nelson Agholor/199 1.50 4.00
13 Marqise Lee/199 1.50 4.00
14 Breshad Perriman/199 1.25 3.00
15 Jason Witten/99 2.50 6.00
16 Antonio Gates/49 2.50 6.00
17 Julio Jones/99 3.00 8.00
18 Sammie Coates/199 1.50 4.00
19 Calvin Johnson/99 3.00 8.00
20 Rob Gronkowski/25 8.00 20.00
21 Travis Kelce/199 2.50 6.00
22 Tyler Lockett/199 2.00 5.00
23 Randall Cobb/25 4.00 10.00
24 Vince Mayle/199 1.50 4.00
25 Jaelen Strong/199 1.50 4.00

2015 Panini Playbook Jerseys Silver

*GOLD/20-25: .6X TO 1.5X BASIC JSY/99
*GOLD/20-25: .5X TO 1.2X BASIC JSY/49
1 Johnny Manziel/99 3.00 8.00
2 Alfred Morris/20 4.00 10.00
3 Sammy Watkins/75 3.00 8.00
4 Jimmy Garoppolo/99 5.00 12.00
5 Donte Moncrief/99 3.00 8.00
6 Carlos Hyde/99 2.50 6.00
7 Demaryius Thomas/25 5.00 12.00
8 Mike Evans/99 3.00 8.00
9 Victor Cruz/49 4.00 10.00
10 Jarvis Landry/99 3.00 8.00
11 Bishop Sankey/99 2.50 6.00
12 Davante Adams/99 3.00 8.00
13 Julius Thomas/49 3.00 8.00
14 Blake Bortles/99 2.50 6.00
15 Keenan Allen/25 5.00 12.00
16 Brandin Cooks/99 3.00 8.00
17 Devonta Freeman/99 3.00 8.00
18 Montee Ball/49 3.00 8.00
19 Patrick Peterson/49 3.00 8.00
20 Jordan Matthews/99 3.00 8.00
21 Tre Mason/99 3.00 8.00
22 Andre Williams/40 3.00 8.00
23 Reggie Bush/49 3.00 8.00
24 Marqise Lee/99 2.50 6.00
27 Jeremy Hill/99 2.50 6.00
28 Cody Latimer/99 2.50 6.00
29 Kelvin Benjamin/99 3.00 8.00

2015 Panini Playbook Jerseys Signatures Silver

*GOLD/35-49: .5X TO 1.2X JSY AU/70-99
*GOLD/25: .6X TO 1.5X JSY AU/70-99
*GOLD/25: .5X TO 1.2X JSY AU/49
*GOLD/15: .5X TO 1.2X JSY AU/25
*PLATINUM/25: .6X TO 1.5X JSY AU/99
*PLATINUM/25: .5X TO 1.2X JSY AU/49
*PLATINUM/15: .5X TO 1.2X JSY AU/20-30
1 Johnny Manziel/25 8.00 20.00
2 Alfred Morris/25 15.00 30.00
3 Sammy Watkins/20
4 Jimmy Garoppolo/99 50.00 100.00
5 Donte Moncrief/49 6.00 15.00
6 Carlos Hyde/49 20.00 40.00
7 Demaryius Thomas/30 8.00 20.00
8 Mike Evans/25
10 Jarvis Landry/49 6.00 15.00
11 Bishop Sankey/25
12 Davante Adams/70 10.00 25.00
14 Blake Bortles/20
15 Keenan Allen/25 8.00 20.00
16 Brandin Cooks/25
17 Devonta Freeman/49 15.00 30.00
18 Montee Ball/49 5.00 12.00
19 Patrick Peterson/99 12.00 30.00
20 Jordan Matthews/49 6.00 15.00
21 Tre Mason/25
22 Andre Williams/49 5.00 12.00
23 Reggie Bush/25 6.00 15.00
24 Marqise Lee/75 4.00 10.00
26 Kenny Stills/25 6.00 15.00
27 Jeremy Hill/49 10.00 25.00
28 Cody Latimer/49 5.00 12.00
29 Kelvin Benjamin/15

2015 Panini Playbook Mammoth Jerseys

*PRIME/50: .5X TO 1.2X BASIC JSY/99
1 Marcus Mariota 6.00 15.00
2 Dorial Green-Beckham 1.50 4.00
3 Jaelen Strong 2.00 5.00
4 Phillip Dorsett 1.50 4.00
5 T.J. Yeldon 1.50 4.00
6 Tevin Coleman 2.00 5.00
7 Devin Funchess 2.50 6.00
8 Garrett Grayson 1.50 4.00
9 Jameis Winston 8.00 20.00
10 Chris Conley 1.50 4.00
11 Amari Cooper 5.00 12.00
12 Melvin Gordon 4.00 10.00
13 David Johnson 4.00 10.00
14 Tyler Lockett 2.50 6.00
15 Sean Mannion 1.50 4.00
16 Todd Gurley 5.00 12.00
17 DeVante Parker 2.50 6.00
18 Bryce Petty 1.50 4.00
19 Nelson Agholor 2.00 5.00
20 Matt Jones 1.50 4.00
21 Breshad Perriman 1.50 4.00
22 Sammie Coates 2.00 5.00
23 Jeremy Langford 1.50 4.00
24 Kevin White 2.00 5.00
25 Ameer Abdullah 2.50 6.00

2015 Panini Playbook Rookie Materials Signatures Silver

51 Marcus Mariota/199 25.00 50.00
52 David Cobb/199 4.00 10.00
53 Dorial Green-Beckham/199 4.00 10.00
54 Jaelen Strong/199 5.00 12.00
55 Phillip Dorsett/199 4.00 10.00
56 T.J. Yeldon/199 4.00 10.00
57 Rashad Greene/199 4.00 10.00
58 Justin Hardy/199 4.00 10.00
59 Tevin Coleman/199 5.00 12.00
60 Devin Funchess/199 6.00 15.00
61 Garrett Grayson/49 6.00 15.00
62 Jameis Winston/199 40.00 80.00
63 Chris Conley/199 4.00 10.00
64 Amari Cooper/99 30.00 60.00
65 Melvin Gordon/199 10.00 25.00
66 David Johnson/199 15.00 40.00
67 Mike Davis/199 4.00 10.00
68 Tyler Lockett/99 8.00 20.00
69 Sean Mannion/199 4.00 10.00
70 Todd Gurley/199 40.00 100.00
71 DeVante Parker/199 6.00 15.00
72 Jay Ajayi/199 6.00 15.00
73 Bryce Petty/199 4.00 10.00
74 Devin Smith/199 4.00 10.00
75 Leonard Williams/199 4.00 10.00
76 Nelson Agholor/199 5.00 12.00
77 Jamison Crowder/199 5.00 12.00
78 Matt Jones/199 4.00 10.00
79 Breshad Perriman/199 4.00 10.00
80 Buck Allen/199 5.00 12.00
81 Maxx Williams/199 4.00 10.00
82 Duke Johnson/199 6.00 15.00
83 Vince Mayle/199 5.00 12.00
84 Sammie Coates/199 5.00 12.00
85 Jeremy Langford/199 4.00 10.00
86 Kevin White/199 5.00 12.00
87 Ameer Abdullah/199 6.00 15.00
88 Brett Hundley/199 4.00 10.00
89 Ty Montgomery/199 12.00 30.00
90 Stefon Diggs/199 10.00 25.00
91 Karlos Williams/199 4.00 10.00

2015 Panini Playbook Rookie Materials Signature Plays

*GREEN/25: .8X TO 2X JSY AU/199
51 Marcus Mariota/25 40.00 80.00
62 Jameis Winston/25 50.00 100.00

2015 Panini Playbook Rookie Materials Signatures Gold

*GOLD/99: .5X TO 1.2X JSY AU/199
*GOLD/49: .5X TO 1.2X JSY AU/99
*GOLD/25: .5X TO 1.2X JSY AU/49
51 Marcus Mariota/99 30.00 60.00
62 Jameis Winston/99 75.00 150.00
70 Todd Gurley/99 75.00 150.00

2015 Panini Playbook Rookie Materials Signatures Green

*GREEN/25: .8X TO 2X JSY AU/199
51 Marcus Mariota/25 40.00 100.00
62 Jameis Winston/25 100.00 200.00
70 Todd Gurley/25 150.00 250.00

2015 Panini Playbook Rookie Materials Signatures Platinum

*PLATINUM/49: .6X TO 1.5X JSY AU/199
*PLATINUM/15: .8X TO 2X JSY AU/99
51 Marcus Mariota/49 30.00 80.00
62 Jameis Winston/49 75.00 150.00

2015 Panini Playbook Rookie X's and O's Signatures

*GOLD/25: .8X TO 2X BASIC AU/199
1 Bud Dupree 4.00 10.00
2 Arik Armstead 3.00 8.00
3 Benardrick McKinney 3.00 8.00
4 Cameron Artis-Payne 3.00 8.00
5 Clive Walford 3.00 8.00
6 Danny Shelton 3.00 8.00
7 Dante Fowler Jr. 5.00 12.00
8 Darren Waller 4.00 10.00
10 Dezmin Lewis 3.00 8.00
11 Eli Harold 3.00 8.00
12 Eric Kendricks 3.00 8.00
13 Eric Rowe 3.00 8.00
14 Byron Jones 8.00 20.00
15 Jalen Collins 3.00 8.00
16 J.J. Nelson 3.00 8.00
17 Josh Robinson 5.00 12.00
18 Jesse James 4.00 10.00
20 Kevin Johnson 3.00 8.00
21 Landon Collins 4.00 10.00
22 Marcus Peters 5.00 12.00
23 Owamagbe Odighizuwa 4.00 10.00
24 Nick O'Leary 3.00 8.00
25 Ronald Darby 3.00 8.00
26 Shane Ray 3.00 8.00
27 Shaq Thompson 4.00 10.00
28 Stephone Anthony 3.00 8.00
29 Trae Waynes 3.00 8.00
30 Vic Beasley Jr. 4.00 10.00

2015 Panini Playbook Signature Materials

1 Tony Romo/25 25.00 50.00
2 Jamaal Charles/49 10.00 25.00
3 Blake Bortles/49 12.00 30.00
4 Ozzie Newsome/49 10.00 25.00
5 Derek Carr/99 20.00 40.00
6 Andrew Luck/12
7 Joseph Randle/199 3.00 8.00
8 Richard Sherman/25 30.00 60.00
9 Tim Brown/25 15.00 30.00
10 Andre Williams/199 3.00 8.00
11 Percy Harvin/49 8.00 20.00
12 Tre Mason/99 5.00 12.00
13 Drew Brees/25 30.00 60.00
14 Cris Collinsworth/25 8.00 20.00
15 Mike Evans/99 5.00 12.00
16 Colin Kaepernick/25 20.00 40.00
17 Rod Woodson/25 20.00 40.00
18 Lorenzo Taliaferro/125 3.00 8.00
19 Jason Witten/25 20.00 40.00
20 DeAndre Hopkins/49 10.00 25.00
21 Teddy Bridgewater/49 20.00 40.00
22 Brandin Cooks/99 5.00 12.00
23 DeSean Jackson/49 6.00 15.00
24 Randall Cobb/49 15.00 30.00
25 Tyler Eifert/99 5.00 12.00
26 Antonio Brown/49 25.00 50.00
27 Ryan Tannehill/49 6.00 15.00
28 Von Miller/99 5.00 12.00
29 Jay Cutler/25 20.00 50.00
30 Manti Te'o/99 5.00 12.00
32 Terrance Williams/99 4.00 10.00
33 Ricky Williams/25 8.00 20.00
34 Jimmy Garoppolo/49 10.00 25.00
35 Michael Strahan/25 20.00 40.00
36 Charles Sims/199 3.00 8.00
38 Marshawn Lynch/25 20.00 40.00
39 Bishop Sankey/99 4.00 10.00
40 Dez Bryant/25 25.00 50.00
41 Terrance West/199 3.00 8.00
42 Jarvis Landry/49 6.00 15.00
43 Cordarrelle Patterson/99 4.00 10.00
44 Charlie Joiner/49 20.00 40.00
45 Matt Ryan/25 12.00 30.00
46 Len Dawson/49 20.00 40.00
47 Geno Smith/49 5.00 12.00
48 DeMarcus Ware/25 8.00 20.00
49 Ha Ha Clinton-Dix/49 5.00 12.00
50 Rob Gronkowski/49 25.00 50.00
51 Darren McFadden/49 5.00 12.00
52 Eric Ebron/99 4.00 10.00
53 Torrey Smith/49
55 Carl Eller/99 10.00 25.00
56 Jordan Matthews/99 5.00 12.00
57 Giovani Bernard/49 5.00 12.00
58 Michael Floyd/49

2015 Panini Playbook Signature Materials Prime

*PRIME AU/25: .8X TO 2X BASIC JSY AU/125-199
*PRIME AU/25: .6X TO 1.5X BASIC JSY AU/99
*PRIME AU/25: .5X TO 1.2X BASIC JSY AU/49

2015 Panini Playbook Storied Signatures

2 Aeneas Williams/25 8.00 20.00
3 James Lofton/25 8.00 20.00
5 Deion Sanders/25 30.00 60.00
6 Jim Kelly/25
7 Derrick Brooks/25 8.00 20.00
8 Kellen Winslow/25 10.00 25.00
10 Steve Largent/25 25.00 50.00

2015 Panini Playbook Triple Threats Jerseys

*PRIME/50: .6X TO 1.5X BASIC JSY/199
*PRIME/50: .5X TO 1.2X BASIC JSY/99
*PRIME/50: .4X TO 1X BASIC JSY/49
*PRIME/15: .8X TO 2X BASIC JSY/99
*PRIME/15: .5X TO 1.2X BASIC JSY/49
1 Wnstn/Grysn/Mrta/199 5.00 12.00
2 Grdn/Yldn/Grly/199 5.00 12.00
3 Whte/Cpr/Prkr/199 4.00 10.00
4 Prmn/Alln/Wllms/199 1.25 3.00
5 Cbb/GrnBckhm/Mrta/199 5.00 12.00
6 Sms/Wnstn/Evns/199 3.00 8.00
7 Flyd/Grdn/Rvrs/99 8.00 20.00
8 Nwtn/Fnchss/Bnjmn/199 2.00 5.00
9 Fvre/Hndly/Rdgrs/25 25.00 50.00
10 Mnzl/Jhnsn/Myle/199 2.00 5.00
11 Pttrsn/Dggs/Brdgwtr/199 3.00 8.00
12 Brwn/Bll/Cts/49 8.00 20.00
13 Wllms/Ptty/Smth/199 1.25 3.00
14 Prkr/Ajyi/Tnnhll/99 2.50 6.00
15 Dltn/Grn/Hll/99 2.50 6.00
16 Rndle/Wllms/Rmo/99 2.00 5.00
17 Mnng/Mntna/Brdy/25 50.00 100.00
18 Wlsn/Lnch/Lcktt/49 15.00 40.00
19 Aghlr/Mtthws/Brdfrd/99 2.00 5.00
20 Wllms/Mnng/Bckhm/49 6.00 15.00
21 Rmo/Akmn/Stbch/49 15.00 40.00
22 Frmn/Jnes/Clmn/99 2.50 6.00
23 Wllms/Grne/Wnstn/199 3.00 8.00
24 Abdllh/Jhnsn/Stffrd/99 2.50 6.00
25 Mnn/Msn/Grly/199 5.00 12.00

2016 Panini Playbook

1 Jason Witten 2.00 5.00
2 T.Y. Hilton 2.00 5.00
3 Antonio Gates 1.50 4.00
4 Matt Forte 1.50 4.00
5 Matt Ryan 2.00 5.00
6 Robert Griffin III 1.50 4.00
7 Jordan Reed 1.50 4.00
8 Colin Kaepernick 2.00 5.00
9 Demaryius Thomas 2.00 5.00
10 Ameer Abdullah 1.50 4.00
11 Antonio Brown 2.50 6.00
12 Delanie Walker 1.50 4.00
13 Doug Baldwin 2.00 5.00
14 Ryan Tannehill 2.00 5.00
15 Jameis Winston 2.50 6.00
16 Aaron Rodgers 5.00 12.00
17 Odell Beckham Jr. 2.50 6.00
18 Ezekiel Ansah 1.50 4.00
19 Latavius Murray 1.50 4.00
20 DeAndre Hopkins 2.00 5.00
21 Andy Dalton 2.00 5.00
22 Blake Bortles 1.50 4.00
23 Carson Palmer 2.00 5.00
24 Brandon Marshall 1.50 4.00
25 Devonta Freeman 2.00 5.00
26 Isaiah Crowell 1.50 4.00
27 Pierre Garcon 2.00 5.00
28 Carlos Hyde 1.50 4.00
29 Von Miller 2.00 5.00
30 Golden Tate III 1.50 4.00
31 Jeremy Hill 1.50 4.00
32 Allen Hurns 1.50 4.00
33 Chris Johnson 1.50 4.00
34 Darrelle Revis 1.50 4.00
35 Julio Jones 2.50 6.00
36 Gary Barnidge 1.50 4.00
37 Sam Bradford 1.50 4.00
38 Navorro Bowman 2.00 5.00
39 Alex Smith 2.00 5.00
40 Jay Cutler 1.50 4.00
41 Jason Pierre-Paul 1.50 4.00
42 J.J. Watt 2.50 6.00
43 Amari Cooper 2.50 6.00
44 Tom Brady 6.00 15.00
45 Cam Newton 2.50 6.00
46 Joe Flacco 2.00 5.00
47 Jarvis Landry 2.00 5.00
48 Todd Gurley 2.50 6.00
49 Doug Martin 2.00 5.00
50 Jordy Nelson 2.00 5.00
51 A.J. Green 2.50 6.00
52 Allen Robinson 2.00 5.00
53 Larry Fitzgerald 2.00 5.00
54 Tyrod Taylor 2.00 5.00
55 Drew Brees 2.50 6.00
56 Teddy Bridgewater 2.00 5.00
57 Jordan Matthews 2.00 5.00
58 Luke Kuechly 2.00 5.00
59 Jamaal Charles 2.00 5.00
60 Jeremy Langford 2.00 5.00
61 Tony Romo 2.00 5.00
62 Andrew Luck 3.00 8.00
63 Philip Rivers 2.50 6.00
64 Rob Gronkowski 2.50 6.00
65 Jonathan Stewart 1.50 4.00
66 Justin Forsett 2.00 5.00
67 Ndamukong Suh 2.00 5.00
68 Kenny Britt 1.50 4.00
69 Mike Evans 2.00 5.00
70 Randall Cobb 2.00 5.00
71 Ben Roethlisberger 2.50 6.00
72 Marcus Mariota 2.50 6.00
73 Russell Wilson 3.00 8.00
74 LeSean McCoy 2.50 6.00
75 Mark Ingram 2.00 5.00
76 Adrian Peterson 2.50 6.00
77 Ryan Mathews 2.00 5.00
78 Khalil Mack 2.50 6.00
79 Jeremy Maclin 1.50 4.00
80 Alshon Jeffery 2.00 5.00
81 Dez Bryant 2.50 6.00
82 Frank Gore 2.00 5.00
83 Melvin Gordon 2.00 5.00
84 Julian Edelman 2.50 6.00
85 Greg Olsen 2.00 5.00
86 Kirk Cousins 2.50 6.00
87 Steve Smith 2.00 5.00
88 Aaron Donald 2.50 6.00
89 Emmanuel Sanders 2.50 6.00
90 Matthew Stafford 2.00 5.00
91 Le'Veon Bell 2.00 5.00
92 DeMarco Murray 2.00 5.00
93 Thomas Rawls 1.50 4.00
94 Sammy Watkins 2.50 6.00
95 Brandin Cooks 2.00 5.00
96 Stefon Diggs 2.00 5.00
97 Eli Manning 2.00 5.00
98 Richard Sherman 2.50 6.00
99 Derek Carr 2.50 6.00
100 Lamar Miller 1.50 4.00
101 Jared Goff JSY AU/99 RC 30.00 80.00
102 Carson Wentz JSY AU/99 RC 100.00 200.00
103 Joey Bosa JSY AU/199 RC 15.00 40.00
104 Ezekiel Elliott JSY AU/99 RC 100.00 200.00
105 Corey Coleman JSY AU/99 RC 8.00 20.00
106 Will Fuller JSY AU/199 RC 12.00 30.00
107 Josh Doctson JSY AU/199 RC 5.00 12.00
108 Laquon Treadwell JSY AU/99 RC 6.00 15.00
109 Paxton Lynch JSY AU/99 RC 5.00 12.00
110 Hunter Henry JSY AU/199 RC 10.00 25.00
111 Sterling Shepard JSY AU/199 RC 15.00 40.00
112 Derrick Henry JSY AU/99 RC 12.00 30.00
113 Michael Thomas JSY AU/99 RC 15.00 40.00
114 Christian Hackenberg JSY AU/199 RC 4.00 10.00
115 Kenyan Drake JSY AU/199 RC 6.00 15.00
116 Braxton Miller JSY AU/199 RC 4.00 10.00
117 Leonte Carroo JSY AU/199 RC 4.00 10.00
118 C.J. Prosise JSY AU/199 RC 4.00 10.00
119 DeAndre Washington JSY AU/199 RC 4.00 10.00
120 Cody Kessler JSY AU/199 RC 4.00 10.00
121 Tyler Boyd JSY AU/199 RC 6.00 15.00
122 Connor Cook JSY AU/99 RC 6.00 15.00
123 Chris Moore JSY AU/199 RC 5.00 12.00
124 Ricardo Louis JSY AU/199 RC 4.00 10.00
125 Pharoh Cooper JSY AU/199 RC 4.00 10.00
126 Tyler Ervin JSY AU/199 RC 4.00 10.00
127 Demarcus Robinson JSY AU/199 RC 4.00 10.00
128 Kenneth Dixon JSY AU/199 RC 4.00 10.00
129 Dak Prescott JSY AU/199 RC 40.00 80.00
130 Devontae Booker JSY AU/199 RC 5.00 12.00
131 Cardale Jones JSY AU/99 RC 5.00 12.00
132 Paul Perkins JSY AU/199 RC 4.00 10.00
133 Jordan Howard JSY AU/199 RC 10.00 25.00
134 Wendell Smallwood JSY AU/199 RC 4.00 10.00
135 Jonathan Williams JSY AU/199 RC 5.00 12.00
136 Kevin Hogan JSY AU/199 RC 5.00 12.00
137 Trevor Davis JSY AU/199 RC 4.00 10.00
138 Alex Collins JSY AU/199 RC 5.00 12.00
139 Keenan Reynolds JSY AU/199 RC 5.00 12.00
140 Moritz Bohringer JSY AU/199 RC 4.00 10.00

2016 Panini Playbook Green

*VETS/25: .8X TO 2X BASIC CARDS/199
*ROOK/25: .8X TO 2X BASIC JSY AU RC/199
*ROOK/25: .6X TO 1.5X BASIC JSY AU RC/99
102 Carson Wentz JSY AU 100.00 200.00
104 Ezekiel Elliott JSY AU 150.00 300.00

2016 Panini Playbook Platinum

*VETS/49: .6X TO 1.5X BASIC CARDS/199
*ROOK/49: .6X TO 1.5X BASIC JSY AU RC/199
*ROOK/49: .5X TO 1.2X BASIC JSY AU RC/99
104 Ezekiel Elliott JSY AU 125.00 250.00

2016 Panini Playbook Rookie Playbook Jersey Autographs Gold

*ROOK/75-99: .5X TO 1.2X BASIC JSY AU RC/199
*ROOK/75-99: .4X TO 1X BASIC JSY AU RC/99
101 Jared Goff/75 60.00 125.00
102 Carson Wentz/75 125.00 250.00
104 Ezekiel Elliott/75 100.00 200.00
129 Dak Prescott/99 60.00 125.00

2016 Panini Playbook Activ8 Rookie Jerseys

*PRIME/25: .6X TO 1.5X BASIC JSY/99
1 Wtz/Elt/Gff/Trdwl/Flr/Clmn/Dtsn/Lch 50.00 100.00
2 Jns/Elt/Wtz/Prct/Bkr/Wlms/Lch/Smlwd 25.00 60.00

2016 Panini Playbook Armory Materials

1 Jared Goff 30.00 80.00
2 Carson Wentz 50.00 125.00
3 Joey Bosa 10.00 25.00
4 Ezekiel Elliott 25.00 60.00
5 Corey Coleman 8.00 20.00
6 Will Fuller 8.00 20.00
7 Josh Doctson 6.00 15.00
8 Laquon Treadwell 6.00 15.00
9 Paxton Lynch 5.00 12.00
10 Derrick Henry 12.00 30.00
11 Christian Hackenberg 5.00 12.00
12 Connor Cook 6.00 15.00

2016 Panini Playbook Down and Dirty Jerseys

1 Jamaal Charles/25 8.00 20.00
2 Emmanuel Sanders/25 10.00 25.00
3 Darren Sproles/25 8.00 20.00
5 Richard Rodgers/25 8.00 20.00
6 Jeremy Hill/25 6.00 15.00
7 Ronnie Hillman/25 6.00 15.00
8 Paul Posluszny/25 6.00 15.00
9 C.J. Anderson/25 8.00 20.00
10 Von Miller/25 8.00 20.00
11 Dontari Poe/25 6.00 15.00
12 Aqib Talib/25 15.00 40.00

2016 Panini Playbook Face 2 Face Materials

1 C.Wentz/J.Goff/99 12.00 30.00
2 D.Henry/E.Elliott/99 15.00 40.00
3 C.Cook/P.Lynch/99 8.00 20.00
4 L.Treadwell/C.Coleman/99 5.00 12.00
5 B.Miller/M.Thomas/99 6.00 15.00
6 J.Winston/M.Mariota/49 8.00 20.00
7 E.Elliott/P.Perkins/99 15.00 40.00
8 C.Coleman/T.Boyd/99 5.00 12.00
9 P.Lynch/J.Bosa/99 8.00 20.00
10 C.Jones/C.Hackenberg/99 3.00 8.00
11 A.Smith/D.Carr/25 10.00 25.00
12 A.Dalton/J.Flacco/25 8.00 20.00

2016 Panini Playbook Game of Inches Jerseys

2 Allen Robinson/25 8.00 20.00
3 Devonta Freeman/25 8.00 20.00
4 Donte Moncrief/25 8.00 20.00
5 Jameis Winston/25 10.00 25.00
6 Kelvin Benjamin/25 8.00 20.00
7 Marcus Mariota/25 10.00 25.00
8 Stefon Diggs/25 8.00 20.00
9 T.Y. Hilton/25 8.00 20.00

2016 Panini Playbook Hot Routes Jersey Signatures

4 Dez Bryant/25 25.00 50.00
5 Kevin White/49 4.00 10.00
6 Laquon Treadwell/99 4.00 10.00
7 Will Fuller/99 5.00 12.00
8 Corey Coleman/99 5.00 12.00
9 Josh Doctson/99
10 Braxton Miller/99 3.00 8.00

2016 Panini Playbook Hot Routes Jerseys

*PRIME/50: .6X TO 1.5X BASIC JSY/199
*PRIME/50: .5X TO 1.2X BASIC JSY/99
*PRIME/25: .8X TO 2X BASIC JSY/199
*PRIME/25: .6X TO 1.5X BASIC JSY/99
1 Braxton Miller/199 2.00 5.00
2 Chris Moore/199 2.50 6.00
3 Corey Coleman/199 3.00 8.00
4 Demarcus Robinson/199 2.00 5.00
5 Josh Doctson/199 2.50 6.00
6 Keenan Reynolds/199 2.50 6.00
7 Laquon Treadwell/199 2.50 6.00
8 Leonte Carroo/199 2.00 5.00
9 Moritz Bohringer/199 2.00 5.00
10 Michael Thomas/199 4.00 10.00
11 Pharoh Cooper/199 2.00 5.00
12 Ricardo Louis/199 2.00 5.00
13 Sterling Shepard/199 2.50 6.00
14 Trevor Davis/199 2.00 5.00
15 Tyler Boyd/199 2.50 6.00
16 Will Fuller/199 3.00 8.00
17 Hunter Henry/199 2.50 6.00
19 Amari Cooper/199 3.00 8.00
20 Odell Beckham Jr./199 3.00 8.00
21 Dez Bryant/49 5.00 12.00
22 Antonio Brown/99 4.00 10.00
23 Demaryius Thomas/99 3.00 8.00
24 Allen Robinson/199 2.50 6.00
25 Travis Kelce/99 4.00 10.00
26 Allen Hurns/99 2.50 6.00
27 Rishard Matthews/199 2.00 5.00
28 A.J. Green/99 4.00 10.00
29 Kenny Stills/199 2.00 5.00
30 Tyler Eifert/199 2.50 6.00
31 Jimmy Graham/49 5.00 12.00
32 Larry Fitzgerald/49 4.00 10.00
33 Julio Jones/49 5.00 12.00
34 Jerry Rice/49 8.00 20.00
35 Calvin Johnson/49 5.00 12.00

2016 Panini Playbook Mammoth Materials

*PRIME/50: .6X TO 1.5X BASIC JSY/199
1 Jared Goff 6.00 15.00
2 Carson Wentz 8.00 20.00
3 Joey Bosa 4.00 10.00
4 Ezekiel Elliott 10.00 25.00
5 Corey Coleman 3.00 8.00
6 Will Fuller 3.00 8.00
7 Josh Doctson 2.50 6.00
8 Laquon Treadwell 2.50 6.00
9 Paxton Lynch 2.00 5.00
10 Cardale Jones 2.00 5.00
11 Christian Hackenberg 2.00 5.00
12 Alex Collins 2.50 6.00
13 C.J. Prosise 2.00 5.00
14 Derrick Henry 5.00 12.00
15 Devontae Booker 2.50 6.00
16 Kevin Hogan 2.50 6.00
17 Cody Kessler 2.00 5.00
18 Connor Cook 2.50 6.00
19 Jonathan Williams 2.50 6.00
20 Jordan Howard 4.00 10.00
21 Kenneth Dixon 2.00 5.00
22 Kenyan Drake 3.00 8.00
23 Paul Perkins 2.00 5.00
24 Tyler Ervin 2.00 5.00
25 Wendell Smallwood 2.00 5.00
26 DeAndre Washington 2.00 5.00
27 Dak Prescott 10.00 25.00
28 Hunter Henry 2.50 6.00
29 Braxton Miller 2.00 5.00
30 Chris Moore 2.50 6.00
31 Demarcus Robinson 2.00 5.00
32 Keenan Reynolds 2.50 6.00
33 Leonte Carroo 2.00 5.00
34 Michael Thomas 4.00 10.00
35 Pharoh Cooper 2.00 5.00
36 Ricardo Louis 2.00 5.00
37 Sterling Shepard 4.00 10.00
38 Trevor Davis 2.00 5.00
39 Tyler Boyd 2.50 6.00
40 Moritz Bohringer 2.00 5.00

2016 Panini Playbook Passport Book Materials

1 Peyton Manning/25 40.00 80.00
3 Brett Favre/25 20.00 50.00
5 Anthony Fasano/99 4.00 10.00
6 Charles Clay/99 4.00 10.00
7 DeSean Jackson/25 8.00 20.00
10 Mike Wallace/99 4.00 10.00

2016 Panini Playbook Playbook Booklet Materials

*GOLD/25: .8X TO 2X BASIC JSY/199
*GOLD/25: .6X TO 1.5X BASIC JSY/99
*GOLD/25: .5X TO 1.2X BASIC JSY/49
1 Amari Cooper/199 3.00 8.00
2 Ameer Abdullah/199 2.00 5.00
3 David Johnson/199 3.00 8.00
4 Dorial Green-Beckham/199 2.00 5.00
5 Jameis Winston/199 3.00 8.00
6 Todd Gurley/199 3.00 8.00
7 Marcus Mariota/199 3.00 8.00
8 Tyler Lockett/199 2.50 6.00
9 Justin Houston/21 5.00 12.00
10 Jamaal Charles/49 4.00 10.00
11 Aqib Talib/99 2.50 6.00
12 Andy Dalton/49 4.00 10.00
13 Russell Wilson/49 6.00 15.00
15 Jeremy Langford/199 2.50 6.00
16 Eric Berry/49 4.00 10.00
17 Chris Harris/99 2.50 6.00
18 Devonta Freeman/199 2.50 6.00
19 Stefon Diggs/199 2.50 6.00
20 Derek Carr/49 5.00 12.00
21 Randall Cobb/99 3.00 8.00
22 Brett Favre/49 10.00 25.00

2016 Panini Playbook Playbook Material Autographs

*GOLD: .5X TO 1.2X BASIC JSY AU
*BLUE: .6X TO 1.5X BASIC JSY AU
*GREEN: .8X TO 2X BASIC JSY AU
3 C.J. Anderson/99 6.00 15.00
4 Alshon Jeffery/25
5 Ameer Abdullah/199 4.00 10.00
11 Brandin Cooks/149 5.00 12.00
15 T.J. Yeldon/99 5.00 12.00
20 Eddie Lacy/25
22 Emmanuel Sanders/99 20.00 50.00
23 Jaelen Strong/149 4.00 10.00
25 Jeremy Hill/149 4.00 10.00
28 Karlos Williams/199 4.00 10.00
30 Matt Jones/199 5.00 12.00
34 Nelson Agholor/149 4.00 10.00
41 Tyler Lockett/199 10.00 25.00
42 Von Miller/25 50.00 100.00

2016 Panini Playbook Red Zone Jerseys

*PRIME/20: .8X TO 2X BASIC JSY/99
*PRIME/20: .6X TO 1.5X BASIC JSY/49
1 Karlos Williams/99 2.50 6.00
2 Brandin Cooks/99 3.00 8.00
3 Todd Gurley/99 4.00 10.00
4 Jarvis Landry/99 3.00 8.00
5 Jeremy Hill/99 2.50 6.00
6 Ameer Abdullah/99 2.50 6.00
7 Andy Dalton/49 4.00 10.00
8 Jeremy Langford/99 3.00 8.00
9 A.J. Green/49 5.00 12.00
10 Blake Bortles/99 2.50 6.00
11 Sammy Watkins/49 5.00 12.00
12 Davante Adams/99 2.50 6.00

2016 Panini Playbook Rookie Jumbo Memorabilia Booklets

*PRIME/25: .8X TO 2X BASIC JSY/149
1 Jared Goff 12.00 30.00
2 Carson Wentz 20.00 50.00
3 Joey Bosa 4.00 10.00
4 Ezekiel Elliott 10.00 25.00
5 Corey Coleman 3.00 8.00
6 Will Fuller 3.00 8.00
7 Josh Doctson 2.50 6.00
8 Laquon Treadwell 2.50 6.00
9 Paxton Lynch 2.00 5.00
10 Cardale Jones 2.00 5.00
11 Sterling Shepard 2.50 6.00
12 Derrick Henry 5.00 12.00
13 Michael Thomas 4.00 10.00
14 Christian Hackenberg 2.00 5.00
15 Dak Prescott 10.00 25.00
16 Braxton Miller 2.00 5.00
17 Kenneth Dixon 2.00 5.00
18 C.J. Prosise 2.00 5.00
19 Connor Cook 2.50 6.00
20 Tyler Boyd 2.50 6.00

2016 Panini Playbook Rookie Jumbo Memorabilia Booklets Signature Plays

1 Jared Goff 50.00 125.00
2 Carson Wentz 100.00 200.00
3 Joey Bosa 15.00 40.00
4 Ezekiel Elliott 100.00 200.00
5 Corey Coleman 12.00 30.00
6 Will Fuller 12.00 30.00
7 Josh Doctson 10.00 25.00
8 Laquon Treadwell 10.00 25.00
9 Paxton Lynch 8.00 20.00
10 Cardale Jones 8.00 20.00
11 Sterling Shepard 10.00 25.00
12 Derrick Henry 20.00 50.00
13 Michael Thomas 15.00 40.00
14 Christian Hackenberg 8.00 20.00
15 Dak Prescott
16 Braxton Miller 8.00 20.00
17 Kenneth Dixon 8.00 20.00
18 C.J. Prosise 8.00 20.00
19 Connor Cook 10.00 25.00
20 Tyler Boyd 10.00 25.00

2016 Panini Playbook Signature Materials

*PRIME/25: .6X TO 1.5X BASIC JSY AU/99
*PRIME/25: .5X TO 1.2X BASIC JSY AU/49
1 Doug Baldwin/49 8.00 20.00
2 Blake Bortles/25 8.00 20.00
4 Champ Bailey/49 8.00 20.00
5 Chris Cooley/25 8.00 20.00
7 Devin Hester/25 10.00 25.00
8 Dorial Green-Beckham/99 5.00 12.00
9 Duke Johnson/99 5.00 12.00
10 Earl Campbell/25 15.00 40.00
12 Jaelen Strong/49 6.00 15.00
13 Jamison Crowder/99 5.00 12.00
15 Joe Theismann/25
17 Karlos Williams/99 5.00 12.00
18 Kurt Warner/25 15.00 40.00
19 Lance Briggs/49 8.00 20.00
21 Matt Jones/99 6.00 15.00
22 Melvin Gordon/25 10.00 25.00
23 Michael Floyd/46 6.00 15.00
25 Nelson Agholor/49 6.00 15.00
27 Stefon Diggs/99 6.00 15.00
28 Teddy Bridgewater/25 15.00 40.00
29 Tyler Lockett/99 10.00 25.00

2016 Panini Playbook Slant Signatures

1 Doug Baldwin/99 8.00 20.00
3 Drew Pearson/49 10.00 25.00
4 Fred Biletnikoff/25 8.00 20.00
5 Jaelen Strong/99 3.00 8.00
6 Jamison Crowder/99 3.00 8.00
7 Michael Thomas/99 6.00 15.00
9 Mike Quick/99 3.00 8.00
10 Nelson Agholor/99 3.00 8.00
11 Dez Bryant/25 25.00 50.00
12 Wes Welker/25 10.00 25.00
13 Stefon Diggs/99 8.00 20.00
14 Tim Brown/25 8.00 20.00
16 Laquon Treadwell/99 4.00 10.00
17 Will Fuller/99 5.00 12.00
18 Corey Coleman/99 5.00 12.00
19 Josh Doctson/99 4.00 10.00
20 Braxton Miller/99 3.00 8.00

2016 Panini Playbook Triple Threats Jerseys

*PRIME/50: .6X TO 1.5X BASIC JSY/199
*PRIME/50: .5X TO 1.2X BASIC JSY/75-99
*PRIME/25: .6X TO 1.5X BASIC JSY/99
1 Brnt/Rmo/Ellt/99 12.00 30.00
3 Mthws/Wntz/Mtthws/99 8.00 20.00
4 Lnch/Andrsn/Thms/99 3.00 8.00
5 Brdgwtr/Ptrsn/Trdwll/49 5.00 12.00
6 Wntz/Gff/Lnch/199 8.00 20.00
7 Prsse/Hnry/Ellt/199 10.00 25.00
8 Clmn/Dctsn/Fllr/199 3.00 8.00
9 Shprd/Trdwll/Thms/199 4.00 10.00
10 Grn/Dltn/Byd/99 4.00 10.00
11 Smth/Rbnsn/Chrls/75 3.00 8.00
13 Ervn/Mllr/Fllr/199 3.00 8.00
14 Rynlds/Mre/Dxn/199 2.50 6.00
15 Ksslr/Clmn/Louis/199 3.00 8.00

2016 Panini Playbook X's and O's Signatures

*GOLD/25: .6X TO 1.5X BASIC AU/99
*GOLD/25: .5X TO 1.2X BASIC AU/49
1 Gary Barnidge/99 3.00 8.00
2 Blake Bortles/15 6.00 15.00
3 Bob Lilly/49 8.00 20.00
5 Charcandrick West/99 3.00 8.00
7 Curtis Martin/15 12.00 30.00
9 Dorial Green-Beckham/99 3.00 8.00
10 Drew Pearson/49 5.00 12.00
11 Duke Johnson/99 3.00 8.00
12 Earl Campbell/25 8.00 20.00
14 Floyd Little/25 5.00 12.00
15 Forrest Gregg/15 12.00 30.00
16 Fred Biletnikoff/25 8.00 20.00
17 Jaelen Strong/99 3.00 8.00
18 Jamal Lewis/99 4.00 10.00
19 Jamison Crowder/99 3.00 8.00
21 Joe Theismann/25 8.00 20.00
23 Kurt Warner/15 12.00 30.00
24 Lance Briggs/49 5.00 12.00
25 Larry Csonka/15 12.00 30.00
27 Matt Jones/99 4.00 10.00
28 Melvin Gordon/25 6.00 15.00
30 Michael Strahan/15 12.00 30.00
31 Paul Hornung/49 12.00 30.00
32 Philip Rivers/15 12.00 30.00
33 Raymond Berry/25 6.00 15.00
34 Reggie Wayne/15 8.00 20.00
35 Richard Sherman/15 25.00 50.00
36 Ricky Williams/49 10.00 25.00
38 Teddy Bridgewater/15 8.00 20.00
39 Tim Brown/15 10.00 25.00

2018 Panini Playbook

1 Tom Brady 2.00 5.00
2 Julian Edelman .75 2.00
3 Rob Gronkowski .75 2.00
4 LeSean McCoy .75 2.00
5 Kelvin Benjamin .60 1.50
6 Zay Jones .50 1.25
7 Ryan Tannehill .60 1.50
8 DeVante Parker .60 1.50
9 Kenyan Drake .50 1.25
10 Robby Anderson .50 1.25
11 Quincy Enunwa .50 1.25
12 Jamal Adams .60 1.50
13 Ben Roethlisberger .75 2.00
14 Le'Veon Bell .60 1.50
15 Antonio Brown .75 2.00
16 JuJu Smith-Schuster .75 2.00
17 Andy Dalton .60 1.50
18 A.J. Green .75 2.00
19 Joe Mixon .60 1.50
20 Blake Bortles .50 1.25
21 Leonard Fournette .75 2.00
22 Jalen Ramsey .60 1.50
23 Marcus Mariota .75 2.00
24 Derrick Henry .75 2.00
25 Corey Davis .60 1.50
26 Andrew Luck 1.00 2.50
27 T.Y. Hilton .60 1.50
28 Deshaun Watson 1.00 2.50
29 DeAndre Hopkins .60 1.50
30 J.J. Watt .75 2.00
31 D'Onta Foreman .50 1.25
32 Patrick Mahomes II 2.00 5.00
33 Kareem Hunt .60 1.50

34 Tyreek Hill .75 2.00
35 Travis Kelce .75 2.00
36 Philip Rivers .75 2.00
37 Melvin Gordon .60 1.50
38 Keenan Allen .60 1.50
39 Derek Carr .75 2.00
40 Khalil Mack .75 2.00
41 Amari Cooper .75 2.00
42 Marshawn Lynch .60 1.50
43 Case Keenum .60 1.50
44 Jordy Nelson .60 1.50
45 Emmanuel Sanders .75 2.00
46 Demaryius Thomas .60 1.50
47 Von Miller .60 1.50
48 Carson Wentz 1.00 2.50
49 Jay Ajayi .60 1.50
50 Zach Ertz .60 1.50
51 Alshon Jeffery .60 1.50
52 Dak Prescott .75 2.00
53 Ezekiel Elliott 1.00 2.50
54 Sean Lee .60 1.50
55 DeMarcus Lawrence .50 1.25
56 Alex Smith .60 1.50
57 Jordan Reed .50 1.25
58 Adrian Peterson .75 2.00
59 Eli Manning .60 1.50
60 Odell Beckham Jr. .75 2.00
61 Landon Collins .50 1.25
62 Kirk Cousins .75 2.00
63 Dalvin Cook .60 1.50
64 Stefon Diggs .60 1.50
65 Adam Thielen .75 2.00
66 Matthew Stafford .60 1.50
67 Marvin Jones Jr. .50 1.25
68 Golden Tate III .50 1.25
69 Aaron Rodgers 1.50 4.00
70 Ty Montgomery .50 1.25
71 Davante Adams .60 1.50
72 Clay Matthews .60 1.50
73 Mitchell Trubisky .75 2.00
74 Jordan Howard .75 2.00
75 Allen Robinson II .60 1.50
76 Drew Brees .75 2.00
77 Alvin Kamara .60 1.50
78 Michael Thomas .75 2.00
79 Marshon Lattimore .50 1.25
80 Cam Newton .75 2.00
81 Christian McCaffrey .75 2.00
82 Devin Funchess .50 1.25
83 Luke Kuechly .60 1.50
84 Matt Ryan .60 1.50
85 Julio Jones .75 2.00
86 Devonta Freeman .60 1.50
87 Jameis Winston .60 1.50
88 Mike Evans .60 1.50
89 Jared Goff .75 2.00
90 Todd Gurley II .75 2.00
91 Brandin Cooks .60 1.50
92 Russell Wilson 1.00 2.50
93 Doug Baldwin .60 1.50
94 Earl Thomas III .60 1.50
95 David Johnson .75 2.00
96 Chandler Jones .50 1.25
97 Larry Fitzgerald .60 1.50
98 Jimmy Garoppolo 1.00 2.50
99 Richard Sherman .75 2.00
100 James Conner .75 2.00
101 Sam Darnold RC 5.00 12.00
102 Braxton Berrios RC .75 2.00
103 Joshua Jackson RC 1.50 4.00
104 Calvin Ridley RC 2.00 5.00
105 James Washington RC 1.50 4.00
106 Ronald Jones II RC .75 2.00
107 Mark Andrews RC 1.25 3.00
108 J.T. Barrett RC 1.25 3.00
109 Sony Michel RC 2.50 6.00
110 Mason Rudolph RC 2.00 5.00
111 Saquon Barkley RC 6.00 15.00
112 Mike White RC 1.00 2.50
113 Mark Walton RC 1.00 2.50
114 Anthony Miller RC 1.25 3.00
115 Kerryon Johnson RC 1.25 3.00
116 Bo Scarbrough RC 1.00 2.50
117 Luke Falk RC 1.00 2.50
118 Damion Ratley RC 1.00 2.50
119 Nick Chubb RC 2.50 6.00
120 Bradley Chubb RC 1.25 3.00
121 Kalen Ballage RC 1.00 2.50
122 Ronnie Harrison RC 1.00 2.50
123 Tremaine Edmunds RC 1.50 4.00
124 Josh Allen RC 3.00 8.00
125 Deontay Burnett RC 1.00 2.50
126 Harold Landry RC .75 2.00
127 Kurt Benkert RC 1.00 2.50
128 Baker Mayfield RC 8.00 20.00
129 Courtland Sutton RC 1.25 3.00
130 Marquez Valdes-Scantling RC 1.00 2.50
131 Minkah Fitzpatrick RC 1.50 4.00
132 John Kelly RC 1.00 2.50
133 Deon Cain RC 1.00 2.50
134 Roquan Smith RC 2.50 6.00
135 Chad Thomas RC .75 2.00
136 Christian Kirk RC 1.25 3.00
137 Kyle Lauletta RC 1.25 3.00
138 Quenton Nelson RC 1.25 3.00
139 D.J. Moore RC 1.50 4.00
140 Derrius Guice RC 1.50 4.00
141 D.J. Chark Jr. RC 1.00 2.50
142 Rashaad Penny RC 1.25 3.00
143 Dante Pettis RC 1.25 3.00
144 Dallas Goedert RC 1.00 2.50
145 Mike Gesicki RC 1.00 2.50
146 Hayden Hurst RC 1.00 2.50
147 Josh Rosen RC 2.50 6.00
148 Lamar Jackson RC 5.00 12.00
149 Derwin James RC 1.50 4.00
150 Marcell Ateman RC 1.00 2.50
151 Nyheim Hines RC 1.00 2.50
152 Michael Gallup RC 1.50 4.00
153 Alex McGough RC 1.00 2.50
154 Allen Lazard RC .75 2.00
155 Arden Key RC .75 2.00
156 Auden Tate RC .75 2.00
157 Carlton Davis RC 1.00 2.50
158 Royce Freeman RC 1.00 2.50
159 Leighton Vander Esch RC 2.50 6.00
160 Ito Smith RC 1.00 2.50
161 Keke Coutee RC 1.00 2.50
162 DaeSean Hamilton RC 1.00 2.50
163 Jaleel Scott RC .75 2.00
164 Jordan Lasley RC .75 2.00
165 Sam Hubbard RC 1.00 2.50
166 Shaquem Griffin RC 1.25 3.00
167 Daron Payne RC 1.25 3.00
168 Isaiah Oliver RC .75 2.00
169 Lorenzo Carter RC .75 2.00
170 Russell Gage RC 1.00 2.50
171 Malik Jefferson RC 1.00 2.50
172 Maurice Hurst RC 1.00 2.50
173 Ogbonnia Okoronkwo RC 1.25 3.00
174 Tarvarus McFadden RC 1.00 2.50
175 Josh Sweat RC 1.00 2.50
176 Avonte Maddox RC 1.00 2.50
177 J'Mon Moore RC .75 2.00
178 Jaylen Samuels RC 1.00 2.50
179 Daurice Fountain RC 1.00 2.50
180 Orlando Brown RC 1.25 3.00
181 Jaire Alexander RC 1.25 3.00
182 Dorance Armstrong Jr. RC .75 2.00
183 Danny Etling RC 1.00 2.50
184 Jordan Thomas RC 1.00 2.50
185 Justin Watson RC 1.00 2.50
186 Rashaan Evans RC 1.25 3.00
187 Antonio Callaway RC 1.00 2.50
188 Tre'Quan Smith RC 1.25 3.00
189 Boston Scott RC 1.00 2.50
190 Denzel Ward RC 2.00 5.00
191 Dalton Schultz RC 1.00 2.50
192 Darius Leonard RC 2.00 5.00
193 Dylan Cantrell RC .75 2.00
194 Marquis Haynes RC .75 2.00
195 Jordan Wilkins RC 1.00 2.50
196 Will Dissly RC 1.00 2.50
197 Phillip Lindsay RC 3.00 8.00
198 Mike Hughes RC 1.25 3.00
199 Lavon Coleman RC 1.00 2.50
200 D.J. Reed RC .75 2.00
201 Sony Michel JSY AU/125 15.00 40.00
202 Baker Mayfield JSY AU/79 100.00 200.00
203 Josh Rosen JSY AU/99 30.00 60.00
204 Saquon Barkley JSY AU/99 75.00 150.00
205 Mason Rudolph JSY AU/125 12.00 30.00
206 Josh Allen JSY AU/99 30.00 60.00
207 Bradley Chubb JSY AU/125 8.00 20.00
208 Nick Chubb JSY AU/99 25.00 50.00
209 Christian Kirk JSY AU/125 8.00 20.00
210 Ronald Jones II JSY AU/125 5.00 12.00
211 Calvin Ridley JSY AU/99 12.00 30.00
212 Courtland Sutton JSY AU/125 8.00 20.00
213 Sam Darnold JSY AU/99 30.00 80.00
214 Anthony Miller JSY AU/125 8.00 20.00
215 D.J. Chark Jr. JSY AU/125 6.00 15.00
216 D.J. Moore JSY AU/125 10.00 25.00
217 J'Mon Moore JSY AU/125 5.00 12.00
218 Mike Gesicki JSY AU/125 6.00 15.00
219 Kyle Lauletta JSY AU/125 8.00 20.00
220 Mike White JSY AU/125 6.00 15.00
221 Mark Walton JSY AU/125 6.00 15.00
222 Royce Freeman JSY AU/125 6.00 15.00
223 Kerryon Johnson JSY AU/125 8.00 20.00
224 Rashaad Penny JSY AU/125 8.00 20.00
225 Kalen Ballage JSY AU/125 6.00 15.00
226 Nyheim Hines JSY AU/125 6.00 15.00
227 Ito Smith JSY AU/125 6.00 15.00
228 James Washington JSY AU/125 10.00 25.00
229 Keke Coutee JSY AU/125 6.00 15.00
230 Michael Gallup JSY AU/125 10.00 25.00
231 Dante Pettis JSY AU/125 8.00 20.00
232 Jaylen Samuels JSY AU/125 6.00 15.00
233 DaeSean Hamilton JSY AU/125 6.00 15.00
234 Tre'Quan Smith JSY AU/125 8.00 20.00
235 Jaleel Scott JSY AU/125 5.00 12.00
236 Marquez Valdes-Scantling JSY AU/125 6.00 15.00
237 Daurice Fountain JSY AU/125 6.00 15.00
238 Hayden Hurst JSY AU/125 6.00 15.00
239 Derrius Guice JSY AU/125 10.00 25.00
240 Lamar Jackson JSY AU/79 50.00 100.00

2018 Panini Playbook Bronze

*VETS: .5X TO 1.2X BASIC CARDS
*ROOKIES: .4X TO 1X BASIC CARDS

2018 Panini Playbook Gold

*GOLD JSY AU/75-99: .4X TO 1X BASIC JSY AU

2018 Panini Playbook Green

*VETS: 2.5X TO 6X BASIC CARDS
*ROOKIES: 1.5X TO 4X BASIC CARDS
*ROOK JSY AU/25: .6X TO 1.5X BASIC JSY AU
*ROOK JSY AU/15: .8X TO 2X BASIC JSY AU
202 Baker Mayfield JSY AU/25 200.00 400.00

2018 Panini Playbook Orange

*VETS: .5X TO 1.2X BASIC CARDS
*ROOKIES: .4X TO 1X BASIC CARDS

2018 Panini Playbook Platinum

*VETS: 2X TO 5X BASIC CARDS
*ROOKIES: 1.2X TO 3X BASIC CARDS
*ROOK JSY AU/35-49: .6X TO 1.5X BASIC JSY AU

2018 Panini Playbook Purple

*VETS: .5X TO 1.2X BASIC CARDS
*ROOKIES: .4X TO 1X BASIC CARDS

2018 Panini Playbook Armory Materials

1 Derrius Guice 8.00 20.00
2 Calvin Ridley 8.00 20.00
3 Lamar Jackson 15.00 40.00
4 Anthony Miller 6.00 15.00
5 Josh Rosen 10.00 25.00
6 Baker Mayfield 40.00 80.00
7 Bradley Chubb 6.00 15.00
8 Josh Allen 10.00 25.00
9 Sam Darnold 15.00 40.00
10 Rashaad Penny 6.00 15.00

2018 Panini Playbook BLITZ

1 Antonio Brown 1.00 2.50
2 Rob Gronkowski 1.00 2.50
3 Adam Thielen 1.00 2.50
4 Odell Beckham Jr. 1.00 2.50
5 Julio Jones 1.00 2.50
6 Drew Brees 1.00 2.50
7 Von Miller .75 2.00
8 JuJu Smith-Schuster 1.00 2.50
9 Khalil Mack 1.00 2.50
10 Matthew Stafford .75 2.00
11 Cam Newton 1.00 2.50
12 Jimmy Garoppolo 1.25 3.00
13 T.J. Watt .75 2.00
14 Le'Veon Bell .75 2.00
15 Mitchell Trubisky 1.00 2.50
16 Ryan Tannehill .75 2.00
17 Joe Flacco .75 2.00
18 Andy Dalton .75 2.00
19 Marcus Mariota 1.00 2.50
20 Andrew Luck 1.25 3.00
21 Jameis Winston .75 2.00
22 Jared Goff 1.00 2.50
23 Mike Evans .75 2.00
24 Zach Ertz .75 2.00
25 Aaron Donald 1.00 2.50

2018 Panini Playbook BLITZ Memorabilia

COMMON CARD 2.50 6.00
SEMISTARS 3.00 8.00
UNLISTED STARS 4.00 10.00
1 Antonio Brown 4.00 10.00
2 Rob Gronkowski 4.00 10.00
3 Adam Thielen 4.00 10.00
4 Odell Beckham Jr. 4.00 10.00
5 Julio Jones 4.00 10.00
6 Drew Brees 4.00 10.00
7 Von Miller 3.00 8.00
8 JuJu Smith-Schuster 4.00 10.00
9 Khalil Mack 4.00 10.00
10 Matthew Stafford 3.00 8.00
11 Cam Newton 4.00 10.00
12 Jimmy Garoppolo 5.00 12.00
14 Le'Veon Bell 3.00 8.00
15 Mitchell Trubisky 4.00 10.00
16 Ryan Tannehill 3.00 8.00
17 Joe Flacco 3.00 8.00
18 Andy Dalton 3.00 8.00
19 Marcus Mariota 4.00 10.00
20 Andrew Luck 5.00 12.00
21 Jameis Winston 3.00 8.00
22 Jared Goff 4.00 10.00
23 Mike Evans 3.00 8.00
24 Zach Ertz 3.00 8.00
25 Aaron Donald 4.00 10.00

2018 Panini Playbook Coaches Quotes

*GOLD/25: .6X TO 1.5X BASIC AU/99
*GOLD/25: .5X TO 1.2X BASIC AU/49
1 Bill Cowher/49 15.00 40.00
2 Marv Levy/99 5.00 12.00
3 Mike Shanahan/40 10.00 25.00
4 Mike Vrabel/99 5.00 12.00
5 Jimmy Johnson/49 30.00 60.00

2018 Panini Playbook Fabled Fabric

*PRIME/46-50: .6X TO 1.5X BASIC JSY/299
*PRIME/25: .8X TO 2X BASIC JSY/299
1 Michael Strahan 2.50 6.00
2 Peyton Manning 6.00 15.00
3 Ozzie Newsome 2.50 6.00
4 Warren Moon 3.00 8.00
5 Michael Irvin 3.00 8.00
6 Terrell Davis 2.50 6.00
7 Jason Witten 2.50 6.00
8 Len Dawson 3.00 8.00
9 LaDainian Tomlinson 2.50 6.00
10 Edgerrin James 2.50 6.00

2018 Panini Playbook Game of Inches Jerseys

1 Marcus Mariota 10.00 25.00
2 Alvin Kamara 8.00 20.00
3 Jordan Howard 10.00 25.00
6 Julio Jones 10.00 25.00
7 Travis Kelce 10.00 25.00
8 Christian McCaffrey 10.00 25.00
12 Antonio Gates 6.00 15.00

2018 Panini Playbook Hail Mary Material Signatures

3 Mitchell Trubisky/25 30.00 60.00
4 Derek Carr/25 15.00 40.00
5 Patrick Mahomes II/49 100.00 200.00
6 Jim Kelly/25 20.00 50.00
7 Carson Wentz/25 40.00 80.00
8 Jared Goff/25 20.00 40.00
9 Deshaun Watson/25 25.00 50.00
10 Jimmy Garoppolo/49 25.00 50.00
11 Chad Pennington/49 6.00 15.00
12 Michael Vick/99 6.00 15.00
13 Len Dawson/75 8.00 20.00
14 Jim Plunkett/99 6.00 15.00
15 Drew Bledsoe/75 12.00 30.00
16 Mark Brunell/199 4.00 10.00
17 Jeff Garcia/190
18 Danny White/49 12.00 30.00
19 Ben Roethlisberger/15 EXCH 75.00 150.00
20 Philip Rivers/15 15.00 40.00

2018 Panini Playbook Hail Mary Material Signatures Prime

*PRIME/25: .8X TO 2X BASIC JSY/190-199
*PRIME/25: .6X TO 1.5X BASIC JSY/75-99
*PRIME/25: .5X TO 1.2X BASIC JSY/49

2018 Panini Playbook Hot Routes Jerseys

*PRIME/50: .6X TO 1.5X BASIC JSY/299
*PRIME/50: .5X TO 1.2X BASIC JSY/125
*PRIME/25: .5X TO 1.2X BASIC JSY/299
1 Julio Jones/299 3.00 8.00
2 Odell Beckham Jr./299 3.00 8.00
3 Michael Thomas/299 3.00 8.00
4 Tyreek Hill/299 3.00 8.00
5 Corey Davis/299 2.50 6.00
6 Antonio Brown/299 3.00 8.00
7 Mike Evans/299 2.50 6.00
8 A.J. Green/299 3.00 8.00
9 DeAndre Hopkins/299 2.50 6.00
10 Keenan Allen/299 2.50 6.00
11 Larry Fitzgerald/299 2.50 6.00
12 Demaryius Thomas/299 2.50 6.00
13 Davante Adams/299 2.50 6.00
14 Doug Baldwin/299 2.50 6.00
15 T.Y. Hilton/299 2.50 6.00
16 Amari Cooper/299 3.00 8.00
17 Adam Thielen/299 3.00 8.00
18 Josh Gordon/125 2.50 6.00
19 Cooper Kupp/299 2.50 6.00
20 Josh Doctson/299 2.00 5.00
21 Devin Funchess/299 2.00 5.00
22 Travis Kelce/299 3.00 8.00
23 Rob Gronkowski/299 3.00 8.00
24 Christian McCaffrey/299 3.00 8.00
25 David Johnson/299 3.00 8.00
26 Le'Veon Bell/299 2.50 6.00
27 Alvin Kamara/299 2.50 6.00
28 Todd Gurley II/299 3.00 8.00
29 Chris Thompson/299 2.00 5.00
30 Kareem Hunt/299 2.50 6.00
31 D.J. Moore/299 4.00 10.00
32 Calvin Ridley/299 5.00 12.00
33 Courtland Sutton/299 3.00 8.00
34 James Washington/299 4.00 10.00
35 Anthony Miller/299 3.00 8.00

2018 Panini Playbook Mammoth Materials

*PRIME/50: .8X TO 2X BASIC JSY/199
1 Lamar Jackson 8.00 20.00
2 Derrius Guice 4.00 10.00
3 Hayden Hurst 2.50 6.00
4 Daurice Fountain 2.50 6.00
5 Marquez Valdes-Scantling 2.50 6.00
6 Jaleel Scott 2.00 5.00
7 Tre'Quan Smith 3.00 8.00
8 DaeSean Hamilton 2.50 6.00
9 Jaylen Samuels 2.50 6.00
10 Dante Pettis 3.00 8.00
11 Michael Gallup 4.00 10.00
12 Keke Coutee 2.50 6.00
13 James Washington 4.00 10.00
14 Ito Smith 2.50 6.00
15 Nyheim Hines 2.50 6.00
16 Kalen Ballage 2.50 6.00
17 Rashaad Penny 3.00 8.00
18 Kerryon Johnson 3.00 8.00
19 Royce Freeman 2.50 6.00
20 Mark Walton 2.50 6.00
21 Mike White 2.50 6.00
22 Kyle Lauletta 3.00 8.00
23 Mike Gesicki 2.50 6.00
24 J'Mon Moore 2.00 5.00
25 D.J. Moore 4.00 10.00
26 D.J. Chark Jr. 2.50 6.00
27 Anthony Miller 3.00 8.00
28 Sam Darnold 8.00 20.00
29 Courtland Sutton 3.00 8.00
30 Calvin Ridley 4.00 10.00
31 Ronald Jones II 2.00 5.00
32 Christian Kirk 3.00 8.00
33 Nick Chubb 6.00 15.00
34 Bradley Chubb 3.00 8.00
35 Josh Allen 5.00 12.00
36 Mason Rudolph 4.00 10.00
37 Saquon Barkley 10.00 25.00
38 Josh Rosen 5.00 12.00
39 Baker Mayfield 8.00 20.00
40 Sony Michel 4.00 10.00

2018 Panini Playbook Nexus Tri Fold Jumbo Jerseys

1 Wnstn/Evns/Jns 12.00 30.00
2 Grn/Dltn/Mxn 15.00 40.00
3 Dvs/Hnry/Mrta 15.00 40.00
4 Frmn/Hpkns/Wtsn 20.00 50.00
5 Thln/Ck/Dggs 15.00 40.00
6 Hnt/Mhms/Hll 40.00 100.00
7 Alln/Grdn/Rvrs 15.00 40.00
8 Chbb/Sttn/Frmn 15.00 40.00
9 Wshngtn/Smls/Rdlph 20.00 50.00
10 Prsctt/Ellt/Gllp 20.00 50.00
11 Rdly/Frmn/Ryn 20.00 50.00
12 Mllr/Hwrd/Trbsky 15.00 40.00
13 Myfld/Jcksn/Drnld 50.00 100.00
14 Pnny/Brkly/Mchl 60.00 125.00

2018 Panini Playbook Play Action

1 Tom Brady 2.50 6.00
2 Ben Roethlisberger 1.00 2.50
3 Deshaun Watson 1.25 3.00
4 Patrick Mahomes II 2.50 6.00
5 Derek Carr 1.00 2.50
6 Carson Wentz 1.25 3.00
7 Dak Prescott 1.00 2.50
8 Aaron Rodgers 2.00 5.00
9 Matt Ryan .75 2.00
10 Russell Wilson 1.25 3.00

2018 Panini Playbook Play Action Swatches

2 Ben Roethlisberger 3.00 8.00
3 Deshaun Watson 4.00 10.00
4 Patrick Mahomes II 8.00 20.00
5 Derek Carr 3.00 8.00
6 Carson Wentz 4.00 10.00
7 Dak Prescott 3.00 8.00
8 Aaron Rodgers 6.00 15.00
9 Matt Ryan 2.50 6.00
10 Russell Wilson 4.00 10.00

2018 Panini Playbook Playbook Material Autographs

1 Aaron Rodgers/25 150.00 250.00
3 Brian Dawkins/49 30.00 60.00
4 Derrick Henry/49 12.00 30.00
5 Adam Thielen/49 30.00 60.00
6 Peyton Manning/25 75.00 150.00
7 Ray Lewis/30 50.00 100.00
8 Russell Wilson/15
9 David Johnson/49 12.00 30.00
10 Rob Gronkowski/49 30.00 60.00

2018 Panini Playbook Playbook Material Autographs Green

*GREEN/25: .5X TO 1.2X BASIC JSY AU/49
*GREEN/25: .4X TO 1X BASIC JSY AU/30
*GREEN/15: .5X TO 1.2X BASIC JSY AU/25
6 Peyton Manning/15 200.00 400.00

2018 Panini Playbook Red Zone Jerseys Prime

1 Leonard Fournette 6.00 15.00
2 Melvin Gordon 5.00 12.00
3 D'Onta Foreman 4.00 10.00
4 Zach Ertz 5.00 12.00
5 Mitchell Trubisky 6.00 15.00
6 Russell Wilson 8.00 20.00
8 Ty Montgomery 4.00 10.00
9 O.J. Howard 4.00 10.00
10 Stefon Diggs 5.00 12.00
11 Kareem Hunt 5.00 12.00
12 Deshaun Watson 8.00 20.00

2018 Panini Playbook Rookie Jumbo Memorabilia Booklets

*PRIME/25: .5X TO 1.2X BASIC JSY/49
1 Lamar Jackson 12.00 30.00
2 Baker Mayfield 12.00 30.00
3 Sony Michel 6.00 15.00
5 Dante Pettis 5.00 12.00
6 Michael Gallup 6.00 15.00
8 James Washington 6.00 15.00
11 Rashaad Penny 5.00 12.00
12 Kerryon Johnson 5.00 12.00
15 Mike White 4.00 10.00
17 Derrius Guice 6.00 15.00
19 D.J. Moore 6.00 15.00
21 Anthony Miller 5.00 12.00
22 Sam Darnold 12.00 30.00
23 Courtland Sutton 5.00 12.00
24 Calvin Ridley 6.00 15.00
26 Christian Kirk 5.00 12.00
27 Nick Chubb 10.00 25.00
28 Bradley Chubb 5.00 12.00
29 Josh Allen 8.00 20.00
30 Mason Rudolph 6.00 15.00
31 Saquon Barkley 15.00 40.00
32 Josh Rosen 8.00 20.00

2018 Panini Playbook Rookie Signatures

101 Sam Darnold 20.00 50.00
102 Braxton Berrios 3.00 8.00
103 Joshua Jackson 6.00 15.00
104 Calvin Ridley 8.00 20.00
105 James Washington 6.00 15.00
106 Ronald Jones II 3.00 8.00
107 Mark Andrews 5.00 12.00
108 J.T. Barrett 5.00 12.00
109 Sony Michel 10.00 25.00
110 Mason Rudolph 8.00 20.00
111 Saquon Barkley 75.00 150.00
112 Mike White 4.00 10.00
113 Mark Walton 4.00 10.00
114 Anthony Miller 5.00 12.00
115 Kerryon Johnson EXCH 5.00 12.00
116 Bo Scarbrough 4.00 10.00
117 Luke Falk 4.00 10.00
118 Damion Ratley 4.00 10.00
119 Nick Chubb 25.00 50.00
120 Bradley Chubb
121 Kalen Ballage 4.00 10.00
122 Ronnie Harrison 4.00 10.00
123 Tremaine Edmunds 6.00 15.00
124 Josh Allen 12.00 30.00
125 Deontay Burnett 4.00 10.00
126 Harold Landry 3.00 8.00
127 Kurt Benkert 4.00 10.00
128 Baker Mayfield 125.00 250.00
129 Courtland Sutton 5.00 12.00
130 Marquez Valdes-Scantling 4.00 10.00
131 Minkah Fitzpatrick 6.00 15.00
132 John Kelly 4.00 10.00
133 Deon Cain 4.00 10.00
134 Roquan Smith 10.00 25.00
135 Chad Thomas 3.00 8.00
136 Christian Kirk 5.00 12.00
137 Kyle Lauletta 5.00 12.00
138 Quenton Nelson 5.00 12.00
139 D.J. Moore 6.00 15.00
140 Derrius Guice
141 D.J. Chark Jr. 4.00 10.00
142 Rashaad Penny 5.00 12.00
143 Dante Pettis 5.00 12.00
144 Dallas Goedert 4.00 10.00
145 Mike Gesicki 4.00 10.00
146 Hayden Hurst 4.00 10.00
147 Josh Rosen 10.00 25.00
148 Lamar Jackson 30.00 60.00
149 Derwin James
150 Marcell Ateman 4.00 10.00
151 Nyheim Hines 4.00 10.00
152 Michael Gallup 6.00 15.00
153 Alex McGough 4.00 10.00
155 Arden Key 3.00 8.00
156 Auden Tate 3.00 8.00
157 Carlton Davis 4.00 10.00
158 Royce Freeman 4.00 10.00
159 Leighton Vander Esch 15.00 40.00
160 Ito Smith 4.00 10.00
161 Keke Coutee 4.00 10.00
162 DaeSean Hamilton 4.00 10.00
163 Jaleel Scott 3.00 8.00
164 Jordan Lasley 3.00 8.00
165 Sam Hubbard 4.00 10.00
166 Shaquem Griffin 5.00 12.00
167 Daron Payne 5.00 12.00
168 Isaiah Oliver 3.00 8.00
169 Lorenzo Carter 3.00 8.00
170 Russell Gage 4.00 10.00
171 Malik Jefferson 4.00 10.00
172 Maurice Hurst 4.00 10.00
173 Ogbonnia Okoronkwo 5.00 12.00
174 Tarvarus McFadden 4.00 10.00
175 Josh Sweat 4.00 10.00
176 Avonte Maddox 4.00 10.00
177 J'Mon Moore 3.00 8.00
178 Jaylen Samuels 6.00 15.00
179 Daurice Fountain 4.00 10.00
180 Orlando Brown 5.00 12.00
181 Jaire Alexander 5.00 12.00
182 Dorance Armstrong Jr. 3.00 8.00
183 Danny Etling 6.00 15.00
184 Jordan Thomas 4.00 10.00
185 Justin Watson 4.00 10.00
186 Rashaan Evans 5.00 12.00
187 Antonio Callaway 4.00 10.00
188 Tre'Quan Smith 5.00 12.00
189 Boston Scott 4.00 10.00
190 Denzel Ward 8.00 20.00
191 Dalton Schultz 4.00 10.00
192 Darius Leonard 40.00 80.00
103 Dylan Cantrell 3.00 8.00
194 Marquis Haynes 3.00 8.00
195 Jordan Wilkins 4.00 10.00
196 Will Dissly 4.00 10.00
197 Phillip Lindsay EXCH 25.00 50.00
198 Mike Hughes 5.00 12.00
199 Lavon Coleman 4.00 10.00
200 D.J. Reed 3.00 8.00

2018 Panini Playbook Rookie Signatures Green

*GREEN/25: .6X TO 1.5X BASIC AU

2018 Panini Playbook Rookie Signatures Platinum

*PLATINUM/49: .5X TO 1.2X BASIC AU

2018 Panini Playbook Signature Materials

*PRIME/25: .8X TO 2X BASIC JSY AU/149-199
*PRIME/25: .6X TO 1.5X BASIC JSY AU/75-125
*PRIME/25: .5X TO 1.2X BASIC JSY AU/49
1 Adam Thielen/75 25.00 50.00
2 John Randle/75 12.00 30.00
3 Christian McCaffrey/99 12.00 30.00
5 Robby Anderson/199 4.00 10.00
6 Plaxico Burress/199 4.00 10.00
7 Ha Ha Clinton-Dix/199 4.00 10.00
8 Isaac Bruce/199 6.00 15.00
9 Ezekiel Elliott/75 30.00 60.00
10 Corey Davis/149 5.00 12.00
11 JuJu Smith-Schuster/199 12.00 30.00
12 Leonard Fournette/25 12.00 30.00
13 Mike Ditka/49
14 Spencer Ware/199 4.00 10.00
15 Ricky Watters/75 6.00 15.00
16 Kenny Golladay/199 4.00 10.00
17 Curtis Martin/25 10.00 25.00
18 Emmanuel Sanders/99
20 LaDainian Tomlinson/25 10.00 25.00
21 Clay Matthews/49 8.00 20.00
22 Ricky Williams/99 6.00 15.00
23 Calais Campbell/149 4.00 10.00
24 Marcus Mariota/25 15.00 40.00
25 Tyreek Hill/99 8.00 20.00
26 Ty Law/49
27 Steven Jackson/49 15.00 40.00
28 Earl Campbell/75 10.00 25.00
29 Warren Moon/49 12.00 30.00
30 Marshawn Lynch/25 10.00 25.00
31 Rob Gronkowski/25 15.00 40.00
32 Travis Kelce/125 8.00 20.00
33 Harry Carson/199 4.00 10.00
34 Ty Montgomery/199 4.00 10.00

2018 Panini Playbook Split 6 Signatures

1 Mfld/Alln/Rsn/Jcksn/Rdph/Dnld 300.00 600.00

2018 Panini Playbook Triple Threats Jerseys

*PRIME/50: .6X TO 1.5X BASIC JSY/299
*PRIME/25: .8X TO 2X BASIC JSY/299
1 Hnt/Mhms/Hll 10.00 25.00
2 Kpp/Gff/Grly 4.00 10.00
3 Brtls/Frntte/Lee 4.00 10.00
4 Mnng/Bckhm/Brkly 12.00 30.00
5 Ck/Csns/Dggs 4.00 10.00
6 Cpr/Crr/Lnch 4.00 10.00
7 Rdly/Jns/Rn 5.00 12.00
8 Frmn/Wtsn/Fllr 5.00 12.00
9 Krk/Jhnsn/Rsn 6.00 15.00
10 Bldwn/Pnny/Wlsn 5.00 12.00
11 Mllr/Hwrd/Trbsky 5.00 12.00
12 Wnstn/Evns/Jns 3.00 8.00
13 Dvs/Hnry/Mrta 4.00 10.00
14 Chbb/Hrrs/Mllr 4.00 10.00
15 Kmra/Brs/Thms 4.00 10.00

2018 Panini Playbook Vault Tri Fold Jersey Autographs

1 Ezekiel Elliott 75.00 150.00
3 Jared Goff
4 Carson Wentz
5 Leonard Fournette 40.00 80.00
6 Mitchell Trubisky
7 Patrick Mahomes II 200.00 400.00
8 JuJu Smith-Schuster
9 Deshaun Watson 75.00 150.00
10 Kareem Hunt
11 Baker Mayfield 500.00 800.00
12 D.J. Moore 60.00 125.00
13 Sony Michel 50.00 100.00
14 Lamar Jackson 125.00 200.00

2018 Panini Playbook X's and O's

1 Sony Michel 2.00 5.00
2 Baker Mayfield 6.00 15.00
3 Josh Rosen 2.00 5.00
4 Saquon Barkley 5.00 12.00
5 Mason Rudolph 1.50 4.00
6 Josh Allen 2.50 6.00
7 Bradley Chubb 1.00 2.50
8 Nick Chubb 2.00 5.00
9 Christian Kirk 1.00 2.50
10 Ronald Jones II .60 1.50
11 Calvin Ridley 1.50 4.00
12 Courtland Sutton 1.00 2.50
13 Sam Darnold 4.00 10.00
14 Anthony Miller 1.00 2.50
15 D.J. Chark Jr. .75 2.00
16 D.J. Moore 1.25 3.00
17 J'Mon Moore .60 1.50
18 Mike Gesicki .75 2.00
19 Kyle Lauletta 1.00 2.50
20 Mike White .75 2.00
21 Mark Walton .75 2.00
22 Royce Freeman .75 2.00
23 Kerryon Johnson 1.00 2.50
24 Rashaad Penny 1.00 2.50
25 Kalen Ballage .75 2.00
26 Nyheim Hines .75 2.00
27 Ito Smith .75 2.00
28 James Washington 1.25 3.00
29 Keke Coutee .75 2.00
30 Michael Gallup 1.25 3.00
31 Dante Pettis 1.00 2.50
32 Jaylen Samuels .75 2.00
33 DaeSean Hamilton .75 2.00
34 Tre'Quan Smith 1.00 2.50
35 Jaleel Scott .60 1.50
36 Marquez Valdes-Scantling .75 2.00
37 Daurice Fountain .75 2.00
38 Hayden Hurst .75 2.00
39 Derrius Guice 1.25 3.00
40 Lamar Jackson 4.00 10.00

2018 Panini Playbook X's and O's Jerseys

1 Sony Michel 4.00 10.00
2 Baker Mayfield 8.00 20.00
3 Josh Rosen 5.00 12.00
4 Saquon Barkley 10.00 25.00
5 Mason Rudolph 4.00 10.00
6 Josh Allen 5.00 12.00
7 Bradley Chubb 3.00 8.00
8 Nick Chubb 6.00 15.00
9 Christian Kirk 3.00 8.00
10 Ronald Jones II 2.00 5.00
11 Calvin Ridley 4.00 10.00
12 Courtland Sutton 3.00 8.00
13 Sam Darnold 8.00 20.00
14 Anthony Miller 3.00 8.00
15 D.J. Chark Jr. 2.50 6.00
16 D.J. Moore 4.00 10.00
17 J'Mon Moore 2.00 5.00
18 Mike Gesicki 2.50 6.00
19 Kyle Lauletta 3.00 8.00
20 Mike White 2.50 6.00
21 Mark Walton 2.50 6.00
22 Royce Freeman 2.50 6.00
23 Kerryon Johnson 3.00 8.00
24 Rashaad Penny 3.00 8.00
25 Kalen Ballage 2.50 6.00
26 Nyheim Hines 2.50 6.00
27 Ito Smith 2.50 6.00
28 James Washington 4.00 10.00
29 Keke Coutee 2.50 6.00
30 Michael Gallup 4.00 10.00
31 Dante Pettis 3.00 8.00
32 Jaylen Samuels 2.50 6.00
33 DaeSean Hamilton 2.50 6.00
34 Tre'Quan Smith 3.00 8.00
35 Jaleel Scott 2.00 5.00
36 Marquez Valdes-Scantling 2.50 6.00
37 Daurice Fountain 2.50 6.00
38 Hayden Hurst 2.50 6.00
39 Derrius Guice 4.00 10.00
40 Lamar Jackson 8.00 20.00

2018 Panini Playbook X's and O's Jersey Autographs

*PRIME/25: .8X TO 2X BASIC AU/149-199
*PRIME/25: .6X TO 1.5X BASIC AU/99
*PRIME/25: .5X TO 1.2X BASIC AU/49
1 Mike Alstott/49 12.00 30.00
2 Marcus Peters/46
5 Matthew Stafford/15
6 Jameis Winston/15 12.00 30.00
7 Antonio Brown/15 30.00 60.00
8 Steve Young/15 20.00 50.00
11 Tevin Coleman/49 6.00 15.00
12 Kenyan Drake/99 5.00 12.00
13 Kyle Rudolph/49 6.00 15.00
14 Danny White/49 12.00 30.00
15 Joe Theismann/49 10.00 25.00
16 Justin Houston/99 5.00 12.00
17 Jurrell Casey/99 5.00 12.00
18 Alex Collins/169 4.00 10.00
19 Larry Johnson/40 6.00 15.00
20 Kareem Hunt/149 5.00 12.00
21 Travis Frederick/199 4.00 10.00
22 Ronnie Brown/49 6.00 15.00
23 Ryan Shazier/49 6.00 15.00
24 Matt Breida/199 5.00 12.00
25 Marlon Mack/149 4.00 10.00
26 Jamal Adams/199 5.00 12.00
27 Alejandro Villanueva/199 20.00 40.00
28 Nelson Agholor/49 6.00 15.00
29 Eric Weddle/49 6.00 15.00
30 Marvin Jones Jr./49 6.00 15.00
31 Desmond Howard/25 8.00 20.00
32 Michael Bennett/49 6.00 15.00
33 Jay Novacek/49 6.00 15.00
34 Greg Olsen/49 8.00 20.00
35 Ozzie Newsome/49 8.00 20.00
36 Don Majkowski/199 5.00 12.00
37 Aqib Talib/149 4.00 10.00
38 Jackie Slater/99 5.00 12.00
39 Ed Reed/25
40 Marcus Allen/25 15.00 40.00

2018 Panini Playbook Zoning Commission

1 LeSean McCoy 1.00 2.50
2 Kenyan Drake .60 1.50
3 James Conner 1.00 2.50
4 Joe Mixon .75 2.00
5 Leonard Fournette 1.00 2.50
6 Derrick Henry 1.00 2.50
7 D'Onta Foreman .60 1.50
8 Kareem Hunt .75 2.00
9 Melvin Gordon .75 2.00
10 Marshawn Lynch .75 2.00
11 Devontae Booker .60 1.50
12 Jay Ajayi .75 2.00
13 Ezekiel Elliott 1.25 3.00
14 Robert Kelley .60 1.50
15 Dalvin Cook .75 2.00
16 Aaron Jones .75 2.00
17 Jordan Howard 1.00 2.50
18 Alvin Kamara .75 2.00
19 Christian McCaffrey 1.00 2.50
20 C.J. Anderson .75 2.00
21 Devonta Freeman .75 2.00
22 Tevin Coleman .60 1.50
23 Todd Gurley II 1.00 2.50
24 David Johnson 1.00 2.50
25 Ty Montgomery .60 1.50

2018 Panini Playbook Zoning Commission Materials

1 LeSean McCoy 3.00 8.00
2 Kenyan Drake 2.00 5.00
3 James Conner 3.00 8.00
4 Joe Mixon 2.50 6.00
5 Leonard Fournette 3.00 8.00
6 Derrick Henry 3.00 8.00
7 D'Onta Foreman 2.00 5.00
8 Kareem Hunt 2.50 6.00
9 Melvin Gordon 2.50 6.00
10 Marshawn Lynch 2.50 6.00
11 Devontae Booker 2.00 5.00
12 Jay Ajayi 2.50 6.00
13 Ezekiel Elliott 4.00 10.00
14 Robert Kelley 2.00 5.00
15 Dalvin Cook 2.50 6.00
17 Jordan Howard 3.00 8.00
18 Alvin Kamara 2.50 6.00
19 Christian McCaffrey 3.00 8.00
20 C.J. Anderson 2.50 6.00
21 Devonta Freeman 2.50 6.00
22 Tevin Coleman 2.00 5.00
23 Todd Gurley II 3.00 8.00
24 David Johnson 3.00 8.00
25 Ty Montgomery 2.00 5.00

2010 Panini Player of the Day

This set was released by Panini to hobby shops participating in the Player of the Day contest in Fall 2010. The first four cards were produced using the basic 2010 Score football design and the fifth is a version of the 2010 Prestige Tim Tebow Rookie Card. Each card features the 2010 Player of the Day logo on the front. A parallel was created, and randomly inserted into 5-card sets, with each card serial numbered to 100 in gold foil. Other than the serial numbering, there are no noticeable differences between the two versions.
COMPLETE SET (5) 2.50 6.00
*SERIAL NUMBERED/100: .6X TO 1.5X
PM1 Peyton Manning .75 2.00
PM2 Peyton Manning .75 2.00
PM3 Peyton Manning .75 2.00
TT1 Tim Tebow .40 1.00
TT2 Tim Tebow .40 1.00

2011 Panini Player of the Day

COMPLETE SET (13) 6.00 15.00
POD1 Sam Bradford .40 1.00
POD2 Joe Flacco .50 1.25
POD3 A.J. Green .60 1.50
POD4 Mark Ingram .40 1.00
POD5 Calvin Johnson .60 1.50
POD6 Julio Jones .75 2.00
POD7 Eli Manning .50 1.25
POD8 Darren McFadden .40 1.00
POD9 Cam Newton 1.25 3.00
POD10 Adrian Peterson .60 1.50
POD11 Matt Ryan .50 1.25
POD12 Ndamukong Suh .50 1.25
POD13 Tim Tebow .60 1.50

2012 Panini Player of the Day

COMPLETE SET (11)
1 Calvin Johnson .40 1.00
2 DeMarco Murray .30 .75
3 Reggie Bush .25 .60
4 Troy Polamalu .40 1.00
5 Tom Brady 1.00 2.50
6 Darren McFadden .25 .60
7 Marshawn Lynch .30 .75
8 Jared Allen .25 .60
9 Julius Peppers .30 .75
10 Aaron Rodgers .60 1.50
11 Andrew Luck 1.50 4.00

2012 Panini Player of the Day National Convention

ISSUED AT 2012 NATIONAL CONVENTION
1 Cam Newton 1.00 2.50
2 Andrew Luck 6.00 15.00
3 Justin Blackmon .60 1.50
4 Kendall Wright .60 1.50
5 Michael Floyd .60 1.50
6 Peyton Manning 2.00 5.00
7 Robert Griffin III .75 2.00
8 Ryan Tannehill 1.00 2.50
9 Tim Tebow 2.00 5.00
10 Trent Richardson .60 1.50
BW Beanie Wells 1.25 3.00

2012 Panini Player of the Day Private Signings

DM Doug Martin 5.00 12.00
EB Earl Bennett 4.00 10.00
ES Emmanuel Sanders 4.00 10.00
JC Jared Cook 3.00 8.00
JS James Starks 3.00 8.00
RB Ryan Broyles 3.00 8.00
RR Ray Rice 6.00 15.00
SL Sean Lee 6.00 15.00

2013 Panini Player of the Day

COMPLETE SET (18) 6.00 15.00
*THICK STOCK: .6X TO 1.5X BASIC CARDS
1 Tom Brady 1.00 2.50
2 Peyton Manning .75 2.00
3 Adrian Peterson .40 1.00
4 Calvin Johnson .40 1.00
5 Colin Kaepernick .30 .75
6 Andrew Luck .60 1.50
7 J.J. Watt .30 .75
8 Joe Flacco .30 .75
9 Robert Griffin III .25 .60
R1 EJ Manuel .15 .40
R2 Geno Smith .15 .40
R3 Giovani Bernard .15 .40
R4 Tavon Austin .20 .50
R5 Eddie Lacy .15 .40
R6 Le'Veon Bell .50 1.25
R7 DeAndre Hopkins .40 1.00
R8 Cordarrelle Patterson .15 .40
R9 Montee Ball .15 .40

2013 Panini Player of the Day Autographs

AB Armon Binns 4.00 10.00
AJ Alshon Jeffery 15.00 40.00
AM Alfred Morris 4.00 10.00
CT Cooper Taylor 4.00 10.00
DB David Bakhtiari 4.00 10.00
DJ1 Datone Jones 4.00 10.00
DJ2 D.J. Fluker 8.00 20.00
EA Ezekiel Ansah 4.00 10.00
ER Eric Reid 8.00 20.00
GA Geno Atkins 25.00 50.00
JC Jamie Collins 4.00 10.00
JC Jonathan Cooper 4.00 10.00
JJ Jarvis Jones 4.00 10.00
JK Jeremy Kerley
KL Kyle Long 60.00 100.00
KV Kenny Vaccaro 4.00 10.00
LJ Lane Johnson 8.00 20.00
MU Max Unger 10.00 25.00
OA Oday Aboushi 4.00 10.00
SF Sharrif Floyd 10.00 25.00
SR Sheldon Richardson 10.00 25.00
TF Travis Frederick 4.00 10.00
TH Trindon Holliday 25.00 50.00

2013 Panini Player of the Day National Convention

COMPLETE SET (6) 2.00 5.00
2 Alfred Morris .30 .75
3 Andre Johnson .30 .75
4 Doug Martin .40 1.00
5 Jamaal Charles .40 1.00
6 Eli Manning .40 1.00

2014 Panini Player of the Day

COMPLETE SET (25) 5.00 12.00
*CRACKED ICE: 1X TO 2.5X BASIC CARDS
*THICK STOCK: .6X TO 1.5X BASIC CARDS
1 Andrew Luck .40 1.00
2 LeSean McCoy .30 .75
3 Richard Sherman .30 .75
4 Jimmy Graham .30 .75
5 Luke Joeckel .20 .50
6 J.J. Watt .30 .75
7 Patrick Peterson .20 .50
8 Ndamukong Suh .25 .60
9 Demaryius Thomas .25 .60
10 Rob Gronkowski .30 .75
11 Dez Bryant .30 .75
12 EJ Manuel .20 .50
13 Antonio Brown .30 .75
RC1 Johnny Manziel .20 .50
RC2 Greg Robinson .12 .30
RC3 Blake Bortles .15 .40
RC4 Sammy Watkins .20 .50
RC5 Khalil Mack .50 1.25
RC6 Jake Matthews .12 .30
RC7 Mike Evans .30 .75
RC8 Odell Beckham Jr. .30 .75
RC9 Brandin Cooks .20 .50
RC10 Eric Ebron .15 .40
RC11 Jadeveon Clowney .15 .40
RC12 Teddy Bridgewater .20 .50

2014 Panini Player of the Day Autographs

AB Anthony Barr 4.00 10.00
BR Bradley Roby
CP Calvin Pryor
DD Darqueze Dennard 5.00 12.00
DE Dominique Easley 4.00 10.00
EE Eric Ebron
GE Gavin Escobar
HCD Ha Ha Clinton-Dix 5.00 12.00
JL Jarvis Landry
JW Jimmie Ward 6.00 15.00

KC Kirk Cousins 6.00 15.00
KF Kyle Fuller 4.00 10.00
KS Kenny Stills 4.00 10.00
MS Marcus Smith
PR Paul Richardson 8.00 20.00
RN Ryan Nassib
RS Ryan Shazier 6.00 15.00
TA Tavon Austin 4.00 10.00

2014 Panini Player of the Day Rookie Materials

AM A.J. McCarron 2.50 6.00
BB Blake Bortles 1.00 2.50
CH Carlos Hyde 1.00 2.50
JC Jadeveon Clowney 1.00 2.50
JG Jimmy Garoppolo 6.00 15.00
JM Johnny Manziel 3.00 8.00
KB Kelvin Benjamin 1.25 3.00
ME Mike Evans 2.00 5.00
OB Odell Beckham Jr. 2.50 6.00
SW Sammy Watkins 1.25 3.00

2015 Panini Player of the Day

*THICK STOCK: .6X TO 1.5X BASIC CARDS
*CRACKED ICE: 1X TO 2.5X BASIC CARDS
1 Andrew Luck .40 1.00
2 Odell Beckham Jr. .30 .75
3 Jimmy Graham .30 .75
4 Jordy Nelson .25 .60
5 Jamaal Charles .25 .60
6 J.J. Watt .30 .75
7 Robert Griffin III .20 .50
8 A.J. Green .30 .75
9 Emmanuel Sanders .25 .60
10 Rob Gronkowski .30 .75
11 Dez Bryant .30 .75
12 Luke Kuechly .25 .60
13 Le'Veon Bell .25 .60
14 LeSean McCoy .30 .75
15 Colin Kaepernick .25 .60
RC1 Jameis Winston .30 .75
RC2 Marcus Mariota .50 1.25
RC3 Leonard Williams .12 .30
RC4 Amari Cooper .40 1.00
RC5 Kevin White .15 .40
RC6 Ameer Abdullah .20 .50
RC7 DeVante Parker .20 .50
RC8 Melvin Gordon .30 .75
RC9 Todd Gurley .50 1.25
RC10 Nelson Agholor .15 .40

2015 Panini Player of the Day Autographs

AA Arik Armstead/75* 2.50 6.00
BO Branden Oliver/30* 5.00 12.00
BP Breshad Perriman/40* 8.00 20.00
DF Devin Funchess/25*
EF Ereck Flowers/75* 3.00 8.00
ER Eric Rowe/25*
ET Earl Thomas/30*
JJ Jackson Jeffcoat 2.50 6.00
KC Ka'Deem Carey/50* 3.00 8.00
MB Malcolm Brown/50* 4.00 10.00
PP Patrick Peterson/50* 6.00 15.00
RN Rajion Neal 2.50 6.00
SR Shane Ray/30* 4.00 10.00
TM Ty Montgomery/40*
TW Trae Waynes/30* 4.00 10.00
TW Terrance West/30* 4.00 10.00
TY T.J. Yeldon/50*
ZM Zack Martin/50* 6.00 15.00
AAB Ameer Abdullah/25* 6.00 15.00
MBY Martavis Bryant/30*

2015 Panini Player of the Day Rookie Materials

1 Jameis Winston 3.00 8.00
2 Marcus Mariota 3.00 8.00
3 DeVante Parker 1.25 3.00
4 Amari Cooper 3.00 8.00
5 Kevin White 1.00 2.50
6 Melvin Gordon 2.50 6.00
7 Tevin Coleman 1.00 2.50
8 Garrett Grayson .75 2.00
9 T.J. Yeldon .75 2.00

2017 Panini Player of the Day

*SQUARES/150: 1.2X TO 3X BASIC CARDS
*CHIMES/75: 2X TO 5X BASIC CARDS
*SPOKES/15: 3X TO 8X BASIC CARDS
1 Tom Brady .75 2.00
2 Stephen Gostkowski .20 .50
3 Dak Prescott .30 .75
4 Ezekiel Elliott .40 1.00
5 Dez Bryant .30 .75
6 Andrew Luck .40 1.00
7 David Johnson .30 .75
8 Matt Ryan .25 .60
9 Danny Woodhead .25 .60
10 LeSean McCoy .30 .75
11 Cam Newton .30 .75
12 Jordan Howard .30 .75
13 A.J. Green .30 .75
14 Von Miller .25 .60
15 Matthew Stafford .25 .60
16 Aaron Rodgers .60 1.50
17 Tyreek Hill .30 .75
18 Philip Rivers .30 .75
19 Todd Gurley II .30 .75
20 Jay Ajayi .25 .60
21 Sam Bradford .20 .50
22 Adrian Peterson .30 .75
23 Odell Beckham Jr. .30 .75
24 Marshawn Lynch .25 .60
25 Carson Wentz .40 1.00
26 Le'Veon Bell .25 .60
27 NaVorro Bowman .25 .60
28 Russell Wilson .40 1.00
29 Marcus Mariota .30 .75
30 Kirk Cousins .30 .75

2017 Panini Player of the Day Autographs

AH Austin Hooper
AJ Adoree' Jackson/15 3.00 8.00
AT Adam Thielen/20 50.00 100.00
CK Cooper Kupp
CS Cameron Sutton/40
CSA Curtis Samuel/25 2.50 6.00
DT Dalvin Tomlinson/35 5.00 12.00
DW Deatrich Wise Jr./40 5.00 12.00
HR Haason Reddick/15
JB Jake Butt/30
JD Jarrad Davis/25
JL Jordan Leggett/20
JY Joseph Yearby
KK Kevin King/30
MH Malik Hooker
MH Marlon Humphrey
ML Marshon Lattimore/15 10.00 25.00
MW Mike Williams/20 4.00 10.00
PM Patrick Mahomes II/15
RM Raekwon McMillan/15 3.00 8.00
RS Ryan Switzer/40 3.00 8.00
SJ Sebastian Janikowski/30 8.00 20.00
SP Samaje Perine/20 5.00 12.00
ST Solomon Thomas/25 6.00 15.00
TB Tyler Boyd
TR Thomas Rawls/10
TW Tre'Davious White

2017 Panini Player of the Day Memorabilia

1 Mitchell Trubisky 5.00 12.00
2 Leonard Fournette 5.00 12.00
3 Christian McCaffrey 5.00 12.00
4 Patrick Mahomes II 15.00 40.00
5 Deshaun Watson 6.00 15.00
6 Dalvin Cook 3.00 8.00
7 O.J. Howard 2.00 5.00
8 DeShone Kizer 1.50 4.00
9 Mike Williams 2.50 6.00
10 Corey Davis 2.50 6.00
11 John Ross III 2.00 5.00
12 Evan Engram 2.00 5.00
13 Joe Mixon 3.00 8.00
14 JuJu Smith-Schuster 4.00 10.00
15 C.J. Beathard 1.50 4.00
16 Davis Webb 1.50 4.00
17 James Conner 3.00 8.00
18 Alvin Kamara 6.00 15.00
19 Kareem Hunt 5.00 12.00
20 D'Onta Foreman 2.00 5.00
21 Amara Darboh 1.50 4.00
22 Cooper Kupp 2.50 6.00
23 Taywan Taylor 1.50 4.00
24 ArDarius Stewart 1.50 4.00
25 Carlos Henderson 1.50 4.00
26 Chris Godwin 2.00 5.00
27 Kenny Golladay 2.50 6.00
28 Samaje Perine 1.50 4.00
29 Joe Williams 1.50 4.00
30 Jamaal Williams 1.50 4.00
31 Wayne Gallman 2.00 5.00
32 Marlon Mack 2.50 6.00
33 R. Joshua Dobbs 2.00 5.00
34 Dede Westbrook 1.50 4.00
35 Josh Reynolds 1.50 4.00
36 Mack Hollins 1.50 4.00
37 Jeremy McNichols 1.50 4.00
38 Nathan Peterman 2.00 5.00
39 Ezekiel Elliott 3.00 8.00
40 Dak Prescott 3.00 8.00
41 Mitchell Trubisky 5.00 12.00
42 Leonard Fournette 5.00 12.00
43 Patrick Mahomes II 15.00 40.00
44 Mike Williams 2.50 6.00
45 Dalvin Cook 3.00 8.00
46 Deshaun Watson 6.00 15.00
47 DeShone Kizer 1.50 4.00
48 Corey Davis 2.50 6.00
49 John Ross III 2.00 5.00
50 O.J. Howard 2.00 5.00

2009 Panini Pop Warner

COMPLETE SET (6) 7.50 15.00
1 Brett Favre 3.00 8.00
2 Tom Brady 2.00 5.00
3 Adrian Peterson .60 1.50
4 Drew Brees .60 1.50
5 Mark Sanchez .20 .50
6 Michael Crabtree .30 .75

2011 Panini Preferred Player of the Day Autographs

DA Danny Amendola 10.00 25.00
JB Jahvid Best 8.00 20.00
JF Jermichael Finley 8.00 20.00
JM Jeremy Maclin 8.00 20.00
MF Matt Forte 8.00 20.00
ML Marshawn Lynch
MW Mike Williams 10.00 25.00
PH Percy Harvin 8.00 20.00
SG Shonn Greene 8.00 20.00
MJD Muarice Jones-Drew 8.00 20.00

2016 Panini Preferred

2 Ameer Abdullah SL JSY AU/99 4.00 10.00
4 Bryce Petty SL JSY AU/99 4.00 10.00
6 Devin Smith SL JSY AU/99 4.00 10.00
8 Emmanuel Sanders SL JSY AU/25 EXCH 10.00 25.00
10 Don Majkowski SL JSY AU/49 10.00 25.00
16 Mike Davis SL JSY AU/99 4.00 10.00
18 Jeremy Hill SL JSY AU/25 6.00 15.00
20 Jaelen Strong SL JSY AU/49 5.00 12.00
22 Jay Ajayi SL JSY AU/99 5.00 12.00
24 David Johnson SL JSY AU/99 12.00 30.00
28 Boomer Esiason SL JSY AU/25 25.00 50.00
30 Jeremy Langford SL JSY AU/49 6.00 15.00
32 Carl Eller SL JSY AU/99 10.00 25.00
34 Matt Jones SL JSY AU/99 5.00 12.00
38 Paul Warfield SL JSY AU/25 15.00 40.00
40 Julius Thomas SL JSY AU/34 5.00 12.00
42 Dorial Green-Beckham SL JSY AU/99 4.00 10.00
44 Sammie Coates SL JSY AU/99 4.00 10.00
46 Byron Jones SL JSY AU/99 8.00 20.00
47 Randy White SL JSY AU/25 25.00 50.00
48 Nelson Agholor SL JSY AU/25 6.00 15.00
50 Dan Hampton SL JSY AU/40 8.00 20.00
52 Kevin White SL JSY AU/25 6.00 15.00
56 Karlos Williams SL JSY AU/99 4.00 10.00
57 Brandin Cooks SL JSY AU/25 8.00 20.00
58 Tyrod Taylor SL JSY AU/49 6.00 15.00
61 Jared Goff SL JSY AU/99 RC 60.00 125.00
62 Carson Wentz SL JSY AU/99 RC 75.00 150.00
63 Joey Bosa SL JSY AU/149 RC 6.00 15.00
64 Ezekiel Elliott SL JSY AU/99 RC 60.00 125.00
65 Corey Coleman SL JSY AU/149 RC 5.00 12.00
66 Will Fuller V SL JSY AU/149 RC 5.00 12.00
67 Josh Doctson SL JSY AU/149 RC 4.00 10.00
68 Laquon Treadwell SL JSY AU/149 RC 4.00 10.00
69 Paxton Lynch SL JSY AU/99 RC 4.00 10.00
70 Derrick Henry SL JSY AU/99 RC 10.00 25.00
71 Connor Cook SL JSY AU/149 RC 4.00 10.00
72 Cardale Jones SL JSY AU/149 RC 3.00 8.00
73 Michael Thomas SL JSY AU/149 RC 6.00 15.00
74 Christian Hackenberg SL JSY AU/149 RC 3.00 8.00
75 C.J. Prosise SL JSY AU/149 RC 3.00 8.00
76 Paul Perkins SL JSY AU/149 RC 3.00 8.00
77 Tyler Boyd SL JSY AU/149 RC 4.00 10.00
78 Braxton Miller SL JSY AU/149 RC 3.00 8.00
79 Cody Kessler SL JSY AU/149 RC 3.00 8.00
80 Sterling Shepard SL JSY AU/199 RC 4.00 10.00
81 Alex Collins SL JSY AU/199 RC 4.00 10.00
82 Jordan Howard SL JSY AU/199 RC 15.00 40.00
83 Pharoh Cooper SL JSY AU/199 RC 3.00 8.00
84 Dak Prescott SL JSY AU/199 RC 40.00 80.00
85 Kenneth Dixon SL JSY AU/199 RC 3.00 8.00
86 DeAndre Washington SL JSY AU/199 RC 3.00 8.00
87 Devontae Booker SL JSY AU/199 RC 4.00 10.00
88 Hunter Henry SL JSY AU/199 RC 4.00 10.00
89 Leonte Carroo SL JSY AU/199 RC 3.00 8.00
90 Chris Moore SL JSY AU/199 RC 4.00 10.00
91 Kenyan Drake SL JSY AU/199 RC 5.00 12.00
92 Ricardo Louis SL JSY AU/199 RC 3.00 8.00
93 Demarcus Robinson SL JSY AU/199 RC 3.00 8.00
94 Jonathan Williams SL JSY AU/199 RC 4.00 10.00
95 Keenan Reynolds SL JSY AU/199 RC 4.00 10.00
96 Kevin Hogan SL JSY AU/199 RC 4.00 10.00
97 Trevor Davis SL JSY AU/199 RC 3.00 8.00
98 Tyler Ervin SL JSY AU/199 RC 3.00 8.00
99 Wendell Smallwood SL JSY AU/199 RC 3.00 8.00
100 Moritz Bohringer SL JSY AU/199 RC 3.00 8.00
101 Rod Woodson PC AU/15 25.00 60.00
102 Emmanuel Sanders PC AU/25 8.00 20.00
104 Paul Warfield PC AU/25 6.00 15.00
106 Don Majkowski PC AU/49 5.00 12.00
108 Jay Ajayi PC AU/49 10.00 25.00
110 Steve Grogan PC AU/49 4.00 10.00
111 Luke Kuechly PC AU/15 8.00 20.00
112 Joe Theismann PC AU/25 8.00 20.00
114 Nelson Agholor PC AU/25 5.00 12.00
116 Dan Hampton PC AU/49 8.00 20.00
118 Carl Eller PC AU/49 4.00 10.00
120 Charcandrick West PC AU/49 4.00 10.00
121 Vincent Jackson PC AU/15 6.00 15.00
122 Brandin Cooks PC AU/25 6.00 15.00
124 Ron Jaworski PC AU/25 6.00 15.00
130 John Hannah PC AU/49 8.00 20.00
132 Andre Reed PC AU/25 6.00 15.00
136 Ameer Abdullah PC AU/49 4.00 10.00
138 Matt Jones PC AU/49 5.00 12.00
141 Randy White PC AU/15 12.00 30.00
142 Jeremy Hill PC AU/25 5.00 12.00
144 Jeremy Langford PC AU/49 5.00 12.00
148 David Johnson PC AU/49 EXCH 12.00 30.00
151 DeAndre Hopkins PC AU/15 8.00 20.00
152 Antonio Freeman PC AU/25 6.00 15.00
154 Julius Thomas PC AU/49 4.00 10.00
156 Kordell Stewart PC AU/49 8.00 20.00
158 Troy Brown PC AU/49 4.00 10.00
159 Doug Flutie PC AU/15 8.00 20.00
167 Josh Doctson PC AU/25 6.00 15.00
168 Laquon Treadwell PC AU/25 6.00 15.00
169 Paxton Lynch PC AU/25 5.00 12.00
170 Derrick Henry PC AU/25 12.00 30.00
171 Connor Cook PC AU/25 6.00 15.00
172 Cardale Jones PC AU/25 5.00 12.00
173 Michael Thomas PC AU/25 10.00 25.00
174 Christian Hackenberg PC AU/49 4.00 10.00
175 C.J. Prosise PC AU/49 4.00 10.00
176 Paul Perkins PC AU/49 4.00 10.00
177 Tyler Boyd PC AU/49 EXCH 5.00 12.00
178 Braxton Miller PC AU/49 4.00 10.00
179 Cody Kessler PC AU/49 4.00 10.00
180 Sterling Shepard PC AU/49 5.00 12.00
181 Alex Collins PC AU/49 5.00 12.00
182 Jordan Howard PC AU/49 10.00 25.00
183 Pharoh Cooper PC AU/49 4.00 10.00
184 Dak Prescott PC AU/99 40.00 80.00
185 Kenneth Dixon PC AU/99 3.00 8.00
186 DeAndre Washington PC AU/99 3.00 8.00
187 Devontae Booker PC AU/99 RC 4.00 10.00
188 Hunter Henry PC AU/99 4.00 10.00
189 Leonte Carroo PC AU/99 3.00 8.00
190 Chris Moore PC AU/99 4.00 10.00
191 Kenyan Drake PC AU/99 5.00 12.00
193 Demarcus Robinson PC AU/99 3.00 8.00
194 Jonathan Williams PC AU/99 4.00 10.00
195 Keenan Reynolds PC AU/99 4.00 10.00
196 Kevin Hogan PC AU/99 4.00 10.00
197 Trevor Davis PC AU/99 RC 3.00 8.00
198 Tyler Ervin PC AU/99 3.00 8.00
199 Wendell Smallwood PC AU/99 3.00 8.00
200 Moritz Bohringer PC AU/99 3.00 8.00
203 Justin Hunter CG AU/25 5.00 12.00
204 Jeff Janis CG AU/49 4.00 10.00
208 Troy Brown CG AU/49 4.00 10.00
209 Jace Amaro CG AU/49 4.00 10.00
210 Jamal Lewis CG AU/25 6.00 15.00
212 Edgerrin James CG AU/25 20.00 40.00
214 Brian Mitchell CG AU/49 4.00 10.00
215 Don Majkowski CG AU/49 5.00 12.00
217 Ickey Woods CG AU/49 4.00 10.00
218 Jim Kiick CG AU/49 4.00 10.00
219 Cameron Artis-Payne CG AU/49 4.00 10.00
220 Carl Eller CG AU/49 4.00 10.00
222 Charles Haley CG AU/49 10.00 25.00
223 Marvin Jones CG AU/49 4.00 10.00
224 Ameer Abdullah CG AU/49 4.00 10.00
229 Dexter Manley CG AU/49 8.00 20.00
230 Jason Verrett CG AU/49 4.00 10.00
231 Trevor Siemian CG AU/49 6.00 15.00
233 Lorenzo Taliaferro CG AU/49 4.00 10.00
234 Ozzie Newsome CG AU/25 6.00 15.00
235 Julius Thomas CG AU/49 4.00 10.00
236 Charlie Joiner CG AU/49 4.00 10.00
237 Charcandrick West CG AU/49 4.00 10.00
238 Steve Grogan CG AU/49 4.00 10.00
243 Matt Jones CG AU/49 5.00 12.00
244 Kony Ealy CG AU/49 4.00 10.00
245 La'el Collins CG AU/49 4.00 10.00
246 Marqise Lee CG AU/25 5.00 12.00
248 Manti Te'o CG AU/25 5.00 12.00
249 Champ Bailey CG AU/25 10.00 25.00
250 Ricky Sanders CG AU/49 4.00 10.00
251 C.J. Fiedorowicz CG AU/49 5.00 12.00
252 Latavius Murray CG AU/49 4.00 10.00
254 Mike Quick CG AU/25 5.00 12.00
255 Brandin Cooks CG AU/25 6.00 15.00
256 Mike Evans CG AU/25 10.00 25.00
257 Tyler Eifert CG AU/25 6.00 15.00
258 Jeremy Langford CG AU/49 5.00 12.00
259 David Carr CG AU/25 5.00 12.00
260 Zach Mettenberger CG AU/49 4.00 10.00
261 Scooby Wright III CG AU/199 RC 2.50 6.00
262 A'Shawn Robinson CG AU/199 RC 2.50 6.00
263 Charone Peake CG AU/199 RC 2.50 6.00
264 Keith Marshall CG AU/199 RC 2.50 6.00
265 Jerell Adams CG AU/199 RC 2.50 6.00
266 Nate Sudfeld CG AU/199 RC 2.50 6.00
267 Jeff Driskel CG AU/199 RC 2.50 6.00
268 Vonn Bell CG AU/199 RC 3.00 8.00
269 Jalen Ramsey CG AU/199 RC 4.00 10.00
271 Eli Apple CG AU/199 RC 3.00 8.00
272 Shilique Calhoun CG AU/199 RC 2.50 6.00
273 Brandon Allen CG AU/199 RC 2.50 6.00
274 Daryl Worley CG AU/199 RC 2.50 6.00
275 Jacoby Brissett CG AU/199 RC 3.00 8.00
276 Maliek Collins CG AU/199 RC 2.50 6.00
277 Nick Vannett CG AU/199 RC 2.50 6.00
278 Xavien Howard CG AU/199 RC 3.00 8.00
279 Austin Johnson CG AU/199 RC 2.50 6.00
280 Mackensie Alexander CG AU/199 RC 2.50 6.00
281 Thomas Duarte CG AU/199 RC 2.50 6.00
282 Byron Marshall CG AU/199 RC 2.50 6.00
283 Emmanuel Ogbah CG AU/199 RC 3.00 8.00
284 Kei'Varae Russell CG AU/199 RC 2.50 6.00
286 Reggie Ragland CG AU/199 RC 2.50 6.00
289 Glenn Gronkowski CG AU/199 RC 2.50 6.00
290 Demarcus Ayers CG AU/199 RC 2.50 6.00
291 Yannick Ngakoue CG AU/199 RC 4.00 10.00
293 Vernon Hargreaves III CG AU/199 RC 4.00 10.00
294 Kendall Fuller CG AU/199 RC 3.00 8.00
295 Tajae Sharpe CG AU/199 RC 3.00 8.00
296 Su'a Cravens CG AU/199 RC 2.50 6.00
298 Kenny Lawler CG AU/199 RC 4.00 10.00
299 Keyarris Garrett CG AU/199 RC 2.50 6.00
300 Aaron Green CG AU/199 RC 2.50 6.00
305 Mohamed Sanu CR AU/49 4.00 10.00
313 Troy Brown CR AU/49 4.00 10.00
317 Edgerrin James CR AU/15 8.00 20.00
320 Don Majkowski CR AU/49 5.00 12.00
321 James White CR AU/49 5.00 12.00
322 Ickey Woods CR AU/49 4.00 10.00
323 Jim Kiick CR AU/49 4.00 10.00
325 Carl Eller CR AU/49 4.00 10.00
327 Charles Haley CR AU/49 10.00 25.00
328 Marvin Jones CR AU/49 4.00 10.00
329 Ameer Abdullah CR AU/49 4.00 10.00
330 Lance Briggs CR AU/15 8.00 20.00
337 Laquon Treadwell GX AU/49 EXCH 5.00 12.00
338 Corey Coleman GX AU/49 6.00 15.00
339 Cardale Jones GX AU/49 4.00 10.00
340 Michael Thomas GX AU/49 8.00 20.00
341 Will Fuller V GX AU/49 6.00 15.00
342 Josh Doctson GX AU/49 5.00 12.00
343 Christian Hackenberg GX AU/49 EXCH 4.00 10.00
344 C.J. Prosise GX AU/49 4.00 10.00
345 Paul Perkins GX AU/49 4.00 10.00
346 Tyler Boyd GX AU/49 EXCH 5.00 12.00
347 Joey Bosa GX AU/49 8.00 20.00
348 Braxton Miller GX AU/49 4.00 10.00
349 Cody Kessler GX AU/49 4.00 10.00
350 Sterling Shepard GX AU/49 5.00 12.00
351 Alex Collins GX AU/49 5.00 12.00
352 Jordan Howard GX AU/49 10.00 25.00
353 Pharoh Cooper GX AU/49 4.00 10.00
354 Dak Prescott GX AU/49 50.00 100.00
355 Kenneth Dixon GX AU/49 4.00 10.00
356 Devontae Booker GX AU/49 5.00 12.00
357 Hunter Henry GX AU/49 5.00 12.00
358 Leonte Carroo GX AU/49 4.00 10.00
359 Chris Moore GX AU/49 5.00 12.00
360 Tajae Sharpe GX AU/49 5.00 12.00
374 Eddie Lacy SM AU/25 5.00 12.00
375 Vincent Jackson SM AU/25 5.00 12.00
376 DeAndre Hopkins SM AU/25 6.00 15.00
377 Brandin Cooks SM AU/49 5.00 12.00
378 Mike Evans SM AU/49 5.00 12.00
379 Tyler Eifert SM AU/49 5.00 12.00
380 Jeremy Langford SM AU/49 5.00 12.00
385 Lance Briggs PS AU/25 6.00 15.00
386 Brett Keisel PS AU/49 15.00 40.00
395 Trevor Siemian PS AU/49 6.00 15.00
396 Ozzie Newsome PS AU/25 6.00 15.00
397 Julius Thomas PS AU/49 4.00 10.00
398 Charlie Joiner PS AU/49 4.00 10.00
399 Charcandrick West PS AU/49 4.00 10.00
400 Steve Grogan PS AU/49 4.00 10.00

2016 Panini Preferred Silhouettes Prime

2 Ameer Abdullah JSY AU/25 6.00 15.00
4 Bryce Petty JSY AU/25 6.00 15.00
6 Devin Smith JSY AU/25 6.00 15.00
16 Mike Davis JSY AU/25 6.00 15.00
20 Jaelen Strong JSY AU/25 6.00 15.00
22 Jay Ajayi JSY AU/25 8.00 20.00
24 David Johnson JSY AU/25 25.00 50.00
30 Jeremy Langford JSY AU/25 8.00 20.00
34 Matt Jones JSY AU/25 8.00 20.00
40 Julius Thomas JSY AU/25 6.00 15.00
42 Dorial Green-Beckham JSY AU/25 6.00 15.00
44 Sammie Coates JSY AU/25 6.00 15.00
46 Byron Jones JSY AU/25 6.00 15.00
56 Karlos Williams JSY AU/25 6.00 15.00
61 Jared Goff JSY AU/25 40.00 100.00
62 Carson Wentz JSY AU/25
63 Joey Bosa JSY AU/25 12.00 30.00
64 Ezekiel Elliott JSY AU/25 150.00 300.00
65 Corey Coleman JSY AU/25 10.00 25.00
66 Will Fuller V JSY AU/25 10.00 25.00
67 Josh Doctson JSY AU/25 15.00 40.00
68 Laquon Treadwell JSY AU/25 15.00 40.00
69 Paxton Lynch JSY AU/25 6.00 15.00
70 Derrick Henry JSY AU/25 15.00 40.00
71 Connor Cook JSY AU/25 8.00 20.00
72 Cardale Jones JSY AU/25 6.00 15.00
73 Michael Thomas JSY AU/25 12.00 30.00
74 Christian Hackenberg JSY AU/25 6.00 15.00
75 C.J. Prosise JSY AU/25 6.00 15.00
76 Paul Perkins JSY AU/25 6.00 15.00
77 Tyler Boyd JSY AU/25 8.00 20.00
78 Braxton Miller JSY AU/25 6.00 15.00
79 Cody Kessler JSY AU/25 6.00 15.00
80 Sterling Shepard JSY AU/25 8.00 20.00
81 Alex Collins JSY AU/25 8.00 20.00
82 Jordan Howard JSY AU/25 40.00 80.00
83 Pharoh Cooper JSY AU/25 6.00 15.00
84 Dak Prescott JSY AU/25 50.00 100.00
85 Kenneth Dixon JSY AU/25 6.00 15.00
86 DeAndre Washington JSY AU/25 6.00 15.00
87 Devontae Booker JSY AU/25 8.00 20.00
88 Hunter Henry JSY AU/25 8.00 20.00
89 Leonte Carroo JSY AU/25 6.00 15.00
90 Chris Moore JSY AU/25 8.00 20.00
91 Kenyan Drake JSY AU/25 10.00 25.00
92 Ricardo Louis JSY AU/25 6.00 15.00
93 Demarcus Robinson JSY AU/25 6.00 15.00
94 Jonathan Williams JSY AU/25 8.00 20.00
95 Keenan Reynolds JSY AU/25 8.00 20.00
96 Kevin Hogan JSY AU/25 8.00 20.00
97 Trevor Davis JSY AU/25 6.00 15.00
98 Tyler Ervin JSY AU/25 6.00 15.00
99 Wendell Smallwood JSY AU/25 6.00 15.00
100 Moritz Bohringer JSY AU/25 6.00 15.00

2016 Panini Preferred Bengals Memorabilia

1 Dnrd/Ika/Bnrd/Grn/Dtn/Pko/Dwsn 5.00 12.00
2 Dtn/Bnrd/Mlga/Efrt/Dlp/Atns/Hll 4.00 10.00

2016 Panini Preferred Broncos Memorabilia

1 Sdrs/Mlr/Tlb/Adsn/Wre/Thms/Mng 10.00 25.00
2 Ry/Grn/Rby/Hrs/Tms/Mng/Wrd 10.00 25.00

2016 Panini Preferred Buffalo Memorabilia

1 Cly/Hghs/Drs/Wds/Wkns/MCy/Tylr 5.00 12.00
2 Drs/Gdwn/Bwn/Wkns/Gmre/MCy/Dby 5.00 12.00

2016 Panini Preferred Championship Fabric

1 Peyton Manning/49 25.00 60.00
2 Von Miller/49 10.00 25.00
3 C.J. Anderson/49 10.00 25.00
4 Demaryius Thomas/99 10.00 25.00
5 Emmanuel Sanders/49 12.00 30.00
6 DeMarcus Ware/49 10.00 25.00
7 Aqib Talib/199 4.00 10.00
8 T.J. Ward/199 4.00 10.00
9 Chris Harris/199 4.00 10.00
10 Shane Ray/199 4.00 10.00

2016 Panini Preferred Chargers Memorabilia

1 Gdn/Ingm/Jnsn/Gts/Whd/Pymn/Alln/Rvrs 5.00 12.00
2 Fld/Teo/Igm/Gts/Ade/Aln/Rvrs/Jnsn 5.00 12.00

2016 Panini Preferred Cowboys Memorabilia

1 Jns/Strt/Ecbr/Rmo/Crh/MFdn/MCln 8.00 20.00
2 Cr/Bsly/Wtn/Wms/Byt/Gry/Mtn 10.00 25.00

2016 Panini Preferred Dolphins Memorabilia

1 Wke/Wlms/Stls/Tnhl/Pkr/Ldy/Cmrn/Msi 4.00 10.00
2 Cmrn/Pcy/Jns/Tnhl/Pkr/Ldy/Jkns/Msi 4.00 10.00

2016 Panini Preferred Jaguars Memorabilia

1 Hrns/Cprn/Lee/Grn/Smth/Btls/Rbsn 3.00 8.00
2 Hse/Tms/Rbsn/Odck/Lws/Plzy/Yldn 4.00 10.00

2016 Panini Preferred KC Chiefs Memorabilia

1 Frd/Bry/Dvs/Hli/Sth/Jnsn/Mcln/Hstn 4.00 10.00
2 Sth/Chls/Mcln/Gns/Jnsn/Pe/Fsr/Hstn 4.00 10.00

2016 Panini Preferred Legends Memorabilia

1 Grse/Tktn/Plkt/Cska/Sbch/Nmth/Hdks 25.00 60.00

2016 Panini Preferred Preferred Pairings Materials

1 A.Hurns/B.Bortles/49 6.00 15.00
2 J.Goff/P.Cooper/199 20.00 50.00
3 O.Beckham Jr./E.Manning/25 12.00 30.00
4 C.Wentz/W.Smallwood/199 30.00 80.00
5 J.Rice/J.Montana/25 30.00 80.00
6 K.Reynolds/C.Moore/199 4.00 10.00
7 J.Jones/M.Ryan/25 12.00 30.00
8 K.Reynolds/K.Dixon/199 4.00 10.00
9 A.Dalton/A.Green/25 12.00 30.00
10 D.Prescott/E.Elliott/199 15.00 40.00
11 J.Charles/J.Maclin/25 10.00 25.00
12 L.Carroo/K.Drake/199 5.00 12.00
13 A.Cooper/D.Carr/49 10.00 25.00
14 H.Henry/J.Bosa/199 6.00 15.00
15 C.Cook/D.Washington/199 4.00 10.00
16 C.Coleman/R.Louis/199 5.00 12.00
17 J.Brissett/M.Mitchell/199 4.00 10.00
18 J.Williams/C.Jones/199 4.00 10.00
19 J.Elway/P.Manning/25 25.00 60.00
20 B.Miller/W.Fuller V/199 6.00 12.00
21 T.Bridgewater/S.Diggs/49 8.00 20.00
22 M.Bohringer/L.Treadwell/199 4.00 10.00
23 C.Wentz/J.Matthews/199 30.00 80.00
24 A.Collins/C.Prosise/199 4.00 10.00
25 M.Evans/J.Winston/49 10.00 25.00
26 T.Ervin/W.Fuller V/199 5.00 12.00
28 C.Coleman/C.Kessler/199 5.00 12.00
29 J.Goff/T.Gurley II/199 20.00 50.00
30 B.Miller/T.Ervin/199 3.00 8.00
32 P.Perkins/S.Shepard/199 4.00 10.00

2016 Panini Preferred Pro Bowl Memorabilia

1 Grn/Wstn/Jns/Wsn/Bgwr/Gly/Frmn 6.00 15.00
2 Cpr/Crr/Mrtn/Mng/Ptsn/Bkhm/Hltn 5.00 12.00
3 Wtn/Stfd/Sdrs/Igm/Bkhm/Cbb/Rmo 12.00 30.00
4 Wtt/Khn/Hltn/Dtn/Wtnr/Nlsn/Frst 5.00 12.00

2016 Panini Preferred Rivals Memorabilia

1 Grn/Dtn/Bwn/Hll/Rbgr/Bll 10.00 25.00

2016 Panini Preferred Rookie Memorabilia

1 Wtz/Hkbrg/Jns/Ck/Gff/Lnch/Clns 30.00 80.00
2 Clns/Hry/Hrd/Dxn/Prse/Elt/Mre 15.00 40.00
3 Mre/Dxn/Ls/Kslr/Clmn/Rnds/Gff 20.00 50.00
4 Gff/Fllr/Wntz/Clmn/Elt/Bsa 30.00 80.00
5 Prct/Hry/Cpr/Clns/Hry/Trwl/ 15.00 40.00

2016 Panini Preferred SB Champs Memorabilia

1 Rgrs/Brs/Mng/Mng/Mlr/Flco/Smth/Brdy 30.00 80.00
2 Rce/Mtna/Elwy/Rgns/Yng/Aln/Lws/Akmn 30.00 80.00

2016 Panini Preferred Seahawks Memorabilia

1 Wgnr/Cclr/Smth/Shmn Wlsn/Bmr/Bdwn/Tms 12.00 30.00

2016 Panini Preferred Wideouts Memorabilia

1 Ryds/Trwl/Ls/Mlr/Rbsn/Dctn/Tms/Cpr 6.00 15.00
2 Mre/Brgr/Clmn/Cro/Shpd/Dvs/Byd/Fllr 5.00 12.00

2017 Panini Preferred

2 Tyler Lockett SL JSY AU/25 8.00 20.00
3 Greg Olsen SL JSY AU/15 10.00 25.00
4 Derek Carr SL JSY AU/15 25.00 50.00
6 Michael Vick SL JSY AU/15 15.00 40.00
8 DeMarco Murray SL JSY AU/15 25.00 50.00
11 Carlos Hyde SL JSY AU/25 6.00 15.00
13 James White SL JSY AU/49 6.00 15.00
14 Thurman Thomas SL JSY AU/25 8.00 20.00
16 Emmanuel Sanders SL JSY AU/15 EXCH 12.00 30.00
17 Aaron Donald SL JSY AU/15 12.00 30.00
20 Malcolm Mitchell SL JSY AU/25 8.00 20.00
22 Tyreek Hill SL JSY AU/25 10.00 25.00
26 Thomas Rawls SL JSY AU/25
27 Rod Woodson SL JSY AU/25 12.00 30.00
29 A.J. Green SL JSY AU/15 12.00 30.00
30 Jordan Howard SL JSY AU/25 10.00 25.00
33 Cole Beasley SL JSY AU/49 EXCH 10.00 25.00
34 David Johnson SL JSY AU/15 12.00 30.00
35 Kiko Alonso SL JSY AU/15 8.00 20.00
36 Mike Evans SL JSY AU/15 10.00 25.00
38 Sterling Shepard SL JSY AU/25 8.00 20.00
40 Travis Kelce SL JSY AU/25 10.00 25.00
44 Joey Bosa SL JSY AU/25
45 Rich Gannon SL JSY AU/25 10.00 25.00
46 Paul Perkins SL JSY AU/49 5.00 12.00
47 Quincy Enunwa SL JSY AU/99 4.00 10.00
48 Golden Tate III SL JSY AU/25 6.00 15.00
49 Carl Eller SL JSY AU/99 EXCH 4.00 10.00
50 Zach Ertz SL JSY AU/49 6.00 15.00
51 Tyler Eifert SL JSY AU/25 8.00 20.00
54 Stefon Diggs SL JSY AU/49
55 Doug Baldwin SL JSY AU/15 10.00 25.00
58 Randall Cobb SL JSY AU/25 8.00 20.00
59 Mark Ingram SL JSY AU/15 10.00 25.00
61 Nathan Peterman SL JSY AU/199 RC 4.00 10.00
62 Zay Jones SL JSY AU/99 RC 5.00 12.00
63 Christian McCaffrey SL JSY AU/99 RC 10.00 25.00
64 Curtis Samuel SL JSY AU/99 RC 5.00 12.00
65 Mitchell Trubisky SL JSY AU/99 RC 25.00 50.00
66 Joe Mixon SL JSY AU/199 RC 6.00 15.00
67 John Ross III SL JSY AU/99 RC 5.00 12.00
68 DeShone Kizer SL JSY AU/99 RC 4.00 10.00
69 Carlos Henderson SL JSY AU/99 RC 4.00 10.00
70 Kenny Golladay SL JSY AU/199 RC 5.00 12.00
71 Jamaal Williams SL JSY AU/199 RC 3.00 8.00
72 Deshaun Watson SL JSY AU/99 RC 50.00 100.00
73 D'Onta Foreman SL JSY AU/99 RC 5.00 12.00
74 Marlon Mack SL JSY AU/199 RC 5.00 12.00
75 Dede Westbrook SL JSY AU/99 RC 4.00 10.00
76 Leonard Fournette SL JSY AU/99 RC 25.00 50.00
77 Kareem Hunt SL JSY AU/199 RC EXCH 6.00 15.00
78 Patrick Mahomes II SL JSY AU/99 RC 150.00 300.00
79 Mike Williams SL JSY AU/99 RC 6.00 15.00
80 Cooper Kupp SL JSY AU/99 RC 6.00 15.00
81 Josh Reynolds SL JSY AU/199 RC 3.00 8.00
82 Dalvin Cook SL JSY AU/99 RC 10.00 25.00
83 Alvin Kamara SL JSY AU/99 RC 25.00 50.00
84 Davis Webb SL JSY AU/99 RC 4.00 10.00
85 Evan Engram SL JSY AU/99 RC EXCH 5.00 12.00
86 Wayne Gallman SL JSY AU/99 RC 5.00 12.00
87 ArDarius Stewart SL JSY AU/99 RC 4.00 10.00
88 Mack Hollins SL JSY AU/199 RC 3.00 8.00
89 James Conner SL JSY AU/199 RC 6.00 15.00
90 JuJu Smith-Schuster SL JSY AU/99 RC 15.00 40.00
91 R. Joshua Dobbs SL JSY AU/199 RC 4.00 10.00
92 C.J. Beathard SL JSY AU/99 RC 4.00 10.00
93 Joe Williams SL JSY AU/199 RC 3.00 8.00
94 Amara Darboh SL JSY AU/99 RC EXCH 4.00 10.00
95 Chris Godwin SL JSY AU/199 RC 4.00 10.00
96 Jeremy McNichols SL JSY AU/199 RC 3.00 8.00
97 O.J. Howard SL JSY AU/99 RC 5.00 12.00
98 Corey Davis SL JSY AU/99 RC EXCH 6.00 15.00
99 Taywan Taylor SL JSY AU/199 RC EXCH 3.00 8.00
100 Samaje Perine SL JSY AU/99 RC 4.00 10.00
101 Charlie Joiner PEN AU/25 5.00 12.00
102 Dan Reeves PEN AU/15 8.00 20.00
103 Lawrence Taylor PEN AU/15 25.00 50.00
105 Jim Zorn PEN AU/15 6.00 15.00
106 Roger Craig PEN AU/25 10.00 25.00
107 Kellen Winslow PEN AU/25 6.00 15.00
108 James Lofton PEN AU/15 8.00 20.00
109 Michael Bennett PEN AU/25 10.00 25.00
110 Earl Campbell PEN AU/25 12.00 30.00
111 Robert Kelley PEN AU/49 4.00 10.00
112 Michael Vick PEN AU/25 6.00 15.00
113 John Brown PEN AU/49 5.00 12.00
114 Dan Hampton PEN AU/49 4.00 10.00
115 Randy White PEN AU/25 10.00 25.00
116 Ty Law PEN AU/15 15.00 40.00
118 Willie McGinest PEN AU/25 5.00 12.00
119 Joe Theismann PEN AU/15 10.00 25.00
120 Priest Holmes PEN AU/49 4.00 10.00
121 Marcus Allen PEN AU/25 10.00 25.00
122 Warren Sapp PEN AU/15 15.00 40.00
123 Ed Too Tall Jones PEN AU/25 5.00 12.00
124 Tim Brown PEN AU/15 10.00 25.00
125 Ozzie Newsome PEN AU/49 5.00 12.00
127 Ron Jaworski PEN AU/25 6.00 15.00
129 Len Dawson PEN AU/25 10.00 25.00
130 Neil Smith PEN AU/49 4.00 10.00
132 Mark Schlereth PEN AU/25 5.00 12.00
133 Steve Atwater PEN AU/25 10.00 25.00
134 Darren Woodson PEN AU/25 12.00 30.00
135 Archie Manning PEN AU/15 30.00 60.00
136 Troy Brown PEN AU/49 EXCH 4.00 10.00
137 Jevon Kearse PEN AU/49 4.00 10.00
138 Kevin Mawae PEN AU/25 5.00 12.00
140 Ronnie Lott PEN AU/25 40.00 80.00
141 Mark Ingram PEN AU/25 6.00 15.00
142 Ed McCaffrey PEN AU/25 10.00 25.00
143 Tedy Bruschi PEN AU/25 12.00 30.00
144 Kyle Rudolph PEN AU/36 4.00 10.00
146 Greg Olsen PEN AU/25 6.00 15.00
147 Jason Witten PEN AU/15 EXCH 30.00 60.00
148 Steve Grogan PEN AU/49 4.00 10.00
149 Cole Beasley PEN AU/49 EXCH 12.00 30.00
150 Eric Dickerson PEN AU/15 10.00 25.00
151 Alan Page PEN AU/25 5.00 12.00
152 Ickey Woods PEN AU/49 4.00 10.00
153 Devonta Freeman PEN AU/25 EXCH 6.00 15.00
154 Ha Ha Clinton-Dix PEN AU/49 10.00 25.00
155 Bob Lilly PEN AU/25 6.00 15.00
156 Landon Collins PEN AU/35 4.00 10.00
157 Heath Miller PEN AU/25 5.00 12.00
158 Fred Taylor PEN AU/15 8.00 20.00
159 Dont'a Hightower PEN AU/49 4.00 10.00
160 Ken Anderson PEN AU/49 8.00 20.00
161 Nathan Peterman PEN AU/99 4.00 10.00
162 Zay Jones PEN AU/99 4.00 10.00
163 Christian McCaffrey PEN AU/25 12.00 30.00
164 Curtis Samuel PEN AU/99 4.00 10.00
166 Joe Mixon PEN AU/49 8.00 20.00
167 John Ross III PEN AU/25 6.00 15.00
169 Carlos Henderson PEN AU/99 3.00 8.00
170 Kenny Golladay PEN AU/99 6.00 15.00
171 Jamaal Williams PEN AU/49 4.00 10.00
173 D'Onta Foreman PEN AU/49 5.00 12.00
174 Marlon Mack PEN AU/49 6.00 15.00
175 Dede Westbrook PEN AU/99 3.00 8.00
177 Kareem Hunt PEN AU/99 6.00 15.00
180 Cooper Kupp PEN AU/49 6.00 15.00
181 Josh Reynolds PEN AU/49 4.00 10.00
182 Dalvin Cook PEN AU/25 12.00 30.00
183 Alvin Kamara PEN AU/99 12.00 30.00
184 Davis Webb PEN AU/25 5.00 12.00
185 Evan Engram PEN AU/99 EXCH 4.00 10.00
186 Wayne Gallman PEN AU/99 4.00 10.00
187 ArDarius Stewart PEN AU/49 4.00 10.00
188 Mack Hollins PEN AU/49 4.00 10.00
189 James Conner PEN AU/49 8.00 20.00
190 JuJu Smith-Schuster PEN AU/25 20.00 40.00
191 R. Joshua Dobbs PEN AU/49 5.00 12.00
192 C.J. Beathard PEN AU/99 3.00 8.00
193 Joe Williams PEN AU/49 4.00 10.00
194 Amara Darboh PEN AU/99 EXCH 3.00 8.00
195 Chris Godwin PEN AU/49 5.00 12.00
196 Jeremy McNichols PEN AU/99 3.00 8.00
197 O.J. Howard PEN AU/99 4.00 10.00
198 Corey Davis PEN AU/25 EXCH 8.00 20.00
199 Taywan Taylor PEN AU/99 EXCH 3.00 8.00
200 Samaje Perine PEN AU/99 3.00 8.00
201 Tim Brown PROM AU/25 10.00 25.00
202 Rod Smith PROM AU/25 6.00 15.00
203 Doug Flutie PROM AU/25 6.00 15.00
204 Kyle Juszczyk PROM AU/25 5.00 12.00
205 Derrick Brooks PROM AU/15 6.00 15.00
207 Drew Pearson PROM AU/25 6.00 15.00
208 Reggie Wayne PROM AU/25 6.00 15.00
210 Steve Largent PROM AU/25 8.00 20.00
212 Aqib Talib PROM AU/25 8.00 20.00
216 Fred Biletnikoff PROM AU/15 10.00 25.00
217 Rod Woodson PROM AU/25 10.00 25.00
218 Stefon Diggs PROM AU/25 12.00 30.00
220 Fran Tarkenton PROM AU/25 25.00 50.00
222 Derrick Henry PROM AU/15
223 Pierre Garcon PROM AU/49 5.00 12.00
224 Paul Hornung PROM AU/25 10.00 25.00
225 Thomas Davis PROM AU/15 6.00 15.00
226 Henry Ellard PROM AU/49 4.00 10.00
228 Andre Reed PROM AU/25 6.00 15.00
229 Ickey Woods PROM AU/25 5.00 12.00
231 Tedy Bruschi PROM AU/25 10.00 25.00
232 Michael Thomas PROM AU/25 8.00 20.00
234 Raymond Berry PROM AU/25 6.00 15.00
238 Y.A. Tittle PROM AU/49 6.00 15.00
239 Jim Plunkett PROM AU/15 8.00 20.00
240 Lamar Miller PROM AU/25 5.00 12.00
241 Bob Griese PROM AU/15 12.00 30.00
242 Donald Driver PROM AU/15
244 Troy Brown PROM AU/49 4.00 10.00
245 Jack Ham PROM AU/25 6.00 15.00
246 Neil Smith PROM AU/49 10.00 25.00
247 Eddie George PROM AU/15 30.00 60.00
248 Mike Singletary PROM AU/25 8.00 20.00
251 Dwight Clark PROM AU/25 12.00 30.00
252 Charley Taylor PROM AU/25 5.00 12.00
253 Bruce Smith PROM AU/15 8.00 20.00
254 LeGarrette Blount PROM AU/25 12.00 30.00
256 Doug Williams PROM AU/25 10.00 25.00
258 Morten Andersen PROM AU/49 4.00 10.00
259 Randall Cunningham PROM AU/15 15.00 40.00
260 Aeneas Williams PROM AU/15 6.00 15.00
261 Solomon Thomas PROM AU/199 2.50 6.00
262 Jamal Adams PROM AU/199 2.50 6.00
263 Marshon Lattimore PROM AU/199 3.00 8.00
264 Haason Reddick PROM AU/199 2.50 6.00
265 Derek Barnett PROM AU/199 EXCH 3.00 8.00
266 Malik Hooker PROM AU/199 2.50 6.00
267 Marlon Humphrey PROM AU/199 2.50 6.00
268 Jonathan Allen PROM AU/99 4.00 10.00
269 Adoree' Jackson PROM AU/199 3.00 8.00
270 Jarrad Davis PROM AU/199 3.00 8.00
271 Charles Harris PROM AU/199 2.50 6.00
272 Gareon Conley PROM AU/199 EXCH 2.50 6.00
273 Jabrill Peppers PROM AU/99 5.00 12.00
274 Chad Williams PROM AU/199 2.50 6.00
275 Tre'Davious White PROM AU/199 2.50 6.00
276 Taco Charlton PROM AU/199 2.50 6.00
277 David Njoku PROM AU/199 3.00 8.00
278 T.J. Watt PROM AU/199 8.00 20.00
279 Chris Carson PROM AU/199 4.00 10.00
280 Gerald Everett PROM AU/199 2.50 6.00
281 Adam Shaheen PROM AU/199 2.50 6.00
282 DeMarcus Walker PROM AU/199 2.50 6.00
283 Raekwon McMillan PROM AU/199 2.50 6.00
284 Obi Melifonwu PROM AU/199 2.50 6.00
285 Malachi Dupre PROM AU/199 EXCH 2.50 6.00
286 Jordan Willis PROM AU/199 2.50 6.00
287 Dalvin Tomlinson PROM AU/199 2.50 6.00
288 Tim Williams PROM AU/199 3.00 8.00
289 Jonnu Smith PROM AU/199 2.50 6.00
290 Cordrea Tankersley PROM AU/199 EXCH 3.00 8.00
291 Josh Malone PROM AU/199 2.50 6.00
292 Donnel Pumphrey PROM AU/199 3.00 8.00
293 Ryan Switzer PROM AU/149 4.00 10.00
294 Chad Hansen PROM AU/199 2.50 6.00
295 Jake Butt PROM AU/199 3.00 8.00
296 Jordan Leggett PROM AU/199 2.50 6.00
297 Brian Hill PROM AU/199 2.50 6.00
298 Shelton Gibson PROM AU/199 2.50 6.00
300 DeAngelo Yancey PROM AU/199 2.50 6.00
301 Mike Evans CR AU/25 6.00 15.00
302 Adam Thielen CR AU/49 25.00 50.00
304 Isaiah Crowell CR AU/49 4.00 10.00
305 Melvin Gordon CR AU/25 6.00 15.00
306 Will Fuller V CR AU/25 5.00 12.00
308 Andre Rison CR AU/25 6.00 15.00
310 Fred Taylor CR AU/15
311 Sterling Shepard CR AU/25 6.00 15.00
312 Tyreek Hill CR AU/25 8.00 20.00
313 Rishard Matthews CR AU/49
314 Ricky Williams CR AU/25 20.00 40.00
315 Torry Holt CR AU/25 6.00 15.00
316 Hines Ward CR AU/15 20.00 40.00
317 Jermaine Kearse CR AU/49 4.00 10.00
318 Tyler Eifert CR AU/25 6.00 15.00
320 Priest Holmes CR AU/25 5.00 12.00
321 Emmanuel Sanders CR AU/25 8.00 20.00
322 Paul Perkins CR AU/49 4.00 10.00
324 Vance Johnson CR AU/25 5.00 12.00
325 Mohamed Sanu CR AU/49 4.00 10.00
326 Jordy Nelson CR AU/15 15.00 40.00
327 Jimmy Garoppolo CR AU/25 30.00 60.00
328 Robert Kelley CR AU/49 4.00 10.00
329 Trevor Siemian CR AU/25 5.00 12.00
330 Brandon Jacobs CR AU/25 5.00 12.00
331 Mitchell Trubisky GX AU/25 30.00 60.00
332 Leonard Fournette GX AU/25 15.00 40.00
333 Corey Davis GX AU/25 EXCH 8.00 20.00
334 Mike Williams GX AU/25
335 Christian McCaffrey GX AU/25 12.00 30.00
336 John Ross III GX AU/25 6.00 15.00
337 Patrick Mahomes II GX AU/25 200.00 400.00
339 O.J. Howard GX AU/49 5.00 12.00
340 Evan Engram GX AU/49 5.00 12.00
341 Zay Jones GX AU/49 5.00 12.00
342 Curtis Samuel GX AU/25 6.00 15.00
343 Dalvin Cook GX AU/25 12.00 30.00
344 Joe Mixon GX AU/49 8.00 20.00
346 JuJu Smith-Schuster GX AU/25 25.00 50.00
347 Alvin Kamara GX AU/49 25.00 50.00
348 Cooper Kupp GX AU/49 6.00 15.00
349 Taywan Taylor GX AU/49 EXCH 4.00 10.00
350 ArDarius Stewart GX AU/49 4.00 10.00
351 Carlos Henderson GX AU/49 4.00 10.00
352 Chris Godwin GX AU/49 5.00 12.00
353 Kareem Hunt GX AU/49 EXCH 8.00 20.00
354 Davis Webb GX AU/25 5.00 12.00
355 D'Onta Foreman GX AU/25 6.00 15.00
356 C.J. Beathard GX AU/49 4.00 10.00
357 James Conner GX AU/49 8.00 20.00
358 Amara Darboh GX AU/49 EXCH 4.00 10.00
359 Dede Westbrook GX AU/25 5.00 12.00
360 R. Joshua Dobbs GX AU/25 6.00 15.00
365 Charles Haley SM AU/25 10.00 25.00
374 Lance Briggs SM AU/15
380 DeSean Jackson SM AU/25 6.00 15.00
381 Daryl Johnston PS AU/25 15.00 40.00
382 Ted Hendricks PS AU/15 6.00 15.00
384 Mike Glennon PS AU/25 6.00 15.00
385 Darius Slay PS AU/49 4.00 10.00
386 Don Majkowski PS AU/25 6.00 15.00
387 Jim Kiick PS AU/25 5.00 12.00
388 Karl Joseph PS AU/49 4.00 10.00
389 Mark Brunell PS AU/25 6.00 15.00
390 Hakeem Nicks PS AU/15
391 Mark Gastineau PS AU/25 5.00 12.00
393 Cameron Brate PS AU/49
394 Haloti Ngata PS AU/49 4.00 10.00
395 Champ Bailey PS AU/25 12.00 30.00
396 Eric Weddle PS AU/25 5.00 12.00
397 Jay Novacek PS AU/25 12.00 30.00
398 Delvin Breaux PS AU/49 4.00 10.00
399 Michael Bennett PS AU/25 10.00 25.00
400 Antonio Freeman PS AU/25 6.00 15.00

2017 Panini Preferred Silhouettes Prime

13 James White JSY AU/25 6.00 15.00
46 Paul Perkins JSY AU/25 5.00 12.00
47 Quincy Enunwa JSY AU/25 5.00 12.00
54 Stefon Diggs JSY AU/25 6.00 15.00
61 Nathan Peterman JSY AU/49 5.00 12.00
62 Zay Jones JSY AU/49 5.00 12.00
63 Christian McCaffrey JSY AU/25 25.00 50.00
64 Curtis Samuel JSY AU/49 5.00 12.00
65 Mitchell Trubisky JSY AU/25 75.00 150.00
66 Joe Mixon JSY AU/49 8.00 20.00
67 John Ross III JSY AU/49 5.00 12.00
68 DeShone Kizer JSY AU/25 5.00 12.00
69 Carlos Henderson JSY AU/49 4.00 10.00
70 Kenny Golladay JSY AU/49 6.00 15.00
71 Jamaal Williams JSY AU/49 4.00 10.00
72 Deshaun Watson JSY AU/25 75.00 150.00
73 D'Onta Foreman JSY AU/49 5.00 12.00
74 Marlon Mack JSY AU/49 6.00 15.00
75 Dede Westbrook JSY AU/49 4.00 10.00
76 Leonard Fournette JSY AU/25 40.00 80.00
77 Kareem Hunt JSY AU/49
78 Patrick Mahomes II JSY AU/25 200.00 400.00
79 Mike Williams JSY AU/25 8.00 20.00
80 Cooper Kupp JSY AU/49 12.00 30.00
81 Josh Reynolds JSY AU/49 4.00 10.00
82 Dalvin Cook JSY AU/49 15.00 40.00
83 Alvin Kamara JSY AU/49 15.00 40.00
84 Davis Webb JSY AU/49 4.00 10.00
85 Evan Engram JSY AU/49 5.00 12.00
86 Wayne Gallman JSY AU/49 5.00 12.00
87 ArDarius Stewart JSY AU/49 4.00 10.00
88 Mack Hollins JSY AU/49 4.00 10.00
89 James Conner JSY AU/49 8.00 20.00
90 JuJu Smith-Schuster JSY AU/49 30.00 60.00
91 R. Joshua Dobbs JSY AU/49 5.00 12.00
92 C.J. Beathard JSY AU/49 4.00 10.00
93 Joe Williams JSY AU/49 4.00 10.00
94 Amara Darboh JSY AU/49 4.00 10.00
95 Chris Godwin JSY AU/49 5.00 12.00
96 Jeremy McNichols JSY AU/49 4.00 10.00
97 O.J. Howard JSY AU/49 5.00 12.00
98 Corey Davis JSY AU/49 10.00 25.00
99 Taywan Taylor JSY AU/49 4.00 10.00
100 Samaje Perine JSY AU/49 4.00 10.00

2017 Panini Preferred Activ8 Rookie Jerseys

1 Brd/Wbb/Wsn/Kzr/Tky/Pmn/Mms/Dbs 15.00 40.00
2 Kra/MCy/Fmn/Ck/Cnr/Mxn/Hnt/Fnte 12.00 30.00

2017 Panini Preferred Armory Materials

1 Mitchell Trubisky 10.00 25.00
2 Deshaun Watson 12.00 30.00
3 Patrick Mahomes II 40.00 100.00
4 Corey Davis 5.00 12.00
5 Mike Williams 5.00 12.00
6 Leonard Fournette 10.00 25.00
7 Christian McCaffrey 10.00 25.00
8 Dalvin Cook 12.00 30.00
9 Evan Engram 4.00 10.00
10 Joe Mixon 6.00 15.00
11 DeShone Kizer 3.00 8.00
12 JuJu Smith-Schuster 8.00 20.00

2017 Panini Preferred Game of Inches Materials

1 Marcus Mariota 8.00 20.00
2 Greg Olsen 6.00 15.00
3 Julio Jones 8.00 20.00
4 Jordan Howard 8.00 20.00
5 Russell Wilson 12.00 30.00
6 Andrew Luck
7 Matthew Stafford 12.00 30.00
8 Odell Beckham Jr. 15.00 40.00
9 Jarvis Landry 6.00 15.00
10 Jameis Winston 6.00 15.00
11 David Johnson 8.00 20.00
12 Ezekiel Elliott

2017 Panini Preferred Preferred Pairings Materials

*PRIME/25: .8X TO 2X BASIC JSY/199
*PRIME/25: .6X TO 1.5X BASIC JSY/99
*PRIME/25: .5X TO 1.2X BASIC JSY/49
1 D.Prescott/E.Elliott/99 25.00 50.00
2 A.Green/M.Stafford/199 4.00 10.00
3 K.Allen/M.Williams/199 4.00 10.00
4 J.Howard/M.Trubisky/199 8.00 20.00
5 C.Newton/L.Kuechly/99 5.00 12.00
6 D.Cook/J.Winston/199 6.00 15.00
7 C.Wentz/M.Hollins/199 5.00 12.00
8 A.Cooper/D.Carr/199 4.00 10.00
9 P.Mahomes II/T.Hill/199 15.00 40.00
10 J.Goff/T.Gurley II/199 4.00 10.00
11 D.Johnson/L.Fitzgerald/49 6.00 15.00
12 E.Engram/O.Beckham Jr./199 4.00 10.00
13 R.Kelley/S.Perine/199 2.50 6.00
14 J.Landry/R.Tannehill/199 3.00 8.00
15 T.Taylor/Z.Jones/49 5.00 12.00
16 A.Luck/C.McCaffrey/199 8.00 20.00
17 B.Bortles/L.Fournette/199 8.00 20.00
18 D.Hopkins/D.Watson/199 8.00 20.00
19 C.Davis/M.Mariota/199 4.00 10.00
20 J.Jones/M.Ryan/199 4.00 10.00
21 A.Kamara/D.Brees/199 8.00 20.00
22 J.Bosa/P.Rivers/199 4.00 10.00
23 D.Baldwin/R.Wilson/199 5.00 12.00

24 J.Hill/L.Fournette/199 8.00 20.00
25 J.Conner/L.Bell/49 8.00 20.00
26 C.Samuel/E.Elliott/49 8.00 20.00
27 D.Kizer/W.Fuller V/199 2.50 6.00
28 J.Doctson/S.Perine/199 2.50 6.00
29 J.Winston/M.Evans/199 3.00 8.00
30 K.Golladay/M.Stafford/199 4.00 10.00

2012 Panini Prizm

COMP.SET w/o RC's (200) 15.00 40.00
ONE ROOKIE PER PACK
1 Larry Fitzgerald .30 .75
2 John Skelton .25 .60
3 Beanie Wells .25 .60
4 Early Doucet .25 .60
5 Patrick Peterson .25 .60
6 LaRod Stephens-Howling .25 .60
7 Matt Ryan .30 .75
8 Roddy White .25 .60
9 Michael Turner .25 .60
10 Julio Jones .40 1.00
11 Jacquizz Rodgers .30 .75
12 Tony Gonzalez .30 .75
13 Anquan Boldin .25 .60
14 Ed Reed .30 .75
15 Joe Flacco .30 .75
16 Ray Lewis .40 1.00
17 Ray Rice .25 .60
18 Terrell Suggs .25 .60
19 Torrey Smith .25 .60
20 Ryan Fitzpatrick .25 .60
21 Fred Jackson .30 .75
22 Mario Williams .25 .60
23 C.J. Spiller .25 .60
24 Steve Johnson .30 .75
25 David Nelson .25 .60
26 Cam Newton .40 1.00
27 DeAngelo Williams .25 .60
28 Jonathan Stewart .25 .60
29 Jon Beason .25 .60
30 Greg Olsen .30 .75
31 Steve Smith .30 .75
32 Brandon Marshall .30 .75
33 Lance Briggs .30 .75
34 Devin Hester .30 .75
35 Jay Cutler .25 .60
36 Julius Peppers .30 .75
37 Matt Forte .25 .60
38 A.J. Green .40 1.00
39 Andy Dalton .30 .75
40 BenJarvus Green-Ellis .30 .75
41 Andrew Hawkins .25 .60
42 Jermaine Gresham .25 .60
43 Greg Little .25 .60
44 Ben Watson .25 .60
45 Joe Haden .25 .60
46 D'Qwell Jackson .25 .60
47 Josh Cribbs .25 .60
48 Mohamed Massaquoi .25 .60
49 DeMarco Murray .30 .75
50 DeMarcus Ware .40 1.00
51 Dez Bryant .40 1.00
52 Jason Witten .30 .75
53 Miles Austin .25 .60
54 Tony Romo .30 .75
55 Brandon Carr .25 .60
56 Champ Bailey .30 .75
57 Demaryius Thomas .40 1.00
58 Elvis Dumervil .25 .60
59 Eric Decker .25 .60
60 Peyton Manning .75 2.00
61 Von Miller .30 .75
62 Willis McGahee .25 .60
63 Brandon Pettigrew .25 .60
64 Calvin Johnson .40 1.00
65 Titus Young .25 .60
66 Stephen Tulloch .25 .60
67 Matthew Stafford .30 .75
68 Ndamukong Suh .30 .75
69 Aaron Rodgers .60 1.50
70 Charles Woodson .40 1.00
71 Clay Matthews .40 1.00
72 Greg Jennings .25 .60
73 Jermichael Finley .25 .60
74 Jordy Nelson .30 .75
75 Andre Johnson .30 .75
76 Arian Foster .30 .75
77 J.J. Watt .40 1.00
78 Kevin Walter .25 .60
79 Matt Schaub .25 .60
80 Owen Daniels .25 .60
81 Donnie Avery .25 .60
82 Delone Carter .25 .60
83 Donald Brown .25 .60
84 Dwight Freeney .25 .60
85 Reggie Wayne .30 .75
86 Robert Mathis .25 .60
87 Blaine Gabbert .25 .60
88 Laurent Robinson .25 .60
89 Cecil Shorts .25 .60
90 Marcedes Lewis .25 .60
91 Maurice Jones-Drew .25 .60
92 Paul Posluszny .25 .60
93 Dwayne Bowe .30 .75
94 Tony Moeaki .25 .60
95 Jamaal Charles .30 .75
96 Matt Cassel .25 .60
97 Peyton Hillis .25 .60
98 Tamba Hali .25 .60
99 Anthony Fasano .25 .60
100 Brian Hartline .30 .75
101 Davone Bess .25 .60
102 Karlos Dansby .25 .60
103 Cameron Wake .30 .75
104 Reggie Bush .25 .60
105 Adrian Peterson .40 1.00
106 Chad Greenway .30 .75
107 Christian Ponder .25 .60
108 Jared Allen .25 .60
109 Percy Harvin .25 .60
110 Toby Gerhart .25 .60
111 Aaron Hernandez .30 .75
112 Brandon Lloyd .25 .60
113 Deion Branch .25 .60
114 Jerod Mayo .25 .60
115 Rob Gronkowski .40 1.00
116 Tom Brady 1.00 2.50
117 Wes Welker .30 .75
118 Drew Brees .40 1.00
119 Darren Sproles .30 .75
120 Jimmy Graham .40 1.00
121 Mark Ingram .30 .75
122 Marques Colston .25 .60
123 Pierre Thomas .25 .60
124 Eli Manning .30 .75
125 Ahmad Bradshaw .25 .60
126 Hakeem Nicks .25 .60
127 Jason Pierre-Paul .25 .60
128 Justin Tuck .25 .60
129 Victor Cruz .30 .75
130 Darrelle Revis .25 .60
131 Joe McKnight .25 .60
132 Dustin Keller .25 .60
133 Mark Sanchez .25 .60
134 Santonio Holmes .25 .60
135 Shonn Greene .25 .60
136 Tim Tebow .40 1.00
137 Carson Palmer .30 .75
138 Darren McFadden .25 .60
139 Darrius Heyward-Bey .25 .60
140 Denarius Moore .25 .60
141 Taiwan Jones .25 .60
142 Jacoby Ford .25 .60
143 Brent Celek .25 .60
144 DeSean Jackson .30 .75
145 Jeremy Maclin .25 .60
146 LeSean McCoy .40 1.00
147 Michael Vick .30 .75
148 Nnamdi Asomugha .25 .60
149 Antonio Brown .40 1.00
150 Ben Roethlisberger .40 1.00
151 James Harrison .30 .75
152 Heath Miller .25 .60
153 Mike Wallace .25 .60
154 Isaac Redman .40 1.00
155 Troy Polamalu .40 1.00
156 Philip Rivers .40 1.00
157 Antonio Gates .30 .75
158 Malcom Floyd .25 .60
159 Eddie Royal .25 .60
160 Robert Meachem .25 .60
161 Ryan Mathews .30 .75
162 NaVorro Bowman .30 .75
163 Alex Smith .30 .75
164 Frank Gore .30 .75
165 Michael Crabtree .25 .60
166 Vernon Davis .25 .60
167 Patrick Willis .30 .75
168 Randy Moss .30 .75
169 Matt Flynn .25 .60
170 Zach Miller .25 .60
171 Golden Tate .25 .60
172 Marshawn Lynch .30 .75
173 Doug Baldwin .40 1.00
174 Sidney Rice .25 .60
175 Steve Smith USC .30 .75
176 Chris Long .25 .60
177 Lance Kendricks .25 .60
178 James Laurinaitis .25 .60
179 Sam Bradford .25 .60
180 Danny Amendola .30 .75
181 Steven Jackson .25 .60
182 Ronde Barber .25 .60
183 Mike Williams .30 .75
184 Dallas Clark .25 .60
185 Josh Freeman .30 .75
186 LeGarrette Blount .30 .75
187 Vincent Jackson .25 .60
188 Chris Johnson .25 .60
189 Jake Locker .40 1.00
190 Kenny Britt .25 .60
191 Michael Griffin .25 .60
192 Jared Cook .25 .60
193 Nate Washington .25 .60
194 Brian Orakpo .30 .75
195 London Fletcher .30 .75
196 Fred Davis .25 .60
197 Pierre Garcon .30 .75
198 Ryan Kerrigan .25 .60
199 Santana Moss .30 .75
200 Leonard Hankerson .25 .60
201 A.J. Jenkins RC .50 1.25
202 Alshon Jeffery RC 1.00 2.50
203A Andrew Luck RC 8.00 20.00
203B Andrew Luck SP 12.00 30.00
204 Bernard Pierce RC .50 1.25
205 Brandon Weeden RC .50 1.25
206 Brian Quick RC .50 1.25
207 Brock Osweiler RC .50 1.25
208 Chris Givens RC .50 1.25
209 Coby Fleener RC .50 1.25
210 David Wilson RC .50 1.25
211 DeVier Posey RC .50 1.25
212A Doug Martin RC .75 2.00
212B Doug Martin SP 1.50 4.00
213 Dwayne Allen RC .50 1.25
214A Isaiah Pead RC .50 1.25
214B Isaiah Pead SP 1.00 2.50
215 Jarius Wright RC .50 1.25
216 Joe Adams RC .50 1.25
217A Justin Blackmon RC .50 1.25
217B Justin Blackmon SP 1.00 2.50
218A Kendall Wright RC .50 1.25
218B Kendall Wright SP 1.00 2.50
219 Lamar Miller RC .75 2.00
220 LaMichael James RC .50 1.25
221 Michael Egnew RC .50 1.25
222 Michael Floyd RC .50 1.25
223 Mohamed Sanu RC .75 2.00
224 Nick Foles RC 1.25 3.00
225 Nick Toon RC .50 1.25
226A Rueben Randle RC .50 1.25
226B Rueben Randle SP 1.00 2.50
227A Robert Griffin III RC .60 1.50
227B Robert Griffin III SP 1.25 3.00
228A Robert Turbin RC .50 1.25
228B Robert Turbin SP 1.00 2.50
229 Ronnie Hillman RC .50 1.25
230A Russell Wilson RC 6.00 12.00
230B Russell Wilson SP 8.00 20.00
231 Ryan Broyles RC .50 1.25
232A Ryan Tannehill RC .75 2.00
232B Ryan Tannehill SP 1.50 4.00
233A Stephen Hill RC .50 1.25
233B Stephen Hill SP 1.00 2.50
234 T.J. Graham RC .50 1.25
235A Trent Richardson RC .50 1.25
235B Trent Richardson SP 1.00 2.50
236A Alfred Morris RC .50 1.25
236B Alfred Morris SP 1.00 2.50
237 Andre Branch RC .50 1.25
238 Greg Zuerlein RC .75 2.00
239 Bobby Wagner RC .75 2.00
240A Brandon Bolden RC .50 1.25
240B Brandon Bolden SP 1.00 2.50
241 Brandon Taylor RC .50 1.25
242 Bruce Irvin RC .60 1.50
243 Bryce Brown RC .50 1.25
244 Brandon Hardin RC .60 1.50
245 Casey Hayward RC .50 1.25
246A Chandler Jones RC .50 1.25
246B Chandler Jones SP 1.00 2.50
247 Damaris Johnson RC .50 1.25
248 Chris Rainey RC .50 1.25
249A Courtney Upshaw RC .60 1.50
249B Courtney Upshaw SP 1.25 3.00
250A Josh Gordon RC 1.25 3.00
250B Josh Gordon SP 2.50 6.00
251 Mike Martin RC .60 1.50
252 Rhett Ellison RC .60 1.50
253 Demario Davis RC .50 1.25
254 Derek Wolfe RC .60 1.50
255 Rishard Matthews RC .50 1.25
256 Devon Wylie RC .50 1.25
257 Dont'a Hightower RC .75 2.00
258 Dontari Poe RC .50 1.25
259 Dre Kirkpatrick RC .50 1.25
260 Bill Bentley RC .60 1.50
261 Jeff Demps RC .60 1.50
262 Josh Cooper RC .60 1.50
263 Fletcher Cox RC .75 2.00
264 Rod Streater RC .75 2.00
265 Harrison Smith RC .50 1.25
266 Jamell Fleming RC .50 1.25
267 James Hanna RC .50 1.25
268 Janoris Jenkins RC .60 1.50
269 Jared Crick RC .50 1.25
270 T.Y. Hilton RC 1.00 2.50
271 Jerel Worthy RC .50 1.25
272 Josh Robinson RC .75 2.00
273 Kellen Moore RC .60 1.50
274 Kendall Reyes RC .50 1.25
275 Keshawn Martin RC .60 1.50
276 Kevin Zeitler RC .50 1.25
277 Kirk Cousins RC 2.00 5.00
278A Lavonte David RC .75 2.00
278B Lavonte David SP 1.50 4.00
279A Luke Kuechly RC 1.25 3.00
279B Luke Kuechly SP 2.50 6.00
280A Mark Barron RC .50 1.25
280B Mark Barron SP 1.00 2.50
281 Tommy Streeter RC .50 1.25
282 Matt Kalil RC .50 1.25
283A Melvin Ingram RC .50 1.25
283B Melvin Ingram SP 1.00 2.50
284A Michael Brockers RC .50 1.25
284B Michael Brockers SP 1.00 2.50
285A Morris Claiborne RC .50 1.25
285B Morris Claiborne SP 1.00 2.50
286 Travis Benjamin RC .50 1.25
287 Nick Perry RC .60 1.50
288 Olivier Vernon RC .75 2.00
289 Quinton Coples RC .50 1.25
290 Riley Reiff RC .50 1.25
291 Trumaine Johnson RC .50 1.25
292 Shea McClellin RC .60 1.50
293 Stephon Gilmore RC .60 1.50
294 Terrance Ganaway RC .60 1.50
295A Zach Brown RC .50 1.25
295B Zach Brown SP 1.00 2.50
296 Tyrone Crawford RC .50 1.25
297 Vick Ballard RC .60 1.50
298 Vinny Curry RC .60 1.50
299A Vontaze Burfict RC .60 1.50
299B Vontaze Burfict SP 1.25 3.00
300 Whitney Mercilus RC .50 1.25

2012 Panini Prizm Prizms

*1-200 VETS: 2.5X TO 6X BASIC CARDS
*201-300 ROOKIES: 1.2X TO 3X BASIC RC
*ROOKIES SP: 1X TO 2.5X BASIC SP
STATED ODDS 3:20

2012 Panini Prizm Prizms Green

*1-200 VETS: 5X TO 12X BASIC CARDS
*201-300 ROOKIES: 2.5X TO 6X BASIC RC
RANDOM INSERTS IN RETAIL PACKS
203 Andrew Luck 90.00 150.00
230 Russell Wilson 60.00 120.00

2012 Panini Prizm Prizms Red

*1-200 VETS: 8X TO 15X BASIC CARDS
*201-300 ROOKIES: 3X TO 8X BASIC RC
STATED ODDS 1:20
203 Andrew Luck 125.00 200.00
230 Russell Wilson 60.00 120.00

2012 Panini Prizm Autographs

EXCH EXPIRATION: 7/30/2014
1 Aaron Hernandez/25 10.00 25.00
4 Antoine Bethea/149 4.00 10.00
5 Antonio Brown/49 15.00 40.00
7 Heath Miller/25 12.00 30.00
9 BenJarvus Green-Ellis/20 12.00 30.00
11 Brandon LaFell/149 4.00 10.00
13 Brandon Pettigrew/49 6.00 15.00
14 Brent Celek/25 8.00 20.00
15 Brian Hartline/15 10.00 25.00
18 James Laurinaitis/25 8.00 20.00
20 Darrius Heyward-Bey/25 8.00 20.00
21 David Nelson/149 4.00 10.00
22 James Starks/149 4.00 10.00
23 DeMarcus Ware/49 15.00 40.00
24 Demaryius Thomas/25 12.00 30.00
25 Denarius Moore/149 4.00 10.00
28 Dwayne Bowe/15 10.00 25.00
29 Fred Davis/99 4.00 10.00
30 Jason Pierre-Paul/49 6.00 15.00
31 Greg Little/49 6.00 15.00
32 Greg Olsen/49 8.00 20.00
33 Jermaine Gresham/49 6.00 15.00
36 Jared Cook/149 4.00 10.00
38 Jermichael Finley/49 6.00 15.00
39 J.J. Watt/49 30.00 60.00
40 Jon Beason/149 4.00 10.00
42 Jonathan Baldwin/49 8.00 20.00
43 Jerod Mayo/49 6.00 15.00
44 Kevin Walter/49 6.00 15.00
46 London Fletcher/49 15.00 40.00
48 Josh Cribbs/49 6.00 15.00
49 Mario Williams/25 8.00 20.00
52 Owen Daniels/49 6.00 15.00
53 Patrick Willis/25 15.00 40.00
55 Pierre Thomas/49 6.00 15.00
56 Kyle Rudolph/149 4.00 10.00
59 Sean Lee/99 8.00 20.00
60 LeGarrette Blount/25 10.00 25.00
63 Torrey Smith/49 6.00 15.00
66 Von Miller/49 10.00 25.00
68 Brian Cushing/49 6.00 15.00
69 Brian Orakpo/25 10.00 25.00
70 Nnamdi Asomugha/49 8.00 20.00
74 Dexter McCluster/149 4.00 10.00
75 Paul Posluszny/49 6.00 15.00
77 Roy Helu/149 4.00 10.00
201 A.J. Jenkins/299 2.50 6.00
202 Alshon Jeffery/250 12.00 30.00
203 Andrew Luck/250 75.00 150.00
204 Bernard Pierce/250 8.00 20.00
205 Brandon Weeden/250 2.50 6.00
206 Brian Quick/299 2.50 6.00
207 Brock Osweiler/250 5.00 12.00
208 Chris Givens/250 2.50 6.00
209 Coby Fleener/250 2.50 6.00
210 David Wilson/250 2.50 6.00
211 DeVier Posey/250 2.50 6.00
212 Doug Martin/250 4.00 10.00
213 Dwayne Allen/250 2.50 6.00
214 Isaiah Pead/250 2.50 6.00
215 Jarius Wright/299 2.50 6.00
216 Joe Adams/250 2.50 6.00
217 Justin Blackmon/499 2.00 5.00
218 Kendall Wright/250 2.50 6.00
219 Lamar Miller/399 3.00 8.00
220 LaMichael James/399 2.00 5.00
221 Michael Egnew/499 2.00 5.00
222 Michael Floyd/250 2.50 6.00
223 Mohamed Sanu/399 3.00 8.00
224 Nick Foles/250 20.00 40.00
225 Nick Toon/250 2.50 6.00
226 Rueben Randle/250 5.00 12.00
227 Robert Griffin III/250 3.00 8.00
228 Robert Turbin/250 2.50 6.00
229 Ronnie Hillman/99 3.00 8.00
230 Russell Wilson/250 75.00 150.00
231 Ryan Broyles/499 2.00 5.00
232 Ryan Tannehill/250 4.00 10.00
233 Stephen Hill/250 2.50 6.00
234 T.J. Graham/250 2.50 6.00
235 Trent Richardson/250 2.50 6.00
236 Alfred Morris/399 2.00 5.00
237 Andre Branch/499 2.00 5.00
238 Greg Zuerlein/399 3.00 8.00
239 Bobby Wagner/99 5.00 12.00
240 Brandon Bolden/399 2.00 5.00
241 Brandon Taylor/499 2.00 5.00
242 Bruce Irvin/499 2.50 6.00
243 Bryce Brown/399 2.00 5.00
244 Brandon Hardin/499 2.50 6.00
245 Casey Hayward/499 2.00 5.00
246 Chandler Jones/499 2.00 5.00
247 Damaris Johnson/399 2.00 5.00
248 Chris Rainey/399 2.00 5.00
249 Courtney Upshaw/399 2.50 6.00
250 Josh Gordon/499 5.00 12.00
251 Mike Martin/499 2.50 6.00
252 Rhett Ellison/499 2.50 6.00
253 Demario Davis/499 2.00 5.00
254 Derek Wolfe/399 2.50 6.00
255 Rishard Matthews/499 2.00 5.00
256 Devon Wylie/299 2.50 6.00
257 Dont'a Hightower/299 4.00 10.00
258 Dontari Poe/299 2.50 6.00
259 Dre Kirkpatrick/299 2.50 6.00
260 Bill Bentley/499 2.50 6.00
261 Jeff Demps/199 3.00 8.00
262 Josh Cooper/299 3.00 8.00
263 Fletcher Cox/299 4.00 10.00
264 Rod Streater/399 3.00 8.00
265 Harrison Smith/199 5.00 12.00
266 Jamell Fleming/499 2.00 5.00
267 James Hanna/299 2.50 6.00
268 Janoris Jenkins/399 2.50 6.00
269 Jared Crick/499 2.00 5.00
270 T.Y. Hilton/399 6.00 15.00
271 Jerel Worthy/299 2.50 6.00
272 Josh Robinson/499 3.00 8.00
273 Kellen Moore/499 2.50 6.00
274 Kendall Reyes/499 2.00 5.00
275 Keshawn Martin/399 2.50 6.00
276 Kevin Zeitler/499 2.00 5.00
277 Kirk Cousins/499 10.00 25.00
278 Lavonte David/399 3.00 8.00
279 Luke Kuechly/299 10.00 25.00
280 Mark Barron/399 2.00 5.00
281 Tommy Streeter/299 2.50 6.00
282 Matt Kalil/499 2.00 5.00
283 Melvin Ingram/399 2.00 5.00
284 Michael Brockers/299 2.50 6.00
285 Morris Claiborne/149 3.00 8.00
286 Travis Benjamin/499 2.00 5.00
287 Nick Perry/499 2.50 6.00
288 Olivier Vernon/499 3.00 8.00
289 Quinton Coples/399 2.00 5.00
290 Riley Reiff/299 2.50 6.00
291 Trumaine Johnson/499 2.00 5.00
292 Shea McClellin/299 3.00 8.00
293 Stephon Gilmore/499 2.50 6.00
294 Terrance Ganaway/499 2.50 6.00
295 Zach Brown/299 2.50 6.00
296 Tyrone Crawford/499 2.00 5.00
297 Vick Ballard/499 5.00 12.00
298 Vinny Curry/499 2.50 6.00
299 Vontaze Burfict/499 2.50 6.00
300 Whitney Mercilus/440 2.00 5.00

2012 Panini Prizm Autographs Prizms

*VETS/25: .8X TO 2X BASIC AU/99-149
*VETS/25: .5X TO 1.2X BASIC AU/49
*ROOKIES/99: .6X TO 1.5X BASIC AU/399-499
*ROOKIES/75-99: .5X TO 1.2X BASIC AU/199-299
*ROOKIES/99: .4X TO 1X BASIC AU/99-149
*ROOKIES/49: .6X TO 1.5X BASIC AU/299
*ROOKIES/49: .5X TO 1.2X BASIC AU/99
*ROOKIES/25: .8X TO 2X BASIC AU/199
*ROOKIES/25: .6X TO 1.5X BASIC AU/99
203 Andrew Luck/99 150.00 300.00
230 Russell Wilson/99 150.00 250.00

2012 Panini Prizm Brilliance

STATED ODDS 1:20
*PRIZM: .6X TO 1.5X BASIC INSERTS
1 Ray Rice 1.00 2.50
2 A.J. Green 1.50 4.00
3 Mike Wallace 1.00 2.50
4 Arian Foster 1.25 3.00
5 Tom Brady 4.00 10.00
6 Peyton Manning 3.00 8.00
7 Darren McFadden 1.00 2.50
8 Brandon Marshall 1.25 3.00
9 Calvin Johnson 1.50 4.00
10 Aaron Rodgers 2.50 6.00
11 Adrian Peterson 1.50 4.00
12 Julio Jones 1.50 4.00
13 Cam Newton 1.50 4.00
14 Drew Brees 1.50 4.00
15 Dez Bryant 1.50 4.00
16 Hakeem Nicks 1.00 2.50
17 Michael Vick 1.25 3.00
18 Larry Fitzgerald 1.25 3.00
19 Randy Moss 1.25 3.00
20 Steven Jackson 1.00 2.50
21 Dwayne Bowe 1.25 3.00
22 Maurice Jones-Drew 1.00 2.50
23 Reggie Wayne 1.25 3.00
24 Philip Rivers 1.50 4.00
25 Chris Johnson 1.00 2.50

2012 Panini Prizm Decade Dominance

STATED ODDS 1:20
*PRIZM: .6X TO 1.5X BASIC INSERTS
1 Jerry Rice 2.50 6.00
2 Jim Brown 2.00 5.00
3 Lawrence Taylor 1.25 3.00
4 Joe Montana 4.00 10.00
5 Walter Payton 3.00 8.00
6 Johnny Unitas 2.50 6.00
7 Reggie White 1.50 4.00
8 Dick Butkus 2.00 5.00
9 Barry Sanders 2.50 6.00
10 Dan Marino 3.00 8.00
11 John Elway 2.50 6.00
12 Emmitt Smith 2.50 6.00
13 Deion Sanders 1.25 3.00
14 Bruce Smith 1.25 3.00
15 Joe Greene 1.50 4.00
16 Earl Campbell 1.50 4.00
17 Deacon Jones 1.25 3.00
18 Mike Singletary 1.50 4.00
19 Jack Lambert 1.50 4.00
20 Terry Bradshaw 2.00 5.00
21 Marshall Faulk 1.25 3.00
22 Marcus Allen 1.50 4.00
23 Ozzie Newsome 1.25 3.00
24 Brett Favre 3.00 8.00
25 Alan Page 1.00 2.50

2012 Panini Prizm Rookie Impact

STATED ODDS 1:20
*PRIZM: 1X TO 2.5X BASIC INSERTS
1 Andrew Luck 6.00 15.00
2 Doug Martin .75 2.00
3 Kendall Wright .50 1.25
4 Rueben Randle .50 1.25
5 Robert Griffin III .60 1.50
6 Robert Turbin .50 1.25
7 Ronnie Hillman .50 1.25
8 Russell Wilson 4.00 10.00
9 Ryan Tannehill .75 2.00
10 Trent Richardson .50 1.25
11 Stephen Hill .50 1.25
12 Alfred Morris .50 1.25
13 Bruce Irvin .60 1.50
14 Chandler Jones .50 1.25
15 Fletcher Cox .75 2.00
16 Janoris Jenkins .60 1.50
17 Lavonte David .75 2.00
18 Mark Barron .50 1.25
19 Matt Kalil .50 1.25
20 Morris Claiborne .50 1.25
21 Nick Perry .60 1.50
22 Quinton Coples .50 1.25
23 Shea McClellin .60 1.50
24 Vontaze Burfict .60 1.50
25 Whitney Mercilus .50 1.25

2013 Panini Prizm

COMP.SET w/o RC's (200) 15.00 40.00
ONE ROOKIE PER PACK
1 Joe Flacco .25 .60
2 Torrey Smith .20 .50
3 Jacoby Jones .20 .50
4 Ray Rice .20 .50
5 Bernard Pierce .20 .50
6 Terrell Suggs .20 .50
7 Andy Dalton .25 .60
8 A.J. Green .30 .75
9 Mohamed Sanu .20 .50
10 Andrew Hawkins .20 .50
11 BenJarvus Green-Ellis .25 .60
12 Jermaine Gresham .25 .60
13 Brandon Weeden .20 .50
14 Josh Gordon .20 .50
15 Greg Little .20 .50
16 Davone Bess .20 .50
17 Trent Richardson .20 .50
18 D'Qwell Jackson .20 .50
19 Ben Roethlisberger .30 .75
20 Antonio Brown .30 .75
21 Emmanuel Sanders .25 .60
22 Plaxico Burress .20 .50
23 Isaac Redman .30 .75
24 Heath Miller .20 .50
25 Troy Polamalu .30 .75
26 Matt Schaub .20 .50
27 Andre Johnson .20 .50
28 Lestar Jean .20 .50
29 Arian Foster .25 .60
30 Ben Tate .20 .50
31 Owen Daniels .20 .50
32 J.J. Watt .25 .60
33 Andrew Luck .50 1.25
34 Reggie Wayne .25 .60
35 T.Y. Hilton .25 .60
36 Vick Ballard .20 .50
37 Donald Brown .20 .50
38 Coby Fleener .20 .50
39 Chad Henne .20 .50
40 Justin Blackmon .20 .50
41 Cecil Shorts III .20 .50
42 Maurice Jones-Drew .20 .50
43 Marcedes Lewis .20 .50
44 Russell Allen .20 .50
45 Jake Locker .25 .60
46 Kenny Britt .20 .50
47 Kendall Wright .20 .50
48 Chris Johnson .20 .50
49 Shonn Greene .20 .50
50 Delanie Walker .20 .50
51 Kevin Kolb .20 .50
52 Steve Johnson .25 .60
53 T.J. Graham .20 .50
54 C.J. Spiller .20 .50
55 Fred Jackson .25 .60
56 Scott Chandler .20 .50
57 Ryan Tannehill .25 .60
58 Mike Wallace .20 .50
59 Brian Hartline .20 .50
60 Lamar Miller .20 .50
61 Daniel Thomas .20 .50
62 Dustin Keller .20 .50
63 Cameron Wake .20 .50
64 Tom Brady .75 2.00
65 Danny Amendola .25 .60
66 Stevan Ridley .20 .50
67 Shane Vereen .25 .60
68 Rob Gronkowski .30 .75
69 Tim Tebow .25 .60
70 Mark Sanchez .20 .50
71 Santonio Holmes .20 .50
72 Jeremy Kerley .20 .50
73 Stephen Hill .20 .50
74 Antonio Cromartie .20 .50
75 Bilal Powell .20 .50
76 Chris Ivory .25 .60
77 Peyton Manning .60 1.50
78 Demaryius Thomas .25 .60
79 Wes Welker .25 .60
80 Eric Decker .20 .50
81 Trindon Holliday .25 .60
82 Von Miller .25 .60
83 Ronnie Hillman .20 .50
84 Alex Smith .25 .60
85 Dwayne Bowe .25 .60
86 Donnie Avery .20 .50
87 Jonathan Baldwin .20 .50
88 Jamaal Charles .25 .60
89 Anthony Fasano .20 .50
90 Matt Flynn .20 .50
91 Denarius Moore .20 .50
92 Rod Streater .20 .50
93 Jacoby Ford .20 .50
94 Darren McFadden .25 .60
95 Rashad Jennings .20 .50
96 Philip Rivers .30 .75
97 Danario Alexander .20 .50
98 Malcom Floyd .20 .50
99 Vincent Brown .20 .50
100 Ryan Mathews .25 .60
101 Antonio Gates .25 .60
102 Jay Cutler .20 .50
103 Brandon Marshall .25 .60
104 Alshon Jeffery .25 .60
105 Matt Forte .20 .50
106 Devin Hester .25 .60
107 Martellus Bennett .20 .50
108 Matthew Stafford .25 .60
109 Calvin Johnson .30 .75
110 Ryan Broyles .25 .60
111 Reggie Bush .20 .50
112 Mikel Leshoure .20 .50
113 Brandon Pettigrew .20 .50
114 Ndamukong Suh .25 .60
115 Aaron Rodgers .50 1.25
116 Jordy Nelson .25 .60
117 James Jones .20 .50
118 Randall Cobb .25 .60
119 Jermichael Finley .20 .50
120 Clay Matthews .30 .75
121 Christian Ponder .20 .50
122 Greg Jennings .20 .50
123 Jarius Wright .20 .50
124 Adrian Peterson .30 .75
125 Kyle Rudolph .20 .50
126 Jared Allen .20 .50
127 Matt Ryan .25 .60
128 Julio Jones .30 .75
129 Roddy White .20 .50
130 Steven Jackson .20 .50
131 Jacquizz Rodgers .25 .60
132 Tony Gonzalez .25 .60
133 Cam Newton .30 .75
134 Steve Smith .25 .60
135 Brandon LaFell .20 .50
136 Jonathan Stewart .20 .50
137 DeAngelo Williams .20 .50
138 Greg Olsen .25 .60
139 Luke Kuechly .25 .60
140 Drew Brees .30 .75
141 Marques Colston .20 .50
142 Lance Moore .20 .50
143 Mark Ingram .25 .60
144 Darren Sproles .25 .60
145 Jimmy Graham .30 .75
146 Josh Freeman .25 .60
147 Vincent Jackson .20 .50
148 Mike Williams .25 .60
149 Kevin Ogletree .20 .50
150 Doug Martin .25 .60
151 Lavonte David .20 .50
152 Tony Romo .25 .60
153 Dez Bryant .30 .75
154 Miles Austin .20 .50
155 DeMarco Murray .25 .60
156 Jason Witten .25 .60
157 DeMarcus Ware .30 .75
158 Morris Claiborne .20 .50
159 Eli Manning .25 .60
160 Hakeem Nicks .20 .50
161 Victor Cruz .25 .60
162 David Wilson .20 .50
163 Andre Brown .25 .60
164 Jason Pierre-Paul .20 .50
165 Michael Vick .25 .60
166 DeSean Jackson .25 .60
167 Jeremy Maclin .20 .50
168 LeSean McCoy .30 .75
169 Bryce Brown .25 .60
170 Brent Celek .20 .50
171 Robert Griffin III .20 .50
172 Pierre Garcon .25 .60
173 Santana Moss .25 .60
174 Josh Morgan .20 .50
175 Alfred Morris .20 .50
176 Fred Davis .20 .50
177 Carson Palmer .25 .60
178 Larry Fitzgerald .25 .60
179 Michael Floyd .20 .50
180 Rashard Mendenhall .20 .50
181 Robert Housler .20 .50
182 Patrick Peterson .20 .50
183 Colin Kaepernick .25 .60
184 Michael Crabtree .20 .50
185 Anquan Boldin .20 .50
186 Frank Gore .25 .60
187 LaMichael James .20 .50
188 Vernon Davis .20 .50
189 Russell Wilson .60 1.50
190 Percy Harvin .20 .50
191 Sidney Rice .20 .50
192 Golden Tate .20 .50
193 Marshawn Lynch .25 .60
194 Richard Sherman .30 .75
195 Sam Bradford .20 .50
196 Brian Quick .20 .50
197 Chris Givens .20 .50
198 Daryl Richardson .20 .50
199 Isaiah Pead .20 .50
200 Jared Cook .20 .50
201 Aaron Dobson RC .40 1.00
202 Aaron Mellette RC .40 1.00
203 Ace Sanders RC .40 1.00
204 Alec Ogletree RC .40 1.00
205 Alex Okafor RC .40 1.00
206 Andre Ellington RC .40 1.00
207 Arthur Brown RC .40 1.00
208 Barkevious Mingo RC .40 1.00
209 Bjoern Werner RC .40 1.00
210 Chance Warmack RC .40 1.00
211 Chris Gragg RC .40 1.00
212 Chris Harper RC .40 1.00
213 Christine Michael RC .40 1.00
214 Cobi Hamilton RC .40 1.00
215 Conner Vernon RC .40 1.00
216 Cordarrelle Patterson RC .40 1.00
217 Corey Fuller RC .40 1.00
218 Cornellius Carradine RC .40 1.00
219 D.J. Hayden RC .40 1.00
220 Damontre Moore RC .40 1.00
221 Da'Rick Rogers RC .40 1.00
222 Darius Slay RC .40 1.00
223 Datone Jones RC .40 1.00
224 David Amerson RC .50 1.25
225 DeAndre Hopkins RC 1.00 2.50
226 Dee Milliner RC .40 1.00
227 Denard Robinson RC .40 1.00
228 Dennis Johnson RC .40 1.00
229 Desmond Trufant RC .40 1.00
230 Dion Jordan RC .40 1.00
231 Dion Sims RC .40 1.00
232 Eddie Lacy RC .40 1.00
233 EJ Manuel RC .40 1.00
234 Eric Fisher RC .40 1.00
235 Eric Reid RC .50 1.25
236 Ezekiel Ansah RC .40 1.00
237 Gavin Escobar RC .40 1.00
238 Geno Smith RC .40 1.00
239 Giovani Bernard RC .40 1.00
240 Jamar Taylor RC .40 1.00
241 Jarvis Jones RC .40 1.00
242 Jasper Collins RC .40 1.00
243 Jawan Jamison RC .40 1.00
244 Johnathan Cyprien RC .40 1.00
245 Johnathan Franklin RC .40 1.00
246 Johnthan Banks RC .40 1.00
247 Jordan Poyer RC .50 1.25
248 Jordan Reed RC .60 1.50
249 Joseph Randle RC .40 1.00
250 Josh Boyce RC .40 1.00
251 Justin Hunter RC .40 1.00
252 Keenan Allen RC .75 2.00
253 Kenjon Barner RC .40 1.00
254 Kenny Stills RC .40 1.00
255 Kenny Vaccaro RC .40 1.00
256 Kevin Minter RC .40 1.00
257 Knile Davis RC .40 1.00
258 Landry Jones RC .40 1.00
259 Le'Veon Bell RC 1.25 3.00
260 Luke Joeckel RC .40 1.00
261 Manti Te'o RC .50 1.25
262 Marcus Davis RC .40 1.00
263 Marcus Lattimore RC .40 1.00
264 Margus Hunt RC .40 1.00
265 Markus Wheaton RC .40 1.00
266 Marquess Wilson RC .60 1.50
267 Marquise Goodwin RC .40 1.00
268 Matt Barkley RC .40 1.00
269 Matt Elam RC .40 1.00
270 Matt Scott RC .40 1.00
271 Mike Gillislee RC .40 1.00
272 Mike Glennon RC .40 1.00
273 Montee Ball RC .50 1.25
274 Nick Kasa RC .40 1.00
275 Onterio McCalebb RC .50 1.25
276 Phillip Thomas RC .40 1.00
277 Quinton Patton RC .40 1.00
278 Rex Burkhead RC .50 1.25
279 Robert Woods RC .60 1.50
280 Rodney Smith RC .40 1.00
281 Ryan Nassib RC .40 1.00
282 Ryan Otten RC .40 1.00
283 Ryan Swope RC .40 1.00
284 Sam Montgomery RC .40 1.00
285 D.J. Fluker RC .40 1.00
286 Stedman Bailey RC .40 1.00
287 Stepfan Taylor RC .40 1.00
288 Tavarres King RC .40 1.00
289 Tavon Austin RC .50 1.25
290 Terrance Williams RC .40 1.00
291 Theo Riddick RC .40 1.00
292 Travis Kelce RC 1.00 2.50
293 Tyler Bray RC .40 1.00
294 Tyler Eifert RC .40 1.00
295 Tyler Wilson RC .40 1.00
296 Tyrann Mathieu RC .60 1.50
297 Vance McDonald RC .50 1.25
298 Xavier Rhodes RC .40 1.00
299 Zac Dysert RC .40 1.00
300 Zach Ertz RC .75 2.00

2013 Panini Prizm Prizms

*1-200 VETS: 2X TO 5X BASIC CARDS
*201-300 ROOKIES: 1X TO 2.5X BASIC RC

2013 Panini Prizm Prizms Blue

*1-200 VETS: 2.5X TO 6X BASIC CARDS
*201-300 ROOKIES: 1.2X TO 3X BASIC RC
FOUR PER WAL-MART BLASTER

2013 Panini Prizm Prizms Blue Pulsar

*1-200 VETS: 2X TO 5X BASIC CARDS
*201-300 ROOKIES: 1X TO 2.5X BASIC RC
THREE PER WAL-MART MULTI-PACK

2013 Panini Prizm Prizms Camo

*1-200 VETS: 2X TO 5X BASIC CARDS
*201-300 ROOKIES: 1X TO 2.5X BASIC RC
THREE PER TARGET RETAIL BLASTER

2013 Panini Prizm Prizms Green

*1-200 VETS: 4X TO 10X BASIC CARDS
*201-300 ROOKIES: 2X TO 5X BASIC RC
ONE PER TARGET RETAIL BOX

2013 Panini Prizm Prizms Light Blue Pulsar

*1-200 VETS: 2X TO 5X BASIC CARDS
*201-300 ROOKIES: 1X TO 2.5X BASIC RC
ONE PER JUMBO PACK

2013 Panini Prizm Prizms Light Blue Die Cut

*1-200 VETS/15: 8X TO 20X BASIC CARDS
*201-300 ROOKIES/15: 4X TO 10X BASIC RC
RANDOM INSERTS IN JUMBO PACKS

2013 Panini Prizm Prizms Orange Die Cut

*1-200 VETS/50: 5X TO 12X BASIC CARDS
*201-300 ROOKIES/50: 2.5X TO 6X BASIC RC

2013 Panini Prizm Prizms Purple Pulsar

*1-200 VETS/40: 5X TO 12X BASIC CARDS
*201-300 ROOKIES/40: 2.5X TO 6X BASIC RC
RANDOM INSERTS IN JUMBO PACKS

2013 Panini Prizm Prizms Red Pulsar

*1-200 VETS: 2X TO 5X BASIC CARDS
*201-300 ROOKIES: 1X TO 2.5X BASIC RC

2013 Panini Prizm Autographs

*BASE VET AU: .25X TO .6X PRIZM/15-25
*BASE ROOK.AU: .25X TO .6X PRIZM/99
EXCH EXPIRATION: 4/23/2015
1 Adrian Peterson SP 50.00 100.00

2013 Panini Prizm Autographs Prizms

5 Andrew Hawkins/25 5.00 12.00
12 Brian Quick/25 5.00 12.00
13 Bryce Brown/25 6.00 15.00
16 Cecil Shorts III/25 8.00 20.00
20 Danario Alexander/25 5.00 12.00
23 David Wilson/25 5.00 12.00
33 Frank Gore/25 8.00 20.00
43 Jeremy Kerley/25 5.00 12.00
45 Jerod Mayo/25 6.00 15.00
47 Joe Adams/25 5.00 12.00
53 Kenny Britt/25 5.00 12.00
54 Kyle Rudolph/25 5.00 12.00
55 Lamar Miller/25 5.00 12.00
58 Luke Kuechly/25 12.00 30.00
61 Mark Ingram/25 6.00 15.00
66 Maurice Jones-Drew/25 5.00 12.00
67 Michael Vick/25 10.00 25.00
70 Nick Foles/25 15.00 40.00
75 Rashard Mendenhall/25 5.00 12.00
79 Robert Griffin III/25 5.00 12.00
80 Robert Turbin/25 5.00 12.00
82 Rueben Randle/25 5.00 12.00
85 Ryan Tannehill/25 12.00 30.00
87 Sean Lee/25 10.00 25.00
95 T.Y. Hilton/25 6.00 15.00
101 A.J. Jenkins/25 5.00 12.00
102 Adrian Clayborn/25 5.00 12.00
103 Adrien Robinson/25 5.00 12.00
104 Alex Green/25 5.00 12.00
105 Ryan Williams/25 5.00 12.00
106 Anthony Spencer/25 5.00 12.00
107 Antoine Bethea/25 5.00 12.00
108 B.J. Coleman/25 5.00 12.00
110 Blair Walsh/25 8.00 20.00
111 Brandon Spikes/25 6.00 15.00
112 Cameron Heyward/25 5.00 12.00
113 Casey Hayward/25 6.00 15.00
114 Charles Clay/25 5.00 12.00
115 Chris Cook/20 5.00 12.00
116 Jorvorskie Lane/25 5.00 12.00
117 Coby Fleener/25 5.00 12.00
118 Courtney Upshaw/25 5.00 12.00
119 D.J. Williams/25 5.00 12.00
120 Da'Quan Bowers/25 5.00 12.00
121 Daryl Richardson/25 5.00 12.00
122 Delone Carter/25 5.00 12.00
123 Ryan Torain/25 5.00 12.00
125 Dion Lewis/25 5.00 12.00
126 Dontari Poe/25 5.00 12.00
127 Dustin Keller/25 5.00 12.00
128 Dwayne Allen/25 5.00 12.00
129 Dwayne Harris/25 6.00 15.00
130 Taiwan Jones/25 5.00 12.00
131 Eric Page/25 5.00 12.00
132 Kealoha Pilares/25 5.00 12.00
133 Fletcher Cox/25 5.00 12.00
134 Gerell Robinson/25 5.00 12.00
135 Golden Tate/25 5.00 12.00
136 Zach Brown/25 5.00 12.00
137 Greg McElroy/25 6.00 15.00
139 Isaiah Pead/25 5.00 12.00
140 Jacquizz Rodgers/25 6.00 15.00
141 Jake Ballard/25 5.00 12.00
142 James Hanna/25 5.00 12.00
143 Janoris Jenkins/25 5.00 12.00
144 Jarius Wright/25 5.00 12.00
146 Josh Cooper/25 5.00 12.00
147 Justin Tucker/25 12.00 30.00
148 Keshawn Martin/25 5.00 12.00
149 Kris Adams/25 5.00 12.00
150 Lance Dunbar/25 5.00 12.00
151 Lance Kendricks/25 5.00 12.00
154 Leonard Hankerson/25 5.00 12.00
155 Tyron Smith/25 5.00 12.00
156 Tyrod Taylor/25 6.00 15.00
157 Tommy Streeter/25 5.00 12.00
158 Mark Barron/25 6.00 15.00
159 Matt Cassel/20 12.00 30.00
160 Melvin Ingram/25 5.00 12.00
164 Mohamed Sanu/25 5.00 12.00
165 Tarvaris Jackson/25 5.00 12.00
166 T.J. Graham/15 5.00 12.00
168 Nick Toon/25 5.00 12.00
170 Pat Angerer/25 20.00 50.00
172 Paul Posluszny/25 5.00 12.00
173 Prince Amukamara/25 5.00 12.00
174 Rahim Moore/25 5.00 12.00
175 Robert Housler/25 5.00 12.00
177 Ronnell Lewis/25 5.00 12.00
178 Shea McClellin/25 6.00 15.00
201 Aaron Dobson/99 3.00 8.00
202 Aaron Mellette/99 3.00 8.00
203 Ace Sanders/99 EXCH 3.00 8.00
204 Alec Ogletree/99 EXCH 3.00 8.00
205 Alex Okafor/99 3.00 8.00
206 Andre Ellington/99 10.00 25.00
207 Arthur Brown/99 3.00 8.00
208 Barkevious Mingo/99 3.00 8.00
209 Bjoern Werner/99 3.00 8.00
210 Chance Warmack/99 3.00 8.00
211 Chris Gragg/99 3.00 8.00
212 Chris Harper/99 3.00 8.00
213 Christine Michael/99 3.00 8.00
214 Cobi Hamilton/99 EXCH 3.00 8.00
215 Conner Vernon/99 3.00 8.00
216 Cordarrelle Patterson/99 3.00 8.00
217 Corey Fuller/99 3.00 8.00
218 Cornellius Carradine/99 5.00 12.00
219 D.J. Hayden/99 3.00 8.00
220 Damontre Moore/99 EXCH 3.00 8.00
221 Da'Rick Rogers/99 3.00 8.00
222 Darius Slay/99 3.00 8.00
223 Datone Jones/99 EXCH 3.00 8.00
224 David Amerson/99 EXCH 3.00 8.00
225 DeAndre Hopkins/99 8.00 20.00
226 Dee Milliner/99 EXCH 3.00 8.00
227 Denard Robinson/99 EXCH 3.00 8.00
228 Dennis Johnson/99 3.00 8.00
229 Desmond Trufant/99 3.00 8.00
230 Dion Jordan/99 3.00 8.00
231 Dion Sims/99 EXCH 3.00 8.00
232 Eddie Lacy/99 3.00 8.00
234 Eric Fisher/99 EXCH 3.00 8.00
235 Eric Reid/99 EXCH 5.00 12.00
236 Ezekiel Ansah/99 3.00 8.00
237 Gavin Escobar/99 3.00 8.00
238 Geno Smith/99 8.00 20.00
239 Giovani Bernard/99 3.00 8.00
240 Jamar Taylor/99 3.00 8.00
241 Jarvis Jones/99 EXCH 3.00 8.00

242 Jasper Collins/99 3.00 8.00
243 Jawan Jamison/99 3.00 8.00
244 Johnathan Cyprien/99 3.00 8.00
245 Johnathan Franklin/99 3.00 8.00
246 Johnthan Banks/99 3.00 8.00
247 Jordan Poyer/99 EXCH 3.00 8.00
248 Jordan Reed/99 8.00 20.00
249 Joseph Randle/99 3.00 8.00
250 Josh Boyce/99 3.00 8.00
251 Justin Hunter/99 EXCH 3.00 8.00
252 Keenan Allen/99 6.00 15.00
253 Kenjon Barner/99 3.00 8.00
254 Kenny Stills/99 3.00 8.00
255 Kenny Vaccaro/99 EXCH 3.00 8.00
256 Kevin Minter/99 EXCH 3.00 8.00
257 Knile Davis/99 3.00 8.00
258 Landry Jones/99 3.00 8.00
259 Le'Veon Bell/99 12.00 30.00
260 Luke Joeckel/99 EXCH 3.00 8.00
261 Manti Te'o/99 4.00 10.00
262 Marcus Davis/99 3.00 8.00
263 Marcus Lattimore/99 10.00 25.00
264 Margus Hunt/99 3.00 8.00
265 Markus Wheaton/99 3.00 8.00
266 Marquess Wilson/99 5.00 12.00
267 Marquise Goodwin/99 3.00 8.00
268 Matt Barkley/99 3.00 8.00
269 Matt Elam/99 3.00 8.00
270 Matt Scott/99 EXCH 3.00 8.00
271 Mike Gillislee/99 EXCH 3.00 8.00
272 Mike Glennon/99 3.00 8.00
273 Montee Ball/99 3.00 8.00
274 Nick Kasa/99 EXCH 3.00 8.00
275 Onterio McCalebb/99 EXCH 4.00 10.00
276 Phillip Thomas/99 EXCH 3.00 8.00
277 Quinton Patton/99 3.00 8.00
278 Rex Burkhead/99 4.00 10.00
279 Robert Woods/99 5.00 12.00
280 Rodney Smith/99 3.00 8.00
281 Ryan Nassib/99 3.00 8.00
282 Ryan Otten/99 3.00 8.00
283 Ryan Swope/99 3.00 8.00
284 Sam Montgomery/99 EXCH 3.00 8.00
285 D.J. Fluker/99 3.00 8.00
286 Stedman Bailey/99 EXCH 3.00 8.00
287 Stepfan Taylor/99 3.00 8.00
288 Tavarres King/99 3.00 8.00
289 Tavon Austin/99 4.00 10.00
290 Terrance Williams/99 3.00 8.00
291 Theo Riddick/99 3.00 8.00
292 Travis Kelce/99 EXCH 25.00 60.00
293 Tyler Bray/99 3.00 8.00
294 Tyler Eifert/99 3.00 8.00
295 Tyler Wilson/99 3.00 8.00
296 Tyrann Mathieu/99 5.00 12.00
297 Vance McDonald/99 4.00 10.00
298 Xavier Rhodes/99 3.00 8.00
299 Zac Dysert/99 3.00 8.00
300 Zach Ertz/99 6.00 15.00
301 Bildi Wreh-Wilson/99 4.00 10.00
302 Brad Sorensen/99 3.00 8.00
303 Chris Thompson/99 3.00 8.00
304 Kerwynn Williams/99 3.00 8.00
305 Mychal Rivera/99 3.00 8.00
306 Robert Alford/99 3.00 8.00

2013 Panini Prizm Brilliance

COMPLETE SET (25) 20.00 40.00
TWO PER HOBBY BOX
*PRIZM: .5X TO 1.2X BASIC INSERTS
*BLUE: .8X TO 2X BASIC INSERTS
*BLUE PULSAR: .6X TO 1.5X BASIC INSERTS
*GREEN: 1.2X TO 3X BASIC INSERTS
*RED PULSAR: .6X TO 1.5X BASIC INSERTS
1 Robert Griffin III .60 1.50
2 Andrew Luck 1.50 4.00
3 Colin Kaepernick .75 2.00
4 Marshawn Lynch .75 2.00
5 Trent Richardson .60 1.50
6 Alfred Morris .60 1.50
7 Rob Gronkowski 1.00 2.50
8 Jimmy Graham 1.00 2.50
9 Jason Witten .75 2.00
10 J.J. Watt .75 2.00
11 DeMarcus Ware 1.00 2.50
12 Richard Sherman 1.00 2.50
13 Patrick Peterson .60 1.50
14 Luke Kuechly .75 2.00
15 Darrelle Revis .60 1.50
16 Russell Wilson 2.00 5.00
17 Wes Welker .75 2.00
18 Andre Johnson .60 1.50
19 Troy Polamalu 1.00 2.50
20 Jamaal Charles .75 2.00
21 C.J. Spiller .60 1.50
22 Jordy Nelson .75 2.00
23 Matthew Stafford .75 2.00
24 LeSean McCoy 1.00 2.50
25 Eli Manning .75 2.00

2013 Panini Prizm Decade Dominance

COMPLETE SET (25) 25.00 50.00
TWO PER HOBBY BOX
*PRIZM: .5X TO 1.2X BASIC INSERTS
*BLUE: .8X TO 2X BASIC INSERTS
*BLUE PULSAR: .6X TO 1.5X BASIC INSERTS
*GREEN: 1.2X TO 3X BASIC INSERTS
*RED PULSAR: .6X TO 1.5X BASIC INSERTS
1 Sonny Jurgensen 1.00 2.50
2 Gale Sayers 1.25 3.00
3 Bob Lilly 1.00 2.50
4 Bart Starr 2.00 5.00
5 Roger Staubach 1.50 4.00
6 Franco Harris 1.25 3.00
7 Dave Casper .75 2.00
8 Jack Ham 1.00 2.50
9 Dan Fouts 1.00 2.50
10 Eric Dickerson 1.00 2.50
11 James Lofton 1.00 2.50
12 Art Monk 1.25 3.00
13 Kellen Winslow 1.00 2.50
14 Randy White 1.00 2.50
15 Troy Aikman 1.50 4.00
16 Steve Young 1.50 4.00
17 Eddie George 1.00 2.50
18 Jerome Bettis 1.25 3.00
19 Michael Irvin 1.25 3.00
20 Rod Woodson 1.00 2.50
21 Shannon Sharpe 1.00 2.50
22 Kurt Warner 1.00 2.50
23 LaDainian Tomlinson 1.00 2.50
24 Randy Moss 1.00 2.50
25 Warren Sapp 1.00 2.50

2013 Panini Prizm HRX Rookies

COMPLETE SET (25) 6.00 15.00
ONE PER PACK
1 Keenan Allen .30 .75
2 Tavon Austin .20 .50
3 Montee Ball .15 .40
4 Matt Barkley .15 .40
5 Giovani Bernard .15 .40
6 Marquise Goodwin .15 .40
7 Aaron Dobson .15 .40
8 DeAndre Hopkins .40 1.00
9 Justin Hunter .15 .40
10 Dion Jordan .15 .40
11 Marcus Lattimore .15 .40
12 Eddie Lacy .15 .40
13 EJ Manuel .15 .40
14 Markus Wheaton .15 .40
15 Cordarrelle Patterson .15 .40
16 Quinton Patton .15 .40
17 Denard Robinson .15 .40
18 Geno Smith .15 .40
19 Kenny Stills .15 .40
20 Terrance Williams .15 .40
21 Robert Woods .25 .60
22 Stedman Bailey .15 .40
23 Tyler Eifert .15 .40
24 Vance McDonald .20 .50
25 INFO card .20 .50

2013 Panini Prizm Monday Night Heroes

COMPLETE SET (25) 15.00 30.00
TWO PER HOBBY BOX
*PRIZM: .5X TO 1.2X BASIC INSERTS
*BLUE: .8X TO 2X BASIC INSERTS
*BLUE PULSAR: .6X TO 1.5X BASIC INSERTS
*GREEN: 1.2X TO 3X BASIC INSERTS
*RED PULSAR: .6X TO 1.5X BASIC INSERTS
1 Joe Flacco .75 2.00
2 Philip Rivers 1.00 2.50
3 Matt Ryan .75 2.00
4 Golden Tate .60 1.50
5 Brandon Marshall .75 2.00
6 Charles Tillman .75 2.00
7 Arian Foster .75 2.00
8 Peyton Manning 2.00 5.00
9 Chris Harris .60 1.50
10 Jay Cutler .60 1.50
11 Michael Crabtree .60 1.50
12 Aldon Smith .60 1.50
13 Drew Brees 1.00 2.50
14 Jimmy Graham 1.00 2.50
15 Brett Keisel .60 1.50
16 Colin Kaepernick .75 2.00
17 NaVorro Bowman .75 2.00
18 Cam Newton 1.00 2.50
19 Luke Kuechly .75 2.00
20 Pierre Garcon .75 2.00
21 Robert Griffin III .60 1.50
22 Tom Brady 2.50 6.00
23 Stevan Ridley .60 1.50
24 Chris Johnson .60 1.50
25 Michael Griffin .60 1.50

2013 Panini Prizm Rated Rookie Patches

ONE PER WAL-MART BLASTER
201 Aaron Dobson 1.50 4.00
202 Aaron Mellette 1.50 4.00
203 Ace Sanders 1.50 4.00
204 Alec Ogletree 1.50 4.00
205 Alex Okafor 1.50 4.00
206 Andre Ellington 1.50 4.00
207 Arthur Brown 1.50 4.00
208 Barkevious Mingo 1.50 4.00
209 Bjoern Werner 1.50 4.00
210 Chance Warmack 1.50 4.00
211 Chris Gragg 1.50 4.00
212 Chris Harper 1.50 4.00
213 Christine Michael 1.50 4.00
214 Cobi Hamilton 1.50 4.00
215 Conner Vernon 1.50 4.00
216 Cordarrelle Patterson 1.50 4.00
217 Corey Fuller 1.50 4.00
218 Cornellius Carradine 1.50 4.00
219 D.J. Hayden 1.50 4.00
220 Damontre Moore 1.50 4.00
221 Da'Rick Rogers 1.50 4.00
222 Darius Slay 1.50 4.00
223 Datone Jones 1.50 4.00
224 David Amerson 1.50 4.00
225 DeAndre Hopkins 4.00 10.00
226 Dee Milliner 1.50 4.00
227 Denard Robinson 1.50 4.00
228 Dennis Johnson 1.50 4.00
229 Desmond Trufant 1.50 4.00
230 Dion Jordan 1.50 4.00
231 Dion Sims 1.50 4.00
232 Eddie Lacy 1.50 4.00
233 EJ Manuel 6.00 15.00
234 Eric Fisher 1.50 4.00
235 Eric Reid 2.00 5.00
236 Ezekiel Ansah 1.50 4.00
237 Gavin Escobar 1.50 4.00
238 Geno Smith 1.50 4.00
239 Giovani Bernard 1.50 4.00
240 Jamar Taylor 1.50 4.00
241 Jarvis Jones 1.50 4.00
242 Jasper Collins 1.50 4.00
243 Jawan Jamison 1.50 4.00
244 Johnathan Cyprien 1.50 4.00
245 Johnathan Franklin 1.50 4.00
246 Johnthan Banks 1.50 4.00
247 Jordan Poyer 1.50 4.00
248 Jordan Reed 2.50 6.00
249 Joseph Randle 1.50 4.00
250 Josh Boyce 1.50 4.00
251 Justin Hunter 1.50 4.00
252 Keenan Allen 3.00 8.00
253 Kenjon Barner 1.50 4.00
254 Kenny Stills 1.50 4.00
255 Kenny Vaccaro 1.50 4.00
256 Kevin Minter 1.50 4.00
257 Knile Davis 1.50 4.00
258 Landry Jones 1.50 4.00
259 Le'Veon Bell 5.00 12.00
260 Luke Joeckel 1.50 4.00
261 Manti Te'o 2.00 5.00
262 Marcus Davis 1.50 4.00
263 Marcus Lattimore 2.00 5.00
264 Margus Hunt 1.50 4.00
265 Markus Wheaton 1.50 4.00
266 Marquess Wilson 2.50 6.00
267 Marquise Goodwin 1.50 4.00
268 Matt Barkley 1.50 4.00
269 Matt Elam 1.50 4.00
270 Matt Scott 1.50 4.00
271 Mike Gillislee 1.50 4.00
272 Mike Glennon 1.50 4.00
273 Montee Ball 1.50 4.00
274 Nick Kasa 1.50 4.00
275 Onterio McCalebb 2.00 5.00
276 Phillip Thomas 1.50 4.00
277 Quinton Patton 1.50 4.00
278 Rex Burkhead 2.00 5.00
279 Robert Woods 2.50 6.00
280 Rodney Smith 1.50 4.00
281 Ryan Nassib 1.50 4.00
282 Ryan Otten 1.50 4.00
283 Ryan Swope 1.50 4.00
284 Sam Montgomery 1.50 4.00
285 D.J. Fluker 1.50 4.00
286 Stedman Bailey 1.50 4.00
287 Stepfan Taylor 1.50 4.00
288 Tavarres King 1.50 4.00
289 Tavon Austin 2.00 5.00
290 Terrance Williams 1.50 4.00
291 Theo Riddick 1.50 4.00
292 Travis Kelce 4.00 10.00
293 Tyler Bray 1.50 4.00
294 Tyler Eifert 1.50 4.00
295 Tyler Wilson 1.50 4.00
296 Tyrann Mathieu 2.50 6.00
297 Vance McDonald 1.50 4.00
298 Xavier Rhodes 1.50 4.00
299 Zac Dysert 1.50 4.00
300 Zach Ertz 2.00 5.00

2013 Panini Prizm Rookie Impact

COMPLETE SET (25) 12.00 30.00
TWO PER HOBBY BOX
*PRIZM: .5X TO 1.2X BASIC INSERTS
*BLUE: .8X TO 2X BASIC INSERTS
*BLUE PULSAR: .6X TO 1.5X BASIC INSERTS
*GREEN: 1.2X TO 3X BASIC INSERTS
*RED PULSAR: .6X TO 1.5X BASIC INSERTS
1 EJ Manuel .40 1.00
2 Tyler Wilson .40 1.00
3 Geno Smith .40 1.00
4 Eddie Lacy .40 1.00
5 Le'Veon Bell 1.25 3.00
6 Giovani Bernard .40 1.00
7 Joseph Randle .40 1.00
8 Johnathan Franklin .40 1.00
9 Knile Davis .40 1.00
10 Montee Ball .40 1.00
11 Mike Gillislee .40 1.00
12 Tavon Austin .40 1.00
13 DeAndre Hopkins 1.00 2.50
14 Robert Woods .60 1.50
15 Markus Wheaton .40 1.00
16 Quinton Patton .40 1.00
17 Cordarrelle Patterson .40 1.00
18 Tyler Eifert .40 1.00
19 Zach Ertz .75 2.00
20 Vance McDonald .40 1.00
21 Tyrann Mathieu .60 1.50
22 Manti Te'o .50 1.25
23 Ezekiel Ansah .40 1.00
24 Dee Milliner .40 1.00

2014 Panini Prizm

COMP.SET w/o RC's (200) 20.00 40.00
1 Steve Smith .25 .60
2 Tom Rathman .20 .50
3 Dez Bryant .30 .75
4 Jerry Rice .50 1.25
5 Torrey Smith .25 .60
6 Cecil Shorts III .20 .50
7 Joe Flacco .25 .60
8 Bruce Smith .25 .60
9 LeSean McCoy .30 .75
10 Maurice Jones-Drew .25 .60
11 Joseph Randle .20 .50
12 Eric Dickerson .25 .60
13 Larry Fitzgerald .30 .75
14 Jake Locker .25 .60
15 Larry Csonka .30 .75
16 Scott Tolzien .20 .50
17 Brett Favre .60 1.50
18 Jason Witten .25 .60
19 Jimmy Graham .30 .75
20 Gale Sayers .30 .75
21 Tamba Hali .20 .50
22 DeMarcus Ware .25 .60
23 Eli Manning .25 .60
24 Riley Cooper .25 .60
25 Hakeem Nicks .20 .50
26 Bob Lilly .20 .50
27 Alshon Jeffery .25 .60
28 Keenan Allen .25 .60
29 Greg Jennings .25 .60
30 Victor Cruz .25 .60
31 Montee Ball .25 .60
32 Frank Gore .25 .60
33 Kurt Warner .25 .60
34 Julian Edelman .30 .75
35 Chris Givens .20 .50
36 Tom Brady .75 2.00
37 Tony Romo .30 .75
38 Philip Rivers .30 .75
39 Jordan Cameron .20 .50
40 Antonio Brown .30 .75
41 John Elway .50 1.25
42 Ray Rice .20 .50
43 Reggie Bush .20 .50
44 Michael Irvin .25 .60
45 Wes Welker .25 .60
46 Jamaal Charles .30 .75
47 Le'Veon Bell .30 .75
48 Marshall Faulk .25 .60
49 Rashad Jennings .20 .50
50 Franco Harris .25 .60
51 Robert Griffin III .25 .60
52 Reggie Wayne .25 .60
53 Frank Gifford .25 .60
54 Greg Little .20 .50
55 Stevan Ridley .20 .50
56 Bob Griese .25 .60
57 Brent Celek .20 .50
58 Peyton Manning .60 1.50
59 Arian Foster .25 .60
60 Jeremy Maclin .25 .60
61 Fred Jackson .25 .60
62 Terrell Davis .12 .30
63 Tavon Austin .25 .60
64 Ndamukong Suh .25 .60
65 Calvin Johnson .30 .75
66 Dan Fouts .25 .60
67 Aaron Rodgers .60 1.50
68 Bo Jackson .40 1.00
69 Terry Bradshaw .40 1.00
70 Andy Dalton .25 .60
71 Steve Johnson .20 .50
72 DeMarco Murray .30 .75
73 Sidney Rice .20 .50
74 Michael Crabtree .25 .60
75 Fran Tarkenton .30 .75
76 Matt Schaub .20 .50
77 Brett Favre .60 1.50
78 Patrick Willis .25 .60
79 Antonio Gates .25 .60
80 Marshawn Lynch .25 .60
81 Brandon Marshall .25 .60
82 Shannon Sharpe .20 .50
83 Ryan Tannehill .25 .60
84 Lamar Miller .25 .60
85 Geno Smith .25 .60
86 Jay Cutler .25 .60
87 Alfred Morris .25 .60
88 Derrick Johnson .20 .50
89 Jonathan Stewart .25 .60
90 Steven Jackson .25 .60
91 Chris Ivory .25 .60
92 Julius Peppers .25 .60
93 Eddie Lacy .30 .75
94 Trent Richardson .20 .50
95 Kyle Rudolph .25 .60
96 Giovani Bernard .25 .60
97 Cris Carter .30 .75
98 Jordy Nelson .30 .75
99 Devin Hester .25 .60
100 Matt Forte .25 .60
101 Kurt Warner .30 .75
102 Pierre Thomas .20 .50
103 Paul Warfield .25 .60
104 Steve Young .40 1.00
105 Dan Hampton .20 .50
106 Zac Stacy .20 .50
107 Mike Wallace .25 .60
108 Santana Moss .25 .60
109 Vincent Jackson .25 .60
110 Eric Decker .25 .60
111 DeAngelo Williams .25 .60
112 Chris Johnson .25 .60
113 Jared Allen .25 .60
114 Greg Olsen .25 .60
115 Adrian Peterson .50 1.25
116 Brett Favre .60 1.50
117 Golden Tate .25 .60
118 Mohamed Sanu .20 .50
119 Cam Newton .30 .75
120 Daunte Culpepper .25 .60
121 Jerome Bettis .30 .75
122 Shonn Greene .20 .50
123 Nick Foles .30 .75
124 Toby Gerhart .20 .50
125 Ryan Mathews .25 .60
126 Demaryius Thomas .30 .75
127 James Lofton .25 .60
128 Ronnie Lott .25 .60
129 Andrew Luck .40 1.00
130 Kiko Alonso .25 .60
131 Nate Washington .20 .50
132 Torrell Suggs .20 .50
133 Clay Matthews .30 .75
134 Brian Hartline .20 .50
135 Ryan Fitzpatrick .20 .50
136 T.Y. Hilton .25 .60
137 Jack Ham .25 .60
138 Russell Wilson .50 1.25
139 C.J. Spiller .25 .60
140 Tyler Eifert .25 .60
141 Carson Palmer .25 .60
142 Mike Glennon .20 .50
143 Matt Ryan .25 .60
144 Kendall Wright .20 .50
145 Knowshon Moreno .25 .60
146 Andre Johnson .25 .60
147 Roger Staubach .40 1.00
148 Lance Alworth .25 .60
149 Chad Henne .20 .50
150 Cordarrelle Patterson .25 .60
151 Josh McCown .20 .50
152 Rob Gronkowski .30 .75
153 John Riggins .25 .60
154 Antrel Rolle .20 .50
155 Emmitt Smith .50 1.25
156 Von Miller .25 .60
157 Percy Harvin .25 .60
158 Willis McGahee .20 .50
159 Dwayne Bowe .20 .50
160 Julius Thomas .25 .60
161 Kenny Stills .25 .60
162 Troy Polamalu .30 .75
163 Chris Long .20 .50
164 Andre Roberts .20 .50
165 Art Monk .25 .60
166 Warren Moon .30 .75
167 Sam Bradford .25 .60
168 Denarius Moore .20 .50
169 Alex Smith .25 .60
170 Ace Sanders .20 .50
171 Matthew Stafford .30 .75
172 Darrelle Revis .25 .60
173 Warren Sapp .25 .60
174 Ben Roethlisberger .30 .75
175 Brian Hoyer .25 .60
176 Michael Vick .25 .60
177 Jacquizz Rodgers .20 .50
178 Julio Jones .30 .75
179 Colin Kaepernick .30 .75
180 Andre Ellington .25 .60
181 Jordan Reed .20 .50
182 Justin Tuck .20 .50
183 Warren Moon .25 .60
184 Zach Ertz .25 .60
185 EJ Manuel .20 .50
186 Darren McFadden .25 .60
187 Dan Marino .60 1.50
188 J.J. Watt .30 .75
189 DeAndre Hopkins .25 .60
190 A.J. Green .30 .75
191 Drew Brees .30 .75
192 Michael Floyd .25 .60
193 Roddy White .25 .60
194 Doug Martin .25 .60
195 Fred Biletnikoff .25 .60
196 Marques Colston .25 .60
197 Earl Campbell .50 1.25
198 Anquan Boldin .25 .60
199 Christian Ponder .25 .60
200 Mxwll/Thms/Chn/Shrm .30 .75
201 Rajion Neal RC .40 1.00
202 Austin Seferian-Jenkins RC .40 1.00
203 Bradley Roby RC .40 1.00
204 Deone Bucannon RC .40 1.00
205 James White RC .75 2.00
206 L'Damian Washington RC .50 1.25
207 Donte Moncrief RC .60 1.50
208 C.J. Mosley RC .50 1.25
209 Ahmad Dixon RC .40 1.00
210 Jerick McKinnon RC .50 1.25
211 Greg Robinson RC .40 1.00
212 Kony Ealy RC .40 1.00
213 TJ Jones RC .50 1.25
214 Carlos Hyde RC .60 1.50
215 Brandon Coleman RC .50 1.25
216A Mike Evans RC 1.00 2.50
216B Mike Evans SP 1.25 3.00
216C Mike Evans SP 1.25 3.00
216D Mike Evans SP 1.25 3.00
216E Mike Evans SP 1.25 3.00
217 Mike Davis RC .40 1.00
218 Khalil Mack RC 1.50 4.00
219 Louis Nix III RC .40 1.00
220 Kevin Norwood RC .40 1.00
221 Kyle Fuller RC .40 1.00
222 Justin Gilbert RC .40 1.00
223 Kelvin Benjamin RC .60 1.50
224 Cody Hoffman RC .40 1.00
225 Jeff Janis RC .60 1.50
226 Ka'Deem Carey RC .40 1.00
227 Troy Niklas RC .40 1.00
228 Aaron Donald RC 1.00 2.50
229A Sammy Watkins RC .60 1.50
229B Sammy Watkins SP .75 2.00
229C Sammy Watkins SP .75 2.00
229D Sammy Watkins SP .75 2.00
229E Sammy Watkins SP .75 2.00
230 Connor Shaw RC .40 1.00
231 Calvin Pryor RC .40 1.00
232 Jalen Saunders RC .40 1.00
233 Jordan Matthews RC .60 1.50
234 Tajh Boyd RC .50 1.25
235A Blake Bortles RC .50 1.25
235B Blake Bortles SP .60 1.50
235C Blake Bortles SP .60 1.50
235D Blake Bortles SP .60 1.50
235E Blake Bortles SP .60 1.50
236 Brandin Cooks RC .60 1.50
237 Matt Hazel RC .40 1.00
238 Devin Street RC .40 1.00
239 Martavis Bryant RC .50 1.25
240 Lamarcus Joyner RC .40 1.00
241 Bruce Ellington RC .40 1.00
242A Teddy Bridgewater RC .60 1.50
242B Teddy Bridgewater SP .75 2.00
242C Teddy Bridgewater SP .75 2.00
242D Teddy Bridgewater SP .75 2.00
242E Teddy Bridgewater SP .75 2.00
243A Jimmy Garoppolo RC 3.00 8.00
243B Jimmy Garoppolo SP 3.00 8.00
243C Jimmy Garoppolo SP 3.00 8.00
244 Ryan Shazier RC .50 1.25
245 Ha Ha Clinton-Dix RC .60 1.50
246 Lache Seastrunk RC .40 1.00
247 Michael Campanaro RC .40 1.00
248 Dri Archer RC .40 1.00
249 Bee Ford RC .40 1.00
250 Aaron Murray RC .40 1.00
251 Jake Matthews RC .40 1.00
252 Paul Richardson RC .40 1.00
253 Bishop Sankey RC .40 1.00
254 Marion Grice RC .40 1.00
255 Cyrus Kouandjio RC .40 1.00
256 James Wilder Jr. RC .50 1.25
257A Derek Carr RC 2.50 6.00
257B Derek Carr SP 3.00 8.00
257C Derek Carr SP 2.50 6.00
258 Logan Thomas RC .40 1.00
259 C.J. Fiedorowicz RC .40 1.00
260A Tom Savage RC .40 1.00
260B Tom Savage SP .50 1.25
260C Tom Savage SP .50 1.25
261 Cody Latimer RC .50 1.25
262 Anthony Barr RC .50 1.25
263 Terrance West RC .40 1.00
264 Michael Sam RC .40 1.00
265 Allen Robinson RC .60 1.50
266 Telvin Reese RC .40 1.00
267 De'Anthony Thomas RC .40 1.00
268 Jared Abbrederis RC .40 1.00
269 Stephon Tuitt RC .60 1.50
270 Chris Borland RC .40 1.00
271 Tyler Gaffney RC .40 1.00
272 Devonta Freeman RC 1.25 1.25
273 Taylor Lewan RC .60 1.50
274 Josh Huff RC .50 1.25
275 Kyle Van Noy RC .50 1.25
276 Darqueze Dennard RC .50 1.25
277 Storm Johnson RC .40 1.00
278 Jace Amaro RC .40 1.00
279 Andre Williams RC .40 1.00
280 Jason Verrett RC .40 1.00
281 Davante Adams RC .60 1.50
282 Odell Beckham Jr. RC 1.00 2.50
283 Jeremy Hill RC .60 1.50
284 Zach Mettenberger RC .40 1.00
285A Jadeveon Clowney RC .50 1.25
285B Jadeveon Clowney SP .60 1.50
285C Jadeveon Clowney SP .60 1.50
286 Isaiah Crowell RC .50 1.25
287A Johnny Manziel RC .60 1.50
287B Johnny Manziel SP .75 2.00
287C Johnny Manziel SP .75 2.00
287D Johnny Manziel SP .75 2.00
287E Johnny Manziel SP .75 2.00
288 Shaq Evans RC .40 1.00
289 Charles Sims RC .40 1.00
290 Robert Herron RC .40 1.00
291 Marqise Lee RC .50 1.25
292 Eric Ebron RC .50 1.25
293A A.J. McCarron RC .40 1.00
293B A.J. McCarron SP .50 1.25
293C A.J. McCarron SP .50 1.25
294 Antonio Andrews RC .40 1.00
295 Jarvis Landry RC .75 2.00
296 Brett Smith RC .40 1.00
297 Zack Martin RC .50 1.25
298 David Yankey RC .40 1.00
299 Tre Mason RC .40 1.00
300 David Fales RC .40 1.00

2014 Panini Prizm Prizms

*VETS: 2X TO 5X BASIC CARDS
*ROOKIES: .6X TO 1.5X BASIC CARDS

2014 Panini Prizm Prizms Blue

*VETS: 2X TO 5X BASIC CARDS
*ROOKIES: .8X TO 2X BASIC RC
RANDOM INSERTS IN WAL-MART PACKS

2014 Panini Prizm Prizms Camo

*VETS: 3X TO 8X BASIC CARDS
*ROOKIES: 1X TO 2.5X BASIC CARDS
INSERTED IN JUMBO BOXES ONLY

2014 Panini Prizm Prizms Green

*VETS: 2X TO 5X BASIC CARDS
*ROOKIES: .8X TO 2X BASIC RC
RANDOM INSERTS IN SPECIAL RETAIL

2014 Panini Prizm Prizms Light Blue Wave

*VETS/99: 5X TO 12X BASIC CARDS
*ROOK/99: 1.5X TO 4X BASIC CARDS

2014 Panini Prizm Prizms Neon Green Yellow

*VETS: 3X TO 8X BASIC CARDS
*ROOKIES: 1X TO 2.5X BASIC CARDS

2014 Panini Prizm Prizms NFL Shield

*VETS/75: 5X TO 12X BASIC CARDS
*ROOK/75: 1.5X TO 4X BASIC CARDS

2014 Panini Prizm Prizms Orange

*VETS: 4X TO 10X BASIC CARDS
*ROOKIES: 1.2X TO 3X BASIC CARDS

2014 Panini Prizm Prizms Pink

*VETS: 3X TO 8X BASIC CARDS
*ROOKIES: 1X TO 2.5X BASIC CARDS
INSERTED IN JUMBO BOXES ONLY

2014 Panini Prizm Prizms Purple

*VETS: 2.5X TO 6X BASIC CARDS
*ROOKIES: 1X TO 2.5X BASIC RC
RANDOM INSERTS IN SPECIAL RETAIL

2014 Panini Prizm Prizms Panini Logo

*VETS: 2.5X TO 6X BASIC CARDS
*ROOKIES: .8X TO 2X BASIC RC

2014 Panini Prizm Prizms Red

*VETS: 2X TO 5X BASIC CARDS
*ROOKIES: .8X TO 2X BASIC RC

2014 Panini Prizm Prizms Red Power

*VETS/125: 4X TO 10X BASIC CARDS
*ROOK/125: 1.2X TO 3X BASIC CARDS

2014 Panini Prizm Prizms Red White and Blue

*VETS: 3X TO 8X BASIC CARDS
*ROOKIES: 1.2X TO 3X BASIC RC
RANDOM INSERTS IN MULTI-PACK RETAIL

2014 Panini Prizm Prizms Team Logo

*VETS/50: 6X TO 15X BASIC CARDS
*ROOKIES/50: 2X TO 5X BASIC RC

2014 Panini Prizm Prizms Tie Dyed

*VETS/25: 10X TO 25X BASIC CARDS
*ROOKIES/25: 3X TO 8X BASIC RC
205 James White 6.00 15.00

2014 Panini Prizm Air Marshalls

*PRIZM: .5X TO 1.2X BASIC INSERTS
1 Tom Brady 2.50 6.00
2 Peyton Manning 2.00 5.00
3 Drew Brees 1.00 2.50
4 Matt Ryan .75 2.00
5 Russell Wilson 1.50 4.00
6 Ben Roethlisberger 1.00 2.50
7 Matthew Stafford .75 2.00
8 Colin Kaepernick .75 2.00
9 Andrew Luck 1.25 3.00
10 Tony Romo .75 2.00
11 Cam Newton 1.00 2.50
12 Jay Cutler .60 1.50

2014 Panini Prizm Autographs

*GRN YEL/50: .6X TO 1.5X BASIC AU/250
*GRN YEL/50: .5X TO 1.2X BASIC AU/75
*GRN YEL/50: .4X TO 1X BASIC AU/35
*PAN.LOG/100: .5X TO 1.2X BASIC AU/250
*PAN.LOG/50: .5X TO 1.2X BASIC AU/75
*PAN.LOG/25: .5X TO 1.2X BASIC AU/35
3 Andy Dalton/15
6 Le'Veon Bell/35 12.00 30.00
8 T.Y. Hilton/15
10 Zac Stacy/250 3.00 8.00
11 Montee Ball/25 6.00 15.00
12 Giovani Bernard/15 8.00 20.00
14 Cordarrelle Patterson/75 4.00 10.00
15 DeMarco Murray/250 4.00 10.00

2014 Panini Prizm Autographs Prizms

*PRIZM/150: .4X TO 1X BASIC AU/250
*PRIZM/25: .5X TO 1.2X BASIC AU/35
10 Zac Stacy/150 3.00 8.00

2014 Panini Prizm Autographs Prizms Camo

1 Brandon Browner/45
6 Le'Veon Bell/15 15.00 40.00
8 T.Y. Hilton/45 6.00 15.00
10 Zac Stacy/30 6.00 15.00
12 Giovani Bernard/20 10.00 25.00
15 DeMarco Murray/50 6.00 15.00

2014 Panini Prizm Believe the Hype

*PRIZM: .5X TO 1.2X BASIC INSERTS
1 Johnny Manziel .60 1.50
2 Blake Bortles .50 1.25
3 Teddy Bridgewater .60 1.50
4 Sammy Watkins .60 1.50
5 Mike Evans 1.00 2.50
6 A.J. McCarron .40 1.00
7 Aaron Murray .40 1.00
8 Tom Savage .40 1.00
9 Jeremy Hill .50 1.25
10 Khalil Mack 1.50 4.00
11 Jadeveon Clowney .50 1.25
12 Odell Beckham Jr. 1.00 2.50
13 Jordan Matthews .60 1.50
14 Cody Latimer .50 1.25
15 Derek Carr 2.50 6.00
16 Jimmy Garoppolo 3.00 8.00

2014 Panini Prizm Class Rings

*PRIZM: .5X TO 1.2X BASIC INSERTS
1 Johnny Manziel .60 1.50
2 Teddy Bridgewater .60 1.50
3 Blake Bortles .50 1.25
4 Derek Carr 2.50 6.00
5 Sammy Watkins .60 1.50
6 Mike Evans 1.00 2.50

2014 Panini Prizm Dirty Laundry

*PRIZM: .5X TO 1.2X BASIC JSY
1 Aaron Murray 1.25 3.00
2 A.J. McCarron 1.25 3.00
3 Allen Robinson 2.00 5.00
4 Andre Williams 1.25 3.00
5 Asa Watson 1.25 3.00
6 Austin Seferian-Jenkins 1.25 3.00
7 Bishop Sankey 1.25 3.00
8 Blake Bortles 1.50 4.00
9 Brandin Cooks 2.00 5.00
10 Carlos Hyde 1.50 4.00
11 Cody Latimer 1.50 4.00
12 Connor Shaw 1.25 3.00
13 Davante Adams 2.00 5.00
14 De'Anthony Thomas 1.25 3.00
15 Devonta Freeman 2.00 5.00
16 Donte Moncrief 1.25 3.00
17 Dri Archer 1.25 3.00
18 Eric Ebron 1.50 4.00
19 Jadeveon Clowney 1.50 4.00
20 Jarvis Landry 2.50 6.00
21 Jeremy Hill 1.50 4.00
22 Jimmy Garoppolo 10.00 25.00
23 Johnny Manziel 2.00 5.00
24 Jordan Matthews 2.00 5.00
25 Ka'Deem Carey 1.25 3.00
26 Kelvin Benjamin 2.00 5.00
27 Khalil Mack 5.00 12.00
28 Logan Thomas 1.25 3.00
29 Marqise Lee 1.50 4.00
30 Mike Evans 3.00 8.00
31 Odell Beckham Jr. 3.00 8.00
32 Paul Richardson 1.50 4.00
33 Sammy Watkins 2.00 5.00
34 Tajh Boyd 1.25 3.00
35 Teddy Bridgewater 5.00 12.00
36 Terrance West 1.25 3.00
37 Tom Savage 1.25 3.00
38 Tre Mason 1.25 3.00
39 Jace Amaro 1.25 3.00
40 Derek Carr 8.00 20.00
41 Adrian Peterson 4.00 10.00
42 Brett Favre 8.00 20.00
43 Calvin Johnson 4.00 10.00
44 Cam Newton 4.00 10.00
45 Colin Kaepernick 3.00 8.00
46 Drew Brees 4.00 10.00
47 Larry Fitzgerald 3.00 8.00
48 Ray Rice 2.50 6.00
49 Tom Brady 10.00 25.00
50 Maurice Jones-Drew 2.50 6.00

2014 Panini Prizm Fresh Faces

*PRIZM: .5X TO 1.2X BASIC INSERTS
1 Johnny Manziel .60 1.50
2 Blake Bortles .50 1.25
3 Teddy Bridgewater .60 1.50
4 Sammy Watkins .60 1.50
5 Mike Evans 1.00 2.50
6 Eric Ebron .50 1.25
7 Derek Carr 2.50 6.00
8 Tom Savage .40 1.00
9 Brandin Cooks .60 1.50
10 Marqise Lee .50 1.25
11 Odell Beckham Jr. 1.00 2.50
12 Davante Adams .60 1.50
13 Khalil Mack 1.50 4.00
14 Jadeveon Clowney .50 1.25
15 Carlos Hyde .50 1.25
16 Jordan Matthews .60 1.50
17 Jimmy Garoppolo 3.00 8.00
18 Jeremy Hill .50 1.25
19 Cody Latimer .50 1.25
20 Bishop Sankey .40 1.00
21 Giovani Bernard .50 1.25
22 Keenan Allen .60 1.50
23 Eddie Lacy .50 1.25
24 Mike Glennon .40 1.00

2014 Panini Prizm Hands Team

*PRIZM: .5X TO 1.2X BASIC INSERTS
1 DeSean Jackson .75 2.00
2 Jordy Nelson .75 2.00
3 Anquan Boldin .60 1.50
4 Larry Fitzgerald .75 2.00
5 Jimmy Graham 1.00 2.50
6 Demaryius Thomas .75 2.00
7 Dez Bryant 1.00 2.50
8 A.J. Green .75 2.00
9 Julian Edelman 1.00 2.50
10 Andre Johnson .75 2.00
11 Antonio Brown 1.00 2.50
12 Pierre Garcon .75 2.00
13 Wes Welker .75 2.00
14 Calvin Johnson 1.00 2.50
15 Brandon Marshall .60 1.50
16 Alshon Jeffery .75 2.00

2014 Panini Prizm Head to Head GOAT

*PRIZM: .5X TO 1.2X BASIC INSERTS
1 E.Smith/W.Payton 5.00 12.00
2 B.Favre/D.Marino 3.00 8.00
3 C.Carter/J.Rice 2.50 6.00
4 A.Peterson/E.Smith 2.50 6.00
5 B.Favre/P.Manning 3.00 8.00
6 C.Johnson/J.Rice 3.00 8.00

2014 Panini Prizm Intros

*PRIZM: .5X TO 1.2X BASIC INSERTS
1 Calvin Johnson 1.25 3.00
2 Frank Gore 1.00 2.50
3 Victor Cruz 1.00 2.50
4 EJ Manuel .75 2.00
5 Keenan Allen 1.00 2.50
6 Steven Jackson .75 2.00
7 J.J. Watt 1.25 3.00
8 Cam Newton 1.25 3.00
9 Jimmy Graham 1.25 3.00
10 Colin Kaepernick 1.25 3.00
11 Brandon Marshall .75 2.00
12 Peyton Manning 2.50 6.00
13 Russell Wilson 2.00 5.00
14 Ben Roethlisberger 1.25 3.00
15 Robert Griffin III .75 2.00
16 Ray Rice .75 2.00
17 Andrew Luck 1.50 4.00
18 James Laurinaitis .75 2.00
19 Tom Brady 3.00 8.00
20 Ray Lewis 1.25 3.00

2014 Panini Prizm Patented Penmanship

2 Aaron Rodgers/5
4 Eli Manning/25 25.00 50.00
5 Sam Bradford/15 15.00 30.00
PPJJ J.J. Watt/50 30.00 60.00

2014 Panini Prizm Rookie Autographs

*BASE AU: .3X TO .8X ORANGE/100-200
*BASE AU: .25X TO .6X ORANGE/75
*BASE AU: .2X TO .5X ORANGE 30-60
ARJF Johnny Manziel 6.00 15.00
ARJG Jimmy Garoppolo 40.00 80.00

2014 Panini Prizm Rookie Autographs Prizms

*PRIZMS/40-60: .4X TO 1X ORANGE/35-60
*PRIZMS/75: .4X TO 1X ORANGE/75
*PRIZMS/100-350: .4X TO 1X ORANGE/100-200
*PRIZMS/40-60: .5X TO 1.2X ORANGE/75
ARJG Jimmy Garoppolo/60 100.00 200.00

2014 Panini Prizm Rookie Autographs Prizms Blue

*BLUE/50-75: .5X TO 1.2X ORNG/100-200
*BLUE/75: .4X TO 1X ORNG/50-75
*BLUE/75: .3X TO .8X ORNG/30
*BLUE/40: .6X TO 1.5X ORNG/100
*BLUE/40: .4X TO 1X ORNG/35
*BLUE/30-40: .5X TO 1.2X ORNG/50-75
ARJG Jimmy Garoppolo/30 100.00 200.00

2014 Panini Prizm Rookie Autographs Prizms Camo

*CAMO/100-200: .4X TO 1X ORNG/100-200
*CAMO/100-200: .5X TO 1.2X ORNG/50-75
*CAMO/150: .6X TO 1.5X ORNG/35
*CAMO/50-75: .4X TO 1X ORNG/50-75
*CAMO/75: .3X TO .8X ORNG/35
*CAMO/40: .5X TO 1.2X ORNG/50
*CAMO/40: .4X TO 1X ORNG/30
*CAMO/25: .6X TO 1.5X ORNG/50
ARJG Jimmy Garoppolo/75 60.00 125.00

2014 Panini Prizm Rookie Autographs Prizms Green

*GREEN/60: .5X TO 1.2X ORNG/100-200
*GREEN/60: .4X TO 1X ORNG/50-75
*GREEN/60: .3X TO .8X ORNG/30
*GREEN/30-35: .6X TO 1.5X ORNG/100
*GREEN/30: .5X TO 1.2X ORNG/50-75
*GREEN/30: .4X TO 1X ORNG/35
*GREEN/25: .6X TO 1.5X ORNG/50-75
ARJC Jadeveon Clowney/20 6.00 15.00
ARJG Jimmy Garoppolo/25 125.00 250.00

2014 Panini Prizm Rookie Autographs Prizms Light Blue Wave

*WAVE/99: .4X TO 1X ORANGE/100-200
*WAVE/50-75: .5X TO 1.2X ORANGE/100-200
*WAVE/50-75: .4X TO 1X ORANGE/50-75
*WAVE/35: .5X TO 1.2X ORANGE/50-75
*WAVE/25: .5X TO 1.2X ORANGE/30-35
ARJG Jimmy Garoppolo/35 100.00 200.00

2014 Panini Prizm Rookie Autographs Prizms Neon Green Yellow

*GRN-YEL/100-150: .4X TO 1X ORNG/100-200
*GRN-YEL/85: .5X TO 1.2X ORNG/100
*GRN-YEL/50-75: .4X TO 1X ORNG/50-75
*GRN-YEL/30-35: .4X TO 1X ORNG/30-35
ARJG Jimmy Garoppolo/50 75.00 150.00

2014 Panini Prizm Rookie Autographs Prizms NFL Shield

*NFL SHLD/50-75: .5X TO 1.2X ORNG/100-200
*NFL SHLD/50-75: .4X TO 1X ORNG/75
*NFL SHLD/35: .5X TO 1.2X ORNG/50-75
*NFL SHLD/25: .6X TO 1.5X ORNG/50-75
*NFL SHLD/15-25: .5X TO 1.2X ORNG/30-35
ARJG Jimmy Garoppolo/25 125.00 250.00

2014 Panini Prizm Rookie Autographs Prizms Orange

ARAA Antonio Andrews/100 2.50 6.00
ARAB Anthony Barr/50 3.00 8.00
ARAD Aaron Donald/50 10.00 25.00
ARAM1 A.J. McCarron/50 3.00 8.00
ARAM2 Aaron Murray/35 4.00 10.00
ARAR Allen Robinson/35 6.00 15.00
ARAS Austin Seferian-Jenkins/30 4.00 10.00
ARAW Andre Williams/50 3.00 8.00
ARBB Blake Bortles/75 4.00 10.00
ARBC1 Brandon Coleman/50 3.00 8.00
ARBC2 Brandin Cooks/35 6.00 15.00
ARBE Bruce Ellington/100 2.50 6.00
ARBR Bradley Roby/50 3.00 8.00
ARBS1 Bishop Sankey/75 3.00 8.00
ARBS2 Brett Smith/150 2.50 6.00
ARCB Chris Borland/125 3.00 8.00
ARCF C.J. Fiedorowicz/200 2.50 6.00
ARCH1 Carlos Hyde/35 5.00 12.00
ARCH2 Cody Hoffman/50 2.50 6.00
ARCL Cody Latimer/100 3.00 8.00
ARCM C.J. Mosley/50 4.00 10.00
ARCP Calvin Pryor/50 3.00 8.00
ARCR Cyril Richardson/75 2.50 6.00
ARCS1 Charles Sims/50 3.00 8.00
ARCS2 Chris Smith/50 2.50 6.00
ARDA Dri Archer/35 4.00 10.00
ARDB Deone Bucannon/75 3.00 8.00
ARDC Derek Carr/50 40.00 100.00
ARDD Darqueze Dennard/125 3.00 8.00
ARDF1 David Fales/60 3.00 8.00
ARDF2 Dee Ford/60 3.00 8.00
ARDM Donte Moncrief/125 2.50 6.00
ARDY David Yankey/150 2.50 6.00
AREE Eric Ebron/50 4.00 10.00
ARER Ed Reynolds/75 2.50 6.00
ARHCD Ha Ha Clinton-Dix/50 4.00 10.00
ARIC Isaiah Crowell/75 3.00 8.00
ARJA1 Jace Amaro/100 2.50 6.00
ARJA2 Jared Abbrederis/125 2.50 6.00
ARJG Jimmy Garoppolo/50 60.00 125.00
ARJH1 Jeremy Hill/50 4.00 10.00
ARJH2 Josh Huff/50 3.00 8.00
ARJJ Jeff Janis/150 2.50 6.00
ARJM1 Jake Matthews/50 3.00 8.00
ARJM2 Jerick McKinnon/60 4.00 10.00
ARJM4 Jordan Matthews/35 6.00 15.00
ARJV Jason Verrett/60 3.00 8.00
ARJW1 James Wilder Jr./150 2.50 6.00
ARJW2 Jimmie Ward/75 4.00 10.00
ARKC Ka'Deem Carey/50 3.00 8.00
ARKE Kony Ealy/50 3.00 8.00
ARKM Khalil Mack/50 25.00 60.00
ARKN Kevin Norwood/50 3.00 8.00
ARLJ Lamarcus Joyner/60 3.00 8.00
ARLN Louis Nix III/50 3.00 8.00
ARLS Lache Seastrunk/75 2.50 6.00
ARLT Logan Thomas/35 4.00 10.00
ARLW L'Damian Washington/200 3.00 8.00
ARMC Michael Campanaro/75 3.00 8.00
ARMD Mike Davis/50 2.50 6.00
ARME Mike Evans/75 8.00 20.00
ARMG Marion Grice/75 3.00 8.00
ARMH Matt Hazel/60 2.50 6.00
ARML Marqise Lee/50 4.00 10.00
ARMR Marcus Roberson/75 4.00 10.00
ARMS1 Marcus Smith/50 3.00 8.00
ARMS2 Michael Sam/150 2.50 6.00
ARPR Paul Richardson/75 6.00 15.00
ARRH1 Ra'Shede Hageman/50 3.00 8.00
ARRH2 Robert Herron/200 2.50 6.00
ARRN Rajion Neal/75 2.50 6.00
ARRS Ryan Shazier/200 4.00 10.00
ARSC Scott Crichton/60 3.00 8.00
ARSE Shaq Evans/50 3.00 8.00
ARSS Shayne Skov/50 3.00 8.00
ARSW Sammy Watkins/75 10.00 25.00
ARTB1 Tajh Boyd/50 3.00 8.00
ARTB2 Teddy Bridgewater/75 5.00 12.00
ARTG Tyler Gaffney/50 3.00 8.00

ARTJ Timmy Jernigan/50 3.00 8.00
ARTL Taylor Lewan/50 3.00 8.00
ARTM Trent Murphy/125 2.50 6.00
ARTN Troy Niklas/50 3.00 8.00
ARTR1 Tevin Reese/50 3.00 8.00
ARTR2 Trevor Reilly/50 3.00 8.00
ARTS1 Telvin Smith/50 3.00 8.00
ARTS2 Tom Savage/100 2.50 6.00
ARTS3 Travis Swanson/50 3.00 8.00
ARTW Terrance West/100 2.50 6.00
ARXS Xavier Su'A-Filo/100 3.00 8.00
ARYS Yawin Smallwood/75 3.00 8.00

2014 Panini Prizm Rookie Autographs Prizms Panini Logo

*PAN.LOGO/125-250: .4X TO 1X ORNG/100-200
*PAN.LOGO/100-125: .3X TO .8X ORNG/50-75
*PAN.LOGO/50-75: .4X TO 1X ORNG/50-75
*PAN.LOGO/50-75: .3X TO .8X ORNG/35
*PAN.LOGO/30: .4X TO 1X ORNG/30
ARJG Jimmy Garoppolo/60 60.00 125.00

2014 Panini Prizm Rookie Autographs Prizms Pink

*PINK/100-150: .4X TO 1X ORNG/100-200
*PINK/100-150: .3X TO .8X ORNG/50-75
*PINK/100-150: .25X TO .6X ORNG/35
*PINK/65: .5X TO 1.2X ORNG/100
*PINK/50-75: .4X TO 1X ORNG/50-75
*PINK/50-65: .5X TO 1.2X ORNG/35
*PINK/35-45: .5X TO 1.2X ORNG/50-75
*PINK/25: .6X TO 1.5X ORNG/50
*PINK/25: .5X TO 1.2X ORNG/30
*PINK/15: .6X TO 1.5X ORNG/50
ARJC Jadeveon Clowney/15 6.00 15.00
ARJG Jimmy Garoppolo/45 75.00 150.00

2014 Panini Prizm Rookie Autographs Prizms Purple

*PURPL/50: .5X TO 1.2X ORNG/100-200
*PURPL/50: .4X TO 1X ORNG/50-75
*PURPL/40: .5X TO 1.2X ORNG/50
*PURPL/40: .4X TO 1X ORNG/30
*PURPL/35: .6X TO 1.5X ORNG/125-200

2014 Panini Prizm Rookie Autographs Prizms Red

*RED/75: .5X TO 1.2X ORNG/100-200
*RED/75: .4X TO 1X ORNG/50-75
*RED/75: .3X TO .8X ORNG/30
*RED/50: .5X TO 1.2X ORNG/100
*RED/40: .6X TO 1.5X ORNG/100
*RED/40: .4X TO 1X ORNG/35
*RED/30-40: .5X TO 1.2X ORNG/50-75
ARJG Jimmy Garoppolo/30 100.00 200.00

2014 Panini Prizm Rookie Autographs Prizms Red Power

*RED PWR/100-125: .4X TO 1X ORNG/125-200
*RED PWR/75: .5X TO 1.2X ORNG/100-200
*RED PWR/50-75: .4X TO 1X ORNG/50-75
*RED PWR/35: .5X TO 1.2X ORNG/50-75
*RED PWR/25: .5X TO 1.2X ORNG/30-35
ARJG Jimmy Garoppolo/35 100.00 200.00

2014 Panini Prizm Rookie Autographs Prizms Team Logo

*TM LOGO/50: .5X TO 1.2X ORNG/100-200
*TM LOGO/50: .4X TO 1X ORNG/75
*TM LOGO/35: .6X TO 1.5X ORNG/100
*TM LOGO/35: .5X TO 1.2X ORNG/50-75
*TM LOGO/25: .6X TO 1.5X ORNG/50-75
*TM LOGO/15-25: .5X TO 1.2X ORNG/30-35
ARJG Jimmy Garoppolo/25 125.00 250.00

2014 Panini Prizm Rookie Autographs Prizms Tie Dyed

*TIE DYE/15-25: .8X TO 2X ORNG/100-200
*TIE DYE/15-25: .6X TO 1.5X ORNG/50-75
*TIE DYE/15-25: .5X TO 1.2X ORNG/30-35
ARDC Derek Carr/25 125.00 200.00
ARJG Jimmy Garoppolo/25 125.00 250.00

2015 Panini Prizm

1 Cam Newton .30 .75
2 Matt Ryan .25 .60
3 Russell Wilson .40 1.00
4 Brett Favre .60 1.50
5 Joe Flacco .25 .60
6 Jay Cutler .20 .50
7 John Elway .50 1.25
8 Troy Aikman .40 1.00
9 Drew Brees .30 .75
10 Eli Manning .25 .60
11 Larry Fitzgerald .25 .60
12 Tom Brady .75 2.00
13 Dan Marino .60 1.50
14 Andy Dalton .25 .60
15 Brandon Marshall .20 .50
16 Joe Montana .75 2.00
17 Philip Rivers .30 .75
18 Peyton Manning .60 1.50
19 Ben Roethlisberger .30 .75
20 Darren McFadden .20 .50
21 Deion Sanders .25 .60
22 Emmitt Smith .50 1.25
23 Arian Foster .25 .60
24 Darrelle Revis .20 .50
25 Richard Sherman .30 .75
26 Rod Woodson .25 .60
27 Eddie Lacy .20 .50
28 Adrian Peterson .30 .75
29 DeMarco Murray .25 .60
30 Terrell Davis .25 .60
31 Kam Chancellor .30 .75
32 Eric Weddle .20 .50
33 Tony Dorsett .30 .75
34 Walter Payton .60 1.50
35 Joique Bell .20 .50
36 Jerome Bettis .30 .75
37 Brent Celek .20 .50
38 Pierre Garcon .25 .60
39 Reggie Bush .20 .50
40 Gale Sayers .30 .75
41 Victor Cruz .25 .60
42 Paul Warfield .25 .60
43 Roger Staubach .40 1.00
44 John Riggins .25 .60
45 Jeremy Hill .20 .50
46 LeGarrette Blount .25 .60
47 Josh McCown .25 .60
48 Justin Houston .20 .50
49 Carson Palmer .25 .60
50 Kiko Alonso .20 .50
51 Frank Gore .25 .60
52 Jonathan Stewart .20 .50
53 Earl Campbell .30 .75
54 Ryan Tannehill .25 .60
55 Colin Kaepernick .25 .60
56 Lawrence Taylor .30 .75
57 Le'Veon Bell .25 .60
58 Randall Cobb .25 .60
59 Rashad Jennings .20 .50
60 Terrance Williams .20 .50
61 Von Miller .25 .60
62 Trent Richardson .20 .50
63 Sam Bradford .20 .50
64 Matthew Stafford .25 .60
65 LeSean McCoy .30 .75
66 Art Monk .30 .75
67 Cordarrelle Patterson .20 .50
68 Doug Martin .25 .60
69 Devonta Freeman .25 .60
70 Michael Crabtree .20 .50
71 Fran Tarkenton .30 .75
72 Kendall Wright .20 .50
73 Martavis Bryant .20 .50
74 Isaiah Crowell .20 .50
75 Jarvis Landry .25 .60
76 Joe Namath .40 1.00
77 Mohamed Sanu .20 .50
78 Tony Romo .25 .60
79 Jordan Reed .20 .50
80 Jerry Rice .50 1.25
81 Calvin Johnson .30 .75
82 Jason Witten .25 .60
83 Johnny Manziel .25 .60
84 Antonio Brown .30 .75
85 Antonio Gates .20 .50
86 Heath Miller .20 .50
87 Rob Gronkowski .30 .75
88 Dez Bryant .30 .75
89 Steve Smith Sr. .25 .60
90 Ndamukong Suh .25 .60
91 Tamba Hali .20 .50
92 James Harrison .25 .60
93 Gerald McCoy .20 .50
94 DeMarcus Ware .25 .60
95 Matt Forte .20 .50
96 Nick Foles .25 .60
97 C.J. Spiller .20 .50
98 Dan Fouts .25 .60
99 J.J. Watt .30 .75
100 Ronnie Lott .25 .60
101 Tavon Austin .20 .50
102 C.J. Anderson .25 .60
103 Terry Bradshaw .40 1.00
104 Blake Bortles .20 .50
105 Brandon LaFell .20 .50
106 Kelvin Benjamin .25 .60
107 Jared Cook .20 .50
108 Mike Wallace .20 .50
109 Alfred Morris .20 .50
110 Percy Harvin .20 .50
111 Torrey Smith .20 .50
112 Aaron Rodgers .60 1.50
113 Emmanuel Sanders .25 .60
114 Khalil Mack .30 .75
115 DeSean Jackson .25 .60
116 Kyle Rudolph .20 .50
117 Earl Thomas .25 .60
118 Malcom Floyd .20 .50
119 Joseph Randle .20 .50
120 Julio Jones .30 .75
121 Clay Matthews .30 .75
122 Bishop Sankey .20 .50
123 Andrew Luck .40 1.00
124 Latavius Murray .20 .50
125 Malcolm Butler .30 .75
126 Bo Jackson .40 1.00
127 Cecil Shorts III .20 .50
128 Warren Moon .30 .75
129 Cris Carter .30 .75
130 Delanie Walker .20 .50
131 Jimmy Graham .30 .75
132 Marshall Faulk .25 .60
133 Jason Pierre-Paul .20 .50
134 Greg Jennings .20 .50
135 Mark Ingram .25 .60
136 Charles Woodson .30 .75
137 Robert Griffin III .20 .50
138 Haloti Ngata .20 .50
139 Kurt Warner .25 .60
140 Riley Cooper .25 .60
141 Brandin Cooks .25 .60
142 Paul Posluszny .20 .50
143 Justin Hunter .20 .50
144 Greg Olsen .25 .60
145 Jordy Nelson .25 .60
146 Barry Sanders .50 1.25
147 Allen Hurns .20 .50
148 Markus Wheaton .20 .50
149 Lavonte David .20 .50
150 Vincent Jackson .20 .50
151 Dwayne Bowe .25 .60
152 Sammy Watkins .25 .60
153 Demaryius Thomas .25 .60
154 Kirk Cousins .30 .75
155 Roddy White .20 .50
156 Chris Ivory .25 .60
157 Tre Mason .25 .60
158 Austin Seferian-Jenkins .20 .50
159 Ryan Mathews .25 .60
160 DeAndre Hopkins .25 .60
161 C.J. Mosley .30 .75
162 Brian Hoyer .20 .50
163 Lamar Miller .20 .50
164 Julius Thomas .20 .50
165 Shannon Sharpe .25 .60
166 De'Anthony Thomas .20 .50
167 Julian Edelman .30 .75
168 Vernon Davis .20 .50
169 Devin Hester .25 .60
170 Michael Floyd .20 .50
171 Julius Peppers .25 .60
172 T.Y. Hilton .25 .60
173 Justin Forsett .25 .60
174 Jeremy Maclin .20 .50
175 Branden Oliver .25 .60
176 Alshon Jeffery .25 .60
177 Carlos Hyde .20 .50
178 Denard Robinson .20 .50
179 Marques Colston .20 .50
180 Anquan Boldin .20 .50
181 Patrick Peterson .20 .50
182 Donte Moncrief .25 .60
183 Jamaal Charles .25 .60
184 Odell Beckham Jr. .30 .75
185 Geno Smith .20 .50
186 Teddy Bridgewater .25 .60
187 Golden Tate .20 .50
188 Eric Dickerson .25 .60
189 Mario Williams .20 .50
190 Eric Decker .20 .50
191 Jordan Matthews .25 .60
192 Doug Baldwin .25 .60
193 Andre Johnson .25 .60
194 Alex Smith .25 .60
195 Mike Evans .25 .60
196 Derek Carr .30 .75
197 A.J. Green .30 .75
198 Marshawn Lynch .25 .60
199 Andre Ellington .20 .50
200 Terrell Suggs .20 .50
201A Amari Cooper RC 1.25 3.00
201B Amari Cooper SP 1.50 4.00
202A Ameer Abdullah RC .60 1.50
202B Ameer Abdullah SP .75 2.00
203 Antwan Goodley RC .40 1.00
204 Arik Armstead RC .40 1.00
205 Ben Koyack RC .60 1.50
206 Benardrick McKinney RC .40 1.00
207 Blake Bell RC .60 1.50
208 Byron Jones RC .60 1.50
209 Breshad Perriman RC .40 1.00
210 Brett Hundley RC .40 1.00
211 Bryan Bennett RC .40 1.00
212 Bryce Petty RC .40 1.00
213 Bud Dupree RC .50 1.25
214 Cameron Artis-Payne RC .40 1.00
215 Carl Davis RC .50 1.25
216 Chris Conley RC .40 1.00
217 Clive Walford RC .40 1.00
218 Danielle Hunter RC .50 1.25
219 Danny Shelton RC .40 1.00
220 Dante Fowler Jr. RC .60 1.50
221 Darren Waller RC .50 1.25
222 DaVaris Daniels RC .40 1.00
223 David Cobb RC .40 1.00
224 David Johnson RC 1.00 2.50
225 DeAndrew White RC .60 1.50
226 Denzel Perryman RC .40 1.00
227 Duron Carter RC .50 1.25
228A DeVante Parker RC .60 1.50
228B DeVante Parker SP .75 2.00
229 Devin Funchess RC .60 1.50
230 Devin Smith RC .40 1.00
231 Dezmin Lewis RC .40 1.00
232 Dorial Green-Beckham RC .40 1.00
233 Jarryd Hayne RC .60 1.50
234 Duke Johnson RC .60 1.50
235 Eddie Goldman RC .40 1.00
236 Eli Harold RC .40 1.00
237 Eric Kendricks RC .40 1.00
238 Eric Rowe RC .40 1.00
239 Garrett Grayson RC .40 1.00
240 Jordan Taylor RC .50 1.25
241 Jaelen Strong RC .50 1.25
242 Jalston Fowler RC .50 1.25
243 Jalen Collins RC .40 1.00
244A Jameis Winston RC 1.00 2.50
244B Jameis Winston SP 1.25 3.00
245 Jamison Crowder RC .50 1.25
246 Buck Allen RC .50 1.25
247 Jay Ajayi RC .60 1.50
248 Jeremy Langford RC .40 1.00
249 Jesse James RC .50 1.25
250 J.J. Nelson RC .40 1.00
251 Josh Harper RC .40 1.00
252 Josh Robinson RC .40 1.00
253 Josh Shaw RC .60 1.50
254 Justin Hardy RC .40 1.00
255 Karlos Williams RC .40 1.00
256 Kenny Bell RC .60 1.50
257 Kevin Johnson RC .40 1.00
258A Kevin White RC .50 1.25
258B Kevin White SP .60 1.50
259 Kwon Alexander RC .50 1.25
260 Landon Collins RC .50 1.25
261 Leonard Williams RC .40 1.00
262 Malcolm Brown RC .50 1.25
263 Malcom Brown RC .40 1.00
264A Marcus Mariota RC 1.50 4.00
two hands on ball
264B Marcus Mariota SP 2.00 5.00
portrait
265 Marcus Peters RC .60 1.50
266 Mario Alford RC .40 1.00
267 Mike Davis RC .40 1.00
268 Matt Jones RC .40 1.00
269 Maxx Williams RC .40 1.00
270A Melvin Gordon RC 1.00 2.50
270B Melvin Gordon SP 1.25 3.00
271 Michael Dyer RC .60 1.50
272A Nelson Agholor RC .50 1.25
272B Nelson Agholor SP .60 1.50
273 Nick O'Leary RC .40 1.00
274 Owamagbe Odighizuwa RC .50 1.25
275 P.J. Williams RC .50 1.25
276A Phillip Dorsett RC .40 1.00
276B Phillip Dorsett SP .50 1.25
277 Randy Gregory RC .40 1.00
278 Rashad Greene RC .40 1.00
279 Ronald Darby RC .40 1.00
280 Sammie Coates RC .50 1.25
281 Sean Mannion RC .40 1.00
282 Shane Carden RC .40 1.00
283 Shane Ray RC .40 1.00
284 Shaq Thompson RC .50 1.25
285 Stefon Diggs RC 1.00 2.50
286 Stephone Anthony RC .40 1.00
287 T.J. Yeldon RC .40 1.00
288 Taylor Heinicke RC .60 1.50
289 Tevin Coleman RC .50 1.25
290 Jahwan Edwards RC .50 1.25
291A Todd Gurley RC 1.50 4.00
291B Todd Gurley SP 2.00 5.00
292 Tony Lippett RC .40 1.00
293 Trae Waynes RC .40 1.00
294 Tre McBride RC .40 1.00
295 Trey Flowers RC .60 1.50
296 Trey Williams RC .50 1.25
297 Ty Montgomery RC .40 1.00
298 Tyler Lockett RC .60 1.50
299 Vic Beasley Jr. RC .50 1.25
300 Vince Mayle RC .50 1.25

2015 Panini Prizm Prizms

*VETS: 2X TO 5X BASIC CARDS
*ROOKIES: .6X TO 1.5X BASIC CARDS

2015 Panini Prizm Prizms Blue

*VETS: 2X TO 5X BASIC CARDS
*ROOKIES: .8X TO 2X BASIC RC

2015 Panini Prizm Prizms Green

*VETS: 2X TO 5X BASIC CARDS
*ROOKIES: .8X TO 2X BASIC RC

2015 Panini Prizm Prizms Green Cracked Ice

*VETS/75: 5X TO 12X BASIC CARDS
*ROOK/75: 1.5X TO 4X BASIC CARDS

2015 Panini Prizm Prizms Light Blue Wave

*VETS/150: 4X TO 10X BASIC CARDS
*ROOK/150: 1.2X TO 3X BASIC CARDS

2015 Panini Prizm Prizms Purple

*VETS: 2.5X TO 6X BASIC CARDS
*ROOKIES: 1X TO 2.5X BASIC RC

2015 Panini Prizm Prizms Purple Mosaic

*VETS/50: 6X TO 15X BASIC CARDS
*ROOKIES/50: 2X TO 5X BASIC RC

2015 Panini Prizm Prizms Red

*VETS: 2X TO 5X BASIC CARDS
*ROOKIES: .8X TO 2X BASIC RC

2015 Panini Prizm Prizms Red Power

*VETS/99: 5X TO 12X BASIC CARDS
*ROOK/99: 1.5X TO 4X BASIC CARDS

2015 Panini Prizm Prizms Red White and Blue

*VETS: 3X TO 8X BASIC CARDS
*ROOKIES: 1.2X TO 3X BASIC RC

2015 Panini Prizm Prizms Tie Dyed

*VETS/25: 10X TO 25X BASIC CARDS
*ROOKIES/25: 3X TO 8X BASIC RC

2015 Panini Prizm Air Marshals

*PRIZM: .5X TO 1.2X BASIC INSERTS
1 Aaron Rodgers 2.00 5.00
2 Peyton Manning 2.00 5.00
3 Andrew Luck 1.25 3.00
4 Ben Roethlisberger 1.00 2.50
5 Matt Ryan .75 2.00
6 Colin Kaepernick .75 2.00
7 Drew Brees 1.00 2.50
8 Tom Brady 2.50 6.00
9 Philip Rivers 1.00 2.50
10 Cam Newton 1.00 2.50
11 Russell Wilson 1.25 3.00
12 Tony Romo .75 2.00
13 Matthew Stafford .75 2.00
14 Eli Manning .75 2.00
15 Joe Flacco .75 2.00

2015 Panini Prizm Fireworks

*PRIZM: .5X TO 1.2X BASIC INSERTS
F1 Tom Brady 2.50 6.00
F2 DeMarco Murray .75 2.00
F3 Andrew Luck 1.25 3.00
F4 LeSean McCoy 1.00 2.50
F5 Peyton Manning 2.00 5.00
F6 Antonio Brown 1.00 2.50
F7 Russell Wilson 1.25 3.00
F8 Julio Jones 1.00 2.50
F9 Cam Newton 1.00 2.50
F10 Jamaal Charles .75 2.00
F11 Marshawn Lynch .75 2.00
F12 Aaron Rodgers 2.00 5.00
F13 Odell Beckham Jr. 1.00 2.50
F14 T.Y. Hilton .75 2.00
F15 Dez Bryant 1.00 2.50

2015 Panini Prizm Hall of Fame

*PRIZM: .5X TO 1.2X BASIC INSERTS
HOFWP Walter Payton 3.00 8.00
HOFBS Barry Sanders 2.50 6.00
HOFDM Dan Marino 3.00 8.00
HOFES Emmitt Smith 2.50 6.00
HOFFH Franco Harris 1.50 4.00
HOFJE John Elway 2.50 6.00
HOFJK Jim Kelly 1.50 4.00
HOFJM Joe Montana 4.00 10.00
HOFJN Joe Namath 2.00 5.00
HOFJR Jerry Rice 2.50 6.00

2015 Panini Prizm Helmets

*PRIZM: .5X TO 1.2X BASIC INSERTS
1 Tom Brady 2.50 6.00
2 Russell Wilson 1.25 3.00
3 Peyton Manning 2.00 5.00
4 Odell Beckham Jr. 1.00 2.50
5 DeMarco Murray .75 2.00
6 Aaron Rodgers 2.00 5.00
7 Dez Bryant 1.00 2.50
8 Andrew Luck 1.25 3.00
9 Colin Kaepernick .75 2.00
10 Ben Roethlisberger 1.00 2.50
11 Jameis Winston 1.00 2.50
12 Marcus Mariota 1.50 4.00
13 Amari Cooper 1.25 3.00
14 Kevin White .50 1.25
15 DeVante Parker .60 1.50
16 Matt Jones .40 1.00
17 Melvin Gordon 1.00 2.50
18 Todd Gurley 1.50 4.00
19 Bryce Petty .40 1.00
20 Maxx Williams .40 1.00

2015 Panini Prizm Intros

*PRIZM: .5X TO 1.2X BASIC INSERTS
1 J.J. Watt 1.00 2.50
2 Cam Newton 1.00 2.50
3 Richard Sherman 1.00 2.50
4 Terrell Suggs .60 1.50
5 Tom Brady 2.50 6.00
6 Calvin Johnson 1.00 2.50
7 Larry Fitzgerald .75 2.00
8 Ben Roethlisberger 1.00 2.50
9 DeSean Jackson .75 2.00
10 Peyton Manning 2.00 5.00
11 Aaron Rodgers 2.00 5.00
12 Teddy Bridgewater .75 2.00
13 Andrew Luck 1.25 3.00
14 Cameron Wake .60 1.50
15 Dez Bryant 1.00 2.50

2015 Panini Prizm Patented Penmanship

2 Eli Manning/25 25.00 50.00
3 Dez Bryant/25
4 Andrew Luck/25
8 Philip Rivers/25 20.00 40.00
15 Franco Harris/25

2015 Panini Prizm Prizm Pairs Jersey Autographs

1 J.Winston/M.Mariota/25 100.00 200.00
2 M.Gordon/T.Gurley/99 25.00 60.00
3 A.Cooper/T.Yeldon/25 60.00 120.00
4 J.Langford/K.White/49 10.00 25.00
5 J.Hardy/T.Coleman/149 6.00 15.00
6 B.Petty/D.Smith/199 5.00 12.00
7 D.Cobb/D.GrnBckhm/199
8 J.Crowder/M.Jones/199 6.00 15.00
9 D.Johnson/V.Mayle/99 10.00 25.00
10 B.Hundley/T.Montgomery/149 5.00 12.00
11 D.Parker/J.Ajayi/149 12.00 30.00
12 G.Grayson/S.Mannion/25 10.00 25.00
13 A.Abdullah/M.Davis/149 8.00 20.00
14 D.Funchess/P.Dorsett/199 8.00 20.00
15 R.Greene/S.Diggs/199
16 C.Conley/S.Coates/199 6.00 15.00
17 B.Allen/N.Agholor/99
18 J.Strong/T.Lockett/149 10.00 25.00
19 B.Perriman/M.Williams/149
20 D.Smith/L.Williams/199

2015 Panini Prizm Prizm Pairs Jersey Autographs Prizms Gold

*GOLD/25: .8X TO 2X BASIC JSY AU/149-199
*GOLD/25: .6X TO 1.5X BASIC JSY AU/99
*GOLD/25: .5X TO 1.2X BASIC JSY AU/49

2015 Panini Prizm Prizm Signatures

1 Eddie Lacy/25 25.00 50.00
2 Andy Dalton/25 6.00 15.00
4 C.J. Anderson/99 4.00 10.00
5 Derek Carr/50 20.00 40.00
6 Mike Evans/25 6.00 15.00
7 Jamaal Charles/25 6.00 15.00
8 Nick Foles/25 6.00 15.00
9 Joseph Randle/50 4.00 10.00
10 Joique Bell/50 4.00 10.00
11 Luke Kuechly/25 20.00 40.00
13 Antonio Brown/25 20.00 40.00
14 Teddy Bridgewater/25 15.00 30.00
15 Patrick Peterson/50 4.00 10.00
20 Ryan Tannehill/25 6.00 15.00

2015 Panini Prizm Rookie Revolution

*PRIZM: .5X TO 1.2X BASIC INSERTS
1 Jameis Winston 1.00 2.50
2 Marcus Mariota 1.50 4.00
3 Amari Cooper 1.25 3.00
4 Kevin White .50 1.25
5 Nelson Agholor .50 1.25
6 DeVante Parker .60 1.50
7 Melvin Gordon 1.00 2.50
8 Todd Gurley 1.50 4.00
9 Phillip Dorsett .40 1.00
10 Breshad Perriman .40 1.00
11 Tevin Coleman .50 1.25
12 Ty Montgomery .40 1.00
13 Devin Smith .40 1.00
14 Ameer Abdullah .60 1.50
15 T.J. Yeldon .40 1.00

2015 Panini Prizm Rookie Autographs

RSAA Ameer Abdullah 3.00 8.00
RSAC Amari Cooper 12.00 30.00
RSAG Antwan Goodley 2.00 5.00
RSAR Arik Armstead 2.00 5.00
RSBA Buck Allen 2.50 6.00
RSBB Blake Bell 3.00 8.00
RSBD Bud Dupree 2.50 6.00
RSBH Brett Hundley 2.00 5.00
RSBJ Byron Jones 3.00 8.00
RSBK Ben Koyack 3.00 8.00
RSBM Benardrick McKinney 2.00 5.00
RSBP1 Breshad Perriman 2.00 5.00
RSBP2 Bryce Petty 2.00 5.00
RSBR Bryan Bennett 2.00 5.00
RSCAP Cameron Artis-Payne 2.00 5.00
RSCC Chris Conley 2.00 5.00
RSCD Carl Davis 2.50 6.00
RSCW Clive Walford 2.00 5.00
RSDA Dres Anderson 2.00 5.00
RSDC David Cobb 2.00 5.00
RSDD DaVaris Daniels 2.00 5.00
RSDF Devin Funchess 3.00 8.00
RSDFJ Dante Fowler Jr. 3.00 8.00
RSDG Deontay Greenberry 2.00 5.00
RSDGR Dorial Green-Beckham [illegible]
RSDH Danielle Hunter 2.00 5.00
RSDJ David Johnson 10.00 25.00
RSDL Dezmin Lewis 2.00 5.00
RSDP DeVante Parker 3.00 8.00
RSDPY Denzel Perryman 2.00 5.00
RSDS Devin Smith 2.00 5.00
RSDS Danny Shelton 2.00 5.00
RSDU Duke Johnson 3.00 8.00
RSDW1 Darren Waller 2.50 6.00
RSDW2 DeAndrew White 3.00 8.00
RSEG Eddie Goldman 2.00 5.00
RSEH Eli Harold 2.00 5.00
RSEK Eric Kendricks 2.00 5.00
RSER Eric Rowe 2.00 5.00
RSGG Garrett Grayson 2.00 5.00
RSJA Jay Ajayi 3.00 8.00
RSJC Jalen Collins 2.00 5.00
RSJCR Jamison Crowder 2.50 6.00
RSJE Jesse James 2.50 6.00
RSJH1 Josh Harper 2.00 5.00
RSJH2 Justin Hardy 2.00 5.00
RSJJ J.J. Nelson 2.00 5.00
RSJL Jeremy Langford 8.00 20.00
RSJR Josh Robinson 2.00 5.00
RSJS Josh Shaw 3.00 8.00
RSJS Jaelen Strong 2.50 6.00
RSJW Jameis Winston 60.00 100.00
RSKA Kwon Alexander 2.50 6.00
RSKB Kenny Bell 3.00 8.00
RSKJ Kevin Johnson 2.00 5.00
RSKW Karlos Williams
RSKWH Kevin White 2.50 6.00
RSLC Landon Collins 2.50 6.00
RSMA1 Marcus Murphy 2.00 5.00
RSMA2 Mario Alford 2.00 5.00
RSMB Malcolm Brown 2.50 6.00
RSMD Mike Davis 2.00 5.00
RSME Mario Edwards Jr. 2.00 5.00
RSMG Melvin Gordon 5.00 12.00
RSMJ Matt Jones 6.00 15.00
RSMM Marcus Mariota 30.00 60.00
RSMP Marcus Peters 3.00 8.00
RSMW Maxx Williams 2.00 5.00
RSNA Nelson Agholor 2.50 6.00
RSNO Nick O'Leary 2.00 5.00
RSOO Owamagbe Odighizuwa 2.50 6.00
RSPA Paul Dawson 2.50 6.00
RSPD Phillip Dorsett 2.00 5.00
RSPJ P.J. Williams 2.50 6.00
RSRA Randy Gregory
RSRD Ronald Darby 2.00 5.00
RSRG Rashad Greene 2.00 5.00
RSRH Rannell Hall 2.00 5.00
RSSA Stephone Anthony 2.00 5.00
RSSC Shane Carden 2.00 5.00
RSSC Sammie Coates 2.50 6.00
RSSD Stefon Diggs 5.00 12.00
RSSM Sean Mannion 2.00 5.00
RSSR Shane Ray 2.00 5.00
RSST Shaq Thompson 2.50 6.00
RSTC Tevin Coleman 2.50 6.00
RSTD Titus Davis 2.50 6.00
RSTF Trey Flowers 3.00 8.00
RSTG Todd Gurley 25.00 50.00
RSTH Taylor Heinicke 3.00 8.00
RSTJ T.J. Yeldon 2.00 5.00
RSTL Tyler Lockett 3.00 8.00
RSTM Tre McBride 2.00 5.00
RSTO Tony Lippett 2.00 5.00
RSTR Trey Williams 2.50 6.00
RSTW Trae Waynes
RSTY Ty Montgomery 2.00 5.00
RSVBJ Vic Beasley Jr.
RSVM Vince Mayle 2.50 6.00

2015 Panini Prizm Rookie Autographs Prizms

*PRIZM/125-350: .5X TO 1.2X BASIC AU
*PRIZM/75-100: .6X TO 1.5X BASIC AU
*PRIZM/35-60: .8X TO 2X BASIC AU
*PRIZM/25: 1X TO 2.5X BASIC AU
RSJW Jameis Winston/99 50.00 100.00

2015 Panini Prizm Rookie Autographs Prizms Blue

*BLUE/125-199: .5X TO 1.2X BASIC AU
*BLUE/75-100: .6X TO 1.5X BASIC AU
*BLUE/30-50: .8X TO 2X BASIC AU
*BLUE/25: 1X TO 2.5X BASIC AU
*BLUE/15: 1.2X TO 3X BASIC AU
RSJW Jameis Winston/99 50.00 100.00

2015 Panini Prizm Rookie Autographs Prizms Green

*GREEN/75-99: .6X TO 1.5X BASIC AU
*GREEN/30-60: .8X TO 2X BASIC AU
*GREEN/25: 1X TO 2.5X BASIC AU
*GREEN/15: 1.2X TO 3X BASIC AU

2015 Panini Prizm Rookie Autographs Prizms Green Cracked Ice

*GRN CRACKED/75: .6X TO 1.5X BASIC AU
*GRN CRACKED/35-60: .8X TO 2X BASIC AU
*GRN CRACKED/25: 1X TO 2.5X BASIC AU

2015 Panini Prizm Rookie Autographs Prizms Light Blue Wave

*BLUE WAVE/125-150: .5X TO 1.2X BASIC AU
*BLUE WAVE/75-100: .6X TO 1.5X BASIC AU
*BLUE WAVE/45-60: .8X TO 2X BASIC AU
*BLUE WAVE/25: 1X TO 2.5X BASIC AU
*BLUE WAVE: 1.2X TO 3X BASIC AU

2015 Panini Prizm Rookie Autographs Prizms Red

*RED/125-299: .5X TO 1.2X BASIC AU
*RED/75-100: .6X TO 1.5X BASIC AU
*RED/35-50: .8X TO 2X BASIC AU
*RED/25: 1X TO 2.5X BASIC AU
*RED/15: 1.2X TO 3X BASIC AU

2015 Panini Prizm Rookie Autographs Prizms Red Power

*RED POW/75-99: .6X TO 1.5X BASIC AU
*RED POW/40-60: .8X TO 2X BASIC AU
*RED POW/25: 1X TO 2.5X BASIC AU
*RED POW/15: 1.2X TO 3X BASIC AU
RSJW Jameis Winston/40 50.00 100.00

2015 Panini Prizm Rookie Autographs Prizms Tie Dyed

*TIE DYE/25: 1X TO 2.5X BASIC AU
RSAC Amari Cooper 40.00 100.00

2015 Panini Prizm Rookie Autographs Prizms Violet

*VIOLET: .5X TO 1.2X BASIC AU

2015 Panini Prizm Rookie Autographs Prizms Violet Mosaic

*VIOLET MOS/30-50: .8X TO 2X BASIC AU
*VIOLET MOS/25: 1X TO 2.5X BASIC AU

2015 Panini Prizm Cyber Monday

STATED PRINT RUN 500 SER.#'d SETS
*PRIZMS/25: 1.2X TO 3X BASIC
8 Jameis Winston 2.00 5.00
9 Marcus Mariota 3.00 8.00
10 Todd Gurley 2.50 6.00
11 Melvin Gordon 1.50 4.00
12 Amari Cooper 2.00 5.00

2016 Panini Prizm

1 Julio Jones .30 .75
2 Tom Brady .75 2.00
3 Mike Evans .25 .60
4 Chris Ivory .25 .60
5 Thomas Rawls .20 .50
6 Travis Kelce .30 .75
7 Andre Williams .20 .50
8 Joe Flacco .25 .60
9 Eddie Royal .20 .50
10 Antonio Brown .30 .75
11 Tevin Coleman .25 .60
12 LeGarrette Blount .25 .60
13 Vincent Jackson .20 .50
14 T.J. Yeldon .20 .50
15 Doug Baldwin .25 .60
16 Derek Carr .30 .75
17 Odell Beckham Jr. .30 .75
18 Justin Forsett .25 .60
19 Zach Miller .20 .50
20 Markus Wheaton .20 .50
21 Devonta Freeman .25 .60
22 Dion Lewis .20 .50
23 Austin Seferian-Jenkins .20 .50
24 Allen Robinson .25 .60
25 Tyler Lockett .25 .60
26 Latavius Murray .20 .50
27 Victor Cruz .25 .60
28 Buck Allen .20 .50
29 Matthew Stafford .25 .60
30 Darrius Heyward-Bey .20 .50
31 Mohamed Sanu .20 .50
32 Danny Amendola .25 .60
33 Carson Palmer .25 .60
34 Allen Hurns .20 .50
35 Jermaine Kearse .20 .50
36 Marcel Reece .20 .50
37 Larry Donnell .20 .50
38 Steve Smith Sr. .25 .60
39 Ameer Abdullah .20 .50
40 Brock Osweiler .20 .50
41 Jacob Tamme .20 .50
42 Julian Edelman .30 .75
43 David Johnson .30 .75
44 Julius Thomas .20 .50
45 Jimmy Graham .30 .75
46 Michael Crabtree .20 .50
47 Sam Bradford .20 .50
48 Kamar Aiken .20 .50
49 Golden Tate III .20 .50
50 Lamar Miller .20 .50
51 Cam Newton .30 .75
52 Rob Gronkowski .30 .75
53 Chris Johnson .20 .50
54 Marcus Mariota .30 .75
55 Darrelle Revis .20 .50
56 Amari Cooper .30 .75
57 Ryan Mathews .25 .60
58 Mike Wallace .20 .50
59 Marvin Jones Jr. .20 .50
60 Alfred Blue .20 .50
61 Jonathan Stewart .20 .50
62 Martellus Bennett .20 .50
63 Larry Fitzgerald .25 .60
64 DeMarco Murray .25 .60
65 Josh Norman .20 .50
66 Philip Rivers .30 .75
67 Darren Sproles .25 .60
68 Andy Dalton .25 .60
69 Brandon Pettigrew .20 .50
70 DeAndre Hopkins .25 .60
71 Devin Funchess .20 .50
72 Ryan Fitzpatrick .20 .50
73 Michael Floyd .20 .50
74 Harry Douglas .20 .50
75 J.J. Watt .30 .75
76 Danny Woodhead .25 .60
77 Jordan Matthews .25 .60
78 Jeremy Hill .20 .50
79 Eric Ebron .20 .50
80 Jaelen Strong .20 .50
81 Kelvin Benjamin .25 .60
82 Matt Forte .20 .50
83 John Brown .25 .60
84 Kendall Wright .20 .50
85 Clay Matthews .30 .75
86 Melvin Gordon .25 .60
87 Nelson Agholor .20 .50
88 Giovani Bernard .20 .50
89 Aaron Rodgers .60 1.50
90 Tyrod Taylor .25 .60
91 Ted Ginn Jr. .20 .50
92 Bilal Powell .20 .50
93 Todd Gurley .30 .75
94 Delanie Walker .20 .50
95 Richard Sherman .30 .75
96 Travis Benjamin .20 .50
97 Brent Celek .20 .50
98 A.J. Green .30 .75
99 Eddie Lacy .20 .50
100 LeSean McCoy .30 .75
101 Greg Olsen .25 .60
102 Brandon Marshall .20 .50
103 Kenny Britt .20 .50
104 Mark Sanchez .20 .50
105 Steve Young .40 1.00
106 Keenan Allen .25 .60
107 Kirk Cousins .30 .75
108 Boomer Esiason .25 .60
109 Jordy Nelson .25 .60
110 Karlos Williams .20 .50
111 Drew Brees .30 .75
112 Eric Decker .20 .50
113 Tavon Austin .20 .50
114 C.J. Anderson .25 .60
115 Brett Favre .60 1.50
116 Antonio Gates .20 .50
117 Matt Jones .25 .60
118 Tyler Eifert .25 .60
119 Randall Cobb .25 .60
120 Sammy Watkins .30 .75
121 Mark Ingram .25 .60
122 Jace Amaro .20 .50
123 Brian Quick .20 .50
124 Ronnie Hillman .20 .50
125 Peyton Manning .60 1.50
126 Tony Romo .25 .60
127 Pierre Garcon .25 .60
128 Robert Griffin III .20 .50
129 Davante Adams .20 .50
130 Robert Woods .25 .60
131 C.J. Spiller .20 .50
132 Andrew Luck .40 1.00
133 Lance Kendricks .20 .50
134 Demaryius Thomas .25 .60
135 Dan Marino .60 1.50
136 Darren McFadden .20 .50
137 DeSean Jackson .25 .60
138 Isaiah Crowell .20 .50
139 Richard Rodgers .25 .60
140 Charles Clay .20 .50
141 Brandin Cooks .25 .60
142 Frank Gore .25 .60
143 Colin Kaepernick .25 .60
144 Emmanuel Sanders .30 .75
145 Michael Irvin .30 .75
146 Dez Bryant .30 .75
147 Jamison Crowder .20 .50
148 Duke Johnson .20 .50
149 Teddy Bridgewater .25 .60
150 Ryan Tannehill .25 .60
151 Willie Snead .25 .60
152 Donte Moncrief .25 .60
153 Carlos Hyde .20 .50
154 Virgil Green .20 .50
155 Joe Namath .40 1.00
156 Terrance Williams .20 .50
157 Jordan Reed .20 .50
158 Brian Hartline .20 .50
159 Adrian Peterson .30 .75
160 Jay Ajayi .25 .60
161 Coby Fleener .20 .50
162 T.Y. Hilton .25 .60
163 Quinton Patton .20 .50
164 Alex Smith .25 .60
165 Barry Sanders .50 1.25
166 Cole Beasley .30 .75
167 Jay Cutler .20 .50
168 Gary Barnidge .20 .50
169 Stefon Diggs .25 .60
170 DeVante Parker .25 .60
171 Jameis Winston .30 .75
172 Phillip Dorsett .20 .50
173 Torrey Smith .20 .50
174 Jamaal Charles .25 .60
175 Troy Aikman .40 1.00
176 Jason Witten .25 .60
177 Jeremy Langford .25 .60
178 Ben Roethlisberger .30 .75
179 Jarius Wright .20 .50
180 Kenny Stills .20 .50
181 Doug Martin .25 .60
182 Dwayne Allen .20 .50
183 Vance McDonald .20 .50
184 Charcandrick West .20 .50
185 Emmitt Smith .50 1.25
186 Eli Manning .25 .60
187 Kevin White .20 .50
188 Le'Veon Bell .25 .60
189 Kyle Rudolph .20 .50
190 Jarvis Landry .25 .60
191 Charles Sims .20 .50
192 Blake Bortles .20 .50
193 Russell Wilson .40 1.00
194 Jeremy Maclin .20 .50
195 Marvin Harrison .25 .60
196 Rashad Jennings .20 .50
197 Alshon Jeffery .25 .60
198 DeAngelo Williams .20 .50
199 Matt Ryan .25 .60
200 Jordan Cameron .20 .50
201 Demarcus Ayers RC .40 1.00
202 Alex Collins RC .50 1.25
203 DeForest Buckner RC .40 1.00
204 Kenyan Drake RC .60 1.50
205 Artie Burns RC .50 1.25
206 Moritz Bohringer RC .40 1.00
207 Rashard Higgins RC .40 1.00
208 Jared Goff RC 2.50 6.00
209 Derek Watt RC .60 1.50
210 Daniel Braverman RC .40 1.00
211 Connor Cook RC .50 1.25
212 Jordan Howard RC 1.00 2.50
213 Ricardo Louis RC .40 1.00
214 Leonard Floyd RC .50 1.25
215 Kenny Clark RC .40 1.00
216 Jeff Driskel RC .40 1.00
217 Andy Janovich RC .50 1.25
218 Carson Wentz RC 4.00 10.00
219 Cody Core RC .40 1.00
220 Cardale Jones RC .40 1.00
221 Dwayne Washington RC .50 1.25
222 Pharoh Cooper RC .40 1.00
223 Eli Apple RC .50 1.25
224 Demarcus Robinson RC .40 1.00
225 Robert Nkemdiche RC .50 1.25
226 Austin Hooper RC .40 1.00
227 Temarrick Hemingway RC .40 1.00
228 Joey Bosa RC .75 2.00
229 Brandon Allen RC .40 1.00
230 Michael Thomas RC .75 2.00
231 Dak Prescott RC 2.00 5.00
232 Daniel Lasco RC .40 1.00
233 Vernon Hargreaves III RC .60 1.50
234 Jonathan Williams RC .50 1.25
235 Vernon Butler RC .40 1.00
236 Nick Vannett RC .40 1.00
237 Jerell Adams RC .40 1.00
238 Ezekiel Elliott RC 2.00 5.00
239 Mike Thomas RC .60 1.50
240 Christian Hackenberg RC .40 1.00
241 Devin Fuller RC .50 1.25
242 Kenneth Dixon RC .40 1.00
243 Sheldon Rankins RC .50 1.25
244 Keenan Reynolds RC .50 1.25
245 Reggie Ragland RC .40 1.00
246 Tyler Higbee RC .40 1.00
247 Jakeem Grant RC .40 1.00
248 Corey Coleman RC .60 1.50
249 Kelvin Taylor RC .40 1.00
250 C.J. Prosise RC .40 1.00
251 Charone Peake RC .40 1.00
252 Devontae Booker RC .50 1.25
253 Karl Joseph RC .40 1.00
254 Kevin Hogan RC .50 1.25
255 Noah Spence RC .40 1.00
256 Seth DeValve RC .50 1.25
257 Nate Sudfeld RC .40 1.00
258 Aaron Burbridge RC .40 1.00
259 Josh Doctson RC .50 1.25
260 Paul Perkins RC .40 1.00
261 Keith Marshall RC .40 1.00
262 Hunter Henry RC .50 1.25
263 Keanu Neal RC .40 1.00
264 Trevor Davis RC .40 1.00
265 Emmanuel Ogbah RC .50 1.25
266 Tajae Sharpe RC .50 1.25
267 David Morgan RC .60 1.50
268 Will Fuller RC .60 1.50
269 Darius Jackson RC .50 1.25
270 Tyler Boyd RC .50 1.25
271 Kenny Lawler RC .60 1.50
272 Leonte Carroo RC .40 1.00
273 Shaq Lawson RC .40 1.00
274 Tyler Ervin RC .40 1.00
275 Kevin Dodd RC .40 1.00
276 DeAndre Washington RC .40 1.00
277 Jake Rudock RC .40 1.00
278 Laquon Treadwell RC .50 1.25
279 Rico Gathers RC .40 1.00
280 Braxton Miller RC .40 1.00
281 Charles Tapper RC .50 1.25
282 Chris Moore RC .50 1.25
283 Darron Lee RC .40 1.00
284 Malcolm Mitchell RC .40 1.00
285 Jaylon Smith RC .40 1.00
286 Jordan Payton RC .40 1.00
287 Kolby Listenbee RC .40 1.00
288 Paxton Lynch RC .40 1.00
289 Brandon Doughty RC .40 1.00
290 Cody Kessler RC .40 1.00
291 Jalen Ramsey RC .60 1.50
292 Jacoby Brissett RC .50 1.25
293 William Jackson III RC .50 1.25
294 Wendell Smallwood RC .40 1.00
295 Myles Jack RC .50 1.25
296 Tyreek Hill RC 1.50 4.00
297 Dan Vitale RC .40 1.00
298 Derrick Henry RC 1.00 2.50
299 Devin Lucien RC .50 1.25
300 Sterling Shepard RC .50 1.25

2016 Panini Prizm Prizms

*VETS: 2X TO 5X BASIC CARDS

2016 Panini Prizm Prizms Blue Wave

*VETS/149: 4X TO 10X BASIC CARDS
*ROOK/149: 1.2X TO 3X BASIC CARDS

2016 Panini Prizm Prizms Camo

*VETS/25: 8X TO 20X BASIC CARDS
*ROOKIES/25: 2.5X TO 6X BASIC RC

2016 Panini Prizm Prizms Green

*VETS: 2.5X TO 6X BASIC CARDS
*ROOKIES: .75X TO 2X BASIC CARDS

2016 Panini Prizm Prizms Green Power

*VETS/49: 6X TO 15X BASIC CARDS
*ROOKIES/49: 2X TO 5X BASIC RC

2016 Panini Prizm Prizms Light Blue

*VETS/199: 4X TO 10X BASIC CARDS
*ROOK/199: 1.2X TO 3X BASIC CARDS

2016 Panini Prizm Prizms Orange
*VETS/299: 3X TO 8X BASIC CARDS
*ROOK/299: 1X TO 2.5X BASIC CARDS

2016 Panini Prizm Prizms Purple Scope
*VETS/99: 5X TO 12X BASIC CARDS
*ROOK/99: 1.5X TO 4X BASIC CARDS

2016 Panini Prizm Prizms Red Crystals
*VETS/75: 5X TO 12X BASIC CARDS
*ROOK/75: 1.5X TO 4X BASIC CARDS

2016 Panini Prizm Prizms Red White and Blue
*VETS: 2X TO 5X BASIC CARDS
*ROOKIES: .8X TO 2X BASIC CARDS

2016 Panini Prizm Dazzle Prizms
1 Cam Newton 5.00 12.00
2 Dez Bryant 5.00 12.00
3 Todd Gurley 5.00 12.00
4 Russell Wilson 6.00 15.00
5 Odell Beckham Jr. 5.00 12.00
6 Aaron Rodgers 10.00 25.00
7 Brandon Marshall 3.00 8.00
8 Andrew Luck 6.00 15.00
9 Adrian Peterson 5.00 12.00
10 Richard Sherman 5.00 12.00
11 Matt Ryan 4.00 10.00
12 Tony Romo 4.00 10.00
13 Marcus Mariota 5.00 12.00
14 Ben Roethlisberger 5.00 12.00
15 Philip Rivers 5.00 12.00
16 Tom Brady 20.00 50.00
17 Eddie Lacy 3.00 8.00
18 Antonio Brown 5.00 12.00
19 Larry Fitzgerald 4.00 10.00
20 Julio Jones 5.00 12.00
21 Joe Flacco 4.00 10.00
22 Darrelle Revis 3.00 8.00
23 Jameis Winston 5.00 12.00
24 Drew Brees 5.00 12.00
25 Clay Matthews 5.00 12.00
26 J.J. Watt 5.00 12.00
27 Amari Cooper 5.00 12.00
28 Rob Gronkowski 5.00 12.00

2016 Panini Prizm Decade of Dominance Prizms
*GREEN: .6X TO 1.5X BASIC INSERTS
1 Roger Staubach 2.00 5.00
2 Dan Marino 3.00 8.00
3 Steve Young 2.00 5.00
4 Troy Aikman 2.00 5.00
5 Terry Bradshaw 2.00 5.00
6 Eric Dickerson 1.25 3.00
7 Emmitt Smith 2.50 6.00
8 Franco Harris 1.50 4.00
9 Peyton Manning 3.00 8.00
10 Barry Sanders 2.50 6.00
11 Tony Dorsett 1.50 4.00
12 Marvin Harrison 1.25 3.00
13 Tom Brady 4.00 10.00
14 Jerry Rice 2.50 6.00
15 Brett Favre 3.00 8.00

2016 Panini Prizm Illumination Prizms
*GREEN: .6X TO 1.5X BASIC INSERTS
1 Cam Newton 1.50 4.00
2 Russell Wilson 2.00 5.00
3 Tom Brady 4.00 10.00
4 Drew Brees 1.50 4.00
5 Eli Manning 1.25 3.00
6 Aaron Rodgers 3.00 8.00
7 Adrian Peterson 1.50 4.00
8 Odell Beckham Jr. 1.50 4.00
9 Antonio Brown 1.50 4.00
10 Julio Jones 1.50 4.00

2016 Panini Prizm Patented Penmanship Prizms
1 Fred Biletnikoff/25 15.00 40.00
3 Teddy Bridgewater/25 12.00 30.00
9 Blake Bortles/25 10.00 25.00
11 Lawrence Taylor/25 15.00 40.00
13 Tim Brown/25 15.00 40.00
19 Jay Cutler/25 10.00 25.00
21 Richard Sherman/25 15.00 40.00
23 Jack Ham/25 12.00 30.00
29 Curtis Martin/25 12.00 30.00
31 Earl Campbell/25 15.00 40.00
37 Kurt Warner/25 25.00 50.00

2016 Panini Prizm Prizm Pairs Jersey Autographs
PPAC A.Collins/C.Prosise 6.00 15.00
PPAJ A.Collins/J.Williams 6.00 15.00
PPBE B.Miller/E.Elliott 75.00 150.00
PPBL B.Miller/L.Carroo 5.00 12.00
PPCK C.Moore/K.Reynolds 6.00 15.00
PPCR C.Coleman/R.Louis 8.00 20.00
PPCW C.Prosise/W.Fuller 8.00 20.00
PPDD D.Prescott/D.Booker 50.00 100.00
PPDK D.Henry/K.Drake 12.00 30.00
PPEJ E.Elliott/J.Bosa 75.00 150.00
PPHJ H.Henry/J.Bosa 10.00 25.00
PPJC C.Wentz/J.Goff 50.00 125.00
PPJL J.Doctson/L.Treadwell 6.00 15.00
PPKD K.Dixon/D.Prescott 50.00 100.00
PPKK K.Dixon/K.Reynolds 6.00 15.00
PPKL K.Drake/L.Carroo 8.00 20.00
PPKT K.Hogan/T.Davis 6.00 15.00
PPSP P.Perkins/S.Shepard 6.00 15.00
PPWB B.Miller/W.Fuller 8.00 20.00
PPWJ W.Fuller/J.Doctson 8.00 20.00

2016 Panini Prizm Prizm Premier Jerseys
*PINK: .5X TO 1.2X BASIC JSY
*PRIME/49: .6X TO 1.5X BASIC JSY
1 Jared Goff 5.00 12.00
2 Carson Wentz 10.00 25.00
3 Joey Bosa 3.00 8.00
4 Ezekiel Elliott 8.00 20.00
5 Corey Coleman 2.50 6.00
6 Josh Doctson 2.00 5.00
7 Will Fuller 2.50 6.00
8 Laquon Treadwell 2.00 5.00
9 Paxton Lynch 1.50 4.00
10 Derrick Henry 4.00 10.00
11 Connor Cook 2.00 5.00
12 Cardale Jones 1.50 4.00
13 Michael Thomas 3.00 8.00
14 Christian Hackenberg 1.50 4.00
15 C.J. Prosise 1.50 4.00
16 Paul Perkins 1.50 4.00
17 Tyler Boyd 2.00 5.00
18 Braxton Miller 1.50 4.00
19 Cody Kessler 1.50 4.00
20 Sterling Shepard 2.00 5.00
21 Alex Collins 2.00 5.00
22 Jordan Howard 4.00 10.00
23 Pharoh Cooper 1.50 4.00
24 Dak Prescott 8.00 20.00
25 Kenneth Dixon 1.50 4.00
26 Devontae Booker 2.00 5.00
27 Hunter Henry 2.00 5.00
28 Leonte Carroo 1.50 4.00
29 Chris Moore 2.00 5.00
30 DeAndre Washington 1.50 4.00
31 Kenyan Drake 2.50 6.00
32 Ricardo Louis 1.50 4.00
33 Demarcus Robinson 1.50 4.00
34 Jonathan Williams 2.00 5.00
35 Keenan Reynolds 2.00 5.00
36 Kevin Hogan 2.00 5.00
37 Trevor Davis 1.50 4.00
38 Tyler Ervin 1.50 4.00
39 Wendell Smallwood 1.50 4.00
40 Moritz Bohringer 1.50 4.00

2016 Panini Prizm Razzle Prizms
1 Cam Newton 5.00 12.00
2 Dez Bryant 5.00 12.00
3 Todd Gurley 5.00 12.00
4 Russell Wilson 6.00 15.00
5 Odell Beckham Jr. 5.00 12.00
6 Aaron Rodgers 10.00 25.00
7 Brandon Marshall 3.00 8.00
8 Andrew Luck 6.00 15.00
9 Adrian Peterson 5.00 12.00
10 Richard Sherman 5.00 12.00
11 Matt Ryan 4.00 10.00
12 Tony Romo 4.00 10.00
13 Marcus Mariota 5.00 12.00
14 Ben Roethlisberger 5.00 12.00
15 Philip Rivers 5.00 12.00
16 Tom Brady 25.00 50.00
17 Eddie Lacy 3.00 8.00
18 Antonio Brown 5.00 12.00
19 Larry Fitzgerald 4.00 10.00
20 Julio Jones 5.00 12.00
21 Joe Flacco 4.00 10.00
22 Darrelle Revis 3.00 8.00
23 Jameis Winston 5.00 12.00
24 Drew Brees 5.00 12.00
25 Clay Matthews 5.00 12.00
26 J.J. Watt 5.00 12.00
27 Amari Cooper 5.00 12.00
28 Rob Gronkowski 5.00 12.00

2016 Panini Prizm Rookie Autographs Prizms Purple Scope
1 Jared Goff 100.00 200.00
2 Charone Peake 3.00 8.00
3 Derrick Henry 8.00 20.00
4 Seth DeValve 4.00 10.00
5 Cody Kessler EXCH 8.00 20.00
7 Kenneth Dixon 3.00 8.00
8 Cyrus Jones 3.00 8.00
10 Cody Core 3.00 8.00
11 Carson Wentz 60.00 125.00
12 Keith Marshall 3.00 8.00
13 Michael Thomas 6.00 15.00
14 Jordan Jenkins 5.00 12.00
15 Nick Vannett 3.00 8.00
18 Vonn Bell 4.00 10.00
20 Brandon Allen 3.00 8.00
21 Ezekiel Elliott EXCH 100.00 200.00
22 Kenny Lawler 5.00 12.00
23 Christian Hackenberg 3.00 8.00
24 Emmanuel Ogbah 4.00 10.00
25 Connor Cook 4.00 10.00
26 Jihad Ward 3.00 8.00
27 Devontae Booker 4.00 10.00
28 Adam Gotsis 3.00 8.00
29 Trevor Davis 3.00 8.00
30 Jeff Driskel 3.00 8.00
31 Corey Coleman 5.00 12.00
32 Jalen Ramsey 5.00 12.00
33 Tyler Boyd 4.00 10.00
34 Kevin Dodd 3.00 8.00
35 Chris Moore 4.00 10.00
36 A'Shawn Robinson 3.00 8.00
37 Cardale Jones 3.00 8.00
40 Kelvin Taylor 3.00 8.00
41 Will Fuller 5.00 12.00
42 Kevon Seymour 3.00 8.00
43 Kenyan Drake 5.00 12.00
44 Jaylon Smith 3.00 8.00
45 Tyler Higbee 3.00 8.00
46 Jarran Reed 3.00 8.00
47 Tajae Sharpe 4.00 10.00
48 Maliek Collins 3.00 8.00
49 Rashard Higgins 3.00 8.00
50 Aaron Burbridge 3.00 8.00
51 Josh Doctson 4.00 10.00
52 Eli Apple 4.00 10.00
53 Austin Hooper 3.00 8.00
54 Myles Jack 4.00 10.00
55 Malcolm Mitchell 3.00 8.00
57 DeAndre Washington 3.00 8.00
59 Moritz Bohringer 3.00 8.00
60 Brandon Doughty 3.00 8.00
61 Laquon Treadwell 4.00 10.00
62 Vernon Hargreaves III 5.00 12.00
63 Braxton Miller 3.00 8.00
64 Chris Jones 5.00 12.00
65 Ricardo Louis 3.00 8.00
66 Su'a Cravens 3.00 8.00
67 Paul Perkins 3.00 8.00
68 Bronson Kaufusi 3.00 8.00
69 Keenan Reynolds 4.00 10.00
70 Demarcus Ayers 3.00 8.00
71 Paxton Lynch 25.00 60.00
72 Keanu Neal 3.00 8.00
73 Leonte Carroo 3.00 8.00
74 Xavien Howard 4.00 10.00
75 Pharoh Cooper 3.00 8.00
76 Mackensie Alexander 3.00 8.00
77 Jordan Howard
78 Darian Thompson 3.00 8.00
79 Jerell Adams 3.00 8.00
80 Daniel Braverman 3.00 8.00
81 Hunter Henry 4.00 10.00
82 Jayron Kearse 3.00 8.00
83 C.J. Prosise 3.00 8.00
84 D.J. Foster 4.00 10.00
85 Tyler Ervin 3.00 8.00
86 T.J. Green 5.00 12.00
87 Wendell Smallwood 3.00 8.00
88 Jonathan Bullard 3.00 8.00
89 Nate Sudfeld 3.00 8.00
90 Thomas Duarte 3.00 8.00
91 Sterling Shepard 10.00 25.00
92 Yannick Ngakoue 5.00 12.00
93 Jacoby Brissett 4.00 10.00
94 Reggie Ragland 3.00 8.00
95 Demarcus Robinson 3.00 8.00
96 Artie Burns 10.00 25.00
97 Jordan Payton 3.00 8.00
98 Joey Bosa 6.00 15.00
99 William Jackson III 4.00 10.00
100 Kevin Byard 3.00 8.00

2016 Panini Prizm Rookie Autographs Prizms
*BASE AU: .25X TO .6X PURPLE AU/99
11 Carson Wentz 60.00 125.00
17 Dak Prescott 40.00 80.00
21 Ezekiel Elliott EXCH 75.00 150.00

2016 Panini Prizm Rookie Autographs Prizms Blue Wave
*BLUE WAVE/149: .3X TO .8X PURPLE AU/99
11 Carson Wentz 75.00 150.00
21 Ezekiel Elliott EXCH 100.00 200.00

2016 Panini Prizm Rookie Autographs Prizms Camo
*CAMO/25: .6X TO 1.5X PURPLE AU/99
1 Jared Goff 150.00 300.00
11 Carson Wentz 150.00 250.00
21 Ezekiel Elliott EXCH 150.00 300.00

2016 Panini Prizm Rookie Autographs Prizms Green Power
*GRN POWER/49: .5X TO 1.2X PURPLE AU/99
11 Carson Wentz 75.00 150.00
21 Ezekiel Elliott EXCH 150.00 250.00

2016 Panini Prizm Rookie Autographs Prizms Red Crystals
*RED/75: .4X TO 1X PURPLE AU/99
11 Carson Wentz 60.00 125.00
21 Ezekiel Elliott EXCH 100.00 200.00

2016 Panini Prizm Rookie Introductions Prizms
1 Jared Goff 4.00 10.00
2 Carson Wentz 6.00 15.00
3 Joey Bosa 1.25 3.00
4 Ezekiel Elliott 10.00 25.00
5 Devontae Booker .75 2.00
6 Corey Coleman 1.00 2.50
7 Josh Doctson .75 2.00
8 Will Fuller 1.00 2.50
9 Laquon Treadwell .75 2.00
10 Paxton Lynch .60 1.50
11 Derrick Henry 1.50 4.00
12 Connor Cook .75 2.00
13 Cardale Jones .60 1.50
14 Michael Thomas 1.25 3.00
15 Christian Hackenberg .60 1.50
16 C.J. Prosise .60 1.50
17 Paul Perkins .60 1.50
18 Tyler Boyd .75 2.00
19 Braxton Miller .60 1.50
20 Sterling Shepard .75 2.00
21 Tyler Ervin .60 1.50
22 Dak Prescott 10.00 25.00
23 Pharoh Cooper .60 1.50
24 Kenyan Drake 1.00 2.50
25 Keenan Reynolds .75 2.00

2016 Panini Prizm Shining Stars Prizms
1 Blake Bortles 1.00 2.50
2 Philip Rivers 1.50 4.00
3 Tony Romo 1.25 3.00
4 Aaron Rodgers 3.00 8.00
5 A.J. Green 1.50 4.00
6 Julio Jones 1.50 4.00
7 Jameis Winston 1.50 4.00
8 Tom Brady 4.00 10.00
9 Todd Gurley 1.50 4.00
10 Drew Brees 1.50 4.00
11 Ryan Tannehill 1.25 3.00
12 Dez Bryant 1.50 4.00
13 Odell Beckham Jr. 1.50 4.00
14 Richard Sherman 1.50 4.00
15 Darrelle Revis 1.00 2.50
16 Matt Ryan 1.25 3.00
17 Cam Newton 1.50 4.00
18 Marcus Mariota 1.50 4.00
19 Antonio Brown 1.50 4.00
20 Ben Roethlisberger 1.50 4.00
21 Eli Manning 1.25 3.00
22 Doug Martin 1.25 3.00
23 Adrian Peterson 1.50 4.00
24 Derek Carr 1.50 4.00
25 J.J. Watt 1.50 4.00
26 Matthew Stafford 1.25 3.00
27 Russell Wilson 2.00 5.00
28 Amari Cooper 1.50 4.00
29 Carson Palmer 1.25 3.00
30 Rob Gronkowski 1.50 4.00

2017 Panini Prizm
1 Aaron Rodgers .60 1.50
2 Eric Ebron .20 .50
3 A.J. Green .30 .75
4 Kirk Cousins .30 .75
5 Odell Beckham Jr. .30 .75
6 Carlos Hyde .20 .50
7 Antonio Gates .20 .50
8 Matt Ryan .25 .60
9 Frank Gore .25 .60
10 Aaron Donald .30 .75
11 Larry Fitzgerald .25 .60
12 Ezekiel Elliott .40 1.00
13 Duke Johnson .20 .50
14 Cody Kessler .20 .50
15 Breshad Perriman .20 .50
16 Julius Thomas .20 .50
17 Emmanuel Sanders .30 .75
18 Derrick Henry .25 .60
19 Jimmy Graham .30 .75
20 Phillip Dorsett .20 .50
21 Terrelle Pryor Sr. .20 .50
22 LeGarrette Blount .25 .60
23 Jay Ajayi .25 .60
24 Tyrell Williams .20 .50
25 David Johnson .30 .75
26 Cole Beasley .30 .75
27 Zach Ertz .25 .60
28 T.J. Yeldon .20 .50
29 Adam Thielen .30 .75
30 Joey Bosa .30 .75
31 Eddie Lacy .20 .50
32 Willie Snead .25 .60
33 Tom Brady .75 2.00
34 Ty Montgomery .20 .50
35 DeVante Parker .25 .60
36 Vance McDonald .20 .50
37 DeMarco Murray .25 .60
38 Allen Hurns .20 .50
39 Gerald McCoy .20 .50
40 Michael Crabtree .20 .50
41 Matthew Stafford .25 .60
42 Devonta Freeman .25 .60
43 Tyrann Mathieu .25 .60
44 Keenan Allen .25 .60
45 Chandler Jones .20 .50
46 Charles Clay .20 .50
47 Torrey Smith .20 .50
48 Cam Newton .30 .75
49 Jadeveon Clowney .20 .50
50 Cameron Meredith .20 .50
51 Will Fuller V .20 .50
52 Luke Kuechly .25 .60
53 Brandin Cooks .25 .60
54 Tom Savage .20 .50
55 Rishard Matthews .20 .50
56 Kelvin Benjamin .25 .60
57 Marquise Goodwin .20 .50
58 Tevin Coleman .25 .60
59 Jared Goff .30 .75
60 Kenny Britt .20 .50
61 Adrian Peterson .30 .75
62 Julio Jones .30 .75
63 Laquon Treadwell .20 .50
64 Von Miller .25 .60
65 Marqise Lee .20 .50
66 Chris Hogan .20 .50
67 Dak Prescott .30 .75
68 Mike Evans .25 .60
69 Jason Witten .25 .60
70 Julian Edelman .30 .75
71 Terrance Williams .20 .50
72 Tavon Austin .20 .50
73 Greg Olsen .25 .60
74 Delanie Walker .20 .50
75 Bruce Ellington .20 .50
76 Alex Smith .25 .60
77 Davante Adams .25 .60
78 Jameis Winston .25 .60
79 Patrick Peterson .20 .50
80 Ben Roethlisberger .30 .75
81 Joe Flacco .25 .60
82 Jarvis Landry .25 .60
83 Philip Rivers .30 .75
84 Marshawn Lynch .25 .60
85 Jesse James .20 .50
86 Jalen Ramsey .20 .50
87 Stefon Diggs .25 .60
88 Carson Palmer .25 .60
89 Andy Dalton .25 .60
90 J.J. Watt .30 .75
91 Robby Anderson .20 .50
92 Brandon LaFell .20 .50
93 Jamison Crowder .20 .50
94 Lorenzo Alexander .20 .50
95 C.J. Mosley .25 .60
96 Kevin White .20 .50
97 Jordan Howard .30 .75
98 Jamaal Charles .25 .60
99 Isaiah Crowell .20 .50
100 Jonathan Stewart .20 .50
101 Doug Martin .25 .60
102 Jordan Matthews .20 .50
103 Julius Peppers .25 .60
104 Jordan Reed .20 .50
105 Tyreek Hill .30 .75
106 Todd Gurley II .30 .75
107 Darrius Heyward-Bey .20 .50
108 Pierre Garcon .25 .60
109 Andrew Luck .40 1.00
110 Robert Kelley .20 .50
111 C.J. Anderson .25 .60
112 Eric Decker .20 .50
113 Alshon Jeffery .25 .60
114 James Harrison .25 .60
115 Demaryius Thomas .25 .60
116 Rob Gronkowski .30 .75
117 Geno Atkins .20 .50
118 Paul Perkins .20 .50
119 LeSean McCoy .30 .75
120 Damon Harrison .20 .50
121 Danny Woodhead .25 .60
122 John Brown .25 .60
123 DeSean Jackson .25 .60
124 Jamie Collins .20 .50
125 Ameer Abdullah .20 .50
126 Dion Lewis .20 .50
127 Russell Wilson .40 1.00
128 Brian Orakpo .20 .50
129 Amari Cooper .30 .75
130 Carson Wentz .40 1.00
131 Randall Cobb .25 .60
132 Jared Cook .20 .50
133 Marcus Mariota .30 .75
134 Antonio Brown .30 .75
135 Dez Bryant .30 .75
136 Donte Moncrief .25 .60
137 Michael Thomas .30 .75
138 Josh Doctson .20 .50
139 Travis Kelce .30 .75
140 Tyrod Taylor .25 .60
141 Eric Berry .25 .60
142 Khalil Mack .30 .75
143 Zach Miller .20 .50
144 Ryan Tannehill .25 .60
145 Jeremy Hill .20 .50
146 Sam Bradford .20 .50
147 Spencer Ware .20 .50
148 Theo Riddick .20 .50
149 Melvin Gordon .25 .60
150 Eli Manning .25 .60
151 Jeremy Langford .25 .60
152 Jeremy Maclin .20 .50
153 Terrell Suggs .20 .50
154 Le'Veon Bell .25 .60
155 Blake Bortles .20 .50
156 Adam Vinatieri .20 .50
157 Richard Sherman .30 .75
158 Mike Wallace .20 .50
159 Sterling Shepard .25 .60
160 Mike Glennon .25 .60
161 Josh McCown .20 .50
162 Mark Ingram .25 .60
163 Darron Lee .20 .50
164 Brian Hoyer .20 .50
165 Justin Houston .20 .50
166 Ted Ginn Jr. .20 .50
167 Kenny Stills .20 .50
168 Sheldon Richardson .20 .50
169 T.Y. Hilton .25 .60
170 Kyle Rudolph .20 .50
171 Tyler Eifert .25 .60
172 Mark Barron .20 .50
173 Thomas Rawls .20 .50
174 Robert Woods .25 .60
175 DeAndre Hopkins .25 .60
176 Golden Tate III .20 .50
177 Marvin Jones Jr. .20 .50
178 Sammy Watkins .30 .75
179 Brandon Marshall .20 .50
180 Matt Forte .20 .50
181 Jordy Nelson .25 .60
182 Allen Robinson .25 .60
183 Derek Carr .30 .75
184 Trevor Siemian .20 .50
185 James White .25 .60
186 Charles Sims .20 .50
187 Doug Baldwin .25 .60
188 Martellus Bennett .20 .50
189 Mohamed Sanu .20 .50
190 Corey Coleman .20 .50
191 Taylor Gabriel .20 .50
192 Drew Brees .30 .75
193 Latavius Murray .20 .50
194 Paul Posluszny .20 .50
195 Quincy Enunwa .20 .50
196 Vic Beasley Jr. .20 .50
197 Bobby Wagner .20 .50
198 Kyle Williams .20 .50
199 Travis Benjamin .20 .50
200 Lamar Miller .20 .50
201 David Njoku RC .50 1.25
202 Malachi Dupre RC .40 1.00
203 Cooper Kupp RC .60 1.50
204 Malik Hooker RC .40 1.00
205 Jonnu Smith RC .40 1.00
206 Taco Charlton RC .40 1.00
207 Josh Malone RC .40 1.00
208 Jeremy McNichols RC .40 1.00
209 Mitchell Trubisky RC 2.00 5.00
210 De'Angelo Henderson RC .40 1.00
211 Zay Jones RC .50 1.25
212 Chris Carson RC .60 1.50
213 Taywan Taylor RC .40 1.00
214 Marlon Humphrey RC .40 1.00
215 C.J. Beathard RC .40 1.00
216 T.J. Watt RC 1.25 3.00
217 Donnel Pumphrey RC .50 1.25
218 Shelton Gibson RC .40 1.00
219 Leonard Fournette RC 1.25 3.00
220 Robert Davis RC .40 1.00
221 Curtis Samuel RC .50 1.25
222 Matthew Dayes RC .40 1.00
223 ArDarius Stewart RC .40 1.00
224 Jonathan Allen RC .50 1.25
225 James Conner RC .75 2.00
226 Reuben Foster RC .40 1.00
227 Ryan Switzer RC .50 1.25
228 Rodney Adams RC .40 1.00
229 Corey Davis RC .60 1.50
230 Brad Kaaya RC .40 1.00
231 Dalvin Cook RC 1.00 2.50
232 Chad Kelly RC .40 1.00
233 Carlos Henderson RC .40 1.00
234 Adoree' Jackson RC .50 1.25
235 Amara Darboh RC .40 1.00
236 Kevin King RC .50 1.25
237 Jamaal Williams RC .40 1.00
238 Nathan Peterman RC .50 1.25
239 Mike Williams RC .60 1.50
240 Stacy Coley RC .40 1.00
241 Gerald Everett RC .40 1.00
242 Myles Garrett RC 1.25 3.00
243 Chris Godwin RC .50 1.25
244 Jarrad Davis RC .50 1.25
245 Dede Westbrook RC .40 1.00
246 Malik McDowell RC .40 1.00
247 R. Joshua Dobbs RC .50 1.25
248 Isaiah McKenzie RC .40 1.00
249 Christian McCaffrey RC 1.00 2.50
250 David Moore RC .40 1.00
251 Adam Shaheen RC .40 1.00
252 Solomon Thomas RC .40 1.00
253 Kareem Hunt RC .75 2.00
254 Charles Harris RC .40 1.00
255 Samaje Perine RC .40 1.00
256 Budda Baker RC .40 1.00
257 Jehu Chesson RC .50 1.25
258 DeAngelo Yancey RC .40 1.00
259 John Ross III RC .50 1.25
260 Isaiah Ford RC .40 1.00
261 Joe Mixon RC .75 2.00
262 Jamal Adams RC .40 1.00
263 Davis Webb RC .40 1.00
264 Gareon Conley RC .40 1.00
265 Josh Reynolds RC .40 1.00
266 Marcus Maye RC .40 1.00
267 Wayne Gallman RC .50 1.25
268 Trent Taylor RC .50 1.25
269 Patrick Mahomes II RC 40.00 80.00
270 Devante Mays RC .40 1.00
271 DeShone Kizer RC .40 1.00
272 Marshon Lattimore RC .50 1.25
273 D'Onta Foreman RC .50 1.25
274 Jabrill Peppers RC .60 1.50
275 Mack Hollins RC .40 1.00
276 Sidney Jones RC .40 1.00
277 Chad Hansen RC .40 1.00
278 T.J. Logan RC .60 1.50
279 Deshaun Watson RC 2.50 6.00
280 Noah Brown RC .50 1.25
281 JuJu Smith-Schuster RC 1.00 2.50
282 Haason Reddick RC .40 1.00
283 Kenny Golladay RC .60 1.50
284 Takkarist McKinley RC .40 1.00
285 Tarik Cohen RC .75 2.00
286 Teez Tabor RC .50 1.25
287 Marlon Mack RC .60 1.50
288 Aaron Jones RC 1.00 2.50
289 O.J. Howard RC .50 1.25
290 Khalfani Muhammad RC .40 1.00
291 Alvin Kamara RC 1.50 4.00
292 Derek Barnett RC .50 1.25
293 Chad Williams RC .40 1.00
294 Tre'Davious White RC .40 1.00
295 Joe Williams RC .40 1.00
296 Raekwon McMillan RC .40 1.00
297 Brian Hill RC .40 1.00
298 Elijah McGuire RC .40 1.00
299 Evan Engram RC .50 1.25
300 Elijah Hood RC .40 1.00

2017 Panini Prizm Prizms
*VETS: 2X TO 5X BASIC CARDS

2017 Panini Prizm Prizms Blue
*VETS: 3X TO 8X BASIC CARDS
*ROOKIES: 1.5X TO 4X BASIC CARDS
269 Patrick Mahomes II 60.00 125.00

2017 Panini Prizm Prizms Blue Wave
*VETS/149: 4X TO 10X BASIC CARDS
*ROOK/149: 2X TO 5X BASIC CARDS
269 Patrick Mahomes II 125.00 250.00

2017 Panini Prizm Prizms Bronze Stars
*VETS: 2.5X TO 6X BASIC CARDS
*ROOKIES: 1.2X TO 3X BASIC CARDS
269 Patrick Mahomes II 75.00 150.00

2017 Panini Prizm Prizms Camo
*VETS/25: 8X TO 20X BASIC CARDS
*ROOK/25: 4X TO 10X BASIC CARDS
269 Patrick Mahomes II 150.00 300.00

2017 Panini Prizm Prizms Disco
*VETS: 2X TO 5X BASIC CARDS
*ROOKIES: 1X TO 2.5X BASIC CARDS
269 Patrick Mahomes II 100.00 200.00

2017 Panini Prizm Prizms Green
*VETS: 2.5X TO 6X BASIC CARDS
*ROOKIES: 1.2X TO 3X BASIC CARDS
269 Patrick Mahomes II 100.00 200.00

2017 Panini Prizm Prizms Green Scope
*VETS/99: 5X TO 12X BASIC CARDS
*ROOK/99: 2.5X TO 6X BASIC CARDS
269 Patrick Mahomes II 200.00 300.00

2017 Panini Prizm Prizms Light Blue
*VETS/199: 4X TO 10X BASIC CARDS
*ROOK/199: 2X TO 5X BASIC CARDS
269 Patrick Mahomes II 125.00 250.00

2017 Panini Prizm Prizms Orange
*VETS/275: 3X TO 8X BASIC CARDS
*ROOK/275: 1.5X TO 4X BASIC CARDS
269 Patrick Mahomes II 125.00 250.00

2017 Panini Prizm Prizms Pink
*VETS: 2X TO 5X BASIC CARDS
*ROOKIES: 1X TO 2.5X BASIC CARDS
269 Patrick Mahomes II 50.00 100.00

2017 Panini Prizm Prizms Purple Crystals
*VETS/75: 5X TO 12X BASIC CARDS
*ROOK/75: 2.5X TO 6X BASIC CARDS
269 Patrick Mahomes II 200.00 300.00

2017 Panini Prizm Prizms Red
*VETS: 3X TO 8X BASIC CARDS
*ROOKIES: 1.5X TO 4X BASIC CARDS
269 Patrick Mahomes II 60.00 125.00

2017 Panini Prizm Prizms Red Power
*VETS/49: 6X TO 15X BASIC CARDS
*ROOKIES/49: 3X TO 8X BASIC RC
269 Patrick Mahomes II 250.00 400.00

2017 Panini Prizm Prizms Red White and Blue
*VETS: 2X TO 5X BASIC CARDS
*ROOKIES: 1X TO 2.5X BASIC CARDS

2017 Panini Prizm Hall of Fame Prizms
*GREEN: .6X TO 1.5X BASIC INSERTS
1 Thurman Thomas 1.25 3.00
2 Howie Long 1.50 4.00
3 Joe Namath 2.00 5.00
4 Barry Sanders 2.50 6.00
5 Kurt Warner 1.25 3.00
6 Dan Marino 3.00 8.00
7 Marshall Faulk 1.25 3.00
8 Eric Dickerson 1.50 4.00
9 Steve Young 2.00 5.00
10 Gale Sayers 1.50 4.00
11 Tony Dorsett 1.50 4.00
12 Jim Kelly 1.50 4.00
13 John Elway 2.50 6.00
14 Brett Favre 3.00 8.00
15 LaDainian Tomlinson 1.25 3.00
16 Michael Strahan 1.25 3.00
17 Michael Irvin 1.50 4.00
18 Fran Tarkenton 1.50 4.00
19 Terrell Davis 1.25 3.00
20 Jerome Bettis 1.50 4.00
21 Troy Aikman 2.00 5.00
22 Joe Montana 4.00 10.00
23 Curtis Martin 1.25 3.00
24 Mike Ditka 1.50 4.00
25 Larry Csonka 1.25 3.00
26 Emmitt Smith 2.50 6.00
27 Franco Harris 1.50 4.00
28 Roger Staubach 2.00 5.00
29 Terry Bradshaw 2.50 6.00
30 Jerry Rice 2.50 6.00

2017 Panini Prizm Illumination Prizms
*GREEN: .6X TO 1.5X BASIC INSERTS
1 Deshaun Watson 4.00 10.00
2 Odell Beckham Jr. 1.00 2.50
3 Patrick Mahomes II 8.00 20.00
4 Aaron Rodgers 2.00 5.00
5 Rob Gronkowski 1.00 2.50
6 Dak Prescott 1.00 2.50
7 Leonard Fournette 2.00 5.00
8 Ezekiel Elliott 1.25 3.00
9 Mitchell Trubisky 3.00 8.00
10 Tom Brady 2.50 6.00

2017 Panini Prizm NFL MVPs Prizms
1 John Elway 2.50 6.00
2 Rich Gannon 1.00 2.50
3 Barry Sanders 2.50 6.00
4 Aaron Rodgers 3.00 8.00
5 Thurman Thomas 1.25 3.00
6 LaDainian Tomlinson 1.25 3.00
7 Earl Campbell 1.50 4.00
8 Cam Newton 1.50 4.00
9 Peyton Manning 3.00 8.00
10 Joe Montana 4.00 10.00
11 Peyton Manning 3.00 8.00
12 Terry Bradshaw 2.50 6.00
13 Matt Ryan 1.25 3.00
14 Emmitt Smith 2.50 6.00
15 Peyton Manning 3.00 8.00
16 Dan Marino 3.00 8.00
17 Steve Young 2.00 5.00
18 Kurt Warner 1.25 3.00
19 Steve Young 2.00 5.00
20 Tom Brady 4.00 10.00
21 Joe Theismann 1.50 4.00
22 Terrell Davis 1.25 3.00
23 Brett Favre 3.00 8.00
24 Tom Brady 4.00 10.00
25 Lawrence Taylor 1.50 4.00
26 Kurt Warner 1.25 3.00
27 Brett Favre 3.00 8.00
28 Aaron Rodgers 3.00 8.00
29 Peyton Manning 3.00 8.00
30 Marcus Allen 1.25 3.00
31 Marshall Faulk 1.25 3.00
32 Brett Favre 3.00 8.00
33 Adrian Peterson 1.50 4.00
34 Joe Montana 4.00 10.00
35 Peyton Manning 3.00 8.00

2017 Panini Prizm Prizm Premier Jerseys
*PINK: .5X TO 1.2X BASIC JSY
*PRIME/25: .8X TO 2X BASIC JSY
1 Carlos Henderson 2.00 5.00
2 Mitchell Trubisky 6.00 15.00
3 D'Onta Foreman 2.50 6.00
4 Christian McCaffrey 6.00 15.00
5 Amara Darboh 2.00 5.00
6 O.J. Howard 2.50 6.00
7 Mack Hollins 2.00 5.00
8 Dalvin Cook 4.00 10.00
9 Wayne Gallman 2.50 6.00
10 Alvin Kamara 5.00 12.00
11 Chris Godwin 2.50 6.00
12 Leonard Fournette 8.00 20.00
13 Kenny Golladay 3.00 8.00
14 John Ross III 2.50 6.00
15 Dede Westbrook 2.00 5.00
16 Evan Engram 2.50 6.00
17 Joe Williams 2.00 5.00
18 Joe Mixon 4.00 10.00
19 Marlon Mack 3.00 8.00
20 Cooper Kupp 3.00 8.00
21 Kareem Hunt 5.00 12.00
22 Corey Davis 3.00 8.00
23 C.J. Beathard 2.00 5.00
24 Patrick Mahomes II 15.00 40.00
25 Samaje Perine 2.00 5.00
26 Zay Jones 2.50 6.00
27 Jamaal Williams 2.00 5.00
28 DeShone Kizer 2.00 5.00
29 Jeremy McNichols 2.00 5.00
30 Taywan Taylor 2.00 5.00
31 Davis Webb 2.00 5.00
32 Mike Williams 3.00 8.00
33 James Conner 4.00 10.00
34 Deshaun Watson 10.00 25.00
35 Josh Reynolds 2.00 5.00
36 R. Joshua Dobbs 2.50 6.00
37 Curtis Samuel 2.50 6.00
38 JuJu Smith-Schuster 4.00 10.00
39 ArDarius Stewart 2.00 5.00
40 Nathan Peterman 2.50 6.00

2017 Panini Prizm Randy Moss Tribute Prizms
1 Randy Moss/84 4.00 10.00
2 Randy Moss/84 4.00 10.00
3 Randy Moss/84 4.00 10.00
4 Randy Moss/84 4.00 10.00
5 Randy Moss/84 4.00 10.00
6 Randy Moss/84 4.00 10.00
7 Randy Moss/84 4.00 10.00
8 Randy Moss/18
9 Randy Moss/18
10 Randy Moss/81 4.00 10.00
11 Randy Moss/81 4.00 10.00
12 Randy Moss/81 4.00 10.00
13 Randy Moss/84 4.00 10.00
14 Randy Moss/84 4.00 10.00

2017 Panini Prizm Rize Up Prizms
*GREEN: .6X TO 1.5X BASIC INSERTS
1 Amari Cooper 1.00 2.50
2 Le'Veon Bell .75 2.00
3 Cam Newton 1.00 2.50
4 Julio Jones 1.00 2.50
5 Julian Edelman 1.00 2.50
6 Russell Wilson 1.25 3.00
7 Von Miller .75 2.00
8 Dez Bryant 1.00 2.50
9 Antonio Brown 1.00 2.50
10 Rob Gronkowski 1.00 2.50
11 Odell Beckham Jr. 1.00 2.50
12 Ezekiel Elliott 1.25 3.00
13 J.J. Watt 1.00 2.50
14 Tyreek Hill 1.00 2.50
15 Richard Sherman 1.00 2.50

2017 Panini Prizm Rookie Autographs Prizms
RASP Samaje Perine 2.00 5.00
RACK Chad Kelly 6.00 15.00
RAJA Jamal Adams 2.00 5.00
RAMH Malik Hooker 2.00 5.00
RAMT Mitchell Trubisky 40.00 80.00
RARM Raekwon McMillan 2.00 5.00
RAZJ Zay Jones 5.00 12.00
RABK Brad Kaaya 2.00 5.00
RACH Carlos Henderson 2.00 5.00
RADK Desmond King 2.50 6.00
RAJR Josh Reynolds 2.00 5.00
RARJN Aaron Jones 12.00 30.00
RAIF Isaiah Ford 2.00 5.00
RASG Shelton Gibson 2.00 5.00
RALF Leonard Fournette 20.00 40.00
RAMD Matthew Dayes 2.00 5.00
RACS Curtis Samuel 2.50 6.00
RAJW Jordan Willis 2.00 5.00
RACG Chris Godwin 2.50 6.00
RAGC Gareon Conley 2.00 5.00
RAMHL Mack Hollins 2.00 5.00
RARA Rodney Adams EXCH
RADN David Njoku 2.50 6.00
RATW Tre'Davious White 2.00 5.00
RACD Corey Davis EXCH 8.00 20.00
RAST Solomon Thomas 2.00 5.00
RADC Dalvin Cook 15.00 40.00
RAJL Jordan Leggett 2.00 5.00
RAKH Kareem Hunt 12.00 30.00
RAMDP Malachi Dupre 2.00 5.00
RAJWL Joe Williams 2.00 5.00
RADH De'Angelo Henderson 2.00 5.00
RAJAL Jonathan Allen 2.50 6.00
RABH Brian Hill 2.00 5.00
RAMW Mike Williams 3.00 8.00
RATJ T.J. Watt 12.00 30.00
RAJM Joe Mixon 8.00 20.00
RAZC Zach Cunningham 2.50 6.00
RADW Davis Webb 2.00 5.00
RACB Caleb Brantley EXCH 2.00 5.00
RAJWS Jamaal Williams 2.00 5.00
RATC Tarik Cohen 8.00 20.00
RATCH Taco Charlton 2.00 5.00
RAML Marshon Lattimore 2.50 6.00
RACM Christian McCaffrey 25.00 50.00
RACL Carl Lawson 2.00 5.00
RADKZ DeShone Kizer 8.00 20.00
RAEQ Elijah Qualls 2.00 5.00
RADF D'Onta Foreman 2.50 6.00
RAJP Jabrill Peppers 3.00 8.00
RAJD R. Joshua Dobbs 2.50 6.00
RAJS Jonnu Smith 2.00 5.00
RAAS Artavis Scott 2.00 5.00
RARS Ryan Switzer 2.50 6.00
RAJRS John Ross III 2.50 6.00
RAEH Elijah Hood 2.00 5.00
RAJJ JuJu Smith-Schuster 15.00 40.00
RASJ Sidney Jones 2.00 5.00
RAKG Kenny Golladay 5.00 12.00
RADB Derek Barnett 2.50 6.00
RAWG Wayne Gallman 2.50 6.00
RAJC Jehu Chesson 2.50 6.00
RAJB Jake Butt 2.50 6.00
RATWL Tim Williams 2.50 6.00
RAPM Patrick Mahomes II 150.00 300.00
RACT Cordrea Tankersley 2.50 6.00
RAAK Alvin Kamara 15.00 40.00
RAAJ Adoree' Jackson 2.50 6.00
RACJ C.J. Beathard 2.00 5.00
RABHD Bucky Hodges 2.00 5.00
RAMM Marlon Mack 4.00 10.00
RANB Noah Brown 2.50 6.00
RAQW Quincy Wilson 2.00 5.00
RAMHP Marlon Humphrey 2.00 5.00
RADWS Deshaun Watson 75.00 150.00
RACHN Chad Hansen 2.00 5.00
RACKP Cooper Kupp 3.00 8.00
RAMMC Malik McDowell
RAJCN James Conner 4.00 10.00
RACW Chad Williams 2.00 5.00
RAJMN Jeremy McNichols 2.00 5.00
RAHR Haason Reddick EXCH 2.00 5.00
RACC Corey Clement 2.50 6.00
RACHR Charles Harris 2.00 5.00
RAOJ O.J. Howard EXCH 2.50 6.00
RAKK Kevin King 2.50 6.00
RATT Taywan Taylor 2.00 5.00
RAJD Jarrad Davis EXCH 2.50 6.00
RAAD Amara Darboh 2.00 5.00
RAASH Adam Shaheen 2.00 5.00
RANP Nathan Peterman 2.50 6.00
RATJL T.J. Logan 3.00 8.00
RATR Travis Rudolph 2.00 5.00
RADWK DeMarcus Walker 2.00 5.00
RAEE Evan Engram 6.00 15.00
RAJML Josh Malone 2.00 5.00
RAAST ArDarius Stewart 2.00 5.00
RADP Donnel Pumphrey 2.50 6.00
RADWB Dede Westbrook 2.00 5.00
RAGE Gerald Everett 2.00 5.00

2017 Panini Prizm Rookie Introductions Prizms
*GREEN: .6X TO 1.5X BASIC AU
1 Davis Webb .75 2.00
2 Patrick Mahomes II 10.00 25.00
3 James Conner 1.50 4.00
4 Evan Engram 1.00 2.50
5 Dalvin Cook 2.00 5.00
6 Mitchell Trubisky 4.00 10.00
7 JuJu Smith-Schuster 2.00 5.00
8 Corey Davis 1.25 3.00
9 Cooper Kupp 1.25 3.00
10 Christian McCaffrey 2.00 5.00
11 D'Onta Foreman 1.00 2.50
12 Dede Westbrook .75 2.00
13 Deshaun Watson 5.00 12.00
14 Jamaal Williams .75 2.00
15 Joe Mixon 1.50 4.00
16 Leonard Fournette 2.50 6.00
17 Alvin Kamara 3.00 8.00
18 Mike Williams 1.25 3.00
19 Kareem Hunt 1.50 4.00
20 John Ross III 1.00 2.50
21 C.J. Beathard .75 2.00
22 O.J. Howard 1.00 2.50
23 Samaje Perine .75 2.00
24 R. Joshua Dobbs 1.00 2.50
25 DeShone Kizer .75 2.00

2017 Panini Prizm Rookie Patch Autographs Prizms
1 Curtis Samuel 5.00 12.00
2 Zay Jones 5.00 12.00
3 Joe Mixon/49 10.00 25.00
4 Dalvin Cook 25.00 50.00
5 JuJu Smith-Schuster 25.00 50.00
6 DeShone Kizer 4.00 10.00
7 Deshaun Watson 100.00 200.00
8 Alvin Kamara 15.00 40.00
9 D'Onta Foreman 5.00 12.00
10 C.J. Beathard 4.00 10.00
11 Leonard Fournette 30.00 60.00
12 Mitchell Trubisky 60.00 125.00
13 Mike Williams 6.00 15.00
14 Corey Davis 6.00 15.00
15 John Ross III 5.00 12.00
16 Christian McCaffrey 10.00 25.00
17 Cooper Kupp 6.00 15.00
18 Patrick Mahomes II 250.00 500.00
19 Evan Engram 5.00 12.00
20 O.J. Howard 5.00 12.00

2017 Panini Prizm Rookie Patch Autographs Prizms Red Power
*RED/15: .8X TO 2X BASIC JSY AU/99
*RED/15: .6X TO 1.5X BASIC JSY AU/49
12 Mitchell Trubisky 125.00 250.00
18 Patrick Mahomes II 600.00 1000.00

2017 Panini Prizm Stained Glass Prizms
1 Mitchell Trubisky 4.00 10.00
2 Aaron Rodgers 2.50 6.00
3 Tom Brady 3.00 8.00
4 Christian McCaffrey 2.00 5.00
5 Ben Roethlisberger 1.25 3.00
6 Deshaun Watson 5.00 12.00
7 Leonard Fournette 2.50 6.00
8 Dalvin Cook 2.00 5.00
9 Ezekiel Elliott 1.50 4.00
10 Patrick Mahomes II 50.00 100.00

2017 Panini Prizm Super Bowl MVPs Prizms
1 Desmond Howard 1.25 3.00
2 Len Dawson 1.50 4.00
3 John Riggins 1.25 3.00
4 Joe Montana 4.00 10.00
5 Franco Harris 1.50 4.00
6 Randy White 1.25 3.00
7 Jerry Rice 2.50 6.00
8 Troy Aikman 2.00 5.00
9 Terry Bradshaw 2.50 6.00

10 Joe Montana 4.00 10.00
11 Emmitt Smith 2.50 6.00
12 Larry Brown 1.00 2.50
13 Drew Brees 1.50 4.00
14 Eli Manning 1.25 3.00
15 Tom Brady 4.00 10.00
16 Kurt Warner 1.25 3.00
17 Tom Brady 4.00 10.00
18 Hines Ward 1.25 3.00
19 Tom Brady 4.00 10.00
20 Eli Manning 1.25 3.00
21 Doug Williams 1.25 3.00
22 Joe Montana 4.00 10.00
23 Terry Bradshaw 2.50 6.00
24 Jim Plunkett 1.25 3.00
25 Joe Namath 2.00 5.00
26 Roger Staubach 2.00 5.00
27 Marcus Allen 1.25 3.00
28 Phil Simms 1.25 3.00
29 Larry Csonka 1.25 3.00
30 Fred Biletnikoff 1.50 4.00
31 Malcolm Smith 1.00 2.50
32 Von Miller 1.25 3.00
33 Tom Brady 4.00 10.00
34 Peyton Manning 3.00 8.00
35 Steve Young 2.00 5.00
36 Terrell Davis 1.25 3.00
37 Aaron Rodgers 3.00 8.00
38 Joe Flacco 1.25 3.00
39 John Elway 2.50 6.00
40 Ray Lewis 1.50 4.00

2018 Panini Prizm

1 Alex Smith .25 .60
2 Josh Doctson .20 .50
3 Vernon Davis .20 .50
4 Josh Norman .20 .50
5 Samaje Perine .20 .50
6 Jordan Reed .20 .50
7 Marcus Mariota .30 .75
8 Corey Davis .25 .60
9 Derrick Henry .30 .75
10 Dion Lewis .20 .50
11 Delanie Walker .20 .50
12 Adoree' Jackson .20 .50
13 Jameis Winston .25 .60
14 Mike Evans .25 .60
15 Gerald McCoy .20 .50
16 O.J. Howard .20 .50
17 Cameron Brate .20 .50
18 DeSean Jackson .25 .60
19 Russell Wilson .40 1.00
20 Earl Thomas III .25 .60
21 Doug Baldwin .25 .60
22 Kam Chancellor .30 .75
23 Brandon Marshall .20 .50
24 Chris Carson .25 .60
25 Jimmy Garoppolo .40 1.00
26 Jerick McKinnon .20 .50
27 Richard Sherman .30 .75
28 Pierre Garcon .25 .60
29 Marquise Goodwin .20 .50
30 Kyle Juszczyk .20 .50
31 Ben Roethlisberger .30 .75
32 Le'Veon Bell .25 .60
33 Antonio Brown .30 .75
34 T.J. Watt .25 .60
35 Cameron Heyward .20 .50
36 JuJu Smith-Schuster .30 .75
37 Alejandro Villanueva .25 .60
38 Carson Wentz .40 1.00
39 Nick Foles .25 .60
40 Jay Ajayi .25 .60
41 Zach Ertz .25 .60
42 Nelson Agholor .20 .50
43 Alshon Jeffery .25 .60
44 Brandon Graham .20 .50
45 Derek Carr .30 .75
46 Amari Cooper .30 .75
47 Khalil Mack .30 .75
48 Marshawn Lynch .25 .60
49 Jordy Nelson .25 .60
50 Bruce Irvin .20 .50
51 Jamal Adams .25 .60
52 Josh McCown .20 .50
53 Isaiah Crowell .20 .50
54 Jermaine Kearse .20 .50
55 Robby Anderson .20 .50
56 Quincy Enunwa .20 .50
57 Eli Manning .25 .60
58 Odell Beckham Jr. .30 .75
59 Jonathan Stewart .20 .50
60 Landon Collins .20 .50
61 Evan Engram .20 .50
62 Sterling Shepard .25 .60
63 Drew Brees .30 .75
64 Alvin Kamara .25 .60
65 Michael Thomas .30 .75
66 Mark Ingram .25 .60
67 Cameron Meredith .20 .50
68 Marshon Lattimore .20 .50
69 Tom Brady .75 2.00
70 Rob Gronkowski .30 .75
71 Devin McCourty .20 .50
72 James White .25 .60
73 Chris Hogan .20 .50
74 Julian Edelman .30 .75
75 Jeremy Hill .20 .50
76 Kirk Cousins .30 .75
77 Xavier Rhodes .20 .50
78 Adam Thielen .30 .75
79 Dalvin Cook .25 .60
80 Stefon Diggs .25 .60
81 Kyle Rudolph .20 .50
82 Harrison Smith .30 .75
83 Ryan Tannehill .25 .60
84 Kenyan Drake .20 .50
85 Kiko Alonso .20 .50
86 Frank Gore .25 .60
87 Danny Amendola .25 .60
88 DeVante Parker .25 .60
89 Todd Gurley II .30 .75
90 Jared Goff .30 .75
91 Aaron Donald .30 .75
92 Robert Woods .25 .60
93 Ndamukong Suh .25 .60
94 Brandin Cooks .25 .60
95 Cooper Kupp .25 .60
96 Philip Rivers .30 .75
97 Melvin Gordon .25 .60
98 Joey Bosa .30 .75
99 Keenan Allen .25 .60
100 Mike Williams .20 .50
101 Melvin Ingram .20 .50
102 Patrick Mahomes II .75 2.00
103 Tyreek Hill .30 .75
104 Kareem Hunt .25 .60
105 Travis Kelce .30 .75
106 Eric Berry .25 .60
107 Justin Houston .20 .50
108 Blake Bortles .20 .50
109 Leonard Fournette .30 .75
110 Jalen Ramsey .25 .60
111 A.J. Bouye .20 .50
112 Calais Campbell .20 .50
113 Marqise Lee .20 .50
114 Andrew Luck .40 1.00
115 Jacoby Brissett .20 .50
116 Marlon Mack .20 .50
117 T.Y. Hilton .25 .60
118 Adam Vinatieri .20 .50
119 Jack Doyle .20 .50
120 Deshaun Watson .40 1.00
121 J.J. Watt .30 .75
122 DeAndre Hopkins .25 .60
123 Jadeveon Clowney .20 .50
124 Will Fuller V .20 .50
125 Lamar Miller .20 .50
126 D'Onta Foreman .20 .50
127 Aaron Rodgers .60 1.50
128 Jimmy Graham .30 .75
129 Davante Adams .25 .60
130 Clay Matthews .25 .60
131 Aaron Jones .25 .60
132 Randall Cobb .25 .60
133 Matthew Stafford .25 .60
134 Golden Tate III .20 .50
135 Ameer Abdullah .20 .50
136 LeGarrette Blount .25 .60
137 Marvin Jones Jr. .20 .50
138 Darius Slay .20 .50
139 Emmanuel Sanders .30 .75
140 Demaryius Thomas .25 .60
141 Case Keenum .25 .60
142 Devontae Booker .20 .50
143 Von Miller .25 .60
144 Marquette King .20 .50
145 Dak Prescott .30 .75
146 Ezekiel Elliott .40 1.00
147 Sean Lee .25 .60
148 Dan Bailey .20 .50
149 Allen Hurns .20 .50
150 DeMarcus Lawrence .20 .50
151 Jabrill Peppers .20 .50
152 Myles Garrett .30 .75
153 Tyrod Taylor .25 .60
154 Carlos Hyde .20 .50
155 Jarvis Landry .25 .60
156 Josh Gordon .20 .50
157 Andy Dalton .25 .60
158 A.J. Green .30 .75
159 Joe Mixon .25 .60
160 Geno Atkins .20 .50
161 Tyler Eifert .25 .60
162 Vontaze Burfict .20 .50
163 Mitchell Trubisky .30 .75
164 Jordan Howard .30 .75
165 Tarik Cohen .25 .60
166 Allen Robinson .25 .60
167 Eddie Jackson .20 .50
168 Leonard Floyd .20 .50
169 Cam Newton .30 .75
170 Luke Kuechly .25 .60
171 Devin Funchess .20 .50
172 Christian McCaffrey .30 .75
173 Greg Olsen .25 .60
174 Torrey Smith .20 .50
175 LeSean McCoy .30 .75
176 A.J. McCarron .20 .50
177 Kelvin Benjamin .25 .60
178 Charles Clay .20 .50
179 Micah Hyde .20 .50
180 Jordan Poyer .20 .50
181 Joe Flacco .25 .60
182 Justin Tucker .20 .50
183 Terrell Suggs .20 .50
184 C.J. Mosley .25 .60
185 Eric Weddle .20 .50
186 Alex Collins .20 .50
187 Michael Crabtree .20 .50
188 Matt Ryan .25 .60
189 Vic Beasley Jr. .20 .50
190 Julio Jones .30 .75
191 Devonta Freeman .25 .60
192 Tevin Coleman .20 .50
193 Mohamed Sanu .20 .50
194 Larry Fitzgerald .25 .60
195 Patrick Peterson .20 .50
196 David Johnson .30 .75
197 Sam Bradford .20 .50
198 Chandler Jones .20 .50
199 Deone Bucannon .20 .50
200 Cole Beasley .25 .60
201 Baker Mayfield RC 12.00 30.00
202 Saquon Barkley RC 4.00 10.00
203 Sam Darnold RC 4.00 10.00
204 Bradley Chubb RC .60 1.50
205 Josh Allen RC 1.50 4.00
206 Josh Rosen RC 1.25 3.00
207 D.J. Moore RC .75 2.00
208 Hayden Hurst RC .50 1.25
209 Calvin Ridley RC 1.00 2.50
210 Rashaad Penny RC .60 1.50
211 Sony Michel RC 1.25 3.00
212 Lamar Jackson RC 2.50 6.00
213 Nick Chubb RC 1.25 3.00
214 Ronald Jones II RC .40 1.00
215 Courtland Sutton RC .60 1.50
216 Mike Gesicki RC .50 1.25
217 Kerryon Johnson RC .60 1.50
218 Dante Pettis RC .60 1.50
219 Christian Kirk RC .60 1.50
220 Anthony Miller RC .60 1.50
221 Derrius Guice RC .75 2.00
222 James Washington RC .75 2.00
223 D.J. Chark Jr. RC .50 1.25
224 Royce Freeman RC .50 1.25
225 Mason Rudolph RC 1.00 2.50
226 Michael Gallup RC .75 2.00
227 Tre'Quan Smith RC .60 1.50
228 Keke Coutee RC .50 1.25
229 Nyheim Hines RC .50 1.25
230 Kyle Lauletta RC .60 1.50
231 Mark Walton RC .50 1.25
232 DaeSean Hamilton RC .50 1.25
233 Ito Smith RC .50 1.25
234 Kalen Ballage RC .50 1.25
235 Jaleel Scott RC .40 1.00
236 J'Mon Moore RC .40 1.00
237 Daurice Fountain RC .50 1.25
238 Jaylen Samuels RC .50 1.25
239 Mike White RC .50 1.25
240 Marquez Valdes-Scantling RC .50 1.25
241 Denzel Ward RC 1.00 2.50
242 Roquan Smith RC 1.25 3.00
243 Minkah Fitzpatrick RC .75 2.00
244 Vita Vea RC .60 1.50
245 Daron Payne RC .60 1.50
246 Marcus Davenport RC .75 2.00
247 Tremaine Edmunds RC .75 2.00
248 Derwin James RC .75 2.00
249 Jaire Alexander RC .60 1.50
250 Leighton Vander Esch RC 1.25 3.00
251 Rashaan Evans RC .60 1.50
252 Terrell Edmunds RC 1.25 3.00
253 Mike Hughes RC .60 1.50
254 Harold Landry RC .40 1.00
255 Joshua Jackson RC .75 2.00
256 M.J. Stewart RC .40 1.00
257 Fred Warner RC .40 1.00
258 Duke Dawson RC .40 1.00
259 Isaiah Oliver RC .40 1.00
260 Carlton Davis RC .50 1.25
261 Tyquan Lewis RC .50 1.25
262 Lorenzo Carter RC .40 1.00
263 Justin Reid RC .40 1.00
264 Jerome Baker RC .50 1.25
265 Derrick Nnadi RC .40 1.00
266 Sam Hubbard RC .50 1.25
267 Arden Key RC .40 1.00
268 Ronnie Harrison RC .50 1.25
269 Jalyn Holmes RC .60 1.50
270 Antonio Callaway RC .50 1.25
271 Christopher Herndon IV RC .40 1.00
272 Da'Shawn Hand RC .40 1.00
273 Justin Watson RC .50 1.25
274 Armani Watts RC .40 1.00
275 Josh Sweat RC .50 1.25
276 Chase Edmonds RC .40 1.00
277 Dalton Schultz RC .50 1.25
278 Richie James RC .40 1.00
279 Shaquem Griffin RC .60 1.50
280 Troy Fumagalli RC .50 1.25
281 Jordan Lasley RC .40 1.00
282 John Kelly RC .50 1.25
283 Ray-Ray McCloud RC .40 1.00
284 Dylan Cantrell RC .40 1.00
285 Luke Falk RC .50 1.25
286 Cedrick Wilson Jr. RC .40 1.00
287 Braxton Berrios RC .40 1.00
288 Marcell Ateman RC .50 1.25
289 Bo Scarbrough RC .50 1.25
290 Ryan Izzo RC .40 1.00
291 Justin Jackson RC .50 1.25
292 Auden Tate RC .40 1.00
293 Trey Quinn RC .40 1.00
294 Allen Lazard RC .40 1.00
295 Deontay Burnett RC .50 1.25
296 Josh Adams RC .75 2.00
297 Riley Ferguson RC .60 1.50
298 Simmie Cobbs Jr. RC .60 1.50
299 Dallas Goedert RC .50 1.25
300 Rasheem Green RC .40 1.00

2018 Panini Prizm Prizms

*VETS: 12X TO 30X BASIC CARDS
*ROOKIES: 6X TO 15X BASIC CARDS
201 Baker Mayfield 75.00 150.00
202 Saquon Barkley 100.00 200.00
203 Sam Darnold 75.00 150.00
212 Lamar Jackson 60.00 125.00

2018 Panini Prizm Prizms Blue

*VETS: 3X TO 8X BASIC CARDS
*ROOKIES: 1.5X TO 4X BASIC CARDS
201 Baker Mayfield 50.00 100.00

2018 Panini Prizm Prizms Blue Scope

*VETS: 5X TO 12X BASIC CARDS
*ROOKIES: 2.5X TO 6X BASIC CARDS
201 Baker Mayfield 150.00 300.00

2018 Panini Prizm Prizms Camo

*VETS: 8X TO 20X BASIC CARDS
*ROOKIES: 4X TO 10X BASIC CARDS
201 Baker Mayfield 125.00 250.00

2018 Panini Prizm Prizms Disco

*VETS: 3X TO 5X BASIC CARDS
*ROOKIES: 1X TO 2.5X BASIC CARDS
201 Baker Mayfield 60.00 125.00

2018 Panini Prizm Prizms Green

*VETS: 2.5X TO 6X BASIC CARDS
*ROOKIES: 1.2X TO 3X BASIC CARDS
201 Baker Mayfield 50.00 100.00

2018 Panini Prizm Prizms Green Crystals

*VETS: 5X TO 12X BASIC CARDS
*ROOKIES: 2.5X TO 6X BASIC CARDS
201 Baker Mayfield 150.00 300.00

2018 Panini Prizm Prizms Hyper

*VETS: 4X TO 10X BASIC CARDS
*ROOKIES: 2X TO 5X BASIC CARDS
201 Baker Mayfield 100.00 200.00

2018 Panini Prizm Prizms Lazer

*VETS: 3X TO 5X BASIC CARDS
*ROOKIES: 1X TO 2.5X BASIC CARDS
201 Baker Mayfield 40.00 80.00

2018 Panini Prizm Prizms Light Blue

*VETS: 4X TO 10X BASIC CARDS
*ROOKIES: 2X TO 5X BASIC CARDS
201 Baker Mayfield 100.00 200.00

2018 Panini Prizm Prizms Neon Green Pulsar

*VETS: 2.5X TO 6X BASIC CARDS
*ROOKIES: 1.2X TO 3X BASIC CARDS
201 Baker Mayfield 50.00 100.00

2018 Panini Prizm Prizms Orange

*VETS: 4X TO 10X BASIC CARDS
*ROOKIES: 2X TO 5X BASIC CARDS
201 Baker Mayfield 100.00 200.00

2018 Panini Prizm Prizms Purple Power

*VETS: 6X TO 15X BASIC CARDS
*ROOKIES: 3X TO 8X BASIC CARDS
201 Baker Mayfield 200.00 375.00

2018 Panini Prizm Prizms Red

*VETS: 3X TO 8X BASIC CARDS
*ROOKIES: 1.5X TO 4X BASIC CARDS
201 Baker Mayfield 30.00 60.00

2018 Panini Prizm Prizms Red Wave

*VETS: 4X TO 10X BASIC CARDS
*ROOKIES: 2X TO 5X BASIC CARDS
201 Baker Mayfield 100.00 200.00

2018 Panini Prizm Prizms Red White and Blue

*VETS: 3X TO 5X BASIC CARDS
*ROOKIES: 1X TO 2.5X BASIC CARDS

2018 Panini Prizm '18 HOF Tribute Prizms

1 Randy Moss 2.50 6.00
2 Randy Moss 2.50 6.00
3 Randy Moss 2.50 6.00
4 Randy Moss 2.50 6.00
5 Brian Urlacher 3.00 8.00
6 Brian Urlacher 3.00 8.00
7 Brian Urlacher 3.00 8.00
8 Brian Urlacher 3.00 8.00
9 Brian Dawkins 3.00 8.00
10 Brian Dawkins 3.00 8.00
11 Brian Dawkins 3.00 8.00
12 Brian Dawkins 3.00 8.00
13 Ray Lewis 3.00 8.00
14 Ray Lewis 3.00 8.00
15 Ray Lewis 3.00 8.00

2018 Panini Prizm Apex Prizms

1 Tom Brady 6.00 15.00
2 Nick Foles 2.00 5.00
3 Von Miller 2.00 5.00
4 Joe Flacco 2.00 5.00
5 Eli Manning 2.00 5.00
6 Aaron Rodgers 5.00 12.00
7 Drew Brees 2.50 6.00
8 James Harrison 2.00 5.00
9 Peyton Manning 5.00 12.00
10 Hines Ward 2.00 5.00
11 Ray Lewis 2.50 6.00
12 Kurt Warner 2.00 5.00
13 John Elway 4.00 10.00
14 Terrell Davis 2.00 5.00
15 James White 2.00 5.00
16 Russell Wilson 3.00 8.00
17 Ben Roethlisberger 2.50 6.00
18 Jordy Nelson 2.00 5.00
19 Steve Young 3.00 8.00
20 Emmitt Smith 4.00 10.00
21 Troy Aikman 3.00 8.00
22 Marcus Allen 2.50 6.00
23 John Riggins 2.00 5.00
24 Joe Montana 6.00 15.00
25 Terry Bradshaw 4.00 10.00

2018 Panini Prizm Grit Prizms

1 Luke Kuechly 2.00 5.00
2 J.J. Watt 2.50 6.00
3 T.J. Watt 2.00 5.00
4 Jason Witten 2.00 5.00
5 Von Miller 2.00 5.00
6 Rob Gronkowski 2.50 6.00
7 Joey Bosa 2.50 6.00
8 Lawrence Taylor 2.50 6.00
9 Brian Urlacher 2.50 6.00
10 Jason Taylor 2.00 5.00
11 Jalen Ramsey 2.00 5.00
12 Howie Long 2.50 6.00
13 Julius Peppers 2.00 5.00
14 Brian Dawkins 2.50 6.00
15 John Lynch 2.00 5.00
16 Khalil Mack 2.50 6.00
17 Tony Gonzalez 2.00 5.00
18 Greg Olsen 2.00 5.00
19 Ray Lewis 2.50 6.00
20 Brett Favre 5.00 12.00

2018 Panini Prizm Hall of Fame Prizms

*GREEN: .6X TO 1.5X BASIC INSERTS
1 Brian Urlacher 1.50 4.00
2 Randy Moss 1.25 3.00
3 Jason Taylor 1.25 3.00
4 Troy Aikman 2.00 5.00
5 Lawrence Taylor 1.50 4.00
6 Emmitt Smith 2.50 6.00
7 Terry Bradshaw 2.50 6.00
8 Jerry Rice 2.50 6.00
9 Steve Young 2.00 5.00
10 Bruce Smith 1.25 3.00
11 Terrell Davis 1.25 3.00
12 Dan Marino 3.00 8.00
13 Curtis Martin 1.25 3.00
14 Jim Kelly 1.50 4.00
15 John Randle 1.25 3.00
16 Tim Brown 1.50 4.00
17 Deion Sanders 1.25 3.00
18 Kurt Warner 1.25 3.00
19 John Riggins 1.25 3.00
20 Barry Sanders 2.50 6.00
21 Marshall Faulk 1.25 3.00
22 Howie Long 1.50 4.00
23 Jerome Bettis 1.50 4.00
24 Roger Staubach 2.00 5.00
25 Brett Favre 3.00 8.00
26 Brian Dawkins 1.50 4.00
27 Charles Haley 1.50 4.00
28 Cris Carter 1.50 4.00
29 Jonathan Ogden 1.25 3.00
30 Warren Sapp 1.25 3.00

2018 Panini Prizm Hype Prizms

*GREEN: .6X TO 1.5X BASIC INSERTS
1 Tom Brady 5.00 12.00
2 Von Miller 1.50 4.00
3 J.J. Watt 2.00 5.00
4 Cam Newton 2.00 5.00
5 Matt Ryan 1.50 4.00
6 Aaron Rodgers 4.00 10.00
7 Derek Carr 2.00 5.00
8 Dak Prescott 2.00 5.00
9 Todd Gurley II 2.00 5.00
10 Jimmy Garoppolo 2.50 6.00
11 Kareem Hunt 1.50 4.00
12 Carson Wentz 2.50 6.00
13 Deshaun Watson 2.50 6.00
14 Odell Beckham Jr. 2.00 5.00
15 Drew Brees 2.00 5.00

2018 Panini Prizm Illumination Prizms

*GREEN: .6X TO 1.5X BASIC INSERTS
1 Tom Brady 5.00 12.00
2 Deshaun Watson 2.50 6.00
3 Alvin Kamara 1.50 4.00
4 Julio Jones 2.00 5.00
5 Le'Veon Bell 1.50 4.00
6 Ezekiel Elliott 2.50 6.00
7 Jimmy Garoppolo 2.50 6.00
8 Jordan Howard 2.00 5.00
9 Derek Carr 2.00 5.00
10 Drew Brees 2.00 5.00

2018 Panini Prizm Instant Impact Prizms

*GREEN: .6X TO 1.5X BASIC INSERTS
1 Baker Mayfield 10.00 25.00
2 Saquon Barkley 8.00 20.00
3 Sam Darnold 6.00 15.00
4 Bradley Chubb 1.50 4.00
5 Josh Allen 4.00 10.00
6 Josh Rosen 3.00 8.00
7 D.J. Moore 2.00 5.00
8 Mason Rudolph 2.50 6.00
9 Calvin Ridley 2.50 6.00
10 Rashaad Penny 1.50 4.00
11 Sony Michel 3.00 8.00
12 Lamar Jackson 6.00 15.00
13 Nick Chubb 3.00 8.00
14 Ronald Jones II 1.00 2.50
15 Courtland Sutton 1.50 4.00
16 Derrius Guice 2.00 5.00
17 Kerryon Johnson 1.50 4.00
18 Dante Pettis 1.50 4.00
19 Christian Kirk 1.50 4.00
20 Anthony Miller 1.50 4.00

2018 Panini Prizm Patented Penmanship Prizms

1 Baker Mayfield/25 EXCH 100.00 200.00
2 Saquon Barkley/25 100.00 200.00
5 Josh Allen/25 25.00 60.00
6 Josh Rosen/25 20.00 50.00
7 D.J. Moore/25 12.00 30.00
10 Rashaad Penny/25 10.00 25.00
11 Sony Michel/25
12 Lamar Jackson/25 75.00 150.00
13 Nick Chubb/25
14 Ronald Jones II/25
15 Courtland Sutton/25 10.00 25.00
17 Kerryon Johnson/25 30.00 60.00
18 Dante Pettis/25 10.00 25.00
20 Anthony Miller/25
22 James Washington/25 12.00 30.00
25 Mason Rudolph/25 50.00 100.00
27 Tre'Quan Smith/25 10.00 25.00
28 Keke Coutee/25 8.00 20.00
29 Nyheim Hines/25 8.00 20.00
30 Kyle Lauletta/25 10.00 25.00
32 DaeSean Hamilton/25 8.00 20.00
33 Ito Smith/25 8.00 20.00
34 Kalen Ballage/25 8.00 20.00
35 Jaleel Scott/25 6.00 15.00
36 J'Mon Moore/25 6.00 15.00
37 Daurice Fountain/25 8.00 20.00
38 Jaylen Samuels/25 8.00 20.00
40 Marquez Valdes-Scantling/25 8.00 20.00

2018 Panini Prizm Prizm Premier Jerseys

*PINK: .5X TO 1.2X BASIC JSY
*PRIME/25: .8X TO 2X BASIC JSY
1 Baker Mayfield 10.00 25.00
2 Saquon Barkley 8.00 20.00
3 Sam Darnold 6.00 15.00
4 Bradley Chubb 2.50 6.00
5 Josh Allen 5.00 12.00
6 Josh Rosen 5.00 12.00
7 D.J. Moore 3.00 8.00
8 Hayden Hurst 2.00 5.00
9 Calvin Ridley 4.00 10.00
10 Rashaad Penny 2.50 6.00
11 Sony Michel 4.00 10.00
12 Lamar Jackson 6.00 15.00
13 Nick Chubb 5.00 12.00
14 Ronald Jones II 1.50 4.00
15 Courtland Sutton 2.50 6.00
16 Mike Gesicki 2.00 5.00
17 Kerryon Johnson 2.50 6.00
18 Dante Pettis 2.50 6.00
19 Christian Kirk 2.50 6.00
20 Anthony Miller 2.50 6.00
21 Derrius Guice 3.00 8.00
22 James Washington 3.00 8.00
23 D.J. Chark Jr. 2.00 5.00
24 Royce Freeman 2.00 5.00
25 Mason Rudolph 4.00 10.00
26 Michael Gallup 3.00 8.00
27 Tre'Quan Smith 2.50 6.00
28 Keke Coutee 2.00 5.00
29 Nyheim Hines 2.00 5.00
30 Kyle Lauletta 2.50 6.00
31 Mark Walton 2.00 5.00
32 DaeSean Hamilton 2.00 5.00
33 Ito Smith 2.00 5.00
34 Kalen Ballage 2.00 5.00
35 Jaleel Scott 1.50 4.00
36 J'Mon Moore 1.50 4.00
37 Daurice Fountain 2.00 5.00
38 Jaylen Samuels 2.00 5.00
39 Mike White 2.00 5.00
40 Marquez Valdes-Scantling 2.00 5.00

2018 Panini Prizm Rookie Autographs Prizms

1 Baker Mayfield EXCH 125.00 400.00
2 Saquon Barkley 100.00 200.00
3 Sam Darnold 50.00 125.00
4 Bradley Chubb EXCH 6.00 15.00
5 Josh Allen 30.00 60.00
6 Josh Rosen 15.00 40.00
7 D.J. Moore 6.00 15.00
9 Calvin Ridley 12.00 30.00
10 Rashaad Penny 3.00 8.00
11 Sony Michel 15.00 40.00
12 Lamar Jackson 60.00 125.00
13 Nick Chubb 12.00 30.00
14 Ronald Jones II 2.00 5.00
15 Courtland Sutton 3.00 8.00
16 Mike Gesicki 2.50 6.00
17 Kerryon Johnson 12.00 30.00
18 Dante Pettis EXCH 3.00 8.00
19 Christian Kirk 3.00 8.00
20 Anthony Miller 3.00 8.00
21 Derrius Guice EXCH 4.00 10.00
22 James Washington 4.00 10.00
24 Royce Freeman 2.50 6.00
25 Mason Rudolph 20.00 40.00
26 Michael Gallup 8.00 20.00
27 Tre'Quan Smith 3.00 8.00
28 Keke Coutee EXCH 2.50 6.00
29 Nyheim Hines 2.50 6.00
30 Kyle Lauletta 6.00 15.00
32 DaeSean Hamilton 2.50 6.00
33 Ito Smith 2.50 6.00
34 Kalen Ballage 2.50 6.00
35 Jaleel Scott 2.00 5.00
36 J'Mon Moore 2.00 5.00
37 Daurice Fountain 2.50 6.00
38 Jaylen Samuels 2.50 6.00
39 Mike White 2.50 6.00
40 Marquez Valdes-Scantling 4.00 10.00
41 Denzel Ward 5.00 12.00
42 Roquan Smith 6.00 15.00
43 Minkah Fitzpatrick 4.00 10.00
44 Vita Vea 3.00 8.00
45 Daron Payne 3.00 8.00
46 Marcus Davenport 4.00 10.00
47 Tremaine Edmunds 4.00 10.00
48 Derwin James 4.00 10.00
49 Jaire Alexander 3.00 8.00
50 Leighton Vander Esch 12.00 30.00
51 Rashaan Evans 3.00 8.00
52 Terrell Edmunds 6.00 15.00
53 Mike Hughes 3.00 8.00
54 Harold Landry 2.00 5.00
55 Joshua Jackson 4.00 10.00
56 M.J. Stewart 2.00 5.00
57 Fred Warner 2.00 5.00
58 Kurt Benkert 2.50 6.00
59 Isaiah Oliver 2.00 5.00
60 Carlton Davis 2.50 6.00
62 Lorenzo Carter 2.00 5.00
63 Deon Cain 2.50 6.00
64 Richie James 2.00 5.00
65 Derrick Nnadi 2.00 5.00
66 Sam Hubbard 2.50 6.00
68 Ronnie Harrison 2.50 6.00
71 Christopher Herndon IV 2.00 5.00
72 Da'Shawn Hand 2.00 5.00
73 Jordan Akins 2.00 5.00
74 Armani Watts 2.00 5.00
75 Josh Sweat 2.50 6.00
76 Russell Gage 2.50 6.00
77 Dalton Schultz 2.50 6.00
78 Maurice Hurst 2.50 6.00
79 Shaquem Griffin 3.00 8.00
81 Jordan Lasley 2.00 5.00
82 John Kelly 2.50 6.00
83 Mark Andrews 3.00 8.00
84 Dylan Cantrell 2.00 5.00
85 Luke Falk 2.50 6.00
86 Cedrick Wilson Jr. 2.00 5.00
87 Alex McGough 2.50 6.00
88 Marcell Ateman 2.50 6.00
89 Bo Scarbrough 2.50 6.00
90 Ryan Izzo 2.00 5.00
91 Justin Jackson 2.50 6.00
93 Danny Etling 2.50 6.00
94 Allen Lazard 2.00 5.00
95 Deontay Burnett 2.50 6.00
96 Josh Adams 4.00 10.00
97 Riley Ferguson 3.00 8.00
98 Simmie Cobbs Jr. 3.00 8.00
99 Dallas Goedert 2.50 6.00
100 Rasheem Green 2.00 5.00

2018 Panini Prizm Rookie Autographs Prizms Blue Scope

*BL. SCOPE/75-99: .8X TO 2X BASIC AU
*BL. SCOPE/25: 1.2X TO 3X BASIC AU
*BL. SCOPE/15: 1.5X TO 4X BASIC AU
1 Baker Mayfield/99 200.00 600.00
2 Saquon Barkley/99 175.00 300.00
3 Sam Darnold/75 100.00 200.00
12 Lamar Jackson/15 250.00 400.00

2018 Panini Prizm Rookie Autographs Prizms Blue Shimmer

*BL. SHIM/25: 1.2X TO 3X BASIC AU
1 Baker Mayfield 400.00 1000.00
2 Saquon Barkley 300.00 600.00
3 Sam Darnold 150.00 300.00
12 Lamar Jackson 200.00 300.00

2018 Panini Prizm Rookie Autographs Prizms Camo

*CAMO/25: 1.2X TO 3X BASIC AU
1 Baker Mayfield/25 400.00 1000.00
2 Saquon Barkley/25 300.00 600.00

2018 Panini Prizm Rookie Autographs Prizms Green Crystals

*GR. CRYSTAL/75: .8X TO 2X BASIC AU
*GR. CRYSTAL/49: 1X TO 2.5X BASIC AU
*GR. CRYSTAL/15: 1.5X TO 4X BASIC AU
1 Baker Mayfield/75 EXCH 400.00 800.00
2 Saquon Barkley/75 200.00 300.00
3 Sam Darnold/49 125.00 250.00

2018 Panini Prizm Rookie Autographs Prizms Purple Power

*PURPLE/49: 1X TO 2.5X BASIC AU
*PURPLE/25: 1.2X TO 3X BASIC AU
1 Baker Mayfield/49 400.00 800.00
2 Saquon Barkley/49 250.00 400.00
3 Sam Darnold/25 150.00 300.00

2018 Panini Prizm Rookie Autographs Prizms Red Wave

*RED WAVE/199: .6X TO 1.5X BASIC AU
*RED WAVE/99: .8X TO 2X BASIC AU
*RED WAVE/49: 1X TO 2.5X BASIC AU
*RED WAVE/25: 1.2X TO 3X BASIC AU
1 Baker Mayfield/199 EXCH 300.00 600.00
2 Saquon Barkley/199 125.00 250.00
3 Sam Darnold/99 100.00 200.00
12 Lamar Jackson/25 200.00 300.00

2018 Panini Prizm Rookie Introduction Prizms

1 Baker Mayfield 10.00 25.00
2 Saquon Barkley 8.00 20.00
3 Sam Darnold 6.00 15.00
4 Bradley Chubb 1.50 4.00
5 Josh Allen 4.00 10.00
6 Josh Rosen 3.00 8.00
7 D.J. Moore 2.00 5.00
8 Hayden Hurst 1.25 3.00
9 Calvin Ridley 2.50 6.00
10 Rashaad Penny 1.50 4.00
11 Sony Michel 3.00 8.00
12 Lamar Jackson 6.00 15.00
13 Nick Chubb 3.00 8.00
14 Ronald Jones II 1.00 2.50
15 Courtland Sutton 1.50 4.00
16 Mike Gesicki 1.25 3.00
17 Kerryon Johnson 1.50 4.00
18 Dante Pettis 1.50 4.00
19 Christian Kirk 1.50 4.00
20 Anthony Miller 1.50 4.00
21 Derrius Guice 2.00 5.00
22 James Washington 2.00 5.00
23 D.J. Chark Jr. 1.25 3.00
24 Royce Freeman 1.25 3.00
25 Mason Rudolph 2.50 6.00

2018 Panini Prizm Rookie Patch Autographs Prizms

*PURPLE/50: .5X TO 1.2X BASIC JSY AU/99
1 Baker Mayfield 100.00 200.00
2 Saquon Barkley 100.00 200.00
3 Sam Darnold 50.00 100.00
4 Ito Smith 6.00 15.00
5 Josh Allen 20.00 50.00
6 Josh Rosen 15.00 40.00
7 D.J. Moore 15.00 40.00
8 Tre'Quan Smith 8.00 20.00
9 Rashaad Penny 8.00 20.00
10 Sony Michel 25.00 60.00
11 Mason Rudolph 12.00 30.00
12 Nick Chubb 15.00 40.00
13 Ronald Jones II 5.00 12.00
14 Courtland Sutton 8.00 20.00
15 Nyheim Hines 6.00 15.00
16 Anthony Miller 8.00 20.00
17 Kerryon Johnson 30.00 60.00
18 James Washington 10.00 25.00
19 J'Mon Moore 5.00 12.00
20 Lamar Jackson 30.00 80.00

2018 Panini Prizm Stained Glass Prizms

1 Tom Brady 10.00 25.00
2 Aaron Rodgers 8.00 20.00
3 Odell Beckham Jr. 4.00 10.00
4 Antonio Brown 4.00 10.00
5 Jimmy Garoppolo 5.00 12.00
6 Baker Mayfield 25.00 60.00
7 Saquon Barkley 20.00 50.00
8 Josh Allen 10.00 25.00
9 Sam Darnold 15.00 40.00
10 Lamar Jackson 15.00 40.00

2018 Panini Prizm Trifecta Prizms

1 Mllr/Hwrd/Trbsky 3.00 8.00
2 Ftzgrld/Jhnsn/Rsn 4.00 10.00
3 Frmn/Jns/Ryn 2.00 5.00
4 McCy/Alln/Bnjmn 4.00 10.00
5 Nwtn/McCffry/Mre 2.50 6.00
6 Grn/Dltn/Mxn 2.00 5.00
7 Myfld/Grdn/Chbb 5.00 12.00
8 Ellt/Prsctt/Gllp 2.50 6.00
9 Chbb/Hrrs/Mllr 2.00 5.00
10 Tte/Jhnsn/Stffrd 2.00 5.00
11 Adms/Grhm/Rdgrs 4.00 10.00
12 Hpkns/Frmn/Wtsn 2.50 6.00
13 Brtls/Chrk/Frntte 2.00 5.00
14 Hltn/Lck/Mck 2.50 6.00
15 Hnt/Mhms/Hll 10.00 25.00
16 Alln/Grdn/Rvrs 2.00 5.00
17 Gff/Grly/Cks 2.00 5.00
18 Drke/Gscki/Tnnhll 1.50 4.00
19 Thln/Ck/Csns 2.00 5.00
20 Gronk/Mchl/Brdy 5.00 12.00
21 Kmra/Brs/Thms 2.00 5.00
22 Mnng/Brkly/Bckhm 6.00 15.00
23 Krse/Pwll/Drnld 5.00 12.00
24 Cpr/Crr/Lnch 2.00 5.00
25 Jffry/Wntz/Ajyi 2.50 6.00
26 Brwn/Bll/Rthlsbrgr 2.00 5.00
27 Grpplo/Gdwn/McKnn 2.50 6.00
28 Wlsn/Bldwn/Pnny 2.50 6.00
29 Wnstn/Evns/Jns 1.50 4.00
30 Smth/Gce/Rd 2.50 6.00

2015 Panini Prizm Draft Picks

1 A.J. Green .30 .75
2 Aaron Rodgers .60 1.50
3 Adrian Peterson .30 .75
4 Alex Smith .25 .60
5 Allen Hurns .20 .50
6 Alshon Jeffery .25 .60
7 Andre Ellington .20 .50
8 Andre Johnson .25 .60
9 Andre Williams .20 .50
10 Andrew Luck .40 1.00
11 Andy Dalton .25 .60
12 Anquan Boldin .20 .50
13 Antonio Brown .30 .75
14 Antonio Gates .20 .50
15 Arian Foster .25 .60
16 Ben Roethlisberger .30 .75
17 Blake Bortles .20 .50
18 Brandon LaFell .20 .50
19 Brandon Marshall .20 .50
20 Carson Palmer .25 .60
21 C.J. Anderson .25 .60
22 Calvin Johnson .30 .75
23 Cam Newton .30 .75
24 Charles Woodson .30 .75
25 Clay Matthews .30 .75
26 Colin Kaepernick .25 .60
27 Danny Amendola .25 .60
28 Darren Sproles .25 .60
29 DeAndre Hopkins .25 .60
30 DeMarco Murray .25 .60
31 Demaryius Thomas .25 .60
32 Derek Carr .30 .75
33 DeSean Jackson .25 .60
34 Dez Bryant .30 .75
35 Drew Brees .30 .75
36 Dwayne Bowe .25 .60
37 Dwight Freeney .20 .50
38 Earl Thomas .25 .60
39 Eddie Lacy .20 .50
40 Eli Manning .25 .60
41 Frank Gore .25 .60
42 J.J. Watt .30 .75
43 Jamaal Charles .25 .60
44 Jason Witten .25 .60
45 Jay Cutler .20 .50
46 Jeremy Hill .20 .50
47 Jimmy Graham .30 .75
48 Joe Flacco .25 .60
49 Johnny Manziel .25 .60
50 Jordan Cameron .20 .50
51 Jordan Matthews .25 .60
52 Jordy Nelson .25 .60
53 Josh Gordon .20 .50
54 Julian Edelman .30 .75
55 Julio Jones .30 .75
56 Julius Peppers .25 .60
57 Julius Thomas .20 .50
58 Justin Forsett .25 .60
59 Justin Houston .20 .50
60 Kam Chancellor .30 .75
61 Keenan Allen .25 .60
62 Kelvin Benjamin .25 .60
63 Kenny Stills .20 .50
64 Khalil Mack .30 .75
65 Larry Fitzgerald .25 .60
66 LeSean McCoy .30 .75
67 Le'Veon Bell .25 .60
68 Luke Kuechly .25 .60
69 Marshawn Lynch .25 .60
70 Martavis Bryant .20 .50
71 Matt Forte .20 .50
72 Matt Ryan .25 .60
73 Matthew Stafford .25 .60
74 Mike Evans .25 .60
75 Mike Wallace .20 .50
76 Ndamukong Suh .25 .60
77 Nick Foles .25 .60
78 Odell Beckham Jr. .30 .75
79 Patrick Peterson .20 .50
80 Paul Posluszny .20 .50
81 Peyton Manning .60 1.50
82 Philip Rivers .30 .75
83 Randall Cobb .25 .60
84 Rashad Jennings .20 .50
85 Reggie Wayne .25 .60
86 Richard Sherman .30 .75
87 Rob Gronkowski .30 .75
88 Robert Griffin III .20 .50
89 Russell Wilson .40 1.00
90 Ryan Tannehill .25 .60
91 LeGarrette Blount .25 .60
92 Sammy Watkins .25 .60
93 Steve Smith .25 .60
94 Teddy Bridgewater .25 .60
95 Terrance Williams .20 .50
96 Tom Brady .75 2.00
97 Tony Romo .25 .60
98 Troy Polamalu .30 .75
99 Vincent Jackson .20 .50
100 Wes Welker .25 .60
101 Amari Cooper RC 1.25 3.00
102 Ameer Abdullah RC .60 1.50
103 Phillip Dorsett RC .40 1.00
104 Vince Mayle RC .50 1.25
105 Benardrick McKinney RC .40 1.00
106 Brett Hundley RC .40 1.00
107 Bryce Petty RC .40 1.00
108 Cameron Artis-Payne RC .40 1.00
109 Clive Walford RC .40 1.00
110 Devin Smith RC .40 1.00
111 Danny Shelton RC .40 1.00
112 Dante Fowler Jr. RC .60 1.50
113 David Cobb RC .40 1.00
114 DeVante Parker RC .60 1.50
115 Devin Funchess RC .60 1.50
116 Bryan Bennett RC .40 1.00
117 Breshad Perriman RC .40 1.00
118 Duke Johnson RC .60 1.50
119 Eddie Goldman RC .40 1.00
120 Garrett Grayson RC .40 1.00
121 Jaelen Strong RC .50 1.25
122 Jameis Winston RC 1.00 2.50
123 Buck Allen RC .50 1.25
124 Jay Ajayi RC .60 1.50
125 Jeremy Langford RC .40 1.00
126 Josh Harper RC .40 1.00
127 Justin Hardy RC .40 1.00
128 Kevin White RC .50 1.25
129 Landon Collins RC .50 1.25
130 Leonard Williams RC .40 1.00
131 Marcus Mariota RC 1.50 4.00
132 Melvin Gordon III RC 1.00 2.50
133 Mike Davis RC .40 1.00
134 Nelson Agholor RC .50 1.25
135 Nick O'Leary RC .40 1.00
136 Randy Gregory RC .40 1.00
137 Rashad Greene RC .40 1.00
138 Sammie Coates RC .50 1.25
139 Shane Carden RC .40 1.00
140 Shane Ray RC .40 1.00
141 Shaq Thompson RC .50 1.25
142 Maxx Williams RC .40 1.00
143 Tony Lippett RC .40 1.00
144 T.J. Yeldon RC .40 1.00
145 Tevin Coleman RC .50 1.25
146 Todd Gurley RC 1.50 4.00
147 Trae Waynes RC .40 1.00
148 Ty Montgomery RC .40 1.00
149 Tyler Lockett RC .60 1.50
150 Vic Beasley Jr. RC .50 1.25
151 Bud Dupree RC .50 1.25
152 Andrus Peat RC .40 1.00
153 Anthony Harris RC .40 1.00
154 Arik Armstead RC .40 1.00
155 Blake Bell RC .60 1.50
156 Bo Wallace RC .40 1.00
157 Taylor Heinicke RC .60 1.50
158 Brandon Scherff RC .60 1.50
159 A.J. Cann RC .50 1.25
160 Da'Ron Brown RC .40 1.00
161 Blake Sims RC .40 1.00
162 Eric Tomlinson RC .50 1.25
163 Cedric Ogbuehi RC .40 1.00
164 Charles Gaines RC .60 1.50
165 Dres Anderson RC .40 1.00
166 Deontay Greenberry RC .40 1.00
167 Cody Fajardo RC .50 1.25
168 Cody Prewitt RC .50 1.25
169 Connor Halliday RC .60 1.50
170 Corey Grant RC .60 1.50
171 Danielle Hunter RC .50 1.25
172 David Johnson RC 1.00 2.50
173 Denzel Perryman RC .40 1.00
174 Ereck Flowers RC .50 1.25
175 Derron Smith RC .40 1.00
176 Devante Davis RC .50 1.25
177 Dezmin Lewis RC .40 1.00
178 Doran Grant RC .60 1.50
179 Kevin White CB RC .50 1.25
180 Dominique Brown RC .40 1.00
181 Dreamius Smith RC 1.00 2.50
182 E.J. Bibbs RC .50 1.25
183 Eric Kendricks RC .40 1.00
184 Chris Conley RC .40 1.00
185 Gary Nova RC .40 1.00
186 Eli Harold RC .40 1.00
187 Gerald Christian RC .50 1.25
188 J.J. Nelson RC .40 1.00
189 Gerod Holliman RC .60 1.50
190 Hau'oli Kikaha RC .50 1.25
191 Hutson Mason RC .40 1.00
192 Ifo Ekpre-Olomu RC .40 1.00
193 Jahwan Edwards RC .50 1.25
194 Jalen Collins RC .40 1.00
195 Jake Waters RC .50 1.25
196 Casey Pierce RC .40 1.00
197 Jesse James RC .50 1.25
198 Jamison Crowder RC .50 1.25
199 Jaquiski Tartt RC .40 1.00
200 Jaxon Shipley RC .40 1.00
201 Jeff Heuerman RC .50 1.25
202 Cameron Erving RC .50 1.25
203 Jordan Taylor RC .50 1.25
204 Jordon James RC .50 1.25
205 Karlos Williams RC .40 1.00
206 Jordan Phillips RC .40 1.00
207 Kenny Bell RC .60 1.50
208 Kevin Johnson RC .40 1.00
209 Kevin Parks RC .40 1.00
210 Kurtis Drummond RC .50 1.25
211 La'el Collins RC .50 1.25

212 Levi Norwood RC .40 1.00
213 Lorenzo Doss RC .40 1.00
214 Lorenzo Mauldin RC .40 1.00
215 Malcolm Agnew RC .40 1.00
216 Malcolm Brown RC .50 1.25
217 Malcom Brown RC .40 1.00
218 Marcus Murphy RC .40 1.00
219 Marcus Peters RC .60 1.50
220 Josh Robinson RC .40 1.00
221 Mario Edwards Jr. RC .40 1.00
222 Markus Golden RC .40 1.00
223 Matt Jones RC .40 1.00
224 Michael Bennett RC .40 1.00
225 Michael Dyer RC .60 1.50
226 MyCole Pruitt RC .40 1.00
227 Nate Orchard RC .40 1.00
228 Nick Boyle RC .40 1.00
229 Nick Marshall RC .60 1.50
230 P.J. Williams RC .50 1.25
231 Antwan Goodley RC .40 1.00
232 Rannell Hall RC .40 1.00
233 Geneo Grissom RC .40 1.00
234 Owamagbe Odighizuwa RC .50 1.25
235 Paul Dawson RC .50 1.25
236 Sean Mannion RC .40 1.00
237 Senquez Golson RC .40 1.00
238 T.J. Clemmings RC .40 1.00
239 Taylor Kelly RC .50 1.25
240 Terrence Magee RC .60 1.50
241 Mario Alford RC .40 1.00
242 Titus Davis RC .50 1.25
243 Stefon Diggs RC 1.00 2.50
244 Preston Smith RC .50 1.25
245 Trey Flowers RC .60 1.50
246 Quinten Rollins RC .75 2.00
247 Tyler Kroft RC .50 1.25
248 Austin Hill RC .40 1.00
249 Kaelin Clay RC .40 1.00
250 Kwon Alexander RC .50 1.25

2015 Panini Prizm Draft Picks Prizms

*VETS: 2X TO 5X BASIC CARDS
*ROOKIES: .6X TO 1.5X BASIC CARDS

2015 Panini Prizm Draft Picks Prizms Blue

*VETS/75: 4X TO 10X BASIC CARDS
*ROOK/75: 1.2X TO 3X BASIC CARDS

2015 Panini Prizm Draft Picks Prizms Camo

*VETS/199: 3X TO 8X BASIC CARDS
*ROOKIES/199: 1X TO 2.5X BASIC CARDS

2015 Panini Prizm Draft Picks Prizms Purple

*VETS/99: 4X TO 10X BASIC CARDS
*ROOK/99: 1.2X TO 3X BASIC CARDS

2015 Panini Prizm Draft Picks Prizms Red White and Blue

*VETS/25: 10X TO 25X BASIC CARDS
*ROOKIES/25: 3X TO 8X BASIC RC

2015 Panini Prizm Draft Picks Prizms Tie Dyed

*VETS/49: 6X TO 15X BASIC CARDS
*ROOKIES/49: 2X TO 5X BASIC RC

2015 Panini Prizm Draft Picks All Americans

1 Tevin Coleman .75 2.00
2 Amari Cooper 2.00 5.00
3 Melvin Gordon III 1.50 4.00
4 Marcus Mariota 2.50 6.00
5 Nick O'Leary .60 1.50
6 Landon Collins .75 2.00
7 Senquez Golson .60 1.50
8 Gerod Holliman 1.00 2.50
9 Hau'oli Kikaha .75 2.00
10 Brandon Scherff 1.00 2.50
11 Malcom Brown .60 1.50
12 Shane Ray .60 1.50
13 Paul Dawson .75 2.00
14 Vic Beasley Jr. .75 2.00
15 Ifo Ekpre-Olomu .60 1.50
16 Tyler Lockett 1.00 2.50
17 Jameis Winston 1.50 4.00
18 Ka'Deem Carey .60 1.50
19 Andre Williams .60 1.50
20 Brandin Cooks .75 2.00
21 Mike Evans .75 2.00
22 Jace Amaro .60 1.50
23 Aaron Donald 1.00 2.50
24 Jackson Jeffcoat .60 1.50
25 Michael Sam .60 1.50
26 Anthony Barr .60 1.50
27 C.J. Mosley 1.00 2.50
28 Trent Murphy .60 1.50
29 Ha Ha Clinton-Dix .60 1.50
30 Darqueze Dennard .60 1.50
31 Justin Gilbert .60 1.50
32 Lamarcus Joyner .60 1.50
33 Ty Montgomery .60 1.50
34 Johnny Manziel .75 2.00
35 Montee Ball .60 1.50
36 Kenjon Barner .60 1.50
37 Marqise Lee .60 1.50
38 Terrance Williams .60 1.50
39 Zach Ertz .75 2.00
40 Jadeveon Clowney .60 1.50
41 Damontre Moore .60 1.50
42 Jarvis Jones .60 1.50
43 Jordan Poyer .60 1.50
44 Bjoern Werner .60 1.50
45 Dee Milliner .60 1.50
46 Eric Reid .75 2.00
47 Phillip Thomas .60 1.50
48 Dri Archer .60 1.50
49 Robert Griffin III .60 1.50
50 Luke Kuechly .75 2.00

2015 Panini Prizm Draft Picks All Americans Autographs

1 Tevin Coleman 3.00 8.00
2 Amari Cooper
3 Melvin Gordon III
4 Marcus Mariota 50.00 100.00
5 Nick O'Leary 2.50 6.00
6 Landon Collins 3.00 8.00
7 Senquez Golson 2.50 6.00
8 Gerod Holliman 4.00 10.00
9 Hau'oli Kikaha 3.00 8.00
10 Brandon Scherff 4.00 10.00
11 Malcom Brown 2.50 6.00
13 Paul Dawson 3.00 8.00
14 Vic Beasley Jr. 3.00 8.00
15 Ifo Ekpre-Olomu 2.50 6.00
16 Tyler Lockett 4.00 10.00
17 Jameis Winston 50.00 100.00
18 Ty Montgomery 2.50 6.00
19 Johnny Manziel 3.00 8.00
20 Jadeveon Clowney 2.50 6.00

2015 Panini Prizm Draft Picks Alumnus Autographs Prizms Camo

*BLUE/75: .5X TO 1.2X CAMO AU/199
*BLUE/25: .4X TO 1X CAMO AU/35
*PURPLE/99: .5X TO 1.2X CAMO AU/199
*PURPLE/30: .4X TO 1X CAMO AU/35
*RED WHITE BLUE/25: .8X TO 2X CAMO AU/199
*RED WHITE BLUE/15: .6X TO 1.5X CAMO AU/35
*TIE DYED/49: .6X TO 1.5X CAMO AU/199
*TIE DYED/20: .6X TO 1.5X CAMO AU/35
3 Allen Hurns/199 3.00 8.00
12 Brandon LaFell/199 3.00 8.00
16 Charles Clay/199 3.00 8.00
37 Jeremy Kerley/199 3.00 8.00
45 Justin Forsett/35 6.00 15.00
46 Justin Houston/35 5.00 12.00
61 Paul Posluszny/35 5.00 12.00
71 Sean Lee/35 15.00 30.00

2015 Panini Prizm Draft Picks Autographs Prizms

101 Amari Cooper 25.00 50.00
102 Ameer Abdullah 3.00 8.00
103 Phillip Dorsett 2.00 5.00
104 Vince Mayle 2.50 6.00
106 Brett Hundley 2.00 5.00
107 Bryce Petty 2.00 5.00
108 Cameron Artis-Payne 2.00 5.00
109 Clive Walford 2.00 5.00
111 Danny Shelton 2.00 5.00
112 Dante Fowler Jr. 3.00 8.00
113 David Cobb 2.00 5.00
114 DeVante Parker 3.00 8.00
115 Devin Funchess 3.00 8.00
116 Bryan Bennett 2.00 5.00
117 Breshad Perriman 2.00 5.00
118 Duke Johnson 3.00 8.00
121 Jaelen Strong 2.50 6.00
122 Jameis Winston SP 30.00 60.00
123 Buck Allen 2.50 6.00
124 Jay Ajayi 3.00 8.00
125 Jeremy Langford 2.00 5.00
126 Josh Harper 2.00 5.00
127 Justin Hardy 2.00 5.00
128 Kevin White 2.50 6.00
129 Landon Collins 2.50 6.00
130 Leonard Williams 2.00 5.00
131 Marcus Mariota SP 40.00 80.00
132 Melvin Gordon III 12.00 30.00
133 Mike Davis 2.00 5.00
134 Nelson Agholor 2.50 6.00
135 Nick O'Leary 2.00 5.00
136 Randy Gregory 2.00 5.00
137 Rashad Greene 2.00 5.00
138 Sammie Coates 2.50 6.00
139 Shane Carden 2.00 5.00
141 Shaq Thompson 2.50 6.00
142 Maxx Williams 2.00 5.00
143 Tony Lippett 2.00 5.00
144 T.J. Yeldon 2.00 5.00
145 Tevin Coleman 2.50 6.00
146 Todd Gurley 20.00 40.00
147 Trae Waynes 2.00 5.00
148 Ty Montgomery 2.00 5.00
149 Tyler Lockett 3.00 8.00
150 Vic Beasley Jr. 2.50 6.00
151 Bud Dupree 2.50 6.00
152 Andrus Peat 2.00 5.00
153 Anthony Harris 2.00 5.00
154 Arik Armstead 2.00 5.00
155 Blake Bell 3.00 8.00
156 Bo Wallace 2.00 5.00
157 Taylor Heinicke 3.00 8.00
158 Brandon Scherff 3.00 8.00
159 A.J. Cann 2.50 6.00
160 Da'Ron Brown 2.00 5.00
161 Blake Sims 2.00 5.00
162 Eric Tomlinson 2.50 6.00
163 Cedric Ogbuehi 2.00 5.00
164 Charles Gaines 3.00 8.00
165 Dres Anderson 2.00 5.00
166 Deontay Greenberry 2.00 5.00
167 Cody Fajardo 2.50 6.00
168 Cody Prewitt 2.50 6.00
169 Connor Halliday 3.00 8.00
170 Corey Grant 3.00 8.00
171 Danielle Hunter 2.50 6.00
172 David Johnson 10.00 25.00
173 Denzel Perryman 2.00 5.00
174 Ereck Flowers 2.50 6.00
175 Derron Smith 2.00 5.00
176 Devante Davis 2.50 6.00
177 Dezmin Lewis 2.00 5.00
179 Kevin White 2.50 6.00
180 Dominique Brown 2.00 5.00
181 Dreamius Smith 5.00 12.00
182 E.J. Bibbs 2.50 6.00
183 Eric Kendricks 2.00 5.00
184 Chris Conley 2.00 5.00
185 Gary Nova 2.00 5.00
186 Eli Harold 2.00 5.00
187 Gerald Christian 2.50 6.00
188 J.J. Nelson 2.00 5.00
189 Gerod Holliman 3.00 8.00
190 Hau'oli Kikaha 2.50 6.00
191 Hutson Mason 2.00 5.00
192 Ifo Ekpre-Olomu 2.00 5.00
193 Johwan Edwards 2.50 6.00
195 Jake Waters 2.50 6.00
196 Casey Pierce 2.00 5.00
197 Jesse James 2.50 6.00
198 Jamison Crowder 2.50 6.00
199 Jaquiski Tartt 2.00 5.00
200 Jaxon Shipley 2.00 5.00
202 Cameron Erving 2.50 6.00
203 Jordan Taylor 2.50 6.00
204 Jordon James 2.50 6.00
205 Karlos Williams 2.00 5.00
206 Jordan Phillips 2.00 5.00
207 Kenny Bell 3.00 8.00
208 Kevin Johnson 2.00 5.00
209 Kevin Parks 2.00 5.00
210 Kurtis Drummond 2.50 6.00
211 La'el Collins 2.50 6.00
212 Levi Norwood 2.00 5.00
213 Lorenzo Doss 2.00 5.00
214 Lorenzo Mauldin 2.00 5.00
215 Malcolm Agnew 2.00 5.00
216 Malcolm Brown 2.50 6.00
217 Malcom Brown 2.00 5.00
218 Marcus Murphy 2.00 5.00
219 Marcus Peters 3.00 8.00
220 Josh Robinson 2.00 5.00
221 Mario Edwards Jr. 2.00 5.00
222 Markus Golden 2.00 5.00
223 Matt Jones 2.00 5.00
225 Michael Dyer 3.00 8.00
226 MyCole Pruitt 2.00 5.00
227 Nate Orchard 2.00 5.00
228 Nick Boyle 2.00 5.00
229 Nick Marshall 3.00 8.00
230 P.J. Williams 2.50 6.00
231 Antwan Goodley 2.50 6.00
232 Rannell Hall 2.00 5.00
233 Geneo Grissom 2.00 5.00
234 Owamagbe Odighizuwa 2.50 6.00
235 Paul Dawson 2.50 6.00
236 Sean Mannion 2.00 5.00
237 Senquez Golson 2.00 5.00
238 T.J. Clemmings 2.00 5.00
239 Taylor Kelly 2.50 6.00
240 Terrence Magee 3.00 8.00
241 Mario Alford 2.00 5.00
242 Titus Davis 2.50 6.00
243 Stefon Diggs 5.00 12.00
245 Trey Flowers 3.00 8.00
247 Tyler Kroft 2.50 6.00
248 Austin Hill 2.00 5.00
249 Kaelin Clay 2.00 5.00
250 Kwon Alexander 2.50 6.00

2015 Panini Prizm Draft Picks Autographs Prizms Blue

*BLUE/75: .6X TO 1.5X BASIC AU
*BLUE/25: 1X TO 2.5X BASIC AU

2015 Panini Prizm Draft Picks Autographs Prizms Camo

*CAMO/140 199: .5X TO 1.2X BASIC AU
*CAMO/99: .6X TO 1.5X BASIC AU
*CAMO/25: 1X TO 2.5X BASIC AU

2015 Panini Prizm Draft Picks Autographs Prizms Purple

*PURPLE/99: .6X TO 1.5X BASIC AU
*PURPLE/30-49: .8X TO 2X BASIC AU
122 Jameis Winston/30 50.00 125.00

2015 Panini Prizm Draft Picks Autographs Prizms Red White and Blue

*RWB/25: 1X TO 2.5X BASIC AU
*RWB/15: 1.2X TO 3X BASIC AU
122 Jameis Winston/15 75.00 150.00

2015 Panini Prizm Draft Picks Autographs Prizms Tie Dyed

*TIE DYE/49: .8X TO 2X BASIC AU
*TIE DYE/20: 1X TO 2.5X BASIC AU
122 Jameis Winston/20 60.00 150.00

2015 Panini Prizm Draft Picks D Fence Die Cuts

1 Leonard Williams .75 2.00
2 Randy Gregory .75 2.00
3 Landon Collins 1.00 2.50
4 Shane Ray .75 2.00
5 Vic Beasley Jr. 1.00 2.50
6 Bud Dupree 1.00 2.50
7 Shaq Thompson 1.00 2.50
8 Dante Fowler Jr. 1.25 3.00
9 Trae Waynes .75 2.00
10 Danny Shelton .75 2.00
11 Eddie Goldman .75 2.00
12 Malcom Brown .75 2.00
13 Benardrick McKinney .75 2.00
14 Nate Orchard .75 2.00
15 Ifo Ekpre-Olomu .75 2.00
16 Danielle Hunter 1.00 2.50
17 Marcus Peters 1.25 3.00
18 Michael Bennett .75 2.00
19 Arik Armstead .75 2.00
20 P.J. Williams 1.00 2.50
21 Eli Harold .75 2.00
22 Lorenzo Mauldin .75 2.00
23 Paul Dawson 1.00 2.50
24 Jalen Collins .75 2.00
25 Hau'oli Kikaha 1.00 2.50
26 Julius Peppers 1.00 2.50
27 Cody Prewitt 1.00 2.50
28 Owamagbe Odighizuwa 1.00 2.50
29 Steven Nelson .75 2.00
30 Eric Kendricks .75 2.00
31 Senquez Golson .75 2.00
32 Mario Edwards Jr. .75 2.00
33 Jordan Phillips .75 2.00
34 Anthony Harris .75 2.00
35 Derron Smith .75 2.00
36 Troy Polamalu 2.00 5.00
37 Kevin Johnson .75 2.00
38 Markus Golden .75 2.00
39 Denzel Perryman .75 2.00
40 Trey Flowers 1.25 3.00
41 Kevin White 1.00 2.50
42 Richard Sherman 2.00 5.00
43 Quinten Rollins 1.50 4.00
44 Jaquiski Tartt .75 2.00
45 Kwon Alexander 1.00 2.50
46 Doran Grant 1.25 3.00
47 Preston Smith 1.00 2.50
48 Lorenzo Doss .75 2.00
49 J.J. Watt 2.00 5.00
50 Charles Woodson 2.00 5.00

2015 Panini Prizm Draft Picks Helmet Die Cuts

1 Bud Dupree 1.00 2.50
2 Amari Cooper 2.50 6.00
3 Ameer Abdullah 1.25 3.00
4 Benardrick McKinney .75 2.00
5 Brett Hundley .75 2.00
6 Bryce Petty .75 2.00
7 Cameron Artis-Payne .75 2.00
8 Clive Walford .75 2.00
9 David Cobb .75 2.00
10 DeVante Parker 1.25 3.00
11 Devin Funchess 1.25 3.00
12 Devin Smith .75 2.00
13 Chris Conley .75 2.00
14 Dres Anderson .75 2.00
15 Duke Johnson 1.25 3.00
16 Garrett Grayson .75 2.00
17 Jaelen Strong 1.00 2.50
18 Jameis Winston 2.00 5.00
19 Buck Allen 1.00 2.50
20 Jay Ajayi 1.25 3.00
21 Jeremy Langford .75 2.00
22 Josh Harper .75 2.00
23 Justin Hardy .75 2.00
24 Kevin White 1.00 2.50
25 Landon Collins 1.00 2.50
26 Leonard Williams .75 2.00
27 Marcus Mariota 3.00 8.00
28 Matt Jones .75 2.00
29 Maxx Williams .75 2.00
30 Melvin Gordon III 2.00 5.00
31 Mike Davis .75 2.00
32 Nelson Agholor 1.00 2.50
33 Nick O'Leary .75 2.00
34 Phillip Dorsett .75 2.00
35 Randy Gregory .75 2.00
36 Rashad Greene .75 2.00
37 Sammie Coates 1.00 2.50
38 Shane Carden .75 2.00
39 Shane Ray .75 2.00
40 Shaq Thompson 1.00 2.50
41 Stefon Diggs 2.00 5.00
42 T.J. Yeldon .75 2.00
43 Tevin Coleman 1.00 2.50
44 Todd Gurley 3.00 8.00
45 Tony Lippett .75 2.00
46 Trae Waynes .75 2.00
47 Ty Montgomery .75 2.00
48 Tyler Lockett 1.25 3.00
49 Vic Beasley Jr. 1.00 2.50
50 Vince Mayle 1.00 2.50

2015 Panini Prizm Draft Picks Stained Glass

1 A.J. Green 1.25 3.00
2 Aaron Rodgers 2.50 6.00
3 Andre Johnson 1.00 2.50
4 Andrew Luck 1.50 4.00
5 Andy Dalton 1.00 2.50
6 Anquan Boldin .75 2.00
7 Arian Foster 1.00 2.50
8 Brandon Marshall .75 2.00
9 Carson Palmer 1.00 2.50
10 C.J. Anderson 1.00 2.50
11 Calvin Johnson 1.25 3.00
12 Cam Newton 1.25 3.00
13 Charles Woodson 1.25 3.00
14 Clay Matthews 1.25 3.00
15 Colin Kaepernick 1.00 2.50
16 DeMarco Murray 1.00 2.50
17 Demaryius Thomas 1.00 2.50
18 DeSean Jackson 1.00 2.50
19 Dez Bryant 1.25 3.00
20 Drew Brees 1.25 3.00
21 Eddie Lacy .75 2.00
22 Eli Manning 1.00 2.50
23 Frank Gore 1.00 2.50
24 J.J. Watt 1.25 3.00
25 Jamaal Charles 1.00 2.50
26 Jason Witten 1.00 2.50
27 Jimmy Graham 1.25 3.00
28 Joe Flacco 1.00 2.50
29 Julio Jones 1.25 3.00
30 Larry Fitzgerald 1.00 2.50
31 LeSean McCoy 1.25 3.00
32 Le'Veon Bell 1.00 2.50
33 Marshawn Lynch 1.00 2.50
34 Matt Forte .75 2.00
35 Matt Ryan 1.00 2.50
36 Matthew Stafford 1.00 2.50
37 Nick Foles 1.00 2.50
38 Odell Beckham Jr. 1.25 3.00
39 Peyton Manning 2.50 6.00
40 Philip Rivers 1.25 3.00
41 Reggie Wayne 1.00 2.50
42 Richard Sherman 1.25 3.00
43 Rob Gronkowski 1.25 3.00
44 Robert Griffin III .75 2.00
45 Russell Wilson 1.50 4.00
46 Tom Brady 3.00 8.00
47 Tony Romo 1.00 2.50
48 Troy Polamalu 1.25 3.00
49 LeGarrette Blount 1.00 2.50
50 Wes Welker 1.00 2.50
51 Amari Cooper 2.50 6.00
52 Ameer Abdullah 1.25 3.00
53 Breshad Perriman .75 2.00
54 Tony Lippett .75 2.00
55 Benardrick McKinney .75 2.00
56 Brett Hundley .75 2.00
57 Bryce Petty .75 2.00
58 Cameron Artis-Payne .75 2.00
59 Clive Walford .75 2.00
60 Maxx Williams .75 2.00
61 Danny Shelton .75 2.00
62 Dante Fowler Jr. 1.25 3.00
63 David Cobb .75 2.00
64 DeVante Parker 1.25 3.00
65 Devin Funchess 1.25 3.00
66 Chris Conley .75 2.00
67 Phillip Dorsett .75 2.00
68 Duke Johnson 1.25 3.00
69 Eddie Goldman .75 2.00
70 Garrett Grayson .75 2.00
71 Jaelen Strong 1.00 2.50
72 Jameis Winston 2.00 5.00
73 Buck Allen 1.00 2.50
74 Jay Ajayi 1.25 3.00
75 Jeremy Langford .75 2.00
76 Josh Harper .75 2.00
77 Justin Hardy .75 2.00
78 Kevin White 1.00 2.50
79 Landon Collins 1.00 2.50
80 Leonard Williams .75 2.00
81 Marcus Mariota 3.00 8.00
82 Melvin Gordon III 2.00 5.00
83 Mike Davis .75 2.00
84 Nelson Agholor 1.00 2.50
85 Nick O'Leary .75 2.00
86 Randy Gregory .75 2.00
87 Rashad Greene .75 2.00
88 Sammie Coates 1.00 2.50
89 Shane Carden .75 2.00
90 Shane Ray .75 2.00
91 Shaq Thompson 1.00 2.50
92 Devin Smith .75 2.00
93 Vince Mayle 1.00 2.50
94 T.J. Yeldon .75 2.00
95 Tevin Coleman 1.00 2.50
96 Todd Gurley 3.00 8.00
97 Trae Waynes .75 2.00
98 Ty Montgomery .75 2.00
99 Tyler Lockett 1.25 3.00
100 Vic Beasley Jr. 1.00 2.50

2015 Panini Prizm Draft Picks Team Trademarks

1 Amari Cooper 2.50 6.00
2 Ameer Abdullah 1.25 3.00
3 Phillip Dorsett .75 2.00
4 Tony Lippett .75 2.00
5 Benardrick McKinney .75 2.00
6 Brett Hundley .75 2.00
7 Bryce Petty .75 2.00
8 Cameron Artis-Payne .75 2.00
9 Clive Walford .75 2.00
10 Maxx Williams .75 2.00
11 Danny Shelton .75 2.00
12 Dante Fowler Jr. 1.25 3.00
13 David Cobb .75 2.00
14 DeVante Parker 1.25 3.00
15 Devin Funchess 1.25 3.00
16 Chris Conley .75 2.00
17 Breshad Perriman .75 2.00
18 Duke Johnson 1.25 3.00
19 Eddie Goldman .75 2.00
20 Garrett Grayson .75 2.00
21 Jaelen Strong 1.00 2.50
22 Jameis Winston 2.00 5.00
23 Buck Allen 1.00 2.50
24 Jay Ajayi 1.25 3.00
25 Jeremy Langford .75 2.00
26 Josh Harper .75 2.00
27 Justin Hardy .75 2.00
28 Kevin White 1.00 2.50
29 Landon Collins 1.00 2.50
30 Leonard Williams .75 2.00
31 Marcus Mariota 3.00 8.00
32 Melvin Gordon III 2.00 5.00
33 Mike Davis .75 2.00
34 Nelson Agholor 1.00 2.50
35 Nick O'Leary .75 2.00
36 Randy Gregory .75 2.00
37 Rashad Greene .75 2.00
38 Sammie Coates 1.00 2.50
39 Shane Carden .75 2.00
40 Shane Ray .75 2.00
41 Shaq Thompson 1.00 2.50
42 Devin Smith .75 2.00
43 Vince Mayle 1.00 2.50
44 T.J. Yeldon .75 2.00
45 Tevin Coleman 1.00 2.50
46 Todd Gurley 3.00 8.00
47 Trae Waynes .75 2.00
48 Ty Montgomery .75 2.00
49 Tyler Lockett 1.25 3.00
50 Vic Beasley Jr. 1.00 2.50

2015 Panini Prizm Draft Picks Team Trademarks Autographs Prizms

1 Amari Cooper 60.00 120.00
2 Ameer Abdullah 4.00 10.00
3 Phillip Dorsett 2.50 6.00
4 Tony Lippett
6 Brett Hundley 2.50 6.00
7 Bryce Petty 2.50 6.00
8 Cameron Artis-Payne 2.50 6.00
9 Clive Walford 2.50 6.00
10 Maxx Williams 2.50 6.00
11 Danny Shelton 2.50 6.00
12 Dante Fowler Jr. 4.00 10.00
13 David Cobb 2.50 6.00
14 DeVante Parker 6.00 15.00
15 Devin Funchess 4.00 10.00
16 Chris Conley 2.50 6.00
17 Breshad Perriman 2.50 6.00
18 Duke Johnson 4.00 10.00
21 Jaelen Strong
22 Jameis Winston 60.00 120.00
23 Buck Allen 3.00 8.00
24 Jay Ajayi 4.00 10.00
25 Jeremy Langford 2.50 6.00
26 Josh Harper 2.50 6.00
27 Justin Hardy 2.50 6.00
28 Kevin White
29 Landon Collins 3.00 8.00
30 Leonard Williams 2.50 6.00
31 Marcus Mariota 50.00 100.00
32 Melvin Gordon III
33 Mike Davis 2.50 6.00
34 Nelson Agholor 10.00 26.00
35 Nick O'Leary 2.50 6.00
36 Randy Gregory 2.50 6.00
37 Rashad Greene 2.50 6.00
38 Sammie Coates 3.00 8.00
39 Shane Carden 2.50 6.00
41 Shaq Thompson 3.00 8.00
43 Vince Mayle 3.00 8.00
44 T.J. Yeldon 2.50 6.00
45 Tevin Coleman 3.00 8.00
46 Todd Gurley 60.00 120.00
47 Trae Waynes 2.50 6.00
48 Ty Montgomery 2.50 6.00
49 Tyler Lockett 4.00 10.00
50 Vic Beasley Jr. 3.00 8.00

2016 Panini Prizm Draft Picks

1 A.J. Green .30 .75
2 Aaron Rodgers .60 1.50
3 Adrian Peterson .30 .75
4 Alex Smith .25 .60
5 Allen Hurns .20 .50
6 Allen Robinson .25 .60
7 Amari Cooper .30 .75
8 Andrew Luck .40 1.00
9 Andy Dalton .25 .60
10 Antonio Brown .30 .75
11 Arian Foster .25 .60
12 Ben Roethlisberger .30 .75
13 Blake Bortles .20 .50
14 Brandon Marshall .20 .50
15 C.J. Anderson .25 .60
16 Calvin Johnson .30 .75
17 Cam Newton .30 .75
18 Cameron Wake .20 .50
19 Carlos Hyde .20 .50
20 Carson Palmer .25 .60
21 Charles Woodson .30 .75
22 Chris Johnson .20 .50
23 Clay Matthews .30 .75
24 Darrelle Revis .20 .50
25 Darren Sproles .25 .60
26 DeAndre Hopkins .25 .60
27 DeMarco Murray .25 .60
28 Demaryius Thomas .25 .60
29 Derek Carr .30 .75
30 DeSean Jackson .25 .60
31 Devonta Freeman .25 .60
32 Dez Bryant .30 .75
33 Doug Martin .25 .60
34 Drew Brees .30 .75
35 Earl Thomas .25 .60
36 Eddie Lacy .20 .50
37 Eli Manning .25 .60
38 Elvis Dumervil .20 .50
39 Emmanuel Sanders .30 .75
40 Frank Gore .25 .60
41 Giovani Bernard .20 .50
42 Greg Olsen .25 .60
43 J.J. Watt .30 .75
44 Jamaal Charles .25 .60
45 Jameis Winston .30 .75
46 James Jones .20 .50
47 Jason Witten .25 .60
48 Jeremy Hill .20 .50
49 Jeremy Maclin .20 .50
50 Jimmy Graham .30 .75
51 Joe Flacco .25 .60
52 Joe Haden .20 .50
53 Jordy Nelson .25 .60
54 Julian Edelman .30 .75
55 Julio Jones .30 .75
56 Julius Thomas .20 .50
57 Justin Forsett .25 .60
58 Justin Houston .20 .50
59 Kam Chancellor .30 .75
60 Keenan Allen .25 .60
61 Khalil Mack .30 .75
62 Kirk Cousins .30 .75
63 Larry Fitzgerald .25 .60
64 Latavius Murray .20 .50
65 LeSean McCoy .30 .75
66 Le'Veon Bell .25 .60
67 Luke Kuechly .25 .60
68 Marcus Mariota .30 .75
69 Mario Williams .20 .50
70 Mark Ingram .25 .60
71 Marshawn Lynch .25 .60
72 Matt Forte .20 .50
73 Matt Ryan .25 .60
74 Matthew Stafford .25 .60
75 Melvin Gordon .25 .60
76 Mike Evans .25 .60
77 Ndamukong Suh .25 .60
78 Nick Foles .25 .60
79 Odell Beckham Jr. .30 .75
80 Patrick Peterson .20 .50
81 Peyton Manning .60 1.50
82 Philip Rivers .30 .75
83 Randall Cobb .25 .60
84 Richard Sherman .30 .75
85 Rob Gronkowski .30 .75
86 Stefon Diggs .25 .60
87 Russell Wilson .40 1.00
88 Ryan Tannehill .25 .60
89 Sam Bradford .20 .50
90 Steve Smith .25 .60
91 Teddy Bridgewater .25 .60
92 Thomas Rawls .20 .50
93 T.J. Yeldon .20 .50
94 Todd Gurley .30 .75
95 Tom Brady .75 2.00
96 Tony Romo .25 .60
97 Travis Benjamin .20 .50
98 Tyrod Taylor .25 .60
99 Von Miller .25 .60
100 Willie Snead .25 .60
101 Joey Bosa RC .75 2.00
102 Jared Goff RC 2.50 6.00
103 Connor Cook RC .50 1.25
104 Laquon Treadwell RC .50 1.25
105 Ezekiel Elliott RC 2.00 5.00
106 Michael Thomas RC .75 2.00
107 Josh Doctson RC .50 1.25
108 Derrick Henry RC 1.00 2.50
109 Cardale Jones RC .40 1.00
110 Christian Hackenberg RC .40 1.00
111 Corey Coleman RC .60 1.50
112 Tyler Boyd RC .50 1.25
113 Hunter Henry RC .50 1.25
114 Demarcus Robinson RC .40 1.00
115 Alex Collins RC .50 1.25
116 Nile Lawrence-Stample RC .50 1.25
117 Paul Perkins RC .40 1.00
118 Jeff Driskel RC .40 1.00
119 Rashard Higgins RC .40 1.00
120 Pharoh Cooper RC .40 1.00
121 Tyler Ervin RC .40 1.00
122 Devontae Booker RC .50 1.25
123 De'Runnya Wilson RC .40 1.00
124 Jordan Williams RC .40 1.00
125 Dak Prescott RC 2.00 5.00
126 Aaron Green RC .40 1.00
127 Carson Wentz RC 4.00 10.00
128 Nick Vannett RC .40 1.00
129 Bronson Kaufusi RC .40 1.00
130 Leonte Carroo RC .40 1.00
131 Tre Madden RC .40 1.00
132 D.J. White RC .40 1.00
133 Brandon Doughty RC .40 1.00
134 Bralon Addison RC .40 1.00
135 Nelson Spruce RC .40 1.00
136 Kenneth Dixon RC .40 1.00
137 Kenyan Drake RC .60 1.50
138 Braxton Miller RC .40 1.00
139 Josh Ferguson RC .40 1.00
140 Cody Kessler RC .40 1.00
141 Devon Cajuste RC .40 1.00
142 Devon Johnson RC .50 1.25
143 D.J. Foster RC .50 1.25
144 Kelvin Taylor RC .40 1.00
145 Sterling Shepard RC .50 1.25
146 Mekale McKay RC .40 1.00
147 Carl Nassib RC .40 1.00
148 Jacoby Brissett RC .50 1.25
149 Paxton Lynch RC .40 1.00
150 Kenny Lawler RC .60 1.50
151 Kyle Carter RC .40 1.00
152 Bryce Williams RC .50 1.25
153 Austin Johnson RC .40 1.00
154 Austin Hooper RC .40 1.00
155 Jerell Adams RC .40 1.00
156 Byron Marshall RC .40 1.00
157 Kevin Hogan RC .50 1.25
158 Jordan Payton RC .40 1.00
159 Demarcus Ayers RC .40 1.00
160 Jonathan Williams RC .50 1.25
161 Jordan Canzeri RC .60 1.50
162 Daniel Braverman RC .40 1.00
163 Kolby Listenbee RC .40 1.00
164 Brandon Allen RC .40 1.00
165 Robert Nkemdiche RC .50 1.25
166 Jalen Ramsey RC .60 1.50
167 Vernon Hargreaves III RC .60 1.50
168 Leonard Floyd RC .50 1.25
169 DeForest Buckner RC .40 1.00
170 Kenny Clark RC .40 1.00
171 Marquise Williams RC .40 1.00
172 Myles Jack RC .50 1.25
173 Reggie Ragland RC .40 1.00
174 Shawn Oakman RC .50 1.25
175 A'Shawn Robinson RC .40 1.00
176 Su'a Cravens RC .40 1.00
177 Emmanuel Ogbah RC .50 1.25
178 DeAndre Washington RC .40 1.00
179 Shilique Calhoun RC .40 1.00
180 Kendall Fuller RC .50 1.25
181 Adolphus Washington RC .40 1.00
182 Andrew Billings RC .50 1.25
183 Vonn Bell RC .50 1.25
184 Jordan Jenkins RC .60 1.50
185 Jaydon Mickens RC .40 1.00
186 DeAndre Houston-Carson RC .40 1.00
187 Daniel Lasco RC .40 1.00
188 Artie Burns RC .50 1.25
189 Jake Coker RC
190 Jordan Howard RC 1.00 2.50
191 Mackensie Alexander RC .40 1.00
192 Trevone Boykin RC .40 1.00
193 Jason Spriggs RC .40 1.00
194 Tra Carson RC .40 1.00
195 Noah Spence RC .40 1.00
196 Steven Scheu RC .40 1.00
197 Dan Vitale RC .40 1.00
198 Jalin Marshall RC .60 1.50
199 Jake McGee RC .50 1.25
200 Eli Apple RC .50 1.25
201 Shaq Lawson RC .40 1.00
202 Jeremy Cash RC .50 1.25
203 Jonathan Bullard RC .40 1.00
204 William Jackson III RC .50 1.25
205 Darian Thompson RC .40 1.00
206 Jayron Kearse RC .40 1.00
207 Joshua Perry RC .40 1.00
208 Deion Jones RC .40 1.00
209 Tyler Higbee RC .40 1.00
210 Antonio Morrison RC .50 1.25
211 Dadi Lhomme Nicolas RC .50 1.25
212 Nate Sudfeld RC .40 1.00
213 Jalen Mills RC .50 1.25
214 Will Redmond RC .60 1.50
215 Dominique Alexander RC .40 1.00
216 Adam Gotsis RC .40 1.00
217 Kevon Seymour RC .40 1.00
218 Briean Boddy-Calhoun RC .40 1.00
219 Kentrell Brothers RC .40 1.00
220 Maliek Collins RC .40 1.00
221 Deon Bush RC .40 1.00
222 Aaron Burbridge RC .40 1.00
223 Maurice Canady RC .40 1.00
224 Scooby Wright RC .40 1.00
225 Derek Watt RC .60 1.50
226 Sheldon Rankins RC .50 1.25
227 Eric Striker RC .50 1.25
228 Charles Tapper RC .50 1.25
229 Jared Norris RC .40 1.00
230 Jason Fanaika RC .40 1.00
231 Laremy Tunsil RC .40 1.00
232 Taylor Decker RC .50 1.25
233 Vadal Alexander RC .40 1.00
234 Germain Ifedi RC .50 1.25
235 Jack Conklin RC .60 1.50
236 Anthony Zettel RC .50 1.25
237 Chris Jones RC .40 1.00
238 Roberto Aguayo RC .40 1.00
239 Jarran Reed RC .40 1.00
240 Luther Maddy RC .40 1.00
241 Cyrus Jones RC .40 1.00
242 Terrance Smith RC .60 1.50
243 Jack Allen RC .50 1.25
244 Eric Murray RC .40 1.00
245 Kyler Fackrell RC .50 1.25
246 Blake Martinez RC .50 1.25
247 Vernon Butler RC .40 1.00
248 Harlan Miller RC .50 1.25
249 Keyarris Garrett RC .40 1.00
250 Vernon Adams Jr. RC .60 1.50

2016 Panini Prizm Draft Picks Prizms

*VETS: 2X TO 5X BASIC CARDS
*ROOKIES: .6X TO 1.5X BASIC CARDS

2016 Panini Prizm Draft Picks Prizms Blue

*VETS: 2.5X TO 6X BASIC CARDS
*ROOKIES: .8X TO 2X BASIC CARDS

2016 Panini Prizm Draft Picks Prizms Camo

*VETS/199: 3X TO 8X BASIC CARDS
*ROOKIES/199: 1X TO 2.5X BASIC CARDS

2016 Panini Prizm Draft Picks Prizms Purple

*VETS/99: 4X TO 10X BASIC CARDS
*ROOKIES/99: 1.2X TO 3X BASIC CARDS

2016 Panini Prizm Draft Picks Prizms Red White and Blue

*VETS/25: 10X TO 25X BASIC CARDS
*ROOKIES/25: 3X TO 8X BASIC RC

2016 Panini Prizm Draft Picks Prizms Tie Dyed

*VETS/49: 6X TO 15X BASIC CARDS
*ROOKIES/49: 2X TO 5X BASIC RC

2016 Panini Prizm Draft Picks All Americans Autographs

1 Joey Bosa
2 Scooby Wright 5.00 12.00
3 Ricky Williams 6.00 15.00
4 Peyton Manning 150.00 300.00
5 Charles Woodson 20.00 40.00
6 Emmitt Smith 75.00 150.00
7 Troy Aikman
8 Bo Jackson
9 Steve Young
10 John Elway
11 Tim Tebow 50.00 100.00
12 Dan Marino
13 Sam Bradford 12.00 30.00
14 Dez Bryant 25.00 50.00
15 Andrew Luck 40.00 80.00
16 Marcus Allen 6.00 15.00
17 Eric Dickerson 6.00 15.00
18 Carson Palmer 6.00 15.00
19 Doug Flutie 6.00 15.00
20 Rashard Higgins 5.00 12.00

2016 Panini Prizm Draft Picks Autographs Prizms

101 Joey Bosa 20.00 40.00
102 Jared Goff 40.00 80.00
103 Connor Cook 20.00 40.00
104 Laquon Treadwell 25.00 50.00
105 Ezekiel Elliott 50.00 100.00
106 Michael Thomas 4.00 10.00
107 Josh Doctson 2.50 6.00
108 Derrick Henry 30.00 60.00
109 Cardale Jones 10.00 25.00
111 Corey Coleman 6.00 15.00
113 Hunter Henry 2.50 6.00
114 Demarcus Robinson 2.00 5.00
115 Alex Collins 2.50 6.00
117 Paul Perkins 2.00 5.00
119 Rashard Higgins 2.00 5.00
120 Pharoh Cooper 2.00 5.00
122 Devontae Booker 2.50 6.00
123 De'Runnya Wilson 2.00 5.00
124 Jordan Williams 2.00 5.00
125 Dak Prescott 25.00 50.00
126 Aaron Green 2.00 5.00
127 Carson Wentz 60.00 125.00
128 Nick Vannett 2.00 5.00
130 Leonte Carroo 2.00 5.00
131 Tre Madden 2.00 5.00
133 Brandon Doughty 2.00 5.00
135 Nelson Spruce 2.00 5.00
137 Kenyan Drake 3.00 8.00
138 Braxton Miller 15.00 30.00
139 Josh Ferguson 2.00 5.00
140 Cody Kessler 2.00 5.00
141 Devon Cajuste 2.00 5.00
142 Devon Johnson 2.50 6.00
143 D.J. Foster 2.50 6.00
144 Kelvin Taylor 2.00 5.00
145 Sterling Shepard 2.50 6.00
146 Mekale McKay 2.00 5.00
149 Paxton Lynch 25.00 50.00
151 Kyle Carter 2.00 5.00
152 Bryce Williams 2.50 6.00
154 Austin Hooper 2.00 5.00
155 Jerell Adams 2.00 5.00
156 Byron Marshall 2.00 5.00
157 Kevin Hogan 2.50 6.00
158 Jordan Payton 2.00 5.00
160 Jonathan Williams 2.50 6.00
162 Daniel Braverman 2.00 5.00
163 Kolby Listenbee 2.00 5.00
164 Brandon Allen 2.00 5.00
167 Vernon Hargreaves III 5.00 12.00
169 DeForest Buckner 2.00 5.00
170 Kenny Clark 2.00 5.00
172 Myles Jack 6.00 15.00
173 Reggie Ragland 2.00 5.00
175 A'Shawn Robinson 2.00 5.00
176 Su'a Cravens 2.00 5.00
177 Emmanuel Ogbah 2.50 6.00
178 DeAndre Washington 2.00 5.00
179 Shilique Calhoun 2.00 5.00
180 Kendall Fuller 2.50 6.00
181 Adolphus Washington 2.00 5.00
182 Andrew Billings 2.50 6.00
183 Vonn Bell 2.50 6.00
184 Jordan Jenkins 3.00 8.00
185 Jaydon Mickens 2.00 5.00
187 Daniel Lasco 2.00 5.00
190 Jordan Howard 5.00 12.00
192 Trevone Boykin 2.00 5.00
193 Jason Spriggs 2.00 5.00
194 Tra Carson 2.00 5.00
195 Noah Spence 2.00 5.00
196 Steven Scheu 2.00 5.00
197 Dan Vitale 2.00 5.00
198 Jalin Marshall 3.00 8.00
199 Jake McGee 2.50 6.00
200 Eli Apple 2.50 6.00
202 Jeremy Cash 2.50 6.00
203 Jonathan Bullard 2.00 5.00
205 Darian Thompson 2.00 5.00
207 Joshua Perry 2.00 5.00
209 Tyler Higbee 2.00 5.00
211 Dadi Lhomme Nicolas 2.50 6.00
213 Jalen Mills 2.50 6.00
215 Dominique Alexander 2.00 5.00
216 Adam Gotsis 2.00 5.00
217 Kevon Seymour 2.00 5.00
218 Briean Boddy-Calhoun 2.00 5.00
219 Kentrell Brothers 2.00 5.00
220 Maliek Collins 2.00 5.00
222 Aaron Burbridge 2.00 5.00
223 Maurice Canady 2.00 5.00
225 Victor Ochi 2.00 5.00
226 Sheldon Rankins 2.50 6.00
227 Eric Striker 2.50 6.00
228 Charles Tapper 2.50 6.00
231 Laremy Tunsil 2.50 6.00
232 Taylor Decker 2.50 6.00
234 Germain Ifedi 2.50 6.00
235 Jack Conklin 3.00 8.00
236 Anthony Zettel 2.50 6.00
237 Chris Jones 2.00 5.00
238 Roberto Aguayo 2.00 5.00
239 Jarran Reed 2.00 5.00
244 Eric Murray 2.00 5.00
245 Kyler Fackrell 2.50 6.00
246 Blake Martinez 2.50 6.00
247 Karl Joseph 2.00 5.00
249 Keyarris Garrett 2.00 5.00
251 Cody Whitehair 3.00 8.00
252 Spencer Drango 2.00 5.00
253 Max Tuerk 2.00 5.00
254 Trent Matthews 2.00 5.00
255 Vernon Adams Jr. 3.00 8.00
257 Jack Allen 2.50 6.00
258 Keenan Reynolds 5.00 12.00
259 Cyrus Jones 2.00 5.00
260 Luther Maddy 2.00 5.00
262 Jordan Lomax 3.00 8.00
264 Jared Norris 2.00 5.00
265 Derek Watt 3.00 8.00
266 Scooby Wright 2.00 5.00
267 Nate Sudfeld 2.00 5.00
271 Jeff Driskel 2.00 5.00
273 Taveze Calhoun 2.00 5.00
275 Terrance Smith 3.00 8.00
276 Nile Lawrence-Stample 2.50 6.00
278 Marteze Waller 3.00 8.00
280 Bronson Kaufusi 2.00 5.00
281 Ken Crawley 2.50 6.00
283 D.J. White 2.00 5.00
285 Carl Nassib 2.00 5.00
286 Kenny Lawler 3.00 8.00
288 Austin Johnson 2.00 5.00
289 Jordan Canzeri 3.00 8.00
290 Jason Fanaika 2.00 5.00
291 Marquise Williams 2.00 5.00
292 DeAndre Houston-Carson 2.00 5.00
293 Mackensie Alexander 2.00 5.00
296 Demarcus Ayers 2.00 5.00
298 Deion Jones 2.00 5.00
299 Antonio Morrison 2.50 6.00

2016 Panini Prizm Draft Picks Autographs Prizms Blue

*BLUE: .5X TO 1.2X BASIC AU
125 Dak Prescott 25.00 60.00

2016 Panini Prizm Draft Picks Autographs Prizms Camo

*CAMO/199: .5X TO 1.2X BASIC AU

127 Carson Wentz 75.00 150.00
149 Paxton Lynch 25.00 60.00

2016 Panini Prizm Draft Picks Autographs Prizms Purple

*PURPLE/99: .6X TO 1.5X BASIC AU
127 Carson Wentz 100.00 200.00

2016 Panini Prizm Draft Picks Autographs Prizms Red White and Blue

*RWB/25: 1X TO 2.5X BASIC AU
102 Jared Goff 125.00 250.00
127 Carson Wentz 150.00 300.00

2016 Panini Prizm Draft Picks Autographs Prizms Tie Dyed

*TIE DYED/49: .8X TO 2X BASIC AU
105 Ezekiel Elliott 100.00 200.00
127 Carson Wentz 125.00 250.00

2016 Panini Prizm Draft Picks Ball Die Cut

1 A.J. Green 1.25 3.00
2 Aaron Rodgers 2.50 6.00
3 Adrian Peterson 1.25 3.00
4 Amari Cooper 1.25 3.00
5 Andrew Luck 1.50 4.00
6 Andy Dalton 1.00 2.50
7 Antonio Brown 1.25 3.00
8 Blake Bortles .75 2.00
9 Calvin Johnson 1.25 3.00
10 Cam Newton 1.25 3.00
11 Charles Woodson 1.25 3.00
12 Clay Matthews 1.25 3.00
13 DeAndre Hopkins 1.00 2.50
14 Derek Carr 1.25 3.00
15 Devonta Freeman 1.00 2.50
16 Dez Bryant 1.25 3.00
17 Drew Brees 1.25 3.00
18 Eddie Lacy .75 2.00
19 Eli Manning 1.00 2.50
20 J.J. Watt 1.25 3.00
21 Jameis Winston 1.25 3.00
22 Jason Witten 1.00 2.50
23 Jimmy Graham 1.25 3.00
24 Julio Jones 1.25 3.00
25 Le'Veon Bell 1.00 2.50
26 Marcus Mariota 1.25 3.00
27 Marshawn Lynch 1.00 2.50
28 Matt Ryan 1.00 2.50
29 Mike Evans 1.00 2.50
30 Odell Beckham Jr. 1.25 3.00
31 Peyton Manning 2.50 6.00
32 Philip Rivers 1.25 3.00
33 Richard Sherman 1.25 3.00
34 Rob Gronkowski 1.25 3.00
35 Russell Wilson 1.50 4.00
36 Teddy Bridgewater 1.00 2.50
37 T.J. Yeldon .75 2.00
38 Todd Gurley 1.25 3.00
39 Tom Brady 3.00 8.00
40 Tony Romo 1.00 2.50
41 Joey Bosa 1.50 4.00
42 Jared Goff 5.00 12.00
43 Connor Cook 1.00 2.50
44 Laquon Treadwell 1.00 2.50
45 Ezekiel Elliott 4.00 10.00
46 Corey Coleman 1.25 3.00
47 Michael Thomas 1.50 4.00
48 Paxton Lynch .75 2.00
49 Josh Doctson 1.00 2.50
50 Derrick Henry 2.00 5.00

2016 Panini Prizm Draft Picks Helmet Die Cut

1 A.J. Green 1.25 3.00
2 Aaron Rodgers 2.50 6.00
3 Adrian Peterson 1.25 3.00
4 Amari Cooper 1.25 3.00
5 Andrew Luck 1.50 4.00
6 Andy Dalton 1.00 2.50
7 Antonio Brown 1.25 3.00
8 Blake Bortles .75 2.00
9 Calvin Johnson 1.25 3.00
10 Cam Newton 1.25 3.00
11 Charles Woodson 1.25 3.00
12 Clay Matthews 1.25 3.00
13 DeAndre Hopkins 1.00 2.50
14 Derek Carr 1.25 3.00
15 Devonta Freeman 1.00 2.50
16 Dez Bryant 1.25 3.00
17 Drew Brees 1.25 3.00
18 Eddie Lacy .75 2.00
19 Eli Manning 1.00 2.50
20 J.J. Watt 1.25 3.00
21 Jameis Winston 1.25 3.00
22 Jason Witten 1.00 2.50
23 Jimmy Graham 1.25 3.00
24 Julio Jones 1.25 3.00
25 Le'Veon Bell 1.00 2.50
26 Marcus Mariota 1.25 3.00
27 Marshawn Lynch 1.00 2.50
28 Matt Ryan 1.00 2.50
29 Mike Evans 1.00 2.50
30 Odell Beckham Jr. 1.25 3.00
31 Peyton Manning 2.50 6.00
32 Philip Rivers 1.25 3.00
33 Richard Sherman 1.25 3.00
34 Rob Gronkowski 1.25 3.00
35 Russell Wilson 1.50 4.00
36 Teddy Bridgewater 1.00 2.50
37 T.J. Yeldon .75 2.00
38 Todd Gurley 1.25 3.00
39 Tom Brady 3.00 8.00
40 Tony Romo 1.00 2.50
41 Joey Bosa 1.50 4.00
42 Jared Goff 5.00 12.00
43 Connor Cook 1.00 2.50
44 Laquon Treadwell 1.00 2.50
45 Ezekiel Elliott 4.00 10.00
46 Corey Coleman 1.25 3.00
47 Michael Thomas 1.50 4.00
48 Paxton Lynch .75 2.00
49 Josh Doctson 1.00 2.50
50 Derrick Henry 2.00 5.00

2016 Panini Prizm Draft Picks Stained Glass

1 A.J. Green 1.25 3.00
2 Aaron Rodgers 2.50 6.00
3 Adrian Peterson 1.25 3.00
4 Alex Smith 1.00 2.50
5 Allen Hurns .75 2.00
6 Allen Robinson 1.00 2.50
7 Amari Cooper 1.25 3.00
8 Andrew Luck 1.50 4.00
9 Andy Dalton 1.00 2.50
10 Antonio Brown 1.25 3.00
11 Arian Foster 1.00 2.50
12 Ben Roethlisberger 1.25 3.00
13 Blake Bortles .75 2.00
14 Brandon Marshall .75 2.00
15 C.J. Anderson 1.00 2.50
16 Calvin Johnson 1.25 3.00
17 Cam Newton 1.25 3.00
18 Carlos Hyde .75 2.00
19 Carson Palmer 1.00 2.50
20 Charles Woodson 1.25 3.00
21 Chris Johnson .75 2.00
22 Clay Matthews 1.25 3.00
23 Darrelle Revis .75 2.00
24 Darren Sproles 1.00 2.50
25 DeAndre Hopkins 1.00 2.50
26 DeMarco Murray 1.00 2.50
27 Demaryius Thomas 1.00 2.50
28 Derek Carr 1.25 3.00
29 DeSean Jackson 1.00 2.50
30 Devonta Freeman 1.00 2.50
31 Dez Bryant 1.25 3.00
32 Drew Brees 1.25 3.00
33 Eddie Lacy .75 2.00
34 Eli Manning 1.00 2.50
35 Emmanuel Sanders 1.25 3.00
36 Frank Gore 1.00 2.50
37 Giovani Bernard .75 2.00
38 Greg Olsen 1.00 2.50
39 J.J. Watt 1.25 3.00
40 Jamaal Charles 1.00 2.50
41 Jameis Winston 1.25 3.00
42 Jason Witten 1.00 2.50
43 Jeremy Hill .75 2.00
44 Jimmy Graham 1.25 3.00
45 Joe Flacco 1.00 2.50
46 Jordy Nelson 1.00 2.50
47 Julian Edelman 1.25 3.00
48 Julio Jones 1.25 3.00
49 Justin Forsett 1.00 2.50
50 Justin Houston .75 2.00
51 Kam Chancellor 1.25 3.00
52 Keenan Allen 1.00 2.50
53 Kirk Cousins 1.25 3.00
54 Larry Fitzgerald 1.00 2.50
55 Latavius Murray .75 2.00
56 LeSean McCoy 1.25 3.00
57 Le'Veon Bell 1.00 2.50
58 Luke Kuechly 1.00 2.50
59 Marcus Mariota 1.25 3.00
60 Mark Ingram 1.00 2.50
61 Marshawn Lynch 1.00 2.50
62 Matt Forte .75 2.00
63 Matt Ryan 1.00 2.50
64 Matthew Stafford 1.00 2.50
65 Melvin Gordon 1.00 2.50
66 Mike Evans 1.00 2.50
67 Ndamukong Suh 1.00 2.50
68 Nick Foles 1.00 2.50
69 Odell Beckham Jr. 1.25 3.00
70 Patrick Peterson .75 2.00
71 Peyton Manning 2.50 6.00
72 Philip Rivers 1.25 3.00
73 Randall Cobb 1.00 2.50
74 Richard Sherman 1.25 3.00
75 Rob Gronkowski 1.25 3.00
76 Stefon Diggs 1.00 2.50
77 Russell Wilson 1.50 4.00
78 Ryan Tannehill 1.00 2.50
79 Sam Bradford .75 2.00
80 Steve Smith 1.00 2.50
81 Teddy Bridgewater 1.00 2.50
82 Thomas Rawls .75 2.00
83 T.J. Yeldon .75 2.00
84 Todd Gurley 1.25 3.00
85 Tom Brady 3.00 8.00
86 Tony Romo 1.00 2.50
87 Travis Benjamin .75 2.00
88 Tyrod Taylor 1.00 2.50
89 Von Miller 1.00 2.50
90 Willie Snead 1.00 2.50
91 Derrick Henry 2.00 5.00
92 Josh Doctson 1.00 2.50
93 Paxton Lynch .75 2.00
94 Michael Thomas 1.50 4.00
95 Corey Coleman 1.25 3.00
96 Ezekiel Elliott 4.00 10.00
97 Laquon Treadwell 1.00 2.50
98 Connor Cook 1.00 2.50
99 Jared Goff 5.00 12.00
100 Joey Bosa 1.50 4.00

2016 Panini Prizm Draft Picks Team Trademarks Autographs Prizms

1 Joey Bosa 20.00 50.00
2 Jared Goff 50.00 100.00
3 Connor Cook 4.00 10.00
4 Laquon Treadwell 4.00 10.00
5 Ezekiel Elliott 150.00 250.00
6 Michael Thomas 6.00 15.00
7 Josh Doctson 12.00 30.00
8 Derrick Henry
9 Cardale Jones 3.00 8.00
11 Corey Coleman 10.00 25.00
13 Hunter Henry 4.00 10.00
14 Demarcus Robinson 3.00 8.00
15 Alex Collins 4.00 10.00
17 Paul Perkins 3.00 8.00
19 Rashard Higgins 3.00 8.00
20 Pharoh Cooper 3.00 8.00
22 Devontae Booker 4.00 10.00
23 De'Runnya Wilson 3.00 8.00
24 Jordan Williams 3.00 8.00
25 Dak Prescott 40.00 80.00
26 Aaron Green 3.00 8.00
27 Paxton Lynch 3.00 8.00
29 Leonte Carroo 3.00 8.00
30 Tre Madden 3.00 8.00
32 Brandon Doughty 3.00 8.00
34 Sterling Shepard 4.00 10.00
35 Kenneth Dixon 3.00 8.00
36 Kenyan Drake 5.00 12.00
37 Carson Wentz
38 Braxton Miller 3.00 8.00
40 Trevone Boykin 3.00 8.00

2019 Panini Prizm Draft Picks

1 A.J. Green .30 .75
2 Aaron Rodgers .60 1.50
3 Bevo .30 .75
4 Adam Thielen .30 .75
5 Adrian Peterson .30 .75
6 Alvin Kamara .25 .60
7 Anthony Miller AA .25 .60
8 Amari Cooper .30 .75
9 Andrew Luck .40 1.00
10 Antonio Brown .30 .75
11 Aaron Rodgers SG .60 1.50
12 Baker Mayfield .50 1.25
13 Barry Sanders .50 1.25
14 Brutus Buckeye .30 .75
15 Bo Jackson .40 1.00
16 Brett Favre .60 1.50
17 Calvin Ridley .25 .60
18 Baker Mayfield AA .50 1.25
19 Cam Newton .30 .75
20 Carson Wentz .40 1.00
21 Christian Kirk .20 .50
22 Baker Mayfield SG .50 1.25
23 Christian McCaffrey .30 .75
24 Dak Prescott .30 .75
25 Big Al .30 .75
26 Dan Marino .60 1.50
27 David Johnson .30 .75
28 DeAndre Hopkins .25 .60
29 Barry Sanders AA .50 1.25
30 Derek Carr .30 .75
31 Derrick Henry .30 .75
32 Deshaun Watson .40 1.00
33 Barry Sanders SG .50 1.25
34 Drew Brees .30 .75
35 Earl Campbell .30 .75
36 Albert .30 .75
37 Emmitt Smith .50 1.25
38 Eric Dickerson .30 .75
39 Ezekiel Elliott .40 1.00
40 Deshaun Watson AA .40 1.00
41 Herschel Walker .30 .75
42 J.J. Watt .30 .75
43 James Conner .30 .75
44 Dan Marino SG .60 1.50
45 Jared Goff .30 .75
46 Jerry Rice .50 1.25
47 Mike The Tiger .30 .75
48 Joe Namath .40 1.00
49 John Elway .50 1.25
50 Josh Allen .30 .75
51 Emmitt Smith AA .50 1.25
52 Josh Rosen .30 .75
53 Julio Jones .30 .75
54 Emmitt Smith SG .50 1.25
55 JuJu Smith-Schuster .30 .75
56 Nittany Lion .30 .75
57 Kerryon Johnson .25 .60
58 Khalil Mack .30 .75
59 Lamar Jackson AA .30 .75
60 Lamar Jackson .30 .75
61 Leonard Fournette .30 .75
62 Le'Veon Bell .25 .60
63 John Elway SG .50 1.25
64 Marcus Allen .30 .75
65 Michael Irvin .40 1.00
66 Michael Thomas .30 .75
67 Sparty .30 .75
68 Mitchell Trubisky .30 .75
69 Nick Chubb .30 .75
70 Leonard Fournette AA .30 .75
71 Odell Beckham Jr. .30 .75
72 Patrick Mahomes II .75 2.00
73 Peyton Manning .60 1.50
74 Peyton Manning SG .60 1.50
75 Philip Rivers .30 .75
76 Phillip Lindsay .30 .75
77 Ray Lewis .30 .75
78 Bucky Badger .30 .75
79 Red Grange .40 1.00
80 Roger Staubach .40 1.00
81 Melvin Gordon III AA .25 .60
82 Royce Freeman .20 .50
83 Russell Wilson .40 1.00
84 Saquon Barkley SG .40 1.00
85 Sam Darnold .30 .75
86 The Duck .30 .75
87 Saquon Barkley .40 1.00
88 Sony Michel .30 .75
89 Terry Bradshaw .50 1.25
90 Rashaad Penny AA .20 .50
91 Tim Tebow .30 .75
92 Todd Gurley II .30 .75
93 Sam Darnold SG .30 .75
94 Tom Brady .75 2.00
95 The Tiger .30 .75
96 Tony Dorsett .30 .75
97 Troy Aikman .40 1.00
98 Peyton Manning AA .60 1.50
99 Tyreek Hill .30 .75
100 Tom Brady SG .75 2.00
101 Kyler Murray 8.00 20.00
102 Marquise Brown 1.25 3.00
103 Bryce Love .60 1.50
104 Will Grier 1.25 3.00
105 A.J. Brown 1.00 2.50
106 Damien Harris 1.00 2.50
107 Ryan Finley .75 2.00
108 N'Keal Harry 1.25 3.00
109 Rodney Anderson .50 1.25
110 Drew Lock 2.00 5.00
111 JJ Arcega-Whiteside .60 1.50
112 Justice Hill .60 1.50
113 Dwayne Haskins 2.00 5.00
114 Kelvin Harmon .60 1.50
115 Trayveon Williams .50 1.25
116 Daniel Jones 2.00 5.00
117 Anthony Johnson .50 1.25
118 David Montgomery 1.50 4.00
119 Jarrett Stidham 1.25 3.00
120 Parris Campbell 1.00 2.50
121 Benny Snell Jr. 1.25 3.00
122 Clayton Thorson .60 1.50
123 Hakeem Butler .75 2.00
124 Devin Singletary .50 1.25
125 Irv Smith Jr. .75 2.00
126 Nick Bosa 1.25 3.00
127 Darrell Henderson 1.00 2.50
128 Riley Ridley .60 1.50
129 Noah Fant .75 2.00
130 Lil'Jordan Humphrey .50 1.25
131 Deebo Samuel 1.00 2.50
132 Myles Gaskin .75 2.00
133 D.K. Metcalf 1.25 3.00
134 Brett Rypien .50 1.25
135 Josh Jacobs 2.00 5.00

2019 Panini Prizm Draft Picks Prizms Blue

*VETS: 1.5X TO 4X BASIC CARDS
*ROOKIES: .8X TO 2X BASIC CARDS

2019 Panini Prizm Draft Picks Prizms Camo

*VETS/25: 8X TO 20X BASIC CARDS
*ROOKIES/25: 2.5X TO 6X BASIC RC

2019 Panini Prizm Draft Picks Prizms Hyper

*VETS/75: 5X TO 12X BASIC CARDS
*ROOKIES/75: 1.5X TO 4X BASIC RC

2019 Panini Prizm Draft Picks Prizms Mojo

*VETS/49: 6X TO 15X BASIC CARDS
*ROOKIES/49: 2X TO 5X BASIC RC

2019 Panini Prizm Draft Picks Prizms Orange

*VETS: 1.5X TO 4X BASIC CARDS
*ROOKIES: .8X TO 2X BASIC CARDS

2019 Panini Prizm Draft Picks Prizms Pink Pulsar

*VETS: 1.2X TO 3X BASIC CARDS
*ROOKIES: .6X TO 1.5X BASIC CARDS

2019 Panini Prizm Draft Picks Prizms Purple

*VETS: 1.5X TO 4X BASIC CARDS
*ROOKIES: .8X TO 2X BASIC CARDS

2019 Panini Prizm Draft Picks Prizms Red

*VETS: 1.5X TO 4X BASIC CARDS
*ROOKIES: .8X TO 2X BASIC CARDS

2019 Panini Prizm Draft Picks Prizms Red White and Blue

*VETS/99: 5X TO 12X BASIC CARDS
*ROOKIES/99: 1.5X TO 4X BASIC RC

2019 Panini Prizm Draft Picks Prizms Silver

*VETS: 2X TO 5X BASIC CARDS
*ROOKIES: .6X TO 1.5X BASIC CARDS

2019 Panini Prizm Draft Picks Prizms White Sparkle

*VETS/15: 10X TO 25X BASIC CARDS
*ROOKIES/15: 3X TO 8X BASIC RC

2019 Panini Prizm Draft Picks Autograph Prizms

101 Kyler Murray 150.00 300.00
102 Marquise Brown EXCH 6.00 15.00
103 Bryce Love 3.00 8.00
104 Will Grier 10.00 80.00
105 A.J. Brown 5.00 12.00
106 Damien Harris 5.00 12.00
107 Ryan Finley 4.00 10.00
108 N'Keal Harry 6.00 15.00
109 Rodney Anderson 2.50 6.00
110 Drew Lock 30.00 60.00
111 JJ Arcega-Whiteside 3.00 8.00
112 Justice Hill 3.00 8.00
113 Dwayne Haskins EXCH 60.00 125.00
114 Kelvin Harmon 3.00 8.00
115 Trayveon Williams 2.50 6.00
116 Daniel Jones 25.00 50.00
117 Anthony Johnson 2.50 6.00
118 David Montgomery 8.00 20.00
119 Jarrett Stidham 6.00 15.00
120 Parris Campbell 5.00 12.00
121 Benny Snell Jr. EXCH 12.00 30.00
122 Clayton Thorson 3.00 8.00
123 Hakeem Butler 4.00 10.00
124 Devin Singletary 2.50 6.00
125 Irv Smith Jr. 4.00 10.00
126 Nick Bosa 30.00 60.00
127 Darrell Henderson 5.00 12.00
128 L.J. Scott 3.00 8.00
129 Noah Fant 4.00 10.00
130 Lil'Jordan Humphrey 2.50 6.00
131 Deebo Samuel 5.00 12.00
132 Myles Gaskin 4.00 10.00
133 D.K. Metcalf 6.00 15.00
134 Brett Rypien 2.50 6.00
135 Josh Jacobs 12.00 30.00
136 Karan Higdon 2.50 6.00
137 Tyree Jackson 5.00 12.00
138 Riley Ridley 3.00 8.00
139 Mike Weber 3.00 8.00
140 Trace McSorley 5.00 12.00
141 Emanuel Hall 2.00 5.00
142 Jalin Moore Jr. 2.00 5.00
144 Miles Boykin 2.50 6.00
145 Elijah Holyfield 3.00 8.00
146 Jordan Ta'amu 5.00 12.00
148 Antoine Wesley 2.00 5.00
149 Alex Barnes 2.50 6.00
150 Preston Williams 2.00 5.00
151 Greedy Williams 6.00 15.00
152 Deandre Baker 5.00 12.00
153 Zach Allen 3.00 8.00
155 Te'Von Coney 6.00 15.00
157 Montez Sweat 6.00 15.00
158 T.J. Edwards 2.00 5.00
159 D'Andre Walker 2.00 5.00
160 Johnathan Abram 2.00 5.00
161 Amani Oruwariye 2.50 6.00
162 Jerry Tillery 2.50 6.00
163 Jaylon Ferguson 2.00 5.00
164 Ben Burr-Kirven 2.50 6.00
165 Oshane Ximines 2.00 5.00
166 Jalen Jelks 2.50 6.00
167 Marvell Tell III 4.00 10.00
168 Jaquan Johnson 4.00 10.00
170 Austin Bryant 4.00 10.00
171 Lukas Denis 2.50 6.00
172 Kendall Joseph 4.00 10.00
173 Chase Winovich 6.00 15.00
174 Ryan Connelly 2.50 6.00
175 Gerald Willis III 4.00 10.00
176 David Blough 2.50 6.00
177 Gardner Minshew II 3.00 8.00
178 Cameron Smith 2.50 6.00
179 Demarcus Christmas 2.50 6.00
180 C.J. Conrad 2.00 5.00
181 Blace Brown 2.00 5.00
182 Terry Beckner Jr. 2.00 5.00
183 Christian Miller 4.00 10.00
184 Isaiah Buggs 5.00 12.00
185 Daniel Wise 2.50 6.00
186 Vosean Joseph 2.50 6.00
187 Tyler Petite 3.00 8.00
188 Porter Gustin 3.00 8.00
189 DaMarkus Lodge 2.00 5.00
190 Carl Granderson 3.00 8.00
191 Keelan Doss 2.50 6.00
192 Germaine Pratt 2.50 6.00
193 Ed Oliver 3.00 8.00
194 Deionte Thompson 2.50 6.00
195 Devin White 6.00 15.00
197 Taylor Rapp 2.00 5.00
198 Julian Love 2.50 6.00
199 Clelin Ferrell 3.00 8.00
200 Dexter Lawrence 3.00 8.00
201 Devin Bush II 8.00 20.00
202 Trayvon Mullen Jr. 3.00 8.00
203 Rashan Gary 4.00 10.00
204 Mack Wilson 2.50 6.00
205 Brent Stockstill 3.00 8.00
206 Taylor Cornelius 4.00 10.00
207 Jeffery Simmons 2.00 5.00
208 Brian Burns 2.50 6.00
209 Dre'Mont Jones 2.50 6.00
210 Tre Lamar 3.00 8.00
211 Kyle Shurmur 4.00 10.00
213 Saivion Smith 2.50 6.00
214 Jace Sternberger 2.50 6.00
216 Joe Jackson 2.50 6.00
218 Kaden Smith 2.00 5.00
219 Chauncey Gardner-Johnson 2.00 5.00
220 Otaro Alaka 3.00 8.00
221 Dre Greenlaw 2.00 5.00
222 Terry McLaurin 2.50 6.00
223 Micky Crum 2.00 5.00
224 Taiwan Deal 2.50 6.00
225 Kris Boyd 2.50 6.00
226 Iman Marshall 2.50 6.00
227 Dexter Williams 2.50 6.00
229 Derrick Baity Jr. 2.50 6.00
230 Marquise Copeland 2.50 6.00
231 Ugo Amadi 2.50 6.00
232 Tyree Kinnel 5.00 12.00
233 Chris Johnson 3.00 8.00
234 Jamel Dean 4.00 10.00
236 Jordan Scarlett 2.00 5.00
237 Chase Hansen 3.00 8.00
238 Darrin Hall 2.50 6.00
239 Ty Johnson 8.00 20.00
241 Khalil Hodge 2.50 6.00
242 Greg Gaines 2.50 6.00
243 Josh Oliver 2.00 5.00
244 Caleb Wilson 2.00 5.00
245 Terry Godwin II 2.50 6.00
246 Andrew Wingard 3.00 8.00
247 Gary Jennings Jr. 3.00 8.00
248 Juan Thornhill 2.00 5.00
249 Jazz Ferguson 2.00 5.00
250 D'Cota Dixon 2.50 6.00
251 Emmanuel Butler 3.00 8.00
252 Hunter Renfrow 4.00 10.00
253 Anthony Ratliff-Williams 4.00 10.00
254 Tommy Sweeney 2.00 5.00
255 Jovon Durante 2.50 6.00
256 Jacques Patrick 2.00 5.00
257 Matt Sokol 3.00 8.00
258 KaVontae Turpin 3.00 8.00
259 Felton Davis III 5.00 12.00
260 Dax Raymond 2.00 5.00
261 Stanley Morgan Jr. 3.00 8.00
262 Nyqwan Murray 3.00 8.00
263 Justice Hansen 2.50 6.00
264 Blessuan Austin 2.50 6.00
265 Jaylen Smith 2.00 5.00
266 Eric Dungey 8.00 20.00
267 Jalen Hurd 2.50 6.00
268 T.J. Hockenson 5.00 12.00
269 Keenen Brown 2.00 5.00
271 Drew Sample 2.00 5.00
272 Zach Gentry 2.00 5.00
273 Foster Moreau 2.00 5.00
274 Travis Homer 2.00 5.00
275 Nick Brossette 2.50 6.00
277 Mecole Hardman Jr. 5.00 12.00
278 Jake Browning 5.00 12.00
280 Andy Isabella 3.00 8.00
281 Darius Slayton 3.00 8.00
282 Jordan Brailford 3.00 8.00
283 Ryquell Armstead 2.00 5.00
284 Tony Pollard 5.00 12.00
285 Travis Fulgham 2.00 5.00
287 Ben Banogu 4.00 10.00
288 Miles Sanders 5.00 12.00
289 David Sills V 6.00 15.00
290 Cody Thompson 2.00 5.00
291 Travon McMillian 3.00 8.00
292 David Long 2.50 6.00
293 Tyre Brady 2.00 5.00
294 Alex Wesley 3.00 8.00
295 Darwin Thompson 3.00 8.00
296 Patrick Laird 4.00 10.00
297 Justin Layne 4.00 10.00
298 Johnnie Dixon 2.50 6.00
299 Mike Edwards 4.00 10.00
300 Darnell Savage Jr. 3.00 8.00

2019 Panini Prizm Draft Picks Autograph Prizms Camo

*CAMO/25: 1X TO 2.5X BASIC AU
*CAMO: 1.2X TO 3X BASIC AU
101 Kyler Murray/15 300.00 600.00
104 Will Grier/15 100.00 200.00
110 Drew Lock/15 100.00 200.00
113 Dwayne Haskins/15 EXCH 125.00 250.00
126 Nick Bosa/25 60.00 150.00

2019 Panini Prizm Draft Picks Autograph Prizms Hyper

*HYPER/75: .6X TO 1.5X BASIC AU
*HYPER/25: 1X TO 2.5X BASIC AU
101 Kyler Murray/25 250.00 450.00
104 Will Grier/25 100.00 200.00
110 Drew Lock/25 60.00 150.00
113 Dwayne Haskins/25 EXCH 100.00 200.00
126 Nick Bosa/75 40.00 100.00

2019 Panini Prizm Draft Picks Autograph Prizms Mojo

*MOJO/49: .8X TO 2X BASIC AU
*MOJO/20: 1.2X TO 3X BASIC AU
101 Kyler Murray/20 300.00 500.00
104 Will Grier/20 100.00 200.00
110 Drew Lock/20 100.00 200.00
113 Dwayne Haskins/20 EXCH 125.00 250.00
126 Nick Bosa/49 50.00 125.00

2019 Panini Prizm Draft Picks Autograph Prizms Red White and Blue

*RWB/99: .6X TO 1.5X BASIC AU
*RWB/49: .8X TO 2X BASIC AU
101 Kyler Murray/49 250.00 400.00
104 Will Grier/99 50.00 100.00
110 Drew Lock/99 40.00 100.00
113 Dwayne Haskins/99 EXCH 75.00 150.00
126 Nick Bosa/99 40.00 100.00

2019 Panini Prizm Draft Picks Crusade Prizms

*BLUE: .5X TO 1.2X BASIC INSERTS
*CAMO/25: 1X TO 2.5X BASIC INSERTS
*HYPER/75: .6X TO 1.5X BASIC INSERTS
*MOJO/49: .8X TO 2X BASIC INSERTS
*ORNAGE: .5X TO 1.2X BASIC INSERTS
*PINK: .5X TO 1.2X BASIC INSERTS
*PURPLE: .5X TO 1.2X BASIC INSERTS
*RED: .5X TO 1.2X BASIC INSERTS
*RWB/99: .6X TO 1.5X BASIC INSERTS
*SPARKLE: 1.2X TO 3X BASIC INSERTS
1 Nick Bosa 1.50 4.00
2 Marquise Brown 1.50 4.00
3 D.K. Metcalf 1.50 4.00
4 Will Grier 1.50 4.00
5 A.J. Brown 1.25 3.00
6 Damien Harris 1.25 3.00
7 Hakeem Butler 1.00 2.50
8 N'Keal Harry 1.50 4.00
9 Parris Campbell 1.25 3.00
10 Drew Lock 2.50 6.00
11 JJ Arcega-Whiteside .75 2.00
12 David Montgomery 2.00 5.00
13 Dwayne Haskins 2.50 6.00
14 Kelvin Harmon .75 2.00
15 Daniel Jones 2.50 6.00

2012 Panini Prominence

1-150 STATED PRINT RUN 897
EXCH EXPIRATION: 3/19/2014
1A Kevin Kolb P .60 1.50
2A Beanie Wells P .60 1.50
3A Larry Fitzgerald P .75 2.00
4A Matt Ryan P .75 2.00
5A Michael Turner P .60 1.50
6A Roddy White P .60 1.50
7A Joe Flacco P .75 2.00
8A Ray Rice P .60 1.50
9A Ray Lewis P 1.00 2.50
10A Ed Reed P .75 2.00
11A Ryan Fitzpatrick P .60 1.50
12A Fred Jackson P .75 2.00
13A Steve Johnson P .75 2.00
14A Cam Newton P 1.00 2.50
15A DeAngelo Williams P .60 1.50
16A Steve Smith P .75 2.00
17A Jay Cutler P .60 1.50
18A Matt Forte P .60 1.50
19A Brandon Marshall P .75 2.00
20A Andy Dalton P .75 2.00
21A BenJarvus Green-Ellis P .75 2.00
22A A.J. Green P 1.00 2.50
23A Miles Austin P .60 1.50
24A Greg Little P .60 1.50
25A Josh Cribbs P .60 1.50
26A Tony Romo P .75 2.00
27A DeMarco Murray P .75 2.00
28A Dez Bryant P 1.00 2.50
29A Peyton Manning P 2.00 5.00
30A Willis McGahee P .60 1.50
31A Eric Decker P .60 1.50
32A Matthew Stafford P .75 2.00
33A Calvin Johnson P 1.00 2.50
34A Ndamukong Suh P .75 2.00
35A Aaron Rodgers P 1.50 4.00
36A Jordy Nelson P .75 2.00
37A Greg Jennings P .60 1.50
38A Matt Schaub P .60 1.50
39A Arian Foster P .75 2.00
40A Andre Johnson P .75 2.00
41A Austin Collie P .60 1.50
42A Reggie Wayne P .75 2.00
43A Donald Brown P .60 1.50
44A Blaine Gabbert P .60 1.50
45A Maurice Jones-Drew P .60 1.50
46A Mike Thomas P .75 2.00
47A Matt Cassel P .60 1.50
48A Jamaal Charles P .75 2.00
49A Dwayne Bowe P .75 2.00
50A Reggie Bush P .60 1.50
51A Karlos Dansby P .60 1.50
52A Anthony Fasano P .60 1.50
53A Christian Ponder P .60 1.50
54A Adrian Peterson P 1.00 2.50
55A Percy Harvin P .60 1.50
56A Tom Brady P 2.50 6.00
57A Aaron Hernandez P .75 2.00
58A Wes Welker P .75 2.00
59A Rob Gronkowski P 1.00 2.50
60A Drew Brees P 1.00 2.50
61A Mark Ingram P .75 2.00
62A Jimmy Graham P 1.00 2.50
63A Eli Manning P .75 2.00
64A Ahmad Bradshaw P .60 1.50
65A Victor Cruz P .75 2.00
66A Hakeem Nicks P .60 1.50
67A Mark Sanchez P .60 1.50
68A Tim Tebow P 1.00 2.50
69A Santonio Holmes P .60 1.50
70A Carson Palmer P .75 2.00
71A Darren McFadden P .60 1.50
72A Darrius Heyward-Bey P .60 1.50
73A Michael Vick P .75 2.00
74A LeSean McCoy P 1.00 2.50
75A DeSean Jackson P .75 2.00
76A Ben Roethlisberger P 1.00 2.50
77A Isaac Redman P 1.00 2.50
78A Mike Wallace P .60 1.50
79A Philip Rivers P 1.00 2.50
80A Ryan Mathews P .75 2.00
81A Antonio Gates P .75 2.00
82A Alex Smith P .75 2.00
83A Frank Gore P .75 2.00
84A Randy Moss P .75 2.00
85A Vernon Davis P .60 1.50
86A Matt Flynn P .60 1.50
87A Marshawn Lynch P .75 2.00
88A Doug Baldwin P 1.00 2.50
89A Sam Bradford P .60 1.50
90A Steven Jackson P .60 1.50
91A James Laurinaitis P .60 1.50
92A Josh Freeman P .75 2.00
93A Dallas Clark P .60 1.50
94A Vincent Jackson P .60 1.50
95A Kenny Britt P .60 1.50
96A Chris Johnson P .60 1.50
97A Nate Washington P .60 1.50
98A Pierre Garcon P .75 2.00
99A Roy Helu P .60 1.50
100A Jabar Gaffney P .60 1.50
101A Art Monk P 1.25 3.00
102A Barry Sanders P 2.00 5.00
103A Bernie Kosar P 1.00 2.50
104A Bo Jackson P 1.50 4.00
105A Boomer Esiason P 1.00 2.50
106A Brett Favre P 2.50 6.00
107A Dan Marino P 2.50 6.00
108A Deion Sanders P 1.00 2.50
109A Doug Flutie P 1.00 2.50
110A Eddie George P 1.00 2.50
111A Emmitt Smith P 2.00 5.00
112A Ernie Davis P 1.00 2.50
113A Floyd Little P .75 2.00
114A Frank Gifford P 1.00 2.50
115A Fred Williamson P .75 2.00
116A Gene Upshaw P .75 2.00
117A Howie Long P 1.25 3.00
118A Irving Fryar P .75 2.00
119A Jerome Bettis P 1.25 3.00
120A Jerry Rice P 2.00 5.00
121A Jim Brown P 1.50 4.00
122A Joe Montana P 3.00 8.00
123A John Elway P 2.00 5.00
124A John Fuqua P 1.00 2.50
125A Junior Seau P 1.00 2.50
126A Keith Jackson P .75 2.00
127A Larry Csonka P 1.25 3.00
128A Marcus Allen P 1.25 3.00
129A Mark Carrier P .75 2.00
130A Michael Strahan P 1.00 2.50
131A Mike Alstott P .75 2.00
132A Ozzie Newsome P 1.00 2.50
133A Phil Simms P 1.00 2.50
134A Randall Cunningham P 1.00 2.50
135A Randy White P 1.00 2.50
136A Reggie White P 1.25 3.00
137A Richard Dent P 1.00 2.50
138A Rod Woodson P 1.00 2.50
139A Ron Mix P .75 2.00
140A Ronnie Lott P 1.00 2.50
141A Sterling Sharpe P 1.00 2.50
142A Steve Bartkowski P 1.00 2.50
143A Terrell Davis P 1.00 2.50
144A Terry Bradshaw P 1.50 4.00
145A Thurman Thomas P 1.00 2.50
146A Tony Dorsett P 1.25 3.00
147A Walter Payton P 2.50 6.00
148A Warren Moon P 1.25 3.00
149A Warren Sapp P 1.00 2.50
150A Willie Brown P .75 2.00
151 Matt Kalil AU/499 RC 2.50 6.00
152 Morris Claiborne AU/99 RC 4.00 10.00
153 Mark Barron AU/499 RC 2.50 6.00
154 Luke Kuechly AU/499 RC 6.00 15.00
155 Stephon Gilmore AU/499 RC 3.00 8.00
156 Dontari Poe AU/169 RC 3.00 8.00
157 Fletcher Cox AU/499 RC 4.00 10.00
158 M.Brockers AU/499 RC 2.50 6.00
159 Bruce Irvin AU/199 RC 4.00 10.00
160 Quinton Coples AU/499 RC 2.50 6.00
161 Kirkpatrick AU/99 RC EXCH 4.00 10.00
162 M.Ingram AU/199 RC 3.00 8.00
163 Shea McClellin AU/199 RC 8.00 20.00
164 Chandler Jones AU/499 RC 2.50 6.00
165 Riley Reiff AU/499 RC 2.50 6.00
166 David DeCastro AU/349 RC 2.50 6.00
167 D.Hightower AU/499 RC 4.00 10.00
168 W.Mercilus AU/298 RC 2.50 6.00
169 Kevin Zeitler AU/499 RC 2.50 6.00
170 Nick Perry AU/499 RC 3.00 8.00
171 Harrison Smith AU/499 RC 5.00 12.00
172 Courtney Upshaw AU/499 RC 3.00 8.00
173 Andre Branch AU/496 RC 2.50 6.00
174 Janoris Jenkins AU/199 RC 4.00 10.00
175 Jonathan Martin AU/499 RC 2.50 6.00
176 Dwight Jones AU/499 RC 2.50 6.00
177 M.Kendricks AU/292 RC 4.00 10.00
178 Bobby Wagner AU/497 RC 4.00 10.00
179 Zach Brown AU/199 RC 3.00 8.00
180 Devon Still AU/286 RC 3.00 8.00
181 Lavonte David AU/199 RC 5.00 12.00
182 Vinny Curry AU/499 RC 3.00 8.00
183 Travis Benjamin AU/199 RC 6.00 15.00
184 Kirk Cousins AU/499 RC 15.00 30.00
185 Devon Wylie AU/199 RC 3.00 8.00
186 Ladarius Green AU/128 RC 4.00 10.00
187 Orson Charles AU/199 RC 3.00 8.00
188 Keshawn Martin AU/199 RC 4.00 10.00
189 Ronnell Lewis AU/199 RC 3.00 8.00
190 Jared Crick AU/499 RC 2.50 6.00
191 Greg Childs AU/199 RC 3.00 8.00
192 Danny Coale AU/199 RC 3.00 8.00
193 Chris Rainey AU/199 RC 3.00 8.00
194 Marvin Jones AU/499 RC 2.50 6.00
195 George Iloka AU/265 RC 2.50 6.00
196 Juron Criner AU/499 RC 2.50 6.00
197 Vick Ballard AU/499 RC 3.00 8.00
198 Alfred Morris AU/499 RC 2.50 6.00
199 Cyrus Gray AU/499 RC 2.50 6.00
200 B.J. Cunningham AU/499 RC 2.50 6.00
201 Ryan Lindley AU/199 RC 3.00 8.00
202 Dan Herron AU/435 RC 2.50 6.00
203 Marvin McNutt AU/173 RC 3.00 8.00
204 T.Streeter AU/99 RC 4.00 10.00
205 T.Ganaway AU/199 RC 4.00 10.00
206 LaVon Brazill AU/499 RC 4.00 10.00
207 Michael Smith AU/99 RC EX 5.00 12.00
208 Rishard Matthews AU/199 RC 3.00 8.00
209 Bryce Brown AU/99 RC 4.00 10.00
210 B.J. Coleman AU/99 RC 4.00 10.00
211 Chandler Harnish AU/499 RC 2.50 6.00
212 Case Keenum AU/499 RC 5.00 12.00
213 Kellen Moore AU/349 RC 3.00 8.00
214 Marquis Maze AU/99 RC 2.50 6.00
215 T.Y. Hilton AU/499 RC 5.00 12.00
216 D.Wilson JSY AU/150 RC 4.00 10.00
217 T.J. Graham JSY AU/240 RC 4.00 10.00
218 D.Posey JSY AU/200 RC 4.00 10.00
219 M.Floyd JSY AU/75 RC 6.00 15.00
220 N.Foles JSY AU/125 RC EX 30.00 60.00
221 Joe Adams JSY AU/175 RC 4.00 10.00
222 R.Randle JSY AU/120 RC 4.00 10.00
223 B.Weeden JSY AU/90 RC 5.00 12.00
224 L.James JSY AU/150 RC 4.00 10.00
225 Broyles JSY AU/245 RC EX 4.00 10.00
226 R.Griffin III JSY AU/70 RC 8.00 20.00
227 Nick Toon JSY AU/200 RC 4.00 10.00
228 R.Tannehill JSY AU/90 RC 8.00 20.00
229 M.Egnew JSY AU/200 RC 4.00 10.00
230 R.Turbin JSY AU/150 RC 4.00 10.00
231 A.Luck JSY AU/80 RC 60.00 125.00
232 D.Martin JSY AU/90 RC 8.00 20.00
233 Hillman JSY AU/210 RC EX 4.00 10.00
234 M.Sanu JSY AU/140 RC 6.00 15.00
235 R.Wilson JSY AU/150 RC 60.00 125.00
236 T.Richardson JSY AU/80 RC 5.00 12.00
237 A.Jenkins JSY AU/175 RC EX 4.00 10.00
238 J.Blackmon JSY AU/80 RC 5.00 12.00
239 Stephen Hill JSY AU/140 RC 4.00 10.00
240 A.Jeffery JSY AU/175 RC 12.00 30.00
241 B.Quick JSY AU/200 RC EX 4.00 10.00
242 K.Wright JSY AU/90 RC EX 5.00 12.00
243 Jarius Wright JSY AU/240 RC 4.00 10.00
244 L.Miller JSY AU/90 RC 8.00 20.00
245 Isaiah Pead JSY AU/140 RC 4.00 10.00
246 B.Osweiler JSY AU/80 RC 5.00 12.00
247 D.Allen JSY AU/200 RC 4.00 10.00
248 Coby Fleener JSY AU/175 RC 4.00 10.00
249 B.Pierce JSY AU/150 RC EX 4.00 10.00
250 Chris Givens JSY AU/240 RC 4.00 10.00

2012 Panini Prominence Apprentice Ink

STATED PRINT RUN 10-99
EXCH EXPIRATION: 3/19/2014
1 Andrew Luck/25 100.00 200.00
2 Robert Griffin III/25 6.00 15.00
3 Trent Richardson/25 5.00 12.00
4 Matt Kalil/99 3.00 8.00
6 Morris Claiborne/25 5.00 12.00
7 Mark Barron/99 4.00 10.00
8 Ryan Tannehill/25 8.00 20.00
9 Luke Kuechly/99 8.00 20.00
10 Stephon Gilmore/99 4.00 10.00
11 Dontari Poe/99 3.00 8.00
12 Fletcher Cox/99 5.00 12.00
13 Michael Floyd/25 5.00 12.00
14 Michael Brockers/99 3.00 8.00
16 Quinton Coples/99 3.00 8.00
21 Chandler Jones/99 3.00 8.00
22 Brandon Weeden/15 5.00 12.00
23 Riley Reiff/99 3.00 8.00
24 David DeCastro/99 3.00 8.00
25 Dont'a Hightower/99 5.00 12.00
26 Whitney Mercilus/99 3.00 8.00
27 Kevin Zeitler/99 3.00 8.00
28 Nick Perry/99 4.00 10.00
29 Harrison Smith/99 6.00 15.00
30 A.J. Jenkins/49
31 Doug Martin/25 8.00 20.00
34 Coby Fleener/25 5.00 12.00
35 Courtney Upshaw/99 4.00 10.00

2012 Panini Prominence Black and Blue Materials

1 Anthony Fasano/170 2.50 6.00
4 Chris Cooley/199 2.50 6.00
5 DeMarco Murray/55 4.00 10.00
6 Devery Henderson/199 2.50 6.00
8 Felix Jones/199 2.50 6.00
9 Haloti Ngata/199 2.50 6.00
10 Jamaal Charles/199 3.00 8.00
11 Anquan Boldin/55 3.00 8.00
12 Jay Cutler/199 2.50 6.00
14 Miles Austin/199 2.50 6.00
15 Ray Lewis/125 4.00 10.00
16 Santana Moss/55 4.00 10.00
17 Tony Gonzalez/10
18 Tony Romo/199 3.00 8.00
19 Will Smith/199 2.50 6.00
20 Kevin Kolb/199 2.50 6.00
21 Knowshon Moreno/185 2.50 6.00
22 Mark Sanchez/199 2.50 6.00
23 Nate Washington/70 3.00 8.00
24 Shawne Merriman/199 2.50 6.00
26 Matt Schaub/199 2.50 6.00
27 Chris Johnson/99 3.00 8.00
28 Devin Hester/199 3.00 8.00
29 Hakeem Nicks/49 3.00 8.00
30 Ryan Mathews/10

2012 Panini Prominence Black and Blue Materials Prime

1 Anthony Fasano/49 4.00 10.00
4 Chris Cooley/25 5.00 12.00
5 DeMarco Murray/49 5.00 12.00
6 Devery Henderson/49 4.00 10.00
7 Ed Reed/49 6.00 15.00
8 Felix Jones/49 4.00 10.00
9 Haloti Ngata /49 4.00 10.00
10 Jamaal Charles/49 5.00 12.00
14 Miles Austin/49 4.00 10.00
16 Santana Moss/49 5.00 12.00
17 Tony Gonzalez/49 5.00 12.00
18 Tony Romo/49 5.00 12.00
19 Will Smith/49 4.00 10.00
25 Antonio Gates/49 5.00 12.00
27 Chris Johnson/49 4.00 10.00
28 Devin Hester/49 5.00 12.00
29 Hakeem Nicks/49 4.00 10.00
30 Ryan Mathews/49 5.00 12.00

2012 Panini Prominence Eminence Materials Signatures

STATED PRINT RUN 25 SER.#'d SETS
1 Andy Dalton 8.00 20.00
3 Michael Turner 6.00 15.00
4 Chris Cooley 10.00 25.00
5 DeMarco Murray 8.00 20.00
6 Dez Bryant 10.00 25.00
8 Eli Manning 50.00 100.00
9 Hakeem Nicks 10.00 25.00
11 Jay Cutler 25.00 50.00
12 Joe Flacco 20.00 50.00

2012 Panini Prominence Eminence Signatures

1 A.J. Green/15 15.00 40.00
2 Aaron Rodgers/5 EXCH
3 Andy Dalton/15 8.00 20.00
4 Anquan Boldin/15 6.00 15.00
5 Asante Samuel/15 10.00 25.00
6 Ben Roethlisberger/5
7 Ben Tate/50 4.00 10.00
8 Blaine Gabbert/15 6.00 15.00
9 Brandon Spikes/15
10 Braylon Edwards/15 6.00 15.00
11 Cam Newton/5
12 Chad Johnson/3
13 Chris Cooley/25 8.00 20.00
14 Christian Ponder/25 5.00 12.00
15 Damian Williams/25 6.00 15.00
16 David Harris/1
17 David Nelson/25
19 Donald Driver/25 20.00 40.00
20 Early Doucet/25 5.00 12.00
21 Golden Tate/19
22 Jimmy Graham/15 12.00 30.00
23 Justin Durant/5
24 Lavelle Hawkins/25 6.00 15.00
25 Marques Colston/25 5.00 12.00
26 Matthew Stafford/25 20.00 40.00
27 Mike Tolbert/7
28 Peyton Manning/25 100.00 175.00
29 Pierre Thomas/25 5.00 12.00
30 Steve Smith/25 8.00 20.00
31 Tim Tebow/5 EXCH
32 Tony Moeaki/25 5.00 12.00
33 Torrey Smith/49
34 Troy Polamalu/25 60.00 100.00
35 Aaron Hernandez/35 8.00 20.00
37 Victor Cruz/35 15.00 40.00
38 Ryan Mathews/5 EXCH
39 Patrick Willis/25 12.00 30.00
40 Ray Rice/25 10.00 25.00
41 Owen Daniels/25 5.00 12.00
42 Alex Smith/5
43 Arian Foster/5
44 Brian Hartline/25 6.00 15.00

45 Brian Orakpo/25 6.00 15.00
46 Calvin Johnson/5
47 DeMarcus Ware/5
48 Greg Jennings/10
49 Jason Pierre-Paul/5
50 LeGarrette Blount/75 5.00 12.00
52 Matt Forte/25 8.00 20.00
53 Eli Manning/25 40.00 80.00
54 James Laurinaitis/25 5.00 12.00
55 Kenny Britt/10
56 Pierre Garcon/25 6.00 15.00
57 Fred Jackson/25 25.00 50.00
58 Ronde Barber/25 8.00 20.00
59 Dwayne Bowe/5 EXCH
60 Jerod Mayo/5

2012 Panini Prominence Illustrious Signatures

STATED PRINT RUN 30 SER.#'d SETS
1 Joe Namath 60.00 120.00
2 Willie Brown 8.00 20.00
3 Jack Lambert 30.00 60.00
4 Jim McMahon 12.00 30.00
5 Frank Gifford 15.00 40.00
6 Randall Cunningham 15.00 40.00
7 Junior Seau 40.00 80.00
8 Boomer Esiason 10.00 25.00
9 Doug Flutie 10.00 25.00
10 Cris Carter 12.00 30.00
11 Keyshawn Johnson 10.00 25.00
12 Joe Montana 100.00 200.00
13 Jerome Bettis 40.00 80.00
14 Michael Irvin 25.00 50.00
15 Ed Too Tall Jones 10.00 25.00
16 Marcus Allen 12.00 30.00
17 Sterling Sharpe 12.00 30.00
18 Thurman Thomas
19 Bo Jackson 40.00 80.00
20 John Elway 50.00 100.00
21 Bernie Kosar 12.00 30.00
22 Archie Manning 12.00 30.00
23 Howie Long 15.00 40.00
24 Phil Simms 12.00 30.00
25 Ronnie Lott 15.00 40.00
26 Rod Woodson 15.00 40.00
27 Danny White 12.00 30.00
28 Mike Curtis 8.00 20.00

2012 Panini Prominence Premiere Materials Signatures

STATED PRINT RUN 25 SER.#'d SETS
EXCH EXPIRATION: 3/19/2014
*PRIME/15: .6X TO 1.5X BASIC JSYAU/25
1 Brock Osweiler 6.00 15.00
2 LaMichael James 6.00 15.00
3 Michael Floyd 6.00 15.00
4 DeVier Posey 6.00 15.00
5 Doug Martin 10.00 25.00
6 Ryan Broyles EXCH 6.00 15.00
7 Bernard Pierce 6.00 15.00
8 Rueben Randle 6.00 15.00
9 Robert Griffin III 8.00 20.00
10 David Wilson 6.00 15.00
11 Dwayne Allen 6.00 15.00
12 Coby Fleener 6.00 15.00
13 Brian Quick 6.00 15.00
14 Nick Foles 25.00 60.00
15 A.J. Jenkins 6.00 15.00
16 Justin Blackmon 6.00 15.00
17 Mohamed Sanu 10.00 25.00
18 Alshon Jeffery 12.00 30.00
19 Isaiah Pead 6.00 15.00
20 Andrew Luck 125.00 250.00
21 Brandon Weeden 6.00 15.00
22 Kendall Wright 6.00 15.00
23 Ronnie Hillman EXCH 6.00 15.00
24 Stephen Hill 6.00 15.00
25 Trent Richardson 6.00 15.00
26 Russell Wilson 100.00 175.00
27 Ryan Tannehill EXCH 10.00 25.00
28 Michael Egnew 6.00 15.00

2012 Panini Prominence Rookie Letter Autographs

*LETTER AU: .5X TO 1.2X BASE JSY AU RC
STATED PRINT RUN 70-245
220 Nick Foles/125 25.00 60.00
226 Robert Griffin III/70 10.00 25.00
231 Andrew Luck/80 125.00 250.00
235 Russell Wilson/150 75.00 135.00

2012 Panini Prominence Rookie NFL Field Autographs

*NFL FIELD AU: .4X TO 1X BASE JSY AU RC
STATED PRINT RUN 70-245
226 Robert Griffin III/70 8.00 20.00
231 Andrew Luck/80 75.00 150.00
235 Russell Wilson/150 50.00 100.00

2012 Panini Prominence Rookie Projection Materials

STATED PRINT RUN 299 SER.#'d SETS
*PRIME/49: .6X TO 1.5X BASIC JSY/299
1 Coby Fleener 1.50 4.00
2 Michael Egnew 1.50 4.00
3 Brock Osweiler 1.50 4.00
4 Ronnie Hillman 1.50 4.00
5 Robert Turbin 1.50 4.00
6 Rueben Randle 1.50 4.00
7 Chris Givens 1.50 4.00
8 Stephen Hill 1.50 4.00
9 Isaiah Pead 1.50 4.00
10 Bernard Pierce 1.50 4.00
11 Trent Richardson 1.50 4.00
12 LaMichael James 1.50 4.00
13 Lamar Miller 2.50 6.00
14 David Wilson 1.50 4.00
15 Doug Martin 2.50 6.00
16 Russell Wilson 8.00 20.00
17 Nick Foles 4.00 10.00
18 Brandon Weeden 1.50 4.00
19 Ryan Tannehill 2.50 6.00
20 Robert Griffin III 2.00 5.00
21 Nick Toon 1.50 4.00
22 Michael Floyd 1.50 4.00
23 Justin Blackmon 1.50 4.00
24 Andrew Luck 12.00 30.00
25 Jarius Wright 1.50 4.00
26 Kendall Wright 1.50 4.00
27 Mohamed Sanu 2.50 6.00
28 Brian Quick 1.50 4.00
29 T.J. Graham 1.50 4.00
30 DeVier Posey 1.50 4.00
31 Ryan Broyles 1.50 4.00
32 Joe Adams 1.50 4.00
33 Alshon Jeffery 3.00 8.00
34 A.J. Jenkins 1.50 4.00
35 Dwayne Allen 1.50 4.00

2012 Panini Prominence Rookie Team Helmet Autographs

*HELMET AU: .4X TO 1X BASE JSY AU RC
STATED PRINT RUN 70-245
231 Andrew Luck/80 125.00 200.00
235 Russell Wilson/150 60.00 120.00

2012 Panini Prominence Rookie Team Logo Autographs

*TEAM LOGO AU: .4X TO 1X BASE JSY AU RC
STATED PRINT RUN 70-245
231 Andrew Luck/80 100.00 200.00
235 Russell Wilson/150 60.00 120.00

2012 Panini Prominence Unlimited Potential Materials Combos

STATED PRINT RUN 249 SER.#'d SETS
PRIME/49: .6X TO 1.5X DUAL JSY/249
1 A.Luck/C.Fleener 6.00 15.00
2 B.Osweiler/R.Wilson 6.00 15.00
3 D.Wilson/I.Pead 1.50 4.00
4 R.Tannehill/B.Weeden 2.50 6.00
5 K.Wright/B.Quick 1.50 4.00
6 R.Griffin III/N.Foles 4.00 10.00
7 S.Hill/D.Posey 1.50 4.00
8 T.Richardson/D.Martin 2.50 6.00
9 J.Blackmon/A.Jenkins 1.50 4.00
10 T.Graham/M.Sanu 2.50 6.00
11 L.Miller/L.James 2.50 6.00
12 D.Allen/R.Hillman 1.50 4.00
13 R.Broyles/J.Wright 1.50 4.00
14 R.Randle/M.Egnew 1.50 4.00
15 M.Floyd/N.Toon 1.50 4.00

2012 Panini Prominence Unlimited Potential Materials Signatures

STATED PRINT RUN 25 SER.#'d SETS
EXCH EXPIRATION: 3/19/2014
*PRIME/15: .6X TO 1.5X BASIC JSYAU/25
1 Lamar Miller 10.00 25.00
2 Jarius Wright 6.00 15.00
3 Andrew Luck 125.00 250.00
4 Robert Turbin 6.00 15.00
5 Isaiah Pead 6.00 15.00
6 Alshon Jeffery 12.00 30.00
7 Mohamed Sanu 10.00 25.00
8 Justin Blackmon 6.00 15.00
9 A.J. Jenkins 6.00 15.00
10 Ronnie Hillman EXCH 6.00 15.00
11 Stephen Hill 6.00 15.00
12 Brandon Weeden 6.00 15.00
13 Ryan Tannehill 10.00 25.00
14 Michael Egnew 6.00 15.00
15 Russell Wilson 90.00 150.00
16 Kendall Wright 6.00 15.00
17 Trent Richardson 6.00 15.00
18 Nick Toon 6.00 15.00
19 T.J. Graham 6.00 15.00
20 Brock Osweiler 6.00 15.00
21 LaMichael James 6.00 15.00
22 Michael Floyd 6.00 15.00
23 Joe Adams 6.00 15.00
24 DeVier Posey 6.00 15.00
25 Doug Martin 10.00 25.00
26 Ryan Broyles EXCH 6.00 15.00
27 Bernard Pierce 6.00 15.00
28 Rueben Randle 6.00 15.00
29 Robert Griffin III 8.00 20.00
30 David Wilson 6.00 15.00
31 Dwayne Allen 6.00 15.00
32 Chris Givens 6.00 15.00
33 Coby Fleener 6.00 15.00
34 Brian Quick 6.00 15.00
35 Nick Foles 30.00 80.00

2013 Panini Prominence

1 Larry Fitzgerald .60 1.50
2 Rashard Mendenhall .50 1.25
3 Patrick Peterson .50 1.25
4 Matt Ryan .60 1.50
5 Julio Jones .75 2.00
6 Steven Jackson .50 1.25
7 Tony Gonzalez .60 1.50
8 Joe Flacco .60 1.50
9 Torrey Smith .50 1.25
10 Ray Rice .50 1.25
11 C.J. Spiller .50 1.25
12 Fred Jackson .60 1.50
13 Steve Johnson .60 1.50
14 Cam Newton .75 2.00
15 Steve Smith .60 1.50
16 Jonathan Stewart .50 1.25
17 Jay Cutler .50 1.25
18 Brandon Marshall .60 1.50
19 Matt Forte .50 1.25
20 Andy Dalton .60 1.50
21 A.J. Green .75 2.00
22 BenJarvus Green-Ellis .60 1.50
23 Brandon Weeden .50 1.25
24 Josh Gordon .50 1.25
25 Trent Richardson .50 1.25
26 Tony Romo .60 1.50
27 Dez Bryant .75 2.00
28 DeMarco Murray .60 1.50
29 Jason Witten .60 1.50
30 Peyton Manning 1.50 4.00
31 Demaryius Thomas .60 1.50
32 Wes Welker .60 1.50
33 Eric Decker .50 1.25
34 Matthew Stafford .60 1.50
35 Calvin Johnson .75 2.00
36 Reggie Bush .50 1.25
37 Aaron Rodgers 1.25 3.00
38 Jordy Nelson .60 1.50
39 Clay Matthews .75 2.00
40 Matt Schaub .50 1.25
41 Andre Johnson .50 1.25
42 Arian Foster .60 1.50
43 Andrew Luck 1.25 3.00
44 Reggie Wayne .60 1.50
45 Vick Ballard .50 1.25
46 Cecil Shorts .50 1.25
47 Justin Blackmon .50 1.25
48 Maurice Jones-Drew .50 1.25
49 Alex Smith .60 1.50
50 Dwayne Bowe .60 1.50
51 Jamaal Charles .60 1.50
52 Ryan Tannehill .60 1.50
53 Mike Wallace .50 1.25
54 Dustin Keller .50 1.25
55 Christian Ponder .50 1.25
56 Greg Jennings .50 1.25
57 Adrian Peterson .75 2.00
58 Tom Brady 2.00 5.00
59 Danny Amendola .60 1.50
60 Rob Gronkowski .75 2.00
61 Drew Brees .75 2.00
62 Marques Colston .50 1.25
63 Jimmy Graham .75 2.00
64 Eli Manning .60 1.50
65 Hakeem Nicks .50 1.25
66 David Wilson .50 1.25
67 Mark Sanchez .50 1.25
68 Santonio Holmes .50 1.25
69 Bilal Powell .50 1.25
70 Matt Flynn .50 1.25
71 Denarius Moore .50 1.25
72 Darren McFadden .60 1.50
73 Michael Vick .60 1.50
74 DeSean Jackson .60 1.50
75 LeSean McCoy .75 2.00
76 Ben Roethlisberger .75 2.00
77 Antonio Brown .75 2.00
78 Jonathan Dwyer .50 1.25
79 Sam Bradford .50 1.25
80 Chris Givens .50 1.25
81 Jared Cook .50 1.25
82 Philip Rivers .75 2.00
83 Antonio Gates .60 1.50
84 Ryan Mathews .60 1.50
85 Colin Kaepernick .60 1.50
86 Michael Crabtree .50 1.25
87 Anquan Boldin .50 1.25
88 Frank Gore .60 1.50
89 Russell Wilson 1.50 4.00
90 Percy Harvin .50 1.25
91 Marshawn Lynch .60 1.50
92 Josh Freeman .60 1.50
93 Vincent Jackson .50 1.25
94 Doug Martin .60 1.50
95 Jake Locker .60 1.50
96 Kenny Britt .50 1.25
97 Chris Johnson .50 1.25
98 Robert Griffin III .50 1.25
99 Pierre Garcon .60 1.50
100 Alfred Morris .50 1.25
101 Aaron Dobson RC .75 2.00
102 Aaron Mellette RC .75 2.00
103 Ace Sanders RC .75 2.00
104 Cornellius Carradine RC .75 2.00
105 Alec Ogletree RC .75 2.00
106 Alex Okafor RC .75 2.00
107 Andre Ellington RC .75 2.00
108 Arthur Brown RC .75 2.00
109 Barkevious Mingo RC .75 2.00
110 Bjoern Werner RC .75 2.00
111 Chance Warmack RC .75 2.00
112 Chris Gragg RC .75 2.00
113 Chris Harper RC .75 2.00
114 Christine Michael RC .75 2.00
115 D.J. Hayden RC .75 2.00
116 Cobi Hamilton RC .75 2.00
117 Conner Vernon RC .75 2.00
118 Cordarrelle Patterson RC .75 2.00
119 Corey Fuller RC .75 2.00
120 Damontre Moore RC .75 2.00
121 Da'Rick Rogers RC .75 2.00
122 Darius Slay RC .75 2.00
123 Datone Jones RC .75 2.00
124 DeAndre Hopkins RC 2.00 5.00
125 Dee Milliner RC .75 2.00
126 Denard Robinson RC .75 2.00
127 Desmond Trufant RC .75 2.00
128 Dion Jordan RC .75 2.00
129 Dion Sims RC .75 2.00
130 Eddie Lacy RC .75 2.00
131 EJ Manuel RC .75 2.00
132 Eric Fisher RC .75 2.00
133 Eric Reid RC 1.00 2.50
134 Ezekiel Ansah RC .75 2.00
135 Gavin Escobar RC .75 2.00
136 Geno Smith RC .75 2.00
137 Giovani Bernard RC .75 2.00
138 Jamar Taylor RC .75 2.00
139 Jarvis Jones RC .75 2.00
140 Jawan Jamison RC .75 2.00
141 Johnathan Franklin RC .75 2.00
142 Dennis Johnson RC .75 2.00
143 Johnthan Banks RC .75 2.00
144 Jordan Poyer RC .75 2.00
145 Jordan Reed RC 1.25 3.00
146 Joseph Randle RC .75 2.00
147 Josh Boyce RC .75 2.00
148 Justin Hunter RC .75 2.00
149 Keenan Allen RC 1.50 4.00
150 Kenjon Barner RC .75 2.00
151 Kenny Stills RC .75 2.00
152 Kenny Vaccaro RC .75 2.00
153 Kevin Minter RC .75 2.00
154 Johnathan Cyprien RC .75 2.00
155 Knile Davis RC .75 2.00
156 Landry Jones RC .75 2.00
157 Le'Veon Bell RC 2.50 6.00
158 Jasper Collins RC .75 2.00
159 Luke Joeckel RC .75 2.00
160 Manti Te'o RC 1.00 2.50
161 Marcus Davis RC .75 2.00
162 Marcus Lattimore RC .75 2.00
163 Margus Hunt RC .75 2.00
164 Markus Wheaton RC .75 2.00
165 Marquess Wilson RC 1.25 3.00
166 Marquise Goodwin RC .75 2.00
167 Matt Barkley RC .75 2.00
168 Matt Elam RC .75 2.00
169 Matt Scott RC .75 2.00
170 Mike Gillislee RC .75 2.00
171 Mike Glennon RC .75 2.00
172 Montee Ball RC .75 2.00
173 Nick Kasa RC .75 2.00
174 Phillip Thomas RC .75 2.00
175 Quinton Patton RC .75 2.00
176 Ray Graham RC .75 2.00
177 Rex Burkhead RC 1.00 2.50
178 Robert Woods RC 1.25 3.00
179 Rodney Smith RC .75 2.00
180 Ryan Nassib RC .75 2.00
181 Ryan Otten RC .75 2.00
182 Ryan Swope RC .75 2.00
183 Sam Montgomery RC .75 2.00
184 Sheldon Richardson RC .75 2.00
185 Onterio McCalebb RC 1.00 2.50
186 Stedman Bailey RC .75 2.00
187 Stepfan Taylor RC .75 2.00
188 Tavarres King RC .75 2.00
189 Tavon Austin RC 1.00 2.50
190 Terrance Williams RC .75 2.00
191 Theo Riddick RC .75 2.00
192 Travis Kelce RC 2.00 5.00
193 Tyler Bray RC .75 2.00
194 Tyler Eifert RC .75 2.00
195 Tyler Wilson RC .75 2.00
196 Tyrann Mathieu RC 1.25 3.00
197 Vance McDonald RC 1.00 2.50
198 Xavier Rhodes RC .75 2.00
199 Zac Dysert RC .75 2.00
200 Zach Ertz RC 1.50 4.00

2013 Panini Prominence Gold

*1-100 VETS/199: 1X TO 2.5X BASIC CARDS
*101-200 ROOKIES/199: .6X TO 1.5X BASIC RC

2013 Panini Prominence Platinum

*1-100 VETS/99: 1.2X TO 3X BASIC CARDS
*101-200 ROOKIES/99: .8X TO 2X BASIC RC

2013 Panini Prominence Eminence Signatures

1 Darren McFadden/49 8.00 20.00
3 DeSean Jackson/25 8.00 20.00
4 Doug Martin/99 6.00 15.00
6 Jay Cutler/49
7 Maurice Jones-Drew/49
8 Andrew Luck/25 90.00 150.00
9 Andrew Hawkins/999 2.50 6.00
10 Jeremy Kerley/999 2.50 6.00
11 Robert Turbin/999 2.50 6.00
12 Rueben Randle/999 4.00 10.00
13 T.Y. Hilton/999 4.00 10.00

2013 Panini Prominence Eminence Signatures Combos

EXCH EXPIRATION: 3/4/2015
1 Kaepernick/RGIII/25 40.00 100.00
3 F.Gore/M.Crabtree/25
4 C.Matthews/R.Cobb/25

2013 Panini Prominence Rookie Gridiron Gems Autographs

*GRID GEM AU/100-225: .4X TO 1X RATED ROOKIE AU
131 EJ Manuel/102 8.00 20.00
136 Geno Smith/100 4.00 10.00

2013 Panini Prominence Rookie Letter Autographs

*LETTER/100-224: .4X TO 1X RATED RK AU
103 Ace Sanders/210 8.00 20.00
111 Chance Warmack/175 10.00 25.00
118 Cordarrelle Patterson/108 4.00 10.00
130 Eddie Lacy/100 4.00 10.00
131 EJ Manuel/102 8.00 20.00
136 Geno Smith/100 4.00 10.00
145 Jordan Reed/200 8.00 20.00
171 Mike Glennon/105 4.00 10.00
172 Montee Ball/100 4.00 10.00
177 Rex Burkhead/208 15.00 40.00
196 Tyrann Mathieu/105 15.00 40.00

2013 Panini Prominence Rookie NFL Field Autographs

*FIELD AU/100-225: .4X TO 1X RATED ROOKIE AU

2013 Panini Prominence Rookie Rated Rookie Patch Autographs

101 Aaron Dobson/102 4.00 10.00
102 Aaron Mellette/208 3.00 8.00
103 Ace Sanders/210 6.00 15.00
104 Cornellius Carradine/180 3.00 8.00
106 Alex Okafor/204 3.00 8.00
107 Andre Ellington/108 4.00 10.00
108 Arthur Brown/225 3.00 8.00
109 Barkevious Mingo/200 3.00 8.00
110 Bjoern Werner/204 3.00 8.00
111 Chance Warmack/175 8.00 20.00
112 Chris Gragg/225 3.00 8.00
113 Chris Harper/204 3.00 8.00
114 Christine Michael/105 4.00 10.00
115 D.J. Hayden/180 8.00 20.00
117 Conner Vernon/204 3.00 8.00
118 Cordarrelle Patterson/108 4.00 10.00
119 Corey Fuller/204 3.00 8.00
120 Damontre Moore/200 3.00 8.00
121 Da'Rick Rogers/102 4.00 10.00
122 Darius Slay/100 4.00 10.00
123 Datone Jones/200 3.00 8.00
124 DeAndre Hopkins/105 12.00 30.00
126 Denard Robinson/208 3.00 8.00
127 Desmond Trufant/210 3.00 8.00
128 Dion Jordan/204 3.00 8.00
129 Dion Sims/200 3.00 8.00
130 Eddie Lacy/100 4.00 10.00
131 EJ Manuel/102 8.00 20.00
132 Eric Fisher/102 4.00 10.00
133 Eric Reid/225 8.00 20.00
135 Gavin Escobar/225 8.00 20.00
136 Geno Smith/100 4.00 10.00
137 Giovani Bernard/105 4.00 10.00
138 Jamar Taylor/225 3.00 8.00
139 Jarvis Jones/100 4.00 10.00
141 Johnathan Franklin/104 4.00 10.00
142 Dennis Johnson/210 3.00 8.00
143 Johnthan Banks/225 6.00 15.00
144 Jordan Poyer/225 3.00 8.00
145 Jordan Reed/200 5.00 12.00
146 Joseph Randle/102 4.00 10.00
147 Josh Boyce/225 3.00 8.00
148 Justin Hunter/102 4.00 10.00
149 Keenan Allen/100 12.00 30.00
150 Kenjon Barner/102 4.00 10.00
151 Kenny Stills/102 4.00 10.00
152 Kenny Vaccaro/105 4.00 10.00
153 Kevin Minter/204 3.00 8.00
154 Johnathan Cyprien/210 3.00 8.00
155 Knile Davis/100 4.00 10.00
156 Landry Jones/100 4.00 10.00
157 Le'Veon Bell/100 12.00 30.00
158 Jasper Collins/105 4.00 10.00
160 Manti Te'o/102 5.00 12.00
161 Marcus Davis/225 3.00 8.00
162 Marcus Lattimore/108 4.00 10.00
163 Margus Hunt/225 3.00 8.00
164 Markus Wheaton/105 4.00 10.00
166 Marquise Goodwin/105 4.00 10.00
167 Matt Barkley/105 4.00 10.00
168 Matt Elam/225 3.00 8.00
169 Matt Scott/100 4.00 10.00
170 Mike Gillislee/108 4.00 10.00
171 Mike Glennon/105 4.00 10.00
172 Montee Ball/100 4.00 10.00
173 Nick Kasa/225 3.00 8.00
174 Phillip Thomas/225 3.00 8.00
175 Quinton Patton/102 4.00 10.00
177 Rex Burkhead/208 12.00 30.00
178 Robert Woods/100 6.00 15.00
179 Rodney Smith/225 3.00 8.00
180 Ryan Nassib/102 4.00 10.00
181 Ryan Otten/100 4.00 10.00
182 Ryan Swope/100 4.00 10.00
183 Sam Montgomery/100 4.00 10.00
185 Onterio McCalebb/100 5.00 12.00
186 Stedman Bailey/102 4.00 10.00
187 Stepfan Taylor/102 4.00 10.00
188 Tavarres King/100 4.00 10.00
189 Tavon Austin/102 5.00 12.00
190 Terrance Williams/104 4.00 10.00
191 Theo Riddick/105 4.00 10.00
192 Travis Kelce/200 15.00 40.00
193 Tyler Bray/100 4.00 10.00
194 Tyler Eifert/102 4.00 10.00
195 Tyler Wilson/102 4.00 10.00
196 Tyrann Mathieu/105 6.00 15.00
197 Vance McDonald/225 4.00 10.00
198 Xavier Rhodes/102 4.00 10.00
199 Zac Dysert/102 4.00 10.00
200 Zach Ertz/100 8.00 20.00

2013 Panini Prominence Rookie Team Helmet Autographs

*HELMET AU/100-225: .4X TO 1X RATED RK AU
201 Blidi Wreh-Wilson/999 3.00 8.00
202 Brad Sorensen/999 2.50 6.00
203 Brice Butler/999 2.50 6.00
204 Chris Thompson/999 5.00 12.00
205 D.J. Fluker/999 2.50 6.00
207 Dustin Hopkins/999 5.00 12.00
208 Jon Bostic/999 8.00 20.00
209 Justin Brown/999 4.00 10.00
210 Kerwynn Williams/999 2.50 6.00
211 Latavius Murray/999 8.00 20.00
212 Mychal Rivera/999 2.50 6.00
213 Robert Alford/999 2.50 6.00

2013 Panini Prominence Rookie Team Logo Patch Signatures

*TEAM LOGO/100-225: .4X TO 1X RATED RK AU

2013 Panini Rookie Crusade

RANDOM INSERTS IN ROOKIES AND STARS
*GOLD/25: 1.2X TO 3X BASIC INSERTS
*PURPLE/49: 1X TO 2.5X BASIC INSERTS
*RED/99: .8X TO 2X BASIC INSERTS
1 Aaron Dobson .75 2.00
2 Andre Ellington .75 2.00
3 Christine Michael .75 2.00
4 Cordarrelle Patterson .75 2.00
5 DeAndre Hopkins 2.00 5.00
6 Denard Robinson .75 2.00
7 Eddie Lacy .75 2.00
8 EJ Manuel .75 2.00
9 Gavin Escobar .75 2.00
10 Geno Smith .75 2.00
11 Giovani Bernard .75 2.00
12 Johnathan Franklin .75 2.00
13 Jordan Reed 1.25 3.00
14 Joseph Randle .75 2.00
15 Justin Hunter .75 2.00
16 Keenan Allen 1.50 4.00
17 Kenny Stills .75 2.00
18 Knile Davis .75 2.00
19 Landry Jones .75 2.00
20 Le'Veon Bell 2.50 6.00
21 Manti Te'o 1.00 2.50
22 Marcus Lattimore .75 2.00
23 Markus Wheaton .75 2.00
24 Marquise Goodwin .75 2.00
25 Matt Barkley .75 2.00
26 Mike Gillislee .75 2.00
27 Mike Glennon .75 2.00
28 Montee Ball .75 2.00
29 Quinton Patton .75 2.00
30 Robert Woods 1.25 3.00
31 Ryan Nassib .75 2.00
32 Stedman Bailey .75 2.00
33 Stepfan Taylor .75 2.00
34 Tavon Austin 1.00 2.50
35 Terrance Williams .75 2.00
36 Dion Jordan .75 2.00
37 Tyler Eifert .75 2.00
38 Tyler Wilson .75 2.00
39 Vance McDonald 1.00 2.50
40 Zach Ertz 1.50 4.00

2013 Panini Pepsi Rookie of the Week

1A Caleb Sturgis .75 2.00
1B Keenan Allen ROY 1.00 2.50
2 EJ Manuel .50 1.25
3 Giovani Bernard .50 1.25
4 Kiko Alonso .60 1.50
5 Geno Smith .50 1.25
6 Keenan Allen 1.00 2.50
7 D.J. Fluker .50 1.25
8 Sio Moore .50 1.25
9 Eddie Lacy .50 1.25
10 Tavon Austin .60 1.50
11 Matt McGloin 1.50 4.00
12 Kennan Allen 1.00 2.50
13 Zach Ertz 1.00 2.50
14 Marlon Brown .75 2.00
15 Keenan Allen 1.00 2.50
16 Le'Veon Bell 1.50 4.00
17 Keenan Allen 1.00 2.50

2014 Panini Pepsi Rookie of the Week

1 Kelvin Benjamin .75 2.00
2 Sammy Watkins .75 2.00
3 Kyle Fuller .50 1.25
4 Teddy Bridgewater .75 2.00
5 Branden Oliver .75 2.00
6 Branden Oliver .75 2.00
7 Sammy Watkins .75 2.00
8 Sammy Watkins .75 2.00
9 Jeremy Hill .60 1.50
10 Chris Borland .50 1.25
11 Chris Borland .50 1.25
12 Odell Beckham Jr. 1.25 3.00
13 Teddy Bridgewater .75 2.00
14 Derek Carr 3.00 8.00
15 Odell Beckham Jr. 1.25 3.00
16 Odell Beckham Jr. 1.25 3.00
17 Odell Beckham Jr. 1.25 3.00
TBROY Teddy Bridgewater ROY .75 2.00

2013 Panini Rookie Premiere Autographs

RANDOM INSERTS IN 2013 CONTENDERS
ANNOUNCED PRINT RUN 50
1 Aaron Dobson 6.00 15.00
2 Andre Ellington 6.00 15.00
3 Christine Michael 6.00 15.00
4 Cordarrelle Patterson 6.00 15.00
5 DeAndre Hopkins 15.00 40.00
6 Denard Robinson 6.00 15.00
7 Dion Jordan 6.00 15.00
8 Eddie Lacy 6.00 15.00
9 EJ Manuel 6.00 15.00
10 Gavin Escobar 6.00 15.00
11 Geno Smith
12 Giovani Bernard 6.00 15.00
13 Johnathan Franklin
14 Jordan Reed
15 Joseph Randle
16 Justin Hunter
17 Keenan Allen 12.00 30.00
18 Kenny Stills 6.00 15.00
19 Knile Davis 6.00 15.00
20 Landry Jones 6.00 15.00
21 Le'Veon Bell
22 Manti Te'o 8.00 20.00
23 Marcus Lattimore 6.00 15.00
24 Markus Wheaton
25 Marquise Goodwin
26 Matt Barkley 6.00 15.00
27 Mike Gillislee 8.00 20.00
28 Mike Glennon 6.00 15.00
29 Montee Ball 10.00 25.00
30 Quinton Patton 10.00 25.00
31 Robert Woods 10.00 25.00
32 Ryan Nassib 6.00 15.00
33 Stedman Bailey 6.00 15.00
34 Stepfan Taylor 6.00 15.00
35 Tavon Austin 8.00 20.00
36 Terrance Williams
37 Tyler Eifert 6.00 15.00
38 Tyler Wilson 6.00 15.00
39 Vance McDonald
40 Zach Ertz

2012 Panini Signatures

INSERTS IN VARIOUS 2012 PANINI RETAIL
1 Aaron Maybin 2.50 6.00
2 Aldrick Robinson
3 Alex Green
4 Alex Henery
5 Andre Roberts 3.00 8.00
7 Armanti Edwards 2.50 6.00
9 Bilal Powell 2.50 6.00
11 Brandon Meriweather
12 Braylon Edwards 2.50 6.00
15 Cameron Jordan 2.50 6.00
16 Cecil Shorts
20 Colin Kaepernick 3.00 8.00
21 Curtis Brinkley 2.50 6.00
24 David Garrard 3.00 8.00
25 Dennis Dixon 4.00 10.00
27 Derrick Harvey 2.50 6.00
29 Dwayne Harris 3.00 8.00
30 Dwight Lowery 2.50 6.00
31 Earl Thomas 4.00 10.00
32 Emmanuel Sanders
34 Gerald McCoy 2.50 6.00
36 Isaiah Stanback
37 Jacob Hester 2.50 6.00
39 Jed Collins
40 Jeremy Horne 2.50 6.00
41 Jerome Felton 2.50 6.00
42 Jimmy Clausen 2.50 6.00
43 Joe McKnight 2.50 6.00
44 John Clay 3.00 8.00
47 Julius Thomas 2.50 6.00
50 Kellen Davis
53 Kregg Lumpkin
54 Kyle Williams 2.50 6.00
57 Lavelle Hawkins
62 Martellus Bennett 3.00 8.00
63 Mason Crosby
68 Mike Kafka
69 Mikel Leshoure
70 Nate Allen 2.50 6.00
71 Nick Folk
76 Quentin Groves 4.00 10.00
77 Quintin Demps
78 Ramses Barden
83 Ryan Mallett 6.00 15.00
87 Sergio Kindle 2.50 6.00
88 Shane Vereen 2.50 6.00
91 Stevan Ridley
92 T.J. Yates 4.00 10.00
97 Zack Bowman 4.00 10.00
98 Tyler Sash 2.50 6.00
99 Phil Taylor 2.50 6.00
100 Tyron Smith 3.00 8.00

2013 Panini Spectra

1 Larry Fitzgerald .60 1.50
2 Michael Floyd .50 1.25
3 Patrick Peterson .50 1.25
4 Julio Jones .75 2.00
5 Matt Ryan .60 1.50
6 Tony Gonzalez .60 1.50
7 Joe Flacco .60 1.50
8 Ray Rice .50 1.25
9 Torrey Smith .50 1.25
10 C.J. Spiller .50 1.25
11 Fred Jackson .60 1.50
12 Steve Johnson .60 1.50
13 Cam Newton .75 2.00
14 Steve Smith .60 1.50
15 Luke Kuechly .60 1.50
16 Brandon Marshall .60 1.50
17 Jay Cutler .50 1.25
18 Matt Forte .50 1.25
19 A.J. Green .75 2.00
20 Andy Dalton .60 1.50
21 BenJarvus Green-Ellis .60 1.50
22 Brandon Weeden .50 1.25
23 Jordan Cameron .50 1.25
24 Josh Gordon .50 1.25
25 DeMarco Murray .60 1.50
26 Dez Bryant .75 2.00
27 Jason Witten .60 1.50
28 Tony Romo .60 1.50
29 Demaryius Thomas .60 1.50
30 Julius Thomas .50 1.25
31 Peyton Manning 3.00 8.00
32 Wes Welker .60 1.50
33 Calvin Johnson .75 2.00
34 Matthew Stafford .60 1.50
35 Reggie Bush .50 1.25
36 Aaron Rodgers 1.25 3.00
37 Clay Matthews .75 2.00
38 Randall Cobb .60 1.50
39 Andre Johnson .50 1.25
40 Arian Foster .60 1.50
41 J.J. Watt .60 1.50
42 Matt Schaub .50 1.25
43 Andrew Luck 1.25 3.00
44 Reggie Wayne .60 1.50
45 T.Y. Hilton .60 1.50
46 Trent Richardson .50 1.25
47 Cecil Shorts III .50 1.25
48 Justin Blackmon .50 1.25
49 Maurice Jones-Drew .50 1.25
50 Alex Smith .60 1.50
51 Dwayne Bowe .60 1.50
52 Jamaal Charles .60 1.50
53 Lamar Miller .50 1.25
54 Mike Wallace .50 1.25
55 Ryan Tannehill .60 1.50
56 Adrian Peterson .75 2.00
57 Greg Jennings .50 1.25
58 Kyle Rudolph .50 1.25
59 Danny Amendola .60 1.50
60 Julian Edelman .75 2.00
61 Rob Gronkowski .75 2.00
62 Tom Brady 2.00 5.00
63 Drew Brees .75 2.00
64 Jimmy Graham .75 2.00
65 Marques Colston .50 1.25
66 David Wilson .50 1.25
67 Eli Manning .60 1.50
68 Victor Cruz .60 1.50
69 Bilal Powell .50 1.25
70 Santonio Holmes .50 1.25
71 Darren McFadden .60 1.50
72 Denarius Moore .50 1.25
73 Terrelle Pryor .60 1.50
74 DeSean Jackson .60 1.50
75 LeSean McCoy .75 2.00
76 Nick Foles .60 1.50
77 Antonio Brown .75 2.00
78 Ben Roethlisberger .75 2.00
79 Troy Polamalu .75 2.00
80 Antonio Gates .60 1.50
81 Eddie Royal .50 1.25
82 Philip Rivers .75 2.00
83 Anquan Boldin .50 1.25
84 Colin Kaepernick .60 1.50
85 Frank Gore .60 1.50
86 Vernon Davis .50 1.25
87 Marshawn Lynch .60 1.50
88 Percy Harvin .50 1.25
89 Richard Sherman .75 2.00
90 Russell Wilson 3.00 8.00
91 Chris Givens .50 1.25
92 Sam Bradford .50 1.25
93 Doug Martin .60 1.50
94 Vincent Jackson .50 1.25
95 Chris Johnson .50 1.25
96 Jake Locker .60 1.50
97 Kendall Wright .50 1.25
98 Alfred Morris .50 1.25
99 Pierre Garcon .60 1.50
100 Robert Griffin III .50 1.25
102 Ace Sanders AU/299 2.00 5.00
103 Alan Bonner AU/299 RC 2.00 5.00
105 Timothy Wright AU/299 RC 2.50 6.00
108 Benny Cunningham AU/299 RC 3.00 8.00
109 B.J. Daniels AU/299 RC 3.00 8.00
111 Brad Sorensen AU/299 RC 2.00 5.00
112 Brice Butler AU/299 RC 2.00 5.00
113 Blidi Wreh-Wilson AU/299 RC 2.50 6.00
114 C.J. Anderson AU/299 RC 8.00 20.00
115 Caleb Sturgis AU/299 RC 3.00 8.00
116 Chance Warmack AU/299 RC 2.00 5.00
117 Chris Gragg AU/99 RC 2.50 6.00
118 Chris Harper AU/299 RC 2.00 5.00
119 Chris Thompson AU/99 RC 2.50 6.00
120 Cierre Wood AU/299 RC 2.00 5.00
121 Cobi Hamilton AU/299 RC 2.00 5.00
122 Corey Fuller AU/299 RC 2.00 5.00
124 D.J. Hayden AU/299 RC 2.00 5.00
126 Da'Rick Rogers AU/299 RC 2.00 5.00
127 Darius Slay AU/299 RC 2.00 5.00
128 Datone Jones AU/299 RC 2.00 5.00
129 David Amerson AU/99 RC 2.50 6.00
130 Dee Milliner AU/99 RC 2.50 6.00
131 Dennis Johnson AU/299 RC 2.00 5.00
132 Desmond Trufant AU/299 RC 2.00 5.00
133 Dion Sims AU/299 RC 2.00 5.00
134 D.J. Swearinger AU/299 RC 2.00 5.00
135 D.J. Fluker AU/299 RC 2.00 5.00
136 Dustin Hopkins AU/299 RC 2.00 5.00
137 Earl Wolff AU/299 RC 3.00 8.00
138 Eric Fisher AU/299 RC 2.00 5.00
139 Eric Reid AU/99 RC 6.00 15.00
140 Ezekiel Ansah AU/99 RC 2.50 6.00
141 Jack Doyle AU/299 RC 2.00 5.00
142 Joseph Fauria AU/299 RC 3.00 8.00
143 Jamie Collins AU/299 RC 2.00 5.00
144 Jaron Brown AU/299 RC 2.00 5.00
145 Jarvis Jones AU/299 RC 2.00 5.00
146 Jawan Jamison AU/299 RC 2.00 5.00
147 Jeff Tuel AU/299 RC 2.00 5.00
148 Johnthan Banks AU/299 RC 2.00 5.00
149 Jon Bostic AU/299 RC 5.00 12.00
150 Johnathan Cyprien AU/299 RC 2.00 5.00
151 Skye Dawson AU/299 RC 3.00 8.00
152 Josh Boyce AU/299 RC 2.00 5.00
153 Justin Brown AU/299 RC 3.00 8.00
154 Kenbrell Thompkins AU/299 3.00 8.00
155 Kenjon Barner AU/299 RC 2.00 5.00
157 Kerwynn Williams AU/299 RC 2.00 5.00
158 Kevin Minter AU/299 RC 2.00 5.00
159 Khiry Robinson AU/299 3.00 8.00
160 Kiko Alonso AU/99 3.00 8.00
161 Latavius Murray AU/299 RC 8.00 20.00
162 Levine Toilolo AU/299 RC 2.50 6.00
163 Luke Joeckel AU/99 RC 2.50 6.00
164 Luke Willson AU/299 5.00 12.00
165 Margus Hunt AU/99 RC 2.50 6.00
166 Marlon Brown AU/99 4.00 10.00
168 Matt Elam AU/99 RC 2.50 6.00
169 Matt McGloin AU/299 RC 6.00 15.00
170 Matt Scott AU/99 RC 2.50 6.00
171 Matt Simms AU/299 RC 2.50 6.00
172 Michael Cox AU/299 RC 2.50 6.00
173 Michael Ford AU/299 RC 3.00 8.00
174 Mike James AU/299 RC 3.00 8.00
175 Mychal Rivera/299 AU 2.00 5.00
176 Nick Kasa AU/299 RC 2.00 5.00
177 Nick Moody AU/299 RC 2.50 6.00
178 Kayvon Webster AU/99 RC 3.00 8.00
179 Phillip Thomas AU/299 RC 2.00 5.00
180 Ray Graham AU/299 RC 2.00 5.00
181 Rex Burkhead AU/299 RC 2.50 6.00
182 Robert Alford AU/299 RC 2.00 5.00
183 Rodney Smith AU/299 RC 2.00 5.00
184 Russell Shepard AU/299 RC 2.00 5.00
185 Ryan Griffin AU/299 RC 2.00 5.00
186 Ryan Griffin AU/299 RC 2.00 5.00
187 Ryan Spadola AU/299 RC 2.50 6.00
188 Sam Montgomery AU/299 RC 2.00 5.00
189 Sharrif Floyd AU/99 RC 2.50 6.00
190 Sio Moore AU/299 RC 2.00 5.00
191 Spencer Ware AU/299 RC 2.00 5.00
192 Tavarres King AU/299 RC 2.00 5.00
193 Theo Riddick AU/299 RC 2.00 5.00
194 Travis Kelce AU/99 RC 20.00 50.00
195 Tyler Bray AU/299 RC 2.00 5.00
196 Tyrann Mathieu AU/299 3.00 8.00
197 Xavier Rhodes AU/99 RC 2.50 6.00
198 Zac Dysert AU/99 RC 5.00 12.00
199 Zac Stacy AU/299 RC 2.00 5.00
200 Zach Sudfeld AU/299 RC 2.00 5.00
201 Aaron Dobson RC 1.00 2.50
202 Andre Ellington RC 1.00 2.50
203 Christine Michael RC 1.00 2.50
204 Cordarrelle Patterson RC 1.00 2.50
205 DeAndre Hopkins RC 2.50 6.00
206 Denard Robinson RC 1.00 2.50
207 Dion Jordan RC 1.00 2.50
208 Eddie Lacy RC 1.00 2.50
209 EJ Manuel RC 1.00 2.50
210 Gavin Escobar RC 1.00 2.50
211 Geno Smith RC 1.00 2.50
212 Giovani Bernard RC 1.00 2.50
213 Johnathan Franklin RC 1.00 2.50
214 Jordan Reed RC 1.50 4.00
215 Joseph Randle RC 1.00 2.50
216 Justin Hunter RC 1.00 2.50
217 Keenan Allen RC 2.00 5.00
218 Kenny Stills RC 1.00 2.50
219 Knile Davis RC 1.00 2.50
220 Landry Jones RC 1.00 2.50
221 Le'Veon Bell RC 3.00 8.00
222 Manti Te'o RC 1.25 3.00
223 Marcus Lattimore RC 1.00 2.50
224 Markus Wheaton RC 1.00 2.50
225 Marquise Goodwin RC 1.00 2.50
226 Matt Barkley RC 1.00 2.50
227 Mike Gillislee RC 1.00 2.50
228 Mike Glennon RC 1.00 2.50
229 Montee Ball RC 1.00 2.50
230 Quinton Patton RC 1.00 2.50
231 Robert Woods RC 1.50 4.00
232 Ryan Nassib RC 1.00 2.50
233 Stedman Bailey RC 1.00 2.50
234 Stepfan Taylor RC 1.00 2.50
235 Tavon Austin RC 1.25 3.00
236 Terrance Williams RC 1.00 2.50
237 Tyler Eifert RC 1.00 2.50
238 Tyler Wilson RC 1.00 2.50
239 Vance McDonald RC 1.25 3.00
240 Zach Ertz RC 2.00 5.00
241 Ace Sanders RC 1.00 2.50
242 Brice Butler RC 1.00 2.50
243 Kenbrell Thompkins RC 1.50 4.00
244 Khiry Robinson RC 1.50 4.00
245 Kiko Alonso RC 1.25 3.00
246 Luke Willson RC 1.50 4.00
247 Marlon Brown RC 1.50 4.00
248 Mychal Rivera RC 1.00 2.50
249 Sheldon Richardson RC 1.00 2.50
250 Tyrann Mathieu RC 1.50 4.00

2013 Panini Spectra Blue

*1-100 VETS/99: 1.5X TO 4X BASIC CARDS
*101-200 ROOK.AU/99: .5X TO 1.2X AU/299
*101-200 ROOK.AU/49: .5X TO 1.2X AU/99
*201-250 ROOKIE/49: .6X TO 1.5X RC/99

2013 Panini Spectra Embossed Green

*EMB. GREEN: 2.5X TO 6X BASIC CARDS

2013 Panini Spectra Embossed Pink

*EMB. PINK: 2.5X TO 6X BASIC CARDS

2013 Panini Spectra Red

*1-100 VETS/25: 2.5X TO 6X BASIC CARDS
*101-200 ROOK.AU/25: .8X TO 2X AU/299
*101-200 ROOK.AU/25: .6X TO 1.5X AU/99
*201-250 ROOKIE/25: .8X TO 2X RC/99

2013 Panini Spectra 50th Anniversary HOF

4 Art Monk 8.00 20.00
6 Barry Sanders 8.00 20.00
8 Bill Parcells 5.00 12.00
10 Bob Griese 5.00 12.00
BL Bob Lilly 4.00 10.00
16 Bruce Smith 4.00 10.00
32 Dan Fouts 4.00 10.00
36 Dave Casper 3.00 8.00
47 Earl Campbell 5.00 12.00
51 Eric Dickerson 4.00 10.00
54 Fran Tarkenton 5.00 12.00
55 Franco Harris 5.00 12.00
56 Frank Gifford 4.00 10.00
57 Fred Biletnikoff 5.00 12.00
59 Gale Sayers 5.00 12.00
65 Jack Ham 4.00 10.00
70 James Lofton 3.00 8.00
85 John Elway 8.00 20.00
92 Kellen Winslow 4.00 10.00
94 Lance Alworth 4.00 10.00
96 Larry Csonka 5.00 12.00
105 Marshall Faulk 4.00 10.00
118 Paul Warfield 4.00 10.00
129 Ronnie Lott 5.00 12.00
132 Shannon Sharpe 4.00 10.00
133 Sonny Jurgensen 4.00 10.00
134 Steve Largent 5.00 12.00
135 Steve Young 6.00 15.00
136 Ted Hendricks 3.00 8.00
143 Warren Moon 5.00 12.00

2013 Panini Spectra 50th Anniversary HOF Signatures

4 Art Monk 30.00 60.00
6 Barry Sanders 100.00 200.00
8 Bill Parcells 30.00 60.00
10 Bob Griese
11 Bob Lilly 25.00 50.00
16 Bruce Smith 30.00 60.00
18 Carl Eller 30.00 60.00
28 Cris Carter 40.00 80.00
30 Curtis Martin 30.00 60.00
32 Dan Fouts 30.00 60.00
33 Dan Hampton 20.00 40.00
34 Dan Marino 125.00 200.00
36 Dave Casper 25.00 50.00
39 Deion Sanders 90.00 150.00
41 Dick Butkus 75.00 125.00
47 Earl Campbell 30.00 60.00
49 Emmitt Smith 125.00 200.00
51 Eric Dickerson 50.00 100.00
53 Forrest Gregg 25.00 50.00
54 Fran Tarkenton 30.00 60.00
55 Franco Harris 30.00 60.00
56 Frank Gifford 30.00 60.00
57 Fred Biletnikoff 30.00 60.00
59 Gale Sayers 40.00 80.00
65 Jack Ham 25.00 50.00
68 Jackie Slater 20.00 40.00
69 Jackie Smith 15.00 40.00
70 James Lofton 60.00 120.00
71 Jan Stenerud 30.00 60.00
72 Jerry Rice 100.00 175.00
74 Jim Kelly 60.00 120.00
82 Joe Montana 125.00 250.00
83 Joe Namath 50.00 100.00
84 John Randle 50.00 100.00
85 John Elway 125.00 250.00
89 John Riggins 30.00 60.00
92 Kellen Winslow 25.00 50.00
94 Lance Alworth 50.00 100.00
96 Larry Csonka 30.00 60.00
RS Roger Staubach 60.00 120.00

100 Len Dawson 25.00 60.00
105 Marshall Faulk 40.00 100.00
108 Michael Irvin 40.00 80.00
115 Ozzie Newsome 60.00 120.00
116 Paul Hornung 40.00 80.00
118 Paul Warfield 25.00 50.00
120 Randy White 25.00 50.00
121 Raymond Berry 20.00 50.00
124 Rod Woodson 50.00 100.00
129 Ronnie Lott 25.00 50.00
132 Shannon Sharpe 40.00 80.00
133 Sonny Jurgensen 25.00 50.00
134 Steve Largent 30.00 60.00
135 Steve Young 50.00 100.00
136 Ted Hendricks 20.00 40.00
137 Terry Bradshaw 75.00 150.00
138 Thurman Thomas 50.00 120.00
141 Tony Dorsett 50.00 100.00
142 Troy Aikman 75.00 150.00
143 Warren Moon 40.00 80.00

2013 Panini Spectra City Limits

*BLUE/49: .5X TO 1.2X BASIC INSERTS
*RED/25: .8X TO 2X BASIC INSERTS
1 A.J. Green 2.50 6.00
2 Aaron Rodgers 4.00 10.00
3 Adrian Peterson 2.50 6.00
4 Alfred Morris 1.50 4.00
5 Andrew Luck 4.00 10.00
6 Andy Dalton 2.00 5.00
7 Antonio Gates 2.00 5.00
8 Arian Foster 2.00 5.00
9 Ben Roethlisberger 2.50 6.00
10 Brandon Marshall 2.00 5.00
11 C.J. Spiller 1.50 4.00
12 Calvin Johnson 2.50 6.00
13 Cam Newton 2.50 6.00
14 Chris Johnson 1.50 4.00
15 Clay Matthews 2.50 6.00
16 Colin Kaepernick 2.00 5.00
17 Darren McFadden 2.00 5.00
18 Dez Bryant 2.50 6.00
19 Doug Martin 2.00 5.00
20 Drew Brees 2.50 6.00
21 Eli Manning 2.00 5.00
22 Frank Gore 2.00 5.00
23 J.J. Watt 2.00 5.00
24 Jamaal Charles 2.00 5.00
25 Jason Witten 2.00 5.00
26 Joe Flacco 2.00 5.00
27 Josh Gordon 1.50 4.00
28 Julio Jones 2.50 6.00
29 Larry Fitzgerald 2.00 5.00
30 LeSean McCoy 2.50 6.00
31 Marshawn Lynch 2.00 5.00
32 Matt Ryan 2.00 5.00
33 Matthew Stafford 2.00 5.00
34 Maurice Jones-Drew 1.50 4.00
35 Percy Harvin 1.50 4.00
36 Peyton Manning 10.00 25.00
37 Philip Rivers 2.50 6.00
38 Ray Rice 1.50 4.00
39 Reggie Wayne 2.00 5.00
40 Rob Gronkowski 2.50 6.00
41 Robert Griffin III 1.50 4.00
42 Russell Wilson 5.00 12.00
43 Ryan Tannehill 2.00 5.00
44 Sam Bradford 1.50 4.00
45 Tom Brady 6.00 15.00
46 Tony Romo 2.00 5.00
47 Troy Polamalu 2.50 6.00
48 Victor Cruz 2.00 5.00
49 Von Miller 2.00 5.00
50 Wes Welker 2.00 5.00
51 Aaron Dobson 1.00 2.50
52 Andre Ellington 1.00 2.50
53 Christine Michael 1.00 2.50
54 Cordarrelle Patterson 1.00 2.50
55 DeAndre Hopkins 2.50 6.00
56 Denard Robinson 1.00 2.50
57 Dion Jordan 1.00 2.50
58 Eddie Lacy 1.00 2.50
59 EJ Manuel 1.00 2.50
60 Gavin Escobar 1.00 2.50
61 Geno Smith 1.00 2.50
62 Giovani Bernard 1.00 2.50
63 Johnathan Franklin 1.00 2.50
64 Jordan Reed 1.50 4.00
65 Joseph Randle 1.00 2.50
66 Justin Hunter 1.00 2.50
67 Keenan Allen 2.00 5.00
68 Kenny Stills 1.00 2.50
69 Knile Davis 1.00 2.50
70 Landry Jones 1.00 2.50
71 Le'Veon Bell 3.00 8.00
72 Manti Te'o 1.25 3.00
73 Marcus Lattimore 1.00 2.50
74 Markus Wheaton 1.00 2.50
75 Marquise Goodwin 1.00 2.50
76 Matt Barkley 1.00 2.50
77 Mike Gillislee 1.00 2.50
78 Mike Glennon 1.00 2.50
79 Montee Ball 1.00 2.50
80 Quinton Patton 1.00 2.50
81 Robert Woods 1.50 4.00
82 Ryan Nassib 1.00 2.50
83 Stedman Bailey 1.00 2.50
84 Stepfan Taylor 1.00 2.50
85 Tavon Austin 2.50 6.00
86 Terrance Williams 1.00 2.50
87 Tyler Eifert 1.00 2.50
88 Tyler Wilson 1.00 2.50
89 Vance McDonald 1.25 3.00
90 Zach Ertz 2.00 5.00
91 Ace Sanders 1.00 2.50
92 Zac Stacy 1.00 2.50
93 Kenbrell Thompkins 1.50 4.00
94 Timothy Wright 1.25 3.00
95 Kiko Alonso 1.25 3.00
96 Luke Willson 1.50 4.00
97 Marlon Brown 1.50 4.00
98 Mychal Rivera 1.00 2.50
99 Sheldon Richardson 1.00 2.50
100 Tyrann Mathieu 1.50 4.00

2013 Panini Spectra Combo Materials

*BLUE/25-99: .5X TO 1.2X BASIC JSY/49-299
*RED/25: .8X TO 2X BASIC JSY/299
*RED/25: .6X TO 1.5X BASIC JSY/99
*RED/15: .5X TO 1.2X BASIC JSY/49
1 M.Ryan/J.Jones/99 5.00 12.00
2 J.Flacco/R.Rice/299 3.00 8.00
3 C.Spiller/F.Jackson/299 3.00 8.00
5 A.Dalton/A.Green/99 5.00 12.00
6 J.Cameron/J.Gordon/299 6.00 15.00
7 P.Manning/W.Welker/99 10.00 25.00
8 D.Thomas/E.Decker/99 4.00 10.00
9 M.Stafford/C.Johnson/99 6.00 15.00
10 A.Smith/J.Charles/199 3.00 8.00
11 R.Tannehill/M.Wallace/299 3.00 8.00
12 D.Brees/J.Graham/49 10.00 25.00
13 A.Gates/P.Rivers/199 4.00 10.00
14 C.Johnson/J.Locker/99 4.00 10.00
15 A.Morris/R.Griffin/99 3.00 8.00

2013 Panini Spectra Materials

*BLUE/99: .5X TO 1.2X BASIC JSY/199-299
*BLUE/99: .4X TO 1X BASIC JSY/99
*BLUE/49: .5X TO 1.2X BASIC JSY/199
*BLUE/49: .4X TO 1X BASIC JSY/99
*BLUE/20-25: .5X TO 1.2X BASIC JSY/99
1 A.J. Green/99 5.00 12.00
3 Adrian Peterson/49 5.00 12.00
4 Alex Smith/299 3.00 8.00
5 Alfred Morris/99 3.00 8.00
6 Andre Johnson/49 3.00 8.00
7 Andrew Luck/49 8.00 20.00
8 Andy Dalton/199 3.00 8.00
9 Antonio Brown/299 4.00 10.00
10 Antonio Gates/49 4.00 10.00
11 BenJarvus Green-Ellis/299 3.00 8.00
12 Bernard Pierce/299 2.50 6.00
13 Brandon Weeden/299 2.50 6.00
14 Brian Hartline/99 3.00 8.00
15 C.J. Spiller/99 3.00 8.00
16 Calvin Johnson/49 5.00 12.00
17 Cam Newton/99 5.00 12.00
18 Cameron Wake/299 2.50 6.00
19 Champ Bailey/299 3.00 8.00
20 Chris Johnson/49 3.00 8.00
21 Colin Kaepernick/299 3.00 8.00
22 Daniel Thomas/299 2.50 6.00
23 Darren McFadden/199 3.00 8.00
24 DeMarco Murray/49 4.00 10.00
25 Demaryius Thomas/49 4.00 10.00
26 Derrick Johnson/299 2.50 6.00
27 Dontari Poe/299 2.50 6.00
28 Doug Martin/299 3.00 8.00
29 D'Qwell Jackson/299 2.50 6.00
30 Drew Brees/99 5.00 12.00
31 Dwayne Bowe/199 3.00 8.00
32 Eric Decker/199 2.50 6.00
33 Frank Gore/99 4.00 10.00
34 Fred Jackson/199 3.00 8.00
35 Geno Atkins/299 2.50 6.00
36 Jake Locker/299 3.00 8.00
37 Jamaal Charles/199 3.00 8.00
38 Jermaine Gresham/299 3.00 8.00
39 Jimmy Graham/99 5.00 12.00
40 Joe Flacco/99 4.00 10.00
41 Jordan Cameron/199 2.50 6.00
42 Josh Gordon/199 2.50 6.00
43 Julio Jones/199 4.00 10.00
44 Justin Houston/299 2.50 6.00
45 Kendall Wright/299 2.50 6.00
46 Kenny Britt/299 2.50 6.00
47 Knowshon Moreno/99 3.00 8.00
48 Lamar Miller/299 2.50 6.00
49 Larry Fitzgerald/199 3.00 8.00
50 Leonard Hankerson/299 2.50 6.00
51 LeSean McCoy/49 5.00 12.00
52 London Fletcher/199 3.00 8.00
53 Malcom Floyd/299 2.50 6.00
54 Marques Colston/199 2.50 6.00
55 Matt Forte/99 3.00 8.00
56 Matt Ryan/199 3.00 8.00
57 Matthew Stafford/99 4.00 10.00
58 Maurice Jones-Drew/199 2.50 6.00
59 Mike Wallace/199 2.50 6.00
60 Nate Washington/299 2.50 6.00
61 Patrick Willis/199 3.00 8.00
62 Peyton Manning/199 8.00 20.00
63 Philip Rivers/299 4.00 10.00
64 Pierre Garcon/99 4.00 10.00
65 Ray Rice/199 2.50 6.00
66 Reshad Jones/299 2.50 6.00
67 Robert Griffin III/99 3.00 8.00
68 Roddy White/99 3.00 8.00
70 Ryan Kerrigan/299 2.50 6.00
71 Ryan Mathews/99 4.00 10.00
72 Ryan Tannehill/199 3.00 8.00
73 Sam Bradford/299 2.50 6.00
74 Santana Moss/199 3.00 8.00
75 Scott Chandler/299 2.50 6.00
76 Steve Johnson/299 3.00 8.00
78 Tamba Hali/199 2.50 6.00
79 Terrell Suggs/199 2.50 6.00
80 Tom Brady/99 12.00 30.00
81 Tony Romo/299 3.00 8.00
82 Torrey Smith/99 3.00 8.00
84 Vontaze Burfict/299 2.50 6.00
85 Wes Welker/49 4.00 10.00

2013 Panini Spectra Rookie Combo Materials

*BLUE/49: .4X TO 1X BASIC COMBO/99
*RED/25: .5X TO 1.2X BASIC COMBO/99
1 G.Smith/E.Manuel/99 2.00 5.00
3 M.Ball/L.Bell/99 6.00 15.00
4 D.Hopkins/C.Patterson/99 5.00 12.00
5 T.Austin/A.Dobson/25 3.00 8.00
6 A.Ellington/S.Taylor/99 2.00 5.00
7 K.Alonso/E.Manuel/99 2.50 6.00
8 M.Goodwin/R.Woods/99 3.00 8.00
9 G.Bernard/T.Eifert/99 2.00 5.00
10 G.Escobar/T.Williams/99 2.00 5.00
12 T.Kelce/K.Davis/99 5.00 12.00
13 M.Barkley/Z.Ertz/49 4.00 10.00
14 L.Bell/M.Wheaton/99 6.00 15.00
15 K.Allen/M.Te'o/99 4.00 10.00
16 Q.Patton/V.McDonald/99 2.50 6.00
17 S.Bailey/T.Austin/99 2.50 6.00

2013 Panini Spectra Rookie Materials

*BLUE/39-49: .5X TO 1.2X BASIC JSY/99
*BLUE/15-25: .6X TO 1.5X BASIC JSY/99
*RED/25: .6X TO 1.5X BASIC JSY/99
101 Aaron Mellette 2.00 5.00
107 Barkevious Mingo 2.00 5.00
110 Bjoern Werner 2.00 5.00
117 Chris Gragg 2.00 5.00
129 David Amerson 2.00 5.00
133 Dion Sims 2.00 5.00
135 D.J. Fluker 2.00 5.00
138 Eric Fisher 2.00 5.00
156 Kenny Vaccaro 2.00 5.00
160 Kiko Alonso 2.50 6.00
163 Luke Joeckel 2.00 5.00
165 Margus Hunt 2.00 5.00
168 Matt Elam 2.00 5.00
189 Sharrif Floyd 2.00 5.00
194 Travis Kelce 5.00 12.00
197 Xavier Rhodes 5.00 12.00
201 Aaron Dobson 2.00 5.00
202 Andre Ellington 2.00 5.00
203 Christine Michael 2.00 5.00
204 Cordarrelle Patterson 2.00 5.00
205 DeAndre Hopkins 5.00 12.00
206 Denard Robinson 2.00 5.00
207 Dion Jordan 2.00 5.00
208 Eddie Lacy 2.00 5.00
209 EJ Manuel 6.00 15.00
210 Gavin Escobar 2.00 5.00
211 Geno Smith 2.00 5.00
212 Giovani Bernard 2.00 5.00
213 Johnathan Franklin 2.00 5.00
214 Jordan Reed 3.00 8.00
215 Joseph Randle 2.00 5.00
216 Justin Hunter 2.00 5.00
217 Keenan Allen 5.00 12.00
218 Kenny Stills 2.00 5.00
219 Knile Davis 2.00 5.00
220 Landry Jones 2.00 5.00
221 Le'Veon Bell 5.00 12.00
222 Manti Te'o 2.50 6.00
223 Marcus Lattimore 2.00 5.00
224 Markus Wheaton 2.00 5.00
225 Marquise Goodwin 2.00 5.00
226 Matt Barkley 2.00 5.00
227 Mike Gillislee 2.00 5.00
228 Mike Glennon 2.00 5.00
229 Montee Ball 2.00 5.00
230 Quinton Patton 2.00 5.00
231 Robert Woods 3.00 8.00
232 Ryan Nassib 2.00 5.00
233 Stedman Bailey 2.00 5.00
234 Stepfan Taylor 2.00 5.00
235 Tavon Austin 2.50 6.00
236 Terrance Williams 2.00 5.00
237 Tyler Eifert 2.00 5.00
238 Tyler Wilson 2.00 5.00
239 Vance McDonald 2.50 6.00
240 Zach Ertz 4.00 10.00
241 Jonathan Cooper 2.00 5.00
242 Lane Johnson 2.50 6.00
243 Nico Johnson 2.50 6.00
244 Bacarri Rambo 2.50 6.00

2013 Panini Spectra Rookie Premiere Date

*BLUE/49: .5X TO 1.2X BASIC INSERTS
*RED/25: .8X TO 2X BASIC INSERTS
1 Cordarrelle Patterson 1.00 2.50
2 DeAndre Hopkins 2.50 6.00
3 Eddie Lacy 1.00 2.50
4 EJ Manuel 1.00 2.50
5 Geno Smith 1.00 2.50
6 Giovani Bernard 1.00 2.50
7 Le'Veon Bell 3.00 8.00
8 Mike Glennon 1.00 2.50
9 Montee Ball 1.00 2.50
10 Tavon Austin 1.25 3.00

2013 Panini Spectra Rookie Revolution

*BLUE/49: .5X TO 1.2X BASIC INSERTS
*RED/25: .8X TO 2X BASIC INSERTS
1 Aaron Dobson 1.00 2.50
2 Andre Ellington 1.00 2.50
3 Christine Michael 1.00 2.50
4 Cordarrelle Patterson 1.00 2.50
5 DeAndre Hopkins 2.50 6.00
6 Denard Robinson 1.00 2.50
7 Dion Jordan 1.00 2.50
8 Eddie Lacy 1.00 2.50
9 EJ Manuel 1.00 2.50
10 Gavin Escobar 1.00 2.50
11 Geno Smith 1.00 2.50
12 Giovani Bernard 1.00 2.50
13 Johnathan Franklin 1.00 2.50
14 Jordan Reed 1.50 4.00
15 Joseph Randle 1.00 2.50
16 Justin Hunter 1.00 2.50
17 Keenan Allen 2.00 5.00
18 Kenny Stills 1.00 2.50
19 Knile Davis 1.00 2.50
20 Landry Jones 1.00 2.50
21 Le'Veon Bell 3.00 8.00
22 Manti Te'o 1.25 3.00
23 Marcus Lattimore 1.00 2.50
24 Markus Wheaton 1.00 2.50
25 Marquise Goodwin 1.00 2.50
26 Matt Barkley 1.00 2.50
27 Mike Gillislee 1.00 2.50
28 Mike Glennon 1.00 2.50
29 Montee Ball 1.00 2.50
30 Quinton Patton 1.00 2.50
31 Robert Woods 1.50 4.00
32 Ryan Nassib 1.00 2.50
33 Stedman Bailey 1.00 2.50
34 Stepfan Taylor 1.00 2.50
35 Tavon Austin 1.25 3.00
36 Terrance Williams 1.00 2.50
37 Tyler Eifert 1.00 2.50
38 Tyler Wilson 1.00 2.50
39 Vance McDonald 1.25 3.00
40 Zach Ertz 2.00 5.00

2013 Panini Spectra Rookie Signature Materials

*BLUE/49: .4X TO 1X BASIC AU/99
*BLUE/25: .6X TO 1.5X BASIC AU/99
*RED/15-25: .6X TO 1.5X BASIC AU/99
*RED/25: .4X TO 1X BASIC AU/20
EXCH EXPIRATION: 9/5/2015
117 Chris Gragg/99 3.00 8.00
119 Chris Thompson/99 3.00 8.00
129 David Amerson/99 3.00 8.00
130 Dee Milliner/20 15.00 40.00
133 Dion Sims/99 3.00 8.00
139 Eric Reid/99 8.00 20.00
140 Ezekiel Ansah/99 3.00 8.00
160 Kiko Alonso/99 4.00 10.00
165 Margus Hunt/99 3.00 8.00
168 Matt Elam/99 3.00 8.00
178 Kayvon Webster/99 4.00 10.00
189 Sharrif Floyd/99 3.00 8.00
194 Travis Kelce/99 30.00 60.00
197 Xavier Rhodes/99 6.00 15.00
201 Aaron Dobson/99 3.00 8.00
202 Andre Ellington/99 8.00 20.00
203 Christine Michael/99 6.00 15.00
204 Cordarrelle Patterson/99 3.00 8.00
205 DeAndre Hopkins/99 8.00 20.00
206 Denard Robinson/99 3.00 8.00
207 Dion Jordan/99 3.00 8.00
208 Eddie Lacy/99 3.00 8.00
209 EJ Manuel/99 12.00 30.00
210 Gavin Escobar/99 6.00 15.00
211 Geno Smith/99 3.00 8.00
212 Giovani Bernard/99 3.00 8.00
213 Johnathan Franklin/99 3.00 8.00
214 Jordan Reed/99 EXCH 5.00 12.00
215 Joseph Randle/99 3.00 8.00
216 Justin Hunter/99 3.00 8.00
217 Keenan Allen/99 12.00 30.00
218 Kenny Stills/99 3.00 8.00
219 Knile Davis/99 3.00 8.00
220 Landry Jones/99 3.00 8.00
221 Le'Veon Bell/99 12.00 30.00
222 Manti Te'o/99 4.00 10.00
223 Marcus Lattimore/99 10.00 25.00
224 Markus Wheaton/99 3.00 8.00
225 Marquise Goodwin/99 3.00 8.00
226 Matt Barkley/99 3.00 8.00
227 Mike Gillislee/99 3.00 8.00
228 Mike Glennon/99 3.00 8.00
229 Montee Ball/99 3.00 8.00
230 Quinton Patton/99 EXCH 3.00 8.00
231 Robert Woods/99 5.00 12.00
232 Ryan Nassib/99 6.00 15.00
233 Stedman Bailey/99 3.00 8.00
234 Stepfan Taylor/99 3.00 8.00
235 Tavon Austin/99 4.00 10.00
236 Terrance Williams/99 3.00 8.00
237 Tyler Eifert/99 6.00 15.00
238 Tyler Wilson/99 3.00 8.00
239 Vance McDonald/99 4.00 10.00
240 Zach Ertz/99 6.00 15.00

2013 Panini Spectra Rookie Signatures

*BLUE/49: .5X TO 1.2X BASIC AU/99
*RED/25: .6X TO 1.5X BASIC AU/99
201 Aaron Dobson 3.00 8.00
202 Andre Ellington 3.00 8.00
203 Christine Michael 3.00 8.00
204 Cordarrelle Patterson 3.00 8.00
205 DeAndre Hopkins 8.00 20.00
206 Denard Robinson 3.00 8.00
207 Dion Jordan 3.00 8.00
208 Eddie Lacy 3.00 8.00
209 EJ Manuel 3.00 8.00
210 Gavin Escobar 3.00 8.00
211 Geno Smith 3.00 8.00
212 Giovani Bernard 3.00 8.00
213 Johnathan Franklin 3.00 8.00
214 Jordan Reed 5.00 12.00
215 Joseph Randle 3.00 8.00
216 Justin Hunter 3.00 8.00
217 Keenan Allen 6.00 15.00
218 Kenny Stills 3.00 8.00
219 Knile Davis 3.00 8.00
220 Landry Jones 3.00 8.00
221 Le'Veon Bell 10.00 25.00
222 Manti Te'o 4.00 10.00
223 Marcus Lattimore 3.00 8.00
224 Markus Wheaton 3.00 8.00
225 Marquise Goodwin 3.00 8.00
226 Matt Barkley 3.00 8.00
227 Mike Gillislee 3.00 8.00
228 Mike Glennon 3.00 8.00
229 Montee Ball 3.00 8.00
230 Quinton Patton 3.00 8.00
231 Robert Woods 5.00 12.00
232 Ryan Nassib 3.00 8.00
233 Stedman Bailey 3.00 8.00
234 Stepfan Taylor 3.00 8.00
235 Tavon Austin 4.00 10.00
236 Terrance Williams 3.00 8.00
237 Tyler Eifert 3.00 8.00
238 Tyler Wilson 3.00 8.00
239 Vance McDonald 4.00 10.00
240 Zach Ertz 6.00 15.00

2013 Panini Spectra Signature Materials

EXCH EXPIRATION: 9/5/2015
1 Adrian Peterson/25 EXCH 75.00 135.00
2 Peyton Manning/49 100.00 175.00
3 Colin Kaepernick/49 EXCH 20.00 50.00
4 Andrew Luck/25 EXCH 90.00 150.00
5 Russell Wilson/25
6 Cam Newton/49 EXCH 30.00 60.00
7 Doug Martin/49 20.00 50.00
8 Alfred Morris/49 EXCH 15.00 40.00
10 Drew Brees/49 EXCH

2013 Panini Spectra Signatures

EXCH EXPIRATION: 9/5/2015
*BLUE/25: .5X TO 1.2X BASIC AU/49
*BLUE/15: .4X TO 1X BASIC AU/25
1 Aaron Rodgers EXCH 125.00 200.00
3 A.J. Green EXCH 15.00 40.00
4 Matt Ryan
7 Ryan Tannehill EXCH 12.00 30.00
8 C.J. Spiller EXCH 10.00 25.00
9 Frank Gore EXCH 15.00 40.00
10 Jason Witten 12.00 30.00

2014 Panini Spectra

1 James Jones 2.50 6.00
2 Giovani Bernard 2.50 6.00
3 Jerome Bettis 5.00 12.00
4 Montee Ball 2.50 6.00
5 Richard Sherman 4.00 10.00
6 J.J. Watt 4.00 10.00
7 Warren Moon 5.00 12.00
8 Carson Palmer 3.00 8.00
9 Mike Wallace 2.50 6.00
10 Robert Woods 3.00 8.00
11 Daryle Lamonica 3.00 8.00
12 Jermaine Gresham 2.50 6.00
13 Philip Rivers 4.00 10.00
14 John Elway 10.00 25.00
15 Steve Largent 5.00 12.00
16 DeAndre Hopkins 3.00 8.00
17 Robert Griffin III 2.50 6.00
18 Larry Fitzgerald 3.00 8.00
19 Knowshon Moreno 2.50 6.00
20 C.J. Spiller 2.50 6.00
21 Geno Smith 2.50 6.00
22 Ken Anderson 4.00 10.00
23 Keenan Allen 3.00 8.00
24 Matthew Stafford 3.00 8.00
25 Sam Bradford 2.50 6.00
26 Andrew Luck 5.00 12.00
27 Pierre Garcon 3.00 8.00
28 Michael Floyd 2.50 6.00
29 Dan Marino 12.00 30.00
30 Fred Jackson 3.00 8.00
31 Eric Decker 2.50 6.00
32 Brian Hoyer 2.50 6.00
33 Ryan Mathews 3.00 8.00
34 Calvin Johnson 4.00 10.00
35 Tavon Austin 2.50 6.00
36 Reggie Wayne 3.00 8.00
37 Alfred Morris 2.50 6.00
38 Andre Ellington 2.50 6.00
39 Matt Cassel 2.50 6.00
40 Jim Kelly 5.00 12.00
41 Chris Ivory 3.00 8.00
42 Ben Tate 2.50 6.00
43 Antonio Gates 2.50 6.00
44 Reggie Bush 2.50 6.00
45 Chris Givens 2.50 6.00
46 Trent Richardson 2.50 6.00
47 DeSean Jackson 3.00 8.00
48 Larry Wilson 3.00 8.00
49 Cordarrelle Patterson 2.50 6.00
50 Cam Newton 4.00 10.00
51 Jeremy Kerley 2.50 6.00
52 Jordan Cameron 2.50 6.00
53 LaDainian Tomlinson 4.00 10.00
54 Golden Tate 3.00 8.00
55 Zac Stacy 2.50 6.00
56 Raymond Berry 4.00 10.00
57 Darrell Green 5.00 12.00
58 Matt Ryan 3.00 8.00
59 Greg Jennings 2.50 6.00
60 Jerricho Cotchery 2.50 6.00
61 Nick Foles 3.00 8.00
62 Ozzie Newsome 3.00 8.00
63 Colin Kaepernick 3.00 8.00
64 Barry Sanders 8.00 20.00
65 Kurt Warner 4.00 10.00
66 Chad Henne 2.50 6.00
67 Drew Brees 4.00 10.00
68 Julio Jones 4.00 10.00
69 Fran Tarkenton 5.00 12.00
70 DeAngelo Williams 2.50 6.00
71 Jeremy Maclin 2.50 6.00
72 Tony Romo 3.00 8.00
73 Anquan Boldin 2.50 6.00
74 Aaron Rodgers 8.00 20.00
75 Josh McCown 2.50 6.00
76 Cecil Shorts III 2.50 6.00
77 Marques Colston 2.50 6.00
78 Roddy White 2.50 6.00
79 Cris Carter 5.00 12.00
80 Greg Olsen 3.00 8.00
81 Riley Cooper 3.00 8.00
82 Dez Bryant 4.00 10.00
83 Michael Crabtree 2.50 6.00
84 Jordy Nelson 3.00 8.00
85 Vincent Jackson 2.50 6.00
86 Toby Gerhart 2.50 6.00
87 Pierre Thomas 2.50 6.00
88 Steven Jackson 2.50 6.00
89 Tom Brady 10.00 25.00
90 Jay Cutler 2.50 6.00
91 LeSean McCoy 4.00 10.00
92 Troy Aikman 6.00 15.00
93 Vernon Davis 2.50 6.00
94 Randall Cobb 3.00 8.00
95 Doug Martin 3.00 8.00
96 Marcedes Lewis 2.50 6.00
97 Jimmy Graham 4.00 10.00
98 Joe Flacco 3.00 8.00
99 Julian Edelman 4.00 10.00
100 Brandon Marshall 2.50 6.00
101 Darren Sproles 3.00 8.00
102 DeMarco Murray 3.00 8.00
103 Frank Gore 3.00 8.00
104 Eddie Lacy 2.50 6.00
105 Warren Sapp 4.00 10.00
106 Alex Smith 3.00 8.00
107 Mark Ingram 3.00 8.00
108 Torrey Smith 2.50 6.00
109 Rob Gronkowski 4.00 10.00
110 Gale Sayers 5.00 12.00
111 Ben Roethlisberger 4.00 10.00
112 Jason Witten 3.00 8.00
113 Joe Montana 12.00 30.00
114 Brett Favre 10.00 25.00
115 Jake Locker 3.00 8.00
116 Dwayne Bowe 3.00 8.00
117 Eli Manning 3.00 8.00
118 Bernard Pierce 2.50 6.00
119 Darrelle Revis 2.50 6.00
120 Matt Forte 2.50 6.00
121 Antonio Brown 4.00 10.00
122 Peyton Manning 10.00 25.00
123 Russell Wilson 6.00 15.00
124 Andre Johnson 3.00 8.00
125 Dexter McCluster 3.00 8.00
126 Jamaal Charles 3.00 8.00
127 Victor Cruz 3.00 8.00
128 Trent Dilfer 3.00 8.00
129 Curtis Martin 4.00 10.00
130 Martellus Bennett 2.50 6.00
131 Le'Veon Bell 3.00 8.00
132 Demaryius Thomas 3.00 8.00
133 Percy Harvin 2.50 6.00
134 Arian Foster 3.00 8.00
135 Kendall Wright 2.50 6.00
136 Len Dawson 5.00 12.00
137 Rashad Jennings 2.50 6.00
138 Steve Smith 3.00 8.00
139 Maurice Jones-Drew 2.50 6.00
140 Andy Dalton 3.00 8.00
141 Troy Polamalu 4.00 10.00
142 Wes Welker 3.00 8.00
143 Marshawn Lynch 3.00 8.00
144 Ryan Fitzpatrick 2.50 6.00
145 Shonn Greene 2.50 6.00
146 Ryan Tannehill 3.00 8.00
147 Frank Gifford 4.00 10.00
148 EJ Manuel 2.50 6.00
149 Darren McFadden 2.50 6.00
150 A.J. Green 4.00 10.00
151 John Brown RC 1.50 4.00
152 Dri Archer RC 1.00 2.50
153 Lorenzo Taliaferro RC 1.00 2.50
154 Jeremy Hill RC 1.25 3.00
155 Kelvin Benjamin RC 1.50 4.00
156 A.J. McCarron RC 1.00 2.50
157 Blake Bortles RC 1.25 3.00
158 Mike Evans RC 2.50 6.00
159 Davante Adams RC 1.50 4.00
160 Teddy Bridgewater RC 1.50 4.00
161 Allen Hurns RC 1.25 3.00
162 Eric Ebron RC 1.25 3.00
163 Alfred Blue RC 1.00 2.50
164 Jimmy Garoppolo RC 8.00 20.00
165 Allen Robinson RC 1.50 4.00
166 Khalil Mack RC 4.00 10.00
167 Brandin Cooks RC 1.50 4.00
168 Odell Beckham Jr. RC 2.50 6.00
169 De'Anthony Thomas RC 1.00 2.50
170 Terrance West RC 1.00 2.50
171 Jadeveon Clowney RC 1.25 3.00
172 Isaiah Crowell RC 1.25 3.00
173 Garrett Gilbert RC 1.00 2.50
174 Johnny Manziel RC 1.50 4.00
175 Andre Williams RC 1.00 2.50
176 Logan Thomas RC 1.00 2.50
177 Carlos Hyde RC 1.25 3.00
178 Paul Richardson RC 1.25 3.00
179 Derek Carr RC 6.00 15.00
180 Tom Savage RC 1.00 2.50
181 Calvin Pryor RC 1.00 2.50
182 Jake Matthews RC 1.00 2.50
183 Zach Mettenberger RC 1.00 2.50
184 Jordan Matthews RC 1.50 4.00
185 Austin Seferian-Jenkins RC 1.00 2.50
186 Marqise Lee RC 1.25 3.00
187 Charles Sims RC 1.00 2.50
188 Sammy Watkins RC 1.50 4.00
189 Devonta Freeman RC 1.50 4.00
190 Tre Mason RC 1.00 2.50
191 Devin Street RC 1.00 2.50
192 Jarvis Landry RC 2.00 5.00
193 Aaron Murray RC 1.00 2.50
194 Ka'Deem Carey RC 1.00 2.50
195 Bishop Sankey RC 1.00 2.50
196 Branden Oliver RC 1.50 4.00
197 Cody Latimer RC 1.25 3.00
198 Silas Redd RC 1.25 3.00
199 Donte Moncrief RC 1.00 2.50
200 Taylor Gabriel RC 1.25 3.00
201 Aaron Murray JSY AU 12.00 30.00
202 Asa Watson JSY AU 4.00 10.00
204 Charles Sims JSY AU 4.00 10.00
205 Devin Street JSY AU 4.00 10.00
206 Logan Thomas JSY AU 4.00 10.00
207 Jeremy Hill JSY AU 5.00 12.00
208 Paul Richardson JSY AU 5.00 12.00
209 Jace Amaro JSY AU 4.00 10.00
211 Davante Adams JSY AU 6.00 15.00
212 Allen Robinson JSY AU 6.00 15.00
213 Dri Archer JSY AU 4.00 10.00
214 Beckham Jr. JSY AU EXCH 50.00 120.00
215 Donte Moncrief JSY AU 4.00 10.00
216 Andre Williams JSY AU 4.00 10.00
217 A.J. McCarron JSY AU 4.00 10.00
218 Jimmy Garoppolo JSY AU 40.00 80.00
219 Jarvis Landry JSY AU 8.00 20.00
220 Khalil Mack JSY AU 15.00 40.00
221 Seferian-Jenkins JSY AU 4.00 10.00
222 Jordan Matthews JSY AU 6.00 15.00
223 De'Anthony Thomas JSY AU 4.00 10.00
224 Eric Ebron JSY AU 5.00 12.00
225 Tre Mason JSY AU 4.00 10.00
226 Bishop Sankey JSY AU 4.00 10.00
227 Cody Latimer JSY AU 5.00 12.00
228 Tom Savage JSY AU 4.00 10.00
229 Marqise Lee JSY AU 5.00 12.00
230 Mike Evans JSY AU 15.00 40.00
231 Sammy Watkins JSY AU 6.00 15.00
232 Ka'Deem Carey JSY AU 4.00 10.00
233 Brandin Cooks JSY AU 6.00 15.00
234 T.Bidgewater JSY AU 6.00 15.00
235 J.Clowney JSY AU 5.00 12.00
236 Kelvin Benjamin JSY AU 6.00 15.00
237 Terrance West JSY AU 4.00 10.00
239 Blake Bortles JSY AU 5.00 12.00
240 Johnny Manziel JSY AU 12.00 30.00
241 A.Barr AU RC/J.McKinnon AU RC 4.00 10.00
242 A.Hurns/.Brown AU RC 5.00 12.00
243 D.Street AU/Z.Martin AU RC 6.00 15.00
244 A.Dixon AU RC/Clinton-Dix AU RC 3.00 8.00
246 I.Crowell AU RC/J.Wilder Jr. AU RC 4.00 10.00
247 D.Dennard AU RC/J.Wright AU RC 4.00 10.00
248 R.Shazier AU RC/K.VanNoy AU RC 5.00 12.00
250 X.Su'A-Filo AU RC/C.Fdrwcz AU RC 4.00 10.00
251 Janis/R.Rodgers AU RC 5.00 12.00
252 K.Wenning AU RC/G.Gilbert AU RC 4.00 10.00
253 R.Hageman AU RC/J.Matthews AU RC 3.00 8.00
254 D.Fales AU RC/R.Ross AU RC 6.00 15.00
255 C.Kouandjio AU RC/P.Brown AU RC 4.00 10.00
256 J.Verrett AU RC/P.Desir AU RC 3.00 8.00
258 A.Donald AU RC/G.Robinson AU RC 6.00 15.00
259 M.Campanaro AU RC/T.Reese AU RC 3.00 8.00
260 C.Parkey AU RC/J.Huff AU RC 4.00 10.00
263 Taylor Lewan AU RC 3.00 8.00
264 Henry Josey AU RC 3.00 8.00
265 Jared Abbrederis AU RC 8.00 20.00
266 Kevin Norwood AU RC 3.00 8.00
267 Louis Nix III AU RC 3.00 8.00
268 Alfred Blue AU 3.00 8.00
269 Orleans Darkwa AU RC 5.00 12.00
270 Scott Crichton AU RC 3.00 8.00
271 Branden Oliver AU 5.00 12.00
272 David Yankey AU RC 3.00 8.00
273 Bruce Ellington AU RC 3.00 8.00
274 Isaiah Burse AU RC 3.00 8.00
276 Kony Ealy AU RC 4.00 10.00
277 Marcus Roberson AU RC 4.00 10.00
278 Anthony Hitchens AU RC 3.00 8.00
280 Brandon Coleman AU RC 3.00 8.00
283 Travis Swanson AU RC 3.00 8.00
284 Jace Amaro AU RC 3.00 8.00
285 Chandler Catanzaro AU RC 4.00 10.00
287 Marcus Smith AU RC 3.00 8.00
288 Antonio Andrews AU RC 3.00 8.00
289 Quincy Enunwa AU RC 5.00 12.00
290 Shayne Skov AU RC 3.00 8.00
291 Calvin Pryor AU 3.00 8.00
292 Deone Bucannon AU RC 3.00 8.00
293 Trent Murphy AU RC 3.00 8.00
295 Christian Kirksey AU RC 3.00 8.00
296 Kyle Van Noy AU RC 4.00 10.00
207 Marion Grice AU RC 3.00 8.00
298 Arthur Lynch AU RC 3.00 8.00
299 Rajion Neal AU RC 3.00 8.00
300 Chris Borland AU RC 3.00 8.00
301 Silas Redd AU 8.00 20.00
302 Dominique Easley AU RC 3.00 8.00
303 Trevor Reilly AU RC 3.00 8.00
304 James White AU RC 6.00 15.00
305 Darrin Reaves AU RC 4.00 10.00
306 Lache Seastrunk AU RC 3.00 8.00
307 Martavis Bryant AU RC 4.00 10.00
308 Asa Watson AU RC 3.00 8.00
310 Crockett Gillmore AU RC 4.00 10.00
312 E.J. Gaines AU RC 3.00 8.00
313 Troy Niklas AU RC 3.00 8.00
314 James Wright AU RC 4.00 10.00
315 Dustin Vaughan AU RC 3.00 8.00
316 Lamarcus Joyner AU RC 4.00 10.00
317 Matt Hazel AU RC 3.00 8.00
318 Glenn Winston AU RC 4.00 10.00
319 Jay Prosch AU RC 5.00 12.00
320 Chris Smith AU RC 3.00 8.00
321 TJ Jones AU RC 5.00 12.00
322 Ed Reynolds AU RC 3.00 8.00
323 Yawin Smallwood AU RC 3.00 8.00
324 Jordan Lynch AU RC 4.00 10.00
325 Juwan Thompson AU RC 5.00 12.00
326 L'Damian Washington AU RC 4.00 10.00
327 Mike Davis AU RC 3.00 8.00
328 Terrance Mitchell AU RC 5.00 12.00
329 Robert Herron AU RC 3.00 8.00
330 Cyril Richardson AU RC 3.00 8.00
331 Taylor Gabriel AU 4.00 10.00
332 Walt Aikens AU RC 4.00 10.00
333 Zach Mettenberger AU 3.00 8.00
334 Ja'Wuan James AU RC 3.00 8.00
335 Walter Powell AU RC 3.00 8.00

2014 Panini Spectra Prizms Blue

*1-150 VETS/49: .5X TO 1.2X BASIC CARDS/75
*151-200 ROOKIES/49: 1X TO 2.5X BASIC RC/149
*201-240 ROOK.JSY AU/49: .5X TO 1.2X BASIC RC/149
*241-335 ROOK.AU/49: .5X TO 1.2X BASIC RC/149
218 Jimmy Garoppolo JSY AU 75.00 150.00

2014 Panini Spectra Prizms Blue Die Cut

*1-150 VETS/25: .6X TO 1.5X BASIC CARDS/75
*151-200 ROOKIES/25: 1.2X TO 3X BASIC RC/149

2014 Panini Spectra Prizms Gold

*1-150 VETS/25: .6X TO 1.5X BASIC CARDS/75
*151-200 ROOKIES/25: 1.2X TO 3X BASIC RC/149
*201-240 ROOK.JSY AU/25: .6X TO 1.5X BASIC RC/149
*241-335 ROOK.AU/25: .6X TO 1.5X BASIC RC/149
214 Odell Beckham Jr. JSY AU EXCH 75.00 150.00
218 Jimmy Garoppolo JSY AU 300.00 500.00

2014 Panini Spectra Aspiring Signature Materials

2 Davante Adams/49 8.00 20.00
3 Dri Archer/49 5.00 12.00
4 Donte Moncrief/49 5.00 12.00
5 Andre Williams/49 5.00 12.00
6 A.J. McCarron/25 6.00 15.00
7 Jordan Matthews/49 8.00 20.00
8 Tre Mason/49 5.00 12.00
9 Bishop Sankey/49 5.00 12.00
10 Marqise Lee/25 8.00 20.00
11 Mike Evans/25 25.00 60.00
12 Sammy Watkins/25 10.00 25.00
13 Brandin Cooks/49 8.00 20.00
14 Teddy Bridgewater/25 10.00 25.00
15 Jadeveon Clowney/25 8.00 20.00
16 Kelvin Benjamin/30 10.00 25.00
17 Terrance West/49 5.00 12.00
18 Derek Carr/25 40.00 100.00
19 Blake Bortles/25 8.00 20.00
20 Johnny Manziel/25

2014 Panini Spectra Building Blocks Prizms Blue

*GOLD/25: .5X TO 1.2X BASIC INSERTS/49
1 Sammy Watkins 2.50 6.00
2 Andre Williams 1.50 4.00
3 Eric Ebron 2.00 5.00
4 Giovani Bernard 1.50 4.00
5 Johnny Manziel 2.50 6.00
6 Geno Smith 1.50 4.00
7 Derek Carr 10.00 25.00
8 Jordan Matthews 2.50 6.00
9 Jadeveon Clowney 2.00 5.00
10 Terrance West 1.50 4.00
11 Khalil Mack 6.00 15.00
12 Eddie Lacy 1.50 4.00
13 Odell Beckham Jr. 4.00 10.00
14 Le'Veon Bell 2.00 5.00
15 Kelvin Benjamin 2.50 6.00
16 EJ Manuel 1.50 4.00
17 Marqise Lee 2.00 5.00
18 Bishop Sankey 1.50 4.00
19 Blake Bortles 2.00 5.00
20 Isaiah Crowell 2.00 5.00
21 Mike Evans 4.00 10.00
22 Keenan Allen 2.00 5.00
23 Cordarrelle Patterson 1.50 4.00
24 Brandin Cooks 2.50 6.00
25 Teddy Bridgewater 2.50 6.00

2014 Panini Spectra Building Blocks Jerseys

*BLUE/49: .6X TO 1.5X BASIC JSY/199
*BLUE/49: .5X TO 1.2X BASIC JSY/199
*GOLD/25: .8X TO 2X BASIC JSY/199
*GOLD/25: .6X TO 1.5X BASIC JSY/199
1 Austin Seferian-Jenkins/199 1.50 4.00
2 Johnny Manziel/199 2.50 6.00
3 Davante Adams/199 2.50 6.00
4 Kelvin Benjamin/199 2.50 6.00
5 Jarvis Landry/199 4.00 10.00
6 Mike Evans/199 4.00 10.00
7 Derek Carr/199 4.00 10.00
8 Bishop Sankey/199 1.50 4.00
9 Khalil Mack/199 6.00 15.00
10 Teddy Bridgewater/199 2.50 6.00
11 Cody Latimer/199 2.00 5.00
12 Eric Ebron/199 2.00 5.00
13 Paul Richardson/199 2.00 5.00
14 Brandin Cooks/199 2.50 6.00
15 Jordan Matthews/199 2.50 6.00
16 Jimmy Garoppolo/199 4.00 10.00
17 Carlos Hyde/199 2.00 5.00
18 Jadeveon Clowney/199 2.00 5.00
19 Blake Bortles/199 2.00 5.00
20 Jeremy Hill/199 2.00 5.00
21 Allen Robinson/199 2.50 6.00
22 Sammy Watkins/199 2.50 6.00
23 Marqise Lee/199 2.00 5.00
24 Odell Beckham Jr./199 8.00 20.00
25 Terrance West/199 1.50 4.00
26 Tre Mason/199 1.50 4.00
27 Donte Moncrief/199 1.50 4.00
28 Andre Williams/199 1.50 4.00
29 Telvin Smith/99 2.00 5.00
30 Storm Johnson/199 1.50 4.00
31 Bradley Roby/199 1.50 4.00
32 Ryan Shazier/99 3.00 8.00
33 Charles Sims/199 1.50 4.00
34 Lorenzo Taliaferro/199 1.50 4.00
35 C.J. Mosley/199 2.00 5.00

2014 Panini Spectra Cornerstones Prizms Blue

*GOLD/25: .5X TO 1.2X BASIC INSERTS/49
1 Lance Briggs 4.00 10.00
2 Eli Manning 4.00 10.00
3 Darnell Dockett 3.00 8.00
4 Tony Romo 4.00 10.00
5 Vince Wilfork 3.00 8.00
6 Reggie Wayne 4.00 10.00
7 Philip Rivers 5.00 12.00
8 Jason Witten 4.00 10.00
9 Aaron Rodgers 10.00 25.00
10 Larry Fitzgerald 4.00 10.00
11 Robert Mathis 3.00 8.00
12 Ben Roethlisberger 5.00 12.00
13 A.J. Hawk 3.00 8.00
14 Heath Miller 3.00 8.00
15 Tom Brady 12.00 30.00
16 Troy Polamalu 5.00 12.00
17 Calvin Johnson 5.00 12.00
18 Antonio Gates 3.00 8.00
19 Charles Tillman 4.00 10.00
20 Andre Johnson 4.00 10.00
21 Tamba Hali 3.00 8.00
22 Roddy White 3.00 8.00
23 Derrick Johnson 3.00 8.00
24 Frank Gore 4.00 10.00
25 Terrell Suggs 3.00 8.00

2014 Panini Spectra Cornerstones Jerseys

*BLUE/49: .5X TO 1.2X BASIC JSY/99-199
*BLUE/25: .5X TO 1.2X BASIC JSY/35-49
*BLUE/15: .4X TO 1X BASIC JSY/15
*GOLD/25: .6X TO 1.5X BASIC JSY/99-199
1 Antonio Gates/99 3.00 8.00
2 Tamba Hali/199 3.00 8.00
3 Lance Briggs/15 6.00 15.00
4 Frank Gore/35 5.00 12.00
5 Reggie Wayne/5
6 Fred Jackson/149 4.00 10.00
7 Robert Mathis/15 5.00 12.00
8 Matt Forte/99 3.00 8.00
9 Troy Polamalu/75 6.00 15.00
10 Brandon Pettigrew/149 3.00 8.00
11 Charles Tillman/49 5.00 12.00
12 Roddy White/99 3.00 8.00
13 Eli Manning/99 4.00 10.00
14 Terrell Suggs/199 3.00 8.00
15 Philip Rivers/199 5.00 12.00
16 Marques Colston/99 3.00 8.00
17 Tom Brady/25 20.00 50.00
18 DeAngelo Williams/49 4.00 10.00
19 Calvin Johnson/49 6.00 15.00
20 Matt Ryan/199 4.00 10.00
21 Andre Johnson/49 5.00 12.00
22 Derrick Johnson/199 3.00 8.00
23 Tony Romo/199 4.00 10.00
24 Dwayne Bowe/199 4.00 10.00
25 =E583&"/"&K583 5.00 12.00

2014 Panini Spectra Dynamic Duos Prizms Blue

*GOLD/25: .5X TO 1.2X BASIC INSERTS/49
1 F.Jackson/C.Spiller 4.00 10.00
2 R.Gronkowski/T.Brady 12.00 30.00
3 K.Moreno/L.Miller 3.00 8.00
4 D.Sproles/L.McCoy 5.00 12.00
5 D.Bryant/T.Romo 5.00 12.00
6 V.Cruz/E.Manning 4.00 10.00
7 A.Green/A.Dalton 5.00 12.00
8 L.Bell/A.Brown 5.00 12.00
9 C.Johnson/M.Stafford 5.00 12.00
10 B.Marshall/J.Cutler 3.00 8.00
11 A.Rodgers/J.Nelson 10.00 25.00
12 K.Wright/J.Locker 4.00 10.00
13 A.Luck/R.Wayne 6.00 15.00
14 J.Jones/M.Ryan 5.00 12.00
15 J.Stewart/D.Williams 3.00 8.00
16 D.Brees/M.Colston 5.00 12.00
17 D.Martin/B.Rainey 4.00 10.00
18 P.Manning/D.Thomas 10.00 25.00
19 K.Allen/P.Rivers 5.00 12.00
20 K.Davis/J.Charles 4.00 10.00
21 D.McFadden/M.Jones-Drew 3.00 8.00
22 C.Palmer/L.Fitzgerald 4.00 10.00
23 R.Wilson/M.Lynch 8.00 20.00
24 B.Cunningham/Z.Stacy 4.00 10.00
25 M.Crabtree/C.Kaepernick/49 4.00 10.00

2014 Panini Spectra Leading Men Signature Materials

2 Ryan Tannehill/49 8.00 20.00
3 Peyton Manning/25 90.00 150.00
4 Eric Decker/49 6.00 15.00
5 Matt Ryan/25 40.00 80.00
6 Doug Martin/49 8.00 20.00
7 Andrew Luck/25 75.00 150.00
8 Andy Dalton/49 8.00 20.00
9 Cam Newton/25 25.00 50.00
10 Tony Romo/25 40.00 80.00
11 Jay Cutler/30 8.00 20.00
12 Matthew Stafford/25 30.00 60.00
13 Jamaal Charles/49 8.00 20.00
14 Antonio Gates/49 6.00 15.00
15 Russell Wilson/15 60.00 100.00
16 Nick Foles/49 8.00 20.00
17 EJ Manuel/49 6.00 15.00
18 Sam Bradford/25 8.00 20.00
19 Arian Foster/49 8.00 20.00
20 Adrian Peterson/25 40.00 80.00

2014 Panini Spectra Next Level Prizms Blue

*GOLD/25: .5X TO 1.2X BASIC INSERTS/49
1 Eric Ebron 2.00 5.00
2 Jeremy Hill 2.00 5.00
3 Odell Beckham Jr. 4.00 10.00
4 Bishop Sankey 1.50 4.00
5 Jerick McKinnon 2.00 5.00
6 Derek Carr 10.00 25.00
7 Sammy Watkins 2.50 6.00
8 Blake Bortles 2.00 5.00
9 John Brown 2.50 6.00
10 Terrance West 1.50 4.00
11 Branden Oliver 2.50 6.00
12 Alfred Blue 1.50 4.00
13 Martavis Bryant 2.00 5.00
14 Lorenzo Taliaferro 1.50 4.00
15 Kelvin Benjamin 2.50 6.00
16 Teddy Bridgewater 2.50 6.00
17 Jordan Matthews 2.50 6.00
18 Johnny Manziel 2.50 6.00
19 Marqise Lee 2.00 5.00
20 Isaiah Crowell 2.00 5.00
21 Brandin Cooks 2.50 6.00
22 Andre Williams 1.50 4.00
23 Tre Mason 1.50 4.00
24 Carlos Hyde 2.00 5.00
25 Mike Evans 4.00 10.00

2014 Panini Spectra Quad Jerseys Prizms Blue

*GOLD/25: .5X TO 1.2X QUAD BLUE/49
*GOLD/15: .4X TO 1X QUAD BLUE/20
*QUAD/199: .25X TO .6X QUAD BLUE/49
*QUAD/65-99: .3X TO .8X QUAD BLUE/49
*QUAD/15-25: .4X TO 1X QUAD BLUE/20
1 Bortles/Mack/Watkins/Clowney/49 10.00 25.00
2 Bortles/Manziel/Carr/Bridgewater/49 15.00 40.00
3 Hyde/Hill/Sankey/Sims/49 3.00 8.00
4 Cooks/Watkins/Evans/Beckham/49 12.00 30.00
6 Marino/Manning/Favre/Brady/20 60.00 120.00
7 Sanders/Martin/Smith/Payton/20 50.00 100.00

9 Morris/Charles/McCoy/Forte/49 6.00 15.00
10 Johnson/Garcon/Brown/Edelman/49 6.00 15.00

2014 Panini Spectra Retired Autographs

*BLUE/25: .5X TO 1.2X BASIC AU/49
1 Terrell Davis/25 25.00 50.00
2 Jackie Slater/49
3 Jerome Bettis/25
6 Carl Eller/49 8.00 20.00
7 Lenny Moore/49 8.00 20.00
8 Dick Butkus/25
11 Tim Brown/25
12 Jackie Smith/49
14 Bob Lilly/49
18 Eric Dickerson/25
19 Steve Largent/25 15.00 40.00
20 Gale Sayers/25
22 Jan Stenerud/49 8.00 20.00
24 Bruce Smith/25 20.00 40.00

2014 Panini Spectra Rookie Combo Jerseys

*BLUE/49: .6X TO 1.5X BASIC CMBO/99-199
*GOLD/25: .8X TO 2X BASIC CMBO/99-199
1 A.Murray/A.McCarron/199 1.25 3.00
2 A.Seferian-Jenkins/B.Sankey/199 3.00 8.00
3 A.Seferian-Jenkins/M.Evans/199 3.00 8.00
4 D.Carr/J.Garoppolo/199 10.00 25.00
5 A.Robinson/B.Bortles/199 2.00 5.00
6 D.Thomas/K.Carey/199 3.00 8.00
7 J.Clowney/K.Mack/199 5.00 12.00
8 J.Landry/S.Watkins/199 2.50 6.00
9 J.Manziel/B.Bortles/99 2.00 5.00
10 O.Beckham/J.Landry/199 3.00 8.00
11 A.McCarron/J.Hill/199 1.50 4.00
12 S.Watkins/K.Benjamin/199 2.00 5.00
13 D.Thomas/A.Murray/199 1.50 4.00
14 M.Lee/P.Richardson/199 2.50 6.00
15 M.Lee/B.Bortles/199 1.50 4.00
16 D.Carr/J.Manziel/99 8.00 20.00
17 J.Clowney/T.Savage/199 1.50 4.00
18 K.Benjamin/D.Freeman/199 2.00 5.00
19 J.Manziel/T.Bridgewater/99 2.00 5.00
20 M.Evans/J.Manziel/99 3.00 8.00
21 J.Manziel/T.West/99 2.00 5.00
22 M.Evans/O.Beckham/199 3.00 8.00
23 A.Williams/O.Beckham/199 3.00 8.00
24 A.Williams/D.Freeman/199 3.00 8.00
25 D.Carr/K.Mack/199 8.00 20.00

2014 Panini Spectra Rookie Jerseys

*BLUE/49: .6X TO 1.5X BASIC JSY/99-199
*GOLD/25: .8X TO 2X BASIC JSY/99-199
*JUMBO/199: .5X TO 1.2X BASIC JSY/99-199
*JUMBO/49: .6X TO 1.5X BASIC JSY/99-199
*JUM.BLU/49: .6X TO 1.5X BASIC JSY/99-199
*JUM.BLU/25: .8X TO 2X BASIC JSY/99-199
*JUM.GOLD/15-25: .8X TO 2X BASIC JSY/99-199
1 Carlos Hyde/199 2.00 5.00
2 Logan Thomas/199 1.50 4.00
3 Davante Adams/199 2.50 6.00
4 Paul Richardson/199 2.00 5.00
5 Donte Moncrief/199 1.50 4.00
6 Tom Savage/199 1.50 4.00
7 Aaron Murray/199 1.50 4.00
8 Jarvis Landry/199 4.00 10.00
9 Austin Seferian-Jenkins/199 1.50 4.00
10 Jordan Matthews/199 2.50 6.00
11 Charles Sims/199 1.50 4.00
12 Marqise Lee/199 2.00 5.00
13 De'Anthony Thomas/199 1.50 4.00
14 Sammy Watkins/199 5.00 12.00
15 Dri Archer/199 1.50 4.00
16 Tre Mason/199 1.50 4.00
17 A.J. McCarron/199 1.50 4.00
18 Bishop Sankey/199 1.50 4.00
19 Jeremy Hill/199 2.00 5.00
20 Ka'Deem Carey/199 1.50 4.00
21 Cody Latimer/199 2.00 5.00
22 Mike Evans/199 4.00 10.00
23 Derek Carr/199 4.00 10.00
24 Teddy Bridgewater/199 2.50 6.00
25 Eric Ebron/199 2.00 5.00
26 Allen Hurns/99 2.00 5.00
27 Allen Robinson/199 2.50 6.00
28 Jimmy Garoppolo/199 4.00 10.00
29 Blake Bortles/199 2.00 5.00
30 Kelvin Benjamin/199 2.50 6.00
31 Connor Shaw/199 1.50 4.00
32 Odell Beckham Jr./199 8.00 20.00
33 Devonta Freeman/199 2.50 6.00
34 Terrance West/199 1.50 4.00
35 Jadeveon Clowney/199 2.00 5.00
36 Storm Johnson/199 1.50 4.00
37 Andre Williams/199 1.50 4.00
38 Johnny Manziel/199 2.50 6.00
39 Brandin Cooks/199 4.00 10.00
40 Khalil Mack/199 6.00 15.00

2014 Panini Spectra Teammates Combo Jerseys

1 J.Maclin/L.McCoy/49 6.00 15.00
2 D.Murray/D.Bryant/99 5.00 12.00
3 C.Kaepernick/M.Crabtree/25 6.00 15.00
4 A.Smith/D.Bowe/199 3.00 8.00
5 A.Morris/R.Griffin III/99 3.00 8.00
6 J.Jones/R.White/99 5.00 12.00
7 T.Brady/J.Edelman/25
8 C.Spiller/F.Jackson/199 3.00 8.00
9 E.Manning/V.Cruz/49 5.00 12.00
11 A.Brown/L.Bell/99 8.00 20.00
12 V.Miller/D.Thomas/99 4.00 10.00
13 D.Martin/M.Evans/99 4.00 10.00
14 B.Hartline/M.Wallace/199 2.50 6.00
15 C.Palmer/L.Fitzgerald/99 4.00 10.00
16 B.Pierce/J.Flacco/99 4.00 10.00
17 P.Thomas/M.Colston/25 5.00 12.00
18 D.Williams/J.Stewart/25 5.00 12.00
19 D.McFadden/M.Jones-Drew/99 3.00 8.00
20 A.Dalton/A.Green/99 5.00 12.00
21 A.Gates/P.Rivers/99 5.00 12.00
22 E.Lacy/J.Nelson/20 6.00 15.00
23 D.Walker/J.Locker/199 3.00 8.00
24 C.Patterson/T.Bridgewater/99 2.50 6.00

2015 Panini Spectra

1 Aaron Rodgers 8.00 20.00
2 Adrian Peterson 4.00 10.00
3 Aeneas Williams 3.00 8.00
4 A.J. Green 4.00 10.00
5 Alfred Morris 2.50 6.00
6 Alshon Jeffery 3.00 8.00
7 Andre Ellington 2.50 6.00
8 Andrew Luck 5.00 12.00
9 Andy Dalton 3.00 8.00
10 Antonio Brown 4.00 10.00
11 Antonio Gates 2.50 6.00
12 Arian Foster 3.00 8.00
13 Barry Sanders 8.00 20.00
14 Ben Roethlisberger 4.00 10.00
15 Blake Bortles 2.50 6.00
16 Bo Jackson 6.00 15.00
17 Bob Griese 5.00 12.00
18 Brandon Marshall 2.50 6.00
19A Brett Favre ATL 10.00 25.00
19B Brett Favre GB 10.00 25.00
19C Brett Favre MINN 10.00 25.00
19D Brett Favre NYJ 10.00 25.00
20 Barkevious Mingo 2.50 6.00
21 Brian Urlacher 5.00 12.00
22 Calvin Johnson 4.00 10.00
23 Cam Newton 4.00 10.00
24 Carlos Hyde 2.50 6.00
25 Colin Kaepernick 3.00 8.00
26A Cris Carter MIA 5.00 12.00
26B Cris Carter MINN 5.00 12.00
26C Cris Carter PHIL 5.00 12.00
27 Cris Collinsworth 4.00 10.00
28 Dan Marino 10.00 25.00
29 Darrelle Revis 2.50 6.00
30 DeAndre Hopkins 3.00 8.00
31A Deion Sanders ATL 4.00 10.00
31B Deion Sanders BALT 4.00 10.00
31C Deion Sanders DAL 4.00 10.00
31D Deion Sanders 49ERS 4.00 10.00
31E Deion Sanders WASH 4.00 10.00
32 DeMarco Murray 3.00 8.00
33 Demaryius Thomas 3.00 8.00
34 Denard Robinson 2.50 6.00
35 Derek Carr 4.00 10.00
36 Derrick Brooks 2.50 6.00
37 DeSean Jackson 3.00 8.00
38 Dez Bryant 4.00 10.00
39A Doug Flutie BUFF 4.00 10.00
39B Doug Flutie CHI 4.00 10.00
39C Doug Flutie NE 4.00 10.00
39D Doug Flutie SD 4.00 10.00
40A Drew Brees NO 4.00 10.00
40B Drew Brees SD 4.00 10.00
41 Dwayne Bowe 3.00 8.00
42A Earl Campbell HOUS 5.00 12.00
42B Earl Campbell NO 5.00 12.00
43 Eli Manning 3.00 8.00
44A Emmitt Smith ARI 8.00 20.00
44B Emmitt Smith DAL 8.00 20.00
45 Frank Gore 3.00 8.00
46 Fred Taylor 2.50 6.00
47 Gale Sayers 5.00 12.00
48 Joique Bell 2.50 6.00
49 J.J. Watt 4.00 10.00
50 Jamaal Charles 3.00 8.00
51 Jeremy Hill 2.50 6.00
52 Jeremy Maclin 2.50 6.00
53A Jerome Bettis LA 5.00 12.00
53B Jerome Bettis PITT 5.00 12.00
54A Jerry Rice OAK 8.00 20.00
54B Jerry Rice 49ERS 8.00 20.00
54C Jerry Rice SEA 8.00 20.00
55 Jim Kelly 5.00 12.00
56 Joe Flacco 3.00 8.00
57 Joe Greene 5.00 12.00
58A Joe Montana KC 12.00 30.00
58B Joe Montana 49ERS 12.00 30.00
59A Joe Namath LA 6.00 15.00
59B Joe Namath NYJ 6.00 15.00
60 John Elway 8.00 20.00
61 Johnny Manziel 3.00 8.00
62 Jordy Nelson 3.00 8.00
63 Julian Edelman 4.00 10.00
64 Julio Jones 4.00 10.00
65 Julius Thomas 2.50 6.00
66 Justin Hunter 2.50 6.00
67 Kelvin Benjamin 3.00 8.00
68A Kurt Warner ARI 4.00 10.00
68B Kurt Warner NYG 4.00 10.00
68C Kurt Warner STL 4.00 10.00
69A LaDainian Tomlinson NYJ 4.00 10.00
69B LaDainian Tomlinson SD 4.00 10.00
70 Larry Fitzgerald 3.00 8.00
71 Lawrence Taylor 5.00 12.00
72 LeSean McCoy 4.00 10.00
73 Le'Veon Bell 3.00 8.00
74 Luke Kuechly 3.00 8.00
75 Marcus Allen 5.00 12.00
76 Mark Ingram 3.00 8.00
77 Marques Colston 2.50 6.00
78A Marshall Faulk INDY 4.00 10.00
78B Marshall Faulk STL 4.00 10.00
79A Marshawn Lynch BUFF 3.00 8.00
79B Marshawn Lynch SEA 3.00 8.00
80 Matt Forte 2.50 6.00
81 Matt Ryan 3.00 8.00
82 Matthew Stafford 3.00 8.00
83 Michael Irvin 5.00 12.00
84 Michael Strahan 4.00 10.00
85 Mike Evans 3.00 8.00
86 Ndamukong Suh 3.00 8.00
87 Nick Foles 3.00 8.00
88 Odell Beckham Jr. 4.00 10.00
89 Ozzie Newsome 4.00 10.00
90 Peyton Manning DEN 8.00 20.00
90B Peyton Manning INDY 8.00 20.00
91 Philip Rivers 4.00 10.00
92 Ricky Williams 4.00 10.00
93 Rob Gronkowski 4.00 10.00
94 Robert Griffin III 2.50 6.00
95 Roger Staubach 6.00 15.00
96 Russell Wilson 5.00 12.00
97 Ryan Tannehill 3.00 8.00
98 Sam Bradford 2.50 6.00
99 Sammy Watkins 3.00 8.00
100A Shannon Sharpe BALT 4.00 10.00
100B Shannon Sharpe DEN 4.00 10.00
101 Sterling Sharpe 4.00 10.00
102 Steve Largent 5.00 12.00
103A Steve Smith BALT 3.00 8.00
103B Steve Smith CAR 3.00 8.00
104A Steve Young 49ERS 6.00 15.00
104B Steve Young TB 6.00 15.00
105 T.Y. Hilton 3.00 8.00
106 Teddy Bridgewater 3.00 8.00
107 Terrance West 2.50 6.00
108 Terrell Davis 4.00 10.00
109A Thurman Thomas BUFF 4.00 10.00
109B Thurman Thomas MIA 4.00 10.00
110 Tim Brown 5.00 12.00
111 Tom Brady 10.00 25.00
112 Tony Romo 3.00 8.00
113 Troy Aikman 6.00 15.00
114A Warren Moon HOUS 5.00 12.00
114B Warren Moon KC 5.00 12.00
114C Warren Moon MINN 5.00 12.00
114D Warren Moon SEA 5.00 12.00
115 Zach Mettenberger 2.50 6.00
116 Jameis Winston RC 2.50 6.00
117 Marcus Mariota RC 4.00 10.00
118 Amari Cooper RC 3.00 8.00
119 Leonard Williams RC 1.00 2.50
120 Kevin White RC 1.25 3.00
121 Todd Gurley RC 4.00 10.00
122 DeVante Parker RC 1.50 4.00
123 Melvin Gordon RC 2.50 6.00
124 Nelson Agholor RC 1.25 3.00
125 Breshad Perriman RC 1.00 2.50
126 Phillip Dorsett RC 1.00 2.50
127 T.J. Yeldon RC 1.00 2.50
128 Devin Smith RC 1.00 2.50
129 Dorial Green-Beckham RC 1.00 2.50
130 Devin Funchess RC 1.50 4.00
131 Ameer Abdullah RC 1.50 4.00
132 Maxx Williams RC 1.00 2.50
133 Tyler Lockett RC 1.50 4.00
134 Jaelen Strong RC 1.25 3.00
135 Tevin Coleman RC 1.25 3.00
136 Garrett Grayson RC 1.00 2.50
137 Chris Conley RC 1.00 2.50
138 Duke Johnson RC 1.50 4.00
139 David Johnson RC 2.50 6.00
140 Sammie Coates RC 1.25 3.00
141 Sean Mannion RC 1.00 2.50
142 Ty Montgomery RC 1.00 2.50
143 Matt Jones RC 1.00 2.50
144 Bryce Petty RC 1.00 2.50
145 Jamison Crowder RC 1.25 3.00
146 Jeremy Langford RC 1.00 2.50
147 Justin Hardy RC 1.00 2.50
148 Vince Mayle RC 1.25 3.00
149 Buck Allen RC 1.25 3.00
150 Mike Davis RC 1.00 2.50
151 David Cobb RC 1.00 2.50
152 Rashad Greene RC 1.00 2.50
153 Stefon Diggs RC 2.50 6.00
154 Brett Hundley RC 1.00 2.50
155 Jay Ajayi RC 1.50 4.00
156 Shane Ray RC 1.00 2.50
157 Randy Gregory RC 1.00 2.50
158 Bud Dupree RC 1.25 3.00
159 Cameron Artis-Payne RC 1.00 2.50
160 Clive Walford RC 1.00 2.50
161 Jameis Winston JSY AU/99 50.00 100.00
162 Marcus Mariota JSY AU/99 40.00 80.00
163 Amari Cooper JSY AU/75 30.00 60.00
165 Kevin White JSY AU/75 5.00 12.00
166 Todd Gurley JSY AU/75 60.00 120.00
167 DeVante Parker JSY AU/99 6.00 15.00
168 Melvin Gordon JSY AU/99 15.00 40.00
169 Nelson Agholor JSY AU/99 5.00 12.00
170 Breshad Perriman JSY AU/99 4.00 10.00
171 Phillip Dorsett JSY AU/99 4.00 10.00
172 T.J. Yeldon JSY AU/99 4.00 10.00
173 Devin Smith JSY AU/99 4.00 10.00
174 Dorial Green-Beckham JSY AU/99 4.00 10.00
175 Devin Funchess JSY AU/99 6.00 15.00
176 Ameer Abdullah JSY AU/99 6.00 15.00
177 Maxx Williams JSY AU/75 4.00 10.00
178 Tyler Lockett JSY AU/99 25.00 50.00
179 Jaelen Strong JSY AU/99 5.00 12.00
180 Tevin Coleman JSY AU/99 5.00 12.00
181 Garrett Grayson JSY AU/75 4.00 10.00
182 Chris Conley JSY AU/99 4.00 10.00
183 Duke Johnson JSY AU/75 6.00 15.00
184 David Johnson JSY AU/99 10.00 25.00
185 Sammie Coates JSY AU/99 5.00 12.00
186 Sean Mannion JSY AU/99 4.00 10.00
187 Ty Montgomery JSY AU/99 4.00 10.00
188 Matt Jones JSY AU/99 4.00 10.00
189 Bryce Petty JSY AU/99 4.00 10.00
191 Jeremy Langford JSY AU/99 4.00 10.00
192 Justin Hardy JSY AU/99 4.00 10.00
193 Vince Mayle JSY AU/99 5.00 12.00
195 Mike Davis JSY AU/99 4.00 10.00
196 David Cobb JSY AU/99 4.00 10.00
197 Rashad Greene JSY AU/99 6.00 15.00
199 Brett Hundley JSY AU/99 4.00 10.00
200 Jay Ajayi JSY AU/99 6.00 15.00
203 Shane Ray AU 3.00 8.00
204 Trae Waynes AU 3.00 8.00
205 Dezmin Lewis AU 3.00 8.00
206 Clive Walford AU 3.00 8.00
207 Shaq Thompson AU 4.00 10.00
208 Dante Fowler Jr. AU 5.00 12.00
209 Bud Dupree AU 4.00 10.00
210 Kevin Johnson AU 3.00 8.00
211 Marcus Peters AU 5.00 12.00
212 Stephone Anthony AU 3.00 8.00
213 Jesse James AU 4.00 10.00
214 Denzel Perryman AU 3.00 8.00
215 MyCole Pruitt AU 3.00 8.00
216 Ben Koyack AU 5.00 12.00
217 Cameron Artis-Payne AU 3.00 8.00
218 Trey Williams AU 4.00 10.00
220 Kenny Bell AU 5.00 12.00
221 Darren Waller AU 4.00 10.00
222 Trey Flowers AU 5.00 12.00
223 Owamagbe Odighizuwa AU 4.00 10.00
224 Eddie Goldman AU 3.00 8.00
225 Mario Alford AU 3.00 8.00
226 Josh Robinson AU 3.00 8.00
227 Benardrick McKinney AU 3.00 8.00
228 Arik Armstead AU 3.00 8.00
229 J.J. Nelson AU 3.00 8.00
230 Vic Beasley Jr. AU 4.00 10.00
231 Carl Davis AU 4.00 10.00
232 D.Hunter AU/E.Kendricks AU 4.00 10.00
233 A.Goodley AU/D.Greenberry AU 3.00 8.00
234 D.Daniels AU/T.Heinicke AU 5.00 12.00
235 J.Shaw AU/P.Dawson AU 5.00 12.00
236 D.Shelton AU/I.Ekpre-Olomu AU 3.00 8.00
237 D.White AU/D.Anderson AU 5.00 12.00
238 B.Bennett AU/S.Carden AU 3.00 8.00
239 P.Williams AU/R.Darby AU 4.00 10.00

2015 Panini Spectra Neon Blue

*1-150 VETS/49: .5X TO 1.2X BASIC CARDS/99
*151-200 ROOKIES/49: 1X TO 2.5X BASIC RC/99
*161-201 ROOK.JSY AU/35-50: .5X TO 1.2X BASIC RC/75-99
*161-201 ROOK.JSY AU/25: .6X TO 1.5X BASIC RC/75-99
*161-201 ROOK.JSY AU/15: .8X TO 2X BASIC RC/75-99
*203-241 ROOK.AU/50: .5X TO 1.2X BASIC RC/99
163 Amari Cooper JSY AU/25 75.00 150.00

2015 Panini Spectra Neon Blue Die Cut

*1-115 VETS/35: .6X TO 1.5X BASIC CARDS/99
*116-160 ROOKIES/35: 1X TO 2.5X BASIC CARDS/99

2015 Panini Spectra Neon Green

*1-150 VETS/49: .6X TO 1.5X BASIC CARDS/99
*151-200 ROOKIES/49: 1.2X TO 3X BASIC RC/99
*161-201 ROOK.JSY AU/35-50: .6X TO 1.5X BASIC RC/75-99
*161-201 ROOK.JSY AU/25: .8X TO 2X BASIC RC/75-99
*161-201 ROOK.JSY AU/15: 1X TO 2.5X BASIC RC/75-99
*203-241 ROOK.AU/50: .6X TO 1.5X BASIC RC/99

2015 Panini Spectra Neon Green Die Cut

*1-115 VETS/15: .8X TO 2X BASIC CARDS/99
*116-160 ROOK/15: 1.5X TO 4X BASIC CARDS/99

2015 Panini Spectra 50th Anniversary Pro Football Hall of Fame Signatures

21 Charlie Joiner 25.00 60.00
81 Joe Greene 40.00 100.00
104 Marcus Allen 25.00 60.00
109 Mike Ditka 40.00 100.00

2015 Panini Spectra Aspiring Patch Autographs

AJAAC Amari Cooper/25 40.00 100.00
AJABH Brett Hundley/25 6.00 15.00
AJABRP Breshad Perriman/49 5.00 12.00
AJABYP Bryce Petty/25 6.00 15.00
AJADAJ David Johnson/99 10.00 25.00
AJADGB Dorial Green-Beckham/49 5.00 12.00
AJADP DeVante Parker/99 6.00 15.00
AJADS Devin Smith/99 4.00 10.00
AJADUJ Duke Johnson/75 6.00 15.00
AJAJA Jay Ajayi/99 6.00 15.00
AJAJS Jaelen Strong/99 5.00 12.00
AJAMD Mike Davis/99 4.00 10.00
AJAMJ Matt Jones/99 12.00 30.00
AJAMM Marcus Mariota/49 40.00 80.00
AJAMW Maxx Williams/49
AJANA Nelson Agholor/99 5.00 12.00
AJASC Sammie Coates/75 5.00 12.00
AJATC Tevin Coleman/99 5.00 12.00
AJATL Tyler Lockett/99
AJAVM Vince Mayle/99 5.00 12.00

2015 Panini Spectra Aspiring Patch Autographs Neon Blue

*BLUE/50: .5X TO 1.2X BASIC JSY AU/75-99
*BLUE/25: .6X TO 1.5X BASIC JSY AU/75-99
*BLUE/25: .5X TO 1.2X BASIC JSY AU/49
*BLUE/15: .6X TO 1.5X BASIC JSY AU/49
AJAMM Marcus Mariota/25 40.00 100.00

2015 Panini Spectra Aspiring Patch Autographs Neon Green

*GREEN/25: .6X TO 1.5X BASIC JSY AU/75-99
*GREEN/15: .6X TO 1.5X BASIC JSY AU/49
*GREEN/15: .8X TO 2X BASIC JSY AU/75-99
AJAMM Marcus Mariota/15 50.00 125.00

2015 Panini Spectra Catalyst Jerseys

*BLUE/50: .5X TO 1.2X BASIC JSY/99-199
*BLUE/25: .6X TO 1.5X BASIC JSY/99-199
*GREEN/25: .6X TO 1.5X BASIC JSY/99-199
CAAH Anthony Hitchens/99 2.50 6.00
CABB Blake Bortles/199 2.50 6.00
CABR Bradley Roby/199 2.50 6.00
CADC Derek Carr/199 4.00 10.00
CADD Darqueze Dennard/199 2.50 6.00
CADF Dee Ford/199 2.50 6.00
CAFR Devonta Freeman/199 3.00 8.00
CAHA Ha Ha Clinton-Dix/99 2.50 6.00
CAJH Jeremy Hill/199 2.50 6.00
CAKB Kelvin Benjamin/199 3.00 8.00
CAME Mike Evans/199 3.00 8.00
CAOB Odell Beckham Jr./199 4.00 10.00
CASJ Storm Johnson/199 2.50 6.00
CASW Sammy Watkins/199 3.00 8.00
CATB Teddy Bridgewater/199 3.00 8.00

2015 Panini Spectra Epic Legends Materials

*BLUE/50: .5X TO 1.2X BASIC JSY/99
*BLUE/25: .5X TO 1.2X BASIC JSY/49
*GREEN/25: .6X TO 1.5X BASIC JSY/99
*GREEN/15: .8X TO 2X BASIC JSY/99
*GREEN/15: .6X TO 1.5X BASIC JSY/49
LMBF Brett Favre 10.00 25.00
LMBG Bob Griese 5.00 12.00
LMBS Barry Sanders 8.00 20.00
LMBU Brian Urlacher 5.00 12.00
LMDM Dan Marino 10.00 25.00
LMDS Deion Sanders 4.00 10.00
LMEC Earl Campbell 5.00 12.00
LMED Eric Dickerson 4.00 10.00
LMFT Fran Tarkenton 5.00 12.00
LMJC Larry Csonka 5.00 12.00
LMJE John Elway 8.00 20.00
LMJK Jim Kelly 5.00 12.00
LMJM Joe Montana 12.00 30.00
LMJN Joe Namath 6.00 15.00
LMJR Jerry Rice 8.00 20.00
LMJT Joe Theismann 5.00 12.00
LMMA Marcus Allen 5.00 12.00
LMMS Michael Strahan 4.00 10.00
LMRC Roger Craig 4.00 10.00
LMTA Troy Aikman 6.00 15.00

2015 Panini Spectra Gigantic Jerseys

*BLUE/50: .5X TO 1.2X BASIC JSY/199
*GREEN/25: .6X TO 1.5X BASIC JSY/199
GJAA Ameer Abdullah 2.50 6.00
GJAC Amari Cooper 5.00 12.00
GJBA Buck Allen 2.00 5.00
GJBH Brett Hundley 1.50 4.00
GJBRP Breshad Perriman 1.50 4.00
GJBYP Bryce Petty 1.50 4.00
GJCC Chris Conley 1.50 4.00
GJDAJ David Johnson 4.00 10.00
GJDC David Cobb 1.50 4.00
GJDF Devin Funchess 2.50 6.00
GJDGB Dorial Green-Beckham 1.50 4.00
GJDP DeVante Parker 2.50 6.00
GJDS Devin Smith 1.50 4.00
GJDUJ Duke Johnson 2.50 6.00
GJGG Garrett Grayson 1.50 4.00
GJJA Jay Ajayi 2.50 6.00
GJJC Jamison Crowder 2.00 5.00
GJJH Justin Hardy 1.50 4.00
GJJL Jeremy Langford 1.50 4.00
GJJS Jaelen Strong 2.00 5.00
GJJW Jameis Winston 8.00 20.00
GJKW Kevin White 2.00 5.00
GJLW Leonard Williams 1.50 4.00
GJMD Mike Davis 1.50 4.00
GJMG Melvin Gordon 4.00 10.00
GJMJ Matt Jones 1.50 4.00
GJMM Marcus Mariota 6.00 15.00
GJMW Maxx Williams 1.50 4.00
GJNA Nelson Agholor 2.00 5.00
GJPD Phillip Dorsett 1.50 4.00
GJRG Rashad Greene 1.50 4.00
GJSC Sammie Coates 2.00 5.00
GJSD Stefon Diggs 4.00 10.00
GJSM Sean Mannion 1.50 4.00
GJTC Tevin Coleman 2.00 5.00
GJTG Todd Gurley 5.00 12.00
GJTL Tyler Lockett 2.50 6.00
GJTM Ty Montgomery 1.50 4.00
GJTY T.J. Yeldon 1.50 4.00
GJVM Vince Mayle 2.00 5.00

2015 Panini Spectra Illustrious Legends

ILBU Brian Urlacher/25 25.00 60.00
ILCC Cris Carter/25 30.00 60.00
ILDE Eric Dickerson/49
ILDH Dan Hampton/99 10.00 25.00
ILDM Dan Marino/15 150.00 250.00
ILDS Deion Sanders/25 60.00
ILEC Earl Campbell/25 25.00 60.00
ILES Emmitt Smith/15 200.00 300.00
ILGS Gale Sayers/49 20.00 50.00
ILJB Jerome Bettis/49 40.00 80.00
ILJOR John Riggins/25 20.00 50.00
ILKW Kurt Warner/25 20.00 50.00
ILLD Len Dawson/25 25.00 60.00
ILLT LaDainian Tomlinson/25 20.00 50.00
ILMF Marshall Faulk/25 20.00 50.00
ILMI Michael Irvin/15 40.00 80.00
ILRS Roger Staubach/15 75.00 150.00
ILRW Rod Woodson/50 15.00 40.00
ILSL Steve Largent/25 15.00 40.00
ILTB Tim Brown/25 25.00 60.00
ILTD Tony Dorsett/15

2015 Panini Spectra Illustrious Legends Neon Blue

*BLUE/50: .5X TO 1.2X BASIC AU/99

2015 Panini Spectra Immense Materials

*BLUE/49-50: .5X TO 1.2X BASIC JSY/99-199
*BLUE/25: .5X TO 1.2X BASIC JSY/49
*BLUE/15: .5X TO 1.2X BASIC JSY/25
*BLUE/15: .6X TO 1.5X BASIC JSY/49
*GREEN/25: .6X TO 1.5X BASIC JSY/99-199
*GREEN/25: .5X TO 1.2X BASIC JSY/49
IMAB Antonio Brown/49 5.00 12.00
IMAG Antonio Gates/49 3.00 8.00
IMAJ A.J. Green/49 5.00 12.00
IMBB Blake Bortles/199 2.50 6.00
IMBC Brandin Cooks/199 3.00 8.00
IMBR B.J. Raji/149 2.50 6.00
IMCH Carlos Hyde/199 2.50 6.00
IMDM Devin McCourty/49 3.00 8.00
IMEM EJ Manuel/199 2.50 6.00
IMES Emmanuel Sanders/99 3.00 8.00
IMGA Geno Atkins/199 2.50 6.00
IMJL Jarvis Landry/199 3.00 8.00
IMJS Jonathan Stewart/99 2.50 6.00
IMKD Knile Davis/199 2.50 6.00
IMLF Larry Fitzgerald/49 4.00 10.00
IMLM Lamar Miller/99 2.50 6.00
IMME Mike Evans/199 3.00 8.00
IMMS Mohamed Sanu/99 2.50 6.00
IMOB Odell Beckham Jr./199 4.00 10.00
IMOS Orlando Scandrick/99 2.50 6.00
IMRG Robert Griffin III/25 4.00 10.00
IMSG Shonn Greene/99 2.50 6.00
IMTB Teddy Bridgewater/199 3.00 8.00
IMTM Tre Mason/199 3.00 8.00
IMVM Von Miller/99 3.00 8.00

2015 Panini Spectra Radiant Rookie Patch Signatures

*PATCH AU/75-99: .3X TO .8X BLUE/50
*PATCH AU/75-99: .25X TO .6X BLUE/25
*PATCH AU/35-49: .3X TO .8X BLUE/25
*PATCH AU/25: .3X TO .8X BLUE/15
RRMSAA Ameer Abdullah/25 10.00 25.00
RRMSJW Jameis Winston/49 75.00 160.00

2015 Panini Spectra Radiant Rookie Patch Signatures Neon Blue

RRMSAA Ameer Abdullah/15 12.00 30.00
RRMSBA Buck Allen/50 6.00 15.00
RRMSCC Chris Conley/15 8.00 20.00
RRMSDC David Cobb/50 5.00 12.00
RRMSDF Devin Funchess/25 10.00 25.00
RRMSGG Garrett Grayson/25
RRMSJC Jamison Crowder/50 10.00 25.00
RRMSJH Justin Hardy/50 5.00 12.00
RRMSJL Jeremy Langford/50 12.00 30.00
RRMSJW Jameis Winston/25 100.00 200.00
RRMSKW Kevin White/15
RRMSLW Leonard Williams/25
RRMSMG Melvin Gordon/15
RRMSPD Phillip Dorsett/25 6.00 15.00
RRMSRG Rashad Greene/25 6.00 15.00
RRMSSD Stefon Diggs/25 15.00 40.00
RRMSSM Sean Mannion/25 6.00 15.00
RRMSTG Todd Gurley/25 100.00 200.00
RRMSTM Ty Montgomery/25 6.00 15.00
RRMSTY T.J. Yeldon/25 6.00 15.00

2015 Panini Spectra Radiant Rookie Patch Signatures Neon Green

*GREEN/25: .5X TO 1.2X BLUE/50
*GREEN/15: .5X TO 1.2X BLUE/25
RRMSJW Jameis Winston/15 125.00 250.00

2015 Panini Spectra Rising Rookie Materials

*BLUE/50: .6X TO 1.5X BASIC JSY/199
*GREEN/25: .6X TO 1.5X BASIC JSY/199
RRAA Ameer Abdullah 2.50 6.00
RRAC Amari Cooper 6.00 15.00
RRBH Brett Hundley 1.50 4.00
RRBRP Breshad Perriman 1.50 4.00
RRBYP Bryce Petty 1.50 4.00
RRCC Chris Conley 1.50 4.00
RRDF Devin Funchess 2.50 6.00
RRDGB Dorial Green-Beckham 1.50 4.00
RRDP DeVante Parker 2.50 6.00
RRDUJ Duke Johnson 2.50 6.00
RRGG Garrett Grayson 1.50 4.00
RRJA Jay Ajayi 2.50 6.00
RRJC Jamison Crowder 2.00 5.00
RRJH Justin Hardy 1.50 4.00
RRJS Jaelen Strong 2.00 5.00
RRJW Jameis Winston 8.00 20.00
RRKW Kevin White 2.00 5.00
RRLW Leonard Williams 1.50 4.00
RRMD Mike Davis 1.50 4.00
RRMG Melvin Gordon 4.00 10.00
RRMM Marcus Mariota 6.00 15.00
RRNA Nelson Agholor 2.00 5.00
RRPD Phillip Dorsett 1.50 4.00
RRSC Sammie Coates 2.00 5.00
RRSD Stefon Diggs 4.00 10.00
RRSM Sean Mannion 1.50 4.00
RRTC Tevin Coleman 2.00 5.00
RRTG Todd Gurley 5.00 12.00
RRTY T.J. Yeldon 1.50 4.00
RRVM Vince Mayle 2.00 5.00

2015 Panini Spectra Rivals Jerseys

*BLUE/50: .5X TO 1.2X BASIC JSY/99
*BLUE/25: .5X TO 1.2X BASIC JSY/49
*GREEN/25: .6X TO 1.5X BASIC JSY/99
*GREEN/25: .5X TO 1.2X BASIC JSY/49
RVBC B.Carr/O.Beckham Jr./99 5.00 12.00
RVBG B.Bortles/M.Griffin/99 3.00 8.00
RVBR D.Revis/T.Brady/49 15.00 40.00
RVBS A.Brown/S.Smith/99 5.00 12.00
RVDH J.Hill/K.Dansby/99 3.00 8.00
RVEC M.Colston/M.Evans/99 4.00 10.00
RVEH A.Ellington/C.Hyde/99 3.00 8.00
RVFH J.Flacco/J.Haden/99 4.00 10.00
RVFS B.Sanders/B.Favre/99 12.00 30.00
RVJB J.Jones/K.Benjamin/99 5.00 12.00
RVJC B.Church/D.Jackson/99 4.00 10.00
RVKL C.Kaepernick/J.Laurinaitis/99 4.00 10.00
RVKM A.Peterson/J.Bell/99 5.00 12.00
RVKM D.Marino/J.Kelly/99 10.00 25.00
RVLI I.Crowell/L.Bell/99 4.00 10.00
RVLW A.Luck/J.Watt/49 8.00 20.00
RVMH J.Houston/P.Manning/99 10.00 25.00
RVMS D.Sproles/E.Manning/99 4.00 10.00
RVMW D.Ware/K.Mack/99 5.00 12.00
RVPA J.Allen/J.Peppers/99 4.00 10.00
RVRC D.Carr/P.Rivers/99 5.00 12.00
RVTA S.Young/T.Aikman/99 6.00 15.00
RVTT J.Theismann/L.Taylor/99 5.00 12.00
RVWB N.Bowman/R.Wilson/49 8.00 20.00
RVWW C.Wake/S.Watkins/99 4.00 10.00

2015 Panini Spectra Rookie Dual Patch Autographs

RDJABW B.Petty/L.Williams/20
RDJACC A.Cooper/S.Coates/25 30.00 60.00
RDJACGB D.Cobb/D.Green-Beckham/25 6.00 15.00
RDJADS D.Smith/P.Dorsett/25 6.00 15.00
RDJAGA A.Abdullah/M.Gordon/25 15.00 40.00
RDJAGY R.Greene/T.Yeldon/25 6.00 15.00
RDJAHM B.Hundley/T.Montgomery/25
RDJAJD D.Johnson/M.Davis/25
RDJAJM D.Johnson/V.Mayle/25 10.00 25.00
RDJALC C.Conley/T.Lockett/25 10.00 25.00
RDJALW J.Langford/K.White/25 20.00 50.00
RDJAMG S.Mannion/T.Gurley/25 25.00 60.00
RDJAPA D.Parker/J.Ajayi/50 8.00 20.00
RDJAPW B.Perriman/M.Williams/25
RDJARS D.Funchess/J.Strong/50 8.00 20.00
RDJAWM J.Winston/M.Mariota/15 100.00 200.00
RJACG G.Grayson/T.Coleman/25 8.00 20.00

2015 Panini Spectra Rookie Dual Patch Autographs Neon Blue

*BLUE/25: .5X TO 1.2X BASIC JSY AU/50
*BLUE/15: .6X TO 1.5X BASIC JSY AU/50
*BLUE/15: .5X TO 1.2X BASIC JSY AU/25
RDJAAA Buck Allen 20.00 50.00
Nelson Agholor/15
RDJACJ Jamison Crowder 25.00 50.00
Matt Jones/25

2015 Panini Spectra Rookie Dual Patch Autographs Neon Green

*GREEN/15: .6X TO 1.5X BASIC JSY AU/50

2015 Panini Spectra Signatures

*BLUE/50: .5X TO 1.2X BASIC AU/75-99
*BLUE/25: .6X TO 1.5X BASIC AU/75-99
*BLUE/25: .5X TO 1.2X BASIC AU/49
*GREEN/25: .6X TO 1.5X BASIC AU/75-99
*GREEN/15: .6X TO 1.5X BASIC AU/49
1 Zach Mettenberger/99 5.00 12.00
2 Rob Gronkowski/49 20.00 40.00
3 Sean Lee/99 6.00 15.00
4 Prince Amukamara/99 5.00 12.00
5 Brock Osweiler/99 5.00 12.00
6 Barkevious Mingo/99 5.00 12.00
7 Allen Hurns/99 5.00 12.00
8 Jeremy Maclin/49 6.00 15.00
9 Luke Kuechly/99 10.00 25.00
10 Derek Carr/99 20.00 40.00
11 Brandon LaFell/99 5.00 12.00
12 Cordarrelle Patterson/75 5.00 12.00
13 Jason Witten/25 15.00 40.00
14 Jimmy Garoppolo/75 30.00 60.00
15 Isaiah Crowell/99 5.00 12.00
16 Jamaal Charles/25 10.00 25.00
18 Don Majkowski/99 10.00 25.00
19 Colin Kaepernick/25 15.00 40.00
20 Coby Fleener/99 5.00 12.00
21 John Brown/99 6.00 15.00
22 Julius Thomas/99 5.00 12.00
24 Martavis Bryant/99 5.00 12.00
26 Mike Evans/99 15.00 30.00
26 Nick Foles/25
27 Ha Ha Clinton-Dix/99 5.00 12.00
28 Earl Thomas/99 10.00 25.00
29 Aeneas Williams/99 5.00 12.00
30 Philly Brown/99 5.00 12.00
31 DeAndre Hopkins/49 8.00 20.00
32 Branden Oliver/99 6.00 15.00
33 Rod Streater/99 5.00 12.00
34 Mark Chmura/99 5.00 12.00
35 Vance McDonald/99 5.00 12.00
36 Andre Williams/99 5.00 12.00
37 Andrew Luck/25 125.00 200.00
38 Joseph Randle/99 5.00 12.00
39 Steve Grogan/99 5.00 12.00
40 Tyler Eifert/99 6.00 15.00
41 Eddie Lacy/49 20.00 50.00
42 Eli Manning/25
43 Arian Foster/25
44 Jordan Matthews/99 6.00 15.00
45 Justin Forsett/99 6.00 15.00
46 Derrick Brooks/99 10.00 25.00
47 Calvin Pryor/99 5.00 12.00
48 Barry Sanders/15 150.00 250.00
49 Eric Ebron/99 5.00 12.00
50 Justin Hunter/99 5.00 12.00

2015 Panini Spectra Sunday Best Jerseys

*BLUE/99-199: .5X TO 1.2X BASIC JSY/50
*BLUE/99-199: .6X TO 1.5X BASIC JSY/25
*BLUE/35-49: .5X TO 1.2X BASIC JSY/25
*GREEN/25: .6X TO 1.5X BASIC JSY/99-199
*GREEN/25: .5X TO 1.2X BASIC JSY/35-49
*GREEN/15: .6X TO 1.5X BASIC JSY/35-49
1 Aaron Rodgers/35 10.00 25.00
2 Tom Brady/49 12.00 30.00
3 Kendall Wright/199 2.50 6.00
4 Andrew Luck/99 5.00 12.00
5 Marshawn Lynch/99 3.00 8.00
6 Teddy Bridgewater/199 3.00 8.00
7 Ryan Tannehill/99 3.00 8.00
8 Alfred Morris/99 2.50 6.00
9 Philip Rivers/149 4.00 10.00
10 A.J. Green/199 4.00 10.00
11 Odell Beckham Jr./199 4.00 10.00
12 Bishop Sankey/199 2.50 6.00
13 Andre Ellington/199 2.50 6.00
14 Andy Dalton/199 3.00 8.00
15 Aqib Talib/199 2.50 6.00
16 Marqise Lee/199 2.50 6.00
17 C.J. Anderson/199 3.00 8.00
18 DeMarco Murray/199 3.00 8.00
19 Khalil Mack/199 4.00 10.00
20 DeMarcus Ware/199 3.00 8.00
21 Matthew Stafford/99 3.00 8.00
22 Denard Robinson/199 2.50 6.00
23 Devin Hester/199 3.00 8.00
24 Demaryius Thomas/199 3.00 8.00
25 Antonio Brown/199 4.00 10.00
26 Malcom Floyd/199 2.50 6.00
27 Vernon Davis/199 2.50 6.00
28 Calvin Johnson/199 4.00 10.00
29 Chris Long/199 2.50 6.00
30 Cam Newton/99 4.00 10.00
31 Dontari Poe/199 2.50 6.00
32 Elvis Dumervil/199 2.50 6.00
33 Sheldon Richardson/199 2.50 6.00
34 Travis Benjamin/199 2.50 6.00
35 Martellus Bennett/199 2.50 6.00
36 Robert Woods/199 3.00 8.00
37 Austin Seferian-Jenkins/199 2.50 6.00
38 Carson Palmer/199 3.00 8.00
39 DeMarcus Lawrence/199 2.50 6.00
40 Cameron Wake/199 3.00 8.00
41 John Kuhn/199 2.50 6.00
42 Rob Gronkowski/49 5.00 12.00
43 Kam Chancellor/199 4.00 10.00
44 J.J. Watt/35 5.00 12.00
45 Delanie Walker/199 2.50 6.00
46 Peyton Manning/99 8.00 20.00
47 Cordarrelle Patterson/199 2.50 6.00
48 Davante Adams/199 3.00 8.00
49 T.Y. Hilton/199 3.00 8.00
50 Eli Manning/99 3.00 8.00

2015 Panini Spectra Synced Swatches

*BLUE/50: .5X TO 1.2X BASIC JSY/199
*GREEN/25: .6X TO 1.5X BASIC JSY/199
1 J.Winston/M.Evans 6.00 15.00
2 A.Cooper/D.Carr 4.00 10.00
3 B.Sankey/M.Mariota 5.00 12.00
4 B.Bortles/T.Yeldon 1.25 3.00
5 D.Parker/J.Landry 2.00 5.00
6 A.Jeffery/K.White 3.00 8.00
7 T.Gurley/T.Mason 4.00 10.00
8 J.Matthews/N.Agholor 1.50 4.00
9 A.Abdullah/E.Ebron 2.00 5.00
10 D.Moncrief/P.Dorsett 1.50 4.00
11 D.Funchess/K.Benjamin 2.00 5.00
12 D.Freeman/T.Coleman 1.50 4.00
13 B.Perriman/M.Williams 1.25 3.00
14 J.Clowney/J.Strong 1.50 4.00
15 B.Cooks/G.Grayson 1.50 4.00
16 D.Johnson/T.West 2.00 5.00
17 A.Brown/S.Coates 2.00 5.00
18 D.Adams/T.Montgomery 1.50 4.00
19 B.Petty/L.Williams 4.00 10.00
20 J.Langford/K.White 3.00 8.00
21 J.Jones/J.Hardy 2.00 5.00
22 C.Hyde/M.Davis 1.25 3.00
23 M.Lee/R.Greene 1.25 3.00
24 S.Diggs/T.Bridgewater 3.00 8.00
25 J.Manziel/V.Mayle 1.50 4.00
26 A.Cooper/O.Beckham Jr. 4.00 10.00
27 J.Winston/M.Mariota 5.00 12.00
28 M.Gordon/T.Gurley 5.00 12.00
29 D.Green-Beckham/M.Mariota 5.00 12.00
30 B.Hundley/J.Winston 6.00 15.00

2015 Panini Spectra Team Trios

*BLUE/50: .5X TO 1.2X BASIC JSY/99-199
*GREEN/25: .6X TO 1.5X BASIC JSY/99-199
1 Sms/Wnstn/Evns 4.00 10.00
2 Cbb/GrnBckhm/Mrta 6.00 15.00
3 Andrsn/Ltmr/Mnng 8.00 20.00
4 Ctlr/Whte/Frte 2.00 5.00
5 Brtls/Lee/Yldn 1.50 4.00
6 Jhnsn/Mnzl/Myle 2.50 6.00
7 Mnl/Wds/Wtkns 2.00 5.00
8 Mtthws/Aghlr/Ertz 2.00 5.00
9 Lck/Mncrf/Drstt 6.00 15.00
10 Prkr/Ajyi/Tnnhll 2.50 6.00
11 Hrdy/Ryn/Clmn 2.00 5.00
12 Hndly/Adms/Mntgmry 2.00 5.00
13 Cpr/Crr/Mck 5.00 12.00
14 Mnn/Grly/Msn 6.00 15.00
15 Prrmn/Alln/Flcco 2.00 5.00

2015 Panini Spectra Vested Veterans Jersey Autographs

*BLUE/50: .5X TO 1.2X BASIC JSY AU/75-99
*BLUE/25: .6X TO 1.5X BASIC JSY AU/75-99
*BLUE/25: .5X TO 1.2X BASIC JSY AU/50
*GREEN/25: .6X TO 1.5X BASIC JSY AU/75-99
2 Antonio Gates/50 6.00 15.00
3 Terrance Williams/75 5.00 12.00
5 Victor Cruz/25
6 Marshawn Lynch/49 20.00 50.00
7 Alshon Jeffery/99 6.00 15.00
8 Matthew Stafford/15
9 Patrick Peterson/99 8.00 20.00
10 Zach Ertz/35
11 DeSean Jackson/50 8.00 20.00
12 Antonio Brown/50
13 Michael Floyd/99 5.00 12.00
14 Randall Cobb/75 8.00 20.00
15 Darren Sproles/50 8.00 20.00
16 Justin Houston/99 8.00 20.00
17 Danny Woodhead/99 10.00 25.00
19 J.J. Watt/25 40.00 80.00
20 Fred Jackson/99 6.00 15.00
21 James Laurinaitis/99 6.00 15.00
23 Robert Woods/99 6.00 15.00
24 Richard Sherman/25 40.00 80.00
25 Paul Posluszny/99 5.00 12.00

2016 Panini Spectra

1 Marvin Harrison 2.50 6.00
2 Drew Brees 3.00 8.00
3 J.J. Watt 3.00 8.00
4 Jamaal Charles 2.50 6.00
5 Larry Fitzgerald 2.50 6.00
6 Amari Cooper 3.00 8.00
7A Cris Carter 3.00 8.00
7B Cris Carter 3.00 8.00
8 Richard Sherman 3.00 8.00
9 Mark Ingram 2.50 6.00
10 Larry Csonka 2.50 6.00
11 Brian Urlacher 3.00 8.00
12 LeSean McCoy 3.00 8.00
13 Darren McFadden 2.00 5.00
14A Dez Bryant 3.00 8.00
ball in left arm
14B Dez Bryant
ball in right arm
15 Adrian Peterson 3.00 8.00
16 Ben Roethlisberger 3.00 8.00
17 Andrew Luck 4.00 10.00
18 Randall Cobb 2.50 6.00
19 Brandon Marshall 2.00 5.00
20 Blake Bortles 2.00 5.00
21A Jerome Bettis 3.00 8.00
21B Jerome Bettis 3.00 8.00
22 Alex Smith 2.50 6.00
23 Chris Ivory 2.50 6.00
24 Chris Johnson 2.00 5.00
25 John Elway 5.00 12.00
26 Marshawn Lynch 2.50 6.00
27 Thurman Thomas 2.50 6.00
28 Tony Dorsett 3.00 8.00
29 Sam Bradford 2.00 5.00
30 Julio Jones 3.00 8.00
31 John Stallworth 2.50 6.00
32 Tony Romo 2.50 6.00
33 Jonathan Stewart 2.00 5.00
34 Teddy Bridgewater 2.50 6.00
35 DeAndre Hopkins 2.50 6.00
36 Jordy Nelson 2.50 6.00
37 Josh Norman 2.00 5.00
38 T.Y. Hilton 2.50 6.00
39 Jordan Reed 2.00 5.00
40 Darrelle Revis 2.00 5.00
41 Bo Jackson 4.00 10.00
42 Carson Palmer 2.50 6.00
43 Calvin Johnson 3.00 8.00
44 Emmitt Smith 5.00 12.00
45A Eric Dickerson 2.50 6.00
45B Eric Dickerson 2.50 6.00
46 Jim Kelly 3.00 8.00
47 Mike Evans 2.50 6.00
48 Devonta Freeman 2.50 6.00
49A Shannon Sharpe 3.00 8.00
49B Shannon Sharpe 3.00 8.00
50 Von Miller 2.50 6.00
51 Bruce Smith 2.50 6.00
52 Gary Barnidge 2.00 5.00
53A James Lofton 2.50 6.00
53B James Lofton 2.50 6.00
54 Lamar Miller 2.00 5.00
55 Greg Olsen 2.50 6.00
56 Frank Gore 2.50 6.00
57 Kirk Cousins 3.00 8.00
58A Rob Gronkowski 3.00 8.00
White jsy
58B Rob Gronkowski
Blue jsy
59 Dan Marino 6.00 15.00
60 Odell Beckham Jr. 3.00 8.00
61A Jim McMahon 2.50 6.00
61B Jim McMahon 2.50 6.00
62A Joe Montana 8.00 20.00
62B Joe Montana 8.00 20.00
63 Tyrod Taylor 2.50 6.00
64A Marcus Allen 2.50 6.00
64B Marcus Allen 2.50 6.00
65 Doug Martin 2.50 6.00
66 Matt Ryan 2.50 6.00
67 Latavius Murray 2.00 5.00
68 Demaryius Thomas 2.50 6.00
69 Michael Irvin 3.00 8.00
70 Keenan Allen 2.50 6.00
71A Fran Tarkenton 3.00 8.00
71B Fran Tarkenton 3.00 8.00
72 Matt Forte 2.00 5.00
73 Doug Baldwin 2.50 6.00
74 Cam Newton 3.00 8.00
75 Jarvis Landry 2.50 6.00
76A Tom Brady 8.00 20.00
running
76B Tom Brady
throwing
77 A.J. Green 3.00 8.00
78 Eli Manning 2.50 6.00
79 Joe Namath 4.00 10.00
80 Joe Flacco 2.50 6.00
81A Doug Flutie 2.50 6.00
81B Doug Flutie 2.50 6.00
82 Franco Harris 3.00 8.00
83 Eric Decker 2.00 5.00
84 Jameis Winston 3.00 8.00
85 Derek Carr 3.00 8.00
86A Peyton Manning 6.00 15.00
86B Peyton Manning 6.00 15.00
87 Jeremy Hill 2.00 5.00
88 Antonio Gates 2.00 5.00
89 Barry Sanders 5.00 12.00
90 Colin Kaepernick 2.50 6.00
91 Tim Brown 3.00 8.00
92 Marcus Mariota 3.00 8.00
93 Ted Ginn Jr. 2.00 5.00
94 Ryan Tannehill 2.50 6.00
95 Andy Dalton 2.50 6.00
96 DeMarco Murray 2.50 6.00
97 Travis Kelce 3.00 8.00
98 Antonio Brown 3.00 8.00
99 Troy Aikman 4.00 10.00
100 Jay Cutler 2.00 5.00
101 Gale Sayers 3.00 8.00
102 Brandin Cooks 2.50 6.00
103 Tyler Lockett 2.50 6.00
104 Jeremy Maclin 2.00 5.00
105 Russell Wilson 4.00 10.00
106 Philip Rivers 3.00 8.00
107 Alshon Jeffery 2.50 6.00
108 Todd Gurley 3.00 8.00
109 Roger Staubach 4.00 10.00
110A Edgerrin James 2.50 6.00
110B Edgerrin James 2.50 6.00
111 Warren Sapp 2.50 6.00
112 Sammy Watkins 3.00 8.00
113 Stefon Diggs 2.50 6.00
114 Jason Witten 2.50 6.00
115 Aaron Rodgers 6.00 15.00
116 Le'Veon Bell 2.50 6.00
117 Allen Hurns 2.00 5.00
118 Matthew Stafford 2.50 6.00
119A Marshall Faulk 2.50 6.00
119B Marshall Faulk 2.50 6.00
120 Allen Robinson 2.50 6.00
121 Braxton Miller RC 1.00 2.50
122 Jacoby Brissett RC 1.25 3.00
123 Temarrick Hemingway RC 1.00 2.50
124 Jarran Reed RC 1.00 2.50
125 Leonte Carroo RC 1.00 2.50
126 Rico Gathers RC 1.00 2.50

127 Chris Jones RC 1.00 2.50
128 Corey Coleman RC 1.50 4.00
129 C.J. Prosise RC 1.00 2.50
130 Jakeem Grant RC 1.00 2.50
131 William Jackson III RC 1.25 3.00
132 Vonn Bell RC 1.25 3.00
133 Will Fuller RC 1.50 4.00
134 Paxton Lynch RC 1.00 2.50
135 A'Shawn Robinson RC 1.00 2.50
136 Seth DeValve RC 1.25 3.00
137 Josh Doctson RC 1.25 3.00
138 Hunter Henry RC 1.25 3.00
139 Artie Burns RC 1.25 3.00
140 Laquon Treadwell RC 1.25 3.00
141 Tyler Boyd RC 1.25 3.00
142 Cyrus Jones RC 1.00 2.50
143 Jake Rudock RC 1.00 2.50
144 Sheldon Rankins RC 1.25 3.00
145 Robert Nkemdiche RC 1.25 3.00
146 Karl Joseph RC 1.00 2.50
147 Jihad Ward RC 1.00 2.50
148 Mike Thomas RC 1.50 4.00
149 Mackensie Alexander RC 1.00 2.50
150 Vernon Butler RC 1.00 2.50
151 Moritz Bohringer RC 1.00 2.50
152 Tyreek Hill RC 4.00 10.00
153 Sterling Shepard RC 1.25 3.00
154 Christian Hackenberg RC 1.00 2.50
155 Kenny Clark RC 1.00 2.50
156 Keenan Reynolds RC 1.25 3.00
157 Derrick Henry RC 2.50 6.00
158 Kenyan Drake RC 1.50 4.00
159 Xavien Howard RC 1.25 3.00
160 Michael Thomas RC 2.00 5.00
161 Jared Goff RC 6.00 15.00
162 Ezekiel Elliott RC 5.00 12.00
163 Austin Johnson RC 1.00 2.50
164 Cody Kessler RC 1.00 2.50
165 Carson Wentz RC 10.00 25.00
166 David Morgan RC 1.50 4.00
167 Keanu Neal RC 1.00 2.50
168 Emmanuel Ogbah RC 1.25 3.00
169 Joey Bosa RC 2.00 5.00
170 Darius Jackson RC 1.25 3.00
171 Jared Goff JSY AU RC 60.00 125.00
172 Carson Wentz JSY AU RC 100.00 200.00
173 Joey Bosa JSY AU RC 8.00 20.00
174 Ezekiel Elliott JSY AU RC 100.00 200.00
175 Corey Coleman JSY AU RC EXCH 6.00 15.00
176 Will Fuller JSY AU RC 12.00 30.00
177 Josh Doctson JSY AU RC 5.00 12.00
178 Laquon Treadwell JSY AU RC 25.00 50.00
179 Paxton Lynch JSY AU RC 4.00 10.00
180 Hunter Henry JSY AU RC EXCH 5.00 12.00
181 Sterling Shepard JSY AU RC 10.00 25.00
182 Derrick Henry JSY AU RC 10.00 25.00
183 Michael Thomas JSY AU RC 8.00 20.00
184 Christian Hackenberg JSY AU RC 4.00 10.00
185 Kenyan Drake JSY AU RC 6.00 15.00
186 Braxton Miller JSY AU RC 4.00 10.00
187 Leonte Carroo JSY AU RC 4.00 10.00
188 C.J. Prosise JSY AU RC 4.00 10.00
189 DeAndre Washington JSY AU RC 4.00 10.00
190 Cody Kessler JSY AU RC 12.00 30.00
191 Tyler Boyd JSY AU RC 12.00 30.00
192 Connor Cook JSY AU RC 5.00 12.00
193 Chris Moore JSY AU RC 5.00 12.00
194 Ricardo Louis JSY AU RC 4.00 10.00
195 Pharoh Cooper JSY AU RC 4.00 10.00
196 Tyler Ervin JSY AU RC 4.00 10.00
197 Demarcus Robinson JSY AU RC 4.00 10.00
198 Kenneth Dixon JSY AU RC 4.00 10.00
199 Dak Prescott JSY AU RC 50.00 100.00
200 Devontae Booker JSY AU RC 5.00 12.00
201 Cardale Jones JSY AU RC 4.00 10.00
202 Paul Perkins JSY AU RC 4.00 10.00
203 Jordan Howard JSY AU RC 12.00 30.00
204 Wendell Smallwood JSY AU RC 4.00 10.00
205 Jonathan Williams JSY AU RC 5.00 12.00
206 Kevin Hogan JSY AU RC 5.00 12.00
207 Trevor Davis JSY AU RC 4.00 10.00
208 Alex Collins JSY AU RC 5.00 12.00
209 Keenan Reynolds JSY AU RC 5.00 12.00
210 Moritz Bohringer JSY AU RC 4.00 10.00
211 Kelvin Taylor AU RC 2.50 6.00
212 Rashard Higgins AU RC 2.50 6.00
213 Aaron Burbridge AU RC 2.50 6.00
214 Kenny Lawler AU RC 4.00 10.00
215 Austin Hooper AU RC 2.50 6.00
216 Nick Vannett AU RC 2.50 6.00
217 Jerell Adams AU RC 2.50 6.00
218 Nate Sudfeld AU RC 2.50 6.00
219 Brandon Allen AU RC 2.50 6.00
220 Brandon Doughty AU RC 2.50 6.00
221 Malcolm Mitchell AU RC 2.50 6.00
222 Jordan Payton AU RC 2.50 6.00
223 KeiVarae Russell AU RC 2.50 6.00
224 Cody Core AU RC 2.50 6.00
225 Daniel Braverman AU RC 2.50 6.00
226 Thomas Duarte AU RC 2.50 6.00
227 Daniel Lasco AU RC 2.50 6.00
228 Tyler Higbee AU RC 2.50 6.00
229 Tajae Sharpe AU RC 6.00 15.00
230 Charone Peake AU RC 2.50 6.00
231 Keith Marshall AU RC 2.50 6.00
232 Demarcus Ayers AU RC 2.50 6.00
233 Derek Watt AU RC 4.00 10.00
234 Jalen Ramsey AU RC 4.00 10.00
235 Vernon Hargreaves III AU RC 4.00 10.00
236 DeForest Buckner AU RC 2.50 6.00
237 Shaq Lawson AU RC 2.50 6.00
238 Rico Gathers AU RC 2.50 6.00
239 Eli Apple AU RC 3.00 8.00
240 William Jackson III AU RC 3.00 8.00

2016 Panini Spectra Neon Blue

*1-120 VETS/60: .5X TO 1.2X BASIC CARDS/99
*121-170 ROOKIES/60: 1X TO 2.5X BASIC RC/99
*171-210 ROOK.JSY AU/60: .5X TO 1.2X BASIC RC/99
*211-240 ROOK.AU/99: .5X TO 1.2X BASIC RC/199
172 Carson Wentz JSY AU 150.00 300.00
174 Ezekiel Elliott JSY AU 125.00 250.00

2016 Panini Spectra Aspiring Patch Autographs

*BLUE/35-60: .5X TO 1.2X BASIC JSY AU/99-199
*BLUE/25: .5X TO 1.2X BASIC JSY AU/35
1 Jared Goff/35 50.00 100.00
2 Joey Bosa/99 8.00 20.00
3 Corey Coleman/35 8.00 20.00
4 Laquon Treadwell/35 30.00 60.00
5 Paxton Lynch/35 5.00 12.00
6 Sterling Shepard/199 12.00 30.00
7 Michael Thomas/35 10.00 25.00
8 Kenyan Drake/199 6.00 15.00
9 Leonte Carroo/199 4.00 10.00
10 DeAndre Washington/199 4.00 10.00
11 Tyler Boyd/99 12.00 30.00
12 Chris Moore/199 5.00 12.00
13 Ricardo Louis/199 4.00 10.00
14 Tyler Ervin/199 4.00 10.00
15 Kenneth Dixon/199 4.00 10.00
16 Devontae Booker/199 5.00 12.00
17 Paul Perkins/99 4.00 10.00
18 Wendell Smallwood/199 4.00 10.00
19 Kevin Hogan/199 5.00 12.00
20 Alex Collins/99 5.00 12.00

2016 Panini Spectra Catalyst Jerseys

*BLUE/99: .4X TO 1X BASIC JSY/199
*BLUE/35. .4X TO 1X BASIC JSY/49
*BLUE/25: .5X TO 1.2X BASIC JSY/35
*BLUE/15: .5X TO 1.2X BASIC JSY/25
*GREEN/25: .6X TO 1.5X BASIC JSY/199
1 Jeremy Maclin/199 2.50 6.00
2 Joe Flacco/35 4.00 10.00
3 Andy Dalton/99 [illegible]
4 Julio Jones/35 5.00 12.00
5 Brian Urlacher/49 5.00 12.00
6 Odell Beckham Jr./199 4.00 10.00
7 Derek Carr/199 4.00 10.00
8 Drew Brees/15 8.00 20.00
10 Jameis Winston/199 4.00 10.00
11 Amari Cooper/199 4.00 10.00
13 Barry Sanders/25 10.00 25.00
14 Matthew Stafford/49 4.00 10.00
15 Dan Marino/49 10.00 25.00
16 Peyton Manning/199 8.00 20.00
17 Devonta Freeman/199 3.00 8.00
18 Eli Manning/49 4.00 10.00
20 Marcus Mariota/199 4.00 10.00

2016 Panini Spectra City 2 City Jerseys

*BLUE/99: .4X TO 1X BASIC JSY/199
*BLUE/60: .5X TO 1.2X BASIC JSY/99
*BLUE/35: .4X TO 1X BASIC JSY/49
*BLUE/25: .5X TO 1.2X BASIC JSY/35
*BLUE/15: .5X TO 1.2X BASIC JSY/25
*GREEN/25: .6X TO 1.5X BASIC JSY/99-199
*GREEN/25: .5X TO 1.2X BASIC JSY/49
*GREEN/15: .6X TO 1.5X BASIC JSY/49
2 Owen Daniels/199 2.50 6.00
3 DeMarcus Ware/99 3.00 8.00
4 Ryan Mathews/49 4.00 10.00
5 Emmanuel Sanders/35 5.00 12.00
6 Jimmy Graham/35 5.00 12.00
7 Anquan Boldin/199 2.50 6.00
8 Jordan Cameron/199 2.50 6.00
9 Brett Favre/25 12.00 30.00
10 LaDainian Tomlinson/49 4.00 10.00
11 Darren McFadden/99 2.50 6.00
12 Percy Harvin/49 3.00 8.00
13 DeSean Jackson/199 3.00 8.00
14 Steve Johnson/199 3.00 8.00
15 Eric Decker/35 3.00 8.00
16 Joe Montana/25 15.00 40.00
17 Brandon Marshall/99 2.50 6.00
18 Julius Thomas/99 2.50 6.00
19 Carson Palmer/49 4.00 10.00
20 LeSean McCoy/49 5.00 12.00
21 Greg Jennings/99 2.50 6.00
22 Ronnie Lott/49 4.00 10.00
23 Elvis Dumervil/99 2.50 6.00
24 Toby Gerhart/199 2.50 6.00
25 Eric Dickerson/49 4.00 10.00

2016 Panini Spectra Epic Legends Materials

*BLUE/60: .6X TO 1.5X BASIC JSY/199
*BLUE/49-60: .5X TO 1.2X BASIC JSY/99
*BLUE/35: .4X TO 1X BASIC JSY/49
*BLUE/25: .5X TO 1.2X BASIC JSY/49
*BLUE/15: .5X TO 1.2X BASIC JSY/25
*GREEN/25: .6X TO 1.5X BASIC JSY/99
1 Bo Jackson/99 6.00 15.00
2 Roger Staubach/15 12.00 30.00
3 Jerry Rice/25 12.00 30.00
4 Tim Tebow/99 5.00 12.00
5 Marshall Faulk/49 5.00 12.00
6 Earl Campbell/49 6.00 15.00
7 Ricky Williams/99 4.00 10.00
8 Jim Kelly/49 6.00 15.00
9 Tom Landry/199 12.00 30.00
11 Rod Woodson/49 5.00 12.00
12 John Elway/25 12.00 30.00
13 Joe Montana/25 20.00 50.00
14 Don Majkowski/199 3.00 8.00
15 Joe Theismann/17
16 Larry Csonka/25 6.00 15.00
17 Brett Favre/25 15.00 40.00
18 Brian Urlacher/99 5.00 12.00
19 Joe Namath/25 10.00 25.00
20 Ozzie Newsome/99 4.00 10.00

2016 Panini Spectra Illustrious Legends Autographs

*BLUE/50: X TO X BASIC AU/99
*GREEN/25: .6X TO 1.5X BASIC AU/99
*GREEN/25: .5X TO 1.2X BASIC AU/49
2 Marcus Allen/25 20.00 50.00
6 Ricky Williams/99 12.00 30.00
7 Joe Greene/25 25.00 60.00
8 Steve Young/15
9 Doug Flutie/99 12.00 30.00
10 Joe Theismann/49 20.00 50.00
11 Franco Harris/25
12 Tony Dorsett/15 30.00 80.00
14 Jim Kelly/15
15 Larry Csonka/15
16 Bo Jackson/25 40.00 80.00
17 Dallas Clark/99 10.00 25.00
19 LaDainian Tomlinson/25 20.00 50.00
20 Rod Smith/49 15.00 40.00
21 Darrell Green/49 15.00 40.00
23 Eric Dickerson/25 20.00 50.00
24 Andre Reed/99 12.00 30.00
25 Gale Sayers/49 20.00 50.00

2016 Panini Spectra Immense Materials

*BLUE/99: .4X TO 1X BASIC JSY/99-199
*BLUE/49-60: .5X TO 1.2X BASIC JSY/99-199
*BLUE/35: .4X TO 1X BASIC JSY/49
*GREEN/25: .5X TO 1.5X BASIC JSY/99-199
1 Jared Goff/199 10.00 25.00
2 Amari Cooper/199 4.00 10.00
3 Andy Dalton/99 3.00 8.00
4 Brian Urlacher/49 5.00 12.00
5 Carlos Hyde/199 2.50 6.00
6 Carson Wentz/199 15.00 40.00
7 Derek Carr/199 4.00 10.00
8 Devonta Freeman/199 3.00 8.00
9 Dorial Green-Beckham/199 2.50 6.00
10 Eric Berry/99 3.00 8.00
11 Derrick Henry/199 4.00 10.00
12 Jarvis Landry/199 3.00 8.00
13 Jeremy Hill/199 2.50 6.00
14 Joe Haden/99 2.50 6.00
15 Ezekiel Elliott/199 8.00 20.00
16 Julius Thomas/99 2.50 6.00
17 Karlos Williams/199 2.50 6.00
18 Kevin White/199 2.50 6.00
19 Marcus Mariota/199 4.00 10.00
20 Melvin Gordon/199 3.00 8.00
21 Nelson Agholor/199 2.50 6.00
22 Jordan Matthews/199 3.00 8.00
23 Paxton Lynch/199 1.50 4.00
24 T.Y. Hilton/99 3.00 8.00
25 Vontaze Burfict/199 2.50 6.00

2016 Panini Spectra Monumental Memorabilia

*BLUE/99: .4X TO 1X BASIC JSY/199
*BLUE/49-60: .5X TO 1.2X BASIC JSY/99
*BLUE/25: .6X TO 1.5X BASIC JSY/99-199
1 Cardale Jones/199 1.50 4.00
2 Allen Robinson/199 3.00 8.00
3 Ameer Abdullah/199 2.50 6.00
4 Blake Bortles/99 2.50 6.00
5 Buck Allen/199 2.50 6.00
6 Davante Adams/199 2.50 6.00
7 Connor Cook/199 2.00 5.00
8 Alex Collins/199 2.00 5.00
9 Donte Moncrief/199 3.00 8.00
10 Duke Johnson/199 2.50 6.00
11 Jadeveon Clowney/199 2.50 6.00
12 Jameis Winston/199 4.00 10.00
13 Jay Ajayi/199 3.00 8.00
14 Jeremy Langford/199 3.00 8.00
15 Jordan Matthews/199 3.00 8.00
16 Joe Haden/99 2.50 6.00
17 C.J. Prosise/199 1.50 4.00
18 Kelvin Benjamin/199 3.00 8.00
19 Cameron Wake/199 2.50 6.00
20 Khalil Mack/199 4.00 10.00
21 Marqise Lee/199 2.50 6.00
22 Mike Evans/140 3.00 8.00
23 Phillip Dorsett/199 2.50 6.00
24 T.J. Yeldon/199 2.50 6.00
25 Todd Gurley/199 4.00 10.00
26 Jared Goff/199 10.00 25.00
27 Carson Wentz/199 15.00 40.00
28 Paxton Lynch/199 1.50 4.00
29 Ezekiel Elliott/199 8.00 20.00
30 Corey Coleman/199 2.50 6.00
31 Will Fuller/199 2.50 6.00
32 Josh Doctson/199 2.00 5.00
33 Laquon Treadwell/199 2.00 5.00
34 Joey Bosa/199 3.00 8.00
35 Hunter Henry/199 2.00 5.00
36 Sterling Shepard/199 2.00 5.00
37 Derrick Henry/199 6.00 15.00
38 Michael Thomas/199 3.00 8.00
39 Christian Hackenberg/199 1.50 4.00
40 Kenyan Drake/199 2.50 6.00

2016 Panini Spectra Next Era Jerseys

*BLUE/99: .4X TO 1X BASIC JSY/199
*GREEN/25: .6X TO 1.5X BASIC JSY/199
1 Jared Goff 10.00 25.00
2 Carson Wentz 15.00 40.00
3 Joey Bosa 3.00 8.00
4 Ezekiel Elliott 8.00 20.00
5 Corey Coleman 2.50 6.00
6 Will Fuller 2.50 6.00
7 Josh Doctson 2.00 5.00
8 Laquon Treadwell 2.00 5.00
9 Paxton Lynch 1.50 4.00
10 Derrick Henry 4.00 10.00

2016 Panini Spectra Radiant Rookie Patch Signatures

1 Ezekiel Elliott/35 100.00 200.00
2 Carson Wentz/35 100.00 200.00
3 Will Fuller/35 8.00 20.00
4 Josh Doctson/35 6.00 15.00
5 Hunter Henry/199 5.00 12.00
6 Derrick Henry/35 12.00 30.00
7 Christian Hackenberg/35 5.00 12.00
8 Braxton Miller/99 4.00 10.00
9 C.J. Prosise/99 4.00 10.00
10 Cody Kessler/99 4.00 10.00
11 Connor Cook/35 6.00 15.00
12 Moritz Bohringer/199 4.00 10.00
13 Pharoh Cooper/199 4.00 10.00
14 Demarcus Robinson/199 4.00 10.00
15 Dak Prescott/199 50.00 100.00
16 Cardale Jones/35 5.00 12.00
17 Jordan Howard/199 10.00 25.00
18 Jonathan Williams/199 5.00 12.00
19 Trevor Davis/199 4.00 10.00
20 Keenan Reynolds/199 5.00 12.00

2016 Panini Spectra Radiant Rookie Patch Signatures Neon Blue

*BLUE/35-60: .5X TO 1.2X BASIC JSY AU/99-199
*BLUE/25: .5X TO 1.2X BASIC JSY AU/35
2 Carson Wentz/25 150.00 250.00
15 Dak Prescott/60 50.00 125.00

2016 Panini Spectra Radiant Rookie Patch Signatures Neon Green

*GREEN/25: .8X TO 2X BASIC JSY AU/199
*GREEN/25: .6X TO 1.5X BASIC JSY AU/99
*GREEN/15: .6X TO 1.5X BASIC JSY AU/35
2 Carson Wentz/15 150.00 300.00

2016 Panini Spectra Rising Rookie Materials

*BLUE/99: .5X TO 1.2X BASIC JSY/199
*GREEN/25: .6X TO 1.5X BASIC JSY/199
1 Jared Goff 10.00 25.00
2 Carson Wentz 15.00 40.00
3 Joey Bosa 3.00 8.00
4 Ezekiel Elliott 8.00 20.00
5 Corey Coleman 2.50 6.00
6 Will Fuller 2.50 6.00
7 Josh Doctson 2.00 5.00
8 Laquon Treadwell 2.00 5.00
9 Paxton Lynch 1.50 4.00
10 Hunter Henry 2.00 5.00
11 Sterling Shepard 2.00 5.00
12 Derrick Henry 6.00 15.00
13 Michael Thomas 3.00 8.00
14 Christian Hackenberg 1.50 4.00
15 Kenyan Drake 2.50 6.00
16 Braxton Miller 1.50 4.00
17 Leonte Carroo 1.50 4.00
18 C.J. Prosise 1.50 4.00
19 Moritz Bohringer 1.50 4.00
20 Cody Kessler 1.50 4.00
21 Tyler Boyd 2.00 5.00
22 Connor Cook 2.00 5.00
23 Chris Moore 2.00 5.00
24 Kenneth Dixon 1.50 4.00
25 Dak Prescott 8.00 20.00
26 Cardale Jones 1.50 4.00
27 Keenan Reynolds 2.00 5.00
28 Kevin Hogan 2.00 5.00
29 Ricardo Louis 1.50 4.00
30 Paul Perkins 1.50 4.00

2016 Panini Spectra Rookie Dual Patch Autographs

1 J.Goff/C.Wentz 125.00 250.00
2 D.Henry/E.Elliott 75.00 150.00
3 D.Henry/K.Drake 15.00 40.00
4 A.Collins/J.Williams 8.00 20.00
5 J.Goff/T.Davis 50.00 100.00
6 W.Fuller/C.Prosise 10.00 25.00
7 E.Elliott/J.Bosa 75.00 150.00
8 B.Miller/C.Jones 6.00 15.00
9 K.Dixon/K.Reynolds 8.00 20.00
10 C.Jones/J.Williams 8.00 20.00
11 T.Boyd/C.Coleman 10.00 25.00
12 D.Prescott/E.Elliott
13 P.Lynch/D.Booker 8.00 20.00
14 B.Miller/W.Fuller 10.00 25.00
15 K.Drake/L.Carroo 10.00 25.00
16 D.Robinson/K.Hogan 8.00 20.00
17 D.Washington/C.Cook 8.00 20.00
18 P.Perkins/S.Shepard 8.00 20.00
19 A.Collins/C.Prosise 8.00 20.00
20 J.Goff/P.Cooper 50.00 100.00

2016 Panini Spectra Rookie Dual Patch Autographs Neon Blue

*BLUE/15: .5X TO 1.2X BASIC JSY AU/25
7 Ezekiel Elliott 125.00 250.00
Joey Bosa
12 Dak Prescott 300.00 600.00
Ezekiel Elliott

2016 Panini Spectra Signatures

*BLUE/50: .5X TO 1.2X BASIC AU/99
*BLUE/25: .5X TO 1.2X BASIC AU/49
*BLUE/15: .5X TO 1.2X BASIC AU/25
1 Tim Brown/49 15.00 40.00
2 Len Dawson/49 10.00 25.00
3 Kurt Warner/25 10.00 25.00
6 Wes Welker/25 10.00 25.00
7 Tyler Lockett/99 6.00 15.00
8 Ameer Abdullah/99 5.00 12.00
9 Robert Mathis/99 5.00 12.00
10 Victor Cruz/49 8.00 20.00
11 Latavius Murray/99 5.00 12.00
12 Eric Ebron/99 5.00 12.00
13 Fred Biletnikoff/49 12.00 30.00
14 Donald Driver/49 8.00 20.00
15 Robert Brooks/99 6.00 15.00
16 Joe Theismann/49 10.00 25.00
17 Michael Strahan/25 15.00 40.00
18 Dan Hampton/99 5.00 12.00
19 Torrey Smith/99 5.00 12.00
20 Jay Cutler/25 8.00 20.00
21 Harold Carmichael/99 5.00 12.00
22 Trent Dilfer/99 5.00 12.00
23 Ricky Sanders/99 5.00 12.00
24 Charles Mann/99 5.00 12.00
25 Charles Sims/99 5.00 12.00
26 Stefon Diggs/99 6.00 15.00
27 Derek Carr/49 15.00 40.00
28 Knile Davis/99 5.00 12.00
29 Brian Urlacher/25 40.00 00.00
30 Melvin Gordon/49 8.00 20.00
31 Torry Holt/99 6.00 15.00
32 David Carr/99 5.00 12.00
33 Marcus Peters/99 5.00 12.00
34 Sammy Watkins/49 10.00 25.00
35 Emmanuel Sanders/99 8.00 20.00
36 Brian Mitchell/99 5.00 12.00
37 Kwon Alexander/99 5.00 12.00
38 Ronald Darby/99 5.00 12.00
40 B.J. Raji/99 5.00 12.00
41 Von Miller/49 8.00 20.00
42 Buck Allen/99 5.00 12.00
43 Larry Csonka/25 10.00 25.00
44 Mark Chmura/99 5.00 12.00
45 Jay Ajayi/99 6.00 15.00
46 Vincent Jackson/49 6.00 15.00
47 Devin Hester/49 8.00 20.00
49 Andy Dalton/49 8.00 20.00
50 Kelvin Benjamin/99 6.00 15.00

2016 Panini Spectra Sunday Spectacle Jerseys

*BLUE/99: .4X TO 1X BASIC JSY/199
*BLUE/49-60: .5X TO 1.2X BASIC JSY/99
*BLUE/35: .4X TO 1X BASIC JSY/49
*BLUE/25: .5X TO 1.2X BASIC JSY/49
*GREEN/25: .6X TO 1.5X BASIC JSY/99-199
*GREEN/25: .5X TO 1.2X BASIC JSY/49
1 Rob Gronkowski/15 8.00 20.00
2 Devonta Freeman/199 3.00 8.00
3 T.Y. Hilton/199 3.00 8.00
4 Jadeveon Clowney/199 2.50 6.00
5 Jeremy Hill/199 2.50 6.00
6 A.J. Green/99 4.00 10.00
7 Karlos Williams/199 2.50 6.00
8 Amari Cooper/199 4.00 10.00
9 Marcus Mariota/199 4.00 10.00
10 Buck Allen/199 2.50 6.00
11 Russell Wilson/15 10.00 25.00
12 Donte Moncrief/199 3.00 8.00
13 Teddy Bridgewater/199 3.00 8.00
14 Jamaal Charles/49 4.00 10.00
15 Jeremy Langford/199 3.00 8.00
17 Kelvin Benjamin/199 3.00 8.00
18 Ameer Abdullah/199 2.50 6.00
19 Melvin Gordon/199 3.00 8.00
20 Carlos Hyde/199 2.50 6.00
21 Jason Witten/199 3.00 8.00
22 Dorial Green-Beckham/199 2.50 6.00
23 Todd Gurley/199 4.00 10.00
24 Jameis Winston/199 4.00 10.00
25 Joe Haden/199 2.50 6.00
26 Adrian Peterson/49 5.00 12.00
27 Kevin White/199 2.50 6.00
28 Jeremy Maclin/199 2.50 6.00
29 Mike Evans/199 3.00 8.00
30 Davante Adams/199 2.50 6.00
31 Stefon Diggs/199 3.00 8.00
32 Duke Johnson/199 2.50 6.00
33 Tyler Lockett/199 3.00 8.00
34 Jamison Crowder/199 2.50 6.00
35 Jordan Matthews/199 3.00 8.00
36 Allen Hurns/99 2.50 6.00
37 Khalil Mack/199 4.00 10.00
38 Antonio Gates/49 3.00 8.00
39 Paul Posluszny/199 2.50 6.00
40 Derek Carr/199 4.00 10.00
41 T.J. Yeldon/199 2.50 6.00
42 Eric Berry/199 3.00 8.00
43 Wes Welker/199 3.00 8.00
44 Jarvis Landry/199 3.00 8.00
45 Julius Thomas/99 2.50 6.00
46 Allen Robinson/199 3.00 8.00
47 LeSean McCoy/49 5.00 12.00
48 Blake Bortles/199 2.50 6.00
49 Phillip Dorsett/199 2.50 6.00
50 Devin Funchess/199 2.50 6.00

2016 Panini Spectra Synced Swatches

1 D.Freeman/M.Ryan/49 4.00 10.00
2 B.Allen/J.Flacco/49 4.00 10.00
3 L.McCoy/S.Watkins/49 5.00 12.00
4 D.Funchess/K.Benjamin/199 3.00 8.00
5 J.Langford/K.White/199 3.00 8.00
6 A.Green/A.Dalton/49 5.00 12.00
7 V.Burfict/G.Atkins/199 2.50 6.00
8 G.Bernard/J.Hill/199 2.50 6.00
9 A.Rodgers/R.Cobb/10
10 D.Moncrief/P.Dorsett/199 3.00 8.00
11 A.Luck/T.Hilton/49 6.00 15.00
12 A.Hurns/A.Robinson/199 3.00 8.00
13 B.Bortles/J.Thomas/99 2.50 6.00
14 D.Johnson/J.Houston/99 2.50 6.00
15 S.Diggs/T.Brdgwtr/199 3.00 8.00
16 T.Brady/R.Grnkwski/10
17 R.Wilson/T.Lockett/199 5.00 12.00
18 J.Winston/M.Evans/199 4.00 10.00
19 D.GrnBckhm/M.Mariota/199 4.00 10.00
20 D.Jackson/K.Cousins/49 5.00 12.00
21 J.Goff/T.Gurley/199 8.00 20.00
22 E.Elliott/T.Romo/199 8.00 20.00
23 T.Brdgwtr/L.Treadwell/199 2.00 5.00
24 D.Jackson/J.Doctson/99 2.00 5.00
25 J.Bosa/M.Te'o/49 4.00 10.00
26 C.Wentz/J.Matthews/199 15.00 40.00
27 C.Kessler/C.Coleman/199 2.50 6.00
28 B.Miller/W.Fuller/199 2.50 6.00
29 K.Drake/L.Carroo/199 2.50 6.00
30 H.Henry/Joey Bosa/199 3.00 8.00

2016 Panini Spectra Vested Veterans Jersey Autographs

1 Blake Bortles/25
2 Derek Carr/49 15.00 40.00
3 Richard Sherman/25 25.00 50.00
4 Demaryius Thomas/49 8.00 20.00
5 Alex Smith/49 8.00 20.00
6 Jason Witten/49 25.00 60.00
10 Greg Olsen/30 10.00 25.00
11 Matthew Stafford/25 20.00 50.00
12 Heath Miller/75 12.00 30.00
13 Darren Sproles/99 6.00 15.00
14 Julius Thomas/99 5.00 12.00
15 Danny Woodhead/99 6.00 15.00
16 Vincent Jackson/75 5.00 12.00
17 Jordy Nelson/75 15.00 40.00
18 Doug Martin/75 6.00 15.00
19 Eddie Lacy/75 5.00 12.00
20 Jeremy Maclin/49 6.00 15.00
21 DeAngelo Williams/15 12.00 30.00
22 DeMarcus Ware/49 8.00 20.00
23 Anquan Boldin/49 6.00 15.00
24 Philip Rivers/25 15.00 40.00
25 Antonio Brown/49 30.00 60.00

2016 Panini Spectra Vested Veterans Jersey Autographs Blue

*BLUE/35-50: .5X TO 1.2X BASIC JSY AU/75-99
*BLUE/20-25: .5X TO 1.2X BASIC JSY AU/49
25 Antonio Brown/25 40.00 100.00

2017 Panini Spectra

1 Ezekiel Elliott 4.00 10.00
2 Dak Prescott 3.00 8.00
3 Cole Beasley 3.00 8.00
4 Dez Bryant 3.00 8.00
5 Eli Manning 2.50 6.00
6 Odell Beckham Jr. 3.00 8.00
7 Brandon Marshall 2.00 5.00
8 Sterling Shepard 2.50 6.00
9 Carson Wentz 4.00 10.00
10 Alshon Jeffery 2.50 6.00
11 Jordan Matthews 2.00 5.00
12 Zach Ertz 2.50 6.00
13 Kirk Cousins 3.00 8.00
14 Robert Kelley 2.00 5.00
15 Jamison Crowder 2.00 5.00
16A John Riggins 2.50 6.00
16B John Riggins 2.50 6.00
17 Carson Palmer 2.50 6.00
18 David Johnson 3.00 8.00
19 Larry Fitzgerald 2.50 6.00
20 Patrick Peterson 2.00 5.00
21 Jared Goff 3.00 8.00
22 Todd Gurley II 3.00 8.00
23 Robert Woods 2.50 6.00
24A Kurt Warner 2.50 6.00
24B Kurt Warner 2.50 6.00
25 Carlos Hyde 2.00 5.00
26 Pierre Garcon 2.50 6.00
27A Steve Young 4.00 10.00
27B Steve Young 4.00 10.00
28 Russell Wilson 4.00 10.00
29 Thomas Rawls 2.00 5.00
30 Michael Bennett 2.00 5.00
31 Richard Sherman 3.00 8.00
32 Mike Glennon 2.50 6.00
33 Jordan Howard 3.00 8.00
34 Kevin White 2.00 5.00
35 Matthew Stafford 2.50 6.00
36 Ameer Abdullah 2.00 5.00
37 Golden Tate III 2.00 5.00
38 Aaron Rodgers 6.00 15.00
39 Ty Montgomery 2.00 5.00
40 Davante Adams 2.50 6.00
41A Brett Favre 6.00 15.00
41B Brett Favre 6.00 15.00
42 Sam Bradford 2.00 5.00
43 Stefon Diggs 2.50 6.00
44 Laquon Treadwell 2.00 5.00
45A Randy Moss 2.50 6.00
45B Randy Moss 2.50 6.00
46 Matt Ryan 2.50 6.00
47 Devonta Freeman 2.50 6.00
48 Julio Jones 3.00 8.00
49A Deion Sanders 2.50 6.00
49B Deion Sanders 2.50 6.00
50 Cam Newton 3.00 8.00
51 Jonathan Stewart 2.00 5.00
52 Kelvin Benjamin 2.50 6.00
53 Julius Peppers 2.50 6.00
54 Drew Brees 3.00 8.00
55 Mark Ingram 2.50 6.00
56 Michael Thomas 3.00 8.00
57 Willie Snead 2.50 6.00
58 Jameis Winston 2.50 6.00
59 Mike Evans 2.50 6.00
60 DeSean Jackson 2.50 6.00
61 Tyrod Taylor 2.50 6.00
62 LeSean McCoy 3.00 8.00
63 Sammy Watkins 3.00 8.00
64A Thurman Thomas 2.50 6.00
64B Thurman Thomas 2.50 6.00
65 Ryan Tannehill 2.50 6.00
66 Jay Ajayi 2.50 6.00
67 Jarvis Landry 2.50 6.00
68A Ricky Williams 2.50 6.00
68B Ricky Williams 2.50 6.00
69 Tom Brady 8.00 20.00
70 James White 2.50 6.00
71 Brandin Cooks 2.50 6.00
72 Rob Gronkowski 3.00 8.00
73 Julian Edelman 3.00 8.00
74 Matt Forte 2.00 5.00
75 Muhammad Wilkerson 2.00 5.00
76A LaDainian Tomlinson 2.50 6.00
76B LaDainian Tomlinson 2.50 6.00
77 Paxton Lynch 2.00 5.00
78 Trevor Siemian 2.00 5.00
79 C.J. Anderson 2.50 6.00
80 Demaryius Thomas 2.50 6.00
81A Ed McCaffrey 2.00 5.00
81B Ed McCaffrey 2.00 5.00
82 Alex Smith 2.50 6.00
83 Tyreek Hill 3.00 8.00
84 Jeremy Maclin 2.00 5.00
85A Priest Holmes 2.00 5.00
85B Priest Holmes 2.00 5.00
86 Philip Rivers 3.00 8.00
87 Melvin Gordon 2.50 6.00
88 Joey Bosa 3.00 8.00
89A Lance Alworth 2.50 6.00
89B Lance Alworth 2.50 6.00
90 Derek Carr 3.00 8.00
91 DeAndre Washington 2.00 5.00
92 Amari Cooper 3.00 8.00
93 Khalil Mack 3.00 8.00
94 Joe Flacco 2.50 6.00
95 Danny Woodhead 2.50 6.00
96 Breshad Perriman 2.00 5.00
97A Ed Reed 2.50 6.00
97B Ed Reed 2.50 6.00
98 Andy Dalton 2.50 6.00
99 Jeremy Hill 2.00 5.00
100 A.J. Green 3.00 8.00
101 Tyler Eifert 2.50 6.00
102 Cody Kessler 2.00 5.00
103 Isaiah Crowell 2.00 5.00
104 Corey Coleman 2.00 5.00
105 Ben Roethlisberger 3.00 8.00
106 Le'Veon Bell 2.50 6.00
107 Antonio Brown 3.00 8.00
108 Lamar Miller 2.00 5.00
109 DeAndre Hopkins 2.50 6.00
110 J.J. Watt 3.00 8.00
111 Andrew Luck 4.00 10.00
112 T.Y. Hilton 2.50 6.00
113 Frank Gore 2.50 6.00
114 Blake Bortles 2.00 5.00
115 Allen Robinson 2.50 6.00
116 Jalen Ramsey 2.00 5.00
117A Mark Brunell 2.50 6.00
117B Mark Brunell 2.50 6.00
118 Marcus Mariota 3.00 8.00
119 DeMarco Murray 2.50 6.00
120A Earl Campbell 3.00 8.00
120B Earl Campbell 3.00 8.00
121 Brad Kaaya RC 1.00 2.50
122 Chad Kelly RC 1.00 2.50
123 Cooper Rush RC 1.25 3.00
124 Corey Clement RC 1.25 3.00
125 Brian Hill RC 1.00 2.50
126 Matthew Dayes RC 1.00 2.50
127 Aaron Jones RC 2.50 6.00
128 Elijah Hood RC 1.00 2.50
129 De'Angelo Henderson RC 1.00 2.50
130 Tarik Cohen RC 2.00 5.00
131 T.J. Logan RC 1.50 4.00
132 Brandon Wilson RC 1.25 3.00
133 Khalfani Muhammad RC 1.00 2.50
134 Devante Mays RC 1.00 2.50
135 Teez Tabor RC 1.25 3.00
136 Sidney Jones RC 1.00 2.50
137 Takkarist McKinley RC 1.00 2.50
138 Gareon Conley RC 1.00 2.50
139 Chidobe Awuzie RC 1.25 3.00
140 Fabian Moreau RC 1.00 2.50
141 Myles Garrett RC 3.00 8.00
142 DeMarcus Walker RC 1.00 2.50
143 Malik McDowell RC 1.00 2.50
144 Dalvin Tomlinson RC 1.00 2.50
145 Reuben Foster RC 1.00 2.50
146 Raekwon McMillan RC 1.00 2.50
147 Zach Cunningham RC 1.25 3.00
148 Tim Williams RC 1.25 3.00
149 Ryan Anderson RC 1.00 2.50
150 Tyus Bowser RC 1.00 2.50
151 Marcus Williams RC 1.00 2.50
152 Marcus Maye RC 1.00 2.50
153 Budda Baker RC 1.00 2.50
154 Jourdan Lewis RC 1.00 2.50
155 Gerald Everett RC 1.00 2.50
156 Jonnu Smith RC 1.00 2.50
157 Jordan Leggett RC 1.00 2.50
158 Michael Roberts RC 1.50 4.00
159 Jeremy Sprinkle RC 1.00 2.50
160 Isaiah Ford RC 1.00 2.50
161 Malachi Dupre RC 1.00 2.50
162 Noah Brown RC 1.25 3.00
163 Rodney Adams RC 1.00 2.50
164 Isaiah McKenzie RC 1.00 2.50
165 Robert Davis RC 1.00 2.50
166 David Moore RC 1.00 2.50
167 Justin Evans RC 1.00 2.50
168 Josh Jones RC 1.00 2.50
169 Obi Melifonwu RC 1.00 2.50
170 Haason Reddick RC 1.00 2.50
171 Donnel Pumphrey AU RC 3.00 8.00
172 Elijah McGuire AU RC 2.50 6.00
173 Marlon Humphrey AU RC 2.50 6.00
174 Marshon Lattimore AU RC 3.00 8.00
175 Quincy Wilson AU RC 2.50 6.00
176 Adoree' Jackson AU RC 3.00 8.00
177 David Njoku AU RC 3.00 8.00
178 Tre'Davious White AU RC 2.50 6.00
179 Kevin King AU RC 3.00 8.00
180 Derek Barnett AU RC 3.00 8.00
181 Charles Harris AU RC 2.50 6.00
182 Taco Charlton AU RC 2.50 6.00
183 Solomon Thomas AU RC 2.50 6.00
184 Jarrad Davis AU RC 3.00 8.00
185 Jabrill Peppers AU RC 4.00 10.00
186 Jonathan Allen AU RC 3.00 8.00
187 Cameron Sutton AU RC 2.50 6.00
188 T.J. Watt AU RC 12.00 30.00
189 Jamal Adams AU RC 2.50 6.00
190 Malik Hooker AU RC 2.50 6.00
191 Jake Butt AU RC 3.00 8.00
192 Adam Shaheen AU RC 2.50 6.00
193 Ryan Switzer AU RC 3.00 8.00
194 Shelton Gibson AU RC 2.50 6.00
195 Josh Malone AU RC 2.50 6.00
196 Jehu Chesson AU RC 3.00 8.00
197 Chad Hansen AU RC 2.50 6.00
199 DeAngelo Yancey AU RC 2.50 6.00
200 Trent Taylor AU RC 3.00 8.00
201 Deshaun Watson JSY AU RC 60.00 125.00
202 Mitchell Trubisky JSY AU RC 60.00 125.00
203 DeShone Kizer JSY AU RC 4.00 10.00
204 Patrick Mahomes II JSY AU RC 250.00 500.00
205 C.J. Beathard JSY AU RC 4.00 10.00
206 Davis Webb JSY AU RC 4.00 10.00
207 Nathan Peterman JSY AU RC 5.00 12.00
208 R. Joshua Dobbs JSY AU RC 5.00 12.00
209 Leonard Fournette JSY AU RC 12.00 30.00
210 Dalvin Cook JSY AU RC 30.00 60.00
211 Christian McCaffrey JSY AU RC 60.00 125.00
212 D'Onta Foreman JSY AU RC 5.00 12.00
213 Alvin Kamara JSY AU RC 15.00 40.00
214 Samaje Perine JSY AU RC 4.00 10.00
215 Wayne Gallman JSY AU RC 5.00 12.00
216 Kareem Hunt JSY AU RC 20.00 50.00
217 Jeremy McNichols JSY AU RC 4.00 10.00
218 James Conner JSY AU RC 8.00 20.00
219 Joe Mixon JSY AU RC 15.00 40.00
220 Marlon Mack JSY AU RC 6.00 15.00
221 O.J. Howard JSY AU RC 5.00 12.00
222 Mike Williams JSY AU RC 6.00 15.00
223 Corey Davis JSY AU RC 6.00 15.00
224 John Ross III JSY AU RC 5.00 12.00
225 JuJu Smith-Schuster JSY AU RC 10.00 25.00
226 Zay Jones JSY AU RC 5.00 12.00
227 Curtis Samuel JSY AU RC 5.00 12.00
228 Dede Westbrook JSY AU RC 4.00 10.00
229 Carlos Henderson JSY AU RC 4.00 10.00
230 Chris Godwin JSY AU RC 5.00 12.00
231 Joe Williams JSY AU RC 4.00 10.00
232 Cooper Kupp JSY AU RC 12.00 30.00
233 Amara Darboh JSY AU RC 4.00 10.00
234 Jamaal Williams JSY AU RC 4.00 10.00
235 ArDarius Stewart JSY AU RC 4.00 10.00
236 Kenny Golladay JSY AU RC 6.00 15.00
237 Josh Reynolds JSY AU RC 4.00 10.00
238 Taywan Taylor JSY AU RC 4.00 10.00
239 Mack Hollins JSY AU RC 4.00 10.00
240 Evan Engram JSY AU RC EXCH 15.00 40.00

2017 Panini Spectra Neon Blue

*VETS/50: .5X TO 1.2X BASIC CARDS/99
*ROOK/50: .5X TO 1.2X BASIC RC/99
*ROOK AU/75: .5X TO 1.2X BASIC RC AU/199
*ROOK JSY AU/75: .4X TO 1X BASIC RC JSY AU/199
201 Deshaun Watson JSY AU 60.00 125.00
202 Mitchell Trubisky JSY AU 75.00 150.00
204 Patrick Mahomes II JSY AU 250.00 500.00

2017 Panini Spectra Neon Blue Die Cut

*VETS/35: .5X TO 1.2X BASIC CARDS/99
*ROOKIES/35: .5X TO 1.2X BASIC RC/99

2017 Panini Spectra Neon Green

*VETS/25: .6X TO 1.5X BASIC CARDS/99
*ROOKIES/25: .6X TO 1.5X BASIC RC/99
*ROOK AU/50: .6X TO 1.5X RC AU/199
*RC JSY AU/50: .5X TO 1.2X RC JSY AU/99
201 Deshaun Watson JSY AU 100.00 200.00
202 Mitchell Trubisky JSY AU 100.00 200.00
204 Patrick Mahomes II JSY AU 300.00 600.00
211 Christian McCaffrey JSY AU 100.00 200.00

2017 Panini Spectra Neon Green Die Cut

*VETS/20: .8X TO 2X BASIC CARDS/99
*ROOKIES: .8X TO 2X BASIC RC/99

2017 Panini Spectra Neon Pink

*VETS/15: .8X TO 2X BASIC CARDS/99
*ROOK/15: .8X TO 2X BASIC RC
*ROOK AU/15: 1X TO 2.5X BASIC RC AU/199
*RC JSY AU/15: .8X TO 2X BASIC JSY AU/99
201 Deshaun Watson JSY AU 150.00 300.00
202 Mitchell Trubisky JSY AU 150.00 300.00
204 Patrick Mahomes II JSY AU 400.00 800.00
211 Christian McCaffrey JSY AU 125.00 250.00

2017 Panini Spectra Aspiring Patch Autographs

1 Mitchell Trubisky/20 75.00 150.00
2 Patrick Mahomes II/20 300.00 600.00
3 Davis Webb/99 4.00 10.00
4 R. Joshua Dobbs/199 4.00 10.00
5 Dalvin Cook/20 20.00 50.00
6 D'Onta Foreman/25 8.00 20.00
7 Samaje Perine/25 6.00 15.00
8 Kareem Hunt/299 EXCH 6.00 15.00
9 James Conner/50 EXCH 10.00 25.00
10 Marlon Mack/299 5.00 12.00
11 Mike Williams/25 10.00 25.00
12 John Ross III/25 8.00 20.00
13 Zay Jones/25 8.00 20.00
14 Dede Westbrook/25 6.00 15.00
15 Chris Godwin/25 8.00 20.00
16 Cooper Kupp/49 0.00 20.00
17 Joe Williams/299 3.00 8.00
18 Jamaal Williams/299 3.00 8.00
19 Taywan Taylor/299 3.00 8.00
20 Evan Engram/199 EXCH 4.00 10.00

2017 Panini Spectra Aspiring Patch Autographs Neon Blue

*BLUE/50: .6X TO 1.5X BASIC JSY AU/199-299
*BLUE/50: .4X TO 1X BASIC JSY AU/50
*BLUE/30: .5X TO 1.2X BASIC JSY AU/49
*BLUE/20: .5X TO 1.2X BASIC JSY AU/25

2017 Panini Spectra Aspiring Patch Autographs Neon Pink

*PINK/15: 1X TO 2.5X BASIC JSY AU/199-299
*PINK/15: .8X TO 2X BASIC JSY AU/99
*PINK/15: .6X TO 1.5X BASIC JSY AU/49-50
*PINK/15: .5X TO 1.2X BASIC JSY AU/25
*PINK/15: .4X TO 1X BASIC JSY AU/20

2017 Panini Spectra Attired Athletes Material Autographs

*BLUE/50: .5X TO 1.2X BASIC JSY/75-99
*BLUE/25: .5X TO 1.2X BASIC JSY/50
*BLUE/15: .5X TO 1.2X BASIC JSY/25
*GREEN/25: .6X TO 1.5X BASIC JSY AU/75-99
*GREEN/15: .8X TO 2X BASIC JSY AU/75-99
*GREEN/15: .6X TO 1.5X BASIC JSY AU/50
*PINK/15: .8X TO 2X BASIC JSY AU/75-99
1 DeMarco Murray/25 8.00 20.00
3 Ricky Williams/50 10.00 25.00
4 Tyler Boyd/50 5.00 12.00
8 Mike Evans/25 8.00 20.00
9 Kenneth Dixon/99 4.00 10.00
10 Will Fuller V/50 5.00 12.00
11 Thomas Rawls/75 4.00 10.00
12 Sterling Sharpe/50 10.00 25.00
14 David Johnson/25 12.00 30.00
15 Paul Warfield/50 6.00 15.00
16 Michael Thomas/50 8.00 20.00
17 Jordan Howard/99 6.00 15.00
18 Tyreek Hill/99 15.00 40.00
19 Mark Brunell/75 5.00 12.00
20 Carson Wentz/25 60.00 125.00
21 Ezekiel Elliott/25 50.00 100.00
22 Matthew Stafford/25 20.00 50.00
23 Tyler Ervin/99 4.00 10.00
24 Cole Beasley/99 6.00 15.00
25 Sterling Shepard/50 6.00 15.00

2017 Panini Spectra Catalysts Jerseys

*BLUE/99: .5X TO 1.2X BASIC JSY/149-199
*BLUE/50: .6X TO 1.5X BASIC JSY/149-199
*BLUE/50: .5X TO 1.2X BASIC JSY/99
*BLUE/15: .4X TO 1X BASIC JSY/20
*GREEN/25: .8X TO 2X BASIC JSY/149-199
*GREEN/15-20: 1X TO 2.5X BASIC JSY/149-199
*PINK/15: 1X TO 2.5X BASIC JSY/149-199
1 Eli Manning/99 4.00 10.00
2 Joe Namath/99 6.00 15.00
3 Champ Bailey/199 3.00 8.00
4 Sterling Sharpe/149 3.00 8.00
5 Aaron Rodgers/20 20.00 50.00
6 Curtis Martin/199 3.00 8.00
7 Chris Johnson/199 2.50 6.00
8 Ricky Williams/199 3.00 8.00
9 Rob Gronkowski/199 4.00 10.00
10 Priest Holmes/199 2.50 6.00
11 Matthew Stafford/199 3.00 8.00
12 Troy Aikman/199 5.00 12.00
13 Tyreek Hill/199 4.00 10.00
14 Russell Wilson/199 5.00 12.00
15 Fred Taylor/199 3.00 8.00
16 Brian Urlacher/199 4.00 10.00
17 David Johnson/199 4.00 10.00
18 Randy Moss/99 4.00 10.00
19 Patrick Peterson/199 2.50 6.00
20 Drew Brees/199 4.00 10.00

2017 Panini Spectra Epic Legends Materials

*BLUE/20: .6X TO 1.5X BASIC JSY/50
1 John Elway 10.00 25.00
2 Steve Young 8.00 20.00
3 Peyton Manning 12.00 30.00
4 Dan Marino 12.00 30.00
5 Jerry Rice 10.00 25.00
6 Paul Hornung 6.00 15.00
7 Jerome Bettis 6.00 15.00
8 Phil Simms 5.00 12.00
9 Tony Romo 5.00 12.00
10 Ray Lewis 6.00 15.00
11 Dwight Clark 5.00 12.00
12 DeMarcus Ware 5.00 12.00
13 Bo Jackson 8.00 20.00
14 Barry Sanders 10.00 25.00
15 Maurice Jones-Drew 4.00 10.00
16 Hines Ward 5.00 12.00
17 Terrell Davis 5.00 12.00
18 Jim Kelly 6.00 15.00
19 Marshall Faulk 5.00 12.00
20 Franco Harris 6.00 15.00

2017 Panini Spectra Illustrious Legends Autographs

1 Warren Moon/50 15.00 40.00
3 Tedy Bruschi/50 10.00 25.00
7 Jay Novacek/50
9 Jevon Kearse/99 5.00 12.00
10 Warren Sapp/15
11 Jim Plunkett/99 6.00 15.00
14 Jim Zorn/99 5.00 12.00
16 Ozzie Newsome/99 6.00 15.00
17 Christian Okoye/99 10.00 25.00
19 Sterling Sharpe/99 6.00 15.00
20 Rodney Harrison/50 15.00 40.00
24 Steve Smith Sr./15 25.00 50.00

2017 Panini Spectra Illustrious Legends Autographs Neon Blue

*BLUE/50: .5X TO 1.2X BASIC AU/99
*BLUE/25: .6X TO 1.5X BASIC AU/99
*BLUE/25: .5X TO 1.2X BASIC AU/50

2017 Panini Spectra Illustrious Legends Autographs Neon Green

*GREEN/25: .6X TO 1.5X BASIC AU/99
*GREEN/15: .8X TO 2X BASIC AU/99
*GREEN/15: .6X TO 1.5X BASIC AU/50

2017 Panini Spectra Illustrious Legends Autographs Neon Pink

*PINK/15: .8X TO 2X BASIC AU/99

2017 Panini Spectra Immense Materials

*BLUE/99: .5X TO 1.2X BASIC JSY/149-199
*BLUE/50: .5X TO 1.2X BASIC JSY/99
*BLUE/25: .5X TO 1.2X BASIC JSY/50
*GREEN/25: .8X TO 2X BASIC JSY/149-199
*GREEN/15: 1X TO 2.5X BASIC JSY/149-199
*PINK/15: 1X TO 2.5X BASIC JSY/149-199
1 Leonard Fournette/199 10.00 25.00
2 Aqib Talib/99 3.00 8.00
3 Christian McCaffrey/199 8.00 20.00
4 Jarvis Landry/199 3.00 8.00
5 Dalvin Cook/199 8.00 20.00
6 Corey Davis/199 4.00 10.00
7 Khalil Mack/199 4.00 10.00
8 Nathan Peterman/199 3.00 8.00
9 Jordan Howard/199 4.00 10.00
10 LeSean McCoy/199 4.00 10.00
11 Patrick Mahomes II/199 15.00 40.00
12 DeMarco Murray/149 3.00 8.00
13 Mack Hollins/199 2.50 6.00
14 Cody Kessler/199 2.50 6.00
15 Joe Williams/199 2.50 6.00
16 Russell Wilson/199 5.00 12.00
17 James Conner/199 5.00 12.00
18 Amari Cooper/199 4.00 10.00
19 Amara Darboh/199 2.50 6.00
20 Luke Kuechly/199 3.00 8.00
21 DeShone Kizer/199 2.50 6.00
22 Matt Ryan/50 5.00 12.00

23 Jamaal Williams/199 2.50 6.00
24 Aaron Rodgers/15 20.00 50.00
25 Kenny Golladay/199 4.00 10.00

2017 Panini Spectra Monumental Memorabilia

*BLUE/99: .5X TO 1.2X BASIC JSY/199
*GREEN/25: .8X TO 2X BASIC JSY/199
*PINK/15: 1X TO 2.5X BASIC JSY/199

2017 Panini Spectra Next Era Jerseys

*BLUE/99: .5X TO 1.2X BASIC JSY/199
*GREEN/25: .8X TO 2X BASIC JSY/199
*PINK/15: 1X TO 2.5X BASIC JSY/199
1 Dalvin Cook 6.00 15.00
2 Patrick Mahomes II 25.00 50.00
3 Leonard Fournette 8.00 20.00
4 John Ross III 5.00 12.00
5 Joe Mixon 5.00 12.00
6 Evan Engram 3.00 8.00
7 Corey Davis 4.00 10.00
8 Christian McCaffrey 8.00 20.00
9 D'Onta Foreman 3.00 8.00
10 O.J. Howard 3.00 8.00

2017 Panini Spectra Radiant Rookie Patch Signatures

1 Deshaun Watson/20 100.00 200.00
2 DeShone Kizer/20 8.00 20.00
3 C.J. Beathard/25 6.00 15.00
4 Nathan Peterman/75 5.00 12.00
5 Leonard Fournette/20 75.00 150.00
6 Christian McCaffrey/25 40.00 80.00
7 Alvin Kamara/50 20.00 50.00
8 Wayne Gallman/299 4.00 10.00
9 Jeremy McNichols/299 3.00 8.00
10 Joe Mixon/50 10.00 25.00
11 O.J. Howard/25 8.00 20.00
12 Corey Davis/25 10.00 25.00
13 JuJu Smith-Schuster/25 15.00 40.00
14 Curtis Samuel/25 8.00 20.00
15 Carlos Henderson/299 3.00 8.00
16 Kenny Golladay/299 5.00 12.00
17 Amara Darboh/299 3.00 8.00
18 ArDarius Stewart/50 5.00 12.00
19 Josh Reynolds/299 3.00 8.00
20 Mack Hollins/299 3.00 8.00

2017 Panini Spectra Radiant Rookie Patch Signatures Neon Blue

*BLUE/50: .6X TO 1.5X BASIC JSY AU/299
*BLUE/50: .4X TO 1X BASIC JSY AU/50
*BLUE/30: .8X TO 2X BASIC JSY AU/299
*BLUE/30: .5X TO 1.2X BASIC JSY AU/50
*BLUE/20: .5X TO 1.2X BASIC JSY AU/25

2017 Panini Spectra Radiant Rookie Patch Signatures Neon Green

*GREEN/25: .8X TO 2X BASIC JSY AU/299
*GREEN/25: .5X TO 1.2X BASIC JSY AU/50
*GREEN/15: 1X TO 2.5X BASIC JSY AU/299
*GREEN/15: .6X TO 1.5X BASIC JSY AU/50

2017 Panini Spectra Radiant Rookie Patch Signatures Neon Pink

*PINK/15: 1X TO 2.5X BASIC JSY AU/299
*PINK/15: .6X TO 1.5X BASIC JSY AU/50
*PINK/15: .5X TO 1.2X BASIC JSY AU/25

2017 Panini Spectra Rising Rookie Materials

*BLUE/99: .5X TO 1.2X BASIC JSY/199
*GREEN/25: .8X TO 2X BASIC JSY/199
*PINK/15: 1X TO 2.5X BASIC JSY/199
1 Deshaun Watson 10.00 25.00
2 Mitchell Trubisky 8.00 20.00
3 DeShone Kizer 2.50 6.00
4 Patrick Mahomes II 20.00 50.00
5 C.J. Beathard 2.50 6.00
6 Davis Webb 2.50 6.00
7 Nathan Peterman 3.00 8.00
8 R. Joshua Dobbs 5.00 12.00
9 Leonard Fournette 10.00 25.00
10 Dalvin Cook 8.00 20.00
11 Christian McCaffrey 8.00 20.00
12 D'Onta Foreman 3.00 8.00
13 Alvin Kamara 5.00 12.00
14 Samaje Perine 2.50 6.00
15 Jeremy McNichols 2.50 6.00
16 James Conner 5.00 12.00
17 Joe Mixon 5.00 12.00
18 Marlon Mack 4.00 10.00
19 O.J. Howard 3.00 8.00
20 Mike Williams 4.00 10.00
21 Corey Davis 6.00 15.00
22 John Ross III 5.00 12.00
23 JuJu Smith-Schuster 5.00 12.00
24 Zay Jones 3.00 8.00
25 Curtis Samuel 3.00 8.00
26 Dede Westbrook 2.50 6.00
27 Joe Williams 2.50 6.00
28 Amara Darboh 2.50 6.00
29 Jamaal Williams 2.50 6.00
30 Evan Engram 3.00 8.00

2017 Panini Spectra Rivals Jerseys

*BLUE/25: .8X TO 2X BASIC JSY/199
*BLUE/25: .6X TO 1.5X BASIC JSY/99
*BLUE/25: .5X TO 1.2X BASIC JSY/50
*GREEN/15: 1X TO 2.5X BASIC JSY/199
1 C.Wentz/D.Prescott/50 8.00 20.00
2 D.Watson/M.Mariota/50 15.00 40.00
3 C.McCaffrey/D.Freeman/199 8.00 20.00
4 A.Rodgers/M.Trubisky/15
5 G.Olsen/O.Howard/99 4.00 10.00
6 C.Davis/D.Hopkins/199 4.00 10.00
7 D.Cook/J.Howard/199 6.00 15.00
8 J.Mixon/L.Bell/50 8.00 20.00
9 J.Ross/J.SmthSchstr/199 5.00 12.00
10 E.Engram/J.Witten/50 5.00 12.00
11 D.Carr/P.Mahomes/50 6.00 15.00
12 D.Henry/L.Fournette/199 8.00 20.00
13 M.Williams/A.Cooper/50 6.00 15.00
14 J.Landry/Z.Jones/199 3.00 8.00
15 A.Kamara/T.Coleman/199 5.00 12.00
16 C.Davis/D.Westbrook/199 4.00 10.00
17 D.Prescott/K.Cousins/50 8.00 20.00
18 C.Samuel/M.Thomas/199 4.00 10.00
19 A.Darboh/C.Kupp/199 4.00 10.00
20 I.Crowell/J.Conner/50 8.00 20.00

2017 Panini Spectra Rookie Dual Patch Autographs

1 D.Watson/D.Foreman 50.00 125.00
2 N.Peterman/Z.Jones 10.00 25.00
3 C.McCaffrey/C.Samuel 20.00 50.00
4 D.Westbrook/L.Fournette 25.00 60.00
5 C.Beathard/J.Williams 8.00 20.00
6 D.Webb/E.Engram 10.00 25.00
7 K.Hunt/P.Mahomes 150.00 300.00
8 D.Cook/J.McNichols 20.00 50.00
9 D.Kizer/J.Williams 8.00 20.00
10 M.Mack/S.Perine 12.00 30.00
11 K.Golladay/M.Trubisky 50.00 100.00
12 C.Henderson/M.Hollins 8.00 20.00
13 A.Darboh/A.Stewart 8.00 20.00
14 W.Gallman/M.Williams 12.00 30.00
15 C.Kupp/J.Reynolds 12.00 30.00
16 C.Godwin/O.Howard 10.00 25.00
17 J.Conner/J.Smith-Schuster 40.00 80.00
18 J.Mixon/J.Ross 15.00 40.00
19 C.Davis/T.Taylor 12.00 30.00
20 A.Kamara/R.J.Dobbs 30.00 80.00

2017 Panini Spectra Rookie Dual Patch Autographs Neon Blue

*BLUE/20: .5X TO 1.2X BASIC JSY AU/25

2017 Panini Spectra Signatures

1 Billy Sims/99 6.00 15.00
2 J.J. Watt/25 30.00 60.00
3 Ahmad Rashad/99 6.00 15.00
4 Peyton Manning/20 60.00 125.00
5 Raymond Berry/50 8.00 20.00
6 Quincy Enunwa/99 5.00 12.00
7 Jamison Crowder/99 5.00 12.00
8 Mark Schlereth/99 5.00 12.00
9 Drew Brees/20 50.00 100.00
10 Bill Bates/99 5.00 12.00
11 Matt Ryan/20 30.00 60.00
13 LeGarrette Blount/99 6.00 15.00
15 Y.A. Tittle/99 8.00 20.00
17 Jeff Garcia/99 5.00 12.00
18 Marcus Mariota/20 40.00 80.00
20 Dan Fouts/20 20.00 50.00
21 Robert Kelley/99 5.00 12.00
23 Hines Ward/49 15.00 40.00
24 Rodney Harrison/49 15.00 40.00
25 Doug Baldwin/25
27 Jeff Saturday/99 6.00 15.00
28 Jameis Winston/20 12.00 30.00
29 Kordell Stewart/99 8.00 20.00
30 Ron Jaworski/99 8.00 20.00
31 Ray Lewis/20 30.00 80.00
32 Carlos Hyde/99 5.00 12.00
33 Jordy Nelson/20 15.00 40.00
35 Chad Pennington/99 5.00 12.00
36 Ty Law/49 10.00 25.00
37 Derek Carr/25 75.00 150.00
38 Priest Holmes/25 8.00 20.00
39 Bert Jones/99 5.00 12.00
40 Gilbert Brown/99 5.00 12.00
41 Ernest Givins/81 5.00 12.00
42 Paxton Lynch/20 8.00 20.00
44 Henry Ellard/99 5.00 12.00
45 Rich Gannon/99 5.00 12.00
46 Isaiah Crowell/99 5.00 12.00
47 Jimmy Garoppolo/99 30.00 60.00
48 Dan Bailey/99 12.00 30.00
49 Steve Largent/25 12.00 30.00
50 John Brown/99 6.00 15.00

2017 Panini Spectra Signatures Neon Blue

*BLUE/50: .5X TO 1.2X BASIC AU/81-99
*BLUE/25: .5X TO 1.5X BASIC AU/49-50
*BLUE/15-20: .6X TO 1.5X BASIC AU/49-50
*BLUE/15-20: .5X TO 1.2X BASIC AU/25
*BLUE/15-20: .4X TO 1X BASIC AU/20

2017 Panini Spectra Signatures Neon Green

*GREEN/25: .6X TO 1.5X BASIC AU/49-50
*GREEN/15-20: .8X TO 2X BASIC AU/81-99
*GREEN/15-20: .6X TO 1.5X BASIC AU/49-50
*GREEN/15-20: .5X TO 1.2X BASIC AU/25

2017 Panini Spectra Signatures Neon Pink

*PINK/15: .8X TO 2X BASIC AU/81-99

2017 Panini Spectra Sunday Spectacle Jerseys

*BLUE/99: .5X TO 1.2X BASIC JSY/199
*BLUE/50: .5X TO 1.2X BASIC JSY/75-99
*BLUE/25: .5X TO 1.2X BASIC JSY/50
*GREEN/25: .8X TO 2X BASIC JSY/199
*GREEN/15: 1X TO 2.5X BASIC JSY/199
*GREEN/15: .8X TO 2X BASIC JSY/99
1 Richard Sherman/99 5.00 12.00
2 Randall Cobb/99 4.00 10.00
3 Matt Forte/99 3.00 8.00
4 J.J. Watt/99 5.00 12.00
5 Philip Rivers/199 4.00 10.00
6 Antonio Brown/99 5.00 12.00
7 David Johnson/199 4.00 10.00
8 Emmanuel Sanders/199 4.00 10.00
9 Jay Ajayi/199 3.00 8.00
10 Tyrod Taylor/199 3.00 8.00
11 A.J. Green/99 5.00 12.00
12 Von Miller/199 3.00 8.00
13 James White/199 3.00 8.00
14 Carlos Hyde/199 2.50 6.00
15 Ameer Abdullah/199 2.50 6.00
16 Devonta Freeman/199 3.00 8.00
17 Tyler Eifert/199 3.00 8.00
18 Allen Robinson/199 3.00 8.00
19 Marcus Mariota/199 4.00 10.00
20 Derek Carr/199 4.00 10.00
21 Jarvis Landry/199 3.00 8.00
22 Andy Dalton/199 3.00 8.00
23 Doug Martin/199 3.00 8.00
24 Jeremy Hill/199 2.50 6.00
25 Julio Jones/99 5.00 12.00
26 Luke Kuechly/199 3.00 8.00
27 LeSean McCoy/199 4.00 10.00
28 Keenan Allen/199 3.00 8.00
29 Drew Brees/199 4.00 10.00
30 Jordan Reed/199 2.50 6.00
31 Odell Beckham Jr./199 4.00 10.00
32 Lamar Miller/199 2.50 6.00
33 T.Y. Hilton/199 3.00 8.00
34 Russell Wilson/199 5.00 12.00
35 Ndamukong Suh/199 3.00 8.00
36 Travis Kelce/199 4.00 10.00
37 Rob Gronkowski/99 5.00 12.00
38 Martavis Bryant/199 2.50 6.00
39 Khalil Mack/199 4.00 10.00
40 Todd Gurley II/199 4.00 10.00
41 Jadeveon Clowney/199 2.50 6.00
42 Dak Prescott/199 4.00 10.00
43 Demaryius Thomas/199 3.00 8.00
44 Andrew Luck/199 5.00 12.00
45 Paxton Lynch/199 2.50 6.00
46 Carson Wentz/199 5.00 12.00
47 Ryan Tannehill/199 3.00 8.00
48 Ezekiel Elliott/199 5.00 12.00
49 Tom Brady/50 15.00 40.00
50 Joey Bosa/199 4.00 10.00

2017 Panini Spectra Synced Swatches

*BLUE/75-99: .5X TO 1.2X BASIC JSY/149-199
*BLUE/75-99: .4X TO 1X BASIC JSY/99
*BLUE/50: .6X TO 1.5X BASIC JSY/149-199
*BLUE/50: .5X TO 1.2X BASIC JSY/99
1 C.McCaffrey/K.Benjamin/149 8.00 20.00
2 C.Davis/D.Henry/199 4.00 10.00
3 C.Kessler/D.Kizer/199 2.50 6.00
4 S.Diggs/D.Cook/149 6.00 15.00
5 L.Fournette/D.Westbrook/199 10.00 25.00
6 D.Hopkins/D.Foreman/199 3.00 8.00
7 J.Ross/J.Mixon/99 6.00 15.00
8 J.SmthSchstr/L.Bell/199 5.00 12.00
9 M.Trubisky/J.Howard/99 10.00 25.00
10 P.Mahomes/T.Hill/99 12.00 30.00
11 S.Watkins/Z.Jones/199 4.00 10.00
12 M.Thomas/A.Kamara/199 5.00 12.00
13 C.Wentz/M.Hollins/199 5.00 12.00
14 A.Robinson/D.Westbrook/199 3.00 8.00
15 M.Williams/M.Gordon/199 4.00 10.00
16 W.Gallman/P.Perkins/199 3.00 8.00
17 D.Prescott/E.Elliott/199 5.00 12.00
18 D.Foreman/D.Watson/199 12.00 30.00
19 A.Darboh/T.Lockett/199 3.00 8.00
20 E.Engram/S.Shepard/199 3.00 8.00
21 O.Howard/J.Winston/149 3.00 8.00
22 N.Peterman/Z.Jones/199 3.00 8.00
23 M.Trubisky/K.White/199 8.00 20.00
24 C.Davis/M.Mariota/199 4.00 10.00
25 J.Williams/D.Adams/199 3.00 8.00
26 A.Luck/M.Mack/199 5.00 12.00
27 A.Green/J.Ross/199 5.00 12.00
28 C.Beasley/D.Prescott/199 5.00 12.00
29 J.Gull/C.Kupp/199 4.00 10.00
30 C.Prosise/R.Wilson/199 5.00 12.00

2017 Panini Spectra Triple Threats Materials

*BLUE/50: .5X TO 1.2X BASIC JSY/75-99
*BLUE/25: .5X TO 1.2X BASIC JSY/50
*BLUE/15-20: .8X TO 2X BASIC JSY/75-99
*BLUE/15-20: .6X TO 1.5X BASIC JSY/50
*BLUE/15-20: .5X TO 1.2X BASIC JSY/25
*GREEN/15-20: .8X TO 2X BASIC JSY/75-99
1 Tom Brady/25 20.00 50.00
2 Dak Prescott/50 6.00 15.00
3 Odell Beckham Jr./75 5.00 12.00
4 Corey Davis/99 5.00 12.00
5 Carlos Hyde/99 3.00 8.00
6 Devonta Freeman/99 4.00 10.00
7 Mike Evans/50 5.00 12.00
8 Derek Carr/50 6.00 15.00
9 Jordan Howard/50 6.00 15.00
10 Le'Veon Bell/50 5.00 12.00
11 Michael Thomas/99 5.00 12.00
12 David Johnson/99 5.00 12.00
13 Russell Wilson/50 8.00 20.00
14 Jay Ajayi/99 4.00 10.00
15 Amari Cooper/50 6.00 15.00
16 Todd Gurley II/99 5.00 12.00
17 Tyler Lockett/99 4.00 10.00
18 Ezekiel Elliott/75 6.00 15.00
19 Joe Mixon/99 6.00 15.00
20 Deshaun Watson/99 12.00 30.00
21 Christian McCaffrey/99 10.00 25.00
22 D'Onta Foreman/99 4.00 10.00
23 Alvin Kamara/99 6.00 15.00
24 JuJu Smith-Schuster/99 6.00 15.00
25 DeShone Kizer/99 3.00 8.00

2018 Panini Spectra

1 Jerick McKinnon 2.00 5.00
2A Jimmy Garoppolo 4.00 10.00
2B Jimmy Garoppolo
3A Joe Montana 8.00 20.00
3B Joe Montana
4A Richard Sherman 3.00 8.00
4B Richard Sherman
5 Allen Robinson 2.50 6.00
6 Brian Urlacher 3.00 8.00
7 Jordan Howard 3.00 8.00
8 Mitchell Trubisky 3.00 8.00
9 A.J. Green 3.00 8.00
10 Andy Dalton 2.50 6.00
11 Joe Mixon 2.50 6.00
12 A.J. McCarron 2.00 5.00
13 Kelvin Benjamin 2.50 6.00
14 LeSean McCoy 3.00 8.00
15 Case Keenum 2.50 6.00
16 Demaryius Thomas 2.50 6.00
17 John Elway 5.00 12.00
18 Von Miller 2.50 6.00
19 Jarvis Landry 2.50 6.00
20 Josh Gordon 2.00 5.00
21 Tyrod Taylor 2.50 6.00
22 Jameis Winston 2.50 6.00
23A John Lynch 2.50 6.00
23B John Lynch
24 Mike Evans 2.50 6.00
25 David Johnson 3.00 8.00
26 Larry Fitzgerald 2.50 6.00
27 Sam Bradford 2.00 5.00
28 Joey Bosa 3.00 8.00
29 Keenan Allen 2.50 6.00
30 Philip Rivers 3.00 8.00
31 Kareem Hunt 2.50 6.00
32 Patrick Mahomes II 8.00 20.00
33 Sammy Watkins 3.00 8.00
34A Tony Gonzalez 2.50 6.00
34B Tony Gonzalez
35 Travis Kelce 3.00 8.00
36 Andrew Luck 4.00 10.00
37 Jacoby Brissett 2.00 5.00
38A Peyton Manning 6.00 15.00
38B Peyton Manning
39 T.Y. Hilton 2.50 6.00
40 Dak Prescott 3.00 8.00
41A Deion Sanders 2.50 6.00
41B Deion Sanders
42 Ezekiel Elliott 4.00 10.00
43 Jason Witten 2.50 6.00
44 Danny Amendola 2.50 6.00
45 Ryan Tannehill 2.50 6.00
46A Zach Thomas 2.50 6.00
46B Zach Thomas
47A Brian Dawkins 3.00 8.00
47B Brian Dawkins
48 Carson Wentz 4.00 10.00
49 Jay Ajayi 2.50 6.00
50 Nick Foles 2.50 6.00
51 Devonta Freeman 2.50 6.00
52 Julio Jones 3.00 8.00
53 Matt Ryan 2.50 6.00
54A Michael Vick 2.50 6.00
54B Michael Vick
55 Eli Manning 2.50 6.00
56 Jeremy Shockey 2.00 5.00
57 Michael Strahan 2.50 6.00
58 Odell Beckham Jr. 3.00 8.00
59 Blake Bortles 2.00 5.00
60 Jalen Ramsey 2.50 6.00
61 Leonard Fournette 3.00 8.00
62 Jamal Adams 2.50 6.00
63 Jermaine Kearse 2.00 5.00
64 Josh McCown 2.00 5.00
65 Barry Sanders 5.00 12.00
66 Marvin Jones Jr. 2.00 5.00
67 Matthew Stafford 2.50 6.00
68 Earl Campbell 3.00 8.00
69 Aaron Rodgers 6.00 15.00
70A Brett Favre 6.00 15.00
70B Brett Favre
71 Davante Adams 2.50 6.00
72 Jimmy Graham 3.00 8.00
73 Cam Newton 3.00 8.00
74 Christian McCaffrey 3.00 8.00
75A Julius Peppers 2.50 6.00
75B Julius Peppers
76 Julian Edelman 3.00 8.00
77 Rob Gronkowski 3.00 8.00
78 Tom Brady 8.00 20.00
79A Ty Law 3.00 8.00
79B Ty Law
80 Charles Woodson 3.00 8.00
80B Charles Woodson
81 Derek Carr 3.00 8.00
82 Jordy Nelson 2.50 6.00
82B Jordy Nelson
83A Marshawn Lynch 2.50 6.00
83B Marshawn Lynch
84 Brandin Cooks 2.50 6.00
85 Jared Goff 3.00 8.00
86A Marshall Faulk 2.50 6.00
86B Marshall Faulk
87 Todd Gurley II 3.00 8.00
88 Alex Collins 2.00 5.00
89 Eric Weddle 2.00 5.00
90 Joe Flacco 2.50 6.00
91 Michael Crabtree 2.00 5.00
92 Alex Smith 2.50 6.00
93 Jamison Crowder 2.00 5.00
94 Josh Norman 2.00 5.00
95 Alvin Kamara 2.50 6.00
96 Drew Brees 3.00 8.00
97 Marshon Lattimore 2.00 5.00
98 Michael Thomas 3.00 8.00
99 Doug Baldwin 2.50 6.00
100 Earl Thomas III 2.50 6.00
101 Russell Wilson 4.00 10.00
102 Shaun Alexander 2.00 5.00
103 Antonio Brown 3.00 8.00
104 Ben Roethlisberger 3.00 8.00
105 Le'Veon Bell 2.50 6.00
106 Ryan Shazier 2.00 5.00
107 Terry Bradshaw 5.00 12.00
108 Deshaun Watson 4.00 10.00
109 D'Onta Foreman 2.00 5.00
110 J.J. Watt 3.00 8.00
111 Tyrann Mathieu 2.50 6.00
112 Corey Davis 2.50 6.00
113 Derrick Henry 3.00 8.00
114 Marcus Mariota 3.00 8.00
115 Vince Young 2.00 5.00
116 Adam Thielen 3.00 8.00
117 Cris Carter 3.00 8.00
118 Dalvin Cook 2.50 6.00
119 Harrison Smith 3.00 8.00
120 Kirk Cousins 3.00 8.00
121 Baker Mayfield RC 25.00 50.00
122 Saquon Barkley RC 15.00 40.00
123 Sam Darnold RC 10.00 25.00
124 Bradley Chubb RC 1.50 4.00
125 Josh Allen RC 4.00 10.00
126 Josh Rosen RC 3.00 8.00
127 D.J. Moore RC 2.00 5.00
128 Hayden Hurst RC 1.25 3.00
129 Calvin Ridley RC 2.50 6.00
130 Rashaad Penny RC 1.50 4.00
131 Sony Michel RC 3.00 8.00
132 Lamar Jackson RC 6.00 15.00
133 Nick Chubb RC 3.00 8.00
134 Ronald Jones II RC 1.00 2.50
135 Courtland Sutton RC 1.50 4.00
136 Dante Pettis RC 1.50 4.00
137 Christian Kirk RC 1.50 4.00
138 Anthony Miller RC 1.50 4.00
139 Derrius Guice RC 2.00 5.00
140 James Washington RC 2.00 5.00
141 Royce Freeman RC 1.25 3.00
142 Mason Rudolph RC 2.50 6.00
143 Michael Gallup RC 2.00 5.00
144 Mike White RC 1.25 3.00
145 Marquez Valdes-Scantling RC 1.25 3.00
146 Braxton Berrios RC 1.00 2.50
147 Mike McGlinchey RC 2.00 5.00
148 Cedrick Wilson Jr. RC 1.00 2.50
149 Uchenna Nwosu RC 1.50 4.00
150 Maurice Hurst RC 1.25 3.00
151 Shaquem Griffin RC 1.50 4.00
152 Arden Key RC 1.00 2.50
153 Da'Shawn Hand RC 1.00 2.50
154 Dorance Armstrong Jr. RC 1.00 2.50
155 Marcus Allen RC 1.50 4.00
156 Equanimeous St. Brown RC 1.50 4.00
157 Taven Bryan RC 1.00 2.50
158 Breeland Speaks RC 1.25 3.00
159 Deon Cain RC 1.25 3.00
160 Marcell Ateman RC 1.25 3.00
161 Dylan Cantrell RC 1.00 2.50
162 Jordan Lasley RC 1.00 2.50
163 Jerome Baker RC 1.25 3.00
164 Lorenzo Carter RC 1.00 2.50
165 Derrick Nnadi RC 1.00 2.50
166 Armani Watts RC 1.00 2.50
167 Troy Fumagalli RC 1.25 3.00
168 Mark Andrews RC 1.50 4.00
169 Kolton Miller RC 1.50 4.00
170 J.T. Barrett RC 1.50 4.00
171 Denzel Ward AU RC 6.00 15.00
172 Quenton Nelson AU RC 4.00 10.00
173 Roquan Smith AU RC 10.00 25.00
174 Minkah Fitzpatrick AU RC 5.00 12.00
175 Vita Vea AU RC 4.00 10.00
176 Daron Payne AU RC 4.00 10.00
177 Marcus Davenport AU RC 5.00 12.00
178 Tremaine Edmunds AU RC 5.00 12.00
179 Derwin James AU RC 5.00 12.00
180 Jaire Alexander AU RC 4.00 10.00
181 Leighton Vander Esch AU RC 8.00 20.00
182 Rashaan Evans AU RC 4.00 10.00
183 Terrell Edmunds AU RC 8.00 20.00
184 Mike Hughes AU RC 4.00 10.00
185 Harold Landry AU RC 5.00 12.00
186 Joshua Jackson AU RC 5.00 12.00
187 Dallas Goedert AU RC 3.00 8.00
188 Shaquem Griffin AU 12.00 30.00
189 Ronnie Harrison AU RC 3.00 8.00
190 Jordan Wilkins AU RC 8.00 20.00
191 Isaiah Oliver AU RC 2.50 6.00
192 Carlton Davis AU RC 3.00 8.00
193 Tyquan Lewis AU RC 3.00 8.00
194 Malik Jefferson AU RC 3.00 8.00
195 Antonio Callaway AU RC EXCH 6.00 15.00
196 Chase Edmonds AU RC 2.50 6.00
197 Dalton Schultz AU RC 3.00 8.00
198 John Kelly AU RC 3.00 8.00
199 Bo Scarbrough AU RC 3.00 8.00
200 Austin Proehl AU RC 2.50 6.00
201 Sam Darnold JSY AU 75.00 150.00
202 Josh Rosen JSY AU 30.00 60.00
203 Baker Mayfield JSY AU 125.00 250.00
204 Josh Allen JSY AU 30.00 60.00
205 Mason Rudolph JSY AU 10.00 25.00
206 Saquon Barkley JSY AU 100.00 200.00
207 Derrius Guice JSY AU 8.00 20.00
208 Nick Chubb JSY AU 12.00 30.00
209 Sony Michel JSY AU 12.00 30.00
210 Ronald Jones II JSY AU 4.00 10.00
211 Calvin Ridley JSY AU 25.00 50.00
212 Courtland Sutton JSY AU 6.00 15.00
213 Christian Kirk JSY AU 6.00 15.00
214 Anthony Miller JSY AU 6.00 15.00
215 D.J. Chark Jr. JSY AU RC 5.00 12.00
216 D.J. Moore JSY AU 8.00 20.00
217 Lamar Jackson JSY AU 50.00 100.00
218 Mike Gesicki JSY AU RC 5.00 12.00
219 Kyle Lauletta JSY AU RC 6.00 15.00
220 Mike White JSY AU 5.00 12.00
221 Mark Walton JSY AU RC 5.00 12.00
222 Royce Freeman JSY AU 5.00 12.00
223 Kerryon Johnson JSY AU RC 6.00 15.00
224 Rashaad Penny JSY AU EXCH 6.00 15.00
225 Kalen Ballage JSY AU RC 5.00 12.00
226 Nyheim Hines JSY AU RC 5.00 12.00
227 Ito Smith JSY AU RC 5.00 12.00
228 James Washington JSY AU 8.00 20.00
229 Keke Coutee JSY AU RC 5.00 12.00
230 J'Mon Moore JSY AU RC 4.00 10.00
231 Michael Gallup JSY AU 8.00 20.00
232 Dante Pettis JSY AU 6.00 15.00
233 Jaylen Samuels JSY AU RC 5.00 12.00
234 DaeSean Hamilton JSY AU RC 5.00 12.00
235 Tre'Quan Smith JSY AU RC 6.00 15.00
236 Jaleel Scott JSY AU RC 4.00 10.00
237 Marquez Valdes-Scantling JSY AU 5.00 12.00
238 Daurice Fountain JSY AU RC 5.00 12.00
239 Hayden Hurst JSY AU EXCH 5.00 12.00
240 Bradley Chubb JSY AU 6.00 15.00

2018 Panini Spectra Neon Blue

*VETS: .4X TO 1X BASIC CARDS/99
*ROOKIES: .4X TO 1X BASIC CARDS/99
*ROOK AU/149: .4X TO 1X BASIC CARDS/199
*ROOK JSY AU/75: .4X TO 1X BASIC CARDS/99
206 Saquon Barkley JSY AU 100.00 200.00

2018 Panini Spectra Neon Blue Die Cut

*VETS/35: .5X TO 1.2X BASIC CARDS/99
*ROOKIES/35: .5X TO 1.2X BASIC CARDS/99

2018 Panini Spectra Neon Green

*VETS/30: .6X TO 1.5X BASIC CARDS/99
*ROOKIES/30: .6X TO 1.5X BASIC CARDS/99
*ROOK AU/99: .5X TO 1.2X BASIC CARDS/199
*ROOK JSY AU/60: .5X TO 1.2X BASIC CARDS/99
206 Saquon Barkley JSY AU/60 125.00 250.00

2018 Panini Spectra Neon Green Die Cut

*VETS/25: .6X TO 1.5X BASIC CARDS/25
*ROOKIES/25: .6X TO 1.5X BASIC CARDS/25

2018 Panini Spectra Neon Pink

*VETS/20: .8X TO 2X BASIC CARDS/99
*ROOKIES/20: X TO X BASIC CARDS/99
*ROOK AU/50: .6X TO 1.5X BASIC CARDS/199
*ROOK JSY AU/25: .6X TO 1.5X BASIC CARDS/99

2018 Panini Spectra Neon Pink Die Cut

*VETS/15: .8X TO 2X BASIC CARDS/99
*ROOKIES/15: X TO X BASIC CARDS/99

2018 Panini Spectra Rookie Patch Autographs Neon Purple

*PURPLE/50: .5X TO 1.2X BASIC JSY AU/99
*PURPLE/25: .6X TO 1.5X BASIC JSY AU/99
206 Saquon Barkley/50 125.00 250.00

2018 Panini Spectra Building Blocks Materials

*BLUE/50: .5X TO 1.2X BASIC JSY/99
*GREEN/25: .6X TO 1.5X BASIC JSY/99
*PINK/15: .8X TO 2X BASIC JSY/99
1 Patrick Mahomes II 12.00 30.00
2 Baker Mayfield 12.00 30.00
3 Saquon Barkley 15.00 40.00
4 Alvin Kamara 4.00 10.00
5 Leonard Fournette 5.00 12.00
6 Sam Darnold 12.00 30.00
7 Josh Allen 10.00 25.00
8 Josh Rosen 12.00 30.00
9 Derrius Guice 6.00 15.00
10 Courtland Sutton 5.00 12.00
11 Lamar Jackson 12.00 30.00
12 Dalvin Cook 4.00 10.00
13 Mitchell Trubisky 5.00 12.00
14 Joe Mixon 4.00 10.00
15 Nick Chubb 10.00 25.00
16 Sony Michel 8.00 20.00
17 Bradley Chubb 5.00 12.00
18 Calvin Ridley 8.00 20.00
19 Christian Kirk 5.00 12.00
20 Rashaad Penny 5.00 12.00
21 Ronald Jones II 3.00 8.00
22 Royce Freeman 4.00 10.00
23 Nyheim Hines 4.00 10.00
24 D.J. Chark Jr. 4.00 10.00
25 Michael Gallup 6.00 15.00

2018 Panini Spectra Cornerstone Materials

*BLUE/99: .5X TO 1.2X BASIC JSY/199
*BLUE/50: .5X TO 1.2X BASIC JSY/75-99
*GREEN/25: .8X TO 2X BASIC JSY/199
*GREEN/25: .6X TO 1.5X BASIC JSY/75-99
*PINK/15: 1X TO 2.5X BASIC JSY/199
*PINK/15: .8X TO 2X BASIC JSY/75-99
1 Aaron Rodgers/99 10.00 25.00
2 Patrick Mahomes II/199 8.00 20.00
3 Jared Goff/199 4.00 10.00
4 Derek Carr/199 4.00 10.00
5 Mitchell Trubisky/199 4.00 10.00
6 Alvin Kamara/199 3.00 8.00
7 Matt Ryan/199 3.00 8.00
8 Earl Thomas III/99 4.00 10.00
9 Deshaun Watson/199 5.00 12.00
10 Luke Kuechly/75 4.00 10.00
11 Rob Gronkowski/199 4.00 10.00
12 Antonio Brown/99 5.00 12.00
13 Matthew Stafford/199 3.00 8.00
14 Andrew Luck/199 5.00 12.00
15 Dak Prescott/199 4.00 10.00
16 Joe Mixon/199 3.00 8.00
17 Dalvin Cook/199 3.00 8.00
18 Leonard Fournette/199 4.00 10.00
19 Jameis Winston/199 3.00 8.00
20 Melvin Gordon/199 3.00 8.00
21 LeSean McCoy/99 5.00 12.00
22 Carson Wentz/199 5.00 12.00
23 Marcus Mariota/199 4.00 10.00
24 Eli Manning/99 4.00 10.00
25 David Johnson/199 4.00 10.00

2018 Panini Spectra Epic Legends Materials

*BLUE/99: .5X TO 1.2X BASIC JSY/199
*BLUE/50: .5X TO 1.2X BASIC JSY/99
*GREEN/25: .8X TO 2X BASIC JSY/199
*PINK/15: 1X TO 2.5X BASIC JSY/199
1 Tom Brady/99 12.00 30.00
2 John Elway/199 6.00 15.00
3 Jerry Rice/199 6.00 15.00
4 Cris Carter/199 4.00 10.00
5 Jim McMahon/199 2.50 6.00
6 Desmond Howard/199 2.50 6.00
7 Brian Dawkins/199 4.00 10.00
8 Michael Irvin/199 4.00 10.00
9 Terrell Davis/199 3.00 8.00
10 James Harrison/199 3.00 8.00
11 Charles Woodson/199 4.00 10.00
12 Peyton Manning/199 8.00 20.00
13 Len Dawson/199 4.00 10.00
14 Barry Sanders/199 6.00 15.00
15 Dan Marino/199 8.00 20.00
16 Rod Woodson/199 4.00 10.00
17 Marcus Allen/199 4.00 10.00
18 Troy Aikman/199 5.00 12.00
19 Steve Largent/199 4.00 10.00
20 Tony Gonzalez/199 3.00 8.00

2018 Panini Spectra Illustrious Legends Autographs

1 Rod Woodson/99 12.00 30.00
2 LaVar Arrington/49 6.00 15.00
3 Bruce Smith/25 10.00 25.00
4 Brian Dawkins/49 40.00 80.00
5 Bruce Matthews/99 5.00 12.00
6 Jason Taylor/25 EXCH 10.00 25.00
7 Ted Johnson/99 5.00 12.00
8 Aaron Rodgers/25 200.00 300.00
9 Roger Staubach/25 40.00 80.00
10 Tony Gonzalez/25 EXCH 25.00 50.00
11 Jack Youngblood/99 5.00 12.00
12 Cris Carter/25 40.00 80.00
13 Rich Gannon/99 EXCH 6.00 15.00
14 Ty Law/49 12.00 30.00
15 Devin Hester/49 12.00 30.00
16 Vinny Testaverde/99 5.00 12.00
17 John Lynch/99 6.00 15.00
18 Shaun Alexander/35 12.00 30.00
19 Mike Alstott/99 12.00 30.00
20 Larry Allen/99 EXCH 8.00 20.00
21 Peyton Manning/15

2018 Panini Spectra Next Era Memorabilia

*BLUE/99: .5X TO 1.2X BASIC JSY/199
*GREEN/25: .8X TO 2X BASIC JSY/199
*PINK/15: 1X TO 2.5X BASIC JSY/199
1 Saquon Barkley 12.00 30.00
2 Mason Rudolph 6.00 15.00
3 Lamar Jackson 10.00 25.00
4 Josh Allen 8.00 20.00
5 Sam Darnold 10.00 25.00
6 Baker Mayfield 10.00 25.00
7 Derrius Guice
8 Josh Rosen 10.00 25.00
9 Calvin Ridley 6.00 15.00
10 Sony Michel 6.00 15.00

2018 Panini Spectra Rising Rookie Materials

*BLUE/99: .5X TO 1.2X BASIC JSY/199
*GREEN/50: .6X TO 1.5X BASIC JSY/199
*PINK/15: 1X TO 2.5X BASIC JSY/199
1 Mason Rudolph 6.00 15.00
2 Josh Allen 8.00 20.00
3 Baker Mayfield 1.00 25.00
4 Josh Rosen 10.00 25.00
5 Sam Darnold 10.00 25.00
6 Ronald Jones II 2.50 6.00
7 Sony Michel 6.00 15.00
8 Nick Chubb 6.00 15.00
9 Derrius Guice 5.00 12.00
10 Saquon Barkley 12.00 30.00
11 Royce Freeman 3.00 8.00
12 Mike White 3.00 8.00
13 Kyle Lauletta 4.00 10.00
14 Mike Gesicki 3.00 8.00
15 Lamar Jackson 10.00 25.00
16 D.J. Chark Jr. 3.00 8.00
17 Anthony Miller 4.00 10.00
18 Christian Kirk 4.00 10.00
19 Courtland Sutton 4.00 10.00
20 Calvin Ridley 6.00 15.00
21 D.J. Moore 5.00 12.00
22 Bradley Chubb 4.00 10.00
23 James Washington 5.00 12.00
24 J'Mon Moore 2.50 6.00
25 Michael Gallup 5.00 12.00
26 Dante Pettis 4.00 10.00
27 Jaylen Samuels 3.00 8.00
28 DaeSean Hamilton 3.00 8.00
29 Rashaad Penny 4.00 10.00
30 Kerryon Johnson 4.00 10.00

2018 Panini Spectra Rivals Jerseys

*BLUE/50: .6X TO 1.5X BASIC JSY/199
*BLUE/50: .5X TO 1.2X BASIC JSY/99
*GREEN/25: .8X TO 2X BASIC JSY/199
*GREEN/25: .6X TO 1.5X BASIC JSY/99
*PINK/15: 1X TO 2.5X BASIC JSY/199
*PINK/15: .8X TO 2X BASIC JSY/99
1 S.Largent/B.Jackson/99 5.00 12.00
2 B.Mayfield/L.Jackson/199 8.00 20.00
3 E.Elliott/S.Barkley/99 12.00 30.00
4 S.Darnold/J.Allen/199 8.00 20.00
5 J.Rosen/J.Goff/199 8.00 20.00
6 C.Ridley/D.Moore/199 5.00 12.00
7 S.Michel/K.Ballage/199 5.00 12.00
8 M.Walton/N.Chubb/199 6.00 15.00
9 D.Chark Jr./K.Coutee/199 2.50 6.00
10 K.Lauletta/M.White/199 3.00 8.00
11 A.Miller/J.Moore/199 3.00 8.00
12 D.Pettis/C.Kirk/199 3.00 8.00
13 B.Chubb/P.Mahomes II/199 8.00 20.00
14 R.Jones II/L.Kuechly/99 3.00 8.00
15 E.Berry/C.Sutton/99 4.00 10.00
16 H.Hurst/J.Peppers/199 2.50 6.00
17 A.Brown/V.Burfict/99 4.00 10.00
18 L.Alexander/M.Gesicki/199 2.50 6.00
19 C.Matthews/K.Johnson/199 3.00 8.00

2018 Panini Spectra Signatures

*BLUE/35-50: .5X TO 1.2X BASIC AU/99
*BLUE/35: .4X TO 1X BASIC AU/49
*BLUE/25: .5X TO 1.2X BASIC AU/35
*BLUE/25: .6X TO 1.5X BASIC AU/49
*BLUE/20: .5X TO 1.2X BASIC AU/25
*GREEN/25: .6X TO 1.5X BASIC AU/99
*GREEN/25: .5X TO 1.2X BASIC AU/49
*GREEN/15: .6X TO 1.5X BASIC AU/35-49
*GREEN/15: .5X TO 1.2X BASIC AU/25
*PINK/15: .8X TO 2X BASIC AU/99
*PINK/15: .6X TO 1.5X BASIC AU/49
*PINK/15: .5X TO 1.2X BASIC AU/25
1 Fletcher Cox/99 5.00 12.00
2 Willis McGahee/99 5.00 12.00
3 Christian McCaffrey/49 10.00 25.00
8 Joe Mixon/99 6.00 15.00
9 JuJu Smith-Schuster/99 12.00 30.00
10 Kareem Hunt/99 6.00 15.00
11 Patrick Mahomes II/49 75.00 150.00
13 Warren Sapp/25 10.00 25.00
14 Jamal Adams/99 6.00 15.00
16 Steve Young/25 40.00 100.00
17 Devin Funchess/99 5.00 12.00
18 Sean Lee/99 6.00 15.00
19 Ezekiel Elliott/49 40.00 80.00
20 Stephen Gostkowski/99 8.00 20.00
21 Xavier Rhodes/99 5.00 12.00
22 Justin Tucker/99 5.00 12.00
23 Alex Collins/99 EXCH 5.00 12.00
24 Justin Houston/99 5.00 12.00
26 Chandler Jones/99 5.00 12.00
27 Carlos Hyde/99 5.00 12.00
28 Greg Olsen/49 8.00 20.00
29 Dan Bailey/99 5.00 12.00
30 Geno Atkins/99 5.00 12.00
31 Aaron Jones/99 6.00 15.00
32 J.J. Watt/15 EXCH 40.00 80.00
33 Sterling Sharpe/99 6.00 15.00
34 Michael Bennett/25 8.00 20.00
35 Stefon Diggs/99 EXCH 10.00 25.00
36 Melvin Ingram/99 5.00 12.00
37 Jordan Howard/99 8.00 20.00
38 Travis Kelce/49 10.00 25.00
39 Bob Lilly/49 8.00 20.00
40 Bo Jackson/25 40.00 80.00
41 Zach Thomas/49 12.00 30.00
42 Darren Woodson/49 8.00 20.00
43 Warrick Dunn/25 15.00 40.00
45 Randy Moss/25
46 Curtis Martin/25 10.00 25.00
47 Mike Singletary/25 12.00 30.00
48 Kirk Cousins/25 75.00 150.00
49 Michael Vick/35 15.00 40.00
50 Brett Keisel/99 5.00 12.00

2018 Panini Spectra Sunday Spectacle Jerseys

*BLUE/99: .5X TO 1.2X BASIC JSY/199
*BLUE/50: .5X TO 1.2X BASIC JSY/75-99
*GREEN/25: .8X TO 2X BASIC JSY/199
*GREEN/25: .6X TO 1.5X BASIC JSY/75-99
*PINK/15: 1X TO 2.5X BASIC JSY/199
*PINK/15: .8X TO 2X BASIC JSY/75-99
1 Stefon Diggs/199 3.00 8.00
2 Tyler Lockett/199 3.00 8.00
3 Devontae Booker/199 2.50 6.00
4 JuJu Smith-Schuster/199 4.00 10.00
5 Von Miller/99 4.00 10.00
6 Ty Montgomery/199 2.50 6.00
7 Dak Prescott/199 4.00 10.00
8 Nelson Agholor/199 2.50 6.00
9 C.J. Mosley/199 3.00 8.00
10 Cooper Kupp/199 3.00 8.00
11 Duke Johnson Jr./199 2.50 6.00
12 Jordan Howard/199 4.00 10.00
13 Larry Fitzgerald/199 3.00 8.00
14 Golden Tate III/199 3.00 8.00
15 Tyler Eifert/199 2.50 6.00
16 Kareem Hunt/199 3.00 8.00
17 Michael Thomas/199 4.00 10.00
18 Zach Ertz/199 3.00 8.00
19 Shaq Lawson/199 2.50 6.00
20 DeSean Jackson/199 3.00 8.00
21 Terrance Williams/199 2.50 6.00
22 Jamison Crowder/199 2.50 6.00
23 Kenny Golladay/199 2.50 6.00
24 Jerry Hughes/199 2.50 6.00
25 Amari Cooper/199 4.00 10.00
26 Cameron Wake/199 2.50 6.00
27 Kenyan Drake/199 2.50 6.00
28 DeAndre Washington/199 2.50 6.00
29 Josh Doctson/199 2.50 6.00
30 Sterling Shepard/199 3.00 8.00
31 Devonta Freeman/199 3.00 8.00
32 Clay Matthews/199 3.00 8.00
33 Marqise Lee/199 2.50 6.00
34 Tevin Coleman/199 2.50 6.00
35 Dede Westbrook/100 2.50 6.00
36 O.J. Howard/199 2.50 6.00
37 T.Y. Hilton/199 3.00 8.00
38 Demaryius Thomas/199
39 Corey Davis/199 3.00 8.00
40 Noah Brown/199 2.50 6.00
41 Devin Funchess/199 2.50 6.00
42 Geno Atkins/199 2.50 6.00
43 Hunter Henry/199 2.50 6.00
44 DeVante Parker/199 3.00 8.00
45 Christian McCaffrey/199 4.00 10.00
46 Joey Bosa/199 4.00 10.00
47 Mike Williams/199 2.50 6.00
48 Derrick Henry/199 4.00 10.00
49 Patrick Peterson/75 3.00 8.00
50 D'Onta Foreman/199 2.50 6.00

2018 Panini Spectra Synced Swatches

*BLUE/75: .4X TO 1X BASIC JSY/99
*GREEN/50: .5X TO 1.2X BASIC JSY/99
*PINK/15: .8X TO 2X BASIC JSY/99
1 R.Freeman/C.Sutton 4.00 10.00
2 N.Chubb/B.Mayfield 10.00 25.00
3 C.Kirk/J.Rosen 10.00 25.00
4 K.Lauletta/S.Barkley 12.00 30.00
5 J.Samuels/M.Rudolph 6.00 15.00
6 J.Scott/L.Jackson 10.00 25.00
7 N.Hines/D.Fountain 3.00 8.00
8 M.White/M.Gallup 5.00 12.00
9 J.Washington/M.Rudolph 6.00 15.00
10 C.Ridley/M.Ryan 6.00 15.00
11 J.Moore/M.Valdes-Scantling 3.00 8.00
12 D.Hamilton/C.Sutton 4.00 10.00
13 P.Mahomes II/K.Hunt 10.00 25.00
14 J.Rosen/L.Fitzgerald 10.00 25.00
15 E.Manning/S.Barkley 12.00 30.00
16 R.Penny/R.Wilson 5.00 12.00
17 R.Jones II/J.Winston 3.00 8.00
18 K.Johnson/M.Stafford 4.00 10.00
19 K.Coutee/D.Watson 5.00 12.00
20 A.Miller/M.Trubisky 4.00 10.00
21 B.Chubb/V.Miller 4.00 10.00
22 M.Thomas/T.Smith 4.00 10.00
23 L.Jackson/H.Hurst 10.00 25.00
24 J.Allen/L.McCoy 8.00 20.00
25 A.Dalton/M.Walton 3.00 8.00
26 M.Gesicki/K.Ballage 3.00 8.00
27 I.Smith/M.Ryan 3.00 8.00
28 D.Chark Jr./L.Fournette 4.00 10.00
29 D.Prescott/M.Gallup 5.00 12.00
30 T.Kelce/P.Mahomes II 10.00 25.00

2015 Panini Super Bowl Highlights

COMPLETE SET (16)
1 Kurt Warner
2 Malcolm Smith
3 Joe Flacco
4 Eli Manning
5 Peyton Manning
6 Drew Brees
7 Santonio Holmes
8 Emmitt Smith
9 John Elway
10 Jerry Rice
11 Troy Aikman
12 Aaron Rodgers
13 Kurt Warner
14 Tom Brady
15 Russell Wilson
16 Tom Brady

2016 Panini Super Bowl 50

1 Super Bowl Logo .60 1.50

2011 Panini Team Colors National Convention

TC1 Jay Cutler 1.25 3.00
TC2 Brian Urlacher 1.25 3.00
TC3 Devin Hester 1.25 3.00
TC4 Matt Forte 1.25 3.00

1988 Panini Stickers

This set of 433 different stickers (457 different subjects including half stickers) was issued in 1988 by Panini. Panini had been producing stickers under Topps license but, beginning with this set, Panini established its own trade name in this country separate from Topps. The stickers measure approximately 2 1/8" by 2 3/4", are numbered on both the front and the back, and are in alphabetical order by team. The album for the set is easily obtainable. It is organized in team order like the sticker numbering. On the inside back cover of the sticker album the company offered (via direct mail-order) up to 30 different stickers of your choice for either ten cents each (only in Canada) or in trade one-for-one for your unwanted extra stickers (only in the United States) plus 1.00 for postage and handling; this is one reason why the values of the most popular players in these sticker sets are somewhat depressed compared to traditional card set prices. Each sticker pack included one foil sticker. Team name foils were produced in pairs; the other member of the pair is listed parenthetically. The team name foils contain a referee signal on the sticker back, the helmet foils have the team's stadium on the back, and the uniform foils include a team "Huddles" cartoon card on the back. The album for the set features John Elway on the cover. Bo Jackson appears in his Rookie Football Card year and Simon Fletcher appears one year prior to his Rookie Cards.

COMPLETE SET (447) 14.00 35.00
1 Super Bowl XXII .04 .10
2 Buffalo Bills Helmet FOIL .04 .10
3 Buffalo Bills Action .04 .10
4 Cornelius Bennett .08 .20
5 Chris Burkett .04 .10
6 Derrick Burroughs .04 .10
7 Shane Conlan .08 .20
8 Ronnie Harmon .04 .10
9 Jim Kelly .30 .75
10 Buffalo Bills FOIL (240) .04 .10
11 Mark Kelso .04 .10
12 Nate Odomes .04 .10
13 Andre Reed .08 .20
14 Fred Smerlas .04 .10
15 Bruce Smith .10 .25
16 Buffalo Bills Uniform FOIL .04 .10
17 Cincinnati Bengals Helmet FOIL .04 .10
18 Cincinnati Bengals Action .04 .10
19 Jim Breech .04 .10
20 James Brooks .04 .10
21 Eddie Brown .04 .10
22 Cris Collinsworth .04 .10
23 Boomer Esiason .08 .20
24 Rodney Holman .04 .10
25 Cincinnati Bengals FOIL (255) .04 .10
26 Larry Kinnebrew .04 .10
27 Tim Krumrie .04 .10
28 Anthony Munoz .08 .20
29 Reggie Williams .04 .10
30 Carl Zander .04 .10
31 Cincinnati Bengals Uniform FOIL .04 .10
32 Cleveland Browns Helmet FOIL .04 .10
33 Cleveland Browns Action .04 .10
34 Earnest Byner .08 .20
35 Hanford Dixon .04 .10

Card	Low	High
36 Bob Golic	.04	.10
37 Mike Johnson	.04	.10
38 Bernie Kosar	.08	.20
39 Kevin Mack	.04	.10
40 Cleveland Browns FOIL (270)	.04	.10
41 Clay Matthews	.04	.10
42 Gerald McNeil	.04	.10
43 Frank Minnifield	.04	.10
44 Ozzie Newsome	.08	.20
45 Cody Risien	.04	.10
46 Cleveland Browns Uniform FOIL	.04	.10
47 Denver Broncos Helmet FOIL	.04	.10
48 Denver Broncos Action	.04	.10
49 Keith Bishop	.04	.10
50 Tony Dorsett	.08	.20
51 John Elway	1.50	4.00
52 Simon Fletcher	.04	.10
53 Mark Jackson	.04	.10
54 Vance Johnson	.04	.10
55 Denver Broncos FOIL (285)	.04	.10
56 Rulon Jones	.04	.10
57 Rich Karlis	.04	.10
58 Karl Mecklenburg	.04	.10
59 Ricky Nattiel	.04	.10
60 Sammy Winder	.04	.10
61 Denver Broncos Uniform FOIL	.04	.10
62 Houston Oilers Helmet FOIL	.04	.10
63 Houston Oilers Action	.08	.20
64 Keith Bostic	.04	.10
65 Steve Brown	.04	.10
66 Ray Childress	.04	.10
67 Jeff Donaldson	.04	.10
68 John Grimsley	.04	.10
69 Robert Lyles	.04	.10
70 Houston Oilers FOIL (300)	.04	.10
71 Drew Hill	.04	.10
72 Warren Moon	.20	.50
73 Mike Munchak	.04	.10
74 Mike Rozier	.04	.10
75 Johnny Meads	.04	.10
76 Houston Oilers Uniform FOIL	.04	.10
77 Indianapolis Colts Helmet FOIL	.04	.10
78 Indianapolis Colts Action	.04	.10
79 Albert Bentley	.04	.10
80 Dean Biasucci	.04	.10
81 Duane Bickett	.04	.10
82 Bill Brooks	.04	.10
83 Johnie Cooks	.04	.10
84 Eric Dickerson	.08	.20
85 Indianapolis Colts FOIL (315)	.04	.10
86 Ray Donaldson	.04	.10
87 Chris Hinton	.04	.10
88 Cliff Odom	.04	.10
89 Barry Krauss	.04	.10
90 Jack Trudeau	.04	.10
91 Indianapolis Colts Uniform FOIL	.04	.10
92 Kansas City Chiefs Helmet FOIL	.04	.10
93 Kansas City Chiefs Action	.04	.10
94 Carlos Carson	.04	.10
95 Deron Cherry	.04	.10
96 Dino Hackett	.04	.10
97 Bill Kenney	.04	.10
98 Albert Lewis	.08	.20
99 Nick Lowery	.04	.10
100 Kansas City Chiefs FOIL (330)	.04	.10
101 Bill Maas	.04	.10
102 Christian Okoye	.08	.20
103 Stephone Paige	.04	.10
104 Paul Palmer	.04	.10
105 Kevin Ross	.04	.10
106 Kansas City Chiefs Uniform FOIL	.04	.10
107 Los Angeles Raiders Helmet FOIL	.04	.10
108 Los Angeles Raiders Action	.08	.20
109 Marcus Allen	.12	.30
110 Todd Christensen	.04	.10
111 Mike Haynes	.04	.10
112 Bo Jackson	.08	.20
113 James Lofton	.08	.20
114 Howie Long	.08	.20
115 Los Angeles Raiders FOIL (345)	.04	.10
116 Rod Martin	.04	.10
117 Vann McElroy	.04	.10
118 Bill Pickel	.04	.10
119 Don Mosebar	.04	.10
120 Stacey Toran	.04	.10
121 Los Angeles Raiders Uniform FOIL	.04	.10
122 Miami Dolphins Helmet FOIL	.04	.10
123 Miami Dolphins Action	.04	.10
124 John Bosa	.04	.10
125 Mark Clayton	.04	.10
126 Mark Duper	.04	.10
127 Lorenzo Hampton	.04	.10
128 William Judson	.04	.10
129 Dan Marino	1.50	4.00
130 Miami Dolphins FOIL (360)	.04	.10
131 John Offerdahl	.04	.10
132 Reggie Roby	.04	.10
133 Jackie Shipp	.04	.10
134 Dwight Stephenson	.04	.10
135 Troy Stradford	.04	.10
136 Miami Dolphins Uniform FOIL	.04	.10
137 New England Patriots Helmet FOIL	.04	.10
138 New England Patriots Action	.04	.10
139 Bruce Armstrong	.04	.10
140 Raymond Clayborn	.04	.10
141 Reggie Dupard	.04	.10
142 Steve Grogan	.04	.10
143 Craig James	.04	.10
144 Ronnie Lippett	.04	.10
145 New England Patriots FOIL (375)	.04	.10
146 Fred Marion	.04	.10
147 Stanley Morgan	.04	.10
148 Mosi Tatupu	.04	.10
149 Andre Tippett	.04	.10
150 Garin Veris	.04	.10
151 New England Patriots Uniform FOIL	.04	.10
152 New York Jets Helmet FOIL	.04	.10
153 New York Jets Action	.04	.10
154 Bob Crable	.04	.10
155 Mark Gastineau	.04	.10
156 Pat Leahy	.04	.10
157 Johnny Hector	.04	.10
158 Marty Lyons	.04	.10
159 Freeman McNeil	.04	.10
160 New York Jets FOIL (390)	.04	.10
161 Ken O'Brien	.04	.10
162 Mickey Shuler	.04	.10
163 Al Toon	.04	.10
164 Roger Vick	.04	.10
165 Wesley Walker	.04	.10
166 New York Jets Uniform FOIL	.04	.10
167 Pittsburgh Steelers Helmet FOIL	.04	.10
168 Pittsburgh Steelers Action	.04	.10
169 Walter Abercrombie	.04	.10
170 Gary Anderson K	.04	.10
171 Todd Blackledge	.04	.10
172 Thomas Everett	.04	.10
173 Delton Hall	.04	.10
174 Bryan Hinkle	.04	.10
175 Pittsburgh Steelers FOIL (405)	.04	.10
176 Earnest Jackson	.04	.10
177 Louis Lipps	.04	.10
178 David Little	.04	.10
179 Mike Merriweather	.04	.10
180 Mike Webster	.04	.10
181 Pittsburgh Steelers Uniform FOIL	.04	.10
182 San Diego Chargers Helmet FOIL	.04	.10
183 San Diego Chargers Action	.04	.10
184 Gary Anderson RB	.04	.10
185 Chip Banks	.04	.10
186 Martin Bayless	.04	.10
187 Chuck Ehin	.04	.10
188 Vencie Glenn	.04	.10
189 Lionel James	.04	.10
190 San Diego Chargers FOIL (420)	.04	.10
191 Mark Malone	.04	.10
192 Ralf Mojsiejenko	.04	.10
193 Billy Ray Smith	.04	.10
194 Lee Williams	.04	.10
195 Kellen Winslow	.08	.20
196 San Diego Chargers Uniform FOIL	.04	.10
197 Seattle Seahawks Helmet FOIL	.04	.10
198 Seattle Seahawks Action	.04	.10
199 Eugene Robinson	.04	.10
200 Jeff Bryant	.04	.10
201 Raymond Butler	.04	.10
202 Jacob Green	.04	.10
203 Norm Johnson	.04	.10
204 Dave Krieg	.04	.10
205 Seattle Seahawks FOIL (435)	.04	.10
206 Steve Largent	.20	.50
207 Joe Nash	.04	.10
208 Curt Warner	.04	.10
209 Bobby Joe Edmonds	.04	.10
210 Daryl Turner	.04	.10
211 Seattle Seahawks Uniform FOIL	.04	.10
212 AFC Logo	.04	.10
213 Bernie Kosar	.08	.20
214 Curt Warner	.04	.10
215 Jerry Rice	.60	1.50
Largent		
216 Mark Bavaro	.04	.10
Munoz		
217 Gary Zimmerman	.08	.20
Fralic		
218 Dwight Stephenson	.04	.10
Munchak		
219 Joe Montana	2.00	5.00
220 Charles White	.10	.25
Dickerson		
221 Morten Andersen	.04	.10
Sikahema		
222 Bruce Smith	.12	.30
R.White DE		
223 Michael Carter	.04	.10
McMichael		
224 Jim Arnold	.04	.10
225 Carl Banks	.04	.10
Tippett		
226 Barry Wilburn	.04	.10
Singletary		
227 Hanford Dixon	.04	.10
Minnifield		
228 Ronnie Lott	.08	.20
Browner		
229 NFC Logo	.04	.10
230 Gary Clark	.08	.20
231 Richard Dent	.08	.20
232 Atlanta Falcons Helmet FOIL	.04	.10
233 Atlanta Falcons Action	.04	.10
234 Rick Bryan	.04	.10
235 Bobby Butler	.04	.10
236 Tony Casillas	.04	.10
237 Floyd Dixon	.04	.10
238 Rick Donnelly	.04	.10
239 Bill Fralic	.04	.10
240 Atlanta Falcons FOIL (10)	.04	.10
241 Mike Gann	.04	.10
242 Chris Miller	.08	.20
243 Robert Moore	.04	.10
244 John Rade	.04	.10
245 Gerald Riggs	.04	.10
246 Atlanta Falcons Uniform FOIL	.04	.10
247 Chicago Bears Helmet FOIL	.04	.10
248 Chicago Bears Action	.04	.10
249 Neal Anderson	.08	.20
250 Jim Covert	.04	.10
251 Richard Dent	.08	.20
252 Dave Duerson	.04	.10
253 Dennis Gentry	.04	.10
254 Jay Hilgenberg	.04	.10
255 Chicago Bears FOIL (25)	.04	.10
256 Jim McMahon	.08	.20
257 Steve McMichael	.04	.10
258 Matt Suhey	.04	.10
259 Mike Singletary	.08	.20
260 Otis Wilson	.04	.10
261 Chicago Bears Uniform FOIL	.04	.10
262 Dallas Cowboys Helmet FOIL	.04	.10
263 Dallas Cowboys Action	.04	.10
264 Bill Bates	.04	.10
265 Doug Cosbie	.04	.10
266 Ron Francis	.04	.10
267 Jim Jeffcoat	.04	.10
268 Ed Too Tall Jones	.08	.20
269 Eugene Lockhart	.04	.10
270 Dallas Cowboys FOIL (40)	.04	.10
271 Danny Noonan	.04	.10
272 Steve Pelluer	.04	.10
273 Herschel Walker	.08	.20
274 Everson Walls	.04	.10
275 Randy White	.08	.20
276 Dallas Cowboys Uniform FOIL	.04	.10
277 Detroit Lions Helmet FOIL	.04	.10
278 Detroit Lions Action	.04	.10
279 Jim Arnold	.04	.10
280 Jerry Ball	.04	.10
281 Michael Cofer	.04	.10
282 Keith Ferguson	.04	.10
283 Dennis Gibson	.04	.10
284 James Griffin	.04	.10
285 Detroit Lions FOIL (55)	.04	.10
286 James Jones FB	.04	.10
287 Chuck Long	.04	.10
288 Pete Mandley	.04	.10
289 Eddie Murray	.04	.10
290 Garry James	.04	.10
291 Detroit Lions Uniform FOIL	.04	.10
292 Green Bay Packers Helmet FOIL	.04	.10
293 Green Bay Packers Action	.04	.10
294 John Anderson	.04	.10
295 Dave Brown DB	.04	.10
296 Alphonso Carreker	.04	.10
297 Kenneth Davis	.04	.10
298 Phillip Epps	.04	.10
299 Brent Fullwood	.04	.10
300 Green Bay Packers FOIL (70)	.04	.10
301 Tim Harris	.04	.10
302 Johnny Holland	.04	.10
303 Mark Murphy	.04	.10
304 Brian Noble	.04	.10
305 Walter Stanley	.04	.10
306 Green Bay Packers Uniform FOIL	.04	.10
307 Los Angeles Rams Helmet FOIL	.04	.10
308 Los Angeles Rams Action	.04	.10
309 Jim Collins	.04	.10
310 Henry Ellard	.10	.25
311 Jim Everett	.08	.20
312 Jerry Gray	.04	.10
313 LeRoy Irvin	.04	.10
314 Mike Lansford	.04	.10
315 Los Angeles Rams FOIL (85)	.04	.10
316 Mel Owens	.04	.10
317 Jackie Slater	.04	.10
318 Doug Smith	.04	.10
319 Charles White	.04	.10
320 Mike Wilcher	.04	.10
321 Los Angeles Rams Uniform FOIL	.04	.10
322 Minnesota Vikings Helmet FOIL	.04	.10
323 Minnesota Vikings Action	.04	.10
324 Joey Browner	.04	.10
325 Anthony Carter	.04	.10
326 Chris Doleman	.08	.20
327 D.J. Dozier	.04	.10
328 Steve Jordan	.04	.10
329 Tommy Kramer	.04	.10
330 Minnesota Vikings FOIL (100)	.04	.10
331 Darrin Nelson	.04	.10
332 Jesse Solomon	.04	.10
333 Scott Studwell	.04	.10
334 Wade Wilson	.04	.10
335 Gary Zimmerman	.08	.20
336 Minnesota Vikings Uniform FOIL	.04	.10
337 New Orleans Saints Helmet FOIL	.04	.10
338 New Orleans Saints Action	.04	.10
339 Morten Andersen	.04	.10
340 Bruce Clark	.04	.10
341 Brad Edelman	.04	.10
342 Bobby Hebert	.04	.10
343 Dalton Hilliard	.04	.10
344 Rickey Jackson	.04	.10
345 New Orleans Saints FOIL (115)	.04	.10
346 Vaughan Johnson	.04	.10
347 Rueben Mayes	.04	.10
348 Sam Mills	.08	.20
349 Pat Swilling	.08	.20
350 Dave Waymer	.04	.10
351 New Orleans Saints Uniform FOIL	.04	.10
352 New York Giants Helmet FOIL	.04	.10
353 New York Giants Action	.04	.10
354 Carl Banks	.04	.10
355 Mark Bavaro	.04	.10
356 Jim Burt	.04	.10
357 Harry Carson	.04	.10
358 Terry Kinard	.04	.10
359 Lionel Manuel	.04	.10
360 New York Giants FOIL (130)	.04	.10
361 Leonard Marshall	.04	.10
362 George Martin	.04	.10
363 Joe Morris	.04	.10
364 Phil Simms	.10	.25
365 George Adams	.04	.10
366 New York Giants Uniform FOIL	.04	.10
367 Philadelphia Eagles Helmet FOIL	.04	.10
368 Philadelphia Eagles Action	.08	.20
369 Jerome Brown	.08	.20
370 Keith Byars	.08	.20
371 Randall Cunningham	.08	.20
372 Terry Hoage	.04	.10
373 Seth Joyner	.08	.20
374 Mike Quick	.04	.10
375 Philadelphia Eagles FOIL (145)	.04	.10
376 Clyde Simmons	.04	.10
377 Anthony Toney	.04	.10
378 Andre Waters	.04	.10
379 Reggie White	.20	.50
380 Roynell Young	.04	.10
381 Philadelphia Eagles Uniform FOIL	.04	.10
382 Phoenix Cardinals Helmet FOIL	.04	.10
383 Phoenix Cardinals Action	.04	.10
384 Robert Awalt	.04	.10
385 Roy Green	.04	.10
386 Neil Lomax	.04	.10
387 Stump Mitchell	.04	.10
388 Niko Noga	.04	.10
389 Freddie Joe Nunn	.04	.10
390 Phoenix Cardinals FOIL (160)	.04	.10
391 Luis Sharpe	.04	.10
392 Vai Sikahema	.04	.10
393 J.T. Smith	.04	.10
394 Leonard Smith	.04	.10
395 Lonnie Young	.04	.10
396 Phoenix Cardinals Uniform FOIL	.04	.10
397 San Francisco 49ers Helmet FOIL	.04	.10
398 San Francisco 49ers Action	.40	1.00
399 Dwaine Board	.04	.10
400 Michael Carter	.04	.10
401 Roger Craig	.04	.10
402 Jeff Fuller	.04	.10
403 Don Griffin	.04	.10
404 Ronnie Lott	.08	.20
405 San Francisco 49ers FOIL (175)	.04	.10
406 Joe Montana	2.00	5.00
407 Tom Rathman	.08	.20
408 Jerry Rice	1.00	2.50
409 Keena Turner	.04	.10
410 Michael Walter	.04	.10
411 San Francisco 49ers Uniform FOIL	.04	.10
412 Tampa Bay Bucs Helmet FOIL	.04	.10
413 Tampa Bay Bucs Action	.04	.10
414 Mark Carrier WR	.08	.20
415 Gerald Carter	.04	.10
416 Ron Holmes	.04	.10
417 Rod Jones CB	.04	.10
418 Calvin Magee	.04	.10
419 Ervin Randle	.04	.10
420 Tampa Bay Buccaneers FOIL (190)	.04	.10
421 Donald Igwebuike	.04	.10
422 Vinny Testaverde	.08	.20
423 Jackie Walker TE	.04	.10
424 Chris Washington	.04	.10
425 James Wilder	.04	.10
426 Tampa Bay Bucs Uniform FOIL	.04	.10
427 Washington Redskins Helmet FOIL	.04	.10
428 Washington Redskins Action	.04	.10
429 Gary Clark	.08	.20
430 Monte Coleman	.04	.10
431 Darrell Green	.08	.20
432 Charles Mann	.04	.10
433 Kelvin Bryant	.04	.10
434 Art Monk	.08	.20
435 Washington Redskins FOIL (205)	.04	.10
436 Ricky Sanders	.08	.20
437 Jay Schroeder	.04	.10
438 Alvin Walton	.04	.10
439 Barry Wilburn	.04	.10
440 Doug Williams	.08	.20
441 Washington Redskins Uniform FOIL	.04	.10
442 Super Bowl action	.04	.10
443 Super Bowl action	.04	.10
444 Doug Williams	.04	.10
445 Super Bowl action	.04	.10
446 Super Bowl action	.04	.10
447 Super Bowl action	.04	.10
NNO Panini Album	1.00	2.50

1989 Panini Stickers

This set of 416 stickers was issued in 1989 by Panini. The stickers measure approximately 1 15/16" by 3" and are numbered on the front and on the back. The album for the set is easily obtainable. It is organized in team order like the sticker numbering. On the inside back cover of the sticker album the company offered (via direct mail-order) up to 30 different stickers of your choice for either ten cents each (only in Canada) or in trade one-for-one for your unwanted extra stickers (only in the United States) plus 1.00 for postage and handling; this is one reason why the values of the most popular players in these sticker sets are somewhat depressed compared to traditional card set prices. The album for the set features Joe Montana on the cover. Tim Brown, Cris Carter, Michael Irvin, Keith Jackson, Jay Novacek, Sterling Sharpe, Thurman Thomas, Rod Woodson appear in their Rookie Card year. The stickers were also issued in a UK version which is distinguished by the presence of stats printed on the sticker backs. The UK version album also features Joe Montana as well as the TV-4 logo.

Card	Low	High
COMPLETE SET (416)	8.00	20.00
COMP.UK SET (416)	100.00	250.00
*UK VERSION: 5X TO 10X		
1 SB XXIII Program	.04	.10
2 SB XXIII Program	.04	.10
3 Floyd Dixon	.04	.10
4 Tony Casillas	.04	.10
5 Bill Fralic	.04	.10
6 Aundray Bruce	.04	.10
7 Scott Case	.04	.10
8 Rick Donnelly	.04	.10
9 Atlanta Falcons Logo FOIL	.04	.10
10 Atlanta Falcons Helmet FOIL	.04	.10
11 Marcus Cotton	.04	.10
12 Chris Miller	.04	.10
13 Robert Moore	.04	.10
14 Bobby Butler	.04	.10
15 Rick Bryan	.04	.10
16 John Settle	.04	.10
17 Jim McMahon	.04	.10
18 Neal Anderson	.04	.10
19 Dave Duerson	.04	.10
20 Steve McMichael	.04	.10
21 Jay Hilgenberg	.04	.10
22 Dennis McKinnon	.04	.10
23 Chicago Bears Logo FOIL	.04	.10
24 Chicago Bears Helmet FOIL	.04	.10
25 Richard Dent	.04	.10
26 Dennis Gentry	.04	.10
27 Mike Singletary	.04	.10
28 Vestee Jackson	.04	.10
29 Mike Tomczak	.04	.10
30 Dan Hampton	.04	.10
31 Michael Irvin	.40	1.00
32 Eugene Lockhart	.04	.10
33 Herschel Walker	.04	.10
34 Kelvin Martin	.04	.10
35 Jim Jeffcoat	.04	.10
36 Everson Walls	.04	.10
37 Dallas Cowboys Logo FOIL	.04	.10
38 Dallas Cowboys Helmet FOIL	.04	.10
39 Danny Noonan	.04	.10
40 Ray Alexander	.04	.10
41 Garry Cobb	.04	.10
42 Ed Too Tall Jones	.04	.10
43 Kevin Brooks	.04	.10
44 Bill Bates	.04	.10
45 Detroit Lions Logo FOIL	.04	.10
46 Chuck Long	.04	.10
47 Jim Arnold	.04	.10
48 Michael Cofer	.04	.10
49 Eddie Murray	.04	.10
50 Keith Ferguson	.04	.10
51 Pete Mandley	.04	.10
52 Detroit Lions Helmet FOIL	.04	.10
53 Jerry Ball	.04	.10
54 Bennie Blades	.04	.10
55 Dennis Gibson	.04	.10
56 Chris Spielman	.08	.20
57 Eric Williams	.04	.10
58 Lomas Brown	.04	.10
59 Johnny Holland	.04	.10
60 Tim Harris	.04	.10
61 Mark Murphy	.04	.10
62 Walter Stanley	.04	.10
63 Brent Fullwood	.04	.10
64 Ken Ruettgers	.04	.10
65 Green Bay Packers Logo FOIL	.04	.10
66 Green Bay Packers	.04	.10
Helmet FOIL		
67 John Anderson	.04	.10
68 Brian Noble	.04	.10
69 Sterling Sharpe	.15	.40
70 Keith Woodside	.04	.10
71 Mark Lee	.04	.10
72 Don Majkowski	.04	.10
73 Aaron Cox	.04	.10
74 LeRoy Irvin	.04	.10
75 Jim Everett	.04	.10
76 Mike Lansford	.04	.10
77 Mike Wilcher	.04	.10
78 Henry Ellard	.08	.20
79 Los Angeles Rams	.04	.10
Helmet FOIL		
80 Jerry Gray	.04	.10
81 Doug Smith	.04	.10
82 Tom Newberry	.04	.10
83 Jackie Slater	.04	.10
84 Greg Bell	.04	.10
85 Kevin Greene	.08	.20
86 Chris Doleman	.04	.10
87 Steve Jordan	.04	.10
88 Jesse Solomon	.04	.10
89 Randall McDaniel	.20	.50
90 Hassan Jones	.04	.10
91 Joey Browner	.04	.10
92 Minnesota Vikings	.04	.10
Logo FOIL		
93 Minnesota Vikings	.04	.10
Helmet FOIL		
94 Anthony Carter	.08	.20
95 Gary Zimmerman	.08	.20
96 Wade Wilson	.04	.10
97 Scott Studwell	.04	.10
98 Keith Millard	.04	.10
99 Carl Lee	.04	.10
100 Morten Andersen	.04	.10
101 Bobby Hebert	.04	.10
102 Rueben Mayes	.04	.10
103 Sam Mills	.04	.10
104 Vaughan Johnson	.04	.10
105 Pat Swilling	.04	.10
106 New Orleans Saints	.04	.10
Logo FOIL		
107 New Orleans Saints	.04	.10
Helmet FOIL		
108 Brad Edelman	.04	.10
109 Craig Heyward	.04	.10
110 Eric Martin	.04	.10
111 Dalton Hilliard	.04	.10
112 Lonzell Hill	.04	.10
113 Rickey Jackson	.04	.10
114 Erik Howard	.04	.10
115 Phil Simms	.04	.10
116 Leonard Marshall	.04	.10
117 Joe Morris	.04	.10
118 Bart Oates	.04	.10
119 Mark Bavaro	.04	.10
120 New York Giants	.04	.10
Logo FOIL		
121 New York Giants	.04	.10
Helmet FOIL		
122 Terry Kinard	.04	.10
123 Carl Banks	.04	.10
124 Lionel Manuel	.04	.10
125 Stephen Baker	.04	.10
126 Pepper Johnson	.04	.10
127 Jim Burt	.04	.10
128 Cris Carter	1.00	2.50
129 Mike Quick	.04	.10
130 Terry Hoage	.04	.10
131 Keith Jackson	.08	.20
132 Clyde Simmons	.04	.10
133 Eric Allen	.04	.10
134 Philadelphia Eagles	.04	.10
Logo FOIL		
135 Philadelphia Eagles	.04	.10
Helmet FOIL		
136 Randall Cunningham	.20	.50
137 Mike Pitts	.04	.10
138 Keith Byars	.04	.10
139 Seth Joyner	.04	.10
140 Jerome Brown	.08	.20
141 Reggie White	.08	.20
142 Jay Novacek	.08	.20
143 Neil Lomax	.04	.10
144 Ken Harvey	.04	.10
145 Freddie Joe Nunn	.04	.10
146 Robert Awalt	.04	.10
147 Niko Noga	.04	.10
148 Phoenix Cardinals	.04	.10
Logo FOIL		
149 Phoenix Cardinals	.04	.10
Helmet FOIL		
150 Tim McDonald	.04	.10
151 Roy Green	.04	.10
152 Stump Mitchell	.04	.10
153 J.T. Smith	.04	.10
154 Luis Sharpe	.04	.10
155 Vai Sikahema	.04	.10
156 Jeff Fuller	.04	.10
157 Joe Montana	1.50	4.00
158 Harris Barton	.04	.10
159 Michael Carter	.04	.10
160 Jeff Fuller	.04	.10
161 Jerry Rice	.60	1.50
162 San Francisco 49ers	.04	.10
Logo FOIL		
163 San Francisco 49ers	.04	.10
Helmet FOIL		
164 Tom Rathman	.04	.10
165 Roger Craig	.08	.20
166 Ronnie Lott	.08	.20
167 Charles Haley	.08	.20
168 John Taylor	.08	.20
169 Michael Walter	.04	.10
170 Ron Hall	.04	.10
171 Ervin Randle	.04	.10
172 James Wilder	.04	.10
173 Ron Holmes	.04	.10
174 Mark Carrier WR	.08	.20
175 William Howard	.04	.10
176 Tampa Bay Bucs	.04	.10
Logo FOIL		
177 Tampa Bay Bucs	.04	.10
Helmet FOIL		
178 Lars Tate	.04	.10
179 Vinny Testaverde	.08	.20
180 Paul Gruber	.04	.10
181 Bruce Hill	.04	.10
182 Reuben Davis	.04	.10
183 Ricky Reynolds	.04	.10
184 Ricky Sanders	.04	.10
185 Gary Clark	.08	.20
186 Mark May	.04	.10
187 Darrell Green	.04	.10
188 Jim Lachey	.04	.10
189 Doug Williams	.04	.10
190 Washington Redskins	.04	.10
Helmet FOIL		
191 Washington Redskins	.04	.10
Logo FOIL		
192 Kelvin Bryant	.04	.10
193 Charles Mann	.04	.10
194 Alvin Walton	.04	.10
195 Art Monk	.08	.20
196 Barry Wilburn	.04	.10
197 Mark Rypien	.04	.10
198 NFC Logo	.04	.10
199 Scott Case	.04	.10
200 Herschel Walker	.04	.10
201 Herschel Walker	.08	.20
202 Henry Ellard	.20	.50
Rice		
203 Bruce Matthews	.04	.10
204 Gary Zimmerman	.08	.20
205 Boomer Esiason	.04	.10
206 Jay Hilgenberg	.04	.10
207 Keith Jackson	.08	.20
208 Reggie White	.08	.20
209 Keith Millard	.04	.10
210 Carl Lee	.04	.10
211 Joey Browner	.04	.10
212 Shane Conlan	.04	.10
213 Mike Singletary	.04	.10
214 Cornelius Bennett	.04	.10
215 AFC Logo	.04	.10
216 Boomer Esiason	.04	.10
217 Erik McMillan	.04	.10
218 Jim Kelly	.15	.40
219 Cornelius Bennett	.04	.10
220 Fred Smerlas	.04	.10
221 Shane Conlan	.04	.10
222 Scott Norwood	.04	.10
223 Mark Kelso	.04	.10
224 Buffalo Bills Logo FOIL	.04	.10
225 Buffalo Bills Helmet FOIL	.04	.10
226 Thurman Thomas	.30	.75
227 Pete Metzelaars	.04	.10
228 Bruce Smith	.08	.20
229 Art Still	.04	.10
230 Kent Hull	.04	.10
231 Andre Reed	.08	.20
232 Tim Krumrie	.04	.10
233 Boomer Esiason	.04	.10
234 Ickey Woods	.04	.10
235 Eric Thomas	.04	.10
236 Rodney Holman	.04	.10
237 Jim Skow	.04	.10
238 Cincinnati Bengals	.04	.10
Helmet FOIL		
239 James Brooks	.04	.10
240 David Fulcher	.04	.10
241 Carl Zander	.04	.10
242 Eddie Brown	.04	.10
243 Max Montoya	.04	.10
244 Anthony Munoz	.08	.20
245 Felix Wright	.04	.10
246 Clay Matthews	.04	.10
247 Hanford Dixon	.04	.10
248 Ozzie Newsome	.04	.10
249 Bernie Kosar	.04	.10
250 Kevin Mack	.04	.10
251 Cincinnati Bengals	.04	.10
Helmet FOIL		
252 Brian Brennan	.04	.10
253 Reggie Langhorne	.04	.10
254 Cody Risien	.04	.10
255 Webster Slaughter	.04	.10
256 Mike Johnson	.04	.10
257 Frank Minnifield	.04	.10
258 Mike Horan	.04	.10
259 Dennis Smith	.04	.10
260 Ricky Nattiel	.04	.10
261 Karl Mecklenburg	.04	.10
262 Keith Bishop	.04	.10
263 John Elway	1.25	3.00
264 Denver Broncos	.04	.10
Helmet FOIL		
265 Denver Broncos	.04	.10
Logo FOIL		
266 Simon Fletcher	.04	.10
267 Vance Johnson	.04	.10
268 Tony Dorsett	.04	.10
269 Greg Kragen	.04	.10
270 Mike Harden	.04	.10
271 Mark Jackson	.04	.10
272 Warren Moon	.08	.20
273 Mike Rozier	.04	.10
274 Houston Oilers Logo FOIL	.04	.10
275 Allen Pinkett	.04	.10
276 Tony Zendejas	.04	.10
277 Alonzo Highsmith	.04	.10
278 Johnny Meads	.04	.10
279 Houston Oilers	.04	.10
Helmet FOIL		
280 Mike Munchak	.04	.10
281 John Grimsley	.04	.10
282 Ernest Givins	.04	.10
283 Drew Hill	.04	.10
284 Bruce Matthews	.04	.10
285 Ray Childress	.04	.10
286 Indianapolis Colts	.04	.10
Logo FOIL		
287 Chris Hinton	.04	.10
288 Clarence Verdin	.04	.10
289 Jon Hand	.04	.10
290 Chris Chandler	.40	1.00
291 Eugene Daniel	.04	.10
292 Dean Biasucci	.04	.10
293 Indianapolis Colts	.04	.10
Helmet FOIL		
294 Duane Bickett	.04	.10
295 Rohn Stark	.04	.10
296 Albert Bentley	.04	.10
297 Bill Brooks	.04	.10
298 O'Brien Alston	.04	.10
299 Ray Donaldson	.04	.10
300 Carlos Carson	.04	.10
301 Lloyd Burruss	.04	.10
302 Steve DeBerg	.04	.10
303 Irv Eatman	.04	.10
304 Dino Hackett	.04	.10
305 Albert Lewis	.04	.10
306 Kansas City Chiefs	.04	.10
Helmet FOIL		
307 Kansas City Chiefs	.04	.10
Logo FOIL		
308 Deron Cherry	.04	.10
309 Paul Palmer	.04	.10
310 Neil Smith	.12	.30
311 Christian Okoye	.08	.20
312 Stephone Paige	.04	.10
313 Bill Maas	.04	.10
314 Marcus Allen	.08	.20
315 Vann McElroy	.04	.10
316 Mervyn Fernandez	.04	.10
317 Bill Pickel	.04	.10
318 Greg Townsend	.04	.10
319 Tim Brown	.50	1.25
320 Los Angeles Raiders	.04	.10
Logo FOIL		
321 Los Angeles Raiders	.04	.10
Helmet FOIL		
322 James Lofton	.08	.20
323 Willie Gault	.04	.10
324 Jay Schroeder	.04	.10
325 Matt Millen	.04	.10
326 Howie Long	.08	.20
327 Bo Jackson	.10	.25
328 Lorenzo Hampton	.04	.10
329 Jarvis Williams	.04	.10
330 Jim C. Jensen	.04	.10
331 Dan Marino	1.25	3.00
332 John Offerdahl	.04	.10
333 Brian Sochia	.04	.10
334 Miami Dolphins Logo FOIL	.04	.10
335 Miami Dolphins	.04	.10
Helmet FOIL		
336 Ferrell Edmunds	.04	.10
337 Mark Brown	.04	.10
338 Mark Duper	.04	.10
339 Troy Stradford	.04	.10
340 T.J. Turner	.04	.10
341 Mark Clayton	.04	.10
342 New England Patriots	.04	.10
Logo FOIL		
343 Johnny Rembert	.04	.10
344 Garin Veris	.04	.10
345 Stanley Morgan	.04	.10
346 John Stephens	.04	.10
347 Fred Marion	.04	.10
348 Irving Fryar	.08	.20
349 New England Patriots	.04	.10
Helmet FOIL		
350 Andre Tippett	.04	.10
351 Roland James	.04	.10
352 Brent Williams	.04	.10
353 Raymond Clayborn	.04	.10
354 Tony Eason	.04	.10
355 Bruce Armstrong	.04	.10
356 New York Jets Logo FOIL	.04	.10
357 Marty Lyons	.04	.10
358 Bobby Humphery	.04	.10
359 Pat Leahy	.04	.10
360 Mickey Shuler	.04	.10
361 James Hasty	.04	.10
362 Ken O'Brien	.04	.10
363 New York Jets	.04	.10
Helmet FOIL		
364 Alex Gordon	.04	.10
365 Al Toon	.04	.10
366 Erik McMillan	.04	.10
367 Johnny Hector	.04	.10
368 Wesley Walker	.04	.10
369 Freeman McNeil	.04	.10
370 Pittsburgh Steelers	.04	.10
Logo FOIL		
371 Gary Anderson K	.04	.10
372 Rodney Carter	.04	.10
373 Merril Hoge	.04	.10
374 David Little	.04	.10
375 Bubby Brister	.12	.30
376 Thomas Everett	.04	.10
377 Pittsburgh Steelers	.04	.10
Helmet FOIL		
378 Rod Woodson	.25	.60
379 Bryan Hinkle	.04	.10
380 Tunch Ilkin	.04	.10
381 Aaron Jones	.04	.10
382 Louis Lipps	.04	.10
383 Warren Williams	.04	.10
384 Anthony Miller	.08	.20
385 Gary Anderson RB	.04	.10
386 Lee Williams	.04	.10
387 Lionel James	.04	.10
388 Gary Plummer	.04	.10
389 Gill Byrd	.04	.10
390 San Diego Chargers	.04	.10
Helmet FOIL		
391 Ralf Mojsiejenko	.04	.10
392 Rod Bernstine	.04	.10
393 Keith Browner	.04	.10
394 Billy Ray Smith	.04	.10
395 Leslie O'Neal	.04	.10
396 Jamie Holland	.04	.10
397 Tony Woods	.04	.10
398 Bruce Scholtz	.04	.10
399 Joe Nash	.04	.10
400 Curt Warner	.04	.10
401 John L. Williams	.04	.10
402 Bryan Millard	.04	.10
403 Seattle Seahawks	.04	.10
Logo FOIL		
404 Seattle Seahawks	.04	.10
Helmet FOIL		
405 Steve Largent	.12	.30
406 Norm Johnson	.04	.10
407 Jacob Green	.04	.10
408 Dave Krieg	.04	.10
409 Paul Moyer	.04	.10
410 Brian Blades	.08	.20
411 SB XXIII	.04	.10
412 Jerry Rice	.60	1.50
413 SB XXIII	.04	.10
414 SB XXIII	.04	.10
415 SB XXIII	.04	.10
416 SB XXIII	.04	.10
NNO Panini Album	1.25	3.00

1990 Panini Stickers

This set contains 396 colorful stickers. The stickers are numbered in team order. Each sticker measures approximately 1 7/8" by 2 15/16". The cover of the album contains pictures of Mike Singletary, Ronnie Lott, and Lawrence Taylor as the theme is "The Hitters." The stickers were also issued in a UK version which is distinguished by the presence of stats printed on the sticker backs.

Card	Low	High
COMPLETE SET (396)	8.00	20.00
COMP.UK SET (396)	100.00	250.00
*UK VERSION: 5X TO 10X		
1 Super Bowl XXIV FOIL	.02	.05
2 Super Bowl XXIV FOIL	.02	.05
3 Buffalo Bills Crest FOIL	.02	.05
4 Thurman Thomas	.10	.30
5 Nate Odomes	.02	.05
6 Jim Kelly	.10	.30
7 Cornelius Bennett	.04	.10
8 Scott Norwood	.02	.05
9 Mark Kelso	.02	.05
10 Kent Hull	.02	.05
11 Jim Ritcher	.02	.05
12 Darryl Talley	.04	.10
13 Bruce Smith	.07	.20
14 Shane Conlan	.04	.10
15 Andre Reed	.07	.20
16 Jason Buck	.02	.05
17 David Fulcher	.02	.05
18 Jim Skow	.02	.05
19 Anthony Munoz	.07	.20
20 Eric Thomas	.02	.05
21 Eric Ball	.02	.05
22 Tim Krumrie	.04	.10
23 James Brooks	.04	.10
24 Cincinnati Bengals Crest FOIL	.02	.05
25 Rodney Holman	.02	.05
26 Boomer Esiason	.04	.10
27 Eddie Brown	.04	.10
28 Tim McGee	.02	.05
29 Cleveland Browns Crest FOIL	.02	.05
30 Mike Johnson	.02	.05
31 David Grayson	.02	.05
32 Thane Gash	.02	.05
33 Robert Banks DE	.02	.05
34 Eric Metcalf	.07	.20
35 Kevin Mack	.02	.05
36 Reggie Langhorne	.02	.05
37 Webster Slaughter	.04	.10
38 Felix Wright	.02	.05
39 Bernie Kosar	.04	.10
40 Frank Minnifield	.02	.05
41 Clay Matthews	.04	.10
42 Vance Johnson	.02	.05
43 Ron Holmes	.02	.05
44 Melvin Bratton	.02	.05
45 Greg Kragen	.02	.05
46 Karl Mecklenburg	.04	.10
47 Dennis Smith	.02	.05
48 Bobby Humphrey	.02	.05
49 Simon Fletcher	.02	.05
50 Denver Broncos Crest FOIL	.02	.05
51 Michael Brooks	.02	.05
52 Steve Atwater	.04	.10
53 John Elway	1.00	2.50
54 David Treadwell	.02	.05
55 Houston Oilers Crest FOIL	.02	.05
56 Bubba McDowell	.04	.10
57 Ray Childress	.04	.10
58 Bruce Matthews	.04	.10
59 Allen Pinkett	.02	.05
60 Warren Moon	.07	.20
61 John Grimsley	.02	.05
62 Alonzo Highsmith	.02	.05
63 Mike Munchak	.04	.10
64 Ernest Givins	.04	.10
65 Johnny Meads	.02	.05
66 Drew Hill	.04	.10
67 William Fuller	.04	.10
68 Duane Bickett	.02	.05
69 Jack Trudeau	.02	.05
70 Jon Hand	.02	.05
71 Chris Hinton	.04	.10
72 Bill Brooks	.04	.10
73 Donnell Thompson	.02	.05
74 Jeff Herrod	.02	.05
75 Andre Rison	.07	.20
76 Indianapolis Colts Crest FOIL	.02	.05
77 Chris Chandler	.10	.30
78 Ray Donaldson	.02	.05
79 Albert Bentley	.02	.05
80 Keith Taylor	.02	.05
81 Kansas City Chiefs	.02	.05
Crest FOIL		
82 Leonard Griffin	.02	.05
83 Dino Hackett	.02	.05
84 Christian Okoye	.04	.10
85 Chris Martin	.02	.05
86 John Alt	.02	.05
87 Kevin Ross	.02	.05
88 Steve DeBerg	.04	.10
89 Albert Lewis	.02	.05
90 Stephone Paige	.02	.05
91 Derrick Thomas	.07	.20
92 Neil Smith	.07	.20
93 Pete Mandley	.02	.05
94 Howie Long	.07	.20
95 Greg Townsend	.04	.10
96 Mervyn Fernandez	.02	.05
97 Scott Davis	.02	.05
98 Steve Beuerlein	.04	.10
99 Mike Dyal	.02	.05
100 Willie Gault	.02	.05
101 Eddie Anderson	.02	.05
102 Los Angeles Raiders	.02	.05
Crest FOIL		
103 Terry McDaniel	.04	.10
104 Bo Jackson	.08	.25
105 Steve Wisniewski	.04	.10
106 Steve Smith	.02	.05
107 Miami Dolphins Crest FOIL	.02	.05
108 Mark Clayton	.04	.10
109 Louis Oliver	.02	.05
110 Jarvis Williams	.02	.05
111 Ferrell Edmunds	.02	.05
112 Jeff Cross	.02	.05
113 John Offerdahl	.02	.05
114 Brian Sochia	.02	.05
115 Dan Marino	1.00	2.50
116 Jim C. Jensen	.02	.05
117 Sammie Smith	.02	.05
118 Reggie Roby	.02	.05
119 Roy Foster	.02	.05
120 Bruce Armstrong	.02	.05
121 Steve Grogan	.04	.10
122 Hart Lee Dykes	.02	.05
123 Andre Tippett	.02	.05
124 Johnny Rembert	.02	.05
125 Ed Reynolds	.02	.05
126 Cedric Jones	.02	.05
127 Vincent Brown	.07	.20

128 New England Patriots Crest FOIL .02 .05
129 Brent Williams .02 .05
130 John Stephens .02 .05
131 Eric Sievers .02 .05
132 Maurice Hurst .02 .05
133 Jets Crest FOIL .02 .05
134 Johnny Hector .02 .05
135 Erik McMillan .02 .05
136 Jeff Lageman .04 .10
137 Al Toon .04 .10
138 James Hasty .02 .05
139 Kyle Clifton .02 .05
140 Ken O'Brien .04 .10
141 Jim Sweeney .02 .05
142 Jo Jo Townsell .02 .05
143 Dennis Byrd .04 .10
144 Mickey Shuler .02 .05
145 Alex Gordon .02 .05
146 Keith Willis .02 .05
147 Louis Lipps .04 .10
148 David Little .02 .05
149 Greg Lloyd .07 .20
150 Carnell Lake .04 .10
151 Tim Worley .02 .05
152 Dwayne Woodruff .02 .05
153 Gerald Williams .02 .05
154 Pittsburgh Steelers Crest FOIL .02 .05
155 Merril Hoge .02 .05
156 Bubby Brister .07 .20
157 Tunch Ilkin .02 .05
158 Rod Woodson .07 .20
159 San Diego Chargers Crest FOIL .02 .05
160 Leslie O'Neal .04 .10
161 Billy Ray Smith .02 .05
162 Marion Butts .04 .10
163 Lee Williams .02 .05
164 Gill Byrd .02 .05
165 Jim McMahon .04 .10
166 Courtney Hall .02 .05
167 Burt Grossman .02 .05
168 Gary Plummer .02 .05
169 Anthony Miller .07 .20
170 Billy Joe Tolliver .02 .05
171 Vencie Glenn .02 .05
172 Andy Heck .02 .05
173 Brian Blades .04 .10
174 Bryan Millard .02 .05
175 Tony Woods .02 .05
176 Rufus Porter .02 .05
177 David Wyman .02 .05
178 John L. Williams .02 .05
179 Jacob Green .02 .05
180 Seattle Seahawks Crest FOIL .02 .05
181 Eugene Robinson .02 .05
182 Jeff Bryant .02 .05
183 Dave Krieg .04 .10
184 Joe Nash .02 .05
185 Christian Okoye LL .02 .05
186 Felix Wright LL .02 .05
187 Rod Woodson LL .07 .20
188 Barry Sanders AP and .50 1.25
189 Jerry Rice St.Sharpe .25 .60
190 Bruce Matthews AP .04 .10
191 Jay Hilgenberg AP .02 .05
192 Tom Newberry AP .02 .05
193 Anthony Munoz AP .07 .20
194 Jim Lachey AP .02 .05
195 Keith Jackson AP .02 .05
196 Joe Montana AP .80 2.00
197 David Fulcher AP and .02 .05
198 Albert Lewis AP and .02 .05
199 Reggie White AP .07 .20
200 Keith Millard AP .02 .05
201 Chris Doleman AP .02 .05
202 Mike Singletary AP .04 .10
203 Tim Harris AP .02 .05
204 Lawrence Taylor AP .07 .20
205 Rich Camarillo AP .02 .05
206 Sterling Sharpe LL .07 .20
207 Chris Doleman LL .02 .05
208 Barry Sanders LL .50 1.25
209 Atlanta Falcons Crest FOIL .02 .05
210 Michael Haynes .07 .20
211 Scott Case .02 .05
212 Marcus Cotton .02 .05
213 Chris Miller .07 .20
214 Keith Jones .02 .05
215 Tim Green .02 .05
216 Deion Sanders .30 .75
217 Shawn Collins .02 .05
218 John Settle .02 .05
219 Bill Fralic .02 .05
220 Aundray Bruce .02 .05
221 Jessie Tuggle .02 .05
222 James Thornton .02 .05
223 Dennis Gentry .02 .05
224 Richard Dent .04 .10
225 Jay Hilgenberg .02 .05
226 Steve McMichael .02 .05
227 Brad Muster .02 .05
228 Donnell Woolford .04 .10
229 Mike Singletary .04 .10
230 Chicago Bears Crest FOIL .02 .05
231 Mark Bortz .02 .05
232 Kevin Butler .02 .05
233 Neal Anderson .04 .10
234 Trace Armstrong .02 .05
235 Dallas Cowboys Crest FOIL .02 .05
236 Mark Tuinei .02 .05
237 Tony Tolbert .04 .10
238 Eugene Lockhart .02 .05
239 Daryl Johnston .07 .20
240 Troy Aikman .60 1.50
241 Jim Jeffcoat .02 .05
242 James Dixon .02 .05
243 Jesse Solomon .02 .05
244 Ken Norton Jr. .07 .20
245 Kelvin Martin .02 .05
246 Danny Noonan .02 .05
247 Michael Irvin .10 .30
248 Eric Williams .02 .05
249 Richard Johnson .02 .05
250 Michael Cofer .02 .05
251 Chris Spielman .07 .20
252 Rodney Peete .04 .10
253 Bennie Blades .02 .05
254 Jerry Ball .02 .05
255 Eddie Murray .02 .05
256 Detroit Lions Crest FOIL .02 .05
257 Barry Sanders 1.20 3.00
258 Jerry Holmes .02 .05
259 Dennis Gibson .02 .05
260 Lomas Brown .02 .05
261 Packers Crest FOIL .02 .05
262 Dave Brown DB .02 .05
263 Mark Murphy .02 .05
264 Perry Kemp .02 .05
265 Don Majkowski .04 .10
266 Chris Jacke .02 .05
267 Keith Woodside .02 .05
268 Tony Mandarich .02 .05
269 Robert Brown .02 .05
270 Sterling Sharpe .07 .20
271 Tim Harris .02 .05
272 Brent Fullwood .02 .05
273 Brian Noble .02 .05
274 Alvin Wright .02 .05
275 Flipper Anderson .04 .10
276 Jackie Slater .02 .05
277 Kevin Greene .04 .10
278 Pete Holohan .02 .05
279 Tom Newberry .02 .05
280 Jerry Gray .02 .05
281 Henry Ellard .04 .10
282 Rams Crest FOIL .02 .05
283 LeRoy Irvin .02 .05
284 Jim Everett .04 .10
285 Greg Bell .02 .05
286 Doug Smith .02 .05
287 Minnesota Vikings Crest FOIL .02 .05
288 Joey Browner .02 .05
289 Wade Wilson .04 .10
290 Chris Doleman .04 .10
291 Al Noga .02 .05
292 Herschel Walker .04 .10
293 Henry Thomas .04 .10
294 Steve Jordan .04 .10
295 Anthony Carter .04 .10
296 Keith Millard .02 .05
297 Carl Lee .02 .05
298 Randall McDaniel .05 .15
299 Gary Zimmerman .04 .10
300 Morten Andersen .02 .05
301 Rickey Jackson .04 .10
302 Sam Mills .04 .10
303 Hoby Brenner .02 .05
304 Dalton Hilliard .02 .05
305 Robert Massey .02 .05
306 John Fourcade .02 .05
307 Lonzell Hill .02 .05
308 Saints Crest FOIL .02 .05
309 Jim Dombrowski .02 .05
310 Pat Swilling .04 .10
311 Vaughan Johnson .04 .10
312 Eric Martin .02 .05
313 Giants Crest FOIL .02 .05
314 Ottis Anderson .04 .10
315 Myron Guyton .02 .05
316 Terry Kinard .02 .05
317 Mark Bavaro .02 .05
318 Phil Simms .04 .10
319 Lawrence Taylor .07 .20
320 Odessa Turner .02 .05
321 Erik Howard .02 .05
322 Mark Collins .02 .05
323 Dave Meggett .04 .10
324 Leonard Marshall .04 .10
325 Carl Banks .04 .10
326 Anthony Toney .02 .05
327 Seth Joyner .04 .10
328 Cris Carter .20 .50
329 Eric Allen .04 .10
330 Keith Jackson .04 .10
331 Clyde Simmons .04 .10
332 Byron Evans .02 .05
333 Keith Byars .04 .10
334 Philadelphia Eagles Crest FOIL .02 .05
335 Reggie White .07 .20
336 Izel Jenkins .02 .05
337 Jerome Brown .04 .10
338 David Alexander .02 .05
339 Phoenix Cardinals Crest FOIL .02 .05
340 Rich Camarillo .02 .05
341 Ken Harvey .04 .10
342 Luis Sharpe .02 .05
343 Timm Rosenbach .02 .05
344 Tim McDonald .02 .05
345 Vai Sikahema .02 .05
346 Freddie Joe Nunn .02 .05
347 Ernie Jones .02 .05
348 J.T. Smith .02 .05
349 Eric Hill .02 .05
350 Roy Green .04 .10
351 Anthony Bell .02 .05
352 Kevin Fagan .02 .05
353 Roger Craig .04 .10
354 Ronnie Lott .04 .10
355 Mike Cofer .02 .05
356 John Taylor .07 .20
357 Joe Montana 1.20 3.00
358 Charles Haley .07 .20
359 Guy McIntyre .02 .05
360 49ers Crest FOIL .02 .05
361 Pierce Holt .02 .05
362 Tom Rathman .04 .10
363 Jerry Rice .50 1.25
364 Michael Carter .02 .05
365 Buccaneers Crest FOIL .02 .05
366 Lars Tate .02 .05
367 Paul Gruber .02 .05
368 Winston Moss .02 .05
369 Reuben Davis .02 .05
370 Mark Robinson .02 .05
371 Bruce Hill .02 .05
372 Kevin Murphy .02 .05
373 Ricky Reynolds .02 .05
374 Harry Hamilton .02 .05
375 Vinny Testaverde .04 .10
376 Mark Carrier WR .04 .10
377 Ervin Randle .02 .05
378 Ricky Sanders .04 .10
379 Charles Mann .04 .10
380 Jim Lachey .02 .05
381 Wilber Marshall .02 .05
382 A.J. Johnson .02 .05
383 Darrell Green .04 .10
384 Mark Rypien .02 .05
385 Gerald Riggs .04 .10
386 Washington Redskins Crest FOIL .02 .05
387 Alvin Walton .02 .05
388 Art Monk .07 .20
389 Gary Clark .07 .20
390 Earnest Byner .04 .10
391 SB XXIV Action FOIL Rice .30 .75
392 SB XXIV Action FOIL/49ers .02 .05
393 SB XXIV Action FOIL Rathman .02 .05
394 SB XXIV Action FOIL Chet Brooks .02 .05
395 SB XXIV Action FOIL Elway .30 .75
396 Joe Montana FOIL 1.60 4.00
NNO Panini Album .80 2.00

2010 Panini Stickers

COMPLETE SET (560) 25.00 50.00
1 NFL LOGO Foil .20 .50
2 NFLPA LOGO Foil .20 .50
3 AFC LOGO Foil .20 .50
4 NFC LOGO Foil .20 .50
5 AFC CHAMP LOGO Foil .20 .50
6 NFC CHAMP LOGO Foil .20 .50
7 PRO BOWL LOGO Foil .20 .50
8 Buffalo HEL/Miami HEL .20 .50
9 New England HEL/Jets HEL .20 .50
10 Baltimore HEL/Cincinnati HEL .20 .50
11 Cleveland HEL/Pittsburgh HEL .20 .50
12 Houston HEL/Indianapolis HEL .20 .50
13 Jacksonville HEL/Tennessee HEL .20 .50
14 Denver HEL/Kansas City HEL .20 .50
15 Oakland HEL/San Diego HEL .20 .50
16 Dallas HEL/NY Giants HEL .20 .50
17 Philadelphia HEL/Washington HEL .20 .50
18 Chicago HEL/Detroit HEL .20 .50
19 Green Bay HEL/Minnesota HEL .20 .50
20 Atlanta HEL/Carolina HEL .20 .50
21 New Orleans HEL/Tampa Bay HEL .20 .50
22 Arizona HEL/San Francisco HEL .20 .50
23 Seattle HEL/St. Louis HEL .20 .50
24 Buffalo Bills LOGO Foil .20 .50
25 Ryan Fitzpatrick .10 .25
26 C.J. Spiller .10 .25
27 Marshawn Lynch .12 .30
28 Fred Jackson .12 .30
29 Lee Evans .12 .30
30 Leodis McKelvin .10 .25
31 Marcus Easley .10 .25
32 Paul Posluszny .10 .25
33 Jairus Byrd .12 .30
34 Marcus Stroud .10 .25
35 Donte Whitner .10 .25
36 George Wilson .10 .25
37 Fred Jackson Foil .25 .60
38 Lee Evans Foil .25 .60
39 Paul Posluszny Foil .20 .50
40 Miami Dolphins LOGO Foil .20 .50
41 Chad Henne .12 .30
42 Ricky Williams .12 .30
43 Ronnie Brown .10 .25
44 Davone Bess .10 .25
45 Lex Hilliard .10 .25
46 Brian Hartline .12 .30
47 Anthony Fasano .10 .25
48 Brandon Marshall .12 .30
49 Yeremiah Bell .10 .25
50 Vontae Davis .10 .25
51 Channing Crowder .10 .25
52 Randy Starks .10 .25
53 Chad Henne Foil .25 .60
54 Ricky Williams Foil .25 .60
55 Ronnie Brown Foil .20 .50
56 New England Patriots LOGO Foil .20 .50
57 Tom Brady .40 1.00
58 Laurence Maroney .10 .25
59 Wes Welker .12 .30
60 Randy Moss .12 .30
61 Julian Edelman .15 .40
62 Taylor Price .10 .25
63 Torry Holt .12 .30
64 Rob Gronkowski .30 .75
65 Brandon Meriweather .10 .25
66 Leigh Bodden .10 .25
67 Tully Banta-Cain .10 .25
68 Jerod Mayo .12 .30
69 Tom Brady Foil .75 2.00
70 Wes Welker Foil .25 .60
71 Randy Moss Foil .25 .60
72 New York Jets LOGO Foil .20 .50
73 Mark Sanchez .10 .25
74 Shonn Greene .10 .25
75 LaDainian Tomlinson .15 .40
76 Joe McKnight .10 .25
77 Jerricho Cotchery .10 .25
78 Braylon Edwards .10 .25
79 Santonio Holmes .10 .25
80 Dustin Keller .10 .25
81 Darrelle Revis .10 .25
82 David Harris .10 .25
83 Calvin Pace .10 .25
84 Shaun Ellis .10 .25
85 Mark Sanchez Foil .20 .50
86 Braylon Edwards Foil .20 .50
87 Darrelle Revis Foil .20 .50
88 Baltimore Ravens LOGO Foil .20 .50
89 Joe Flacco .12 .30
90 Ray Rice .10 .25
91 Derrick Mason .10 .25
92 Willis McGahee .10 .25
93 Mark Clayton .10 .25
94 Anquan Boldin .10 .25
95 Todd Heap .10 .25
96 Michael Oher .12 .30
97 Ray Lewis .15 .40
98 Ed Reed .12 .30
99 Terrell Suggs .10 .25
100 Dawan Landry .10 .25
101 Joe Flacco Foil .25 .60
102 Ray Rice Foil .20 .50
103 Ray Lewis Foil .30 .75
104 Cincinnati Bengals LOGO Foil .20 .50
105 Carson Palmer .12 .30
106 Cedric Benson .10 .25
107 Bernard Scott .10 .25
108 Chad Ochocinco .10 .25
109 Andre Caldwell .10 .25
110 Jordan Shipley .10 .25
111 Jermaine Gresham .10 .25
112 Terrell Owens .12 .30
113 Johnathan Joseph .10 .25
114 Leon Hall .10 .25
115 Dhani Jones .10 .25
116 Matt Jones .10 .25
117 Carson Palmer Foil .25 .60
118 Cedric Benson Foil .20 .50
119 Chad Ochocinco Foil .20 .50
120 Cleveland Browns LOGO Foil .20 .50
121 Jake Delhomme .10 .25
122 Jerome Harrison .10 .25
123 Montario Hardesty .10 .25
124 Mohamed Massaquoi .12 .30
125 Colt McCoy .12 .30
126 Josh Cribbs .10 .25
127 Joe Thomas .10 .25
128 James Davis .10 .25
129 Eric Wright .10 .25
130 Abram Elam .15 .40
131 David Bowens .10 .25
132 Joe Haden .15 .40
133 Jerome Harrison Foil .20 .50
134 Mohamed Massaquoi Foil .25 .60
135 Josh Cribbs Foil .20 .50
136 Pittsburgh Steelers LOGO Foil .20 .50
137 Ben Roethlisberger .15 .40
138 Rashard Mendenhall .10 .25
139 Jonathan Dwyer .10 .25
140 Hines Ward .12 .30
141 Mike Wallace .10 .25
142 Emmanuel Sanders .15 .40
143 Heath Miller .10 .25
144 Troy Polamalu .15 .40
145 James Harrison .15 .40
146 LaMarr Woodley .10 .25
147 Lawrence Timmons .10 .25
148 James Farrior .10 .25
149 Ben Roethlisberger Foil .30 .75
150 Rashard Mendenhall Foil .20 .50
151 Troy Polamalu Foil .30 .75
152 Houston Texans LOGO Foil .20 .50
153 Matt Schaub .10 .25
154 Steve Slaton .10 .25
155 Ben Tate .10 .25
156 Andre Johnson .12 .30
157 Kevin Walter .12 .30
158 Owen Daniels .10 .25
159 Jacoby Jones .10 .25
160 Brian Cushing .10 .25
161 DeMeco Ryans .10 .25
162 Mario Williams .12 .30
163 Kareem Jackson .10 .25
164 Bernard Pollard .10 .25
165 Matt Schaub Foil .20 .50
166 Andre Johnson Foil .25 .60
167 Brian Cushing Foil .20 .50
168 Indianapolis Colts LOGO Foil .20 .50
169 Peyton Manning .40 1.00
170 Robert Mathis .10 .25
171 Joseph Addai .10 .25
172 Donald Brown .10 .25
173 Reggie Wayne .12 .30
174 Austin Collie .10 .25
175 Pierre Garcon .12 .30
176 Dallas Clark .10 .25
177 Clint Session .10 .25
178 Dwight Freeney .10 .25
179 Bob Sanders .12 .30
180 Antoine Bethea .10 .25
181 Peyton Manning Foil .75 2.00
182 Joseph Addai Foil .20 .50
183 Dallas Clark Foil .20 .50
184 Jacksonville Jaguars LOGO Foil .20 .50
185 David Garrard .10 .25
186 Maurice Jones-Drew .10 .25
187 Rashad Jennings .10 .25
188 Mike Sims-Walker .10 .25
189 Aaron Kampman .12 .30
190 Marcedes Lewis .10 .25
191 Zach Miller .12 .30
192 Mike Thomas .12 .30
193 Daryl Smith .10 .25
194 Justin Durant .10 .25
195 Derrick Harvey .10 .25
196 Kirk Morrison .10 .25
197 David Garrard Foil .20 .50
198 Maurice Jones-Drew Foil .20 .50
199 Mike Sims-Walker Foil .20 .50
200 Tennessee Titans LOGO Foil .20 .50
201 Vince Young .10 .25
202 Chris Johnson .10 .25
203 Kenny Britt .10 .25
204 Nate Washington .10 .25
205 Bo Scaife .10 .25
206 Justin Gage .10 .25
207 Damian Williams .10 .25
208 Stephen Tulloch .10 .25
209 Rob Bironas .10 .25
210 Cortland Finnegan .10 .25
211 Michael Griffin .10 .25
212 Javon Ringer .10 .25
213 Vince Young Foil .20 .50
214 Chris Johnson Foil .20 .50
215 Cortland Finnegan Foil .20 .50
216 Denver Broncos LOGO Foil .20 .50
217 Kyle Orton .10 .25
218 Knowshon Moreno .10 .25
219 Jabar Gaffney .10 .25
220 Eddie Royal .10 .25
221 Correll Buckhalter .10 .25
222 Demaryius Thomas .25 .60
223 Eric Decker .12 .30
224 Tim Tebow .30 .75
225 Brian Dawkins .10 .25
226 Champ Bailey .12 .30
227 Elvis Dumervil .10 .25
228 D.J. Williams .10 .25
229 Kyle Orton Foil .20 .50
230 Knowshon Moreno Foil .20 .50
231 Champ Bailey Foil .25 .60
232 Kansas City Chiefs LOGO Foil .20 .50
233 Matt Cassel .10 .25
234 Jamaal Charles .12 .30
235 Thomas Jones .10 .25
236 Dexter McCluster .12 .30
237 Chris Chambers .10 .25
238 Dwayne Bowe .12 .30
239 Leonard Pope .10 .25
240 Eric Berry .15 .40
241 Brandon Flowers .10 .25
242 Tamba Hali .10 .25
243 Derrick Johnson .10 .25
244 Demorrio Williams .10 .25
245 Matt Cassel Foil .20 .50
246 Jamaal Charles Foil .25 .60
247 Dwayne Bowe Foil .25 .60
248 Oakland Raiders LOGO Foil .20 .50
249 Jason Campbell .10 .25
250 Michael Bush .10 .25
251 Darren McFadden .10 .25
252 Louis Murphy .10 .25
253 Chaz Schilens .10 .25
254 Darrius Heyward-Bey .12 .30
255 Zach Miller .10 .25
256 Rolando McClain .10 .25
257 Shane Lechler .10 .25
258 Nnamdi Asomugha .10 .25
259 Tyvon Branch .10 .25
260 Trevor Scott .10 .25
261 Darren McFadden Foil .20 .50
262 Zach Miller Foil .20 .50
263 Nnamdi Asomugha Foil .20 .50
264 San Diego Chargers LOGO Foil .20 .50
265 Philip Rivers .15 .40
266 Ryan Mathews .10 .25
267 Darren Sproles .12 .30
268 Vincent Jackson .10 .25
269 Malcom Floyd .10 .25
270 Legedu Naanee .10 .25
271 Antonio Gates .12 .30
272 Stephen Cooper .10 .25
273 Eric Weddle .10 .25
274 Shawne Merriman .10 .25
275 Shaun Phillips .10 .25
276 Quentin Jammer .10 .25
277 Philip Rivers Foil .30 .75
278 Antonio Gates Foil .25 .60
279 Shaun Phillips Foil .20 .50
280 Dallas Cowboys LOGO Foil .20 .50
281 Tony Romo .12 .30
282 Felix Jones .10 .25
283 Marion Barber .12 .30
284 Tashard Choice .10 .25
285 Miles Austin .10 .25
286 Dez Bryant .25 .60
287 Jason Witten .12 .30
288 Roy Williams WR .10 .25
289 Bradie James .10 .25
290 DeMarcus Ware .12 .30
291 Jay Ratliff .12 .30
292 Mike Jenkins .10 .25
293 Tony Romo Foil .25 .60
294 Jason Witten Foil .25 .60
295 DeMarcus Ware Foil .25 .60
296 New York Giants LOGO Foil .20 .50
297 Eli Manning .12 .30
298 Brandon Jacobs .10 .25
299 Ahmad Bradshaw .10 .25
300 Mario Manningham .10 .25
301 Steve Smith USC .10 .25
302 Hakeem Nicks .10 .25
303 Kevin Boss .10 .25
304 Terrell Thomas .10 .25
305 Justin Tuck .10 .25
306 Kenny Phillips .10 .25
307 Osi Umenyiora .10 .25
308 Jason Pierre-Paul .15 .40
309 Eli Manning Foil .25 .60
310 Brandon Jacobs Foil .20 .50
311 Steve Smith USC Foil .20 .50
312 Philadelphia Eagles LOGO Foil .20 .50
313 Kevin Kolb .10 .25
314 Michael Vick .12 .30
315 LeSean McCoy .15 .40
316 Leonard Weaver .10 .25
317 DeSean Jackson .12 .30
318 Jeremy Maclin .10 .25
319 Brent Celek .10 .25
320 Quintin Mikell .10 .25
321 Trent Cole .10 .25
322 Asante Samuel .10 .25
323 Jason Avant .10 .25
324 Nate Allen .15 .40
325 LeSean McCoy Foil .30 .75
326 DeSean Jackson Foil .25 .60
327 Brent Celek Foil .20 .50
328 Washington Redskins LOGO Foil .20 .50
329 Donovan McNabb .12 .30
330 Clinton Portis .10 .25
331 Santana Moss .12 .30
332 Devin Thomas .10 .25
333 Chris Cooley .10 .25
334 Fred Davis .10 .25
335 London Fletcher .12 .30
336 Rocky McIntosh .10 .25
337 LaRon Landry .10 .25
338 Chris Horton .10 .25
339 Albert Haynesworth .10 .25
340 Trent Williams .12 .30
341 Clinton Portis Foil .20 .50
342 Santana Moss Foil .25 .60
343 Chris Cooley Foil .20 .50
344 Chicago Bears LOGO Foil .20 .50
345 Jay Cutler .10 .25
346 Matt Forte .10 .25
347 Chester Taylor .10 .25
348 Devin Hester .12 .30
349 Earl Bennett .12 .30
350 Johnny Knox .10 .25
351 Greg Olsen .12 .30
352 Lance Briggs .12 .30
353 Brian Urlacher .15 .40
354 Julius Peppers .12 .30
355 Zack Bowman .10 .25
356 Danieal Manning .10 .25
357 Jay Cutler Foil .20 .50
358 Matt Forte Foil .20 .50
359 Brian Urlacher Foil .30 .75
360 Detroit Lions LOGO Foil .20 .50
361 Matthew Stafford .12 .30
362 Kevin Smith .10 .25
363 Jahvid Best .10 .25
364 Calvin Johnson .15 .40
365 Bryant Johnson .10 .25
366 Brandon Pettigrew .10 .25
367 Dennis Northcutt .10 .25
368 Nate Burleson .10 .25
369 Louis Delmas .10 .25
370 Kyle Vanden Bosch .10 .25
371 Julian Peterson .10 .25
372 Ndamukong Suh .40 1.00
373 Matthew Stafford Foil .25 .60
374 Calvin Johnson Foil .30 .75
375 Brandon Pettigrew Foil .20 .50
376 Green Bay Packers LOGO Foil .20 .50
377 Aaron Rodgers .30 .75
378 Ryan Grant .12 .30
379 Brandon Jackson .10 .25
380 Greg Jennings .10 .25
381 Donald Driver .12 .30
382 Jermichael Finley .10 .25
383 James Jones .10 .25
384 Jordy Nelson .12 .30
385 Nick Barnett .10 .25
386 A.J. Hawk .10 .25
387 Charles Woodson .15 .40
388 Clay Matthews .15 .40
389 Aaron Rodgers Foil .60 1.50
390 Ryan Grant Foil .25 .60
391 Donald Driver Foil .25 .60
392 Minnesota Vikings LOGO Foil .20 .50
393 Brett Favre .30 .75
394 Adrian Peterson .15 .40
395 Toby Gerhart .10 .25
396 Bernard Berrian .10 .25
397 Sidney Rice .10 .25
398 Percy Harvin .10 .25
399 Visanthe Shiancoe .12 .30
400 Jared Allen .10 .25
401 Chad Greenway .10 .25
402 Cedric Griffin .10 .25
403 Ray Edwards .10 .25
404 Kevin Williams .10 .25
405 Brett Favre Foil .60 1.50
406 Adrian Peterson Foil .30 .75
407 Jared Allen Foil .20 .50
408 Atlanta Falcons LOGO Foil .20 .50
409 Matt Ryan .12 .30
410 Michael Turner .10 .25
411 Roddy White .10 .25
412 Michael Jenkins .10 .25
413 Jerious Norwood .10 .25
414 Tony Gonzalez .12 .30
415 Jason Snelling .12 .30
416 Curtis Lofton .10 .25
417 Jonathan Babineaux .10 .25
418 Brent Grimes .10 .25
419 Erik Coleman .10 .25
420 Mike Peterson .10 .25
421 Matt Ryan Foil .25 .60
422 Roddy White Foil .20 .50
423 Tony Gonzalez Foil .25 .60
424 Carolina Panthers LOGO Foil .20 .50
425 Matt Moore .10 .25
426 DeAngelo Williams .10 .25
427 Jonathan Stewart .10 .25
428 Steve Smith .12 .30
429 Jimmy Clausen .10 .25
430 Armanti Edwards .12 .30
431 Brandon LaFell .15 .40
432 Dante Rosario .10 .25
433 Dwayne Jarrett .10 .25
434 Jon Beason .10 .25
435 Richard Marshall .10 .25
436 Chris Gamble .10 .25
437 DeAngelo Williams Foil .20 .50
438 Jonathan Stewart Foil .20 .50
439 Steve Smith Foil .25 .60
440 New Orleans Saints LOGO Foil .20 .50
441 Drew Brees .15 .40
442 Pierre Thomas .10 .25
443 Reggie Bush .10 .25
444 Marques Colston .10 .25
445 Robert Meachem .10 .25
446 Jeremy Shockey .10 .25
447 Devery Henderson .10 .25
448 Garrett Hartley .10 .25
449 Jonathan Vilma .10 .25
450 Roman Harper .10 .25
451 Darren Sharper .10 .25
452 Will Smith .10 .25
453 Drew Brees Foil .30 .75
454 Marques Colston Foil .20 .50
455 Darren Sharper Foil .20 .50
456 Tampa Bay Buccaneers LOGO Foil .20 .50
457 Josh Freeman .12 .30
458 Cadillac Williams .10 .25
459 Derrick Ward .10 .25
460 Sammie Stroughter .10 .25
461 Mike Williams .10 .25
462 Kellen Winslow Jr. .10 .25
463 Arrelious Benn .10 .25
464 Maurice Stovall .10 .25
465 Gerald McCoy .10 .25
466 Barrett Ruud .10 .25
467 Tanard Jackson .10 .25
468 Ronde Barber .10 .25
469 Josh Freeman Foil .25 .60
470 Cadillac Williams Foil .20 .50
471 Kellen Winslow Jr. Foil .20 .50
472 Arizona Cardinals LOGO Foil .20 .50
473 Matt Leinart .10 .25
474 Larry Fitzgerald .12 .30
475 Chris Wells .10 .25
476 Steve Breaston .10 .25
477 Tim Hightower .10 .25
478 Early Doucet .10 .25
479 Andre Roberts .12 .30
480 LaRod Stephens-Howling .12 .30
481 Adrian Wilson .10 .25
482 Dominique Rodgers-Cromartie .10 .25
483 Joey Porter .10 .25
484 Calais Campbell .10 .25
485 Matt Leinart Foil .20 .50
486 Larry Fitzgerald Foil .25 .60
487 Chris Wells Foil .20 .50
488 San Francisco 49ers LOGO Foil .20 .50
489 Alex Smith QB .12 .30
490 Frank Gore .12 .30
491 Brian Westbrook .10 .25
492 Michael Crabtree .10 .25
493 Josh Morgan .12 .30
494 Vernon Davis .10 .25
495 Ted Ginn .10 .25
496 Patrick Willis .12 .30
497 Manny Lawson .10 .25
498 Justin Smith .12 .30
499 Dashon Goldson .10 .25
500 Takeo Spikes .10 .25
501 Frank Gore Foil .25 .60
502 Vernon Davis Foil .20 .50
503 Patrick Willis Foil .25 .60
504 Seattle Seahawks LOGO Foil .20 .50
505 Matt Hasselbeck .10 .25
506 Julius Jones .10 .25
507 Justin Forsett .12 .30
508 Leon Washington .10 .25
509 T.J. Houshmandzadeh .10 .25
510 Deion Branch .10 .25
511 John Carlson .10 .25
512 Golden Tate .12 .30
513 Aaron Curry .12 .30
514 Josh Wilson .10 .25
515 Lofa Tatupu .10 .25
516 Earl Thomas .25 .60
517 Matt Hasselbeck Foil .20 .50
518 Julius Jones Foil .20 .50
519 T.J. Houshmandzadeh Foil .20 .50
520 St. Louis Rams LOGO Foil .20 .50
521 Sam Bradford .12 .30
522 Steven Jackson .10 .25
523 Donnie Avery .10 .25
524 Brandon Gibson .10 .25
525 Mardy Gilyard .10 .25
526 Donnie Jones .10 .25
527 Daniel Fells .15 .40
528 Danny Amendola .15 .40
529 James Laurinaitis .12 .30
530 C.J. Ah You .10 .25
531 Chris Long .10 .25
532 James Butler .10 .25
533 Steven Jackson .10 .25
534 Danny Amendola .15 .40
535 James Laurinaitis .12 .30
536 Matt Schaub LL .10 .25
537 Chris Johnson LL .10 .25
538 Andre Johnson LL .12 .30
539 Patrick Willis LL .12 .30
540 Elvis Dumervil LL .10 .25
541 Jairus Byrd LL .12 .30
542 Shane Lechler LL .10 .25
543 Danny Amendola LL .15 .40
544 Nate Kaeding LL .10 .25
545 Adrian Peterson LL .15 .40
546 Darrelle Revis LL .10 .25
547 Drew Brees LL .15 .40
548 Wes Welker LL .12 .30
549 David Akers LL .10 .25
550 New Orleans Saints LL .10 .25
551 New York Jets LL .10 .25
552 Super Bowl XLV Foil .20 .50
553 Super Bowl XLV Foil .20 .50
554 Super Bowl XLV Foil .20 .50
555 Super Bowl I Foil .20 .50
556 Super Bowl IX Foil .20 .50
557 Super Bowl XVIII Foil .20 .50
558 Super Bowl XXVII Foil .20 .50
559 Super Bowl XXXVI Foil .20 .50
560 Super Bowl XLIV Foil .20 .50

2011 Panini Stickers

1 NFL Logo .10 .25
2 TBD .10 .25
3 AFC Logo .10 .25
4 NFC Logo .10 .25
5 Buffalo Bills Foil .20 .50
6 Steve Johnson .10 .25
7 Paul Posluszny .10 .25
8 Ryan Fitzpatrick .10 .25
9 Lee Evans .12 .30
10 Roscoe Parrish .10 .25
11 C.J. Spiller .10 .25
12 Fred Jackson .10 .25
13 David Nelson .12 .30
14 Jairus Byrd .10 .25
15 Marcell Dareus .10 .25
16 Steve Johnson FOIL .20 .50
17 Paul Posluszny FOIL .20 .50
18 Ryan Fitzpatrick FOIL .20 .50
19 Miami Dolphins FOIL .20 .50
20 Brandon Marshall .12 .30
21 Jake Long .10 .25
22 Ronnie Brown .12 .30
23 Anthony Fasano .10 .25
24 Cameron Wake .12 .30
25 Chad Henne .12 .30
26 Davone Bess .10 .25
27 Ricky Williams .12 .30
28 Karlos Dansby .10 .25
29 Yeremiah Bell .10 .25
30 Brandon Marshall FOIL .25 .60
31 Jake Long FOIL .20 .50
32 Cameron Wake FOIL .25 .60
33 New England Patriots FOIL .20 .50
34 Tom Brady .40 1.00
35 Wes Welker .12 .30
36 Devin McCourty .10 .25
37 Jerod Mayo .10 .25
38 Danny Woodhead .12 .30
39 Rob Gronkowski .15 .40
40 Deion Branch .10 .25
41 BenJarvus Green-Ellis .10 .25
42 Vince Wilfork .10 .25
43 Aaron Hernandez .12 .30
44 Tom Brady FOIL .75 2.00
45 Wes Welker FOIL .25 .60
46 Jerod Mayo FOIL .20 .50
47 New York Jets FOIL .20 .50
48 Darrelle Revis .10 .25
49 Mark Sanchez .10 .25
50 Brad Smith .10 .25
51 David Harris .10 .25
52 Braylon Edwards .10 .25
53 Dustin Keller .12 .30
54 Jerricho Cotchery .10 .25
55 LaDainian Tomlinson .15 .40
56 Santonio Holmes .10 .25
57 Shonn Greene .10 .25
58 Darrelle Revis FOIL .20 .50
59 Mark Sanchez FOIL .20 .50
60 LaDainian Tomlinson FOIL .30 .75
61 Baltimore Ravens FOIL .20 .50
62 Ray Lewis .15 .40
63 Joe Flacco .12 .30
64 Anquan Boldin .10 .25
65 Derrick Mason .10 .25
66 Ed Reed .12 .30
67 Michael Oher .10 .25
68 Ray Rice FOIL .10 .25
69 Terrell Suggs .10 .25
70 Todd Heap .10 .25
71 Haloti Ngata .10 .25
72 Ray Lewis FOIL .30 .75
73 Joe Flacco FOIL .25 .60
74 Ray Rice FOIL .20 .50
75 Cincinnati Bengals Foil .20 .50
76 Carson Palmer .12 .30
77 Chad Ochocinco .10 .25
78 Cedric Benson .10 .25
79 Terrell Owens .12 .30
80 Andy Dalton .20 .50
81 Dhani Jones .10 .25
82 Jermaine Gresham .10 .25
83 A.J. Green .25 .60
84 Jordan Shipley .10 .25
85 Leon Hall .10 .25
86 Carson Palmer FOIL .25 .60
87 Chad Ochocinco FOIL .20 .50
88 Cedric Benson FOIL .20 .50
89 Cleveland Browns FOIL .20 .50
90 Peyton Hillis .10 .25
91 Colt McCoy .10 .25
92 Abram Elam .10 .25
93 Ben Watson .10 .25
94 Joe Haden .10 .25
95 T.J. Ward .10 .25
96 Joe Thomas .10 .25
97 Josh Cribbs .10 .25
98 Mohamed Massaquoi .10 .25
99 Scott Fujita .10 .25
100 Peyton Hillis FOIL .20 .50
101 Colt McCoy FOIL .20 .50
102 Josh Cribbs FOIL .20 .50
103 Pittsburgh Steelers FOIL .20 .50
104 Troy Polamalu .15 .40
105 Ben Roethlisberger .15 .40
106 Brett Keisel .12 .30
107 LaMarr Woodley .10 .25
108 Lawrence Timmons .10 .25
109 Heath Miller .10 .25
110 Hines Ward .12 .30
111 James Harrison .12 .30
112 Mike Wallace .10 .25
113 Rashard Mendenhall .10 .25
114 Troy Polamalu FOIL .30 .75
115 Ben Roethlisberger FOIL .30 .75
116 Hines Ward FOIL .25 .60
117 Houston Texans FOIL .20 .50
118 Andre Johnson .12 .30
119 Arian Foster .10 .25
120 Mario Williams .10 .25
121 Matt Schaub .10 .25
122 Brian Cushing .10 .25
123 DeMeco Ryans .10 .25
124 Jacoby Jones .10 .25
125 Kevin Walter .10 .25
126 Owen Daniels .10 .25
127 Bernard Pollard .10 .25
128 Andre Johnson FOIL .25 .60
129 Arian Foster FOIL .20 .50
130 Mario Williams FOIL .20 .50
131 Indianapolis Colts FOIL .20 .50
132 Peyton Manning .30 .75
133 Dwight Freeney .10 .25
134 Reggie Wayne .12 .30
135 Antoine Bethea .10 .25
136 Pierre Garcon .12 .30
137 Austin Collie .10 .25
138 Dallas Clark .10 .25
139 Donald Brown .10 .25
140 Joseph Addai .10 .25
141 Robert Mathis .10 .25
142 Peyton Manning FOIL .60 1.50
143 Dwight Freeney FOIL .20 .50
144 Reggie Wayne FOIL .25 .60
145 Jacksonville Jaguars FOIL .20 .50
146 Maurice Jones-Drew .10 .25
147 David Garrard .10 .25
148 Daryl Smith .10 .25
149 Kirk Morrison .10 .25
150 Marcedes Lewis .10 .25
151 Mike Sims-Walker .12 .30
152 Mike Thomas .12 .30
153 Rashad Jennings .10 .25
154 Rashean Mathis .10 .25
155 Blaine Gabbert .10 .25
156 Maurice Jones-Drew FOIL .20 .50
157 David Garrard FOIL .20 .50
158 Mike Thomas FOIL .25 .60
159 Tennessee Titans FOIL .20 .50
160 Chris Johnson .10 .25
161 Michael Griffin .10 .25
162 Bo Scaife .10 .25
163 Cortland Finnegan .10 .25
164 Jake Locker .10 .25
165 Marc Mariani .12 .30
166 Kenny Britt .10 .25
167 Nate Washington .10 .25
168 Stephen Tulloch .10 .25
169 Vince Young .10 .25
170 Chris Johnson FOIL .20 .50
171 Michael Griffin FOIL .20 .50
172 Kenny Britt FOIL .20 .50
173 Denver Broncos FOIL .20 .50
174 Tim Tebow .15 .40
175 Champ Bailey .12 .30
176 Brandon Lloyd .10 .25
177 Brian Dawkins .10 .25
178 D.J. Williams .10 .25
179 Jabar Gaffney .10 .25
180 Von Miller .15 .40
181 Elvis Dumervil .10 .25
182 Knowshon Moreno .10 .25
183 Kyle Orton .10 .25
184 Tim Tebow FOIL .30 .75
185 Champ Bailey FOIL .25 .60
186 Brandon Lloyd FOIL .20 .50
187 Kansas City Chiefs FOIL .20 .50
188 Jamaal Charles .12 .30
189 Dwayne Bowe .12 .30
190 Brandon Flowers .10 .25
191 Dexter McCluster .10 .25
192 Eric Berry .12 .30
193 Derrick Johnson .10 .25
194 Tony Moeaki .10 .25
195 Matt Cassel .10 .25
196 Jonathan Baldwin .10 .25
197 Thomas Jones .10 .25
198 Jamaal Charles FOIL .25 .60
199 Dwayne Bowe FOIL .25 .60
200 Matt Cassel FOIL .20 .50
201 Oakland Raiders FOIL .20 .50
202 Darren McFadden .10 .25
203 Nnamdi Asomugha .10 .25
204 Jacoby Ford .12 .30
205 Louis Murphy .10 .25
206 Jason Campbell .10 .25
207 Michael Bush .10 .25
208 Richard Seymour .10 .25
209 Rolando McClain .10 .25
210 Tyvon Branch .10 .25
211 Zach Miller .10 .25
212 Darren McFadden FOIL .20 .50
213 Richard Seymour FOIL .20 .50
214 Jason Campbell FOIL .20 .50
215 San Diego Chargers FOIL .20 .50
216 Philip Rivers .15 .40
217 Antonio Gates .10 .25
218 Darren Sproles .12 .30
219 Antoine Cason .10 .25
220 Eric Weddle .10 .25
221 Malcom Floyd .10 .25
222 Quentin Jammer .10 .25
223 Ryan Mathews .12 .30
224 Shaun Phillips .10 .25
225 Vincent Jackson .10 .25
226 Philip Rivers FOIL .30 .75
227 Antonio Gates FOIL .20 .50
228 Vincent Jackson FOIL .20 .50
229 Dallas Cowboys FOIL .20 .50
230 Tony Romo .12 .30
231 DeMarcus Ware .12 .30
232 Anthony Spencer .10 .25
233 Bradie James .10 .25
234 Dez Bryant .15 .40
235 Felix Jones .10 .25
236 Jason Witten .12 .30
237 Mike Jenkins .10 .25
238 Jay Ratliff .12 .30
239 Miles Austin .10 .25
240 Tony Romo FOIL .25 .60
241 DeMarcus Ware FOIL .25 .60
242 Jason Witten FOIL .25 .60
243 New York Giants FOIL .20 .50
244 Eli Manning .12 .30
245 Osi Umenyiora .10 .25
246 Ahmad Bradshaw .10 .25

247 Brandon Jacobs .10 .25
248 Hakeem Nicks .10 .25
249 Justin Tuck .10 .25
250 Kevin Boss .10 .25
251 Mario Manningham .10 .25
252 Steve Smith USC .10 .25
253 Terrell Thomas .10 .25
254 Eli Manning FOIL .25 .60
255 Osi Umenyiora FOIL .20 .50
256 Steve Smith USC FOIL .20 .50
257 Philadelphia Eagles FOIL .20 .50
258 Michael Vick .12 .30
259 DeSean Jackson .12 .30
260 Brent Celek .10 .25
261 Asante Samuel .10 .25
262 Nate Allen .10 .25
263 Jeremy Maclin .10 .25
264 Kevin Kolb .10 .25
265 LeSean McCoy .15 .40
266 Quintin Mikell .10 .25
267 Trent Cole .10 .25
268 Michael Vick FOIL .25 .60
269 DeSean Jackson FOIL .25 .60
270 LeSean McCoy FOIL .30 .75
271 Washington Redskins FOIL .20 .50
272 Chris Cooley .10 .25
273 London Fletcher .12 .30
274 Brian Orakpo .12 .30
275 DeAngelo Hall .10 .25
276 Keiland Williams .10 .25
277 Donovan McNabb .12 .30
278 LaRon Landry .10 .25
279 Ryan Torain .10 .25
280 Santana Moss .12 .30
281 Anthony Armstrong .12 .30
282 Chris Cooley FOIL .20 .50
283 London Fletcher FOIL .25 .60
284 DeAngelo Hall FOIl .20 .50
285 Chicago Bears FOIL .20 .50
286 Brian Urlacher .15 .40
287 Devin Hester .12 .30
288 Jay Cutler .10 .25
289 Julius Peppers .12 .30
290 Matt Forte .10 .25
291 Danieal Manning .10 .25
292 Earl Bennett .10 .25
293 Greg Olsen .12 .30
294 Johnny Knox .10 .25
295 Lance Briggs .12 .30
296 Brian Urlacher FOIL .30 .75
297 Devin Hester FOIL .25 .60
298 Jay Cutler FOIl .20 .50
299 Detroit Lions .20 .50
300 Ndamukong Suh .12 .30
301 Calvin Johnson .15 .40
302 Brandon Pettigrew .10 .25
303 Shaun Hill .10 .25
304 Jahvid Best .10 .25
305 Kyle Vanden Bosch .10 .25
306 Louis Delmas .10 .25
307 Nick Fairley .10 .25
308 Matthew Stafford .12 .30
309 Nate Burleson .10 .25
310 Ndamukong Suh FOIL .25 .60
311 Calvin Johnson FOIL .30 .75
312 Matthew Stafford FOIL .25 .60
313 Green Bay Packers FOIL .30 .75
314 Aaron Rodgers .25 .60
315 Clay Matthews .15 .40
316 Charles Woodson .15 .40
317 Donald Driver .12 .30
318 Greg Jennings .10 .25
319 Jermichael Finley .10 .25
320 Nick Collins .10 .25
321 A.J. Hawk .10 .25
322 Ryan Grant .10 .25
323 Tramon Williams .10 .25
324 Aaron Rodgers FOIL .50 1.25
325 Clay Matthews FOIL .30 .75
326 Charles Woodson FOIL .30 .75
327 Minnesota Vikings FOIL .20 .50
328 Adrian Peterson .15 .40
329 Jared Allen .10 .25
330 Sidney Rice .10 .25
331 Antoine Winfield .10 .25
332 Christian Ponder .10 .25
333 E.J. Henderson .10 .25
334 Percy Harvin .10 .25
335 Toby Gerhart .12 .30
336 Joe Webb .10 .25
337 Visanthe Shiancoe .12 .30
338 Adrian Peterson FOIL .30 .75
339 Jared Allen FOIL .20 .50
340 Sidney Rice FOIL .20 .50
341 Atlanta Falcons FOIL .20 .50
342 Matt Ryan .12 .30
343 Michael Turner .10 .25
344 Roddy White .10 .25
345 Julio Jones .30 .75
346 Curtis Lofton .10 .25
347 Jason Snelling .10 .25
348 Eric Weems .10 .25
349 John Abraham .10 .25
350 Brent Grimes .10 .25
351 Tony Gonzalez .12 .30
352 Matt Ryan FOIL .25 .60
353 Michael Turner FOIL .20 .50
354 Roddy White FOIL .20 .50
355 Carolina Panthers FOIL .20 .50
356 Steve Smith .12 .30
357 DeAngelo Williams .10 .25
358 Charles Johnson .10 .25
359 Chris Gamble .10 .25
360 Cam Newton .50 1.25
361 Jimmy Clausen .10 .25
362 Jon Beason .10 .25
363 Jonathan Stewart .10 .25
364 James Anderson .10 .25
365 Mike Goodson .10 .25
366 Steve Smith FOIL .25 .60
367 DeAngelo Williams FOIL .20 .50
368 Jon Beason FOIL .20 .50
369 New Orleans Saints FOIL .20 .50
370 Drew Brees .15 .40
371 Jonathan Vilma .10 .25
372 Chris Ivory .12 .30
373 Robert Meachem .10 .25
374 Mark Ingram .15 .40
375 Marques Colston .10 .25
376 Pierre Thomas .10 .25
377 Reggie Bush .10 .25
378 Roman Harper .10 .25
379 Tracy Porter .10 .25
380 Drew Brees FOIL .30 .75
381 Jonathan Vilma FOIl .20 .50
382 Marques Colston FOIL .20 .50
383 Tampa Bay Buccaneers FOIL .20 .50
384 Josh Freeman .12 .30
385 Ronde Barber .10 .25
386 Aqib Talib .10 .25
387 Barrett Ruud .10 .25
388 Cadillac Williams .10 .25
389 Mike Williams .12 .30
390 Stylez White .10 .25
391 Gerald McCoy .10 .25
392 Kellen Winslow Jr. .10 .25
393 LeGarrette Blount .12 .30
394 Josh Freeman FOIL .25 .60
395 Ronde Barber FOIL .20 .50
396 Mike Williams FOIL .25 .60
397 Arizona Cardinals FOIL .20 .50
398 Adrian Wilson .10 .25
399 Larry Fitzgerald .12 .30
400 Paris Lenon .10 .25
401 Beanie Wells .10 .25
402 Darnell Dockett .10 .25
403 Dominique Rodgers-Cromartie .10 .25
404 Steve Breaston .10 .25
405 Tim Hightower .10 .25
406 John Skelton .10 .25
407 Patrick Peterson .20 .50
408 Adrian Wilson FOIL .20 .50
409 Larry Fitzgerald FOIL .25 .60
410 Dominique Rodgers-Cromartie FOIL .20 .50
411 St. Louis Rams FOIL .20 .50
412 Sam Bradford .10 .25
413 Steven Jackson .10 .25
414 Chris Long .10 .25
415 Daniel Fells .12 .30
416 Danny Amendola .12 .30
417 Donnie Avery .10 .25
418 James Laurinaitis .10 .25
419 Kenneth Darby .10 .25
420 Mark Clayton .10 .25
421 James Hall .10 .25
422 Sam Bradford FOIL .20 .50
423 Steven Jackson FOIL .20 .50
424 Danny Amendola FOIL .25 .60
425 San Francisco 49ers FOIL .20 .50
426 Patrick Willis .12 .30
427 Frank Gore .12 .30
428 Alex Smith QB .12 .30
429 Justin Smith .10 .25
430 Troy Smith .10 .25
431 Josh Morgan .10 .25
432 Colin Kaepernick .15 .40
433 Michael Crabtree .10 .25
434 Takeo Spikes .10 .25
435 Vernon Davis .10 .25
436 Patrick Willis FOIL .25 .60
437 Frank Gore FOIL .25 .60
438 Vernon Davis FOIL .20 .50
439 Seattle Seahawks FOIL .20 .50
440 Matt Hasselbeck .10 .25
441 Aaron Curry .10 .25
442 Chris Clemons .10 .25
443 Leon Washington .10 .25
444 Mike Williams USC .10 .25
445 John Carlson .10 .25
446 Earl Thomas .12 .30
447 Marshawn Lynch .12 .30
448 Justin Forsett .12 .30
449 Lofa Tatupu .10 .25
450 Matt Hasselbeck FOIL .20 .50
451 Aaron Curry FOIL .20 .50
452 Mike Williams USC FOIL .20 .50
453 Cam Newton FOIL .75 2.00
454 Von Miller FOIL .25 .60
455 Marcell Dareus FOIL .15 .40
456 A.J. Green FOIL .40 1.00
457 Patrick Peterson FOIL .30 .75
458 Julio Jones FOIL .50 1.25
459 Jake Locker FOIL .15 .40
460 Blaine Gabbert FOIL .15 .40
461 Christian Ponder FOIL .15 .40
462 Jonathan Baldwin FOIL .15 .40
463 Mark Ingram FOIL .25 .60
464 Andy Dalton FOIL .30 .75
465 Ben Roethlisberger AFC Champs .15 .40
466 Aaron Rodgers NFC Champs .25 .60
467 DeAngelo Hall PB .10 .25
468 AFC Divisional Playoff .10 .25
469 AFC Divisional Playoff .10 .25
470 Aaron Rodgers Div. Playoff .25 .60
471 NFC Divisional Playoff .10 .25
472 Super Bowl XLV .10 .25
473 Aaron Rodgers SB MVP .25 .60
474 Jordy Nelson SB .12 .30
475 Super Bowl XLV .15 .40
476 Elijah Pitts SB .10 .25
477 Super Bowl II .10 .25
478 Reggie White SB .15 .40
479 Super Bowl XLV .10 .25
480 Pop Warner Football .10 .25
481 Pop Warner Football .10 .25
482 Pop Warner Football .10 .25
483 Pop Warner Football .10 .25
484 Tim Tebow PW .15 .40
485 Pop Warner Football .10 .25
486 Adrenalyn Bowl Logo .10 .25
487 Marshall Faulk HOF .12 .30
488 Deion Sanders HOF .12 .30
489 Shannon Sharpe HOF .12 .30
490 Chris Hanburger HOF UER .10 .25
491 Les Richter HOF .10 .25
492 Richard Dent HOF .10 .25
493 Ed Sabol HOF .10 .25
494 Hall of Fame Logo .10 .25

2012 Panini Stickers

1 NFL Logo .10 .25
2 NFLPA Logo .10 .25
3 AFC Logo .10 .25
4 NFC Logo .10 .25
5 Buffalo Bills Logo FOIL .20 .50
6 Ryan Fitzpatrick .10 .25
7 Fred Jackson .12 .30
8 Mario Williams .10 .25
9 David Nelson .10 .25
10 Ryan Fitzpatrick SS FOIL .20 .50
11 C.J. Spiller .10 .25
12 Jairus Byrd .10 .25
13 Marcell Dareus .10 .25
14 Steve Johnson .12 .30
15 Nick Barnett .10 .25
16 Scott Chandler .10 .25
17 Fred Jackson SS FOIL .25 .60
18 Mario Williams SS FOIL .20 .50
19 Miami Dolphins Logo FOIL .20 .50
20 Reggie Bush .10 .25
21 Cameron Wake SS FOIL .25 .60
22 Jake Long .10 .25
23 Daniel Thomas .10 .25
24 Reggie Bush SS FOIL .20 .50
25 Davone Bess .10 .25
26 Karlos Dansby .10 .25
27 David Garrard .10 .25
28 Brian Hartline .12 .30
29 Ryan Tannehill .15 .40
30 Vontae Davis .10 .25
31 Cameron Wake SS FOIL .25 .60
32 Jake Long SS FOIL .20 .50
33 New England Patriots Logo FOIL .20 .50
34 Tom Brady .40 1.00
35 Wes Welker .12 .30
36 Rob Gronkowski .15 .40
37 Aaron Hernandez .12 .30
38 Tom Brady SS FOIL .75 2.00
39 Deion Branch .10 .25
40 Danny Woodhead .12 .30
41 Patrick Chung .10 .25
42 Brandon Lloyd .10 .25
43 Jerod Mayo .10 .25
44 Vince Wilfork .10 .25
45 Wes Welker SS FOIL .25 .60
46 Rob Gronkowski SS FOIL .30 .75
47 New York Jets Logo FOIL .20 .50
48 Darrelle Revis .10 .25
49 Mark Sanchez .10 .25
50 Tim Tebow .15 .40
51 David Harris .10 .25
52 Darrelle Revis SS FOIL .20 .50
53 Santonio Holmes .10 .25
54 D'Brickashaw Ferguson .10 .25
55 Nick Mangold .10 .25
56 LaRon Landry .10 .25
57 Shonn Greene .10 .25
58 Dustin Keller .10 .25
59 Mark Sanchez SS FOIL .20 .50
60 Tim Tebow SS FOIL .30 .75
61 Baltimore Ravens Logo FOIL .20 .50
62 Ray Rice .10 .25
63 Ray Lewis .15 .40
64 Joe Flacco .12 .30
65 Anquan Boldin .10 .25
66 Ray Rice SS FOIL .20 .50
67 Ed Reed .12 .30
68 Haloti Ngata .10 .25
69 Vonta Leach .10 .25
70 Michael Oher .12 .30
71 Terrell Suggs .10 .25
72 Torrey Smith .10 .25
73 Ray Lewis SS FOIL .30 .75
74 Joe Flacco SS FOIL .25 .60
75 Cincinnati Bengals Logo FOIL .20 .50
76 Andy Dalton .12 .30
77 A.J. Green .15 .40
78 Rey Maualuga .10 .25
79 Geno Atkins .15 .40
80 Andy Dalton SS FOIL .25 .60
81 Jermaine Gresham .10 .25
82 Dre Kirkpatrick .10 .25
83 Bernard Scott .10 .25
84 Leon Hall .10 .25
85 BenJarvus Green-Ellis .12 .30
86 Reggie Nelson .10 .25
87 A.J. Green SS FOIL .30 .75
88 Rey Maualuga SS FOIL .20 .50
89 Cleveland Browns Logo FOIL .20 .50
90 Josh Cribbs .10 .25
91 D'Qwell Jackson .10 .25
92 Trent Richardson .10 .25
93 Colt McCoy .12 .30
94 Josh Cribbs SS FOIL .20 .50
95 Ben Watson .10 .25
96 Greg Little .10 .25
97 Joe Haden .10 .25
98 Joe Thomas .10 .25
99 Brandon Weeden .10 .25
100 T.J. Ward .12 .30
101 D'Qwell Jackson SS FOIL .20 .50
102 Trent Richardson SS FOIL .15 .40
103 Pittsburgh Steelers Logo FOIL .20 .50
104 Troy Polamalu .15 .40
105 Ben Roethlisberger .15 .40
106 Mike Wallace .10 .25
107 Antonio Brown .15 .40
108 Troy Polamalu SS FOIL .30 .75
109 Heath Miller .10 .25
110 Ryan Clark .10 .25
111 James Harrison .12 .30
112 LaMarr Woodley .10 .25
113 Lawrence Timmons .10 .25
114 Rashard Mendenhall .10 .25
115 Ben Roethlisberger SS FOIL .30 .75
116 Mike Wallace SS FOIL .20 .50
117 Houston Texans FOIL .20 .50
118 Andre Johnson .12 .30
119 Arian Foster .12 .30
120 Matt Schaub .10 .25
121 Brian Cushing .10 .25
122 Andre Johnson SS FOIL .12 .30
123 Johnathan Joseph .20 .50
124 Kevin Walter .10 .25
125 Connor Barwin .10 .25
126 J.J. Watt .15 .40
127 Ben Tate .10 .25
128 Owen Daniels .10 .25
129 Arian Foster SS FOIL .25 .60
130 Matt Schaub SS FOIL .20 .50
131 Indianapolis Colts Logo FOIL .20 .50
132 Reggie Wayne .12 .30
133 Dwight Freeney .10 .25
134 Andrew Luck 1.00 2.50
135 Antoine Bethea .10 .25
136 Reggie Wayne SS FOIL .25 .60
137 Robert Mathis .10 .25
138 Austin Collie .10 .25
139 Delone Carter .10 .25
140 Donald Brown .10 .25
141 Pat Angerer .10 .25
142 Adam Vinatieri .10 .25
143 Dwight Freeney SS FOIL .20 .50
144 Andrew Luck SS FOIL 1.50 4.00
145 Jacksonville Jaguars FOIL .20 .50
146 Maurice Jones-Drew .10 .25
147 Paul Posluszny .10 .25
148 Justin Blackmon .10 .25
149 Blaine Gabbert .10 .25
150 Maurice Jones-Drew SS FOIL .20 .50
151 Daryl Smith .10 .25
152 Marcedes Lewis .10 .25
153 Jeremy Mincey .10 .25
154 Laurent Robinson .10 .25
155 Chad Henne .10 .25
156 Aaron Ross .10 .25
157 Paul Posluszny SS FOIL .20 .50
158 Justin Blackmon SS FOIL .15 .40
159 Tennessee Titans Logo FOIL .20 .50
160 Chris Johnson .10 .25
161 Nate Washington .10 .25
162 Kenny Britt .10 .25
163 Jason McCourty .15 .40
164 Chris Johnson SS FOIL .20 .50
165 Jake Locker .15 .40
166 Jared Cook .10 .25
167 Marc Mariani .10 .25
168 Kamerion Wimbley .10 .25
169 Matt Hasselbeck .10 .25
170 Michael Griffin .10 .25
171 Nate Washington SS FOIL .20 .50
172 Kenny Britt SS FOIL .20 .50
173 Denver Broncos Logo FOIL .20 .50
174 Peyton Manning .30 .75
175 Champ Bailey .12 .30
176 Von Miller .12 .30
177 D.J. Williams .10 .25
178 Peyton Manning SS FOIL .60 1.50
179 Demaryius Thomas .15 .40
180 Elvis Dumervil .10 .25
181 Knowshon Moreno .10 .25
182 Jacob Tamme .10 .25
183 Eric Decker .10 .25
184 Willis McGahee .10 .25
185 Champ Bailey SS FOIL .25 .60
186 Von Miller SS FOIL .25 .60
187 Kansas City Chiefs FOIL .20 .50
188 Derrick Johnson .10 .25
189 Dwayne Bowe .12 .30
190 Jamaal Charles .12 .30
191 Brandon Flowers .10 .25
192 Derrick Johnson SS FOIL .20 .50
193 Eric Berry .12 .30
194 Dexter McCluster .10 .25
195 Matt Cassel .10 .25
196 Steve Breaston .10 .25
197 Peyton Hillis .10 .25
198 Tamba Hali .10 .25
199 Dwayne Bowe SS FOIL .25 .60
200 Jamaal Charles SS FOIL .25 .60
201 Oakland Raiders Logo FOIL .20 .50
202 Darren McFadden .10 .25
203 Richard Seymour .10 .25
204 Carson Palmer .12 .30
205 Sebastian Janikowski .12 .30
206 Darren McFadden SS FOIL .20 .50
207 Darrius Heyward-Bey .10 .25
208 Louis Murphy .10 .25
209 Denarius Moore .10 .25
210 Shane Lechler .10 .25
211 Tyvon Branch .10 .25
212 Rolando McClain .10 .25
213 Richard Seymour SS FOIL .20 .50
214 Carson Palmer 33 FOIL .25 .60
215 San Diego Chargers Logo FOIL .20 .50
216 Philip Rivers .15 .40
217 Antonio Gates .12 .30
218 Ryan Mathews .12 .30
219 Donald Butler .10 .25
220 Philip Rivers SS FOIL .30 .75
221 Eric Weddle .10 .25
222 Malcolm Floyd .12 .30
223 Eddie Royal .10 .25
224 Robert Meachem .10 .25
225 Antwan Barnes .10 .25
226 Takeo Spikes .10 .25
227 Antonio Gates SS FOIL .25 .60
228 Ryan Mathews SS FOIL .25 .60
229 Dallas Cowboys Logo FOIL .20 .50
230 Tony Romo .12 .30
231 DeMarcus Ware .15 .40
232 Dez Bryant .15 .40
233 Brandon Carr .10 .25
234 Tony Romo SS FOIL .25 .60
235 DeMarco Murray .12 .30
236 Morris Claiborne .10 .25
237 Jason Witten .12 .30
238 Jay Ratliff .12 .30
239 Miles Austin .10 .25
240 Sean Lee .15 .40
241 DeMarcus Ware SS FOIL .30 .75
242 Dez Bryant SS FOIL .30 .75
243 New York Giants Logo FOIL .20 .50
244 Eli Manning .12 .30
245 Victor Cruz .12 .30
246 Jason Pierre-Paul .10 .25
247 Ahmad Bradshaw .10 .25
248 Eli Manning SS FOIL .25 .60
249 Corey Webster .10 .25
250 Michael Boley .10 .25
251 Hakeem Nicks .10 .25
252 Justin Tuck .10 .25
253 Osi Umenyiora .10 .25
254 Antrel Rolle .10 .25
255 Victor Cruz SS FOIL .25 .60
256 Jason Pierre-Paul SS FOIL .20 .50
257 Philadelphia Eagles Logo FOIL .20 .50
258 Michael Vick .12 .30
259 LeSean McCoy .15 .40
260 Jason Babin .10 .25
261 Dominique Rodgers-Cromartie .10 .25
262 Michael Vick SS FOIL .25 .60
263 Brent Celek .10 .25
264 DeMeco Ryans .10 .25
265 DeSean Jackson .12 .30
266 Nnamdi Asomugha .10 .25
267 Jeremy Maclin .10 .25
268 Trent Cole .10 .25
269 LeSean McCoy SS FOIL .30 .75
270 Jason Babin .10 .25
271 Washington Redskins Logo FOIL .20 .50
272 Brian Orakpo .12 .30
273 Roy Helu .10 .25
274 Robert Griffin III .12 .30
275 Pierre Garcon .12 .30
276 Brian Orakpo SS FOIL .25 .60
277 DeAngelo Hall .10 .25
278 Josh Morgan .12 .30
279 Fred Davis .10 .25
280 Santana Moss .12 .30
281 London Fletcher .12 .30
282 Ryan Kerrigan .10 .25
283 Roy Helu SS FOIL .20 .50
284 Robert Griffin III SS FOIL .20 .50
285 Chicago Bears Logo FOIL .20 .50
286 Brian Urlacher .15 .40
287 Devin Hester .12 .30
288 Matt Forte .10 .25
289 Charles Tillman .12 .30
290 Brian Urlacher SS FOIL .30 .75
291 Johnny Knox .10 .25
292 Julius Peppers .12 .30
293 Lance Briggs .12 .30
294 Michael Bush .10 .25
295 Jay Cutler .10 .25
296 Brandon Marshall .12 .30
297 Devin Hester SS FOIL .25 .60
298 Matt Forte SS FOIL .20 .50
299 Detroit Lions Logo FOIL .20 .50
300 Matthew Stafford .12 .30
301 Calvin Johnson .15 .40
302 Ndamukong Suh .12 .30
303 Brandon Pettigrew .10 .25
304 Matthew Stafford SS FOIL .25 .60
305 Jahvid Best .10 .25
306 Kyle Vanden Bosch .10 .25
307 Chris Houston .10 .25
308 Nate Burleson .10 .25
309 Stephen Tulloch .10 .25
310 Cliff Avril .10 .25
311 Calvin Johnson SS FOIL .30 .75
312 Ndamukong Suh SS FOIL .25 .60
313 Green Bay Packers Logo FOIL .20 .50
314 Aaron Rodgers .25 .60
315 Clay Matthews .15 .40
316 Charles Woodson .15 .40
317 B.J. Raji .10 .25
318 Aaron Rodgers SS FOIL .50 1.25
319 Greg Jennings .10 .25
320 Jermichael Finley .10 .25
321 Jordy Nelson .12 .30
322 John Kuhn .10 .25
323 Ryan Grant .10 .25
324 Tramon Williams .10 .25
325 Clay Matthews SS FOIL .30 .75
326 Charles Woodson SS FOIL .30 .75
327 Minnesota Vikings Logo FOIL .20 .50
328 Adrian Peterson .15 .40
329 Jared Allen .10 .25
330 Christian Ponder .10 .25
331 Antoine Winfield .10 .25
332 Adrian Peterson SS FOIL .30 .75
333 Chad Greenway .12 .30
334 E.J. Henderson .10 .25
335 Michael Jenkins .10 .25
336 Percy Harvin .10 .25
337 Toby Gerhart .10 .25
338 Visanthe Shiancoe .10 .25
339 Jared Allen SS FOIL .20 .50
340 Christian Ponder SS FOIL .20 .50
341 Atlanta Falcons Logo FOIL .20 .50
342 Matt Ryan .12 .30
343 Michael Turner .10 .25
344 Roddy White .10 .25
345 Brent Grimes .10 .25
346 Matt Ryan SS FOIL .25 .60
347 Sean Weatherspoon .10 .25
348 Tyson Clabo .10 .25
349 Jacquizz Rodgers .12 .30
350 John Abraham .10 .25
351 Julio Jones .15 .40
352 Tony Gonzalez .12 .30
353 Michael Turner SS FOIL .20 .50
354 Roddy White SS FOIL .20 .50
355 Carolina Panthers FOIL .20 .50
356 Cam Newton .15 .40
357 Steve Smith .12 .30
358 DeAngelo Williams .10 .25
359 Charles Johnson .10 .25
360 Cam Newton SS FOIL .30 .75
361 Chris Gamble .10 .25
362 Greg Olsen .12 .30
363 James Anderson .10 .25
364 Ryan Kalil .10 .25
365 Jon Beason .10 .25
366 Jonathan Stewart .10 .25
367 Steve Smith SS FOIL .25 .60
368 DeAngelo Williams SS FOIL .20 .50
369 New Orleans Saints Logo FOIL .20 .50
370 Drew Brees .15 .40
371 Jimmy Graham .15 .40
372 Darren Sproles .12 .30
373 Marques Colston .10 .25
374 Drew Brees SS FOIL .30 .75
375 Mark Ingram .12 .30
376 Pierre Thomas .10 .25
377 Lance Moore .10 .25
378 Curtis Lofton .10 .25
379 Roman Harper .10 .25
380 Jahri Evans .10 .25
381 Jimmy Graham SS FOIL .30 .75
382 Darren Sproles SS FOIL .25 .60
383 Tampa Bay Buccaneers Logo FOIL .20 .50
384 Josh Freeman .12 .30
385 Dallas Clark .10 .25
386 Vincent Jackson .10 .25
387 Dezmon Briscoe .10 .25
388 Josh Freeman SS FOIL .25 .60
389 Adrian Clayborn .10 .25
390 Mike Williams .12 .30
391 LeGarrette Blount .12 .30
392 Ronde Barber .10 .25
393 Carl Nicks .10 .25
394 Aqib Talib .10 .25
395 Dallas Clark SS FOIL .20 .50
396 Vincent Jackson SS FOIL .20 .50
397 Arizona Cardinals Logo FOIL .20 .50
398 Larry Fitzgerald .12 .30
399 Beanie Wells .10 .25
400 Patrick Peterson .10 .25
401 Adrian Wilson .10 .25
402 Larry Fitzgerald SS FOIL .25 .60
403 Andre Roberts .12 .30
404 Calais Campbell .10 .25
405 Michael Floyd .10 .25
406 Paris Lenon .10 .25
407 Kevin Kolb .10 .25
408 Todd Heap .12 .30
409 Beanie Wells SS FOIL .20 .50
410 Patrick Peterson SS FOIL .20 .50
411 San Francisco 49ers Logo FOIL .20 .50
412 Patrick Willis .12 .30
413 Frank Gore .12 .30
414 Vernon Davis .10 .25
415 Alex Smith .12 .30
416 Patrick Willis SS FOIL .25 .60
417 Carlos Rogers .10 .25
418 Justin Smith .10 .25
419 Aldon Smith .10 .25
420 Michael Crabtree .10 .25
421 Randy Moss .12 .30
422 Navorro Bowman .12 .30
423 Frank Gore SS FOIL .25 .60
424 Vernon Davis SS FOIL .20 .50
425 St. Louis Rams Logo FOIL .20 .50
426 Steven Jackson .10 .25
427 Chris Long .10 .25
428 Sam Bradford .10 .25
429 Danario Alexander .10 .25
430 Steven Jackson SS FOIL .20 .50
431 Danny Amendola .12 .30
432 Lance Kendricks .10 .25
433 James Laurinaitis .10 .25
434 Cortland Finnegan .10 .25
435 Greg Salas .10 .25
436 Quintin Mikell .10 .25
437 Chris Long SS FOIL .20 .50
438 Sam Bradford SS FOIL .20 .50
439 Seattle Seahawks Logo FOIL .20 .50
440 Marshawn Lynch .12 .30
441 Earl Thomas .12 .30
442 Sidney Rice .10 .25
443 Chris Clemons .10 .25
444 Marshawn Lynch SS FOIL .25 .60
445 Doug Baldwin .15 .40
446 Tarvaris Jackson .10 .25
447 Matt Flynn .10 .25
448 David Hawthorne .10 .25
449 Kellen Winslow Jr. .10 .25
450 Brandon Browner .10 .25
451 Earl Thomas SS FOIL .25 .60
452 Sidney Rice SS FOIL .20 .50
453 NFL Draft Logo .10 .25
454 Andrew Luck FOIL 1.50 4.00
455 Justin Blackmon FOIL .15 .40
456 Kendall Wright FOIL .15 .40
457 Brandon Weeden FOIL .15 .40
458 Michael Floyd FOIL .15 .40
459 Morris Claiborne FOIL .15 .40
460 Ryan Tannehill FOIL .25 .60
461 Robert Griffin III FOIL .20 .50
462 Rueben Randle FOIL .15 .40
463 Trent Richardson FOIL .15 .40
464 A.J. Jenkins FOIL .15 .40
465 Coby Fleener FOIL .15 .40
466 NFL Playoffs Logo .10 .25
467 Giants vs. Packers .10 .25
468 Texans vs. Ravens .10 .25
469 Patriots vs. Broncos .10 .25
470 Saints vs. 49ers .10 .25
471 Patriots vs. Ravens .10 .25
472 Giants vs. 49ers .10 .25
473 New York Giants .10 .25
474 Jeff Hostetler .10 .25
475 New York Giants .10 .25
476 Eli Manning .12 .30
477 Eli Manning .12 .30
478 Giants vs. Patriots .10 .25
479 Andy Dalton .12 .30
480 Super Bowl XLVII .10 .25
481 Pop Warner Logo .10 .25
482 Pop Warner Logo .10 .25
483 Matt Ryan PW .12 .30
484 Ray Rice PW .10 .25
485 Pop Warner Eastern WR .10 .25
486 Pop Warner Southern Players .10 .25
487 Pop Warner Eastern WR .10 .25
488 Hall of Fame Logo .10 .25
489 Jack Butler HOF .10 .25
490 Dermontti Dawson HOF .10 .25
491 Chris Doleman HOF .10 .25
492 Cortez Kennedy HOF .10 .25
493 Curtis Martin HOF .12 .30
494 Willie Roaf HOF .12 .30

2013 Panini Stickers

1 Panini Knight Logo .10 .25
2 NFL Logo .10 .25
3 Baltimore Ravens .12 .30
Joe Flacco
Ray Rice
4 Rush Zone Logo .10 .25
5 Buffalo Bills Logo FOIL .10 .25
6 Buffalo Bills Rusher .10 .25
7 C.J. Spiller FOIL .20 .50
8 Steve Johnson FOIL .25 .60
9 Fred Jackson FOIL .25 .60
10 Kevin Kolb .10 .25
11 EJ Manuel .10 .25
12 C.J. Spiller .10 .25
13 Fred Jackson .12 .30
14 Scott Chandler .10 .25
15 Steve Johnson .12 .30
16 Mario Williams .10 .25
17 Jairus Byrd .10 .25
18 Stephon Gilmore .10 .25
19 Miami Dolphins Logo FOIL .10 .25
20 Miami Dolphins Rusher .10 .25
21 Ryan Tannehill FOIL .25 .60
22 Mike Wallace FOIL .20 .50
23 Cameron Wake FOIL .20 .50
24 Ryan Tannehill .12 .30
25 Lamar Miller .10 .25
26 Daniel Thomas .10 .25
27 Marcus Thigpen .10 .25
28 Dustin Keller .10 .25
29 Brian Hartline .10 .25
30 Mike Wallace .10 .25
31 Cameron Wake .10 .25
32 Dion Jordan .10 .25
33 New England Patriots Logo FOIL .10 .25
34 New England Patriots Rusher .10 .25
35 Tom Brady FOIL .75 2.00
36 Rob Gronkowski FOIL .30 .75
37 Stevan Ridley FOIL .20 .50
38 Tom Brady .40 1.00
39 Stevan Ridley .10 .25
40A Aaron Hernandez .30 .75
issued in packs
40B Tim Tebow .30 .75
issued via mail redemption
41 Aaron Dobson .10 .25
42 Danny Amendola .12 .30
43 Rob Gronkowski .15 .40
44 Vince Wilfork .10 .25
45 Jerod Mayo .12 .30
46 Devin McCourty .10 .25
47 New York Jets Logo FOIL .10 .25
48 New York Jets Rusher .10 .25
49 Santonio Holmes FOIL .20 .50
50 Mark Sanchez FOIL .20 .50
51 Bilal Powell FOIL .20 .50
52 Mark Sanchez .10 .25
53 Geno Smith .10 .25
54 Bilal Powell .10 .25
55 Mike Goodson .10 .25
56 Jeremy Kerley .10 .25
57 Santonio Holmes .10 .25
58 Quinton Coples .10 .25
59 David Harris .10 .25
60 Antonio Cromartie .10 .25
61 Baltimore Ravens Logo FOIL .10 .25
62 Baltimore Ravens Rusher .10 .25
63 Joe Flacco FOIL .25 .60
64 Ray Rice FOIL .20 .50
65 Torrey Smith FOIL .20 .50
66 Joe Flacco .12 .30
67 Bernard Pierce .10 .25
68 Ray Rice .10 .25
69 Jacoby Jones .10 .25
70 Dennis Pitta .10 .25
71 Torrey Smith .10 .25
72 Haloti Ngata .10 .25
73 Elvis Dumervil .10 .25
74 Terrell Suggs .10 .25
75 Cincinnati Bengals Logo FOIL .10 .25
76 Cincinnati Bengals Rusher .10 .25
77 A.J. Green FOIL .30 .75
78 Andy Dalton FOIL .25 .60
79 BenJarvus Green-Ellis FOIL .25 .60
80 Andy Dalton .12 .30
81 BenJarvus Green-Ellis .12 .30
82 Giovani Bernard .10 .25
83 Andrew Hawkins .10 .25
84 Jermaine Gresham .12 .30
85 A.J. Green .15 .40
86 Mohamed Sanu .10 .25
87 Vontaze Burfict .10 .25
88 Rey Maualuga .10 .25
89 Cleveland Browns Logo FOIL .10 .25
90 Cleveland Browns Rusher .10 .25
91 Trent Richardson FOIL .20 .50
92 Josh Gordon FOIL .20 .50
93 Brandon Weeden FOIL .20 .50
94 Brandon Weeden .10 .25
95 Montario Hardesty .10 .25
96 Trent Richardson .10 .25
97 Greg Little .10 .25
98 Josh Gordon .10 .25
99 Barkevious Mingo .10 .25
100 Jabaal Sheard .10 .25
101 D'Qwell Jackson .10 .25
102 Joe Haden .10 .25
103 Pittsburgh Steelers Logo FOIL .10 .25
104 Pittsburgh Steelers Rusher .10 .25
105 Ben Roethlisberger FOIL .30 .75
106 Troy Polamalu FOIL .30 .75
107 Antonio Brown FOIL .30 .75
108 Ben Roethlisberger .15 .40
109 Jonathan Dwyer .10 .25
110 Heath Miller .10 .25
111 Emmanuel Sanders .12 .30
112 Antonio Brown .15 .40
113 Jarvis Jones .10 .25
114 Lawrence Timmons .10 .25
115 LaMarr Woodley .10 .25
116 Troy Polamalu .15 .40
117 Houston Texans Logo FOIL .10 .25
118 Houston Texans Rusher .10 .25
119 Arian Foster FOIL .25 .60
120 Andre Johnson FOIL .20 .50
121 J.J. Watt FOIL .25 .60
122 Matt Schaub .10 .25
123 Ben Tate .10 .25
124 Arian Foster .12 .30
125 Owen Daniels .10 .25
126 Andre Johnson .10 .25
127 DeAndre Hopkins .25 .60
128 J.J. Watt .12 .30
129 Brian Cushing .10 .25
130 Ed Reed .12 .30
131 Indianapolis Colts Logo FOIL .10 .25
132 Indianapolis Colts Rusher .10 .25
133 Andrew Luck FOIL .50 1.25
134 Reggie Wayne FOIL .25 .60
135 Antoine Bethea FOIL .20 .50
136 Andrew Luck .25 .60
137 Vick Ballard .10 .25
138 Darrius Heyward-Bey .10 .25
139 Dwayne Allen .10 .25
140 T.Y. Hilton .12 .30
141 Reggie Wayne .12 .30
142 Jerrell Freeman .15 .40
143 Antoine Bethea .10 .25
144 Adam Vinatieri .10 .25
145 Jacksonville Jaguars Logo FOIL .10 .25
146 Jacksonville Jaguars Rusher .10 .25
147 Maurice Jones-Drew FOIL .20 .50
148 Justin Blackmon FOIL .20 .50
149 Paul Posluszny FOIL .20 .50
150 Blaine Gabbert .10 .25
151 Maurice Jones-Drew .10 .25
152 Denard Robinson .10 .25
153 Marcedes Lewis .10 .25
154 Cecil Shorts .10 .25
155 Justin Blackmon .10 .25
156 Jason Babin .10 .25
157 Russell Allen .10 .25
158 Paul Posluszny .10 .25
159 Tennessee Titans Logo FOIL .10 .25
160 Tennessee Titans Rusher .10 .25
161 Chris Johnson FOIL .20 .50
162 Kenny Britt FOIL .20 .50
163 Jake Locker FOIL .25 .60
164 Jake Locker .12 .30
165 Ryan Fitzpatrick .10 .25
166 Chris Johnson .10 .25
167 Shonn Greene .10 .25
168 Nate Washington .10 .25
169 Kendall Wright .10 .25
170 Kenny Britt .10 .25
171 Justin Hunter .10 .25
172 Akeem Ayers .10 .25
173 Denver Broncos Logo FOIL .10 .25
174 Denver Broncos Rusher .10 .25
175 Peyton Manning FOIL .60 1.50
176 Demaryius Thomas FOIL .25 .60
177 Von Miller FOIL .25 .60
178 Peyton Manning .30 .75
179 Knowshon Moreno .10 .25
180 Willis McGahee .10 .25
181 Montee Ball .10 .25
182 Eric Decker .10 .25
183 Wes Welker .12 .30
184 Demaryius Thomas .12 .30
185 Von Miller .12 .30
186 Champ Bailey .12 .30
187 Kansas City Chiefs Logo FOIL .10 .25
188 Kansas City Chiefs Rusher .10 .25
189 Jamaal Charles FOIL .25 .60
190 Dwayne Bowe FOIL .25 .60
191 Alex Smith FOIL .25 .60
192 Alex Smith .12 .30
193 Jamaal Charles .12 .30
194 Anthony Fasano .10 .25
195 Dexter McCluster .12 .30
196 Dwayne Bowe .12 .30
197 Tamba Hali .10 .25
198 Derrick Johnson .10 .25
199 Eric Berry .12 .30
200 Eric Fisher .10 .25
201 Oakland Raiders Logo FOIL .10 .25
202 Oakland Raiders Rusher .10 .25
203 Darren McFadden FOIL .25 .60
204 Matt Flynn FOIL .20 .50
205 Sebastian Janikowski FOIL .20 .50
206 Matt Flynn .10 .25
207 Marcel Reece .10 .25
208 Darren McFadden .12 .30
209 Denarius Moore .10 .25
210 Jacoby Ford .10 .25
211 Miles Burris .10 .25
212 Tyvon Branch .10 .25
213 D.J. Hayden .10 .25
214 Sebastian Janikowski .10 .25
215 San Diego Chargers Logo FOIL .10 .25
216 San Diego Chargers Rusher .10 .25
217 Philip Rivers FOIL .30 .75
218 Antonio Gates FOIL .25 .60
219 Ryan Mathews FOIL .25 .60
220 Philip Rivers .15 .40
221 Danny Woodhead .12 .30
222 Ryan Mathews .12 .30
223 Eddie Royal .10 .25
224 Malcom Floyd .10 .25
225 Robert Meachem .10 .25
226 Antonio Gates .12 .30
227 Manti Te'o .12 .30
228 Eric Weddle .10 .25
229 Dallas Cowboys Logo FOIL .10 .25
230 Dallas Cowboys Rusher .10 .25
231 Tony Romo FOIL .25 .60
232 Dez Bryant FOIL .30 .75
233 DeMarcus Ware FOIL .30 .75
234 Tony Romo .12 .30
235 DeMarco Murray .12 .30
236 Miles Austin .10 .25
237 Jason Witten .12 .30
238 Dez Bryant .15 .40
239 Terrance Williams .10 .25
240 Sean Lee .12 .30
241 DeMarcus Ware .15 .40
242 Morris Claiborne .10 .25
243 New York Giants Logo FOIL .10 .25
244 New York Giants Rusher .10 .25
245 Eli Manning FOIL .25 .60
246 Victor Cruz FOIL .25 .60
247 Jason Pierre-Paul FOIL .20 .50
248 Eli Manning .12 .30
249 Ryan Nassib .10 .25
250 Andre Brown .12 .30
251 David Wilson .10 .25
252 Brandon Myers .12 .30
253 Victor Cruz .12 .30
254 Hakeem Nicks .10 .25
255 Justin Tuck .10 .25
256 Jason Pierre-Paul .10 .25
257 Philadelphia Eagles Logo FOIL .10 .25
258 Philadelphia Eagles Rusher .10 .25
259 LeSean McCoy FOIL .30 .75
260 Michael Vick FOIL .25 .60
261 DeSean Jackson FOIL .25 .60
262 Michael Vick .12 .30
263 Matt Barkley .10 .25
264 Bryce Brown .12 .30
265 LeSean McCoy .15 .40
266 Brent Celek .10 .25
267 Jeremy Maclin .10 .25
268 DeSean Jackson .12 .30
269 Fletcher Cox .10 .25
270 DeMeco Ryans .10 .25
271 Washington Redskins Logo FOIL .10 .25
272 Washington Redskins Rusher .10 .25
273 Robert Griffin III FOIL .20 .50
274 Alfred Morris FOIL .20 .50
275 Pierre Garcon FOIL .25 .60
276 Robert Griffin III .10 .25
277 Kirk Cousins .15 .40
278 Alfred Morris .10 .25
279 Fred Davis .10 .25
280 Santana Moss .12 .30
281 Pierre Garcon .12 .30
282 Brian Orakpo .12 .30
283 Ryan Kerrigan .10 .25
284 London Fletcher .12 .30
285 Chicago Bears Logo FOIL .10 .25
286 Chicago Bears Rusher .10 .25
287 Brandon Marshall FOIL .25 .60
288 Jay Cutler FOIL .20 .50
289 Matt Forte FOIL .20 .50
290 Jay Cutler .10 .25
291 Michael Bush .10 .25
292 Matt Forte .10 .25
293 Alshon Jeffery .12 .30
294 Brandon Marshall .12 .30
295 Julius Peppers .12 .30
296 Lance Briggs .12 .30
297 Charles Tillman .12 .30
298 Tim Jennings .10 .25
299 Detroit Lions Logo FOIL .10 .25
300 Detroit Lions Rusher .10 .25
301 Calvin Johnson FOIL .30 .75
302 Matthew Stafford FOIL .25 .60
303 Ndamukong Suh FOIL .25 .60
304 Matthew Stafford .12 .30
305 Mikel Leshoure .10 .25
306 Reggie Bush .10 .25
307 Ryan Broyles .12 .30
308 Brandon Pettigrew .10 .25
309 Calvin Johnson .15 .40
310 Stephen Tulloch .10 .25
311 Nick Fairley .10 .25
312 Ndamukong Suh .12 .30
313 Green Bay Packers Logo FOIL .10 .25
314 Green Bay Packers Rusher .10 .25
315 Aaron Rodgers FOIL .50 1.25
316 Clay Matthews FOIL .30 .75
317 Jordy Nelson FOIL .25 .60
318 Aaron Rodgers .25 .60
319 DuJuan Harris .15 .40
320 Eddie Lacy .10 .25
321 James Jones .10 .25
322 Randall Cobb .12 .30
323 Jordy Nelson .12 .30
324 Jermichael Finley .10 .25
325 A.J. Hawk .10 .25
326 Clay Matthews .15 .40
327 Minnesota Vikings Logo FOIL .10 .25
328 Minnesota Vikings Rusher .10 .25
329 Adrian Peterson FOIL .30 .75
330 Jared Allen FOIL .20 .50
331 Greg Jennings FOIL .20 .50
332 Christian Ponder .10 .25
333 Adrian Peterson .15 .40
334 Toby Gerhart .10 .25
335 Cordarrelle Patterson .10 .25
336 Jarius Wright .10 .25
337 Kyle Rudolph .10 .25
338 Greg Jennings .10 .25
339 Jared Allen .10 .25
340 Harrison Smith .10 .25
341 Atlanta Falcons Logo FOIL .10 .25
342 Atlanta Falcons Rusher .10 .25
343 Matt Ryan FOIL .25 .60

344 Roddy White FOIL .20 .50
345 Julio Jones FOIL .30 .75
346 Matt Ryan .12 .30
347 Jacquizz Rodgers .12 .30
348 Steven Jackson .10 .25
349 Tony Gonzalez .12 .30
350 Roddy White .10 .25
351 Julio Jones .15 .40
352 Osi Umenyiora .10 .25
353 Sean Weatherspoon .10 .25
354 Asante Samuel .10 .25
355 Carolina Panthers Logo FOIL .10 .25
356 Carolina Panthers Rusher .10 .25
357 Cam Newton FOIL .30 .75
358 Steve Smith FOIL .25 .60
359 Luke Kuechly FOIL .25 .60
360 Cam Newton .15 .40
361 DeAngelo Williams .10 .25
362 Jonathan Stewart .10 .25
363 Greg Olsen .12 .30
364 Brandon LaFell .10 .25
365 Steve Smith .12 .30
366 Star Lotulelei .12 .30
367 Thomas Davis .10 .25
368 Luke Kuechly .12 .30
369 New Orleans Saints Logo FOIL .10 .25
370 New Orleans Saints Rusher .10 .25
371 Drew Brees FOIL .30 .75
372 Jimmy Graham FOIL .30 .75
373 Darren Sproles FOIL .25 .60
374 Drew Brees .15 .40
375 Mark Ingram .12 .30
376 Darren Sproles .12 .30
377 Lance Moore .10 .25
378 Marques Colston .10 .25
379 Jimmy Graham .15 .40
380 Cameron Jordan .10 .25
381 Curtis Lofton .10 .25
382 Kenny Vaccaro .10 .25
383 Tampa Bay Buccaneers Logo FOIL .10 .25
384 Tampa Bay Buccaneers Rusher .10 .25
385 Doug Martin FOIL .25 .60
386 Vincent Jackson FOIL .20 .50
387 Josh Freeman FOIL .25 .60
388 Josh Freeman .12 .30
389 Mike Glennon .10 .25
390 Doug Martin .12 .30
391 Vincent Jackson .10 .25
392 Mike Williams .12 .30
393 Lavonte David .10 .25
394 Mason Foster .10 .25
395 Darrelle Revis .10 .25
396 Mark Barron .12 .30
397 Arizona Cardinals Logo FOIL .10 .25
398 Arizona Cardinals Rusher .10 .25
399 Larry Fitzgerald FOIL .25 .60
400 Patrick Peterson FOIL .20 .50
401 Carson Palmer FOIL .25 .60
402 Carson Palmer .12 .30
403 Rashard Mendenhall .10 .25
404 Rob Housler .10 .25
405 Andre Roberts .10 .25
406 Michael Floyd .10 .25
407 Larry Fitzgerald .12 .30
408 Calais Campbell .10 .25
409 Tyrann Mathieu .15 .40
410 Patrick Peterson .10 .25
411 St. Louis Rams Logo FOIL .10 .25
412 St. Louis Rams Rusher .10 .25
413 Sam Bradford FOIL .20 .50
414 James Laurinaitis FOIL .25 .60
415 Greg Zuerlein FOIL .20 .50
416 Sam Bradford .10 .25
417 Daryl Richardson .10 .25
418 Tavon Austin .12 .30
419 Jared Cook .10 .25
420 Chris Long .10 .25
421 James Laurinaitis .12 .30
422 Cortland Finnegan .10 .25
423 Janoris Jenkins .10 .25
424 Greg Zuerlein .10 .25
425 San Francisco 49ers Logo FOIL .10 .25
426 San Francisco 49ers Rusher .10 .25
427 Colin Kaepernick FOIL .25 .60
428 Michael Crabtree FOIL .20 .50
429 Frank Gore FOIL .25 .60
430 Colin Kaepernick .12 .30
431 LaMichael James .10 .25
432 Frank Gore .12 .30
433 Anquan Boldin .10 .25
434 Vernon Davis .10 .25
435 Michael Crabtree .10 .25
436 Quinton Patton .10 .25
437 Aldon Smith .10 .25
438 Patrick Willis .12 .30
439 Seattle Seahawks Logo FOIL .10 .25
440 Seattle Seahawks Rusher .10 .25
441 Russell Wilson FOIL .60 1.50
442 Percy Harvin FOIL .20 .50
443 Marshawn Lynch FOIL .25 .60
444 Russell Wilson .30 .75
445 Marshawn Lynch .12 .30
446 Chris Harper .10 .25
447 Golden Tate .10 .25
448 Sidney Rice .10 .25
449 Percy Harvin .10 .25
450 Bobby Wagner .10 .25
451 Richard Sherman .15 .40
452 Kam Chancellor .20 .50
453 Panini Clinic Logo .10 .25
454 POP Warner Logo .10 .25
455 Pop Warner Action 1 .10 .25
456 Pop Warner Action 2 .10 .25
457 Pop Warner Action 3 .10 .25
458 Pop Warner Action 4 .10 .25
459 Andrew Luck PW .25 .60
460 Alfred Morris PW .10 .25
461 Tavon Austin PW .12 .30
462 Dave Robinson HOF .10 .25
463 Bill Parcells HOF .15 .40
464 Jonathan Ogden HOF .10 .30
465 Larry Allen HOF .10 .30
466 Warren Sapp HOF .12 .30
467 Curley Culp HOF .10 .25
468 Cris Carter HOF .15 .40
469 AFC Championship .10 .25
Ray Rice
470 NFC Championship .12 .30
Colin Kaepernick
471 Super Bowl XLVII .10 .25
472 Super Bowl XLVII .12 .30
Joe Flacco
Derrick Brooks
473 Super Bowl XLVII .10 .25
474 Super Bowl XLVII .10 .25
475 Super Bowl XLVII .12 .30
Joe Flacco celebration
476 Super Bowl XLVIII Logo .10 .25
477 Rush Zone Troy .10 .25
478 Rush Zone Ricky .10 .25
479 Rush Zone Cartoon .10 .25
480 Rush Zone Cartoon .10 .25
481 Rush Zone Ash .10 .25
482 Rush Zone Tua .10 .25
483 Rush Zone Ish .10 .25
484 Rush Zone Marty .10 .25
485 Rush Zone Cartoon .10 .25
486 Rush Zone Cartoon .10 .25
487 Rush Zone Cartoon .10 .25
488 Rush Zone Cartoon .10 .25

2015 Panini Stickers

1 Odell Beckham Jr. ROY .15 .40
2 NFL Honors .10 .25
3 Aaron Donald ROY .15 .40
4 Larry Fitzgerald .12 .30
Art Rooney Award
5 Thomas Davis .10 .25
Walter Payton MOY
6 DeMarco Murray .12 .30
Offensive POY
7 Aaron Rodgers .30 .75
NFL MVP
8 J.J. Watt .15 .40
Defensive POY
9 NFL Draft Logo .10 .25
10 NFL Draft 3rd Pick .10 .25
11 NFL Draft 5th Pick .10 .25
12 NFL Draft 6th Pick .10 .25
13 NFL Draft 7th Pick .10 .25
14 NFL Draft 8th Pick .10 .25
15 Buffalo Bills Logo FOIL .20 .50
16 Sammy Watkins FOIL .25 .60
17 LeSean McCoy FOIL .30 .75
18 Mario Williams FOIL .20 .50
19 EJ Manuel .10 .25
20 Fred Jackson .12 .30
21 LeSean McCoy .15 .40
22 Sammy Watkins .12 .30
23 Robert Woods .12 .30
24 Percy Harvin .10 .25
25 Chris Hogan .12 .30
26 Marcell Dareus .10 .25
27 Mario Williams .10 .25
28 2 Time Super Bowl Champs .10 .25
29 Miami Dolphins Logo FOIL .20 .50
30 Ryan Tannehill FOIL .25 .60
31 Jarvis Landry FOIL .25 .60
32 Ndamukong Suh FOIL .25 .60
33 Ryan Tannehill .12 .30
34 Lamar Miller .10 .25
35 Jarvis Landry .12 .30
36 DeVante Parker .15 .40
37 Ndamukong Suh .12 .30
38 Cameron Wake .10 .25
39 Olivier Vernon .10 .25
40 Jelani Jenkins .10 .25
41 Brent Grimes .10 .25
42 Four Time Super Bowl Champs .10 .25
43 New England Patriots Logo FOIL .20 .50
44 Tom Brady FOIL .75 2.00
45 Rob Gronkowski FOIL .30 .75
46 Julian Edelman FOIL .30 .75
47 Tom Brady .40 1.00
48 LeGarrette Blount .12 .30
49 Julian Edelman .15 .40
50 Rob Gronkowski .15 .40
51 Dont'a Hightower .10 .25
52 Chandler Jones .10 .25
53 Rob Ninkovich .10 .25
54 Devin McCourty .10 .25
55 Stephen Gostkowski .12 .30
56 One Time Super Bowl Champs .10 .25
57 New York Jets Logo FOIL .20 .50
58 Brandon Marshall FOIL .20 .50
59 Darrelle Revis FOIL .20 .50
60 Antonio Cromartie FOIL .20 .50
61 Geno Smith .10 .25
62 Chris Ivory .12 .30
63 Brandon Marshall .10 .25
64 Eric Decker .10 .25
65 Jeremy Kerley .10 .25
66 Darrelle Revis .10 .25
67 Antonio Cromartie .10 .25
68 Sheldon Richardson .10 .25
69 Nick Folk .10 .25
70 Two Time Super Bowl Champs .10 .25
71 Baltimore Ravens Logo FOIL .20 .50
72 Joe Flacco FOIL .25 .60
73 Steve Smith FOIL .25 .60
74 Justin Forsett FOIL .25 .60
75 Joe Flacco .12 .30
76 Justin Forsett .12 .30
77 Breshad Perriman .10 .25
78 Steve Smith .12 .30
79 Dennis Pitta .10 .25
80 Elvis Dumervil .10 .25
81 C.J. Mosley .15 .40
82 Terrell Suggs .10 .25
83 Justin Tucker .10 .25
84 Cincinnati Bengals Logo FOIL .20 .50
85 Andy Dalton FOIL .25 .60
86 Jeremy Hill FOIL .20 .50
87 A.J. Green FOIL .30 .75
88 Andy Dalton .12 .30
89 Jeremy Hill .10 .25
90 Giovani Bernard .10 .25
91 A.J. Green .15 .40
92 Mohamed Sanu .10 .25
93 Vontaze Burfict .10 .25
94 Carlos Dunlap .10 .25
95 Vincent Rey .10 .25
96 Geno Atkins .10 .25
97 Cleveland Browns Logo FOIL .20 .50
98 Terrance West FOIL .20 .50
99 Tashaun Gipson FOIL .25 .60
100 Paul Kruger FOIL .20 .50
101 Johnny Manziel .12 .30
102 Terrance West .10 .25
103 Isaiah Crowell .10 .25
104 Andrew Hawkins .10 .25
105 Taylor Gabriel .10 .25
106 Karlos Dansby .10 .25
107 Tashaun Gipson .12 .30
108 Joe Haden .10 .25
109 Paul Kruger .10 .25
110 Six Time Super Bowl Champs .10 .25
111 Pittsburgh Steelers Logo FOIL .20 .50
112 Ben Roethlisberger FOIL .30 .75
113 Le'Veon Bell FOIL .25 .60
114 Antonio Brown FOIL .30 .75
115 Ben Roethlisberger .15 .40
116 Le'Veon Bell .12 .30
117 Antonio Brown .15 .40
118 Heath Miller .10 .25
119 Markus Wheaton .10 .25
120 Martavis Bryant .10 .25
121 Lawrence Timmons .10 .25
122 Cameron Heyward .10 .25
123 James Harrison .12 .30
124 Houston Texans Logo FOIL .20 .50
125 Arian Foster FOIL .25 .60
126 DeAndre Hopkins FOIL .25 .60
127 J.J. Watt FOIL .30 .75
128 Ryan Mallett .12 .30
129 Arian Foster .12 .30
130 DeAndre Hopkins .12 .30
131 Damaris Johnson .10 .25
132 Garrett Graham .10 .25
133 J.J. Watt .15 .40
134 Johnathan Joseph .10 .25
135 Whitney Mercilus .10 .25
136 Jadeveon Clowney .10 .25
137 Two Time Super Bowl Champs .10 .25
138 Indianapolis Colts Logo FOIL .20 .50
139 Andrew Luck FOIL .40 1.00
140 T.Y. Hilton FOIL .25 .60
141 D'Qwell Jackson FOIL .20 .50
142 Andrew Luck .20 .50
143 Frank Gore .12 .30
144 T.Y. Hilton .12 .30
145 Andre Johnson .12 .30
146 Coby Fleener .10 .25
147 Vontae Davis .10 .25
148 D'Qwell Jackson .10 .25
149 Bjoern Werner .10 .25
150 Adam Vinatieri .10 .25
151 Jacksonville Jaguars Logo FOIL .20 .50
152 Blake Bortles FOIL .20 .50
153 Julius Thomas FOIL .20 .50
154 Denard Robinson FOIL .20 .50
155 Blake Bortles .10 .25
156 Toby Gerhart .10 .25
157 Denard Robinson .10 .25
158 Allen Hurns .10 .25
159 Julius Thomas .10 .25
160 Johnathan Cyprien .10 .25
161 Sen'Derrick Marks .10 .25
162 Paul Posluszny .10 .25
163 Josh Scobee .10 .25
164 Tennessee Titans Logo FOIL .20 .50
165 Kendall Wright FOIL .20 .50
166 Bishop Sankey FOIL .20 .50
167 Delanie Walker FOIL .20 .50
168 Zach Mettenberger .10 .25
169 Marcus Mariota .40 1.00
170 Bishop Sankey .10 .25
171 Shonn Greene .10 .25
172 Kendall Wright .10 .25
173 Justin Hunter .10 .25
174 Delanie Walker .10 .25
175 Michael Griffin .10 .25
176 Jurrell Casey .10 .25
177 Two Time Super Bowl Champs .10 .25
178 Denver Broncos Logo FOIL .20 .50
179 Peyton Manning FOIL .60 1.50
180 Demaryius Thomas FOIL .25 .60
181 Von Miller FOIL .25 .60
182 Peyton Manning .30 .75
183 C.J. Anderson .12 .30
184 Montee Ball .10 .25
185 Demaryius Thomas .12 .30
186 Emmanuel Sanders .12 .30
187 Von Miller .12 .30
188 Brandon Marshall .10 .25
189 DeMarcus Ware .12 .30
190 Aqib Talib .10 .25
191 One Time Super Bowl Champs .10 .25
192 Kansas City Chiefs Logo FOIL .20 .50
193 Alex Smith FOIL .25 .60
194 Jamaal Charles FOIL .25 .60
195 Justin Houston FOIL .20 .50
196 Alex Smith .12 .30
197 Jamaal Charles .12 .30
198 Knile Davis .10 .25
199 Jeremy Maclin .10 .25
200 Travis Kelce .15 .40
201 Justin Houston .10 .25
202 Tamba Hali .10 .25
203 Dontari Poe .10 .25
204 Derrick Johnson .10 .25
205 Three Time Super Bowl Champs .10 .25
206 Oakland Raiders Logo FOIL .20 .50
207 Derek Carr FOIL .30 .75
208 Charles Woodson FOIL .30 .75
209 Khalil Mack FOIL .30 .75
210 Derek Carr .15 .40
211 Latavius Murray .10 .25
212 Marcel Reece .10 .25
213 Amari Cooper .30 .75
214 Mychal Rivera .10 .25
215 Justin Tuck .10 .25
216 Charles Woodson .15 .40
217 Khalil Mack .15 .40
218 Sebastian Janikowski .10 .25
219 San Diego Chargers Logo FOIL .20 .50
220 Philip Rivers FOIL .30 .75
221 Antonio Gates FOIL .20 .50
222 Keenan Allen FOIL .25 .60
223 Philip Rivers .15 .40
224 Melvin Gordon III .25 .60
225 Danny Woodhead .12 .30
226 Keenan Allen .12 .30
227 Malcom Floyd .10 .25
228 Antonio Gates .10 .25
229 Eric Weddle .10 .25
230 Brandon Flowers .10 .25
231 Nick Novak .10 .25
232 Five Time Super Bowl Champs .10 .25
233 Dallas Cowboys Logo FOIL .20 .50
234 Tony Romo FOIL .25 .60
235 Dez Bryant FOIL .30 .75
236 Jason Witten FOIL .25 .60
237 Tony Romo .12 .30
238 Joseph Randle .10 .25
239 Dez Bryant .15 .40
240 Terrance Williams .10 .25
241 Cole Beasley .15 .40
242 Jason Witten .12 .30
243 Barry Church .12 .30
244 Orlando Scandrick .10 .25
245 Dan Bailey .10 .25
246 Four Time Super Bowl Champs .10 .25
247 New York Giants Logo FOIL .20 .50
248 Eli Manning FOIL .25 .60
249 Odell Beckham Jr. FOIL .30 .75
250 Jason Pierre-Paul FOIL .20 .50
251 Eli Manning .12 .30
252 Rashad Jennings .10 .25
253 Andre Williams .10 .25
254 Odell Beckham Jr. .15 .40
255 Victor Cruz .12 .30
256 Rueben Randle .10 .25
257 Jason Pierre-Paul .10 .25
258 Jameel McClain .10 .25
259 Dominique Rodgers-Cromartie .10 .25
260 Philadelphia Eagles Logo FOIL .20 .50
261 DeMarco Murray FOIL .25 .60
262 Darren Sproles FOIL .25 .60
263 Connor Barwin FOIL .20 .50
264 Sam Bradford .10 .25
265 DeMarco Murray .12 .30
266 Darren Sproles .12 .30
267 Riley Cooper .12 .30
268 Nelson Agholor .12 .30
269 Zach Ertz .12 .30
270 Connor Barwin .10 .25
271 Mychal Kendricks .10 .25
272 Fletcher Cox .10 .25
273 Three Time Super Bowl Champs .10 .25
274 Washington Redskins Logo FOIL .20 .50
275 Alfred Morris FOIL .20 .50
276 DeSean Jackson FOIL .25 .60
277 Ryan Kerrigan FOIL .20 .50
278 Robert Griffin III .10 .25
279 Kirk Cousins .15 .40
280 Alfred Morris .10 .25
281 Pierre Garcon .12 .30
282 DeSean Jackson .12 .30
283 Jordan Reed .10 .25
284 DeAngelo Hall .12 .30
285 Ryan Kerrigan .10 .25
286 Perry Riley Jr. .10 .25
287 One Time Super Bowl Champs .10 .25
288 Chicago Bears Logo FOIL .20 .50
289 Matt Forte FOIL .20 .50
290 Alshon Jeffery FOIL .25 .60
291 Jay Cutler FOIL .20 .50
292 Jay Cutler .10 .25
293 Matt Forte .10 .25
294 Alshon Jeffery .12 .30
295 Kevin White .12 .30
296 Martellus Bennett .10 .25
297 Jared Allen .10 .25
298 Willie Young .10 .25
299 Kyle Fuller .10 .25
300 Ryan Mundy .10 .25
301 Detroit Lions Logo FOIL .20 .50
302 Matthew Stafford FOIL .25 .60
303 Calvin Johnson FOIL .30 .75
304 Golden Tate FOIL .20 .50
305 Matthew Stafford .12 .30
306 Joique Bell .10 .25
307 Ameer Abdullah .15 .40
308 Calvin Johnson .15 .40
309 Golden Tate .10 .25
310 Eric Ebron .10 .25
311 DeAndre Levy .10 .25
312 Ezekiel Ansah .10 .25
313 Glover Quin .10 .25
314 Four Time Super Bowl Champs .10 .25
315 Green Bay Packers Logo FOIL .20 .50
316 Aaron Rodgers FOIL .60 1.50
317 Jordy Nelson FOIL .25 .60
318 Clay Matthews FOIL .30 .75
319 Aaron Rodgers .30 .75
320 Eddie Lacy .10 .25
321 Jordy Nelson .12 .30
322 Randall Cobb .12 .30
323 Davante Adams .12 .30
324 Clay Matthews .15 .40
325 Julius Peppers .12 .30
326 Morgan Burnett .10 .25
327 Mason Crosby .10 .25
328 Minnesota Vikins Logo FOIL .20 .50
329 Teddy Bridgewater FOIL .25 .60
330 Kyle Rudolph FOIL .20 .50
331 Harrison Smith FOIL .20 .50
332 Teddy Bridgewater .12 .30
333 Matt Asiata .10 .25
334 Jerick McKinnon .10 .25
335 Mike Wallace .10 .25
336 Charles Johnson .10 .25
337 Kyle Rudolph .10 .25
338 Chad Greenway .10 .25
339 Everson Griffen .10 .25
340 Harrison Smith .10 .25
341 Atlanta Falcons Logo FOIL .20 .50
342 Matt Ryan FOIL .25 .60
343 Julio Jones FOIL .30 .75
344 Roddy White FOIL .20 .50
345 Matt Ryan .12 .30
346 Devonta Freeman .12 .30
347 Tevin Coleman .12 .30
348 Julio Jones .15 .40
349 Roddy White .10 .25
350 Devin Hester .12 .30
351 Paul Worrilow .10 .25
352 Jonathan Babineaux .10 .25
353 Matt Bryant .10 .25
354 Carolina Panthers Logo FOIL .20 .50
355 Cam Newton FOIL .30 .75
356 Kelvin Benjamin FOIL .25 .60
357 Luke Kuechly FOIL .25 .60
358 Cam Newton .15 .40
359 Jonathan Stewart .10 .25
360 Kelvin Benjamin .12 .30
361 Jerricho Cotchery .10 .25
362 Greg Olsen .12 .30
363 Luke Kuechly .12 .30
364 Thomas Davis .10 .25
365 Roman Harper .10 .25
366 Charles Johnson .10 .25
367 One Time Super Bowl Champs .10 .25
368 New Orleans Saints Logo FOIL .20 .50
369 Drew Brees FOIL .30 .75
370 Mark Ingram FOIL .25 .60
371 Marques Colston FOIL .20 .50
372 Drew Brees .15 .40
373 Mark Ingram .12 .30
374 Marques Colston .10 .25
375 Brandin Cooks .12 .30
376 Benjamin Watson .10 .25
377 David Hawthorne .10 .25
378 Junior Galette .10 .25
379 Cameron Jordan .10 .25
380 Kenny Vaccaro .10 .25
381 One Time Super Bowl Champs .10 .25
382 Tampa Bay Buccaneers Logo FOIL .20 .50
383 Vincent Jackson FOIL .20 .50
384 Mike Evans FOIL .25 .60
385 Lavonte David FOIL .20 .50
386 Mike Glennon .12 .30
387 Jameis Winston .25 .60
388 Doug Martin .12 .30
389 Bobby Rainey .10 .25
390 Vincent Jackson .10 .25
391 Mike Evans .12 .30
392 Lavonte David .10 .25
393 Gerald McCoy .10 .25
394 Alterraun Verner .10 .25
395 Arizona Cardinals Logo FOIL .20 .50
396 Larry Fitzgerald FOIL .25 .60
397 Andre Ellington FOIL .20 .50
398 Patrick Peterson FOIL .20 .50
399 Carson Palmer .12 .30
400 Drew Stanton .15 .40
401 Andre Ellington .10 .25
402 Larry Fitzgerald .12 .30
403 John Brown .12 .30
404 Michael Floyd .10 .25
405 Alex Okafor .10 .25
406 Tyrann Mathieu .12 .30
407 Patrick Peterson .10 .25
408 One Time Super Bowl Champs .10 .25
409 St. Louis Rams Logo FOIL .20 .50
410 Tre Mason FOIL .25 .60
411 Robert Quinn FOIL .25 .60
412 Aaron Donald FOIL .30 .75
413 Nick Foles .12 .30
414 Tre Mason .12 .30
415 Todd Gurley .40 1.00
416 Kenny Britt .10 .25
417 Tavon Austin .10 .25
418 Jared Cook .10 .25
419 Alec Ogletree .10 .25
420 Robert Quinn .12 .30
421 Aaron Donald .15 .40
422 Five Time Super Bowl Champs .10 .25
423 San Francisco 49ers Logo FOIL .20 .50
424 Colin Kaepernick FOIL .25 .60
425 Anquan Boldin FOIL .20 .50
426 Antoine Bethea FOIL .20 .50
427 Colin Kaepernick .12 .30
428 Carlos Hyde .10 .25
429 Anquan Boldin .10 .25
430 Torrey Smith .10 .25
431 Vernon Davis .10 .25
432 NaVorro Bowman .12 .30
433 Ahmad Brooks .10 .25
434 Antoine Bethea .10 .25
435 Bruce Ellington .10 .25
436 One Time Super Bowl Champs .10 .25
437 Seattle Seahawks Logo FOIL .20 .50
438 Russell Wilson FOIL .40 1.00
439 Marshawn Lynch FOIL .25 .60
440 Richard Sherman FOIL .30 .75
441 Russell Wilson .20 .50
442 Marshawn Lynch .12 .30
443 Doug Baldwin .12 .30
444 Jimmy Graham .15 .40
445 Bobby Wagner .10 .25
446 Cliff Avril .10 .25
447 Michael Bennett .10 .25
448 Richard Sherman .15 .40
449 Kam Chancellor .15 .40
450 Pop Warner Action 1 .10 .25
451 Pop Warner Action 2 .10 .25
452 Pop Warner Action 3 .10 .25
453 Pop Warner Action 4 .10 .25
454 Pop Warner Action 5 .10 .25
455 Pop Warner Action 6 .10 .25
456 Pop Warner Action 7 .10 .25
457 Pro Football Hall of Fame Logo .10 .25
458 Jerome Bettis HOF .15 .40
459 Tim Brown HOF .15 .40
460 Charles Haley HOF .15 .40
461 Junior Seau HOF .12 .30
462 Will Shields HOF .10 .25
463 Mick Tingelhoff HOF .10 .25
464 Super Bowl XLIX .12 .30
Marshawn Lynch
465 Super Bowl XLIX .12 .30
Danny Amendola
466 Super Bowl XLIX .15 .40
Rob Gronkowski
467 Super Bowl XLIX .15 .40
Julian Edelman
468 Super Bowl XLIX .10 .25
Jermaine Kearse
469 Super Bowl XLIX .15 .40
Malcolm Butler
470 Super Bowl XLIX .12 .30
Robert Kraft
471 Super Bowl XLIX .40 1.00
Tom Brady
472 NFL Logo .10 .25
473 Super Bowl 50 Puzzle .10 .25
474 Super Bowl 50 Puzzle .10 .25
475 Super Bowl 50 Puzzle .10 .25
476 Super Bowl 50 Puzzle .10 .25
477 Panini Logo FOIL .20 .50

2016 Panini Stickers

1 AFC West .10 .25
2 AFC North .10 .25
3 AFC South .10 .25
4 AFC East .10 .25
5 NFC West .10 .25
6 NFC North .10 .25
7 NFC South .10 .25
8 NFC East .10 .25
9 Jared Goff DRAFT .60 1.50
10 Carson Wentz DRAFT 1.00 2.50
11 Joey Bosa DRAFT .20 .50
12 Ezekiel Elliott DRAFT .50 1.25
13 Josh Doctson DRAFT .12 .30
14 Laquon Treadwell DRAFT .12 .30
15 Buffalo Bills Logo FOIL .20 .50
16 Buffalo Bills Mascot .10 .25
17 Karlos Williams FOIL .20 .50
18 Tyrod Taylor FOIL .25 .60
19 LeSean McCoy FOIL .30 .75
20 Tyrod Taylor .12 .30
21 Karlos Williams .10 .25
22 LeSean McCoy .15 .40
23 Robert Woods .12 .30
24 Sammy Watkins ILL .15 .40
25 Sammy Watkins .15 .40
26 Charles Clay .10 .25
27 Marcell Dareus .10 .25
28 Ronald Darby .10 .25
29 Miami Dolphins Logo FOIL .20 .50
30 Miami Dolphins Mascot .10 .25
31 Ryan Tannehill FOIL .25 .60
32 Ndamukong Suh FOIL .25 .60
33 Cameron Wake FOIL .20 .50
34 Ryan Tannehill .12 .30
35 Jay Ajayi .12 .30
36 DeVante Parker .12 .30
37 Jarvis Landry .12 .30
38 Jarvis Landry ILL .12 .30
39 Ndamukong Suh .12 .30
40 Cameron Wake .10 .25
41 Kenyan Drake .15 .40
42 Reshad Jones .10 .25
43 New England Patriots Logo FOIL .20 .50
44 New England Patriots Mascot .10 .25
45 Tom Brady FOIL .75 2.00
46 Malcolm Butler FOIL .30 .75
47 Julian Edelman FOIL .30 .75
48 Tom Brady .40 1.00
49 Dion Lewis .10 .25
50 Julian Edelman .15 .40
51 Rob Gronkowski .15 .40
52 Rob Gronkowski ILL .15 .40
53 Martellus Bennett .10 .25
54 Rob Ninkovich .10 .25
55 Jamie Collins .10 .25
56 Malcolm Butler .15 .40
57 New York Jets Logo FOIL .20 .50
58 New York Jets Mascot .10 .25
59 Darrelle Revis FOIL .20 .50
60 Matt Forte FOIL .20 .50
61 Brandon Marshall FOIL .20 .50
62 Christian Hackenberg .10 .25
63 Matt Forte .10 .25
64 Nick Mangold .10 .25
65 Brandon Marshall .10 .25
66 Eric Decker ILL .10 .25
67 Eric Decker .10 .25
68 Leonard Williams .10 .25
69 Muhammad Wilkerson .10 .25
70 Darrelle Revis .10 .25
71 Baltimore Ravens Logo FOIL .20 .50
72 Baltimore Ravens Mascot .10 .25
73 Joe Flacco FOIL .25 .60
74 Terrell Suggs FOIL .20 .50
75 Justin Forsett FOIL .25 .60
76 Joe Flacco .12 .30
77 Buck Allen .10 .25
78 Justin Forsett .12 .30
79 Kamar Aiken .10 .25
80 Steve Smith Sr. ILL .12 .30
81 Steve Smith Sr. .12 .30
82 Terrell Suggs .10 .25
83 C.J. Mosley .12 .30
84 Elvis Dumervil .10 .25
85 Cincinnati Bengals Logo FOIL .20 .50
86 Cincinnati Bengals Mascot .10 .25
87 Tyler Eifert FOIL .25 .60
88 Jeremy Hill FOIL .20 .50
89 Andy Dalton FOIL .25 .60
90 Andy Dalton .12 .30
91 Giovani Bernard .10 .25
92 Jeremy Hill .10 .25
93 A.J. Green .15 .40
94 A.J. Green ILL .15 .40
95 Tyler Boyd .12 .30
96 Tyler Eifert .12 .30
97 Geno Atkins .10 .25
98 Carlos Dunlap .10 .25
99 Cleveland Browns Logo FOIL .20 .50
100 Cleveland Browns Mascot .10 .25
101 Joe Haden FOIL .20 .50
102 Duke Johnson FOIL .20 .50
103 Robert Griffin III FOIL .20 .50
104 Robert Griffin III .10 .25
105 Duke Johnson .10 .25
106 Isaiah Crowell .10 .25
107 Corey Coleman .15 .40
108 Gary Barnidge ILL .10 .25
109 Gary Barnidge .10 .25
110 Joe Thomas .10 .25
111 Danny Shelton .10 .25
112 Joe Haden .10 .25
113 Pittsburgh Steelers Logo FOIL .20 .50
114 Pittsburgh Steelers Mascot .10 .25
115 Ben Roethlisberger FOIL .30 .75
116 James Harrison FOIL .25 .60
117 Le'Veon Bell FOIL .25 .60
118 Ben Roethlisberger .15 .40
119 DeAngelo Williams .10 .25
120 Le'Veon Bell .12 .30
121 Ladarius Green .10 .25
122 Antonio Brown ILL .15 .40
123 Markus Wheaton .10 .25
124 Antonio Brown .15 .40
125 Lawrence Timmons .12 .30
126 James Harrison .12 .30
127 Houston Texans Logo FOIL .20 .50
128 Houston Texans Mascot .10 .25
129 Brock Osweiler FOIL .20 .50
130 DeAndre Hopkins FOIL .25 .60
131 J.J. Watt FOIL .30 .75
132 Brock Osweiler .10 .25
133 Lamar Miller .10 .25
134 DeAndre Hopkins .12 .30
135 Will Fuller .15 .40
136 J.J. Watt ILL .15 .40
137 J.J. Watt .15 .40
138 Jadeveon Clowney .10 .25
139 Brian Cushing .10 .25
140 Whitney Mercilus .10 .25
141 Indianapolis Colts Logo FOIL .20 .50
142 Indianapolis Colts Mascot .10 .25
143 Andrew Luck FOIL .40 1.00
144 Donte Moncrief FOIL .25 .60
145 Frank Gore FOIL .25 .60
146 Andrew Luck .20 .50
147 Frank Gore .12 .30
148 Donte Moncrief .12 .30
149 Phillip Dorsett .10 .25
150 T.Y. Hilton ILL .12 .30
151 T.Y. Hilton .12 .30
152 Dwayne Allen .10 .25
153 Vontae Davis .10 .25
154 Adam Vinatieri .12 .30
155 Jacksonville Jaguars Logo FOIL .20 .50
156 Jacksonville Jaguars Mascot .10 .25
157 Julius Thomas FOIL .20 .50
158 Allen Hurns FOIL .20 .50
159 Blake Bortles FOIL .20 .50
160 Blake Bortles .10 .25
161 Chris Ivory .12 .30
162 T.J. Yeldon .10 .25
163 Allen Hurns .10 .25
164 Allen Robinson ILL .12 .30
165 Allen Robinson .12 .30
166 Marqise Lee .10 .25
167 Julius Thomas .10 .25
168 Paul Posluszny .10 .25
169 Tennessee Titans Logo FOIL .20 .50
170 Tennessee Titans Mascot .10 .25
171 Marcus Mariota FOIL .30 .75
172 Delanie Walker FOIL .20 .50
173 DeMarco Murray FOIL .25 .60
174 Marcus Mariota .15 .40
175 DeMarco Murray .12 .30
176 Derrick Henry .25 .60
177 Dorial Green-Beckham .10 .25
178 Dorial Green-Beckham ILL .10 .25
179 Harry Douglas .10 .25
180 Kendall Wright .10 .25
181 Delanie Walker .10 .25
182 Taylor Lewan .10 .25
183 Denver Broncos Logo FOIL .20 .50
184 Denver Broncos Mascot .10 .25
185 Emmanuel Sanders FOIL .30 .75
186 Von Miller FOIL .25 .60
187 C.J. Anderson FOIL .25 .60
188 Paxton Lynch .10 .25
189 C.J. Anderson .12 .30
190 Demaryius Thomas .12 .30
191 Emmanuel Sanders .15 .40
192 Demaryius Thomas ILL .12 .30
193 Ronnie Hillman .10 .25
194 DeMarcus Ware .12 .30
195 Von Miller .12 .30
196 Chris Harris Jr. .10 .25
197 Kansas City Chiefs Logo FOIL .20 .50
198 Kansas City Chiefs Mascot .10 .25
199 Jeremy Maclin FOIL .20 .50
200 Alex Smith FOIL .25 .60
201 Jamaal Charles FOIL .25 .60
202 Alex Smith .12 .30
203 Jamaal Charles .12 .30
204 Jeremy Maclin .10 .25
205 Travis Kelce .15 .40
206 Travis Kelce ILL .15 .40
207 Justin Houston .10 .25
208 Tamba Hali .10 .25
209 Marcus Peters .10 .25
210 Eric Berry .12 .30
211 Oakland Raiders Logo FOIL .20 .50
212 Oakland Raiders Mascot .10 .25
213 Derek Carr FOIL .30 .75
214 Latavius Murray FOIL .20 .50
215 Khalil Mack FOIL .30 .75
216 Derek Carr .15 .40
217 Latavius Murray .10 .25
218 Marcel Reece .10 .25
219 Amari Cooper .15 .40
220 Amari Cooper ILL .15 .40
221 Michael Crabtree .10 .25
222 Seth Roberts .12 .30
223 Clive Walford .10 .25
224 Khalil Mack .15 .40
225 San Diego Chargers Logo FOIL .20 .50
226 San Diego Chargers Mascot .10 .25
227 Antonio Gates FOIL .20 .50
228 Philip Rivers FOIL .30 .75
229 Melvin Gordon FOIL .25 .60
230 Philip Rivers .15 .40
231 Danny Woodhead .12 .30
232 Melvin Gordon .12 .30
233 Keenan Allen .12 .30
234 Keenan Allen ILL .12 .30
235 Steve Johnson .12 .30
236 Antonio Gates .10 .25
237 Travis Benjamin .10 .25
238 Joey Bosa .20 .50
239 Tony Romo .12 .30
240 Darren McFadden .10 .25
241 Alfred Morris .10 .25
242 Ezekiel Elliott .50 1.25
243 Dez Bryant ILL .15 .40
244 Dez Bryant .15 .40
245 Terrance Williams .10 .25
246 Jason Witten .12 .30
247 Byron Jones .10 .25
248 Darren McFadden FOIL .20 .50
249 Jason Witten FOIL .25 .60
250 Tony Romo FOIL .25 .60
251 Dallas Cowboys Mascot .10 .25
252 Dallas Cowboys Logo FOIL .20 .50
253 Eli Manning .12 .30
254 Rashad Jennings .10 .25
255 Dwayne Harris .10 .25
256 Odell Beckham Jr. .15 .40
257 Odell Beckham Jr. ILL .15 .40
258 Sterling Shepard .12 .30
259 Victor Cruz .12 .30
260 Will Tye
261 Landon Collins .10 .25
262 Rashad Jennings FOIL .20 .50
263 Eli Manning FOIL .25 .60
264 Victor Cruz FOIL .25 .60
265 New York Giants Mascot .10 .25
266 New York Giants Logo FOIL .20 .50
267 Sam Bradford .10 .25
268 Carson Wentz 1.00 2.50
269 Darren Sproles .12 .30
270 Ryan Mathews .12 .30
271 Zach Ertz ILL .12 .30
272 Jordan Matthews .12 .30
273 Brent Celek .10 .25
274 Zach Ertz .12 .30
275 Fletcher Cox .10 .25
276 Jordan Matthews FOIL .25 .60
277 Sam Bradford FOIL .20 .50
278 Fletcher Cox FOIL .20 .50
279 Philadelphia Eagles Mascot .10 .25
280 Philadelphia Eagles Logo FOIL .20 .50
281 Kirk Cousins .15 .40
282 Matt Jones .12 .30
283 DeSean Jackson .12 .30
284 Jamison Crowder .10 .25
285 Jordan Reed ILL .10 .25
286 Josh Doctson .12 .30
287 Jordan Reed .10 .25
288 Trent Williams .10 .25
289 Ryan Kerrigan .10 .25
290 Kirk Cousins FOIL .30 .75
291 DeSean Jackson FOIL .25 .60
292 Matt Jones FOIL .25 .60
293 Washington Redskins Mascot .10 .25
294 Washington Redskins Logo FOIL .20 .50
295 Jay Cutler .10 .25
296 Jeremy Langford .12 .30
297 Alshon Jeffery .12 .30
298 Kevin White .10 .25
299 Alshon Jeffery ILL .12 .30
300 Kyle Long .10 .25
301 Zach Miller .10 .25
302 Kyle Fuller .10 .25
303 Robbie Gould .10 .25
304 Kevin White FOIL .20 .50
305 Jeremy Langford FOIL .25 .60
306 Jay Cutler FOIL .20 .50
307 Chicago Bears Mascot .10 .25
308 Chicago Bears Logo FOIL .20 .50
309 Matthew Stafford .12 .30
310 Ameer Abdullah .10 .25
311 Marvin Jones .10 .25
312 Golden Tate .10 .25
313 Ameer Abdullah ILL .10 .25
314 Eric Ebron .10 .25
315 Ezekiel Ansah .10 .25
316 DeAndre Levy .10 .25
317 Glover Quin .10 .25
318 Golden Tate FOIL .20 .50
319 Matthew Stafford FOIL .25 .60
320 Ameer Abdullah FOIL .20 .50
321 Detroit Lions Mascot .10 .25
322 Detroit Lions Logo FOIL .20 .50
323 Aaron Rodgers .30 .75
324 Eddie Lacy .10 .25
325 James Starks .10 .25
326 John Kuhn .10 .25
327 Clay Matthews ILL .15 .40
328 Jordy Nelson .12 .30
329 Randall Cobb .12 .30
330 Julius Peppers .12 .30
331 Clay Matthews .15 .40
332 Aaron Rodgers FOIL .60 1.50
333 Randall Cobb FOIL .25 .60
334 Jordy Nelson FOIL .25 .60
335 Green Bay Packers Mascot .10 .25
336 Green Bay Packers Logo FOIL .20 .50
337 Teddy Bridgewater .12 .30
338 Adrian Peterson .15 .40
339 Laquon Treadwell .12 .30
340 Stefon Diggs .12 .30
341 Adrian Peterson ILL .15 .40
342 Kyle Rudolph .10 .25
343 Anthony Barr .10 .25
344 Eric Kendricks .10 .25
345 Harrison Smith .10 .25
346 Stefon Diggs FOIL .25 .60
347 Kyle Rudolph FOIL .20 .50
348 Teddy Bridgewater FOIL .25 .60
349 Minnesota Vikings Mascot .10 .25
350 Minnesota Vikings Logo FOIL .20 .50
351 Matt Ryan .12 .30
352 Devonta Freeman .12 .30
353 Tevin Coleman .12 .30
354 Julio Jones .15 .40
355 Julio Jones ILL .15 .40
356 Jacob Tamme .10 .25
357 Devin Hester .12 .30
358 Paul Worrilow .10 .25
359 Desmond Trufant .10 .25
360 Matt Ryan FOIL .25 .60
361 Devonta Freeman FOIL .25 .60
362 Desmond Trufant FOIL .20 .50
363 Atlanta Falcons Mascot .10 .25
364 Atlanta Falcons Logo FOIL .20 .50
365 Cam Newton .15 .40
366 Jonathan Stewart .10 .25
367 Kelvin Benjamin .12 .30
368 Ted Ginn Jr. .10 .25
369 Cam Newton ILL .15 .40
370 Greg Olsen .12 .30
371 Luke Kuechly .12 .30
372 Thomas Davis .10 .25
373 Kawann Short .10 .25
374 Ted Ginn Jr. FOIL .20 .50
375 Greg Olsen FOIL .25 .60
376 Luke Kuechly FOIL .25 .60
377 Carolina Panthers Mascot .10 .25
378 Carolina Panthers Logo FOIL .20 .50
379 Drew Brees .15 .40
380 Mark Ingram .12 .30
381 Brandin Cooks .12 .30
382 Willie Snead .12 .30
383 Brandin Cooks ILL .12 .30
384 Michael Thomas .20 .50
385 Cameron Jordan .10 .25
386 Stephone Anthony .10 .25
387 Delvin Breaux .12 .30
388 Drew Brees FOIL .30 .75
389 Mark Ingram FOIL .25 .60
390 Willie Snead FOIL .25 .60
391 New Orleans Saints Mascot .10 .25
392 New Orleans Saints Logo FOIL .20 .50
393 Jameis Winston .15 .40
394 Charles Sims .10 .25
395 Doug Martin .12 .30
396 Mike Evans .12 .30
397 Mike Evans ILL .12 .30
398 Vincent Jackson .10 .25
399 Austin Seferian-Jenkins .10 .25
400 Gerald McCoy .10 .25
401 Lavonte David .10 .25
402 Jameis Winston FOIL .30 .75
403 Austin Seferian-Jenkins FOIL .20 .50
404 Doug Martin FOIL .25 .60
405 Tampa Bay Buccaneers Mascot .10 .25
406 Tampa Bay Buccaneers Logo FOIL .20 .50
407 Carson Palmer .12 .30
408 Chris Johnson .10 .25
409 David Johnson .15 .40
410 John Brown .12 .30
411 Larry Fitzgerald ILL .12 .30
412 Larry Fitzgerald .12 .30
413 Michael Floyd .10 .25
414 Patrick Peterson .10 .25
415 Tyrann Mathieu .12 .30
416 Carson Palmer FOIL .25 .60
417 David Johnson FOIL .30 .75
418 Patrick Peterson FOIL .20 .50
419 Arizona Cardinals Mascot .10 .25
420 Arizona Cardinals Logo FOIL .20 .50
421 Case Keenum .12 .30
422 Jared Goff .60 1.50
423 Todd Gurley .15 .40
424 Kenny Britt .10 .25
425 Todd Gurley ILL .15 .40
426 Tavon Austin .10 .25
427 Aaron Donald .15 .40
428 Alec Ogletree .10 .25
429 Mark Barron .10 .25
430 Case Keenum FOIL .25 .60
431 Aaron Donald FOIL .30 .75
432 Tavon Austin FOIL .20 .50
433 Los Angeles Rams Mascot .10 .25
434 Los Angeles Rams Logo FOIL .20 .50
435 Colin Kaepernick .12 .30
436 Blaine Gabbert .10 .25
437 Carlos Hyde .10 .25
438 Torrey Smith .10 .25
439 Carlos Hyde ILL .10 .25
440 Vance McDonald .10 .25
441 Aaron Lynch .10 .25
442 NaVorro Bowman .12 .30
443 Eric Reid .12 .30
444 Colin Kaepernick FOIL .25 .60
445 NaVorro Bowman FOIL .25 .60
446 Torrey Smith FOIL .20 .50
447 San Francisco 49ers Mascot .10 .25
448 San Francisco 49ers Logo FOIL .20 .50
449 Russell Wilson .20 .50
450 Thomas Rawls .10 .25

451 Doug Baldwin .12 .30
452 Tyler Lockett .12 .30
453 Richard Sherman ILL .15 .40
454 Jimmy Graham .15 .40
455 Bobby Wagner .10 .25
456 Richard Sherman .15 .40
457 Kam Chancellor .15 .40
458 Russell Wilson FOIL .40 1.00
459 Thomas Rawls FOIL .20 .50
460 Tyler Lockett FOIL .25 .60
461 Seattle Seahawks Mascot .10 .25
462 Seattle Seahawks Logo FOIL .20 .50
463 Pop Warner Action 1 .10 .25
464 Pop Warner Action 2 .10 .25
465 Pop Warner Action 3 .10 .25
466 Pop Warner Action 4 .10 .25
467 Pop Warner Action 5 .10 .25
468 Pop Warner Action 6 .10 .25
469 Pop Warner Football Logo FOIL .20 .20
470 Brett Favre HOF .30 .75
471 Kevin Greene HOF .15 .40
472 Marvin Harrison HOF .12 .30
473 Orlando Pace HOF .10 .25
474 Ken Stabler HOF .15 .40
475 Dick Stanfel HOF .10 .25
476 Pro Football Hall of Fame Logo FOIL .20 .50
477 Super Bowl 50 .12 .30
Von Miller
478 Super Bowl 50 .12 .30
Luke Kuechly
479 Super Bowl 50 .15 .40
Emmanuel Sanders
480 Super Bowl 50 .10 .25
Jonathan Stewart
481 Super Bowl 50 .15 .40
Cam Newton
482 Super Bowl 50 .30 .75
Peyton Manning
483 Super Bowl 50 .12 .30
C.J. Anderson
484 NFL Logo FOIL .20 .50
485 Official NFL Football FOIL .20 .50

2018 Panini Stickers

1 Robert Brazile .10 .25
2 Brian Dawkins .15 .40
3 Jerry Kramer .10 .25
4 Ray Lewis .15 .40
5 Randy Moss .12 .30
6 Terrell Owens .12 .30
7 Brian Urlacher .15 .40
8 Denzel Ward .25 .60
9 Marcus Davenport .20 .50
10 Tremaine Edmunds .20 .50
11 Jaire Alexander .15 .40
12 Leighton Vander Esch .30 .75
13 Calvin Ridley .25 .60
14 Mike Hughes .15 .40
15 Lamar Jackson .60 1.50
16 Courtland Sutton .15 .40
17 Derrius Guice .20 .50
18 Panini Logo FOIL .20 .50
19 Buffalo Bills Logo FOIL .20 .50
20 LeSean McCoy FOIL .30 .75
21 Kelvin Benjamin FOIL .25 .60
22 Zay Jones .10 .25
23 A.J. McCarron .10 .25
24 Josh Allen .40 1.00
25 LeSean McCoy .15 .40
26 Mike Tolbert .10 .25
27 Kelvin Benjamin .12 .30
28 Zay Jones .10 .25
29 Charles Clay .10 .25
30 Jerry Hughes .10 .25
31 Tre'Davious White .10 .25
32 Miami Dolphins Logo FOIL .20 .50
33 DeVante Parker FOIL .25 .60
34 Kenyan Drake FOIL .20 .50
35 Kenny Stills .10 .25
36 Ryan Tannehill .12 .30
37 Kenyan Drake .10 .25
38 DeVante Parker .12 .30
39 Kenny Stills .10 .25
40 Mike Gesicki .12 .30
41 Cameron Wake .10 .25
42 Kiko Alonso .10 .25
43 Minkah Fitzpatrick .20 .50
44 Reshad Jones .10 .25
45 New England Patriots Logo FOIL .20 .50
46 Tom Brady FOIL .75 2.00
47 Rob Gronkowski FOIL .30 .75
48 Julian Edelman .15 .40
49 Tom Brady .40 1.00
50 James White .12 .30
51 Mike Gillislee .10 .25
52 Sony Michel .30 .75
53 Julian Edelman .15 .40
54 Chris Hogan .10 .25
55 Rob Gronkowski .15 .40
56 Devin McCourty .10 .25
57 Stephen Gostkowski .10 .25
58 New York Jets Logo FOIL .20 .50
59 Robby Anderson FOIL .20 .50
60 Bilal Powell FOIL .20 .50
61 Jermaine Kearse .10 .25
62 Josh McCown .10 .25
63 Sam Darnold .60 1.50
64 Bilal Powell .10 .25
65 Elijah McGuire .10 .25
66 Robby Anderson .10 .25
67 Jermaine Kearse .10 .25
68 Darron Lee .10 .25
69 Jamal Adams .12 .30
70 Marcus Maye .10 .25
71 Baltimore Ravens Logo FOIL .20 .50
72 Joe Flacco FOIL .25 .60
73 Alex Collins FOIL .20 .50
74 Terrell Suggs .10 .25
75 Joe Flacco .12 .30
76 Alex Collins .10 .25
77 Buck Allen .10 .25
78 Michael Crabtree .10 .25
79 Hayden Hurst .12 .30
80 Terrell Suggs .10 .25
81 C.J. Mosley .12 .30
82 Eric Weddle .10 .25
83 Justin Tucker .10 .25
84 Cincinnati Bengals Logo FOIL .20 .50
85 A.J. Green FOIL .30 .75
86 Joe Mixon FOIL .25 .60
87 Giovani Bernard .10 .25
88 Andy Dalton .12 .30
89 Joe Mixon .12 .30
90 Giovani Bernard .10 .25
91 A.J. Green .15 .40
92 Brandon LaFell .10 .25
93 Tyler Boyd .10 .25
94 Alex Erickson .10 .25
95 Geno Atkins .10 .25
96 Darqueze Dennard .10 .25
97 Cleveland Browns Logo FOIL .20 .50
98 Corey Coleman FOIL .20 .50
99 Duke Johnson FOIL .20 .50
100 David Njoku .10 .25
101 Baker Mayfield 1.00 2.50
102 Duke Johnson .10 .25
103 Carlos Hyde .10 .25
104 Josh Gordon .10 .25
105 Corey Coleman .10 .25
106 Jarvis Landry .12 .30
107 David Njoku .10 .25
108 Myles Garrett .15 .40
109 Jabrill Peppers .10 .25
110 Pittsburgh Steelers Logo FOIL .20 .50
111 Le'Veon Bell FOIL .25 .60
112 Antonio Brown FOIL .30 .75
113 Ben Roethlisberger .15 .40
114 Ben Roethlisberger .15 .40
115 Le'Veon Bell .12 .30
116 James Conner .15 .40
117 Antonio Brown .15 .40
118 JuJu Smith-Schuster .15 .40
119 James Washington .20 .50
120 Jesse James .10 .25
121 Cameron Heyward .10 .25
122 T.J. Watt .12 .30
123 Houston Texans Logo FOIL .20 .50
124 DeShaun Watson FOIL .40 1.00
125 DeAndre Hopkins FOIL .25 .60
126 Lamar Miller .10 .25
127 DeShaun Watson .20 .50
128 Lamar Miller .10 .25
129 D'onta Foreman .10 .25
130 DeAndre Hopkins .12 .30
131 Will Fuller .10 .25
132 Stephen Anderson .10 .25
133 J.J. Watt .15 .40
134 Jadeveon Clowney .10 .25
135 Benardrick McKinney .10 .25
136 Indianapolis Colts Logo FOIL .20 .50
137 T.Y. Hilton FOIL .25 .60
138 Andrew Luck FOIL .40 1.00
139 Jack Doyle .10 .25
140 Andrew Luck .20 .50
141 Jacoby Brissett .10 .25
142 Marlon Mack .10 .25
143 T.Y. Hilton .12 .30
144 Chester Rogers .10 .25
145 Jack Doyle .10 .25
146 Jabaal Sheard .10 .25
147 Antonio Morrison .10 .25
148 Adam Vinatieri .10 .25
149 Jacksonville Jaguars Logo FOIL .20 .50
150 Leonard Fournette FOIL .30 .75
151 Blake Bortles FOIL .20 .50
152 Keelan Cole .10 .25
153 Blake Bortles .10 .25
154 Leonard Fournette .15 .40
155 T.J. Yeldon .10 .25
156 Keelan Cole .10 .25
157 Dede Westbrook .10 .25
158 Yannick Ngakoue .10 .25
159 Calais Campbell .10 .25
160 A.J. Bouye .10 .25
161 Jalen Ramsey .12 .30
162 Tennessee Titans Logo FOIL .20 .50
163 Marcus Mariota FOIL .30 .75
164 Derrick Henry FOIL .30 .75
165 Corey Davis .12 .30
166 Marcus Mariota .15 .40
167 Derrick Henry .15 .40
168 Dion Lewis .10 .25
169 Corey Davis .12 .30
170 Rishard Matthews .10 .25
171 Delanie Walker .10 .25
172 Jonnu Smith .10 .25
173 Jurrell Casey .10 .25
174 Kevin Byard .10 .25
175 Denver Broncos Logo FOIL .20 .50
176 Demaryius Thomas FOIL .25 .60
177 Von Miller FOIL .25 .60
178 Emmanuel Sanders .15 .40
179 Case Keenum .12 .30
180 DeVontae Booker .10 .25
181 Demaryius Thomas .12 .30
182 Emmanuel Sanders .15 .40
183 Bennie Fowler .10 .25
184 Bradley Chubb .15 .40
185 Von Miller .12 .30
186 Brandon Marshall .10 .25
187 Chris Harris Jr. .10 .25
188 Kansas City Chiefs Logo FOIL .20 .50
189 Tyreek Hill FOIL .30 .75
190 Kareem Hunt FOIL .25 .60
191 Travis Kelce .15 .40
192 Patrick Mahomes .40 1.00
193 Kareem Hunt .12 .30
194 Charcandrick West .10 .25
195 Tyreek Hill .15 .40
196 Sammy Watkins .15 .40
197 Travis Kelce .15 .40
198 Justin Houston .10 .25
199 Reggie Ragland .10 .25
200 Eric Berry .12 .30
201 Los Angeles Chargers Logo FOIL .20 .50
202 Keenan Allen FOIL .25 .60
203 Philip Rivers FOIL .30 .75
204 Melvin Gordon .12 .30
205 Philip Rivers .15 .40
206 Melvin Gordon .12 .30
207 Austin Ekeler .10 .25
208 Keenan Allen .12 .30
209 Tyrell Williams .10 .25
210 Hunter Henry .10 .25
211 Joey Bosa .15 .40
212 Melvin Ingram .10 .25
213 Derwin James .20 .50
214 Oakland Raiders Logo FOIL .20 .50
215 Derek Carr FOIL .30 .75
216 Amari Cooper FOIL .30 .75
217 Marshawn Lynch .12 .30
218 Derek Carr .15 .40
219 Marshawn Lynch .12 .30
220 Jalen Richard .10 .25
221 Doug Martin .12 .30
222 Amari Cooper .15 .40
223 Jordy Nelson .12 .30
224 Jared Cook .10 .25
225 Khalil Mack .15 .40
226 Karl Joseph .10 .25
227 Dallas Cowboys Logo FOIL .20 .50
228 Ezekiel Elliott FOIL .40 1.00
229 Sean Lee FOIL .25 .60
230 Dak Prescott .15 .40
231 Dak Prescott .15 .40
232 Ezekiel Elliott .20 .50
233 Rod Smith .12 .30
234 Allen Hurns .10 .25
235 Cole Beasley .12 .30
236 Terrance Williams .10 .25
237 DeMarcus Lawrence .10 .25
238 Sean Lee .12 .30
239 Dan Bailey .10 .25
240 New York Giants Logo FOIL .20 .50
241 Evan Engram FOIL .20 .50
242 Odell Beckham Jr. FOIL .30 .75
243 Sterling Shepard .12 .30
244 Eli Manning .12 .30
245 Wayne Gallman .10 .25
246 Saquon Barkley .75 2.00
247 Odell Beckham Jr. .15 .40
248 Sterling Shepard .12 .30
249 Roger Lewis .10 .25
250 Evan Engram .10 .25
251 Olivier Vernon .10 .25
252 Landon Collins .10 .25
253 Philadelphia Eagles Logo FOIL .20 .50
254 Carson Wentz FOIL .40 1.00
255 Zach Ertz FOIL .25 .60
256 Alshon Jeffery .12 .30
257 Carson Wentz .20 .50
258 Nick Foles .12 .30
259 Jay Ajayi .12 .30
260 Corey Clement .10 .25
261 Alshon Jeffery .12 .30
262 Nelson Agholor .10 .25
263 Zach Ertz .12 .30
264 Fletcher Cox .10 .25
265 Brandon Graham .10 .25
266 Washington Redskins Logo FOIL .20 .50
267 Ryan Kerrigan FOIL .20 .50
268 Jordan Reed FOIL .20 .50
269 Alex Smith .12 .30
270 Alex Smith .12 .30
271 Samaje Perine .10 .25
272 Chris Thompson .10 .25
273 Jamison Crowder .10 .25
274 Josh Doctson .10 .25
275 Jordan Reed .10 .25
276 Daron Payne .15 .40
277 Ryan Kerrigan .10 .25
278 Josh Norman .10 .25
279 Chicago Bears Logo FOIL .20 .50
280 Jordan Howard FOIL .30 .75
281 Mitchell Trubisky FOIL .30 .75
282 Tarik Cohen .12 .30
283 Mitchell Trubisky .15 .40
284 Jordan Howard .15 .40
285 Tarik Cohen .12 .30
286 Josh Bellamy .10 .25
287 Allen Robinson .12 .30
288 Akiem Hicks .15 .40
289 Roquan Smith .30 .75
290 Danny Trevathan .10 .25
291 Eddie Jackson .10 .25
292 Detroit Lions Logo FOIL .20 .50
293 Matthew Stafford FOIL .25 .60
294 Golden Tate FOIL .20 .50
295 Marvin Jones Jr. .10 .25
296 Matthew Stafford .12 .30
297 Ameer Abdullah .10 .25
298 Theo Riddick .10 .25
299 LeGarrette Blount .12 .30
300 Marvin Jones Jr. .10 .25
301 Golden Tate .10 .25
302 Ezekiel Ansah .10 .25
303 Darius Slay .10 .25
304 Jamal Agnew .10 .25
305 Green Bay Packers Logo FOIL .20 .50
306 Aaron Rodgers FOIL .60 1.50
307 DaVante Adams FOIL .25 .60
308 Clay Matthews .12 .30
309 Aaron Rodgers .30 .75
310 Jamal Williams .12 .30
311 Aaron Jones .12 .30
312 TY Montgomery .10 .25
313 DaVante Adams .12 .30
314 Randall Cobb .12 .30
315 Jimmy Graham .15 .40
316 Clay Matthews .12 .30
317 Mason Crosby .10 .25
318 Minnesota Vikings Logo FOIL .20 .50
319 Dalvin Cook FOIL .25 .60
320 Adam Thielen FOIL .30 .75
321 Stefon Diggs .12 .30
322 Kirk Cousins .15 .40
323 Dalvin Cook .12 .30
324 Latavius Murray .10 .25
325 Adam Thielen .15 .40
326 Stefon Diggs .12 .30
327 Kyle Rudolph .10 .25
328 Everson Griffen .10 .25
329 Eric Kendricks .10 .25
330 Harrison Smith .15 .40
331 Atlanta Falcons Logo FOIL .20 .50
332 Julio Jones FOIL .30 .75
333 Matt Ryan FOIL .25 .60
334 DeVonta Freeman .12 .30
335 Matt Ryan .12 .30
336 DeVonta Freeman .12 .30
337 Tevin Coleman .10 .25
338 Julio Jones .15 .40
339 Mohamed Sanu .10 .25
340 Austin Hooper .10 .25
341 Deion Jones .10 .25
342 Desmond Trufant .10 .25
343 Keanu Neal .10 .25
344 Carolina Panthers Logo FOIL .20 .50
345 Christian McCaffrey FOIL .30 .75
346 Cam Newton FOIL .30 .75
347 Devin Funchess .10 .25
348 Cam Newton .15 .40
349 Christian McCaffrey .15 .40
350 Devin Funchess .10 .25
351 Curtis Samuel .10 .25
352 D.J. Moore .20 .50
353 Greg Olsen .12 .30
354 Kawann Short .10 .25
355 Mario Addison .10 .25
356 Luke Kuechly .12 .30
357 New Orleans Saints Logo FOIL .20 .50
358 Drew Brees FOIL .30 .75
359 Alvin Kamara FOIL .25 .60
360 Mark Ingram .12 .30
361 Drew Brees .15 .40
362 Mark Ingram .12 .30
363 Alvin Kamara .12 .30
364 Michael Thomas .15 .40
365 Ted Ginn Jr. .10 .25
366 Brandon Coleman .10 .25
367 Cameron Jordan .10 .25
368 Marshon Lattimore .10 .25
369 Marcus Williams .10 .25
370 Tampa Bay Buccaneers Logo FOIL .20 .50
371 Mike Evans FOIL .25 .60
372 Jameis Winston FOIL .25 .60
373 DeSean Jackson .12 .30
374 Jameis Winston .12 .30
375 Peyton Barber .10 .25
376 Mike Evans .12 .30
377 DeSean Jackson .12 .30
378 Adam Humphries .10 .25
379 O.J. Howard .10 .25
380 Cameron Brate .10 .25
381 Vita Vea .15 .40
382 Gerald McCoy .10 .25
383 Arizona Cardinals Logo FOIL .20 .50
384 Larry Fitzgerald FOIL .25 .60
385 David Johnson FOIL .30 .75
386 Patrick Peterson .10 .25
387 Sam Bradford .10 .25
388 Josh Rosen .30 .75
389 David Johnson .15 .40
390 Larry Fitzgerald .12 .30
391 J.J. Nelson .10 .25
392 Christian Kirk .15 .40
393 Jermaine Gresham .10 .25
394 Chandler Jones .10 .25
395 Patrick Peterson .10 .25
396 Los Angeles Rams Logo FOIL .20 .50
397 Jared Goff FOIL .30 .75
398 Todd Gurley FOIL .30 .75
399 Cooper Kupp .12 .30
400 Jared Goff .15 .40
401 Todd Gurley .15 .40
402 Cooper Kupp .12 .30
403 Robert Woods .12 .30
404 Brandin Cooks .12 .30
405 Aaron Donald .15 .40
406 Ndamukong Suh .12 .30
407 Mark Barron .10 .25
408 Greg Zuerlein .10 .25
409 San Francisco 49ers Logo FOIL .20 .50
410 Jimmy Garoppolo FOIL .40 1.00
411 Marquise Goodwin FOIL .20 .50
412 Pierre Garcon .12 .30
413 Jimmy Garoppolo .20 .50
414 Matt Breida .12 .30
415 Jerick McKinnon .10 .25
416 Marquise Goodwin .10 .25
417 Pierre Garcon .12 .30
418 George Kittle .10 .25
419 DeForest Buckner .10 .25
420 Richard Sherman .15 .40
421 Robbie Gould .10 .25
422 Seattle Seahawks Logo FOIL .20 .50
423 Russell Wilson FOIL .40 1.00
424 Doug Baldwin FOIL .25 .60
425 Bobby Wagner .10 .25
426 Russell Wilson .20 .50
427 Chris Carson .12 .30
428 Rashaad Penny .15 .40
429 Doug Baldwin .12 .30
430 Tyler Lockett .12 .30
431 Frank Clark .10 .25
432 K.J. Wright .10 .25
433 Bobby Wagner .10 .25
434 Earl Thomas .12 .30
435 Pop Warner Redshirt Runner .10 .25
436 Pop Warner Blackshirt Runner .10 .25
437 Pop Warner Whiteshirt Catch .10 .25
438 Pop Warner Purpleshirt QB .10 .25
439 Pop Warner Goldshirt Runner .10 .25
440 Pop Warner Goldshirt Falling .10 .25
441 Pop Warner Up For Grabs .10 .25
442 James White PLAYOFFS .12 .30
443 Nick Foles PLAYOFFS .12 .30
444 Tom Brady PLAYOFFS .40 1.00
445 Blake Bortles PLAYOFFS .10 .25
446 LeGarrette Blount PLAYOFFS .12 .30
447 Stefon Diggs PLAYOFFS .12 .30
448 Marcus Mariota PLAYOFFS .15 .40
449 Leonard Fournette PLAYOFFS .15 .40
450 Matt Ryan PLAYOFFS .12 .30
451 Drew Brees PLAYOFFS .15 .40
452 Alshon Jeffery SB LII .12 .30
453 Trey Burton SB LII .10 .25
454 Rob Gronkowski SB LII .15 .40
455 Zach Ertz SB LII .12 .30
456 Tom Brady SB LII .40 1.00
457 Tom Brady SB LII .40 1.00
458 Nick Foles SB LII .12 .30
459 Marcedes Lewis LONDON .10 .25
460 Tony Jefferson LONDON .10 .25
461 Cordrea Tankersley LONDON .10 .25
462 Alvin Kamara LONDON .12 .30
463 Todd Gurley LONDON .15 .40
464 Todd Gurley LONDON .15 .40
465 Adam Thielen LONDON .15 .40
466 Adam Thielen LONDON .15 .40
467 Tom Brady MEXICO .40 1.00
468 Tom Brady MEXICO .40 1.00

1989 Panini Super Bowl Stickers

COMPLETE SET (23) 4.00 10.00
A Super Bowl I .20 .50
B Super Bowl II .20 .50
C Super Bowl III .20 .50
D Super Bowl IV .20 .50
E Super Bowl V .20 .50
F Super Bowl VI .20 .50
G Super Bowl VII .20 .50
H Super Bowl VIII .20 .50
I Super Bowl IX .20 .50
J Super Bowl X .20 .50
K Super Bowl XI .20 .50
L Super Bowl XII .20 .50
M Super Bowl XIII .20 .50
N Super Bowl XIV .20 .50
O Super Bowl XV .20 .50
P Super Bowl XVI .20 .50
Q Super Bowl XVII .20 .50
R Super Bowl XVIII .20 .50
S Super Bowl XIX .20 .50
T Super Bowl XX .20 .50
U Super Bowl XXI .20 .50
V Super Bowl XXII .20 .50
W Super Bowl XXIII .20 .50

2011 Panini Super Bowl XLV Promos

These three cards were released at the 2011 Super Bowl Card Show in Dallas as part of a wrapper redemption program at the Panini booth. The basic design was modeled after the 2010 Classics set.

COMPLETE SET (3) 5.00 12.00
SBRK1 Dez Bryant 2.50 6.00
SBMVP1 Troy Aikman 2.00 5.00
SBMVP2 Randy White 1.25 3.00

2013 Panini Super Bowl XLVII Private Signings

AR Andre Reed/25 20.00 40.00
DB Drew Brees/15 50.00 100.00
EG Eddie George/25 20.00 40.00
HL Howie Long/25 20.00 40.00
HW Hines Ward/15
JB Jerome Bettis/25 40.00 80.00
JG Joe Greene/25 30.00 60.00
JM Jim McMahon/25
JP Jim Plunkett/25 15.00 30.00
MI Michael Irvin/25 20.00 40.00
PS Phil Simms/25 20.00 40.00
RW Rod Woodson/25 30.00 60.00
TD Terrell Davis/25 20.00 40.00

2013 Panini Super Bowl XLVII Rookie Patch Autographs

AL Andrew Luck/20
BW Brandon Weeden/25
JB Justin Blackmon/25
RT Ryan Tannehill/25
RW Russell Wilson/15

2010 Panini Threads

COMP.SET w/o RC's (150) 8.00 20.00
151-200 ROOKIE AUTO PRINT RUN 220-500
1 Chris Wells .20 .50
2 Larry Fitzgerald .25 .60
3 Matt Leinart .20 .50
4 Steve Breaston .20 .50
5 Matt Ryan .25 .60
6 Michael Turner .20 .50
7 Roddy White .20 .50
8 Tony Gonzalez .25 .60
9 Anquan Boldin .20 .50
10 Derrick Mason .20 .50
11 Joe Flacco .25 .60
12 Ray Rice .20 .50
13 Willis McGahee .20 .50
14 Fred Jackson .25 .60
15 Lee Evans .25 .60
16 Marshawn Lynch .25 .60
17 Ryan Fitzpatrick .20 .50
18 DeAngelo Williams .20 .50
19 Jonathan Stewart .20 .50
20 Matt Moore .20 .50
21 Steve Smith .25 .60
22 Brian Urlacher .30 .75
23 Devin Hester .25 .60
24 Greg Olsen .25 .60
25 Jay Cutler .20 .50
26 Matt Forte .20 .50
27 Andre Caldwell .20 .50
28 Antonio Bryant .20 .50
29 Carson Palmer .25 .60
30 Cedric Benson .20 .50
31 Chad Ochocinco .20 .50
32 Ben Watson .20 .50
33 Jake Delhomme .20 .50
34 Jerome Harrison .20 .50
35 Josh Cribbs .20 .50
36 Mohamed Massaquoi .25 .60
37 Felix Jones .20 .50
38 Jason Witten .25 .60
39 Marion Barber .25 .60
40 Miles Austin .20 .50
41 Tony Romo .25 .60
42 Eddie Royal .20 .50
43 Jabar Gaffney .20 .50
44 Knowshon Moreno .20 .50
45 Kyle Orton .20 .50
46 Brandon Pettigrew .20 .50
47 Calvin Johnson .30 .75
48 Matthew Stafford .25 .60
49 Nate Burleson .20 .50
50 Aaron Rodgers .60 1.50
51 Donald Driver .25 .60
52 Greg Jennings .20 .50
53 Jermichael Finley .20 .50
54 Ryan Grant .25 .60
55 Andre Johnson .25 .60
56 Kevin Walter .25 .60
57 Matt Schaub .20 .50
58 Owen Daniels .20 .50
59 Steve Slaton .20 .50
60 Dallas Clark .20 .50
61 Joseph Addai .20 .50
62 Peyton Manning .75 2.00
63 Pierre Garcon .25 .60
64 Reggie Wayne .25 .60
65 David Garrard .20 .50
66 Maurice Jones-Drew .20 .50
67 Mike Sims-Walker .20 .50
68 Mike Thomas .25 .60
69 Chris Chambers .20 .50
70 Dwayne Bowe .25 .60
71 Jamaal Charles .25 .60
72 Matt Cassel .20 .50
73 Thomas Jones .20 .50
74 Brandon Marshall .25 .60
75 Brian Hartline .25 .60
76 Chad Henne .25 .60
77 Davone Bess .20 .50
78 Greg Camarillo .20 .50
79 Ronnie Brown .20 .50
80 Adrian Peterson .30 .75
81 Brett Favre 1.25 3.00
82 Percy Harvin .20 .50
83 Sidney Rice .20 .50
84 Visanthe Shiancoe .25 .60
85 Laurence Maroney .20 .50
86 Randy Moss .25 .60
87 Tom Brady .75 2.00
88 Torry Holt .25 .60
89 Wes Welker .25 .60
90 Devery Henderson .20 .50
91 Drew Brees .30 .75
92 Jeremy Shockey .20 .50
93 Marques Colston .20 .50
94 Pierre Thomas .20 .50
95 Brandon Jacobs .20 .50
96 Eli Manning .25 .60
97 Hakeem Nicks .20 .50
98 Kevin Boss .20 .50
99 Steve Smith USC .20 .50
100 Braylon Edwards .20 .50
101 LaDainian Tomlinson .30 .75
102 Mark Sanchez .20 .50
103 Santonio Holmes .20 .50
104 Shonn Greene .20 .50
105 Chaz Schilens .20 .50
106 Darren McFadden .20 .50
107 Jason Campbell .20 .50
108 Louis Murphy .20 .50
109 Zach Miller .20 .50
110 Brent Celek .20 .50
111 DeSean Jackson .25 .60
112 Jeremy Maclin .20 .50
113 Kevin Kolb .20 .50
114 LeSean McCoy .30 .75
115 Ben Roethlisberger .30 .75
116 Heath Miller .20 .50
117 Hines Ward .25 .60
118 Rashard Mendenhall .20 .50
119 Troy Polamalu .30 .75
120 Antonio Gates .25 .60
121 Darren Sproles .25 .60
122 Philip Rivers .30 .75
123 Vincent Jackson .20 .50
124 Alex Smith QB .25 .60
125 Frank Gore .25 .60
126 Patrick Willis .25 .60
127 Michael Crabtree .20 .50
128 Vernon Davis .20 .50
129 Deion Branch .20 .50
130 John Carlson .20 .50
131 Julius Jones .20 .50
132 Matt Hasselbeck .20 .50
133 T.J. Houshmandzadeh .20 .50
134 Danny Amendola .30 .75
135 Donnie Avery .20 .50
136 James Laurinaitis .25 .60
137 Steven Jackson .20 .50
138 Cadillac Williams .20 .50
139 Josh Freeman .25 .60
140 Kellen Winslow Jr. .20 .50
141 Sammie Stroughter .20 .50
142 Bo Scaife .20 .50
143 Chris Johnson .20 .50
144 Kenny Britt .20 .50
145 Vince Young .20 .50
146 Chris Cooley .20 .50
147 Clinton Portis .20 .50
148 Donovan McNabb .25 .60
149 Larry Johnson .20 .50
150 Santana Moss .25 .60
151 A.Hernandez AU/441 RC 15.00 40.00
152 Andre Roberts AU/385 RC 6.00 15.00
153 Anthony McCoy AU/325 RC 5.00 12.00
154 Armanti Edwards AU/455 RC 6.00 15.00
155 Arrelious Benn AU/280 RC 5.00 12.00
156 Ben Tate AU/280 RC 5.00 12.00
157 Brandon LaFell AU/360 RC 8.00 20.00
158 Brandon Spikes AU/360 RC 6.00 15.00
159 C.J. Spiller AU/280 RC 5.00 12.00
160 Carlos Dunlap AU/360 RC 5.00 12.00
161 Carlton Mitchell AU/440 RC 5.00 12.00
162 Colt McCoy AU/250 RC 6.00 15.00
163 Damian Williams AU/440 RC 5.00 12.00
164 Dan LeFevour AU/440 RC 5.00 12.00
165 D.Thomas AU/360 RC 12.00 30.00
166 Derrick Morgan AU/360 RC 5.00 12.00
167 D.McCluster AU/450 RC 6.00 15.00
168 Dez Bryant AU/270 RC 40.00 80.00
169 Dezmon Briscoe AU/385 RC 5.00 12.00
170 Earl Thomas AU/360 RC 15.00 40.00
171 E.Sanders AU/350 RC 8.00 20.00
172 Eric Berry AU/325 RC 8.00 20.00
173 Eric Decker AU/330 RC 12.00 30.00
174 Gerald McCoy AU/325 RC 5.00 12.00
175 Golden Tate AU/240 RC 6.00 15.00
176 Jacoby Ford AU/280 RC 5.00 12.00
177 Jahvid Best AU/220 RC 5.00 12.00
178 J.Gresham AU/385 RC 5.00 12.00
179 Jimmy Clausen AU/280 RC 5.00 12.00
180 Joe Haden AU/325 RC 10.00 25.00
181 Joe McKnight AU/385 RC 5.00 12.00
182 John Skelton AU/280 RC 6.00 15.00
183 J.Crompton AU/440 RC 5.00 12.00
184 Jonathan Dwyer AU/225 RC 5.00 12.00
185 Jordan Shipley AU/385 RC 5.00 12.00
186 Marcus Easley AU/330 RC 5.00 12.00
187 Mardy Gilyard AU/385 RC 5.00 12.00
188 Mike Kafka AU/375 RC 6.00 15.00
189 Mike Williams AU/440 RC 5.00 12.00
190 M.Hardesty AU/440 RC 5.00 12.00
191 Ndamukong Suh AU/255 RC 10.00 25.00
192 Ricky Sapp AU/280 RC 5.00 12.00
193 R.Gronkowski AU/500 RC 40.00 80.00
194 Rolando McClain AU/385 RC 5.00 12.00
195 Ryan Mathews AU/280 RC 5.00 12.00
196 Sam Bradford AU/280 RC 6.00 15.00
197 Taylor Mays AU/280 RC 5.00 12.00
198 Taylor Price AU/325 RC 5.00 12.00
199 Tim Tebow AU/250 RC 25.00 60.00
200 Toby Gerhart AU/385 RC 5.00 12.00
201 A.J. Edds RC 1.25 3.00
202 Alterraun Verner RC 1.25 3.00
203 Amari Spievey RC 1.00 2.50
204 Andre Anderson RC 1.00 2.50
205 Anthony Davis RC 1.25 3.00
206 Anthony Dixon RC 1.00 2.50
207 Antonio Brown RC 8.00 20.00
208 Blair White RC 1.00 2.50
209 Brandon Ghee RC 1.00 2.50
210 Brandon Graham RC 1.25 3.00
211 Brian Price RC 1.00 2.50
212 Bryan Bulaga RC 1.00 2.50
213 Chad Jones RC 1.00 2.50
214 Charles Scott RC 1.00 2.50
215 Chris Cook RC 1.00 2.50
216 Chris McGaha RC 1.00 2.50
217 Corey Wootton RC 1.00 2.50
218 Dan Williams RC 1.00 2.50
219 Darrell Stuckey RC 1.00 2.50
220 Darryl Sharpton RC 1.00 2.50
221 Daryl Washington RC 1.00 2.50
222 David Gettis RC 1.00 2.50
223 David Reed RC 1.00 2.50
224 Deji Karim RC 1.25 3.00
225 Dennis Pitta RC 1.00 2.50
226 Devin McCourty RC 1.25 3.00
227 Dominique Franks RC 1.00 2.50
228 Donald Butler RC 1.00 2.50
229 Ed Dickson RC 1.00 2.50
230 Ed Wang RC 1.50 4.00
231 Everson Griffen RC 1.00 2.50
232 Freddie Barnes RC 1.00 2.50
233 Garrett Graham RC 1.00 2.50
234 James Starks RC 1.25 3.00
235 Jared Odrick RC 1.25 3.00
236 Jarrett Brown RC 1.00 2.50
237 Jason Pierre-Paul RC 1.50 4.00
238 Jason Worilds RC 1.00 2.50
239 Javier Arenas RC 1.00 2.50
240 Jeremy Williams RC 1.00 2.50
241 Jermaine Cunningham RC 1.00 2.50
242 Jerome Murphy RC 1.25 3.00
243 Jerry Hughes RC 1.00 2.50
244 Jevan Snead RC 1.00 2.50
245 Jimmy Graham RC 2.50 6.00
246 Joe Webb RC 1.00 2.50
247 John Conner RC 1.00 2.50
248 Joique Bell RC 1.00 2.50
249 Kareem Jackson RC 1.00 2.50
250 Kerry Meier RC 1.25 3.00
251 Kevin Thomas RC 1.25 3.00
252 Koa Misi RC 1.25 3.00
253 Kyle Williams RC 1.50 4.00
254 Kyle Wilson RC 1.00 2.50
255 Lamarr Houston RC 1.25 3.00
256 LeGarrette Blount RC 2.00 5.00
257 Levi Brown RC 1.00 2.50
258 Linval Joseph RC 1.00 2.50
259 Lonyae Miller RC 1.25 3.00
260 Major Wright RC 1.00 2.50
261 Marc Mariani RC 1.50 4.00
262 Maurkice Pouncey RC 1.25 3.00
263 Mike Iupati RC 1.50 4.00
264 Mike Neal RC 1.50 4.00
265 Morgan Burnett RC 1.25 3.00
266 Myron Lewis RC 1.25 3.00
267 Nate Allen RC 1.50 4.00
268 NaVorro Bowman RC 2.00 5.00
269 Pat Angerer RC 1.00 2.50
270 Pat Paschall RC 1.00 2.50
271 Patrick Robinson RC 1.25 3.00
272 Perrish Cox RC 1.25 3.00
273 Perry Riley RC 1.25 3.00
274 Phillip Dillard RC 1.00 2.50
275 Rennie Curran RC 1.00 2.50
276 Riley Cooper RC 1.00 2.50
277 Rodger Saffold RC 1.00 2.50
278 Russell Okung RC 1.00 2.50
279 Rusty Smith RC 1.50 4.00
280 Sean Canfield RC 1.00 2.50
281 Sean Lee RC 2.00 5.00
282 Sean Weatherspoon RC 1.00 2.50
283 Sergio Kindle RC 1.00 2.50
284 Seyi Ajirotutu RC 1.00 2.50
285 Shay Hodge RC 1.00 2.50
286 T.J. Ward RC 1.50 4.00
287 Terrence Austin RC 1.25 3.00
288 Terrence Cody RC 1.00 2.50
289 Thaddeus Gibson RC 1.25 3.00
290 Timothy Toone RC 1.25 3.00
291 Tony Moeaki RC 1.25 3.00
292 Tony Pike RC 1.00 2.50
293 Torell Troup RC 1.00 2.50
294 Trent Williams RC 1.25 3.00
295 Trevard Lindley RC 1.00 2.50
296 Trindon Holliday RC 3.00 8.00
297 Tyson Alualu RC 1.00 2.50
298 Walter Thurmond RC 1.00 2.50
299 Zac Robinson RC 1.25 3.00
300 Zane Beadles RC 1.25 3.00

2010 Panini Threads Gold Holofoil

*VETS: 3X TO 8X BASIC CARDS
*ROOKIES: .8X TO 2X BASIC CARDS
STATED PRINT RUN 100 SER.#'d SETS

2010 Panini Threads Platinum Holofoil

*VETS: 5X TO 12X BASIC CARDS
*ROOKIES: 1.2X TO 3X BASIC CARDS
STATED PRINT RUN 25 SER.#'d SETS

2010 Panini Threads Silver Holofoil

*VETS 1-150: 2X TO 5X BASIC CARDS
*ROOKIES 201-300: .5X TO 1.2X BASIC CARDS
STATED PRINT RUN 250 SER.#'d SETS

2010 Panini Threads 2009 All Rookie Team

COMPLETE SET (5) 6.00 15.00
1 Mark Sanchez 1.00 2.50
2 Knowshon Moreno 1.00 2.50
3 Percy Harvin 1.00 2.50
4 Chris Wells 1.00 2.50
5 Brian Cushing 1.00 2.50

2010 Panini Threads 2009 All Rookie Team Threads

STATED PRINT RUN 299 SER.#'d SETS
*PRIME/50: .6X TO 1.5X BASIC JSY/299
1 Mark Sanchez 2.00 5.00
2 Knowshon Moreno 2.00 5.00
3 Percy Harvin 2.00 5.00
4 Chris Wells 2.00 5.00

2010 Panini Threads Autographs Silver

5-148 VETERAN PRINT RUN 1-100
204-299 ROOKIE PRINT RUN 399-499
EXCH EXPIRATION: 3/8/2012
30 Cedric Benson/15
31 Chad Ochocinco/15
62 Peyton Manning/18 75.00 150.00
66 Maurice Jones-Drew/15 8.00 20.00
95 Brandon Jacobs/15 8.00 20.00
103 Santonio Holmes/25 8.00 20.00
108 Louis Murphy/100 6.00 15.00
113 Kevin Kolb/25 8.00 20.00
119 Troy Polamalu/25 75.00 150.00
120 Antonio Gates/15 12.00 30.00
127 Michael Crabtree/35 12.00 30.00
144 Kenny Britt/25 8.00 20.00
204 Andre Anderson/499 3.00 8.00
206 Anthony Dixon/399 3.00 8.00
207 Antonio Brown/499 30.00 60.00
208 Blair White/499 3.00 8.00
210 Brandon Graham/499 4.00 10.00
212 Bryan Bulaga/499 3.00 8.00
213 Chad Jones/499 3.00 8.00
214 Charles Scott/499 3.00 8.00
216 Chris McGaha/499 3.00 8.00
217 Corey Wootton/499 3.00 8.00
222 David Gettis/499 3.00 8.00
226 Devin McCourty/499 6.00 15.00
229 Ed Dickson/499 3.00 8.00
231 Everson Griffen/499 3.00 8.00
232 Freddie Barnes/499 3.00 8.00
233 Garrett Graham/499 3.00 8.00
234 James Starks/499 4.00 10.00
236 Jarrett Brown/499 3.00 8.00
237 Jason Pierre-Paul/499 5.00 12.00
238 Jason Worilds/499 3.00 8.00
240 Jeremy Williams/499 3.00 8.00
243 Jerry Hughes/499 3.00 8.00
244 Jevan Snead/499 3.00 8.00
245 Jimmy Graham/499 8.00 20.00
248 Joique Bell/499 3.00 8.00
249 Kareem Jackson/399 3.00 8.00
256 LeGarrette Blount/499 6.00 15.00
259 Lonyae Miller/499 4.00 10.00
265 Morgan Burnett/499 4.00 10.00
271 Patrick Robinson/499 4.00 10.00
272 Perrish Cox/499 4.00 10.00
276 Riley Cooper/499 3.00 8.00
280 Sean Canfield/499 3.00 8.00
281 Sean Lee/499 6.00 15.00
282 Sean Weatherspoon/499 3.00 8.00
284 Seyi Ajirotutu/499 3.00 8.00
285 Shay Hodge/499 3.00 8.00
292 Tony Pike/499 3.00 8.00
299 Zac Robinson/399 4.00 10.00

2010 Panini Threads Century Legends

COMPLETE SET (14) 12.00 30.00
*HOLOFOIL/100: .6X TO 1.5X BASIC INSERTS
1 John Taylor 1.00 2.50
2 Art Monk 1.50 4.00
3 Len Dawson 1.50 4.00
4 Steve Young 2.00 5.00
5 Lenny Moore 1.00 2.50
6 Randall Cunningham 1.25 3.00
7 Frank Gifford 1.25 3.00
8 Joe Namath 2.00 5.00
10 Daryle Lamonica 1.00 2.50
11 Rod Woodson 1.25 3.00
12 Bo Jackson 2.00 5.00
13 Roger Craig 1.25 3.00
14 Terry Bradshaw 2.00 5.00
15 Dan Fouts 1.25 3.00

2010 Panini Threads Century Legends Materials

STATED PRINT RUN 50-175
*PRIME/15-25: .8X TO 2X BASIC JSY/160-175
*PRIME/15-25: .6X TO 1.5X BASIC JSY/100
*PRIME/15-25: .5X TO 1.2X BASIC JSY/50
1 John Taylor/175 3.00 8.00
2 Art Monk/160 6.00 15.00
3 Len Dawson/100 6.00 15.00
4 Steve Young/175 6.00 15.00
5 Lenny Moore/175 3.00 8.00
6 Randall Cunningham/175 4.00 10.00
7 Frank Gifford/100 5.00 12.00
8 Joe Namath/50 10.00 25.00
10 Daryle Lamonica/165 3.00 8.00
11 Rod Woodson/100 5.00 12.00
12 Bo Jackson/100 8.00 20.00
13 Roger Craig/50 6.00 15.00
14 Terry Bradshaw/175 6.00 15.00
15 Dan Fouts/175 4.00 10.00

2010 Panini Threads Century Stars

COMPLETE SET (25) 10.00 25.00
*HOLOFOIL/100: .6X TO 1.5X BASIC INSERTS
1 Antonio Gates 1.00 2.50
2 Carson Palmer 1.00 2.50
3 Brandon Jacobs .75 2.00
4 Philip Rivers 1.25 3.00
5 Clinton Portis .75 2.00
6 Donald Driver 1.00 2.50
7 Drew Brees 1.25 3.00
8 Eli Manning 1.00 2.50
9 Frank Gore 1.00 2.50
10 Darrelle Revis .75 2.00
11 Maurice Jones-Drew .75 2.00
12 Wes Welker 1.00 2.50
13 Ed Reed 1.00 2.50
14 Matt Hasselbeck .75 2.00
15 Dallas Clark .75 2.00
16 Chris Johnson .75 2.00
17 Troy Polamalu 1.25 3.00
18 Michael Turner .75 2.00
19 Jason Witten 1.00 2.50
20 Steven Jackson .75 2.00
21 Brian Urlacher 1.25 3.00
22 Reggie Wayne 1.00 2.50
23 Chad Ochocinco .75 2.00
24 Vernon Davis .75 2.00
25 Steve Smith 1.00 2.50

2010 Panini Threads Century Stars Materials Prime

STATED PRINT RUN 3-50
1 Antonio Gates/50 4.00 10.00
3 Brandon Jacobs/50 3.00 8.00
4 Philip Rivers/25 6.00 15.00
5 Clinton Portis/50 3.00 8.00
6 Donald Driver/50 4.00 10.00
8 Eli Manning/50 4.00 10.00
9 Frank Gore/50 4.00 10.00
10 Darrelle Revis/50 3.00 8.00
11 Maurice Jones-Drew/50 3.00 8.00
12 Wes Welker/50 4.00 10.00
14 Matt Hasselbeck/50 3.00 8.00
15 Dallas Clark/50 3.00 8.00
16 Chris Johnson/50 3.00 8.00
17 Troy Polamalu/60 5.00 12.00

18 Michael Turner/50 3.00 8.00
19 Jason Witten/50 4.00 10.00
20 Steven Jackson/50 3.00 8.00
21 Brian Urlacher/50 5.00 12.00
22 Reggie Wayne/50 4.00 10.00
23 Chad Ochocinco/50 3.00 8.00
24 Vernon Davis/50 3.00 8.00
25 Steve Smith/50 4.00 10.00

2010 Panini Threads Franchise Fabrics

STATED PRINT RUN 80-299
*PRIME/50: .6X TO 1.5X BASIC JSY/150-299
*PRIME/50: .5X TO 1.2X BASIC JSY/80-125
*PRIME/15-25: .8X TO 2X BASIC JSY/150-299
*PRIME/15-25: .6X TO 1.5X BASIC JSY/80-125
2 Calvin Johnson/299 3.00 8.00
3 Larry Fitzgerald/80 3.00 8.00
5 Vince Young/299 2.00 5.00
6 Chris Cooley/299 2.00 5.00
7 LeSean McCoy/190 3.00 8.00
8 Andre Johnson/299 2.50 6.00
9 Mark Sanchez/150 2.00 5.00
10 Darren Sproles/150 2.50 6.00
11 Matt Ryan/299 2.50 6.00
12 Ray Lewis/299 4.00 10.00
13 Matt Forte/299 2.00 5.00
14 Adrian Peterson/150 3.00 8.00
15 Joe Flacco/299 2.50 6.00
16 Sidney Rice/299 3.00 8.00
17 Peyton Manning/125 10.00 25.00
18 Tony Romo/100 3.00 8.00
19 DeAngelo Williams/299 2.00 5.00
20 Tom Brady/299 8.00 20.00

2010 Panini Threads Game Day Jerseys

STATED PRINT RUN 115-299
*PRIME/50: .6X TO 1.5X BASIC JSY/150-299
*PRIME/50: .5X TO 1.2X BASIC JSY/115-140
2 Chris Wells/150 2.00 5.00
3 Braylon Edwards/299 2.00 5.00
5 Cadillac Williams/299 2.00 5.00
6 Devery Henderson/299 2.00 5.00
7 Dwayne Bowe/299 2.50 6.00
8 Knowshon Moreno/115 2.50 6.00
9 Ladell Betts/299 2.00 5.00
10 Louis Murphy/150 2.00 5.00
11 Reggie Bush/299 2.00 5.00
12 Tony Romo/299 2.50 6.00
14 Kevin Boss/299 3.00 8.00
15 Josh Cribbs/140 5.00 12.00
16 Ronnie Brown/299 2.00 5.00
17 Tony Gonzalez/175 2.50 6.00
19 Matthew Stafford/200 2.50 6.00
20 Dustin Keller/299 2.00 5.00
21 Darren McFadden/299 2.00 5.00
22 Bernard Berrian/299 2.00 5.00
23 Percy Harvin/299 2.00 5.00
24 Greg Olsen/299 2.50 6.00
25 Greg Jennings/250 2.00 5.00

2010 Panini Threads Game Day Jerseys Autographs

AUTO STATED PRINT RUN 1-15
3 Braylon Edwards/15 10.00 25.00
5 Cadillac Williams/15 10.00 25.00
7 Dwayne Bowe/15 12.00 30.00
10 Louis Murphy/15 10.00 25.00
22 Bernard Berrian/15 10.00 25.00

2010 Panini Threads Generations

COMPLETE SET (15) 12.00 30.00
*HOLOFOIL/100: .6X TO 1.5X BASIC INSERTS
1 B.Jones/V.Davis .75 2.00
2 J.McMahon/J.Cutler 1.00 2.50
3 P.Holmes/R.Rice .75 2.00
4 C.Carter/S.Rice 1.25 3.00
5 J.Seau/S.Merriman 1.00 2.50
6 F.Tarkenton/B.Favre 2.50 6.00
7 R.Woodson/T.Polamalu 1.25 3.00
8 J.Namath/M.Sanchez 1.50 4.00
9 T.Bradshaw/B.Roethlisberger 1.50 4.00
10 B.Starr/A.Rodgers 2.50 6.00
11 E.George/C.Johnson 1.00 2.50
12 B.Jackson/D.McFadden 1.50 4.00
13 D.Fouts/P.Rivers 1.25 3.00
14 R.Craig/F.Gore 1.00 2.50
15 M.Irvin/M.Austin 1.25 3.00

2010 Panini Threads Generations Materials

STATED PRINT RUN 50-200
*PRIME/30-50: .6X TO 1.5X BASIC JSY/200
*PRIME/25: .8X TO 2X BASIC JSY/200
*PRIME/25: .6X TO 1.5X BASIC JSY/100
1 B.Jones/V.Davis 4.00 10.00
2 J.McMahon/J.Cutler 8.00 20.00
4 C.Carter/S.Rice 6.00 15.00
5 J.Seau/S.Merriman 5.00 12.00
7 R.Woodson/T.Polamalu 8.00 20.00
8 J.Namath/M.Sanchez 10.00 25.00
9 T.Bradshaw/B.Roethlisberger 8.00 20.00
11 E.George/C.Johnson 5.00 12.00
12 B.Jackson/D.McFadden 8.00 20.00
13 D.Fouts/P.Rivers 6.00 15.00
14 R.Craig/F.Gore 6.00 15.00

2010 Panini Threads Gridiron Kings

*FRAMED BLACK/10: 1.5X TO 4X BASIC INS
*FRAMED BLUE/50: .8X TO 2X BASIC INS
*FRAMED GREEN/25: 1X TO 2.5X BASIC INS
*FRAMED RED/100: .6X TO 1.5X BASIC INSERTS
1 Bobby Bell 1.00 2.50
2 Jim McMahon 1.25 3.00
3 Johnny Morris 1.00 2.50
4 Art Monk 1.50 4.00
5 Jimmy Orr 1.00 2.50
6 Larry Little 1.00 2.50
7 Bart Starr 2.50 6.00
8 Paul Krause 1.00 2.50
9 Daryle Lamonica 1.00 2.50
10 Dan Fouts 1.25 3.00
11 Rick Casares 1.00 2.50
12 Priest Holmes 1.00 2.50
13 Fran Tarkenton 1.50 4.00
14 Eddie George 1.25 3.00
15 John Taylor 1.00 2.50
16 Steve Young 2.00 5.00
18 Willie Davis 1.00 2.50
19 Junior Seau 1.25 3.00
20 Mark Duper 1.00 2.50
21 Len Dawson 1.50 4.00
22 Boyd Dowler 1.00 2.50
23 Lenny Moore 1.00 2.50
24 Dante Lavelli 1.00 2.50
25 Frank Gifford 1.25 3.00
26 Lem Barney 1.00 2.50
27 Billy Howton 1.00 2.50
28 Cris Carter 1.50 4.00
29 Lydell Mitchell 1.00 2.50
30 Fred Williamson 1.00 2.50
31 Harlon Hill 1.00 2.50
32 Joe Namath 2.00 5.00
33 Brent Jones 1.00 2.50
34 Gary Collins 1.00 2.50
35 Mike Curtis 1.00 2.50
36 Phil Simms 1.25 3.00
37 Randall Cunningham 1.25 3.00
38 Charley Trippi 1.00 2.50
39 Jan Stenerud 1.00 2.50
40 Roger Craig 1.25 3.00
41 Rod Woodson 1.25 3.00
42 Terry Bradshaw 2.00 5.00
43 Cliff Harris 1.00 2.50
44 Lee Roy Selmon 1.00 2.50
45 Dub Jones 1.00 2.50
46 Hugh McElhenny 1.00 2.50
47 Leroy Kelly 1.25 3.00
48 Michael Irvin 1.50 4.00
49 Pete Retzlaff 1.00 2.50
50 Bo Jackson 2.00 5.00

2010 Panini Threads Gridiron Kings Autographs

STATED PRINT RUN 5-50
1 Bobby Bell/50 12.00 30.00
3 Johnny Morris/25 10.00 25.00
5 Jimmy Orr/50 8.00 20.00
6 Larry Little/50 8.00 20.00
8 Paul Krause/25 10.00 25.00
9 Daryle Lamonica/50 8.00 20.00
11 Rick Casares/50 8.00 20.00
18 Willie Davis/50 20.00 40.00
20 Mark Duper/50 8.00 20.00
21 Len Dawson/50 12.00 30.00
22 Boyd Dowler/50 8.00 20.00
23 Lenny Moore/50 8.00 20.00
24 Dante Lavelli/25 15.00 40.00
26 Lem Barney/50 8.00 20.00
27 Billy Howton/50 10.00 25.00
29 Lydell Mitchell/50 8.00 20.00
30 Fred Williamson/50 8.00 20.00
31 Harlon Hill/50 8.00 20.00
32 Joe Namath/25 60.00 120.00
34 Gary Collins/19 10.00 25.00
35 Mike Curtis/50 8.00 20.00
38 Charley Trippi/50 8.00 20.00
39 Jan Stenerud/50 8.00 20.00
40 Roger Craig/35 10.00 25.00
43 Cliff Harris/50 8.00 20.00
44 Lee Roy Selmon/50 8.00 20.00
45 Dub Jones/50 8.00 20.00
46 Hugh McElhenny/25 10.00 25.00
47 Leroy Kelly/50 12.00 30.00
49 Pete Retzlaff/50 8.00 20.00

2010 Panini Threads Gridiron Kings Materials

STATED PRINT RUN 15-299
2 Jim McMahon/200 4.00 10.00
4 Art Monk/200 6.00 15.00
7 Bart Starr/299 8.00 20.00
10 Dan Fouts/150 6.00 15.00
12 Priest Holmes/50 5.00 12.00
13 Fran Tarkenton/50 8.00 20.00
14 Eddie George/299 4.00 10.00
15 John Taylor/150 3.00 8.00
16 Steve Young/299 6.00 15.00
19 Junior Seau/299 4.00 10.00
23 Lenny Moore/100 4.00 10.00
25 Frank Gifford/50 6.00 15.00
26 Lem Barney/50 5.00 12.00
28 Cris Carter/299 5.00 12.00
32 Joe Namath/15 12.00 30.00
33 Brent Jones/50 5.00 12.00
36 Phil Simms/150 4.00 10.00
37 Randall Cunningham/65 5.00 12.00
42 Terry Bradshaw/150 6.00 15.00
43 Cliff Harris/50 5.00 12.00
44 Lee Roy Selmon/30 6.00 15.00
46 Hugh McElhenny/100 4.00 10.00
48 Michael Irvin/100 6.00 15.00
50 Bo Jackson/150 6.00 15.00

2010 Panini Threads Gridiron Kings Materials Prime

STATED PRINT RUN 1-50
4 Art Monk/50 12.00 30.00
12 Priest Holmes/50 6.00 15.00
14 Eddie George/50 8.00 20.00
15 John Taylor/25 8.00 20.00
16 Steve Young/15 15.00 40.00
19 Junior Seau/50 8.00 20.00
28 Cris Carter/50 10.00 25.00
33 Brent Jones/25 8.00 20.00
41 Rod Woodson/25 10.00 25.00
42 Terry Bradshaw/50 12.00 30.00
48 Michael Irvin/50 10.00 25.00

2010 Panini Threads Gridiron Kings Materials Autographs

STATED PRINT RUN 15-25
EXCH EXPIRATION: 3/8/2012
2 Jim McMahon/25 25.00 50.00
4 Art Monk/25 25.00 50.00
7 Bart Starr/15 100.00 175.00
8 Paul Krause/25 10.00 25.00
9 Daryle Lamonica/25 12.00 30.00
10 Dan Fouts/25 30.00 60.00
12 Priest Holmes/25 10.00 25.00
13 Fran Tarkenton/25 40.00 80.00
14 Eddie George/25 20.00 50.00
15 John Taylor/25 12.00 25.00
16 Steve Young/15 40.00 80.00
19 Junior Seau/25 40.00 80.00
20 Mark Duper/25 10.00 25.00
21 Len Dawson/25 20.00 40.00
23 Lenny Moore/25
25 Frank Gifford/25 20.00 40.00
26 Lem Barney/25 10.00 25.00
32 Joe Namath/25 75.00 150.00
33 Brent Jones/25
36 Phil Simms/25 15.00 40.00
37 Randall Cunningham/25 25.00 50.00
39 Jan Stenerud/25 10.00 25.00
40 Roger Craig/25 12.00 30.00
41 Rod Woodson/25 40.00 80.00
42 Terry Bradshaw/25 60.00 120.00
43 Cliff Harris/25 10.00 25.00
44 Lee Roy Selmon/25 15.00 40.00
46 Hugh McElhenny/25 10.00 25.00
47 Leroy Kelly/20 20.00 40.00
48 Michael Irvin/15 25.00 50.00
50 Bo Jackson/25 40.00 80.00

2010 Panini Threads Jerseys Prime

STATED PRINT RUN 10-50
1 Chris Wells/45 4.00 10.00
2 Larry Fitzgerald/25 6.00 15.00
5 Matt Ryan/50 5.00 12.00
6 Michael Turner/50 4.00 10.00
7 Roddy White/50 4.00 10.00
8 Tony Gonzalez/50 5.00 12.00
11 Joe Flacco/15 6.00 15.00
13 Willis McGahee/50 4.00 10.00
15 Lee Evans/15 6.00 15.00
16 Marshawn Lynch/50 5.00 12.00
18 DeAngelo Williams/50 4.00 10.00
19 Jonathan Stewart/50 4.00 10.00
21 Steve Smith/50 5.00 12.00
22 Brian Urlacher/30 8.00 20.00
23 Devin Hester/50 5.00 12.00
24 Greg Olsen/50 5.00 12.00
25 Jay Cutler/35 4.00 10.00
26 Matt Forte/50 4.00 10.00
30 Cedric Benson/50 4.00 10.00
31 Chad Ochocinco/50 4.00 10.00
35 Josh Cribbs/25 5.00 12.00
37 Felix Jones/50 4.00 10.00
38 Jason Witten/50 5.00 12.00
39 Marion Barber/50 5.00 12.00
41 Tony Romo/10
42 Eddie Royal/50 4.00 10.00
44 Knowshon Moreno/50 4.00 10.00
45 Kyle Orton/40 4.00 10.00
47 Calvin Johnson/50 6.00 15.00
51 Donald Driver/50 5.00 12.00
52 Greg Jennings/50 4.00 10.00
54 Ryan Grant/50 5.00 12.00
55 Andre Johnson/50 5.00 12.00
58 Owen Daniels/50 4.00 10.00
59 Steve Slaton/50 4.00 10.00
60 Dallas Clark/50 4.00 10.00
61 Joseph Addai/50 4.00 10.00
62 Peyton Manning/25 20.00 50.00
64 Reggie Wayne/50 5.00 12.00
65 David Garrard/50 4.00 10.00
66 Maurice Jones-Drew/50 4.00 10.00
70 Dwayne Bowe/50 5.00 12.00
71 Jamaal Charles/50 5.00 12.00
79 Ronnie Brown/50 4.00 10.00
80 Adrian Peterson/50 6.00 15.00
82 Percy Harvin/50 4.00 10.00
83 Sidney Rice/50 4.00 10.00
84 Visanthe Shiancoe/50 5.00 12.00
85 Laurence Maroney/50 4.00 10.00
86 Randy Moss/50 5.00 12.00
87 Tom Brady/50 15.00 40.00
89 Wes Welker/50 5.00 12.00
90 Devery Henderson/50 4.00 10.00
92 Jeremy Shockey/50 4.00 10.00
93 Marques Colston/50 4.00 10.00
95 Brandon Jacobs/50 4.00 10.00
96 Eli Manning/50 5.00 12.00
98 Kevin Boss/50 4.00 10.00
99 Steve Smith USC/50 4.00 10.00
100 Braylon Edwards/50 4.00 10.00
102 Mark Sanchez/25 5.00 12.00
104 Shonn Greene/50 4.00 10.00
106 Darren McFadden/50 4.00 10.00
108 Louis Murphy/50 4.00 10.00
112 Jeremy Maclin/50 4.00 10.00
114 LeSean McCoy/50 6.00 15.00
115 Ben Roethlisberger/10
116 Heath Miller/50 4.00 10.00
117 Hines Ward/50 8.00 20.00
118 Rashard Mendenhall/50 4.00 10.00
119 Troy Polamalu/50 6.00 15.00
120 Antonio Gates/50 5.00 12.00
121 Darren Sproles/50 5.00 12.00
122 Philip Rivers/25 8.00 20.00
123 Vincent Jackson/50 4.00 10.00
124 Alex Smith QB/50 5.00 12.00
125 Frank Gore/50 5.00 12.00
126 Patrick Willis/20 6.00 15.00
127 Michael Crabtree/50 4.00 10.00
128 Vernon Davis/50 4.00 10.00
129 Deion Branch/50 4.00 10.00
132 Matt Hasselbeck/50 4.00 10.00
137 Steven Jackson/50 4.00 10.00
138 Cadillac Williams/50 4.00 10.00
139 Josh Freeman/50 5.00 12.00
143 Chris Johnson/50 4.00 10.00
144 Kenny Britt/50 4.00 10.00
145 Vince Young/50 4.00 10.00
146 Chris Cooley/50 4.00 10.00
147 Clinton Portis/50 4.00 10.00
150 Santana Moss/50 5.00 12.00

2010 Panini Threads Rookie Autographs Combo

STATED PRINT RUN 25 SER.#'d SETS
EXCH EXPIRATION: 3/8/2012
1 A.Roberts/J.Skelton 12.00 30.00
2 S.Weatherspoon/D.Franks 8.00 20.00
3 S.Kindle/E.Dickson 12.00 30.00
4 P.Robinson/J.Graham
5 C.Wootton/D.LeFevour 10.00 25.00
6 J.Gresham/C.Dunlap 12.00 30.00
7 J.Haden/M.Hardesty 15.00 40.00
8 D.Bryant/S.Lee 60.00 120.00
9 B.Bulaga/M.Burnett
10 K.Jackson/B.Tate 10.00 25.00

2010 Panini Threads Rookie Autographs Triple

STATED PRINT RUN 15 SER.#'d SETS
EXCH EXPIRATION: 3/8/2012
1 Grshm/Dnlp/Shply
2 Wash/Rbrts/Skltn 15.00 40.00
3 Haden/Hardesty/McCoy 40.00 80.00
4 Cook/Gerhart/Griffen
5 Grhm/Allen/Kafka EXCH 10.00 25.00
6 Mays/Bwmn/Dixon
7 Okung/Thomas/Tate 25.00 60.00
8 Haden/Thomas/Jackson
9 Will/Okng/Bulaga
10 Grahm/Prre-Paul/Morgn 15.00 40.00

2010 Panini Threads Rookie Collection Materials

STATED PRINT RUN 299 SER.#'d SETS
*PRIME/50: .6X TO 1.5X BASIC JSY/299
1 Andre Roberts 2.50 6.00
2 Armanti Edwards 2.50 6.00
3 Arrelious Benn 2.00 5.00
4 Ben Tate 2.00 5.00
5 Brandon LaFell 3.00 8.00
6 C.J. Spiller 2.00 5.00
7 Colt McCoy 6.00 15.00
8 Damian Williams 2.00 5.00
9 Demaryius Thomas 5.00 12.00
10 Dexter McCluster 2.50 6.00
11 Dez Bryant 6.00 15.00
12 Emmanuel Sanders 3.00 8.00
13 Eric Berry 3.00 8.00
14 Eric Decker 2.50 6.00
15 Gerald McCoy 2.00 5.00
16 Golden Tate 2.50 6.00
17 Jahvid Best 2.00 5.00
18 Jermaine Gresham 2.00 5.00
19 Jimmy Clausen 2.00 5.00
20 Joe McKnight 2.00 5.00
21 Jonathan Dwyer 2.00 5.00
22 Jordan Shipley 2.00 5.00
23 Marcus Easley 2.00 5.00
24 Mardy Gilyard 2.00 5.00
25 Mike Kafka 2.50 6.00
26 Mike Williams 2.00 5.00
27 Montario Hardesty 2.00 5.00
28 Ndamukong Suh 4.00 10.00
29 Rob Gronkowski 6.00 15.00
30 Rolando McClain 2.00 5.00
31 Ryan Mathews 2.00 5.00
32 Sam Bradford 2.50 6.00
33 Taylor Price 2.00 5.00
34 Tim Tebow 6.00 15.00
35 Toby Gerhart 2.00 5.00

2010 Panini Threads Rookie Collection Materials Autographs

STATED PRINT RUN 25 SER.#'d SETS
*PRIME/15: .6X TO 1.5X BASIC JSY AU/25
EXCH EXPIRATION: 3/8/2012
1 Andre Roberts 8.00 20.00
2 Armanti Edwards 8.00 20.00
3 Arrelious Benn 6.00 15.00
4 Ben Tate 6.00 15.00
5 Brandon LaFell 10.00 25.00
6 C.J. Spiller 6.00 15.00
7 Colt McCoy 8.00 20.00
8 Damian Williams 6.00 15.00
9 Demaryius Thomas 15.00 40.00
10 Dexter McCluster 8.00 20.00
11 Dez Bryant 50.00 100.00
12 Emmanuel Sanders 10.00 25.00
13 Eric Berry 15.00 40.00
14 Eric Decker 8.00 20.00
15 Gerald McCoy 6.00 15.00
16 Golden Tate 8.00 20.00
17 Jahvid Best 6.00 15.00
18 Jermaine Gresham 6.00 15.00
19 Jimmy Clausen 6.00 15.00
20 Joe McKnight 6.00 15.00
21 Jonathan Dwyer 6.00 15.00
22 Jordan Shipley 6.00 15.00
23 Marcus Easley 6.00 15.00
24 Mardy Gilyard 6.00 15.00
25 Mike Kafka 8.00 20.00
26 Mike Williams 12.00 30.00
27 Montario Hardesty 6.00 15.00
28 Ndamukong Suh 12.00 30.00
29 Rob Gronkowski 30.00 60.00
30 Rolando McClain 6.00 15.00
31 Ryan Mathews 6.00 15.00
32 Sam Bradford 8.00 20.00
33 Taylor Price 6.00 15.00
34 Tim Tebow 40.00 100.00
35 Toby Gerhart 6.00 15.00

2010 Panini Threads Rookie Collection Materials Combo

STATED PRINT RUN 299 SER.#'d SETS
*PRIME/25: .8X TO 2X BASIC COMBO/299
1 C.Spiller/M.Easley 2.00 5.00
2 T.Tebow/D.Thomas 12.00 30.00
3 J.Gresham/J.Shipley 2.00 5.00
4 E.Berry/D.McCluster 2.50 6.00
5 J.Clausen/B.LaFell 3.00 8.00
6 E.Sanders/J.Dwyer 3.00 8.00
7 G.McCoy/A.Benn 2.00 5.00
8 C.McCoy/M.Hardesty 2.50 6.00
9 S.Bradford/M.Gilyard 2.50 6.00
10 N.Suh/J.Best 6.00 15.00
11 R.Gronkowski/T.Price 6.00 15.00
12 N.Suh/G.McCoy 6.00 15.00
13 D.Thomas/D.Bryant 8.00 20.00
14 C.Spiller/R.Mathews 2.00 5.00
15 S.Bradford/T.Tebow 6.00 15.00

2010 Panini Threads Rookie Collection Materials Quad

STATED PRINT RUN 299 SER.#'d SETS
*PRIME/25: .6X TO 1.5X BASIC QUAD/299
1 Brdfrd/Suh/G.McCy/Brry 5.00 12.00
2 Spllr/Mthws/Best/Gerhrt 2.50 6.00
3 Thms/Brynt/McClstr/Benn 6.00 15.00
4 Brdfrd/Tebw/Clsn/C.McCy 8.00 20.00
5 Suh/McCoy/Berry/McClain 5.00 12.00

2010 Panini Threads Triple Threat

COMPLETE SET (10) 10.00 25.00
*HOLOFOIL/100: .6X TO 1.5X BASIC INSERTS
1 Favre/Peterson/Rice 2.50 6.00
2 Smith/Williams/Stewart 1.00 2.50
3 Brees/Bush/Colston 1.25 3.00
4 Sanchez/Edwards/Cotchery .75 2.00
5 Romo/Jones/Austin 1.00 2.50
6 Davis/Gore/Crabtree 1.00 2.50
7 McNabb/Moss/Portis 1.00 2.50
8 Flacco/Rice/McGahee 1.00 2.50
9 Cutler/Forte/Knox .75 2.00
10 Palmer/Ochocinco/Benson 1.00 2.50

2010 Panini Threads Triple Threat Materials

STATED PRINT RUN 85-200
3 Brees/Bush/Colston 6.00 15.00
4 Sanchez/Edwards/Cotchery 3.00 8.00
6 Davis/Gore/Crabtree 4.00 10.00
7 McNabb/Moss/Portis 6.00 15.00
9 Cutler/Forte/Knox 6.00 15.00
10 Palmer/Ochocinco/Benson 4.00 10.00

2010 Panini Threads Triple Threat Materials Prime

STATED PRINT RUN 7-25
2 Smith/Williams/Stewart 10.00 25.00
3 Brees/Bush/Colston 12.00 30.00
4 Sanchez/Edwards/Cotchery 8.00 20.00
6 Davis/Gore/Crabtree 10.00 25.00
9 Cutler/Forte/Knox 15.00 40.00
10 Palmer/Ochocinco/Benson

2011 Panini Threads

COMP.SET w/o AU's (250) 40.00 80.00
COMP.SET w/o RC's (150) 8.00 20.00
ROOKIE AUTO PRINT RUN 200 500
1 Beanie Wells .20 .50
2 Larry Fitzgerald .25 .60
3 Steve Breaston .20 .50
4 Tim Hightower .20 .50
5 Jason Snelling .20 .50
6 Matt Ryan .25 .60
7 Michael Turner .20 .50
8 Roddy White .20 .50
9 Tony Gonzalez .25 .60
10 Anquan Boldin .20 .50
11 Joe Flacco .25 .60
12 Ray Lewis .30 .75
13 Ray Rice .20 .50
14 Todd Heap .20 .50
15 C.J. Spiller .20 .50
16 Fred Jackson .20 .50
17 Lee Evans .25 .60
18 Ryan Fitzpatrick .20 .50
19 Steve Johnson .20 .50
20 DeAngelo Williams .20 .50
21 Jimmy Clausen .20 .50
22 Jonathan Stewart .20 .50
23 Steve Smith .25 .60
24 Brian Urlacher .30 .75
25 Devin Hester .25 .60
26 Jay Cutler .20 .50
27 Johnny Knox .20 .50
28 Matt Forte .20 .50
29 Carson Palmer .25 .60
30 Cedric Benson .20 .50
31 Chad Ochocinco .20 .50
32 Jordan Shipley .20 .50
33 Terrell Owens .25 .60
34 Ben Watson .20 .50
35 Colt McCoy .20 .50
36 Josh Cribbs .20 .50
37 Peyton Hillis .20 .50
38 Dez Bryant .30 .75
39 Felix Jones .20 .50
40 Jason Witten .25 .60
41 Miles Austin .20 .50
42 Tony Romo .25 .60
43 Brandon Lloyd .20 .50
44 Eddie Royal .20 .50
45 Jabar Gaffney .20 .50
46 Knowshon Moreno .20 .50
47 Tim Tebow .30 .75
48 Brandon Pettigrew .20 .50
49 Calvin Johnson .30 .75
50 Jahvid Best .20 .50
51 Matthew Stafford .25 .60
52 Nate Burleson .20 .50
53 Aaron Rodgers .50 1.25
54 Clay Matthews .30 .75
55 Donald Driver .25 .60
56 Greg Jennings .20 .50
57 Jordy Nelson .25 .60
58 Andre Johnson .25 .60
59 Arian Foster .20 .50
60 Brian Cushing .20 .50
61 Kevin Walter .20 .50
62 Matt Schaub .20 .50
63 Austin Collie .20 .50
64 Dallas Clark .20 .50
65 Joseph Addai .20 .50
66 Peyton Manning .60 1.50
67 Reggie Wayne .25 .60
68 David Garrard .20 .50
69 Marcedes Lewis .20 .50
70 Maurice Jones-Drew .20 .50
71 Mike Sims-Walker .25 .60
72 Mike Thomas .25 .60
73 Dwayne Bowe .25 .60
74 Jamaal Charles .25 .60
75 Matt Cassel .20 .50
76 Tony Moeaki .20 .50
77 Brandon Marshall .25 .60
78 Brian Hartline .25 .60
79 Chad Henne .25 .60
80 Devone Bess .20 .50
81 Ronnie Brown .25 .60
82 Adrian Peterson .30 .75
83 Percy Harvin .20 .50
84 Sidney Rice .20 .50
85 Joe Webb .20 .50
86 Visanthe Shiancoe .25 .60
87 BenJarvus Green-Ellis .20 .50
88 Danny Woodhead .25 .60
89 Deion Branch .20 .50
90 Tom Brady .75 2.00
91 Wes Welker .25 .60
92 Drew Brees .30 .75
93 Lance Moore .20 .50
94 Marques Colston .20 .50
95 Pierre Thomas .20 .50
96 Reggie Bush .20 .50
97 Ahmad Bradshaw .20 .50
98 Eli Manning .25 .60
99 Hakeem Nicks .20 .50
100 Mario Manningham .20 .50
101 Steve Smith USC .20 .50
102 Braylon Edwards .20 .50
103 LaDainian Tomlinson .30 .75
104 Mark Sanchez .20 .50
105 Santonio Holmes .20 .50
106 Shonn Greene .20 .50
107 Darren McFadden .20 .50
108 Jacoby Ford .25 .60
109 Louis Murphy .20 .50
110 Zach Miller .20 .50
111 DeSean Jackson .25 .60
112 Jeremy Maclin .20 .50
113 LeSean McCoy .30 .75
114 Michael Vick .25 .60
115 Ben Roethlisberger .30 .75
116 Hines Ward .25 .60
117 Mike Wallace .20 .50
118 Rashard Mendenhall .20 .50
119 Troy Polamalu .30 .75
120 Antonio Gates .20 .50
121 Malcom Floyd .20 .50
122 Mike Tolbert .20 .50
123 Philip Rivers .30 .75
124 Ryan Mathews .25 .60
125 Frank Gore .25 .60
126 Michael Crabtree .20 .50
127 Patrick Willis .25 .60
128 Vernon Davis .20 .50
129 John Carlson .20 .50
130 Marshawn Lynch .25 .60
131 Matt Hasselbeck .20 .50
132 Mike Williams USC .20 .50
133 Danny Amendola .25 .60
134 Donnie Avery .20 .50
135 Sam Bradford .20 .50
136 Steven Jackson .20 .50
137 Cadillac Williams .20 .50
138 Josh Freeman .25 .60
139 Kellen Winslow Jr. .20 .50
140 LeGarrette Blount .25 .60
141 Mike Williams .25 .60
142 Bo Scaife .20 .50
143 Chris Johnson .20 .50
144 Kenny Britt .20 .50
145 Nate Washington .20 .50
146 Randy Moss .25 .60
147 Chris Cooley .20 .50
148 Donovan McNabb .25 .60
149 Ryan Torain .20 .50
150 Santana Moss .25 .60
151 Aaron Williams RC .60 1.50
152 Adrian Clayborn RC .60 1.50
153 Ahmad Black RC .75 2.00
154 Akeem Ayers RC .60 1.50
155 Aldon Smith RC .60 1.50
156 Aldrick Robinson RC .75 2.00
157 Allen Bradford RC .60 1.50
158 Anthony Allen RC .60 1.50
159 Anthony Castonzo RC .60 1.50
160 Anthony Sherman RC .60 1.50
161 Baron Batch RC .75 2.00
162 Terrelle Pryor RC 1.00 2.50
163 Brandon Harris RC .60 1.50
164 Brandon Hogan RC .60 1.50
165 Brooks Reed RC .75 2.00
166 Bruce Carter RC .60 1.50
167 Cameron Heyward RC .75 2.00
168 Cameron Jordan RC .75 2.00
169 Casey Matthews RC .60 1.50
170 Chimdi Chekwa RC .75 2.00
171 Chris Conte RC .60 1.50
172 Chris Culliver RC .60 1.50
173 Corey Liuget RC .60 1.50
174 Curtis Brown RC .60 1.50
175 Curtis Marsh RC .75 2.00
176 Danny Watkins RC .60 1.50
177 Da'Rel Scott RC .60 1.50
178 David Ausberry RC .60 1.50
179 DeMarco Sampson RC .60 1.50
180 DeMarcus Van Dyke RC .75 2.00
181 Denarius Moore RC .60 1.50
182 Derek Sherrod RC .60 1.50
183 Dion Lewis RC .75 2.00
184 Dontay Moch RC .60 1.50
185 Dwayne Harris RC .60 1.50
186 Evan Royster RC .60 1.50
187 Gabe Carimi RC .75 2.00
188 Greg Jones RC .75 2.00
189 Greg McElroy RC 1.00 2.50
190 J.J. Watt RC 3.00 8.00
191 Jabaal Sheard RC .60 1.50
192 Jah Reid RC .60 1.50
193 Jaiquawn Jarrett RC .60 1.50
194 James Carpenter RC .75 2.00
195 Jarvis Jenkins RC .60 1.50
196 Jay Finley RC .75 2.00
197 Jimmy Smith RC .60 1.50
198 Johnny Patrick RC .75 2.00
199 Johnny White RC .60 1.50
200 Jonas Mouton RC .75 2.00
201 Jordan Cameron RC .75 2.00
202 Julius Thomas RC .75 2.00
203 Justin Houston RC .75 2.00
204 Kealoha Pilares RC .60 1.50
205 Kelvin Sheppard RC .60 1.50
206 Kris Durham RC .60 1.50
207 Lance Kendricks RC .60 1.50
208 Lee Smith RC .75 2.00
209 Luke Stocker RC .60 1.50
210 Malcolm Williams RC .60 1.50
211 Marcus Cannon RC .60 1.50
212 Marcus Gilbert RC 1.00 2.50
213 Marcus Gilchrist RC .60 1.50
214 Martez Wilson RC .60 1.50
215 Marvin Austin RC .60 1.50
216 Mason Foster RC .60 1.50
217 Matt Bosher RC .60 1.50
218 Mike Pouncey RC 1.00 2.50
219 Muhammad Wilkerson RC .60 1.50
220 Nate Irving RC .75 2.00
221 Nate Solder RC .60 1.50
222 Nathan Enderle RC .60 1.50
223 Orlando Franklin RC .75 2.00
224 Owen Marecic RC .60 1.50
225 Phil Taylor RC .60 1.50
226 Quan Sturdivant RC .75 2.00
227 Quinton Carter RC .60 1.50
228 Rahim Moore RC .60 1.50
229 Ras-I Dowling RC .60 1.50
230 Richard Gordon RC .60 1.50
231 Robert Housler RC .60 1.50
232 Robert Sands RC .60 1.50
233 Rodney Hudson RC .60 1.50
234 Ronald Johnson RC .60 1.50
235 Ross Homan RC .75 2.00
236 Ryan Kerrigan RC .75 2.00
237 Ryan Whalen RC .60 1.50
238 Scotty McKnight RC .60 1.50
239 Shane Bannon RC .60 1.50
240 Shareece Wright RC .75 2.00
241 Stanley Havili RC .60 1.50
242 Stefen Wisniewski RC 1.00 2.50
243 Stephen Burton RC .60 1.50
244 Stephen Paea RC .60 1.50
245 T.J. Yates RC .60 1.50
246 Terrell McClain RC .75 2.00
247 Tyler Sash RC .60 1.50
248 Tyrod Taylor RC 1.25 3.00
249 Tyron Smith RC .75 2.00
250 Virgil Green RC .60 1.50
251 M.Dareus AU/300 RC 5.00 12.00
252 Von Miller AU/300 RC 12.00 30.00
253 Andy Dalton AU/300 RC 15.00 40.00
254 B.Gabbert AU/350 RC 5.00 12.00
255 Cam Newton AU/300 RC 50.00 120.00
256 C.Ponder AU/300 RC 5.00 12.00
257 C.Kaepernick AU/500 RC 8.00 20.00
258 Jake Locker AU/300 RC 5.00 12.00
259 Ryan Mallett AU/350 RC 5.00 12.00
260 Bilal Powell AU/450 RC 6.00 15.00
261 Daniel Thomas AU/300 RC 5.00 12.00
262 Delone Carter AU/300 RC 5.00 12.00
263 D.Murray AU/300 RC 10.00 25.00
264 Jamie Harper AU/300 RC 5.00 12.00
265 Jordan Todman AU/300 RC 5.00 12.00
266 Kendall Hunter AU/300 RC 10.00 25.00
267 Mark Ingram AU/300 RC 8.00 20.00
268 Mikel Leshoure AU/400 RC 5.00 12.00
269 Ryan Williams AU/400 RC 5.00 12.00
270 Shane Vereen AU/300 RC 6.00 15.00
271 Stevan Ridley AU/360 RC 5.00 12.00
272 Taiwan Jones AU/250 RC 10.00 25.00
273 Kyle Rudolph AU/350 RC 5.00 12.00
274 A.J. Green AU/250 RC 30.00 60.00
275 Austin Pettis AU/450 RC 5.00 12.00
276 Greg Little AU/450 RC 10.00 25.00
277 Jerrel Jernigan AU/400 RC 5.00 12.00
278 J.Baldwin AU/350 RC 10.00 25.00
279 Julio Jones AU/250 RC 20.00 50.00
280 L.Hankerson AU/450 RC 5.00 12.00
281 Randall Cobb AU/200 RC 8.00 20.00
282 Titus Young AU/480 RC 5.00 12.00
283 Torrey Smith AU/250 RC 5.00 12.00
284 Vincent Brown AU/375 RC 5.00 12.00
285 Clyde Gates AU/300 RC 5.00 12.00
286 Alex Green AU/360 RC 10.00 25.00
287 D.Bowers AU/300 RC 5.00 12.00
288 Ricky Stanzi AU/300 RC 5.00 12.00
289 J.Rodgers AU/350 RC 5.00 12.00
290 Niles Paul AU/300 RC 5.00 12.00
291 Tandon Doss AU/300 RC 5.00 12.00
292 Prince Amukamara AU/450 RC 5.00 12.00
293 Roy Helu AU/280 RC 5.00 12.00
294 D.J. Williams AU/400 RC 10.00 25.00
295 Cecil Shorts AU/450 RC 5.00 12.00
296 Jeremy Kerley AU/450 RC 8.00 20.00
297 Greg Salas AU/375 RC 5.00 12.00
298 Patrick Peterson/400 RC 4.00 10.00
299 Robert Quinn/250 RC 2.00 5.00
300 Nick Fairley/350 RC 2.00 5.00

2011 Panini Threads Gold

*1-150 VETS/100: 3X TO 8X BASIC CARDS
*151-250 ROOKIES/100: 1X TO 2.5X BASIC CARDS

2011 Panini Threads Platinum

*1-150 VETS/25: 5X TO 12X BASIC CARDS
*151-250 ROOKIES/25: 1.5X TO 4X BASIC CARDS

2011 Panini Threads Silver

*1-150 VETS/250: 2X TO 5X BASIC CARDS
*151-250 ROOKIES/250: .6X TO 1.5X BASIC CARDS

2011 Panini Threads 2010 All Rookie Team

*HOLOFOIL/100: .5X TO 1.2X BASIC INSERTS
1 Colt McCoy 1.00 2.50
2 Dez Bryant 1.50 4.00
3 Jahvid Best 1.00 2.50
4 Jermaine Gresham 1.00 2.50
5 Mike Williams 1.25 3.00
6 Ndamukong Suh 1.25 3.00
7 Rob Gronkowski 1.50 4.00
8 Ryan Mathews 1.25 3.00
9 Sam Bradford 1.00 2.50
10 Tim Tebow 1.50 4.00

2011 Panini Threads 2010 All Rookie Team Autographs

STATED PRINT RUN 5-15
1 Colt McCoy/15
2 Dez Bryant/15 10.00 25.00
3 Jahvid Best/15 6.00 15.00
4 Jermaine Gresham/15 6.00 15.00
5 Mike Williams/15 8.00 20.00
10 Tim Tebow/15 50.00 120.00

2011 Panini Threads 2010 All Rookie Team Threads

STATED PRINT RUN 299 SER.#'d SETS
9 Sam Bradford 2.50 6.00
10 Tim Tebow 4.00 10.00

2011 Panini Threads 2010 All Rookie Team Threads Prime

STATED PRINT RUN 5-99
1 Colt McCoy/99 4.00 10.00
2 Dez Bryant/99 6.00 15.00
3 Jahvid Best/99 4.00 10.00
4 Jermaine Gresham/99 4.00 10.00
5 Mike Williams/99 5.00 12.00
6 Ndamukong Suh/99 5.00 12.00
7 Rob Gronkowski/99 6.00 15.00
8 Ryan Mathews/99 5.00 12.00
9 Sam Bradford/99 4.00 10.00

2011 Panini Threads Autographs Silver

VETERAN AU PRINT RUN 1-100
ROOKIE AU STATED PRINT RUN 299
11 Joe Flacco/15 10.00 25.00
21 Jimmy Clausen/35 10.00 25.00
31 Chad Ochocinco/20
37 Peyton Hillis/25 15.00 40.00
43 Brandon Lloyd/25 8.00 20.00
46 Knowshon Moreno/25 12.00 30.00
56 Greg Jennings/20
59 Arian Foster/20 20.00 50.00
61 Kevin Walter/30 6.00 15.00
78 Brian Hartline/25 10.00 25.00
87 BenJarvus Green-Ellis/25 30.00 60.00
107 Darren McFadden/25 12.00 30.00
113 LeSean McCoy/25 12.00 30.00
122 Mike Tolbert/100 4.00 10.00
123 Philip Rivers/25 20.00 40.00
151 Aaron Williams 4.00 10.00
152 Adrian Clayborn 4.00 10.00
153 Ahmad Black 5.00 12.00
154 Akeem Ayers 4.00 10.00
155 Aldon Smith 4.00 10.00
156 Aldrick Robinson 5.00 12.00
158 Anthony Allen 4.00 10.00
159 Anthony Castonzo 5.00 12.00
163 Brandon Harris 4.00 10.00
167 Cameron Heyward 5.00 12.00
168 Cameron Jordan 5.00 12.00
173 Corey Liuget 4.00 10.00
177 Da'Rel Scott 4.00 10.00
181 Denarius Moore 12.00 30.00
183 Dion Lewis 5.00 12.00
185 Dwayne Harris 4.00 10.00
186 Evan Royster 4.00 10.00
188 Greg Jones 5.00 12.00
190 J.J. Watt 50.00 80.00
197 Jimmy Smith 4.00 10.00
199 Johnny White 4.00 10.00
201 Jordan Cameron 5.00 12.00
202 Julius Thomas 5.00 12.00
203 Justin Houston 5.00 12.00
204 Kealoha Pilares 4.00 10.00
206 Kris Durham 4.00 10.00
207 Lance Kendricks 4.00 10.00
209 Luke Stocker 4.00 10.00
211 Marcus Cannon 4.00 10.00
214 Martez Wilson 4.00 10.00
225 Phil Taylor 4.00 10.00
227 Quinton Carter 4.00 10.00
228 Rahim Moore 4.00 10.00
234 Ronald Johnson 4.00 10.00
236 Ryan Kerrigan 5.00 12.00
238 Scotty McKnight 4.00 10.00
241 Stanley Havili 4.00 10.00
243 Stephen Burton 4.00 10.00
244 Stephen Paea 4.00 10.00
245 T.J. Yates 4.00 10.00
247 Tyler Sash 4.00 10.00
248 Tyrod Taylor 8.00 20.00
249 Tyron Smith 5.00 12.00

2011 Panini Threads Franchise Fabrics

STATED PRINT RUN 15-299
*PRIME/50: .8X TO 2X BASIC JSY/150-299
*PRIME/20-25: 1X TO 2.5X BASIC JSY/150-299
1 Aaron Rodgers/299 10.00 25.00
2 Andre Johnson/299 2.50 6.00
3 Antonio Gates/299 2.00 5.00
5 Calvin Johnson/299 3.00 8.00
6 Chris Cooley/299 3.00 8.00
7 Chris Johnson/299 2.00 5.00
8 Darrelle Revis/299 2.00 5.00
9 Hakeem Nicks/150 2.00 5.00
10 Joe Flacco/299 2.50 6.00
11 Larry Fitzgerald/220 2.50 6.00
12 Mark Sanchez/299 2.00 5.00
13 Marques Colston/299 2.00 5.00
15 Michael Vick/299 2.50 6.00
16 Miles Austin/299 3.00 8.00
17 Reggie Wayne/299 2.50 6.00
18 Steve Smith/170 2.50 6.00
19 Vernon Davis/299 2.00 5.00

2011 Panini Threads Game Day Jerseys

STATED PRINT RUN 290-299
1 Adrian Peterson/299 3.00 8.00
2 Ahmad Bradshaw/290 2.00 5.00
3 Brent Celek/299 2.00 5.00
4 Carson Palmer/299 2.50 6.00
5 Cedric Benson/299 2.00 5.00
6 Devin Hester/299 2.50 6.00
8 Donovan McNabb/299 2.50 6.00
9 Drew Brees/299 3.00 8.00
10 Eli Manning/299 2.50 6.00
11 Jason Witten/299 3.00 8.00
12 Jay Cutler/299 2.00 5.00
13 Jeremy Maclin/299 2.00 5.00
14 Jonathan Stewart/299 2.00 5.00
15 LaDainian Tomlinson/299 3.00 8.00
16 Matt Forte/299 2.00 5.00
17 Matt Schaub/299 2.00 5.00
18 Maurice Jones-Drew/299 2.00 5.00
19 Michael Turner/299 2.00 5.00
20 Peyton Manning/299 6.00 15.00
21 Reggie Bush/299 2.00 5.00
22 Roddy White/299 2.00 5.00
23 Steven Jackson/299 2.00 5.00
24 Tony Gonzalez/299 2.50 6.00
25 Tony Romo/299 2.50 6.00

2011 Panini Threads Game Day Jerseys Prime

*PRIME/30-50: .8X TO 2X BASIC JSY
*PRIME/25: 1X TO 2.5X BASIC JSY
STATED PRINT RUN 25-50
7 Donald Driver/50 5.00 12.00

2011 Panini Threads Game Day Jerseys Autographs

STATED PRINT RUN 15 SER.#'d SETS
EXCH EXPIRATION: 2/24/2013
1 Adrian Peterson 75.00 150.00
2 Ahmad Bradshaw 10.00 25.00
6 Devin Hester EXCH 12.00 30.00
8 Donovan McNabb
9 Drew Brees EXCH 50.00 100.00
10 Eli Manning 40.00 80.00
11 Jason Witten 12.00 30.00
12 Jay Cutler 10.00 25.00
13 Jeremy Maclin 10.00 25.00
14 Jonathan Stewart 10.00 25.00
15 LaDainian Tomlinson 20.00 40.00
16 Matt Forte 10.00 25.00
17 Matt Schaub 10.00 25.00
18 Maurice Jones-Drew 10.00 25.00
19 Michael Turner 10.00 25.00
20 Peyton Manning 75.00 150.00
21 Reggie Bush 12.00 30.00
22 Roddy White 10.00 25.00
23 Steven Jackson 15.00 40.00
25 Tony Romo 40.00 80.00

2011 Panini Threads Generations

*HOLOFOIL/100: .6X TO 1.5X BASIC INSERTS
1 A.Page/J.Allen .75 2.00
2 J.Brown/E.Davis 1.50 4.00
3 M.Faulk/S.Jackson 1.00 2.50
4 J.Perry/F.Gore 1.00 2.50
5 R.Dent/J.Peppers 1.00 2.50
6 M.Irvin/D.Bryant 1.25 3.00
7 J.Elway/T.Tebow 2.00 5.00
8 P.Manning/S.Bradford 2.50 6.00
9 E.Reed/D.Revis 1.00 2.50
10 S.Bartkowski/M.Ryan 1.00 2.50

2011 Panini Threads Generations Materials

STATED PRINT RUN 200-299
1 A.Page/J.Allen/299 4.00 10.00
2 J.Brown/E.Davis/299 15.00 30.00
3 Faulk/S.Jackson/230 5.00 12.00
4 J.Perry/F.Gore/200 5.00 12.00
5 R.Dent/J.Peppers/299 6.00 15.00
7 J.Elway/T.Tebow/299 10.00 25.00
8 P.Mann/Bradford/299 12.00 30.00
9 E.Reed/D.Revis/299 5.00 12.00
10 Bartkowski/Ryan/299 5.00 12.00

2011 Panini Threads Generations Materials Prime

*PRIME/49-50: .6X TO 1.5X BASIC JSY/230-299
*PRIME/25: .8X TO 2X BASIC JSY/200
STATED PRINT RUN 25-50
6 M.Irvin/D.Bryant/50 12.00 30.00

2011 Panini Threads Gridiron Kings

*FRMD BLACK/10: 1.5X TO 4X BASIC INSERTS
*FRAMED BLUE/50: .8X TO 2X BASIC INSERTS
*FRMD GREEN/25: 1X TO 2.5X BASIC INSERTS
*FRAMED RED/100: .6X TO 1.5X BASIC INSERTS
1 Vincent Jackson 1.00 2.50
2 Roy Williams WR 1.00 2.50
3 Bo Scaife 1.00 2.50
4 Anquan Boldin 1.00 2.50
5 Brian Urlacher 1.50 4.00
6 Chad Henne 1.25 3.00
7 DeAngelo Williams 1.00 2.50
8 Julius Peppers 1.25 3.00
9 Jared Allen 1.00 2.50
10 Ray Lewis 1.50 4.00
11 C.J. Spiller 1.00 2.50
12 Dwight Freeney 1.00 2.50
13 Asante Samuel 1.00 2.50
14 Dustin Keller 1.25 3.00
15 Darren Sproles 1.25 3.00
16 Shonn Greene 1.00 2.50

17 Pierre Thomas 1.00 2.50
18 Heath Miller 1.00 2.50
19 Dallas Clark 1.00 2.50
20 David Harris 1.00 2.50
21 Hines Ward 1.25 3.00
22 Cortland Finnegan 1.00 2.50
23 Patrick Willis 1.25 3.00
24 Steve Smith USC 1.00 2.50
25 London Fletcher 1.25 3.00
26 Ryan Grant 1.00 2.50
27 Sidney Rice 1.00 2.50
28 James Laurinaitis 1.00 2.50
29 Malcom Floyd 1.00 2.50
30 Michael Crabtree 1.00 2.50
31 Ryan Fitzpatrick 1.00 2.50
32 Lee Evans 1.25 3.00
33 Visanthe Shiancoe 1.25 3.00
34 Todd Heap 1.00 2.50
35 Matt Cassel 1.00 2.50
36 Ed Reed 1.25 3.00
37 Brian Cushing 1.00 2.50
38 David Garrard 1.00 2.50
39 Santonio Holmes 1.00 2.50
40 Ryan Mathews 1.25 3.00
41 Kevin Boss 1.00 2.50
42 Devery Henderson 1.00 2.50
43 Matthew Stafford 1.25 3.00
44 Ndamukong Suh 1.25 3.00
45 Troy Polamalu 1.50 4.00
46 Josh Cribbs 1.00 2.50
47 Eddie Royal 1.00 2.50
48 Brandon Jacobs 1.00 2.50
49 Rashard Mendenhall 1.00 2.50
50 Greg Olsen 1.25 3.00

2011 Panini Threads Gridiron Kings Autographs

STATED PRINT RUN 1-100
9 Jared Allen/25 20.00 40.00
17 Pierre Thomas/15
20 David Harris/100 5.00 12.00
25 London Fletcher/35 8.00 20.00
26 Ryan Grant/25 12.00 30.00
28 James Laurinaitis/25
37 Brian Cushing/35 6.00 15.00
50 Greg Olsen/25 10.00 25.00

2011 Panini Threads Gridiron Kings Materials

STATED PRINT RUN 98-299
1 Vincent Jackson/299 2.00 5.00
2 Roy Williams WR/299 2.00 5.00
3 Bo Scaife/299 2.00 5.00
4 Anquan Boldin/299 2.00 5.00
5 Brian Urlacher/299 3.00 8.00
6 Chad Henne/225 2.50 6.00
7 DeAngelo Williams/299 2.00 5.00
9 Jared Allen/299 3.00 8.00
10 Ray Lewis/299 3.00 8.00
11 C.J. Spiller/299 2.00 5.00
12 Dwight Freeney/299 2.00 5.00
13 Asante Samuel/190 2.00 5.00
14 Dustin Keller/299 2.50 6.00
15 Darren Sproles/299 2.50 6.00
16 Shonn Greene/299 2.00 5.00
18 Heath Miller/299 2.00 5.00
19 Dallas Clark/299 2.00 5.00
20 David Harris/299 2.00 5.00
21 Hines Ward/299 3.00 8.00
22 Cortland Finnegan/299 2.00 5.00
23 Patrick Willis/299 2.50 6.00
24 Steve Smith USC/299 2.00 5.00
25 London Fletcher/299 2.50 6.00
27 Sidney Rice/299 2.00 5.00
28 James Laurinaitis/98 2.50 6.00
29 Malcom Floyd/299 2.00 5.00
30 Michael Crabtree/299 2.00 5.00
31 Ryan Fitzpatrick/299 2.00 5.00
32 Lee Evans/299 2.50 6.00
33 Visanthe Shiancoe/299 2.50 6.00
34 Todd Heap/299 2.00 5.00
35 Matt Cassel/299 2.00 5.00
36 Ed Reed/299 3.00 8.00
38 David Garrard/299 2.00 5.00
39 Santonio Holmes/299 2.00 5.00
40 Ryan Mathews/299 2.50 6.00
41 Kevin Boss/299 2.00 5.00
42 Devery Henderson/299 2.00 5.00
43 Matthew Stafford/230 2.50 6.00
44 Ndamukong Suh/299 2.50 6.00
45 Troy Polamalu/299 3.00 8.00
46 Josh Cribbs/200 2.00 5.00
47 Eddie Royal/299 2.00 5.00
48 Brandon Jacobs/299 2.00 5.00
49 Rashard Mendenhall/299 2.00 5.00
50 Greg Olsen/299 2.50 6.00

2011 Panini Threads Gridiron Kings Materials Prime

*PRIME/90-99: .5X TO 1.2X BASIC JSY/190-299
*PRIME/99: .5X TO 1.2X BASIC JSY/98
*PRIME/50-60: .6X TO 1.5X BASIC JSY/190-299
*PRIME/25: .8X TO 2X BASIC JSY/225-299
PRIME STATED PRINT RUN 25-99
17 Pierre Thomas/99 3.00 8.00

2011 Panini Threads Gridiron Kings Materials Autographs

STATED PRINT RUN 9-25
EXCH EXPIRATION: 2/24/2013
3 Bo Scaife/20 10.00 25.00
4 Anquan Boldin/15
6 Chad Henne/15 12.00 30.00
7 DeAngelo Williams/15 10.00 25.00
9 Jared Allen/15 30.00 60.00
11 C.J. Spiller/15
16 Shonn Greene/15 10.00 25.00
18 Heath Miller/20
19 Dallas Clark/15 EXCH
20 David Harris/25
21 Hines Ward/15 30.00 60.00
23 Patrick Willis/15 15.00 40.00
25 London Fletcher/15 25.00 50.00
27 Sidney Rice/15 10.00 25.00
28 James Laurinaitis/15
29 Malcom Floyd/15
30 Michael Crabtree/15
35 Matt Cassel/15
38 David Garrard/15
39 Santonio Holmes/15 10.00 25.00
42 Devery Henderson/15 EXCH
43 Matthew Stafford/15
45 Troy Polamalu/15 125.00 200.00
49 Rashard Mendenhall/15 10.00 25.00
50 Greg Olsen/15 12.00 30.00

2011 Panini Threads Heritage Collection

*HOLOFOIL/100: .6X TO 1.5X BASIC INSERTS
1 Barry Sanders 2.50 6.00
2 Buck Buchanan 1.00 2.50
3 Knute Rockne 1.50 4.00
4 Bernie Kosar 1.25 3.00
5 John Brodie 1.00 2.50
6 Sam Huff 1.25 3.00
7 Bob Hayes 1.50 4.00
8 Franco Harris 1.50 4.00
9 Jay Novacek 1.25 3.00
10 Jim Parker 1.00 2.50
11 Lamar Lundy 1.00 2.50
12 Terrell Davis 1.25 3.00
13 Willie Brown 1.00 2.50
14 Y.A. Tittle 1.50 4.00
15 Mark Carrier 1.00 2.50

2011 Panini Threads Heritage Collection Materials

*PRIME/50: .6X TO 1.5X BASIC JSY
*PRIME/25: .8X TO 2X BASIC JSY
1 Barry Sanders 8.00 20.00
2 Buck Buchanan 3.00 8.00
3 Knute Rockne 10.00 25.00
4 Bernie Kosar 4.00 10.00
5 John Brodie 6.00 15.00
6 Sam Huff 4.00 10.00
7 Bob Hayes 6.00 15.00
8 Franco Harris 6.00 15.00
9 Jay Novacek 5.00 12.00
10 Jim Parker 3.00 8.00
12 Terrell Davis 4.00 10.00
13 Willie Brown 3.00 8.00
14 Y.A. Tittle 5.00 12.00
15 Mark Carrier 3.00 8.00

2011 Panini Threads Jerseys Prime

STATED PRINT RUN 10-99
1 Beanie Wells/99 3.00 8.00
2 Larry Fitzgerald/65 4.00 10.00
6 Matt Ryan/99 4.00 10.00
7 Michael Turner/99 3.00 8.00
8 Roddy White/99 3.00 8.00
9 Tony Gonzalez/99 4.00 10.00
10 Anquan Boldin/99 3.00 8.00
11 Joe Flacco/35 5.00 12.00
12 Ray Lewis/99 5.00 12.00
13 Ray Rice/99 3.00 8.00
14 Todd Heap/99 3.00 8.00
15 C.J. Spiller/99 3.00 8.00
16 Fred Jackson/99 6.00 15.00
17 Lee Evans/99 4.00 10.00
18 Ryan Fitzpatrick/99 3.00 8.00
20 DeAngelo Williams/99 3.00 8.00
21 Jimmy Clausen/25 5.00 12.00
22 Jonathan Stewart/99 3.00 8.00
23 Steve Smith/99 4.00 10.00
24 Brian Urlacher/99 5.00 12.00
25 Devin Hester/99 4.00 10.00
26 Jay Cutler/10 6.00 15.00
27 Johnny Knox/99 3.00 8.00
28 Matt Forte/99 3.00 8.00
29 Carson Palmer/99 4.00 10.00
30 Cedric Benson/99 3.00 8.00
31 Chad Ochocinco/99 3.00 8.00
32 Jordan Shipley/50 4.00 10.00
36 Josh Cribbs/60 3.00 8.00
37 Peyton Hillis/99 3.00 8.00
38 Dez Bryant/55 6.00 15.00
39 Felix Jones/99 3.00 8.00
40 Jason Witten/99 5.00 12.00
41 Miles Austin/99 5.00 12.00
42 Tony Romo/99 4.00 10.00
43 Brandon Lloyd/99 3.00 8.00
44 Eddie Royal/99 3.00 8.00
45 Jabar Gaffney/99 3.00 8.00
46 Knowshon Moreno/99 3.00 8.00
47 Tim Tebow/25 8.00 20.00
49 Calvin Johnson/99 5.00 12.00
50 Jahvid Best/99 3.00 8.00
51 Matthew Stafford/99 4.00 10.00
53 Aaron Rodgers/15 20.00 50.00
54 Clay Matthews/99 6.00 15.00
55 Donald Driver/99 5.00 12.00
58 Andre Johnson/99 4.00 10.00
59 Arian Foster/99 5.00 12.00
62 Matt Schaub/25 5.00 12.00
64 Dallas Clark/99 3.00 8.00
65 Joseph Addai/99 3.00 8.00
66 Peyton Manning/25 15.00 40.00
67 Reggie Wayne/99 4.00 10.00
68 David Garrard/65 3.00 8.00
69 Marcedes Lewis/99 3.00 8.00
70 Maurice Jones-Drew/99 3.00 8.00
72 Mike Thomas/99 4.00 10.00
73 Dwayne Bowe/99 4.00 10.00
74 Jamaal Charles/99 4.00 10.00
75 Matt Cassel/30 4.00 10.00
77 Brandon Marshall/99 4.00 10.00
79 Chad Henne/24 6.00 15.00
81 Ronnie Brown/99 4.00 10.00
82 Adrian Peterson/99 5.00 12.00
83 Percy Harvin/99 3.00 8.00
84 Sidney Rice/99 3.00 8.00
86 Visanthe Shiancoe/49 5.00 12.00
87 BenJarvus Green-Ellis/99 3.00 8.00
88 Danny Woodhead/99 10.00 25.00
90 Tom Brady/99 10.00 25.00
91 Wes Welker/99 4.00 10.00
92 Drew Brees/15 8.00 20.00
94 Marques Colston/99 3.00 8.00
95 Pierre Thomas/30 4.00 10.00
96 Reggie Bush/99 3.00 8.00
97 Ahmad Bradshaw/99 3.00 8.00
98 Eli Manning/99 4.00 10.00
99 Hakeem Nicks/99 3.00 8.00
101 Steve Smith USC/99 3.00 8.00
102 Braylon Edwards/99 3.00 8.00
103 LaDainian Tomlinson/55 6.00 15.00
104 Mark Sanchez/25 5.00 12.00
105 Santonio Holmes/99 3.00 8.00
106 Shonn Greene/20 5.00 12.00
107 Darren McFadden/99 3.00 8.00
108 Jacoby Ford/99 4.00 10.00
109 Louis Murphy/99 3.00 8.00
110 Zach Miller/99 3.00 8.00
111 DeSean Jackson/99 4.00 10.00
112 Jeremy Maclin/99 3.00 8.00
113 LeSean McCoy/65 5.00 12.00
114 Michael Vick/25 6.00 15.00
115 Ben Roethlisberger/99 8.00 20.00
116 Hines Ward/99 5.00 12.00
117 Mike Wallace/40 4.00 10.00
118 Rashard Mendenhall/99 3.00 8.00
119 Troy Polamalu/75 5.00 12.00
120 Antonio Gates/99 3.00 8.00
121 Malcom Floyd/45 4.00 10.00
123 Philip Rivers/99 5.00 12.00
124 Ryan Mathews/99 4.00 10.00
125 Frank Gore/99 4.00 10.00
126 Michael Crabtree/99 3.00 8.00
127 Patrick Willis/99 4.00 10.00
128 Vernon Davis/99 3.00 8.00
135 Sam Bradford/50 4.00 10.00
136 Steven Jackson/99 3.00 8.00
137 Cadillac Williams/70 3.00 8.00
138 Josh Freeman/70 4.00 10.00
139 Kellen Winslow Jr./99 3.00 8.00
142 Bo Scaife/99 3.00 8.00
143 Chris Johnson/99 3.00 8.00
144 Kenny Britt/99 3.00 8.00
145 Nate Washington/99 3.00 8.00
146 Randy Moss/99 4.00 10.00
147 Chris Cooley/99 5.00 12.00
148 Donovan McNabb/99 4.00 10.00
150 Santana Moss/99 4.00 10.00

2011 Panini Threads Rookie Autographs Combo

STATED PRINT RUN 15 SER.#'d SETS
1 C.Newton/K.Pilares 100.00 200.00
2 A.Green/A.Dalton 50.00 100.00
3 J.Locker/A.Ayers
4 B.Gabbert/C.Shorts 8.00 20.00
5 J.Jones/J.Rodgers 50.00 100.00
6 V.Miller/R.Moore 30.00 60.00
7 C.Ponder/K.Rudolph 40.00 80.00
8 M.Dareus/A.Williams
9 T.Smith/D.Murray 20.00 50.00
10 M.Ingram/M.Wilson

2011 Panini Threads Rookie Collection Materials

STATED PRINT RUN 299 SER.#'d SETS
*PRIME/50: .8X TO 2X BASIC JSY/299
1 A.J. Green 4.00 10.00
2 Alex Green 4.00 10.00
3 Andy Dalton 3.00 8.00
4 Austin Pettis 1.50 4.00
5 Bilal Powell 2.00 5.00
6 Blaine Gabbert 1.50 4.00
7 Cam Newton 8.00 20.00
8 Christian Ponder 1.50 4.00
9 Colin Kaepernick 2.50 6.00
10 Daniel Thomas 1.50 4.00
11 Delone Carter 1.50 4.00
12 DeMarco Murray 3.00 8.00
13 Greg Little 2.00 5.00
14 Jake Locker 1.50 4.00
15 Jamie Harper 1.50 4.00
16 Jerrel Jernigan 1.50 4.00
17 Jonathan Baldwin 1.50 4.00
18 Jordan Todman 1.50 4.00
19 Julio Jones 5.00 12.00
20 Kendall Hunter 1.50 4.00
21 Kyle Rudolph 1.50 4.00
22 Leonard Hankerson 1.50 4.00
23 Marcell Dareus 1.50 4.00
24 Mark Ingram 2.50 6.00
25 Mikel Leshoure 1.50 4.00
26 Randall Cobb 2.50 6.00
27 Ryan Mallett 1.50 4.00
28 Ryan Williams 1.50 4.00
29 Shane Vereen 2.00 5.00
30 Stevan Ridley 1.50 4.00
31 Taiwan Jones 1.50 4.00
32 Titus Young 1.50 4.00
33 Torrey Smith 1.50 4.00
34 Vincent Brown 1.50 4.00
35 Von Miller 2.50 6.00
36 Clyde Gates 1.50 4.00

2011 Panini Threads Rookie Collection Materials Autographs

STATED PRINT RUN 25 SER.#'d SETS
*PRIME AU/15: .6X TO 1.5X BASIC AU/25
1 A.J. Green 30.00 60.00
2 Alex Green 15.00 40.00
3 Andy Dalton 20.00 50.00
4 Austin Pettis 6.00 15.00
5 Bilal Powell 8.00 20.00
6 Blaine Gabbert 6.00 15.00
7 Cam Newton 100.00 200.00
8 Christian Ponder 6.00 15.00
9 Colin Kaepernick 10.00 25.00
10 Daniel Thomas 6.00 15.00
11 Delone Carter 6.00 15.00
12 DeMarco Murray
13 Greg Little 8.00 20.00
14 Jake Locker 6.00 15.00
15 Jamie Harper 6.00 15.00
16 Jerrel Jernigan 6.00 15.00
17 Jonathan Baldwin 6.00 15.00
18 Jordan Todman 6.00 15.00
19 Julio Jones 40.00 80.00
20 Kendall Hunter 6.00 15.00
21 Kyle Rudolph 6.00 15.00
22 Leonard Hankerson 6.00 15.00
23 Marcell Dareus 6.00 15.00
24 Mark Ingram 10.00 25.00
25 Mikel Leshoure 6.00 15.00
26 Randall Cobb 10.00 25.00
27 Ryan Mallett 6.00 15.00
28 Ryan Williams 6.00 15.00
29 Shane Vereen 8.00 20.00
30 Stevan Ridley 6.00 15.00
31 Taiwan Jones 6.00 15.00
32 Titus Young 6.00 15.00
33 Torrey Smith 6.00 15.00
34 Vincent Brown 6.00 15.00
35 Von Miller 15.00 40.00
36 Clyde Gates 6.00 15.00

2011 Panini Threads Rookie Collection Materials Combo

STATED PRINT RUN 299 SER.#'d SETS
*PRIME/50: .6X TO 1.5X BASIC JSY/299
1 C.Newton/M.Ingram 12.00 30.00
2 R.Cobb/A.Green 4.00 10.00
3 J.Todman/V.Brown 2.50 6.00
4 Leshoure/T.Young 2.50 6.00
5 R.Mallett/S.Vereen 3.00 8.00
6 C.Ponder/K.Rudolph 2.50 6.00
7 J.Locker/J.Harper 2.50 6.00
8 A.Green/A.Dalton 6.00 15.00
9 Kaepernick/K.Hunter 4.00 10.00
10 M.Ingram/J.Jones 8.00 20.00
11 C.Newton/J.Locker 12.00 30.00
12 M.Ingram/R.Williams 4.00 10.00
13 A.Green/J.Jones 10.00 25.00
14 C.Ponder/A.Dalton 5.00 12.00
15 V.Miller/M.Dareus 4.00 10.00

2011 Panini Threads Rookie Collection Materials Quad

STATED PRINT RUN 299 SER.#'d SETS
*PRIME/50: .8X TO 2X BASIC QUAD/299
1 Newton/Lockr/Gabbrt/Pondr 12.00 30.00
2 Ingram/Will/Vereen/Leshre 4.00 10.00
3 Green/Jones/Baldwn/Yng 8.00 20.00
4 Newton/Lockr/Green/Jnes 12.00 30.00
5 Newtn/Miller/Dareus/Green 12.00 30.00

2011 Panini Threads Star Factor

*HOLOFOIL/100: .6X TO 1.5X BASIC INSERTS
1 Arian Foster .75 2.00
2 Braylon Edwards .75 2.00
3 Chad Ochocinco .75 2.00
4 Clay Matthews 1.25 3.00
5 Danny Woodhead 1.00 2.50
6 Darren McFadden .75 2.00
7 DeSean Jackson 1.00 2.50
8 Dez Bryant 1.25 3.00
9 Dwayne Bowe 1.00 2.50
10 Felix Jones .75 2.00
11 Frank Gore 1.00 2.50
12 Greg Jennings .75 2.00
13 Jamaal Charles 1.00 2.50
14 Josh Freeman 1.00 2.50
15 Kenny Britt .75 2.00
16 Knowshon Moreno .75 2.00
17 LeSean McCoy 1.25 3.00
18 Michael Turner .75 2.00
19 Mike Wallace .75 2.00
20 Percy Harvin .75 2.00
21 Philip Rivers 1.25 3.00
22 Ray Rice .75 2.00
23 Sam Bradford .75 2.00
24 Tim Tebow 1.25 3.00
25 Tom Brady 3.00 8.00

2011 Panini Threads Star Factor Materials Prime

STATED PRINT RUN 25-99
1 Arian Foster/99 4.00 10.00
2 Braylon Edwards/99 4.00 10.00
3 Chad Ochocinco/99 4.00 10.00
4 Clay Matthews/90 8.00 20.00
5 Danny Woodhead/99 5.00 12.00
6 Darren McFadden/99 4.00 10.00
7 DeSean Jackson/99 5.00 12.00
8 Dez Bryant/90 8.00 20.00
9 Dwayne Bowe/99 5.00 12.00
10 Felix Jones/99 4.00 10.00
11 Frank Gore/99 5.00 12.00
13 Jamaal Charles/99 5.00 12.00
14 Josh Freeman/80 5.00 12.00
15 Kenny Britt/99 4.00 10.00
16 Knowshon Moreno/99 4.00 10.00
17 LeSean McCoy/99 6.00 15.00
18 Michael Turner/99 4.00 10.00
19 Mike Wallace/25 6.00 15.00
20 Percy Harvin/99 4.00 10.00
21 Philip Rivers/99 6.00 15.00
22 Ray Rice/99 4.00 10.00
23 Sam Bradford/99 4.00 10.00
24 Tim Tebow/25 10.00 25.00
25 Tom Brady/99 15.00 40.00

2011 Panini Threads Triple Threat

*HOLOFOIL/100: .6X TO 1.5X BASIC INSERTS
1 Lewis/Reed/Suggs 1.25 3.00
2 Cassel/Bowe/Charles 1.00 2.50
3 Orakpo/Landry/Fletcher 1.00 2.50
4 Vick/McCoy/D.Jacksn 1.25 3.00
5 Rivers/Gates/V.Jacksn 1.25 3.00
6 Bradford/S.Jcksn/Amend 1.00 2.50
7 Rodgers/Driver/Jennings 2.50 6.00
8 Ryan/Turner/R.White 1.00 2.50
9 Garrard/Jons-Drw/Thoms 1.00 2.50
10 Schaub/A.Jhnsn/Foster 1.00 2.50

2011 Panini Threads Triple Threat Materials

*PRIME/25: 1X TO 2.5X BASIC JSY/125-200
1 Lewis/Reed/Suggs/200 6.00 15.00
2 Cassel/Bowe/Charles/200 5.00 12.00
3 Orkp/Lndry/Fletcher/125 6.00 15.00
4 Vick/McCoy/D.Jacksn/200 6.00 15.00
5 Rivrs/Gats/V.Jacksn/200 6.00 15.00
7 Rodgrs/Drivr/Jenngs/75 25.00 50.00
8 Ryan/Turner/R.White/200 5.00 12.00
9 Garrd/Jns-Drw/Thoms/200 5.00 12.00
10 Schb/A.Jhnsn/Foster/200 5.00 12.00

2016 Panini Unparalleled

1 Drew Brees .40 1.00
2 Joe Namath .50 1.25
3 Cris Carter .40 1.00
4 Eli Manning .30 .75
5 Bradley Roby .25 .60
6 Jarvis Landry .30 .75
7 T.J. Yeldon .25 .60
8 Geno Smith .25 .60
9 Ricky Williams .30 .75
10 Edgerrin James .30 .75
11 Brandin Cooks .30 .75
12 DeMarcus Ware .30 .75
13 Warren Sapp .30 .75
14 Philip Rivers .40 1.00
15 Jaelen Strong .25 .60
16 Cameron Wake .25 .60
17 Kenny Stills .25 .60
18 Blake Bortles .25 .60
19 Joe Montana 1.00 2.50
20 Eric Ebron .25 .60
21 Brian Urlacher .40 1.00
22 Peyton Manning .75 2.00
23 Colin Kaepernick .30 .75
24 Roger Staubach .50 1.25
25 Jameis Winston .40 1.00
26 Chris Conley .25 .60
27 Emmitt Smith .60 1.50
28 Bob Griese .40 1.00
29 Teddy Bridgewater .30 .75
30 Rod Smith .30 .75
31 Bruce Smith .30 .75
32 Fred Taylor .25 .60
33 Manti Te'o .25 .60
34 Earl Campbell .40 1.00
35 Nelson Agholor .25 .60
36 Emmanuel Sanders .40 1.00
37 Jamison Crowder .25 .60
38 Anquan Boldin .25 .60
39 Curtis Martin .30 .75
40 Stefon Diggs .30 .75
41 Ben Roethlisberger .40 1.00
42 Vincent Jackson .25 .60
43 Kendall Wright .25 .60
44 Jim Kelly .40 1.00
45 Ahman Green .30 .75
46 Devin Funchess .25 .60
47 Jimmy Garoppolo .50 1.25
48 Matt Jones .30 .75
49 Marshall Faulk .30 .75
50 Dorial Green-Beckham .25 .60
51 Tony Romo .30 .75
52 Michael Floyd .25 .60
53 Shane Ray .25 .60
54 Dan Marino .75 2.00
55 Jeremy Langford .30 .75
56 Melvin Gordon .30 .75
57 Tyler Lockett .30 .75
58 Matthew Stafford .30 .75
59 Jerome Bettis .40 1.00
60 Antonio Brown .40 1.00
61 Russell Wilson .50 1.25
62 Brett Hundley .25 .60
63 Jerry Rice .60 1.50
64 A.J. McCarron .25 .60
65 Devin Smith .25 .60
66 Brett Favre .75 2.00
67 Derek Carr .40 1.00
68 Jay Ajayi .30 .75
69 Kevin White .25 .60
70 Kurt Warner .30 .75
71 Bryce Petty .25 .60
72 Austin Seferian-Jenkins .25 .60
73 Justin Hardy .25 .60
74 Davante Adams .25 .60
75 Willie Snead .30 .75
76 Barkevious Mingo .25 .60
77 Jordan Cameron .25 .60
78 John Elway .60 1.50
79 Jay Cutler .25 .60
80 Kelvin Benjamin .30 .75
81 John Riggins .30 .75
82 Karlos Williams .25 .60
83 Clinton Portis .25 .60
84 Amari Cooper .40 1.00
85 A.J. Green .40 1.00
86 David Johnson .40 1.00
87 Allen Robinson .30 .75
88 Ameer Abdullah .25 .60
89 Dez Bryant .40 1.00
90 Marcus Mariota .40 1.00
91 Andrew Luck .50 1.25
92 Todd Gurley .40 1.00
93 Rob Gronkowski .40 1.00
94 Odell Beckham Jr. .40 1.00
95 Khalil Mack .40 1.00
96 Joe Haden .25 .60
97 J.J. Watt .40 1.00
98 Barry Sanders .60 1.50
99 Tom Brady 1.00 2.50
100 Cam Newton .40 1.00
101 Troy Aikman .50 1.25
102 Larry Csonka .30 .75
103 Lawrence Taylor .40 1.00
104 Tim Brown .40 1.00
105 Marcus Allen .30 .75
106 Paul Warfield .30 .75
107 Michael Irvin .40 1.00
108 Kellen Winslow .30 .75
109 Antonio Freeman .30 .75
110 Champ Bailey .30 .75
111 Warrick Dunn .25 .60
112 Andre Rison .30 .75
113 Trent Dilfer .25 .60
114 Mark Chmura .25 .60
115 Andre Reed .30 .75
116 Bubba Franks .25 .60
117 Donald Driver .30 .75
118 Michael Strahan .30 .75
119 Aeneas Williams .25 .60
120 Jack Ham .30 .75
121 Aaron Rodgers .75 2.00
122 DeAngelo Williams .25 .60
123 Lance Briggs .30 .75
124 Adrian Peterson .40 1.00
125 Darren McFadden .25 .60
126 Matt Ryan .30 .75
127 Jordy Nelson .30 .75
128 Sam Bradford .25 .60
129 Victor Cruz .30 .75
130 Doug Williams .30 .75
131 Torrey Smith .25 .60
132 Richard Sherman .40 1.00
133 Case Keenum .30 .75
134 Lamar Miller .25 .60
135 Alshon Jeffery .30 .75
136 T.Y. Hilton .30 .75
137 Tyler Eifert .30 .75
138 Zach Ertz .30 .75
139 Charles Sims .25 .60
140 Devonta Freeman .30 .75
141 Marqise Lee .25 .60
142 Brandon Coleman .25 .60
143 Crockett Gillmore .25 .60
144 Kony Ealy .25 .60
145 David Cobb .25 .60
146 Rashad Greene .25 .60
147 Breshad Perriman .25 .60
148 Thomas Rawls .25 .60
149 Charcandrick West .25 .60
150 Latavius Murray .25 .60
151 Aaron Burbridge RC .60 1.50
152 Artie Burns RC .75 2.00
153 A'Shawn Robinson RC .60 1.50
154 Austin Hooper RC .60 1.50
155 Brandon Allen RC .60 1.50
156 Brandon Doughty RC .60 1.50
157 Charone Peake RC .60 1.50
158 Daniel Braverman RC .60 1.50
159 Daniel Lasco RC .60 1.50
160 Darron Lee RC .60 1.50
161 DeForest Buckner RC .60 1.50
162 Devin Lucien RC .75 2.00
163 Eli Apple RC .75 2.00
164 Germain Ifedi RC .75 2.00
165 Jack Conklin RC 1.00 2.50
166 Jalen Ramsey RC 1.00 2.50
167 James Bradberry RC .75 2.00
168 Jarran Reed RC .60 1.50
169 Jaylon Smith RC .60 1.50
170 Jeff Driskel RC .60 1.50
171 Joshua Garnett RC .60 1.50
172 Karl Joseph RC .60 1.50
173 Keanu Neal RC .60 1.50
174 Keith Marshall RC .60 1.50
175 Kelvin Taylor RC .60 1.50
176 Kendall Fuller RC .75 2.00
177 Kenny Clark RC .60 1.50
178 Kolby Listenbee RC .60 1.50
179 Leonard Floyd RC .75 2.00
180 Mackensie Alexander RC .60 1.50
181 Myles Jack RC .75 2.00
182 Nick Vannett RC .60 1.50
183 Noah Spence RC .60 1.50
184 Reggie Ragland RC .60 1.50
185 Robert Nkemdiche RC .75 2.00
186 Roberto Aguayo RC .60 1.50
187 Ronnie Stanley RC .75 2.00
188 Ryan Kelly RC 1.00 2.50
189 Sean Davis RC .60 1.50
190 Shaq Lawson RC .60 1.50
191 Sheldon Rankins RC .75 2.00
192 Su'a Cravens RC .60 1.50
193 T.J. Green RC 1.00 2.50
194 Tajae Sharpe RC .75 2.00
195 Taylor Decker RC .75 2.00
196 Tyler Higbee RC .60 1.50
197 Vernon Butler RC .60 1.50
198 Vernon Hargreaves III RC 1.00 2.50
199 Vonn Bell RC .75 2.00
200 William Jackson III RC .75 2.00
201 Jared Goff JSY AU/99 RC 50.00 100.00
202 Carson Wentz JSY AU/99 RC 60.00 125.00
203 Joey Bosa JSY AU/99 RC 8.00 20.00
204 Ezekiel Elliott JSY AU/99 RC EXCH 50.00 100.00
205 Corey Coleman JSY AU/99 RC 6.00 15.00
206 Will Fuller JSY AU/99 RC 6.00 15.00
207 Josh Doctson JSY AU/99 RC 5.00 12.00
208 Laquon Treadwell JSY AU/99 RC 25.00 50.00
209 Paxton Lynch JSY AU/99 RC 30.00 60.00
210 Hunter Henry JSY AU/199 RC 4.00 10.00
211 Sterling Shepard JSY AU/199 RC 12.00 30.00
212 Derrick Henry JSY AU/99 RC 40.00 80.00
213 Michael Thomas JSY AU/199 RC 6.00 15.00
214 Christian Hackenberg JSY AU/199 RC 8.00 20.00
215 Kenyan Drake JSY AU/199 RC 10.00 25.00
216 Braxton Miller JSY AU/199 RC 3.00 8.00
217 Leonte Carroo JSY AU/199 RC 3.00 8.00
218 C.J. Prosise JSY AU/199 RC 3.00 8.00
219 DeAndre Washington JSY AU/199 RC 3.00 8.00
220 Cody Kessler JSY AU/199 RC 3.00 8.00
221 Tyler Boyd JSY AU/199 RC 12.00 30.00
222 Connor Cook JSY AU/199 RC 4.00 10.00
223 Chris Moore JSY AU/199 RC 4.00 10.00
224 Ricardo Louis JSY AU/199 RC 3.00 8.00
225 Pharoh Cooper JSY AU/199 RC 3.00 8.00
226 Tyler Ervin JSY AU/199 RC 3.00 8.00
227 Demarcus Robinson JSY AU/199 RC 3.00 8.00
228 Kenneth Dixon JSY AU/199 RC 3.00 8.00
229 Dak Prescott JSY AU/199 RC UER 30.00 60.00
230 Devontae Booker JSY AU/199 RC 8.00 20.00
231 Cardale Jones JSY AU/199 RC 3.00 8.00
232 Paul Perkins JSY AU/199 RC 3.00 8.00
233 Jordan Howard JSY AU/199 RC 8.00 20.00
234 Wendell Smallwood JSY AU/199 RC 3.00 8.00
235 Jonathan Williams JSY AU/199 RC 4.00 10.00
236 Kevin Hogan JSY AU/199 RC 4.00 10.00
237 Trevor Davis JSY AU/199 RC 3.00 8.00
238 Alex Collins JSY AU/199 RC 4.00 10.00
239 Keenan Reynolds JSY AU/199 RC 4.00 10.00
240 Moritz Bohringer JSY AU/199 RC 6.00 15.00

2016 Panini Unparalleled Blue

*VETS/25: 3X TO 8X BASIC CARDS
*ROOKIES/25: 1.2X TO 3X BASIC CARDS

2016 Panini Unparalleled Orange

*VETS/99: 2X TO 5X BASIC CARDS
*ROOKIES/99: .8X TO 2X BASIC CARDS
*ROOK JSY AU/49: .6X TO 1.5X BASIC JSY AU/199
*ROOK JSY AU/49: .5X TO 1.2X BASIC JSY AU/99

2016 Panini Unparalleled Purple

*VETS(1-150): 1X TO 2.5X BASIC CARDS
*ROOK(151-200): .5X TO 1.2X BASIC CARDS

2016 Panini Unparalleled Red

*VETS: 2.5X TO 6X BASIC CARDS
*ROOKIES: 1X TO 2.5X BASIC CARDS
*ROOK JSY AU/25: .8X TO 2X BASIC JSY AU/199
*ROOK JSY AU/25: .6X TO 1.5X BASIC JSY AU/99

2016 Panini Unparalleled Teal

*VETS(1-150): 1.2X TO 3X BASIC CARDS
*ROOK(151-200): .6X TO 1.5X BASIC CARDS

2016 Panini Unparalleled All Pros

*ORANGE/99: .6X TO 1.5X BASIC INSERTS
*RED/49: 1X TO 2.5X BASIC INSERTS
*BLUE/25: 2X TO 5X BASIC INSERTS
1 Cam Newton 1.00 2.50
2 Adrian Peterson 1.00 2.50
3 Doug Martin .75 2.00
4 Josh Norman .60 1.50
5 Tyrann Mathieu .75 2.00
6 Eric Berry .75 2.00
7 Von Miller .75 2.00
8 Khalil Mack 1.00 2.50
9 J.J. Watt 1.00 2.50
10 Aaron Donald 1.00 2.50
11 Tyler Lockett .75 2.00
12 Stephen Gostkowski .75 2.00
13 Antonio Brown 1.00 2.50
14 Julio Jones 1.00 2.50
15 Rob Gronkowski 1.00 2.50
16 Thomas Davis .60 1.50
17 Patrick Peterson .60 1.50
18 Joe Thomas .60 1.50
19 Luke Kuechly .75 2.00
20 Navorro Bowman .75 2.00

2016 Panini Unparalleled Autographs Blue

3 Cris Carter/25 25.00 50.00
4 Eli Manning/25 40.00 80.00
5 Bradley Roby/49 5.00 12.00
7 T.J. Yeldon/49 5.00 12.00
8 Geno Smith/49 5.00 12.00
9 Ricky Williams/49 12.00 30.00
10 Edgerrin James/49 6.00 15.00
12 DeMarcus Ware/15
13 Warren Sapp/49 6.00 15.00
14 Philip Rivers/25 10.00 25.00
15 Jaelen Strong/99 4.00 10.00
17 Kenny Stills/99 4.00 10.00
18 Blake Bortles/49 10.00 25.00
20 Eric Ebron/99 4.00 10.00
21 Brian Urlacher/15
23 Colin Kaepernick/49 6.00 15.00
25 Jameis Winston/25 25.00 60.00
26 Chris Conley/99 4.00 10.00
28 Bob Griese/25 15.00 40.00
29 Teddy Bridgewater/49 15.00 40.00
30 Rod Smith/25 20.00 50.00
31 Bruce Smith/25 8.00 20.00
32 Fred Taylor/25 6.00 15.00
33 Manti Te'o/99 4.00 10.00
34 Earl Campbell/49 20.00 50.00
35 Nelson Agholor/99 4.00 10.00
36 Emmanuel Sanders/25 10.00 25.00
37 Jamison Crowder/99 4.00 10.00
38 Anquan Boldin/49 5.00 12.00
39 Curtis Martin/25 8.00 20.00
42 Vincent Jackson/49 5.00 12.00
44 Jim Kelly/25 12.00 30.00
46 Devin Funchess/25 6.00 15.00
47 Jimmy Garoppolo/99 30.00 60.00
48 Matt Jones/99 5.00 12.00
49 Marshall Faulk/25 15.00 40.00
50 Dorial Green-Beckham/99 4.00 10.00
52 Michael Floyd/99 4.00 10.00
56 Melvin Gordon/49 6.00 15.00
57 Tyler Lockett/99 5.00 12.00
58 Matthew Stafford/25 12.00 30.00
59 Jerome Bettis/25 30.00 60.00
61 Russell Wilson/15 40.00 80.00
62 Brett Hundley/49 5.00 12.00
64 A.J. McCarron/25 6.00 15.00
65 Devin Smith/99 4.00 10.00
67 Derek Carr/49 15.00 40.00
68 Jay Ajayi/99 5.00 12.00
69 Kevin White/49 5.00 12.00
70 Kurt Warner/25 25.00 50.00
71 Bryce Petty/99 4.00 10.00
72 Austin Seferian-Jenkins/25 6.00 15.00
73 Justin Hardy/99 4.00 10.00
74 Davante Adams/15 8.00 20.00
75 Willie Snead/25 8.00 20.00
76 Barkevious Mingo/49 5.00 12.00
77 Jordan Cameron/25 6.00 15.00
79 Jay Cutler/25 6.00 15.00
80 Kelvin Benjamin/49 6.00 15.00
82 Karlos Williams/25 6.00 15.00
83 Clinton Portis/25 6.00 15.00
101 Troy Aikman/25 30.00 60.00
102 Larry Csonka/49 25.00 50.00
103 Lawrence Taylor/49 25.00 60.00
104 Tim Brown/49 25.00 50.00
106 Paul Warfield/25 8.00 20.00
107 Michael Irvin/25 30.00 60.00
108 Kellen Winslow/15 10.00 25.00
109 Antonio Freeman/25 8.00 20.00
110 Champ Bailey/99 10.00 25.00
111 Warrick Dunn/49 12.00 30.00
112 Andre Rison/75 10.00 25.00
113 Trent Dilfer/25 12.00 30.00
114 Mark Chmura/49 5.00 12.00
115 Andre Reed/49 6.00 15.00
116 Bubba Franks/99 4.00 10.00
117 Donald Driver/49 15.00 40.00
118 Michael Strahan/25 25.00 50.00
119 Aeneas Williams/49 5.00 12.00
120 Jack Ham/49 15.00 40.00
122 DeAngelo Williams/49 15.00 40.00
123 Lance Briggs/99 5.00 12.00
125 Darren McFadden/49 5.00 12.00
127 Jordy Nelson/25 8.00 20.00
128 Sam Bradford/25 6.00 15.00
129 Victor Cruz/49 15.00 40.00
131 Torrey Smith/49 5.00 12.00
132 Richard Sherman/49 15.00 40.00
133 Case Keenum/99 5.00 12.00
134 Lamar Miller/15 8.00 20.00
137 Tyler Eifert/99 5.00 12.00
138 Zach Ertz/99 5.00 12.00
139 Charles Sims/99 4.00 10.00
140 Devonta Freeman/25 8.00 20.00
141 Marqise Lee/99 4.00 10.00
142 Brandon Coleman/99 4.00 10.00
143 Crockett Gillmore/99 4.00 10.00
144 Kony Ealy/99 4.00 10.00
145 David Cobb/99 4.00 10.00
146 Rashad Greene/99 4.00 10.00
147 Breshad Perriman/99 4.00 10.00
148 Thomas Rawls/99 4.00 10.00
149 Charcandrick West/99 4.00 10.00
150 Latavius Murray/99 4.00 10.00
151 Aaron Burbridge/199 3.00 8.00
153 A'Shawn Robinson/199 3.00 8.00
154 Austin Hooper/99 4.00 10.00
155 Brandon Allen/199 3.00 8.00
156 Brandon Doughty/199 3.00 8.00
157 Charone Peake/199 3.00 8.00
158 Daniel Braverman/199 3.00 8.00
159 Daniel Lasco/199 3.00 8.00
161 DeForest Buckner/199 3.00 8.00
163 Eli Apple/199 4.00 10.00
164 Germain Ifedi/199 4.00 10.00
165 Jack Conklin/199 5.00 12.00
166 Jalen Ramsey/199 5.00 12.00
169 Jaylon Smith/99 4.00 10.00
170 Jeff Driskel/199 3.00 8.00
172 Karl Joseph/199 3.00 8.00
173 Keanu Neal/199 3.00 8.00
174 Keith Marshall/199 3.00 8.00
175 Kelvin Taylor/199 3.00 8.00
176 Kendall Fuller/199 4.00 10.00
177 Kenny Clark/99 4.00 10.00
178 Kolby Listenbee/99 4.00 10.00
180 Mackensie Alexander/199 3.00 8.00
181 Myles Jack/199 4.00 10.00
182 Nick Vannett/199 3.00 8.00
184 Reggie Ragland/199 3.00 8.00
185 Robert Nkemdiche/99 5.00 12.00
187 Ronnie Stanley/199 4.00 10.00
188 Ryan Kelly/199 5.00 12.00
192 Su'a Cravens/199 3.00 8.00
193 T.J. Green/199 5.00 12.00
194 Tajae Sharpe/199 4.00 10.00
195 Taylor Decker/199 4.00 10.00
196 Tyler Higbee/99 4.00 10.00
197 Vernon Butler/199 3.00 8.00
198 Vernon Hargreaves III/199 5.00 12.00
199 Vonn Bell/199 4.00 10.00
200 William Jackson III/99 5.00 12.00

2016 Panini Unparalleled Draft Diamonds

1 Michael Strahan .75 2.00
2 Terrell Davis .75 2.00
3 Joe Montana 2.50 6.00
4 Tom Brady 2.50 6.00
5 Roger Staubach 1.25 3.00
6 Antonio Brown 1.00 2.50
7 Kam Chancellor 1.00 2.50
8 Brandon Marshall .60 1.50
9 Robert Mathis .60 1.50
10 Jason Witten .75 2.00
11 Shannon Sharpe 1.00 2.50
12 Richard Dent .60 1.50
13 Rob Gronkowski 1.00 2.50
14 Jack Lambert .60 1.50
15 Russell Wilson 1.25 3.00
16 Drew Brees 1.00 2.50
17 Dan Fouts .75 2.00
18 Andre Reed .75 2.00
19 Curtis Martin .75 2.00
20 Richard Sherman 1.00 2.50
21 Jamaal Charles .75 2.00
22 Stefon Diggs .75 2.00
23 Frank Gore .75 2.00
24 Kirk Cousins 1.00 2.50
25 Josh Norman .60 1.50

2016 Panini Unparalleled Dual Jerseys

4 Eli Manning/25 5.00 12.00
5 Bradley Roby/99 2.50 6.00
6 Jarvis Landry/99 3.00 8.00
7 T.J. Yeldon/99 2.50 6.00
8 Geno Smith/25 4.00 10.00
11 Brandin Cooks/99 3.00 8.00
12 DeMarcus Ware/49 4.00 10.00
14 Philip Rivers/25 6.00 15.00
15 Jaelen Strong/99 2.50 6.00
16 Cameron Wake/99 2.50 6.00
17 Kenny Stills/49 3.00 8.00
18 Blake Bortles/99 2.50 6.00
19 Joe Montana/25 15.00 40.00
20 Eric Ebron/99 2.50 6.00
21 Brian Urlacher/25 6.00 15.00
25 Jameis Winston/99 4.00 10.00
26 Chris Conley/99 2.50 6.00
29 Teddy Bridgewater/99 3.00 8.00
35 Nelson Agholor/99 2.50 6.00
36 Emmanuel Sanders/49 5.00 12.00
37 Jamison Crowder/99 2.50 6.00
38 Anquan Boldin/49 3.00 8.00
40 Stefon Diggs/99 3.00 8.00
43 Kendall Wright/25 4.00 10.00
46 Devin Funchess/99 2.50 6.00
47 Jimmy Garoppolo/99 8.00 20.00
48 Matt Jones/99 3.00 8.00
50 Dorial Green-Beckham/99 2.50 6.00
53 Shane Ray/99 2.50 6.00
55 Jeremy Langford/99 3.00 8.00
56 Melvin Gordon/99 3.00 8.00
57 Tyler Lockett/99 3.00 8.00
59 Jerome Bettis/25 6.00 15.00
60 Antonio Brown/25 6.00 15.00
61 Russell Wilson/25 8.00 20.00
62 Brett Hundley/99 2.50 6.00
65 Devin Smith/99 2.50 6.00
67 Derek Carr/99 4.00 10.00
68 Jay Ajayi/99 3.00 8.00
69 Kevin White/99 2.50 6.00
71 Bryce Petty/99 2.50 6.00
73 Justin Hardy/99 2.50 6.00
74 Davante Adams/99 2.50 6.00
75 Willie Snead/25 5.00 12.00
77 Jordan Cameron/99 2.50 6.00
80 Kelvin Benjamin/99 3.00 8.00
82 Karlos Williams/99 2.50 6.00
83 Clinton Portis/25 4.00 10.00
84 Amari Cooper/99 4.00 10.00
85 A.J. Green/49 5.00 12.00
87 Allen Robinson/99 3.00 8.00
88 Ameer Abdullah/99 2.50 6.00
89 Dez Bryant/25 6.00 15.00
90 Marcus Mariota/99 4.00 10.00
92 Todd Gurley/99 4.00 10.00
95 Khalil Mack/99 4.00 10.00
96 Joe Haden/99 2.50 6.00

2016 Panini Unparalleled High Flyers

*ORANGE/99: .6X TO 1.5X BASIC INSERTS
*RED/49: 1X TO 2.5X BASIC INSERTS
*BLUE/25: 2X TO 5X BASIC INSERTS
1 A.J. Green .60 1.50
2 Odell Beckham Jr. .60 1.50
3 Mike Evans .50 1.25
4 Sammy Watkins .60 1.50
5 DeAndre Hopkins .50 1.25
6 Amari Cooper .60 1.50
7 T.Y. Hilton .50 1.25
8 Julio Jones .60 1.50
9 Alshon Jeffery .50 1.25
10 Brandon Marshall .40 1.00
11 Antonio Brown .60 1.50
12 DeVante Parker .50 1.25
13 Allen Robinson .50 1.25
14 Stefon Diggs .50 1.25
15 Dez Bryant .60 1.50

2016 Panini Unparalleled In the Moment

*ORANGE/99: .6X TO 1.5X BASIC INSERTS
*RED/49: 1X TO 2.5X BASIC INSERTS
*BLUE/25: 2X TO 5X BASIC INSERTS
1 J.J. Watt 1.00 2.50
2 Rob Gronkowski 1.00 2.50
3 Andrew Luck 1.25 3.00
4 Derrick Johnson .60 1.50
5 Von Miller .75 2.00
6 Philip Rivers 1.00 2.50
7 Khalil Mack 1.00 2.50
8 Ndamukong Suh .75 2.00
9 Ben Roethlisberger 1.00 2.50
10 Andy Dalton .75 2.00
11 Steve Smith Sr. .75 2.00
12 Joe Haden .60 1.50
13 Richard Sherman 1.00 2.50
14 Todd Gurley 1.00 2.50
15 Jay Cutler .60 1.50
16 Julius Peppers .75 2.00
17 Kirk Cousins 1.00 2.50
18 Mark Ingram .75 2.00
19 Cam Newton 1.00 2.50
20 Travis Kelce 1.00 2.50
21 Jameis Winston 1.00 2.50
22 Carson Palmer .75 2.00
23 Brandon Marshall .60 1.50
24 Jason Witten .75 2.00
25 Devonta Freeman .75 2.00

2016 Panini Unparalleled Jerseys

1 Drew Brees/49 5.00 12.00
2 Joe Namath/25 8.00 20.00
3 Cris Carter/99 4.00 10.00
4 Eli Manning/99 3.00 8.00
5 Bradley Roby/199 2.00 5.00
6 Jarvis Landry/199 2.50 6.00
7 T.J. Yeldon/199 2.00 5.00
8 Geno Smith/99 2.50 6.00

11 Brandin Cooks/199 2.50 6.00
12 DeMarcus Ware/199 2.50 6.00
14 Philip Rivers/99 4.00 10.00
15 Jaelen Strong/199 2.00 5.00
16 Cameron Wake/199 2.00 5.00
17 Kenny Stills/199 2.00 5.00
18 Blake Bortles/199 2.00 5.00
19 Joe Montana/49 12.00 30.00
20 Eric Ebron/199 2.00 5.00
21 Brian Urlacher/99 4.00 10.00
22 Peyton Manning/49 10.00 25.00
23 Colin Kaepernick/49 4.00 10.00
24 Roger Staubach/49 6.00 15.00
25 Jameis Winston/199 3.00 8.00
26 Chris Conley/199 2.00 5.00
27 Emmitt Smith/25 10.00 25.00
28 Bob Griese/25 6.00 15.00
29 Teddy Bridgewater/199 2.50 6.00
31 Bruce Smith/199 2.50 6.00
33 Manti Te'o/99 2.50 6.00
34 Earl Campbell/99 4.00 10.00
35 Nelson Agholor/199 2.00 5.00
36 Emmanuel Sanders/199 3.00 8.00
37 Jamison Crowder/199 2.00 5.00
38 Anquan Boldin/99 2.50 6.00
39 Curtis Martin/25 5.00 12.00
40 Stefon Diggs/199 2.50 6.00
41 Ben Roethlisberger/49 5.00 12.00
42 Vincent Jackson/99 2.50 6.00
43 Kendall Wright/99 2.50 6.00
44 Jim Kelly/99 4.00 10.00
46 Devin Funchess/199 2.00 5.00
47 Jimmy Garoppolo/199 4.00 10.00
48 Matt Jones/199 2.50 6.00
49 Marshall Faulk/99 3.00 8.00
50 Dorial Green-Beckham/199 2.00 5.00
51 Tony Romo/99 3.00 8.00
52 Michael Floyd/199 2.00 5.00
53 Shane Ray/199 2.00 5.00
54 Dan Marino/99 8.00 20.00
55 Jeremy Langford/199 2.50 6.00
56 Melvin Gordon/199 2.50 6.00
57 Tyler Lockett/199 2.50 6.00
58 Matthew Stafford/99 3.00 8.00
59 Jerome Bettis/99 4.00 10.00
60 Antonio Brown/49 5.00 12.00
61 Russell Wilson/49 6.00 15.00
62 Brett Hundley/199 2.00 5.00
63 Jerry Rice/49 8.00 20.00
65 Devin Smith/199 2.00 5.00
66 Brett Favre/99 8.00 20.00
67 Derek Carr/199 3.00 8.00
68 Jay Ajayi/199 2.50 6.00
69 Kevin White/199 2.00 5.00
70 Kurt Warner/49 4.00 10.00
71 Bryce Petty/199 2.00 5.00
73 Justin Hardy/199 2.00 5.00
74 Davante Adams/199 2.00 5.00
75 Willie Snead/49 4.00 10.00
77 Jordan Cameron/199 2.00 5.00
78 John Elway/99 6.00 15.00
79 Jay Cutler/199 2.00 5.00
80 Kelvin Benjamin/199 2.50 6.00
81 John Riggins/99 3.00 8.00
82 Karlos Williams/199 2.00 5.00
83 Clinton Portis/49 3.00 8.00
84 Amari Cooper/199 3.00 8.00
85 A.J. Green/99 4.00 10.00
86 David Johnson/199 3.00 8.00
87 Allen Robinson/199 2.50 6.00
88 Ameer Abdullah/199 2.00 5.00
89 Dez Bryant/49 5.00 12.00
90 Marcus Mariota/199 3.00 8.00
91 Andrew Luck/49 6.00 15.00
92 Todd Gurley/199 3.00 8.00
93 Rob Gronkowski/25 6.00 15.00
94 Odell Beckham Jr./199 3.00 8.00
95 Khalil Mack/199 3.00 8.00
96 Joe Haden/199 2.00 5.00
97 J.J. Watt/49 5.00 12.00
98 Barry Sanders/49 8.00 20.00
99 Tom Brady/49 12.00 30.00
100 Cam Newton/49 5.00 12.00

2016 Panini Unparalleled Jumbo Jerseys

6 Jarvis Landry/25 6.00 15.00
7 T.J. Yeldon/25 5.00 12.00
15 Jaelen Strong/25 5.00 12.00
16 Cameron Wake/25 5.00 12.00
20 Eric Ebron/25 5.00 12.00
25 Jameis Winston/25 8.00 20.00
26 Chris Conley/25 5.00 12.00
29 Teddy Bridgewater/25 6.00 15.00
35 Nelson Agholor/25 5.00 12.00
37 Jamison Crowder/25 5.00 12.00
46 Devin Funchess/25 5.00 12.00
47 Jimmy Garoppolo/25 15.00 40.00
48 Matt Jones/25 6.00 15.00
50 Dorial Green-Beckham/25 5.00 12.00
53 Shane Ray/25 5.00 12.00
55 Jeremy Langford/25 6.00 15.00
56 Melvin Gordon/25 6.00 15.00
57 Tyler Lockett/25 6.00 15.00
62 Brett Hundley/25 5.00 12.00
65 Devin Smith/25 5.00 12.00
67 Derek Carr/25 8.00 20.00
68 Jay Ajayi/25 6.00 15.00
71 Bryce Petty/25 5.00 12.00
73 Justin Hardy/25 5.00 12.00
74 Davante Adams/25 5.00 12.00
77 Jordan Cameron/25 5.00 12.00
80 Kelvin Benjamin/25 6.00 15.00
82 Karlos Williams/25 5.00 12.00
87 Allen Robinson/25 6.00 15.00
88 Ameer Abdullah/25 5.00 12.00
90 Marcus Mariota/25 8.00 20.00
92 Todd Gurley/25 8.00 20.00
95 Khalil Mack/25 8.00 20.00
96 Joe Haden/25 5.00 12.00

2016 Panini Unparalleled Perfect Pairs

*ORANGE/99: .6X TO 1.5X BASIC INSERTS
*RED/49: 1X TO 2.5X BASIC INSERTS
*BLUE/25: 2X TO 5X BASIC INSERTS
1 P.Peterson/T.Mathieu .75 2.00
2 E.Thomas/K.Chancellor 1.00 2.50
3 C.Newton/T.Ginn Jr. 1.00 2.50
4 M.Ryan/J.Jones 1.00 2.50
5 S.Diggs/T.Bridgewater .75 2.00
6 M.Evans/J.Winston 1.00 2.50
7 E.Manning/O.Beckham Jr. 1.00 2.50
8 A.Hurns/A.Robinson .75 2.00
9 D.Ware/V.Miller .75 2.00
10 G.Bernard/J.Hill .60 1.50
11 A.Brown/B.Roethlisberger 1.00 2.50
12 A.Cooper/D.Carr 1.00 2.50
13 T.Brady/R.Gronkowski 2.50 6.00
14 J.Landry/R.Tannehill .75 2.00
15 K.Williams/L.McCoy 1.00 2.50
16 B.Marshall/E.Decker .60 1.50
17 A.Luck/T.Hilton 1.25 3.00
18 J.Watt/J.Clowney 1.00 2.50

2016 Panini Unparalleled Pivotal Drive

*ORANGE/99: .6X TO 1.5X BASIC INSERTS
*RED/49: 1X TO 2.5X BASIC INSERTS
*BLUE/25: 2X TO 5X BASIC INSERTS
1 Plmr/Jhnsn/Ftzgrld 1.00 2.50
2 Frmn/Jns/Ryn 1.00 2.50
3 Flcco/Frstt/Akn .75 2.00
4 Hrvn/Tylr/McCy 1.00 2.50
5 Nwtn/Olsn/Stwrt 1.00 2.50
6 Ctlr/Lngfrd/Mllr .75 2.00
7 Grfi/Dlth/Bmrd 1.00 2.50
8 Jhnsn/Brndge/McCwn .60 1.50
9 McFddn/Wttn/Rmo .75 2.00
10 Sndrs/Thms/Mnng 2.00 5.00
11 Stffrd/Tte/Mre .75 2.00
12 Jns/Rdgrs/Rdgrs 2.00 5.00
13 Hpkns/Ble/Shrts .75 2.00
14 Mncrf/Hltn/Lck 1.25 3.00
15 Hrns/Rbnsn/Brtls .75 2.00
16 Smth/Wst/Klce 1.00 2.50
17 Lndry/Cmrn/Tnnhll .75 2.00
18 Dggs/Brdgwtr/Ptrsn 1.00 2.50
19 Edlmn/Grnkwski/Brdy 2.50 6.00
20 Cks/Brs/Spllr 1.00 2.50
21 Mnng/Bckhm/Jnngs 1.00 2.50
22 Mrshll/Ftzptrck/Dckr .60 1.50
23 Mrry/Cpr/Crr 1.00 2.50
24 Sprls/Brdfrd/Mtthws .75 2.00
25 Brwn/Rthlsbrgr/Wllms 1.00 2.50
26 Wdhd/Alln/Rvrs 1.00 2.50
27 Bldn/Hyde/Kprnck .75 2.00
28 Grhm/Bldwn/Wlsn 1.25 3.00
29 Knm/Grly/Astn 1.00 2.50
30 Mrtn/Evns/Wnstn 1.00 2.50
31 GrnBckhm/Mrta/Fsno 1.00 2.50
32 Rd/Csns/Jns 1.00 2.50
33 Grn/Fvre/Frmn 2.00 5.00
34 Thms/Lftn/Klly 1.00 2.50
35 Hrrs/Fqua/Brdshw 1.25 3.00
36 Vntri/Brnch/Brdy 2.50 6.00
37 Clrk/Hrrsn/Mnng 2.00 5.00
38 Mntna/Rce/Crg 2.50 6.00
39 Irvn/Smth/Akmn 1.50 4.00
40 Elwy/Smth/Dvs 1.50 4.00

2016 Panini Unparalleled Rookie Dual Memorabilia

1 C.Wentz/J.Goff 10.00 25.00
2 D.Henry/K.Drake 4.00 10.00
3 B.Miller/C.Jones 1.50 4.00
4 P.Perkins/S.Shepard 2.00 5.00
5 C.Coleman/J.Doctson 2.50 6.00
6 D.Booker/P.Lynch 2.00 5.00
7 E.Elliott/D.Prescott 15.00 40.00
8 C.Hackenberg/C.Kessler 1.50 4.00
9 M.Bohringer/L.Treadwell 2.00 5.00
10 A.Collins/C.Prosise 2.00 5.00
11 C.Cook/K.Hogan 2.00 5.00
12 J.Bosa/M.Thomas 3.00 8.00
13 K.Reynolds/K.Dixon 2.00 5.00
14 C.Cook/D.Washington 2.00 5.00
15 T.Ervin/W.Fuller 2.50 6.00
16 R.Louis/C.Kessler 1.50 4.00
17 L.Carroo/T.Boyd 2.00 5.00
18 J.Howard/W.Smallwood 4.00 10.00
19 A.Collins/H.Henry 2.00 5.00
20 J.Goff/P.Cooper 6.00 15.00

2016 Panini Unparalleled Rookie Jerseys

1 Jared Goff 10.00 25.00
2 Carson Wentz 6.00 15.00
3 Joey Bosa 3.00 8.00
4 Ezekiel Elliott 8.00 20.00
5 Corey Coleman 2.50 6.00
6 Will Fuller 2.50 6.00
7 Josh Doctson 2.00 5.00
8 Laquon Treadwell 2.00 5.00
9 Paxton Lynch 6.00 15.00
10 Hunter Henry 2.00 5.00
11 Sterling Shepard 2.00 5.00
12 Derrick Henry 6.00 15.00
13 Michael Thomas 3.00 8.00
14 Christian Hackenberg 1.50 4.00
15 Kenyan Drake 2.50 6.00
16 Braxton Miller 1.50 4.00
17 Leonte Carroo 1.50 4.00
18 C.J. Prosise 1.50 4.00
19 DeAndre Washington 1.50 4.00
20 Cody Kessler 1.50 4.00
21 Tyler Boyd 2.00 5.00
22 Connor Cook 2.00 5.00
23 Chris Moore 2.00 5.00
24 Ricardo Louis 1.50 4.00
25 Pharoh Cooper 1.50 4.00
26 Tyler Ervin 1.50 4.00
27 Demarcus Robinson 1.50 4.00
28 Kenneth Dixon 1.50 4.00
29 Dak Prescott 8.00 20.00
30 Devontae Booker 2.00 5.00
31 Cardale Jones 1.50 4.00
32 Paul Perkins 1.50 4.00
33 Jordan Howard 4.00 10.00
34 Wendell Smallwood 1.50 4.00
35 Jonathan Williams 2.00 5.00
36 Kevin Hogan 2.00 5.00
37 Trevor Davis 1.50 4.00
38 Alex Collins 2.00 5.00
39 Keenan Reynolds 2.00 5.00
40 Moritz Bohringer 1.50 4.00

2016 Panini Unparalleled Rookie Jerseys Dual

1 Jared Goff 10.00 25.00
2 Carson Wentz 6.00 15.00
3 Joey Bosa 3.00 8.00
4 Ezekiel Elliott 8.00 20.00
5 Corey Coleman 2.50 6.00
6 Will Fuller 2.50 6.00
7 Josh Doctson 2.00 5.00
8 Laquon Treadwell 2.00 5.00
9 Paxton Lynch 6.00 15.00
10 Hunter Henry 2.00 5.00
11 Sterling Shepard 2.00 5.00
12 Derrick Henry 8.00 20.00
13 Michael Thomas 3.00 8.00
14 Christian Hackenberg 1.50 4.00
15 Kenyan Drake 2.50 6.00
16 Braxton Miller 1.50 4.00
17 Leonte Carroo 1.50 4.00
18 C.J. Prosise 1.50 4.00
19 DeAndre Washington 1.50 4.00
20 Cody Kessler 1.50 4.00
21 Tyler Boyd 2.00 5.00
22 Connor Cook 2.00 5.00
23 Chris Moore 2.00 5.00
25 Ricardo Louis 1.50 4.00
26 Pharoh Cooper 1.50 4.00
27 Tyler Ervin 1.50 4.00
28 Demarcus Robinson 1.50 4.00
29 Kenneth Dixon 1.50 4.00
30 Dak Prescott 12.00 30.00
31 Devontae Booker 2.00 5.00
32 Cardale Jones 1.50 4.00
33 Paul Perkins 1.50 4.00
34 Jordan Howard 4.00 10.00
35 Wendell Smallwood 1.50 4.00
36 Jonathan Williams 2.00 5.00
37 Kevin Hogan 2.00 5.00
38 Trevor Davis 1.50 4.00
39 Alex Collins 2.00 5.00
40 Keenan Reynolds 2.00 5.00
41 Moritz Bohringer 1.50 4.00

2016 Panini Unparalleled Rookie Jerseys Triple

1 Jared Goff 12.00 30.00
2 Carson Wentz
3 Joey Bosa 8.00 20.00
4 Ezekiel Elliott 20.00 50.00
5 Corey Coleman 6.00 15.00
6 Will Fuller 6.00 15.00
7 Josh Doctson 5.00 12.00
8 Laquon Treadwell 5.00 12.00
9 Paxton Lynch 15.00 40.00
10 Hunter Henry 5.00 12.00
11 Sterling Shepard 5.00 12.00
12 Derrick Henry 15.00 40.00
13 Michael Thomas 8.00 20.00
14 Christian Hackenberg 4.00 10.00
15 Kenyan Drake 6.00 15.00
16 Braxton Miller 4.00 10.00
17 Leonte Carroo 4.00 10.00
18 C.J. Prosise 4.00 10.00
19 DeAndre Washington 4.00 10.00
20 Cody Kessler 4.00 10.00
21 Tyler Boyd 5.00 12.00
22 Connor Cook 5.00 12.00
23 Chris Moore 5.00 12.00
25 Ricardo Louis 4.00 10.00
26 Pharoh Cooper 4.00 10.00
27 Tyler Ervin 4.00 10.00
28 Demarcus Robinson 4.00 10.00
29 Kenneth Dixon 4.00 10.00
30 Dak Prescott 20.00 50.00
31 Devontae Booker 5.00 12.00
32 Cardale Jones 4.00 10.00
33 Paul Perkins 4.00 10.00
34 Jordan Howard 10.00 25.00
35 Wendell Smallwood 4.00 10.00
36 Jonathan Williams 5.00 12.00
37 Kevin Hogan 5.00 12.00
38 Trevor Davis 4.00 10.00
39 Alex Collins 5.00 12.00
40 Keenan Reynolds 5.00 12.00
41 Moritz Bohringer 4.00 10.00

2016 Panini Unparalleled Triple Jerseys

5 Bradley Roby/49 4.00 10.00
6 Jarvis Landry/49 5.00 12.00
7 T.J. Yeldon/49 4.00 10.00
11 Brandin Cooks/49 5.00 12.00
12 DeMarcus Ware/25 6.00 15.00
15 Jaelen Strong/49 4.00 10.00
16 Cameron Wake/49 4.00 10.00
18 Blake Bortles/49 4.00 10.00
20 Eric Ebron/49 4.00 10.00
25 Jameis Winston/49 6.00 15.00
26 Chris Conley/49 4.00 10.00
29 Teddy Bridgewater/49 5.00 12.00
35 Nelson Agholor/49 4.00 10.00
36 Emmanuel Sanders/25 8.00 20.00
37 Jamison Crowder/49 4.00 10.00
38 Anquan Boldin/25 5.00 12.00
40 Stefon Diggs/49 5.00 12.00
45 Ahman Green/25 6.00 15.00
46 Devin Funchess/49 4.00 10.00
47 Jimmy Garoppolo/49 8.00 20.00
48 Matt Jones/49 5.00 12.00
50 Dorial Green-Beckham/49 4.00 10.00
53 Shane Ray/49 4.00 10.00
55 Jeremy Langford/49 5.00 12.00
56 Melvin Gordon/49 5.00 12.00
57 Tyler Lockett/49 5.00 12.00
62 Brett Hundley/49 4.00 10.00
65 Devin Smith/49 4.00 10.00
67 Derek Carr/49 6.00 15.00
68 Jay Ajayi/49 5.00 12.00
69 Kevin White/49 4.00 10.00
71 Bryce Petty/49 4.00 10.00
73 Justin Hardy/49 4.00 10.00
74 Davante Adams/49 4.00 10.00
77 Jordan Cameron/49 4.00 10.00
80 Kelvin Benjamin/49 5.00 12.00
82 Karlos Williams/49 4.00 10.00
84 Amari Cooper/49 6.00 15.00
85 A.J. Green/25 8.00 20.00
87 Allen Robinson/49 5.00 12.00
88 Ameer Abdullah/49 4.00 10.00
90 Marcus Mariota/49 6.00 15.00
92 Todd Gurley/49 6.00 15.00
95 Khalil Mack/49 6.00 15.00
96 Joe Haden/49 4.00 10.00

2016 Panini Unparalleled World Class Records

*ORANGE/99: .6X TO 1.5X BASIC INSERTS
*RED/49: 1X TO 2.5X BASIC INSERTS
*BLUE/25: 2X TO 5X BASIC INSERTS
1 Peyton Manning 2.00 5.00
2 Emmitt Smith 1.50 4.00
3 Jerry Rice 1.50 4.00
4 Brett Favre 2.00 5.00
5 Tom Brady 2.50 6.00
6 Bruce Smith .75 2.00
7 Devin Hester .75 2.00
8 Adrian Peterson 1.00 2.50
9 Drew Brees 1.00 2.50
10 Julio Jones 1.00 2.50

2016 Panini Unparalleled Zoned In

*ORANGE/99: .6X TO 1.5X BASIC INSERTS
*RED/49: 1X TO 2.5X BASIC INSERTS
*BLUE/25: 2X TO 5X BASIC INSERTS
1 J.J. Watt 1.00 2.50
2 Carlos Hyde .60 1.50
3 Larry Fitzgerald .75 2.00
4 Matt Jones .75 2.00
5 Devonta Freeman .75 2.00
6 A.J. Green 1.00 2.50
7 Philip Rivers 1.00 2.50
8 Allen Hurns .60 1.50
9 Eli Manning .75 2.00
10 Cameron Wake .60 1.50
11 DeAndre Hopkins .75 2.00
12 Todd Gurley 1.00 2.50
13 Khalil Mack 1.00 2.50
14 Tom Brady 2.50 6.00
15 Drew Brees 1.00 2.50
16 Sammy Watkins 1.00 2.50
17 Antonio Brown 1.00 2.50
18 Jeremy Langford .75 2.00
19 Adrian Peterson 1.00 2.50
20 Thomas Rawls .60 1.50
21 Derek Carr 1.00 2.50
22 Justin Houston .60 1.50
23 Marcus Mariota 1.00 2.50
24 Allen Robinson .75 2.00
25 Tyler Lockett .75 2.00
26 Odell Beckham Jr. 1.00 2.50
27 David Johnson 1.00 2.50
28 Aaron Donald 1.00 2.50
29 Jordan Reed .60 1.50
30 Doug Baldwin .75 2.00
31 Demaryius Thomas .75 2.00
32 Luke Kuechly .75 2.00

2017 Panini Unparalleled

1 Tom Brady 1.00 2.50
2 Rob Gronkowski .40 1.00
3 Julian Edelman .40 1.00
4 Brandin Cooks .30 .75
5 Joe Thuney .30 .75
6 David Andrews RC .25 .60
7 Ryan Tannehill .30 .75
8 Jay Ajayi .30 .75
9 Jarvis Landry .30 .75
10 Reshad Jones .25 .60
11 Jermon Bushrod RC .25 .60
12 Michael Thomas .40 1.00
13 Tyrod Taylor .30 .75
14 LeSean McCoy .40 1.00
15 Sammy Watkins .40 1.00
16 Shaq Lawson .25 .60
17 Richie Incognito .25 .60
18 Patrick DiMarco RC .30 .75
19 Sheldon Richardson .25 .60
20 Darron Lee .25 .60
21 Matt Forte .25 .60
22 Muhammad Wilkerson .25 .60
23 Wesley Johnson RC .25 .60
24 Brian Winters RC .25 .60
25 Ben Roethlisberger .40 1.00
26 Antonio Brown .40 1.00
27 Lo'Von Bell .30 .75
28 James Harrison .30 .75
29 Ross Cockrell .25 .60
30 Ramon Foster .25 .60
31 Mike Wallace .25 .60
32 Joe Flacco .30 .75
33 Terrell Suggs .25 .60
34 Justin Tucker .25 .60
35 Albert McClellan RC .25 .60
36 Brandon Williams RC .25 .60
37 Andy Dalton .30 .75
38 A.J. Green .40 1.00
39 Jeremy Hill .25 .60
40 Vontaze Burfict .25 .60
41 Russell Bodine RC .25 .60
42 Clint Boling RC .25 .60
43 Isaiah Crowell .25 .60
44 Corey Coleman .25 .60
45 Gary Barnidge .25 .60
46 Jamie Collins .25 .60
47 Ibraheim Campbell RC .30 .75
48 Jamie Meder RC .25 .60
49 J.J. Watt .40 1.00
50 Jadeveon Clowney .25 .60
51 DeAndre Hopkins .30 .75
52 Lamar Miller .25 .60
53 Greg Mancz RC .25 .60
54 Andre Hal RC .30 .75
55 Marcus Mariota .40 1.00
56 Derrick Henry .30 .75
57 DeMarco Murray .30 .75
58 Delanie Walker .25 .60
59 Quinton Spain RC .25 .60
60 DaQuan Jones .25 .60
61 Andrew Luck .50 1.25
62 T.Y. Hilton .30 .75
63 Jack Doyle .25 .60
64 Frank Gore .30 .75
65 David Parry RC .25 .60
66 Joe Haeg .25 .60
67 Allen Robinson .30 .75
68 Jalen Ramsey .25 .60
69 Myles Jack .25 .60
70 Blake Bortles .25 .60
71 A.J. Bouye RC .25 .60
72 Malik Jackson RC .25 .60
73 Eric Berry .30 .75
74 Alex Smith .30 .75
75 Travis Kelce .40 1.00
76 Derrick Johnson .25 .60
77 Cairo Santos RC .25 .60
78 Daniel Sorensen RC .25 .60
79 Derek Carr .40 1.00
80 Khalil Mack .40 1.00
81 Amari Cooper .40 1.00
82 Marshawn Lynch .30 .75
83 Donald Penn RC .25 .60
84 Jamize Olawale RC .30 .75
85 Von Miller .30 .75
86 Demaryius Thomas .30 .75
87 Emmanuel Sanders .40 1.00
88 Derek Wolfe .25 .60
89 Matt Paradis RC .30 .75
90 Darian Stewart RC .40 1.00
91 Philip Rivers .40 1.00
92 Melvin Gordon .30 .75
93 Hunter Henry .25 .60
94 Keenan Allen .30 .75
95 Joe Barksdale RC .25 .60
96 Josh Lambo RC .25 .60
97 Dak Prescott .40 1.00
98 Ezekiel Elliott .50 1.25
99 Jason Witten .30 .75
100 Dez Bryant .40 1.00
101 Anthony Brown RC .40 1.00
102 David Irving RC .40 1.00
103 Eli Manning .30 .75
104 Odell Beckham Jr. .40 1.00
105 Brandon Marshall .25 .60
106 Landon Collins .25 .60
107 Damon Harrison RC .25 .60
108 Bobby Hart RC .25 .60
109 Kirk Cousins .40 1.00
110 Terrelle Pryor Sr. .25 .60
111 Robert Kelley .25 .60
112 Junior Galette RC .25 .60
113 Spencer Long RC .25 .60
114 Will Compton RC .25 .60
115 Carson Wentz .50 1.25
116 Alshon Jeffery .30 .75
117 Zach Ertz .30 .75
118 Fletcher Cox .25 .60
119 Rodney McLeod RC .30 .75
120 Jason Kelce RC .25 .60
121 Aaron Rodgers .75 2.00
122 Jordy Nelson .30 .75
123 Clay Matthews .30 .75
124 Blake Martinez .25 .60
125 Geronimo Allison .30 .75
126 David Bakhtiari RC .30 .75
127 Matthew Stafford .30 .75
128 Golden Tate III .25 .60
129 Ameer Abdullah .25 .60
130 Ezekiel Ansah .25 .60
131 Kerry Hyder .25 .60
132 Larry Warford RC .25 .60
133 Sam Bradford .25 .60
134 Stefon Diggs .30 .75
135 Harrison Smith .25 .60
136 Danielle Hunter .25 .60
137 Andrew Sendejo RC .30 .75
138 Joe Berger RC .25 .60
139 Kai Forbath RC .25 .60
140 Jordan Howard .40 1.00
141 Kevin White .25 .60
142 Leonard Floyd .25 .60
143 Mike Glennon .30 .75
144 Akiem Hicks RC 6.00 15.00
145 Daniel Brown RC .25 .60
146 Matt Ryan .30 .75
147 Julio Jones .40 1.00
148 Devonta Freeman .30 .75
149 Tevin Coleman .30 .75
150 Chris Chester RC .25 .60
151 Brian Poole RC .30 .75
152 Ricardo Allen RC .40 1.00
153 Jameis Winston .30 .75
154 Mike Evans .30 .75
155 DeSean Jackson .30 .75
156 Cameron Brate .25 .60
157 Donovan Smith RC .25 .60
158 Ali Marpet .25 .60
159 Drew Brees .40 1.00
160 Michael Thomas .40 1.00
161 Mark Ingram .30 .75
162 John Kuhn .25 .60
163 Wil Lutz RC .25 .60
164 Craig Robertson RC .25 .60
165 Cam Newton .40 1.00
166 Greg Olsen .30 .75
167 Luke Kuechly .30 .75
168 Julius Peppers .30 .75
169 Kurt Coleman .30 .75
170 Trai Turner RC .25 .60
171 Russell Wilson .50 1.25
172 Eddie Lacy .25 .60
173 Richard Sherman .40 1.00
174 Bobby Wagner .25 .60
175 Jeremy Lane RC .40 1.00
176 Kasen Williams RC .30 .75
177 Will Tukuafu RC .40 1.00
178 Carson Palmer .30 .75
179 Larry Fitzgerald .30 .75
180 David Johnson .40 1.00
181 Tyrann Mathieu .30 .75
182 Chandler Jones .25 .60
183 Jared Veldheer RC .25 .60
184 Justin Bethel RC .30 .75
185 Jared Goff .40 1.00
186 Todd Gurley II .40 1.00
187 Tavon Austin .25 .60
188 Aaron Donald .40 1.00
189 Cody Davis RC .25 .60
190 Jake McQuaide RC .25 .60
191 Carlos Hyde .25 .60
192 Navorro Bowman .30 .75
193 Kyle Juszczyk .25 .60
194 Joe Staley .25 .60
195 Jeremy Zuttah RC .25 .60
196 Trenton Brown RC .25 .60
197 Ben Jones RC .25 .60
198 Kelvin Beachum Jr. RC .25 .60
199 Aaron Ripkowski RC .40 1.00
200 Christian Kirksey RC .25 .60
201 Chad Kelly RC .60 1.50
202 Brad Kaaya RC .60 1.50
203 Brian Hill RC .60 1.50
204 Matthew Dayes RC .60 1.50
205 Elijah Hood RC .60 1.50
206 Donnel Pumphrey RC .75 2.00
207 Tarik Cohen RC 1.25 3.00
208 Dalvin Tomlinson RC .60 1.50
209 Haason Reddick RC .60 1.50
210 De'Veon Smith RC 1.50 4.00
211 Jake Butt RC .75 2.00
212 Bucky Hodges RC .60 1.50
213 Jordan Leggett RC .60 1.50
214 Obi Melifonwu RC .60 1.50
215 Adam Shaheen RC .60 1.50
216 Malachi Dupre RC .60 1.50
217 Ryan Switzer RC .75 2.00
218 Shelton Gibson RC .60 1.50
219 Stacy Coley RC .60 1.50
220 Gerald Everett RC .60 1.50
221 Isaiah Ford RC .60 1.50
222 Josh Malone RC .60 1.50
223 Chad Hansen RC .60 1.50
224 Marlon Humphrey RC .60 1.50
225 Marshon Lattimore RC .75 2.00
226 Quincy Wilson RC .60 1.50
227 Teez Tabor RC .75 2.00
228 Adoree' Jackson RC .75 2.00
229 Sidney Jones RC .60 1.50
230 Desmond King RC .75 2.00
231 Jourdan Lewis RC .60 1.50
232 Cordrea Tankersley RC .75 2.00
233 Tre'Davious White RC .60 1.50
234 Cameron Sutton RC .60 1.50
235 Gareon Conley RC .60 1.50
236 Jonathan Allen RC .75 2.00
237 Myles Garrett RC 2.00 5.00
238 Derek Barnett RC .75 2.00
239 Carl Lawson RC .60 1.50
240 Charles Harris RC .60 1.50
241 Taco Charlton RC .60 1.50
242 Jordan Willis RC .60 1.50
243 DeMarcus Walker RC .60 1.50
244 Solomon Thomas RC .60 1.50
245 Malik McDowell RC .60 1.50
246 Elijah Qualls RC .60 1.50
247 Caleb Brantley RC .60 1.50
248 Reuben Foster RC .60 1.50
249 Raekwon McMillan RC .60 1.50
250 Zach Cunningham RC .75 2.00
251 Jarrad Davis RC .75 2.00
252 Jabrill Peppers RC 1.00 2.50
253 Tim Williams RC .75 2.00
254 Jerod Evans RC .75 2.00
255 T.J. Watt RC 2.00 5.00
256 Chad Williams RC .60 1.50
257 Jamal Adams RC .60 1.50
258 Malik Hooker RC .60 1.50
259 T.J. Logan RC 1.00 2.50
260 Greg Ward Jr. RC .60 1.50
261 Cooper Rush RC .75 2.00
262 Elijah McGuire RC .60 1.50
263 Aaron Jones RC 1.50 4.00
264 Fabian Moreau RC .60 1.50
265 Rasul Douglas RC .75 2.00
266 Deatrich Wise Jr. RC 1.00 2.50
267 Chidobe Awuzie RC .75 2.00
268 Kevin King RC .75 2.00
269 Marquez White RC .60 1.50
270 Dawuane Smoot RC .60 1.50
271 Daeshon Hall RC .60 1.50
272 Tanoh Kpassagnon RC .75 2.00
273 Chris Wormley RC .60 1.50
274 Carlos Watkins RC .60 1.50
275 Montravius Adams RC .75 2.00
276 Jaleel Johnson RC 1.25 3.00
277 Ryan Glasgow RC .60 1.50
278 Kendell Beckwith RC .60 1.50
279 Anthony Walker Jr. RC .60 1.50
280 Ryan Anderson RC .60 1.50
281 Tyus Bowser RC .60 1.50
282 Duke Riley RC .60 1.50
283 Josh Jones RC .60 1.50
284 Marcus Williams RC .60 1.50
285 Budda Baker RC .60 1.50
286 Marcus Maye RC .60 1.50
287 Justin Evans RC .60 1.50
288 Eddie Jackson RC .75 2.00
289 Eddie Vanderdoes RC .60 1.50
290 Jeremy Sprinkle RC .60 1.50
291 Noah Brown RC .75 2.00
292 Jehu Chesson RC .75 2.00
293 Derek Rivers RC .75 2.00
294 Trent Taylor RC .75 2.00
295 DeAngelo Yancey RC .60 1.50
296 De'Angelo Henderson RC .60 1.50
297 Chris Carson RC 1.00 2.50
298 Nazair Jones RC .60 1.50
299 Jonnu Smith RC .60 1.50
300 David Njoku RC .75 2.00
301 Deshaun Watson JSY AU/99 RC 50.00 100.00
302 Mitchell Trubisky JSY AU/99 RC 50.00 100.00
303 DeShone Kizer JSY AU/99 RC 4.00 10.00
304 Patrick Mahomes II JSY AU/99 RC 200.00 400.00
305 C.J. Beathard JSY AU/199 RC 3.00 8.00
306 R. Joshua Dobbs JSY AU/99 RC 5.00 12.00
307 Davis Webb JSY AU/199 RC 3.00 8.00
308 Leonard Fournette JSY AU/99 RC 30.00 60.00
309 Dalvin Cook JSY AU/99 RC 25.00 60.00
310 Christian McCaffrey JSY AU/99 RC 30.00 60.00
311 D'Onta Foreman JSY AU/199 RC 4.00 10.00
312 Samaje Perine JSY AU/199 RC 3.00 8.00
313 Alvin Kamara JSY AU/99 RC 15.00 40.00
314 Joe Mixon JSY AU/99 RC 8.00 20.00
315 Kareem Hunt JSY AU/199 RC 12.00 30.00
316 Wayne Gallman JSY AU/199 RC 4.00 10.00
317 James Conner JSY AU/99 RC 8.00 20.00
318 Joe Williams JSY AU/99 RC 4.00 10.00
319 Marlon Mack JSY AU/99 RC 6.00 15.00
320 O.J. Howard JSY AU/99 RC 5.00 12.00
321 Evan Engram JSY AU/99 RC 5.00 12.00
322 Mike Williams JSY AU/99 RC 6.00 15.00
323 John Ross III JSY AU/99 RC 5.00 12.00
324 Corey Davis JSY AU/99 RC 5.00 12.00
325 JuJu Smith-Schuster JSY AU/99 RC 10.00 25.00
326 Dede Westbrook JSY AU/99 RC 3.00 8.00
327 Curtis Samuel JSY AU/199 RC 4.00 10.00
328 Amara Darboh JSY AU/199 RC 3.00 8.00
329 Taywan Taylor JSY AU/199 RC 3.00 8.00
330 Carlos Henderson JSY AU/199 RC 3.00 8.00
331 Chris Godwin JSY AU/99 RC 5.00 12.00
332 Zay Jones JSY AU/99 RC 5.00 12.00
333 Cooper Kupp JSY AU/99 RC 6.00 15.00
334 Kenny Golladay JSY AU/199 RC 5.00 12.00
335 Josh Reynolds JSY AU/199 RC 3.00 8.00
336 Mack Hollins JSY AU/199 RC 3.00 8.00
337 Jamaal Williams JSY AU/99 RC 4.00 10.00
338 Jeremy McNichols JSY AU/199 RC 3.00 8.00
339 ArDarius Stewart JSY AU/99 RC 4.00 10.00
340 Nathan Peterman JSY AU/149 RC 4.00 10.00

2017 Panini Unparalleled Blue

*RC'S(201-300): 2X TO 5X BASIC CARDS

2017 Panini Unparalleled Lime Green

*VETS: .8X TO 2X BASIC CARDS
*ROOKIES/499: .5X TO 1.2X BASIC CARDS

2017 Panini Unparalleled Orange

*VETS: 3X TO 8X BASIC CARDS
*ROOKIES: 1X TO 2.5X BASIC CARDS
*ROOK JSY AU/49: .6X TO 1.5X BASIC JSY AU/199
*ROOK JSY AU/25: .8X TO 2X BASIC JSY AU/199
*ROOK JSY AU/15: .8X TO 2X BASIC JSY AU/99
302 Mitchell Trubisky JSY AU/15 125.00 250.00
304 Patrick Mahomes II JSY AU/15 400.00 800.00

2017 Panini Unparalleled Pink

*VETS: 1X TO 2.5X BASIC CARDS
*ROOKIES/299: .6X TO 1.5X BASIC CARDS

2017 Panini Unparalleled Purple

*VETS: 2X TO 5X BASIC CARDS
*ROOKIES: .8X TO 2X BASIC CARDS
*ROOK JSY AU/99: .5X TO 1.2X BASIC JSY AU/199
*ROOK JSY AU/49: .6X TO 1.5X BASIC JSY AU/199
*ROOK JSY AU/25: .6X TO 1.5X BASIC JSY AU/99
301 Deshaun Watson JSY AU/25 75.00 150.00
304 Patrick Mahomes II JSY AU/25 300.00 600.00

2017 Panini Unparalleled Red

*VETS/15: 5X TO 12X BASIC CARDS
*ROOKIES/25: 1.5X TO 4X BASIC CARDS

2017 Panini Unparalleled Teal

*VETS/25: 4X TO 10X BASIC CARDS
*ROOKIES/49: 1.2X TO 3X BASIC CARDS
*TEAL JSY AU/25: .8X TO 2X JSY AU/199

2017 Panini Unparalleled Yellow

*VETS: 2X TO 5X BASIC CARDS
*ROOKIES: .8X TO 2X BASIC CARDS

2017 Panini Unparalleled High Flyers

*LIME GREEN/199: .5X TO 1.2X BASIC INSERTS
*PINK/99: .6X TO 1.5X BASIC INSERTS
*PURPLE/49: .8X TO 2X BASIC INSERTS
*ORANGE/25: 1X TO 2.5X BASIC INSERTS
*TEAL/15: 1.2X TO 3X BASIC INSERTS
1 Jerry Rice 1.00 2.50
2 Sterling Sharpe .50 1.25
3 Reggie Wayne .50 1.25
4 Hines Ward .50 1.25
5 Fred Biletnikoff .60 1.50
6 Steve Largent .60 1.50
7 Michael Irvin .60 1.50
8 Tim Brown .60 1.50
9 Randy Moss .50 1.25
10 Mike Evans .50 1.25
11 Julio Jones .60 1.50
12 Odell Beckham Jr. .60 1.50
13 Antonio Brown .60 1.50
14 Jordy Nelson .50 1.25
15 Brandin Cooks .50 1.25
16 Amari Cooper .60 1.50
17 Julian Edelman .60 1.50
18 Doug Baldwin .50 1.25
19 Kelvin Benjamin .50 1.25
20 Larry Fitzgerald .50 1.25

2017 Panini Unparalleled High Flyers Autographs Red

*BLUE/25: .6X TO 1.5X BASIC AU/99
*BLUE/25: .4X TO 1X BASIC AU/25
1 Jerry Rice/25 100.00 200.00
2 Sterling Sharpe/99 8.00 20.00
3 Reggie Wayne/25
4 Hines Ward/25 30.00 60.00
5 Fred Biletnikoff/25 10.00 25.00
6 Steve Largent/25 10.00 25.00
7 Michael Irvin/25 30.00 60.00
8 Tim Brown/25
9 Randy Moss/25
10 Mike Evans/25 8.00 20.00
14 Jordy Nelson/49
15 Brandin Cooks/15
18 Doug Baldwin/15

2017 Panini Unparalleled Perfect Pairs

*LIME GREEN/199: .5X TO 1.2X BASIC INSERTS
*PINK/99: .6X TO 1.5X BASIC INSERTS
*PURPLE/49: .8X TO 2X BASIC INSERTS
*ORANGE/25: 1X TO 2.5X BASIC INSERTS
*TEAL/15: 1.2X TO 3X BASIC INSERTS
1 D.Prescott/E.Elliott 1.25 3.00
2 W.Fuller/D.Hopkins .75 2.00
3 O.Beckham/S.Shepard 1.00 2.50
4 J.Landry/J.Ajayi .75 2.00
5 B.Cooks/T.Brady 2.50 6.00
6 J.Howard/K.White 1.00 2.50
7 A.Talib/C.Harris .60 1.50
8 D.Murray/D.Henry .75 2.00
9 D.Jackson/M.Evans .75 2.00
10 E.Thomas/K.Chancellor 1.00 2.50
11 E.Lacy/T.Rawls .60 1.50
12 R.Quinn/A.Donald 1.00 2.50
13 L.Kuechly/T.Davis .75 2.00
14 L.Bell/D.Williams .75 2.00
15 N.Suh/C.Wake .75 2.00

2017 Panini Unparalleled Perfect Pairs Dual Jerseys Red

*BLUE/25: .4X TO 1X BASIC JSY/25
1 Dak Prescott 8.00 20.00
Ezekiel Elliott
2 DeAndre Hopkins 5.00 12.00
Will Fuller V
3 Odell Beckham Jr. 6.00 15.00
Sterling Shepard
4 Jarvis Landry 5.00 12.00
Jay Ajayi
5 Brandin Cooks 25.00 50.00
Tom Brady
6 Jordan Howard 6.00 15.00
Kevin White
7 Chris Harris 4.00 10.00
Aqib Talib
8 DeMarco Murray 5.00 12.00
Derrick Henry
10 Kam Chancellor 6.00 15.00
Earl Thomas III
12 Aaron Donald 6.00 15.00
Robert Quinn
14 DeAngelo Williams 5.00 12.00
Le'Veon Bell
15 Ndamukong Suh 5.00 12.00
Cameron Wake

2017 Panini Unparalleled Rookie Autographs

201 Chad Kelly/199 10.00 25.00
202 Brad Kaaya/199 2.50 6.00
203 Brian Hill/199 2.50 6.00
204 Matthew Dayes/199 2.50 6.00
205 Elijah Hood/199 2.50 6.00
206 Donnel Pumphrey/199 3.00 8.00
207 Tarik Cohen/199 20.00 50.00
208 Dalvin Tomlinson/199 2.50 6.00
209 Haason Reddick/199 2.50 6.00
210 De'Veon Smith/199 6.00 15.00
211 Jake Butt/199 3.00 8.00
212 Bucky Hodges/199 2.50 6.00
213 Jordan Leggett/199 2.50 6.00
214 Obi Melifonwu/199 2.50 6.00
215 Adam Shaheen/199 2.50 6.00
216 Malachi Dupre/199 2.50 6.00
217 Ryan Switzer/199 3.00 8.00
218 Shelton Gibson/199 2.50 6.00
219 Stacy Coley/199 2.50 6.00
220 Gerald Everett/199 2.50 6.00
221 Isaiah Ford/199 2.50 6.00
222 Josh Malone/199 2.50 6.00
223 Chad Hansen/199 2.50 6.00
224 Marlon Humphrey/199 2.50 6.00
225 Marshon Lattimore/199 3.00 8.00
226 Quincy Wilson/199 2.50 6.00
228 Adoree' Jackson/199 3.00 8.00
229 Sidney Jones/199 2.50 6.00
230 Desmond King/199 3.00 8.00
232 Cordrea Tankersley/199 3.00 8.00
233 Tre'Davious White/199 2.50 6.00
234 Cameron Sutton/199 2.50 6.00
235 Gareon Conley/199 2.50 6.00
236 Jonathan Allen/199 3.00 8.00
238 Derek Barnett/199 10.00 25.00
239 Carl Lawson/199 2.50 6.00
240 Charles Harris/199 2.50 6.00
241 Taco Charlton/199 2.50 6.00
242 Jordan Willis/199 2.50 6.00
243 DeMarcus Walker/199 2.50 6.00
244 Solomon Thomas/199 6.00 15.00
245 Malik McDowell/199 2.50 6.00
246 Elijah Qualls/199 2.50 6.00
247 Caleb Brantley/49 4.00 10.00
249 Raekwon McMillan/199 2.50 6.00
250 Zach Cunningham/199 3.00 8.00
251 Jarrad Davis/199 3.00 8.00
252 Jabrill Peppers/199 4.00 10.00
253 Tim Williams/199 3.00 8.00
254 Jerod Evans/199 3.00 8.00
255 T.J. Watt/199 25.00 50.00
257 Jamal Adams/199 2.50 6.00
258 Malik Hooker/199 2.50 6.00
259 T.J. Logan/49 6.00 15.00
260 Greg Ward Jr./49 4.00 10.00
261 Cooper Rush/49 5.00 12.00
262 Elijah McGuire/99 3.00 8.00
263 Aaron Jones/49 10.00 25.00
264 Fabian Moreau/49 4.00 10.00
265 Rasul Douglas/49 5.00 12.00
266 Deatrich Wise Jr./49 6.00 15.00
267 Chidobe Awuzie/49 5.00 12.00
268 Kevin King/49 8.00 20.00
269 Marquez White/49 4.00 10.00
270 Dawuane Smoot/49 4.00 10.00
271 Daeshon Hall/49 4.00 10.00
272 Tanoh Kpassagnon/49 5.00 12.00
273 Chris Wormley/49 4.00 10.00
274 Carlos Watkins/49 4.00 10.00
275 Montravius Adams/49 5.00 12.00
276 Jaleel Johnson/49
277 Ryan Glasgow/49 4.00 10.00
278 Kendell Beckwith/49 4.00 10.00
279 Anthony Walker Jr./49 4.00 10.00
280 Ryan Anderson/49 4.00 10.00
281 Tyus Bowser/49 4.00 10.00
282 Duke Riley/49 4.00 10.00
283 Josh Jones/49 4.00 10.00
284 Marcus Williams/49 4.00 10.00
285 Budda Baker/49
286 Marcus Maye/49 4.00 10.00
287 Justin Evans/49 4.00 10.00
288 Eddie Jackson/49 5.00 12.00
289 Eddie Vanderdoes/49 4.00 10.00
290 Jeremy Sprinkle/49 4.00 10.00
291 Noah Brown/49 5.00 12.00
292 Jehu Chesson/49 5.00 12.00
293 Derek Rivers/49 5.00 12.00
294 Trent Taylor/49 5.00 12.00
295 DeAngelo Yancey/49 4.00 10.00
296 De'Angelo Henderson/49 4.00 10.00
297 Chris Carson/49 6.00 15.00
298 Nazair Jones/49 4.00 10.00
299 Jonnu Smith/49 4.00 10.00
300 David Njoku/149 EXCH 3.00 8.00

2017 Panini Unparalleled Rookie Autographs Orange

*ORANGE/49: .6X TO 1.5X BASIC AU/199
*ORANGE/25: .8X TO 2X BASIC AU/149
*ORANGE/15: .8X TO 2X BASIC AU/49
*ORANGE/15: .6X TO 1.5X BASIC AU/49

2017 Panini Unparalleled Rookie Autographs Purple

*PURPLE/75-99: .5X TO 1.2X BASIC AU/149-199
*PURPLE/25: .6X TO 1.5X BASIC AU/99
*PURPLE/25: .5X TO 1.5X BASIC AU/49

2017 Panini Unparalleled Rookie Autographs Red

*RED/15: 1X TO 2.5X BASIC AU/199

2017 Panini Unparalleled Rookie Autographs Teal

*TEAL/25: .8X TO 2X BASIC AU/199
*TEAL/15: 1X TO 2.5X BASIC AU/149

2017 Panini Unparalleled Rookie Autographs Yellow

*YELLOW/149: .4X TO 1X BASIC AU/199
*YELLOW/99: .5X TO 1.2X BASIC AU/149
*YELLOW/49: .5X TO 1.2X BASIC AU/99
*YELLOW/49: .4X TO 1X BASIC AU/49

2017 Panini Unparalleled Rookie Stitches Dual Jerseys

*PURPLE/99: .5X TO 1.2X BASIC JSY/199
*ORANGE/49: .6X TO 1.5X BASIC JSY/199
*TEAL/25: .8X TO 2X BASIC JSY/199
1 Deshaun Watson 12.00 30.00
2 Mitchell Trubisky 10.00 25.00
3 Patrick Mahomes II 20.00 50.00
4 Leonard Fournette 10.00 25.00
5 Dalvin Cook 10.00 25.00
6 Christian McCaffrey 10.00 25.00
7 D'Onta Foreman 3.00 8.00
8 Joe Mixon 6.00 15.00
9 James Conner 5.00 12.00
10 Joe Williams 2.50 6.00
11 O.J. Howard 3.00 8.00
12 Evan Engram 3.00 8.00
13 Mike Williams 4.00 10.00
14 John Ross III 6.00 15.00
15 Corey Davis 4.00 10.00
16 JuJu Smith-Schuster 6.00 15.00
17 Curtis Samuel 3.00 8.00
18 Chris Godwin 3.00 8.00
19 Zay Jones 3.00 8.00
20 Jeremy McNichols 2.50 6.00

2017 Panini Unparalleled Rookie Stitches Jerseys

*PURPLE/99: .6X TO 1.5X BASIC JSY/199
*ORANGE/49: .6X TO 1.5X BASIC JSY/199
*TEAL/25: .8X TO 2X BASIC JSY/199
1 Deshaun Watson 12.00 30.00
2 Mitchell Trubisky 10.00 25.00
3 DeShone Kizer 2.50 6.00
4 Patrick Mahomes II 20.00 50.00
5 C.J. Beathard 2.50 6.00
6 R. Joshua Dobbs 6.00 15.00
7 Davis Webb 2.50 6.00
8 Leonard Fournette 10.00 25.00
9 Dalvin Cook 10.00 25.00
10 Christian McCaffrey 10.00 25.00
11 D'Onta Foreman 3.00 8.00
12 Samaje Perine 2.50 6.00
13 Alvin Kamara 6.00 15.00
14 Joe Mixon 6.00 15.00
15 Kareem Hunt 5.00 12.00
16 Wayne Gallman 3.00 8.00
17 James Conner 5.00 12.00
18 Joe Williams 2.50 6.00
19 Marlon Mack 4.00 10.00
20 O.J. Howard 3.00 8.00

21 Evan Engram 3.00 8.00
22 Mike Williams 4.00 10.00
23 John Ross III 6.00 15.00
24 Corey Davis 4.00 10.00
25 JuJu Smith-Schuster 6.00 15.00
26 Dede Westbrook 2.50 6.00
27 Curtis Samuel 3.00 8.00
28 Amara Darboh 2.50 6.00
29 Taywan Taylor 2.50 6.00
30 Carlos Henderson 2.50 6.00
31 Chris Godwin 3.00 8.00
32 Zay Jones 3.00 8.00
33 Cooper Kupp 4.00 10.00
34 Kenny Golladay 4.00 10.00
35 Josh Reynolds 2.50 6.00
36 Mack Hollins 2.50 6.00
37 Jamaal Williams 2.50 6.00
38 Jeremy McNichols 2.50 6.00
39 ArDarius Stewart 2.50 6.00
40 Nathan Peterman 3.00 8.00

2017 Panini Unparalleled Star Factor

*LIME GREEN/199: .5X TO 1.2X BASIC INSERTS
*PINK/99: .6X TO 1.5X BASIC INSERTS
*PURPLE/49: .8X TO 2X BASIC INSERTS
*ORANGE/25: 1X TO 2.5X BASIC INSERTS
*TEAL/15: 1.2X TO 3X BASIC INSERTS
1 Peyton Manning 2.00 5.00
2 John Elway 1.50 4.00
3 Brett Favre 2.00 5.00
4 Steve Young 1.25 3.00
5 Dan Marino 2.00 5.00
6 Troy Aikman 1.25 3.00
7 Priest Holmes .60 1.50
8 Terry Bradshaw 1.50 4.00
9 Aaron Rodgers 2.00 5.00
10 Drew Brees 1.00 2.50
11 Matt Ryan .75 2.00
12 Andrew Luck 1.25 3.00
13 Russell Wilson 1.25 3.00
14 Derek Carr 1.00 2.50
15 Marcus Mariota 1.00 2.50
16 Barry Sanders 1.50 4.00
17 Emmitt Smith 1.50 4.00
18 Bo Jackson 1.25 3.00
19 Jerome Bettis 1.00 2.50
20 Marshawn Lynch .75 2.00
21 Ezekiel Elliott 1.25 3.00
22 Adrian Peterson 1.00 2.50
23 DeMarco Murray .75 2.00
24 Le'Veon Bell .75 2.00
25 David Johnson 1.00 2.50

2017 Panini Unparalleled Star Factor Autographs Red

*BLUE/25: .6X TO 1.5X BASIC AU/99
*BLUE/15: .5X TO 1.2X BASIC AU/25
2 John Elway/15 75.00 125.00
3 Brett Favre/15 75.00 150.00
4 Steve Young/25 25.00 50.00
5 Dan Marino/25 60.00 125.00
6 Troy Aikman/25 40.00 80.00
7 Priest Holmes/99 4.00 10.00
9 Aaron Rodgers/15 150.00 300.00
10 Drew Brees/15 60.00 125.00
11 Matt Ryan/25 25.00 50.00
12 Andrew Luck/15 30.00 60.00
13 Russell Wilson/15 50.00 100.00
14 Derek Carr/49 40.00 80.00
15 Marcus Mariota/25 40.00 80.00
16 Barry Sanders/25 40.00 80.00
17 Emmitt Smith/15 90.00 150.00
18 Bo Jackson/25 25.00 50.00
19 Jerome Bettis/25 25.00 50.00
20 Marshawn Lynch/25 15.00 40.00
21 Ezekiel Elliott/49 50.00 100.00
23 DeMarco Murray/25 15.00 40.00
25 David Johnson/25 10.00 25.00

2017 Panini Unparalleled Year 2

*LIME GREEN/199: .5X TO 1.2X BASIC INSERTS
*PINK/99: .6X TO 1.5X BASIC INSERTS
*PURPLE/49: .8X TO 2X BASIC INSERTS
*ORANGE/25: 1X TO 2.5X BASIC INSERTS
*TEAL/15: 1.2X TO 3X BASIC INSERTS
1 Ezekiel Elliott 1.25 3.00
2 Dak Prescott 1.00 2.50
3 Sterling Shepard .75 2.00
4 Joey Bosa 1.00 2.50
5 Kenneth Dixon .60 1.50
6 Leonard Floyd .60 1.50
7 Jordan Howard 1.00 2.50
8 Paxton Lynch .60 1.50
9 Andy Janovich .60 1.50
10 Tyreek Hill 1.00 2.50
11 Michael Thomas 1.00 2.50
12 Shaq Lawson .60 1.50
13 DeAndre Washington .60 1.50
14 Jalen Ramsey .60 1.50
15 Kenyan Drake .60 1.50
16 Malcolm Mitchell .75 2.00
17 Carson Wentz 1.25 3.00
18 Derrick Henry .75 2.00
19 Tajae Sharpe .60 1.50
20 Keanu Neal .60 1.50
21 Tyler Boyd .60 1.50
22 Will Fuller V .60 1.50
23 Jared Goff 1.00 2.50
24 Robert Kelley .60 1.50
25 Corey Coleman .60 1.50

2017 Panini Unparalleled Zoned In

*LIME GREEN/199: .5X TO 1.2X BASIC INSERTS
*PINK/99: .6X TO 1.5X BASIC INSERTS
*PURPLE/49: .8X TO 2X BASIC INSERTS
*ORANGE/25: 1X TO 2.5X BASIC INSERTS
*TEAL/15: 1.2X TO 3X BASIC INSERTS
1 A.J. Green 1.00 2.50
2 Stefon Diggs .75 2.00
3 Jameis Winston .75 2.00
4 Julio Jones 1.00 2.50
5 T.Y. Hilton .75 2.00
6 Odell Beckham Jr. 1.00 2.50
7 Jay Ajayi .75 2.00
8 Derek Carr 1.00 2.50
9 Melvin Gordon .75 2.00
10 Russell Wilson 1.25 3.00
11 Ezekiel Elliott 1.25 3.00
12 Justin Houston .60 1.50
13 Eric Berry .75 2.00
14 Vic Beasley Jr. .60 1.50
15 Drew Brees 1.00 2.50

2017 Panini Unparalleled Zoned In Jerseys Blue

*RED/25: .4X TO 1X BLUE JSY/25
1 A.J. Green 4.00 10.00
2 Stefon Diggs 3.00 8.00
3 Jameis Winston 3.00 8.00
4 Julio Jones 4.00 10.00
5 T.Y. Hilton 3.00 8.00
6 Odell Beckham Jr. 4.00 10.00
7 Jay Ajayi 3.00 8.00
8 Derek Carr 4.00 10.00
9 Melvin Gordon 3.00 8.00
10 Russell Wilson 5.00 12.00
11 Ezekiel Elliott 5.00 12.00
12 Justin Houston 2.50 6.00
13 Eric Berry 3.00 8.00
14 Vic Beasley Jr. 2.50 6.00
15 Drew Brees 4.00 10.00

2018 Panini Unparalleled

1 Sam Bradford .25 .60
2 David Johnson .40 1.00
3 Larry Fitzgerald .30 .75
4 Patrick Peterson .25 .60
5 Olsen Pierre RC .25 .60
6 Aaron Brewer RC .25 .60
7 Matt Ryan .30 .75
8 Julio Jones .40 1.00
9 Devonta Freeman .30 .75
10 Tevin Coleman .25 .60
11 Vic Beasley Jr. .25 .60
12 Marvin Hall RC .25 .60
13 Josh Harris RC .25 .60
14 Joe Flacco .30 .75
15 Michael Crabtree .25 .60
16 Terrell Suggs .25 .60
17 Alex Collins .25 .60
18 Patrick Ricard RC .25 .60
19 James Hurst RC .25 .60
20 A.J. McCarron .25 .60
21 LeSean McCoy .40 1.00
22 Zay Jones .25 .60
23 Vontae Davis .25 .60
24 Dion Dawkins .25 .60
25 Brandon Reilly RC .25 .60
26 Cam Newton .40 1.00
27 Christian McCaffrey .40 1.00
28 Greg Olsen .30 .75
29 Devin Funchess .25 .60
30 Mose Frazier RC .25 .60
31 Tyler Larsen RC .25 .60
32 Mitchell Trubisky .40 1.00
33 Jordan Howard .40 1.00
34 Allen Robinson .30 .75
35 Kyle Long .25 .60
36 Eric Kush RC .25 .60
37 John Timu RC .25 .60
38 Andy Dalton .30 .75
39 A.J. Green .40 1.00
40 Joe Mixon .30 .75
41 Tyler Eifert .30 .75
42 Alex Erickson RC .25 .60
43 Jarveon Williams RC .25 .60
44 Tyrod Taylor .30 .75
45 Josh Gordon .25 .60
46 Jarvis Landry .30 .75
47 Jabrill Peppers .25 .60
48 Dan Vitale .25 .60
49 Joel Bitonio .25 .60
50 Dak Prescott .40 1.00
51 Ezekiel Elliott .50 1.25
52 Dez Bryant .40 1.00
53 Allen Hurns .25 .60
54 Sean Lee .30 .75
55 Justin March-Lillard RC .25 .60
56 Rod Smith .30 .75
57 Case Keenum .30 .75
58 Von Miller .30 .75
59 Devontae Booker .25 .60
60 Demaryius Thomas .30 .75
61 Todd Davis RC .25 .60
62 Austin Traylor RC .25 .60
63 Matthew Stafford .30 .75
64 Golden Tate III .25 .60
65 Ezekiel Ansah .25 .60
66 LeGarrette Blount .30 .75
67 Graham Glasgow RC .25 .60
68 Bradley Marquez RC .25 .60
69 Aaron Rodgers .75 2.00
70 Davante Adams .30 .75
71 Clay Matthews .30 .75
72 Jimmy Graham .40 1.00
73 Randall Cobb .30 .75
74 Corey Linsley RC .25 .60
75 Joe Kerridge RC .25 .60
76 Deshaun Watson .50 1.25
77 D'Onta Foreman .25 .60
78 DeAndre Hopkins .30 .75
79 J.J. Watt .40 1.00
80 Brennan Scarlett RC .25 .60
81 Stephen Anderson .25 .60
82 Jacoby Brissett .25 .60
83 Marlon Mack .25 .60
84 T.Y. Hilton .30 .75
85 Andrew Luck .50 1.25
86 Phillip Walker RC .25 .60
87 K.J. Brent RC .25 .60
88 Blake Bortles .25 .60
89 Leonard Fournette .40 1.00
90 Jalen Ramsey .30 .75
91 Myles Jack .25 .60
92 Brandon Linder RC .25 .60
93 Jaydon Mickens .25 .60
94 Patrick Mahomes II 1.00 2.50
95 Travis Kelce .40 1.00
96 Kareem Hunt .30 .75
97 Tyreek Hill .40 1.00
98 Eric Berry .30 .75
99 Marcus Kemp RC .25 .60
100 Demetrius Harris RC .25 .60
101 Jared Goff .40 1.00
102 Todd Gurley II .40 1.00
103 Sam Shields .25 .60
104 Aaron Donald .40 1.00
105 Ndamukong Suh .30 .75
106 Rob Havenstein RC .25 .60
107 Cory Littleton RC .30 .75
108 Philip Rivers .40 1.00
109 Melvin Gordon .30 .75
110 Keenan Allen .30 .75
111 Joey Bosa .40 1.00
112 Drew Kaser RC .25 .60
113 Nick Dzubnar RC .25 .60
114 Ryan Tannehill .30 .75
115 Cameron Wake .25 .60
116 DeVante Parker .30 .75
117 Frank Gore .30 .75
118 Mike Hull RC .25 .60
119 Matt Haack RC .25 .60
120 Kirk Cousins .40 1.00
121 Dalvin Cook .30 .75
122 Stefon Diggs .30 .75
123 Adam Thielen .40 1.00
124 Ryan Quigley RC .25 .60
125 Kentrell Brothers .25 .60
126 Tom Brady 1.00 2.50
127 Rob Gronkowski .40 1.00
128 Patrick Chung .25 .60
129 Rex Burkhead .25 .60
130 Chris Hogan .25 .60
131 Shaq Mason RC .25 .60
132 Ryan Allen .25 .60
133 Drew Brees .40 1.00
134 Alvin Kamara .30 .75
135 Michael Thomas .40 1.00
136 Marshon Lattimore .25 .60
137 Ken Crawley .25 .60
138 Justin Hardee RC .25 .60
139 Eli Manning .30 .75
140 Odell Beckham Jr. .40 1.00
141 Jonathan Stewart .25 .60
142 Landon Collins .25 .60
143 Aldrick Rosas RC .25 .60
144 Kalif Raymond RC .25 .60
145 Teddy Bridgewater .30 .75
146 Robby Anderson .25 .60
147 Bilal Powell .25 .60
148 Quincy Enunwa .25 .60
149 Lac Edwards RC .25 .60
150 Neal Sterling RC .25 .60
151 Derek Carr .40 1.00
152 Marshawn Lynch .30 .75
153 Khalil Mack .40 1.00
154 Amari Cooper .40 1.00
155 Giorgio Tavecchio RC .25 .60
156 Treyvon Hester RC .25 .60
157 Carson Wentz .50 1.25
158 Jay Ajayi .30 .75
159 Alshon Jeffery .30 .75
160 Fletcher Cox .25 .60
161 Jason Peters .25 .60
162 Brandon Brooks RC .25 .60
163 Adam Zaruba RC .25 .60
164 Ben Roethlisberger .40 1.00
165 Le'Veon Bell .30 .75
166 Antonio Brown .40 1.00
167 JuJu Smith-Schuster .40 1.00
168 T.J. Watt .30 .75
169 Roosevelt Nix RC .25 .60
170 Chris Boswell .25 .60
171 Jimmy Garoppolo .50 1.25
172 Jerick McKinnon .25 .60
173 Richard Sherman .40 1.00
174 Marquise Goodwin .25 .60
175 DeAndre Carter RC .25 .60
176 Elijah Lee RC .25 .60
177 Russell Wilson .50 1.25
178 Chris Carson .30 .75
179 Earl Thomas III .30 .75
180 Doug Baldwin .30 .75
181 J.D. McKissic .25 .60
182 Cyril Grayson RC .25 .60
183 Jameis Winston .30 .75
184 Mike Evans .30 .75
185 Peyton Barber .25 .60
186 DeSean Jackson .30 .75
187 Bobo Wilson RC .25 .60
188 Antony Auclair RC .25 .60
189 Marcus Mariota .40 1.00
190 Derrick Henry .40 1.00
191 Rishard Matthews .25 .60
192 Malcolm Butler .40 1.00
193 Phillip Supernaw RC .25 .60
194 Darius Jennings RC .25 .60
195 Alex Smith .30 .75
196 Josh Norman .25 .60
197 Jordan Reed .25 .60
198 Chris Thompson .25 .60
199 Nick Sundberg RC .25 .60
200 Tress Way RC .25 .60
201 Minkah Fitzpatrick RC 1.25 3.00
202 Denzel Ward RC 1.50 4.00
203 Bradley Chubb RC 1.00 2.50
204 Harold Landry RC .60 1.50
205 Josh Rosen RC 2.00 5.00
206 Sam Darnold RC 4.00 10.00
207 Josh Allen RC 2.50 6.00
208 Baker Mayfield RC 6.00 15.00
209 Lamar Jackson RC 4.00 10.00
210 Mason Rudolph RC 1.50 4.00
211 Deontay Burnett RC .75 2.00
212 Riley Ferguson RC 1.00 2.50
213 Saquon Barkley RC 5.00 12.00
214 Derrius Guice RC 1.25 3.00
215 Ronald Jones II RC .60 1.50
216 Nick Chubb RC 2.00 5.00
217 Kerryon Johnson RC 1.00 2.50
218 Sony Michel RC 2.00 5.00
219 John Kelly RC .75 2.00
220 Rashaad Penny RC 1.00 2.50
221 Calvin Ridley RC 1.50 4.00
222 Christian Kirk RC 1.00 2.50
223 Courtland Sutton RC 1.00 2.50
224 James Washington RC 1.25 3.00
225 Anthony Miller RC 1.00 2.50
226 Brian O'Neill RC .60 1.50
227 Michael Gallup RC 1.25 3.00
228 D.J. Chark RC .75 2.00
229 Dallas Goedert RC .75 2.00
230 Deon Cain RC .75 2.00
231 Uchenna Nwosu RC 1.00 2.50
232 Lorenzo Carter RC .60 1.50
233 Arden Key RC .60 1.50
234 Quadree Henderson RC .75 2.00
235 Marquez Valdes-Scantling RC .75 2.00
236 Maurice Hurst RC .75 2.00
237 Vita Vea RC 1.00 2.50
238 Roquan Smith RC 2.00 5.00
239 Malik Jefferson RC .75 2.00
240 Rashaan Evans RC 1.00 2.50
241 Tremaine Edmunds RC 1.25 3.00
242 Justin Jackson RC .75 2.00
243 Luke Falk RC .75 2.00
244 Mike White RC .75 2.00
245 Simmie Cobbs Jr. RC 1.00 2.50
246 Trey Quinn RC .60 1.50
247 Kemoko Turay RC .75 2.00
248 Bo Scarbrough RC .75 2.00
249 Royce Freeman RC .75 2.00
250 Josh Adams RC 1.25 3.00
251 Kalen Ballage RC .75 2.00
252 Joshua Jackson RC 1.25 3.00
253 Derwin James RC 1.25 3.00
254 Ronnie Harrison RC .75 2.00
255 Mark Andrews RC 1.00 2.50
256 Mike Gesicki RC .75 2.00
257 D.J. Moore RC 1.25 3.00
258 Marcell Ateman RC .75 2.00
259 Daron Payne RC 1.00 2.50
260 Breeland Speaks RC .75 2.00
261 Dante Pettis RC 1.00 2.50
262 Jaleel Scott RC .60 1.50
263 Jordan Lasley RC .60 1.50
264 Braxton Berrios RC .60 1.50
265 Ito Smith RC .75 2.00
266 Carlton Davis RC .75 2.00
267 Jaire Alexander RC 1.00 2.50
268 B.J. Hill RC .75 2.00
269 Lavon Coleman RC .75 2.00
270 Dorance Armstrong Jr. RC .60 1.50
271 Josh Sweat RC .75 2.00
272 Ryan Izzo RC .60 1.50
273 Jordan Whitehead RC .60 1.50
274 Austin Proehl RC .60 1.50
275 J'Mon Moore RC .60 1.50
276 Connor Williams RC 1.25 3.00
277 Orlando Brown RC 1.00 2.50
278 Tanner Lee RC .75 2.00
279 Jessie Bates RC 1.00 2.50
280 M.J. Stewart RC .60 1.50
281 Nathan Shepherd RC .60 1.50
282 Dalton Schultz RC .75 2.00
283 Will Hernandez RC .75 2.00
284 Auden Tate RC .60 1.50
285 Hayden Hurst RC .75 2.00
286 Duke Dawson RC .60 1.50
287 Kyle Allen RC .75 2.00
288 Sam Hubbard RC .75 2.00
289 Taven Bryan RC .60 1.50
290 Justin Reid RC .60 1.50
291 Donte Jackson RC 1.00 2.50
292 Leighton Vander Esch RC 2.00 5.00
293 Mike Hughes RC 1.00 2.50
294 Tre'Quan Smith RC 1.00 2.50
295 Korey Robertson RC .75 2.00
296 Antonio Callaway RC .75 2.00
297 Equanimeous St. Brown RC 1.00 2.50
298 Cedrick Wilson Jr. RC .60 1.50
299 Marcus Davenport RC 1.25 3.00
300 Quenton Nelson RC 1.00 2.50

2018 Panini Unparalleled Astral

*VETS/200: 1.5X TO 4X BASIC CARDS
*ROOKIES/200: .8X TO 2X BASIC CARDS

2018 Panini Unparalleled Galactic

*VETS: 4X TO 10X BASIC CARDS
*ROOKIES: 3X TO 8X BASIC CARDS
126 Tom Brady 100.00 200.00
171 Jimmy Garoppolo 50.00 100.00
205 Josh Rosen 50.00 100.00
209 Lamar Jackson 50.00 100.00

2018 Panini Unparalleled Hyper

*VETS/25: 4X TO 10X BASIC CARDS
*ROOKIES/25: 1.5X TO 4X BASIC CARDS

2018 Panini Unparalleled Impact

*VETS/75: 2.5X TO 6X BASIC CARDS
*ROOKIES/75: 1X TO 2.5X BASIC CARDS

2018 Panini Unparalleled Superplaid

*VETS/150: 2.5X TO 6X BASIC CARDS
*ROOK/150: 1X TO 2.5X BASIC CARDS

2018 Panini Unparalleled Whirl

*VETS/100: 2.5X TO 6X BASIC CARDS
*ROOK/100: 1X TO 2.5X BASIC CARDS

2018 Panini Unparalleled Bright Futures

*ASTRAL/200: 1X TO 2.5X BASIC INSERTS
*WHIRL/100: 1.2X TO 3X BASIC INSERTS
*HYPER/25: 2X TO 5X BASIC INSERTS
1 Dak Prescott .60 1.50
2 Sterling Shepard .50 1.25
3 Patrick Mahomes II 1.50 4.00
4 Corey Coleman .40 1.00
5 Evan Engram .40 1.00
6 Davante Adams .50 1.25
7 Chris Godwin .40 1.00
8 Jordan Howard .60 1.50
9 Kenny Stills .40 1.00
10 Carson Wentz .75 2.00
11 Jared Goff .60 1.50
12 Devonta Freeman .50 1.25
13 Amari Cooper .60 1.50
14 Michael Thomas .60 1.50
15 Marcus Mariota .60 1.50
16 Deshaun Watson .75 2.00
17 Ameer Abdullah .40 1.00
18 Kareem Hunt .50 1.25
19 Stefon Diggs .50 1.25
20 Le'Veon Bell .50 1.25

2018 Panini Unparalleled Bright Futures Memorabilia

*WHIRL/50: .6X TO 1.5X BASIC JSY
*HYPER/25: .8X TO 2X BASIC AU
1 Dak Prescott 3.00 8.00
2 Sterling Shepard 2.50 6.00
3 Patrick Mahomes II 8.00 20.00
4 Corey Coleman 2.00 5.00
5 Evan Engram 2.00 5.00
6 Davante Adams 2.50 6.00
7 Chris Godwin 2.00 5.00
8 Jordan Howard 3.00 8.00
9 Kenny Stills 2.00 5.00
10 Carson Wentz 4.00 10.00
11 Jared Goff 3.00 8.00
12 Devonta Freeman 2.50 6.00
13 Amari Cooper 3.00 8.00
14 Michael Thomas 3.00 8.00
15 Marcus Mariota 3.00 8.00
16 Deshaun Watson 4.00 10.00
17 Ameer Abdullah 2.00 5.00
18 Kareem Hunt 2.50 6.00
19 Stefon Diggs 2.50 6.00
20 Le'Veon Bell 2.50 6.00

2018 Panini Unparalleled High Flyers

*ASTRAL/200: 1X TO 2.5X BASIC INSERTS
*WHIRL/100: 1.2X TO 3X BASIC INSERTS
*HYPER/25: 2X TO 5X BASIC INSERTS
1 Antonio Brown .60 1.50
2 Larry Fitzgerald .50 1.25
3 Odell Beckham Jr. .60 1.50
4 Mike Evans .50 1.25
5 A.J. Green .60 1.50
6 Rob Gronkowski .60 1.50
7 Julio Jones .60 1.50
8 DeAndre Hopkins .50 1.25
9 Amari Cooper .60 1.50
10 Devin Funchess .40 1.00
11 T.Y. Hilton .50 1.25
12 Alshon Jeffery .50 1.25
13 Keenan Allen .50 1.25
14 Doug Baldwin .50 1.25
15 Davante Adams .50 1.25
16 Golden Tate III .40 1.00
17 Cooper Kupp .50 1.25
18 Stefon Diggs .50 1.25

2018 Panini Unparalleled High Flyers Memorabilia

*WHIRL/50: .6X TO 1.5X BASIC JSY
*HYPER/25: .8X TO 2X BASIC AU
1 Antonio Brown 3.00 8.00
2 Larry Fitzgerald 2.50 6.00
3 Odell Beckham Jr. 3.00 8.00
4 Mike Evans 2.50 6.00
5 A.J. Green 3.00 8.00
6 Rob Gronkowski 3.00 8.00
7 Julio Jones 3.00 8.00
8 DeAndre Hopkins 2.50 6.00
9 Amari Cooper 3.00 8.00
10 Devin Funchess 2.00 5.00
11 T.Y. Hilton 2.50 6.00
13 Keenan Allen 2.50 6.00
14 Doug Baldwin 2.50 6.00
15 Davante Adams 2.50 6.00
16 Golden Tate III 2.00 5.00
17 Cooper Kupp 2.50 6.00
18 Stefon Diggs 2.50 6.00

2018 Panini Unparalleled Pioneers

*ASTRAL/200: 1X TO 2.5X BASIC INSERTS
*WHIRL/100: 1.2X TO 3X BASIC INSERTS
*HYPER/25: 2X TO 5X BASIC INSERTS
1 Jim Kelly .60 1.50
2 Michael Strahan .50 1.25
3 Mike Singletary .60 1.50
4 Terry Bradshaw 1.00 2.50
5 Mike Ditka .60 1.50
6 Emmitt Smith 1.00 2.50
7 LeRoy Butler .40 1.00
8 Ron Jaworski .50 1.25
9 Joe Namath .75 2.00
10 Dan Marino 1.25 3.00
11 Tim Brown .60 1.50
12 Jack Lambert .40 1.00
13 Brett Favre 1.25 3.00
14 Tony Gonzalez .50 1.25
15 Roger Wehrli .40 1.00
16 Peyton Manning 1.25 3.00

2018 Panini Unparalleled Rookie Autographs

201 Minkah Fitzpatrick 5.00 12.00
202 Denzel Ward 6.00 15.00
204 Harold Landry 2.50 6.00
205 Josh Rosen
206 Sam Darnold 60.00 125.00
207 Josh Allen
208 Baker Mayfield
210 Mason Rudolph 12.00 30.00
211 Deontay Burnett 3.00 8.00
212 Riley Ferguson 4.00 10.00
213 Saquon Barkley
214 Derrius Guice 5.00 12.00
215 Ronald Jones II 2.50 6.00
216 Nick Chubb
217 Kerryon Johnson 4.00 10.00
218 Sony Michel 12.00 30.00
219 John Kelly 3.00 8.00
221 Calvin Ridley 12.00 30.00
222 Christian Kirk 4.00 10.00
223 Courtland Sutton 4.00 10.00
224 James Washington 5.00 12.00
225 Anthony Miller 4.00 10.00
229 Dallas Goedert 3.00 8.00
232 Lorenzo Carter 2.50 6.00
233 Arden Key 2.50 6.00
234 Quadree Henderson 3.00 8.00
236 Maurice Hurst 3.00 8.00
237 Vita Vea 4.00 10.00
238 Roquan Smith 8.00 20.00
239 Malik Jefferson 3.00 8.00
240 Rashaan Evans 4.00 10.00
241 Tremaine Edmunds 5.00 12.00
242 Justin Jackson 3.00 8.00
243 Luke Falk 3.00 8.00
245 Simmie Cobbs Jr. 4.00 10.00
246 Trey Quinn 2.50 6.00
248 Bo Scarbrough 3.00 8.00
250 Josh Adams 5.00 12.00
252 Joshua Jackson 5.00 12.00
253 Derwin James 5.00 12.00
254 Ronnie Harrison 3.00 8.00
255 Mark Andrews 4.00 10.00
257 D.J. Moore 5.00 12.00
258 Marcell Ateman 3.00 8.00
259 Daron Payne 4.00 10.00
261 Dante Pettis 4.00 10.00
262 Jaleel Scott 2.50 6.00
263 Jordan Lasley 2.50 6.00
265 Ito Smith 3.00 8.00
266 Carlton Davis 3.00 8.00
267 Jaire Alexander 4.00 10.00
269 Lavon Coleman 3.00 8.00
270 Dorance Armstrong Jr. 2.50 6.00
271 Josh Sweat 3.00 8.00
272 Ryan Izzo 2.50 6.00
273 Jordan Whitehead 2.50 6.00
274 Austin Proehl 2.50 6.00
275 J'Mon Moore 2.50 6.00
276 Connor Williams 5.00 12.00
280 M.J. Stewart 2.50 6.00
282 Dalton Schultz 3.00 8.00
287 Kyle Allen 3.00 8.00
288 Sam Hubbard 3.00 8.00
289 Taven Bryan 2.50 6.00
290 Justin Reid 2.50 6.00
292 Leighton Vander Esch 8.00 20.00
293 Mike Hughes 4.00 10.00
294 Tre'Quan Smith 4.00 10.00
298 Cedrick Wilson Jr. 2.50 6.00
299 Marcus Davenport 5.00 12.00
300 Quenton Nelson 4.00 10.00

2018 Panini Unparalleled Rookie Focus

*ASTRAL/200: 1X TO 2.5X BASIC INSERTS
*WHIRL/100: 1.2X TO 3X BASIC INSERTS
*HYPER/25: 2X TO 5X BASIC INSERTS
1 Dante Pettis .60 1.50
2 Bradley Chubb .60 1.50
3 James Washington .75 2.00
4 Lamar Jackson 2.50 6.00
5 Sam Darnold 2.50 6.00
6 Josh Rosen 1.25 3.00
7 Baker Mayfield 4.00 10.00
8 Saquon Barkley 3.00 8.00
9 Mason Rudolph 1.00 2.50
10 Josh Allen 1.50 4.00
11 Derrius Guice .75 2.00
12 Nick Chubb 1.25 3.00
13 Sony Michel 1.25 3.00
14 Calvin Ridley 1.00 2.50
15 Christian Kirk .60 1.50
16 D.J. Moore .75 2.00

2018 Panini Unparalleled Rookie Focus Memorabilia

*WHIRL/50: .6X TO 1.5X BASIC JSY
*HYPER/25: .8X TO 2X BASIC AU
1 Dante Pettis 3.00 8.00
2 Bradley Chubb 3.00 8.00
3 James Washington 4.00 10.00
4 Lamar Jackson 8.00 20.00
5 Sam Darnold 8.00 20.00
6 Josh Rosen 8.00 20.00
7 Baker Mayfield 8.00 20.00
8 Saquon Barkley 10.00 25.00
9 Mason Rudolph 5.00 12.00
10 Josh Allen 6.00 15.00
11 Derrius Guice 4.00 10.00
12 Nick Chubb 6.00 15.00
13 Sony Michel 5.00 12.00
14 Calvin Ridley 5.00 12.00
15 Christian Kirk 3.00 8.00
16 D.J. Moore 4.00 10.00

2018 Panini Unparalleled Rookie Jersey Autographs

1 Bradley Chubb 6.00 15.00
2 Dante Pettis 6.00 15.00
3 James Washington 8.00 20.00
4 Rashaad Penny EXCH 6.00 15.00
5 Kerryon Johnson 6.00 15.00
6 Lamar Jackson 50.00 100.00
7 Sam Darnold 50.00 100.00
8 Josh Rosen 40.00 80.00
9 Baker Mayfield 50.00 100.00
10 Josh Allen 50.00 100.00
11 Saquon Barkley 90.00 150.00
12 Mason Rudolph 10.00 25.00
13 Nick Chubb 12.00 30.00
14 Derrius Guice 8.00 20.00
15 Sony Michel 12.00 30.00
16 Ronald Jones II 4.00 10.00
17 Calvin Ridley 10.00 25.00
18 Christian Kirk 6.00 15.00
19 Courtland Sutton 6.00 15.00
20 D.J. Moore 8.00 20.00
21 Anthony Miller 6.00 15.00
22 D.J. Chark EXCH 5.00 12.00
23 Mike Gesicki 5.00 12.00
24 Kyle Lauletta 6.00 15.00
25 Mark Walton 5.00 12.00
26 Mike White 5.00 12.00
27 Royce Freeman 5.00 12.00
28 Kalen Ballage 5.00 12.00
29 Nyheim Hines 5.00 12.00
30 Ito Smith 5.00 12.00
31 Keke Coutee 5.00 12.00
32 J'Mon Moore 4.00 10.00
33 Michael Gallup 8.00 20.00
34 Jaylen Samuels 5.00 12.00
35 Tre'Quan Smith 6.00 15.00
36 Jaleel Scott 4.00 10.00
37 Hayden Hurst 5.00 12.00
38 DaeSean Hamilton 5.00 12.00

2018 Panini Unparalleled Rookie Jersey Autographs Hyper

*HYPER/25: .6X TO 1.5X BASIC JSY AU
6 Lamar Jackson 90.00 150.00
7 Sam Darnold 100.00 200.00
10 Josh Allen 100.00 200.00
11 Saquon Barkley 125.00 250.00

2018 Panini Unparalleled Rookie Jersey Autographs Impact

*IMPACT/75: .5X TO 1.2X BASIC JSY AU
7 Sam Darnold 60.00 125.00
9 Baker Mayfield 75.00 150.00
10 Josh Allen 75.00 150.00
11 Saquon Barkley 100.00 200.00

2018 Panini Unparalleled Star Factor

*ASTRAL/200: 1X TO 2.5X BASIC INSERTS
*WHIRL/100: 1.2X TO 3X BASIC INSERTS
*HYPER/25: 2X TO 5X BASIC INSERTS
1 Odell Beckham Jr. .60 1.50
2 Ezekiel Elliott .75 2.00
3 Antonio Brown .60 1.50
4 Todd Gurley II .60 1.50
5 Tom Brady 1.50 4.00
6 Julio Jones .60 1.50
7 Le'Veon Bell .50 1.25
8 Kareem Hunt .50 1.25
9 Rob Gronkowski .60 1.50
10 Aaron Rodgers 1.25 3.00

2018 Panini Unparalleled Star Signatures

*IMPACT/15: .4X TO 1X BASIC AU/20
*IMPACT/20: .6X TO 1.5X BASIC AU/35
*IMPACT/20: .8X TO 2X BASIC AU/99
15 Jimmy Garoppolo/20 50.00 100.00
16 Charles Haley/35 8.00 20.00
17 Ed Too Tall Jones/35 10.00 25.00
18 Alvin Kamara/99 10.00 25.00

2018 Panini Unparalleled Undeniable Autographs

*IMPACT/25: .5X TO 1.2X BASIC AU/35
1 Eddie George/15 25.00 50.00
2 Maurice Jones-Drew/15 8.00 20.00
3 Rod Smith/15 40.00 80.00
4 Clay Matthews/15
5 Ricky Williams/35 10.00 25.00
6 Andre Reed/35 6.00 15.00
7 Sterling Sharpe/35
8 Larry Allen/35 8.00 20.00
9 Vinny Testaverde/35 5.00 12.00
10 Steve Atwater/35 6.00 15.00
11 Willis McGahee/35 5.00 12.00

2018 Panini Unparalleled Victorious

*ASTRAL/200: 1X TO 2.5X BASIC INSERTS
*WHIRL/100: 1.2X TO 3X BASIC INSERTS
*HYPER/25: 2X TO 5X BASIC INSERTS
1 Jared Goff .60 1.50
2 Alvin Kamara .50 1.25
3 Jordan Howard .60 1.50
4 Ezekiel Elliott .75 2.00
5 Deshaun Watson .75 2.00
6 Mitchell Trubisky .60 1.50
7 Melvin Gordon .50 1.25
8 JuJu Smith-Schuster .60 1.50
9 Matt Ryan .50 1.25
10 Chris Hogan .40 1.00
11 Zach Ertz .50 1.25
12 Christian McCaffrey .60 1.50
13 LeSean McCoy .60 1.50
14 Josh Gordon .40 1.00
15 Patrick Mahomes II 1.50 4.00
16 Kenny Golladay .40 1.00
17 Will Fuller V .40 1.00
18 Leonard Fournette .60 1.50
19 Andy Dalton .50 1.25
20 Amari Cooper .60 1.50

2018 Panini Unparalleled Victorious Memorabilia

*WHIRL/50: .6X TO 1.5X BASIC JSY
*HYPER/25: .8X TO 2X BASIC AU
1 Jared Goff 3.00 8.00
2 Alvin Kamara 2.50 6.00
3 Jordan Howard 3.00 8.00
4 Ezekiel Elliott 4.00 10.00
5 Deshaun Watson 4.00 10.00
6 Mitchell Trubisky 3.00 8.00
7 Melvin Gordon 2.50 6.00
8 JuJu Smith-Schuster 3.00 8.00
9 Matt Ryan 2.50 6.00
11 Zach Ertz 2.50 6.00
12 Christian McCaffrey 3.00 8.00
13 LeSean McCoy 3.00 8.00
14 Josh Gordon 2.00 5.00
15 Patrick Mahomes II 8.00 20.00
16 Kenny Golladay 2.00 5.00
17 Will Fuller V 2.00 5.00
18 Leonard Fournette 3.00 8.00
19 Andy Dalton 2.50 6.00
20 Amari Cooper 3.00 8.00

2017 Panini Vertex

1 Joe Flacco .75 2.00
2 Jeremy Maclin .60 1.50
3 Terrell Suggs .60 1.50
4 Tyrod Taylor .75 2.00
5 LeSean McCoy 1.00 2.50
6 Jordan Matthews .60 1.50
7 Andy Dalton .75 2.00
8 A.J. Green 1.00 2.50
9 Tyler Eifert .75 2.00
10 Corey Coleman .60 1.50
11 Myles Garrett RC 3.00 8.00
12 Demaryius Thomas .75 2.00
13 C.J. Anderson .75 2.00
14 Von Miller .75 2.00
15 Lamar Miller .60 1.50
16 DeAndre Hopkins .75 2.00
17 J.J. Watt 1.00 2.50
18 Andrew Luck 1.25 3.00
19 T.Y. Hilton .75 2.00
20 Donte Moncrief .75 2.00
21 Blake Bortles .60 1.50
22 Allen Hurns .60 1.50
23 Jalen Ramsey .60 1.50
24 Alex Smith .75 2.00
25 Tyreek Hill 1.00 2.50
26 Travis Kelce 1.00 2.50
27 Philip Rivers 1.00 2.50
28 Melvin Gordon .75 2.00
29 Hunter Henry .60 1.50
30 Jay Cutler .60 1.50
31 Jay Ajayi .75 2.00
32 Jarvis Landry .75 2.00
33 Tom Brady 2.50 6.00
34 Chris Hogan .60 1.50
35 Rob Gronkowski 1.00 2.50
36 Robby Anderson .60 1.50
37 Matt Forte .60 1.50
38 Derek Carr 1.00 2.50
39 Marshawn Lynch .75 2.00
40 Amari Cooper 1.00 2.50
41 Khalil Mack 1.00 2.50
42 Ben Roethlisberger 1.00 2.50
43 Le'Veon Bell .75 2.00
44 Antonio Brown 1.00 2.50
45 James Harrison .75 2.00
46 Marcus Mariota 1.00 2.50
47 DeMarco Murray .75 2.00
48 Eric Decker .60 1.50
49 Delanie Walker .60 1.50
50 Carson Palmer .75 2.00
51 David Johnson 1.00 2.50
52 Larry Fitzgerald .75 2.00
53 Matt Ryan .75 2.00
54 Devonta Freeman .75 2.00
55 Tevin Coleman .75 2.00
56 Julio Jones 1.00 2.50
57 Cam Newton 1.00 2.50
58 Kelvin Benjamin .75 2.00
59 Luke Kuechly .75 2.00
60 Jordan Howard 1.00 2.50
61 Leonard Floyd .60 1.50
62 Kendall Wright .60 1.50
63 Dak Prescott 1.00 2.50
64 Ezekiel Elliott 1.25 3.00
65 Jason Witten .75 2.00
66 Cole Beasley 1.00 2.50
67 Matthew Stafford .75 2.00
68 Ameer Abdullah .60 1.50
69 Golden Tate III .60 1.50
70 Aaron Rodgers 2.00 5.00
71 Aaron Jones 1.50 4.00
72 Jordy Nelson .75 2.00
73 Clay Matthews .75 2.00
74 Jared Goff 1.00 2.50
75 Todd Gurley II 1.00 2.50
76 Teddy Bridgewater .75 2.00
77 Stefon Diggs .75 2.00
78 Drew Brees 1.00 2.50
79 Mark Ingram .75 2.00
80 Adrian Peterson 1.00 2.50
81 Michael Thomas 1.00 2.50
82 Eli Manning .75 2.00
83 Paul Perkins .60 1.50
84 Odell Beckham Jr. 1.00 2.50
85 Brandon Marshall .60 1.50
86 Carson Wentz 1.25 3.00
87 Alshon Jeffery .75 2.00
88 Zach Ertz .75 2.00
89 Carlos Hyde .60 1.50
90 Jimmy Garoppolo 10.00 25.00
91 Russell Wilson 1.25 3.00
92 Thomas Rawls .60 1.50
93 Doug Baldwin .75 2.00
94 Richard Sherman 1.00 2.50
95 Jameis Winston .75 2.00
96 Mike Evans .75 2.00
97 DeSean Jackson .75 2.00
98 Kirk Cousins 1.00 2.50
99 Chris Thompson .60 1.50
100 Jamison Crowder .60 1.50
101 Mitchell Trubisky CAP JSY AU RC
102 Deshaun Watson CAP JSY AU RC 100.00 200.00
103 DeShone Kizer CAP JSY AU RC 5.00 12.00
104 Patrick Mahomes II CAP JSY AU RC 100.00 200.00
105 Nathan Peterman CAP JSY AU RC 6.00 15.00
106 Davis Webb CAP JSY AU RC 5.00 12.00
107 R. Joshua Dobbs CAP JSY AU RC 6.00 15.00
108 C.J. Beathard CAP JSY AU RC 5.00 12.00
109 Leonard Fournette CAP JSY AU RC EXCH 15.00 40.00
110 Christian McCaffrey CAP JSY AU RC
111 Dalvin Cook CAP JSY AU RC EXCH 30.00 60.00
112 Joe Mixon CAP JSY AU RC 10.00 25.00
113 Alvin Kamara CAP JSY AU RC 90.00 150.00
114 Samaje Perine CAP JSY AU RC 5.00 12.00
115 Marlon Mack CAP JSY AU RC 8.00 20.00
116 Wayne Gallman CAP JSY AU RC 6.00 15.00
117 Kareem Hunt CAP JSY AU RC 20.00 50.00
118 D'Onta Foreman CAP JSY AU RC 6.00 15.00
119 James Conner CAP JSY AU RC 10.00 25.00
120 Jeremy McNichols CAP JSY AU RC 5.00 12.00
121 Joe Williams CAP JSY AU RC 5.00 12.00
122 Corey Davis CAP JSY AU RC 8.00 20.00
123 Mike Williams CAP JSY AU RC 8.00 20.00
124 John Ross III CAP JSY AU RC 6.00 15.00
125 JuJu Smith-Schuster CAP JSY AU RC 40.00 80.00
126 Dede Westbrook CAP JSY AU RC 5.00 12.00
127 Curtis Samuel CAP JSY AU RC 6.00 15.00
128 Zay Jones CAP JSY AU RC 6.00 15.00
129 Amara Darboh CAP JSY AU RC 5.00 12.00
130 Carlos Henderson CAP JSY AU RC 5.00 12.00
131 Cooper Kupp CAP JSY AU RC 8.00 20.00
132 Josh Reynolds CAP JSY AU RC 5.00 12.00
133 ArDarius Stewart CAP JSY AU RC 5.00 12.00
134 Chris Godwin CAP JSY AU RC 6.00 15.00
135 Taywan Taylor CAP JSY AU RC 5.00 12.00
136 Kenny Golladay CAP JSY AU RC 8.00 20.00
137 Mack Hollins CAP JSY AU RC 5.00 12.00
138 Jamaal Williams CAP JSY AU RC 5.00 12.00
139 O.J. Howard CAP JSY AU RC 6.00 15.00
140 Evan Engram CAP JSY AU RC 6.00 15.00
141 Adoree' Jackson ASC AU/49 RC EXCH 6.00 15.00
142 Charles Harris ASC AU/49 RC 5.00 12.00
143 David Njoku ASC AU/99 RC 5.00 12.00
144 Derek Barnett ASC AU/99 RC 5.00 12.00
145 Gareon Conley ASC AU/99 RC 4.00 10.00
146 Haason Reddick ASC AU/99 RC 4.00 10.00
147 Jabrill Peppers ASC AU/49 RC 8.00 20.00
148 Jamal Adams ASC AU/49 RC 5.00 12.00
149 Jarrad Davis ASC AU/199 RC 5.00 12.00
150 Jonathan Allen ASC AU/49 RC 6.00 15.00
152 Marlon Humphrey ASC AU/99 RC 4.00 10.00
153 Marshon Lattimore ASC AU/49 RC 6.00 15.00
154 Solomon Thomas ASC AU/49 RC 5.00 12.00
155 T.J. Watt ASC AU/99 RC 12.00 30.00
156 Taco Charlton ASC AU/99 RC 4.00 10.00
157 Tre'Davious White ASC AU/99 RC 4.00 10.00
158 Adam Shaheen ASC AU/99 RC 4.00 10.00
159 Eddie Vanderdoes ASC AU/199 RC 4.00 10.00
160 Derek Rivers ASC AU/99 RC 5.00 12.00
161 Dalvin Tomlinson ASC AU/199 RC 4.00 10.00
164 Josh Jones ASC AU/199 RC 5.00 12.00
165 Justin Evans ASC AU/199 RC 4.00 10.00
166 Duke Riley ASC AU/99 RC 4.00 10.00
167 Malik McDowell ASC AU/99 RC 4.00 10.00
168 Marcus Maye ASC AU/199 RC 4.00 10.00
169 Marcus Williams ASC AU/199 RC 4.00 10.00
170 Eddie Jackson ASC AU/99 RC 5.00 12.00
171 Quincy Wilson ASC AU/49 RC 5.00 12.00
172 Raekwon McMillan ASC AU/49 RC 5.00 12.00
173 Ryan Anderson ASC AU/99 RC 4.00 10.00
174 Sidney Jones ASC AU/99 RC 4.00 10.00
175 Tanoh Kpassagnon ASC AU/199 RC 5.00 12.00
176 Tyus Bowser ASC AU/99 RC 4.00 10.00
177 Zach Cunningham ASC AU/49 RC 6.00 15.00
178 Cameron Sutton ASC AU/49 RC 5.00 12.00
179 Chad Williams ASC AU/99 RC 4.00 10.00
181 Tim Williams ASC AU/99 RC 5.00 12.00
182 Chad Hansen ASC AU/99 RC 4.00 10.00
183 Donnel Pumphrey ASC AU/99 RC 5.00 12.00
184 Jordan Leggett ASC AU/99 RC 4.00 10.00
185 Josh Malone ASC AU/49 RC 5.00 12.00
186 Ryan Switzer ASC AU/99 RC 5.00 12.00
187 Chris Carson ASC AU/99 RC 6.00 15.00
188 Jake Butt ASC AU/49 RC 6.00 15.00
189 Brad Kaaya ASC AU/49 RC 5.00 12.00
190 Matt Breida ASC AU/49 RC 8.00 20.00

2017 Panini Vertex Granite

*ROOK JSY AU/25: .6X TO 1.5X BASIC JSY AU/99
102 Deshaun Watson CAP JSY AU 400.00 800.00
104 Patrick Mahomes II CAP JSY AU 300.00 600.00

2017 Panini Vertex Quartz

*VETS/99: .6X TO 1.5X BASIC CARDS
*ROOK JSY AU/49: .5X TO 1.2X BASIC JSY AU/99
102 Deshaun Watson CAP JSY AU 250.00 350.00
104 Patrick Mahomes II CAP JSY AU 250.00 500.00
113 Alvin Kamara CAP JSY AU 100.00 200.00

2017 Panini Vertex Air Supremacy

1 Dak Prescott 1.25 3.00
2 Eli Manning 1.00 2.50
3 Carson Wentz 1.50 4.00
4 Kirk Cousins 1.25 3.00
5 Carson Palmer 1.00 2.50
6 Jared Goff 1.25 3.00
7 Russell Wilson 1.50 4.00
8 Mitchell Trubisky 4.00 10.00
9 Matthew Stafford 1.00 2.50
10 Aaron Rodgers 2.50 6.00
11 Matt Ryan 1.00 2.50
12 Cam Newton 1.25 3.00
13 Drew Brees 1.25 3.00
14 Jameis Winston 1.00 2.50
15 Tyrod Taylor 1.00 2.50
16 Dan Marino 2.50 6.00
17 Tom Brady 3.00 8.00
18 Peyton Manning 2.50 6.00
19 Jimmy Garoppolo 10.00 25.00
20 Alex Smith 1.00 2.50
21 Patrick Mahomes II 10.00 25.00
22 Philip Rivers 1.25 3.00
23 Derek Carr 1.25 3.00
24 Joe Flacco 1.00 2.50
25 Andy Dalton 1.00 2.50
26 DeShone Kizer .75 2.00
27 Ben Roethlisberger 1.25 3.00
28 Deshaun Watson 5.00 12.00
29 Andrew Luck 1.50 4.00
30 Marcus Mariota 1.25 3.00

2017 Panini Vertex Apogee Autographs

*GRANITE/25: .6X TO 1.5X BASIC AU/99
*GRANITE/15: .8X TO 2X BASIC AU/99
*GRANITE/15: .6X TO 1.5X BASIC AU/49-64
2 Alvin Kamara/99 60.00 125.00
3 Zay Jones/99 4.00 10.00
4 Taywan Taylor/99 3.00 8.00
5 Samaje Perine/99 [illegible] [illegible]

6 O.J. Howard/99 4.00 10.00
7 Mack Hollins/99 3.00 8.00
8 Kareem Hunt/99 6.00 15.00
9 Jeremy McNichols/99 3.00 8.00
11 Christian Okoye/99 3.00 8.00
12 Dalvin Cook/15 25.00 50.00
13 Christian McCaffrey/15
16 Corey Davis/25 8.00 20.00
17 Kiko Alonso/99 3.00 8.00
18 Jack Ham/99 20.00 50.00
21 LaDainian Tomlinson/15
22 Gerald McCoy/50 4.00 10.00
24 Tevin Coleman/49 5.00 12.00
25 Jordan Howard/49 6.00 15.00
26 Steve Largent/49 12.00 30.00
27 Delanie Walker/99 3.00 8.00
28 Kyle Juszczyk/99 3.00 8.00
30 Ryan Shazier/99 3.00 8.00
31 Hunter Henry/99 3.00 8.00
32 Fletcher Cox/49 4.00 10.00
33 Michael Bennett/99 3.00 8.00
34 Aaron Donald/99 5.00 12.00
35 Mike Vrabel/99 15.00 40.00
37 Chris Spielman/99 4.00 10.00
38 Lenny MooreA•64 4.00 10.00
40 Randy White/99 12.00 30.00

2017 Panini Vertex Capstones Jersey Autographs

*QUARTZ/49: .5X TO 1.2X BASIC JSY AU/99
*QUARTZ/25: .6X TO 1.5X BASIC JSY AU/99
*QUARTZ/25: .5X TO 1.2X BASIC JSY AU/49
*QUARTZ/15: .5X TO 1.2X BASIC JSY AU/25
*QUARTZ/15: .4X TO 1X BASIC JSY AU/20
*GRANITE/25: .6X TO 1.5X BASIC JSY AU/99
*GRANITE/15: .8X TO 2X BASIC JSY AU/99
*GRANITE/15: .6X TO 1.5X BASIC JSY AU/49
1 DeMarco Murray/99 5.00 12.00
2 Mike Evans/99 10.00 25.00
4 Drew Brees/15
5 A.J. Green/25 15.00 40.00
6 Ameer Abdullah/99 4.00 10.00
7 Carson Wentz/15
8 Doug Baldwin/99 10.00 25.00
9 Joey Bosa/99 25.00 50.00
10 Eddie Lacy/99 4.00 10.00
11 Matt Ryan/15
12 Jameis Winston/15 25.00 50.00
13 Jason Witten/99 EXCH 40.00 80.00
14 Quincy Enunwa/99 4.00 10.00
15 Isaiah Crowell/99 4.00 10.00
17 Derek Carr/25
18 Thomas Rawls/99 4.00 10.00
19 James White/99 5.00 12.00
20 Mark Ingram/99 12.00 30.00
21 Tevin Coleman/99 8.00 20.00
22 Dan Bailey/99 10.00 25.00
23 Danny Woodhead/99 5.00 12.00
24 Sterling Shepard/99 5.00 12.00
25 Tyler Lockett/99 5.00 12.00
26 Earl Thomas III/99 10.00 25.00
27 Tyreek Hill/99 12.00 30.00
28 Cole Beasley/99 EXCH 10.00 25.00
29 Marcus Mariota/20 40.00 80.00
30 Geno Atkins/99 4.00 10.00
31 Ezekiel Elliott/25 EXCH 60.00 125.00
32 Dak Prescott/49 EXCH 8.00 20.00
34 Latavius Murray/99 EXCH 4.00 10.00
35 Jordan Howard/99 6.00 15.00
36 Gerald McCoy/99 4.00 10.00
37 Melvin Gordon/99 15.00 40.00
38 Carlos Hyde/99 4.00 10.00
39 Zach Ertz/99 12.00 30.00
40 Terrelle Pryor/99 4.00 10.00

2017 Panini Vertex Championship Ink

1 James White/25 6.00 15.00
2 C.J. Anderson/20 8.00 20.00

2017 Panini Vertex Closers Jerseys

*GRANITE/25: .6X TO 1.5X BASIC JSY/99
*GRANITE/25: .5X TO 1.2X BASIC JSY/35-49
1 Tom Brady/35 12.00 30.00
2 Troy Aikman/49 6.00 15.00
3 Ray Lewis/49 5.00 12.00
4 Lawrence Taylor/49 5.00 12.00
5 Joe Namath/49 6.00 15.00
6 Aaron Rodgers/49 10.00 25.00
7 Eli Manning/49 4.00 10.00
8 Peyton Manning/49 10.00 25.00
9 John Elway/49 8.00 20.00
10 Joe Montana/49 12.00 30.00
11 Jerry Rice/49 8.00 20.00
12 Steve Young/49 6.00 15.00
13 Kurt Warner/49 4.00 10.00
14 Adam Vinatieri/49 3.00 8.00
15 Jason Witten/49 4.00 10.00
16 Russell Wilson/99 5.00 12.00
17 Terry Bradshaw/49 8.00 20.00
18 Terrell Davis/49 4.00 10.00
19 John Riggins/49 4.00 10.00
20 Phil Simms/99 3.00 8.00

2017 Panini Vertex Difference Makers Autographs

1 Bill Cowher/25 25.00 50.00
2 Mike Shanahan/25 6.00 15.00
3 Ozzie Newsome/25
5 Dan Bailey/49 4.00 10.00
6 Dick Anderson/49 8.00 20.00
7 Ed McCaffrey/25 5.00 12.00
8 Mark Moseley/99 3.00 8.00
9 Wayne Gallman/199 3.00 8.00
10 Sebastian Janikowski/25 15.00 40.00
11 Zach Thomas/25 25.00 50.00
13 Gerald McCoy/99 3.00 8.00
14 Elijah Hood/199 2.50 6.00
15 Samaje Perine/99 3.00 8.00
16 Jack Doyle/99 3.00 8.00
17 O.J. Howard/49 5.00 12.00
18 James White/99 4.00 10.00
19 Tevin Coleman/49 5.00 12.00
20 Jordan Howard/49 10.00 25.00
21 Marshon Lattimore/99 4.00 10.00
22 Steve Tasker/25 5.00 12.00
23 Terrelle Pryor/25 5.00 12.00
24 Delanie Walker/25 5.00 12.00
25 Jamaal Williams/199 2.50 6.00
26 Carlos Hyde/25 5.00 12.00
27 Hunter Henry/25 5.00 12.00
28 John Kuhn/99 3.00 8.00
29 Aaron Donald/49 6.00 15.00
31 Ed Too Tall Jones/49 4.00 10.00
32 Tyreek Hill/49 6.00 15.00
34 Troy Brown/99 3.00 8.00
35 Amara Darboh/49 4.00 10.00
36 Taywan Taylor/199 2.50 6.00
37 Zay Jones/99 4.00 10.00
38 Kenny Golladay/99 5.00 12.00
39 Brett Keisel/25 5.00 12.00
40 Kareem Hunt/199 5.00 12.00
42 Isaiah Crowell/99 3.00 8.00
43 Steve McMichael/99 3.00 8.00
44 Quincy Enunwa/99 3.00 8.00
45 Louis Lipps/99 3.00 8.00
46 Evan Engram/99 4.00 10.00
47 LeGarrette Blount/49 5.00 12.00
48 Cliff Branch/49 4.00 10.00
49 Jamal Adams/99 3.00 8.00
50 Adoree' Jackson/199 3.00 8.00

2017 Panini Vertex Domination Jerseys

*GRANITE/25: .6X TO 1.5X BASIC JSY/99
*GRANITE/25: .5X TO 1.2X BASIC JSY/35-49
1 Joey Bosa/35 5.00 12.00
2 Justin Houston/75 2.50 6.00
3 Harrison Smith/35 3.00 8.00
4 Geno Atkins/99 2.50 6.00
5 Ndamukong Suh/35 4.00 10.00
6 Jadeveon Clowney/99 2.50 6.00
7 Vic Beasley Jr./35 3.00 8.00
8 Aqib Talib/35 3.00 8.00
9 Richard Sherman/75 4.00 10.00
10 Luke Kuechly/49 4.00 10.00
11 Aaron Donald/49 5.00 12.00
12 Eric Berry/35 4.00 10.00
13 Von Miller/35 4.00 10.00
14 J.J. Watt/35 5.00 12.00
15 Khalil Mack/49 5.00 12.00

2017 Panini Vertex Ground Control

1 LeSean McCoy 1.25 3.00
2 Jay Ajayi 1.00 2.50
3 C.J. Anderson 1.00 2.50
4 Kareem Hunt 1.50 4.00
5 Melvin Gordon 1.00 2.50
6 Marshawn Lynch 1.00 2.50
7 Joe Mixon 1.50 4.00
8 Isaiah Crowell .75 2.00
9 Lamar Miller .75 2.00
10 Marlon Mack 1.25 3.00
11 Leonard Fournette 2.50 6.00
12 DeMarco Murray 1.00 2.50
13 Derrick Henry 1.00 2.50
14 Ezekiel Elliott 1.50 4.00
15 Le'Veon Bell 1.00 2.50
16 LeGarrette Blount 1.00 2.50
17 Chris Thompson .75 2.00
18 Samaje Perine .75 2.00
19 David Johnson 1.25 3.00
20 Todd Gurley II 1.25 3.00
21 Carlos Hyde .75 2.00
22 Chris Carson 1.25 3.00
23 Tarik Cohen 1.50 4.00
24 Jordan Howard 1.25 3.00
25 Dalvin Cook 2.00 5.00
26 Devonta Freeman 1.00 2.50
27 Alex Collins .75 2.00
28 Christian McCaffrey 2.00 5.00
29 Mark Ingram 1.00 2.50
30 Adrian Peterson 1.25 3.00

2017 Panini Vertex Highly Revered Autographs

1 Jim Kelly/49 20.00 50.00
3 Ty Law/99 12.00 30.00
4 Jason Taylor/99 15.00 40.00
5 Warren Moon/99 20.00 50.00
6 Tim Brown/99 6.00 15.00
11 Steve Young/49 50.00 100.00
12 Adam Vinatieri/49 15.00 40.00
13 Bruce Smith/99 15.00 40.00
17 Dan Fouts/25 12.00 30.00
18 Eric Dickerson/99 15.00 40.00
20 Jerome Bettis/49 25.00 50.00
21 Joe Greene/99 15.00 40.00
22 Jevon Kearse/99 4.00 10.00
23 Dan Reeves/99 12.00 30.00
24 Randy White/99 10.00 25.00
25 Brian Dawkins/99 100.00 200.00
26 Franco Harris/99 15.00 40.00
27 Chris Spielman/99 5.00 12.00
31 Lawrence Taylor/99 25.00 50.00
34 LaDainian Tomlinson/99 8.00 20.00
36 Ray Lewis/25 75.00 150.00
38 Bo Jackson/99 40.00 80.00
39 Ed Reed/40 15.00 40.00

2017 Panini Vertex Legendary Capstones Jersey Autographs

*QUARTZ/49: .5X TO 1.2X BASIC JSY AU/75-99
*QUARTZ/25: .6X TO 1.5X BASIC JSY AU/75-99
*QUARTZ/25: .5X TO 1.2X BASIC JSY AU/49
*GRANITE/25: .6X TO 1.5X BASIC JSY AU/75-99
*GRANITE/20: .8X TO 2X BASIC JSY AU/75-99
3 Ray Lewis/15 100.00 200.00
4 Dan Marino/15 75.00 150.00
5 Steve Young/15 EXCH 100.00 200.00
6 Jim Kelly
7 Warren Moon/99 30.00 60.00
8 Lawrence Taylor/49 50.00 100.00
9 Barry Sanders/15 EXCH 25.00 60.00
11 LaDainian Tomlinson/49 20.00 40.00
12 Champ Bailey/75 EXCH 20.00 50.00
13 Jeff Saturday/99 8.00 20.00
14 Hines Ward/99 30.00 60.00
15 Jim Plunkett/99 6.00 15.00
16 Joe Theismann/15 25.00 50.00
17 Thurman Thomas/99 12.00 30.00
18 Mark Brunell/99 6.00 15.00
19 Andre Reed/99 6.00 15.00

2017 Panini Vertex Nemeses

1 J.Norman/O.Beckham Jr. 1.50 4.00
2 R.Sherman/T.Brady 4.00 10.00
3 J.Montana/J.Elway 4.00 10.00
4 B.Favre/W.Sapp 3.00 8.00
5 D.Revis/R.Moss 1.25 3.00
6 E.George/R.Lewis 1.50 4.00
7 B.Sanders/E.Smith 2.50 6.00
8 J.Winston/M.Mariota 1.50 4.00
9 D.Sanders/J.Rice 2.50 6.00
10 C.Newton/V.Miller 1.50 4.00
11 D.Marino/J.Kelly 3.00 8.00
12 P.Manning/T.Brady 4.00 10.00
13 R.Staubach/T.Bradshaw 2.50 6.00
14 M.Crabtree/R.Sherman 1.50 4.00
15 B.Dawkins/M.Irvin 1.50 4.00
16 A.Luck/J.Watt 2.00 5.00
17 E.Manning/R.Harrison 1.25 3.00
18 S.Young/T.Aikman 2.00 5.00
19 D.Bryant/J.Norman 1.50 4.00
20 A.Brown/V.Burfict 1.50 4.00

2017 Panini Vertex Past and Present

1 E.Elliott/L.Taylor 2.00 5.00
2 L.Bell/R.Lewis 1.50 4.00
3 B.Sanders/C.Matthews 2.50 6.00
4 J.Elway/K.Mack 2.50 6.00
5 J.Rice/R.Sherman 2.50 6.00
6 J.Watt/P.Manning 3.00 8.00
7 D.Sanders/O.Beckham Jr. 1.50 4.00
8 C.Newton/W.Sapp 1.50 4.00
9 A.Rodgers/M.Singletary 3.00 8.00
10 B.Smith/T.Brady 4.00 10.00
11 J.Lynch/K.Hunt 2.00 5.00
12 A.Luck/M.Faulk 2.00 5.00
13 E.Dickerson/J.Goff 1.50 4.00
14 D.Marino/J.Ajayi 3.00 8.00
15 B.Jackson/D.Carr 2.00 5.00
16 C.Hyde/J.Montana 4.00 10.00
17 E.George/M.Mariota 1.50 4.00
18 D.Freeman/M.Vick 1.25 3.00
19 D.Prescott/E.Smith 2.50 6.00
20 L.Bell/T.Bradshaw 2.50 6.00

2017 Panini Vertex Portraits Jerseys

*GRANITE/25: .6X TO 1.5X BASIC JSY/99
*GRANITE/25: .5X TO 1.2X BASIC JSY/35-49
1 Josh Reynolds/99 2.50 6.00
2 Dalvin Cook/49 6.00 15.00
3 Alvin Kamara/49 12.00 30.00
4 Davis Webb/99 2.50 6.00
5 Wayne Gallman/99 3.00 8.00
6 Evan Engram/49 4.00 10.00
7 ArDarius Stewart/99 2.50 6.00
8 Mack Hollins/99 2.50 6.00
9 R. Joshua Dobbs/49 4.00 10.00
10 James Conner/49 6.00 15.00
11 JuJu Smith-Schuster/49 6.00 15.00
12 C.J. Beathard/49 3.00 8.00
13 Joe Williams/49 3.00 8.00
14 Amara Darboh/99 2.50 6.00
15 Derek Carr/99 4.00 10.00
16 Chris Godwin/40 4.00 10.00
17 O.J. Howard/49 4.00 10.00
18 Corey Davis/49 6.00 15.00
19 Taywan Taylor/49 3.00 8.00
20 Samaje Perine/99 2.50 6.00
21 Ezekiel Elliott/49 6.00 15.00
22 Dak Prescott/49 6.00 15.00
23 Dez Bryant/49 5.00 12.00
24 Carlos Hyde/49 3.00 8.00
25 Latavius Murray/99 2.50 6.00
26 Andy Dalton/49 4.00 10.00
27 Shaq Lawson/99 2.50 6.00
28 Isaiah Crowell/49 3.00 8.00
29 Marcus Mariota/49 5.00 12.00
30 Tyler Lockett/99 3.00 8.00
31 Jameis Winston/49 4.00 10.00
32 Tony Romo/49 4.00 10.00
33 Golden Tate III/49 3.00 8.00
34 Malcolm Mitchell/99 3.00 8.00
35 Doug Baldwin/49 4.00 10.00
36 Matt Ryan/49 4.00 10.00
37 Stefon Diggs/49 4.00 10.00
38 Sterling Shepard/99 3.00 8.00
39 Derrick Henry/49 4.00 10.00
40 Jared Goff/49 5.00 12.00
41 Carson Wentz/49 6.00 15.00
42 Joey Bosa/49 5.00 12.00
43 Kenyan Drake/99 2.50 6.00
44 Hunter Henry/99 2.50 6.00
45 Jordan Howard/49 5.00 12.00
46 Michael Thomas/49 5.00 12.00
47 Laquon Treadwell/49 3.00 8.00
48 Ameer Abdullah/99 2.50 6.00
49 Nelson Agholor/49 3.00 8.00
50 Jay Ajayi/49 4.00 10.00

2017 Panini Vertex Startups Jerseys

*GRANITE/25: .6X TO 1.5X BASIC JSY/99
1 Mitchell Trubisky 8.00 20.00
2 Deshaun Watson 10.00 25.00
3 DeShone Kizer 2.50 6.00
4 Patrick Mahomes II 30.00 60.00
5 Nathan Peterman 3.00 8.00
6 Davis Webb 2.50 6.00
7 R. Joshua Dobbs 3.00 8.00
8 C.J. Beathard 2.50 6.00
9 Leonard Fournette 8.00 20.00
10 Christian McCaffrey 6.00 15.00
11 Dalvin Cook 5.00 12.00
12 Joe Mixon 5.00 12.00
13 Alvin Kamara 10.00 25.00
14 Samaje Perine 2.50 6.00
15 Marlon Mack 4.00 10.00
16 Wayne Gallman 3.00 8.00
17 Kareem Hunt 5.00 12.00
18 D'Onta Foreman 3.00 8.00
19 James Conner 5.00 12.00
20 Amara Darboh 2.50 6.00
21 Joe Williams 2.50 6.00
22 Corey Davis 5.00 12.00
23 Mike Williams 4.00 10.00
24 John Ross III 3.00 8.00
25 JuJu Smith-Schuster 5.00 12.00
26 Dede Westbrook 2.50 6.00
27 Curtis Samuel 3.00 8.00
28 Zay Jones 3.00 8.00
29 David Njoku 3.00 8.00
30 Carlos Henderson 2.50 6.00
31 Cooper Kupp 4.00 10.00
32 Ryan Switzer 3.00 8.00
33 ArDarius Stewart 2.50 6.00
34 Chris Godwin 3.00 8.00
35 Taywan Taylor 2.50 6.00
36 Kenny Golladay 4.00 10.00
37 Mack Hollins 2.50 6.00
38 Jamaal Williams 2.50 6.00
39 O.J. Howard 3.00 8.00
40 Evan Engram 3.00 8.00

2017 Panini Vertex Unbreakable Jerseys

*GRANTE/25: .5X TO 1.2X BASIC JSY/49
1 Joe Thomas 3.00 8.00
2 Matthew Stafford 4.00 10.00
3 Barry Sanders 8.00 20.00
4 Jerome Bettis 5.00 12.00
5 Demaryius Thomas 4.00 10.00
6 Joe Flacco 4.00 10.00
7 Jeff Saturday 3.00 8.00
8 Marcus Allen 4.00 10.00
9 Derrick Brooks 3.00 8.00
10 Andre Reed 4.00 10.00
11 Len Dawson 5.00 12.00
12 Hines Ward 4.00 10.00
13 Emmitt Smith 8.00 20.00
14 Dan Marino 10.00 25.00
15 Charles Woodson 5.00 12.00
16 Brett Favre 10.00 25.00
17 Heath Miller 3.00 8.00
18 Drew Brees 5.00 12.00
19 Antonio Gates 3.00 8.00
20 Terrell Suggs 3.00 8.00
21 Larry Fitzgerald 4.00 10.00
22 Ben Roethlisberger 5.00 12.00
23 Philip Rivers 5.00 12.00
24 Derrick Johnson 3.00 8.00
25 Jason Witten 4.00 10.00

2017 Panini Vertex Upper Tier Signatures

2 Jay Novacek/99 10.00 25.00
4 Priest Holmes/99 4.00 10.00
5 Ed McCaffrey/99 4.00 10.00
6 Steve Largent/99 6.00 15.00
7 Charles Haley/99 6.00 15.00
8 Sterling Sharpe/99 5.00 12.00
9 Roger Craig/99 12.00 30.00
10 Ricky Williams/99 8.00 20.00
11 Ron Jaworski/99 5.00 12.00
12 Rod Woodson/99 15.00 40.00
13 Raymond Berry/49 6.00 15.00
15 Paul Warfield/99 5.00 12.00
16 Bill Bates/99 4.00 10.00
17 Steve Atwater/99 5.00 12.00
18 Bob Lilly/99 5.00 12.00
19 Joe Theismann/49 10.00 25.00
20 Andre Reed/99 5.00 12.00
21 Drew Pearson/99 EXCH 5.00 12.00
22 Zach Thomas/99 EXCH 15.00 40.00
23 Archie Manning/49 15.00 40.00
24 Fred Taylor/49 6.00 15.00
25 Jim Plunkett/49 6.00 15.00
27 Alan Page/99 8.00 20.00
28 Hines Ward/15 30.00 60.00
29 Heath Miller/99 4.00 10.00
30 Troy Brown/99 4.00 10.00
31 Mike Vrabel/99 4.00 10.00
32 Christian Okoye/99 4.00 10.00
33 Howie Long/15 25.00 50.00
34 Dan Hampton/99 4.00 10.00
35 Ozzie Newsome/99 5.00 12.00
37 Brett Keisel/99 20.00 40.00
38 Marcus Allen/15 20.00 50.00
39 Rod Smith/49 6.00 15.00
40 Jeremy Shockey/49 EXCH 5.00 12.00

2017 Panini Vertex Vertex Materials

*GRANITE/25: .6X TO 1.5X BASIC JSY/99
*GRANITE/25: .5X TO 1.2X BASIC JSY/35-49
1 Dwight Clark/99 3.00 8.00
2 Mitchell Trubisky/49 10.00 25.00
3 Julius Peppers/99 3.00 8.00
4 Joe Mixon/49 6.00 15.00
5 John Ross III/99 3.00 8.00
6 Nathan Peterman/99 3.00 8.00
7 Zay Jones/49 4.00 10.00
8 LeSean McCoy/49 5.00 12.00
9 Carlos Henderson/99 2.50 6.00
10 Jamaal Charles/75 3.00 8.00
11 Derek Wolfe/99 2.50 6.00
12 Andy Janovich/75 2.50 6.00
13 Brandon McManus/99 2.50 6.00
14 C.J. Anderson/75 3.00 8.00
15 DeShone Kizer/49 3.00 8.00
16 David Johnson/49 5.00 12.00
17 Mike Williams/75 4.00 10.00
18 Melvin Gordon/49 4.00 10.00
19 Patrick Mahomes II/75 30.00 80.00
20 Kareem Hunt/49 6.00 15.00
21 Marlon Mack/99 4.00 10.00
22 Zack Martin/75 2.50 6.00
23 DeVante Parker/49 4.00 10.00
24 Laremy Tunsil/99 3.00 8.00
25 Jarvis Landry/49 4.00 10.00
26 Michael Vick/49 4.00 10.00
27 Tevin Coleman/49 4.00 10.00
28 Devonta Freeman/49 4.00 10.00
29 Julio Jones/49 5.00 12.00
30 Leonard Fournette/49 10.00 25.00
31 Dede Westbrook/49 3.00 8.00
32 T.J. Yeldon/49 3.00 8.00
33 Jalen Ramsey/49 3.00 8.00
34 Mark Brunell/49 4.00 10.00
35 Blake Bortles/49 3.00 8.00
36 Leonard Williams/99 2.50 6.00
37 Kenny Golladay/99 4.00 10.00
38 Jamaal Williams/49 3.00 8.00
39 Ty Montgomery/49 3.00 8.00
40 Christian McCaffrey/49 8.00 20.00
41 Curtis Samuel/99 3.00 8.00
42 Kelvin Benjamin/49 4.00 10.00
43 Cooper Kupp/49 5.00 12.00
44 Todd Gurley II/49 5.00 12.00
45 Jamison Crowder/49 3.00 8.00
46 Earl Thomas III/49 4.00 10.00
47 Sammie Coates/99 2.50 6.00
48 Deshaun Watson/49 12.00 30.00
49 D'Onta Foreman/49 4.00 10.00
50 Teddy Bridgewater/49 4.00 10.00

2017 Panini Vertex Vertex Signatures

*GRANTE/25: .8X TO 2X BASIC AU/199
*GRANTE/15: 1X TO 2.5X BASIC AU/199
*GRANTE/15: .8X TO 2X BASIC AU/99
1 Brian Hill/99 3.00 8.00
2 Matt Breida/99 5.00 12.00
3 Adoree' Jackson/49 5.00 12.00
6 Carl Lawson/99 3.00 8.00
7 Chad Hansen/99 3.00 8.00
8 Chad Kelly/49 12.00 30.00
9 Chris Carson/199 4.00 10.00
10 Cole Hikutini/199 2.50 6.00
12 Damontae Kazee/199 3.00 8.00
14 Deatrich Wise Jr./199 4.00 10.00
16 Derek Barnett/49 5.00 12.00
17 Derek Rivers/199 3.00 8.00
18 Donnel Pumphrey/49 5.00 12.00
19 Eddie Vanderdoes/199 2.50 6.00
20 Elijah Hood/99 3.00 8.00
21 Gareon Conley/99 3.00 8.00
22 Greg Ward Jr./99 3.00 8.00
23 Haason Reddick/49 4.00 10.00
24 Jabrill Peppers/25 8.00 20.00
25 Jake Butt/99 4.00 10.00
26 Jordan Leggett/99 3.00 8.00
27 Josh Malone/49 4.00 10.00
28 Marcus Williams/99 3.00 8.00
29 Marlon Humphrey/49 4.00 10.00
30 Jamal Adams/49 4.00 10.00
31 Marshon Lattimore/25 6.00 15.00
32 Matthew Dayes/99 3.00 8.00
33 Montravius Adams/199 3.00 8.00
34 Quincy Wilson/99 3.00 8.00
35 Raekwon McMillan/99 3.00 8.00
37 Robert Davis/99 3.00 8.00
38 Ryan Switzer/49 5.00 12.00
39 Sam Rogers/199 2.50 6.00
40 Sidney Jones/99 3.00 8.00
41 Solomon Thomas/49 4.00 10.00
42 T.J. Logan/99 5.00 12.00
43 T.J. Watt/99 10.00 25.00
44 Taco Charlton/49 4.00 10.00
45 Tanoh Kpassagnon/199 3.00 8.00
46 Tim Williams/199 3.00 8.00
47 Travis Rudolph/199 2.50 6.00
48 Tre'Davious White/199 2.50 6.00
49 Tyus Bowser/199 2.50 6.00
50 Zach Cunningham/199 3.00 8.00

2017 Panini XR

1 Carson Palmer .30 .75
2 Larry Fitzgerald .30 .75
3 David Johnson .40 1.00
4 Patrick Peterson .25 .60
5 Julio Jones .40 1.00
6 Matt Ryan .30 .75
7 Vic Beasley Jr. .25 .60
8 Devonta Freeman .30 .75
9 Joe Flacco .30 .75
10 Mike Wallace .25 .60
11 Terrell Suggs .25 .60
12 LeSean McCoy .40 1.00
13 Tyrod Taylor .30 .75
14 Sammy Watkins .40 1.00
15 Cam Newton .40 1.00
16 Luke Kuechly .30 .75
17 Greg Olsen .30 .75
18 Kelvin Benjamin .30 .75
19 Mike Glennon .30 .75
20 Leonard Floyd .25 .60
21 Jordan Howard .40 1.00
22 Andy Dalton .30 .75
23 Tyler Eifert .30 .75
24 A.J. Green .40 1.00
25 Corey Coleman .25 .60
26 Isaiah Crowell .25 .60
27 Ezekiel Elliott .50 1.25
28 Dak Prescott .40 1.00
29 Dez Bryant .40 1.00
30 Jason Witten .30 .75
31 Von Miller .30 .75
32 Emmanuel Sanders .40 1.00
33 Devontae Booker .25 .60
34 Demaryius Thomas .30 .75
35 Zach Zenner .25 .60
36 Matthew Stafford .30 .75
37 Golden Tate III .25 .60
38 Aaron Rodgers .75 2.00
39 Clay Matthews .30 .75
40 Jordy Nelson .30 .75
41 J.J. Watt .40 1.00
42 DeAndre Hopkins .30 .75
43 Jadeveon Clowney .25 .60
44 Andrew Luck .50 1.25
45 T.Y. Hilton .30 .75
46 Frank Gore .30 .75
47 Blake Bortles .25 .60
48 Allen Robinson .30 .75
49 Marqise Lee .25 .60
50 Eric Berry .30 .75
51 Alex Smith .30 .75
52 Tyreek Hill .40 1.00
53 Chris Conley .25 .60
54 Philip Rivers .40 1.00
55 Antonio Gates .25 .60
56 Keenan Allen .30 .75
57 Joey Bosa .40 1.00
58 Todd Gurley II .40 1.00
59 Jared Goff .40 1.00
60 Aaron Donald .40 1.00
61 Ryan Tannehill .30 .75
62 Jarvis Landry .30 .75
63 Jay Ajayi .30 .75
64 Tom Brady 1.00 2.50
65 Rob Gronkowski .40 1.00
66 Julian Edelman .40 1.00
67 Adrian Peterson .40 1.00
68 Drew Brees .40 1.00
69 Mark Ingram .30 .75
70 Eli Manning .30 .75
71 Paul Perkins .25 .60
72 Odell Beckham Jr. .40 1.00
73 Brandon Marshall .25 .60
74 Matt Forte .25 .60
75 Quincy Enunwa .25 .60
76 Leonard Williams .25 .60
77 Derek Carr .40 1.00
78 Amari Cooper .40 1.00
79 Khalil Mack .40 1.00
80 Carson Wentz .50 1.25
81 Jordan Matthews .25 .60
82 Alshon Jeffery .30 .75
83 Antonio Brown .40 1.00
84 Le'Veon Bell .30 .75
85 Ben Roethlisberger .40 1.00
86 Navorro Bowman .30 .75
87 Carlos Hyde .25 .60
88 Russell Wilson .50 1.25
89 Doug Baldwin .30 .75
90 Kam Chancellor .40 1.00
91 Jameis Winston .30 .75
92 Mike Evans .30 .75
93 Gerald McCoy .25 .60
94 Marcus Mariota .40 1.00
95 DeMarco Murray .30 .75
96 Rishard Matthews .25 .60
97 Josh Norman .25 .60
98 Kirk Cousins .40 1.00
99 Ryan Kerrigan .25 .60
100 Jordan Reed .25 .60
101 Myles Garrett RC 2.00 5.00
102 Josh Malone RC .60 1.50
103 Chad Hansen RC .60 1.50
104 Donnel Pumphrey RC .75 2.00
105 Ryan Switzer RC .75 2.00
106 Brian Hill RC .60 1.50
107 Shelton Gibson RC .60 1.50
108 Chad Williams RC .60 1.50
109 Jehu Chesson RC .75 2.00
110 Tarik Cohen RC 1.25 3.00
111 Rodney Adams RC .60 1.50
112 Isaiah McKenzie RC .60 1.50
113 DeAngelo Yancey RC .60 1.50
114 Trent Taylor RC .75 2.00
115 T.J. Logan RC 1.00 2.50
116 Solomon Thomas RC .60 1.50
117 Jamal Adams RC .60 1.50
118 Marshon Lattimore RC .75 2.00
119 Haason Reddick RC .60 1.50
120 Derek Barnett RC .75 2.00
121 Malik Hooker RC .60 1.50
122 Marlon Humphrey RC .60 1.50
123 Jonathan Allen RC .75 2.00
124 Adoree' Jackson RC .75 2.00
125 Garett Bolles RC .60 1.50
126 Jarrad Davis RC .75 2.00
127 Charles Harris RC .60 1.50
128 Gareon Conley RC .60 1.50
129 Jabrill Peppers RC 1.00 2.50
130 Takkarist McKinley RC .60 1.50
131 Tre'Davious White RC .60 1.50
132 Taco Charlton RC .60 1.50
133 David Njoku RC .75 2.00
134 T.J. Watt RC 2.00 5.00
135 Reuben Foster RC .60 1.50
136 Jake Butt RC .75 2.00
137 Kevin King RC .75 2.00
138 Cam Robinson RC .60 1.50
139 Budda Baker RC .60 1.50
140 Marcus Maye RC .60 1.50
141 Marcus Williams RC .60 1.50
142 Sidney Jones RC .60 1.50
143 Gerald Everett RC .60 1.50
144 Adam Shaheen RC .60 1.50
145 Quincy Wilson RC .60 1.50
146 Tyus Bowser RC .60 1.50
147 Ryan Anderson RC .60 1.50
148 Justin Evans RC .60 1.50
149 DeMarcus Walker RC .60 1.50
150 Teez Tabor RC .75 2.00
151 Raekwon McMillan RC .60 1.50
152 Dalvin Tomlinson RC .60 1.50
153 Obi Melifonwu RC .60 1.50
154 Zach Cunningham RC .75 2.00
155 Tanoh Kpassagnon RC .75 2.00
156 Chidobe Awuzie RC .75 2.00
157 Josh Jones RC .60 1.50
158 Chris Wormley RC .60 1.50
159 Jordan Willis RC .60 1.50
160 Duke Riley RC .60 1.50
161 Mitchell Trubisky JSY AU/25 RC 50.00 100.00
162 Deshaun Watson JSY AU/25 RC 75.00 150.00
163 DeShone Kizer JSY AU/25 RC 6.00 15.00
164 Patrick Mahomes II JSY AU/25 RC 125.00 250.00
165 Davis Webb JSY AU/49 RC 5.00 12.00
166 C.J. Beathard JSY AU/99 RC 4.00 10.00
167 R. Joshua Dobbs JSY AU/99 RC 5.00 12.00
168 Nathan Peterman JSY AU/99 RC 5.00 12.00
169 Leonard Fournette JSY AU/25 RC 20.00 50.00
170 Dalvin Cook JSY AU/49 RC 12.00 30.00
171 Christian McCaffrey JSY AU/25 RC 15.00 40.00
172 D'Onta Foreman JSY AU/99 RC 5.00 12.00
173 Alvin Kamara JSY AU/199 RC 12.00 30.00
174 Samaje Perine JSY AU/199 RC 3.00 8.00
175 Marlon Mack JSY AU/99 RC 6.00 15.00
176 Kareem Hunt JSY AU/199 RC 20.00 50.00
177 Wayne Gallman JSY AU/199 RC 4.00 10.00
178 James Conner JSY AU/99 RC 8.00 20.00
179 Joe Mixon JSY AU/99 RC 8.00 20.00
180 Mack Hollins JSY AU/99 RC 4.00 10.00
181 O.J. Howard JSY AU/199 RC 4.00 10.00
182 Mike Williams JSY AU/25 RC
183 Corey Davis JSY AU/99 RC 6.00 15.00
184 John Ross III JSY AU/99 RC 5.00 12.00
185 JuJu Smith-Schuster JSY AU/99 RC 10.00 25.00
186 Zay Jones JSY AU/199 RC 4.00 10.00
187 Curtis Samuel JSY AU/199 RC 4.00 10.00
188 Dede Westbrook JSY AU/199 RC 3.00 8.00
189 Carlos Henderson JSY AU/199 RC 3.00 8.00
190 Chris Godwin JSY AU/99 RC 5.00 12.00
191 Kenny Golladay JSY AU/99 RC 6.00 15.00
192 Cooper Kupp JSY AU/99 RC 6.00 15.00
193 Amara Darboh JSY AU/199 RC 3.00 8.00
194 Jeremy McNichols JSY AU/199 RC 3.00 8.00
195 ArDarius Stewart JSY AU/99 RC 4.00 10.00
196 Joe Williams JSY AU/99 RC 4.00 10.00
197 Josh Reynolds JSY AU/99 RC 4.00 10.00
198 Taywan Taylor JSY AU/199 RC 3.00 8.00
199 Evan Engram JSY AU/199 RC 4.00 10.00
200 Jamaal Williams JSY AU/99 RC 4.00 10.00

2017 Panini XR Blue

*VETS: 1.5X TO 4X BASIC CARDS
*ROOKIES: .6X TO 1.5X BASIC CARDS
*ROOK JSY AU/49: .6X TO 1.5X BASIC JSY AU/199
*ROOK JSY AU/49: .5X TO 1.2X BASIC JSY AU/99
*ROOK JSY AU/25: .5X TO 1.2X BASIC JSY AU/49

2017 Panini XR Orange

*VETS: 2X TO 5X BASIC CARDS
*ROOKIES: .8X TO 2X BASIC CARDS
*ROOK JSY AU/25: .8X TO 2X BASIC JSY AU/199
*ROOK JSY AU/25: .6X TO 1.5X BASIC JSY AU/99

2017 Panini XR Red

*VETS: 1.2X TO 3X BASIC CARDS
*ROOKIES: .5X TO 1.2X BASIC CARDS
*ROOK JSY AU/75: .5X TO 1.2X BASIC JSY AU/199
*ROOK JSY AU/75: .4X TO 1X BASIC JSY AU/99
*ROOK JSY AU/35: .4X TO 1X BASIC JSY AU/49
*ROOK JSY AU/15: .5X TO 1.2X BASIC JSY AU/25
162 Deshaun Watson JSY AU/15 100.00 200.00
164 Patrick Mahomes II JSY AU/15 200.00 400.00

2017 Panini XR Autographs

*ORANGE/49: .6X TO 1.5X BASIC AU/199
*ORANGE/49: .5X TO 1.2X BASIC AU/99
8 Devonta Freeman/20 8.00 20.00
16 Luke Kuechly/20 8.00 20.00
17 Greg Olsen/20 8.00 20.00
23 Tyler Eifert/20 8.00 20.00
25 Corey Coleman/20 6.00 15.00
26 Isaiah Crowell/20 6.00 15.00
32 Emmanuel Sanders/20 10.00 25.00
33 Devontae Booker/20 6.00 15.00
37 Golden Tate III/20 6.00 15.00
40 Jordy Nelson/20 8.00 20.00
48 Allen Robinson/20 8.00 20.00
49 Marqise Lee/20 6.00 15.00
50 Eric Berry/20 8.00 20.00
52 Tyreek Hill/20 10.00 25.00
56 Keenan Allen/20 8.00 20.00
57 Joey Bosa/15 10.00 25.00
71 Paul Perkins/20 6.00 15.00
87 Carlos Hyde/20 6.00 15.00
89 Doug Baldwin/20 8.00 20.00
92 Mike Evans/20 8.00 20.00
96 Rishard Matthews/20 6.00 15.00
102 Josh Malone/199 2.50 6.00
103 Chad Hansen/99 3.00 8.00
105 Ryan Switzer/199 3.00 8.00
106 Brian Hill/99 3.00 8.00
107 Shelton Gibson/199 2.50 6.00
109 Jehu Chesson/199 3.00 8.00
110 Tarik Cohen/199 5.00 12.00
113 DeAngelo Yancey/199 2.50 6.00
114 Trent Taylor/199 3.00 8.00
115 T.J. Logan/199 4.00 10.00
116 Solomon Thomas/99 3.00 8.00
117 Jamal Adams/99 3.00 8.00
118 Marshon Lattimore/99 4.00 10.00
119 Haason Reddick/199 2.50 6.00
121 Malik Hooker/99 3.00 8.00
122 Marlon Humphrey/99 3.00 8.00
123 Jonathan Allen/99 4.00 10.00
124 Adoree' Jackson/99 4.00 10.00
125 Garett Bolles/199 2.50 6.00
126 Jarrad Davis/199 3.00 8.00
127 Charles Harris/199 2.50 6.00
128 Gareon Conley/199 2.50 6.00
129 Jabrill Peppers/99 5.00 12.00
131 Tre'Davious White/199 2.50 6.00
132 Taco Charlton/199 2.50 6.00
133 David Njoku/99 4.00 10.00
134 T.J. Watt/199 8.00 20.00
136 Jake Butt/199 3.00 8.00
137 Kevin King/199 3.00 8.00
140 Marcus Maye/199 2.50 6.00
141 Marcus Williams/199 2.50 6.00
142 Sidney Jones/199 2.50 6.00
143 Gerald Everett/199 2.50 6.00
144 Adam Shaheen/199 2.50 6.00
145 Quincy Wilson/99 3.00 8.00
146 Tyus Bowser/199 2.50 6.00
147 Ryan Anderson/199 2.50 6.00
148 Justin Evans/199 2.50 6.00
149 DeMarcus Walker/199 2.50 6.00
151 Raekwon McMillan/199 2.50 6.00
152 Dalvin Tomlinson/199 2.50 6.00
153 Obi Melifonwu/199 2.50 6.00
154 Zach Cunningham/199 3.00 8.00
155 Tanoh Kpassagnon/199 3.00 8.00
157 Josh Jones/199 2.50 6.00
158 Chris Wormley/199 2.50 6.00
160 Duke Riley/199 2.50 6.00

2017 Panini XR Gilded Greats

*BLUE/49: .5X TO 1.2X BASIC INSERTS/99
*ORANGE/25: .6X TO 1.5X BASIC INSERTS/99
1 Joe Namath 2.00 5.00
2 Emmitt Smith 2.50 6.00
3 Brett Favre 3.00 8.00
4 Jerome Bettis 1.50 4.00
5 Michael Strahan 1.25 3.00
6 Warren Sapp 1.25 3.00
7 Deion Sanders 1.25 3.00
8 Marshall Faulk 1.25 3.00
9 Bruce Smith 1.25 3.00
10 Troy Aikman 2.00 5.00
11 Steve Young 2.00 5.00
12 Barry Sanders 2.50 6.00
13 John Elway 2.50 6.00
14 Terry Bradshaw 2.50 6.00
15 Dan Marino 3.00 8.00
16 Howie Long 1.50 4.00
17 Mike Singletary 1.50 4.00
18 Roger Staubach 2.00 5.00
19 Earl Campbell 1.50 4.00
20 Eric Dickerson 1.50 4.00

2017 Panini XR Illustrious

*BLUE/49: .5X TO 1.2X BASIC INSERTS/99
*ORANGE/25: .6X TO 1.5X BASIC INSERTS/99
1 Rob Gronkowski 1.50 4.00
2 Antonio Brown 1.50 4.00
3 Greg Olsen 1.25 3.00
4 A.J. Green 1.50 4.00
5 Dez Bryant 1.50 4.00
6 Odell Beckham Jr. 1.50 4.00
7 Jordy Nelson 1.25 3.00
8 Julio Jones 1.50 4.00
9 Michael Thomas 1.50 4.00
10 Jarvis Landry 1.25 3.00
11 Amari Cooper 1.50 4.00
12 Larry Fitzgerald 1.25 3.00
13 Doug Baldwin 1.25 3.00
14 Jordan Matthews 1.00 2.50
15 Sammy Watkins 1.50 4.00
16 Rishard Matthews 1.00 2.50
17 T.Y. Hilton 1.25 3.00
18 Mike Evans 1.25 3.00
19 Travis Kelce 1.50 4.00
20 Golden Tate III 1.00 2.50

2017 Panini XR Luminous Endorsements

1 Mitchell Trubisky/49 50.00 100.00
2 Deshaun Watson/49 75.00 150.00
3 DeShone Kizer/49 4.00 10.00
4 Patrick Mahomes II/49 125.00 250.00
5 Davis Webb/99 3.00 8.00
6 C.J. Beathard/99 3.00 8.00
7 R. Joshua Dobbs/99 4.00 10.00
8 Nathan Peterman/99 4.00 10.00
9 Leonard Fournette/49 40.00 80.00
10 Dalvin Cook/49
11 Christian McCaffrey/49 10.00 25.00
12 D'Onta Foreman/99 4.00 10.00
13 Alvin Kamara/99 12.00 30.00
14 Samaje Perine/99 3.00 8.00
15 Marlon Mack/99 5.00 12.00
16 Kareem Hunt/99 25.00 60.00
17 Wayne Gallman/99 4.00 10.00
18 James Conner/99 6.00 15.00
19 Joe Mixon/99 6.00 15.00
20 Mack Hollins/99 3.00 8.00
21 O.J. Howard/99 4.00 10.00
22 Mike Williams/49 6.00 15.00
23 Corey Davis/99 5.00 12.00
24 John Ross III/99 4.00 10.00
25 JuJu Smith-Schuster/99 8.00 20.00
26 Zay Jones/99 4.00 10.00
27 Curtis Samuel/99 4.00 10.00
28 Dede Westbrook/99 3.00 8.00
29 Carlos Henderson/99 3.00 8.00
30 Chris Godwin/99 4.00 10.00
31 Kenny Golladay/99 5.00 12.00
32 Cooper Kupp/99 5.00 12.00
33 Amara Darboh/99 3.00 8.00
34 Jeremy McNichols/99 3.00 8.00
35 ArDarius Stewart/99 3.00 8.00
36 Joe Williams/99 3.00 8.00
37 Josh Reynolds/99 3.00 8.00
38 Taywan Taylor/99 3.00 8.00
39 Evan Engram/99 4.00 10.00
40 Jamaal Williams/99 3.00 8.00

2017 Panini XR Luminous Endorsements Blue

*BLUE/49: .5X TO 1.2X BASIC AU/99
*BLUE/25: .5X TO 1.2X BASIC AU/49
2 Deshaun Watson/25 100.00 200.00

2017 Panini XR Luminous Endorsements Orange

*ORANGE/25: .6X TO 1.5X BASIC AU

2017 Panini XR Maximal Materials

*BLUE/49: .5X TO 1.2X BASIC JSY/75-99
*BLUE/25: .5X TO 1.2X BASIC JSY/49
*ORANGE/25: .6X TO 1.5X BASIC JSY/75-99
*ORANGE/25: .4X TO 1X BASIC JSY/25
1 Dak Prescott/99 4.00 10.00
2 Ezekiel Elliott/99 5.00 12.00
3 Jordan Howard/99 4.00 10.00
4 Cam Newton/49 5.00 12.00
5 Jameis Winston/75 3.00 8.00
6 Marcus Mariota/75 4.00 10.00
7 Andy Dalton/25 5.00 12.00
8 Ryan Tannehill/75 3.00 8.00
9 Joey Bosa/99 4.00 10.00
10 DeMarco Murray/75 3.00 8.00
11 Steve Young/25 8.00 20.00
12 Bo Jackson/49 6.00 15.00
13 David Johnson/75 4.00 10.00
14 Jim Kelly/49 5.00 12.00
15 John Elway/49 8.00 20.00
16 Jerome Bettis/49 5.00 12.00
17 Jerry Rice/49 8.00 20.00
18 Barry Sanders/75 6.00 15.00
19 Dan Marino/49 10.00 25.00
20 Franco Harris/25 6.00 15.00
21 Jay Ajayi/75 3.00 8.00
22 Matthew Stafford/25 5.00 12.00
23 Jadeveon Clowney/75 2.50 6.00
24 Amari Cooper/99 4.00 10.00
25 Odell Beckham Jr./75 4.00 10.00
26 Le'Veon Bell/75 3.00 8.00
27 Kirk Cousins/25 6.00 15.00
28 Dan Bailey/25 4.00 10.00
29 Carson Wentz/99 5.00 12.00
30 Paxton Lynch/99 2.50 6.00

2017 Panini XR Mirrored

*RED/25: .5X TO 1.2X BASIC INSERTS
*BLUE/15: .6X TO 1.5X BASIC INSERTS
1 M.Trubisky/M.Stafford 4.00 10.00
2 D.Watson/M.Mariota 5.00 12.00
3 D.Kizer/W.Moon 1.25 3.00
4 D.Carr/P.Mahomes 1.25 3.00
5 D.Webb/E.Manning 1.00 2.50
6 C.Beathard/K.Cousins 1.25 3.00
7 D.Prescott/R.Dobbs 1.25 3.00
8 J.Garoppolo/N.Peterman 4.00 10.00
9 B.Jackson/L.Fournette 2.50 6.00
10 E.James/D.Cook 2.00 5.00
11 C.McCaffrey/E.McCaffrey 2.00 5.00
12 D.Foreman/R.Williams 1.00 2.50
13 D.Williams/A.Kamara 3.00 8.00
14 B.Sims/S.Perine 1.00 2.50
15 F.Gore/M.Mack 1.25 3.00
16 P.Holmes/K.Hunt 1.50 4.00
17 P.Perkins/W.Gallman 1.00 2.50
18 J.Conner/L.Bell 1.50 4.00
19 A.Peterson/J.Mixon 1.50 4.00
20 J.Matthews/M.Hollins .75 2.00
21 J.Thomas/O.Howard 1.00 2.50
22 M.Williams/D.Hopkins 1.25 3.00
23 C.Davis/C.Johnson 1.25 3.00
24 D.Jackson/J.Ross 1.00 2.50
25 J.Smith-Schuster/A.Boldin 2.00 5.00
26 S.Watkins/Z.Jones 1.25 3.00
27 C.Samuel/E.Elliott 1.50 4.00
28 D.Westbrook/A.Hurns .75 2.00
29 C.Henderson/E.Sanders 1.25 3.00
30 C.Godwin/M.Evans 1.00 2.50
31 K.Golladay/M.Jones 1.25 3.00
32 C.Kupp/J.Edelman 1.25 3.00
33 A.Darboh/D.Baldwin 1.00 2.50
34 D.Martin/J.McNichols 1.00 2.50
35 A.Cooper/A.Stewart 1.25 3.00
36 C.Hyde/J.Williams .75 2.00
37 T.Austin/J.Reynolds .75 2.00
38 S.Diggs/T.Taylor 1.00 2.50
39 E.Engram/R.Gronkowski 1.25 3.00
40 J.Williams/M.Forte .75 2.00

2017 Panini XR Notorious

*BLUE/49: .5X TO 1.2X BASIC INSERTS/99
*ORANGE/25: .6X TO 1.5X BASIC INSERTS
1 Tom Brady 4.00 10.00
2 Ben Roethlisberger 1.50 4.00
3 Cam Newton 1.50 4.00
4 Andy Dalton 1.25 3.00
5 Dak Prescott 1.50 4.00
6 Eli Manning 1.25 3.00
7 Aaron Rodgers 3.00 8.00
8 Matt Ryan 1.25 3.00
9 Drew Brees 1.50 4.00
10 Ryan Tannehill 1.25 3.00
11 Derek Carr 1.50 4.00
12 Carson Palmer 1.25 3.00
13 Russell Wilson 2.00 5.00
14 Carson Wentz 2.00 5.00
15 Tyrod Taylor 1.25 3.00
16 Marcus Mariota 1.50 4.00
17 Andrew Luck 2.00 5.00
18 Jameis Winston 1.25 3.00
19 Alex Smith 1.25 3.00
20 Matthew Stafford 1.25 3.00

2017 Panini XR Rookie Jumbo Materials

*BLUE/49: .5X TO 1.2X BASIC JSY/75
*ORANGE/25: .6X TO 1.5X BASIC JSY/75
1 Mitchell Trubisky 12.00 20.00
2 Deshaun Watson 12.00 30.00
3 DeShone Kizer 2.50 6.00
4 Patrick Mahomes II 6.00 15.00
5 Davis Webb 2.50 6.00
6 C.J. Beathard 2.50 6.00
7 R. Joshua Dobbs 5.00 12.00
8 Nathan Peterman 3.00 8.00
9 Leonard Fournette 10.00 25.00
10 Dalvin Cook 6.00 15.00
11 Christian McCaffrey 8.00 20.00
12 D'Onta Foreman 3.00 8.00
13 Alvin Kamara 5.00 12.00
14 Samaje Perine 2.50 6.00
15 Marlon Mack 4.00 10.00
16 Kareem Hunt 6.00 15.00
17 Wayne Gallman 3.00 8.00
18 James Conner 5.00 12.00
19 Joe Mixon 5.00 12.00
20 Mack Hollins 2.50 6.00
21 O.J. Howard 3.00 8.00
22 Mike Williams 4.00 10.00
23 Corey Davis 4.00 10.00
24 John Ross III 5.00 12.00
25 JuJu Smith-Schuster 5.00 12.00
26 Zay Jones 3.00 8.00
27 Curtis Samuel 3.00 8.00
28 Dede Westbrook 2.50 6.00
29 Carlos Henderson 2.50 6.00
30 Chris Godwin 3.00 8.00
31 Kenny Golladay 4.00 10.00
32 Cooper Kupp 4.00 10.00
33 Amara Darboh 2.50 6.00
34 Jeremy McNichols 2.50 6.00

35 ArDarius Stewart 2.50 6.00
36 Joe Williams 2.50 6.00
37 Josh Reynolds 2.50 6.00
38 Taywan Taylor 2.50 6.00
39 Evan Engram 3.00 8.00
40 Jamaal Williams 2.50 6.00

2017 Panini XR Rookie Jumbo Swatch Autographs Blue

*BLUE/49: .5X TO 1.2X BASIC JSY AU/99
*BLUE/25: .6X TO 1.5X BASIC JSY AU/99
*BLUE/25: .5X TO 1.2X BASIC JSY AU/49
*BLUE/15: .6X TO 1.5X BASIC JSY AU/49

2017 Panini XR Rookie Jumbo Swatch Autographs Orange

*ORANGE/25: .6X TO 1.5X BASIC JSY AU/99

2017 Panini XR Rookie Jumbo Swatch Autographs Red

*RED/75: .4X TO 1X BASIC JSY AU/99
*RED/35: .5X TO 1.2X BASIC JSY AU/99
*RED/35: .4X TO 1X BASIC JSY AU/49
*RED/25: .5X TO 1.2X BASIC JSY AU/49
*RED/15: .5X TO 1.2X BASIC JSY AU/25

2017 Panini XR Rookie Swatch Autographs Blue

*BLUE/49: .6X TO 1.5X BASIC JSY AU/199
*BLUE/49: .5X TO 1.2X BASIC JSY AU/99
*BLUE/25: .6X TO 1.5X BASIC JSY AU/99
*BLUE/25: .5X TO 1.2X BASIC JSY AU/49
*BLUE/15: .6X TO 1.5X BASIC JSY AU/49

2017 Panini XR Rookie Triple Threats Materials

*BLUE/49: .5X TO 1.2X BASIC JSY/99
*ORANGE/25: .6X TO 1.5X BASIC JSY/99
1 Mitchell Trubisky 8.00 20.00
2 Deshaun Watson 12.00 30.00
3 DeShone Kizer 2.50 6.00
4 Patrick Mahomes II 6.00 15.00
5 Davis Webb 2.50 6.00
6 C.J. Beathard 2.50 6.00
7 R. Joshua Dobbs 5.00 12.00
8 Nathan Peterman 3.00 8.00
9 Leonard Fournette 10.00 25.00
10 Dalvin Cook 6.00 15.00
11 Christian McCaffrey 8.00 20.00
12 D'Onta Foreman 3.00 8.00
13 Alvin Kamara 5.00 12.00
14 Samaje Perine 2.50 6.00
15 Marlon Mack 4.00 10.00
16 Kareem Hunt 5.00 12.00
17 Wayne Gallman 3.00 8.00
18 James Conner 5.00 12.00
19 Joe Mixon 5.00 12.00
20 Mack Hollins 2.50 6.00
21 O.J. Howard 3.00 8.00
22 Mike Williams 4.00 10.00
23 Corey Davis 4.00 10.00
24 John Ross III 5.00 12.00
25 JuJu Smith-Schuster 5.00 12.00
26 Zay Jones 3.00 8.00
27 Curtis Samuel 3.00 8.00
28 Dede Westbrook 2.50 6.00
29 Carlos Henderson 2.50 6.00
30 Chris Godwin 3.00 8.00
31 Kenny Golladay 4.00 10.00
32 Cooper Kupp 4.00 10.00
33 Amara Darboh 2.50 6.00
34 Jeremy McNichols 2.50 6.00
35 ArDarius Stewart 2.50 6.00
36 Joe Williams 2.50 6.00
37 Josh Reynolds 2.50 6.00
38 Taywan Taylor 2.50 6.00
39 Evan Engram 3.00 8.00
40 Jamaal Williams 2.50 6.00

2017 Panini XR Team Trios Materials

*BLUE/49: .5X TO 1.2X BASIC JSY/99
*ORANGE/25: .6X TO 1.5X BASIC JSY/99
*ORANGE/25: .5X TO 1.2X BASIC JSY/49
*ORANGE/20: .8X TO 2X BASIC JSY/99
1 Hwrd/Trbsky/Cllr/99 10.00 25.00
2 Tte/Glldy/Sffrd/99 5.00 12.00
3 Wtsn/Clwny/Hpkns/99 12.00 30.00
4 Kzr/Clmn/Crwll/99 3.00 8.00
5 Mhms/Hll/Hnt/99 15.00 40.00
6 Shprd/Bckhm/Gllmn/99 5.00 12.00
7 Bthrd/Hde/Wllms/99 3.00 8.00
8 Rthlsbrgr/Cnnr/Bll/99 6.00 15.00
9 McCy/Ptrmn/Tylr/49 6.00 15.00
10 Rbnsn/Brtls/Frntte/99 8.00 20.00
11 Ck/Trdwll/Dggs/99 8.00 20.00
12 McCffry/Kchly/Nwtn/99 8.00 20.00
13 Kmra/Brs/Ingrm/99 10.00 25.00
14 Krrgn/Csns/Prne/49 6.00 15.00
15 Lck/Mck/Hltn/99
16 Grn/Dltn/Mxn/25 10.00 25.00
17 Wntz/Mtthws/Hllns/99 6.00 15.00
18 Wnstn/Evns/Hwrd/99 4.00 10.00
19 Bsa/Wllms/Rvrs/99 5.00 12.00
20 Dvs/Hnry/Mrta/99 5.00 12.00
21 Brwn/SmthSctr/Dbbs/99 8.00 20.00
22 Wtkns/Tylr/Jns/99 5.00 12.00
23 Nwtn/Sml/Bnjmn/99 5.00 12.00
24 Hndrsn/Lnch/Mllr/99 4.00 10.00
25 Kpp/Gff/Grly/99 5.00 12.00
26 Drbh/Wlsn/Lcktt/99 6.00 15.00
27 Hcknbrg/Frte/Stwrt/99 3.00 8.00
28 Wllms/Nlsn/Rdgrs/25 15.00 40.00
29 Prsctt/Brnt/Ellt/99 6.00 15.00
30 Flcco/Dxn/Lws/25 8.00 20.00

2017 Panini XR X-Alted Signatures

1 Maurkice Pouncey/20 12.00 30.00
2 Muhammad Wilkerson/20
4 Michael Vick/20 15.00 40.00
7 Lamar Miller/20
9 Jeff Garcia/20
12 Ickey Woods/20 6.00 15.00
16 Danny Woodhead/20 12.00 30.00
17 Thomas Davis/20
18 Y.A. Tittle/20
19 Landon Collins/20

2017 Panini XR Xtreme Rookies

*BLUE/49: .5X TO 1.2X BASIC INSERTS
*ORANGE/25: .6X TO 1.5X BASIC INSERTS
1 Mitchell Trubisky 3.00 8.00
2 Deshaun Watson 4.00 10.00
3 DeShone Kizer .60 1.50
4 Patrick Mahomes II 8.00 20.00
5 Davis Webb .60 1.50
6 C.J. Beathard .60 1.50
7 R. Joshua Dobbs .75 2.00
8 Nathan Peterman .75 2.00
9 Leonard Fournette 2.00 5.00
10 Dalvin Cook 1.50 4.00
11 Christian McCaffrey 1.50 4.00
12 D'Onta Foreman .75 2.00
13 Alvin Kamara 2.50 6.00
14 Samaje Perine .60 1.50
15 Marlon Mack 1.00 2.50
16 Kareem Hunt 1.25 3.00
17 Wayne Gallman .75 2.00
18 James Conner 1.25 3.00
19 Joe Mixon 1.25 3.00
20 Mack Hollins .60 1.50
21 O.J. Howard .75 2.00
22 Mike Williams 1.00 2.50
23 Corey Davis 1.00 2.50
24 John Ross III .75 2.00
25 JuJu Smith-Schuster 1.50 4.00
26 Zay Jones .75 2.00
27 Curtis Samuel .75 2.00
28 Dede Westbrook .60 1.50
29 Carlos Henderson .60 1.50
30 Chris Godwin .75 2.00
31 Kenny Golladay 1.00 2.50
32 Cooper Kupp 1.00 2.50
33 Amara Darboh .60 1.50
34 Jeremy McNichols .60 1.50
35 ArDarius Stewart .60 1.50
36 Joe Williams .60 1.50
37 Josh Reynolds .60 1.50
38 Taywan Taylor .60 1.50
39 Evan Engram .75 2.00
40 Jamaal Williams .60 1.50

2018 Panini XR

1 LeSean McCoy .40 1.00
2 A.J. McCarron .25 .60
3 Kelvin Benjamin .30 .75
4 Ryan Tannehill .30 .75
5 Kenyan Drake .25 .60
6 Kiko Alonso .25 .60
7 Tom Brady 1.00 2.50
8 Julian Edelman .40 1.00
9 Rob Gronkowski .40 1.00
10 Jermaine Kearse .25 .60
11 Leonard Williams .25 .60
12 Jamal Adams .30 .75
13 Joe Flacco .30 .75
14 C.J. Mosley .30 .75
15 Terrell Suggs .25 .60
16 Andy Dalton .30 .75
17 A.J. Green .40 1.00
18 Joe Mixon .30 .75
19 Tyrod Taylor .30 .75
20 Jarvis Landry .30 .75
21 Josh Gordon .25 .60
22 Ben Roethlisberger .40 1.00
23 Antonio Brown .40 1.00
24 Le'Veon Bell .30 .75
25 JuJu Smith-Schuster .40 1.00
26 Deshaun Watson .50 1.25
27 DeAndre Hopkins .30 .75
28 J.J. Watt .40 1.00
29 Andrew Luck .50 1.25
30 T.Y. Hilton .30 .75
31 Marlon Mack .25 .60
32 Blake Bortles .25 .60
33 Leonard Fournette .40 1.00
34 Jalen Ramsey .30 .75
35 Marcus Mariota .40 1.00
36 Derrick Henry .40 1.00
37 Corey Davis .30 .75
38 Case Keenum .30 .75
39 Demaryius Thomas .30 .75
40 Von Miller .30 .75
41 Philip Rivers .40 1.00
42 Melvin Gordon .30 .75
43 Hunter Henry .25 .60
44 Joey Bosa .40 1.00
45 Derek Carr .40 1.00
46 Marshawn Lynch .30 .75
47 Amari Cooper .40 1.00
48 Khalil Mack .40 1.00
49 Dak Prescott .40 1.00
50 Ezekiel Elliott .50 1.25
51 DeMarcus Lawrence .25 .60
52 Eli Manning .30 .75
53 Odell Beckham Jr. .40 1.00
54 Sterling Shepard .30 .75
55 Carson Wentz .50 1.25
56 Alshon Jeffery .30 .75
57 Jay Ajayi .30 .75
58 Alex Smith .30 .75
59 Jamison Crowder .25 .60
60 Josh Norman .25 .60
61 Mitchell Trubisky .40 1.00
62 Jordan Howard .40 1.00
63 Allen Robinson .30 .75
64 Matthew Stafford .30 .75
65 Marvin Jones Jr. .25 .60
66 Golden Tate III .25 .60
67 Aaron Rodgers .75 2.00
68 Davante Adams .30 .75
69 Jimmy Graham .40 1.00
70 Kirk Cousins .40 1.00
71 Adam Thielen .40 1.00
72 Dalvin Cook .30 .75
73 Harrison Smith .40 1.00
74 Matt Ryan .30 .75
75 Julio Jones .40 1.00
76 Devonta Freeman .30 .75
77 Cam Newton .40 1.00
78 Christian McCaffrey .40 1.00
79 Luke Kuechly .30 .75
80 Drew Brees .40 1.00
81 Alvin Kamara .30 .75
82 Michael Thomas .40 1.00
83 Jameis Winston .30 .75
84 Mike Evans .30 .75
85 Gerald McCoy .25 .60
86 Sam Bradford .25 .60
87 David Johnson .40 1.00
88 Larry Fitzgerald .30 .75
89 Jared Goff .40 1.00
90 Todd Gurley II .40 1.00
91 Brandin Cooks .30 .75
92 Russell Wilson .50 1.25
93 Doug Baldwin .30 .75
94 Earl Thomas III .30 .75
95 Jimmy Garoppolo .50 1.25
96 Marquise Goodwin .25 .60
97 Richard Sherman .40 1.00
98 Aaron Donald .40 1.00
99 Stefon Diggs .30 .75
100 Clay Matthews .30 .75
101 Quenton Nelson RC 1.00 2.50
102 Kurt Benkert RC .75 2.00
103 Deontay Burnett RC .75 2.00
104 Simmie Cobbs Jr. RC 1.00 2.50
105 Shaquem Griffin RC 1.00 2.50
106 Denzel Ward RC 1.50 4.00
107 Luke Falk RC .75 2.00
108 Mike Hughes RC 1.00 2.50
109 Kemoko Turay RC .75 2.00
110 Carlton Davis RC .75 2.00
111 Taven Bryan RC .60 1.50
112 Tremaine Edmunds RC 1.25 3.00
113 J.T. Barrett RC 1.00 2.50
114 Roquan Smith RC 2.00 5.00
115 Minkah Fitzpatrick RC 1.25 3.00
116 Vita Vea RC 1.00 2.50
117 Marcus Davenport RC 1.25 3.00
118 Derwin James RC 1.25 3.00
119 Daron Payne RC 1.00 2.50
120 Leighton Vander Esch RC 2.00 5.00
121 Braxton Berrios RC .60 1.50
122 Jaire Alexander RC 1.00 2.50
123 Rashaan Evans RC 1.00 2.50
124 Terrell Edmunds RC 2.00 5.00
125 Harold Landry RC .60 1.50
126 Joshua Jackson RC 1.25 3.00
127 M.J. Stewart RC .60 1.50
128 Mark Andrews RC 1.00 2.50
129 Duke Dawson RC .60 1.50
130 Isaiah Oliver RC .60 1.50
131 Tyquan Lewis RC .75 2.00
132 Lorenzo Carter RC .60 1.50
133 Fred Warner RC .60 1.50
134 Chad Thomas RC .60 1.50
135 Malik Jefferson RC .75 2.00
136 Jerome Baker RC .75 2.00
137 Justin Reid RC .60 1.50
138 Rasheem Green RC .60 1.50
139 Sam Hubbard RC .75 2.00
140 Arden Key RC .60 1.50
141 Ronnie Harrison RC .75 2.00
142 Ian Thomas RC .60 1.50
143 Jalyn Holmes RC 1.00 2.50
144 Josey Jewell RC .75 2.00
145 Tyler Conklin RC .60 1.50
146 Jordan Lasley RC .60 1.50
147 Dallas Goedert RC .75 2.00
148 John Kelly RC .75 2.00
149 Antonio Callaway RC .75 2.00
150 Ray-Ray McCloud RC .60 1.50
151 Dylan Cantrell RC .60 1.50
152 Cedrick Wilson Jr. RC .60 1.50
153 Richie James RC .60 1.50
154 Josh Adams RC 1.25 3.00
155 Marcell Ateman RC .75 2.00
156 Bo Scarbrough RC .75 2.00
157 Ryan Izzo RC .60 1.50
158 Auden Tate RC .60 1.50
159 Austin Proehl RC .60 1.50
160 Trey Quinn RC .60 1.50
161 Baker Mayfield JSY AU/25 RC EXCH 75.00 150.00
162 Saquon Barkley JSY AU/25 RC 75.00 150.00
163 Sam Darnold JSY AU/25 RC 40.00 100.00
164 Bradley Chubb JSY AU/99 RC 6.00 15.00
165 Josh Allen JSY AU/25 RC 25.00 60.00
166 Josh Rosen JSY AU/25 RC 20.00 50.00
167 D.J. Moore JSY AU/49 RC 10.00 25.00
168 Hayden Hurst JSY AU/99 RC 5.00 12.00
169 Calvin Ridley JSY AU/49 RC 12.00 30.00
170 Rashaad Penny JSY AU/99 RC 6.00 15.00
171 Sony Michel JSY AU/49 RC 15.00 40.00
172 Lamar Jackson JSY AU/15 RC 75.00 150.00
173 Nick Chubb JSY AU/49 RC 15.00 40.00
174 Ronald Jones II JSY AU/99 RC 4.00 10.00
175 Courtland Sutton JSY AU/99 RC 6.00 15.00
176 Mike Gesicki JSY AU/199 RC 4.00 10.00
177 Kerryon Johnson JSY AU/199 RC 10.00 25.00
178 Dante Pettis JSY AU/99 RC 6.00 15.00
179 Christian Kirk JSY AU/99 RC 6.00 15.00
180 Anthony Miller JSY AU/199 RC 5.00 12.00
181 Derrius Guice JSY AU/49 RC 10.00 25.00
182 James Washington JSY AU/99 RC 8.00 20.00
183 D.J. Chark Jr. JSY AU/199 RC 4.00 10.00
184 Royce Freeman JSY AU/199 RC 4.00 10.00
185 Mason Rudolph JSY AU/99 RC 10.00 25.00
186 Michael Gallup JSY AU/199 RC 6.00 15.00
187 Tre'Quan Smith JSY AU/199 RC 5.00 12.00
188 Keke Coutee JSY AU/199 RC EXCH 4.00 10.00
189 Nyheim Hines JSY AU/199 RC 4.00 10.00
190 Kyle Lauletta JSY AU/199 RC 5.00 12.00
191 Mark Walton JSY AU/199 RC 4.00 10.00
192 DaeSean Hamilton JSY AU/199 RC 4.00 10.00
193 Ito Smith JSY AU/199 RC 4.00 10.00
194 Kalen Ballage JSY AU/199 RC 4.00 10.00
195 Jaleel Scott JSY AU/199 RC 3.00 8.00
196 J'Mon Moore JSY AU/199 RC 3.00 8.00
197 Daurice Fountain JSY AU/199 RC 4.00 10.00
198 Jaylen Samuels JSY AU/199 RC 4.00 10.00
199 Mike White JSY AU/199 RC 4.00 10.00
200 Marquez Valdes-Scantling JSY AU/199 RC 4.00 10.00

2018 Panini XR Blue

*VETS: 1.5X TO 4X BASIC CARDS
*ROOKIES: .6X TO 1.5X BASIC CARDS
*ROOK JSY AU/49: .6X TO 1.5X BASIC JSY AU/199
*ROOK JSY AU/49: .5X TO 1.2X BASIC JSY AU/99
*ROOK JSY AU/25: .6X TO 1.5X BASIC JSY AU/99
*ROOK JSY AU/25: .5X TO 1.2X BASIC JSY AU/49
*ROOK JSY AU/15: .6X TO 1.5X BASIC JSY AU/49

2018 Panini XR Orange

*VETS: 2X TO 5X BASIC CARDS
*ROOKIES: .8X TO 2X BASIC CARDS
*ROOK JSY AU/25: .8X TO 2X BASIC JSY AU/199
*ROOK JSY AU/25: .6X TO 1.5X BASIC JSY AU/99

2018 Panini XR Red

*VETS/299: 1.2X TO 3X BASIC CARDS
*ROOKIES/299: .5X TO 1.2X BASIC CARDS
*ROOK JSY AU/75: .5X TO 1.2X BASIC JSY AU/199
*ROOK JSY AU/75: .4X TO 1X BASIC JSY AU/99
*ROOK JSY AU/49: .5X TO 1.2X BASIC JSY AU/99
*ROOK JSY AU/35: .4X TO 1X BASIC JSY AU/49
*ROOK JSY AU/25: .5X TO 1.2X BASIC JSY AU/49
*ROOK JSY AU/15: .5X TO 1.2X BASIC JSY AU/25
161 Baker Mayfield JSY AU/15 EXCH 100.00 200.00
162 Saquon Barkley JSY AU/15 100.00 200.00

2018 Panini XR Acclaimed Autographs

1 Donald Driver/20
2 Ron Jaworski/20 8.00 20.00
3 Tedy Bruschi/20 10.00 25.00
4 Trent Dilfer/20 6.00 15.00
6 Rodney Harrison/20 8.00 20.00
8 LaVar Arrington/20 6.00 15.00
9 Mark Brunell/20 6.00 15.00
10 Hines Ward/20
12 Tony Gonzalez/20 15.00 40.00
14 Dick LeBeau/20 6.00 15.00
15 John Lynch/20 8.00 20.00
16 Shaun Alexander/20 6.00 15.00
17 Bo Jackson/20
18 Champ Bailey/20
19 Steve Largent/20 10.00 25.00

2018 Panini XR Autograph Swatches

1 John Randle/20 15.00 40.00
2 Aaron Donald/20 12.00 30.00
3 Alvin Kamara/20 10.00 25.00
4 O.J. Howard/20 8.00 20.00
5 Hunter Henry/20 8.00 20.00
7 Adam Thielen/20 25.00 50.00
8 Ozzie Newsome/20 10.00 25.00
9 Joe Mixon/20 10.00 25.00
16 David Johnson/20 25.00 50.00
18 Travis Kelce/20
19 Jordan Howard/20 12.00 30.00
20 JuJu Smith-Schuster/20 12.00 30.00
21 Stefon Diggs/20 EXCH 15.00 40.00
22 Brian Dawkins/20 40.00 80.00
25 Jeff Saturday/20 8.00 20.00
26 Rich Gannon/20
28 Jeff Garcia/20 8.00 20.00
29 Quincy Enunwa/20 8.00 20.00

2018 Panini XR Autographs Orange

*ORANGE/49: .6X TO 1.5X BASIC AU/199
*ORANGE/49: .5X TO 1.2X BASIC AU/99

2018 Panini XR Gilded Greats

*BLUE/49: .5X TO 1.2X BASIC INSERTS/99
*ORANGE/25: .6X TO 1.5X BASIC INSERTS/99
1 Morten Andersen 1.00 2.50
2 Jonathan Ogden 1.25 3.00
3 Curtis Martin 1.25 3.00
4 Michael Strahan 1.25 3.00
5 Tim Brown 1.50 4.00
6 Jason Taylor 1.25 3.00
7 Kurt Warner 1.25 3.00
8 LaDainian Tomlinson 1.25 3.00
9 Terrell Davis 1.25 3.00
10 Harry Carson 1.00 2.50
11 Joe Montana 4.00 10.00
12 Jim Kelly 1.50 4.00
13 Michael Irvin 1.50 4.00
14 Thurman Thomas 1.25 3.00
15 John Randle 1.25 3.00
16 Jerry Rice 2.50 6.00
17 Franco Harris 1.50 4.00
18 John Riggins 1.25 3.00
19 Tony Dorsett 1.50 4.00
20 Steve Largent 1.50 4.00

2018 Panini XR Luminous Endorsements

1 Baker Mayfield/49 60.00 125.00
2 Saquon Barkley/49 60.00 125.00
3 Sam Darnold/49 40.00 80.00
4 Bradley Chubb/99 5.00 12.00
5 Josh Allen/49 15.00 40.00
6 Josh Rosen/49 12.00 30.00
7 D.J. Moore/99 6.00 15.00
8 Hayden Hurst/99 4.00 10.00
9 Calvin Ridley/49 10.00 25.00
10 Rashaad Penny/49 6.00 15.00
11 Sony Michel/99 12.00 30.00
12 Lamar Jackson/49 25.00 60.00
13 Nick Chubb/49 12.00 30.00
14 Ronald Jones II/99 3.00 8.00
15 Courtland Sutton/49 6.00 15.00
16 Mike Gesicki/99 4.00 10.00
17 Kerryon Johnson/99 5.00 12.00
18 Dante Pettis/99 5.00 12.00
19 Christian Kirk/49 6.00 15.00
20 Anthony Miller/99 5.00 12.00
21 Derrius Guice/49 8.00 20.00
22 James Washington/99 6.00 15.00
23 D.J. Chark Jr./99 4.00 10.00
24 Royce Freeman/99 4.00 10.00
25 Mason Rudolph/49 10.00 25.00
26 Michael Gallup/99 6.00 15.00
27 Tre'Quan Smith/99 5.00 12.00
28 Keke Coutee/99 4.00 10.00
29 Nyheim Hines/99 4.00 10.00
30 Kyle Lauletta/99 5.00 12.00
31 Mark Walton/99 4.00 10.00
32 DaeSean Hamilton/99 4.00 10.00
33 Ito Smith/99 4.00 10.00
34 Kalen Ballage/99 4.00 10.00
35 Jaleel Scott/99 3.00 8.00
36 J'Mon Moore/99 3.00 8.00
37 Daurice Fountain/99 4.00 10.00
38 Jaylen Samuels/99 4.00 10.00
39 Mike White/99 4.00 10.00
40 Marquez Valdes-Scantling/99 4.00 10.00

2018 Panini XR Luminous Endorsements Blue

*BLUE/49: .5X TO 1.2X BASIC AU/99
*BLUE/25: .5X TO 1.2X BASIC AU/49

2018 Panini XR Luminous Endorsements Orange

*ORANGE/25: .6X TO 1.5X BASIC AU/99

2018 Panini XR Mirrored

*RED/35: .5X TO 1.2X BASIC INSERTS/75
*BLUE/25: .6X TO 1.5X BASIC INSERTS/75
1 B.Mayfield/R.Wilson 6.00 15.00
2 D.Johnson/S.Barkley 5.00 12.00
3 A.Luck/S.Darnold 4.00 10.00
4 B.Chubb/V.Miller 1.00 2.50
5 J.Kelly/J.Allen 2.50 6.00
6 A.Rodgers/J.Rosen 2.00 5.00
7 D.Moore/S.Diggs 1.25 3.00
8 H.Hurst/R.Gronkowski 1.00 2.50
9 C.Ridley/J.Jones 1.50 4.00
10 M.Lynch/R.Penny 1.00 2.50
11 A.Kamara/S.Michel 2.00 5.00
12 L.Jackson/M.Vick 4.00 10.00
13 N.Chubb/T.Gurley II 2.00 5.00
14 J.Charles/R.Jones II .60 1.50
15 C.Sutton/D.Thomas 1.00 2.50
16 J.Witten/M.Gesicki .75 2.00
17 K.Johnson/L.Bell 1.00 2.50
18 D.Pettis/D.Hester 1.00 2.50
19 C.Kirk/J.Edelman 1.00 2.50
20 A.Miller/A.Brown 1.00 2.50
21 D.Guice/L.Fournette 1.25 3.00
22 D.Bryant/J.Washington 1.25 3.00
23 D.Chark Jr./O.Beckham Jr. 1.00 2.50
24 M.Lynch/R.Freeman .75 2.00
25 B.Roethlisberger/M.Rudolph 1.50 4.00
26 M.Gallup/S.Watkins 1.25 3.00
27 M.Thomas/T.Smith 1.00 2.50
28 D.Hopkins/K.Coutee .75 2.00
29 M.Jones-Drew/N.Hines .75 2.00
30 E.Manning/K.Lauletta 1.00 2.50
31 F.Gore/M.Walton .75 2.00
32 D.Hamilton/E.Sanders 1.00 2.50
33 D.Johnson Jr./I.Smith .75 2.00
34 D.Henry/K.Ballage 1.00 2.50
35 J.Scott/M.Crabtree .60 1.50
36 D.Adams/J.Moore .75 2.00
37 D.Fountain/T.Hilton .75 2.00
38 J.Samuels/J.Bettis 1.00 2.50
39 M.White/T.Romo .75 2.00
40 M.Valdes-Scantling/M.Jones Jr. .75 2.00

2018 Panini XR Rookie Jumbo Materials

*BLUE/49: .5X TO 1.2X BASIC JSY/99
*ORANGE/25: .6X TO 1.5X BASIC JSY/99
1 Baker Mayfield 10.00 25.00
2 Saquon Barkley 12.00 30.00
3 Sam Darnold 10.00 25.00
4 Bradley Chubb 4.00 10.00
5 Josh Allen 8.00 20.00
6 Josh Rosen 10.00 25.00
7 D.J. Moore 5.00 12.00
8 Hayden Hurst 3.00 8.00
9 Calvin Ridley 6.00 15.00
10 Rashaad Penny 4.00 10.00
11 Sony Michel 6.00 15.00
12 Lamar Jackson 10.00 25.00
13 Nick Chubb 6.00 15.00
14 Ronald Jones II 2.50 6.00
15 Courtland Sutton 4.00 10.00
16 Mike Gesicki 3.00 8.00
17 Kerryon Johnson 4.00 10.00
18 Dante Pettis 4.00 10.00
19 Christian Kirk 4.00 10.00
20 Anthony Miller 4.00 10.00
21 Derrius Guice 5.00 12.00
22 James Washington 5.00 12.00
23 D.J. Chark Jr. 3.00 8.00
24 Royce Freeman 3.00 8.00
25 Mason Rudolph 6.00 15.00
26 Michael Gallup 5.00 12.00
27 Tre'Quan Smith 4.00 10.00
28 Keke Coutee 3.00 8.00
29 Nyheim Hines 3.00 8.00
30 Kyle Lauletta 4.00 10.00
31 Mark Walton 3.00 8.00
32 DaeSean Hamilton 3.00 8.00
33 Ito Smith 3.00 8.00
34 Kalen Ballage 3.00 8.00
35 Jaleel Scott 2.50 6.00
36 J'Mon Moore 2.50 6.00
37 Daurice Fountain 3.00 8.00
38 Jaylen Samuels 3.00 8.00
39 Mike White 3.00 8.00
40 Marquez Valdes-Scantling 3.00 8.00

2018 Panini XR Rookie Jumbo Swatch Autographs

1 Baker Mayfield/25 125.00 250.00
2 Sam Darnold/25 50.00 100.00
3 Josh Rosen/25 20.00 50.00
4 Josh Allen/25 50.00 100.00
5 Saquon Barkley/25 75.00 150.00
6 Derrius Guice/49 10.00 25.00
7 Calvin Ridley/49 12.00 30.00
8 Courtland Sutton/99 6.00 15.00
9 D.J. Moore/99 8.00 20.00
10 Sony Michel/49 15.00 40.00
11 Nick Chubb/49 15.00 40.00
12 Ronald Jones II/99 4.00 10.00
13 Christian Kirk/49 8.00 20.00
14 James Washington/99 8.00 20.00
15 Anthony Miller/99 6.00 15.00
16 Mason Rudolph/49 12.00 30.00
17 Rashaad Penny/99 6.00 15.00
18 Michael Gallup/99 8.00 20.00
19 Dante Pettis/99 6.00 15.00
20 Royce Freeman/99 5.00 12.00

2018 Panini XR Rookie Jumbo Swatch Autographs Blue

*BLUE/49: .5X TO 1.2X BASIC JSY/99
*BLUE/25: .5X TO 1.2X BASIC JSY/49
*BLUE/20: .6X TO 1.5X BASIC JSY/49

2018 Panini XR Rookie Jumbo Swatch Autographs Orange

*ORANGE/25: .6X TO 1.5X BASIC JSY AU/99

2018 Panini XR Rookie Jumbo Swatch Autographs Red

*RED/75: .4X TO 1X BASIC JSY AU/99
*RED/35: .4X TO 1X BASIC JSY AU/49
*RED/25: .5X TO 1.2X BASIC JSY AU/49
*RED/15: .5X TO 1.2X BASIC JSY AU/25

2018 Panini XR Rookie Swatch Autographs

1 Baker Mayfield/25 125.00 250.00
2 Saquon Barkley/25 75.00 150.00
3 Sam Darnold/25 50.00 100.00
4 Bradley Chubb/99 6.00 15.00
5 Josh Allen/25 50.00 100.00
6 Josh Rosen/25 20.00 50.00
7 D.J. Moore/99 8.00 20.00
8 Hayden Hurst/99 5.00 12.00
9 Calvin Ridley/49 12.00 30.00
10 Rashaad Penny/99 6.00 15.00
11 Sony Michel/49 15.00 40.00
13 Nick Chubb/49 15.00 40.00
14 Ronald Jones II/99 4.00 10.00
15 Courtland Sutton/99 6.00 15.00
16 Mike Gesicki/99 5.00 12.00
17 Kerryon Johnson/99 10.00 25.00
18 Dante Pettis/99 6.00 15.00
19 Christian Kirk/49 8.00 20.00
20 Anthony Miller/99 6.00 15.00
21 Derrius Guice/49 10.00 25.00
22 James Washington/99 8.00 20.00
23 D.J. Chark Jr./199 4.00 10.00
24 Royce Freeman/199 4.00 10.00
25 Mason Rudolph/49 12.00 30.00
26 Michael Gallup/199 6.00 15.00
27 Tre'Quan Smith/199 5.00 12.00
28 Keke Coutee/199 4.00 10.00
29 Nyheim Hines/199 4.00 10.00
30 Kyle Lauletta/199 5.00 12.00
31 Mark Walton/199 4.00 10.00
32 DaeSean Hamilton/199 4.00 10.00
33 Ito Smith/199 4.00 10.00
34 Kalen Ballage/199 4.00 10.00
35 Jaleel Scott/199 3.00 8.00
36 J'Mon Moore/199 3.00 8.00
37 Daurice Fountain/199 4.00 10.00
38 Jaylen Samuels/199 4.00 10.00
39 Mike White/199 4.00 10.00
40 Marquez Valdes-Scantling/199 4.00 10.00

2018 Panini XR Rookie Swatch Autographs Blue

*BLUE/49: .6X TO 1.5X BASIC JSY AU/199
*BLUE/49: .5X TO 1.2X BASIC JSY AU/99
*BLUE/25: .6X TO 1.5X BASIC JSY AU/99
*BLUE/25: .5X TO 1.2X BASIC JSY AU/49
*BLUE/15: .8X TO 2X BASIC JSY AU/99
*BLUE/15: .6X TO 1.5X BASIC JSY AU/49

2018 Panini XR Rookie Swatch Autographs Orange

*ORANGE/25: .8X TO 2X BASIC JSY AU/199
*ORANGE/25: .6X TO 1.5X BASIC JSY AU/99
*ORANGE/15: .8X TO 2X BASIC JSY AU/99

2018 Panini XR Rookie Swatch Autographs Red

*RED/75: .5X TO 1.2X BASIC JSY AU/199
*RED/75: .4X TO 1X BASIC JSY AU/99
*RED/35: .5X TO 1.2X BASIC JSY AU/99
*RED/35: .4X TO 1X BASIC JSY AU/49
*RED/25: .5X TO 1.2X BASIC JSY AU/49
*RED/15: .5X TO 1.2X BASIC JSY AU/25

2018 Panini XR Rookie Triple Threats Materials

*BLUE/75: .4X TO 1X BASIC JSY/99
*ORANGE/25: .6X TO 1.5X BASIC JSY/99
1 Baker Mayfield 10.00 25.00
2 Saquon Barkley 12.00 30.00
3 Sam Darnold 10.00 25.00
4 Bradley Chubb 4.00 10.00
5 Josh Allen 8.00 20.00
6 Josh Rosen 10.00 25.00
7 D.J. Moore 5.00 12.00
8 Hayden Hurst 3.00 8.00
9 Calvin Ridley 6.00 15.00
10 Rashaad Penny 4.00 10.00
11 Sony Michel 6.00 15.00
12 Lamar Jackson 10.00 25.00
13 Nick Chubb 8.00 20.00
14 Ronald Jones II 2.50 6.00
15 Courtland Sutton 4.00 10.00
16 Mike Gesicki 3.00 8.00
17 Kerryon Johnson 4.00 10.00
18 Dante Pettis 4.00 10.00
19 Christian Kirk 4.00 10.00
20 Anthony Miller 4.00 10.00
21 Derrius Guice 5.00 12.00
22 James Washington 5.00 12.00
23 D.J. Chark Jr. 3.00 8.00
24 Royce Freeman 3.00 8.00
25 Mason Rudolph 6.00 15.00
26 Michael Gallup 5.00 12.00
27 Tre'Quan Smith 4.00 10.00
28 Keke Coutee 3.00 8.00
29 Nyheim Hines 3.00 8.00
30 Kyle Lauletta 4.00 10.00
31 Mark Walton 3.00 8.00
32 DaeSean Hamilton 3.00 8.00
33 Ito Smith 3.00 8.00
34 Kalen Ballage 3.00 8.00
35 Jaleel Scott 2.50 6.00
36 J'Mon Moore 2.50 6.00
37 Daurice Fountain 3.00 8.00
38 Jaylen Samuels 3.00 8.00
39 Mike White 3.00 8.00
40 Marquez Valdes-Scantling 3.00 8.00

2018 Panini XR Team Trios Materials

*BLUE/49: .5X TO 1.2X BASIC JSY/99
*ORANGE/25: .6X TO 1.5X BASIC JSY/99
1 Krk/Jhnsn/Rsn 12.00 30.00
2 Rdly/Frmn/Ryn 8.00 20.00
3 Hrst/Flcco/Jcksn 12.00 30.00
4 Alln/McCy/Jns 10.00 25.00
5 Nwtn/McCffry/Mre 6.00 15.00
6 Mllr/Hwrd/Trbsky 5.00 12.00
7 Grn/Dltn/Wltn 5.00 12.00
8 Myfld/Njku/Chbb 12.00 30.00
9 Prsctt/Ellt/Gllp 6.00 15.00
10 Chbb/Mrshll/Mllr 5.00 12.00
11 Rdgrs/Adms/Mre 8.00 20.00
12 Frmn/Wtsn/Ctee 6.00 15.00
13 Lck/Hns/Hltn 6.00 15.00
14 Brtls/Chrk/Frntte 5.00 12.00
15 Hnt/Mhms/Hll 12.00 30.00
16 Bsa/Grdn/Rvrs 5.00 12.00
17 Bllge/Drke/Tnnhll 4.00 10.00
18 White/Grnkwski/Mchl 8.00 20.00
19 Kmra/Thms/Smth 5.00 12.00
20 Mnng/Lltta/Brkly 15.00 40.00
21 Cpr/Crr/Lnch 5.00 12.00
22 Brwn/Rthlsbgr/Rdlph 8.00 20.00
23 Brwn/Wshngtn/SmthSchstr 6.00 15.00
24 Dldwn/Pnny/Wlsn 6.00 15.00
25 Wnstn/Evns/Jns 4.00 10.00
26 Sttn/Thms/Sndrs 5.00 12.00
27 Dvs/Hnry/Mrta 5.00 12.00
28 Gce/Rd/Dctsn 6.00 15.00
29 Wntz/Aghlr/Ertz 6.00 15.00
30 Jhnsn/Jns/Stffrd 5.00 12.00

2018 Panini XR Vanguard

*BLUE/49: .5X TO 1.2X BASIC INSERTS/99
*ORANGE/25: .6X TO 1.5X BASIC INSERTS/99
1 Kyle Long 1.00 2.50
2 Jason Kelce 1.00 2.50
3 David DeCastro 1.00 2.50
4 Alejandro Villanueva 1.25 3.00
5 Zack Martin 1.00 2.50
6 Alex Mack 1.00 2.50
7 Travis Frederick 1.00 2.50
8 Lane Johnson 1.00 2.50
9 Brandon Scherff 1.00 2.50
10 Taylor Lewan 1.00 2.50
11 Maurkice Pouncey 1.00 2.50
12 Trent Williams 1.00 2.50
13 T.J. Lang 1.00 2.50
14 Jonathan Ogden 1.25 3.00
15 Walter Jones 1.00 2.50
16 John Hannah 1.00 2.50
17 Larry Allen 1.50 4.00
18 Art Shell 1.00 2.50
19 Mark Schlereth 1.00 2.50
20 Ron Yary 1.00 2.50

2018 Panini XR X-Factor

*BLUE/49: .5X TO 1.2X BASIC INSERTS/99
*ORANGE/25: .6X TO 1.5X BASIC INSERTS/99
1 Tom Brady 4.00 10.00
2 Jimmy Garoppolo 2.00 5.00
3 Russell Wilson 2.00 5.00
4 Ezekiel Elliott 2.00 5.00
5 Antonio Brown 1.50 4.00
6 Deshaun Watson 2.00 5.00
7 Patrick Mahomes II 4.00 10.00
8 Aaron Rodgers 3.00 8.00
9 Matt Ryan 1.25 3.00
10 Carson Wentz 2.00 5.00
11 Von Miller 1.25 3.00
12 Odell Beckham Jr. 1.50 4.00
13 David Johnson 1.50 4.00
14 Drew Brees 1.50 4.00
15 Cam Newton 1.50 4.00
16 Matthew Stafford 1.25 3.00
17 Jordan Howard 1.50 4.00
18 Adam Thielen 1.50 4.00
19 Marcus Mariota 1.50 4.00
20 A.J. Green 1.50 4.00

1995 Panthers SkyBox

This 21-card set of the Carolina Panthers features borderless color action player photos with the player's name and position in team color stripes at the bottom. The backs carry another color player picture along with player biographical information. The set includes 20 numbered player cards and one unnumbered cover/checklist card.
COMPLETE SET (21) 6.00 15.00
1 John Kasay .40 1.00
2 Kerry Collins 2.00 5.00
3 Frank Reich .40 1.00
4 Rod Smith .60 1.50
5 Tim McKyer .30 .75
6 Randy Baldwin .30 .75
7 Bubba McDowell .30 .75
8 Tyrone Poole .60 1.50
9 Sam Mills .50 1.25
10 Carlton Bailey .30 .75
11 Darion Conner .30 .75
12 Lamar Lathon .40 1.00
13 Blake Brockermeyer .40 1.00
14 Mike Fox .30 .75
15 Don Beebe .40 1.00
16 Mark Carrier WR .60 1.50
17 Pete Metzelaars .30 .75
18 Shawn King .30 .75
19 Howard Griffith .30 .75
20 Bob Christian .40 1.00
NNO Cover Card CL .30 .75

1996 Panthers Fleer/SkyBox Impact Promo Sheet

Fleer/SkyBox distributed this promo sheet primarily at the NFL Experience Card Show at the Charlotte Convention Center August 29-31, 1996. The sheet features six Panthers' players with individual card numbers CP1-CP6.
NNO Uncut Promo Sheet 2.00 5.00

1997 Panthers Collector's Choice

Upper Deck released several team sets in 1997 in a blister pack wrapper. Each of the 14-cards in this set are very similar to the base Collector's Choice cards except for the card numbering on the cardback. A cover/checklist card was added featuring the team helmet.
COMPLETE SET (14) 1.20 3.00
CA1 Wesley Walls .05 .15
CA2 Mark Carrier WR .08 .25
CA3 Muhsin Muhammad .05 .15
CA4 John Kasay .02 .10
CA5 Anthony Johnson .02 .10
CA6 Kerry Collins .40 1.00
CA7 Kevin Greene .05 .15
CA8 Sam Mills .02 .10
CA9 Rae Carruth .02 .10
CA10 Micheal Barrow .02 .10
CA11 Ernie Mills .02 .10
CA12 Tim Biakabutuka .05 .15
CA13 Winslow Oliver .02 .10
CA14 Panthers Logo Checklist .20 .50

1997 Panthers Score

This 15-card set of the Carolina Panthers was distributed in five-card packs with a suggested retail price of $1.99. The fronts feature color action player photos with white borders and the player's name and team logo printed in team color foil at the bottom. The backs carry player information and career statistics. Platinum Team parallel cards were randomly seeded in packs featuring all foil cardfronts.
COMPLETE SET (15) 2.40 6.00
*PLATINUM TEAMS: 1X TO 2X
1 Kerry Collins .60 1.50
2 Mark Carrier WR .15 .40
3 Tim Biakabutuka .30 .75
4 Anthony Johnson .08 .25
5 Kevin Greene .15 .40
6 Eric Davis .08 .25
7 Muhsin Muhammad .15 .40
8 Micheal Barrow .08 .25
9 Wesley Walls .15 .40
10 Winslow Oliver .08 .25
11 Lamar Lathon .08 .25
12 Sam Mills .08 .25
13 Chad Cota .08 .25
14 Michael Bates .08 .25
15 John Kasay .08 .25

2006 Panthers Topps

COMPLETE SET (12) 3.00 6.00
CAR1 Keary Colbert .15 .40
CAR2 Jake Delhomme .25 .60
CAR3 Dan Morgan .25 .60
CAR4 Chris Gamble .25 .60
CAR5 Julius Peppers .30 .75
CAR6 Steve Smith .40 1.00
CAR7 DeShaun Foster .30 .75
CAR8 Drew Carter .25 .60
CAR9 Keyshawn Johnson .30 .75
CAR10 Nick Goings .25 .60
CAR11 Brad Hoover .25 .60
CAR12 DeAngelo Williams .30 .75

2007 Panthers Topps

COMPLETE SET (12) 2.50 5.00
1 Julius Peppers .50 1.25
2 Jake Delhomme .40 1.00
3 DeAngelo Williams .40 1.00
4 Steve Smith .50 1.25
5 Dwayne Jarrett .50 1.25
6 DeShaun Foster .50 1.25
7 Drew Carter .40 1.00
8 Chris Gamble .40 1.00
9 David Carr .40 1.00
10 John Kasay .40 1.00
11 Dan Morgan .40 1.00
12 Jon Beason .40 1.00

2008 Panthers Topps

COMPLETE SET (12) 2.50 5.00
1 Steve Smith .50 1.25
2 DeAngelo Williams .40 1.00
3 Jeff King .40 1.00
4 Julius Peppers .50 1.25
5 Jon Beason .40 1.00
6 Matt Moore .40 1.00
7 Jake Delhomme .40 1.00
8 Richard Marshall
9 Chris Harris .40 1.00
10 Chris Gamble .40 1.00
11 Jonathan Stewart .60 1.50
12 Dan Connor .40 1.00

1998 Paramount

The 1998 Pacific Paramount set was issued in one series totalling 250 cards. The cards were issued in six card packs with 36 packs per box and 20 boxes per case. Each pack had a suggested retail of $1.49 per pack. The full border fronts feature an action photo on most of the cards with the "Pacific Paramount" logo on the upper left and the players name and position on the lower left. The teams logo is on the bottom right. The back has a color portait, biographical information, seasonal and career statistics as well as some personal information
COMPLETE SET (250) 30.00 60.00
1 Larry Centers .07 .20
2 Chris Gedney .07 .20
3 Rob Moore .10 .30
4 Jake Plummer .20 .50
5 Simeon Rice .10 .30
6 Frank Sanders .10 .30
7 Mark Smith DE .07 .20
8 Eric Swann .07 .20
9 Jamal Anderson .20 .50
10 Chris Chandler .10 .30
11 Bert Emanuel .10 .30
12 Tony Graziani .07 .20
13 Byron Hanspard .07 .20
14 Terance Mathis .10 .30
15 O.J. Santiago .07 .20
16 Chuck Smith .07 .20
17 Derrick Alexander WR .10 .30
18 Peter Boulware .07 .20
19 Jay Graham .07 .20
20 Priest Holmes RC 4.00 10.00
21 Michael Jackson .07 .20
22 Byron Bam Morris .07 .20
23 Vinny Testaverde .10 .30
24 Eric Zeier .10 .30
25 Todd Collins .07 .20
26 Quinn Early .07 .20
27 Bryce Paup .07 .20
28 Andre Reed .10 .30
29 Jay Riemersma .07 .20
30 Antowain Smith .20 .50
31 Bruce Smith .10 .30
32 Thurman Thomas .20 .50
33 Michael Bates .07 .20
34 Mark Carrier WR .07 .20
35 Rae Carruth .07 .20
36 Kerry Collins .10 .30
37 Fred Lane .07 .20
38 Lamar Lathon .07 .20
39 Muhsin Muhammad .10 .30
40 Wesley Walls .10 .30
41 Darnell Autry .07 .20
42 Curtis Conway .10 .30
43 Raymont Harris .07 .20
44 Tyrone Hughes .07 .20
45 Chris Penn .07 .20
46 Ricky Proehl .07 .20
47 Steve Stenstrom .07 .20
48 Ryan Wetnight RC .07 .20
49 Jeff Blake .10 .30
50 Ki-Jana Carter .07 .20
51 Corey Dillon .20 .50
52 David Dunn .07 .20
53 Boomer Esiason .07 .20
54 Brian Milne .07 .20
55 Carl Pickens .10 .30
56 Darnay Scott .10 .30
57 Troy Aikman .40 1.00
58 Eric Bjornson .07 .20
59 Michael Irvin .20 .50
60 Daryl Johnston .10 .30
61 Anthony Miller .07 .20
62 Deion Sanders .20 .50
63 Emmitt Smith .60 1.50
64 Omar Stoutmire RC .07 .20
65 Sherman Williams .07 .20
66 Terrell Davis .20 .50
67 John Elway .75 2.00
68 Darrien Gordon .07 .20
69 Ed McCaffrey .10 .30
70 Bill Romanowski .07 .20
71 Shannon Sharpe .10 .30
72 Neil Smith .10 .30
73 Rod Smith WR .10 .30
74 Maa Tanuvasa .07 .20
75 Tommie Boyd .07 .20
76 Glyn Milburn .07 .20
77 Scott Mitchell .10 .30
78 Herman Moore .10 .30
79 Johnnie Morton .10 .30
80 Robert Porcher .07 .20
81 Barry Sanders .60 1.50
82 Bryant Westbrook .07 .20
83 Robert Brooks .10 .30
84 LeRoy Butler .07 .20
85 Mark Chmura .10 .30
86 Brett Favre .75 2.00
87 Antonio Freeman .20 .50
88 Dorsey Levens .20 .50
89 Eugene Robinson .07 .20
90 Bill Schroeder RC .60 1.50
91 Reggie White .20 .50
92 Aaron Bailey .07 .20
93 Quentin Coryatt .07 .20
94 Zack Crockett .07 .20
95 Sean Dawkins .07 .20
96 Ken Dilger .07 .20
97 Marshall Faulk .25 .60
98 Jim Harbaugh .10 .30
99 Marvin Harrison .20 .50
100 Bryan Barker .07 .20
101 Tony Boselli .07 .20
102 Tony Brackens .07 .20
103 Mark Brunell .20 .50
104 Mike Hollis .07 .20
105 Keenan McCardell .10 .30
106 Natrone Means .10 .30
107 Jimmy Smith .10 .30
108 James Stewart .10 .30

109 Marcus Allen .20 .50
110 Kimble Anders .10 .30
111 Dale Carter .07 .20
112 Tony Gonzalez .20 .50
113 Elvis Grbac .10 .30
114 Greg Hill .07 .20
115 Andre Rison .10 .30
116 Will Shields .07 .20
117 Derrick Thomas .20 .50
118 Karim Abdul-Jabbar .20 .50
119 Trace Armstrong .07 .20
120 Damon Huard RC .75 2.00
121 Charles Jordan .07 .20
122 Dan Marino .75 2.00
123 O.J. McDuffie .10 .30
124 Irving Spikes .07 .20
125 Zach Thomas .20 .50
126 Cris Carter .20 .50
127 Charles Woodson RC 1.50 4.00
128 Brad Johnson .20 .50
129 Randall McDaniel .07 .20
130 John Randle .10 .30
131 Jake Reed .10 .30
132 Robert Smith .20 .50
133 Todd Steussie .07 .20
134 Bruce Armstrong .07 .20
135 Drew Bledsoe .30 .75
136 Ben Coates .10 .30
137 Derrick Cullors RC .07 .20
138 Terry Glenn .20 .50
139 Shawn Jefferson .07 .20
140 Curtis Martin .20 .50
141 Chris Slade .07 .20
142 Larry Whigham .07 .20
143 Troy Davis .07 .20
144 Andre Hastings .07 .20
145 Randal Hill .07 .20
146 Sammy Knight RC .20 .50
147 William Roaf .07 .20
148 Heath Shuler .07 .20
149 Danny Wuerffel .10 .30
150 Ray Zellars .07 .20
151 Jessie Armstead .07 .20
152 Tiki Barber .20 .50
153 Chris Calloway .07 .20
154 Danny Kanell .10 .30
155 David Patten RC .50 1.25
156 Michael Strahan .10 .30
157 Charles Way .07 .20
158 Tyrone Wheatley .10 .30
159 Kyle Brady .07 .20
160 Wayne Chrebet .20 .50
161 Glenn Foley .10 .30
162 Aaron Glenn .07 .20
163 Leon Johnson .07 .20
164 Adrian Murrell .10 .30
165 Neil O'Donnell .10 .30
166 Dedric Ward .07 .20
167 Tim Brown .20 .50
168 Rickey Dudley .07 .20
169 Jeff George .10 .30
170 Desmond Howard .10 .30
171 James Jett .10 .30
172 Napoleon Kaufman .20 .50
173 Chester McGlockton .07 .20
174 Darrell Russell .07 .20
175 Ty Detmer .10 .30
176 Irving Fryar .10 .30
177 Charlie Garner .10 .30
178 Bobby Hoying .10 .30
179 Chad Lewis .10 .30
180 Duce Staley .25 .60
181 Kevin Turner .07 .20
182 Ricky Watters .10 .30
183 Jerome Bettis .20 .50
184 Will Blackwell .07 .20
185 Charles Johnson .07 .20
186 George Jones .07 .20
187 Levon Kirkland .07 .20
188 Carnell Lake .07 .20
189 Kordell Stewart .20 .50
190 Yancey Thigpen .07 .20
191 Tony Banks .10 .30
192 Isaac Bruce .20 .50
193 Ernie Conwell .07 .20
194 Craig Heyward .07 .20
195 Eddie Kennison .10 .30
196 Amp Lee .07 .20
197 Orlando Pace .07 .20
198 Torrance Small .07 .20
199 Gary Brown .07 .20
200 Kenny Bynum RC .07 .20
201 Freddie Jones .07 .20
202 Tony Martin .10 .30
203 Eric Metcalf .07 .20
204 Junior Seau .20 .50
205 Craig Whelihan RC .07 .20
206 William Floyd .07 .20
207 Merton Hanks .07 .20
208 Garrison Hearst .20 .50
209 Brent Jones .07 .20
210 Terrell Owens .20 .50
211 Jerry Rice .40 1.00
212 J.J. Stokes .10 .30
213 Rod Woodson .10 .30
214 Steve Young .20 .50
215 Steve Broussard .07 .20
216 Joey Galloway .10 .30
217 Cortez Kennedy .07 .20
218 Jon Kitna .20 .50
219 James McKnight .20 .50
220 Warren Moon .20 .50
221 Michael Sinclair .07 .20
222 Ryan Leaf RC .50 1.25
223 Darryl Williams .07 .20
224 Mike Alstott .20 .50
225 Reidel Anthony .10 .30
226 Derrick Brooks .20 .50
227 Horace Copeland .07 .20
228 Trent Dilfer .20 .50
229 Warrick Dunn .20 .50
230 Hardy Nickerson .07 .20
231 Warren Sapp .10 .30
232 Karl Williams .07 .20
233 Blaine Bishop .07 .20
234 Willie Davis .07 .20
235 Eddie George .20 .50
236 Derrick Mason .10 .30
237 Bruce Matthews .07 .20
238 Steve McNair .20 .50
239 Chris Sanders .07 .20
240 Rodney Thomas .07 .20
241 Frank Wycheck .07 .20
242 Terry Allen .20 .50
243 Jamie Asher .07 .20
244 Larry Bowie .07 .20
245 Albert Connell .07 .20
246 Stephen Davis .07 .20
247 Gus Frerotte .07 .20
248 Ken Harvey .07 .20
249 Leslie Shepherd .07 .20
250 Michael Westbrook .10 .30
S1 Mark Brunell Sample .40 1.00

1998 Paramount Copper

COMP.COPPER SET (250) 40.00 80.00
*COPPER STARS: 1.5X TO 3X HI COL.
*COPPER RCs: .6X TO 1.5X
COPPER STATED ODDS 1:1 HOBBY

1998 Paramount Platinum Blue

*PLAT.BLUE STARS: 5X TO 12X
*PLAT.BLUE ROOKIES: 2X TO 5X
PLAT.BLUE STATED ODDS 1:73

1998 Paramount Red

COMP.RED SET (250) 60.00 120.00
*RED STARS: 1.5X TO 4X HI COL.
*RED RCs: .8X TO 2X
ONE PER SPECIAL RETAIL

1998 Paramount Silver

COMP.SILVER SET (250) 40.00 80.00
*SILVER STARS: 1.5X TO 3X HI COL.
*SILVER RCs: .6X TO 1.5X
ONE PER RETAIL PACK

1998 Paramount Kings of the NFL

This 20 card set features some leading NFL players. These cards were inserted into packs at a rate of one every 73 packs. The fronts feature a player photo against a gold background with the words "Kings of the NFL". The backs feature another portrait along with some player information. A "Kings of the NFL Proof" parallel set was also issued. These cards had a limited production of 20 sets.

COMPLETE SET (20) 50.00 120.00
STATED ODDS 1:73
*PROOF CARDS: 5X TO 12X BASIC INSERTS
PROOFS STATED PRINT RUN 20 SETS
1 Antowain Smith 2.00 5.00
2 Corey Dillon 2.00 5.00
3 Troy Aikman 4.00 10.00
4 Emmitt Smith 6.00 15.00
5 Terrell Davis 2.00 5.00
6 John Elway 8.00 20.00
7 Barry Sanders 6.00 15.00
8 Brett Favre 8.00 20.00
9 Dorsey Levens 2.00 5.00
10 Reggie White 2.00 5.00
11 Mark Brunell 2.00 5.00
12 Dan Marino 8.00 20.00
13 Curtis Martin 2.00 5.00
14 Drew Bledsoe 3.00 8.00
15 Jerome Bettis 2.00 5.00
16 Kordell Stewart 2.00 5.00
17 Jerry Rice 4.00 10.00
18 Steve Young 2.00 5.00
19 Warrick Dunn 2.00 5.00
20 Eddie George 2.00 5.00

1998 Paramount Personal Bests

This 36 card set was inserted four every 37 packs. These fully foiled and etched cards feature a player photo against a solid shiny background. The players name is spelled vertically on the left side of the card. The horizontal back has another photo as well as more player information.

COMPLETE SET (36) 25.00 60.00
STATED ODDS 4:37
1 Jake Plummer .60 1.50
2 Antowain Smith .40 1.00
3 Kerry Collins .40 1.00
4 Raymont Harris .25 .60
5 Corey Dillon .60 1.50
6 Troy Aikman 1.25 3.00
7 Deion Sanders .60 1.50
8 Emmitt Smith 2.00 5.00
9 Terrell Davis .60 1.50
10 John Elway 2.50 6.00
11 Shannon Sharpe .40 1.00
12 Herman Moore .25 .60
13 Barry Sanders 2.00 5.00
14 Brett Favre 2.50 6.00
15 Antonio Freeman .40 1.00
16 Dorsey Levens .40 1.00
17 Marshall Faulk .75 2.00
18 Mark Brunell .60 1.50
19 Dan Marino 2.50 6.00
20 Robert Smith .40 1.00
21 Curtis Martin .60 1.50
22 Drew Bledsoe 1.00 2.50
23 Danny Kanell .25 .60
24 Adrian Murrell .25 .60
25 Napoleon Kaufman .40 1.00
26 Jerome Bettis .60 1.50
27 Kordell Stewart .60 1.50
28 Terrell Owens .60 1.50
29 Jerry Rice 1.25 3.00
30 Steve Young .75 2.00
31 Warren Moon .60 1.50
32 Mike Alstott .60 1.50
33 Trent Dilfer .40 1.00
34 Warrick Dunn .60 1.50
35 Eddie George .60 1.50
36 Steve McNair .60 1.50

1998 Paramount Pro Bowl Die Cuts

This 20-card set features players who participated in the 1998 Pro Bowl. Using a design based on "Hawaiian" objects, the card is die cut and features a canoe design along with a player photo on the front. The back has some personal information as well as another color photo.

COMPLETE SET (20) 40.00 100.00
STATED ODDS 1:37
1 Terrell Davis 2.50 6.00
2 John Elway 10.00 25.00
3 Shannon Sharpe 1.50 4.00
4 Herman Moore 1.50 4.00
5 Barry Sanders 8.00 20.00
6 Mark Chmura 1.50 4.00
7 Brett Favre 10.00 25.00
8 Dorsey Levens 2.50 6.00
9 Mark Brunell 2.50 6.00
10 Andre Rison 1.50 4.00
11 Cris Carter 2.50 6.00
12 Drew Bledsoe 4.00 10.00
13 Ben Coates 1.50 4.00
14 Jerome Bettis 2.50 6.00
15 Steve Young 2.50 6.00
16 Warren Moon 2.50 6.00
17 Mike Alstott 2.50 6.00
18 Trent Dilfer 2.50 6.00
19 Warrick Dunn 2.50 6.00
20 Eddie George 2.50 6.00

1998 Paramount Super Bowl XXXII

These 10 cards feature key figures in Super Bowl XXXII. They were issued two every 37 packs and feature a player's portrait against a background which includes Super Bowl XXXII logos. The back explains the significance of each player in the set.

COMPLETE SET (10) 30.00 60.00
STATED ODDS 2:37
1 Terrell Davis 2.00 5.00
2 John Elway 8.00 20.00
3 John Elway 8.00 20.00
4 Brett Favre 8.00 20.00
5 Antonio Freeman 2.00 5.00
6 Dorsey Levens 2.00 5.00
7 Ed McCaffrey 1.25 3.00
8 Eugene Robinson .75 2.00
9 Bill Romanowski .75 2.00
10 Darren Sharper 1.25 3.00

1999 Paramount

This 250 card set was issued in six card packs and released in July, 1999. The set is sequenced in alphabetical order which is also in team order. Notable Rookie Cards in this set include Tim Couch, Edgerrin James and Ricky Williams.

COMPLETE SET (250) 20.00 50.00
1 David Boston RC .20 .50
2 Larry Centers .12 .30
3 Joel Makovicka RC .20 .50
4 Eric Metcalf .12 .30
5 Rob Moore .12 .30
6 Adrian Murrell .12 .30
7 Jake Plummer .12 .30
8 Frank Sanders .12 .30
9 Aeneas Williams .12 .30
10 Morten Andersen .12 .30
11 Jamal Anderson .15 .40
12 Chris Chandler .15 .40
13 Tim Dwight .15 .40
14 Terance Mathis .12 .30
15 Jeff Paulk RC .20 .50
16 O.J. Santiago .12 .30
17 Chuck Smith .12 .30
18 Peter Boulware .12 .30
19 Priest Holmes .12 .30
20 Michael Jackson .12 .30
21 Jermaine Lewis .12 .30
22 Ray Lewis .20 .50
23 Michael McCrary .12 .30
24 Bennie Thompson .12 .30
25 Rod Woodson .20 .50
26 Shawn Bryson RC .20 .50
27 Doug Flutie .20 .50
28 Eric Moulds .12 .30
29 Peerless Price RC .20 .50
30 Andre Reed .20 .50
31 Jay Riemersma .12 .30
32 Antowain Smith .12 .30
33 Bruce Smith .15 .40
34 Michael Bates .12 .30
35 Steve Beuerlein .15 .40
36 Tim Biakabutuka .15 .40
37 Kevin Greene .20 .50
38 Anthony Johnson .12 .30
39 Fred Lane .12 .30
40 Muhsin Muhammad .12 .30
41 Wesley Walls .15 .40
42 D'Wayne Bates RC .20 .50
43 Edgar Bennett .15 .40
44 Marty Booker RC .20 .50
45 Curtis Conway .15 .40
46 Bobby Engram .12 .30
47 Curtis Enis .12 .30
48 Erik Kramer .15 .40
40 Cade McNown RC .20 .50
50 Jeff Blake .15 .40
51 Scott Covington RC .20 .50
52 Corey Dillon .12 .30
53 Quincy Jackson RC .20 .50
54 Carl Pickens .15 .40
55 Darnay Scott .12 .30
56 Akili Smith RC .20 .50
57 Craig Yeast RC .20 .50
58 Jerry Ball .12 .30
59 Darrin Chiaverini RC .20 .50
60 Tim Couch RC .25 .60
61 Ty Detmer .12 .30
62 Kevin Johnson RC .25 .60
63 Terry Kirby .12 .30
64 Daylon McCutcheon RC .20 .50
65 Irv Smith .12 .30
66 Troy Aikman .25 .60
67 Ebenezer Ekuban RC .20 .50
68 Michael Irvin .20 .50
69 Daryl Johnston .15 .40
70 Wane McGarity RC .20 .50
71 Dat Nguyen RC .30 .75
72 Deion Sanders .15 .40
73 Emmitt Smith .30 .75
74 Bubby Brister .12 .30
75 Terrell Davis .15 .40
76 Jason Elam .12 .30
77 Olandis Gary RC .30 .75
78 Brian Griese .12 .30
79 Ed McCaffrey .15 .40
80 Travis McGriff RC .20 .50
81 Shannon Sharpe .15 .40
82 Rod Smith .15 .40
83 Charlie Batch .12 .30
84 Chris Claiborne RC .20 .50
85 Germane Crowell .12 .30
86 Sedrick Irvin RC .20 .50
87 Herman Moore .15 .40
88 Johnnie Morton .15 .40
89 Barry Sanders .30 .75
90 Robert Brooks .15 .40
91 Aaron Brooks RC .25 .60
92 Mark Chmura .12 .30
93 Brett Favre .40 1.00
94 Antonio Freeman .15 .40
95 Vonnie Holliday .12 .30
96 Dorsey Levens .15 .40
97 De'Mond Parker RC .20 .50
98 Ken Dilger .12 .30
99 Marvin Harrison .15 .40
100 Edgerrin James RC .30 .75
101 Peyton Manning .60 1.50
102 Jerome Pathon .12 .30
103 Mike Peterson RC .20 .50
104 Marcus Pollard .12 .30
105 Tavian Banks .12 .30
106 Reggie Barlow .12 .30
107 Tony Boselli .15 .40
108 Mark Brunell .15 .40
109 Keenan McCardell .15 .40
110 Bryce Paup .12 .30
111 Jimmy Smith .15 .40
112 Fred Taylor .12 .30
113 Dave Thomas RC .25 .60
114 Kimble Anders .12 .30
115 Donnell Bennett .12 .30
116 Mike Cloud RC .20 .50
117 Tony Gonzalez .15 .40
118 Elvis Grbac .12 .30
119 Larry Parker RC .25 .60
120 Andre Rison .15 .40
121 Brian Shay RC .20 .50
122 Karim Abdul-Jabbar .12 .30
123 Oronde Gadsden .12 .30
124 James Johnson RC .20 .50
125 Rob Konrad RC .20 .50
126 Dan Marino .40 1.00
127 O.J. McDuffie .15 .40
128 Zach Thomas .15 .40
129 Cris Carter .20 .50
130 Daunte Culpepper RC .30 .75
131 Randall Cunningham .15 .40
132 Matthew Hatchette .15 .40
133 Leroy Hoard .12 .30
134 Randy Moss .15 .40
135 John Randle .20 .50
136 Jake Reed .15 .40
137 Robert Smith .12 .30
138 Michael Bishop RC .25 .60
139 Drew Bledsoe .15 .40
140 Ben Coates .15 .40
141 Kevin Faulk RC .20 .50
142 Terry Glenn .15 .40
143 Shawn Jefferson .12 .30
144 Andy Katzenmoyer RC .25 .60
145 Tony Simmons .12 .30
146 Cuncho Brown RC .20 .50
147 Cam Cleeland .12 .30
148 Mark Fields .12 .30
149 La'Roi Glover RC .30 .75
150 Andre Hastings .12 .30
151 Billy Joe Hobert .12 .30
152 William Roaf .12 .30
153 Billy Joe Tolliver .12 .30
154 Ricky Williams RC .30 .75
155 Jessie Armstead .15 .40
156 Tiki Barber .15 .40
157 Gary Brown .12 .30
158 Kent Graham .12 .30
159 Ike Hilliard .12 .30
160 Joe Montgomery RC .20 .50
161 Amani Toomer .12 .30
162 Charles Way .12 .30
163 Wayne Chrebet .12 .30
164 Bryan Cox .15 .40
165 Aaron Glenn .12 .30
166 Keyshawn Johnson .15 .40
167 Leon Johnson .12 .30
168 Curtis Martin .15 .40
169 Vinny Testaverde .12 .30
170 Dedric Ward .12 .30
171 Tim Brown .20 .50
172 Dameane Douglas RC .20 .50
173 Rickey Dudley .12 .30
174 James Jett .12 .30
175 Napoleon Kaufman .12 .30
176 Darrell Russell .12 .30
177 Harvey Williams .12 .30
178 Charles Woodson .20 .50
179 Na Brown RC .20 .50
180 Hugh Douglas .15 .40
181 Cecil Martin RC .20 .50
182 Donovan McNabb RC 1.50 4.00
183 Duce Staley .12 .30
184 Kevin Turner .12 .30
185 Jerome Bettis .20 .50
186 Troy Edwards RC .20 .50
187 Jason Gildon .15 .40
188 Courtney Hawkins .12 .30
189 Malcolm Johnson RC .20 .50
190 Kordell Stewart .12 .30
191 Jerame Tuman RC .20 .50
192 Amos Zereoue RC .20 .50
193 Isaac Bruce .20 .50
194 Kevin Carter .12 .30
195 Jeremaine Copeland RC .25 .60
196 Joe Germaine RC .25 .60
197 Az-Zahir Hakim .12 .30
198 Torry Holt RC .40 1.00
199 Amp Lee .12 .30
200 Ricky Proehl .12 .30
201 Charlie Jones .12 .30
202 Freddie Jones .12 .30
203 Ryan Leaf .15 .40
204 Natrone Means .15 .40
205 Mikhael Ricks .12 .30
206 Junior Seau .15 .40
207 Bryan Still .12 .30
208 Garrison Hearst .12 .30
209 Terry Jackson RC .20 .50
210 R.W. McQuarters .12 .30
211 Ken Norton Jr. .12 .30
212 Terrell Owens .15 .40
213 Jerry Rice .50 1.25
214 J.J. Stokes .12 .30
215 Tai Streets RC .25 .60
216 Steve Young .25 .60
217 Karsten Bailey RC .20 .50
218 Chad Brown .12 .30
219 Joey Galloway .15 .40
220 Ahman Green .15 .40
221 Brock Huard RC .20 .50
222 Cortez Kennedy .15 .40
223 Jon Kitna .12 .30
224 Shawn Springs .12 .30
225 Ricky Watters .15 .40
226 Mike Alstott .12 .30
227 Reidel Anthony .12 .30
228 Trent Dilfer .12 .30
229 Warrick Dunn .12 .30
230 Bert Emanuel .15 .40
231 Martin Gramatica RC .20 .50
232 Jacquez Green .12 .30
233 Shaun King RC .20 .50
234 Anthony McFarland RC .25 .60
235 Warren Sapp .15 .40
236 Willie Davis .12 .30
237 Kevin Dyson .12 .30
238 Eddie George .15 .40
239 Darran Hall RC .20 .50
240 Jackie Harris .15 .40
241 Steve McNair .15 .40
242 Yancey Thigpen .12 .30
243 Frank Wycheck .15 .40
244 Stephen Alexander .12 .30
245 Champ Bailey RC .40 1.00
246 Stephen Davis .12 .30
247 Darrell Green .20 .50
248 Skip Hicks .12 .30
249 Brian Mitchell .15 .40
250 Michael Westbrook .12 .30

1999 Paramount Copper

COMPLETE SET (250) 60.00 120.00
*COPPER STARS: 1.2X TO 3X BASIC CARDS
*COPPER RCs: .5X TO 1.2X
ONE PER HOBBY PACK

1999 Paramount Premiere Date

*PREM.DATE STARS: 15X TO 40X BASIC CARDS
*PREMIERE DATE ROOKIES: 4X TO 10X
PREM.DATE STATED ODDS 1:37 HOB
PREMIERE DATE PRINT RUN 62 SER.#'d SETS

1999 Paramount Gold

COMPLETE SET (250) 60.00 120.00
*GOLD STARS: 1.2X TO 3X
*GOLD RCs: .5X TO 1.2X
GOLDS ONE PER RETAIL PACK

1999 Paramount HoloGold

*HOLO.GOLD STARS: 8X TO 20X BASIC CARDS
*HOLO.GOLD ROOKIES: 2.5X TO 6X
HOLO.GOLD PRINT RUN 199 SERIAL #'d SETS
HOLO.GOLDS INSERTED IN RETAIL PACKS

1999 Paramount HoloSilver

*HOLO.SILVER STARS: 12X TO 30X BASIC CARDS
*HOLO.SILVER ROOKIES: 4X TO 10X
HOLO.SILVER PRINT RUN 99 SERIAL #'d SETS
HOLO.SILVER INSERTED IN HOBBY PACKS

1999 Paramount Platinum Blue

*PLAT.BLUE STARS: 8X TO 20X BASIC CARDS
*PLATINUM BLUE ROOKIES: 2.5X TO 6X
PLATINUM BLUE STATED ODDS 1:73

1999 Paramount Canton Bound

Issued at a rate of one in 361 packs, this 10 card fully foiled and etched card set featured players destined for the Hall of Fame.

COMPLETE SET (10) 60.00 150.00
STATED ODDS 1:361
*PROOFS: 1.2X TO 3X HI COL.
PROOFS STATED PRINT RUN 20 SER.#'d SETS
1 Troy Aikman 8.00 20.00
2 Emmitt Smith 8.00 20.00
3 Terrell Davis 4.00 10.00
4 Barry Sanders 12.50 30.00
5 Brett Favre 12.50 30.00
6 Dan Marino 12.50 30.00
7 Randy Moss 10.00 25.00
8 Drew Bledsoe 5.00 12.00
9 Jerry Rice 8.00 20.00
10 Steve Young 5.00 12.00

1999 Paramount End Zone Net-Fusions

Inserted one every 73 packs, these 20 card set was produced using a format including actual netting behind the player's photo.

COMPLETE SET (20) 60.00 150.00
STATED ODDS 1:73
1 Jake Plummer 1.50 4.00
2 Jamal Anderson 2.50 6.00
3 Doug Flutie 2.50 6.00
4 Tim Couch 1.50 4.00
5 Troy Aikman 5.00 12.00
6 Emmitt Smith 5.00 12.00
7 Terrell Davis 2.50 6.00
8 Barry Sanders 8.00 20.00
9 Brett Favre 8.00 20.00
10 Peyton Manning 8.00 20.00
11 Mark Brunell 2.50 6.00
12 Fred Taylor 2.50 6.00
13 Dan Marino 8.00 20.00
14 Randy Moss 6.00 15.00
15 Drew Bledsoe 3.00 8.00
16 Ricky Williams 3.00 8.00
17 Jerry Rice 5.00 12.00
18 Steve Young 3.00 8.00
19 Jon Kitna 2.50 6.00
20 Eddie George 2.50 6.00

1999 Paramount Personal Bests

Inserted one every 37 packs, this 36 card set features leading players featured on holographic patterned foil. The backs have another player photo as well as some interesting player facts.

COMPLETE SET (36) 50.00 120.00
STATED ODDS 1:37
1 Jake Plummer .75 2.00
2 Jamal Anderson 1.25 3.00
3 Priest Holmes 2.00 5.00
4 Doug Flutie 1.25 3.00
5 Antowain Smith 1.25 3.00
6 Corey Dillon 1.25 3.00
7 Akili Smith .40 1.00
8 Tim Couch .60 1.50
9 Troy Aikman 2.50 6.00
10 Emmitt Smith 2.50 6.00
11 Terrell Davis 1.25 3.00
12 Barry Sanders 4.00 10.00
13 Brett Favre 4.00 10.00
14 Antonio Freeman 1.25 3.00
15 Edgerrin James 2.50 6.00
16 Peyton Manning 4.00 10.00
17 Mark Brunell 1.25 3.00
18 Fred Taylor 1.25 3.00
19 Dan Marino 4.00 10.00
20 Randall Cunningham 1.25 3.00
21 Randy Moss 3.00 8.00
22 Drew Bledsoe 1.50 4.00
23 Kevin Faulk .60 1.50
24 Ricky Williams 1.25 3.00
25 Curtis Martin 1.25 3.00
26 Napoleon Kaufman 1.25 3.00
27 Donovan McNabb 3.00 8.00
28 Jerome Bettis 1.25 3.00
29 Kordell Stewart .75 2.00
30 Terrell Owens 1.25 3.00
31 Jerry Rice 2.50 6.00
32 Steve Young 1.50 4.00
33 Jon Kitna 1.25 3.00
34 Warrick Dunn 1.25 3.00
35 Eddie George 1.25 3.00
36 Steve McNair 1.25 3.00

1999 Paramount Team Checklists

Inserted at a rate of two in 37, these full foil cards feature a star from each team in action on the front. The backs have the main set checklist for each team.

COMPLETE SET (31) 40.00 100.00
STATED ODDS 2:37
1 Jake Plummer 1.00 2.50
2 Jamal Anderson 1.50 4.00
3 Priest Holmes 2.50 6.00
4 Doug Flutie 1.50 4.00
5 Muhsin Muhammad 1.00 2.50
6 Cade McNown .50 1.25
7 Corey Dillon 1.50 4.00
8 Tim Couch .75 2.00
9 Troy Aikman 3.00 8.00
10 Terrell Davis 1.50 4.00
11 Barry Sanders 5.00 12.00
12 Brett Favre 5.00 12.00
13 Peyton Manning 5.00 12.00
14 Fred Taylor 1.50 4.00
15 Elvis Grbac 1.00 2.50
16 Dan Marino 5.00 12.00
17 Randy Moss 4.00 10.00
18 Drew Bledsoe 2.00 5.00
19 Ricky Williams 1.50 4.00
20 Ike Hilliard .60 1.50
21 Curtis Martin 1.50 4.00
22 Napoleon Kaufman 1.50 4.00
23 Donovan McNabb 4.00 10.00
24 Jerome Bettis 1.50 4.00
25 Torry Holt 2.00 5.00
26 Natrone Means 1.00 2.50
27 Jerry Rice 3.00 8.00
28 Jon Kitna 1.50 4.00
29 Warrick Dunn 1.50 4.00
30 Eddie George 1.50 4.00
31 Skip Hicks .60 1.50

2000 Paramount

Released as a 249-card base set, Paramount cards are numbered from 1-250. Shortly before release, card number 242 was intended to have been pulled from production, but apparently a very small number of cards packed out. Base cards feature a white border with full color player action photography and a background colored to match the featured player's team colors. Paramount was packaged in 36-pack boxes with packs containing six cards each.

COMPLETE SET (249) 15.00 40.00
1 David Boston .12 .30
2 Thomas Jones RC .25 .60
3 Rob Moore .12 .30
4 Jake Plummer .12 .30
5 Simeon Rice .15 .40
6 Frank Sanders .12 .30
7 Raynoch Thompson RC .20 .50
8 Jamal Anderson .15 .40
9 Chris Chandler .15 .40
10 Bob Christian .12 .30
11 Tim Dwight .15 .40
12 Byron Hanspard .12 .30
13 Terance Mathis .12 .30
14 Mareno Philyaw RC .20 .50
15 Tony Banks .12 .30
16 Priest Holmes .12 .30
17 Qadry Ismail .12 .30
18 Pat Johnson .12 .30
19 Jamal Lewis RC .30 .75
20 Chris Redman RC .20 .50
21 Shannon Sharpe .15 .40
22 Travis Taylor RC .20 .50
23 Erik Flowers RC .20 .50
24 Doug Flutie .15 .40
25 Rob Johnson .15 .40
26 Jonathan Linton .12 .30
27 Corey Moore RC .20 .50
28 Eric Moulds .12 .30
29 Peerless Price .15 .40
30 Jay Riemersma .12 .30
31 Antowain Smith .15 .40
32 Rashard Anderson RC .20 .50
33 Steve Beuerlein .15 .40
34 Tim Biakabutuka .15 .40
35 Donald Hayes .12 .30
36 Patrick Jeffers .12 .30
37 Jeff Lewis .12 .30
38 Muhsin Muhammad .12 .30
39 Wesley Walls .12 .30
40 Bobby Engram .12 .30
41 Curtis Enis .12 .30
42 Cade McNown .12 .30
43 Jim Miller .12 .30
44 Marcus Robinson .15 .40
45 Brian Urlacher RC 1.00 2.50
46 Dez White RC .20 .50
47 Michael Basnight .12 .30
48 Corey Dillon .12 .30
49 Ron Dugans RC .20 .50
50 Willie Jackson .12 .30
51 Darnay Scott .15 .40
52 Akili Smith .12 .30
53 Peter Warrick RC .20 .50
54 Courtney Brown RC .25 .60
55 Darrin Chiaverini .12 .30
56 Tim Couch .15 .40
57 Kevin Johnson .12 .30
58 Terry Kirby .12 .30
59 Dennis Northcutt RC .20 .50
60 Travis Prentice RC .20 .50
61 Leslie Shepherd .12 .30
62 Troy Aikman .25 .60
63 Joey Galloway .15 .40
64 Rocket Ismail .15 .40
65 David LaFleur .12 .30
66 Emmitt Smith .30 .75
67 Jason Tucker .12 .30
68 Chris Warren .12 .30
69 Michael Wiley RC .20 .50
70 Desmond Clark .12 .30
71 Chris Cole RC .25 .60
72 Terrell Davis .15 .40
73 Olandis Gary .15 .40
74 Brian Griese .12 .30
75 Jarious Jackson RC .25 .60
76 Ed McCaffrey .15 .40
77 Deltha O'Neal RC .20 .50
78 Rod Smith .15 .40
79 Charlie Batch .12 .30
80 Germane Crowell .12 .30
81 Reuben Droughns RC .20 .50
82 Terry Fair .12 .30
83 Herman Moore .12 .30
84 Johnnie Morton .15 .40
85 Barry Sanders .30 .75
86 James Stewart .12 .30
87 Corey Bradford .12 .30
88 Tyrone Davis .12 .30
89 Brett Favre .40 1.00
90 Bubba Franks RC .20 .50
91 Antonio Freeman .15 .40
92 Matt Hasselbeck .12 .30
93 Dorsey Levens .15 .40
94 Anthony Lucas RC .20 .50
95 Bill Schroeder .15 .40
96 Ken Dilger .12 .30
97 E.G. Green .12 .30
98 Marvin Harrison .15 .40
99 Edgerrin James .15 .40
100 Peyton Manning .50 1.25
101 Jerome Pathon .12 .30
102 Marcus Washington RC .25 .60
103 Terrence Wilkins .12 .30
104 Kyle Brady .12 .30
105 Mark Brunell .15 .40
106 Kevin Hardy .12 .30
107 Keenan McCardell .15 .40
108 Jimmy Smith .15 .40
109 R.Jay Soward RC .20 .50
110 Shyrone Stith RC .20 .50
111 Fred Taylor .12 .30
112 Alvis Whitted .12 .30
113 Derrick Alexander .12 .30
114 Kimble Anders .12 .30
115 Donnell Bennett .12 .30
116 Tony Gonzalez .15 .40
117 Elvis Grbac .12 .30
118 Kevin Lockett .12 .30
119 Sylvester Morris RC .20 .50
120 Tony Richardson RC .20 .50
121 Deon Dyer RC .20 .50
122 Oronde Gadsden .15 .40
123 Damon Huard .12 .30
124 James Johnson .12 .30
125 Dan Marino .40 1.00
126 Tony Martin .15 .40
127 O.J. McDuffie .15 .40
128 Zach Thomas .15 .40
129 Cris Carter .20 .50
130 Daunte Culpepper .15 .40
131 Leroy Hoard .12 .30
132 Chris Hovan RC .25 .60
133 Randy Moss .15 .40
134 John Randle .20 .50
135 Robert Smith .12 .30
136 Troy Walters RC .20 .50
137 Drew Bledsoe .15 .40
138 Tom Brady RC 40.00 80.00
139 Troy Brown .12 .30
140 Kevin Faulk .12 .30
141 Terry Glenn .15 .40
142 J.R. Redmond RC .20 .50
143 Tony Simmons .12 .30
144 David Stachelski RC .20 .50
145 Jeff Blake .15 .40
146 Marc Bulger RC .25 .60
147 Cam Cleeland .12 .30
148 Sherrod Gideon RC .20 .50
149 Darren Howard RC .20 .50
150 Chad Morton RC .25 .60
151 Keith Poole .12 .30
152 Ricky Williams .15 .40
153 Tiki Barber .15 .40
154 Kerry Collins .12 .30
155 Ron Dayne RC .30 .75
156 Ike Hilliard .12 .30
157 Joe Jurevicius .12 .30
158 Pete Mitchell .12 .30
159 Joe Montgomery .12 .30
160 Amani Toomer .12 .30
161 John Abraham RC .30 .75
162 Anthony Becht RC .20 .50
163 Wayne Chrebet .12 .30
164 Laveranues Coles RC .25 .60
165 Ray Lucas .12 .30
166 Curtis Martin .15 .40
167 Chad Pennington RC .25 .60
168 Vinny Testaverde .12 .30
169 Dedric Ward .12 .30
170 Tim Brown .20 .50
171 Rich Gannon .15 .40
172 Bobby Hoying .12 .30
173 James Jett .15 .40
174 Napoleon Kaufman .15 .40
175 Jerry Porter RC .30 .75
176 Tyrone Wheatley .12 .30
177 Charles Woodson .20 .50
178 Dameane Douglas .12 .30
179 Charles Johnson .12 .30
180 Donovan McNabb .15 .40
181 Todd Pinkston RC .20 .50
182 Gari Scott RC .20 .50
183 Torrance Small .12 .30
184 Duce Staley .12 .30
185 Jerome Bettis .20 .50
186 Plaxico Burress RC .25 .60
187 Troy Edwards .12 .30
188 Danny Farmer RC .20 .50
189 Richard Huntley .12 .30
190 Tee Martin RC .20 .50
191 Kordell Stewart .12 .30
192 Hines Ward .15 .40
193 Isaac Bruce .20 .50
194 Trung Canidate RC .20 .50
195 Marshall Faulk .15 .40
196 Az-Zahir Hakim .12 .30
197 Torry Holt .15 .40
198 Tony Horne .12 .30
199 Ricky Proehl .12 .30
200 Kurt Warner .30 .75
201 Jermaine Fazande .12 .30
202 Trevor Gaylor RC .20 .50
203 Jeff Graham .12 .30
204 Jim Harbaugh .15 .40
205 Freddie Jones .12 .30
206 Mikhael Ricks .12 .30
207 Junior Seau .15 .40
208 Fred Beasley .12 .30
209 Giovanni Carmazzi RC .20 .50
210 Jeff Garcia .12 .30
211 Charlie Garner .15 .40
212 Terrell Owens .15 .40
213 Tim Rattay RC .25 .60
214 Jerry Rice .50 1.25
215 J.J. Stokes .15 .40
216 Steve Young .25 .60
217 Shaun Alexander RC .30 .75
218 Sean Dawkins .12 .30
219 Darrell Jackson RC .20 .50
220 Jon Kitna .12 .30
221 Derrick Mayes .12 .30
222 Charlie Rogers .12 .30
223 Shawn Springs .12 .30
224 Ricky Watters .15 .40
225 Mike Alstott .12 .30
226 Reidel Anthony .12 .30
227 Warrick Dunn .12 .30
228 Jacquez Green .12 .30
229 Joe Hamilton RC .20 .50
230 Keyshawn Johnson .15 .40
231 Shaun King .12 .30
232 Warren Sapp .15 .40
233 Keith Bulluck RC .25 .60
234 Kevin Dyson .15 .40
235 Eddie George .15 .40
236 Jevon Kearse .12 .30
237 Erron Kinney RC .20 .50
238 Steve McNair .15 .40
239 Neil O'Donnell .12 .30
240 Yancy Thigpen .12 .30
241 Frank Wycheck .15 .40
242 Julian Peterson SP RC 20.00 40.00
243 Champ Bailey .15 .40
244 Larry Centers .12 .30
245 Albert Connell .12 .30
246 Stephen Davis .12 .30
247 Todd Husak RC .20 .50
248 Brad Johnson .15 .40
249 Chris Samuels RC .30 .75
250 Michael Westbrook .12 .30

2000 Paramount Draft Picks 325

*ROOKIES/325: 2.5X TO 6X BASIC CARDS
STATED PRINT RUN 325 SERIAL #'d SETS
138 Tom Brady 100.00 175.00

2000 Paramount HoloGold

*VETS: 6X TO 15X BASIC CARDS
*ROOKIES: 4X TO 10X BASIC CARDS
RETAIL HOLOGOLD PRINT RUN 130
138 Tom Brady 400.00 800.00

2000 Paramount HoloSilver

*VETS: 10X TO 25X BASIC CARDS
*ROOKIES: 6X TO 15X BASIC CARDS
HOBBY HOLOSILVER PRINT RUN 85
138 Tom Brady 500.00 1000.00

2000 Paramount Platinum Blue

*VETS: 10X TO 25X BASIC CARDS
*ROOKIES: 6X TO 15X BASIC CARDS
PLATINUM BLUE PRINT RUN 75
138 Tom Brady 500.00 1000.00

2000 Paramount Premiere Date

*VETERANS: 10X TO 25X BASIC CARDS
*ROOKIES: 6X TO 15X BASIC CARDS
HOBBY PREM.DATE PRINT RUN 79
138 Tom Brady 500.00 1000.00

2000 Paramount Draft Report

Randomly inserted in packs at the rate of two in 37, this 31-card set features top draft picks from the 2000 NFL Draft with player photos in full color on a bronze background sporting each player's draft team logo.

COMPLETE SET (31) 25.00 60.00
STATED ODDS 2:37
*NATIONAL LOGO/20: 8X TO 20X BASIC INSERT
1 Thomas Jones .50 1.25
2 Mareno Philyaw .40 1.00
3 Jamal Lewis .60 1.50
4 Erik Flowers .40 1.00
5 Rashard Anderson .40 1.00
6 Dez White .40 1.00
7 Peter Warrick .40 1.00
8 Dennis Northcutt .40 1.00
9 Michael Wiley .40 1.00
10 Deltha O'Neal .40 1.00
11 Reuben Droughns .40 1.00
12 Anthony Lucas .40 1.00
13 Marcus Washington UER .50 1.25
14 R.Jay Soward .40 1.00
15 Sylvester Morris .40 1.00
16 Deon Dyer .40 1.00
17 Troy Walters .40 1.00
18 J.R. Redmond .40 1.00
19 Marc Bulger .50 1.25
20 Ron Dayne .60 1.50
21 Chad Pennington .50 1.25
22 Jerry Porter .60 1.50
23 Todd Pinkston .40 1.00
24 Plaxico Burress .50 1.25
25 Trung Canidate .40 1.00
26 Trevor Gaylor .40 1.00
27 Giovanni Carmazzi .40 1.00
28 Shaun Alexander .60 1.50
29 Joe Hamilton .40 1.00
30 Erron Kinney .40 1.00
31 Todd Husak .40 1.00

2000 Paramount End Zone Net-Fusions

Randomly inserted in packs at the rate of one in 73, this 20-card set features action photograpy on a die cut card that features actual "netting" in the background.

COMPLETE SET (20) 30.00 80.00
STATED ODDS 1:73
1 Jake Plummer 1.00 2.50
2 Cade McNown 1.00 2.50
3 Tim Couch 1.25 3.00
4 Troy Aikman 2.00 5.00
5 Emmitt Smith 2.50 6.00
6 Terrell Davis 1.25 3.00
7 Brett Favre 3.00 8.00
8 Edgerrin James 1.25 3.00
9 Peyton Manning 4.00 10.00
10 Mark Brunell 1.25 3.00
11 Fred Taylor 1.00 2.50
12 Drew Bledsoe 1.25 3.00
13 Ricky Williams 1.25 3.00
14 Randy Moss 1.25 3.00
15 Marshall Faulk 1.25 3.00
16 Kurt Warner 2.50 6.00
17 Jerry Rice 4.00 10.00
18 Jon Kitna 1.00 2.50
19 Eddie George 1.25 3.00
20 Stephen Davis 1.00 2.50

2000 Paramount Game Used Footballs

Randomly inserted in packs, this 10-card set features full color player action photos coupled with a swatch of a game used football. Photos are on the left side of the card and set against a tan and green background of a crowd at a game. The football swatch appears on the right side of the card and is oval in shape.

1 Troy Aikman 3.00 8.00
2 Emmitt Smith 4.00 10.00
3 Olandis Gary 2.00 5.00
4 Brett Favre 5.00 12.00
5 Edgerrin James 2.00 5.00
6 Peyton Manning 6.00 15.00
7 Randy Moss 2.00 5.00
8 Drew Bledsoe 2.00 5.00
9 Kurt Warner 4.00 10.00
10 Jerry Rice 6.00 15.00

2000 Paramount Sculptures
Randomly inserted in packs at the rate of one in 361, this 10-card set features circular embossed player portraits in bronze set against a "woodgrain" background shaped like the NFL shield logo.
COMPLETE SET (10) 50.00 120.00
STATED ODDS 1:361
*PROOF/20: 1.2X TO 3X BASIC INSERTS
PROOF PRINT RUN 20 SER.#'d SETS
UNPRICED CANVAS PRINT RUN 1
1 Peter Warrick 1.50 4.00
2 Tim Couch 2.00 5.00
3 Emmitt Smith 10.00 25.00
4 Edgerrin James 2.00 5.00
5 Mark Brunell 2.00 5.00
6 Fred Taylor 1.50 4.00
7 Randy Moss 2.00 5.00
8 Kurt Warner 4.00 10.00
9 Eddie George 2.00 5.00
10 Stephen Davis 1.50 4.00

2000 Paramount Zoned In
Randomly inserted in packs at the rate of one in 37, this 36-card set features cards with an orange border along the top and a blue and silver border along the bottom with close-up action shots of players on a silver foil card stock.
COMPLETE SET (36) 60.00 120.00
STATED ODDS 1:37
1 Thomas Jones 1.00 2.50
2 Jake Plummer 1.00 2.50
3 Jamal Lewis 1.25 3.00
4 Cade McNown 1.00 2.50
5 Marcus Robinson 1.25 3.00
6 Peter Warrick .75 2.00
7 Tim Couch 1.25 3.00
8 Troy Aikman 2.00 5.00
9 Emmitt Smith 2.50 6.00
10 Barry Sanders 2.50 6.00
11 Terrell Davis 1.25 3.00
12 Brian Griese 1.00 2.50
13 Brett Favre 3.00 8.00
14 Marvin Harrison 1.25 3.00
15 Edgerrin James 1.25 3.00
16 Peyton Manning 4.00 10.00
17 Mark Brunell 1.25 3.00
18 Fred Taylor 1.00 2.50
19 Drew Bledsoe 1.25 3.00
20 Ricky Williams 1.25 3.00
21 Ron Dayne 1.25 3.00
22 Chad Pennington 1.00 2.50
23 Randy Moss 1.25 3.00
24 Donovan McNabb 1.25 3.00
25 Plaxico Burress 1.00 2.50
26 Isaac Bruce 1.50 4.00
27 Marshall Faulk 1.25 3.00
28 Kurt Warner 2.50 6.00
29 Jerry Rice 4.00 10.00
30 Shaun Alexander 1.25 3.00
31 Jon Kitna 1.00 2.50
32 Shaun King 1.00 2.50
33 Eddie George 1.25 3.00
34 Steve McNair 1.25 3.00
35 Stephen Davis 1.00 2.50
36 Brad Johnson 1.25 3.00

1989 Parker Brothers Talking Football
Measuring approximately 2 5/8" by 3", this 34-card set was licensed only by the NFL Players Association. When players are shown together on a card, it relates to their respective position(s). The cards are unnumbered so they are listed below in alphabetical order according to the AFC (1-17) and the NFC (18-34). For cards with more than one subject, those players are in turn alphabetically listed so that they can be alphabetized consistently along with the single player cards.
COMPLETE SET (34) 150.00 300.00
1 AFC Team Roster 2.50 6.00
2 Marcus Allen 8.00 20.00
3 Cornelius Bennett 3.00 8.00
4 Keith Bishop 2.50 6.00
5 Keith Bostic 2.50 6.00
6 Carlos Carson 2.50 6.00
7 Todd Christensen 2.50 6.00
8 Eric Dickerson 4.00 10.00
9 Ray Donaldson 2.50 6.00
10 Jacob Green 2.50 6.00
11 Mark Haynes 2.50 6.00
12 Chris Hinton 2.50 6.00
13 Steve Largent 6.00 15.00
14 Howie Long 5.00 12.00
15 Nick Lowery 2.50 6.00
16 Dan Marino 40.00 80.00
17 Karl Mecklenburg 3.00 8.00
18 NFC Team Roster 2.50 6.00
19 Morten Andersen 2.50 6.00
20 Carl Banks 3.00 8.00
21 Mark Bavaro 2.50 6.00
22 Joey Browner 2.50 6.00
23 Anthony Carter 12.00 30.00
24 Gary Clark 3.00 8.00
25 Richard Dent 3.00 8.00
26 Brad Edelman 2.50 6.00
27 Carl Ekern 2.50 6.00
Rickey Jackson
28 Jerry Gray 2.50 6.00
29 Mel Gray 2.50 6.00
30 Dexter Manley 3.00 8.00
31 Rueben Mayes 2.50 6.00
32 Joe Montana 40.00 80.00
33 Jackie Slater 2.50 6.00
34 Herschel Walker 4.00 10.00

1968-70 Partridge Meats
These black and white (with some red trim and text) photo-like cards feature players from all three Cincinnati major league sports teams of that time: Cincinnati Reds baseball (BB1-BB20), Cincinnati Bengals football (FB1-FB5), and Cincinnati Royals basketball (BK1-BK2). The cards measure approximately 4" by 5" or 3-3/4" by 5-1/2" and were issued over a period of years. The cards are blank backed and a "Mr. Whopper" card was also issued in honor of the 7'-3" company spokesperson. The Tom Rhoads football card was only recently discovered, in 2012, adding to the prevailing thought that these cards were issued over a period of years since its format matches some of the baseball cards and not the other four more well-known football cards in the set. Joe Morgan was also recently added to the checklist indicating that more cards could turn up in the future. This card follows the same format as Gullett, May, Perez, and Tolan (all measuring 3-3/4" by 5-1/2") missing the team's logo on the cap, missing the team's nickname in the text, and missing the company's slogan below the image. Some collectors believe this style to be consistent with a 1972 release.
COMPLETE SET (14) 400.00 800.00
FB1 Bob Johnson 6.00 15.00
(measures 4" x 5")
FB2 Paul Robinson SP 25.00 50.00
FB3 John Stofa SP 25.00 50.00
(measures 4" x 5")
FB4 Bob Trumpy 6.00 15.00
(measures 4" x 5")
FB5 Tom Rhoads SP 75.00 150.00
(measures 4" x 5")

1961 Patriots Team Issue
The Patriots issued these photos around 1961. Each measures roughly 8" by 10" and includes a black and white player image with the player's name and team name (Boston Patriots) to the left and the team logo and address to the right below the image. The backs are blank.
COMPLETE SET 50.00 100.00
1 Ron Burton 7.50 15.00
2 Gerry Delucca 6.00 12.00
3 Mike Holovak 7.50 15.00
4 Jim Hunt 6.00 12.00
5 Harry Jacobs 6.00 12.00
6 Dick Klein 6.00 12.00
7 Tommy Stephens 6.00 12.00
8 Clyde Washington 6.00 12.00

1965 Patriots Team Issue
1 Tom Addison 7.50 15.00
All-League Linebacker
2 Houston Antwine DT 6.00 12.00
3 Jim Boudreaux 6.00 12.00
Tackle
4 John Charles 6.00 12.00
Defensive Back
5 Jim Colclough 6.00 12.00
Offensive End
6 Jay Cunningham DB 6.00 12.00
7 Tom Fussell 6.00 12.00
Defensive End
8 J.D. Garrett 6.00 12.00
Halfback
9 Art Graham 7.50 15.00
Split End
10 White Graves DB 6.00 12.00
11 Tom Hennessey DB 6.00 12.00
12 John Huarte 7.50 15.00
Quarterback
13 Ray Ilg 6.00 12.00
Linebacker
14 LeRoy Mitchell 6.00 12.00
Defensive Back
15 Don Oakes T. 6.00 12.00
16 Babe Parilli Q.B. 7.50 15.00
(team name under player name)
17 Vic Purvis DB 6.00 12.00
18 Chuck Shonta 6.00 12.00
Defensive Back
19 Terry Swanson 6.00 12.00
Punter
20 Don Webb DB 6.00 12.00
21 Jim Whalen E 6.00 12.00

1967 Patriots Team Issue
The Patriots issued this set of photos and distributed them to fans through mail requests. Each measures roughly 8" by 10 1/8" and includes a black and white player photo. The cards are unnumbered and checklisted below in alphabetical order.
COMPLETE SET (8) 50.00 100.00
1 Houston Antwine 6.00 12.00
2 Gino Cappelletti 7.50 15.00
3 John Charles 6.00 12.00
4 Jim Hunt 6.00 12.00
5 Leroy Mitchell 6.00 12.00
6 Babe Parilli 7.50 15.00
7 Don Trull 6.00 12.00
8 Jim Whalen 6.00 12.00

1971 Patriots Team Sheets
The New England Patriots issued these sheets of black-and-white player photos around 1971. Each measures roughly 8" by 10 1/8" and was printed on glossy stock with white borders. Each sheet includes photos of 4-players with the player's names, positions, team name and logo grouped below the photos. The coaches photo is a simple group shot with their names and positions listed below. The photo sheets are blankbacked.
COMPLETE SET (10) 50.00 100.00
1 Houston Antwine 5.00 10.00
2 Randall Edmunds 5.00 10.00
3 Halvor Hagen 5.00 10.00
4 Jon Morris 5.00 10.00
5 Jim Nance 6.00 12.00
6 John Outlaw 5.00 10.00
7 Jim Plunkett 7.50 15.00
8 Perry Pruett 5.00 10.00
9 Sam Rutigliano CO 5.00 10.00
10 Ron Sellers 5.00 10.00

1974 Patriots Linnett
Noted sports Artist Charles Linnett drew these charcoal portraits of New England Patriots players. The 8 1/2" by 11" portraits were sold three per pack. Each is blankbacked and includes the player's name below the artwork.
COMPLETE SET (9) 35.00 60.00
1 Jim Plunkett 6.00 12.00
2 Jon Morris 3.00 6.00
3 Julius Adams 3.00 6.00
4 Randy Vataha 3.00 6.00
5 Sam Cunningham 4.00 8.00
6 Reggie Rucker 4.00 8.00
7 Tom Neville 3.00 6.00
8 Mack Herron 3.00 6.00
9 John Smith 3.00 6.00

1974 Patriots Team Issue
The Patriots issued this set of player photos for the purpose of media use only. The 4 7/8" by 7 1/8" black and white photos are blankbanked and unnumbered and checklisted below in alphabetical order.
COMPLETE SET (29) 75.00 150.00
1 Bob Adams 3.00 6.00
2 Julius Adams 3.00 6.00
3 Sam Adams 4.00 8.00
4 Josh Ashton 3.00 6.00
5 Bruce Barnes 3.00 6.00
6 Sam Cunningham 5.00 10.00
7 Sandy Durko 3.00 6.00
8 Allen Gallaher 3.00 6.00
9 Neil Graff 3.00 6.00
10 Leon Gray 4.00 8.00
11 John Hannah 7.50 15.00
12 Craig Hanneman 3.00 6.00
13 Andy Johnson 3.00 6.00
14 Steve King 3.00 6.00
15 Bill Lenkaitis 3.00 6.00
16 Prentice McCray 3.00 6.00
17 Jack Mildren 3.00 6.00
18 Arthur Moore 3.00 6.00
19 Jon Morris 3.00 6.00
20 Reggie Rucker 4.00 8.00
21 John Sanders 3.00 6.00
22 Steve Schubert 3.00 6.00
23 John Smith 3.00 6.00
24 John Tanner 3.00 6.00
25 John Tarver 3.00 6.00
26 Randy Vataha 3.00 6.00
27 George Webster 4.00 8.00
28 Joe Wilson 3.00 6.00
29 Bob Windsor 3.00 6.00

1976 Patriots Frito Lay
The New England Patriots issued this set sponsored by Frito Lay. The cards are blankbacked, measure approximately 5" by 7", and feature black and white player photos. The cards can be distinguished from other Patriots Frito Lay issues by the notation "Compliments of Frito Lay" contained at the bottom of the cardfront along with the "FL" logo. The left and right hand borders are much wider than the 1977-78 release. The player's are not identified on the photos and each appears in a kneeling (one hand on helmet) pose. Any additions to the list below are appreciated.
COMPLETE SET (44)
1 Julius Adams 3.00 8.00
2 Sam Adams 4.00 10.00
3 Pete Barnes 3.00 8.00
4 Doug Beaudoin 3.00 8.00
5 Richard Bishop 3.00 8.00
6 Marlin Briscoe 3.00 8.00
7 Peter Brock 3.00 8.00
8 Steve Burks 3.00 8.00
9 Don Calhoun 3.00 8.00
10 Al Chandler 3.00 8.00
11 Dick Conn 3.00 8.00
12 Sam Cunningham 4.00 10.00
13 Ike Forte 3.00 8.00
14 Tim Fox 4.00 10.00
15 Russ Francis 5.00 12.00
16 Willie Germany 3.00 8.00
17 Leon Gray 3.00 8.00
18 Steve Grogan 6.00 15.00
19 Ray Hamilton 3.00 8.00
20 John Hannah 8.00 20.00
21 Mike Haynes 5.00 12.00
22 Bob Howard 3.00 8.00
23 Sam Hunt 3.00 8.00
24 Andy Johnson 3.00 8.00
25 Steve King 3.00 8.00
26 Bill Lenkaitis 3.00 8.00
27 Prentice McCray 3.00 8.00
28 Tony McGee 4.00 10.00
29 Bob McKay 3.00 8.00
30 Arthur Moore 3.00 8.00
31 Steve Nelson 3.00 8.00
32 Tom Neville 3.00 8.00
33 Tom Owen 3.00 8.00
34 Mike Patrick 3.00 8.00
35 Jess Phillips 3.00 8.00
36 Jim Romaniszyn 3.00 8.00
37 John Smith 3.00 8.00
38 Darryl Stingley 4.00 10.00
39 Fred Sturt 3.00 8.00
40 Randy Vataha 3.00 8.00
41 George Webster 3.00 8.00
42 Steve Zabel 3.00 8.00
43 R.Miller 3.00 8.00
Erhardt
Perkins
Dotsch
44 Team Photo 3.00 8.00

1977-78 Patriots Frito Lay
The New England Patriots issued this set sponsored by Frito Lay. The cards are blankbacked, measure approximately 5" by 7", and feature black and white player photos. The cards can be distinguished from other Patriots Frito Lay issues by the simple notation "Compliments of Frito Lay" contained at the bottom of the cardfront along with the "FL" logo. The left and right hand borders around the image are much thinner than the 1976 release, but otherwise the photos look the same. The player's are not identified on the photos and each appears in a kneeling (one hand on helmet) pose unless noted. Any additions to the list below are appreciated.
1 Richard Bishop 3.00 8.00
2 Sam Cunningham 4.00 10.00
3 Tim Fox 3.00 8.00
4 Leon Gray 3.00 8.00
5A Steve Grogan kneeling 6.00 15.00
5B Steve Grogan snap 6.00 15.00
5C Steve Grogan pass 6.00 15.00
6A Don Hasselbeck kneeling 3.00 8.00
6B Don Hasselbeck action 3.00 8.00
7A Stanley Morgan kneeling 5.00 12.00
7B Stanley Morgan action 5.00 12.00
8 Steve Nelson 3.00 8.00
9 Mike Patrick 3.00 8.00

1979 Patriots Frito Lay
The New England Patriots issued this set sponsored by Frito Lay. The cards are blankbacked, measure approximately 3 7/8" by 5 3/4", and contain black and white player photos. The cards can be distinguished from other Patriots Frito Lay issues by the notation "A WINNING TEAM" in all caps contained at the bottom of the cardfront. Each player's name is also printed below the photo with full first and last names. Any additions to the list below are appreciated.
COMPLETE SET (27) 100.00 200.00
1 Julius Adams 4.00 8.00
2 Sam Adams 4.00 8.00
3 Doug Beaudoin 4.00 8.00
4 Richard Bishop 4.00 8.00
5 Mark Buben 4.00 8.00
6 Matt Cavanaugh 5.00 10.00
7 Allan Clark 4.00 8.00
8 Ray Costict 4.00 8.00
9 Sam Cunningham 5.00 10.00
10 Russ Francis 5.00 10.00
11 Bob Golic 5.00 10.00
12 Ray Hamilton 4.00 8.00
13 John Hannah 6.00 12.00
14 Eddie Hare 4.00 8.00
15 Mike Hawkins 4.00 8.00
16 Horace Ivory 4.00 8.00
17 Harold Jackson 6.00 12.00
18 Andy Johnson 4.00 8.00
19 Shelby Jordan 4.00 8.00
20 Bill Lenkaitis 4.00 8.00
21 Bill Matthews 4.00 8.00
22 Stanley Morgan 4.00 8.00
23 Steve Nelson 4.00 8.00
24 Tom Owen 4.00 8.00
25 Carlos Pennywell 4.00 8.00
26 John Smith 4.00 8.00
27 Mosi Tatupu 4.00 8.00

1981 Patriots Frito Lay
The New England Patriots issued this set sponsored by Frito Lay. The cards are blankbacked, measure approximately 4" by 6", and contain black and white player photos. The cards can be distinguished from other Patriots Frito Lay issues by the title line "A Winning Team" contained at the top of the cardfront. Nearly all cards in this issue contain two player photos instead of one. The photos were issued before the season so they feature some players who never made the final roster.
COMPLETE SET (55) 200.00 400.00
1 Julius Adams 3.00 8.00
2 Richard Bishop 3.00 8.00
3 Don Blackmon 3.00 8.00
4 Pete Brock 3.00 8.00
5 Preston Brown 3.00 8.00
6 Mark Buben 3.00 8.00
7 Don Calhoun 3.00 8.00
8 Rich Camarillo 3.00 8.00
9 Matt Cavanaugh 4.00 10.00
10 Allan Clark 3.00 8.00
11 Steve Clark 3.00 8.00
12 Raymond Clayborn 4.00 10.00
13 Tony Collins 3.00 8.00
14 Charles Cook 3.00 8.00
15 Bob Cryder 3.00 8.00
16 Sam Cunningham 4.00 10.00
17 Lin Dawson 3.00 8.00
18 Ron Erhardt 3.00 8.00
19 Vagas Ferguson 3.00 8.00
20 Tim Fox 3.00 8.00
21 Bob Golic 4.00 10.00
22 Steve Grogan 6.00 15.00
23 Ray Hamilton 3.00 8.00
24 John Hannah 6.00 15.00
25 Don Hasselbeck 3.00 8.00
26 Mike Hawkins 3.00 8.00
27 Mike Haynes 6.00 15.00
28 Brian Holloway 3.00 8.00
29 Harold Jackson 4.00 10.00
30 Roland James 3.00 8.00
31 Andy Johnson 3.00 8.00
32 Shelby Jordan 3.00 8.00
33 Steve King 3.00 8.00
34 Keith Lee 3.00 8.00
35 Bill Lenkaitis UER 3.00 8.00
36 Bill Matthews 3.00 8.00
37 Tony McGee 3.00 8.00
38 Larry McGrew 3.00 8.00
39 Stanley Morgan 5.00 12.00
40 Steve Nelson 3.00 8.00
41 Tom Owen 3.00 8.00
42 Carlos Pennywell 3.00 8.00
43 Garry Puetz 3.00 8.00
44 Rick Sanford 3.00 8.00
45 Rod Shoate 3.00 8.00
46 John Smith 3.00 8.00
47 Mosi Tatupu 3.00 8.00
48 John Tautolo 3.00 8.00
49 Ken Toler 3.00 8.00
50 Richard Villella 3.00 8.00
51 Don Westbrook 3.00 8.00
52 Dwight Wheeler 3.00 8.00
53 Ron Wooten 3.00 8.00
54 Gary Wright 3.00 8.00
55 John Zamberlin 3.00 8.00

1982 Patriots Frito Lay
The New England Patriots issued this set sponsored by Frito Lay. The cards are blankbacked, measure approximately 4" by 6", and contain black and white player photos. The cards can be distinguished from other Patriots Frito Lay issues by the title line "get up for it" contained at the top of the cardfront. Each player's name is printed with first initial and full last name below the photo. The photos were issued before the season so they feature some players who never made the final roster. Any additions to the list below are appreciated.
COMPLETE SET (35) 125.00 250.00
1 Julius Adams 3.00 8.00
2 Pete Brock 3.00 8.00
3 Preston Brown 3.00 8.00
4 Mark Buben 3.00 8.00
5 Don Calhoun 3.00 8.00
6 Matt Cavanaugh 4.00 10.00
7 Allan Clark 3.00 8.00
8 Raymond Clayborn 3.00 8.00
9 Bob Cryder 3.00 8.00
10 Bill Currier 3.00 8.00
11 Vagas Ferguson 3.00 8.00
12 Chuck Foreman 5.00 12.00
13 Tim Fox 3.00 8.00
14 Russ Francis 5.00 12.00
15 Steve Grogan 6.00 15.00
16 Ray Hamilton 3.00 8.00
17 John Hannah 6.00 15.00
18 Don Hasselbeck 3.00 8.00
19 Mike Haynes 6.00 15.00
20 Mike Hubach 3.00 8.00
21 Horace Ivory 3.00 8.00
22 Harold Jackson 4.00 10.00
23 Roland James 3.00 8.00
24 Andy Johnson 3.00 8.00
25 Steve King 3.00 8.00
26 Bill Matthews 3.00 8.00
27 Tony McGee 3.00 8.00
28 Stanley Morgan 6.00 15.00
29 Steve Nelson 3.00 8.00
30 Garry Puetz 3.00 8.00
31 Rick Sanford 3.00 8.00
32 Rod Shoate 3.00 8.00
33 John Smith 3.00 8.00
34 Mosi Tatupu 3.00 8.00
35 Dwight Wheeler 3.00 8.00

1985 Patriots Frito Lay
The New England Patriots issued this set sponsored by Frito Lay. The cards are blankbacked, measure approximately 4" by 6", and contain black and white player photos. The cards can be distinguished from other Patriots Frito Lay issues by the lack of any set title something commonly found on the other releases. Any additions to this list would be appreciated.
COMPLETE SET (16) 60.00 120.00
1 Tony Collins 4.00 10.00
2 Rich Camarillo 3.00 8.00
3 Paul Dombroski 3.00 8.00
4 Tim Golden 3.00 8.00
5 Darryl Haley 3.00 8.00
6 Brian Ingram 3.00 8.00
7 Cedric Jones WR 3.00 8.00
8 Ronnie Lippett 3.00 8.00
9 Larry McGrew 3.00 8.00
10 Steve Moore 3.00 8.00
11 Stanley Morgan 4.00 10.00
12 Steve Nelson 3.00 8.00
13 Tom Ramsey 3.00 8.00
15 Kenneth Sims 3.00 8.00
16 Stephen Starring 3.00 8.00
17 Clayton Weishuhn 3.00 8.00

1986 Patriots Frito Lay
The New England Patriots issued this set sponsored by Frito Lay. The cards are blankbacked, measure approximately 4" by 6", and contain black and white player photos. The cards can be distinguished from other Patriots Frito Lay issues by the title "Together We Win" printed at the bottom of the cardfront. The set is thought to be complete at 42-cards. Any additions to the list would be appreciated.
COMPLETE SET (42) 125.00 250.00
1 Greg Baty 3.00 8.00
2 Raymond Berry CO 5.00 12.00
3 Don Blackmon 3.00 8.00
4 Jim Bowman 3.00 8.00
5 Pete Brock 3.00 8.00
6 Raymond Clayborn 3.00 8.00
7 Tony Collins 4.00 10.00
8 Rich Camarillo 3.00 8.00
9 Steve Doig 3.00 8.00
10 Reggie Dupard 3.00 8.00
11 Tony Eason 4.00 10.00
12 Sean Farrell 3.00 8.00
13 Tony Franklin 3.00 8.00
14 Ernest Gibson 3.00 8.00
15 Steve Grogan 5.00 12.00
16 Greg Hawthorne 3.00 8.00
17 Brian Holloway 3.00 8.00
18 Craig James 6.00 15.00
19 Roland James 3.00 8.00
20 Eric Jordan 3.00 8.00
21 Ronnie Lippett 4.00 10.00
22 Fred Marion 3.00 8.00
23 Trevor Matich 3.00 8.00
24 Rod McSwain 3.00 8.00
25 Guy Morriss 3.00 8.00
26 Steve Nelson 3.00 8.00
27 Dennis Owens 3.00 8.00
28 Eugene Profit 3.00 8.00
29 Tom Ramsey 3.00 8.00
30 Johnny Rembert 3.00 8.00
31 Ed Reynolds 3.00 8.00
32 Mike Ruth 3.00 8.00
33 Stephen Starring 3.00 8.00
34 Willie Scott 3.00 8.00
35 Mosi Tatupu 3.00 8.00
36 Andre Tippett 5.00 12.00
37 Garin Veris 3.00 8.00
38 Robert Weathers 3.00 8.00
39 Brent Williams 3.00 8.00
40 Derwin Williams 3.00 8.00
41 Toby Williams 3.00 8.00
42 Ron Wooten 3.00 8.00

1987 Patriots Team Issue
Each photo in this series measures roughly 8" by 10" and features a group of two to four different black and white images of each player on the fronts. The player's name, the team name, and his position are included below the images in a variety of type styles. The backs are blank and the photos are listed below alphabetically.
COMPLETE SET (8) 20.00 40.00
1 Reggie Dupard 2.50 6.00
2 Cedric Jones 2.50 6.00
3 Ronnie Lippett 3.00 8.00
4 Trevor Matich 2.50 6.00
5 Kenneth Sims 2.50 6.00
6 Mosi Tatupu 3.00 8.00
7 Garin Veris 2.50 6.00
8 Ron Wooten 2.50 6.00

1988 Patriots Ace Fact Pack
Cards from this 33-card set measure approximately 2 1/4" by 3 5/8". This set consists of 22-player cards and 11-additional informational cards about the Patriots team. We've checklisted the cards alphabetically beginning with the 22-players. The cards have square corners (as opposed to rounded like the 1987 sets) and a playing card design on the back printed in blue. These cards were manufactured in West Germany (by Ace Fact Pack) and released primarily in Great Britain.
COMPLETE SET (33) 60.00 120.00
1 Bruce Armstrong 1.50 4.00
2 Raymond Clayborn 1.50 4.00
3 Reggie Dupard 1.50 4.00
4 Tony Eason 2.00 5.00
5 Sean Farrell 1.50 4.00
6 Tony Franklin 1.50 4.00
7 Irving Fryar 3.00 8.00
8 Steve Grogan 3.00 8.00
9 Craig James UER 2.00 5.00
(listed as James Craig)
10 Ronnie Lippett 1.50 4.00
11 Fred Marion 1.50 4.00
12 Larry McGrew 1.50 4.00
13 Steve Moore 1.50 4.00
14 Stanley Morgan 3.00 8.00
15 Robert Perryman 1.50 4.00
16 Kenneth Sims 1.50 4.00
17 Stephen Starring 2.00 5.00
18 Mosi Tatupu 1.50 4.00
19 Andre Tippett 2.00 5.00
20 Garin Veris 1.50 4.00
21 Toby Williams 1.50 4.00
22 Ron Wooten 1.50 4.00
23 1987 Team Statistics 1.50 4.00
24 All-Time Greats 1.50 4.00
25 Career Record Holders 1.50 4.00
26 Coaching History 1.50 4.00
27 Game Record Holders 1.50 4.00
28 Patriots Helmet 1.50 4.00
(Cover Card)
29 Patriots Helmet 1.50 4.00
(Informational Card)
30 Patriots Uniform 1.50 4.00
31 Record 1968-87 1.50 4.00
32 Season Record Holders 1.50 4.00
33 Sullivan Stadium 1.50 4.00

1988 Patriots Holsum
This 12-card standard-size full-color set features players of the New England Patriots; cards were available only in Holsum Bread packages. The set was co-produced by Mike Schechter Associates on behalf of the NFL Players Association. Card fronts have a color photo within a green border and the backs are printed in black ink on white card stock.
COMPLETE SET (12) 25.00 60.00
1 Andre Tippett 2.50 6.00
2 Stanley Morgan 3.00 8.00
3 Steve Grogan 3.00 8.00
4 Ronnie Lippett 2.00 5.00
5 Kenneth Sims 2.00 5.00
6 Pete Brock 2.00 5.00
7 Sean Farrell 2.00 5.00
8 Garin Veris 2.00 5.00
9 Mosi Tatupu 2.00 5.00
10 Raymond Clayborn 2.50 6.00
11 Tony Franklin 2.00 5.00
12 Reggie Dupard 2.00 5.00

1990 Patriots Knudsen/Sealtest
This six-card set (of bookmarks) which measures approximately 2" by 8" was produced by Knudsen's and Sealtest to help promote readership by people under 15 years old in the New England area. Between the Knudsen or Sealtest company name, the front features a color action photo of the player superimposed on a football stadium. The field is green, the bleachers are yellow with gray print, and the scoreboard above the player reads "The Reading Team". The box below the player gives brief biographical information and player highlights. The back has logos of the sponsors and describes two books that are available at the public library. We have checklisted this set in alphabetical order because they are otherwise unnumbered except for the player's uniform number displayed on the card front.
COMPLETE SET (6) 12.00 30.00
1 Steve Grogan 2.40 6.00
2 Ronnie Lippett 2.00 5.00
3 Eric Sievers 2.00 5.00
4 Mosi Tatupu 2.00 5.00
5 Andre Tippett 2.40 6.00
6 Garin Veris 2.00 5.00

1997 Patriots Score
This 15-card set of the New England Patriots was distributed in five-card packs with a suggested retail price of $1.99. The fronts feature color action player photos with white borders and the player's name and team logo printed in team color foil at the bottom. The backs carry player information and career statistics. Platinum Team parallel cards were randomly seeded in packs featuring all foil cardfronts.
COMPLETE SET (15) 2.80 7.00
*PLATINUM TEAMS: 1X TO 2X
1 Drew Bledsoe .80 2.00
2 Curtis Martin .80 2.00
3 Terry Glenn .30 .75
4 Shawn Jefferson .08 .25
5 Ben Coates .15 .40
6 Willie McGinest .08 .25
7 Keith Byars .08 .25
8 Chris Slade .08 .25
9 Tedy Bruschi .30 .75
10 Ty Law .15 .40
11 Devin Wyman .08 .25
12 Sam Gash .08 .25
13 Dave Meggett .08 .25
14 Ferric Collons .08 .25
15 Willie Clay .08 .25

2005 Patriots Topps Super Bowl Champions
This set was issued by Topps in factory set form right after the Patriots victory in Super Bowl XXXIX. 38-different players are included in the set with 2-players appearing for the first time on cards. The set is rounded out by several Season Highlight cards and one jumbo card. Factory sets initially retailed for $19.95.
COMPLETE SET (56) 15.00 25.00
1 Corey Dillon .40 1.00
2 Ty Warren .20 .50
3 Adam Vinatieri .40 1.00
4 Troy Brown .40 1.00
5 Christian Fauria .20 .50
6 Tom Brady 1.25 3.00
7 Willie McGinest .30 .75
8 Deion Branch .40 1.00
9 David Patten .30 .75
10 Rodney Harrison .30 .75
11 Kevin Faulk .30 .75
12 Mike Vrabel .40 1.00
13 Tedy Bruschi .40 1.00
14 Josh Miller .20 .50
15 Ty Law .40 1.00
16 Roman Phifer .20 .50
17 David Givens .30 .75
18 Eugene Wilson .20 .50
19 Patrick Pass .20 .50
20 Bethel Johnson .30 .75
21 Keith Traylor .20 .50
22 Randall Gay .20 .50
23 Rohan Davey .30 .75
24 Richard Seymour .30 .75
25 Ted Johnson .30 .75
26 Asante Samuel .20 .50
27 Steve Neal .20 .50
28 Rosevelt Colvin .20 .50
29 Larry Izzo .20 .50
30 Daniel Graham .30 .75
31 Tully Banta-Cain .20 .50
32 Jarvis Green .20 .50
33 Vince Wilfork .40 1.00
34 Matt Light .20 .50
35 Joe Andruzzi .20 .50
36 Dan Koppen .20 .50
37 Brandon Gorin .20 .50
38 Rabih Abdullah .20 .50
39 Tom Brady HL .75 2.00
40 Pats 19th Win .30 .75
41 Ty Law HL .30 .75
42 Adam Vinatieri HL .40 1.00
43 Corey Dillon HL .40 1.00
44 Tedy Bruschi HL .40 1.00
45 Corey Dillon HL .40 1.00
46 Tom Brady HL .75 2.00
47 Deion Branch HL .40 1.00
48 Rodney Harrison HL .30 .75
49 Tom Brady HL .75 2.00
50 Mike Vrabel HL .40 1.00
51 Deion Branch HL .40 1.00
52 Rodney Harrison HL .30 .75
53 Super Bowl XXXIX Champs .40 1.00
54 Team Card .20 .50
55 Deion Branch MVP .40 1.00
NNO Jumbo Team Card .30 .75

2005 Patriots Upper Deck Super Bowl Champions
This set was issued by Upper Deck in factory set form after the Patriots victory in Super Bowl XXXIX. Forty different players are included in the set with 2-players appearing for the first time on cards. The set is rounded out by several Season Highlight cards and one jumbo card. Factory sets initially retailed for $19.95.
COMPLETE SET (51) 15.00 25.00
1 Tom Ashworth .20 .50
2 Tom Brady 1.25 3.00
3 Deion Branch .40 1.00
4 Troy Brown .40 1.00
5 Tedy Bruschi .40 1.00
6 Je'Rod Cherry .20 .50
7 Rohan Davey .30 .75
8 Don Davis .20 .50
9 Corey Dillon .40 1.00
10 Kevin Faulk .30 .75
11 Christian Fauria .20 .50
12 Randall Gay .20 .50
13 David Givens .30 .75
14 Daniel Graham .30 .75
15 Rodney Harrison .30 .75
16 Russ Hochstein .20 .50
17 Larry Izzo .20 .50
18 Bethel Johnson .30 .75
19 Ted Johnson .30 .75
20 Dan Koppen .20 .50
21 Ty Law .40 1.00
22 Matt Light .20 .50
23 Willie McGinest .30 .75
24 Ben Watson .50 1.25
25 Josh Miller .20 .50
26 Steve Neal .20 .50
27 Patrick Pass .20 .50
28 David Patten .30 .75
29 Lonie Paxton .20 .50
30 Roman Phifer .20 .50
31 Tyrone Poole .30 .75
32 Asante Samuel .20 .50
33 Richard Seymour .30 .75
34 Keith Traylor .20 .50
35 Adam Vinatieri .40 1.00
36 Mike Vrabel .40 1.00
37 Ty Warren .20 .50
38 Jed Weaver .20 .50
39 Vince Wilfork .40 1.00
40 Eugene Wilson .20 .50
41 Tom Brady HL .75 2.00
42 Corey Dillon HL .40 1.00
43 David Givens HL .30 .75
44 Adam Vinatieri HL .40 1.00
45 Deion Branch HL .40 1.00
SH1 Tom Brady MM .75 2.00
SH2 Corey Dillon MM .40 1.00
SH3 David Givens MM .30 .75
SH4 Rodney Harrison MM .30 .75
MVP Deion Branch MVP .40 1.00
SBC Jumbo Patriots Team .30 .75

2006 Patriots Topps
COMPLETE SET (12) 4.00 8.00
NE1 Kevin Faulk .25 .60
NE2 Corey Dillon .25 .60
NE3 Ben Watson .25 .60
NE4 Tom Brady 1.25 3.00
NE5 Tedy Bruschi .30 .75
NE6 Deion Branch .25 .60
NE7 Mike Vrabel .30 .75
NE8 Daniel Graham .25 .60
NE9 Rodney Harrison .25 .60
NE10 Richard Seymour .25 .60
NE11 Laurence Maroney 1.00 2.50
NE12 Chad Jackson .25 .60

2006 Patriots Upper Deck Boston Globe
This set was produced by Upper Deck and issued by the Boston Glode in 12-card sheets over the course of three weeks in November 2006. Cards #1-12 released November 12, cards #13-24 on November 19, and cards #14-36 on November 26.
COMPLETE SET (36) 7.50 15.00
1 Tom Brady 1.00 2.50
2 Vince Wilfork .30 .75
3 Dan Koppen .25 .60
4 Ben Watson .30 .75
5 Stephen Gostkowski .40 1.00
6 Logan Mankins .25 .60
7 Eugene Wilson .30 .75
8 Chad Jackson .75 2.00
9 Tully Banta-Cain .25 .60
10 Junior Seau .50 1.25
11 Artrell Hawkins .25 .60
12 Heath Evans .25 .60
13 Tedy Bruschi .50 1.25
14 Matt Light .25 .60
15 Mike Vrabel .30 .75
16 Corey Dillon .30 .75
17 Rodney Harrison .30 .75
18 Ty Warren .25 .60
19 Rosevelt Colvin .30 .75
20 Steve Neal .25 .60
21 Ryan O'Callaghan .25 .60
22 Don Davis .25 .60
23 David Thomas .50 1.25
24 Matt Cassel .75 2.00
25 Richard Seymour .30 .75
26 Troy Brown .30 .75
27 Asante Samuel .30 .75
28 Daniel Graham .25 .60
29 Laurence Maroney 1.25 3.00
30 Ellis Hobbs .25 .60
31 Larry Izzo .25 .60
32 Reche Caldwell .30 .75
33 Kevin Faulk .30 .75
34 Jarvis Green .25 .60
35 Mike Wright .25 .60
36 James Sanders .25 .60

2007 Patriots Topps
COMPLETE SET (12) 3.00 6.00
1 Tom Brady 2.00 5.00
2 Laurence Maroney .50 1.25
3 Kevin Faulk .40 1.00
4 Reche Caldwell .40 1.00
5 Ben Watson .40 1.00
6 Richard Seymour .40 1.00
7 Wes Welker .50 1.25
8 Donte' Stallworth .50 1.25
9 Tedy Bruschi .50 1.25
10 Adalius Thomas .40 1.00
11 Rodney Harrison .40 1.00
12 Randy Moss .50 1.25

2007 Patriots Upper Deck Boston Globe
This set was produced by Upper Deck and issued by the Boston Glode in 12-card sheets over the course of three weeks in the fall of 2007.
COMPLETE SET (36) 7.50 15.00
1 Larry Izzo .25 .60
2 Ellis Hobbs .25 .60
3 Matt Light .25 .60
4 Donte Stallworth .30 .75
5 Tom Brady 1.25 3.00
6 Junior Seau .40 1.00
7 Wes Welker .30 .75
8 Rosevelt Colvin .25 .60
9 Stephen Gostkowski .30 .75
10 Troy Brown .25 .60
11 Mike Vrabel .30 .75
12 Nick Kaczur .25 .60
13 Dan Koppen .25 .60
14 Kevin Faulk .25 .60
15 Jabar Gaffney .25 .60
16 Laurence Maroney .30 .75
17 Richard Seymour .25 .60
18 Adalius Thomas .25 .60
19 Vince Wilfork .25 .60
20 Steve Neal .25 .60
21 Ben Watson .25 .60
22 Ty Warren .25 .60
23 Eugene Wilson .25 .60
24 Rodney Harrison .25 .60
25 Kyle Brady .25 .60
26 Sammy Morris .25 .60
27 Asante Samuel .25 .60
28 Brandon Meriweather .30 .75
29 Randy Moss .30 .75
30 Tedy Bruschi .30 .75
31 James Sanders .25 .60
32 Randall Gay .25 .60
33 Jarvis Green .25 .60
34 Mike Wright .25 .60
35 Heath Evans .25 .60
36 Logan Mankins .25 .60

2008 Patriots Topps
COMPLETE SET (12) 2.50 5.00
1 Tom Brady 2.00 5.00
2 Randy Moss .50 1.25
3 Laurence Maroney .50 1.25
4 Wes Welker .50 1.25
5 Mike Vrabel .40 1.00
6 Sammy Morris .40 1.00
7 Ben Watson .40 1.00
8 Vince Wilfork .40 1.00
9 Jabar Gaffney .40 1.00
10 Tedy Bruschi .50 1.25
11 Kevin O'Connell .40 1.00
12 Jerod Mayo .60 1.50

2014 Patriots Topps 5x7 Super Bowl XLIX
COMPLETE SET (9) 12.00 20.00
52 Tom Brady 4.00 10.00
104 Darrelle Revis 1.00 2.50
128 Stephen Gostkowski 1.25 3.00
144 Shane Vereen 1.25 3.00
148 Julian Edelman 1.50 4.00
215 Brandon Lafell 1.00 2.50
258 Rob Gronkowski 1.50 4.00
310 Chandler Jones 1.00 2.50
313 Danny Amendola 1.25 3.00

2014 Patriots Topps 5x7 Super Bowl XLIX Champions
COMPLETE SET (10) 15.00 30.00
1 Tom Brady MVP 3.00 8.00
2 Julian Edelman 1.25 3.00
3 Rob Gronkowski 1.25 3.00
4 Rob Ninkovich 1.00 2.50
5 Danny Amendola 1.00 2.50
6 Malcolm Butler 4.00 10.00
7 Brandon Lafell .75 2.00
8 Duron Harmon .75 2.00
9 Super Bowl Champions .60 1.50
10 Tom Brady 3.00 8.00

2014 Patriots Topps 5x7 Super Bowl XLIX Champions Limited
COMPLETE SET (12) 75.00 150.00
*1-10 LIMITED/49: 1.2X TO 3X BASIC CARDS
11 Tom Brady 15.00 30.00
12 Super Bowl Trophy 4.00 10.00

2015 Patriots Panini Super Bowl XLIX
COMPLETE SET (10) 12.50 25.00
1 Tom Brady 3.00 8.00
2 Julian Edelman 1.25 3.00
3 Brandon LaFell .75 2.00
4 Rob Gronkowski 1.25 3.00
5 Brandon Browner .75 2.00
6 Darrelle Revis .75 2.00
7 Jamie Collins .75 2.00
8 Chandler Jones .75 2.00
9 Vince Wilfork .75 2.00
10 Stephen Gostkowski 1.00 2.50

2002 Peoria Pirates AF2
COMPLETE SET (24) 15.00 30.00
1 Brandon Campbell .60 1.50
2 Ronnie Gordon .60 1.50
3 Todd Kurz .60 1.50
4 Jerome Hurd .60 1.50
5 Geral Neasman .60 1.50
6 Lincoln Dupree .60 1.50
7 Walter Church .60 1.50
8 Titcus Pettigrew .75 2.00
9 Frank West .60 1.50
10 Robert Meyer .60 1.50
11 Tim Simpson .60 1.50
12 Jon Verdegan .60 1.50
13 Jason Hennigh .60 1.50
14 Demond Gibson .60 1.50
15 Cornell Craig .60 1.50
16 Jermaine Sheffield .60 1.50
17 Eric Johnson .60 1.50
18 Terence Cook .60 1.50
19 Rasche Hill .75 2.00
20 Ken Bouie .60 1.50
21 Bruce Cowdrey CO .60 1.50
22 Tony Johnson Asst.CO .60 1.50
23 Tony Johnson Asst.CO .60 1.50
Treasure Life
24 Cover Card .60 1.50
Jermaine Sheffield
Cornell Craig

2003 Peoria Pirates AFL
This 30-card set was produced by Multi-Ad and distributed at a 2003 Pirates home game to attendees. Each includes a color photo of a Pirates player on the front with a bio and year of issue on the back.
COMPLETE SET (30) 15.00 30.00
1 Bryan Archibald .50 1.25
2 Kraig Baker .50 1.25
3 Anthony Chiaravalle .50 1.25
4 Nick Cosontino .50 1.25
5 Bruce Cowdrey .50 1.25
6 Michael Cunningham .50 1.25
7 Bryan Eakin .50 1.25
8 Troy Edwards .60 1.50
9 Steve Fickert .50 1.25
10 Thomas Guynes .50 1.25

11 Torrance Heggie .50 1.25
12 Davaren Hightower .50 1.25
13 Rasche Hill .60 1.50
14 Eric Johnson .50 1.25
15 Jay Johnson .50 1.25
16 Tony Johnson .50 1.25
17 David Knott .50 1.25
18 Michael Leaks .60 1.50
19 Chris Martin .50 1.25
20 Eddie McKennie .50 1.25
21 Gerald Neasman .50 1.25
22 Charlie Peterson .50 1.25
23 Matt Pike .75 2.00
24 Ted Schmitz .50 1.25
25 Jon Verdegan .50 1.25
26 Frank West .50 1.25
27 Tyshaun Whitson .50 1.25
28 Jack Wilson .50 1.25
29 Checklist .50 1.25
30 Cover Card .50 1.25

2004 Peoria Pirates AFL

Cards in this set were produced by Multi-Ad and were given away four or five at a time to fans attending Pirates games in Peoria. We've catalogued those cards using a series number followed by a card number below. Also, at the last game of the year on July 31, 2004, a full 31-card set was issued with all of the cards being re-numbered (#1-31). We've cataloged those below with the prefix "T" to indicate team set. Two players were added to this "team set" version in place of two players dropped from the set. Cards in this version of the set are slightly different (in addition to the different card numbers) in that they have a different placement of the sponsor logo or the logo is printed in a different color. We've included the date of release for each card issued throughout the season when known. The cardfronts feature a larger action photo on the right side and a smaller head shot on the left. The backs include a short player bio. The cards in the weekly series are numbered 1 through 4 or 1 through 5 with each new series starting over. We've listed those below in alphabetical order for ease in cataloging.

COMP.TEAM T SET (31) 15.00 30.00
1-1 Louie Aguiar 4/9 .75 2.00
1-2 Lucas Brigman 4/9 .60 1.50
1-3 Troy Edwards 4/9 .75 2.00
1-4 Jerry Samuels 4/9 .60 1.50
1-5 Enoch Smith 4/9 .60 1.50
2-1 Brandon Campbell 5/15 .75 2.00
2-2 Tony Pryor 5/15 .75 2.00
2-3 Casey Urlacher 5/15 3.00 8.00
2-4 Frank West 5/15 .60 1.50
3-1 Kevin Brown 5/29 .60 1.50
3-2 Lawrence Mathews 5/29 1.25 3.00
3-3 Ben Sanderson 5/29 .60 1.50
3-4 Paul Steffeck 5/29 .60 1.50
4-1 Talmadge Hill 6/12 1.25 3.00
4-2 Joe Laudano 6/12 .60 1.50
4-3 Joe Peters 6/12 .60 1.50
4-4 Chris Robinson 6/12 1.25 3.00
5-1 Louie Aguiar RB 7/17 .75 2.00
5-2 Ken Bouie RB 7/17 .60 1.50
5-3 Bruce Cowdrey CO 7/17 .60 1.50
5-4 Casey Urlacher RB 7/17 2.00 5.00
5-6 Frank West RB 7/17 .60 1.50
5-7 Team Mascot CL 7/17 .60 1.50
T1 Louie Aguiar .75 2.00
T2 Ken Bouie .60 1.50
T3 Milt Bowen .60 1.50
T4 Lucas Brigman .60 1.50
T5 Kevin Brown .60 1.50
T6 Brandon Campbell .75 2.00
T7 Mike Cunningham .60 1.50
T8 Troy Edwards .75 2.00
T9 Sameer Hamood .60 1.50
T10 Talmadge Hill 1.25 3.00
T11 Colin Johnson .60 1.50
T12 Eric Johnson .60 1.50
T13 Joe Laudano .60 1.50
T14 Lawrence Mathews 1.25 3.00
T15 Joe Peters .60 1.50
T16 Tony Pryor .75 2.00
T17 Andrew Webb 1.25 3.00
T18 Chris Robinson 1.25 3.00
T19 Jerald Burley 1.25 3.00
T20 Ben Sanderson .60 1.50
T21 Enoch Smith .60 1.50
T22 Mike Souza .75 2.00
T23 Paul Steffeck .60 1.50
T24 Casey Urlacher 3.00 8.00
T25 Frank West .60 1.50
T26 Louie Aguiar RB .75 2.00
T27 Casey Urlacher RB 2.00 5.00
T28 Frank West RB .60 1.50
T29 Ken Bouie RB .60 1.50
T30 Bruce Cowdrey CO .60 1.50
T31 Team Mascot CL .60 1.50

1976 Pepsi Discs

The 1976 Pepsi Discs set contains 40 numbered discs, each measuring approximately 3 1/2" in diameter. Each disc has a player photo, biographical information, and 1975 statistics. Disc numbers 1-20 are from many different teams and are known as "All-Stars." Numbers 21-40 feature Cincinnati Bengals, since this set was a regional issue produced in the Cincinnati area. Numbers 1, 5, 7, 8, and 14 are much scarcer than the other 35 and are marked SP in the checklist below. Ed Marinaro also exists as a New York Jet, which is very difficult to find. It has been reported that Ed Marinaro may be a sixth SP. The checklist for the set is printed on the tab; the checklist below values the discs with the tabs intact as that is the way they are most commonly found.

COMPLETE SET (40) 75.00 150.00
1 Steve Bartkowski SP 10.00 20.00
2 Lydell Mitchell 1.25 3.00
3 Wally Chambers 1.00 2.50
4 Doug Buffone 1.00 2.50
5 Jerry Sherk SP 7.50 15.00
6 Drew Pearson 1.50 4.00
7 Otis Armstrong SP 7.50 15.00
8 Charlie Sanders SP 7.50 15.00
9 John Brockington 1.25 3.00
10 Curley Culp 1.25 3.00
11 Jan Stenerud 1.25 3.00
12 Lawrence McCutchen 1.25 3.00
13 Chuck Foreman 1.25 3.00
14 Bob Pollard SP 7.50 15.00
15 Ed Marinaro 2.00 5.00
16 Jack Lambert 4.00 8.00
17 Terry Metcalf 1.25 3.00
18 Mel Gray 1.25 3.00
19 Russ Washington 1.00 2.50
20 Charley Taylor 1.50 4.00
21 Ken Anderson 2.00 5.00
22 Bob Brown DT 1.00 2.50
23 Ron Carpenter 1.00 2.50
24 Tommy Casanova 1.00 2.50
25 Boobie Clark 1.00 2.50
26 Isaac Curtis 1.25 3.00
27 Lenvil Elliott 1.00 2.50
28 Stan Fritts 1.00 2.50
29 Vern Holland 1.00 2.50
30 Bob Johnson 1.25 3.00
31 Ken Johnson DT 1.00 2.50
32 Bill Kollar 1.00 2.50
33 Jim LeClair 1.00 2.50
34 Chip Myers 1.00 2.50
35 Lemar Parrish 1.25 3.00
36 Ron Pritchard 1.00 2.50
37 Bob Trumpy 1.25 3.00
38 Sherman White 1.00 2.50
39 Archie Griffin 1.50 4.00
40 John Shinners 1.00 2.50

1964 Philadelphia

The 1964 Philadelphia Gum set of 198 standard-size cards, featuring National Football League players, is the first of four annual issues released by the company. The cards were issued in one-card penny packs, five-card nickel packs, as well as cello packs. Each card has a question about that player in a cartoon at the bottom of the reverse; the answer is given upside down in blue ink. Each team has a team picture card as well as a card diagramming one of the team's plays; this "play card" shows a small black and white picture of the team's coach on the front of the card. The card backs are printed in blue and black on a gray card stock. Within each team group the players are arranged alphabetically by last name. The two checklist cards erroneously say "Official 1963 Checklist" at the top. The key Rookie Cards in this set are Herb Adderley, Willie Davis, Jim Johnson, John Mackey and Merlin Olsen. Tatoo Transfers sheets were included as inserts in packs.

COMPLETE SET (198) 600.00 900.00
WRAPPER (1-CENT) 35.00 60.00
WRAPPER (5-CENT) 10.00 20.00
1 Raymond Berry 10.00 20.00
2 Tom Gilburg 1.25 2.50
3 John Mackey RC 20.00 40.00
4 Gino Marchetti 2.50 5.00
5 Jim Martin 1.25 2.50
6 Tom Matte RC 3.00 6.00
7 Jimmy Orr 1.50 3.00
8 Jim Parker 2.00 4.00
9 Bill Pellington 1.25 2.50
10 Alex Sandusky 1.25 2.50
11 Dick Szymanski 1.25 2.50
12 Johnny Unitas 25.00 50.00
13 Baltimore Colts 1.50 3.00
14 Colts Play 20.00 35.00
Don Shula
15 Doug Atkins 2.50 5.00
16 Ronnie Bull 1.25 2.50
17 Mike Ditka 25.00 40.00
18 Joe Fortunato 1.25 2.50
19 Willie Galimore 1.50 3.00
20 Joe Marconi 1.25 2.50
21 Bennie McRae RC 1.25 2.50
22 Johnny Morris 1.25 2.50
23 Richie Petitbon 1.25 2.50
24 Mike Pyle RC 1.25 2.50
25 Roosevelt Taylor RC 2.00 4.00
26 Bill Wade 1.50 3.00
27 Chicago Bears 1.50 3.00
28 Bears Play 6.00 12.00
George Halas
29 Johnny Brewer RC 1.25 2.50
30 Jim Brown 50.00 90.00
31 Gary Collins RC 4.00 8.00
32 Vince Costello 1.25 2.50
33 Galen Fiss 1.25 2.50
34 Bill Glass 1.25 2.50
35 Ernie Green RC 1.50 3.00
36 Rich Kreitling 1.25 2.50
37 John Morrow 1.25 2.50
38 Frank Ryan 1.50 3.00
39 Charlie Scales RC 1.25 2.50
40 Dick Schafrath RC 1.25 2.50
41 Cleveland Browns 1.50 3.00
42 Cleveland Browns Play 1.25 2.50
43 Don Bishop 1.25 2.50
44 Frank Clarke RC 1.50 3.00
45 Mike Connelly 1.25 2.50
46 Lee Folkins RC 1.25 2.50
47 Cornell Green RC 4.00 8.00
48 Bob Lilly 25.00 40.00
49 Amos Marsh 1.25 2.50
50 Tommy McDonald 2.50 5.00
51 Don Meredith 20.00 35.00
52 Pettis Norman RC 1.50 3.00
53 Don Perkins 2.00 4.00
54 Guy Reese RC 1.25 2.50
55 Dallas Cowboys 2.00 4.00
56 Cowboys Play 12.00 20.00
T.Landry
57 Terry Barr 1.25 2.50
58 Roger Brown 1.50 3.00
59 Gail Cogdill 1.25 2.50
60 John Gordy RC 1.25 2.50
61 Dick Lane 2.00 4.00
62 Yale Lary 2.00 4.00
63 Dan Lewis 1.25 2.50
64 Darris McCord 1.25 2.50
65 Earl Morrall 1.50 3.00
66 Joe Schmidt 2.50 5.00
67 Pat Studstill RC 1.50 3.00
68 Wayne Walker RC 1.50 3.00
69 Detroit Lions 1.50 3.00
70 Detroit Lions 1.25 2.50
71 Herb Adderley RC 20.00 35.00
72 Willie Davis RC 18.00 30.00
73 Forrest Gregg 2.50 5.00
74 Paul Hornung 20.00 35.00
75 Hank Jordan 2.50 5.00
76 Jerry Kramer 3.00 6.00
77 Tom Moore 1.50 3.00
78 Jim Ringo 2.50 5.00
79 Bart Starr 35.00 60.00
80 Jim Taylor 15.00 25.00
81 Jesse Whittenton RC 1.50 3.00
82 Willie Wood 4.00 8.00
83 Green Bay Packers 3.00 6.00
84 Packers Play 20.00 35.00
Lombardi
85 Jon Arnett 1.25 2.50
86 Pervis Atkins RC 1.25 2.50
87 Dick Bass 1.50 3.00
88 Carroll Dale 2.00 4.00
89 Roman Gabriel 3.00 6.00
90 Ed Meador 1.25 2.50
91 Merlin Olsen RC 30.00 50.00
92 Jack Pardee RC 2.00 4.00
93 Jim Phillips 1.25 2.50
94 Carver Shannon RC 1.25 2.50
95 Frank Varrichione 1.25 2.50
96 Danny Villanueva 1.25 2.50
97 Los Angeles Rams 1.50 3.00
98 Los Angeles Rams Play 1.25 2.50
99 Grady Alderman RC 1.50 3.00
100 Larry Bowie RC 1.25 2.50
101 Bill Brown RC 3.00 6.00
102 Paul Flatley RC 1.25 2.50
103 Rip Hawkins 1.25 2.50
104 Jim Marshall 4.00 8.00
105 Tommy Mason 1.50 3.00
106 Jim Prestel 1.25 2.50
107 Jerry Reichow 1.25 2.50
108 Ed Sharockman 1.25 2.50
109 Fran Tarkenton 20.00 35.00
110 Mick Tingelhoff RC 3.00 6.00
111 Minnesota Vikings 1.50 3.00
112 Vikings Play 2.00 4.00
Van Brock.
113 Erich Barnes 1.25 2.50
114 Roosevelt Brown 2.00 4.00
115 Don Chandler 1.25 2.50
116 Darrell Dess 1.25 2.50
117 Frank Gifford 20.00 35.00
118 Dick James 1.25 2.50
119 Jim Katcavage 1.25 2.50
120 John Lovetere RC 1.25 2.50
121 Dick Lynch RC 1.50 3.00
122 Jim Patton 1.25 2.50
123 Del Shofner 1.25 2.50
124 Y.A.Tittle 10.00 20.00
125 New York Giants 1.50 3.00
126 New York Giants Play 1.25 2.50
127 Sam Baker 1.25 2.50
128 Maxie Baughan 1.25 2.50
129 Timmy Brown 1.50 3.00
130 Mike Clark RC 1.25 2.50
131 Irv Cross RC 2.00 4.00
132 Ted Dean 1.25 2.50
133 Ron Goodwin RC 1.25 2.50
134 King Hill 1.25 2.50
135 Clarence Peaks 1.25 2.50
136 Pete Retzlaff 1.50 3.00
137 Jim Schrader 1.25 2.50
138 Norm Snead 1.50 3.00
139 Philadelphia Eagles 1.50 3.00
140 Philadelphia Eagles Play 1.25 2.50
141 Gary Ballman RC 1.25 2.50
142 Charley Bradshaw RC 1.25 2.50
143 Ed Brown 1.50 3.00
144 John Henry Johnson 2.00 4.00
145 Joe Krupa 1.25 2.50
146 Bill Mack 1.25 2.50
147 Lou Michaels 1.25 2.50
148 Buzz Nutter 1.25 2.50
149 Myron Pottios 1.25 2.50
150 John Reger 1.25 2.50
151 Mike Sandusky 1.25 2.50
152 Clendon Thomas 1.25 2.50
153 Pittsburgh Steelers 1.50 3.00
154 Pittsburgh Steelers Play 1.25 2.50
155 Kermit Alexander RC 1.50 3.00
156 Bernie Casey 1.50 3.00
157 Dan Colchico 1.25 2.50
158 Clyde Conner 1.25 2.50
159 Tommy Davis 1.25 2.50
160 Matt Hazeltine 1.25 2.50
161 Jim Johnson RC 15.00 25.00
162 Don Lisbon RC 1.25 2.50
163 Lamar McHan 1.25 2.50
164 Bob St.Clair 2.00 4.00
165 J.D. Smith 1.25 2.50
166 Abe Woodson 1.25 2.50
167 San Francisco 49ers 1.50 3.00
168 San Francisco 49ers Play 1.25 2.50
169 Garland Boyette UER RC 1.25 2.50
170 Bobby Joe Conrad 1.50 3.00
171 Bob DeMarco RC 1.25 2.50
172 Ken Gray RC 1.25 2.50
173 Jimmy Hill 1.25 2.50
174 Charley Johnson 1.50 3.00
175 Ernie McMillan 1.25 2.50
176 Dale Meinert RC 1.25 2.50
177 Luke Owens RC 1.25 2.50
178 Sonny Randle 1.25 2.50
179 Joe Robb RC 1.25 2.50
180 Bill Stacy 1.25 2.50
181 St. Louis Cardinals 1.50 3.00
182 St. Louis Cardinals Play 1.25 2.50
183 Bill Barnes 1.25 2.50
184 Don Bosseler 1.25 2.50
185 Sam Huff 3.00 6.00
186 Sonny Jurgensen 10.00 20.00
187 Bob Khayat RC 1.25 2.50
188 Riley Mattson 1.25 2.50
189 Bobby Mitchell 3.00 6.00
190 John Nisby 1.25 2.50
191 Vince Promuto 1.25 2.50
192 Joe Rutgens RC 1.25 2.50
193 Lonnie Sanders RC 1.25 2.50
194 Jim Steffen RC 1.25 2.50
195 Washington Redskins 1.50 3.00
196 Washington Redskins Play 1.25 2.50
197 Checklist 1 UER 18.00 30.00
198 Checklist 2 UER 30.00 55.00

1965 Philadelphia

The 1965 Philadelphia Gum set of NFL players consists of 198 standard-size cards. The cards were issued in five-card nickel packs and cello packs. The card fronts have the player's name, team name and position in a black box beneath the photo. The NFL logo is at bottom right. The card backs feature statistics and a question and answer section that requires a coin to rub and reveal the answer. The card backs are printed in maroon on a gray card stock. Each team has a team picture card as well as a card featuring a diagram of one of the team's plays; this play card shows a small coach's picture in black and white on the front of the card. The card backs are printed in maroon on a gray card stock. The cards are numbered within team with the players arranged alphabetically by last name. The key Rookie Cards in this set are Carl Eller, Paul Krause, Mel Renfro, Charley Taylor, and Paul Warfield. Comic Transfers sheets were included as inserts into packs.

COMPLETE SET (198) 500.00 800.00
WRAPPER (5-CENT) 10.00 20.00
1 Colts Team 7.50 15.00
2 Raymond Berry 5.00 10.00
3 Bob Boyd DB 1.00 2.00
4 Wendell Harris 1.00 2.00
5 Jerry Logan RC 1.00 2.00
6 Tony Lorick RC 1.00 2.00
7 Lou Michaels 1.00 2.00
8 Lenny Moore 4.00 8.00
9 Jimmy Orr 1.50 3.00
10 Jim Parker 2.00 4.00
11 Dick Szymanski 1.00 2.00
12 Johnny Unitas 25.00 40.00
13 Bob Vogel RC 1.00 2.00
14 Colts Play 12.00 20.00
Don Shula
15 Chicago Bears 1.50 3.00
16 Jon Arnett 1.00 2.00
17 Doug Atkins 2.50 5.00
18 Rudy Bukich RC 1.50 3.00
19 Mike Ditka 25.00 40.00
20 Dick Evey RC 1.00 2.00
21 Joe Fortunato 1.00 2.00
22 Bobby Joe Green RC 1.00 2.00
23 Johnny Morris 1.00 2.00
24 Mike Pyle 1.00 2.00
25 Roosevelt Taylor 1.50 3.00
26 Bill Wade 1.50 3.00
27 Bob Wetoska RC 1.00 2.00
28 Bears Play 4.00 8.00
George Halas
29 Cleveland Browns 1.50 3.00
30 Walter Beach RC 1.00 2.00
31 Jim Brown 50.00 80.00
32 Gary Collins 1.50 3.00
33 Bill Glass 1.00 2.00
34 Ernie Green 1.00 2.00
35 Jim Houston RC 1.00 2.00
36 Dick Modzelewski 1.00 2.00
37 Bernie Parrish 1.00 2.00
38 Walter Roberts RC 1.00 2.00
39 Frank Ryan 1.50 3.00
40 Dick Schafrath 1.00 2.00
41 Paul Warfield RC 50.00 90.00
42 Cleveland Browns 1.00 2.00
43 Dallas Cowboys 1.50 3.00
44 Frank Clarke 1.50 3.00
45 Mike Connelly 1.00 2.00
46 Buddy Dial 1.00 2.00
47 Bob Lilly 20.00 35.00
48 Tony Liscio RC 1.00 2.00
49 Tommy McDonald 2.50 5.00
50 Don Meredith 15.00 25.00
51 Pettis Norman 1.00 2.00
52 Don Perkins 2.00 4.00
53 Mel Renfro RC 35.00 50.00
54 Jim Ridlon 1.00 2.00
55 Jerry Tubbs 1.00 2.00
56 Cowboys Play 7.50 15.00
T.Landry
57 Detroit Lions 1.50 3.00
58 Terry Barr 1.00 2.00
59 Roger Brown 1.00 2.00
60 Gail Cogdill 1.00 2.00
61 Jim Gibbons 1.00 2.00
62 John Gordy 1.00 2.00
63 Yale Lary 2.00 4.00
64 Dick LeBeau RC 25.00 40.00
65 Earl Morrall 1.50 3.00
66 Nick Pietrosante 1.00 2.00
67 Pat Studstill 1.00 2.00
68 Wayne Walker 1.50 3.00
69 Tom Watkins RC 1.00 2.00
70 Detroit Lions 1.50 3.00
71 Green Bay Packers 4.00 8.00
72 Herb Adderley 4.00 8.00
73 Willie Davis DE 4.00 8.00
74 Boyd Dowler 2.00 4.00
75 Forrest Gregg 2.50 5.00
76 Paul Hornung 20.00 35.00
77 Hank Jordan 2.50 5.00
78 Tom Moore 1.50 3.00
79 Ray Nitschke 12.00 20.00
80 Elijah Pitts RC 4.00 8.00
81 Bart Starr 30.00 50.00
82 Jim Taylor 12.00 20.00
83 Willie Wood 3.00 6.00
84 Packers Play 12.00 20.00
Lombardi
85 Los Angeles Rams 1.50 3.00
86 Dick Bass 1.50 3.00
87 Roman Gabriel 2.50 5.00
88 Roosevelt Grier 2.00 4.00
89 Deacon Jones 5.00 10.00
90 Lamar Lundy RC 2.00 4.00
91 Marlin McKeever 1.00 2.00
92 Ed Meador 1.00 2.00
93 Bill Munson RC 2.00 4.00
94 Merlin Olsen 7.50 15.00
95 Bobby Smith RC 1.00 2.00
96 Frank Varrichione 1.00 2.00
97 Ben Wilson RC 1.00 2.00
98 Los Angeles Rams 1.00 2.00
99 Minnesota Vikings 1.50 3.00
100 Grady Alderman 1.00 2.00
101 Hal Bedsole RC 1.00 2.00
102 Bill Brown 1.50 3.00
103 Bill Butler RC 1.00 2.00
104 Fred Cox RC 1.50 3.00
105 Carl Eller RC 18.00 30.00
106 Paul Flatley 1.00 2.00
107 Jim Marshall 3.00 6.00
108 Tommy Mason 1.00 2.00
109 George Rose RC 1.00 2.00
110 Fran Tarkenton 15.00 25.00
111 Mick Tingelhoff 1.50 3.00
112 Vikings Play 2.00 4.00
Van Brock.
113 New York Giants 1.50 3.00
114 Erich Barnes 1.00 2.00
115 Roosevelt Brown 2.00 4.00
116 Clarence Childs RC 1.00 2.00
117 Jerry Hillebrand 1.00 2.00
118 Greg Larson RC 1.00 2.00
119 Dick Lynch 1.00 2.00
120 Joe Morrison RC 2.00 4.00
121 Lou Slaby RC 1.00 2.00
122 Aaron Thomas RC 1.00 2.00
123 Steve Thurlow RC 1.00 2.00
124 Ernie Wheelwright RC 1.00 2.00
125 Gary Wood RC 1.50 3.00
126 New York Giants 1.00 2.00
127 Philadelphia Eagles 1.50 3.00
128 Sam Baker 1.00 2.00
129 Maxie Baughan 1.00 2.00
130 Timmy Brown 1.50 3.00
131 Jack Concannon RC 1.00 2.00
132 Irv Cross 1.50 3.00
133 Earl Gros 1.00 2.00
134 Dave Lloyd RC 1.00 2.00
135 Floyd Peters RC 1.00 2.00
136 Nate Ramsey RC 1.00 2.00
137 Pete Retzlaff 1.50 3.00
138 Jim Ringo 2.00 4.00
139 Norm Snead 2.00 4.00
140 Philadelphia Eagles 1.00 2.00
141 Pittsburgh Steelers 1.50 3.00
142 John Baker 1.00 2.00
143 Gary Ballman 1.00 2.00
144 Charley Bradshaw 1.00 2.00
145 Ed Brown 1.00 2.00
146 Dick Haley 1.00 2.00
147 John Henry Johnson 2.00 4.00
148 Brady Keys RC 1.00 2.00
149 Ray Lemek 1.00 2.00
150 Ben McGee RC 1.00 2.00
151 Clarence Peaks UER 1.00 2.00
152 Myron Pottios 1.00 2.00
153 Clendon Thomas 1.00 2.00
154 Pittsburgh Steelers 1.00 2.00
155 St. Louis Cardinals 1.50 3.00
156 Jim Bakken RC 1.50 3.00
157 Joe Childress 1.00 2.00
158 Bobby Joe Conrad 1.50 3.00
159 Bob DeMarco 1.00 2.00
160 Pat Fischer RC 2.00 4.00
161 Irv Goode RC 1.00 2.00
162 Ken Gray 1.00 2.00
163 Charley Johnson 1.50 3.00
164 Bill Koman 1.00 2.00
165 Dale Meinert 1.00 2.00
166 Jerry Stovall RC 1.50 3.00
167 Abe Woodson 1.00 2.00
168 St. Louis Cardinals 1.00 2.00
169 San Francisco 49ers 1.50 3.00
170 Kermit Alexander 1.00 2.00
171 John Brodie 5.00 10.00
172 Bernie Casey 1.50 3.00
173 John David Crow 1.50 3.00
174 Tommy Davis 1.00 2.00
175 Matt Hazeltine 1.00 2.00
176 Jim Johnson 2.00 4.00
177 Charlie Krueger RC 1.00 2.00
178 Roland Lakes RC 1.00 2.00
179 George Mira RC 1.50 3.00
180 Dave Parks RC 1.50 3.00
181 John Thomas RC 1.00 2.00
182 49ers Play 1.00 2.00
Christiansen
183 Washington Redskins 1.50 3.00
184 Pervis Atkins 1.00 2.00
185 Preston Carpenter 1.00 2.00
186 Angelo Coia 1.00 2.00
187 Sam Huff 3.00 6.00
188 Sonny Jurgensen 7.50 15.00
189 Paul Krause RC 20.00 40.00
190 Jim Martin 1.00 2.00
191 Bobby Mitchell 2.50 5.00
192 John Nisby 1.00 2.00
193 John Paluck 1.00 2.00
194 Vince Promuto 1.00 2.00
195 Charley Taylor RC 30.00 50.00
196 Washington Redskins 1.00 2.00
197 Checklist 1 15.00 30.00
198 Checklist 2 UER 25.00 50.00

1966 Philadelphia

The 1966 Philadelphia Gum football card set contains 198 standard-size cards featuring NFL players. The cards were issued in five-card nickel packs which came 24 packs to a box and cello packs. The card fronts feature the player's name, team name and position in a color bar above the photo. The NFL logo is at upper left. The card backs are printed in green and black on a white card stock. The backs contain the player's name, a card number, a short biography, and a "Guess Who" quiz. The quiz answer is found on another card. The last two cards in the set are checklist cards. Each team's "play card" shows a color photo of actual game action, described on the back. The cards are numbered within team with the players arranged alphabetically by last name. The set features the debut of Hall of Fame Chicago Bears' greats Dick Butkus and Gale Sayers. Other Rookie Cards include Cowboys Bob Hayes and Chuck Howley. Comic Transfers sheets were included as inserts into packs.

COMPLETE SET (198) 600.00 900.00
WRAPPER (5-CENT) 10.00 20.00
1 Atlanta Falcons Logo 6.00 12.00
2 Larry Benz RC 1.00 2.00
3 Dennis Claridge RC 1.00 2.00
4 Perry Lee Dunn RC 1.00 2.00
5 Dan Grimm RC 1.00 2.00
6 Alex Hawkins 1.00 2.00
7 Ralph Heck RC 1.00 2.00
8 Frank Lasky RC 1.00 2.00
9 Guy Reese 1.00 2.00
10 Bob Richards RC 1.00 2.00
11 Ron Smith RC 1.00 2.00
12 Ernie Wheelwright 1.00 2.00
13 Atlanta Falcons Roster 1.50 3.00
14 Baltimore Colts Team 1.50 3.00
15 Raymond Berry 4.00 8.00
16 Bob Boyd DB 1.00 2.00
17 Jerry Logan 1.00 2.00
18 John Mackey 3.00 6.00
19 Tom Matte 2.00 4.00
20 Lou Michaels 1.00 2.00
21 Lenny Moore 4.00 8.00
22 Jimmy Orr 1.50 3.00
23 Jim Parker 2.00 4.00
24 Johnny Unitas 30.00 50.00
25 Bob Vogel 1.00 2.00
26 Colts Play 2.00 4.00
Lenny Moore
Jim Parker
27 Chicago Bears Team 1.50 3.00
28 Doug Atkins 2.00 4.00
29 Rudy Bukich 1.00 2.00
30 Ronnie Bull 1.00 2.00
31 Dick Butkus RC 150.00 250.00
32 Mike Ditka 20.00 35.00
33 Joe Fortunato 1.00 2.00
34 Bobby Joe Green 1.00 2.00
35 Roger LeClerc 1.00 2.00
36 Johnny Morris 1.00 2.00
37 Mike Pyle 1.00 2.00
38 Gale Sayers RC 125.00 225.00
39 Bears Play 20.00 35.00
Gale Sayers
40 Cleveland Browns Team 1.50 3.00
41 Jim Brown 50.00 80.00
42 Gary Collins 1.50 3.00
43 Ross Fichtner RC 1.00 2.00
44 Ernie Green 1.00 2.00
45 Gene Hickerson RC 15.00 25.00
46 Jim Houston 1.00 2.00
47 John Morrow 1.00 2.00
48 Walter Roberts 1.00 2.00
49 Frank Ryan 1.50 3.00
50 Dick Schafrath 1.00 2.00
51 Paul Wiggin RC 1.00 2.00
52 Cleveland Browns Play 1.00 2.00
53 Dallas Cowboys Team 1.50 3.00
54 George Andrie UER RC 2.00 4.00
55 Frank Clarke 1.50 3.00
56 Mike Connelly 1.00 2.00
57 Cornell Green 2.00 4.00
58 Bob Hayes RC 45.00 75.00
59 Chuck Howley RC 15.00 30.00
60 Bob Lilly 12.00 20.00
61 Don Meredith 15.00 30.00
62 Don Perkins 1.50 3.00
63 Mel Renfro 7.50 15.00
64 Danny Villanueva 1.00 2.00
65 Dallas Cowboys Play 1.00 2.00
66 Detroit Lions Team 1.50 3.00
67 Roger Brown 1.00 2.00
68 John Gordy 1.00 2.00
69 Alex Karras 5.00 10.00
70 Dick LeBeau 3.00 6.00
71 Amos Marsh 1.00 2.00
72 Milt Plum 1.50 3.00
73 Bobby Smith 1.00 2.00
74 Wayne Rasmussen RC 1.00 2.00
75 Pat Studstill 1.00 2.00
76 Wayne Walker 1.00 2.00
77 Tom Watkins 1.00 2.00
78 Detroit Lions Play 1.00 2.00
79 Green Bay Packers Team 3.00 6.00
80 Herb Adderley 3.00 6.00
81 Lee Roy Caffey RC 2.00 4.00
82 Don Chandler 1.50 3.00
83 Willie Davis DE 3.00 6.00
84 Boyd Dowler 2.00 4.00
85 Forrest Gregg 2.00 4.00
86 Tom Moore 1.50 3.00
87 Ray Nitschke 7.50 15.00
88 Bart Starr 30.00 50.00
89 Jim Taylor 12.00 20.00
90 Willie Wood 3.00 6.00
91 Green Bay Packers Play 1.00 2.00
92 Los Angeles Rams Team 1.50 3.00
93 Willie Brown RC 1.00 2.00
94 Roman Gabriel 2.00 4.00
Dick Bass
95 Bruce Gossett RC 1.50 3.00
96 Deacon Jones 3.00 6.00
97 Tommy McDonald 2.50 5.00
98 Marlin McKeever 1.00 2.00
99 Aaron Martin RC 1.00 2.00
100 Ed Meador 1.00 2.00
101 Bill Munson 1.50 3.00
102 Merlin Olsen 4.00 8.00
103 Jim Stiger RC 1.00 2.00
104 Rams Play 1.50 3.00
Willie Brown
105 Minnesota Vikings Team 1.50 3.00
106 Grady Alderman 1.00 2.00
107 Bill Brown 1.50 3.00
108 Fred Cox 1.00 2.00
109 Paul Flatley 1.00 2.00
110 Rip Hawkins 1.00 2.00
111 Tommy Mason 1.00 2.00
112 Ed Sharockman 1.00 2.00
113 Gordon Smith RC 1.00 2.00
114 Fran Tarkenton 15.00 30.00
115 Mick Tingelhoff 1.50 3.00
116 Bobby Walden RC 1.00 2.00
117 Minnesota Vikings Play 1.00 2.00
118 New York Giants Team 1.50 3.00
119 Roosevelt Brown 2.00 4.00
120 Henry Carr RC 1.50 3.00
121 Clarence Childs 1.00 2.00
122 Tucker Frederickson RC 1.50 3.00
123 Jerry Hillebrand 1.00 2.00
124 Greg Larson 1.00 2.00
125 Spider Lockhart RC 1.50 3.00
126 Dick Lynch 1.00 2.00
127 Earl Morrall 1.50 3.00
Bob Scholtz
128 Joe Morrison 1.00 2.00
129 Steve Thurlow 1.00 2.00
130 New York Giants Play 1.00 2.00
131 Philadelphia Eagles Team 1.50 3.00
132 Sam Baker 1.00 2.00
133 Maxie Baughan 1.00 2.00
134 Bob Brown OT RC 7.50 15.00
135 Timmy Brown 1.50 3.00
136 Irv Cross 1.50 3.00
137 Earl Gros 1.00 2.00
138 Ray Poage RC 1.00 2.00
139 Nate Ramsey 1.00 2.00
140 Pete Retzlaff 1.50 3.00
141 Jim Ringo 2.00 4.00
142 Norm Snead 2.00 4.00
143 Philadelphia Eagles Play 1.00 2.00
144 Pittsburgh Steelers Team 1.50 3.00
145 Gary Ballman 1.00 2.00
146 Jim Bradshaw 1.00 2.00
147 Jim Butler RC 1.00 2.00
148 Mike Clark 1.00 2.00
149 Dick Hoak RC 1.00 2.00
150 Roy Jefferson RC 1.50 3.00
151 Frank Lambert RC 1.00 2.00
152 Mike Lind RC 1.00 2.00
153 Bill Nelsen RC 2.00 4.00
154 Clarence Peaks 1.00 2.00
155 Clendon Thomas 1.00 2.00
156 Pittsburgh Steelers Play 1.00 2.00
157 St. Louis Cardinals Team 1.50 3.00
158 Jim Bakken 1.00 2.00
159 Bobby Joe Conrad 1.50 3.00
160 Willis Crenshaw RC 1.00 2.00
161 Bob DeMarco 1.00 2.00
162 Pat Fischer 1.50 3.00
163 Charley Johnson 1.50 3.00
164 Dale Meinert 1.00 2.00
165 Sonny Randle 1.00 2.00
166 Sam Silas RC 1.00 2.00
167 Bill Triplett RC 1.00 2.00
168 Larry Wilson 2.00 4.00
169 St. Louis Cardinals Play 1.00 2.00
170 San Francisco 49ers Team 1.50 3.00
171 Kermit Alexander 1.00 2.00
172 Bruce Bosley 1.00 2.00
173 John Brodie 3.00 6.00
174 Bernie Casey 1.50 3.00
175 John David Crow 2.00 4.00
176 Tommy Davis 1.00 2.00
177 Jim Johnson 2.00 4.00
178 Gary Lewis RC 1.00 2.00
179 Dave Parks 1.00 2.00
180 Walter Rock RC 1.50 3.00
181 Ken Willard RC 2.00 4.00
182 San Francisco 49ers Play 1.00 2.00
183 Washington Redskins Team 1.50 3.00
184 Rickie Harris RC 1.00 2.00
185 Sonny Jurgensen 4.00 8.00
186 Paul Krause 3.00 6.00
187 Bobby Mitchell 3.00 6.00
188 Vince Promuto 1.00 2.00
189 Pat Richter RC 1.00 2.00
190 Joe Rutgens 1.00 2.00
191 Johnny Sample 1.00 2.00
192 Lonnie Sanders 1.00 2.00
193 Jim Steffen 1.00 2.00
194 Charley Taylor 7.50 15.00
195 Washington Redskins Play 1.00 2.00
196 Referee Signals 1.50 3.00
197 Checklist 1 12.50 25.00
198 Checklist 2 UER 25.00 50.00

1967 Philadelphia

The 1967 Philadelphia Gum set of NFL players consists of 198 standard-size cards. It was the company's last issue. Cards were issued in five-card nickel packs and cello packs. This set is easily distinguished from the other Philadelphia football sets by its yellow border on the fronts of the cards. The player's name, team name and position are at the bottom in a color bar. The NFL logo is at the top right or left. Horizontally designed backs are printed in brown on a white card stock. The left side of the back contains a trivia question that requires a coin to scratch to reveal the answer. The right side has a brief write-up. The cards are numbered within team with players arranged alphabetically by last name. The key Rookie Cards in this set are Lee Roy Jordan, Leroy Kelly, Tommy Nobis, Dan Reeves and Jackie Smith.

COMPLETE SET (198) 400.00 650.00
WRAPPER (5-CENT) 10.00 20.00
1 Falcons Team 5.00 10.00
2 Junior Coffey RC 1.50 3.00
3 Alex Hawkins 1.00 2.00
4 Randy Johnson RC 1.50 3.00
5 Lou Kirouac RC 1.00 2.00
6 Billy Martin RC 1.00 2.00
7 Tommy Nobis RC 10.00 20.00
8 Jerry Richardson RC 2.00 4.00
9 Marion Rushing RC 1.00 2.00
10 Ron Smith 1.00 2.00
11 Ernie Wheelwright UER 1.00 2.00
12 Atlanta Falcons 1.00 2.00
13 Baltimore Colts 1.50 3.00
14 Raymond Berry UER 3.50 7.00
15 Bob Boyd DB 1.00 2.00
16 Ordell Braase RC 1.00 2.00
17 Alvin Haymond RC 1.00 2.00
18 Tony Lorick 1.00 2.00
19 Lenny Lyles RC 1.00 2.00
20 John Mackey 2.50 5.00
21 Tom Matte 1.50 3.00
22 Lou Michaels 1.00 2.00
23 Johnny Unitas 25.00 40.00
24 Baltimore Colts 1.00 2.00
25 Chicago Bears 1.50 3.00
26 Rudy Bukich UER 1.00 2.00
27 Ronnie Bull 1.00 2.00
28 Dick Butkus 45.00 75.00
29 Mike Ditka 18.00 30.00
30 Dick Gordon RC 1.50 3.00
31 Roger LeClerc 1.00 2.00
32 Bennie McRae 1.00 2.00
33 Richie Petitbon 1.00 2.00
34 Mike Pyle 1.00 2.00
35 Gale Sayers 45.00 75.00
36 Chicago Bears 1.00 2.00
37 Cleveland Browns 1.50 3.00
38 Johnny Brewer 1.00 2.00
39 Gary Collins 1.50 3.00
40 Ross Fichtner 1.00 2.00
41 Ernie Green 1.00 2.00
42 Gene Hickerson 2.50 5.00
43 Leroy Kelly RC 25.00 50.00
44 Frank Ryan 1.50 3.00
45 Dick Schafrath 1.00 2.00
46 Paul Warfield 10.00 18.00
47 John Wooten RC 1.00 2.00
48 Cleveland Browns 1.00 2.00
49 Dallas Cowboys 1.50 3.00
50 George Andrie 1.00 2.00
51 Cornell Green 1.50 3.00
52 Bob Hayes 10.00 20.00
53 Chuck Howley 2.00 4.00
54 Lee Roy Jordan RC 12.00 20.00
55 Bob Lilly 7.50 15.00
56 Dave Manders RC 1.00 2.00
57 Don Meredith 15.00 25.00
58 Dan Reeves RC 18.00 30.00
59 Mel Renfro 3.00 6.00
60 Dallas Cowboys 1.50 3.00
61 Detroit Lions 1.50 3.00
62 Roger Brown 1.50 3.00
63 Gail Cogdill 1.00 2.00
64 John Gordy 1.00 2.00
65 Ron Kramer 1.00 2.00
66 Dick LeBeau 2.00 4.00
67 Mike Lucci RC 2.00 4.00
68 Amos Marsh 1.00 2.00
69 Tom Nowatzke RC 1.00 2.00
70 Pat Studstill 1.00 2.00
71 Karl Sweetan RC 1.00 2.00
72 Detroit Lions 1.00 2.00
73 Green Bay Packers 2.50 5.00
74 Herb Adderley UER 3.00 6.00
75 Lee Roy Caffey 1.50 3.00
76 Willie Davis DE 2.50 5.00
77 Forrest Gregg 2.00 4.00
78 Hank Jordan 2.00 4.00
79 Ray Nitschke 6.00 12.00
80 Dave Robinson RC 18.00 30.00
81 Bob Skoronski RC 1.50 3.00
82 Bart Starr 30.00 50.00
83 Willie Wood 2.50 5.00
84 Green Bay Packers 1.50 3.00
85 Los Angeles Rams 1.50 3.00
86 Dick Bass 1.50 3.00
87 Maxie Baughan 1.00 2.00
88 Roman Gabriel 2.00 4.00
89 Bruce Gossett 1.00 2.00
90 Deacon Jones 2.50 5.00
91 Tommy McDonald 2.50 5.00
92 Marlin McKeever 1.00 2.00
93 Tom Moore 1.00 2.00
94 Merlin Olsen 3.00 6.00
95 Clancy Williams RC 1.00 2.00
96 Los Angeles Rams 1.00 2.00
97 Minnesota Vikings 1.50 3.00
98 Grady Alderman 1.00 2.00
99 Bill Brown 1.50 3.00
100 Fred Cox 1.00 2.00
101 Paul Flatley 1.00 2.00
102 Dale Hackbart RC 1.00 2.00
103 Jim Marshall 2.00 4.00
104 Tommy Mason 1.00 2.00
105 Milt Sunde RC 1.00 2.00
106 Fran Tarkenton 10.00 20.00
107 Mick Tingelhoff 1.50 3.00
108 Minnesota Vikings 1.00 2.00
109 New York Giants 1.50 3.00
110 Henry Carr 1.00 2.00
111 Clarence Childs 1.00 2.00
112 Allen Jacobs RC 1.00 2.00
113 Homer Jones RC 1.50 3.00
114 Tom Kennedy RC 1.00 2.00
115 Spider Lockhart 1.00 2.00
116 Joe Morrison 1.00 2.00
117 Francis Peay RC 1.00 2.00
118 Jeff Smith LB RC 1.00 2.00
119 Aaron Thomas 1.00 2.00
120 New York Giants 1.00 2.00
121 Saints Insignia 1.50 3.00
122 Charley Bradshaw 1.00 2.00
123 Paul Hornung 12.50 25.00
124 Elbert Kimbrough RC 1.00 2.00
125 Earl Leggett RC 1.00 2.00
126 Obert Logan RC 1.00 2.00
127 Riley Mattson 1.00 2.00
128 John Morrow 1.00 2.00
129 Bob Scholtz RC 1.00 2.00
130 Dave Whitsell RC 1.00 2.00
131 Gary Wood 1.00 2.00
132 Saints Roster UER 121 1.50 3.00
133 Philadelphia Eagles 1.50 3.00
134 Sam Baker 1.00 2.00
135 Bob Brown OT 2.00 5.00
136 Timmy Brown 1.50 3.00
137 Earl Gros 1.00 2.00
138 Dave Lloyd 1.00 2.00
139 Floyd Peters 1.00 2.00
140 Pete Retzlaff 1.50 3.00
141 Joe Scarpati RC 1.00 2.00
142 Norm Snead 1.50 3.00
143 Jim Skaggs RC 1.00 2.00
144 Philadelphia Eagles 1.00 2.00
145 Pittsburgh Steelers 1.50 3.00
146 Bill Asbury RC 1.00 2.00
147 John Baker 1.00 2.00
148 Gary Ballman 1.00 2.00
149 Mike Clark 1.00 2.00
150 Riley Gunnels 1.00 2.00
151 John Hilton RC 1.00 2.00
152 Roy Jefferson 1.50 3.00
153 Brady Keys 1.00 2.00
154 Ben McGee 1.00 2.00
155 Bill Nelsen 1.50 3.00
156 Pittsburgh Steelers 1.00 2.00
157 St. Louis Cardinals 1.50 3.00
158 Jim Bakken 1.00 2.00
159 Bobby Joe Conrad 1.50 3.00
160 Ken Gray 1.00 2.00
161 Charley Johnson 1.50 3.00
162 Joe Robb 1.00 2.00
163 Johnny Roland RC 1.50 3.00
164 Roy Shivers RC 1.00 2.00
165 Jackie Smith RC 10.00 20.00
166 Jerry Stovall 1.00 2.00
167 Larry Wilson 2.00 4.00
168 St. Louis Cardinals 1.00 2.00
169 San Francisco 49ers 1.50 3.00
170 Kermit Alexander 1.00 2.00
171 Bruce Bosley 1.00 2.00
172 John Brodie 3.00 6.00
173 Bernie Casey 1.50 3.00
174 Tommy Davis 1.00 2.00
175 Howard Mudd RC 2.00 4.00
176 Dave Parks 1.00 2.00
177 John Thomas 1.00 2.00
178 Dave Wilcox RC 12.50 25.00
179 Ken Willard 1.50 3.00
180 San Francisco 49ers 1.00 2.00
181 Washington Redskins 1.50 3.00
182 Charlie Gogolak RC 1.00 2.00
183 Chris Hanburger RC 7.50 15.00
184 Len Hauss RC 1.50 3.00
185 Sonny Jurgensen 3.50 7.00
186 Bobby Mitchell 2.50 5.00
187 Brig Owens RC 1.00 2.00
188 Jim Shorter RC 1.00 2.00
189 Jerry Smith RC 1.50 3.00
190 Charley Taylor 4.00 8.00
191 A.D. Whitfield RC 1.00 2.00
192 Washington Redskins 1.00 2.00
193 Browns Play 3.00 6.00
Leroy Kelly
194 New York Giants PC 1.00 2.00
195 Atlanta Falcons PC 1.00 2.00
196 Referee Signals 1.50 3.00
197 Checklist 1 12.00 20.00
198 Checklist 2 UER 20.00 40.00

2009 Philadelphia

COMP.SET w/o SP's (200) 25.00 50.00
1 Kurt Warner .25 .60
2 Matt Leinart .20 .50
3 Edgerrin James .25 .60
4 Tim Hightower .20 .50
5 Larry Fitzgerald .25 .60
6 Anquan Boldin .20 .50
7 Karlos Dansby .20 .50
8 Steve Breaston .25 .60
9 Matt Ryan .25 .60
10 Michael Turner .25 .60
11 Jerious Norwood .20 .50
12 Roddy White .20 .50
13 John Abraham .20 .50
14 Harry Douglas .20 .50
15 Michael Jenkins .20 .50
16 Joe Flacco .25 .60
17 Willis McGahee .20 .50
18 Ray Rice .20 .50
19 Derrick Mason .20 .50
20 Ray Lewis .30 .75
21 Terrell Suggs .20 .50
22 Trent Edwards .25 .60
23 Marshawn Lynch .25 .60
24 Lee Evans .20 .50
25 Josh Reed .20 .50
26 Paul Posluszny .20 .50
27 Jake Delhomme .20 .50
28 Jonathan Stewart .25 .60
29 DeAngelo Williams .25 .60
30 Steve Smith .25 .60
31 Muhsin Muhammad .20 .50
32 Jon Beason .20 .50
33 Julius Peppers .20 .50
34 Kyle Orton .20 .50

35 Matt Forte .20 .50
36 Devin Hester .25 .60
37 Brian Urlacher .30 .75
38 Lance Briggs .25 .60
39 Charles Tillman .25 .60
40 Greg Olsen .25 .60
41 Carson Palmer .25 .60
42 Chris Perry .20 .50
43 T.J. Houshmandzadeh .20 .50
44 Chad Ocho Cinco .20 .50
45 Dhani Jones .20 .50
46 Brady Quinn .20 .50
47 Jamal Lewis .25 .60
48 Braylon Edwards .20 .50
49 Kellen Winslow .20 .50
50 D'Qwell Jackson .20 .50
51 Shaun Rogers .20 .50
52 Tony Romo .25 .60
53 Marion Barber .25 .60
54 Jason Witten .25 .60
55 Terrell Owens .25 .60
56 Felix Jones .20 .50
57 Roy Williams WR .20 .50
58 DeMarcus Ware .25 .60
59 Zach Thomas .25 .60
60 Jay Cutler .20 .50
61 Tony Schettler .20 .50
62 Brandon Marshall .25 .60
63 Eddie Royal .20 .50
64 D.J. Williams .20 .50
65 Ronald Curry .20 .50
66 Kevin Smith .20 .50
67 Rudi Johnson .20 .50
68 Calvin Johnson .30 .75
69 Ernie Sims .20 .50
70 DeWayne White .20 .50
71 Aaron Rodgers .60 1.50
72 Ryan Grant .25 .60
73 Greg Jennings .20 .50
74 Donald Driver .25 .60
75 A.J. Hawk .20 .50
76 Aaron Kampman .25 .60
77 Nick Collins .20 .50
78 Matt Schaub .20 .50
79 Steve Slaton .20 .50
80 Andre Johnson .25 .60
81 Owen Daniels .20 .50
82 Kevin Walter .25 .60
83 Mario Williams .25 .60
84 Peyton Manning .75 2.00
85 Joseph Addai .20 .50
86 Reggie Wayne .25 .60
87 Dwight Freeney .20 .50
88 Anthony Gonzalez .20 .50
89 Dallas Clark .20 .50
90 Robert Mathis .20 .50
91 David Garrard .20 .50
92 Maurice Jones-Drew .20 .50
93 Marcedes Lewis .20 .50
94 Rashean Mathis .20 .50
95 Mike Peterson .20 .50
96 Matt Cassel .20 .50
97 Larry Johnson .20 .50
98 Jamaal Charles .25 .60
99 Dwayne Bowe .25 .60
100 Tony Gonzalez .25 .60
101 Chad Pennington .20 .50
102 Ronnie Brown .20 .50
103 Ted Ginn .20 .50
104 Greg Camarillo .25 .60
105 Joey Porter .25 .60
106 Adrian Peterson .30 .75
107 Bernard Berrian .20 .50
108 Bobby Wade .20 .50
109 Kevin Williams .20 .50
110 Jared Allen .20 .50
111 Gus Frerotte .20 .50
112 Tom Brady 1.00 2.50
113 Sammy Morris .20 .50
114 Randy Moss .25 .60
115 Wes Welker .25 .60
116 Jerod Mayo .25 .60
117 Brandon Meriweather .20 .50
118 Drew Brees .30 .75
119 Reggie Bush .20 .50
120 Robert Meachem .20 .50
121 Devery Henderson .20 .50
122 Lance Moore .20 .50
123 Jeremy Shockey .20 .50
124 Jonathan Vilma .20 .50
125 Marques Colston .20 .50
126 Eli Manning .25 .60
127 Brandon Jacobs .20 .50
128 Osi Umenyiora .20 .50
129 Steve Smith USC .25 .60
130 Justin Tuck .20 .50
131 Mathias Kiwanuka .20 .50
132 Bart Scott .20 .50
133 Thomas Jones .20 .50
134 Laveranues Coles .20 .50
135 Jerricho Cotchery .20 .50
136 Chansi Stuckey .20 .50
137 JaMarcus Russell .20 .50
138 Darren McFadden .30 .75
139 Zach Miller .20 .50
140 Gibril Wilson .20 .50
141 Justin Fargas .20 .50
142 Donovan McNabb .25 .60
143 Brian Westbrook .20 .50
144 Correll Buckhalter .20 .50
145 DeSean Jackson .25 .60
146 Quintin Mikell RC .30 .75
147 Asante Samuel .20 .50
148 Hank Baskett .20 .50
149 Ben Roethlisberger .30 .75
150 Willie Parker .20 .50
151 Santonio Holmes .20 .50
152 Hines Ward .25 .60
153 James Harrison .30 .75
154 Troy Polamalu .30 .75
155 LaMarr Woodley .20 .50
156 Philip Rivers .30 .75
157 LaDainian Tomlinson .30 .75
158 Vincent Jackson .20 .50
159 Antonio Gates .25 .60
160 Chris Chambers .20 .50
161 Antonio Cromartie .20 .50
162 Shaun Hill .20 .50
163 Frank Gore .25 .60
164 Isaac Bruce .30 .75
165 Patrick Willis .25 .60
166 Takeo Spikes .20 .50
167 Arnaz Battle .20 .50
168 Matt Hasselbeck .20 .50
169 Julius Jones .20 .50
170 John Carlson .25 .60
171 Lofa Tatupu .20 .50
172 Julian Peterson .20 .50
173 Patrick Kerney .20 .50
174 Marc Bulger .20 .50
175 Steven Jackson .20 .50
176 Donnie Avery .20 .50
177 Torry Holt .25 .60
178 Chris Long .25 .60
179 Oshiomogho Atogwe .20 .50
180 Leonard Little .20 .50
181 Jeff Garcia .20 .50
182 Earnest Graham .20 .50
183 Warrick Dunn .20 .50
184 Antonio Bryant .20 .50
185 Barrett Ruud .20 .50
186 Ronde Barber .20 .60
187 Vince Young .20 .50
188 Kerry Collins .20 .50
189 Chris Johnson .20 .50
190 LenDale White .20 .50
191 Bo Scaife .20 .50
192 Albert Haynesworth .20 .50
193 Cortland Finnegan .20 .50
194 Jason Campbell .20 .50
195 Clinton Portis .20 .50
196 Santana Moss .25 .60
197 Chris Cooley .20 .50
198 Antwaan Randle El .20 .50
199 London Fletcher .25 .60
200 DeAngelo Hall .20 .50
201 Matthew Stafford RC 5.00 12.00
202 Knowshon Moreno RC 1.00 2.50
203 Patrick Turner RC 1.00 2.50
204 Mike Goodson RC 1.25 3.00
205 Darrius Heyward-Bey RC 1.50 4.00
206 Javon Ringer RC 1.00 2.50
207 Aaron Curry RC 1.50 4.00
208 Brian Orakpo RC 1.25 3.00
209 Brandon Pettigrew RC 1.00 2.50
210 Michael Johnson RC 1.00 2.50
211 Rey Maualuga RC 1.50 4.00
212 William Moore RC 1.00 2.50
213 James Laurinaitis RC 1.00 2.50
214 Brian Cushing RC 1.00 2.50
215 Malcolm Jenkins RC 1.00 2.50
216 Alphonso Smith RC 1.00 2.50
217 Chase Coffman RC 1.00 2.50
218 Brian Robiskie RC 1.00 2.50
219 Marcus Freeman RC 1.00 2.50
220 Juaquin Iglesias RC 1.00 2.50
221 Vontae Davis RC 1.00 2.50
222 Michael Crabtree RC 1.50 4.00
223 Chris Wells RC 1.00 2.50
224 Mark Sanchez RC 1.00 2.50
225 Jeremy Maclin RC 1.25 3.00
226 Nathan Brown RC 1.25 3.00
227 LeSean McCoy RC 2.50 6.00
228 Percy Harvin RC 1.00 2.50
229 Jarett Dillard RC .75 2.00
230 Travis Beckum RC 1.00 2.50
231 Devin Moore RC 1.00 2.50
232 Graham Harrell RC 1.00 2.50
233 Demetrius Byrd RC 1.25 3.00
234 Aaron Kelly RC 1.00 2.50
235 Pat White RC 1.25 3.00
236 Shonn Greene RC 1.00 2.50
237 James Davis RC 1.00 2.50
238 P.J. Hill RC 1.00 2.50
239 Eben Britton RC 1.25 3.00
240 B.J. Raji RC 1.25 3.00
241 Ian Johnson RC 1.00 2.50
242 Quan Cosby RC 1.00 2.50
243 Darius Butler RC 1.25 3.00
244 Kenny Britt RC 1.50 4.00
245 Curtis Painter RC 1.00 2.50
246 Sen'Derrick Marks RC 1.00 2.50
247 Larry English RC 1.25 3.00
248 Sean Smith RC 1.00 2.50
249 Victor Harris RC 1.25 3.00
250 Everette Brown RC 1.00 2.50
251 Darry Beckwith RC 1.00 2.50
252 Mike Wallace RC 1.50 4.00
253 Derrick Williams RC 1.00 2.50
254 Clint Sintim RC 1.00 2.50
255 Mike Mickens RC 1.00 2.50
256 Patrick Chung RC 1.00 2.50
257 Aaron Maybin RC 1.25 3.00
258 Matt Shaughnessy RC 1.25 3.00
259 Fili Moala RC 1.00 2.50
260 Tyson Jackson RC 1.00 2.50
261 Peria Jerry RC 1.00 2.50
262 Rhett Bomar RC 1.00 2.50
263 Michael Oher RC 1.50 4.00
264 Eugene Monroe RC 1.00 2.50
265 Alex Mack RC 1.00 2.50
266 Duke Robinson RC 1.00 2.50
267 Josh Freeman RC 1.00 2.50
268 Jason Smith RC 1.00 2.50
269 Herman Johnson RC 1.25 3.00
270 Stephen McGee RC 1.00 2.50
271 Hakeem Nicks RC 1.25 3.00
272 Alex Boone RC 1.50 4.00
273 Rashad Jennings RC 1.25 3.00
274 Brandon Tate RC 1.25 3.00
275 Donald Brown RC 1.00 2.50
276 Alan Page 1.50 4.00
277 Lem Barney 1.50 4.00
278 Phil Simms 2.00 5.00
279 Jim Kelly 2.50 6.00
280 Jack Youngblood 1.50 4.00
281 Alex Karras 2.00 5.00
282 Fred Biletnikoff 2.50 6.00
283 Earl Campbell 2.50 6.00
284 Darrell Green 2.00 5.00
285 Steve Young 3.00 8.00
286 Ron Yary 1.50 4.00
287 Thurman Thomas 2.00 5.00
288 Lawrence Taylor 2.50 6.00
289 Steve Largent 2.50 6.00
290 Roger Staubach 3.00 8.00
291 Troy Aikman 3.00 8.00
292 John Elway 4.00 10.00
293 Tom Rathman 1.50 4.00
294 Fran Tarkenton 2.50 6.00
295 Terry Bradshaw 3.00 8.00
296 Barry Sanders 4.00 10.00
297 Merlin Olsen 1.50 4.00
298 Roger Craig 2.00 5.00
299 Ken Anderson 2.00 5.00
300 Jerry Rice 5.00 12.00
301 Barack Obama 1.50 4.00
302 Barack Obama 1.50 4.00
303 Barack Obama 1.50 4.00
304 Barack Obama 1.50 4.00
305 Barack Obama 1.50 4.00
306 Barack Obama 1.50 4.00
307 Barack Obama 1.50 4.00
308 Barack Obama 1.50 4.00
309 Barack Obama 1.50 4.00
310 Barack Obama 1.50 4.00
311 Barack Obama 1.50 4.00
312 Barack Obama 1.50 4.00
313 Barack Obama 1.50 4.00
314 Barack Obama 1.50 4.00
315 Barack Obama 1.50 4.00
316 Barack Obama 1.50 4.00
317 Barack Obama 1.50 4.00
318 Barack Obama 1.50 4.00
319 Barack Obama 1.50 4.00
320 Barack Obama 1.50 4.00
321 Barack Obama 1.50 4.00
322 Barack Obama 1.50 4.00
323 Barack Obama 1.50 4.00
324 Barack Obama 1.50 4.00
325 Barack Obama 1.50 4.00
326 Woodstock 40th Anniversary 1.25 3.00
327 Woodstock 40th Anniversary 1.25 3.00
328 Woodstock 40th Anniversary 1.25 3.00
329 Woodstock 40th Anniversary 1.25 3.00
330 Woodstock 40th Anniversary 1.25 3.00
331 The Vietnam War 1.25 3.00
332 The Vietnam War 1.25 3.00
333 The Vietnam War 1.25 3.00
334 The Vietnam War 1.25 3.00
335 The Vietnam War 1.25 3.00
336 The Vietnam War 1.25 3.00
337 The Vietnam War 1.25 3.00
338 The Vietnam War 1.25 3.00
339 The Vietnam War 1.25 3.00
340 The Vietnam War 1.25 3.00
341 Humphrey/McCarthy 1.25 3.00
342 Goldwater/Rockefeller 1.25 3.00
343 Rockefeller/Reagan 2.00 5.00
344 R.Nixon/Rockefeller 1.50 4.00
345 L.Johnson/Lodge 1.25 3.00
346 S.Agnew/E.Muskie 1.25 3.00
347 J.F.Kennedy/Humphrey 2.00 5.00
348 P.Brown/R.Nixon 1.50 4.00
349 R.Reagan/P.Brown 2.00 5.00
350 Humphrey/W.Miller 1.25 3.00
351 J.F.Kennedy/R.Nixon 2.00 5.00
352 Anquan Boldin IA 1.00 2.50
353 Kurt Warner IA 1.25 3.00
354 Larry Fitzgerald IA 1.25 3.00
355 Roddy White IA 1.00 2.50
356 Matt Ryan IA 1.25 3.00
357 Michael Turner IA 1.00 2.50
358 Ray Lewis IA 1.50 4.00
359 Marshawn Lynch IA 1.25 3.00
360 DeAngelo Williams IA 1.00 2.50
361 Steve Smith IA 1.25 3.00
362 Julius Peppers IA 1.25 3.00
363 Brian Urlacher IA 1.50 4.00
364 T.J. Houshmandzadeh IA 1.00 2.50
365 DeMarcus Ware IA 1.25 3.00
366 Tony Romo IA 1.25 3.00
367 Marion Barber IA 1.25 3.00
368 Brandon Marshall IA 1.25 3.00
369 Jay Cutler IA 1.00 2.50
370 Calvin Johnson IA 1.50 4.00
371 Greg Jennings IA 1.00 2.50
372 Andre Johnson IA 1.25 3.00
373 Peyton Manning IA 4.00 10.00
374 Bob Sanders IA 1.25 3.00
375 Reggie Wayne IA 1.25 3.00
376 Maurice Jones-Drew IA 1.00 2.50
377 Dwayne Bowe IA 1.25 3.00
378 Ronnie Brown IA 1.00 2.50
379 Adrian Peterson IA 1.50 4.00
380 Randy Moss IA 1.25 3.00
381 Tom Brady IA 5.00 12.00
382 Drew Brees IA 1.50 4.00
383 Justin Tuck IA 1.00 2.50
384 Eli Manning IA 1.25 3.00
385 Brett Favre IA 3.00 8.00
386 Darren McFadden IA 1.50 4.00
387 Brian Dawkins IA 1.00 2.50
388 Donovan McNabb IA 1.25 3.00
389 Brian Westbrook IA 1.00 2.50
390 Troy Polamalu IA 1.50 4.00
391 Ben Roethlisberger IA 1.50 4.00
392 Philip Rivers IA 1.50 4.00
393 LaDainian Tomlinson IA 1.50 4.00
394 Frank Gore IA 1.25 3.00
395 Julian Peterson IA 1.00 2.50
396 Steven Jackson IA 1.00 2.50
397 Derrick Brooks IA 1.00 2.50
398 Darren Sproles IA 1.25 3.00
399 Chris Johnson IA 1.00 2.50
400 Clinton Portis IA 1.00 2.50

2009 Philadelphia Fabric

STATED ODDS 1:10 HOB, 1:24 RET
PFAG Antonio Gates 3.00 8.00
PFAJ Andre Johnson 3.00 8.00
PFAS Alex Smith 4.00 10.00
PFAV Adam Vinatieri 4.00 10.00
PFBA Ronde Barber 2.50 6.00
PFBE Braylon Edwards 2.50 6.00
PFBM Brandon Marshall 3.00 8.00
PFBQ Brady Quinn 2.50 6.00
PFBU Brian Urlacher 4.00 10.00
PFCA Jason Campbell 2.50 6.00
PFCB Champ Bailey 3.00 8.00
PFCP Carson Palmer 3.00 8.00
PFCT Chester Taylor 2.50 6.00
PFDB Drew Brees 4.00 10.00
PFDD Donald Driver 3.00 8.00
PFDE Deuce McAllister 3.00 8.00
PFDG David Garrard 2.50 6.00
PFDH Devin Hester 3.00 8.00
PFDM Donovan McNabb 3.00 8.00
PFDS Darren Sproles 3.00 8.00
PFDW DeAngelo Williams 2.50 6.00
PFEJ Edgerrin James 3.00 8.00
PFFG Frank Gore 3.00 8.00
PFHA Marvin Harrison 3.00 8.00
PFHO Torry Holt 3.00 8.00
PFJA Joseph Addai 2.50 6.00
PFJC Jay Cutler 2.50 6.00
PFJL Jamal Lewis 3.00 8.00
PFJP Julius Peppers 3.00 8.00
PFJT Jason Taylor 3.00 8.00
PFLE Lee Evans 3.00 8.00
PFLJ Larry Johnson 2.50 6.00
PFMC Marques Colston 2.50 6.00
PFMH Matt Hasselbeck 2.50 6.00
PFMJ Maurice Jones-Drew 2.50 6.00
PFML Marshawn Lynch 3.00 8.00
PFPB Plaxico Burress 2.50 6.00
PFRB Ronnie Brown 2.50 6.00
PFRC Ronald Curry 2.50 6.00
PFRG Ryan Grant 3.00 8.00
PFRL Ray Lewis 4.00 10.00
PFSH Santonio Holmes 2.50 6.00
PFSM Shawne Merriman 2.50 6.00
PFSS Steve Smith 3.00 8.00
PFTG Tony Gonzalez 3.00 8.00
PFTH T.J. Houshmandzadeh 2.50 6.00
PFTR Tony Romo
PFVJ Vincent Jackson 2.50 6.00
PFVY Vince Young 2.50 6.00
PFWP Willie Parker 2.50 6.00

2009 Philadelphia Jumbos

ONE JUMBO PER HOBBY BOX
RC1 Brandon Marshall 2.00 5.00
RC2 Brett Favre 5.00 12.00
RC3 Brian Westbrook 1.50 4.00
RC4 Calvin Johnson 2.50 6.00
RC5 Dallas Clark 1.50 4.00
RC6 Devin Hester 2.00 5.00
RC7 Drew Brees 2.50 6.00
RC8 Frank Gore 2.00 5.00
RC9 Hines Ward 2.00 5.00
RC10 Jay Cutler 1.50 4.00
RC11 A.J. Hawk 1.50 4.00
RC12 Chris Cooley 1.50 4.00
RC13 Greg Jennings 1.50 4.00
RC14 Patrick Willis 2.00 5.00
RC15 Anquan Boldin 1.50 4.00
RC16 Roman Gabriel 1.50 4.00
RC17 Joe Greene 2.50 6.00
RC18 Steve Young 3.00 8.00
RC19 Archie Manning 2.00 5.00
RC20 Paul Hornung 2.50 6.00
RC21 Jim Kelly 2.50 6.00
RC22 Don Maynard 2.00 5.00
RC23 Deion Sanders 2.00 5.00
RC24 Dick Butkus 3.00 8.00
RC25 Mike Singletary 2.50 6.00
RC26 Rey Maualuga 2.00 5.00
RC27 Malcolm Jenkins 1.25 3.00
RC28 LeSean McCoy 3.00 8.00
RC29 Michael Crabtree 2.00 5.00
RC30 Chris Wells 1.25 3.00
RC31 Brian Orakpo 1.50 4.00
RC32 William Moore 1.25 3.00
RC33 Knowshon Moreno 1.25 3.00
RC34 James Laurinaitis 1.25 3.00
RC35 Jeremy Maclin 1.50 4.00
RC36 Aaron Curry 2.00 5.00
RC37 Shonn Greene 1.25 3.00
RC38 Brandon Pettigrew 1.25 3.00
RC39 Darrius Heyward-Bey 2.00 5.00
RC40 Percy Harvin 1.25 3.00
RC41 Brian Cushing 1.25 3.00
RC42 Matthew Stafford 6.00 15.00
RC43 Darius Butler 1.50 4.00
RC44 D.J. Moore 1.50 4.00
RC45 Javon Ringer 1.25 3.00
RC46 Alphonso Smith 1.25 3.00
RC47 Mark Sanchez 1.25 3.00
RC48 Donald Brown 1.25 3.00
RC49 Josh Freeman 1.25 3.00
RC50 Nate Davis 1.25 3.00

2009 Philadelphia Jumbos Autographs

OVERALL AUTO STATED ODDS 1:20
RC1 Brandon Marshall
RC2 Brett Favre
RC3 Brian Westbrook
RC4 Calvin Johnson
RC5 Dallas Clark
ΠC6 Devin Hester
RC7 Drew Brees
RC8 Frank Gore
RC9 Hines Ward
RC10 Jay Cutler
RC11 A.J. Hawk
RC12 Chris Cooley
RC13 Greg Jennings
RC14 Patrick Willis 20.00 40.00
RC15 Anquan Boldin
RC16 Roman Gabriel
RC17 Joe Greene
RC18 Steve Young
RC19 Archie Manning
RC20 Paul Hornung 25.00 50.00
RC21 Jim Kelly
RC22 Don Maynard 20.00 40.00
RC23 Deion Sanders
RC24 Dick Butkus
RC25 Mike Singletary
RC26 Rey Maualuga 10.00 25.00
RC27 Malcolm Jenkins
RC28 LeSean McCoy 15.00 40.00
RC29 Michael Crabtree 10.00 25.00
RC30 Chris Wells 6.00 15.00
RC31 Brian Orakpo 8.00 20.00
RC32 William Moore EXCH 6.00 15.00
RC33 Knowshon Moreno 6.00 15.00
RC34 James Laurinaitis 6.00 15.00
RC35 Jeremy Maclin 8.00 20.00
RC36 Aaron Curry 10.00 25.00
RC37 Shonn Greene 6.00 15.00
RC38 Brandon Pettigrew 6.00 15.00
RC39 Darrius Heyward-Bey
RC40 Percy Harvin 6.00 15.00
RC41 Brian Cushing
RC42 Matthew Stafford 50.00 100.00
RC43 Darius Butler EXCH 8.00 20.00
RC44 D.J. Moore 8.00 20.00
RC45 Javon Ringer 6.00 15.00
RC46 Alphonso Smith 6.00 15.00
RC47 Mark Sanchez 40.00 80.00
RC48 Donald Brown 6.00 15.00
RC49 Josh Freeman 6.00 15.00
RC50 Nate Davis 6.00 15.00

2009 Philadelphia National Chicle

STATED ODDS 1:5
NC1 John F. Kennedy 2.50 10.00
NC2 Spiro Agnew 2.50 6.00
NC3 Pat Brown 2.50 6.00
NC4 Henry Cabot Lodge 2.50 6.00
NC5 Lyndon Johnson 2.50 6.00
NC6 Richard Nixon 2.50 8.00
NC7 Hubert Humphrey 2.50 6.00
NC8 Barry Goldwater 2.50 6.00
NC9 William Miller 2.50 6.00
NC10 Ronald Reagan 2.50 8.00
NC11 Eugene McCarthy 2.50 6.00
NC12 Edmund Muskie 2.50 6.00
NC13 Nelson Rockefeller 2.50 6.00
NC14 Robert Kennedy 2.50 8.00
NC15 Adlai Stevenson 2.50 6.00
NC16 William Scranton 2.50 6.00
NC17 George McGovern 2.50 6.00
NC18 Margaret Chase Smith 2.50 6.00
NC19 Ted Kennedy 2.50 6.00
NC20 Dodge Dart 2.50 6.00
NC21 Chevrolet Bel Air 2.50 6.00
NC22 Chevrolet El Camino 2.50 6.00
NC23 Dodge Charger 2.50 6.00
NC24 Chevrolet Corvette 2.50 6.00
NC25 Ford Mustang 2.50 6.00
NC26 Ford Thunderbird 2.50 6.00
NC27 Pontiac Bonneville 2.50 6.00
NC28 Pontiac GTO 2.50 6.00
NC29 Plymouth Barracuda 2.50 6.00
NC30 Martin B-26 Marauder 2.50 6.00
NC31 North American F-86 Sabre 2.50 6.00
NC32 Consolidated B-24 Liberator 2.50 6.00
NC33 FG-1D Corsair 2.50 6.00
NC34 Curtiss P-40 Warhawk 2.50 6.00
NC35 Northrop P-61 Black Widow 2.50 6.00
NC36 Boeing B-17 Flying Fortress 2.50 6.00
NC37 P51 Mustang 2.50 6.00
NC38 McDonnell FD-FH Phantom 2.50 6.00
NC39 Lockheed P-58 Chain Lightning 2.50 6.00
NC40 Golden Arrow Train 2.50 6.00
NC41 The 20th Century Ltd Train 2.50 6.00
NC42 Super Chief Train 2.50 6.00
NC43 Pioneer Zephyr Train 2.50 6.00
NC44 Flying Scotsman Train 2.50 6.00
NC45 Blue Train 2.50 6.00
NC46 TGV Train 2.50 6.00
NC47 Orient Express Train 2.50 6.00
NC48 Bullet Train 2.50 6.00
NC49 Indian Pacific Train 2.50 6.00
NC50 Brandon Marshall 1.50 4.00
NC51 Brett Favre 4.00 10.00
NC52 Brian Westbrook 1.25 3.00
NC53 Calvin Johnson 2.00 5.00
NC54 Dallas Clark 1.25 3.00
NC55 Devin Hester 1.50 4.00
NC56 Drew Brees 2.00 5.00
NC57 Frank Gore 1.50 4.00
NC58 Hines Ward 1.50 4.00
NC59 Jay Cutler 1.25 3.00
NC60 LaDainian Tomlinson 2.00 5.00
NC61 Marvin Harrison 1.50 4.00
NC62 Patrick Willis 1.50 4.00
NC63 Philip Rivers 2.00 5.00
NC64 Kurt Warner 1.50 4.00
NC65 T.J. Houshmandzadeh 1.25 3.00
NC66 Tony Romo 1.50 4.00
NC67 Brian Urlacher 2.00 5.00
NC68 Adrian Peterson 2.00 5.00
NC69 Anquan Boldin 1.25 3.00
NC70 Ben Roethlisberger 2.00 5.00
NC71 Clinton Portis 1.25 3.00
NC72 Eli Manning 1.50 4.00
NC73 Jason Witten 1.50 4.00
NC74 Larry Fitzgerald 1.50 4.00
NC75 Peyton Manning 5.00 12.00
NC76 Matthew Stafford 4.00 10.00
NC77 Nate Davis .75 2.00
NC78 Brian Orakpo 1.00 2.50
NC79 Michael Crabtree 1.25 3.00
NC80 Jeremy Maclin 1.00 2.50
NC81 Aaron Curry 1.25 3.00
NC82 Rey Maualuga 1.25 3.00
NC83 James Laurinaitis .75 2.00
NC84 Chris Wells .75 2.00
NC85 Brandon Pettigrew .75 2.00
NC86 Percy Harvin .75 2.00
NC87 LeSean McCoy 2.00 5.00
NC88 Darrius Heyward-Bey 1.25 3.00
NC89 Aaron Maybin 1.00 2.50
NC90 Brian Cushing .75 2.00
NC91 Everette Brown .75 2.00
NC92 Donald Brown .75 2.00
NC93 Knowshon Moreno .75 2.00
NC94 Chase Coffman .75 2.00
NC95 Malcolm Jenkins .75 2.00
NC96 Vontae Davis .75 2.00
NC97 Hakeem Nicks 1.00 2.50
NC98 Mark Sanchez .75 2.00
NC99 Andre Smith .75 2.00
NC100 Michael Oher 1.25 3.00

2009 Philadelphia National Chicle Autographs

NC51-NC75 VETS TOO SCARCE TO PRICE
OVERALL AUTO STATED ODDS 1:20
ROOKIE PRINT RUN 97-100
NC60 LaDainian Tomlinson/21
NC76 Matthew Stafford/100 50.00 120.00
NC77 Nate Davis/100 6.00 15.00
NC78 Brian Orakpo/100 8.00 20.00
NC79 Michael Crabtree/100 10.00 25.00
NC80 Jeremy Maclin/99 8.00 20.00
NC81 Aaron Curry/100 10.00 25.00
NC82 Rey Maualuga/100 10.00 25.00
NC83 James Laurinaitis/100 6.00 15.00
NC84 Chris Wells/100 20.00 50.00
NC85 Brandon Pettigrew/100 6.00 15.00
NC86 Percy Harvin/100 6.00 15.00
NC87 LeSean McCoy/98 15.00 40.00
NC88 Darrius Heyward-Bey/100 10.00 25.00
NC90 Brian Cushing/96 6.00 15.00
NC92 Donald Brown/100 6.00 15.00
NC93 Knowshon Moreno/100 6.00 15.00
NC94 Chase Coffman/100 6.00 15.00
NC95 Malcolm Jenkins/100 6.00 15.00
NC96 Vontae Davis/100 6.00 15.00
NC97 Hakeem Nicks/99 8.00 20.00
NC98 Mark Sanchez/100 30.00 80.00
NC99 Andre Smith/100 6.00 15.00
NC100 Michael Oher/100 30.00 80.00

2009 Philadelphia Signatures

OVERALL AUTO ODDS 1:20 H, 1:1500 R
PSAG Andre Gurode EXCH 6.00 15.00
PSAH Albert Haynesworth 5.00 12.00
PSAJ A.J. Hawk 8.00 20.00
PSAP Adrian Peterson 90.00 150.00
PSAW Adrian Wilson
PSBD Brian Dawkins
PSBF Brett Favre
PSBM Brandon Marshall 6.00 15.00
PSBO Dwayne Bowe 6.00 15.00
PSBR Ben Roethlisberger
PSBU Brian Urlacher
PSBW Brian Westbrook
PSCC Chris Cooley
PSCJ Calvin Johnson
PSCO Jerricho Cotchery 5.00 12.00
PSDB Drew Brees
PSDC Dallas Clark 8.00 20.00
PSDF Dwight Freeney
PSDH Devin Hester
PSDJ DeSean Jackson 8.00 20.00
PSDQ D'Qwell Jackson 5.00 12.00
PSDV Donovan McNabb
PSDW DeMarcus Ware 8.00 20.00
PSEM Eli Manning 60.00 100.00
PSER Ed Reed
PSFG Frank Gore 6.00 15.00
PSGC Greg Camarillo 8.00 20.00
PSJA Jared Allen 12.00 30.00
PSJF Joe Flacco
PSJH James Harrison
PSJM Jerod Mayo 6.00 15.00
PSJO Chris Johnson 15.00 30.00
PSJP Joey Porter 8.00 20.00
PSJS Jonathan Stewart 15.00 30:00
PSJW Jason Witten
PSLB Lance Briggs 10.00 25.00
PSLC Laveranues Coles
PSLE Lee Evans 6.00 15.00
PSLT LaDainian Tomlinson
PSMB Marion Barber
PSMC Matt Cassel 8.00 20.00
PSMF Matt Forte 10.00 25.00
PSMJ Maurice Jones-Drew 5.00 12.00
PSMR Matt Ryan 25.00 60.00
PSMT Michael Turner
PSMW Mario Williams 6.00 15.00
PSPM Peyton Manning 50.00 100.00
PSPW Patrick Willis 8.00 20.00
PSQJ Quentin Jammer 5.00 12.00
PSRL Ray Lewis
PSRW Roddy White
PSSS Steve Slaton 5.00 12.00
PSTB Tom Brady
PSTH T.J. Houshmandzadeh
PSTP Troy Polamalu
PSTR Tony Romo
PSWJ Walter Jones

1974 Philadelphia Bell WFL Team Issue

These photos were issued by the team for promotional purposes and fan mail requests. Each includes a black and white image printed above the subject's name and team logo. Each measures 5 1/2" by 7."

COMPLETE SET (8) 50.00 100.00
1 John Bosacco Pres. 6.00 12.00
2 Jim Corcoran 6.00 12.00
3 Richard Iannarella GM 6.00 12.00
4 J.J. Jennings 6.00 12.00
5 Ted Kwalick 6.00 12.00
6 Tim Rossovich 6.00 12.00
7 Claude Watts 6.00 12.00
8 Willie Wood 7.50 15.00

1992 Philadelphia Daily News

This nine-card set, which is aptly subtitled "Great Moments in Philadelphia Sports," was sponsored by the Philadelphia Daily News. The fronts of the standard-size cards have red borders and feature miniature reproductions of newspaper front pages with famous headlines and memorable photos. Each card captures a great moment in the history of Philadelphia sports. Sports represented are baseball, (cards 1 and 7-8) hockey, (2) basketball, (3-4) football, (5-6) and boxing (9). The backs are printed in gray, black and white and provide text relating to the event commemorated on the card.

COMPLETE SET (9) 1.40 3.50
5 Eagles Seek New CO, QB .10 .25
(Eagles win NFL Championship
6 Super .10 .25
Eagles win NFC Championship

1984 Philadelphia Stars USFL Team Issue

Each of these blankbacked photos was issued by the team, measures roughly 5" x 7" and features a black and white image of a player. The player's name, his position, and the team name are listed below the image to the left and the Stars' logo is oriented to the right below the image.

1 Jon Brooks 4.00 10.00
2 Kelvin Bryant 5.00 12.00
3 Frank Case 4.00 10.00
4 Willie Collier 4.00 10.00
5 Chuck Commiskey 4.00 10.00
6 George Cooper 4.00 10.00
7 Tom Donovan 4.00 10.00
8 Steve Folsom 4.00 10.00
9 Antonio Gibson 4.00 10.00
10 George Gilbert 4.00 10.00
11 Joe Happe 4.00 10.00
12 Allen Harvin 4.00 10.00
13 Glenn Howard 4.00 10.00
14 Sean Landeta 5.00 12.00
15 Sam Mills 5.00 12.00
16 Buddy Moor 4.00 10.00
17 Brad Oates 4.00 10.00
18 Dave Opfar 4.00 10.00
19 David Riley 4.00 10.00
20 Booker Russell 4.00 10.00
21 David Trout 4.00 10.00
22 Scott Woerner 4.00 10.00

1981-82 Philip Morris

This 18-card standard-size set was included in the Champions of American Sport program and features major stars from a variety of sports. The program was issued in conjunction with a traveling exhibition organized by the National Portrait Gallery and the Smithsonian Institution and sponsored by Philip Morris and Miller Brewing Company. The cards are either reproductions of works of art (paintings) or famous photographs of the time. The cards are frequently found with a perforated edge on at least one side. The cards were actually obtained from two perforated pages in the program. There is no notation anywhere on the cards indicating the manufacturer or sponsor.

COMPLETE SET (18) 40.00 100.00
11 Joe Namath 6.00 15.00
13 Knute Rockne 5.00 12.00
18 Johnny Unitas 6.00 15.00

1972 Phoenix Blazers Shamrock Dairy

The Shamrock Dairy issued these cards on the sides of milk cartons in 1972. Each features a member of the Phoenix Blazers minor league football team and was printed in green ink. The blankbacked cards when cut cleanly to the edges of the carton measure roughly 3 3/4" by 7 1/2" and include a brief player bio and Blazers home schedule. Any additions to this list are appreicated.

1 Darby Jones 10.00 20.00
2 Joe Spagnola 10.00 20.00

1999 Pinheads

These pins were produced by Pinheads Promotions and measure roughly 1" by 1 1/2" each. Each pin features an artist's rendering of the player with a typical pin style back along with the year and "Pinheads First Edition."

COMPLETE SET (12) 12.00 30.00
1 Troy Aikman 1.20 3.00
2 Drew Bledsoe 1.20 3.00
3 Terrell Davis 1.20 3.00
4 Brett Favre 1.20 3.00
5 Doug Flutie 1.00 2.50
6 Keyshawn Johnson 1.00 2.50
7 Peyton Manning 1.60 4.00
8 Dan Marino 1.60 4.00
9 Jerry Rice 1.20 3.00
10 Kordell Stewart 1.20 3.00
11 Ricky Williams 1.20 3.00
12 Steve Young 1.00 2.50

1991 Pinnacle Promo Panels

These (approximately) 5" by 7" promo panels each feature four cards to show the design of the 1991 Pinnacle series cards. They were introduced and initially distributed at the Super Bowl XXVI Card Show. The cards, which would measure the standard size if cut, display two color photos on a black panel with white borders. The backs carry a color cut-out action shot, biography, player profile, and statistics. The cards are numbered on the back as in the regular series; the panels themselves, however, are unnumbered. The panels are listed below alphabetically according to the player's name on the card featured at upper left corner of each panel.

1 John Alt 1.25 3.00
2 Morten Andersen 12.50 25.00
John Elway
Mike Merriweather
Ronnie Lott
3 Bruce Armstrong 15.00 30.00
4 Don Beebe 1.50 4.00
5 Duane Bickett 1.25 3.00
6 Mark Bortz 1.50 4.00
7 Roger Craig 1.25 3.00
8 Wendell Davis 1.25 3.00
9 Dermontti Dawson 1.25 3.00
10 Cris Dishman 1.25 3.00
Bill Fralic
John L. Williams
Simon Fletcher
11 Chris Doleman 10.00 20.00
12 Rodney Hampton 1.50 4.00
Bubby Brister
Johnny Bailey
Christian Okoye
13 Darryl Henley 1.50 4.00
14 Mark Higgs 1.50 4.00
15 Jay Hilgenburg 15.00 30.00
16 Louis Lipps 1.50 4.00
17 Greg McMurtry 1.50 4.00
18 Chris Miller 1.25 3.00
James Brooks
Eric Ball
Gerald Williams
19 Nate Odomes 1.25 3.00
20 Andre Rison 1.50 4.00
21 E.Smith/B.Brooks/Hebert/D.Smith 15.00 30.00
22 Rohn Stark 1.50 4.00
Neal Anderson
Barry Foster
Steve DeBerg
23 Reyna Thompson 1.50 4.00
24 Lorenzo White 1.50 4.00
Jeff Herrod
Cornelius Bennett
Jessie Tuggle
25 Will Wolford 3.00 8.00
Tom Tupa
Derrick Thomas
Derrick Fenner

1991 Pinnacle

The premier edition of the 1991 Pinnacle set contains 415 standard-size cards. Cards were issued in 12-card packs. The front design of the veteran player cards features two color photos, an action photo and a head shot, on a black background with white borders. The card backs have a color action shot superimposed on a black background. The rookie cards have the same design, except with a green background on the front, and head shots rather than action shots on the back. The backs also include a biography, player profile, and statistics (where appropriate). The set includes 58 rookies (253, 281-336, 393) and four special cards. Special subsets featured are Head to Head (351-355), Technicians (356-362), Gamewinners (363-371), Idols (372-386), and Sideline (394-415). A patented anti-counterfeit device appears on the bottom border of each card back. Rookie Cards in this set include Bryan Cox, Lawrence Dawsey, Ricky Ervins, Jeff Graham, Randal Hill, Russell Maryland, Bryce Paup, Erric Pegram, Mike Pritchard, Leonard Russell, and Harvey Williams. An Emmitt Smith promo card was produced as well and listed below. It can be differentiated from the regular issue Smith card by the mention of his "holdout" on the cardback.

COMPLETE SET (415) 7.50 20.00
1 Warren Moon .15 .40
2 Morten Andersen .02 .10
3 Rohn Stark .02 .10
4 Mark Bortz .02 .10
5 Mark Higgs RC .02 .10
6 Troy Aikman .75 2.00
7 John Elway 1.25 3.00
8 Neal Anderson .07 .20
9 Chris Doleman .02 .10
10 Jay Schroeder .02 .10
11 Sterling Sharpe .15 .40
12 Steve DeBerg .02 .10
13 Ronnie Lott .07 .20
14 Sean Landeta .02 .10
15 Jim Everett .07 .20
16 Jim Breech .02 .10
17 Barry Foster .07 .20
18 Mike Merriweather .02 .10
19 Eric Metcalf .07 .20
20 Mark Carrier DB .07 .20
21 James Brooks .07 .20
22 Nate Odomes .02 .10
23 Rodney Hampton .15 .40
24 Chris Miller .07 .20
25 Roger Craig .07 .20
26 Louis Oliver .02 .10
27 Allen Pinkett .02 .10
28 Bubby Brister .02 .10
29 Reyna Thompson .02 .10
30 Issiac Holt .02 .10
31 Steve Broussard .02 .10
32 Christian Okoye .07 .20
33 Dave Meggett .07 .20
34 Andre Reed .07 .20
35 Shane Conlan .02 .10
36 Eric Ball .02 .10
37 Johnny Bailey .02 .10
38 Don Majkowski .02 .10
39 Gerald Williams .02 .10
40 Kevin Mack .02 .10
41 Jeff Herrod .02 .10
42 Emmitt Smith 2.50 6.00
43 Wendell Davis .02 .10
44 Lorenzo White .02 .10
45 Andre Rison .07 .20
46 Jerry Gray .02 .10
47 Dennis Smith .02 .10
48 Gaston Green .02 .10
49 Dermontti Dawson .08 .20
50 Jeff Hostetler .07 .20
51 Nick Lowery .02 .10
52 Merril Hoge .02 .10
53 Bobby Hebert .02 .10
54 Scott Case .02 .10
55 Jack Del Rio .07 .20
56 Cornelius Bennett .07 .20
57 Tony Mandarich .02 .10
58 Bill Brooks .02 .10
59 Jessie Tuggle .02 .10
60 Hugh Millen RC .02 .10
61 Tony Bennett .07 .20
62 Cris Dishman RC .02 .10
63 Darryl Henley RC .02 .10
64 Duane Bickett .02 .10
65 Jay Hilgenberg .02 .10
66 Joe Montana 1.25 3.00
67 Bill Fralic .02 .10
68 Sam Mills .02 .10
69 Bruce Armstrong .02 .10
70 Dan Marino 1.25 3.00
71 Jim Lachey .02 .10
72 Rod Woodson .15 .40
73 Simon Fletcher .02 .10
74 Bruce Matthews .07 .20
75 Howie Long .15 .40
76 John Friesz .15 .40
77 Karl Mecklenburg .02 .10
78 John L. Williams UER .02 .10
79 Rob Burnett RC .07 .20
80 Anthony Carter .07 .20
81 Henry Ellard .07 .20
82 Don Beebe .02 .10
83 Louis Lipps .02 .10
84 Greg McMurtry .02 .10
85 Will Wolford .02 .10
86 Eric Green .02 .10
87 Irving Fryar .07 .20
88 John Offerdahl .02 .10
89 John Alt .02 .10
90 Tom Tupa .02 .10
91 Don Mosebar .02 .10
92 Jeff George .20 .50
93 Vinny Testaverde .07 .20
94 Greg Townsend .02 .10
95 Derrick Fenner .02 .10
96 Brian Mitchell .07 .20
97 Herschel Walker .07 .20
98 Ricky Proehl .02 .10
99 Mark Clayton .07 .20
100 Derrick Thomas .15 .40
101 Jim Harbaugh .15 .40
102 Barry Word .02 .10
103 Jerry Rice .75 2.00
104 Keith Byars .02 .10
105 Marion Butts .07 .20
106 Rich Moran .02 .10
107 Thurman Thomas .15 .40
108 Stephone Paige .02 .10
109 D.J. Johnson .02 .10
110 William Perry .07 .20
111 Haywood Jeffires .07 .20
112 Rodney Peete .07 .20
113 Andy Heck .02 .10
114 Kevin Ross .02 .10
115 Michael Carter .02 .10
116 Tim McKyer .02 .10
117 Kenneth Davis .02 .10
118 Richmond Webb .02 .10
119 Rich Camarillo .02 .10
120 James Francis .02 .10
121 Craig Heyward .07 .20
122 Hardy Nickerson .07 .20
123 Michael Brooks .02 .10
124 Fred Barnett .15 .40
125 Cris Carter .40 1.00
126 Brian Jordan .07 .20
127 Pat Leahy .02 .10
128 Kevin Greene .07 .20
129 Trace Armstrong .02 .10
130 Eugene Lockhart .02 .10
131 Albert Lewis .02 .10
132 Ernie Jones .02 .10
133 Eric Martin .02 .10
134 Anthony Thompson .02 .10
135 Tim Krumrie .02 .10
136 James Lofton .07 .20
137 John Taylor .07 .20
138 Jeff Cross .02 .10
139 Tommy Kane .02 .10
140 Robb Thomas .02 .10
141 Gary Anderson K .02 .10
142 Mark Murphy .02 .10
143 Rickey Jackson .02 .10
144 Ken O'Brien .02 .10
145 Ernest Givins .07 .20
146 Jessie Hester .02 .10
147 Deion Sanders .30 .75
148 Keith Henderson RC .02 .10
149 Chris Singleton .02 .10
150 Rod Bernstine .02 .10
151 Quinn Early .07 .20
152 Boomer Esiason .07 .20
153 Mike Gann .02 .10
154 Dino Hackett .02 .10
155 Perry Kemp .02 .10
156 Mark Ingram .07 .20
157 Daryl Johnston .30 .75
158 Eugene Daniel .02 .10
159 Dalton Hilliard .02 .10
160 Rufus Porter .02 .10

161 Tunch Ilkin .02 .10
162 James Hasty .02 .10
163 Keith McKeller .02 .10
164 Heath Sherman .02 .10
165 Vai Sikahema .02 .10
166 Pat Terrell .02 .10
167 Anthony Munoz .07 .20
168 Brad Edwards RC .02 .10
169 Tom Rathman .02 .10
170 Steve McMichael .07 .20
171 Vaughan Johnson .02 .10
172 Nate Lewis RC .02 .10
173 Mark Rypien .07 .20
174 Rob Moore .20 .50
175 Tim Green .02 .10
176 Tony Casillas .02 .10
177 Jon Hand .02 .10
178 Todd McNair .02 .10
179 Toi Cook RC .02 .10
180 Eddie Brown .02 .10
181 Mark Jackson .02 .10
182 Pete Stoyanovich .02 .10
183 Bryce Paup RC .15 .40
184 Anthony Miller .07 .20
185 Dan Saleaumua .02 .10
186 Guy McIntyre .02 .10
187 Broderick Thomas .02 .10
188 Frank Warren .02 .10
189 Drew Hill .02 .10
190 Reggie White .15 .40
191 Chris Hinton .02 .10
192 David Little .02 .10
193 David Fulcher .02 .10
194 Clarence Verdin .02 .10
195 Junior Seau .25 .60
196 Blair Thomas .02 .10
197 Stan Brock .02 .10
198 Gary Clark .15 .40
199 Michael Irvin .15 .40
200 Ronnie Harmon .02 .10
201 Steve Young .75 2.00
202 Brian Noble .02 .10
203 Dan Stryzinski .02 .10
204 Darryl Talley .02 .10
205 David Alexander .02 .10
206 Pat Swilling .07 .20
207 Gary Plummer .02 .10
208 Robert Delpino .02 .10
209 Norm Johnson .02 .10
210 Mike Singletary .07 .20
211 Anthony Johnson .15 .40
212 Eric Allen .02 .10
213 Gill Fenerty .02 .10
214 Neil Smith .15 .40
215 Joe Phillips .02 .10
216 Ottis Anderson .07 .20
217 LeRoy Butler .07 .20
218 Ray Childress .02 .10
219 Rodney Holman .02 .10
220 Kevin Fagan .02 .10
221 Bruce Smith .15 .40
222 Brad Muster .02 .10
223 Mike Horan .02 .10
224 Steve Atwater .02 .10
225 Rich Gannon .20 .50
226 Anthony Pleasant .02 .10
227 Steve Jordan .02 .10
228 Lomas Brown .02 .10
229 Jackie Slater .02 .10
230 Brad Baxter .02 .10
231 Joe Morris .02 .10
232 Marcus Allen .15 .40
233 Chris Warren .15 .40
234 Johnny Johnson .02 .10
235 Phil Simms .07 .20
236 Dave Krieg .07 .20
237 Jim McMahon .07 .20
238 Richard Dent .07 .20
239 John Washington RC .02 .10
240 Sammie Smith .02 .10
241 Brian Brennan .02 .10
242 Cortez Kennedy .15 .40
243 Tim McDonald .02 .10
244 Charles Haley .07 .20
245 Joey Browner .02 .10
246 Eddie Murray .02 .10
247 Bob Golic .02 .10
248 Myron Guyton .02 .10
249 Dennis Byrd .02 .10
250 Barry Sanders 1.25 3.00
251 Clay Matthews .07 .20
252 Pepper Johnson .02 .10
253 Eric Swann RC .15 .40
254 Lamar Lathon .02 .10
255 Andre Tippett .02 .10
256 Tom Newberry .02 .10
257 Kyle Clifton .02 .10
258 Leslie O'Neal .07 .20
259 Bubba McDowell .02 .10
260 Scott Davis .02 .10
261 Wilber Marshall .02 .10
262 Marv Cook .02 .10
263 Jeff Lageman .02 .10
264 Michael Young .02 .10
265 Gary Zimmerman .02 .10
266 Mike Munchak .07 .20
267 David Treadwell .02 .10
268 Steve Wisniewski .02 .10
269 Mark Duper .07 .20
270 Chris Spielman .07 .20
271 Brett Perriman .15 .40
272 Lionel Washington .02 .10
273 Lawrence Taylor .15 .40
274 Mark Collins .02 .10
275 Mark Carrier WR .15 .40
276 Paul Gruber .02 .10
277 Earnest Byner .02 .10
278 Andre Collins .02 .10
279 Reggie Cobb .02 .10
280 Art Monk .07 .20
281 Henry Jones RC .07 .20
282 Mike Pritchard RC .15 .40
283 Moe Gardner RC .02 .10
284 Chris Zorich RC .15 .40
285 Keith Traylor RC .02 .10
286 Mike Dumas RC .02 .10
287 Ed King RC .02 .10
288 Russell Maryland RC .15 .40
289 Alfred Williams RC .02 .10
290 Derek Russell RC .02 .10
291 Vinnie Clark RC .02 .10
292 Mike Croel RC .02 .10
293 Todd Marinovich RC .02 .10
294 Phil Hansen RC .02 .10
295 Aaron Craver RC .02 .10
296 Nick Bell RC .02 .10
297 Kenny Walker RC .02 .10
298 Roman Phifer RC .02 .10
299 Kanavis McGhee RC .02 .10
300 Ricky Ervins RC .07 .20
301 Jim Price RC .02 .10
302 John Johnson RC .02 .10
303 George Thornton RC .02 .10
304 Huey Richardson RC .02 .10
305 Harry Colon RC .02 .10
306 Antone Davis RC .02 .10
307 Todd Lyght RC .02 .10
308 Bryan Cox RC .15 .40
309 Brad Goebel RC .02 .10
310 Eric Moten RC .02 .10
311 John Kasay RC .07 .20
312 Esera Tuaolo RC .02 .10
313 Bobby Wilson RC .02 .10
314 Mo Lewis RC .07 .20
315 Harvey Williams RC .15 .40
316 Mike Stonebreaker RC .02 .10
317 Charles McRae RC .02 .10
318 John Flannery RC .02 .10
319 Ted Washington RC .02 .10
320 Stanley Richard RC .02 .10
321 Browning Nagle RC .02 .10
322 Ed McCaffrey RC 2.00 5.00
323 Jeff Graham RC .15 .40
324 Stan Thomas .02 .10
325 Lawrence Dawsey RC .07 .20
326 Eric Bieniemy RC .02 .10
327 Tim Barnett RC .02 .10
328 Erric Pegram RC .15 .40
329 Lamar Rogers RC .02 .10
330 Ernie Mills RC .07 .20
331 Pat Harlow RC .02 .10
332 Greg Lewis RC .02 .10
333 Jarrod Bunch RC .02 .10
334 Dan McGwire RC .02 .10
335 Randal Hill RC .07 .20
336 Leonard Russell RC .15 .40
337 Carnell Lake .02 .10
338 Brian Blades .07 .20
339 Darrell Green .02 .10
340 Bobby Humphrey .02 .10
341 Mervyn Fernandez .02 .10
342 Ricky Sanders .02 .10
343 Keith Jackson .07 .20
344 Carl Banks .02 .10
345 Gill Byrd .02 .10
346 Al Toon .07 .20
347 Stephen Baker .02 .10
348 Randall Cunningham .15 .40
349 Flipper Anderson .02 .10
350 Jay Novacek .15 .40
351 Steve Young .15 .40
B.Smith HH
352 Barry Sanders .30 .75
Browner HH
353 Joe Montana .30 .75
M.Carrier HH
354 Thurman Thomas .07 .20
L.Taylor
355 Jerry Rice .20 .50
Darr.Green HH
356 Warren Moon Tech .07 .20
357 Anthony Munoz TECH .02 .10
358 Barry Sanders Tech .50 1.25
359 Jerry Rice Tech .50 1.25
360 Joey Browner TECH .02 .10
361 Morten Andersen TECH .02 .10
362 Sean Landeta TECH .02 .10
363 Thurman Thomas GW .15 .40
364 Emmitt Smith GW 1.25 3.00
365 Gaston Green GW .02 .10
366 Barry Sanders GW .50 1.25
367 Christian Okoye GW .02 .10
368 Earnest Byner GW .02 .10
369 Neal Anderson GW .02 .10
370 Herschel Walker GW .07 .20
371 Rodney Hampton GW .15 .40
372 Darryl Talley IDOL .02 .10
373 Mark Carrier IDOL .02 .10
374 Jim Breech IDOL .02 .10
375 R.Hampton .02 .10
O.Anderson ID
376 Kevin Mack IDOL .02 .10
377 S.Jordan .02 .10
O.Robertson ID
378 B.Esiason .02 .10
B.Jones ID
379 Steve DeBerg IDOL .07 .20
300 Al Toon IDOL .02 .10
381 Ronnie Lott .07 .20
C.Taylor ID
382 Henry Ellard IDOL .02 .10
383 Troy Aikman .50 1.25
Staubach ID
384 T.Thomas .15 .40
E.Campbell ID
385 Dan Marino .60 1.50
Bradshaw ID
386 Howie Long .07 .20
Joe Greene ID
387 Franco Harris IR .07 .20
388 Esera Tuaolo .02 .10
389 Super Bowl XXVI .02 .10
390 Charles Mann .02 .10
391 Kenny Walker Succeed .02 .10
392 Reggie Roby .02 .10
393 Bruce Pickens RC .02 .10
394 Ray Childress SIDE .02 .10
395 Karl Mecklenburg SIDE .02 .10
396 Dean Biasucci SIDE .02 .10
397 John Alt SIDE .02 .10
398 Marcus Allen SL .07 .20
399 John Offerdahl SIDE .02 .10
400 Richard Tardits RC .02 .10
401 Al Toon SIDE .02 .10
402 Joey Browner SIDE .02 .10
403 Spencer Tillman RC .02 .10
404 Jay Novacek SIDE .07 .20
405 Stephen Braggs SIDE .02 .10
406 Mike Tice RC .02 .10
407 Kevin Greene SIDE .07 .20
408 Reggie White SIDE .07 .20
409 Brian Noble SIDE .02 .10
410 Bart Oates SIDE .02 .10
411 Art Monk SIDE .07 .20
412 Ron Wolfley SIDE .02 .10
413 Louis Lipps SIDE .02 .10
414 Dante Jones SIDE RC .07 .20
415 Kenneth Davis SIDE .02 .10
P1 Emmitt Smith Promo 12.50 25.00

1992 Pinnacle Samples

This six-card sample standard-size set features action color player photos on a black card face. The image of the player is partially cut out and extends beyond the photo background. A thin white line forms a frame near the card edge. The player's name appears at the bottom in a gradated bar that reflects the team's color. The horizontally oriented backs have white borders and black backgrounds. A gradated purple bar at the top contains the player's name, the word "sample," and the card number. A close-up player photo appears in the center. The back is rounded out with biography, statistics (1991 and career), player profile, and a picture of the team helmet in a circular format.

COMPLETE SET (6) 2.00 5.00
1 Reggie White .80 2.00
5 Pepper Johnson .30 .75
19 Chris Spielman .30 .75
59 Mike Croel .30 .75
100 Bobby Hebert .30 .75
102 Rodney Hampton .50 1.25

1992 Pinnacle

The 1992 Pinnacle set consists of 360 standard-size cards. Cards were issued in 16-card and 27-card super packs. The set closes with the following subsets: Rookies (314-330), Sidelines (331-334), Gamewinners (335-344), Hall of Famers (345-347), and Idols (348-357). Rookie Cards include Steve Bono, Edgar Bennett, Amp Lee and Tommy Vardell. An eight-card Promo Panel was produced and distributed at the Super Bowl XXVII Card Show in Pasadena.

COMPLETE SET (360) 12.50 25.00
1 Reggie White .20 .50
2 Eric Green .05 .15
3 Craig Heyward .10 .30
4 Phil Simms .10 .30
5 Pepper Johnson .05 .15
6 Sean Landeta .05 .15
7 Dino Hackett .05 .15
8 Andre Ware .05 .15
9 Ricky Nattiel .05 .15
10 Jim Price .05 .15
11 Jim Ritcher .05 .15
12 Kelly Stouffer .05 .15
13 Ray Crockett .05 .15
14 Steve Tasker .10 .30
15 Barry Sanders 1.25 3.00
16 Pat Swilling .05 .15
17 Moe Gardner .05 .15
18 Steve Young .75 2.00
19 Chris Spielman .10 .30
20 Richard Dent .10 .30
21 Anthony Munoz .10 .30
22 Thurman Thomas .20 .50
23 Ricky Sanders .05 .15
24 Steve Atwater .05 .15
25 Tony Tolbert .05 .15
26 Haywood Jeffires .10 .30
27 Duane Bickett .05 .15
28 Tim McDonald .05 .15
29 Cris Carter .30 .75
30 Derrick Thomas .20 .50
31 Hugh Millen .05 .15
32 Bart Oates .05 .15
33 Darryl Talley .05 .15
34 Marion Butts .05 .15
35 Pete Stoyanovich .05 .15
36 Ronnie Lott .10 .30
37 Simon Fletcher .05 .15
38 Morten Andersen .05 .15
39 Clyde Simmons .05 .15
40 Mark Rypien .05 .15
41 Henry Ellard .10 .30
42 Michael Irvin .20 .50
43 Louis Lipps .05 .15
44 John L. Williams .05 .15
45 Broderick Thomas .05 .15
46 Don Majkowski .05 .15
47 William Perry .10 .30
48 David Fulcher .05 .15
49 Tony Bennett .05 .15
50 Clay Matthews .10 .30
51 Warren Moon .20 .50
52 Bruce Armstrong .05 .15
53 Bill Brooks .05 .15
54 Greg Townsend .05 .15
55 Steve Broussard .05 .15
56 Mel Gray .10 .30
57 Kevin Mack .05 .15
58 Emmitt Smith 2.00 4.00
59 Mike Croel .05 .15
60 Brian Mitchell .10 .30
61 Bennie Blades .05 .15
62 Carnell Lake .05 .15
63 Cornelius Bennett .10 .30
64 Darrell Thompson .05 .15
65 Jessie Hester .05 .15
66 Marv Cook .05 .15
67 Tim Brown .20 .50
68 Mark Duper .05 .15
69 Robert Delpino .05 .15
70 Eric Martin .05 .15
71 Wendell Davis .05 .15
72 Vaughan Johnson .05 .15
73 Brian Blades .10 .30
74 Ed King .05 .15
75 Gaston Green .05 .15
76 Christian Okoye .05 .15
77 Rohn Stark .05 .15
78 Kevin Greene .10 .30
79 Jay Novacek .10 .30
80 Chip Lohmiller .05 .15
81 Cris Dishman .05 .15
82 Ethan Horton .05 .15
83 Pat Harlow .05 .15
84 Mark Ingram .05 .15
85 Mark Carrier DB .05 .15
86 Sam Mills .05 .15
87 Mark Higgs .05 .15
88 Keith Jackson .10 .30
89 Gary Anderson K .05 .15
90 Ken Harvey .05 .15
91 Anthony Carter .10 .30
92 Randall McDaniel .05 .15
93 Johnny Johnson .05 .15
94 Shane Conlan .05 .15
95 Sterling Sharpe .20 .50
96 Guy McIntyre .05 .15
97 Albert Lewis .05 .15
98 Chris Doleman .05 .15
99 Andre Rison .10 .30
100 Bobby Hebert .05 .15
101 Dan Owens .05 .15
102 Rodney Hampton .10 .30
103 Ernie Jones .05 .15
104 Reggie Cobb .05 .15
105 Wilber Marshall .05 .15
106 Mike Munchak .10 .30
107 Cortez Kennedy .10 .30
108 Todd Lyght .05 .15
109 Burt Grossman .05 .15
110 Ferrell Edmunds .05 .15
111 Jim Everett .10 .30
112 Hardy Nickerson .10 .30
113 Andre Tippett .05 .15
114 Ronnie Harmon .05 .15
115 Andre Waters .05 .15
116 Ernest Givins .10 .30
117 Eric Hill .05 .15
118 Erric Pegram .10 .30
119 Jarrod Bunch .05 .15
120 Marcus Allen .20 .50
121 Barry Foster .10 .30
122 Kent Hull .05 .15
123 Neal Anderson .05 .15
124 Stephen Braggs .05 .15
125 Nick Lowery .05 .15
126 Jeff Hostetler .10 .30
127 Michael Carter .05 .15
128 Don Warren .05 .15
129 Brad Baxter .05 .15
130 John Taylor .10 .30
131 Harold Green .05 .15
132 Mike Merriweather .05 .15
133 Gary Clark .20 .50
134 Vince Buck .05 .15
135 Dan Saleaumua .05 .15
136 Gary Zimmerman .05 .15
137 Richmond Webb .05 .15
138 Art Monk .10 .30
139 Mervyn Fernandez .05 .15
140 Mark Jackson .05 .15
141 Freddie Joe Nunn .05 .15
142 Jeff Lageman .05 .15
143 Kenny Walker .05 .15
144 Mark Carrier WR .10 .30
145 Jon Vaughn .05 .15
146 Greg Davis .05 .15
147 Bubby Brister .05 .15
148 Mo Lewis .05 .15
149 Howie Long .20 .50
150 Rod Bernstine .05 .15
151 Nick Bell .05 .15
152 Terry Allen .20 .50
153 William Fuller .05 .15
154 Dexter Carter .05 .15
155 Gene Atkins .05 .15
156 Don Beebe .05 .15
157 Mark Collins .05 .15
158 Jerry Ball .05 .15
159 Fred Barnett .20 .50
160 Rodney Holman .05 .15
161 Stephen Baker .05 .15
162 Jeff Graham .20 .50
163 Leonard Russell .10 .30
164 Jeff Gossett .05 .15
165 Vinny Testaverde .10 .30
166 Maurice Hurst .05 .15
167 Louis Oliver .05 .15
168 Jim Morrissey .05 .15
169 Greg Kragen .05 .15
170 Andre Collins .05 .15
171 Dave Meggett .10 .30
172 Keith Henderson .05 .15
173 Vince Newsome .05 .15
174 Chris Hinton .05 .15
175 James Hasty .05 .15
176 John Offerdahl .05 .15
177 Lomas Brown .05 .15
178 Neil O'Donnell .10 .30
179 Leonard Marshall .05 .15
180 Bubba McDowell .05 .15
181 Herman Moore .20 .50
182 Rob Moore .10 .30
183 Earnest Byner .05 .15
184 Keith McCants .05 .15
185 Floyd Turner .05 .15
186 Steve Jordan .05 .15
187 Nate Odomes .05 .15
188 Jeff Herrod .05 .15
189 Jim Harbaugh .20 .50
190 Jessie Tuggle .05 .15
191 Al Smith .05 .15
192 Lawrence Dawsey .10 .30
193 Steve Bono RC .20 .50
194 Greg Lloyd .10 .30
195 Steve Wisniewski .05 .15
196 Larry Kelm .05 .15
197 Tommy Kane .05 .15
198 Mark Schlereth RC .05 .15
199 Ray Childress .05 .15
200 Vincent Brown .05 .15
201 Rodney Peete .10 .30
202 Dennis Smith .05 .15
203 Bruce Matthews .05 .15
204 Rickey Jackson .05 .15
205 Eric Allen .05 .15
206 Rich Camarillo .05 .15
207 Jim Lachey .05 .15
208 Kevin Ross .05 .15
209 Irving Fryar .10 .30
210 Mark Clayton .10 .30
211 Keith Byars .05 .15
212 John Elway 1.25 3.00
213 Harris Barton .05 .15
214 Aeneas Williams .10 .30
215 Rich Gannon .20 .50
216 Toi Cook .05 .15
217 Rod Woodson .20 .50
218 Gary Anderson RB .05 .15
219 Reggie Roby .05 .15
220 Karl Mecklenburg .05 .15
221 Rufus Porter .05 .15
222 Jon Hand .05 .15
223 Tim Barnett .05 .15
224 Eric Swann .10 .30
225 Eugene Robinson .05 .15
226 Michael Young .05 .15
227 Frank Warren .05 .15
228 Mike Kenn .05 .15
229 Tim Green .05 .15
230 Barry Word .05 .15
231 Mike Pritchard .10 .30
232 John Kasay .05 .15
233 Derek Russell .05 .15
234 Jim Breech .05 .15
235 Pierce Holt .05 .15
236 Tim Krumrie .05 .15
237 William Roberts .05 .15
238 Erik Kramer .10 .30
239 Brett Perriman .20 .50
240 Reyna Thompson .05 .15
241 Chris Miller .10 .30
242 Drew Hill .05 .15
243 Curtis Duncan .05 .15
244 Seth Joyner .05 .15
245 Ken Norton Jr. .10 .30
246 Calvin Williams .10 .30
247 James Joseph .05 .15
248 Bennie Thompson RC .05 .15
249 Tunch Ilkin .05 .15
250 Brad Edwards .05 .15
251 Jeff Jaeger .05 .15
252 Gill Byrd .05 .15
253 Jeff Feagles .05 .15
254 Jamie Dukes RC .05 .15
255 Greg McMurtry .05 .15
256 Anthony Johnson .10 .30
257 Lamar Lathon .05 .15
258 John Roper .05 .15
259 Lorenzo White .05 .15
260 Brian Noble .05 .15
261 Chris Singleton .05 .15
262 Todd Marinovich .05 .15
263 Jay Hilgenberg .05 .15
264 Kyle Clifton .05 .15
265 Tony Casillas .05 .15
266 James Francis .05 .15
267 Eddie Anderson .05 .15
268 Tim Harris .05 .15
269 James Lofton .10 .30
270 Jay Schroeder .05 .15
271 Ed West .05 .15
272 Don Mosebar .05 .15
273 Jackie Slater .05 .15
274 Fred McAfee RC .05 .15
275 Steve Sewell .05 .15
276 Charles Mann .05 .15
277 Ron Hall .05 .15
278 Darrell Green .05 .15
279 Jeff Cross .05 .15
280 Jeff Wright .05 .15
281 Issiac Holt .05 .15
282 Dermontti Dawson .10 .30
283 Michael Haynes .10 .30
284 Tony Mandarich .05 .15
285 Leroy Hoard .10 .30
286 Darryl Henley .05 .15
287 Tim McGee .05 .15
288 Willie Gault .10 .30
289 Dalton Hilliard .05 .15
290 Tim McKyer .05 .15
291 Tom Waddle .05 .15
292 Eric Thomas .05 .15
293 Herschel Walker .10 .30
294 Donnell Woolford .05 .15
295 James Brooks .10 .30
296 Brad Muster .05 .15
297 Brent Jones .10 .30
298 Erik Howard .05 .15
299 Alvin Harper .10 .30
300 Joey Browner .05 .15
301 Jack Del Rio .05 .15
302 Cleveland Gary .05 .15
303 Brett Favre 3.00 6.00
304 Freeman McNeil .05 .15
305 Willie Green .05 .15
306 Percy Snow .05 .15
307 Neil Smith .20 .50
308 Eric Bieniemy .05 .15
309 Keith Traylor .05 .15
310 Ernie Mills .05 .15
311 Will Wolford .05 .15
312 Robert Young .05 .15
313 Anthony Smith .05 .15
314 Robert Porcher RC .20 .50
315 Leon Searcy RC .05 .15
316 Amp Lee RC .05 .15
317 Siran Stacy RC .05 .15
318 Patrick Rowe RC .05 .15
319 Chris Mims RC .05 .15
320 Matt Elliott RC .05 .15
321 Ricardo McDonald RC .05 .15
322 Keith Hamilton RC .10 .30
323 Edgar Bennett RC .20 .50
324 Chris Hakel RC .05 .15
325 Dexter McNabb RC .05 .15
326 Rod Milstead RC .05 .15
327 Joe Bowden RC .05 .15
328 Brian Bollinger RC .05 .15
329 Darryl Williams RC .05 .15
330 Tommy Vardell RC .05 .15
331 Glenn Parker SIDE .05 .15
332 Herschel Walker SIDE .05 .15
333 Mike Cofer SIDE .05 .15
334 Mark Rypien SIDE .05 .15
335 Andre Rison GW .10 .30
336 Henry Ellard GW .05 .15
337 Rob Moore GW .05 .15
338 Fred Barnett GW .05 .15
339 Mark Clayton GW .05 .15
340 Eric Martin GW .05 .15
341 Irving Fryar GW .05 .15
342 Tim Brown GW .10 .30
343 Sterling Sharpe GW .10 .30
344 Gary Clark GW .05 .15
345 John Mackey HOF .05 .15
346 Lem Barney HOF .05 .15
347 John Riggins HOF .10 .30
348 Marion Butts IDOL .05 .15
349 Jeff Lageman IDOL .05 .15
350 Eric Green IDOL .05 .15
351 Reggie White .10 .30
Bob.Jones I
352 Marv Cook IDOL .05 .15
353 John Elway .50 1.25
Staubach ID
354 Steve Tasker IDOL .05 .15
355 Nick Lowery IDOL .05 .15
356 Mark Clayton .05 .15
Warfield ID
357 Warren Moon .10 .30
R.Gabriel ID
358 Eric Metcalf .10 .30
359 Charles Haley .10 .30
360 Terrell Buckley RC .05 .15
P1 Promo Panel 2.00 5.00

1992 Pinnacle Team Pinnacle

These 13 standard-size cards feature paintings by sports artist Christopher Greco. The cards were randomly inserted into Pinnacle packs at an approximate rate of one in 36. One side showcases the best offensive player by position while the other side has his defensive counterpart. On both sides, a gold foil stripe carrying the player's name and position and a black stripe appear beneath the portrait. The card number is printed on the back in the black stripe.

COMPLETE SET (13) 25.00 60.00
RANDOM INSERTS IN FOIL PACKS
1 M.Rypien 2.50 6.00
R.Lott
2 B.Sanders 6.00 15.00
D.Thomas
3 T.Thomas 3.00 8.00
P.Swilling
4 E.Green 2.50 6.00
S.Atwater
5 H.Jeffires 2.50 6.00
D.Green
6 M.Irvin 3.00 8.00
E.Allen
7 B.Matthews 1.50 4.00
J.Ball
8 S.Wisniewski 1.50 4.00
P.Johnson
9 W.Roberts 1.50 4.00
K.Mecklen.
10 J.Lachey 1.50 4.00
W.Fuller
11 A.Munoz 3.00 8.00
Reg.White
12 M.Gray 2.50 6.00
S.Tasker
13 J.Jaeger 1.50 4.00
J.Gossett

1992 Pinnacle Team 2000

This 30-card standard-size set focuses on young players who were expected to be the NFL's major stars in the year 2000. The cards were inserted two per 27-card jumbo pack.

COMPLETE SET (30) 7.50 15.00
TWO PER JUMBO PACK
1 Todd Marinovich .02 .10
2 Rodney Hampton .08 .25
3 Mike Croel .02 .10
4 Leonard Russell .08 .25
5 Herman Moore .15 .40
6 Rob Moore .08 .25
7 Jon Vaughn .02 .10
8 Lamar Lathon .02 .10
9 Ed King .02 .10
10 Moe Gardner .02 .10
11 Barry Foster .08 .25
12 Eric Green .02 .10
13 Kenny Walker .02 .10
14 Tim Barnett .02 .10
15 Derrick Thomas .15 .40
16 Steve Atwater .02 .10
17 Nick Bell .02 .10
18 John Friesz .02 .10
19 Emmitt Smith 1.50 3.00
20 Eric Swann .08 .25
21 Barry Sanders 1.25 2.50
22 Mark Carrier DB .02 .10
23 Brett Favre 2.50 5.00
24 James Francis .02 .10
25 Lawrence Dawsey .08 .25
26 Keith McCants .02 .10
27 Broderick Thomas .02 .10
28 Mike Pritchard .08 .25
29 Bruce Pickens .02 .10
30 Todd Lyght .02 .10

1993 Pinnacle Samples

This sample panel measures approximately 7 1/2" by 7" and features two rows of three cards each. If cut, the cards would measure the standard size. The fronts display color action player photos on a black card face accented by thin white picture frames. The team name and the player's name are printed above and below the picture respectively; the gold-foil stamped Pinnacle logo at the lower right corner rounds out the card face. On a black background, the horizontal backs carry a color close-up photo, biography, career summary, and 1992 season statistics. The cards are numbered at the upper left corner, and the word "Sample" is printed just below Score's anti-counterfeiting device.

COMPLETE SET (6) 3.20 8.00
1 Brett Favre 2.00 5.00
2 Tommy Vardell .30 .75
3 Jarrod Bunch .30 .75
4 Mike Croel .30 .75
5 Morten Andersen .30 .75
6 Barry Foster .30 .75

1993 Pinnacle

The 1993 Pinnacle set consists of 360 standard-size cards that were issued in 15 and 27-card packs. The set closes with the Hall of Fame (353-356) and Hometown Hero (357-360) subsets. Rookie Cards include Dave Brown. For each order of 20 boxes, Pinnacle would send one of 3,000 autographed cards of its spokesman, Franco Harris.

COMPLETE SET (360) 7.50 20.00
1 Brett Favre 1.25 3.00
2 Tommy Vardell .02 .10
3 Jarrod Bunch .02 .10
4 Mike Croel .02 .10
5 Morten Andersen .02 .10
6 Barry Foster .07 .20
7 Chris Spielman .07 .20
8 Jim Jeffcoat .02 .10
9 Ken Ruettgers .02 .10
10 Cris Dishman .02 .10
11 Ricky Watters .15 .40
12 Alfred Williams .02 .10
13 Mark Kelso .02 .10
14 Moe Gardner .02 .10
15 Terry Allen .15 .40
16 Willie Gault .02 .10
17 Bubba McDowell .02 .10
18 Brian Mitchell .07 .20
19 Karl Mecklenburg .02 .10
20 Jim Everett .07 .20
21 Bobby Humphrey .02 .10
22 Tim Krumrie .02 .10
23 Ken Norton Jr. .07 .20
24 Wendell Davis .02 .10
25 Brad Baxter .02 .10
26 Mel Gray .07 .20
27 Jon Vaughn .02 .10
28 James Hasty .02 .10
29 Chris Warren .07 .20
30 Tim Harris .02 .10
31 Eric Metcalf .07 .20
32 Rob Moore .07 .20
33 Charles Haley .07 .20
34 Leonard Marshall .02 .10
35 Jeff Graham .07 .20
36 Eugene Robinson .02 .10
37 Darryl Talley .02 .10
38 Brent Jones .07 .20
39 Reggie Roby .02 .10
40 Bruce Armstrong .02 .10
41 Audray McMillian .02 .10
42 Bern Brostek .02 .10
43 Tony Bennett .02 .10
44 Albert Lewis .02 .10
45 Derrick Thomas .15 .40
46 Cris Carter .15 .40
47 Richmond Webb .02 .10
48 Sean Landeta .02 .10
49 Cleveland Gary .02 .10
50 Mark Carrier DB .02 .10
51 Lawrence Dawsey .02 .10
52 Lamar Lathon .02 .10
53 Nick Bell .02 .10
54 Curtis Duncan .02 .10
55 Irving Fryar .07 .20
56 Seth Joyner .02 .10
57 Jay Novacek .07 .20
58 John L. Williams .02 .10
59 Amp Lee .02 .10
60 Marion Butts .02 .10
61 Clyde Simmons .02 .10
62 Rich Gannon .15 .40
63 Anthony Johnson .07 .20
64 Dave Meggett .02 .10
65 James Francis .02 .10
66 Trace Armstrong .02 .10
67 Mo Lewis .02 .10
68 Cornelius Bennett .07 .20
69 Mark Duper .02 .10
70 Frank Reich .07 .20
71 Eric Green .02 .10
72 Bruce Matthews .02 .10
73 Steve Broussard .02 .10
74 Anthony Carter .07 .20
75 Sterling Sharpe .15 .40
76 Mike Kenn .02 .10
77 Andre Rison .07 .20
78 Todd Marinovich .02 .10
79 Vincent Brown .02 .10
80 Harold Green .02 .10
81 Art Monk .07 .20
82 Reggie Cobb .02 .10
83 Johnny Johnson .02 .10
84 Tommy Kane .02 .10
85 Rohn Stark .02 .10
86 Steve Tasker .07 .20
87 Ronnie Harmon .02 .10
88 Pepper Johnson .02 .10
89 Hardy Nickerson .07 .20
90 Alvin Harper .07 .20
91 Louis Oliver .02 .10
92 Rod Woodson .15 .40
93 Sam Mills .02 .10
94 Randall McDaniel .05 .15
95 Johnny Holland .02 .10
96 Jackie Slater .02 .10
97 Don Mosebar .02 .10
98 Andre Ware .02 .10
99 Kelvin Martin .02 .10
100 Emmitt Smith 1.00 2.50
101 Michael Brooks .02 .10
102 Dan Saleaumua .02 .10
103 John Elway 1.00 2.50
104 Henry Jones .02 .10
105 William Perry .07 .20
106 James Lofton .07 .20
107 Carnell Lake .02 .10
108 Chip Lohmiller .02 .10
109 Andre Tippett .02 .10
110 Barry Word .02 .10
111 Haywood Jeffires .07 .20
112 Kenny Walker .02 .10
113 John Randle .07 .20
114 Donnell Woolford .02 .10
115 Johnny Bailey .02 .10
116 Marcus Allen .15 .40
117 Mark Jackson .02 .10
118 Ray Agnew .02 .10
119 Gill Byrd .02 .10
120 Kyle Clifton .02 .10
121 Marv Cook .02 .10
122 Jerry Ball .02 .10
123 Steve Jordan .02 .10
124 Shannon Sharpe .15 .40
125 Brian Blades .07 .20
126 Rodney Hampton .07 .20
127 Bobby Hebert .02 .10
128 Jessie Tuggle .02 .10
129 Tom Newberry .02 .10
130 Keith McCants .02 .10
131 Richard Dent .07 .20
132 Herman Moore .15 .40
133 Michael Irvin .15 .40
134 Ernest Givins .07 .20
135 Mark Rypien .02 .10
136 Leonard Russell .07 .20
137 Reggie White .15 .40
138 Thurman Thomas .15 .40
139 Nick Lowery .02 .10
140 Al Smith .02 .10
141 Jackie Harris .02 .10
142 Duane Bickett .02 .10
143 Lawyer Tillman .02 .10
144 Steve Wisniewski .02 .10
145 Derrick Fenner .02 .10
146 Harris Barton .02 .10
147 Rich Camarillo .02 .10
148 John Offerdahl .02 .10
149 Mike Johnson .02 .10
150 Ricky Reynolds .02 .10
151 Fred Barnett .07 .20
152 Nate Newton .07 .20
153 Chris Doleman .02 .10
154 Todd Scott .02 .10
155 Tim McKyer .02 .10
156 Ken Harvey .02 .10
157 Jeff Feagles .02 .10
158 Vince Workman .02 .10
159 Bart Oates .02 .10
160 Chris Miller .07 .20
161 Pete Stoyanovich .02 .10
162 Steve Wallace .02 .10
163 Dermontti Dawson .08 .20
164 Kenneth Davis .02 .10
165 Mike Munchak .07 .20
166 George Jamison .02 .10
167 Christian Okoye .02 .10
168 Chris Hinton .02 .10
169 Vaughan Johnson .02 .10
170 Gaston Green .02 .10
171 Kevin Greene .07 .20
172 Rob Burnett .02 .10
173 Norm Johnson .02 .10
174 Eric Hill .02 .10
175 Lomas Brown .02 .10
176 Chip Banks .02 .10
177 Greg Townsend .02 .10
178 David Fulcher .02 .10
179 Gary Anderson RB .02 .10
180 Brian Washington .02 .10
181 Brett Perriman .15 .40
182 Chris Chandler .07 .20
183 Phil Hansen .02 .10
184 Mark Clayton .02 .10
185 Frank Warren .02 .10
186 Tim Brown .15 .40
187 Mark Stepnoski .02 .10
188 Bryan Cox .02 .10
189 Gary Zimmerman .02 .10
190 Neil O'Donnell .15 .40
191 Anthony Smith .02 .10
192 Craig Heyward .07 .20
193 Keith Byars .02 .10
194 Sean Salisbury .02 .10
195 Todd Lyght .02 .10
196 Jessie Hester .02 .10
197 Rufus Porter .02 .10
198 Steve Christie .02 .10
199 Nate Lewis .02 .10
200 Barry Sanders .75 2.00
201 Michael Haynes .07 .20
202 John Taylor .07 .20
203 John Friesz .07 .20
204 William Fuller .02 .10
205 Dennis Smith .02 .10
206 Adrian Cooper .02 .10
207 Henry Thomas .02 .10
208 Gerald Williams .02 .10
209 Chris Burkett .02 .10
210 Broderick Thomas .02 .10
211 Marvin Washington .02 .10
212 Bennie Blades .02 .10
213 Tony Casillas .02 .10
214 Bubby Brister .02 .10
215 Don Griffin .02 .10
216 Jeff Cross .02 .10
217 Derrick Walker .02 .10
218 Lorenzo White .02 .10
219 Ricky Sanders .02 .10
220 Rickey Jackson .02 .10
221 Simon Fletcher .02 .10
222 Troy Vincent .02 .10
223 Gary Clark .07 .20
224 Stanley Richard .02 .10
225 Dave Krieg .07 .20
226 Warren Moon .15 .40
227 Reggie Langhorne .02 .10
228 Kent Hull .02 .10
229 Ferrell Edmunds .02 .10
230 Cortez Kennedy .07 .20
231 Hugh Millen .02 .10
232 Eugene Chung .02 .10
233 Rodney Peete .02 .10
234 Tom Waddle .02 .10
235 David Klingler .02 .10
236 Mark Carrier WR .07 .20
237 Jay Schroeder .02 .10
238 James Jones DT .02 .10
239 Phil Simms .07 .20
240 Steve Atwater .02 .10
241 Jeff Herrod .02 .10
242 Dale Carter .02 .10
243 Glenn Cadrez RC .02 .10
244 Wayne Martin .02 .10
245 Willie Davis .15 .40
246 Lawrence Taylor .15 .40
247 Stan Humphries .07 .20
248 Byron Evans .02 .10
249 Wilber Marshall .02 .10
250 Michael Bankston RC .02 .10
251 Steve McMichael .07 .20
252 Brad Edwards .02 .10
253 Will Wolford .02 .10
254 Paul Gruber .02 .10
255 Steve Young .50 1.25
256 Chuck Cecil .02 .10
257 Pierce Holt .02 .10
258 Anthony Miller .07 .20
259 Carl Banks .02 .10
260 Brad Muster .02 .10
261 Clay Matthews .07 .20
262 Rod Bernstine .02 .10
263 Tim Barnett .02 .10
264 Greg Lloyd .07 .20
265 Sean Jones .02 .10
266 J.J. Birden .02 .10
267 Tim McDonald .02 .10
268 Charles Mann .02 .10
269 Bruce Smith .15 .40
270 Sean Gilbert .07 .20
271 Ricardo McDonald .02 .10
272 Jeff Hostetler .07 .20
273 Russell Maryland .02 .10
274 Dave Brown RC .15 .40
275 Ronnie Lott .07 .20
276 Jim Kelly .15 .40
277 Joe Montana 1.00 2.50
278 Eric Allen .02 .10
279 Browning Nagle .02 .10
280 Neal Anderson .02 .10
281 Troy Aikman .50 1.25
282 Ed McCaffrey .15 .40
283 Robert Jones .02 .10
284 Dalton Hilliard .02 .10
285 Johnny Mitchell .02 .10
286 Jay Hilgenberg .02 .10
287 Eric Martin .02 .10
288 Steve Emtman .02 .10
289 Vaughn Dunbar .02 .10
290 Mark Wheeler .02 .10
291 Leslie O'Neal .07 .20
292 Jerry Rice .60 1.50
293 Neil Smith .15 .40
294 Kerry Cash .02 .10
295 Dan McGwire .02 .10
296 Carl Pickens .07 .20
297 Terrell Buckley .02 .10
298 Randall Cunningham .15 .40
299 Santana Dotson .07 .20
300 Keith Jackson .07 .20

301 Jim Lachey .02 .10
302 Dan Marino 1.00 2.50
303 Lee Williams .02 .10
304 Burt Grossman .02 .10
305 Kevin Mack .02 .10
306 Pat Swilling .02 .10
307 Arthur Marshall RC .02 .10
308 Jim Harbaugh .15 .40
309 Kurt Barber .02 .10
310 Harvey Williams .07 .20
311 Ricky Ervins .02 .10
312 Flipper Anderson .02 .10
313 Bernie Kosar .07 .20
314 Boomer Esiason .07 .20
315 Deion Sanders .30 .75
316 Ray Childress .02 .10
317 Howie Long .15 .40
318 Henry Ellard .07 .20
319 Marco Coleman .02 .10
320 Chris Mims .02 .10
321 Quentin Coryatt .07 .20
322 Jason Hanson .02 .10
323 Ricky Proehl .02 .10
324 Randal Hill .02 .10
325 Vinny Testaverde .07 .20
326 Jeff George .15 .40
327 Junior Seau .15 .40
328 Earnest Byner .02 .10
329 Andre Reed .07 .20
330 Phillippi Sparks .02 .10
331 Kevin Ross .02 .10
332 Clarence Verdin .02 .10
333 Darryl Henley .02 .10
334 Dana Hall .02 .10
335 Greg McMurtry .02 .10
336 Ron Hall .02 .10
337 Darrell Green .02 .10
338 Carlton Bailey .02 .10
339 Irv Eatman .02 .10
340 Greg Kragen .02 .10
341 Wade Wilson .02 .10
342 Klaus Wilmsmeyer .02 .10
343 Derek Brown TE .02 .10
344 Erik Williams .02 .10
345 Jim McMahon .07 .20
346 Mike Sherrard .02 .10
347 Mark Bavaro .02 .10
348 Anthony Munoz .07 .20
349 Eric Dickerson .07 .20
350 Steve Beuerlein .07 .20
351 Tim McGee .02 .10
352 Terry McDaniel .02 .10
353 Dan Fouts HOF .02 .10
354 Chuck Noll HOF .07 .20
355 Bill Walsh HOF RC .07 .20
356 Larry Little HOF .02 .10
357 Todd Marinovich HH .02 .10
358 Jeff George HH .15 .40
359 Bernie Kosar HH .07 .20
360 Rob Moore HH .07 .20
NNO Franco Harris AU/3000 12.50 30.00

1993 Pinnacle Men of Autumn

The 1993 Pinnacle Men of Autumn set consists of 55 standard-size cards. Not available in regular Pinnacle packs, one of these cards was inserted into each 16-card 1993 Score football foil pack. The cards are arranged in alphabetical order within an alphabetical team order.

COMPLETE SET (55) 4.00 10.00
ONE PER SCORE FOIL AND JUMBO PACK
1 Andre Rison .05 .15
2 Thurman Thomas .10 .30
3 Wendell Davis .02 .10
4 Harold Green .02 .10
5 Eric Metcalf .05 .15
6 Michael Irvin .10 .30
7 John Elway 1.00 2.00
8 Barry Sanders .75 1.50
9 Sterling Sharpe .10 .30
10 Warren Moon .10 .30
11 Rohn Stark .02 .10
12 Derrick Thomas .10 .30
13 Terry McDaniel .02 .10
14 Cleveland Gary .02 .10
15 Dan Marino 1.00 2.00
16 Terry Allen .10 .30
17 Marv Cook .02 .10
18 Bobby Hebert .02 .10
19 Rodney Hampton .05 .15
20 Brad Baxter .02 .10
21 Reggie White .10 .30
22 Ricky Proehl .02 .10
23 Barry Foster .05 .15
24 Junior Seau .10 .30
25 Steve Young .40 1.00
26 Cortez Kennedy .05 .15
27 Reggie Cobb .02 .10
28 Mark Rypien .02 .10
29 Deion Sanders .25 .60
30 Bruce Smith .10 .30
31 Richard Dent .05 .15
32 Alfred Williams .02 .10
33 Clay Matthews .05 .15
34 Emmitt Smith 1.00 2.00
35 Simon Fletcher .02 .10
36 Chris Spielman .05 .15
37 Brett Favre 1.25 2.50
38 Bruce Matthews .02 .10
39 Jeff Herrod .02 .10
40 Nick Lowery .02 .10
41 Steve Wisniewski .02 .10
42 Jim Everett .05 .15
43 Keith Jackson .05 .15
44 Chris Doleman .02 .10
45 Irving Fryar .05 .15
46 Rickey Jackson .02 .10
47 Pepper Johnson .02 .10
48 Randall Cunningham .10 .30
49 Rich Camarillo .02 .10
50 Rod Woodson .10 .30
51 Ronnie Harmon .02 .10
52 Ricky Watters .10 .30
53 Chris Warren .05 .15
54 Lawrence Dawsey .02 .10
55 Wilber Marshall .02 .10

1993 Pinnacle Rookies

The 1993 Pinnacle Rookies set consists of 25 standard-size cards, which were randomly inserted in one of approximately every 36 1993 Pinnacle foil packs. The cards are numbered on the back "X of 25."

COMPLETE SET (25) 100.00 200.00
STATED ODDS 1:36 HOB/RET
1 Drew Bledsoe 15.00 40.00
2 Garrison Hearst 6.00 15.00
3 John Copeland 2.50 6.00
4 Eric Curry 3.00 8.00
5 Curtis Conway 4.00 10.00
6 Lincoln Kennedy 2.50 6.00
7 Jerome Bettis 20.00 50.00
8 Dan Williams 2.50 6.00
9 Patrick Bates 2.50 6.00
10 Brad Hopkins 2.50 6.00
11 Wayne Simmons 2.50 6.00
12 Rick Mirer 4.00 10.00
13 Tom Carter 2.50 6.00
14 Irv Smith 3.00 8.00
15 Marvin Jones 2.50 6.00
16 Deon Figures 2.50 6.00
17 Leonard Renfro 2.50 6.00
18 O.J.McDuffie 4.00 10.00
19 Dana Stubblefield 4.00 10.00
20 Carlton Gray 2.50 6.00
21 Demetrius DuBose 2.50 6.00
22 Troy Drayton 2.50 6.00
23 Natrone Means 4.00 10.00
24 Reggie Brooks 3.00 8.00
25 Glyn Milburn 4.00 10.00

1993 Pinnacle Super Bowl XXVII

The 1993 Pinnacle Super Bowl XXVII set consists of ten standard-size cards commemorating the 1993 Super Bowl Champion Dallas Cowboys. The cards were issued one per hobby box. The cards are numbered on the back "X of 10."

COMPLETE SET (10) 40.00 100.00
ONE PER SEALED HOBBY FOIL BOX
1 Rose Bowl 1.50 4.00
2 Thomas Everett 1.50 4.00
3 Emmitt Smith 12.00 30.00
4 Ken Norton Jr. 2.00 5.00
5 Michael Irvin 5.00 12.00
6 Jay Novacek 2.50 6.00
7 Charles Haley 3.00 8.00
8 Leon Lett 2.00 5.00
9 Alvin Harper 2.50 6.00
10 Tony Casillas 2.00 5.00

1993 Pinnacle Team Pinnacle

The 1993 Pinnacle Team Pinnacle set consists of 13 two-player standard-size cards. One side showcases the best player by position for the AFC, while the flip side carries his NFC counterpart. The cards were randomly inserted in 1993 Pinnacle foil packs at an insertion rate of at least one in 90 packs. Both sides display black-bordered color action player paintings framed by a thin white line. The player's name, position, and conference designation appear on a gray stripe along the bottom of the portrait. Both sides of the card are numbered "X of 13."

COMPLETE SET (13) 60.00 150.00
STATED ODDS 1:90 HOB/RET
1 T.Aikman J.Montana 20.00 50.00
2 E.Smith T.Thomas 12.50 30.00
3 R.Hampton B.Foster 5.00 12.00
4 St.Sharpe A.Miller 5.00 12.00
5 M.Irvin H.Jeffires 5.00 12.00
6 K.Jackson J.Novacek 5.00 12.00
7 R.Webb S.Wallace 3.00 8.00
8 R.White L.O'Neal 5.00 12.00
9 C.Kennedy S.Gilbert 3.00 8.00
10 D.Thomas W.Marshall 5.00 12.00
11 J.Seau S.Mills 5.00 12.00
12 D.Sanders R.Woodson 6.00 15.00
13 S.Atwater T.McDonald 3.00 8.00

1993 Pinnacle Team 2001

The 1993 Pinnacle Team 2001 set consists of 30 standard-size cards showcasing the league's young players who were expected to be the NFL's major stars in the year 2001. The cards were inserted one per 27-card super pack of 1993 Pinnacle. The cards are numbered on the back "X of 30."

COMPLETE SET (30) 7.50 15.00
ONE PER JUMBO PACK
1 Junior Seau .30 .75
2 Cortez Kennedy .15 .40
3 Carl Pickens .15 .40
4 David Klingler .07 .20
5 Santana Dotson .15 .40
6 Sean Gilbert .15 .40
7 Brett Favre 3.00 6.00
8 Steve Emtman .07 .20
9 Rodney Hampton .15 .40
10 Browning Nagle .07 .20
11 Amp Lee .07 .20
12 Vaughn Dunbar .07 .20
13 Quentin Coryatt .15 .40
14 Marco Coleman .07 .20
15 Johnny Mitchell .07 .20
16 Arthur Marshall .07 .20
17 Dale Carter .07 .20
18 Henry Jones .07 .20
19 Terrell Buckley .07 .20
20 Tommy Vardell .07 .20
21 Tommy Maddox .07 .20
22 Barry Foster .15 .40
23 Herman Moore .30 .75
24 Ricky Watters .30 .75
25 Mike Croel .07 .20
26 Russell Maryland .07 .20
27 Terry Allen .30 .75
28 Jon Vaughn .07 .20
29 Todd Marinovich .07 .20
30 Jeff Graham .15 .40

1993 Pinnacle Power

This card was given to dealers who attended the Pinnacle Brands factory tour during the 1993 SCAI Convention. It measures approximately 3 1/2" by 5", and came in a hard plastic holder with a black velvet case that carries the word "Pinnacle" in yellow letters. According to Score, only 200 cards exist, the remainder of the print run having been shredded following distribution of the gift. The horizontal front features color head shots of Pinnacle spokesmen, Alexander Daigle, Franco Harris, and Eric Lindros, on a red background with a thin gold border, and a slightly thicker black border around it. The words "Pinnacle Power" on a red bar on the bottom of the card complete the front. On a shaded red to black background, the horizontal back carries biographical information about all three players.

1 Alexandre Daigle/200 Franco Harris Eric Lindros 60.00 150.00

1994 Pinnacle Samples

This ten-card standard-size set was issued to promote the 1994 Pinnacle football series. The cards are virtually identical to their counterparts in the regular series, with only a very slight difference when examined closely. We've noted the minor differences below. The sample cards also are punched in one corner to indicate that they are promotional samples not for sale.

COMPLETE SET (11) 3.20 8.00
1 Deion Sanders .60 1.50
3 Barry Sanders 1.60 4.00
24 Sean Gilbert .20 .50
30 Alvin Harper .20 .50
32 Derrick Thomas .30 .75
85 James Jett .30 .75
214 Chuck Levy .20 .50
DP8 William Floyd .30 .75
NNO Ad Card Hobby .20 .50
NNO Pick Pinnacle .20 .50
NNO Ad Card Retail .20 .50

1994 Pinnacle

The 1994 Pinnacle football set consists of 270 standard-size cards. The fronts feature full-bleed photos with the player's name and Pinnacle logo in gold foil at the bottom. Horizontal backs have a player photo, a brief write-up and statistics. Cards 190-221 comprise of a Rookies subset. Card 271, Jerry Rice, was issued only in jumbo packs. The set is considered complete without it. Odds of finding the Drew Bledsoe Pinnacle Passer were one in approximately 360 hobby packs. Key Rookie Cards in this set include Trent Dilfer and Marshall Faulk. The Franco Harris signed card was randomly seeded in cases of Pinnacle and Pinnacle Canton Bound.

COMPLETE SET (270) 8.00 20.00
1 Deion Sanders .20 .50
2 Eric Metcalf .07 .20
3 Barry Sanders .75 2.00
4 Ernest Givins .07 .20
5 Phil Simms .07 .20
6 Rod Woodson .07 .20
7 Michael Irvin .15 .40
8 Cortez Kennedy .07 .20
9 Eric Martin .02 .10
10 Jeff Hostetler .07 .20
11 Sterling Sharpe .07 .20
12 John Elway 1.00 2.50
13 Neal Anderson .02 .10
14 Terry Kirby .15 .40
15 Jim Everett .07 .20
16 Lawrence Dawsey .02 .10
17 Kelvin Martin .02 .10
18 Tim McGee .02 .10
19 Cris Carter .20 .50
20 Ronnie Harmon .02 .10
21 Jim Kelly .15 .40
22 Steve Young .40 1.00
23 Johnny Johnson .02 .10
24 Sean Gilbert .02 .10
25 Brian Mitchell .02 .10
26 Carl Pickens .07 .20
27 Tim Brown .15 .40
28 Reggie Langhorne .02 .10
29 Webster Slaughter .02 .10
30 Alvin Harper .07 .20
31 Andre Rison .07 .20
32 Derrick Thomas .15 .40
33 Irving Fryar .07 .20
34 Vinny Testaverde .07 .20
35 Steve Beuerlein .07 .20
36 Brett Favre 1.00 2.50
37 Barry Foster .02 .10
38 Vaughan Johnson .02 .10
39 Carlton Bailey .02 .10
40 Steve Emtman .02 .10
41 Anthony Miller .07 .20
42 Jeff Cross .02 .10
43 Trace Armstrong .02 .10
44 Derek Russell .02 .10
45 Vincent Brisby .07 .20
46 Mark Jackson .02 .10
47 Eugene Robinson .02 .10
48 John Friesz .07 .20
49 Scott Mitchell .07 .20
50 Steve Atwater .02 .10
51 Ken Norton .07 .20
52 Vincent Brown .02 .10
53 Morten Andersen .02 .10
54 Gary Anderson K .02 .10
55 Eric Curry .02 .10
56 Henry Jones .02 .10
57 Flipper Anderson .02 .10
58 Pat Swilling .02 .10
59 Erric Pegram .02 .10
60 Bruce Matthews .02 .10
61 Willie Davis .07 .20
62 O.J.McDuffie .15 .40
63 Qadry Ismail .15 .40
64 Anthony Smith .02 .10
65 Eric Allen .02 .10
66 Marion Butts .02 .10
67 Chris Miller .02 .10
68 Terrell Buckley .02 .10
69 Thurman Thomas .15 .40
70 Roosevelt Potts .02 .10
71 Tony McGee .02 .10
72 Jason Hanson .02 .10
73 Victor Bailey .02 .10
74 Albert Lewis .02 .10
75 Nate Odomes .02 .10
76 Ben Coates .07 .20
77 Warren Moon .15 .40
78 Derek Brown RBK .02 .10
79 David Klingler .02 .10
80 Cleveland Gary .02 .10
81 Emmitt Smith .75 2.00
82 Jay Novacek .07 .20
83 Dana Stubblefield .07 .20
84 Michael Brooks .02 .10
85 James Jett .02 .10
86 J.J. Birden .02 .10
87 William Fuller .02 .10
88 Glyn Milburn .07 .20
89 Tim Worley .02 .10
90 Brett Perriman .07 .20
91 Randall Cunningham .15 .40
92 Drew Bledsoe .40 1.00
93 Jerome Bettis .25 .60
94 Boomer Esiason .07 .20
95 Garrison Hearst .15 .40
96 Bruce Smith .15 .40
97 Jackie Harris .02 .10
98 Jeff George .15 .40
99 Tom Waddle .02 .10
100 John Copeland .02 .10
101 Bobby Hebert .02 .10
102 Joe Montana 1.00 2.50
103 Herman Moore .15 .40
104 Rick Mirer .15 .40
105 Ricky Watters .07 .20
106 Neil O'Donnell .15 .40
107 Herschel Walker .07 .20
108 Rob Moore .07 .20
109 Reggie Brooks .07 .20
110 Tommy Vardell .02 .10
111 Eric Green .02 .10
112 Stan Humphries .07 .20
113 Greg Robinson .02 .10
114 Eric Swann .07 .20
115 Courtney Hawkins .02 .10
116 Andre Reed .07 .20
117 Steve McMichael .07 .20
118 Gary Brown .02 .10
119 Terry Allen .07 .20
120 Dan Marino 1.00 2.50
121 Gary Clark .07 .20
122 Chris Warren .07 .20
123 Pierce Holt .02 .10
124 Anthony Carter .07 .20
125 Quentin Coryatt .02 .10
126 Harold Green .02 .10
127 Leonard Russell .02 .10
128 Tim McDonald .02 .10
129 Chris Spielman .07 .20
130 Cody Carlson .02 .10
131 Ronald Moore .02 .10
132 Renaldo Turnbull .02 .10
133 Ronnie Lott .07 .20
134 Natrone Means .15 .40
135 Keith Byars .02 .10
136 Henry Ellard .07 .20
137 Steve Jordan .02 .10
138 Calvin Williams .07 .20
139 Brian Blades .07 .20
140 Michael Jackson .07 .20
141 Charles Haley .07 .20
142 Curtis Conway .15 .40
143 Nick Lowery .02 .10
144 Bill Brooks .02 .10
145 Michael Haynes .07 .20
146 Willie Green .02 .10
147 Duane Bickett .02 .10
148 Shannon Sharpe .07 .20
149 Ricky Proehl .02 .10
150 Troy Aikman .50 1.25
151 Mike Sherrard .02 .10
152 Reggie Cobb .02 .10
153 Norm Johnson .02 .10
154 Neil Smith .07 .20
155 James Francis .02 .10
156 Greg McMurtry .02 .10
157 Greg Townsend .02 .10
158 Mel Gray .02 .10
159 Rocket Ismail .07 .20
160 Leslie O'Neal .02 .10
161 Johnny Mitchell .02 .10
162 Brent Jones .07 .20
163 Chris Doleman .02 .10
164 Seth Joyner .02 .10
165 Marco Coleman .02 .10
166 Mark Higgs .02 .10
167 John L. Williams .02 .10
168 Darrell Green .02 .10
169 Mark Carrier WR .07 .20
170 Reggie White .15 .40
171 Darryl Talley .02 .10
172 Russell Maryland .02 .10
173 Mark Collins .02 .10
174 Chris Jacke .02 .10
175 Richard Dent .07 .20
176 John Taylor .07 .20
177 Rodney Hampton .07 .20
178 Dwight Stone .02 .10
179 Cornelius Bennett .07 .20
180 Cris Dishman .02 .10
181 Jerry Rice .50 1.25
182 Rod Bernstine .02 .10
183 Keith Hamilton .02 .10
184 Keith Jackson .02 .10
185 Craig Erickson .02 .10
186 Marcus Allen .15 .40
187 Marcus Robertson .02 .10
188 Junior Seau .15 .40
189 LeShon Johnson RC .07 .20
190 Perry Klein RC .02 .10
191 Bryant Young RC .25 .60
192 Byron Bam Morris RC .07 .20
193 Jeff Cothran RC .02 .10
194 Lamar Smith RC .60 1.50
195 Calvin Jones RC .02 .10
196 James Bostic RC .15 .40
197 Dan Wilkinson RC .07 .20
198 Marshall Faulk RC 2.50 6.00
199 Heath Shuler RC .15 .40
200 Willie McGinest RC .15 .40
201 Trev Alberts RC .07 .20
202 Trent Dilfer RC .60 1.50
203 Sam Adams RC .07 .20
204 Charles Johnson RC .15 .40
205 Johnnie Morton RC .60 1.50
206 Thomas Lewis RC .07 .20
207 Greg Hill RC .15 .40
208 William Floyd RC .15 .40
209 Derrick Alexander WR RC .15 .40
210 Darnay Scott RC .30 .75
211 Lake Dawson RC .07 .20
212 Errict Rhett RC .15 .40
213 Kevin Lee RC .02 .10
214 Chuck Levy RC .02 .10
215 David Palmer RC .15 .40
216 Ryan Yarborough RC .02 .10
217 Charlie Garner RC .60 1.50
218 Mario Bates RC .15 .40
219 Jamir Miller RC .07 .20
220 Bucky Brooks RC .02 .10
221 Donnell Bennett RC .15 .40
222 Kevin Greene .07 .20
223 LeRoy Butler .02 .10
224 Anthony Pleasant .02 .10
225 Steve Christie .02 .10
226 Bill Romanowski .02 .10
227 Darren Carrington .02 .10
228 Chester McGlockton .02 .10
229 Jack Del Rio .02 .10
230 Kevin Smith .02 .10
231 Chris Zorich .02 .10
232 Donnell Woolford .02 .10
233 Tony Casillas .02 .10
234 Terry McDaniel .02 .10
235 Ray Childress .02 .10
236 John Randle .07 .20
237 Clyde Simmons .02 .10
238 Dante Jones .02 .10
239 Karl Mecklenburg .02 .10
240 Daryl Johnston .07 .20
241 Hardy Nickerson .07 .20
242 Jeff Lageman .02 .10
243 Lewis Tillman .02 .10
244 Jim McMahon .07 .20
245 Mike Pritchard .02 .10
246 Harvey Williams .07 .20
247 Sean Jones .02 .10
248 Stevon Moore .02 .10
249 Pete Metzelaars .02 .10
250 Mike Johnson .02 .10
251 Chris Slade .02 .10
252 Jessie Hester .02 .10
253 Louis Oliver .02 .10
254 Ken Harvey .02 .10
255 Bryan Cox .02 .10
256 Erik Kramer .07 .20
257 Andy Harmon .02 .10
258 Rickey Jackson .02 .10
259 Mark Carrier DB .02 .10
260 Greg Lloyd .07 .20
261 Robert Brooks .15 .40
262 Dave Brown .07 .20
263 Dennis Smith .02 .10
264 Michael Dean Perry .07 .20
265 Dan Saleaumua .02 .10
266 Mo Lewis .02 .10
267 AFC Checklist .02 .10
268 AFC Checklist .02 .10
269 NFC Checklist .02 .10
270 NFC Checklist .02 .10
271SP Jerry Rice TD King SP 4.00 8.00
AU Franco Harris AU 10.00 25.00
NNO Drew Bledsoe Pin.Passer 15.00 40.00

1994 Pinnacle Trophy Collection

COMPLETE SET (270) 100.00 200.00
*STARS: 3X TO 8X BASIC CARDS
*RCs: 2X TO 5X BASIC CARDS

1994 Pinnacle Draft Pinnacle

Randomly inserted in hobby packs only, this 10-card standard-size set features ten top draft choices in their NFL uniforms. Odds of finding a Draft Pinnacle card are approximately one in every 24 hobby packs. The cards also have a dufex parallel that could be obtained through the "Pick Pinnacle" redemption program.

COMPLETE SET (10) 15.00 40.00
STATED ODDS 1:24 HOBBY
*DUFEX CARDS: SAME PRICE
DUFEX: PRIZES FOR PICK PINN.WINNERS
PICK PINNACLE STATED ODDS 1:80
DP1 Dan Wilkinson .40 1.00
DP2 Marshall Faulk 15.00 30.00
DP3 Heath Shuler 1.00 2.00
DP4 Trent Dilfer 4.00 8.00
DP5 Charles Johnson 1.00 2.00
DP6 Johnnie Morton 4.00 8.00
DP7 Darnay Scott 2.00 4.00
DP8 William Floyd 1.00 2.00
DP9 Errict Rhett 1.00 2.00
DP10 Chuck Levy .20 .50

1994 Pinnacle Performers

Randomly inserted in jumbo packs at a rate of one in four, this 18-card standard-size set spotlights some of the NFL's superstars. Card fronts feature a player photo superimposed over an enlarged Pinnacle gold pyramid logo. The back has a small color photo and highlights over a ghosted black and white photo. The cards are numbered on the back with a "PP" prefix.

COMPLETE SET (18) 10.00 25.00
STATED ODDS 1:4 JUMBO
PP1 Troy Aikman 1.50 3.00
PP2 Emmitt Smith 2.50 5.00
PP3 Sterling Sharpe .20 .50
PP4 Barry Sanders 2.50 5.00
PP5 Jerry Rice 1.50 3.00
PP6 Steve Young 1.25 2.50
PP7 John Elway 3.00 6.00
PP8 Michael Irvin .40 1.00
PP9 Jerome Bettis .75 1.50
PP10 Tim Brown .40 1.00
PP11 Joe Montana 3.00 6.00
PP12 Reggie Brooks .20 .50
PP13 Brett Favre 3.00 6.00
PP14 Drew Bledsoe 1.25 2.50
PP15 Ricky Watters .20 .50
PP16 Garrison Hearst .40 1.00
PP17 Rodney Hampton .20 .50
PP18 Dan Marino 3.00 6.00

1994 Pinnacle Team Pinnacle

Randomly inserted in retail and hobby packs at a rate of one in 90, this 10-card standard-size set showcases a top AFC player on one side with his NFC counterpart on the flipside. With a Dufex design, the horizontally designed cards have two player photos -- one on either side. The cards were printed with only one side in Dufex and the other with a flat gold finish, but two versions of each card were made with either side Dufexed.

COMPLETE SET (10) 25.00 60.00
*DUFEX BACK: .4X TO 1X BASIC CARDS
STATED ODDS 1:90
TP1 T.Aikman J.Montana 5.00 12.00
TP2 B.Favre R.Mirer 5.00 12.00
TP3 E.Smith T.Thomas 4.00 10.00
TP4 B.Sanders B.Foster 4.00 10.00
TP5 J.Bettis N.Means 2.50 6.00
TP6 St.Sharpe T.Brown 1.25 3.00
TP7 J.Rice A.Miller 3.00 8.00
TP8 M.Irvin J.Jett 2.00 5.00
TP9 R.White B.Smith 2.00 5.00
TP10 S.Gilbert C.Kennedy .75 2.00

1994 Pinnacle Canton Bound

These 25 standard-size cards feature Pinnacle's picks for future Hall of Fame inductees. Production was limited to 100,000 sets, and each set contained a numbered certificate of authenticity. The fronts feature color player action shots that are borderless, and carry the player's name in vertical gold-foil lettering near the right edge. On a borderless back composed of multiple player photos, the back carries the player's biography, career highlights, and statistics. A Ronnie Lott Sample card was produced as well and is listed below, but is not considered part of the set.

COMP.FACT SET (25) 4.00 10.00
1 Troy Aikman .50 1.25
2 Emmitt Smith 1.00 2.50
3 Barry Sanders 1.00 2.50
4 Jerry Rice .50 1.25
5 Sterling Sharpe .10 .30
6 Ronnie Lott .10 .30
7 John Elway 1.00 2.50
8 Joe Montana 1.00 2.50
9 Reggie White .10 .30
10 Thurman Thomas .20 .50
11 Bruce Smith .05 .15
12 Cortez Kennedy .05 .15
13 Dan Marino 1.00 2.50
14 Andre Rison .10 .30
15 Art Monk .10 .30
16 Warren Moon .10 .30
17 Barry Foster .05 .15
18 Steve Young .40 1.00
19 Phil Simms .10 .30
20 Richard Dent .05 .15
21 Marcus Allen .10 .30
22 Junior Seau .10 .30
23 Michael Irvin .20 .50
24 Deion Sanders .30 .75
25 Jerome Bettis .20 .50
S1 Ronnie Lott Sample .40 1.00

1994 Pinnacle/Sportflics Super Bowl

This seven-card 1994 Magic Motion standard-size set was issued by Pinnacle Brands, Inc. (Score) at the 1994 Super Bowl Card Show in Atlanta. Cards were distributed individually by exchanging three Pinnacle Brands wrappers from foil packs. The cards were produced and distributed in the following quantities: 3,000 for Gary Brown and Emmitt Smith; 2,000 for Sterling Sharpe, Jerome Bettis/Reggie Brooks, and Drew Bledsoe/Rick Mirer; and 1,000 for Jerry Rice and Deion Sanders. The "Magic Motion" process is an improved version of the old Sportflics. An "S" prefix and a "B" suffix appear on either side of the card number printed on a yellow oval on the card back.

COMPLETE SET (7) 110.00 275.00
1 Gary Brown/3000 4.80 12.00
2 Emmitt Smith/3000 20.00 50.00
3 Sterling Sharpe/2000 8.00 20.00
4 Jerome Bettis R.Brooks/2000 12.00 30.00
5 Drew Bledsoe Mirer/2000 16.00 40.00
6 Jerry Rice/1000 30.00 75.00
7 Deion Sanders/1000 20.00 50.00

1994 Pinnacle Team Histories

Cards from this set were issued in blister pack format along with a metal lapel pin featuring the team's logo. The card/pin combos were released to commemorate historic franchises for the NFL's 75th anniversary.

COMPLETE SET (12) 8.00 20.00
1 Dallas Cowboys 1.25 3.00
2 Miami Dolphins 1.00 2.50
3 Kansas City Chiefs 1.00 2.50
4 San Francisco 49ers 1.25 3.00
5 Los Angeles Raiders 1.00 2.50
6 New York Giants 1.00 2.50
7 Green Bay Packers 1.25 3.00
8 Philadelphia Eagles 1.00 2.50
9 Chicago Bears 1.00 2.50
10 Pittsburgh Steelers 1.25 3.00
11 Buffalo Bills 1.00 2.50
12 Washington Redskins 1.00 2.50

1995 Pinnacle Promos

These four cards were produced to promote the 1995 Pinnacle release. They include two base brand cards, one Showcase insert and an ad card.

COMPLETE SET (4) 3.20 8.00
1 Dan Marino 1.60 4.00
39 Barry Sanders 1.60 4.00
62 Steve Young .50 1.25
NNO Ad Card .20 .50

1995 Pinnacle

This 250 card set was issued by Pinnacle Brands and was available in 12 card packs for hobby and retail. Jumbo packs were also available. A special Deion Sanders card was issued only in jumbo packs and numbered 251SP. It features Sanders with his new team - the Dallas Cowboys. The set also contains a parallel called Trophy Collection, which features the same player shots with an all-foil dufex background. Trophy Collection cards were randomly inserted into packs at a rate of one in four. The Joe Montana Trophy Collection card (#193) is unique from the other cards because it does not have an Artist Proof parallel. Rookie Cards include Jeff Blake, Ki-Jana Carter, Kerry Collins, Joey Galloway, Steve McNair, Rashaan Salaam, Kordell Stewart, J.J. Stokes and Michael Westbrook

COMPLETE SET (250) 8.00 20.00
1 Reggie White .15 .40
2 Troy Aikman .40 1.00
3 Willie Davis .07 .20
4 Jerry Rice .40 1.00
5 Bruce Smith .15 .40
6 Keith Byars .02 .10
7 Chris Warren .07 .20
8 Erik Kramer .02 .10
9 Leon Lett .02 .10
10 Greg Lloyd .07 .20
11 Jackie Harris .02 .10
12 Irving Fryar .07 .20
13 Rodney Hampton .07 .20
14 Michael Irvin .15 .40
15 Michael Haynes .07 .20
16 Irving Spikes .07 .20
17 Calvin Williams .07 .20
18 Ken Norton Jr. .07 .20
19 Herman Moore .15 .40
20 Lewis Tillman .02 .10
21 Cortez Kennedy .07 .20
22 Dan Marino .75 2.00
23 Erric Pegram .07 .20
24 Tim Brown .15 .40
25 Jeff Blake RC .30 .75
26 Brett Favre .75 2.00
27 Garrison Hearst .15 .40
28 Ronnie Harmon .02 .10
29 Qadry Ismail .07 .20
30 Ben Coates .07 .20
31 Deion Sanders .25 .60
32 John Elway .75 2.00
33 Natrone Means .07 .20
34 Derrick Alexander WR .15 .40
35 Craig Heyward .07 .20
36 Jake Reed .07 .20
37 Steve Walsh .02 .10
38 John Randle .07 .20
39 Barry Sanders .60 1.50
40 Tydus Winans .02 .10
41 Thomas Lewis .07 .20
42 Jim Kelly .15 .40
43 Gus Frerotte .07 .20
44 Cris Carter .15 .40
45 Kevin Williams WR .07 .20
46 Dave Meggett .02 .10
47 Pat Swilling .02 .10
48 Neil O'Donnell .07 .20
49 Terance Mathis .07 .20
50 Desmond Howard .07 .20
51 Bryant Young .07 .20
52 Stan Humphries .07 .20
53 Alvin Harper .02 .10
54 Henry Ellard .07 .20
55 Jessie Hester .02 .10
56 Lorenzo White .02 .10
57 John Friesz .07 .20
58 Anthony Smith .02 .10
59 Bert Emanuel .15 .40
60 Gary Clark .02 .10
61 Bill Brooks .02 .10
62 Steve Young .30 .75
63 Jerome Bettis .15 .40
64 John Taylor .02 .10
65 Ricky Proehl .02 .10
66 Junior Seau .15 .40
67 Bubby Brister .02 .10
68 Neil Smith .07 .20
69 Dan McGwire .02 .10
70 Brett Perriman .07 .20
71 Chris Spielman .07 .20
72 Jeff George .07 .20
73 Emmitt Smith .40 1.00
74 Chris Penn .02 .10
75 Derrick Fenner .02 .10
76 Reggie Brooks .07 .20
77 Chris Chandler .07 .20
78 Rod Woodson .07 .20
79 Isaac Bruce .25 .60
80 Reggie Cobb .02 .10
81 Bryce Paup .07 .20
82 Warren Moon .07 .20
83 Bryan Reeves .02 .10
84 Lake Dawson .07 .20
85 Larry Centers .07 .20
86 Marshall Faulk .50 1.25
87 Jim Harbaugh .07 .20
88 Ray Childress .02 .10
89 Eric Metcalf .07 .20
90 Ernie Mills .02 .10
91 Lamar Lathon .02 .10
92 Errict Rhett .07 .20
93 David Klingler .07 .20
94 Vincent Brown .02 .10
95 Andre Rison .07 .20
96 Brian Mitchell .02 .10
97 Mark Rypien .02 .10
98 Eugene Robinson .02 .10
99 Eric Green .02 .10
100 Rocket Ismail .07 .20
101 Flipper Anderson .02 .10
102 Randall Cunningham .15 .40
103 Ricky Watters .07 .20
104 Amp Lee .02 .10
105 Ernest Givins .02 .10
106 Daryl Johnston .07 .20
107 Dave Krieg .02 .10
108 Dana Stubblefield .07 .20
109 Torrance Small .02 .10
110 Yancey Thigpen RC .07 .20
111 Chester McGlockton .07 .20
112 Craig Erickson .02 .10
113 Herschel Walker .07 .20
114 Mike Sherrard .02 .10
115 Tony McGee .02 .10
116 Adrian Murrell .07 .20
117 Frank Reich .02 .10
118 Hardy Nickerson .02 .10
119 Andre Reed .07 .20
120 Leonard Russell .02 .10
121 Eric Allen .02 .10
122 Jeff Hostetler .07 .20
123 Barry Foster .07 .20
124 Anthony Miller .07 .20
125 Shawn Jefferson .02 .10
126 Richie Anderson RC .20 .50
127 Steve Bono .07 .20
128 Seth Joyner .02 .10
129 Darnay Scott .07 .20
130 Johnny Mitchell .02 .10
131 Eric Swann .07 .20
132 Drew Bledsoe .25 .60
133 Marcus Allen .15 .40
134 Carl Pickens .07 .20
135 Michael Brooks .02 .10
136 John L. Williams .02 .10
137 Steve Beuerlein .07 .20
138 Robert Smith .15 .40
139 O.J. McDuffie .15 .40
140 Haywood Jeffires .02 .10
141 Aeneas Williams .02 .10
142 Rick Mirer .07 .20
143 William Floyd .07 .20
144 Fred Barnett .07 .20
145 Leroy Hoard .02 .10
146 Terry Kirby .07 .20
147 Boomer Esiason .07 .20
148 Ken Harvey .02 .10
149 Cleveland Gary .02 .10
150 Brian Blades .07 .20
151 Eric Turner .02 .10
152 Vinny Testaverde .07 .20
153 Ronald Moore UER .02 .10
154 Curtis Conway .15 .40
155 Johnnie Morton .07 .20
156 Kenneth Davis .02 .10
157 Scott Mitchell .07 .20
158 Sean Gilbert .07 .20
159 Shannon Sharpe .07 .20
160 Mark Seay .07 .20
161 Cornelius Bennett .07 .20
162 Heath Shuler .07 .20
163 Byron Bam Morris .02 .10
164 Robert Brooks .15 .40
165 Glyn Milburn .02 .10
166 Gary Brown .02 .10
167 Jim Everett .02 .10
168 Steve Atwater .02 .10
169 Darren Woodson .07 .20
170 Mark Ingram .02 .10
171 Donnell Woolford .02 .10
172 Trent Dilfer .15 .40
173 Charlie Garner .15 .40
174 Charles Johnson .07 .20
175 Mike Pritchard .02 .10
176 Derek Brown RBK .02 .10
177 Chris Miller .02 .10
178 Charles Haley .07 .20
179 J.J. Birden .02 .10
180 Jeff Graham .02 .10
181 Bernie Parmalee .07 .20
182 Mark Brunell .25 .60
183 Greg Hill .07 .20
184 Michael Timpson .02 .10
185 Terry Allen .07 .20
186 Ricky Ervins .02 .10
187 Dave Brown .07 .20
188 Dan Wilkinson .07 .20
189 Jay Novacek .07 .20
190 Harvey Williams .02 .10
191 Mario Bates .07 .20
192 Steve Young LAW .20 .50
193 Joe Montana .75 2.00
194 Steve Young PP .20 .50
195 Troy Aikman PP .25 .60
196 Drew Bledsoe PP .15 .40
197 Dan Marino PP .40 1.00
198 John Elway PP .40 1.00
199 Brett Favre PP .40 1.00
200 Heath Shuler PP .07 .20
201 Warren Moon PP .02 .10
202 Jim Kelly PP .15 .40
203 Jeff Hostetler PP .07 .20
204 Rick Mirer PP .07 .20
205 Dave Brown PP .07 .20
206 Randall Cunningham PP .07 .20
207 Neil O'Donnell PP .07 .20
208 Jim Everett PP .02 .10
209 Ki-Jana Carter RC .15 .40
210 Steve McNair RC 1.25 3.00
211 Michael Westbrook RC .15 .40
212 Kerry Collins RC .75 2.00
213 Joey Galloway RC .60 1.50
214 Kyle Brady RC .15 .40
215 J.J. Stokes RC .15 .40
216 Tyrone Wheatley RC .50 1.25
217 Rashaan Salaam RC .07 .20
218 Napoleon Kaufman RC .50 1.25
219 Frank Sanders RC .15 .40
220 Stoney Case RC .02 .10
221 Todd Collins RC .50 1.25
222 Warren Sapp RC .60 1.50
223 Sherman Williams RC .02 .10
224 Rob Johnson RC .40 1.00
225 Mark Bruener RC .07 .20
226 Derrick Brooks RC .60 1.50
227 Chad May RC .02 .10
228 James A.Stewart RC .02 .10
229 Ray Zellars RC .07 .20
230 Dave Barr RC .02 .10
231 Kordell Stewart RC .60 1.50
232 Jimmy Oliver RC .02 .10
233 Tony Boselli RC .15 .40
234 James O. Stewart RC .50 1.25
235 Derrick Alexander DE RC .02 .10
236 Lovell Pinkney RC .02 .10
237 John Walsh RC .02 .10
238 Tyrone Davis RC .02 .10
239 Joe Aska RC .02 .10
240 Korey Stringer RC .10 .30
241 Hugh Douglas RC .15 .40
242 Christian Fauria RC .07 .20
243 Terrell Fletcher RC .02 .10
244 Dan Marino CL .25 .60
245 Drew Bledsoe CL .15 .40
246 John Elway CL .15 .40
247 Emmitt Smith CL .20 .50
248 Steve Young CL .15 .40
249 Barry Sanders CL .25 .60
250 Jerry Rice Seau CL .15 .40
251SP Deion Sanders SP 1.50 4.00

1995 Pinnacle Artist's Proofs

COMPLETE SET (249) 150.00 300.00
*AP STARS: 7.5X TO 20X
*AP RCs: 4X TO 10X
STATED ODDS 1:48

1995 Pinnacle Trophy Collection

COMPLETE SET (250) 50.00 120.00
*TC STARS: 2X TO 5X BASIC CARDS
*RCs: 1.25X TO 3X BASIC CARDS
193 Joe Montana 25.00 50.00

1995 Pinnacle Black 'N Blue

Inserted at a rate of one in 18 jumbo packs only, this 30 card set features an all-foil silver dufex background with the "Black 'N' Blue" logo at the bottom left of the card. The player's name is listed directly to the right of the logo. Card backs are numbered out of 30 and feature a player shot on the left side of the card with a brief commentary to the right.

COMPLETE SET (30) 30.00 60.00
STATED ODDS 1:18 JUMBO
1 Junior Seau 1.00 2.50
2 Byron Bam Morris .25 .60
3 Craig Heyward .50 1.25
4 Drew Bledsoe 1.50 4.00
5 Barry Sanders 4.00 10.00
6 Jerome Bettis 1.00 2.50
7 William Floyd .50 1.25
8 Greg Lloyd .50 1.25
9 John Elway 6.00 12.00
10 Jerry Rice 2.50 6.00
11 Kevin Greene .25 .60
12 Errict Rhett .50 1.25
13 Steve Young 2.00 5.00
14 Bruce Smith 1.00 2.50

Card	Low	High
15 Steve Atwater	.25	.60
16 Natrone Means	.50	1.25
17 Ben Coates	.50	1.25
18 Reggie White	1.00	2.50
19 Ken Harvey	.25	.60
20 Dan Marino	5.00	12.00
21 Marshall Faulk	3.00	8.00
22 Seth Joyner	.25	.60
23 Rod Woodson	.50	1.25
24 Hardy Nickerson	.25	.60
25 Brett Favre	5.00	12.00
26 Bryan Cox	.25	.60
27 Rodney Hampton	.50	1.25
28 Jeff Hostetler	.50	1.25
29 Brent Jones	.25	.60
30 Emmitt Smith	2.50	6.00

1995 Pinnacle Clear Shots

Inserted at a rate of one in 60 hobby and one in 33 retail packs, this 10 card set features eight of the league's hottest veteran players and two promising rookies using a clear plastic card stock overprinted with rainbow holographic foil. Cards are numbered out of 10.

Card	Low	High
COMPLETE SET (10)	25.00	60.00
STATED ODDS 1:60 HOB, 1:33 RETAIL		
1 Jerry Rice	2.50	6.00
2 Dan Marino	5.00	12.00
3 Steve Young	2.00	5.00
4 Drew Bledsoe	1.50	4.00
5 Emmitt Smith	2.50	6.00
6 Barry Sanders	4.00	10.00
7 Marshall Faulk	3.00	8.00
8 Troy Aikman	2.50	6.00
9 Ki-Jana Carter	.50	1.25
10 Steve McNair	4.00	10.00

1995 Pinnacle Gamebreakers

This 15 card set was randomly inserted into packs at a rate of one in 24 hobby packs. Card fronts feature the shot of the player against different color dufexed backgrounds. Cards are numbered out of 15.

Card	Low	High
COMPLETE SET (15)	12.00	30.00
STATED ODDS 1:24 HOBBY		
1 Marshall Faulk	2.50	5.00
2 Emmitt Smith	2.00	4.00
3 Steve Young	1.50	3.00
4 Ki-Jana Carter	.30	.75
5 Drew Bledsoe	1.25	2.50
6 Troy Aikman	2.00	4.00
7 Rashaan Salaam	.15	.40
8 Tyrone Wheatley	1.25	2.50
9 Dan Marino	4.00	8.00
10 Natrone Means	.30	.75
11 Barry Sanders	3.00	6.00
12 Jerry Rice	2.00	4.00
13 Byron Bam Morris	.15	.40
14 Steve McNair	3.00	6.00
15 Kerry Collins	1.50	4.00

1995 Pinnacle Showcase

This 21 card black and white set was randomly inserted into one in every 18 hobby, one in every 10 retail packs and one in every 14 jumbo packs.

Card	Low	High
COMPLETE SET (21)	15.00	30.00
STATED ODDS 1:18 HOB,1:14 JUM,1:10 RET		
1 Drew Bledsoe	.75	1.50
2 Joey Galloway	.75	1.50
3 Steve Young	1.00	2.00
4 Joe Aska	.02	.10
5 Barry Sanders	2.00	4.00
6 Troy Aikman	1.25	2.50
7 Dan Marino	2.50	5.00
8 Randall Cunningham	.40	1.00
9 John Elway	2.50	5.00
10 Brett Favre	2.50	5.00
11 Jim Kelly	.40	1.00
12 Warren Moon	.20	.50
13 Dave Brown	.20	.50
14 Jeff Hostetler	.20	.50
15 Rick Mirer	.20	.50
16 Ki-Jana Carter	.15	.40
17 Kerry Collins	.75	2.00
18 J.J. Stokes	.15	.40
19 Kordell Stewart	2.00	4.00
20 Michael Westbrook	.15	.40
21 Todd Collins	.40	1.00

1995 Pinnacle Team Pinnacle

Inserted one in every 90 hobby and one in every 49 retail packs, this 10 card set features the hottest NFC and AFC players back-to-back by position. Each card features one side printed with all-foil dufex. The cards have an orange/brown/yellow color with the player's team logo in the background. The "Team Pinnacle" logo, player's name and position is located on the bottom left of the card against a green and black marble background. Cards are numbered out of 10.

Card	Low	High
COMPLETE SET (10)	30.00	80.00
STATED ODDS 1:90 HOBBY, 1:49 RETAIL		
*DUFEX BACK: .4X TO 1X BASIC CARDS		
1 S.Young D.Bledsoe	4.00	10.00
2 E.Smith M.Faulk	5.00	12.00
3 B.Sanders N.Means	4.00	10.00
4 D.Marino T.Aikman	5.00	12.00
5 J.Rice T.Brown	4.00	10.00
6 E.Rhett B.Morris	2.00	5.00
7 B.Favre J.Elway	6.00	15.00
8 R.Salaam Ki.Carter	2.00	5.00
9 K.Collins S.McNair	3.00	8.00
10 J.Galloway M.Westbrook	2.00	5.00

1995 Pinnacle Dial Corporation

This 30-card standard-size set was sponsored by Dial and Purex and carries a Pinnacle '95 logo. It could be obtained by sending in UPC symbols from three Dial soap and Purex laundry products plus 2.50 to cover shipping and handling. The offer expired 1/31/96, or earlier if supplies became exhausted. The fronts feature full-bleed color action photos, with biography and statistical information on the backs. As part of a Dial Soap Super Bowl Contest, uncut sheets of the cards were issued as prizes. These sheets include 90-cards (3 complete sets) with one of the Bruce Smith cards autographed.

Card	Low	High
COMPLETE SET (30)	12.00	30.00
DC1 Troy Aikman	.80	2.00
DC2 Frank Reich	.08	.25
DC3 Drew Bledsoe	.80	2.00
DC4 Bubby Brister	.20	.50
DC5 Dave Brown	.08	.25
DC6 Randall Cunningham	.30	.75
DC7 John Elway	1.60	4.00
DC8 Boomer Esiason	.08	.25
DC9 Jim Everett	.08	.25
DC10 Bruce Smith	.20	.50
DC11 Brett Favre	1.60	4.00
DC12 Jim Harbaugh	.30	.75
DC13 Jeff Hostetler	.08	.25
DC14 Michael Irvin	.30	.75
DC15 Jim Kelly	.30	.75
DC16 David Klingler	.08	.25
DC17 Bernie Kosar	.08	.25
DC18 Dan Marino	1.60	4.00
DC19 Chris Miller	.08	.25
DC20 Rick Mirer	.20	.50
DC21 Warren Moon	.30	.75
DC22 Neil O'Donnell	.20	.50
DC23 Jerry Rice	.80	2.00
DC24 Mark Rypien	.08	.25
DC25 Barry Sanders	1.60	4.00
DC26 Junior Seau	.30	.75
DC27 Heath Shuler	.20	.50
DC28 Phil Simms	.08	.25
DC29 Emmitt Smith	1.20	3.00
DC30 Steve Young	.60	1.50
P1 Uncut Sheet Prize	15.00	40.00

1996 Pinnacle

The 1996 Pinnacle set was issued in one series totalling 200 cards with each base card printed with gold foil highlights. The 10-card packs retail for $2.49 each. The following subsets are included in the set: Rookies (153-182), Bid for 6 (183-194) and Checklists (195-199). A number of parallel sets were produced for this release with varying insertion ratios and packaging types.

Card	Low	High
COMPLETE SET (200)	8.00	20.00
1 Emmitt Smith	.60	1.50
2 Robert Brooks	.15	.40
3 Joey Galloway	.15	.40
4 Dan Marino	.75	2.00
5 Frank Sanders	.07	.20
6 Cris Carter	.15	.40
7 Jeff Blake	.15	.40
8 Steve McNair	.30	.75
9 Tamarick Vanover	.07	.20
10 Andre Reed	.07	.20
11 Junior Seau	.15	.40
12 Alvin Harper	.02	.10
13 Trent Dilfer	.15	.40
14 Kordell Stewart	.15	.40
15 Kyle Brady	.02	.10
16 Charles Haley	.07	.20
17 Greg Lloyd	.07	.20
18 Mario Bates	.07	.20
19 Shannon Sharpe	.07	.20
20 Scott Mitchell	.07	.20
21 Craig Heyward	.02	.10
22 Marcus Allen	.15	.40
23 Curtis Martin	.30	.75
24 Drew Bledsoe	.25	.60
25 Jerry Rice	.40	1.00
26 Charlie Garner	.07	.20
27 Michael Irvin	.15	.40
28 Curtis Conway	.15	.40
29 Terrell Davis	.30	.75
30 Jeff Hostetler	.02	.10
31 Neil O'Donnell	.07	.20
32 Errict Rhett	.07	.20
33 Stan Humphries	.07	.20
34 Jeff Graham	.02	.10
35 Floyd Turner	.02	.10
36 Vincent Brisby	.02	.10
37 Steve Young	.30	.75
38 Carl Pickens	.07	.20
39 Terance Mathis	.02	.10
40 Brett Favre	.75	2.00
41 Ki-Jana Carter	.07	.20
42 Jim Everett	.02	.10
43 Marshall Faulk	.20	.50
44 William Floyd	.07	.20
45 Deion Sanders	.25	.60
46 Garrison Hearst	.07	.20
47 Chris Sanders	.07	.20
48 Isaac Bruce	.15	.40
49 Natrone Means	.07	.20
50 Troy Aikman	.40	1.00
51 Ben Coates	.07	.20
52 Tony Martin	.07	.20
53 Rod Woodson	.07	.20
54 Edgar Bennett	.07	.20
55 Eric Zeier	.02	.10
56 Steve Bono	.02	.10
57 Tim Brown	.15	.40
58 Kevin Williams	.02	.10
59 Erik Kramer	.02	.10
60 Jim Kelly	.15	.40
61 Larry Centers	.07	.20
62 Terrell Fletcher	.02	.10
63 Michael Westbrook	.15	.40
64 Kerry Collins	.15	.40
65 Jay Novacek	.02	.10
66 J.J. Stokes	.15	.40
67 John Elway	.75	2.00
68 Jim Harbaugh	.07	.20
69 Aeneas Williams	.02	.10
70 Tyrone Wheatley	.07	.20
71 Chris Warren	.07	.20
72 Rodney Thomas	.02	.10
73 Jeff George	.07	.20
74 Rick Mirer	.07	.20
75 Yancey Thigpen	.07	.20
76 Herman Moore	.07	.20
77 Gus Frerotte	.07	.20
78 Anthony Miller	.07	.20
79 Ricky Watters	.07	.20
80 Sherman Williams	.02	.10
81 Hardy Nickerson	.02	.10
82 Henry Ellard	.02	.10
83 Aaron Craver	.02	.10
84 Rodney Peete	.02	.10
85 Eric Metcalf	.02	.10
86 Brian Blades	.02	.10
87 Rob Moore	.07	.20
88 Kimble Anders	.07	.20
89 Harvey Williams	.02	.10
90 Thurman Thomas	.15	.40
91 Dave Brown	.02	.10
92 Terry Allen	.07	.20
93 Ken Norton Jr.	.02	.10
94 Reggie White	.15	.40
95 Mark Chmura	.07	.20
96 Bert Emanuel	.07	.20
97 Brett Perriman	.02	.10
98 Antonio Freeman	.15	.40
99 Brian Mitchell	.02	.10
100 Orlando Thomas	.02	.10
101 Aaron Hayden	.02	.10
102 Quinn Early	.02	.10
103 Lovell Pinkney	.02	.10
104 Napoleon Kaufman	.15	.40
105 Daryl Johnston	.07	.20
106 Steve Tasker	.02	.10
107 Brent Jones	.02	.10
108 Mark Brunell	.25	.60
109 Leslie O'Neal	.02	.10
110 Irving Fryar	.07	.20
111 Jim Miller	.15	.40
112 Sean Dawkins	.02	.10
113 Boomer Esiason	.07	.20
114 Heath Shuler	.07	.20
115 Bruce Smith	.07	.20
116 Russell Maryland	.02	.10
117 Jake Reed	.07	.20
118 O.J. McDuffie	.07	.20
119 Erik Williams	.02	.10
120 Willie McGinest	.02	.10
121 Terry Kirby	.07	.20
122 Fred Barnett	.02	.10
123 Andre Hastings	.02	.10
124 Dale Hellestrae	.02	.10
125 Darren Woodson	.07	.20
126 Steve Atwater	.02	.10
127 Quentin Coryatt	.02	.10
128 Derrick Thomas	.15	.40
129 Nate Newton	.02	.10
130 Kevin Greene	.07	.20
131 Barry Sanders	.60	1.50
132 Warren Moon	.07	.20
133 Rashaan Salaam	.07	.20
134 Rodney Hampton	.07	.20
135 James O.Stewart	.07	.20
136 Erric Pegram	.02	.10
137 Bryan Cox	.02	.10
138 Adrian Murrell	.07	.20
139 Robert Smith	.07	.20
140 Bernie Parmalee	.02	.10
141 Bryce Paup	.02	.10
142 Darick Holmes	.02	.10
143 Hugh Douglas	.07	.20
144 Ken Dilger	.07	.20
145 Derek Loville	.02	.10
146 Horace Copeland	.02	.10
147 Wayne Chrebet	.25	.60
148 Andre Coleman	.02	.10
149 Greg Hill	.07	.20
150 Eric Swann	.02	.10
151 Tyrone Hughes	.02	.10
152 Ernie Mills	.02	.10
153 Terry Glenn RC	.50	1.25
154 Cedric Jones RC	.02	.10
155 Leeland McElroy RC	.07	.20
156 Bobby Engram RC	.15	.40
157 Willie Anderson RC	.02	.10
158 Mike Alstott RC	.50	1.25
159 Alex Van Dyke RC	.07	.20
160 Jeff Lewis RC	.07	.20
161 Keyshawn Johnson RC	.50	1.25
162 Regan Upshaw RC	.02	.10
163 Eric Moulds RC	.60	1.50
164 Tim Biakabutuka RC	.15	.40
165 Kevin Hardy RC	.15	.40
166 Marvin Harrison RC	1.25	3.00
167 Karim Abdul-Jabbar RC	.15	.40
168 Tony Brackens RC	.15	.40
169 Stepfret Williams RC	.07	.20
170 Eddie George RC	.60	1.50
171 Lawrence Phillips RC	.15	.40
172 Danny Kanell RC	.15	.40
173 Derrick Mayes RC	.15	.40
174 Daryl Gardener RC	.02	.10
175 Jonathan Ogden RC	.40	1.00
176 Alex Molden RC	.02	.10
177 Chris Darkins RC	.02	.10
178 Stephen Davis RC	.75	2.00
179 Rickey Dudley RC	.15	.40
180 Eddie Kennison RC	.15	.40
181 Simeon Rice RC	.40	1.00
182 Bobby Hoying RC	.15	.40
183 Troy Aikman BF6	.20	.50
184 Emmitt Smith BF6	.40	1.00
185 Michael Irvin BF6	.07	.20
186 Deion Sanders BF6	.15	.40
187 Daryl Johnston BF6	.07	.20
188 Jay Novacek BF6	.02	.10
189 Steve Young BF6	.15	.40
190 Jerry Rice BF6	.20	.50
191 J.J. Stokes BF6	.15	.40
192 Ken Norton BF6	.02	.10
193 William Floyd BF6	.07	.20
194 Brent Jones BF6	.02	.10
195 Dan Marino CL	.15	.40
196 Brett Favre CL	.15	.40
197 Emmitt Smith CL	.15	.40
198 Barry Sanders CL	.15	.40
199 ESmith Mar Fav BSand CL	.15	.40
200 Brett Favre PackBack	.75	2.00

1996 Pinnacle Artist's Proofs

*AP STARS: 5X TO 12X HI COLUMN
*AP RCs: 2.5X TO 6X HI
STATED ODDS 1:48 HOB, 1:12 PS, 1:67 JUM

1996 Pinnacle Foil

Card	Low	High
COMP.FOIL SET (200)	8.00	20.00
*FOILS. SAME PRICE AS BASIC CARDS		
RANDOM INSERTS IN RETAIL JUMBOS		

1996 Pinnacle Premium Stock Silver

Card	Low	High
COMPLETE SET (200)	12.50	30.00
*PREMIUM STOCK: .6X TO 1.5X		

1996 Pinnacle Trophy Collection

Card	Low	High
COMPLETE SET (200)	60.00	150.00
*TC STARS: 2.5X TO 6X		
*TC RCs: 1.2X TO 3X		
STATED ODDS 1:5		

1996 Pinnacle Black 'N Blue

Randomly inserted in magazine all-foil packs only at a rate of one in 33, this 25-card set features borderless color player photos on the top two-thirds of the all-foil fronts with a black-and-white player image at the bottom.

Card	Low	High
COMPLETE SET (25)	100.00	200.00
STATED ODDS 1:33 JUMBO		
1 Steve Young	5.00	12.00
2 Troy Aikman	6.00	15.00
3 Dan Marino	12.50	30.00
4 Michael Irvin	2.50	6.00
5 Jerry Rice	6.00	15.00
6 Emmitt Smith	10.00	25.00
7 Brett Favre	12.50	30.00
8 Drew Bledsoe	4.00	10.00
9 John Elway	12.50	30.00
10 Barry Sanders	10.00	25.00
11 Cris Carter	2.50	6.00
12 Jeff Blake	2.50	6.00
13 Chris Warren	1.25	3.00
14 Kerry Collins	2.50	6.00
15 Natrone Means	1.25	3.00
16 Herman Moore	1.25	3.00
17 Steve McNair	5.00	12.00
18 Ricky Watters	1.25	3.00
19 Tamarick Vanover	1.25	3.00
20 Deion Sanders	4.00	10.00
21 Terrell Davis	5.00	12.00
22 Rodney Thomas	.60	1.50
23 Rashaan Salaam	1.25	3.00
24 Darick Holmes	.60	1.50
25 Eric Zeier	.60	1.50

1996 Pinnacle Die Cut Jerseys

Randomly inserted in hobby packs only at a rate of one in 24, this 20-card set features action color player images printed on a die cut card of the player's game jersey as background. A parallel exclusive rainbow holographic foil version of this set was randomly inserted in Pinnacle Premium Stock packs at the rate of one in six.

Card	Low	High
COMPLETE SET (20)	75.00	150.00
STATED ODDS 1:24 HOBBY		
*HOLOFOILS: .6X TO 1.5X BASIC INSERTS		
HOLOFOIL STATED ODDS 1:6 PREM.STOCK		
1 Errict Rhett	1.00	2.50
2 Marshall Faulk	2.50	6.00
3 Isaac Bruce	2.00	5.00
4 William Floyd	1.00	2.50
5 Heath Shuler	1.00	2.50
6 Kerry Collins	2.00	5.00
7 Kordell Stewart	2.00	5.00
8 Rashaan Salaam	1.00	2.50
9 Terrell Davis	4.00	10.00
10 Rodney Thomas	.75	2.00
11 Curtis Martin	4.00	10.00
12 Steve McNair	4.00	10.00
13 J.J. Stokes	2.00	5.00
14 Joey Galloway	2.00	5.00
15 Michael Westbrook	2.00	5.00
16 Keyshawn Johnson	3.00	6.00
17 Lawrence Phillips	.75	2.00
18 Terry Glenn	3.00	6.00
19 Tim Biakabutuka	.75	2.00
20 Eddie George	4.00	8.00

1996 Pinnacle Double Disguise

Randomly inserted in packs at a rate of one in 18, this double-sided 20-card set features color photos of five players in different combinations with each other and an opaque peel-off wrapper covering both sides of the cards. Prices below are for peeled cards.

Card	Low	High
COMPLETE SET (20)	40.00	100.00
STATED ODDS 1:18 HOB, 1:5 PS, 1:25 JUM		
1 E.Smith E.Smith	3.00	8.00
2 E.Smith D.Marino	4.00	10.00
3 E.Smith B.Favre	4.00	10.00
4 E.Smith S.Young	3.00	8.00
5 D.Marino D.Marino	4.00	10.00
6 D.Marino E.Smith	4.00	10.00
7 D.Marino K.Collins	3.00	8.00
8 D.Marino S.Young	3.00	8.00
9 K.Collins K.Collins	2.50	6.00
10 K.Collins D.Marino	3.00	8.00
11 K.Collins B.Favre	3.00	8.00
12 K.Collins S.Young	2.50	6.00
13 B.Favre B.Favre	4.00	10.00
14 B.Favre K.Collins	3.00	8.00
15 B.Favre D.Marino	4.00	10.00
16 B.Favre E.Smith	4.00	10.00
17 S.Young S.Young	1.50	4.00
18 S.Young B.Favre	3.00	8.00
19 S.Young E.Smith	3.00	8.00
20 S.Young K.Collins	2.50	6.00

1996 Pinnacle On The Line

Randomly inserted in retail packs only at a rate of one in 23, this Dufex printed 15-card set features color player photos of top NFL receivers.

Card	Low	High
COMPLETE SET (15)	20.00	50.00
STATED ODDS 1:23 RETAIL		
1 Michael Irvin	3.00	8.00
2 Robert Brooks	3.00	8.00
3 Herman Moore	1.50	4.00
4 Cris Carter	3.00	8.00
5 Chris Sanders	1.50	4.00
6 Jerry Rice	8.00	20.00
7 Michael Westbrook	3.00	8.00
8 Carl Pickens	1.50	4.00
9 Bobby Engram	.60	1.50
10 Alex Van Dyke	.30	.75
11 Keyshawn Johnson	2.00	5.00
12 Terry Glenn	2.00	5.00
13 Eric Moulds	2.50	6.00
14 Marvin Harrison	5.00	12.00
15 Eddie Kennison	.60	1.50

1996 Pinnacle Team Pinnacle

Randomly inserted in packs at a rate of one in 90, this 10-card set features color player images of the best AFC player at each position with the top NFC position player on the flip side with each image set on a facsimile football background.

Card	Low	High
COMPLETE SET (10)	40.00	100.00
STATED ODDS 1:90 H/R,1:20 PREM.STOCK		
1 T.Aikman D.Bledsoe	5.00	12.00
2 S.Young J.Blake	4.00	10.00
3 B.Favre J.Elway	10.00	25.00
4 K.Collins D.Marino	6.00	15.00
5 E.Smith C.Martin	6.00	15.00
6 B.Sanders C.Warren	5.00	12.00
7 E.Rhett M.Faulk	4.00	10.00
8 J.Rice C.Pickens	5.00	12.00
9 M.Irvin J.Galloway	3.00	8.00
10 I.Bruce K.Stewart	3.00	8.00

1996 Pinnacle Bimbo Bread

These small (approximately 1 1/2" by 2 1/2") magic motion cards were distributed in Mexico through Bimbo Bakery snack products. The cardfronts feature a magic motion action photo of the player with the Bimbo logo. The backs are green with a player photo and player bio written in spanish.

Card	Low	High
COMPLETE SET (30)	60.00	120.00
1 Troy Aikman	4.00	10.00
2 Michael Irvin	2.00	5.00
3 Emmitt Smith	4.80	12.00
4 Jim Kelly	2.00	5.00
5 John Elway	6.00	15.00
6 Barry Sanders	6.00	15.00
7 Brett Favre	6.00	15.00
8 Jim Harbaugh	1.20	3.00
9 Dan Marino	6.00	15.00
10 Warren Moon	2.00	5.00
11 Drew Bledsoe	3.20	8.00
12 Jim Everett	.80	2.00
13 Jeff Hostetler	.80	2.00
14 Neil O'Donnell	.80	2.00
15 Junior Seau	1.20	3.00
16 Jerry Rice	4.00	10.00
17 Steve Young	3.20	8.00
18 Rick Mirer	1.20	3.00
19 Jeff Blake	1.20	3.00
20 David Klingler	.80	2.00
21 Boomer Esiason	1.20	3.00
22 Heath Shuler	.80	2.00
23 Dave Brown	.80	2.00
24 Bernie Kosar	.80	2.00
25 Kordell Stewart	2.40	6.00
26 Mark Brunell	3.20	8.00
27 Kerry Collins	2.00	5.00
28 Scott Mitchell	1.20	3.00
29 Erik Kramer	.80	2.00
30 Jeff George	1.20	3.00

1996 Pinnacle Super Bowl Card Show

This 15-card standard-size set features color action player photos on a metallic dufex background. The player's last name is printed in a metalic gold band with the Super Bowl XXX Card Show logo at the bottom. The horizontal backs carry the player's name, team, a career highlight, nickname, and sponsor logos on a dark blue marblized background. Pinnacle offered three-card packs to each Card Show attendee in exchange for two football card wrappers from 1995 Pinnacle football products. Although the cards carry a 1995 copyright date, the cards were released in January 1996 at the Tempe, Arizona Super Bowl Card Show.

Card	Low	High
COMPLETE SET (15)	6.00	15.00
1 Steve Young	.50	1.25
2 Dan Marino	1.20	3.00
3 Troy Aikman	.60	1.50
4 Drew Bledsoe	.50	1.25
5 John Elway	1.20	3.00
6 Brett Favre	1.20	3.00
7 Jim Harbaugh	.15	.40
8 Jeff Hostetler	.15	.40
9 Michael Irvin	.30	.75
10 Jim Kelly	.30	.75
11 Warren Moon	.30	.75
12 Jerry Rice	.60	1.50
13 Barry Sanders	1.20	3.00
14 Junior Seau	.30	.75
15 Emmitt Smith	1.00	2.50

1997 Pinnacle

The 1997 Pinnacle set was issued in one series totalling 200 cards and was distributed in 10-card packs with a suggested retail price of $2.99. The fronts feature borderless color action player photos. The backs carry player information.

Card	Low	High
COMPLETE SET (200)	7.50	20.00
1 Brett Favre	.75	2.00
2 Dan Marino	.75	2.00
3 Emmitt Smith	.60	1.50
4 Steve Young	.25	.60
5 Drew Bledsoe	.25	.60
6 Eddie George	.20	.50
7 Barry Sanders	.60	1.50
8 Jerry Rice	.40	1.00
9 John Elway	.75	2.00
10 Troy Aikman	.40	1.00
11 Kerry Collins	.20	.50
12 Rick Mirer	.07	.20
13 Jim Harbaugh	.10	.30
14 Elvis Grbac	.10	.30
15 Gus Frerotte	.07	.20
16 Neil O'Donnell	.10	.30
17 Jeff George	.10	.30
18 Kordell Stewart	.20	.50
19 Junior Seau	.20	.50
20 Vinny Testaverde	.10	.30
21 Terry Glenn	.20	.50
22 Anthony Johnson	.07	.20
23 Boomer Esiason	.10	.30
24 Terrell Owens	.25	.60
25 Natrone Means	.10	.30
26 Marcus Allen	.20	.50
27 James Jett	.10	.30
28 Chris T. Jones	.07	.20
29 Stan Humphries	.10	.30
30 Keith Byars	.07	.20
31 John Friesz	.07	.20
32 Mike Alstott	.20	.50
33 Eddie Kennison	.10	.30
34 Eric Moulds	.20	.50
35 Frank Sanders	.10	.30
36 Daryl Johnston	.10	.30
37 Cris Carter	.20	.50
38 Errict Rhett	.07	.20
39 Ben Coates	.10	.30
40 Shannon Sharpe	.10	.30
41 Jamal Anderson	.20	.50
42 Tim Biakabutuka	.10	.30
43 Jeff Blake	.10	.30
44 Michael Irvin	.20	.50
45 Terrell Davis	.25	.60
46 Byron Bam Morris	.07	.20
47 Rashaan Salaam	.07	.20
48 Adrian Murrell	.10	.30
49 Ty Detmer	.10	.30
50 Terry Allen	.20	.50
51 Mark Brunell	.25	.60
52 O.J. McDuffie	.10	.30
53 Willie McGinest	.07	.20
54 Chris Warren	.10	.30
55 Trent Dilfer	.20	.50
56 Jerome Bettis	.20	.50
57 Tamarick Vanover	.10	.30
58 Ki-Jana Carter	.07	.20
59 Ray Zellars	.07	.20
60 J.J. Stokes	.10	.30
61 Cornelius Bennett	.07	.20
62 Scott Mitchell	.10	.30
63 Tyrone Wheatley	.10	.30
64 Steve McNair	.25	.60
65 Tony Banks	.10	.30
66 James O.Stewart	.10	.30
67 Robert Smith	.10	.30
68 Thurman Thomas	.20	.50
69 Mark Chmura	.10	.30
70 Napoleon Kaufman	.20	.50
71 Ken Norton	.07	.20
72 Herschel Walker	.10	.30
73 Joey Galloway	.10	.30
74 Neil Smith	.10	.30
75 Simeon Rice	.10	.30
76 Michael Jackson	.10	.30
77 Muhsin Muhammad	.10	.30
78 Kevin Hardy	.07	.20
79 Irving Fryar	.10	.30
80 Eric Swann	.07	.20
81 Yancey Thigpen	.07	.20
82 Jim Everett	.07	.20
83 Karim Abdul-Jabbar	.20	.50
84 Garrison Hearst	.10	.30
85 Lawrence Phillips	.07	.20
86 Bryan Cox	.07	.20
87 Larry Centers	.10	.30
88 Wesley Walls	.10	.30
89 Curtis Conway	.10	.30
90 Darnay Scott	.10	.30
91 Anthony Miller	.07	.20
92 Edgar Bennett	.10	.30
93 Willie Green	.07	.20
94 Kent Graham	.07	.20
95 Dave Brown	.07	.20
96 Wayne Chrebet	.20	.50
97 Ricky Watters	.10	.30
98 Tony Martin	.10	.30
99 Warren Moon	.20	.50
100 Curtis Martin	.25	.60
101 Dorsey Levens	.20	.50
102 Jim Pyne	.07	.20
103 Antonio Freeman	.20	.50
104 Leeland McElroy	.07	.20
105 Isaac Bruce	.20	.50
106 Chris Sanders	.07	.20
107 Tim Brown	.20	.50
108 Greg Lloyd	.07	.20
109 Terrell Buckley	.07	.20
110 Deion Sanders	.20	.50
111 Carl Pickens	.10	.30
112 Bobby Engram	.10	.30
113 Andre Reed	.10	.30
114 Terance Mathis	.10	.30
115 Herman Moore	.10	.30
116 Robert Brooks	.10	.30
117 Ken Dilger	.07	.20
118 Keenan McCardell	.10	.30
119 Andre Hastings	.07	.20
120 Willie Davis	.07	.20
121 Bruce Smith	.10	.30
122 Rob Moore	.10	.30
123 Johnnie Morton	.10	.30
124 Sean Dawkins	.07	.20
125 Mario Bates	.07	.20
126 Henry Ellard	.07	.20
127 Derrick Alexander WR	.10	.30
128 Kevin Greene	.10	.30
129 Derrick Thomas	.20	.50
130 Rod Woodson	.10	.30
131 Rodney Hampton	.10	.30
132 Marshall Faulk	.25	.60
133 Michael Westbrook	.10	.30
134 Erik Kramer	.07	.20
135 Todd Collins	.07	.20
136 Bill Romanowski	.07	.20
137 Jake Reed	.10	.30
138 Heath Shuler	.07	.20
139 Keyshawn Johnson	.20	.50
140 Marvin Harrison	.20	.50
141 Andre Rison	.10	.30
142 Zach Thomas	.20	.50
143 Eric Metcalf	.10	.30
144 Amani Toomer	.10	.30
145 Desmond Howard	.10	.30
146 Jimmy Smith	.10	.30
147 Brad Johnson	.20	.50
148 Troy Vincent	.07	.20
149 Bryce Paup	.07	.20
150 Reggie White	.20	.50
151 Jake Plummer RC	.75	2.00
152 Darnell Autry RC	.10	.30
153 Tiki Barber RC	1.25	3.00
154 Pat Barnes RC	.20	.50
155 Orlando Pace RC	.20	.50
156 Peter Boulware RC	.20	.50
157 Shawn Springs RC	.10	.30
158 Troy Davis RC	.10	.30
159 Ike Hilliard RC	.30	.75
160 Jim Druckenmiller RC	.10	.30
161 Warrick Dunn RC	.50	1.50
162 James Farrior RC	.20	.50
163 Tony Gonzalez RC	.75	2.00
164 Darrell Russell RC	.07	.20
165 Byron Hanspard RC	.10	.30
166 Corey Dillon RC	.75	2.00
167 Kenny Holmes RC	.20	.50
168 Walter Jones RC	.30	.75
169 Danny Wuerffel RC	.20	.50
170 Tom Knight RC	.07	.20
171 David LaFleur RC	.07	.20
172 Kevin Lockett RC	.10	.30
173 Will Blackwell RC	.10	.30
174 Reidel Anthony RC	.20	.50
175 Dwayne Rudd RC	.20	.50
176 Yatil Green RC	.10	.30
177 Antowain Smith RC	.50	1.25
178 Rae Carruth RC	.07	.20
179 Bryant Westbrook RC	.07	.20
180 Reinard Wilson RC	.10	.30
181 Joey Kent RC	.20	.50
182 Renaldo Wynn RC	.07	.20
183 Brett Favre I	.40	1.00
184 Emmitt Smith I	.30	.75
185 Dan Marino I	.40	1.00
186 Troy Aikman I	.20	.50
187 Jerry Rice I	.20	.50
188 Drew Bledsoe I	.10	.30
189 Eddie George I	.20	.50
190 Terry Glenn I	.10	.30
191 John Elway I	.40	1.00
192 Steve Young I	.10	.30
193 Mark Brunell I	.20	.50
194 Barry Sanders I	.30	.75
195 Kerry Collins I	.10	.30
196 Curtis Martin I	.20	.50
197 Terrell Davis I	.20	.50
198 Bledsoe KCollins Marino CL	.20	.50
199 SYoung Brunell JGeorge CL	.07	.20
200 Aikman Elway Mirer CL	.07	.20

1997 Pinnacle Artist's Proofs

*AP STARS: 8X TO 20X BASIC CARDS
*AP RCs: 4X TO 10X BASIC CARDS
STATED ODDS 1:39 HOBBY

1997 Pinnacle Trophy Collection

Card	Low	High
COMPLETE SET (100)	125.00	250.00
*STARS: 3X TO 8X BASIC CARDS		
*RC'S: 1.5X TO 4X BASIC CARDS		
STATED ODDS 1:9 HOBBY		

1997 Pinnacle Power Pack Jumbos

This set of 24-cards was inserted one per special Power Pack Pinnacle retail packs in 1997. Each measures roughly 3 1/2" by 4 7/8" and is essentially a parallel to the player's base 1997 Pinnacle card with a unique card numbering of 24.

Card	Low	High
COMPLETE SET (24)	20.00	50.00
1 Brett Favre	2.00	5.00
2 Dan Marino	2.00	5.00
3 Emmitt Smith	1.60	4.00
4 Steve Young	.80	2.00
5 Drew Bledsoe	1.00	2.50
6 Eddie George	.80	2.00
7 Barry Sanders	2.00	5.00
8 Jerry Rice	1.00	2.50
9 John Elway	2.00	5.00
10 Troy Aikman	1.00	2.50
11 Kerry Collins	.30	.75
12 Jim Harbaugh	.30	.75
13 Elvis Grbac	.15	.40
14 Gus Frerotte	.15	.40
15 Terrell Davis	1.60	4.00
16 Jeff George	.30	.75
17 Kordell Stewart	.80	2.00
18 Terry Glenn	.40	1.00
19 Jeff Blake	.30	.75
20 Michael Irvin	.40	1.00
21 Tony Banks	.30	.75
22 Curtis Martin	.80	2.00
23 Deion Sanders	.60	1.50
24 Herman Moore	.30	.75

1997 Pinnacle Scoring Core

Randomly inserted in hobby packs only at the rate of one in 89, this 24-card set features color player images of the three-man offensive core of six different teams printed on a full micro-etched foil interlocking die cut card design. A 3-card Promo set featuring three Dallas Cowboys and a Mark Brunell preview card were released through hobby outlets and card shows throughout the year.

Card	Low	High
COMPLETE SET (24)	200.00	400.00
STATED ODDS 1:89 HOBBY		
1 Emmitt Smith	12.50	30.00
2 Troy Aikman	8.00	20.00
3 Michael Irvin	4.00	10.00
4 Robert Brooks	2.50	6.00
5 Brett Favre	12.00	30.00
6 Antonio Freeman	4.00	10.00
7 Curtis Martin	5.00	12.00
8 Drew Bledsoe	5.00	12.00
9 Terry Glenn	4.00	10.00
10 Tim Biakabutuka	2.50	6.00
11 Kerry Collins	4.00	10.00
12 Muhsin Muhammad	2.50	6.00
13 Karim Abdul-Jabbar	4.00	10.00
14 Dan Marino	15.00	40.00
15 O.J. McDuffie	2.50	6.00
16 Terrell Davis	5.00	12.00
17 John Elway	15.00	40.00
18 Shannon Sharpe	2.50	6.00
19 Garrison Hearst	2.50	6.00
20 Steve Young	5.00	12.00
21 Jerry Rice	8.00	20.00
22 Natrone Means	2.50	6.00
23 Mark Brunell	5.00	12.00
24 Keenan McCardell	2.50	6.00
P1 Emmitt Smith Promo	.75	2.00
P2 Troy Aikman Promo	.50	1.25
P3 Michael Irvin Promo	.20	.50
PV Mark Brunell Preview	.40	1.00

1997 Pinnacle Team Pinnacle

Randomly inserted in packs at the rate of one in 240, this 10-card set features color photos of the top AFC and NFC players by position printed on holographic double-fronted cards. Two versions of the base insert were printed with silver foil stock used on either the front side of the card or the back. Additionally, a Holographic Mirror version was also produced.

Card	Low	High
COMPLETE SET (10)	100.00	200.00
*FOIL BACK: .4X TO 1X FOIL FRONT		
STATED ODDS 1:240 HOBBY		
*HOLO.MIRROR: .8X TO 2X BASIC INSERTS		
HOLOGRAPHIC MIRROR RANDOM INSERTS IN PACKS		
1 D.Marino T.Aikman	12.50	30.00
2 D.Bledsoe B.Favre	12.50	30.00
3 M.Brunell K.Collins	4.00	10.00
4 J.Elway S.Young	12.50	30.00
5 T.Davis E.Smith	12.50	30.00
6 C.Martin B.Sanders	12.50	30.00
7 E.George T.Biakabutuka	4.00	10.00
8 K.Abdul-Jabbar L.Phillips	4.00	10.00
9 T.Glenn J.Rice	7.50	20.00
10 J.Galloway M.Irvin	4.00	10.00

1997 Pinnacle Tins

This set of tins was actually released as retail packaging for 1997 Score football cards. Each tin carried a random assortment of 150-Score cards. The featured player's photo is on the lid of the tin with the other five players around the sides of the can.

Card	Low	High
COMPLETE SET (6)	4.80	12.00
1 Troy Aikman	.60	1.50
2 Drew Bledsoe	.60	1.50
3 John Elway	1.20	3.00
4 Brett Favre	1.20	3.00
5 Dan Marino	1.20	3.00
6 Steve Young	.50	1.25

1997 Pinnacle Epix

Randomly inserted in packs at the rate of one in 19, this 24-card set features color action photos that highlight Games, Seasons and Moments related to the featured player. Each card was produced in progressively scarce color versions: orange (easiest), purple, and emerald (toughest).

Card	Low	High
COMP.ORANGE SET (24)	75.00	150.00
*PURPLE CARDS: .6X TO 1.5X ORANGE		
OVERALL STATED ODDS 1:19 HOBBY		
*EMERALD CARDS: 1.2X TO 3X ORANGE		
ONLY ORANGE CARDS PRICED BELOW		
E1 E.Smith GAME	5.00	12.00
E2 T.Aikman GAME	3.00	8.00
E3 T.Davis GAME	2.50	6.00
E4 D.Bledsoe GAME	2.00	5.00
E5 Jeff George GAME	1.00	2.50
E6 K.Collins GAME	1.00	2.50
E7 A.Freeman GAME	2.00	5.00
E8 Herman Moore GAME	1.00	2.50
E9 B.Sanders MOMENT	6.00	15.00
E10 B.Favre MOMENT	7.50	20.00
E11 Michael Irvin MOMENT	1.25	3.00
E12 S.Young MOMENT	4.00	10.00
E13 M.Brunell MOMENT	3.00	8.00
E14 J.Bettis MOMENT	1.25	3.00
E15 D.Sanders MOMENT	3.00	8.00
E16 Jeff Blake MOMENT	1.25	3.00
E17 D.Marino SEASON	6.00	15.00
E18 E.George SEASON	1.50	4.00
E19 J.Rice SEASON	4.00	10.00
E20 J.Elway SEASON	6.00	15.00
E21 C.Martin SEASON	3.00	8.00
E22 K.Stewart SEASON	1.50	4.00
E23 J.Seau SEASON	1.50	4.00
E24 R.White SEASON	1.50	4.00

1997 Pinnacle Magic Motion Puzzles

Pinnacle produced these large Magic Motion puzzles for traditional retailers in 1997. Each features a member of the Quarterback Club and was produced with 25-pieces mounted on a backer board. The overall size of each puzzle is 10 3/4" by 14." Any additions to the checklist below are appreciated.

Card	Low	High
1 Brett Favre	3.20	8.00
2 Steve Young	2.00	5.00

1997 Pinnacle Rembrandt

Pinnacle produced this set of nine-cards distributed by Rembrandt, Inc. with their line of Ultra-PRO plastic sheets. Each included a player photo with a bronze colored foil section to the right of the photo containing the Pinnacle and QB Club logos. One card was inserted into each box of sheets. There were also Silver and Gold parallel sets produced. As part of the promotion, collectors who assembled a complete Gold set could send the set to Rembrandt for $250 cash. A set of Silver cards could be redeemed for a gift box of Ultra-PRO products. A set of Bronze cards could be redeemed for a gold/silver/bronze set of one of the nine players. All sets sent in were returned with a cancelled stamp.

Card	Low	High
COMPLETE SET (9)	4.80	12.00
*GOLD CARDS: 5X TO 10X BASIC CARDS		
*SILVER CARDS: 2.5X TO 5X BASIC CARDS		
1 Brett Favre	.80	2.00
2 Troy Aikman	.40	1.00
3 John Elway	.80	2.00
4 Dan Marino	.80	2.00
5 Drew Bledsoe	.40	1.00
6 Emmitt Smith	.60	1.50
7 Jerry Rice	.40	1.00
8 Barry Sanders	.80	2.00
9 Mark Brunell	.40	1.00

1998 Pinnacle Fanfest Elway

This one card set, issued at the All-Star FanFest in Denver in 1998 honored long time Denver Bronco hero, John Elway. The front of the card features him in an Oneonta Yankee uniform while the back has a brief biography; a ghosted photo of Elway as a Bronco and his career minor league stats. The card was available for a small charity donation at the Pinnacle Booth.

Card	Low	High
NNO John Elway	8.00	20.00

1998 Pinnacle Jerry Rice Jumbo

This card was released at the 1998 Super Bowl Card Show. It was sponsored by Breathe Right nasal strips and produced by Pinnacle Brands. It measures roughly 3 1/2" by 5."

Card	Low	High
NNO Jerry Rice	1.50	4.00

1998 Pinnacle Team Pinnacle Collector's Club Promos

This four-card set originally to have been issued to members of the Pinnacle Collector's Club. Ultimately the cards were released after the company's bankruptcy. Each card reads "Team Pinnacle" at the bottom of the cardfront with the player's name above the image on the front.

Card	Low	High
COMPLETE SET (4)	15.00	30.00
1 John Elway	3.00	8.00

1998 Pinnacle Team Pinnacle Collector's Club

Card	Low	High
COMPLETE SET		
SEMISTARS		
UNLISTED STARS		
F1 Dan Marino	3.00	8.00
F2 Brett Favre	3.00	8.00
F3 Emmitt Smith	2.50	6.00
F4 Drew Bledsoe	1.00	2.50
F5 Eddie George	.75	2.00
F6 Barry Sanders	2.00	5.00
F7 Terrell Davis	1.25	3.00
F8 Mark Brunell	.75	2.00
F9 Jerry Rice	2.00	5.00
F10 Kordell Stewart	.75	2.00

2010-11 Pinnacle Fans of the Game
COMPLETE SET (3) 4.00 10.00
2 Sam Bradford 2.50 6.00

2010-11 Pinnacle Fans of the Game Autographs
2 Sam Bradford 40.00 80.00

1997 Pinnacle Certified Promos
COMPLETE SET (3) 1.50 4.00
1 Emmitt Smith .40 1.00
2 Dan Marino .75 2.00
4 Steve Young .30 .75

1997 Pinnacle Certified
The 1997 Pinnacle Certified set was issued in one series totalling 150 cards and distributed in three-card hobby packs with a suggested price of $5.99. The cards feature color player photos printed on premium 24-point, silver foil card stock with bronze foil stamping.
COMPLETE SET (150) 15.00 40.00
1 Emmitt Smith .60 1.50
2 Dan Marino 1.25 3.00
3 Brett Favre .75 2.00
4 Steve Young .50 1.25
5 Kerry Collins .25 .60
6 Troy Aikman .50 1.25
7 Drew Bledsoe .30 .75
8 Eddie George .30 .75
9 Jerry Rice .75 2.00
10 John Elway 1.25 3.00
11 Barry Sanders .60 1.50
12 Mark Brunell .30 .75
13 Elvis Grbac .30 .75
14 Tony Banks .30 .75
15 Vinny Testaverde .25 .60
16 Rick Mirer .25 .60
17 Carl Pickens .30 .75
18 Deion Sanders .30 .75
19 Terry Glenn .30 .75
20 Heath Shuler .25 .60
21 Dave Brown .25 .60
22 Keyshawn Johnson .30 .75
23 Jeff George .30 .75
24 Ricky Watters .30 .75
25 Kordell Stewart .25 .60
26 Junior Seau .30 .75
27 Terrell Owens .40 1.00
28 Warren Moon .40 1.00
29 Isaac Bruce .40 1.00
30 Steve McNair .40 1.00
31 Gus Frerotte .25 .60
32 Trent Dilfer .40 1.00
33 Shannon Sharpe .30 .75
34 Scott Mitchell .30 .75
35 Antonio Freeman .40 1.00
36 Jim Harbaugh .30 .75
37 Natrone Means .30 .75
38 Marcus Allen .40 1.00
39 Karim Abdul-Jabbar .25 .60
40 Tim Biakabutuka .30 .75
41 Jeff Blake .25 .60
42 Michael Irvin .40 1.00
43 Herschel Walker .40 1.00
44 Curtis Martin .40 1.00
45 Eddie Kennison .25 .60
46 Napoleon Kaufman .25 .60
47 Larry Centers .25 .60
48 Jamal Anderson .30 .75
49 Derrick Alexander WR .25 .60
50 Bruce Smith .30 .75
51 Wesley Walls .25 .60
52 Rod Smith WR .40 1.00
53 Keenan McCardell .30 .75
54 Robert Brooks .30 .75
55 Willie Green .25 .60
56 Jake Reed .30 .75
57 Joey Galloway .30 .75
58 Eric Metcalf .30 .75
59 Chris Sanders .25 .60
60 Jeff Hostetler .25 .60
61 Kevin Greene .40 1.00
62 Frank Sanders .25 .60
63 Dorsey Levens .30 .75
64 Sean Dawkins .25 .60
65 Cris Carter .40 1.00
66 Andre Hastings .25 .60
67 Amani Toomer .25 .60
68 Adrian Murrell .30 .75
69 Ty Detmer .25 .60
70 Yancey Thigpen .25 .60
71 Jim Everett .25 .60
72 Todd Collins .25 .60
73 Curtis Conway .30 .75
74 Herman Moore .30 .75
75 Neil O'Donnell .30 .75
76 Rod Woodson .40 1.00
77 Tony Martin .30 .75
78 Kent Graham .25 .60
79 Andre Reed .40 1.00
80 Reggie White .40 1.00
81 Thurman Thomas .30 .75
82 Garrison Hearst .25 .60
83 Chris Warren .25 .60
84 Wayne Chrebet .25 .60
85 Chris T. Jones .25 .60
86 Anthony Miller .25 .60
87 Chris Chandler .30 .75
88 Terrell Davis .30 .75
89 Mike Alstott .30 .75
90 Terry Allen .30 .75
91 Jerome Bettis .40 1.00
92 Stan Humphries .30 .75
93 Andre Rison .30 .75
94 Marshall Faulk .30 .75
95 Erik Kramer .25 .60
96 O.J. McDuffie .30 .75
97 Robert Smith .25 .60
98 Keith Byars .25 .60
99 Rodney Hampton .30 .75
100 Desmond Howard .30 .75
101 Lawrence Phillips .25 .60
102 Michael Westbrook .30 .75
103 Johnnie Morton .30 .75
104 Ben Coates .30 .75
105 J.J. Stokes .25 .60
106 Terance Mathis .25 .60
107 Errict Rhett .25 .60
108 Tim Brown .40 1.00
109 Marvin Harrison .30 .75
110 Muhsin Muhammad .30 .75
111 Byron Bam Morris .25 .60
112 Mario Bates .25 .60
113 Jimmy Smith .30 .75
114 Irving Fryar .30 .75
115 Tamarick Vanover .30 .75
116 Brad Johnson .30 .75
117 Rashaan Salaam .25 .60
118 Ki-Jana Carter .25 .60
119 Tyrone Wheatley .30 .75
120 John Friesz .25 .60
121 Orlando Pace RC .50 1.25
122 Jim Druckenmiller RC .30 .75
123 Byron Hanspard RC .30 .75
124 David LaFleur RC .25 .60
125 Reidel Anthony RC .30 .75
126 Antowain Smith RC .50 1.25
127 Bryant Westbrook RC .25 .60
128 Fred Lane RC .30 .75
129 Tiki Barber RC 1.25 3.00
130 Shawn Springs RC .30 .75
131 Ike Hilliard RC .40 1.00
132 James Farrior RC .40 1.00
133 Darrell Russell RC .25 .60
134 Walter Jones RC .40 1.00
135 Tom Knight RC .25 .60
136 Yatil Green RC .25 .60
137 Joey Kent RC .25 .60
138 Kevin Lockett RC .30 .75
139 Troy Davis RC .25 .60
140 Darnell Autry RC .25 .60
141 Pat Barnes RC .25 .60
142 Rae Carruth RC .25 .60
143 Will Blackwell RC .25 .60
144 Warrick Dunn RC .75 2.00
145 Corey Dillon RC .60 1.50
146 Dwayne Rudd RC .30 .75
147 Reinard Wilson RC .25 .60
148 Peter Boulware RC .25 .60
149 Tony Gonzalez RC 1.00 2.50
150 Danny Wuerffel RC .40 1.00

1997 Pinnacle Certified Mirror Blue
*MIRROR BLUE: 5X TO 12X BASIC CARDS
STATED ODDS 1:199

1997 Pinnacle Certified Mirror Gold
*MIRROR GOLD: 10X TO 25X BASIC CARDS
STATED ODDS 1:299

1997 Pinnacle Certified Mirror Red
COMPLETE SET (150) 400.00 800.00
*MIRROR RED: 4X TO 10X BASIC CARDS
STATED ODDS 1:99

1997 Pinnacle Certified Red
COMPLETE SET (150) 75.00 150.00
*CERT.RED: 1.5X TO 4X BASIC CARDS
STATED ODDS 1:5

1997 Pinnacle Certified Certified Team
Randomly inserted in packs at the rate of one in 19, this 20-card set features action photos of top stars printed on silver-frosted mirror mylar cards.
COMPLETE SET (20) 25.00 60.00
SILVER STATED ODDS 1:19
*GOLDS: 1.5X TO 4X BASIC INSERTS
GOLD STATED ODDS 1:119
*MIRROR GOLDS: 12X TO 30X BASIC INSERTS
MIRROR GOLD STATED PRINT RUN 25 SETS
1 Brett Favre 2.50 6.00
2 Dan Marino 4.00 10.00
3 Emmitt Smith 3.00 8.00
4 Eddie George 1.00 2.50
5 Jerry Rice 2.00 5.00
6 Troy Aikman 2.00 5.00
7 Barry Sanders 3.00 8.00
8 Terrell Davis 1.25 3.00
9 Drew Bledsoe 1.25 3.00
10 Curtis Martin 1.25 3.00
11 Terry Glenn 1.00 2.50
12 Kerry Collins 1.00 2.50
13 John Elway 4.00 10.00
14 Kordell Stewart 1.00 2.50
15 Karim Abdul-Jabbar .60 1.50
16 Steve Young 1.25 3.00
17 Steve McNair 1.25 3.00
18 Terrell Owens 1.25 3.00
19 Keyshawn Johnson 1.00 2.50
20 Mark Brunell 1.25 3.00

1997 Pinnacle Certified Epix
Randomly inserted in packs at the rate of one in 19, this 24-card set features action player photos that highlight the player's career Games, Seasons or Moments with each category produced in different print runs. Games were the easiest to pull overall and Moments the most difficult. Additionally, each card was produced in progressively scarce color versions: Orange (easiest), Purple, and Emerald (toughest).
COMP.ORANGE SET (24) 150.00 300.00
*PURPLE CARDS: .6X TO 1.5X ORANGE
OVERALL STATED ODDS 1:15
*EMERALD CARDS: 1.2X TO 3X ORANGE
ONLY ORANGE CARDS PRICED BELOW
E1 E.Smith MOMENT 15.00 30.00
E2 T.Aikman MOMENT 7.50 20.00
E3 T.Davis MOMENT 5.00 12.00
E4 D.Bledsoe MOMENT 5.00 12.00
E5 Jeff George MOMENT 2.50 6.00
E6 K.Collins MOMENT 2.50 6.00
E7 A.Freeman MOMENT 5.00 10.00
E8 Herman Moore MOMENT 2.50 6.00
E9 B.Sanders SEASON 7.50 20.00
E10 B.Favre SEASON 10.00 25.00
E11 Michael Irvin SEASON 2.00 5.00
E12 S.Young SEASON 5.00 12.00
E13 M.Brunell SEASON 4.00 10.00
E14 Jerome Bettis SEASON 2.00 5.00
E15 D.Sanders SEASON 4.00 10.00
E16 Jeff Blake SEASON 2.00 5.00
E17 D.Marino GAME 7.50 20.00
E18 E.George GAME 1.50 4.00
E19 J.Rice GAME 5.00 12.00
E20 J.Elway GAME 7.50 20.00
E21 C.Martin GAME 3.00 8.00
E22 K.Stewart GAME 1.50 4.00
E23 Junior Seau GAME 1.50 4.00
E24 Reggie White GAME 1.50 4.00

1995 Pinnacle Club Collection
This debut set contains 261-cards with members of the NFL Quarterback Club having nine cards each. Basic card fronts feature an all bleed photograph with the "Quarterback Club" logo and the player's name listed at the bottom against a gold foil background. Card backs are horizontal with the player's statistical information in yellow at the top and a statistical summary in yellow at the bottom. The cards are numbered against a blue marble background in the upper left corner of the card. The packs also included 20 Pin Redemption cards that were randomly inserted at a rate of one in 24. Collectors could receive a collectible pin of the Quarterback Club member pictured on the card by exchanging it with $1.95 before February 28, 1996. A John Elway signed card (75 autographed) was released as part of the prize list for Arms Race contest winners. The card is virtually identical to card #68 of the base set except for the gold foil being printed with a holographic foil pattern.
COMPLETE SET (261) 5.00 12.00
COMMON STEVE YOUNG .07 .20
COMMON DAN MARINO .20 .50
COMMON TROY AIKMAN .08 .25
COMMON DREW BLEDSOE .08 .25
COMMON BUDDY BRISTER .01 .05
COMMON DAVE BROWN .01 .05
COMMON RA.CUNNINGHAM .05 .15
COMMON JOHN ELWAY .20 .50
COMMON BOOMER ESIASON .02 .10
COMMON JIM EVERETT .01 .05
COMMON BRETT FAVRE .20 .50
COMMON JIM HARBAUGH .01 .05
COMMON JEFF HOSTETLER .01 .05
COMMON MICHAEL IRVIN .05 .15
COMMON JIM KELLY .05 .15
COMMON DAVID KLINGLER .01 .05
COMMON BERNIE KOSAR .01 .05
COMMON CHRIS MILLER .01 .05
COMMON RICK MIRER .01 .05
COMMON WARREN MOON .02 .10
COMMON NEIL O'DONNELL .01 .05
COMMON JERRY RICE .08 .25
COMMON MARK RYPIEN .01 .05
COMMON BARRY SANDERS .15 .40
COMMON JUNIOR SEAU .05 .15
COMMON EMMITT SMITH .10 .30
COMMON PHIL SIMMS .02 .10
COMMON HEATH SHULER .01 .05
COMMON FRANK REICH .01 .05
AU68 John Elway AUTO/75 100.00 175.00

1995 Pinnacle Club Collection Spotlight
This five card set was randomly inserted at a rate of one in 90 packs and is a set focused on the five Quarterback Club superstars who are not quarterbacks. Card fronts feature an all-foil dufex silver background.
COMPLETE SET (5) 10.00 25.00
STATED ODDS 1:90
1 Emmitt Smith 3.00 8.00
2 Barry Sanders 4.00 10.00
3 Jerry Rice 2.50 6.00
4 Michael Irvin 1.50 4.00
5 Junior Seau 1.50 4.00

1995 Pinnacle Club Collection Aerial Assault
Inserted one in every 36 packs, this 18 card set features members of the Quarterback Club against a silver all-foil dufex "X-ed" background. Cards are numbered with an "AA" prefix.
COMPLETE SET (18) 20.00 50.00
STATED ODDS 1:36
AA1 Troy Aikman 2.50 6.00
AA2 Dave Brown .50 1.25
AA3 Drew Bledsoe 2.50 6.00
AA4 Randall Cunningham 1.50 4.00
AA5 Jim Everett .50 1.25
AA6 Jeff Hostetler .50 1.25
AA7 David Klingler .50 1.25
AA8 Dan Marino 5.00 12.00
AA9 Rick Mirer .50 1.25
AA10 Neil O'Donnell .50 1.25
AA11 Brett Favre 5.00 12.00
AA12 Boomer Esiason 1.00 2.50
AA13 Jim Harbaugh .50 1.25
AA14 John Elway 5.00 12.00
AA15 Steve Young 2.00 5.00
AA16 Warren Moon 1.00 2.50
AA17 Jim Kelly 1.50 4.00
AA18 Heath Shuler .50 1.25

1995 Pinnacle Club Collection Arms Race
This 18 card interactive set was randomly inserted into packs at a rate of one in 18. Card backs feature a head shot against a bullseye background with basic information about the interactive element at the bottom. Basic information about the game: each quarterback would accumulate points for touchdown passes, victories, leading the AFC or NFC in any of six statistical categories, and Playoff, Conference Championship and Super Bowl appearances. Consumers that collected the card of the highest point total player could exchange that card for a chance to win a trip to the Foot Action NFL Quarterback Challenge and signed memorabilia. There was only one grand prize of the trip, 50 first prizes of official NFL footballs bearing the signatures of all the members of the Quarterback Club and 75 second prizes of John Elway signed cards.
COMPLETE SET (18) 8.00 20.00
STATED ODDS 1:18
1 Steve Young 1.00 2.50
2 Troy Aikman 1.25 3.00
3 John Elway 2.50 6.00
4 Dan Marino 2.50 6.00
5 Brett Favre WIN 2.50 6.00
6 Heath Shuler .25 .60
7 Jim Kelly .75 2.00
8 Randall Cunningham .75 2.00
9 Dave Brown .25 .60
10 Jim Everett .25 .60
11 Drew Bledsoe 1.25 3.00
12 Rick Mirer .25 .60
13 Jeff Hostetler .25 .60
14 Neil O'Donnell .25 .60
15 Warren Moon .50 1.25
16 Boomer Esiason .50 1.25
17 Chris Miller .25 .60
18 David Klingler .25 .60

1995 Pinnacle Club Collection Pin Redemption
These cards were issued in packs and could be exchanged for a metal pin featuring the player. The exchange card itself has an image of the player as well as the pin. The exchange expiration date was 2/28/1996.
1 Troy Aikman 1.50 4.00
2 Dave Brown .75 2.00
3 Brett Favre 4.00 10.00
4 Jeff Hostetler .75 2.00
5 Michael Irvin 1.25 3.00
6 Chris Miller .75 2.00
7 Heath Shuler .75 2.00
8 Emmitt Smith 2.50 6.00
9 Steve Young 1.50 4.00

1995 Pinnacle Club Collection Promos
Issued in a cello pack, this 4-card standard-size set promoted the 1995 Pinnacle Club Collection series. The set features two regular issue cards, one "Arms Race" card, and an ad card. The backs of the player cards are clearly marked by the word "Promo" in white block lettering.
COMPLETE SET (4) 4.00 10.00
1 Steve Young .80 2.00
11 Dan Marino 2.00 5.00
AR11 Drew Bledsoe 1.20 3.00
NNO Pinnacle Ad Card .20 .50

1997 Pinnacle Inscriptions Promos
2 Steve Young .50 1.25
13 Dan Marino 1.50 4.00
20 Barry Sanders 1.25 3.00

1997 Pinnacle Inscriptions
This 50-card standard-size set was issued by Pinnacle. The cards feature a metallic player photo against a solid background. The players name and position is located on the bottom left of the front. The backs feature a player photo along with some brief information and a smattering of statistics.
COMPLETE SET (50) 7.50 20.00
1 Mark Brunell .50 1.25
2 Steve Young .50 1.25
3 Rick Mirer .15 .40
4 Brett Favre 1.50 4.00
5 Tony Banks .25 .60
6 Elvis Grbac .25 .60
7 John Elway 1.50 4.00
8 Troy Aikman .75 2.00
9 Neil O'Donnell .25 .60
10 Kordell Stewart .40 1.00
11 Drew Bledsoe .50 1.25
12 Kerry Collins .40 1.00
13 Dan Marino 1.50 4.00
14 Jeff George .25 .60
15 Scott Mitchell .25 .60
16 Jim Harbaugh .25 .60
17 Dave Brown .15 .40
18 Jeff Blake .25 .60
19 Trent Dilfer .40 1.00
20 Barry Sanders 1.25 3.00
21 Jerry Rice .75 2.00
22 Emmitt Smith 1.25 3.00
23 Vinny Testaverde .25 .60
24 Warren Moon .40 1.00
25 Junior Seau .40 1.00
26 Gus Frerotte .15 .40
27 Heath Shuler .15 .40
28 Erik Kramer .15 .40
29 Boomer Esiason .25 .60
30 Jim Kelly .40 1.00
31 Mark Brunell TNL .40 1.00
32 Steve Young TNL .40 1.00
33 Brett Favre TNL 1.00 2.50
34 Tony Banks TNL .25 .60
35 John Elway TNL 1.00 2.50
36 Troy Aikman TNL .50 1.25
37 Kordell Stewart TNL .40 1.00
38 Drew Bledsoe TNL .40 1.00
39 Kerry Collins TNL .25 .60
40 Dan Marino TNL 1.00 2.50
41 Jim Harbaugh TNL .25 .60
42 Jeff Blake TNL .25 .60
43 Barry Sanders TNL .75 2.00
44 Jerry Rice TNL .50 1.25
45 Emmitt Smith TNL .75 2.00
46 Rick Mirer TNL .15 .40
47 Jeff George TNL .15 .40
48 Neil O'Donnell TNL .25 .60
49 Elvis Grbac TNL .25 .60
50 Scott Mitchell TNL .15 .40

1997 Pinnacle Inscriptions Artist's Proofs
COMPLETE SET (50) 100.00 200.00
*AP STARS: 4X TO 10X BASIC CARDS
ARTIST PROOF STATED ODDS 1:35

1997 Pinnacle Inscriptions Challenge Collection
COMPLETE SET (50) 40.00 80.00
*CHALL.COLL.STARS: 2X TO 4X HI
STATED ODDS 1:7

1997 Pinnacle Inscriptions Autographs
This set features autographed cards of players in the Pinnacle Inscriptions set. Each player signed a certain amount of cards and that number is featured immediately after the players name. The odds of finding an autograph card was reported by the manufacturer to be one every 23 packs across the entire Inscriptions print run. On many cards there are blue ink and black ink variations, although the signing numbers are not known. A Barry Sanders card appeared on the secondary market later, but was never included in packs.
STATED ODDS 1:23
1 Tony Banks/1925 6.00 15.00
2 Jeff Blake/1470 6.00 15.00
3 Drew Bledsoe/1970 6.00 15.00
4 Dave Brown/1970 5.00 12.00
5 Mark Brunell/2000 8.00 20.00
6 Kerry Collins/1300 8.00 20.00
7 Trent Dilfer/1950 8.00 20.00
8 John Elway/1975 40.00 75.00
9 Jim Everett/2000 6.00 15.00
10 Brett Favre/215 125.00 250.00
11 Gus Frerotte/1975 8.00 20.00
12 Jeff George/1935 8.00 20.00
13 Elvis Grbac/1985 6.00 15.00
14 Jim Harbaugh/1975 12.00 30.00
15 Jeff Hostetler/2000 6.00 15.00
16 Jim Kelly/1925 12.50 30.00
17 Bernie Kosar/1975 8.00 20.00
18 Erik Kramer/2000 5.00 12.00
19 Dan Marino/440 50.00 100.00
20 Rick Mirer/2000 6.00 15.00
21 Scott Mitchell/1995 6.00 15.00
22 Warren Moon/1975 8.00 20.00
23 Neil O'Donnell/1990 6.00 15.00
24 Jerry Rice/950 30.00 80.00
25 Barry Sanders/2053 40.00 75.00
26 Junior Seau/1900 20.00 50.00
27 Heath Shuler/1865 6.00 15.00
28 Emmitt Smith/220 100.00 200.00
29 Kordell Stewart/1495 8.00 20.00
30 Vinny Testaverde/1975 8.00 20.00
31 Steve Young/1900 12.00 30.00

1997 Pinnacle Inscriptions V2
This eighteen card insert set was issued one every 11 Inscription packs. The horizontal cards feature two photos of each player. One is a standard color photo while the other "photo" is actually a picture, produced with lenticular technology, which moves and gives two different images of the player. The player is identified on the top and the words "V2" and the team name are on the bottom. The backs feature seasonal and career stats as well as some text about the players accomplishments. Each card is issued with a "peelable" front.
COMPLETE SET (18) 25.00 60.00
STATED ODDS 1:11
V1 Mark Brunell 1.25 3.00
V2 Steve Young 1.25 3.00
V3 Brett Favre 4.00 10.00
V4 Tony Banks .60 1.50
V5 John Elway 4.00 10.00
V6 Troy Aikman 2.00 5.00
V7 Kordell Stewart 1.00 2.50
V8 Drew Bledsoe 1.25 3.00
V9 Kerry Collins 1.00 2.50
V10 Dan Marino 4.00 10.00
V11 Barry Sanders 3.00 8.00
V12 Jerry Rice 2.00 5.00
V13 Emmitt Smith 3.00 8.00
V14 Neil O'Donnell .60 1.50
V15 Scott Mitchell .60 1.50
V16 Jim Harbaugh .60 1.50
V17 Jeff Blake .60 1.50
V18 Trent Dilfer 1.00 2.50

1998 Pinnacle Inscriptions Promos
Pinnacle created several promo cards in 1998 for sets that were never officially released. We've listed all known cards below for the Inscriptions product. Any additions to the list below are appreciated.
33 John Elway 4.00 10.00
36 Steve Young 1.50 4.00
71 Barry Sanders 3.00 8.00

1998 Pinnacle Inscriptions Pen Pals
This set was originally scheduled to be released with the 1998 Pinnacle Inscriptions product. Due to the bankruptcy of Pinnacle Brands, the product was never released. However, these cards made their way onto the secondary market. Each card was signed by one, both or even none of the featured players and was printed on silver and gold foil stock. We've designed with an "AU" after the player's name each one that originally signed the card. The cards were also hand serial numbered of 50-cards each. Also please note that some of the signed and unsigned cards the serial number area on the card back is blank.
COMPLETE SET (11) 750.00 1500.00
1 T.Aikman AU/K.Collins AU 75.00 125.00
2 Aikman AU 30.00 80.00
Irvin
Smith
3 D.Bledsoe AU/K.Stewart AU 50.00 100.00
4 J.Elway AU 75.00 150.00
T.Davis
5 J.Elway AU/B.Favre AU 250.00 400.00
6 J.Elway AU/D.Marino AU 250.00 400.00
7 Favre AU/B.Sanders No AU 75.00 150.00
8A R.Leaf AU/P.Manning AU 100.00 200.00
8B R.Leaf 2.00 5.00
P.Manning No Auto
9 S.Mitchell AU 12.50 30.00
B.Sanders
10 J.Rice AU/S.Young AU 150.00 250.00
11 B.Sanders 4.00 10.00
E.Smith

1997 Pinnacle Inside
The 1997 Pinnacle Inside set was issued in one series totalling 150-cards and was distributed in 10-card packs inside 28 different collectible player cans. The cardfronts feature color player photos with a thin team colored player photo as the left border. The backs carry a small player head photo with a black-and-white player photo and player information.
COMPLETE SET (150) 7.50 20.00
1 Troy Aikman .40 1.00
2 Dan Marino .75 2.00
3 Barry Sanders .60 1.50
4 Drew Bledsoe .25 .60
5 Kerry Collins .20 .50
6 Emmitt Smith .60 1.50
7 Brett Favre .75 2.00
8 John Elway .75 2.00
9 Jerry Rice .40 1.00
10 Mark Brunell .25 .60
11 Elvis Grbac .10 .30
12 Junior Seau .20 .50
13 Eddie George .20 .50
14 Steve Young .25 .60
15 Terrell Davis .25 .60
16 Thurman Thomas .20 .50
17 Deion Sanders .20 .50
18 Terrell Owens .25 .60
19 Neil O'Donnell .10 .30
20 Carl Pickens .10 .30
21 Marcus Allen .20 .50
22 Ricky Watters .10 .30
23 Vinny Testaverde .10 .30
24 Kordell Stewart .20 .50
25 Tony Banks .20 .50
26 Terry Glenn .20 .50
27 Todd Collins .07 .20
28 Robert Brooks .10 .30
29 Heath Shuler .07 .20
30 Shannon Sharpe .10 .30
31 Michael Westbrook .10 .30
32 Reggie White .20 .50
33 Brad Johnson .20 .50
34 Tamarick Vanover .10 .30
35 Larry Centers .10 .30
36 Terance Mathis .10 .30
37 Hardy Nickerson .07 .20
38 Jamal Anderson .20 .50
39 Kevin Hardy .07 .20
40 Stan Humphries .10 .30
41 Chris Warren .10 .30
42 Tim Brown .20 .50
43 Joey Galloway .10 .30
44 Boomer Esiason .10 .30
45 Jake Reed .10 .30
46 Kent Graham .07 .20
47 Marshall Faulk .25 .60
48 Sean Dawkins .07 .20
49 Dave Brown .07 .20
50 Willie Green .07 .20
51 Andre Hastings .07 .20
52 Erik Kramer .07 .20
53 Michael Irvin .20 .50
54 Gus Frerotte .07 .20
55 Winslow Oliver .07 .20
56 Jimmy Smith .10 .30
57 Derrick Alexander WR .10 .30
58 Adrian Murrell .10 .30
59 Ki-Jana Carter .07 .20
60 Garrison Hearst .10 .30
61 Chris Sanders .07 .20
62 Johnnie Morton .10 .30
63 Lawrence Phillips .07 .20
64 Bobby Engram .10 .30
65 Tim Biakabutuka .10 .30
66 Anthony Johnson .07 .20
67 Keyshawn Johnson .20 .50
68 Jeff George .10 .30
69 Errict Rhett .07 .20
70 Cris Carter .20 .50
71 Chris T. Jones .07 .20
72 Eric Moulds .20 .50
73 Rick Mirer .07 .20
74 Keenan McCardell .10 .30
75 Simeon Rice .10 .30
76 Eddie Kennison .10 .30
77 Herman Moore .10 .30
78 Jim Harbaugh .10 .30
79 Robert Smith .10 .30
80 Bruce Smith .10 .30
81 John Friesz .07 .20
82 Irving Fryar .10 .30
83 Edgar Bennett .10 .30
84 Ty Detmer .10 .30
85 Curtis Conway .10 .30
86 Napoleon Kaufman .20 .50
87 Tony Martin .10 .30
88 Amani Toomer .10 .30
89 Willie McGinest .07 .20
90 Daryl Johnston .10 .30
91 Stanley Pritchett .07 .20
92 Chris Chandler .10 .30
93 Natrone Means .10 .30
94 Kimble Anders .10 .30
95 Steve McNair .25 .60
96 Curtis Martin .25 .60
97 O.J. McDuffie .10 .30
98 Ben Coates .10 .30
99 Jerome Bettis .20 .50
100 Andre Reed .10 .30
101 Jeff Blake .10 .30
102 Wesley Walls .10 .30
103 Warren Moon .20 .50
104 Isaac Bruce .20 .50
105 Terry Allen .20 .50
106 Rodney Hampton .10 .30
107 Karim Abdul-Jabbar .20 .50
108 Marvin Harrison .20 .50
109 Dorsey Levens .20 .50
110 Rashaan Salaam .07 .20
111 Scott Mitchell .10 .30
112 Darnay Scott .10 .30
113 Aeneas Williams .07 .20
114 Trent Dilfer .20 .50
115 Antonio Freeman .20 .50
116 Jim Everett .07 .20
117 Muhsin Muhammad .10 .30
118 Rickey Dudley .10 .30
119 Mike Alstott .20 .50
120 Jim Druckenmiller RC .10 .30
121 Tiki Barber RC 1.25 3.00
122 Ike Hilliard RC .30 .75
123 Orlando Pace RC .20 .50
124 Jake Plummer RC .75 2.00
125 Yatil Green RC .10 .30
126 Byron Hanspard RC .10 .30
127 James Farrior RC .20 .50
128 Corey Dillon RC .75 2.00
129 Pat Barnes RC .20 .50
130 Kenny Holmes RC .20 .50
131 Rae Carruth RC .07 .20
132 Danny Wuerffel RC .20 .50
133 Darnell Autry RC .10 .30
134 Reidel Anthony RC .20 .50
135 Darrell Russell RC .07 .20
136 Will Blackwell RC .10 .30
137 Peter Boulware RC .20 .50
138 Shawn Springs RC .10 .30
139 Joey Kent RC .20 .50
140 Troy Davis RC .10 .30
141 Antowain Smith RC .50 1.25
142 Walter Jones RC .30 .75
143 Tony Gonzalez RC .75 2.00
144 David LaFleur RC .07 .20
145 Warrick Dunn RC .60 1.50
146 Bryant Westbrook RC .07 .20
147 Dwayne Rudd RC .20 .50
148 Tom Knight RC .07 .20
149 Kevin Lockett RC .10 .30
150 Checklist .07 .20
P1 Troy Aikman Promo .40 1.00
P2 Dan Marino Promo .75 2.00
P7 Brett Favre Promo .75 2.00

1997 Pinnacle Inside Gridiron Gold
COMPLETE SET (150) 500.00 1000.00
*STARS: 15X TO 40X HI COLUMN
*RCs: 6X TO 15X HI
STATED ODDS 1:63 HOB/RET

1997 Pinnacle Inside Silver Lining
COMPLETE SET (150) 125.00 250.00
*STARS: 5X TO 12X HI COLUMN
*RCs: 2X TO 5X HI COLUMN
STATED ODDS 1:7 HOB/RET

1997 Pinnacle Inside Autographs
Randomly inserted in cans at the rate of one in 251, this set features color photos of members of the Quarterback Club with their genuine autographs displayed on the card. The unnumbered backs carry another player photo and player information. Several of the cards were only available via a mail-in redemptions that were inserted into packs. The redemption card was to be exchanged for a random signed card. The offer expired March 31, 1998. Barry Sanders and Jerry Rice signed cards surfaced on the secondary market long after the promotion was over.
STATED ODDS 1:251 HOB/RET
1 Tony Banks 10.00 25.00
2 Jeff Blake 10.00 25.00
3 Drew Bledsoe 20.00 40.00
4 Dave Brown 7.50 20.00
5 Mark Brunell 15.00 40.00
6 Kerry Collins 12.50 30.00
7 Trent Dilfer 12.50 30.00
8 John Elway 60.00 150.00
9 Jim Everett 7.50 20.00
10 Brett Favre 100.00 175.00
11 Gus Frerotte 7.50 20.00
12 Jeff George 10.00 25.00
13 Elvis Grbac 10.00 25.00
14 Jim Harbaugh 20.00 40.00
15 Jeff Hostetler 7.50 20.00
16 Jim Kelly 30.00 60.00
17 Bernie Kosar 7.50 20.00
18 Erik Kramer 7.50 20.00
19 Scott Mitchell 10.00 25.00
20 Rick Mirer 7.50 20.00
21 Warren Moon 12.50 30.00
23 Barry Sanders 75.00 150.00
22 Jerry Rice SP
24 Junior Seau 25.00 50.00
25 Heath Shuler 7.50 20.00
26 Kordell Stewart 12.50 30.00
27 Vinny Testaverde 10.00 25.00
28 Steve Young 30.00 80.00

1997 Pinnacle Inside Cans
This set was essentially the "wrappers" for the 1997 Pinnacle Inside product. Each features a color photo of the player reproduced as the can labels painted directly on the metal. There are star cans, rookie cans, a Brett Favre MVP can, a Dan Marino passing record can and a can that privides a tribute to the 25th anniversary of the Ice Bowl (Dallas vs. Green Bay). Shopko Stores in the Green Bay area also received an exclusive 'Showdown in Titledown' can featuring the Packers and Cowboys helmet logos and historical record.
COMPLETE SET (28) 5.00 12.00
*OPENED GOLD CANS: 3X TO 6X
GOLD CAN STATED ODDS 1:47
1 Ice Bowl .02 .10
2 Dan Marino RB .60 1.25
3 Brett Favre MVP .60 1.25
4 Jerome Bettis .10 .30
5 Tony Banks .10 .30
6 Deion Sanders .10 .30
7 Drew Bledsoe .15 .40
8 Jim Harbaugh .07 .20
9 Keyshawn Johnson .10 .30
10 Jeff George .07 .20
11 Karim Abdul-Jabbar .10 .30
12 Rick Mirer .02 .10
13 Kordell Stewart .10 .30
14 Jeff Blake .07 .20
15 Eddie George .10 .30
16 Terry Glenn .10 .30
17 Curtis Martin .15 .40
18 Terrell Davis .15 .40
19 Jerry Rice .25 .60
20 Steve Young .15 .40
21 John Elway .60 1.25
22 Mark Brunell .15 .40
23 Kerry Collins .10 .30
24 Barry Sanders .40 1.00
25 Troy Aikman .25 .60
26 Emmitt Smith .40 1.00
27 Dan Marino .60 1.25
28 Brett Favre .60 1.25
P1 Cowboys vs. Packers .02 .10

1997 Pinnacle Inside Fourth and Goal
Randomly inserted in cans at the rate of one in 23, this 20-card set features color action photos of superstar players printed on full silver foil card stock with foil stamping.
COMPLETE SET (20) 125.00 250.00
STATED ODDS 1:23 HOB/RET
1 Brett Favre 12.50 30.00
2 Drew Bledsoe 4.00 10.00
3 Troy Aikman 6.00 15.00
4 Mark Brunell 4.00 10.00
5 Steve Young 4.00 10.00
6 Vinny Testaverde 2.00 5.00
7 Dan Marino 12.50 30.00
8 Kerry Collins 3.00 8.00
9 John Elway 12.50 30.00
10 Emmitt Smith 10.00 25.00
11 Barry Sanders 10.00 25.00
12 Eddie George 3.00 8.00
13 Terrell Davis 4.00 10.00
14 Curtis Martin 4.00 10.00
15 Terry Glenn 3.00 8.00
16 Jerry Rice 6.00 15.00
17 Herman Moore 2.00 5.00
18 Jeff Blake 2.00 5.00
19 Warrick Dunn 5.00 12.00
20 Antowain Smith 4.00 10.00

1998 Pinnacle Inside Stand Up Guys Promos
These promos, for a product never issued, were released after Pinnacle ceased operations and old card inventory was liquidated. The Stand Up Guys cards include a cut out slot in which two cards featuring the same players were to be slid together to form a cross shaped pair.
1AB Dan Marino 6.00 15.00
John Elway
Brett Favre
Troy Aikman
1CD Dan Marino 6.00 15.00
John Elway
Brett Favre
Troy Aikman
2AB Steve Young 3.00 8.00
Kordell Stewart
Mark Brunell
Drew Bledsoe
2CD Steve Young 3.00 8.00
Kordell Stewart
Mark Brunell
Drew Bledsoe
3AB McNair/Plummer/B.Johnson/K.Collins 2.50 6.00
3CD McNair/Plummer/B.Johnson/K.Collins 2.50 6.00
4AB B.Sanders/E.Smith/T.Davis/Levens 5.00 12.00
4CD B.Sanders/E.Smith/T.Davis/Levens 5.00 12.00
5AB Bettis/C.Martin/Jabbar/Watters 3.00 8.00
5CD Bettis/C.Martin/Jabbar/Watters 3.00 8.00
9AB Tim Brown 4.00 10.00
Keenan McCardell
Michael Jackson
Andre Rison
9CD Tim Brown 4.00 10.00
Keenan McCardell
Michael Jackson
Andre Rison
10AB John Elway 6.00 15.00
Terrell Davis
Shannon Sharpe
Rod Smith
10CD John Elway 6.00 15.00
Terrell Davis
Shannon Sharpe
Rod Smith
12AB Kordell Stewart 3.00 8.00
Jerome Bettis
Charles Johnson
12CD Kordell Stewart 3.00 8.00
Jerome Bettis
Charles Johnson
14AB Ben Coates 2.50 6.00
Drew Bledsoe
Willie McGinest
Terry Glenn
14CD Ben Coates 2.50 6.00
Drew Bledsoe
Willie McGinest
Terry Glenn
15AB Scott Mitchell 2.00 5.00
Herman Moore
Johnnie Morton
15CD Scott Mitchell 2.00 5.00
Herman Moore
Johnnie Morton
16AB Trent Dilfer 2.00 5.00
Reidel Anthony
Warrick Dunn
Mike Alstott
16CD Trent Dilfer 2.00 5.00
Reidel Anthony
Warrick Dunn
Mike Alstott
17AB Karim Adbul-Jabbar 2.00 5.00
Yatil Green
Troy Drayton
17CD Karim Adbul-Jabbar 2.00 5.00
Yatil Green
Troy Drayton
18AB Elvis Grbac 2.50 6.00
Andre Rison
Marcus Allen
18CD Elvis Grbac 2.50 6.00
Andre Rison
Marcus Allen
20AB Steve Young
Garrison Hearst
Jerry Rice
Terrell Owens
20CD Steve Young
Garrison Hearst
Jerry Rice
Terrell Owens
21AB Cris Carter 4.00 10.00
Robert Smith
Brad Johnson
Jake Reed
21CD Cris Carter 4.00 10.00
Robert Smith
Brad Johnson
Jake Reed
22AB Peyton Manning 6.00 15.00
Brian Griese
Ryan Leaf
Thad Busby
22CD Peyton Manning 6.00 15.00
Brian Griese
Ryan Leaf
Thad Busby
23AB Curtis Enis 2.00 5.00
Fred Taylor
Ahman Green
Robert Edwards
23CD Curtis Enis 2.00 5.00
Fred Taylor
Ahman Green
Robert Edwards
24AB Randy Moss 3.00 8.00
Germane Crowell
Jacquez Green
Kevin Dyson
24CD Randy Moss 3.00 8.00
Germane Crowell
Jacquez Green
Kevin Dyson
25AB Dan Marino/Brett Favre 6.00 15.00
Terrell Davis/Barry Sanders
25CD Dan Marino/Brett Favre 6.00 15.00
Terrell Davis/Barry Sanders

1996 Pinnacle Mint
The 1996 Pinnacle Mint Collection set was issued in one series of 30-cards and 30-coins. The two-coin/three-card packs carried a suggested retail price of $3.99 each. The challenge was to fit the coins with the die-cut cards that pictured the same player. Two die-cut cards and two coins were inserted in each pack. Either one bronze, silver or gold card was also included in each pack. The fronts feature color action player photos with a cut-out area for the matching coin. Die cut cards are listed below.
COMP.DIE CUT SET (30) 4.00 10.00
1 Troy Aikman .30 .75
2 John Elway .60 1.50
3 Jim Kelly .10 .30
4 Dan Marino .60 1.50
5 Warren Moon .05 .15
6 Steve Young .25 .60
7 Boomer Esiason .05 .15
8 Jim Everett .02 .08
9 Brett Favre .60 1.50
10 Jim Harbaugh .05 .15
11 Jeff Hostetler .02 .08
12 Neil O'Donnell .05 .15
13 Drew Bledsoe .20 .50
14 Rick Mirer .05 .15
15 Emmitt Smith .50 1.25
16 Jerry Rice .30 .75
17 Barry Sanders .50 1.25
18 Junior Seau .10 .30
19 Dave Brown .02 .08
20 Heath Shuler .05 .15
21 Jeff Blake .10 .30
22 Kerry Collins .10 .30
23 Scott Mitchell .05 .15
24 Kordell Stewart .10 .30
25 Jeff George .05 .15
26 Mark Brunell .20 .50
27 Erik Kramer .02 .08
28 Bernie Kosar .02 .08
29 Frank Reich .02 .08
30 Randall Cunningham .10 .30
S2 John Elway Sample .40 1.00
S13 Drew Bledsoe Sample .20 .50
S14 Rick Mirer Sample .08 .25

1996 Pinnacle Mint Bronze
COMP.BRONZE SET (30) 20.00 40.00
*BRONZE CARDS: .8X TO 2X DIE CUTS

1996 Pinnacle Mint Gold
COMP.GOLD SET (30) 150.00 300.00
*GOLD CARDS: 4X TO 10X DIE CUTS
STATED ODDS 1:48

1996 Pinnacle Mint Silver
COMP.SILVER SET (30) 75.00 150.00
*SILVER CARDS: 2.5X TO 6X DIE CUTS
STATED ODDS 1:20

1996 Pinnacle Mint Coins Brass
Each pack of Pinnacle Mint contained two coins: a mixture of Brass, Nickel (1:20 packs) and Gold Plated (1:48 packs). The Brass coins were the most common. This set features coins minted in brass with embossed player heads and were made to be matched with the die cut card version of the same player. A Solid Silver version of the coins was also randomly seeded in packs. It was the most difficult version to pull.
COMP.BRASS SET (30) 12.50 30.00
BRASS STATED ODDS 2:1
*NICKEL COINS: 1.5X TO 4X BRASS
NICKEL STATED ODDS 1:20
*GOLD PLATED: 3X TO 8X BRASS
GOLD STATED ODDS 1:48
TWO COINS PER PACK

1 Troy Aikman .75 2.00
2 John Elway 1.50 4.00
3 Jim Kelly .30 .75
4 Dan Marino 1.50 4.00
5 Warren Moon .15 .40
6 Steve Young .60 1.50
7 Boomer Esiason .15 .40
8 Jim Everett .07 .20
9 Brett Favre 1.50 4.00
10 Jim Harbaugh .15 .40
11 Jeff Hostetler .07 .20
12 Neil O'Donnell .15 .40
13 Drew Bledsoe .50 1.25
14 Rick Mirer .15 .40
15 Emmitt Smith 1.25 3.00
16 Jerry Rice .75 2.00
17 Barry Sanders 1.25 3.00
18 Junior Seau .30 .75
19 Dave Brown .07 .20
20 Heath Shuler .15 .40
21 Jeff Blake .30 .75
22 Kerry Collins .30 .75
23 Scott Mitchell .15 .40
24 Kordell Stewart .30 .75
25 Jeff George .15 .40
26 Mark Brunell .50 1.25
27 Erik Kramer .07 .20
28 Bernie Kosar .07 .20
29 Frank Reich .07 .20
30 David Klingler .30 .75
SP1 Randall Cunningham 1.25 3.00

1997 Pinnacle Mint

The 1997 Pinnacle Mint set was issued in one series totalling 30-cards and 30-coins and was distributed in packs with one die-cut card, two random coins minted in brass, nickel-silver, solid silver or solid gold plated versions, and two foil stamped cards. The cards feature color action player photos with either a cut-out area for the matching coin or a replica foil coin. The set contains the topical subset: Minted Highlights (21-30). The bronze version of the cards is priced below.

COMPLETE SET (30) 6.00 15.00
1 Brett Favre .75 2.00
2 Drew Bledsoe .25 .60
3 Mark Brunell .25 .60
4 Kerry Collins .15 .40
5 Troy Aikman .40 1.00
6 Steve Young .25 .60
7 Dan Marino .75 2.00
8 Barry Sanders .60 1.50
9 John Elway .75 2.00
10 Emmitt Smith .60 1.50
11 Rick Mirer .05 .15
12 Kordell Stewart .15 .40
13 Tony Banks .08 .25
14 Jeff George .08 .25
15 Jerry Rice .40 1.00
16 Jeff Blake .08 .25
17 Jim Harbaugh .08 .25
18 Heath Shuler .05 .15
19 Scott Mitchell .05 .15
20 Neil O'Donnell .05 .15
21 Brett Favre MH .40 1.00
22 Drew Bledsoe MH .15 .40
23 Mark Brunell MH .15 .40
24 Kerry Collins MH .08 .25
25 Troy Aikman MH .20 .50
26 Dan Marino MH .40 1.00
27 Barry Sanders MH .30 .75
28 Emmitt Smith MH .30 .75
29 Tony Banks MH .05 .15
30 John Elway MH .40 1.00
P2 Drew Bledsoe Promo .40 1.00
P6 Steve Young Promo .40 1.00

1997 Pinnacle Mint Die Cuts

COMPLETE SET (30) 10.00 25.00
*DIE CUTS: .5X TO 1.2X BRONZE CARDS
STATED ODDS 2:1 HOB/RET

1997 Pinnacle Mint Gold Team Pinnacle

COMPLETE SET (30) 100.00 250.00
*GOLD TEAM PINN: 5X TO 12X BRONZES
STATED ODDS 1:47 HOB/1:71 RET

1997 Pinnacle Mint Silver Team Pinnacle

COMPLETE SET (30) 48.00 120.00
*SILVER TEAM PINN: 2X TO 5X BRONZE
STATED ODDS 1:1 HOB/RET

1997 Pinnacle Mint Coins Brass

Each hobby pack of Pinnacle Mint contained two coins and each retail pack contained one coin. This set features coins minted in brass with embossed player heads and were made to be matched with the die-cut card version of the same player. While the Brass coins were the most common, a number of parallels were produced: Brass Proofs (1:79 hobby packs, 1:159 retail packs), Gold Plated (1:47 hobby, 1:95 retail), Gold Proofs (1:425 hobby, 1:850 retail, 100-sets made), Nickel (1:20 hobby, 1:41 retail), Silver Proofs (1:170 hobby, 1:340 retail, 250-sets made), and Solid Silver (1:2880 hobby, 1:4600 retail).

COMP.BRASS SET (30) 12.50 30.00
BRASS COINS 2 PER HOBBY, 1 PER RETAIL
*BRASS PROOFS: 3X TO 8X BRASS
BRASS PROOF/500 ODDS 1:79H, 1:159R
BRASS PROOF PRINT RUN 500 #'d SETS
*GOLD PLATED: 2X TO 5X BRASS
GOLD PLATED ODDS 1:47H, 1:95R
*GOLD PROOFS: 12X TO 30X BRASS
GOLD PROOF/100 ODDS 1:425H, 1:850R
GOLD PROOF PRINT RUN 100 #'d SETS
*NICKEL COINS: 1.2X TO 3X BRASS
NICKEL ODDS 1:20H, 1:41R
*SILVER PROOFS: 5X TO 12X BRASS
SILVER PROOF ODDS 1:170H, 1:340R
SILVER PROOF PRINT RUN 250 #'d SETS
*SOLID SILVERS: 25X TO 50X BRASS
SOLID SILVER ODDS 1:2880H, 1:4600R
1 Brett Favre 2.00 5.00
2 Drew Bledsoe .60 1.50
3 Mark Brunell .60 1.50
4 Kerry Collins .40 1.00
5 Troy Aikman 1.00 2.50
6 Steve Young .60 1.50
7 Dan Marino 2.00 5.00
8 Barry Sanders 1.50 4.00
9 John Elway 2.00 5.00
10 Emmitt Smith 1.50 4.00
11 Rick Mirer .15 .40
12 Kordell Stewart .40 1.00
13 Tony Banks .25 .60
14 Jeff George .25 .60
15 Jerry Rice 1.00 2.50
16 Jeff Blake .25 .60
17 Jim Harbaugh .25 .60
18 Heath Shuler .15 .40
19 Scott Mitchell .15 .40
20 Neil O'Donnell .15 .40
21 Brett Favre MH 1.00 2.50
22 Drew Bledsoe MH .40 1.00
23 Mark Brunell MH .40 1.00
24 Kerry Collins MH .25 .60
25 Troy Aikman MH .50 1.25
26 Dan Marino MH 1.00 2.50
27 Barry Sanders MH .75 2.00
28 Emmitt Smith MH .75 2.00
29 Tony Banks MH .15 .40
30 John Elway MH 1.00 2.50

1997 Pinnacle Mint Commemorative Cards

Randomly inserted in hobby packs at the rate of one in 31 and in retail packs at the rate of one in 47, this six-card set features color photos of some of the most memorable events of the 1996 season with full silver-foil highlights.

COMPLETE SET (6) 20.00 50.00
STATED ODDS 1:31 HOB, 1:47 RET
1 Barry Sanders 5.00 12.00
2 Brett Favre 6.00 15.00
3 Mark Brunell 2.00 5.00
4 Emmitt Smith 5.00 12.00
5 Dan Marino 6.00 15.00
6 Jerry Rice 3.00 8.00

1997 Pinnacle Mint Commemorative Coins

Randomly inserted in hobby packs only at the rate of one in 31, this double-sized brass coin set is parallel to the Pinnacle Mint Commemorative Collection and features embossed images on brass coins commemorating the top six moments from the 1996 season.

COMPLETE SET (6) 50.00 120.00
STATED ODDS 1:31 HOBBY
1 Barry Sanders 10.00 25.00
2 Brett Favre 12.50 30.00
3 Mark Brunell 4.00 10.00
4 Emmitt Smith 10.00 25.00
5 Dan Marino 12.50 30.00
6 Jerry Rice 6.00 15.00

1998 Pinnacle Mint

Each of the 33-players in this set had three card versions within the set. The first 33-cards are die cut which could hold the coin, the next 33-cards are the base product, and the last 33-cards featured a portrait style photo on front and player profile information on back.

COMPLETE SET (100) 12.50 30.00
1 John Elway DC .40 1.00
2 Barry Sanders DC .30 .75
3 Brett Favre DC .40 1.00
4 Drew Bledsoe DC .20 .50
5 Steve Young DC .10 .30
6 Kordell Stewart DC .10 .30
7 Dan Marino DC .40 1.00
8 Troy Aikman DC .20 .50
9 Jake Plummer DC .20 .50
10 Jerry Rice DC .20 .50
11 Rick Mirer DC .07 .20
12 Elvis Grbac DC .07 .20
13 Trent Dilfer DC .10 .30
14 Jeff George DC .07 .20
15 Junior Seau DC .10 .30
16 Warren Moon DC .10 .30
17 Tony Banks DC .07 .20
18 Scott Mitchell DC .07 .20
19 Steve McNair DC .10 .30
20 Gus Frerotte DC .07 .20
21 Michael Irvin DC .10 .30
22 Kerry Collins DC .07 .20
23 Jim Harbaugh DC .07 .20
24 Neil O'Donnell DC .07 .20
25 Jeff Blake DC .07 .20
26 Vinny Testaverde DC .07 .20
27 Erik Kramer DC .07 .20
28 Heath Shuler DC .07 .20
29 Terrell Davis DC .20 .50
30 Randall Cunningham DC .10 .30
31 Ryan Leaf DC .20 .50
32 Brad Johnson DC .10 .30
33 Peyton Manning DC 4.00 10.00
34 John Elway .75 2.00
35 Barry Sanders .60 1.50
36 Brett Favre .75 2.00
37 Drew Bledsoe .30 .75
38 Steve Young .20 .50
39 Kordell Stewart .20 .50
40 Dan Marino .75 2.00
41 Troy Aikman .40 1.00
42 Jake Plummer .20 .50
43 Jerry Rice .40 1.00
44 Rick Mirer .07 .20
45 Elvis Grbac .10 .30
46 Trent Dilfer .20 .50
47 Jeff George .10 .30
48 Junior Seau .20 .50
49 Warren Moon .20 .50
50 Tony Banks .20 .50
51 Scott Mitchell .10 .30
52 Steve McNair .20 .50
53 Gus Frerotte .07 .20
54 Michael Irvin .20 .50
55 Kerry Collins .10 .30
56 Jim Harbaugh .10 .30
57 Neil O'Donnell .10 .30
58 Jeff Blake .10 .30
59 Vinny Testaverde .10 .30
60 Erik Kramer .07 .20
61 Heath Shuler .07 .20
62 Terrell Davis .20 .50
63 Randall Cunningham .20 .50
64 Ryan Leaf .30 .75
65 Brad Johnson .20 .50
66 Peyton Manning 3.00 8.00
67 John Elway PRO .60 1.50
68 Barry Sanders PRO .50 1.25
69 Brett Favre PRO .60 1.50
70 Drew Bledsoe PRO .20 .50
71 Steve Young PRO .20 .50
72 Kordell Stewart PRO .10 .30
73 Dan Marino PRO .60 1.50
74 Troy Aikman PRO .30 .75
75 Jake Plummer PRO .20 .50
76 Jerry Rice PRO .30 .75
77 Rick Mirer PRO .07 .20
78 Elvis Grbac PRO .07 .20
79 Trent Dilfer PRO .10 .30
80 Jeff George PRO .10 .30
81 Junior Seau PRO .20 .50
82 Warren Moon PRO .20 .50
83 Tony Banks PRO .10 .30
84 Scott Mitchell PRO .10 .30
85 Steve McNair PRO .10 .30
86 Gus Frerotte PRO .07 .20
87 Michael Irvin PRO .10 .30
88 Kerry Collins PRO .10 .30
89 Jim Harbaugh PRO .10 .30
90 Neil O'Donnell PRO .10 .30
91 Jeff Blake PRO .10 .30
92 Vinny Testaverde PRO .10 .30
93 Erik Kramer PRO .07 .20
94 Heath Shuler PRO .07 .20
95 Terrell Davis PRO .20 .50
96 Randall Cunningham PRO .10 .30
97 Ryan Leaf PRO .20 .50
98 Brad Johnson PRO .10 .30
99 Peyton Manning PRO 2.50 6.00
100 Checklist Card .02 .10

1998 Pinnacle Mint Silver

COMPLETE SET (99) 50.00 120.00
*SILVER STARS: 1.2X TO 3X BASIC CARDS
*SILVER ROOKIES: .6X TO 1.5X BASE CARDS
STATED ODDS 1:7 HOB, 1:9 RET

1998 Pinnacle Mint Coins Brass

This 33 coin series is of a brass alloy and features the same players as the card set. They were inserted one per pack.

COMP.BRASS SET (33) 12.00 30.00
ONE COIN PER PACK
*NICKEL: 3X TO 8X BRASS COINS
NICKEL COIN ODDS 1:15H, 1:23R
UNPRICED 24K GOLD COINS ISSUED
1 John Elway 1.50 4.00
2 Barry Sanders 1.25 3.00
3 Brett Favre 1.50 4.00
4 Drew Bledsoe .60 1.50
5 Steve Young .50 1.25
6 Kordell Stewart .40 1.00
7 Dan Marino 1.50 4.00
8 Troy Aikman .75 2.00
9 Jake Plummer .40 1.00
10 Jerry Rice .75 2.00
11 Rick Mirer .15 .40
12 Elvis Grbac .25 .60
13 Trent Dilfer .40 1.00
14 Jeff George .25 .60
15 Junior Seau .40 1.00
16 Warren Moon .40 1.00
17 Tony Banks .40 1.00
18 Scott Mitchell .25 .60
19 Steve McNair .40 1.00
20 Gus Frerotte .15 .40
21 Michael Irvin .40 1.00
22 Kerry Collins .25 .60
23 Jim Harbaugh .25 .60
24 Neil O'Donnell .25 .60
25 Jeff Blake .25 .60
26 Vinny Testaverde .25 .60
27 Erik Kramer .15 .40
28 Heath Shuler .15 .40
29 Terrell Davis .40 1.00
30 Randall Cunningham .40 1.00
31 Ryan Leaf .40 1.00
32 Brad Johnson .40 1.00
33 Peyton Manning 6.00 15.00
NNO P.Manning 1.00 2.50
R.Leaf

1998 Pinnacle Mint Gems

Randomly inserted in packs at a rate of one in 17 retail packs; and one in 11 hobby packs. The fronts feature color action photography with diamond-cut designs that read "Mint" and "Gems" on either side of the featured player.

COMPLETE SET (15) 30.00 80.00
STATED ODDS 1:11H, 1:17R
*PROMOS: .2X TO .5X BASIC INSERTS
1 Brett Favre 5.00 12.00
2 Dan Marino 5.00 12.00
3 Kordell Stewart .75 2.00
4 Peyton Manning 8.00 20.00
5 Ryan Leaf .75 2.00
6 Drew Bledsoe 2.00 5.00
7 Troy Aikman 2.50 6.00
8 John Elway 5.00 12.00
9 Barry Sanders 4.00 10.00
10 Steve Young 1.50 4.00
11 Steve McNair 1.25 3.00
12 Trent Dilfer .75 2.00
13 Terrell Davis 1.25 3.00
14 Jerry Rice 2.50 6.00
15 Jake Plummer 1.25 3.00

1998 Pinnacle Mint Impeccable

Randomly inserted in packs at a rate of one in 23 retail packs; and one in 15 hobby packs. The set is printed on foilboard and enhanced with foil stamping. The fronts feature color action photography.

COMPLETE SET (10) 25.00 60.00
STATED ODDS 1:15H, 1:23R
*PROMOS: .2X TO .5X BASIC INSERTS
1 John Elway 5.00 12.00
2 Brett Favre 5.00 12.00
3 Troy Aikman 2.50 6.00
4 Kordell Stewart .75 2.00
5 Jerry Rice 2.50 6.00
6 Barry Sanders 4.00 10.00
7 Dan Marino 5.00 12.00
8 Jake Plummer 1.25 3.00
9 Terrell Davis 1.25 3.00
10 Drew Bledsoe 1.25 3.00

1998 Pinnacle Mint Lasting Impressions

Randomly inserted in packs at a rate of one in 23 retail packs; and one in 15 hobby packs, this set includes 10 cards printed with gold foil highlights.

COMPLETE SET (10) 25.00 60.00
STATED ODDS 1:15H, 1:23R
*PROMOS: .2X TO .5X BASIC INSERTS
1 Brett Favre 5.00 12.00
2 John Elway 5.00 12.00
3 Barry Sanders 4.00 10.00
4 Dan Marino 5.00 12.00
5 Steve Young 1.50 4.00
6 Terrell Davis 1.25 3.00
7 Kordell Stewart .75 2.00
8 Troy Aikman 2.50 6.00
9 Jake Plummer 1.25 3.00
10 Jerry Rice 2.50 6.00

1998 Pinnacle Mint Minted Moments

Randomly inserted in packs at a rate of one in 17 retail packs; and 1:11 hobby packs. The fronts feature color action photography printed on foilboard and enhanced with foil stamping. The words "Minted Moments" are written below the picture.

COMPLETE SET (15) 30.00 80.00
STATED ODDS 1:11H, 1:17R
*PROMO CARDS: .2X TO .5X BASE INSERTS
1 Peyton Manning 8.00 20.00
2 Ryan Leaf .75 2.00
3 John Elway 5.00 12.00
4 Brett Favre 5.00 12.00
5 Drew Bledsoe 2.00 5.00
6 Kordell Stewart .75 2.00
7 Dan Marino 5.00 12.00
8 Jerry Rice 2.50 6.00
9 Barry Sanders 4.00 10.00
10 Jake Plummer 1.25 3.00
11 Troy Aikman 2.50 6.00
12 Trent Dilfer .75 2.00
13 Warren Moon 1.25 3.00
14 Steve Young 1.25 3.00
15 Terrell Davis 1.25 3.00

1998 Pinnacle Mint Team Pinnacle Points

COMPLETE SET (11) 2.00 5.00
*FIVE POINTS: .5X TO 1.2X
*TEN POINTS: .6X TO 1.5X
1 Troy Aikman .30 .75
2 Drew Bledsoe .15 .40
3 Warrick Dunn .08 .25
4 John Elway .50 1.25
5 Brett Favre .60 1.50
6 Ryan Leaf .08 .25
7 Dan Marino .60 1.50
8 Jake Plummer .08 .25
9 Barry Sanders .40 1.00
10 Kordell Stewart .08 .25
11 Steve Young .25 .60

1998 Pinnacle Performers Big Bang Promos

Pinnacle issued several promo cards in 1998 for sets that were never officially released. We've listed all known cards below for the Pinnacle Performers product. Any additions to the list below are appreciated.

9 Eddie George 1.25 3.00
10 John Elway 3.00 8.00
11 Steve Young 2.00 5.00
12 Drew Bledsoe 1.50 4.00

1998 Pinnacle Plus A Piece of the Game Promos

Pinnacle issued several promo cards in 1998 for sets that were never officially released. We've listed all known cards so any additions to the list below are appreciated.

1 Warrick Dunn 1.25 3.00
2 Dan Marino 5.00 12.00
3 Eddie George 1.25 3.00
6 Troy Aikman 2.50 6.00

1998 Pinnacle Plus Go To Guys Promos

Pinnacle issued several promo cards in 1998 for sets that were never officially released. We've listed all known cards so any additions to the list below are appreciated.

1 Jake Plummer 1.25 3.00
2 Emmitt Smith 5.00 12.00
3 Fred Lane 1.00 2.50
4 Curtis Conway 1.25 3.00
6 Barry Sanders 5.00 12.00
7 Brett Favre 6.00 15.00
8 Brad Johnson 1.00 2.50
9 Danny Wuerffel 1.25 3.00
10 Danny Kanell 1.00 2.50
11 Bobby Hoying 1.25 3.00
13 Tony Banks 1.00 2.50
17 Rob Johnson 1.25 3.00
18 Corey Dillon 2.00 4.00
19 John Elway 5.00 12.00
20 Marshall Faulk 2.00 5.00
23 Dan Marino 6.00 15.00
26 Napoleon Kaufman 1.00 2.50
28 Natrone Means 1.25 3.00
30 Eddie George 1.25 3.00

1998 Pinnacle Plus Selected Promos

Pinnacle issued several promo cards in 1998 for sets that were never officially released. We've listed all known cards so any additions to the list below are appreciated.

1 Brett Favre 6.00 15.00
10 Steve Young 2.50 6.00

1998 Pinnacle Plus Sunday's Best Promos

Pinnacle issued several promo cards in 1998 for sets that were never officially released. We've listed all known cards so any additions to the list below are appreciated.

2 John Elway 5.00 12.00
3 Emmitt Smith 5.00 12.00
4 Steve Young 2.50 6.00
8 Corey Dillon 1.50 4.00
9 Dan Marino 6.00 15.00
10 Barry Sanders 5.00 12.00
11 Brett Favre 6.00 15.00
13 Eddie George 1.50 4.00
15 Terrell Davis 2.00 5.00

1997 Pinnacle Totally Certified Platinum Red

This 150 card set is parallel to regular base Certified set. However, it is the "base" set for the Totally Certified set. The totally certified set was issued only through Pinnacle hobby channels. It was issued in four box cases with three cards per pack. Each card in the three parallel version of this set (Platinum Blue, Red and Gold) are all individually serial numbered. The platinum red cards were issued two per pack and are sequentially numbered to 4,999.

COMPLETE SET (150) 60.00 150.00
*PROMOS: .25X TO .6X BASIC RED
1 Emmitt Smith 2.50 6.00
2 Dan Marino 5.00 12.00
3 Brett Favre 3.00 8.00
4 Steve Young 2.00 5.00
5 Kerry Collins 1.00 2.50
6 Troy Aikman 2.00 5.00
7 Drew Bledsoe 1.25 3.00
8 Eddie George 1.25 3.00
9 Jerry Rice 3.00 8.00
10 John Elway 5.00 12.00
11 Barry Sanders 2.50 6.00
12 Mark Brunell 1.25 3.00
13 Elvis Grbac 1.25 3.00
14 Tony Banks 1.25 3.00
15 Vinny Testaverde 1.00 2.50
16 Rick Mirer 1.00 2.50
17 Carl Pickens 1.25 3.00
18 Deion Sanders 1.25 3.00
19 Terry Glenn 1.25 3.00
20 Heath Shuler 1.00 2.50
21 Dave Brown 1.00 2.50
22 Keyshawn Johnson 1.25 3.00
23 Jeff George 1.25 3.00
24 Ricky Watters 1.25 3.00
25 Kordell Stewart 1.00 2.50
26 Junior Seau 1.25 3.00
27 Terrell Owens 1.50 4.00
28 Warren Moon 1.50 4.00
29 Isaac Bruce 1.50 4.00
30 Steve McNair 1.50 4.00
31 Gus Frerotte 1.00 2.50
32 Trent Dilfer 1.50 4.00
33 Shannon Sharpe 1.25 3.00
34 Scott Mitchell 1.25 3.00
35 Antonio Freeman 1.50 4.00
36 Jim Harbaugh 1.25 3.00
37 Natrone Means 1.25 3.00
38 Marcus Allen 1.50 4.00
39 Karim Abdul-Jabbar 1.00 2.50
40 Tim Biakabutuka 1.25 3.00
41 Jeff Blake 1.00 2.50
42 Michael Irvin 1.50 4.00
43 Herschel Walker 1.50 4.00
44 Curtis Martin 1.50 4.00
45 Eddie Kennison 1.00 2.50
46 Napoleon Kaufman 1.00 2.50
47 Larry Centers 1.00 2.50
48 Jamal Anderson 1.25 3.00
49 Derrick Alexander WR 1.00 2.50
50 Bruce Smith 1.25 3.00
51 Wesley Walls 1.00 2.50
52 Rod Smith WR 1.50 4.00
53 Keenan McCardell 1.25 3.00
54 Robert Brooks 1.25 3.00
55 Willie Green 1.00 2.50
56 Jake Reed 1.25 3.00
57 Joey Galloway 1.25 3.00
58 Eric Metcalf 1.25 3.00
59 Chris Sanders 1.00 2.50
60 Jeff Hostetler 1.00 2.50
61 Kevin Greene 1.50 4.00
62 Frank Sanders 1.00 2.50
63 Dorsey Levens 1.25 3.00
64 Sean Dawkins 1.00 2.50
65 Cris Carter 1.50 4.00
66 Andre Hastings 1.00 2.50
67 Amani Toomer 1.00 2.50
68 Adrian Murrell 1.25 3.00
69 Ty Detmer 1.00 2.50
70 Yancey Thigpen 1.00 2.50
71 Jim Everett 1.00 2.50
72 Todd Collins 1.00 2.50
73 Curtis Conway 1.25 3.00
74 Herman Moore 1.25 3.00
75 Neil O'Donnell 1.25 3.00
76 Rod Woodson 1.50 4.00
77 Tony Martin 1.25 3.00
78 Kent Graham 1.00 2.50
79 Andre Reed 1.50 4.00
80 Reggie White 1.50 4.00
81 Thurman Thomas 1.25 3.00
82 Garrison Hearst 1.00 2.50
83 Chris Warren 1.00 2.50
84 Wayne Chrebet 1.00 2.50
85 Chris T. Jones 1.00 2.50
86 Anthony Miller 1.00 2.50
87 Chris Chandler 1.25 3.00
88 Terrell Davis 1.25 3.00
89 Mike Alstott 1.25 3.00
90 Terry Allen 1.25 3.00
91 Jerome Bettis 1.50 4.00
92 Stan Humphries 1.25 3.00
93 Andre Rison 1.25 3.00
94 Marshall Faulk 1.25 3.00
95 Erik Kramer 1.00 2.50
96 O.J. McDuffie 1.25 3.00
97 Robert Smith 1.00 2.50
98 Keith Byars 1.00 2.50
99 Rodney Hampton 1.25 3.00
100 Desmond Howard 1.25 3.00
101 Lawrence Phillips 1.00 2.50
102 Michael Westbrook 1.25 3.00
103 Johnnie Morton 1.25 3.00
104 Ben Coates 1.50 4.00
105 J.J. Stokes 1.00 2.50
106 Terance Mathis 1.00 2.50
107 Errict Rhett 1.00 2.50
108 Tim Brown 1.50 4.00
109 Marvin Harrison 1.25 3.00
110 Muhsin Muhammad 1.25 3.00
111 Byron Bam Morris 1.00 2.50
112 Mario Bates 1.00 2.50
113 Jimmy Smith 1.25 3.00
114 Irving Fryar 1.25 3.00
115 Tamarick Vanover 1.25 3.00
116 Brad Johnson 1.25 3.00
117 Rashaan Salaam 1.00 2.50
118 Ki-Jana Carter 1.00 2.50
119 Tyrone Wheatley 1.25 3.00
120 John Friesz 1.00 2.50
121 Orlando Pace RC 2.00 5.00
122 Jim Druckenmiller RC 1.25 3.00
123 Byron Hanspard RC 1.25 3.00
124 David LaFleur RC 1.00 2.50
125 Reidel Anthony RC 1.25 3.00
126 Antowain Smith RC 2.00 5.00
127 Bryant Westbrook RC 1.00 2.50
128 Fred Lane RC 1.25 3.00
129 Tiki Barber RC 5.00 12.00
130 Shawn Springs RC 1.25 3.00
131 Ike Hilliard RC 1.50 4.00
132 James Farrior RC 1.50 4.00
133 Darrell Russell RC 1.00 2.50
134 Walter Jones RC 1.50 4.00
135 Tom Knight RC 1.00 2.50
136 Yatil Green RC 1.00 2.50
137 Joey Kent RC 1.00 2.50
138 Kevin Lockett RC 1.25 3.00
139 Troy Davis RC 1.00 2.50
140 Darnell Autry RC 1.00 2.50
141 Pat Barnes RC 1.00 2.50
142 Rae Carruth RC 1.00 2.50
143 Will Blackwell RC 1.00 2.50
144 Warrick Dunn RC 3.00 8.00
145 Corey Dillon RC 2.50 6.00
146 Dwayne Rudd RC 1.25 3.00
147 Reinard Wilson RC 1.00 2.50
148 Peter Boulware RC 1.00 2.50
149 Tony Gonzalez RC 4.00 10.00
150 Danny Wuerffel RC 1.50 4.00

1997 Pinnacle Totally Certified Platinum Blue

COMPLETE SET (150) 200.00 400.00
*BLUE/2499: .8X TO 2X RED/4999
STATED PRINT RUN 2499 SER.#'d SETS
STATED ODDS ONE PER PACK
*PROMOS: .2X TO .5X BASIC BLUE

1997 Pinnacle Totally Certified Platinum Gold

*PLAT.GOLD/30: 6X TO 15X RED/4999
GOLD PRINT RUN 30 SER.#'d SETS
STATED ODDS 1:79
*PROMOS: .1X TO .25X BASIC GOLD

1997 Pinnacle X-Press

The 1997 Pinnacle X-Press released was issued in one series totaling 150-cards and distributed in eight card packs plus one Pursuit of Paydirt card for a suggested retail price of $1.99. The fronts feature color player photos while the backs carry player information.

COMPLETE SET (150) 7.50 20.00
1 Drew Bledsoe .25 .60
2 Steve Young .25 .60
3 Brett Favre .75 2.00
4 John Elway .75 2.00
5 Dan Marino .75 2.00
6 Jerry Rice .40 1.00
7 Tony Banks .10 .30
8 Kerry Collins .20 .50
9 Mark Brunell .25 .60
10 Troy Aikman .40 1.00
11 Barry Sanders .60 1.50
12 Elvis Grbac .10 .30
13 Eddie George .20 .50
14 Terry Glenn .20 .50
15 Kordell Stewart .20 .50
16 Junior Seau .20 .50
17 Herman Moore .10 .30
18 Gus Frerotte .07 .20
19 Warren Moon .20 .50
20 Emmitt Smith .60 1.50
21 Henry Ellard .07 .20
22 Rashaan Salaam .07 .20
23 Sean Dawkins .07 .20
24 Tyrone Wheatley .10 .30
25 Lawrence Phillips .07 .20
26 Ty Detmer .10 .30
27 Vinny Testaverde .10 .30
28 Dorsey Levens .20 .50
29 Ricky Watters .10 .30
30 Natrone Means .10 .30
31 Curtis Conway .10 .30
32 Larry Centers .10 .30
33 Johnnie Morton .10 .30
34 Desmond Howard .10 .30
35 Marcus Allen .20 .50
36 Cris Carter .20 .50
37 James O.Stewart .10 .30
38 Frank Sanders .10 .30
39 Bruce Smith .10 .30
40 Carl Pickens .10 .30
41 Neil O'Donnell .10 .30
42 Trent Dilfer .20 .50
43 Rodney Peete .07 .20
44 Terance Mathis .10 .30
45 Muhsin Muhammad .10 .30
46 Jake Reed .10 .30
47 Jim Harbaugh .10 .30
48 Todd Collins .07 .20
49 Ki-Jana Carter .07 .20
50 Scott Mitchell .10 .30
51 Kevin Hardy .07 .20
52 Stanley Pritchett .07 .20
53 Dave Brown .07 .20
54 Jeff George .10 .30
55 Stan Humphries .10 .30
56 Isaac Bruce .20 .50
57 Eric Moulds .20 .50
58 Robert Brooks .10 .30
59 Steve McNair .25 .60
60 Adrian Murrell .10 .30
61 Rodney Hampton .10 .30
62 Michael Jackson .10 .30
63 Tamarick Vanover .10 .30
64 Edgar Bennett .10 .30
65 Andre Hastings .07 .20
66 Robert Smith .10 .30
67 Thurman Thomas .20 .50
68 Tim Biakabutuka .10 .30
69 Rick Mirer .07 .20
70 Deion Sanders .20 .50
71 Curtis Martin .25 .60
72 Garrison Hearst .10 .30
73 Kent Graham .07 .20
74 Anthony Johnson .07 .20
75 Antonio Freeman .20 .50
76 Marshall Faulk .25 .60
77 O.J. McDuffie .10 .30
78 Heath Shuler .07 .20
79 Napoleon Kaufman .20 .50
80 Aeneas Williams .07 .20
81 Hardy Nickerson .07 .20
82 Keenan McCardell .10 .30
83 Erik Kramer .07 .20
84 Ben Coates .10 .30
85 Shannon Sharpe .10 .30
86 Tony Martin .10 .30
87 Chris Sanders .07 .20
88 Jamal Anderson .20 .50
89 Karim Abdul-Jabbar .20 .50
90 Keyshawn Johnson .20 .50
91 Terrell Owens .25 .60
92 Michael Irvin .20 .50
93 John Friesz .07 .20
94 Chris Warren .10 .30
95 Errict Rhett .07 .20
96 Terry Allen .20 .50
97 Michael Westbrook .10 .30
98 Simeon Rice .10 .30
99 Willie Green .07 .20
100 Jerome Bettis .20 .50
101 Reggie White .20 .50
102 Bert Emanuel .10 .30
103 Zach Thomas .20 .50
104 Tim Brown .20 .50
105 Darnay Scott .10 .30
106 Terrell Davis .25 .60
107 Andre Reed .10 .30
108 Amani Toomer .10 .30
109 Irving Fryar .10 .30
110 Joey Galloway .10 .30
111 Marvin Harrison .20 .50
112 Derrick Alexander WR .10 .30
113 Jeff Blake .10 .30
114 Brad Johnson .20 .50
115 Eddie Kennison .10 .30
116 Rae Carruth RC .07 .20
117 Tony Gonzalez RC .60 1.50
118 Joey Kent RC .20 .50
119 Peter Boulware RC .20 .50
120 Orlando Pace RC .20 .50
121 David LaFleur RC .07 .20
122 Darnell Autry RC .10 .30
123 Tiki Barber RC 1.00 2.50
124 Troy Davis RC .10 .30
125 Jim Druckenmiller RC .10 .30
126 Corey Dillon RC .60 1.50
127 Ike Hilliard RC .25 .60
128 Reidel Anthony RC .20 .50
129 Byron Hanspard RC .10 .30
130 Antowain Smith RC .40 1.00
131 Jake Plummer RC .60 1.50
132 Warrick Dunn RC .50 1.25
133 Bryant Westbrook RC .07 .20
134 Darrell Russell RC .07 .20
135 Yatil Green RC .10 .30
136 Shawn Springs RC .10 .30
137 Danny Wuerffel RC .20 .50
138 Brett Favre PP .40 1.00
139 Emmitt Smith PP .30 .75
140 Barry Sanders PP .30 .75
141 Troy Aikman PP .20 .50
142 Drew Bledsoe PP .20 .50
143 Jerry Rice PP .20 .50
144 Dan Marino PP .40 1.00
145 John Elway PP .40 1.00
146 Kerry Collins PP .10 .30
147 Mark Brunell PP .20 .50
148 Brett Favre CL .20 .50
149 Dan Marino CL .20 .50
150 Troy Aikman CL .20 .50

1997 Pinnacle X-Press Autumn Warriors

COMPLETE SET (150) 100.00 200.00
*STARS: 4X TO 10X BASIC CARDS
*RCs: 2X TO 5X BASIC CARDS
STATED ODDS 1:7 HOBBY

1997 Pinnacle X-Press Bombs Away

Randomly inserted in packs at the rate of one in 19, this 18-card set features color photos of top quarterbacks printed on full foil, micro-etched card stock.

COMPLETE SET (18) 50.00 100.00
STATED ODDS 1:19
1 Brett Favre 8.00 20.00
2 Dan Marino 8.00 20.00
3 Troy Aikman 4.00 10.00
4 Drew Bledsoe 2.50 6.00
5 Kerry Collins 2.00 5.00
6 Mark Brunell 2.50 6.00
7 John Elway 8.00 20.00
8 Steve Young 2.50 6.00
9 Jeff Blake 1.25 3.00
10 Kordell Stewart 2.00 5.00
11 Jeff George 1.25 3.00
12 Rick Mirer .75 2.00
13 Neil O'Donnell 1.25 3.00
14 Scott Mitchell 1.25 3.00
15 Jim Harbaugh 1.25 3.00
16 Warren Moon 2.00 5.00
17 Trent Dilfer 2.00 5.00
18 Jim Druckenmiller 1.00 2.00

1997 Pinnacle X-Press Divide and Conquer

Randomly inserted in packs at the rate of one in 299, this 20-card set features color photos of the NFL's elite printed on full foil micro-etched card stock. Each card was serially numbered to 500. A Promo version of each card was also produced. The Promos were not serial numbered.

COMPLETE SET (20) 150.00 400.00
STATED ODDS 1:299
STATED PRINT RUN 500 SERIAL #'d SETS
*PROMO CARDS: .1X TO .25X BASIC INSERTS
1 Tim Biakabutuka 4.00 10.00
2 Karim Abdul-Jabbar 6.00 15.00
3 Jerome Bettis 6.00 15.00
4 Eddie George 6.00 15.00
5 Terrell Davis 8.00 20.00
6 Barry Sanders 20.00 50.00
7 Emmitt Smith 20.00 50.00
8 Brett Favre 25.00 60.00
9 Dan Marino 25.00 60.00
10 Troy Aikman 12.50 30.00
11 Jerry Rice 12.50 30.00
12 Drew Bledsoe 8.00 20.00
13 Kerry Collins 6.00 15.00
14 Mark Brunell 8.00 20.00
15 John Elway 25.00 60.00
16 Steve Young 8.00 20.00
17 Warrick Dunn 10.00 25.00
18 Byron Hanspard 2.50 6.00
19 Troy Davis 2.50 6.00
20 Jeff Blake 4.00 10.00

1997 Pinnacle X-Press Metal Works

Inserted one in every $14.99 X-Press Metal Works special box, this 20-card set features images of top players printed on heavy Bronze metal stock. Redemption cards for single Silver (400-sets made) and Gold (200-sets made) metal versions were also produced and randomly inserted in packs. The redemption offer expired 7/1/98. We've priced only the real metal cards below for all three metal types.

COMP.BRONZE SET (20) 50.00 120.00
ONE BRONZE PER MASTER DECK
*SILVER/400: 2.5X TO 6X BRONZE
SILVER REDEMPTION/400 ODDS 1:470
SILVER PRINT RUN 400 SERIAL #'d SETS
*GOLD/200: 4X TO 10X BRONZE
GOLD REDEMPTION/200 ODDS 1:950
GOLD PRINT RUN 200 SERIAL #'d SETS
1 Troy Aikman 4.00 10.00
2 Emmitt Smith 6.00 15.00
3 Dan Marino 8.00 20.00
4 Brett Favre 8.00 20.00
5 Barry Sanders 6.00 15.00
6 Drew Bledsoe 2.50 6.00
7 Kerry Collins 2.00 5.00
8 Mark Brunell 2.50 6.00
9 John Elway 8.00 20.00
10 Steve Young 2.50 6.00
11 Jerry Rice 4.00 10.00
12 Terrell Davis 2.50 6.00
13 Curtis Martin 2.50 6.00
14 Terry Glenn 2.00 5.00
15 Eddie George 2.00 5.00
16 Jerome Bettis 2.00 5.00
17 Jeff Blake 1.25 3.00
18 Kordell Stewart 2.00 5.00
19 Jeff George 1.25 3.00
20 Deion Sanders 2.00 5.00

1997 Pinnacle X-Press Pursuit of Paydirt

These unnumbered cards were inserted one per pack of 1998 Pinnacle X-Press along with "Booster" points cards of each of the players. The top NFL running backs and quarterbacks each had one card in the set and a multitude of Booster points cards. At season's end, the top player at each position in terms of TDs scored was exchangable, along with the appropriate number of Booster points cards, for a signed Eddie George Pursuit of Paydirt card.

COMPLETE SET (60) 15.00 40.00
STATED ODDS 1:2
1 K.Abdul-Jabbar WIN .75 2.00
2 Troy Aikman .75 2.00
3 Marcus Allen .40 1.00
4 Terry Allen .40 1.00
5 Jamal Anderson .40 1.00
6 Tony Banks .25 .60
7 Tiki Barber 2.00 5.00
8 Jerome Bettis .40 1.00
9 Tim Biakabutuka .25 .60
10 Jeff Blake .25 .60
11 Drew Bledsoe .50 1.25
12 Dave Brown .15 .40
13 Mark Brunell .50 1.25
14 Ki-Jana Carter .15 .40
15 Chris Chandler .15 .40
16 Kerry Collins .40 1.00
17 Todd Collins .15 .40
18 Terrell Davis .50 1.25
19 Troy Davis .25 .60
20 Trent Dilfer .40 1.00
21 Jim Druckenmiller .25 .60
22 John Elway 1.50 4.00
23 Marshall Faulk .50 1.25
24 Brett Favre WIN 2.50 5.00
25 Gus Frerotte .15 .40
26A Eddie George .40 1.00
26B Eddie George AUTO 10.00 25.00
27 Jeff George .25 .60
28 Elvis Grbac .25 .60
29 Byron Hanspard .25 .60
30 Jim Harbaugh .25 .60
31 Garrison Hearst .25 .60
32 Greg Hill .15 .40
33 Stan Humphries .25 .60
34 Brad Johnson .40 1.00
35 Napoleon Kaufman .40 1.00
36 Dorsey Levens .40 1.00
37 Dan Marino 1.50 4.00
38 Curtis Martin .50 1.25
39 Steve McNair .50 1.25
40 Natrone Means .25 .60
41 Rick Mirer .15 .40
42 Scott Mitchell .25 .60
43 Warren Moon .40 1.00
44 Neil O'Donnell .25 .60
45 Rodney Peete .15 .40
46 Lawrence Phillips .15 .40
47 Errict Rhett .15 .40
48 Rashaan Salaam .15 .40
49 Barry Sanders 1.25 3.00
50 Heath Shuler .15 .40
51 Emmitt Smith 1.25 3.00
52 Robert Smith .25 .60
53 James O.Stewart .25 .60
54 Kordell Stewart .40 1.00
55 Vinny Testaverde .25 .60
56 Thurman Thomas .40 1.00
57 Chris Warren .25 .60
58 Ricky Watters .25 .60
59 Tyrone Wheatley .25 .60
60 Steve Young .50 1.25

1992 Playoff Promos

These seven standard-size cards were issued to give collectors a preview of the forthcoming 1992 Playoff series. These cards are distinguished from other cards by the Tekchrome printing process, which enhances the action photography and gives the cards a three-dimensional appearance, and by their thicker (22 point) card stock. The fronts feature glossy full-bleed color player photos that exhibit a metallic-like sheen. The player's name appears in silver lettering in a black bar toward the bottom of the photo. The backs have a full-bleed color close-up photo with the player's name in a team color-coded vertical bar that descends from the top edge. The cards are numbered on the back "X of 6 Promo".

COMPLETE SET (7) 4.80 12.00
1 Calvin Williams .20 .50
2 John Elway 2.00 5.00
3 Dalton Hilliard .20 .50
4 Steve Young 1.00 2.50
5 Emmitt Smith 2.40 6.00
6 Mike Golic .20 .50
NNO Header .20 .50
Intro Card

1992 Playoff

The 150 standard-size cards were issued in eight-card packs. The fronts display full-bleed, metallic player photos accented by the player's name in a black bar near the bottom. The backs have a full-bleed color close-up photo with the player's name in a team color-coded vertical bar that descends from the top edge. A black box centered at the bottom presents a detailed look at the player's performance during a key game in the 1992 season. Twelve different versions of the display box were produced, each featuring a different football player. Rookie Cards in this set include Steve Bono, Terrell Buckley, Willie Davis and Amp Lee.

COMPLETE SET (150) 10.00 25.00
1 Emmitt Smith 4.00 8.00
2 Steve Young 1.50 3.00
3 Jack Del Rio .08 .25
4 Bobby Hebert .08 .25
5 Shannon Sharpe .30 .75
6 Gary Clark .30 .75
7 Christian Okoye .08 .25
8 Ernest Givins .15 .40
9 Mike Horan .08 .25
10 Dennis Gentry .08 .25
11 Michael Irvin .30 .75
12 Eric Floyd .08 .25
13 Brent Jones .15 .40
14 Anthony Carter .15 .40
15 Tony Martin .15 .40
16 Greg Lewis UER .08 .25
17 Todd McNair .08 .25

18 Earnest Byner .08 .25
19 Steve Beuerlein .15 .40
20 Roger Craig .15 .40
21 Mark Higgs .08 .25
22 Guy McIntyre .08 .25
23 Don Warren .08 .25
24 Alvin Harper .15 .40
25 Mark Jackson .08 .25
26 Chris Doleman .08 .25
27 Jesse Sapolu .08 .25
28 Tony Tolbert .08 .25
29 Wendell Davis .08 .25
30 Dan Saleaumua .08 .25
31 Jeff Bostic .08 .25
32 Jay Novacek .15 .40
33 Cris Carter .40 1.00
34 Tony Paige .08 .25
35 Greg Kragen .08 .25
36 Jeff Dellenbach .08 .25
37 Keith DeLong .08 .25
38 Todd Scott .08 .25
39 Jeff Feagles .08 .25
40 Mike Saxon .08 .25
41 Martin Mayhew .08 .25
42 Steve Bono RC .30 .75
43 Willie Davis RC .15 .40
44 Mark Stepnoski .15 .40
45 Harry Newsome .08 .25
46 Thane Gash .08 .25
47 Gaston Green .08 .25
48 James Washington .08 .25
49 Kenny Walker .08 .25
50 Jeff Davidson RC .08 .25
51 Shane Conlan .08 .25
52 Richard Dent .15 .40
53 Haywood Jeffires .15 .40
54 Harry Galbreath .08 .25
55 Terry Allen .30 .75
56 Tommy Barnhardt .08 .25
57 Mike Golic .08 .25
58 Dalton Hilliard .08 .25
59 Danny Copeland .08 .25
60 Jerry Fontenot RC .08 .25
61 Kelvin Martin .08 .25
62 Mark Kelso .08 .25
63 Wymon Henderson .08 .25
64 Mark Rypien .08 .25
65 Bobby Humphrey .08 .25
66 Rich Gannon UER .30 .75
67 Darren Lewis .08 .25
68 Barry Foster .15 .40
69 Ken Norton Jr. .15 .40
70 James Lofton .15 .40
71 Trace Armstrong .08 .25
72 Vestee Jackson .08 .25
73 Clyde Simmons .08 .25
74 Brad Muster .08 .25
75 Cornelius Bennett .15 .40
76 Mike Merriweather .08 .25
77 John Elway 1.50 4.00
78 Herschel Walker .15 .40
79 Hassan Jones UER .08 .25
80 Jim Harbaugh .30 .75
81 Issiac Holt .08 .25
82 David Alexander .08 .25
83 Brian Mitchell .15 .40
84 Mark Tuinei .08 .25
85 Tom Rathman .08 .25
86 Reggie White .30 .75
87 William Perry .15 .40
88 Jeff Wright .08 .25
89 Keith Kartz .08 .25
90 Andre Waters .08 .25
91 Darryl Talley .08 .25
92 Morten Andersen .08 .25
93 Tom Waddle .08 .25
94 Felix Wright UER .08 .25
95 Keith Jackson .15 .40
96 Art Monk .15 .40
97 Seth Joyner .08 .25
98 Steve McMichael .15 .40
99 Thurman Thomas .30 .75
100 Warren Moon .30 .75
101 Tony Casillas .08 .25
102 Vance Johnson .08 .25
103 Doug Dawson RC .08 .25
104 Bill Maas .08 .25
105 Mark Clayton .15 .40
106 Hoby Brenner .08 .25
107 Gary Anderson K .08 .25
108 Marc Logan .08 .25
109 Ricky Sanders .08 .25
110 Vai Sikahema .08 .25
111 Neil Smith .30 .75
112 Cody Carlson .08 .25
113 Jimmie Jones .08 .25
114 Pat Swilling .08 .25
115 Neil O'Donnell .15 .40
116 Chip Lohmiller .08 .25
117 Mike Croel .08 .25
118 Pete Metzelaars .08 .25
119 Ray Childress .08 .25
120 Fred Banks .08 .25
121 Derek Kennard .08 .25
122 Daryl Johnston .30 .75
123 Lorenzo White UER .08 .25
124 Hardy Nickerson .15 .40
125 Derrick Thomas .30 .75
126 Steve Walsh .08 .25
127 Doug Widell .08 .25
128 Calvin Williams .15 .40
129 Tim Harris .08 .25
130 Rod Woodson .30 .75
131 Craig Heyward .15 .40
132 Barry Word .08 .25
133 Mark Duper .08 .25
134 Tim Johnson .08 .25
135 John Gesek .08 .25
136 Steve Jackson .08 .25
137 Dave Krieg .15 .40
138 Barry Sanders 1.50 4.00
139 Michael Haynes .15 .40
140 Eric Metcalf .15 .40
141 Stan Humphries .30 .75
142 Sterling Sharpe .30 .75
143 Todd Marinovich .08 .25
144 Rodney Hampton .15 .40
145 Rodney Peete .15 .40
146 Darryl Williams RC .08 .25
147 Darren Perry RC .08 .25
148 Terrell Buckley RC .08 .25
149 Amp Lee RC .08 .25
150 Ricky Watters .30 .75

1993 Playoff Promos

Measuring the standard-size, these six cards were issued to preview the design of the 1993 Playoff Collectors Edition football set. Printed on a thicker (22 point) card using the Tekchrome printing process, the action player photos on the fronts are full-bleed and have a metallic sheen to them. The cards are numbered "X of 6 Promo."

COMPLETE SET (6) 4.80 12.00
1 Emmitt Smith 2.40 6.00
2 Barry Foster .30 .75
3 Quinn Early .30 .75
4 Tim Brown .50 1.25
5 Steve Young 1.20 3.00
6 Sterling Sharpe .30 .75

1993 Playoff

The 1993 Playoff set consists of 315 standard-size cards that were issued in eight-card packs. Subsets featured include The Backs (277-282), Connections (283-292), and Rookies (293-315). Rookie Cards include Jerome Bettis, Drew Bledsoe, Reggie Brooks, Curtis Conway, Garrison Hearst, O.J. McDuffie, Rick Mirer, and Kevin Williams.

COMPLETE SET (315) 10.00 25.00
1 Troy Aikman .60 1.50
2 Jerry Rice .75 2.00
3 Keith Jackson .07 .20
4 Sean Gilbert .07 .20
5 Jim Kelly .15 .40
6 Junior Seau .15 .40
7 Deion Sanders .40 1.00
8 Joe Montana 1.25 3.00
9 Terrell Buckley .02 .10
10 Emmitt Smith 1.25 3.00
11 Pete Stoyanovich .02 .10
12 Randall Cunningham .15 .40
13 Boomer Esiason .07 .20
14 Mike Saxon .02 .10
15 Chuck Cecil .02 .10
16 Vinny Testaverde .07 .20
17 Jeff Hostetler .07 .20
18 Mark Clayton .02 .10
19 Nick Bell .02 .10
20 Frank Reich .07 .20
21 Henry Ellard .07 .20
22 Andre Reed .07 .20
23 Mark Ingram .02 .10
24 Mike Brim .02 .10
25A Bernie Kosar ERR Kozar .07 .20
25B Bernie Kosar COR .07 .20
26 Jeff George .15 .40
27 Tommy Maddox .15 .40
28 Kent Graham RC .15 .40
29 David Klingler .02 .10
30 Robert Delpino .02 .10
31 Kevin Fagan .02 .10
32 Mark Bavaro .02 .10
33 Harold Green .02 .10
34 Shawn McCarthy .02 .10
35 Ricky Proehl .02 .10
36 Eugene Robinson .02 .10
37 Phil Simms .07 .20
38 David Lang .02 .10
39 Santana Dotson .07 .20
40 Brett Perriman .15 .40
41 Jim Harbaugh .15 .40
42 Keith Byars .02 .10
43 Quentin Coryatt .07 .20
44 Louis Oliver .02 .10
45 Howie Long .15 .40
46 Mike Sherrard .02 .10
47 Earnest Byner .02 .10
48 Neil Smith .15 .40
49 Audray McMillian .02 .10
50 Vaughn Dunbar .02 .10
51 Ronnie Lott .07 .20
52 Clyde Simmons .02 .10
53 Kevin Scott .02 .10
54 Bubby Brister .02 .10
55 Randal Hill .02 .10
56 Pat Swilling .02 .10
57 Steve Beuerlein .07 .20
58 Gary Clark .07 .20
59 Brian Noble .02 .10
60 Leslie O'Neal .07 .20
61 Vincent Brown .02 .10
62 Edgar Bennett .15 .40
63 Anthony Carter .07 .20
64 Glenn Cadrez UER RC .02 .10
65 Dalton Hilliard .02 .10
66 James Lofton .07 .20
67 Walter Stanley .02 .10
68 Tim Harris .02 .10
69 Carl Banks .02 .10
70 Andre Ware .02 .10
71 Karl Mecklenburg .02 .10
72 Russell Maryland .02 .10
73 Leroy Thompson .02 .10
74 Tommy Kane .02 .10
75 Dan Marino 1.25 3.00
76 Darrell Fullington .02 .10
77 Jessie Tuggle .02 .10
78 Bruce Smith .15 .40
79 Neal Anderson .02 .10
80 Kevin Mack .02 .10
81 Shane Dronett .02 .10
82 Nick Lowery .02 .10
83 Sheldon White .02 .10
84 Flipper Anderson .02 .10
85 Jeff Herrod .02 .10
86 Dwight Stone .02 .10
87 Dave Krieg .07 .20
88 Bryan Cox .02 .10
89 Greg McMurtry .02 .10
90 Rickey Jackson .02 .10
91 Ernie Mills .02 .10
92 Browning Nagle .02 .10
93 John Taylor .07 .20
94 Eric Dickerson .07 .20
95 Johnny Holland .02 .10
96 Anthony Miller .07 .20
97 Fred Barnett .07 .20
98 Ricky Ervins UER .02 .10
99 Leonard Russell .07 .20
100 Lawrence Taylor .15 .40
101 Tony Casillas .02 .10
102 John Elway 1.25 3.00
103 Bennie Blades .02 .10
104 Harry Sydney .02 .10
105 Bubba McDowell .02 .10
106 Todd McNair .02 .10
107 Steve Smith .02 .10
108 Jim Everett .07 .20
109 Bobby Humphrey .02 .10
110 Rich Gannon .15 .40
111 Marv Cook .02 .10
112 Wayne Martin .02 .10
113 Sean Landeta .02 .10
114 Brad Baxter UER .02 .10
115 Reggie White .15 .40
116 Johnny Johnson .02 .10
117 Jeff Graham .07 .20
118 Darren Carrington RC .02 .10
119 Ricky Watters .15 .40
120 Art Monk .07 .20
121 Cornelius Bennett .07 .20
122 Wade Wilson .02 .10
123 Daniel Stubbs .02 .10
124 Brad Muster .02 .10
125 Mike Tomczak .02 .10
126 Jay Novacek .07 .20
127 Shannon Sharpe .15 .40
128 Rodney Peete .02 .10
129 Daryl Johnston .15 .40
130 Warren Moon .15 .40
131 Willie Gault .02 .10
132 Tony Martin .15 .40
133 Terry Allen .15 .40
134 Hugh Millen .02 .10
135 Rob Moore .07 .20
136 Andy Harmon RC .07 .20
137 Kelvin Martin .02 .10
138 Rod Woodson .15 .40
139 Nate Lewis .02 .10
140 Darryl Talley .02 .10
141 Guy McIntyre .02 .10
142 John L. Williams .02 .10
143 Brad Edwards .02 .10
144 Trace Armstrong .02 .10
145 Kenneth Davis .02 .10
146 Clay Matthews .07 .20
147 Gaston Green .02 .10
148 Chris Spielman .07 .20
149 Cody Carlson .02 .10
150 Derrick Thomas .15 .40
151 Terry McDaniel .02 .10
152 Kevin Greene .07 .20
153 Roger Craig .07 .20
154 Craig Heyward .07 .20
155 Rodney Hampton .07 .20
156 Heath Sherman .02 .10
157 Mark Stepnoski .02 .10
158 Chris Chandler .07 .20
159 Rod Bernstine .02 .10
160 Pierce Holt .02 .10
161 Wilber Marshall .02 .10
162 Reggie Cobb .02 .10
163 Tom Rathman .02 .10
164 Michael Haynes .07 .20
165 Nate Odomes .02 .10
166 Tom Waddle .02 .10
167 Eric Ball .02 .10
168 Brett Favre 1.50 4.00
169 Michael Jackson .07 .20
170 Lorenzo White .02 .10
171 Cleveland Gary .02 .10
172 Jay Schroeder .02 .10
173 Tony Paige .02 .10
174 Jack Del Rio .02 .10
175 Jon Vaughn .02 .10
176 Morten Andersen UER .02 .10
177 Chris Burkett .02 .10
178 Vai Sikahema .02 .10
179 Ronnie Harmon .02 .10
180 Amp Lee .02 .10
181 Chip Lohmiller .02 .10
182 Steve Broussard .02 .10
183 Don Beebe .02 .10
184 Tommy Vardell .02 .10
185 Keith Jennings .02 .10
186 Simon Fletcher .02 .10
187 Mel Gray .07 .20
188 Vince Workman .02 .10
189 Haywood Jeffires .07 .20
190 Barry Word .02 .10
191 Ethan Horton .02 .10
192 Mark Higgs .02 .10
193 Irving Fryar .07 .20
194 Charles Haley .07 .20
195 Steve Bono .07 .20
196 Mike Golic .02 .10
197 Gary Anderson K .02 .10
198 Sterling Sharpe .15 .40
199 Andre Tippett .02 .10
200 Thurman Thomas .15 .40
201 Chris Miller .07 .20
202 Henry Jones .02 .10
203 Mo Lewis .02 .10
204 Marion Butts .02 .10
205 Mike Johnson .02 .10
206 Alvin Harper .07 .20
207 Ray Childress .02 .10
208 Anthony Johnson .07 .20
209 Tony Bennett .02 .10
210 Anthony Newman RC .02 .10
211 Christian Okoye .02 .10
212 Marcus Allen .15 .40
213 Jackie Harris .02 .10
214 Mark Duper .02 .10
215 Cris Carter .15 .40
216 John Stephens .02 .10
217 Barry Sanders 1.00 2.50
218A H.Moore ERR Sherman .50 1.25
218B Herman Moore COR 1.00 2.50
219 Marvin Washington .02 .10
220 Calvin Williams .07 .20
221 John Randle .07 .20
222 Marco Coleman .02 .10
223 Eric Martin .02 .10
224 Dave Meggett .02 .10
225 Brian Washington .02 .10
226 Barry Foster .07 .20
227 Michael Zordich .02 .10
228 Stan Humphries .07 .20
229 Mike Cofer .02 .10
230 Chris Warren .07 .20
231 Keith McCants .02 .10
232 Mark Rypien .02 .10
233 James Francis .02 .10
234 Andre Rison .07 .20
235 William Perry .07 .20
236 Chip Banks .02 .10
237 Willie Davis .15 .40
238 Chris Doleman .02 .10
239 Tim Brown .15 .40
240 Darren Perry .02 .10
241 Johnny Bailey .02 .10
242 Ernest Givins .07 .20
243 John Carney .02 .10
244 Cortez Kennedy .07 .20
245 Lawrence Dawsey .02 .10
246 Martin Mayhew .02 .10
247 Shane Conlan .02 .10
248 J.J. Birden .02 .10
249 Quinn Early .07 .20
250 Michael Irvin .15 .40
251 Neil O'Donnell .15 .40
252 Stan Gelbaugh .02 .10
253 Drew Hill .02 .10
254 Wendell Davis .02 .10
255 Tim Johnson .02 .10
256 Seth Joyner .02 .10
257 Derrick Fenner .02 .10
258 Steve Young .60 1.50
259 Jackie Slater .02 .10
260 Eric Metcalf .07 .20
261 Rufus Porter .02 .10
262 Ken Norton Jr. .07 .20
263 Tim McDonald .02 .10
264 Mark Jackson .02 .10
265 Hardy Nickerson .07 .20
266 Anthony Munoz .07 .20
267 Mark Carrier WR .07 .20
268 Mike Pritchard .07 .20
269 Steve Emtman .02 .10
270 Ricky Sanders .02 .10
271 Robert Massey .02 .10
272 Pete Metzelaars .02 .10
273 Reggie Langhorne .02 .10
274 Tim McGee .02 .10
275 Reggie Rivers RC .02 .10
276 Jimmie Jones .02 .10
277 Lorenzo White TB .02 .10
278 Emmitt Smith TB .75 2.00
279 Thurman Thomas TB .15 .40
280 Barry Sanders TB .60 1.50
281 Rodney Hampton TB .07 .20
282 Barry Foster TB .07 .20
283 Troy Aikman PC .40 1.00
284 Michael Irvin PC .07 .20
285 Brett Favre PC 1.00 2.50
286 Sterling Sharpe PC .07 .20
287 Steve Young PC .40 1.00
288 Jerry Rice PC .50 1.25
289 Stan Humphries PC .07 .20
290 Anthony Miller PC .07 .20
291 Dan Marino PC .75 2.00
292 Keith Jackson PC .02 .10
293 Patrick Bates RC .02 .10
294 Jerome Bettis RC 4.00 10.00
295 Drew Bledsoe RC 2.50 6.00
296 Tom Carter RC .07 .20
297 Curtis Conway RC .40 1.00
298 John Copeland RC .07 .20
299 Eric Curry RC .02 .10
300 Reggie Brooks RC .07 .20
301 Steve Everitt RC .02 .10
302 Deon Figures RC .02 .10
303 Garrison Hearst RC .75 2.00
304 Qadry Ismail UER RC .15 .40
305 Marvin Jones RC .02 .10
306 Lincoln Kennedy RC .02 .10
307 O.J.McDuffie RC .15 .40
308 Rick Mirer RC .15 .40
309 Wayne Simmons RC .02 .10
310 Irv Smith RC .02 .10
311 Robert Smith RC 1.25 3.00
312 Dana Stubblefield RC .15 .40
313 George Teague RC .07 .20
314 Dan Williams RC .02 .10
315 Kevin Williams RC WR .15 .40
NNO Santa Claus .75 2.00

1993 Playoff Checklists

These eight standard-size cards were randomly inserted in packs. The fronts feature full-bleed color action player photos. Overlaying the picture at the bottom is a silver box edged on its left by a black stripe carrying the words "Check It Out." The silver box carries statistical highlights on the featured player(s). The checklist on the backs is printed on a white panel bordered on the top by a red stripe and on the bottom by a black stripe.

COMPLETE SET (8) 2.50 6.00
1A Warren Moon ERR Kozar .30 .75
1B Warren Moon COR Kosar .30 .75
2 Barry Sanders 1.25 3.00
3 Deion Sanders .50 1.25
4 Rod Woodson .20 .50
5 Junior Seau .40 1.00
6 Mark Rypien .20 .50
7 Derrick Thomas .30 .75
8 M.Irvin .40 1.00
Harper
Johnston

1993 Playoff Club

Featuring all-time great, still active football players, this seven-card, standard-size set was available in both hobby and retail packs. On the fronts, the color head shots inside a picture frame contrast with the black-and-white surrounding photo. The gold Playoff Club emblem appears at the lower left corner, and the player's signature is inscribed in gold ink across the picture. On the backs, a career summary is overprinted on a white panel with a gray Playoff Club emblem. The cards are numbered on the back with a "PC" prefix.

COMPLETE SET (7) 6.00 15.00
PC1 Joe Montana 5.00 12.00
PC2 Art Monk .30 .75
PC3 Lawrence Taylor .60 1.50
PC4 Ronnie Lott .30 .75
PC5 Reggie White .60 1.50
PC6 Anthony Munoz .30 .75
PC7 Jackie Slater .15 .40

1993 Playoff Brett Favre

Randomly inserted in hobby packs, these five standard-size cards trace the career of Brett Favre, quarterback of the Green Bay Packers. The cards are numbered on the back as "X of 5."

COMPLETE SET (5) 12.50 30.00
COMMON FAVRE (1-5) 4.00 10.00
RANDOM INSERTS IN HOBBY PACKS

1993 Playoff Headliners Redemption

A special trade card randomly inserted in retail foil packs, entitled collector to receive these six standard-size cards. The redemption offer expired July 31, 1994. A similar card randomly inserted in hobby foil packs entitled the collector to receive a ten-card Rookie Roundup set. According to the card back, 48,475 trade cards were produced for random insertion. The cards are numbered on the back with an "H" prefix.

COMPLETE SET (6) 4.00 10.00
ONE SET PER REDEMPTION CARD BY MAIL
H1 Brett Favre 3.00 6.00
H2 Sterling Sharpe .25 .60
H3 Emmitt Smith 2.50 5.00
H4 Jerry Rice 1.50 3.00
H5 Thurman Thomas .25 .60
H6 David Klingler .05 .15
NNO Headliner Redemp.Expired .10 .30

1993 Playoff Promo Inserts

One Playoff Promo Insert (or Playoff Ricky Watters card) was inserted in every special retail pack of 1993 Playoff. The six standard-size promos feature borderless player action shots on their fronts. The cards are numbered on the back as "Promo X of 6" and do not feature a player image on the back.

COMPLETE SET (6) 4.00 10.00
1 Michael Irvin .80 2.00
2 Barry Foster .60 1.50
3 Quinn Early .60 1.50
4 Tim Brown .80 2.00
5 Reggie White .80 2.00
6 Sterling Sharpe .60 1.50

1993 Playoff Rookie Roundup Redemption

A special insert card (1993 Playoff Rookie Roundup Redemption) found in hobby foil packs could be redeemed through a mail-in offer for this ten-card, standard-size set. The expiration date was July 3, 1994. These cards showcase the ten hottest rookies of the 1993 NFL season. According to the card back, 15,683 trade cards were produced. The cards are numbered on the back with an "R" prefix.

COMPLETE SET (10) 7.50 20.00
ONE SET PER REDEMPTION CARD BY MAIL
R1 Jerome Bettis 8.00 20.00
R2 Drew Bledsoe 5.00 12.00
R3 Reggie Brooks .15 .40
R4 Derek Brown RBK .07 .20
R5 Garrison Hearst 1.50 4.00
R6 Terry Kirby .07 .20
R7 Glyn Milburn .07 .20
R8 Rick Mirer .30 .75
R9 Roosevelt Potts .07 .20
R10 Dana Stubblefield .30 .75
NNO Rookie Redempt.Expired .20 .50

1993 Playoff Ricky Watters

Randomly inserted in retail packs, these five standard-size cards trace the career of San Francisco running back Ricky Watters. The cards are numbered on the back as "X of 5."

COMPLETE SET (5) 4.00 10.00
COMMON WATTERS (1-5) 1.00 2.50
RANDOM INSERTS IN RETAIL

1994 Playoff Prototypes

These six standard-size prototypes feature on their fronts borderless metallic color player action shots. The player's name appears within an oval emblem in one corner. The borderless back carries a color closeup with the player's name, team helmet, and career highlights. Note that there is no mention of prototype on the cards themselves. Each is unnumbered and checklisted below in alphabetical order.

COMPLETE SET (6) 3.20 8.00
1 Marcus Allen .40 1.00
2 Rick Mirer .30 .75
3 Barry Sanders 1.20 3.00
4 Junior Seau .30 .75
5 Sterling Sharpe .30 .75
6 Emmitt Smith 1.00 2.50

1994 Playoff

These 336 standard-size feature borderless card fronts with metallic color player action shots. The cards were issued in eight-card hobby, retail and four-star packs. The player's name appears within an oval emblem in one corner. The borderless backs carry a color closeup with the player's name, team helmet, and career highlights. Topical subsets featured are Sack Pack (226-232), Ground Attack (233-262), Summerall's Best (263-290), and Rookies (291-336). Rookie Cards include Derrick Alexander, Isaac Bruce, Trent Dilfer, Marshall Faulk, William Floyd, Greg Hill, Charles Johnson, Errict Rhett, Darnay Scott and Heath Shuler.

COMPLETE SET (336) 12.50 30.00
1 Joe Montana 1.50 4.00
2 Derrick Thomas .20 .50
3 Dan Marino 1.50 4.00
4 Cris Carter .30 .75
5 Boomer Esiason .10 .30
6 Bruce Smith .20 .50
7 Andre Rison .10 .30
8 Curtis Conway .20 .50
9 Michael Irvin .20 .50
10 Shannon Sharpe .10 .30
11 Pat Swilling .05 .15
12 John Parrella .05 .15
13 Mel Gray .05 .15
14 Ray Childress .05 .15
15 Willie Davis .10 .30
16 Rocket Ismail .10 .30
17 Jim Everett .10 .30
18 Mark Higgs .05 .15
19 Trace Armstrong .05 .15
20 Jim Kelly .20 .50
21 Rob Burnett .05 .15
22 Jay Novacek .10 .30
23 Robert Delpino .05 .15
24 Brett Perriman .10 .30
25 Troy Aikman .75 2.00
26 Reggie White .20 .50
27 Lorenzo White .05 .15
28 Bubba McDowell .05 .15
29 Steve Emtman .05 .15
30 Brett Favre 1.50 4.00
31 Derek Russell .05 .15
32 Jeff Hostetler .10 .30
33 Henry Ellard .10 .30
34 Jack Del Rio .05 .15
35 Mike Saxon .05 .15
36 Rickey Jackson .05 .15
37 Phil Simms .10 .30
38 Quinn Early .10 .30
39 Russell Copeland .05 .15
40 Carl Pickens .10 .30
41 Lance Gunn .05 .15
42 Bernie Kosar .10 .30
43 John Elway 1.50 4.00
44 George Teague .05 .15
45 Nick Lowery .05 .15
46 Haywood Jeffires .10 .30
47 Will Shields .05 .15
48 Daryl Johnston .10 .30
49 Pete Metzelaars .05 .15
50 Warren Moon .20 .50
51 Cornelius Bennett .10 .30
52 Vinny Testaverde .10 .30
53 John Mangum RC .05 .15
54 Tommy Vardell .05 .15
55 Lincoln Coleman RC .05 .15
56 Karl Mecklenburg .05 .15
57 Jackie Harris .05 .15
58 Curtis Duncan .05 .15
59 Quentin Coryatt .05 .15
60 Tim Brown .20 .50
61 Irving Fryar .10 .30
62 Sean Gilbert .05 .15
63 Qadry Ismail .20 .50
64 Irv Smith .05 .15
65 Mark Jackson .05 .15
66 Ronnie Lott .10 .30
67 Henry Jones .05 .15
68 Horace Copeland .05 .15
69 John Copeland .05 .15
70 Mark Carrier WR .10 .30
71 Michael Jackson .10 .30
72 Jason Elam .10 .30
73 Rod Bernstine .05 .15
74 Wayne Simmons .05 .15
75 Cody Carlson .05 .15
76 Alexander Wright .05 .15
77 Shane Conlan .05 .15
78 Keith Jackson .05 .15
79 Sean Salisbury .05 .15
80 Vaughan Johnson .05 .15
81 Rob Moore .10 .30
82 Andre Reed .10 .30
83 David Klingler .05 .15
84 Jim Harbaugh .20 .50
85 John Jett RC .05 .15
86 Sterling Sharpe .10 .30
87 Webster Slaughter .05 .15
88 J.J. Birden .05 .15-
89 O.J.McDuffie .20 .50
90 Andre Tippett .05 .15
91 Don Beebe .05 .15
92 Mark Stepnoski .05 .15
93 Neil Smith .10 .30
94 Terry Kirby .20 .50
95 Wade Wilson .05 .15
96 Darryl Talley .05 .15
97 Anthony Smith .05 .15
98 Willie Roaf .05 .15
99 Mo Lewis .05 .15
100 James Washington .05 .15
101 Nate Odomes .05 .15
102 Chris Gedney .05 .15
103 Joe Walter .05 .15
104 Alvin Harper .10 .30
105 Simon Fletcher .05 .15
106 Rodney Peete .05 .15
107 Terrell Buckley .05 .15
108 Jeff George .20 .50
109 James Jett .05 .15
110 Tony Casillas .05 .15
111 Marco Coleman .05 .15
112 Anthony Carter .10 .30
113 Lincoln Kennedy .05 .15
114 Chris Calloway .05 .15
115 Randall Cunningham .20 .50
116 Steve Beuerlein .10 .30
117 Neil O'Donnell .20 .50
118 Stan Humphries .10 .30
119 John Taylor .10 .30
120 Cortez Kennedy .10 .30
121 Santana Dotson .10 .30
122 Thomas Smith .05 .15
123 Kevin Williams WR .10 .30
124 Andre Ware .05 .15
125 Ethan Horton .05 .15
126 Mike Sherrard .05 .15
127 Fred Barnett .10 .30
128 Ricky Proehl .05 .15
129 Kevin Greene .10 .30
130 John Carney .05 .15
131 Tim McDonald .05 .15
132 Rick Mirer .20 .50
133 Blair Thomas .05 .15
134 Hardy Nickerson .10 .30
135 Heath Sherman .05 .15
136 Andre Hastings .10 .30
137 Randal Hill .05 .15
138 Mike Cofer .05 .15
139 Brian Blades .10 .30
140 Earnest Byner .05 .15
141 Bill Bates .10 .30
142 Junior Seau .20 .50
143 Johnny Bailey .05 .15
144 Dwight Stone .05 .15
145 Todd Kelly .05 .15
146 Tyrone Montgomery .05 .15
147 Herschel Walker .10 .30
148 Gary Clark .10 .30
149 Eric Green .05 .15
150 Steve Young .60 1.50
151 Anthony Miller .10 .30
152 Dana Stubblefield .10 .30
153 Dean Wells RC .05 .15
154 Vincent Brisby .10 .30
155 Chris Chandler .10 .30
156 Clyde Simmons .05 .15
157 Rod Woodson .10 .30
158 Nate Lewis .05 .15
159 Martin Harrison .05 .15
160 Kelvin Martin .05 .15
161 Craig Erickson .05 .15
162 Johnny Mitchell .05 .15
163 Calvin Williams .10 .30
164 Deon Figures .05 .15
165 Tom Rathman .05 .15
166 Rick Hamilton .05 .15
167 John L. Williams .05 .15
168 Demetrius DuBose .05 .15
169 Michael Brooks .05 .15
170 Marion Butts .05 .15
171 Brent Jones .10 .30
172 Bobby Hebert .05 .15
173 Brad Edwards .05 .15
174 David Wyman .05 .15
175 Herman Moore .20 .50
176 LeRoy Butler .05 .15
177 Reggie Langhorne .05 .15
178 Dave Krieg .10 .30
179 Patrick Bates .05 .15
180 Erik Kramer .10 .30
181 Troy Drayton .05 .15
182 Dave Meggett .05 .15
183 Eric Allen .05 .15
184 Mark Bavaro .05 .15
185 Leslie O'Neal .05 .15
186 Jerry Rice .75 2.00
187 Desmond Howard .10 .30
188 Deion Sanders .30 .75
189 Bill Maas .05 .15
190 Frank Wycheck RC .75 2.00
191 Ernest Givins .10 .30
192 Terry McDaniel .05 .15
193 Bryan Cox .05 .15
194 Guy McIntyre .05 .15
195 Pierce Holt .05 .15
196 Fred Stokes .05 .15
197 Mike Pritchard .05 .15
198 Terry Obee .05 .15
199 Mark Collins .05 .15
200 Drew Bledsoe .50 1.25
201 Barry Word .05 .15
202 Derrick Lassic .05 .15
203 Chris Spielman .10 .30
204 John Jurkovic RC .10 .30
205 Ken Norton Jr. .10 .30
206 Dale Carter .05 .15
207 Chris Doleman .05 .15
208 Keith Hamilton .05 .15
209 Andy Harmon .05 .15
210 John Friesz .10 .30
211 Steve Bono .10 .30
212 Mark Rypien .05 .15
213 Ricky Sanders .05 .15
214 Michael Haynes .10 .30
215 Todd McNair .05 .15
216 Leon Lett .05 .15
217 Scott Mitchell .10 .30
218 Mike Morris RC .05 .15
219 Darrin Smith .05 .15
220 Jim McMahon .10 .30
221 Garrison Hearst .20 .50
222 Leroy Thompson .05 .15
223 Darren Carrington .05 .15
224 Pete Stoyanovich .05 .15
225 Chris Miller .05 .15
226 Bruce Smith SP .10 .30
227 Simon Fletcher SP .05 .15
228 Reggie White SP .20 .50
229 Neil Smith SP .10 .30
230 Chris Doleman SP .05 .15
231 Keith Hamilton SP .05 .15
232 Dana Stubblefield SP .05 .15
233 Eric Pegram GA .05 .15
234 Thurman Thomas GA .20 .50
235 Lewis Tillman GA .05 .15
236 Harold Green GA .05 .15
237 Eric Metcalf GA .10 .30
238 Emmitt Smith GA 1.25 3.00
239 Glyn Milburn GA .10 .30
240 Barry Sanders GA 1.25 3.00
241 Edgar Bennett GA .10 .30
242 Gary Brown GA .05 .15
243 Roosevelt Potts GA .05 .15
244 Marcus Allen GA .20 .50
245 Greg Robinson GA .05 .15
246 Jerome Bettis GA .30 .75
247 Keith Byars GA .05 .15
248 Robert Smith GA .20 .50
249 Leonard Russell GA .05 .15
250 Derek Brown RBK GA .05 .15
251 Rodney Hampton GA .10 .30
252 Johnny Johnson GA .05 .15
253 Vaughn Hebron GA .05 .15
254 Ronald Moore GA .05 .15
255 Barry Foster GA .05 .15
256 Natrone Means GA .20 .50
257 Ricky Watters GA .10 .30
258 Chris Warren GA .20 .50
259 Vince Workman GA .05 .15
260 Reggie Brooks GA .05 .15
261 Carolina Panthers .15 .40
262 Jacksonville Jaguars .15 .40
263 Troy Aikman SB .40 1.00
264 Barry Sanders SB .60 1.50
265 Emmitt Smith SB .60 1.50
266 Michael Irvin SB .20 .50
267 Jerry Rice SB .40 1.00
268 Shannon Sharpe SB .10 .30
269 Bob Kratch SB .05 .15
270 Howard Ballard SB .05 .15
271 Erik Williams SB .05 .15
272 Guy McIntyre SB .05 .15
273 Kevin Williams WR SB .10 .30
274 Mel Gray SB .05 .15
275 Eddie Murray SB .05 .15
276 Mark Stepnoski SB .05 .15
277 Tommy Barnhardt SB .05 .15
278 Derrick Thomas SB .10 .30
279 Ken Norton Jr. SB .10 .30
280 Chris Spielman SB .05 .15
281 Deion Sanders SB .20 .50
282 Mark Collins SB .05 .15
283 Bruce Smith SB .10 .30
284 Reggie White SB .20 .50
285 Sean Gilbert SB .05 .15
286 Cortez Kennedy SB .10 .30
287 Steve Atwater SB .05 .15
288 Tim McDonald SB .05 .15
289 Jerome Bettis SB .30 .75
290 Dana Stubblefield SB .10 .30
291 Bert Emanuel RC .20 .50
292 Jeff Burris RC .10 .30
293 Bucky Brooks RC .05 .15
294 Dan Wilkinson RC .10 .30
295 Darnay Scott RC .40 1.00
296 Derrick Alexander WR RC .20 .50
297 Antonio Langham RC .10 .30
298 Shante Carver RC .05 .15
299 Shelby Hill RC .05 .15
300 Larry Allen RC 6.00 15.00
301 Johnnie Morton RC .75 2.00
302 Van Malone RC .05 .15
303 Aaron Taylor RC .05 .15
304 Marshall Faulk RC 2.50 6.00
305 Eric Mahlum RC .05 .15
306 Trev Alberts RC .10 .30
307 Greg Hill RC .20 .50
308 Donnell Bennett RC .20 .50
309 Rob Fredrickson RC .10 .30
310 James Folston RC .05 .15
311 Isaac Bruce RC 2.00 5.00
312 Tim Ruddy RC .05 .15
313 Aubrey Beavers RC .05 .15
314 David Palmer RC .20 .50
315 Dewayne Washington RC .10 .30
316 Willie McGinest RC .20 .50
317 Mario Bates RC .20 .50
318 Kevin Lee RC .05 .15
319 Jason Sehorn RC .30 .75
320 Thomas Randolph RC .05 .15
321 Ryan Yarborough RC .05 .15
322 Bernard Williams RC .05 .15
323 Chuck Levy RC .05 .15
324 Jamir Miller RC .10 .30
325 Charles Johnson RC .20 .50
326 Bryant Young RC .30 .75
327 William Floyd RC .20 .50
328 Kevin Mitchell RC .05 .15
329 Sam Adams RC .10 .30
330 Kevin Mawae RC .20 .50
331 Errict Rhett RC .20 .50
332 Trent Dilfer RC .60 1.50
333 Heath Shuler RC .20 .50
334 Aaron Glenn RC .20 .50
335 Todd Steussie RC .10 .30
336 Toby Wright RC .05 .15
NNO Gale Sayers Play.Club 1.50 4.00
NNO Gale Sayers AUTO 25.00 60.00

1994 Playoff Jerome Bettis

Randomly inserted in regular issue hobby packs, this standard-size five-card set highlights Jerome Bettis. The cards are numbered on the back with "x of 5".

COMPLETE SET (5) 15.00 40.00
COMMON BETTIS (1-5) 4.00 10.00
RANDOM INSERTS IN HOBBY PACKS

1994 Playoff Checklists

Randomly inserted in regular issue packs, these ten standard-size cards feature on their fronts borderless metallic color action shots with player information in a silver foil box at the bottom. The backs carry the set's checklists. The cards are numbered on the back as "X of 10".

COMPLETE SET (10) 2.00 5.00
1 Keith Cash .20 .50
2 Kerry Cash .20 .50
3 Qadry Ismail .40 1.00
4 Rocket Ismail .40 1.00
5 Bruce Matthews .20 .50
6 Clay Matthews .20 .50
7 Shannon Sharpe .40 1.00
8 Sterling Sharpe .40 1.00
9 John Taylor .20 .50
10 Keith Taylor .20 .50

1994 Playoff Club

Randomly inserted in packs at a rate of one in 20, these six standard-size cards feature metallic color action shots. The cards are numbered on the back with a "PC" prefix.

COMPLETE SET (6) 6.00 15.00
STATED ODDS 1:20
PC8 Jerry Rice 6.00 12.00
PC9 Marcus Allen 1.25 3.00
PC10 Howie Long 1.25 3.00
PC11 Clay Matthews .40 1.00
PC12 Richard Dent .75 2.00
PC13 Morten Andersen .40 1.00

1994 Playoff Headliners Redemption

Issued one set per redemption card, this set consists of six standard-size cards of player that reached milestones in 1994. Full-bleed prism fronts have the Headliners logo and player name at the bottom. Horizontal backs have a close-up photo with a brief write-up on the milestone.

COMPLETE SET (6) 3.00 6.00
ONE SET PER TRADE CARD BY MAIL
1 Tim Brown .75 1.50
2 Bernie Parmalee .20 .50
3 Sterling Sharpe .40 1.00
4 Natrone Means .75 1.50
5 Alvin Harper .40 1.00
6 Deion Sanders 1.25 2.50
NNO Headliners Redemp. .20 .50

1994 Playoff Jerry Rice

Randomly inserted in retail packs, this five-card standard-size set chronicles the career of the 49ers Jerry Rice. Card fronts feature an action photo superimposed over a silver background. The backs detail highlights of his career.

COMPLETE SET (5) 25.00 60.00
COMMON RICE (1-5) 5.00 12.00
RANDOM INSERTS IN RETAIL PACKS

1994 Playoff Rookie Roundup Redemption

A special trade card randomly inserted in packs, could be redeemed through a mail-in offer by the collector for this nine-card, standard-size set. This set was redeemable until December 31, 1995. Popular rookies in this set include Marshall Faulk, Errict Rhett and Heath Shuler.

COMPLETE SET (9) 12.50 30.00
ONE SET PER TRADE CARD BY MAIL
1 Heath Shuler 1.25 3.00
2 David Palmer 1.25 3.00
3 Dan Wilkinson 1.00 2.50
4 Marshall Faulk 5.00 12.00
5 Charlie Garner 2.00 5.00
6 Errict Rhett 1.25 3.00
7 Trent Dilfer 1.50 4.00
8 Antonio Langham 1.00 2.50
9 Gus Frerotte 2.50 6.00
NNO Redemption Card .20 .50

1994 Playoff Barry Sanders

Randomly inserted in four star packs, this five-card standard-size set chronicles the career of Lions running back Barry Sanders. Card fronts have an action photo superimposed over a silver background. The backs detail different parts of his career.

COMPLETE SET (5) 40.00 80.00
COMMON B.SANDERS (1-5) 7.50 20.00
RANDOM INSERTS IN 4 STAR PACKS

1994 Playoff Super Bowl Redemption

A special trade card randomly inserted in packs could be redeemed through a mail-in offer by the collector for a special six-card standard-size set. This set was redeemable until December 31, 1995. The Dallas Cowboys won Super Bowl XXVIII, therefore Cowboy players are featured in this set. The borderless fronts have metallic color player action photos while the backs describe personal highlights from the contest.

COMPLETE SET (6) 8.00 20.00
ONE SET PER TRADE CARD BY MAIL
1 Troy Aikman 3.00 8.00
2 Emmitt Smith 5.00 12.00
3 Leon Lett .25 .60
4 Michael Irvin .75 2.00
5 James Washington .25 .60
6 Darrin Smith .25 .60
NNO Super Bowl Redemp. .20 .50

1994 Playoff Julie Bell Art

This six-card standard-size set was available through mail redemption. Full-bleed, metallic card fronts contain Julie Bell's artwork of top players. The backs contain a quote from Bell that ties in with the theme on the front. A version marked

"SAMPLE" on the back was also produced.
COMPLETE SET (6) 6.00 15.00
*SAMPLE: .4X TO 1X BASIC CARDS
1 Emmitt Smith 5.00 6.00
2 Marcus Allen .80 2.00
3 Junior Seau .50 1.25
4 Barry Sanders 3.00 6.00
5 Rick Mirer .50 1.25
6 Sterling Sharpe .50 1.25

1994 Playoff Super Bowl Promos

This six-card standard-size set was issued by Playoff to commemorate the 1994 Super Bowl. The fronts display borderless color action shots that have a metallic sheen. The player's name appears above and below the Playoff logo, both within a silver-colored oval in a lower corner. The white backs carry the 1994 Super Bowl logo in the center. The cards are numbered in the upper right corner with the word "Promo" printed below the number.

COMPLETE SET (6) 4.80 12.00
1 Jerry Rice 2.00 5.00
2 Daryl Johnston .50 1.25
3 Herschel Walker .50 1.25
4 Reggie White .80 2.00
5 Scott Mitchell .50 1.25
6 Thurman Thomas .80 2.00

1995 Playoff Night of the Stars

This six-card standard-size was given away during the Tuesday night Trade Show preceding the National Sports Collectors Convention in St. Louis. Collectors could also obtain the set by exchanging ten wrappers for one of the six cards at the Playoff Booth. The pro players are pictured in their pro uniforms, and the rookies in their collegiate uniforms. Though each back sports the same geometric design in a different color, all display on a black panel an advertisement for the National Sports Collectors Convention.

COMPLETE SET (6) 8.00 20.00
1 Jerome Bettis 1.20 3.00
2 Ben Coates .80 2.00
3 Deion Sanders 1.60 4.00
4 Ki-Jana Carter .80 2.00
5 Steve McNair 4.00 10.00
6 Errict Rhett .80 2.00

1995 Playoff Super Bowl Card Show

This eight-card standard-size set were given away during the Super Bowl XXIX Card Show. The fronts feature borderless metallic color action player cutouts superposed over a metallic red, silver and gold background. The player's name in silver-foil letters appears in the top left corner. On a black background, the backs carry the player's name, season highlights and the Super Bowl XXIX logo. Only 3,000 of each card was produced.

COMPLETE SET (8) 8.00 20.00
1 Marshall Faulk 3.20 8.00
2 Heath Shuler .80 2.00
3 David Palmer .50 1.25
4 Errict Rhett 1.20 3.00
5 Charlie Garner .80 2.00
6 Irving Spikes .50 1.25
7 Shante Carver .50 1.25
8 Greg Hill 1.00 2.50

1996 Playoff Felt

This set was produced for and sold exclusively for QVC television shopping network. Each features a top player produced with an all felt cardfront finish and a player bio on the back. Each player was produced with three different felt colors as listed below.

COMPLETE SET (9) 40.00 80.00
1A Barry Sanders Blue 6.00 15.00
1B Barry Sanders Gray 6.00 15.00
1C Barry Sanders Green 6.00 15.00
2A Deion Sanders Beige 3.00 8.00
2B Deion Sanders Blue 3.00 8.00
2C Deion Sanders Green 3.00 8.00
3A Drew Bledsoe Beige 3.00 8.00
3B Drew Bledsoe Orange 3.00 8.00
3C Drew Bledsoe Red 3.00 8.00

1996 Playoff Leatherbound

This set of leather cards was issued for QVC television shopping network. Each card was produced in both a silver and gold foil version and features a 1996 Leatherbound logo on the cardfront.

COMPLETE SET (6) 30.00 60.00
*GOLD CARDS: 1X TO 2X SILVERS
1 Eddie George 6.00 15.00
2 John Elway 15.00 30.00
3 Marshall Faulk 6.00 15.00
4 Reggie White 3.00 8.00
5 Kordell Stewart 3.00 8.00
6 Jerome Bettis 3.00 8.00

1996 Playoff National Promos

This seven-card set was distributed at the 1996 National Sports Collectors Convention in Anaheim as part of a wrapper redemption program. Collectors could redeem three wrappers from any Playoff product for one card, or a foil box worth of wrappers for a complete set. The Kordell Stewart card was only available as part of the complete set offer.

COMPLETE SET (7) 16.00 40.00
1 Kordell Stewart 3.20 8.00
2 Curtis Martin 3.20 8.00
3 Tyrone Wheatley 2.00 5.00
4 Joey Galloway 3.20 8.00
5 Steve McNair 3.20 8.00
6 Kerry Collins 1.20 3.00
7 Napoleon Kaufman 2.40 6.00

1996 Playoff Super Bowl Card Show

This six-card set features borderless color action player photos superimposed over an Arizona desert background. The player's name and Super Bowl Card Show logo rounds out the front design. The backs carry the card name, player's name, and a highlight from the 1995 season. Playoff offered one card to each Card Show attendee each day in exchange for one Playoff football card wrapper. Ten wrappers were good for a complete set any day of the show. Although the cards carry a 1995 copyright date, the cards were released in January 1996 at the Tempe, Arizona Super Bowl Card Show. Reportedly, 5500 sets were produced.

COMPLETE SET (6) 6.00 15.00
1 Deion Sanders 1.20 3.00
2 Rashaan Salaam .50 1.25
3 Garrison Hearst .50 1.25
4 Robert Brooks .50 1.25
5 Barry Sanders 3.20 8.00
6 Errict Rhett .50 1.25

1997 Playoff Sports Cards Picks

Playoff produced this set distributed by Sports Cards magazine as a subscription premium. It includes a short dream pick line-up of the staff's favorite players.

COMPLETE SET (6) 3.20 8.00
1 Brett Favre .80 2.00
2 Barry Sanders .80 2.00
3 Terrell Davis .80 2.00
4 Jerry Rice .40 1.00
5 Deion Sanders .30 .75
6 Kordell Stewart .40 1.00

1997 Playoff Super Bowl Card Show

Playoff produced this seven-card set released at the 1997 Super Bowl Card Show in New Orleans. All cards, except Terrell Davis, were available each day of the show in exchange for three Playoff card wrappers opened at the Playoff booth. Two different players were made available each day Thursday through Saturday with all six available on Sunday. Terrell Davis was only available by opening and redeeming a foil box worth of wrappers for a complete seven-card set. The cards are unnumbered and listed below alphabetically.

COMPLETE SET (7) 8.00 20.00
*HOLOFOIL: .4X TO 1X BASIC CARD
1 Terry Allen 1.00 2.50
2 Jerome Bettis 1.00 2.50
3 Terrell Davis 3.20 8.00
4 Marshall Faulk 1.50 4.00
5 Eddie George 1.50 4.00
6 Deion Sanders 1.25 3.00
7 Reggie White 1.00 2.50

1998 Playoff Super Bowl Card Show

Playoff produced this seven-card set for release at the 1998 Super Bowl Card Show in San Diego. The cards were available each day of the show in exchange for various Playoff card wrappers opened at the Playoff booth.

COMPLETE SET (7) 8.00 20.00
1 Trent Dilfer .50 1.25
2 Tony Martin .30 .75
3 Terrell Davis 3.20 8.00
4 Antonio Freeman 1.00 2.50
5 Herschel Walker .30 .75
6 Kordell Stewart 1.60 4.00
7 Drew Bledsoe 1.60 4.00

1998 Playoff Unsung Heroes Banquet

The 1998 Playoff Unsung Heroes Banquet set consisted of 31 player cards and a checklist card. These standard-sized cards are horizontal and have "Unsung" ghosted on the top of the card and "Hero" overprinted on the bottom, with the players name in script in the lower right hand corner. The back of the cards have the players name on the top and a short description why they were the unsung hero for 1997 on their team. This set was also sponsored by Sports Cards Magazine and EA Sports. There were reportedly only 1250 sets available, and those were distributed at the banquet. This set is noteworthy in that it contains an Eddie Robinson card, which is one of the few collector items that he has graced during his legendary career.

COMPLETE SET (32) 8.00 20.00
1 Frank Sanders .75 2.00
2 Chuck Smith .25 .60
3 Earnest Byner .25 .60
4 Phil Hansen .25 .60
5 Greg Kragen .25 .60
6 Carl Reeves .25 .60
7 Eric Bieniemy .25 .60
8 Darren Woodson .40 1.00
9 Howard Griffith .25 .60
10 Kevin Glover .25 .60
11 William Henderson .25 .60
12 Jason Belser .25 .60
13 Keenan McCardell .40 1.00
14 Kimble Anders .40 1.00
15 O.J. McDuffie .40 1.00
16 Randall McDaniel .25 .60
17 Troy Brown .40 1.00
18 Richard Harvey .25 .60
19 Charles Way .40 1.00
20 Mo Lewis .25 .60
21 Russell Maryland .25 .60
22 Michael Zordich .25 .60
23 Tim Lester .25 .60
24 Ryan McNeil .25 .60
25 Rodney Harrison .40 1.00
26 Gary Plummer .25 .60
27 Dean Wells .25 .60
28 Brad Culpepper .25 .60
29 Rodney Thomas .25 .60
30 Marvcus Patton .25 .60
NNO Checklist .25 .60
NNO Eddie Robinson CO .75 2.00

1999 Playoff Sanders/Williams/Davis Promo

Playoff Corporation issued this promo card featuring Barry Sanders, Ricky Williams, and Terrell Davis primarily to distributors in 1999. The card features the three players along with logos for the Donruss, Leaf, Playoff, and Score card brands. Each was serial numbered of 500-cards with just 50 being autographed by all three players.

1 Sanders Williams Davis 7.50 15.00
1AU Sanders Williams Davis AU/50* 200.00 400.00

2000 Playoff Hawaii Promo Autographs

This set of signed cards was produced by Playoff and released as Promos to attendees of the Kit Young Hawaii Trade Conference. Each card features an authentic signature from one or more star players along with Playoff's four brand logos across the top of the cardfront against a Green background. The cardbacks contain the four logos again with "Hawaii 2000" in large letters with serial numbering of 10-sets made. A brief bio on each player also is included. A Gold (serial numbered of 1) parallel set of each card was also produced.

1 John Elway 300.00 500.00
2 Brett Favre 250.00 400.00
3 Edgerrin James 175.00 300.00
4 Peyton Manning 250.00 400.00
5 Dan Marino 300.00 500.00
6 Randy Moss 250.00 400.00
7 Jerry Rice 250.00 400.00
8 Emmitt Smith 250.00 400.00
9 Kurt Warner 250.00 400.00
10 Ricky Williams 175.00 300.00
11 John Elway Brett Favre 240.00 600.00
12 John Elway Dan Marino 240.00 600.00
13 John Elway Jerry Rice 300.00 600.00
14 Brett Favre Jerry Rice 300.00 600.00
15 Brett Favre Emmitt Smith 240.00 600.00
16 Edgerrin James Peyton Manning 240.00 600.00
17 Edgerrin James Emmitt Smith 200.00 500.00
18 Edgerrin James Ricky Williams 200.00 500.00
19 Peyton Manning Dan Marino 240.00 600.00
20 Peyton Manning Kurt Warner 240.00 600.00
21 Dan Marino Kurt Warner 240.00 600.00
22 Randy Moss Jerry Rice 200.00 500.00
23 Randy Moss Kurt Warner 240.00 600.00
24 Randy Moss Ricky Williams 200.00 500.00
25 Emmitt Smith Ricky Williams 200.00 500.00
26 Marino Rice Emmitt Smith 400.00 700.00
27 Moss/Warner/Ricky Williams 280.00 700.00
28 James/Manning/Moss 300.00 750.00
29 Elway/Favre/Marino 300.00 750.00
30 Elway/Manning/Warner 280.00 700.00
31 James/E.Smith/R.Williams 240.00 600.00
32 Favre/Moss/Rice 400.00 700.00
33 Elway/Manning/Marino 300.00 750.00
34 Elway/Marino/Rice/Smith 320.00 800.00
35 James/Moss/Warner/Williams 280.00 700.00
36 Favre/Moss/Rice/Warner 300.00 750.00
37 James/Manning/Smith/Williams 300.00 750.00

2000 Playoff Super Bowl Card Show

Playoff produced this seven-card set for release at the 2000 Super Bowl Card Show. The cards were available each day of the show in exchange for wrappers from various 2000 Playoff products opened at the Playoff booth.

COMPLETE SET (7) 6.00 12.00
SB1 Dan Marino 1.00 2.50
SB2 Peyton Manning .75 2.00
SB3 Kurt Warner 1.50 4.00
SB4 Emmitt Smith .60 1.50
SB5 Fred Taylor .40 1.00
SB6 Steve McNair .40 1.00
SB7 Ricky Williams .60 1.50

2000 Playoff Unsung Heroes Banquet

The 2000 Playoff Unsung Heroes Banquet set consists of 31-player cards. They were released at the April 7, 2000 Unsung Heroes Banquet.

COMPLETE SET (31) 25.00 50.00
UH1 Ronald McKinnon .75 2.00
UH2 Tim Dwight 1.25 3.00
UH3 Bennie Thompson .75 2.00
UH4 Phil Hansen .75 2.00
UH5 Patrick Jeffers 1.25 3.00
UH6 Marcus Robinson 1.25 3.00
UH7 Oliver Gibson .75 2.00
UH8 Lomas Brown .75 2.00
UH9 Dexter Coakley .75 2.00
UH10 Olandis Gary 1.50 4.00
UH11 James Jones .75 2.00
UH12 Corey Bradford 1.25 3.00
UH13 Ken Dilger .75 2.00
UH14 Lonnie Marts .75 2.00
UH15 Tony Gonzalez 1.50 4.00
UH16 Damon Huard 1.25 3.00
UH17 Robert Griffith .75 2.00
UH18 Troy Brown 1.25 3.00
UH19 La'Roi Glover .75 2.00
UH20 Sam Garnes .75 2.00
UH21 Kevin Mawae .75 2.00
UH22 Lincoln Kennedy .75 2.00
UH23 Eric Bieniemy .75 2.00
UH24 Josh Miller .75 2.00
UH25 John Parrella .75 2.00
UH26 Charlie Garner 1.25 3.00
UH27 Walter Jones .75 2.00
UH28 Kurt Warner 4.00 8.00
UH29 Shaun King .75 2.00
UH30 Jason Fisk .75 2.00
UH31 Sam Shade .75 2.00

2001 Playoff Unsung Heroes Banquet

This set was issued to attendees of the annual Playoff Unsung Heroes banquet. These cards feature one player from each team who had been designated as that team's unsung hero. These cards were issued to a stated print run of 2000 serial numbered sets.

COMPLETE SET (31) 25.00 50.00
UH1 Bob Christian .75 2.00
UH2 Ronald McKinnon .75 2.00
UH3 Trent Dilfer 1.25 3.00
UH4 Shawn Price .75 2.00
UH5 Mike Minter 1.25 3.00
UH6 Brian Urlacher 5.00 10.00
UH7 Takeo Spikes .75 2.00
UH8 Wali Rainer .75 2.00
UH9 Larry Allen .75 2.00
UH10 Howard Griffith .75 2.00
UH11 James Jones .75 2.00
UH12 Russell Maryland .75 2.00
UH13 Tarik Glenn .75 2.00
UH14 Daimon Shelton .75 2.00
UH15 Mike Maslowski .75 2.00
UH16 Brian Walker .75 2.00
UH17 Chris Walsh .75 2.00
UH18 Tedy Bruschi 2.00 5.00
UH19 La'Roi Glover .75 2.00
UH20 Greg Comella .75 2.00
UH21 Richie Anderson .75 2.00
UH22 Greg Biekert .75 2.00
UH23 Cecil Martin .75 2.00
UH24 John Fiala .75 2.00
UH25 John Parrella .75 2.00
UH26 Bryant Young .75 2.00
UH27 Fabien Bownes .75 2.00
UH28 Ray Agnew .75 2.00
UH29 John Lynch 1.25 3.00
UH30 Lorenzo Neal .75 2.00
UH31 James Thrash 1.25 3.00

2004 Playoff Super Bowl XXXVIII Jerseys

These three cards were released by Donruss Playoff at the 2004 Super Bowl XXXVIII Card Show in Houston. Each features a swatch(s) from an actual game used jersey(s) for the featured two players.

COMPLETE SET (3) 30.00 60.00
*PRIME: .6X TO 1.5X BASIC JSY
SB1 David Carr 12.00 20.00
SB2 Warren Moon 12.00 20.00
SB3 David Carr/Warren Moon 18.00 30.00

2007 Playoff Pop Warner Super Bowl Promos

1 Tony Romo 1.25 3.00
2 Brett Favre 2.00 5.00
3 Vince Young .60 1.50
4 Adrian Peterson 1.50 4.00
5 Randy Moss .75 2.00
6 Calvin Johnson 2.00 5.00

2008 Playoff Super Bowl XLII Card Show

COMPLETE SET (12) 8.00 20.00
1 Vince Young .50 1.25
2 Brett Favre 1.50 4.00
3 Tony Romo .60 1.50
4 Peyton Manning 2.00 5.00
5 Randy Moss .60 1.50
6 Ben Roethlisberger .75 2.00
7 LaDainian Tomlinson .75 2.00
8 Brian Urlacher .75 2.00
9 Brady Quinn .50 1.25
10 Calvin Johnson .75 2.00
11 Adrian Peterson .75 2.00
12 Reggie Bush .50 1.25

2016 Playoff

1 Carson Palmer .25 .60
2 David Johnson .30 .75
3 Larry Fitzgerald .25 .60
4 Michael Floyd .20 .50
5 Patrick Peterson .20 .50
6 Tyrann Mathieu .25 .60
7 Matt Ryan .25 .60
8 Devonta Freeman .25 .60
9 Julio Jones .30 .75
10 Mohamed Sanu .20 .50
11 Tevin Coleman .25 .60
12 Joe Flacco .25 .60
13 Justin Forsett .25 .60
14 Buck Allen .20 .50
15 Steve Smith .25 .60
16 Mike Wallace .20 .50
17 Eric Weddle .20 .50
18 C.J. Mosley .25 .60
19 Terrell Suggs .20 .50
20 Tyrod Taylor .25 .60
21 LeSean McCoy .30 .75
22 Mike Gillislee .20 .50
23 Sammy Watkins .30 .75
24 Marcell Dareus .20 .50
25 Charles Clay .20 .50
26 Cam Newton .30 .75
27 Jonathan Stewart .20 .50
28 Kelvin Benjamin .25 .60
29 Greg Olsen .25 .60
30 Luke Kuechly .25 .60
31 Thomas Davis .20 .50
32 Ted Ginn Jr. .20 .50
33 Jay Cutler .20 .50
34 Jeremy Langford .25 .60
35 Alshon Jeffery .25 .60
36 Kevin White .20 .50
37 Zach Miller .20 .50
38 Andy Dalton .25 .60
39 Giovani Bernard .20 .50
40 Jeremy Hill .20 .50
41 A.J. Green .30 .75
42 Tyler Eifert .25 .60
43 Rey Maualuga .20 .50
44 Robert Griffin III .20 .50
45 Duke Johnson .20 .50
46 Isaiah Crowell .20 .50
47 Gary Barnidge .20 .50
48 Joe Haden .20 .50
49 Tony Romo .25 .60
50 Darren McFadden .20 .50
51 Alfred Morris .20 .50
52 Dez Bryant .30 .75
53 Jason Witten .25 .60
54 Sean Lee .25 .60
55 Cole Beasley .30 .75
56 Trevor Siemian .20 .50
57 C.J. Anderson .25 .60
58 Demaryius Thomas .25 .60
59 Emmanuel Sanders .30 .75
60 Von Miller .25 .60
61 Chris Harris .20 .50
62 Matthew Stafford .25 .60
63 Ameer Abdullah .20 .50
64 Golden Tate III .20 .50
65 Eric Ebron .20 .50
66 Ezekiel Ansah .20 .50
67 Aaron Rodgers .60 1.50
68 Eddie Lacy .20 .50
69 James Starks .20 .50
70 Jordy Nelson .25 .60
71 Randall Cobb .25 .60
72 Clay Matthews .30 .75
73 Jared Cook .20 .50
74 Brock Osweiler .20 .50
75 Lamar Miller .20 .50
76 DeAndre Hopkins .25 .60
77 Brian Cushing .20 .50
78 J.J. Watt .30 .75
79 Andrew Luck .40 1.00
80 Frank Gore .25 .60
81 T.Y. Hilton .25 .60
82 Donte Moncrief .25 .60
83 Dwayne Allen .20 .50
84 Robert Mathis .20 .50
85 Phillip Dorsett .20 .50
86 Vontae Davis .20 .50
87 Blake Bortles .20 .50
88 T.J. Yeldon .20 .50
89 Chris Ivory .25 .60
90 Allen Robinson .25 .60
91 Allen Hurns .20 .50
92 Julius Thomas .20 .50
93 Alex Smith .25 .60
94 Jamaal Charles .25 .60
95 Jeremy Maclin .20 .50
96 Travis Kelce .30 .75
97 Marcus Peters .20 .50
98 Eric Berry .25 .60
99 Ryan Tannehill .25 .60
100 Jay Ajayi .25 .60
101 Jarvis Landry .25 .60
102 DeVante Parker .25 .60
103 Ndamukong Suh .25 .60
104 Cameron Wake .20 .50
105 Teddy Bridgewater .25 .60
106 Adrian Peterson .30 .75
107 Stefon Diggs .25 .60
108 Harrison Smith .20 .50
109 Tom Brady .75 2.00
110 LeGarrette Blount .25 .60
111 Julian Edelman .30 .75
112 Rob Gronkowski .30 .75
113 Martellus Bennett .20 .50
114 Dion Lewis .20 .50
115 Chris Hogan .20 .50
116 Drew Brees .30 .75
117 Mark Ingram .25 .60
118 Brandin Cooks .25 .60
119 Coby Fleener .20 .50
120 Eli Manning .25 .60
121 Odell Beckham Jr. .30 .75
122 Victor Cruz .25 .60
123 Rashad Jennings .20 .50
124 Matt Forte .20 .50
125 Brandon Marshall .20 .50
126 Eric Decker .20 .50
127 Muhammad Wilkerson .20 .50
128 Darrelle Revis .20 .50
129 Derek Carr .30 .75
130 Latavius Murray .20 .50
131 Amari Cooper .30 .75
132 Michael Crabtree .20 .50
133 Khalil Mack .30 .75
134 Bruce Irvin .20 .50
135 Sam Bradford .20 .50
136 Ryan Mathews .25 .60
137 Darren Sproles .25 .60
138 Jordan Matthews .25 .60
139 Nelson Agholor .20 .50
140 Ben Roethlisberger .30 .75
141 Le'Veon Bell .25 .60
142 DeAngelo Williams .20 .50
143 Antonio Brown .30 .75
144 Markus Wheaton .20 .50
145 Kenny Britt .20 .50
146 Todd Gurley .30 .75
147 Tavon Austin .20 .50
148 Aaron Donald .30 .75
149 Philip Rivers .30 .75
150 Melvin Gordon .25 .60
151 Danny Woodhead .25 .60
152 Antonio Gates .20 .50
153 Keenan Allen .25 .60
154 Travis Benjamin .20 .50
155 Colin Kaepernick .25 .60
156 Carlos Hyde .20 .50
157 Torrey Smith .20 .50
158 Navorro Bowman .25 .60
159 Russell Wilson .40 1.00
160 Thomas Rawls .20 .50
161 Jimmy Graham .30 .75
162 Doug Baldwin .25 .60
163 Tyler Lockett .25 .60
164 Richard Sherman .30 .75
165 Kam Chancellor .30 .75
166 Earl Thomas III .25 .60
167 Jameis Winston .30 .75
168 Doug Martin .25 .60
169 Mike Evans .25 .60
170 Vincent Jackson .20 .50
171 Gerald McCoy .20 .50
172 Marcus Mariota .30 .75
173 DeMarco Murray .25 .60
174 Delanie Walker .20 .50
175 Kendall Wright .20 .50
176 Dorial Green-Beckham .20 .50
177 Kirk Cousins .30 .75
178 Matt Jones .25 .60
170 Jordan Reed .20 .60
180 DeSean Jackson .25 .60
181 Kurt Warner .25 .60
182 Ray Lewis .30 .75
183 Jim Kelly .30 .75
184 Gale Sayers .30 .75
185 Emmitt Smith .50 1.25
186 John Elway .50 1.25
187 Barry Sanders .50 1.25
188 Brett Favre .60 1.50
189 Peyton Manning .60 1.50
190 Steve Young .40 1.00
191 Dan Marino .60 1.50
192 Cris Carter .30 .75
193 Phil Simms .25 .60
194 Joe Namath .40 1.00
195 Marcus Allen .25 .60
196 Terry Bradshaw .40 1.00
197 Dan Fouts .25 .60
198 Jerry Rice .50 1.25
199 Marshall Faulk .25 .60
200 Warren Moon .30 .75
201 Jared Goff RC 3.00 8.00
202 Carson Wentz RC 5.00 12.00
203 Joey Bosa RC 1.00 2.50
204 Ezekiel Elliott RC 2.50 6.00
205 Jalen Ramsey RC .75 2.00
206 Ronnie Stanley RC .60 1.50
207 DeForest Buckner RC .50 1.25
208 Jack Conklin RC .75 2.00
209 Leonard Floyd RC .60 1.50
210 Eli Apple RC .60 1.50
211 Vernon Hargreaves III RC .75 2.00
212 Sheldon Rankins RC .60 1.50
213 Laremy Tunsil RC .50 1.25
214 Karl Joseph RC .50 1.25
215 Corey Coleman RC .75 2.00
216 Taylor Decker RC .60 1.50
217 Keanu Neal RC .50 1.25
218 Ryan Kelly RC .75 2.00
219 Shaq Lawson RC .50 1.25
220 Darron Lee RC .50 1.25
221 Will Fuller RC .75 2.00
222 Josh Doctson RC .60 1.50
223 Laquon Treadwell RC .60 1.50
224 William Jackson III RC .60 1.50
225 Artie Burns RC .60 1.50
226 Paxton Lynch RC .50 1.25
227 Kenny Clark RC .50 1.25
228 Robert Nkemdiche RC .60 1.50
229 Vernon Butler RC .50 1.25
230 Germain Ifedi RC .60 1.50
231 Emmanuel Ogbah RC .60 1.50
232 Kevin Dodd RC .50 1.25
233 Jaylon Smith RC .50 1.25
234 Hunter Henry RC .60 1.50
235 Myles Jack RC .60 1.50
236 Noah Spence RC .50 1.25
237 Sterling Shepard RC .60 1.50
238 Reggie Ragland RC .50 1.25
239 Derrick Henry RC 1.25 3.00
240 Michael Thomas RC 1.00 2.50
241 Christian Hackenberg RC .50 1.25
242 Mackensie Alexander RC .50 1.25
243 Tyler Boyd RC .60 1.50
244 T.J. Green RC .75 2.00
245 Roberto Aguayo RC .50 1.25
246 Cyrus Jones RC .50 1.25
247 Vonn Bell RC .60 1.50
248 James Bradberry RC .60 1.50
249 Kenyan Drake RC .75 2.00
250 Austin Hooper RC .50 1.25
251 Braxton Miller RC .50 1.25
252 Leonte Carroo RC .50 1.25
253 Kyler Fackrell RC .60 1.50
254 C.J. Prosise RC .50 1.25
255 Jacoby Brissett RC .60 1.50
256 Cody Kessler RC .50 1.25
257 Nick Vannett RC .50 1.25
258 Vincent Valentine RC .50 1.25
259 Connor Cook RC .60 1.50
260 Charles Tapper RC .60 1.50
261 Sheldon Day RC .50 1.25
262 Chris Moore RC .60 1.50
263 Tyler Higbee RC .50 1.25
264 Malcolm Mitchell RC .50 1.25
265 Ricardo Louis RC .50 1.25
266 Hassan Ridgeway RC .50 1.25
267 Pharoh Cooper RC .50 1.25
268 Tyler Ervin RC .50 1.25
269 Demarcus Robinson RC .50 1.25
270 Blake Martinez RC .60 1.50
271 Kenneth Dixon RC .50 1.25
272 Dak Prescott RC 2.50 6.00
273 Devontae Booker RC .60 1.50
274 Cardale Jones RC .50 1.25
275 Tajae Sharpe RC .60 1.50
276 DeAndre Washington RC .50 1.25
277 Paul Perkins RC .50 1.25
278 Jordan Howard RC 1.25 3.00
279 Wendell Smallwood RC .50 1.25
280 Jonathan Williams RC .60 1.50
281 Kevin Hogan RC .60 1.50
282 Trevor Davis RC .50 1.25
283 Tyreek Hill RC 2.00 5.00
284 Alex Collins RC .60 1.50
285 Rashard Higgins RC .50 1.25
286 Moritz Bohringer RC .50 1.25
287 Keenan Reynolds RC .60 1.50
288 Nate Sudfeld RC .50 1.25
289 Jake Rudock RC .50 1.25
290 Kolby Listenbee RC .50 1.25
291 Cody Core RC .50 1.25
292 Jeff Driskel RC .50 1.25
293 Kelvin Taylor RC .50 1.25
294 Rico Gathers RC .50 1.25
295 Devin Lucien RC .60 1.50
296 Daniel Braverman RC .50 1.25
297 Daniel Lasco RC .50 1.25
298 Devin Fuller RC .60 1.50
299 Charone Peake RC .50 1.25
300 Keith Marshall RC .50 1.25

2016 Playoff 1st Down

*VETS/99: 2.5X TO 6X BASIC CARDS
*ROOKIES/99: 1X TO 2.5X BASIC CARDS

2016 Playoff 2nd Down

*VETS/49: 3X TO 8X BASIC CARDS
*ROOKIES/49: 1.2X TO 3X BASIC CARDS

2016 Playoff 3rd Down

*VETS/25: 4X TO 10X BASIC CARDS
*ROOKIES/25: 1.5X TO 4X BASIC CARDS

2016 Playoff Goal Line

*VETS: 1X TO 2.5X BASIC CARDS
*ROOKIES: .5X TO 1.2X BASIC CARDS

2016 Playoff Kickoff

*VETS/199: 2X TO 5X BASIC CARDS
*ROOKIES: .75X TO 2X BASIC CARDS

2016 Playoff Air Command

*KICK/199: .6X TO 1.5X BASIC INSERTS
*1ST/99: .75X TO 2X BASIC INSERTS
*2ND/49: 1X TO 2.5X BASIC INSERTS
*3RD/25: 1.2X TO 3X BASIC INSERTS
ACAD Andy Dalton .40 1.00
ACAL Andrew Luck .60 1.50
ACAR Aaron Rodgers 1.00 2.50
ACBB Blake Bortles .30 .75
ACBR Ben Roethlisberger .50 1.25
ACCN Cam Newton .50 1.25
ACCP Carson Palmer .40 1.00
ACDB Drew Brees .50 1.25
ACDC Derek Carr .50 1.25
ACEM Eli Manning .40 1.00
ACJC Jay Cutler .30 .75
ACJF Joe Flacco .40 1.00
ACKC Kirk Cousins .50 1.25
ACMR Matt Ryan .40 1.00
ACMS Matthew Stafford .40 1.00
ACPR Philip Rivers .50 1.25
ACRT Ryan Tannehill .40 1.00
ACRW Russell Wilson .60 1.50
ACTB Tom Brady 1.25 3.00
ACTR Tony Romo .40 1.00

2016 Playoff Boss Hoggs

*KICK/199: .6X TO 1.5X BASIC INSERTS
*1ST/99: .75X TO 2X BASIC INSERTS
*2ND/49: 1X TO 2.5X BASIC INSERTS
*3RD/25: 1.2X TO 3X BASIC INSERTS
BHAP Adrian Peterson .50 1.25
BHCA C.J. Anderson .40 1.00
BHCH Carlos Hyde .30 .75
BHDF Devonta Freeman .40 1.00
BHDH Derrick Henry .75 2.00
BHDJ David Johnson .50 1.25
BHDM Doug Martin .40 1.00
BHEE Ezekiel Elliott 1.50 4.00
BHEL Eddie Lacy .30 .75
BHFG Frank Gore .40 1.00
BHJC Jamaal Charles .40 1.00
BHJL Jeremy Langford .40 1.00
BHJS Jonathan Stewart .30 .75
BHLA Lamar Miller .30 .75
BHLB LeGarrette Blount .40 1.00
BHLB Le'Veon Bell .40 1.00
BHLH Jeremy Hill .30 .75
BHLM Latavius Murray .30 .75
BHLS LeSean McCoy .50 1.25
BHMF Matt Forte .30 .75
BHMI Mark Ingram .40 1.00
BHMJ Matt Jones .40 1.00
BHTG Todd Gurley .50 1.25
BHTR Thomas Rawls .30 .75
BHTY T.J. Yeldon .30 .75

2016 Playoff Class Reunion

*KICK/199: .6X TO 1.5X BASIC INSERTS
*1ST/99: .75X TO 2X BASIC INSERTS
*2ND/49: 1X TO 2.5X BASIC INSERTS
*3RD/25: 1.2X TO 3X BASIC INSERTS
CRBS D.Brees/S.Smith .60 1.50
CRBT D.Bryant/D.Thomas .60 1.50
CRBU T.Brady/B.Urlacher 1.50 4.00
CREM D.Marino/J.Elway 1.25 3.00
CRLH M.Harrison/R.Lewis .60 1.50
CRLW A.Luck/R.Wilson .75 2.00
CRMD C.Martin/T.Davis .50 1.25
CRMR B.Roethlisberger/E.Manning .60 1.50
CRMW P.Manning/H.Ward 1.25 3.00
CRNM C.Newton/V.Miller .60 1.50
CRPR A.Peterson/D.Revis .60 1.50
CRPW C.Palmer/J.Witten .50 1.25
CRRC J.Charles/M.Ryan .50 1.25
CRRR J.Rice/A.Reed 1.00 2.50
CRRW A.Rodgers/D.Ware 1.25 3.00
CRSA B.Sanders/T.Aikman 1.00 2.50
CRSB J.Bettis/M.Strahan .60 1.50
CRSM C.Matthews/M.Stafford .60 1.50
CRSS E.Smith/S.Sharpe 1.00 2.50
CRTS L.Taylor/M.Singletary .60 1.50

2016 Playoff Headliners Jerseys

*KICK/75-99: .5X TO 1.2X BASIC JSY
*KICK/49-50: .6X TO 1.5X BASIC JSY
*KICK/25: .75X TO 2X BASIC JSY
*1ST/25: .75X TO 2X BASIC JSY
1 Von Miller 2.00 5.00
2 Peyton Manning 10.00 25.00
4 Aaron Rodgers 8.00 20.00
5 Eric Berry 2.00 5.00
7 Devonta Freeman 2.00 5.00
8 Jameis Winston 2.50 6.00
9 Brock Osweiler 1.50 4.00
10 Drew Brees 2.50 6.00
11 Antonio Brown 2.50 6.00
12 David Johnson 2.50 6.00
14 A.J. Green 2.50 6.00
16 Cam Newton 2.50 6.00
17 Marcus Mariota 2.50 6.00
19 Todd Gurley 2.50 6.00
20 J.J. Watt 2.50 6.00

2016 Playoff Pennants

1 Aaron Rodgers 3.00 8.00
2 Adrian Peterson 1.50 4.00
3 A.J. Green 1.50 4.00
4 Alex Smith 1.25 3.00
5 Allen Robinson 1.25 3.00
6 Alshon Jeffery 1.25 3.00
7 Amari Cooper 1.50 4.00
8 Andrew Luck 2.00 5.00
9 Andy Dalton 1.25 3.00
10 Antonio Brown 1.50 4.00
11 Ben Roethlisberger 1.50 4.00
12 Blake Bortles 1.00 2.50
13 Brandin Cooks 1.25 3.00
14 Brandon Marshall 1.00 2.50
15 Brock Osweiler 1.00 2.50
16 Cam Newton 1.50 4.00
17 Carlos Hyde 1.00 2.50
18 Carson Palmer 1.25 3.00
19 Carson Wentz 10.00 25.00
20 Clay Matthews 1.50 4.00
21 Colin Kaepernick 1.25 3.00
22 Corey Coleman 1.50 4.00
23 Danny Woodhead 1.25 3.00
24 David Johnson 1.50 4.00
25 DeAndre Hopkins 1.25 3.00
26 DeMarco Murray 1.25 3.00
27 Demaryius Thomas 1.25 3.00
28 Derek Carr 1.50 4.00
29 Derrick Henry 2.50 6.00
30 DeVante Parker 1.25 3.00
31 Devonta Freeman 1.25 3.00
32 Dez Bryant 1.50 4.00
33 Doug Baldwin 1.25 3.00
34 Doug Martin 1.25 3.00
35 Drew Brees 1.50 4.00
36 Duke Johnson 1.00 2.50
37 Eddie Lacy 1.00 2.50
38 Eli Manning 1.25 3.00
39 Emmanuel Sanders 1.50 4.00
40 Eric Decker 1.00 2.50
41 Ezekiel Elliott 5.00 12.00
42 Giovani Bernard 1.00 2.50
43 Golden Tate III 1.00 2.50
44 Jamaal Charles 1.25 3.00
45 Jameis Winston 1.50 4.00
46 Jared Goff 6.00 15.00
47 Jarvis Landry 1.25 3.00
48 Jason Witten 1.25 3.00
49 Jay Cutler 1.00 2.50
50 Jeremy Hill 1.00 2.50
51 Jeremy Langford 1.25 3.00
52 J.J. Watt 1.50 4.00
53 Joe Flacco 1.25 3.00
54 Jonathan Stewart 1.00 2.50
55 Jordan Matthews 1.25 3.00
56 Jordan Reed 1.00 2.50
57 Jordy Nelson 1.25 3.00
58 Josh Doctson 1.25 3.00
59 Julian Edelman 1.50 4.00
60 Julio Jones 1.50 4.00
61 Karlos Williams 1.00 2.50
62 Keenan Allen 1.25 3.00
63 Kelvin Benjamin 1.25 3.00
64 Khalil Mack 1.50 4.00
65 Kirk Cousins 1.50 4.00
66 Lamar Miller 1.00 2.50
67 Laquon Treadwell 1.25 3.00
68 Larry Fitzgerald 1.25 3.00
69 Latavius Murray 1.00 2.50
70 Le'Veon Bell 1.25 3.00
71 Marcus Mariota 1.50 4.00
72 Mark Ingram 1.25 3.00
73 Mark Sanchez 1.00 2.50
74 Matt Forte 1.00 2.50
75 Matt Jones 1.25 3.00
76 Matt Ryan 1.25 3.00
77 Matthew Stafford 1.25 3.00
78 Mike Evans 1.25 3.00
79 Odell Beckham Jr. 1.50 4.00
80 Paxton Lynch 1.00 2.50
81 Philip Rivers 1.50 4.00
82 Rob Gronkowski 1.50 4.00
83 Robert Griffin III 1.00 2.50
84 Russell Wilson 2.00 5.00
85 Ryan Tannehill 1.25 3.00
86 Sam Bradford 1.00 2.50
87 Sammy Watkins 1.50 4.00
88 Stefon Diggs 1.25 3.00
89 Steve Smith 1.25 3.00
90 Teddy Bridgewater 1.25 3.00
91 Thomas Rawls 1.00 2.50
92 T.J. Yeldon 1.00 2.50
93 Todd Gurley 1.50 4.00
94 Tom Brady 4.00 10.00
95 Tony Romo 1.25 3.00
96 Travis Kelce 1.50 4.00
97 T.Y. Hilton 1.25 3.00
98 Tyrod Taylor 1.25 3.00
99 Von Miller 1.25 3.00
100 Will Fuller 1.50 4.00

2016 Playoff Playoff Pairings Jerseys

*KICK/50: .5X TO 1.2X BASIC JSY/90
*KICK/25: .5X TO 1.2X BASIC JSY/50
*KICK/15: .5X TO 1.2X BASIC JSY/25
1 M.Ryan/R.Wilson/25
2 D.Johnson/E.Lacy/90 3.00 8.00
4 R.Gronkowski/E.Berry/50 4.00 10.00
5 A.Luck/J.Flacco/90 4.00 10.00
6 D.Brees/M.Stafford/50 4.00 10.00
7 C.Kaepernick/R.Wilson/50 5.00 12.00
8 R.Cobb/T.Williams/90 2.50 6.00
9 K.Allen/D.Thomas/50 3.00 8.00
10 P.Manning/T.Brady/25 30.00 60.00

2016 Playoff Rookie Autographs

1 Jared Goff/199 30.00 60.00
2 Carson Wentz/199 50.00 100.00
3 Joey Bosa/99 6.00 15.00
4 Ezekiel Elliott/199 75.00 150.00
5 Corey Coleman/199 4.00 10.00
6 Will Fuller/199 4.00 10.00
7 Josh Doctson/199 3.00 8.00
8 Laquon Treadwell/199 3.00 8.00
9 Paxton Lynch/199 2.50 6.00
10 Hunter Henry/199 3.00 8.00
11 Sterling Shepard/199 3.00 8.00
12 Derrick Henry/199 12.00 30.00
13 Michael Thomas/199 20.00 40.00
14 Christian Hackenberg/199 2.50 6.00
15 Kenyan Drake/199 4.00 10.00
16 Braxton Miller/199 2.50 6.00
17 Leonte Carroo/199 2.50 6.00
18 C.J. Prosise/99 3.00 8.00
19 Cody Kessler/199 2.50 6.00
20 Tyler Boyd/199 3.00 8.00
21 Connor Cook/199 3.00 8.00
22 Chris Moore/199 3.00 8.00
23 Ricardo Louis/199 2.50 6.00
24 Pharoh Cooper/199 2.50 6.00
25 Tyler Ervin/199 2.50 6.00
26 Demarcus Robinson/199 2.50 6.00
27 Kenneth Dixon/199 2.50 6.00
28 Dak Prescott/199 40.00 80.00
29 Devontae Booker/199 3.00 8.00
30 Cardale Jones/199 2.50 6.00
31 Paul Perkins/199 2.50 6.00
32 Jordan Howard/199 6.00 15.00
33 Wendell Smallwood/199 2.50 6.00
35 Kevin Hogan/50 5.00 12.00
36 Trevor Davis/199 2.50 6.00
37 Alex Collins/199 3.00 8.00
38 Keenan Reynolds/199 3.00 8.00
39 Moritz Bohringer/199 2.50 6.00
40 DeAndre Washington/199 2.50 6.00

2016 Playoff Rookie Autographs Kickoff

*KICK/49: .6X TO 1.5X BASIC AU/199
*KICK/25: .6X TO 1.5X BASIC AU/99
4 Ezekiel Elliott/49 100.00 200.00

2016 Playoff Rookie Recall Jerseys

*KICK/49: .5X TO 1.2X BASIC JSY/99
*KICK/49: .4X TO 1X BASIC JSY/60
*1ST/25: .6X TO 1.5X BASIC JSY/99
*1ST/25: .5X TO 1.2X BASIC JSY/60
*1ST/15: .75X TO 2X BASIC JSY/99
1 Jameis Winston/99 2.50 6.00
2 Marcus Mariota/99 2.50 6.00
3 Amari Cooper/99 2.50 6.00
4 Todd Gurley/99 2.50 6.00
5 David Johnson/99 2.50 6.00
6 Odell Beckham Jr./99 2.50 6.00
7 Blake Bortles/99 1.50 4.00
8 Teddy Bridgewater/99 2.00 5.00
9 Derek Carr/99 2.50 6.00
10 Brandin Cooks/99 2.00 5.00
11 Sammy Watkins/60 3.00 8.00
12 Devonta Freeman/99 2.00 5.00
13 Eddie Lacy/99 1.50 4.00
14 DeAndre Hopkins/99 2.00 5.00
15 Le'Veon Bell/99 2.00 5.00
16 Keenan Allen/99 2.00 5.00
17 Andrew Luck/99 3.00 8.00
18 Russell Wilson/99 3.00 8.00
19 Ryan Tannehill/99 2.00 5.00
20 Alshon Jeffery/99 2.00 5.00

2016 Playoff Rookie Signatures

*KICK/49: .6X TO 1.5X BASIC AU/199
1 Blake Martinez 3.00 8.00
2 Cody Core 2.50 6.00
3 Su'a Cravens 2.50 6.00
4 Keith Marshall 2.50 6.00
5 Eli Apple 3.00 8.00
6 DeForest Buckner 2.50 6.00
7 Vernon Hargreaves III 4.00 10.00
8 Daniel Lasco 2.50 6.00
9 Austin Hooper 2.50 6.00
10 Jonathan Bullard 2.50 6.00
11 Mackensie Alexander 2.50 6.00
12 Rico Gathers 2.50 6.00
13 Charone Peake 2.50 6.00
14 Nate Sudfeld 2.50 6.00
15 Kevin Dodd 2.50 6.00
19 Kenny Lawler 4.00 10.00
20 Brandon Doughty 2.50 6.00
22 William Jackson III 3.00 8.00
23 Jalen Ramsey 4.00 10.00
25 Jeremy Cash 3.00 8.00
26 Jake Rudock 2.50 6.00
27 James Bradberry 3.00 8.00
28 Jayron Kearse 2.50 6.00
29 Artie Burns 3.00 8.00
30 Seth DeValve 3.00 8.00
31 Jaylon Smith 2.50 6.00
32 Myles Jack 3.00 8.00
33 Glenn Gronkowski 2.50 6.00
34 Scooby Wright III 2.50 6.00
35 Brandon Allen 2.50 6.00
36 Aaron Burbridge 2.50 6.00
38 Vonn Bell 3.00 8.00
39 Daniel Braverman 2.50 6.00
40 Tajae Sharpe 3.00 8.00
41 Kevin Byard 2.50 6.00
42 Kevon Seymour 2.50 6.00
43 Jalin Marshall 4.00 10.00

44 Shilique Calhoun 2.50 6.00
45 Thomas Duarte 2.50 6.00
46 Kolby Listenbee 2.50 6.00
47 Jerell Adams 2.50 6.00
48 Ryan Kelly 4.00 10.00
50 Jack Conklin 4.00 10.00
51 Taylor Decker 3.00 8.00
52 Ronnie Stanley 3.00 8.00
53 Kenny Clark 2.50 6.00
54 Germain Ifedi 3.00 8.00
55 Keanu Neal 2.50 6.00
56 Karl Joseph 2.50 6.00
57 Nick Vannett 2.50 6.00
58 Tyler Higbee 2.50 6.00
59 Rashard Higgins 2.50 6.00
60 Robert Nkemdiche 3.00 8.00

2016 Playoff Rookie Stallions Jerseys

*KICK/49: .6X TO 1.5X BASIC JSY/149
*1ST/25: .75X TO 2X BASIC JSY/149
RSAC Alex Collins 2.00 5.00
RSBM Braxton Miller 1.50 4.00
RSCC Corey Coleman 2.50 6.00
RSCH Christian Hackenberg 1.50 4.00
RSCJ Cardale Jones 1.50 4.00
RSCK Cody Kessler 1.50 4.00
RSCM Chris Moore 2.00 5.00
RSCO Connor Cook 2.00 5.00
RSCP C.J. Prosise 1.50 4.00
RSCW Carson Wentz 6.00 15.00
RSDB Devontae Booker 2.00 5.00
RSDH Derrick Henry 5.00 12.00
RSDI Kenneth Dixon 1.50 4.00
RSDP Dak Prescott 8.00 20.00
RSDR Demarcus Robinson 1.50 4.00
RSDW DeAndre Washington 1.50 4.00
RSEE Ezekiel Elliott 8.00 20.00
RSHH Hunter Henry 2.00 5.00
RSJB Joey Bosa 3.00 8.00
RSJD Josh Doctson 2.00 5.00
RSJG Jared Goff 5.00 12.00
RSJH Jordan Howard 4.00 10.00
RSJW Jonathan Williams 2.00 5.00
RSKD Kenyan Drake 2.50 6.00
RSKR Keenan Reynolds 2.00 5.00
RSLC Leonte Carroo 1.50 4.00
RSLT Laquon Treadwell 2.00 5.00
RSMB Moritz Bohringer 1.50 4.00
RSMT Michael Thomas 3.00 8.00
RSPC Pharoh Cooper 1.50 4.00
RSPL Paxton Lynch 5.00 12.00
RSPP Paul Perkins 1.50 4.00
RSRL Ricardo Louis 1.50 4.00
RSSS Sterling Shepard 2.00 5.00
RSTB Tyler Boyd 2.00 5.00
RSTD Trevor Davis 1.50 4.00
RSTE Tyler Ervin 1.50 4.00
RSWF Will Fuller 2.50 6.00
RSWS Wendell Smallwood 1.50 4.00

2016 Playoff Star Gazing

*KICK/199: .6X TO 1.5X BASIC INSERTS
*1ST/99: .75X TO 2X BASIC INSERTS
*2ND: 1X TO 2.5X BASIC INSERTS
*3RD: 1.2X TO 3X BASIC INSERTS
SGAC Amari Cooper .50 1.25
SGAD Andy Dalton .40 1.00
SGAJ Alshon Jeffery .40 1.00
SGAL Andrew Luck .60 1.50
SGAP Adrian Peterson .50 1.25
SGAR Aaron Rodgers 1.00 2.50
SGBB Blake Bortles .30 .75
SGBR Ben Roethlisberger .50 1.25
SGCN Cam Newton .50 1.25
SGDB Drew Brees .50 1.25
SGDF Devonta Freeman .40 1.00
SGDH DeAndre Hopkins .40 1.00
SGJC Jamaal Charles .40 1.00
SGJE Julian Edelman .50 1.25
SGJW Jameis Winston .50 1.25
SGLF Larry Fitzgerald .40 1.00
SGMF Matt Forte .30 .75
SGMM Marcus Mariota .50 1.25
SGOB Odell Beckham Jr. .50 1.25
SGPR Philip Rivers .50 1.25
SGRT Ryan Tannehill .40 1.00
SGRW Russell Wilson .60 1.50
SGSW Sammy Watkins .50 1.25
SGTG Todd Gurley .50 1.25
SGTR Tony Romo .40 1.00

2016 Playoff Throwbacks Jerseys

*KICK: .5X TO 1.2X BASIC JSY
*1ST: .6X TO 1.5X BASIC JSY
1 Todd Gurley/99 2.50 6.00
2 Rob Gronkowski/99 2.50 6.00
3 Antonio Brown/99 4.00 10.00
4 Jordan Reed/99 1.50 4.00
5 Philip Rivers/99 2.50 6.00
6 Doug Martin/99 2.00 5.00
7 Aaron Rodgers/49 8.00 20.00
8 Julio Jones/99 2.50 6.00
9 Sammy Watkins/99 2.50 6.00
10 Dez Bryant/99 2.50 6.00

2016 Playoff Thunder and Lightning

*KICK/199: .6X TO 1.5X BASIC INSERTS
*1ST/99: .75X TO 2X BASIC INSERTS
*2ND/49: 1X TO 2.5X BASIC INSERTS
*3RD: 1.2X TO 3X BASIC INSERTS
TLBG R.Gronkowski/T.Brady 1.50 4.00
TLBR B.Bortles/A.Robinson .50 1.25
TLCC A.Cooper/D.Carr .60 1.50
TLLH A.Luck/T.Hilton .75 2.00
TLMB O.Beckham Jr./E.Manning .60 1.50
TLMW D.Ware/V.Miller .50 1.25
TLRB D.Bryant/T.Romo .60 1.50
TLRJ J.Jones/M.Ryan .60 1.50
TLRN A.Rodgers/J.Nelson 1.25 3.00
TLST R.Sherman/E.Thomas III .60 1.50

2017 Playoff

1 David Johnson .30 .75
2 Larry Fitzgerald .25 .60
3 Patrick Peterson .20 .50
4 Devonta Freeman .25 .60
5 Julio Jones .30 .75
6 Matt Ryan .25 .60
7 Vic Beasley Jr. .20 .50
8 Joe Flacco .25 .60
9 Terrell Suggs .20 .50
10 Tyrod Taylor .25 .60
11 LeSean McCoy .30 .75
12 Sammy Watkins .30 .75
13 Cam Newton .30 .75
14 Luke Kuechly .25 .60
15 Greg Olsen .25 .60
16 Jordan Howard .30 .75
17 Mike Glennon .25 .60
18 A.J. Green .30 .75
19 Andy Dalton .25 .60
20 Isaiah Crowell .20 .50
21 Joe Thomas .20 .50
22 Dak Prescott .30 .75
23 Ezekiel Elliott .40 1.00
24 Dez Bryant .30 .75
25 Jason Witten .25 .60
26 Von Miller .25 .60
27 Aqib Talib .20 .50
28 Matthew Stafford .25 .60
29 Marvin Jones Jr. .20 .50
30 Clay Matthews .25 .60
31 Aaron Rodgers .60 1.50
32 Jordy Nelson .25 .60
33 J.J. Watt .30 .75
34 Jadeveon Clowney .20 .50
35 DeAndre Hopkins .25 .60
36 Andrew Luck .40 1.00
37 T.Y. Hilton .25 .60
38 Frank Gore .25 .60
39 Blake Bortles .20 .50
40 Allen Robinson .25 .60
41 Eric Berry .25 .60
42 Alex Smith .25 .60
43 Tyreek Hill .30 .75
44 Travis Kelce .30 .75
45 Aaron Donald .30 .75
46 Todd Gurley II .30 .75
47 Jared Goff .30 .75
48 Jarvis Landry .25 .60
49 Jay Ajayi .25 .60
50 Jay Cutler .20 .50
51 Sam Bradford .20 .50
52 Harrison Smith .20 .50
53 Xavier Rhodes .20 .50
54 Tom Brady .75 2.00
55 Rob Gronkowski .30 .75
56 Malcolm Mitchell .25 .60
57 Brandin Cooks .25 .60
58 Adrian Peterson .30 .75
59 Drew Brees .30 .75
60 Landon Collins .20 .50
61 Odell Beckham Jr. .30 .75
62 Brandon Marshall .20 .50
63 Eli Manning .25 .60
64 Leonard Williams .20 .50
65 Matt Forte .20 .50
66 Amari Cooper .30 .75
67 Derek Carr .30 .75
68 Khalil Mack .30 .75
69 Carson Wentz .40 1.00
70 Alshon Jeffery .25 .60
71 Jordan Matthews .20 .50
72 Antonio Brown .30 .75
73 Ben Roethlisberger .30 .75
74 Le'Veon Bell .25 .60
75 Casey Hayward .20 .50
76 Philip Rivers .30 .75
77 Antonio Gates .20 .50
78 Joey Bosa .30 .75
79 Carlos Hyde .20 .50
80 Navorro Bowman .25 .60
81 Doug Baldwin .25 .60
82 Russell Wilson .40 1.00
83 Richard Sherman .30 .75
84 Earl Thomas III .25 .60
85 Jameis Winston .25 .60
86 Mike Evans .25 .60
87 Doug Martin .25 .60
88 Marcus Mariota .30 .75
89 Delanie Walker .20 .50
90 DeMarco Murray .25 .60
91 Jordan Reed .20 .50
92 Josh Norman .20 .50
93 Kirk Cousins .30 .75
94 Danny Woodhead .25 .60
95 Kevin White .20 .50
96 Tyler Eifert .25 .60
97 Demaryius Thomas .25 .60
98 Golden Tate III .20 .50
99 Pierre Garcon .25 .60
100 Michael Thomas .30 .75
101 Ray Lewis .30 .75
102 Ed Reed .25 .60
103 Kurt Warner .25 .60
104 Emmitt Smith .50 1.25
105 Michael Vick .25 .60
106 Deion Sanders .25 .60
107 Morten Andersen .20 .50
108 Jim Kelly .30 .75
109 Bruce Smith .25 .60
110 Kevin Greene .25 .60
111 Steve Smith Sr. .25 .60
112 Brian Urlacher .30 .75
113 Jim McMahon .25 .60
114 Dan Hampton .20 .50
115 Mike Singletary .30 .75
116 Ickey Woods .20 .50
117 Boomer Esiason .25 .60
118 Jim Brown .40 1.00
119 Ozzie Newsome .25 .60
120 Troy Aikman .40 1.00
121 Roger Staubach .40 1.00
122 Michael Irvin .30 .75
123 Tony Romo .25 .60
124 Tony Dorsett .30 .75
125 Terrell Davis .25 .60
126 Ed McCaffrey .20 .50
127 John Elway .50 1.25
128 Calvin Johnson .30 .75
129 Barry Sanders .50 1.25
130 Brett Favre .60 1.50
131 Paul Hornung .30 .75
132 Peyton Manning .60 1.50
133 Marshall Faulk .25 .60
134 Raymond Berry .25 .60
135 Mark Brunell .25 .60
136 Fred Taylor .25 .60
137 Marcus Allen .25 .60
138 Len Dawson .30 .75
139 Torry Holt .25 .60
140 Jerome Bettis .30 .75
141 Dan Fouts .25 .60
142 LaDainian Tomlinson .25 .60
143 Dan Marino .60 1.50
144 Larry Csonka .25 .60
145 Paul Warfield .25 .60
146 Thurman Thomas .25 .60
147 Randy Moss .30 .75
148 Fran Tarkenton .30 .75
149 Tedy Bruschi .30 .75
150 Willie McGinest .20 .50
151 Mike Vrabel .20 .50
152 Ricky Williams .25 .60
153 Archie Manning .25 .60
154 Phil Simms .25 .60
155 Lawrence Taylor .30 .75
156 Michael Strahan .25 .60
157 Jeremy Shockey .20 .50
158 Don Maynard .25 .60
159 Curtis Martin .25 .60
160 John Riggins .25 .60
161 Howie Long .30 .75
162 Jim Plunkett .25 .60
163 Ray Guy .20 .50
164 Fred Biletnikoff .30 .75
165 Randall Cunningham .25 .60
166 Terry Bradshaw .50 1.25
167 Franco Harris .30 .75
168 Hines Ward .25 .60
169 Heath Miller .20 .50
170 Rod Woodson .25 .60
171 Joe Greene .30 .75
172 Steve Young .40 1.00
173 Jerry Rice .50 1.25
174 Roger Craig .25 .60
175 Ronnie Lott .25 .60
176 Jim Zorn .20 .50
177 Steve Largent .30 .75
178 Warren Sapp .25 .60
179 Derrick Brooks .20 .50
180 Warren Moon .30 .75
181 Eddie George .25 .60
182 Earl Campbell .30 .75
183 Joe Theismann .30 .75
184 Alan Page .20 .50
185 Bo Jackson .40 1.00
186 Bob Lilly .25 .60
187 Champ Bailey .25 .60
188 Christian Okoye .20 .50
189 Doug Williams .25 .60
190 Edgerrin James .25 .60
191 Gale Sayers .30 .75
192 Jeff Garcia .20 .50
193 Jeff Saturday .20 .50
194 Kabeer Gbaja-Biamila .20 .50
195 Maurice Jones-Drew .20 .50
196 Reggie Wayne .25 .60
197 Tim Brown .30 .75
198 Steve Grogan .20 .50
199 Rodney Harrison .20 .50
200 Priest Holmes .20 .50
201 Deshaun Watson RC 3.00 8.00
202 Mitchell Trubisky RC 2.50 6.00
203 DeShone Kizer RC .50 1.25
204 Patrick Mahomes II RC 6.00 15.00
205 Nathan Peterman RC .60 1.50
206 Davis Webb RC .50 1.25
207 C.J. Beathard RC .50 1.25
208 R. Joshua Dobbs RC .60 1.50
209 Leonard Fournette RC 1.50 4.00
210 Dalvin Cook RC 1.25 3.00
211 Christian McCaffrey RC 1.25 3.00
212 D'Onta Foreman RC .60 1.50
213 Alvin Kamara RC 2.00 5.00
214 Samaje Perine RC .50 1.25
215 Wayne Gallman RC .60 1.50
216 Kareem Hunt RC 1.00 2.50
217 Kenny Golladay RC .75 2.00
218 James Conner RC 1.00 2.50
219 Joe Mixon RC 1.00 2.50
220 Evan Engram RC .60 1.50
221 O.J. Howard RC .60 1.50
222 Mike Williams RC .75 2.00
223 Corey Davis RC .75 2.00
224 John Ross III RC .60 1.50
225 JuJu Smith-Schuster RC 1.25 3.00
226 Zay Jones RC .60 1.50
227 Curtis Samuel RC .60 1.50
228 Dede Westbrook RC .50 1.25
229 Carlos Henderson RC .50 1.25
230 Chris Godwin RC .60 1.50
231 Mack Hollins RC .50 1.25
232 Cooper Kupp RC .75 2.00
233 Amara Darboh RC .50 1.25
234 Marlon Mack RC .75 2.00
235 ArDarius Stewart RC .50 1.25
236 Joe Williams RC .50 1.25
237 Jamaal Williams RC .50 1.25
238 Taywan Taylor RC .50 1.25
239 Jeremy McNichols RC .50 1.25
240 Josh Reynolds RC .50 1.25
241 DeAngelo Yancey RC .50 1.25
242 Myles Garrett RC 1.50 4.00
243 Solomon Thomas RC .50 1.25
244 Jamal Adams RC .50 1.25
245 Marshon Lattimore RC .60 1.50
246 Haason Reddick RC .50 1.25
247 Derek Barnett RC .60 1.50
248 Malik Hooker RC .50 1.25
249 Marlon Humphrey RC .50 1.25
250 Jonathan Allen RC .60 1.50
251 Adoree' Jackson RC .60 1.50
252 Jarrad Davis RC .60 1.50
253 Gareon Conley RC .50 1.25
254 Jabrill Peppers RC .75 2.00
255 Taco Charlton RC .50 1.25
256 David Njoku RC .60 1.50
257 Reuben Foster RC .50 1.25
258 Kevin King RC .60 1.50
259 Malik McDowell RC .50 1.25
260 Adam Shaheen RC .50 1.25
261 Tarik Cohen RC 1.00 2.50
262 Budda Baker RC .50 1.25
263 Ryan Switzer RC .60 1.50
264 Marcus Maye RC .50 1.25
265 Marcus Williams RC .50 1.25
266 Cooper Rush RC .60 1.50
267 Gerald Everett RC .50 1.25
268 Quincy Wilson RC .50 1.25
269 Tyus Bowser RC .50 1.25
270 Ryan Anderson RC .50 1.25
271 DeMarcus Walker RC .50 1.25
272 Teez Tabor RC .60 1.50
273 Obi Melifonwu RC .50 1.25
274 Zach Cunningham RC .60 1.50
275 Josh Jones RC .60 1.50
276 Duke Riley RC .50 1.25
277 Tim Williams RC .60 1.50
278 Chris Carson RC .75 2.00
279 Daeshon Hall RC .50 1.25
280 Tarell Basham RC .50 1.25
281 Fabian Moreau RC .50 1.25
282 Derek Rivers RC .60 1.50
283 Shaquill Griffin RC .60 1.50
284 T.J. Watt RC 1.50 4.00
285 John Johnson RC .60 1.50
286 Jourdan Lewis RC .50 1.25
287 Montravius Adams RC .60 1.50
288 Cameron Sutton RC .50 1.25
289 Delano Hill RC .60 1.50
290 Cordrea Tankersley RC .60 1.50
291 Rasul Douglas RC .60 1.50
292 Jonnu Smith RC .50 1.25
293 Brendan Langley RC .50 1.25
294 Nazair Jones RC .50 1.25
295 Trey Hendrickson RC .60 1.50
296 Kendell Beckwith RC .50 1.25
297 Matt Breida RC .75 2.00
298 Eddie Jackson RC .60 1.50
299 Chad Kelly RC .50 1.25
300 Jake Butt RC .60 1.50

2017 Playoff 1st Down

*VETS/99: 2.5X TO 6X BASIC CARDS
*ROOK/99: 1X TO 2.5X BASIC CARDS

2017 Playoff 2nd Down

*VETS/49: 3X TO 8X BASIC CARDS
*ROOK/49: 1.2X TO 3X BASIC CARDS

2017 Playoff 3rd Down

*VETS/25: 4X TO 10X BASIC CARDS
*ROOK/25: 1.5X TO 4X BASIC CARDS

2017 Playoff Goal Line

*VETS: 1X TO 2.5X BASIC CARDS
*ROOKIES: .5X TO 1.2X BASIC CARDS

2017 Playoff Kickoff

*VETS/299: 2X TO 5X BASIC CARDS
*ROOK/199: .8X TO 2X BASIC CARDS

2017 Playoff Red Zone

*VETS: 1X TO 2.5X BASIC CARDS
*ROOKIES: .5X TO 1.2X BASIC CARDS

2017 Playoff Air Command Jerseys

*KICK/49: .5X TO 1.2X BASIC JSY/99
*1ST/25: .6X TO 1.5X BASIC JSY/99
1 Christian Hackenberg 2.00 5.00
2 Dak Prescott 3.00 8.00
3 Andy Dalton 2.50 6.00
4 Mitchell Trubisky 6.00 15.00
5 Patrick Mahomes II 5.00 12.00
6 Deshaun Watson 10.00 25.00
7 Matthew Stafford 2.50 6.00
8 Aaron Rodgers 6.00 15.00
9 DeShone Kizer 2.00 5.00
10 Ben Roethlisberger 3.00 8.00
11 Andrew Luck 4.00 10.00
12 Matt Ryan 2.50 6.00
13 Cam Newton 3.00 8.00
14 Blake Bortles 2.00 5.00
15 Marcus Mariota 3.00 8.00
16 Jameis Winston 2.50 6.00
17 Russell Wilson 4.00 10.00
18 Derek Carr 3.00 8.00
19 Tom Brady 8.00 20.00
20 Ryan Tannehill 2.50 6.00

2017 Playoff Boss Hoggs

*KICK/199: .6X TO 1.5X BASIC INSERTS
*1ST/99: .75X TO 2X BASIC INSERTS
*2ND/49: 1X TO 2.5X BASIC INSERTS
*3RD/25: 1.2X TO 3X BASIC INSERTS
1 Ezekiel Elliott .60 1.50
2 Adrian Peterson .50 1.25
3 David Johnson .50 1.25
4 LeSean McCoy .50 1.25
5 DeMarco Murray .40 1.00
6 Jay Ajayi .40 1.00
7 Devonta Freeman .40 1.00
8 Lamar Miller .30 .75
9 Marshawn Lynch .40 1.00
10 Melvin Gordon .40 1.00
11 Jordan Howard .50 1.25
12 Todd Gurley II .50 1.25
13 Mark Ingram .40 1.00
14 Carlos Hyde .30 .75
15 Derrick Henry .40 1.00

2017 Playoff City Limits Jerseys

*KICK/25: .5X TO 1.2X BASIC JSY/99
*1ST/25: .6X TO 1.5X BASIC JSY/99
1 Ezekiel Elliott 4.00 10.00
2 Jameis Winston 2.50 6.00
3 Joey Bosa 3.00 8.00
4 Jordan Howard 3.00 8.00
5 Odell Beckham Jr. 3.00 8.00
6 Jay Ajayi 2.50 6.00
7 Von Miller 2.50 6.00
8 Julio Jones 3.00 8.00
9 Matthew Stafford 2.50 6.00
10 Derrick Henry 2.50 6.00

2017 Playoff Flea Flicker

*KICK/199: .6X TO 1.5X BASIC INSERTS
*1ST/99: .75X TO 2X BASIC INSERTS
*2ND/49: 1X TO 2.5X BASIC INSERTS
*3RD/25: 1.2X TO 3X BASIC INSERTS
1 Brynt/Ellt/Prsctt .75 2.00
2 Hll/Grn/Dltn .60 1.50
3 Rthlsbrgr/Brwn/Bll .60 1.50
4 Mntgmry/Rdgrs/Nlsn 1.25 3.00
5 Frmn/Jns/Ryn .60 1.50
6 Ptrsn/Brs/Thms .60 1.50
7 Evns/Mrtn/Wnstn .50 1.25
8 Bckhm/Prkns/Mnng .60 1.50
9 Jffry/Sprls/Wntz .75 2.00
10 Csns/Klly/Rd .60 1.50
11 Lndry/Ajyi/Tnnhll .50 1.25
12 Cly/McCy/Tylr .60 1.50
13 Hll/Smth/Hnt .75 2.00
14 Gts/Grdn/Rvrs .60 1.50
15 Cpr/Crr/Lnch .60 1.50
16 Plmr/Jhnsn/Ftzgrld .60 1.50
17 Bldwn/Wlsn/Rwls .75 2.00
18 Abdllh/Stffrd/Tte .50 1.25
19 Stwrt/Nwtn/Olsn .60 1.50
20 Lck/Gre/Hltn .75 2.00

2017 Playoff Gridiron Force

*KICK/199: .6X TO 1.5X BASIC INSERTS
*1ST/99: .75X TO 2X BASIC INSERTS
*2ND/49: 1X TO 2.5X BASIC INSERTS
*3RD/25: 1.2X TO 3X BASIC INSERTS
1 J.J. Watt .50 1.25
2 Luke Kuechly .40 1.00
3 Kam Chancellor .50 1.25
4 Justin Houston .30 .75
5 Von Miller .40 1.00
6 Richard Sherman .50 1.25
7 Ndamukong Suh .40 1.00
8 Gerald McCoy .30 .75
9 Harrison Smith .30 .75
10 Ray Lewis .50 1.25
11 Khalil Mack .50 1.25
12 Terrell Suggs .30 .75
13 Derrick Brooks .30 .75
14 Bruce Smith .40 1.00
15 Deion Sanders .40 1.00
16 Michael Strahan .40 1.00
17 Charles Woodson .50 1.25
18 Brian Urlacher .50 1.25
19 Ed Reed .40 1.00
20 Eric Berry .40 1.00

2017 Playoff Hall of Fame Autographs

2 Len Dawson/25 10.00 25.00
3 Marcus Allen/25 8.00 20.00
4 Emmitt Smith/25 50.00 100.00
5 Lance Alworth/25 8.00 20.00
6 James Lofton/25 8.00 20.00
8 Mike Singletary/25 10.00 25.00
9 Jack Youngblood/25 6.00 15.00
10 Deion Sanders/25

2017 Playoff Headliners Jerseys

*KICK/49: .5X TO 1.2X BASIC JSY/99
1 Odell Beckham Jr. 3.00 8.00
2 Ezekiel Elliott 4.00 10.00
3 Jordan Howard 3.00 8.00
4 LeSean McCoy 3.00 8.00
5 Jay Ajayi 2.50 6.00
6 Matt Forte 2.00 5.00
7 Paxton Lynch 2.00 5.00
8 Tyreek Hill 3.00 8.00
9 Joey Bosa 3.00 8.00
10 Amari Cooper 3.00 8.00
11 Robert Kelley 2.00 5.00
12 Luke Kuechly 2.50 6.00
13 Julio Jones 3.00 8.00
14 Jadeveon Clowney 2.00 5.00
15 Devonta Freeman 2.50 6.00
16 Le'Veon Bell 2.50 6.00
17 Antonio Brown 8.00 20.00
18 A.J. Green 3.00 8.00
19 Malcolm Mitchell 2.50 6.00
20 Melvin Gordon 2.50 6.00

2017 Playoff Heads Up

1 Tom Brady 4.00 10.00
2 J.J. Watt 1.50 4.00
3 Dak Prescott 1.50 4.00
4 Ezekiel Elliott 2.00 5.00
5 Carson Wentz 2.00 5.00
6 Aaron Rodgers 3.00 8.00
7 Rob Gronkowski 1.50 4.00
8 Antonio Brown 1.50 4.00
9 Julio Jones 1.50 4.00
10 Von Miller 1.25 3.00
11 Cam Newton 1.50 4.00
12 Odell Beckham Jr. 1.50 4.00
13 Adrian Peterson 1.50 4.00
14 Ben Roethlisberger 1.50 4.00
15 Russell Wilson 2.00 5.00
16 Derek Carr 1.50 4.00
17 Drew Brees 1.50 4.00
18 Eli Manning 1.25 3.00
19 Philip Rivers 1.50 4.00
20 Andrew Luck 2.00 5.00

2017 Playoff Momentum

*KICK/199: .6X TO 1.5X BASIC INSERTS
*1ST/99: .75X TO 2X BASIC INSERTS
*2ND/49: 1X TO 2.5X BASIC INSERTS
*3RD/25: 1.2X TO 3X BASIC INSERTS
1 Julio Jones .50 1.25
2 Antonio Brown .50 1.25
3 Hines Ward .40 1.00
4 Tyreek Hill .50 1.25
5 Rob Gronkowski .50 1.25
6 Dez Bryant .50 1.25
7 Jordy Nelson .40 1.00
8 Jerry Rice .75 2.00
9 Randy Moss .40 1.00
10 DeAndre Hopkins .40 1.00
11 Michael Irvin .50 1.25
12 Reggie Wayne .40 1.00
13 Doug Baldwin .40 1.00
14 Larry Fitzgerald .40 1.00
15 Tim Brown .50 1.25

2017 Playoff Pedigree Jerseys

*KICK/49: .5X TO 1.2X BASIC JSY/99
*1ST/25: .6X TO 1.5X BASIC JSY/99
1 Russell Wilson 4.00 10.00
2 Jadeveon Clowney 2.00 5.00
3 Jarvis Landry 2.50 6.00
4 Devonta Freeman 2.50 6.00
5 Tevin Coleman 2.50 6.00
6 Ben Roethlisberger 3.00 8.00
7 James White 2.50 6.00
8 Travis Kelce 3.00 8.00
9 Larry Fitzgerald 2.50 6.00
10 Cam Newton 3.00 8.00

2017 Playoff Rookie Autographs

*KICK/99: .5X TO 1.2X BASIC AU/199
*KICK/75: .4X TO 1X BASIC AU/99
*KICK/15: .6X TO 1.5X BASIC AU/49
1 Mitchell Trubisky/99 25.00 50.00
2 Leonard Fournette/99 25.00 50.00
3 Corey Davis/199 4.00 10.00
4 Mike Williams/99 5.00 12.00
5 Christian McCaffrey/99 20.00 40.00
6 John Ross III/199 3.00 8.00
7 Patrick Mahomes II/99 150.00 300.00
8 Deshaun Watson/99 40.00 80.00
9 O.J. Howard/199 3.00 8.00
10 Evan Engram/199 3.00 8.00
11 Zay Jones/199 3.00 8.00
12 Curtis Samuel/199 3.00 8.00
13 Dalvin Cook/199 6.00 15.00
14 Joe Mixon/49 EXCH 8.00 20.00
15 DeShone Kizer/99 3.00 8.00
16 JuJu Smith-Schuster/199 8.00 20.00
17 Alvin Kamara/199 20.00 40.00
18 Cooper Kupp/49 6.00 15.00
19 Taywan Taylor/199 2.50 6.00
20 ArDarius Stewart/49 4.00 10.00
21 Carlos Henderson/199 2.50 6.00
22 Chris Godwin/49 5.00 12.00
23 Kareem Hunt/199 EXCH 5.00 12.00
24 Davis Webb/199 2.50 6.00
25 D'Onta Foreman/199 3.00 8.00
26 C.J. Beathard/199 2.50 6.00
27 James Conner/49
28 Amara Darboh/199
29 Kenny Golladay/49 6.00 15.00
30 Dede Westbrook/199 2.50 6.00
31 Samaje Perine/199 2.50 6.00
32 Josh Reynolds/49 4.00 10.00
33 Mack Hollins/199 2.50 6.00
34 Joe Williams/49
35 Jamaal Williams/49 4.00 10.00
36 R. Joshua Dobbs/49 5.00 12.00
37 Wayne Gallman/199 3.00 8.00
38 Marlon Mack/49 6.00 15.00
39 Jeremy McNichols/199 2.50 6.00
40 Nathan Peterman/199 3.00 8.00

2017 Playoff Rookie Signatures

*KICK/99: .5X TO 1.2X BASIC AU/199
1 Adoree' Jackson 3.00 8.00
2 Cameron Sutton 2.50 6.00
3 Marshon Lattimore 3.00 8.00
4 Marlon Humphrey 2.50 6.00
5 Budda Baker
6 Sidney Jones 2.50 6.00
7 Malachi Dupre 2.50 6.00
8 Jeremy Sprinkle 12.00 30.00
9 Isaiah Ford 2.50 6.00
10 Tre'Davious White 2.50 6.00
11 Tim Williams 3.00 8.00
12 Solomon Thomas 2.50 6.00
13 Takkarist McKinley 2.50 6.00
14 Zach Cunningham 3.00 8.00
15 Kevin King
16 Jonathan Allen 3.00 8.00
17 Robert Davis 2.50 6.00
18 Dalvin Tomlinson 2.50 6.00
19 Adam Shaheen 2.50 6.00
20 Gareon Conley 2.50 6.00
21 T.J. Logan 4.00 10.00
22 Malik Hooker 2.50 6.00
23 Derek Rivers 3.00 8.00
24 Jordan Leggett 2.50 6.00
25 Raekwon McMillan 2.50 6.00
26 Chad Kelly 2.50 6.00
27 Malik McDowell 2.50 6.00
28 Jordan Willis 2.50 6.00
29 Noah Brown 3.00 8.00
30 Jehu Chesson 3.00 8.00
31 Charles Harris 2.50 6.00
32 Jabrill Peppers 4.00 10.00
33 Stacy Coley 2.50 6.00
34 Brad Kaaya 2.50 6.00
35 Derek Barnett 3.00 8.00
36 Obi Melifonwu 2.50 6.00
37 DeMarcus Walker 2.50 6.00
38 Cordrea Tankersley
39 Dawuane Smoot 2.50 6.00
40 Matthew Dayes 2.50 6.00
41 Haason Reddick 2.50 6.00
42 T.J. Watt 8.00 20.00
43 Gerald Everett 2.50 6.00
44 Jarrad Davis 3.00 8.00
45 De'Angelo Henderson 2.50 6.00
46 Jonnu Smith 2.50 6.00
47 Ahkello Witherspoon 3.00 8.00
48 Josh Jones 3.00 8.00
49 Quincy Wilson 2.50 6.00
50 Elijah Hood 2.50 6.00
51 Shelton Gibson 2.50 6.00
52 Chris Wormley 2.50 6.00
53 Rodney Adams 2.50 6.00
54 George Kittle 10.00 25.00
55 Elijah Qualls 2.50 6.00
56 Brian Hill 2.50 6.00
57 Jamal Adams 2.50 6.00
58 Jake Butt 3.00 8.00
59 Ryan Anderson 2.50 6.00
60 Taco Charlton 2.50 6.00

2017 Playoff Rookie Stallions Jerseys

*KICK/49: .6X TO 1.5X BASIC JSY/149
*1ST/25: .8X TO 2X BASIC JSY/149
1 Mitchell Trubisky 5.00 12.00
2 Leonard Fournette 6.00 15.00
3 Corey Davis 2.50 6.00
4 Mike Williams 2.50 6.00
5 Christian McCaffrey 5.00 12.00
6 John Ross III 2.00 5.00
7 Patrick Mahomes II 10.00 25.00
8 Deshaun Watson 8.00 20.00
9 O.J. Howard 2.00 5.00
10 Evan Engram 2.00 5.00
11 Zay Jones 2.00 5.00
12 Curtis Samuel 2.00 5.00
13 Dalvin Cook 3.00 8.00
14 Joe Mixon 3.00 8.00
15 DeShone Kizer 1.50 4.00
16 JuJu Smith-Schuster 3.00 8.00
17 Alvin Kamara 5.00 12.00
18 Cooper Kupp 2.50 6.00
19 Taywan Taylor 1.50 4.00
20 ArDarius Stewart 1.50 4.00
21 Carlos Henderson 1.50 4.00
22 Chris Godwin 2.00 5.00
23 Kareem Hunt 4.00 10.00
24 Davis Webb 1.50 4.00
25 D'Onta Foreman 2.00 5.00
26 C.J. Beathard 1.50 4.00
27 James Conner 3.00 8.00
28 Amara Darboh 1.50 4.00
29 Kenny Golladay 2.50 6.00
30 Dede Westbrook 1.50 4.00
31 Samaje Perine 1.50 4.00
32 Josh Reynolds 1.50 4.00
33 Mack Hollins 1.50 4.00
34 Joe Williams 1.50 4.00
35 Jamaal Williams 1.50 4.00
36 R. Joshua Dobbs 2.00 5.00
37 Wayne Gallman 2.00 5.00
38 Marlon Mack 2.50 6.00
39 Jeremy McNichols 1.50 4.00
40 Nathan Peterman 2.00 5.00

2017 Playoff Star Gazing

*KICK/199: .6X TO 1.5X BASIC INSERTS
*1ST/99: .75X TO 2X BASIC INSERTS
*2ND/49: 1X TO 2.5X BASIC INSERTS
*3RD/25: 1.2X TO 3X BASIC INSERTS
1 Dak Prescott .50 1.25
2 Ezekiel Elliott .60 1.50
3 Tom Brady 1.25 3.00
4 Von Miller .40 1.00
5 Julio Jones .50 1.25
6 Antonio Brown .50 1.25
7 Aaron Rodgers 1.00 2.50
8 Odell Beckham Jr. .50 1.25
9 Le'Veon Bell .40 1.00
10 Matt Ryan .40 1.00
11 Derek Carr .50 1.25
12 David Johnson .50 1.25
13 Drew Brees .50 1.25
14 A.J. Green .50 1.25
15 Ben Roethlisberger .50 1.25
16 Rob Gronkowski .50 1.25
17 Russell Wilson .60 1.50
18 Travis Kelce .50 1.25
19 LeSean McCoy .50 1.25
20 Matthew Stafford .40 1.00

2017 Playoff Thunder and Lightning

*KICK/199: .6X TO 1.5X BASIC INSERTS
*1ST/99: .75X TO 2X BASIC INSERTS
*2ND/49: 1X TO 2.5X BASIC INSERTS
*3RD: 1.2X TO 3X BASIC INSERTS
1 D.Prescott/E.Elliott .75 2.00
2 D.Freeman/J.Jones .60 1.50
3 A.Rodgers/J.Nelson 1.25 3.00
4 A.Brown/L.Bell .60 1.50
5 B.Cooks/T.Brady 1.50 4.00
6 J.Winston/M.Evans .50 1.25
7 E.Manning/O.Beckham .60 1.50
8 A.Cooper/M.Lynch .60 1.50
9 A.Dalton/A.Green .60 1.50
10 J.Landry/J.Ajayi .50 1.25

2018 Playoff

1 Sam Bradford .20 .50
2 David Johnson .30 .75
3 Larry Fitzgerald .25 .60
4 Patrick Peterson .20 .50
5 J.J. Nelson .20 .50
6 Chandler Jones .20 .50
7 Matt Ryan .25 .60
8 Devonta Freeman .25 .60
9 Tevin Coleman .20 .50
10 Julio Jones .30 .75
11 Mohamed Sanu .20 .50
12 Vic Beasley Jr. .20 .50
13 Desmond Trufant .20 .50
14 Joe Flacco .25 .60
15 Alex Collins .20 .50
16 Michael Crabtree .20 .50
17 Terrell Suggs .20 .50
18 John Brown .25 .60
19 Justin Tucker .20 .50
20 A.J. McCarron .20 .50
21 LeSean McCoy .30 .75
22 Zay Jones .20 .50
23 Charles Clay .20 .50
24 Kelvin Benjamin .25 .60
25 Vontae Davis .20 .50
26 Cam Newton .30 .75
27 Christian McCaffrey .30 .75
28 Devin Funchess .20 .50
29 Julius Peppers .25 .60
30 Torrey Smith .20 .50
31 Luke Kuechly .25 .60
32 Mitchell Trubisky .30 .75
33 Jordan Howard .30 .75
34 Tarik Cohen .25 .60
35 Allen Robinson .25 .60
36 Trey Burton .20 .50
37 Khalil Mack .30 .75
38 Andy Dalton .25 .60
39 Joe Mixon .25 .60
40 A.J. Green .30 .75
41 Tyler Eifert .25 .60
42 Geno Atkins .20 .50
43 John Ross III .25 .60
44 Tyrod Taylor .25 .60
45 Carlos Hyde .20 .50
46 Jarvis Landry .25 .60
47 Josh Gordon .20 .50
48 David Njoku .20 .50
49 Myles Garrett .30 .75
50 Dak Prescott .30 .75
51 Ezekiel Elliott .40 1.00
52 Allen Hurns .20 .50
53 Cole Beasley .25 .60
54 Sean Lee .25 .60
55 DeMarcus Lawrence .20 .50
56 Tavon Austin .20 .50
57 Case Keenum .25 .60
58 Devontae Booker .20 .50
59 Von Miller .25 .60
60 Demaryius Thomas .25 .60
61 Emmanuel Sanders .30 .75
62 Chris Harris Jr. .20 .50
63 Matthew Stafford .25 .60
64 LeGarrette Blount .25 .60
65 Golden Tate III .20 .50
66 Marvin Jones Jr. .20 .50
67 Darius Slay .20 .50
68 Ezekiel Ansah .20 .50
69 Aaron Rodgers .60 1.50
70 Aaron Jones .25 .60
71 Jimmy Graham .30 .75
72 Davante Adams .25 .60
73 Randall Cobb .25 .60
74 Clay Matthews .25 .60
75 Ty Montgomery .20 .50
76 Deshaun Watson .40 1.00
77 Lamar Miller .20 .50
78 DeAndre Hopkins .25 .60
79 Will Fuller V .20 .50
80 J.J. Watt .30 .75
81 Tyrann Mathieu .25 .60
82 Andrew Luck .40 1.00
83 Marlon Mack .20 .50
84 T.Y. Hilton .25 .60
85 Ryan Grant .20 .50
86 Eric Ebron .20 .50
87 Malik Hooker .20 .50
88 Blake Bortles .20 .50
89 Leonard Fournette .30 .75
90 Marqise Lee .20 .50
91 Jalen Ramsey .25 .60
92 Keelan Cole .20 .50
93 Dede Westbrook .20 .50
94 Patrick Mahomes II .75 2.00
95 Kareem Hunt .25 .60
96 Travis Kelce .30 .75
97 Tyreek Hill .30 .75
98 Eric Berry .25 .60
99 Sammy Watkins .30 .75
100 Jared Goff .30 .75
101 Todd Gurley II .30 .75
102 Cooper Kupp .25 .60
103 Aaron Donald .30 .75
104 Brandin Cooks .25 .60
105 Ndamukong Suh .25 .60
106 Robert Woods .25 .60
107 Philip Rivers .30 .75
108 Melvin Gordon .25 .60
109 Keenan Allen .25 .60
110 Mike Williams .20 .50
111 Joey Bosa .30 .75
112 Melvin Ingram .20 .50
113 Ryan Tannehill .25 .60
114 Kenyan Drake .20 .50
115 Danny Amendola .25 .60
116 Cameron Wake .20 .50
117 DeVante Parker .25 .60
118 Kenny Stills .20 .50
119 Kirk Cousins .30 .75
120 Dalvin Cook .25 .60
121 Stefon Diggs .25 .60
122 Adam Thielen .30 .75
123 Xavier Rhodes .20 .50
124 Kyle Rudolph .20 .50
125 Tom Brady .75 2.00
126 James White .25 .60
127 Rob Gronkowski .30 .75
128 Julian Edelman .30 .75
129 Chris Hogan .20 .50
130 Rex Burkhead .20 .50
131 Dont'a Hightower .20 .50
132 Drew Brees .30 .75
133 Alvin Kamara .25 .60
134 Michael Thomas .30 .75
135 Mark Ingram .25 .60
136 Marshon Lattimore .20 .50
137 Cameron Meredith .20 .50
138 Eli Manning .25 .60
139 Odell Beckham Jr. .30 .75
140 Sterling Shepard .25 .60
141 Paul Perkins .20 .50
142 Landon Collins .20 .50
143 Jonathan Stewart .20 .50
144 Janoris Jenkins .20 .50
145 Josh McCown .20 .50
146 Bilal Powell .20 .50
147 Robby Anderson .20 .50
148 Terrelle Pryor Sr. .20 .50
149 Jermaine Kearse .20 .50
150 Leonard Williams .20 .50
151 Derek Carr .30 .75
152 Marshawn Lynch .25 .60
153 Amari Cooper .30 .75
154 Jordy Nelson .25 .60
155 Doug Martin .25 .60
156 Bruce Irvin .20 .50
157 Seth Roberts .20 .50
158 Carson Wentz .40 1.00
159 Jay Ajayi .25 .60
160 Alshon Jeffery .25 .60
161 Zach Ertz .25 .60
162 Fletcher Cox .20 .50
163 Nelson Agholor .20 .50
164 Ben Roethlisberger .30 .75
165 Le'Veon Bell .25 .60
166 Antonio Brown .30 .75
167 JuJu Smith-Schuster .30 .75
168 Jesse James .20 .50
169 T.J. Watt .25 .60
170 Joe Haden .20 .50
171 Jimmy Garoppolo .40 1.00
172 Matt Breida .25 .60
173 Marquise Goodwin .20 .50
174 Richard Sherman .30 .75
175 Pierre Garcon .25 .60
176 George Kittle .20 .50
177 Russell Wilson .40 1.00
178 Doug Baldwin .25 .60
179 Tyler Lockett .25 .60
180 Bobby Wagner .20 .50
181 Brandon Marshall .20 .50
182 Earl Thomas III .25 .60
183 Jameis Winston .25 .60
184 Mike Evans .25 .60
185 DeSean Jackson .25 .60
186 Cameron Brate .20 .50
187 Peyton Barber .20 .50
188 Adam Humphries .20 .50
189 Marcus Mariota .30 .75
190 Derrick Henry .30 .75
191 Dion Lewis .20 .50
192 Delanie Walker .20 .50
193 Rishard Matthews .20 .50
194 Corey Davis .25 .60
195 Alex Smith .25 .60
196 Jordan Reed .20 .50
197 Josh Doctson .20 .50
198 Chris Thompson .20 .50
199 Josh Norman .20 .50
200 Jamison Crowder .20 .50
201 Saquon Barkley RC 4.00 10.00
202 Baker Mayfield RC 5.00 12.00
203 Sam Darnold RC 3.00 8.00
204 Bradley Chubb RC .75 2.00
205 Josh Allen RC 2.00 5.00
206 Josh Rosen RC 1.50 4.00
207 D.J. Moore RC 1.00 2.50
208 Hayden Hurst RC .60 1.50
209 Calvin Ridley RC 1.25 3.00
210 Rashaad Penny RC .75 2.00
211 Sony Michel RC 1.50 4.00
212 Lamar Jackson RC 3.00 8.00
213 Nick Chubb RC 1.50 4.00
214 Ronald Jones II RC .50 1.25
215 Courtland Sutton RC .75 2.00
216 Mike Gesicki RC .60 1.50
217 Kerryon Johnson RC .75 2.00
218 Dante Pettis RC .75 2.00
219 Christian Kirk RC .75 2.00
220 Anthony Miller RC .75 2.00
221 Derrius Guice RC 1.00 2.50
222 James Washington RC 1.00 2.50
223 D.J. Chark Jr. RC .60 1.50
224 Royce Freeman RC .60 1.50
225 Mason Rudolph RC 1.25 3.00
226 Michael Gallup RC 1.00 2.50
227 Tre'Quan Smith RC .75 2.00
228 Keke Coutee RC .60 1.50
229 Nyheim Hines RC .60 1.50
230 Kyle Lauletta RC .75 2.00
231 Mark Walton RC .60 1.50
232 DaeSean Hamilton RC .60 1.50
233 Ito Smith RC .60 1.50
234 Kalen Ballage RC .60 1.50
235 Jaleel Scott RC .50 1.25
236 J'Mon Moore RC .50 1.25
237 Daurice Fountain RC .60 1.50
238 Jaylen Samuels RC .60 1.50
239 Mike White RC .60 1.50
240 Marquez Valdes-Scantling RC .60 1.50
241 Denzel Ward RC 1.25 3.00
242 Roquan Smith RC 1.50 4.00
243 Minkah Fitzpatrick RC 1.00 2.50
244 Vita Vea RC .75 2.00
245 Daron Payne RC .75 2.00
246 Marcus Davenport RC 1.00 2.50
247 Tremaine Edmunds RC 1.00 2.50
248 Derwin James RC 1.00 2.50
249 Jaire Alexander RC .75 2.00
250 Leighton Vander Esch RC 1.50 4.00
251 Rashaan Evans RC .75 2.00
252 Terrell Edmunds RC 1.50 4.00
253 Mike Hughes RC .75 2.00
254 Harold Landry RC .50 1.25
255 Joshua Jackson RC 1.00 2.50
256 Tyler Conklin RC .50 1.25
257 Jordan Wilkins RC .60 1.50
258 Ian Thomas RC .50 1.25

259 Isaiah Oliver RC .50 1.25
260 Carlton Davis RC .60 1.50
261 Malik Jefferson RC .60 1.50
262 Mark Andrews RC .75 2.00
263 Justin Reid RC .50 1.25
264 Kurt Benkert RC .60 1.50
265 Jalyn Holmes RC .75 2.00
266 Richie James RC .50 1.25
267 Justin Watson RC .60 1.50
268 Ronnie Harrison RC .60 1.50
269 Equanimeous St. Brown RC .75 2.00
270 John Kelly RC .60 1.50
271 Christopher Herndon IV RC .50 1.25
272 Da'Shawn Hand RC .50 1.25
273 Damion Ratley RC .60 1.50
274 Armani Watts RC .50 1.25
275 Josh Sweat RC .60 1.50
276 Chase Edmonds RC .50 1.25
277 Dalton Schultz RC .60 1.50
278 Javon Wims RC .50 1.25
279 Shaquem Griffin RC .75 2.00
280 Danny Etling RC .60 1.50
281 Jordan Lasley RC .50 1.25
282 Antonio Callaway RC .60 1.50
283 Ray-Ray McCloud RC .50 1.25
284 Dylan Cantrell RC .50 1.25
285 Jerome Baker RC .60 1.50
286 Cedrick Wilson Jr. RC .50 1.25
287 Braxton Berrios RC .50 1.25
288 Marcell Ateman RC .60 1.50
289 Bo Scarbrough RC .60 1.50
290 Ryan Izzo RC .50 1.25
291 Lorenzo Carter RC .50 1.25
292 Auden Tate RC .50 1.25
293 Trey Quinn RC .50 1.25
294 Allen Lazard RC .50 1.25
295 Fred Warner RC .50 1.25
296 Josh Adams RC 1.00 2.50
297 Deon Cain RC .60 1.50
298 Simmie Cobbs Jr. RC .75 2.00
299 Dallas Goedert RC .60 1.50
300 Rasheem Green RC .50 1.25

2018 Playoff 1st Down

*VETS/99: 2.5X TO 6X BASIC CARDS
*ROOK/99: 1X TO 2.5X BASIC CARDS

2018 Playoff 2nd Down

*VETS/49: 3X TO 8X BASIC CARDS
*ROOK/49: 1.2X TO 3X BASIC CARDS

2018 Playoff 3rd Down

*VETS/25: 4X TO 10X BASIC CARDS
*ROOK/25: 1.5X TO 4X BASIC CARDS

2018 Playoff Goal Line

*VETS: 1X TO 2.5X BASIC CARDS
*ROOKIES: .5X TO 1.2X BASIC CARDS

2018 Playoff Kickoff

*VETS: 1.5X TO 4X BASIC CARDS
*ROOK: .6X TO 1.5X BASIC CARDS

2018 Playoff Accolades Jerseys

*PRIME/50: .6X TO 1.5X BASIC JSY
1 Terry Bradshaw 4.00 10.00
2 Aaron Rodgers 5.00 12.00
3 Von Miller 2.00 5.00
4 Peyton Manning 5.00 12.00
5 Tony Gonzalez 2.00 5.00
6 Brett Favre 5.00 12.00
7 Jerry Rice 4.00 10.00
8 Drew Brees 2.50 6.00
9 Todd Gurley II 2.50 6.00
10 Matt Ryan 2.00 5.00
11 LaDainian Tomlinson 2.00 5.00
12 Aaron Donald 2.50 6.00
13 Khalil Mack 2.50 6.00
14 Clay Matthews 2.00 5.00
15 Joe Flacco 2.00 5.00
16 Alvin Kamara 2.00 5.00
17 Derek Carr 2.50 6.00
18 Tyreek Hill 2.50 6.00
19 Travis Kelce 2.50 6.00
20 T.Y. Hilton 2.00 5.00

2018 Playoff Air Command

1 Carson Wentz .60 1.50
2 Ben Roethlisberger .50 1.25
3 Matt Ryan .40 1.00
4 Dak Prescott .50 1.25
5 Drew Brees .50 1.25
6 Philip Rivers .50 1.25
7 Eli Manning .40 1.00
8 Russell Wilson .60 1.50
9 Aaron Rodgers 1.00 2.50
10 Kirk Cousins .50 1.25
11 Alex Smith .40 1.00
12 Tom Brady 1.25 3.00
13 Jared Goff .50 1.25
14 Cam Newton .50 1.25
15 Matthew Stafford .40 1.00
16 Jimmy Garoppolo .60 1.50
17 Derek Carr .50 1.25
18 Marcus Mariota .50 1.25
19 Deshaun Watson .60 1.50
20 Andy Dalton .40 1.00

2018 Playoff Game Day Memorabilia

*PRIME/50: .6X TO 1.5X BASIC JSY
1 Aaron Rodgers 5.00 12.00
2 Matthew Stafford 2.00 5.00
3 Deshaun Watson 3.00 8.00
4 Alvin Kamara 2.00 5.00
5 Kareem Hunt 2.00 5.00
6 A.J. Green 2.50 6.00
7 Christian McCaffrey 2.50 6.00
8 Jordan Howard 2.50 6.00
9 Dak Prescott 2.50 6.00
10 Leonard Fournette 2.50 6.00
11 Patrick Mahomes II 6.00 15.00
12 Jared Goff 2.50 6.00
13 Dalvin Cook 2.00 5.00
14 Evan Engram 1.50 4.00
15 Carson Wentz 3.00 8.00
16 Jameis Winston 2.00 5.00
17 Marcus Mariota 2.50 6.00
18 Davante Adams 2.00 5.00
19 Demaryius Thomas 2.00 5.00
20 Mitchell Trubisky 2.50 6.00

2018 Playoff Game Day Signatures

1 Patrick Mahomes II/50 75.00 150.00
2 David Njoku/75 3.00 8.00
3 Christian McCaffrey/35
4 Robby Anderson/75 3.00 8.00
5 Tarik Cohen/75 4.00 10.00
6 Corey Davis/50 5.00 12.00
7 Leonard Fournette/25 8.00 20.00
8 Devin Funchess/50 4.00 10.00
9 Nelson Agholor/50 4.00 10.00
10 Jerick McKinnon/50 4.00 10.00
11 Xavier Rhodes/75 3.00 8.00
12 C.J. Anderson/50 5.00 12.00
13 Malik Hooker/75 3.00 8.00
14 Aaron Rodgers/10
15 Ty Montgomery/75 3.00 8.00
16 Aqib Talib/50 4.00 10.00
17 Stephen Gostkowski/50 4.00 10.00
18 Marcus Mariota/35 40.00 80.00
19 Alex Smith/15
20 Zay Jones/50 4.00 10.00

2018 Playoff Hall of Fame Autographs

1 Marcus Allen 12.00 30.00
2 Curtis Martin 12.00 30.00
3 Paul Hornung
4 Charles Haley 10.00 25.00
5 Bob Griese 15.00 40.00
6 Bruce Smith
7 Ozzie Newsome
8 Jack Lambert
9 Fred Biletnikoff 10.00 25.00
10 Lawrence Taylor 40.00 80.00
11 Len Dawson
12 Dan Hampton 8.00 20.00
13 Troy Aikman
14 Don Maynard 8.00 20.00
15 Eric Dickerson
16 James Lofton 6.00 15.00
17 Warren Sapp 8.00 20.00
18 Andre Reed 8.00 20.00
19 Michael Strahan
20 Jan Stenerud 6.00 15.00

2018 Playoff Hidden Gems

1 Tom Brady 1.25 3.00
2 Antonio Brown .50 1.25
3 Richard Sherman .50 1.25
4 Rodney Harrison .40 1.00
5 Terrell Davis .40 1.00
6 Zach Thomas .40 1.00
7 Joe Klecko .30 .75
8 Roger Staubach .60 1.50
9 Julian Edelman .50 1.25
10 Donald Driver .40 1.00
11 Pierre Garcon .40 1.00
12 Josh Norman .30 .75
13 Kam Chancellor .50 1.25
14 Bo Jackson .60 1.50
15 Chris Hanburger .30 .75
16 Raymond Berry .40 1.00

2018 Playoff Playoff Heroes

1 Tom Brady 1.25 3.00
2 Russell Wilson .60 1.50
3 Ben Roethlisberger .50 1.25
4 Eli Manning .40 1.00
5 Kurt Warner .40 1.00
6 Nick Foles .40 1.00
7 Troy Aikman .60 1.50
8 Dan Marino 1.00 2.50
9 Drew Brees .50 1.25
10 Aaron Rodgers 1.00 2.50
11 Matt Ryan .40 1.00
12 Peyton Manning 1.00 2.50

2018 Playoff Rookie Autograph Variations

201 Saquon Barkley/50
202 Baker Mayfield/50 EXCH
203 Sam Darnold/15
205 Josh Allen/50 15.00 40.00
206 Josh Rosen/50
207 D.J. Moore/50 8.00 20.00
209 Calvin Ridley/15 15.00 40.00
210 Rashaad Penny/15 10.00 25.00
211 Sony Michel/50 12.00 30.00
212 Lamar Jackson/25 60.00 125.00
213 Nick Chubb/50 20.00 50.00
214 Ronald Jones II/15 6.00 15.00
215 Courtland Sutton/50 6.00 15.00
217 Kerryon Johnson/15 EXCH 10.00 25.00
219 Christian Kirk/25 8.00 20.00
220 Anthony Miller/15 10.00 25.00
222 James Washington/15 12.00 30.00
224 Royce Freeman/25 6.00 15.00
225 Mason Rudolph/50 10.00 25.00
226 Michael Gallup/15 12.00 30.00
228 Keke Coutee/50 8.00 20.00
229 Nyheim Hines/50 5.00 12.00
233 Ito Smith/50 5.00 12.00
237 Daurice Fountain/50 5.00 12.00
241 Denzel Ward/25 12.00 30.00
242 Roquan Smith/50 12.00 30.00
243 Minkah Fitzpatrick/50 8.00 20.00
244 Vita Vea/50 6.00 15.00
253 Mike Hughes/50 6.00 15.00
255 Joshua Jackson/50 8.00 20.00
257 Jordan Wilkins/50 5.00 12.00
266 Richie James/50 4.00 10.00
267 Justin Watson/50 5.00 12.00
270 John Kelly/50 5.00 12.00
277 Dalton Schultz/50 5.00 12.00
279 Shaquem Griffin/25 8.00 20.00
280 Danny Etling/50 5.00 12.00
284 Dylan Cantrell/50 4.00 10.00
286 Cedrick Wilson Jr./50 4.00 10.00
288 Marcell Ateman/50 5.00 12.00
289 Bo Scarbrough/25 6.00 15.00
296 Josh Adams/50 8.00 20.00
297 Deon Cain/50 5.00 12.00
290 Simmie Cobbs Jr./50 6.00 15.00
299 Dallas Goedert/50 5.00 12.00

2018 Playoff Rookie Autographs

201 Saquon Barkley 60.00 125.00
202 Baker Mayfield EXCH 50.00 100.00
203 Sam Darnold 15.00 40.00
205 Josh Allen 10.00 25.00
206 Josh Rosen 8.00 20.00
207 D.J. Moore 5.00 12.00
209 Calvin Ridley 6.00 15.00
210 Rashaad Penny 4.00 10.00
211 Sony Michel 8.00 20.00
212 Lamar Jackson 30.00 60.00
213 Nick Chubb 12.00 30.00
214 Ronald Jones II 2.50 6.00
216 Mike Gesicki 3.00 8.00
217 Kerryon Johnson EXCH 4.00 10.00
219 Christian Kirk 4.00 10.00
220 Anthony Miller 4.00 10.00
222 James Washington 5.00 12.00
223 D.J. Chark Jr. 3.00 8.00
224 Royce Freeman 3.00 8.00
225 Mason Rudolph 6.00 15.00
226 Michael Gallup 5.00 12.00
227 Tre'Quan Smith 4.00 10.00
229 Nyheim Hines 3.00 8.00
230 Kyle Lauletta 4.00 10.00
231 Mark Walton 3.00 8.00
232 DaeSean Hamilton 3.00 8.00
233 Ito Smith 3.00 8.00
234 Kalen Ballage 3.00 8.00
235 Jaleel Scott 2.50 6.00
236 J'Mon Moore 2.50 6.00
237 Daurice Fountain 3.00 8.00
238 Jaylen Samuels 3.00 8.00
239 Mike White 3.00 8.00
240 Marquez Valdes-Scantling 3.00 8.00
241 Denzel Ward 6.00 15.00
242 Roquan Smith 8.00 20.00
243 Minkah Fitzpatrick 5.00 12.00
244 Vita Vea 4.00 10.00
245 Daron Payne 4.00 10.00
246 Marcus Davenport 5.00 12.00
247 Tremaine Edmunds
249 Jaire Alexander
250 Leighton Vander Esch 12.00 30.00
251 Rashaan Evans 4.00 10.00
253 Mike Hughes 4.00 10.00
254 Harold Landry 2.50 6.00
255 Joshua Jackson 5.00 12.00
257 Jordan Wilkins 3.00 8.00
259 Isaiah Oliver 2.50 6.00
261 Malik Jefferson 3.00 8.00
262 Mark Andrews 4.00 10.00
263 Justin Reid 2.50 6.00
264 Kurt Benkert 3.00 8.00
266 Richie James 2.50 6.00
267 Justin Watson 3.00 8.00
268 Ronnie Harrison 3.00 8.00
270 John Kelly 3.00 8.00
271 Christopher Herndon IV 2.50 6.00
272 Da'Shawn Hand 2.50 6.00
273 Damion Ratley 3.00 8.00
274 Armani Watts 2.50 6.00
275 Josh Sweat 3.00 8.00
276 Chase Edmonds 2.50 6.00
277 Dalton Schultz 3.00 8.00
279 Shaquem Griffin 4.00 10.00
280 Danny Etling 3.00 8.00
281 Jordan Lasley 2.50 6.00
283 Ray-Ray McCloud 2.50 6.00
286 Cedrick Wilson Jr. 2.50 6.00
287 Braxton Berrios 2.50 6.00
288 Marcell Ateman 3.00 8.00
289 Bo Scarbrough 3.00 8.00
290 Ryan Izzo 2.50 6.00
293 Trey Quinn 2.50 6.00
294 Allen Lazard 2.50 6.00
296 Josh Adams 5.00 12.00
297 Deon Cain 3.00 8.00
298 Simmie Cobbs Jr. 4.00 10.00
299 Dallas Goedert 3.00 8.00
300 Rasheem Green 2.50 6.00

2018 Playoff Rookie Stallions Jerseys

*PRIME/50: .6X TO 1.5X BASIC JSY/50
1 Saquon Barkley 8.00 20.00
2 Baker Mayfield 6.00 15.00
3 Sam Darnold 6.00 15.00
4 Bradley Chubb 2.50 6.00
5 Josh Allen 4.00 10.00
6 Josh Rosen 4.00 10.00
7 D.J. Moore 3.00 8.00
8 Hayden Hurst 2.00 5.00
9 Calvin Ridley 4.00 10.00
10 Rashaad Penny 2.50 6.00
11 Sony Michel 4.00 10.00
12 Lamar Jackson 6.00 15.00
13 Nick Chubb 5.00 12.00
14 Ronald Jones II 1.50 4.00
15 Courtland Sutton 2.50 6.00
16 Mike Gesicki 2.00 5.00
17 Kerryon Johnson 2.50 6.00
18 Dante Pettis 2.50 6.00
19 Christian Kirk 2.50 6.00
20 Anthony Miller 2.50 6.00
21 Derrius Guice 3.00 8.00
22 James Washington 3.00 8.00
23 D.J. Chark Jr. 2.00 5.00
24 Royce Freeman 2.00 5.00
25 Mason Rudolph 4.00 10.00
26 Michael Gallup 3.00 8.00
27 Tre'Quan Smith 2.50 6.00
28 Keke Coutee 2.00 5.00
29 Nyheim Hines 2.00 5.00
30 Kyle Lauletta 2.50 6.00
31 Mark Walton 2.00 5.00
32 DaeSean Hamilton 2.00 5.00
33 Ito Smith 2.00 5.00
34 Kalen Ballage 2.00 5.00
35 Jaleel Scott 1.50 4.00
36 J'Mon Moore 1.50 4.00
37 Daurice Fountain 2.00 5.00
38 Jaylen Samuels 2.00 5.00
39 Mike White 2.00 5.00
40 Marquez Valdes-Scantling 2.00 5.00

2018 Playoff Rookie Wave

1 Baker Mayfield 6.00 15.00
2 Saquon Barkley 5.00 12.00
3 Josh Rosen 2.00 5.00
4 Josh Allen 2.50 6.00
5 Calvin Ridley 1.50 4.00
6 Courtland Sutton 1.00 2.50
7 Lamar Jackson 4.00 10.00
8 Bradley Chubb 1.00 2.50
9 D.J. Moore 1.25 3.00
10 Sony Michel 2.00 5.00
11 Sam Darnold 4.00 10.00
12 Michael Gallup 1.25 3.00
13 Nyheim Hines .75 2.00
14 Derrius Guice
15 Anthony Miller 1.00 2.50

2018 Playoff Star Gazing

1 Odell Beckham Jr. .50 1.25
2 Julio Jones .50 1.25
3 Aaron Rodgers 1.00 2.50
4 Ezekiel Elliott .60 1.50
5 Le'Veon Bell .40 1.00

2018 Playoff Thunder and Lightning

1 L.Bell/A.Brown .60 1.50
2 C.Beasley/E.Elliott .75 2.00
3 D.Freeman/J.Jones .60 1.50
4 O.Beckham/E.Engram .60 1.50
5 T.Eifert/A.Green .60 1.50
6 K Allen/M Gordon .50 1.25
7 K.Hunt/T.Hill .60 1.50
8 C.Kupp/T.Gurley .60 1.50
9 C.Matthews/H.ClintonDix .50 1.25
10 M.Jones/G.Tate .40 1.00
11 D.Hopkins/L.Miller .50 1.25
12 R.Grnkwski/C.Hogan .60 1.50
13 A.Kamara/M.Ingram .50 1.25
14 B.Irvin/E.Thomas .50 1.25
15 A.Jeffery/J.Ajayi .50 1.25
16 A.Bouye/J.Ramsey .50 1.25
17 T.Lockett/D.Baldwin .50 1.25
18 D.Jackson/M.Evans .50 1.25
19 D.Walker/D.Henry .60 1.50
20 A.Thielen/S.Diggs .60 1.50

2018 Playoff Touchdown Sensations

1 Ezekiel Elliott .60 1.50
2 Odell Beckham Jr. .50 1.25
3 Julio Jones .50 1.25
4 Antonio Brown .50 1.25
5 Le'Veon Bell .40 1.00
6 Davante Adams .40 1.00
7 Michael Thomas .50 1.25
8 Todd Gurley II .50 1.25
9 Travis Kelce .50 1.25
10 DeAndre Hopkins .40 1.00
11 Adam Thielen .50 1.25
12 Kareem Hunt .40 1.00

2018 Playoff Turning Pro Memorabilia

*PRIME/50: .6X TO 1.5X BASIC JSY
1 Baker Mayfield 6.00 15.00
2 Josh Allen 4.00 10.00
3 Josh Rosen 4.00 10.00
4 Dante Pettis 2.50 6.00
5 Sam Darnold 6.00 15.00
6 D.J. Moore 3.00 8.00
7 Anthony Miller 2.50 6.00
8 Derrius Guice 3.00 8.00
9 D.J. Chark Jr. 2.00 5.00
10 Nyheim Hines 2.00 5.00
11 James Washington 3.00 8.00
12 Lamar Jackson 6.00 15.00
13 Bradley Chubb 2.50 6.00
14 Sony Michel 4.00 10.00
15 Nick Chubb 5.00 12.00
16 Calvin Ridley 4.00 10.00
17 Jaylen Samuels 2.00 5.00
18 Mike Gesicki 2.00 5.00
19 Saquon Barkley 8.00 20.00
20 Courtland Sutton 2.50 6.00

1993 Playoff Contenders Promos

This six-card standard-size set was issued to herald the release of the 150-card 1993 Playoff Contenders set. The fronts display borderless color action shots that have a metallic sheen. The player's name appears below the Playoff logo, both within a silver-colored box in a lower corner. The horizontal back carries a color player close-up on the left, and a broad team color-coded stripe on the right, in which appears the player's name, his team's helmet, and season highlights. The cards are numbered on the back by Roman numerals.

COMPLETE SET (6) 4.00 10.00
1 Drew Bledsoe 1.00 2.50
2 Neil Smith .20 .50
3 Rick Mirer .30 .75
4 Rodney Hampton .20 .50
5 Barry Sanders 1.20 3.00
6 Emmitt Smith 1.20 3.00

1993 Playoff Contenders

This 150-card standard-size set has fronts that display borderless color action shots that have a metallic sheen. Cards were issued in eight-card packs. Rookie Cards include Jerome Bettis, Drew Bledsoe, Vincent Brisby, Reggie Brooks, Curtis Conway, Garrison Hearst, Terry Kirby, Natrone Means, O.J. McDuffie, Rick Mirer, Ron Moore, Robert Smith and Kevin Williams.

COMPLETE SET (150) 7.50 20.00
1 Brett Favre 1.50 3.00
2 Thurman Thomas .15 .40
3 Barry Word .02 .10
4 Herman Moore .15 .40
5 Reggie Langhorne .02 .10
6 Wilber Marshall .02 .10
7 Ricky Watters .15 .40
8 Marcus Allen .15 .40
9 Jeff Hostetler .07 .20
10 Steve Young .40 1.00
11 Bobby Hebert .02 .10
12 David Klingler .02 .10
13 Craig Heyward .07 .20
14 Andre Reed .07 .20
15 Tommy Vardell .02 .10
16 Anthony Carter .07 .20
17 Mel Gray .07 .20
18 Dan Marino 1.00 2.50
19 Haywood Jeffires .07 .20
20 Joe Montana 1.00 2.50
21 Tim Brown .15 .40
22 Jim McMahon .07 .20
23 Scott Mitchell .15 .40
24 Rickey Jackson .02 .10
25 Troy Aikman .60 1.50
26 Rodney Hampton .07 .20
27 Fred Barnett .07 .20
28 Gary Clark .07 .20
29 Barry Foster .07 .20
30 Brian Blades .07 .20
31 Tim McDonald .02 .10
32 Kelvin Martin .02 .10
33 Henry Jones .02 .10
34 Erric Pegram .07 .20
35 Don Beebe .02 .10
36 Eric Metcalf .07 .20
37 Charles Haley .07 .20
38 Robert Delpino .02 .10
39 Leonard Russell UER .07 .20
40 Jackie Harris .02 .10
41 Ernest Givins .07 .20
42 Willie Davis .15 .40
43 Alexander Wright .02 .10
44 Keith Byars .02 .10
45 Dave Meggett .02 .10
46 Johnny Johnson .02 .10
47 Mark Bavaro .02 .10
48 Seth Joyner .02 .10
49 Junior Seau .15 .40
50 Emmitt Smith 1.25 2.50
51 Shannon Sharpe .15 .40
52 Rodney Peete .02 .10
53 Andre Rison .07 .20
54 Cornelius Bennett .07 .20
55 Mark Carrier WR .07 .20
56 Mark Clayton .02 .10
57 Warren Moon .15 .40
58 J.J. Birden .02 .10
59 Howie Long .15 .40
60 Irving Fryar .07 .20
61 Mark Jackson .02 .10
62 Eric Martin .02 .10
63 Herschel Walker .07 .20
64 Cortez Kennedy .07 .20
65 Steve Beuerlein .07 .20
66 Jim Kelly .15 .40
67 Bernie Kosar Cowboys .07 .20
68 Pat Swilling .02 .10
69 Michael Irvin .15 .40
70 Harvey Williams .07 .20
71 Steve Smith .02 .10
72 Wade Wilson .02 .10
73 Phil Simms .07 .20
74 Vinny Testaverde .07 .20
75 Barry Sanders 1.00 2.50
76 Ken Norton Jr. .07 .20
77 Rod Woodson .15 .40
78 Webster Slaughter .02 .10
79 Derrick Thomas .15 .40
80 Mike Sherrard .02 .10
81 Calvin Williams .07 .20
82 Jay Novacek .07 .20
83 Michael Brooks .02 .10
84 Randall Cunningham .15 .40
85 Chris Warren .07 .20
86 Johnny Mitchell .02 .10
87 Jim Harbaugh .15 .40
88 Rod Bernstine .02 .10
89 John Elway 1.00 2.50
90 Jerry Rice .60 1.50
91 Brent Jones .07 .20
92 Cris Carter .15 .40
93 Alvin Harper .07 .20
94 Horace Copeland RC .07 .20
95 Rocket Ismail .07 .20
96 Darrin Smith RC .07 .20
97 Reggie Brooks RC .07 .20
98 Demetrius DuBose RC .02 .10
99 Eric Curry RC .02 .10
100 Rick Mirer RC .15 .40
101 Carlton Gray UER RC .02 .10
102 Dana Stubblefield RC .15 .40
103 Todd Kelly RC .02 .10
104 Natrone Means RC .15 .40
105 Darrien Gordon RC .02 .10
106 Deon Figures RC .02 .10
107 Garrison Hearst RC .50 1.25
108 Ronald Moore RC .07 .20
109 Leonard Renfro RC .02 .10
110 Lester Holmes .02 .10
111 Vaughn Hebron RC .02 .10
112 Marvin Jones RC .02 .10
113 Irv Smith RC .02 .10
114 Willie Roaf RC .25 .60
115 Derek Brown RBK RC .07 .20
116 Vincent Brisby RC .15 .40
117 Drew Bledsoe RC 1.50 4.00
118 Gino Torretta RC .07 .20
119 Robert Smith RC .75 2.00
120 Qadry Ismail RC .15 .40
121 O.J.McDuffie RC .15 .40
122 Terry Kirby RC .15 .40
123 Troy Drayton RC .07 .20
124 Jerome Bettis RC 2.50 6.00
125 Patrick Bates RC .02 .10
126 Roosevelt Potts RC .02 .10
127 Tom Carter RC .07 .20
128 Patrick Robinson RC .02 .10
129 Brad Hopkins RC .02 .10
130 George Teague RC .07 .20
131 Wayne Simmons RC .02 .10
132 Mark Brunell RC 1.00 2.50
(Error name misspelled on front)
133 Ryan McNeil RC .15 .40
134 Dan Williams RC .02 .10
135 Glyn Milburn RC .15 .40
136 Kevin Williams RC WR .15 .40
137 Derrick Lassic RC .02 .10
138 Steve Everitt RC .02 .10
139 Lance Gunn RC .02 .10
140 John Copeland RC .07 .20
141 Curtis Conway RC .40 1.00
142 Thomas Smith RC .07 .20
143 Russell Copeland RC .07 .20
144 Lincoln Kennedy RC .02 .10
145 Boomer Esiason CL .02 .10
146 Neil Smith CL .02 .10
147 Jack Del Rio CL .02 .10
148 Morten Andersen CL .02 .10
149 Sterling Sharpe CL .07 .20
150 Reggie White CL .07 .20

1993 Playoff Contenders Rick Mirer

Randomly inserted in 1993 Playoff Contenders packs at an approximate rate of one in 80, these five standard-size cards feature borderless fronts with color player action photos that have a metallic sheen. The player's name appears in a black box at the bottom. On a blue panel displaying a ghosted version of Mirer's photo on card number 3, the back presents career highlights. The cards are numbered on the back as "X of 5".

COMPLETE SET (5) 6.00 15.00
COMMON MIRER (1-5) 1.50 4.00

1993 Playoff Contenders Rookie Contenders

Randomly inserted in packs at an approximate rate of one in 40, these ten standard-size cards feature on their fronts borderless color player action shots that have a metallic sheen and blurred backgrounds, which serves to focus attention on the rookie. The cards are numbered on the back as "X of 10."

COMPLETE SET (10) 20.00 50.00
STATED ODDS 1:40
1 Jerome Bettis 15.00 40.00
2 Drew Bledsoe UER 10.00 25.00
3 Reggie Brooks .50 1.25
4 Derek Brown RBK .50 1.25
5 Garrison Hearst 3.00 8.00
6 Vaughn Hebron .25 .60
7 Qadry Ismail 1.00 2.50
8 Derrick Lassic .25 .60
9 Glyn Milburn 1.00 2.50
10 Dana Stubblefield 1.00 2.50

1994 Playoff Contenders Promos

This seven-card standard-size set was issued to herald the release of the 120-card 1994 Playoff Contenders series. The fronts display borderless color action shots that have a metallic sheen. The player's name in silver foil appears in a grass border on the bottom. The team name is printed in the upper portion of the photo. The backs carry a color player close-up with season highlights. The cards are unnumbered and checklisted below in alphabetical order.

COMPLETE SET (7) 2.00 5.00
1 Qadry Ismail .40 1.00
2 Daryl Johnston .40 1.00
3 John Jurkovic .20 .50
4 Eric Metcalf .40 1.00
5 Andre Reed .40 1.00
6 Calvin Williams .20 .50
7 Title Card .20 .50

1994 Playoff Contenders

Distributed through hobby stores in the U.S. and Canada only, this 120-card set measures the standard size. A subset "Draft Picks" (94-120) is featured in this set. Rookie Cards include Derrick Alexander, Lake Dawson, Trent Dilfer, Bert Emanuel, Marshall Faulk, William Floyd, Gus Frerotte, Greg Hill, Charles Johnson, Byron Bam Morris, Errict Rhett and Heath Shuler.

COMPLETE SET (120) 7.50 20.00
1 Drew Bledsoe .40 1.00
2 Barry Sanders 1.00 2.50
3 Jerry Rice .60 1.50
4 Rod Woodson .07 .20
5 Irving Fryar .07 .20
6 Charles Haley .07 .20
7 Chris Warren .07 .20
8 Craig Erickson .02 .10
9 Eric Metcalf .07 .20
10 Marcus Allen .15 .40
11 Chris Miller .02 .10
12 Andre Rison .07 .20
13 Art Monk .07 .20
14 Calvin Williams .07 .20
15 Shannon Sharpe .07 .20
16 Rodney Hampton .07 .20
17 Marion Butts .02 .10
18 John Jurkovic RC .07 .20
19 Jim Kelly .15 .40
20 Emmitt Smith 1.00 2.50
21 Jeff Hostetler .07 .20
22 Barry Foster .02 .10
23 Boomer Esiason .07 .20
24 Jim Harbaugh .15 .40
25 Joe Montana 1.25 3.00
26 Jeff George .15 .40
27 Warren Moon .15 .40
28 Steve Young .50 1.25
29 Randall Cunningham .15 .40
30 Shawn Jefferson .02 .10
31 Cortez Kennedy .07 .20
32 Reggie Brooks .07 .20
33 Alvin Harper .07 .20
34 Brent Jones .07 .20
35 O.J.McDuffie .15 .40
36 Jerome Bettis .25 .60
37 Daryl Johnston .07 .20
38 Herman Moore .15 .40
39 Dave Meggett .02 .10
40 Reggie White .15 .40
41 Junior Seau .15 .40
42 Dan Marino 1.25 3.00
43 Scott Mitchell .07 .20
44 John Elway 1.25 3.00
45 Troy Aikman .60 1.50
46 Terry Allen .07 .20
47 David Klingler .02 .10
48 Stan Humphries .07 .20
49 Rick Mirer .15 .40
50 Neil O'Donnell .15 .40
51 Keith Jackson .02 .10
52 Ricky Watters .07 .20
53 Dave Brown .07 .20
54 Neil Smith .07 .20
55 Johnny Mitchell .02 .10
56 Jackie Harris .02 .10
57 Terry Kirby .15 .40
58 Willie Davis .07 .20
59 Rob Moore .07 .20
60 Nate Newton .02 .10
61 Deion Sanders .30 .75
62 John Taylor .07 .20
63 Sterling Sharpe .07 .20
64 Natrone Means .15 .40
65 Steve Beuerlein .07 .20
66 Erik Kramer .07 .20
67 Qadry Ismail .15 .40
68 Johnny Johnson .02 .10
69 Herschel Walker .07 .20
70 Mark Stepnoski .02 .10
71 Brett Favre 1.25 3.00
72 Dana Stubblefield .07 .20
73 Bruce Smith .15 .40
74 Leroy Hoard .02 .10
75 Steve Walsh .02 .10
76 Jay Novacek .07 .20
77 Derrick Thomas .15 .40
78 Keith Byars .02 .10
79 Ben Coates .07 .20
80 Lorenzo Neal .02 .10
81 Ronnie Lott .07 .20
82 Tim Brown .15 .40
83 Michael Irvin .15 .40
84 Ronald Moore .02 .10
85 Andre Reed .07 .20
86 James Jett .02 .10
87 Curtis Conway .15 .40
88 Bernie Parmalee RC .15 .40
89 Keith Cash .02 .10
90 Russell Copeland .02 .10
91 Kevin Williams WR .07 .20
92 Gary Brown .02 .10
93 Thurman Thomas .15 .40
94 Jamir Miller RC .07 .20
95 Bert Emanuel RC .15 .40
96 Bucky Brooks RC .02 .10
97 Jeff Burris RC .07 .20
98 Antonio Langham RC .07 .20
99 Derrick Alexander WR RC .15 .40
100 Dan Wilkinson RC .07 .20
101 Shante Carver RC .02 .10
102 Johnnie Morton RC .75 2.00
103 LeShon Johnson RC .07 .20
104 Marshall Faulk RC 2.50 6.00
105 Greg Hill RC .15 .40
106 Lake Dawson RC .07 .20
107 Irving Spikes RC .07 .20
108 David Palmer RC .15 .40
109 Willie McGinest RC .15 .40
110 Joe Johnson RC .02 .10
111 Aaron Glenn RC .15 .40
112 Charlie Garner RC .60 1.50
113 Charles Johnson RC .15 .40
114 Byron Bam Morris RC .07 .20
115 Bryant Young RC .25 .60
116 William Floyd RC .15 .40
117 Trent Dilfer RC .60 1.50
118 Errict Rhett RC .15 .40
119 Heath Shuler RC .15 .40
120 Gus Frerotte RC .75 2.00

1994 Playoff Contenders Back-to-Back

Randomly inserted at a rate of one in 24, this 60-card standard-size set pairs two players with a photo on either side. In essence, it parallels the 120-card basic Playoff Contenders set. The difference being the two photo format. Either side is metallic with an action photo that is bordered at the bottom by the player's name and a silver Playoff Contenders logo.

COMPLETE SET (60) 400.00 800.00
STATED ODDS 1:24
1 J.Montana/D.Marino 40.00 100.00
2 D.Bledsoe/J.Elway 20.00 50.00
3 J.Rice/St.Sharpe 15.00 40.00
4 B.Sanders/E.Smith 50.00 100.00
5 T.Aikman/S.Young 25.00 60.00
6 E.Kramer/S.Walsh 3.00 8.00
7 N.Newton/B.Smith 4.00 10.00
8 J.Mitchell/T.Brown 6.00 15.00
9 N.O'Donnell/J.Novacek 3.00 8.00
10 H.Moore/Ca.Williams 6.00 15.00
11 M.Irvin/A.Harper 6.00 15.00
12 J.Harbaugh/C.Conway 4.00 10.00
13 B.Favre/L.Johnson 20.00 50.00
14 M.Faulk/E.Metcalf 10.00 20.00
15 Q.Ismail/D.Palmer 4.00 10.00
16 D.Sanders/A.Rison 7.50 20.00
17 E.Rhett/J.Harris 4.00 10.00
18 K.Jackson/I.Spikes 3.00 8.00
19 D.Meggett/J.Burris 3.00 8.00
20 W.Floyd/D.Stubblefield 4.00 10.00
21 Cunningham/R.White 6.00 15.00
22 Sh.Sharpe/Ke.Cash 3.00 8.00
23 M.Allen/D.Thomas 6.00 15.00
24 I.Fryar/R.Copeland 3.00 8.00
25 Jo.Johnson/B.Coates 3.00 8.00
26 J.Taylor/B.Jones 4.00 10.00
27 T.Kirby/B.Parmalee 4.00 10.00
28 R.Watters/R.Lott 6.00 15.00
29 S.Mitchell/J.Jett 3.00 8.00
30 O.J.McDuffie/K.Byars 4.00 10.00
31 S.Jefferson/A.Reed 4.00 10.00
32 R.Hampton/Lo.Neal 4.00 10.00
33 C.Miller/Ron.Moore 3.00 8.00
34 C.Haley/T.Thomas 6.00 15.00
35 H.Walker/L.Hoard 3.00 8.00
36 N.Means/S.Humphries 4.00 10.00
37 W.Davis/K.Williams 4.00 10.00
38 D.Brown/G.Brown 3.00 8.00
39 J.Bettis/T.Allen 7.50 20.00
40 C.Kennedy/J.Seau 6.00 15.00
41 Klingler/Alexander WR 4.00 10.00
42 C.Warren/Buc.Brooks 4.00 10.00
43 M.Stepnoski/G.Hill 4.00 10.00
44 S.Beuerlein/J.Morton 6.00 15.00
45 Rob Moore/A. Glenn 4.00 10.00
46 N.Smith/L.Dawson 4.00 10.00
47 R.Mirer/B.Young 4.00 10.00
48 D.Johnston/C.Garner 6.00 15.00
49 G.Frerotte/Re.Brooks 5.00 12.00
50 B.Foster/B.Morris 4.00 10.00
51 H.Shuler/A.Monk 6.00 15.00
52 C.Erickson/T.Dilfer 6.00 15.00
53 J.George/B.Emanuel 4.00 10.00
54 R.Woodson/A.Langham 4.00 10.00
55 M.Butts/W.McGinest 6.00 15.00
56 J.Jurkovic/Wilkinson 3.00 8.00
57 J.Kelly/S.Carver 6.00 15.00
58 J.Hostetler/C.Johnson 3.00 8.00
59 B.Esiason/J.Miller 3.00 8.00
60 W.Moon/Joe Johnson 4.00 10.00

1994 Playoff Contenders Rookie Contenders

Randomly inserted in packs at a rate of one in 48, this six-card standard-size set spotlights some of the top rookies from 1994. Metallic card fronts have an action photo superimposed over a silver prismatic background with a thick deep purple left border. The backs have a small player photo and highlights.

COMPLETE SET (6) 20.00 40.00
STATED ODDS 1:48
1 Heath Shuler 1.50 4.00
2 Trent Dilfer 2.50 6.00
3 David Palmer 1.00 2.50
4 Marshall Faulk 10.00 25.00
5 Charlie Garner 2.50 6.00
6 Dan Wilkinson 1.00 2.50

1994 Playoff Contenders Sophomore Contenders

Randomly inserted at a rate of one in 48, this six-card standard-size set spotlights some of the top second year players. An action photo is superimposed over a background that consists of a prismatic silver border and a deep purple upper border. Dark blue backs have a small player photo and brief highlights.

COMPLETE SET (6) 12.50 30.00
STATED ODDS 1:48
1 Drew Bledsoe 6.00 15.00
2 Jerome Bettis 4.00 10.00
3 Reggie Brooks 1.25 3.00
4 Rick Mirer 2.50 6.00
5 Natrone Means 2.50 6.00
6 O.J.McDuffie 2.50 6.00

1994 Playoff Contenders Throwbacks

Randomly inserted in packs at a rate of one in 12, this 30-card standard-size set takes a look at Throwback uniforms that were occasionally worn by each NFL team during the 1994 campaign. This was done to help celebrate the National Football League's 75th Anniversary. Full-bleed metallic fronts with purplish backgrounds feature the player in his Throwback uniform emerging from a generic game action photo. The backs have a close-up of the player with a brief write-up.

COMPLETE SET (30) 40.00 100.00
STATED ODDS 1:12
1 Larry Centers .40 1.00
2 Andre Rison .40 1.00
3 Jim Kelly .75 2.00
4 Curtis Conway .75 2.00
5 David Klingler .20 .50
6 Vinny Testaverde .75 2.00
7 Troy Aikman 3.00 8.00
8 Emmitt Smith 5.00 12.00
9 John Elway 6.00 15.00
10 Barry Sanders 5.00 12.00
11 Sterling Sharpe .40 1.00
12 Gary Brown .20 .50
13 Jim Harbaugh .75 2.00
14 Joe Montana 6.00 15.00
15 Tim Brown .75 2.00
16 Chris Miller .20 .50
17 Dan Marino 6.00 15.00
18 Terry Allen .40 1.00
19 Marion Butts .20 .50
20 Jim Everett .20 .50
21 Dave Brown .40 1.00
22 Johnny Johnson .20 .50
23 Randall Cunningham .75 2.00
24 Barry Foster .20 .50
25 Stan Humphries .40 1.00
26 Jerry Rice 3.00 8.00
27 Steve Young 2.50 6.00
28 Chris Warren .40 1.00
29 Errict Rhett .75 2.00
30 John Friesz .20 .50

1995 Playoff Contenders

The 1995 Playoff Contenders was issued in one series totalling 150 cards. The six-card pack retailed for $3.75. The set features the topical subset: Rookies (121-150). Rookie Cards include Kerry Collins, Terrell Davis, Joey Galloway, Curtis Martin, Steve McNair, Rashaan Salaam, Kordell Stewart, J.J. Stokes, Yancey Thigpen, Tamarick Vanover and Michael Westbrook.

COMPLETE SET (150) 10.00 25.00
1 Steve Young .40 1.00
2 Jeff Blake RC .30 .75
3 Rick Mirer .07 .20
4 Brett Favre 1.25 2.50
5 Heath Shuler .07 .20
6 Steve Bono .07 .20
7 John Elway 1.00 2.50
8 Troy Aikman .50 1.25
9 Rodney Peete .02 .10
10 Gus Frerotte .07 .20
11 Drew Bledsoe .30 .75
12 Jim Kelly .15 .40
13 Dan Marino 1.00 2.50
14 Errict Rhett .07 .20
15 Jeff Hostetler .07 .20
16 Erik Kramer .02 .10
17 Jim Everett .02 .10
18 Elvis Grbac .15 .40
19 Scott Mitchell .07 .20
20 Barry Sanders .75 2.00
21 Deion Sanders .30 .75
22 Emmitt Smith .75 2.00
23 Garrison Hearst .15 .40
24 Mario Bates .07 .20
25 Mark Brunell .30 .75
26 Robert Smith .15 .40
27 Rodney Hampton .07 .20
28 Marshall Faulk .60 1.50
29 Greg Hill .07 .20
30 Bernie Parmalee .07 .20
31 Natrone Means .07 .20
32 Marcus Allen .15 .40
33 Byron Bam Morris .02 .10
34 Edgar Bennett .07 .20
35 Vincent Brisby .02 .10
36 Jerome Bettis .15 .40
37 Craig Heyward .07 .20
38 Anthony Miller .07 .20
39 Curtis Conway .15 .40
40 William Floyd .07 .20
41 Chris Warren .07 .20
42 Terry Kirby .07 .20
43 Herschel Walker .07 .20
44 Eric Metcalf .07 .20
45 Darnay Scott .07 .20
46 Jackie Harris .02 .10
47 Dana Stubblefield .07 .20
48 Daryl Johnston .07 .20
49 Dave Meggett .02 .10
50 Ricky Watters .07 .20
51 Ken Norton .07 .20
52 Boomer Esiason .07 .20
53 Lake Dawson .07 .20
54 Eric Green .02 .10
55 Junior Seau .15 .40
56 Yancey Thigpen RC .15 .40
57 James Jett .07 .20
58 Leonard Russell .02 .10
59 Brent Jones .02 .10
60 Trent Dilfer .15 .40
61 Terance Mathis .07 .20
62 Jeff George .07 .20
63 Alvin Harper .02 .10
64 Terry Allen .07 .20
65 Stan Humphries .07 .20
66 Robert Green .02 .10
67 Bryce Paup .07 .20
68 Tamarick Vanover RC .15 .40
69 Desmond Howard .07 .20
70 Derek Loville .02 .10
71 Dave Brown .07 .20
72 Carl Pickens .07 .20
73 Gary Clark .02 .10
74 Gary Brown .02 .10
75 Brett Perriman .07 .20
76 Charlie Garner .15 .40
77 Ben Coates .07 .20
78 Bruce Smith .15 .40
79 Erric Pegram .07 .20
80 Jerry Rice .50 1.25
81 Tim Brown .15 .40
82 John Taylor .02 .10
83 Will Moore .02 .10
84 Jay Novacek .07 .20
85 Kevin Williams .07 .20
86 Rocket Ismail .07 .20
87 Robert Brooks .15 .40
88 Michael Irvin .15 .40
89 Mark Chmura .15 .40
90 Shannon Sharpe .07 .20
91 Henry Ellard .07 .20
92 Reggie White .15 .40
93 Isaac Bruce .30 .75
94 Charles Haley .07 .20
95 Jake Reed .07 .20
96 Pete Metzelaars .02 .10
97 Dave Krieg .02 .10
98 Tony Martin .07 .20
99 Charles Jordan RC .07 .20
100 Bert Emanuel .15 .40
101 Andre Rison .07 .20
102 Jeff Graham .02 .10
103 O.J. McDuffie .15 .40
104 Randall Cunningham .15 .40
105 Harvey Williams .02 .10
106 Cris Carter .15 .40
107 Irving Fryar .07 .20
108 Jim Harbaugh .07 .20
109 Bernie Kosar .02 .10

110 Charles Johnson .07 .20
111 Warren Moon .07 .20
112 Neil O'Donnell .07 .20
113 Fred Barnett .07 .20
114 Herman Moore .15 .40
115 Chris Miller .02 .10
116 Vinny Testaverde .07 .20
117 Craig Erickson .02 .10
118 Qadry Ismail .07 .20
119 Willie Davis .07 .20
120 Michael Jackson .07 .20
121 Stoney Case RC .15 .40
122 Frank Sanders RC .15 .40
123 Todd Collins RC 1.00 2.50
124 Kerry Collins RC .75 2.00
125 Sherman Williams RC .02 .10
126 Terrell Davis RC 1.00 2.50
127 Luther Elliss RC .02 .10
128 Steve McNair RC 1.25 3.00
129 Chris Sanders RC .15 .40
130 Ki-Jana Carter RC .15 .40
131 Rodney Thomas RC .15 .40
132 Tony Boselli RC .15 .40
133 Rob Johnson RC .40 1.00
134 James O. Stewart RC .50 1.25
135 Chad May RC .02 .10
136 Eric Bjornson RC .07 .20
137 Tyrone Wheatley RC .50 1.25
138 Kyle Brady RC .15 .40
139 Curtis Martin RC 1.25 3.00
140 Eric Zeier RC .15 .40
141 Ray Zellars RC .07 .20
142 Napoleon Kaufman RC .50 1.25
143 Mike Mamula RC .07 .20
144 Mark Bruener RC .07 .20
145 Kordell Stewart RC .60 1.50
146 J.J. Stokes RC .15 .40
147 Joey Galloway RC .60 1.50
148 Warren Sapp RC .60 1.50
149 Michael Westbrook RC .15 .40
150 Rashaan Salaam RC .15 .40

1995 Playoff Contenders Back-to-Back

Randomly inserted in packs at a rate of one in 19, this 75 card parallel set features 150 of the regular player cards including the Rookies subset. The cards have a gold embossed bar at the top and a silver embossed bar at the bottom. The players are featured against a black background in the center.

COMPLETE SET (75) 150.00 400.00
STATED ODDS 1:19
1 D.Marino 10.00 25.00
T.Aikman
2 E.Smith 10.00 25.00
M.Faulk
3 B.Favre 12.50 30.00
J.Elway
4 S.Young 6.00 15.00
D.Bledsoe
5 B.Sanders 7.50 20.00
E.Rhett
6 J.Rice 6.00 15.00
D.Sanders
7 Jeff Blake 3.00 8.00
Mirer
8 Michael Irvin 3.00 8.00
T.Brown
9 R.Watters 2.00 5.00
C.Warren
10 Herman Moore 3.00 8.00
Brisby
11 E.Metcalf 2.00 5.00
J.Jett
12 T.Mathis 2.00 5.00
H.Ellard
13 I.Bruce 5.00 12.00
C.Conway
14 J.Hostetler 2.00 5.00
S.Bono
15 H.Williams 2.00 5.00
G.Hill
16 J.Bettis 4.00 10.00
G.Hearst
17 B.Jones 2.00 5.00
J.Novacek
18 B.Smith 3.00 8.00
R.White
19 S.Sharpe 2.00 5.00
E.Green
20 J.George 2.00 5.00
G.Frerotte
21 S.Mitchell 1.25 3.00
E.Kramer
22 J.Kelly 3.00 8.00
W.Moon
23 B.Coates 2.00 5.00
M.Chmura
24 Heath Shuler 3.00 8.00
T.Dilfer
25 E.Bennett 2.00 5.00
C.Heyward
26 D.Brown 1.25 3.00
J.Everett
27 A.Rison 1.25 3.00
B.Emanuel
28 A.Harper 1.25 3.00
R.Brooks
29 T.Martin 2.00 5.00
D.Howard
30 F.Barnett 1.25 3.00
R.Peete
31 W.Floyd 2.00 5.00
N.Means
32 R.Ismail 1.25 3.00
B.Perriman
33 I.Fryar 2.00 5.00
C.Carter
34 Tam.Vanover 2.00 5.00
D.Scott
35 D.Stubblefield 2.00 5.00
C.Haley
36 K.Norton 1.25 3.00
B.Paup
37 H.Walker 3.00 8.00
M.Allen
38 T.Allen 1.25 3.00
L.Russell
39 D.Loville 3.00 8.00
J.Seau
40 C.Johnson 2.00 5.00
L.Dawson
41 C.Jordan 1.25 3.00
K.Williams
42 C.Pickens 2.00 5.00
J.Graham
43 O.J.McDuffie 2.00 5.00
A.Miller
44 J.Harbaugh 2.00 5.00
E.Grbac
45 T.Kirby 2.00 5.00
D.Meggett
46 S.Humphries 1.25 3.00
D.Krieg
47 B.Esiason 4.00 10.00
M.Brunell
48 V.Testaverde 1.25 3.00
C.Erickson
49 B.Kosar 1.25 3.00
R.Cunningham
50 C.Conner 1.25 3.00
E.Pegram
51 G.Clark 1.25 3.00
W.Moore
52 W.Davis 2.00 5.00
Q.Ismail
53 C.Miller 1.25 3.00
N.O'Donnell
54 R.Smith 2.00 5.00
M.Bates
55 B.Parmalee 2.00 5.00
R.Hampton
56 D.Johnston 2.00 5.00
B.Morris
57 J.Reed 1.25 3.00
J.Harris
58 P.Metzelaars 1.25 3.00
J.Taylor
59 Yan.Thigpen 3.00 8.00
M.Jackson
60 R.Green 1.25 3.00
G.Brown
61 N.Kaufman 3.00 8.00
R.Salaam
62 K.Brady 1.25 3.00
M.Bruener
63 Ki-Jana Carter 3.00 8.00
R.Thomas
64 S.McNair 7.50 20.00
C.May
65 J.J.Stokes 3.00 8.00
F.Sanders
66 W.Sapp 1.25 3.00
M.Mamula
67 K.Stewart 3.00 8.00
St.Case
68 C.Martin 10.00 25.00
T.Davis
69 Chris Sanders 3.00 8.00
S.Williams
70 E.Bjornson 2.00 5.00
J.Stewart
71 T.Wheatley 3.00 8.00
R.Zellars
72 L.Elliss 3.00 8.00
T.Boselli
73 T.Collins 6.00 15.00
R.Johnson
74 Kerry Collins 2.00 5.00
Zeier
75 M.Westbrook 3.00 8.00
J.Galloway

1995 Playoff Contenders Hog Heaven

Randomly inserted in packs at a rate of one in 48, this 30-card set features a leather-shaped football on the front with a foil branded player image and team logo. The player's name and the "Playoff" symbol are in gold at the bottom of the front. Card backs are all brown leather with the player's image in black and the player's name, position and team. Card backs are numbered with a "HH" prefix.

COMPLETE SET (30) 100.00 250.00
STATED ODDS 1:48
HH1 Troy Aikman 8.00 20.00
HH2 Marcus Allen 2.50 6.00
HH3 Jeff Blake 5.00 12.00
HH4 Drew Bledsoe 5.00 12.00
HH5 Steve Bono 1.25 3.00
HH6 Isaac Bruce 5.00 12.00
HH7 Trent Dilfer 2.50 6.00
HH8 John Elway 12.00 30.00
HH9 Marshall Faulk 10.00 25.00
HH10 Brett Favre 12.00 30.00
HH11 Gus Frerotte 1.25 3.00
HH12 Irving Fryar 1.25 3.00
HH13 Jeff George 1.25 3.00
HH14 Rodney Hampton 1.25 3.00
HH15 Garrison Hearst 2.50 6.00
HH16 Michael Irvin 2.50 6.00
HH17 Erik Kramer .60 1.50
HH18 Dan Marino 12.00 30.00
HH19 Natrone Means 1.25 3.00
HH20 Errict Rhett 1.25 3.00
HH21 Jerry Rice 8.00 20.00
HH22 Barry Sanders 12.50 30.00
HH23 Deion Sanders 5.00 12.00
HH24 Shannon Sharpe 1.25 3.00
HH25 Emmitt Smith 12.50 30.00
HH26 Robert Smith 2.50 6.00
HH27 Chris Warren 1.25 3.00
HH28 Reggie White 2.50 6.00
HH29 Harvey Williams .60 1.50
HH30 Steve Young 6.00 15.00

1995 Playoff Contenders Rookie Kickoff

Randomly inserted in packs at a rate of one in 24, this 30-card set features a plastic die-cut football shaped top with a green background at the bottom. Card backs are blank outside of a light shading at the bottom of the card which features the card number with a "RKO" prefix.

COMPLETE SET (30) 50.00 120.00
STATED ODDS 1:24
RKO1 Eric Bjornson .25 .60
RKO2 Tony Boselli .50 1.25
RKO3 Kyle Brady .50 1.25
RKO4 Mark Bruener .25 .60
RKO5 Ki-Jana Carter .50 1.25
RKO6 Stoney Case .50 1.25
RKO7 Kerry Collins 2.50 6.00
RKO8 Todd Collins 1.50 4.00
RKO9 Terrell Davis 3.00 8.00
RKO10 Luther Elliss .10 .30
RKO11 Joey Galloway 2.00 5.00
RKO12 Rob Johnson 1.25 3.00
RKO13 Napoleon Kaufman 1.50 4.00
RKO14 Mike Mamula .25 .60
RKO15 Curtis Martin 4.00 10.00
RKO16 Chad May .10 .30
RKO17 Steve McNair 4.00 10.00
RKO18 Rashaan Salaam .50 1.25
RKO19 Chris Sanders .50 1.25
RKO20 Frank Sanders .50 1.25
RKO21 Warren Sapp 2.00 5.00
RKO22 James O. Stewart 1.50 4.00
RKO23 Kordell Stewart 2.00 5.00
RKO24 J.J. Stokes .50 1.25
RKO25 Rodney Thomas .50 1.25
RKO26 Michael Westbrook .50 1.25
RKO27 Tyrone Wheatley 1.50 4.00
RKO28 Sherman Williams .10 .30
RKO29 Eric Zeier .50 1.25
RKO30 Ray Zellars .25 .60

1996 Playoff Contenders Leather

The 1996 Playoff Contenders Leather set was issued in one series totalling 100 cards. The three-card packs retail for $6.99 each, and contained one Leather, one parallel Pennant, and one parallel Open Field card. The fronts of the Leather cards feature a player image on a genuine leather background with a borderless player portrait on the backs. The set is divided into three color-coded insertion ratios: 50 "Scarce" greens which are the most common, 25 "Rare" purples with a ration of 1:11, and 25 "Ultra Rare" reds with a 1:22 ratio.

COMPLETE SET (100) 100.00 250.00
1 Brett Favre R 12.50 30.00
2 Steve Young P 4.00 10.00
3 Herman Moore P 1.00 2.50
4 Jim Harbaugh P 1.00 2.50
5 Curtis Martin R 5.00 12.00
6 Junior Seau G 1.00 2.50
7 John Elway R 10.00 25.00
8 Troy Aikman R 6.00 15.00
9 Terry Allen G .60 1.50
10 Kordell Stewart R 2.50 6.00
11 Drew Bledsoe R 4.00 10.00
12 Jim Kelly R 2.50 6.00
13 Dan Marino R 12.50 30.00
14 Andre Rison G .60 1.50
15 Jeff Hostetler G .30 .75
16 Scott Mitchell G .60 1.50
17 Carl Pickens G .60 1.50
18 Larry Centers R 1.25 3.00
19 Craig Heyward G .30 .75
20 Barry Sanders R 10.00 25.00
21 Deion Sanders P 3.00 8.00
22 Emmitt Smith R 10.00 25.00
23 Rashaan Salaam P 1.00 2.50
24 Mario Bates G .60 1.50
25 Lawrence Phillips R 1.25 3.00
26 Napoleon Kaufman P 1.50 4.00
27 Rodney Hampton G .60 1.50
28 Marshall Faulk R 3.00 8.00
29 Trent Dilfer G 1.00 2.50
30 Leeland McElroy G .60 1.50
31 Marcus Allen G 1.00 2.50
32 Ricky Watters R 1.25 3.00
33 Karim Abdul-Jabbar R 2.50 6.00
34 Herschel Walker G .60 1.50
35 Thurman Thomas G 1.00 2.50
36 Jerome Bettis G 1.00 2.50
37 Gus Frerotte P 1.00 2.50
38 Neil O'Donnell P 1.00 2.50
39 Rick Mirer G .60 1.50
40 Mike Alstott P 2.50 6.00
41 Vinny Testaverde P 1.00 2.50
42 Derek Loville G .30 .75
43 Ben Coates G .60 1.50
44 Steve McNair G 2.00 5.00
45 Bobby Engram G 1.00 2.50
46 Yancey Thigpen G .60 1.50
47 Lake Dawson G .30 .75
48 Terrell Davis G 2.00 5.00
49 Kerry Collins P 1.50 4.00
50 Eric Metcalf G .30 .75
51 Stanley Pritchett P .50 1.25
52 Robert Brooks G 1.00 2.50
53 Isaac Bruce R 2.50 6.00
54 Tim Brown G 1.00 2.50
55 Edgar Bennett G .60 1.50
56 Warren Moon G .60 1.50
57 Jerry Rice R 6.00 15.00
58 Michael Westbrook G 1.00 2.50
59 Keyshawn Johnson R 2.50 6.00
60 Steve Bono G .30 .75
61 Derrick Mayes G .60 1.50
62 Erik Kramer G .30 .75
63 Rodney Peete G .30 .75
64 Eddie Kennison P 1.50 4.00
65 Derrick Thomas G 1.00 2.50
66 Joey Galloway P 1.50 4.00
67 Amani Toomer G 1.00 2.50
68 Reggie White P 1.50 4.00
69 Heath Shuler R 1.25 3.00
70 Dave Brown R .75 2.00
71 Tony Banks G 1.00 2.50
72 Chris Warren R 1.25 3.00
73 J.J. Stokes R 2.50 6.00
74 Rickey Dudley G 1.00 2.50
75 Stan Humphries G .60 1.50
76 Jason Dunn G .30 .75
77 Tyrone Wheatley P 1.50 4.00
78 Jim Everett R .75 2.00
79 Cris Carter P 1.50 4.00
80 Alex Van Dyke G .60 1.50
81 O.J. McDuffie G .60 1.50
82 Mark Chmura G .60 1.50
83 Terry Glenn G 1.00 2.50
84 Boomer Esiason G .60 1.50
85 Bruce Smith G .60 1.50
86 Curtis Conway P 1.50 4.00
87 Ki-Jana Carter G .60 1.50
88 Tamarick Vanover G .60 1.50
89 Michael Jackson G .60 1.50
90 Mark Brunell P 4.00 10.00
91 Tim Biakabutuka P 1.50 4.00
92 Anthony Miller P .50 1.25
93 Marvin Harrison P 5.00 12.00
94 Jeff George R 1.25 3.00
95 Jeff Blake P 1.50 4.00
96 Eddie George R 4.00 10.00
97 Eric Moulds G 1.00 2.50
98 Mike Tomczak P .50 1.25
99 Chris Sanders P 1.00 2.50
100 Chris Chandler G .60 1.50

1996 Playoff Contenders Leather Accents

COMMON CARD (1-100) 3.00 8.00
SEMISTARS 6.00 15.00
UNLISTED STARS 10.00 25.00
STATED ODDS 1:216
1 Brett Favre 40.00 100.00
2 Steve Young 15.00 40.00
5 Curtis Martin 12.50 30.00
7 John Elway 40.00 100.00
8 Troy Aikman 20.00 50.00
11 Drew Bledsoe 12.50 30.00
13 Dan Marino 40.00 100.00
20 Barry Sanders 30.00 80.00
21 Deion Sanders 12.50 30.00
22 Emmitt Smith 30.00 80.00
28 Marshall Faulk 12.50 30.00
44 Steve McNair 12.50 30.00
48 Terrell Davis 12.50 30.00
57 Jerry Rice 20.00 50.00
93 Marvin Harrison 12.50 30.00

1996 Playoff Contenders Open Field Foil

The 1996 Playoff Contenders Open Field Foil set was issued in one series totalling 100 cards. The three-card packs retail for $6.99 each, and contained one Open Field Foil, one parallel Pennant, and one parallel Leather card. This holographic mini card set features a color player image on a football field background. The set is divided into three color-coded insertion ratios: 50 "Scarce" greens which are the most common, 25 "Rare" purples with a ration of 1:11, and 25 "Ultra Rare" reds with a 1:22 ratio.

COMPLETE SET (100) 50.00 120.00
1 Brett Favre P 5.00 12.00
2 Steve Young R 4.00 10.00
3 Herman Moore P .60 1.50
4 Jim Harbaugh G .50 1.25
5 Curtis Martin P 2.00 5.00
6 Junior Seau P 1.25 3.00
7 John Elway P 5.00 12.00
8 Troy Aikman R 5.00 12.00
9 Terry Allen G .50 1.25
10 Kordell Stewart P 1.25 3.00
11 Drew Bledsoe G 1.25 3.00
12 Jim Kelly G .75 2.00
13 Dan Marino R 8.00 20.00
14 Andre Rison P .60 1.50
15 Jeff Hostetler G .30 .75
16 Scott Mitchell R 1.25 3.00
17 Carl Pickens G .50 1.25
18 Larry Centers G .50 1.25
19 Craig Heyward R .60 1.50
20 Barry Sanders R 7.50 20.00
21 Deion Sanders P 1.50 4.00
22 Emmitt Smith P 4.00 10.00
23 Rashaan Salaam R 1.25 3.00
24 Mario Bates P .40 1.00
25 Lawrence Phillips P .60 1.50
26 Napoleon Kaufman G .75 2.00
27 Rodney Hampton G .50 1.25
28 Marshall Faulk R 2.00 5.00
29 Trent Dilfer G .75 2.00
30 Leeland McElroy R 1.25 3.00
31 Marcus Allen G .75 2.00
32 Ricky Watters P .60 1.50
33 Karim Abdul-Jabbar P 1.25 3.00
34 Herschel Walker R 1.25 3.00
35 Thurman Thomas G .75 2.00
36 Jerome Bettis G .75 2.00
37 Gus Frerotte R 1.25 3.00
38 Neil O'Donnell G .50 1.25
39 Rick Mirer G .50 1.25
40 Mike Alstott G 1.00 2.50
41 Vinny Testaverde G .50 1.25
42 Derek Loville G .30 .75
43 Ben Coates G .50 1.25
44 Steve McNair G 1.25 3.00
45 Bobby Engram R 2.00 5.00
46 Yancey Thigpen G .50 1.25
47 Lake Dawson P .40 1.00
48 Terrell Davis G 1.25 3.00
49 Kerry Collins P 1.25 3.00
50 Eric Metcalf G .30 .75
51 Stanley Pritchett G .30 .75
52 Robert Brooks P .60 1.50
53 Isaac Bruce P 1.25 3.00
54 Tim Brown P 1.25 3.00
55 Edgar Bennett G .50 1.25
56 Warren Moon P 1.25 3.00
57 Jerry Rice P 2.50 6.00
58 Michael Westbrook G .75 2.00
59 Keyshawn Johnson P 1.25 3.00
60 Steve Bono G .30 .75
61 Derrick Mayes R 2.00 5.00
62 Erik Kramer G .30 .75
63 Rodney Peete G .30 .75
64 Eddie Kennison G .75 2.00
65 Derrick Thomas G .75 2.00
66 Joey Galloway R 1.25 3.00
67 Amani Toomer R 2.50 6.00
68 Reggie White R 2.00 5.00
69 Heath Shuler P .60 1.50
70 Dave Brown G .30 .75
71 Tony Banks R 2.00 5.00
72 Chris Warren G .50 1.25
73 J.J. Stokes G .75 2.00
74 Rickey Dudley R 2.00 5.00
75 Stan Humphries G .50 1.25
76 Jason Dunn R .60 1.50
77 Tyrone Wheatley G .50 1.25
78 Jim Everett G .30 .75
79 Cris Carter G .75 2.00
80 Alex Van Dyke R 1.25 3.00
81 O.J. McDuffie P 1.25 3.00
82 Mark Chmura G .50 1.25
83 Terry Glenn R 2.00 5.00
84 Boomer Esiason G .50 1.25
85 Bruce Smith G .50 1.25
86 Curtis Conway G .50 1.25
87 Ki-Jana Carter R 1.25 3.00
88 Tamarick Vanover P .60 1.50
89 Michael Jackson R 1.25 3.00
90 Mark Brunell G 1.25 3.00
91 Tim Biakabutuka G .75 2.00
92 Anthony Miller G .50 1.25
93 Marvin Harrison G 2.50 6.00
94 Jeff George G .50 1.25
95 Jeff Blake G .75 2.00
96 Eddie George P 1.50 4.00
97 Eric Moulds R 2.50 6.00
98 Mike Tomczak R .60 1.50
99 Chris Sanders G .50 1.25
100 Chris Chandler G .50 1.25

1996 Playoff Contenders Pennants

The 1996 Playoff Contenders Pennants set was issued in one series totalling 100 cards. The three-card packs retail for $6.99 each, and contained one Pennant, one parallel Open Field Foil, and one parallel Leather card. The fronts of this Pennant set feature a color player image on a felt-like pennant shaped card with the player's name and team name on the back. The set is divided into three color-coded insertion ratios: 50 "Scarce" greens which are the most common, 25 "Rare" purples with a ratio of 1:11, and 25 "Ultra Rare" reds with a 1:22 ratio. These three colors refer to the Playoff logo on the cardfront that reads "1996 Pennants" and not the color of the actual felt on the front. The felt color can vary for the same player (but generally is a team color) as a number of different colors were used to produce the cards.

COMPLETE SET (100) 50.00 120.00
1 Brett Favre R 10.00 25.00
2 Steve Young R 3.00 8.00
3 Herman Moore R 1.50 4.00
4 Jim Harbaugh R 1.50 4.00
5 Curtis Martin R 5.00 12.00
6 Junior Seau G 1.00 2.50
7 John Elway R 12.50 30.00
8 Troy Aikman P 3.00 8.00
9 Terry Allen G .60 1.50
10 Kordell Stewart R 2.50 6.00
11 Drew Bledsoe G 2.00 5.00
12 Jim Kelly P 1.25 3.00
13 Dan Marino P 4.00 10.00
14 Andre Rison G .60 1.50
15 Jeff Hostetler G .30 .75
16 Scott Mitchell G .60 1.50
17 Carl Pickens R 1.50 4.00
18 Larry Centers P .40 1.00
19 Craig Heyward G .30 .75
20 Barry Sanders P 5.00 12.00
21 Deion Sanders R 4.00 10.00
22 Emmitt Smith R 10.00 25.00
23 Rashaan Salaam R 1.50 4.00
24 Mario Bates G .60 1.50
25 Lawrence Phillips G 1.00 2.50
26 Napoleon Kaufman G 1.00 2.50
27 Rodney Hampton G .60 1.50
28 Marshall Faulk P 1.50 4.00
29 Trent Dilfer G 1.00 2.50
30 Leeland McElroy P .75 2.00
31 Marcus Allen P 1.25 3.00
32 Ricky Watters G .60 1.50
33 Karim Abdul-Jabbar G 1.00 2.50
34 Herschel Walker P .75 2.00
35 Thurman Thomas R 2.50 6.00
36 Jerome Bettis P 1.25 3.00
37 Gus Frerotte G .60 1.50
38 Neil O'Donnell G .60 1.50
39 Rick Mirer G .60 1.50
40 Mike Alstott R 2.50 6.00
41 Vinny Testaverde R 1.50 4.00
42 Derek Loville G .30 .75
43 Ben Coates G .60 1.50
44 Steve McNair R 5.00 12.00
45 Bobby Engram P 1.25 3.00
46 Yancey Thigpen G .60 1.50
47 Lake Dawson G .30 .75
48 Terrell Davis P 3.00 8.00
49 Kerry Collins R 2.50 6.00
50 Eric Metcalf G .30 .75
51 Stanley Pritchett R .75 2.00
52 Robert Brooks R 1.50 4.00
53 Isaac Bruce G 1.00 2.50
54 Tim Brown G 1.00 2.50
55 Edgar Bennett P .40 1.00
56 Warren Moon G .60 1.50
57 Jerry Rice R 6.00 15.00
58 Michael Westbrook G 1.00 2.50
59 Keyshawn Johnson G 1.00 2.50
60 Steve Bono R .30 .75
61 Derrick Mayes P 1.25 3.00
62 Erik Kramer P .40 1.00
63 Rodney Peete G .30 .75
64 Eddie Kennison G 1.00 2.50
65 Derrick Thomas G 1.00 2.50
66 Joey Galloway R 2.50 6.00
67 Amani Toomer P 1.25 3.00
68 Reggie White G 1.00 2.50
69 Heath Shuler G .60 1.50
70 Dave Brown G .30 .75
71 Tony Banks P 1.25 3.00
72 Chris Warren G .60 1.50
73 J.J. Stokes G 1.00 2.50
74 Rickey Dudley P 1.25 3.00
75 Stan Humphries G .60 1.50
76 Jason Dunn P .40 1.00
77 Tyrone Wheatley G .60 1.50
78 Jim Everett G .30 .75
79 Cris Carter P 1.25 3.00
80 Alex Van Dyke P .40 1.00
81 O.J. McDuffie G .60 1.50
82 Mark Chmura P .40 1.00
83 Terry Glenn P 1.25 3.00
84 Boomer Esiason R 1.50 4.00
85 Bruce Smith G .60 1.50
86 Curtis Conway G .60 1.50
87 Ki-Jana Carter G .60 1.50
88 Tamarick Vanover G .60 1.50
89 Michael Jackson G .60 1.50
90 Mark Brunell G 2.00 5.00
91 Tim Biakabutuka R 2.50 6.00
92 Anthony Miller G .60 1.50
93 Marvin Harrison R 6.00 15.00
94 Jeff George P .75 2.00
95 Jeff Blake R 2.50 6.00
96 Eddie George G 1.50 4.00
97 Eric Moulds P 1.50 4.00
98 Mike Tomczak G .30 .75
99 Chris Sanders G .60 1.50
100 Chris Chandler G .60 1.50

1996 Playoff Contenders Air Command

Randomly inserted in hobby packs at a rate of one in 96, this eight-card set features images of the game's hottest quarterbacks on holographic mini cards measuring approximately 2 1/4" by 3 1/8".

COMPLETE SET (8) 50.00 100.00
STATED ODDS 1:96
AC1 Dan Marino 8.00 20.00
AC2 Brett Favre 15.00 40.00
AC3 Troy Aikman 4.00 10.00
AC4 Mike Tomczak .40 1.00
AC5 John Elway 15.00 40.00
AC6 Jeff George 1.00 2.50
AC7 Chris Chandler .75 2.00
AC8 Steve Bono .40 1.00

1996 Playoff Contenders Ground Hogs

Randomly inserted in packs at a rate of one in 144, this eight-card set features color action images of football's top running backs on a leather background. The backs carry a borderless player action photo.

COMPLETE SET (8) 60.00 120.00
STATED ODDS 1:144
GH1 Emmitt Smith 12.50 30.00
GH2 Barry Sanders 12.50 30.00
GH3 Marshall Faulk 12.50 25.00
GH4 Curtis Martin 7.50 20.00
GH5 Chris Warren 6.00 15.00
GH6 Ricky Watters 6.00 15.00
GH7 Thurman Thomas 7.50 20.00
GH8 Terrell Davis 7.50 20.00

1996 Playoff Contenders Honors

Randomly inserted in hobby packs at a rate of one in 7200, this three-card set is a continuation of the 1996 Playoff Prime Honors set and features color player images on a holographic design. The backs carry a borderless player photo.

COMPLETE SET (3) 50.00 120.00
STATED ODDS 1:7200
PH4 Dan Marino 30.00 80.00
PH5 Deion Sanders 15.00 40.00
PH6 Marcus Allen 15.00 40.00

1996 Playoff Contenders Pennant Flyers

Randomly inserted in hobby packs at a rate of one in 48, this eight-card set features color images of the NFL's best receivers on a felt-like pennant shaped card. The backs carry the player's team logo.

COMPLETE SET (8) 60.00 120.00
STATED ODDS 1:48
PF1 Jerry Rice 10.00 25.00
PF2 Joey Galloway 7.50 15.00
PF3 Isaac Bruce 7.50 15.00
PF4 Herman Moore 7.50 15.00
PF5 Carl Pickens 5.00 10.00
PF6 Yancey Thigpen 5.00 10.00
PF7 Deion Sanders 10.00 20.00
PF8 Robert Brooks 7.50 15.00

1997 Playoff Contenders

Distributed in four-card packs, this 150-card set features color player photos printed on super-premium 30 pt. card stock with two-sided action foil etching. The fronts display a double-etched pattern with a silver holographic starburst behind the player. The backs carry the player's name stamped in silver across the card with the etch adding movement and light.

COMPLETE SET (150) 15.00 40.00
UNPRICED GOLD PRINT RUN 1
1 Kent Graham .15 .40
2 Leeland McElroy .15 .40
3 Rob Moore .25 .60
4 Frank Sanders .25 .60
5 Jake Plummer RC 1.50 4.00
6 Chris Chandler .25 .60
7 Bert Emanuel .25 .60
8 O.J. Santiago RC .25 .60
9 Byron Hanspard RC .25 .60
10 Vinny Testaverde .25 .60
11 Michael Jackson .25 .60
12 Earnest Byner .15 .40
13 Jermaine Lewis .40 1.00
14 Derrick Alexander WR .25 .60
15 Jay Graham RC .25 .60
16 Todd Collins .15 .40
17 Thurman Thomas .40 1.00
18 Bruce Smith .25 .60
19 Andre Reed .25 .60
20 Quinn Early .15 .40
21 Antowain Smith RC 1.00 2.50
22 Kerry Collins .40 1.00
23 Tim Biakabutuka .25 .60
24 Anthony Johnson .15 .40
25 Wesley Walls .25 .60
26 Fred Lane RC .25 .60
27 Rae Carruth RC .15 .40
28 Raymont Harris .15 .40
29 Rick Mirer .15 .40
30 Darnell Autry RC .25 .60
31 Jeff Blake .25 .60
32 Ki-Jana Carter .15 .40
33 Carl Pickens .25 .60
34 Darnay Scott .25 .60
35 Corey Dillon RC 1.50 4.00
36 Troy Aikman .75 2.00
37 Emmitt Smith 1.25 3.00
38 Michael Irvin .40 1.00
39 Deion Sanders .40 1.00
40 Anthony Miller .15 .40
41 Eric Bjornson .15 .40
42 David LaFleur RC .15 .40
43 John Elway 1.50 4.00
44 Terrell Davis .40 1.00
45 Shannon Sharpe .25 .60
46 Ed McCaffrey .25 .60
47 Rod Smith WR .40 1.00
48 Scott Mitchell .25 .60
49 Barry Sanders 1.25 3.00
50 Herman Moore .25 .60
51 Brett Favre 1.50 4.00
52 Dorsey Levens .40 1.00
53 William Henderson .25 .60
54 Derrick Mayes .25 .60
55 Antonio Freeman .40 1.00
56 Robert Brooks .25 .60
57 Mark Chmura .25 .60
58 Reggie White .40 1.00
59 Darren Sharper RC 8.00 20.00
60 Jim Harbaugh .25 .60
61 Marshall Faulk .40 1.00
62 Marvin Harrison .40 1.00
63 Mark Brunell .40 1.00
64 Natrone Means .25 .60
65 Jimmy Smith .25 .60
66 Keenan McCardell .25 .60
67 Elvis Grbac .25 .60
68 Greg Hill .15 .40
69 Marcus Allen .40 1.00
70 Andre Rison .25 .60
71 Kimble Anders .25 .60
72 Tony Gonzalez RC 1.50 4.00
73 Pat Barnes RC .40 1.00
74 Dan Marino 1.50 4.00
75 Karim Abdul-Jabbar .25 .60
76 Zach Thomas .40 1.00
77 O.J. McDuffie .25 .60
78 Brian Manning RC .15 .40
79 Brad Johnson .40 1.00
80 Cris Carter .40 1.00
81 Jake Reed .25 .60
82 Robert Smith .25 .60
83 Drew Bledsoe .40 1.00
84 Curtis Martin .40 1.00
85 Ben Coates .25 .60
86 Terry Glenn .40 1.00
87 Shawn Jefferson .15 .40
88 Heath Shuler .15 .40
89 Mario Bates .15 .40
90 Andre Hastings .15 .40
91 Troy Davis RC .25 .60
92 Danny Wuerffel RC .40 1.00
93 Dave Brown .15 .40
94 Chris Calloway .15 .40
95 Tiki Barber RC 2.50 6.00
96 Mike Cherry RC .15 .40
97 Neil O'Donnell .25 .60
98 Keyshawn Johnson .40 1.00
99 Adrian Murrell .25 .60
100 Wayne Chrebet .40 1.00
101 Dedric Ward RC .25 .60
102 Leon Johnson RC .25 .60
103 Jeff George .25 .60
104 Napoleon Kaufman .40 1.00
105 Tim Brown .40 1.00
106 James Jett .25 .60
107 Ty Detmer .25 .60
108 Ricky Watters .25 .60
109 Irving Fryar .25 .60
110 Michael Timpson .15 .40
111 Chad Lewis RC .40 1.00
112 Kordell Stewart .40 1.00
113 Jerome Bettis .40 1.00
114 Charles Johnson .25 .60
115 George Jones RC .25 .60
116 Will Blackwell RC .25 .60
117 Stan Humphries .25 .60
118 Junior Seau .40 1.00
119 Freddie Jones RC .25 .60
120 Steve Young .60 1.50
121 Jerry Rice .75 2.00
122 Garrison Hearst .25 .60
123 William Floyd .25 .60
124 Terrell Owens .40 1.00
125 J.J. Stokes .25 .60
126 Marc Edwards RC .15 .40
127 Jim Druckenmiller RC .25 .60
128 Warren Moon .40 1.00
129 Chris Warren .25 .60
130 Joey Galloway .25 .60
131 Shawn Springs RC .25 .60
132 Tony Banks .25 .60
133 Lawrence Phillips .15 .40
134 Isaac Bruce .40 1.00
135 Eddie Kennison .25 .60
136 Orlando Pace RC .40 1.00
137 Trent Dilfer .40 1.00
138 Mike Alstott .40 1.00
139 Horace Copeland .15 .40
140 Jackie Harris .15 .40
141 Warrick Dunn RC 1.25 3.00
142 Reidel Anthony RC .40 1.00
143 Steve McNair .40 1.00
144 Eddie George .40 1.00
145 Chris Sanders .15 .40
146 Gus Frerotte .15 .40
147 Terry Allen .40 1.00
148 Henry Ellard .15 .40
149 Leslie Shepherd .15 .40
150 Michael Westbrook .25 .60
S1 Terrell Davis Sample .75 2.00

1997 Playoff Contenders Blue

COMPLETE SET (150) 150.00 300.00
*BLUE VETS: 1.2X TO 3X BASIC CARDS
*BLUE ROOKIES: .6X TO 1.5X
BLUE STATED ODDS 1:4

1997 Playoff Contenders Red

*RED VETS: 15X TO 40X BASIC CARDS
*RED ROOKIES: 8X TO 20X
RED PRINT RUN 25 SER.#'d SETS
59 Darren Sharper 50.00 120.00

1997 Playoff Contenders Clash

Randomly inserted in packs at the rate of one in 48, this 12-card set features photos of two players who are top season match-ups printed on etched die-cut cards.

COMPLETE SET (12) 50.00 120.00
SILVER STATED ODDS 1:48
*BLUES: .8X TO 2X SILVERS
BLUE STATED ODDS 1:192
1 B.Favre 12.50 30.00
T.Aikman
2 B.Sanders 10.00 25.00
B.Johnson
3 C.Martin 5.00 12.00
W.Dunn
4 S.Young 12.50 30.00
J.Elway
5 J.Rice 7.50 20.00
M.Allen
6 D.Marino 12.50 30.00
D.Bledsoe
7 T.Davis 5.00 12.00
N.Kaufman
8 E.George 12.50 30.00
E.Smith
9 M.Brunell 5.00 12.00
T.Brown
10 K.Collins 4.00 10.00
R.White
11 D.Sanders 4.00 10.00
C.Pickens
12 M.Alstott 4.00 10.00
K.Johnson

1997 Playoff Contenders Leather Helmet Die Cuts

Randomly inserted in packs at the rate of one in 24, this 18-card set features color photos of top NFL players alongside a genuine leather die-cut helmet resembling the football helments used in the glory days of the NFL.

COMPLETE SET (18) 75.00 150.00
SILVER STATED ODDS 1:24
*BLUE: 1.2X TO 3X BASIC INSERTS
*RED/25: 3X TO 8X BASIC INSERTS
1 Dan Marino 10.00 25.00
2 Troy Aikman 5.00 12.00
3 Brett Favre 10.00 25.00
4 Barry Sanders 8.00 20.00
5 Drew Bledsoe 3.00 8.00
6 Deion Sanders 3.00 8.00
7 Curtis Martin 3.00 8.00
8 Warrick Dunn 2.50 6.00
9 Napoleon Kaufman 2.00 5.00
10 Eddie George 2.50 6.00
11 Antowain Smith 2.00 5.00
12 Emmitt Smith 8.00 20.00
13 John Elway 10.00 25.00
14 Steve Young 4.00 10.00
15 Mark Brunell 2.50 6.00
16 Terrell Davis 3.00 8.00
17 Terry Glenn 2.50 6.00
18 Terrell Owens 3.00 8.00

1997 Playoff Contenders Pennants Black Felt

Randomly inserted in packs at the rate of one in 12, this 36-card set features color player images on a felt pennant design with silver borders. Reportedly, six different colors of felt were used for each card: black, orange, light green, blue, red, and purple.

COMPLETE SET (36) 125.00 250.00
SILVER STATED ODDS 1:12
*BLUES: .8X TO 2X BASIC INSERTS
BLUE STATED ODDS 1:72
1 Dan Marino 8.00 20.00
2 Kordell Stewart 2.00 5.00
3 Drew Bledsoe 2.50 6.00
4 Kerry Collins 2.00 5.00
5 John Elway 8.00 20.00
6 Trent Dilfer 2.00 5.00
7 Jerry Rice 4.00 10.00
8 Emmitt Smith 6.00 15.00
9 Jeff George 1.25 3.00
10 Eddie George 2.00 5.00
11 Terrell Davis 2.50 6.00
12 Mike Alstott 2.00 5.00
13 Jim Druckenmiller .75 2.00
14 Antowain Smith 2.00 5.00
15 Marcus Allen 2.00 5.00
16 Jerome Bettis 2.00 5.00
17 Terrell Owens 2.50 6.00
18 Gus Frerotte .75 2.00
19 Troy Aikman 4.00 10.00
20 Andre Rison 1.25 3.00
21 Mark Brunell 2.00 5.00
22 Antonio Freeman 2.00 5.00
23 Brett Favre 8.00 20.00
24 Steve McNair 2.50 6.00
25 Barry Sanders 6.00 15.00
26 Steve Young 2.50 6.00
27 Curtis Martin 2.50 6.00
28 Napoleon Kaufman 2.00 5.00
29 Deion Sanders 2.00 5.00
30 Terry Glenn 2.00 5.00
31 Warrick Dunn 2.50 6.00
32 Danny Wuerffel .75 2.00
33 Elvis Grbac 1.25 3.00
34 Cris Carter 2.00 5.00
35 Joey Galloway 1.25 3.00
36 Corey Dillon 5.00 12.00

1997 Playoff Contenders Performer Plaques

Randomly inserted in packs at the rate of one in 12, this 45-card set features color player photos printed on die-cut cards shaped as plaques with silver foil stamping.

COMPLETE SET (45) 125.00 250.00
SILVER STATED ODDS 1:12
*BLUES: .8X TO 2X BASIC INSERTS
BLUE STATED ODDS 1:36
1 Jim Druckenmiller .75 2.00
2 Danny Wuerffel .75 2.00
3 Antowain Smith 2.00 5.00
4 Warrick Dunn 2.50 6.00
5 Terrell Owens 2.50 6.00
6 Elvis Grbac 1.25 3.00
7 Andre Rison 1.25 3.00
8 Tim Brown 2.00 5.00
9 Trent Dilfer 2.00 5.00
10 Brad Johnson 2.00 5.00
11 Deion Sanders 2.00 5.00
12 Dan Marino 8.00 20.00
13 Kerry Collins 2.00 5.00
14 Steve McNair 2.50 6.00
15 Eddie George 2.00 5.00
16 Ricky Watters 1.25 3.00
17 Jerome Bettis 2.00 5.00
18 Robert Brooks 1.25 3.00
19 Keyshawn Johnson 2.00 5.00
20 Antonio Freeman 2.00 5.00
21 Eddie Kennison 1.25 3.00
22 Mike Alstott 2.00 5.00
23 Brett Favre 8.00 20.00
24 Troy Aikman 4.00 10.00
25 Emmitt Smith 6.00 15.00
26 Terrell Davis 2.50 6.00
27 John Elway 8.00 20.00
28 Barry Sanders 6.00 15.00
29 Steve Young 2.50 6.00
30 Curtis Martin 2.50 6.00
31 Cris Carter 2.00 5.00
32 Drew Bledsoe 2.50 6.00
33 Mark Brunell 2.50 6.00
34 Kordell Stewart 2.00 5.00
35 Tony Banks 1.25 3.00
36 Napoleon Kaufman 2.00 5.00
37 Marcus Allen 2.00 5.00
38 Terry Glenn 2.00 5.00
39 Herman Moore 1.25 3.00
40 Michael Irvin 2.00 5.00
41 Joey Galloway 1.25 3.00
42 Karim Abdul-Jabbar 1.25 3.00
43 Reggie White 2.00 5.00
44 Jerry Rice 4.00 10.00
45 Gus Frerotte .75 2.00

1997 Playoff Contenders Rookie Wave Pennants Black Felt

Randomly inserted in packs at the rate of one in six, this 27-card set features color images of top rookies on a wave-design background with silver borders. Each pennant was issued in four different felt colors.

COMPLETE SET (27) 40.00 80.00
*BLUE: .4X TO 1X BLACK FELT
*GREEN: .4X TO 1X BLACK FELT
*ORANGE: .4X TO 1X BLACK FELT
OVERALL STATED ODDS 1:6
1 Jim Druckenmiller 1.00 2.50
2 Antowain Smith 2.00 5.00
3 Will Blackwell 1.00 2.50
4 Tiki Barber 5.00 12.00
5 Rae Carruth .75 2.00
6 Jay Graham 1.00 2.50
7 Darnell Autry 1.00 2.50
8 David LaFleur .75 2.00
9 Tony Gonzalez 4.00 10.00
10 Chad Lewis 1.25 3.00
11 Freddie Jones 1.00 2.50
12 Shawn Springs 1.00 2.50
13 Danny Wuerffel 1.25 3.00
14 Warrick Dunn 2.50 6.00
15 Troy Davis 1.00 2.50
16 Reidel Anthony 1.25 3.00
17 Jake Plummer 3.00 8.00
18 Byron Hanspard 1.00 2.50
19 Fred Lane 1.00 2.50
20 Corey Dillon 3.00 8.00
21 Darren Sharper 4.00 10.00
22 Pat Barnes 1.25 3.00
23 Mike Cherry .75 2.00

24 Leon Johnson 1.00 2.50
25 George Jones 1.00 2.50
26 Marc Edwards .75 2.00
27 Orlando Pace 1.25 3.00

1998 Playoff Contenders Leather

This 100-card set features color action player images silhouetted on a die-cut football background and printed on actual leather. The backs carry player information.

COMPLETE SET (100) 100.00 200.00
1 Adrian Murrell .60 1.50
2 Michael Pittman 1.00 2.50
3 Jake Plummer 1.00 2.50
4 Andre Wadsworth .60 1.50
5 Jamal Anderson 1.00 2.50
6 Chris Chandler .60 1.50
7 Tim Dwight 1.00 2.50
8 Pat Johnson .60 1.50
9 Jermaine Lewis .60 1.50
10 Doug Flutie 1.00 2.50
11 Antowain Smith 1.00 2.50
12 Muhsin Muhammad .60 1.50
13 Bobby Engram .60 1.50
14 Curtis Enis .30 .75
15 Alonzo Mayes .30 .75
16 Corey Dillon 1.00 2.50
17 Carl Pickens .60 1.50
18 Troy Aikman 2.00 5.00
19 Michael Irvin 1.00 2.50
20 Deion Sanders 1.00 2.50
21 Emmitt Smith 3.00 8.00
22 Terrell Davis 1.00 2.50
23 John Elway 4.00 10.00
24 Brian Griese 1.50 4.00
25 Rod Smith WR .60 1.50
26 Charlie Batch 1.00 2.50
27 Germane Crowell .30 .75
28 Terry Fair .30 .75
29 Herman Moore .60 1.50
30 Barry Sanders 3.00 8.00
31 Brett Favre 4.00 10.00
32 Antonio Freeman 1.00 2.50
33 Vonnie Holliday .60 1.50
34 Reggie White 1.00 2.50
35 Marshall Faulk 1.00 2.50
36 Marvin Harrison 1.00 2.50
37 Peyton Manning 10.00 25.00
38 Jerome Pathon 1.00 2.50
39 Tavian Banks .60 1.50
40 Mark Brunell .60 1.50
41 Keenan McCardell .60 1.50
42 Fred Taylor 1.50 4.00
43 Elvis Grbac .60 1.50
44 Andre Rison .60 1.50
45 Rashaan Shehee .30 .75
46 Karim Abdul-Jabbar 1.00 2.50
47 John Avery .30 .75
48 Dan Marino 4.00 10.00
49 O.J. McDuffie .60 1.50
50 Cris Carter 1.00 2.50
51 Brad Johnson 1.00 2.50
52 Randy Moss 6.00 15.00
53 Robert Smith 1.00 2.50
54 Drew Bledsoe 1.00 2.50
55 Ben Coates .60 1.50
56 Robert Edwards .60 1.50
57 Chris Floyd .30 .75
58 Terry Glenn 1.00 2.50
59 Cameron Cleeland .30 .75
60 Kerry Collins .60 1.50
61 Danny Kanell .60 1.50
62 Charles Way .40 1.00
63 Glenn Foley .40 1.00
64 Keyshawn Johnson 1.00 2.50
65 Curtis Martin 1.00 2.50
66 Tim Brown 1.00 2.50
67 Jeff George .60 1.50
68 Napoleon Kaufman 1.00 2.50
69 Charles Woodson 4.00 10.00
70 Irving Fryar .60 1.50
71 Bobby Hoying .60 1.50
72 Jerome Bettis 1.00 2.50
73 Kordell Stewart 1.00 2.50
74 Hines Ward 5.00 10.00
75 Ryan Leaf 1.00 2.50
76 Natrone Means .60 1.50
77 Mikhael Ricks .30 .75
78 Junior Seau 1.00 2.50
79 Garrison Hearst 1.00 2.50
80 Terrell Owens 1.00 2.50
81 Jerry Rice 2.00 5.00
82 Steve Young 1.25 3.00
83 Joey Galloway .60 1.50
84 Ahman Green 2.50 6.00
85 Warren Moon 1.00 2.50
86 Ricky Watters .60 1.50
87 Tony Banks .60 1.50
88 Isaac Bruce 1.00 2.50
89 Robert Holcombe .60 1.50
90 Mike Alstott 1.00 2.50
91 Trent Dilfer 1.00 2.50
92 Warrick Dunn 1.00 2.50
93 Jacquez Green .60 1.50
94 Kevin Dyson 1.00 2.50
95 Eddie George 1.00 2.50
96 Steve McNair 1.00 2.50
97 Yancey Thigpen .40 1.00
98 Terry Allen 1.00 2.50
99 Skip Hicks .60 1.50
100 Michael Westbrook .60 1.50

1998 Playoff Contenders Leather Gold

*STARS/70-94: 6X TO 15X BASIC CARDS
*STARS/45-69: 8X TO 20X BASIC CARDS
*RCs/45-69: 4X TO 10X BASIC CARDS
*STARS/30-44: 10X TO 25X BASIC CARDS
*RCs/30-44: 5X TO 12X BASIC CARDS
*STARS/20-29: 12X TO 30X BASIC CARDS
*RCs/20-29: 6X TO 15X BASIC CARDS
*STARS/16-19: 20X TO 50X BASIC CARDS
37 Peyton Manning/36 150.00 300.00
52 Randy Moss/25 75.00 150.00

1998 Playoff Contenders Leather Red

COMP.RED SET (100) 200.00 400.00
*RED STARS: 1X TO 2.5X BASIC LEATHER
*RED ROOKIES: .6X TO 1.5X BASIC LEATHER
STATED ODDS 1:9 HOBBY

1998 Playoff Contenders Leather Registered Exchange

COMPLETE SET (100) 400.00 800.00
*REGISTERED STARS: 2X TO 5X BASIC CARDS
*REGISTERED ROOKIES: 1X TO 2.5X BASIC CARDS
ANNOUNCED PRINT RUN 51 SETS

1998 Playoff Contenders Pennants Blue Felt

This 100-card set features color action player photos printed on die-cut pennant-shaped conventional card stock with silver foil stamping and felt-like flocking. Each card was also produced in 6-different felt colors (blue, green, orange, purple, red, and yellow) all with silver foil highlights. The backs carry player information. A red foil parallel version with an insertion rate of 1:9 and a gold foil parallel version sequentially numbered to 98 were also produced.

COMPLETE SET (100) 60.00 150.00
ONE PENNANT PER PACK
EACH CARD ISSUED IN 6-FELT COLORS
6-FELT COLOR VARIATIONS SAME PRICE
1 Jake Plummer 1.00 2.50
2 Frank Sanders .40 1.00
3 Jamal Anderson 1.00 2.50
4 Tim Dwight 1.00 2.50
5 Jammi German .30 .75
6 Tony Martin .60 1.50
7 Jim Harbaugh .60 1.50
8 Rod Woodson .60 1.50
9 Rob Johnson .60 1.50
10 Eric Moulds 1.00 2.50
11 Antowain Smith 1.00 2.50
12 Steve Beuerlein .60 1.50
13 Fred Lane .40 1.00
14 Curtis Enis .30 .75
15 Corey Dillon 1.00 2.50
16 Neil O'Donnell .60 1.50
17 Carl Pickens .60 1.50
18 Darnay Scott .60 1.50
19 Takeo Spikes 1.00 2.50
20 Troy Aikman 2.00 5.00
21 Michael Irvin 1.00 2.50
22 Deion Sanders 1.00 2.50
23 Emmitt Smith 3.00 8.00
24 Chris Warren .60 1.50
25 Terrell Davis 1.00 2.50
26 John Elway 4.00 10.00
27 Brian Griese 2.00 5.00
28 Ed McCaffrey 1.00 2.50
29 Marcus Nash .30 .75
30 Shannon Sharpe .60 1.50
31 Rod Smith WR .60 1.50
32 Charlie Batch 1.00 2.50
33 Germane Crowell .30 .75
34 Herman Moore .60 1.50
35 Barry Sanders 3.00 8.00
36 Mark Chmura .40 1.00
37 Brett Favre 4.00 10.00
38 Antonio Freeman 1.00 2.50
39 Reggie White 1.00 2.50
40 Marshall Faulk 1.00 2.50
41 E.G. Green .30 .75
42 Peyton Manning 15.00 40.00
43 Jerome Pathon 1.00 2.50
44 Mark Brunell 1.00 2.50
45 Jonathan Quinn .60 1.50
46 Fred Taylor 1.50 4.00
47 Tony Gonzalez 1.00 2.50
48 Andre Rison .60 1.50
49 Karim Abdul-Jabbar 1.00 2.50
50 John Avery .30 .75
51 Dan Marino 4.00 10.00
52 Cris Carter 1.00 2.50
53 Randall Cunningham 1.00 2.50
54 Brad Johnson 1.00 2.50
55 Randy Moss 8.00 20.00
56 Robert Smith 1.00 2.50
57 Drew Bledsoe 1.00 2.50
58 Robert Edwards .60 1.50
59 Terry Glenn 1.00 2.50
60 Tony Simmons .60 1.50
61 Tiki Barber 1.00 2.50
62 Joe Jurevicius 1.00 2.50
63 Danny Kanell .60 1.50
64 Keyshawn Johnson 1.00 2.50
65 Curtis Martin 1.00 2.50
66 Vinny Testaverde .60 1.50
67 Tim Brown 1.00 2.50
68 Jeff George .60 1.50
69 Napoleon Kaufman 1.00 2.50
70 Jon Ritchie .60 1.50
71 Charles Woodson 4.00 10.00
72 Irving Fryar .60 1.50
73 Duce Staley 1.00 2.50
74 Jerome Bettis 1.00 2.50
75 Chris Fuamatu-Ma'afala .60 1.50
76 Kordell Stewart 1.00 2.50
77 Hines Ward 5.00 12.00
78 Ryan Leaf 1.00 2.50
79 Natrone Means .60 1.50
80 Mikhael Ricks .30 .75
81 Garrison Hearst 1.00 2.50
82 R.W. McQuarters .30 .75
83 Jerry Rice 2.00 5.00
84 J.J. Stokes .60 1.50
85 Steve Young 1.25 3.00
86 Joey Galloway .60 1.50
87 Ahman Green 3.00 8.00
88 Warren Moon 1.00 2.50
89 Ricky Watters .60 1.50
90 Isaac Bruce 1.00 2.50
91 Robert Holcombe .60 1.50
92 Mike Alstott 1.00 2.50
93 Trent Dilfer 1.00 2.50
94 Warrick Dunn 1.00 2.50
95 Jacquez Green .60 1.50
96 Kevin Dyson 1.00 2.50
97 Eddie George 1.00 2.50
98 Steve McNair 1.00 2.50
99 Terry Allen 1.00 2.50
100 Skip Hicks .60 1.50

1998 Playoff Contenders Pennants Gold Foil

*GOLD STARS: 4X TO 10X BASIC PENNANTS
*GOLD ROOKIES: 3X TO 7X BASIC PENNANTS
STATED PRINT RUN 98 SERIAL #'d SETS

1998 Playoff Contenders Pennants Red Foil

COMP.RED SET (100) 200.00 400.00
*RED STARS: 1X TO 2.5X BASIC PENNANT
*RED ROOKIES: .6X TO 1.5X BASIC PENNANT
STATED ODDS 1:9 HOBBY

1998 Playoff Contenders Pennants Registered Exchange

COMPLETE SET (100) 400.00 800.00
*REGISTERED STARS: 2X TO 5X BASIC CARDS
*REGISTERED ROOKIES: 1X TO 2.5X BASIC CARDS
ANNOUNCED PRINT RUN 51 SETS

1998 Playoff Contenders Ticket

This 99-card skip-numbered set features color action player photos printed on conventional card stock with foil stamping in a ticket design. The draft picks subset featured authentic player autographs on the cards. Playoff later anounced the print runs for each of those cards. A red foil parallel version of this set was produced and seeded in packs at 1:9. A gold foil parallel version was issued and sequentially numbered to just 25. Please note the following card numbers were never released: 84, 91, 101, and 102.

COMP.SET w/o SPs (80) 25.00 60.00
1 Rob Moore .50 1.25
2 Jake Plummer .75 2.00
3 Jamal Anderson .75 2.00
4 Terance Mathis .50 1.25
5 Priest Holmes RC 10.00 25.00
6 Michael Jackson .30 .75
7 Eric Zeier .50 1.25
8 Andre Reed .50 1.25
9 Antowain Smith .75 2.00
10 Bruce Smith .50 1.25
11 Thurman Thomas .75 2.00
12 Rocket Ismail .30 .75
13 Wesley Walls .50 1.25
14 Curtis Conway .50 1.25
15 Jeff Blake .50 1.25
16 Corey Dillon .75 2.00
17 Carl Pickens .50 1.25
18 Troy Aikman 1.50 4.00
19 Michael Irvin .75 2.00
20 Ernie Mills .30 .75
21 Deion Sanders .75 2.00
22 Emmitt Smith 2.50 6.00
23 Terrell Davis .75 2.00
24 John Elway 3.00 8.00
25 Neil Smith .50 1.25
26 Rod Smith WR .50 1.25
27 Herman Moore .50 1.25
28 Johnnie Morton .50 1.25
29 Barry Sanders 2.50 6.00
30 Robert Brooks .50 1.25
31 Brett Favre 2.50 6.00
32 Antonio Freeman .75 2.00
33 Dorsey Levens .75 2.00
34 Reggie White .75 2.00
35 Marshall Faulk .75 2.00
36 Mark Brunell .75 2.00
37 Jimmy Smith .50 1.25
38 James Stewart .50 1.25
39 Donnell Bennett .30 .75
40 Andre Rison .50 1.25
41 Derrick Thomas .75 2.00
42 Karim Abdul-Jabbar .75 2.00
43 Dan Marino 3.00 8.00
44 Cris Carter .75 2.00
45 Brad Johnson .75 2.00
46 Robert Smith .75 2.00
47 Drew Bledsoe .75 2.00
48 Terry Glenn .75 2.00
49 Lamar Smith .50 1.25
50 Ike Hilliard .50 1.25
51 Danny Kanell .50 1.25
52 Wayne Chrebet .75 2.00
53 Keyshawn Johnson .75 2.00
54 Curtis Martin .75 2.00
55 Tim Brown .75 2.00
56 Rickey Dudley .30 .75
57 Jeff George .50 1.25
58 Napoleon Kaufman .75 2.00
59 Irving Fryar .50 1.25
60 Jerome Bettis .75 2.00
61 Charles Johnson .30 .75
62 Kordell Stewart .75 2.00
63 Natrone Means .50 1.25
64 Bryan Still .30 .75
65 Garrison Hearst .75 2.00
66 Jerry Rice 1.50 4.00
67 Steve Young 1.00 2.50
68 Joey Galloway .50 1.25
69 Warren Moon .75 2.00
70 Ricky Watters .50 1.25
71 Isaac Bruce .75 2.00
72 Mike Alstott .75 2.00
73 Reidel Anthony .50 1.25
74 Trent Dilfer .75 2.00
75 Warrick Dunn .75 2.00
76 Warren Sapp .50 1.25
77 Eddie George .75 2.00
78 Steve McNair .75 2.00
79 Terry Allen .75 2.00
80 Gus Frerotte .30 .75
81 Andre Wadsworth AU/500* 8.00 20.00
82 Tim Dwight AU/500* 12.00 30.00
83 Curtis Enis AU/400* 15.00 40.00
85 Charlie Batch AU/500* 15.00 40.00
86 Germane Crowell AU/500* 8.00 20.00
87 Peyton Manning AU/200* 2500.00 4000.00
88 Jerome Pathon AU/500* 10.00 25.00
89 Fred Taylor AU/500* 25.00 60.00
90 Tavian Banks AU/500* 10.00 25.00
92 Randy Moss AU/300* 400.00 800.00
93 Robert Edwards AU/500* 10.00 25.00
94 Hines Ward AU/500* 75.00 150.00
95 Ryan Leaf AU/200* 25.00 50.00
96 Mikhael Ricks AU/500* 10.00 25.00
97 Ahman Green AU/500* 15.00 40.00
98 Jacquez Green AU/500* 8.00 20.00
99 Kevin Dyson AU/500* 12.00 30.00
100 Skip Hicks AU/500* 8.00 20.00
103 C.Fuamatu-Ma'afala AU/500* 10.00 25.00

1998 Playoff Contenders Ticket Gold

*VETS: 12X TO 30X BASIC CARDS
5 Priest Holmes 60.00 150.00
81 Andre Wadsworth 12.50 30.00
82 Tim Dwight 25.00 60.00
83 Curtis Enis 15.00 40.00
85 Charlie Batch 25.00 60.00
86 Germane Crowell 10.00 25.00
87 Peyton Manning 500.00 800.00
88 Jerome Pathon 15.00 40.00
89 Fred Taylor 40.00 100.00
90 Tavian Banks 12.50 30.00
92 Randy Moss 200.00 400.00
93 Robert Edwards 15.00 40.00
94 Hines Ward 150.00 250.00
95 Ryan Leaf 25.00 60.00
96 Mikhael Ricks 12.50 30.00
97 Ahman Green 60.00 120.00
98 Jacquez Green 15.00 40.00
99 Kevin Dyson 15.00 40.00
100 Skip Hicks 12.50 30.00
103 Chris Fuamatu-Ma'afala 15.00 40.00

1998 Playoff Contenders Ticket Red

*RED STARS: 1X TO 2.5X HI COL.
RED TICKET STATED ODDS 1:9 HOB
5 Priest Holmes 20.00 50.00
81 Andre Wadsworth 2.50 6.00
82 Tim Dwight 3.00 8.00
83 Curtis Enis 2.00 5.00
85 Charlie Batch 3.00 8.00
86 Germane Crowell 2.50 6.00
87 Peyton Manning 150.00 225.00
88 Jerome Pathon 3.00 8.00
89 Fred Taylor 6.00 15.00
90 Tavian Banks 2.50 6.00
92 Randy Moss 25.00 60.00
93 Robert Edwards 2.50 6.00
94 Hines Ward 20.00 50.00
95 Ryan Leaf 3.00 8.00
96 Mikhael Ricks 2.50 6.00
97 Ahman Green 10.00 25.00
98 Jacquez Green 2.50 6.00
99 Kevin Dyson 3.00 8.00
100 Skip Hicks 2.50 6.00
103 Chris Fuamatu-Ma'afala 2.50 6.00

1998 Playoff Contenders Checklist Jumbos

Inserted one per hobby box, this 30-card set measures approximately 3" by 5" and features color action photos of a top star from each club printed on foil/mirror board stock with a set checklist of each player from that team on the back.

COMPLETE SET (30) 75.00 150.00
ONE PER HOBBY BOX
1 Jake Plummer 2.00 5.00
2 Jamal Anderson 2.00 5.00
3 Jermaine Lewis 1.25 3.00
4 Antowain Smith 2.00 5.00
5 Muhsin Muhammad 1.25 3.00
6 Curtis Enis .75 2.00
7 Corey Dillon 2.00 5.00
8 Deion Sanders 2.00 5.00
9 Terrell Davis 2.00 5.00
10 Barry Sanders 6.00 15.00
11 Brett Favre 8.00 20.00
12 Peyton Manning 10.00 25.00
13 Mark Brunell 2.00 5.00
14 Andre Rison 1.25 3.00
15 Dan Marino 8.00 20.00
16 Randy Moss 6.00 15.00
17 Drew Bledsoe 3.00 8.00
18 Kerry Collins 1.25 3.00
19 Danny Kanell 1.25 3.00
20 Curtis Martin 2.00 5.00
21 Tim Brown 2.00 5.00
22 Irving Fryar 1.25 3.00
23 Kordell Stewart 2.00 5.00
24 Natrone Means 1.25 3.00
25 Steve Young 2.50 6.00
26 Isaac Bruce 2.00 5.00
27 Warren Moon 2.00 5.00
28 Warrick Dunn 2.00 5.00
29 Eddie George 2.00 5.00
30 Terry Allen 2.00 5.00

1998 Playoff Contenders Honors

Randomly inserted in hobby packs at the rate of one in 3,241, this three-card set features color action player images silhouetted over the word "Playoff" and printed on die-cut two foil cards.

COMPLETE SET (3) 50.00 100.00
STATED ODDS 1:3241 HOBBY
19 Dan Marino 30.00 80.00
20 Jerry Rice 15.00 40.00
21 Mark Brunell 10.00 25.00

1998 Playoff Contenders MVP Contenders

Randomly inserted in hobby packs at the rate of one in 19, this 36-card set features color action images of players who are contenters for the MVP honor printed on all holographic card stock with an MVP graphic stamped in gold foil.

COMPLETE SET (36) 75.00 150.00
STATED ODDS 1:19 HOBBY
1 Terrell Davis 2.00 5.00
2 Jerry Rice 4.00 10.00
3 Jerome Bettis 2.00 5.00
4 Brett Favre 8.00 20.00
5 Natrone Means 1.25 3.00
6 Steve Young 2.50 6.00
7 John Elway 8.00 20.00
8 Troy Aikman 4.00 10.00
9 Steve McNair 2.00 5.00
10 Kordell Stewart 2.00 5.00
11 Drew Bledsoe 3.00 8.00
12 Tim Brown 2.00 5.00
13 Dan Marino 8.00 20.00
14 Mark Brunell 2.00 5.00
15 Marshall Faulk 2.50 6.00
16 Jake Plummer 2.00 5.00
17 Corey Dillon 2.00 5.00
18 Carl Pickens 1.25 3.00
19 Keyshawn Johnson 2.00 5.00
20 Barry Sanders 6.00 15.00
21 Deion Sanders 2.00 5.00
22 Emmitt Smith 6.00 15.00
23 Antowain Smith 2.00 5.00
24 Curtis Martin 2.00 5.00
25 Cris Carter 2.00 5.00
26 Napoleon Kaufman 2.00 5.00
27 Eddie George 2.00 5.00
28 Warrick Dunn 2.00 5.00
29 Antonio Freeman 2.00 5.00
30 Joey Galloway 1.25 3.00
31 Herman Moore 1.25 3.00
32 Jamal Anderson 2.00 5.00
33 Terry Glenn 2.00 5.00
34 Garrison Hearst 2.00 5.00
35 Robert Smith 2.00 5.00
36 Mike Alstott 2.00 5.00

1998 Playoff Contenders Rookie of the Year

Randomly inserted in hobby packs at the rate of one in 55, this 12-card set features color action photos of top rookies printed on conventional paper stock with a simulated wood-look finish and two types of foil stamping.

COMPLETE SET (12) 50.00 120.00
STATED ODDS 1:55 HOBBY
1 Tim Dwight 2.50 6.00
2 Curtis Enis 1.50 4.00
3 Charlie Batch 2.50 6.00
4 Peyton Manning 20.00 50.00
5 Fred Taylor 4.00 10.00
6 John Avery 1.50 4.00
7 Randy Moss 12.00 30.00
8 Robert Edwards 1.50 4.00
9 Charles Woodson 5.00 12.00
10 Ryan Leaf 2.50 6.00
11 Jacquez Green 1.50 4.00
12 Kevin Dyson 2.50 6.00

1998 Playoff Contenders Rookie Stallions

Randomly inserted in hobby packs at the rate of one in 19, this 18-card set features color action photos of top NFL draftees printed on all micro-etched foil card stock with silver foil stamping.

COMPLETE SET (18) 40.00 100.00
STATED ODDS 1:19 HOBBY
1 Tim Dwight 1.25 3.00
2 Curtis Enis .75 2.00
3 Brian Griese 2.50 6.00
4 Charlie Batch 1.25 3.00
5 Germane Crowell .75 2.00
6 Peyton Manning 12.00 30.00
7 Tavian Banks .75 2.00
8 Fred Taylor 2.00 5.00
9 Rashaan Shehee .75 2.00
10 John Avery .75 2.00
11 Randy Moss 8.00 20.00
12 Robert Edwards .75 2.00
13 Charles Woodson 3.00 8.00
14 Ryan Leaf 1.25 3.00
15 Ahman Green 3.00 8.00
16 Jacquez Green .75 2.00
17 Kevin Dyson 1.25 3.00
18 Skip Hicks .75 2.00

1998 Playoff Contenders Super Bowl Leather

Randomly inserted in hobby packs at the rate of one in 2,401, this six-card set features color action player photos printed on conventional card stock with foil stamping and an actual game-used football piece from Super Bowl XXXII embedded in the card. The unnumbered card backs carry a replica of the letter from the NFL verifying the authenticity of the ball.

STATED ODDS 1:2401 HOBBY
1 Robert Brooks 12.50 30.00
2 Terrell Davis 25.00 60.00
3 John Elway 75.00 200.00
4 Brett Favre 60.00 150.00
5 Antonio Freeman 25.00 60.00
6 Rod Smith 20.00 50.00

1998 Playoff Contenders Touchdown Tandems

Randomly inserted in hobby packs at the rate of one in 19, this 24-card set features color action photos of two teammates who consistently score paired together on holographic foil card stock with foil stamping.

COMPLETE SET (24) 75.00 150.00
STATED ODDS 1:19 HOBBY
1 B.Favre 7.50 20.00
A.Freeman
2 D.Marino 7.50 20.00
K.Abdul-Jabbar
3 E.Smith 6.00 15.00
T.Aikman
4 B.Sanders 6.00 15.00
H.Moore
5 E.George 3.00 8.00
S.McNair
6 R.Edwards 3.00 8.00
D.Bledsoe
7 T.Davis 3.00 8.00
R.Smith
8 M.Brunell 3.00 8.00
F.Taylor
9 J.Rice 4.00 10.00
S.Young
10 J.Bettis 3.00 8.00
K.Stewart
11 C.Martin 3.00 8.00
K.Johnson
12 M.Alstott 3.00 8.00
W.Dunn
13 I.Bruce 3.00 8.00
T.Banks
14 A.Murrell 3.00 8.00
J.Plummer
15 T.Brown 3.00 8.00
N.Kaufman
16 C.Carter 6.00 15.00
R.Moss
17 J.Galloway 2.00 5.00
R.Watters
18 P.Manning 8.00 20.00
M.Faulk
19 R.Leaf 3.00 8.00
N.Means
20 C.Pickens 3.00 8.00
C.Dillon
21 D.Flutie 3.00 8.00
A.Smith
22 R.Cunningham 2.00 5.00
R.Smith
23 C.Chandler 3.00 8.00
J.Anderson
24 J.Elway 7.50 20.00
E.McCaffrey

1999 Playoff Contenders SSD

Released as a 200-card base set, the 1999 Playoff Contenders SSD contains 145 veteran cards, 44 rookie tickets featuring authentic player autographs, and 15 Quarterback Club Playoff tickets seeded at one in seven packs. The cards were printed on thick 30-point card stock with a rainbow holofoil effect. Many of the autographed rookies were issued via mail redemption cards that carried an expiration date of 12/31/2000. While most of those were issued as planned, 3-players did not sign any cards for the set -- Chris McAlister, Shaun King, and James Johnson. Playoff issued these three cards with "No Autograph" printed on the fronts along with another card of the same number signed by a replacement player.

COMPLETE SET (205) 750.00 1500.00
COMP.SET w/o SP's (141) 25.00 60.00
1 Randy Moss .50 1.25
2 Randall Cunningham .50 1.25
3 Cris Carter .60 1.50
4 Robert Smith .40 1.00
5 Jake Reed .50 1.25
6 Albert Connell .40 1.00
7 Jeff George .40 1.00
8 Brett Favre 1.25 3.00
9 Antonio Freeman .50 1.25
10 Dorsey Levens .50 1.25
11 Mark Chmura .40 1.00
12 Mike Alstott .40 1.00
13 Warrick Dunn .40 1.00
14 Trent Dilfer .40 1.00
15 Jacquez Green .40 1.00
16 Reidel Anthony .40 1.00
17 Warren Sapp .50 1.25
18 Amani Toomer .40 1.00
19 Curtis Enis .40 1.00
20 Curtis Conway .50 1.25
21 Bobby Engram .40 1.00
22 Barry Sanders 1.00 2.50
23 Charlie Batch .40 1.00
24 Herman Moore .50 1.25
25 Johnnie Morton .50 1.25
26 Greg Hill .40 1.00
27 Germane Crowell .40 1.00
28 Kerry Collins .40 1.00
29 Ike Hilliard .40 1.00
30 Joe Jurevicius .40 1.00
31 Stephen Davis .40 1.00
32 Brad Johnson .50 1.25
33 Skip Hicks .40 1.00
34 Michael Westbrook .40 1.00
35 Jake Plummer .40 1.00
36 Adrian Murrell .40 1.00
37 Frank Sanders .40 1.00
38 Rob Moore .40 1.00
39 Gary Brown .40 1.00
40 Duce Staley .40 1.00
41 Charles Johnson .40 1.00
42 Emmitt Smith 1.00 2.50
43 Troy Aikman .75 2.00
44 Michael Irvin .60 1.50
45 Deion Sanders .50 1.25
46 Rocket Ismail .50 1.25
47 Jerry Rice 1.50 4.00
48 Terrell Owens .50 1.25
49 Steve Young .75 2.00
50 Garrison Hearst .40 1.00
51 J.J. Stokes .40 1.00
52 Lawrence Phillips .50 1.25
53 Jamal Anderson .50 1.25
54 Chris Chandler .50 1.25
55 Terance Mathis .40 1.00
56 Tim Dwight .50 1.25
57 Charlie Garner .50 1.25
58 Chris Calloway .40 1.00
59 Eddie Kennison .50 1.25
60 Billy Joe Hobert .40 1.00
61 Tim Biakabutuka .50 1.25
62 Muhsin Muhammad .40 1.00
63 Olandis Gary AU/1825* RC 5.00 12.00
64 Wesley Walls .50 1.25
65 Isaac Bruce .60 1.50
66 Marshall Faulk .50 1.25
67 Kordell Stewart .40 1.00
68 Jerome Bettis .60 1.50
69 Hines Ward .50 1.25
70 Corey Dillon .40 1.00
71 Carl Pickens .50 1.25
72 Darnay Scott .40 1.00
73 Steve McNair .50 1.25
74 Eddie George .50 1.25
75 Yancey Thigpen .40 1.00
76 Kevin Dyson .40 1.00
77 Fred Taylor .40 1.00
78 Mark Brunell .50 1.25
79 Jimmy Smith .50 1.25
80 Keenan McCardell .50 1.25
81 James Stewart .40 1.00
82 Jermaine Lewis .40 1.00
83 Priest Holmes .40 1.00
84 Stoney Case .40 1.00
85 Errict Rhett .40 1.00
86 Bill Schroeder .50 1.25
87 Terry Kirby .40 1.00
88 Leslie Shepherd .40 1.00
89 Terrence Wilkins AU/825* RC 4.00 10.00
90 Dan Marino 1.25 3.00
91 O.J. McDuffie .50 1.25
92 Karim Abdul-Jabbar .40 1.00
93 Zach Thomas .50 1.25
94 Terry Allen .50 1.25
95 Tony Martin .50 1.25
96 Drew Bledsoe .50 1.25
97 Terry Glenn .50 1.25
98 Ben Coates .50 1.25
99 Tony Simmons .40 1.00
100 Curtis Martin .50 1.25
101 Keyshawn Johnson .50 1.25
102 Vinny Testaverde .40 1.00
103 Wayne Chrebet .40 1.00
104 Peyton Manning 2.00 5.00
105 Marvin Harrison .50 1.25
106 E.G. Green .40 1.00
107 Doug Flutie .60 1.50
108 Thurman Thomas .50 1.25
109 Andre Reed .60 1.50
110 Eric Moulds .40 1.00
111 Antowain Smith .40 1.00
112 Bruce Smith .50 1.25
113 Terrell Davis .50 1.25
114 John Elway 1.00 2.50
115 Ed McCaffrey .50 1.25
116 Rod Smith .50 1.25
117 Shannon Sharpe .50 1.25
118 Jeff Garcia AU/325* RC 25.00 50.00
119 Brian Griese .40 1.00
120 Justin Watson AU/325* RC 6.00 15.00
121 Bubby Brister .40 1.00
122 Ryan Leaf .50 1.25
123 Natrone Means .50 1.25
124 Mikhael Ricks .40 1.00
125 Junior Seau .50 1.25
126 Jim Harbaugh .50 1.25
127 Andre Rison .50 1.25
128 Elvis Grbac .40 1.00
129 Bam Morris .40 1.00
130 Rashaan Shehee .40 1.00
131 Warren Moon .60 1.50
132 Tony Gonzalez .50 1.25
133 Derrick Alexander .40 1.00
134 Jon Kitna .40 1.00
135 Ricky Watters .50 1.25
136 Joey Galloway .50 1.25
137 Ahman Green .50 1.25
138 Derrick Mayes .40 1.00
139 Tyrone Wheatley .50 1.25
140 Napoleon Kaufman .40 1.00
141 Tim Brown .60 1.50
142 Charles Woodson .60 1.50
143 Rich Gannon .50 1.25
144 Rickey Dudley .40 1.00
145 Az-Zahir Hakim .40 1.00
146 Kurt Warner AU/1825* RC 100.00 200.00
147 Sean Bennett AU/1325* RC 3.00 8.00
148 B.Stokley AU/1325* RC 6.00 15.00
149 Amos Zereoue AU/1325* RC 3.00 8.00
150 Brock Huard AU/1325* RC 3.00 8.00
151 Tim Couch AU/1025* RC 4.00 10.00
152 Ricky Williams AU/725* RC 15.00 30.00
153 D.McNabb AU/525* RC 10.00 25.00
154 Edgerrin James AU/525* RC 15.00 30.00
155 Torry Holt AU/1025* RC 12.00 30.00
156 D.Culpepper AU/1025* RC 12.00 30.00
157 Akili Smith AU/1025* RC 3.00 8.00
158 Champ Bailey AU/1725* RC 15.00 40.00
159 C.Claiborne AU/1825* RC 3.00 8.00
160A C McAlister No AU/1825* RC 3.00 8.00
160B Jason Tucker AU/1825* 4.00 10.00
161 Troy Edwards AU/1225* RC 3.00 8.00
162 Jevon Kearse AU/325* RC 15.00 40.00
163 D.McDonald AU/1825* RC 3.00 8.00
164 David Boston AU/1025* RC 3.00 8.00
165 Peerless Price AU/1325* RC 3.00 8.00
166 Cecil Collins AU/1025* RC 3.00 8.00
167 Rob Konrad AU/1325* RC 3.00 8.00
168 Cade McNown AU/1025* RC 3.00 8.00
169 Shawn Bryson AU/1825* RC 3.00 8.00
170 Kevin Faulk AU/1325* RC 6.00 15.00
171 Corby Jones AU/1825* RC 3.00 8.00
172A J.Johnson No AU/1325* RC 3.00 8.00
172B Patrick Jeffers AU/1325* 5.00 12.00
173 Autry Denson AU/1825* RC 3.00 8.00
174 Sedrick Irvin AU/1825* RC 3.00 8.00
175 M.Bishop AU/1825* RC 4.00 10.00
176 Joe Germaine AU/825* RC 4.00 10.00
177 D.Parker AU/1325* RC 3.00 8.00
178A Shaun King No AU/1825* RC 3.00 8.00
178B Ray Lucas AU/1825* 4.00 10.00
179 D'Wayne Bates AU/1825* RC 3.00 8.00
180 Tal Streets AU/1825* RC 4.00 10.00
181 Na Brown AU/1825* RC 3.00 8.00
182 Desmond Clark AU/1825* RC 4.00 10.00
183 Jim Kleinsasser AU/1825* RC 5.00 12.00
184 Kevin Johnson AU/1325* RC 4.00 10.00
185 Joe Montgomery AU/1325* RC 3.00 8.00
186 John Elway PT 1.50 4.00
187 Dan Marino PT 2.00 5.00
188 Jerry Rice PT 2.50 6.00
189 Barry Sanders PT 1.50 4.00
190 Steve Young PT 1.25 3.00
191 Doug Flutie PT 1.00 2.50
192 Troy Aikman PT 1.25 3.00
193 Drew Bledsoe PT .75 2.00
194 Brett Favre PT 2.00 5.00
195 Randall Cunningham PT .75 2.00
196 Terrell Davis PT .75 2.00
197 Kordell Stewart PT .60 1.50
198 Keyshawn Johnson PT .75 2.00
199 Jake Plummer PT .60 1.50
200 Peyton Manning PT 3.00 8.00
201 Jay Fiedler AU/1825* 5.00 12.00
202 Kevin Daft AU/325* 6.00 15.00

1999 Playoff Contenders SSD Finesse Gold

*VETS/25: 10X TO 25X BASIC CARDS
*ROOK.AU/25: 1.2X TO 3X AU RC/725-1875
*ROOK.AU/25: 1X TO 2.5X AU RC/325-525
*PT VETS/25: 6X TO 15X BASIC CARDS
STATED PRINT RUN 25 SER.#'d SETS
146 Kurt Warner 150.00 300.00

1999 Playoff Contenders SSD Power Blue

*VETS/50: 5X TO 12X BASIC CARDS
*ROOK.AU/50: .6X TO 1.5X AU RC/725-1875
*ROOK.AU/50: .5X TO 1.2X AU RC/325-525
*PT VETS/50: 3X TO 8X BASIC CARDS
STATED PRINT RUN 50 SER.#'d SETS
146 Kurt Warner 125.00 200.00

1999 Playoff Contenders SSD Speed Red

*VETS/100: 4X TO 10X BASIC CARDS
*ROOK.AU/100: .5X TO 1.2X AU RC/725-1875
*ROOK.AU/100: .4X TO 1X AU RC/325-525
*PT VETS/100: 2.5X TO 6X BASIC CARDS
STATED PRINT RUN 100 SER.#'d SETS
146 Kurt Warner 100.00 175.00

1999 Playoff Contenders SSD Game Day Souvenirs

Randomly inserted in packs at the rate of one in 308, this 15-card set features swatches of 1998-99 game-dated game-used footballs on the card fronts. Card backs carry a "GS" prefix.

STATED ODDS 1:308
GS1 Terrell Owens 15.00 40.00
GS2 Jerry Rice 25.00 60.00
GS3 Steve Young 20.00 50.00
GS4 Akili Smith 10.00 25.00
GS5 Tim Couch 12.00 30.00
GS6 Mark Brunell 12.00 30.00
GS7 Eddie George 12.00 30.00
GS8 Dorsey Levens 12.00 30.00
GS9 Brett Favre 25.00 60.00
GS10 Antonio Freeman 12.00 30.00
GS11 Ricky Williams 15.00 40.00
GS12 Steve McNair 15.00 40.00
GS13 Kurt Warner 25.00 60.00
GS14 John Elway 40.00 100.00
GS15 Terrell Davis 15.00 40.00

1999 Playoff Contenders SSD MVP Contenders

Randomly seeded in packs at the rate of one in 43, this 20-card set features the most likely candidates for the 1999 NFL MVP award on a die-cut card stock placing foreground action shots against a football background. Card backs carry an "MC" prefix.

COMPLETE SET (20) 75.00 150.00
STATED ODDS 1:43
MC1 Jamal Anderson 3.00 8.00
MC2 Eddie George 3.00 8.00
MC3 Emmitt Smith 6.00 15.00
MC4 Jerry Rice 6.00 15.00
MC5 Barry Sanders 10.00 25.00
MC6 Keyshawn Johnson 3.00 8.00
MC7 Brett Favre 10.00 25.00
MC8 Randy Moss 8.00 20.00
MC9 Mark Brunell 3.00 8.00
MC10 Fred Taylor 3.00 8.00
MC11 Dan Marino 10.00 25.00
MC12 Peyton Manning 10.00 25.00
MC13 Drew Bledsoe 4.00 10.00
MC14 Antonio Freeman 3.00 8.00
MC15 Steve Young 4.00 10.00
MC16 Terrell Davis 3.00 8.00
MC17 Terrell Owens 3.00 8.00
MC18 Troy Aikman 6.00 15.00
MC19 Steve McNair 3.00 8.00
MC20 Jake Plummer 2.00 5.00

1999 Playoff Contenders SSD Quads

Randomly inserted in packs at the rate of one in 57, this 12-card set features two potential playoff opponents on each side of the card in this dual sided holographic micro-etched insert set. Card backs carry a "CQ" prefix.

COMPLETE SET (12) 100.00 200.00
STATED ODDS 1:57
CQ1 Plmmr/Boston/ESmith/Aik. 5.00 12.00
CQ2 Rice/Yng/And/Chand 7.50 20.00
CQ3 Moss/Cart/Favre/Freeman 12.50 30.00
CQ4 Dunn/Alst/Davis/Johnson 5.00 12.00
CQ5 McNown/Enis/Sanders/Batch 12.50 30.00
CQ6 Williams/Kenn/Faulk/Holt 7.50 20.00
CQ7 Stewart/Bett/George/McNair 5.00 12.00
CQ8 Flutie/Mlds/Bledsoe/Glenn 5.00 12.00
CQ9 Marino/Collins/Keysh/Martin 12.50 30.00
CQ10 Davis/Griese/Brun/Taylor 5.00 12.00
CQ11 Kitna/Gall/Kauf/Brown 5.00 12.00
CQ12 Manning/James/Couch/Jhnsn 25.00 50.00

1999 Playoff Contenders SSD Round Numbers Autographs

Randomly inserted in packs at the rate of one in 109, this 10-card set features autographs from one of ten pairs of rookies drafted from the same round. Card backs carry an "RN" prefix.

STATED ODDS 1:109
RN1 K.Johnson/P.Price 10.00 25.00
RN2 R.Williams/E.James 25.00 60.00
RN3 D.McNabb/A.Smith 30.00 80.00
RN4 S.Bennett/B.Stokley 10.00 25.00
RN5 T.Couch/C.McNown 12.00 30.00
RN6 D.Boston/T.Edwards 10.00 25.00
RN7 D.Culpepper/T.Holt 12.00 30.00
RN8 K.Faulk/J.Fazande 10.00 25.00
RN9 J.Montgomery/R.Konrad 8.00 20.00
RN10 C.Collins/D.Parker 8.00 20.00

1999 Playoff Contenders SSD ROY Contenders

Randomly inserted in packs at the rate of one in 29, this 12-card set features the most likely candidates for the 1999 Rookie of the Year. Card backs carry an "ROYC" prefix.

COMPLETE SET (12) 50.00 100.00
STATED ODDS 1:29
1 Tim Couch 2.00 5.00
2 Donovan McNabb 6.00 15.00
3 Akili Smith 2.00 5.00
4 Daunte Culpepper 5.00 12.00
5 Cade McNown 2.00 5.00
6 Edgerrin James 5.00 12.00
7 Ricky Williams 2.50 6.00
8 Cecil Collins 2.00 5.00
9 Torry Holt 3.00 8.00
10 David Boston 2.00 5.00
11 Troy Edwards 2.00 5.00
12 Champ Bailey 2.50 6.00

1999 Playoff Contenders SSD ROY Contenders Autographs

Randomly inserted in packs, this 12-card set parallels the base Rookie of the Year Contenders insert set but contains authentic autographs. Each card is sequentially numbered to 100, and card backs carry an "ROCY" prefix.

STATED PRINT RUN 100 SER.#'d SETS
1 Tim Couch 8.00 20.00
2 Donovan McNabb 40.00 80.00
3 Akili Smith 6.00 15.00
4 Daunte Culpepper 10.00 25.00
5 Cade McNown 6.00 15.00
6 Edgerrin James 10.00 25.00
7 Ricky Williams 10.00 25.00
8 Cecil Collins 6.00 15.00
9 Torry Holt 12.00 30.00
10 David Boston 6.00 15.00
11 Troy Edwards 6.00 15.00
12 Champ Bailey 12.00 30.00

1999 Playoff Contenders SSD Touchdown Tandems

Randomly inserted in packs at the rate of one in 15, this 24-card set features two touchdown scoring teammates on this dual-sided holographic foil card. A parallel version of this set was released also.

COMPLETE SET (24) 50.00 100.00
STATED ODDS 1:15
T1 K.Johnson 1.25 3.00
C.Martin
T2 D.Marino 5.00 12.00
T.Martin
T3 D.Bledsoe 2.00 5.00
T.Glenn
T4 P.Manning 4.00 10.00
M.Harrison
T5 D.Flutie 1.50 4.00
T.Thomas
T6 S.McNair 1.50 4.00
E.George
T7 K.Stewart 1.25 3.00
J.Bettis
T8 A.Smith 1.25 3.00
C.Pickens
T9 M.Brunell 1.50 4.00
J.Smith
T10 J.Kitna 1.25 3.00
J.Galloway
T11 J.Elway 4.00 10.00
T.Davis
T12 N.Kaufman 1.25 3.00
T.Brown
T13 T.Aikman 3.00 8.00
E.Smith
T14 J.Plummer 1.25 3.00
R.Moore
T15 D.McNabb 3.00 8.00
C.Johnson
T16 B.Johnson 1.25 3.00
M.Westbrook
T17 B.Favre 4.00 10.00
A.Freeman
T18 R.Cunningham 3.00 8.00
R.Moss
T19 M.Alstott 1.25 3.00
W.Dunn
T20 C.McNown 1.25 3.00
C.Enis
T21 B.Sanders 4.00 10.00
H.Moore
T22 S.Young 3.00 8.00
J.Rice
T23 C.Chandler 1.25 3.00
J.Anderson
T24 M.Faulk 2.50 6.00
I.Bruce

1999 Playoff Contenders SSD Touchdown Tandems Die Cuts

T1 K.Johnson 20.00 40.00
C.Martin/20

T2 D.Marino 50.00 100.00
T.Martin/29
T3 D.Bledsoe 25.00 50.00
T.Glenn/23
T4 P.Manning 40.00 100.00
M.Harrison/33
T5 D.Flutie 20.00 40.00
T.Thomas/24
T6 S.McNair 20.00 40.00
E.George/25
T7 K.Stewart 20.00 50.00
J.Bettis/16
T8 A.Smith 6.00 15.00
C.Pickens/41
T9 M.Brunell 25.00 50.00
J.Smith/28
T10 J.Kitna 15.00 40.00
J.Galloway/18
T11 J.Elway 20.00 50.00
T.Davis/46
T12 N.Kaufman 30.00 60.00
T.Brown/11
T13 T.Aikman 40.00 80.00
E.Smith/29
T14 J.Plummer 12.50 30.00
R.Moore/26
T15 D.McNabb 12.50 30.00
C.Johnson/37
T16 B.Johnson 20.00 50.00
M.Westbrook/13
T17 B.Favre 20.00 50.00
A.Freeman/46
T18 R.Cunningham 15.00 40.00
R.Moss/52
T19 M.Alstott 30.00 60.00
W.Dunn/11
T20 C.McNown 10.00 25.00
C.Enis/28
T21 B.Sanders 150.00 250.00
H.Moore/9
T22 S.Young 12.50 30.00
J.Rice/51
T23 C.Chandler 6.00 15.00
J.Anderson/43
T24 M.Faulk 50.00 100.00
I.Bruce/11

1999 Playoff Contenders SSD Triple Threat

Randomly seeded in packs at the rate of one in 15, this 20-card set showcases teammate trios on a silver mirror-board card.

COMPLETE SET (20) 30.00 60.00
STATED ODDS 1:15
TT1 Plummer/Boston/Sanders 1.00 2.50
TT2 Deion/Aikman/E.Smith 2.50 6.00
TT3 Owens/J.Rice/S.Young 2.00 5.00
TT4 Marino/McDuffie/C.Collins 3.00 8.00
TT5 Keyshawn/Chrebet/C.Martin 1.00 2.50
TT6 Anderson/Chandler/Mathis 1.00 2.50
TT7 Griese/T.Davis/S.Sharpe 1.00 2.50
TT8 Taylor/Brunell/McCardell 1.00 2.50
TT9 Moss/C.Carter/Cunningham 3.00 8.00
TT10 Freeman/Favre/Levens 3.00 8.00
TT11 B.Johnson/Hicks/Bailey 1.25 3.00
TT12 B.Sanders/H.Moore/Batch 3.00 8.00
TT13 E.George/McNair/Thigpen 1.00 2.50
TT14 K.Stewart/Bettis/Edwards 1.00 2.50
TT15 Ant.Smith/Moulds/Flutie 1.00 2.50
TT16 Glenn/K.Faulk/Bledsoe 1.50 4.00
TT17 M.Alstott/W.Dunn/S.King 1.00 2.50
TT18 Manning/Harrison/E.James 6.00 15.00
TT19 Dillon/Ak.Smith/Pickens 1.00 2.50
TT20 Bruce/Holt/M.Faulk 3.00 8.00

1999 Playoff Contenders SSD Triple Threat Red

TT4 Dan Marino/23 75.00 200.00
TT7 Brian Griese/33 25.00 60.00
TT11 Brad Johnson/48 7.50 20.00
TT12 Barry Sanders/73 25.00 60.00
TT13 Eddie George/37 12.50 30.00
TT16 Terry Glenn/86 5.00 12.00
TT18 Peyton Manning/26 75.00 200.00
TT19 Corey Dillon/66 6.00 15.00
TT20 Isaac Bruce/80 5.00 12.00
TT23 Jerry Rice/75 15.00 40.00
TT24 O.J. McDuffie/90 2.50 6.00
TT25 Wayne Chrebet/63 6.00 15.00
TT26 Chris Chandler/25 15.00 40.00
TT27 Terrell Davis/21 30.00 60.00
TT28 Mark Brunell/20 35.00 80.00
TT30 Brett Favre/31 60.00 150.00
TT32 Herman Moore/82 5.00 12.00
TT35 Eric Moulds/84 5.00 12.00
TT37 Warrick Dunn/50 7.50 20.00
TT38 Marvin Harrison/61 6.00 15.00
TT39 Akili Smith/32 15.00 40.00
TT41 Frank Sanders/89 2.50 6.00
TT43 Steve Young/36 35.00 80.00
TT44 Cecil Collins/28 15.00 40.00
TT45 Curtis Martin/60 6.00 15.00
TT48 Keenan McCardell/67 3.00 8.00
TT49 Randall Cunningham/34 12.50 30.00
TT50 Dorsey Levens/50 7.50 20.00
TT51 Champ Bailey/22 20.00 50.00
TT52 Charlie Batch/98 3.00 8.00
TT54 Troy Edwards/27 15.00 40.00
TT55 Doug Flutie/20 35.00 80.00
TT56 Drew Bledsoe/20 35.00 80.00
TT57 Shaun King/36 15.00 40.00
TT59 Carl Pickens/67 3.00 8.00
TT60 Marshall Faulk/78 7.50 20.00

2000 Playoff Contenders

Released in mid January 2001, The 200-card contenders set is divided into 100-base cards, 50-autographed Rookie Tickets, 40-autographed NFL Europe prospect cards and 10-autographed Playoff Tickets. Base cards feature player action photography set against a colored background designed to match team colors. A silver foil enhanced "ticket" on the right side containing the player's name. All autographed cards feature an embossed Playoff Authentic Signature stamp on the card front and a color shift to gold on the ticket part of the card. Some RCs were issued in packs as redemption cards which carried an expiration date of 12/31/2002. Four of those players, Thomas Jones, Derrick Ham, Ronnie Powell, and Fred Taylor PT, never signed for the set but unsigned Thomas Jones cards were released at a later date. The NFL Europe cards have player photos on the right and tickets on the left. Contenders was packaged in 12-pack boxes with each pack containing five cards and carried a suggested retail price of $9.99.

COMP.SET w/o SP's (100) 7.50 20.00
1 David Boston .20 .50
2 Jake Plummer .20 .50
3 Chris Chandler .25 .60
4 Jamal Anderson .25 .60
5 Tim Dwight .25 .60
6 Qadry Ismail .20 .50
7 Tony Banks .20 .50
8 Lamar Smith .20 .50
9 Doug Flutie .25 .60
10 Eric Moulds .20 .50
11 Peerless Price .25 .60
12 Rob Johnson .25 .60
13 Muhsin Muhammad .20 .50
14 Reggie White .30 .75
15 Steve Beuerlein .25 .60
16 Cade McNown .20 .50
17 Derrick Alexander .20 .50
18 Marcus Robinson .25 .60
19 Akili Smith .20 .50
20 Corey Dillon .20 .50
21 Kevin Johnson .20 .50
22 Tim Couch .25 .60
23 Emmitt Smith .50 1.25
24 Joey Galloway .25 .60
25 Rocket Ismail .25 .60
26 Troy Aikman .40 1.00
27 Brian Griese .20 .50
28 Ed McCaffrey .25 .60
29 John Elway .50 1.25
30 Olandis Gary .25 .60
31 Rod Smith .25 .60
32 Terrell Davis .25 .60
33 Charlie Batch .20 .50
34 Germane Crowell .20 .50
35 James Stewart .20 .50
36 Barry Sanders .50 1.25
37 Antonio Freeman .25 .60
38 Brett Favre .60 1.50
39 Dorsey Levens .25 .60
40 Edgerrin James .25 .60
41 Marvin Harrison .25 .60
42 Peyton Manning .75 2.00
43 Fred Taylor .20 .50
44 Jimmy Smith .25 .60
45 Mark Brunell .25 .60
46 Elvis Grbac .20 .50
47 Tony Gonzalez .25 .60
48 Dan Marino .60 1.50
49 Joe Horn .25 .60
50 Jay Fiedler .25 .60
51 Thurman Thomas .25 .60
52 Cris Carter .30 .75
53 Daunte Culpepper .25 .60
54 Randy Moss .25 .60
55 Robert Smith .20 .50
56 Drew Bledsoe .25 .60
57 Terry Glenn .25 .60
58 Ricky Williams .25 .60
59 Amani Toomer .20 .50
60 Kerry Collins .20 .50
61 Curtis Martin .25 .60
62 Vinny Testaverde .20 .50
63 Wayne Chrebet .20 .50
64 Rich Gannon .25 .60
65 Tim Brown .30 .75
66 Tyrone Wheatley .20 .50
67 Donovan McNabb .25 .60
68 Duce Staley .20 .50
69 Jerome Bettis .30 .75
70 Jermaine Fazande .20 .50
71 Junior Seau .25 .60
72 Donald Hayes .20 .50
73 Charlie Garner .25 .60
74 Jeff Garcia .20 .50
75 Jerry Rice .75 2.00
76 Steve Young .40 1.00
77 Terrell Owens .25 .60
78 Tiki Barber .25 .60
79 Tim Biakabutuka .25 .60
80 Ricky Watters .25 .60
81 Isaac Bruce .30 .75
82 Kurt Warner .50 1.25
83 Marshall Faulk .25 .60
84 Torry Holt .25 .60
85 Keyshawn Johnson .25 .60
86 Mike Alstott .20 .50
87 Shaun King .20 .50
88 Warren Sapp .25 .60
89 Warrick Dunn .20 .50
90 Eddie George .25 .60
91 Jevon Kearse .20 .50
92 Steve McNair .25 .60
93 Carl Pickens .25 .60
94 Albert Connell .20 .50
95 Brad Johnson .25 .60
96 Bruce Smith .25 .60
97 Deion Sanders .25 .60
98 Jeff George .25 .60
99 Michael Westbrook UER .20 .50
100 Stephen Davis UER .20 .50
101 Courtney Brown AU RC 3.00 8.00
102 Corey Simon AU RC 3.00 8.00
103 Brian Urlacher AU RC 30.00 80.00
104 Deon Grant AU RC 2.50 6.00
105 Peter Warrick AU RC 2.50 6.00
106 Jamal Lewis AU RC 4.00 10.00
107 Thomas Jones No AU RC 4.00 10.00
108 Plaxico Burress AU RC 3.00 8.00
109 Travis Taylor AU RC 2.50 6.00
110 Ron Dayne AU RC 4.00 10.00
111 Bubba Franks AU RC 2.50 6.00
112 Chad Pennington AU RC 4.00 10.00
113 Shaun Alexander AU RC 10.00 25.00
114 Sylvester Morris AU RC 2.50 6.00
115 Mike Anderson AU RC 2.50 6.00
116 R.Jay Soward AU RC 2.50 6.00
117 Trung Canidate AU RC 2.50 6.00
118 Dennis Northcutt AU RC 2.50 6.00
119 Todd Pinkston AU RC 2.50 6.00
120 Jerry Porter AU RC 4.00 10.00
121 Travis Prentice AU RC 2.50 6.00
122 Giovanni Carmazzi AU RC 2.50 6.00
123 Ron Dugans AU RC 2.50 6.00
124 Dez White AU RC 2.50 6.00
125 Chris Cole AU RC 3.00 8.00
126 Ron Dixon AU RC 2.50 6.00
127 Chris Redman AU RC 2.50 6.00
128 J.R. Redmond AU RC 2.50 6.00
129 Laveranues Coles AU RC 3.00 8.00
130 JaJuan Dawson AU RC 2.50 6.00
131 Darrell Jackson AU RC 2.50 6.00
132 Reuben Droughns AU RC 2.50 6.00
133 Doug Chapman AU RC 2.50 6.00
134 Curtis Keaton AU RC 2.50 6.00
135 Gari Scott AU RC 2.50 6.00
136 Danny Farmer AU RC 2.50 6.00
137 Trevor Gaylor AU RC 2.50 6.00
138 Avion Black AU RC 2.50 6.00
139 Michael Wiley AU RC 2.50 6.00
140 Sammy Morris AU RC 2.50 6.00
141 Tee Martin AU RC 2.50 6.00
142 Troy Walters AU RC 2.50 6.00
143 Marc Bulger AU RC 4.00 10.00
144 Tom Brady AU RC 5000.00 8000.00
145 Todd Husak AU RC 2.50 6.00
146 Tim Rattay AU RC 3.00 8.00
147 Jarious Jackson AU RC 3.00 8.00
148 Joe Hamilton AU RC 2.50 6.00
149 Shyrone Stith AU RC 2.50 6.00
150 Kwame Cavil AU RC 2.50 6.00
151 Antonio Banks ET AU RC 2.00 5.00
152 Jonathan Brown ET AU RC 2.00 5.00
153 Ontiwaun Carter ET AU RC 2.00 5.00
154 Jeremaine Copeland ET 2.00 5.00
155 Ralph Dawkins ET AU RC 2.00 5.00
156 Marques Douglas ET AU RC 2.00 5.00
157 Kevin Drake ET AU RC 2.00 5.00
158 Damon Dunn ET AU RC 2.00 5.00
159 Todd Floyd ET AU RC 2.00 5.00
160 Tony Graziani ET AU 2.50 6.00
162 Duane Hawthorne ET AU RC 2.00 5.00
163 Alonzo Johnson ET AU RC 2.00 5.00
164 Mark Kacmarynski ET AU RC 2.00 5.00
165 Eric Kresser ET AU 2.00 5.00
166 Jim Kubiak ET AU RC 2.00 5.00
167 Blaine McElmurry ET AU RC 2.00 5.00
168 Scott Milanovich ET AU 2.00 5.00
169 Norman Miller ET AU RC 2.00 5.00
170 Sean Morey ET AU RC 2.00 5.00
171 Jeff Ogden ET AU 2.00 5.00
172 Pepe Pearson ET AU RC 2.00 5.00
173 Ron Powlus ET AU RC 3.00 8.00
174 Jason Shelley ET AU RC 2.00 5.00
175 Ben Snell ET AU RC 2.00 5.00
176 Aaron Stecker ET AU RC 2.00 5.00
177 L.C. Stevens ET AU 2.00 5.00
178 Mike Sutton ET AU RC 2.00 5.00
179 Damian Vaughn ET AU RC 2.00 5.00
180 Ted White ET AU 2.00 5.00
181 Marcus Crandell ET AU RC 2.00 5.00
182 Darryl Daniel ET AU RC 2.00 5.00
183 Jesse Haynes ET AU 2.00 5.00
184 Matt Lytle ET AU RC 2.00 5.00
185 Deon Mitchell ET AU RC 2.00 5.00
186 Kendrick Nord ET AU RC 2.00 5.00
188 Selucio Sanford ET AU RC 2.00 5.00
189 Corey Thomas ET AU 2.00 5.00
190 Vershan Jackson ET AU RC 2.00 5.00
191 Jake Plummer PT AU 6.00 15.00
192 Jim Kelly PT AU 20.00 40.00
193 Bernie Kosar PT AU 10.00 25.00
194 Marvin Harrison PT AU 15.00 40.00
196 Kerry Collins PT AU 6.00 15.00
197 Kurt Warner PT AU 30.00 60.00
198 Jevon Kearse PT AU 6.00 15.00
199 Brad Johnson PT AU 8.00 20.00
200 Jeff George PT AU 8.00 20.00

2000 Playoff Contenders Championship Ticket

*VETS 1-100: 4X TO 10X BASIC CARDS
*ROOKIE AU 101-150: 1X TO 2.5X BASIC CARDS
*ET AU 151-190: .6X TO 1.5X BASIC CARDS
*PT AU 191-200: .5X TO 1.2X BASIC CARDS
CHAMP.TICKET PRINT RUN 100 SER.#'d SETS
144 Tom Brady AU 6000.00 10000.00

2000 Playoff Contenders Championship Fabric

Randomly inserted in packs, this 45-card set features six different versions. Pant-Single cards, numbers 1-10, are sequentially numbered to 300, Jersey-Single cards, numbers 11-20, are sequentially numbered to 300, Pants/Jersey-Single cards, numbers 21-30, sequentially numbered to 100, Pant-Double cards, numbers 31-35, sequentially numbered to 25, Jersey-Double cards, numbers 36-40, sequentially numbered to 25, and Pant/Jersey Combo-Double cards, numbers 41-45, which are sequentially numbered to 25. All cards contain circular swatches of game used memorabilia, and color action photograps. A few cards were issued as redemptions and those cards could be redeemed until August 31, 2002.

STATED PRINT RUN 25-300
CF1 Az-Zahir Hakim P/300 5.00 12.00
CF2 Grant Wistrom P/300 5.00 12.00
CF3 Isaac Bruce P/300 15.00 40.00
CF4 Kevin Carter P/300 5.00 12.00
CF5 Kurt Warner P/75* 20.00 50.00
CF5A Kurt Warner P AU/25* 100.00 200.00
CF6 Marshall Faulk P/300 6.00 15.00
CF7 Tony Horne P/300 5.00 12.00
CF8 Robert Holcombe P/300 5.00 12.00
CF9 Todd Collins P/300 5.00 12.00
CF10 Torry Holt P/300 6.00 15.00
CF11 Az-Zahir Hakim J/300 5.00 12.00
CF12 Grant Wistrom J/300 5.00 12.00
CF13 Isaac Bruce J/300 8.00 20.00
CF14 Kevin Carter J/300 5.00 12.00
CF15 Kurt Warner J/250* 12.00 30.00
CF15A Kurt Warner J AU/50* 75.00 150.00
CF16 Marshall Faulk J/300 12.00 30.00
CF17 Tony Horne J/300 8.00 20.00
CF18 Robert Holcombe J/300 5.00 12.00
CF19 Todd Collins J/300 5.00 12.00
CF20 Torry Holt J/300 6.00 15.00
CF21 Az-Zahir Hakim P/J/100 8.00 20.00
CF22 Grant Wistrom P/J/100 8.00 20.00
CF23 Isaac Bruce P/J/100 12.00 30.00
CF24 Kevin Carter P/J/100 8.00 20.00
CF25 Kurt Warner P/J/75* 20.00 50.00
CF25A Kurt Warner P/J AU/25* 100.00 200.00
CF26 Marshall Faulk P/J/100 15.00 40.00
CF27 Tony Horne P/J/100 8.00 20.00
CF28 Robert Holcombe P/J/100 8.00 20.00
CF29 Todd Collins P/J/100 8.00 20.00
CF30 Torry Holt P/J/100 10.00 25.00
CF31 K.Warner/T.Holt P/25 30.00 80.00
CF32 M.Faulk/I.Bruce P/25 20.00 50.00
CF33 T.Horne/A.Hakim P/25 12.00 30.00
CF34 G.Wistrom/R.Holcombe P/25 12.00 30.00
CF35 T.Collins/K.Carter P/25 12.00 30.00
CF36 K.Warner/M.Faulk J/25 40.00 100.00
CF37 I.Bruce/T.Holt J/25 20.00 50.00
CF38 K.Carter/A.Hakim J/25 12.00 30.00
CF39 G.Wistrom/R.Holcombe J/25 12.00 30.00
CF40 T.Collins/T.Horne J/25 12.00 30.00
CF41 I.Bruce/K.Warner P/J/25 30.00 80.00
CF42 T.Holt/M.Faulk P/J/25 15.00 40.00
CF43 A.Hakim/R.Holcombe P/J/25 12.00 30.00
CF44 K.Carter/T.Horne P/J/25 12.00 30.00
CF45 G.Wistrom/T.Collins P/J/25 12.00 30.00

2000 Playoff Contenders Hawaii 5-0

Randomly inserted in packs at the rate of one in 11, this 50-card set features the top 50 players to appear in the pro bowl this season. Base cards have a curved red background with an ocean view and a map of Hawaii in the background. Card backs carry "H50" prefix.

COMPLETE SET (50) 30.00 80.00
STATED ODDS 1:11
1 Steve Beuerlein .75 2.00
2 Muhsin Muhammad .60 1.50
3 Jim Kelly 1.00 2.50
4 Doug Flutie .75 2.00
5 Reggie White 1.00 2.50
6 Corey Dillon .60 1.50
7 Emmitt Smith 1.50 4.00
8 Troy Aikman 1.25 3.00
9 Randall Cunningham .75 2.00
10 John Elway 1.50 4.00
11 Terrell Davis .75 2.00
12 Barry Sanders 1.50 4.00
13 Herman Moore .60 1.50
14 Brett Favre 2.00 5.00
15 Dorsey Levens .75 2.00
16 Antonio Freeman .75 2.00
17 Peyton Manning 2.50 6.00
18 Edgerrin James .75 2.00
19 Marvin Harrison .75 2.00
20 Mark Brunell .75 2.00
21 Jimmy Smith .75 2.00
22 Warren Moon 1.00 2.50
23 Dan Marino 2.00 5.00
24 Randy Moss .75 2.00
25 Cris Carter 1.00 2.50
26 Robert Smith .60 1.50
27 Drew Bledsoe .75 2.00
28 Tony Gonzalez .75 2.00
29 Rich Gannon .75 2.00
30 Curtis Martin .75 2.00
31 Vinny Testaverde .60 1.50
32 Frank Wycheck .75 2.00
33 Jerome Bettis 1.00 2.50
34 Junior Seau .75 2.00
35 Jerry Rice 2.50 6.00
36 Steve Young 1.25 3.00
37 Ricky Watters .75 2.00
38 Kurt Warner 1.50 4.00
39 Marshall Faulk .75 2.00
40 Isaac Bruce 1.00 2.50
41 Keyshawn Johnson .75 2.00
42 Mike Alstott .60 1.50
43 Warren Sapp .75 2.00
44 Eddie George .75 2.00
45 Jevon Kearse .60 1.50
46 Carl Pickens .75 2.00
47 Terry Glenn .75 2.00
48 Brad Johnson .75 2.00
49 Bruce Smith .75 2.00
50 Deion Sanders .75 2.00

2000 Playoff Contenders MVP Contenders

Randomly inserted in packs at the rate of one in 35, this 30-card set features all green foil cards with color player action shots centered and silver foil highlights.

COMPLETE SET (30) 40.00 100.00
STATED ODDS 1:35
MVP1 Cade McNown .75 2.00
MVP2 Tim Couch 1.00 2.50
MVP3 Troy Aikman 1.50 4.00
MVP4 Terrell Davis 1.00 2.50
MVP5 Drew Bledsoe 1.00 2.50
MVP6 Ricky Williams 1.00 2.50
MVP7 Jerry Rice 3.00 8.00
MVP8 Jamal Anderson 1.00 2.50
MVP9 Dorsey Levens 1.00 2.50
MVP10 Cris Carter 1.25 3.00
MVP11 Emmitt Smith 2.00 5.00
MVP12 Brett Favre 2.50 6.00
MVP13 Peyton Manning 3.00 8.00
MVP14 Edgerrin James 1.00 2.50
MVP15 Fred Taylor .75 2.00
MVP16 Randy Moss 1.00 2.50
MVP17 Curtis Martin 1.00 2.50
MVP18 Marshall Faulk 1.00 2.50
MVP19 Steve McNair 1.00 2.50
MVP20 Stephen Davis .75 2.00
MVP21 Mark Brunell 1.00 2.50
MVP22 Daunte Culpepper 1.00 2.50
MVP23 Kurt Warner 2.00 5.00
MVP24 Eddie George 1.00 2.50
MVP25 Marvin Harrison 1.00 2.50
MVP26 Isaac Bruce 1.25 3.00
MVP27 Shaun King .75 2.00
MVP28 Keyshawn Johnson 1.00 2.50
MVP29 Brad Johnson 1.00 2.50
MVP30 Jimmy Smith 1.00 2.50

2000 Playoff Contenders Quads

Randomly inserted in packs at the rate of one in 59, this 15-card set features four players on each card. Card fronts and backs feature two players and team logos in the background.

COMPLETE SET (15) 30.00 80.00
STATED ODDS 1:59
*ULTIMATE/80-159: .8X TO 2X BASIC INSERTS
*ULTIMATE/44-60: 1X TO 2.5X BASIC INSERTS
*ULTIMATE/25: 1.5X TO 4X BASIC INSERTS
ULTIMATE QUAD PRINT RUN 8-159
CQ1 Plaxico Burress/Jerome Bettis 1.25 3.00
Travis Prentice/Tim Couch
CQ2 Aikmn/Emmitt/Jhnsn/Dvis 2.00 5.00
CQ3 Mrtin/Penn/Jmes/P.Mann 3.00 8.00
CQ4 Shaun King/Keyshawn Johnson 1.00 2.50
Daunte Culpepper/Randy Moss
CQ5 Fred Taylor/Eddie George 1.00 2.50
Mark Brunell/Steve McNair
CQ6 Ricky Watters/Jerry Porter 1.25 3.00
Tim Brown/Shaun Alexander
CQ7 Frman/Favre/Rob/McNwn 2.50 6.00
CQ8 Donovan McNabb/Duce Staley 1.25 3.00
Kerry Collins/Ron Dayne
CQ9 Jamal Lewis/Akili Smith 1.25 3.00
Peter Warrick/Travis Taylor
CQ10 Blake/Will/Jnes/Plummr 1.00 2.50
CQ11 Rice/TO/Faulk/Warner 3.00 8.00
CQ12 Drew Bledsoe/Peerless Price 1.00 2.50
Terry Glenn/Eric Moulds
CQ13 Terrell Davis/Brian Griese 1.00 2.50
Sylvester Morris/Elvis Grbac
CQ14 Steve Beuerlein 1.00 2.50
Muhsin Muhammad/Jamal Anderson/Chris Chandler
CQ15 Ryan Leaf/Jermaine Fazande 1.00 2.50
Jay Fiedler/Damon Huard

2000 Playoff Contenders Round Numbers Autographs

Randomly inserted in packs at the rate of one in 173, this 15-card set features dual player signed cards. Base cards feature the number of the round each featured player was dragted in on a foil board card stock. Player photos appear inside a circular frame coupled with an authentic autograph. Some cards were issued via mail redemptions that carried an expiration date of 12/31/2002.

STATED ODDS 1:173
1 J.Lewis/T.Taylor 15.00 40.00
2 T.Jones/S.Alexander 10.00 25.00
4 Syl.Morris AU/R.Soward No AU 6.00 15.00
5 T.Pinkston/J.Porter 10.00 25.00
7 G.Carmazzi/C.Redman 6.00 15.00
8 T.Prentice/J.Dawson 6.00 15.00
9 R.Dugans/L.Coles 8.00 20.00
10 C.Simon/B.Urlacher 20.00 50.00
11 T.Brady/M.Bulger 500.00 800.00
12 T.Rattay/J.Hamilton 8.00 20.00
13 T.Gaylor/A.Black 6.00 15.00
15 C.Keaton/G.Scott 6.00 15.00

2000 Playoff Contenders Round Numbers Autographs Gold

Randomly inserted in packs, this 15-card set parallels the base Round numbers set enhanced with gold borders around the palayer's draft round and team logo. Each card is sequentially numbered to the round in which each player was drafted times ten. Most cards were issued via mail redemptions that carried an expiration date of 12/31/2002.

STATED PRINT RUN 10-70
5 Pinkston/Porter/20 25.00 60.00
6 Redmond/Chapman/30 12.00 30.00
7 Carmaz/Redman/30 12.00 30.00
8 T.Prentice/J.Dawson/30 12.00 30.00
9 R.Dugans/L.Coles/30 15.00 40.00
11 Bulger/Brady/60 400.00 800.00
12 Rattay/Hamilton/70 12.00 30.00
13 T.Gaylor/A.Black/40 12.00 30.00
15 C.Keaton/Scott/40 12.00 30.00

2000 Playoff Contenders ROY Contenders

Randomly inserted in packs at the rate of one in 23, this 20-card set features player action photos framed by the NFL shield logo and are enhanced with silver foil.

COMPLETE SET (20) 20.00 50.00
STATED ODDS 1:23
ROY1 Thomas Jones .60 1.50
ROY2 Jamal Lewis .75 2.00
ROY3 Travis Taylor .50 1.25
ROY4 Brian Urlacher 2.50 6.00
ROY5 Peter Warrick .50 1.25
ROY6 Travis Prentice .50 1.25
ROY7 Courtney Brown .60 1.50
ROY8 Bubba Franks .50 1.25
ROY9 R.Jay Soward .50 1.25
ROY10 Sylvester Morris .50 1.25
ROY11 J.R. Redmond .50 1.25
ROY12 Ron Dayne .75 2.00
ROY13 Chad Pennington .60 1.50
ROY14 Laveranues Coles .60 1.50
ROY15 Jerry Porter .75 2.00
ROY16 Todd Pinkston .50 1.25
ROY17 Corey Simon .60 1.50
ROY18 Plaxico Burress .60 1.50
ROY19 Shaun Alexander .75 2.00
ROY20 Darrell Jackson .50 1.25

2000 Playoff Contenders ROY Contenders Autographs

Randomly seeded in packs, this 20-card set parallels the base ROY Contenders insert set with a gold foil shift from the base silver and are enhanced with authentic player autographs. Each card is sequentially numbered to 100 with some being issued via mail-in redemption cards. The expiration date for those was 12/31/2002.

STATED PRINT RUN 100 SER.#'d SETS
ROY1 Thomas Jones 8.00 20.00
ROY2 Jamal Lewis 10.00 25.00
ROY3 Travis Taylor 6.00 15.00
ROY4 Brian Urlacher 30.00 80.00
ROY5 Peter Warrick 6.00 15.00
ROY6 Travis Prentice 6.00 15.00
ROY7 Courtney Brown 8.00 20.00
ROY8 Bubba Franks 6.00 15.00
ROY10 Sylvester Morris 6.00 15.00
ROY13 Chad Pennington 8.00 20.00
ROY14 Laveranues Coles 8.00 20.00
ROY15 Jerry Porter 10.00 25.00
ROY16 Todd Pinkston 6.00 15.00
ROY17 Corey Simon 8.00 20.00
ROY19 Shaun Alexander 10.00 25.00
ROY20 Darrell Jackson 6.00 15.00

2000 Playoff Contenders Touchdown Tandems

Randomly inserted in packs at the rate of one in 11, this 30-card set features all foil dual player cards. Each side features a player with a small circular portrait in the lower left hand corner of the player that appears on the card's other side.

COMPLETE SET (30) 25.00 60.00
STATED ODDS 1:11
*TOTALS/67: 2X TO 5X BASIC INSERTS
*TOTALS/30-39: 3X TO 8X BASIC INSERTS
*TOTALS/20-28: 4X TO 10X BASIC INSERTS
*TOTALS/10-19: 5X TO 12X BASIC INSERTS
TOTALS STATED PRINT RUN 7-67
TD1 R.Moss .60 1.50
M.Harrison
TD2 K.Warner 2.00 5.00
P.Manning
TD3 M.Faulk .60 1.50
E.James
TD4 E.George .60 1.50
F.Taylor
TD5 E.Smith 1.25 3.00
S.Davis
TD6 I.Bruce 2.00 5.00
J.Rice
TD7 A.Freeman .75 2.00
C.Carter
TD8 D.Bledsoe .60 1.50
M.Brunell
TD9 J.Plummer .60 1.50
S.McNair
TD10 C.Martin .60 1.50
D.Staley
TD11 Key.Johnson .60 1.50
M.Robinson
TD12 D.Marino 1.50 4.00
S.Young
TD13 B.Favre 1.50 4.00
T.Aikman
TD14 T.Brown .75 2.00
E.Moulds
TD15 J.Bettis .75 2.00
M.Alstott
TD16 D.Levens .60 1.50
J.Stewart
TD17 O.Gary .60 1.50
R.Watters
TD18 B.Griese .50 1.25
C.Batch
TD19 T.Owens .60 1.50
T.Holt
TD20 J.Smith .60 1.50
J.Galloway
TD21 Kev.Johnson .50 1.25
Westbrook
TD22 C.Dillon .60 1.50
R.Williams
TD23 D.McNabb .60 1.50
A.Smith
TD24 T.Couch .60 1.50
C.McNown
TD25 S.King .50 1.25
J.Kitna
TD26 P.Warrick .60 1.50
P.Burress
TD27 J.Lewis .75 2.00
S.Alexander
TD28 R.Dayne .75 2.00
T.Jones
TD29 Syl.Morris .50 1.25
T.Taylor
TD30 C.Pennington .60 1.50
C.Redman

2001 Playoff Contenders Samples

*VETS 1-100: .8X TO 2X BASIC CARDS
COMMON ROOKIE (101-200) .75 2.00
ROOKIE SEMISTARS 1.00 2.50
ROOKIE UNL.STARS 1.25 3.00
*GOLD VETS: 1X TO 2.5X SILVER
*GOLD ROOKIES: 1.2X TO 3X SILVER
GOLD ANNOUNCED PRINT RUN 30
113 Chad Johnson 1.25 3.00
114 Chris Chambers .75 2.00
123 Deuce McAllister 1.25 3.00
124 Drew Brees 5.00 12.00
150 LaDainian Tomlinson 4.00 10.00
157 Michael Vick 2.00 5.00
166 Reggie Wayne 1.50 4.00
175 Santana Moss 1.25 3.00
177 T.J. Houshmandzadeh 1.00 2.50
190 Steve Smith 2.50 6.00

2001 Playoff Contenders

Released in January, 2002 this 200 card set, issued in five-card packs, featured a mix of 100 leading veterans and 100 rookies who had (or were expected to later have) an impact in the NFL. In addition, nearly all of the Rookie Cards were autographed. However, a few players did not return their cards in time for inclusion in packs. Those cards were issued via mail redemptions that could be redeemed until April 2, 2003. Playoff announced some print run totals on the signed RCs as noted below.

COMP.SET w/o RC's (100) 10.00 25.00
1 David Boston .20 .50
2 Jake Plummer .20 .50
3 Jamal Anderson .25 .60
4 Chris Chandler .25 .60
5 Elvis Grbac .25 .60
6 Brandon Stokley .20 .50
7 Travis Taylor .20 .50
8 Ray Lewis .30 .75
9 Rob Johnson .25 .60
10 Eric Moulds .20 .50
11 Tim Biakabutuka .20 .50
12 Muhsin Muhammad .20 .50
13 James Allen .20 .50
14 Brian Urlacher .40 1.00
15 Peter Warrick .20 .50
16 Corey Dillon .20 .50
17 Tim Couch .20 .50
18 Kevin Johnson .20 .50
19 Rickey Dudley .20 .50
20 Emmitt Smith .50 1.25
21 Joey Galloway .25 .60
22 Brian Griese .20 .50
23 Terrell Davis .25 .60
24 Mike Anderson .20 .50
25 Ed McCaffrey .25 .60
26 Rod Smith .25 .60
27 Charlie Batch .20 .50
28 James Stewart .20 .50
29 Germane Crowell .20 .50
30 Johnnie Morton .25 .60
31 Brett Favre .60 1.50
32 Ahman Green .25 .60
33 Antonio Freeman .30 .75
34 Peyton Manning .75 2.00
35 Edgerrin James .25 .60
36 Marvin Harrison .25 .60
37 Jerome Pathon .20 .50
38 Mark Brunell .25 .60
39 Fred Taylor .20 .50
40 Keenan McCardell .25 .60
41 Jimmy Smith .25 .60
42 Trent Green .20 .50
43 Priest Holmes .20 .50
44 Tony Gonzalez .25 .60
45 Derrick Alexander .20 .50
46 Jay Fiedler .25 .60
47 Lamar Smith .25 .60
48 Zach Thomas .25 .60
49 Oronde Gadsden .20 .50
50 Daunte Culpepper .25 .60
51 Randy Moss .25 .60
52 Cris Carter .30 .75
53 Drew Bledsoe .25 .60
54 J.R. Redmond .20 .50
55 Troy Brown .20 .50
56 Aaron Brooks .20 .50
57 Ricky Williams .25 .60
58 Joe Horn .20 .50
59 Kerry Collins .20 .50
60 Tiki Barber .25 .60
61 Ron Dayne .25 .60
62 Ike Hilliard .20 .50
63 Vinny Testaverde .20 .50
64 Curtis Martin .25 .60
65 Wayne Chrebet .20 .50
66 Laveranues Coles .25 .60
67 Rich Gannon .25 .60
68 Tyrone Wheatley .25 .60
69 Tim Brown .30 .75
70 Jerry Rice .60 1.50
71 Donovan McNabb .25 .60
72 Duce Staley .20 .50
73 Todd Pinkston .20 .50
74 Kordell Stewart .20 .50
75 Jerome Bettis .30 .75
76 Plaxico Burress .20 .50
77 Doug Flutie .25 .60
78 Junior Seau .25 .60
79 Jeff Garcia .20 .50
80 Garrison Hearst .25 .60
81 Terrell Owens .25 .60
82 Matt Hasselbeck .20 .50
83 Ricky Watters .20 .50
84 Shaun Alexander .25 .60
85 Darrell Jackson .25 .60
86 Kurt Warner .50 1.25
87 Marshall Faulk .25 .60
88 Isaac Bruce .30 .75
89 Torry Holt .25 .60
90 Brad Johnson .25 .60
91 Keyshawn Johnson .25 .60
92 Warrick Dunn .20 .50
93 Warren Sapp .25 .60
94 Steve McNair .25 .60
95 Eddie George .30 .75
96 Derrick Mason .20 .50
97 Jevon Kearse .20 .50
98 Stephen Davis .20 .50
99 Bruce Smith .25 .60
100 Michael Westbrook .20 .50
101 Adam Archuleta/50* RC 30.00 80.00
102 Alex Bannister AU RC 3.00 8.00
103 Alge Crumpler AU RC 6.00 15.00
104 Andre Carter AU/100* RC 15.00 40.00
105 Anthony Thomas AU/600* RC 5.00 12.00
106 Ben Leard AU RC 3.00 8.00
107 Bobby Newcombe AU RC 4.00 10.00
108 Brian Allen AU RC 3.00 8.00
109 Carlos Polk AU RC 3.00 8.00
110 Casey Hampton No Auto RC 5.00 12.00
111 Cedric Scott AU RC 3.00 8.00
112 Cedrick Wilson AU RC 4.00 10.00
113 Chad Johnson AU RC 12.00 30.00
114 C.Chambers AU/170* RC 30.00 80.00
115 Chris Weinke AU/350* RC 5.00 12.00
116 C.Buckhalter AU/590* RC 8.00 20.00
117 Damione Lewis AU RC 4.00 10.00
118 Dan Morgan AU RC 6.00 15.00
119 Daniel Guy AU RC 3.00 8.00
120 David Allen AU RC 3.00 8.00
121 David Terrell AU/500* RC 4.00 10.00
122 Ken Lucas AU/276* RC 4.00 10.00
123 D.McAllister AU/500* RC 12.00 30.00
124 Drew Brees AU/500* RC 2500.00 5000.00
125 Eddie Berlin AU RC 3.00 8.00
126 Boo Williams AU/50* RC 15.00 40.00
127 Ennis Davis AU RC 3.00 8.00
128 Freddie Mitchell AU RC 3.00 8.00
129 Gary Baxter AU RC 3.00 8.00
130 Gerard Warren AU/200* RC 6.00 15.00
131 Hakim Akbar AU RC 3.00 8.00
132 Heath Evans AU RC 4.00 10.00
133 Jabari Holloway AU RC 3.00 8.00
134 Jamal Reynolds AU/500* RC 3.00 8.00
135 James Jackson AU RC 3.00 8.00
136 Jamie Winborn AU RC 4.00 10.00
137 Javon Green AU RC 3.00 8.00
138 Jesse Palmer AU RC 4.00 10.00
139 Dominic Rhodes AU/300* RC 8.00 20.00
140 Josh Heupel AU/150* RC 15.00 40.00
141 Justin Smith AU RC 10.00 20.00
142 Karon Riley AU RC 3.00 8.00
143 Keith Adams/50* RC 25.00 60.00
144 Kendrell Bell AU RC 5.00 12.00
145 Kenny Smith AU RC 3.00 8.00
146 Ken.Walker AU/50* RC 25.00 60.00
147 Ken-Yon Rambo AU RC 3.00 8.00
148 Kevan Barlow AU RC 4.00 10.00
149 Koren Robinson AU/400* RC 4.00 10.00
150 L.Tomlinson AU/600 RC 100.00 200.00
151 LaMont Jordan AU/50* RC 20.00 50.00
152 Leonard Davis/50* RC 25.00 60.00
153 Marcus Stroud AU RC 4.00 10.00
154 Marques Tuiasosopo AU RC 4.00 10.00
155 Snoop Minnis AU/295* RC 3.00 8.00
156 Michael Bennett AU/600* RC 4.00 10.00
157 Michael Vick AU/327* RC 30.00 80.00
158 Mike McMahon AU/529* RC 4.00 10.00
159 Moran Norris AU RC 3.00 8.00
160 Morlon Greenwood AU RC 3.00 8.00
161 Nate Clements/50* RC 30.00 80.00
162 Quincy Carter AU SP RC 15.00 40.00
163 Quincy Morgan AU RC 4.00 10.00
164 Jamar Fletcher/50* RC 25.00 60.00
165 Reggie Germany AU RC 3.00 8.00
166 Reggie Wayne AU/400* RC 25.00 60.00
167 Reggie White AU RC 3.00 8.00
168 Richard Seymour/50* RC 40.00 100.00
169 Robert Carswell/50* RC 25.00 60.00
170 Robert Ferguson AU RC 5.00 12.00
171 Rod Gardner AU/75* RC 30.00 80.00
172 Ronney Daniels AU RC 3.00 8.00
173 Rudi Johnson AU RC 15.00 40.00
174 Sage Rosenfels AU/400* RC 12.50 25.00
175 Santana Moss AU/500* RC 8.00 20.00
176 Shaun Rogers AU RC 5.00 12.00
177 Houshmandzadeh AU RC 4.00 10.00
178 Tim Hasselbeck AU RC 4.00 10.00
179 Todd Heap AU/169* RC 20.00 50.00
180 Tony Stewart AU RC 4.00 10.00
181 Torrance Marshall AU RC 3.00 8.00
182 Travis Henry AU/369* RC 10.00 25.00
183 Travis Minor AU RC 4.00 10.00
184 Vinny Sutherland AU RC 3.00 8.00
185 Will Allen AU RC 5.00 12.00
186 Willie Howard AU RC 3.00 8.00
187 W.Middlebrooks/50* RC 30.00 80.00
188 Derrick Blaylock AU/200* RC 6.00 15.00
189 A.J. Feeley AU/200* RC 6.00 15.00
190 Steve Smith AU/300* RC 60.00 120.00
191 Onome Ojo AU/200* RC 5.00 12.00
192 Dee Brown AU/300* RC 3.00 8.00
193 Kevin Kasper AU/200* RC 5.00 12.00
194 Dave Dickenson AU/300* RC 4.00 10.00
195 Chris Barnes AU/200* RC 5.00 12.00
196 Scotty Anderson AU/300* RC 3.00 8.00
197 Chris Taylor AU/300* RC 3.00 8.00
198 Cedric James AU/300* RC 3.00 8.00
199 Justin McCareins AU/200* RC 6.00 15.00
200 Tommy Polley AU/200* RC 5.00 12.00

2001 Playoff Contenders Championship Ticket

*VETS 1-100: 3X TO 8X BASIC CARDS
COMMON ROOKIE (101-200) 3.00 8.00
ROOKIE SEMISTARS 4.00 10.00
ROOKIE UNL.STARS 5.00 12.00
STATED PRINT RUN 100 SER.#'d SETS
113 Chad Johnson 5.00 12.00
114 Chris Chambers 3.00 8.00
123 Deuce McAllister 5.00 12.00
124 Drew Brees 1800.00 2500.00
150 LaDainian Tomlinson 40.00 100.00
157 Michael Vick 50.00 100.00
166 Reggie Wayne 6.00 15.00
175 Santana Moss 5.00 12.00
177 T.J. Houshmandzadeh 4.00 10.00
190 Steve Smith 10.00 25.00

2001 Playoff Contenders Hawaii 2002

Cards from this parallel set were distributed at the 2002 Hawaii Trade Conference. Each card is a basic issue 2001 Playoff Contenders card or insert with the "2002 Hawaii Trade Conference" logo stamped on the fronts in silver foil. Each card was also serial numbered on the front in silver foil of 15 (for veterans) and silver foil on the backs of 10 (for signed rookies). Not all cards from the base Contenders set were issued in this parallel form. Due to scarcity, a stable secondary market price cannot be established.

2001 Playoff Contenders Legendary Contenders Autographs

Randomly inserted in packs, these cards feature autographs of leading NFL retired players. According to Donruss/Playoff a few players signed 50 cards or less. These cards with the supplied print runs are notated in our checklist. Some cards were issued via mail redemptions that carried an expiration date of 4/2/2003.

PRINT RUNS ANNC'd BY PLAYOFF
1 Archie Griffin 15.00 40.00
2 Archie Manning/50* 15.00 40.00
3 Art Monk/25* 50.00 100.00
4 Bart Starr/25* 150.00 300.00
5 Billy Sims 12.00 30.00
6 Bob Griese/25* 40.00 80.00
7 Charlie Joiner/50* 15.00 40.00
8 Charley Taylor/50* 15.00 40.00
9 Cris Collinsworth/50* 15.00 40.00
10 Craig Morton 12.00 30.00
11 Dan Fouts/25* 50.00 100.00
12 Deacon Jones/25* 30.00 80.00
13 Dick Butkus/225* 30.00 60.00
14 Don Maynard/25* 30.00 80.00
15 Drew Pearson/25* 15.00 40.00
16 Dwight Clark/50* 15.00 40.00
17 Earl Campbell/225* 25.00 60.00
18 Eric Dickerson/25* 30.00 80.00
19 Fran Tarkenton/25* 50.00 100.00
20 Franco Harris/50* 50.00 80.00
21 Frank Gifford/25* 50.00 100.00
22 Fred Biletnikoff/125* 15.00 40.00
23 John Fuqua 15.00 40.00
24 Gale Sayers/125* 40.00 80.00
25 George Blanda/125* 25.00 50.00
26 Harvey Martin No Auto 3.00 8.00
27 Henry Ellard 10.00 25.00
28 Irving Fryar 12.00 30.00
29 James Lofton/25* 30.00 80.00
30 Jim Brown/150* 50.00 100.00
31 Jim Plunkett/125* 15.00 40.00
32 Joe Greene/125* 40.00 80.00
33 Joe Montana/50* 100.00 175.00
34 Joe Namath/100* 50.00 120.00
35 Joe Theismann/125* 15.00 40.00
36 John Hadl 10.00 25.00
37 John Stallworth/50* 40.00 80.00
38 Johnny Unitas/25* 200.00 350.00
39 Kellen Winslow 10.00 25.00
40 Ken Anderson/50* 15.00 40.00
41 Ken Stabler/100* 40.00 80.00
42 Lance Alworth/125* 25.00 50.00
43 Warren Moon/72* 20.00 50.00
44 Mike Singletary/125* 25.00 50.00
45 Otto Graham/125* 25.00 50.00
46 Ozzie Newsome/25* 30.00 60.00
47 Paul Hornung/125* 30.00 60.00
48 Paul Warfield/125* 15.00 40.00
49 Raymond Berry/125* 12.00 30.00
50 Rocky Bleier 25.00 50.00
51 Roger Craig/25* 20.00 50.00
52 Roger Staubach/25* 100.00 175.00
53 Ronnie Lott/50* 30.00 60.00
54 Sammy Baugh/125* 50.00 100.00
55 Sonny Jurgensen/25* 60.00 100.00
56 Steve Largent/25* 50.00 100.00
57 Terry Bradshaw/25* 100.00 175.00
58 Todd Christensen 12.00 30.00
59 Tony Dorsett/25* 60.00 120.00
60 Y.A. Tittle/125* 30.00 60.00
61 Larry Csonka/225* 25.00 50.00
62 Lawrence Taylor/52* 40.00 80.00
63 Marcus Allen/50* 25.00 60.00
64 Barry Sanders/50* 100.00 175.00
65 Boomer Esiason/159* 12.00 30.00
66 Dan Marino/59* 75.00 150.00
67 Jim Kelly/58* 40.00 80.00
68 John Elway/53* 100.00 175.00
69 Michael Irvin 15.00 40.00
70 Phil Simms/57* 30.00 60.00
71 Steve Young/54* 40.00 80.00

2001 Playoff Contenders MVP Contenders

Inserted at a stated rate of one in 16, these 20 cards feature players expected to compete for the MVP award.

COMPLETE SET (20) 15.00 40.00
STATED ODDS 1:16
1 Brett Favre 1.50 4.00
2 Brian Griese .50 1.25
3 Corey Dillon .50 1.25
4 Cris Carter .75 2.00
5 Daunte Culpepper .60 1.50
6 Drew Bledsoe .60 1.50
7 Eddie George .75 2.00
8 Edgerrin James .60 1.50
9 Emmitt Smith 1.25 3.00
10 Isaac Bruce .75 2.00
11 Aaron Brooks .50 1.25
12 Jerry Rice 1.50 4.00
13 Kurt Warner 1.25 3.00
14 Mark Brunell .60 1.50
15 Marshall Faulk .60 1.50
16 Peyton Manning 2.00 5.00
17 Randy Moss .60 1.50
18 Ray Lewis .75 2.00
19 Ricky Williams .60 1.50
20 Stephen Davis .50 1.25

2001 Playoff Contenders MVP Contenders Autographs

Randomly inserted in packs, these cards feature autographs on stickers that have been attached to basic MVP Contenders inserts. The signed cards have a stated print run of 25 and due to market scarcity no pricing is provided. Some players did not return their cards in time for inclusion

in packs and those cards could be redeemed until April 2, 2003.
STATED PRINT RUN 25 SER.#'d SETS
1 Brett Favre 250.00 400.00
2 Brian Griese 25.00 60.00
3 Corey Dillon 25.00 60.00
4 Cris Carter 40.00 100.00
5 Daunte Culpepper 15.00 40.00
6 Drew Bledsoe 30.00 80.00
7 Eddie George 40.00 100.00
8 Edgerrin James 30.00 80.00
9 Emmitt Smith 150.00 300.00
10 Isaac Bruce 25.00 60.00
11 Aaron Brooks 25.00 60.00
12 Jerry Rice 175.00 300.00
13 Kurt Warner 50.00 120.00
14 Mark Brunell 30.00 80.00
15 Marshall Faulk 30.00 80.00
16 Peyton Manning 125.00 250.00
17 Randy Moss 60.00 120.00
18 Ray Lewis 60.00 120.00
19 Ricky Williams 30.00 80.00
20 Stephen Davis 25.00 60.00

2001 Playoff Contenders Round Numbers Autographs

Randomly inserted in packs, these 15 cards feature signed copies of both rookies featured on the card. Some players did not return their cards in time for pack insertion and those cards have an expiration of April 2, 2003. Two cards were redeemed with only one or no player autographs as noted below.
*GOLD/20: .0X TO 2X DASIC AU
*GOLD/30: .6X TO 1.5X BASIC AU
GOLD PRINT RUN 10-30
1 M.Vick/L.Tomlinson 100.00 200.00
2 D.McAllister/M.Bennett 15.00 40.00
3 D.Terrell/K.Robinson 10.00 25.00
4 N.Clements/W.Allen No Auto 7.50 20.00
5 T.Heap/R.Wayne 25.00 60.00
6 Seymour No AU/J.Smith AU 7.50 20.00
7 D.Brees/Q.Carter 200.00 400.00
8 A.Thomas/T.Henry 12.00 30.00
9 C.Johnson/Q.Morgan 15.00 40.00
10 R.Ferguson/C.Chambers 15.00 40.00
11 S.Rogers/K.Bell 10.00 25.00
12 K.Barlow/T.Minor 10.00 25.00
13 J.Jackson/S.Minnis 7.50 20.00
14 R.Johnson/C.Buckhalter 15.00 40.00
15 C.Weinke/J.Palmer 10.00 25.00

2001 Playoff Contenders ROY Contenders

Inserted into packs at stated odds of one in 32, these 20 cards feature players who were expected to be the leading contenders for the Rookie of the Year award.
COMPLETE SET (20) 20.00 50.00
STATED ODDS 1:32
1 Anthony Thomas .75 2.00
2 Chad Johnson .75 2.00
3 Chris Chambers .50 1.25
4 Chris Weinke .60 1.50
5 David Terrell .60 1.50
6 Deuce McAllister .75 2.00
7 Drew Brees 25.00 50.00
8 Freddie Mitchell .50 1.25
9 James Jackson .50 1.25
10 Kevan Barlow .60 1.50
11 Koren Robinson .60 1.50
12 LaDainian Tomlinson 2.50 6.00
13 Snoop Minnis .50 1.25
14 Michael Bennett .60 1.50
15 Michael Vick 1.25 3.00
16 Quincy Carter .60 1.50
17 Quincy Morgan .75 2.00
18 Reggie Wayne 1.00 2.50
19 Travis Henry .60 1.50
20 Travis Minor .60 1.50

2001 Playoff Contenders ROY Contenders Autographs

Randomly inserted into packs, these cards parallel the ROY Contenders insert set. These cards have a stated print run of 50 cards. A few players did not return their cards in time for pack out and those cards could be redeemed until April 2, 2003.
STATED PRINT RUN 50 SER.#'d SETS
1 Anthony Thomas 12.00 30.00
2 Chad Johnson 12.00 30.00
3 Chris Chambers 8.00 20.00
4 Chris Weinke 10.00 25.00
5 David Terrell 10.00 25.00
6 Douco McAllistor 12.00 30.00
7 Drew Brees 900.00 1600.00
8 Freddie Mitchell 8.00 20.00
9 James Jackson 8.00 20.00
10 Kevan Barlow 10.00 25.00
11 Koren Robinson 10.00 25.00
12 LaDainian Tomlinson 125.00 250.00
13 Snoop Minnis 8.00 20.00
14 Michael Bennett 10.00 25.00
15 Michael Vick 60.00 120.00
16 Quincy Morgan 10.00 25.00
17 Quincy Carter 10.00 25.00
18 Reggie Wayne 50.00 80.00
19 Travis Henry 10.00 25.00
20 Travis Minor 10.00 25.00

2001 Playoff Contenders Chicago Collection

NOT PRICED DUE TO SCARCITY

2002 Playoff Contenders Samples

*1-100 VETS: .8X TO 2X BASIC CARDS
*1-100 GOLD VETS: 1X TO 2.5X SILVER
*101-186 ROOKIES : .8X TO 2X SILVER
UNPRICED EMERALD ANNC'D PRINT RUN 1
101 Adrian Peterson 1.00 2.50
102 Albert Haynesworth 1.25 3.00
103 Alex Brown 1.25 3.00
104 Andra Davis .75 2.00
105 Andre Davis .75 2.00
106 Andre Lott .75 2.00
107 Anthony Weaver .75 2.00
108 Antonio Bryant 1.25 3.00
109 Antwaan Randle El 1.00 2.50
110 Ashley Lelie .75 2.00
111 Brian Poli-Dixon .75 2.00
112 Brian Westbrook 1.50 4.00
113 Bryant McKinnie .75 2.00
114 Chad Hutchinson .75 2.00
115 Charles Grant 1.25 3.00
116 Chester Taylor 1.25 3.00
117 Cliff Russell .75 2.00
118 Clinton Portis 1.25 3.00
119 Randy McMichael 1.25 3.00
120 Damien Anderson .75 2.00
121 Daniel Graham 1.00 2.50
122 David Carr .75 2.00
123 David Garrard 1.00 2.50
124 Deion Branch 1.25 3.00
125 John Simon .75 2.00
126 DeShaun Foster 1.25 3.00
127 Donte Stallworth 1.25 3.00
128 Dwight Freeney 1.50 4.00
129 Ed Reed 5.00 12.00
130 Eric Crouch 1.25 3.00
131 Freddie Milons .75 2.00
132 Jabar Gaffney .75 2.00
133 Javon Walker 1.25 3.00
134 Jeremy Shockey 1.25 3.00
135 Jerramy Stevens 1.25 3.00
136 Joey Harrington .75 2.00
137 John Henderson 1.00 2.50
138 Jonathan Wells 1.00 2.50
139 Josh McCown 1.25 3.00
140 Josh Reed 1.00 2.50
141 Josh Scobey 1.00 2.50
142 Julius Peppers 2.00 5.00
143 Kalimba Edwards 1.00 2.50
144 Kelly Campbell 1.00 2.50
145 Ken Simonton .75 2.00
146 Keyuo Craver .75 2.00
147 Kahlil Hill .75 2.00
148 Kurt Kittner .75 2.00
149 Ladell Betts 1.25 3.00
150 Lamar Gordon 1.00 2.50
151 Levar Fisher .75 2.00
152 Lito Sheppard 1.25 3.00
153 Luke Staley .75 2.00
154 Marquise Walker .75 2.00
155 Maurice Morris 1.00 2.50
156 Mike Rumph .75 2.00
157 Mike Williams .75 2.00
158 Najeh Davenport .75 2.00
159 Napoleon Harris 1.00 2.50
160 Patrick Ramsey 1.00 2.50
161 Phillip Buchanon 1.25 3.00
162 Quentin Jammer 1.25 3.00
163 Randy Fasani .75 2.00
164 Reche Caldwell 1.00 2.50
165 Robert Thomas .75 2.00
166 Rocky Calmus 1.00 2.50
167 Rohan Davey 1.25 3.00
168 Ron Johnson 1.00 2.50
169 Roy Williams .75 2.00
170 Ryan Sims 1.25 3.00
171 Tavon Mason .75 2.00
172 Terry Charles .75 2.00
173 T.J. Duckett .75 2.00
174 Tim Carter 1.00 2.50
175 Travis Stephens .75 2.00
176 Trev Faulk .75 2.00
177 Wendell Bryant .75 2.00
178 William Green 1.00 2.50
179 Woody Dantzler 1.00 2.50
180 Tony Fisher .75 2.00
181 Javin Hunter .75 2.00
182 Daryl Jones .75 2.00
183 Jesse Chatman .75 2.00
184 J.T. O'Sullivan 1.00 2.50
185 Josh Norman .75 2.00
186 James Mungro 1.25 3.00

2002 Playoff Contenders

Issued in late December 2002, this 186 card set is composed of 100 veteran and 86 rookie ticket segentially numbered autograph cards. Some of the autographed tickets were issued via redemption card only. Cards were packaged in a larger box with 2 sealed mini boxes inside containing 10 packs per mini box with 5 cards per pack. Each mini box contained one rookie ticket autograph card on average. Exchange deadline for rookie ticket cards was 6/23/2004.
COMP.SET w/o SP's (100) 10.00 25.00
ROOKIE AUTO PRINT RUN 40-900
1 Drew Bledsoe .25 .60
2 Travis Henry .20 .50
3 Eric Moulds .20 .50
4 Chris Chambers .20 .50
5 Ricky Williams .25 .60
6 Zach Thomas .25 .60
7 Tom Brady 1.50 4.00
8 Antowain Smith .25 .60
9 Troy Brown .20 .50
10 Curtis Martin .25 .60
11 Vinny Testaverde .20 .50
12 Chad Pennington .20 .50
13 Jeff Blake .25 .60
14 Jamal Lewis .25 .60
15 Ray Lewis .30 .75
16 Michael Westbrook .20 .50
17 Corey Dillon .20 .50
18 Peter Warrick .20 .50
19 Tim Couch .20 .50
20 Quincy Morgan .20 .50
21 Kevin Johnson .20 .50
22 Kordell Stewart .20 .50
23 Plaxico Burress .20 .50
24 Jerome Bettis .30 .75
25 James Allen .20 .50
26 Corey Bradford .20 .50
27 Mark Brunell .25 .60
28 Fred Taylor .20 .50
29 Jimmy Smith .25 .60
30 Peyton Manning .75 2.00
31 Reggie Wayne .25 .60
32 Marvin Harrison .25 .60
33 Edgerrin James .25 .60
34 Steve McNair .25 .60
35 Eddie George .25 .60
36 Jevon Kearse .20 .50
37 Derrick Mason .20 .50
38 Brian Griese .20 .50
39 Terrell Davis .25 .60
40 Ed McCaffrey .25 .60
41 Rod Smith .25 .60
42 Trent Green .20 .50
43 Priest Holmes .20 .50
44 Johnnie Morton .25 .60
45 Tony Gonzalez .25 .60
46 Rich Gannon .25 .60
47 Tim Brown .30 .75
48 Jerry Rice .60 1.50
49 Charlie Garner .25 .60
50 Drew Brees .60 1.50
51 LaDainian Tomlinson .30 .75
52 Junior Seau .25 .60
53 Quincy Carter .20 .50
54 Emmitt Smith .50 1.25
55 Joey Galloway .25 .60
56 Kerry Collins .20 .50
57 Tiki Barber .25 .60
58 Michael Strahan .25 .60
59 Donovan McNabb .25 .60
60 Duce Staley .20 .50
61 Antonio Freeman .30 .75
62 Derrius Thompson .20 .50
63 Stephen Davis .20 .50
64 Rod Gardner .20 .50
65 Anthony Thomas .25 .60
66 Marty Booker .20 .50
67 Brian Urlacher .30 .75
68 James Stewart .20 .50
69 Az-Zahir Hakim .20 .50
70 Brett Favre .60 1.50
71 Ahman Green .25 .60
72 Donald Driver .25 .60
73 Daunte Culpepper .25 .60
74 Michael Bennett .20 .50
75 Randy Moss .25 .60
76 Michael Vick .25 .60
77 Warrick Dunn .20 .50
78 Chris Weinke .20 .50
79 Lamar Smith .20 .50
80 Steve Smith .30 .75
81 Aaron Brooks .20 .50
82 Deuce McAllister .25 .60
83 Joe Horn .20 .50
84 Brad Johnson .25 .60
85 Keyshawn Johnson .25 .60
86 Mike Alstott .20 .50
87 Warren Sapp .25 .60
88 Jake Plummer .20 .50
89 Thomas Jones .20 .50
90 David Boston .20 .50
91 Kurt Warner .25 .60
92 Marshall Faulk .25 .60
93 Isaac Bruce .30 .75
94 Torry Holt .25 .60
95 Jeff Garcia .20 .50
96 Garrison Hearst .20 .50
97 Kevan Barlow .20 .50
98 Terrell Owens .25 .60
99 Trent Dilfer .20 .50
100 Shaun Alexander .20 .50
101 Adrian Peterson AU/360 RC 8.00 20.00
102 A.Haynesworth No Auto RC 8.00 20.00
103 Alex Brown AU/410 RC 6.00 15.00
104 Andra Davis AU/510 RC 3.00 8.00
105 Andre Davis AU/360 RC 4.00 10.00
106 Andre Lott AU/750 RC 3.00 8.00
107 Anthony Weaver AU/450 RC 3.00 8.00
108 Antonio Bryant AU/165 RC 15.00 40.00
109 Antw Randle El AU/135 RC 15.00 40.00
110 Ashley Lelie AU/360 RC 4.00 10.00
111 Brian Poli-Dixon AU/460 RC 3.00 8.00
112 Brian Westbrook AU/600 RC 12.00 30.00
113 Bryant McKinnie AU/600 RC 3.00 8.00
114 C Hutchinson AU/450 RC 3.00 8.00
115 Charles Grant AU/450 RC 5.00 12.00
116 Chester Taylor AU/315 RC 12.00 30.00
117 Cliff Russell AU/545 RC 3.00 8.00
118 Clinton Portis AU/360 RC 12.00 30.00
119 R.McMichael AU/400 RC 6.00 15.00
120 Damien Anderson AU/460 RC 3.00 8.00
121 Daniel Graham AU/185 RC 6.00 15.00
122 David Carr AU/250 RC 10.00 25.00
123 David Garrard AU/310 RC 10.00 25.00
124 Deion Branch AU/650 RC 10.00 20.00
125 John Simon AU/400 RC 4.00 10.00
126 DeShaun Foster AU/310 RC 8.00 20.00
127 Donte Stallworth AU/302 RC 6.00 15.00
128 Dwight Freeney AU/410 RC 30.00 60.00
129 Ed Reed AU/550 RC 60.00 100.00
130 Eric Crouch AU/280 RC 8.00 20.00
131 Freddie Milons AU/380 RC 4.00 10.00
132 Jabar Gaffney AU/315 RC 4.00 10.00
133 Javon Walker AU/435 RC 6.00 15.00
134 Jeremy Shockey AU/160 RC 15.00 40.00
135 Jerramy Stevens AU/250 RC 8.00 20.00
136 Joey Harrington AU/250 RC 5.00 12.00
137 John Henderson AU/560 RC 4.00 10.00
138 Jonathan Wells AU/485 RC 4.00 10.00
139 Josh McCown AU/595 RC 8.00 20.00
140 Josh Reed AU/290 RC 6.00 15.00
141 Josh Scobey AU/615 RC 4.00 10.00
142 Julius Peppers AU/40 RC 350.00 600.00
143 Kalimba Edwards AU/510 RC 4.00 10.00
144 Kelly Campbell AU/360 RC 5.00 12.00
145 Ken Simonton AU/650 RC 3.00 8.00
146 Keyuo Craver AU/850 RC 3.00 8.00
147 Kahlil Hill AU/850 RC 3.00 8.00
148 Kurt Kittner AU/235 RC 5.00 12.00
149 Ladell Betts AU/600 RC 8.00 20.00
150 Lamar Gordon AU/600 RC 4.00 10.00
151 Levar Fisher AU/760 RC 3.00 8.00
152 Lito Sheppard AU/410 RC 10.00 25.00
153 Luke Staley AU/360 RC 4.00 10.00
154 Marquise Walker AU/330 RC 4.00 10.00
155 Maurice Morris AU/153 RC 15.00 40.00
156 Mike Rumph AU/510 RC 3.00 8.00
157 Mike Williams AU/500 RC 3.00 8.00
158 Najeh Davenport AU/460 RC 3.00 8.00
159 Napoleon Harris AU/900 RC 4.00 10.00
160 Patrick Ramsey AU/575 RC 4.00 10.00
161 Buchanon No AU/310 RC 10.00 25.00
162 Quentin Jammer AU/300 RC 8.00 20.00
163 Randy Fasani AU/500 RC 3.00 8.00
164 Reche Caldwell AU/340 RC 5.00 12.00
165 Robert Thomas AU/460 RC 3.00 8.00
166 Rocky Calmus AU/385 RC 5.00 12.00
167 Rohan Davey AU/295 RC 8.00 20.00
168 Ron Johnson AU/385 RC 5.00 12.00
169 Roy Williams AU/250 RC 20.00 40.00
170 Ryan Sims No AU/360 RC 6.00 15.00
171 Tavon Mason AU/690 RC 3.00 8.00
172 Terry Charles AU/750 RC 3.00 8.00
173 T.J. Duckett AU/335 RC 8.00 20.00
174 Tim Carter AU/600 RC 4.00 10.00
175 Travis Stephens AU/170 RC 5.00 12.00
176 Trev Faulk AU/600 RC 3.00 8.00
177 Wendell Bryant AU/560 RC 3.00 8.00
178 William Green AU/317 RC 5.00 12.00
179 Woody Dantzler AU/185 RC 6.00 15.00
180 Tony Fisher AU/340 RC 4.00 10.00
181 Javin Hunter AU/400 RC 4.00 10.00
182 Daryl Jones AU/400 RC 4.00 10.00
183 Jesse Chatman AU/400 RC 4.00 10.00
184 J.T. O'Sullivan AU/340 RC 5.00 12.00
185 Josh Norman AU/340 RC 4.00 10.00
186 James Mungro AU/100 RC 5.00 12.00
NNO1 Santa Claus Red Ink
NNO2 St. Nick Green Ink

2002 Playoff Contenders 10th Anniversary

UNPRICED 10th ANNIV PRINT RUN 10

2002 Playoff Contenders Championship Ticket

*VETS 1-100: 2.5X TO 6X BASIC CARDS
1-100 VETERAN PRINT RUN 250
COMMON ROOKIE (101-186) 5.00 12.00
ROOKIE SEMISTARS 6.00 15.00
ROOKIE UNL.STARS 7.50 20.00
101-186 ROOKIE PRINT RUN 50
108 Antonio Bryant 8.00 20.00
112 Brian Westbrook 10.00 25.00
116 Chester Taylor 8.00 20.00
118 Clinton Portis 8.00 20.00
123 David Garrard 6.00 15.00
128 Dwight Freeney 10.00 25.00
129 Ed Reed 30.00 80.00
134 Jeremy Shockey 8.00 20.00
142 Julius Peppers 12.00 30.00
169 Roy Williams 5.00 12.00

2002 Playoff Contenders Hawaii 2003

*VETS 1-100 : 15X TO 40X BASIC CARDS
1-100 VETERAN PRINT RUN 15
UNPRICED 101-150 ROOKIE AU PRINT RUN 5

2002 Playoff Contenders All-Time Contenders

Inserted in packs at a rate of 1:12,this 33 card set features top NFL stars at all positions.
STATED ODDS 1:12
AT1 Corey Dillon 1.00 2.50
AT2 Ray Lewis 1.50 4.00
AT3 Mark Brunell 1.25 3.00
AT4 Eric Moulds 1.00 2.50
AT5 Tony Gonzalez 1.25 3.00
AT6 Marcus Robinson 1.25 3.00
AT7 Tim Brown 1.50 4.00
AT8 Brian Griese 1.00 2.50
AT9 Cris Carter 1.50 4.00
AT10 Tony Banks 1.00 2.50
AT11 Jamal Lewis 1.25 3.00
AT12 Jimmy Smith 1.25 3.00
AT13 Michael Strahan 1.25 3.00
AT14 David Boston 1.00 2.50
AT15 Marvin Harrison 1.25 3.00
AT16 Emmitt Smith 2.50 6.00
AT17 Robert Ferguson 1.25 3.00
AT18 Boo Williams 1.00 2.50
AT19 Mike Anderson 1.00 2.50
AT20 Isaac Bruce 1.50 4.00
AT21 Shaun Rogers 1.00 2.50
AT22 Jamal Anderson 1.25 3.00
AT23 Torry Holt 1.25 3.00
AT24 Aaron Brooks 1.00 2.50
AT25 Drew Bledsoe 1.25 3.00
AT26 Jake Plummer 1.00 2.50
AT27 Jevon Kearse 1.00 2.50
AT28 Kerry Collins 1.00 2.50
AT29 Terrell Davis 1.25 3.00
AT30 Jeff Blake 1.25 3.00
AT31 Randall Cunningham 1.25 3.00
AT32 Ricky Williams 1.25 3.00
AT33 Brett Favre 3.00 8.00

2002 Playoff Contenders All-Time Contenders Autographs

Randomly inserted in packs, this 33-card set parallels the base All-Time Contenders set featuring an autograph on the card front. The cards were autographed to various quantities of each as noted below.
STATED PRINT RUN 8-140
SERIAL #'d UNDER 15 NOT PRICED
AT1 Corey Dillon/15 12.00 30.00
AT3 Mark Brunell/25 15.00 40.00
AT4 Eric Moulds/20 12.00 30.00
AT5 Tony Gonzalez/25 15.00 40.00
AT6 Marcus Robinson/135 10.00 25.00
AT7 Tim Brown/28 30.00 80.00
AT8 Brian Griese/25 12.00 30.00
AT9 Cris Carter/25 30.00 80.00
AT10 Tony Banks/100 8.00 20.00
AT11 Jamal Lewis/20 15.00 40.00
AT12 Jimmy Smith/50 10.00 25.00
AT13 Michael Strahan/25 15.00 40.00
AT14 David Boston/19 12.00 30.00
AT15 Marvin Harrison/25 30.00 80.00
AT18 Boo Williams/50 8.00 20.00
AT19 Mike Anderson/32 12.00 30.00
AT20 Isaac Bruce/57 12.00 30.00
AT21 Shaun Rogers/20 12.00 30.00
AT23 Torry Holt/25 15.00 40.00
AT24 Aaron Brooks/15 12.00 30.00
AT26 Jake Plummer/15 12.00 30.00
AT28 Kerry Collins/18 12.00 30.00
AT30 Jeff Blake/140 10.00 25.00
AT31 Randall Cunningham/140 10.00 25.00
AT32 Ricky Williams/46 25.00 60.00
AT33 Brett Favre/15 150.00 300.00

2002 Playoff Contenders Legendary Contenders

Inserted in packs at a rate of 1:12,this 15 card set features NFL greats of the past.
STATED ODDS 1:12
LC1 Boomer Esiason 1.25 3.00
LC2 Dan Marino 3.00 8.00
LC3 Jim Kelly 1.50 4.00
LC4 John Elway 2.50 6.00
LC5 Phil Simms 1.25 3.00
LC6 Steve Young 2.00 5.00
LC7 Troy Aikman 2.00 5.00
LC8 Warren Moon 1.50 4.00
LC9 Barry Sanders 2.50 6.00
LC10 Joe Montana 5.00 12.00
LC11 John Riggins 1.25 3.00
LC12 Ronnie Lott 1.25 3.00
LC13 Thurman Thomas 1.25 3.00
LC14 Ozzie Newsome 1.25 3.00
LC15 Jack Lambert 1.50 4.00

2002 Playoff Contenders Legendary Contenders Autographs

Randomly inserted in packs, this 15-card set parallels the base Legendary Contenders set along with a hand signed autograph which varied in different quantities signed per player.
STATED PRINT RUN 10-143
SERIAL #'d UNDER 15 NOT PRICED
LC1 Boomer Esiason/17 25.00 50.00
LC2 Dan Marino/15 100.00 200.00
LC3 Jim Kelly/15 50.00 100.00
LC4 John Elway/15 100.00 200.00
LC5 Phil Simms/75 25.00 60.00
LC6 Steve Young/50 50.00 100.00
LC7 Troy Aikman/25 60.00 120.00
LC9 Barry Sanders/19 75.00 150.00
LC10 Joe Montana/63 60.00 150.00
LC11 John Riggins/141 20.00 50.00
LC13 Thurman Thomas/25 15.00 40.00
LC14 Ozzie Newsome/125 15.00 30.00
LC15 Jack Lambert/125 40.00 80.00

2002 Playoff Contenders MVP Contenders

Inserted in packs at a rate of 1:12, this 10-card set features current NFL Players who are worthy of becoming the league's MVP. An autographed version of each card was also produced and serial numbered of 25.
COMPLETE SET (10) 15.00 40.00
STATED ODDS 1:12
MVP1 Brett Favre 2.50 6.00
MVP2 Jerry Rice 2.50 6.00
MVP3 Ricky Williams 1.00 2.50
MVP4 Edgerrin James 1.00 2.50
MVP5 Emmitt Smith 2.00 5.00
MVP6 Kurt Warner 1.00 2.50
MVP7 Marshall Faulk 1.00 2.50
MVP8 Randy Moss 1.00 2.50
MVP9 Jeff Garcia .75 2.00
MVP10 Ahman Green 1.00 2.50

2002 Playoff Contenders MVP Contenders Autographs

Randomly inserted in packs,this 10 card set parallels the base MVP Contenders set along with a certified autograph and serial numbered on card back to 25.
STATED PRINT RUN 25 SER.#'d SETS
MVP1 Brett Favre 150.00 300.00
MVP2 Jerry Rice 125.00 250.00
MVP3 Ricky Williams 20.00 50.00
MVP4 Edgerrin James 20.00 50.00
MVP5 Emmitt Smith 200.00 350.00
MVP6 Kurt Warner 30.00 80.00
MVP7 Marshall Faulk 25.00 60.00
MVP8 Randy Moss 50.00 100.00
MVP9 Jeff Garcia 15.00 40.00
MVP10 Ahman Green 20.00 50.00

2002 Playoff Contenders Rookie Idols

Inserted in packs at a rate of 1:12, this 10 card set features current NFL rookies paired with another NFL star whom he admires. An autographed version of each card was also produced and serial numbered of 25.
COMPLETE SET (10) 15.00 40.00
STATED ODDS 1:12
RI1 L.Betts/T.Thomas 1.00 2.50
RI2 A.Bryant/M.Irvin 1.00 2.50
RI3 D.Garrard/P.Simms .75 2.00
RI4 E.Crouch/J.Elway 1.50 4.00
RI5 W.Green/B.Sanders 1.50 4.00
RI6 J.McCown/B.Favre 2.00 5.00
RI7 J.Harrington/D.Marino 2.00 5.00
RI8 D.Stallworth/J.Rice 2.00 5.00
RI9 J.Gaffney/T.Brown 1.00 2.50
RI10 R.Davey/D.Culpepper 1.00 2.50

2002 Playoff Contenders Rookie Idols Autographs

Randomly inserted in packs,this 10 card set parallels the base Rookie Idols set with cards also being hand signed on each side of the card by each respective player and serial numbered to 25. Some cards were issued via redemption cards that carried an expiration date of June 23, 2004.
STATED PRINT RUN 25 SER.#'d SETS
RI1 L.Betts/T.Thomas 25.00 60.00
RI2 A.Bryant/M.Irvin 25.00 60.00
RI3 D.Garrard/P.Simms 20.00 50.00
RI4 E.Crouch/J.Elway 75.00 150.00
RI5 W.Green/B.Sanders 75.00 150.00
RI6 J.McCown/B.Favre 125.00 250.00
RI7 J.Harrington/D.Marino 60.00 150.00
RI8 D.Stallworth/J.Rice 75.00 150.00
RI9 J.Gaffney/T.Brown 25.00 60.00
RI10 R.Davey/D.Culpepper 25.00 60.00

2002 Playoff Contenders Round Numbers Autographs

Randomly inserted in packs,this 10 card set features NFL rookies who were drafted in the same round. Cards are hand signed by each player one on each side of the card and are serial numbered to 75. Some cards were issued via exchange card only. Exchange expiration was 6/23/2004.
STATED PRINT RUN 75 SER.#'d SETS
*GOLD/20-30: .5X TO 1.2X BASIC AU
*GOLD/40-60: .4X TO 1X BASIC AU
GOLD STATED PRINT RUN 10-40
RN1 D.Carr/J.Harrington 10.00 25.00
RN2 Q.Jammer/R.Williams 15.00 40.00
RN3 J.Gaffney/R.Caldwell 12.00 30.00
RN4 A.Bryant/J.Reed 15.00 40.00
RN5 J.McCown/E.Crouch 15.00 40.00
RN6 M.Walker/C.Russell 10.00 25.00
RN7 J.Wells/T.Stephens 12.00 30.00
RN8 D.Garrard/R.Davey 15.00 40.00
RN9 R.Fasani/K.Kittner 10.00 25.00
RN10 J.Scobey/C.Taylor 15.00 40.00

2002 Playoff Contenders ROY Contenders

Inserted in packs at a rate of 1:12, this 10-card set features current NFL rookies who had a realistic chance at being awarded rookie of the year honors. An autographed version of each card was also produced and serial numbered of 25.
COMPLETE SET (10) 8.00 20.00
STATED ODDS 1:12
ROY1 Antonio Bryant 1.00 2.50
ROY2 Ashley Lelie .60 1.50
ROY3 David Carr .60 1.50
ROY4 DeShaun Foster 1.00 2.50
ROY5 Donte Stallworth 1.00 2.50
ROY6 Joey Harrington .60 1.50
ROY7 Quentin Jammer 1.00 2.50
ROY8 Patrick Ramsey .75 2.00
ROY9 T.J. Duckett .60 1.50
ROY10 William Green .75 2.00

2002 Playoff Contenders ROY Contenders Autographs

Randomly inserted in packs, this 10-card set parallels the base ROY Contenders inserts along with an authentic signature on the cardfronts. The cards were also serial numbered on the back to 25.
STATED PRINT RUN 25 SER.#'d SETS
ROY1 Antonio Bryant 15.00 40.00
ROY2 Ashley Lelie 10.00 25.00
ROY3 David Carr 10.00 25.00
ROY4 DeShaun Foster 15.00 40.00
ROY5 Donte Stallworth 15.00 40.00
ROY6 Joey Harrington 10.00 25.00
ROY7 Quentin Jammer 15.00 40.00
ROY8 Patrick Ramsey 12.00 30.00
ROY9 T.J. Duckett 10.00 25.00
ROY10 William Green 12.00 30.00

2002 Playoff Contenders Sophomore Contenders

Inserted in packs at a rate of 1 in 12 packs, this 20 card set features top notch players in their second season in the NFL.
STATED ODDS 1:12
SC1 Chad Johnson .50 1.25
SC2 Chris Chambers .50 1.25
SC3 David Terrell .50 1.25
SC4 Jesse Palmer .50 1.25
SC5 Kevan Barlow .50 1.25
SC6 Koren Robinson .50 1.25
SC7 LaMont Jordan .60 1.50
SC8 Michael Bennett .50 1.25
SC9 Quincy Carter .50 1.25
SC10 Santana Moss .60 1.50
SC11 Mike McMahon .50 1.25
SC12 Ken-Yon Rambo .50 1.25
SC13 Will Allen .50 1.25
SC14 Todd Heap .50 1.25
SC15 T.J. Houshmandzadeh .50 1.25
SC16 Travis Henry .50 1.25
SC17 Sage Rosenfels .60 1.50
SC18 Torrance Marshall .50 1.25
SC19 Rudi Johnson .50 1.25
SC20 Travis Minor .50 1.25

2002 Playoff Contenders Sophomore Contenders Autographs

Randomly inserted in packs, this 20 card set features top notch players in their second season in the NFL. Cards also contain a hand signed autograph on card front and were serial numbered to various quantaties signed per player.
STATED PRINT RUN 16-400
SC1 Chad Johnson/26 10.00 25.00
SC2 Chris Chambers/28 10.00 25.00
SC3 David Terrell/188 6.00 15.00
SC4 Jesse Palmer/300 6.00 15.00
SC5 Kevan Barlow/200 6.00 15.00
SC6 Koren Robinson/40 8.00 20.00
SC7 LaMont Jordan/250 8.00 20.00
SC8 Michael Bennett/34 10.00 25.00
SC9 Quincy Carter/300 6.00 15.00
SC10 Santana Moss/400 8.00 20.00
SC11 Mike McMahon/16 12.00 30.00
SC12 Ken-Yon Rambo/300 6.00 15.00
SC13 Will Allen/130 6.00 15.00
SC14 Todd Heap/61 8.00 20.00
SC15 T.J. Houshmandzadeh/220 6.00 15.00
SC16 Damione Lewis/400 6.00 15.00
SC17 Sage Rosenfels/70 10.00 25.00
SC18 Torrance Marshall/50 8.00 20.00
SC19 Rudi Johnson/350 6.00 15.00
SC20 Travis Minor/35 10.00 25.00

2003 Playoff Contenders

Released in January of 2004, this set consists of 200 cards including 100 veterans and 100 rookie ticket autographs. Within the rookie ticket autographs subset are 95 players and 5 coaches. Each rookie ticket is serial numbered to various quantities as noted below. Many players signed a number of cards in both black and blue ink. Playoff announced the print runs of many of those color variations in April 2004. We've noted below just those variations for key players with a significant print run difference. Several rookies were only issued in packs as exchange cards with an expiration date of 7/1/2005. Boxes contained 24 packs of 5 cards. SRP was $6 per pack.
COMP.SET w/o SP's (100) 7.50 20.00
1 Roy Williams .20 .50
2 Antonio Bryant .20 .50
3 Jeremy Shockey .20 .50
4 Kerry Collins .20 .50
5 Tiki Barber .25 .60
6 Michael Strahan .25 .60
7 Donovan McNabb .25 .60
8 Duce Staley .20 .50
9 Todd Pinkston .20 .50
10 Patrick Ramsey .25 .60
11 Laveranues Coles .20 .50
12 Rod Gardner .20 .50
13 Drew Bledsoe .25 .60
14 Travis Henry .20 .50
15 Eric Moulds .20 .50
16 Josh Reed .20 .50
17 Ricky Williams .25 .60
18 Jay Fiedler .20 .50
19 Chris Chambers .20 .50
20 Zach Thomas .25 .60
21 Junior Seau .25 .60
22 Tom Brady 1.25 3.00
23 Troy Brown .20 .50
24 Chad Pennington .20 .50
25 Curtis Martin .25 .60
26 Santana Moss .25 .60
27 Emmitt Smith .50 1.25
28 Jeff Garcia .20 .50
29 Terrell Owens .25 .60
30 Kevan Barlow .20 .50
31 Shaun Alexander .20 .50
32 Matt Hasselbeck .20 .50
33 Koren Robinson .25 .60
34 Kurt Warner .25 .60
35 Marshall Faulk .25 .60
36 Torry Holt .25 .60
37 Isaac Bruce .30 .75
38 Clinton Portis .20 .50
39 Jake Plummer .20 .50
40 Rod Smith .25 .60
41 Ed McCaffrey .25 .60
42 Ashley Lelie .20 .50
43 Priest Holmes .20 .50
44 Trent Green .20 .50
45 Tony Gonzalez .25 .60
46 Jerry Rice .60 1.50
47 Rich Gannon .25 .60
48 Tim Brown .30 .75
49 Jerry Porter .20 .50
50 Charles Woodson .30 .75
51 LaDainian Tomlinson .30 .75
52 Drew Brees .30 .75
53 David Boston .20 .50
54 Brian Urlacher .30 .75
55 Kordell Stewart .20 .50
56 Marty Booker .20 .50
57 Joey Harrington .20 .50
58 Brett Favre .60 1.50
59 Ahman Green .25 .60
60 Donald Driver .25 .60
61 Javon Walker .25 .60
62 Randy Moss .25 .60
63 Daunte Culpepper .25 .60
64 Michael Bennett .20 .50
65 Jamal Lewis .25 .60
66 Ray Lewis .30 .75
67 Corey Dillon .20 .50
68 Chad Johnson .20 .50
69 William Green .20 .50
70 Tim Couch .20 .50
71 Quincy Morgan .20 .50
72 Plaxico Burress .20 .50
73 Tommy Maddox .20 .50
74 Hines Ward .25 .60
75 Antwaan Randle El .20 .50
76 Michael Vick .25 .60
77 Peerless Price .20 .50
78 Warrick Dunn .20 .50
79 T.J. Duckett .20 .50
80 Julius Peppers .30 .75
81 Stephen Davis .20 .50
82 Deuce McAllister .25 .60
83 Aaron Brooks .20 .50
84 Joe Horn .20 .50
85 Donte Stallworth .20 .50
86 Mike Alstott .20 .50
87 Brad Johnson .25 .60
88 Keyshawn Johnson .30 .75
89 Warren Sapp .25 .60
90 David Carr .20 .50
91 Jabar Gaffney .20 .50
92 Peyton Manning .75 2.00
93 Edgerrin James .25 .60
94 Marvin Harrison .25 .60
95 Mark Brunell .25 .60
96 Fred Taylor .20 .50
97 Jimmy Smith .25 .60
98 Steve McNair .25 .60
99 Eddie George .25 .60
100 Jevon Kearse .20 .50
101 Lee Suggs AU/499 RC 4.00 10.00
102 Charles Rogers AU/204 RC 15.00 40.00
103 Brandon Lloyd AU/589 RC 12.00 30.00
104 Terrence Edwards AU/399 RC 4.00 10.00
105 Mike Pinkard AU/849 RC 4.00 10.00
106 DeWayne White AU/524 RC 4.00 10.00
107 J.McDougle AU/339 RC 4.00 10.00
108 Jimmy Kennedy AU/514 RC 5.00 12.00
109 William Joseph AU/764 RC 4.00 10.00
110 E.J. Henderson AU/774 RC 5.00 12.00
111 Mike Doss AU/574 RC 6.00 15.00
112A C.Simms Blu AU/310 RC 12.00 30.00
112B C.Simms Blk AU/79 RC 40.00 80.00
113 Cecil Sapp AU/474 RC 4.00 10.00
114 Justin Gage AU/579 RC 5.00 12.00
115 Sam Aiken AU/664 RC 5.00 12.00
116 Doug Gabriel AU/389 RC 5.00 12.00
117 Jason Witten AU/599 RC 100.00 175.00
118 Bennie Joppru AU/449 RC 4.00 10.00
119 Chris Kelsay AU/864 RC 5.00 12.00
120 Johnathan Sullivan/924 RC 2.50 6.00
121 Kevin Williams AU/764 RC 10.00 20.00
122 Rien Long AU/849 RC 4.00 10.00
123 Kenny Peterson/674 RC 3.00 8.00
124 Boss Bailey AU/564 RC 5.00 12.00
125 Dennis Weathersby AU/774 RC 4.00 10.00
126A C.Palmer Blk AU/36 RC 150.00 300.00
126B C.Palmer Blu AU/158 RC 100.00 200.00
127 Byron Leftwich AU/169 RC 20.00 50.00
128 Kyle Boller AU/439 RC 4.00 10.00
129 Rex Grossman AU/494 RC 5.00 12.00
130 Dave Ragone AU/344 RC 4.00 10.00
131 Brian St.Pierre AU/554 RC 4.00 10.00
132 Kliff Kingsbury AU/879 RC 6.00 15.00
133 Seneca Wallace AU/864 RC 10.00 25.00
134 Larry Johnson AU/344 RC 12.00 30.00
135 Will McGahee AU/369 RC 12.00 30.00
136 Justin Fargas AU/354 RC 10.00 25.00
137 Onterrio Smith AU/414 RC 4.00 10.00
138 Chris Brown AU/279 RC 7.50 20.00
139 Musa Smith AU/379 RC 4.00 10.00
140 Artose Pinner AU/364 RC 4.00 10.00
141 Andre Johnson AU/199 RC 100.00 200.00
142 K.Washington AU/472 RC 4.00 10.00
143 Taylor Jacobs AU/349 RC 4.00 10.00
144 Bryant Johnson AU/389 RC 6.00 15.00
145 Tyrone Calico AU/499 RC 4.00 10.00
146 Anquan Boldin AU/524 RC 25.00 50.00
147 Bethel Johnson AU/484 RC 4.00 10.00
148 Nate Burleson AU/549 RC 5.00 12.00
149 Kevin Curtis AU/455 RC 10.00 25.00
150 Dallas Clark AU/539 RC 6.00 15.00
151 Teyo Johnson AU/389 RC 5.00 12.00
152 Terrell Suggs AU/564 RC 15.00 40.00
153 DeWayne Robertson/689 RC 3.00 8.00
154 Terence Newman AU/364 RC 10.00 25.00
155 Marcus Trufant AU/739 RC 5.00 12.00
156 Tony Romo AU/999 RC 100.00 200.00
157 Brooks Bollinger AU/974 RC 5.00 12.00
158 Ken Dorsey AU/774 RC 5.00 12.00
159 Kirk Farmer AU/999 RC 5.00 12.00
160 Jason Gesser AU/999 RC 5.00 12.00
161 Brock Forsey AU/999 RC 5.00 12.00
162 Quentin Griffin AU/999 RC 5.00 12.00
163 Avon Cobourne AU/974 RC 4.00 10.00
164 Domanick Davis AU/999 RC 5.00 12.00
165 Tony Hollings AU/974 RC 5.00 12.00
166 L.Toefield AU/799 RC 4.00 10.00
167 Arlen Harris AU/974 RC 4.00 10.00
168 Sultan McCullough AU/989 RC 4.00 10.00
169 V.Shiancoe AU/999 RC 10.00 20.00
170 L.J. Smith AU/974 RC 6.00 15.00
171 LaTarence Dunbar AU/999 RC 4.00 10.00
172 Walter Young AU/889 RC 4.00 10.00
173 Bobby Wade AU/989 RC 5.00 12.00
174 Zuriel Smith AU/989 RC 4.00 10.00
175 Adrian Madise AU/999 RC 4.00 10.00
176 Ken Hamlin AU/989 RC 6.00 15.00
177 Carl Ford AU/999 RC 4.00 10.00
178 Cortez Hankton AU/989 RC 5.00 12.00
179 J.R. Tolver AU/889 RC 5.00 12.00
180 Keenan Howry AU/999 RC 4.00 10.00
181 Billy McMullen AU/899 RC 4.00 10.00
182 Arnaz Battle AU/989 RC 7.50 20.00
183 Shaun McDonald AU/899 RC 5.00 12.00
184 Andre Woolfolk AU/989 RC 4.00 10.00
185 Sammy Davis AU/999 RC 5.00 12.00
186 Calvin Pace AU/999 RC 4.00 10.00
187 Michael Haynes AU/999 RC 4.00 10.00
188 Ty Warren AU/999 RC 5.00 12.00
189 Nick Barnett AU/999 RC 6.00 15.00
190 Troy Polamalu AU/989 RC 150.00 300.00
191 Eric Parker AU/589 RC 6.00 15.00
192 Justin Griffith AU/589 RC 5.00 12.00
193 David Tyree AU/599 RC 10.00 25.00
194 Pisa Tinoisamoa/599 RC 4.00 10.00
195 Rashean Mathis AU/589 RC 4.00 10.00
196 Mike Sherman AU/574 RC 6.00 15.00
197 Dave Wannstedt AU/574 RC 7.50 20.00
198 Dick Vermeil AU/574 RC 15.00 30.00
199 Tony Dungy AU/574 RC 25.00 50.00
200 Mike Martz AU/574 RC 7.50 20.00

2003 Playoff Contenders Championship Ticket

UNPRICED CHAMPIONSHIP PRINT RUN 1
NOT PRICED DUE TO SCARCITY

2003 Playoff Contenders Hawaii 2004

*VETS 1-100: 8X TO 20X BASIC CARDS
UNPRICED ROOKIE AU PRINT RUN 5-10

2003 Playoff Contenders Orange County

UNPRICED ORANGE COUNTY PRINT RUN 5

2003 Playoff Contenders Playoff Ticket

*VETS: 4X TO 10X BASIC CARDS
1-100 VET STATED PRINT RUN 150
101-200 ROOKIE PRINT RUN 30
101 Lee Suggs 8.00 20.00
102 Charles Rogers 10.00 25.00
103 Brandon Lloyd 12.00 30.00
104 Terrence Edwards 8.00 20.00
105 Mike Pinkard 8.00 20.00
106 DeWayne White 8.00 20.00
107 Jerome McDougle 8.00 20.00
108 Jimmy Kennedy 10.00 25.00
109 William Joseph 8.00 20.00
110 E.J. Henderson 10.00 25.00
111 Mike Doss 12.00 30.00
112 Chris Simms 8.00 20.00
113 Cecil Sapp 8.00 20.00
114 Justin Gage 10.00 25.00
115 Sam Aiken 10.00 25.00
116 Doug Gabriel 10.00 25.00
117 Jason Witten 30.00 80.00
118 Bennie Joppru 8.00 20.00
119 Chris Kelsay 10.00 25.00
120 Johnathan Sullivan 8.00 20.00
121 Kevin Williams 12.00 30.00
122 Rien Long 8.00 20.00
123 Kenny Peterson 10.00 25.00
124 Boss Bailey 10.00 25.00
125 Dennis Weathersby 8.00 20.00
126 Carson Palmer 15.00 40.00
127 Byron Leftwich 10.00 25.00
128 Kyle Boller 8.00 20.00
129 Rex Grossman 10.00 25.00
130 Dave Ragone 8.00 20.00
131 Brian St.Pierre 8.00 20.00
132 Kliff Kingsbury 12.00 30.00
133 Seneca Wallace 10.00 25.00
134 Larry Johnson 10.00 25.00
135 Willis McGahee 15.00 40.00
136 Justin Fargas 12.00 30.00
137 Onterrio Smith 8.00 20.00
138 Chris Brown 8.00 20.00
139 Musa Smith 8.00 20.00
140 Artose Pinner 8.00 20.00
141 Andre Johnson 20.00 50.00
142 Kelley Washington 8.00 20.00
143 Taylor Jacobs 8.00 20.00
144 Bryant Johnson 12.00 30.00
145 Tyrone Calico 8.00 20.00
146 Anquan Boldin 12.00 30.00
147 Bethel Johnson 8.00 20.00
148 Nate Burleson 10.00 25.00
149 Kevin Curtis 8.00 20.00
150 Dallas Clark 12.00 30.00
151 Teyo Johnson 10.00 25.00
152 Terrell Suggs 10.00 25.00
153 DeWayne Robertson 10.00 25.00
154 Terence Newman 12.00 30.00
155 Marcus Trufant 10.00 25.00
156 Tony Romo 125.00 250.00
157 Brooks Bollinger 10.00 25.00
158 Ken Dorsey 10.00 25.00
159 Kirk Farmer 10.00 25.00
160 Jason Gesser 10.00 25.00
161 Brock Forsey 10.00 25.00
162 Quentin Griffin 10.00 25.00
163 Avon Cobourne 8.00 20.00
164 Domanick Davis 10.00 25.00
165 Tony Hollings 10.00 25.00
166 LaBrandon Toefield 8.00 20.00
167 Arlen Harris 8.00 20.00
168 Sultan McCullough 8.00 20.00
169 Visanthe Shiancoe 12.00 30.00
170 L.J. Smith 12.00 30.00
171 LaTarence Dunbar 8.00 20.00
172 Walter Young 8.00 20.00
173 Bobby Wade 10.00 25.00
174 Zuriel Smith 8.00 20.00
175 Adrian Madise 8.00 20.00
176 Ken Hamlin 12.00 30.00
177 Carl Ford 8.00 20.00
178 Cortez Hankton 10.00 25.00
179 J.R. Tolver 10.00 25.00
180 Keenan Howry 8.00 20.00
181 Billy McMullen 8.00 20.00
182 Arnaz Battle 12.00 30.00
183 Shaun McDonald 10.00 25.00
184 Andre Woolfolk 8.00 20.00
185 Sammy Davis 10.00 25.00
186 Calvin Pace 8.00 20.00
187 Michael Haynes 8.00 20.00
188 Ty Warren 10.00 25.00
189 Nick Barnett 12.00 30.00
190 Troy Polamalu 150.00 250.00
191 Eric Parker 12.00 30.00
192 Justin Griffith 10.00 25.00
193 David Tyree 10.00 25.00
194 Pisa Tinoisamoa 12.00 30.00
195 Rashean Mathis 8.00 20.00
196 Mike Sherman 12.00 30.00
197 Dave Wannstedt 10.00 25.00
198 Dick Vermeil 12.00 30.00
199 Tony Dungy
200 Mike Martz 10.00 25.00

2003 Playoff Contenders Legendary Contenders

COMPLETE SET (10) 15.00 30.00
STATED ODDS 1:24
LC1 Barry Sanders 2.50 6.00
LC2 Franco Harris 2.00 5.00
LC3 Jim Brown 2.00 5.00
LC4 Jim Kelly 1.50 4.00
LC5 Joe Greene 1.50 4.00
LC6 Larry Csonka 1.50 4.00
LC7 Reggie White 1.50 4.00
LC8 Roger Staubach 2.00 5.00
LC9 Steve Largent 1.50 4.00
LC10 Cris Carter 1.60 4.00

2003 Playoff Contenders Legendary Contenders Autographs
Randomly inserted into packs, this set features authentic player autographs on silver foil stickers. Each card is serial numbered to 25.

STATED PRINT RUN 25 SERIAL #'d SETS
LC1 Barry Sanders 100.00 175.00
LC2 Franco Harris 40.00 80.00
LC3 Jim Brown 60.00 120.00
LC4 Jim Kelly 40.00 80.00
LC5 Joe Greene 35.00 60.00
LC6 Larry Csonka 40.00 80.00
LC7 Reggie White 125.00 225.00
LC8 Roger Staubach 50.00 100.00
LC9 Steve Largent 50.00 100.00
LC10 Cris Carter 30.00 60.00

2003 Playoff Contenders MVP Contenders
COMPLETE SET (15) 15.00 40.00
STATED ODDS 1:24
MVP1 Brett Favre 2.50 6.00
MVP2 Brian Urlacher 1.25 3.00
MVP3 Chad Pennington .75 2.00
MVP4 Clinton Portis .75 2.00
MVP5 Drew Bledsoe 1.00 2.50
MVP6 Jeff Garcia .75 2.00
MVP7 Jerry Rice 2.50 6.00
MVP8 Joey Harrington .75 2.00
MVP9 Kurt Warner 1.00 2.50
MVP10 LaDainian Tomlinson 1.25 3.00
MVP11 Marvin Harrison 1.00 2.50
MVP12 Michael Vick 1.00 2.50
MVP13 Randy Moss 1.00 2.50
MVP14 Ricky Williams 1.00 2.50
MVP15 Tom Brady 5.00 12.00

2003 Playoff Contenders MVP Contenders Autographs
Randomly inserted into packs, this set features authentic player autographs on silver foil stickers. Each card is serial numbered to 25. Please note that Tom Brady, Jeff Garcia, Chad Pennington, Michael Vick and Kurt Warner were issued in packs as exchange cards with an expiration date of 7/1/2005.

STATED PRINT RUN 25 SER.#'d SETS
MVP1 Brett Favre 175.00 300.00
MVP2 Brian Urlacher 25.00 60.00
MVP3 Chad Pennington 15.00 40.00
MVP4 Clinton Portis 15.00 40.00
MVP5 Drew Bledsoe 20.00 50.00
MVP6 Jeff Garcia 15.00 40.00
MVP7 Jerry Rice 150.00 250.00
MVP8 Joey Harrington 15.00 40.00
MVP9 Kurt Warner 20.00 50.00
MVP10 LaDainian Tomlinson 75.00 135.00
MVP11 Marvin Harrison 20.00 50.00
MVP12 Michael Vick 60.00 100.00
MVP13 Randy Moss 100.00 200.00
MVP14 Ricky Williams 20.00 50.00
MVP15 Tom Brady 175.00 300.00

2003 Playoff Contenders Rookie Round Up
PRINT RUN 375 SERIAL #'d SETS
RR1 Anquan Boldin 1.50 4.00
RR2 Bryant Johnson 1.50 4.00
RR3 Kyle Boller 1.00 2.50
RR4 Musa Smith 1.00 2.50
RR5 Terrell Suggs 1.25 3.00
RR6 Sam Aiken 1.25 3.00
RR7 Willis McGahee 1.25 3.00
RR8 Walter Young 1.00 2.50
RR9 Rex Grossman 1.25 3.00
RR10 Carson Palmer 2.00 5.00
RR11 Kelley Washington 1.00 2.50
RR12 Ken Hamlin 1.50 4.00
RR13 Terence Newman 1.50 4.00
RR14 Adrian Madise 1.00 2.50
RR15 Artose Pinner 1.00 2.50
RR16 Boss Bailey 1.25 3.00
RR17 Charles Rogers 1.25 3.00
RR18 Eugene Wilson 1.50 4.00
RR19 Nick Barnett 1.50 4.00
RR20 Andre Johnson 2.50 6.00
RR21 Dave Ragone 1.00 2.50
RR22 Domanick Davis 1.25 3.00
RR23 Tony Hollings 1.25 3.00
RR24 Dallas Clark 1.50 4.00
RR25 Mike Doss 1.50 4.00
RR26 Byron Leftwich 1.25 3.00
RR27 LaBrandon Toefield 1.00 2.50
RR28 Larry Johnson 1.25 3.00
RR29 J.R. Tolver 1.25 3.00
RR30 Nate Burleson 1.25 3.00
RR31 Onterrio Smith 1.00 2.50
RR32 Bethel Johnson 1.00 2.50
RR33 Cortez Hankton 1.25 3.00
RR34 B.J. Askew 1.25 3.00
RR35 DeWayne Robertson 1.25 3.00
RR36 Justin Fargas 1.50 4.00
RR37 Teyo Johnson 1.25 3.00
RR38 Billy McMullen 1.00 2.50
RR39 Jerome McDougle 1.00 2.50
RR40 Troy Polamalu 15.00 30.00
RR41 Sammy Davis 1.25 3.00
RR42 Arnaz Battle 1.50 4.00
RR43 Brandon Lloyd 1.50 4.00
RR44 Marcus Trufant 1.25 3.00
RR45 Seneca Wallace 1.25 3.00
RR46 Kevin Curtis 1.00 2.50
RR47 Shaun McDonald 1.25 3.00
RR48 Chris Simms 1.00 2.50
RR49 Tyrone Calico 1.00 2.50
RR50 Taylor Jacobs 1.00 2.50

2003 Playoff Contenders Round Numbers Autographs
Randomly inserted into packs, this set features authentic player autographs on silver foil stickers. Cards R1-R10 are serial numbered to 100, while cards R11-R15 are serial numbered to 50.

RN1-RN10 DUAL AU PRINT RUN 100
RN11-RN15 QUAD AU PRINT RUN 50
*RN1-RN10 GOLD/20-30: .8X TO 2X
*RN11-RN15 GOLD/20-30: .5X TO 1.2X
GOLD STATED PRINT RUN 10-30
RN1 C.Palmer/B.Leftwich 20.00 50.00
RN2 C.Rogers/Br.Johnson 15.00 40.00
RN3 K.Boller/R.Grossman 12.00 30.00
RN4 W.McGahee/L.Johnson 12.00 30.00
RN5 T.Jacobs/A.Boldin 20.00 50.00
RN6 Be.Johnson/T.Calico 10.00 25.00
RN7 D.Ragone/C.Simms 10.00 25.00
RN8 M.Smith/C.Brown 10.00 25.00
RN9 J.Fargas/K.Curtis 15.00 40.00
RN10 K.Washington/N.Burleson 12.00 30.00
RN11 Palm/Left/Rogrs/A.Jhnsn 50.00 120.00
RN12 Boll/Gros/McGa/L.Jhnsn 8.00 20.00
RN13 Jac/Bold/Be.Jhnsn/Calico 40.00 100.00
RN14 Rag/Simm/M.Smith/Brown 20.00 50.00
RN15 Farg/Curt/Wash/Burles 12.00 30.00

2003 Playoff Contenders ROY Contenders
COMPLETE SET (10) 12.00 30.00
STATED ODDS 1:24
ROY1 Carson Palmer 1.25 3.00
ROY2 Byron Leftwich .75 2.00
ROY3 Charles Rogers .75 2.00
ROY4 Andre Johnson 1.50 4.00
ROY5 DeWayne Robertson .75 2.00
ROY6 Terence Newman 1.00 2.50
ROY7 Terrell Suggs .75 2.00
ROY8 Kyle Boller .60 1.50
ROY9 Rex Grossman .75 2.00

2003 Playoff Contenders ROY Contenders Autographs
Randomly inserted into packs, this set features authentic player autographs on silver foil stickers. Each card is serial numbered to 25. Please note that DeWayne Robertson was issued in packs as an exchange card with an expiration date of 7/1/2005.

STATED PRINT RUN 25 SER.#'d SETS
ROY1 Carson Palmer 60.00 150.00
ROY2 Byron Leftwich 12.00 30.00
ROY3 Charles Rogers 12.00 30.00
ROY4 Andre Johnson 100.00 200.00
ROY5 De.Robertson No Auto 6.00 15.00
ROY6 Terence Newman 15.00 40.00
ROY7 Terrell Suggs 30.00 60.00
ROY8 Kyle Boller 10.00 25.00
ROY9 Rex Grossman 12.00 30.00
ROY10 Larry Johnson 12.00 30.00

2004 Playoff Contenders
Playoff Contenders initially released in mid-January 2005 and was once-again one of the most popular releases of the 2004 season. The base set consists of 200-cards including 100-autographed rookie cards. While the signed cards are not serial numbered this year, Playoff did publicly announce print runs on many of the cards as noted below. Hobby boxes contained 24-packs of 4-cards and carried an S.R.P. of $6 per pack. Two parallel sets and a variety of inserts can be found seeded in packs highlighted by the Legendary Contenders Autographs, the MVP Contenders Autographs, and the ROY Contenders Autograph inserts.

COMP.SET w/o SP's (100) 7.50 20.00
1 Anquan Boldin .20 .50
2 Emmitt Smith .50 1.25
3 Josh McCown .25 .60
4 Michael Vick .25 .60
5 Peerless Price .20 .50
6 T.J. Duckett .20 .50
7 Warrick Dunn .20 .50
8 Jamal Lewis .25 .60
9 Kyle Boller .20 .50
10 Ray Lewis .30 .75
11 Drew Bledsoe .25 .60
12 Eric Moulds .20 .50
13 Travis Henry .20 .50
14 Willis McGahee .20 .50
15 DeShaun Foster .25 .60
16 Jake Delhomme .20 .50
17 Stephen Davis .20 .50
18 Steve Smith .30 .75
19 Brian Urlacher .30 .75
20 Rex Grossman .20 .50
21 Thomas Jones .20 .50
22 Carson Palmer .25 .60
23 Chad Johnson .20 .50
24 Rudi Johnson .20 .50
25 Jeff Garcia .20 .50
26 Lee Suggs .25 .60
27 William Green .20 .50
28 Keyshawn Johnson .25 .60
29 Roy Williams S .20 .50
30 Eddie George .25 .60
31 Ashley Lelie .20 .50
32 Jake Plummer .20 .50
33 Quentin Griffin .20 .50
34 Rod Smith .25 .60
35 Charles Rogers .20 .50
36 Joey Harrington .20 .50
37 Ahman Green .25 .60
38 Brett Favre .60 1.50
39 Javon Walker .20 .50
40 Andre Johnson .25 .60
41 David Carr .20 .50
42 Domanick Davis .20 .50
43 Edgerrin James .25 .60
44 Marvin Harrison .25 .60
45 Peyton Manning .75 2.00
46 Byron Leftwich .20 .50
47 Fred Taylor .20 .50
48 Jimmy Smith .25 .60
49 Priest Holmes .20 .50
50 Tony Gonzalez .25 .60
51 Trent Green .20 .50
52 A.J. Feeley .20 .50
53 Chris Chambers .20 .50
54 Deion Sanders .25 .60
55 Daunte Culpepper .25 .60
56 Michael Bennett .20 .50
57 Randy Moss .25 .60
58 Corey Dillon .20 .50
59 Deion Branch .20 .50
60 Tom Brady 1.25 3.00
61 Aaron Brooks .20 .50
62 Deuce McAllister .25 .60
63 Donte Stallworth .20 .50
64 Joe Horn .20 .50
65 Amani Toomer .20 .50
66 Jeremy Shockey .20 .50
67 Michael Strahan .25 .60
68 Tiki Barber .25 .60
69 Chad Pennington .20 .50
70 Curtis Martin .25 .60
71 Santana Moss .25 .60
72 Jerry Porter .20 .50
73 Jerry Rice .60 1.50
74 Warren Sapp .25 .60
75 Brian Westbrook .20 .50
76 Donovan McNabb .25 .60
77 Jevon Kearse .20 .50
78 Terrell Owens .25 .60
79 Antwaan Randle El .20 .50
80 Hines Ward .25 .60
81 Jerome Bettis .30 .75
82 LaDainian Tomlinson .30 .75
83 Kevan Barlow .20 .50
84 Tim Rattay .20 .50
85 Koren Robinson .20 .50
86 Matt Hasselbeck .20 .50
87 Shaun Alexander .20 .50
88 Isaac Bruce .30 .75
89 Marc Bulger .20 .50
90 Marshall Faulk .25 .60
91 Torry Holt .25 .60
92 Brad Johnson .25 .60
93 Mike Alstott .20 .50
94 Chris Brown .20 .50
95 Derrick Mason .20 .50
96 Steve McNair .25 .60
97 Clinton Portis .20 .50
98 LaVar Arrington .20 .50
99 Laveranues Coles .20 .50
100 Mark Brunell .25 .60
101 Adimchinobe Echemandu AU RC 5.00 12.00
102 Ahmad Carroll AU/574* RC 4.00 10.00
103 Andy Hall AU RC 4.00 10.00
104 B.J. Johnson AU RC 4.00 10.00
105 B.J. Symons AU RC 4.00 10.00
106 Roethlisberger AU/541* RC 400.00 800.00
107 Ben Troupe AU/540* RC 4.00 10.00
108 Ben Watson AU/660* RC 5.00 12.00
110 Brandon Miree AU RC 4.00 10.00
111 Bruce Perry AU RC 4.00 10.00
112 Carlos Francis AU RC 4.00 10.00
113 Casey Bramlet AU RC 4.00 10.00
114 Cedric Cobbs AU/630* RC 4.00 10.00
115 Chris Gamble AU/490* RC 4.00 10.00
116 Chris Perry AU/478* RC 6.00 15.00
117 Clarence Moore AU RC 4.00 10.00
118 Cody Pickett AU RC 4.00 10.00
119 Craig Krenzel AU RC 4.00 10.00
120 D.J. Hackett AU/325* RC 8.00 20.00
121 D.J. Williams AU/490* RC 6.00 15.00
122 Darius Watts AU RC 4.00 10.00
123 DeAngelo Hall AU RC 10.00 25.00
124 Derrick Hamilton AU/373* RC 5.00 12.00
125 Derrick Ward AU RC 6.00 15.00
126 Devard Darling AU/325* RC 5.00 12.00
127 D.Henderson AU/475* RC 10.00 25.00
128 Drew Carter AU RC 5.00 12.00
129 Drew Henson AU/415* RC 4.00 10.00
130 D.Robinson AU/660* RC 4.00 10.00
131 Eli Manning AU/372* RC 150.00 300.00
132 Ernest Wilford AU/365* RC 6.00 15.00
133 Greg Jones AU/553* RC 6.00 15.00
134 J.P. Losman AU/358* RC 8.00 20.00
135 Jamaar Taylor AU RC 4.00 10.00
136 Jared Lorenzen AU RC 5.00 12.00
137 Jarrett Payton AU RC 5.00 12.00
138 Jason Babin AU RC 6.00 15.00
139 Jeff Smoker AU RC 5.00 12.00
140 J.Cotchery AU/325* RC 8.00 20.00
141 Jim Sorgi AU RC 5.00 12.00
142 John Navarre AU RC 4.00 10.00
143 Johnnie Morant AU/325* RC 5.00 12.00
144 Jonathan Vilma AU SP RC 5.00 12.00
145 Josh Harris AU/555* RC 4.00 10.00
146 Julius Jones AU/252* RC 10.00 25.00
147 Keary Colbert AU/495* RC 4.00 10.00
148 Kel.Winslow AU/135* RC 20.00 50.00
149 Kenechi Udeze AU/475* RC 5.00 12.00
150 Kevin Jones AU/327* RC 8.00 20.00
151 L.Fitzgerald AU/50* RC 500.00 800.00
152 Lee Evans AU/375* RC 10.00 25.00
153 Luke McCown AU/543* RC 4.00 10.00
154 Matt Mauck AU RC 4.00 10.00
155 Matt Schaub AU/367* RC 12.00 30.00
156 Maurice Mann AU RC 4.00 10.00
157 Mewelde Moore AU/435* RC 8.00 20.00
158 Michael Clayton AU/325* RC 8.00 20.00
159 Michael Jenkins AU/412* RC 8.00 20.00
160 M.Turner AU/535* RC 12.00 30.00
161 P.K. Sam AU/300* RC 5.00 12.00
162 Philip Rivers AU/556* RC 250.00 500.00
163 Quincy Wilson AU/350* RC 5.00 12.00
164 Ran Carthon AU RC 4.00 10.00
165 Rashaun Woods AU RC 4.00 10.00
166 Re.Williams AU/336* RC 8.00 20.00
167 R.Colclough AU/640* RC 4.00 10.00
168 Robert Gallery AU/310* RC 10.00 25.00
169 Roy Williams AU/564* RC 6.00 15.00
170 Samie Parker AU/356* RC 5.00 12.00
171 Sean Jones AU RC 4.00 10.00
172 S.Taylor/575* RC No Auto 10.00 25.00
173 Sloan Thomas AU RC 5.00 12.00
174 Steven Jackson AU/333* RC 15.00 40.00
175 Tatum Bell AU/539* RC 6.00 15.00
176 Tommie Harris AU/365* RC 6.00 15.00
177 Triandos Luke AU RC 4.00 10.00
178 Troy Fleming AU RC 4.00 10.00
179 Vince Wilfork AU/315* RC 25.00 50.00
180 Will Smith AU/565* RC 5.00 12.00
181 Marcus Tubbs AU RC 4.00 10.00
182 Michael Boulware AU RC 6.00 15.00
183 Kris Wilson AU RC 5.00 12.00
184 Richard Smith AU RC 4.00 10.00
185 Teddy Lehman AU RC 4.00 10.00
186 Chris Cooley AU RC 6.00 15.00
187 Thomas Tapeh AU RC 5.00 12.00
188A Willie Parker Blk AU RC 10.00 25.00
188B Willie Parker Blu AU RC 15.00 40.00
189 Patrick Crayton AU RC 8.00 20.00
190 Kendrick Starling AU RC 4.00 10.00
191 B.J. Sams AU RC 4.00 10.00
192 Derick Armstrong AU 4.00 10.00
193 Wes Welker AU RC 25.00 60.00
194 Erik Coleman AU RC 5.00 12.00
195 Gibril Wilson AU RC 6.00 15.00
196 Andy Reid AU/335* RC 15.00 30.00
197 Brian Billick AU/585* RC 6.00 15.00
198 Jeff Fisher AU/585* RC 8.00 20.00
199 Jon Gruden AU/585* RC 12.00 30.00
200 Marvin Lewis AU/585* RC 6.00 15.00

2004 Playoff Contenders Playoff Ticket
1-100 PRINT RUN 150 SER.#'d SETS
COMMON ROOKIE 101-200 3.00 8.00
ROOKIE SEMISTARS 4.00 10.00
ROOKIE UNL.STARS 5.00 12.00
101-200 PRINT RUN 50 SER.#'d SETS
106 Ben Roethlisberger 40.00 100.00
116 Chris Perry 3.00 8.00
123 DeAngelo Hall 5.00 12.00
131 Eli Manning 25.00 60.00
134 J.P. Losman 3.00 8.00
146 Julius Jones 3.00 8.00
148 Kellen Winslow Jr. 3.00 8.00
151 Larry Fitzgerald 12.00 30.00
152 Lee Evans 5.00 12.00
155 Matt Schaub 3.00 8.00
160 Michael Turner 3.00 8.00
162 Philip Rivers 10.00 25.00
169 Roy Williams WR 3.00 8.00
174 Steven Jackson 5.00 12.00
188 Willie Parker 5.00 12.00
189 Patrick Crayton 5.00 12.00
193 Wes Welker 20.00 40.00
196 Andy Reid 5.00 12.00
197 Brian Billick 5.00 12.00
198 Jeff Fisher 5.00 12.00
199 Jon Gruden 5.00 12.00
200 Marvin Lewis 5.00 12.00

2004 Playoff Contenders Hawaii 2005
*SINGLES: 6X TO 15X BASIC CARDS
STATED PRINT RUN 25 SER.#'d SETS

2004 Playoff Contenders Legendary Contenders Orange
ORANGE PRINT RUN 2000 SER.#'d SETS
*BLUE/250: .6X TO 1.5X ORNG/2000
BLUE PRINT RUN 250 SER.#'d SETS
*GREEN/100: 1X TO 2.5X ORNG/2000
GREEN PRINT RUN 100 SER.#'d SETS
*RED/750: .5X TO 1.2X ORNG/2000
RED PRINT RUN 750 SER.#'d SETS
LC1 Barry Sanders 1.25 3.00
LC2 Don Shula .75 2.00
LC3 Gale Sayers .75 2.00
LC4 Herman Edwards .60 1.50
LC5 Joe Montana 2.50 6.00
LC6 Joe Namath 1.25 3.00
LC7 Larry Csonka .75 2.00
LC8 Mark Bavaro .50 1.25
LC9 Michael Irvin .75 2.00
LC10 Roger Staubach 1.00 2.50

2004 Playoff Contenders Legendary Contenders Autographs
AUTOS PRINT RUN 25 SER.#'d SETS
LC1 Barry Sanders 100.00 175.00
LC2 Don Shula 30.00 60.00
LC3 Gale Sayers 40.00 80.00
LC4 Herman Edwards 25.00 50.00
LC5 Joe Montana 125.00 250.00
LC6 Joe Namath 75.00 150.00
LC7 Larry Csonka 30.00 60.00
LC8 Mark Bavaro 25.00 50.00
LC9 Michael Irvin 40.00 80.00
LC10 Roger Staubach 60.00 120.00

2004 Playoff Contenders MVP Contenders Red
RED PRINT RUN 1250 SER.#'d SETS
*BLUE/100: 1X TO 2.5X RED/1250
BLUE PRINT RUN 100 SER.#'d SETS
*GREEN/250: .6X TO 1.5X RED/1250
GREEN PRINT RUN 250 SER.#'d SETS
*ORANGE/500: .5X TO 1.2X RED/1250
ORANGE PRINT RUN 500 SER.#'d SETS
MC1 Ahman Green .60 1.50
MC2 Brett Favre 1.50 4.00
MC3 Clinton Portis .50 1.25
MC4 Deuce McAllister .60 1.50
MC5 Donovan McNabb .60 1.50
MC6 LaDainian Tomlinson .75 2.00
MC7 Matt Hasselbeck .50 1.25
MC8 Priest Holmes .50 1.25
MC9 Brian Urlacher .75 2.00
MC10 Jake Delhomme .50 1.25
MC11 Shaun Alexander .50 1.25
MC12 Stephen Davis .50 1.25
MC13 Steve McNair .60 1.50
MC14 Tom Brady 3.00 8.00
MC15 Torry Holt .60 1.50

2004 Playoff Contenders MVP Contenders Autographs
AUTOS PRINT RUN 25 SER.#'d SETS
MC1 Ahman Green 12.00 30.00
MC2 Brett Favre 150.00 250.00
MC3 Clinton Portis 10.00 25.00
MC4 Deuce McAllister 12.00 30.00
MC5 Donovan McNabb 25.00 60.00
MC6 LaDainian Tomlinson 40.00 80.00
MC7 Matt Hasselbeck 10.00 25.00
MC8 Priest Holmes 10.00 25.00
MC9 Brian Urlacher 30.00 80.00
MC10 Jake Delhomme 10.00 25.00
MC11 Shaun Alexander 10.00 25.00
MC12 Stephen Davis 10.00 25.00
MC13 Steve McNair 30.00 60.00
MC14 Tom Brady 150.00 250.00
MC15 Torry Holt 12.00 30.00

2004 Playoff Contenders Rookie Round Up
STATED PRINT RUN 375 SER.#'d SETS
RU1 Eli Manning 5.00 12.00
RU2 Robert Gallery .75 2.00
RU3 Larry Fitzgerald 2.50 6.00
RU4 Philip Rivers 2.00 5.00
RU5 Sean Taylor 4.00 10.00
RU6 Kellen Winslow Jr. .60 1.50
RU7 Roy Williams WR .60 1.50
RU8 DeAngelo Hall 1.00 2.50
RU9 Reggie Williams .60 1.50
RU10 Dunta Robinson .60 1.50
RU11 Ben Roethlisberger 5.00 12.00
RU12 Jonathan Vilma .75 2.00
RU13 Lee Evans 1.00 2.50
RU14 Tommie Harris .75 2.00
RU15 Michael Clayton .75 2.00
RU16 D.J. Williams 1.00 2.50
RU17 Will Smith .75 2.00
RU18 Kenechi Udeze .75 2.00
RU19 Vince Wilfork 1.00 2.50
RU20 J.P. Losman .60 1.50
RU21 Marcus Tubbs .60 1.50
RU22 Steven Jackson 1.00 2.50
RU23 Ahmad Carroll .60 1.50
RU24 Chris Perry .60 1.50
RU25 Jason Babin 1.00 2.50
RU26 Chris Gamble .60 1.50
RU27 Michael Jenkins .60 1.50
RU28 Kevin Jones .75 2.00
RU29 Rashaun Woods .60 1.50
RU30 Ben Watson .75 2.00
RU31 Karlos Dansby .75 2.00
RU32 Teddy Lehman .60 1.50
RU33 Ricardo Colclough .60 1.50
RU34 Daryl Smith .60 1.50
RU35 Ben Troupe .60 1.50
RU36 Tatum Bell .60 1.50
RU37 Julius Jones .60 1.50
RU38 Erik Coleman .75 2.00
RU39 Dontarrious Thomas .75 2.00
RU40 Keiwan Ratliff .60 1.50
RU41 Devery Henderson .60 1.50
RU42 Michael Boulware 1.00 2.50
RU43 Darius Watts .60 1.50
RU44 Greg Jones .60 1.50
RU45 Madieu Williams .60 1.50
RU46 Shawntae Spencer .60 1.50
RU47 Courtney Watson .60 1.50
RU48 Keary Colbert .60 1.50
RU49 Cedric Cobbs .60 1.50
RU50 Drew Henson .60 1.50

2004 Playoff Contenders Round Numbers Blue
RN1-RN10 BLUE PRINT RUN 1500 SETS
RN11-RN15 BLUE PRINT RUN 1000 SETS
*GREEN: .5X TO 1.2X BLUE
RN1-RN10 GREEN PRINT RUN 750 SETS
RN11-RN15 GREEN PRINT RUN 500 SETS
*ORANGE: .6X TO 1.5X BLUE
RN1-RN10 ORANGE PRINT RUN 500 SETS
RN11-RN15 ORANGE PRINT RUN 250 SETS
*RED: .8X TO 2X BLUE
RN1-RN10 RED PRINT RUN 250 SETS
RN11-RN15 RED PRINT RUN 100 SETS
RN1 E.Manning/P.Rivers 4.00 10.00
RN2 Roethlisberger/Losman 4.00 10.00
RN3 Ro.Williams/Re.Williams .50 1.25
RN4 M.Clayton/M.Jenkins .60 1.50
RN5 S.Jackson/K.Jones .75 2.00
RN6 B.Troupe/G.Jones .50 1.25
RN7 T.Bell/J.Jones .50 1.25
RN8 D.Watts/K.Colbert .50 1.25
RN9 D.Hamilton/M.Schaub .50 1.25
RN10 B.Berrian/D.Darling .50 1.25
RN11 Eli/Rvrs/Roeth/Lsmn 5.00 12.00
RN12 Re.Wil/Prry/Jcksn/K.Jns 1.00 2.50
RN13 Ro.Wil/Evns/Clytn/Jnkns 1.00 2.50
RN14 Bell/J.Jns/G.Jns/Clbrt .60 1.50
RN15 Hamil/Schb/Berr/Darl .60 1.50

2004 Playoff Contenders Round Numbers Autographs
RN1-RN10 PRINT RUN 100 SER.#'d SETS
RN11-RN15 PRINT RUN 50 SER.#'d SETS
*GOLD/30: .5X TO 1.2X BASIC INSERTS
*GOLD/20: .6X TO 1.5X BASIC INSERTS
GOLD/10 TOO SCARCE TO PRICE
RN1 E.Manning/P.Rivers 75.00 150.00
RN2 Roethlisberger/Losman 75.00 150.00
RN3 Ro.Williams/Re.Williams 8.00 20.00
RN4 M.Clayton/M.Jenkins 10.00 25.00
RN5 S.Jackson/K.Jones 12.00 30.00
RN6 B.Troupe/G.Jones 8.00 20.00
RN7 T.Bell/J.Jones 8.00 20.00
RN8 D.Watts/K.Colbert 8.00 20.00
RN9 D.Hamilton/M.Schaub 25.00 60.00
RN10 B.Berrian/D.Darling 8.00 20.00
RN11 Eli/Rvrs/Roeth/Lsmn 200.00 400.00
RN12 Re.Wil/Prry/Jcksn/K.Jns 12.00 30.00
RN13 Ro.Wil/Evns/Clytn/Jnkns 20.00 50.00
RN14 Bell/J.Jns/G.Jns/Clbrt 20.00 50.00
RN15 Hamil/Schb/Berr/Darl 12.50 30.00

2004 Playoff Contenders ROY Contenders Green
GREEN PRINT RUN 2000 SER.#'d SETS
*BLUE/750: .6X TO 1.5X GREEN/2000
BLUE PRINT RUN 750 SER.#'d SETS
*ORANGE/100: 1.2X TO 3X GRN/2000
ORANGE PRINT RUN 100 SER.#'d SETS
*RED/250: .8X TO 2X GREEN/2000
RED PRINT RUN 250 SER.#'d SETS
ROY1 Ben Roethlisberger 3.00 8.00
ROY2 DeAngelo Hall .60 1.50
ROY3 Drew Henson .40 1.00
ROY4 Eli Manning 3.00 8.00
ROY5 Kellen Winslow Jr. .40 1.00
ROY6 Kevin Jones .50 1.25
ROY7 Philip Rivers 1.25 3.00
ROY8 Reggie Williams .40 1.00
ROY9 Roy Williams WR .40 1.00
ROY10 Steven Jackson .60 1.50

2004 Playoff Contenders ROY Contenders Autographs
AUTO PRINT RUN 25 SER.#'d SETS
ROY1 Ben Roethlisberger 100.00 175.00
ROY2 DeAngelo Hall 20.00 50.00
ROY3 Drew Henson 12.00 30.00
ROY4 Eli Manning 100.00 175.00
ROY5 Kellen Winslow Jr. 12.00 30.00
ROY6 Kevin Jones 15.00 40.00
ROY7 Philip Rivers 100.00 200.00
ROY8 Reggie Williams 12.00 30.00
ROY9 Roy Williams WR 12.00 30.00
ROY10 Steven Jackson 20.00 50.00

2004 Playoff Contenders Toe 2 Toe
STATED PRINT RUN 375 SER.#'d SETS
TT1 A.Boldin/T.Holt 1.25 3.00
TT2 M.Bulger/M.Hasselbeck 1.00 2.50
TT3 S.Alexander/K.Barlow 1.00 2.50
TT4 E.Smith/M.Faulk 2.50 6.00
TT5 B.Favre/R.Grossman 3.00 8.00
TT6 I.Bruce/K.Robinson 1.50 4.00
TT7 J.Harrington/D.Culpepper 1.25 3.00
TT8 M.Bennett/A.Green 1.25 3.00
TT9 R.Moss/Ro.Will.WR .60 1.50
TT10 K.Jones/B.Urlacher .75 2.00
TT11 A.Brooks/M.Vick 1.25 3.00
TT12 D.McAllister/S.Davis 1.25 3.00
TT13 B.Johnson/J.Delhomme 1.25 3.00
TT14 J.Horn/S.Smith 1.50 4.00
TT15 M.Clayton/M.Jenkins .60 1.50
TT16 J.Jones/T.Barber .60 1.50
TT17 E.Manning/M.Brunell 4.00 10.00
TT18 L.Coles/A.Toomer 1.00 2.50
TT19 T.Owens/Ke.Johnson 1.25 3.00
TT20 Ro.Will.S/S.Taylor 6.00 15.00
TT21 B.Westbrook/C.Portis 1.00 2.50
TT22 D.McNabb/E.George 1.25 3.00
TT23 J.Kearse/M.Strahan 1.25 3.00
TT24 J.Shockey/L.Arrington 1.00 2.50
TT25 L.Tomlinson/P.Holmes 1.50 4.00
TT26 P.Rivers/T.Green 1.50 4.00
TT27 R.Smith/J.Rice 3.00 8.00
TT28 A.Gates/T.Gonzalez 1.50 4.00
TT29 C.Woodson/C.Bailey 1.50 4.00
TT30 J.Lewis/R.Johnson 1.25 3.00
TT31 J.Garcia/C.Palmer 1.25 3.00
TT32 K.Boller/B.Roethlisberger 4.00 10.00
TT33 K.Bell/R.Lewis 1.50 4.00
TT34 T.Heap/K.Winslow Jr. .50 1.25
TT35 H.Ward/C.Johnson 1.25 3.00
TT36 P.Warrick/A.Randle El 1.00 2.50
TT37 A.Johnson/M.Harrison 1.25 3.00
TT38 D.Carr/B.Leftwich 1.00 2.50
TT39 P.Manning/S.McNair 4.00 10.00
TT40 E.James/F.Taylor 1.25 3.00
TT41 D.Davis/C.Brown 1.00 2.50
TT42 T.Calico/Re.Williams 1.00 2.50
TT43 T.Brady/D.Bledsoe 6.00 15.00
TT44 C.Pennington/A.Feeley 1.00 2.50
TT45 W.McGahee/C.Martin 1.25 3.00
TT46 C.Dillon/T.Henry 1.00 2.50
TT47 S.Moss/C.Chambers 1.25 3.00
TT48 Z.Thomas/T.Bruschi 1.25 3.00
TT49 D.Branch/L.Evans .75 2.00
TT50 J.McCareins/E.Moulds 1.00 2.50

2005 Playoff Contenders
This 200-card set was released in January, 2006. The set was issued through the hobby in five-card packs which came 24 packs to a box. Cards numbered 1-100 feature veterans mainly in alphabetical order by team while cards numbered 101-200 feature signed rookies. A few players signed less cards for this product and playoff announced the print runs for those players signatures. A few players did not return their signatures in time for pack out and those cards could be redeemed until August 1, 2007.

COMP.SET w/o RC's (100) 7.50 20.00
AU PRINT RUNS ANNOUNCED BY PLAYOFF
UNPRICED CHAMPION.PRINT RUN 1 SET
1 Anquan Boldin .20 .50
2 Kurt Warner .25 .60
3 Larry Fitzgerald .30 .75
4 Michael Vick .25 .60
5 T.J. Duckett .20 .50
6 Warrick Dunn .20 .50
7 Derrick Mason .20 .50
8 Jamal Lewis .25 .60
9 Kyle Boller .20 .50
10 Ray Lewis .30 .75
11 J.P. Losman .20 .50
12 Lee Evans .25 .60
13 Willis McGahee .20 .50
14 DeShaun Foster .25 .60
15 Jake Delhomme .20 .50
16 Steve Smith .30 .75
17 Brian Urlacher .30 .75
18 Muhsin Muhammad .20 .50
19 Rex Grossman .20 .50
20 Carson Palmer .25 .60
21 Chad Johnson .20 .50
22 Rudi Johnson .20 .50
23 Lee Suggs .20 .50
24 Trent Dilfer .20 .50
25 Drew Bledsoe .25 .60
26 Jason Witten .25 .60
27 Julius Jones .20 .50
28 Keyshawn Johnson .25 .60
29 Ashley Lelie .20 .50
30 Jake Plummer .20 .50
31 Rod Smith .25 .60
32 Tatum Bell .20 .50
33 Joey Harrington .20 .50
34 Kevin Jones .20 .50
35 Roy Williams WR .20 .50
36 Ahman Green .25 .60
37 Brett Favre .60 1.50
38 Javon Walker .20 .50
39 Andre Johnson .25 .60
40 David Carr .20 .50
41 Domanick Davis .20 .50
42 Edgerrin James .25 .60
43 Marvin Harrison .25 .60
44 Peyton Manning .75 2.00
45 Reggie Wayne .25 .60
46 Byron Leftwich .20 .50
47 Fred Taylor .20 .50
48 Jimmy Smith .25 .60
49 Priest Holmes .20 .50
50 Tony Gonzalez .25 .60
51 Trent Green .20 .50
52 Chris Chambers .20 .50
53 Ricky Williams .25 .60
54 Daunte Culpepper .25 .60
55 Michael Bennett .20 .50
56 Nate Burleson .20 .50
57 Corey Dillon .20 .50
58 Deion Branch .20 .50
59 Tom Brady 1.25 3.00
60 Aaron Brooks .20 .50
61 Deuce McAllister .25 .60
62 Joe Horn .20 .50
63 Eli Manning .50 1.25
64 Jeremy Shockey .20 .50
65 Plaxico Burress .20 .50
66 Tiki Barber .25 .60
67 Chad Pennington .20 .50
68 Curtis Martin .25 .60
69 Laveranues Coles .20 .50
70 Kerry Collins .20 .50
71 LaMont Jordan .25 .60
72 Randy Moss .25 .60
73 Brian Westbrook .20 .50
74 Donovan McNabb .25 .60
75 Terrell Owens .25 .60
76 Ben Roethlisberger .50 1.25
77 Duce Staley .20 .50
78 Hines Ward .25 .60
79 Jerome Bettis .30 .75
80 Antonio Gates .30 .75
81 Drew Brees .30 .75
82 LaDainian Tomlinson .30 .75
83 Brandon Lloyd .20 .50
84 Kevan Barlow .20 .50
85 Darrell Jackson .20 .50
86 Matt Hasselbeck .20 .50
87 Shaun Alexander .20 .50
88 Isaac Bruce .30 .75
89 Marc Bulger .20 .50
90 Steven Jackson .20 .50
91 Torry Holt .25 .60
92 Brian Griese .20 .50
93 Derrick Brooks .20 .50
94 Chris Brown .20 .50
95 Drew Bennett .25 .60
96 Steve McNair .25 .60
97 Travis Henry .20 .50
98 Clinton Portis .20 .50
99 LaVar Arrington .20 .50
100 Santana Moss .25 .60
101 Aaron Rodgers AU/530* RC 700.00 1000.00
102 Adam Jones AU RC 4.00 10.00
103 A.McPherson AU/365* RC 10.00 25.00
104 Alvin Pearman AU RC 4.00 10.00
105 Airese Currie AU RC 4.00 10.00
106 Alex Smith QB AU/401* RC 40.00 100.00
107 Andrew Walter AU/99* RC 50.00 100.00
108 Anthony Davis AU/366* RC 5.00 12.00
109 Antrel Rolle AU RC 6.00 15.00
110 Brandon Jacobs AU RC 10.00 25.00
111 Brandon Jones AU RC 5.00 12.00
112 Braylon Edwards AU RC 6.00 15.00
113 Bryant McFadden AU/315* RC 6.00 15.00
114 Carlos Rogers AU RC 6.00 15.00
115 Cad.Williams AU/380* RC 10.00 25.00
116 Cedric Benson AU/289* RC 12.00 30.00
117 C.Houston AU/116* RC 40.00 100.00
118 Chad Owens AU RC 4.00 10.00
119 Charlie Frye AU RC 4.00 10.00
120 Chris Henry AU RC 5.00 12.00
121 Ciatrick Fason AU RC 4.00 10.00
122 Courtney Roby AU RC 4.00 10.00
123 Craig Bragg AU/425* RC 5.00 12.00
124 C.Thorpe AU/416* RC 5.00 12.00
125 Damien Nash AU RC 5.00 12.00
126 Dan Cody AU/315* RC 5.00 12.00
127 Dan Orlovsky AU RC 4.00 10.00
128 Dante Ridgeway AU/373* RC 5.00 12.00
129 Darren Sproles AU/454* RC 12.00 30.00
130 David Greene AU RC 4.00 10.00
131 David Pollack AU RC 4.00 10.00
132 Deandra Cobb AU/440* RC 5.00 12.00
133 DeMarcus Ware AU RC 15.00 40.00
134 Derek Anderson AU/450* RC 6.00 15.00
135 Derrick Johnson AU RC 6.00 15.00
136 Erasmus James AU RC 4.00 10.00
137 Eric Shelton AU RC 4.00 10.00
138 Fabian Washington AU RC 4.00 10.00
139 Frank Gore AU RC 25.00 50.00
140 Fred Gibson AU/476* RC 5.00 12.00
141 Heath Miller AU/510* RC 20.00 50.00
142 J.J. Arrington AU/465* RC 6.00 15.00
143 J.R. Russell AU/489* RC 5.00 12.00
144 Jason Campbell AU RC 10.00 25.00
145 Jason White AU RC 6.00 15.00
146 Jerome Mathis AU/416* RC 8.00 20.00
147 Josh Davis AU RC 4.00 10.00
148 Kay-Jay Harris AU RC 4.00 10.00
149 Kyle Orton AU RC 8.00 20.00
150 Larry Brackins AU RC 4.00 10.00
151 Lionel Gates AU/241* RC 8.00 20.00
152 Marion Barber AU RC 8.00 20.00
153 Mark Bradley AU RC 4.00 10.00
154 Mark Clayton AU/494* RC 5.00 12.00
155 Marlin Jackson AU RC 4.00 10.00
156 Matt Jones AU/165* RC 12.00 30.00
157 Matt Roth AU RC 4.00 10.00
158 Maurice Clarett AU/89* 25.00 60.00
159 Mike Williams AU/73* 25.00 60.00
160 Paris Warren AU/241* RC 10.00 25.00
161 Rasheed Marshall AU RC 5.00 12.00
162 Reggie Brown AU/528* RC 5.00 12.00
163 Roddy White AU RC 8.00 20.00
164 Ronnie Brown AU/550* RC 6.00 15.00
165 Roscoe Parrish AU RC 4.00 10.00
166 Royd.Williams AU/491* RC 6.00 15.00
167 R.Fitzpatrick AU/284* RC 10.00 25.00
168 Ryan Moats AU RC 4.00 10.00
169 Shaun Cody AU RC 5.00 12.00
170 Shawne Merriman AU RC 6.00 15.00
171 Stefan LeFors AU RC 4.00 10.00
172 Steve Savoy AU RC 4.00 10.00
173 T.A. McLendon AU RC 4.00 10.00
174 Tab Perry AU RC 4.00 10.00
175 Taylor Stubblefield AU RC 4.00 10.00
176 Terrence Murphy AU RC 4.00 10.00
177 Thomas Davis AU RC 4.00 10.00
178 Travis Johnson AU RC 4.00 10.00
179 T.Williamson AU/402* RC 10.00 25.00
180 Vernand Morency AU RC 4.00 10.00
181 Vincent Jackson AU RC 6.00 15.00
182 Alex Smith TE AU RC 4.00 10.00
183 Channing Crowder AU RC 5.00 12.00
184 Darrent Williams AU RC 12.00 30.00
185 Derrick Wimbush AU RC 5.00 12.00
186 James Kilian AU RC 4.00 10.00
187 Josh Cribbs AU RC 12.00 30.00
188 LeRon McCoy AU RC 4.00 10.00
189 Luis Castillo AU RC 5.00 12.00
190 Matt Cassel AU RC 10.00 25.00
191 Mike Patterson AU RC 4.00 10.00
192 Nate Washington AU RC 6.00 15.00
193 Noah Herron AU RC 4.00 10.00
194 Otis Amey AU RC 4.00 10.00
195 Tyson Thompson AU RC 4.00 10.00
196 Mike Nugent AU RC 5.00 12.00
197 Odell Thurman AU RC 6.00 15.00
198 Chris Carr AU RC 4.00 10.00
199 Bo Scaife AU RC 5.00 12.00
200 Billy Bajema AU RC 4.00 10.00

2005 Playoff Contenders Playoff Ticket
*VETERANS 1-100: 2.5X TO 6X BASIC CARDS
1-100 PRINT RUN 199 SER.#'d SETS
COMMON ROOKIE (101-200) 4.00 10.00
ROOKIE SEMISTARS 5.00 12.00
ROOKIE UNL.STARS 6.00 15.00
101-200 ROOK.PRINT RUN 25 SER.#'d SETS
101 Aaron Rodgers 75.00 135.00
106 Alex Smith QB 10.00 25.00
110 Brandon Jacobs 5.00 12.00
112 Braylon Edwards 4.00 10.00
115 Cadillac Williams 4.00 10.00
133 DeMarcus Ware 10.00 25.00
134 Derek Anderson 5.00 12.00
139 Frank Gore 8.00 20.00
141 Heath Miller 8.00 20.00
144 Jason Campbell 15.00 30.00
152 Marion Barber 4.00 10.00
156 Matt Jones 4.00 10.00
164 Ronnie Brown 5.00 12.00
170 Shawne Merriman 6.00 15.00
181 Vincent Jackson 6.00 15.00
187 Josh Cribbs 40.00 80.00
190 Matt Cassel 4.00 10.00
195 Tyson Thompson 4.00 10.00
198 Chris Carr 4.00 10.00

2005 Playoff Contenders Autographs
ANNOUNCED PRINT RUN 2-50
15 Jake Delhomme/250* 10.00 25.00
16 Steve Smith/41* 15.00 40.00
25 Drew Bledsoe/46* 40.00 80.00
28 Keyshawn Johnson/40* 15.00 40.00
39 Andre Johnson/250* 12.00 30.00
41 Domanick Davis/250* 10.00 25.00
69 Laveranues Coles/25* 15.00 40.00
93 Derrick Brooks/250* 10.00 25.00
95 Drew Bennett/250* 12.00 30.00

2005 Playoff Contenders Legendary Contenders Blue
BLUE PRINT RUN 2000 SER.#'d SETS
*GOLD: .8X TO 2X BASIC BLUE
GOLD PRINT RUN 250 SER.#'d SETS
*GREEN: .5X TO 1.2X BASIC BLUE
GREEN PRINT RUN 750 SER.#'d SETS
*RED: 1X TO 2.5X BASIC BLUE
RED PRINT RUN 100 SER.#'d SETS
1 Bo Jackson 2.00 5.00
2 Bob Griese 1.50 4.00
3 Deacon Jones 1.25 3.00
4 Don Meredith 1.50 4.00
5 Don Shula 1.50 4.00
6 Earl Campbell 1.50 4.00
7 Fran Tarkenton 1.50 4.00
8 Franco Harris 1.50 4.00
9 Jack Lambert 1.50 4.00
10 Jim Brown 2.00 5.00
11 Jim Kelly 1.50 4.00
12 Joe Namath 2.50 6.00
13 Len Dawson 1.50 4.00
14 Sonny Jurgensen 1.25 3.00
15 Tony Dorsett 1.50 4.00

2005 Playoff Contenders Legendary Contenders Autographs
STATED PRINT RUN 25-150
1 Bo Jackson/25 50.00 100.00
2 Bob Griese/95 15.00 40.00
3 Deacon Jones/25 15.00 40.00
4 Don Meredith/25 50.00 100.00
5 Don Shula/103 25.00 50.00
6 Earl Campbell/25 25.00 50.00
7 Fran Tarkenton/25 30.00 60.00
8 Franco Harris/65 30.00 60.00
9 Jack Lambert/25 50.00 100.00
10 Jim Brown/150 40.00 80.00
11 Jim Kelly/25 40.00 80.00
12 Joe Namath/175 40.00 80.00
13 Len Dawson/150 25.00 50.00
14 Sonny Jurgensen/25 30.00 60.00
15 Tony Dorsett/25 30.00 60.00

2005 Playoff Contenders MVP Contenders Gold
GOLD PRINT RUN 1250 SER.#'d SETS
*BLUE: .6X TO 1.5X BASIC GOLD
BLUE PRINT RUN 250 SER.#'d SETS
*GREEN: 1X TO 2.5X BASIC GOLD
GREEN PRINT RUN 100 SER.#'d SETS
*RED: .5X TO 1.2X BASIC GOLD
RED PRINT RUN 500 SER.#'d SETS
1 Ben Roethlisberger 2.00 5.00
2 Brett Favre 2.50 6.00
3 Byron Leftwich .75 2.00
4 Chad Pennington .75 2.00
5 Donovan McNabb 1.00 2.50
6 Eli Manning 2.00 5.00
7 Julius Jones .75 2.00
8 Michael Vick 1.00 2.50
9 Priest Holmes .75 2.00
10 Willis McGahee .75 2.00

2005 Playoff Contenders MVP Contenders Autographs
STATED PRINT RUN 25 SER.#'d SETS
1 Ben Roethlisberger 100.00 200.00
2 Brett Favre 125.00 250.00
3 Byron Leftwich 8.00 20.00
4 Chad Pennington 8.00 20.00
5 Donovan McNabb 20.00 50.00
6 Eli Manning 50.00 120.00
7 Julius Jones 8.00 20.00
8 Michael Vick 30.00 80.00
9 Priest Holmes 8.00 20.00
10 Willis McGahee 8.00 20.00

2005 Playoff Contenders Rookie Round Up
STATED PRINT RUN 450 SER.#'d SETS
1 Alex Smith QB 2.50 6.00
2 Ronnie Brown .75 2.00
3 Braylon Edwards .60 1.50
4 Cedric Benson .60 1.50
5 Cadillac Williams .60 1.50
6 Adam Jones .75 2.00
7 Troy Williamson .60 1.50
8 Antrel Rolle 1.00 2.50
9 Carlos Rogers 1.00 2.50
10 Mike Williams .75 2.00
11 DeMarcus Ware 2.00 5.00
12 Shawne Merriman 1.00 2.50
13 Thomas Davis .60 1.50
14 Derrick Johnson .75 2.00
15 Travis Johnson .60 1.50
16 David Pollack .60 1.50
17 Erasmus James .60 1.50
18 Marcus Spears .60 1.50
19 Matt Jones .60 1.50
20 Mark Clayton .60 1.50
21 Aaron Rodgers 20.00 40.00
22 Jason Campbell .60 1.50
23 Roddy White 1.00 2.50
24 Heath Miller 1.25 3.00
25 Reggie Brown .60 1.50
26 Mark Bradley .60 1.50
27 J.J. Arrington .75 2.00
28 Eric Shelton .60 1.50
29 Roscoe Parrish .60 1.50
30 Terrence Murphy .60 1.50
31 Vincent Jackson 1.00 2.50
32 Frank Gore 1.25 3.00
33 Charlie Frye .60 1.50
34 Courtney Roby .60 1.50
35 Andrew Walter .60 1.50
36 Vernand Morency .60 1.50
37 Ryan Moats .75 2.00
38 Chris Henry .75 2.00
39 David Greene .60 1.50
40 Brandon Jones .75 2.00
41 Luis Castillo .75 2.00
42 Kyle Orton .60 1.50
43 Marion Barber .60 1.50
44 Brandon Jacobs .75 2.00
45 Ciatrick Fason .60 1.50
46 Jerome Mathis 1.00 2.50
47 Stefan LeFors .60 1.50
48 Alvin Pearman .60 1.50
49 Darren Sproles 1.00 2.50
50 Mike Patterson .60 1.50

2005 Playoff Contenders Round Numbers Green

RN1-RN10 PRINT RUN 1500 SER.#'d SETS
RN11-RN15 PRINT RUN 1000 SER.#'d SETS
*BLUE: .5X TO 1.2X BASIC GREEN
BLUE RN1-RN10 PRINT RUN 750 SER.#'d SETS
BLUE RN11-RN15 PRINT RUN 500 SETS
*GOLD: .8X TO 2X BASIC GREEN
GOLD RN1-RN10 PRINT RUN 250 SER.#'d SETS
GOLD RN11-RN15 PRINT RUN 100 SETS
*RED: .6X TO 1.5X BASIC GREEN
RED RN1-RN10 PRINT RUN 500 SER.#'d SETS
RED RN11-RN15 PRINT RUN 250 SER.#'d SETS
RN1 A.Smith QB/A.Rodgers 6.00 15.00
RN2 J.Campbell/C.Rogers .75 2.00
RN3 Ro.Brown/C.Williams .60 1.50
RN4 B.Edwards/T.Williamson .50 1.25
RN5 C.Benson/H.Miller 1.00 2.50
RN6 M.Clayton/R.White .75 2.00
RN7 J.Arrington/E.Shelton .60 1.50
RN8 Re.Brown/V.Jackson .75 2.00
RN9 C.Frye/D.Greene .50 1.25
RN10 K.Orton/S.LeFors .50 1.25
RN11 Smith/Rodg/Bens/Clayt 8.00 20.00
RN12 Brown/Will/Cam/Rog 1.00 2.50
RN13 Edw/Will/Williams/Jones .75 2.00
RN14 Arring/Shelt/Brown/Jacks 1.00 2.50
RN15 Frye/Greene/Gore/Moats 1.25 3.00

2005 Playoff Contenders Round Numbers Autographs

RN1-RN10 PRINT RUN 50 SER.#'d SETS
RN11-RN15 PRINT RUN 25 SER.#'d SETS
UNPRICED GOLD PRINT RUN 5-20 CARDS
RN1 A.Smith QB/A.Rodgers 175.00 300.00
RN2 J.Campbell/C.Rogers 12.00 30.00
RN3 Ro.Brown/C.Williams 10.00 25.00
RN4 B.Edwards/T.Williamson 8.00 20.00
RN5 C.Benson/H.Miller 15.00 40.00
RN6 M.Clayton/R.White 12.00 30.00
RN7 J.Arrington/E.Shelton 10.00 25.00
RN8 Re.Brown/V.Jackson 12.00 30.00
RN9 C.Frye/D.Greene 8.00 20.00
RN10 K.Orton/S.LeFors 8.00 20.00
RN11 Smith/Rodg/Bens/Clayt 200.00 350.00
RN12 Brown/Will/Cam/Rog 125.00 250.00
RN13 Edw/Will/Williams/Jones 60.00 150.00
RN14 Arring/Shelt/Brown/Jacks 30.00 80.00
RN15 Frye/Greene/Gore/Moats 30.00 80.00

2005 Playoff Contenders ROY Contenders Red

RED PRINT RUN 2000 SER.#'d SETS
*BLUE: 1X TO 2.5X BASIC REDS
BLUE PRINT RUN 100 SER.#'d SETS
*GOLD: .5X TO 1.2X BASIC REDS
GOLD PRINT RUN 750 SER.#'d SETS
*GREEN: .6X TO 1.5X BASIC REDS
GREEN PRINT RUN 250 SER.#'d SETS
1 Alex Smith QB 2.00 5.00
2 Braylon Edwards .50 1.25
3 Cadillac Williams .50 1.25
4 Cedric Benson .50 1.25
5 J.J. Arrington .60 1.50
6 Mark Clayton .50 1.25
7 Matt Jones .50 1.25
8 Mike Williams .60 1.50
9 Ronnie Brown .60 1.50
10 Troy Williamson .50 1.25

2005 Playoff Contenders ROY Contenders Autographs

STATED PRINT RUN 25 SER.#'d SETS
1 Alex Smith QB 75.00 150.00
2 Braylon Edwards 12.00 30.00
3 Cadillac Williams 12.00 30.00
4 Cedric Benson 12.00 30.00
5 J.J. Arrington 15.00 40.00
6 Mark Clayton 12.00 30.00
7 Matt Jones 12.00 30.00
8 Mike Williams 15.00 40.00
9 Ronnie Brown 30.00 120.00
10 Troy Williamson 12.00 30.00

2005 Playoff Contenders Toe to Toe

STATED PRINT RUN 450 SER.#'d SETS
1 E.James/J.Lewis 1.25 3.00
2 A.Lelie/C.Chambers 1.00 2.50
3 M.Vick/D.McNabb 1.25 3.00
4 K.Jones/C.Benson 1.00 2.50
5 D.Branch/S.Smith 1.50 4.00
6 C.Portis/J.Jones 1.00 2.50
7 C.Pennington/B.Loftwich 1.00 2.50
8 R.Moss/T.Owens 1.25 3.00
9 A.Brooks/D.Culpepper 1.25 3.00
10 C.Johnson/A.Johnson 1.25 3.00
11 P.Manning/S.McNair 4.00 10.00
12 B.Favre/J.Delhomme 3.00 8.00
13 A.Green/D.McAllister 1.25 3.00
14 Roethlisberger/D.Brees 2.50 6.00
15 Muhammad/Williamson 1.00 2.50
16 Ro.Brown/C.Williams 1.25 3.00
17 S.Alexander/D.Davis 1.00 2.50
18 M.Harrison/T.Holt 1.25 3.00
19 J.Walker/N.Burleson 1.00 2.50
20 R.Lewis/B.Urlacher 1.50 4.00
21 L.Jordan/W.McGahee 1.25 3.00
22 P.Holmes/L.Tomlinson 1.50 4.00
23 F.Taylor/S.Jackson 1.00 2.50
24 D.Mason/H.Ward 1.25 3.00
25 T.Green/K.Collins 1.00 2.50
26 D.Jackson/A.Boldin 1.00 2.50
27 A.Smith QB/E.Manning 4.00 10.00
28 L.Arrington/D.Brooks 1.00 2.50
29 R.Williams WR/Fitzgerald 1.50 4.00
30 M.Bulger/M.Hasselbeck 1.00 2.50
31 B.Westbrook/T.Barber 1.25 3.00
32 K.Johnson/M.Williams 1.25 3.00
33 J.Porter/S.Moss 1.25 3.00
34 D.Bledsoe/J.Plummer 1.25 3.00
35 J.Horn/L.Coles 1.00 2.50
36 M.Bennett/L.Suggs 1.00 2.50
37 J.Shockey/J.Witten 1.25 3.00
38 R.Johnson/D.Staley 1.00 2.50
39 K.Boller/D.Carr 1.00 2.50
40 R.Wayne/J.Smith 1.25 3.00
41 T.Brady/J.Losman 6.00 15.00
42 K.Warner/P.Ramsey 1.25 3.00
43 E.Kennison/P.Burress 1.00 2.50
44 Rod Smith/L.Evans 1.25 3.00
45 C.Palmer/J.Harrington 1.25 3.00
46 A.Gates/T.Gonzalez 1.50 4.00
47 Mi.Clayton/R.White 1.50 4.00
48 C.Dillon/C.Martin 1.25 3.00
49 D.Bennett/M.Jones 1.25 3.00
50 Ma.Clayton/B.Edwards 1.00 2.50

2006 Playoff Contenders

This 242-card set was released in January, 2007. The set was issued into the hobby in five-card packs, with a $6 SRP, which came 24 packs to a box. Cards numbered 1-100 feature veterans in team alphabetical order while cards numbered 101-242. A few players signed less cards then other players in the set and we have notated the announced print runs of those players in our checklist.

COMP.SET w/o RC's (100) 8.00 20.00
1 Anquan Boldin .20 .50
2 Edgerrin James .25 .60
3 Larry Fitzgerald .25 .60
4 Alge Crumpler .25 .60
5 Michael Vick .25 .60
6 Warrick Dunn .20 .50
7 Steve McNair .25 .60
8 Mark Clayton .20 .50
9 Derrick Mason .20 .50
10 Lee Evans .25 .60
11 Willis McGahee .20 .50
12 Jake Delhomme .20 .50
13 Keyshawn Johnson .25 .60
14 Steve Smith .30 .75
15 Cedric Benson .20 .50
16 Brian Urlacher .30 .75
17 Thomas Jones .20 .50
18 Carson Palmer .25 .60
19 Chad Johnson .20 .50
20 Rudi Johnson .20 .50
21 T.J. Houshmandzadeh .20 .50
22 Charlie Frye .25 .60
23 Braylon Edwards .20 .50
24 Reuben Droughns .25 .60
25 Tony Romo .75 2.00
26 Julius Jones .20 .50
27 Roy Williams S .20 .50
28 Terrell Owens .25 .60
29 Javon Walker .25 .60
30 Rod Smith .25 .60
31 Tatum Bell .20 .50
32 Roy Williams WR .20 .50
33 Kevin Jones .20 .50
34 Brett Favre .60 1.50
35 Robert Ferguson .20 .50
36 Samkon Gado .20 .50
37 Andre Johnson .25 .60
38 David Carr .20 .50
39 Domanick Davis .20 .50
40 Eric Moulds .20 .50
41 Dallas Clark .20 .50
42 Marvin Harrison .25 .60
43 Peyton Manning .75 2.00
44 Reggie Wayne .25 .60
45 Matt Jones .20 .50
46 Byron Leftwich .20 .50
47 Fred Taylor .20 .50
48 Larry Johnson .20 .50
49 Priest Holmes .20 .50
50 Tony Gonzalez .25 .60
51 Trent Green .20 .50
52 Chris Chambers .20 .50
53 Daunte Culpepper .25 .60
54 Ronnie Brown .25 .60
55 Chester Taylor .25 .60
56 Brad Johnson .25 .60
57 Corey Dillon .20 .50
58 Deion Branch .20 .50
59 Tom Brady 1.00 2.50
60 Tedy Bruschi .25 .60
61 Deuce McAllister .25 .60
62 Donte Stallworth .20 .50
63 Drew Brees .30 .75
64 Eli Manning .25 .60
65 Jeremy Shockey .20 .50
66 Tiki Barber .25 .60
67 Chad Pennington .20 .50
68 Curtis Martin .25 .60
69 Laveranues Coles .20 .50
70 Randy Moss .25 .60
71 LaMont Jordan .25 .60
72 Jerry Porter .20 .50
73 Donovan McNabb .25 .60
74 Reggie Brown .20 .50
75 Ben Roethlisberger .40 1.00
76 Hines Ward .25 .60
77 Willie Parker .25 .60
78 Antonio Gates .30 .75
79 Philip Rivers .30 .75
80 LaDainian Tomlinson .30 .75
81 Alex Smith QB .25 .60
82 Antonio Bryant .20 .50
83 Kevan Barlow .20 .50
84 Darrell Jackson .25 .60
85 Matt Hasselbeck .20 .50
86 Nate Burleson .20 .50
87 Shaun Alexander .20 .50
88 Marc Bulger .20 .50
89 Steven Jackson .20 .50
90 Isaac Bruce .30 .75
91 Torry Holt .25 .60
92 Cadillac Williams .25 .60
93 Chris Simms .20 .50
94 Joey Galloway .25 .60
95 Chris Brown .20 .50
96 David Givens .25 .60
97 Drew Bennett .25 .60
98 Clinton Portis .20 .50
99 Santana Moss .25 .60
100 Mark Brunell .25 .60
101 Malcom Floyd AU RC 12.00 30.00
102 Bart Scott AU RC 8.00 20.00
103 Reggie McNeal AU/457* RC 4.00 10.00
104 Domenik Hixon AU/586* RC 8.00 20.00
105 Vince Young AU/487* RC 5.00 12.00
106 Marcedes Lewis AU RC 4.00 10.00
107 Wali Lundy AU400* RC 5.00 12.00
108 Tarvaris Jackson AU RC 4.00 10.00
109 Ko Simpson AU RC 5.00 12.00
110 Jason Allen AU RC 5.00 12.00
111 Anthony Fasano AU RC 4.00 10.00
112 Joe Klopfenstein AU RC 4.00 10.00
113 Marques Hagans AU RC 4.00 10.00
114 Jason Avant AU RC 4.00 10.00
115 Santonio Holmes AU RC 8.00 20.00
116 Marcus Vick AU/149* RC 15.00 40.00
117 A.Cromartie AU/322* RC 10.00 25.00
118 DeAngelo Williams AU RC 10.00 25.00
119 Laurence Maroney AU RC 4.00 10.00
120 Daniel Bullocks AU RC 4.00 10.00
121 Jonathan Orr AU RC 5.00 12.00
122 Mike Bell AU RC 4.00 10.00
123 Kellen Clemens AU RC 4.00 10.00
124 Tim Jennings AU RC 6.00 15.00
125 Cory Rodgers AU RC 4.00 10.00
126 Jerome Harrison AU RC 4.00 10.00
127 Brad Smith AU/570* RC 8.00 20.00
128 Jeff Webb AU/250* RC 5.00 12.00
129 Will Blackmon AU RC 4.00 10.00
130 Quinton Ganther AU RC 4.00 10.00
131 Drew Olson AU RC 4.00 10.00
132 Omar Jacobs AU RC 4.00 10.00
133 Adam Jennings AU RC 5.00 12.00
134 Cedric Humes AU RC 4.00 10.00
135 Derrick Ross AU/250* RC 40.00 80.00
136 Charlie Whitehurst AU RC 8.00 20.00
137 Bobby Carpenter AU RC 4.00 10.00
138 Darryl Tapp AU RC 5.00 12.00
139 A.J. Hawk AU/399* RC 12.00 30.00
140 Bruce Gradkowski AU RC 5.00 12.00
141 Chad Greenway AU RC 6.00 15.00
142 J.Washington AU RC 4.00 10.00
143 Kamerion Wimbley AU RC 5.00 12.00
144 LenDale White AU/549* RC 5.00 12.00
145 J.Joseph AU/549* RC 5.00 12.00
146 Maurice Drew AU RC 12.00 30.00
147 B.Marshall AU/608* RC 12.00 30.00
148 Vernon Davis AU/537* RC 6.00 15.00
149 Joseph Addai AU RC 8.00 20.00
150 Bennie Brazell AU RC 5.00 12.00
151 D.J. Shockley AU RC 5.00 12.00
152 Jay Cutler AU/501* RC 6.00 15.00
153 Wendell Mathis AU RC 5.00 12.00
154 Demetrius Williams AU RC 4.00 10.00
155 Dusty Dvoracek AU RC 6.00 15.00
156 DeMario Minter AU RC 5.00 12.00
157 Marcus Maxey AU RC 5.00 12.00
158 Brodie Croyle AU RC 6.00 15.00
159 Jeremy Bloom AU/473* RC 5.00 12.00
160 Todd Watkins AU RC 4.00 10.00
161 Cory Ross AU RC 6.00 15.00
162 Tamba Hali AU/500* RC 10.00 25.00
163 P.J. Daniels AU/555* RC 4.00 10.00
164 Brandon Williams AU RC 4.00 10.00
165 Devin Hester AU RC 10.00 25.00
166 Kelly Jennings AU/393* RC 5.00 12.00
167 Dawan Landry AU RC 6.00 15.00
168 Greg Jennings AU RC 6.00 15.00
169 Mathias Kiwanuka AU RC 8.00 20.00
170 Leon Washington AU RC 8.00 20.00
171 Richard Marshall AU RC 4.00 10.00
172 Haloti Ngata AU RC 8.00 20.00
173 Sinorice Moss AU RC 4.00 10.00
174 Greg Blue AU RC 5.00 12.00
175 Chris Barclay AU RC 5.00 12.00
176 D'Qwell Jackson AU RC 4.00 10.00
177 Eric Smith AU RC 5.00 12.00
178 Ethan Kilmer AU RC 5.00 12.00
179 Mike Hass AU RC 4.00 10.00
180 Derek Hagan AU RC 5.00 12.00
181 Travis Wilson AU RC 4.00 10.00
182 Reggie Bush AU/645* RC 10.00 25.00
183 Maurice Stovall AU/579* RC 5.00 12.00
184 Skyler Green AU RC 4.00 10.00
185 Calvin Lowry AU RC 6.00 15.00
186 Jerious Norwood AU RC 4.00 10.00
187 Brodrick Bunkley AU/518* RC 5.00 12.00
188 Ernie Sims AU/611* RC 4.00 10.00
189 Ingle Martin AU RC 5.00 12.00
190 Anthony Mix AU RC 5.00 12.00
191 Patrick Cobbs AU RC 5.00 12.00
192 Delanie Walker AU/212* RC 25.00 60.00
193 Gabe Watson AU RC 4.00 10.00
194 Willie Reid AU/515* RC 5.00 12.00
195 Michael Huff AU RC 5.00 12.00
196 Mario Williams AU/395* RC 12.00 30.00
197 Chad Jackson AU RC 4.00 10.00
198 David Kirtman AU RC 5.00 12.00
199 Brian Calhoun AU/407* RC 5.00 12.00
200 M.Robinson AU/512* RC 8.00 20.00
201 D.Ferguson AU/386* RC 5.00 12.00
202 Donte Whitner AU/518* RC 5.00 12.00
203 Roman Harper AU RC 5.00 12.00
204 Manny Lawson AU RC 5.00 12.00
205 DeMeco Ryans AU RC 8.00 20.00
206 Anthony Smith AU RC 8.00 20.00
207 Thomas Howard AU RC 4.00 10.00
208 John McCargo AU RC 4.00 10.00
209 David Pittman AU RC 5.00 12.00
210 Danieal Manning AU RC 6.00 15.00
211 Nate Salley AU RC 5.00 12.00
212 Jimmy Williams AU/524* RC 4.00 10.00
213 Rocky McIntosh AU RC 4.00 10.00
214 Montell Owens AU RC 5.00 12.00
215 Devin Aromashodu AU RC 10.00 25.00
216 Ben Obomanu AU RC 5.00 12.00
217 David Anderson AU RC 5.00 12.00
218 Marques Colston AU RC 6.00 15.00
219 Miles Austin AU RC 8.00 20.00
220 Tony Scheffler AU/526* RC 10.00 25.00
221 Leonard Pope AU/495* RC 6.00 15.00
222 David Thomas AU RC 4.00 10.00
223 Dominique Byrd AU RC 4.00 10.00
224 Owen Daniels AU RC 6.00 15.00
225 Garrett Mills AU RC 5.00 12.00
226 Hank Baskett AU RC 4.00 10.00
227 Jason Carter AU RC 5.00 12.00
228 Sam Hurd AU RC 4.00 10.00
229 Charles Sharon AU/250* RC 40.00 80.00
230 Chris Hannon AU RC 5.00 12.00
231 John Madsen AU RC 5.00 12.00
232 Shaun Bodiford AU RC 5.00 12.00
233 Mike Espy AU RC 5.00 12.00
234 Abdul Hodge AU RC 4.00 10.00
235 Anthony Montgomery AU RC 5.00 12.00
236 Matt Leinart AU/567* RC 8.00 20.00
237 Bernard Pollard AU/307* RC 10.00 25.00
238 Pat Watkins AU/343* RC 6.00 15.00
239 Cedric Griffin AU/357* RC 8.00 20.00
240 A.J. Nicholson AU RC 4.00 10.00
241 Claude Wroten AU/306* RC 8.00 20.00
242 Tyc Hill AU/368* RC 8.00 20.00

2006 Playoff Contenders Championship Ticket

UNPRICED CHAMP.TICKET PRINT RUN 1

2006 Playoff Contenders Playoff Ticket

*VETS/199: 2.5X TO 6X BASIC CARDS
COMMON ROOKIE (101-242) 4.00 10.00
ROOKIE SEMISTARS 6.00 15.00
ROOKIE UNL.STARS 8.00 20.00
1-100 PRINT RUN 199 SER.#'d SETS
101-242 AU PRINT RUN 25 SER.#'d SETS
25 Tony Romo 6.00 15.00
102 Bart Scott 15.00 40.00
104 Domenik Hixon 8.00 20.00
105 Vince Young 5.00 12.00
115 Santonio Holmes 6.00 15.00
118 DeAngelo Williams 8.00 20.00
119 Laurence Maroney 5.00 12.00
123 Kellen Clemens 5.00 12.00
139 A.J. Hawk 6.00 15.00
140 Bruce Gradkowski 6.00 15.00
144 LenDale White 5.00 12.00
146 Maurice Drew 12.00 30.00
149 Joseph Addai 5.00 12.00
152 Jay Cutler 6.00 15.00
158 Brodie Croyle 5.00 12.00
165 Devin Hester 10.00 25.00
168 Greg Jennings 8.00 20.00
169 Mathias Kiwanuka 8.00 20.00
170 Leon Washington 5.00 12.00
182 Reggie Bush 8.00 20.00
186 Jerious Norwood 5.00 12.00
188 Ernie Sims 5.00 12.00
196 Mario Williams 8.00 20.00
205 DeMeco Ryans 6.00 15.00
218 Marques Colston 8.00 20.00
219 Miles Austin 6.00 15.00
228 Sam Hurd 5.00 12.00
236 Matt Leinart 5.00 12.00

2006 Playoff Contenders Award Winners

STATED PRINT RUN 1000 SER.#'d SETS
*GOLD/250: .5X TO 1.2X BASIC INSERTS
GOLD PRINT RUN 250 SER.#'d SETS
*HOLOFOIL/100: .8X TO 2X BASIC INSERTS
HOLOFOIL PRINT RUN 100 SER.#'d SETS
18 Marcus Allen 2.00 5.00
19 Terry Baker 1.50 4.00
20 Joe Bellino 1.50 4.00
21 Billy Cannon 1.50 4.00
22 John Cappelletti 1.50 4.00
23 Howard Cassady 2.00 5.00
24 Eric Crouch 2.00 5.00
25 John David Crow 1.50 4.00
26 Tony Dorsett 2.50 6.00
27 Paul Hornung 2.00 5.00
28 John Huarte 1.50 4.00
29 Dick Kazmaier 1.50 4.00
30 John Lattner 1.50 4.00
31 John Lujack 2.00 5.00
32 Steve Owens 2.00 5.00
33 Johnny Rodgers 2.00 5.00
34 Billy Sims 2.00 5.00
35 Jason White 2.00 5.00
36 Eddie George 2.00 5.00
37 Doc Blanchard 2.00 5.00
38 Dawkins/Blanchard 2.00 5.00
39 R.Staubach/J.Bellino 4.00 10.00
40 Rozier/Crouch/Rodgers 2.50 6.00
41 Huar/Horn/Lattner/Lujack 2.00 5.00
42 Owens/Sims/White 2.50 6.00
43 Griffin/Cassady/George 2.00 5.00
44 Garrett/White/Allen 2.50 6.00
45 M.Leinart/R.Bush 2.00 5.00

2006 Playoff Contenders Award Winners Autographs

STATED PRINT RUN 50-200
18 Marcus Allen 20.00 50.00
19 Terry Baker 15.00 40.00
20 Joe Bellino 10.00 25.00
21 Billy Cannon 12.00 30.00
22 John Cappelletti 10.00 25.00
23 Howard Cassady 10.00 25.00
24 Eric Crouch 12.00 30.00
25 John David Crow 15.00 40.00
26 Tony Dorsett 20.00 50.00
27 Paul Hornung 15.00 40.00
28 John Huarte 25.00 50.00
29 Richard Kazmaier 12.00 30.00
30 John Lattner 12.00 30.00
31 John Lujack 15.00 40.00
32 Steve Owens 12.00 30.00
33 Johnny Rodgers 12.00 30.00
34 Billy Sims 12.00 30.00
35 Jason White 10.00 25.00
36 Eddie George 15.00 40.00
39 R.Staubach/J.Bellino/50 60.00 120.00
40 Rozier/Crouch/Rodgers/50 40.00 80.00
41 Huar/Horn/Latt/Lujack/50 60.00 120.00
42 Owens/Sims/White/50 30.00 80.00
43 Griffin/Cass/George/50 50.00 100.00
44 Garrett/White/Allen/50 50.00 100.00

2006 Playoff Contenders Draft Class

STATED PRINT RUN 1000 SER.#'d SETS
*HOLOFOIL/100: .8X TO 2X BASIC INSERTS
HOLOFOIL PRINT RUN 100 SER.#'d SETS
*GOLD/250: .5X TO 1.2X BASIC INSERTS
GOLD PRINT RUN 250 SER.#'d SETS
UNPRICED AUTO PRINT RUN 10
1 M.Williams/W.Lundy 2.00 5.00
2 R.Bush/M.Colston 1.50 4.00
3 V.Young/L.White 1.00 2.50
4 D.Ferguson/B.Smith 1.25 3.00
5 A.Hawk/G.Jennings 4.00 10.00
6 V.Davis/M.Robinson 2.00 5.00
7 M.Huff/D.Bing 1.50 4.00
8 D.Whitner/J.McCargo 1.25 3.00
9 E.Sims/B.Calhoun 1.50 4.00
10 M.Leinart/L.Pope 1.50 4.00
11 J.Cutler/T.Scheffler 1.50 4.00
12 H.Ngata/D.Williams 1.50 4.00
13 T.Wilson/J.Harrison 1.25 3.00
14 B.Bunkley/J.Avant 1.25 3.00
15 T.Hill/D.Byrd 1.25 3.00
16 J.Allen/D.Hagan 1.25 3.00
17 C.Greenway/T.Jackson 1.50 4.00
18 B.Carpenter/A.Fasano 1.50 4.00
19 A.Cromartie/C.Whitehurst 1.25 3.00
20 T.Hali/B.Croyle 2.00 5.00
21 L.Maroney/C.Jackson 1.00 2.50
22 B.Williams/M.Lawson 1.25 3.00
23 M.Stovall/B.Gradkowski 1.50 4.00
24 J.Joseph/A.Nicholson 1.00 2.50
25 O.Jacobs/S.Holmes 2.50 6.00
26 D.Manning/D.Hester 2.50 6.00
27 D.Williams/R.Marshall 1.25 3.00
28 M.Lewis/M.Drew 3.00 8.00
29 R.McIntosh/A.Montgomery 1.25 3.00
30 J.Addai/T.Jennings 1.50 4.00
31 K.Jennings/D.Kirtman 1.25 3.00
32 M.Kiwanuka/S.Moss 1.50 4.00

2006 Playoff Contenders Legendary Contenders

STATED PRINT RUN 1000 SER.#'d SETS
*HOLOFOIL/100: .8X TO 2X BASIC INSERTS
HOLOFOIL PRINT RUN 100 SER.#'d SETS
*GOLD/250: .5X TO 1.2X BASIC INSERTS
GOLD PRINT RUN 250 SER.#'d SETS
1 Troy Aikman 2.00 5.00
2 Dan Marino 3.00 8.00
3 John Elway 2.50 6.00
4 Don Meredith 1.50 4.00
5 Bob Griese 1.50 4.00
6 Dave Casper 1.00 2.50
7 Fran Tarkenton 1.50 4.00
8 Ickey Woods 1.00 2.50
9 Jim Otto 1.00 2.50
10 Jim Plunkett 1.25 3.00
11 Phil Simms 1.25 3.00
12 Lee Roy Selmon 1.00 2.50
13 Ozzie Newsome 1.25 3.00
14 Paul Krause 1.00 2.50
15 Paul Lowe 1.00 2.50
16 Len Dawson 1.50 4.00
17 Steve Largent 1.50 4.00
18 Jim Kelly 1.50 4.00
19 Tony Dorsett 1.50 4.00
20 Jerry Rice 3.00 8.00
21 Steve Young 2.00 5.00
22 Thurman Thomas 1.25 3.00
23 Y.A. Tittle 1.50 4.00
24 Terrell Davis 1.25 3.00
25 Sonny Jurgensen 1.25 3.00
26 Willie Brown 1.00 2.50

2006 Playoff Contenders Legendary Contenders Autographs

STATED PRINT RUN 10-100
SERIAL #'d UNDER 25 NOT PRICED
1 Troy Aikman/25 60.00 120.00
2 Dan Marino/30 100.00 200.00
3 John Elway/25 75.00 150.00
4 Don Meredith/100 40.00 80.00
5 Bob Griese/75 20.00 40.00
6 Dave Casper/50 20.00 40.00
7 Fran Tarkenton/50 25.00 50.00
8 Ickey Woods/100 12.50 25.00
9 Jim Otto/35 20.00 40.00
10 Jim Plunkett/25 20.00 40.00
11 Phil Simms/50 15.00 40.00
12 Lee Roy Selmon/75 20.00 50.00
13 Ozzie Newsome/50 12.50 25.00
14 Paul Krause/40 12.50 25.00
15 Paul Lowe/100 10.00 20.00
16 Len Dawson/50 20.00 40.00
17 Steve Largent/75 20.00 40.00
18 Jim Kelly/50 35.00 60.00
19 Tony Dorsett/25 30.00 60.00
20 Jerry Rice/25 100.00 200.00
25 Sonny Jurgensen/25 20.00 40.00
26 Willie Brown/100 15.00 30.00

2006 Playoff Contenders MVP Contenders

STATED PRINT RUN 1000 SER.#'d SETS
*HOLOFOIL/100: .8X TO 2X BASIC INSERTS
HOLOFOIL PRINT RUN 100 SER.#'d SETS
*GOLD/250: .5X TO 1.2X BASIC INSERTS
GOLD PRINT RUN 250 SER.#'d SETS
1 Larry Johnson 1.50 4.00
2 Shaun Alexander 1.50 4.00
3 Peyton Manning 2.50 6.00
4 LaDainian Tomlinson 1.50 4.00
5 Eli Manning 2.00 5.00
6 Tiki Barber 1.50 4.00
7 Edgerrin James 1.50 4.00
8 Steve Smith 1.50 4.00
9 Donovan McNabb 1.50 4.00
10 Carson Palmer 1.50 4.00
11 Steven Jackson 1.50 4.00
12 Brett Favre 3.00 8.00
13 Chad Johnson 1.00 2.50
14 Larry Fitzgerald 1.50 4.00
15 Cadillac Williams 1.25 3.00

2006 Playoff Contenders MVP Contenders Autographs

STATED PRINT RUN 4-25
SERIAL #'d UNDER 25 NOT PRICED
2 Shaun Alexander/25 20.00 50.00
3 Peyton Manning/25 175.00 300.00
4 LaDainian Tomlinson/25 40.00 80.00
5 Eli Manning/25 60.00 100.00
7 Edgerrin James/25 20.00 50.00
9 Donovan McNabb/25 20.00 50.00
10 Carson Palmer/25 30.00 60.00
11 Steven Jackson/25 20.00 50.00
12 Brett Favre/25 100.00 200.00
13 Chad Johnson/25 20.00 50.00
14 Larry Fitzgerald/25 20.00 50.00
15 Cadillac Williams/25 20.00 50.00

2006 Playoff Contenders Round Numbers

STATED PRINT RUN 1000 SER.#'d SETS
*HOLOFOIL/100: .8X TO 2X BASIC INSERTS
HOLOFOIL PRINT RUN 100 SER.#'d SETS
*GOLD/250: .5X TO 1.2X BASIC INSERTS
GOLD PRINT RUN 250 SER.#'d SETS
UNPRICED AU PRINT RUN 5-10
1 R.Bush/V.Young 1.00 2.50
2 M.Leinart/J.Cutler .75 2.00
3 A.Hawk/B.Carpenter .75 2.00
4 M.Williams/D.Ferguson 1.00 2.50
5 J.Addai/L.Maroney .60 1.50
6 V.Davis/M.Lewis .75 2.00
7 K.Clemens/T.Jackson .60 1.50
8 C.Jackson/S.Moss .60 1.50
9 L.White/M.Drew 1.00 2.50
10 A.Fasano/J.Klopfenstein .60 1.50
11 D.Ryans/R.McIntosh .75 2.00
12 B.Williams/M.Stovall .60 1.50
13 C.Whitehurst/B.Croyle .60 1.50
14 D.Thomas/D.Byrd .60 1.50
15 B.Calhoun/J.Norwood .60 1.50
16 Bush/Yng/Leint/Cutler 1.00 2.50
17 Ngata/Wimb/Bunk/Hali 1.00 2.50
18 Huff/Whitner/Hill/Allen .75 2.00
19 Davis/Hlms/Will/Hawk .75 2.00
20 Hstr/Jenn/Schef/Fasano 1.25 3.00
21 Wlsn/Whthrst/Hagan/Croy .75 2.00
22 Robin/Smith/Rdgrs/Will .75 2.00
23 Wash/Mrshll/Green/Avant 1.25 3.00
24 Hrrsn/Bloom/Mrtn/Jcbs .75 2.00
25 Lundy/Hass/McN/Gradk .75 2.00

2006 Playoff Contenders ROY Contenders

STATED PRINT RUN 1000 SER.#'d SETS
*HOLOFOIL/100: .8X TO 2X BASIC INSERTS
HOLOFOIL PRINT RUN 100 SER.#'d SETS
*GOLD/250: .5X TO 1.2X BASIC INSERTS
GOLD PRINT RUN 250 SER.#'d SETS
1 Reggie Bush 1.00 2.50
2 Joseph Addai .60 1.50
3 LenDale White .60 1.50
4 Santonio Holmes .75 2.00
5 Laurence Maroney .60 1.50
6 Jay Cutler .75 2.00
7 Jerious Norwood .60 1.50
0 Vince Young .80 1.50
9 Vernon Davis .75 2.00
10 Mario Williams 1.00 2.50
11 Leon Washington .60 1.50
12 DeAngelo Williams .75 2.00
13 Matt Leinart .60 1.50
14 Jason Avant .60 1.50
15 A.J. Hawk .75 2.00
16 Mike Bell 1.50 4.00
17 Marques Colston 1.00 2.50
18 Michael Robinson .60 1.50
19 Chad Jackson .60 1.50
20 Greg Jennings 1.00 2.50
21 D'Qwell Jackson .60 1.50
22 Manny Lawson .75 2.00
23 Kamerion Wimbley .75 2.00
24 Wali Lundy .60 1.50
25 Maurice Drew 1.00 2.50
26 Jerome Harrison .60 1.50
27 Demetrius Williams .60 1.50
28 Tamba Hali 1.00 2.50
29 Haloti Ngata .75 2.00
30 Dawan Landry 1.00 2.50
31 Ernie Sims .60 1.50
32 Devin Hester 1.25 3.00

2006 Playoff Contenders ROY Contenders Autographs

STATED PRINT RUN 25 SER.#'d SETS
1 Reggie Bush 12.00 30.00
2 Joseph Addai 20.00 50.00
3 LenDale White 8.00 20.00
4 Santonio Holmes 10.00 25.00
5 Laurence Maroney 8.00 20.00
6 Jay Cutler 10.00 25.00
7 Jerious Norwood 15.00 40.00
8 Vince Young 12.00 30.00
9 Vernon Davis 10.00 25.00
10 Mario Williams 12.00 30.00
11 Leon Washington 20.00 50.00
12 DeAngelo Williams 30.00 80.00
13 Matt Leinart 20.00 50.00
14 Jason Avant 8.00 20.00
15 A.J. Hawk 10.00 25.00
16 Mike Bell 8.00 20.00
17 Marques Colston 12.00 30.00
18 Michael Robinson 8.00 20.00
19 Chad Jackson 8.00 20.00
20 Greg Jennings 12.00 30.00
21 D'Qwell Jackson 8.00 20.00
22 Manny Lawson 10.00 25.00
23 Kamerion Wimbley 10.00 25.00
24 Wali Lundy 8.00 20.00
25 Maurice Drew 12.00 30.00
26 Jerome Harrison 8.00 20.00
27 Demetrius Williams 8.00 20.00
28 Tamba Hali 12.00 30.00
29 Haloti Ngata 10.00 25.00
30 Dawan Landry 10.00 25.00
31 Ernie Sims 8.00 20.00
32 Devin Hester 15.00 40.00

2007 Playoff Contenders

COMP.SET w/o RC's (100) 8.00 20.00
1 Edgerrin James .25 .60
2 Larry Fitzgerald .25 .60
3 Anquan Boldin .20 .50
4 Matt Leinart .20 .50
5 Joey Harrington .25 .60
6 Warrick Dunn .20 .50
7 Joe Horn .20 .50
8 Steve McNair .25 .60
9 Willis McGahee .20 .50
10 Derrick Mason .20 .50
11 J.P. Losman .20 .50
12 Lee Evans .25 .60
13 Josh Reed .20 .50
14 Jake Delhomme .20 .50
15 DeShaun Foster .25 .60
16 Steve Smith .25 .60
17 Rex Grossman .20 .50
18 Bernard Berrian .20 .50
19 Cedric Benson .20 .50
20 Carson Palmer .25 .60
21 Chad Johnson .20 .50
22 T.J. Houshmandzadeh .20 .50
23 Rudi Johnson .20 .50
24 Braylon Edwards .20 .50
25 Kellen Winslow .20 .50
26 Jamal Lewis .25 .60
27 Tony Romo .40 1.00
28 Terrell Owens .25 .60
29 Jason Witten .25 .60
30 Julius Jones .20 .50
31 Jay Cutler .20 .50
32 Javon Walker .25 .60
33 Travis Henry .25 .60
34 Jon Kitna .20 .50
35 Roy Williams WR .20 .50
36 Tatum Bell .20 .50
37 Brett Favre .60 1.50
38 Donald Driver .25 .60
39 Greg Jennings .20 .50
40 Matt Schaub .20 .50
41 Ahman Green .25 .60
42 Andre Johnson .25 .60
43 Peyton Manning .75 2.00
44 Joseph Addai .20 .50
45 Marvin Harrison .25 .60
46 Reggie Wayne .25 .60
47 David Garrard .20 .50
48 Fred Taylor .20 .50
49 Maurice Jones-Drew .20 .50
50 Larry Johnson .20 .50
51 Damon Huard .25 .60
52 Tony Gonzalez .25 .60
53 Trent Green .20 .50
54 Ronnie Brown .20 .50
55 Chris Chambers .20 .50
56 Troy Williamson .20 .50
57 Tarvaris Jackson .20 .50
58 Chester Taylor .20 .50
59 Tom Brady 1.00 2.50
60 Randy Moss .25 .60
61 Laurence Maroney .25 .60
62 Drew Brees .30 .75
63 Deuce McAllister .25 .60
64 Reggie Bush .20 .50
65 Eli Manning .25 .60
66 Brandon Jacobs .20 .50
67 Plaxico Burress .20 .50
68 Chad Pennington .20 .50
69 Laveranues Coles .20 .50
70 Thomas Jones .20 .50
71 Ronald Curry .20 .50
72 LaMont Jordan .25 .60
73 Jerry Porter .25 .60
74 Donovan McNabb .25 .60
75 Brian Westbrook .20 .50
76 Ben Roethlisberger .30 .75
77 Willie Parker .25 .60
78 Hines Ward .25 .60
79 LaDainian Tomlinson .30 .75
80 Philip Rivers .30 .75
81 Antonio Gates .30 .75
82 Alex Smith QB .25 .60
83 Frank Gore .25 .60
84 Darrell Jackson .20 .50
85 Vernon Davis .20 .50
86 Deion Branch .20 .50
87 Matt Hasselbeck .20 .50
88 Shaun Alexander .20 .50
89 Marc Bulger .20 .50
90 Steven Jackson .20 .50
91 Torry Holt .25 .60
92 Jeff Garcia .20 .50
93 Cadillac Williams .25 .60
94 Joey Galloway .25 .60
95 Vince Young .20 .50
96 Chris Brown .20 .50
97 Brandon Jones .20 .50
98 Jason Campbell .20 .50
99 Clinton Portis .20 .50
100 Santana Moss .25 .60
101 Aaron Ross AU RC 10.00 25.00
102 Aaron Rouse AU RC 5.00 12.00
103 Adam Carriker AU/333* RC 15.00 40.00
104 A.Peterson AU/355* RC 150.00 300.00
105 Ahmad Bradshaw No AU RC 3.00 8.00
106 Alan Branch No AU RC 1.00 2.50
107 Amobi Okoye AU RC 6.00 15.00
108 Anthony Gonzalez AU RC 5.00 12.00
109 Anthony Spencer AU RC 10.00 25.00
110 Antonio Pittman AU RC 5.00 12.00
111 Aundrae Allison AU RC 5.00 12.00
112 Ben Patrick AU RC 6.00 15.00
113 Biren Ealy AU RC 6.00 15.00
114 Bobby Sippio AU RC 6.00 15.00
115 Brady Quinn AU/534* RC 5.00 12.00
116 Brandon Jackson AU RC 12.50 25.00
117 Brandon Mebane AU RC 6.00 15.00
118 Brandon Meriweather AU RC 6.00 15.00
119 Brandon Siler AU RC 5.00 12.00
120 Brian Leonard AU RC 5.00 12.00
121 Brian Robison AU RC 8.00 20.00
122 Buster Davis AU/246* RC 15.00 40.00
123 C.Johnson AU/525* RC 125.00 250.00
124 Chansi Stuckey AU/502* RC 6.00 15.00
125 Charles Johnson No AU RC 2.00 5.00
126 Chris Davis AU RC 5.00 12.00
127 Chris Henry RB AU RC 5.00 12.00
128 Chris Houston AU RC 5.00 12.00
129 Clifton Ryan AU RC 6.00 15.00
130 Clifton Dawson AU RC 8.00 20.00
131 Courtney Taylor AU RC 5.00 12.00
132 Craig Buster Davis No AU RC 1.00 2.50
133 Dallas Baker AU RC 5.00 12.00
134 Dan Bazuin AU/198* RC 15.00 40.00
135 D.Hughes AU/383* RC 10.00 25.00
136 Dante Rosario AU RC 8.00 20.00
137 David Irons AU/198* RC 15.00 40.00
138 Darrelle Revis AU/533* RC 15.00 40.00
139 David Clowney AU/410* RC 5.00 12.00
140 David Harris AU RC 5.00 12.00
141 DeShawn Wynn AU/429* RC 5.00 12.00
142 Drew Stanton AU RC 5.00 12.00
143 Dwayne Bowe AU RC 5.00 12.00
144 Dwayne Jarrett AU/484* RC 6.00 15.00
145 Dwayne Wright AU/410* RC 5.00 12.00
146 Ed Johnson AU RC 6.00 15.00
147 Eric Frampton AU/452* RC 6.00 15.00
148 Eric Weddle AU RC 6.00 15.00
149 Eric Wright No AU RC 1.00 2.50
150 Fred Bennett AU RC 5.00 12.00
151 Gaines Adams AU RC 6.00 15.00
152 Garrett Wolfe AU RC 10.00 25.00
153 Glenn Holt AU RC 6.00 15.00
154 Glenn Martinez AU RC 8.00 20.00
155 Greg Olsen AU RC 8.00 20.00
156 Greg Peterson AU RC 6.00 15.00
157 H.B. Blades AU/383* RC 5.00 12.00
158 I.Alama-Francis AU/222* RC 15.00 40.00
159 Isaiah Stanback AU/510* RC 5.00 12.00
160 Jacoby Jones AU/435* RC 12.50 25.00
161 J.Anderson AU/123* RC SP 20.00 50.00
162 JaMarcus Russell AU RC 8.00 20.00
163 James Jones AU RC 5.00 12.00
164 J.Zabransky AU/347* RC 15.00 40.00
165 Jarvis Moss AU/227* RC 15.00 40.00
166 Jason Hill AU RC SP 5.00 12.00
167 Jeff Rowe AU/362* RC 10.00 25.00
168 Joe Thomas AU/129* RC 30.00 60.00
169 Joel Filani AU/483* RC 5.00 12.00
170 John Beck AU RC 5.00 12.00
171 John Broussard AU RC 6.00 15.00
172 Johnnie Lee Higgins AU RC 5.00 12.00
173 Jon Beason AU RC 6.00 15.00
174 Jonathan Wade No AU RC 1.50 4.00
175 Jordan Kent AU RC 6.00 15.00
176 Josh Wilson AU/501* RC 6.00 15.00
177 Justin Durant AU RC 8.00 20.00
178 Kenneth Darby AU RC 5.00 12.00
179 Kenny Irons No AU/50* RC 100.00 200.00
180 Kenton Keith AU RC 6.00 15.00
181 Kevin Kolb AU RC 6.00 15.00
182 Keyunta Dawson AU RC 6.00 15.00
183 Kolby Smith AU/444* RC 5.00 12.00
184 LaMarr Woodley AU RC 10.00 25.00
185 LaRon Landry AU RC 12.00 30.00
186 Laurent Robinson AU RC 10.00 25.00
187 Lawrence Timmons AU RC 8.00 20.00
188 Legedu Naanee AU RC 12.50 25.00
189 Leon Hall AU RC 5.00 12.00
190 Levi Brown AU/369* RC 5.00 12.00
191 Lorenzo Booker AU RC 6.00 15.00
192 M.McCauley AU/386* RC 15.00 40.00
193 Marcus Thomas AU RC 6.00 15.00
194 M.Lynch AU/533* RC 40.00 80.00
195 Martrez Milner AU RC 5.00 12.00
196 Mason Crosby AU RC 8.00 20.00
197 Matt Gutierrez AU RC 8.00 20.00
198 Matt Moore AU RC 8.00 20.00
199 Matt Spaeth AU/237* RC 15.00 40.00
200 Michael Bush AU RC 5.00 12.00
201 Michael Griffin AU RC 5.00 12.00
202 Michael Okwo AU/261* RC 10.00 25.00
203 Mike Walker AU/248* RC 15.00 40.00
204 Nick Folk AU RC 8.00 20.00
205 Patrick Willis AU/239* RC 30.00 80.00
206 Paul Posluszny AU RC 8.00 20.00
207 Paul Williams AU RC 5.00 12.00
208 Pierre Thomas AU RC 8.00 20.00
209 Quentin Moses AU/498* RC 5.00 12.00
210 Ray McDonald AU/519* RC 6.00 15.00
211 Reggie Ball AU RC 6.00 15.00
212 Reggie Nelson AU RC 5.00 12.00
213 Robert Meachem AU RC 6.00 15.00
214 Roy Hall AU RC 8.00 20.00
215 Rufus Alexander AU RC 5.00 12.00
216 Ryne Robinson AU/430* RC 6.00 15.00
217 Sabby Piscitelli AU/337* RC 10.00 25.00
218 Scott Chandler AU RC 8.00 20.00
219 Selvin Young No AU RC 2.00 5.00
220 Sidney Rice AU/529* RC 8.00 20.00
221 Stephen Nicholas AU RC 6.00 15.00
222 Steve Breaston AU/274* RC 15.00 40.00
223 Steve Smith AU/541 RC 10.00 25.00
224 Stewart Bradley AU RC 5.00 12.00
225 Syndric Steptoe AU/149* RC 20.00 50.00
226 Tanard Jackson No AU RC 1.00 2.50
227 Ted Ginn AU/519 RC 6.00 15.00
228 Thomas Clayton AU RC 6.00 15.00
229 Tim Crowder AU/454* RC 6.00 15.00
230 Tim Shaw AU/408* RC 6.00 15.00
231 Tony Hunt AU RC 5.00 12.00
232 Trent Edwards AU RC 5.00 12.00
233 Troy Smith AU RC 10.00 25.00
234 Turk McBride AU RC 6.00 15.00
235 Tyler Palko AU RC 10.00 25.00
236 Tyler Thigpen AU RC 8.00 20.00
237 Victor Abiamiri AU/449* RC 5.00 12.00
238 Yamon Figurs AU RC 5.00 12.00
239 Zak DeOssie AU RC 6.00 15.00
240 Zach Miller AU RC 5.00 12.00

2007 Playoff Contenders Championship Ticket

UNPRICED CHAMP.TICKET PRINT RUN 1

2007 Playoff Contenders Playoff Ticket

*VETS 1-100: 2.5X TO 6X BASIC CARDS
COMMON ROOKIE (101-240) 2.50 6.00
ROOKIE SEMISTARS 3.00 8.00
ROOKIE UNL.STARS 4.00 10.00
STATED PRINT RUN 99-199 SER.#'d SETS
104 Adrian Peterson 8.00 20.00
105 Ahmad Bradshaw 4.00 10.00
108 Anthony Gonzalez 2.50 6.00
115 Brady Quinn 2.50 6.00
123 Calvin Johnson 8.00 20.00
138 Darrelle Revis 3.00 8.00
143 Dwayne Bowe 2.50 6.00
155 Greg Olsen 4.00 10.00
181 Kevin Kolb 3.00 8.00
194 Marshawn Lynch 5.00 12.00
198 Matt Moore 4.00 10.00
205 Patrick Willis 4.00 10.00
208 Pierre Thomas 4.00 10.00
220 Sidney Rice 4.00 10.00
223 Steve Smith USC 2.50 6.00
227 Ted Ginn Jr. 3.00 8.00
232 Trent Edwards 2.50 6.00
233 Troy Smith 2.50 6.00

2007 Playoff Contenders Draft Class

STATED PRINT RUN 1000 SER.#'d SETS
*GOLD HOLO/250: .5X TO 1.2X BASIC INSERTS
GOLD HOLOFOIL PRINT RUN 250 SER.#'d SETS
*BLACK/100: .8X TO 2X BASIC INSERTS
BLACK PRINT RUN 100 SER.#'d SETS
1 A.Branch/L.Brown .50 1.25
2 Robinson/J.Anderson .75 2.00
3 T.Smith/Y.Figurs .50 1.25
4 Posluszny/Edwards .50 1.25
5 D.Wright/M.Lynch 1.00 2.50
6 J.Beason/D.Jarrett .60 1.50
7 G.Wolfe/G.Olsen .75 2.00
8 L.Hall/J.Rowe .50 1.25
9 B.Quinn/E.Wright .50 1.25
10 I.Stanback/A.Spencer .60 1.50
11 S.Young/T.Crowder .60 1.50
12 C.Johnson/I.Alama 1.50 4.00
13 B.Jackson/J.Jones .50 1.25
14 J.Jones/A.Okoye .60 1.50
15 A.Gonzalez/D.Hughes .60 1.50
16 D.Bowe/K.Smith .50 1.25
17 T.Ginn Jr./L.Booker .60 1.50
18 A.Peterson/S.Rice 1.50 4.00
19 S.Smith USC/A.Ross .50 1.25
20 R.Meachem/T.Palko .75 2.00
21 D.Revis/D.Harris .60 1.50
22 J.Russell/J.Higgins .50 1.25
23 K.Kolb/T.Hunt .60 1.50
24 M.Spaeth/L.Woodley 1.00 2.50
25 C.Davis/S.Chandler .75 2.00
26 P.Willis/J.Hill .75 2.00
27 C.Taylor/J.Wilson .60 1.50
28 B.Leonard/A.Carriker .50 1.25
29 G.Adams/S.Piscitelli .60 1.50
30 C.Henry RB/M.Griffin .50 1.25
31 P.Williams/C.Davis .50 1.25
32 L.Landry/H.Blades .75 2.00

2007 Playoff Contenders Draft Class Autographs

STATED PRINT RUN 25 SER.#'d SETS
2 Robinson/Anderson 12.00 25.00
4 Posluszny/Edwards 8.00 20.00
5 D.Wright/M.Lynch 15.00 40.00
6 J.Beason/D.Jarrett 10.00 25.00
7 G.Wolfe/G.Olsen 12.00 30.00
8 L.Hall/J.Rowe 8.00 20.00
10 I.Stanback/A.Spencer 10.00 25.00
12 C.Johnson/I.Alama 40.00 100.00
13 B.Jackson/J.Jones 8.00 20.00
14 J.Jones/A.Okoye 10.00 25.00
15 A.Gonzalez/D.Hughes 8.00 20.00
16 D.Bowe/K.Smith 8.00 20.00
17 T.Ginn Jr./L.Booker 10.00 25.00
18 A.Peterson/S.Rice 75.00 150.00
19 S.Smith USC/A.Ross 8.00 20.00
20 R.Meachem/T.Palko 12.00 30.00
21 D.Revis/D.Harris 10.00 25.00
22 J.Russell/J.Higgins 8.00 20.00
23 K.Kolb/T.Hunt 10.00 25.00
24 M.Spaeth/L.Woodley 25.00 60.00
26 P.Willis/J.Hill 40.00 80.00
27 C.Taylor/J.Wilson 10.00 25.00
28 B.Leonard/A.Carriker 8.00 20.00

29 G.Adams/S.Piscitelli 10.00 25.00
30 C.Henry RB/M.Griffin 8.00 20.00
31 P.Williams/C.Davis 8.00 20.00
32 L.Landry/H.Blades 12.00 30.00

2007 Playoff Contenders Legendary Contenders

STATED PRINT RUN 1000 SER.#'d SETS
*GOLD HOLO/250: .5X TO 1.2X BASIC INSERTS
GOLD HOLOFOIL PRINT RUN 250 SER.#'d SETS
*BLACK/100: .8X TO 2X BASIC INSERTS
BLACK PRINT RUN 100 SER.#'d SETS
1 Barry Sanders 1.50 4.00
2 Bill Bates .60 1.50
3 Charlie Joiner .60 1.50
4 Cris Collinsworth .75 2.00
5 Dan Fouts .75 2.00
6 Dan Marino 2.00 5.00
7 Dave Casper .60 1.50
8 Don Perkins .60 1.50
9 Eric Dickerson .75 2.00
10 Gene Upshaw .60 1.50
11 Jim Brown 1.25 3.00
12 Joe Montana 3.00 8.00
13 Lenny Moore .60 1.50
14 Paul Warfield .75 2.00
15 Steve Young 1.25 3.00
16 Thurman Thomas .75 2.00
17 Tim Brown 1.00 2.50

2007 Playoff Contenders Legendary Contenders Autographs

STATED PRINT RUN 10-100
SERIAL #'d UNDER 25 NOT PRICED
2 Bill Bates/50 12.50 25.00
3 Charlie Joiner/75 12.50 25.00
4 Cris Collinsworth/75 12.50 25.00
5 Dan Fouts/100 20.00 40.00
7 Dave Casper/75 12.50 25.00
8 Don Perkins/100 20.00 40.00
9 Eric Dickerson/25 25.00 50.00
10 Gene Upshaw/100 12.50 25.00
11 Jim Brown/25 60.00 120.00
13 Lenny Moore/50 12.50 25.00
14 Paul Warfield/75 10.00 25.00
16 Thurman Thomas/75 15.00 30.00
17 Tim Brown/75 15.00 30.00

2007 Playoff Contenders MVP Contenders

STATED PRINT RUN 1000 SER.#'d SETS
*GOLD HOLO/250: .5X TO 1.2X BASIC INSERTS
GOLD HOLOFOIL PRINT RUN 250 SER.#'d SETS
*BLACK/100: .8X TO 2X BASIC INSERTS
BLACK PRINT RUN 100 SER.#'d SETS
1 Frank Gore .75 2.00
2 Peyton Manning 2.50 6.00
3 LaDainian Tomlinson 1.00 2.50
4 Drew Brees 1.00 2.50
5 Vince Young .60 1.50
6 Chad Johnson .60 1.50
7 Reggie Bush .60 1.50
8 Larry Johnson .60 1.50
9 Steve Smith .75 2.00
10 Carson Palmer .75 2.00
11 Tony Romo 1.25 3.00
12 Brett Favre 2.00 5.00
13 Tom Brady 3.00 8.00
14 Steven Jackson .60 1.50
15 Joseph Addai .60 1.50

2007 Playoff Contenders MVP Contenders Autographs

STATED PRINT RUN 10-25
SERIAL #'d UNDER 25 NOT PRICED
1 Frank Gore/25 10.00 25.00
4 Drew Brees/25 40.00 80.00
6 Chad Johnson/25 8.00 20.00
8 Larry Johnson/25 8.00 20.00
9 Steve Smith/25 10.00 25.00
14 Steven Jackson/25 8.00 20.00
15 Joseph Addai/25

2007 Playoff Contenders Rookie Roll Call

STATED PRINT RUN 1000 SER.#'d SETS
*GOLD HOLO/250: .5X TO 1.2X BASIC INSERTS
GOLD HOLOFOIL PRINT RUN 250 SER.#'d SETS
*BLACK/100: .8X TO 2X BASIC INSERTS
BLACK PRINT RUN 100 SER.#'d SETS
1 Calvin Johnson 1.25 3.00
2 LaRon Landry .60 1.50
3 Adrian Peterson 4.00 10.00
4 Ted Ginn Jr. .50 1.25
5 Patrick Willis .60 1.50
6 Marshawn Lynch .75 2.00
7 Brady Quinn .40 1.00
8 Dwayne Bowe .40 1.00
9 Robert Meachem .50 1.25
10 Craig Buster Davis .40 1.00
11 Greg Olsen .60 1.50
12 Anthony Gonzalez .40 1.00
13 Sidney Rice .50 1.25
14 Steve Smith USC .40 1.00
15 Brian Leonard .40 1.00
16 Brandon Jackson .40 1.00
17 Lorenzo Booker .50 1.25
18 Jacoby Jones .40 1.00
19 Yamon Figurs .40 1.00
20 JaMarcus Russell .40 1.00
21 Jason Hill .40 1.00
22 Matt Spaeth .60 1.50
23 James Jones .40 1.00
24 Paul Williams .40 1.00
25 Trent Edwards .40 1.00
26 Garrett Wolfe .40 1.00
27 Johnnie Lee Higgins .40 1.00
28 DeShawn Wynn .40 1.00
29 Kevin Kolb .50 1.25
30 Dwayne Jarrett .50 1.25
31 Chris Henry RB .40 1.00
32 Chris Davis .40 1.00

2007 Playoff Contenders Rookie Roll Call Autographs

STATED PRINT RUN 25 SER.#'d SETS
1 Calvin Johnson 75.00 150.00
2 LaRon Landry 12.00 30.00
3 Adrian Peterson 150.00 300.00
4 Ted Ginn Jr. 10.00 25.00
5 Patrick Willis 30.00 80.00
6 Marshawn Lynch 40.00 80.00
7 Brady Quinn 8.00 20.00
8 Dwayne Bowe 8.00 20.00
9 Robert Meachem 10.00 25.00
11 Greg Olsen 12.00 30.00
12 Anthony Gonzalez 8.00 20.00
13 Sidney Rice 10.00 25.00
14 Steve Smith USC 8.00 20.00
15 Brian Leonard 8.00 20.00
16 Brandon Jackson 8.00 20.00
17 Lorenzo Booker 10.00 25.00
18 Jacoby Jones 8.00 20.00
19 Yamon Figurs 8.00 20.00
20 JaMarcus Russell 8.00 20.00
21 Jason Hill 8.00 20.00
22 Matt Spaeth 12.00 30.00
23 James Jones 8.00 20.00
24 Paul Williams 8.00 20.00
25 Trent Edwards 8.00 20.00
26 Garrett Wolfe 8.00 20.00
27 Johnnie Lee Higgins 8.00 20.00
28 DeShawn Wynn 8.00 20.00
29 Kevin Kolb 10.00 25.00
30 Dwayne Jarrett 10.00 25.00
31 Chris Henry RB 8.00 20.00
32 Chris Davis 8.00 20.00

2007 Playoff Contenders Round Numbers

STATED PRINT RUN 1000 SER.#'d SETS
*GOLD HOLO/250: .5X TO 1.2X BASIC INSERTS
GOLD HOLOFOIL PRINT RUN 250 SER.#'d SETS
*BLACK/100: .8X TO 2X BASIC INSERTS
BLACK PRINT RUN 100 SER.#'d SETS
1 C.Johnson/A.Peterson 1.50 4.00
2 J.Russell/B.Quinn .50 1.25
3 G.Adams/A.Spencer .60 1.50
4 T.Ginn/M.Lynch 1.00 2.50
5 L.Landry/D.Revis .75 2.00
6 M.Griffin/A.Ross .50 1.25
7 D.Bowe/R.Meachem .60 1.50
8 C.Davis/A.Gonzalez .50 1.25
9 B.Meriweather/G.Olsen .75 2.00
10 J.Thomas/L.Brown .75 2.00
11 P.Willis/J.Beason .75 2.00
12 L.Hall/R.Nelson .50 1.25
13 J.Anderson/A.Carriker .60 1.50
14 K.Kolb/J.Beck .60 1.50
15 C.Henry/B.Jackson .50 1.25
16 P.Posluszny/D.Harris .50 1.25
17 S.Rice/D.Jarrett .60 1.50
18 S.Smith/B.Leonard .50 1.25
19 Z.Miller/S.Piscitelli .50 1.25
20 L.Booker/T.Hunt .60 1.50
21 J.Jones/P.Williams .50 1.25
22 M.Spaeth/J.Higgins .75 2.00
23 J.Jones/Y.Figurs .50 1.25
24 L.Robinson/J.Hill .75 2.00
25 T.Edwards/G.Wolfe .50 1.25
26 J.Wade/A.Rouse .50 1.25
27 A.Pittman/D.Wright .50 1.25
28 C.Davis/S.Chandler .75 2.00
29 A.Allison/K.Smith .50 1.25
30 T.Shaw/T.Smith .60 1.50
31 H.Blades/C.Taylor .50 1.25
32 D.Wynn/A.Bradshaw .75 2.00

2007 Playoff Contenders Round Numbers Autographs

STATED PRINT RUN 25 SER.#'d SETS
1 C.Johnson/A.Peterson 175.00 350.00
2 J.Russell/B.Quinn 8.00 20.00
3 G.Adams/A.Spencer 10.00 25.00
4 T.Ginn/M.Lynch 25.00 50.00
5 L.Landry/D.Revis 12.00 30.00
6 M.Griffin/A.Ross 8.00 20.00
7 D.Bowe/R.Meachem 10.00 25.00
9 B.Meriweather/G.Olsen 12.00 30.00
10 J.Thomas/L.Brown 12.00 30.00
11 P.Willis/J.Beason 40.00 80.00
12 L.Hall/R.Nelson 8.00 20.00
13 J.Anderson/A.Carriker 10.00 25.00
14 K.Kolb/J.Beck 10.00 25.00
15 C.Henry/B.Jackson 20.00 40.00
16 P.Posluszny/D.Harris 8.00 20.00
17 S.Rice/D.Jarrett 10.00 25.00
18 S.Smith USC/B.Leonard 15.00 40.00
19 Z.Miller/S.Piscitelli 8.00 20.00
20 L.Booker/T.Hunt 10.00 25.00
21 J.Jones/P.Williams 8.00 20.00
22 M.Spaeth/J.Higgins 12.00 30.00
23 J.Jones/Y.Figurs 15.00 40.00
24 L.Robinson/J.Hill 12.00 30.00
25 T.Edwards/G.Wolfe 8.00 20.00
26 J.Wade/A.Rouse 8.00 20.00
27 A.Pittman/D.Wright 8.00 20.00
28 C.Davis/S.Chandler 12.00 30.00
30 T.Shaw/T.Smith 10.00 25.00
31 H.Blades/C.Taylor 8.00 20.00
32 D.Wynn/A.Bradshaw 12.00 30.00

2007 Playoff Contenders ROY Contenders

STATED PRINT RUN 1000 SER.#'d SETS
*GOLD HOLO/250: .5X TO 1.2X BASIC INSERTS
GOLD HOLOFOIL PRINT RUN 250 SER.#'d SETS
*BLACK/100: .8X TO 2X BASIC INSERTS
BLACK PRINT RUN 100 SER.#'d SETS
1 Aaron Rouse .40 1.00
2 Adrian Peterson 1.25 3.00
3 Anthony Gonzalez .40 1.00
4 Anthony Spencer .50 1.25
5 Brady Quinn .40 1.00
6 Brandon Jackson .40 1.00
7 Brandon Meriweather .50 1.25
8 Calvin Johnson 1.25 3.00
9 Chris Henry RB .40 1.00
10 Darrelle Revis .50 1.25
11 Dwayne Bowe .40 1.00
12 Dwayne Jarrett .50 1.25
13 Gaines Adams .50 1.25
14 Greg Olsen .60 1.50
15 Jacoby Jones .40 1.00
16 JaMarcus Russell .40 1.00
17 James Jones .40 1.00
18 Jason Hill .40 1.00
19 John Beck .40 1.00
20 LaMarr Woodley .75 2.00
21 LaRon Landry .60 1.50
22 Lorenzo Booker .50 1.25
23 Marshawn Lynch .75 2.00
24 Matt Spaeth .60 1.50
25 Michael Griffin .40 1.00
26 Patrick Willis .60 1.50
27 Paul Posluszny .40 1.00
28 Paul Williams .40 1.00
29 Reggie Nelson .40 1.00
30 Steve Smith USC .40 1.00
31 Ted Ginn Jr. .50 1.25
32 Trent Edwards .40 1.00

2007 Playoff Contenders ROY Contenders Autographs

STATED PRINT RUN 50 SER.#'d SETS
1 Aaron Rouse 6.00 15.00
2 Adrian Peterson 125.00 250.00
3 Anthony Gonzalez 6.00 15.00
4 Anthony Spencer 8.00 20.00
5 Brady Quinn 6.00 15.00
6 Brandon Jackson 6.00 15.00
7 Brandon Meriweather 8.00 20.00
8 Calvin Johnson 75.00 150.00
9 Chris Henry RB 6.00 15.00
10 Darrelle Revis 8.00 20.00
11 Dwayne Bowe 6.00 15.00
12 Dwayne Jarrett 8.00 20.00
13 Gaines Adams 8.00 20.00
14 Greg Olsen 10.00 25.00
15 Jacoby Jones 6.00 15.00
16 JaMarcus Russell 6.00 15.00
17 James Jones 6.00 15.00
18 Jason Hill 6.00 15.00
19 John Beck 6.00 15.00
20 LaMarr Woodley 12.00 30.00
21 LaRon Landry 10.00 25.00
22 Lorenzo Booker 8.00 20.00
23 Marshawn Lynch 12.00 30.00
24 Matt Spaeth 10.00 25.00
25 Michael Griffin 6.00 15.00
26 Patrick Willis 25.00 60.00
27 Paul Posluszny 6.00 15.00
28 Paul Williams 6.00 15.00
29 Reggie Nelson 6.00 15.00
30 Steve Smith USC 6.00 15.00
31 Ted Ginn Jr. 8.00 20.00
32 Trent Edwards 6.00 15.00

2008 Playoff Contenders

This set was released on January 7, 2009. The base set consists of 225 cards. Cards 1-100 feature veterans, and cards 101-225 are autographed rookies. Some rookies were issued via mail redemption cards. Playoff also announced actual print runs on the short-printed signed RCs with a production run of 250 or less.
COMP.SET w/o RC's (100) 8.00 20.00
PLAYOFF ANNOUNCED SOME PRINT RUNS
1 Kurt Warner .25 .60
2 Larry Fitzgerald .25 .60
3 Anquan Boldin .20 .50
4 Edgerrin James .25 .60
5 Jerious Norwood .20 .50
6 Roddy White .20 .50
7 Michael Turner .20 .50
8 Willis McGahee .20 .50
9 Derrick Mason .20 .50
10 Le'Ron McClain .30 .75
11 Trent Edwards .20 .50
12 Marshawn Lynch .25 .60
13 Lee Evans .25 .60
14 Steve Smith .25 .60
15 DeAngelo Williams .20 .50
16 Jake Delhomme .20 .50
17 Greg Olsen .25 .60
18 Devin Hester .25 .60
19 Kyle Orton .20 .50
20 Carson Palmer .25 .60
21 Chad Johnson .20 .50
22 T.J. Houshmandzadeh .20 .50
23 Chris Perry .20 .50
24 Derek Anderson .20 .50
25 Jamal Lewis .25 .60
26 Braylon Edwards .20 .50
27 Tony Romo .25 .60
28 Terrell Owens .25 .60
29 Marion Barber .20 .50
30 Jason Witten .25 .60
31 Jay Cutler .20 .50
32 Selvin Young .20 .50
33 Brandon Marshall .25 .60
34 Jon Kitna .20 .50
35 Roy Williams WR .20 .50
36 Calvin Johnson .30 .75
37 Aaron Rodgers .60 1.50
38 Ryan Grant .25 .60
39 Greg Jennings .20 .50
40 Matt Schaub .20 .50
41 Ahman Green .25 .60
42 Andre Johnson .25 .60
43 Peyton Manning .75 2.00
44 Joseph Addai .20 .50
45 Reggie Wayne .25 .60
46 David Garrard .20 .50
47 Fred Taylor .20 .50
48 Maurice Jones-Drew .20 .50
49 Brodie Croyle .25 .60
50 Larry Johnson .20 .50
51 Tony Gonzalez .25 .60
52 Chad Pennington .20 .50
53 Ronnie Brown .20 .50
54 Ted Ginn Jr. .20 .50
55 Tarvaris Jackson .20 .50
56 Adrian Peterson .30 .75
57 Chester Taylor .20 .50
58 Tom Brady 1.00 2.50
59 Randy Moss .25 .60
60 Laurence Maroney .25 .60
61 Drew Brees .30 .75
62 Reggie Bush .20 .50
63 Marques Colston .20 .50
64 Eli Manning .25 .60
65 Plaxico Burress .20 .50
66 Brandon Jacobs .20 .50
67 Brett Favre 1.50 4.00
68 Leon Washington .20 .50
69 Laveranues Coles .20 .50
70 Javon Walker .25 .60
71 JaMarcus Russell .20 .50
72 Justin Fargas .20 .50
73 Donovan McNabb .25 .60
74 Brian Westbrook .20 .50
75 Kevin Curtis .20 .50
76 Ben Roethlisberger .30 .75
77 Willie Parker .25 .60
78 Santonio Holmes .20 .50
79 Philip Rivers .30 .75
80 LaDainian Tomlinson .30 .75
81 Vincent Jackson .20 .50
82 Antonio Gates .25 .60
83 J.T. O'Sullivan .20 .50
84 Frank Gore .25 .60
85 Isaac Bruce .30 .75
86 Matt Hasselbeck .20 .50
87 Deion Branch .20 .50
88 Julius Jones .20 .50
89 Marc Bulger .20 .50
90 Steven Jackson .20 .50
91 Torry Holt .25 .60
92 Warrick Dunn .20 .50
93 Jeff Garcia .20 .50
94 Joey Galloway .25 .60
95 Vince Young .20 .50
96 LenDale White .20 .50
97 Justin Gage .20 .50
98 Jason Campbell .20 .50
99 Clinton Portis .20 .50
100 Chris Cooley .20 .50
101 Adrian Arrington AU RC 5.00 12.00
102 Ali Highsmith AU/214* RC 15.00 40.00
103 Allen Patrick AU RC 5.00 12.00
104 Andre Caldwell AU RC 5.00 12.00
105 Andre Woodson AU/250* RC 12.00 30.00
106 Antoine Cason AU RC 6.00 15.00
107 Aqib Talib AU RC 8.00 20.00
108 Brad Cottam AU/132* RC 30.00 60.00
109 B.Flowers AU/192* RC 25.00 50.00
110 Brian Brohm AU RC 10.00 25.00
111 Calais Campbell AU RC 6.00 15.00
112 Chad Henne AU RC 8.00 20.00
113 C.Washington AU/114* RC 25.00 60.00
114 Chevis Jackson AU RC 5.00 12.00
115 Chris Johnson AU RC 10.00 25.00
116 Chris Long AU RC 6.00 15.00
117 Colt Brennan AU RC 6.00 15.00
118 Craig Steltz AU RC 5.00 12.00
119 Curtis Lofton AU RC 6.00 15.00
120 Dan Connor AU RC 5.00 12.00
121 Dantrell Savage AU/76* RC 20.00 50.00
122 Darius Reynaud AU RC 5.00 12.00
123 Darren McFadden AU RC 5.00 12.00
124 Davone Bess AU RC 6.00 15.00
125 Dennis Dixon AU RC 15.00 40.00
126 Derrick Harvey AU RC 5.00 12.00
127 DeSean Jackson AU RC 10.00 25.00
128 Devin Thomas AU RC 5.00 12.00
129 Dexter Jackson AU RC 8.00 20.00
130 D.Rodgers-Cromartie AU RC 6.00 15.00
131 Donnie Avery AU RC 6.00 15.00
132 Dustin Keller AU RC 6.00 15.00
133 Earl Bennett AU RC 8.00 20.00
134 Early Doucet AU/113* RC 20.00 50.00
135 Eddie Royal AU RC 5.00 12.00
136 Erik Ainge AU/107* RC 12.00 30.00
137 Erin Henderson AU/158* RC 15.00 40.00
138 Felix Jones AU RC 5.00 12.00
139 Fred Davis AU RC 5.00 12.00
140 Glenn Dorsey AU RC 5.00 12.00
141 Harry Douglas AU RC 6.00 15.00
142 Jacob Hester AU RC 5.00 12.00
143 Jacob Tamme AU RC 10.00 25.00
144 Jake Long AU/163* RC 15.00 40.00
145 Jamaal Charles AU RC 30.00 60.00
146 James Hardy AU RC 5.00 12.00
147 Jed Collins AU/30* RC 150.00 300.00
148 J.Finley AU/231* RC 5.00 12.00
149 Jerod Mayo AU RC 10.00 25.00
150 Jerome Simpson AU RC 6.00 15.00
151 Joe Flacco AU/220* RC 40.00 80.00
152 John Carlson AU RC 5.00 12.00
153 John David Booty AU RC 5.00 12.00
154A J.Stewart AU Blk RC 15.00 40.00
154B J.Stewart AU Blu RC 20.00 50.00
155 Jordon Dizon AU/188* RC 20.00 40.00
156 Jordy Nelson AU RC 25.00 50.00
157 Josh Johnson AU RC 5.00 12.00
158 Josh Morgan AU RC 5.00 12.00
159 Justin Forsett AU RC 15.00 30.00
160 Keenan Burton AU RC 5.00 12.00
161 Keith Rivers AU RC 5.00 12.00
162 Kellen Davis AU RC 5.00 12.00
163 Kenny Phillips AU RC 5.00 12.00
164 Kentwan Balmer AU RC 5.00 12.00
165 Kevin O'Connell AU RC 5.00 12.00
166 Kevin Smith AU RC 5.00 12.00
167 Lavelle Hawkins AU RC 6.00 15.00
168 Lawrence Jackson AU RC 5.00 12.00
169 Leodis McKelvin AU RC 6.00 15.00
170 Limas Sweed AU RC 5.00 12.00
171 Malcolm Kelly AU/141* RC 15.00 40.00
173 Marcus Thomas AU/165* RC 12.00 30.00
174 Mario Manningham AU RC 10.00 25.00
175 Martellus Bennett AU RC 6.00 15.00
176 Martin Rucker AU RC 5.00 12.00
177 Matt Flynn AU RC 5.00 12.00
178 Matt Forte AU RC 15.00 40.00
179 Matt Ryan AU/246* RC 300.00 500.00
180 Mike Hart AU RC 5.00 12.00
181 Mike Jenkins AU RC 5.00 12.00
182 Owen Schmitt AU RC 5.00 12.00
183 Pat Sims AU RC 6.00 15.00
184 Peyton Hillis AU/113* RC 30.00 80.00
185 Phillip Merling AU/100* RC 20.00 50.00
186 Quentin Groves AU RC 6.00 15.00
187 Rashard Mendenhall AU RC 8.00 20.00
188 Ray Rice AU RC 8.00 20.00
189 Reggie Smith AU/196* RC 15.00 40.00
190 Ryan Torain AU/70* RC 50.00 100.00
191 Sedrick Ellis AU RC 5.00 12.00
192 Steve Slaton AU RC 5.00 12.00
193 Tashard Choice AU RC 5.00 12.00
194 Terrell Thomas AU RC 5.00 12.00
195 Thomas Brown AU/151* RC 20.00 40.00
196 Tim Hightower AU RC 6.00 15.00
197 Vernon Gholston AU RC 5.00 12.00
198 Will Franklin AU RC 6.00 15.00
199 Xavier Adibi AU RC 5.00 12.00
200 B.Witherspoon AU/150* RC 20.00 50.00
201 Caleb Hanie AU RC 8.00 20.00
202 Charles Godfrey AU RC 5.00 12.00
203 Chaz Schilens AU RC 10.00 25.00
204 Chris Horton AU RC 8.00 20.00
205 Derek Fine AU RC 5.00 12.00
206 Zackary Bowman AU RC 6.00 15.00
207 Dwight Lowery AU RC 6.00 15.00
208 Jalen Parmele AU RC 6.00 15.00
209 Jerome Felton AU RC 5.00 12.00
210 Kendall Langford AU RC 6.00 15.00
211 Kregg Lumpkin AU RC 8.00 20.00
212 Marcus Henry AU RC 5.00 12.00
213 Matt Slater AU RC 6.00 15.00
214 Mike Cox AU RC 6.00 15.00
215 Mike Tolbert AU/199* RC 20.00 50.00
216 Pierre Garcon AU RC 10.00 25.00
217 Quintin Demps AU RC 6.00 15.00
218 Sam Baker AU RC 5.00 12.00
219 Steve Johnson AU RC 8.00 20.00
220 Tavares Gooden AU RC 5.00 12.00
221 Terrence Wheatley AU RC 5.00 12.00
222 Tom Santi AU RC 6.00 15.00
223 Tom Zbikowski AU/149* RC 20.00 50.00
224 Tyvon Branch AU RC 6.00 15.00
225 Xavier Omon AU/124* RC 20.00 50.00

2008 Playoff Contenders Championship Ticket

UNPRICED CHAMPIONSHIP PRINT RUN 1

2008 Playoff Contenders Playoff Ticket

*VETS 1-100: 3X TO 8X BASIC CARDS
COMMON ROOKIE (101-225) 2.00 5.00
ROOKIE SEMISTARS 2.50 6.00
ROOKIE UNL.STARS 3.00 8.00
STATED PRINT RUN 99 SER.#'d SETS
67 Brett Favre 5.00 12.00
110 Brian Brohm 2.00 5.00
112 Chad Henne 2.50 6.00
115 Chris Johnson 2.50 6.00
116 Chris Long 2.50 6.00
117 Colt Brennan 2.50 6.00
123 Darren McFadden 2.00 5.00
124 Davone Bess 2.50 6.00
127 DeSean Jackson 4.00 10.00
131 Donnie Avery 2.50 6.00
135 Eddie Royal 2.00 5.00
138 Felix Jones 2.00 5.00
140 Glenn Dorsey 2.00 5.00
144 Jake Long 3.00 8.00
145 Jamaal Charles 3.00 8.00
149 Jerod Mayo 3.00 8.00
151 Joe Flacco 4.00 10.00
154 Jonathan Stewart 3.00 8.00
156 Jordy Nelson 6.00 15.00
165 Kevin O'Connell 2.00 5.00
166 Kevin Smith 2.00 5.00
170 Limas Sweed 2.00 5.00
177 Matt Flynn 2.00 5.00
178 Matt Forte 3.00 8.00
179 Matt Ryan 6.00 15.00
180 Mike Hart 2.00 5.00
184 Peyton Hillis 3.00 8.00
187 Rashard Mendenhall 2.00 5.00
188 Ray Rice 2.00 5.00
192 Steve Slaton 2.00 5.00
196 Tim Hightower 2.50 6.00
201 Caleb Hanie 3.00 8.00
204 Chris Horton 3.00 8.00
216 Pierre Garcon 4.00 10.00
223 Tom Zbikowski 2.50 6.00

2008 Playoff Contenders College Rookie Ticket Playoff Ticket

*ROOK/99: .4X TO 1X BASE PLAY.TICKET
STATED PRINT RUN 99 SER.#'d SETS
1 Brian Brohm 2.00 5.00
2 Brandon Flowers 2.50 6.00
3 Chad Henne 2.50 6.00
4 Chris Long 2.50 6.00
5 Chris Johnson 2.50 6.00
6 Dan Connor 2.00 5.00
7 Darren McFadden 2.00 5.00
8 DeSean Jackson 4.00 10.00
9 Devin Thomas 2.00 5.00
10 Donnie Avery 2.50 6.00
11 Dustin Keller 2.50 6.00
12 Early Doucet 2.00 5.00
13 Felix Jones 2.00 5.00
14 Glenn Dorsey 2.00 5.00
15 Jake Long 3.00 8.00
16 Jamaal Charles 3.00 8.00
17 James Hardy 2.00 5.00
18 Jerod Mayo 3.00 8.00
19 Joe Flacco 4.00 10.00
20 John David Booty 2.00 5.00
21 John Carlson 2.00 5.00
22 Jonathan Stewart 3.00 8.00
23 Jordon Dizon 2.00 5.00
24 Jordy Nelson 6.00 15.00
25 Kenny Phillips 2.00 5.00
26 Kevin Smith 2.00 5.00
27 Limas Sweed 2.00 5.00
28 Malcolm Kelly 2.00 5.00
29 Matt Ryan 6.00 15.00
30 Matt Forte 3.00 8.00
31 Phillip Merling 2.00 5.00
32 Rashard Mendenhall 2.00 5.00
33 Ray Rice 2.00 5.00
34 Steve Slaton 2.00 5.00
35 Vernon Gholston 2.00 5.00

2008 Playoff Contenders College Rookie Ticket Autographs

UNPRICED CHAMPIONSHIP PRINT RUN 1
1 Brian Brohm 12.00 30.00
2 Brandon Flowers 15.00 40.00
3 Chad Henne 15.00 40.00
4 Chris Long 15.00 40.00
5 Chris Johnson 25.00 60.00
6 Dan Connor 12.00 30.00
7 Darren McFadden 12.00 30.00
8 DeSean Jackson 25.00 60.00
9 Devin Thomas EXCH 12.00 30.00
10 Donnie Avery 15.00 40.00
11 Dustin Keller 15.00 40.00
12 Early Doucet 12.00 30.00
13 Felix Jones 12.00 30.00
14 Glenn Dorsey 12.00 30.00
15 Jake Long 20.00 50.00
16 Jamaal Charles 40.00 80.00
17 James Hardy 12.00 30.00
18 Jerod Mayo 20.00 50.00
19 Joe Flacco 75.00 150.00
20 John David Booty 12.00 30.00
21 John Carlson 12.00 30.00
22 Jonathan Stewart 40.00 80.00
23 Jordon Dizon 12.00 30.00
24 Jordy Nelson 40.00 80.00
25 Kenny Phillips 12.00 30.00
26 Kevin Smith 12.00 30.00
27 Limas Sweed 12.00 30.00
28 Malcolm Kelly 12.00 30.00
29 Matt Ryan 300.00 600.00
30 Matt Forte 50.00 120.00
31 Phillip Merling 12.00 30.00
32 Rashard Mendenhall 20.00 50.00
33 Ray Rice 25.00 60.00
34 Steve Slaton 12.00 30.00
35 Vernon Gholston 12.00 30.00

2008 Playoff Contenders Draft Class

STATED PRINT RUN 500 SER.#'d SETS
*GOLD/100: .5X TO 1.2X BASIC INSERTS
GOLD PRINT RUN 100 SER.#'d SETS
*BLACK/50: .6X TO 1.5X BASIC INSERTS
BLACK PRINT RUN 50 SER.#'d SETS
UNPRICED AUTO PRINT RUN 10
1 E.Doucet/D.Rodgers-Cromartie .75 2.00
2 M.Ryan/C.Lofton 2.00 5.00
3 C.Jackson/H.Douglas .75 2.00
4 J.Flacco/R.Rice 1.25 3.00
5 L.McKelvin/J.Hardy .75 2.00
6 J.Stewart/D.Connor 1.00 2.50
7 M.Forte/E.Bennett 1.00 2.50
8 K.Rivers/J.Simpson .60 1.50
9 A.Caldwell/P.Sims .75 2.00
10 M.Rucker/P.Hubbard .60 1.50
11 F.Jones/M.Jenkins .60 1.50
12 M.Bennett/T.Choice .75 2.00
13 E.Royal/R.Torain .60 1.50
14 J.Dizon/K.Smith .60 1.50
15 J.Nelson/B.Brohm 2.00 5.00
16 S.Slaton/X.Adibi .60 1.50
17 J.Tamme/M.Hart .75 2.00
18 D.Harvey/Q.Groves .75 2.00
19 G.Dorsey/J.Charles 1.00 2.50
20 V.Gholston/D.Keller .75 2.00
21 J.Long/C.Henne 1.00 2.50
22 J.Mayo/K.O'Connell 1.00 2.50
23 S.Ellis/T.Porter .75 2.00
24 K.Phillips/M.Manningham .60 1.50
25 D.McFadden/T.Branch .75 2.00
26 D.Jackson/J.Collins 1.25 3.00
27 R.Mendenhall/L.Sweed .60 1.50
28 A.Cason/J.Hester .75 2.00
29 K.Balmer/R.Smith .60 1.50
30 L.Jackson/J.Carlson .60 1.50
31 C.Long/D.Avery .75 2.00
32 A.Talib/D.Jackson 1.00 2.50
33 C.Johnson/L.Hawkins .75 2.00
34 D.Thomas/F.Davis .60 1.50
35 M.Kelly/C.Brennan .75 2.00

2008 Playoff Contenders ROY Contenders

STATED PRINT RUN 500 SER.#'d SETS
*GOLD/100: .5X TO 1.2X BASIC INSERTS
GOLD PRINT RUN 100 SER.#'d SETS
*BLACK/50: .6X TO 1.5X BASIC INSERTS
BLACK PRINT RUN 50 SER.#'d SETS
1 Chris Long 1.00 2.50
2 Matt Ryan 2.50 6.00
3 Darren McFadden .75 2.00
4 Glenn Dorsey .75 2.00
5 Vernon Gholston .75 2.00
6 Sedrick Ellis .75 2.00
7 Derrick Harvey .75 2.00
8 Keith Rivers .75 2.00
9 Jerod Mayo 1.25 3.00
10 Jonathan Stewart 1.25 3.00
11 Joe Flacco 1.50 4.00
12 Felix Jones .75 2.00
13 Rashard Mendenhall .75 2.00
14 Chris Johnson 1.00 2.50
15 Dustin Keller 1.00 2.50
16 Kenny Phillips .75 2.00
17 Donnie Avery 1.00 2.50
18 Devin Thomas .75 2.00
19 John Carlson .75 2.00
20 Fred Davis .75 2.00
21 Eddie Royal .75 2.00
22 Jordy Nelson 2.50 6.00
23 Matt Forte 1.25 3.00
24 Chad Henne 1.00 2.50
25 Jerome Simpson 1.00 2.50
26 James Hardy .75 2.00
27 Ray Rice .75 2.00
28 Limas Sweed .75 2.00
29 DeSean Jackson 1.50 4.00
30 Malcolm Kelly .75 2.00
31 Leodis McKelvin 1.00 2.50
32 Kevin Smith .75 2.00
33 Dominique Rodgers-Cromartie 1.00 2.50
34 Aqib Talib 1.25 3.00
35 Antoine Cason 1.00 2.50

2008 Playoff Contenders ROY Contenders Autographs

STATED PRINT RUN 25 SER.#'d SETS
1 Chris Long 10.00 25.00
2 Matt Ryan 200.00 400.00
3 Darren McFadden 8.00 20.00
4 Glenn Dorsey 8.00 20.00
5 Vernon Gholston 8.00 20.00
6 Sedrick Ellis 8.00 20.00
7 Derrick Harvey 8.00 20.00
8 Keith Rivers 8.00 20.00
9 Jerod Mayo 12.00 30.00
10 Jonathan Stewart 12.00 30.00
11 Joe Flacco 40.00 80.00
12 Felix Jones 8.00 20.00
13 Rashard Mendenhall 8.00 20.00
14 Chris Johnson 10.00 25.00
15 Dustin Keller 10.00 25.00
16 Kenny Phillips 8.00 20.00
17 Donnie Avery 10.00 25.00
18 Devin Thomas EXCH 8.00 20.00
19 John Carlson 8.00 20.00
20 Fred Davis 8.00 20.00
21 Eddie Royal 8.00 20.00
22 Jordy Nelson 30.00 60.00
23 Matt Forte 12.00 30.00
24 Chad Henne 10.00 25.00
25 Jerome Simpson 10.00 25.00
26 James Hardy 8.00 20.00
27 Ray Rice 8.00 20.00
28 Limas Sweed 8.00 20.00
29 DeSean Jackson 15.00 40.00
30 Malcolm Kelly 8.00 20.00
31 Leodis McKelvin 10.00 25.00
32 Kevin Smith 8.00 20.00
33 Dominique Rodgers-Cromartie 10.00 25.00
34 Aqib Talib 12.00 30.00
35 Antoine Cason 10.00 25.00

2008 Playoff Contenders Rookie Roll Call

STATED PRINT RUN 500 SER.#'d SETS
*GOLD/100: .5X TO 1.2X BASIC INSERTS
GOLD PRINT RUN 100 SER.#'d SETS
*BLACK/50: .6X TO 1.5X BASIC INSERTS
BLACK PRINT RUN 50 SER.#'d SETS
1 Vernon Gholston .75 2.00
2 Donnie Avery 1.00 2.50
3 Chris Johnson 1.00 2.50
4 Devin Thomas .75 2.00
5 Rashard Mendenhall .75 2.00
6 Kenny Phillips .75 2.00
7 Brandon Flowers 1.00 2.50
8 Jordy Nelson 2.50 6.00
9 Felix Jones .75 2.00
10 Jonathan Stewart 1.25 3.00
11 Joe Flacco 1.50 4.00
12 James Hardy .75 2.00
13 Jerome Simpson 1.00 2.50
14 Matt Forte 1.25 3.00
15 Eddie Royal .75 2.00
16 Limas Sweed .75 2.00
17 DeSean Jackson 1.50 4.00
18 Fred Davis .75 2.00
19 Malcolm Kelly .75 2.00
20 Matt Ryan 2.50 6.00
21 Leodis McKelvin 1.00 2.50
22 Keith Rivers .75 2.00
23 Glenn Dorsey .75 2.00
24 Jake Long 1.25 3.00
25 Jerod Mayo 1.25 3.00
26 Darren McFadden .75 2.00
27 Chris Long 1.00 2.50
28 Colt Brennan 1.00 2.50
29 Jordon Dizon .75 2.00
30 Martellus Bennett 1.00 2.50
31 Brian Brohm .75 2.00
32 Jamaal Charles 1.25 3.00
33 Ray Rice .75 2.00
34 Chad Henne 1.00 2.50
35 Dan Connor .75 2.00

2008 Playoff Contenders Rookie Roll Call Autographs

STATED PRINT RUN 25 SER.#'d SETS
1 Vernon Gholston 8.00 20.00
2 Donnie Avery 10.00 25.00
3 Chris Johnson 10.00 25.00
4 Devin Thomas 8.00 20.00
5 Rashard Mendenhall 8.00 20.00
6 Kenny Phillips 8.00 20.00
7 Brandon Flowers 10.00 25.00
8 Jordy Nelson 30.00 60.00
9 Felix Jones 8.00 20.00
10 Jonathan Stewart 12.00 30.00
11 Joe Flacco 40.00 80.00
12 James Hardy 8.00 20.00
13 Jerome Simpson 10.00 25.00
14 Matt Forte 12.00 30.00
15 Eddie Royal 8.00 20.00
16 Limas Sweed 8.00 20.00
17 DeSean Jackson 15.00 40.00
18 Fred Davis 8.00 20.00
19 Malcolm Kelly 8.00 20.00
20 Matt Ryan 100.00 200.00
21 Leodis McKelvin 10.00 25.00
22 Keith Rivers 8.00 20.00
23 Glenn Dorsey 8.00 20.00
24 Jake Long 12.00 30.00
25 Jerod Mayo 12.00 30.00
26 Darren McFadden 8.00 20.00
27 Chris Long 10.00 25.00
28 Colt Brennan 10.00 25.00
29 Jordon Dizon 8.00 20.00
30 Martellus Bennett 10.00 25.00
31 Brian Brohm 8.00 20.00
32 Jamaal Charles 12.00 30.00
33 Ray Rice 8.00 20.00
34 Chad Henne 10.00 25.00
35 Dan Connor 8.00 20.00

2008 Playoff Contenders Round Numbers

STATED PRINT RUN 500 SER.#'d SETS
*GOLD/100: .5X TO 1.2X BASIC INSERTS
GOLD PRINT RUN 100 SER.#'d SETS
*BLACK/50: .6X TO 1.5X BASIC INSERTS
BLACK PRINT RUN 50 SER.#'d SETS
UNPRICED AUTO PRINT RUN 10
1 J.Long/C.Long 1.25 3.00
2 M.Ryan/D.McFadden 2.50 6.00
3 G.Dorsey/V.Gholston .75 2.00
4 J.Stewart/J.Flacco 1.50 4.00
5 K.Rivers/J.Mayo .75 2.00
6 L.McKelvin/D.Rodgers-Cromartie 1.00 2.50
7 F.Jones/R.Mendenhall .75 2.00
8 D.Keller/K.Phillips 1.00 2.50
9 S.Ellis/D.Harvey .75 2.00
10 M.Jenkins/A.Cason 1.00 2.50
11 D.Avery/D.Thomas 1.00 2.50
12 E.Royal/J.Nelson .75 2.00
13 J.Simpson/J.Hardy .75 2.00
14 M.Forte/C.Henne 1.25 3.00
15 J.Carlson/F.Davis .75 2.00
16 D.Jackson/M.Kelly 1.50 4.00
17 L.Sweed/R.Rice .75 2.00
18 D.Connor/S.Crable .75 2.00
19 K.O'Connell/K.Smith .75 2.00
20 J.Charles/S.Slaton 1.25 3.00
21 B.Cottam/J.Finley .75 2.00
22 E.Bennett/E.Doucet 1.25 3.00
23 H.Douglas/M.Manningham 1.00 2.50
24 W.Franklin/M.Smith 1.00 2.50
25 M.Rucker/J.Tamme 1.00 2.50
26 L.Hawkins/K.Burton 1.00 2.50
27 J.Booty/D.Dixon .75 2.00
28 J.Johnson/E.Ainge .75 2.00
29 T.Hightower/R.Torain 1.00 2.50
30 C.Brennan/A.Woodson 1.00 2.50
31 T.Brown/M.Hart .75 2.00
32 J.Morgan/K.Robinson .75 2.00
33 M.Flynn/C.Washington .75 2.00
34 C.Boyd/A.Patrick .75 2.00
35 A.Arrington/P.Hillis .75 2.00

2009 Playoff Contenders

COMP.SET w/o RC's (100) 10.00 25.00
OVERALL AUTOGRAPH ODDS 1:6
PANINI ANNOUNCED SOME PRINT RUNS
1 Kurt Warner .25 .60
2 Larry Fitzgerald .25 .60
3 Tim Hightower .20 .50
4 Matt Ryan .25 .60
5 Michael Turner .20 .50
6 Roddy White .20 .50
7 Tony Gonzalez .25 .60
8 Joe Flacco .25 .60
9 Mark Clayton .20 .50
10 Willis McGahee .20 .50
11 Lee Evans .25 .60
12 Marshawn Lynch .25 .60
13 Terrell Owens .25 .60
14 DeAngelo Williams .20 .50
15 Jake Delhomme .20 .50
16 Steve Smith .25 .60
17 Devin Hester .25 .60
18 Greg Olsen .25 .60
19 Jay Cutler .20 .50
20 Matt Forte .20 .50
21 Carson Palmer .25 .60
22 Chad Ochocinco .20 .50
23 Cedric Benson .20 .50
24 Josh Cribbs .20 .50
25 Braylon Edwards .20 .50
26 Jamal Lewis .25 .60
27 Roy Williams WR .20 .50
28 Marion Barber .25 .60
29 Tony Romo .25 .60
30 Brandon Marshall .25 .60
31 Eddie Royal .20 .50
32 Kyle Orton .20 .50
33 Calvin Johnson .30 .75
34 Bryant Johnson .20 .50
35 Kevin Smith .20 .50
36 Aaron Rodgers .60 1.50
37 Greg Jennings .20 .50
38 Ryan Grant .25 .60
39 Andre Johnson .25 .60
40 Matt Schaub .20 .50
41 Steve Slaton .20 .50
42 Anthony Gonzalez .20 .50
43 Joseph Addai .20 .50
44 Peyton Manning .75 2.00
45 Reggie Wayne .25 .60
46 David Garrard .20 .50
47 Maurice Jones-Drew .20 .50
48 Torry Holt .25 .60
49 Dwayne Bowe .25 .60
50 Jamaal Charles .25 .60
51 Matt Cassel .20 .50
52 Chad Henne .25 .60
53 Ted Ginn .20 .50
54 Ronnie Brown .20 .50
55 Adrian Peterson .30 .75
56 Bernard Berrian .20 .50
57 Brett Favre 4.00 10.00
58 Randy Moss .25 .60
59 Tom Brady 1.00 2.50
60 Laurence Maroney .25 .60
61 Drew Brees .30 .75
62 Marques Colston .20 .50
63 Reggie Bush .20 .50
64 Brandon Jacobs .20 .50
65 Eli Manning .25 .60
66 Steve Smith USC .25 .60
67 Jerricho Cotchery .20 .50
68 Leon Washington .20 .50
69 Thomas Jones .20 .50
70 Darren McFadden .30 .75
71 JaMarcus Russell .20 .50
72 Zach Miller .20 .50
73 Brian Westbrook .20 .50
74 DeSean Jackson .25 .60
75 Donovan McNabb .25 .60
76 Ben Roethlisberger .30 .75
77 Santonio Holmes .20 .50
78 Willie Parker .20 .50
79 Antonio Gates .25 .60
80 LaDainian Tomlinson .30 .75
81 Philip Rivers .30 .75
82 Vincent Jackson .20 .50
83 Frank Gore .25 .60
84 Josh Morgan .20 .50
85 Vernon Davis .20 .50
86 Julius Jones .20 .50
87 Matt Hasselbeck .20 .50
88 T.J. Houshmandzadeh .20 .50
89 Donnie Avery .20 .50
90 Marc Bulger .20 .50
91 Steven Jackson .20 .50
92 Antonio Bryant .20 .50
93 Derrick Ward .20 .50
94 Kellen Winslow Jr. .20 .50
95 Bo Scaife .20 .50
96 Chris Johnson .20 .50
97 Kerry Collins .20 .50
98 Chris Cooley .20 .50
99 Clinton Portis .20 .50
100 Santana Moss .25 .60
101 M.Stafford AU/540* RC 40.00 100.00
102 Jason Smith AU/237* RC 15.00 40.00
103 Tyson Jackson AU/443* RC 4.00 10.00
104 Aaron Curry AU RC 10.00 25.00
105 Mark Sanchez AU RC 8.00 20.00
106 D.Heyward-Bey AU RC 6.00 15.00
107 M.Crabtree AU/539* RC 6.00 15.00
108 K.Moreno AU/445* RC 4.00 10.00
109 Josh Freeman AU RC 4.00 10.00
110 Jeremy Maclin AU/278* RC 10.00 25.00
111 Brandon Pettigrew AU RC 4.00 10.00
112 Percy Harvin AU/497* RC 10.00 25.00
113 Donald Brown AU/465* RC 8.00 20.00
114 Hakeem Nicks AU/318* RC 5.00 12.00
115 Kenny Britt AU RC 6.00 15.00
116 Chris Wells AU/531* RC 12.00 30.00
117 Brian Robiskie AU RC 4.00 10.00
118 Pat White AU RC 5.00 12.00
119 M.Massaquoi AU RC 10.00 25.00
120 LeSean McCoy AU RC 15.00 40.00
121 Shonn Greene AU RC 4.00 10.00
122 Glen Coffee AU RC 4.00 10.00
123 Derrick Williams AU RC 4.00 10.00
124 Mike Wallace AU RC 6.00 15.00
125 Ramses Barden AU RC 8.00 20.00
126 Patrick Turner AU RC 4.00 10.00
127 Deon Butler AU RC 4.00 10.00
128 J.Iglesias AU/467* RC 4.00 10.00
129 Stephen McGee AU RC 4.00 10.00
130 Mike Thomas AU RC 4.00 10.00
131 Andre Brown AU/363* RC 10.00 20.00
132 Rhett Bomar AU RC 4.00 10.00
133 Nate Davis AU RC 10.00 25.00
134 Javon Ringer AU RC 4.00 10.00
135 Aaron Brown AU RC 6.00 15.00
136 Aaron Kelly AU/21* RC 300.00 500.00
137 Aaron Maybin AU/99* RC 20.00 50.00
138 Alphonso Smith AU/99* RC 20.00 50.00
139 Anthony Hill AU RC 4.00 10.00
140 Vontae Davis AU RC 4.00 10.00
141 Austin Collie AU RC 4.00 10.00
142 B.J. Raji AU RC 10.00 25.00
143 Bernard Scott AU RC 6.00 15.00
144 Brandon Gibson AU RC 5.00 12.00
145 Brandon Myers AU/99* RC 35.00 60.00
146 Brandon Tate AU RC 5.00 12.00
147 Brian Cushing AU/151* RC 20.00 50.00
148 Brian Hartline AU RC 6.00 15.00
149 Brian Hoyer AU RC 8.00 20.00
150 Brian Orakpo AU/199* RC 15.00 40.00
151 Brooks Foster AU RC 4.00 10.00
152 Cameron Morrah AU RC 4.00 10.00
153 Captain Munnerlyn AU RC 5.00 12.00
161 Chaoo Coffman AU RC 4.00 10.00
155 Chase Daniel AU RC 15.00 30.00
156 Clay Matthews AU RC 30.00 60.00
157 Clint Sintim AU/247* RC 4.00 10.00
158 Cornelius Ingram AU RC 4.00 10.00
159 Curtis Painter AU RC 4.00 10.00

Card	Low	High
160 David Johnson AU RC	5.00	12.00
161 Demetrius Byrd AU/505* RC	5.00	12.00
162 Dominique Edison AU RC	4.00	10.00
163 Everette Brown AU RC	4.00	10.00
164 Frank Summers AU RC	6.00	15.00
165 Gartrell Johnson AU RC	5.00	12.00
166 Hunter Cantwell AU/281* RC	4.00	10.00
167 Jake O'Connell AU RC	4.00	10.00
168 James Casey AU RC	5.00	12.00
169 James Laurinaitis AU RC	4.00	10.00
170 Jared Cook AU RC	5.00	12.00
171 Jarett Dillard AU RC	4.00	10.00
172 Zach Miller AU RC	5.00	12.00
173 John Nalbone AU RC	4.00	10.00
174 John Phillips AU RC	6.00	15.00
175 Johnny Knox AU RC	5.00	12.00
176 Julian Edelman AU RC	100.00	200.00
177 Keith Null AU RC	5.00	12.00
178 Kenny McKinley AU RC	4.00	10.00
179 Kevin Ogletree AU/493* RC	5.00	12.00
180 Kory Sheets AU/449* RC	5.00	12.00
181 Lardarius Webb AU RC	6.00	15.00
182 L.Stephens-Howling AU RC	8.00	20.00
183 Larry English AU/510* RC	5.00	12.00
184 Louis Delmas AU RC	5.00	12.00
185 Louis Murphy AU/99* RC	30.00	80.00
186 Malcolm Jenkins AU/393* RC	4.00	10.00
187 Manuel Johnson AU RC	4.00	10.00
188 Marko Mitchell AU RC	4.00	10.00
189 Mike Teel AU RC	4.00	10.00
190 Goodson AU/99* RC EXCH	20.00	50.00
191 Nick Miller AU RC	4.00	10.00
192 P.J. Hill AU RC	4.00	10.00
193 Quan Cosby AU/311* RC	12.00	30.00
194 Quinn Johnson AU RC	4.00	10.00
195 Rashad Jennings AU RC	5.00	12.00
196 Rey Maualuga AU/157* RC	12.00	30.00
197 Richard Quinn AU RC	5.00	12.00
198 Mouton AU/99* RC EXCH	20.00	50.00
199 Sammie Stroughter AU RC	4.00	10.00
200 Sean Smith AU RC	4.00	10.00
201 Nelson AU/99* RC EXCH	20.00	50.00
202 Sherrod Martin AU RC	4.00	10.00
203 Stefan Logan AU RC	6.00	15.00
204 Brandstater AU/63* RC	20.00	50.00
205 Tony Fiammetta AU RC	4.00	10.00
206 Travis Beckum AU RC	4.00	10.00
207 Tyrell Sutton AU/440* RC	8.00	20.00
208 James Davis AU/99* RC	20.00	50.00
209 Michael Oher AU/99* RC	25.00	50.00

2009 Playoff Contenders Playoff Ticket

*VETS 1-100: 3X TO 8X BASIC CARDS

Card	Low	High
COMMON ROOKIE (101-209)	1.50	4.00
ROOKIE SEMISTARS	2.00	5.00
ROOKIE UNL.STARS	2.50	6.00

STATED PRINT RUN 99 SER.#'d SETS

Card	Low	High
57 Brett Favre	10.00	25.00
101 Matthew Stafford	8.00	15.00
104 Aaron Curry	2.50	6.00
105 Mark Sanchez	3.00	8.00
106 Darrius Heyward-Bey	2.50	6.00
107 Michael Crabtree	2.50	6.00
108 Knowshon Moreno	1.50	4.00
109 Josh Freeman	1.50	4.00
110 Jeremy Maclin	2.00	5.00
111 Brandon Pettigrew	1.50	4.00
112 Percy Harvin	1.50	4.00
113 Donald Brown	1.50	4.00
114 Hakeem Nicks	2.00	5.00
115 Kenny Britt	2.50	6.00
116 Chris Wells	1.50	4.00
118 Pat White	2.00	5.00
120 LeSean McCoy	4.00	10.00
121 Shonn Greene	1.50	4.00
122 Glen Coffee	1.50	4.00
124 Mike Wallace	2.50	6.00
141 Austin Collie	1.50	4.00
142 B.J. Raji	2.00	5.00
145 Brandon Myers	4.00	10.00
147 Brian Cushing	1.50	4.00
149 Brian Hoyer	2.50	6.00
150 Brian Orakpo	2.00	5.00
155 Chase Daniel	2.00	5.00
156 Clay Matthews	8.00	20.00
169 James Laurinaitis	1.50	4.00
175 Johnny Knox	2.00	5.00
176 Julian Edelman	6.00	15.00
182 LaRod Stephens-Howling	3.00	8.00
196 Rey Maualuga	2.50	6.00
209 Michael Oher	2.50	6.00

2009 Playoff Contenders College Rookie Ticket Autographs

OVERALL AUTOGRAPH ODDS 1:6
PANINI ANNOUNCED SOME PRINT RUNS

Card	Low	High
1 Mark Sanchez/64*	12.00	30.00
2 Knowshon Moreno/65*	12.00	30.00
3 Brandon Pettigrew/50*	12.00	30.00
4 Kenny Britt/55*	20.00	50.00
5 Matthew Stafford/61*	60.00	120.00
6 Derrick Williams/55*	12.00	30.00
7 Deon Butler/51*	12.00	30.00
8 Andre Brown/64*	15.00	40.00
9 Javon Ringer/65*	12.00	30.00
10 Stephen McGee/60*	12.00	30.00
11 Mike Wallace/80*	30.00	60.00
12 LeSean McCoy/55*	30.00	60.00
13 Brian Robiskie/55*	12.00	30.00
14 Mohamed Massaquoi/59*	12.00	30.00
15 Michael Crabtree/55*	20.00	50.00
16 Jeremy Maclin/65*	15.00	40.00
17 Percy Harvin/55*	12.00	30.00
18 Hakeem Nicks/55*	15.00	40.00
19 Shonn Greene/68*	12.00	30.00
20 Patrick Turner/64*	12.00	30.00
21 Rhett Bomar/65*	12.00	30.00
22 Aaron Curry/64*	20.00	50.00
23 Donald Brown/65*	12.00	30.00
24 Glen Coffee/55*	12.00	30.00
25 Juaquin Iglesias/66*	12.00	30.00
26 Nate Davis/68*	12.00	30.00
27 Ramses Barden/63*	12.00	30.00
28 Chris Wells/63*	12.00	30.00
29 Pat White/65*	15.00	40.00
30 Josh Freeman/65*	12.00	30.00
31 Darrius Heyward-Bey/65*	20.00	50.00
32 Mike Thomas/64*	12.00	30.00

2009 Playoff Contenders College Rookie Ticket Playoff Ticket

STATED PRINT RUN 99 SER.#'d SETS

Card	Low	High
1 Mark Sanchez	1.50	4.00
2 Knowshon Moreno	1.50	4.00
3 Brandon Pettigrew	1.50	4.00
4 Kenny Britt	2.50	6.00
5 Matthew Stafford	6.00	15.00
6 Derrick Williams	1.50	4.00
7 Deon Butler	1.50	4.00
8 Andre Brown	2.00	5.00
9 Javon Ringer	1.50	4.00
10 Stephen McGee	1.50	4.00
11 Mike Wallace	2.50	6.00
12 LeSean McCoy	4.00	10.00
13 Brian Robiskie	1.50	4.00
14 Mohamed Massaquoi	1.50	4.00
15 Michael Crabtree	2.50	6.00
16 Jeremy Maclin	2.00	5.00
17 Percy Harvin	1.50	4.00
18 Hakeem Nicks	2.00	5.00
19 Shonn Greene	1.50	4.00
20 Patrick Turner	1.50	4.00
21 Rhett Bomar	1.50	4.00
22 Aaron Curry	2.50	6.00
23 Donald Brown	1.50	4.00
24 Glen Coffee	1.50	4.00
25 Juaquin Iglesias	1.50	4.00
26 Nate Davis	1.50	4.00
27 Ramses Barden	1.50	4.00
28 Chris Wells	1.50	4.00
29 Pat White	2.00	5.00
30 Josh Freeman	1.50	4.00
31 Darrius Heyward-Bey	2.50	6.00
32 Mike Thomas	1.50	4.00

2009 Playoff Contenders Draft Class

*BLACK/50: .6X TO 1.5X BASIC INSERTS
*GOLD/100: .5X TO 1.2X BASIC INSERTS

Card	Low	High
1 A.Maybin/S.Nelson	.75	2.00
2 E.Brown/M.Goodson	.75	2.00
3 J.Iglesias/J.Knox	.75	2.00
4 R.Maualuga/C.Coffman	1.00	2.50
5 B.Robiskie/M.Massaquoi	.60	1.50
6 S.McGee/K.Ogletree	.75	2.00
7 K.Moreno/K.McKinley	.60	1.50
8 M.Stafford/B.Pettigrew	3.00	8.00
9 B.Raji/C.Matthews	1.25	3.00
10 B.Cushing/J.Casey	.60	1.50
11 D.Brown/A.Collie	.60	1.50
12 M.Thomas/J.Dillard	.60	1.50
13 V.Davis/P.White	.75	2.00
14 M.Jenkins/P.Hill	.60	1.50
15 H.Nicks/C.Sintim	.75	2.00
16 M.Sanchez/S.Greene	.60	1.50
17 D.Heyward-Bey/L.Murphy	1.00	2.50
18 J.Maclin/L.McCoy	1.50	4.00
19 L.English/D.Byrd	.75	2.00
20 M.Crabtree/C.Coffee	1.00	2.50
21 A.Curry/D.Butler	1.00	2.50
22 J.Smith/J.Laurinaitis	.60	1.50
23 K.Britt/J.Cook	1.00	2.50
24 A.Brown/R.Bomar	.75	2.00
25 C.Ingram/B.Gibson	.75	2.00

2009 Playoff Contenders Legendary Contenders

*GOLD/100: .5X TO 1.2X BASIC INSERTS

Card	Low	High
1 Alan Page	1.00	2.50
2 Andre Reed	1.25	3.00
3 Archie Manning	1.25	3.00
4 Bart Starr	2.50	6.00
5 Bert Jones	1.00	2.50
6 Billy Sims	1.25	3.00
7 Bob Lilly	1.25	3.00
8 Bobby Bell	1.00	2.50
9 Boyd Dowler	1.00	2.50
10 Brett Favre	3.00	8.00
11 Carl Eller	1.00	2.50
12 Charley Trippi	1.00	2.50
13 Charlie Joiner	1.00	2.50
14 Chuck Bednarik	1.25	3.00
15 Chuck Foreman	1.00	2.50
16 Ace Parker	1.00	2.50
17 Cris Collinsworth	1.25	3.00
18 Dan Fouts	1.25	3.00
19 Dan Hampton	1.00	2.50
20 Dan Marino	3.00	8.00
21 Danny White	1.25	3.00
22 Daryl Johnston	1.25	3.00
23 Dave Casper	1.00	2.50
24 Deion Sanders	1.25	3.00
25 Del Shofner	1.00	2.50
26 Dick Butkus	2.00	5.00
27 Dub Jones	1.00	2.50
28 Earl Campbell	1.50	4.00
29 Emmitt Smith	2.50	6.00
30 Forrest Gregg	1.00	2.50
31 Franco Harris	1.50	4.00
32 Frank Gifford	1.50	4.00
33 Fred Dryer	1.00	2.50
34 Gale Sayers	1.50	4.00
35 Garo Yepremian	1.00	2.50
36 George Blanda	1.25	3.00
37 Harlon Hill	1.00	2.50
38 Howie Long	1.50	4.00
39 Hugh McElhenny	1.00	2.50
40 Jack Youngblood	1.00	2.50
41 James Lofton	1.00	2.50
42 Jan Stenerud	1.00	2.50
43 Jay Novacek	1.25	3.00
44 Jethro Pugh	1.00	2.50
45 Jim Brown	2.00	5.00
46 Jim McMahon	1.25	3.00
47 Jimmy Orr	1.00	2.50
48 Joe Greene	1.50	4.00
49 Joe Klecko	1.00	2.50
50 Joe Namath	2.00	5.00
51 John Elway	2.50	6.00
52 John Mackey	1.25	3.00
53 John Riggins	1.25	3.00
54 John Stallworth	1.25	3.00
55 Johnny Morris	1.00	2.50
56 Ken Stabler	1.50	4.00
57 Lance Alworth	1.25	3.00
58 Lee Roy Selmon	1.00	2.50
59 Lem Barney	1.00	2.50
60 Lenny Moore	1.00	2.50
61 Lydell Mitchell	1.00	2.50
62 Marcus Allen	1.50	4.00
63 Michael Irvin	1.50	4.00
64 Mike Curtis	1.00	2.50
65 Mike Singletary	1.50	4.00
66 Ozzie Newsome	1.25	3.00
67 Paul Hornung	1.50	4.00
68 Paul Warfield	1.25	3.00
69 Randall Cunningham	1.25	3.00
70 Randy White	1.50	4.00
71 Raymond Berry	1.25	3.00
72 Rick Casares	1.00	2.50
73 Roger Craig	1.25	3.00
74 Roger Staubach	2.00	5.00
75 Ronnie Lott	1.25	3.00
76 Sterling Sharpe	1.25	3.00
77 Ted Hendricks	1.00	2.50
78 Tiki Barber	1.25	3.00
79 Tim Brown	1.50	4.00
80 Tommy McDonald	1.00	2.50
81 Troy Aikman	2.00	5.00
82 Warren Moon	1.50	4.00
83 Yale Lary	1.00	2.50
84 Y.A. Tittle	1.50	4.00

2009 Playoff Contenders Legendary Contenders Autographs

OVERALL AUTOGRAPH ODDS 1:6
PANINI ANNC'D SOME PRINT RUNS

Card	Low	High
1 Alan Page	12.00	30.00
2 Andre Reed	10.00	25.00
3 Archie Manning/35*	25.00	50.00
4 Bart Starr/62*	90.00	150.00
5 Bert Jones/33*	12.00	30.00
6 Billy Sims	10.00	25.00
7 Bob Lilly	12.00	30.00
8 Bobby Bell/24*	20.00	40.00
9 Boyd Dowler/77*	12.00	30.00
10 Brett Favre/4*		
11 Carl Eller	10.00	25.00
12 Charley Trippi/29*	12.00	30.00
13 Charlie Joiner	8.00	20.00
14 Chuck Bednarik	10.00	25.00
15 Chuck Foreman	8.00	20.00
16 Ace Parker	12.00	30.00
17 Cris Collinsworth/99*	10.00	25.00
18 Dan Fouts/60*	35.00	60.00
19 Dan Hampton	15.00	40.00
20 Dan Marino/2*		
21 Danny White/85*	20.00	40.00
22 Daryl Johnston/94*	20.00	40.00
23 Dave Casper	8.00	20.00
24 Deion Sanders/58*	50.00	80.00
25 Del Shofner/5*		
26 Dick Butkus	35.00	60.00
27 Dub Jones	8.00	20.00
28 Earl Campbell/47*	12.00	30.00
29 Emmitt Smith/11*		
30 Forrest Gregg	25.00	50.00
31 Franco Harris	25.00	50.00
32 Frank Gifford/66*	25.00	50.00
33 Fred Dryer/45*	12.00	30.00
34 Gale Sayers/84*	20.00	50.00
35 Garo Yepremian/14*		
36 George Blanda/55*	20.00	40.00
37 Harlon Hill	8.00	20.00
38 Howie Long	25.00	50.00
39 Hugh McElhenny/25*	12.00	30.00
40 Jack Youngblood	8.00	20.00
41 James Lofton	8.00	20.00
42 Jan Stenerud/65*	10.00	25.00
43 Jay Novacek	10.00	25.00
44 Jethro Pugh	8.00	20.00
45 Jim Brown/60*	40.00	80.00
46 Jim McMahon/62*	20.00	40.00
47 Jimmy Orr/67*	10.00	25.00
48 Joe Greene/27*	30.00	50.00
49 Joe Klecko	8.00	20.00
50 Joe Namath/30*	50.00	100.00
51 John Elway/4*		
52 John Mackey	12.00	30.00
53 John Riggins/57*	20.00	40.00
54 John Stallworth/86*	20.00	40.00
55 Johnny Morris	8.00	20.00
56 Ken Stabler/25*	30.00	60.00
57 Lance Alworth/41*	35.00	60.00
58 Lee Roy Selmon/31*	25.00	50.00
59 Lem Barney/6*		
60 Lenny Moore	8.00	20.00
61 Lydell Mitchell/57*	12.00	30.00
62 Marcus Allen/6*		
63 Michael Irvin/33*	35.00	60.00
64 Mike Curtis/44*	20.00	40.00
65 Mike Singletary/91*	20.00	40.00
66 Ozzie Newsome	10.00	25.00
67 Paul Hornung	12.00	30.00
68 Paul Warfield/38*	12.00	30.00
69 Randall Cunningham/54*	20.00	40.00
70 Randy White	12.00	30.00
71 Raymond Berry	12.00	30.00
72 Rick Casares/18*	25.00	50.00
73 Roger Craig	10.00	25.00
74 Roger Staubach/66*	50.00	100.00
75 Ronnie Lott/26*	40.00	80.00
76 Sterling Sharpe/82*	20.00	40.00
77 Ted Hendricks	10.00	25.00
78 Tiki Barber	10.00	25.00
79 Tim Brown/46*	35.00	60.00
80 Tommy McDonald	10.00	25.00
81 Troy Aikman/39*	40.00	80.00
82 Warren Moon	15.00	40.00
83 Yale Lary/6*		
84 Y.A. Tittle/25*	20.00	40.00

2009 Playoff Contenders Rookie Roll Call

*BLACK/50: .6X TO 1.5X BASIC INSERTS
*GOLD/100: .5X TO 1.2X BASIC INSERTS

Card	Low	High
1 Ramses Barden	.60	1.50
2 Brian Robiskie	.60	1.50
3 Jeremy Maclin	.75	2.00
4 Matthew Stafford	3.00	8.00
5 Chris Wells	.60	1.50
6 Malcolm Jenkins	.60	1.50
7 Rey Maualuga	1.00	2.50
8 Shonn Greene	.60	1.50
9 Aaron Curry	1.00	2.50
10 Donald Brown	.60	1.50
11 Brian Cushing	.60	1.50
12 LeSean McCoy	1.50	4.00
13 Darrius Heyward-Bey	1.00	2.50
14 Percy Harvin	.60	1.50
15 Kenny Britt	1.00	2.50
16 Mark Sanchez	.60	1.50
17 Vontae Davis	.60	1.50
18 Derrick Williams	.60	1.50
19 Brian Orakpo	.75	2.00
20 Mohamed Massaquoi	.60	1.50
21 Michael Crabtree	1.00	2.50
22 Josh Freeman	.60	1.50
23 Hakeem Nicks	.75	2.00
24 Knowshon Moreno	.60	1.50
25 James Laurinaitis	.60	1.50

2009 Playoff Contenders Round Numbers

*BLACK/50: .6X TO 1.5X BASIC INSERTS
*GOLD/100: .5X TO 1.2X BASIC INSERTS

Card	Low	High
1 M.Stafford/J.Smith	3.00	8.00
2 T.Jackson/A.Curry	1.00	2.50
3 M.Sanchez/D.Heyward-Bey	1.00	2.50
4 B.Raji/M.Crabtree	1.00	2.50
5 A.Maybin/K.Moreno	.75	2.00
6 B.Orakpo/M.Jenkins	.75	2.00
7 B.Cushing/L.English	.60	1.50
8 J.Freeman/J.Maclin	.75	2.00
9 B.Pettigrew/P.Harvin	.60	1.50
10 V.Davis/C.Matthews	2.50	6.00
11 D.Brown/H.Nicks	.75	2.00
12 K.Britt/C.Wells	1.00	2.50
13 J.Laurinaitis/B.Robiskie	.60	1.50
14 R.Maualuga/E.Brown	1.00	2.50
15 M.Massaquoi/L.McCoy	1.50	4.00
16 S.Greene/G.Coffee	.60	1.50
17 D.Williams/B.Tate	.75	2.00
18 M.Wallace/R.Barden	1.00	2.50
19 P.Turner/J.Cook	.75	2.00
20 D.Butler/C.Coffman	.60	1.50
21 J.Iglesias/T.Beckum	.60	1.50
22 S.McGee/M.Thomas	.60	1.50
23 S.Nelson/L.Murphy	.60	1.50
24 T.Fiammetta/A.Brown	.75	2.00
25 K.McKinley/J.Dillard	.60	1.50

2009 Playoff Contenders ROY Contenders

*BLACK/50: .6X TO 1.5X BASIC INSERTS
*GOLD/100: .5X TO 1.2X BASIC INSERTS

Card	Low	High
1 Percy Harvin	.60	1.50
2 Ramses Barden	.60	1.50
3 B.J. Raji	.75	2.00
4 Matthew Stafford	3.00	8.00
5 Johnny Knox	.75	2.00
6 Brian Robiskie	.60	1.50
7 James Laurinaitis	.60	1.50
8 Kenny Britt	1.00	2.50
9 Mark Sanchez	.60	1.50
10 Aaron Curry	1.00	2.50
11 Brandon Pettigrew	.60	1.50
12 Hakeem Nicks	.75	2.00
13 Derrick Williams	.60	1.50
14 Mohamed Massaquoi	.60	1.50
15 Shonn Greene	.60	1.50
16 Brian Orakpo	.75	2.00
17 Chris Wells	.60	1.50
18 Darrius Heyward-Bey	1.00	2.50
19 Jeremy Maclin	.75	2.00
20 Tyson Jackson	.60	1.50
21 Josh Freeman	.60	1.50
22 Brian Cushing	.60	1.50
23 LeSean McCoy	1.50	4.00
24 Knowshon Moreno	.60	1.50
25 Donald Brown	.60	1.50

2010 Playoff Contenders

Card	Low	High
COMP.SET w/o RC's (100)	8.00	20.00

EXCH EXPIRATION: 8/16/2012

Card	Low	High
1 Larry Fitzgerald	.25	.60
2 Steve Breaston	.20	.50
3 Tim Hightower	.20	.50
4 Matt Ryan	.25	.60
5 Michael Turner	.20	.50
6 Roddy White	.20	.50
7 Anquan Boldin	.20	.50
8 Joe Flacco	.25	.60
9 Ray Rice	.20	.50
10 Lee Evans	.25	.60
11 Fred Jackson	.25	.60
12 Ryan Fitzpatrick	.20	.50
13 DeAngelo Williams	.20	.50
14 Jonathan Stewart	.20	.50
15 Steve Smith	.25	.60
16 Jay Cutler	.20	.50
17 Johnny Knox	.20	.50
18 Matt Forte	.20	.50
19 Carson Palmer	.25	.60
20 Cedric Benson	.20	.50
21 Chad Ochocinco	.20	.50
22 Ben Watson	.20	.50
23 Josh Cribbs	.20	.50
24 Peyton Hillis	.25	.60
25 Jason Witten	.25	.60
26 Miles Austin	.20	.50
27 Tony Romo	.25	.60
28 Brandon Lloyd	.20	.50
29 Knowshon Moreno	.20	.50
30 Kyle Orton	.20	.50
31 Calvin Johnson	.30	.75
32 Matthew Stafford	.25	.60
33 Brandon Pettigrew	.20	.50
34 Aaron Rodgers	.40	1.00
35 Clay Matthews	.30	.75
36 Donald Driver	.25	.60
37 Andre Johnson	.25	.60
38 Arian Foster	.25	.60
39 Matt Schaub	.20	.50
40 Dallas Clark	.20	.50
41 Peyton Manning	.75	2.00
42 Reggie Wayne	.25	.60
43 David Garrard	.20	.50
44 Maurice Jones-Drew	.20	.50
45 Mike Sims-Walker	.20	.50
46 Dwayne Bowe	.25	.60
47 Jamaal Charles	.25	.60
48 Matt Cassel	.20	.50
49 Brandon Marshall	.25	.60
50 Chad Henne	.25	.60
51 Ronnie Brown	.20	.50
52 Adrian Peterson	.30	.75
53 Brett Favre	.60	1.50
54 Percy Harvin	.20	.50
55 Randy Moss	.25	.60
56 Danny Woodhead RC	2.50	6.00
57 BenJarvus Green-Ellis	.30	.75
58 Tom Brady	.75	2.00
59 Wes Welker	.25	.60
60 Drew Brees	.30	.75
61 Marques Colston	.20	.50
62 Reggie Bush	.20	.50
63 Ahmad Bradshaw	.20	.50
64 Eli Manning	.25	.60
65 Hakeem Nicks	.20	.50
66 Braylon Edwards	.20	.50
67 Mark Sanchez	.20	.50
68 Shonn Greene	.20	.50
69 Bruce Gradkowski	.20	.50
70 Darren McFadden	.20	.50
71 Darrius Heyward-Bey	.25	.60
72 DeSean Jackson	.25	.60
73 Jeremy Maclin	.20	.50
74 LeSean McCoy	.30	.75
75 Michael Vick	.25	.60
76 Ben Roethlisberger	.30	.75
77 Mike Wallace	.20	.50
78 Rashard Mendenhall	.20	.50
79 Troy Polamalu	.30	.75
80 Antonio Gates	.25	.60
81 Malcom Floyd	.20	.50
82 Philip Rivers	.30	.75
83 Frank Gore	.25	.60
84 Michael Crabtree	.20	.50
85 Vernon Davis	.20	.50
86 Mike Williams USC	.20	.50
87 Marshawn Lynch	.25	.60
88 Matt Hasselbeck	.20	.50
89 Danny Amendola	.30	.75
90 Mark Clayton	.20	.50
91 Steven Jackson	.20	.50
92 Cadillac Williams	.20	.50
93 Josh Freeman	.25	.60
94 Kellen Winslow Jr.	.20	.50
95 Chris Johnson	.20	.50
96 Kenny Britt	.20	.50
97 Vince Young	.20	.50
98 Chris Cooley	.20	.50
99 Donovan McNabb	.25	.60
100 Anthony Armstrong RC	1.50	4.00
101 Aaron Hernandez AU RC	12.00	30.00
102 Andrew Quarless AU RC	4.00	10.00
103 Anthony Dixon AU/360* RC	10.00	25.00
104 Anthony McCoy AU RC	4.00	10.00
105 Antonio Brown AU RC	250.00	500.00
106 Blair White AU/75* RC	40.00	100.00
107 Brandon Banks AU/500* RC	8.00	20.00
108 Brandon Graham AU/306* RC	6.00	15.00
109 Brandon Spikes AU/500* RC	8.00	20.00
110 Brody Eldridge AU RC	8.00	20.00
111 Bryan Bulaga AU RC	4.00	10.00
112 Carlos Dunlap AU RC	10.00	25.00
113 Carlton Mitchell AU/496* RC	10.00	25.00
114 Chris Cook AU RC	6.00	15.00
115 Chris Ivory AU/500* RC	8.00	20.00
116 Chris McGaha AU/441* RC	6.00	15.00
117 Clay Harbor AU RC	4.00	10.00
118 Corey Wootton AU RC	4.00	10.00
119 Dan LeFevour AU/455* RC	8.00	20.00
120 Dan Williams AU RC	4.00	10.00
121 D.Alexander AU/300* RC	10.00	25.00
122 David Gettis AU RC	5.00	12.00
123 David Nelson AU/500* RC	10.00	20.00
124 David Reed AU RC	6.00	15.00
125 Deji Karim AU RC	5.00	12.00
126 Dennis Pitta AU/500* RC	8.00	20.00
127 Derrick Morgan AU RC	4.00	10.00
128 Devin McCourty AU RC	6.00	15.00
129 Briscoe AU/495* RC EXCH	10.00	25.00
130 D.Curry AU/190* RC	30.00	80.00
131 Dominique Franks AU RC	4.00	10.00
132 Donald Jones AU RC	8.00	20.00
133 Dorin Dickerson AU RC	8.00	20.00
134 Duke Calhoun AU RC	6.00	15.00
135 Earl Thomas AU RC	20.00	40.00
136 Ed Dickson AU RC	4.00	10.00
137 Ed Wang AU/500* RC	8.00	20.00
138 Everson Griffen AU RC	5.00	12.00
139 Fendi Onobun AU RC	6.00	15.00
140 Garrett Graham AU RC	4.00	10.00
141 Jacoby Ford AU RC	4.00	10.00
142 James Starks AU RC	5.00	12.00
143 Jared Odrick AU RC	8.00	20.00
144 Jason Pierre-Paul AU RC	10.00	25.00
145 Jason Worilds AU RC	4.00	10.00
146 Javier Arenas AU RC	4.00	10.00
147 Jeremy Horne AU/500* RC	10.00	25.00
148 J.Williams AU/194* RC	20.00	50.00
149A Jerry Hughes AU RC	4.00	10.00
149B Joique Bell AU/161* RC	4.00	10.00
150 Jim Dray AU RC	5.00	12.00
151 Jimmy Graham AU/358* RC	40.00	80.00
152 Joe Haden AU RC	8.00	20.00
153 Joe Webb AU RC	8.00	20.00
154 John Conner AU RC	4.00	10.00
155 John Skelton AU RC	12.00	30.00
157 K.Jackson AU/500* RC	12.00	30.00
158 Keiland Williams AU/500* RC	5.00	12.00
159 Keith Toston AU RC	6.00	15.00
160 Kerry Meier AU RC	5.00	12.00
161 Koa Misi AU/190* RC	12.00	30.00
162 Kyle Williams AU/436* RC	10.00	25.00
163 Sergio Kindle AU RC	4.00	10.00
164 L.Houston AU/500* RC	5.00	12.00
165 L.Blount AU/287* RC	20.00	40.00
166 Lonyae Miller AU/412* RC	10.00	25.00
167 Marc Mariani AU RC	6.00	15.00
168 Marlon Moore AU/500* RC	6.00	15.00
169 Max Hall AU/401* RC	6.00	15.00
170 Max Komar No AU/500* RC	2.50	6.00
171 Hoomanawanui AU RC	8.00	20.00
172 Mickey Shuler AU RC	6.00	15.00
173 Morgan Burnett AU RC	5.00	12.00
174 Nate Allen AU RC	8.00	20.00
175 Nate Byham AU RC	5.00	12.00
176 NaVorro Bowman AU RC	8.00	20.00
177 Patrick Robinson AU RC	6.00	15.00
178 Perrish Cox AU RC	5.00	12.00
179 Preston Parker AU/190* RC	12.00	30.00
180 Ricky Sapp AU RC	4.00	10.00
181 Riley Cooper AU RC	8.00	20.00
182 Roberto Wallace AU RC	6.00	15.00
183 Russell Okung AU/174* RC	20.00	50.00
184 Rusty Smith AU/190* RC	12.00	30.00
185 Michael Palmer AU RC	8.00	20.00
186 Sean Lee AU RC	12.00	30.00
187 S.Weatherspoon AU RC	5.00	12.00
188 C.Gronkwski AU/500* RC	10.00	25.00
189 Seyi Ajirotutu AU/384* RC	4.00	10.00
190 Shay Hodge AU RC	4.00	10.00
191 Stephen Williams AU RC	5.00	12.00
192 T.J. Ward AU/500* RC	6.00	15.00
193 Taylor Mays AU RC	4.00	10.00
194 T.Lewis AU/190* RC	15.00	40.00
195 Tony Moeaki AU RC	8.00	20.00
196 Tony Pike AU RC	8.00	20.00
197 T.Williams AU/500* RC	12.00	30.00
198 Tyson Alualu AU/190* RC	25.00	60.00
199 Victor Cruz AU RC	15.00	40.00
200 Z.Robinson AU/340* RC	20.00	50.00
201A A.Roberts RJ AU/498* RC	6.00	15.00
201B A.Roberts WJ AU/498* RC	6.00	15.00
202A A.Edwards BJ AU RC	5.00	12.00
202B A.Edwards WJ AU RC	5.00	12.00
203A A.Benn RJ AU/285* RC	4.00	10.00
203B A.Benn WJ AU/285* RC	4.00	10.00
204A Ben Tate Cut AU RC	4.00	10.00
204B Ben Tate Stnd AU RC	4.00	10.00
205A B.LaFell BJ AU/312* RC	6.00	15.00
205B B.LaFell WJ AU/312* RC	6.00	15.00
206A C.Spiller BJ AU/372* RC	4.00	10.00
206B C.Spiller WJ AU/372* RC	4.00	10.00
207A C.McCoy BJ AU/394* RC	8.00	20.00
207B C.McCoy WJ AU/394* RC	8.00	20.00
208A D.Williams BJ AU/412* RC	5.00	12.00
208B D.Williams WJ AU/412* RC	5.00	12.00
209A D.Thomas Cut AU RC	20.00	50.00
209B D.Thomas Frwd AU RC	30.00	50.00
210A D.McCluster RJ AU RC	5.00	12.00
210B D.McCluster WJ AU RC	5.00	12.00
211A D.Bryant BJ AU/360* RC	40.00	80.00
211B D.Bryant BJ AU/360* RC	40.00	80.00
212A E.Sanders BJ AU RC	10.00	25.00
212B E.Sanders WJ AU RC	10.00	25.00
213A E.Berry Stnd AU/97* RC	20.00	50.00
213B E.Berry Run AU/97* RC	20.00	50.00
214A E.Decker BJ AU/492* RC	5.00	12.00
214B E.Decker OJ AU/492* RC	5.00	12.00
215A G.McCoy RJ AU/82* RC	10.00	25.00
215B G.McCoy WJ AU/82* RC	10.00	25.00
216A G.Tate Cut AU RC	8.00	20.00
216B G.Tate Run AU RC	8.00	20.00
217A Jahvid Best BJ AU RC	4.00	10.00
217B Jahvid Best WJ AU RC	4.00	10.00
218A Gresham BJ AU/500* RC	6.00	15.00
218B J.Gresham WJ AU/500* RC	6.00	15.00
219A J.Clausen BJ AU/403* RC	6.00	15.00
219B J.Clausen WJ AU/403* RC	6.00	15.00
220A McKnight GJ AU/392* RC	4.00	10.00
220B J.McKnight WJ AU/392* RC	4.00	10.00
221A J.Dwyer fwd AU/439* RC	4.00	10.00
221B J.Dwyer side AU/439* RC	4.00	10.00
222A J.Shipley BJ AU/499* RC	6.00	15.00
222B J.Shipley WJ AU/499* RC	6.00	15.00
223A M.Easley Cut AU RC	4.00	10.00
223B M.Easley Fwd AU RC	4.00	10.00
224A M.Gilyard Cut AU RC	4.00	10.00
224B MGilyard Fwd AU RC	4.00	10.00
225A Mike Kafka GJ AU RC	6.00	15.00
225B Mike Kafka WJ AU RC	6.00	15.00
226A M.Williams AU/391* RJ RC	4.00	10.00
226B M.Williams AU/391* WJ RC	4.00	10.00
227A M.Hardesty Jsy# AU RC	4.00	10.00
227B M.Hardesty No# AU RC	4.00	10.00
228A N.Suh BJ AU/326* RC	12.00	30.00
228B N.Suh WJ AU/326* RC	12.00	30.00
229A R.Grnkwski BJ AU/499* RC	100.00	200.00
229B R.Gronkowski WJ AU/499* RC	100.00	200.00
230A R.McClain Run AU/378* RC	4.00	10.00
230B R.McClain Set AU/378* RC	4.00	10.00
231A Mathews Shld AU/300* RC	8.00	20.00
231B Mathews No Shld AU/300* RC	8.00	20.00
232A Bradford Fwd AU/377* RC	20.00	40.00
232B Bradford Lft AU/377* RC	20.00	40.00
233A Taylor Price Fwd AU RC	4.00	10.00
233B Taylor Price Rgt AU RC	4.00	10.00
234A T.Tebow BJ AU/400* RC	30.00	80.00
234B Tim Tebow WJ AU/400* RC	30.00	80.00
235A Gerhart Jsy# AU/495* RC	4.00	10.00
235B T.Gerhart No# AU/495* RC	4.00	10.00

2010 Playoff Contenders Playoff Ticket

*1-99 VETS: 3X TO 8X BASIC CARDS

Card	Low	High
COMMON ROOKIE (100-200)	2.50	6.00
ROOKIE SEMISTAR 100-200	3.00	8.00
ROOKIE UNL.STAR 100-200	4.00	10.00
COMMON ROOKIE (201-235)	2.50	6.00
ROOKIE UNL.STAR 201-235	3.00	8.00

201-235 HAVE TWO CARDS OF EQUAL VALUE
STATED PRINT RUN 99 SER.#'d SETS

Card	Low	High
56 Danny Woodhead	12.00	30.00
100 Anthony Armstrong	5.00	12.00
101 Aaron Hernandez	3.00	8.00
102 Andrew Quarless	2.50	6.00
107 Brandon Banks	5.00	12.00
109 Brandon Spikes	2.50	6.00
115 Chris Ivory	5.00	12.00
117 Clay Harbor	2.50	6.00
123 David Nelson	4.00	10.00
128 Devin McCourty	3.00	8.00
142 James Starks	3.00	8.00
153 Joe Webb	2.50	6.00
158 Keiland Williams	3.00	8.00
165 LeGarrette Blount	5.00	12.00
167 Marc Mariani	4.00	10.00
169 Max Hall	4.00	10.00
172 Mickey Shuler	4.00	10.00
188 Chris Gronkowski	4.00	10.00
195 Tony Moeaki	3.00	8.00
197 Trent Williams	3.00	8.00
206A C.J. Spiller	2.00	5.00
207A Colt McCoy	2.50	6.00
209A Demaryius Thomas	5.00	12.00
210A Dexter McCluster	2.50	6.00
211A Dez Bryant	5.00	12.00
212A Emmanuel Sanders	3.00	8.00
213A Eric Berry	3.00	8.00
215A Gerald McCoy	2.50	6.00
216A Golden Tate	4.00	10.00
217A Jahvid Best	2.00	5.00
218A Jermaine Gresham	2.00	5.00
219A Jimmy Clausen	2.00	5.00
222A Jordan Shipley	2.00	5.00
226A Mike Williams	2.00	5.00
228A Ndamukong Suh	8.00	20.00
229A Rob Gronkowski	6.00	15.00
230A Rolando McClain	2.00	5.00
231A Ryan Mathews	2.00	5.00
232A Sam Bradford	10.00	25.00
234A Tim Tebow	12.00	30.00
235A Toby Gerhart	2.00	5.00

2010 Playoff Contenders Draft Class

*BLACK/50: .8X TO 2X BASIC INSERTS
*GOLD/100: .6X TO 1.5X BASIC INSERTS

Card	Low	High
1 S.Bradford/T.Tebow	1.50	4.00
2 C.Spiller/R.Mathews	.50	1.25
3 D.Thomas/D.Bryant	2.00	5.00
4 J.Gresham/R.Gronkowski	1.50	4.00
5 M.Gilyard/S.Bradford	.60	1.50
6 J.Best/N.Suh	1.00	2.50
7 J.Gresham/J.Shipley	.50	1.25
8 B.LaFell/J.Clausen	.75	2.00
9 G.Tate/J.Clausen	.60	1.50
10 J.Gresham/S.Bradford	.60	1.50
11 C.McCoy/J.Shipley	.60	1.50
12 D.Thomas/T.Tebow	1.25	3.00
13 D.McCluster/T.Moeaki	.60	1.50
14 A.Benn/M.Williams	.50	1.25
15 A.Hernandez/R.Gronkowski	1.50	4.00
16 G.McCoy/N.Suh	1.00	2.50
17 R.Okung/T.Williams	.60	1.50
18 E.Berry/J.Haden	.75	2.00
19 B.Graham/R.McClain	.60	1.50
20 D.Morgan/J.Pierre-Paul	.75	2.00
21 C.McCoy/J.Clausen	.60	1.50
22 D.McCluster/J.Best	.60	1.50
23 A.Benn/G.Tate	.60	1.50
24 A.Hernandez/T.Moeaki	.60	1.50
25 D.Bryant/S.Lee	2.00	5.00

2010 Playoff Contenders Golden Ticket

2010 Playoff Contenders packs included 52 redemption cards called Golden Tickets that could be redeemed for an actual gold "card" containing 11 grams of 14K gold. Each gold prize card was serial numbered 1/1 and encased in a BGS card slab.
EXCH EXPIRATION: 8/16/2012

2010 Playoff Contenders Legendary Contenders

*BLACK/50: .8X TO 2X BASIC INSERTS
*GOLD/100: .6X TO 1.5X BASIC INSERTS

Card	Low	High
1 Joe Namath	1.50	4.00
2 Lydell Mitchell	.75	2.00
3 Jim Brown	1.50	4.00
4 Charley Taylor	.75	2.00
5 Steve Largent	1.25	3.00
6 Pete Retzlaff	.75	2.00
7 Barry Sanders	2.00	5.00
8 Todd Christensen	.75	2.00
9 Joe Montana	4.00	10.00
10 Rick Casares	.75	2.00
11 John Elway	2.00	5.00
12 Randall Cunningham	1.00	2.50
13 Bart Starr	2.00	5.00
14 Fred Biletnikoff	1.25	3.00
15 Art Monk	1.25	3.00
16 Dave Casper	.75	2.00
17 Floyd Little	.75	2.00
18 Jim Kelly	1.25	3.00
19 Michael Irvin	1.25	3.00
20 Daryle Lamonica	.75	2.00
21 Leroy Kelly	1.00	2.50
22 Jim Plunkett	1.00	2.50
23 Jim Taylor	1.25	3.00
24 Fran Tarkenton	1.25	3.00
25 Don Maynard	1.00	2.50

2010 Playoff Contenders Legendary Contenders Autographs

PANINI ANNOUNCED PRINT RUNS 15-250

Card	Low	High
1 Joe Namath/25*	50.00	100.00
2 Lydell Mitchell/250*	8.00	20.00
3 Jim Brown/25*	40.00	80.00
4 Charley Taylor/200*	8.00	20.00
5 Steve Largent/65*	12.00	30.00
6 Pete Retzlaff/250*	8.00	20.00
7 Barry Sanders/25*	75.00	150.00
8 Todd Christensen/100*	10.00	25.00
9 Joe Montana/20*	75.00	150.00
10 Rick Casares/250*	8.00	20.00
11 John Elway/20*	100.00	175.00
12 Randall Cunningham/45*	20.00	50.00
13 Bart Starr/40	75.00	150.00
14 Fred Biletnikoff/55*	20.00	40.00
15 Art Monk/35*	30.00	60.00
16 Dave Casper/40*	12.00	30.00
17 Floyd Little/50*	10.00	25.00
18 Jim Kelly/25*	30.00	60.00
19 Michael Irvin/15*	50.00	100.00
20 Daryle Lamonica/55*	12.00	30.00
21 Leroy Kelly/75*	10.00	25.00
22 Jim Plunkett/100*	10.00	25.00
23 Jim Taylor/60*	30.00	60.00
24 Fran Tarkenton/45*	25.00	50.00
25 Don Maynard/40*	10.00	25.00

2010 Playoff Contenders Rookie Ink

ANNOUNCED PRINT RUN 50
EXCH EXPIRATION: 8/16/2012

Card	Low	High
1 Colt McCoy	8.00	20.00
2 Jahvid Best	6.00	15.00
3 Taylor Price	6.00	15.00
4 Toby Gerhart	12.00	30.00
5 Andre Roberts	8.00	20.00
6 Emmanuel Sanders	10.00	25.00
7 Rob Gronkowski	30.00	60.00
8 Brandon LaFell	10.00	25.00
9 Rolando McClain	10.00	25.00
10 Jordan Shipley	6.00	15.00
11 Dexter McCluster	8.00	20.00
12 Armanti Edwards	8.00	20.00
13 Jermaine Gresham	6.00	15.00
14 Eric Berry	10.00	25.00
15 Sam Bradford	50.00	100.00
16 Ndamukong Suh	30.00	60.00
17 Demaryius Thomas	15.00	40.00
18 Arrelious Benn	6.00	15.00
19 Tim Tebow	50.00	120.00
20 Ryan Mathews	6.00	15.00
21 Mardy Gilyard	6.00	15.00
22 Eric Decker	8.00	20.00
23 Golden Tate	8.00	20.00
24 C.J. Spiller	6.00	15.00
25 Dez Bryant	50.00	100.00
26 Damian Williams	6.00	15.00
27 Gerald McCoy	20.00	40.00
28 Jonathan Dwyer	6.00	15.00
29 Jimmy Clausen	6.00	15.00
30 Mike Williams	6.00	15.00

2010 Playoff Contenders Rookie Roll Call

*BLACK/50: .8X TO 2X BASIC INSERTS
*GOLD/100: .6X TO 1.5X BASIC INSERTS

Card	Low	High
1 Sam Bradford	.60	1.50
2 Tim Tebow	1.50	4.00
3 Jimmy Clausen	.50	1.25
4 Colt McCoy	.60	1.50
5 C.J. Spiller	.50	1.25
6 Ryan Mathews	.50	1.25
7 Jahvid Best	.50	1.25
8 Ndamukong Suh	1.00	2.50
9 Demaryius Thomas	1.25	3.00
10 Dez Bryant	1.25	3.00
11 Golden Tate	.60	1.50
12 Dexter McCluster	.60	1.50
13 Jermaine Gresham	.50	1.25
14 Rob Gronkowski	1.50	4.00
15 Arrelious Benn	.50	1.25
16 Marc Mariani	.75	2.00
17 Mardy Gilyard	.50	1.25
18 Eric Decker	.60	1.50
19 Toby Gerhart	.50	1.25
20 Tony Moeaki	.60	1.50
21 Jordan Shipley	.50	1.25
22 Mike Williams	.50	1.25
23 Aaron Hernandez	.50	1.25
24 Max Hall	.75	2.00
25 Rolando McClain	.50	1.25

2010 Playoff Contenders ROY Contenders

*BLACK/50: .8X TO 2X BASIC INSERTS
*GOLD/100: .6X TO 1.5X BASIC INSERTS

Card	Low	High
1 Sam Bradford	.60	1.50
2 Aaron Hernandez	.50	1.25
3 Jahvid Best	.50	1.25
4 Jimmy Clausen	.50	1.25
5 Ryan Mathews	.50	1.25
6 C.J. Spiller	.50	1.25
7 Mike Williams	.50	1.25
8 Dexter McCluster	.60	1.50
9 Jordan Shipley	.50	1.25
10 Golden Tate	.60	1.50
11 Rob Gronkowski	1.50	4.00
12 Dez Bryant	1.25	3.00
13 Demaryius Thomas	1.25	3.00
14 Marc Mariani	.75	2.00
15 Brandon LaFell	.75	2.00
16 T.J. Ward	.75	2.00
17 Mardy Gilyard	.50	1.25
18 Tony Moeaki	.60	1.50
19 Arrelious Benn	.50	1.25
20 Max Hall	.75	2.00
21 Nate Allen	.75	2.00
22 Ndamukong Suh	1.00	2.50
23 Rolando McClain	.50	1.25
24 Brandon Graham	.60	1.50
25 Sean Weatherspoon	.50	1.25

2010 Playoff Contenders Super Bowl Ticket

*BLACK/50: .8X TO 2X BASIC INSERTS
*GOLD/100: .6X TO 1.5X BASIC INSERTS

Card	Low	High
1 Bart Starr	2.50	6.00
2 Jim Taylor	1.50	4.00
3 Willie Wood	1.25	3.00
4 Bart Starr	2.50	6.00
5 Willie Davis	1.25	3.00
6 Boyd Dowler	1.25	3.00
7 Joe Namath	2.00	5.00
8 Don Maynard	1.25	3.00
9 Len Dawson	1.50	4.00
10 Willie Lanier	1.00	2.50
11 Bobby Bell	1.00	2.50
12 Jan Stenerud	1.00	2.50
13 Chuck Howley	1.00	2.50
14 Roger Staubach	2.00	5.00
15 Cliff Harris	1.00	2.50
16 John Niland	1.00	2.50
17 Bob Lilly	1.25	3.00
18 Lee Roy Jordan	1.25	3.00
19 Mel Renfro	1.00	2.50
20 Larry Little	1.00	2.50
21 Paul Warfield	1.25	3.00
22 Jack Lambert	1.50	4.00
23 L.C. Greenwood	1.00	2.50
24 Fred Biletnikoff	1.50	4.00
25 Willie Brown	1.00	2.50
26 Dave Casper	1.00	2.50
27 Ken Stabler	1.50	4.00
28 Randy White	1.25	3.00
29 Tony Dorsett	1.50	4.00
30 Ed Too Tall Jones	1.00	2.50
31 D.D. Lewis	1.00	2.50
32 Terry Bradshaw	2.00	5.00
33 Terry Bradshaw	2.00	5.00
34 Jim Plunkett	1.25	3.00
35 Joe Montana	5.00	12.00
36 Russ Grimm	1.00	2.50
37 Jim Plunkett	1.25	3.00
38 Joe Montana	5.00	12.00
39 William Perry	1.00	2.50
40 Jim McMahon	1.25	3.00
41 Phil Simms	1.25	3.00
42 Doug Williams	1.25	3.00
43 Jerry Rice	2.50	6.00
44 Joe Montana	5.00	12.00
45 Tom Rathman	1.00	2.50
46 Ottis Anderson	1.00	2.50
47 Art Monk	1.50	4.00
48 Troy Aikman	2.00	5.00
49 Mark Stepnoski	1.00	2.50
50 Emmitt Smith	2.50	6.00
51 Michael Irvin	1.50	4.00
52 Darren Woodson	1.25	3.00
53 Steve Young	2.00	5.00
54 Brent Jones	1.00	2.50
55 John Taylor	1.00	2.50
56 Deion Sanders	1.25	3.00
57 Rod Woodson	1.25	3.00
58 Brett Favre	3.00	8.00
59 Terrell Davis	1.25	3.00
60 Ed McCaffrey	1.00	2.50
61 John Elway	2.50	6.00
62 Marshall Faulk	1.25	3.00
63 Tom Brady	4.00	10.00
64 Tom Brady	4.00	10.00
65 Tom Brady	4.00	10.00
66 Ben Roethlisberger	1.50	4.00
67 Peyton Manning	4.00	10.00
68 Reggie Wayne	1.25	3.00
69 Eli Manning	1.25	3.00
70 Brandon Jacobs	1.00	2.50
71 Ben Roethlisberger	1.50	4.00
72 Santonio Holmes	1.00	2.50
73 Drew Brees	1.50	4.00
74 Keyshawn Johnson	1.00	2.50
75 Marques Colston	1.00	2.50

2010 Playoff Contenders Super Bowl Ticket Autographs

PANINI ANNOUNCED PRINT RUNS 1-250

Card	Low	High
5 Willie Davis/250*	15.00	40.00
6 Boyd Dowler/250*	10.00	25.00
7 Joe Namath/25*	50.00	100.00
8 Don Maynard/15*	15.00	40.00
9 Len Dawson/15*	25.00	50.00
10 Willie Lanier/65*	12.00	30.00
11 Bobby Bell/35*	12.00	30.00
12 Jan Stenerud/75*	10.00	25.00
15 Cliff Harris/75*	12.00	30.00
16 John Niland/65*	10.00	25.00
17 Bob Lilly/100*	12.00	30.00
18 Lee Roy Jordan/35*	12.00	30.00
19 Mel Renfro/25*	15.00	40.00
20 Larry Little/50*	10.00	25.00
21 Paul Warfield/15*	15.00	40.00
22 Jack Lambert/75*	40.00	80.00
23 L.C. Greenwood/45*	15.00	40.00
24 Fred Biletnikoff/50*	20.00	50.00
25 Willie Brown/75*	10.00	25.00
26 Dave Casper/20*	12.00	30.00
27 Ken Stabler/25*	20.00	50.00

28 Randy White/30* 15.00 40.00
29 Tony Dorsett/33* 30.00 60.00
30 Ed Too Tall Jones/15* 20.00 50.00
31 D.D. Lewis/20* 12.00 30.00
34 Jim Plunkett/35* 12.00 30.00
35 Joe Montana/20* 125.00 200.00
36 Russ Grimm/65* 12.00 30.00
39 William Perry/45* 12.00 30.00
40 Jim McMahon/25* 30.00 60.00
42 Doug Williams/25* 25.00 50.00
45 Tom Rathman/35* 15.00 40.00
46 Ottis Anderson/50* 12.00 30.00
47 Art Monk/15* 90.00 150.00
49 Mark Stepnoski/25* 15.00 40.00
52 Darren Woodson/15* 20.00 50.00
53 Steve Young/15* 75.00 150.00
60 Ed McCaffrey/25* 25.00 50.00
61 John Elway/20* 75.00 150.00
62 Marshall Faulk/25* 30.00 80.00
70 Brandon Jacobs/15* 12.00 30.00
72 Santonio Holmes/50* 25.00 50.00
74 Keyshawn Johnson/25* 15.00 40.00

2011 Playoff Contenders

COMP.SET w/o RC's (100) 8.00 20.00
OVERALL AUTO ODDS 4 PER HOBBY BOX
1 Fred Jackson .20 .50
2 Ryan Fitzpatrick .20 .50
3 Steve Johnson .20 .50
4 Brandon Marshall .25 .60
5 Chad Henne .25 .60
6 Reggie Bush .20 .50
7 Chad Ochocinco .20 .50
8 Deion Branch .20 .50
9 Tom Brady .75 2.00
10 Wes Welker .25 .60
11 Mark Sanchez .20 .50
12 Santonio Holmes .20 .50
13 Shonn Greene .20 .50
14 Anquan Boldin .20 .50
15 Joe Flacco .25 .60
16 Lee Evans .25 .60
17 Ray Rice .20 .50
18 Andre Caldwell .20 .50
19 Cedric Benson .20 .50
20 Rey Maualuga .20 .50
21 Ben Watson .20 .50
22 Colt McCoy .20 .50
23 Peyton Hillis .20 .50
24 Ben Roethlisberger .30 .75
25 Mike Wallace .20 .50
26 Rashard Mendenhall .20 .50
27 Andre Johnson .25 .60
28 Arian Foster .20 .50
29 Matt Schaub .20 .50
30 Dallas Clark .20 .50
31 Peyton Manning .60 1.50
32 Reggie Wayne .25 .60
33 Marcedes Lewis .20 .50
34 Maurice Jones-Drew .25 .60
35 Mike Thomas .20 .50
36 Chris Johnson .20 .50
37 Kenny Britt .20 .50
38 Matt Hasselbeck .20 .50
39 Knowshon Moreno .20 .50
40 Kyle Orton .20 .50
41 Willis McGahee .20 .50
42 Dwayne Bowe .25 .60
43 Jamaal Charles .25 .60
44 Matt Cassel .20 .50
45 Darren McFadden .20 .50
46 Carson Palmer .25 .60
47 Michael Bush .20 .50
48 Malcom Floyd .20 .50
49 Philip Rivers .30 .75
50 Vincent Jackson .20 .50
51 Dez Bryant .30 .75
52 Felix Jones .20 .50
53 Miles Austin .20 .50
54 Tony Romo .25 .60
55 Eli Manning .25 .60
56 Hakeem Nicks .20 .50
57 Mario Manningham .20 .50
58 DeSean Jackson .25 .60
59 LeSean McCoy .30 .75
60 Michael Vick .25 .60
61 DeAngelo Hall .20 .50
62 Santana Moss .25 .60
63 Tim Hightower .20 .50
64 Jay Cutler .20 .50
65 Marion Barber .20 .50
66 Matt Forte .20 .50
67 Calvin Johnson .30 .75
68 Jahvid Best .20 .50
69 Matthew Stafford .25 .60
70 Ndamukong Suh .25 .60
71 Aaron Rodgers .50 1.25
72 Greg Jennings .20 .50
73 Jermichael Finley .20 .50
74 Adrian Peterson .30 .75
75 Michael Jenkins .20 .50
76 Percy Harvin .20 .50
77 Matt Ryan .25 .60
78 Michael Turner .20 .50
79 Roddy White .20 .50
80 DeAngelo Williams .20 .50
81 Jon Beason .20 .50
82 Steve Smith .25 .60
83 Drew Brees .30 .75
84 Marques Colston .20 .50
85 Pierre Thomas .20 .50
86 Josh Freeman .25 .60
87 LeGarrette Blount .25 .60
88 Mike Williams .25 .60
89 Beanie Wells .20 .50
90 Kevin Kolb .20 .50
91 Larry Fitzgerald .25 .60
92 Alex Smith QB .25 .60
93 Frank Gore .25 .60
94 Vernon Davis .20 .50
95 Marshawn Lynch .25 .60
96 Sidney Rice .20 .50
97 Tarvaris Jackson .20 .50
98 Danny Amendola .25 .60
99 Sam Bradford .20 .50
100 Steven Jackson .20 .50
101 Terrelle Pryor AU RC 6.00 15.00
102 Aaron Williams AU/99* RC 30.00 80.00
103 A.Clayborn AU/114* SP RC 12.00 30.00
104 Ahmad Black AU RC 5.00 12.00
105 Akeem Ayers AU/188* RC 10.00 25.00
106 Ald.Smith AU/102* SP RC 40.00 100.00
107 Aldrick Robinson AU RC 5.00 12.00
108 Alex Henery AU RC 5.00 12.00
109 Allen Bradford AU RC 4.00 10.00
110 Anthony Allen AU RC 4.00 10.00
111 Anthony Castonzo AU RC 4.00 10.00
112 Anthony Sherman AU RC 4.00 10.00
113 Armond Smith AU RC 5.00 12.00
114 Brandon Harris AU RC 4.00 10.00
115 C.Heyward AU/99* RC 40.00 80.00
116 Cameron Jordan AU/99* RC 40.00 80.00
117 Casey Matthews AU RC 4.00 10.00
118 Cecil Shorts AU/99* RC 20.00 50.00
119 Charles Clay AU/99* RC 30.00 60.00
120 Colin Cochart AU RC 4.00 10.00
121 Corey Liuget AU RC 4.00 10.00
122 D.J. Williams AU/171* RC 15.00 40.00
123 Da'Quan Bowers AU RC 4.00 10.00
124 Da'Rel Scott AU RC 4.00 10.00
125 D.Sanzenbacher AU RC 4.00 10.00
126 Darron Evans AU RC 6.00 12.00
127 David Ausberry AU RC 4.00 10.00
128 DeMarco Sampson AU/99* RC 20.00 50.00
129 Denarius Moore AU RC 4.00 10.00
130 Dion Lewis AU/224* RC 12.00 30.00
131 Doug Baldwin AU RC 15.00 30.00
132 Mark Herzlich AU RC 4.00 10.00
133 Evan Royster AU RC 4.00 10.00
134 Greg Jones AU RC 5.00 12.00
135 Greg McElroy AU/204* RC 6.00 15.00
136 Greg Salas AU RC 4.00 10.00
137 J.J. Watt AU RC 75.00 150.00
138 Jacquizz Rodgers AU RC 4.00 10.00
139 Jamar Newsome AU RC 4.00 10.00
140 Jeremy Kerley AU/82* RC 25.00 60.00
141 Jimmy Smith AU/173* RC 12.00 30.00
142 Joe Lefeged AU RC 5.00 12.00
143 Johnny White AU RC 4.00 10.00
144 Jordan Cameron AU RC 5.00 12.00
145 Josh Portis AU RC 6.00 15.00
146 Julius Thomas AU/99* RC 15.00 40.00
147 Justin Houston AU RC 5.00 12.00
148 Kealoha Pilares AU/128* RC 15.00 40.00
149 Kris Durham AU RC 4.00 10.00
150 Kyle Adams AU RC 4.00 10.00
151 Lance Kendricks/298* AU RC 4.00 10.00
152 LaQuan Williams AU RC 5.00 12.00
153 Lee Smith AU RC 5.00 12.00
154 Luke Stocker AU RC 4.00 10.00
155 J.Ballard AU/99* RC 20.00 50.00
156 Marcus Gilchrist AU RC 4.00 10.00
157 Martez Wilson AU/134* RC 15.00 40.00
158 Mason Foster AU RC 4.00 10.00
159 Bruce Miller AU RC 5.00 12.00
160 Nathan Enderle AU/99* RC 25.00 60.00
161 Niles Paul AU/152* RC 4.00 10.00
162 O.Marecic AU/99* RC EXCH 40.00 80.00
163 Phil Taylor AU/371* RC 4.00 10.00
164 Phillip Tanner AU RC 6.00 15.00
165 P.Amukamara AU/213* RC 4.00 10.00
166 Quinton Carter AU RC 4.00 10.00
167 Rahim Moore AU/316* RC 12.00 30.00
168 Richard Gordon AU RC 4.00 10.00
169 Ricky Stanzi AU RC 4.00 10.00
170 Robert Housler AU RC 4.00 10.00
171 Ronald Johnson AU/192* RC 12.00 30.00
172 Roy Helu AU RC 4.00 10.00
173 Ryan Kerrigan AU RC 5.00 12.00
174 Ryan Taylor AU RC 5.00 12.00
175 Ryan Whalen AU RC 4.00 10.00
176 Jackie Battle AU RC 6.00 15.00
177 Shane Bannon AU RC 4.00 10.00
178 Stanley Havili AU RC 4.00 10.00
179 Stephen Burton AU/140* RC 15.00 40.00
180 Stephen Paea AU RC 4.00 10.00
181 T.J. Yates AU RC 4.00 10.00
182 Tandon Doss AU RC 4.00 10.00
183 Tyler Sash AU/193* RC 10.00 25.00
184 Tyrod Taylor AU RC 8.00 20.00
185 Tyron Smith AU/23* RC 500.00 800.00
186 Virgil Green AU RC 4.00 10.00
187 W.Saunders AU/99* RC EXCH 75.00 150.00
188 Curtis Brinkley AU RC 6.00 15.00
189 Zack Pianalto AU RC 5.00 12.00
190 Buster Skrine AU RC 5.00 12.00
191 Chimdi Chekwa AU RC 5.00 12.00
192 Chris Harris AU RC 5.00 12.00
193 Chris White AU RC 5.00 12.00
194 Dan Bailey AU RC 10.00 25.00
195 Henry Hynoski AU RC 6.00 15.00
196 J.Williams AU/99* RC EXCH 50.00 100.00
197 K.J. Wright AU RC 6.00 15.00
199 Patrick Peterson AU/343* RC 8.00 20.00
200 Robert Quinn AU RC 15.00 30.00
201A Marcell Dareus AU RC EXCH 4.00 10.00
202A Randall Cobb AU RC 6.00 15.00
202B R.Cobb no logo AU/250* 10.00 25.00
203A Ryan Mallett AU RC 4.00 10.00
203B Ryan Mallett no logo AU/25* 30.00 60.00
204A Greg Little AU RC 5.00 12.00
205A Christian Ponder AU RC 4.00 10.00
205B C.Ponder no logo AU/50* 20.00 50.00
206A Jamie Harper AU RC 4.00 10.00
206B J.Harper no logo AU/250* 5.00 12.00
207A Alex Green AU RC 4.00 10.00
208A Austin Pettis AU RC 4.00 10.00
208B Austin Pettis no logo AU/50* 12.00 30.00
209A Ryan Williams AU RC 4.00 10.00
209B R.Williams no logo AU/250* 6.00 15.00
210A Taiwan Jones AU RC 4.00 10.00
210B Taiwan Jones no logo AU/25* 50.00 100.00
211A Jake Locker AU RC 4.00 10.00
211B J.Locker no shldr # AU/50* 25.00 60.00
212A Blaine Gabbert AU RC 4.00 10.00
212B B.Gabbert no logo AU/25*
213A Mark Ingram AU RC 6.00 15.00
213B Mark Ingram no logo AU/100* 12.00 30.00
214A Stevan Ridley AU RC EXCH 15.00 40.00
215A Daniel Thomas AU RC 4.00 10.00
216A Jordan Todman AU RC 4.00 10.00
216B J.Todman no logo AU/250* 6.00 15.00
217A Shane Vereen AU RC 5.00 12.00
217B Shane Vereen no logo AU/250* 8.00 20.00
218A Titus Young AU RC 4.00 10.00
218B T.Young no logo AU/250* 6.00 15.00
219A Jonathan Baldwin AU RC 4.00 10.00
219B J.Baldwin no logo AU/250* 6.00 15.00
220A Von Miller AU RC 25.00 50.00
220B Von Miller no logo AU/100* 40.00 80.00
221A Julio Jones AU RC 75.00 150.00
222A A.J. Green AU RC 20.00 50.00
222B A.J. Green no logo AU/25* 60.00 120.00
223A Bilal Powell AU RC 5.00 12.00
223B Bilal Powell no logo AU/25* 25.00 50.00
224A Kyle Rudolph AU RC 4.00 10.00
224B Rudolph no watch AU/100* 8.00 20.00
225A Andy Dalton AU RC 20.00 40.00
225B A.Dalton no logo AU/100* 30.00 80.00
226A Clyde Gates AU RC 4.00 10.00
226B Clyde Gates no logo AU/50* 12.00 30.00
227A Colin Kaepernick AU RC 15.00 40.00
227B Kaepernick no logo AU/250* 25.00 60.00
228A Cam Newton AU RC 100.00 200.00
228B Cam Newton no logo AU/25* 250.00 400.00
229A Mikel Leshoure AU RC 4.00 10.00
229B M.Leshoure no logo AU/250* 15.00 40.00
230A Torrey Smith AU RC 4.00 10.00
230B T.Smith no logo AU/250* 6.00 15.00
231A DeMarco Murray AU RC 8.00 20.00
231B D.Murray no logo AU/250* 25.00 60.00
232A Kendall Hunter AU RC 4.00 10.00
232B K.Hunter no logo AU/100* 12.00 30.00
233A Vincent Brown AU RC 4.00 10.00
233B V.Brown no logo AU/250* 6.00 15.00
234A Leonard Hankerson AU RC 4.00 10.00
234B L.Hankerson no logo AU/100* 8.00 20.00
235A Jerrel Jernigan AU RC 4.00 10.00
235B Jerrel Jernigan no logo AU/50* 8.00 20.00
236A Delone Carter AU RC 4.00 10.00
236B Delone Carter no logo AU/100* 8.00 20.00

2011 Playoff Contenders Playoff Ticket

*1-100 VETS/99: 3X TO 8X BASIC CARDS
COMMON ROOKIE (101-236) 2.50 6.00
ROOKIE SEMISTARS 3.00 8.00
ROOKIE UNL.STARS 4.00 10.00
STATED PRINT RUN 99 SER.#'d SETS
101 Terrelle Pryor 4.00 10.00
106 Aldon Smith 2.50 6.00
129 Denarius Moore 2.50 6.00
131 Doug Baldwin 6.00 15.00
137 J.J. Watt 12.00 30.00
155 Jake Ballard 8.00 20.00
169 Ricky Stanzi 2.50 6.00
172 Roy Helu 2.50 6.00
174 Ryan Taylor 3.00 8.00
176 Jackie Battle 4.00 10.00
181 T.J. Yates 2.50 6.00
185 Tyron Smith 3.00 8.00
187 Weslye Saunders 12.00 30.00
195 Henry Hynoski 4.00 10.00
196 Jacquian Williams 4.00 10.00
198 Nick Fairley 2.50 6.00
199 Patrick Peterson 5.00 12.00
202 Randall Cobb 4.00 10.00
203 Ryan Mallett 2.50 6.00
205 Christian Ponder 2.50 6.00
209 Ryan Williams 2.50 6.00
211 Jake Locker 2.50 6.00
212 Blaine Gabbert 2.50 6.00
213 Mark Ingram 4.00 10.00
215 Daniel Thomas 2.50 6.00
218 Titus Young 2.50 6.00
220 Von Miller 4.00 10.00
221 Julio Jones 8.00 20.00
222 A.J. Green 6.00 15.00
225 Andy Dalton 5.00 12.00
227 Colin Kaepernick 15.00 40.00
228 Cam Newton 12.00 30.00
230 Torrey Smith 2.50 6.00
231 DeMarco Murray 5.00 12.00

2011 Playoff Contenders Draft Class

*BLACK/50: .8X TO 2X BASIC INSERTS
*GOLD/100: .6X TO 1.5X BASIC INSERTS
1 C.Kaepernick/K.Hunter .75 2.00
2 A.Green/A.Dalton 1.25 3.00
3 M.Dareus/A.Williams .50 1.25
4 V.Miller/R.Moore .75 2.00
5 G.Little/J.Cameron .60 1.50
6 A.Clayborn/D.Bowers .50 1.25
7 V.Brown/J.Todman .50 1.25
8 J.Baldwin/R.Stanzi .50 1.25
9 D.Thomas/C.Gates .50 1.25
10 J.Jones/J.Rodgers 1.50 4.00
11 J.Jernigan/D.Scott .50 1.25
12 B.Gabbert/C.Shorts .50 1.25
13 J.Kerley/S.McKnight .75 2.00
14 B.Powell/G.McElroy .75 2.00
15 R.Cobb/A.Green .75 2.00
16 C.Ponder/K.Rudolph .50 1.25
17 S.Vereen/S.Ridley .60 1.50
18 T.Jones/D.Moore .50 1.25
19 A.Pettis/G.Salas .50 1.25
20 T.Smith/T.Doss .50 1.25
21 L.Hankerson/N.Paul 1.00 2.50
22 R.Helu/E.Royster .50 1.25
23 C.Jordan/M.Ingram .75 2.00
24 J.Watt/B.Harris 2.50 6.00
25 J.Locker/J.Harper .50 1.25

2011 Playoff Contenders Legendary Contenders

*BLACK/50: .8X TO 2X BASIC INSERTS
*GOLD/100: .6X TO 1.5X BASIC INSERTS
1 Art Monk 1.25 3.00
2 Earl Campbell 1.25 3.00
3 Bill Bates .75 2.00
4 Cris Collinsworth 1.00 2.50
5 Emmitt Smith 2.00 5.00
6 Bruce Smith 1.00 2.50
7 Steve Largent 1.25 3.00
8 Gale Sayers 1.25 3.00
9 Darrell Green 1.00 2.50
10 Don Maynard 1.00 2.50
11 Larry Csonka 1.00 2.50
12 Dick Lane .75 2.00
13 Fred Biletnikoff 1.25 3.00
14 Barry Sanders 2.00 5.00
15 Alan Page .75 2.00
16 Henry Ellard .75 2.00
17 Bo Jackson 1.50 4.00
18 John Randle 1.00 2.50
19 Brent Jones .75 2.00
20 Curtis Martin 1.00 2.50
21 Deacon Jones 1.00 2.50
22 Tom Rathman .75 2.00
23 Danny White 1.00 2.50
24 Junior Seau 1.00 2.50
25 Irving Fryar .75 2.00

2011 Playoff Contenders Legendary Contenders Autographs

ANNOUNCED PRINT RUN 5-25
3 Bill Bates/25* 15.00 40.00
7 Steve Largent/25* 15.00 40.00
15 Alan Page/25* 15.00 40.00
16 Henry Ellard/25* 10.00 25.00
17 Bo Jackson/25* 50.00 100.00
18 John Randle/25* 15.00 40.00
19 Brent Jones/25* 10.00 25.00
20 Curtis Martin/25* 30.00 60.00
21 Deacon Jones/25* 15.00 40.00
22 Tom Rathman/25* 15.00 40.00
23 Danny White/25* 25.00 50.00
25 Irving Fryar/25* 15.00 40.00

2011 Playoff Contenders Rookie Ink

ANNOUNCED AU PRINT RUN 25-100
EXCH EXPIRATION: 8/8/2013
1 Jamie Harper/100* 6.00 15.00
2 Ryan Williams/100* 6.00 15.00
3 Julio Jones/100* 25.00 60.00
4 Delone Carter/100* 6.00 15.00
5 Colin Kaepernick/100* 40.00 100.00
6 Bilal Powell/25* 15.00 40.00
7 Marcell Dareus/50* EXCH
8 Blaine Gabbert/25* 8.00 20.00
9 Jonathan Baldwin/100* 12.00 30.00
10 Kendall Hunter/100* 15.00 40.00
11 Clyde Gates/50* 6.00 15.00
12 Ryan Mallett/25* 12.00 30.00
13 Taiwan Jones/25* 15.00 40.00
14 Kyle Rudolph/100* 6.00 15.00
15 Vincent Brown/100* 6.00 15.00
16 Andy Dalton/100* 25.00 60.00
17 Randall Cobb/100* 10.00 25.00
18 Austin Pettis/50* 6.00 15.00
19 Shane Vereen/100* 8.00 20.00
20 Mark Ingram/100* 25.00 60.00
21 Mikel Leshoure/100* 12.00 30.00
22 Cam Newton/25* 125.00 250.00
23 Leonard Hankerson/100* 6.00 15.00
24 Greg Little/50* 8.00 20.00
25 Jake Locker/50* 6.00 15.00
26 Torrey Smith/100* 6.00 15.00
27 Jerrel Jernigan/50* 6.00 15.00
28 DeMarco Murray/100* 12.00 30.00
29 Christian Ponder/50* 6.00 15.00
30 A.J. Green/25* 30.00 80.00
31 Von Miller/100* 15.00 40.00
32 Alex Green/100* 6.00 15.00
33 Titus Young/100* EXCH 6.00 15.00
34 Daniel Thomas/100* 6.00 15.00
35 Jordan Todman/100* 6.00 15.00
36 Stevan Ridley/50* 6.00 15.00

2011 Playoff Contenders Rookie Roll Call

COMPLETE SET (25) 15.00 40.00
*GOLD/100: 1X TO 2.5X BASIC INSERTS
1 Alex Green .50 1.25
2 Bilal Powell .60 1.50
3 Cam Newton 2.50 6.00
4 Christian Ponder .50 1.25
5 Delone Carter .50 1.25
6 DeMarco Murray 1.00 2.50
7 Jake Locker .50 1.25
8 Jamie Harper .50 1.25
9 Jordan Todman .50 1.25
10 Mikel Leshoure .50 1.25
11 Randall Cobb .75 2.00
12 Ryan Mallett .50 1.25
13 Ryan Williams .50 1.25
14 Shane Vereen .60 1.50
15 Stevan Ridley .50 1.25
16 Taiwan Jones .50 1.25
17 Titus Young .50 1.25
18 Aaron Williams .50 1.25
19 Aldon Smith .50 1.25
20 Corey Liuget .50 1.25
21 Jimmy Smith .50 1.25
22 Lance Kendricks .50 1.25
23 Prince Amukamara .50 1.25
24 Ryan Kerrigan .60 1.50
25 Terrelle Pryor .75 2.00

2011 Playoff Contenders ROY Contenders

COMPLETE SET (25) 15.00 40.00
*GOLD/100: 1X TO 2.5X BASIC INSERTS
1 A.J. Green 1.25 3.00
2 Andy Dalton 1.00 2.50
3 Austin Pettis .50 1.25
4 Blaine Gabbert .50 1.25
5 Cam Newton 2.50 6.00
6 Daniel Thomas .50 1.25
7 Greg Little .60 1.50
8 Julio Jones 1.50 4.00
9 Kyle Rudolph .50 1.25
10 Marcell Dareus .50 1.25
11 Mark Ingram .75 2.00
12 Torrey Smith .50 1.25
13 Dane Sanzenbacher .50 1.25
14 Von Miller .75 2.00
15 Roy Helu .50 1.25
16 Denarius Moore .50 1.25
17 Mason Foster .50 1.25
18 Stevan Ridley .50 1.25
19 Clyde Gates .50 1.25
20 Ryan Kerrigan .60 1.50
21 Delone Carter .50 1.25
22 Kendall Hunter .50 1.25
23 Adrian Clayborn .50 1.25
24 Aldon Smith .50 1.25
25 J.J. Watt 2.50 6.00

2011 Playoff Contenders ROY Contenders Black

*BLACK/50: 1.2X TO 3X BASIC INSERTS
BLACK PRINT RUN 50 SER.#'d SETS

2011 Playoff Contenders Signs of Greatness

ANNOUNCED PRINT RUN 5-25
EXCH EXPIRATION: 8/8/2013
5 Hakeem Nicks/25* 10.00 25.00
6 Jahvid Best/25* 10.00 25.00
15 Shonn Greene/25* 10.00 25.00
16 Sidney Rice/25* 10.00 25.00
18 Tony Moeaki/25* 10.00 25.00
19 BenJarvus Green-Ellis/25* 15.00 40.00
30 Matt Forte/25* 15.00 40.00
32 Ryan Torain/25* 12.00 30.00
35 Danny Amendola/25* 12.00 30.00
36 Ron Mix/25* 10.00 25.00
37 Harlon Hill/25* 15.00 40.00
38 Boyd Dowler/25* 15.00 40.00
39 Mike Curtis/25* 10.00 25.00
40 Willie Brown/25* 10.00 25.00
42 Rick Casares/25* 12.00 30.00
44 Paul Krause/25* 10.00 25.00
46 Lydell Mitchell/25* 10.00 25.00
49 Leroy Kelly/25* 12.00 30.00
50 Rosey Grier/25* 12.00 30.00

2011 Playoff Contenders Super Bowl Tickets

*BLACK/50: .8X TO 2X BASIC INSERTS
*GOLD/100: .6X TO 1.5X BASIC INSERTS
UNPRICED AUTO ANNC'D PRINT RUN 10
1 Aaron Rodgers 2.50 6.00
2 Greg Jennings 1.00 2.50
3 Donald Driver 1.25 3.00
4 Pierre Thomas 1.00 2.50
5 Larry Fitzgerald 1.25 3.00
6 Ahmad Bradshaw 1.00 2.50
7 Dallas Clark 1.00 2.50
8 Hines Ward 1.25 3.00
9 Troy Polamalu 1.50 4.00
10 Donovan McNabb 1.25 3.00
11 Steve Smith 1.25 3.00
12 Mike Alstott 1.00 2.50
13 Charles Woodson 1.50 4.00
14 Eddie George 1.25 3.00
15 Rod Smith 1.00 2.50
16 Shannon Sharpe 1.25 3.00
17 Ronnie Lott 1.25 3.00
18 Mike Singletary 1.50 4.00
19 Marcus Allen 1.50 4.00
20 John Riggins 1.25 3.00
21 Franco Harris 1.50 4.00
22 John Stallworth 1.25 3.00
23 Joe Greene 1.50 4.00
24 Bob Griese 1.50 4.00
25 John Mackey 1.25 3.00

1997 Playoff First and Ten Prototypes

This set was issued to promote the 1997 Playoff First and Ten brand. The cards appear very similar to their regular issue counterparts and can be distinguished primarily by the different card numbering.

COMPLETE SET (6) 1.60 4.00
1 Antonio Freeman .20 .50
2 Terry Allen .20 .50
3 Terrell Davis .80 2.00
4 Eddie George .50 1.25
5 Karim Abdul-Jabbar .20 .50
6 Curtis Martin .30 .75

1997 Playoff First and Ten

The 1997 Playoff First and Ten set was issued in one series totalling 250-cards and was distributed in nine-card packs plus one "Chip Shot" or plastic token with a suggested retail price of $1.99. The cards feature player photos printed in full-color on high-gloss coated card stock.

COMPLETE SET (250) 7.50 20.00
1 Marcus Allen .20 .50
2 Eric Bieniemy .07 .20
3 Jason Dunn .07 .20
4 Jim Harbaugh .10 .30
5 Michael Westbrook .10 .30
6 Tiki Barber RC 1.25 3.00
7 Frank Reich .07 .20
8 Irving Fryar .10 .30
9 Courtney Hawkins .07 .20
10 Eric Zeier .10 .30
11 Kent Graham .07 .20
12 Trent Dilfer .20 .50
13 Neil O'Donnell .10 .30
14 Reidel Anthony RC .20 .50
15 Jeff Hostetler .07 .20
16 Lawrence Phillips .07 .20
17 Dave Brown .07 .20
18 Mike Tomczak .07 .20
19 Jake Reed .10 .30
20 Anthony Miller .07 .20
21 Eric Metcalf .10 .30
22 Sedrick Shaw RC .10 .30
23 Anthony Johnson .07 .20
24 Mario Bates .07 .20
25 Dorsey Levens .20 .50
26 Stan Humphries .10 .30
27 Ben Coates .10 .30
28 Tyrone Wheatley .10 .30
29 Adrian Murrell .10 .30
30 William Henderson .10 .30
31 Warrick Dunn RC .60 1.50
32 LeShon Johnson .07 .20
33 James O.Stewart .10 .30
34 Edgar Bennett .10 .30
35 Raymont Harris .07 .20
36 LeRoy Butler .07 .20
37 Darren Woodson .07 .20
38 Darnell Autry RC .10 .30
39 Johnnie Morton .10 .30
40 William Floyd .10 .30
41 Terrell Fletcher .07 .20
42 Leonard Russell .07 .20
43 Henry Ellard .07 .20
44 Terrell Owens .25 .60
45 John Friesz .07 .20
46 Antowain Smith RC .50 1.25
47 Charles Johnson .10 .30
48 Rickey Dudley .10 .30
49 Lake Dawson .07 .20
50 Bert Emanuel .10 .30
51 Zach Thomas .20 .50
52 Earnest Byner .07 .20
53 Yatil Green RC .10 .30
54 Chris Spielman .07 .20
55 Muhsin Muhammad .10 .30
56 Bobby Engram .10 .30
57 Eric Bjornson .07 .20
58 Willie Green .07 .20
59 Derrick Mayes .10 .30
60 Chris Sanders .07 .20
61 Jimmy Smith .10 .30
62 Tony Gonzalez RC .75 2.00
63 Rich Gannon .20 .50
64 Stanley Pritchett .07 .20
65 Brad Johnson .20 .50
66 Rodney Peete .07 .20
67 Sam Gash .07 .20
68 Chris Calloway .07 .20
69 Chris T. Jones .07 .20
70 Will Blackwell RC .10 .30
71 Mark Bruener .07 .20
72 Terry Kirby .10 .30
73 Brian Blades .07 .20
74 Craig Heyward .07 .20
75 Jamie Asher .07 .20
76 Terance Mathis .10 .30
77 Troy Davis RC .10 .30
78 Bruce Smith .10 .30
79 Simeon Rice .10 .30
80 Fred Barnett .07 .20
81 Tim Brown .20 .50
82 James Jett .10 .30
83 Mark Carrier WR .07 .20
84 Shawn Jefferson .07 .20
85 Ken Dilger .07 .20
86 Rae Carruth RC .07 .20
87 Keenan McCardell .10 .30
88 Michael Irvin .20 .50
89 Mark Chmura .10 .30
90 Derrick Alexander WR .10 .30
91 Andre Reed .10 .30
92 Ed McCaffrey .10 .30
93 Erik Kramer .07 .20
94 Albert Connell RC .20 .50
95 Frank Wycheck .07 .20
96 Zack Crockett .07 .20
97 Jim Everett .07 .20
98 Michael Haynes .07 .20
99 Jeff Graham .07 .20
100 Brent Jones .10 .30
101 Troy Aikman .40 1.00
102 Byron Hanspard RC .10 .30
103 Robert Brooks .10 .30
104 Karim Abdul-Jabbar .20 .50
105 Drew Bledsoe .25 .60
106 Napoleon Kaufman .20 .50
107 Steve Young .25 .60
108 Leeland McElroy .07 .20
109 Jamal Anderson .20 .50
110 David LaFleur RC .07 .20
111 Vinny Testaverde .10 .30
112 Eric Moulds .20 .50
113 Tim Biakabutuka .10 .30
114 Rick Mirer .07 .20
115 Jeff Blake .10 .30
116 Jim Schwantz RC .07 .20
117 Herman Moore .10 .30
118 Ike Hilliard RC .30 .75
119 Reggie White .20 .50
120 Steve McNair .25 .60
121 Marshall Faulk .25 .60
122 Natrone Means .10 .30
123 Greg Hill .07 .20
124 O.J. McDuffie .10 .30
125 Robert Smith .10 .30
126 Bryant Westbrook RC .07 .20
127 Ray Zellars .07 .20
128 Rodney Hampton .10 .30
129 Wayne Chrebet .20 .50
130 Desmond Howard .10 .30
131 Ty Detmer .10 .30
132 Erric Pegram .07 .20
133 Yancey Thigpen .10 .30
134 Danny Wuerffel RC .20 .50
135 Charlie Jones .10 .30
136 Chris Warren .10 .30
137 Isaac Bruce .20 .50
138 Errict Rhett .07 .20
139 Gus Frerotte .07 .20
140 Frank Sanders .10 .30
141 Todd Collins .07 .20
142 Jake Plummer RC .75 2.00
143 Darnay Scott .10 .30
144 Rashaan Salaam .07 .20
145 Terrell Davis .25 .60
146 Scott Mitchell .10 .30
147 Junior Seau .20 .50
148 Warren Moon .20 .50
149 Wesley Walls .10 .30
150 Daryl Johnston .10 .30
151 Brett Favre .75 2.00
152 Emmitt Smith .60 1.50
153 Dan Marino .75 2.00
154 Larry Centers .10 .30
155 Michael Jackson .10 .30
156 Kerry Collins .20 .50
157 Curtis Conway .10 .30
158 Peter Boulware RC .20 .50
159 Carl Pickens .10 .30
160 Shannon Sharpe .10 .30
161 Brett Perriman .07 .20
162 Eddie George .20 .50
163 Mark Brunell .25 .60
164 Tamarick Vanover .10 .30
165 Cris Carter .20 .50
166 Corey Dillon RC .75 2.00
167 Curtis Martin .25 .60
168 Amani Toomer .10 .30
169 Jeff George .10 .30
170 Kordell Stewart .20 .50
171 Garrison Hearst .10 .30
172 Tony Banks .10 .30
173 Mike Alstott .20 .50
174 Jim Druckenmiller RC .10 .30
175 Chris Chandler .10 .30
176 Byron Bam Morris .07 .20
177 Billy Joe Hobert .10 .30
178 Ernie Mills .07 .20
179 Ki-Jana Carter .07 .20
180 Deion Sanders .20 .50
181 Ricky Watters .10 .30
182 Shawn Springs RC .10 .30
183 Barry Sanders .60 1.50
184 Antonio Freeman .20 .50
185 Marvin Harrison .20 .50
186 Elvis Grbac .10 .30
187 Terry Glenn .20 .50
188 Willie Roaf .07 .20
189 Keyshawn Johnson .20 .50
190 Orlando Pace RC .20 .50
191 Jerome Bettis .20 .50
192 Tony Martin .10 .30
193 Jerry Rice .40 1.00
194 Joey Galloway .10 .30
195 Terry Allen .20 .50
196 Eddie Kennison .10 .30
197 Thurman Thomas .20 .50
198 Darrell Russell RC .07 .20
199 Rob Moore .10 .30
200 John Elway .75 2.00
201 Quinn Early .07 .20
202 Kevin Greene .10 .30
203 Robert Green .07 .20
204 Tony Carter .07 .20
205 Michael Timpson .07 .20
206 Kevin Smith .07 .20
207 Herschel Walker .10 .30
208 Steve Atwater .07 .20
209 Tyrone Braxton .07 .20
210 Willie Davis .07 .20
211 Lamont Warren .07 .20
212 Sean Dawkins .07 .20
213 Dale Carter .07 .20
214 Kimble Anders .10 .30
215 Derrick Thomas .20 .50
216 Chris Penn .07 .20
217 Irving Spikes .07 .20
218 Amp Lee .07 .20
219 Qadry Ismail .10 .30
220 Dave Meggett .07 .20
221 Tyrone Hughes .07 .20
222 Haywood Jeffires .07 .20
223 Torrance Small .07 .20
224 Danny Kanell .10 .30
225 Thomas Lewis .07 .20
226 Kyle Brady .07 .20
227 Harvey Williams .07 .20
228 Bobby Hoying .10 .30
229 Charlie Garner .10 .30
230 Andre Hastings .07 .20
231 Heath Shuler .07 .20
232 J.J. Stokes .10 .30
233 Ken Norton .07 .20
234 Steve Walsh .07 .20
235 Harold Green .07 .20
236 Reggie Brooks .07 .20
237 Robb Thomas .07 .20
238 Brian Mitchell .07 .20
239 Bill Brooks .07 .20
240 Leslie Shepherd .07 .20
241 Jay Graham RC .10 .30
242 Kevin Lockett RC .10 .30
243 Derrick Mason RC .50 1.25
244 Marc Edwards RC .07 .20
245 Joey Kent RC .20 .50
246 Pat Barnes RC .20 .50
247 Sherman Williams .07 .20
248 Ray Brown G .07 .20
249 Stephen Davis .20 .50
250 Lamar Smith .20 .50

1997 Playoff First and Ten Kickoff

COMPLETE SET (250) 100.00 200.00
*KICKOFF STARS: 4X TO 10X BASIC CARDS
*KICKOFF RCs: 2X TO 5X BASIC CARDS
STATED ODDS 1:9

1997 Playoff First and Ten Chip Shots Green

COMPLETE SET (250) 125.00 250.00
*1-200: .4X TO 1X ABSOLUTE CHIP SHOTS
1-200: ONE PER PACK
201-250: ONE PER SPECIAL RETAIL PACK
WITH WHITE STRIPES ON COIN'S EDGE
EACH PRINTED IN GREEN, YELLOW, AND RED
201 Quinn Early .25 .60
202 Kevin Greene .25 .60
203 Robert Green .25 .60
204 Tony Carter .25 .60
205 Michael Timpson .25 .60
206 Kevin Smith .25 .60
207 Herschel Walker .40 1.00
208 Steve Atwater .25 .60
209 Tyrone Braxton .25 .60
210 Willie Davis .25 .60
211 Lamont Warren .25 .60
212 Sean Dawkins .25 .60
213 Dale Carter .25 .60
214 Kimble Anders .25 .60
215 Derrick Thomas .75 2.00
216 Chris Penn .25 .60
217 Irving Spikes .25 .60
218 Amp Lee .25 .60
219 Qadry Ismail .40 1.00
220 Dave Meggett .25 .60
221 Tyrone Hughes .25 .60
222 Haywood Jeffires .25 .60
223 Torrance Small .25 .60
224 Danny Kanell .25 .60
225 Thomas Lewis .25 .60
226 Kyle Brady .75 2.00
227 Harvey Williams .25 .60
228 Bobby Hoying .75 2.00
229 Charlie Garner .40 1.00
230 Andre Hastings .25 .60
231 Heath Shuler .25 .60
232 J.J. Stokes .40 1.00
233 Ken Norton .25 .60
234 Steve Walsh .25 .60
235 Harold Green .25 .60
236 Reggie Brooks .25 .60
237 Robb Thomas .25 .60
238 Brian Mitchell .25 .60
239 Bill Brooks .25 .60
240 Leslie Shepherd .25 .60
241 Jay Graham .25 .60
242 Kevin Lockett .25 .60
243 Derrick Mason .75 2.00
244 Marc Edwards .25 .60
245 Joey Kent .25 .60
246 Pat Barnes .25 .60
247 Sherman Williams .25 .60
248 Ray Brown .25 .60
249 Stephen Davis .75 2.00
250 Lamar Smith .75 2.00

1997 Playoff First and Ten Hot Pursuit

Randomly inserted in packs at the rate of one in 180, this 100-card set features color photos of top players printed on 24-pt. mirror board.

COMPLETE SET (100) 350.00 700.00
STATED ODDS 1:180
1 Brett Favre 20.00 50.00
2 Dorsey Levens 5.00 12.00
3 Antonio Freeman 5.00 12.00
4 Robert Brooks 3.00 8.00
5 Mark Chmura 3.00 8.00
6 Reggie White 5.00 12.00
7 Drew Bledsoe 6.00 15.00
8 Curtis Martin 6.00 15.00
9 Ben Coates 3.00 8.00
10 Terry Glenn 5.00 12.00
11 Kerry Collins 5.00 12.00
12 Tim Biakabutuka 3.00 8.00
13 Anthony Johnson 2.00 5.00
14 Wesley Walls 3.00 8.00
15 Muhsin Muhammad 3.00 8.00
16 Mark Brunell 6.00 15.00
17 Natrone Means 3.00 8.00
18 Jimmy Smith 3.00 8.00
19 John Elway 20.00 50.00
20 Terrell Davis 6.00 15.00
21 Anthony Miller 2.00 5.00
22 Shannon Sharpe 3.00 8.00
23 Steve Young 6.00 15.00
24 Garrison Hearst 3.00 8.00
25 Jerry Rice 10.00 25.00
26 Troy Aikman 10.00 25.00
27 Deion Sanders 5.00 12.00
28 Emmitt Smith 15.00 40.00
29 Michael Irvin 5.00 12.00
30 Kordell Stewart 5.00 12.00
31 Jerome Bettis 5.00 12.00
32 Charles Johnson 3.00 8.00
33 Ty Detmer 3.00 8.00
34 Ricky Watters 3.00 8.00
35 Irving Fryar 3.00 8.00
36 Todd Collins 2.00 5.00
37 Thurman Thomas 5.00 12.00
38 Bruce Smith 3.00 8.00
39 Eric Moulds 5.00 12.00
40 Brad Johnson 5.00 12.00
41 Robert Smith 3.00 8.00
42 Cris Carter 5.00 12.00
43 Elvis Grbac 3.00 8.00
44 Greg Hill 2.00 5.00
45 Marcus Allen 5.00 12.00
46 Gus Frerotte 2.00 5.00
47 Terry Allen 5.00 12.00
48 Michael Westbrook 3.00 8.00
49 Jim Harbaugh 3.00 8.00
50 Marshall Faulk 6.00 15.00
51 Marvin Harrison 5.00 12.00
52 Jeff Blake 3.00 8.00
53 Ki-Jana Carter 2.00 5.00
54 Carl Pickens 3.00 8.00
55 Junior Seau 5.00 12.00
56 Tony Martin 3.00 8.00
57 Dan Marino 20.00 50.00
58 Karim Abdul-Jabbar 5.00 12.00
59 Stanley Pritchett 2.00 5.00
60 Zach Thomas 5.00 12.00
61 Steve McNair 6.00 15.00
62 Eddie George 5.00 12.00
63 Chris Sanders 2.00 5.00
64 Rick Mirer 2.00 5.00
65 Rashaan Salaam 2.00 5.00
66 Curtis Conway 3.00 8.00
67 Bobby Engram 3.00 8.00
68 Kent Graham 2.00 5.00
69 Leeland McElroy 2.00 5.00
70 Larry Centers 3.00 8.00
71 Frank Sanders 3.00 8.00
72 Jeff George 3.00 8.00
73 Napoleon Kaufman 5.00 12.00
74 Desmond Howard 3.00 8.00
75 Tim Brown 5.00 12.00
76 John Friesz 2.00 5.00
77 Chris Warren 3.00 8.00
78 Joey Galloway 3.00 8.00
79 Tony Banks 3.00 8.00
80 Lawrence Phillips 2.00 5.00
81 Isaac Bruce 5.00 12.00
82 Eddie Kennison 3.00 8.00
83 Errict Rhett 2.00 5.00
84 Mike Alstott 5.00 12.00
85 Rodney Hampton 3.00 8.00
86 Amani Toomer 3.00 8.00
87 Scott Mitchell 3.00 8.00
88 Barry Sanders 15.00 40.00
89 Herman Moore 3.00 8.00
90 Vinny Testaverde 3.00 8.00
91 Byron Bam Morris 2.00 5.00
92 Michael Jackson 3.00 8.00
93 Chris Chandler 3.00 8.00
94 Eric Metcalf 3.00 8.00
95 Jamal Anderson 5.00 12.00
96 Jim Everett 2.00 5.00
97 Mario Bates 2.00 5.00
98 Wayne Chrebet 5.00 12.00
99 Adrian Murrell 3.00 8.00
100 Keyshawn Johnson 5.00 12.00

1997 Playoff First and Ten Xtra Point

Randomly inserted in packs at the rate of one in 432, this 10-card set features color photos of the NFL's impact players printed on felt-like cards in various color backgrounds. Autographed cards, signed in gold ink, of Tony Banks and Terrell Davis were randomly inserted in packs at the rate of one in 4454.

STATED ODDS 1:432
AUTOGRAPHS STATED ODDS 1:4454
XP1R Kordell Stewart RED 5.00 12.00
XP2R Dan Marino RED 20.00 50.00
XP3G Brett Favre GREEN 15.00 40.00
XP4G Emmitt Smith GREEN 15.00 40.00
XP5B John Elway BLUE 15.00 40.00
XP6B Eddie George BLUE 5.00 12.00
XP7 Karim Abdul-Jabbar 5.00 12.00
XP8B Terry Glenn BLUE 5.00 12.00
XP9 Curtis Martin 6.00 15.00
XP10B Joey Galloway BLUE 5.00 12.00
XPA1 Tony Banks AU 10.00 25.00
XPA2 Terrell Davis AU 30.00 80.00

2003 Playoff Hogg Heaven

Released in October of 2003, this set consists of 230 cards including 150 veterans and 80 rookies. Rookies 151-200 are serial numbered to 1000. Rookies 201-250 feature event worn jersey swatches and are serial numbered to 750. Boxes contained 20 packs of 5 cards. SRP was $6.00.

COMP.SET w/o SP's (150) 12.50 30.00
151-200 ROOKIE PRINT RUN 1000
201-230 ROOKIE JSY PRINT RUN 750
1 Emmitt Smith .60 1.50
2 Marcel Shipp .25 .60
3 Michael Vick .30 .75
4 Warrick Dunn .25 .60
5 T.J. Duckett .25 .60
6 Peerless Price .25 .60
7 Brian Finneran .25 .60
8 Chris Redman .25 .60
9 Jamal Lewis .30 .75
10 Todd Heap .25 .60
11 Travis Taylor .25 .60
12 Ray Lewis .40 1.00
13 Peter Boulware .30 .75
14 Ed Reed .30 .75
15 Drew Bledsoe .30 .75
16 Travis Henry .25 .60
17 Eric Moulds .25 .60
18 Josh Reed .25 .60
19 Takeo Spikes .25 .60
20 Julius Peppers .40 1.00
21 Stephen Davis .25 .60
22 Muhsin Muhammad .25 .60
23 Wesley Walls .30 .75
24 Anthony Thomas .30 .75
25 Brian Urlacher .40 1.00
26 Marty Booker .25 .60
27 Mike Brown .25 .60
28 Kordell Stewart .25 .60
29 Dez White .25 .60
30 Corey Dillon .25 .60
31 Chad Johnson .25 .60
32 Peter Warrick .25 .60
33 Tim Couch .25 .60
34 William Green .25 .60
35 Andre Davis .25 .60
36 Quincy Morgan .25 .60
37 Kevin Johnson .25 .60
38 Dennis Northcutt .25 .60
39 Antonio Bryant .25 .60
40 Terry Glenn .30 .75
41 Joey Galloway .30 .75

42 Roy Williams .25 .60
43 Darren Woodson .30 .75
44 Jake Plummer .25 .60
45 Clinton Portis .25 .60
46 Mike Anderson .25 .60
47 Rod Smith .30 .75
48 Ed McCaffrey .30 .75
49 Ashley Lelie .25 .60
50 Shannon Sharpe .30 .75
51 Al Wilson .25 .60
52 Joey Harrington .25 .60
53 James Stewart .25 .60
54 Brett Favre .75 2.00
55 Ahman Green .30 .75
56 Darren Sharper .25 .60
57 Donald Driver .30 .75
58 Javon Walker .30 .75
59 Robert Ferguson .25 .60
60 David Carr .25 .60
61 Jabar Gaffney .25 .60
62 Stacey Mack .25 .60
63 Marvin Harrison .30 .75
64 Peyton Manning 1.00 2.50
65 Edgerrin James .30 .75
66 Reggie Wayne .30 .75
67 Fred Taylor .25 .60
68 Mark Brunell .30 .75
69 Jimmy Smith .30 .75
70 Hugh Douglas .25 .60
71 Priest Holmes .25 .60
72 Trent Green .25 .60
73 Tony Gonzalez .30 .75
74 Marc Boerigter .25 .60
75 Ricky Williams .30 .75
76 Jay Fiedler .25 .60
77 Chris Chambers .25 .60
78 Zach Thomas .30 .75
79 Jason Taylor .30 .75
80 Junior Seau .30 .75
81 Randy McMichael .25 .60
82 Patrick Surtain .25 .60
83 Randy Moss .30 .75
84 Michael Bennett .25 .60
85 Daunte Culpepper .30 .75
86 Tom Brady 1.50 4.00
87 Troy Brown .25 .60
88 Ty Law .40 1.00
89 Aaron Brooks .25 .60
90 Deuce McAllister .30 .75
91 Donte Stallworth .25 .60
92 Joe Horn .25 .60
93 Michael Strahan .30 .75
94 Kerry Collins .25 .60
95 Tiki Barber .30 .75
96 Amani Toomer .25 .60
97 Jeremy Shockey .25 .60
98 Chad Pennington .25 .60
99 Curtis Martin .30 .75
100 Santana Moss .30 .75
101 Rich Gannon .30 .75
102 Jerry Rice .75 2.00
103 Tim Brown .40 1.00
104 Jerry Porter .25 .60
105 Charlie Garner .30 .75
106 Charles Woodson .40 1.00
107 Donovan McNabb .30 .75
108 Duce Staley .25 .60
109 James Thrash .25 .60
110 Chad Lewis .30 .75
111 Troy Vincent .30 .75
112 Tommy Maddox .25 .60
113 Plaxico Burress .25 .60
114 Hines Ward .30 .75
115 Antwaan Randle El .25 .60
116 Jerome Bettis .40 1.00
117 Kendrell Bell .25 .60
118 LaDainian Tomlinson .40 1.00
119 Drew Brees .40 1.00
120 David Boston .25 .60
121 Jeff Garcia .25 .60
122 Terrell Owens .30 .75
123 Tai Streets .25 .60
124 Kevan Barlow .25 .60
125 Matt Hasselbeck .25 .60
126 Koren Robinson .30 .75
127 Shaun Alexander .25 .60
128 Kurt Warner .30 .75
129 Marc Bulger .25 .60
130 Marshall Faulk .30 .75
131 Torry Holt .30 .75
132 Isaac Bruce .40 1.00
133 Brad Johnson .30 .75
134 Keyshawn Johnson .40 1.00
135 Warren Sapp .30 .75
136 Derrick Brooks .25 .60
137 John Lynch .30 .75
138 Michael Pittman .25 .60
139 Mike Alstott .25 .60
140 Steve McNair .30 .75
141 Eddie George .30 .75
142 Jevon Kearse .25 .60
143 Keith Bulluck .25 .60
144 Derrick Mason .25 .60
145 Patrick Ramsey .30 .75
146 Ladell Betts .25 .60
147 Laveranues Coles .25 .60
148 Rod Gardner .25 .60
149 Champ Bailey .30 .75
150 Bruce Smith .30 .75
151 Ken Dorsey RC 2.00 5.00
152 Lee Suggs RC 1.50 4.00
153 Domanick Davis RC 2.00 5.00
154 Quentin Griffin RC 2.00 5.00
155 LaBrandon Toefield RC 1.50 4.00
156 B.J. Askew RC 2.00 5.00
157 Jason Witten RC 6.00 15.00
158 Bennie Joppru RC 1.50 4.00
159 L.J. Smith RC 2.50 6.00
160 Billy McMullen RC 1.50 4.00
161 Shaun McDonald RC 2.00 5.00
162 Brandon Lloyd RC 2.50 6.00
163 Sam Aiken RC 2.00 5.00
164 Bobby Wade RC 2.00 5.00
165 Justin Gage RC 2.00 5.00
166 Doug Gabriel RC 2.00 5.00
167 David Kircus RC 2.00 5.00
168 Arnaz Battle RC 2.50 6.00
169 Kareem Kelly RC 1.50 4.00
170 Talman Gardner RC 1.50 4.00
171 Ryan Hoag RC 1.50 4.00
172 LaTarence Dunbar RC 1.50 4.00
173 Johnathan Sullivan RC 1.50 4.00
174 Kevin Williams RC 2.50 6.00
175 Jimmy Kennedy RC 2.00 5.00
176 Ty Warren RC 2.00 5.00
177 William Joseph RC 1.50 4.00
178 Michael Haynes RC 1.50 4.00
179 Jerome McDougle RC 1.50 4.00
180 Calvin Pace RC 1.50 4.00
181 Tyler Brayton RC 2.00 5.00
182 Chris Kelsay RC 2.00 5.00
183 DeWayne White RC 1.50 4.00
184 E.J. Henderson RC 2.00 5.00
185 Charles Rogers RC 2.00 5.00
186 Terry Pierce RC 1.50 4.00
187 Nick Barnett RC 2.50 6.00
188 Boss Bailey RC 2.00 5.00
189 Pisa Tinoisamoa RC 2.50 6.00
190 Chaun Thompson RC 1.50 4.00
191 Andre Woolfolk RC 1.50 4.00
192 Sammy Davis RC 2.00 5.00
193 Eugene Wilson RC 2.50 6.00
194 Drayton Florence RC 2.50 6.00
195 Ricky Manning RC 2.00 5.00
196 Donald Strickland RC 1.50 4.00
197 Dennis Weathersby RC 1.50 4.00
198 Troy Polamalu RC 12.50 25.00
199 Ken Hamlin RC 2.50 6.00
200 Mike Doss RC 2.50 6.00
201 Carson Palmer JSY RC 4.00 10.00
202 Byron Leftwich JSY RC 2.50 6.00
203 Kyle Boller JSY RC 2.00 5.00
204 Rex Grossman JSY RC 2.50 6.00
205 Andre Johnson JSY RC 5.00 12.00
206 Bryant Johnson JSY RC 3.00 8.00
207 Larry Johnson JSY RC 2.50 6.00
208 Taylor Jacobs JSY RC 2.00 5.00
209 Bethel Johnson JSY RC 2.00 5.00
210 Anquan Boldin JSY RC 3.00 8.00
211 Tyrone Calico JSY RC 2.00 5.00
212 Teyo Johnson JSY RC 2.50 6.00
213 Kelley Washington JSY RC 2.00 5.00
214 Musa Smith JSY RC 2.00 5.00
215 Chris Brown JSY RC 2.00 5.00
216 Justin Fargas JSY RC 3.00 8.00
217 Artose Pinner JSY RC 2.00 5.00
218 Onterrio Smith JSY RC 2.00 5.00
219 Brian St.Pierre JSY RC 2.00 5.00
220 Dave Ragone JSY RC 2.00 5.00
221 Dallas Clark JSY RC 3.00 8.00
222 Seneca Wallace JSY RC 2.50 6.00
223 Terrell Suggs JSY RC 2.50 6.00
224 Terence Newman JSY RC 3.00 8.00
225 DeWayne Robertson JSY RC 2.50 6.00
226 Marcus Trufant JSY RC 2.50 6.00
227 Kliff Kingsbury JSY RC 3.00 8.00
228 Kevin Curtis JSY RC 2.00 5.00
229 Willis McGahee JSY RC 2.50 6.00
230 Nate Burleson JSY RC 2.50 6.00

2003 Playoff Hogg Heaven Hogg Wild

*VETS: 3X TO 8X BASIC CARDS
1-150 VETERAN PRINT RUN 150
*ROOKIES 151-200: .8X TO 2X
151-200 ROOKIE PRINT RUN 100
*ROOKIE JSY 201-230: 1.2X TO 3X
201-230 ROOKIE JSY PRINT RUN 25

2003 Playoff Hogg Heaven Accent

STATED PRINT RUN 25 SER.#'d SETS
A1 Michael Vick 8.00 20.00
A2 Donovan McNabb 8.00 20.00
A3 Peyton Manning 25.00 60.00
A4 Brett Favre 20.00 50.00
A5 Rich Gannon 8.00 20.00
A6 Jeff Garcia 6.00 15.00
A7 LaDainian Tomlinson 10.00 25.00
A8 Marshall Faulk 8.00 20.00
A9 Emmitt Smith 15.00 40.00
A10 Edgerrin James 8.00 20.00
A11 Ricky Williams 8.00 20.00
A12 Deuce McAllister 8.00 20.00
A13 Priest Holmes 6.00 15.00
A14 Ahman Green 8.00 20.00
A15 Marvin Harrison 8.00 20.00
A16 Terrell Owens 8.00 20.00
A17 Randy Moss 8.00 20.00
A18 Jerry Rice 20.00 50.00
A19 Tim Brown 10.00 25.00
A20 Jeremy Shockey 6.00 15.00

2003 Playoff Hogg Heaven Branded

STATED ODDS 1:19
B1 Michael Vick 1.50 4.00
B2 Donovan McNabb 1.50 4.00
B3 Peyton Manning 5.00 12.00
B4 Brett Favre 4.00 10.00
B5 Drew Bledsoe 1.50 4.00
B6 Tom Brady 8.00 20.00
B7 LaDainian Tomlinson 2.00 5.00
B8 Edgerrin James 1.50 4.00
B9 Ricky Williams 1.50 4.00
B10 Deuce McAllister 1.50 4.00
B11 Ahman Green 1.50 4.00
B12 Marshall Faulk 1.50 4.00
B13 Priest Holmes 1.25 3.00
B14 Marvin Harrison 1.50 4.00
B15 Terrell Owens 1.50 4.00
B16 Randy Moss 1.50 4.00
B17 Jerry Rice 4.00 10.00
B18 David Boston 1.25 3.00
B19 Tony Gonzalez 1.50 4.00
B20 Jeremy Shockey 1.25 3.00
B21 Warren Sapp 1.50 4.00
B22 Brian Urlacher 2.00 5.00
B23 Zach Thomas 1.50 4.00
B24 Ray Lewis 2.00 5.00
B25 Charles Woodson 2.00 5.00

2003 Playoff Hogg Heaven Hogg of Fame

PRINT RUN 500 SERIAL #'d SETS
HF1 Dan Marino 3.00 8.00
HF2 John Riggins 1.25 3.00
HF3 Steve Young 2.00 5.00
HF4 Brett Favre 3.00 8.00
HF5 Jerry Rice 3.00 8.00
HF6 Emmitt Smith 2.50 6.00
HF7 Tim Brown 1.50 4.00
HF8 Cris Carter 1.50 4.00
HF9 Peyton Manning 4.00 10.00
HF10 Marvin Harrison 1.25 3.00
HF11 Edgerrin James 1.25 3.00
HF12 Randy Moss 1.25 3.00
HF13 Terrell Owens 1.25 3.00
HF14 Ricky Williams 1.25 3.00
HF15 Michael Vick 1.25 3.00
HF16 Donovan McNabb 1.25 3.00
HF17 Clinton Portis 1.00 2.50
HF18 Priest Holmes 1.00 2.50
HF19 Marshall Faulk 1.25 3.00
HF20 Brian Urlacher 1.50 4.00
HF21 Ray Lewis 1.50 4.00
HF22 Jeremy Shockey 1.00 2.50
HF23 LaDainian Tomlinson 1.50 4.00
HF24 Deuce McAllister 1.25 3.00
HF25 Kurt Warner 1.25 3.00
HF26 Tom Brady 6.00 15.00
HF27 Drew Bledsoe 1.25 3.00
HF28 Drew Brees 1.50 4.00

2003 Playoff Hogg Heaven Hogg of Fame Materials Bronze

Randomly inserted in packs, this set features game worn jersey swatches. Each card is serial numbered to 125.
BRONZE PRINT RUN 125 SER.#'d SETS
*SILVER/75: .5X TO 1.2X BRONZE/125
SILVER PRINT RUN 75 SER.#'d SETS
*GOLD/25: .8X TO 2X BRONZE/125
GOLD PRINT RUN 25 SER.#'d SETS
HF1 Dan Marino 8.00 20.00
HF2 John Riggins 3.00 8.00
HF3 Steve Young 5.00 12.00
HF4 Brett Favre 8.00 20.00
HF5 Jerry Rice 8.00 20.00
HF6 Emmitt Smith 6.00 15.00
HF7 Tim Brown 4.00 10.00
HF8 Cris Carter 4.00 10.00
HF9 Peyton Manning 10.00 25.00
HF10 Marvin Harrison 3.00 8.00
HF11 Edgerrin James 3.00 8.00
HF12 Randy Moss 3.00 8.00
HF13 Terrell Owens 3.00 8.00
HF14 Ricky Williams 3.00 8.00
HF15 Michael Vick 3.00 8.00
HF16 Donovan McNabb 3.00 8.00
HF17 Clinton Portis 2.50 6.00
HF18 Priest Holmes 2.50 6.00
HF19 Marshall Faulk 3.00 8.00
HF20 Brian Urlacher 4.00 10.00
HF21 Ray Lewis 4.00 10.00
HF22 Jeremy Shockey 2.50 6.00
HF23 LaDainian Tomlinson 4.00 10.00
HF24 Deuce McAllister 3.00 0.00
HF25 Kurt Warner 3.00 8.00
HF26 Tom Brady 15.00 40.00
HF27 Drew Bledsoe 3.00 8.00
HF28 Drew Brees 4.00 10.00

2003 Playoff Hogg Heaven Leather in Leather

Randomly inserted in packs, this set features event used football swatches. Each card is serial numbered to 250.
STATED PRINT RUN 250 SER.#'d SETS
*LACES/25: .8X TO 2X LEATHER/250
LACES PRINT RUN 25 SERIAL #'d SETS
LL1 Emmitt Smith 8.00 20.00
LL2 Donovan McNabb 4.00 10.00
LL3 Steve McNair 4.00 10.00
LL4 Drew Bledsoe 4.00 10.00
LL5 Kurt Warner 4.00 10.00
LL6 Aaron Brooks 3.00 8.00
LL7 Tom Brady 10.00 25.00
LL8 Marvin Harrison 4.00 10.00
LL9 Chad Pennington 3.00 8.00
LL10 Randy Moss 4.00 10.00
LL11 Carson Palmer 6.00 15.00
LL12 Byron Leftwich 4.00 10.00
LL13 Kyle Boller 3.00 8.00
LL14 Rex Grossman 2.50 6.00
LL15 Andre Johnson 5.00 12.00
LL16 Bryant Johnson 3.00 8.00
LL17 Larry Johnson 2.50 6.00
LL18 Taylor Jacobs 2.00 5.00
LL19 Bethel Johnson 2.00 5.00
LL20 Anquan Boldin 3.00 8.00
LL21 Tyrone Calico 2.00 5.00
LL22 Teyo Johnson 2.50 6.00
LL23 Kelley Washington 2.00 5.00
LL24 Musa Smith 2.00 5.00
LL25 Chris Brown 2.00 5.00
LL26 Justin Fargas 3.00 8.00
LL27 Artose Pinner 2.00 5.00
LL28 Onterrio Smith 2.00 5.00
LL29 Brian St.Pierre 2.00 5.00
LL30 Dave Ragone 2.00 5.00
LL31 Dallas Clark 3.00 8.00
LL32 Seneca Wallace 2.50 6.00
LL33 Terrell Suggs 2.50 6.00
LL34 Terence Newman 3.00 8.00
LL35 DeWayne Robertson 2.50 6.00
LL36 Marcus Trufant 2.50 6.00
LL37 Kliff Kingsbury 3.00 8.00
LL38 Kevin Curtis 2.00 5.00
LL39 Willis McGahee 2.50 6.00
LL40 Nate Burleson 2.50 6.00

2003 Playoff Hogg Heaven Material Hoggs Bronze

Randomly inserted in packs, this set features game worn jersey swatches. Each card is serial numbered to 200.
BRONZE PRINT RUN 200 SER.#'d SETS
*SILVER/125: .5X TO 1.2X BRONZE/200
SILVER PRINT RUN 125 SER.#'d SETS
*GOLD/25: 1X TO 2.5X BRONZE/200
GOLD PRINT RUN 25 SER.#'d SETS
MH1 Emmitt Smith 8.00 20.00
MH2 Jerry Rice 10.00 25.00
MH3 Donovan McNabb 4.00 10.00
MH4 Peyton Manning 12.00 30.00
MH5 Brett Favre 10.00 25.00
MH6 Michael Vick 4.00 10.00
MH7 Aaron Brooks 3.00 8.00
MH8 Ahman Green 4.00 10.00
MH9 Antwaan Randle El 3.00 8.00
MH10 Brian Urlacher 5.00 12.00
MH11 Chad Pennington 3.00 8.00
MH12 Chris Chambers 3.00 8.00
MH13 Clinton Portis 3.00 8.00
MH14 Corey Dillon 3.00 8.00
MH15 Curtis Martin 4.00 10.00
MH16 Daunte Culpepper 4.00 10.00
MH17 David Boston 3.00 8.00
MH18 David Carr 3.00 8.00
MH19 Deuce McAllister 4.00 10.00
MH20 Donald Driver 4.00 10.00
MH21 Donte Stallworth 3.00 8.00
MH22 Drew Bledsoe 4.00 10.00
MH23 Drew Brees 5.00 12.00
MH24 Ed McCaffrey 4.00 10.00
MH25 Eddie George 4.00 10.00
MH26 Edgerrin James 4.00 10.00
MH27 Eric Moulds 3.00 8.00
MH28 Fred Taylor 3.00 8.00
MH29 Garrison Hearst 3.00 8.00
MH30 Hines Ward 4.00 10.00
MH31 Isaac Bruce 5.00 12.00
MH32 Jake Plummer 3.00 8.00
MH33 Chris Redman 3.00 8.00
MH34 Jeff Garcia 3.00 8.00
MH35 Jeremy Shockey 3.00 8.00
MH36 Jerome Bettis 6.00 15.00
MH37 Jevon Kearse 3.00 8.00
MH38 Jimmy Smith 4.00 10.00
MH39 Joey Harrington 3.00 8.00
MH40 Julius Peppers 5.00 12.00
MH41 Kurt Warner 4.00 10.00
MH42 Laveranues Coles 3.00 8.00
MH43 Mark Brunell 4.00 10.00
MH44 Marshall Faulk 4.00 10.00
MH45 Marvin Harrison 4.00 10.00
MH46 Jamal Lewis 4.00 10.00
MH47 Plaxico Burress 3.00 8.00
MH48 Ricky Williams 4.00 10.00
MH49 Santana Moss 4.00 10.00
MH50 Terrell Davis 4.00 10.00

2003 Playoff Hogg Heaven Pig Pens Autographs

Randomly inserted in packs, this set features authentic player autographs on foil stickers. Cards are serial numbered to varying quantities. Please note that Kurt Warner, Michael Vick, Roy Williams, Terrell Owens, E.J.Henderson, and Zach Thomas were issued in packs as exchange cards with an expiration date of 4/15/2005.
STATED PRINT RUN 25-250
PP1 Kurt Warner/200 15.00 40.00
PP2 Michael Vick/25 50.00 80.00
PP3 Dan Marino/50 90.00 150.00
PP4 John Riggins/100 15.00 40.00
PP5 Carson Palmer/50 40.00 100.00
PP6 Byron Leftwich/75 25.00 60.00
PP7 Kendrell Bell/25 12.00 30.00
PP8 Deuce McAllister/25 15.00 40.00
PP9 David Carr/25 12.00 30.00
PP10 Patrick Ramsey/25 15.00 40.00
PP11 Roy Williams/50 8.00 20.00
PP12 Joey Harrington/25 12.00 30.00
PP13 Anthony Thomas/50 10.00 25.00
PP14 Derrick Mason/70 8.00 20.00
PP15 Donald Driver/35 30.00 60.00
PP16 Marty Booker/30 12.00 30.00
PP17 Bethel Johnson/35 12.00 30.00
PP18 Antowain Smith/50 10.00 25.00
PP19 Garrison Hearst/75 8.00 20.00
PP20 Hines Ward/50 25.00 50.00
PP21 Jerome Bettis/50 50.00 80.00
PP22 Joe Horn/100 6.00 15.00
PP23 Deion Branch/75 8.00 20.00
PP24 Laveranues Coles/45 8.00 20.00
PP25 Marvin Harrison/50 15.00 40.00
PP26 Mike Alstott/50 8.00 20.00
PP27 Priest Holmes/25 12.00 30.00
PP28 Randy Moss/35 50.00 100.00
PP29 Rod Gardner/50 8.00 20.00
PP30 Sonny Jurgensen/141 15.00 40.00
PP31 Terrell Owens/25 20.00 50.00
PP32 Tommy Maddox/75 8.00 20.00
PP33 Zach Thomas/75 15.00 40.00
PP34 Charley Taylor/208 6.00 15.00
PP35 Jimmy Smith/75 10.00 25.00
PP36 E.J. Henderson/250 6.00 15.00
PP37 Musa Smith/250 5.00 12.00
PP38 Chris Brown/250 5.00 12.00
PP39 Dennis Weathersby/250 5.00 12.00
PP40 Kyle Boller/155 5.00 12.00
PP41 Marc Boerigter/250 5.00 12.00
PP42 Taylor Jacobs/200 5.00 12.00
PP43 Terrence Edwards/250 5.00 12.00
PP44 DeWayne White/250 5.00 12.00
PP45 Jerome McDougle/250 5.00 12.00
PP46 Kevin Curtis/250 5.00 12.00
PP47 Sam Aiken/250 6.00 15.00
PP48 Doug Gabriel/250 6.00 15.00
PP49 Chris Kelsay/250 6.00 15.00
PP50 Kevin Williams/250 8.00 20.00

2003 Playoff Hogg Heaven Rival Hoggs

PRINT RUN 500 SERIAL #'d SETS
RH1 B.Favre/R.Moss 2.50 6.00
RH2 J.Harrington/B.Urlacher 1.25 3.00
RH3 D.Bledsoe/T.Brady 5.00 12.00
RH4 R.Williams/D.McAllister 1.00 2.50
RH5 P.Burress/R.Lewis 1.25 3.00
RH6 M.Strahan/W.Sapp 1.00 2.50
RH7 E.Smith/T.Owens 2.00 5.00
RH8 L.Tomlinson/C.Portis 1.25 3.00
RH9 P.Holmes/M.Faulk 1.00 2.50
RH10 P.Manning/S.McNair 3.00 8.00
RH11 W.Green/J.Bettis 1.25 3.00
RH12 T.Henry/Z.Thomas 1.00 2.50
RH13 S.Alexander/A.Green 1.00 2.50
RH14 J.Kearse/J.Peppers 1.25 3.00
RH15 M.Vick/D.McNabb 1.00 2.50
RH16 A.Bryant/R.Gardner .75 2.00
RH17 J.Lewis/K.Bell 1.00 2.50
RH18 M.Harrison/J.Rice 2.50 6.00
RH19 J.Shockey/T.Gonzalez 1.00 2.50
RH20 K.Warner/J.Garcia 1.00 2.50
RH21 T.Brown/D.Boston 1.25 3.00
RH22 D.Brees/R.Gannon 1.25 3.00
RH23 D.Culpepper/K.Stewart 1.00 2.50
RH24 E.James/E.George 1.00 2.50
RH25 D.Carr/M.Brunell 1.00 2.50
RH26 W.Payton/E.Smith 4.00 10.00
RH27 T.Duckett/M.Alstott .75 2.00
RH28 A.Brooks/Br.Johnson .75 2.00
RH29 H.Ward/Key.Johnson 1.25 3.00
RH30 M.Bennett/A.Thomas 1.00 2.50

2003 Playoff Hogg Heaven Rival Hoggs Materials

Randomly inserted in packs, this set features two game worn swatches. Each card is serial numbered to 125.
PRINT RUN 125 SERIAL #'d SETS
RH1 B.Favre/R.Moss 12.00 30.00
RH2 J.Harrington/B.Urlacher 6.00 15.00
RH3 D.Bledsoe/T.Brady 25.00 60.00
RH4 R.Williams/D.McAllister 5.00 12.00
RH5 P.Burress/R.Lewis 6.00 15.00
RH6 M.Strahan/W.Sapp 5.00 12.00
RH7 E.Smith/T.Owens 10.00 25.00
RH8 L.Tomlinson/C.Portis 6.00 15.00
RH9 P.Holmes/M.Faulk 5.00 12.00
RH10 P.Manning/S.McNair 15.00 40.00
RH11 W.Green/J.Bettis 6.00 15.00
RH12 T.Henry/Z.Thomas 5.00 12.00
RH13 S.Alexander/A.Green 5.00 12.00
RH14 J.Kearse/J.Peppers 6.00 15.00
RH15 M.Vick/D.McNabb 5.00 12.00
RH16 A.Bryant/R.Gardner 4.00 10.00
RH17 J.Lewis/K.Bell 5.00 12.00
RH18 M.Harrison/J.Rice 12.00 30.00
RH19 J.Shockey/T.Gonzalez 5.00 12.00
RH20 K.Warner/J.Garcia 5.00 12.00
RH21 T.Brown/D.Boston 6.00 15.00
RH22 D.Brees/R.Gannon 6.00 15.00
RH23 D.Culpepper/K.Stewart 5.00 12.00
RH24 E.James/E.George 5.00 12.00
RH25 D.Carr/M.Brunell 5.00 12.00
RH26 W.Payton/E.Smith 30.00 80.00
RH27 T.Duckett/M.Alstott 4.00 10.00
RH28 A.Brooks/B.Johnson 4.00 10.00
RH29 H.Ward/K.Johnson 6.00 15.00
RH30 M.Bennett/A.Thomas 5.00 12.00

2003 Playoff Hogg Heaven Rookie Hoggs

STATED ODDS 1:19
RCH1 Carson Palmer 2.00 5.00
RCH2 Byron Leftwich 1.25 3.00
RCH3 Kyle Boller 1.00 2.50
RCH4 Chris Simms 1.00 2.50
RCH5 Rex Grossman 1.25 3.00
RCH6 Willis McGahee 1.25 3.00
RCH7 Larry Johnson 1.25 3.00
RCH8 Lee Suggs 1.00 2.50
RCH9 Musa Smith 1.00 2.50
RCH10 Chris Brown 1.00 2.50
RCH11 Charles Rogers 1.25 3.00
RCH12 Andre Johnson 2.50 6.00
RCH13 Taylor Jacobs 1.00 2.50
RCH14 Kelley Washington 1.00 2.50
RCH15 Bryant Johnson 1.50 4.00
RCH16 Brandon Lloyd 1.50 4.00
RCH17 Tyrone Calico 1.00 2.50
RCH18 Jason Witten 4.00 10.00
RCH19 Dallas Clark 1.50 4.00
RCH20 Terrell Suggs 1.25 3.00
RCH21 DeWayne Robertson 1.25 3.00
RCH22 Jimmy Kennedy 1.25 3.00
RCH23 Boss Bailey 1.25 3.00
RCH24 Terence Newman 1.50 4.00
RCH25 Marcus Trufant 1.25 3.00

2003 Playoff Hogg Heaven National Previews

Distributed by Playoff at the 2003 National Convention in Atlantic City, this set consists of 6 NFL superstars. Sets were randomly distributed to collectors visiting the Donruss/Playoff booth.
COMPLETE SET (6) 2.50 6.00
1 Brett Favre .75 2.00
2 Jeff Garcia .25 .60
3 Clinton Portis .25 .60
4 Jeremy Shockey .25 .60
5 Michael Vick .30 .75
6 Ricky Williams .30 .75

2004 Playoff Hogg Heaven

Playoff Hogg Heaven initially released in early September 2004. The base set consists of 180-cards including 50-rookies serial numbered to 750 and 30-rookie jersey cards numbered of 750. Hobby boxes contained 12-packs of 5-cards and carried an S.R.P. of $6 per pack. One parallel set and a variety of inserts can be found seeded in packs highlighted by a large number of jersey card inserts and the Rookie Hoggs and Pig Pens Autograph inserts.
COMP.SET w/o SP's (100) 12.50 30.00
101-150 RC PRINT RUN 750 SER.#'d SETS
151-180 RPH RC PRINT RUN 750 SER.#'d SETS
1 Anquan Boldin .25 .60
2 Emmitt Smith .60 1.50
3 Josh McCown .30 .75
4 Michael Vick .30 .75
5 Peerless Price .25 .60
6 T.J. Duckett .25 .60
7 Jamal Lewis .30 .75
8 Kyle Boller .25 .60
9 Ray Lewis .40 1.00
10 Terrell Owens .30 .75
11 Drew Bledsoe .30 .75
12 Eric Moulds .25 .60
13 Travis Henry .25 .60
14 Jake Delhomme .25 .60
15 Stephen Davis .25 .60
16 Steve Smith .40 1.00
17 Anthony Thomas .30 .75
18 Brian Urlacher .40 1.00
19 Rex Grossman .25 .60
20 Carson Palmer .30 .75
21 Chad Johnson .25 .60
22 Peter Warrick .25 .60
23 Rudi Johnson .25 .60
24 Andre Davis .25 .60
25 Lee Suggs .30 .75
26 Keyshawn Johnson .30 .75
27 Quincy Carter .25 .60
28 Roy Williams S .25 .60
29 Ashley Lelie .25 .60
30 Jake Plummer .25 .60
31 Rod Smith .30 .75
32 Charles Rogers .25 .60
33 Joey Harrington .25 .60
34 Ahman Green .30 .75
35 Brett Favre .75 2.00
36 Javon Walker .25 .60
37 Andre Johnson .30 .75
38 David Carr .25 .60
39 Domanick Davis .25 .60
40 Edgerrin James .30 .75
41 Marvin Harrison .30 .75
42 Peyton Manning 1.00 2.50
43 Reggie Wayne .30 .75
44 Byron Leftwich .25 .60
45 Fred Taylor .25 .60
46 Jimmy Smith .30 .75
47 Priest Holmes .25 .60
48 Tony Gonzalez .30 .75
49 Trent Green .25 .60
50 A.J. Feeley .25 .60
51 Chris Chambers .25 .60
52 Ricky Williams .30 .75
53 Zach Thomas .30 .75
54 Daunte Culpepper .30 .75
55 Michael Bennett .25 .60
56 Randy Moss .30 .75
57 Deion Branch .25 .60
58 Tom Brady 1.50 4.00
59 Ty Law .40 1.00
60 Aaron Brooks .25 .60
61 Deuce McAllister .30 .75
62 Joe Horn .25 .60
63 Jeremy Shockey .25 .60
64 Kerry Collins .25 .60
65 Michael Strahan .30 .75
66 Tiki Barber .30 .75
67 Chad Pennington .25 .60
68 Curtis Martin .30 .75
69 Santana Moss .30 .75
70 Jerry Rice .75 2.00
71 Rich Gannon .30 .75
72 Tim Brown .40 1.00
73 Brian Westbrook .25 .60
74 Donovan McNabb .30 .75
75 Jevon Kearse .25 .60
76 Hines Ward .30 .75
77 Jerome Bettis .40 1.00
78 Kendrell Bell .25 .60
79 David Boston .25 .60
80 Drew Brees .40 1.00
81 LaDainian Tomlinson .40 1.00
82 Jeff Garcia .25 .60
83 Kevan Barlow .25 .60
84 Tim Rattay .25 .60
85 Koren Robinson .25 .60
86 Matt Hasselbeck .25 .60
87 Shaun Alexander .25 .60
88 Isaac Bruce .40 1.00
89 Marc Bulger .25 .60
90 Marshall Faulk .30 .75
91 Torry Holt .30 .75
92 Brad Johnson .30 .75
93 Keenan McCardell .25 .60
94 Warren Sapp .30 .75
95 Derrick Mason .25 .60
96 Steve McNair .30 .75
97 Eddie George .30 .75
98 Clinton Portis .25 .60
99 Laveranues Coles .25 .60
100 Mark Brunell .30 .75
101 Adimchinobe Echemandu RC 1.25 3.00
102 Ahmad Carroll RC 1.00 2.50
103 Andy Hall RC 1.00 2.50
104 B.J. Symons RC 1.00 2.50
105 Bradlee Van Pelt RC 1.25 3.00
106 Brandon Miree RC 1.00 2.50
107 Bruce Perry RC 1.00 2.50
108 Carlos Francis RC 1.00 2.50
109 Casey Bramlet RC 1.00 2.50
110 Chris Gamble RC 1.00 2.50
111 Clarence Moore RC 1.00 2.50
112 Cody Pickett RC 1.00 2.50
113 Craig Krenzel RC 1.00 2.50
114 D.J. Hackett RC 1.00 2.50
115 D.J. Williams RC 1.50 4.00
116 Derrick Ward RC 1.50 4.00
117 Drew Carter RC 1.25 3.00
118 Ernest Wilford RC 1.25 3.00
119 Drew Henson RC 1.00 2.50
120 Jamaar Taylor RC 1.00 2.50
121 Jared Lorenzen RC 1.25 3.00
122 Jarrett Payton RC 1.25 3.00
123 Jason Babin RC 1.50 4.00
124 Jeff Smoker RC 1.25 3.00
125 Jeris McIntyre RC 1.00 2.50
126 Jerricho Cotchery RC 1.25 3.00
127 Jim Sorgi RC 1.25 3.00
128 John Navarre RC 1.00 2.50
129 Johnnie Morant RC 1.00 2.50
130 Sean Taylor RC 6.00 15.00
131 Jonathan Vilma RC 1.25 3.00
132 Josh Harris RC 1.00 2.50
133 Kenechi Udeze RC 1.25 3.00
134 Marcus Tubbs RC 1.00 2.50
135 Mark Jones RC 1.00 2.50
136 Matt Mauck RC 1.00 2.50
137 Maurice Mann RC 1.00 2.50
138 Michael Turner RC 1.00 2.50
139 P.K. Sam RC 1.00 2.50
140 Patrick Crayton RC 1.50 4.00
141 Quincy Wilson RC 1.00 2.50
142 Ran Carthon RC 1.00 2.50
143 Ryan Krause RC 1.00 2.50
144 Samie Parker RC 1.00 2.50
145 Sloan Thomas RC 1.25 3.00
146 Tommie Harris RC 1.25 3.00
147 Triandos Luke RC 1.00 2.50
148 Troy Fleming RC 1.00 2.50
149 Vince Wilfork RC 1.50 4.00
150 Will Smith RC 1.25 3.00
151 Larry Fitzgerald RPH RC 6.00 15.00
152 DeAngelo Hall RPH RC 2.50 6.00
153 Matt Schaub RPH RC 1.50 4.00
154 Michael Jenkins RPH RC 1.50 4.00
155 Devard Darling RPH RC 1.50 4.00
156 J.P. Losman RPH RC 1.50 4.00
157 Lee Evans RPH RC 2.50 6.00
158 Keary Colbert RPH RC 1.50 4.00
159 Bernard Berrian RPH RC 1.50 4.00
160 Chris Perry RPH RC 1.50 4.00
161 Kellen Winslow RPH RC 1.50 4.00
162 Luke McCown RPH RC 1.50 4.00
163 Julius Jones RPH RC 1.50 4.00
164 Darius Watts RPH RC 1.50 4.00
165 Tatum Bell RPH RC 1.50 4.00
166 Kevin Jones RPH RC 2.00 5.00
167 Roy Williams RPH RC 1.50 4.00
168 Greg Jones RPH RC 1.50 4.00
169 Reggie Williams RPH RC 1.50 4.00
170 Ben Watson RPH RC 2.00 5.00
171 Cedric Cobbs RPH RC 1.50 4.00
172 D.Henderson RPH RC 1.50 4.00
173 Eli Manning RPH RC 12.00 30.00
174 Roethlisberger RPH RC 12.00 30.00
175 Philip Rivers RPH RC 5.00 12.00
176 Derrick Hamilton RPH RC 1.50 4.00
177 Rashaun Woods RPH RC 1.50 4.00
178 Steven Jackson RPH RC 2.50 6.00
179 Michael Clayton RPH RC 2.00 5.00
180 Ben Troupe RPH RC 1.50 4.00

2004 Playoff Hogg Heaven Hogg Wild

*1-100 VETS/250: 3X TO 8X BASIC CARDS
*101-150 ROOKIES/125: .8X TO 2X BASIC RC
*151-180 ROOKIES/25: 1.2X TO 3X BASIC RC

2004 Playoff Hogg Heaven Accent

ACCENT PRINT RUN 25 SETS
A1 Andre Johnson 5.00 12.00
A2 Brian Urlacher 6.00 15.00
A3 Byron Leftwich 4.00 10.00
A4 Carson Palmer 5.00 12.00
A5 Clinton Portis 4.00 10.00
A6 Daunte Culpepper 5.00 12.00
A7 David Carr 4.00 10.00
A8 Deuce McAllister 5.00 12.00
A9 Edgerrin James 5.00 12.00
A10 Emmitt Smith 10.00 25.00
A11 Jake Delhomme 4.00 10.00
A12 Jeremy Shockey 4.00 10.00
A13 Jerry Rice 12.00 30.00
A14 Joey Harrington 4.00 10.00
A15 LaDainian Tomlinson 6.00 15.00
A16 Marvin Harrison 5.00 12.00
A17 Matt Hasselbeck 4.00 10.00
A18 Michael Vick 5.00 12.00
A19 Peyton Manning 15.00 40.00
A20 Priest Holmes 4.00 10.00
A21 Randy Moss 5.00 12.00
A22 Roy Williams S 4.00 10.00
A23 Santana Moss 5.00 12.00
A24 Stephen Davis 4.00 10.00
A25 Tom Brady 25.00 60.00

2004 Playoff Hogg Heaven Branded

COMPLETE SET (25) 20.00 50.00
STATED PRINT RUN 1250 SER.#'d SETS
B1 Ahman Green 1.00 2.50
B2 Andre Johnson 1.00 2.50
B3 Anquan Boldin .75 2.00
B4 Brian Urlacher 1.25 3.00
B5 Byron Leftwich .75 2.00
B6 Carson Palmer 1.00 2.50
B7 Clinton Portis .75 2.00
B8 Daunte Culpepper 1.00 2.50
B9 David Carr .75 2.00
B10 Deuce McAllister 1.00 2.50
B11 Edgerrin James 1.00 2.50
B12 Jake Delhomme .75 2.00
B13 Jeremy Shockey .75 2.00
B14 Joey Harrington .75 2.00
B15 LaDainian Tomlinson 1.25 3.00
B16 Marvin Harrison 1.00 2.50
B17 Matt Hasselbeck .75 2.00
B18 Priest Holmes .75 2.00
B19 Randy Moss 1.00 2.50
B20 Roy Williams S .75 2.00
B21 Santana Moss 1.00 2.50
B22 Shaun Alexander .75 2.00
B23 Stephen Davis .75 2.00
B24 Tom Brady 5.00 12.00
B25 Torry Holt 1.00 2.50

2004 Playoff Hogg Heaven Hogg of Fame

COMPLETE SET (25) 20.00 50.00
STATED ODDS 1:12
HF1 Brett Favre 2.00 5.00
HF2 Chad Pennington .60 1.50
HF3 Clinton Portis .60 1.50
HF4 David Carr .60 1.50
HF5 Deion Sanders .75 2.00
HF6 Donovan McNabb .75 2.00
HF7 Drew Bledsoe .75 2.00
HF8 Emmitt Smith 1.50 4.00
HF9 Jamal Lewis .75 2.00
HF10 Jerry Rice 2.00 5.00
HF11 Jim Kelly 1.00 2.50
HF12 Joe Montana 3.00 8.00
HF13 Joey Harrington .60 1.50
HF14 Marshall Faulk .75 2.00
HF15 Marvin Harrison .75 2.00
HF16 Michael Irvin 1.00 2.50
HF17 Michael Vick .75 2.00
HF18 Mike Singletary 1.00 2.50
HF19 Peyton Manning 2.50 6.00
HF20 Ricky Williams .75 2.00
HF21 Steve McNair .75 2.00
HF22 Terrell Davis .75 2.00
HF23 Terrell Owens .75 2.00
HF24 Tom Brady 4.00 10.00
HF25 Warren Moon 1.00 2.50

2004 Playoff Hogg Heaven Hogg of Fame Jerseys Bronze

BRONZE PRINT RUN 150 SER.#'d SETS
*GOLD/25: 1X TO 2.5X BRONZE
GOLD PRINT RUN 25 SER.#'d SETS
UNPRICED PLATINUM PRINT RUN 1 SET
*SILVER/75: .5X TO 1.2X BRONZE
SILVER PRINT RUN 75 SER.#'d SETS
HF1 Brett Favre 6.00 15.00
HF2 Chad Pennington 2.00 5.00
HF3 Clinton Portis 2.00 5.00
HF4 David Carr 2.00 5.00
HF5 Deion Sanders 2.50 6.00
HF6 Donovan McNabb 2.50 6.00
HF7 Drew Bledsoe 2.50 6.00
HF8 Emmitt Smith 5.00 12.00
HF9 Jamal Lewis 2.50 6.00
HF10 Jerry Rice 6.00 15.00
HF11 Jim Kelly 3.00 8.00
HF12 Joe Montana 10.00 25.00
HF13 Joey Harrington 2.00 5.00
HF14 Marshall Faulk 2.50 6.00
HF15 Marvin Harrison 2.50 6.00
HF16 Michael Irvin 3.00 8.00
HF17 Michael Vick 2.50 6.00
HF18 Mike Singletary 3.00 8.00
HF19 Peyton Manning 8.00 20.00
HF20 Ricky Williams 2.50 6.00
HF21 Steve McNair 2.50 6.00
HF22 Terrell Davis 2.50 6.00
HF23 Terrell Owens 2.50 6.00
HF24 Tom Brady 12.00 30.00
HF25 Warren Moon 3.00 8.00

2004 Playoff Hogg Heaven Leather in Leather

LEATHER PRINT RUN 250 SER.#'d SETS
*LACE VETS/25: 1.2X TO 3X LEATHER
*LACE ROOKIE/25: 1X TO 2.5X LEATHER
LACES PRINT RUN 25 SER.#'d SETS
LL1 Ahman Green 2.50 6.00
LL2 Anquan Boldin 2.00 5.00
LL3 Chad Johnson 2.00 5.00
LL4 Donovan McNabb 2.50 6.00
LL5 Emmitt Smith 5.00 12.00
LL6 Jamal Lewis 2.50 6.00
LL7 Jeff Garcia 2.00 5.00
LL8 Kevan Barlow 2.00 5.00
LL9 Koren Robinson 2.00 5.00
LL10 Marc Bulger 2.00 5.00
LL11 Matt Hasselbeck 2.00 5.00
LL12 Randy Moss 2.50 6.00
LL13 Ray Lewis 3.00 8.00
LL14 Ricky Williams 2.50 6.00
LL15 Rudi Johnson 2.00 5.00
LL16 Shaun Alexander 2.00 5.00
LL17 Steve McNair 2.50 6.00
LL18 Steve Smith 3.00 8.00
LL19 Terrell Owens 2.50 6.00
LL20 Terrell Suggs 2.00 5.00
LL21 Eli Manning 15.00 40.00
LL22 Philip Rivers 6.00 15.00
LL23 Ben Roethlisberger 15.00 40.00
LL24 J.P. Losman 2.00 5.00
LL25 Larry Fitzgerald 8.00 20.00
LL26 Roy Williams WR 2.00 5.00
LL27 Reggie Williams 2.00 5.00
LL28 Lee Evans 3.00 8.00
LL29 Steven Jackson 3.00 8.00
LL30 Chris Perry 2.00 5.00
LL31 Kevin Jones 2.50 6.00
LL32 Tatum Bell 2.00 5.00
LL33 Michael Clayton 2.50 6.00
LL34 Kellen Winslow Jr. 2.00 5.00
LL35 Michael Jenkins 2.00 5.00
LL36 Julius Jones 2.00 5.00
LL37 Matt Schaub 2.00 5.00
LL38 Luke McCown 2.00 5.00
LL39 Rashaun Woods 2.00 5.00
LL40 Greg Jones 2.00 5.00

2004 Playoff Hogg Heaven Leather Quads

STATED PRINT RUN 1250 SER.#'d SETS
LQ1 McCown/Boldin/Johnson/Shipp 1.00 2.50
LQ2 Vick/Price/Duckett/Dunn 1.00 2.50
LQ3 Boller/Lewis/Lewis/Heap 1.25 3.00
LQ4 Bledsoe/Henry/Moulds/Reed 1.00 2.50
LQ5 Gross/Thom/Urlac/Terrell 1.25 3.00
LQ6 Couch/Green/Holcomb/Northcutt 1.00 2.50
LQ7 Favre/Green/Driver/Walker 2.50 6.00
LQ8 Mann/James/Harris/Wayne 3.00 8.00
LQ9 Green/Holmes/Hall/Gonz 1.00 2.50
LQ10 Fdler/Will/Chmbrs/Thmas 1.00 2.50
LQ11 Brks/McAll/Stllwrth/Horn 1.00 2.50
LQ12 Collin/Barb/Toom/Shock 1.00 2.50
LQ13 Pennin/Martin/Abra/Ellis 1.00 2.50
LQ14 Gan/Rice/Brown/Wdson 2.50 6.00
LQ15 McNabb/Buck/Mitchell/Pink 1.00 2.50
LQ16 Bettis/Ward/Bell/Burress 1.25 3.00
LQ17 Flutie/Tomlin/Brees/Bstn 1.25 3.00
LQ18 Warner/Faulk/Bruce/Holt 1.25 3.00
LQ19 Johnson/Alstott/Johnson/Sapp 1.00 2.50
LQ20 McNair/Grge/Krse/Mason 1.00 2.50
LQ21 Rams/Coles/Gard/Arring 1.00 2.50
LQ22 E.Man/River/Roeth/Losman 4.00 10.00
LQ23 Fitzg/Ro.Will/Re.Will/Evans 2.00 5.00
LQ24 Jackson/Perry/Jones/Bell .75 2.00
LQ25 Clayt/Winsl/Jenkin/J.Jones 1.00 2.50

2004 Playoff Hogg Heaven Leather Quads Jerseys Single

SINGLE PRINT RUN 150 SER.#'d SETS
*DOUBLE/100: .5X TO 1.2X SINGLE
DOUBLE PRINT RUN 100 SER.#'d SETS
*TRIPLE/50: .8X TO 2X SINGLE
TRIPLE PRINT RUN 50 SER.#'d SETS
*QUADS/25: 1X TO 2.5X SINGLE
QUAD PRINT RUN 25 SER.#'d SETS
LQ1 McCown/Boldin/Johnson/Shipp 3.00 8.00
LQ2 Vick/Price/Duckett/Dunn 3.00 8.00
LQ3 Boller/Lewis/Lewis/Heap 4.00 10.00
LQ4 Bledsoe/Henry/Moulds/Reed 3.00 8.00
LQ5 Grssmn/Thmas/Urlac/Trrell 4.00 10.00
LQ6 Couch/Green/Holcomb/Northcutt 3.00 8.00
LQ7 Favre/Green/Driver/Walker 8.00 20.00
LQ8 Mann/James/Harris/Wayne 10.00 25.00
LQ9 Green/Holmes/Hall/Gonzalez 3.00 8.00
LQ10 Fiedler/Williams/Chambers/Thomas 3.00 8.00
LQ11 Brooks/McAllister/Stallworth/Horn 3.00 8.00
LQ12 Cllns/Brbr/Tmer/Shcky 3.00 8.00
LQ13 Pennin/Martin/Abra/Ellis 3.00 8.00
LQ14 Gann/Rce/Brwn/Wdsn 6.00 15.00
LQ15 McNbb/Buck/Mtchl/Pink 3.00 8.00
LQ16 Bettis/Ward/Bell/Burress 4.00 10.00
LQ17 Flutie/Tomlin/Brees/Bstn 4.00 10.00
LQ18 Warner/Faulk/Bruce/Holt 4.00 10.00
LQ19 John/Alstott/John/Spp 3.00 8.00
LQ20 McNair/Grge/Krse/Mason 3.00 8.00
LQ21 Ramsey/Coles/Gardner/Arrington 3.00 8.00
LQ22 E.Mnn/River/Roeth/Lsmn 12.00 30.00
LQ23 Fitz/Ro.Wll/Re.Wll/Evns 6.00 15.00
LQ24 Jacksn/Prry/K.Jnes/Bell 2.50 6.00
LQ25 Clayt/Wnsl/Jnkns/J.Jnes 4.00 10.00

2004 Playoff Hogg Heaven Material Hoggs Bronze

BRONZE PRINT RUN 150 SER.#'d SETS
*GOLD/25: 1X TO 2.5X BRONZE/150
GOLD PRINT RUN 25 SER.#'d SETS
UNPRICED PLATINUM PRINT RUN 1
*SILVER/75: .5X TO 1.2X BRONZE/150
SILVER PRINT RUN 75 SER.#'d SETS
MH1 Aaron Brooks 2.50 6.00
MH2 Anquan Boldin 2.50 6.00
MH3 Brett Favre 8.00 20.00
MH4 Brian Urlacher 4.00 10.00
MH5 Bruce Smith 3.00 8.00
MH6 Byron Leftwich 2.50 6.00
MH7 Chad Johnson 2.50 6.00
MH8 Chad Pennington 2.50 6.00
MH9 Charles Rogers 2.50 6.00
MH10 Clinton Portis 2.50 6.00
MH11 Curtis Martin 3.00 8.00
MH12 Daunte Culpepper 3.00 8.00
MH13 David Carr 2.50 6.00
MH14 Deuce McAllister 3.00 8.00
MH15 Donovan McNabb 3.00 8.00
MH16 Eddie George 3.00 8.00
MH17 Edgerrin James 3.00 8.00
MH18 Emmitt Smith 6.00 15.00
MH19 Fred Taylor 2.50 6.00
MH20 Jamal Lewis 3.00 8.00
MH21 Jeff Garcia 2.50 6.00
MH22 Jeremy Shockey 2.50 6.00
MH23 Jerome Bettis 4.00 10.00
MH24 Jerry Rice 8.00 20.00
MH25 Jevon Kearse 2.50 6.00
MH26 Joey Harrington 2.50 6.00
MH27 Josh McCown 3.00 8.00
MH28 Kendrell Bell 2.50 6.00
MH29 Keyshawn Johnson 3.00 8.00
MH30 Kurt Warner 3.00 8.00
MH31 LaDainian Tomlinson 4.00 10.00
MH32 Mark Brunell 3.00 8.00
MH33 Marshall Faulk 3.00 8.00
MH34 Marvin Harrison 3.00 8.00
MH35 Michael Bennett 2.50 6.00
MH36 Michael Vick 3.00 8.00
MH37 Patrick Ramsey 3.00 8.00
MH38 Peyton Manning 10.00 25.00
MH39 Priest Holmes 2.50 6.00
MH40 Randy Moss 3.00 8.00
MH41 Ricky Williams 3.00 8.00
MH42 Roy Williams S 2.50 6.00
MH43 Santana Moss 3.00 8.00
MH44 Shaun Alexander 2.50 6.00
MH45 Steve McNair 3.00 8.00
MH46 Terrell Owens 3.00 8.00

MH47 Terrell Davis 3.00 8.00
MH48 Tiki Barber 3.00 8.00
MH49 Tim Brown 4.00 10.00
MH50 Torry Holt 3.00 8.00

2004 Playoff Hogg Heaven Pig Pals

STATED PRINT RUN 1050 SER.#'d SETS
PP1 A.Boldin/E.Smith 2.50 6.00
PP2 M.Vick/P.Price 1.25 3.00
PP3 J.Lewis/R.Lewis 1.50 4.00
PP4 D.Bledsoe/E.Moulds 1.25 3.00
PP5 S.Davis/J.Peppers 1.25 3.00
PP6 B.Urlacher/R.Grossman 1.50 4.00
PP7 C.Johnson/P.Warrick 1.00 2.50
PP8 R.Williams S/T.Newman 1.25 3.00
PP9 J.Plummer/C.Portis 1.00 2.50
PP10 J.Harrington/C.Rogers 1.00 2.50
PP11 B.Favre/A.Green 3.00 8.00
PP12 D.Carr/A.Johnson 1.25 3.00
PP13 P.Manning/E.James 4.00 10.00
PP14 B.Leftwich/J.Smith 1.25 3.00
PP15 P.Holmes/T.Gonzalez 1.25 3.00
PP16 R.Williams/Z.Thomas 1.25 3.00
PP17 R.Moss/M.Bennett 1.25 3.00
PP18 T.Brady/T.Law 6.00 15.00
PP19 A.Brooks/D.McAllister 1.25 3.00
PP20 K.Collins/M.Strahan 1.25 3.00
PP21 C.Pennington/C.Martin 1.25 3.00
PP22 J.Rice/T.Brown 3.00 8.00
PP23 D.McNabb/C.Buckhalter 1.25 3.00
PP24 J.Bettis/H.Ward 1.50 4.00
PP25 D.Brees/L.Tomlinson 1.50 4.00
PP26 M.Hasselbeck/K.Robinson 1.00 2.50
PP27 M.Bulger/I.Bruce 1.50 4.00
PP28 B.Johnson/W.Sapp 1.25 3.00
PP29 S.McNair/E.George 1.25 3.00
PP30 P.Ramsey/L.Coles 1.25 3.00

2004 Playoff Hogg Heaven Pig Pals Jerseys

STATED PRINT RUN 100 SER.#'d SETS
UNPRICED PRIME PRINT RUN 1 SET
PP1 A.Boldin/E.Smith 10.00 25.00
PP2 M.Vick/P.Price 8.00 20.00
PP3 J.Lewis/R.Lewis 6.00 15.00
PP4 D.Bledsoe/E.Moulds 5.00 12.00
PP5 S.Davis/J.Peppers 5.00 12.00
PP6 B.Urlacher/R.Grossman 6.00 15.00
PP7 C.Johnson/P.Warrick 4.00 10.00
PP8 R.Williams S/T.Newman 5.00 12.00
PP9 J.Plummer/C.Portis 4.00 10.00
PP10 J.Harrington/C.Rogers 4.00 10.00
PP11 B.Favre/A.Green 12.00 30.00
PP12 D.Carr/A.Johnson 5.00 12.00
PP13 P.Manning/E.James 15.00 40.00
PP14 B.Leftwich/J.Smith 5.00 12.00
PP15 P.Holmes/T.Gonzalez 5.00 12.00
PP16 R.Williams/Z.Thomas 5.00 12.00
PP17 R.Moss/M.Bennett 5.00 12.00
PP18 T.Brady/T.Law 25.00 60.00
PP19 A.Brooks/D.McAllister 5.00 12.00
PP20 K.Collins/M.Strahan 5.00 12.00
PP21 C.Pennington/C.Martin 5.00 12.00
PP22 J.Rice/T.Brown 12.00 30.00
PP23 D.McNabb/C.Buckhalter 5.00 12.00
PP24 J.Bettis/H.Ward 6.00 15.00
PP25 D.Brees/L.Tomlinson 6.00 15.00
PP26 M.Hasselbeck/K.Robinson 4.00 10.00
PP27 M.Bulger/I.Bruce 6.00 15.00
PP28 B.Johnson/W.Sapp 5.00 12.00
PP29 S.McNair/E.George 5.00 12.00
PP30 P.Ramsey/L.Coles 5.00 12.00

2004 Playoff Hogg Heaven Pig Pens Autographs

STATED PRINT RUN 50-250
PP51 ISSUED AS EXCH REPLACEMENT
PP1 Aaron Brooks/50 8.00 20.00
PP2 Ahman Green/50 10.00 25.00
PP3 Anquan Boldin/100 6.00 15.00
PP4 Dante Hall/50 8.00 20.00
PP5 Deuce McAllister/50 10.00 25.00
PP6 Domanick Davis/250 6.00 15.00
PP7 George Blanda/100 25.00 50.00
PP8 Ickey Woods/150 10.00 25.00
PP9 James Lofton/170 10.00 25.00
PP10 Jim Brown/50 50.00 100.00
PP11 Jim Plunkett/50 12.00 30.00
PP12 Joe Greene/50 25.00 50.00
PP13 Joe Namath/100 40.00 80.00
PP14 John Riggins/100 20.00 50.00
PP16 Kyle Boller/150 6.00 15.00
PP17 Matt Hasselbeck/75 8.00 20.00
PP18 Mel Blount/53 12.00 30.00
PP19 Ozzie Newsome/187 12.00 30.00
PP20 Patrick Ramsey/50 10.00 25.00
PP21 Priest Holmes/50 8.00 20.00
PP23 Roy Williams S/50 8.00 20.00
PP24 Rudi Johnson/100 6.00 15.00
PP25 Sammy Baugh/150 No Auto 10.00 25.00
PP26 Shaun Alexander/50 8.00 20.00
PP27 Steve Smith/150 10.00 25.00
PP28 Terence Newman/150 8.00 20.00
PP29 Todd Heap/89 8.00 20.00
PP30 Warren Moon/75 15.00 40.00
PP31 Ahmad Carroll/141 6.00 15.00
PP32 Bernard Berrian/125 15.00 40.00
PP33 Cedric Cobbs/150 6.00 15.00
PP34 D.J. Hackett/150 6.00 15.00
PP35 D.J. Williams/150 10.00 25.00
PP36 Devard Darling/150 6.00 15.00
PP37 Dunta Robinson/150 6.00 15.00
PP38 Ernest Wilford/75 10.00 25.00
PP39 Jerricho Cotchery/150 8.00 20.00
PP40 Johnnie Morant/100 6.00 15.00
PP41 Jonathan Vilma/150 8.00 20.00
PP42 Josh Harris/150 6.00 15.00
PP43 Julius Jones/100 6.00 15.00
PP44 Luke McCown/150 6.00 15.00
PP45 Mewelde Moore/150 8.00 20.00
PP46 Michael Jenkins/125 6.00 15.00
PP47 Philip Rivers/150 15.00 40.00
PP48 Ricardo Colclough/150 6.00 15.00
PP49 Tatum Bell/61 8.00 20.00
PP51 T.J. Houshmandzadeh/150 8.00 20.00

2004 Playoff Hogg Heaven Rookie Hoggs

STATED PRINT RUN 750 SER.#'d SETS
RH1 Eli Manning 6.00 15.00
RH2 Robert Gallery 1.00 2.50
RH3 Larry Fitzgerald 3.00 8.00
RH4 Philip Rivers 2.50 6.00
RH5 Sean Taylor 5.00 12.00
RH6 Kellen Winslow Jr. .75 2.00
RH7 Roy Williams WR .75 2.00
RH8 DeAngelo Hall 1.25 3.00
RH9 Reggie Williams .75 2.00
RH10 Dunta Robinson .75 2.00
RH11 Ben Roethlisberger 6.00 15.00
RH12 Jonathan Vilma 1.00 2.50
RH13 Lee Evans 1.25 3.00
RH14 Tommie Harris 1.00 2.50
RH15 Michael Clayton 1.00 2.50
RH16 D.J. Williams 1.25 3.00
RH17 Will Smith 1.00 2.50
RH18 Kenechi Udeze 1.00 2.50
RH19 Vince Wilfork 1.25 3.00
RH20 J.P. Losman .75 2.00
RH21 Marcus Tubbs .75 2.00
RH22 Steven Jackson 1.25 3.00
RH23 Ahmad Carroll .75 2.00
RH24 Chris Perry .75 2.00
RH25 Jason Babin 1.25 3.00
RH26 Chris Gamble .75 2.00
RH27 Michael Jenkins .75 2.00
RH28 Kevin Jones 1.00 2.50
RH29 Rashaun Woods .75 2.00
RH30 Ben Watson 1.00 2.50
RH31 Ben Troupe .75 2.00
RH32 Tatum Bell .75 2.00
RH33 Julius Jones .75 2.00
RH34 Ernest Wilford 1.00 2.50
RH35 Devery Henderson .75 2.00
RH36 Darius Watts .75 2.00
RH37 Greg Jones .75 2.00
RH38 Sean Jones .75 2.00
RH39 Keary Colbert .75 2.00
RH40 Derrick Hamilton .75 2.00
RH41 Bernard Berrian .75 2.00
RH42 Devard Darling .75 2.00
RH43 Matt Schaub .75 2.00
RH44 Carlos Francis .75 2.00
RH45 Samie Parker .75 2.00
RH46 Luke McCown .75 2.00
RH47 Jerricho Cotchery 1.00 2.50
RH48 Mewelde Moore 1.00 2.50
RH49 Cedric Cobbs .75 2.00
RH50 Drew Henson .75 2.00

2004 Playoff Hogg Heaven Rookie Hoggs Autographs

STATED PRINT RUN 150 SER.#'d SETS
RH2 Robert Gallery 6.00 15.00
RH4 Philip Rivers 15.00 40.00
RH7 Roy Williams WR 5.00 12.00
RH8 DeAngelo Hall 8.00 20.00
RH10 Dunta Robinson 5.00 12.00
RH13 Lee Evans 8.00 20.00
RH15 Michael Clayton 6.00 15.00
RH20 J.P. Losman 5.00 12.00
RH24 Chris Perry 5.00 12.00
RH27 Michael Jenkins 5.00 12.00
RH30 Ben Watson 6.00 15.00
RH31 Ben Troupe 5.00 12.00
RH32 Tatum Bell 5.00 12.00
RH33 Julius Jones 5.00 12.00
RH35 Devery Henderson 5.00 12.00
RH36 Darius Watts 5.00 12.00
RH37 Greg Jones 5.00 12.00
RH39 Keary Colbert 5.00 12.00
RH40 Derrick Hamilton 5.00 12.00
RH41 Bernard Berrian 5.00 12.00
RH42 Devard Darling 5.00 12.00
RH46 Luke McCown 5.00 12.00
RH48 Mewelde Moore 6.00 15.00
RH49 Cedric Cobbs 5.00 12.00

2004 Playoff Hogg Heaven Unsung Hoggs

COMPLETE SET (25) 20.00 50.00
STATED PRINT RUN 1250 SER.#'d SETS
UH1 Keith Brooking 1.25 3.00
UH2 Ed Reed 1.50 4.00
UH3 Takeo Spikes 1.25 3.00
UH4 Kris Jenkins 1.50 4.00
UH5 Marty Booker 1.25 3.00
UH6 Quincy Morgan 1.25 3.00
UH7 Dat Nguyen 1.25 3.00
UH8 Al Wilson 1.25 3.00
UH9 Kabeer Gbaja-Biamila 1.25 3.00
UH10 Dwight Freeney 1.25 3.00
UH11 Marcus Stroud 1.25 3.00
UH12 Tony Richardson 1.25 3.00
UH13 Patrick Surtain 1.25 3.00
UH14 Jim Kleinsasser 1.25 3.00
UH15 Tedy Bruschi 1.50 4.00
UH16 Michael Lewis 1.50 4.00
UH17 Tyrone Wheatley 1.50 4.00
UH18 Brian Dawkins 1.25 3.00
UH19 Joey Porter 1.50 4.00
UH20 Julian Peterson 1.50 4.00
UH21 Darrell Jackson 1.50 4.00
UH22 Keenan McCardell 1.25 3.00
UH23 Joe Jurevicius 1.25 3.00
UH24 Keith Bulluck 1.25 3.00
UH25 Darnerien McCants 1.25 3.00

2001 Playoff Honors

Released as a 232-card set, this product was issued 16 packs per box with 6 cards per pack. This set includes 100 veterans and 132 rookies. The first 100 rookies (101-200) are serial numbered to 250, and the remaining rookies are numbered to 725. Cards numbered 201 through 235 contained swatches of game used memorabilia. Cards number 209, 211 and 221 were not produced.

COMP.SET w/o RC's (100) 10.00 25.00
201-235 ROOKIE JSY PRINT RUN 725
1 Rob Johnson .30 .75
2 Eric Moulds .25 .60
3 Marvin Harrison .30 .75
4 Edgerrin James .30 .75
5 Peyton Manning 1.00 2.50
6 Jay Fiedler .30 .75
7 Lamar Smith .30 .75
8 Zach Thomas .30 .75
9 Dan Marino .75 2.00
10 Drew Bledsoe .30 .75
11 Terry Glenn .30 .75
12 Wayne Chrebet .25 .60
13 Curtis Martin .30 .75
14 Chad Pennington .25 .60
15 Vinny Testaverde .25 .60
16 Corey Dillon .25 .60
17 Jon Kitna .25 .60
18 Akili Smith .25 .60
19 Peter Warrick .25 .60
20 Kevin Johnson .25 .60
21 Tim Couch .25 .60
22 Eddie George .40 1.00
23 Steve McNair .30 .75
24 Jevon Kearse .25 .60
25 Jerome Bettis .40 1.00
26 Kordell Stewart .25 .60
27 Plaxico Burress .25 .60
28 Mark Brunell .30 .75
29 Keenan McCardell .30 .75
30 Jimmy Smith .30 .75
31 Fred Taylor .25 .60
32 Elvis Grbac .30 .75
33 Jamal Lewis .40 1.00
34 Ray Lewis .40 1.00
35 Mike Anderson .25 .60
36 Terrell Davis .30 .75
37 John Elway .60 1.50
38 Brian Griese .25 .60
39 Ed McCaffrey .30 .75
40 Tony Gonzalez .30 .75
41 Trent Green .25 .60
42 Sylvester Morris .25 .60
43 Tim Brown .40 1.00
44 Rich Gannon .30 .75
45 Charlie Garner .30 .75
46 Tyrone Wheatley .30 .75
47 Charles Woodson .40 1.00
48 Tim Dwight .30 .75
49 Doug Flutie .30 .75
50 Junior Seau .30 .75
51 Shaun Alexander .25 .60
52 Matt Hasselbeck .25 .60
53 Ricky Watters .30 .75
54 Tony Banks .25 .60
55 Joey Galloway .30 .75
56 Emmitt Smith .60 1.50
57 Troy Aikman .50 1.25
58 Kerry Collins .25 .60
59 Ron Dayne .30 .75
60 Donovan McNabb .30 .75
61 Duce Staley .25 .60
62 David Boston .25 .60
63 Thomas Jones .25 .60
64 Jake Plummer .25 .60
65 Stephen Davis .25 .60
66 Jeff George .30 .75
67 Michael Westbrook .25 .60
68 Deion Sanders .30 .75
69 James Allen .25 .60
70 Cade McNown .30 .75
71 Marcus Robinson .30 .75
72 Brian Urlacher .50 1.25
73 Germane Crowell .25 .60
74 Charlie Batch .25 .60
75 James Stewart .25 .60
76 Brett Favre .75 2.00
77 Antonio Freeman .40 1.00
78 Ahman Green .30 .75
79 Cris Carter .40 1.00
80 Daunte Culpepper .30 .75
81 Randy Moss .30 .75
82 Mike Alstott .25 .60
83 Warrick Dunn .25 .60
84 Brad Johnson .30 .75
85 Keyshawn Johnson .30 .75
86 Warren Sapp .30 .75
87 Jamal Anderson .30 .75
88 Chris Chandler .30 .75
89 Isaac Bruce .40 1.00
90 Marshall Faulk .30 .75
91 Torry Holt .30 .75
92 Kurt Warner .60 1.50
93 Aaron Brooks .25 .60
94 Albert Connell .25 .60
95 Ricky Williams .30 .75
96 Jeff Garcia .25 .60
97 Terrell Owens .30 .75
98 Steve Young .50 1.25
99 Jerry Rice .75 2.00
100 Jeff Lewis .25 .60
101 Rashard Casey RC 2.00 5.00
102 A.J. Feeley RC 2.50 6.00
103 Josh Booty RC 2.50 6.00
104 LaMont Jordan RC 3.00 8.00
105 Ben Leard RC 2.00 5.00
106 David Rivers RC 2.00 5.00
107 Tim Hasselbeck RC 2.50 6.00
108 Jason McKinley RC 2.00 5.00
109 Correll Buckhalter RC 2.00 5.00
110 Dan Alexander RC 2.50 6.00
111 Derrick Blaylock RC 2.50 6.00
112 Chris Barnes RC 2.00 5.00
113 Dee Brown RC 2.00 5.00
114 Derek Combs RC 2.00 5.00
115 David Allen RC 2.00 5.00
116 DeAngelo Evans RC 2.50 6.00
117 Reggie White RC 2.00 5.00
118 Heath Evans RC 2.50 6.00
119 George Layne RC 2.00 5.00
120 Moran Norris RC 2.00 5.00
121 Bhawoh Jue RC 2.50 6.00
122 Dustin McClintock RC 2.50 6.00
123 Ja'Mar Toombs RC 2.00 5.00
124 Steve Smith RC 6.00 15.00
125 Milton Wynn RC 2.00 5.00
126 Justin McCareins RC 2.50 6.00
127 Jarrod Cooper RC 2.50 6.00
128 Vinny Sutherland RC 2.00 5.00
129 Alex Bannister RC 2.00 5.00
130 Scotty Anderson RC 2.00 5.00
131 Onome Ojo RC 2.00 5.00
132 Darnerien McCants RC 2.50 6.00
133 Eddie Berlin RC 2.00 5.00
134 Jonathan Carter RC 2.00 5.00
135 Bobby Newcombe RC 2.50 6.00
136 Cedrick Wilson RC 2.50 6.00
137 Kevin Kasper RC 2.00 5.00
138 Francis St. Paul RC 2.00 5.00
139 David Martin RC 2.00 5.00
140 T.J. Houshmandzadeh RC 2.50 6.00
141 John Capel RC 2.00 5.00
142 Reggie Germany RC 2.00 5.00
143 Chris Taylor RC 2.00 5.00
144 Ken-Yon Rambo RC 2.00 5.00
145 Richmond Flowers RC 2.00 5.00
146 Quentin McCord RC 2.50 6.00
147 Andre King RC 2.00 5.00
148 Boo Williams RC 2.00 5.00
149 Daniel Guy RC 2.00 5.00
150 Javon Green RC 2.00 5.00
151 Ronney Daniels RC 2.00 5.00
152 Alge Crumpler RC 3.00 8.00
153 Tony Driver RC 2.50 6.00
154 Shad Meier RC 2.00 5.00
155 Jabari Holloway RC 2.00 5.00
156 Ryan Pickett RC 2.00 5.00
157 Cedric James RC 2.00 5.00
158 Tony Stewart RC 2.50 6.00
159 Sean Brewer RC 2.00 5.00
160 Orlando Huff RC 2.00 5.00
161 Nate Clements RC 2.50 6.00
162 Will Allen RC 3.00 8.00
163 Willie Middlebrooks RC 2.50 6.00
164 Jamar Fletcher RC 2.00 5.00
165 Ken Lucas RC 2.50 6.00
166 Fred Smoot RC 2.50 6.00
167 Michael Stone RC 2.00 5.00
168 Tony Dixon RC 2.00 5.00
169 Andre Dyson RC 2.00 5.00
170 Gary Baxter RC 2.00 5.00
171 Adam Archuleta RC 2.50 6.00
172 Derrick Gibson RC 2.00 5.00
173 Edgerton Hartwell RC 2.00 5.00
174 Jamal Reynolds RC 2.00 5.00
175 Richard Seymour RC 3.00 8.00
176 B.Manumaleuna RC 2.50 6.00
177 Idrees Bashir RC 2.00 5.00
178 DeLawrence Grant RC 2.00 5.00
179 Karon Riley RC 2.00 5.00
180 Cedric Scott RC 2.00 5.00
181 Damione Lewis RC 2.50 6.00
182 Marcus Stroud RC 2.50 6.00
183 Casey Hampton RC 3.00 8.00
184 Willie Howard RC 2.00 5.00
185 Shaun Rogers RC 3.00 8.00
186 Kenny Smith RC 2.00 5.00
187 Marcus Bell DT RC 2.00 5.00
188 Mario Fatafehi RC 2.00 5.00
189 Kendrell Bell RC 3.00 8.00
190 Tommy Polley RC 2.00 5.00
191 Jamie Winborn RC 2.50 6.00
192 Sedrick Hodge RC 2.00 5.00
193 Torrance Marshall RC 2.00 5.00
194 Eric Westmoreland RC 2.00 5.00
195 Brian Allen RC 2.00 5.00
196 Morlon Greenwood RC 2.00 5.00
197 Brandon Spoon RC 2.50 6.00
198 Carlos Polk RC 2.00 5.00
199 Alex Lincoln RC 2.00 5.00
200 Keith Adams RC 2.00 5.00
201 Kevan Barlow JSY RC 2.50 6.00
202 Michael Bennett JSY RC 2.50 6.00
203 Drew Brees JSY RC 25.00 50.00
204 Quincy Carter JSY RC 2.50 6.00
205 Andre Carter JSY RC 2.50 6.00
206 Chris Chambers JSY RC 2.00 5.00
207 Robert Ferguson JSY RC 3.00 8.00
208 Rod Gardner JSY RC 2.50 6.00
210 Travis Henry JSY RC 2.50 6.00
212 Chad Johnson JSY RC 3.00 8.00
213 Rudi Johnson JSY RC 3.00 8.00
214 Sage Rosenfels JSY RC 2.50 6.00
215 Deuce McAllister JSY RC 3.00 8.00
216 Mike McMahon JSY RC 2.50 6.00
217 Snoop Minnis JSY RC 2.00 5.00
218 Travis Minor JSY RC 2.50 6.00
219 Freddie Mitchell JSY RC 2.00 5.00
220 Quincy Morgan JSY RC 2.50 6.00
222 Santana Moss JSY RC 3.00 8.00
223 Jesse Palmer JSY RC 2.50 6.00
224 Koren Robinson JSY RC 2.50 6.00
225 Josh Heupel JSY RC [illegible]
226 Justin Smith JSY RC 4.00 10.00
227 David Terrell JSY RC 2.50 6.00
228 Anthony Thomas JSY RC 3.00 8.00
229 L.Tomlinson JSY RC 10.00 25.00
230 M.Tuiasosopo JSY RC 2.50 6.00
231 Michael Vick JSY RC 5.00 12.00
232 Gerard Warren JSY RC 2.50 6.00
233 Reggie Wayne JSY RC 4.00 10.00
234 Chris Weinke JSY RC 2.50 6.00
235 Leonard Davis JSY RC 3.00 8.00

2001 Playoff Honors Chicago Collection

NOT PRICED DUE TO SCARCITY

2001 Playoff Honors X's and O's

*VETS/200-300: 3X TO 8X BASIC CARDS
*VETS/140-199: 4X TO 10X BASIC CARDS
*VETS/100-139: 5X TO 12X BASIC CARDS
*VETS/70-99: 6X TO 15X BASIC CARDS
*ROOKIES/70-80: .4X TO 1X
*VETS/50-69: 8X TO 20X BASIC CARDS
*ROOKIES/50-60: .5X TO 1.2X
*ROOKIES JSY/50-60: .8X TO 2X
*VETS/30-45: 10X TO 25X BASIC CARDS
*ROOKIES/30-40: .6X TO 1.5X
*ROOKIES JSY/30-40: 1X TO 2.5X
*VETS/21-29: 12X TO 30X BASIC CARDS
*ROOKIES/20: 1X TO 2.5X
*ROOKIES JSY/20: 1.5X TO 4X
*VETS/10-19: 15X TO 40X BASIC CARDS
*ROOKIES/10: 1.2X TO 3X
*ROOKIES JSY/10: 2X TO 5X
203 Drew Brees JSY/20 100.00 250.00

2001 Playoff Honors Alma Mater Materials

Randomly inserted in packs at a rate of 1 in 32 packs, this 15 card set features collegiate game worn jersey cards of top past and present NFL superstars such as Edgerrin James, Ricky Williams and Earl Campbell. A few cards were printed in smaller quantities and we have notated that information in our checklist.

STATED ODDS 1:32
*VARSITY PATCH/50: .8X TO 2X BASIC JSY
VARSITY PATCH PRINT RUN 50
AM1 Shaun Alexander 10.00 25.00
AM2 Drew Bledsoe 15.00 30.00
AM3 Earl Campbell 6.00 15.00
AM4 Sam Cowart 5.00 12.00
AM5 Terrell Davis 6.00 15.00
AM6 Tony Dorsett 12.50 30.00
AM7 John Elway SP 25.00 60.00
AM8 Eddie George SP 30.00 60.00
AM9 Edgerrin James 6.00 15.00
AM10 Keyshawn Johnson 6.00 15.00
AM11 Jevon Kearse 5.00 12.00
AM12 Fred Taylor SP 5.00 12.00
AM13 Ricky Williams SP 6.00 15.00
AM14 Olandis Gary 5.00 12.00
AM15 E.G. Green 5.00 12.00

2001 Playoff Honors Alma Mater Materials Varsity Patch Autographs

Randomly inserted in packs , this 3-card set features hand autographed collegiate game worn jersey patch cards of top past and present NFL superstarsl. These cards have a stated print run of 25 serial numbered sets.

STATED PRINT RUN 25 SER.#'d SETS
AM3 Earl Campbell 75.00 125.00
AM6 Tony Dorsett 90.00 150.00
AM9 Edgerrin James 60.00 100.00

2001 Playoff Honors Game Day Jerseys

Randomly inserted in packs at a rate of 1 in 16 packs, these game worn jersey swatch cards are cut out in a round swatch with a tan colored background. Cards are full color action shots of some of the hottest NFL stars such as Jerry Rice and Troy Aikman. Fifteen cards were also produced in an Autographed version with each card serial numbered of 25.

STATED ODDS 1:16
*SOUVENIRS/25: 1X TO 2.5X JERSEY
SOUVENIRS PRINT RUN 25 SER.#'d SETS
GD1 Troy Aikman 8.00 20.00
GD2 Mike Alstott 4.00 10.00
GD3 Jerome Bettis 6.00 15.00
GD4 Drew Bledsoe 5.00 12.00
GD5 Jamal Anderson 5.00 12.00
GD6 Isaac Bruce 6.00 15.00
GD7 Tim Brown 6.00 15.00
GD8 Mark Brunell 5.00 12.00
GD9 Cris Carter 6.00 15.00
GD10 Kerry Collins 4.00 10.00
GD11 Tim Couch 4.00 10.00
GD12 Daunte Culpepper 5.00 12.00
GD13 Stephen Davis 4.00 10.00
GD14 Terrell Davis 5.00 12.00
GD15 Ron Dayne 5.00 12.00
GD16 Corey Dillon 4.00 10.00
GD17 Warrick Dunn 4.00 10.00
GD18 Johnnie Morton 5.00 12.00
GD19 Marshall Faulk 5.00 12.00
GD20 Brett Favre 12.00 30.00
GD21 Eddie George 6.00 15.00
GD22 Brian Griese 4.00 10.00
GD23 Marvin Harrison 5.00 12.00
GD24 Torry Holt 5.00 12.00
GD25 Edgerrin James 5.00 12.00
GD26 Keyshawn Johnson 5.00 12.00
GD27 Jevon Kearse 4.00 10.00
GD28 Charlie Batch 4.00 10.00
GD29 Peyton Manning 15.00 40.00
GD30 Dan Marino 12.00 30.00
GD31 Curtis Martin 5.00 12.00
GD32 Donovan McNabb 5.00 12.00
GD33 Steve McNair 5.00 12.00
GD34 Joe Montana 20.00 50.00
GD35 Randy Moss 5.00 12.00
GD36 Eric Moulds 4.00 10.00
GD37 Jake Plummer 4.00 10.00
GD38 Jerry Rice 12.00 30.00
GD39 Charles Woodson 8.00 15.00
GD40 Deion Sanders 5.00 12.00
GD41 Warren Sapp 5.00 12.00
GD42 Junior Seau 5.00 12.00
GD43 Emmitt Smith 10.00 25.00
GD44 Fred Taylor 4.00 10.00
GD45 Frank Sanders 4.00 10.00
GD46 Lamar Smith 5.00 12.00
GD47 Kurt Warner 10.00 25.00
GD48 Peter Warrick 4.00 10.00
GD49 Ricky Williams 5.00 12.00
GD50 Steve Young 8.00 20.00

2001 Playoff Honors Game Day Jerseys Autographs

Randomly inserted in packs these game worn jersey autograph swatch cards are cut out in a round swatch with a tan colored background. Cards are full color action shots of some of the hottest NFL stars. These hand signed autograph versions are limited to 25 of each card signed

ANNOUNCED PRINT RUN 25 SETS
GD5 Jamal Anderson 25.00 60.00
GD7 Tim Brown 30.00 80.00
GD22 Brian Griese 20.00 50.00
GD23 Marvin Harrison 25.00 60.00
GD24 Torry Holt
GD28 Charlie Batch 20.00 50.00
GD30 Dan Marino 200.00 350.00
GD36 Eric Moulds 20.00 50.00
GD42 Junior Seau 50.00 100.00
GD43 Emmitt Smith 200.00 350.00
GD47 Kurt Warner 40.00 100.00
GD48 Peter Warrick 20.00 50.00
GD49 Ricky Williams 25.00 60.00
GD50 Steve Young [illegible]

2001 Playoff Honors Honor Roll Autographs

Inserted at a rate of 1 in 48 packs this set features hand serial numbered autographed cards issued in various quantities using cards from years and brands of the past. Please note that some cards were issued in autograph form in previous products, but have been hand numbered separately for this release.

STATED ODDS 1:48
20 J.Bettis 99PreCL/60 40.00 80.00
40 F.Bownes 01PlaUH/31 7.50 20.00
41 T.Brown 99PreCL/61 12.50 30.00
42 I.Bruce 98Mom/30 20.00 40.00
45 T.Bruschi 01PlaUH/37 100.00 175.00
48 B.Christian 01PlaUH/32 7.50 20.00
51 G.Comella 01PlaUH/20 7.50 20.00
53 G.Crowell 98Con/165 7.50 20.00
70 R.Cunningham 99Mom/70 10.00 25.00
71 R.Cunningham 00Abs/92 10.00 25.00
72 R.Cunningham 00AbsCA/25 12.50 30.00
73 R.Cunningham 00ConHFO/34 12.50 30.00
74 R.Cunningham 00Pre/56 10.00 25.00
76 T.Davis 99AbsTS/28 20.00 50.00
77 T.Davis 99AbsTS/50 20.00 50.00
78 T.Davis 99AbsTS/41 20.00 50.00
79 T.Davis 99AbsTS/33 20.00 50.00
92 C.Dillon 99PreCL/29 15.00 30.00
99 K.Faulk 99PreCL/25 20.00 40.00
108 J.Fiala 01PlaUH/30 7.50 20.00
111 C.Fuamatu 98ConTic/20 12.50 30.00
113 J.Galloway 99PreCL/49 12.50 30.00
115 O.Gary 99Con/55 12.50 30.00
119 T.Glenn 01PlaUH/35 10.00 25.00
123 J.Green 98ConTic/196 10.00 25.00
130 B.Huard 99Con/25 12.50 30.00
140 Kev.Johnson 99PreCL/25 12.50 30.00
150 J.Lynch 01PlaUH/35 12.50 30.00
151 P.Manning 98Abs/43 75.00 150.00
157 P.Manning 98PreHob/33 75.00 150.00
158 P.Manning 98PreRet/26 75.00 150.00
165 D.Marino 99MomSG/125 40.00 80.00
172 Cec.Martin 01PlaUH/32 7.50 20.00
173 R.Maryland 01PlaUH/37 7.50 20.00
176 R.McKinnon 01PlaUH/37 7.50 20.00
177 D.McNabb 99Con/25 100.00 200.00
184 C.McNown 99PreCL/97 7.50 20.00
185 C.McNown 99PreEXP/32 12.50 30.00
190 C.McNown 00Pre/24 12.50 30.00
216 W.Moon 99Con/61 12.50 30.00
220 W.Moon 00Abs/47 15.00 40.00
222 W.Moon 00ConHFO/34 15.00 40.00
223 W.Moon 00Pre/32 15.00 40.00
230 J.Plummer 97Abs/29 12.50 30.00
239 J.Plummer PT 99Con/22 15.00 40.00
244 J.Plummer 99PreCL/26 12.50 30.00
245 J.Plummer 00Abs/45 12.50 30.00
246 J.Plummer 00Con/43 12.50 30.00
247 J.Plummer 00Mom/70 10.00 25.00
248 J.Plummer 00Pre/35 12.50 30.00
259 B.Sanders 99Mom/26 60.00 120.00
260 B.Sanders 99PreCL/21 60.00 120.00
262 B.Sanders 00Abs/49 60.00 120.00
263 B.Sanders 00Mom/72 30.00 60.00
264 B.Sanders 00Pre/30 50.00 100.00
268 A.Smith 99ConROY/20 10.00 25.00
271 T.Spikes 01PlaUH/37 7.50 20.00
273 K.Stewart 99MomSG/20 12.50 30.00
279 F.Taylor 99MomSG/50 20.00 40.00
280 F.Taylor 99PreCL/28 20.00 50.00
289 V.Testaverde 97Abs/44 12.50 30.00
296 V.Testaverde 99Con/68 10.00 25.00
299 V.Testaverde 00Con/41 12.50 30.00
300 V.Testaverde 00ConHFO/32 12.50 30.00
301 V.Testaverde 00Mom/66 10.00 25.00
302 V.Testaverde 00Pre/27 12.50 30.00
303 J.Thrash 01PlaUH/24 12.50 30.00
305 B.Urlacher 01PlaUH/31 40.00 80.00
307 C.Walsh 01PlaUH/34 7.50 20.00
310 R.Williams 99AbsEXP/34 30.00 80.00
313 R.Williams 99PreCL/34 30.00 80.00
315 R.Williams 99PreEXP/37 30.00 80.00
317 B.Young 01PlaUH/24 12.50 30.00

2001 Playoff Honors Rookie Hidden Gems Autographs

Randomly inserted in packs of Playoff Honors this autographed set features rookie autographs on pull out oversized jersey swatch cards. The first 50 cards of the set feature hand autographed versions of the rookie jerseys.

STATED PRINT RUN 50 SER.#'d SETS
201 Kevan Barlow 12.00 30.00
202 Michael Bennett 12.00 30.00
203 Drew Brees 200.00 400.00
204 Quincy Carter 12.00 30.00
205 Andre Carter 12.00 30.00
206 Chris Chambers 10.00 25.00
207 Robert Ferguson 15.00 40.00
208 Rod Gardner 12.00 30.00
210 Travis Henry 12.00 30.00
212 Chad Johnson 15.00 40.00
213 Rudi Johnson 15.00 40.00
214 Sage Rosenfels 12.00 30.00
215 Deuce McAllister 15.00 40.00
216 Mike McMahon 12.00 30.00
217 Snoop Minnis 10.00 25.00
218 Travis Minor 12.00 30.00
219 Freddie Mitchell 10.00 25.00
220 Quincy Morgan 12.00 30.00
222 Santana Moss 15.00 40.00
223 Jesse Palmer 12.00 30.00
224 Koren Robinson 12.00 30.00
225 Josh Heupel 15.00 40.00
226 Justin Smith 20.00 50.00
227 David Terrell 12.00 30.00
228 Anthony Thomas 15.00 40.00
229 LaDainian Tomlinson 75.00 150.00
230 Marques Tuiasosopo 12.00 30.00
231 Michael Vick 25.00 60.00
232 Gerard Warren 12.00 30.00
233 Reggie Wayne 20.00 50.00
234 Chris Weinke 12.00 30.00
235 Leonard Davis 15.00 40.00

2001 Playoff Honors Rookie Quad Footballs

Randomly inserted in packs, these cards feature 4 rookie players on each card front with four pieces of event worn football swatches per card. Cards have full color phots. Cards have two players with two swatches on both card front and back

OVERALL QUAD/TANDEM ODDS 1:16
*JERSEY QUAD: .5X TO 1.2X FB QUAD
*JSY/FB QUAD/25: .8X TO 2X FB QUAD
JERSEY/BALL COMBOS SER.#'d OF 25
RQ1 Vick/Q.Crtr/Weinke/McMhn 10.00 25.00
RQ2 Brees/Tmlsn/A.Thmas/Terr 12.00 30.00
RQ3 Rsfls/Grdr/R.Jhsn/C.Jhsn 6.00 15.00
RQ4 Heupel/Minor/Jacksn/Mrgn 6.00 15.00
RQ5 Rbsn/Wayne/Mtchell/Moss 8.00 20.00
RQ6 [illegible]
RQ7 Chmbs/Mnnis/Frgsn/Heap 6.00 15.00
RQ8 Tuiaso/Palmr/Smith/Warren 8.00 20.00

2001 Playoff Honors Rookie Tandem Footballs

Randomly inserted in packs, these cards feature two leading rookies as well as swatches of footballs.

OVERALL QUAD/TANDEM ODDS 1:16
*JERSEYS: .5X TO 1.2X BALLS
*JSY/FR/100: .8X TO 2X FOOTBALL
JERSEY/FB COMBOS #'d OF 100
RT1 M.Vick/Q.Carter 8.00 20.00
RT2 C.Weinke/M.McMahon 4.00 10.00
RT3 D.Brees/L.Tomlinson 15.00 40.00
RT4 A.Thomas/D.Terrell 5.00 12.00
RT5 S.Rosenfels/R.Gardner 4.00 10.00
RT6 R.Johnson/C.Johnson 5.00 12.00
RT7 J.Heupel/T.Minor 5.00 12.00
RT8 J.Jackson/Q.Morgan 4.00 10.00
RT9 K.Robinson/R.Wayne 6.00 15.00
RT10 F.Mitchell/S.Moss 5.00 12.00
RT11 M.Bennett/D.McAllister 5.00 12.00
RT12 T.Henry/K.Barlow 4.00 10.00
RT13 C.Chambers/S.Minnis 3.00 8.00
RT14 R.Ferguson/T.Heap 5.00 12.00
RT15 M.Tuiasosopo/J.Palmer 4.00 10.00
RT16 J.Smith/G.Warren 6.00 15.00
RT17 A.Carter/D.Morgan 4.00 10.00

2001 Playoff Honors Souvenirs

Inserted in packs at a rate of one in 108, these 10 cards feature past and present stars along with a memorabilia piece relating to their career. Most of these cards are jersey cards but a few cards have different types of memorabilia which we have notated in our checklist. A signed version serial numbered of 25 was issued for each player except Payton Manning whos "Signs of Greatness" version was issued unsigned.

STATED ODDS 1:108
PB1 Jerry Rice 12.00 30.00
PB2 Mark Brunell 5.00 12.00
PB3 John Elway 10.00 25.00
PB4 Jimmy Smith 5.00 12.00
PB5 Peyton Manning 10.00 25.00
PB6 Eddie George 6.00 15.00
PB7 Roger Staubach FB 10.00 25.00
PB8 Bob Griese FB 8.00 20.00
PB9 Drew Bledsoe 5.00 12.00
PB10 Jamal Lewis Pylon 6.00 15.00

2001 Playoff Honors Souvenirs Signs of Greatness

Randomly inserted in packs, these 10 cards feature authentic autographs of the featured players. Some players did not return their cards in time for release with the product and these cards could be redeemed until May 1,2003. Twenty-five of each card was signed for this promotion. Please note that Peyton Manning did not sign for this set and his cards contain "no autograph" on the card front

STATED PRINT RUN 25 SER.#'d SETS
PB1 Jerry Rice 175.00 300.00
PB2 Mark Brunell 25.00 60.00
PB3 John Elway 200.00 350.00
PB4 Jimmy Smith 25.00 60.00
PB5 Peyton Manning No Auto 10.00 25.00
PB6 Eddie George 30.00 80.00
PB7 Roger Staubach 125.00 200.00
PB8 Bob Griese 30.00 80.00
PB9 Drew Bledsoe 50.00 120.00
PB10 Jamal Lewis 30.00 80.00

2002 Playoff Honors Samples

*SAMPLE SILVER: .8X TO 2X BASE CARDS
*SAMPLE GOLD: 1.2X TO 3X BASE CARDS

2002 Playoff Honors

Released in late November as a 232-card set, this product was issued with two mini boxes containing 12 packs each with 6 cards per pack. SRP per pack was 5.99. This set includes 100 veterans and 132 rookies. The first 100 rookies (101-200) are serial numbered to 1000, and the remaining rookies are numbered to 725. Cards numbered 201 through 232 contained swatches of game used memorabilia.

COMP.SET w/o SP's (100) 10.00 25.00
201-232 ROOKIE JSY PRINT RUN 650
1 David Boston .25 .60
2 Jake Plummer .25 .60
3 Warrick Dunn .25 .60
4 Michael Vick .30 .75
5 Jamal Lewis .30 .75
6 Chris Redman .25 .60
7 Ray Lewis .40 1.00
8 Drew Bledsoe .30 .75
9 Travis Henry .25 .60
10 Eric Moulds .25 .60
11 Lamar Smith .25 .60
12 Steve Smith .40 1.00
13 Chris Weinke .25 .60
14 Chris Chandler .30 .75
15 David Terrell .25 .60
16 Anthony Thomas .30 .75
17 Brian Urlacher .40 1.00
18 Corey Dillon .25 .60
19 Peter Warrick .25 .60
20 Tim Couch .25 .60
21 James Jackson .25 .60
22 Kevin Johnson .25 .60
23 Quincy Carter .25 .60
24 Joey Galloway .30 .75
25 Emmitt Smith .60 1.50
26 Terrell Davis .30 .75
27 Brian Griese .25 .60
28 Rod Smith .30 .75
29 Germane Crowell .25 .60
30 Az-Zahir Hakim .25 .60
31 Mike McMahon .25 .60
32 Brett Favre .75 2.00
33 Terry Glenn .30 .75
34 Ahman Green .30 .75
35 James Allen .25 .60
36 Corey Bradford .25 .60
37 Marvin Harrison .30 .75
38 Peyton Manning 1.00 2.50
39 Edgerrin James .30 .75
40 Reggie Wayne .30 .75
41 Mark Brunell .30 .75
42 Fred Taylor .25 .60
43 Jimmy Smith .30 .75
44 Tony Gonzalez .30 .75
45 Trent Green .25 .60
46 Priest Holmes .25 .60
47 Snoop Minnis .25 .60
48 Chris Chambers .25 .60
49 Jay Fiedler .30 .75
50 Ricky Williams .30 .75
51 Zach Thomas .30 .75
52 Randy Moss .30 .75
53 Daunte Culpepper .30 .75
54 Michael Bennett .25 .60
55 Tom Brady 2.00 5.00
56 Troy Brown .25 .60
57 Antowain Smith .30 .75
58 Aaron Brooks .25 .60
59 Deuce McAllister .30 .75
60 Tiki Barber .30 .75
61 Kerry Collins .25 .60
62 Amani Toomer .25 .60
63 Michael Strahan .30 .75
64 Curtis Martin .30 .75
65 Vinny Testaverde .25 .60
66 Chad Pennington .25 .60
67 Laveranues Coles .30 .75
68 Tim Brown .40 1.00
69 Rich Gannon .30 .75
70 Jerry Rice .75 2.00
71 Donovan McNabb .30 .75
72 Freddie Mitchell .25 .60
73 [illegible]
74 Jerome Bettis .40 1.00
75 Plaxico Burress .25 .60
76 Kordell Stewart .25 .60
77 Drew Brees .75 2.00
78 Doug Flutie .30 .75
79 LaDainian Tomlinson .40 1.00
80 Jeff Garcia .25 .60
81 Garrison Hearst .25 .60
82 Terrell Owens .30 .75
83 Shaun Alexander .25 .60
84 Trent Dilfer .25 .60
85 Koren Robinson .25 .60
86 Isaac Bruce .40 1.00
87 Marshall Faulk .30 .75
88 Torry Holt .30 .75
89 Kurt Warner .30 .75
90 Mike Alstott .25 .60
91 Brad Johnson .30 .75
92 Keyshawn Johnson .30 .75
93 Keenan McCardell .30 .75
94 Steve McNair .30 .75
95 Eddie George .30 .75
96 Jevon Kearse .25 .60
97 Derrick Mason .25 .60
98 Stephen Davis .25 .60
99 Sage Rosenfels .30 .75
100 Rod Gardner .25 .60
101 Randy Fasani RC 1.00 2.50
102 Kurt Kittner RC 1.00 2.50
103 Brandon Doman RC 1.00 2.50
104 Craig Nall RC 1.25 3.00
105 J.T. O'Sullivan RC 1.25 3.00
106 Seth Burford RC 1.00 2.50
107 Jeff Kelly RC 1.00 2.50
108 Ronald Curry RC 1.00 2.50
109 Wes Pate RC 1.00 2.50
110 Chad Hutchinson RC 1.00 2.50
111 Major Applewhite RC 1.50 4.00
112 Preston Parsons RC 1.00 2.50
113 David Priestley RC 1.00 2.50
114 Lamar Gordon RC 1.25 3.00
115 Brian Westbrook RC 2.00 5.00
116 Jonathan Wells RC 1.25 3.00
117 Omar Easy RC 1.25 3.00
118 Verron Haynes RC 1.00 2.50
119 Josh Scobey RC 1.25 3.00
120 Larry Ned RC 1.00 2.50
121 Adrian Peterson RC 1.25 3.00
122 Brian Allen RC 1.00 2.50
123 Chester Taylor RC 1.50 4.00
124 Luke Staley RC 1.00 2.50
125 Antwoine Womack RC 1.00 2.50
126 Leonard Henry RC 1.00 2.50
127 Jesse Chatman RC 1.00 2.50
128 Damien Anderson RC 1.00 2.50
129 Eric McCoo RC 1.00 2.50
130 Tellis Redmon RC 1.00 2.50
131 Joe Burns RC 1.00 2.50
132 Delvon Flowers RC 1.00 2.50
133 Ken Simonton RC 1.00 2.50
134 Ricky Williams RC 1.25 3.00
135 Dicenzo Miller RC 1.00 2.50
136 James Mungro RC 1.50 4.00
137 Randy McMichael RC 1.50 4.00
138 Deion Branch RC 1.50 4.00
139 Terry Charles RC 1.00 2.50
140 Herb Haygood RC 1.00 2.50
141 Jason McAddley RC 1.25 3.00
142 Jake Schifino RC 1.00 2.50
143 Freddie Milons RC 1.00 2.50
144 Kahlil Hill RC 1.00 2.50
145 Lamont Brightful RC 1.00 2.50
146 Chris Luzar RC 1.00 2.50
147 Daryl Jones RC 1.00 2.50
148 Woody Dantzler RC 1.25 3.00
149 Kelly Campbell RC 1.25 3.00
150 Brian Poli-Dixon RC 1.00 2.50
151 Atrews Bell RC 1.00 2.50
152 Jarrod Baxter RC 1.00 2.50
153 Eddie Drummond RC 1.00 2.50
154 Jerramy Stevens RC 1.50 4.00
155 Doug Jolley RC 1.00 2.50
156 Jamar Martin RC 1.25 3.00
157 Najeh Davenport RC 1.00 2.50
158 Dwight Freeney RC 2.00 5.00
159 Bryan Thomas RC 1.00 2.50
160 Charles Grant RC 1.50 4.00
161 Kalimba Edwards RC 1.25 3.00
162 Ryan Denney RC 1.00 2.50
163 Will Overstreet RC 1.00 2.50
164 Dennis Johnson RC 1.00 2.50
165 Alex Brown RC 1.50 4.00
166 Kenyon Coleman RC 1.00 2.50
167 Ryan Sims RC 1.50 4.00
168 John Henderson RC 1.25 3.00
169 Wendell Bryant RC 1.00 2.50
170 Albert Haynesworth RC 1.50 4.00
171 Larry Tripplett RC 1.00 2.50
172 Eddie Freeman RC 1.00 2.50
173 Anthony Weaver RC 1.00 2.50
174 Quentin Jammer RC 1.50 4.00
175 Phillip Buchanon RC 1.50 4.00
176 Lito Sheppard RC 1.50 4.00
177 Mike Rumph RC 1.00 2.50
178 Roosevelt Williams RC 1.00 2.50
179 Derek Ross RC 1.25 3.00
180 Mike Echols RC 1.00 2.50
181 Keyou Craver RC 1.00 2.50
182 Ed Reed RC 7.50 15.00
183 Lamont Thompson RC 1.25 3.00
184 Tank Williams RC 1.25 3.00
185 Michael Lewis RC 1.25 3.00
186 Napoleon Harris RC 1.25 3.00
187 Robert Thomas RC 1.00 2.50
188 Raonall Smith RC 1.00 2.50
189 Levar Fisher RC 1.00 2.50
190 Rocky Calmus RC 1.25 3.00
191 Andra Davis RC 1.00 2.50
192 Nick Rolovich RC 1.00 2.50
193 Zak Kustok RC 1.00 2.50
194 Dusty Bonner RC 1.00 2.50
195 Tony Fisher RC 1.00 2.50
196 Sam Simmons RC 1.00 2.50
197 Lee Mays RC 1.00 2.50
198 Jamin Elliott RC 1.00 2.50
199 Javin Hunter RC 1.00 2.50
200 Kendall Newson RC 1.00 2.50
201 Ladell Betts JSY RC 3.00 8.00
202 Antonio Bryant JSY RC 3.00 8.00
203 Reche Caldwell JSY RC 2.50 6.00
204 David Carr JSY RC 2.00 5.00
205 Tim Carter JSY RC 2.50 6.00
206 Eric Crouch JSY RC 3.00 8.00
207 Rohan Davey JSY RC 3.00 8.00
208 Andre Davis JSY RC 2.00 5.00
209 T.J. Duckett JSY RC 2.00 5.00
210 DeShaun Foster JSY RC 3.00 8.00
211 Jabar Gaffney JSY RC 2.00 5.00
212 David Garrard JSY RC 2.50 6.00
213 Daniel Graham JSY RC 2.50 6.00
214 William Green JSY RC 2.50 6.00
215 Joey Harrington JSY RC 2.00 5.00
216 Ron Johnson JSY RC 2.50 6.00
217 Ashley Lelie JSY RC 2.00 5.00
218 Josh McCown JSY RC 3.00 8.00
219 Maurice Morris JSY RC 2.50 6.00
220 Julius Peppers JSY RC 5.00 12.00
221 Clinton Portis JSY RC 3.00 8.00
222 Patrick Ramsey JSY RC 2.50 6.00
223 Antwaan Randle El JSY RC 2.50 6.00
224 Josh Reed JSY RC 2.50 6.00
225 Cliff Russell JSY RC 2.00 5.00
226 Jeremy Shockey JSY RC 3.00 8.00
227 Donte Stallworth JSY RC 3.00 8.00
228 Travis Stephens JSY RC [illegible]
229 Javon Walker JSY RC 3.00 8.00

230 Marquise Walker JSY RC 2.00 5.00
231 Roy Williams JSY RC 2.00 5.00
232 Mike Williams JSY RC 2.00 5.00
RWH1 Payton/Smith JSY/250 40.00 100.00
RWH1A Payton/Smith AUTO/22 200.00 400.00

2002 Playoff Honors O's

*1-100 VETS: 4X TO 10X BASIC CARDS
1-100 VETERAN PRINT RUN 100
*101-200 ROOKIES: 1X TO 2.5X
101-200 ROOKIE PRINT RUN 50
*201-232 ROOKIE JSY: 1.5X TO 4X
201-232 ROOKIE JSY PRINT RUN 25
RANDOM INSERTS IN RETAIL PACKS

2002 Playoff Honors X's

*1-100 VETS: 4X TO 10X BASIC CARDS
1-100 VETERAN PRINT RUN 100
*101-200 ROOKIES: 1X TO 2.5X
101-200 ROOKIE PRINT RUN 50
*201-232 ROOKIE JSY: 1.5X TO 4X
201-232 ROOKIE JSY PRINT RUN 25

2002 Playoff Honors Rookie Hidden Gems Autographs

Randomly inserted in packs,this 32 card set features Playoff's unique pull out swatch of game worn jersey containing an autograph directly on the swatch. The first 50 cards of the 650 jersey print run were signed.
STATED PRINT RUN 50 SER.#'d SETS
201 Ladell Betts 20.00 50.00
202 Antonio Bryant 20.00 50.00
203 Reche Caldwell 15.00 40.00
204 David Carr 12.00 30.00
205 Tim Carter 15.00 40.00
206 Eric Crouch 20.00 50.00
207 Rohan Davey 20.00 50.00
208 Andre Davis 12.00 30.00
209 T.J. Duckett 12.00 30.00
210 DeShaun Foster 20.00 50.00
211 Jabar Gaffney 12.00 30.00
212 David Garrard 15.00 40.00
213 Daniel Graham 15.00 40.00
214 William Green 15.00 40.00
215 Joey Harrington 12.00 30.00
216 Ron Johnson 15.00 40.00
217 Ashley Lelie 12.00 30.00
218 Josh McCown 20.00 50.00
219 Maurice Morris 15.00 40.00
220 Julius Peppers 50.00 100.00
221 Clinton Portis 20.00 50.00
222 Patrick Ramsey 15.00 40.00
223 Antwaan Randle El 15.00 40.00
224 Josh Reed 15.00 40.00
225 Cliff Russell 12.00 30.00
226 Jeremy Shockey 20.00 50.00
227 Donte Stallworth 20.00 50.00
228 Travis Stephens 12.00 30.00
229 Javon Walker 20.00 50.00
230 Marquise Walker 12.00 30.00
231 Roy Williams 12.00 30.00
232 Mike Williams 12.00 30.00

2002 Playoff Honors Alma Mater Materials

Randomly inserted in packs, this 15-card set features various cards which contained pieces of collegiate alma mater game used memorabilia such as jerseys, shoes, helmets and gloves. A Varsity Patch version was also issued for each player with each being serial numbered of 25.
STATED PRINT RUN 25-400
AM1 Doug Flutie JSY/150 4.00 10.00
AM2 Ahman Green JSY/150 4.00 10.00
AM3 Travis Minor Shoes/100 3.00 8.00
AM4 Laverneus Coles JSY/250 3.00 8.00
AM5 Drew Brees Shoes/100 10.00 25.00
AM6 Terrell Davis HEL/75 5.00 12.00
AM7 Javon Walker Shoes/100 5.00 12.00
AM8 James Jackson JSY/250 2.50 6.00
AM9 Reggie Wayne JSY/400 3.00 8.00
AM10 Champ Bailey HEL/75 5.00 12.00
AM11 Snoop Minnis GLV/25 5.00 12.00
AM12 Dan Morgan JSY/25 5.00 12.00
AM13 Peyton Manning HEL/75 15.00 40.00
AM14 Santana Moss JSY/250 3.00 8.00
AM15 Peter Warrick GLV/25 5.00 12.00

2002 Playoff Honors Alma Mater Materials Varsity Patches

Randomly inserted in packs, this 15-card set features various cards which contained pieces of collegiate alma mater game used memorabilia such as jerseys, shoes, helmets and gloves. The cards were serial numbered to 25 with some being hand signed.
STATED PRINT RUN 25 SER.#'d SETS
AM1 Doug Flutie JSY 6.00 15.00
AM2 Ahman Green JSY AU 20.00 50.00
AM3 Travis Minor Shoes AU 15.00 40.00
AM4 Laverneus Coles JSY 6.00 15.00
AM5 Drew Brees Shoes AU 60.00 120.00
AM6 Terrell Davis HEL AU 20.00 50.00
AM7 Javon Walker Shoes 8.00 20.00
AM8 James Jackson JSY AU
AM9 Reggie Wayne JSY AU 20.00 50.00
AM10 Champ Bailey HEL 6.00 15.00
AM11 Snoop Minnis GLV 5.00 12.00
AM12 Dan Morgan JSY AU 15.00 40.00
AM13 Peyton Manning HEL 20.00 50.00
AM14 Santana Moss JSY AU 20.00 50.00
AM15 Peter Warrick GLV AU 15.00 40.00
AM13S Peyton Manning HEL Sample 30.00 60.00

2002 Playoff Honors Award Winning Materials

Randomly inserted in packs,this 12 card set features game worn jerseys which were cut out in the shape of the year the award was won. The cards were serial numbered to 150.
STATED PRINT RUN 150 SER.#'d SETS
UNPRICED AUTO PRINT RUN 10
AW1 Anthony Thomas 4.00 10.00
AW2 Edgerrin James 4.00 10.00
AW3 Randy Moss 4.00 10.00
AW4 Curtis Martin 4.00 10.00
AW5 Eddie George 4.00 10.00
AW6 Marshall Faulk 4.00 10.00
AW7 Kurt Warner 4.00 10.00
AW8 Terrell Davis 4.00 10.00
AW9 Barry Sanders 8.00 20.00
AW10 Brett Favre 10.00 25.00
AW11 Emmitt Smith 8.00 20.00
AW12 Steve Young 6.00 15.00

2002 Playoff Honors Game Day Souvenirs

Randomly inserted in packs, this 6 card set features game used footballs along with a swatch of game worn jersey. Cards were serial numbered to 250.
STATED PRINT RUN 250 SER.#'d SETS
GD1 Donovan McNabb 3.00 8.00
GD2 Emmitt Smith 6.00 15.00
GD3 Jerry Rice 8.00 20.00
GD4 Jeff Garcia 2.50 6.00
GD5 Brian Urlacher 4.00 10.00
GD6 Brett Favre 8.00 20.00

2002 Playoff Honors Honorable Signatures

Randomly inserted in packs, this 50 card set features color action shots of top NFL stars along with hand signed autographs. The cards were oriented horizontally. In 2005, Donruss/Playoff made an announcement of print runs for many older autographed sets including this one. Those announced print runs are included below.
ANNOUNCED PRINT RUNS BELOW
HS1 Barry Sanders/50* 75.00 150.00
HS2 Joe Montana 60.00 120.00
HS3 Joe Namath 45.00 80.00
HS4 Jeff Blake 8.00 13.00
HS5 Kerry Collins 8.00 20.00
HS6 Randall Cunningham 8.00 20.00
HS7 Anthony Thomas 6.00 15.00
HS8 Damione Lewis 5.00 12.00
HS9 Dan Morgan 5.00 12.00
HS10 LaMont Jordan 6.00 15.00
HS11 Jesse Palmer 5.00 12.00
HS12 Boo Williams 5.00 12.00
HS13 Isaac Bruce 8.00 20.00
HS14 Jimmy Smith 6.00 15.00
HS15 Santana Moss 6.00 15.00
HS16 Quincy Carter 5.00 12.00
HS17 Sage Rosenfels 6.00 15.00
HS18 T.J. Houshmandzadeh 5.00 12.00
HS19 Robert Ferguson 6.00 15.00
HS20 Aaron Brooks/100* 8.00 20.00
HS21 Brett Favre/50* 150.00 250.00
HS22 Cade McNown 6.00 15.00
HS23 Drew Bledsoe/100* 15.00 40.00
HS24 Jerry Rice/49* 100.00 200.00
HS25 Junior Seau/75* 30.00 60.00
HS26 Kordell Stewart/75* 8.00 20.00
HS27 Tony Banks 5.00 12.00
HS28 Chris Chambers/50* 8.00 20.00
HS29 David Terrell 5.00 12.00
HS30 Edgerrin James/51* 10.00 25.00
HS31 Gerard Warren 5.00 12.00
HS32 Jamal Anderson/45* 10.00 25.00
HS33 Jamal Lewis/100* 10.00 25.00
HS34 Justin Smith 6.00 15.00
HS35 Ken-Yon Rambo 5.00 12.00
HS36 Kurt Warner/100* 20.00 50.00
HS37 Marcus Robinson 6.00 15.00
HS38 Mark Brunell/100* 10.00 25.00
HS39 Marshall Faulk/50* 15.00 40.00
HS40 Mike McMahon/75* 8.00 20.00
HS41 Peter Warrick/100* 8.00 20.00
HS42 Quincy Morgan 5.00 12.00
HS43 Rudi Johnson 5.00 12.00
HS44 Shaun Rogers/100* 8.00 20.00
HS45 Stephen Davis/41* 8.00 20.00
HS46 Tim Brown/50* 12.00 30.00
HS47 Travis Minor/100* 8.00 20.00
HS48 Warren Moon/25* 25.00 50.00
HS49 Dan Marino/25* 75.00 150.00
HS50 John Elway /25* 60.00 120.00

2002 Playoff Honors Rookie Class Jerseys

Randomly inserted in packs,this 12 card set features three top NFL classmates with one swatch of game worn jersey per player on card front. Cards are serial numbered to 50.
STATED PRINT RUN 50 SER.#'d SETS
RC1 E.Smith/Seau/George 10.00 25.00
RC2 Conway/Bledsoe/Brunell 5.00 12.00
RC3 Bettis/Strahan/McDuffie 6.00 15.00
RC4 Dilfer/Garner/Bruce 6.00 15.00
RC5 K.Collins/C.Martin/T.Davis 5.00 12.00
RC6 Key.Johnson/Owens/Glenn 5.00 12.00
RC7 Manning/Dyson/Leaf 15.00 40.00
RC8 Griese/Moss/F.Taylor 5.00 12.00
RC9 James/McNabb/Garcia 5.00 12.00
RC10 Warner/R.Willms/Culpepper 5.00 12.00
RC11 Brady/Urlacher/Alexander 30.00 80.00
RC12 Vick/Tomlinson/Thomas 6.00 15.00

2002 Playoff Honors Rookie Stallion Autographs

Randomly inserted in packs,this 50 card set features top NFL rookies with color action shots. Cards are also hand signed and serial numbered to 100. Please note that some cards were only available via redemption. Those cards could be redeemed until May 6, 2004.
STATED PRINT RUN 100 SER.#'d SETS
RS2 Alex Brown 8.00 20.00
RS3 Andra Davis 5.00 12.00
RS4 Andre Lott 5.00 12.00
RS5 Antwaan Randle El 6.00 15.00
RS6 Ashley Lelie 5.00 12.00
RS7 Brian Westbrook 40.00 80.00
RS8 Bryant McKinnie 5.00 12.00
RS9 Chad Hutchinson 5.00 12.00
RS10 Cliff Russell 5.00 12.00
RS11 Cortlen Johnson 5.00 12.00
RS12 Damien Anderson 5.00 12.00
RS13 David Garrard 6.00 15.00
RS14 Deion Branch 10.00 25.00
RS15 Mike Williams 5.00 12.00
RS16 Donte Stallworth 8.00 20.00
RS17 Ed Reed 50.00 100.00
RS18 Eric Crouch 8.00 20.00
RS19 Freddie Milons 5.00 12.00
RS20 Jabar Gaffney 5.00 12.00
RS21 Javon Walker 8.00 20.00
RS22 Jerramy Stevens 8.00 20.00
RS23 John Henderson 6.00 15.00
RS25 Josh McCown 8.00 20.00
RS26 Josh Scobey 6.00 15.00
RS27 Levar Fisher 5.00 12.00
RS28 Kalimba Edwards 6.00 15.00
RS29 Ken Simonton 5.00 12.00
RS30 Keyuo Craver 5.00 12.00
RS31 Kurt Kittner 5.00 12.00
RS32 Lito Sheppard 8.00 20.00
RS33 Marquise Walker 5.00 12.00
RS34 Mike Rumph 5.00 12.00
RS35 Najeh Davenport 5.00 12.00
RS36 Patrick Ramsey 6.00 15.00
RS37 Randy Fasani 5.00 12.00
RS38 Robert Thomas 5.00 12.00
RS39 Rocky Calmus 6.00 15.00
RS40 Tavon Mason 5.00 12.00
RS41 Terry Charles 5.00 12.00
RS42 T.J. Duckett 5.00 12.00
RS43 Tim Carter 6.00 15.00
RS44 Trev Faulk 5.00 12.00
RS45 Wendall Bryant 5.00 12.00
RS46 William Green 6.00 15.00
RS47 Kahlil Hill 5.00 12.00
RS48 Ladell Betts 8.00 20.00
RS49 Lamar Gordon 6.00 15.00
RS50 Napoleon Harris 6.00 15.00

2002 Playoff Honors Rookie Stallions

Inserted in packs at a rate of 1:12, this 50 card set features top rookies with color action shots done with team color in background.
COMPLETE SET (50) 25.00 60.00
STATED ODDS 1:12
RS1 Albert Haynesworth .75 2.00
RS2 Alex Brown .75 2.00
RS3 Andra Davis .50 1.25
RS4 Andre Lott .50 1.25
RS5 Antwaan Randle El .60 1.50
RS6 Ashley Lelie .50 1.25
RS7 Brian Westbrook 1.00 2.50
RS8 Bryant McKinnie .50 1.25
RS9 Chad Hutchinson .50 1.25
RS10 Cliff Russell .50 1.25
RS11 Cortlen Johnson .50 1.25
RS12 Damien Anderson .50 1.25
RS13 David Garrard .60 1.50
RS14 Deion Branch .75 2.00
RS15 Mike Williams .50 1.25
RS16 Donte Stallworth .75 2.00
RS17 Ed Reed 3.00 8.00
RS18 Eric Crouch .75 2.00
RS19 Freddie Milons .50 1.25
RS20 Jabar Gaffney .50 1.25
RS21 Javon Walker .75 2.00
RS22 Jerramy Stevens .75 2.00
RS23 John Henderson .60 1.50
RS24 Jonathan Wells .60 1.50
RS25 Josh McCown .75 2.00
RS26 Josh Scobey .60 1.50
RS27 Levar Fisher .50 1.25
RS28 Kalimba Edwards .60 1.50
RS29 Ken Simonton .50 1.25
RS30 Keyuo Craver .50 1.25
RS31 Kurt Kittner .50 1.25
RS32 Lito Sheppard .75 2.00
RS33 Marquise Walker .50 1.25
RS34 Mike Rumph .50 1.25
RS35 Najeh Davenport .50 1.25
RS36 Patrick Ramsey .60 1.50
RS37 Randy Fasani .50 1.25
RS38 Robert Thomas .50 1.25
RS39 Rocky Calmus .60 1.50
RS40 Tavon Mason .50 1.25
RS41 Terry Charles .50 1.25
RS42 T.J. Duckett .50 1.25
RS43 Tim Carter .60 1.50
RS44 Trev Faulk .50 1.25
RS45 Wendall Bryant .50 1.25
RS46 William Green .60 1.50
RS47 Kahlil Hill .50 1.25
RS48 Ladell Betts .75 2.00
RS49 Lamar Gordon .60 1.50
RS50 Napoleon Harris .60 1.50

2002 Playoff Honors Rookie Tandems/Quads

Randomly inserted in packs, this 22-card set features top NFL rookie tandems with dual event-used footballs on the card fronts. Four-player Tandem quads were also produced with 2-pieces of event-used footballs on both the card fronts and backs; serial numbered to 500.
RQ16-RQ22 STATED PRINT RUN 500
*RT1-RT15 GOLD: .6X TO 1.5X BASIC DUAL
RT1-RT15 TANDEM GOLD PRINT RUN 250
RQ16-RQ22 QUAD GOLD PRINT RUN 25
RT1 D.Carr/J.Gaffney 2.00 5.00
RT2 T.Stephens/M.Walker 2.00 5.00
RT3 P.Ramsey/C.Russell 2.50 6.00
RT4 A.Bryant/R.Williams 3.00 8.00
RT5 C.Portis/A.Lelie 3.00 8.00
RT6 M.Morris/A.Davis 2.50 6.00
RT7 D.Foster/J.Peppers 5.00 12.00
RT8 E.Crouch/A.Randle El 3.00 8.00
RT9 J.Harrington/D.Garrard 2.50 6.00
RT10 J.McCown/R.Davey 3.00 8.00
RT11 D.Stallworth/R.Caldwell 3.00 8.00
RT12 J.Walker/R.Johnson 3.00 8.00
RT13 J.Reed/T.Carter 2.50 6.00
RT14 T.J.Duckett/L.Betts 3.00 8.00
RT15 J.Shockey/D.Graham 3.00 8.00
RQ16 Carr/Gaff/Steph/Walk 2.50 6.00
RQ17 Rams/Russ/Bryant/Willms 4.00 10.00
RQ18 Portis/Lelie/Morris/Davis 4.00 10.00
RQ19 Fost/Pepp/Crou/RandleEl 6.00 15.00
RQ20 Harr/Garr/McCwn/Davey 4.00 10.00
RQ21 Stall/Cald/Walker/Johns 4.00 10.00
RQ22 Reed/Cart/Duck/Betts 4.00 10.00

2002 Playoff Honors Player of the Week

ANNOUNCED PRINT RUN 100 SETS
*PANELIST/10: .8X TO 2X
1 Priest Holmes 2.00 5.00
2 Drew Bledsoe 2.50 6.00
3 Tom Brady 15.00 40.00
4 Shaun Alexander 2.00 5.00
5 Rich Gannon 2.50 6.00
6 Drew Brees 6.00 15.00
7 Marshall Faulk 2.50 6.00
8 Michael Vick 2.50 6.00
9 Brad Johnson 2.50 6.00
10 Rich Gannon 2.50 6.00
11 Donovan McNabb 2.50 6.00
12 Priest Holmes 2.00 5.00
13 LaDainian Tomlinson 3.00 8.00
14 Ricky Williams 2.50 6.00
15 Clinton Portis 3.00 8.00
16 Amani Toomer 2.00 5.00
17 Clinton Portis 3.00 8.00
18 Jeff Garcia 2.00 5.00
19 Steve McNair 2.50 6.00
20 Rich Gannon 2.50 6.00
21 Dexter Jackson 3.00 8.00

2003 Playoff Honors

Released in November of 2003, this set consists of 230 cards, including 100 veterans and 130 rookies. Rookies 101-150, found only in hobby packs, are serial numbered to 550. Rookies 151-200, found only in retail packs, are serial numbered to 200. Rookies 201-230 feature event worn jerseys and are serial numbered to 700. Each box contained two 10-pack mini-boxes. SRP was $6 per 6 card in pack.
COMP.SET w/o SP's (100) 7.50 20.00
1 Aaron Brooks .20 .50
2 Ahman Green .25 .60
3 Amani Toomer .20 .50
4 Anthony Thomas .25 .60
5 Antonio Bryant .20 .50
6 Antwaan Randle El .20 .50
7 Ashley Lelie .20 .50
8 Brad Johnson .25 .60
9 Brett Favre .60 1.50
10 Brian Urlacher .30 .75
11 Bruce Smith .25 .60
12 Chad Johnson .20 .50
13 Chad Pennington .20 .50
14 Charlie Garner .25 .60
15 Chris Chambers .20 .50
16 Clinton Portis .20 .50
17 Corey Dillon .20 .50
18 Curtis Martin .25 .60
19 Daunte Culpepper .25 .60
20 David Boston .20 .50
21 David Carr .20 .50
22 Deuce McAllister .25 .60
23 Donald Driver .25 .60
24 Donovan McNabb .25 .60
25 Donte Stallworth .20 .50
26 Drew Bledsoe .25 .60
27 Drew Brees .30 .75
28 Duce Staley .20 .50
29 Ed McCaffrey .25 .60
30 Eddie George .25 .60
31 Edgerrin James .25 .60
32 Emmitt Smith .50 1.25
33 Eric Moulds .20 .50
34 Fred Taylor .20 .50
35 Garrison Hearst .20 .50
36 Hines Ward .25 .60
37 Isaac Bruce .30 .75
38 Jabar Gaffney .20 .50
39 Jake Plummer .20 .50
40 Jamal Lewis .25 .60
41 Jay Fiedler .20 .50
42 Jeff Garcia .20 .50
43 Jeremy Shockey .20 .50
44 Jerome Bettis .30 .75
45 Jerry Porter .20 .50
46 Jerry Rice .60 1.50
47 Jevon Kearse .20 .50
48 Jimmy Smith .25 .60
49 Joe Horn .20 .50
50 Joey Harrington .20 .50
51 Josh Reed .20 .50
52 Julius Peppers .30 .75
53 Kendrell Bell .20 .50
54 Kerry Collins .20 .50
55 Keyshawn Johnson .30 .75
56 Kordell Stewart .20 .50
57 Koren Robinson .25 .60
58 Kurt Warner .25 .60
59 LaDainian Tomlinson .30 .75
60 Laveranues Coles .20 .50
61 Mark Brunell .25 .60
62 Marshall Faulk .25 .60
63 Marvin Harrison .25 .60
64 Matt Hasselbeck .20 .50
65 Michael Bennett .20 .60
66 Michael Strahan .25 .60
67 Michael Vick .25 .60
68 Mike Alstott .20 .50
69 Patrick Ramsey .25 .60
70 Peerless Price .20 .50
71 Peyton Manning .75 2.00
72 Plaxico Burress .20 .50
73 Priest Holmes .20 .50
74 Randy Moss .25 .60
75 Ray Lewis .30 .75
76 Rich Gannon .25 .60
77 Ricky Williams .25 .60
78 Rod Gardner .20 .50
79 Rod Smith .25 .60
80 Roy Williams .20 .50
81 Shaun Alexander .20 .50
82 Stephen Davis .20 .50
83 Steve McNair .25 .60
84 T.J. Duckett .20 .50
85 Terrell Owens .25 .60
86 Tiki Barber .25 .60
87 Tim Brown .30 .75
88 Tim Couch .20 .50
89 Todd Heap .20 .50
90 Tom Brady 1.25 3.00
91 Tommy Maddox .20 .50
92 Tony Gonzalez .25 .60
93 Torry Holt .25 .60
94 Travis Henry .20 .50
95 Trent Green .20 .50
96 Troy Brown .20 .50
97 Warren Sapp .25 .60
98 Warrick Dunn .20 .50
99 William Green .20 .50
100 Zach Thomas .25 .60
101 Chris Simms RC 1.25 3.00
102 Brooks Bollinger RC 1.50 4.00
103 Gibran Hamdan RC 1.25 3.00
104 Ken Dorsey RC 1.50 4.00
105 Jason Gesser RC 1.50 4.00
106 Brad Banks RC 1.50 4.00
107 Tony Romo RC 20.00 50.00
108 B.J. Askew RC 1.50 4.00
109 Domanick Davis RC 1.50 4.00
110 Lee Suggs RC 1.25 3.00
111 LaBrandon Toefield RC 1.25 3.00
112 Brock Forsey RC 1.50 4.00
113 Malaefou MacKenzie RC 1.25 3.00
114 Andrew Pinnock RC 1.50 4.00
115 Ahmaad Galloway RC 1.50 4.00
116 Tony Hollings RC 1.50 4.00
117 Charles Rogers RC 1.50 4.00
118 Billy McMullen RC 1.25 3.00
119 Shaun McDonald RC 1.50 4.00
120 Brandon Lloyd RC 2.00 5.00
121 Sam Aiken RC 1.50 4.00
122 Bobby Wade RC 1.50 4.00
123 Justin Gage RC 1.50 4.00
124 Adrian Madise RC 1.25 3.00
125 Jon Olinger RC 1.25 3.00
126 Doug Gabriel RC 1.50 4.00
127 J.R. Tolver RC 1.50 4.00
128 David Kircus RC 1.50 4.00
129 Zuriel Smith RC 1.25 3.00
130 LaTarence Dunbar RC 1.25 3.00
131 Arnaz Battle RC 2.00 5.00
132 Willie Ponder RC 1.25 3.00
133 Kareem Kelly RC 1.25 3.00
134 David Tyree RC 1.50 4.00
135 Keenan Howry RC 1.25 3.00
136 Taco Wallace RC 1.25 3.00
137 Walter Young RC 1.25 3.00
138 Talman Gardner RC 1.25 3.00
139 DeAndrew Rubin RC 1.25 3.00
140 Kevin Walter RC 3.00 8.00
141 Carl Ford RC 1.25 3.00
142 Travis Anglin RC 1.25 3.00
143 Ryan Hoag RC 1.25 3.00
144 Terrence Edwards RC 1.25 3.00
145 Bennie Joppru RC 1.25 3.00
146 L.J. Smith RC 2.00 5.00
147 Jason Witten RC 5.00 12.00
148 Andre Woolfolk RC 1.25 3.00
149 Nnamdi Asomugha RC 2.00 5.00
150 Troy Polamalu RC 15.00 30.00
151 Nate Hybl RC 3.00 8.00
152 Curt Anes RC 2.50 6.00
153 Avon Cobourne RC 2.50 6.00
154 Cecil Sapp RC 2.50 6.00
155 Casey Urlacher RC 4.00 10.00
156 Dwone Hicks RC 2.50 6.00
157 Jeremi Johnson RC 2.50 6.00
158 Kirk Farmer RC 3.00 8.00
159 James MacPherson RC 3.00 8.00
160 Chris Davis RC 3.00 8.00
161 Brandon Drumm RC 2.50 6.00
162 J.T. Wall RC 2.50 6.00
163 Casey Moore RC 2.50 6.00
164 Mike Seidman RC 2.50 6.00
165 Visanthe Shiancoe RC 4.00 10.00
166 George Wrighster RC 2.50 6.00
167 Dan Curley RC 2.50 6.00
168 Donald Lee RC 3.00 8.00
169 Aaron Walker RC 3.00 8.00
170 Trent Smith RC 3.00 8.00
171 Spencer Nead RC 2.50 6.00
172 Richard Angulo RC 2.50 6.00
173 Mike Pinkard RC 2.50 6.00
174 Johnathan Sullivan RC 2.50 6.00
175 Kevin Williams RC 4.00 10.00
176 Jimmy Kennedy RC 3.00 8.00
177 Ty Warren RC 3.00 8.00
178 William Joseph RC 2.50 6.00
179 Michael Haynes RC 2.50 6.00
180 Jerome McDougle RC 2.50 6.00
181 Calvin Pace RC 2.50 6.00
182 Tyler Brayton RC 3.00 8.00
183 Chris Kelsay RC 3.00 8.00
184 Osi Umenyiora RC 5.00 12.00
185 Alonzo Jackson RC 2.50 6.00
186 DeWayne White RC 2.50 6.00
187 Kenny Peterson RC 3.00 8.00
188 Nick Barnett RC 4.00 10.00
189 Boss Bailey RC 3.00 8.00
190 E.J. Henderson RC 3.00 8.00
191 Pisa Tinoisamoa RC 4.00 10.00
192 Sammy Davis RC 3.00 8.00
193 Charles Tillman RC 15.00 30.00
194 Eugene Wilson RC 4.00 10.00
195 Drayton Florence RC 4.00 10.00
196 Ricky Manning RC 3.00 8.00
197 Rashean Mathis RC 2.50 6.00
198 Ken Hamlin RC 4.00 10.00
199 Mike Doss RC 4.00 10.00
200 Julian Battle RC 3.00 8.00
201 Andre Johnson JSY RC 5.00 12.00
202 Anquan Boldin JSY RC 3.00 8.00
203 Artose Pinner JSY RC 2.00 5.00
204 Bethel Johnson JSY RC 2.00 5.00
205 Brian St.Pierre JSY RC 2.00 5.00
206 Bryant Johnson JSY RC 3.00 8.00
207 Byron Leftwich JSY RC 2.50 6.00
208 Carson Palmer JSY RC 4.00 10.00
209 Chris Brown JSY RC 2.00 5.00
210 Dallas Clark JSY RC 3.00 8.00
211 Dave Ragone JSY RC 2.00 5.00
212 DeWayne Robertson JSY RC 2.50 6.00
213 Justin Fargas JSY RC 3.00 8.00
214 Kelley Washington JSY RC 2.00 5.00
215 Kevin Curtis JSY RC 2.00 5.00
216 Kliff Kingsbury JSY RC 3.00 8.00
217 Kyle Boller JSY RC 2.00 5.00
218 Larry Johnson JSY RC 2.50 6.00
219 Marcus Trufant JSY RC 2.50 6.00
220 Musa Smith JSY RC 2.00 5.00
221 Nate Burleson JSY RC 2.50 6.00
222 Onterrio Smith JSY RC 2.00 5.00
223 Rex Grossman JSY RC 2.50 6.00
224 Seneca Wallace JSY RC 2.50 6.00
225 Taylor Jacobs JSY RC 2.00 5.00
226 Terrell Suggs JSY RC 2.50 6.00
227 Terence Newman JSY RC 3.00 8.00
228 Teyo Johnson JSY RC 2.50 6.00
229 Tyrone Calico JSY RC 2.00 5.00
230 Willis McGahee JSY RC 2.50 6.00

2003 Playoff Honors O's

*VETS 1-100: 4X TO 10X BASIC CARDS
1-100 VETERAN PRINT RUN 100
*ROOKIES 151-200: .6X TO 1.5X
151-200 ROOKIE PRINT RUN 50
*ROOKIE JSY 201-230: 1.2X TO 3X
201-230 JSY PRINT RUN 25
O's FOUND ONLY IN RETAIL PACKS

2003 Playoff Honors X's

*VETS 1-100: 2X TO 5X BASIC CARDS
1-100 VETERAN PRINT RUN 250
*ROOKIES 101-150: 1X TO 2.5X
101-150 ROOKIE PRINT RUN 100
*ROOKIE JSY 201-230: 1.2X TO 3X
201-230 JSY PRINT RUN 25
X's FOUND ONLY IN HOBBY PACKS
107 Tony Romo 40.00 100.00
150 Troy Polamalu 60.00 100.00

2003 Playoff Honors Rookie Hidden Gems Autographs

Randomly inserted in packs,this set features Playoff's unique pull out swatch of game worn jersey swatch containing an autograph directly on the swatch. The first 50 cards of the 700 jersey print run were signed.
FIRST 50 BASE CARDS SIGNED
201 Andre Johnson JSY 25.00 60.00
202 Anquan Boldin JSY 15.00 40.00
203 Artose Pinner JSY 10.00 25.00
204 Bethel Johnson JSY 10.00 25.00
205 Brian St.Pierre JSY 10.00 25.00
206 Bryant Johnson JSY 15.00 40.00
207 Byron Leftwich JSY 12.00 30.00
208 Carson Palmer JSY 25.00 60.00
209 Chris Brown JSY 10.00 25.00
210 Dallas Clark JSY 15.00 40.00
211 Dave Ragone JSY 10.00 25.00
212 DeWayne Robertson JSY 12.00 30.00
213 Justin Fargas JSY 15.00 40.00
214 Kelley Washington JSY 10.00 25.00
215 Kevin Curtis JSY 10.00 25.00
216 Kliff Kingsbury JSY 15.00 40.00
217 Kyle Boller JSY 10.00 25.00
218 Larry Johnson JSY 12.00 30.00
219 Marcus Trufant JSY 12.00 30.00
220 Musa Smith JSY 10.00 25.00
221 Nate Burleson JSY 12.00 30.00
222 Onterrio Smith JSY 10.00 25.00
223 Rex Grossman JSY 12.00 30.00
224 Seneca Wallace JSY 12.00 30.00
225 Taylor Jacobs JSY 10.00 25.00
226 Terrell Suggs JSY 25.00 50.00
227 Terence Newman JSY 15.00 40.00
228 Teyo Johnson JSY 12.00 30.00
229 Tyrone Calico JSY 10.00 25.00
230 Willis McGahee JSY 12.00 30.00

2003 Playoff Honors Alma Mater Materials

Randomly inserted in packs, this set features single, double, and triple player cards with swatches of their collegiate alma mater game used jerseys. Each card is serial numbered.
STATED PRINT RUN 25-400
AM1 Fred Taylor/400 4.00 10.00
AM2 Jevon Kearse/150 5.00 12.00
AM3 Michael Pittman/400 4.00 10.00
AM4 Ahman Green/250 5.00 12.00
AM5 Eddie George/150 6.00 15.00
AM6 Shaun Alexander/200 4.00 10.00
AM7 Terrell Davis/150 6.00 15.00
AM8 Frank Wycheck/400 4.00 10.00
AM9 Laveranues Coles/250 4.00 10.00
AM10 Edgerrin James/300 5.00 12.00
AM11 Reggie Wayne/400 5.00 12.00
AM12 Dan Morgan/400 5.00 12.00
AM13 Santana Moss/300 5.00 12.00
AM14 Jeremy Shockey/150 5.00 12.00
AM15 Clinton Portis/50 6.00 15.00
AM16 Tony Dorsett/25 20.00 50.00
AM16AU Tony Dorsett/25 AU 50.00 100.00
AM17 Earl Campbell/125 10.00 25.00
AM17AU Earl Campbell/125 AU 40.00 80.00
AM18 Ricky Williams/150 6.00 15.00
AM19 Drew Bledsoe/150 6.00 15.00
AM20 Doug Flutie/250 5.00 12.00
AM21 Curtis Martin/200 5.00 12.00
AM22 Anquan Boldin/350 4.00 10.00
AM23 Keyshawn Johnson/200 6.00 15.00
AM24 Tyrone Calico/400 4.00 10.00
AM25 Kyle Boller/200 4.00 10.00
AM26 F.Taylor/J.Kearse/100 5.00 12.00
AM27 A.Green/E.George/100 6.00 15.00
AM28 S.Alexander/T.Davis/100 6.00 15.00
AM29 E.James/C.Portis/100 6.00 15.00
AM30 S.Moss/J.Shockey/100 6.00 15.00
AM31 L.Coles/R.Wayne/100 6.00 15.00
AM32 Campbell/Ric.Will./100 10.00 25.00
AM33 D.Bledsoe/D.Flutie/100 6.00 15.00
AM34 C.Martin/A.Boldin/100 5.00 12.00
AM35 Key.Johnson/T.Calico/100 8.00 20.00
AM36 F.Taylor/S.Alex/T.Dav/25 15.00 40.00
AM37 A.Grn/Cmpbll/Ric.Will./25 25.00 60.00
AM38 James/Portis/Shock/25 15.00 40.00
AM39 Bledsoe/Flutie/Boller/25 15.00 40.00
AM40 Dorsett/Martin/Grge/25 25.00 60.00

2003 Playoff Honors Class Reunion Tandems

Randomly inserted in packs, this set features two game worn jersey swatches of players who are members of the same draft class. Each card is serial numbered to 150.
PRINT RUN 150 SERIAL #'d SETS
CRT1 E.Smith/J.Seau 10.00 25.00
CRT2 B.Favre/E.McCaffrey 12.00 30.00
CRT3 R.Smith/J.Smith 5.00 12.00
CRT4 D.Bledsoe/J.Bettis 6.00 15.00
CRT5 M.Faulk/I.Bruce 6.00 15.00
CRT6 T.Davis/C.Martin 5.00 12.00
CRT7 S.McNair/W.Sapp 5.00 12.00
CRT8 Key.Johnson/E.Moulds 6.00 15.00
CRT9 T.Owens/M.Harrison 5.00 12.00
CRT10 R.Lewis/Z.Thomas 6.00 15.00
CRT11 T.Gonzalez/T.Barber 5.00 12.00
CRT12 P.Manning/P.Holmes 15.00 40.00
CRT13 R.Moss/H.Ward 5.00 12.00
CRT14 A.Green/F.Taylor 5.00 12.00
CRT15 E.James/Ric.Williams 5.00 12.00
CRT16 D.McNabb/D.Culpepper 5.00 12.00
CRT17 T.Holt/D.Boston 5.00 12.00
CRT18 T.Brown/S.Sharpe 6.00 15.00
CRT19 A.Brooks/D.Driver 5.00 12.00
CRT20 L.Coles/C.Pennington 4.00 10.00
CRT21 J.Lewis/S.Alexander 5.00 12.00
CRT22 P.Burress/B.Urlacher 6.00 15.00
CRT23 M.Vick/D.Brees 6.00 15.00
CRT24 L.Tomlinson/D.McAllister 6.00 15.00
CRT25 K.Robinson/R.Gardner 5.00 12.00
CRT26 M.Bennett/T.Henry 4.00 10.00
CRT27 C.Chambers/K.Bell 4.00 10.00
CRT28 D.Carr/J.Harrington 4.00 10.00
CRT29 J.Shockey/C.Portis 4.00 10.00
CRT30 D.Stallworth/A.Randle El 4.00 10.00

2003 Playoff Honors Game Day Souvenirs Bronze

Randomly inserted in packs, the cards in this set features a game used jersey and football swatch. Each card is serial numbered to 150. There is also a Silver and Gold parallel to this set. The Silver parallel cards are serial numbered to 75, and the Gold parallel cards are serial numbered to 25.
BRONZE PRINT RUN 150
*SILVER/75: .5X TO 1.2X BRONZE/150
SILVER PRINT RUN 75 SER.#'d SETS
*GOLD/25: 1X TO 2.5X BRONZE/150
GOLD PRINT RUN 25 SER.#'d SETS
GDS1 Emmitt Smith 6.00 15.00
GDS2 Donovan McNabb 3.00 8.00
GDS3 Steve McNair 3.00 8.00
GDS4 Curtis Martin 3.00 8.00
GDS5 Edgerrin James 3.00 8.00
GDS6 Rich Gannon 3.00 8.00
GDS7 Kurt Warner 3.00 8.00
GDS8 Aaron Brooks 2.50 6.00
GDS9 LaDainian Tomlinson 4.00 10.00
GDS10 Peyton Manning 10.00 25.00
GDS11 David Boston 2.50 6.00
GDS12 Michael Vick 3.00 8.00

2003 Playoff Honors Jersey Quads

Randomly inserted in packs, each card in this set features four top NFL rookies along with an event used jersey swatch for each player. Each card is serial numbered to 250. A Football swatch parallel and a Football-Jersey dual swatch parallel was also produced.
JSY PRINT RUN 250 SER.#'d SETS
*FB/50: .5X TO 1.2X JSY QUAD/250
FOOTBALL STATED PRINT RUN 50
*JSY-FB/25: .8X TO 2X JSY QUAD/250
JSY-FOOTBALL STATED PRINT RUN 25
JQ1 Palm/Wash/Left/Clark 5.00 12.00
JQ2 LJ/Pinn/Burl/Smith 3.00 8.00
JQ3 A.Jhns/Rag/Brwn/Calic 6.00 15.00
JQ4 St.Pier/Wall/Gross/Jac 3.00 8.00
JQ5 Be.John/Bold/McGah/Curt 4.00 10.00
JQ6 Fargas/Johns/Boll/Smith 4.00 10.00
JQ7 King/Be.Jhn/Suggs/Nwmn 4.00 10.00

2003 Playoff Honors Jersey Tandems

Randomly inserted in packs, each card in this set features two top NFL rookies along with an event used jersey swatch for each player. A Football swatch parallel and a Football-Jersey dual swatch parallel was also produced.
*FB/100: .5X TO 1.2X JSY TANDEM
FOOTBALL STATED PRINT RUN 100
*JSY-FB/75: .6X TO 1.5X JSY TANDEM
JSY-FOOTBALL STATED PRINT RUN 75
JT1 C.Palmer/K.Washington 4.00 10.00
JT2 B.Leftwich/D.Clark 3.00 8.00
JT3 L.Johnson/A.Pinner 2.50 6.00
JT4 N.Burleson/O.Smith 2.50 6.00
JT5 A.Johnson/D.Ragone 5.00 12.00
JT6 C.Brown/T.Calico 2.00 5.00
JT7 B.St.Pierre/S.Wallace 2.50 6.00
JT8 R.Grossman/T.Jacobs 2.50 6.00
JT9 Br.Johnson/A.Boldin 3.00 8.00
JT10 W.McGahee/K.Curtis 2.50 6.00
JT11 J.Fargas/T.Johnson 3.00 8.00
JT12 K.Boller/M.Smith 2.00 5.00
JT13 K.Kingsbury/Be.Johnson 3.00 8.00
JT14 D.Robertson/T.Suggs 2.50 6.00
JT15 T.Newman/M.Trufant 3.00 8.00

2003 Playoff Honors Patches

Randomly inserted in packs, this set features game worn patches taken from the number section of the player's jersey. Each card is serial numbered to 75.
PATCH PRINT RUN 75 SER.#'d SETS
*PLATE/40-65: .5X TO 1.2X PATCH/75
*PLATE/30-38: .6X TO 1.5X PATCH/75
*PLATE/20-29: .8X TO 2X PATCH/75
PLATES PRINT RUN 1-65
*PLATE-PATCH/45: .6X TO 1.5X PATCH/75
*PLATE-PATCH/31-34: .8X TO 2X PATCH/75
*PLATE-PATCH/20-28: 1X TO 2.5X PATCH/75
PLATE-PATCH PRINT RUN 3-45
SERIAL #'d UNDER 20 NOT PRICED
PP1 Michael Vick 4.00 10.00
PP2 Brett Favre 10.00 25.00
PP3 Peyton Manning 12.00 30.00
PP4 Donovan McNabb 4.00 10.00
PP5 Daunte Culpepper 4.00 10.00
PP6 Jeff Garcia 3.00 8.00
PP7 David Carr 3.00 8.00
PP8 Joey Harrington 3.00 8.00
PP9 Kurt Warner 4.00 10.00
PP10 Drew Brees 5.00 12.00
PP11 Drew Bledsoe 4.00 10.00
PP12 Tom Brady 20.00 50.00
PP13 LaDainian Tomlinson 5.00 12.00
PP14 Deuce McAllister 4.00 10.00
PP15 Ricky Williams 4.00 10.00
PP16 Marshall Faulk 4.00 10.00
PP17 Edgerrin James 4.00 10.00
PP18 Travis Henry 3.00 8.00
PP19 Michael Bennett 3.00 8.00
PP20 Emmitt Smith 8.00 20.00
PP21 Priest Holmes 3.00 8.00
PP22 Clinton Portis 3.00 8.00
PP23 William Green 3.00 8.00
PP24 T.J. Duckett 3.00 8.00
PP25 Randy Moss 4.00 10.00
PP26 Jerry Rice 10.00 25.00
PP27 Terrell Owens 4.00 10.00
PP28 David Boston 3.00 8.00
PP29 Marvin Harrison 4.00 10.00
PP30 Tim Brown 5.00 12.00
PP31 Donte Stallworth 3.00 8.00
PP32 Ashley Lelie 3.00 8.00
PP33 Antwaan Randle El 3.00 8.00
PP34 Tony Gonzalez 4.00 10.00
PP35 Jeremy Shockey 3.00 8.00
PP36 Brian Urlacher 5.00 12.00
PP37 Kendrell Bell 3.00 8.00
PP38 Zach Thomas 4.00 10.00
PP39 Warren Sapp 4.00 10.00
PP40 Julius Peppers 5.00 12.00

2003 Playoff Honors Prime Signatures

Randomly inserted in packs, this set features authentic player autographs on foil stickers. Please note that K.Warner, J.Smith, M.Vick, C.Garner, C.Dillon, Z.Thomas, P.Price, R.Williams, J.Bettis, M.Alstott, S.Wallace, A.Boldin, Be.Johnson, N.Buleson, O.Smith, and K.Peterson were issued as exchange cards in packs with an expiration date of 5/1/2005. Corey Dillon (#PS10) and Kenny Peterson (#PS60) did not sign cards for the set and their Exchange cards were eventually redeemed by Playoff for other autographed cards.
STATED PRINT RUN 1-300
PS1 Kurt Warner/300 15.00 40.00
PS2 Eric Moulds/81 8.00 20.00
PS3 Marc Boerigter/95 8.00 20.00
PS4 Tim Brown/88 12.00 30.00
PS5 Ahman Green/75 12.00 30.00
PS7 Jimmy Smith/95 10.00 25.00
PS8 Michael Vick/70 15.00 40.00
PS9 Charlie Garner/75 12.00 30.00
PS11 Jamal Lewis/50 12.00 30.00
PS12 Jerry Rice/40 75.00 150.00
PS14 Shaun Alexander/70 10.00 25.00
PS15 Steve McNair/59 12.00 30.00
PS16 Tommy Maddox/70 10.00 25.00
PS17 Chris Chambers/60 10.00 25.00
PS18 Tom Jackson/55 12.00 30.00
PS19 David Carr/50 10.00 25.00
PS20 Deuce McAllister/50 12.00 30.00
PS21 Jeff Garcia/50 10.00 25.00
PS22 Torry Holt/50 12.00 30.00
PS23 Zach Thomas/95 10.00 25.00
PS24 Anthony Thomas/70 12.00 30.00
PS25 Eddie George/45 12.00 30.00
PS26 Marty Booker/45 10.00 25.00
PS27 Priest Holmes/45 10.00 25.00
PS28 Peerless Price/70 12.00 30.00
PS29 Ricky Williams/25 15.00 40.00
PS30 Brett Favre/21 125.00 250.00
PS31 Drew Bledsoe/20 15.00 40.00
PS33 Jerome Bettis/45 40.00 80.00
PS35 Kendrell Bell/20 10.00 25.00
PS36 LaDainian Tomlinson/20 40.00 80.00
PS37 Laveranues Coles/45 10.00 25.00
PS38 Dan Marino/32 100.00 200.00
PS39 Mike Alstott/45 10.00 25.00
PS40 Rod Gardner/45 10.00 25.00
PS41 Carson Palmer/20 20.00 50.00
PS42 Byron Leftwich/20 12.00 30.00
PS43 Kliff Kingsbury/300 6.00 15.00
PS44 Seneca Wallace/300 5.00 12.00
PS45 Anquan Boldin/300 6.00 15.00
PS46 Bethel Johnson/300 4.00 10.00
PS47 Nate Burleson/300 5.00 12.00
PS48 Onterrio Smith/300 4.00 10.00
PS49 Bryant Johnson/290 6.00 15.00
PS50 Terrence Edwards/300 4.00 10.00
PS51 Teyo Johnson/300 5.00 12.00
PS52 DeWayne White/300 4.00 10.00
PS53 Jerome McDougle/300 4.00 10.00
PS54 Terrell Suggs/300 10.00 25.00
PS55 Terence Newman/300 6.00 15.00
PS56 Brian St.Pierre/300 4.00 10.00
PS57 Artose Pinner/250 4.00 10.00
PS58 Cecil Sapp/300 4.00 10.00
PS59 Doug Gabriel/300 5.00 12.00

2003 Playoff Honors Rookie Year Jerseys

Randomly inserted in packs, this set features game used jersey swatches taken from the player's rookie year jersey. Each card is serial numbered to 100.
STATED PRINT RUN 100 SER.#'d SETS
RYJ1 Curtis Martin 3.00 8.00
RYJ2 Isaac Bruce 4.00 10.00
RYJ3 Keyshawn Johnson 4.00 10.00
RYJ4 Mark Brunell 3.00 8.00
RYJ5 Peyton Manning 10.00 25.00
RYJ6 Randy Moss 3.00 8.00
RYJ7 Ricky Williams 3.00 8.00
RYJ8 Tim Couch 2.50 6.00
RYJ9 LaDainian Tomlinson 4.00 10.00
RYJ10 Chris Chambers 2.50 6.00
RYJ11 Koren Robinson 3.00 8.00
RYJ12 Michael Vick 3.00 8.00
RYJ13 Anthony Thomas 3.00 8.00
RYJ14 David Terrell 2.50 6.00
RYJ15 Joey Harrington 2.50 6.00
RYJ16 Clinton Portis 2.50 6.00
RYJ17 Jeremy Shockey 2.50 6.00
RYJ18 David Carr 2.50 6.00
RYJ19 Antwaan Randle El 2.50 6.00
RYJ20 Donte Stallworth 2.50 6.00

2004 Playoff Honors

Playoff Honors initially released in mid-October 2004. The base set consists of 233-cards including 50-rookies inserted in hobby packs, 50-rookies inserted in retail packs and 33 rookie jersey cards serial numbered of 750. Hobby boxes contained 12-packs of 6-cards and carried an S.R.P. of $6 per pack. Two parallel sets and a variety of inserts can be found seeded in packs highlighted by the Rookie Hidden Gems Autographs inserts.
COMP.SET w/o SP's (100) 7.50 20.00
1 Anquan Boldin .25 .60
2 Emmitt Smith .60 1.50
3 Josh McCown .30 .75
4 Michael Vick .30 .75
5 Peerless Price .25 .60
6 T.J. Duckett .25 .60
7 Warrick Dunn .25 .60
8 Jamal Lewis .30 .75
9 Kyle Boller .25 .60
10 Ray Lewis .40 1.00
11 Drew Bledsoe .30 .75
12 Eric Moulds .25 .60
13 Travis Henry .25 .60
14 DeShaun Foster .30 .75
15 Jake Delhomme .25 .60
16 Steve Smith .40 1.00
17 Stephen Davis .25 .60
18 Brian Urlacher .40 1.00
19 Rex Grossman .25 .60
20 Thomas Jones .25 .60
21 Carson Palmer .30 .75
22 Chad Johnson .25 .60
23 Rudi Johnson .25 .60
24 Jeff Garcia .25 .60
25 Lee Suggs .30 .75
26 Keyshawn Johnson .30 .75
27 Quincy Carter .25 .60
28 Roy Williams S .25 .60
29 Jake Plummer .25 .60
30 Quentin Griffin .25 .60
31 Rod Smith .30 .75
32 Charles Rogers .25 .60
33 Joey Harrington .25 .60
34 Ahman Green .30 .75
35 Brett Favre .75 2.00
36 Javon Walker .25 .60
37 Andre Johnson .30 .75
38 David Carr .25 .60
39 Domanick Davis .25 .60
40 Edgerrin James .30 .75
41 Marvin Harrison .30 .75
42 Peyton Manning 1.00 2.50
43 Byron Leftwich .25 .60
44 Fred Taylor .25 .60
45 Jimmy Smith .30 .75
46 Priest Holmes .25 .60
47 Tony Gonzalez .30 .75
48 Trent Green .25 .60
49 A.J. Feeley .25 .60
50 Chris Chambers .25 .60
51 Ricky Williams .30 .75
52 Daunte Culpepper .30 .75
53 Michael Bennett .25 .60
54 Randy Moss .30 .75
55 Corey Dillon .25 .60
56 Deion Branch .25 .60
57 Tom Brady 1.50 4.00
58 Aaron Brooks .25 .60
59 Deuce McAllister .30 .75
60 Joe Horn .25 .60
61 Jeremy Shockey .25 .60
62 Michael Strahan .30 .75
63 Tiki Barber .30 .75
64 Chad Pennington .25 .60
65 Curtis Martin .30 .75
66 Santana Moss .30 .75
67 Jerry Rice .75 2.00
68 Justin Fargas .30 .75
69 Kerry Collins .25 .60
70 Tim Brown .40 1.00
71 Brian Westbrook .25 .60
72 Donovan McNabb .30 .75
73 Jevon Kearse .25 .60
74 Torrell Owens .30 .75
75 Duce Staley .25 .60
76 Hines Ward .30 .75
77 Jerome Bettis .40 1.00

78 Tommy Maddox .25 .60
79 Drew Brees .40 1.00
80 LaDainian Tomlinson .40 1.00
81 Kevan Barlow .25 .60
82 Tim Rattay .25 .60
83 Koren Robinson .25 .60
84 Matt Hasselbeck .25 .60
85 Shaun Alexander .25 .60
86 Isaac Bruce .40 1.00
87 Marc Bulger .25 .60
88 Marshall Faulk .30 .75
89 Torry Holt .30 .75
90 Brad Johnson .30 .75
91 Charlie Garner .30 .75
92 Keenan McCardell .25 .60
93 Chris Brown .25 .60
94 Derrick Mason .25 .60
95 Eddie George .30 .75
96 Steve McNair .30 .75
97 Clinton Portis .25 .60
98 LaVar Arrington .25 .60
99 Laveranues Coles .25 .60
100 Mark Brunell .30 .75
101 Drew Henson RC 1.25 3.00
102 Craig Krenzel RC 1.25 3.00
103 Andy Hall RC 1.25 3.00
104 Josh Harris RC 1.25 3.00
105 Jim Sorgi RC 1.50 4.00
106 Jeff Smoker RC 1.50 4.00
107 John Navarre RC 1.25 3.00
108 Cody Pickett RC 1.25 3.00
109 Casey Bramlet RC 1.25 3.00
110 Matt Mauck RC 1.25 3.00
111 B.J. Symons RC 1.25 3.00
112 Bradlee Van Pelt RC 1.50 4.00
113 Michael Turner RC 1.25 3.00
114 Troy Fleming RC 1.25 3.00
115 Adimchinobe Echemandu RC 1.50 4.00
116 Quincy Wilson RC 1.25 3.00
117 Derrick Ward RC 2.00 5.00
118 Bruce Perry RC 1.25 3.00
119 Brandon Miree RC 1.25 3.00
120 Carlos Francis RC 1.25 3.00
121 Samie Parker RC 1.25 3.00
122 Jerricho Cotchery RC 1.50 4.00
123 Ernest Wilford RC 1.50 4.00
124 Johnnie Morant RC 1.25 3.00
125 Maurice Mann RC 1.25 3.00
126 D.J. Hackett RC 1.25 3.00
127 Drew Carter RC 1.50 4.00
128 P.K. Sam RC 1.25 3.00
129 Jamaar Taylor RC 1.25 3.00
130 Ryan Krause RC 1.25 3.00
131 Triandos Luke RC 1.25 3.00
132 Jeris McIntyre RC 1.25 3.00
133 Clarence Moore RC 1.25 3.00
134 Mark Jones RC 1.25 3.00
135 Sloan Thomas RC 1.50 4.00
136 Jonathan Smith RC 1.25 3.00
137 Patrick Crayton RC 2.00 5.00
138 Derek Abney RC 1.25 3.00
139 Kris Wilson RC 1.50 4.00
140 Sean Taylor RC 8.00 20.00
141 Jonathan Vilma RC 1.50 4.00
142 Tommie Harris RC 1.50 4.00
143 D.J. Williams RC 2.00 5.00
144 Will Smith RC 1.50 4.00
145 Kenechi Udeze RC 1.50 4.00
146 Vince Wilfork RC 2.00 5.00
147 Marcus Tubbs RC 1.25 3.00
148 Ahmad Carroll RC 1.25 3.00
149 Jason Babin RC 2.00 5.00
150 Chris Gamble RC 1.25 3.00
151 Willie Parker RC 3.00 8.00
152 Darnell Dockett RC 3.00 8.00
153 Nate Poole RC 2.00 5.00
154 Matt Kegel RC 3.00 8.00
155 Kendrick Starling RC 2.00 5.00
156 Tramon Douglas RC 2.00 5.00
157 Ryan Dinwiddie RC 2.00 5.00
158 Brian Gaither RC 2.00 5.00
159 Ran Carthon RC 2.00 5.00
160 Derick Armstrong 2.00 5.00
161 Chris Cooley RC 2.50 6.00
162 Casey Clausen RC 2.50 6.00
163 Omar Jenkins RC 2.00 5.00
164 Justin Jenkins RC 2.00 5.00
165 Wes Welker RC 10.00 25.00
166 Terrance Copper RC 3.00 8.00
167 Jarrett Payton RC 2.50 6.00
168 Zamir Cobb RC 2.00 5.00
169 Derrick Knight RC 2.00 5.00
170 Romby Bryant RC 2.00 5.00
171 Larry Croom RC 2.00 5.00
172 Thomas Tapeh RC 2.50 6.00
173 Brock Lesnar RC 15.00 30.00
174 Richard Smith RC 2.00 5.00
175 Ricky Ray RC 3.00 8.00
176 John Booth RC 2.00 5.00
177 Huey Whittaker RC 2.00 5.00
178 Fred Russell RC 2.50 6.00
179 Ben Hartsock RC 2.00 5.00
180 Tim Euhus RC 2.00 5.00
181 Ricardo Colclough RC 2.00 5.00
182 Keiwan Ratliff RC 2.00 5.00
183 Shawntae Spencer RC 2.00 5.00
184 Joey Thomas RC 2.00 5.00
185 Keith Smith RC 2.00 5.00
186 Derrick Strait RC 2.00 5.00
187 Jeremy LeSueur RC 2.00 5.00
188 Matt Ware RC 3.00 8.00
189 Rich Gardner RC 2.50 6.00
190 Daryl Smith RC 2.00 5.00
191 Dontarrious Thomas RC 2.50 6.00
192 Courtney Watson RC 2.00 5.00
193 Karlos Dansby RC 2.50 6.00
194 Teddy Lehman RC 2.00 5.00
195 Michael Boulware RC 3.00 8.00
196 Bob Sanders RC 4.00 10.00
197 Travis LaBoy RC 2.50 6.00
198 Antwan Odom RC 2.00 5.00
199 Marquise Hill RC 2.00 5.00
200 Terry Johnson RC 2.00 5.00
201 Larry Fitzgerald JSY RC 5.00 12.00
202 DeAngelo Hall JSY RC 2.00 5.00
203 Matt Schaub JSY RC 1.25 3.00
204 Michael Jenkins JSY RC 1.25 3.00
205 Devard Darling JSY RC 1.25 3.00
206 J.P. Losman JSY RC 1.25 3.00
207 Lee Evans JSY RC 2.00 5.00
208 Keary Colbert JSY RC 1.25 3.00
209 Bernard Berrian JSY RC 1.25 3.00
210 Chris Perry JSY RC 1.25 3.00
211 Kellen Winslow JSY RC 1.25 3.00
212 Luke McCown JSY RC 1.25 3.00
213 Julius Jones JSY RC 1.25 3.00
214 Darius Watts JSY RC 1.25 3.00
215 Tatum Bell JSY RC 1.25 3.00
216 Kevin Jones JSY RC 1.50 4.00
217 Roy Williams JSY RC 1.25 3.00
218 Dunta Robinson JSY RC 1.25 3.00
219 Greg Jones JSY RC 1.25 3.00
220 Reggie Williams JSY RC 1.25 3.00
221 Mewelde Moore JSY RC 1.50 4.00
222 Ben Watson JSY RC 1.50 4.00
223 Cedric Cobbs JSY RC 1.25 3.00
224 Devery Henderson JSY RC 1.25 3.00
225 Eli Manning JSY RC 10.00 25.00
226 Robert Gallery JSY RC 1.50 4.00
227 B.Roethlisberger JSY RC 10.00 25.00
228 Philip Rivers JSY RC 4.00 10.00
229 Derrick Hamilton JSY RC 1.25 3.00
230 Rashaun Woods JSY RC 1.25 3.00
231 Steven Jackson JSY RC 2.00 5.00
232 Michael Clayton JSY RC 1.50 4.00
233 Ben Troupe JSY RC 1.25 3.00

2004 Playoff Honors O's

*VETS 1-100: 2.5X TO 6X BASIC CARDS
1-100 VETERAN PRINT RUN 175
*ROOKIES 151-200: .6X TO 1.5X BASE CARDS
151-200 ROOKIE PRINT RUN 100
*ROOKIE JSY 201-233: 1.5X TO 4X
201-233 ROOKIE JSY PRINT RUN 25
INSERTS IN RETAIL PACKS ONLY

2004 Playoff Honors X's

*VETS 1-100: 2X TO 5X BASE CARD HI
1-100 VETERAN PRINT RUN 199
*ROOKIES 101-150: .6X TO 1.5X
101-150 ROOKIE PRINT RUN 99
*ROOK.JSY 201-233: 1.5X TO 4X
201-233 ROOKIE JSY PRINT RUN 25
INSERTS IN HOBBY PACKS ONLY

2004 Playoff Honors Accolades

STATED PRINT RUN 1000 SER.#'d SETS
UNPRICED DIE CUT PRINT RUN 5
A1 Aaron Brooks 1.25 3.00
A2 Ahman Green 1.50 4.00
A3 Andre Johnson 1.50 4.00
A4 Anquan Boldin 1.25 3.00
A5 Barry Sanders 3.00 8.00
A6 Brett Favre 4.00 10.00
A7 Brian Urlacher 2.00 5.00
A8 Byron Leftwich 1.25 3.00
A9 Carson Palmer 1.50 4.00
A10 Chad Johnson 1.25 3.00
A11 Chad Pennington 1.25 3.00
A12 Chris Chambers 1.25 3.00
A13 Clinton Portis 1.25 3.00
A14 Daunte Culpepper 1.50 4.00
A15 David Carr 1.25 3.00
A16 Deuce McAllister 1.50 4.00
A17 Domanick Davis 1.25 3.00
A18 Donovan McNabb 1.50 4.00
A19 Drew Bledsoe 1.50 4.00
A20 Edgerrin James 1.50 4.00
A21 Emmitt Smith 3.00 8.00
A22 Fred Taylor 1.25 3.00
A23 Jack Lambert 2.50 6.00
A24 Jake Delhomme 1.25 3.00
A25 Jake Plummer 1.25 3.00
A26 Jamal Lewis 1.50 4.00
A27 Jeremy Shockey 1.25 3.00
A28 Jerry Rice 4.00 10.00
A29 Jim Brown 2.50 6.00
A30 Joe Namath 3.00 8.00
A31 Joey Harrington 1.25 3.00
A32 John Riggins 1.50 4.00
A33 LaDainian Tomlinson 2.00 5.00
A34 Marc Bulger 1.25 3.00
A35 Marshall Faulk 1.50 4.00
A36 Marvin Harrison 1.50 4.00
A37 Matt Hasselbeck 1.25 3.00
A38 Michael Vick 1.50 4.00
A39 Peyton Manning 5.00 12.00
A40 Priest Holmes 1.25 3.00
A41 Randy Moss 1.50 4.00
A42 Ray Lewis 2.00 5.00
A43 Rex Grossman 1.25 3.00
A44 Ricky Williams 1.50 4.00
A45 Shaun Alexander 1.25 3.00
A46 Steve McNair 1.50 4.00
A47 Terrell Owens 1.50 4.00
A48 Tom Brady 8.00 20.00
A49 Torry Holt 1.50 4.00
A50 Travis Henry 1.25 3.00

2004 Playoff Honors Alma Mater Materials

AM1-AM25 STATED ODDS 1:50
AM26-AM35 PRINT RUN 100 SER.#'d SETS
AM36-AM40 PRINT RUN 25 SER.#'d SETS
AM1 Aaron Brooks 2.50 6.00
AM2 Anquan Boldin 2.50 6.00
AM3 Laveranues Coles 2.50 6.00
AM4 Ahman Green 3.00 8.00
AM5 Barry Sanders 6.00 15.00
AM6 Ricky Williams 3.00 8.00
AM7 Drew Bledsoe 3.00 8.00
AM8 Reggie Williams 2.50 6.00
AM9 Marshall Faulk 3.00 8.00
AM10 Steven Jackson 4.00 10.00
AM11 DeShaun Foster 3.00 8.00
AM12 Keyshawn Johnson 3.00 8.00
AM13 Carson Palmer 3.00 8.00
AM14 Kyle Boller 2.50 6.00
AM15 Doug Flutie 3.00 8.00
AM16 Edgerrin James 3.00 8.00
AM17 Clinton Portis 2.50 6.00
AM18 Jeremy Shockey 2.50 6.00
AM19 Santana Moss 3.00 8.00
AM20 Curtis Martin 3.00 8.00
AM21 Andre Johnson 3.00 8.00
AM22 Herschel Walker 4.00 10.00
AM23 Shaun Alexander 2.50 6.00
AM24 Fred Taylor 2.50 6.00
AM25 Eddie George 6.00 15.00
AM26 A.Boldin/A.Brooks 3.00 8.00
AM27 B.Sanders/A.Green 8.00 20.00
AM28 D.Bledsoe/Re.Williams 4.00 10.00
AM29 M.Faulk/S.Jackson 5.00 12.00
AM30 D.Morgan/D.Foster 4.00 10.00
AM31 C.Palmer/K.Boller 4.00 10.00
AM32 E.James/An.Johnson 4.00 10.00
AM33 L.Coles/C.Portis 3.00 8.00
AM34 J.Shockey/S.Moss 4.00 10.00
AM35 H.Walker/S.Alexander 12.00 30.00
AM36 Brooks/Boldin/Coles 3.00 8.00
AM37 B.Sanders/Green/Ri.Will. 30.00 80.00
AM38 Bledsoe/Re.Will./S.Jackson 15.00 40.00
AM39 Palmer/Boller/Flutie 12.50 30.00
AM40 James/Shockey/Portis 12.50 30.00

2004 Playoff Honors Class Reunion

STATED PRINT RUN 1500 SER.#'d SETS
CR1 E.Smith/S.Sharpe 2.00 5.00
CR2 B.Favre/K.McCardell 2.50 6.00
CR3 J.Bettis/M.Brunell 1.25 3.00
CR4 M.Faulk/C.Garner 1.00 2.50
CR5 S.McNair/T.Law 1.25 3.00
CR6 T.Owens/R.Lewis 1.25 3.00
CR7 M.Harrison/E.Moulds 1.00 2.50
CR8 E.George/S.Davis 1.00 2.50
CR9 A.Green/M.Hasselbeck 1.00 2.50
CR10 P.Holmes/C.Woodson 1.25 3.00
CR11 P.Manning/F.Taylor 3.00 8.00
CR12 R.Moss/H.Ward 1.00 2.50
CR13 Ri.Williams/D.Boston 1.00 2.50
CR14 D.McNabb/J.Kearse 1.00 2.50
CR15 D.Culpepper/A.Brooks 1.00 2.50
CR16 E.James/T.Holt 1.00 2.50
CR17 T.Brady/C.Pennington 5.00 12.00
CR18 M.Bulger/S.Alexander .75 2.00
CR19 L.Arrington/L.Coles .75 2.00
CR20 J.Lewis/K.Bulluck 1.00 2.50
CR21 B.Urlacher/T.Jones 1.25 3.00
CR22 M.Vick/D.McAllister 1.00 2.50
CR23 L.Tomlinson/T.Henry 1.25 3.00
CR24 C.Portis/J.Shockey .75 2.00
CR25 J.Harrington/J.Walker .75 2.00
CR26 D.Carr/J.McCown 1.00 2.50
CR27 A.Johnson/C.Rogers 1.00 2.50
CR28 A.Boldin/T.Suggs .75 2.00
CR29 B.Leftwich/T.Calico 1.00 2.50
CR30 K.Boller/R.Grossman .75 2.00

2004 Playoff Honors Class Reunion Jerseys

STATED PRINT RUN 150 SER.#'d SETS
CR1 E.Smith/S.Sharpe 6.00 15.00
CR2 B.Favre/K.McCardell 8.00 20.00
CR3 J.Bettis/M.Brunell 4.00 10.00
CR4 M.Faulk/C.Garner 3.00 8.00
CR5 S.McNair/T.Law 4.00 10.00
CR6 T.Owens/R.Lewis 4.00 10.00
CR7 M.Harrison/E.Moulds 3.00 8.00
CR8 E.George/S.Davis 3.00 8.00
CR9 A.Green/M.Hasselbeck 3.00 8.00
CR10 P.Holmes/C.Woodson 4.00 10.00
CR11 P.Manning/F.Taylor 10.00 25.00
CR12 R.Moss/H.Ward 3.00 8.00
CR13 Ri.Williams/D.Boston 3.00 8.00
CR14 D.McNabb/J.Kearse 3.00 8.00
CR15 D.Culpepper/A.Brooks 3.00 8.00
CR16 E.James/T.Holt 3.00 8.00
CR17 T.Brady/C.Pennington 15.00 40.00
CR18 M.Bulger/S.Alexander 2.50 6.00
CR19 L.Arrington/L.Coles 2.50 6.00
CR20 J.Lewis/K.Bulluck 3.00 8.00
CR21 B.Urlacher/T.Jones 4.00 10.00
CR22 M.Vick/D.McAllister 3.00 8.00
CR23 L.Tomlinson/T.Henry 4.00 10.00
CR24 C.Portis/J.Shockey 2.50 6.00
CR25 J.Harrington/J.Walker 2.50 6.00
CR26 D.Carr/J.McCown 3.00 8.00
CR27 A.Johnson/C.Rogers 3.00 8.00
CR28 A.Boldin/T.Suggs 2.50 6.00
CR29 B.Leftwich/T.Calico 3.00 8.00
CR30 K.Boller/R.Grossman 2.50 6.00

2004 Playoff Honors Fans of the Game Silver

COMPLETE SET (6) 4.00 10.00
*HOLOGOLD: .5X TO 1.2X SILVER
234 Ray Romano Jets 1.00 2.50
234 Ray Romano Giants 1.00 2.50
235 Darius Rucker .75 2.00
236 Mel Kiper .75 2.00
237 Chris Mortensen .75 2.00
238 John O'Hurley .75 2.00

2004 Playoff Honors Fans of the Game Autographs

234 Ray Romano Giants SP 75.00 150.00
234 Ray Romano Jets SP 75.00 150.00
235 Darius Rucker 20.00 50.00
236A Mel Kiper 12.00 30.00
236B Mel Kiper The Viper 15.00 40.00
237 Chris Mortensen 12.00 30.00
238 John O'Hurley 12.00 30.00

2004 Playoff Honors Game Day

STATED PRINT RUN 1750 SER.#'d SETS
GS1 Ahman Green .75 2.00
GS2 Anquan Boldin .60 1.50
GS3 Brett Favre 2.00 5.00
GS4 Chad Johnson .60 1.50
GS5 Daunte Culpepper .75 2.00
GS6 Donovan McNabb .75 2.00
GS7 Eddie George .75 2.00
GS8 Emmitt Smith 1.50 4.00
GS9 Jamal Lewis .75 2.00
GS10 Jerry Rice 2.00 5.00
GS11 Koren Robinson .60 1.50
GS12 LaDainian Tomlinson 1.00 2.50
GS13 LaVar Arrington .60 1.50
GS14 Marc Bulger .60 1.50
GS15 Marshall Faulk .75 2.00
GS16 Matt Hasselbeck .60 1.50
GS17 Michael Vick .75 2.00
GS18 Randy Moss .75 2.00
GS19 Ray Lewis 1.00 2.50
GS20 Ricky Williams .75 2.00
GS21 Shaun Alexander .60 1.50
GS22 Stephen Davis .60 1.50
GS23 Steve McNair .75 2.00
GS24 Terrell Suggs .60 1.50
GS25 Torry Holt .75 2.00

2004 Playoff Honors Game Day Souvenirs

STATED PRINT RUN 250 SER.#'d SETS
*PRIME/25: 1X TO 2.5X DUAL/250
PRIME PRINT RUN 25 SER.#'d SETS
GS1 Ahman Green 3.00 8.00
GS2 Anquan Boldin 2.50 6.00
GS3 Brett Favre 8.00 20.00
GS4 Chad Johnson 2.50 6.00
GS5 Daunte Culpepper 3.00 8.00
GS6 Donovan McNabb 3.00 8.00
GS7 Eddie George 3.00 8.00
GS8 Emmitt Smith 6.00 15.00
GS9 Jamal Lewis 3.00 8.00
GS10 Jerry Rice 8.00 20.00
GS11 Koren Robinson 2.50 6.00
GS12 LaDainian Tomlinson 4.00 10.00
GS13 LaVar Arrington 2.50 6.00
GS14 Marc Bulger 2.50 6.00
GS15 Marshall Faulk 3.00 8.00
GS16 Matt Hasselbeck 2.50 6.00
GS17 Michael Vick 3.00 8.00
GS18 Randy Moss 3.00 8.00
GS19 Ray Lewis 4.00 10.00
GS20 Ricky Williams 3.00 8.00
GS21 Shaun Alexander 2.50 6.00
GS22 Stephen Davis 2.50 6.00
GS23 Steve McNair 3.00 8.00
GS24 Terrell Suggs 2.50 6.00
GS25 Torry Holt 3.00 8.00

2004 Playoff Honors Patches

PATCHES PRINT RUN 75 SER.#'d SETS
*PLATES/41-50: .5X TO 1.2X PATCHES
*PLATES/31-39: .6X TO 1.5X PATCHES
*PLATES/20-25: .8X TO 2X PATCHES
*PLATES/10-19: 1X TO 2.5X PATCHES
*PLATE&PATCH/10: 1.2X TO 3X PATCHES
PLATES AND PATCHES PRINT RUN 10
PP1 Anquan Boldin 4.00 10.00
PP2 Brett Favre 12.00 30.00
PP3 Brian Urlacher 6.00 15.00
PP4 Chad Johnson 4.00 10.00
PP5 Chad Pennington 4.00 10.00
PP6 Clinton Portis 4.00 10.00
PP7 Daunte Culpepper 5.00 12.00
PP8 Deuce McAllister 5.00 12.00
PP9 Donovan McNabb 5.00 12.00
PP10 Drew Bledsoe 5.00 12.00
PP11 Edgerrin James 5.00 12.00
PP12 Emmitt Smith 10.00 25.00
PP13 Jerry Rice 12.00 30.00
PP14 LaDainian Tomlinson 6.00 15.00
PP15 LaVar Arrington 4.00 10.00
PP16 Marc Bulger 4.00 10.00
PP17 Marshall Faulk 5.00 12.00
PP18 Matt Hasselbeck 4.00 10.00
PP19 Peyton Manning 15.00 40.00
PP20 Priest Holmes 4.00 10.00
PP21 Randy Moss 5.00 12.00
PP22 Ricky Williams 5.00 12.00
PP23 Shaun Alexander 4.00 10.00
PP24 Steve McNair 5.00 12.00
PP25 Tom Brady 25.00 60.00

2004 Playoff Honors Prime Signature Previews

STATED PRINT RUN 999 SER.#'d SETS
PS1 Aaron Brooks .75 2.00
PS2 Adam Vinatieri .75 2.00
PS3 Deacon Jones 1.25 3.00
PS4 Domanick Davis .75 2.00
PS5 Don Maynard 1.25 3.00
PS6 George Blanda 1.50 4.00
PS7 Herschel Walker 1.50 4.00
PS8 Jack Lambert 2.00 5.00
PS9 Jim Brown 2.00 5.00
PS10 Jim Plunkett 1.25 3.00
PS11 Joe Greene 1.50 4.00
PS12 Joe Namath 2.50 6.00
PS13 L.C. Greenwood 1.00 2.50
PS14 Laveranues Coles .75 2.00
PS15 Leroy Kelly 1.25 3.00
PS16 Mel Blount 1.25 3.00
PS17 Michael Strahan 1.00 2.50
PS18 Paul Warfield 1.25 3.00
PS19 Richard Dent 1.00 2.50
PS20 Sonny Jurgensen 1.25 3.00
PS21 Steve Smith 1.25 3.00
PS22 Tom Brady 5.00 12.00
PS23 Ernest Wilford 1.00 2.50
PS24 Philip Rivers 1.50 4.00
PS25 Samie Parker .75 2.00

2004 Playoff Honors Prime Signature Previews Autographs

STATED PRINT RUN 25-300
PS1 Aaron Brooks/25 10.00 25.00
PS2 Adam Vinatieri/200 30.00 60.00
PS3 Deacon Jones/125 12.00 30.00
PS4 Domanick Davis/300 6.00 15.00
PS5 Don Maynard/100 12.00 30.00
PS7 Herschel Walker/25 20.00 50.00
PS8 Jack Lambert/25 40.00 100.00
PS9 Jim Brown/34 40.00 80.00
PS10 Jim Plunkett/25 15.00 40.00
PS11 Joe Greene/25 40.00 80.00
PS12 Joe Namath/70 50.00 100.00
PS14 Laveranues Coles/100 8.00 20.00
PS15 Leroy Kelly/206 15.00 40.00
PS17 Michael Strahan/25 12.00 30.00
PS18 Paul Warfield/25 15.00 40.00
PS20 Sonny Jurgensen/25 15.00 40.00
PS21 Steve Smith/300 10.00 25.00
PS22 Tom Brady/25 150.00 250.00
PS23 Ernest Wilford/300 8.00 20.00
PS24 Philip Rivers/300 60.00 125.00
PS25 Samie Parker/300 6.00 15.00

2004 Playoff Honors Rookie Hidden Gems Autographs

STATED PRINT RUN 50 SER.#'d SETS
201 Larry Fitzgerald JSY 40.00 100.00
202 DeAngelo Hall JSY 20.00 50.00
203 Matt Schaub JSY 12.00 30.00
204 Michael Jenkins JSY 12.00 30.00
205 Devard Darling JSY 12.00 30.00
206 J.P. Losman JSY 12.00 30.00
207 Lee Evans JSY 20.00 50.00
208 Keary Colbert JSY 12.00 30.00
209 Bernard Berrian JSY 12.00 30.00
210 Chris Perry JSY 12.00 30.00
211 Kellen Winslow Jr. JSY 12.00 30.00
212 Luke McCown JSY 12.00 30.00
213 Julius Jones JSY 12.00 30.00
214 Darius Watts JSY 12.00 30.00
215 Tatum Bell JSY 12.00 30.00
216 Kevin Jones JSY 15.00 40.00
217 Roy Williams WR JSY 12.00 30.00
218 Dunta Robinson JSY 12.00 30.00
219 Greg Jones JSY 12.00 30.00
220 Reggie Williams JSY 12.00 30.00
221 Mewelde Moore JSY 15.00 40.00
222 Ben Watson JSY 15.00 40.00
223 Cedric Cobbs JSY 12.00 30.00
224 Devery Henderson JSY 12.00 30.00
225 Eli Manning JSY 100.00 200.00
226 Robert Gallery JSY 15.00 40.00
227 Ben Roethlisberger JSY 150.00 300.00
228 Philip Rivers JSY 50.00 100.00
229 Derrick Hamilton JSY 12.00 30.00
230 Rashaun Woods JSY 12.00 30.00
231 Steven Jackson JSY 20.00 50.00
232 Michael Clayton JSY 15.00 40.00
233 Ben Troupe JSY 12.00 30.00

2004 Playoff Honors Rookie Quad

STATED PRINT RUN 1250 SER.#'d SETS
RQ1 E.Mann/J.Jones/Clayt/Colb 6.00 15.00
RQ2 Fitzg/Hall/Jenkins/Schaub 3.00 8.00
RQ3 Rivers/Hender/Bell/Watts 2.50 6.00
RQ4 Roeth/Darl/Win/McCwn 6.00 15.00
RQ5 K.Jones/Ro.Will/Berr/Moore 1.00 2.50
RQ6 G.Jones/Re.Will/Rob/Trpe .75 2.00
RQ7 Losman/Evans/Cobbs/Wats 1.25 3.00
RQ8 S.Jack/Perry/Woods/Hamil 1.25 3.00

2004 Playoff Honors Rookie Quad Jerseys

JERSEY PRINT RUN 250 SER.#'d SETS
*FOOTBALL/75: .6X TO 1.5X JSY/250
FOOTBALLS PRINT RUN 75 SER.#'d SETS
*JSY-FB/25: 1X TO 2.5X QUAD JSY/250
JSY/FB PRINT RUN 25 SER.#'d SETS
RQ1 E.Mann/J.Jones/Clayt/Colb 6.00 15.00
RQ2 Fitzg/Hall/Jenkins/Schaub 10.00 25.00
RQ3 Rivers/Hender/Bell/Watts 8.00 20.00
RQ4 Roeth/Drlng/Wins/McCwn 8.00 20.00
RQ5 K.Jones/Ro.Will/Berr/Moore 3.00 8.00
RQ6 G.Jones/Re.Will/Rob/Trpe 2.50 6.00
RQ7 Losman/Evans/Cobbs/Wats 4.00 10.00
RQ8 S.Jack/Perry/Woods/Hamil 4.00 10.00

2004 Playoff Honors Rookie Tandem

STATED ODDS 1:13
RT1 E.Manning/J.Jones 4.00 10.00
RT2 M.Clayton/K.Colbert .60 1.50
RT3 L.Fitzgerald/D.Hall 2.00 5.00
RT4 M.Jenkins/M.Schaub .50 1.25
RT5 P.Rivers/D.Henderson 1.50 4.00
RT6 T.Bell/D.Watts .50 1.25
RT7 B.Roethlisberger/D.Darling 4.00 10.00
RT8 K.Winslow Jr./L.McCown .50 1.25
RT9 K.Jones/Ro.Williams .60 1.50
RT10 B.Berrian/M.Moore .60 1.50
RT11 G.Jones/Re.Williams .50 1.25
RT12 D.Robinson/B.Troupe .75 2.00
RT13 J.P.Losman/L.Evans .75 2.00
RT14 C.Cobbs/B.Watson .60 1.50
RT15 S.Jackson/C.Perry .75 2.00
RT16 R.Woods/D.Hamilton .50 1.25

2004 Playoff Honors Rookie Tandem Jerseys

STATED ODDS 1:68
*FOOTBALL/125: .6X TO 1.5X TANDEM JSY
FOOTBALLS PRINT RUN 125 SER.#'d SETS
*JSY-FB/50: .8X TO 2X TANDEM JSY
JERSEY AND FOOTBALL PRINT RUN 50
RT1 E.Manning/J.Jones 6.00 15.00
RT2 M.Clayton/K.Colbert 2.50 6.00
RT3 L.Fitzgerald/D.Hall 8.00 20.00
RT4 M.Jenkins/M.Schaub 2.00 5.00
RT5 P.Rivers/D.Henderson 6.00 15.00
RT6 T.Bell/D.Watts 2.00 5.00
RT7 B.Roethlisberger/D.Darling 10.00 25.00
RT8 K.Winslow Jr./L.McCown 2.00 5.00
RT9 K.Jones/Ro.Williams WR 2.50 6.00
RT10 B.Berrian/M.Moore 2.50 6.00
RT11 G.Jones/Re.Williams 2.00 5.00
RT12 D.Robinson/B.Troupe 2.00 5.00
RT13 J.P.Losman/L.Evans 3.00 8.00
RT14 C.Cobbs/B.Watson 2.50 6.00
RT15 S.Jackson/C.Perry 3.00 8.00
RT16 R.Woods/D.Hamilton 2.00 5.00

2004 Playoff Honors Rookie Year

STATED ODDS 1:12
RY1 Curtis Martin 1.00 2.50
RY2 David Carr .75 2.00
RY3 Jeremy Shockey .75 2.00
RY4 Joey Harrington .75 2.00
RY5 John Riggins 1.00 2.50
RY6 Koren Robinson .75 2.00
RY7 LaDainian Tomlinson 1.25 3.00
RY8 Mark Brunell 1.00 2.50
RY9 Keyshawn Johnson 1.00 2.50
RY10 Peyton Manning 3.00 8.00
RY11 Randy Moss 1.00 2.50
RY12 Ricky Williams 1.00 2.50
RY13 Roy Williams S .75 2.00
RY14 Quincy Carter .75 2.00
RY15 Andre Johnson 1.00 2.50
RY16 Anquan Boldin .75 2.00
RY17 Byron Leftwich .75 2.00
RY18 Kyle Boller .75 2.00
RY19 Rex Grossman .75 2.00
RY20 Terrell Suggs .75 2.00

2004 Playoff Honors Rookie Year Jerseys

STATED PRINT RUN 150 SER.#'d SETS
RY1 Curtis Martin 3.00 8.00
RY2 David Carr 2.50 6.00
RY3 Jeremy Shockey 2.50 6.00
RY4 Joey Harrington 2.50 6.00
RY5 John Riggins 3.00 8.00
RY6 Koren Robinson 2.50 6.00
RY7 LaDainian Tomlinson 4.00 10.00
RY8 Mark Brunell 3.00 8.00
RY9 Keyshawn Johnson 3.00 8.00
RY10 Peyton Manning 10.00 25.00
RY11 Randy Moss 3.00 8.00
RY12 Ricky Williams 3.00 8.00
RY13 Roy Williams S 2.50 6.00
RY14 Quincy Carter 2.50 6.00
RY15 Andre Johnson 3.00 8.00
RY16 Anquan Boldin 2.50 6.00
RY17 Byron Leftwich 2.50 6.00
RY18 Kyle Boller 2.50 6.00
RY19 Rex Grossman 2.50 6.00
RY20 Terrell Suggs 2.50 6.00

2005 Playoff Honors

This 229-card set was released in October, 2005. The set was issued through the hobby in six-card packs with an $5 SRP which came 12 packs to a box. Cards numbered 1-99 feature veterans sequenced in alphabetical order by team while cards numbered 101-229 all feature rookies. In that rookie grouping, cards numbered 201-229 all have a player-worn swatch. The rookies are split up thusly: Cards numbered 101-150 were issued to a stated print run of 699 serial numbered packs; cards numbered 151-200 were issued to a stated print run of 399 serial numbered sets and cards numbered 201-229 were issued to a stated print run of 750 serial numbered sets.

COMP.SET w/o SP's (100) 7.50 20.00
101-150 INSERTED IN HOBBY PACKS
101-150 PRINT RUN 699 SER.#'d SETS
151-200 INSERTED IN RETAIL PACKS
151-200 PRINT RUN 399 SER.#'d SETS
ROOKIE JSY PRINT RUN 750 SER.#'d SETS
1 Anquan Boldin .25 .60
2 Larry Fitzgerald .40 1.00
3 Kurt Warner .30 .75
4 Michael Vick .30 .75
5 Alge Crumpler .30 .75
6 Warrick Dunn .25 .60
7 Jamal Lewis .30 .75
8 Kyle Boller .25 .60
9 Ray Lewis .40 1.00
10 Derrick Mason .25 .60
11 Eric Moulds .25 .60
12 J.P. Losman .25 .60
13 Willis McGahee .25 .60
14 Jake Delhomme .25 .60
15 Steve Smith .40 1.00
16 DeShaun Foster .30 .75
17 Rex Grossman .25 .60
18 Brian Urlacher .40 1.00
19 Muhsin Muhammad .25 .60
20 Carson Palmer .30 .75
21 Chad Johnson .25 .60
22 Rudi Johnson .25 .60
23 Lee Suggs .25 .60
24 Trent Dilfer .25 .60
25 Reuben Droughns .25 .60
26 Drew Bledsoe .30 .75
27 Julius Jones .25 .60
28 Keyshawn Johnson .30 .75
29 Roy Williams S .25 .60
30 Ashley Lelie .25 .60
31 Jake Plummer .25 .60
32 Rod Smith .30 .75
33 Tatum Bell .25 .60
34 Joey Harrington .25 .60
35 Kevin Jones .25 .60
36 Roy Williams WR .25 .60
37 Ahman Green .30 .75
38 Brett Favre .75 2.00
39 Javon Walker .25 .60
40 Andre Johnson .30 .75
41 David Carr .25 .60
42 Domanick Davis .25 .60
43 Marvin Harrison .30 .75
44 Edgerrin James .30 .75
45 Peyton Manning 1.00 2.50
46 Reggie Wayne .30 .75
47 Fred Taylor .25 .60
48 Byron Leftwich .25 .60
49 Jimmy Smith .30 .75
50 Priest Holmes .25 .60
51 Tony Gonzalez .30 .75
52 Trent Green .25 .60
53 A.J. Feeley .25 .60
54 Chris Chambers .25 .60
55 Daunte Culpepper .30 .75
56 Nate Burleson .25 .60
57 Michael Bennett .25 .60
58 Corey Dillon .25 .60
59 Deion Branch .25 .60
60 Tedy Bruschi .30 .75
61 Tom Brady 1.50 4.00
62 Aaron Brooks .25 .60
63 Deuce McAllister .30 .75
64 Joe Horn .25 .60
65 Eli Manning .60 1.50
66 Tiki Barber .30 .75
67 Plaxico Burress .25 .60
68 Jeremy Shockey .25 .60
69 Chad Pennington .25 .60
70 Curtis Martin .30 .75
71 Laveranues Coles .25 .60
72 Kerry Collins .25 .60
73 Randy Moss .30 .75
74 LaMont Jordan .30 .75
75 Brian Westbrook .25 .60
76 Donovan McNabb .30 .75
77 Terrell Owens .30 .75
78 Ben Roethlisberger .60 1.50
79 Hines Ward .30 .75
80 Duce Staley .25 .60
81 Jerome Bettis .40 1.00
82 Drew Brees .40 1.00
83 LaDainian Tomlinson .40 1.00
84 Antonio Gates .40 1.00
85 Kevan Barlow .25 .60
86 Brandon Lloyd .25 .60
87 Darrell Jackson .25 .60
88 Matt Hasselbeck .25 .60
89 Shaun Alexander .25 .60
90 Marc Bulger .25 .60
91 Torry Holt .30 .75
92 Steven Jackson .25 .60
93 Brian Griese .25 .60
94 Michael Clayton .25 .60
95 Drew Bennett .30 .75
96 Steve McNair .30 .75
97 Chris Brown .25 .60
98 Clinton Portis .25 .60
99 LaVar Arrington .25 .60
100 Santana Moss .30 .75
101 Cedric Benson RC 1.25 3.00
102 Mike Williams 1.50 4.00
103 DeMarcus Ware RC 4.00 10.00
104 Shawne Merriman RC 2.00 5.00
105 Thomas Davis RC 1.25 3.00
106 Derrick Johnson RC 1.50 4.00
107 David Pollack RC 1.25 3.00
108 Erasmus James RC 1.25 3.00
109 Marcus Spears RC 1.25 3.00
110 Fabian Washington RC 1.25 3.00
111 Aaron Rodgers RC 20.00 40.00
112 Marlin Jackson RC 1.25 3.00
113 Heath Miller RC 2.50 6.00
114 Alex Smith TE RC 1.25 3.00
115 Chris Henry RC 1.50 4.00
116 David Greene RC 1.25 3.00
117 Brandon Jones RC 1.50 4.00
118 Marion Barber RC 1.25 3.00
119 Brandon Jacobs RC 1.50 4.00
120 Jerome Mathis RC 2.00 5.00
121 Craphonso Thorpe RC 1.25 3.00
122 Manuel White RC 1.50 4.00
123 Alvin Pearman RC 1.25 3.00
124 Darren Sproles RC 2.00 5.00
125 Fred Gibson RC 1.25 3.00
126 Roydell Williams RC 1.50 4.00
127 Airese Currie RC 1.25 3.00
128 Damien Nash RC 1.50 4.00
129 Dan Orlovsky RC 1.25 3.00
130 Adrian McPherson RC 1.25 3.00
131 Larry Brackins RC 1.25 3.00
132 Rasheed Marshall RC 1.50 4.00
133 Cedric Houston RC 2.00 5.00
134 Chad Owens RC 1.25 3.00
135 Tab Perry RC 1.25 3.00
136 Dante Ridgeway RC UER 1.25 3.00
137 Craig Bragg RC 1.25 3.00
138 Deandra Cobb RC 1.25 3.00
139 Derek Anderson RC 1.50 4.00
140 Travis Johnson RC 1.25 3.00
141 Paris Warren RC 1.50 4.00
142 LeRon McCoy RC 1.25 3.00
143 James Kilian RC 1.25 3.00
144 Matt Cassel RC 1.25 3.00
145 Lionel Gates RC 1.25 3.00
146 Harry Williams RC 1.50 4.00
147 Anthony Davis RC 1.25 3.00
148 Noah Herron RC 1.25 3.00
149 Ryan Fitzpatrick RC 2.00 5.00
150 J.R. Russell RC 1.25 3.00
151 Cole Magner RC 1.50 4.00
152 Luis Castillo RC 2.00 5.00
153 Mike Patterson RC 1.50 4.00
154 Brodney Pool RC 2.00 5.00
155 Barrett Ruud RC 2.00 5.00
156 Shaun Cody RC 2.00 5.00
157 Stanford Routt RC 2.00 5.00
158 Josh Bullocks RC 2.00 5.00
159 Kevin Burnett RC 2.00 5.00
160 Corey Webster RC 2.00 5.00
161 Lofa Tatupu RC 2.00 5.00
162 Matt Roth RC 1.50 4.00
163 Mike Nugent RC 2.00 5.00
164 Odell Thurman RC 2.50 6.00
165 Ronald Bartell RC 2.00 5.00
166 Nick Collins RC 2.50 6.00
167 Dan Cody RC 1.50 4.00
168 Darrent Williams RC 2.50 6.00
169 Justin Miller RC 1.50 4.00
170 Jerome Collins RC 2.00 5.00
171 Justin Green RC 2.50 6.00
172 Eric Green RC 1.50 4.00
173 Joel Dreessen RC 2.00 5.00
174 Bo Scaife RC 2.00 5.00
175 Antonio Perkins RC 2.00 5.00
176 Nehemiah Broughton RC 2.00 5.00
177 Patrick Estes RC 1.50 4.00
178 Billy Bajema RC 1.50 4.00
179 Madison Hedgecock RC 2.50 6.00
180 Roscoe Crosby RC 1.50 4.00
181 Kendrick Mosley RC 1.50 4.00
182 Tyson Thompson RC 1.50 4.00
183 Fred Amey RC 1.50 4.00
184 Brock Berlin RC 1.50 4.00
185 Gino Guidugli RC 1.50 4.00
186 Walter Reyes RC 1.50 4.00
187 Lydell Ross RC 2.00 5.00
188 Carlyle Holiday RC 2.00 5.00
189 Bryan Randall RC 2.00 5.00
190 Derrick Tinsley RC 2.00 5.00
191 Ryan Grant RC 15.00 40.00
192 Bobby Purify RC 2.00 5.00
193 Leonard Weaver RC 1.50 4.00
194 Vincent Fuller RC 2.00 5.00
195 Tony Brown RC 2.00 5.00
196 Zach Tuiasosopo RC 1.50 4.00
197 Craig Ochs RC 2.00 5.00
198 Ruvell Martin RC 2.50 6.00
199 Manuel Wright RC 2.00 5.00
200 Travis Daniels RC 2.00 5.00
201 Adam Jones JSY RC 2.00 5.00
202 Alex Smith QB JSY RC 10.00 25.00
203 Andrew Walter JSY RC 2.00 5.00
204 Antrel Rolle JSY RC 3.00 8.00
205 Braylon Edwards JSY RC 2.00 5.00
206 Cadillac Williams JSY RC 2.00 5.00
207 Carlos Rogers JSY RC 3.00 8.00
208 Charlie Frye JSY RC 2.00 5.00
209 Ciatrick Fason JSY RC 2.00 5.00
210 Courtney Roby JSY RC 2.00 5.00
211 Eric Shelton JSY RC 2.00 5.00
212 Frank Gore JSY RC 6.00 15.00
213 J.J. Arrington JSY RC 2.50 6.00
214 Jason Campbell JSY RC 2.00 5.00
215 Kyle Orton JSY RC 2.00 5.00
216 Mark Bradley JSY RC 2.00 5.00
217 Mark Clayton JSY RC 2.00 5.00
218 Matt Jones JSY RC 2.00 5.00
219 Maurice Clarett JSY 2.00 5.00
220 Reggie Brown JSY RC 2.00 5.00
221 Ronnie Brown JSY RC 2.50 6.00
222 Roddy White JSY RC 3.00 8.00
223 Ryan Moats JSY RC 2.00 5.00
224 Roscoe Parrish JSY RC 2.00 5.00
225 Stefan LeFors JSY RC 2.00 5.00
226 Terrence Murphy JSY RC 2.00 5.00
227 Troy Williamson JSY RC 2.00 5.00
228 Vernand Morency JSY RC 2.00 5.00
229 Vincent Jackson JSY RC 3.00 8.00

2005 Playoff Honors O's

*VETERANS: 2X TO 5X BASIC CARDS
1-100 PRINT RUN 150 SER.#'d SETS
*ROOKIES 151-200: .8X TO 2X BASIC CARDS
151-200 PRINT RUN 99 SER.#'d SETS
*JSY 201-229: 1.5X TO 4X BASIC JSYs
201-229 JSY PRINT RUN 25 SER.#'d SETS
O's INSERTED IN RETAIL PACKS ONLY
191 Ryan Grant 15.00 40.00

2005 Playoff Honors Vanguard

*VETERANS 1-100: 2.5X TO 6X BASIC CARDS
1-100 PRINT RUN 99 SER.#'d SETS
*ROOKIES 151-200: 1X TO 2.5X BASIC CARDS
151-200 PRINT RUN 50 SER.#'d SETS
VANGUARD INSERTED IN BLASTER PACKS
191 Ryan Grant 20.00 50.00

2005 Playoff Honors X's

*VETERANS 1-100: 1.5X TO 4X BASIC CARDS
1-100 PRINT RUN 299 SER.#'d SETS
*ROOKIES 101-150: .8X TO 2X BASIC CARDS
101-150 PRINT RUN 99 SER.#'d SETS
*JSY 201-229: 1.5X TO 4X BASIC JSYs
201-229 JSY PRINT RUN 25 SER.#'d SETS
X's INSERTED IN HOBBY PACKS ONLY

2005 Playoff Honors Accolades

STATED PRINT RUN 699 SER.#'d SETS
A1 Alex Smith QB 3.00 8.00
A2 Antonio Gates 1.25 3.00
A3 Ben Roethlisberger 2.00 5.00
A4 Braylon Edwards .75 2.00
A5 Brett Favre 2.50 6.00
A6 Brian Urlacher 1.25 3.00
A7 Byron Leftwich .75 2.00
A8 Cadillac Williams .75 2.00
A9 Carson Palmer 1.00 2.50
A10 Cedric Benson .75 2.00
A11 Chad Pennington .75 2.00
A12 Clinton Portis .75 2.00
A13 Corey Dillon .75 2.00
A14 Curtis Martin 1.00 2.50
A15 Daunte Culpepper 1.00 2.50
A16 David Carr .75 2.00
A17 Deion Sanders 1.00 2.50
A18 Deuce McAllister 1.00 2.50
A19 Domanick Davis .75 2.00
A20 Donovan McNabb 1.00 2.50
A21 Edgerrin James 1.00 2.50
A22 Eli Manning 2.00 5.00
A23 J.P. Losman .75 2.00
A24 Jake Delhomme .75 2.00
A25 Jake Plummer .75 2.00
A26 Jamal Lewis 1.00 2.50
A27 Javon Walker .75 2.00
A28 Jerome Bettis 1.25 3.00
A29 Jerry Rice 2.50 6.00
A30 Jim Brown 1.50 4.00
A31 Joe Montana 4.00 10.00
A32 Joe Namath 2.00 5.00
A33 Julius Jones .75 2.00
A34 Kevin Jones .75 2.00
A35 LaDainian Tomlinson 1.25 3.00
A36 Larry Fitzgerald 1.25 3.00
A37 LaVar Arrington .75 2.00
A38 Marc Bulger .75 2.00
A39 Matt Hasselbeck .75 2.00
A40 Michael Vick 1.00 2.50
A41 Peyton Manning 3.00 8.00
A42 Priest Holmes .75 2.00
A43 Randy Moss 1.00 2.50
A44 Ronnie Brown 1.00 2.50
A45 Rudi Johnson .75 2.00
A46 Roy Williams WR .75 2.00
A47 Steven Jackson .75 2.00
A48 Terrell Owens 1.00 2.50
A49 Tom Brady 5.00 12.00
A50 Willis McGahee .75 2.00

2005 Playoff Honors Alma Mater Materials

DUAL PRINT RUN 100 SER.#'d SETS
OVERALL STATED ODDS 1:147
AM1 Aaron Brooks 1.50 4.00
AM2 Ahman Green 2.00 5.00
AM3 Cadillac Williams 1.50 4.00
AM4 Carson Palmer 2.00 5.00
AM5 Cedric Benson 1.50 4.00
AM6 DeShaun Foster 2.00 5.00
AM7 Doug Flutie 2.00 5.00
AM8 Drew Bledsoe 2.00 5.00
AM9 Hines Ward SP 2.00 5.00
AM10 Jevon Kearse 1.50 4.00
AM11 John Elway 4.00 10.00
AM12 Julius Jones 1.50 4.00
AM13 Kyle Boller 1.50 4.00
AM14 Lee Suggs 1.50 4.00
AM15 Marshall Faulk 2.00 5.00
AM16 Michael Clayton 1.50 4.00
AM17 Michael Vick 2.00 5.00
AM18 Mike Singletary 2.50 6.00
AM19 Reggie Williams 1.50 4.00
AM20 Roy Williams S 1.50 4.00
AM21 Santana Moss 2.00 5.00
AM22 Steven Jackson 1.50 4.00
AM23 Tony Dorsett 2.50 6.00
AM24 Tyrone Calico 1.50 4.00
AM25 Willis McGahee 1.50 4.00
AM26 C.Portis/S.Moss/100 3.00 8.00
AM27 M.Vick/L.Suggs/100 3.00 8.00
AM28 J.Elway/D.Bledsoe/100 6.00 15.00
AM29 A.Johnson/R.Wayne/100 3.00 8.00
AM30 C.Palmer/S.Jackson/100 3.00 8.00
AM31 W.McGahee/A.Boldin/100 2.50 6.00
AM32 D.Flutie/M.Faulk/100 3.00 8.00
AM33 H.Ward/Ca.Williams/100 3.00 8.00
AM34 T.Dorsett/J.Jones/100 4.00 10.00
AM35 C.Benson/B.Sanders/100 6.00 15.00
AM36 Wayne/Shock/McG/25 5.00 12.00
AM37 Elway/Bledsoe/Palmer/25 10.00 25.00
AM38 Dorsett/Jones/Will S/25 6.00 15.00
AM39 Vick/Flutie/Brooks/25 5.00 12.00
AM40 Benson/Sand/Green/25 10.00 25.00

2005 Playoff Honors Award Winners

STATED ODDS 1:12 HOB, 1:24 RET
*FOIL: .5X TO 1.2X BASIC INSERTS
FOIL PRINT RUN 250 SER.#'d SETS
*HOLOFOIL: .8X TO 2X BASIC INSERTS
HOLOFOIL PRINT RUN 100 SER.#'d SETS
AW1 Andre Ware .75 2.00
AW2 Archie Griffin 1.25 3.00
AW3 Charles White .75 2.00
AW4 Danny Wuerffel .75 2.00
AW5 Chris Weinke .75 2.00
AW6 Doug Flutie 1.25 3.00
AW7 Gary Beban .75 2.00
AW8 George Rogers 1.50 4.00
AW9 Gino Torretta .75 2.00
AW10 Glenn Davis .75 2.00
AW11 Mike Garrett .75 2.00
AW12 Mike Rozier 1.25 3.00
AW13 Pat Sullivan .75 2.00
AW14 Pete Dawkins 1.25 3.00
AW15 Roger Staubach 2.50 6.00
AW16 Rashaan Salaam .75 2.00
AW17 Ty Detmer .75 2.00

2005 Playoff Honors Award Winners Autographs

STATED PRINT RUN 300 SER.#'d SETS
AW1 Andre Ware 7.50 20.00
AW2 Archie Griffin 15.00 40.00
AW3 Charles White 7.50 20.00
AW4 Danny Wuerffel 10.00 25.00
AW5 Chris Weinke 6.00 15.00
AW6 Doug Flutie 15.00 30.00
AW7 Gary Beban 10.00 25.00
AW8 George Rogers 12.50 30.00
AW9 Gino Torretta 10.00 25.00
AW10 Glenn Davis 20.00 50.00
AW11 Mike Garrett 15.00 40.00
AW12 Mike Rozier 12.50 30.00
AW13 Pat Sullivan 10.00 25.00
AW14 Pete Dawkins 15.00 40.00

AW15 Roger Staubach 30.00 60.00
AW16 Rashaan Salaam 6.00 15.00
AW17 Ty Detmer 6.00 15.00

2005 Playoff Honors Class Reunion

STATED ODDS 1:9 HOB, 1:24 RET
*FOIL/250: .5X TO 1.2X BASIC INSERTS
*HOLOFOIL/100: .6X TO 1.5X BASIC INSERTS
CR1 K.Johnson/E.George .60 1.50
CR2 T.Owens/M.Harrison .60 1.50
CR3 P.Manning/B.Griese 2.00 5.00
CR4 A.Green/F.Taylor .60 1.50
CR5 R.Moss/C.Woodson .75 2.00
CR6 D.McNabb/D.Culpepper .60 1.50
CR7 E.James/A.Brooks .60 1.50
CR8 T.Holt/P.Price .60 1.50
CR9 B.Urlacher/T.Jones .75 2.00
CR10 S.Alexander/L.Arrington .50 1.25
CR11 L.Coles/C.Pennington .50 1.25
CR12 P.Burress/J.Lewis .60 1.50
CR13 M.Bulger/T.Brady 3.00 8.00
CR14 M.Vick/L.Tomlinson .75 2.00
CR15 S.Moss/R.Wayne .60 1.50
CR16 T.Heap/D.McAllister
CR17 C.Chambers/Ch.Johnson .50 1.25
CR18 R.Johnson/D.Brees .75 2.00
CR19 D.Carr/J.Harrington .50 1.25
CR20 C.Portis/J.Walker .50 1.25
CR21 P.Ramsey/A.Lelie .60 1.50
CR22 C.Palmer/B.Leftwich .60 1.50
CR23 K.Boller/R.Grossman .50 1.25
CR24 W.McGahee/C.Brown .50 1.25
CR25 A.Johnson/A.Boldin .60 1.50
CR26 L.Fitzgerald/M.Clayton .75 2.00
CR27 R.Williams WR/K.Jones .50 1.25
CR28 E.Manning/B.Roethlisberger 1.25 3.00
CR29 S.Jackson/J.Jones .50 1.25
CR30 L.Evans/J.Losman .60 1.50

2005 Playoff Honors Class Reunion Materials

STATED PRINT RUN 150 SER.#'d SETS
*PRIME/25: .8X TO 2X BASIC JSY/150
CR1 K.Johnson/E.George 4.00 10.00
CR2 T.Owens/M.Harrison 4.00 10.00
CR3 P.Manning/B.Griese 12.00 30.00
CR4 A.Green/F.Taylor 4.00 10.00
CR5 R.Moss/C.Woodson 5.00 12.00
CR6 D.McNabb/D.Culpepper 4.00 10.00
CR7 E.James/A.Brooks 4.00 10.00
CR8 T.Holt/P.Price 4.00 10.00
CR9 B.Urlacher/T.Jones 5.00 12.00
CR10 S.Alexander/L.Arrington 3.00 8.00
CR11 L.Coles/C.Pennington 3.00 8.00
CR12 P.Burress/J.Lewis 4.00 10.00
CR13 M.Bulger/T.Brady 20.00 50.00
CR14 M.Vick/L.Tomlinson 5.00 12.00
CR15 S.Moss/R.Wayne 4.00 10.00
CR16 T.Heap/D.McAllister 4.00 10.00
CR17 C.Chambers/Ch.Johnson 3.00 8.00
CR18 R.Johnson/D.Brees 5.00 12.00
CR19 D.Carr/J.Harrington 3.00 8.00
CR20 C.Portis/J.Walker 3.00 8.00
CR21 P.Ramsey/A.Lelie 4.00 10.00
CR22 C.Palmer/B.Leftwich 4.00 10.00
CR23 K.Boller/R.Grossman 3.00 8.00
CR24 W.McGahee/C.Brown 3.00 8.00
CR25 A.Johnson/A.Boldin 4.00 10.00
CR26 L.Fitzgerald/M.Clayton 5.00 12.00
CR27 R.Williams WR/K.Jones 3.00 8.00
CR28 E.Manning/B.Roethlisberger 8.00 20.00
CR29 S.Jackson/J.Jones 3.00 8.00
CR30 L.Evans/J.Losman 4.00 10.00

2005 Playoff Honors Game Day

STATED ODDS 1:9 HOB, 1:24 RET
*FOIL/250: .5X TO 1.2X BASIC INSERTS
*HOLOFOIL/100: .6X TO 1.5X BASIC INSERTS
GD1 Anquan Boldin .50 1.25
GD2 Larry Fitzgerald .75 2.00
GD3 Chad Pennington .50 1.25
GD4 Tom Brady 3.00 8.00
GD5 Corey Dillon .50 1.25
GD6 Curtis Martin .60 1.50
GD7 Matt Hasselbeck .50 1.25
GD8 Shaun Alexander .50 1.25
GD9 Koren Robinson .50 1.25
GD10 Michael Clayton .50 1.25
GD11 Tiki Barber .60 1.50
GD12 Jeremy Shockey .50 1.25
GD13 Aaron Brooks .50 1.25
GD14 Deuce McAllister .60 1.50
GD15 Marc Bulger .50 1.25
GD16 Torry Holt .60 1.50
GD17 Steven Jackson .50 1.25
GD18 Donovan McNabb .60 1.50
GD19 Chris Chambers .50 1.25
GD20 Brian Urlacher .75 2.00
GD21 Steve McNair .60 1.50
GD22 Peyton Manning 2.00 5.00
GD23 Jamal Lewis .60 1.50
GD24 Todd Heap .50 1.25
GD25 Michael Strahan .60 1.50

2005 Playoff Honors Game Day Souvenirs

STATED PRINT RUN 250 SER.#'d SETS
*PRIME: 1X TO 2.5X BASIC INSERTS
PRIME PRINT RUN 25 SER.#'d SETS
GD1 Anquan Boldin 2.00 5.00
GD2 Larry Fitzgerald 3.00 8.00
GD3 Chad Pennington 2.00 5.00
GD4 Tom Brady 12.00 30.00
GD5 Corey Dillon 2.00 5.00
GD6 Curtis Martin 2.50 6.00
GD7 Matt Hasselbeck 2.00 5.00
GD8 Shaun Alexander 2.00 5.00
GD9 Koren Robinson 2.00 5.00
GD10 Michael Clayton 2.00 5.00
GD11 Tiki Barber 2.50 6.00
GD12 Jeremy Shockey 2.00 5.00
GD13 Aaron Brooks 2.00 5.00
GD14 Deuce McAllister 2.50 6.00
GD15 Marc Bulger 2.00 5.00
GD16 Torry Holt 2.50 6.00
GD17 Steven Jackson 2.00 5.00
GD18 Donovan McNabb 2.50 6.00
GD19 Chris Chambers 2.00 5.00
GD20 Brian Urlacher 3.00 8.00
GD21 Steve McNair 2.50 6.00
GD22 Peyton Manning 8.00 20.00
GD23 Jamal Lewis 2.50 6.00
GD24 Todd Heap 2.00 5.00
GD25 Michael Strahan 2.50 6.00

2005 Playoff Honors Honorable Signatures

HS1 Aaron Brooks/100 6.00 15.00
HS2 Andre Johnson/75 10.00 25.00
HS3 Antonio Gates/100 12.50 30.00
HS4 Ben Roethlisberger/25 100.00 175.00
HS6 Domanick Davis/25 10.00 25.00
HS7 Donnie Edwards/100 10.00 25.00
HS8 Michael Vick/25 40.00 80.00
HS9 Rex Grossman/25 25.00 50.00
HS10 Rudi Johnson/25 12.00 30.00
HS11 Tatum Bell/25 10.00 25.00
HS12 Terence Newman/100 10.00 25.00
HS13 Todd Heap/100 6.00 15.00
HS14 Christian Okoye/150 6.00 15.00
HS15 Ickey Woods/150 10.00 25.00
HS16 John Taylor/100 7.50 20.00
HS17 Richard Dent/150 6.00 15.00
HS18 Alex Smith QB/50 60.00 120.00
HS19 Adrian McPherson/150 7.50 20.00
HS20 Cadillac Williams/50 20.00 50.00
HS21 Fred Gibson/150 6.00 15.00
HS22 J.J. Arrington/100 7.50 20.00
HS23 Jason Campbell/50 20.00 40.00
HS24 Ronnie Brown/100 15.00 40.00
HS25 Troy Williamson/50 20.00 40.00

2005 Playoff Honors Patches

*PLATES/35-45: .5X TO 1.2X PATCHES/75-99
*PLATES/25-30: .6X TO 1.5X PATCHES/75-99
*PLATES/25-30: .5X TO 1.2X PATCHES/50-65
*PLATES/15-20: .8X TO 2X PATCHES/75-99
*PLATES/15-20: .6X TO 1.5X PATCHES/50-65
PP1 Anquan Boldin/75 2.50 6.00
PP2 Ben Roethlisberger/50 8.00 20.00
PP3 Brett Favre/75 8.00 20.00
PP4 Carson Palmer/75 3.00 8.00
PP5 Chad Johnson/75 2.50 6.00
PP6 Chad Pennington/50 3.00 8.00
PP7 Daunte Culpepper/99 3.00 8.00
PP8 Deuce McAllister/99 3.00 8.00
PP9 Donovan McNabb/75 3.00 8.00
PP10 Edgerrin James/99 3.00 8.00
PP11 Eli Manning/65 8.00 20.00
PP12 Joey Harrington/75 2.50 6.00
PP13 Julius Jones/75 2.50 6.00
PP14 LaDainian Tomlinson/75 4.00 10.00
PP15 Kevin Jones/50 3.00 8.00
PP16 Larry Fitzgerald/75 4.00 10.00
PP17 LaVar Arrington/75 2.50 6.00
PP18 Marvin Harrison/99 3.00 8.00
PP19 Michael Clayton/75 2.50 6.00
PP20 Peyton Manning/89 10.00 25.00
PP21 Randy Moss/75 3.00 8.00
PP22 Steven Jackson/75 2.50 6.00
PP23 Terrell Owens/75 3.00 8.00
PP24 Trent Green/75 2.50 6.00
PP25 Tom Brady/50 20.00 50.00

2005 Playoff Honors Rookie Hidden Gems Autographs

STATED PRINT RUN 50 SER.#'d SETS
201 Adam Jones JSY 12.00 30.00
202 Alex Smith QB JSY 60.00 120.00
203 Andrew Walter JSY 12.00 30.00
204 Antrel Rolle JSY 20.00 50.00
205 Braylon Edwards JSY 25.00 60.00
206 Cadillac Williams JSY 12.00 30.00
207 Carlos Rogers JSY 20.00 50.00
208 Charlie Frye JSY 12.00 30.00
209 Ciatrick Fason JSY 12.00 30.00
210 Courtney Roby JSY 12.00 30.00
211 Eric Shelton JSY 12.00 30.00
212 Frank Gore JSY 40.00 80.00
213 J.J. Arrington JSY 15.00 40.00
214 Jason Campbell JSY 12.00 30.00
215 Kyle Orton JSY 12.00 30.00
216 Mark Bradley JSY
217 Mark Clayton JSY 12.00 30.00
218 Matt Jones JSY 12.00 30.00
219 Maurice Clarett JSY 12.00 30.00
220 Reggie Brown JSY 12.00 30.00
221 Ronnie Brown JSY 25.00 60.00
222 Roddy White JSY 20.00 50.00
223 Ryan Moats JSY 12.00 30.00
224 Roscoe Parrish JSY 12.00 30.00
225 Stefan LeFors JSY 12.00 30.00
226 Terrence Murphy JSY 12.00 30.00
227 Troy Williamson JSY 12.00 30.00
228 Vernand Morency JSY 12.00 30.00
229 Vincent Jackson JSY 20.00 50.00

2005 Playoff Honors Rookie Tandem

STATED ODDS 1:12 HOB, 1:24 RET
*FOIL: .5X TO 1.2X BASIC INSERTS
FOIL PRINT RUN 250 SER.#'d SETS
*HOLOFOIL: .6X TO 1.5X BASIC INSERTS
HOLOFOIL PRINT RUN 100 SER.#'d SETS
RT1 A.Smith QB/F.Gore 2.00 5.00
RT2 Ro.Brown/Ca.Williams .60 1.50
RT3 B.Edwards/C.Frye .50 1.25
RT4 A.Jones/C.Roby .50 1.25
RT5 T.Williamson/C.Fason .50 1.25
RT6 A.Rolle/J.Arrington .75 2.00
RT7 M.Jones/M.Clayton .50 1.25
RT8 R.White/T.Murphy .75 2.00
RT9 C.Rogers/J.Campbell .75 2.00
RT10 R.Parrish/V.Jackson .75 2.00
RT11 Re.Brown/R.Moats .50 1.25
RT12 M.Bradley/K.Orton .50 1.25
RT13 E.Shelton/S.LeFors .50 1.25
RT14 V.Morency/M.Clarett .50 1.25
RT15 A.Smith QB/A.Walter 2.00 5.00

2005 Playoff Honors Rookie Tandem Jerseys

*FOOTBALL/125: .5X TO 1.2X JSY
*COMBO/50: .8X TO 2X JERSEYS
RT1 A.Smith QB/F.Gore 10.00 25.00
RT2 Ro.Brown/Ca.Williams 3.00 8.00
RT3 B.Edwards/C.Frye 2.50 6.00
RT4 A.Jones/C.Roby 2.50 6.00
RT5 T.Williamson/C.Fason 2.50 6.00
RT6 A.Rolle/J.Arrington 4.00 10.00
RT7 M.Jones/M.Clayton 2.50 6.00
RT8 R.White/T.Murphy 4.00 10.00
RT9 C.Rogers/J.Campbell 4.00 10.00
RT10 R.Parrish/V.Jackson 4.00 10.00
RT11 Re.Brown/R.Moats 2.50 6.00
RT12 M.Bradley/K.Orton 2.50 6.00
RT13 E.Shelton/S.LeFors 2.50 6.00
RT14 V.Morency/M.Clarett 2.50 6.00
RT15 A.Smith QB/A.Walter 10.00 25.00

2005 Playoff Honors Rookie Quad

STATED PRINT RUN 250 SER.#'d SETS
*FOIL: .5X TO 1.2X BASIC INSERTS
FOIL PRINT RUN 100 SER.#'d SETS
*HOLOFOIL: .8X TO 2X BASIC INSERTS
HOLOFOIL PRINT RUN 25 SER.#'d SETS
RQ1 Smith QB/Gore/Rolle/J.J. 5.00 12.00
RQ2 Rgrs/Camp/Ro.Brwn/Carn 2.00 5.00
RQ3 Edwards/Frye/Will/Fason 4.00 10.00
RQ4 A.Jns/Roby/M.Jns/Clayton 1.25 3.00
RQ5 Walter/Clarett/Parrish/Jack 2.00 5.00
RQ6 Re.Brwn/Moats/Brdly/Orton 1.25 3.00
RQ7 White/Murphy/Shel/LeFors 2.00 5.00

2005 Playoff Honors Rookie Quad Jerseys

JERSEY PRINT RUN 250 SER.#'d SETS
*FOOTBALLS: .6X TO 1.5X JERSEYS
FOOTBALLS PRINT RUN 75 SER.#'d SETS
*COMBOS: .8X TO 2X JERSEYS
COMBOS PRINT RUN 25 SER.#'d SETS
RQ1 Smith QB/Gore/Rolle/J.J. 15.00 40.00
RQ2 Rgrs/Camp/Ro.Brwn/Carn 20.00 50.00
RQ3 Edwards/Frye/Will/Fason 10.00 25.00
RQ4 A.Jns/Roby/M.Jns/Clayton 7.50 20.00
RQ5 Walter/Clarett/Parrish/Jack 6.00 15.00
RQ6 Re.Brwn/Moats/Brdly/Orton 6.00 15.00
RQ7 White/Murphy/Shel/LeFors 6.00 15.00

2005 Playoff Honors Touchdown Tandems

STATED ODDS 1:12 RET, 1:24 RET
*FOIL: .5X TO 1.2X BASIC INSERTS
FOIL PRINT RUN 250 SER.#'d SETS
*HOLOFOIL: .6X TO 1.5X BASIC INSERTS
HOLOFOIL PRINT RUN 100 SER.#'d SETS
TT1 M.Vick/A.Crumpler .75 2.00
TT2 J.Losman/L.Evans .75 2.00
TT3 J.Delhomme/S.Smith 1.00 2.50
TT4 C.Palmer/C.Johnson .75 2.00
TT5 M.Irvin/T.Aikman 1.50 4.00
TT6 J.Plummer/A.Lelie .60 1.50
TT7 J.Harrington/R.Williams WR .60 1.50
TT8 B.Favre/J.Walker 2.00 5.00
TT9 D.Carr/A.Johnson .75 2.00
TT10 P.Manning/M.Harrison 2.50 6.00
TT11 B.Leftwich/J.Smith .75 2.00
TT12 T.Green/T.Gonzalez .75 2.00
TT13 D.Culpepper/N.Burleson .75 2.00
TT14 T.Brady/D.Branch 4.00 10.00
TT15 E.Manning/J.Shockey 1.50 4.00
TT16 C.Pennington/L.Coles .60 1.50
TT17 K.Collins/J.Porter .60 1.50
TT18 D.McNabb/T.Owens .75 2.00
TT19 B.Roethlisberger/H.Ward 1.50 4.00
TT20 D.Brees/A.Gates 1.00 2.50
TT21 J.Montana/J.Rice 4.00 10.00
TT22 M.Bulger/T.Holt .75 2.00
TT23 M.Hasselbeck/D.Jackson .60 1.50
TT24 S.McNair/D.Bennett .75 2.00
TT25 A.Brooks/J.Horn .60 1.50

2005 Playoff Honors Touchdown Tandems Materials

MATERIAL PRINT RUN 125 SER.#'d SETS
*PRIME: .8X TO 2X BASIC MATERIALS/125
PRIME PRINT RUN 25 SER.#'d SETS
TT1 M.Vick/A.Crumpler 4.00 10.00
TT2 J.Losman/L.Evans 4.00 10.00
TT3 J.Delhomme/S.Smith 5.00 12.00
TT4 C.Palmer/C.Johnson 4.00 10.00
TT5 M.Irvin/T.Aikman 6.00 15.00
TT6 J.Plummer/A.Lelie 3.00 8.00
TT7 J.Harrington/R.Williams WR 3.00 8.00
TT8 B.Favre/J.Walker 10.00 25.00
TT9 D.Carr/A.Johnson 4.00 10.00
TT10 P.Manning/M.Harrison 12.00 30.00
TT11 B.Leftwich/J.Smith 4.00 10.00
TT12 T.Green/T.Gonzalez 4.00 10.00
TT13 D.Culpepper/N.Burleson 4.00 10.00
TT14 T.Brady/D.Branch 12.00 30.00
TT15 E.Manning/J.Shockey 8.00 20.00
TT16 C.Pennington/L.Coles 3.00 8.00
TT17 K.Collins/J.Porter 3.00 8.00
TT18 D.McNabb/T.Owens 4.00 10.00
TT19 B.Roethlisberger/H.Ward 8.00 20.00
TT20 D.Brees/A.Gates 5.00 12.00
TT21 J.Montana/J.Rice 15.00 40.00
TT22 M.Bulger/T.Holt 4.00 10.00
TT23 M.Hasselbeck/D.Jackson 3.00 8.00
TT24 S.McNair/D.Bennett 4.00 10.00
TT25 A.Brooks/J.Horn 3.00 8.00

1996 Playoff Illusions

This 120-card 1996 Playoff Illusions set was distributed in five-card packs with a suggested retail price of $4.39. The set features six different designs representing the six NFL divisions. Cards 1-63 appear four cards per pack and cards 64-120 appear one per pack. The fonts display color player photos with tie-dyed color graphics.

COMPLETE SET (120) 20.00 50.00
COMP.SERIES 1 (63) 4.00 10.00
COMP.SERIES 2 (57) 15.00 40.00
1 Troy Aikman .60 1.50
2 Larry Centers .10 .30
3 Terance Mathis .08 .20
4 Michael Irvin .25 .60
5 Jim Kelly .25 .60
6 Tim Biakabutuka RC .25 .60
7 Rashaan Salaam .10 .30
8 Ki-Jana Carter .10 .30
9 Anthony Miller .10 .30
10 Deion Sanders .30 .75
11 Scott Mitchell .10 .30
12 Robert Brooks .25 .60
13 Willie Davis .08 .20
14 Zack Crockett .08 .20
15 James O.Stewart .10 .30
16 Tamarick Vanover .10 .30
17 Stanley Pritchett .08 .20
18 Warren Moon .10 .30
19 Shawn Jefferson .08 .20
20 Shannon Sharpe .10 .30
21 Jim Everett .08 .20
22 Dave Brown .08 .20
23 Adrian Murrell .10 .30
24 Rickey Dudley RC .25 .60
25 Chris T. Jones .10 .30
26 Andre Hastings .08 .20
27 Stan Humphries .10 .30
28 Steve Young .50 1.25
29 Joey Galloway .25 .60
30 Jim Harbaugh .10 .30
31 Eddie Kennison RC .25 .60
32 Mike Alstott RC .75 2.00
33 Michael Westbrook .25 .60
34 Leeland McElroy RC .10 .30
35 Erik Kramer .08 .20
36 Mark Chmura .10 .30
37 Cris Carter .25 .60
38 Ben Coates .10 .30
39 Wayne Chrebet .40 1.00
40 Jerome Bettis .25 .60
41 Tim Brown .25 .60
42 Jason Dunn RC .10 .30
43 William Henderson .25 .60
44 Rick Mirer .10 .30
45 J.J. Stokes .25 .60
46 Rodney Peete .08 .20
47 Neil O'Donnell .10 .30
48 Tyrone Wheatley .10 .30
49 Terry Glenn RC .75 2.00
50 Junior Seau .25 .60
51 Jake Reed .10 .30
52 O.J. McDuffie .10 .30
53 Steve Bono .08 .20
54 Steve McNair .50 1.25
55 Antonio Freeman .25 .60
56 Johnnie Morton .10 .30
57 Eric Metcalf .08 .20
58 Andre Reed .10 .30
59 Bobby Engram RC .25 .60
60 Gus Frerotte .10 .30
61 Jeff Blake .25 .60
62 Erric Pegram .08 .20
63 Jeff Hostetler .08 .20
64 Edgar Bennett .25 .60
65 Eddie George RC 1.50 4.00
66 Marvin Harrison RC 3.00 8.00
67 LeShon Johnson .15 .40
68 Jamal Anderson RC .60 1.50
69 Thurman Thomas .50 1.25
70 Barry Sanders 2.00 5.00
71 Muhsin Muhammad RC 1.25 3.00
72 Robert Green .15 .40
73 Garrison Hearst .25 .60
74 John Elway 2.50 6.00
75 Herman Moore .25 .60
76 Chris Chandler 15.00 .40
77 Marshall Faulk .60 1.50
78 Mark Brunell .75 2.00
79 Tony Banks RC .50 1.25
80 Terrell Davis 1.00 2.50
81 Marcus Allen .50 1.25
82 Dan Marino 2.50 6.00
83 Robert Smith .25 .60
84 Curtis Martin 1.00 2.50
85 Amani Toomer RC 1.50 4.00
86 Napoleon Kaufman .25 .60
87 Ricky Watters .25 .60
88 Kordell Stewart .50 1.25
89 Keyshawn Johnson RC 1.25 3.00
90 Emmitt Smith 2.00 5.00
91 Chris Warren .25 .60
92 Isaac Bruce .50 1.25
93 Terry Allen .25 .60
94 Trent Dilfer .25 .60
95 Vinny Testaverde .25 .60
96 Bruce Smith .50 1.25
97 Kerry Collins .50 1.25
98 Curtis Conway .50 1.25
99 Karim Abdul-Jabbar RC .50 1.25
100 Brett Favre 2.50 6.00
101 Carl Pickens .25 .60
102 Brett Perriman .15 .40
103 Keith Jackson .15 .40
104 Drew Bledsoe .75 2.00
105 Rodney Hampton .15 .40
106 Ray Zellars .15 .40
107 Jeff Graham .15 .40
108 Irving Fryar .25 .60
109 Lawrence Phillips RC .50 1.25
110 Jerry Rice 1.25 3.00
111 Mike Tomczak .15 .40
112 Tony Martin .25 .60
113 Brian Blades .25 .60
114 Bill Brooks .15 .40
115 Rob Moore .25 .60
116 Quinn Early .15 .40
117 Darnay Scott .25 .60
118 Ken Dilger .15 .40
119 Derek Loville .15 .40
120 Reggie White .50 1.25
P1 Robert Brooks Promo .30 .75

1996 Playoff Illusions Spectralusion Dominion

*1-63 DOMINION: 10X TO 25X BASIC CARDS
*64-120 DOMINION: 5X TO 12X BASIC CARDS
STATED ODDS 1:192

1996 Playoff Illusions Spectralusion Elite

COMP.SPECT.ELITE (120) 175.00 300.00
*1-63 ELITE: 2.5X TO 6X BASIC CARDS
*64-120 ELITE: 1.2X TO 3X BASIC CARDS
STATED ODDS 1:5

1996 Playoff Illusions XXXI

*1-63 XXXI: 4X TO 10X BASIC CARDS
*64-120 XXXI: 2X TO 5X BASIC CARDS
STATED ODDS 1:12

1996 Playoff Illusions XXXI Spectralusion

*1-63 XXXI SPEC: 10X TO 25X BASIC CARDS
*64-120 XXXI SPEC: 5X TO 12X BASIC CARDS
STATED ODDS 1:96

1996 Playoff Illusions Optical Illusions

Randomly inserted in packs at the rate of one in 96, this 18-card set features color player images of fantasy tandems that likely will never happen.

COMPLETE SET (18) 125.00 300.00
STATED ODDS 1:96
1 B.Favre / J.Rice 20.00 50.00
2 T.Aikman / B.Sanders 20.00 50.00
3 D.Marino / E.Smith 20.00 50.00
4 W.Moon / C.Pickens 3.00 8.00
5 J.Elway / H.Moore 15.00 40.00
6 S.Young / A.Miller 10.00 25.00
7 J.Harbaugh / T.Davis 6.00 15.00
8 K.Stewart / K.Stewart 3.00 8.00
9 D.Sanders / D.Sanders 7.50 20.00
10 K.Collins / C.Martin 6.00 15.00
11 S.Mitchell / R.Brooks 3.00 8.00
12 J.Blake / T.Martin 3.00 8.00
13 M.Brunell / M.Faulk 7.50 20.00
14 D.Bledsoe / J.Bettis 10.00 25.00
15 G.Frerotte / K.Abdul-Jabbar 6.00 15.00
16 S.Bono / R.Watters 3.00 8.00
17 C.Chandler / T.Allen 3.00 8.00
18 T.Banks / K.Johnson 3.00 8.00

1998 Playoff Momentum Hobby

This 250-card Playoff Momentum Hobby set was issued in one series totalling 250 cards and distributed in five-card packs. The set features color action player photos printed on doublesided metalized mylar topped cards with double micro-ethcing on both sides. A red parallel set was also produced and inserted at a rate of one in 4. A limited edition gold parallel set was produced and sequentially numbered to 25.

COMPLETE SET (250) 100.00 250.00
1 Jake Plummer 1.00 2.50
2 Eric Metcalf .40 1.00
3 Adrian Murrell .60 1.50
4 Larry Centers .40 1.00
5 Frank Sanders .60 1.50
6 Rob Moore .60 1.50
7 Andre Wadsworth RC 1.50 4.00
8 Chris Chandler .60 1.50
9 Jamal Anderson 1.00 2.50
10 Tony Martin .60 1.50
11 Terance Mathis .60 1.50
12 Tim Dwight RC 2.00 5.00
13 Jammi German RC 1.00 2.50
14 O.J. Santiago .40 1.00
15 Jim Harbaugh .60 1.50
16 Eric Zeier .60 1.50
17 Duane Starks RC 1.00 2.50
18 Rod Woodson .60 1.50
19 Errict Rhett .60 1.50
20 Jay Graham .40 1.00
21 Ray Lewis 1.00 2.50
22 Michael Jackson .40 1.00
23 Jermaine Lewis .60 1.50
24 Patrick Johnson RC 1.50 4.00
25 Eric Green .40 1.00
26 Doug Flutie 1.00 2.50
27 Rob Johnson .60 1.50
28 Antowain Smith 1.00 2.50
29 Thurman Thomas 1.00 2.50
30 Jonathan Linton RC 1.50 4.00
31 Bruce Smith .60 1.50
32 Eric Moulds 1.00 2.50
33 Kevin Williams .40 1.00
34 Andre Reed .60 1.50
35 Steve Beuerlein .60 1.50
36 Kerry Collins .60 1.50
37 Anthony Johnson .40 1.00
38 Fred Lane .40 1.00
39 William Floyd .40 1.00
40 Rocket Ismail .40 1.00
41 Wesley Walls .60 1.50
42 Muhsin Muhammad .60 1.50
43 Hae Carruth .40 1.00
44 Kevin Greene .60 1.50
45 Greg Lloyd .40 1.00
46 Moses Moreno RC 1.00 2.50
47 Erik Kramer .40 1.00
48 Edgar Bennett .40 1.00
49 Curtis Enis RC 1.00 2.50
50 Curtis Conway .60 1.50
51 Bobby Engram .60 1.50
52 Alonzo Mayes RC 1.00 2.50
53 Jeff Blake .60 1.50
54 Neil O'Donnell .60 1.50
55 Corey Dillon 1.00 2.50
56 Takeo Spikes RC 2.00 5.00
57 Carl Pickens .60 1.50
58 Tony McGee .40 1.00
59 Darnay Scott .60 1.50
60 Troy Aikman 2.00 5.00
61 Deion Sanders 1.00 2.50
62 Emmitt Smith 3.00 8.00
63 Darren Woodson .40 1.00
64 Chris Warren .60 1.50
65 Daryl Johnston .60 1.50
66 Ernie Mills .40 1.00
67 Billy Davis .40 1.00
68 Michael Irvin 1.00 2.50
69 David LaFleur .40 1.00
70 John Elway 4.00 10.00
71 Brian Griese RC 4.00 10.00
72 Steve Atwater .40 1.00
73 Terrell Davis 1.00 2.50
74 Rod Smith .60 1.50
75 Marcus Nash RC 1.00 2.50
76 Shannon Sharpe .60 1.50
77 Ed McCaffrey .60 1.50
78 Neil Smith .60 1.50
79 Charlie Batch RC 2.00 5.00
80 Germane Crowell RC 1.50 4.00
81 Scott Mitchell .60 1.50
82 Barry Sanders 3.00 8.00
83 Terry Fair RC 1.50 4.00
84 Herman Moore .60 1.50
85 Johnnie Morton .60 1.50
86 Brett Favre 4.00 10.00
87 Rick Mirer .40 1.00
88 Dorsey Levens 1.00 2.50
89 William Henderson .60 1.50
90 Derrick Mayes .60 1.50
91 Antonio Freeman 1.00 2.50
92 Robert Brooks .60 1.50
93 Mark Chmura .60 1.50
94 Vonnie Holliday RC 1.50 4.00
95 Reggie White 1.00 2.50
96 E.G. Green RC 1.50 4.00
97 Jerome Pathon RC 2.00 5.00
98 Peyton Manning RC 20.00 50.00
99 Marshall Faulk 1.25 3.00
100 Zack Crockett .40 1.00
101 Ken Dilger .40 1.00
102 Marvin Harrison 1.00 2.50
103 Mark Brunell 1.00 2.50
104 Jonathan Quinn RC 2.00 5.00
105 Tavian Banks RC 1.50 4.00
106 Fred Taylor RC 3.00 8.00
107 James Stewart .60 1.50
108 Jimmy Smith .60 1.50
109 Keenan McCardell .60 1.50
110 Elvis Grbac .60 1.50
111 Rich Gannon 1.00 2.50
112 Rashaan Shehee RC 1.50 4.00
113 Donnell Bennett .40 1.00
114 Kimble Anders .60 1.50
115 Derrick Thomas 1.00 2.50
116 Kevin Lockett .40 1.00
117 Derrick Alexander WR .60 1.50
118 Tony Gonzalez 1.00 2.50
119 Andre Rison .60 1.50
120 Craig Erickson .40 1.00
121 Dan Marino 2.50 6.00
122 John Avery RC 1.50 4.00
123 Karim Abdul-Jabbar 1.00 2.50
124 Zach Thomas 1.00 2.50
125 O.J. McDuffie .60 1.50
126 Troy Drayton .40 1.00
127 Randall Cunningham 1.00 2.50
128 Brad Johnson 1.00 2.50
129 Robert Smith 1.00 2.50
130 Cris Carter 1.00 2.50
131 Randy Moss RC 12.00 30.00
132 Jake Reed .60 1.50
133 John Randle .60 1.50
134 Drew Bledsoe 1.50 4.00
135 Tony Simmons RC 1.50 4.00
136 Sedrick Shaw .40 1.00
137 Chris Floyd RC 1.00 2.50
138 Robert Edwards RC 1.50 4.00
139 Rod Rutledge RC 1.00 2.50
140 Shawn Jefferson .40 1.00
141 Ben Coates .60 1.50
142 Terry Glenn 1.00 2.50
143 Heath Shuler .40 1.00
144 Danny Wuerffel .60 1.50
145 Troy Davis .40 1.00
146 Qadry Ismail .60 1.50
147 Ray Zellars .40 1.00
148 Lamar Smith .60 1.50
149 Cameron Cleeland RC 1.00 2.50
150 Sean Dawkins .40 1.00
151 Andre Hastings .40 1.00
152 Danny Kanell .60 1.50
153 Tiki Barber 1.00 2.50
154 Tyrone Wheatley .60 1.50
155 Charles Way .40 1.00
156 Gary Brown .40 1.00
157 Shaun Williams RC 1.50 4.00
158 Chris Calloway .40 1.00
159 Amani Toomer .60 1.50
160 Brian Alford RC 1.00 2.50
161 Joe Jurevicius RC 2.00 5.00
162 Ike Hilliard .60 1.50
163 Michael Strahan .60 1.50
164 Glenn Foley .60 1.50
165 Vinny Testaverde .60 1.50
166 Keyshawn Johnson 1.00 2.50
167 Curtis Martin 1.00 2.50
168 Leon Johnson .40 1.00
169 Keith Byars .40 1.00
170 Wayne Chrebet 1.00 2.50
171 Kyle Brady .40 1.00
172 Dedric Ward .40 1.00
173 Jeff George .60 1.50
174 Charles Woodson RC 4.00 10.00
175 Napoleon Kaufman 1.00 2.50
176 Jon Ritchie RC 1.50 4.00
177 Tim Brown 1.00 2.50
178 James Jett .60 1.50
179 Rickey Dudley .40 1.00
180 Bobby Hoying .60 1.50
181 Duce Staley 1.25 3.00
182 Charlie Garner .60 1.50
183 Irving Fryar .60 1.50
184 Jeff Graham .40 1.00
185 Jason Dunn .40 1.00
186 Kordell Stewart 1.00 2.50
187 Jerome Bettis 1.00 2.50
188 Andre Coleman .40 1.00
189 Chris Fuamatu-Ma'afala RC 1.50 4.00
190 Charles Johnson .40 1.00
191 Hines Ward RC 10.00 20.00
192 Mark Bruener .40 1.00
193 Courtney Hawkins .40 1.00
194 Will Blackwell .40 1.00
195 Levon Kirkland .40 1.00
196 Mikhael Ricks RC 1.50 4.00
197 Ryan Leaf RC 2.00 5.00
198 Natrone Means .60 1.50
199 Junior Seau 1.00 2.50
200 Bryan Still .40 1.00
201 Freddie Jones .40 1.00
202 Steve Young 1.25 3.00
203 Jim Druckenmiller .40 1.00
204 Garrison Hearst 1.00 2.50
205 R.W. McQuarters RC 1.50 4.00
206 Merton Hanks .40 1.00
207 Marc Edwards .40 1.00
208 Jerry Rice 2.00 5.00
209 Terrell Owens 1.00 2.50
210 J.J. Stokes .60 1.50
211 Tony Banks .60 1.50
212 Robert Holcombe RC 1.50 4.00
213 Greg Hill .40 1.00
214 Amp Lee .40 1.00
215 Jerald Moore .40 1.00
216 Isaac Bruce 1.00 2.50
217 Az-Zahir Hakim RC 2.00 5.00
218 Eddie Kennison .60 1.50
219 Grant Wistrom RC 1.50 4.00
220 Warren Moon 1.00 2.50
221 Ahman Green RC 4.00 10.00
222 Steve Broussard .40 1.00
223 Ricky Watters .60 1.50
224 James McKnight 1.00 2.50
225 Joey Galloway .60 1.50
226 Mike Pritchard .40 1.00
227 Trent Dilfer 1.00 2.50
228 Warrick Dunn 1.00 2.50
229 Mike Alstott 1.00 2.50
230 John Lynch .60 1.50
231 Jacquez Green RC 1.50 4.00
232 Reidel Anthony .60 1.50
233 Bert Emanuel .60 1.50
234 Warren Sapp .60 1.50
235 Steve McNair 1.00 2.50
236 Eddie George 1.00 2.50
237 Chris Sanders .40 1.00
238 Yancey Thigpen .40 1.00
239 Willie Davis .40 1.00
240 Kevin Dyson RC 2.00 5.00
241 Frank Wycheck .40 1.00
242 Trent Green 1.00 2.50
243 Gus Frerotte .40 1.00
244 Skip Hicks RC 1.50 4.00
245 Terry Allen 1.00 2.50
246 Stephen Davis .40 1.00
247 Stephen Alexander RC 1.50 4.00
248 Michael Westbrook .60 1.50
249 Dana Stubblefield SP 1.00 2.50
250 Dan Wilkinson SP 1.00 2.50

1998 Playoff Momentum Hobby Gold

*GOL VETS: 12X TO 30X BASIC CARDS
*GOLD ROOKIES: 2.5X TO 6X
STATED PRINT RUN 25 SERIAL #'d SETS
98 Peyton Manning 200.00 350.00

1998 Playoff Momentum Hobby Red

COMPLETE SET (250) 400.00 800.00
*RED VETS: 1.5X TO 3X BASIC CARDS
*RED ROOKIES: .6X TO 1.2X BASIC CARDS
STATED ODDS 1:4 HOB/RET

1998 Playoff Momentum Retail

COMPLETE SET (250) 75.00 150.00
ROOKIE SUBSET ODDS 1:3 RETAIL
1 Karim Abdul-Jabbar .30 .75
2 Troy Aikman .60 1.50
3 Derrick Alexander .20 .50
4 Stephen Alexander .50 1.25
5 Brian Alford RC .50 1.25
6 Terry Allen .30 .75
7 Mike Alstott .30 .75
8 Kimble Anders .20 .50
9 Jamal Anderson .30 .75
10 Reidel Anthony .20 .50
11 Steve Atwater .10 .30
12 John Avery RC .75 2.00
13 Tavian Banks RC .75 2.00
14 Tony Banks .20 .50
15 Tiki Barber .30 .75
16 Charlie Batch RC 1.00 2.50
17 Donnell Bennett .10 .30
18 Edgar Bennett .10 .30
19 Jerome Bettis .30 .75
20 Steve Beuerlein .20 .50
21 Will Blackwell .10 .30
22 Jeff Blake .20 .50
23 Drew Bledsoe .50 1.25
24 Kyle Brady .10 .30
25 Robert Brooks .20 .50
26 Steve Broussard .10 .30
27 Gary Brown .10 .30
28 Tim Brown .30 .75
29 Isaac Bruce .30 .75
30 Mark Bruener .10 .30
31 Mark Brunell .30 .75
32 Keith Byars .10 .30
33 Chris Calloway .10 .30
34 Rae Carruth .10 .30
35 Cris Carter .30 .75
36 Larry Centers .10 .30
37 Chris Chandler .20 .50
38 Mark Chmura .20 .50
39 Wayne Chrebet .30 .75
40 Cameron Cleeland RC .50 1.25
41 Ben Coates .20 .50
42 Kerry Collins .20 .50
43 Andre Coleman .10 .30
44 Curtis Conway .20 .50
45 Zack Crockett .10 .30
46 Germane Crowell RC .75 2.00
47 Randall Cunningham .30 .75
48 Billy Davis .10 .30
49 Stephen Davis .10 .30
50 Terrell Davis .30 .75
51 Troy Davis .10 .30
52 Willie Davis .10 .30
53 Sean Dawkins .10 .30
54 Trent Dilfer .30 .75
55 Ken Dilger .10 .30
56 Corey Dillon .30 .75
57 Troy Drayton .10 .30
58 Jim Druckenmiller .10 .30
59 Rickey Dudley .10 .30
60 Jason Dunn .10 .30
61 Warrick Dunn .30 .75
62 Tim Dwight RC 1.00 2.50
63 Kevin Dyson RC 1.00 2.50
64 Marc Edwards .10 .30
65 Robert Edwards RC .75 2.00
66 John Elway 1.25 3.00
67 Bert Emanuel .20 .50
68 Bobby Engram .20 .50
69 Curtis Enis RC .50 1.25
70 Craig Erickson .10 .30
71 Terry Fair RC .75 2.00
72 Marshall Faulk .40 1.00
73 Brett Favre 1.25 3.00
74 Chris Floyd .30 .75
75 William Floyd .10 .30
76 Doug Flutie .30 .75
77 Glenn Foley .20 .50
78 Antonio Freeman .30 .75
79 Gus Frerotte .10 .30
80 Irving Fryar .20 .50
81 Chris Fuamatu-Ma'afala RC .75 2.00
82 Joey Galloway .20 .50
83 Rich Gannon .30 .75
84 Charlie Garner .20 .50
85 Eddie George .30 .75
86 Jeff George .20 .50
87 Jammi German RC .50 1.25
88 Terry Glenn .30 .75
89 Tony Gonzalez .30 .75
90 Jay Graham .10 .30
91 Jeff Graham .10 .30
92 Elvis Grbac .20 .50
93 Ahman Green RC 2.00 5.00
94 E.G. Green RC .75 2.00
95 Eric Green .10 .30
96 Jacquez Green RC .75 2.00
97 Trent Green .30 .75
98 Kevin Greene .20 .50
99 Brian Griese RC 2.00 5.00
100 Az-Zahir Hakim RC 1.00 2.50
101 Merton Hanks .10 .30
102 Jim Harbaugh .20 .50
103 Marvin Harrison .30 .75
104 Andre Hastings .10 .30
105 Courtney Hawkins .10 .30
106 Garrison Hearst .30 .75
107 William Henderson .20 .50
108 Skip Hicks RC .75 2.00
109 Greg Hill .10 .30
110 Ike Hilliard .20 .50
111 Robert Holcombe RC .75 2.00
112 Vonnie Holliday RC .75 2.00
113 Bobby Hoying .20 .50
114 Michael Irvin .30 .75
115 Qadry Ismail .20 .50
116 Rocket Ismail .10 .30
117 Michael Jackson .10 .30
118 Shawn Jefferson .10 .30
119 James Jett .20 .50
120 Anthony Johnson .10 .30
121 Brad Johnson .30 .75
122 Charles Johnson .10 .30
123 Keyshawn Johnson .30 .75
124 Leon Johnson .10 .30
125 Pat Johnson RC .75 2.00
126 Rob Johnson .20 .50
127 Daryl Johnston .20 .50
128 Freddie Jones .10 .30
129 Joe Jurevicius RC 1.00 2.50
130 Danny Kanell .20 .50
131 Napoleon Kaufman .30 .75
132 Eddie Kennison .20 .50
133 Levon Kirkland .10 .30
134 Erik Kramer .10 .30
135 David LaFleur .10 .30
136 Fred Lane .10 .30
137 Ryan Leaf RC 1.00 2.50
138 Amp Lee .10 .30
139 Dorsey Levens .30 .75
140 Jermaine Lewis .20 .50
141 Ray Lewis .30 .75
142 Jonathan Linton RC .75 2.00
143 Greg Lloyd .10 .30
144 Kevin Lockett .10 .30
145 John Lynch .20 .50
146 Peyton Manning RC 8.00 20.00
147 Dan Marino 1.25 3.00
148 Curtis Martin .30 .75
149 Tony Martin .20 .50
150 Terance Mathis .20 .50
151 Alonzo Mayes RC .50 1.25
152 Derrick Mayes .20 .50
153 Ed McCaffrey .20 .50
154 Keenan McCardell .20 .50
155 O.J. McDuffie .20 .50
156 Tony McGee .10 .30
157 James McKnight .30 .75
158 Steve McNair .30 .75
159 R.W. McQuarters RC .75 2.00
160 Natrone Means .20 .50
161 Eric Metcalf .10 .30
162 Ernie Mills .10 .30
163 Rick Mirer .10 .30
164 Scott Mitchell .20 .50
165 Warren Moon .30 .75
166 Herman Moore .20 .50
167 Jerald Moore .10 .30
168 Rob Moore .20 .50
169 Moses Moreno RC .50 1.25
170 Johnnie Morton .20 .50
171 Randy Moss RC 6.00 15.00
172 Eric Moulds .30 .75
173 Muhsin Muhammad .20 .50
174 Adrian Murrell .20 .50
175 Marcus Nash RC .50 1.25
176 Neil O'Donnell .20 .50
177 Terrell Owens .30 .75
178 Jerome Pathon RC 1.00 2.50
179 Carl Pickens .20 .50
180 Jake Plummer .30 .75
181 Mike Pritchard .10 .30
182 Jonathan Quinn RC 1.00 2.50
183 John Randle .20 .50
184 Andre Reed .20 .50
185 Jake Reed .20 .50
186 Errict Rhett .20 .50
187 Jerry Rice .60 1.50
188 Mikhael Ricks RC .75 2.00
189 Andre Rison .20 .50
190 Jon Ritchie RC .75 2.00
191 Rod Rutledge .30 .75
192 Barry Sanders 1.00 2.50
193 Chris Sanders .10 .30
194 Deion Sanders .30 .75
195 Frank Sanders .20 .50
196 O.J. Santiago .10 .30
197 Warren Sapp .20 .50
198 Darnay Scott .20 .50
199 Junior Seau .30 .75
200 Shannon Sharpe .20 .50
201 Sedrick Shaw .10 .30
202 Rashaan Shehee RC .75 2.00
203 Heath Shuler .10 .30
204 Tony Simmons RC .75 2.00
205 Antowain Smith .30 .75
206 Bruce Smith .20 .50
207 Emmitt Smith 1.00 2.50
208 Jimmy Smith .20 .50
209 Lamar Smith .20 .50
210 Neil Smith .20 .50
211 Robert Smith .30 .75
212 Rod Smith .20 .50
213 Takeo Spikes RC 1.00 2.50
214 Duce Staley .40 1.00
215 Duane Starks RC .50 1.25
216 James Stewart .20 .50
217 Kordell Stewart .30 .75
218 Bryan Still .10 .30
219 J.J. Stokes .20 .50
220 Michael Strahan .20 .50
221 Dana Stubblefield .10 .30
222 Fred Taylor RC 1.50 4.00
223 Vinny Testaverde .20 .50
224 Yancey Thigpen .10 .30
225 Derrick Thomas .30 .75
226 Thurman Thomas .30 .75
227 Zach Thomas .30 .75
228 Amani Toomer .20 .50
229 Andre Wadsworth RC .75 2.00
230 Wesley Walls .20 .50
231 Dedric Ward .10 .30
232 Hines Ward RC 4.00 10.00
233 Chris Warren .20 .50
234 Ricky Watters .20 .50
235 Charles Way .10 .30
236 Michael Westbrook .20 .50
237 Tyrone Wheatley .20 .50
238 Reggie White .30 .75
239 Dan Wilkinson .10 .30
240 Kevin Williams .10 .30
241 Shaun Williams RC .75 2.00
242 Grant Wistrom RC .75 2.00
243 Charles Woodson RC 2.00 5.00
244 Darren Woodson .10 .30
245 Rod Woodson .20 .50
246 Danny Wuerffel .20 .50
247 Frank Wycheck .10 .30
248 Steve Young .40 1.00

249 Eric Zeier .20 .50
250 Ray Zellars .10 .30

1998 Playoff Momentum Retail Red

COMPLETE SET (250) 125.00 250.00
*RED VETS: 1.5X TO 3X BASIC CARDS
*RED ROOKIES: .6X TO 1.2X BASIC CARDS
STATED ODDS 1:4 RETAIL
146 Peyton Manning 12.00 30.00

1998 Playoff Momentum 7-11

This 100-card set is a special version of the Playoff Momentum Retail set made specifically for 7-11 stores. This cards are essentially a back-to-back parallel set of the basic issue Momentum Retail with no additional distinguishing features. The unnumbered cards have been arranged below alphabetically according to which player on each card is alphabetized first.

COMPLETE SET (100) 24.00 60.00
1 K.Abdul / M.Brunell .80 2.00
2 T.Aikman / I.Fryar 1.20 3.00
3 D.Alexander / E.Bennett .25 .60
4 T.Allen / J.Jett .25 .60
5 M.Alstott / B.Favre 1.60 4.00
6 K.Anders / G.Hill .10 .30
7 J.Anderson / G.Brown .50 1.25
8 R.Anthony / M.Hanks .10 .30
9 S.Atwater / J.Blake .50 1.25
10 T.Banks / B.Coates .50 1.25
11 T.Barber / K.Collins .50 1.25
12 D.Bennett / C.Dillon .50 1.25
13 J.Bettis / C.Calloway .50 1.25
14 S.Beuerlein / R.Gannon .50 1.25
15 W.Blackwell / K.Johnson .50 1.25
16 D.Bledsoe / W.Chrebet .60 1.50
17 K.Brady / E.Green .10 .30
18 R.Brooks / R.Cunningham .50 1.25
19 S.Broussard / J.Dunn .10 .30
20 T.Brown / C.Chandler .50 1.25
21 I.Bruce / T.Glenn .50 1.25
22 M.Bruener / T.Dilfer .25 .60
23 K.Byars / J.Galloway .50 1.25
24 R.Carruth / A.Johnson .10 .30
25 C.Carter / W.Floyd .50 1.25
26 L.Centers / I.Hilliard .10 .30
27 M.Chmura / J.Harbaugh .25 .60
28 A.Coleman / M.Jackson .10 .30
29 C.Conway / C.Erickson .25 .60
30 Z.Crockett / G.Hearst .25 .60
31 B.Davis / T.Green .50 1.25
32 S.Davis / B.Emanuel .50 1.25
33 Ter.Davis / A.Hastings .80 2.00
34 Troy Davis / C.Johnson .10 .30
35 W.Davis / G.Foley .10 .30
36 S.Dawkins / M.Irvin .25 .60
37 K.Dilger / G.Frerotte .25 .60
38 T.Drayton / S.Jefferson .10 .30
39 J.Druckenmiller / M.Faulk .50 1.25
40 R.Dudley / W.Henderson .25 .60
41 W.Dunn / K.Green .50 1.25
42 M.Edwards / A.Freeman .50 1.25
43 J.Elway / Q.Ismail 1.60 4.00
44 B.Engram / J.Graham .25 .60
45 D.Flutie / E.George .60 1.50
46 C.Garner / B.Johnson .50 1.25
47 J.George / B.Hoying .25 .60
48 T.Gonzalez / M.Harrison .50 1.25
49 J.Graham / R.Ismail .25 .60
50 E.Grbac / C.Hawkins .25 .60
51 L.Johnson / E.McCaffrey .25 .60
52 R.Johnson / D.Levens .50 1.25
53 D.Johnston / A.Murrell .25 .60
54 F.Jones / R.Zellars .10 .30
55 D.Kanell / R.Smith .50 1.25
56 N.Kaufman / D.Sanders .50 1.25
57 E.Kennison / H.Moore .25 .60
58 L.Kirkland / F.Wycheck .10 .30
59 E.Kramer / G.Lloyd .10 .30
60 D.LaFleur / C.Pickens .25 .60
61 F.Lane / D.Mayes .10 .30
62 A.Lee / K.McCardell .25 .60
63 J.Lewis / D.Thomas .25 .60
64 R.Lewis / E.Mills .50 1.25
65 K.Lockett / R.Watters .25 .60
66 J.Lynch / T.Owens .50 1.25
67 D.Marino / K.Williams 1.60 4.00
68 C.Martin / D.Staley .50 1.25
69 T.Martin / O.J. Mc... .25 .60
70 T.Mathis / R.Moore .25 .60
71 O.J. McDuffie / M.Muhammad .25 .60
72 T.McGee / T.Wheatley .25 .60
73 J.McKnight / N.Smith .50 1.25
74 S.McNair / C.Sanders .50 1.25
75 N.Means / W.Moon .50 1.25
76 E.Metcalf / D.Wuerffel .10 .30
77 R.Mirer / H.Shuler .25 .60
78 S.Mitchell / V.Testaverde .25 .60
79 J.Moore / D.Ward .10 .30
80 J.Morton / E.Rhett .25 .60
81 E.Moulds / B.Still .25 .60
82 N.O'Donnell / T.Thomas .25 .60
83 J.Plummer / E.Smith 1.20 3.00
84 M.Pritchard / J.Rice .80 2.00
85 J.Randle / D.Woodson .25 .60
86 A.Reed / J.Stewart .50 1.25
87 J.Reed / W.Sapp .25 .60
88 A.Rison / S.Shaw .25 .60
89 B.Sanders / E.Zeier 1.60 4.00
90 F.Sanders / W.Walls .25 .60
91 J.Seau / C.Way .25 .60
92 D.Scott / B.Smith .25 .60
93 S.Sharpe / J.Smith .25 .60
94 A.Smith / K.Stewart .50 1.25
95 L.Smith / M.Strahan .25 .60
96 Rod Smith / A.Toomer .25 .60
97 J.J.Stokes / M.Westbrook .25 .60
98 Y.Thigpen / R.Woodson .25 .60
99 Z.Thomas / R.White .50 1.25
100 C.Warren / S.Young .60 1.50

1998 Playoff Momentum Class Reunion Quads

Randomly inserted in hobby packs only at the rate of one in 81, this 16-card set features color photos of four players drafted from the same year printed two on front and two on back on thick doublesided mirror foil stock with micro-etching on each side and gold foil stamping. A parallel jumbo set was also produced measuring approximately 3 1/2" x 5" printed in a "box topper" style and inserted one per hobby box.

COMPLETE SET (16) 125.00 300.00
STATED ODDS 1:81 HOBBY
*JUMBOS: .1X TO .25X HI COL.
JUMBOS: ONE PER HOBBY BOX
1 Marino/Elway/Matt/D.Green 20.00 50.00
2 SYoung/Fryar/RWhite/Host. 7.50 20.00
3 Rice/BSmith/AReed/Flutie 10.00 25.00
4 Byars/O'Neal/Joyner/R.Brown 4.00 10.00
5 CCarter/Testa/Harb/R.Wood 5.00 12.00
6 TBrown/Chand/Irvin/N.Smith 5.00 12.00
7 Aikman/BSand/DSand/Rison 20.00 50.00
8 ESmith/JGeor/O'Donn/S.Shar. 12.50 30.00
9 Favre/HMoore/Thigpen/Watt. 15.00 40.00
10 Chmu./BJohn/Pick/R.Brooks 5.00 12.00
11 Bledsoe/Bettis/Brun/Hearst 12.50 30.00
12 Dilfer/Levens/Faulk/Bruce 10.00 25.00
13 TDavis/KStew/Kauf/C.Martin 7.50 20.00
14 EGeorge/KJohn/Abdul/Glenn 6.00 15.00
15 WDunn/Dill/Plumm/A.Smith 6.00 15.00
16 Manning/Leaf/Enis/Moss 12.00 30.00

1998 Playoff Momentum Class Reunion Tandems

Randomly inserted in retail packs only at the rate of one in 121, this 16-card set features color action photos of two NFL players from the same draft printed on two-sided conventional card stock with foil stamped logo and draft year on both sides.

COMPLETE SET (16) 250.00 500.00
STATED ODDS 1:121 RETAIL
1 D.Marino / J.Elway 30.00 80.00
2 S.Young / R.White 12.50 30.00
3 J.Rice / B.Smith 15.00 40.00
4 K.Byars / L.O'Neil 6.00 15.00
5 C.Carter / V.Testaverde 10.00 25.00
6 T.Brown / M.Irvin 10.00 25.00
7 T.Aikman / B.Sanders 30.00 80.00
8 E.Smith / J.George 20.00 50.00
9 B.Favre / H.Moore 25.00 60.00
10 B.Johnson / C.Pickens 10.00 25.00
11 D.Bledsoe / M.Brunell 20.00 50.00
12 D.Levens / I.Bruce 12.50 30.00
13 T.Davis / K.Stewart 10.00 25.00
14 E.George / K.Johnson 10.00 25.00
15 W.Dunn / J.Plummer 10.00 25.00
16 P.Manning / R.Leaf 15.00 40.00

1998 Playoff Momentum Endzone X-press

Randomly inserted in retail packs at the rate of one in 13 and in hobby packs at the rate of one in nine, this 29-card set features color action player photos printed on plastic stock with holofoil stamping. The hobby version is die-cut and printed on clear plastic card stock with holographic foil stamping.

COMPLETE DIE CUT SET (29) 60.00 120.00
DIE CUT STATED ODDS 1:9 HOBBY
*NON-DIE CUTS: .4X TO .8X DIE CUTS
NON-DIE CUT STATED ODDS 1:13 RETAIL
1 Jake Plummer 1.60 4.00
2 Herman Moore 1.00 2.50
3 Terrell Davis 1.50 4.00
4 Antowain Smith 1.50 4.00
5 Curtis Enis .30 .75
6 Corey Dillon 1.50 4.00
7 Troy Aikman 3.00 8.00
8 John Elway 6.00 15.00
9 Barry Sanders 5.00 12.00
10 Brett Favre 6.00 15.00
11 Peyton Manning 12.00 30.00
12 Mark Brunell 1.50 4.00
13 Andre Rison 1.00 2.50
14 Dan Marino 6.00 15.00
15 Randy Moss 4.00 10.00
16 Drew Bledsoe 2.50 6.00
17 Jerome Bettis 1.50 4.00
18 Tim Brown 1.50 4.00
19 Antonio Freeman 1.50 4.00
20 Napoleon Kaufman 1.50 4.00
21 Emmitt Smith 5.00 12.00
22 Kordell Stewart 1.50 4.00
23 Curtis Martin 1.50 4.00
24 Ryan Leaf .50 1.50
25 Jerry Rice 3.00 8.00
26 Joey Galloway 1.00 2.50
27 Warrick Dunn 1.50 4.00
28 Eddie George 1.50 4.00
29 Steve McNair 1.50 4.00

1998 Playoff Momentum Headliners

Randomly inserted in hobby packs only at the rate of one in 49, this 23-card set features color action images of top players with a newspaper headline background stating the milestone event that made them the league's best and is printed on holographic card stock with foil stamping. The retail version of this set has an insertion rate of one in 73 and is printed on holofoil board with red color overlay and black foil.

COMPLETE SET (23) 100.00 200.00
BLUE STATED ODDS 1:49 HOBBY
*RED: .3X TO .8X BLUE
RED STATED ODDS 1:73 RETAIL
1 Brett Favre 10.00 25.00
2 Jerry Rice 6.00 15.00
3 Barry Sanders 8.00 20.00
4 Troy Aikman 5.00 12.00
5 Warrick Dunn 2.50 6.00
6 Dan Marino 10.00 25.00
7 John Elway 8.00 20.00
8 Drew Bledsoe 3.00 8.00
9 Kordell Stewart 2.50 6.00
10 Mark Brunell 2.50 6.00
11 Eddie George 2.50 6.00
12 Terrell Davis 3.00 8.00
13 Emmitt Smith 8.00 20.00
14 Steve McNair 2.50 6.00
15 Mike Alstott 2.50 6.00
16 Peyton Manning 10.00 25.00
17 Antonio Freeman 2.50 6.00
18 Curtis Martin 3.00 8.00
19 Terry Glenn 2.50 6.00
20 Brad Johnson 2.50 6.00
21 Karim Abdul-Jabbar 2.50 6.00
22 Ryan Leaf 2.00 5.00
23 Jerome Bettis 3.00 8.00

1998 Playoff Momentum Headliners Gold

*GOLD/65-166: 1.2X TO 3X BLUE
*GOLD/32-49: 2X TO 5X BLUE
*GOLD/19-24: 2.5X TO 6X BLUE
16 Peyton Manning/33 150.00 250.00

1998 Playoff Momentum Honors

Randomly inserted in hobby packs only at the rate of one in 3841, this three-card set features color action player photos printed on two-foil die-cut cards. These cards are the next three cards in the ever-continuing cross-brand insert set.

COMPLETE SET (3) 50.00 120.00
STATED ODDS 1:3841 HOBBY
PH16 Brett Favre 30.00 80.00
PH17 Kordell Stewart 10.00 25.00
PH18 Troy Aikman 25.00 50.00

1998 Playoff Momentum NFL Rivals

Randomly inserted in hobby packs at the rate of one in 49 and in retail packs at the rate of one in 73, this 22-card set features color action images of two NFL players from rival teams printed on mirror foil board stock. The hobby version has gold foil stamping. The retail version has silver foil stamping.

COMP.HOBBY SET (22) 100.00 200.00
STATED ODDS 1:49 HOBBY
*RETAIL SILVER: .3X TO .8X HOBBY
SILVER STATED ODDS 1:73 RETAIL
1 M.Brunell/J.Elway 7.50 20.00
2 J.Bettis/E.George 3.00 8.00
3 B.Sanders/E.Smith 10.00 25.00
4 D.Marino/D.Bledsoe 7.50 20.00
5 T.Aikman/J.Plummer 3.00 8.00
6 T.Davis/N.Kaufman 3.00 8.00
7 C.Carter/H.Moore 2.00 5.00
8 W.Dunn/D.Levens 3.00 8.00
9 K.Stewart/S.McNair 3.00 8.00
10 C.Martin/A.Smith 3.00 8.00
11 J.Rice/M.Irvin 5.00 12.00
12 S.Young/B.Favre 10.00 25.00
13 C.Dillon/F.Taylor 3.00 8.00
14 T.Brown/A.Rison 3.00 8.00
15 M.Alstott/R.Smith 2.00 5.00
16 B.Johnson/S.Mitchell 2.00 5.00
17 R.Edwards/J.Avery 3.00 8.00
18 D.Sanders/R.Moore 3.00 8.00
19 A.Freeman/R.Moss 10.00 25.00
20 P.Manning/R.Leaf 12.00 30.00
21 C.Enis/J.Green 2.00 5.00
22 K.Johnson/T.Glenn 2.00 5.00

1998 Playoff Momentum Rookie Double Feature Hobby

Randomly inserted in hobby packs only at the rate of one in 17, this 20-card set features color action photos of two rookies with similar styles of play printed one on each side on doublesided foil board with three patterned micro-etches on each side.

COMPLETE SET (20) 60.00 120.00
STATED ODDS 1:17 HOBBY
1 P.Manning / B.Griese 15.00 40.00
2 R.Leaf / C.Batch 2.00 5.00
3 C.Woodson / T.Fair 4.00 10.00
4 C.Enis / T.Banks 1.00 2.50
5 F.Taylor / J.Avery 2.50 6.00
6 K.Dyson / E.G.Green 2.00 5.00
7 R.Edwards / C.Fuamatu 1.50 4.00
8 R.Moss / T.Dwight 10.00 25.00
9 M.Nash / J.Jurevicius 2.00 5.00
10 J.Pathon / A.Hakim 2.00 5.00
11 J.Green / T.Simmons 1.50 4.00
12 R.Holcombe / J.Ritchie 1.50 4.00
13 C.Cleeland / A.Mayes 1.00 2.50
14 P.Johnson / M.Ricks 1.50 4.00
15 G.Crowell / H.Ward 6.00 12.00
16 S.Hicks / C.Floyd 1.50 4.00
17 B.Alford / J.German 1.00 2.50
18 A.Green / R.Shehee 4.00 10.00
19 J.Quinn / M.Moreno 1.50 4.00
20 R.W.McQuarters / D.Starks 1.00 2.50

1998 Playoff Momentum Rookie Double Feature Retail

Randomly inserted in retail packs only at the rate of one in 25, this 40-card set features color action player photos printed on singlesided foil board with three micro-etched patterns. The same image from the front appears in color on the back with film laminant.

COMPLETE SET (40) 75.00 150.00
STATED ODDS 1:25 RETAIL
R1 Peyton Manning 10.00 25.00
R2 Ryan Leaf .60 1.50
R3 Charles Woodson 2.50 6.00
R4 Curtis Enis .60 1.50
R5 Fred Taylor 1.50 4.00
R6 Kevin Dyson 1.00 2.50
R7 Robert Edwards .60 1.50
R8 Randy Moss 6.00 15.00
R9 Marcus Nash .30 .75
R10 Jerome Pathon .60 1.50
R11 Jacquez Green .60 1.50
R12 Robert Holcombe .30 .75
R13 Cameron Cleeland .30 .75
R14 Pat Johnson .30 .75
R15 Germane Crowell .60 1.50
R16 Skip Hicks .30 .75
R17 Brian Alford .30 .75
R18 Ahman Green 2.50 6.00
R19 Jonathan Quinn .30 .75
R20 R.W. McQuarters .30 .75
R21 Brian Griese 2.00 5.00
R22 Charlie Batch 1.00 2.50
R23 Terry Fair .30 .75
R24 Tavian Banks .30 .75
R25 John Avery .30 .75
R26 E.G. Green .30 .75
R27 Chris Fuamatu-Ma'afala .30 .75
R28 Tim Dwight 1.00 2.50
R29 Joe Jurevicius 1.00 2.50
R30 Az-Zahir Hakim .60 1.50
R31 Tony Simmons .30 .75
R32 Jon Ritchie .30 .75
R33 Alonzo Mayes .30 .75
R34 Mikhael Ricks .30 .75
R35 Hines Ward 4.00 10.00
R36 Chris Floyd .30 .75
R37 Jammi German .30 .75
R38 Rashaan Shehee .30 .75
R39 Moses Moreno .30 .75
R40 Duane Starks .30 .75

1998 Playoff Momentum Team Threads Home

Randomly inserted in hobby packs only at the rate of one in 33, this 20-card set features color action player photos with foil stamping and a replica home jersey swatch (not game used) inserted in the die-cut section of the card.

HOME STATED ODDS 1:33 HOBBY
*AWAY: .6X TO 1.5X HOME
AWAY STATED ODDS 1:65 HOBBY
*RETAIL HOME: .3X TO .8X HOBBY HOME
RETAIL HOME STATED ODDS 1:49
*RETAIL AWAY: .3X TO .8X HOBBY HOME
RETAIL AWAY STATED ODDS 1:97
1 Jerry Rice 10.00 25.00
2 Terrell Davis 3.00 8.00
3 Warrick Dunn 2.50 6.00
4 Brett Favre 6.00 15.00
5 Napoleon Kaufman 2.50 6.00
6 Corey Dillon 2.50 6.00
7 John Elway 6.00 15.00
8 Troy Aikman 5.00 12.00
9 Mark Brunell 3.00 8.00
10 Kordell Stewart 2.50 6.00
11 Drew Bledsoe 3.00 8.00
12 Curtis Martin 3.00 8.00
13 Dan Marino 8.00 20.00
14 Jerome Bettis 6.00 15.00
15 Eddie George 3.00 8.00
16 Ryan Leaf 3.00 8.00
17 Jake Plummer 2.50 6.00
18 Peyton Manning 15.00 40.00
19 Steve Young 5.00 12.00
20 Barry Sanders 6.00 15.00

1999 Playoff Momentum

The 1999 Playoff Momentum set was issued as a 200 card set done a plastic card stock with color action photos. Cards numbered one through 100 were issued at a rate of four in every pack. Cards numbered 101 through 150 were available one per pack and cards numbered 151 through 200 were the short printed rookie cards and were available at a rate of one in five packs. Also inserted were game used Barry Sanders cards featuring pieces of Game worn Jerseys and Helmets. Also inserted were the Star Gazing Red Certified hand signed cards.

COMPLETE SET (200) 150.00 300.00
COMP.SHORT SET (150) 50.00 100.00
1 Rob Moore .20 .50
2 Adrian Murrell .20 .50
3 Frank Sanders .20 .50
4 Andre Wadsworth .20 .50
5 Tim Dwight .25 .60
6 Terance Mathis .20 .50
7 Priest Holmes .20 .50
8 Jermaine Lewis .20 .50
9 Scott Mitchell .20 .50
10 Patrick Johnson .20 .50
11 Tony Banks .25 .60
12 Thurman Thomas .25 .60
13 Andre Reed .30 .75
14 Bruce Smith .25 .60
15 Tim Biakabutuka .25 .60
16 Muhsin Muhammad .20 .50
17 Wesley Walls .25 .60
18 Rae Carruth .20 .50
19 Curtis Conway .25 .60
20 Bobby Engram .20 .50
21 Jeff Blake .25 .60
22 Darnay Scott .20 .50
23 Ty Detmer .20 .50
24 Leslie Shepherd .20 .50
25 Sedrick Shaw .20 .50
26 Michael Irvin .30 .75
27 Rocket Ismail .25 .60
28 Ed McCaffrey .25 .60
29 Marcus Nash .20 .50
30 Shannon Sharpe .25 .60
31 Neil Smith .20 .50
32 Rod Smith .25 .60
33 Bubby Brister .20 .50
34 Germane Crowell .20 .50
35 Johnnie Morton .25 .60
36 Bill Schroeder .25 .60
37 Mark Chmura .20 .50
38 Marvin Harrison .25 .60
39 E.G. Green .20 .50
40 Jerome Pathon .20 .50
41 Keenan McCardell .25 .60
42 Jimmy Smith .25 .60
43 Kyle Brady .20 .50
44 Tavian Banks .20 .50
45 Warren Moon .30 .75
46 Derrick Alexander WR .20 .50
47 Elvis Grbac .20 .50
48 Andre Rison .25 .60
49 Byron Bam Morris .20 .50
50 Rashaan Shehee .20 .50
51 Karim Abdul-Jabbar .20 .50
52 John Avery .20 .50
53 Tony Martin .25 .60
54 O.J. McDuffie .25 .60
55 Oronde Gadsden .20 .50
56 Robert Smith .20 .50
57 Jeff George .20 .50
58 Jake Reed .25 .60
59 Leroy Hoard .20 .50
60 Terry Allen .25 .60
61 Terry Glenn .25 .60
62 Ben Coates .25 .60
63 Tony Simmons .20 .50
64 Cameron Cleeland .20 .50
65 Eddie Kennison .25 .60
66 Billy Joe Hobert .20 .50
67 Amani Toomer .20 .50
68 Kerry Collins .20 .50
69 Ike Hilliard .20 .50
70 Gary Brown .20 .50
71 Joe Jurevicius .20 .50
72 Wayne Chrebet .20 .50
73 Vinny Testaverde .20 .50
74 Charles Woodson .30 .75
75 James Jett .20 .50
76 Charles Johnson .20 .50
77 Duce Staley .20 .50
78 Hines Ward .25 .60
79 Jim Harbaugh .25 .60
80 Ryan Leaf .25 .60
81 Junior Seau .25 .60
82 Mikhael Ricks .20 .50
83 Garrison Hearst .20 .50
84 J.J. Stokes .20 .50
85 Lawrence Phillips .25 .60
86 Derrick Mayes .20 .50
87 Mike Pritchard .20 .50
88 Ahman Green .25 .60
89 Ricky Watters .25 .60
90 Robert Holcombe .20 .50
91 Isaac Bruce .30 .75
92 Trent Dilfer .20 .50
93 Reidel Anthony .20 .50
94 Jacquez Green .20 .50
95 Warren Sapp .25 .60
96 Kevin Dyson .20 .50
97 Yancey Thigpen .20 .50
98 Stephen Davis .20 .50
99 Irving Fryar .25 .60
100 Michael Westbrook .20 .50
101 Jake Plummer .30 .75
102 Jamal Anderson .40 1.00
103 Chris Chandler .40 1.00
104 Doug Flutie .50 1.25
105 Eric Moulds .30 .75
106 Antowain Smith .30 .75
107 Jonathan Linton .30 .75
108 Curtis Enis .30 .75
109 Corey Dillon .30 .75
110 Carl Pickens .40 1.00
111 Emmitt Smith .75 2.00
112 Troy Aikman .60 1.50
113 Deion Sanders .40 1.00
114 John Elway .75 2.00
115 Terrell Davis .40 1.00
116 Brian Griese .30 .75
117 Barry Sanders .75 2.00
118 Charlie Batch .30 .75
119 Herman Moore .40 1.00
120 Brett Favre 1.00 2.50
121 Antonio Freeman .40 1.00
122 Dorsey Levens .40 1.00
123 Peyton Manning 1.50 4.00
124 Fred Taylor .30 .75
125 Mark Brunell .40 1.00
126 Dan Marino 1.00 2.50
127 Randy Moss .40 1.00
128 Cris Carter .50 1.25
129 Randall Cunningham .40 1.00
130 Drew Bledsoe .40 1.00
131 Keyshawn Johnson .40 1.00
132 Curtis Martin .40 1.00
133 Tim Brown .50 1.25
134 Napoleon Kaufman .30 .75
135 Kordell Stewart .30 .75
136 Jerome Bettis .50 1.25
137 Natrone Means .40 1.00
138 Jerry Rice 1.25 3.00
139 Steve Young .60 1.50
140 Terrell Owens .40 1.00
141 Joey Galloway .40 1.00
142 Jon Kitna .30 .75
143 Marshall Faulk .40 1.00
144 Kurt Warner RC 5.00 12.00
145 Warrick Dunn .30 .75
146 Mike Alstott .30 .75
147 Eddie George .40 1.00
148 Steve McNair .40 1.00
149 Brad Johnson .40 1.00
150 Skip Hicks .30 .75
151 Tim Couch RC 1.50 4.00
152 Donovan McNabb RC 4.00 10.00
153 Akili Smith RC 1.25 3.00
154 Edgerrin James RC 2.00 5.00
155 Ricky Williams RC 2.00 5.00
156 Torry Holt RC 2.50 6.00
157 Champ Bailey RC 2.50 6.00
158 David Boston RC 1.25 3.00
159 Chris Claiborne RC 1.25 3.00
160 Chris McAlister RC 1.25 3.00
161 Daunte Culpepper RC 2.00 5.00
162 Cade McNown RC 1.25 3.00
163 Troy Edwards RC 1.25 3.00
164 Jevon Kearse RC 1.50 4.00
165 Kevin Johnson RC 1.50 4.00
166 James Johnson RC 1.25 3.00
167 Reginald Kelly RC 1.25 3.00
168 Rob Konrad RC 1.25 3.00
169 Jim Kleinsasser RC 2.00 5.00
170 Kevin Faulk RC 1.25 3.00
171 Joe Montgomery RC 1.25 3.00
172 Shaun King RC 1.25 3.00
173 Peerless Price RC 1.25 3.00
174 Mike Cloud RC 1.25 3.00
175 Jermaine Fazande RC 1.25 3.00
176 D'Wayne Bates RC 1.25 3.00
177 Brock Huard RC 1.25 3.00
178 Marty Booker RC 1.25 3.00
179 Karsten Bailey RC 1.25 3.00
180 Shawn Bryson RC 1.25 3.00
181 Jeff Paulk RC 1.25 3.00
182 Travis McGriff RC 1.25 3.00
183 Amos Zereoue RC 1.25 3.00
184 Craig Yeast RC 1.25 3.00
185 Joe Germaine RC 1.50 4.00
186 Dameane Douglas RC 1.25 3.00
187 Sedrick Irvin RC 1.25 3.00
188 Brandon Stokley RC 1.50 4.00
189 Larry Parker RC 1.50 4.00
190 Sean Bennett RC 1.25 3.00
191 Wane McGarity RC 1.25 3.00
192 Olandis Gary RC 2.00 5.00
193 Na Brown RC 1.25 3.00
194 Aaron Brooks RC 1.50 4.00
195 Cecil Collins RC 1.25 3.00
196 Darrin Chiaverini RC 1.25 3.00
197 Kevin Daft RC 1.25 3.00
198 Darnell McDonald RC 1.25 3.00
199 Joel Makovicka RC 1.25 3.00
200 Michael Bishop RC 1.50 4.00

1999 Playoff Momentum SSD O's

*1-100 STARS: 30X TO 80X HI COL.
*101-150 STARS: 20X TO 50X HI COL.
*144/151-200 RCs: 2X TO 5X
STATED PRINT RUN 25 SERIAL #'d SETS

1999 Playoff Momentum SSD X's

*1-100 STARS: 4X TO 10X HI COL.
*101-150 STARS: 2.5X TO 6X HI COL.
*144/151-200 RCs: .8X TO 2X
STATED PRINT RUN 300 SERIAL #'d SETS

1999 Playoff Momentum SSD Chart Toppers

Randomly inserted at a rate of one in 33 packs, This 24 card insert set features star players who are at the top of the charts such as Dan Marino and Eddie George.

COMPLETE SET (24) 75.00 150.00
STATED ODDS 1:33
CT1 Donovan McNabb 5.00 12.00
CT2 Randy Moss 5.00 12.00
CT3 Cade McNown .75 2.00
CT4 Brett Favre 6.00 15.00
CT5 Edgerrin James 4.00 10.00
CT6 Dan Marino 6.00 15.00
CT7 Jamal Anderson 2.00 5.00
CT8 Barry Sanders 6.00 15.00
CT9 Kordell Stewart 1.25 3.00
CT10 John Elway 6.00 15.00
CT11 Eddie George 1.25 3.00
CT12 Terrell Davis 2.00 5.00
CT13 Ricky Williams 3.00 8.00
CT14 Peyton Manning 6.00 15.00
CT15 Tim Couch 1.25 3.00
CT16 Emmitt Smith 4.00 10.00
CT17 Doug Flutie 1.25 3.00
CT18 Troy Aikman 4.00 10.00
CT19 Steve Young 2.50 6.00
CT20 Jerry Rice 4.00 10.00
CT21 Mark Brunell 1.25 3.00
CT22 Fred Taylor 2.00 5.00
CT23 Jake Plummer 1.25 3.00
CT24 Drew Bledsoe 2.50 6.00

1999 Playoff Momentum SSD Terrell Davis Salute

Randomly inserted in packs, This five card insert set features Terrell Davis on the card front in five different card designs. 150 cards for each design were hand signed and serial numbered.

COMPLETE SET (5) 20.00 50.00
COMMON CARD (TD11-TD15) 4.00 10.00
STATED ODDS 1:255
COMMON AUTO (TD11-TD15) 12.00 30.00
AUTO STATED PRINT RUN 150

1999 Playoff Momentum SSD Gridiron Force

Randomly inserted at a rate of one in one in 17 packs, This 24 card insert set features stars such as Troy Aikman and Dan Marino. Cards are done with a color action shot with a gold foil stamping on card front.

COMPLETE SET (24) 40.00 80.00
STATED ODDS 1:17
GF1 Cris Carter 1.25 3.00
GF2 Brett Favre 4.00 10.00
GF3 Jamal Anderson 1.25 3.00
GF4 Dan Marino 4.00 10.00
GF5 Deion Sanders 1.25 3.00
GF6 Barry Sanders 4.00 10.00
GF7 Jerome Bettis 1.25 3.00
GF8 John Elway 4.00 10.00
GF9 Eddie George .75 2.00
GF10 Peyton Manning 4.00 10.00
GF11 Warrick Dunn 1.25 3.00
GF12 Troy Aikman 2.50 6.00
GF13 Keyshawn Johnson 1.25 3.00
GF14 Jerry Rice 2.50 6.00
GF15 Terrell Owens 1.25 3.00
GF16 Randy Moss 3.00 8.00
GF17 Fred Taylor 1.25 3.00
GF18 Mark Brunell .75 2.00
GF19 Steve Young 1.50 4.00
GF20 Drew Bledsoe 1.50 4.00
GF21 Kordell Stewart .75 2.00
GF22 Emmitt Smith 2.50 6.00
GF23 Terrell Davis 1.25 3.00
GF24 Jake Plummer .75 2.00

1999 Playoff Momentum SSD Hog Heaven

Randomly inserted at a rate of one in 81 packs, This 12 card die-cut insert set features color action shots with a real football leather background featuring such stars as Jake Plummer and Jerry Rice.

COMPLETE SET (12) 100.00 200.00
STATED ODDS 1:81
HH1 Ricky Williams 5.00 12.00
HH2 Terrell Davis 4.00 10.00
HH3 Emmitt Smith 7.50 20.00
HH4 Brett Favre 12.50 30.00
HH5 Fred Taylor 4.00 10.00
HH6 Tim Couch 4.00 10.00
HH7 John Elway 12.50 30.00
HH8 Dan Marino 12.50 30.00
HH9 Randy Moss 7.50 20.00
HH10 Barry Sanders 12.50 30.00
HH11 Jerry Rice 7.50 20.00
HH12 Jake Plummer 4.00 10.00

1999 Playoff Momentum SSD Rookie Quads

Randomly inerted at a rate of one in 97 packs, This quad player card features two rookie players on the card front as well on the card back with a mirror-like finish.

COMPLETE SET (12) 100.00 200.00
STATED ODDS 1:97
*GOLDS: 1X TO 2.5X HI COL.
GOLDS STATED PRINT RUN 50 SER.#'d SETS
1 Couch/Brooks/King/Bishop 5.00 12.00
2 James/Cloud/Paulk/Mak 12.50 30.00
3 Holt/Kelly/Booker/Doug 7.50 20.00
4 Bailey/Claib/McAli/McFar 4.00 10.00
5 Boston/Kleins/Bailey/Stok 4.00 10.00
6 Williams/Zer/Coll/Azum 6.00 15.00
7 McNabb/Huard/Culp/Cov 12.50 30.00
8 Johnson/Faz/Irvin/Benn 4.00 10.00
9 Edwards/Price/McGriff/Prkr 4.00 10.00
10 Konrad/Flk/Mont/Bryson 4.00 10.00
11 McNown/Germ/Smith/Greis 4.00 10.00
12 Johnson/Bates/Yst/McGar 7.50 20.00

1999 Playoff Momentum SSD Rookie Recall

Randomly inserted at a rate of one in 49 packs, This 30 card insert set features a current action shot on the card front and a rookie action shot on the card back. Set features such stars as John Elway and Emmitt Smith.

COMPLETE SET (30) 100.00 200.00
STATED ODDS 1:49
1 Jerome Bettis 2.50 6.00
2 Tim Brown 2.50 6.00
3 Cris Carter 2.50 6.00
4 Marshall Faulk 3.00 8.00
5 Doug Flutie 1.50 4.00
6 Randall Cunningham 1.50 4.00
7 Brett Favre 8.00 20.00
8 Dan Marino 8.00 20.00
9 Barry Sanders 8.00 20.00
10 John Elway 8.00 20.00
11 Emmitt Smith 5.00 12.00
12 Troy Aikman 5.00 12.00
13 Jerry Rice 5.00 12.00
14 Steve Young 3.00 8.00
15 Randy Moss 5.00 12.00
16 Peyton Manning 6.00 15.00
17 Fred Taylor 2.50 6.00
18 Jake Plummer 1.50 4.00
19 Drew Bledsoe 3.00 8.00
20 Mark Brunell 1.50 4.00
21 Charlie Batch 1.00 2.50
22 Antonio Freeman 1.50 4.00
23 Curtis Martin 2.50 6.00
24 Eddie George 1.50 4.00
25 Kordell Stewart 1.50 4.00
26 Jamal Anderson 1.50 4.00
27 Curtis Enis 1.00 2.50
28 Terrell Davis 2.50 6.00
29 Eric Moulds 1.50 4.00
30 Terrell Owens 2.50 6.00

1999 Playoff Momentum SSD Barry Sanders Commemorative

Randomly inserted in packs at a rate of one in 275 packs, This five card insert set is a continuation to the Barry Sanders Run for the Record set which was available in several Playoff products. A Game Jersey card (#RR1) was also produced and serial numbered of 300-cards made.

COMPLETE SET (5) 20.00 50.00
COMMON CARD (RR7-RR11) 5.00 12.00
STATED ODDS 1:275

1999 Playoff Momentum SSD Barry Sanders Memorabilia

Randomly inserted in packs, this two card set features either a swatch of a game used jersey numbered out of 300, or a game used helmet numbered out of 125.

JERSEY PRINT RUN 300 SERIAL #'d CARDS
HELMET PRINT RUN 125 SERIAL #'d CARDS
RR1 Barry Sanders Jsy/300 12.00 30.00
RR5 Barry Sanders Hel/125 25.00 60.00

1999 Playoff Momentum SSD Star Gazing

Randomly inserted in packs The Star Gazing insert set came in three tiered colors: Blue cards (SG9-SG30) were inserted at a rate of one in 17 packs, Red cards (SG1-SG8) were hand signed by each player and available one in 185 packs, and finally Green cards (SG31-SG45) were inserted at the rate of 1:65. Also inserted was a parallel gold version of each insert with each card serial numbered to only 50. Some signed cards were issued via mail redemptions that carried an expiration date of 10/31/2000.

COMPLETE SET (45) 200.00 400.00
SG1-SG8 RED AUTO STATED ODDS 1:185
SG9-SG30 BLUE STATED ODDS 1:17
SG31-SG45 GREEN STATED ODDS 1:65
GOLD STATED PRINT RUN 50 SER.#'d SETS
SG1 Terrell Davis AU 10.00 25.00
SG2 Dan Marino AU 40.00 80.00
SG3 Joey Galloway AU 7.50 20.00
SG4 Steve McNair AU 8.00 20.00
SG5 Doug Flutie AU 12.50 30.00
SG6 Kordell Stewart AU 7.50 20.00
SG7 Fred Taylor AU 10.00 25.00
SG8 Jamal Anderson AU 7.50 20.00
SG9 Karim Abdul-Jabbar .50 1.25
SG10 Mike Alstott .50 1.25
SG11 Jerome Bettis .50 1.25
SG12 Carl Pickens .50 1.25
SG13 Cris Carter .50 1.25
SG14 Randall Cunningham .50 1.25
SG15 Corey Dillon .50 1.25
SG16 Tim Dwight .50 1.25
SG17 Cade McNown .50 1.25
SG18 Marshall Faulk 1.25 3.00
SG19 Napoleon Kaufman .50 1.25
SG20 Antonio Freeman .50 1.25
SG21 Edgerrin James 1.50 4.00
SG22 Terrell Owens .75 2.00
SG23 Garrison Hearst .50 1.25
SG24 Keyshawn Johnson .50 1.25
SG25 Akili Smith .50 1.25
SG26 Curtis Martin .50 1.25
SG27 Dorsey Levens .50 1.25
SG28 Deion Sanders .50 1.25
SG29 Herman Moore .50 1.25
SG30 Eric Moulds .50 1.25
SG31 Randy Moss 3.00 8.00
SG32 Eddie George 1.50 4.00
SG33 Barry Sanders 5.00 12.00
SG34 John Elway 5.00 12.00
SG35 Peyton Manning 4.00 10.00
SG36 Emmitt Smith 3.00 8.00
SG37 Troy Aikman 3.00 8.00
SG38 Jerry Rice 3.00 8.00
SG39 Mark Brunell 2.00 5.00
SG40 Steve Young 2.00 5.00
SG41 Tim Couch 2.00 5.00
SG42 Ricky Williams 3.00 8.00
SG43 Donovan McNabb 5.00 12.00
SG44 Drew Bledsoe 2.00 5.00
SG45 Brett Favre 5.00 12.00

1999 Playoff Momentum SSD Star Gazing Gold

*SG9-SG30 STARS: 3X TO 8X BASIC INSERTS
*SG9-SG30 ROOKIES: 1.5X TO 4X BASIC INS.
*SG31-SG45 STARS: 2X TO 5X BASIC INSERTS
*SG31-SG45 ROOKIES: 1.2X TO 3X BASIC INS.
SG1 Terrell Davis 10.00 25.00
SG2 Dan Marino 40.00 80.00
SG3 Joey Galloway 7.50 20.00
SG4 Steve McNair 8.00 20.00
SG5 Doug Flutie 12.50 25.00
SG6 Kordell Stewart 7.50 20.00
SG7 Fred Taylor 10.00 25.00
SG8 Jamal Anderson 7.50 20.00

1999 Playoff Momentum SSD Team Thread Checklists

Randomly inserted at a rate of one in 17 packs, This 31 card set features a swatch of NFL team jersey on the card front.

COMPLETE SET (31) 100.00 250.00
STATED ODDS 1:17
TTC1 Dan Marino 10.00 25.00
TTC2 Drew Bledsoe 4.00 10.00
TTC3 Keyshawn Johnson 3.00 8.00
TTC4 Eric Moulds 3.00 8.00
TTC5 Peyton Manning 8.00 20.00
TTC6 Natrone Means 2.00 5.00
TTC7 Jon Kitna 2.00 5.00
TTC8 Byron Bam Morris .75 2.00
TTC9 Tim Brown 3.00 8.00
TTC10 Terrell Davis 3.00 8.00
TTC11 Kordell Stewart 2.00 5.00
TTC12 Fred Taylor 2.50 6.00
TTC13 Tim Couch 2.00 5.00
TTC14 Eddie George 2.00 5.00
TTC15 Priest Holmes 2.50 6.00
TTC16 Akili Smith .30 .75
TTC17 Emmitt Smith 6.00 15.00
TTC18 Skip Hicks 1.00 2.50
TTC19 Jake Plummer 2.00 5.00
TTC20 Donovan McNabb 8.00 20.00
TTC21 Ike Hilliard .75 2.00
TTC22 Barry Sanders 10.00 25.00
TTC23 Cade McNown 1.50 4.00
TTC24 Randy Moss 6.00 15.00
TTC25 Brett Favre 10.00 25.00
TTC26 Mike Alstott 3.00 8.00
TTC27 Marshall Faulk 4.00 10.00
TTC28 Ricky Williams 3.00 8.00
TTC29 Jamal Anderson 3.00 8.00
TTC30 Jerry Rice 6.00 15.00
TTC31 Tim Biakabutuka 1.25 3.00

2000 Playoff Momentum

Released as a 200-card set, Momentum is comprised of 100 base veteran cards and 100 short printed rookie cards sequentially numbered to 750. Base cards were etched silver foil with a border along the left side of the card and an oval

nameplate centered along the bottom. One or two Beckett Grading Services cards were included as a box topper, where 210 of each veteran were graded and 175 of each rookie were graded. Momentum was packaged in 16-pack boxes with each pack containing six cards.
COMP.SET w/o RC's (100) 6.00 15.00
1 David Boston .15 .40
2 Jake Plummer .15 .40
3 Chris Chandler .20 .50
4 Jamal Anderson .20 .50
5 Tim Dwight .20 .50
6 Qadry Ismail .15 .40
7 Peerless Price .20 .50
8 Antowain Smith .20 .50
9 Eric Moulds .15 .40
10 Rob Johnson .20 .50
11 Natrone Means .20 .50
12 Muhsin Muhammad .15 .40
13 Steve Beuerlein .20 .50
14 Patrick Jeffers .15 .40
15 Curtis Enis .15 .40
16 Cade McNown .15 .40
17 Marcus Robinson .20 .50
18 Corey Dillon .15 .40
19 Akili Smith .15 .40
20 Carl Pickens .20 .50
21 Tim Couch .20 .50
22 Kevin Johnson .15 .40
23 Troy Aikman .30 .75
24 Emmitt Smith .40 1.00
25 Joey Galloway .20 .50
26 Rocket Ismail .20 .50
27 Olandis Gary .20 .50
28 John Elway .40 1.00
29 Brian Griese .15 .40
30 Ed McCaffrey .20 .50
31 Terrell Davis .20 .50
32 Charlie Batch .15 .40
33 James Stewart .15 .40
34 Germane Crowell .15 .40
35 Barry Sanders .40 1.00
36 Herman Moore .15 .40
37 Antonio Freeman .20 .50
38 Dorsey Levens .20 .50
39 Brett Favre .50 1.25
40 Edgerrin James .20 .50
41 Marvin Harrison .20 .50
42 Peyton Manning .60 1.50
43 Fred Taylor .15 .40
44 Keenan McCardell .20 .50
45 Mark Brunell .20 .50
46 Jimmy Smith .20 .50
47 Elvis Grbac .15 .40
48 Tony Gonzalez .20 .50
49 James Johnson .15 .40
50 Dan Marino .50 1.25
51 Thurman Thomas .20 .50
52 Cris Carter .25 .60
53 Robert Smith .15 .40
54 Randy Moss .20 .50
55 Daunte Culpepper .20 .50
56 Terry Glenn .20 .50
57 Kevin Faulk .15 .40
58 Drew Bledsoe .20 .50
59 Ricky Williams .20 .50
60 Amani Toomer .15 .40
61 Kerry Collins .15 .40
62 Vinny Testaverde .15 .40
63 Curtis Martin .20 .50
64 Rich Gannon .20 .50
65 Tyrone Wheatley .15 .40
66 Napoleon Kaufman .20 .50
67 Tim Brown .25 .60
68 Duce Staley .15 .40
69 Donovan McNabb .20 .50
70 Kordell Stewart .15 .40
71 Troy Edwards .15 .40
72 Jerome Bettis .25 .60
73 Jim Harbaugh .20 .50
74 Jermaine Fazande .15 .40
75 Steve Young .30 .75
76 Charlie Garner .20 .50
77 Terrell Owens .20 .50
78 Jerry Rice .60 1.50
79 Jeff Garcia .15 .40
80 Ricky Watters .20 .50
81 Jon Kitna .15 .40
82 Marshall Faulk .20 .50
83 Isaac Bruce .25 .60
84 Torry Holt .20 .50
85 Kurt Warner .40 1.00
86 Keyshawn Johnson .20 .50
87 Warrick Dunn .15 .40
88 Mike Alstott .15 .40
89 Warren Sapp .20 .50
90 Shaun King .15 .40
91 Eddie George .20 .50
92 Steve McNair .20 .50
93 Jevon Kearse .15 .40
94 Bruce Smith .20 .50
95 Deion Sanders .20 .50
96 Albert Connell .15 .40
97 Michael Westbrook .15 .40
98 Brad Johnson .20 .50
99 Jeff George .20 .50
100 Stephen Davis .15 .40
101 Peter Warrick RC 2.00 5.00
102 Jamal Lewis RC 3.00 8.00
103 Thomas Jones RC 2.50 6.00
104 Plaxico Burress RC 2.50 6.00
105 Travis Taylor RC 2.00 5.00
106 Ron Dayne RC 3.00 8.00
107 Bubba Franks RC 2.00 5.00
108 Sebastian Janikowski RC 3.00 8.00
109 Chad Pennington RC 2.50 6.00
110 Shaun Alexander RC 3.00 8.00
111 Sylvester Morris RC 2.00 5.00
112 Anthony Becht RC 2.00 5.00
113 R.Jay Soward RC 2.00 5.00
114 Trung Canidate RC 2.00 5.00
115 Dennis Northcutt RC 2.00 5.00
116 Todd Pinkston RC 2.00 5.00
117 Jerry Porter RC 3.00 8.00
118 Travis Prentice RC 2.00 5.00
119 Giovanni Carmazzi RC 2.00 5.00
120 Ron Dugans RC 2.00 5.00
121 Erron Kinney RC 2.00 5.00
122 Dez White RC 2.00 5.00
123 Chris Cole RC 2.50 6.00
124 Ron Dixon RC 2.00 5.00
125 Chris Redman RC 2.00 5.00
126 J.R. Redmond RC 2.00 5.00
127 Laveranues Coles RC 2.50 6.00
128 JaJuan Dawson RC 2.00 5.00
129 Darrell Jackson RC 2.00 5.00
130 Reuben Droughns RC 2.00 5.00
131 Doug Chapman RC 2.00 5.00
132 Terrelle Smith RC 2.00 5.00
133 Curtis Keaton RC 2.00 5.00
134 Gari Scott RC 2.00 5.00
135 Courtney Brown RC 2.50 6.00
136 Corey Simon RC 2.50 6.00
137 Brian Urlacher RC 10.00 25.00
138 Shaun Ellis RC 2.50 6.00
139 John Abraham RC 3.00 8.00
140 Deltha O'Neal RC 2.00 5.00
141 Rashard Anderson RC 2.00 5.00
142 Ahmed Plummer RC 2.00 5.00
143 Chris Hovan RC 2.50 6.00
144 Erik Flowers RC 2.00 5.00
145 Rob Morris RC 2.50 6.00
146 Keith Bulluck RC 2.50 6.00
147 Darren Howard RC 2.00 5.00
148 John Engelberger RC 2.00 5.00
149 Ian Gold RC 2.00 5.00
150 Raynoch Thompson RC 2.00 5.00
151 Cornelius Griffin RC 2.00 5.00
152 Rogers Beckett RC 2.00 5.00
153 Dwayne Goodrich RC 2.00 5.00
154 Barrett Green RC 2.00 5.00
155 Kevin Thompson RC 2.00 5.00
156 Ben Kelly RC 2.00 5.00
157 Danny Farmer RC 2.00 5.00
158 Aaron Shea RC 2.50 6.00
159 Trevor Gaylor RC 2.00 5.00
160 Mike Brown RC 2.00 5.00
161 Frank Moreau RC 2.00 5.00
162 Deon Dyer RC 2.00 5.00
163 Avion Black RC 2.00 5.00
164 Spergon Wynn RC 2.00 5.00
165 Billy Volek RC 3.00 8.00
166 Michael Wiley RC 2.00 5.00
167 Dante Hall RC 2.00 5.00
168 Ronney Jenkins RC 2.00 5.00
169 Sammy Morris RC 2.00 5.00
170 Kevin McDougal RC 2.00 5.00
171 Tee Martin RC 2.00 5.00
172 Troy Walters RC 2.00 5.00
173 Chad Morton RC 2.50 6.00
174 Jamel White RC 2.00 5.00
175 Shockmain Davis RC 2.00 5.00
176 Mario Edwards RC 2.00 5.00
177 Brandon Short RC 2.00 5.00
178 James Williams RC 2.00 5.00
179 Mike Anderson RC 2.00 5.00
180 Tom Brady RC 500.00 1000.00
181 Na'il Diggs RC 2.00 5.00
182 Todd Husak RC 2.00 5.00
183 JaJuan Seider RC 2.00 5.00
184 Tim Rattay RC 2.50 6.00
185 Jarious Jackson RC 2.50 6.00
186 Joe Hamilton RC 2.00 5.00
187 Shyrone Stith RC 2.00 5.00
188 Mondriel Fulcher RC 2.00 5.00
189 Bashir Yamini RC 2.00 5.00
190 Herbert Goodman RC 2.00 5.00
191 Mike Green RC 2.50 6.00
192 Demario Brown RC 2.00 5.00
193 Charles Lee RC 2.00 5.00
194 Doug Johnson RC 2.00 5.00
195 Windrell Hayes RC 2.00 5.00
196 Julian Peterson RC 3.00 8.00
197 Kwame Cavil RC 2.00 5.00
198 Hank Poteat RC 2.00 5.00
199 Clint Stoerner RC 3.00 8.00
200 Mark Simoneau RC 2.00 5.00

2000 Playoff Momentum O's

*VETS/120: 6X TO 15X BASIC CARD
*VETS/60-90: 8X TO 20X BASIC CARD
*ROOKIES/60-90: .6X TO 1.5X
*VETS/40-50: 10X TO 25X BASIC CARD
*ROOKIES/40-50: .8X TO 2X
*VETS/30: 12X TO 30X BASIC CARD
*ROOKIES/30: 1X TO 2.5X
*VETS/20: 15X TO 40X BASIC CARD
*ROOKIES/20: 1.2X TO 3X
*VETS/10: 20X TO 50X BASIC CARD
*ROOKIES/10: 1.5X TO 4X
STATED PRINT RUN 10-120
180 Tom Brady/60 1500.00 3000.00

2000 Playoff Momentum X's

*VETS/201-326: 5X TO 12X BASIC CARD
*ROOKIES/200-326: .4X TO 1X
*VETS/100-199: 6X TO 15X BASIC CARD
*ROOKIES/100-199: .5X TO 1.2X
*VETS/60-99: 8X TO 20X BASIC CARD
*ROOKIES/60-99: .6X TO 1.5X
*VETS/40-53: 10X TO 25X BASIC CARD
*ROOKIES/40-53: .8X TO 2X
*VETS/30-39: 12X TO 30X BASIC CARD
*ROOKIES/30-39: 1X TO 2.5X
*VETS/21-29: 15X TO 40X BASIC CARD
*ROOKIES/21-29: 1.2X TO 3X
*VETS/10-19: 20X TO 50X BASIC CARD
*ROOKIES/10: 1.5X TO 4X
STATED PRINT RUN 10-326
180 Tom Brady/199 800.00 1400.00

2000 Playoff Momentum Game Day Jerseys

Randomly inserted in Hobby packs, this 45-card set paralles the base Game Day Souvenirs set enhanced with a swatch of a game worn jersey. Single player cards, numbers 1-30 are sequentially numbered to 75, and dual player cards, numbers 31-45, are sequentially numbered to 25. Ronnie Lott and Howie Long both signed the first 25-cards of each of their 75-basic inserts.
GDS1-GDS30 SINGLE JSY PRINT RUN 50-75
FIRST 25 LOTT AND LONG CARDS SIGNED
GDS31-GDS45 DUAL JSY PRINT RUN 25
GDS1 Joe Montana 30.00 80.00
GDS2 Dan Marino 20.00 50.00
GDS3 Joe Montana 30.00 80.00
GDS4 John Elway 15.00 40.00
GDS5 Terry Bradshaw 25.00 60.00
GDS6 Roger Staubach 12.00 30.00
GDS7 Bob Griese 10.00 25.00
GDS8 Fran Tarkenton 10.00 25.00
GDS9 Phil Simms 10.00 25.00
GDS10 Lawrence Taylor 10.00 25.00
GDS11 Ronnie Lott 10.00 25.00
GDS11A Ronnie Lott AU/25 60.00 120.00
GDS12 Boomer Esiason 10.00 25.00
GDS13 Joe Namath 20.00 50.00
GDS14 Don Maynard 8.00 20.00
GDS15 Howie Long 10.00 25.00
GDS15A Howie Long AU/25 90.00 150.00
GDS16 Marcus Allen 10.00 25.00
GDS17 Jim Kelly 10.00 25.00
GDS18 Thurman Thomas 8.00 20.00
GDS19 Fred Taylor 5.00 12.00
GDS20 Mark Brunell 6.00 15.00
GDS21 Randy Moss 6.00 15.00
GDS22 Antonio Freeman 6.00 15.00
GDS23 Ricky Williams 6.00 15.00
GDS24 Tim Couch 6.00 15.00
GDS25 Kurt Warner 12.00 30.00
GDS26 Eddie George 6.00 15.00
GDS27 Troy Aikman 10.00 25.00
GDS28 Steve Young 15.00 40.00
GDS29 Dorsey Levens 6.00 15.00
GDS30 Barry Sanders 12.00 30.00
GDS31 J.Montana/D.Marino 150.00 300.00
GDS32 J.Montana/J.Elway 100.00 200.00
GDS33 T.Bradshaw/R.Staubach 30.00 80.00
GDS34 Bob Griese/F.Tarkenton 20.00 50.00
GDS35 P.Simms/L.Taylor 20.00 50.00
GDS36 R.Lott/B.Esiason 20.00 50.00
GDS37 J.Namath/D.Maynard 40.00 100.00
GDS38 H.Long/M.Allen 20.00 50.00
GDS39 J.Kelly/T.Thomas 20.00 50.00
GDS41 R.Moss/A.Freeman 12.00 30.00
GDS42 R.Williams/T.Couch 12.00 30.00
GDS43 K.Warner/E.George 25.00 60.00
GDS44 T.Aikman/S.Young 30.00 80.00
GDS45 D.Levens/B.Sanders 25.00 60.00

2000 Playoff Momentum Game Day Signatures

Randomly inserted in packs, this 45-card set parallels the base Game Day Souvenirs insert set enhanced with player autographs. Single player cards are sequentially numbered to 75 and dual player cards are sequentially numbered to 25. Some cards were issued in packs via redemption cards and a few players never did sign cards for the set. Those have been removed from our checklist below.
GDS1-GDS30 PRINT RUN 75
GDS31-GDS45 PRINT RUN 25
GDS1 Joe Montana 40.00 100.00
GDS2 Dan Marino 60.00 120.00
GDS3 Joe Montana 40.00 100.00
GDS4 John Elway 60.00 120.00
GDS5 Terry Bradshaw 40.00 100.00
GDS6 Roger Staubach 40.00 100.00
GDS7 Bob Griese 12.00 30.00
GDS8 Fran Tarkenton 25.00 50.00
GDS9 Phil Simms 12.00 30.00
GDS10 Lawrence Taylor 25.00 50.00
GDS11 Ronnie Lott 30.00 60.00
GDS12 Boomer Esiason 12.00 30.00
GDS13 Joe Namath 50.00 120.00
GDS14 Don Maynard 10.00 25.00
GDS15 Howie Long 50.00 100.00
GDS17 Jim Kelly 20.00 40.00
GDS18 Thurman Thomas 10.00 25.00
GDS19 Fred Taylor 6.00 15.00
GDS20 Mark Brunell 10.00 25.00
GDS22 Antonio Freeman 10.00 25.00
GDS23 Ricky Williams 10.00 25.00
GDS24 Tim Couch 10.00 25.00
GDS25 Kurt Warner 25.00 50.00
GDS26 Eddie George 12.00 30.00
GDS27 Troy Aikman 35.00 80.00
GDS28 Steve Young 40.00 80.00
GDS29 Dorsey Levens 8.00 20.00
GDS30 Barry Sanders 60.00 120.00
GDS31 J.Montana/D.Marino 200.00 400.00
GDS32 J.Montana/J.Elway 200.00 400.00
GDS33 T.Bradshaw/R.Staubach 150.00 300.00
GDS34 Bo.Griese/F.Trkntn 60.00 120.00
GDS35 P.Simms/L.Taylor 60.00 120.00
GDS36 R.Lott/B.Esiason 40.00 80.00
GDS37 J.Namath/D.Maynard 75.00 150.00
GDS38 H.Long/M.Allen
GDS39 J.Kelly/T.Thomas 125.00 250.00
GDS40 F.Taylor/M.Brunell 25.00 60.00
GDS42 Williams/Couch EXCH
GDS43 K.Warner/E.George 40.00 80.00
GDS44 T.Aikman/S.Young 75.00 150.00
GDS45 D.Levens/B.Sanders 60.00 150.00

2000 Playoff Momentum Game Day Souvenirs

Released as a two tier insert set, this 45-card set features single player cards inserted at the rate of one in 15 and dual player cards inserted at the rate of one in 47. Base cards are designed to represent a Game Day Program and are highlighted with silver foil stamping.
COMPLETE SET (45) 60.00 120.00
GDS1-GDS30 STATED ODDS 1:15
GDS31-GDS45 STATED ODDS 1:47
GDS1 Joe Montana 3.00 8.00
GDS2 Dan Marino 2.00 5.00
GDS3 Joe Montana 3.00 8.00
GDS4 John Elway 1.50 4.00
GDS5 Terry Bradshaw 2.50 6.00
GDS6 Roger Staubach 1.25 3.00
GDS7 Bob Griese 1.00 2.50
GDS8 Fran Tarkenton 1.00 2.50
GDS9 Phil Simms 1.00 2.50
GDS10 Lawrence Taylor 1.00 2.50
GDS11 Ronnie Lott 1.00 2.50
GDS12 Boomer Esiason 1.00 2.50
GDS13 Joe Namath 2.00 5.00
GDS14 Don Maynard .75 2.00
GDS15 Howie Long 1.00 2.50
GDS16 Marcus Allen 1.00 2.50
GDS17 Jim Kelly 1.00 2.50
GDS18 Thurman Thomas .75 2.00
GDS19 Fred Taylor .60 1.50
GDS20 Mark Brunell .75 2.00
GDS21 Randy Moss .75 2.00
GDS22 Antonio Freeman .75 2.00
GDS23 Ricky Williams .75 2.00
GDS24 Tim Couch .75 2.00
GDS25 Kurt Warner 1.50 4.00
GDS26 Eddie George .75 2.00
GDS27 Troy Aikman 1.25 3.00
GDS28 Steve Young 1.25 3.00
GDS29 Dorsey Levens .75 2.00
GDS30 Barry Sanders 1.50 4.00
GDS31 J.Montana D.Marino 4.00 10.00
GDS32 J.Montana J.Elway 4.00 10.00
GDS33 T.Bradshaw R.Staubach 3.00 8.00
GDS34 Bob Griese F.Tarkenton 1.25 3.00
GDS35 P.Simms L.Taylor 1.25 3.00
GDS36 R.Lott B.Esiason 1.25 3.00
GDS37 J.Namath D.Maynard 2.50 6.00
GDS38 H.Long M.Allen 1.25 3.00
GDS39 J.Kelly T.Thomas 1.25 3.00
GDS40 F.Taylor M.Brunell 1.00 2.50
GDS41 R.Moss A.Freeman 1.00 2.50
GDS42 R.Williams T.Couch 1.00 2.50
GDS43 K.Warner E.George 2.00 5.00
GDS44 T.Aikman S.Young 1.50 4.00
GDS45 D.Levens B.Sanders 2.00 5.00

2000 Playoff Momentum Generations

Randomly inserted in packs at the rate of one in eight, this 50-card set features top players in action on an all foil insert card. To the right of each player there is a picture of the respective team logo.
COMPLETE SET (50) 30.00 80.00
STATED ODDS 1:8
*GOLD/50: 3X TO 8X BASIC INSERTS
GOLD PRINT RUN 50 SER.#'d SETS
GN1 Jake Plummer .40 1.00
GN2 Tim Couch .50 1.25
GN3 Emmitt Smith 1.00 2.50
GN4 Troy Aikman .75 2.00
GN5 John Elway 1.00 2.50
GN6 Terrell Davis .50 1.25
GN7 Barry Sanders 1.00 2.50
GN8 Brett Favre 1.25 3.00
GN9 Peyton Manning 1.50 4.00
GN10 Edgerrin James .50 1.25
GN11 Mark Brunell .50 1.25
GN12 Fred Taylor .40 1.00
GN13 Dan Marino 1.25 3.00
GN14 Randy Moss .50 1.25
GN15 Drew Bledsoe .50 1.25
GN16 Ricky Williams .50 1.25
GN17 Jerry Rice 1.50 4.00
GN18 Steve Young .75 2.00
GN19 Kurt Warner 1.00 2.50
GN20 Eddie George .50 1.25
GN21 Eric Moulds .40 1.00
GN22 Cade McNown .40 1.00
GN23 Corey Dillon .40 1.00
GN24 Kevin Johnson .40 1.00
GN25 Joey Galloway .50 1.25
GN26 Dorsey Levens .50 1.25
GN27 Antonio Freeman .50 1.25
GN28 Marvin Harrison .50 1.25
GN29 Daunte Culpepper .50 1.25
GN30 Cris Carter .60 1.50
GN31 Curtis Martin .50 1.25
GN32 Tim Brown .60 1.50
GN33 Donovan McNabb .50 1.25
GN34 Terrell Owens .50 1.25
GN35 Peter Warrick .40 1.00
GN36 Jamal Lewis .60 1.50
GN37 Thomas Jones .50 1.25
GN38 Plaxico Burress .60 1.25
GN39 Travis Taylor .40 1.00
GN40 Ron Dayne .60 1.50
GN41 Chad Pennington .50 1.25
GN42 Shaun Alexander .60 1.50
GN43 Marshall Faulk .50 1.25
GN44 Keyshawn Johnson .50 1.25
GN45 Steve McNair .50 1.25
GN46 Stephen Davis .40 1.00
GN47 Brad Johnson .50 1.25
GN48 Akili Smith .40 1.00
GN49 Brian Griese .40 1.00
GN50 Isaac Bruce .60 1.50

2000 Playoff Momentum Rookie Quads

Randomly inserted in packs at the rate of one in 159, this 12-card set places four top rookies on each card. Basic card design consists of two circles on each card side framing the featured players.
COMPLETE SET (12) 40.00 80.00
STATED ODDS 1:159
RQ1 Warrick/Blk/Dgns/Lee 1.50 4.00
RQ2 Brrss/Gaylr/Dwsn/White 2.00 5.00
RQ3 Tylr/Frmr/Porter/Coles 2.50 6.00
RQ4 Sctt/Syl.Mrrs/Pnkstn/Dixon 1.50 4.00
RQ5 Jcksn/Swrd/Nrthctt/Cole 2.00 5.00
RQ6 Lewis/Jnkin/Chpmn/Drghn 2.50 6.00
RQ7 Jones/Mrtn/Rdmnd/Keatn 2.00 5.00
RQ8 Dne/Sm.Mrrs/Prntc/Moru 2.50 6.00
RQ9 Alxndr/Hall/Canidt/Wiley 2.50 6.00
RQ10 Pnngtn/Husak/Mrtn/Volek 2.50 6.00
RQ11 Carm/Rttay/Rdmn/Brady 150.00 250.00
RQ12 Brwn/Ellis/Simon/Urlacher 8.00 20.00

2000 Playoff Momentum Rookie Tandems

Randomly seeded in packs at the rate of one in 95 Retail, this 24-card set pairs top 2000 rookies on an all foil insert card. One player appears on the front, while the other on the back. Action photos are set inside a circular fram with a shield shaped Rookie Tandem logo centered right below the player picture.
COMPLETE SET (24) 40.00 80.00
STATED ODDS 1:95 RETAIL
RT1 P.Warrick A.Black .75 2.00
RT2 R.Dugans C.Lee .75 2.00
RT3 P.Burress T.Gaylor 1.00 2.50
RT4 D.White J.Dawson .75 2.00
RT5 T.Taylor D.Farmer .75 2.00
RT6 J.Porter L.Coles 1.25 3.00
RT7 Syl.Morris G.Scott .75 2.00
RT8 T.Pinkston R.Dixon .75 2.00
RT9 R.Soward D.Jackson .75 2.00
RT10 D.Northcutt C.Cole 1.00 2.50
RT11 J.Lewis R.Jenkins 1.25 3.00
RT12 R.Droughns D.Chapman .75 2.00
RT13 T.Jones C.Morton 1.00 2.50
RT14 J.Redmond C.Keaton .75 2.00
RT15 R.Dayne Sm.Morris 1.25 3.00
RT16 T.Prentice F.Moreau .75 2.00
RT17 S.Alexander D.Hall 1.25 3.00
RT18 T.Canidate M.Wiley .75 2.00
RT19 C.Pennington T.Husak 1.00 2.50
RT20 T.Martin B.Volek 1.25 3.00
RT21 G.Carmazzi T.Rattay 1.00 2.50
RT22 C.Redman T.Brady 100.00 200.00
RT23 C.Brown S.Ellis 1.00 2.50
RT24 C.Simon B.Urlacher 4.00 10.00

2000 Playoff Momentum Signing Bonus Quads

Randomly inserted in packs at the rate of one in 684 packs, this three card set showcases four top rookies on each all foil insert card in the same format as the Rookie Quads insert set. Each card contains all four of the featured player's autographs. RQ3 was sent out without a Thomas Jones autograph.
STATED ODDS 1:684
RQ1 Warr/Swrd/Burres/Morris 20.00 50.00
RQ2 Lewis/White/Alxndr/Taylor 20.00 50.00
RQ3 Dyn/Pen/Rdm/T.Jns No AU 10.00 25.00

2000 Playoff Momentum Signing Bonus Tandems

Raondomly inserted in retail packs at the rate of 1:675, this set utilizes the card design from the Rookie Tandems insert set and is enhanced with authentic player autographs. The cards were released through exchange inserts that carried an expiration date of August 31, 2002.
STATED ODDS 1:675 RETAIL
RT3 J.Lewis/D.White 12.00 30.00
RT4 T.Taylor/S.Alexander 12.00 30.00
RT5 T.Jones/C.Redman 10.00 25.00
RT6 R.Dayne/C.Pennington 12.00 30.00

2000 Playoff Momentum Star Gazing Green

Randomly inserted in packs at the rate of one in 15, this 100-card insert set features players set against an outer space background. The base insert cards have green foil highlights.
GREEN STATED ODDS 1:15
*GREEN DIE CUT/25: 3X TO 8X GREEN
GREEN DIE CUT PRINT RUN 25
*BLUE: .6X TO 1.5X GREEN
BLUE STATED ODDS 1:47
*BLUE DIE CUT/50: 2X TO 5X GREEN
BLUE DIE CUT PRINT RUN 50 SER.#'d SETS
*RED: 1X TO 2.5X GREEN
RED STATED ODDS 1:95
*RED DIE CUT/75: 1.5X TO 4X GREEN
RED DIE CUT PRINT RUN 75 SER.#'d SETS
SG1 Jake Plummer .60 1.50
SG2 Tim Couch .75 2.00
SG3 Emmitt Smith 1.50 4.00
SG4 Troy Aikman 1.25 3.00
SG5 John Elway 1.50 4.00
SG6 Terrell Davis .75 2.00
SG7 Charlie Batch .60 1.50
SG8 Barry Sanders 1.50 4.00
SG9 Brett Favre 2.00 5.00
SG10 Peyton Manning 2.50 6.00
SG11 Edgerrin James .75 2.00
SG12 Mark Brunell .75 2.00
SG13 Fred Taylor .60 1.50
SG14 Dan Marino 2.00 5.00
SG15 Randy Moss .75 2.00
SG16 Drew Bledsoe .75 2.00
SG17 Ricky Williams .75 2.00
SG18 Jerry Rice 2.50 6.00
SG19 Steve Young 1.25 3.00
SG20 Kurt Warner 1.50 4.00
SG21 Eddie George .75 2.00
SG22 Jamal Anderson .75 2.00
SG23 Eric Moulds .60 1.50
SG24 Antowain Smith .75 2.00
SG25 Curtis Enis .60 1.50
SG26 Cade McNown .60 1.50
SG27 Deion Sanders .75 2.00
SG28 Joey Galloway .75 2.00
SG29 Olandis Gary .75 2.00
SG30 Dorsey Levens .75 2.00
SG31 Antonio Freeman .75 2.00
SG32 Marvin Harrison .75 2.00
SG33 Daunte Culpepper .75 2.00
SG34 Cris Carter 1.00 2.50
SG35 Robert Smith .60 1.50
SG36 Terry Glenn .75 2.00
SG37 Curtis Martin .75 2.00
SG38 Napoleon Kaufman .75 2.00
SG39 Tim Brown 1.00 2.50
SG40 Duce Staley .60 1.50
SG41 Donovan McNabb .75 2.00
SG42 Kordell Stewart .60 1.50
SG43 Jerome Bettis 1.00 2.50
SG44 Terrell Owens .75 2.00
SG45 Jon Kitna .60 1.50
SG46 Marshall Faulk .75 2.00
SG47 Torry Holt .75 2.00
SG48 Mike Alstott .60 1.50
SG49 Shaun King .60 1.50
SG50 Keyshawn Johnson .75 2.00
SG51 Steve McNair .75 2.00
SG52 Stephen Davis .60 1.50
SG53 Brad Johnson .75 2.00
SG54 David Boston .60 1.50
SG55 Chris Chandler .75 2.00
SG56 Qadry Ismail .60 1.50
SG57 Peerless Price .75 2.00
SG58 Rob Johnson .75 2.00
SG59 Muhsin Muhammad .60 1.50
SG60 Steve Beuerlein .75 2.00
SG61 Patrick Jeffers .60 1.50
SG62 Marcus Robinson .75 2.00
SG63 Akili Smith .60 1.50
SG64 Rocket Ismail .75 2.00
SG65 Ed McCaffrey .75 2.00
SG66 Brian Griese .60 1.50
SG67 Germane Crowell .60 1.50
SG68 James Stewart .60 1.50
SG69 Keenan McCardell .75 2.00
SG70 Jimmy Smith .75 2.00
SG71 Elvis Grbac .60 1.50
SG72 Thurman Thomas .75 2.00
SG73 Amani Toomer .60 1.50
SG74 Vinny Testaverde .60 1.50
SG75 Tyrone Wheatley .60 1.50
SG76 Rich Gannon .75 2.00
SG77 Troy Edwards .60 1.50
SG78 Jim Harbaugh .75 2.00
SG79 Jermaine Fazande .60 1.50
SG80 Natrone Means .75 2.00
SG81 Charlie Garner .75 2.00
SG82 Jeff Garcia .60 1.50
SG83 Ricky Watters .75 2.00
SG84 Isaac Bruce 1.00 2.50
SG85 Warren Sapp .75 2.00
SG86 Jevon Kearse .60 1.50
SG87 Bruce Smith .75 2.00
SG88 Michael Westbrook .60 1.50
SG89 Albert Connell .60 1.50
SG90 Jeff George .75 2.00
SG91 Peter Warrick .60 1.50
SG92 Jamal Lewis 1.00 2.50
SG93 Thomas Jones .75 2.00
SG94 Plaxico Burress .75 2.00
SG95 Travis Taylor .60 1.50
SG96 Ron Dayne 1.00 2.50
SG97 Chad Pennington .75 2.00
SG98 Shaun Alexander 1.00 2.50
SG99 Corey Dillon .60 1.50
SG100 Kevin Johnson .60 1.50

2000 Playoff Momentum Super Bowl Souvenirs

Super Bowl Souvenirs was released as a three tier parallel set. Single player cards are sequentially numbered to 100, dual player cards are sequentially numbered to 50, and triple player cards are sequentially numbered to 25. Cards feature between one and three player action shots, and one swatch of a game used football for each player appearing on the card front. Swatches are either football leather or football and laces.
SB1-SB24 PRINT RUN 100 SER.#'d SETS
SB25-SB36 PRINT RUN 50 SER.#'d SETS
SB37-SB40 PRINT RUN 25 SER.#'d SETS
SB1 Bob Griese 12.00 30.00
SB2 Roger Staubach 15.00 40.00
SB3 Larry Csonka 12.00 30.00
SB4 Fran Tarkenton 12.00 30.00
SB5 Terry Bradshaw 30.00 80.00
SB6 Franco Harris 20.00 50.00
SB7 Terry Bradshaw 30.00 80.00
SB8 Roger Staubach 15.00 40.00
SB9 Ken Stabler 15.00 40.00
SB10 Fran Tarkenton 12.00 30.00
SB11 Franco Harris 20.00 50.00
SB12 Joe Greene 12.00 30.00
SB13 Walter Payton 50.00 125.00
SB14 Jim McMahon 15.00 40.00
SB15 John Elway 20.00 50.00
SB16 Darrell Green 10.00 25.00
SB17 Joe Montana 40.00 100.00
SB18 John Elway 30.00 80.00
SB19 Steve Young 15.00 40.00
SB20 Jerry Rice 30.00 80.00
SB21 Kurt Warner 20.00 50.00
SB22 Steve McNair 10.00 25.00
SB23 Marshall Faulk 10.00 25.00
SB24 Eddie George 10.00 25.00
SB25 Bob Griese/R.Staubach 30.00 80.00
SB26 L.Csonka/F.Tarkenton 15.00 40.00
SB27 T.Bradshaw/F.Harris 40.00 100.00
SB28 Bradshaw/Staubach 60.00 120.00
SB29 K.Stabler/F.Tarkenton 20.00 50.00
SB30 F.Harris/J.Greene 15.00 40.00
SB31 W.Payton/J.McMahon 60.00 150.00
SB32 J.Elway/D.Green 25.00 60.00
SB33 J.Montana/J.Elway 125.00 250.00
SB34 S.Young/J.Rice 40.00 100.00
SB35 K.Warner/S.McNair 25.00 60.00
SB36 M.Faulk/E.George 12.00 30.00
SB37 Stabch/Trkntn/Brdshw 100.00 200.00
SB38 Wrner/Elway/Montana 100.00 200.00
SB39 Stablr/B.Griese/Young 75.00 150.00
SB40 Harris/Payton/George 100.00 200.00

2000 Playoff Momentum Super Bowl Souvenirs Signs of Greatness

STATED PRINT RUN 25 SER.#'d SETS
SB1 Bob Griese 40.00 80.00
SB2 Roger Staubach 100.00 200.00
SB3 Larry Csonka 90.00 150.00
SB4 Fran Tarkenton 60.00 120.00
SB5 Terry Bradshaw 125.00 200.00
SB6 Franco Harris 60.00 120.00
SB7 Terry Bradshaw 125.00 200.00
SB8 Roger Staubach 100.00 200.00
SB9 Ken Stabler 100.00 200.00
SB10 Fran Tarkenton 60.00 120.00
SB11 Franco Harris 60.00 120.00
SB12 Joe Greene 40.00 80.00
SB13 Walter Payton No AU 60.00 150.00
SB14 Jim McMahon 60.00 120.00
SB15 John Elway 125.00 250.00
SB17 Joe Montana 200.00 325.00
SB18 John Elway 125.00 250.00
SB19 Steve Young 75.00 150.00
SB20 Jerry Rice 125.00 200.00
SB21 Kurt Warner 75.00 150.00
SB22 Steve McNair 40.00 80.00
SB23 Marshall Faulk 60.00 120.00
SB24 Eddie George 30.00 60.00

2006 Playoff National Treasures

This 200-card set was released in January, 2007. The set was issued into the hobby in seven-card packs (boxes) with a $500 SRP. Cards numbered 1-100 feature a mix of active and retired NFL greats while cards numbered 101-200 feature 2006 rookies. Cards numbered 1-100 were issued to a stated print run of 125 serial numbered sets. The rookies have the following subsets: 101-146 have both player-worn swatches as well as an autograph and those cards were issued to a stated print run of 99 serial numbered sets, cards 147-188 were signed by the player and had a stated print run of 200 serial numbered sets and cards numbered 189-200 were signed by the player and also had a stated print run of 99 serial numbered sets. Some players did not return their signatures in time for pack out and those cards could be redeemed until August 1, 2008.
1-100 PRINT RUN 125 SER.#'d SETS
101-146 JSY AU PRINT RUN 99
147-188 AU RC PRINT RUN 200
189-200 AU RC PRINT RUN 99
UNPRICED PLATINUM PRINT RUN 1
1 Barry Sanders 8.00 20.00
2 Bo Jackson 6.00 15.00
3 Cadillac Williams 4.00 10.00
4 Cedric Benson 3.00 8.00
5 Charley Taylor 4.00 10.00
6 Clinton Portis 3.00 8.00
7 Curtis Martin 4.00 10.00
8 Dutch Clark 4.00 10.00
9 Earl Campbell 5.00 12.00
10 Edgerrin James 4.00 10.00
11 Ernie Nevers 4.00 10.00
12 Frank Gifford 4.00 10.00
13 Jim Thorpe 12.00 30.00
14 Hugh McElhenny 4.00 10.00
15 Jim Brown 6.00 15.00
16 Jim Taylor 5.00 12.00
17 John Henry Johnson 4.00 10.00
18 John Riggins 4.00 10.00
19 Julius Jones 3.00 8.00
20 Kevin Jones 3.00 8.00
21 LaDainian Tomlinson 5.00 12.00
22 Larry Johnson 3.00 8.00
23 Lenny Moore 3.00 8.00
24 Leroy Kelly 4.00 10.00
25 Ollie Matson 4.00 10.00
26 Paul Hornung 5.00 12.00
27 Red Grange 6.00 15.00
28 Ronnie Brown 4.00 10.00
29 Shaun Alexander 3.00 8.00
30 Steve Van Buren 4.00 10.00
31 Steven Jackson 3.00 8.00
32 Terrell Davis 4.00 10.00
33 Tiki Barber 4.00 10.00
34 Tony Dorsett 5.00 12.00
35 Willie Parker 4.00 10.00
36 Willis McGahee 3.00 8.00
37 Deion Sanders 4.00 10.00
38 Lawrence Taylor 5.00 12.00
39 Anquan Boldin 3.00 8.00
40 Bobby Mitchell 4.00 10.00
41 Braylon Edwards 3.00 8.00
42 Chad Johnson 3.00 8.00
43 Charlie Joiner 3.00 8.00
44 Cliff Branch 3.00 8.00
45 Dante Lavelli 4.00 10.00
46 Don Maynard 4.00 10.00
47 Hines Ward 4.00 10.00
48 James Lofton 3.00 8.00
49 Jerry Rice 10.00 25.00
50 Jimmy Johnson 3.00 8.00
51 Lance Alworth 4.00 10.00
52 Larry Fitzgerald 4.00 10.00
53 Marvin Harrison 4.00 10.00
54 Matt Jones 3.00 8.00
55 Paul Warfield 4.00 10.00
56 Randy Moss 4.00 10.00
57 Raymond Berry 4.00 10.00
58 Roy Williams WR 3.00 8.00
59 Steve Largent 5.00 12.00
60 Steve Smith 5.00 12.00
61 Terrell Owens 4.00 10.00
62 Tommy McDonald 3.00 8.00
63 Torry Holt 4.00 10.00
64 Antonio Gates 5.00 12.00
65 Dave Casper 3.00 8.00
66 John Mackey 4.00 10.00
67 Ozzie Newsome 4.00 10.00
68 Aaron Rodgers 12.00 30.00
69 Alex Smith QB 4.00 10.00
70 Ben Roethlisberger 6.00 15.00
71 Bill Dudley 4.00 10.00
72 Bob Griese 5.00 12.00
73 Brett Favre 10.00 25.00
74 Carson Palmer 4.00 10.00
75 Charley Trippi 3.00 8.00
76 Johnny Unitas 8.00 20.00
77 Dan Marino 10.00 25.00
78 Daunte Culpepper 4.00 10.00
79 Don Meredith 5.00 12.00
80 Donovan McNabb 4.00 10.00
81 Drew Bledsoe 4.00 10.00
82 Eli Manning 4.00 10.00
83 Fran Tarkenton 5.00 12.00
84 George Blanda 4.00 10.00
85 Jim Kelly 5.00 12.00
86 Joe Montana 15.00 40.00
87 Len Dawson 5.00 12.00
88 Michael Vick 4.00 10.00
89 Otto Graham 4.00 10.00
90 Peyton Manning 12.00 30.00
91 Philip Rivers 5.00 12.00
92 Roger Staubach 6.00 15.00
93 Sonny Jurgensen 4.00 10.00
94 Steve McNair 4.00 10.00
95 Steve Young 6.00 15.00
96 Terry Bradshaw 6.00 15.00
97 Tom Brady 15.00 40.00
98 Troy Aikman 6.00 15.00
99 Warren Moon 5.00 12.00
100 Y.A. Tittle 5.00 12.00
101 Anthony Fasano JSY AU RC 10.00 25.00
102 B.Carpenter JSY AU RC 10.00 25.00
103 D.Ferguson JSY AU RC 10.00 25.00
104 Jay Cutler JSY AU RC 15.00 40.00
105 Joe Klopfenstein JSY AU RC 10.00 25.00
106 J.D.Washington JSY AU RC 10.00 25.00
107 Joseph Addai JSY AU RC 10.00 25.00
108 L.Maroney JSY AU RC 10.00 25.00
109 Mario Williams JSY AU RC 15.00 40.00
110 M.Kiwanuka JSY AU RC 15.00 40.00
111 Matt Leinart JSY AU RC 10.00 25.00
112 S.Holmes JSY AU RC 12.00 30.00
113 Sinorice Moss JSY AU RC 10.00 25.00
114 Tye Hill JSY AU RC 10.00 25.00
115 Vince Young JSY AU RC 10.00 25.00
116 B.Marshall JSY AU RC 20.00 50.00
117 Brandon Williams JSY AU RC 10.00 25.00
118 Brian Calhoun JSY AU RC 10.00 25.00
119 Omar Jacobs JSY AU RC 10.00 25.00
120 A.J. Hawk JSY AU RC 12.00 30.00
121 Chad Jackson JSY AU RC 10.00 25.00
122 DeA.Williams JSY AU RC 12.00 30.00
123 Dem.Williams JSY AU RC 10.00 25.00
124 Derek Hagan JSY AU RC 12.00 30.00
125 Jason Avant JSY AU RC 10.00 25.00
126 J.Norwood JSY AU RC 10.00 25.00
127 Kellen Clemens JSY AU RC 10.00 25.00
128 LenDale White JSY AU RC 10.00 25.00
129 L.Washington JSY AU RC 10.00 25.00
130 Marcedes Lewis JSY AU RC 10.00 25.00
131 Maurice Drew JSY AU RC 40.00 80.00
132 Maurice Stovall JSY AU RC 10.00 25.00
133 Michael Huff JSY AU RC 12.00 30.00
134 M.Robinson JSY AU RC 10.00 25.00
135 Tarvaris Jackson JSY AU RC 10.00 25.00
136 Travis Wilson JSY AU RC 10.00 25.00
137 Vernon Davis JSY AU RC 12.00 30.00
138 C.Whitehurst JSY AU RC 10.00 25.00
139 Brad Smith JSY AU RC 12.00 30.00
140 B.Gradkowski JSY AU RC 12.00 30.00
141 Hank Baskett JSY AU RC 10.00 25.00
142 Mike Bell JSY AU RC 10.00 25.00
143 Reggie Bush JSY AU RC 15.00 40.00
144 Devin Hester JSY AU RC 20.00 50.00
145 Jerome Harrison JSY AU RC 10.00 25.00
146 Brodie Croyle JSY AU RC 10.00 25.00
147 Greg Jennings AU RC 8.00 20.00
148 Marques Colston AU RC 12.00 30.00
149 Sam Hurd AU RC 5.00 12.00
150 Wali Lundy AU RC 5.00 12.00
151 Skyler Green AU RC 5.00 12.00
152 Ingle Martin AU RC 6.00 15.00
153 Adam Jennings AU RC 6.00 15.00
154 Antonio Cromartie AU RC 6.00 15.00
155 Brodrick Bunkley AU RC 6.00 15.00
156 Cedric Humes AU RC 5.00 12.00
157 Chad Greenway AU RC 8.00 20.00
158 Marcus Vick AU RC 5.00 12.00
159 David Thomas AU RC 5.00 12.00
160 Delanie Walker AU RC 10.00 25.00
161 Derrick Ross AU RC 6.00 15.00
162 Domenik Hixon AU RC 8.00 20.00
163 Ethan Kilmer AU RC 6.00 15.00
164 Haloti Ngata AU RC 6.00 15.00
165 Jason Allen AU RC 6.00 15.00
166 Jeff Webb AU RC 6.00 15.00
167 Jeremy Bloom AU RC 5.00 12.00
168 John McCargo AU RC 5.00 12.00
169 Johnathan Joseph AU RC 6.00 15.00
170 Jonathan Orr AU RC 6.00 15.00
171 Kelly Jennings AU RC 6.00 15.00
172 Leonard Pope AU RC 8.00 20.00
173 Manny Lawson AU RC 6.00 15.00
174 Mike Hass AU RC 5.00 12.00
175 Miles Austin AU RC 6.00 15.00
176 P.J. Daniels AU RC 5.00 12.00
177 Patrick Cobbs AU RC 6.00 15.00
178 Quinton Ganther AU RC 5.00 12.00
179 Tamba Hali AU RC 8.00 20.00
180 Tony Scheffler AU RC 8.00 20.00
181 Will Blackmon AU RC 5.00 12.00
182 D.J. Shockley AU RC 6.00 15.00
183 Dominique Byrd AU RC 5.00 12.00
184 Donte Whitner AU RC 6.00 15.00
185 Ernie Sims AU RC 5.00 12.00
186 Kamerion Wimbley AU RC 6.00 15.00
187 Marques Hagans AU RC 5.00 12.00
188 Willie Reid AU RC 6.00 15.00
189 Reggie McNeal AU/99 RC 8.00 20.00
190 Drew Olson AU/99 RC 8.00 20.00
191 Owen Daniels AU/99 RC 12.00 30.00
192 Garrett Mills AU/99 RC 10.00 25.00
193 D'Qwell Jackson AU/99 RC 8.00 20.00
194 DeMeco Ryans AU/99 RC 10.00 25.00
195 Rocky McIntosh AU/99 RC 8.00 20.00
196 Thomas Howard AU/99 RC 8.00 20.00
197 Roman Harper AU/99 RC 10.00 25.00
198 Abdul Hodge AU/99 RC 8.00 20.00
199 Richard Marshall AU/99 RC 8.00 20.00
200 Dawan Landry AU/99 RC 12.00 30.00

2006 Playoff National Treasures Gold

*VETS/25: .8X TO 2X BASIC CARDS
VETERANS PRINT RUN 25 SER.#'d SETS
*ROOKIE JSY AU/30: .5X TO 1.2X
*ROOKIE AU/52: .6X TO 1.5X BASIC CARDS
*ROOKIE AU/25: .5X TO 1.2X BASIC CARDS
ROOKIES PRINT RUN 25 52 SER.#'d SETS

2006 Playoff National Treasures Rookie Signature Gold

*SIG GOLD/15: .4X TO 1X BASE JSY AU RCs

2006 Playoff National Treasures Rookie Signature Silver

*SIG SILVER: .25X TO .6X BASE JSY AU RCs
STATED PRINT RUN 30 SER.#'d SETS
UNPRICED GOLD PRINT RUN 5-15
UNPRICED PLATINUM PRINT RUN 1
101 Anthony Fasano 6.00 15.00
102 Bobby Carpenter 6.00 15.00
103 D'Brickashaw Ferguson 6.00 15.00
104 Jay Cutler 8.00 20.00
105 Joe Klopfenstein 6.00 15.00
106 John David Washington 6.00 15.00
107 Joseph Addai 6.00 15.00
108 Laurence Maroney 6.00 15.00
109 Mario Williams 10.00 25.00
110 Mathias Kiwanuka 10.00 25.00
111 Matt Leinart 6.00 15.00
112 Santonio Holmes 8.00 20.00
113 Sinorice Moss 6.00 15.00
114 Tye Hill 6.00 15.00
115 Vince Young 6.00 15.00
116 Brandon Marshall 12.00 30.00
117 Brandon Williams 6.00 15.00
119 Omar Jacobs 6.00 15.00
120 A.J. Hawk 8.00 20.00
121 Chad Jackson 6.00 15.00
122 DeAngelo Williams 8.00 20.00
123 Demetrius Williams 6.00 15.00
124 Derek Hagan 8.00 20.00
125 Jason Avant 6.00 15.00
126 Jerious Norwood 6.00 15.00
127 Kellen Clemens 6.00 15.00
128 LenDale White 6.00 15.00
129 Leon Washington 6.00 15.00
130 Marcedes Lewis 6.00 15.00
131 Maurice Drew 10.00 25.00
132 Maurice Stovall 6.00 15.00
133 Michael Huff 8.00 20.00
134 Michael Robinson 6.00 15.00
135 Tarvaris Jackson 6.00 15.00
136 Travis Wilson 6.00 15.00
137 Vernon Davis 8.00 20.00
138 Charlie Whitehurst 6.00 15.00
139 Brad Smith 8.00 20.00
140 Bruce Gradkowski 8.00 20.00
141 Hank Baskett 6.00 15.00
142 Mike Bell 6.00 15.00
143 Reggie Bush 10.00 25.00
144 Devin Hester 12.00 30.00
145 Jerome Harrison 6.00 15.00
146 Brodie Croyle 6.00 15.00

2006 Playoff National Treasures Rookie Signature Material Gold

*GOLD/25: .6X TO 1.5X BASE JSY AU RCs
GOLD PRINT RUN 25 SER.#'d SETS

2006 Playoff National Treasures Rookie Signature Material Silver

*SILVER/49: .5X TO 1.2X BASE JSY AU RCs
SILVER PRINT RUN 49 SER.#'d SETS
UNPRICED PLATINUM PRINT RUN 1

101 Anthony Fasano 12.00 30.00
102 Bobby Carpenter 12.00 30.00
103 D'Brickashaw Ferguson 12.00 30.00
104 Jay Cutler 15.00 40.00
105 Joe Klopfenstein 12.00 30.00
106 John David Washington 12.00 30.00
107 Joseph Addai 12.00 30.00
108 Laurence Maroney 12.00 30.00
109 Mario Williams 20.00 50.00
110 Mathias Kiwanuka 20.00 50.00
111 Matt Leinart 12.00 30.00
112 Santonio Holmes 15.00 40.00
113 Sinorice Moss 12.00 30.00
114 Tye Hill 12.00 30.00
115 Vince Young 15.00 40.00
116 Brandon Marshall 25.00 60.00
117 Brandon Williams 12.00 30.00
118 Brian Calhoun 12.00 30.00
119 Omar Jacobs 12.00 30.00
120 A.J. Hawk 15.00 40.00
121 Chad Jackson 12.00 30.00
122 DeAngelo Williams 15.00 40.00
123 Demetrius Williams 12.00 30.00
124 Derek Hagan 15.00 40.00
125 Jason Avant 12.00 30.00
126 Jerious Norwood 12.00 30.00
127 Kellen Clemens 12.00 30.00
128 LenDale White 12.00 30.00
129 Leon Washington 12.00 30.00
130 Marcedes Lewis 12.00 30.00
131 Maurice Drew 20.00 50.00
132 Maurice Stovall 12.00 30.00
133 Michael Huff 15.00 40.00
134 Michael Robinson 12.00 30.00
135 Tarvaris Jackson 12.00 30.00
136 Travis Wilson 12.00 30.00
137 Vernon Davis 15.00 40.00
138 Charlie Whitehurst 12.00 30.00
139 Brad Smith 15.00 40.00
140 Bruce Gradkowski 15.00 40.00
141 Hank Baskett 12.00 30.00
142 Mike Bell 12.00 30.00
143 Reggie Bush 20.00 50.00
144 Devin Hester 25.00 60.00
145 Jerome Harrison 12.00 30.00
146 Brodie Croyle 12.00 30.00

2006 Playoff National Treasures 50th Anniversary Team Materials

STATED PRINT RUN 49 SER.#'d SETS
*PRIME/25: .5X TO 1.2X BASIC INSERTS
PRIME PRINT RUN 25 SER.#'d SETS
GS Gale Sayers 15.00 40.00
JB Jim Brown 15.00 40.00
JT Jim Thorpe/25 150.00 250.00
RN Ray Nitschke 12.00 30.00

2006 Playoff National Treasures 50th Anniversary Team Materials Signature

UNPRICED SIGNATURE PRINT RUN 15
*PRIME/20-25: .6X TO 1.2X BASIC INSERTS
GS Gale Sayers 40.00 80.00
JB Jim Brown 60.00 120.00

2006 Playoff National Treasures 50th Anniversary Team Signature

STATED PRINT RUN 10-25 SER.#'d SETS
JM John Mackey/25 25.00 50.00

2006 Playoff National Treasures 75th Anniversary Team Materials

STATED PRINT RUN 49 SER.#'d SETS
*PRIME/25: .5X TO 1.2X BASIC INSERTS
PRIME PRINT RUN 3-25
GS Gale Sayers 15.00 40.00
JB Jim Brown 15.00 40.00
JM Joe Montana 25.00 60.00
JR Jerry Rice 12.00 30.00
JU Johnny Unitas 20.00 50.00
OG Otto Graham 25.00 50.00
RB Raymond Berry 10.00 25.00
WP Walter Payton 25.00 60.00

2006 Playoff National Treasures 75th Anniversary Team Materials Signature

STATED PRINT RUN 5-25
UNPRICED PRIME PRINT RUN 1-16
JB Jim Brown/25 60.00 120.00

2006 Playoff National Treasures 75th Anniversary Team Signatur

STATED PRINT RUN 1-25
JB Jim Brown/25 50.00 100.00
SB Sammy Baugh/22 60.00 100.00

2006 Playoff National Treasures Canton Classics Materials

STATED PRINT RUN 1-99
*PRIME/25: .6X TO 1.5X BASIC INSERTS
PRIME PRINT RUN 1-25
*JUMBO JERSEY/25: .6X TO 1.5X
JUMBO JERSEY PRINT RUN 1-25
*JUMBO JSY PRIME/25: .8X TO 2X
JUMBO JERSEY PRIME PRINT RUN 1-25
SERIAL #'d UNDER 25 NOT PRICED
BG Bob Griese 10.00 25.00
CJ Charlie Joiner 8.00 20.00
CT Charley Taylor 8.00 20.00
DJ Deacon Jones 8.00 20.00
DM Dan Marino 20.00 50.00
EC Earl Campbell 10.00 25.00
FG Forrest Gregg 6.00 15.00
FT Fran Tarkenton 12.00 30.00
GB George Blanda 8.00 20.00
GS Gale Sayers 12.00 30.00
HM Hugh McElhenny 8.00 20.00
JB Jim Brown/32 15.00 40.00
JE John Elway 15.00 40.00
JG Joe Greene 10.00 25.00
JK Jim Kelly 12.00 30.00
JM Joe Montana 15.00 40.00
JO Jim Otto 6.00 15.00
JR John Riggins 10.00 25.00
JU Johnny Unitas/50 20.00 50.00
JY Jack Youngblood 8.00 20.00
LB Lem Barney 8.00 20.00
LD Len Dawson 10.00 25.00
LK Leroy Kelly/50 10.00 25.00
LM Lenny Moore 8.00 20.00
LS Lee Roy Selmon 8.00 20.00
LT Lawrence Taylor 10.00 25.00
OG Otto Graham 12.00 30.00
ON Ozzie Newsome 8.00 20.00
PH Paul Hornung 10.00 25.00
PK Paul Krause 6.00 15.00
RB Raymond Berry 8.00 20.00
RS Roger Staubach 15.00 40.00
SJ Sonny Jurgensen/50 10.00 25.00
SL Steve Largent 10.00 25.00
SY Steve Young 12.00 30.00
TA Troy Aikman 8.00 20.00
TB Terry Bradshaw/90 15.00 40.00
TD Tony Dorsett 10.00 25.00
TH Ted Hendricks 8.00 20.00
WB Willie Brown 8.00 20.00
WM Warren Moon 10.00 25.00
WP Walter Payton 15.00 40.00
YT Y.A. Tittle 10.00 25.00
BSA Barry Sanders 15.00 40.00
BST Bart Starr 15.00 40.00
DCA Dave Casper 6.00 15.00
DOM Don Maynard 8.00 20.00
JLA Jack Lambert 10.00 25.00
JLO James Lofton/22

2006 Playoff National Treasures Canton Classics Materials Signature

STATED PRINT RUN 25 SER.#'d SETS
CJ Charlie Joiner 15.00 40.00
CT Charley Taylor 10.00 25.00
DC Dave Casper 15.00 40.00
DJ Deacon Jones 15.00 40.00
DM Dan Marino 125.00 250.00
DOM Don Maynard 15.00 40.00
GB George Blanda 40.00 80.00
GS Gale Sayers 40.00 80.00
HM Hugh McElhenny 15.00 40.00
JB Jim Brown 60.00 120.00
JE John Elway 75.00 150.00
JG Joe Greene 40.00 80.00
JLA Jack Lambert/20
JLO James Lofton 20.00 50.00
JM Joe Montana 100.00 200.00
JR John Riggins 20.00 50.00
JY Jack Youngblood 20.00 50.00
LB Lem Barney 15.00 40.00
LD Len Dawson 30.00 60.00
LK Leroy Kelly 15.00 40.00
LM Lenny Moore 20.00 50.00
LT Lawrence Taylor 40.00 80.00
ON Ozzie Newsome 20.00 50.00
PH Paul Hornung 40.00 100.00
PK Paul Krause 15.00 40.00
PW Paul Warfield/15
RB Raymond Berry 20.00 50.00
RS Roger Staubach 50.00 120.00
SJ Sonny Jurgensen 40.00 80.00
SL Steve Largent 25.00 60.00
SY Steve Young 60.00 120.00
TB Terry Bradshaw 60.00 120.00
TD Tony Dorsett 30.00 60.00
TH Ted Hendricks 30.00 60.00
WB Willie Brown 15.00 40.00
WM Warren Moon 20.00 50.00
YT Y.A. Tittle 20.00 50.00

2006 Playoff National Treasures Canton Classics Materials Signature Prime

*PRIME/15-25: .6X TO 1.2X BASIC INSERTS
DME Don Meredith/15 60.00 120.00
FT Fran Tarkenton/15 30.00 60.00
JO Jim Otto/15 20.00 50.00

2006 Playoff National Treasures Canton Classics Materials Signature Jersey Number

STATED PRINT RUN 1-87
CJ Charlie Joiner/18 20.00 50.00
CT Charley Taylor/42 10.00 25.00
DC Dave Casper/87 20.00 50.00
DJ Deacon Jones/75 12.00 30.00
FG Frank Gifford/16 40.00 80.00
GB George Blanda/16 40.00 80.00
HM Hugh McElhenny/39 20.00 50.00
JB Jim Brown/32 50.00 120.00
JG Joe Greene/75 30.00 60.00
JL James Lofton/80 12.00 30.00
JM Joe Montana/16 100.00 200.00
JR John Riggins/44 20.00 50.00
JY Jack Youngblood/85 15.00 40.00
LB Lem Barney/20 15.00 40.00
LD Len Dawson/16 40.00 80.00
LM Lenny Moore/24 20.00 50.00
LT Lawrence Taylor/56 30.00 60.00
ON Ozzie Newsome/82 15.00 40.00
PK Paul Krause/22
RB Raymond Berry/82 15.00 40.00
SL Steve Largent/80 30.00 60.00
TD Tony Dorsett/33 30.00 60.00
TH Ted Hendricks/83 20.00 50.00
WB Willie Brown/24 15.00 40.00
YL Yale Lary/28 20.00 40.00
BSA Barry Sanders/20 100.00 175.00
DME Don Meredith/17 60.00 120.00

2006 Playoff National Treasures Canton Classics Materials Signature Jersey Number Prime

*PRIME/24-85: .6X TO 1.2X BASIC INSERTS
PRIME PRINT RUN 1-85 SER.#'d SETS
EC Earl Campbell/34 40.00 80.00
GS Gale Sayers/40 50.00 100.00
JL Jack Lambert/58 50.00 100.00
LK Leroy Kelly/44 20.00 40.00

2006 Playoff National Treasures Canton Classics Materials Signature Position

POSITION PRINT RUN 5-25
*PRIME/25: .75X TO 1.5X MATERIAL SIG
POSITION PRIME PRINT RUN 1-25
CJ Charlie Joiner 25.00 50.00
CT Charley Taylor 12.00 30.00
DC Dave Casper 25.00 50.00
DJ Deacon Jones 25.00 50.00
DM Dan Marino 125.00 250.00
FT Fran Tarkenton 30.00 60.00
GB George Blanda 40.00 80.00
GS Gale Sayers 50.00 100.00
HM Hugh McElhenny 25.00 50.00
JB Jim Brown 75.00 150.00
JE John Elway 100.00 200.00
JG Joe Greene 50.00 100.00
JM Joe Montana 100.00 200.00
JR John Riggins 30.00 60.00
JY Jack Youngblood 30.00 60.00
LB Lem Barney 25.00 50.00
LD Len Dawson 40.00 80.00
LK Leroy Kelly 25.00 50.00
LM Lenny Moore 30.00 60.00
LT Lawrence Taylor 50.00 100.00
ON Ozzie Newsome 30.00 60.00
PH Paul Hornung 60.00 120.00
PK Paul Krause 25.00 50.00
RB Raymond Berry 30.00 60.00
RS Roger Staubach 60.00 120.00
SJ Sonny Jurgensen 50.00 100.00
SL Steve Largent 50.00 100.00
SY Steve Young 75.00 150.00
TB Terry Bradshaw 75.00 150.00
TD Tony Dorsett 40.00 80.00
TH Ted Hendricks 40.00 80.00
WB Willie Brown 25.00 50.00
WM Warren Moon 30.00 60.00
YL Yale Lary 20.00 40.00
YT Y.A. Tittle 30.00 60.00
BSA Barry Sanders 75.00 150.00
DME Don Meredith/24 60.00 120.00
DOM Don Maynard 25.00 50.00
FGI Frank Gifford 25.00 50.00
FGR Forrest Gregg 30.00 60.00
JLO James Lofton 30.00 60.00

2006 Playoff National Treasures Canton Classics Signature

STATED PRINT RUN 1-99
BD Bill Dudley/50 25.00 60.00
CJ Charlie Joiner/18 12.00 30.00
DC Dave Casper/25 15.00 40.00
DJ Deacon Jones/20 12.00 30.00
HM Hugh McElhenny/99 15.00 40.00
JB Jim Brown/32 50.00 100.00
JG Joe Greene/89 25.00 50.00
JJ Jimmy Johnson/99 12.00 30.00
JL James Lofton/80 10.00 25.00
JO Jim Otto/77 12.00 30.00
JP Joe Perry/99 20.00 40.00
JR John Riggins/99 15.00 40.00
JT Jim Taylor/50 26.00 60.00
JY Jack Youngblood/70 12.00 30.00
LB Lem Barney/96 10.00 25.00
LK Leroy Kelly/44 12.00 30.00
LM Lenny Moore/24 20.00 40.00
PH Paul Hornung/86 20.00 50.00
PK Paul Krause/39 12.00 30.00
TH Ted Hendricks/54 20.00 50.00
TM Tommy McDonald/99 12.00 30.00
WB Willie Brown/99 12.00 30.00
WM Warren Moon/99 15.00 40.00
YL Yale Lary/99 12.00 30.00
CTT Charley Trippi/65 15.00 40.00
DME Don Meredith/99 50.00 80.00
DOM Don Maynard/99 10.00 25.00
JHJ John Henry Johnson/99 No AU 10.00 25.00
JMA John Mackey/99 15.00 40.00
JMO Joe Montana/16 75.00 150.00

2006 Playoff National Treasures Canton Classics Signature Cuts

STATED PRINT RUN 1-99
RBR Roosevelt Brown/99 25.00 50.00

2006 Playoff National Treasures Charter Class Signature Cuts

STATED PRINT RUN 1-102
BB Bert Bell/35 100.00 200.00
BN Bronko Nagurski/102 250.00 400.00
SB Sammy Baugh/100 75.00 150.00

2006 Playoff National Treasures Charter Class Materials

STATED PRINT RUN 10-50
UNPRICED CUT AUTO PRINT RUN 1-4
JT Jim Thorpe/50 90.00 150.00

2006 Playoff National Treasures Face Masks

STATED PRINT RUN 25 SER.#'d SETS
1 Barry Sanders 20.00 50.00
6 Clinton Portis 12.00 30.00
7 Curtis Martin 12.00 30.00
9 Earl Campbell 12.00 30.00
21 LaDainian Tomlinson 12.00 30.00
29 Shaun Alexander 12.00 30.00
32 Terrell Davis 12.00 30.00
34 Tony Dorsett 12.00 30.00
36 Willis McGahee 12.00 30.00
38 Lawrence Taylor 12.00 30.00
47 Hines Ward 12.00 30.00
49 Jerry Rice 20.00 50.00
53 Marvin Harrison 12.00 30.00
56 Randy Moss 12.00 30.00
60 Steve Smith 12.00 30.00
63 Torry Holt 10.00 25.00
73 Brett Favre 25.00 60.00
74 Carson Palmer 12.00 30.00
77 Dan Marino 25.00 60.00
80 Donovan McNabb 12.00 30.00
82 Eli Manning 15.00 40.00
85 Jim Kelly 15.00 40.00
86 Joe Montana 25.00 60.00
87 Len Dawson 12.00 30.00
88 Michael Vick 12.00 30.00
90 Peyton Manning 20.00 50.00
92 Roger Staubach 20.00 50.00
95 Steve Young 15.00 40.00
97 Tom Brady 20.00 50.00
98 Troy Aikman 15.00 40.00

2006 Playoff National Treasures Face Masks Signature

STATED PRINT RUN 5-25
9 Earl Campbell/25 30.00 60.00
32 Terrell Davis/25 25.00 50.00

2006 Playoff National Treasures Helmets

*HELMET/15-25: .4X TO 1X FACE MASK
HELMET PRINT RUN 1-25
7 Curtis Martin/25 12.00 30.00
32 Terrell Davis/25 12.00 30.00
53 Marvin Harrison/25 12.00 30.00
85 Jim Kelly/25 15.00 40.00
87 Len Dawson/25 12.00 30.00
88 Michael Vick/25 12.00 30.00

2006 Playoff National Treasures Helmets Signature

STATED PRINT RUN 1-25
32 Terrell Davis/25 30.00 60.00

2006 Playoff National Treasures Historical Cuts

STATED PRINT RUN 1-60
SERIAL #'d UNDER 25 NOT PRICED
DW1 DeAngelo Williams/50 12.00 30.00
DW2 DeAngelo Williams/55 12.00 30.00
LM1 Laurence Maroney/60 10.00 25.00
LM2 Laurence Maroney/60 10.00 25.00
RB1 Reggie Bush/50 12.00 30.00
RB2 Reggie Bush/54 12.00 30.00

2006 Playoff National Treasures HOF Greatness Material Jumbo Jersey

*JUMBO/25: .5X TO 1.2X TRIPLE MATERIAL
STATED PRINT RUN 25 SER.#'d SETS
UNPRICED PRIME PRINT RUN 10
BS Barry Sanders 30.00 80.00
JK Jim Kelly 20.00 50.00
SL Steve Largent 20.00 50.00

2006 Playoff National Treasures HOF Greatness Material Triple

STATED PRINT RUN 49 SER.#'d SETS
*PRIME/25: .5X TO 1.2X BASIC INSERTS
PRIME PRINT RUN 1-25
*FIVE MATER/40: .5X TO 1.2X BASIC INSERTS
*FIVE MAT PRIME/25: .6X TO 1.5X
UNPRICED SIX MATERIAL PRINT RUN 1-5
*QUAD MAT/25-49: .5X TO 1.2X
*QUAD MAT.PRIME/25: .6X TO 1.5X
DM Dan Marino 30.00 80.00
EC Earl Campbell 15.00 40.00
ED Eric Dickerson 12.00 30.00
JE John Elway/24 25.00 60.00
JM Joe Montana 30.00 80.00
MA Marcus Allen 15.00 40.00
RL Ronnie Lott 12.00 30.00
RS Roger Staubach 20.00 50.00
SY Steve Young 20.00 50.00
TB Terry Bradshaw 25.00 60.00
TD Tony Dorsett 15.00 40.00

2006 Playoff National Treasures HOF Greatness Material Signature Quad

STATED PRINT RUN 7-49
*PRIME/25: .6X TO 1.2X BASIC INSERTS
PRIME PRINT RUN 1-25
SL Steve Largent/49 50.00 100.00

2006 Playoff National Treasures HOF Greatness Material Signature Triple

STATED PRINT RUN 2-49
*PRIME/25: .6X TO 1.2X BASIC INSERTS
PRIME PRINT RUN 1-25
EC Earl Campbell/49 40.00 80.00
JM Joe Montana/49 100.00 200.00
MA Marcus Allen/49 40.00 80.00
RL Ronnie Lott/49 40.00 80.00
RS Roger Staubach/30 75.00 150.00
SL Steve Largent/49 40.00 80.00
SY Steve Young/49 60.00 120.00
TB Terry Bradshaw/49 75.00 150.00

2006 Playoff National Treasures Material Jersey Numbers

STATED PRINT RUN 1-89
*PRIME/24-89: .5X TO 1.2X BASIC INSERTS
2 Bo Jackson/34 15.00 40.00
4 Cedric Benson/32 12.00 30.00
5 Charley Taylor/42 10.00 25.00
6 Clinton Portis/26 12.00 30.00
7 Curtis Martin/28 12.00 30.00
9 Earl Campbell/34 12.00 30.00
14 Hugh McElhenny/39 10.00 25.00
15 Jim Brown/32 15.00 40.00
18 John Riggins/44 12.00 30.00
20 Kevin Jones/34 12.00 30.00
22 Larry Johnson/27 12.00 30.00
24 Leroy Kelly/44 10.00 25.00
29 Shaun Alexander/37 12.00 30.00
31 Steven Jackson/39 12.00 30.00
32 Terrell Davis/30 12.00 30.00
34 Tony Dorsett/33 12.00 30.00
35 Willie Parker/39 10.00 25.00
38 Lawrence Taylor/56 10.00 25.00
39 Anquan Boldin/81 6.00 15.00
42 Chad Johnson/85 4.00 10.00
49 Jerry Rice/80 15.00 40.00
53 Marvin Harrison/88 10.00 25.00
55 Paul Warfield/42 10.00 25.00
57 Raymond Berry/82 8.00 20.00
59 Steve Largent/80 10.00 25.00
60 Steve Smith/89 10.00 25.00
63 Torry Holt/81 6.00 15.00
64 Antonio Gates/85 10.00 25.00
65 Dave Casper/87 6.00 15.00
67 Ozzie Newsome/82 8.00 20.00

2006 Playoff National Treasures Material Prime

STATED PRINT RUN 25 SER.#'d SETS
UNPRICED BRAND LOGO PRINT RUN 1-10
UNPRICED BUTTON PRINT RUN 4
UNPRICED LAUNDRY TAG PRINT RUN 1-10
UNPRICED NFL LOGO PRINT RUN 1
1 Barry Sanders 25.00 60.00
2 Bo Jackson 20.00 50.00
3 Cadillac Williams 12.00 30.00
5 Charley Taylor 12.00 30.00
6 Clinton Portis 15.00 40.00
7 Curtis Martin 15.00 40.00
9 Earl Campbell 15.00 40.00
15 Jim Brown 20.00 50.00
18 John Riggins 15.00 40.00
19 Julius Jones 15.00 40.00
20 Kevin Jones 15.00 40.00
21 LaDainian Tomlinson 15.00 40.00
22 Larry Johnson 15.00 40.00
23 Lenny Moore 12.00 30.00
28 Ronnie Brown 15.00 40.00
29 Shaun Alexander 15.00 40.00
31 Steven Jackson 15.00 40.00
32 Terrell Davis 15.00 40.00
33 Tiki Barber 15.00 40.00
34 Tony Dorsett 15.00 40.00
35 Willie Parker 12.00 30.00
36 Willis McGahee 15.00 40.00
37 Deion Sanders 20.00 50.00
38 Lawrence Taylor 15.00 40.00
41 Braylon Edwards/24 15.00 40.00
42 Chad Johnson 8.00 20.00
43 Charlie Joiner 12.00 30.00
47 Hines Ward 15.00 40.00
49 Jerry Rice 20.00 50.00
52 Larry Fitzgerald 15.00 40.00
53 Marvin Harrison 15.00 40.00
54 Matt Jones 15.00 40.00
56 Randy Moss 12.00 30.00
58 Roy Williams WR 15.00 40.00
59 Steve Largent 15.00 40.00
60 Steve Smith 15.00 40.00
63 Torry Holt 12.00 30.00
64 Antonio Gates 15.00 40.00
68 Aaron Rodgers 30.00 80.00
69 Alex Smith QB 15.00 40.00
70 Ben Roethlisberger 25.00 60.00
72 Bob Griese 15.00 40.00
73 Brett Favre 30.00 80.00
74 Carson Palmer 15.00 40.00
76 Johnny Unitas 25.00 60.00
77 Dan Marino 30.00 80.00
80 Donovan McNabb 15.00 40.00
82 Eli Manning 20.00 50.00
83 Fran Tarkenton 20.00 50.00
85 Jim Kelly 20.00 50.00
86 Joe Montana 30.00 80.00
88 Michael Vick 15.00 40.00
90 Peyton Manning 25.00 60.00
91 Philip Rivers 15.00 40.00
92 Roger Staubach 25.00 60.00
95 Steve Young 20.00 50.00
97 Tom Brady 25.00 60.00
98 Troy Aikman 20.00 50.00

2006 Playoff National Treasures Material Signature Jersey Numbers

STATED PRINT RUN 1-82
1 Barry Sanders/20 75.00 150.00
2 Bo Jackson/34 60.00 120.00
3 Cadillac Williams/24 20.00 50.00
4 Cedric Benson/32 15.00 40.00
14 Hugh McElhenny/39 20.00 50.00
15 Jim Brown/32 60.00 120.00
18 John Riggins/44 20.00 50.00
19 Julius Jones/21
20 Kevin Jones/34 15.00 40.00
23 Lenny Moore/24 20.00 50.00
29 Shaun Alexander/37 15.00 40.00
31 Steven Jackson/39 20.00 50.00
35 Willie Parker/39 15.00 40.00
37 Deion Sanders/21 40.00 80.00
41 Braylon Edwards/17
44 Cliff Branch/21 12.00 30.00
57 Raymond Berry/82 15.00 40.00
79 Don Meredith/17 50.00 100.00
84 George Blanda/16 50.00 100.00
86 Joe Montana/16 100.00 200.00
87 Len Dawson/16
90 Peyton Manning/18 90.00 150.00
91 Philip Rivers/17 50.00 100.00

2006 Playoff National Treasures Material Signature Jersey Numbers Prime

*PRIME/24-88: .6X TO 1.2X BASIC INSERTS
PRIME PRINT RUN 1-88
1 Barry Sanders/20 100.00 175.00
5 Charley Taylor/42 15.00 40.00
9 Earl Campbell/34 30.00 60.00
24 Leroy Kelly/44 20.00 50.00
32 Terrell Davis/30 20.00 50.00
34 Tony Dorsett/33 30.00 60.00
37 Deion Sanders/21 40.00 80.00
38 Lawrence Taylor/56 30.00 60.00
53 Marvin Harrison/88 30.00 60.00
55 Paul Warfield/42 20.00 50.00
59 Steve Largent/80 30.00 60.00
65 Dave Casper/87 20.00 50.00
67 Ozzie Newsome/82 15.00 40.00
86 Joe Montana/16 100.00 200.00
87 Len Dawson/16 40.00 80.00
90 Peyton Manning/18 100.00 200.00
91 Philip Rivers/17 40.00 80.00

2006 Playoff National Treasures Material Signature Prime

STATED PRINT RUN 1-25
5 Charley Taylor/25 20.00 50.00
15 Jim Brown/25 75.00 150.00
23 Lenny Moore/25 20.00 50.00
26 Paul Hornung/25 40.00 100.00
31 Steven Jackson/25 25.00 60.00
35 Willie Parker/25 20.00 50.00
36 Willis McGahee/25 20.00 50.00
37 Deion Sanders/25 40.00 80.00
44 Cliff Branch/15 25.00 60.00
59 Steve Largent/25 50.00 100.00
67 Ozzie Newsome/25 20.00 50.00
81 Drew Bledsoe/25 25.00 60.00
83 Fran Tarkenton/25 40.00 80.00
85 Jim Kelly/25 50.00 100.00
86 Joe Montana/25 125.00 250.00
87 Len Dawson/25 40.00 80.00
92 Roger Staubach/25 75.00 150.00
95 Steve Young/25 50.00 100.00
96 Terry Bradshaw/25 75.00 150.00
100 Y.A. Tittle/20 40.00 80.00

2006 Playoff National Treasures Material Quads

STATED PRINT RUN 25 SER.#'d SETS
*PRIME/25: .5X TO 1.2X BASIC INSERTS
PRIME PRINT RUN 2-25
BGMM Brry/Giff/McElh/Moore 30.00 60.00
BJOG Bled/Jnes/Owens/Glenn 30.00 60.00
BKGN Brwn/Kelly/Grah/News 50.00 100.00
CBBO Casp/Bilet/Blanda/Otto 40.00 80.00
CBSS Camp/Brad/Stblr/Staub 30.00 60.00
DJYE Dickr/Jnes/Yngbld/Ellrd 30.00 60.00
GJBU Gross/Jnes/Brsn/Urlach 30.00 60.00
HKSB Hrng/Kelly/Syers/Brown 40.00 80.00
MBSB Eli/Barber/Shock/Brress 30.00 60.00
MHWC P.Mnn/Hrrsn/Wyne/Clark 60.00 120.00
MMYT McElh/Mont/Yng/Tittle 50.00 120.00
MWBB McNbb/Wstbk/Brwn/Buck 20.00 50.00
PJJH Palmr/Chad/Rudi/Hshmn 20.00 50.00
RPWP Roeth/Prkr/Ward/Polam 50.00 100.00
SDLS Staub/Drsett/Lilly/Smith 30.00 80.00
SGHN Strr/Grgg/Horn/Nitsch 50.00 100.00
SLGG Stall/Lamb/Grne/Grnwd 60.00 120.00
SLWC Sndrs/Lyne/Wlkr/Clark 60.00 120.00
STHL Single/LT/Hndrks/Lamb 30.00 60.00

2006 Playoff National Treasures Material Trios

STATED PRINT RUN 25 SER.#'d SETS
*PRIME/25: .6X TO 1.2X BASIC INSERTS
PRIME PRINT RUN 1-25
*HOF/25: .5X TO 1X BASIC INSERTS
*HOF PRIME/25: .6X TO 1.2X BASIC INSERTS
*NFL/25: .5X TO 1X BASIC INSERTS
*NFL PRIME/25: .6X TO 1.2X BASIC INSERTS
CKS Casper/Kelly/Stallworth 20.00 40.00
DNT Dicker/Nwsme/Taylor 20.00 40.00
EFS Elway/Favre/Sanders 40.00 80.00
GCM Griese/Csonka/Marino 40.00 80.00
HBS Harris/Brad/Stllworth 30.00 80.00
JSU Jurgensen/Starr/Unitas 40.00 80.00
SDA Staubach/Dorsett/Aikman 30.00 60.00
SDT Sanders/Davis/Thom/20 25.00 50.00
SSB Sanders/Sims/Barney 30.00 60.00
TBS Turner/Butkus/Singletary 20.00 50.00
TJS Taylor/Jurgensen/Starr 30.00 60.00
TRJ Taylor/Riggins/Jurgen 20.00 40.00
UMB Unitas/Moore/Berry 40.00 80.00

2006 Playoff National Treasures Rookie Autographed Letters

STATED PRINT RUN 70-80
AH A.J. Hawk/80 10.00 25.00
CJ Chad Jackson/70 8.00 20.00
DW DeAngelo Williams/80 10.00 25.00
JA Joseph Addai/80 8.00 20.00
JC Jay Cutler/80 10.00 25.00
LM Laurence Maroney/80 8.00 20.00
LW LenDale White/80 8.00 20.00
MB Mike Bell/80 8.00 20.00
MC Marques Colston/80 12.00 30.00
ML Matt Leinart/80 8.00 20.00
RB Reggie Bush/80 12.00 30.00
SH Santonio Holmes/80 10.00 25.00
SM Sinorice Moss/80 8.00 20.00
VD Vernon Davis/80 10.00 25.00
VY Vince Young/80 8.00 20.00

2006 Playoff National Treasures Rookie Jumbo Material Silver

STATED PRINT RUN 25 SER.#'d SETS
UNPRICED GOLD PRINT RUN 10
UNPRICED PLATINUM PRINT RUN 1
101 Anthony Fasano 4.00 10.00
102 Bobby Carpenter 4.00 10.00
103 D'Brickashaw Ferguson 4.00 10.00
104 Jay Cutler 5.00 12.00
105 Joe Klopfenstein 4.00 10.00
106 John David Washington 4.00 10.00
107 Joseph Addai 4.00 10.00
108 Laurence Maroney 4.00 10.00
109 Mario Williams 6.00 15.00
110 Mathias Kiwanuka 6.00 15.00
111 Matt Leinart 4.00 10.00
112 Santonio Holmes 5.00 12.00
113 Sinorice Moss 4.00 10.00
114 Tye Hill 4.00 10.00
115 Vince Young 4.00 10.00
116 Brandon Marshall 8.00 20.00
117 Brandon Williams 4.00 10.00
118 Brian Calhoun 4.00 10.00
119 Omar Jacobs 4.00 10.00
120 A.J. Hawk 5.00 12.00
121 Chad Jackson 4.00 10.00
122 DeAngelo Williams 5.00 12.00
123 Demetrius Williams 4.00 10.00
124 Derek Hagan 5.00 12.00
125 Jason Avant 4.00 10.00
126 Jerious Norwood 4.00 10.00
127 Kellen Clemens 4.00 10.00
128 LenDale White 4.00 10.00
129 Leon Washington 4.00 10.00
130 Marcedes Lewis 4.00 10.00
131 Maurice Drew 6.00 15.00
132 Maurice Stovall 4.00 10.00
133 Michael Huff 5.00 12.00
134 Michael Robinson 4.00 10.00
135 Tarvaris Jackson 4.00 10.00
136 Travis Wilson 4.00 10.00
137 Vernon Davis 5.00 12.00
138 Charlie Whitehurst 4.00 10.00
139 Brad Smith 5.00 12.00
140 Bruce Gradkowski 5.00 12.00
141 Hank Baskett 4.00 10.00
142 Mike Bell 4.00 10.00
143 Reggie Bush 6.00 15.00
144 Devin Hester 8.00 20.00
145 Jerome Harrison 4.00 10.00
146 Brodie Croyle 4.00 10.00

2006 Playoff National Treasures Signature Gold

*GOLD: .5X TO 1.2X SILVER SIG
GOLD PRINT RUN 1-62
SERIAL #'d UNDER 24 NOT PRICED
15 Jim Brown/32 50.00 100.00
35 Willie Parker/39 15.00 40.00
75 Charley Trippi/62 12.00 30.00
84 George Blanda/49 30.00 60.00
93 Sonny Jurgensen/49 15.00 40.00

2006 Playoff National Treasures Signature Silver

SILVER PRINT RUN 7-99
UNPRICED PLATINUM PRINT RUN 1
SERIAL #'d UNDER 25 NOT PRICED
10 Edgerrin James/61 12.00 30.00
16 Jim Taylor/59 25.00 60.00
18 John Riggins/99 15.00 40.00
23 Lenny Moore/71 12.00 30.00
26 Paul Hornung/69 20.00 50.00
31 Steven Jackson/99 15.00 40.00
40 Bobby Mitchell/99 10.00 25.00
41 Braylon Edwards/55 12.00 30.00
44 Cliff Branch/59 12.00 30.00
45 Dante Lavelli/65 20.00 50.00
46 Don Maynard/99 10.00 25.00
48 James Lofton/80 10.00 25.00
50 Jimmy Johnson/81 12.00 30.00
53 Marvin Harrison/43 25.00 50.00
62 Tommy McDonald/91 12.00 30.00
66 John Mackey/74 12.00 30.00
71 Bill Dudley/66 25.00 60.00
74 Carson Palmer/23
79 Don Meredith/99 50.00 100.00
80 Donovan McNabb/34 20.00 50.00
86 Joe Montana/68 60.00 120.00
88 Michael Vick/32 30.00 80.00
93 Sonny Jurgensen/32 20.00 50.00
95 Steve Young/57 50.00 100.00
99 Warren Moon/75 15.00 40.00

2006 Playoff National Treasures Signature Combos

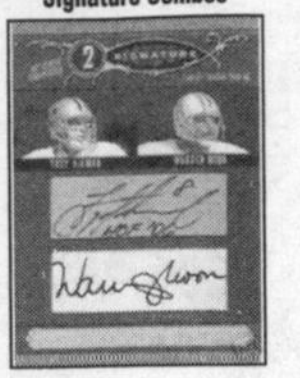

STATED PRINT RUN 5-25
SERIAL #'d UNDER 25 NOT PRICED
1 J.Brown/Y.Tittle 75.00 150.00
2 D.Lavelli/L.Moore 30.00 60.00
3 L.Barney/J.Riggins 40.00 80.00
4 S.Largent/L.Selmon 50.00 100.00
5 J.Montana/R.Lott 150.00 250.00
6 M.Allen/J.Lofton 40.00 80.00
7 J.Elway/B.Sanders 75.00 150.00
8 D.Marino/S.Young 150.00 250.00
9 T.Aikman/W.Moon 50.00 100.00
10 J.Kelly/J.Stallworth/24 40.00 100.00
11 E.Dickerson/L.Taylor 40.00 80.00
12 M.Singletary/P.Krause 30.00 60.00
13 L.Kelly/J.Smith 20.00 40.00
14 G.Sayers/F.Gregg 50.00 100.00
15 D.Jones/B.Lilly 30.00 60.00
17 F.Gifford/R.Berry/24 40.00 80.00

2006 Playoff National Treasures Signature Trios

STATED PRINT RUN 1-25
BSS Brdshw/Stblr/Stbch/15 125.00 250.00
CBA Cspr/Bltnkft/Alln/25 60.00 120.00
DJB Ddly/Jhn No AU/Brdsw/25 60.00 120.00
DJM Dwsn/Jhnsn/Mynrd EXCH/16 30.00 80.00
DNT Dckrsn/Nwsme/Tylr/15 30.00 80.00
EFS Elwy/Fvre/Sndrs/15 250.00 400.00
GMW Grse/Mrno/Wrfld/19 100.00 200.00
JMW Jurgensen/Mitchell/Warfield/25 30.00 80.00
KLD Kavanaugh/Lavelli/Dudley/25 30.00 80.00
LBK Lavelli/Brown/Kelly/25 60.00 120.00
MMB Mackey/Moore/Berry/25 60.00 120.00
MTJ Mitchell/Taylor/Jurgensen/25 30.00 80.00
MYT Montana/Young/Tittle/25 125.00 250.00
SBS Sanders/Barney/Sims/25 125.00 200.00
SBT Sayers/Brown/Taylor/25 125.00 200.00
SDA Stbch/Drstt/Akmn/15 125.00 250.00
SHK Starr/Hornung/Kelly/15 125.00 250.00
STH2 Starr/Taylor/Hornung/15 150.00 300.00
STH1 Sngltry/Tylr/Hndrcks/15 40.00 100.00
TMJ Taylor/Mackey/Jurgensen/17 30.00 80.00

2006 Playoff National Treasures Timeline Material AFC/NFC

STATED PRINT RUN 2-25
*PRIME/15-25: .5X TO 1.2X AFC/NFC/20-25
PRIME PRINT RUN 1-25
BE Boomer Esiason/25 12.00 30.00
BF Brett Favre/25 30.00 80.00
BJ Bo Jackson/25 20.00 50.00
BLI Bob Lilly/25 12.00 30.00
BS Barry Sanders/20 25.00 60.00
BT Bulldog Turner/25 15.00 40.00
CJ Charlie Joiner/25 10.00 25.00
CT Charley Taylor/25 12.00 30.00
DB Dick Butkus/25 20.00 50.00
DC Dave Casper/25 10.00 25.00
DJ Deacon Jones/25 12.00 30.00
DL Daryle Lamonica/25 10.00 25.00
DM Dan Marino/25 30.00 80.00
DS Deion Sanders/25 12.00 30.00
DW Doak Walker/25 15.00 40.00
EC Earl Campbell/25 15.00 40.00
ED Eric Dickerson/25 12.00 30.00
FGR Forrest Gregg/25 10.00 25.00
FT Fran Tarkenton/25 15.00 40.00
GB George Blanda/25 12.00 30.00
GS Gale Sayers/25 15.00 40.00
HM Hugh McElhenny/25 12.00 30.00
HW Hines Ward/25 12.00 30.00
JB Jerome Bettis/25 25.00 60.00
JE John Elway/25 25.00 60.00
JER Jerry Rice/25 30.00 80.00
JK Jim Kelly/25 15.00 40.00
JM Joe Montana/25 50.00 125.00
JO Jim Otto/25 10.00 25.00
JP Jim Plunkett/25 12.00 30.00
JSM Jackie Smith/25 10.00 25.00
JST John Stallworth/25 12.00 30.00
JT Joe Theismann/25 15.00 40.00
JU Johnny Unitas/25 25.00 60.00
LB Lem Barney/25 12.00 30.00
LD Len Dawson/25 15.00 40.00
LM Lenny Moore/25 10.00 25.00
LS Lee Roy Selmon/25 10.00 25.00
LT Lawrence Taylor/25 15.00 40.00
MA Marcus Allen/25 15.00 40.00
MS Mike Singletary/25 15.00 40.00
OG Otto Graham/25 20.00 50.00
ON Ozzie Newsome/25 12.00 30.00
PK Paul Krause/25 10.00 25.00
PM Peyton Manning/25 40.00 100.00
PS Phil Simms/25 12.00 30.00
RB Raymond Berry/25 12.00 30.00
RN Ray Nitschke/25 25.00 50.00
RS Roger Staubach/25 15.00 40.00
RW Reggie White/25 20.00 50.00
SA Shaun Alexander/25 10.00 25.00
SL Steve Largent/25 15.00 40.00
SY Steve Young/25 20.00 50.00
TA Troy Aikman/25 20.00 50.00
TDA Terrell Davis/20 12.00 30.00
TDO Tony Dorsett/25 15.00 40.00
WB Willie Brown/25 10.00 25.00
WM Warren Moon/25 15.00 40.00
WP Walter Payton/25 30.00 80.00

2006 Playoff National Treasures Timeline Material HOF

HOF JERSEY PRINT RUN 2-25
*PRIME/15-25: .5X TO 1.2X HOF JSY/20-25
BLI Bob Lilly/25 12.00 30.00
BS Barry Sanders/20 25.00 60.00
BST Bart Starr/25 25.00 60.00
BT Bulldog Turner/25 15.00 40.00
CT Charley Taylor/25 12.00 30.00
DB Dick Butkus/25 20.00 50.00
DJ Deacon Jones/25 12.00 30.00
DM Dan Marino/25 30.00 80.00
DW Doak Walker/25 15.00 40.00
EC Earl Campbell/25 15.00 40.00
ED Eric Dickerson/25 12.00 30.00
FGR Forrest Gregg/25 10.00 25.00
FT Fran Tarkenton/25 15.00 40.00
GB George Blanda/25 12.00 30.00
GS Gale Sayers/25 15.00 40.00
HM Hugh McElhenny/25 12.00 30.00
JB Jim Brown/25 20.00 50.00
JE John Elway/25 25.00 60.00
JK Jim Kelly/25 15.00 40.00
JM Joe Montana/25 50.00 125.00
JO Jim Otto/25 10.00 25.00
JSM Jackie Smith/25 10.00 25.00
JST John Stallworth/25 12.00 30.00
JU Johnny Unitas/25 25.00 60.00
LB Lem Barney/25 12.00 30.00
LD Len Dawson/25 15.00 40.00
LM Lenny Moore/25 10.00 25.00
LS Lee Roy Selmon/25 10.00 25.00
LT Lawrence Taylor/25 15.00 40.00
MA Marcus Allen/25 15.00 40.00
MS Mike Singletary/25 15.00 40.00
OG Otto Graham/25 20.00 50.00
ON Ozzie Newsome/25 12.00 30.00
PH Paul Hornung/25 15.00 40.00
PK Paul Krause/25 10.00 25.00
RB Raymond Berry/25 12.00 30.00
RN Ray Nitschke/25 25.00 50.00
RS Roger Staubach/25 15.00 40.00
RW Reggie White/25 20.00 50.00
SL Steve Largent/25 15.00 40.00
SY Steve Young/25 20.00 50.00
TA Troy Aikman/25 20.00 50.00
TDO Tony Dorsett/25 15.00 40.00
WB Willie Brown/25 10.00 25.00
WM Warren Moon/25 15.00 40.00
WP Walter Payton/25 30.00 80.00

2006 Playoff National Treasures Timeline Material Jumbo Jersey

JUMBO JERSEY PRINT RUN 1-25
*PRIME/15-25: .5X TO 1.2X JUMBO/15-25
PRIME PRINT RUN 1-25
BE Boomer Esiason/25 12.00 30.00
BF Brett Favre/25 30.00 80.00
BJ Bo Jackson/25 20.00 50.00
BLA Bobby Layne/20 20.00 50.00
BLI Bob Lilly/25 12.00 30.00
BS Barry Sanders/25 25.00 60.00
BST Bart Starr/25 25.00 60.00
BT Bulldog Turner/25 15.00 40.00
CJ Charlie Joiner/25 10.00 25.00
CT Charley Taylor/25 12.00 30.00
DB Dick Butkus/25 20.00 50.00
DC Dave Casper/25 10.00 25.00
DM Dan Marino/25 30.00 80.00
DS Deion Sanders/25 12.00 30.00
EC Earl Campbell/25 15.00 40.00
ED Eric Dickerson/25 12.00 30.00
FGR Forrest Gregg/25 10.00 25.00
FT Fran Tarkenton/25 15.00 40.00
GS Gale Sayers/15 15.00 40.00
HM Hugh McElhenny/25 12.00 30.00
JB Jerome Bettis/25 25.00 60.00
JB Jim Brown/25 20.00 50.00
JE John Elway/25 25.00 60.00
JER Jerry Rice/17 30.00 80.00
JK Jim Kelly/25 15.00 40.00
JM Joe Montana/25 50.00 125.00
JO Jim Otto/25 10.00 25.00
JP Jim Plunkett/25 12.00 30.00
JSM Jackie Smith/25 10.00 25.00
JST John Stallworth/25 12.00 30.00
JT Joe Theismann/25 15.00 40.00
LB Lem Barney/25 12.00 30.00
LM Lenny Moore/25 10.00 25.00
LS Lee Roy Selmon/25 10.00 25.00
LT Lawrence Taylor/25 15.00 40.00
MA Marcus Allen/25 15.00 40.00
MS Mike Singletary/25 15.00 40.00
OG Otto Graham/25 20.00 50.00
PM Peyton Manning/25 40.00 100.00
PS Phil Simms/25 12.00 30.00
RB Raymond Berry/25 12.00 30.00
RN Ray Nitschke/25 25.00 50.00
RS Roger Staubach/25 15.00 40.00
RW Reggie White/25 20.00 50.00
SA Shaun Alexander/25 10.00 25.00
SL Steve Largent/25 15.00 40.00
SY Steve Young/25 20.00 50.00
TA Troy Aikman/25 20.00 50.00
TDO Tony Dorsett/25 15.00 40.00
WB Willie Brown/25 10.00 25.00
WM Warren Moon/25 15.00 40.00
WP Walter Payton/25 30.00 80.00

2006 Playoff National Treasures Timeline Material MVP

STATED PRINT RUN 2-25
*PRIME/15-25: .5X TO 1.2X MVP/20-25
BE Boomer Esiason/25 12.00 30.00
BF Brett Favre/25 30.00 80.00
BS Barry Sanders/20 25.00 60.00
BST Bart Starr/25 25.00 60.00
DM Dan Marino/25 30.00 80.00
EC Earl Campbell/25 15.00 40.00
FT Fran Tarkenton/25 15.00 40.00
HW Hines Ward/25 12.00 30.00
JB Jim Brown/25 20.00 50.00
JE John Elway/25 25.00 60.00
JM Joe Montana/25 50.00 125.00
JP Jim Plunkett/25 12.00 30.00
JT Joe Theismann/25 15.00 40.00
JU Johnny Unitas/25 25.00 60.00
LD Len Dawson/25 15.00 40.00
LT Lawrence Taylor/25 15.00 40.00
MA Marcus Allen/25 15.00 40.00
PH Paul Hornung/25 15.00 40.00
PM Peyton Manning/25 40.00 100.00
PS Phil Simms/25 12.00 30.00
RS Roger Staubach/25 15.00 40.00
SA Shaun Alexander/25 10.00 25.00
SY Steve Young/25 15.00 40.00
TA Troy Aikman/25 20.00 50.00
TD Terrell Davis/20 12.00 30.00
WP Walter Payton/25 30.00 80.00
JER Jerry Rice/25 30.00 80.00

2006 Playoff National Treasures Timeline Material NFL

COMMON CARD/60-99 6.00 15.00
SEMISTARS/60-99 8.00 20.00
UNL.STARS/60-99 10.00 25.00
COMMON CARD/30-50 10.00 25.00
UNL.STARS/30-50 12.00 30.00
COMMON CARD/16-29 10.00 25.00
SEMISTARS/16-29 12.00 30.00
UNL.STARS/16-29 15.00 40.00
STATED PRINT RUN 4-99
*PRIME/15-25: .5X TO 1.2X AFC/NFC
BE Boomer Esiason/30 10.00 25.00
BF Brett Favre/99 20.00 50.00
BJ Bo Jackson/99 12.00 30.00
BT Bulldog Turner/99 10.00 25.00
CJ Charlie Joiner/99 6.00 15.00
CT Charley Taylor/99 8.00 20.00
DB Dick Butkus/99 12.00 30.00
DC Dave Casper/99 6.00 15.00
DL Daryle Lamonica/75 6.00 15.00
DM Dan Marino/99 20.00 50.00
DS Deion Sanders/99 8.00 20.00
DW Doak Walker/37 12.00 30.00
EC Earl Campbell/99 10.00 25.00
ED Eric Dickerson/29 12.00 30.00
FT Fran Tarkenton/99 10.00 25.00
GB George Blanda/16 12.00 30.00
GS Gale Sayers/40 12.00 30.00
HM Hugh McElhenny/99 8.00 20.00
HW Hines Ward/60 8.00 20.00
JE John Elway/50 20.00 50.00
JK Jim Kelly/49 12.00 30.00
JM Joe Montana/50 40.00 100.00
JO Jim Otto/99 6.00 15.00
JP Jim Plunkett/99 8.00 20.00
JU Johnny Unitas/19 25.00 60.00
LB Lem Barney/99 8.00 20.00

LD Len Dawson/45 12.00 30.00
LM Lenny Moore/99 6.00 15.00
LS Lee Roy Selmon/50 8.00 20.00
LT Lawrence Taylor/99 10.00 25.00
MA Marcus Allen/99 10.00 25.00
MS Mike Singletary/50 12.00 30.00
OG Otto Graham/99 8.00 20.00
ON Ozzie Newsome/50 10.00 25.00
PK Paul Krause/22 10.00 25.00
PM Peyton Manning/99 25.00 60.00
PS Phil Simms/99 8.00 20.00
RB Raymond Berry/99 8.00 20.00
RN Ray Nitschke/66 12.00 30.00
RS Roger Staubach/99 12.00 30.00
RW Reggie White/92 12.00 30.00
SA Shaun Alexander/99 6.00 15.00
SL Steve Largent/99 10.00 25.00
SY Steve Young/99 12.00 30.00
TA Troy Aikman/99 12.00 30.00
WB Willie Brown/99 6.00 15.00
WM Warren Moon/99 10.00 25.00
WP Walter Payton/50 25.00 60.00
BLI Bob Lilly/99 8.00 20.00
BS Barry Sanders/50 20.00 50.00
BST Bart Starr/50 20.00 50.00
FGR Forrest Gregg/99 6.00 15.00
JBE Jerome Bettis/99 15.00 40.00
JBR Jim Brown/32 15.00 40.00
JER Jerry Rice/99 20.00 50.00
JOT Joe Theismann/99 10.00 25.00
JSM Jackie Smith/99 6.00 15.00
JST John Stallworth/99 8.00 20.00
TDA Terrell Davis/20 12.00 30.00
TDO Tony Dorsett/99 10.00 25.00

2006 Playoff National Treasures Timeline Material Signature AFC/NFC

STATED PRINT RUN 1-25
*PRIME/15-25: .6X TO 1.2X AFC/NFC SIG
PRIME PRINT RUN 1-25
SERIAL #'d UNDER 20 NOT PRICED
BE Boomer Esiason/15 20.00 50.00
BJ Bo Jackson/20 40.00 80.00
BL Bob Lilly/20 20.00 50.00
BS Barry Sanders/15 75.00 150.00
CJ Charlie Joiner/25 15.00 40.00
DB Dick Butkus/25 60.00 120.00
DC Dave Casper/20 20.00 50.00
DJ Deacon Jones/25 15.00 40.00
DL Daryle Lamonica/25 15.00 40.00
DS Deion Sanders/25 30.00 60.00
ED Eric Dickerson/25 40.00 80.00
FB Fred Biletnikoff/15 30.00 60.00
HM Hugh McElhenny/25 15.00 40.00
JB Jerome Bettis/25 60.00 120.00
JE John Elway/15 75.00 150.00
JM Joe Montana/16 75.00 150.00
JO Jim Otto/15 20.00 50.00
JP Jim Plunkett/16 20.00 50.00
JT Joe Theismann/25 40.00 80.00
LB Lem Barney/25 15.00 40.00
LM Lenny Moore/25 20.00 50.00
LS Lee Roy Selmon/15 20.00 50.00
LT Lawrence Taylor/25 40.00 80.00
MA Marcus Allen/25 30.00 60.00
MS Mike Singletary/20 25.00 60.00
ON Ozzie Newsome/15 20.00 50.00
PK Paul Krause/25 15.00 40.00
PS Phil Simms/25 25.00 60.00
RB Raymond Berry/25 20.00 50.00
RL Ronnie Lott/15 30.00 80.00
RS Roger Staubach/25 60.00 120.00
SJ Sonny Jurgensen/20 40.00 80.00
SL Steve Largent/25 40.00 80.00
SY Steve Young/15 40.00 80.00
TD Terrell Davis/15 20.00 50.00
WB Willie Brown/25 15.00 40.00
WM Warren Moon/15 40.00 80.00
JLO James Lofton/15 20.00 50.00
JOR John Riggins/25 20.00 50.00
JSM Jackie Smith/25 15.00 40.00
JST John Stallworth/25 40.00 80.00
TDO Tony Dorsett/25 30.00 60.00

2006 Playoff National Treasures Timeline Material Signature HOF

STATED PRINT RUN 1-25
*PRIME/15-25: .6X TO 1.2X AFC/NFC SIG
PRIME PRINT RUN 1-25
SERIAL #'d UNDER 15 NOT PRICED
DB Dick Butkus/25 60.00 120.00
DJ Deacon Jones/25 15.00 40.00
ED Eric Dickerson/25 40.00 80.00
HM Hugh McElhenny/25 15.00 40.00
JB Jim Brown/23 60.00 120.00
JR John Riggins/25 20.00 50.00
LB Lem Barney/25 15.00 40.00
LM Lenny Moore/25 20.00 50.00
LT Lawrence Taylor/25 40.00 80.00
MA Marcus Allen/25 30.00 60.00
MS Mike Singletary/20 25.00 60.00
PH Paul Hornung/25 30.00 80.00
PK Paul Krause/25 15.00 40.00
RB Raymond Berry/25 20.00 50.00
RS Roger Staubach/25 60.00 120.00
SL Steve Largent/25 40.00 80.00
TD Tony Dorsett/25 30.00 60.00
WB Willie Brown/25 15.00 40.00
BLI Bob Lilly/20 20.00 50.00
JSM Jackie Smith/25 15.00 40.00
JST John Stallworth/25 40.00 80.00

2006 Playoff National Treasures Timeline Material Signature MVP

*MVP/15-25: .4X TO 1X AFC/NFC SIG
MVP PRINT RUN 2-25
*PRIME/15-25: .6X TO 1.2X AFC/NFC SIG
PRIME PRINT RUN 1-25
SERIAL #'d UNDER 15 NOT PRICED
BE Boomer Esiason/15 20.00 50.00
FB Fred Biletnikoff/15 25.00 60.00
JB Jim Brown/25 60.00 120.00
JE John Elway/15 75.00 150.00
JM Joe Montana/16 75.00 150.00
JP Jim Plunkett/16 20.00 50.00
JT Joe Theismann/25 40.00 80.00
LT Lawrence Taylor/25 40.00 80.00
MA Marcus Allen/25 30.00 60.00
PH Paul Hornung/25 30.00 80.00
PM Peyton Manning/18
PS Phil Simms/25 30.00 60.00
RS Roger Staubach/25 60.00 120.00
SY Steve Young/15 40.00 80.00
TD Terrell Davis/15 20.00 50.00
BSA Barry Sanders/15 75.00 150.00
JOR John Riggins/25 20.00 50.00

2006 Playoff National Treasures Timeline Material Signature NFL

*NFL/15-25: .4X TO 1X AFC/NFC SIG
NFL PRINT RUN 1-25
*PRIME/15-25: .6X TO 1.2X AFC/NFC SIG
PRIME PRINT RUN 1-25
SERIAL #'d UNDER 15 NOT PRICED
PH Paul Hornung/25 30.00 80.00

2006 Playoff National Treasures Timeline Signature

STATED PRINT RUN 1-99
SERIAL #'d UNDER 24 NOT PRICED
UNPRICED SIG CUT PRINT RUN 1-10
DB Dick Butkus/60 30.00 80.00
DL Daryle Lamonica/76 12.00 30.00
FB Fred Biletnikoff/30 25.00 60.00
HM Hugh McElhenny/29 20.00 50.00
JBE Jerome Bettis/87 50.00 100.00
JBR Jim Brown/32 50.00 100.00
JL James Lofton/80 10.00 25.00
JOR John Riggins/99 15.00 40.00
JS Jackie Smith/64 12.00 30.00
JT Joe Theismann/99 15.00 40.00
LB Lem Barney/99 10.00 25.00
LK Leroy Kelly/25 15.00 40.00
LM Lenny Moore/24 15.00 40.00
MA Marcus Allen/99 20.00 50.00
PS Phil Simms/44 20.00 50.00
RB Raymond Berry/30 15.00 40.00
RL Ronnie Lott/49 20.00 50.00
SJ Sonny Jurgensen/95 15.00 40.00
TDA Terrell Davis/26 20.00 50.00
WB Willie Brown/99 12.00 30.00
YL Yale Lary/54 15.00 40.00
YT Y.A. Tittle/22 30.00 80.00

2007 Playoff National Treasures

This 200-card set was released in January, 2008. The set was issued in seven-card pack (boxes) with an $500 SRP: Cards numbered 1-54 feature veterans while cards numbered 55-100 feature retired greats. All cards numbered 1-100 were issued to a stated print run of 100 serial numbered sets. Cards numbered 101-134 are 2007 NFL rookies and feature both player-worn jersey swatches and a signature and those cards were issued to a stated print run of 99 serial numbered sets. Cards numbered 135-200 are also NFL rookies and those were signed and issued to a stated print run of 99 serial numbered sets. A few players did not return their cards in time for pack out and those cards could be redeemed until August 1, 2009.

1-100 PRINT RUN 100 SER.#'d SETS
101-134 JSY AU RC PRINT RUN 99
135-200 AU RC PRINT RUN 99-299
UNPRICED GOLD PRINT RUN 5
UNPRICED PLATINUM PRINT RUN 1
1 Tom Brady 12.00 30.00
2 Brett Favre 8.00 20.00
3 Tony Romo 5.00 12.00
4 Carson Palmer 3.00 8.00
5 Eli Manning 3.00 8.00
6 Peyton Manning 10.00 25.00
7 Philip Rivers 4.00 10.00
8 Donovan McNabb 3.00 8.00
9 Vince Young 2.50 6.00
10 Drew Brees 4.00 10.00
11 Ben Roethlisberger 4.00 10.00
12 Jay Cutler 2.50 6.00
13 Brian Westbrook 2.50 6.00
14 Willie Parker 3.00 8.00
15 LaDainian Tomlinson 4.00 10.00
16 Ronnie Brown 2.50 6.00
17 Willis McGahee 2.50 6.00
18 Steven Jackson 2.50 6.00
19 Larry Johnson 2.50 6.00
20 Laurence Maroney 3.00 8.00
21 Clinton Portis 2.50 6.00
22 Shaun Alexander 2.50 6.00
23 Maurice Jones-Drew 2.50 6.00
24 Frank Gore 3.00 8.00
25 Cadillac Williams 3.00 8.00
26 Edgerrin James 3.00 8.00
27 Brandon Jacobs 2.50 6.00
28 Marion Barber 3.00 8.00
29 Cedric Benson 2.50 6.00
30 Fred Taylor 2.50 6.00
31 Randy Moss 3.00 8.00
32 Chad Johnson 2.50 6.00
33 Antonio Gates 4.00 10.00
34 Larry Fitzgerald 3.00 8.00
35 Plaxico Burress 2.50 6.00
36 Kellen Winslow 2.50 6.00
37 T.J. Houshmandzadeh 2.50 6.00
38 Steve Smith 3.00 8.00
39 Terrell Owens 3.00 8.00
40 Tony Gonzalez 3.00 8.00
41 Roy Williams WR 2.50 6.00
42 Donald Driver 3.00 8.00
43 Torry Holt 3.00 8.00
44 Hines Ward 3.00 8.00
45 Reggie Wayne 3.00 8.00
46 Marvin Harrison 3.00 8.00
47 Laveranues Coles 2.50 6.00
48 Jeremy Shockey 2.50 6.00
49 Anquan Boldin 2.50 6.00
50 Dallas Clark 3.00 8.00
51 Devin Hester 3.00 8.00
52 Joey Galloway 3.00 8.00
53 Andre Johnson 3.00 8.00
54 Reggie Bush 2.50 6.00
55 Joe Montana 12.00 30.00
56 Joe Namath 5.00 12.00
57 John Elway 6.00 15.00
58 Johnny Morris 2.50 6.00
59 Ken Strong 2.50 6.00
60 Larry Csonka 4.00 10.00
61 Lawrence Taylor 4.00 10.00
62 Mel Hein 2.50 6.00
63 Michael Irvin 4.00 10.00
64 Paul Krause 2.50 6.00
65 Randall Cunningham 3.00 8.00
66 Rick Casares 2.50 6.00
67 Emmitt Smith 6.00 15.00
68 Lydell Mitchell 2.50 6.00
69 Roger Craig 3.00 8.00
70 Sam Huff 3.00 8.00
71 Sammy Baugh 4.00 10.00
72 Sid Luckman 4.00 10.00
73 Sonny Jurgensen 3.00 8.00
74 Walter Payton 8.00 20.00
75 Steve Largent 4.00 10.00
76 Thurman Thomas 3.00 8.00
77 Tommy McDonald 2.50 6.00
78 Bob Waterfield 2.50 6.00
79 Tom Fears 2.50 6.00
80 Dick Lane 2.50 6.00
81 Jim Parker 2.50 6.00
82 Norm Van Brocklin 3.00 8.00
83 Ollie Matson 3.00 8.00
84 Tom Landry 5.00 12.00
85 Barry Sanders 6.00 15.00
86 Bo Jackson 5.00 12.00
87 Bob Griese 4.00 10.00
88 Red Grange 5.00 12.00
89 Yale Lary 2.50 6.00
90 Cris Collinsworth 3.00 8.00
91 Daryle Lamonica 2.50 6.00
92 Doak Walker 3.00 8.00
93 Fred Biletnikoff 4.00 10.00
94 George Blanda 3.00 8.00
95 Harlon Hill 2.50 6.00
96 Marion Motley 2.50 6.00
97 Jimmy Orr 2.50 6.00
98 Jim Thorpe 5.00 12.00
99 Ernie Nevers 3.00 8.00
100 Otto Graham 3.00 8.00
101 A.Peterson JSY AU RC 300.00 500.00
102 A.Gonzalez JSY AU RC 12.00 30.00
103 Antonio Pittman JSY AU RC 12.00 30.00
104 Brady Quinn JSY AU RC 12.00 30.00
105 B.Jackson JSY AU RC 12.00 30.00
106 Brian Leonard JSY AU RC 12.00 30.00
107 Cal.Johnson JSY AU RC 250.00 400.00
108 Chris Henry JSY AU RC 12.00 30.00
109 Drew Stanton JSY AU RC 12.00 30.00
110 Dwayne Jarrett JSY AU RC 15.00 40.00
111 Dwayne Bowe JSY AU RC 12.00 30.00
112 Gaines Adams JSY AU RC 15.00 40.00
113 Garrett Wolfe JSY AU RC 12.00 30.00
114 Greg Olsen JSY AU RC 20.00 50.00
115 J.Russell JSY AU RC 12.00 30.00
116 Jason Hill JSY AU RC 12.00 30.00
117 Joe Thomas JSY AU RC 20.00 50.00
118 John Beck JSY AU RC 12.00 30.00
119 J.Lee Higgins JSY AU RC 12.00 30.00
120 Kenny Irons JSY No AU RC 5.00 12.00
121 Kevin Kolb JSY AU RC 15.00 40.00
122 L.Booker JSY AU RC 15.00 40.00
123 M.Lynch JSY AU RC 40.00 80.00
124 Michael Bush JSY AU RC 12.00 30.00
125 Patrick Willis JSY AU RC 30.00 80.00
126 Paul Williams JSY AU RC 12.00 30.00
127 R. Meachem JSY AU RC 15.00 40.00
128 Sidney Rice JSY AU RC 30.00 60.00
129 Steve Smith JSY AU RC 12.00 30.00
130 Ted Ginn JSY AU RC 15.00 40.00
131 Tony Hunt JSY AU RC 12.00 30.00
132 T.Edwards JSY AU RC 12.00 30.00
133 Troy Smith JSY AU RC 12.00 30.00
134 Yamon Figurs JSY AU RC 12.00 30.00
135 Darrelle Revis AU RC 6.00 15.00
136 Aaron Ross AU RC 5.00 12.00
137 LaRon Landry AU RC 8.00 20.00
138 James Jones AU RC 5.00 12.00
139 Michael Griffin AU RC 5.00 12.00
140 Aundrae Allison AU RC 5.00 12.00
141 Craig Buster Davis No AU RC 2.00 5.00
142 David Harris AU RC 5.00 12.00
143 DeShawn Wynn AU RC 5.00 12.00
144 Dwayne Wright AU RC 5.00 12.00
145 Jacoby Jones AU/299 RC 4.00 10.00
146 J.Broussard AU/299 RC 5.00 12.00
147 Jon Beason AU/299 RC 4.00 10.00
148 Kenton Keith AU RC 6.00 15.00
149 Kolby Smith AU RC 5.00 12.00
150 Leon Hall AU RC 5.00 12.00
151 Reggie Nelson AU RC 5.00 12.00
152 Roy Hall AU/299 RC 6.00 15.00
153 R.Robinson AU/299 RC 5.00 12.00
154 Selvin Young AU RC 5.00 12.00
155 Steve Breaston AU/243 RC 4.00 10.00
156 Chris Davis AU RC 5.00 12.00
157 Glenn Holt AU RC 6.00 15.00
158 Kenneth Darby AU RC 5.00 12.00
159 Mike Walker AU/299 RC 6.00 15.00
160 Chris Houston AU RC 5.00 12.00
161 David Clowney AU RC 5.00 12.00
162 Mason Crosby AU/299 RC 10.00 25.00
163 Bobby Sippio AU/299 RC 5.00 12.00
164 Biren Ealy AU RC 6.00 15.00
166 Laurent Robinson AU RC 8.00 20.00
167 Lawrence Timmons AU RC 8.00 20.00
168 Legedu Naanee AU RC 6.00 15.00
169 Brandon Meriweather AU RC 6.00 15.00
170 Brian Robison AU RC 8.00 20.00
171 Greg Peterson AU RC 6.00 15.00
172 Alama-Francis AU/190 RC 6.00 15.00
173 Isaiah Stanback AU RC 5.00 12.00
174 Ed Johnson AU RC 6.00 15.00
175 Eric Frampton AU/299 RC 5.00 12.00
176 Eric Weddle AU/299 RC 5.00 12.00
177 Fred Bennett AU/299 RC 4.00 10.00
178 Dante Rosario AU RC 8.00 20.00
179 C.Dawson AU/299 RC 6.00 15.00
180 Jeff Rowe AU/299 RC 4.00 10.00
181 Justin Durant AU RC 8.00 20.00
182 Charles Johnson No AU RC 2.00 5.00
183 Paul Posluszny AU RC 5.00 12.00
184 Pierre Thomas AU RC 8.00 20.00
185 Quentin Moses AU/299 RC 4.00 10.00
186 Ray McDonald AU RC 6.00 15.00
187 Sabby Piscitelli AU/299 RC 4.00 10.00
188 Scott Chandler AU RC 8.00 20.00
189 Matt Gutierrez AU RC 8.00 20.00
190 Matt Moore AU RC 8.00 20.00
191 Martrez Milner AU RC 5.00 12.00
192 Amobi Okoye AU RC 6.00 15.00
193 Adam Carriker AU RC 5.00 12.00
194 Alan Branch AU RC EXCH 2.00 5.00
195 A.Spencer AU/299 RC 8.00 20.00
196 Tyler Thigpen AU RC 8.00 20.00
197 V Abiamiri AU/299 RC 4.00 10.00
198 Zach Miller AU RC 5.00 12.00
199 Jarvis Moss AU/199 RC 4.00 10.00
200 LaMarr Woodley AU RC 12.50 25.00

2007 Playoff National Treasures Silver

*VETS: 1X TO 2.5X BASIC CARDS
SILVER PRINT RUN 25 SER.#'d SETS

2007 Playoff National Treasures All Decade Material Jumbo

JUMBO PRINT RUN 1-25
*BASE MAT/15-25: .3X TO .8X JUMBO/15-25
BASE MATERIAL PRINT RUN 1-25
*JUMBO PRIME/15-25: .6X TO 1.5X JUMBO/15-25
JUMBO PRIME PRINT RUN 1-25
SER.#'d UNDER 15 NOT PRICED
AP Alan Page 15.00 40.00
BF Brett Favre 30.00 80.00
BS Barry Sanders 25.00 60.00
BST Bart Starr 25.00 60.00
BT Bulldog Turner 15.00 40.00
CB Chuck Bednarik 12.00 30.00
CH Cliff Harris 12.00 30.00
CT Charley Taylor 10.00 25.00
DB Dick Butkus 20.00 50.00
DC Dave Casper 10.00 25.00
DG Darrell Green 15.00 40.00
DH Dan Hampton 12.00 30.00
DJ Deacon Jones 12.00 30.00
EC Earl Campbell 15.00 40.00
ED Eric Dickerson 12.00 30.00
ES Emmitt Smith/22 25.00 60.00
FG Forrest Gregg 10.00 25.00
GS Gale Sayers 15.00 40.00
GU Gene Upshaw/15 10.00 25.00
HM Hugh McElhenny 12.00 30.00
JE John Elway 25.00 60.00
JLO James Lofton 10.00 25.00
JL Jack Lambert 15.00 40.00
JMO Joe Montana 50.00 120.00
JM John Mackey 12.00 30.00
JP Jim Parker 10.00 25.00
JR John Riggins 12.00 30.00
JU Johnny Unitas 25.00 60.00
JY Jack Youngblood 12.00 30.00
KS Ken Stabler 20.00 50.00
KSG Ken Strong 15.00 40.00
LB Lem Barney 12.00 30.00
LK Leroy Kelly/15 12.00 30.00
LM Lenny Moore 10.00 25.00
LS Lee Roy Selmon/20 10.00 25.00
LT Lawrence Taylor 15.00 40.00
MH Mel Hein 15.00 40.00
MM Marion Motley 15.00 40.00
MS Mike Singletary 15.00 40.00
NV Norm Van Brocklin 25.00 60.00
OG Otto Graham 12.00 30.00
OM Ollie Matson/15 12.00 30.00
ON Ozzie Newsome 12.00 30.00
PW Paul Warfield 12.00 30.00
RB Roosevelt Brown 10.00 25.00
RL Ronnie Lott 12.00 30.00
RN Ray Nitschke 15.00 40.00
SB Sammy Baugh 20.00 50.00
SJ Sonny Jurgensen 12.00 30.00
SL Sid Luckman 20.00 50.00
SLA Steve Largent 15.00 40.00
TB Tim Brown 15.00 40.00
TF Tom Fears/15 10.00 25.00
TH Ted Hendricks 12.00 30.00
TT Thurman Thomas 12.00 30.00
WP Walter Payton 30.00 80.00

2007 Playoff National Treasures All Decade Material Quads

BASE QUAD PRINT RUN 1-25
*PRIME/22-25: .5X TO 1.2X BASIC QUAD/25
PRIME PRINT RUN 1-25
BIGL Brwn/Irvn/Grn/Ltt 25.00 60.00
BLWT Bgh/Lckmn/Wtrfld/Tnr 40.00 100.00
EFSS Elwy/Fvre/Sndrs/Smth 50.00 120.00
FHVM Frs/Hrs/Brck/Mtsn 40.00 80.00
GLMB Grhm/Lyne/McElh/Brry 30.00 60.00
JBON Jnes/Btks/Olsn/Ntsc 30.00 60.00
JSMT Jrgn/Str/Mcky/Tylr 40.00 100.00
LHLH Litle/Hnd/Lmbrt/Hrrs 30.00 60.00
MFDR Mntna/Fts/Dckrsn/Rgg 25.00 60.00
SCHP Stub/Cmbll/Hrrs/Pytn 30.00 80.00
SHST Slmn/Hmp/Sngly/Tylr 20.00 50.00
YGLP Yngbld/Grne/Lily/Pge 20.00 50.00

2007 Playoff National Treasures All Decade Material Signature

MATERIAL SIG PRINT RUN 1-25
*POSITION/25: .4X TO 1X BASE MATERIAL SIG
POSITION MAT.SIG PRINT RUN 1-25
SER.#'d UNDER 25 NOT PRICED
AP Alan Page/25 25.00 60.00
DH Dan Hampton/25 20.00 50.00
JE John Elway/25 75.00 150.00
JM Joe Montana/25 100.00 200.00
LM Lenny Moore/25 20.00 50.00
LT Lawrence Taylor/25 30.00 80.00
MI Michael Irvin/25 40.00 80.00
RS Roger Staubach/25 50.00 100.00
SL Steve Largent/25 25.00 60.00
TB Tim Brown/25 25.00 60.00

2007 Playoff National Treasures All Decade Material Signature Jersey Numbers

STATED PRINT RUN 4-99
SER.#'d UNDER 22 NOT PRICED
LM Lenny Moore/24 20.00 50.00
CH Cliff Harris/43 20.00 50.00
DH Dan Hampton/99 15.00 40.00
ED Eric Dickerson/29 25.00 60.00
ES Emmitt Smith/22 150.00 250.00
LT Lawrence Taylor/56 25.00 60.00
ON Ozzie Newsome/82 15.00 40.00
PW Paul Warfield/42 15.00 40.00
RL Ronnie Lott/42 20.00 50.00
SL Steve Largent/80 20.00 50.00

2007 Playoff National Treasures All Decade Material Trios

BASE TRIO JSY PRINT RUN 2-25
*PRIME/25: .6X TO 1.5X BASE JSY/25
PRIME PRINT RUN 1-25
*HOF/25: .4X TO 1X BASE JSY/25
HOF TRIO PRINT RUN 2-25
*HOF PRIME/25: .6X TO 1.5X BASE JSY/25
HOF TRIO PRIME PRINT RUN 1-25
*NFL TRIO/25: .4X TO 1X BASE JSY/25
NFL TRIO PRINT RUN 2-25
*NFL PRIME/25: .6X TO 1.5X BASE JSY/25
NFL TRIO PRIME PRINT RUN 1-25
SER.#'d UNDER 25 NOT PRICED
BLW Baugh/Luckman/Waterfield 30.00 80.00
BFH Berry/Fears/Hirsch 15.00 40.00
BNB Butkus/Nitschke/Barney 25.00 50.00
BPB Brown/Parker/Bednarik 15.00 40.00
CHP Campbell/Harris/Payton 30.00 80.00
EFI Elway/Favre/Irvin 30.00 80.00
FRN Fouts/Riggins/Newsome 15.00 40.00
GJO Gregg/Jones/Olsen 15.00 40.00
GLV Graham/Layne/Van Brocklin 12.00 30.00
JSM Jurgensen/Starr/Mackey 25.00 60.00
MMM Matson/McElhenny/Moore 15.00 40.00
PHL Page/Hendricks/Lambert 15.00 40.00
RLL Rice/Largent/Lofton 25.00 60.00
SST Sanders/Smith/Thomas 30.00 80.00
STL Singletary/Taylor/Lott 15.00 40.00
TMK Taylor/Mackey/Kelly 15.00 40.00
YGL Youngblood/Greene/Lilly 15.00 40.00

2007 Playoff National Treasures All Decade Signature

STATED PRINT RUN 1-99
SERIAL #'d UNDER 20 NOT PRICED
DL Dante Lavelli 12.00 30.00
AP Alan Page 15.00 40.00
BD Boyd Dowler 12.00 30.00
BL Bob Lilly/21 20.00 50.00
BS Bart Starr/35 90.00 150.00
CB Chuck Bednarik/50 15.00 40.00
CT Charley Trippi 12.00 30.00
CT Charley Taylor 12.00 30.00
DC Dave Casper 10.00 25.00
DF Dan Fouts/50 15.00 40.00
DH Dan Hampton/42 12.00 30.00
DJ Deacon Jones 12.00 30.00
FG Forrest Gregg/24 25.00 60.00
GS Gale Sayers 26.00 60.00
GU Gene Upshaw 15.00 40.00
HM Hugh McElhenny 12.00 30.00
JB Jim Brown 40.00 80.00
JL James Lofton/23 15.00 40.00
JM Joe Montana/16 100.00 200.00
JR John Riggins 15.00 40.00
KW Kellen Winslow Sr./75 12.00 30.00
LB Lem Barney 10.00 25.00
LL Larry Little 10.00 25.00
LM Lenny Moore 12.00 30.00
LS Lee Roy Selmon 12.00 30.00
LT Lawrence Taylor 20.00 50.00
PH Paul Hornung 20.00 50.00
PW Paul Warfield/66 12.00 30.00
RB Raymond Berry 12.00 30.00
RC Roger Craig 10.00 25.00
SH Sam Huff/83 15.00 40.00
SJ Sonny Jurgensen/75 15.00 40.00
SL Steve Largent/82 15.00 40.00
WB Willie Brown 12.00 30.00
YL Yale Lary 10.00 25.00

2007 Playoff National Treasures All Decade Signature Cuts

STATED PRINT RUN 1-100
AP Alan Page/25 25.00 60.00
AW Alex Wojciechowicz/36 75.00 150.00
BF Brett Favre/21 150.00 250.00
BS Barry Sanders/25 100.00 200.00
BST Bart Starr/29 125.00 200.00
BT Bulldog Turner/100 40.00 100.00
BWA Bob Waterfield/39 40.00 100.00
BW Byron White/16 90.00 150.00
CB Cliff Battles/41 125.00 225.00
CBE Chuck Bednarik/25 40.00 80.00
CT Charley Trippi/50 20.00 50.00
DC Dutch Clark/30 175.00 300.00
DF Dan Fortmann/21 125.00 250.00
DFO Dan Fouts/25 25.00 60.00
DJ Deacon Jones/50 20.00 50.00
DL Dick Lane/32 125.00 250.00
DLV Dante Lavelli/25 40.00 80.00
EC Earl Campbell/50 25.00 60.00
ED Eric Dickerson/60 25.00 60.00
EH Ed Healey/22 150.00 300.00
EN Ernie Nevers/21 250.00 400.00
ES Ernie Stautner/100 25.00 60.00
FH Franco Harris/50 30.00 80.00
GC George Connor/70 20.00 50.00
GM George McAfee/56 30.00 80.00
GS Gale Sayers/59 30.00 80.00
GT George Trafton/67 125.00 250.00
HM Hugh McElhenny/50 20.00 50.00
JB Jim Brown/25 60.00 120.00
JE John Elway/25 75.00 150.00
JG Joe Greene/15 30.00 80.00
JL Jack Lambert/25 75.00 150.00
JLO James Lofton/30 15.00 40.00
JM Joe Montana/25 75.00 150.00
JR John Riggins/25 30.00 80.00
JU Johnny Unitas/19 200.00 350.00
KST Ken Strong/40 40.00 100.00
LM Lenny Moore/59 20.00 50.00
MH Mel Hein/61 60.00 120.00
MS Mike Singletary/50 25.00 60.00
OG Otto Graham/100 25.00 60.00
OM Ollie Matson/21 40.00 80.00
ON Ozzie Newsome/50 15.00 40.00
PH Paul Hornung/50 40.00 80.00
PP Pete Pihos/32 50.00 100.00
RBE Raymond Berry/50 25.00 60.00
RB Roosevelt Brown/50 25.00 60.00
RG Red Grange/40 250.00 500.00
RN Ray Nitschke/19 90.00 150.00
RS Roger Staubach/15 90.00 150.00
SB Sammy Baugh/50 75.00 150.00
SJ Sonny Jurgensen/25 25.00 60.00
SL Steve Largent/50 40.00 80.00
SLU Sid Luckman/42 100.00 200.00
SV Steve Van Buren/32 100.00 200.00
TC Tony Canadeo/100 40.00 100.00
TT Thurman Thomas/15 25.00 60.00
WP Walter Payton/34 200.00 400.00

2007 Playoff National Treasures Fearsome Foursome

STATED PRINT RUN 100
*PRIME/25: .6X TO 1.5X BASE JSY/100
PRIME PRINT RUN 25
1 Lundy/Grier/Olsen/Jones 15.00 40.00

2007 Playoff National Treasures Material Face Mask

STATED PRINT RUN 3-25
SERIAL #'d UNDER 25 NOT PRICED
1 Tom Brady 40.00 100.00
2 Brett Favre 25.00 60.00
4 Carson Palmer 10.00 25.00
5 Eli Manning 10.00 25.00
6 Peyton Manning 30.00 80.00
8 Donovan McNabb 10.00 25.00
10 Drew Brees 12.00 30.00
15 LaDainian Tomlinson 12.00 30.00
21 Clinton Portis 8.00 20.00
22 Shaun Alexander 8.00 20.00
26 Edgerrin James 10.00 25.00
38 Steve Smith 10.00 25.00
44 Hines Ward 10.00 25.00
46 Marvin Harrison 10.00 25.00
48 Jeremy Shockey/39 8.00 20.00
53 Andre Johnson 10.00 25.00
55 Joe Montana 40.00 100.00
57 John Elway 20.00 50.00
65 Randall Cunningham 10.00 25.00
69 Roger Craig 10.00 25.00
76 Thurman Thomas 10.00 25.00

2007 Playoff National Treasures Material Helmet

STATED PRINT RUN 1-25
SERIAL #'d UNDER 25 NOT PRICED
46 Marvin Harrison/25 10.00 25.00
92 Doak Walker/25 60.00 100.00

2007 Playoff National Treasures Material Jersey Numbers

STATED PRINT RUN 4-89
SERIAL #'d UNDER 20 NOT PRICED
13 Brian Westbrook/36 5.00 12.00
14 Willie Parker/39 6.00 15.00
15 LaDainian Tomlinson/21 10.00 25.00
16 Ronnie Brown/23 6.00 15.00
18 Steven Jackson/39 5.00 12.00
19 Larry Johnson/27 6.00 15.00
20 Laurence Maroney/39 6.00 15.00
21 Clinton Portis/26 6.00 15.00
22 Shaun Alexander/37 5.00 12.00
23 Maurice Jones-Drew/32 5.00 12.00
24 Frank Gore/21 8.00 20.00
25 Cadillac Williams/24 8.00 20.00
27 Brandon Jacobs/27 6.00 15.00
28 Marion Barber/24 8.00 20.00
29 Cedric Benson/32 5.00 12.00
30 Fred Taylor/28 6.00 15.00
31 Randy Moss/81 5.00 12.00
32 Chad Johnson/85 4.00 10.00
33 Antonio Gates/85 6.00 15.00
37 T.J. Houshmandzadeh/84 4.00 10.00
38 Steve Smith/89 5.00 12.00
39 Terrell Owens/81 5.00 12.00
40 Tony Gonzalez/88 5.00 12.00
42 Donald Driver/80 5.00 12.00
43 Torry Holt/81 5.00 12.00
44 Hines Ward/86 10.00 25.00
45 Reggie Wayne/87 5.00 12.00
46 Marvin Harrison/88 5.00 12.00
47 Laveranues Coles/87 4.00 10.00
48 Jeremy Shockey/80 4.00 10.00
49 Anquan Boldin/81 4.00 10.00
50 Dallas Clark/44 6.00 15.00
51 Devin Hester/23 8.00 20.00
52 Joey Galloway/84 5.00 12.00
53 Andre Johnson/80 5.00 12.00
54 Reggie Bush/25 6.00 15.00
59 Ken Strong/50 12.00 30.00
60 Larry Csonka/39 10.00 25.00
61 Lawrence Taylor/56 8.00 20.00
63 Michael Irvin/88 8.00 20.00
67 Emmitt Smith/22 20.00 50.00
71 Sammy Baugh/33 10.00 25.00
74 Walter Payton/34 20.00 50.00
75 Steve Largent/80 8.00 20.00
76 Thurman Thomas/34 8.00 20.00
77 Tommy McDonald/25 8.00 20.00
79 Tom Fears/55 5.00 12.00
83 Ollie Matson/33 8.00 20.00
84 Tom Landry/49 12.00 30.00
85 Barry Sanders/20 20.00 50.00
86 Bo Jackson/34 12.00 30.00
90 Cris Collinsworth/80 6.00 15.00
93 Fred Biletnikoff/25 12.00 30.00
96 Marion Motley/36 10.00 25.00

2007 Playoff National Treasures Material Prime

STATED PRINT RUN 4-25
SERIAL #'d UNDER 25 NOT PRICED
UNPRICED BRAND LOGO PRINT RUN 1-10
UNPRICED BUTTON PRINT RUN 3-5
UNPRICED LAUN.TAG PRINT RUN 1-10
UNPRICED NFL LOGO PRINT RUN 1
1 Tom Brady 40.00 100.00
2 Brett Favre 25.00 60.00
3 Tony Romo 15.00 40.00
4 Carson Palmer 10.00 25.00
5 Eli Manning 10.00 25.00
6 Peyton Manning 30.00 80.00
7 Philip Rivers 12.00 30.00
8 Donovan McNabb 10.00 25.00
9 Vince Young 8.00 20.00
11 Ben Roethlisberger 12.00 30.00
12 Jay Cutler 8.00 20.00
13 Brian Westbrook 8.00 20.00
14 Willie Parker 10.00 25.00
15 LaDainian Tomlinson 12.00 30.00
16 Ronnie Brown 8.00 20.00
18 Steven Jackson 8.00 20.00
19 Larry Johnson 8.00 20.00
20 Laurence Maroney 10.00 25.00
21 Clinton Portis 8.00 20.00
22 Shaun Alexander 8.00 20.00
23 Maurice Jones-Drew 8.00 20.00
24 Frank Gore 10.00 25.00
25 Cadillac Williams 10.00 25.00
27 Brandon Jacobs 8.00 20.00
28 Marion Barber 12.00 30.00
29 Cedric Benson 8.00 20.00
30 Fred Taylor 8.00 20.00
31 Randy Moss 10.00 25.00
32 Chad Johnson 8.00 20.00
33 Antonio Gates 12.00 30.00
35 Plaxico Burress 8.00 20.00
36 Kellen Winslow 8.00 20.00
37 T.J. Houshmandzadeh 8.00 20.00
38 Steve Smith 10.00 25.00
39 Terrell Owens 10.00 25.00
40 Tony Gonzalez 10.00 25.00
41 Roy Williams WR 8.00 20.00
42 Donald Driver 10.00 25.00
43 Torry Holt 10.00 25.00
44 Hines Ward 10.00 25.00
45 Reggie Wayne 10.00 25.00
46 Marvin Harrison 10.00 25.00
47 Laveranues Coles 8.00 20.00
48 Jeremy Shockey 8.00 20.00
49 Anquan Boldin 8.00 20.00
50 Dallas Clark 10.00 25.00
51 Devin Hester 10.00 25.00
52 Joey Galloway 10.00 25.00
53 Andre Johnson 10.00 25.00
54 Reggie Bush 8.00 20.00
55 Joe Montana 50.00 120.00
57 John Elway 25.00 60.00
59 Ken Strong 15.00 40.00
61 Lawrence Taylor 15.00 40.00
62 Mel Hein 15.00 40.00
63 Michael Irvin 15.00 40.00
67 Emmitt Smith 25.00 60.00
75 Steve Largent 15.00 40.00
85 Barry Sanders 25.00 60.00
86 Bo Jackson 20.00 50.00
90 Cris Collinsworth 12.00 30.00
93 Fred Biletnikoff 15.00 40.00
96 Marion Motley 15.00 40.00
100 Otto Graham 12.00 30.00

2007 Playoff National Treasures Material Quads

STATED PRINT RUN 5-25
*PRIME/25: .5X TO 1.2X BASE QUAD JSY
PRIME PRINT RUN 25 SER.#'d SETS
SERIAL #'d UNDER 25 NOT PRICED
1 Smith/Payton/Sanders/Brown 75.00 150.00
2 Smith/Allen/Payton/Tomlin 60.00 120.00
3 Rice/Brown/Lofton/Harrison 30.00 80.00
4 Favre/Marino/Elway/Moon 60.00 120.00
5 Lilly/Harris/Lambert/Greene 25.00 60.00
6 Aikman/Irvin/Montana/Rice 40.00 100.00
8 Tark/Page/Dawson/Stene 25.00 60.00
9 Landry/Staub/Stram/Dawson 50.00 120.00
10 Staub/Mntna/Aikman/Young 50.00 120.00
11 Aikman/Smith/Kelly/Thomas 30.00 80.00
12 Greene/Page/Olsen/Lilly 20.00 50.00
14 Otto/Parker/Mix/Bednarik 20.00 50.00
15 Van Brck/Wtrfld/Lyne/Grhm 40.00 100.00

2007 Playoff National Treasures Material Signature Face Mask

STATED PRINT RUN 1-25
UNPRICED HELMET PRINT RUN 1-18
SERIAL #'d UNDER 20 NOT PRICED
5 Eli Manning/25 60.00 120.00
6 Peyton Manning/25 75.00 150.00
10 Drew Brees/25 40.00 80.00
38 Steve Smith/25 20.00 50.00
61 Lawrence Taylor/25 30.00 80.00
65 Randall Cunningham/25 25.00 60.00
67 Emmitt Smith/22 125.00 250.00
69 Roger Craig/25 15.00 40.00

2007 Playoff National Treasures Material Signature Jersey Numbers

STATED PRINT RUN 4-87
UNPRICED BRAND LOGO PRINT RUN 1
UNPRICED BUTTON PRINT RUN 1
UNPRICED LAUN.TAG PRINT RUN 1
UNPRICED NFL LOGO PRINT RUN 1
SERIAL #'d UNDER 18 NOT PRICED
6 Peyton Manning/18 100.00 175.00
13 Brian Westbrook/36 20.00 50.00
15 LaDainian Tomlinson/21 60.00 120.00
16 Ronnie Brown/23 20.00 50.00
18 Steven Jackson/39 15.00 40.00
19 Larry Johnson/27
20 Laurence Maroney/39 20.00 50.00
23 Maurice Jones-Drew/32 20.00 50.00
24 Frank Gore/21 20.00 50.00
25 Cadillac Williams/24
27 Brandon Jacobs/27 30.00 60.00
28 Marion Barber/24 25.00 60.00
29 Cedric Benson/32 15.00 40.00
30 Fred Taylor/28 20.00 50.00
37 T.J. Houshmandzadeh/84 15.00 40.00
43 Torry Holt/81 15.00 40.00
45 Reggie Wayne/87 20.00 50.00
51 Devin Hester/23 50.00 100.00
54 Reggie Bush/25 40.00 100.00
61 Lawrence Taylor/56 30.00 60.00
67 Emmitt Smith/22 125.00 250.00
75 Steve Largent/80 20.00 50.00
76 Thurman Thomas/34 20.00 50.00
77 Tommy McDonald/25 15.00 40.00
86 Bo Jackson/34 40.00 80.00
90 Cris Collinsworth/80 12.00 30.00
93 Fred Biletnikoff/20 40.00 80.00

2007 Playoff National Treasures Material Trios

STATED PRINT RUN 25 SER.#'d SETS
*HOF/25: .4X TO 1X BASE TRIO
HOF PRINT RUN 25
*HOF PRIME/25: .6X TO 1.5X BASE TRIO
HOF PRIME PRINT RUN 25
*NFL/25: .4X TO 1X BASE TRIO
NFL PRINT RUN 25
*NFL PRIME/25: .6X TO 1.5X BASE TRIO
NFL PRIME PRINT RUN 25
*PRIME/25: .6X TO 1.5X BASE TRIO
PRIME PRINT RUN 25
1 Manning/Brady/Favre 50.00 120.00
2 Smith/Payton/Sanders 40.00 100.00
3 Favre/Marino/Elway 50.00 100.00
4 Jurgensen/Staubach/Montana 30.00 80.00
5 Harrison/Johnson/Owens 15.00 40.00
6 Manning/Manning/Manning 50.00 100.00
7 Irvin/Brown/Largent 20.00 50.00
8 Starr/Namath/Unitas 50.00 120.00
9 Landry/Staubach/Dorsett 50.00 100.00
10 Stram/Dawson/Stenerud 15.00 40.00
11 Fears/Parker/Lane 15.00 40.00
12 Campbell/Harris/Payton 30.00 80.00
13 Brown/Campbell/Sanders 30.00 80.00
14 Sharpe/Irvin/Rice/15 25.00 60.00
15 Namath/Tarkenton/Manning 25.00 60.00

2007 Playoff National Treasures Notable Nicknames Signature

STATED PRINT RUN 25-126
10 Joe Greene/54 30.00 60.00
AP Adrian Peterson/28 300.00 600.00
BD Bill Dudley/54 20.00 50.00
FB Fred Biletnikoff/52 25.00 50.00
JN Joe Namath/55 90.00 150.00
LM Lenny Moore/126 20.00 50.00
MD Mark Duper/74 16.00 40.00
SM Shawne Merriman/25 30.00 60.00
WL Willie Lanier/85 20.00 50.00
WL Willie Lanier/38 25.00 60.00

2007 Playoff National Treasures Pen Pals

STATED PRINT RUN 12-30
GG T.Ginn Jr./A.Gonzalez
JM C.Johnson/R.Meachem/29 40.00 80.00
JO C.Johnson/G.Olsen 60.00 120.00
JS D.Jarrett/S.Smith USC 15.00 40.00
PL A.Peterson/M.Lynch 75.00 150.00
RQ J.Russell/B.Quinn 20.00 50.00
SP T.Smith/A.Pittman 20.00 50.00

2007 Playoff National Treasures Rookie Jumbo Material

STATED PRINT RUN 49 SER.#'d SETS
UNPRICED BRAND LOGO PRINT RUN 10
UNPRICED PRIME PRINT RUN 1
UNPRICED LAUNDRY TAG PRINT RUN 10
UNPRICED NFL SHIELD PRINT RUN 1
101 Adrian Peterson 8.00 20.00
102 Anthony Gonzalez 2.50 6.00
103 Antonio Pittman 2.50 6.00
104 Brady Quinn 2.50 6.00
105 Brandon Jackson 2.50 6.00
106 Brian Leonard 2.50 6.00
107 Calvin Johnson 8.00 20.00
108 Chris Henry RB 2.50 6.00
109 Drew Stanton 2.50 6.00
110 Dwayne Jarrett 3.00 8.00
111 Dwayne Bowe 2.50 6.00
112 Gaines Adams 3.00 8.00
113 Garrett Wolfe 2.50 6.00
114 Greg Olsen 4.00 10.00
115 JaMarcus Russell 2.50 6.00
116 Jason Hill 2.50 6.00
117 Joe Thomas 4.00 10.00
118 John Beck 2.50 6.00
119 Johnnie Lee Higgins 2.50 6.00
120 Kenny Irons 2.50 6.00
121 Kevin Kolb 3.00 8.00
122 Lorenzo Booker 3.00 8.00
123 Marshawn Lynch 5.00 12.00
124 Michael Bush 3.00 8.00
125 Patrick Willis 4.00 10.00
126 Paul Williams 2.50 6.00
127 Robert Meachem 3.00 8.00
128 Sidney Rice 3.00 8.00
129 Steve Smith USC 2.50 6.00
130 Ted Ginn Jr. 3.00 8.00
131 Tony Hunt 2.50 6.00
132 Trent Edwards 2.50 6.00
133 Troy Smith 2.50 6.00
134 Yamon Figurs 2.50 6.00

2007 Playoff National Treasures Rookie Signature Combo Material Silver

*SILV.COMBO/25: .3X TO .8X BASE JSY AU/99
SILVER COMBO PRINT RUN 25
UNPRICED GOLD PRINT RUN 10
UNPRICED PLATINUM PRINT RUN 1
101 Adrian Peterson 200.00 400.00
107 Calvin Johnson 125.00 250.00

2007 Playoff National Treasures Rookie Signature Jumbo Material Gold

GOLD JUMBO PRINT RUN 25
*GOLD JUMBO/25: .4X TO 1X BASE JSY AU/99
UNPRICED PLATINUM PRINT RUN 5
UNPRICED BLACK PRINT RUN 1
101 Adrian Peterson 250.00 500.00
107 Calvin Johnson 125.00 250.00

2007 Playoff National Treasures Rookie Signature Material Gold

*GOLD: .3X TO .8X BASE JSY AU/99
GOLD PRINT RUN 25 SER.#'d SETS
101 Adrian Peterson 200.00 400.00
107 Calvin Johnson 125.00 250.00

2007 Playoff National Treasures Rookie Signature Material Silver

*SILVER/49: .25X TO .6X BASE JSY AU/99
SILVER PRINT RUN 49 SER.#'d SETS
UNPRICED PLATINUM PRINT RUN 1
101 Adrian Peterson 150.00 300.00
107 Calvin Johnson 50.00 100.00

2007 Playoff National Treasures Signature Combos

STATED PRINT RUN 20 SER.#'d SETS
UNPRICED SIG TRIOS PRINT RUN 15
1 L.Tomlinson/M.Turner 40.00 80.00
2 R.Craig/F.Gore 15.00 40.00
3 J.Kelly/T.Thomas 40.00 80.00
4 P.Simms/E.Manning 75.00 125.00
5 F.Taylor/M.Jones-Drew 20.00 50.00
6 J.Namath/D.Maynard 60.00 120.00
7 W.Moon/E.Campbell 50.00 100.00
8 D.Driver/G.Jennings 25.00 50.00
9 S.Smith/D.Williams 15.00 40.00
10 M.Allen/T.Brown 50.00 100.00
11 E.Dickerson/S.Jackson 50.00 100.00
12 S.McNair/W.McGahee 25.00 60.00
13 J.Stallworth/H.Ward 60.00 120.00
14 F.Tarkenton/P.Krause 40.00 100.00
15 C.Harris/B.Bates 25.00 50.00

2007 Playoff National Treasures Signature Gold

GOLD PRINT RUN 4-49
SER.#'d UNDER 25 NOT PRICED
5 Eli Manning 50.00 100.00
10 Drew Brees 50.00 100.00
13 Brian Westbrook 20.00 50.00
16 Ronnie Brown 12.00 30.00
17 Willis McGahee 12.00 30.00
18 Steven Jackson 12.00 30.00
19 Larry Johnson 12.00 30.00
20 Laurence Maroney 15.00 40.00
23 Maurice Jones-Drew 15.00 40.00
24 Frank Gore 15.00 40.00
25 Cadillac Williams 15.00 40.00
27 Brandon Jacobs 12.00 30.00
28 Marion Barber 20.00 50.00
29 Cedric Benson 12.00 30.00
34 Larry Fitzgerald 25.00 60.00
37 T.J. Houshmandzadeh 12.00 30.00
38 Steve Smith 15.00 40.00
41 Roy Williams WR 12.00 30.00
43 Torry Holt 15.00 40.00
58 Johnny Morris 12.00 30.00
61 Lawrence Taylor 25.00 60.00
63 Michael Irvin 30.00 60.00
64 Paul Krause 15.00 40.00
65 Randall Cunningham 20.00 50.00
66 Rick Casares 20.00 50.00
68 Lydell Mitchell 12.00 30.00
69 Roger Craig 15.00 40.00
70 Sam Huff 15.00 40.00
73 Sonny Jurgensen 30.00 80.00
75 Steve Largent 20.00 50.00
77 Tommy McDonald 12.00 30.00
86 Bo Jackson 40.00 80.00
89 Yale Lary 12.00 30.00
90 Cris Collinsworth 15.00 40.00
91 Daryle Lamonica 20.00 50.00
94 George Blanda 20.00 50.00
95 Harlon Hill 12.00 30.00
97 Jimmy Orr 12.00 30.00
101 Adrian Peterson 125.00 250.00
102 Anthony Gonzalez 20.00 50.00
103 Antonio Pittman 6.00 15.00
104 Brady Quinn 6.00 15.00

105 Brandon Jackson 6.00 15.00
106 Brian Leonard 6.00 15.00
107 Calvin Johnson 75.00 150.00
108 Chris Henry RB 6.00 15.00
109 Drew Stanton 6.00 15.00
110 Dwayne Jarrett 8.00 20.00
111 Dwayne Bowe 6.00 15.00
112 Gaines Adams 8.00 20.00
113 Garrett Wolfe 6.00 15.00
114 Greg Olsen 10.00 25.00
115 JaMarcus Russell 6.00 15.00
116 Jason Hill 6.00 15.00
117 Joe Thomas 12.00 30.00
118 John Beck 6.00 15.00
119 Johnnie Lee Higgins 6.00 15.00
121 Kevin Kolb 8.00 20.00
122 Lorenzo Booker 8.00 20.00
123 Marshawn Lynch 30.00 60.00
124 Michael Bush 6.00 15.00
125 Patrick Willis 25.00 60.00
126 Paul Williams 6.00 15.00
127 Robert Meachem 15.00 40.00
128 Sidney Rice 8.00 20.00
129 Steve Smith USC 6.00 15.00
130 Ted Ginn Jr. 20.00 50.00
131 Tony Hunt 6.00 15.00
132 Trent Edwards 6.00 15.00
133 Troy Smith 6.00 15.00
134 Yamon Figurs 6.00 15.00
135 Darrelle Revis 25.00 50.00
136 Aaron Ross No AU 6.00 15.00
137 LaRon Landry 8.00 20.00
138 James Jones 5.00 12.00
139 Michael Griffin 5.00 12.00
140 Aundrae Allison 5.00 12.00
143 DeShawn Wynn 5.00 12.00
144 Dwayne Wright 5.00 12.00
145 Jacoby Jones 12.00 30.00
146 John Broussard 6.00 15.00
147 Jon Beason 5.00 12.00
148 Kenton Keith 6.00 15.00
149 Kolby Smith 5.00 12.00
150 Leon Hall 5.00 12.00
151 Reggie Nelson 5.00 12.00
152 Roy Hall 8.00 20.00
153 Ryne Robinson 6.00 15.00
154 Selvin Young 5.00 12.00
155 Steve Breaston 5.00 12.00
156 Chris Davis 5.00 12.00
157 Glenn Holt 6.00 15.00
158 Kenneth Darby 5.00 12.00
159 Mike Walker 8.00 20.00
160 Chris Houston 5.00 12.00
161 David Clowney 5.00 12.00
162 Mason Crosby 12.00 30.00
163 Bobby Sippio 6.00 15.00
164 Biren Ealy 6.00 15.00
166 Laurent Robinson 10.00 25.00
167 Lawrence Timmons 8.00 20.00
168 Legedu Naanee 6.00 15.00
169 Brandon Meriweather 6.00 15.00
170 Brian Robison 8.00 20.00
171 Greg Peterson 6.00 15.00
172 Ikaika Alama-Francis 8.00 20.00
173 Isaiah Stanback 5.00 12.00
174 Ed Johnson 6.00 15.00
175 Eric Frampton 6.00 15.00
176 Eric Weddle 6.00 15.00
177 Fred Bennett 5.00 12.00
178 Dante Rosario 8.00 20.00
179 Clifton Dawson 8.00 20.00
180 Jeff Rowe 5.00 12.00
181 Justin Durant 8.00 20.00
183 Paul Posluszny 5.00 12.00
184 Pierre Thomas 8.00 20.00
185 Quentin Moses 5.00 12.00
186 Ray McDonald 6.00 15.00
187 Sabby Piscitelli 5.00 12.00
188 Scott Chandler 8.00 20.00
189 Matt Gutierrez 8.00 20.00
190 Matt Moore 8.00 20.00
191 Martrez Milner 5.00 12.00
192 Amobi Okoye 6.00 15.00
193 Adam Carriker 5.00 12.00
195 Anthony Spencer 6.00 15.00
196 Tyler Thigpen 8.00 20.00
197 Victor Abiamiri 5.00 12.00
198 Zach Miller 5.00 12.00
199 Jarvis Moss 5.00 12.00
200 LaMarr Woodley 12.00 30.00

2007 Playoff National Treasures Signature Silver

SILVER PRINT RUN 12-50
UNPRICED PLATINUM PRINT RUN 1
SER.#'d UNDER 20 NOT PRICED
5 Eli Manning 40.00 80.00
6 Peyton Manning/25 60.00 120.00
10 Drew Brees 40.00 80.00
12 Jay Cutler/20 25.00 60.00
13 Brian Westbrook 15.00 40.00
16 Ronnie Brown 10.00 25.00
17 Willis McGahee 10.00 25.00
18 Steven Jackson 10.00 25.00
19 Larry Johnson 10.00 25.00
20 Laurence Maroney 12.00 30.00
23 Maurice Jones-Drew 12.00 30.00
24 Frank Gore 12.00 30.00
25 Cadillac Williams 12.00 30.00
27 Brandon Jacobs 10.00 25.00
28 Marion Barber 15.00 40.00
29 Cedric Benson 10.00 25.00
30 Fred Taylor/31 10.00 25.00
34 Larry Fitzgerald/49 20.00 50.00
37 T.J. Houshmandzadeh 10.00 25.00
41 Roy Williams WR 10.00 25.00
42 Donald Driver/35 25.00 50.00
55 Joe Montana/20 75.00 150.00
56 Joe Namath/25 60.00 120.00
58 Johnny Morris 10.00 25.00
61 Lawrence Taylor 20.00 50.00
63 Michael Irvin 20.00 50.00
64 Paul Krause 12.00 30.00
65 Randall Cunningham 15.00 40.00
66 Rick Casares 15.00 40.00
68 Lydell Mitchell 10.00 25.00
69 Roger Craig 12.00 30.00
70 Sam Huff 12.00 30.00
73 Sonny Jurgensen 25.00 60.00
75 Steve Largent 15.00 40.00
77 Tommy McDonald 10.00 25.00
86 Bo Jackson 30.00 60.00
87 Bob Griese/38 15.00 30.00
89 Yale Lary 10.00 25.00
90 Cris Collinsworth 12.00 30.00
91 Daryle Lamonica 15.00 40.00
94 George Blanda 15.00 40.00
95 Harlon Hill 10.00 25.00
97 Jimmy Orr 10.00 25.00
101 Adrian Peterson 100.00 200.00
102 Anthony Gonzalez 5.00 12.00
103 Antonio Pittman 5.00 12.00
104 Brady Quinn 10.00 25.00
105 Brandon Jackson 5.00 12.00
106 Brian Leonard 5.00 12.00
107 Calvin Johnson 100.00 200.00
108 Chris Henry RB 5.00 12.00
109 Drew Stanton 5.00 12.00
110 Dwayne Jarrett 6.00 15.00
111 Dwayne Bowe 5.00 12.00
112 Gaines Adams 6.00 15.00
113 Garrett Wolfe 5.00 12.00
114 Greg Olsen 8.00 20.00
115 JaMarcus Russell 5.00 12.00
116 Jason Hill 5.00 12.00
117 Joe Thomas 8.00 20.00
118 John Beck 5.00 12.00
119 Johnnie Lee Higgins 5.00 12.00
121 Kevin Kolb 6.00 15.00
122 Lorenzo Booker 6.00 15.00
123 Marshawn Lynch 25.00 50.00
124 Michael Bush 6.00 15.00
125 Patrick Willis 15.00 40.00
126 Paul Williams 5.00 12.00
127 Robert Meachem 10.00 25.00
128 Sidney Rice 20.00 40.00
129 Steve Smith USC 5.00 12.00
130 Ted Ginn Jr. 6.00 15.00
131 Tony Hunt 5.00 12.00
132 Trent Edwards/34 5.00 12.00
133 Troy Smith 5.00 12.00
134 Yamon Figurs 5.00 12.00

2007 Playoff National Treasures Signature Trios

SIGNATURE TRIOS PRINT RUN 15
2 Tomlinson/Turner/Merriman 50.00 100.00
3 Berrian/Benson/Hester 25.00 50.00
5 Dawson/Lanier/Stenerud 30.00 60.00
6 Manning/Harrison/Addai 75.00 150.00
7 Griese/Csonka/Warfield 75.00 150.00
8 Favre/Jennings/Hawk 100.00 200.00
10 Bush/McAllister/Colston 40.00 80.00
11 Tarkenton/Krause/Page 75.00 150.00
14 Smith/Sanders/Brown 250.00 400.00

2007 Playoff National Treasures Super Bowl Signatures Cuts

STATED PRINT RUN 1-50
DM Dan Marino/25 125.00 200.00
FT Fran Tarkenton/25 40.00 80.00
JE John Elway/15 75.00 200.00
JE John Elway/15 75.00 200.00
JK Jim Kelly/25 50.00 100.00
JL Jack Lambert/25 90.00 150.00
JN Joe Namath/25 60.00 120.00
JR John Riggins/25 30.00 80.00
LD Len Dawson/50 30.00 60.00
MA Marcus Allen/25 20.00 50.00
MI Michael Irvin/34 40.00 80.00
RS Roger Staubach/29 50.00 100.00
SY Steve Young/50 50.00 100.00
TD Tony Dorsett/50 40.00 80.00
WP Walter Payton/34 200.00 400.00

2007 Playoff National Treasures Super Bowl Material

STATED PRINT RUN 10-49
*PRIME/25: .5X TO 1.2X BASE JSY/40-49
*PRIME/25: .4X TO 1X BASE JSY/20-30
PRIME PRINT RUN 1-25
SERIAL #'d UNDER 19 NOT PRICED
BF Brett Favre 40.00 100.00
BG Bob Griese 20.00 50.00
BS Bart Starr 30.00 80.00
CT Charley Taylor 12.00 30.00
DB Deion Branch 12.00 30.00
DG Darrell Green 20.00 50.00
DH Devin Hester 15.00 40.00
DL Daryle Lamonica 15.00 40.00
DM Dan Marino 40.00 100.00
ES1 Emmitt Smith 30.00 80.00
ES2 Emmitt Smith 30.00 80.00
FB Fred Biletnikoff 20.00 50.00
FT Fran Tarkenton 20.00 50.00
HW Hines Ward 15.00 40.00
JE1 John Elway/25 40.00 100.00
JE2 John Elway/25 40.00 100.00
JK Jim Kelly/25 25.00 60.00
JL Jack Lambert 20.00 50.00
JM2 Joe Montana/19 80.00 200.00
JM3 Joe Montana/24 80.00 200.00
JMA John Mackey 15.00 40.00
JMC Jim McMahon/25 30.00 80.00
JN Joe Namath/25 30.00 80.00
JP Jim Plunkett 15.00 40.00
JR1 Jerry Rice/30 50.00 125.00
JR2 Jerry Rice/30 50.00 125.00
JRI John Riggins/44 15.00 40.00
KW Kurt Warner 15.00 40.00
LC Larry Csonka/25 25.00 60.00
LD Len Dawson 20.00 50.00
MA Mike Alstott/48 12.00 30.00
MI Michael Irvin 20.00 50.00
PM Peyton Manning 50.00 125.00
PS Phil Simms 12.00 30.00
RL Ray Lewis 20.00 50.00
RS Roger Staubach/25 30.00 80.00
SS Steve Smith 15.00 40.00
SY Steve Young 25.00 60.00
TA Troy Aikman 25.00 60.00
TD Tony Dorsett 20.00 50.00
TO Terrell Owens 15.00 40.00
TT Thurman Thomas 15.00 40.00
WP Walter Payton/40 40.00 100.00
MAL Marcus Allen 20.00 50.00
TB1 Tom Brady/20 80.00 200.00
TB2 Tom Brady/20 80.00 200.00
WPA Willie Parker 15.00 40.00

2007 Playoff National Treasures Super Bowl Material Signatures

STATED PRINT RUN 1-25
SER.#'d UNDER 20 NOT PRICED
DM Dan Marino/25 125.00 250.00
FB Fred Biletnikoff/20 40.00 80.00
FT Fran Tarkenton/25 40.00 80.00
JM Joe Montana/24 125.00 200.00
MI Michael Irvin/25 40.00 100.00
PM Peyton Manning/25 125.00 200.00
PS Phil Simms/25 40.00 80.00
RS Roger Staubach/25 60.00 120.00
SS Steve Smith/25 25.00 60.00
SY Steve Young/25 50.00 100.00
TD Tony Dorsett/25 50.00 100.00

2007 Playoff National Treasures Super Bowl Signatures

STATED PRINT RUN 5-33
BS Bart Starr/15 100.00 175.00
CT Charley Taylor/25 15.00 40.00
DL Daryle Lamonica/25 20.00 50.00
DM Dan Marino/25 100.00 200.00
FT Fran Tarkenton/25 25.00 60.00
JM Joe Montana/16 100.00 175.00
JM Joe Montana/24 75.00 150.00
JM Joe Montana/19 100.00 200.00
JM John Mackey/25 20.00 50.00
JN Joe Namath/25 60.00 120.00
JR John Riggins/25 25.00 60.00
LD Len Dawson/25 20.00 50.00
PM Peyton Manning/18 60.00 120.00
SS Steve Smith/15 20.00 50.00
SY Steve Young/29 30.00 80.00
TD Tony Dorsett/33 25.00 60.00

2007 Playoff National Treasures Timeline Material NFL

*AFC/NFC/25: .6X TO 1.5X NFL JSY/50-99
*AFC/NFC/25: .4X TO 1X BASE NFL JSY/15-25
*AFC/NFC PRM/25: .8X TO 2X NFL JSY/50-99
*HOF/25: .6X TO 1.5X NFL JSY/50-99
*HOF/25: .5X TO 1X NFL JSY/15-25
*HOF PRIME/25: .8X TO 2X NFL JSY/50-99
*JUMBO/21-25: .6X TO 1.5X NFL JSY/50-99
*JUMBO/21-25: .4X TO 1X NFL JSY/15-25
*JUMBO PRIME/25: 1X TO 2.5X NFL JSY/50-99
*JUMBO PRIME/25: .6X TO 1.5X NFL JSY/15-25
*NFL PRIME/25: .8X TO 2X NFL JSY/50-99
*MVP/25: .6X TO 1.5X NFL JSY/50-99
*MVP/25: .4X TO 1X BASE NFL JSY/25
*MVP PRIME/20-25: .8X TO 2X NFL JSY/50-99
*MVP PRIME/25: .5X TO 1.2X NFL JSY/25
MVP PRIME PRINT RUN 3-25
AM Archie Manning 8.00 20.00
AP Alan Page 10.00 25.00
BB Bill Bates 6.00 15.00
BF Brett Favre 20.00 50.00
BL Bob Lilly/15 12.00 30.00
BR Ben Roethlisberger 10.00 25.00
BS Barry Sanders 15.00 40.00
BW Bob Waterfield/25 12.00 30.00
CB Chuck Bednarik 8.00 20.00
CH Cliff Harris 8.00 20.00
CJ Chad Johnson/20 10.00 25.00
DF Dan Fouts/25 12.00 30.00
DG Darrell Green 10.00 25.00
DL Dick Lane/25 10.00 25.00
DM Don Maynard/25 12.00 30.00
EH Elroy Hirsch/25 12.00 30.00
ES Emmitt Smith 15.00 40.00
GU Gene Upshaw 6.00 15.00
HS Hank Stram 15.00 30.00
JB Jim Brown/25 20.00 50.00
JG Joe Greene/50 10.00 25.00
JH John Hannah 6.00 15.00
JK Jim Kelly/25 15.00 40.00
JL James Lofton 6.00 15.00
JM Jim McMahon/50 12.00 30.00
JN Joe Namath/25 20.00 50.00
JO Jim Otto/50 6.00 15.00
JP Jim Parker/50 6.00 15.00
JR Jerry Rice/25 30.00 80.00
JS Jan Stenerud/20 10.00 25.00
JT Jim Thorpe/25 125.00 200.00
JY Jack Youngblood 8.00 20.00
KS Ken Stabler 12.00 30.00
LA Lance Alworth/25 12.00 30.00
LC Larry Csonka/25 15.00 40.00
LG Lou Groza 8.00 20.00
LL Larry Little/10 8.00 20.00
LT LaDainian Tomlinson/50 10.00 25.00
MD Mark Duper/50 6.00 15.00
MI Michael Irvin 10.00 25.00
MO Merlin Olsen/50 6.00 15.00
NV Norm Van Brocklin 15.00 40.00
OM Ollie Matson 8.00 20.00
PM Peyton Manning 25.00 60.00
PS Phil Simms 8.00 20.00
RB Reggie Bush 6.00 15.00
RC Randall Cunningham 8.00 20.00
RG Rosey Grier 6.00 15.00
RM Randy Moss 8.00 20.00
RS Roger Staubach 12.00 30.00
SA Shaun Alexander 6.00 15.00
SB Sammy Baugh 12.00 30.00
SJ Sonny Jurgensen 8.00 20.00
SL Sid Luckman 12.00 30.00
TB Tom Brady/50 30.00 80.00
TF Tom Fears 8.00 20.00
TL Tom Landry 25.00 50.00
TM Tommy McDonald 10.00 25.00
TR Tony Romo 12.00 30.00
TT Thurman Thomas 8.00 20.00
VY Vince Young 10.00 25.00
WL Willie Lanier 8.00 20.00
WP Walter Payton/50 20.00 50.00
BLA Bobby Layne/25 12.00 30.00
JTH Joe Theismann 10.00 25.00
KST Ken Strong 10.00 25.00
RMI Ron Mix/50 6.00 15.00
TBA Tiki Barber 8.00 20.00
TBR Tim Brown 10.00 25.00

2007 Playoff National Treasures Timeline Material Signature AFC/NFC Prime

AFC/NFC PRIME PRINT RUN 1-25
*NFL PRM/15-25: .4X TO 1X AFC/NFC PRM/15-25
NFL PRIME PRINT RUN 1-25
JT Joe Theismann/25 50.00 100.00
AM Archie Manning/25 30.00 80.00
BB Bill Bates/25 30.00 80.00
CH Cliff Harris/15 20.00 50.00
JO Jim Otto/25 25.00 60.00
MD Mark Duper/25 20.00 50.00
MI Michael Irvin/25 50.00 100.00
PM Peyton Manning/25 125.00 250.00
PS Phil Simms/15 25.00 60.00
RB Reggie Bush/15 30.00 80.00
RS Roger Staubach/25 60.00 120.00
SS Sterling Sharpe/25 25.00 60.00
TB Tim Brown/25 30.00 80.00
TB Tiki Barber/25 25.00 60.00

2007 Playoff National Treasures Timeline Material Signature HOF

STATED PRINT RUN 1-25
*PRIME/25: .5X TO 1.2X BASE HOF SIG
PRIME PRINT RUN 1-25
AP Alan Page 25.00 60.00
BL Bob Lilly 25.00 60.00
CB Chuck Bednarik 40.00 80.00
DF Dan Fouts 25.00 60.00
DM Don Maynard 20.00 50.00
GU Gene Upshaw 15.00 40.00
JL James Lofton 20.00 50.00
JN Joe Namath 75.00 150.00
JO Jim Otto 25.00 60.00
JS Jan Stenerud/20 15.00 40.00
JY Jack Youngblood 25.00 50.00
LA Lance Alworth 40.00 80.00
LL Larry Little 15.00 40.00
MI Michael Irvin 30.00 80.00
RM Ron Mix 15.00 40.00
RS Roger Staubach 50.00 100.00
SJ Sonny Jurgensen 25.00 60.00
TM Tommy McDonald 15.00 40.00
WL Willie Lanier 20.00 50.00

2007 Playoff National Treasures Timeline Material Signature MVP

MVP PRINT RUN 3-25
*PRIME/15-25: .5X TO 1.2X BASE MVP SIG
MVP PRIME PRINT RUN 1-25
AP Alan Page/25 25.00 60.00
DF Dan Fouts/25 25.00 60.00
JB Jim Brown/25 60.00 120.00
JN Joe Namath/25 75.00 150.00
JR Jerry Rice/15 125.00 200.00
JT Joe Theismann/25 25.00 60.00
LT LaDainian Tomlinson/15 30.00 80.00
PM Peyton Manning/25 100.00 200.00
RC Randall Cunningham/25 30.00 60.00
RS Roger Staubach/25 50.00 100.00
TT Thurman Thomas/15 30.00 80.00

2007 Playoff National Treasures Timeline Signature

STATED PRINT RUN 1-99
SER.#'d UNDER 25 NOT PRICED
AM Archie Manning/99 20.00 50.00
AP Alan Page/85 15.00 40.00
BD Bill Dudley/99 20.00 50.00
BD Boyd Dowler/99 12.00 30.00
BH Billy Howton/99 12.00 30.00
CB Chuck Bednarik/75 15.00 40.00
DF Dan Fouts/50 15.00 40.00
DM Don Maynard/99 10.00 25.00
GU Gene Upshaw/99 10.00 25.00
JB Jim Brown/56 40.00 80.00
JN Joe Namath/25 60.00 120.00
JO Jim Otto/99 15.00 40.00
JS Jan Stenerud/99 10.00 25.00
KW Kellen Winslow Sr./58 12.00 30.00
LA Lance Alworth/30 20.00 50.00
LL Larry Little/47 12.00 30.00
MD Mark Duper/99 10.00 25.00
MO Merlin Olsen/30 15.00 40.00
RC Randall Cunningham/99 15.00 40.00
RG Rosey Grier/92 15.00 40.00
RM Ron Mix/99 10.00 25.00
SJ Sonny Jurgensen/75 15.00 40.00
SS Sterling Sharpe/99 12.00 30.00
TB Tim Brown/33 20.00 50.00
TB Tiki Barber/32 12.00 30.00
WL Willie Lanier/45 12.00 30.00
YL Yale Lary/99 10.00 25.00

2007 Playoff National Treasures Timeline Signature Cuts

STATED PRINT RUN 1-100
AP Alan Page/25 20.00 50.00
BF Brett Favre/25 150.00 250.00
BH Billy Howton/50 15.00 40.00
BS Barry Sanders/34 100.00 175.00
BW Bob Waterfield/100 60.00 120.00
CB Chuck Bednarik/25 25.00 60.00
DF Dan Fouts/25 25.00 60.00
DL Dick Lane/40 100.00 200.00
DM Don Maynard/50 15.00 40.00
JB Jim Brown/25 60.00 120.00
JK Jim Kelly/25 50.00 100.00
JL James Lofton/30 15.00 40.00
JN Joe Namath/25 60.00 120.00
JO Jim Otto/50 20.00 50.00
LA Lance Alworth/25 30.00 60.00
OM Ollie Matson/20 25.00 50.00
RB Reggie Bush/50 20.00 50.00
RS Roger Staubach/15 50.00 100.00
SB Sammy Baugh/50 50.00 120.00
SJ Sonny Jurgensen/25 40.00 80.00
SL Sid Luckman/35 125.00 250.00
TT Thurman Thomas/20 25.00 50.00
WP Walter Payton/34 175.00 350.00

2008 Playoff National Treasures

This set was released on January 28, 2009. The base set consists of 200 cards. Cards 1-100 feature veterans serial numbered of 99, and cards 101-200 are autographed rookies serial numbered of 99. This product was released with 7 cards per pack and 1 pack per hobby box.
1-100 STATED PRINT RUN 99
101-134 JSY AU RC PRINT RUN 99
135-200 AU RC PRINT RUN 49-99
UNPRICED GOLD 1-100 PRINT RUN 5
UNPRICED PLATINUM 1-100 PRINT RUN 1
UNPRICED ROOKIE SIG PLAT.PRINT RUN 1
UNPRICED SIG.PLATINUM PRINT RUN 1
1 LaDainian Tomlinson 3.00 8.00
2 Adrian Peterson 3.00 8.00
3 Brian Westbrook 2.00 5.00
4 Willie Parker 2.50 6.00
5 Clinton Portis 2.00 5.00
6 Fred Taylor 2.00 5.00
7 Marshawn Lynch 2.50 6.00
8 Frank Gore 2.50 6.00
9 Joseph Addai 2.00 5.00
10 Steven Jackson 2.00 5.00
11 Brandon Jacobs 2.00 5.00
12 Marion Barber 2.00 5.00
13 Ryan Grant 2.50 6.00
14 Selvin Young 2.00 5.00
15 Larry Johnson 2.00 5.00
16 Tom Brady 10.00 25.00
17 Drew Brees 3.00 8.00
18 Tony Romo 2.50 6.00
19 Brett Favre 6.00 15.00
20 Peyton Manning 8.00 20.00
21 Jay Cutler 2.00 5.00
22 Eli Manning 2.50 6.00
23 Donovan McNabb 2.50 6.00
24 Ben Roethlisberger 3.00 8.00
25 Philip Rivers 3.00 8.00
26 Trent Edwards 2.00 5.00
27 Carson Palmer 2.50 6.00
28 Reggie Wayne 2.50 6.00
29 Randy Moss 2.50 6.00
30 Chad Johnson 2.00 5.00
31 Larry Fitzgerald 2.50 6.00
32 Terrell Owens 2.50 6.00
33 Brandon Marshall 2.50 6.00
34 Braylon Edwards 2.00 5.00
35 Marques Colston 2.00 5.00
36 Roddy White 2.00 5.00
37 Torry Holt 2.50 6.00
38 Wes Welker 2.50 6.00
39 Tony Gonzalez 2.50 6.00
40 T.J. Houshmandzadeh 2.00 5.00
41 Jerricho Cotchery 2.00 5.00
42 Laveranues Coles 2.00 5.00
43 Kellen Winslow 2.00 5.00
44 Jason Witten 2.50 6.00
45 Donald Driver 2.50 6.00
46 Greg Jennings 2.00 5.00
47 Plaxico Burress 2.00 5.00
48 Steve Smith 2.50 6.00
49 Jake Delhomme 2.00 5.00
50 Hines Ward 2.50 6.00
51 Anquan Boldin 2.00 5.00
52 Dwayne Bowe 2.50 6.00
53 Antonio Gates 2.50 6.00
54 Lee Evans 2.50 6.00
55 Santana Moss 2.00 5.00
56 Chris Cooley 2.00 5.00
57 Calvin Johnson 3.00 8.00
58 Reggie Bush 2.00 5.00
59 Anthony Gonzalez 2.00 5.00
60 Michael Turner 2.00 5.00
61 Earnest Graham 2.00 5.00
62 Kevin Curtis 2.00 5.00
63 Dallas Clark 2.00 5.00
64 Laurence Maroney 2.50 6.00
65 Santonio Holmes 2.00 5.00
66 Sidney Rice 2.00 5.00
67 Vincent Jackson 2.00 5.00
68 Barry Sanders 5.00 12.00
69 Bert Jones 2.00 5.00
70 Bill Dudley 2.00 5.00
71 Billy Howton 2.00 5.00
72 Dan Marino 6.00 15.00
73 Dave Casper 2.00 5.00
74 Earl Campbell 3.00 8.00
75 Franco Harris 3.00 8.00
76 Gale Sayers 3.00 8.00
77 Jack Lambert 3.00 8.00
78 James Lofton 2.00 5.00
79 Jim Brown 4.00 10.00
80 Joe Montana 10.00 25.00
81 John Elway 5.00 12.00
82 Bobby Bell 2.00 5.00
83 Charley Trippi 2.00 5.00
84 Ace Clarence Parker 2.00 5.00
85 Dante Lavelli 2.00 5.00
86 Del Shofner 2.00 5.00
87 Dub Jones 2.00 5.00
88 Fred Williamson 2.00 5.00
89 Gary Collins 2.00 5.00
90 Hugh McElhenny 2.00 5.00
91 Jim Taylor 3.00 8.00
92 Lydell Mitchell 2.00 5.00
93 Mike Curtis 2.00 5.00
94 Paul Krause 2.00 5.00
95 Pete Retzlaff 2.00 5.00
96 William Perry 2.00 5.00
97 Willie Davis 2.00 5.00
98 Don Perkins 2.00 5.00
99 Willie Wood 2.00 5.00
100 Yale Lary 2.00 5.00
101 D.McFadden JSY AU RC 10.00 25.00
102 J.Stewart JSY AU RC 25.00 60.00
103 Felix Jones JSY AU RC 10.00 25.00
104 R.Mendenhall JSY AU RC 10.00 25.00
105 C.Johnson JSY AU RC EXCH 40.00 80.00
106 Matt Forte JSY AU RC 40.00 100.00
107 Ray Rice JSY AU RC 25.00 60.00
108 Kevin Smith JSY AU RC 10.00 25.00
109 Jamaal Charles JSY AU RC 25.00 50.00
110 Steve Slaton JSY AU RC 10.00 25.00
111 Matt Ryan JSY AU RC 200.00 300.00
112 Joe Flacco JSY AU RC 75.00 150.00
113 Brian Brohm JSY AU RC 10.00 25.00
114 Chad Henne JSY AU RC 12.00 30.00
115 Kevin O'Connell JSY AU RC 10.00 25.00
116 J.Booty JSY AU RC 10.00 25.00
117 Andre Caldwell JSY AU RC 10.00 25.00
118 Donnie Avery JSY AU RC 12.00 30.00
119 Devin Thomas JSY AU RC 10.00 25.00
120 Jordy Nelson JSY AU RC 75.00 125.00
121 James Hardy JSY AU RC 10.00 25.00
122 Eddie Royal JSY AU RC 10.00 25.00
123 Jerome Simpson JSY AU RC 12.00 30.00
124 DeSean Jackson JSY AU RC 30.00 80.00
125 Malcolm Kelly JSY AU RC 10.00 25.00
127 Dexter Jackson JSY AU RC 15.00 40.00
128 Earl Bennett JSY AU RC 15.00 40.00
129 Early Doucet JSY AU RC 10.00 25.00
130 Harry Douglas JSY AU RC 12.00 30.00
131 M.Manningham JSY AU RC 20.00 50.00
132 Dustin Keller JSY AU RC 12.00 30.00
133 Glenn Dorsey JSY AU RC 10.00 25.00
134 Jake Long JSY AU RC 15.00 40.00
135 Adrian Arrington AU RC 5.00 12.00
136 Ali Highsmith AU RC 5.00 12.00
137 Antoine Cason AU RC 6.00 15.00
138 Aqib Talib AU RC 8.00 20.00
139 Brad Cottam AU RC 5.00 12.00
140 Brandon Flowers AU RC 6.00 15.00
141 B.Witherspoon AU/49 RC 6.00 15.00
142 Calais Campbell AU RC 6.00 15.00
143 C.Washington AU/49 RC 6.00 15.00
144 Chaz Schilens AU RC 6.00 15.00
145 Chevis Jackson AU RC 5.00 12.00
146 Chris Long AU RC 6.00 15.00
147 Colt Brennan AU RC 6.00 15.00
148 Curtis Lofton AU RC 6.00 15.00
149 Dan Connor AU RC 5.00 12.00
150 Dantrell Savage AU/49 RC 6.00 15.00
151 Davone Bess AU RC 6.00 15.00
152 Dennis Dixon AU RC 20.00 50.00
153 Derrick Harvey AU RC 5.00 12.00
154 D.Rodgers-Cromartie AU RC 10.00 25.00
155 Erik Ainge AU RC 5.00 12.00
156 Erin Henderson AU RC 6.00 15.00
157 Fred Davis AU RC 5.00 12.00
158 Jacob Hester AU RC 5.00 12.00
159 Jacob Tamme AU RC 10.00 25.00
160 Jermichael Finley AU RC 5.00 12.00
161 Jerod Mayo AU RC 12.00 30.00
162 John Carlson AU RC 5.00 12.00
163 Jordon Dizon AU RC 5.00 12.00
164 Josh Johnson AU RC 5.00 12.00
165 Josh Morgan AU RC 5.00 12.00
166 Justin Forsett AU RC 10.00 25.00
167 Keenan Burton AU RC 5.00 12.00
168 Keith Rivers AU RC 5.00 12.00
169 Kellen Davis AU RC 5.00 12.00
170 Kenny Phillips AU RC 5.00 12.00
171 Kentwan Balmer AU RC 5.00 12.00
172 Kregg Lumpkin AU RC 8.00 20.00
173 Lavelle Hawkins AU RC 6.00 15.00
174 Lawrence Jackson AU RC 5.00 12.00
175 Leodis McKelvin AU RC 6.00 15.00
176 Marcus Henry AU RC 5.00 12.00
177 Marcus Smith AU/49 RC 6.00 15.00
178 Marcus Thomas AU RC 6.00 15.00
179 Martellus Bennett AU RC 6.00 15.00
180 Martin Rucker AU RC 5.00 12.00
181 Matt Flynn AU RC 15.00 40.00
182 Matt Slater AU/49 RC 8.00 20.00
183 Mike Hart AU RC 5.00 12.00
184 Mike Jenkins AU RC 5.00 12.00
185 Owen Schmitt AU RC 10.00 25.00
186 Pat Sims AU RC 6.00 15.00
187 Phillip Merling AU RC 5.00 12.00
188 Pierre Garcon AU/49 RC 75.00 150.00
189 Quentin Groves AU RC 6.00 15.00
190 Reggie Smith AU RC 5.00 12.00
191 Ryan Torain AU/49 RC 25.00 60.00
192 Sedrick Ellis AU RC 5.00 12.00
193 Steve Johnson AU RC 20.00 50.00
194 Tashard Choice AU RC 5.00 12.00
195 Terrell Thomas AU RC 5.00 12.00
196 Tim Hightower AU RC 12.00 30.00
197 Vernon Gholston AU RC 5.00 12.00
198 Will Franklin AU RC 6.00 15.00
199 Xavier Adibi AU RC 5.00 12.00
200 Xavier Omon AU/49 RC 5.00 12.00

2008 Playoff National Treasures 50th Anniversary Material

STATED PRINT RUN 25 SER.#'d SETS
*PRIME/14-25: .6X TO 1.5X MATERIAL/25
PRIME PRINT RUN 3-25
UNPRICED SIGN PRINT RUN 10
1 Jim Brown 10.00 25.00
2 Gale Sayers 8.00 20.00
3 Hugh McElhenny 5.00 12.00
4 John Mackey 5.00 12.00
5 Chuck Bednarik 6.00 15.00
6 Ray Nitschke 8.00 20.00
7 Raymond Berry 6.00 15.00
8 Norm Van Brocklin 15.00 40.00
9 Mel Hein 10.00 25.00
10 Lenny Moore 5.00 12.00

2008 Playoff National Treasures 75th Anniversary Material

STATED PRINT RUN 4-25
UNPRICED SIG PRINT RUN 1-10
3 Joe Montana 25.00 60.00
5 Marion Motley 12.00 30.00
6 Walter Payton 25.00 60.00
7 Gale Sayers 15.00 40.00
8 Lance Alworth 20.00 50.00
9 Raymond Berry 10.00 25.00
10 Jerry Rice 15.00 40.00
11 Mike Ditka 20.00 50.00
14 Gene Upshaw 8.00 20.00
17 Reggie White 15.00 40.00
18 Joe Greene 15.00 40.00
19 Bob Lilly 10.00 25.00
20 Merlin Olsen 10.00 25.00
21 Dick Butkus/20 20.00 50.00
23 Jack Lambert/15 20.00 50.00
28 Ronnie Lott 15.00 40.00
29 Jan Stenerud 10.00 25.00

2008 Playoff National Treasures All Pros Material NFL

BASIC MATERIAL PRINT RUN 1-25
*JUMBO MAT/13-25: .4X TO 1X MATERIAL/25
JUMBO MATERIAL PRINT RUN 1-25
*HOF MAT/25: .4X TO 1X MATERIAL/25
HOF MATERIAL PRINT RUN 1-25
*MVP MAT/25: .4X TO 1X MATERIAL/25
MVP MATERIAL PRINT RUN 1-25
SERIAL #'d UNDER 13 NOT PRICED
3 Andre Reed/25 12.00 30.00
9 Carl Eller/25 10.00 25.00
11 Charlie Joiner/25 10.00 25.00
21 Jim Kelly/25 15.00 40.00
24 Joe Klecko/25 10.00 25.00
27 Emmitt Smith/25 25.00 60.00
33 Ollie Matson/22 12.00 30.00
36 Randall Cunningham/25 12.00 30.00
39 Sterling Sharpe/25 12.00 30.00
41 Tiki Barber/25 12.00 30.00

2008 Playoff National Treasures All Pros Material Quads

STATED PRINT RUN 25 SER.#'d SETS
*PRIME/15-25: .5X TO 1.2X BASIC QUAD/25
PRIME PRINT RUN 15-25
1 Sanders/Smith/Bruce/Rice 30.00 80.00
2 Elway/Young/Rice/Brown 50.00 100.00
4 Seau/Gnzalz/Moss/Owens 15.00 40.00
5 McAll/Shcky/Rice/Owens 15.00 40.00
6 P.Mann/Crmplr/Ward/Hrrisn 20.00 50.00
7 Tmlinsn/Gnzalz/Jhnsn/Owns 15.00 40.00
8 Brady/Alexndr/Cooley/Smith 20.00 50.00
9 Hester/Gates/Johnson/Holt 12.00 30.00
10 Wstbrk/F.Tylr/Tmlinsn/Prkr 15.00 40.00

2008 Playoff National Treasures All Pros Material Signature NFL

STATED PRINT RUN 1-25
*HOF/25: .4X TO 1X MATER.SIG/25
HOF MAT.SIG PRINT RUN 1-25
*MVP/25: .4X TO 1X MATER.SIG/25
MVP MAT.SIG PRINT RUN 1-25
SERIAL #'d UNDER 15 NOT PRICED
2 Alex Karras/25 50.00 100.00
3 Andre Reed/25 25.00 50.00
9 Carl Eller/25 30.00 60.00
11 Charlie Joiner/25 30.00 60.00
17 Fred Dryer/15 30.00 60.00
19 Howie Long/25 75.00 135.00
21 Jim Kelly/25 60.00 100.00
24 Joe Klecko/25 20.00 40.00
27 Emmitt Smith/22 125.00 200.00
32 Mark Gastineau/18 20.00 40.00
36 Randall Cunningham/25 25.00 60.00
39 Sterling Sharpe/25 25.00 50.00
41 Tiki Barber/25 25.00 50.00

2008 Playoff National Treasures All Pros Material Trios

STATED PRINT RUN 25 SER.#'d SETS
*PRIME/25: .5X TO 1.2X BASIC TRIO/25
PRIME PRINT RUN 25 SER.#'d SETS
*NFL/25: .4X TO 1X BASIC TRIO/25
NFL TRIO PRINT RUN 22-25
*NFL PRIME/25: .5X TO 1.2X BASIC TRIO/25
NFL PRIME PRINT RUN 25
1 Elway/Allen/Irvin 25.00 60.00
2 Marino/Smith/Rice 50.00 100.00
3 Marino/Aikman/Young 30.00 80.00
4 Sanders/Smith/Rice 30.00 80.00
5 Favre/Elway/Young 30.00 80.00
6 Sanders/Young/Moss 20.00 50.00
7 Bruce/Harrison/Seau 10.00 25.00
9 Warner/Green/Owens 12.00 30.00
10 Williams/Gonzalez/Moss 10.00 25.00
11 Favre/Westbrook/Holt 20.00 50.00
12 Manning/Ward/Witten 12.00 30.00
13 Hasselbeck/Johnson/Harrison 10.00 25.00
14 Manning/Tomlinson/Johnson 15.00 40.00
15 Brady/Peterson/Owens 20.00 50.00

2008 Playoff National Treasures All Pros Signature Cuts

STATED PRINT RUN 1-50
SERIAL #'d UNDER 15 NOT PRICED
6 Bob Waterfield/35 60.00 120.00
8 Bulldog Turner/58 30.00 80.00
15 Doak Walker/29 100.00 200.00
25 Johnny Unitas/25 200.00 350.00
31 Lou Groza/15 30.00 60.00
45 Y.A. Tittle/50 30.00 60.00

2008 Playoff National Treasures Champions Cuts

UNPRICED CUT AU PRINT RUN 1-22
6 Dan Marino/22

2008 Playoff National Treasures Champions Material Jumbo

MATERIAL JUMBO PRINT RUN 25
*JUM.PRIME/15-25: .5X TO 1.2X MAT.JUMB/25
JUMBO PRIME PRINT RUN 10-25
*MATER/14-25: .3X TO .8X MAT.JUMBO/25
BASIC MATERIAL PRINT RUN 1-25
1 Barry Sanders 20.00 50.00
2 Bo Jackson 20.00 50.00
3 Cliff Harris 10.00 25.00
4 Cris Collinsworth 10.00 25.00
5 Dan Fouts 15.00 40.00
6 Dan Marino 30.00 80.00
7 Danny White 15.00 40.00
11 Don Maynard 10.00 25.00
12 Earl Campbell 12.00 30.00
13 Eric Dickerson 12.00 30.00
15 Garo Yepremian 10.00 25.00
16 Jack Youngblood 10.00 25.00
17 Jay Novacek 12.00 30.00
18 John Matuszak 12.00 30.00
19 Knute Rockne Jkt 40.00 80.00
22 Paul Hornung 15.00 40.00
24 Tom Landry 20.00 50.00
25 Willie Brown 10.00 25.00

2008 Playoff National Treasures Champions Signature Material

STATED PRINT RUN 1-25
SERIAL #'d UNDER 23 NOT PRICED
1 Barry Sanders 75.00 150.00
2 Bo Jackson 60.00 120.00
3 Cliff Harris 20.00 50.00
4 Cris Collinsworth 15.00 40.00
5 Dan Fouts 40.00 80.00
6 Dan Marino 125.00 250.00
7 Danny White 25.00 60.00
12 Earl Campbell 40.00 80.00
13 Eric Dickerson 40.00 80.00
15 Garo Yepremian 15.00 40.00
17 Jay Novacek 30.00 60.00
21 Mark Duper 15.00 40.00
22 Paul Hornung/23 25.00 60.00
25 Willie Brown 15.00 40.00

2008 Playoff National Treasures Championships Material VS

MATERIAL VS PRINT RUN 10-50
UNPRICED MAT.VS PRIME PRINT RUN 2-10
UNPRICED MAT.SCORE PRINT RUN 1-5
UNPRICED MAT.YR PRINT RUN 1-10
1 B.Turner/M.Hein/50 15.00 40.00
2 S.Baugh/S.Luckman/50 20.00 50.00
3 L.Groza/B.Waterfield/50 10.00 25.00
4 O.Graham/T.Fears/50 10.00 25.00
5 B.Layne/O.Graham/50 10.00 25.00
6 D.Walker/O.Graham/50 15.00 40.00
7 N.Van Brocklin/O.Graham/50 10.00 25.00
8 B.Layne/J.Brown/50 15.00 40.00

2008 Playoff National Treasures College Material

STATED PRINT RUN 25-99
1 Lee Evans 8.00 20.00
2 Edgerrin James 8.00 20.00
3 Darren McFadden/99 4.00 10.00
4 Larry Fitzgerald 8.00 20.00
5 Dwayne Bowe 8.00 20.00
6 Brady Quinn 6.00 15.00
7 Jay Cutler 6.00 15.00
8 Felix Jones 5.00 12.00
9 Adrian Peterson/99 5.00 12.00
10 Braylon Edwards 12.00 30.00

2008 Playoff National Treasures College Material Signature

STATED PRINT RUN 2-25
SERIAL #'d UNDER 22 NOT PRICED
7 Jay Cutler/22 40.00 80.00
8 Felix Jones 10.00 25.00
9 Adrian Peterson 90.00 150.00
10 Braylon Edwards 25.00 50.00

2008 Playoff National Treasures Heisman Cuts

STATED PRINT RUN 1-63
2 Larry Kelley/26 50.00 120.00
6 Angelo Bertelli/47 40.00 100.00
8 Glenn Davis/51 40.00 100.00
10 Leon Hart/35 40.00 100.00
11 Vic Janowicz/63 60.00 125.00

2008 Playoff National Treasures Notable Nicknames Signature

STATED PRINT RUN 25-50
1 Lenny Moore/25 25.00 50.00
2 Dante Lavelli/25 20.00 40.00
3 Joe Montana/50 100.00 175.00
4 Chuck Bednarik/25 25.00 50.00
5 Del Shofner/27 30.00 60.00
6 Paul Hornung/25 50.00 100.00
7 Lance Alworth/25 60.00 120.00
8 Tommy McDonald/36 25.00 50.00
9 Randy White/50 20.00 50.00
10 Mike Singletary/50 30.00 60.00
11 Pete Retzlaff/26 20.00 40.00

2008 Playoff National Treasures Pen Pals

1 F.Jones/D.McFadden 20.00 50.00
2 J.Charles/L.Sweed 15.00 40.00
3 J.Simpson/A.Caldwell 12.00 30.00
4 H.Douglas/B.Brohm 15.00 40.00
5 M.Forte/E.Bennett 20.00 50.00
6 C.Henne/J.Long 25.00 50.00
7 J.Nelson/B.Brohm 25.00 50.00
8 J.Flacco/R.Rice 30.00 60.00
9 D.Thomas/M.Kelly 15.00 40.00
10 D.Avery/C.Long
11 R.Mendenhall/L.Sweed 20.00 50.00
12 Long/Dorsey/Long EXCH
13 Manningham/Henne/Long 20.00 50.00
14 Royl/Smpsn/De.Jcksn/Klly 25.00 60.00
15 Avery/D.Thms/Nlsn/Hrdy
16 McFad/Stwrt/F.Jns/Mendn 25.00 60.00
17 Ryan/Flacco/Brohm/Henne 100.00 200.00
18 Sweed/Dx.Jcksn/Bnntt/Dcet 20.00 50.00

2008 Playoff National Treasures Rookie Combo Material

STATED PRINT RUN 25 SER.#'d SETS
UNPRICED BRAND LOGO PRINT RUN 1-10
UNPRICED LAUNDRY TAG PRINT RUN 1-10
UNPRICED NFL SHIELDS PRINT RUN 1-9
1 H.Douglas/B.Brohm 4.00 10.00
2 R.Mendenhall/J.Stewart 6.00 15.00
3 G.Dorsey/E.Doucet 4.00 10.00
4 C.Henne/M.Manningham 5.00 12.00
5 M.Ryan/J.Flacco 12.00 30.00
6 J.Charles/L.Sweed 6.00 15.00
7 M.Ryan/D.McFadden 12.00 30.00
8 B.Brohm/C.Henne 5.00 12.00
9 D.McFadden/F.Jones 4.00 10.00
10 E.Royal/J.Hardy 4.00 10.00
11 J.Charles/S.Slaton 6.00 15.00
12 J.Stewart/F.Jones 6.00 15.00
13 J.Long/G.Dorsey 6.00 15.00
14 M.Forte/R.Rice 6.00 15.00
15 D.Avery/D.Thomas 5.00 12.00
16 R.Mendenhall/C.Johnson 5.00 12.00
17 D.Thomas/J.Nelson 12.00 30.00
18 D.Thomas/M.Manningham 4.00 10.00
19 D.Avery/K.Smith 5.00 12.00
20 D.Keller/D.Avery 5.00 12.00
21 D.Jackson/M.Kelly 8.00 20.00
22 R.Rice/S.Slaton 4.00 10.00
23 M.Ryan/E.Royal 4.00 10.00
24 C.Johnson/M.Forte 6.00 15.00
25 D.Jackson/K.O'Connell 8.00 20.00
26 J.Charles/G.Dorsey 6.00 15.00
27 B.Brohm/J.Nelson 12.00 30.00
28 C.Henne/J.Long 6.00 15.00
29 D.Thomas/M.Kelly 4.00 10.00
30 M.Forte/E.Bennett 6.00 15.00
31 M.Ryan/H.Douglas 12.00 30.00
32 R.Mendenhall/L.Sweed 4.00 10.00
33 A.Caldwell/J.Simpson 6.00 15.00
34 R.Rice/J.Flacco 8.00 20.00

2008 Playoff National Treasures Rookie Signature Jumbo Material Gold

*GLD JMBO/25: .5X TO 1.2X BASE JSY AU RC
STATED PRINT RUN 25 SER.#'d SETS
UNPRICED BLACK JUMBO PRINT RUN 1
UNPRICED PLATINUM JUMBO PRINT RUN 5
111 Matt Ryan 300.00 500.00
112 Joe Flacco 200.00 300.00

2008 Playoff National Treasures Rookie Signature Material Gold

*MAT.GOLD/25: .4X TO 1X BASE JSY AU RC
GOLD PRINT RUN 25 SER.#'d SETS
UNPRICED PLATINUM PRINT RUN 1
UNPRICED SIG. BRAND LOGO PRINT RUN 1
UNPRICED SIG.COMBO MAT. PRINT RUN 10
UNPRICED SIG.COMBO PLAT. PRINT RUN 1
UNPRICED SIG.LAUN.TAG PRINT RUN 1
101 Darren McFadden 10.00 25.00
102 Jonathan Stewart 15.00 40.00
105 Chris Johnson 50.00 120.00
106 Matt Forte 40.00 100.00
108 Kevin Smith 10.00 25.00
109 Jamaal Charles 40.00 100.00
110 Steve Slaton 10.00 25.00
111 Matt Ryan 300.00 500.00
112 Joe Flacco 75.00 150.00
113 Brian Brohm 10.00 25.00
114 Chad Henne 12.00 30.00
115 Kevin O'Connell 10.00 25.00
116 John David Booty 10.00 25.00
117 Andre Caldwell 10.00 25.00
118 Donnie Avery 12.00 30.00
119 Devin Thomas 10.00 25.00
120 Jordy Nelson 75.00 125.00
121 James Hardy 10.00 25.00
122 Eddie Royal 10.00 25.00
123 Jerome Simpson 12.00 30.00
124 DeSean Jackson 40.00 100.00
125 Malcolm Kelly 10.00 25.00
126 Limas Sweed 10.00 25.00
127 Dexter Jackson 15.00 40.00
128 Earl Bennett 15.00 40.00
129 Early Doucet 10.00 25.00
130 Harry Douglas 12.00 30.00
131 Mario Manningham 20.00 50.00
132 Dustin Keller 12.00 30.00
133 Glenn Dorsey 10.00 25.00
134 Jake Long 12.00 30.00

2008 Playoff National Treasures Signature Patches College

STATED PRINT RUN 24-52
1 Troy Aikman/25 50.00 100.00
2 Ace Clarence Parker/25 25.00 60.00
3 Lee Roy Selmon/26 15.00 40.00
4 Charley Trippi/26 15.00 40.00
5 Warren Moon/26 25.00 60.00
6 Lenny Moore/26 15.00 40.00
7 Jack Youngblood/26 15.00 40.00

8 Earl Campbell/50 40.00 80.00
17 Gary Collins/24 15.00 40.00
18 Dan Fouts/25 20.00 50.00
19 Dante Lavelli/25 15.00 40.00
20 John Mackey/25 15.00 40.00
21 Dan Hampton/25 15.00 40.00
22 Len Dawson/25 25.00 60.00
23 Alan Page/25 15.00 40.00
24 Charley Taylor/25 15.00 40.00
25 Dave Casper/25 15.00 40.00
26 Joe Montana/25 125.00 200.00
27 Rosey Grier/25 15.00 40.00
28 Lawrence Taylor/26 40.00 80.00
29 Bob Griese/26 25.00 60.00
46 Paul Hornung/24 25.00 60.00
47 Daryle Lamonica/25 20.00 50.00
49 Danny White/26 25.00 60.00
50 Fran Tarkenton/26 25.00 60.00
51 Fred Biletnikoff/26 40.00 80.00
52 George Blanda/26 20.00 50.00
53 Jim Otto/26 25.00 60.00
54 Jim Taylor/26 25.00 60.00
55 Lance Alworth/28 50.00 100.00
56 Michael Irvin/26 25.00 60.00
57 Roger Staubach/26 40.00 80.00
58 Steve Largent/26 25.00 60.00
59 Tommy McDonald/26 20.00 50.00
60 Dick Butkus/26 50.00 100.00
61 Franco Harris/26 25.00 60.00
62 Gale Sayers/26 40.00 80.00
63 Hugh McElhenny/26 15.00 40.00
64 Jim Brown/26 50.00 100.00
65 Randy White/26 20.00 50.00
66 Roger Craig/26 20.00 50.00
67 Thurman Thomas/27 20.00 50.00
69 Ken Stabler/26 25.00 60.00
70 Lydell Mitchell/26 15.00 40.00
71 John Elway/27 75.00 150.00
73 John Riggins/50 20.00 50.00
74 Billy Sims/51 15.00 40.00
75 Bert Jones/52 15.00 40.00
80 Ozzie Newsome/52 15.00 40.00
83 Y.A. Tittle/26 25.00 60.00
84 Daryl Johnston/25 25.00 60.00
85 James Lofton/26 15.00 40.00
93 Emmitt Smith/26 100.00 200.00
95 Barry Sanders/25 75.00 150.00
97 Dan Marino/26 100.00 200.00
99 Howie Long/26 40.00 100.00
100 Marcus Allen/26 25.00 60.00
101 Mark Gastineau/26 15.00 40.00
102 Ronnie Lott/26 20.00 50.00
103 Tim Brown/26 40.00 80.00
104 Tony Dorsett/26 25.00 60.00
105 Mike Curtis/26 15.00 40.00
106 Archie Manning/26 20.00 50.00
107 Bo Jackson/25 100.00 200.00
110 Willie Wood/25 20.00 50.00
112 Frank Gifford/50 25.00 60.00
135 Jim Kelly/25 40.00 80.00

2008 Playoff National Treasures Signature Patches NFL

STATED PRINT RUN 25-53
1 Troy Aikman/25 40.00 100.00
9 John Stallworth/25 20.00 50.00
10 Willie Brown/26 15.00 40.00
11 Bobby Bell/25 15.00 40.00
12 Forrest Gregg/25 20.00 50.00
13 Joe Klecko/25 15.00 40.00
14 Randall Cunningham/25 20.00 50.00
15 Raymond Berry/25 20.00 50.00
16 Merlin Olsen/25 15.00 40.00
17 Gary Collins/25 15.00 40.00
18 Dan Fouts/25 20.00 50.00
19 Dante Lavelli/25 15.00 40.00
20 John Mackey/25 15.00 40.00
21 Dan Hampton/25 20.00 50.00
22 Len Dawson/25 25.00 60.00
23 Alan Page/25 15.00 40.00
24 Charley Taylor/25 15.00 40.00
25 Dave Casper/25 15.00 40.00
26 Joe Montana/25 100.00 175.00
27 Rosey Grier/25 20.00 50.00
28 Lawrence Taylor/25 40.00 80.00
29 Bob Griese/25 25.00 60.00
30 Bob Lilly/26 20.00 50.00
31 Carl Eller/26 15.00 40.00
32 Chuck Bednarik/26 20.00 50.00
33 Don Maynard/26 15.00 40.00
34 Joe Greene/26 25.00 60.00
35 Larry Little/26 15.00 40.00
36 Leroy Kelly/26 20.00 50.00
37 Paul Krause/26 15.00 40.00
38 Steve Young/26 60.00 100.00
39 Willie Davis/26 15.00 40.00
40 Alex Karras/26 20.00 50.00
41 Charlie Joiner/26 20.00 50.00
42 Lem Barney/26 15.00 40.00
43 Del Shofner NY/26 15.00 40.00
44 Del Shofner Rams/26 15.00 40.00
45 Jan Stenerud/26 15.00 40.00
46 Paul Hornung/26 25.00 60.00
47 Daryle Lamonica/26 20.00 50.00
48 Paul Warfield/26 20.00 50.00
49 Danny White/26 40.00 80.00
50 Fran Tarkenton/26 25.00 60.00
51 Fred Biletnikoff/26 40.00 80.00
52 George Blanda/26 20.00 50.00
53 Jim Otto/26 25.00 60.00
54 Jim Taylor/26 25.00 60.00
55 Lance Alworth/26 50.00 100.00
56 Michael Irvin/26 40.00 80.00
57 Roger Staubach/26 60.00 100.00
58 Steve Largent/26 25.00 60.00
59 Tommy McDonald/26 15.00 40.00
60 Dick Butkus/26 50.00 100.00
61 Franco Harris/26 40.00 80.00
62 Gale Sayers/26 40.00 80.00
63 Hugh McElhenny/26 15.00 40.00
64 Jim Brown/26 50.00 100.00
65 Randy White/26 40.00 80.00
66 Roger Craig/26 20.00 50.00
67 Thurman Thomas/26 20.00 50.00
68 Jim McMahon/27 25.00 60.00
69 Ken Stabler/25 25.00 60.00
70 Lydell Mitchell/27 15.00 40.00
71 John Elway/27 75.00 150.00
72 Fred Williamson/50 15.00 40.00
73 John Riggins/50 25.00 60.00
74 Billy Sims/51 15.00 40.00
75 Bert Jones/51 20.00 40.00
76 Dub Jones/52 15.00 40.00
77 Jerry Rice/52 75.00 150.00
78 Willie Lanier/52 15.00 40.00
79 Billy Howton/52 15.00 40.00
80 Ozzie Newsome/52 15.00 40.00
81 Mike Singletary/53 25.00 60.00
82 Mark Duper/53 15.00 40.00
83 Y.A. Tittle/26 25.00 60.00
84 Daryl Johnston/26 25.00 60.00
85 James Lofton/53 15.00 40.00
86 Jay Novacek/26 25.00 60.00
88 William Perry/25 25.00 60.00
92 Darrell Green/26 50.00 80.00
93 Emmitt Smith/26 125.00 200.00
95 Barry Sanders/26 75.00 150.00
97 Dan Marino/26 125.00 250.00
98 Fred Dryer/26 15.00 40.00
99 Howie Long/26 60.00 120.00
100 Marcus Allen/26 25.00 60.00
101 Mark Gastineau/26 15.00 40.00
102 Ronnie Lott/26 20.00 50.00
103 Tim Brown/26 40.00 80.00
104 Tony Dorsett/26 30.00 80.00
105 Mike Curtis/26 15.00 40.00
106 Archie Manning/26 25.00 60.00
107 Bo Jackson/25 60.00 120.00
110 Willie Wood/25 20.00 50.00
112 Frank Gifford/50 20.00 50.00
114 Tony Romo/25 60.00 120.00
133 Jermichael Finley/25 10.00 25.00
135 Jim Kelly/25 40.00 80.00
136 Mike Ditka Bears/26 50.00 100.00
137 Mike Ditka Cowboys/26 50.00 100.00

2008 Playoff National Treasures Signature Patches NFL Logo

STATED PRINT RUN 2-25
SERIAL #'d UNDER 25 NOT PRICED
2 Ace Clarence Parker/25 30.00 60.00

2008 Playoff National Treasures Super Bowl Material Final Score

MATERIAL FINAL SCORE PRINT RUN 14-25
UNPRICED FNL SCR PRME PRINT RUN 1-10
*SB MATERIAL/15-25: .4X TO 1X FINAL SCORE
SUPER BOWL MATERIAL PRINT RUN 1-25
UNPRICED MATERIAL YR PRINT RUN 1-10
UNPRICED MATERIAL MVP PRINT RUN 2-10
UNPRICED MATERIAL PRIME PRINT RUN 2-10
1 Bart Starr 40.00 80.00
2 Len Dawson 15.00 40.00
3 Franco Harris 15.00 40.00
4 Roger Staubach 20.00 50.00
5 Fred Biletnikoff 15.00 40.00
6 Randy White 12.00 30.00
7 John Riggins/14 12.00 30.00
8 Joe Montana 50.00 120.00
9 Jerry Rice 20.00 50.00
10 Marcus Allen 15.00 40.00
11 Phil Simms 12.00 30.00
12 Steve Young 20.00 50.00
13 Troy Aikman 20.00 50.00
14 Emmitt Smith 25.00 60.00
15 John Elway 25.00 60.00
16 Bob Griese 15.00 40.00
17 Tony Dorsett 15.00 40.00
18 John Stallworth 15.00 40.00
19 Roger Craig 12.00 30.00
20 Jim McMahon 15.00 40.00
21 Mike Singletary/15 15.00 40.00
22 Thurman Thomas 12.00 30.00
23 Michael Irvin 15.00 40.00
24 Joe Greene 15.00 40.00
25 Lawrence Taylor 15.00 40.00
26 Tom Landry 30.00 60.00
27 Kurt Warner 12.00 30.00
28 Tom Brady 50.00 125.00
29 Peyton Manning 40.00 100.00
30 Eli Manning 12.00 30.00

2008 Playoff National Treasures Super Bowl Signature Cuts

STATED PRINT RUN 1-27
SERIAL #'d UNDER 27 NOT PRICED
4 Roger Staubach/27 60.00 100.00
15 John Elway/27 75.00 150.00
23 Michael Irvin/27 30.00 60.00

2008 Playoff National Treasures Promos

CJ Chris Johnson .75 2.00
DJ DeSean Jackson 1.25 3.00
DM Darren McFadden .60 1.50
ER Eddie Royal .60 1.50
FJ Felix Jones .60 1.50
JF Joe Flacco 1.25 3.00
JS Jonathan Stewart 1.00 2.50
MF Matt Forte 1.00 2.50
MR Matt Ryan 2.00 5.00
SS Steve Slaton .60 1.50

2009 Playoff National Treasures

STATED PRINT RUN 99 SER.#'d SETS
EXCH EXPIRATION: 8/3/2011
1 Kurt Warner 2.50 6.00
2 Larry Fitzgerald 2.50 6.00
3 Tim Hightower 2.00 5.00
4 Matt Ryan 2.50 6.00
5 Michael Turner 2.00 5.00
6 Roddy White 2.00 5.00
7 Tony Gonzalez 2.50 6.00
8 Joe Flacco 2.50 6.00
9 Derrick Mason 2.00 5.00
10 Ray Rice 2.00 5.00
11 Trent Edwards 2.00 5.00
12 Lee Evans 2.50 6.00
13 Terrell Owens 2.50 6.00
14 DeAngelo Williams 2.00 5.00
15 Jonathan Stewart 2.00 5.00
16 Muhsin Muhammad 2.00 5.00
17 Devin Hester 2.50 6.00
18 Greg Olsen 2.50 6.00
19 Jay Cutler 2.00 5.00
20 Matt Forte 2.00 5.00
21 Carson Palmer 2.50 6.00
22 Chad Ochocinco 2.00 5.00
23 Cedric Benson 2.00 5.00
24 Derek Anderson 2.00 5.00
25 Braylon Edwards 2.00 5.00
26 Jamal Lewis 2.50 6.00
27 Jason Witten 2.50 6.00
28 Marion Barber 2.50 6.00
29 Tony Romo 2.50 6.00
30 Brandon Marshall 2.50 6.00
31 Brandon Stokley 2.00 5.00
32 Correll Buckhalter 2.00 5.00
33 Calvin Johnson 3.00 8.00
34 Bryant Johnson 2.00 5.00
35 Kevin Smith 2.00 5.00
36 Aaron Rodgers 6.00 15.00
37 Greg Jennings 2.00 5.00
38 Ryan Grant 2.50 6.00
39 Andre Johnson 2.50 6.00
40 Owen Daniels 2.00 5.00
41 Steve Slaton 2.00 5.00
42 Anthony Gonzalez 2.00 5.00
43 Joseph Addai 2.00 5.00
44 Peyton Manning 6.00 15.00
45 Reggie Wayne 2.50 6.00
46 David Garrard 2.00 5.00
47 Maurice Jones-Drew 2.00 5.00
48 Torry Holt 2.50 6.00
49 Dwayne Bowe 2.50 6.00
50 Jamaal Charles 2.50 6.00
51 Matt Cassel 2.00 5.00
52 Chad Henne 2.50 6.00
53 Ronnie Brown 2.00 5.00
54 Ricky Williams 2.50 6.00
55 Adrian Peterson 12.50 25.00
56 Bernard Berrian 2.00 5.00
57 Brett Favre 12.00 30.00
58 Laurence Maroney 2.50 6.00
59 Randy Moss 2.50 6.00
60 Tom Brady 6.00 15.00
61 Wes Welker 2.50 6.00
62 Drew Brees 3.00 8.00
63 Marques Colston 2.00 5.00
64 Devery Henderson 2.00 5.00
65 Brandon Jacobs 2.00 5.00
66 Eli Manning 2.50 6.00
67 Steve Smith 2.50 6.00
68 Jerricho Cotchery 2.00 5.00
69 Thomas Jones 2.00 5.00
70 Darren McFadden 3.00 8.00
71 JaMarcus Russell 2.00 5.00
72 Zach Miller 2.00 5.00
73 Brian Westbrook 2.00 5.00
74 Michael Vick 2.50 6.00
75 Donovan McNabb 2.50 6.00
76 Ben Roethlisberger 3.00 8.00
77 Santonio Holmes 2.00 5.00
78 Willie Parker 2.00 5.00
79 Antonio Gates 2.50 6.00
80 LaDainian Tomlinson 3.00 8.00
81 Philip Rivers 3.00 8.00
82 Vincent Jackson 2.00 5.00
83 Frank Gore 2.50 6.00
84 Isaac Bruce 3.00 8.00
85 Vernon Davis 2.00 5.00
86 Julius Jones 2.00 5.00
87 Matt Hasselbeck 2.00 5.00
88 T.J. Houshmandzadeh 2.00 5.00
89 Donnie Avery 2.00 5.00
90 Marc Bulger 2.00 5.00
91 Steven Jackson 2.00 5.00
92 Antonio Bryant 2.00 5.00
93 Cadillac Williams 2.50 6.00
94 Kellen Winslow Jr. 2.00 5.00
95 Chris Johnson 2.00 5.00
96 Justin Gage 2.00 5.00
97 Vince Young 2.00 5.00
98 Chris Cooley 2.00 5.00
99 Clinton Portis 2.00 5.00
100 Jason Campbell 2.00 5.00
101 Aaron Curry JSY AU RC 15.00 40.00
102 Andre Brown JSY AU RC 20.00 40.00
103 B.Pettigrew JSY AU RC 10.00 25.00
104 B.Robiskie JSY AU RC 10.00 25.00
105 Chris Wells JSY AU RC 25.00 60.00
106 D.Heyward-Bey JSY AU RC 15.00 40.00
107 Deon Butler JSY AU RC 10.00 25.00
108 Derrick Williams JSY AU RC 10.00 25.00
109 D.Brown JSY AU RC 10.00 25.00
110 Glen Coffee JSY AU RC 10.00 25.00
111 Hakeem Nicks JSY AU RC 12.00 30.00
112 Jason Smith JSY AU RC 10.00 25.00
113 Javon Ringer JSY AU RC 10.00 25.00
114 Jeremy Maclin JSY AU RC 20.00 50.00
115 Josh Freeman JSY AU RC 10.00 25.00
116 Juaquin Iglesias JSY AU RC 10.00 25.00
117 Kenny Britt JSY AU RC 10.00 25.00
118 K.Moreno JSY AU RC 10.00 25.00
119 LeSean McCoy JSY AU RC 75.00 150.00
120 Mark Sanchez JSY AU RC 10.00 25.00
121 M.Stafford JSY AU RC 200.00 400.00
122 M.Crabtree JSY AU RC 15.00 40.00
123 Mike Thomas JSY AU RC 10.00 25.00
124 Mike Wallace JSY AU RC 15.00 40.00
125 M.Massaquoi JSY AU RC 10.00 25.00
126 Nate Davis JSY AU RC 10.00 25.00
127 Pat White JSY AU RC 12.00 30.00
128 Patrick Turner JSY AU RC 10.00 25.00
129 Percy Harvin JSY AU RC 10.00 25.00
130 Ramses Barden JSY AU RC 10.00 25.00
131 Rhett Bomar JSY AU RC 10.00 25.00
132 Shonn Greene JSY AU RC 10.00 25.00
133 Stephen McGee JSY AU RC 10.00 25.00
134 Tyson Jackson JSY AU RC 10.00 25.00
135 Aaron Brown AU RC 6.00 15.00
136 Aaron Maybin AU RC 6.00 15.00
137 Alphonso Smith AU RC 5.00 12.00
138 Austin Collie AU RC 5.00 12.00
139 B.J. Raji AU RC 10.00 25.00
140 Bernard Scott AU RC 10.00 25.00
141 Brandon Gibson AU RC 6.00 15.00
142 Brandon Tate AU RC 6.00 15.00
143 Brian Cushing AU RC 5.00 12.00
144 Brian Hartline AU RC 8.00 20.00
145 Brian Hoyer AU RC 20.00 50.00
146 Brian Orakpo AU RC 6.00 15.00
147 Brooks Foster AU RC 5.00 12.00
148 Chase Coffman AU RC 5.00 12.00
149 Chase Daniel AU RC 15.00 40.00
150 Clay Matthews AU RC 50.00 100.00
151 Clint Sintim AU RC 5.00 12.00
152 Everette Brown AU RC 5.00 12.00
153 Frank Summers AU RC 8.00 20.00
154 Gartrell Johnson AU RC 5.00 12.00
155 James Casey AU RC 6.00 15.00
156 James Davis AU RC 10.00 25.00
157 James Laurinaitis AU RC 10.00 25.00
158 Jared Cook AU RC 6.00 15.00
159 Jarett Dillard AU RC 5.00 12.00
160 Johnny Knox AU RC 6.00 15.00
161 Julian Edelman AU RC 100.00 200.00
162 Keith Null AU RC 6.00 15.00
163 Kenny McKinley AU RC 5.00 12.00
164 Kory Sheets AU RC 6.00 15.00
165 Lardarius Webb AU RC 8.00 20.00
166 L.Stephens-Howling AU RC 10.00 25.00
167 Larry English AU RC 6.00 15.00
168 Louis Delmas AU RC 6.00 15.00
169 Louis Murphy AU RC 5.00 12.00
170 Malcolm Jenkins AU RC 5.00 12.00
171 Mike Teel AU RC 5.00 12.00
172 M.Goodson AU RC EXCH 2.50 6.00
173 Quinn Johnson AU RC 5.00 12.00
174 Rashad Jennings AU RC 12.00 30.00
175 Rey Maualuga AU RC 8.00 20.00
176 Richard Quinn AU RC 6.00 15.00
177 Sammie Stroughter AU RC 5.00 12.00
178 Sean Smith AU RC 5.00 12.00
179 S.Nelson AU RC EXCH 2.00 5.00
180 Stefan Logan AU RC 8.00 20.00
181 Tom Brandstater AU RC 6.00 15.00
182 Tony Fiammetta AU RC 5.00 12.00
183 Travis Beckum AU RC 5.00 12.00
184 Vontae Davis AU RC 5.00 12.00
185 Alex Karras 2.50 6.00
186 Andre Reed 2.50 6.00
187 Archie Manning 2.50 6.00
188 Billy Howton 2.00 5.00
189 Bob Lilly 2.50 6.00
190 Boyd Dowler 2.00 5.00
191 Charley Taylor 2.00 5.00
192 Cliff Harris 2.50 6.00
193 Danny White 2.50 6.00
194 Dante Lavelli 2.00 5.00
195 Dave Casper 2.00 5.00
196 Del Shofner 2.00 5.00
197 Don Perkins 2.00 5.00
198 Dub Jones 2.00 5.00
199 Gary Collins 2.00 5.00
200 Harlon Hill 2.00 5.00
201 Jim Taylor 3.00 8.00
202 Joe Klecko 2.00 5.00
203 Johnny Morris 2.00 5.00
204 Johnny Unitas 5.00 12.00
205 Kellen Winslow Sr. 2.00 5.00
206 Lee Roy Selmon 2.00 5.00
207 Leroy Kelly 2.50 6.00
208 Mark Gastineau 2.00 5.00
209 Mike Curtis 2.00 5.00
210 Ozzie Newsome 2.50 6.00
211 Roger Craig 2.50 6.00
212 Rosey Grier 2.00 5.00
213 Sonny Jurgensen 2.50 6.00
214 Sterling Sharpe 3.00 8.00
215 Tiki Barber 2.50 6.00
216 William Perry 2.00 5.00
217 Willie Wood 2.50 6.00
218 Jim Thorpe 8.00 20.00
219 Deion Sanders 2.50 6.00
220 Jim Brown 4.00 10.00
221 Jim McMahon 2.50 6.00
222 Joe Namath 4.00 10.00
223 Sammy Baugh 3.00 8.00
224 Tony Dorsett 3.00 8.00
225 Lawrence Taylor 3.00 8.00
226 John Elway 5.00 12.00
227 Thurman Thomas 2.50 6.00
228 Bo Jackson 4.00 10.00
229 Walter Payton 5.00 12.00
230 Barry Sanders 6.00 15.00
231 Joe Greene 3.00 8.00
232 Len Dawson 3.00 8.00
233 Paul Warfield 2.50 6.00
234 Steve Young 4.00 10.00

2009 Playoff National Treasures AFL 50th Anniversary Materials

STATED PRINT RUN 30-99
*PRIME/15-35: .8X TO 2X BASIC JSY
PRIME PRINT RUN 1-35
1 George Blanda/99 8.00 20.00
3 Don Maynard/99 4.00 10.00
4 Joe Namath/30 10.00 25.00
5 Jim Otto/99 3.00 8.00
6 Willie Brown/99 3.00 8.00
7 Lance Alworth/99 8.00 20.00
9 Len Dawson/99 5.00 12.00
10 Daryle Lamonica/99 [illegible] 8.00
11 Bob Griese/90 5.00 12.00
12 Charlie Joiner/99 3.00 8.00
13 Fred Biletnikoff/99 5.00 12.00
14 Gene Upshaw/99 3.00 8.00
15 Jan Stenerud/35 4.00 10.00
16 Larry Csonka/99 5.00 12.00
17 Larry Little/90 3.00 8.00
18 Ron Mix/50 4.00 10.00
19 Willie Lanier/99 3.00 8.00

2009 Playoff National Treasures AFL 50th Anniversary Signature Materials

STATED PRINT RUN 12-50
*PRIME/17-25: X TO X BASIC JSY AU
SERIAL #'d UNDER 17 NOT PRICED
1 George Blanda/50 25.00 50.00
3 Don Maynard/35 15.00 40.00
4 Joe Namath/15 50.00 100.00
5 Jim Otto/50 15.00 40.00
6 Willie Brown/35 12.00 30.00
7 Lance Alworth/50 40.00 80.00
9 Len Dawson/25 30.00 60.00
10 Daryle Lamonica/50 15.00 40.00
11 Bob Griese/25 20.00 50.00
12 Charlie Joiner/50 12.00 30.00
13 Fred Biletnikoff/50 30.00 60.00
15 Jan Stenerud/50 12.00 30.00
18 Ron Mix/50 12.00 30.00
19 Willie Lanier/50 12.00 30.00
20 Ken Stabler/40 40.00 80.00

2009 Playoff National Treasures Biography Materials

STATED PRINT RUN 20-50
*PRIME/25: .8X TO 2X BASIC JSY
PRIME PRINT RUN 1-25
1 Alex Karras 5.00 12.00
2 Bill Bates 4.00 10.00
3 Cris Collinsworth 5.00 12.00
4 Darrell Green 8.00 20.00
5 Deacon Jones 5.00 12.00
6 Dick Lane 4.00 10.00
7 Doak Walker 10.00 25.00
8 Elroy Hirsch 5.00 12.00
9 Fred Dryer 4.00 10.00
10 Howie Long 6.00 15.00
11 James Lofton 4.00 10.00
12 Joe Theismann 6.00 15.00
13 John Mackey 5.00 12.00
14 Ken Strong 8.00 20.00
15 Lem Barney 6.00 15.00
16 Marion Motley 10.00 25.00
17 Ollie Matson 5.00 12.00
18 Paul Krause/20 6.00 15.00
19 Tommy McDonald 4.00 10.00
20 Reggie White 10.00 25.00
21 Walter Payton 10.00 25.00
22 Randall Cunningham 5.00 12.00

2009 Playoff National Treasures Biography Materials Signature

STATED PRINT RUN 4-50
*PRIME/25: .5X TO 1.2X BASIC JSY
PRIME PRINT RUN 1-25
SERIAL #'d UNDER 15 NOT PRICED
1 Alex Karras/15 15.00 40.00
2 Bill Bates/40 10.00 25.00
3 Cris Collinsworth/50 12.00 30.00
4 Darrell Green/17 30.00 60.00
9 Fred Dryer/50 12.00 30.00
10 Howie Long/50 25.00 60.00
11 James Lofton/50 10.00 25.00
12 Joe Theismann/41 15.00 40.00
13 John Mackey/50 12.00 30.00
15 Lem Barney/50 10.00 25.00
19 Tommy McDonald/50 12.00 30.00
22 Randall Cunningham/50 12.00 30.00

2009 Playoff National Treasures Century Material Prime

STATED PRINT RUN 1-50
SERIAL #'d UNDER 15 NOT PRICED
2 Larry Fitzgerald/50 5.00 12.00
5 Michael Turner/30 4.00 10.00
6 Roddy White/40 4.00 10.00
11 Trent Edwards/50 4.00 10.00
12 Lee Evans/50 5.00 12.00
14 DeAngelo Williams/50 4.00 10.00
16 Muhsin Muhammad/50 4.00 10.00
17 Devin Hester/15 6.00 15.00
18 Greg Olsen/30 5.00 12.00
21 Carson Palmer/30 5.00 12.00
22 Chad Ochocinco/50 4.00 10.00
24 Derek Anderson/50 4.00 10.00
26 Jamal Lewis/50 5.00 12.00
27 Jason Witten/40 5.00 12.00
28 Marion Barber/50 5.00 12.00
29 Tony Romo/50 5.00 12.00
31 Brandon Stokley/23 5.00 12.00
33 Calvin Johnson/30 6.00 15.00
36 Aaron Rodgers/50 12.00 30.00
37 Greg Jennings/50 4.00 10.00
38 Ryan Grant/50 5.00 12.00
39 Andre Johnson/50 5.00 12.00
43 Joseph Addai/50 4.00 10.00
44 Peyton Manning/15 15.00 40.00
45 Reggie Wayne/50 5.00 12.00
46 David Garrard/30 4.00 10.00
47 Maurice Jones-Drew/50 4.00 10.00
49 Dwayne Bowe/30 5.00 12.00
53 Ronnie Brown/50 4.00 10.00
54 Ricky Williams/50 5.00 12.00
55 Adrian Peterson/50 6.00 15.00
58 Laurence Maroney/50 5.00 12.00
59 Randy Moss/50 5.00 12.00
60 Tom Brady/50 20.00 50.00
61 Wes Welker/50 5.00 12.00
62 Drew Brees/50 8.00 20.00
65 Brandon Jacobs/50 4.00 10.00
67 Steve Smith/50 5.00 12.00
68 Jerricho Cotchery/30 4.00 10.00
69 Thomas Jones/50 4.00 10.00
70 Darren McFadden/30 6.00 15.00
71 JaMarcus Russell/50 4.00 10.00
72 Zach Miller/30 4.00 10.00
73 Brian Westbrook/40 4.00 10.00
77 Santonio Holmes/50 4.00 10.00
78 Willie Parker/50 4.00 10.00
79 Antonio Gates/50 5.00 12.00
80 LaDainian Tomlinson/50 6.00 15.00
81 Philip Rivers/15 8.00 20.00
82 Vincent Jackson/50 4.00 10.00
83 Frank Gore/50 5.00 12.00
85 Vernon Davis/35 4.00 10.00
87 Matt Hasselbeck/30 4.00 10.00
90 Marc Bulger/40 4.00 10.00
91 Steven Jackson/50 4.00 10.00
93 Cadillac Williams/50 5.00 12.00
95 Chris Johnson/50 4.00 10.00
96 Justin Gage /50 4.00 10.00
98 Chris Cooley/50 4.00 10.00
99 Clinton Portis/50 4.00 10.00
100 Jason Campbell/35 4.00 10.00
186 Andre Reed/25 8.00 20.00
204 Johnny Unitas/25 40.00 80.00
214 Sterling Sharpe/25 8.00 20.00
215 Tiki Barber/25 8.00 20.00
216 William Perry/25 6.00 15.00
219 Deion Sanders/25 12.00 30.00
222 Joe Namath/25 12.00 30.00
225 Lawrence Taylor/25 10.00 25.00
226 John Elway/25 15.00 40.00
229 Walter Payton/25 15.00 40.00
230 Barry Sanders/25 15.00 40.00
234 Steve Young/25 12.00 30.00

2009 Playoff National Treasures Century Material Signature Prime

PRIME PRINT RUN 1-25
SERIAL #'d UNDER 15 NOT PRICED
12 Lee Evans/16 12.00 30.00
63 Marques Colston/25 12.00 30.00
186 Andre Reed/25 15.00 40.00
191 Charley Taylor/25 12.00 30.00
214 Sterling Sharpe/25 20.00 50.00
215 Tiki Barber/25 15.00 40.00
216 William Perry/15 20.00 50.00
219 Deion Sanders/25 50.00 100.00
225 Lawrence Taylor/25 30.00 60.00
227 Thurman Thomas/15 20.00 50.00
228 Bo Jackson/22 40.00 80.00
234 Steve Young/25 50.00 100.00

2009 Playoff National Treasures Champions Materials Combo

STATED PRINT RUN 50-99
*PRIME/25: .6X TO 1.5X BASIC DUAL
PRIME PRINT RUN 2-25
1 S.Luckman/C.Turner 15.00 30.00
2 F.Gifford/R.Brown 8.00 20.00
3 R.Berry/L.Moore 6.00 15.00
4 D.Lamonica/F.Biletnikoff 10.00 25.00
5 J.Namath/D.Maynard 12.00 30.00
6 L.Dawson/W.Lanier 10.00 25.00
7 G.Upshaw/T.Hendricks 8.00 20.00
8 J.Montana/R.Lott 30.00 80.00
9 P.Simms/L.Taylor 10.00 25.00
10 T.Aikman/E.Smith 15.00 40.00

2009 Playoff National Treasures Champions Materials Quads

STATED PRINT RUN 50-99
*PRIME/25: .6X TO 1.5X BASIC QUAD
PRIME PRINT RUN 1-25
1 Blanda/Bilet/Lmnica/Otto 12.00 30.00
2 Griese/Csnka/Wrfld/Lttle/50 12.00 30.00
3 Harris/Stllwrth/Grne/Lmbert 20.00 50.00
4 McMhn/Paytn/Sngle/Hmptn 20.00 50.00
5 Montana/Rice/Lott/Young 30.00 80.00
6 Aikman/Smith/Irvin/Novacek 20.00 50.00
7 Landry/Staubch/Drstt/Whte 20.00 50.00
8 Roeth/Ward/Parker/Randle 10.00 25.00
9 P.Mann/Wayn/Clark/Sandrs 25.00 60.00
10 Eli/Jacobs/Ross/Toomer 8.00 20.00

2009 Playoff National Treasures Champions Materials Trios

STATED PRINT RUN 30-99
*PRIME/25: .6X TO 1.5X BASIC TRIO
PRIME TRIO PRINT RUN 10-25
1 Montana/Rice/Lott 40.00 100.00
2 Harris/Stallworth/Greene 12.00 30.00
3 Biletnikoff/Brown/Hendricks 12.00 30.00
4 Starr/Hornung/Gregg/30 25.00 60.00
5 Parker/Berry/Moore 8.00 20.00

2009 Playoff National Treasures Champions Signatures

STATED PRINT RUN 5-99
1 Dante Lavelli/99 12.00 30.00
2 Charley Trippi/50 10.00 25.00
3 Yale Lary/30 10.00 25.00
4 Rick Casares/99 10.00 25.00
5 Daryle Lamonica/99 12.00 30.00
7 Lawrence Taylor/99 15.00 40.00
8 Ronnie Lott/99 15.00 40.00
9 Frank Gifford/50 15.00 40.00

2009 Playoff National Treasures Champions Signature Combo

COMBO AUTO PRINT RUN 5-50
1 D.Jones/D.Lavelli/40 20.00 50.00
3 R.Berry/L.Moore/50 20.00 50.00

2009 Playoff National Treasures Champions Signature Quads

1 Str/Hrnng/Grgg/Dwlr/15 175.00 300.00
2 Tylr/Wd/Grgg/Hrnng/15 100.00 200.00
4 Blnda/Bltnkf/Lmnca/Oto/15 60.00 120.00
5 Bll/Dwsn/Lnr/Stnrd/15 50.00 100.00
6 Stbch/Pgh/Llly/Alwrth/15 90.00 150.00
8 Mchn/Hmptn/Sngltry/Prry/15 90.00 150.00

2009 Playoff National Treasures College Material

STATED PRINT RUN 10-99
2 Larry Csonka/99 8.00 20.00
3 Roger Staubach/99 10.00 25.00
4 Lawrence Taylor/99 8.00 20.00
5 Thurman Thomas/99 6.00 15.00
7 Dan Marino/45 20.00 50.00
9 Joe Greene/99 8.00 20.00
10 Steve Largent/99 8.00 20.00
11 Eric Dickerson/99 8.00 20.00
12 John Elway/15 40.00 80.00
13 Peyton Manning/55 20.00 50.00
14 Marcus Allen/99 10.00 25.00
15 Adrian Peterson/99 5.00 12.00
22 Knute Rockne/99 15.00 40.00
30 Hugh McElhenny/99 5.00 12.00

2009 Playoff National Treasures College Material Prime

PRIME PRINT RUN 50 SER.#'d SETS
2 Larry Csonka 12.00 30.00
4 Lawrence Taylor 12.00 30.00
5 Thurman Thomas 10.00 25.00
6 Barry Sanders 20.00 50.00
7 Dan Marino 25.00 60.00
10 Steve Largent 12.00 30.00
11 Eric Dickerson 10.00 25.00
14 Marcus Allen 10.00 25.00
15 Adrian Peterson 6.00 15.00
22 Knute Rockne 25.00 50.00

2009 Playoff National Treasures College Material Signature

STATED PRINT RUN 1-99
*PRIME/15: .8X TO 2X BASIC JSY AU/25-35
PRIME PRINT RUN 1-15
SERIAL #'d UNDER 25 NOT PRICED
3 Roger Staubach/25 40.00 80.00
4 Lawrence Taylor/25 30.00 60.00
5 Thurman Thomas/25 20.00 40.00
8 Tony Dorsett/30 30.00 60.00
9 Joe Greene/35 25.00 50.00
30 Hugh McElhenny/99 12.00 30.00

2009 Playoff National Treasures College Materials Quad

STATED PRINT RUN 25-99
*PRIME/15-25: .5X TO 1.2X BASIC QUAD
QUAD PRIME PRINT RUN 1-25
1 Campbll/Will/Bensn/Charles 20.00 50.00
2 Dickrsn/Sandrs/Drstt/Allen 20.00 50.00
3 Staubch/Mrino/Elwy/P.Mann 30.00 80.00
4 Portis/Wayne/McGahee/Moss 10.00 25.00
5 Allen/Palmer/Bush/Leinart 12.00 30.00

2009 Playoff National Treasures College Signature

STATED PRINT RUN 1-99
1 Mike Singletary/15 25.00 50.00
4 Lawrence Taylor/15 30.00 60.00
8 Tony Dorsett/20 25.00 50.00
9 Joe Greene/25 20.00 50.00
16 Ace Parker/25 20.00 50.00
17 Billy Sims/99 10.00 25.00
19 Bo Jackson/18 40.00 80.00
20 Deion Sanders/25 40.00 80.00
21 Joe Namath/25 60.00 120.00
23 Lydell Mitchell/99 8.00 20.00
24 Tim Brown/50 25.00 50.00
25 Carl Eller/99 8.00 20.00
26 Troy Aikman/20 40.00 80.00
28 Rick Casares/99 10.00 25.00
30 Hugh McElhenny/99 8.00 20.00

2009 Playoff National Treasures Colossal Materials

STATED PRINT RUN 2-99
1 Adrian Peterson/99 5.00 12.00
2 Andre Johnson/99 4.00 10.00
3 LaDainian Tomlinson/25 6.00 15.00
4 Ben Roethlisberger/25 6.00 15.00
5 Brian Westbrook/25 4.00 10.00
7 Dallas Clark/15 4.00 10.00
8 DeAngelo Williams/25 4.00 10.00
9 Drew Brees/50 8.00 20.00
10 Peyton Manning/15 15.00 40.00
11 Tony Romo/99 4.00 10.00
12 Frank Gore/45 4.00 10.00
14 Lee Evans/25 5.00 12.00
15 Matt Ryan/50 4.00 10.00
17 Michael Turner/65 3.00 8.00

2009 Playoff National Treasures Colossal Materials Jersey Numbers

STATED PRINT RUN 2-80
1 Adrian Peterson/28 6.00 15.00
2 Andre Johnson/80 4.00 10.00
3 LaDainian Tomlinson/21 6.00 15.00
5 Brian Westbrook/36 4.00 10.00
6 Chad Ochocinco/65 3.00 8.00
7 Dallas Clark/44 3.00 8.00
8 DeAngelo Williams/34 4.00 10.00
10 Peyton Manning/18 15.00 40.00
12 Frank Gore/21 5.00 12.00
14 Lee Evans/25 5.00 12.00
16 Maurice Jones-Drew/32 4.00 10.00
17 Michael Turner/33 4.00 10.00
20 Willie Parker/39 3.00 8.00

2009 Playoff National Treasures Colossal Materials Position

STATED PRINT RUN 5-99
2 Andre Johnson/99 4.00 10.00
3 LaDainian Tomlinson/25 6.00 15.00
4 Ben Roethlisberger/25 6.00 15.00
5 Brian Westbrook/25 4.00 10.00
7 Dallas Clark/15 4.00 10.00
8 DeAngelo Williams/25 4.00 10.00
9 Drew Brees/50 5.00 12.00
10 Peyton Manning/25 15.00 40.00
11 Tony Romo/99 4.00 10.00
12 Frank Gore/50 4.00 10.00
14 Lee Evans/25 5.00 12.00
15 Matt Ryan/50 4.00 10.00
16 Maurice Jones-Drew/34 4.00 10.00

2009 Playoff National Treasures Colossal Materials Position Prime

POSITION PRIME PRINT RUN 1-20
6 Chad Ochocinco/20 6.00 15.00
8 DeAngelo Williams/20 6.00 15.00
14 Lee Evans/20 8.00 20.00
20 Willie Parker/20 6.00 15.00

2009 Playoff National Treasures Colossal Materials Signature

UNPRICED SIG JSY NUM PRIME 1-10
UNPRICED SIG POSITION PRIME 1-10

2009 Playoff National Treasures Combo Material

STATED PRINT RUN 80-95
*PRIME/25: .8X TO 2X BASIC COMBO
1 B.Sanders/E.Dickerson 12.00 30.00
2 M.Allen/R.Bush 8.00 20.00
3 L.Fitzgerald/R.Williams WR 6.00 15.00

2009 Playoff National Treasures League Leaders Materials

STATED PRINT RUN 50-99
*PRIME/17-25: .8X TO 2X BASIC JSY/50-99
PRIME PRINT RUN 5-25
1 Emmitt Smith/99 12.00 30.00
2 Eric Dickerson/99 6.00 15.00
3 Jerry Rice/75 8.00 20.00
4 Jim Brown/50 10.00 25.00
5 Michael Irvin/99 8.00 20.00
6 Norm Van Brocklin/99 6.00 15.00
7 Otto Graham/99 8.00 20.00
8 Sammy Baugh/99 10.00 25.00
9 Tom Brady/50 20.00 50.00
10 Walter Payton/99 12.00 30.00

2009 Playoff National Treasures League Leaders Materials Combo

STATED PRINT RUN 80-99
*PRIME/20-25: .8X TO 2X BASIC INSERTS
PRIME PRINT RUN 3-25
1 S.Luckman/B.Waterfield/80 10.00 25.00
2 B.Layne/T.Fears/99 10.00 25.00
3 J.Brown/G.Sayers/99 12.00 30.00
4 B.Jones/F.Tarkenton/99 8.00 20.00
5 E.Campbell/W.Payton/99 12.00 30.00
6 S.Largent/J.Stallworth/99 10.00 25.00
7 D.Fouts/J.Montana/99 25.00 60.00
8 D.Marino/E.Dickerson/99 15.00 40.00
9 E.Dickerson/W.Payton/99 12.00 30.00
10 D.Marino/J.Elway/99 15.00 40.00
11 B.Sanders/T.Thomas/99 12.00 30.00
12 D.Marino/E.Smith/99 15.00 40.00
13 J.Rice/M.Irvin/99 10.00 25.00
14 E.Smith/B.Sanders/99 12.00 30.00
15 D.Brees/P.Manning/99 20.00 50.00

2009 Playoff National Treasures League Leaders Materials Quads

STATED PRINT RUN 10-99
*PRIME/25: .6X TO 1.5X BASIC QUAD
1 Moon/Kelly/Smith/Sanders 15.00 40.00
2 Marino/Young/Kelly/Aikman 20.00 50.00
3 Holt/Moss/Boldin/Ochocinco 6.00 15.00
4 Moss/Holt/Chmbrs/Gnzalz/35 8.00 20.00
5 Brady/Brees/Romo/Favre 25.00 60.00
6 Tomlinsn/Petrsn/Wstbrk/Prkr 12.00 30.00
7 Wyne/Moss/Ochocinco/Fitz 6.00 15.00
9 Petrsn/Turner/Willms/Portis 12.00 30.00
10 Johnson/Fitzgerald/Smith/White 6.00 15.00

2009 Playoff National Treasures League Leaders Materials Trios

STATED PRINT RUN 70-99
*PRIME/25: .6X TO 1.5X BASIC TRIO
1 Harris/Foreman/Payton 15.00 40.00
2 Payton/Dorsett/Harris 15.00 40.00
3 Fouts/Campbell/Largent 10.00 25.00
4 Dickerson/Riggins/Allen 10.00 25.00
5 Marino/Dickerson/Rice 20.00 50.00
6 Moon/Sanders/Rice 20.00 50.00
7 Smith/Sanders/Thomas 15.00 40.00
8 Elway/Young/Moon 12.00 30.00
9 Young/Favre/Marino 20.00 50.00
10 Favre/Smith/Rice 20.00 50.00
11 Favre/Young/Manning 20.00 50.00
12 Manning/James/Holt 10.00 25.00
13 Warner/Manning/Favre 20.00 50.00
14 Tomlinson/Johnson/Gore 8.00 20.00
15 Ochocinco/Harrison/Wayne/70 6.00 15.00

2009 Playoff National Treasures League Leaders Signatures

STATED PRINT RUN 3-99
SERIAL #'d UNDER 25 NOT PRICED
1 Ace Parker/50 12.50 30.00
8 Johnny Morris/99 8.00 20.00
10 Michael Irvin/25 25.00 50.00

2009 Playoff National Treasures League Leaders Signature Combo

STATED PRINT RUN 5-15
3 J.Brown/D.Shofner/15 50.00 100.00
4 J.Brown/L.Moore/15 60.00 125.00
5 S.Jurgensen/T.McDonald/15 25.00 50.00
6 T.McDonald/D.Shofner/15 20.00 40.00
7 J.Brown/D.Perkins/15 50.00 100.00
8 S.Jurgensen/G.Sayers/15 40.00 80.00
9 G.Sayers/L.Kelly/15 40.00 80.00
10 S.Jurgensen/F.Tarkenton/15 40.00 80.00
11 B.Jones/F.Tarkenton/15 40.00 80.00
14 D.Marino/J.Elway/15 150.00 250.00
15 J.Rice/M.Irvin/15 100.00 200.00

2009 Playoff National Treasures League Leaders Signature Materials

STATED PRINT RUN 15-50
1 Emmitt Smith/22 100.00 175.00
2 Eric Dickerson/15 30.00 60.00
3 Jerry Rice/15 100.00 200.00
4 Jim Brown/32 50.00 100.00
5 Michael Irvin/50 25.00 50.00

2009 Playoff National Treasures Pen Pals

1 M.Crabtree/B.Pettigrew 12.00 30.00
2 M.Stafford/B.Pettigrew 30.00 80.00
3 M.Stafford/M.Sanchez 60.00 150.00
4 K.Moreno/C.Wells 15.00 40.00
5 M.Crabtree/J.Maclin 20.00 50.00
6 D.Brown/L.McCoy 25.00 50.00
7 D.Heyward-Bey/P.Harvin 20.00 50.00
8 B.Robiskie/M.Massaquoi 12.00 30.00
9 P.White/P.Turner 12.00 30.00
10 M.Sanchez/S.Greene 30.00 80.00
11 L.McCoy/J.Maclin 25.00 50.00
12 G.Coffee/M.Crabtree 15.00 40.00
13 A.Curry/D.Butler 12.00 30.00
14 H.Nicks/B.Tate 20.00 40.00
15 S.McGee/R.Bomar 10.00 25.00
16 B.Wells/B.Robiskie 20.00 50.00
17 K.Britt/J.Ringer 12.00 30.00
18 Stafford/Sanchez/Freeman 75.00 150.00
19 Moreno/Wells/Brown 40.00 80.00
20 Heywrd-By/Crbtree/Maclin 20.00 50.00
21 Moreno/Massaq/Stafford 50.00 120.00
22 Thomas/Williams/Butler
23 Turner/Butler/Iglesias 20.00 50.00
24 Staffrd/Pettigrw/Willms 50.00 120.00
25 Davis/Crabtree/Coffee 15.00 40.00
26 Staff/Snchz/Frmn/Whte 75.00 150.00
27 Moreno/Wlls/Brwn/McCy 60.00 120.00
28 Crab/Macln/Hywrd/Hrvn 20.00 50.00
29 Stffrd/Snchz/Crab/Mcln 75.00 150.00
30 Stffrd/Moren/Crab/Pttigw 50.00 120.00
31 Moren/Wlls/Crab/Maclin 20.00 50.00
32 Willms/Tate/Wllce/Bardn 40.00 80.00
33 Nicks/Bardn/Bomar/Brwn 20.00 50.00

2009 Playoff National Treasures Retired Materials Jersey Numbers Prime

PRIME PRINT RUN 1-25
1 Jim Kelly/25 15.00 40.00
2 Otto Graham/25 15.00 40.00
5 Jim Parker/25 10.00 25.00
6 Raymond Berry/25 12.00 30.00
11 Dan Marino/20 20.00 50.00
14 Don Maynard/15 12.00 30.00
15 Dan Fouts/25 12.00 30.00
16 Earl Campbell/25 12.00 30.00
17 Walter Payton/25 25.00 60.00
24 Mel Hein/25 25.00 50.00
26 Y.A. Tittle/25 15.00 40.00
29 Lawrence Taylor/25 15.00 40.00
31 Bob Waterfield/25 12.00 30.00
32 Merlin Olsen/25 10.00 25.00
35 Joe Montana/25 30.00 80.00
36 Steve Largent/25 15.00 40.00

2009 Playoff National Treasures Retired Materials Signature Jersey Numbers Prime

SIGNATURE PRIME PRINT RUN 2-25
1 Jim Kelly/25 50.00 100.00
6 Raymond Berry/25 30.00 60.00
9 Willie Lanier/25 25.00 50.00
15 Dan Fouts/25 40.00 100.00
16 Earl Campbell/25 40.00 80.00
22 Fran Tarkenton/15 50.00 100.00
26 Y.A. Tittle/25 40.00 80.00
27 Frank Gifford/16 40.00 80.00
29 Lawrence Taylor/20 40.00 80.00
32 Merlin Olsen/25 30.00 60.00

2009 Playoff National Treasures Rookie Colossal Materials

STATED PRINT RUN 50 SER.#'d SETS
*PRIME/25: .6X TO 1.5X BASIC JSY/50
*BRAND LOGO/14-15: 1X TO 2.5X BASIC INSERTS
*JSY NMBR/25: .6X TO 1.5X BASIC JSY/50
*POSITION/25: .6X TO 1.5X BASIC JSY/50
*PRIME TAG/50: .6X TO 1.5X BASIC JSY/50
1 Mark Sanchez 2.00 5.00
2 Matthew Stafford 10.00 25.00
3 LeSean McCoy 5.00 12.00
4 Knowshon Moreno 2.00 5.00
5 Kenny Britt 3.00 8.00
6 Juaquin Iglesias 2.00 5.00
7 Josh Freeman 2.00 5.00
8 Jeremy Maclin 2.50 6.00
9 Javon Ringer 2.00 5.00
10 Jason Smith 2.00 5.00
11 Hakeem Nicks 2.50 6.00
12 Glen Coffee 2.00 5.00
13 Michael Crabtree 3.00 8.00
14 Aaron Curry 3.00 8.00
15 Andre Brown 2.50 6.00
16 Brandon Pettigrew 2.00 5.00
17 Brian Robiskie 2.00 5.00
18 Chris Wells 2.00 5.00
19 Darrius Heyward-Bey 3.00 8.00
20 Deon Butler 2.00 5.00
21 Derrick Williams 2.00 5.00
22 Donald Brown 2.00 5.00
23 Tyson Jackson 2.00 5.00
24 Stephen McGee 2.00 5.00
25 Shonn Greene 2.00 5.00
26 Rhett Bomar 2.00 5.00

27 Ramses Barden 2.00 5.00
28 Percy Harvin 2.00 5.00
29 Patrick Turner 2.00 5.00
30 Pat White 2.50 6.00
31 Nate Davis 2.00 5.00
32 Mohamed Massaquoi 2.00 5.00
33 Mike Wallace 3.00 8.00
34 Mike Thomas 2.00 5.00

2009 Playoff National Treasures Rookie Colossal Materials Signatures Jersey Numbers

JERSEY NUMBERS PRINT RUN 26-50
*BASE MAT SIG/50: .4X TO 1X JSY NUM
MATERIAL SIGN PRINT RUN 11-50
*POSITION/50: .4X TO 1X JSY NUM
1 Mark Sanchez/50 30.00 80.00
2 Matthew Stafford/50 30.00 80.00
3 LeSean McCoy/50 40.00 80.00
4 Knowshon Moreno/50 6.00 15.00
5 Kenny Britt/50 10.00 25.00
6 Juaquin Iglesias/50 6.00 15.00
7 Josh Freeman/50 6.00 15.00
8 Jeremy Maclin/50 8.00 20.00
9 Javon Ringer/50 6.00 15.00
10 Jason Smith/50 6.00 15.00
11 Hakeem Nicks/50 8.00 20.00
12 Glen Coffee/50 6.00 15.00
13 Michael Crabtree/50 10.00 25.00
14 Aaron Curry/50 10.00 25.00
15 Andre Brown/50 8.00 20.00
16 Brandon Pettigrew/50 6.00 15.00
17 Brian Robiskie/50 6.00 15.00
18 Chris Wells/50 6.00 15.00
19 Darrius Heyward-Bey/26 10.00 25.00
20 Deon Butler/50 6.00 15.00
21 Derrick Williams/50 6.00 15.00
22 Donald Brown/50 6.00 15.00
23 Tyson Jackson/32 6.00 15.00
24 Stephen McGee/50 6.00 15.00
25 Shonn Greene/50 6.00 15.00
26 Rhett Bomar/50 6.00 15.00
27 Ramses Barden/50 6.00 15.00
28 Percy Harvin/50 6.00 15.00
29 Patrick Turner/50 6.00 15.00
30 Pat White/50 8.00 20.00
31 Nate Davis/50 6.00 15.00
32 Mohamed Massaquoi/50 6.00 15.00
33 Mike Wallace/50 10.00 25.00
34 Mike Thomas/50 6.00 15.00

2009 Playoff National Treasures Rookie Signature Material Gold

*ROOKIE JSY AU: .5X TO 1.2X BASIC JSY AU
STATED PRINT RUN 25 SER.#'d SETS
EXCH EXPIRATION: 8/3/2011
115 Josh Freeman 12.00 30.00
119 LeSean McCoy 125.00 250.00
120 Mark Sanchez 100.00 200.00
121 Matthew Stafford 300.00 600.00

2009 Playoff National Treasures Signature Patches College

STATED PRINT RUN 2-86
1 Anthony Gonzalez/26 12.00 30.00
2 Bart Starr/27 90.00 150.00
4 Braylon Edwards/26 12.00 30.00
6 Brian Cushing/50 8.00 20.00
8 Chad Ochocinco/26 12.00 30.00
9 Cris Collinsworth/28 20.00 50.00
11 Drew Brees/26 50.00 100.00
12 Frank Gore/27 15.00 40.00
13 Fred Taylor/26 20.00 50.00
14 James Casey/35 12.00 30.00
15 Jason Witten/27 40.00 80.00
16 Jermichael Finley/26 12.00 30.00
17 Joe Theismann/25 20.00 50.00
18 Joseph Addai/26 12.00 30.00
20 Justin Fargas/31 12.00 30.00
22 Malcolm Jenkins/51 8.00 20.00
24 Marshawn Lynch/24 15.00 40.00
25 Paul Hornung/50 20.00 50.00
28 Reggie Wayne/25 25.00 50.00
29 Ronnie Brown/26 30.00 60.00
30 Shonn Greene/86 8.00 20.00
31 Troy Aikman/25 40.00 80.00
32 Wes Welker/26 30.00 60.00
33 Willie Parker/26 12.00 30.00
34 Yale Lary/26 15.00 40.00
36 Joe Montana/16 125.00 200.00
38 Joe Namath/26 60.00 120.00
39 Emmitt Smith/22 100.00 200.00

2009 Playoff National Treasures Signature Patches NFL

STATED PRINT RUN 22-106
1 Anthony Gonzalez/26 12.00 30.00
2 Bart Starr/27 125.00 200.00
3 Ben Roethlisberger/26 50.00 100.00
5 Brett Favre/25 125.00 250.00
8 Chad Ochocinco/27 12.00 30.00
9 Cris Collinsworth/54 12.00 30.00
10 Donald Driver/26 20.00 50.00
11 Drew Brees/27 60.00 100.00
12 Frank Gore/27 15.00 40.00
15 Jason Witten/27 30.00 60.00
18 Joseph Addai/26 15.00 40.00
20 Justin Fargas/26 12.00 30.00
23 Marion Barber/51 15.00 40.00
24 Marshawn Lynch/25 12.00 30.00
25 Paul Hornung/50 20.00 50.00
28 Reggie Wayne/26 20.00 50.00
29 Ronnie Brown/26 20.00 50.00
31 Troy Aikman/25 40.00 80.00
32 Wes Welker/26 30.00 60.00
33 Willie Parker/26 12.00 30.00
34 Yale Lary/26 15.00 40.00
35 Cliff Harris/106 15.00 40.00
36 Joe Montana/26 60.00 120.00
37 Joe Montana/26 60.00 120.00
38 Joe Namath/26 75.00 150.00
39 Emmitt Smith/22 100.00 200.00

2009 Playoff National Treasures Signature Patches NFL Logo

STATED PRINT RUN 1-45
6 Brian Cushing/35 15.00 40.00
21 LeSean McCoy/25 50.00 100.00
22 Malcolm Jenkins/35 15.00 30.00
30 Shonn Greene/45 20.00 50.00

2009 Playoff National Treasures Timeline Materials Player Name

STATED PRINT RUN 1-99
1 Dan Marino/25 25.00 60.00
2 Brett Favre/99 12.00 30.00
3 John Elway/99 12.00 30.00
5 Jim Brown/32 12.00 30.00
8 Peyton Manning/18 15.00 40.00
9 LaDainian Tomlinson/15 8.00 20.00
10 Troy Aikman/99 10.00 25.00
11 Joe Montana/99 25.00 60.00
12 Jerry Rice/25 20.00 50.00
14 Walter Payton/50 20.00 50.00
15 Reggie White/99 10.00 25.00
16 Adrian Peterson/28 8.00 20.00
17 Clinton Portis/99 4.00 10.00
19 Andre Johnson/20 6.00 15.00
20 Brian Westbrook/25 5.00 12.00

2009 Playoff National Treasures Timeline Materials Player Name Prime

NAME PRIME PRINT RUN 1-50
*TEAM PRIME/21-50: .4X TO 1X NAMES PRIME
2 Brett Favre/15 20.00 50.00
4 Barry Sanders/50 15.00 40.00
[illegible] 25.00 60.00
9 LaDainian Tomlinson/20 12.00 30.00
10 Troy Aikman/20 15.00 40.00
17 Clinton Portis/50 6.00 15.00
20 Brian Westbrook/50 6.00 15.00

2009 Playoff National Treasures Timeline Materials Team Name

*TEAM NAME/15-99: .4X TO 1X NAMES
TEAM NICKNAME PRINT RUN 1-99
1 Dan Marino/15 20.00 50.00
2 Brett Favre/99 12.00 30.00
3 John Elway/99 12.00 30.00
4 Barry Sanders/25 15.00 40.00
5 Jim Brown/32 12.00 30.00
8 Peyton Manning/25 20.00 50.00
10 Troy Aikman/99 10.00 25.00
11 Joe Montana/99 25.00 60.00
12 Jerry Rice/25 20.00 50.00
14 Walter Payton/50 20.00 50.00
15 Reggie White/99 10.00 25.00
16 Adrian Peterson/28 8.00 20.00
17 Clinton Portis/50 4.00 10.00
19 Andre Johnson/25 6.00 15.00
20 Brian Westbrook/25 5.00 12.00

2009 Playoff National Treasures Timeline Materials Signature Player Name

PLAYER NAME AU PRINT RUN 2-25
*TEAM NAME/15-25: .4X TO 1X SIG/15-25
*PLYR NAME PRIME/15: .5X TO 1.2X SIG/15
*TEAM NAME PRIME/25: .5X TO 1.2X SIG/25
1 Dan Marino/15 125.00 250.00
5 Jim Brown/25 50.00 100.00
10 Troy Aikman/25 50.00 100.00
12 Jerry Rice/15 100.00 200.00
13 Tim Brown/25 30.00 60.00

2010 Playoff National Treasures

STATED PRINT RUN 99 SER.#'d SETS
EXCH EXPIRATION: 9/2/2012
1 Chris Wells 2.00 5.00
2 Larry Fitzgerald 2.50 6.00
3 Steve Breaston 2.00 5.00
4 Tim Hightower 2.00 5.00
5 Curtis Lofton 2.00 5.00
6 Matt Ryan 2.50 6.00
7 Michael Turner 2.00 5.00
8 Roddy White 2.00 5.00
9 Anquan Boldin 2.00 5.00
10 Joe Flacco 2.50 6.00
11 Ray Lewis 3.00 8.00
12 Ray Rice 2.00 5.00
13 Todd Heap 2.00 5.00
14 Willis McGahee 2.00 5.00
15 Fred Jackson 2.50 6.00
16 Lee Evans 2.50 6.00
17 Roscoe Parrish 2.00 5.00
18 Ryan Fitzpatrick 2.00 5.00
19 Steve Johnson 2.50 6.00
20 DeAngelo Williams 2.00 5.00
21 Dwayne Jarrett 2.00 5.00
22 Jonathan Stewart 2.00 5.00
23 Steve Smith 2.50 6.00
24 Brian Urlacher 3.00 8.00
26 Devin Hester 2.50 6.00
26 Jay Cutler 2.00 5.00
27 Johnny Knox 2.00 5.00
28 Matt Forte 2.00 5.00
29 Carson Palmer 2.50 6.00
30 Cedric Benson 2.00 5.00
31 Chad Ochocinco 2.00 5.00
32 Terrell Owens 2.50 6.00
33 Ben Watson 2.00 5.00
34 Josh Cribbs 2.00 5.00
35 Mohamed Massaquoi 2.50 6.00
36 Peyton Hillis 2.50 6.00
37 DeMarcus Ware 2.50 6.00
38 Felix Jones 2.00 5.00
39 Jason Witten 2.50 6.00
40 Miles Austin 2.00 5.00
41 Tony Romo 2.50 6.00
42 Brandon Lloyd 2.00 5.00
43 Eddie Royal 2.00 5.00
44 Knowshon Moreno 2.00 5.00
45 Kyle Orton 2.00 5.00
46 Brandon Pettigrew 2.00 5.00
47 Calvin Johnson 3.00 8.00
48 Matthew Stafford 2.50 6.00
49 Nate Burleson 2.00 5.00
50 Aaron Rodgers 8.00 20.00
51 Charles Woodson 3.00 8.00
52 Clay Matthews 3.00 8.00
53 Donald Driver 2.50 6.00
54 Greg Jennings 2.00 5.00
55 Andre Johnson 2.50 6.00
56 Arian Foster 2.50 6.00
57 Kevin Walter 2.50 6.00
58 Matt Schaub 2.00 5.00
59 Owen Daniels 2.00 5.00
60 Austin Collie 2.00 5.00
61 Dallas Clark 2.00 5.00
62 Joseph Addai 2.00 5.00
63 Peyton Manning 8.00 20.00
64 Reggie Wayne 2.50 6.00
65 David Garrard 2.00 5.00
66 Marcedes Lewis 2.00 5.00
67 Maurice Jones-Drew 2.00 5.00
68 Mike Sims-Walker 2.00 5.00
69 Chris Chambers 2.00 5.00
70 Dwayne Bowe 2.50 6.00
71 Jamaal Charles 2.50 6.00
72 Matt Cassel 2.00 5.00
73 Thomas Jones 2.00 5.00
74 Anthony Fasano 2.00 5.00
75 Brandon Marshall 2.50 6.00
76 Brian Hartline 2.50 6.00
77 Chad Henne 2.50 6.00
78 Ronnie Brown 2.00 5.00
79 Adrian Peterson 8.00 20.00
80 Bernard Berrian 2.00 5.00
81 Brett Favre 12.50 25.00
82 Percy Harvin 2.00 5.00
83 Randy Moss 2.50 6.00
84 Visanthe Shiancoe 2.50 6.00
85 BenJarvus Green-Ellis 3.00 8.00
86 Brandon Meriweather 2.00 5.00
87 Deion Branch 2.00 5.00
88 Tom Brady 6.00 15.00
89 Wes Welker 2.50 6.00
90 Devery Henderson 2.00 5.00
91 Drew Brees 3.00 8.00
92 Marques Colston 2.00 5.00
93 Pierre Thomas 2.00 5.00
94 Reggie Bush 2.00 5.00
95 Robert Meachem 2.00 5.00
96 Ahmad Bradshaw 2.00 5.00
97 Brandon Jacobs 2.00 5.00
98 Eli Manning 2.50 6.00
99 Hakeem Nicks 2.00 5.00
100 Steve Smith USC 2.00 5.00
101 Braylon Edwards 2.00 5.00
102 Darrelle Revis 2.00 5.00
103 LaDainian Tomlinson 3.00 8.00
104 Mark Sanchez 2.00 5.00
105 Shonn Greene 2.00 5.00
106 Darren McFadden 2.00 5.00
107 Darrius Heyward-Bey 2.50 6.00
108 Jason Campbell 2.00 5.00
109 Louis Murphy 2.00 5.00
110 Zach Miller 2.00 5.00
111 DeSean Jackson 2.50 6.00
112 Jeremy Maclin 2.00 5.00
113 Kevin Kolb 2.00 5.00
114 LeSean McCoy 3.00 8.00
115 Michael Vick 2.50 6.00
116 Ben Roethlisberger 3.00 8.00
117 Heath Miller 2.00 5.00
118 Hines Ward 2.50 6.00
119 Mike Wallace 2.00 5.00
120 Rashard Mendenhall 2.00 5.00
121 Troy Polamalu 3.00 8.00
122 Antonio Gates 2.50 6.00
123 Darren Sproles 2.50 6.00
124 Malcom Floyd 2.00 5.00
125 Philip Rivers 3.00 8.00
126 Frank Gore 2.50 6.00
127 Michael Crabtree 2.00 5.00
128 Patrick Willis 2.50 6.00
129 Vernon Davis 2.00 5.00
130 John Carlson 2.00 5.00
131 Marshawn Lynch 2.50 6.00
132 Matt Hasselbeck 2.00 5.00
133 Mike Williams USC 2.00 5.00
134 Danny Amendola 3.00 8.00
135 James Laurinaitis 2.50 6.00
136 Brandon Gibson 2.00 5.00
137 Steven Jackson 2.00 5.00
138 Cadillac Williams 2.00 5.00
139 Josh Freeman 2.50 6.00
140 Kellen Winslow Jr. 2.00 5.00
141 Ronde Barber 2.00 5.00
142 Bo Scaife 2.00 5.00
143 Chris Johnson 2.00 5.00
144 Kenny Britt 2.00 5.00
145 Nate Washington 2.00 5.00
146 Vince Young 2.00 5.00
147 Chris Cooley 2.00 5.00
148 Clinton Portis 2.00 5.00
149 Donovan McNabb 2.50 6.00
150 Santana Moss 2.50 6.00
151 Deion Sanders 3.00 8.00
152 Thurman Thomas 3.00 8.00
153 Tom Landry 5.00 12.00
154 Walter Payton 6.00 15.00
155 Andre Reed 3.00 8.00
156 Frank Gifford 3.00 8.00
157 Jack Lambert 4.00 10.00
158 Jan Stenerud 2.50 6.00
159 Joe Greene 4.00 10.00
160 Joe Klecko 2.50 6.00
161 Kellen Winslow 3.00 8.00
162 Lem Barney 2.50 6.00
163 Leroy Kelly 3.00 8.00
164 Mark Duper 2.50 6.00
165 Paul Krause 2.50 6.00
166 Chuck Bednarik 3.00 8.00
167 Billy Howton 2.50 6.00
168 Bobby Bell 2.50 6.00
169 Boyd Dowler 2.50 6.00
170 Marshall Faulk 3.00 8.00
171 Dante Lavelli 2.50 6.00
172 Ottis Anderson 2.50 6.00
173 Don Perkins 2.50 6.00
174 Doug Williams 3.00 8.00
175 Dub Jones 2.50 6.00
176 Everson Walls 2.50 6.00
177 Floyd Little 2.50 6.00
178 Fred Williamson 2.50 6.00
179 Gary Collins 2.50 6.00
180 Harlon Hill 2.50 6.00
181 Jim Taylor 4.00 10.00
182 Jimmy Orr 2.50 6.00
183 Johnny Morris 2.50 6.00
184 Lee Roy Jordan 3.00 8.00
185 Lydell Mitchell 2.50 6.00
186 Mel Renfro 2.50 6.00
187 Mike Curtis 2.50 6.00
188 Pete Retzlaff 2.50 6.00
189 Rayfield Wright 2.50 6.00
190 Rick Casares 2.50 6.00
191 Russ Grimm 2.50 6.00
192 Willie Davis 2.50 6.00
193 Cliff Harris 2.50 6.00
194 Joe Namath 5.00 12.00
195 Ed McCaffrey 2.50 6.00
196 Archie Manning 3.00 8.00
197 Art Monk 4.00 10.00
198 Jack Youngblood 2.50 6.00
199 Roosevelt Grier 2.50 6.00
200 Vince Lombardi 6.00 15.00
201 Aaron Hernandez AU RC 12.00 30.00
202 Andrew Quarless AU RC 5.00 12.00
203 Anthony Dixon AU RC 5.00 12.00
204 Anthony McCoy AU RC 5.00 12.00
205 Antonio Brown AU RC 200.00 400.00
206 Blair White AU RC 5.00 12.00
207 Brandon Banks AU RC 10.00 25.00
208 Brandon Graham AU RC 6.00 15.00
209 Brandon Spikes AU RC 5.00 12.00
210 Brody Eldridge AU RC 8.00 20.00
211 Bryan Bulaga AU RC 5.00 12.00
212 Carlos Dunlap AU RC 5.00 12.00
213 Carlton Mitchell AU RC 5.00 12.00
214 Chris Cook AU RC 5.00 12.00
215 Chris Ivory AU RC 12.00 30.00
216 Chris McGaha AU RC 5.00 12.00
217 Clay Harbor AU RC 6.00 15.00
218 Corey Wootton AU RC 5.00 12.00
219 Dan LeFevour AU RC 5.00 12.00
220 Dan Williams AU RC 5.00 12.00
221 Danario Alexander AU RC 12.00 30.00
222 David Gettis AU RC 5.00 12.00
223 David Nelson AU RC 8.00 20.00
224 David Reed AU RC 5.00 12.00
225 Deji Karim AU RC 6.00 15.00
226 Dennis Pitta AU RC 5.00 12.00
227 Derrick Morgan AU RC 5.00 12.00
228 Devin McCourty AU RC 10.00 25.00
229 Dezmon Briscoe AU RC 5.00 12.00
230 Dominique Curry AU RC 6.00 15.00
231 Dominique Franks AU RC 5.00 12.00
232 Donald Jones AU RC 10.00 25.00
233 Dorin Dickerson AU RC 5.00 12.00
234 Duke Calhoun AU RC 6.00 15.00
235 Earl Thomas AU RC 20.00 40.00
236 Ed Dickson AU RC 5.00 12.00
237 Ed Wang AU RC 8.00 20.00
238 Everson Griffen AU RC 5.00 12.00
239 Fendi Onobun AU RC 6.00 15.00
240 Garrett Graham AU RC 5.00 12.00
241 Jacoby Ford AU RC 5.00 12.00
242 James Starks AU RC 6.00 15.00
243 Jared Odrick AU RC 6.00 15.00
244 Jason Pierre-Paul AU RC 8.00 20.00
245 Jason Worilds AU RC 5.00 12.00
246 Javier Arenas AU RC 10.00 25.00
247 Jeremy Horne AU RC 6.00 15.00
248 Jeremy Williams AU RC 5.00 12.00
249 Jerry Hughes AU RC 5.00 12.00
250 Jim Dray AU RC 6.00 15.00
251 Jimmy Graham AU RC 30.00 60.00
252 Joe Haden AU RC 10.00 25.00
253 Joe Webb AU RC 5.00 12.00
254 John Conner AU RC 5.00 12.00
255 John Skelton AU RC 12.00 30.00
256 Joique Bell AU RC 5.00 12.00
257 Kareem Jackson AU RC 5.00 12.00
258 Keiland Williams AU RC 6.00 15.00
259 Keith Toston AU RC 8.00 20.00
260 Kerry Meier AU RC 6.00 15.00
261 Koa Misi AU RC 6.00 15.00
262 Kyle Williams AU RC 8.00 20.00
263 Sergio Kindle AU RC 5.00 12.00
264 Lamarr Houston AU RC 6.00 15.00
265 LeGarrette Blount AU RC 25.00 60.00
266 Lonyae Miller AU RC 6.00 15.00
267 Marc Mariani AU RC 8.00 20.00
268 Marlon Moore AU RC 8.00 20.00
269 Max Hall AU RC 8.00 20.00
270 Max Komar AU RC 8.00 20.00
271 M.Hoomanawanui AU RC 8.00 20.00
272 Mickey Shuler AU RC 8.00 20.00
273 Morgan Burnett AU RC 6.00 15.00
274 Nate Allen AU RC 8.00 20.00
275 Nate Byham AU RC 5.00 12.00
276 NaVorro Bowman AU RC 25.00 60.00
277 Patrick Robinson AU RC 6.00 15.00
278 Perrish Cox AU RC 6.00 15.00
279 Preston Parker AU RC 6.00 15.00
280 Ricky Sapp AU RC 5.00 12.00
281 Riley Cooper AU RC 12.50 25.00
282 Roberto Wallace AU RC 6.00 15.00
283 Russell Okung AU RC 10.00 25.00
284 Rusty Smith AU RC 8.00 20.00
285 Michael Palmer AU RC 6.00 15.00
286 Sean Lee AU RC 20.00 40.00
287 S.Weatherspoon AU RC 5.00 12.00
288 Chris Gronkowski AU RC 8.00 20.00
289 Seyi Ajirotutu AU RC 5.00 12.00
290 Shay Hodge AU RC 8.00 20.00
291 Stephen Williams AU RC 6.00 15.00
292 T.J. Ward AU RC 6.00 15.00
293 Taylor Mays AU RC 5.00 12.00
294 Thaddeus Lewis AU RC 12.50 25.00
295 Tony Moeaki AU RC 6.00 15.00
296 Tony Pike AU RC 5.00 12.00
297 Trent Williams AU RC 6.00 15.00
298 Tyson Alualu AU RC 5.00 12.00
299 Victor Cruz AU RC 10.00 25.00
300 Zac Robinson AU RC 6.00 15.00
301 A.Roberts JSY AU RC 12.00 30.00
302 A.Edwards JSY AU RC 15.00 40.00
303 A.Benn JSY AU RC 12.00 30.00
304 Ben Tate JSY AU RC 12.00 30.00
305 B.LaFell JSY AU RC 30.00 60.00
306 C.J. Spiller JSY AU RC 30.00 80.00
307 Colt McCoy JSY AU RC 25.00 60.00
308 D.Williams JSY AU RC 12.00 30.00
309 D.Thomas JSY AU RC 75.00 150.00
310 D.McCluster JSY AU RC EXCH 15.00 40.00
311 Dez Bryant JSY AU RC 175.00 300.00
312 E.Sanders JSY AU RC 20.00 50.00
313 Eric Berry JSY AU RC 20.00 50.00
314 Eric Decker JSY AU RC 15.00 40.00
315 Gerald McCoy JSY AU RC 12.00 30.00
316 Golden Tate JSY AU RC 30.00 60.00
317 Jahvid Best JSY AU RC 15.00 40.00
318 J.Gresham JSY AU RC 12.00 30.00
319 Jimmy Clausen JSY AU RC 12.00 30.00
320 Joe McKnight JSY AU RC 12.00 30.00
321 Jonathan Dwyer JSY AU RC 15.00 40.00
322 Jordan Shipley JSY AU RC 12.00 30.00
323 Marcus Easley JSY AU RC 12.00 30.00
324 Mardy Gilyard JSY AU RC 12.00 30.00
325 Mike Kafka JSY AU RC 15.00 40.00
326 Mike Williams JSY AU RC 12.00 30.00
327 M.Hardesty JSY AU RC 10.00 25.00
328 N.Suh JSY AU RC 50.00 100.00
329 R.Gronkowski JSY AU RC 100.00 200.00
330 R.McClain JSY AU RC 15.00 40.00
331 R.Mathews JSY AU RC 12.00 30.00
332 Sam Bradford JSY AU RC 100.00 200.00
333 T.Price JSY AU RC EXCH 20.00 50.00
334 Tim Tebow JSY AU RC 125.00 250.00
335 Toby Gerhart JSY AU RC 12.00 30.00

2010 Playoff National Treasures Century Silver

*1-150 VETS: .8X TO 2X BASIC CARDS
*151-200 LEGENDS: .6X TO 1.5X BASIC CARDS
STATED PRINT RUN 25 SER.#'d SETS

2010 Playoff National Treasures Rookie Signature Material Gold

*GOLD/25: .6X TO 1.5X BASE JSY AU/99
GOLD JSY AU PRINT RUN 25
309 Demaryius Thomas 150.00 250.00
311 Dez Bryant 200.00 400.00
329 Rob Gronkowski 200.00 400.00
332 Sam Bradford 100.00 200.00
334 Tim Tebow 250.00 500.00

2010 Playoff National Treasures Century Gold Signature

1-200 GOLD AU PRINT RUN 5-25
*201-300 ROOK/25: .6X TO 1.5X BASE RC AU/99
201-300 ROOKIE GOLD AU PRINT RUN 25
22 Jonathan Stewart/25 12.00 30.00
34 Josh Cribbs/25 12.00 30.00
50 Aaron Rodgers/21 175.00 300.00
60 Austin Collie/25 15.00 40.00
63 Peyton Manning/25 125.00 200.00
64 Reggie Wayne/17 15.00 40.00
78 Ronnie Brown/25 12.00 30.00
109 Louis Murphy/25 10.00 25.00
116 Ben Roethlisberger/18 60.00 120.00
117 Heath Miller/25 12.00 30.00
120 Rashard Mendenhall/25 12.00 30.00
127 Michael Crabtree/25 15.00 40.00
138 Cadillac Williams/25 10.00 25.00
155 Andre Reed/25 10.00 25.00
158 Jan Stenerud/25 10.00 25.00
160 Joe Klecko/25 10.00 25.00
161 Kellen Winslow/25 10.00 25.00
162 Lem Barney/25 10.00 25.00
163 Leroy Kelly/25 12.00 30.00
164 Mark Duper/25 10.00 25.00
166 Chuck Bednarik/25 12.00 30.00
167 Billy Howton/25 12.00 30.00
168 Bobby Bell/25 15.00 40.00
169 Boyd Dowler/25 12.00 30.00
172 Ottis Anderson/25 12.00 30.00
173 Don Perkins/25 12.00 30.00
175 Dub Jones/25 10.00 25.00
176 Everson Walls/25 10.00 25.00
179 Gary Collins/25 10.00 25.00
180 Harlon Hill/25 15.00 40.00
182 Jimmy Orr/25 10.00 25.00
183 Johnny Morris/25 10.00 25.00
185 Lydell Mitchell/25 12.00 30.00
186 Mel Renfro/25 12.00 30.00
187 Mike Curtis/25 10.00 25.00
188 Pete Retzlaff/25 10.00 25.00
190 Rick Casares/25 12.00 30.00
192 Willie Davis/25 12.00 30.00
196 Archie Manning/25 15.00 40.00
198 Jack Youngblood/25 10.00 25.00
251 Jimmy Graham/25 60.00 125.00
299 Victor Cruz/25 15.00 40.00

2010 Playoff National Treasures Century Material

STATED PRINT RUN 1-99
1 Chris Wells/99 2.50 6.00
6 Matt Ryan/99 3.00 8.00
7 Michael Turner/99 2.50 6.00
8 Roddy White/25 4.00 10.00
11 Ray Lewis/25 6.00 15.00
12 Ray Rice/25 4.00 10.00
16 Lee Evans/99 3.00 8.00
20 DeAngelo Williams/25 4.00 10.00
23 Steve Smith/30 4.00 10.00
24 Brian Urlacher/25 6.00 15.00
26 Jay Cutler/25 4.00 10.00
26 Devin Hester/99 3.00 8.00
28 Matt Forte/25 4.00 10.00
29 Carson Palmer/25 5.00 12.00
31 Chad Ochocinco/99 2.50 6.00
37 DeMarcus Ware/99 3.00 8.00
38 Felix Jones/25 4.00 10.00
39 Jason Witten/99 3.00 8.00
40 Miles Austin/25 4.00 10.00
41 Tony Romo/25 5.00 12.00
45 Kyle Orton/99 2.50 6.00
47 Calvin Johnson/99 4.00 10.00
48 Matthew Stafford/99 3.00 8.00
50 Aaron Rodgers/25 12.00 30.00
53 Donald Driver/35 4.00 10.00
54 Greg Jennings/25 4.00 10.00
55 Andre Johnson/99 3.00 8.00
58 Matt Schaub/99 2.50 6.00
61 Dallas Clark/99 2.50 6.00
63 Peyton Manning/25 15.00 40.00
64 Reggie Wayne/99 3.00 8.00
65 David Garrard/99 2.50 6.00
70 Dwayne Bowe/99 3.00 8.00
72 Matt Cassel/99 2.50 6.00
78 Ronnie Brown/29 4.00 10.00
79 Adrian Peterson/28 6.00 15.00
81 Brett Favre/25 12.00 30.00
82 Percy Harvin/99 2.50 6.00
88 Tom Brady/49 12.00 30.00
90 Devery Henderson/99 2.50 6.00
91 Drew Brees/99 4.00 10.00
94 Reggie Bush/25 4.00 10.00
96 Ahmad Bradshaw/99 2.50 6.00
97 Brandon Jacobs/49 3.00 8.00
98 Eli Manning/99 3.00 8.00
100 Steve Smith USC/99 2.50 6.00
101 Braylon Edwards/99 2.50 6.00
103 LaDainian Tomlinson/99 4.00 10.00
104 Mark Sanchez/99 2.50 6.00
105 Shonn Greene/99 2.50 6.00
106 Darren McFadden/99 2.50 6.00
115 Michael Vick/99 8.00 20.00
120 Rashard Mendenhall/99 2.50 6.00
121 Troy Polamalu/83 4.00 10.00
122 Antonio Gates/99 3.00 8.00
125 Philip Rivers/49 5.00 12.00
126 Frank Gore/99 3.00 8.00
127 Michael Crabtree/89 2.50 6.00
132 Matt Hasselbeck/99 2.50 6.00
137 Steven Jackson/99 2.50 6.00
138 Cadillac Williams/99 2.50 6.00
142 Bo Scaife/99 2.50 6.00
147 Chris Cooley/99 2.50 6.00
148 Clinton Portis/99 2.50 6.00
149 Donovan McNabb/99 4.00 10.00
150 Santana Moss/99 3.00 8.00
151 Deion Sanders/99 6.00 15.00
152 Thurman Thomas/99 4.00 10.00
153 Tom Landry/99 12.00 30.00
154 Walter Payton/99 12.00 30.00
155 Andre Reed/99 4.00 10.00
157 Jack Lambert/25 8.00 20.00
170 Marshall Faulk/99 4.00 10.00
194 Joe Namath/25 10.00 25.00
195 Ed McCaffrey/70 3.00 8.00
196 Archie Manning/99 4.00 10.00
198 Jack Youngblood/25 5.00 12.00
199 Roosevelt Grier/15 5.00 12.00

2010 Playoff National Treasures Century Material Prime

STATED PRINT RUN 1-50
6 Matt Ryan/50 5.00 12.00
7 Michael Turner/50 4.00 10.00
8 Roddy White/50 4.00 10.00
10 Joe Flacco/40 5.00 12.00
11 Ray Lewis/50 6.00 15.00
12 Ray Rice/25 5.00 12.00
13 Todd Heap/50 4.00 10.00
16 Lee Evans/50 5.00 12.00
20 DeAngelo Williams/25 5.00 12.00
24 Brian Urlacher/50 6.00 15.00
26 Devin Hester/50 5.00 12.00
26 Jay Cutler/50 4.00 10.00
28 Matt Forte/50 4.00 10.00
29 Carson Palmer/50 5.00 12.00
30 Cedric Benson/50 4.00 10.00
31 Chad Ochocinco/50 4.00 10.00
37 DeMarcus Ware/50 5.00 12.00
38 Felix Jones/50 4.00 10.00
39 Jason Witten/50 5.00 12.00
40 Miles Austin/50 4.00 10.00
41 Tony Romo/50 5.00 12.00
44 Knowshon Moreno/50 4.00 10.00
45 Kyle Orton/50 4.00 10.00
47 Calvin Johnson/50 6.00 15.00
50 Aaron Rodgers/50 20.00 50.00
51 Charles Woodson/15 8.00 20.00
53 Donald Driver/35 5.00 12.00
58 Matt Schaub/50 4.00 10.00
61 Dallas Clark/50 4.00 10.00
62 Joseph Addai/50 4.00 10.00
64 Reggie Wayne/50 5.00 12.00
65 David Garrard/50 4.00 10.00
67 Maurice Jones-Drew/50 4.00 10.00
70 Dwayne Bowe/50 5.00 12.00
71 Jamaal Charles/50 5.00 12.00
78 Ronnie Brown/23 5.00 12.00
79 Adrian Peterson/50 6.00 15.00
80 Bernard Berrian/50 4.00 10.00
82 Percy Harvin/50 4.00 10.00
83 Randy Moss/50 5.00 12.00
84 Visanthe Shiancoe/50 5.00 12.00
88 Tom Brady/50 15.00 40.00
89 Wes Welker/35 5.00 12.00
90 Devery Henderson/50 4.00 10.00
91 Drew Brees/50 6.00 15.00
92 Marques Colston/50 4.00 10.00
94 Reggie Bush/50 4.00 10.00
96 Ahmad Bradshaw/50 4.00 10.00
97 Brandon Jacobs/50 4.00 10.00
98 Eli Manning/50 5.00 12.00
100 Steve Smith USC/30 4.00 10.00
101 Braylon Edwards/50 4.00 10.00
102 Darrelle Revis/50 4.00 10.00
103 LaDainian Tomlinson/50 6.00 15.00
104 Mark Sanchez/50 4.00 10.00
105 Shonn Greene/50 4.00 10.00
106 Darren McFadden/50 4.00 10.00
111 DeSean Jackson/50 5.00 12.00
112 Jeremy Maclin/50 4.00 10.00
113 Kevin Kolb/50 4.00 10.00
114 LeSean McCoy/50 6.00 15.00
118 Hines Ward/50 8.00 20.00
120 Rashard Mendenhall/30 4.00 10.00
121 Troy Polamalu/50 6.00 15.00
122 Antonio Gates/50 5.00 12.00
123 Darren Sproles/50 5.00 12.00
125 Philip Rivers/50 6.00 15.00
128 Patrick Willis/50 5.00 12.00
129 Vernon Davis/50 4.00 10.00
132 Matt Hasselbeck/50 4.00 10.00
137 Steven Jackson/50 4.00 10.00
138 Cadillac Williams/25 5.00 12.00
143 Chris Johnson/50 4.00 10.00
144 Kenny Britt/50 4.00 10.00
147 Chris Cooley/50 4.00 10.00
148 Clinton Portis/50 4.00 10.00
149 Donovan McNabb/15 6.00 15.00
150 Santana Moss/50 5.00 12.00
151 Deion Sanders/50 10.00 25.00
152 Thurman Thomas/50 6.00 15.00
154 Walter Payton/50 20.00 50.00
157 Jack Lambert/50 8.00 20.00
158 Jan Stenerud/50 5.00 12.00
159 Joe Greene/50 8.00 20.00
164 Mark Duper/50 5.00 12.00
170 Marshall Faulk/50 6.00 15.00
194 Joe Namath/50 12.00 30.00
195 Ed McCaffrey/50 5.00 12.00

2010 Playoff National Treasures Century Material Signature Prime

PRIME JSY AU PRINT RUN 1-25
1 Chris Wells/20 12.00 30.00
7 Michael Turner/20 12.00 30.00
20 DeAngelo Williams/20 12.00 30.00
26 Jay Cutler/20 30.00 60.00
37 DeMarcus Ware/20 15.00 40.00
53 Donald Driver/20 30.00 80.00
56 Arian Foster/20 40.00 80.00
64 Reggie Wayne/20 15.00 40.00
67 Maurice Jones-Drew/20 15.00 40.00
80 Bernard Berrian/20 15.00 40.00
84 Visanthe Shiancoe/20
97 Brandon Jacobs/20 12.00 30.00
98 Eli Manning/20 40.00 80.00
101 Braylon Edwards/20 12.00 30.00
104 Mark Sanchez/20 15.00 40.00
105 Shonn Greene/20 15.00 40.00
112 Jeremy Maclin/20 15.00 40.00
113 Kevin Kolb/20 15.00 40.00
114 LeSean McCoy/20 20.00 50.00
120 Rashard Mendenhall/20 15.00 40.00
123 Darren Sproles/20 12.00 30.00
144 Kenny Britt/20 15.00 40.00
151 Deion Sanders/20 50.00 100.00
152 Thurman Thomas/20 20.00 50.00
157 Jack Lambert/20 50.00 100.00
158 Jan Stenerud/20 15.00 40.00
159 Joe Greene/20 30.00 60.00
164 Mark Duper/20 15.00 40.00
170 Marshall Faulk/25 50.00 100.00
194 Joe Namath/20 150.00 250.00
195 Ed McCaffrey/20 20.00 50.00

2010 Playoff National Treasures Colossal Materials

STATED PRINT RUN 8-50
1 Aaron Rodgers/15 25.00 50.00
2 Adrian Peterson/50 6.00 15.00
3 Andre Johnson/50 5.00 12.00
4 Antonio Gates/50 5.00 12.00
5 Arian Foster/50 8.00 20.00
7 Brandon Jacobs/50 4.00 10.00
8 Braylon Edwards/50 4.00 10.00
9 Brent Celek/50 4.00 10.00
10 Brett Favre/50 12.00 30.00
11 Brian Urlacher/50 6.00 15.00
12 Calvin Johnson/50 6.00 15.00
14 Carson Palmer/50 5.00 12.00
15 Cedric Benson/50 4.00 10.00
17 Chris Cooley/50 4.00 10.00
18 Chris Johnson/50 4.00 10.00
19 Clinton Portis/50 4.00 10.00
20 Dallas Clark/50 4.00 10.00
21 Darrelle Revis/40 4.00 10.00
22 Darren Sproles/50 5.00 12.00
23 Darren McFadden/50 4.00 10.00
24 DeAngelo Williams/50 4.00 10.00
25 DeSean Jackson/50 5.00 12.00
27 Donovan McNabb/50 5.00 12.00
28 Eli Manning/50 5.00 12.00
29 Felix Jones/50 4.00 10.00
30 Frank Gore/50 5.00 12.00
31 Devin Hester/50 5.00 12.00
32 Jamaal Charles/50 5.00 12.00
33 Heath Miller/15 5.00 12.00
34 Jason Witten/50 5.00 12.00
35 Joe Flacco/25 6.00 15.00
36 Knowshon Moreno/50 4.00 10.00
37 LaDainian Tomlinson/50 6.00 15.00
38 Lee Evans/50 5.00 12.00
39 Mark Sanchez/50 4.00 10.00
40 Matt Forte/50 4.00 10.00
41 Matt Ryan/50 5.00 12.00
42 Matt Schaub/50 4.00 10.00
43 Percy Harvin/50 4.00 10.00
44 Peyton Manning/50 12.00 30.00
45 Philip Rivers/50 6.00 15.00
46 Randy Moss/50 5.00 12.00
48 Ray Lewis/50 8.00 20.00
49 Ray Rice/50 4.00 10.00
50 Reggie Bush/50 4.00 10.00
51 Reggie Wayne/50 5.00 12.00
52 Roddy White/50 4.00 10.00
54 Shonn Greene/50 4.00 10.00
55 Steven Jackson/50 4.00 10.00
56 Tom Brady/50 12.00 30.00
57 Tony Romo/50 5.00 12.00
60 Wes Welker/50 5.00 12.00

2010 Playoff National Treasures Colossal Materials Jersey Numbers Prime

*JSY # PRIME/15-25: .4X TO 1X PRIME/15-25
STATED PRINT RUN 4-25
5 Arian Foster/25 12.00 30.00

2010 Playoff National Treasures Colossal Materials Position Prime

*POS.PRIME/15-25: .4X TO 1X PRIME/15-25
STATED PRINT RUN 5-25
5 Arian Foster/25 12.00 30.00

2010 Playoff National Treasures Colossal Materials Prime

STATED PRINT RUN 2-25
2 Adrian Peterson/25 10.00 25.00
4 Antonio Gates/25 8.00 20.00
7 Brandon Jacobs/25 6.00 15.00
8 Braylon Edwards/15 6.00 15.00
9 Brent Celek/24 6.00 15.00
11 Brian Urlacher/25 10.00 25.00
12 Calvin Johnson/25 10.00 25.00
14 Carson Palmer/25 8.00 20.00
15 Cedric Benson/15 6.00 15.00
16 Chad Ochocinco/25 6.00 15.00
17 Chris Cooley/25 6.00 15.00
18 Chris Johnson/25 6.00 15.00
19 Clinton Portis/25 6.00 15.00
21 Darrelle Revis/25 6.00 15.00
22 Darren Sproles/25 8.00 20.00
24 DeAngelo Williams/25 6.00 15.00
25 DeSean Jackson/25 8.00 20.00
26 Devery Henderson/25 6.00 15.00
28 Eli Manning/25 8.00 20.00
29 Felix Jones/25 6.00 15.00
30 Frank Gore/25 8.00 20.00
31 Devin Hester/25 8.00 20.00
32 Jamaal Charles/25 8.00 20.00
34 Jason Witten/25 8.00 20.00
36 Knowshon Moreno/15 6.00 15.00
37 LaDainian Tomlinson/25 10.00 25.00
38 Lee Evans/25 8.00 20.00
39 Mark Sanchez/15 6.00 15.00
40 Matt Forte/25 6.00 15.00
42 Matt Schaub/25 6.00 15.00
46 Randy Moss/15 8.00 20.00
48 Ray Lewis/25 15.00 40.00
49 Ray Rice/15 6.00 15.00
50 Reggie Bush/25 6.00 15.00
54 Shonn Greene/15 6.00 15.00
55 Steven Jackson/25 6.00 15.00
56 Tom Brady/25 20.00 50.00
57 Tony Romo/25 8.00 20.00
59 Vernon Davis/25 6.00 15.00
60 Wes Welker/25 8.00 20.00

2010 Playoff National Treasures Colossal Materials Signature

STATED PRINT RUN 1-25
9 Brent Celek/25 15.00 40.00

2010 Playoff National Treasures Emblems of the Hall

STATED PRINT RUN 99 SER.#'d SETS
1 Terry Bradshaw 5.00 12.00
2 Johnny Unitas 6.00 15.00
3 Bob Hayes 4.00 10.00
4 Mike Singletary 4.00 10.00
5 Michael Irvin 4.00 10.00
6 Earl Campbell 4.00 10.00
7 Bruce Smith 3.00 8.00
8 Barry Sanders 6.00 15.00
9 Bart Starr 6.00 15.00
10 Dan Fouts 3.00 0.00
12 Emmitt Smith 8.00 20.00
14 Jerry Rice 6.00 15.00
15 Jim Brown 5.00 12.00
16 Joe Montana 12.00 30.00
17 Joe Namath 5.00 12.00
18 Joe Perry 3.00 8.00
19 John Elway 6.00 15.00
20 Rickey Jackson 2.50 6.00

2010 Playoff National Treasures Emblems of the Hall Materials

STATED PRINT RUN 47-99
*PRIME/23-25: .8X TO 2X BASE JSY/55-99
1 Terry Bradshaw/99 8.00 20.00
2 Johnny Unitas/99 10.00 25.00
3 Bob Hayes/99 8.00 20.00
4 Mike Singletary/99 6.00 15.00
5 Michael Irvin/99 6.00 15.00
6 Earl Campbell/47 8.00 20.00
7 Bruce Smith/55 5.00 12.00
8 Barry Sanders/99 10.00 25.00
9 Bart Starr/99 10.00 25.00
10 Dan Fouts/99 5.00 12.00
12 Emmitt Smith/99 12.00 30.00
14 Jerry Rice/99 10.00 25.00
15 Jim Brown/99 8.00 20.00
16 Joe Montana/99 15.00 40.00
17 Joe Namath/99 8.00 20.00
18 Joe Perry/99 5.00 12.00
19 John Elway/99 10.00 25.00
20 Rickey Jackson/99 6.00 15.00

2010 Playoff National Treasures Emblems of the Hall Signature Materials

STATED PRINT RUN 10-25
4 Mike Singletary/20 20.00 50.00
5 Michael Irvin/25 40.00 80.00
6 Earl Campbell/25 40.00 80.00
7 Bruce Smith/25 30.00 60.00
8 Barry Sanders/25 100.00 200.00
9 Bart Starr/25 100.00 200.00
10 Dan Fouts/25 50.00 100.00
12 Emmitt Smith/10
14 Jerry Rice/12
15 Jim Brown/25 50.00 100.00
16 Joe Montana/25 125.00 200.00
17 Joe Namath/25 60.00 120.00
18 Joe Perry/25 15.00 40.00
19 John Elway/25 75.00 150.00
20 Rickey Jackson/25 20.00 50.00

2010 Playoff National Treasures Emblems of the Hall Signature Materials Prime

*PRIME/15: .5X TO 1.2X BASIC JSY/20-25
PRIME STATED PRINT RUN 2-15
12 Emmitt Smith/15 150.00 250.00

2010 Playoff National Treasures Emblems of the Hall Signatures

STATED PRINT RUN 5-50
5 Michael Irvin/18 30.00 60.00
6 Earl Campbell/50 30.00 60.00
7 Bruce Smith/50 20.00 50.00
8 Barry Sanders/50 75.00 135.00
9 Bart Starr/50 75.00 150.00
10 Dan Fouts/99 25.00 60.00
15 Jim Brown/39 40.00 80.00
16 Joe Montana/16 100.00 175.00
18 Joe Perry/50 12.00 30.00
20 Rickey Jackson/50 15.00 40.00

2010 Playoff National Treasures NFL Gear Prime

PRIME PRINT RUN 49 SER.#'d SETS
*BASE NFL GEAR/25: .4X TO 1X PRIME/49
*LAUNDRY TAG/15: .6X TO 1.5X PRIME/49
*TRIPLE NFL GEAR/25: .4X TO 1X PRIME/49
*TRIPLE GEAR PRIME/49: .4X TO 1X PRIME/49
1 Tim Tebow 10.00 25.00
2 Sam Bradford 4.00 10.00
3 C.J. Spiller 3.00 8.00
4 Dez Bryant 12.00 30.00
5 Eric Berry 5.00 12.00
6 Jahvid Best 3.00 8.00
7 Jordan Shipley 3.00 8.00
8 Jimmy Clausen 3.00 8.00
9 Joe McKnight 3.00 8.00
10 Andre Roberts 4.00 10.00
11 Arrelious Benn 3.00 8.00
12 Brandon LaFell 5.00 12.00
13 Ryan Mathews 3.00 8.00
14 Rolando McClain 3.00 8.00
15 Mike Williams 3.00 8.00
16 Montario Hardesty 3.00 8.00
17 Jonathan Dwyer 3.00 8.00
18 Mardy Gilyard 3.00 8.00
19 Eric Decker 4.00 10.00
20 Armanti Edwards 4.00 10.00
21 Demaryius Thomas 8.00 20.00
22 Emmanuel Sanders 5.00 12.00
23 Jermaine Gresham 3.00 8.00
24 Toby Gerhart 3.00 8.00
25 Ben Tate 3.00 8.00
26 Mike Kafka 4.00 10.00
27 Rob Gronkowski 10.00 25.00
28 Taylor Price 3.00 8.00
29 Marcus Easley 3.00 8.00
30 Ndamukong Suh 12.00 30.00
31 Gerald McCoy 3.00 8.00
32 Golden Tate 4.00 10.00
33 Colt McCoy 4.00 10.00
34 Dexter McCluster 4.00 10.00
35 Damian Williams 3.00 8.00

2010 Playoff National Treasures NFL Gear Signatures Prime

DUAL PRIME AU PRINT RUN 25 SER.#'d SETS
20.00
*TRIPLE PRIME/19-25: .5X TO 1.2X PRIME DUAL/25
1 Tim Tebow 60.00 150.00
2 Sam Bradford 50.00 100.00
3 C.J. Spiller 5.00 12.00
4 Dez Bryant 60.00 120.00
5 Eric Berry 12.00 30.00
6 Jahvid Best 10.00 25.00
7 Jordan Shipley 5.00 12.00
8 Jimmy Clausen 5.00 12.00
9 Joe McKnight 5.00 12.00
10 Andre Roberts 6.00 15.00
11 Arrelious Benn 5.00 12.00
12 Brandon LaFell 8.00 20.00
13 Ryan Mathews 5.00 12.00
14 Rolando McClain 6.00 15.00
15 Mike Williams 10.00 25.00
16 Montario Hardesty 5.00 12.00
17 Jonathan Dwyer 5.00 12.00
18 Mardy Gilyard 5.00 12.00
19 Eric Decker 15.00 30.00
20 Armanti Edwards 6.00 15.00
21 Demaryius Thomas 12.00 30.00
22 Emmanuel Sanders 8.00 20.00
23 Jermaine Gresham 5.00 12.00
24 Toby Gerhart 15.00 40.00
25 Ben Tate 10.00 25.00
26 Mike Kafka 6.00 15.00
27 Rob Gronkowski 75.00 150.00
28 Taylor Price 5.00 12.00
29 Marcus Easley 5.00 12.00
31 Gerald McCoy 5.00 12.00
32 Golden Tate 6.00 15.00
33 Colt McCoy 6.00 15.00
34 Dexter McCluster No AU 6.00 15.00
35 Damian Williams 5.00 12.00

2010 Playoff National Treasures NFL Greatest

STATED PRINT RUN 99 SER.#'d SETS
1 Deacon Jones 3.00 8.00
2 Charlie Joiner 2.50 6.00
3 Sonny Jurgensen 3.00 8.00

4 Hugh McElhenny 2.50 6.00
5 Jim Kelly 4.00 10.00
6 George Blanda 3.00 8.00
7 James Lofton 2.50 6.00
8 Charley Taylor 2.50 6.00
9 Larry Little 2.50 6.00
10 Dave Casper 2.50 6.00
11 Willie Lanier 2.50 6.00
12 Merlin Olsen 2.50 6.00
13 Gale Sayers 4.00 10.00
14 Paul Hornung 4.00 10.00
15 Roger Staubach 5.00 12.00
16 Raymond Berry 3.00 8.00
17 Forrest Gregg 2.50 6.00
18 Sammy Baugh 4.00 10.00
19 Bob Griese 4.00 10.00
20 Junior Seau 3.00 8.00
21 Ron Mix 2.50 6.00
22 Alan Page 3.00 8.00
23 Bob Lilly 3.00 8.00
24 Dan Marino 8.00 20.00
25 Dick Butkus 5.00 12.00
26 Don Maynard 3.00 8.00
27 Fran Tarkenton 4.00 10.00
28 Franco Harris 4.00 10.00
29 Fred Biletnikoff 4.00 10.00
30 Howie Long 4.00 10.00
31 Jim Otto 2.50 6.00
32 John Randle 3.00 8.00
33 Lee Roy Selmon 2.50 6.00
34 Len Dawson 4.00 10.00
35 Lenny Moore 2.50 6.00

2010 Playoff National Treasures NFL Greatest Materials

STATED PRINT RUN 20-99
*PRIME/35-49: .6X TO 1.5X BASIC JSY
*PRIME/49: .5X TO 1.2X BASIC JSY/49
*PRIME/15-29: .8X TO 2X BASIC JSY
1 Deacon Jones/90 4.00 10.00
2 Charlie Joiner/99 3.00 8.00
3 Sonny Jurgensen/99 5.00 12.00
4 Hugh McElhenny/99 6.00 15.00
5 Jim Kelly/99 5.00 12.00
6 George Blanda/99 5.00 12.00
7 James Lofton/50 3.00 8.00
8 Charley Taylor/99 3.00 8.00
9 Larry Little/99 3.00 8.00
11 Willie Lanier/20 5.00 12.00
12 Merlin Olsen/99 3.00 8.00
13 Gale Sayers/99 5.00 12.00
14 Paul Hornung/99 6.00 15.00
15 Roger Staubach/99 8.00 20.00
16 Raymond Berry/99 4.00 10.00
17 Forrest Gregg/99 5.00 12.00
18 Sammy Baugh/99 8.00 20.00
19 Bob Griese/99 5.00 12.00
20 Junior Seau/49 4.00 10.00
22 Alan Page/99 5.00 12.00
23 Bob Lilly/99 4.00 10.00
24 Dan Marino/99 10.00 25.00
25 Dick Butkus/99 6.00 15.00
26 Don Maynard/99 4.00 10.00
27 Fran Tarkenton/99 6.00 15.00
28 Franco Harris/99 6.00 15.00
29 Fred Biletnikoff/99 5.00 12.00
30 Howie Long/99 5.00 12.00
31 Jim Otto/99 4.00 10.00
32 John Randle/99 5.00 12.00
33 Lee Roy Selmon/99 5.00 12.00
34 Len Dawson/99 5.00 12.00
35 Lenny Moore/99 5.00 12.00

2010 Playoff National Treasures NFL Greatest Signature Materials

STATED PRINT RUN 8-25
1 Deacon Jones/25 15.00 40.00
2 Charlie Joiner/25 20.00 50.00
3 Sonny Jurgensen/25 15.00 40.00
4 Hugh McElhenny/25 15.00 40.00
5 Jim Kelly/25 30.00 60.00
6 George Blanda/25 25.00 50.00
7 James Lofton/25 15.00 40.00
8 Charley Taylor/25 12.00 30.00
9 Larry Little/25 15.00 40.00
11 Willie Lanier/25 12.00 30.00
13 Gale Sayers/25 40.00 80.00
14 Paul Hornung/25 15.00 40.00
15 Roger Staubach/15 40.00 80.00
16 Raymond Berry/25 20.00 50.00
17 Forrest Gregg/25 20.00 50.00
19 Bob Griese/25 20.00 50.00
20 Junior Seau/25 40.00 80.00
22 Alan Page/25 15.00 40.00
23 Bob Lilly/25 15.00 40.00
24 Dan Marino/8
25 Dick Butkus/10
26 Don Maynard/25 15.00 40.00
27 Fran Tarkenton/25 30.00 60.00
28 Franco Harris/25 20.00 50.00
29 Fred Biletnikoff/25 30.00 60.00
30 Howie Long/25 20.00 50.00
31 Jim Otto/25 15.00 40.00
32 John Randle/25 15.00 40.00
33 Lee Roy Selmon/25 15.00 40.00
34 Len Dawson/25 25.00 50.00
35 Lenny Moore/25 15.00 40.00

2010 Playoff National Treasures NFL Greatest Signature Materials Prime

*PRIME AU/14-15: .5X TO 1.2X JSY AU/15-25
PRIME JSY AU PRINT RUN 3-15
21 Ron Mix/15 15.00 40.00
25 Dick Butkus/15 50.00 100.00

2010 Playoff National Treasures NFL Greatest Signatures

STATED PRINT RUN 1-15
2 Charlie Joiner/15 20.00 50.00
17 Forrest Gregg/15 15.00 40.00

2010 Playoff National Treasures Notable Numbers

STATED PRINT RUN 99 SER.#'d SETS
1 Bo Jackson 5.00 12.00
2 Bernie Kosar 4.00 10.00
3 Brent Jones 2.50 6.00
4 Eddie George 3.00 8.00
5 William Perry 2.50 6.00
6 L.C. Greenwood 2.50 6.00
7 Rod Smith 2.50 6.00
8 Irving Fryar 2.50 6.00
9 Boomer Esiason 3.00 8.00
10 John Taylor 2.50 6.00
11 Buck Buchanan 2.50 6.00
12 Chuck Howley 2.50 6.00
13 Cris Carter 4.00 10.00
14 Curtis Martin 3.00 8.00
15 Daryle Lamonica 2.50 6.00
16 Ernie Davis 5.00 12.00
17 Walter Payton 8.00 20.00
18 Michael Strahan 3.00 8.00
19 Ed Too Tall Jones 2.50 6.00
20 Mike Alstott 2.50 6.00
21 Phil Simms 3.00 8.00
22 Priest Holmes 2.50 6.00
23 Randall Cunningham 3.00 8.00
24 Roger Craig 3.00 8.00
25 Ozzie Newsome 3.00 8.00
26 Paul Warfield 3.00 8.00
27 Randy White 3.00 8.00
28 Rod Woodson 3.00 8.00
29 Steve Largent 4.00 10.00
30 Steve Young 5.00 12.00
31 Tony Dorsett 4.00 10.00
32 Troy Aikman 5.00 12.00
33 Craig James 2.50 6.00
34 Willie Brown 2.50 6.00
35 Ronnie Lott 3.00 8.00

2010 Playoff National Treasures Notable Numbers Materials

STATED PRINT RUN 9-99
1 Bo Jackson/99 8.00 20.00
3 Brent Jones/99 4.00 10.00
4 Eddie George/99 4.00 10.00
7 Rod Smith/99 3.00 8.00
8 Irving Fryar/99 4.00 10.00
9 Boomer Esiason/99 4.00 10.00
11 Buck Buchanan/99 4.00 10.00
12 Chuck Howley/99 3.00 8.00
13 Cris Carter/99 5.00 12.00
14 Curtis Martin/99 4.00 10.00
15 Daryle Lamonica/99 4.00 10.00
16 Ernie Davis/99 15.00 30.00
17 Walter Payton/99 10.00 25.00
18 Michael Strahan/99 4.00 10.00
19 Ed Too Tall Jones/99 3.00 8.00
20 Mike Alstott/99 4.00 10.00
21 Phil Simms/99 4.00 10.00
22 Priest Holmes/99 3.00 8.00
23 Randall Cunningham/99 5.00 12.00
24 Roger Craig/99 4.00 10.00
25 Ozzie Newsome/99 4.00 10.00
26 Paul Warfield/99 4.00 10.00
27 Randy White/99 5.00 12.00
28 Rod Woodson/99 4.00 10.00
29 Steve Largent/99 5.00 12.00
30 Steve Young/99 6.00 15.00
31 Tony Dorsett/99 6.00 15.00
32 Troy Aikman/99 6.00 15.00
33 Craig James/99 3.00 8.00
34 Willie Brown/99 3.00 8.00
35 Ronnie Lott/99 4.00 10.00

2010 Playoff National Treasures Notable Numbers Materials Prime

*PRIME/30-50: .5X TO 1.2X BASIC JSY/99
*PRIME/25: .6X TO 1.5X BASIC JSY/99
PRIME STATED PRINT RUN 11-50
5 William Perry/50 5.00 12.00

2010 Playoff National Treasures Notable Numbers Signature Materials

STATED PRINT RUN 5-25
1 Bo Jackson/25 40.00 80.00
2 Bernie Kosar/25 20.00 50.00
3 Brent Jones/25 12.00 30.00
4 Eddie George/25 30.00 60.00
5 William Perry/25 20.00 50.00
6 L.C. Greenwood/25 30.00 60.00
7 Rod Smith/25 15.00 40.00
8 Irving Fryar/25 12.00 30.00
9 Boomer Esiason/25 15.00 40.00
12 Chuck Howley/25 12.00 30.00
14 Curtis Martin/25 25.00 60.00
15 Daryle Lamonica/25 15.00 40.00
18 Michael Strahan/25 15.00 40.00
20 Mike Alstott/25 25.00 60.00
21 Phil Simms/25 15.00 40.00
22 Priest Holmes/25 12.00 30.00
23 Randall Cunningham/25 25.00 50.00
24 Roger Craig/25 15.00 40.00
25 Ozzie Newsome/25 15.00 40.00
26 Paul Warfield/25 15.00 40.00
27 Randy White/25 15.00 40.00
28 Rod Woodson/25 40.00 80.00
29 Steve Largent/25 20.00 50.00
30 Steve Young/25 50.00 100.00
31 Tony Dorsett/25 30.00 60.00
33 Craig James/25 12.00 30.00
34 Willie Brown/25 12.00 30.00
35 Ronnie Lott/25 20.00 50.00

2010 Playoff National Treasures Notable Numbers Signature Materials Prime

*PRIME AU/15/25: .5X TO 1.2X JSY AU/25
PRIME JSY AU PRINT RUN 1-15
10 John Taylor/15 30.00 60.00
32 Troy Aikman/15 50.00 100.00

2010 Playoff National Treasures Pen Pals

1 McCy/Shp/Brd/Grsh 30.00 60.00
2 Clsn/Tate/McKn/Will 15.00 40.00
3 C.Spiller/M.Easley 25.00 50.00
4 Clausn/LaFell/Edwrds 12.00 30.00
5 J.Gresham/J.Shipley 20.00 40.00
6 C.McCoy/M.Hardesty 25.00 60.00
7 Tebow/Thmas/Deckr 60.00 150.00
8 N.Suh/J.Best 40.00 100.00
9 Gronkowski/T.Price 25.00 50.00
10 S.Bradford/M.Gilyard 40.00 80.00
11 Brdfrd/Tbw/Clsn/McCy 40.00 80.00
12 Thmas/Brynt/McCl/Bnn 60.00 120.00
13 Spill/Mthws/Bst/Grhrt 50.00 120.00
14 Brdfrd/Tebw and six rookies
15 Tebow and seven rookies 60.00 150.00
16 C.McCoy and seven rookies 40.00 100.00
17 Brdfrd/Suh/Mthws/five others
18 Rookie QBs and RBs

2010 Playoff National Treasures Ring of Honor

STATED PRINT RUN 99 SER.#'d SETS
1 Bart Starr 8.00 20.00
2 Jim Taylor 5.00 12.00
3 Willie Davis 3.00 8.00
4 Joe Namath 6.00 15.00
5 Len Dawson 5.00 12.00
6 Chuck Howley 3.00 8.00
7 Roger Staubach 6.00 15.00
8 Larry Little 3.00 8.00
9 Paul Warfield 4.00 10.00
10 Jack Lambert 5.00 12.00
11 L.C. Greenwood 3.00 8.00
12 Fred Biletnikoff 5.00 12.00
13 Randy White 3.00 8.00
14 Ed Too Tall Jones 3.00 8.00
15 Terry Bradshaw 6.00 15.00
16 Terry Bradshaw 6.00 15.00
17 Jim Plunkett 4.00 10.00
18 Joe Montana 15.00 40.00
19 Russ Grimm 3.00 8.00
20 Jim Plunkett 4.00 10.00
21 Joe Montana 15.00 40.00
22 William Perry 3.00 8.00
23 Phil Simms 4.00 10.00
24 Doug Williams 4.00 10.00
25 Jerry Rice 8.00 20.00
26 Joe Montana 12.00 30.00
27 Ottis Anderson 3.00 8.00
28 Art Monk 5.00 12.00
29 Troy Aikman 6.00 15.00
30 Emmitt Smith 8.00 20.00
31 Steve Young 6.00 15.00
32 John Taylor 3.00 8.00
33 Deion Sanders 4.00 10.00
34 Brett Favre 10.00 25.00
35 Terrell Davis 4.00 10.00
36 John Elway 8.00 20.00
37 Rod Smith 3.00 8.00
38 Marshall Faulk 4.00 10.00
39 Rod Woodson 4.00 10.00
40 Tom Brady 6.00 15.00
41 Mike Alstott 4.00 10.00
42 Keyshawn Johnson 3.00 8.00
43 Tom Brady 6.00 15.00
44 Tom Brady 6.00 15.00
45 Ben Roethlisberger 5.00 12.00
46 Peyton Manning 12.00 30.00
47 Reggie Wayne 4.00 10.00
48 [illegible] 4.00 10.00
49 Santonio Holmes 3.00 8.00
50 Drew Brees 5.00 12.00

2010 Playoff National Treasures Ring of Honor Signatures

STATED PRINT RUN 4-50
1 Bart Starr/50 75.00 150.00
2 Jim Taylor/35 30.00 80.00
3 Willie Davis/50 15.00 40.00
5 Len Dawson/25 25.00 50.00
8 Larry Little/25 12.00 30.00
9 Paul Warfield/50 12.00 30.00
10 Jack Lambert/50 40.00 80.00
11 L.C. Greenwood/50 20.00 50.00
12 Fred Biletnikoff/50 15.00 40.00
13 Randy White/45 12.00 30.00
17 Jim Plunkett/15 25.00 50.00
18 Joe Montana/16 100.00 175.00
19 Russ Grimm/50 15.00 40.00
20 Jim Plunkett/15 25.00 50.00
21 Joe Montana/19 100.00 175.00
22 William Perry/50 15.00 40.00
23 Phil Simms/21 15.00 40.00
24 Doug Williams/50 15.00 40.00
26 Joe Montana/24 100.00 175.00
27 Ottis Anderson/50 12.00 30.00
28 Art Monk/50 30.00 60.00
30 Emmitt Smith/22 125.00 250.00
32 John Taylor/50 12.00 30.00
33 Deion Sanders/27 40.00 80.00
36 John Elway/25 75.00 150.00
37 Rod Smith/33 12.00 30.00
38 Marshall Faulk/50 20.00 50.00
39 Rod Woodson/35 25.00 60.00
41 Mike Alstott/50 25.00 50.00
42 Keyshawn Johnson/50 15.00 40.00
45 Ben Roethlisberger/25 60.00 120.00
46 Peyton Manning/18 100.00 200.00
49 Santonio Holmes/50 15.00 40.00

2010 Playoff National Treasures Souvenir Cuts

CUT AU STATED PRINT RUN 1-88
2 Bill Dudley/35 20.00 50.00
7 Hank Stram/16 20.00 50.00
9 Johnny Unitas/40 200.00 350.00
11 Kyle Rote/88 20.00 50.00
14 Paul Brown/62 40.00 80.00
17 Walter Payton/61 175.00 300.00
18 Weeb Ewbank/74 20.00 50.00

2010 Playoff National Treasures Timeline Materials Player Name

STATED PRINT RUN 5-99
1 Alex Karras/99 5.00 12.00
3 Danny White/99 5.00 12.00
4 Warren Moon/99 6.00 15.00
5 D.D. Lewis/99 5.00 12.00
6 Doug Flutie/99 5.00 12.00
7 Henry Ellard/55 4.00 10.00
8 Paul Hornung/99 6.00 15.00
9 Jim McMahon/99 6.00 15.00
10 Y.A. Tittle/99 6.00 15.00
12 Ken Stabler/99 8.00 20.00
14 Steve McNair/99 5.00 12.00
15 Terrell Davis/99 5.00 12.00
16 Tiki Barber/30 6.00 15.00
17 Todd Christensen/99 4.00 10.00
18 Tom Rathman/99 4.00 10.00
20 Derrick Thomas/99 20.00 50.00

2010 Playoff National Treasures Timeline Materials Player Name Prime

*PRIME/20-25: .6X TO 1.5X BASIC JSY/99
PRIME STATED PRINT RUN 1-50
13 Keyshawn Johnson/50 5.00 12.00

2010 Playoff National Treasures Timeline Materials Team Name

*TEAM/85-99: .4X TO 1X PLAYER/55-99
STATED PRINT RUN 5-99
2 Jim Plunkett/89 5.00 12.00
16 Tiki Barber/21 8.00 20.00
18 Tom Rathman/20 6.00 15.00

2010 Playoff National Treasures Timeline Materials Signature Team Name

TEAM NAME AU PRINT RUN 4-25
*TN PRIME/15: .5X TO 1.2X TN JSY AU/15-25
*PLY.NME/15-25: .4X TO 1X TEAM JSY AU/15-25
*PN PRIME/15: .5X TO 1.2X TN JSY AU/19-25
1 Alex Karras/25 15.00 40.00
2 Jim Plunkett/20 15.00 40.00
3 Danny White/25 15.00 40.00
4 Warren Moon/25 30.00 80.00
5 D.D. Lewis/15 12.00 30.00
6 Doug Flutie/25 15.00 40.00
7 Henry Ellard/25 15.00 40.00
8 Paul Hornung/25 15.00 40.00
9 Jim McMahon/25 30.00 60.00
10 Y.A. Tittle/25 20.00 50.00
12 Ken Stabler/20 30.00 60.00
13 Keyshawn Johnson/19 20.00 50.00
15 Terrell Davis/15 40.00 80.00
16 Tiki Barber/25 12.00 30.00
17 Todd Christensen/25 15.00 40.00
18 Tom Rathman/25 15.00 40.00
19 Wayne Chrebet/25 15.00 40.00

2010 Playoff National Treasures Timeline Materials Team Name Prime

*PRIME/24-25: .6X TO 1.5X TEAM NAME JSY/99
PRIME STATED PRINT RUN 1-25
13 Keyshawn Johnson/50 5.00 12.00

2011 Playoff National Treasures

STATED PRINT RUN 99 SER.#'d SETS
EACH EXPIRATION: 10/4/2013
1 Beanie Wells 2.00 5.00
2 Early Doucet 2.00 5.00
3 Kevin Kolb 2.00 5.00
4 Larry Fitzgerald 2.50 6.00
5 Curtis Lofton 2.00 5.00
6 Matt Ryan 2.50 6.00
7 Michael Turner 2.00 5.00
8 Roddy White 2.00 5.00
9 Tony Gonzalez 2.50 6.00
10 Anquan Boldin 2.00 5.00
11 Joe Flacco 2.50 6.00
12 Lee Evans 2.50 6.00
13 Ray Rice 2.00 5.00
14 Ricky Williams 2.50 6.00
15 C.J. Spiller 2.00 5.00
16 David Nelson 2.50 6.00
17 Fred Jackson 2.00 5.00
18 Ryan Fitzpatrick 2.00 5.00
19 Steve Johnson 2.00 5.00
20 Brandon LaFell 2.00 5.00
21 DeAngelo Williams 2.00 5.00
22 Greg Olsen 2.50 6.00
23 Jonathan Stewart 2.00 5.00
24 Steve Smith 2.50 6.00
25 Brian Urlacher 3.00 8.00
26 Devin Hester 2.50 6.00
27 Jay Cutler 2.00 5.00
28 Johnny Knox 2.00 5.00
29 Matt Forte 2.00 5.00
30 Cedric Benson 2.00 5.00
31 Jermaine Gresham 2.00 5.00
32 Jerome Simpson 2.00 5.00
33 Jordan Shipley 2.00 5.00
34 Colt McCoy 2.00 5.00
35 Josh Cribbs 2.00 5.00
36 Mohamed Massaquoi 2.00 5.00
37 Peyton Hillis 2.00 5.00
38 Dez Bryant 3.00 8.00
39 Felix Jones 2.00 5.00
40 Jason Witten 2.50 6.00
41 Miles Austin 2.00 5.00
42 Tony Romo 2.50 6.00
43 Brandon Lloyd 2.00 5.00
44 Eric Decker 2.00 5.00
45 Knowshon Moreno 2.00 5.00
46 Kyle Orton 2.00 5.00
47 Willis McGahee 2.00 5.00
48 Calvin Johnson 3.00 8.00
49 Jahvid Best 2.00 5.00
50 Matthew Stafford 2.50 6.00
51 Nate Burleson 2.00 5.00
52 Ndamukong Suh 2.50 6.00
53 Aaron Rodgers 12.00 30.00
54 Greg Jennings 2.00 5.00
55 James Starks 2.00 5.00
56 Jermichael Finley 2.00 5.00
57 Jordy Nelson 2.50 6.00
58 Andre Johnson 2.50 6.00
59 Arian Foster 2.00 5.00
60 Ben Tate 2.00 5.00
61 Matt Schaub 2.00 5.00
62 Owen Daniels 2.00 5.00
63 Dallas Clark 2.00 5.00
64 Joseph Addai 2.00 5.00
65 Peyton Manning 8.00 20.00
66 Pierre Garcon 2.50 6.00
67 Reggie Wayne 2.50 6.00
68 Marcedes Lewis 2.00 5.00
69 Maurice Jones-Drew 2.00 5.00
70 Mike Thomas 2.50 6.00
71 Paul Posluszny 2.00 5.00
72 Dexter McCluster 2.00 5.00
73 Dwayne Bowe 2.50 6.00
74 Jamaal Charles 2.50 6.00
75 Matt Cassel 2.00 5.00
76 Thomas Jones 2.00 5.00
77 Anthony Fasano 2.00 5.00
78 Brandon Marshall 2.50 6.00
79 Chad Henne 2.50 6.00
80 Davone Bess 2.00 5.00
81 Reggie Bush 2.00 5.00
82 Adrian Peterson 3.00 8.00
83 Toby Gerhart 2.50 6.00
84 Jared Allen 2.00 5.00
85 Percy Harvin 2.00 5.00
86 Visanthe Shiancoe 2.50 6.00
87 Aaron Hernandez 2.50 6.00
88 BenJarvus Green-Ellis 2.00 5.00
89 Chad Ochocinco 2.00 5.00
90 Rob Gronkowski 3.00 8.00
91 Tom Brady 6.00 15.00
92 Wes Welker 2.50 6.00
93 Darren Sproles 2.50 6.00
94 Drew Brees 3.00 8.00
95 Jimmy Graham 3.00 8.00
96 Marques Colston 2.00 5.00
97 Pierre Thomas 2.00 5.00
98 Ahmad Bradshaw 2.00 5.00
99 Brandon Jacobs 2.00 5.00
100 Eli Manning 2.50 6.00
101 Hakeem Nicks 2.00 5.00
102 Mario Manningham 2.00 5.00
103 Dustin Keller 2.50 6.00
104 Mark Sanchez 2.00 5.00
105 Plaxico Burress 2.00 5.00
106 Santonio Holmes 2.00 5.00
107 Shonn Greene 2.00 5.00
108 Darren McFadden 2.00 5.00
109 Jacoby Ford 2.50 6.00
110 Carson Palmer 2.50 6.00
111 Michael Bush 2.00 5.00
112 DeSean Jackson 2.50 6.00
113 Jeremy Maclin 2.00 5.00
114 LeSean McCoy 3.00 8.00
115 Michael Vick 2.50 6.00
116 Nnamdi Asomugha 2.00 5.00
117 Antonio Brown 3.00 8.00
118 Ben Roethlisberger 3.00 8.00
119 Mike Wallace 2.00 5.00
120 Rashard Mendenhall 2.00 5.00
121 Troy Polamalu 3.00 8.00
122 Antonio Gates 2.00 5.00
123 Mike Tolbert 2.00 5.00
124 Philip Rivers 3.00 8.00
125 Ryan Mathews 2.50 6.00
126 Vincent Jackson 2.00 5.00
127 Alex Smith QB 2.50 6.00
128 Braylon Edwards 2.00 5.00
129 Frank Gore 2.50 6.00
130 Vernon Davis 2.00 5.00
131 Marshawn Lynch 2.50 6.00
132 Sidney Rice 2.00 5.00
133 Tarvaris Jackson 2.00 5.00
134 Zach Miller 2.00 5.00
135 Brandon Gibson 2.00 5.00
136 Cadillac Williams 2.00 5.00
137 Sam Bradford 2.00 5.00
138 Steven Jackson 2.00 5.00
139 Josh Freeman 2.50 6.00
140 Kellen Winslow Jr. 2.00 5.00
141 LeGarrette Blount 2.50 6.00
142 Mike Williams 2.50 6.00
143 Chris Johnson 2.00 5.00
144 Kenny Britt 2.00 5.00
145 Matt Hasselbeck 2.00 5.00
146 Nate Washington 2.00 5.00
147 Fred Davis 2.00 5.00
148 Rex Grossman 2.00 5.00
149 Santana Moss 2.50 6.00
150 Tim Hightower 2.00 5.00
151 Art Monk 3.00 8.00
152 Bernie Kosar 2.50 6.00
153 Boomer Esiason 2.50 6.00
154 Chuck Howley 2.00 5.00
155 Ernie Davis 2.50 6.00
156 Floyd Little 2.00 5.00
157 Forrest Gregg 2.00 5.00
158 Fred Biletnikoff 3.00 8.00
159 Fred Williamson 2.00 5.00
160 Garo Yepremian 2.00 5.00
161 Gene Upshaw 2.00 5.00
162 Hugh McElhenny 2.00 5.00
163 Irving Fryar 2.00 5.00
164 Jay Novacek 2.50 6.00
165 Jerome Bettis 3.00 8.00
166 Jim Plunkett 2.50 6.00
167 John Brodie 2.00 5.00
168 John Fuqua 2.00 5.00
169 John Hadl 2.00 5.00
170 John Hannah 2.00 5.00
171 John Matuszak 2.00 5.00
172 Junior Seau 2.50 6.00
173 Keith Jackson 2.00 5.00
174 Ken Anderson 2.50 6.00
175 Knute Rockne 3.00 8.00
176 Larry Csonka 2.50 6.00
177 Mark Carrier 2.00 5.00
178 Merlin Olsen 2.50 6.00
179 Mike Alstott 2.00 5.00
180 Ozzie Newsome 2.50 6.00
181 Paul Krause 2.00 5.00
182 Paul Warfield 2.50 6.00
183 Pete Retzlaff 2.00 5.00
184 Randall Cunningham 2.50 6.00
185 Randy White 2.50 6.00
186 Richard Dent 2.00 5.00
187 Rickey Jackson 2.00 5.00
188 Rod Woodson 2.50 6.00
189 Roger Craig 2.50 6.00
190 Ron Mix 2.00 5.00
191 Ronnie Lott 2.50 6.00
192 Sterling Sharpe 2.50 6.00
193 Bo Jackson 4.00 10.00
194 Steve Bartkowski 2.50 6.00
195 Ted Hendricks 2.00 5.00
196 Tony Dorsett 3.00 8.00
197 Eddie George 2.50 6.00
198 Warren Sapp 2.50 6.00
199 Willie Brown 2.00 5.00
200 Y.A. Tittle 3.00 8.00
201 Aaron Williams AU RC 5.00 12.00
202 Adrian Clayborn AU RC 5.00 12.00
203 Ahmad Black AU RC 6.00 15.00
204 Akeem Ayers AU RC EXCH 5.00 12.00
205 Aldon Smith AU RC EXCH
206 Aldrick Robinson AU RC 6.00 15.00
207 Alex Henery AU RC 6.00 15.00
208 Allen Bradford AU RC 5.00 12.00
209 Anthony Allen AU RC 5.00 12.00
210 Anthony Castonzo AU RC 5.00 12.00
211 Anthony Sherman AU RC 5.00 12.00
212 Armond Smith AU RC 6.00 15.00
213 Brandon Harris AU RC 5.00 12.00
214 Bruce Miller AU RC 6.00 15.00
215 Buster Skrine AU RC 6.00 15.00
216 Cameron Heyward AU RC 6.00 15.00
217 Cameron Jordan AU RC 6.00 15.00
218 Casey Matthews AU RC 5.00 12.00
219 Cecil Shorts AU RC 12.00 30.00
220 Charles Clay AU RC 10.00 25.00
221 Chimdi Chekwa AU RC 6.00 15.00
222 Chris Harris AU RC 6.00 15.00
223 Chris White AU RC 6.00 15.00
224 Colin Cochart AU RC 5.00 12.00
225 Corey Liuget AU RC 5.00 12.00
226 D.J. Williams AU RC 5.00 12.00
227 D.Bowers AU RC 5.00 12.00
228 Da'Rel Scott AU RC 5.00 12.00
229 Dan Bailey AU RC 10.00 25.00
230 D.Sanzenbacher AU RC 5.00 12.00
231 Darren Evans AU RC 6.00 15.00
232 David Ausberry AU RC 5.00 12.00
233 D.Sampson AU RC 5.00 12.00
234 D.Moore AU RC 20.00 40.00
235 Dion Lewis AU RC 20.00 40.00
236 Doug Baldwin AU RC 25.00 50.00
237 Mark Herzlich AU RC 5.00 12.00
238 Evan Royster AU RC 5.00 12.00
239 Greg Jones AU RC 6.00 15.00
240 Greg McElroy AU RC 15.00 40.00
241 Greg Salas AU RC 5.00 12.00
242 Henry Hynoski AU RC 8.00 20.00
243 J.J. Watt AU RC 175.00 300.00
244 J.Williams AU RC EXCH 8.00 20.00
245 Jacquizz Rodgers AU RC 10.00 25.00
246 Jamar Newsome AU RC 5.00 12.00
247 Jeremy Kerley AU RC 8.00 20.00
248 Jimmy Smith AU RC 5.00 12.00
249 Joe Lefeged AU RC 6.00 15.00
250 Johnny White AU RC 5.00 12.00
251 Jordan Cameron AU RC 6.00 15.00
252 Josh Portis AU RC 8.00 20.00
253 Julius Thomas AU RC 6.00 15.00
254 Justin Houston AU RC 15.00 30.00
255 K.J. Wright AU RC 10.00 25.00
256 Kealoha Pilares AU RC 5.00 12.00
257 Kris Durham AU RC 5.00 12.00
258 Kyle Adams AU RC 5.00 12.00
259 Lance Kendricks AU RC 5.00 12.00
260 LaQuan Williams AU RC 6.00 15.00
261 Lee Smith AU RC 6.00 15.00
262 Luke Stocker AU RC 5.00 12.00
263 Marcus Cannon AU RC 5.00 12.00
264 Marcus Gilchrist AU RC 5.00 12.00
266 Mason Foster AU RC 5.00 12.00
267 N.Enderle AU RC 5.00 12.00
268 Niles Paul AU RC 5.00 12.00
269 O.Marecic AU RC EXCH 5.00 12.00
270 Phil Taylor AU RC 5.00 12.00
271 Phillip Tanner AU RC 8.00 20.00
272 Prince Amukamara AU RC 5.00 12.00
273 Quinton Carter AU RC 5.00 12.00
274 Rahim Moore AU RC 5.00 12.00
275 Richard Gordon AU RC 5.00 12.00
276 Ricky Stanzi AU RC 5.00 12.00
277 Robert Housler AU RC 5.00 12.00
279 Roy Helu AU RC 5.00 12.00
280 Ryan Kerrigan AU RC 6.00 15.00
281 Ryan Taylor AU RC 6.00 15.00
282 Ryan Whalen AU RC 5.00 12.00
283 S.Tolzien AU RC EXCH
284 Shane Bannon AU RC 5.00 12.00
285 Stanley Havili AU RC 5.00 12.00
286 Stephen Burton AU RC 5.00 12.00
287 Stephen Paea AU RC 5.00 12.00
288 T.J. Yates AU RC 15.00 30.00
289 Tandon Doss AU RC 5.00 12.00
290 Terrelle Pryor AU RC 8.00 20.00
291 Tyler Sash AU RC 5.00 12.00
292 Tyrod Taylor AU RC 30.00 60.00
293 Tyron Smith AU RC 10.00 25.00
294 Virgil Green AU RC 5.00 12.00
295 W.Saunders AU RC EXCH 8.00 20.00
296 W.Yeatman AU RC EXCH 6.00 15.00
297 Zack Pianalto AU RC 6.00 15.00
299 Patrick Peterson AU RC 10.00 25.00
300 Robert Quinn AU RC 5.00 12.00
301 Christian Ponder JSY AU RC 12.00 30.00
302 Clyde Gates JSY AU RC 12.00 30.00
303 Jamie Harper JSY AU RC 12.00 30.00
304 Blaine Gabbert JSY AU RC 12.00 30.00
305 M.Leshoure JSY AU RC EXCH 12.00 30.00
306 Stevan Ridley JSY AU RC 12.00 30.00
307 Von Miller JSY AU RC 40.00 80.00
308 L.Hankerson JSY AU RC 12.00 30.00
309 Delone Carter JSY AU RC 12.00 30.00
310 Kyle Rudolph JSY AU RC 12.00 30.00
311 Austin Pettis JSY AU RC 12.00 30.00
312 Daniel Thomas JSY AU RC 12.00 30.00
313 Torrey Smith JSY AU RC 12.00 30.00
314 Marcell Dareus JSY AU RC 12.00 30.00
315 Ryan Mallett JSY AU RC 12.00 30.00
316 Alex Green JSY AU RC 12.00 30.00
317 Jerrel Jernigan JSY AU RC 12.00 30.00
318 Mark Ingram JSY AU RC 20.00 50.00
319 Vincent Brown JSY AU RC 12.00 30.00
320 Titus Young JSY AU RC 12.00 30.00
321 Bilal Powell JSY AU RC 15.00 40.00
322 Kendall Hunter JSY AU RC 12.00 30.00
323 J.Jones JSY AU RC EXCH 250.00 400.00
324 Jordan Todman JSY AU RC 12.00 30.00
325 Jake Locker JSY AU RC 12.00 30.00
326 Andy Dalton JSY AU RC 75.00 150.00
327 C.Kaepernick JSY AU RC 60.00 125.00
328 Cam Newton JSY AU RC 500.00 800.00
329 A.J. Green JSY AU RC 100.00 200.00
330 Randall Cobb JSY AU RC 20.00 50.00
331 DeMarco Murray JSY AU RC 25.00 60.00
332 Taiwan Jones JSY AU RC 12.00 30.00
333 Greg Little JSY AU RC 15.00 40.00
334 Ryan Williams JSY AU RC 12.00 30.00
335 J.Baldwin JSY AU RC 12.00 30.00
336 Shane Vereen JSY AU RC 15.00 40.00

2011 Playoff National Treasures Century Silver

*SLVER/25: .8X TO 2X BASIC CARDS
STATED PRINT RUN 25 SER.#'d SETS

2011 Playoff National Treasures 1958 Goal Post

1 Johnny Unitas/58 40.00 80.00

2011 Playoff National Treasures Century Black Signature

1-199 UNPRICED PRINT RUN 1-10
*201-300 ROOKIE AU/25: .6X TO 1.5X BASIC AU/99
201-300 ROOKIE AU PRINT RUN 25
205 Aldon Smith/25 EXCH
243 J.J. Watt/25 350.00 500.00
290 Terrelle Pryor/25 12.00 30.00

2011 Playoff National Treasures Century Gold Signature

1-200 VETERAN PRINT RUN 1-25
*201-300 GOLD AU/49: .5X TO 1.2X AU RC/99
201-300 ROOKIE AU PRINT RUN 49
95 Jimmy Graham/25 12.00 30.00
205 Aldon Smith/49 EXCH
290 Terrelle Pryor/49 10.00 25.00

2011 Playoff National Treasures Century Material Prime

STATED PRINT RUN 1-49
8 Roddy White/49 4.00 10.00
9 Tony Gonzalez/49 5.00 12.00
10 Anquan Boldin/49 4.00 10.00
11 Joe Flacco/49 5.00 12.00
13 Ray Rice/49 4.00 10.00
15 C.J. Spiller/25 5.00 12.00
18 Ryan Fitzpatrick/49 4.00 10.00
25 Brian Urlacher/49 6.00 15.00
26 Devin Hester/49 5.00 12.00
29 Matt Forte/49 4.00 10.00
30 Cedric Benson/49 4.00 10.00
35 Josh Cribbs/49 4.00 10.00
38 Dez Bryant/49 6.00 15.00
39 Felix Jones/49 4.00 10.00
41 Miles Austin/49 4.00 10.00
42 Tony Romo/49 5.00 12.00
48 Calvin Johnson/15 8.00 20.00
52 Ndamukong Suh/24 6.00 15.00
66 Pierre Garcon/26 6.00 15.00
69 Maurice Jones-Drew/49 4.00 10.00
70 Mike Thomas/39 5.00 12.00
72 Dexter McCluster/49 4.00 10.00
73 Dwayne Bowe/15 6.00 15.00
74 Jamaal Charles/49 5.00 12.00
75 Matt Cassel/23 5.00 12.00
77 Anthony Fasano/49 4.00 10.00
78 Brandon Marshall/25 6.00 15.00
88 BenJarvus Green-Ellis/25 5.00 12.00
92 Wes Welker/49 8.00 20.00
94 Drew Brees/49 8.00 20.00
96 Marques Colston/49 4.00 10.00
97 Pierre Thomas/49 4.00 10.00
98 Ahmad Bradshaw/49 4.00 10.00
99 Brandon Jacobs/49 4.00 10.00
101 Hakeem Nicks/49 4.00 10.00
102 Mario Manningham/49 4.00 10.00
105 Plaxico Burress/49 4.00 10.00
107 Shonn Greene/49 4.00 10.00
108 Darren McFadden/25 5.00 12.00
116 Nnamdi Asomugha/49 4.00 10.00
122 Antonio Gates/49 4.00 10.00
125 Ryan Mathews/49 5.00 12.00
126 Vincent Jackson/49 4.00 10.00
129 Frank Gore/49 5.00 12.00
134 Zach Miller/49 4.00 10.00
138 Steven Jackson/49 4.00 10.00
143 Chris Johnson/49 4.00 10.00
145 Matt Hasselbeck/24 5.00 12.00
149 Santana Moss/49 5.00 12.00
152 Bernie Kosar/49 6.00 15.00
164 Jay Novacek/49 8.00 20.00
165 Jerome Bettis/22 15.00 40.00
166 Jim Plunkett/49 6.00 15.00
167 John Brodie/49 8.00 20.00
168 John Fuqua/49 6.00 15.00
169 John Hadl/49 5.00 12.00
171 John Matuszak/18 6.00 15.00
173 Keith Jackson/49 8.00 20.00
174 Ken Anderson/49 6.00 15.00
175 Knute Rockne/49 25.00 50.00
177 Mark Carrier/40 5.00 12.00
179 Mike Alstott/49 5.00 12.00
180 Ozzie Newsome/49 6.00 15.00
182 Paul Warfield/25 8.00 20.00
184 Randall Cunningham/49 6.00 15.00
185 Randy White/49 8.00 20.00
186 Richard Dent/49 8.00 20.00
187 Rickey Jackson/49 5.00 12.00
188 Rod Woodson/48 8.00 20.00
191 Ronnie Lott/49 8.00 20.00
194 Steve Bartkowski/49 6.00 15.00
195 Ted Hendricks/49 5.00 12.00
196 Tony Dorsett/49 8.00 20.00
197 Eddie George/49 8.00 20.00

2011 Playoff National Treasures Century Material Signature Prime

PRIME STATED PRINT RUN 1-15
10 Anquan Boldin/15 12.00 30.00
15 C.J. Spiller/15 12.00 30.00
29 Matt Forte/15 12.00 30.00
41 Miles Austin/15 20.00 50.00
42 Tony Romo/15 40.00 80.00
69 Maurice Jones-Drew/15 20.00 50.00
75 Matt Cassel/15 12.00 30.00
96 Marques Colston/15 12.00 30.00
97 Pierre Thomas/15 20.00 50.00
104 Mark Sanchez/15 15.00 40.00
107 Shonn Greene/15 12.00 30.00
116 Nnamdi Asomugha/15 12.00 30.00
122 Antonio Gates/15 12.00 30.00
126 Vincent Jackson/15 12.00 30.00
149 Santana Moss/15 12.00 30.00
152 Bernie Kosar/15 20.00 50.00
165 Jerome Bettis/15 125.00 200.00
166 Jim Plunkett/15 20.00 50.00
167 John Brodie/15 30.00 60.00
177 Mark Carrier/15 15.00 40.00
179 Mike Alstott/15 20.00 50.00
182 Paul Warfield/15 20.00 50.00
184 Randall Cunningham/15 30.00 60.00
186 Richard Dent/15 30.00 60.00
187 Rickey Jackson/15 20.00 50.00
188 Rod Woodson/15 50.00 100.00
191 Ronnie Lott/15 30.00 60.00

2011 Playoff National Treasures Colossal Materials

STATED PRINT RUN 14-99
1 Adrian Peterson/18 6.00 15.00
2 Antonio Gates/50 3.00 8.00
4 Cedric Benson/5 4.00 10.00
5 Chris Johnson/99 3.00 8.00
6 Danny Amendola/99 4.00 10.00
7 DeAngelo Williams/99 3.00 8.00
8 Eli Manning/99 4.00 10.00
9 Felix Jones/99 3.00 8.00
10 Frank Gore/85 4.00 10.00
11 Jason Witten/14 5.00 12.00
12 Jermaine Gresham/85 3.00 8.00
13 Knowshon Moreno/99 3.00 8.00
14 LaDainian Tomlinson/15 6.00 15.00
15 LeSean McCoy/71 5.00 12.00
16 Mark Sanchez/99 3.00 8.00
17 Matt Cassel/99 3.00 8.00
19 Maurice Jones-Drew/15 4.00 10.00
20 Michael Turner/15 4.00 10.00
21 Miles Austin/99 3.00 8.00
23 Roddy White/5 4.00 10.00
24 Santana Moss/99 4.00 10.00
26 Jason Campbell/99 3.00 8.00
29 Troy Polamalu/99 5.00 12.00
30 Vernon Davis/30 4.00 10.00
31 Jerod Mayo/99 3.00 8.00
32 Montell Owens/99 3.00 8.00
33 Roman Harper/99 3.00 8.00
34 David Akers/99 3.00 8.00
35 Ray Lewis/99 6.00 15.00
36 Matt Light/99 4.00 10.00
37 Jeff Saturday/99 4.00 10.00
38 Terrell Suggs/99 3.00 8.00
39 [illegible] 4.00 10.00
40 John Abraham/99 3.00 8.00
41 Antrel Rolle/90 3.00 8.00
42 Ryan Kalil/99 3.00 8.00
43 Alex Mack/99 3.00 8.00
44 London Fletcher/99 4.00 10.00
45 Jamaal Charles/99 4.00 10.00
46 Eric Weems/99 3.00 8.00
47 Billy Cundiff/99 3.00 8.00
48 Dwayne Bowe/99 4.00 10.00
49 Darrelle Revis/99 3.00 8.00
50 Zach Miller/99 3.00 8.00
51 Tony Gonzalez/99 4.00 10.00
52 John Denney/99 3.00 8.00
53 Michael Griffin/99 3.00 8.00
54 Drew Brees/99 5.00 12.00
55 Arian Foster/99 3.00 8.00
56 Joe Thomas/99 4.00 10.00
57 Brian Waters/99 3.00 8.00
58 Jay Ratliff/99 4.00 10.00
59 Larry Fitzgerald/99 4.00 10.00
60 Adrian Wilson/99 3.00 8.00
61 Ovie Mughelli/99 3.00 8.00
62 Vonta Leach/99 3.00 8.00
63 Marc Mariani/99 5.00 12.00
64 Carl Nicks/99 3.00 8.00
65 Michael Vick/99 4.00 10.00
66 Steven Jackson/99 3.00 8.00
67 Jonathan Vilma/99 3.00 8.00
68 Mat McBriar/99 3.00 8.00
69 Devin McCourty/99 3.00 8.00
70 Jahri Evans/99 3.00 8.00

2011 Playoff National Treasures Colossal Materials Prime

PRIME STATED PRINT RUN 6-49
1 Adrian Peterson/35 8.00 20.00
2 Antonio Gates/49 5.00 12.00
3 DeAngelo Hall/25 6.00 15.00
4 Cedric Benson/44 5.00 12.00
5 Chris Johnson/49 5.00 12.00
6 Danny Amendola/40 6.00 15.00
7 DeAngelo Williams/49 5.00 12.00
8 Eli Manning/15 8.00 20.00
9 Felix Jones/49 5.00 12.00
10 Frank Gore/20 8.00 20.00
12 Jermaine Gresham/37 5.00 12.00
14 LaDainian Tomlinson/17 10.00 25.00
18 Matt Forte/18 6.00 15.00
19 Maurice Jones-Drew/49 8.00 20.00
20 Michael Turner/40 5.00 12.00
21 Miles Austin/49 8.00 20.00
22 Philip Rivers/40 8.00 20.00
23 Roddy White/39 5.00 12.00
24 Santana Moss/49 6.00 15.00
25 Santonio Holmes/20 6.00 15.00
27 Dexter McCluster/25 6.00 15.00
28 Brian Hartline/49 6.00 15.00
31 Jerod Mayo/49 5.00 12.00
32 Montell Owens/49 5.00 12.00
33 Roman Harper/49 5.00 12.00
34 David Akers/49 5.00 12.00
35 Ray Lewis/49 10.00 25.00
36 Matt Light/49 6.00 15.00
37 Jeff Saturday/49 6.00 15.00
38 Terrell Suggs/49 5.00 12.00
39 Reggie Wayne/49 6.00 15.00
40 John Abraham/49 5.00 12.00
41 Antrel Rolle/49 5.00 12.00
42 Ryan Kalil/49 5.00 12.00
43 Alex Mack/49 5.00 12.00
44 London Fletcher/49 6.00 15.00
45 Jamaal Charles/49 6.00 15.00
46 Eric Weems/49 5.00 12.00
47 Billy Cundiff/49 5.00 12.00
48 Dwayne Bowe/49 6.00 15.00
49 Darrelle Revis/49 5.00 12.00
50 Zach Miller/49 5.00 12.00
51 Tony Gonzalez/49 6.00 15.00
52 John Denney/49 5.00 12.00
53 Michael Griffin/49 5.00 12.00
54 Drew Brees/25 12.00 30.00
55 Arian Foster/49 5.00 12.00
56 Joe Thomas/49 6.00 15.00
57 Brian Waters/49 5.00 12.00
58 Jay Ratliff/49 6.00 15.00
59 Larry Fitzgerald/35 6.00 15.00
60 Adrian Wilson/49 5.00 12.00
61 Ovie Mughelli/49 5.00 12.00
62 Vonta Leach/49 5.00 12.00
63 Marc Mariani/49 8.00 20.00
64 Carl Nicks/49 5.00 12.00
65 Michael Vick/13 8.00 20.00
66 Steven Jackson/49 5.00 12.00
67 Jonathan Vilma/49 5.00 12.00
68 Mat McBriar/43 5.00 12.00
69 Devin McCourty/49 5.00 12.00
70 Jahri Evans/49 5.00 12.00

2011 Playoff National Treasures Colossal Materials Signature

STATED PRINT RUN 2-49
6 Danny Amendola/9 8.00 20.00
7 DeAngelo Williams/20 10.00 25.00
12 Jermaine Gresham/49 6.00 15.00
17 Matt Cassel/15 10.00 25.00
28 Brian Hartline/35 10.00 25.00
31 Jerod Mayo/9 6.00 15.00

2011 Playoff National Treasures Colossal Materials Signature Prime

PRIME STATED PRINT RUN 1-25
3 DeAngelo Hall/25 12.00 30.00
6 Danny Amendola/25 15.00 40.00
12 Jermaine Gresham/25 12.00 30.00
18 Matt Forte/20 20.00 50.00
28 Brian Hartline/25 15.00 40.00

2011 Playoff National Treasures Emblems of the Hall

STATED PRINT RUN 99 SER.#'d SETS
1 Deion Sanders 2.50 6.00
2 Fran Tarkenton 3.00 8.00
3 Jim Parker 2.00 5.00
4 Shannon Sharpe 2.50 6.00
5 Chris Hanburger 2.00 5.00
6 Les Richter 2.00 5.00
7 Ozzie Newsome 2.50 6.00
8 Bobby Layne 2.50 6.00
9 Carl Eller 2.00 5.00
10 Buck Buchanan 2.00 5.00
11 Dan Hampton 2.00 5.00
12 Deacon Jones 2.50 6.00
13 Eric Dickerson 2.50 6.00
14 Darrell Green 3.00 8.00
15 Derrick Thomas 15.00 30.00
16 Lou Groza 2.50 6.00
17 Richard Dent 2.00 5.00
18 Sam Huff 2.50 6.00
19 Steve Largent 3.00 8.00
20 Jan Stenerud 2.00 5.00
21 Jack Youngblood 2.00 5.00
22 Jack Lambert 3.00 8.00

23 Joe Greene 3.00 8.00
24 Don Maynard 2.50 6.00
25 Gale Sayers 3.00 8.00
26 Bob Griese 3.00 8.00
27 Chuck Bednarik 2.50 6.00
28 Frank Gifford 2.50 6.00
29 Jim Kelly 3.00 8.00
30 John Mackey 2.50 6.00

2011 Playoff National Treasures Emblems of the Hall Materials

STATED PRINT RUN 1-99
1 Deion Sanders/99 8.00 20.00
2 Fran Tarkenton/99 6.00 15.00
3 Jim Parker/99 4.00 10.00
4 Shannon Sharpe/57 5.00 12.00
7 Ozzie Newsome/99 5.00 12.00
9 Carl Eller/99 4.00 10.00
10 Buck Buchanan/99 4.00 10.00
11 Dan Hampton/49 5.00 12.00
14 Darrell Green/99 6.00 15.00
18 Sam Huff/47 5.00 12.00
19 Steve Largent/99 6.00 15.00
20 Jan Stenerud/99 4.00 10.00
23 Joe Greene/99 6.00 15.00
24 Don Maynard/99 5.00 12.00
25 Gale Sayers/49 6.00 15.00
26 Bob Griese/99 6.00 15.00
29 Jim Kelly/99 6.00 15.00

2011 Playoff National Treasures Emblems of the Hall Materials Prime

*PRIME/25: .8X TO 2X BASIC JSY/47-99
PIRME STATED PRINT RUN 1-25
15 Derrick Thomas/25 90.00 150.00

2011 Playoff National Treasures Emblems of the Hall Signature Materials

STATED PRINT RUN 2-25
*PRIME/15: .6X TO 1.5X BASIC JSY/15-25
2 Fran Tarkenton/25 20.00 50.00
4 Shannon Sharpe/25 20.00 50.00
9 Carl Eller/15 12.00 30.00
18 Sam Huff/25 15.00 40.00
19 Steve Largent/25 15.00 40.00
20 Jan Stenerud/25 12.00 30.00
23 Joe Greene/25 20.00 50.00
26 Bob Griese/25 20.00 50.00
29 Jim Kelly/25 20.00 50.00

2011 Playoff National Treasures Emblems of the Hall Signatures

STATED PRINT RUN 5-99
2 Fran Tarkenton/25 25.00 50.00
4 Shannon Sharpe/99 20.00 40.00
12 Deacon Jones/49 15.00 40.00
13 Eric Dickerson/25 25.00 50.00
18 Sam Huff/99 10.00 25.00
19 Steve Largent/49 12.00 30.00
21 Jack Youngblood/38 12.00 30.00
22 Jack Lambert/49 30.00 60.00
23 Joe Greene/25 25.00 50.00
25 Gale Sayers/25 30.00 60.00
26 Bob Griese/15 15.00 40.00
27 Chuck Bednarik/25 12.00 30.00
28 Frank Gifford/25 20.00 40.00

2011 Playoff National Treasures Fans of the Game

EXCH EXPIRATION: 10/4/2013
1 Alyssa Milano 1.50 4.00
1AU Alyssa Milano AU 75.00 125.00

2011 Playoff National Treasures Hall of Fame Leather Autographs

STATED PRINT RUN 5-53
1 Barry Sanders/20 90.00 150.00
2 Bart Starr/50 60.00 120.00
3 Bob Griese/27 25.00 50.00
5 Deion Sanders/25 40.00 80.00
7 Eric Dickerson/27 30.00 60.00
8 Forrest Gregg/27 20.00 40.00
9 Franco Harris/18 30.00 60.00
10 Jim Kelly/25 25.00 50.00
11 Joe Greene/26 30.00 60.00
12 Joe Namath/49 60.00 120.00
14 Michael Irvin/25 30.00 60.00
15 Paul Hornung/26 20.00 40.00
16 Paul Warfield/26 15.00 30.00
17 Raymond Berry/27 20.00 40.00
18 Bobby Bell/37 15.00 30.00
19 Chuck Bednarik/35 20.00 40.00
20 Frank Gifford/17 25.00 50.00
21 Hugh McElhenny/38 15.00 30.00
22 Kellen Winslow/37 20.00 40.00
23 Larry Little/35 15.00 30.00
24 Lenny Moore/37 15.00 30.00
25 Marcus Allen/53 20.00 40.00

2011 Playoff National Treasures HOF Patch Autographs

STATED PRINT RUN 20-45
1 Dick Butkus/21 40.00 80.00
2 Frank Gifford/20 25.00 50.00
3 Howie Long/21 30.00 60.00
4 John Riggins/21 25.00 50.00
5 Ronnie Lott/21 30.00 60.00
6 Steve Largent/26 20.00 40.00
7 Alan Page/36 20.00 40.00
8 Barry Sanders/32 75.00 150.00
9 Bart Starr/45 60.00 120.00
10 Bob Griese/40 25.00 50.00
11 Dan Marino/45 100.00 200.00
12 Deion Sanders/30 50.00 100.00
13 Emmitt Smith/37 125.00 200.00
14 Eric Dickerson/40 30.00 60.00
15 Forrest Gregg/30 20.00 40.00
16 Franco Harris/40 25.00 50.00
17 Jim Kelly/40 25.00 50.00
18 Joe Greene/35 30.00 60.00
19 Joe Montana/26 100.00 175.00
20 Joe Namath/45 60.00 120.00
21 John Elway/30 90.00 150.00
22 Lenny Moore/30 20.00 40.00
23 Marcus Allen/30 25.00 50.00
24 Michael Irvin/40 25.00 50.00
25 Paul Hornung/40 20.00 40.00
26 Paul Warfield/40 15.00 30.00
27 Raymond Berry/25 20.00 40.00

2011 Playoff National Treasures NFL Gear Combos

STATED PRINT RUN 99 SER.#'d SETS
*TRIPLE/99: .5X TO 1.2X COMBO/99
2 Alex Green 2.00 5.00
3 Andy Dalton 4.00 10.00
4 Austin Pettis 2.00 5.00
5 Bilal Powell 2.50 6.00
6 Blaine Gabbert 2.00 5.00
7 Cam Newton 10.00 25.00
9 Clyde Gates 2.00 5.00
10 Colin Kaepernick 3.00 8.00
11 Daniel Thomas 2.00 5.00
12 Delone Carter 2.00 5.00
13 DeMarco Murray 4.00 10.00
14 Greg Little 2.50 6.00
15 Jake Locker 2.00 5.00
16 Jamie Harper 2.00 5.00
17 Jerrel Jernigan 2.00 5.00
18 Jonathan Baldwin 2.00 5.00
19 Jordan Todman 2.00 5.00
20 Julio Jones 6.00 15.00
21 Kendall Hunter 2.00 5.00
23 Leonard Hankerson 2.00 5.00
24 Marcell Dareus 2.00 5.00
25 Mark Ingram 3.00 8.00
26 Mikel Leshoure 2.00 5.00
27 Randall Cobb 3.00 8.00
28 Ryan Mallett 2.00 5.00
29 Ryan Williams 2.00 5.00
30 Shane Vereen 2.50 6.00
31 Stevan Ridley 2.00 5.00
32 Taiwan Jones 2.00 5.00
33 Titus Young 2.00 5.00
34 Torrey Smith 2.00 5.00
35 Vincent Brown 2.00 5.00
36 Von Miller 3.00 8.00

2011 Playoff National Treasures NFL Gear Combos Prime

*PRIME/49: .6X TO 1.5X BASIC JSY/99
PRIME STATED PRINT RUN 49
*TRIPLE PRIME/49: .5X TO 1.2X PRIME/49
1 A.J. Green 8.00 20.00
8 Christian Ponder 3.00 8.00

2011 Playoff National Treasures NFL Gear Combos ID Tag Signatures

STATED PRINT RUN 1-25
3 Andy Dalton/25 40.00 100.00
5 Bilal Powell/20 20.00 50.00
8 Christian Ponder/15 25.00 60.00
9 Clyde Gates/15 15.00 40.00
15 Jake Locker/25 15.00 40.00
34 Torrey Smith/20 15.00 40.00
35 Vincent Brown/25 15.00 40.00
36 Von Miller/25 40.00 100.00

2011 Playoff National Treasures NFL Gear Combos Laundry Tag Signatures

STATED PRINT RUN 3-25
3 Andy Dalton/15 40.00 100.00
5 Bilal Powell/25 20.00 50.00
9 Clyde Gates/15 15.00 40.00
10 Colin Kaepernick/25 25.00 60.00
15 Jake Locker/25 15.00 40.00
16 Jamie Harper/20 15.00 40.00
18 Jonathan Baldwin/25 15.00 40.00
25 Mark Ingram/15 25.00 60.00
26 Mikel Leshoure/25 15.00 40.00
28 Ryan Mallett/25 15.00 40.00
30 Shane Vereen/25 20.00 50.00
31 Stevan Ridley/25 15.00 40.00
33 Titus Young/25 15.00 40.00
34 Torrey Smith/25 15.00 40.00
36 Von Miller/25 40.00 100.00

2011 Playoff National Treasures NFL Gear Combos Signatures

STATED PRINT RUN 25-49
*TRIPLE/25-49: .5X TO 1.2X COMBO/25-49
2 Alex Green/49 5.00 12.00
3 Andy Dalton/49 30.00 60.00
4 Austin Pettis/49 5.00 12.00
5 Bilal Powell/49 6.00 15.00
6 Blaine Gabbert/49 5.00 12.00
7 Cam Newton/25 125.00 250.00
9 Clyde Gates/49 5.00 12.00
10 Colin Kaepernick/49 60.00 120.00
15 Jake Locker/49 5.00 12.00
17 Jerrel Jernigan/49 5.00 12.00
18 Jonathan Baldwin/49 5.00 12.00
19 Jordan Todman/49 5.00 12.00
21 Kendall Hunter/49 5.00 12.00
23 Leonard Hankerson/49 5.00 12.00
25 Mark Ingram/25 10.00 25.00
26 Mikel Leshoure/49 5.00 12.00
27 Randall Cobb/49 8.00 20.00
28 Ryan Mallett/49 5.00 12.00
29 Ryan Williams/49 5.00 12.00
30 Shane Vereen/49 6.00 15.00
31 Stevan Ridley/49 5.00 12.00
32 Taiwan Jones/49 5.00 12.00
34 Torrey Smith/49 5.00 12.00
35 Vincent Brown/49 5.00 12.00

2011 Playoff National Treasures NFL Gear Combos Signatures Prime

*PRIME/25: .8X TO 2X COMBO AU/25-49
PRIME STATED PRINT RUN 10-25
*TRIP.PRIME/25: .4X TO 1X CMBO PRIME/25
1 A.J. Green/25 50.00 100.00

2011 Playoff National Treasures NFL Greatest

STATED PRINT RUN 99 SER.#'d SETS
1 Walter Payton 6.00 15.00
2 Randy Moss 2.00 5.00
3 Brett Favre 5.00 12.00
4 Joe Montana 8.00 20.00
5 Roger Staubach 4.00 10.00
6 Warren Moon 3.00 8.00
7 Barry Sanders 5.00 12.00
8 Bruce Smith 2.50 6.00
9 Doak Walker 3.00 8.00
10 Franco Harris 3.00 8.00
11 Jerry Rice 5.00 12.00
12 Jim Brown 4.00 10.00
13 Jim Thorpe 4.00 10.00
14 Johnny Unitas 5.00 12.00
15 Reggie White 3.00 8.00
16 Terry Bradshaw 4.00 10.00
17 Troy Aikman 4.00 10.00
18 Dan Fouts 2.50 6.00
19 Dan Marino 6.00 15.00
20 Emmitt Smith 5.00 12.00
21 Steve Young 4.00 10.00
22 John Elway 5.00 12.00
23 Dick Butkus 4.00 10.00
24 Tom Brady 6.00 15.00
25 Peyton Manning 5.00 12.00
26 Sammy Baugh 3.00 8.00
27 Dick Lane 2.00 5.00
28 Mike Singletary 3.00 8.00
29 Lee Roy Selmon 2.00 5.00
30 Jim Otto 2.00 5.00
31 Ray Nitschke 2.50 6.00
32 Otto Graham 2.50 6.00

2011 Playoff National Treasures NFL Greatest Materials

STATED PRINT RUN 25-99
3 Brett Favre/99 10.00 25.00
4 Joe Montana/99 12.00 30.00
5 Roger Staubach/99 8.00 20.00
6 Warren Moon/99 5.00 12.00
9 Doak Walker/99 8.00 20.00
10 Franco Harris/99 5.00 12.00
11 Jerry Rice/99 8.00 20.00
12 Jim Brown/99 6.00 15.00
15 Reggie White/77 8.00 20.00
16 Terry Bradshaw/99 6.00 15.00
17 Troy Aikman/99 6.00 15.00
18 Dan Fouts/99 4.00 10.00
19 Dan Marino/5 15.00 40.00
20 Emmitt Smith/99 8.00 20.00
21 Steve Young/99 6.00 15.00
22 John Elway/99 8.00 20.00
23 Dick Butkus/99 6.00 15.00
24 Tom Brady/99 12.00 30.00
26 Sammy Baugh/57 10.00 25.00
27 Dick Lane/99 5.00 12.00
29 Lee Roy Selmon/99 3.00 8.00
30 Jim Otto/99 3.00 8.00
31 Ray Nitschke/99 8.00 20.00
32 Otto Graham/99 8.00 20.00

2011 Playoff National Treasures NFL Greatest Materials Prime

STATED PRINT RUN 4-49
1 Walter Payton/49 15.00 40.00
2 Randy Moss/49 6.00 15.00
4 Joe Montana/20 25.00 60.00
5 Roger Staubach/49 12.00 30.00
7 Barry Sanders/25 15.00 40.00
8 Bruce Smith/49 6.00 15.00
11 Jerry Rice/49 15.00 40.00
17 Troy Aikman/49 10.00 25.00
18 Dan Fouts/49 6.00 15.00
19 Dan Marino/25 20.00 50.00
20 Emmitt Smith/49 12.00 30.00
21 Steve Young/49 10.00 25.00
28 Mike Singletary/45 8.00 20.00
29 Lee Roy Selmon/49 6.00 15.00
30 Jim Otto/25 6.00 15.00

2011 Playoff National Treasures NFL Greatest Signature Materials

STATED PRINT RUN 5-25
3 Brett Favre/25 100.00 200.00
4 Joe Montana/25 90.00 150.00
6 Warren Moon/25 25.00 50.00
22 John Elway/25 90.00 150.00
30 Jim Otto/25 15.00 30.00

2011 Playoff National Treasures NFL Greatest Signature Materials Prime

*PRIME/15: .6X TO 1.5X BASIC JSY AU/25
PRIME STATED PRINT RUN 5-15
21 Steve Young/15 50.00 100.00

2011 Playoff National Treasures NFL Greatest Signatures

STATED PRINT RUN 5-25
3 Brett Favre/15 100.00 200.00
4 Joe Montana/25 75.00 125.00
6 Warren Moon/24 20.00 40.00
7 Barry Sanders/25 75.00 135.00
30 Jim Otto/25 12.50 25.00

2011 Playoff National Treasures NFL Leather Autographs

STATED PRINT RUN 6-103
1 Archie Manning/50 25.00 50.00
2 Bo Jackson/25 50.00 100.00
3 Brandon Lloyd/27 10.00 25.00
4 Danny White/27 20.00 40.00
5 Don Perkins/53 12.00 30.00
6 Doug Flutie/50 20.00 40.00
7 Ed Too Tall Jones/27 12.00 30.00
8 Henry Ellard/35 12.00 30.00
10 Jim McMahon/27 25.00 50.00
11 Keyshawn Johnson/27 10.00 25.00
12 Larry Fitzgerald/27 40.00 80.00
13 Lydell Mitchell/103 8.00 20.00
14 Mark Sanchez/25 15.00 40.00
15 Matt Ryan/27 25.00 50.00
17 Miles Austin/25 25.00 50.00
19 Priest Holmes/27 20.00 40.00
20 Randall Cunningham/26 25.00 50.00
21 Sam Bradford/22 25.00 60.00
23 Tony Romo/27 40.00 80.00
24 Troy Polamalu/27 100.00 175.00

2011 Playoff National Treasures NFL MVPs Leather Autographs

STATED PRINT RUN 7-38
2 Bart Starr/23 90.00 150.00
3 Dan Marino/14 150.00 250.00
4 Emmitt Smith/17 125.00 200.00
6 Adrian Peterson/27 90.00 150.00
7 Alan Page/38 20.00 40.00
8 Ben Roethlisberger/27 50.00 100.00
9 Boomer Esiason/26 25.00 50.00
10 Curtis Martin/26 25.00 50.00
11 Frank Gifford/20 20.00 40.00
12 LaDainian Tomlinson/26 25.00 50.00

2011 Playoff National Treasures Pen Pals

STATED PRINT RUN 15-25
1 Kaepernick/Hunter/25 75.00 125.00
2 A.Dalton/A.Green/25 30.00 80.00
3 J.Todman/V.Brown/25 12.00 30.00
4 M.Leshoure/T.Young/25 20.00 40.00
5 A.Green/R.Cobb/25 12.00 30.00
6 Mallett/Vereen/Ridley/25 25.00 60.00
7 C.Ponder/K.Rudolph/25 12.00 30.00
8 M.Dareus/V.Miller/25 20.00 40.00
9 Six Rookie QBs/15 75.00 150.00
10 Six Rookie RBs/15 25.00 60.00
11 Six Rookie RBs/15 20.00 50.00
12 Six Rookie WRs/15 60.00 120.00
13 Six Rookie WRs/15 125.00 250.00
14 Eight Rookies/15 50.00 100.00
15 Eight Rookies/15 25.00 60.00
16 Eight Rookies/15 15.00 40.00
17 Eight Rookies/15 60.00 150.00
18 Eight Rookies/15 40.00 80.00
19 Eight Rookies/15 100.00 200.00
20 Eight Rookies/15 25.00 60.00

2011 Playoff National Treasures Pro Bowl Materials

STATED PRINT RUN 99 SER.#'d SETS
*PRIME/49: .6X TO 1.5X BASIC JSY/99
1 John Abraham 3.00 8.00
2 Ray Lewis 5.00 12.00
3 Darrelle Revis 3.00 8.00
4 Larry Fitzgerald 4.00 10.00
5 Steven Jackson 3.00 8.00
6 Dwayne Bowe 4.00 10.00
7 Tony Gonzalez 4.00 10.00
8 Drew Brees 5.00 12.00
9 Jerod Mayo 3.00 8.00
10 Reggie Wayne 4.00 10.00
11 Vonta Leach 3.00 8.00
12 Devin McCourty 3.00 8.00
13 Terrell Suggs 3.00 8.00
14 Jamaal Charles 4.00 10.00
15 Michael Vick 4.00 10.00
16 Michael Griffin 3.00 8.00
17 Zach Miller 3.00 8.00
18 London Fletcher 4.00 10.00
19 Arian Foster 3.00 8.00
20 Adrian Wilson 3.00 8.00

2011 Playoff National Treasures Pro Bowl Signature Materials

STATED PRINT RUN 10-25
9 Jerod Mayo/25 10.00 25.00
18 London Fletcher/25 15.00 40.00

2011 Playoff National Treasures Ring of Honor

STATED PRINT RUN 99 SER.#'d SETS
1 Bart Starr 5.00 12.00
2 Bob Lilly 2.50 6.00
3 John Stallworth 2.50 6.00
4 Russ Grimm 2.00 5.00
5 Terrell Davis 2.50 6.00
6 Jim McMahon 2.50 6.00
7 Ken Stabler 3.00 8.00
8 Cliff Branch 2.00 5.00
9 Raymond Berry 2.50 6.00
10 Doug Williams 2.50 6.00
11 Joe Namath 4.00 10.00
12 Larry Little 2.00 5.00
13 Len Dawson 3.00 8.00
14 Howie Long 3.00 8.00
15 Jim Taylor 2.50 6.00
16 Michael Strahan 2.50 6.00

2011 Playoff National Treasures Ring of Honor Signatures

STATED PRINT RUN 5-49
1 Bart Starr/15 75.00 150.00
4 Russ Grimm/49 12.00 30.00
5 Terrell Davis/30 26.00 50.00
6 Jim McMahon/49 25.00 50.00
9 Raymond Berry/49 15.00 40.00
10 Doug Williams/17 25.00 50.00
12 Larry Little/49 12.00 30.00
13 Len Dawson/15 25.00 50.00
14 Howie Long/49 25.00 50.00
15 Jim Taylor/49 25.00 50.00
16 Michael Strahan/49 20.00 40.00

2011 Playoff National Treasures Rookie Signature Material Black

*BLACK/25: .6X TO 1.5X BASIC JSY AU/99
STATED PRINT RUN 25 SER.#'d SETS
323 Julio Jones EXCH 300.00 600.00
325 Jake Locker 250.00 500.00
326 Andy Dalton 125.00 250.00
327 Colin Kaepernick 200.00 400.00
328 Cam Newton 1500.00 2500.00
329 A.J. Green 250.00 400.00
331 DeMarco Murray 40.00 100.00

2011 Playoff National Treasures Rookie Signature Material Gold

*GOLD/49: .5X TO 1.2X BASIC JSY AU/99
STATED PRINT RUN 49 SER.#'d SETS
323 Julio Jones EXCH 250.00 500.00
325 Jake Locker 100.00 200.00
326 Andy Dalton 100.00 200.00
327 Colin Kaepernick 150.00 300.00
328 Cam Newton 500.00 1000.00
329 A.J. Green 125.00 250.00
331 DeMarco Murray 30.00 80.00

2011 Playoff National Treasures Souvenir Cuts

STATED PRINT RUN 1-49
1 Bob Waterfield/26 60.00 120.00
3 Joe Perry/49 20.00 40.00
5 Dante Lavelli/14 30.00 60.00
6 Frank Gatski/20 20.00 40.00

2011 Playoff National Treasures Stamp Jumbo Material

2 Knute Rockne/19 60.00 120.00

2011 Playoff National Treasures Super Bowl MVPs Leather Autographs

STATED PRINT RUN 2-52
5 John Elway/33 75.00 150.00
6 Aaron Rodgers/27 200.00 300.00
7 Drew Brees/27 90.00 150.00
9 Jim Plunkett/27 15.00 40.00
10 Peyton Manning/52 125.00 200.00
11 Ottis Anderson/35 15.00 40.00
12 Terrell Davis/27 30.00 60.00

2011 Playoff National Treasures Timeline Materials Custom Names

STATED PRINT RUN 50-99
*PRIME/15: .8X TO 2X BASIC JSY/99
*TEAM/50-99: .4X TO 1X CUSTOM/50-99
1 Dan Fouts/99 5.00 12.00
2 Dan Marino/99 12.00 30.00
3 Emmitt Smith/50 10.00 25.00
4 George Blanda/99 5.00 12.00
5 Keyshawn Johnson/50 5.00 12.00
6 Marshall Faulk/99 5.00 12.00
7 Phil Simms/99 5.00 12.00
8 Steve Young/99 8.00 20.00
9 John Elway/99 10.00 25.00
10 Dick Butkus/50 8.00 20.00

2011 Playoff National Treasures Timeline Materials Signature Custom Names

STATED PRINT RUN 22-25
*TEAM/25: .4X TO 1X CUSTOM/25
2 Dan Marino/25 125.00 200.00
3 Emmitt Smith/22 125.00 200.00
5 Keyshawn Johnson/25 10.00 25.00
7 Phil Simms/25 15.00 40.00
8 Steve Young/25 50.00 100.00
9 John Elway/25 90.00 150.00
10 Dick Butkus/25 40.00 80.00

2006 Playoff NFL Playoffs

This 150-card set was released in factory set form in December, 2006. The set was issued with an $100 SRP price tag. Cards numbered 1-70 feature veterans, most of whom were sequenced in first name alphabetical order while cards numbered 71-150 feature 2006 rookies.

COMP.FACT SET (155) 60.00 100.00
COMPLETE SET (150) 20.00 50.00
1 Alex Smith QB .25 .60
2 Alge Crumpler .25 .60
3 Andre Johnson .25 .60
4 Anquan Boldin .20 .50
5 Antonio Gates .30 .75
6 Ben Roethlisberger .40 1.00
7 Braylon Edwards .20 .50
8 Brian Urlacher .30 .75
9 Brett Favre .60 1.50
10 Byron Leftwich .20 .50
11 Cadillac Williams .25 .60
12 Carson Palmer .25 .60
13 Cedric Benson .20 .50
14 Chad Johnson .20 .50
15 Charlie Frye .25 .60
16 Chris Brown .20 .50
17 Chris Chambers .20 .50
18 Clinton Portis .20 .50
19 Dallas Clark .20 .50
20 Darrell Jackson .25 .60
21 Deion Branch .20 .50
22 Domanick Davis .20 .50
23 Donovan McNabb .25 .60
24 Drew Bennett .25 .60
25 Drew Bledsoe .25 .60
26 Edgerrin James .25 .60
27 Eli Manning .25 .60
28 Hines Ward .25 .60
29 Jake Delhomme .20 .50
30 Jerry Porter .20 .50
31 Julius Jones .20 .50
32 Kevin Jones .20 .50
33 LaDainian Tomlinson .30 .75
34 LaMont Jordan .25 .60
35 Larry Fitzgerald .25 .60
36 Larry Johnson .20 .50
37 Lee Evans .25 .60
38 Marc Bulger .20 .50
39 Mark Clayton .20 .50
40 Matt Hasselbeck .20 .50
41 Marvin Harrison .25 .60
42 Matt Jones .20 .50
43 Michael Vick .25 .60
44 Nate Burleson .20 .50
45 Peyton Manning .75 2.00
46 Philip Rivers .30 .75
47 Priest Holmes .20 .50
48 Reggie Brown .20 .50
49 Reggie Wayne .25 .60
50 Robert Ferguson .20 .50
51 Ronnie Brown .25 .60
52 Roy Williams S .20 .50
53 Roy Williams WR .20 .50
54 Rudi Johnson .20 .50
55 Samkon Gado .20 .50
56 Santana Moss .25 .60
57 Shaun Alexander .20 .50
58 Steven Jackson .20 .50
59 Steve Smith .30 .75
60 T.J. Houshmandzadeh .20 .50
61 Tatum Bell .20 .50
62 Thomas Jones .20 .50
63 Tiki Barber .25 .60
64 Torry Holt .25 .60
65 Tedy Bruschi .25 .60
66 Willie Parker .25 .60
67 Willis McGahee .20 .50
68 Drew Brees .30 .75
69 Dominic Rhodes .20 .50
70 Brian Westbrook .20 .50
71 Reggie Bush RC 1.00 2.50
72 Matt Leinart RC .60 1.50
73 Vince Young RC .60 1.50
74 Jay Cutler RC .75 2.00
75 DeAngelo Williams RC .75 2.00
76 LenDale White RC .60 1.50
77 Laurence Maroney RC .60 1.50
78 Santonio Holmes RC .75 2.00
79 Brodie Croyle RC .60 1.50
80 Sinorice Moss RC .60 1.50
81 Jeremy Bloom RC .60 1.50
82 A.J. Hawk RC .75 2.00
83 Joseph Addai RC .60 1.50
84 Vernon Davis RC .75 2.00
85 Michael Huff RC .75 2.00
86 Mario Williams RC 1.00 2.50
87 Demetrius Williams RC .60 1.50
88 Donte Whitner RC .75 2.00
89 Haloti Ngata RC .75 2.00
90 Tamba Hali RC 1.00 2.50
91 Omar Jacobs RC .60 1.50
92 Leonard Pope RC 1.00 2.50
93 Chad Jackson RC .60 1.50
94 Maurice Stovall RC .60 1.50
95 D'Brickashaw Ferguson RC .60 1.50
96 Charlie Whitehurst RC .60 1.50
97 Ingle Martin RC .75 2.00
98 Brian Calhoun RC .60 1.50
99 Leon Washington RC .60 1.50
100 Marcedes Lewis RC .60 1.50
101 Anthony Fasano RC .60 1.50
102 Derek Hagan RC .75 2.00
103 Devin Hester RC 1.25 3.00
104 Bobby Carpenter RC .60 1.50
105 Brodrick Bunkley RC .75 2.00
106 Maurice Drew RC 1.00 2.50
107 P.J. Daniels RC .60 1.50
108 Marques Hagans RC .60 1.50
109 Joe Klopfenstein RC .60 1.50
110 Tony Scheffler RC 1.00 2.50
111 Cory Rodgers RC .60 1.50
112 Tye Hill RC .60 1.50
113 Johnathan Joseph RC .75 2.00
114 John McCargo RC .60 1.50
115 Kamerion Wimbley RC .75 2.00
116 Jerious Norwood RC .60 1.50
117 Michael Robinson RC .60 1.50
118 Jason Avant RC .60 1.50
119 Manny Lawson RC .75 2.00
120 Mathias Kiwanuka RC 1.00 2.50
121 Kellen Clemens RC .60 1.50
122 Jerome Harrison RC .60 1.50
123 Dominique Byrd RC .60 1.50
124 Travis Wilson RC .60 1.50
125 Brandon Williams RC .60 1.50
126 Brandon Marshall RC 1.25 3.00
127 Greg Jennings RC 1.00 2.50
128 Brad Smith RC .75 2.00
129 Domenik Hixon RC 1.00 2.50
130 Kelly Jennings RC .75 2.00
131 Ernie Sims RC .60 1.50
132 Jason Allen RC .75 2.00
133 Tarvaris Jackson RC .60 1.50
134 David Thomas RC .60 1.50
135 Willie Reid RC .75 2.00
136 Skyler Green RC .60 1.50
137 Antonio Cromartie RC .75 2.00
138 Chad Greenway RC 1.00 2.50
139 Owen Daniels RC 1.00 2.50
140 Garrett Mills RC .75 2.00
141 Will Blackmon RC .60 1.50
142 David Kirtman RC .75 2.00
143 DeMeco Ryans RC .75 2.00
144 D'Qwell Jackson RC .60 1.50
145 Rocky McIntosh RC .60 1.50
146 Wali Lundy RC .60 1.50
147 Mike Bell RC .60 1.50
148 Daniel Bullocks RC .60 1.50
149 Marques Colston RC 1.00 2.50
150 Roman Harper RC .75 2.00

2006 Playoff NFL Playoffs Gold Proof

*VETERANS: 5X TO 12X BASIC CARDS
*ROOKIES: 1.2X TO 3X BASIC CARDS
STATED PRINT RUN 100 SER.#'d SETS

2006 Playoff NFL Playoffs Red

*VETERANS: 2X TO 5X BASIC CARDS
*ROOKIES: .5X TO 1.2X BASIC CARDS

2006 Playoff NFL Playoffs Platinum

UNPRICED PLATINUM PRINT RUN 1

2006 Playoff NFL Playoffs Silver Proof

*VETERANS: 3X TO 8X BASIC CARDS
*ROOKIES: .8X TO 2X BASIC CARDS
STATED PRINT RUN 250 SER.#'d SETS

2006 Playoff NFL Playoffs Jersey Signature Proofs Silver

SILVER PRINT RUN 10-100
*GOLD: .5X TO 1.2X SLVR JSY AU
GOLD PRINT RUN 4-50
UNPRICED PLATINUM PRINT RUN 1
SERIAL #'d UNDER 24 NOT PRICED
2 Alge Crumpler/25
5 Antonio Gates/25
6 Ben Roethlisberger/25 60.00 120.00
7 Braylon Edwards/25
8 Brian Urlacher/50 20.00 50.00
9 Brett Favre/25 125.00 250.00
14 Chad Johnson/25 15.00 40.00
15 Charlie Frye/25
16 Chris Brown/25 7.50 20.00
19 Dallas Clark/25
20 Darrell Jackson/25
21 Deion Branch/25 15.00 40.00
22 Domanick Davis/100 7.50 20.00
24 Drew Bennett/100 7.50 20.00
30 Jerry Porter/24
35 Larry Fitzgerald/25 25.00 50.00
37 Lee Evans/25
39 Mark Clayton/25
40 Matt Hasselbeck/25
45 Peyton Manning/25 75.00 150.00
49 Reggie Wayne/25 15.00 40.00
51 Ronnie Brown/25
52 Roy Williams S/25
54 Rudi Johnson/25
55 Samkon Gado/100 8.00 20.00
58 Steven Jackson/25 10.00 25.00
60 T.J. Houshmandzadeh/25
61 Tatum Bell/25
62 Thomas Jones/25
63 Tiki Barber/25
65 Tedy Bruschi/25 50.00 100.00
66 Willie Parker/25
71 Reggie Bush/25 20.00 50.00
72 Matt Leinart/25
73 Vince Young/25 40.00 100.00
75 DeAngelo Williams/50 25.00 60.00
76 LenDale White/25
77 Laurence Maroney/25 20.00 50.00
78 Santonio Holmes/25 15.00 40.00
80 Sinorice Moss/25
82 A.J. Hawk/25
84 Vernon Davis/25
85 Michael Huff/75 12.00 30.00
86 Mario Williams/75 15.00 40.00
87 Demetrius Williams/25
91 Omar Jacobs/60 12.50 30.00
93 Chad Jackson/25
94 Maurice Stovall/25
96 Charlie Whitehurst/25 12.50 30.00
98 Brian Calhoun/25
99 Leon Washington/49 12.00 30.00
100 Marcedes Lewis/100 7.50 20.00
102 Derek Hagan/100 7.50 20.00
106 Maurice Drew/25 40.00 80.00
109 Joe Klopfenstein/100 6.00 15.00
116 Jerious Norwood/100 10.00 25.00
117 Michael Robinson/25
118 Jason Avant/25 12.50 30.00
121 Kellen Clemens/25
124 Travis Wilson/50 12.00 30.00
125 Brandon Williams/25
126 Brandon Marshall/50 15.00 40.00
133 Tarvaris Jackson/25

2006 Playoff NFL Playoffs Signature Proofs Silver

1-70 SILVER PRINT RUN 7-150
71-150 SILVER PRINT RUN 148-150
*GOLD VETS: .5X TO 1.2X SILVER AU
*GOLD ROOKIES: .6X TO 1.5X SILVER AU
GOLD PRINT RUN 4-50
UNPRICED PLATINUM PRINT RUN 1
SERIAL #'d UNDER 24 NOT PRICED
2 Alge Crumpler/86 10.00 20.00
3 Andre Johnson/150 10.00 25.00
4 Anquan Boldin/25 10.00 25.00
5 Antonio Gates/50 10.00 25.00
6 Ben Roethlisberger/25 60.00 120.00
7 Braylon Edwards/25 15.00 40.00
8 Brian Urlacher/150 15.00 40.00
9 Brett Favre/25 100.00 200.00
10 Byron Leftwich/75 8.00 20.00
11 Cadillac Williams/25 15.00 40.00
13 Cedric Benson/25 10.00 25.00
14 Chad Johnson/25 12.00 30.00
15 Charlie Frye/148 10.00 25.00
16 Chris Brown/47 8.00 20.00
17 Chris Chambers/100 8.00 20.00
19 Dallas Clark/150 8.00 20.00
20 Darrell Jackson/50 6.00 15.00
21 Deion Branch/86 8.00 20.00
22 Domanick Davis/150 6.00 15.00
24 Drew Bennett/150 6.00 15.00
29 Jake Delhomme/25 12.00 30.00
35 Larry Fitzgerald/25 20.00 50.00
36 Larry Johnson/25 15.00 40.00
37 Lee Evans/140 6.00 15.00
38 Marc Bulger/62 8.00 20.00
39 Mark Clayton/50 10.00 25.00
40 Matt Hasselbeck/25 15.00 40.00
44 Nate Burleson/75 10.00 25.00
45 Peyton Manning/25 75.00 150.00
46 Philip Rivers/25 20.00 50.00
49 Reggie Wayne/50 12.50 30.00
53 Roy Williams WR/25 10.00 25.00
54 Rudi Johnson/50 10.00 25.00
55 Samkon Gado/150 8.00 20.00
56 Santana Moss/98 10.00 25.00
58 Steven Jackson/25 15.00 40.00
59 Steve Smith/25 15.00 40.00
60 T.J. Houshmandzadeh/150 8.00 20.00
61 Tatum Bell/50 8.00 20.00
62 Thomas Jones/50 8.00 20.00
63 Tiki Barber/25 10.00 25.00
65 Tedy Bruschi/50 30.00 60.00
66 Willie Parker/50 12.00 30.00
67 Willis McGahee/25 10.00 25.00
68 Drew Brees/40 30.00 60.00
69 Dominic Rhodes/24 15.00 40.00
71 Reggie Bush 6.00 15.00
72 Matt Leinart 10.00 25.00
73 Vince Young 10.00 25.00
74 Jay Cutler 5.00 12.00
75 DeAngelo Williams 15.00 40.00
76 LenDale White 4.00 10.00
77 Laurence Maroney 4.00 10.00
78 Santonio Holmes 5.00 12.00
79 Brodie Croyle 4.00 10.00
80 Sinorice Moss 4.00 10.00
81 Jeremy Bloom 4.00 10.00
82 A.J. Hawk 12.00 30.00
83 Joseph Addai 4.00 10.00
84 Vernon Davis 5.00 12.00
85 Michael Huff 5.00 12.00
86 Mario Williams 6.00 15.00
87 Demetrius Williams 4.00 10.00
88 Donte Whitner 5.00 12.00
89 Haloti Ngata 5.00 12.00
90 Tamba Hali 6.00 15.00
91 Omar Jacobs 4.00 10.00
92 Leonard Pope 6.00 15.00
93 Chad Jackson 4.00 10.00
94 Maurice Stovall 4.00 10.00
95 D'Brickashaw Ferguson 4.00 10.00
96 Charlie Whitehurst 4.00 10.00
97 Ingle Martin 5.00 12.00
98 Brian Calhoun 4.00 10.00
99 Leon Washington 4.00 10.00
100 Marcedes Lewis 4.00 10.00
101 Anthony Fasano 4.00 10.00
102 Derek Hagan 5.00 12.00
103 Devin Hester 8.00 20.00
104 Bobby Carpenter 4.00 10.00
105 Brodrick Bunkley 5.00 12.00
106 Maurice Drew 12.00 30.00
107 P.J. Daniels 4.00 10.00
108 Marques Hagans 4.00 10.00
109 Joe Klopfenstein 4.00 10.00
110 Tony Scheffler 6.00 15.00
111 Cory Rodgers 4.00 10.00
112 Tye Hill 4.00 10.00
113 Johnathan Joseph 5.00 12.00
114 John McCargo 4.00 10.00
115 Kamerion Wimbley 5.00 12.00
116 Jerious Norwood 4.00 10.00
117 Michael Robinson 4.00 10.00
118 Jason Avant 4.00 10.00
119 Manny Lawson 5.00 12.00
120 Mathias Kiwanuka 6.00 15.00
121 Kellen Clemens 4.00 10.00
122 Jerome Harrison 4.00 10.00
123 Dominique Byrd 4.00 10.00
124 Travis Wilson 4.00 10.00
125 Brandon Williams 4.00 10.00
126 Brandon Marshall 12.50 25.00
127 Greg Jennings 6.00 15.00
128 Brad Smith 5.00 12.00
129 Domenik Hixon 6.00 15.00
130 Kelly Jennings 5.00 12.00
131 Ernie Sims 4.00 10.00
132 Jason Allen 5.00 12.00
133 Tarvaris Jackson 4.00 10.00
134 David Thomas 4.00 10.00
135 Willie Reid 5.00 12.00
136 Skyler Green 4.00 10.00
137 Antonio Cromartie 5.00 12.00
138 Chad Greenway 6.00 15.00
139 Owen Daniels 6.00 15.00
140 Garrett Mills 5.00 12.00
141 Will Blackmon 4.00 10.00
142 David Kirtman 6.00 12.00
143 DeMeco Ryans/148 5.00 12.00
144 D'Qwell Jackson 4.00 10.00
145 Rocky McIntosh 4.00 10.00
146 Wali Lundy 4.00 10.00
147 Mike Bell 4.00 10.00
148 Daniel Bullocks 4.00 10.00
149 Marques Colston 6.00 15.00
150 Roman Harper 5.00 12.00

2007 Playoffs NFL Playoffs Preview

This set was issued in a foil wrapper through the Shop at Home Network to preview the 2007 Playoff NFL Playoffs product.

COMPLETE SET (6) 15.00 30.00
P1 JaMarcus Russell .50 1.25
P2 Adrian Peterson 1.50 4.00
P3 Calvin Johnson 1.50 4.00
P4 Brady Quinn .50 1.25
P5 Marshawn Lynch 1.00 2.50
P6 Ted Ginn Jr. .60 1.50

2007 Playoffs NFL Playoffs Preview Bonus

This set was issued in a foil wrapper through the Shop at Home Network. Each card was produced in the style of the 2006 NFL Playoffs product with an udated player photo and a 2007 copyright line on the back. Red foil highlights appear at the top of the basic cards with a series of parallels issued in different foil colors. One Jersey card and one parallel card was issued in each foil pack along with the basic 10-card red foil set.

COMPLETE SET (10) 6.00 12.00
*GOLD/300: 1X TO 2.5X RED FOIL
*GREEN/125: 1.5X TO 4X RED FOIL
*BLUE/600: .8X TO 2X RED FOIL
UNPRICED BLACK PRINT RUN 1
B1 Reggie Bush .40 1.00
B2 Vince Young .40 1.00
B3 Maurice Jones-Drew .40 1.00
B4 Matt Leinart .40 1.00
B5 Laurence Maroney .50 1.25
B6 Vernon Davis .40 1.00
B7 DeAngelo Williams .40 1.00
B8 Joseph Addai .40 1.00
B9 Leon Washington .40 1.00
B10 Santonio Holmes .40 1.00

2007 Playoffs NFL Playoffs Preview Bonus Jerseys Red

COMPLETE SET (10) 50.00 100.00
*BLUE/500: .5X TO 1.2X RED FOIL
*GOLD/250: .8X TO 2X RED FOIL
*GREEN/50: 1.5X TO 4X RED FOIL
UNPRICED BLACK PRINT RUN 1
B1 Reggie Bush 2.50 6.00
B2 Vince Young 2.50 6.00
B3 Maurice Jones-Drew 2.50 6.00
B4 Matt Leinart 2.50 6.00
B5 Laurence Maroney 3.00 8.00
B6 Vernon Davis 2.50 6.00
B7 DeAngelo Williams 2.50 6.00
B8 Joseph Addai 2.50 6.00
B9 Leon Washington 2.50 6.00
B10 Santonio Holmes 2.50 6.00

2007 Playoff NFL Playoffs

This 180-card set was released in December, 2007. The set was issued as part of a factory set with an $100 SRP. The first 100 cards in this set are in alphabetical team order while the final 80 cards in the set feature 2007 NFL rookies.

COMP.FACT.SET (180) 60.00 100.00
COMPLETE SET (184) 15.00 40.00
UNPRICED BLACK PROOF PRINT RUN 5
UNPRICED BLACK HOLOFOIL PRINT RUN 10
UNPRICED GOLD PROOF PRINT RUN 10
UNPRICED PLATINUM PRINT RUN 1
UNPRICED PLATINUM HOLOFOIL PRINT RUN 1
UNPRICED PLATINUM METAL PRINT RUN 1
UNPRICED PLATINUM PROOF PRINT RUN 1
1 Anquan Boldin .20 .50
2 Larry Fitzgerald .25 .60
3 Edgerrin James .25 .60
4 Matt Leinart .20 .50
5 Alge Crumpler .25 .60
6 Jerious Norwood .20 .50
7 Warrick Dunn .20 .50
8 Steve McNair .25 .60
9 Demetrius Williams .20 .50
10 Willis McGahee .20 .50
11 J.P. Losman .20 .50
12 Lee Evans .25 .60
13 Steve Smith .25 .60
14 DeAngelo Williams .20 .50
15 Jake Delhomme .20 .50
16 Bernard Berrian .20 .50
17 Cedric Benson .20 .50
18 Rex Grossman .20 .50
19 Chad Johnson .20 .50
20 Rudi Johnson .20 .50
21 T.J. Houshmandzadeh .20 .50
22 Carson Palmer .25 .60
23 Braylon Edwards .20 .50
24 Kellen Winslow .20 .50
25 Terrell Owens .25 .60
26 Julius Jones .20 .50
27 Marion Barber .25 .60
28 Tony Romo .40 1.00
29 Jay Cutler .20 .50
30 Mike Bell .25 .60
31 Brandon Marshall .25 .60
32 Jon Kitna .20 .50
33 Roy Williams WR .20 .50
34 Mike Furrey .25 .60
35 Brett Favre .60 1.50
36 Donald Driver .25 .60
37 Greg Jennings .20 .50
38 A.J. Hawk .20 .50
39 Andre Johnson .25 .60
40 Matt Schaub .20 .50
41 Ahman Green .25 .60
42 Peyton Manning .75 2.00
43 Joseph Addai .20 .50
44 Marvin Harrison .25 .60
45 Reggie Wayne .25 .60
46 Fred Taylor .20 .50
47 David Garrard .20 .50
48 Maurice Jones-Drew .20 .50
49 Larry Johnson .20 .50
50 Tony Gonzalez .25 .60
51 Trent Green .20 .50
52 Chris Chambers .20 .50
53 Ronnie Brown .20 .50
54 Chester Taylor .20 .50
55 Tarvaris Jackson .20 .50
56 Tom Brady 1.00 2.50
57 Randy Moss .25 .60
58 Laurence Maroney .25 .60
59 Deuce McAllister .25 .60
60 Drew Brees .30 .75
61 Marques Colston .20 .50
62 Reggie Bush .20 .50
63 Jeremy Shockey .20 .50
64 Plaxico Burress .20 .50
65 Brandon Jacobs .20 .50
66 Eli Manning .25 .60
67 Chad Pennington .20 .50
68 Jerricho Cotchery .20 .50
69 Leon Washington .20 .50
70 Thomas Jones .20 .50
71 LaMont Jordan .25 .60
72 Daunte Culpepper .25 .60
73 Brian Westbrook .20 .50
74 Donovan McNabb .25 .60
75 Hank Baskett .25 .60
76 Hines Ward .25 .60
77 Willie Parker .25 .60
78 Santonio Holmes .20 .50
79 Ben Roethlisberger .30 .75
80 Antonio Gates .30 .75
81 LaDainian Tomlinson .30 .75
82 Philip Rivers .30 .75
83 Shawne Merriman .20 .50
84 Vincent Jackson .20 .50

85 Alex Smith QB .25 .60
86 Frank Gore .25 .60
87 Vernon Davis .20 .50
88 Deion Branch .20 .50
89 Matt Hasselbeck .20 .50
90 Shaun Alexander .20 .50
91 Marc Bulger .20 .50
92 Torry Holt .25 .60
93 Steven Jackson .20 .50
94 Joey Galloway .25 .60
95 Cadillac Williams .25 .60
96 LenDale White .25 .60
97 Vince Young .20 .50
98 Clinton Portis .20 .50
99 Jason Campbell .20 .50
100 Ladell Betts .20 .50
101 Adrian Peterson RC 5.00 12.00
102 Anthony Gonzalez RC .50 1.25
103 Yamon Figurs RC .50 1.25
104 Brady Quinn RC .50 1.25
105 Brandon Jackson RC .50 1.25
106 Brian Leonard RC .50 1.25
107 Calvin Johnson RC 1.50 4.00
108 Chris Henry RB RC .50 1.25
109 Drew Stanton RC .50 1.25
110 Dwayne Bowe RC .50 1.25
111 Dwayne Jarrett RC .60 1.50
112 Gaines Adams RC .60 1.50
113 Garrett Wolfe RC .50 1.25
114 Greg Olsen RC .75 2.00
115 JaMarcus Russell RC .50 1.25
116 Jason Hill RC .50 1.25
117 Joe Thomas RC .75 2.00
118 John Beck RC .50 1.25
119 Johnnie Lee Higgins RC .50 1.25
120 Kenny Irons RC .50 1.25
121 Kevin Kolb RC .60 1.50
122 Lorenzo Booker RC .60 1.50
123 Marshawn Lynch RC 1.00 2.50
124 Michael Bush RC .50 1.25
125 Patrick Willis RC .75 2.00
126 Paul Williams RC .50 1.25
127 Robert Meachem RC .60 1.50
128 Sidney Rice RC .60 1.50
129 Steve Smith RC .50 1.25
130 Ted Ginn Jr. RC .60 1.50
131 Tony Hunt RC .50 1.25
132 Trent Edwards RC .50 1.25
133 Troy Smith RC .50 1.25
134 Antonio Pittman RC .50 1.25
135 Levi Brown RC .50 1.25
136 LaRon Landry RC .75 2.00
137 Jamaal Anderson RC .60 1.50
138 Amobi Okoye RC .60 1.50
139 Adam Carriker RC .50 1.25
140 Darrelle Revis RC .60 1.50
141 Lawrence Timmons RC .75 2.00
142 Leon Hall RC .50 1.25
143 Michael Griffin RC .50 1.25
144 Aaron Ross RC .50 1.25
145 Reggie Nelson RC .50 1.25
146 Brandon Meriweather RC .60 1.50
147 Jon Beason RC .50 1.25
148 Chris Davis RC .50 1.25
149 Jeff Rowe RC .50 1.25
150 Courtney Taylor RC .50 1.25
151 Dallas Baker RC .50 1.25
152 Roy Hall RC .75 2.00
153 Jordan Kent RC .60 1.50
154 David Clowney RC .50 1.25
155 Scott Chandler RC .75 2.00
156 Anthony Spencer RC .60 1.50
157 Paul Posluszny RC .50 1.25
158 Craig Buster Davis RC .50 1.25
159 Zach Miller RC .50 1.25
160 Alan Branch RC .50 1.25
161 Chris Houston RC .50 1.25
162 Laurent Robinson RC .75 2.00
163 LaMarr Woodley RC 1.00 2.50
164 James Jones RC .50 1.25
165 David Harris RC .50 1.25
166 Mike Walker RC .75 2.00
167 Eric Wright RC .50 1.25
168 Isaiah Stanback RC .50 1.25
169 Josh Wilson RC .60 1.50
170 Dwayne Wright RC .50 1.25
171 Tim Crowder RC .60 1.50
172 Ryne Robinson RC .60 1.50
173 Jacoby Jones RC .50 1.25
174 Steve Breaston RC .50 1.25
175 Dan Bazuin RC .60 1.50
176 Aundrae Allison RC .50 1.25
177 Sabby Piscitelli RC .50 1.25
178 Kolby Smith RC .50 1.25
179 Matt Spaeth RC .75 2.00
180 DeShawn Wynn RC .50 1.25

2007 Playoff NFL Playoffs Black

*VETS/199: 2.5X TO 6X BASIC CARDS
*ROOKIES/199: 1X TO 2.5X BASIC CARDS
STATED PRINT RUN 199 SER.#'d SETS

2007 Playoff NFL Playoffs Black Metalized

*VETS/49: 4X TO 10X BASIC CARDS
*ROOKIES/49: 1.5X TO 4X BASIC CARDS
STATED PRINT RUN 49 SER.#'d SETS

2007 Playoff NFL Playoffs Gold

*VETS/299: 2X TO 5X BASIC CARDS
*ROOKIES/299: .8X TO 2X BASIC CARDS
STATED PRINT RUN 299 SER.#'d SETS

2007 Playoff NFL Playoffs Gold Holofoil

*VETS/25: 8X TO 12X BASIC CARDS
*ROOKIES/25: 2X TO 5X BASIC CARDS
STATED PRINT RUN 25 SER.#'d SETS

2007 Playoff NFL Playoffs Gold Metalized

*VETS/ 149: 2.5X TO 6X BASIC CARDS
*ROOKIES/149: 1X TO 2.5X BASIC CARDS
STATED PRINT RUN 149 SER.#'d SETS

2007 Playoff NFL Playoffs Red Holofoil

*VETS/125: 3X TO 8X BASIC CARDS
*ROOKIES/125: 1.2X TO 3X BASIC CARDS
STATED PRINT RUN 125 SER.#'d SETS

2007 Playoff NFL Playoffs Red Metalized

*VETS/399: 1.5X TO 4X BASIC CARDS
*ROOKIES/399: .6X TO 1.5X BASIC CARDS
STATED PRINT RUN 399 SER.#'d SETS

2007 Playoff NFL Playoffs Red Proof

*VETERANS: 1.5X TO 4X BASIC CARDS
*ROOKIES: .6X TO 1.5X BASIC CARDS

2007 Playoff NFL Playoffs Silver Holofoil

*VETS/99: 3X TO 8X BASIC CARDS
*ROOKIES/99: 1.2X TO 3X BASIC CARDS
STATED PRINT RUN 99 SER.#'d SETS

2007 Playoff NFL Playoffs Silver Metalized

*VETS/249: 2X TO 5X BASIC CARDS
*ROOKIES/249: .8X TO 2X BASIC CARDS
STATED PRINT RUN 249 SER.#'d SETS

2007 Playoff NFL Playoffs Silver Proof

*VETS/50: 4X TO 10X BASIC CARDS
*ROOKIES/50: 1.5X TO 4X BASIC CARDS
STATED PRINT RUN 50 SER.#'d SETS

2007 Playoff NFL Playoffs Material Signatures Red

RED PRINT RUN 50 SER.#'d SETS
*RED PRIME/50: .5X TO 1.2X RED/50
RED PRIME PRINT RUN 50 SER.#'d SETS
*SILVER/25: .5X TO 1.2X RED/50
SILVER PRINT RUN 25 SER.#'d SETS
*SILVER PRIME/20-25: .6X TO 1.5X RED/50
SILVER PRIME PRINT RUN 20-25
UNPRICED GOLD PRINT RUN 10
UNPRICED GOLD PRIME PRINT RUN 10
UNPRICED BLACK PRINT RUN 5
UNPRICED BLACK PRIME PRINT RUN 5
UNPRICED PLATINUM PRINT RUN 1
UNPRICED PLATINUM PRIME PRINT RUN 1
101 Adrian Peterson 60.00 120.00
102 Anthony Gonzalez 8.00 20.00
103 Yamon Figurs 8.00 20.00
104 Brady Quinn 8.00 20.00
105 Brandon Jackson 8.00 20.00
106 Brian Leonard 8.00 20.00
107 Calvin Johnson 25.00 60.00
108 Chris Henry RB 8.00 20.00
109 Drew Stanton 8.00 20.00
110 Dwayne Bowe 8.00 20.00
111 Dwayne Jarrett 10.00 25.00
112 Gaines Adams 10.00 25.00
113 Garrett Wolfe 8.00 20.00
114 Greg Olsen 12.00 30.00
115 JaMarcus Russell 8.00 20.00
116 Jason Hill 8.00 20.00
117 Joe Thomas 12.00 30.00
118 John Beck 8.00 20.00
119 Johnnie Lee Higgins 8.00 20.00
120 Kenny Irons No AU 5.00 12.00
121 Kevin Kolb 10.00 25.00
122 Lorenzo Booker 10.00 25.00
123 Marshawn Lynch 20.00 50.00
124 Michael Bush 8.00 20.00
125 Patrick Willis 20.00 50.00
126 Paul Williams 8.00 20.00
127 Robert Meachem 10.00 25.00
128 Sidney Rice 10.00 25.00
129 Steve Smith USC 8.00 20.00
130 Ted Ginn Jr. 10.00 25.00
131 Tony Hunt 8.00 20.00
132 Trent Edwards 8.00 20.00
133 Troy Smith 8.00 20.00

2007 Playoff NFL Playoffs Materials Gold

GOLD PRINT RUN 10-25
*RED/100: .25X TO .6X GOLD/25
RED PRINT RUN 100 SER.#'d SETS
*SILVER/50: .3X TO .8X GOLD/25
SILVER PRINT RUN 50 SER.#'d SETS
*RED PRIME: .5X TO 1.2X GOLD/25
*SLVR PRIME/13-15: .6X TO 1.5X GOLD/25
UNPRICED GOLD PRIME PRINT RUN 10
UNPRICED BLACK PRINT RUN 5-10
UNPRICED BLACK PRIME PRINT RUN 5
UNPRICED PLATINUM PRINT RUN 1
UNPRICED PLATINUM PRIME PRINT RUN 1
1 Anquan Boldin 4.00 10.00
2 Larry Fitzgerald 5.00 12.00
3 Edgerrin James 5.00 12.00
4 Matt Leinart 4.00 10.00
5 Alge Crumpler 5.00 12.00
6 Jerious Norwood 4.00 10.00
7 Warrick Dunn 4.00 10.00
8 Steve McNair 5.00 12.00
9 Demetrius Williams 4.00 10.00
11 J.P. Losman 4.00 10.00
12 Lee Evans 5.00 12.00
13 Steve Smith 5.00 12.00
14 DeAngelo Williams 4.00 10.00
15 Jake Delhomme 4.00 10.00
16 Bernard Berrian 4.00 10.00
17 Cedric Benson 4.00 10.00
18 Rex Grossman 4.00 10.00
19 Chad Johnson 4.00 10.00
20 Rudi Johnson 4.00 10.00
21 T.J. Houshmandzadeh 4.00 10.00
22 Carson Palmer 5.00 12.00
23 Braylon Edwards 4.00 10.00
24 Kellen Winslow 4.00 10.00
25 Terrell Owens 5.00 12.00
26 Julius Jones 4.00 10.00
27 Marion Barber 5.00 12.00
28 Tony Romo 8.00 20.00
29 Jay Cutler 4.00 10.00
30 Mike Bell 5.00 12.00
31 Brandon Marshall 5.00 12.00
32 Jon Kitna 4.00 10.00
33 Roy Williams WR 4.00 10.00
34 Mike Furrey 5.00 12.00
35 Brett Favre 12.00 30.00
36 Donald Driver 5.00 12.00
37 Greg Jennings 4.00 10.00
38 A.J. Hawk 4.00 10.00
39 Andre Johnson 5.00 12.00
42 Peyton Manning 15.00 40.00
43 Joseph Addai 4.00 10.00
44 Marvin Harrison 5.00 12.00
45 Reggie Wayne 5.00 12.00
46 Fred Taylor 4.00 10.00
48 Maurice Jones-Drew 4.00 10.00
49 Larry Johnson 4.00 10.00
50 Tony Gonzalez 5.00 12.00
52 Chris Chambers 4.00 10.00
53 Ronnie Brown 4.00 10.00
54 Chester Taylor 4.00 10.00
55 Tarvaris Jackson 4.00 10.00
56 Tom Brady 20.00 50.00
57 Randy Moss 5.00 12.00
58 Laurence Maroney 5.00 12.00
59 Deuce McAllister 5.00 12.00
60 Drew Brees 6.00 15.00
61 Marques Colston 5.00 12.00
62 Reggie Bush 4.00 10.00
63 Jeremy Shockey 4.00 10.00
64 Plaxico Burress 4.00 10.00
65 Brandon Jacobs 4.00 10.00
66 Eli Manning 5.00 12.00
67 Chad Pennington 4.00 10.00
68 Jerricho Cotchery 4.00 10.00
69 Leon Washington 4.00 10.00
71 LaMont Jordan 5.00 12.00
73 Brian Westbrook 4.00 10.00
74 Donovan McNabb 5.00 12.00
75 Hank Baskett 5.00 12.00
76 Hines Ward 5.00 12.00
77 Willie Parker 5.00 12.00
78 Santonio Holmes 4.00 10.00
79 Ben Roethlisberger 6.00 15.00
80 Antonio Gates 6.00 15.00
81 LaDainian Tomlinson 6.00 15.00
82 Philip Rivers 6.00 15.00
83 Shawne Merriman 4.00 10.00
84 Vincent Jackson 4.00 10.00
85 Alex Smith QB 5.00 12.00
86 Frank Gore 5.00 12.00
87 Vernon Davis 4.00 10.00
88 Deion Branch 4.00 10.00
89 Matt Hasselbeck 4.00 10.00
90 Shaun Alexander 4.00 10.00
91 Marc Bulger 4.00 10.00
92 Torry Holt 5.00 12.00
93 Steven Jackson 4.00 10.00
94 Joey Galloway 5.00 12.00
95 Cadillac Williams 5.00 12.00
96 LenDale White 5.00 12.00
97 Vince Young 4.00 10.00
98 Clinton Portis 4.00 10.00
99 Jason Campbell 4.00 10.00
100 Ladell Betts 4.00 10.00
101 Adrian Peterson 8.00 20.00
102 Anthony Gonzalez 2.50 6.00
103 Yamon Figurs 2.50 6.00
104 Brady Quinn 2.50 6.00
105 Brandon Jackson 2.50 6.00
106 Brian Leonard 2.50 6.00
107 Calvin Johnson 8.00 20.00
108 Chris Henry RB 2.50 6.00
109 Drew Stanton 2.50 6.00
110 Dwayne Bowe 2.50 6.00
111 Dwayne Jarrett 3.00 8.00
112 Gaines Adams 3.00 8.00
113 Garrett Wolfe 2.50 6.00
114 Greg Olsen 4.00 10.00
115 JaMarcus Russell 2.50 6.00
116 Jason Hill 2.50 6.00
117 Joe Thomas 4.00 10.00
118 John Beck 2.50 6.00
119 Johnnie Lee Higgins 2.50 6.00
120 Kenny Irons 2.50 6.00
121 Kevin Kolb 3.00 8.00
122 Lorenzo Booker 3.00 8.00
123 Marshawn Lynch 5.00 12.00
124 Michael Bush 2.50 6.00
125 Patrick Willis 4.00 10.00
126 Paul Williams 2.50 6.00
127 Robert Meachem 3.00 8.00
128 Sidney Rice 3.00 8.00
129 Steve Smith USC 2.50 6.00
130 Ted Ginn Jr. 3.00 8.00
131 Tony Hunt 2.50 6.00
132 Trent Edwards 2.50 6.00
133 Troy Smith 2.50 6.00

2007 Playoff NFL Playoffs Signatures Red

STATED PRINT RUN 15-100 SER.#'d SETS
*SILVER/25: .6X TO 1.5X RED AUTO/91-100
*SILVER/25: .5X TO 1.2X RED AUTO/34-52
*SILVER/25: .4X TO 1X RED AUTO/25
SILVER PRINT RUN 10-25
UNPRICED GOLD PRINT RUN 10
UNPRICED BLACK PRINT RUN 5
UNPRICED PLATINUM PRINT RUN 1
101 Adrian Peterson/25 125.00 250.00
102 Anthony Gonzalez/25 8.00 20.00
103 Yamon Figurs/15 8.00 20.00
104 Brady Quinn/25 8.00 20.00
105 Brandon Jackson/25 8.00 20.00
106 Brian Leonard/100 5.00 12.00
107 Calvin Johnson/25 25.00 60.00
108 Chris Henry RB/25 8.00 20.00
109 Drew Stanton/25 8.00 20.00
110 Dwayne Bowe/25 8.00 20.00
111 Dwayne Jarrett/25 10.00 25.00
112 Gaines Adams/50 8.00 20.00
113 Garrett Wolfe/100 5.00 12.00
114 Greg Olsen/25 12.00 30.00
115 JaMarcus Russell/25 8.00 20.00
116 Jason Hill/100 5.00 12.00
117 Joe Thomas/100
118 John Beck/100 5.00 12.00
119 Johnnie Lee Higgins/100 5.00 12.00
121 Kevin Kolb/25 10.00 25.00
122 Lorenzo Booker/50 8.00 20.00
123 Marshawn Lynch/25 15.00 40.00
124 Michael Bush/25 8.00 20.00
125 Patrick Willis/41 10.00 25.00
126 Paul Williams/100 5.00 12.00
127 Robert Meachem/25 10.00 25.00
128 Sidney Rice/25 10.00 25.00
129 Steve Smith USC/50 6.00 15.00
130 Ted Ginn Jr./25 10.00 25.00
131 Tony Hunt/50 6.00 15.00
132 Trent Edwards/50 6.00 15.00
133 Troy Smith/25 8.00 20.00
134 Antonio Pittman/100 5.00 12.00
135 Levi Brown/100 5.00 12.00
136 LaRon Landry/100 8.00 20.00
137 Jamaal Anderson/52 8.00 20.00
138 Amobi Okoye/100 6.00 15.00
139 Adam Carriker/100 5.00 12.00
140 Darrelle Revis/100 6.00 15.00
141 Lawrence Timmons/100 8.00 20.00
142 Leon Hall/100 5.00 12.00
143 Michael Griffin/34 6.00 15.00
144 Aaron Ross/91 5.00 12.00
145 Reggie Nelson/100 5.00 12.00
146 Brandon Meriweather/100 6.00 15.00
147 Jon Beason/100 5.00 12.00
148 Chris Davis/100 5.00 12.00
149 Jeff Rowe/100 5.00 12.00
150 Courtney Taylor/100 5.00 12.00
151 Dallas Baker/100 5.00 12.00
152 Roy Hall/100 8.00 20.00
153 Jordan Kent/100 6.00 15.00
154 David Clowney/100 5.00 12.00
155 Scott Chandler/100 8.00 20.00
156 Anthony Spencer/100 6.00 15.00
157 Paul Posluszny/100 5.00 12.00
159 Zach Miller/100 5.00 12.00
161 Chris Houston/100 5.00 12.00
162 Laurent Robinson/100 8.00 20.00
163 LaMarr Woodley/100 10.00 25.00
164 James Jones/100 5.00 12.00
165 David Harris/100 5.00 12.00
166 Mike Walker/100 8.00 20.00
168 Isaiah Stanback/100 5.00 12.00
169 Josh Wilson/100 6.00 15.00
170 Dwayne Wright/100 5.00 12.00
171 Tim Crowder/100 6.00 15.00
172 Ryne Robinson/100 6.00 15.00
173 Jacoby Jones/100 5.00 12.00
174 Steve Breaston/100 5.00 12.00
175 Dan Bazuin/100 6.00 15.00
176 Aundrae Allison/100 5.00 12.00
177 Sabby Piscitelli/100 5.00 12.00
178 Kolby Smith/100 5.00 12.00
179 Matt Spaeth/100 8.00 20.00
180 DeShawn Wynn/100 5.00 12.00

2002 Playoff Piece of the Game

Released in October 2002, this set contains 75 veterans, 25 rookies #'d to 500, and 32 rookies #'d to 500 that feature a jersey swatch. Boxes contained 6 packs of 5 cards, with each pack containing 4 base cards and one memorabilia card.
COMP.SET w/o SP's (75) 30.00 50.00
76-132 ROOKIE PRINT RUN 500
1 Daunte Culpepper .40 1.00
2 Tim Couch .30 .75
3 Michael Vick .40 1.00
4 Brett Favre 1.00 2.50
5 Drew Bledsoe .40 1.00
6 Mark Brunell .40 1.00
7 Jake Plummer .30 .75
8 Mike McMahon .30 .75
9 Brian Griese .30 .75
10 Aaron Brooks .30 .75
11 Chris Weinke .30 .75
12 Peyton Manning 1.25 3.00
13 Trent Green .30 .75
14 Quincy Carter .30 .75
15 Tom Brady 2.50 6.00
16 Vinny Testaverde .30 .75
17 Drew Brees 1.00 2.50
18 Kordell Stewart .30 .75
19 Kerry Collins .30 .75
20 Kurt Warner .40 1.00
21 Rich Gannon .40 1.00
22 Jeff Garcia .30 .75
23 Shaun Alexander .30 .75
24 Doug Flutie .40 1.00
25 Donovan McNabb .40 1.00
26 Steve McNair .40 1.00
27 Michael Bennett .30 .75
28 Jamal Lewis .40 1.00
29 Marshall Faulk .40 1.00
30 Curtis Martin .40 1.00
31 James Jackson .30 .75
32 Terrell Davis .40 1.00
33 Travis Henry .30 .75
34 Corey Dillon .30 .75
35 Deuce McAllister .40 1.00
36 Priest Holmes .30 .75
37 Antowain Smith .40 1.00
38 Anthony Thomas .40 1.00
39 Ricky Williams .40 1.00
40 Charlie Garner .40 1.00
41 Jerome Bettis .50 1.25
42 Ahman Green .40 1.00
43 Emmitt Smith .75 2.00
44 Edgerrin James .40 1.00
45 Warrick Dunn .30 .75
46 LaDainian Tomlinson .50 1.25
47 Fred Taylor .30 .75
48 Eddie George .40 1.00
49 Garrison Hearst .30 .75
50 Stephen Davis .30 .75
51 Snoop Minnis .30 .75
52 Troy Brown .30 .75
53 Cris Carter .50 1.25
54 Jerry Rice 1.00 2.50
55 Terry Glenn .40 1.00
56 Plaxico Burress .30 .75
57 David Boston .30 .75
58 Marvin Harrison .40 1.00
59 Randy Moss .40 1.00
60 Eric Moulds .30 .75
61 Rod Smith .40 1.00
62 Freddie Mitchell .30 .75
63 Chris Chambers .30 .75
64 Keyshawn Johnson .40 1.00
65 Terrell Owens .40 1.00
66 Isaac Bruce .50 1.25
67 Tim Brown .50 1.25
68 Tony Gonzalez .40 1.00
69 Jevon Kearse .30 .75
70 Warren Sapp .40 1.00
71 Junior Seau .40 1.00
72 Michael Strahan .40 1.00
73 Ray Lewis .50 1.25
74 Zach Thomas .40 1.00
75 Brian Urlacher .50 1.25
76 Quentin Jammer RC 2.00 5.00
77 Kurt Kittner RC 1.25 3.00
78 Chad Hutchinson RC 1.25 3.00
79 Randy Fasani RC 1.25 3.00
80 Lamar Gordon RC 1.50 4.00
81 Brian Westbrook RC 2.50 6.00
82 Josh Scobey RC 1.50 4.00
83 Chester Taylor RC 2.00 5.00
84 Luke Staley RC 1.25 3.00
85 Deion Branch RC 2.00 5.00
86 Terry Charles RC 1.25 3.00
87 Kahlil Hill RC 1.25 3.00
88 Freddie Milons RC 1.25 3.00
89 Woody Dantzler RC 1.50 4.00
90 Kelly Campbell RC 1.50 4.00
91 Dwight Freeney RC 2.50 6.00
92 Bryan Thomas RC 1.25 3.00
93 Ryan Sims RC 2.00 5.00
94 John Henderson RC 1.50 4.00
95 Wendell Bryant RC 1.25 3.00
96 Albert Haynesworth RC 2.00 5.00
97 Phillip Buchanon RC 2.00 5.00
98 Lito Sheppard RC 2.00 5.00
99 Ed Reed RC 7.50 15.00
100 Napoleon Harris RC 1.50 4.00
101 David Carr JSY RC 2.50 6.00
102 Rohan Davey JSY RC 4.00 10.00
103 Joey Harrington JSY RC 2.50 6.00
104 Josh McCown JSY RC 4.00 10.00
105 Patrick Ramsey JSY RC 3.00 8.00
106 Ladell Betts JSY RC 4.00 10.00
107 T.J. Duckett JSY RC 2.50 6.00
108 DeShaun Foster JSY RC 4.00 10.00
109 William Green JSY RC 3.00 8.00
110 Maurice Morris JSY RC 3.00 8.00
111 Clinton Portis JSY RC 4.00 10.00
112 Travis Stephens JSY RC 2.50 6.00
113 Antonio Bryant JSY RC 4.00 10.00
114 Reche Caldwell JSY RC 3.00 8.00
115 Tim Carter JSY RC 3.00 8.00
116 Eric Crouch JSY RC 4.00 10.00
117 Andre Davis JSY RC 2.50 6.00
118 Jabar Gaffney JSY RC 2.50 6.00
119 Ron Johnson JSY RC 3.00 8.00
120 Ashley Lelie JSY RC 2.50 6.00
121 Antwaan Randle El JSY RC 3.00 8.00
122 Josh Reed JSY RC 3.00 8.00
123 Cliff Russell JSY RC 2.50 6.00
124 Donte Stallworth JSY RC 4.00 10.00
125 Javon Walker JSY RC 4.00 10.00
126 Marquise Walker JSY RC 2.50 6.00
127 Jeremy Shockey JSY RC 4.00 10.00
128 Daniel Graham JSY RC 3.00 8.00
129 David Garrard JSY RC 3.00 8.00
130 Roy Williams JSY RC 2.50 6.00
131 Julius Peppers JSY RC 6.00 15.00
132 Mike Williams JSY RC 2.50 6.00

2002 Playoff Piece of the Game Materials

Inserted one per pack, this set features game used material, including jerseys, footballs, and pants. Cards 1-58 contain single swatches, while cards 59-63 contain swatches from both players featured, and cards 64-68 feature two swatches from the featured player.
59-63 DUAL PLAYER PRINT RUN 500
64-68 DUAL SWATCH PRINT RUN 250
*1-58 1st DOWN/250: .5X TO 1.2X
*59-63 1st DOWN/100: .5X TO 1.2X
*64-68 1st DOWN/50: .6X TO 1.5X
FIRST DOWN PRINT RUN 50-250
*1-58 2nd DOWN/150: .6X TO 1.5X
*59-63 2nd DOWN/50: .6X TO 1.5X
*64-68 2nd DOWN/25 : 1X TO 2.5X
SECOND DOWN PRINT RUN 25-150
*1-58 3rd DOWN/50: .8X TO 2X
*59-63 3rd DOWN/25 : 1X TO 2.5X
64-68 3rd DOWN/10 NOT PRICED
THIRD DOWN PRINT RUN 10-50
*1-58 4th DOWN/25 : 1.2X TO 3X
64-68 4th DOWN/5 NOT PRICED
OVERALL MATERIAL ODDS ONE PER PACK
1F Ahman Green FB 3.00 8.00
1J Ahman Green JSY SP 4.00 10.00
2F Antonio Freeman FB 4.00 10.00
2J Antonio Freeman JSY 4.00 10.00
3J Barry Sanders JSY 8.00 20.00
4F Brett Favre FB 8.00 20.00
4J Brett Favre JSY 8.00 20.00
5F Brian Griese FB 2.50 6.00
5J Brian Griese JSY 2.50 6.00
6J Charles Woodson JSY 4.00 10.00
7F Chris Chambers FB 2.50 6.00
7J Chris Chambers JSY 2.50 6.00
8F Corey Dillon FB 2.50 6.00
8J Corey Dillon JSY 2.50 6.00
9J Cory Schlesinger JSY 2.50 6.00
10F Cris Carter FB 4.00 10.00
10J Cris Carter JSY 4.00 10.00
11F Curtis Martin FB SP 4.00 10.00
11J Curtis Martin JSY 3.00 8.00
11P Curtis Martin Pants 3.00 8.00
12J Dan Marino JSY 10.00 25.00
13J Darren Woodson JSY 3.00 8.00
14F Daunte Culpepper FB 3.00 8.00
14J Daunte Culpepper JSY 3.00 8.00
15F David Boston FB SP 3.00 8.00
15J David Boston JSY 2.50 6.00
15P David Boston Pants 2.50 6.00
16F Donovan McNabb FB SP 4.00 10.00
16J Donovan McNabb JSY 3.00 8.00
17J Ed McCaffrey JSY 3.00 8.00
18F Eddie George FB 3.00 8.00
18J Eddie George JSY 3.00 8.00
19F Edgerrin James FB 3.00 8.00
19J Edgerrin James JSY 3.00 8.00
20F Emmitt Smith FB SP 8.00 20.00
20J Emmitt Smith JSY 6.00 15.00
21P Frank Wycheck Pants SP 3.00 8.00
22J Fred Taylor JSY 2.50 6.00
23J Isaac Bruce JSY 4.00 10.00
24J Jake Plummer JSY 2.50 6.00
24P Jake Plummer Pants 2.50 6.00
25F Jeff Garcia FB SP 3.00 8.00
25J Jeff Garcia JSY 2.50 6.00
26J Jerome Bettis JSY SP 8.00 20.00
27J Jerry Rice JSY 6.00 15.00
28J Jevon Kearse JSY 2.50 6.00
29J Jim Kelly JSY 5.00 12.00
30J Jimmy Smith JSY SP 4.00 10.00
31J John Elway JSY 8.00 20.00
32J Junior Seau JSY 3.00 8.00
33J Kevin Johnson JSY 2.50 6.00
33P Kevin Johnson Pants 2.50 6.00
34J Kordell Stewart JSY 2.50 6.00
35F Kurt Warner FB SP 4.00 10.00
35J Kurt Warner JSY 3.00 8.00
35P Kurt Warner Pants 3.00 8.00
36F LaDainian Tomlinson FB 4.00 10.00
36J LaDainian Tomlinson JSY 4.00 10.00
37J Mark Brunell JSY 3.00 8.00
38J Marshall Faulk JSY 3.00 8.00
39F Marvin Harrison FB 3.00 8.00
39J Marvin Harrison JSY 3.00 8.00
40J Michael Irvin JSY 5.00 12.00
41J Mike Alstott JSY 2.50 6.00
42J Peyton Manning JSY SP 12.00 30.00
43F Randy Moss FB 3.00 8.00
43J Randy Moss JSY 3.00 8.00
44F Rich Gannon FB 3.00 8.00
44J Rich Gannon JSY 3.00 8.00
45F Ron Dayne FB SP 4.00 10.00
45J Ron Dayne JSY 3.00 8.00
46F Stephen Davis FB 2.50 6.00
46J Stephen Davis JSY 2.50 6.00
47F Steve McNair FB 3.00 8.00
47J Steve McNair JSY 3.00 8.00
48J Steve Young JSY 6.00 15.00
49F Terrell Davis FB 3.00 8.00
49J Terrell Davis JSY 3.00 8.00
50F Terrell Owens FB 3.00 8.00
50J Terrell Owens JSY 3.00 8.00
51J Thurman Thomas JSY 3.00 8.00
52F Tim Brown FB 4.00 10.00
52J Tim Brown JSY 4.00 10.00
53F Tim Couch FB SP 3.00 8.00
53J Tim Couch JSY 2.50 6.00
54F Tony Gonzalez FB 3.00 8.00
54J Tony Gonzalez JSY 3.00 8.00
55J Troy Aikman JSY 6.00 15.00
56F Vinny Testaverde FB 2.50 6.00
56J Vinny Testaverde JSY 2.50 6.00
57J Warren Sapp JSY 3.00 8.00
58J Zach Thomas JSY 3.00 8.00
59J McNair/George JSY/500 5.00 12.00
60J Griese/Davis JSY/500 5.00 12.00
61J Manning/James JSY/500 15.00 40.00
62J Warner/Faulk JSY/500 5.00 12.00
63J Aikman/Emmitt JSY/500 12.00 30.00
64J Cris Carter JSY/250 6.00 15.00
65J Jeff Garcia JSY/250 4.00 10.00
66J Emmitt Smith JSY/250 10.00 25.00
67J Kurt Warner JSY/250 5.00 12.00
68J Randy Moss JSY/250 5.00 12.00

2001 Playoff Preferred Samples

*SILVERS: .5X TO 1.2X BASE CARDS
*GOLD: 1X TO 2.5X SILVER

2001 Playoff Preferred

Released as a 225-card set, this product was issued 12 packs per box, with three cards per pack. This set includes 100 veterans and 125 rookies. The first 100 rookies are serial numbered to 1100, and the remaining rookies have stated print runs numbered to 400, 600, or 750. Those shorter printed cards have swatches of game used jerseys or footballs on the card front.
COMP.SET w/o RC's (100) 30.00 60.00
1 Elvis Grbac .40 1.00
2 Ray Lewis .50 1.25
3 Travis Taylor .30 .75
4 Rob Johnson .40 1.00
5 Eric Moulds .30 .75
6 Corey Dillon .30 .75
7 Peter Warrick .30 .75
8 Tim Couch .30 .75
9 Kevin Johnson .30 .75
10 Brian Griese .30 .75
11 Mike Anderson .30 .75
12 Rod Smith .40 1.00
13 Terrell Davis .40 1.00
14 Olandis Gary .30 .75
15 Peyton Manning 1.25 3.00
16 Edgerrin James .40 1.00
17 Marvin Harrison .40 1.00
18 Terrence Wilkins .30 .75
19 Mark Brunell .40 1.00
20 Fred Taylor .30 .75
21 Keenan McCardell .40 1.00
22 Jimmy Smith .40 1.00
23 Stacey Mack .30 .75
24 Trent Green .30 .75
25 Priest Holmes .30 .75
26 Tony Gonzalez .40 1.00
27 Jay Fiedler .40 1.00
28 Lamar Smith .40 1.00
29 Zach Thomas .40 1.00
30 Drew Bledsoe .40 1.00
31 Antowain Smith .40 1.00
32 Troy Brown .30 .75
33 Tom Brady 4.00 10.00
34 Vinny Testaverde .30 .75
35 Wayne Chrebet .30 .75
36 Curtis Martin .40 1.00
37 Rich Gannon .40 1.00
38 Tyrone Wheatley .40 1.00
39 Jerry Rice 1.00 2.50
40 Tim Brown .50 1.25
41 Charles Woodson .50 1.25
42 Charlie Garner .40 1.00
43 Kordell Stewart .30 .75
44 Jerome Bettis .50 1.25
45 Doug Flutie .40 1.00
46 Junior Seau .40 1.00
47 Matt Hasselbeck .30 .75
48 Trent Dilfer .30 .75
49 Shaun Alexander .30 .75
50 Ricky Watters .40 1.00
51 Eddie George .50 1.25
52 Steve McNair .40 1.00
53 Jevon Kearse .30 .75
54 David Boston .30 .75
55 Jake Plummer .30 .75
56 Chris Chandler .40 1.00
57 Maurice Smith .30 .75
58 Muhsin Muhammad .30 .75
59 Wesley Walls .30 .75
60 James Allen .30 .75
61 Marcus Robinson .40 1.00
62 Brian Urlacher .60 1.50
63 Clint Stoerner .40 1.00
64 Ryan Leaf .30 .75
65 Emmitt Smith .75 2.00
66 Joey Galloway .40 1.00
67 Charlie Batch .30 .75
68 James Stewart .30 .75
69 Brett Favre 1.00 2.50
70 Ahman Green .40 1.00
71 Bill Schroeder .40 1.00
72 Bubba Franks .30 .75
73 Daunte Culpepper .40 1.00
74 Randy Moss .40 1.00
75 Cris Carter .50 1.25
76 Aaron Brooks .30 .75
77 Ricky Williams .40 1.00
78 Albert Connell .30 .75
79 Kerry Collins .30 .75
80 Ron Dayne .40 1.00
81 Jason Sehorn .40 1.00
82 Amani Toomer .30 .75
83 Donovan McNabb .40 1.00
84 James Thrash .40 1.00
85 Duce Staley .30 .75
86 Jeff Garcia .30 .75
87 Garrison Hearst .40 1.00
88 Terrell Owens .40 1.00
89 Kurt Warner .75 2.00
90 Marshall Faulk .40 1.00
91 Torry Holt .40 1.00
92 Isaac Bruce .50 1.25
93 Brad Johnson .40 1.00
94 Warrick Dunn .30 .75
95 Mike Alstott .30 .75
96 Keyshawn Johnson .40 1.00
97 Warren Sapp .40 1.00
98 Tony Banks .30 .75
99 Stephen Davis .30 .75
100 Champ Bailey .40 1.00
101 Michael Vick RC 3.00 8.00
102 Drew Brees RC 40.00 80.00
103 Marques Tuiasosopo RC 1.25 3.00
104 Sage Rosenfels RC 1.25 3.00
105 Jesse Palmer RC 1.25 3.00
106 Mike McMahon RC 1.25 3.00
107 A.J. Feeley RC 1.25 3.00
108 Josh Booty RC 1.25 3.00
109 Josh Heupel RC 1.50 4.00
110 Henry Burris RC 1.50 4.00
111 Roderick Robinson RC 1.00 2.50
112 Tory Woodbury RC 1.00 2.50
113 Dave Dickenson RC 1.25 3.00
114 Deuce McAllister RC 1.50 4.00
115 Michael Bennett RC 1.25 3.00
116 Rudi Johnson RC 1.50 4.00
117 Derrick Blaylock RC 1.25 3.00
118 Dee Brown RC 1.00 2.50
119 Eric Kelly RC 1.00 2.50
120 Dominic Rhodes RC 1.25 3.00
121 Jason Brookins RC 1.50 4.00
122 Nick Goings RC 1.50 4.00
123 Markus Steele RC 1.00 2.50
124 Benjamin Gay RC 1.25 3.00
125 Tony Taylor RC 1.00 2.50
126 Elvis Joseph RC 1.00 2.50
127 Tay Cody RC 1.00 2.50
128 Heath Evans RC 1.25 3.00
129 George Layne RC 1.00 2.50
130 Moran Norris RC 1.00 2.50
131 Jameel Cook RC 1.25 3.00
132 Patrick Washington RC 1.00 2.50
133 Chad Johnson RC 1.50 4.00
134 Santana Moss RC 1.50 4.00
135 Reggie Wayne RC 2.00 5.00
136 Robert Ferguson RC 1.50 4.00
137 Steve Smith RC 3.00 8.00
138 Justin McCareins RC 1.25 3.00
139 Vinny Sutherland RC 1.00 2.50
140 Alex Bannister RC 1.00 2.50
141 Scotty Anderson RC 1.00 2.50
142 Onome Ojo RC 1.00 2.50
143 Damerien McCants RC 1.25 3.00
144 Eddie Berlin RC 1.00 2.50
145 Cedrick Wilson RC 1.25 3.00
146 Kevin Kasper RC 1.00 2.50
147 T.J. Houshmandzadeh RC 1.25 3.00
148 Reggie Germany RC 1.00 2.50
149 Chris Taylor RC 1.00 2.50
150 Ken-Yon Rambo RC 1.00 2.50
151 Quentin McCord RC 1.25 3.00
152 Andre King RC 1.00 2.50
153 Arnold Jackson RC 1.00 2.50
154 Tim Baker RC 1.00 2.50
155 Drew Bennett RC 1.50 4.00
156 Cedric James RC 1.00 2.50
157 Todd Heap RC 1.25 3.00
158 Alge Crumpler RC 1.50 4.00
159 Sean Brewer RC 1.00 2.50
160 Shad Meier RC 1.00 2.50
161 B.Manumaleuna RC 1.25 3.00
162 Tony Stewart RC 1.25 3.00
163 David Martin RC 1.00 2.50
164 Matt Dominguez RC 1.00 2.50
165 Boo Williams RC 1.00 2.50
166 Justin Smith RC 2.00 5.00
167 Andre Carter RC 1.25 3.00
168 Jamal Reynolds RC 1.00 2.50
169 Ryan Pickett RC 1.00 2.50
170 Aaron Schobel RC 1.50 4.00
171 Derrick Burgess RC 1.50 4.00
172 DeLawrence Grant RC 1.00 2.50
173 Karon Riley RC 1.00 2.50
174 Richard Seymour RC 1.50 4.00
175 Marcus Stroud RC 1.25 3.00
176 Casey Hampton RC 1.50 4.00
177 Shaun Rogers RC 1.50 4.00
178 Kris Jenkins RC 1.50 4.00
179 Eric Downing RC 1.00 2.50
180 Kenny Smith RC 1.00 2.50
181 Marcus Bell RC 1.00 2.50
182 Dan Morgan RC 1.25 3.00
183 Kendrell Bell RC 1.50 4.00
184 Tommy Polley RC 1.00 2.50
185 Jamie Winborn RC 1.25 3.00
186 Quinton Caver RC 1.00 2.50
187 Sedrick Hodge RC 1.00 2.50
188 Brian Allen RC 1.00 2.50
189 Torrance Marshall RC 1.00 2.50
190 Willie Middlebrooks RC 1.25 3.00
191 Jamar Fletcher RC 1.00 2.50
192 Ken Lucas RC 1.25 3.00
193 Fred Smoot RC 1.25 3.00
194 Andre Dyson RC 1.00 2.50
195 Anthony Henry RC 1.50 4.00
196 Adam Archuleta RC 1.25 3.00
197 Idrees Bashir RC 1.00 2.50
198 Adrian Wilson RC 4.00 10.00
199 Cory Bird RC 1.25 3.00
200 Jarrod Cooper RC 1.25 3.00
201 L.Tomlinson JSY/400 RC 12.00 30.00
202 Chris Weinke JSY/400 RC 3.00 8.00
203 Anthony Thomas FB/400 RC 4.00 10.00
204 Koren Robinson JSY/400 RC 3.00 8.00
205 James Jackson JSY/400 RC 2.50 6.00
206 Kevan Barlow FB/400 RC 3.00 8.00
207 Quincy Morgan JSY/400 RC 3.00 8.00
208 Nate Clements JSY/400 RC 3.00 8.00
209 Travis Henry JSY/400 RC 3.00 8.00
210 Damione Lewis FB/400 RC 3.00 8.00
211 Snoop Minnis FB/400 RC 2.50 6.00
212 David Terrell FB/600 RC 2.50 6.00
213 Gerard Warren JSY/600 RC 2.50 6.00
214 Chris Chambers JSY/600 RC 2.00 5.00
215 Will Allen FB/750 RC 3.00 8.00
216 Leonard Davis JSY/750 RC 3.00 8.00
217 Travis Minor JSY/750 RC 2.50 6.00
218 Will Peterson FB/750 RC 2.50 6.00
219 Rod Gardner FB/750 RC 2.50 6.00
220 Freddie Mitchell FB/750 RC 2.00 5.00
221 Derrick Gibson FB/750 RC 2.00 5.00
222 Vanden Bosch JSY/750 RC 3.00 8.00
223 LaMont Jordan FB/750 RC 3.00 8.00
224 Quincy Carter FB/750 RC 2.50 6.00
225 C.Buckhalter FB/750 RC 2.00 5.00

2001 Playoff Preferred National Treasures Gold

*VETS 1-100: 3X TO 8X BASIC CARDS
1-100 VETERAN PRINT RUN 100
*ROOKIES 101-200: 1.5X TO 4X
101-200 ROOKIE PRINT RUN 50
*ROOKIE JSY: 1.5X TO 4X JSY/FB/400
*ROOKIE JSY: 2X TO 5X JSY/FB/600-750
201-225 ROOKIE JSY PRINT RUN 10

2001 Playoff Preferred National Treasures Silver

*VETS 1-100: 1.2X TO 3X BASIC CARDS
1-100 VETERAN PRINT RUN 400
*ROOKIES 101-200: .8X TO 2X
101-200 ROOKIE PRINT RUN 275
*ROOKIE JSY: 1X TO 2.5X BASE JSY/400
*ROOK.JSY: 1.2X TO 3X BASE JSY/600-750
201-225 ROOKIE JSY PRINT RUN 25

2001 Playoff Preferred Materials

Randomly inserted in packs, this 50 card sets features game worn jerseys on the card front of both past and present NFL stars. Cards are serial numbered in different quantities which vary from 100 to 600 of each card made.
STATED PRINT RUN 100-600
1 Barry Sanders/100 10.00 25.00
2 Dan Marino/100 12.00 30.00
3 Warren Moon/100 10.00 25.00
4 Walter Payton/100 40.00 100.00
5 Brett Favre/100 12.00 30.00
6 Daunte Culpepper/100 5.00 12.00
7 Eddie George/100 6.00 15.00
8 Edgerrin James/100 5.00 12.00
9 Steve McNair/100 5.00 12.00
10 Terrell Owens/100 5.00 12.00
11 Troy Aikman/100 8.00 20.00
12 Randy Moss/100 5.00 12.00
13 Peyton Manning/100 15.00 40.00
14 Emmitt Smith/100 10.00 25.00
15 Marshall Faulk/100 5.00 12.00
16 Jevon Kearse/100 4.00 10.00
17 Jake Plummer/100 4.00 10.00
18 Jim Kelly/100 10.00 25.00
19 Boomer Esiason/250 6.00 15.00
20 John Elway/250 15.00 40.00
21 Brian Griese/250 3.00 8.00
22 Cris Carter/250 5.00 12.00
23 Isaac Bruce/250 5.00 12.00
24 Ricky Williams/250 4.00 10.00
25 Kurt Warner/250 8.00 20.00
26 Corey Dillon/250 3.00 8.00
27 Tyrone Wheatley/250 4.00 10.00
28 Rod Smith/250 4.00 10.00
29 Earl Campbell/400 6.00 15.00
30 Curtis Martin/400 3.00 8.00
31 Donovan McNabb/400 3.00 8.00
32 Lamar Smith/400 3.00 8.00
33 Tim Couch/400 2.50 6.00
34 Mark Brunell/400 3.00 8.00
35 Stephen Davis/400 2.50 6.00
36 Charles Woodson/400 5.00 12.00
37 Eric Moulds/400 2.50 6.00
38 Jay Fiedler/400 3.00 8.00
39 Jason Sehorn/400 3.00 8.00
40 Steve Young/500 8.00 20.00
41 Drew Bledsoe/500 3.00 8.00
42 Mike Alstott/500 2.50 6.00
43 Ron Dayne/500 3.00 8.00
44 Jeff Garcia/500 2.50 6.00
45 Torry Holt/500 3.00 8.00
46 Warren Sapp/500 3.00 8.00
47 Junior Seau/500 3.00 8.00
48 Wayne Chrebet/600 2.50 6.00
49 Jimmy Smith/600 3.00 8.00
50 David Boston/600 2.50 6.00

2001 Playoff Preferred Signatures Bronze

Randomly inserted in packs, this 81-card set features hand signed holographic stickers on the card fronts. The cards are full color action shots of past and future NFL stars produced with a bronze refractor-like finish. Some cards were issued in packs via mail redemption cards that carried an expiration date of 1/2/2004. In 2005, Donruss/Playoff made an announcement of print runs for many older autographed sets including this one. Those announced print runs are included below.
1 A.J. Feeley 5.00 12.00
2 Alan Page 15.00 30.00
3 Andre Carter/75* 6.00 15.00
10 Cedric James 4.00 10.00
11 Charlie Batch 4.00 10.00
12 Chris Barnes 4.00 10.00
13 Chris Chambers 12.50 30.00
16 Corey Dillon/50* 5.00 12.00
17 Damione Lewis 5.00 12.00
18 Dan Alexander 5.00 12.00
19 Dan Fouts/45* 20.00 40.00
21 Dave Dickenson 5.00 12.00
23 Dee Brown 4.00 10.00
24 Derrick Blaylock/45* 6.00 15.00
27 Earl Campbell/30* 20.00 50.00
32 Frank Gifford/37* 20.00 40.00
35 George Blanda/50* 30.00 60.00
39 Joe Montana/25* 75.00 150.00
40 Joe Namath/25* 40.00 80.00
43 Jonathan Carter 4.00 10.00
44 Josh Booty 5.00 12.00
46 Kellen Winslow/50* 8.00 20.00
47 Kevin Kasper/45* 5.00 12.00
50 Larry Csonka/60* 30.00 60.00
51 Lawrence Taylor/52* 35.00 60.00
53 Marshall Faulk25* 20.00 50.00
54 Marvin Harrison/25* 20.00 50.00
56 Onome Ojo/45* 5.00 12.00
58 Ozzie Newsome/25* 12.00 30.00
59 Paul Hornung/25* 20.00 50.00
61 Ray Lewis/25* 40.00 80.00
64 Roger Craig/25* 20.00 50.00
66 Ronnie Lott/25* 15.00 40.00
71 Steve Smith 25.00 60.00
72 Terry Bradshaw/29* 40.00 80.00
73 Tim Brown/50* 15.00 30.00
74 Tommy Polley 4.00 10.00
75 Tony Dorsett/54* 25.00 50.00
76 Tony Gonzalez/25* 10.00 25.00
77 Torry Holt 5.00 12.00
79 Chad Pennington 4.00 10.00
80 Cris Carter/25* 15.00 40.00
81 Laveranues Coles 5.00 12.00
82 Correll Buckhalter 4.00 10.00
83 Jamal Anderson/32* 10.00 25.00
85 Marcus Robinson 5.00 12.00
87 Wesley Walls 4.00 10.00
88 Terrell Owens/25* 25.00 60.00
89 Thurman Thomas/25* 20.00 50.00
90 Doug Johnson 4.00 10.00
91 Ron Dugans 4.00 10.00
93 Kenyatta Walker 4.00 10.00
94 Reggie Germany 4.00 10.00

96 Justin Smith 8.00 20.00
97 Heath Evans 5.00 12.00
100 Alge Crumpler 10.00 25.00
101 Shaun Rogers 6.00 15.00
102 Will Allen 6.00 15.00
103 Moran Norris 4.00 10.00
104 Travis Minor 5.00 12.00
105 Brian Allen/75* 5.00 12.00
109 Anthony Thomas/50* 8.00 20.00
110 James Jackson 4.00 10.00

2001 Playoff Preferred Signatures Silver

Randomly inserted in packs, this 57-card set features hand signed holographic stickers on the fronts. The cards are full color action shots of past and future NFL stars produced with a silver refractor-like finish. Each is serial numbered in gold on the card back to 100.

STATED PRINT RUN 100 SER.#'d SETS
1 A.J. Feeley 8.00 20.00
2 Alan Page 10.00 25.00
3 Andre Carter 8.00 20.00
5 Archie Manning 20.00 40.00
6 Art Monk 20.00 40.00
11 Charlie Batch 6.00 15.00
13 Chris Chambers 6.00 15.00
14 Chris Taylor 6.00 15.00
16 Corey Dillon 6.00 15.00
17 Damione Lewis 8.00 20.00
18 Dan Alexander 8.00 20.00
19 Dan Fouts 15.00 40.00
21 Dave Dickenson 8.00 20.00
23 Dee Brown 6.00 15.00
28 Boo Williams 6.00 15.00
30 Eric Dickerson 20.00 40.00
31 Fran Tarkenton 20.00 40.00
35 George Blanda 25.00 50.00
43 Jonathan Carter 6.00 15.00
44 Josh Booty 8.00 20.00
50 Larry Csonka 30.00 60.00
52 Marcus Allen 20.00 50.00
58 Ozzie Newsome 12.00 30.00
65 Roger Staubach 50.00 100.00
68 Scotty Anderson 6.00 15.00
69 Sonny Jurgensen 20.00 40.00
70 Steve Largent 20.00 40.00
71 Steve Smith 30.00 80.00
74 Tommy Polley 6.00 15.00
76 Tony Gonzalez 8.00 20.00
77 Torry Holt 8.00 20.00
79 Chad Pennington 6.00 15.00
80 Cris Carter 20.00 40.00
82 Correll Buckhalter 6.00 15.00
85 Marcus Robinson 8.00 20.00
87 Wesley Walls 6.00 15.00
88 Terrell Owens 15.00 40.00
90 Doug Johnson 6.00 15.00
91 Ron Dugans 6.00 15.00
94 Reggie Germany 6.00 15.00
95 Mike McMahon 8.00 20.00
96 Justin Smith 12.00 30.00
97 Heath Evans 8.00 20.00
98 Eddie Berlin 6.00 15.00
100 Alge Crumpler 10.00 25.00
101 Shaun Rogers 10.00 25.00
102 Will Allen 10.00 25.00
103 Moran Norris 6.00 15.00
104 Travis Minor 8.00 20.00
105 Brian Allen 6.00 15.00
108 Alex Bannister 6.00 15.00
109 Anthony Thomas 10.00 25.00
110 James Jackson 6.00 15.00

2001 Playoff Preferred Signatures Gold

Randomly inserted in packs, this 99-card set features hand signed holographic stickers on the card fronts. The cards are full color action shots of past and future NFL stars produced with a gold refractor-like finish. Each is serial numbered in gold foil on the card back to 25. Some cards were initially issued in packs as redemption cards with an expiration date of 1/2/2004.

STATED PRINT RUN 25 SER.#'d SETS
1 A.J. Feeley 15.00 40.00
2 Alan Page 15.00 40.00
3 Andre Carter 15.00 40.00
4 Archie Griffin 15.00 40.00
6 Art Monk 40.00 100.00
7 Bart Starr 125.00 250.00
8 Bob Griese 40.00 80.00
9 Brian Griese 12.00 30.00
10 Cedric James 12.00 30.00
11 Charlie Batch 12.00 30.00
13 Chris Chambers 25.00 60.00
14 Chris Taylor 12.00 30.00
15 Chris Weinke 15.00 40.00
16 Corey Dillon 12.00 30.00
17 Damione Lewis 15.00 40.00
18 Dan Alexander 15.00 40.00
19 Dan Fouts 20.00 50.00
21 Dave Dickenson 15.00 40.00
22 Deacon Jones 20.00 50.00
25 Don Maynard 20.00 50.00
26 Drew Pearson 20.00 50.00
27 Earl Campbell 40.00 80.00
29 Edgerrin James 15.00 40.00
30 Eric Dickerson 40.00 80.00
31 Fran Tarkenton 50.00 100.00
33 Fred Biletnikoff 20.00 50.00
35 George Blanda 40.00 80.00
36 James Lofton 15.00 40.00
38 Jim Plunkett 20.00 50.00
39 Joe Montana 100.00 200.00
40 Joe Namath 100.00 200.00
41 Joe Theismann 25.00 60.00
42 Johnny Unitas 200.00 350.00
43 Jonathan Carter 12.00 30.00
44 Josh Booty 15.00 40.00
45 Justin McCareins 15.00 40.00
49 Lance Alworth 40.00 80.00
50 Larry Csonka 40.00 80.00
51 Lawrence Taylor 25.00 60.00
54 Marvin Harrison 15.00 40.00
55 Mike Singletary 50.00 100.00
57 Otto Graham 50.00 100.00
60 Paul Warfield 20.00 50.00
61 Ray Lewis 50.00 100.00
63 Rod Gardner 15.00 40.00
64 Roger Craig 20.00 50.00
65 Roger Staubach 75.00 150.00
66 Ronnie Lott 40.00 80.00
67 Sammy Baugh 75.00 150.00
68 Scotty Anderson 12.00 30.00
69 Sonny Jurgensen 25.00 60.00
70 Steve Largent 40.00 80.00
71 Steve Smith 40.00 100.00
72 Terry Bradshaw 75.00 150.00
74 Tommy Polley 12.00 30.00
75 Tony Dorsett 60.00 120.00
76 Tony Gonzalez 15.00 40.00
77 Torry Holt 15.00 40.00
78 Y.A. Tittle 20.00 50.00
79 Chad Pennington 12.00 30.00
80 Cris Carter 20.00 50.00
81 Laveranues Coles 15.00 40.00
82 Correll Buckhalter 12.00 30.00
83 Jamal Anderson 15.00 40.00
85 Marcus Robinson 15.00 40.00
86 Mark Brunell 15.00 40.00
87 Wesley Walls 12.00 30.00
88 Terrell Owens 15.00 40.00
89 Thurman Thomas 30.00 80.00
90 Doug Johnson 12.00 30.00
91 Ron Dugans 12.00 30.00
92 Eddie George 20.00 50.00
93 Kenyatta Walker 12.00 30.00
94 Reggie Germany 12.00 30.00

97 Heath Evans 15.00 40.00
98 Eddie Berlin 12.00 30.00
99 Jerome Bettis 40.00 80.00
100 Alge Crumpler 20.00 50.00
101 Shaun Rogers 20.00 50.00
102 Will Allen 20.00 50.00
103 Moran Norris 12.00 30.00
105 Brian Allen 12.00 30.00
106 Emmitt Smith 125.00 250.00
107 Kurt Warner 40.00 80.00
108 Alex Bannister 12.00 30.00
109 Anthony Thomas 20.00 50.00
110 James Jackson 12.00 30.00

1998 Playoff Prestige Samples

Playoff produced this six-card set to promote the upcoming Prestige football cards. Each card was produced with a textured foil cardfront and resembles the base card of the same player.

COMPLETE SET (6) 3.20 8.00
1 Eddie George .80 2.00
2 Napoleon Kaufman .40 1.00
3 Dorsey Levens .40 1.00
4 Jerome Bettis .40 1.00
5 Corey Dillon .80 2.00
6 Terrell Davis 1.20 3.00

1998 Playoff Prestige Hobby

The 1998 Playoff Prestige SSD (signed, sealed, and delivered) set was issued in one series totalling 200-cards and was distributed in five-card packs to the hobby market. The fronts feature borderless color action player photos printed on 30-point etched silver foil stock. A retail version of the product was released at a later date printed on thinner stock with different foil highlights than the hobby version.

COMP.HOBBY SET (200) 40.00 100.00
1 John Elway 3.00 8.00
2 Steve Atwater .30 .75
3 Terrell Davis .75 2.00
4 Bill Romanowski .30 .75
5 Rod Smith .50 1.25
6 Shannon Sharpe .50 1.25
7 Ed McCaffrey .50 1.25
8 Neil Smith .50 1.25
9 Brett Favre 3.00 8.00
10 Dorsey Levens .75 2.00
11 LeRoy Butler .30 .75
12 Antonio Freeman .75 2.00
13 Robert Brooks .50 1.25
14 Mark Chmura .50 1.25
15 Gilbert Brown .30 .75
16 Kordell Stewart .75 2.00
17 Jerome Bettis .75 2.00
18 Carnell Lake .30 .75
19 Dermontti Dawson .60 1.50
20 Charles Johnson .30 .75
21 Greg Lloyd .30 .75
22 Levon Kirkland .30 .75
23 Steve Young 1.00 2.50
24 Jim Druckenmiller .30 .75
25 Garrison Hearst .75 2.00
26 Merton Hanks .30 .75
27 Ken Norton .30 .75
28 Jerry Rice 1.50 4.00
29 Terrell Owens .75 2.00
30 J.J. Stokes .50 1.25
31 Trent Dilfer .75 2.00
32 Warrick Dunn .75 2.00
33 Mike Alstott .75 2.00
34 Reidel Anthony .50 1.25
35 Warren Sapp .50 1.25
36 Elvis Grbac .50 1.25
37 Kimble Anders .50 1.25
38 Ted Popson .30 .75
39 Derrick Thomas .75 2.00
40 Tony Gonzalez .75 2.00
41 Andre Rison .50 1.25
42 Derrick Alexander .50 1.25
43 Brad Johnson .75 2.00
44 Robert Smith .75 2.00
45 Randall McDaniel .30 .75
46 Cris Carter .75 2.00
47 Jake Reed .50 1.25
48 John Randle .50 1.25
49 Drew Bledsoe 1.25 3.00
50 Willie Clay .30 .75
51 Chris Slade .30 .75
52 Willie McGinest .30 .75
53 Shawn Jefferson .30 .75
54 Ben Coates .50 1.25
55 Terry Glenn .75 2.00
56 Jason Hanson .30 .75
57 Scott Mitchell .50 1.25
58 Barry Sanders 2.50 6.00
59 Herman Moore .50 1.25
60 Johnnie Morton .50 1.25
61 Mark Brunell .75 2.00
62 James Stewart .50 1.25
63 Tony Boselli .30 .75
64 Jimmy Smith .50 1.25
65 Keenan McCardell .50 1.25
66 Dan Marino 3.00 8.00
67 Troy Drayton .30 .75
68 Bernie Parmalee .30 .75
69 Karim Abdul-Jabbar .75 2.00
70 Zach Thomas .75 2.00
71 O.J. McDuffie .50 1.25
72 Tim Bowens .30 .75
73 Danny Kanell .50 1.25
74 Tiki Barber .75 2.00
75 Tyrone Wheatley .50 1.25
76 Charles Way .30 .75
77 Jason Sehorn .50 1.25
78 Ike Hilliard .50 1.25
79 Michael Strahan .50 1.25
80 Troy Aikman 1.50 4.00
81 Deion Sanders .75 2.00
82 Emmitt Smith 2.50 6.00
83 Darren Woodson .30 .75
84 Daryl Johnston .50 1.25
85 Michael Irvin .75 2.00
86 David LaFleur .30 .75
87 Glenn Foley .50 1.25
88 Neil O'Donnell .50 1.25
89 Keyshawn Johnson .75 2.00
90 Aaron Glenn .30 .75
91 Wayne Chrebet .75 2.00
92 Curtis Martin .75 2.00
93 Steve McNair .75 2.00
94 Eddie George .75 2.00
95 Bruce Matthews .30 .75
96 Frank Wycheck .30 .75
97 Yancey Thigpen .30 .75
98 Gus Frerotte .30 .75
99 Terry Allen .75 2.00
100 Michael Westbrook .50 1.25
101 Jamie Asher .30 .75
102 Marshall Faulk 1.00 2.50
103 Zack Crockett .30 .75
104 Ken Dilger .30 .75
105 Marvin Harrison .75 2.00
106 Chris Chandler .50 1.25
107 Byron Hanspard .30 .75
108 Jamal Anderson .75 2.00
109 Terance Mathis .50 1.25
110 Peter Boulware .30 .75
111 Michael Jackson .30 .75
112 Jim Harbaugh .50 1.25
113 Errict Rhett .50 1.25
114 Antowain Smith .75 2.00
115 Thurman Thomas .75 2.00
116 Bruce Smith .50 1.25
117 Doug Flutie .75 2.00
118 Rob Johnson .50 1.25
119 Kerry Collins .50 1.25
120 Fred Lane .30 .75
121 Wesley Walls .50 1.25
122 William Floyd .30 .75
123 Kevin Greene .50 1.25
124 Erik Kramer .30 .75
125 Darnell Autry .30 .75
126 Curtis Conway .50 1.25
127 Edgar Bennett .30 .75
128 Jeff Blake .50 1.25
129 Corey Dillon .75 2.00
130 Carl Pickens .50 1.25
131 Darnay Scott .50 1.25
132 Jake Plummer .75 2.00
133 Larry Centers .30 .75
134 Frank Sanders .50 1.25
135 Rob Moore .50 1.25
136 Adrian Murrell .50 1.25
137 Troy Davis .30 .75
138 Ray Zellars .30 .75
139 Willie Roaf .30 .75
140 Andre Hastings .30 .75
141 Jeff George .50 1.25
142 Napoleon Kaufman .75 2.00
143 Desmond Howard .50 1.25
144 Tim Brown .75 2.00
145 James Jett .50 1.25
146 Rickey Dudley .30 .75
147 Bobby Hoying .50 1.25
148 Duce Staley 1.00 2.50
149 Charlie Garner .50 1.25
150 Irving Fryar .50 1.25
151 Chris T. Jones .30 .75
152 Tony Banks .50 1.25
153 Craig Heyward .30 .75
154 Isaac Bruce .75 2.00
155 Eddie Kennison .50 1.25
156 Junior Seau .75 2.00
157 Tony Martin .50 1.25
158 Freddie Jones .30 .75
159 Natrone Means .50 1.25
160 Warren Moon .75 2.00
161 Steve Broussard .30 .75
162 Joey Galloway .50 1.25
163 Brian Blades .30 .75
164 Ricky Watters .50 1.25
165 Peyton Manning RC 12.00 30.00
166 Ryan Leaf RC 1.25 3.00
167 Andre Wadsworth RC 1.00 2.50
168 Charles Woodson RC 2.50 6.00
169 Curtis Enis RC .60 1.50
170 Fred Taylor RC 2.00 5.00
171 Kevin Dyson RC 1.25 3.00
172 Robert Edwards RC 1.00 2.50
173 Randy Moss RC 6.00 15.00
174 R.W. McQuarters RC 1.00 2.50
175 John Avery RC 1.00 2.50
176 Marcus Nash RC .60 1.50
177 Jerome Pathon RC 1.25 3.00
178 Jacquez Green RC 1.00 2.50
179 Robert Holcombe RC 1.00 2.50
180 Pat Johnson RC 1.00 2.50
181 Germane Crowell RC 1.00 2.50
182 Tony Simmons RC 1.00 2.50
183 Joe Jurevicius RC 1.25 3.00
184 Mikhail Ricks RC 1.00 2.50
185 Charlie Batch RC 1.25 3.00
186 Jon Ritchie RC 1.00 2.50
187 Scott Frost RC .60 1.50
188 Skip Hicks RC 1.00 2.50
189 Brian Alford RC .60 1.50
190 E.G. Green RC 1.00 2.50
191 Jammi German RC .60 1.50
192 Ahman Green RC 2.50 6.00
193 Chris Floyd RC .60 1.50
194 Larry Shannon RC .60 1.50
195 Jonathan Quinn RC 1.25 3.00
196 Rashaan Shehee RC 1.00 2.50
197 Brian Griese RC 2.50 6.00
198 Hines Ward RC 5.00 10.00
199 Michael Pittman RC 2.00 4.00
200 Az-Zahir Hakim RC 1.25 3.00

1998 Playoff Prestige Hobby Gold

*GOLD STARS: 12X TO 30X HI COL.
*GOLD RCs: 4X TO 10X
GOLDS PRINT RUN 25 SERIAL #'d SETS
165 Peyton Manning 200.00 350.00

1998 Playoff Prestige Hobby Red

COMP.RED SET (200) 300.00 600.00
*RED STARS: 1X TO 2.5X HI COL.
*RED RCs: .6X TO 1.5X
RED STATED ODDS 1:3 HOBBY

1998 Playoff Prestige Retail

COMPLETE SET (200) 40.00 80.00
*RETAIL: .25X TO .5X HOBBY

1998 Playoff Prestige Retail Green

COMPLETE SET (200) 150.00 300.00
*GREEN VETS: 1.5X TO 3X BASIC RETAIL
*GREEN ROOKIES: .8X TO 2X BASIC CARDS

1998 Playoff Prestige Retail Red

COMP.RED SET (200) 150.00 300.00
*RED STARS: 1.5X TO 3X HI COL.
*RED RCs: .8X TO 2X
RED STATED ODDS 1:3 RETAIL

1998 Playoff Prestige 7-Eleven

*STARS: .6X TO 1.5X BASIC RETAIL

1998 Playoff Prestige Alma Maters

Randomly inserted in packs at the rate of one in 17, this 28-card set features three player images to a card printed on foil board with foil stamped highlights.

COMP.SILVER SET (28) 175.00 350.00
SILVER STATED ODDS 1:17 HOBBY
*BLUE CARDS: .3X TO .6X SILVERS
BLUE STATED ODDS 1:25 RETAIL
1 Favre/M.Jackson/P.Carter 15.00 40.00
2 Irvin/Maryland/Testaverde 3.00 8.00
3 Dunn/Wadsworth/Boulware 5.00 12.00
4 DSanders/Benn/B.Johnson 5.00 12.00
5 E.Smith/F.Taylor/Anthony 12.50 25.00
6 A.Smith/Anders/Lathon 4.00 10.00
7 BSanders/TThom/McQuart 15.00 40.00
8 Leaf/Bledsoe/Hansen 7.50 20.00
9 Brunell/Moon/R.Shehee 5.00 12.00
10 Kaufman/Dillon/J.Pathon 5.00 12.00
11 Manning/Pickens/R.White 15.00 30.00
12 KStewart/Carruth/Westbr. 3.00 8.00
13 Enis/Collins/McDuffie 5.00 12.00
14 E.George/Hoying/Dudley 5.00 12.00
15 C.Carter/Glenn/Galloway 3.00 8.00
16 Grbac/Harb/C.Woodson 3.00 8.00
17 Elway/McCaffrey/Milburn 15.00 40.00
18 T.Davis/Hearst/R.Edwards 5.00 12.00
19 Walker/Hastings/H.Ward 10.00 20.00
20 Marino/C.Martin/Heyward 15.00 40.00
21 Aikman/Stokes/Hicks 10.00 20.00
22 Seau/K.Johnson/Morton 5.00 12.00
23 Bettis/T.Brown/Watters 3.00 8.00
24 Faulk/Scott/Hakim 7.50 20.00
25 BSmith/Druck/Freeman 4.00 10.00
26 Plummer/Woodson/Bates 5.00 12.00
27 H.Moore/Barber/Way 5.00 12.00
28 Avery/Walls/Bowens 3.00 8.00

1998 Playoff Prestige Award Winning Performers

Randomly inserted in packs at the rate of one in 65, this 22-card set features color player photos printed on silver foil board and die-cut in the shape of a trophy.

COMP.SILVER SET (22) 125.00 300.00
SILVER STATED ODDS 1:65 HOBBY
*BLUE: .25X TO .6X SILVER
BLUE STATED ODDS 1:97 RETAIL
1 Terrell Davis 5.00 12.00
2 Troy Aikman 10.00 25.00
3 Brett Favre 20.00 50.00
4 Barry Sanders 15.00 40.00
5 Warrick Dunn 5.00 12.00
6 John Elway 20.00 50.00
7 Jerome Bettis 5.00 12.00
8 Jake Plummer 5.00 12.00
9 Corey Dillon 5.00 12.00
10 Jerry Rice 10.00 25.00
11 Steve Young 6.00 15.00
12 Mark Brunell 5.00 12.00
13 Drew Bledsoe 7.50 20.00
14 Dan Marino 20.00 50.00
15 Kordell Stewart 5.00 12.00
16 Emmitt Smith 15.00 40.00
17 Deion Sanders 5.00 12.00
18 Mike Alstott 5.00 12.00
19 Herman Moore 5.00 12.00
20 Cris Carter 5.00 12.00
21 Eddie George 5.00 12.00
22 Dorsey Levens 5.00 12.00

1998 Playoff Prestige Best of the NFL

Randomly inserted in packs at the rate of one in 33, this 24-card set features color action player images printed on silver board with a die-cut NFL shield as background.

COMP.DIE CUT SET (24) 125.00 250.00
DIE CUT STATED ODDS 1:33 HOBBY
*NON-DIE CUTS: .3X TO .6X DIE CUTS
NON-DIE CUT STATED ODDS 1:49 RETAIL
1 Terrell Davis 3.00 8.00
2 Troy Aikman 6.00 15.00
3 Brett Favre 12.50 30.00
4 Barry Sanders 10.00 25.00
5 Warrick Dunn 3.00 8.00
6 John Elway 12.50 30.00
7 Jerome Bettis 3.00 8.00
8 Jake Plummer 3.00 8.00
9 Corey Dillon 3.00 8.00
10 Jerry Rice 6.00 15.00
11 Steve Young 4.00 10.00
12 Mark Brunell 3.00 8.00
13 Drew Bledsoe 5.00 12.00
14 Dan Marino 12.50 30.00
15 Kordell Stewart 3.00 8.00
16 Emmitt Smith 10.00 25.00
17 Deion Sanders 3.00 8.00
18 Mike Alstott 3.00 8.00
19 Herman Moore 2.00 5.00
20 Cris Carter 3.00 8.00
21 Eddie George 3.00 8.00
22 Dorsey Levens 3.00 8.00
23 Peyton Manning 15.00 40.00
24 Ryan Leaf 2.00 5.00

1998 Playoff Prestige Checklists

Randomly inserted in packs at the rate of one in 17, this 30-card set features color action player photos printed on silver foil. A gold foil parallel version of this set was also produced. The cards are unnumbered and listed below in alphabetical order.

COMPLETE SET (30) 125.00 250.00
SILVER STATED ODDS 1:17 HOBBY
*GOLD CARDS: .2X TO .5X SILVERS
GOLD STATED ODDS 1:17 RETAIL
1 Troy Aikman 6.00 15.00
2 Drew Bledsoe 5.00 12.00
3 Isaac Bruce 3.00 8.00
4 Mark Brunell 3.00 8.00
5 Cris Carter 3.00 8.00
6 Troy Davis 1.25 3.00
7 Corey Dillon 3.00 8.00
8 Warrick Dunn 3.00 8.00
9 John Elway 12.50 30.00
10 Brett Favre 12.50 30.00
11 Glenn Foley 2.00 5.00
12 Gus Frerotte 1.25 3.00
13 Joey Galloway 2.00 5.00
14 Eddie George 3.00 8.00
15 Byron Hanspard 1.25 3.00
16 Bobby Hoying 2.00 5.00
17 Michael Jackson 1.25 3.00
18 Danny Kanell 2.00 5.00
19 Napoleon Kaufman 3.00 8.00
20 Erik Kramer 1.25 3.00
21 Ryan Leaf 1.50 4.00
22 Peyton Manning 12.00 30.00
23 Dan Marino 12.50 30.00
24 Jake Plummer 3.00 8.00
25 Jerry Rice 6.00 15.00
26 Andre Rison 2.00 5.00
27 Barry Sanders 10.00 25.00
28 Antowain Smith 3.00 8.00
29 Kordell Stewart 3.00 8.00
30 Wesley Walls 2.00 5.00

1998 Playoff Prestige Draft Picks

Randomly inserted one in every nine hobby packs, this 33-card set features color player photos printed on etched silver foil board. Several parallel sets were produced as well and randomly distributed in retail or special retail packs or boxes.

COMPLETE SILVER SET (33) 50.00 120.00
SILVER STATED ODDS 1:9 HOBBY
*SILVER JUMBOS: .5X TO 1.2X HI COL.
SILVER JUMBOS ONE PER HOBBY BOX
*BRONZE CARDS: .2X TO .5X SILVERS
BRONZE STATED ODDS 1:9 RETAIL
*BRONZE JUMBOS: .5X TO 1.2X SILVERS
BRONZE JUMBOS ONE PER RETAIL BOX
*BRON.JUMBOS LIM.EDITION: 2X TO 5X SILV.
BRON.JUMBO LIM.EDITION 50 SER.#'d SETS
*GREEN CARDS: .4X TO .8X SILVERS
GREEN ODDS 1 PER SPECIAL RETAIL BOX
*GREEN JUMBOS: .4X TO .8X BASIC INSERTS
GREEN JUMBOS ONE PER SPECIAL RET.BOX
*GREEN LIMIT.EDITION: 4X TO 10X SILVERS
GREEN LIMIT.EDITION PRINT RUN 25 SETS
1 Peyton Manning 10.00 25.00
2 Ryan Leaf 1.25 3.00
3 Andre Wadsworth 1.00 2.50
4 Charles Woodson 2.50 6.00
5 Curtis Enis .60 1.50
6 Fred Taylor 2.00 5.00
7 Kevin Dyson 1.25 3.00
8 Robert Edwards 1.00 2.50
9 Randy Moss 6.00 15.00
10 R.W. McQuarters 1.00 2.50
11 John Avery 1.00 2.50
12 Marcus Nash .60 1.50
13 Jerome Pathon 1.25 3.00
14 Jacquez Green 1.00 2.50
15 Robert Holcombe 1.00 2.50
16 Pat Johnson 1.00 2.50
17 Germane Crowell 1.00 2.50
18 Tony Simmons 1.00 2.50
19 Joe Jurevicius 1.25 3.00
20 Mikhael Ricks 1.00 2.50
21 Charlie Batch 1.25 3.00
22 Jon Ritchie 1.00 2.50
23 Scott Frost .60 1.50
24 Skip Hicks 1.00 2.50
25 Brian Alford .60 1.50
26 E.G. Green 1.00 2.50
27 Jammi German .60 1.50
28 Ahman Green 2.50 6.00
29 Chris Floyd .60 1.50
30 Larry Shannon .60 1.50
31 Jonathan Quinn 1.25 3.00
32 Rashaan Shehee 1.00 2.50
33 Brian Griese 2.50 6.00

1998 Playoff Prestige Honors

Randomly inserted in hobby packs at the rate of one in 3200, this three card set features color player images on a die-cut Playoff logo background printed in black over holographic foil.

COMPLETE SET (3) 40.00 100.00
STATED ODDS 1:3200 HOBBY
1 Terrell Davis 12.50 30.00
2 Warrick Dunn 10.00 25.00
3 Barry Sanders 25.00 60.00

1998 Playoff Prestige Inside the Numbers

Randomly inserted in packs at the rate of one in 49, this 18-card set features action color photos of top players printed on a background of die-cut numbers on bright silver foil.

COMP.DIE CUT (18) 150.00 300.00
DIE CUT STATED ODDS 1:49 HOBBY
*NON-DIE CUTS: .3X TO .6X DIE CUTS
NON-DIE CUT STATED ODDS 1:72 RETAIL
1 Barry Sanders 15.00 40.00
2 Terrell Davis 6.00 15.00
3 Jerry Rice 10.00 25.00
4 Kordell Stewart 4.00 10.00
5 Dan Marino 20.00 50.00
6 Warrick Dunn 6.00 15.00
7 Corey Dillon UER 6.00 15.00
8 Drew Bledsoe 7.50 20.00
9 Herman Moore 4.00 10.00
10 Troy Aikman 10.00 25.00
11 Brett Favre 20.00 50.00
12 Mark Brunell 6.00 15.00
13 Tim Brown 6.00 15.00
14 Jerome Bettis 6.00 15.00
15 Eddie George 6.00 15.00
16 Dorsey Levens 6.00 15.00
17 Napoleon Kaufman 6.00 15.00
18 John Elway 20.00 50.00

1998 Playoff Prestige Dan Marino Milestone Autographs

This cards from this set, featuring highlights of Dan Marino's career, were randomly inserted into packs at a rate of one every 321. Each of the five cards were personally signed by Marino. A 15-photo Promo sheet was distributed at the 1998 National Card Collector's Convention in Chicago. The sheet was blankbacked and featured a Playoff Chicago 1998 logo stamped in gold foil.

COMMON CARD (1-5) 40.00 100.00
STATED ODDS 1:321
P1 Dan Marino Promo 2.00 5.00

1999 Playoff Prestige EXP

This 200 card retail only set was issued in August, 1999. The set has a rookie subset for the first 40 cards. There is also a special Barry Sanders commemorative card at the end of these listings, that card honors Sanders' chase for the all-time rushing record and was inserted one every 289 packs. Notable Rookie Cards inlcude Tim Couch, Edgerrin James and Ricky Williams.

COMPLETE SET (200) 25.00 50.00
1 Anthony McFarland RC .40 1.00
2 Al Wilson RC .50 1.25
3 Jevon Kearse RC .40 1.00
4 Aaron Brooks RC .40 1.00
5 Travis McGriff RC .30 .75
6 Jeff Paulk RC .30 .75
7 Shawn Bryson RC .30 .75
8 Karsten Bailey RC .30 .75
9 Mike Cloud RC .30 .75
10 James Johnson RC .30 .75
11 Tai Streets RC .40 1.00
12 Jermaine Fazande RC .30 .75
13 Ebenezer Ekuban RC .30 .75
14 Joe Montgomery RC .30 .75
15 Craig Yeast RC .30 .75
16 Joe Germaine RC .40 1.00
17 Andy Katzenmoyer RC .40 1.00
18 Kevin Faulk RC .30 .75
19 Chris McAlister RC .30 .75
20 Sedrick Irvin RC .30 .75
21 Brock Huard RC .30 .75
22 Cade McNown RC .30 .75
23 Shaun King RC .30 .75
24 Amos Zereoue RC .30 .75
25 Dameane Douglas RC .30 .75
26 D'Wayne Bates RC .30 .75
27 Kevin Johnson RC .40 1.00
28 Rob Konrad RC .30 .75
29 Troy Edwards RC .30 .75
30 Peerless Price RC .30 .75
31 Daunte Culpepper RC .50 1.25
32 Akili Smith RC .30 .75
33 David Boston RC .30 .75
34 Chris Claiborne RC .30 .75
35 Torry Holt RC .60 1.50
36 Champ Bailey RC .60 1.50
37 Edgerrin James RC .50 1.25
38 Donovan McNabb RC 1.00 2.50
39 Ricky Williams RC .50 1.25
40 Tim Couch RC .40 1.00
41 Charles Woodson RP .30 .75
42 Skip Hicks RP .20 .50
43 Brian Griese RP .20 .50
44 Tim Dwight RP .25 .60
45 Ryan Leaf RP .25 .60
46 Curtis Enis RP .20 .50
47 Charlie Batch RP .20 .50
48 Fred Taylor RP .20 .50
49 Peyton Manning RP 1.00 2.50
50 Randy Moss RP .25 .60
51 Jim Harbaugh .25 .60
52 Warren Moon .30 .75
53 Jeff George .20 .50
54 Rich Gannon .25 .60
55 Scott Mitchell .20 .50
56 Kerry Collins .20 .50
57 Brad Johnson .25 .60
58 Charles Johnson .20 .50
59 Chris Calloway .20 .50
60 Tyrone Wheatley .25 .60
61 Michael Westbrook .20 .50
62 Skip Hicks .20 .50
63 Terry Allen .25 .60
64 Albert Connell .20 .50
65 Kevin Dyson .20 .50
66 Frank Wycheck .25 .60
67 Yancey Thigpen .20 .50
68 Steve McNair .25 .60
69 Eddie George .25 .60
70 Eric Zeier .20 .50
71 Jacquez Green .20 .50
72 Reidel Anthony .20 .50
73 Warren Sapp .25 .60
74 Mike Alstott .20 .50
75 Warrick Dunn .20 .50
76 Trent Dilfer .20 .50
77 Ahman Green .25 .60
78 Joey Galloway .25 .60
79 Ricky Watters .25 .60
80 Jon Kitna .20 .50
81 Amp Lee .20 .50
82 Isaac Bruce .30 .75
83 Robert Holcombe .20 .50
84 Greg Hill .20 .50
85 Marshall Faulk .25 .60
86 Trent Green .20 .50
87 J.J. Stokes .20 .50
88 Terrell Owens .25 .60
89 Jerry Rice .75 2.00
90 Garrison Hearst .20 .50
91 Steve Young .40 1.00
92 Junior Seau .25 .60
93 Mikhael Ricks .20 .50
94 Natrone Means .25 .60
95 Ryan Leaf .25 .60
96 Courtney Hawkins .20 .50
97 Chris Fuamatu-Ma'afala UER .20 .50
98 Jerome Bettis .30 .75
99 Kordell Stewart .20 .50
100 Bobby Hoying .20 .50
101 Charlie Garner .25 .60
102 Duce Staley .20 .50
103 Charles Woodson .30 .75
104 James Jett .20 .50
105 Rickey Dudley .20 .50
106 Tim Brown .30 .75
107 Napoleon Kaufman .20 .50
108 Wayne Chrebet .20 .50
109 Keyshawn Johnson .25 .60
110 Vinny Testaverde .20 .50
111 Curtis Martin .25 .60
112 Joe Jurevicius .20 .50
113 Tiki Barber .25 .60
114 Ike Hilliard .20 .50
115 Kent Graham .20 .50
116 Gary Brown .20 .50
117 Lamar Smith .20 .50
118 Eddie Kennison .25 .60
119 Cam Cleeland .20 .50
120 Tony Simmons .20 .50
121 Ben Coates .25 .60
122 Darick Holmes .20 .50
123 Terry Glenn .25 .60
124 Drew Bledsoe .25 .60
125 Leroy Hoard .20 .50
126 Jake Reed .25 .60
127 Randy Moss .25 .60
128 Cris Carter .30 .75
129 Robert Smith .20 .50
130 Randall Cunningham .25 .60
131 Lamar Thomas .20 .50
132 John Avery .20 .50
133 O.J. McDuffie .25 .60
134 Dan Marino .60 1.50
135 Karim Abdul-Jabbar .20 .50
136 Rashaan Shehee .20 .50
137 Derrick Alexander WR .20 .50
138 Byron Bam Morris .20 .50
139 Andre Rison .25 .60
140 Elvis Grbac .20 .50
141 Tavian Banks .20 .50
142 Keenan McCardell .25 .60
143 Jimmy Smith .25 .60
144 Fred Taylor .20 .50
145 Mark Brunell .25 .60
146 Jerome Pathon .20 .50
147 Marvin Harrison .25 .60
148 Peyton Manning 1.00 2.50
149 Robert Brooks .25 .60
150 Mark Chmura .20 .50
151 Antonio Freeman .25 .60
152 Dorsey Levens .25 .60
153 Brett Favre .60 1.50
154 Johnnie Morton .25 .60
155 Germane Crowell .20 .50
156 Barry Sanders .50 1.25
157 Herman Moore .25 .60
158 Charlie Batch .20 .50
159 Marcus Nash .20 .50
160 Shannon Sharpe .25 .60
161 Rod Smith .25 .60
162 Ed McCaffrey .25 .60
163 Terrell Davis .25 .60
164 John Elway .50 1.25
165 Ernie Mills .20 .50
166 Michael Irvin .30 .75
167 Deion Sanders .25 .60
168 Emmitt Smith .50 1.25
169 Troy Aikman .40 1.00
170 Chris Spielman .25 .60
171 Terry Kirby .20 .50
172 Ty Detmer .20 .50
173 Leslie Shepherd .20 .50
174 Darnay Scott .20 .50
175 Jeff Blake .25 .60
176 Carl Pickens .25 .60
177 Corey Dillon .20 .50
178 Bobby Engram .20 .50
179 Curtis Conway .25 .60
180 Curtis Enis .20 .50
181 Muhsin Muhammad .20 .50
182 Steve Beuerlein .25 .60
183 Tim Biakabutuka .25 .60
184 Bruce Smith .25 .60
185 Andre Reed .30 .75
186 Thurman Thomas .25 .60
187 Eric Moulds .20 .50
188 Antowain Smith .20 .50
189 Doug Flutie .30 .75
190 Jermaine Lewis .20 .50
191 Priest Holmes .20 .50
192 O.J. Santiago .20 .50
193 Tim Dwight .25 .60
194 Terance Mathis .20 .50
195 Chris Chandler .25 .60
196 Jamal Anderson .25 .60
197 Rob Moore .20 .50
198 Frank Sanders .20 .50
199 Adrian Murrell .20 .50
200 Jake Plummer .20 .50
RR1 Barry Sanders RFR 7.50 20.00

1999 Playoff Prestige EXP Reflections Gold

COMPLETE SET (200) 125.00 250.00
*GOLD STARS: 2X TO 5X HI COL.
*GOLD RCs: 1.2X TO 3X
GOLD STATED PRINT RUN 1000 SER.#'d SETS

1999 Playoff Prestige EXP Reflections Silver

COMPLETE SET (200) 60.00 120.00
*SILVER STARS: 1X TO 2.5X HI COL.
*SILVER RCs: .6X TO 1.5X
SILVER PRINT RUN 3250 SERIAL #'d SETS

1999 Playoff Prestige EXP Alma Maters

Inserted one every 25 packs, these 30 cards feature two players from the same college featured on mirror board with green foil stamping. The cards have a "AM" prefix.

COMPLETE SET (30) 50.00 100.00
STATED ODDS 1:25
AM1 P.Holmes / R.Williams 1.00 2.50
AM2 T.Couch / D.Dawson .50 1.25
AM3 T.Davis / G.Hearst 1.00 2.50
AM4 T.Brown / R.Moss 2.50 6.00
AM5 B.Sanders / T.Thomas 3.00 8.00
AM6 E.Smith / F.Taylor 2.00 5.00
AM7 D.Flutie / B.Romanowski 1.00 2.50
AM8 B.Favre / M.Jackson 3.00 8.00
AM9 C.Batch / R.Rice 1.00 2.50
AM10 M.Brunell / C.Chandler 1.00 2.50
AM11 W.Dunn / D.Sanders 1.00 2.50
AM12 C.Carter / E.George 1.00 2.50
AM13 D.Bledsoe / R.Leaf 1.25 3.00
AM14 C.Dillon / N.Kaufman 1.00 2.50
AM15 J.Bettis / T.Brown 1.00 2.50
AM16 M.Faulk / D.Scott 1.25 3.00
AM17 T.Barber / H.Moore 1.00 2.50
AM18 J.Anderson / C.Fuamat. 1.00 2.50
AM19 T.Aikman / C.McNown 2.00 5.00
AM20 B.Griese / C.Woodson 1.00 2.50
AM21 C.Johnson / K.Stewart .60 1.50
AM22 K.Faulk / E.Kennison .50 1.25
AM23 D.McNabb / R.Moore 2.50 6.00
AM24 S.McNair / J.Thierry 1.00 2.50
AM25 M.Irvin / V.Testaverde .60 1.50
AM26 R.Cunnin. / K.McCard. 1.00 2.50
AM27 Key.Johnson / J.Seau 1.00 2.50
AM28 K.Abdul-Jabbar / S.Hicks .60 1.50
AM29 C.Enis / O.J. McDuffie .60 1.50
AM30 J.Galloway / R.Smith .60 1.50

1999 Playoff Prestige EXP Checklists

Inserted at a rate of one in 25, this 31 card set features the top player from each NFL team on mirror board with silver foil stamping.

COMPLETE SET (31) 50.00 100.00
STATED ODDS 1:25
CL1 Jake Plummer .75 2.00
CL2 Chris Chandler .75 2.00
CL3 Priest Holmes 2.00 5.00
CL4 Doug Flutie 1.25 3.00
CL5 Wesley Walls .75 2.00
CL6 Curtis Enis .50 1.25
CL7 Corey Dillon 1.25 3.00
CL8 Kevin Johnson .60 1.50
CL9 Troy Aikman 2.50 6.00
CL10 Terrell Davis 1.25 3.00
CL11 Barry Sanders 4.00 10.00
CL12 Antonio Freeman 1.25 3.00
CL13 Peyton Manning 4.00 10.00
CL14 Fred Taylor 1.25 3.00
CL15 Andre Rison .75 2.00
CL16 Dan Marino 4.00 10.00
CL17 Randy Moss 3.00 8.00
CL18 Kevin Faulk .60 1.50
CL19 Ricky Williams 1.25 3.00
CL20 Joe Montgomery .40 1.00
CL21 Vinny Testaverde .75 2.00
CL22 Tim Brown 1.25 3.00
CL23 Duce Staley 1.25 3.00
CL24 Jerome Bettis 1.25 3.00
CL25 Natrone Means .75 2.00
CL26 Terrell Owens 1.25 3.00
CL27 Joey Galloway .75 2.00
CL28 Isaac Bruce 1.25 3.00
CL29 Mike Alstott 1.25 3.00
CL30 Eddie George 1.25 3.00
CL31 Skip Hicks .50 1.25

1999 Playoff Prestige EXP Crowd Pleasers

Inserted at a rate of one in 49, these 30 cards featuring some of the NFL hottest players were printed on foil board with foil stamping. The cards have a "CP" prefix.

COMPLETE SET (30) 100.00 200.00
STATED ODDS 1:49
CP1 Terrell Davis 2.00 5.00
CP2 Fred Taylor 2.00 5.00
CP3 Corey Dillon 2.00 5.00
CP4 Eddie George 2.00 5.00
CP5 Napoleon Kaufman 2.00 5.00
CP6 Jamal Anderson 2.00 5.00
CP7 Tim Couch .75 2.00
CP8 Emmitt Smith 4.00 10.00
CP9 Deion Sanders 2.00 5.00
CP10 Garrison Hearst 1.25 3.00
CP11 Peyton Manning 6.00 15.00
CP12 Ricky Williams 1.50 4.00
CP13 Barry Sanders 6.00 15.00
CP14 Jerry Rice 4.00 10.00
CP15 Jake Plummer 1.25 3.00
CP16 Tim Brown 2.00 5.00
CP17 Terrell Owens 2.00 5.00
CP18 Dan Marino 6.00 15.00
CP19 Chris Chandler 1.25 3.00
CP20 Drew Bledsoe 2.50 6.00
CP21 Charlie Batch 2.00 5.00
CP22 Mark Brunell 2.00 5.00
CP23 Troy Aikman 4.00 10.00
CP24 John Elway 6.00 15.00
CP25 Jon Kitna 2.00 5.00
CP26 Jerome Bettis 2.00 5.00
CP27 Brett Favre 6.00 15.00
CP28 Steve Young 2.50 6.00
CP29 Randy Moss 5.00 12.00
CP30 Antonio Freeman 2.00 5.00

1999 Playoff Prestige EXP Draft Picks

Inserted at a rate of one in 13, these 30 cards feature top rookies from the NFL draft and are highlighted on micro-etched mirror board with foil stamping.

COMPLETE SET (30) 35.00 70.00
STATED ODDS 1:13
DP1 Tim Couch .50 1.25
DP2 Ricky Williams 1.00 2.50
DP3 Donovan McNabb 2.50 6.00
DP4 Edgerrin James 2.00 5.00
DP5 Champ Bailey .60 1.50
DP6 Torry Holt 1.25 3.00
DP7 Chris Claiborne .20 .50
DP8 David Boston .50 1.25
DP9 Akili Smith .30 .75
DP10 Daunte Culpepper 2.00 5.00
DP11 Peerless Price .50 1.25
DP12 Troy Edwards .30 .75
DP13 Rob Konrad .50 1.25
DP14 Kevin Johnson .50 1.25
DP15 D'Wayne Bates .30 .75
DP16 Cecil Collins .20 .50
DP17 Amos Zereoue .50 1.25
DP18 Shaun King .30 .75
DP19 Cade McNown .30 .75
DP20 Brock Huard .50 1.25
DP21 Sedrick Irvin .20 .50
DP22 Chris McAlister .30 .75
DP23 Kevin Faulk .50 1.25
DP24 Jevon Kearse .75 2.00
DP25 Joe Germaine .30 .75
DP26 Andy Katzenmoyer .30 .75
DP27 Joe Montgomery .30 .75
DP28 Al Wilson .20 .50
DP29 Jermaine Fazande .30 .75
DP30 Ebenezer Ekuban .20 .50

1999 Playoff Prestige EXP Performers

Inserted at a rate of one in 97, these 24 cards featuring top performers of 1998 were printed on foil board with foil stamping. The cards have a "PP" prefix.

COMPLETE SET (24) 100.00 200.00

STATED ODDS 1:97
PP1 Marshall Faulk 4.00 10.00
PP2 Jake Plummer 2.00 5.00
PP3 Antonio Freeman 3.00 8.00
PP4 Brett Favre 10.00 25.00
PP5 Troy Aikman 6.00 15.00
PP6 Randy Moss 8.00 20.00
PP7 John Elway 10.00 25.00
PP8 Mark Brunell 3.00 8.00
PP9 Jamal Anderson 3.00 8.00
PP10 Doug Flutie 3.00 8.00
PP11 Drew Bledsoe 4.00 10.00
PP12 Barry Sanders 10.00 25.00
PP13 Dan Marino 10.00 25.00
PP14 Randall Cunningham 3.00 8.00
PP15 Steve Young 4.00 10.00
PP16 Carl Pickens 2.00 5.00
PP17 Peyton Manning 10.00 25.00
PP18 Herman Moore 2.00 5.00
PP19 Eddie George 3.00 8.00
PP20 Fred Taylor 3.00 8.00
PP21 Garrison Hearst 2.00 5.00
PP22 Emmitt Smith 6.00 15.00
PP23 Jerry Rice 6.00 15.00
PP24 Terrell Davis 3.00 8.00

1999 Playoff Prestige EXP Stars of the NFL

Inserted one every 73 packs, these 20 cards are printed on clear plastic with stars die-cit behind the featured player.
COMPLETE SET (20) 75.00 150.00
STATED ODDS 1:73
ST1 Jerry Rice 5.00 12.00
ST2 Steve Young 3.00 8.00
ST3 Drew Bledsoe 3.00 8.00
ST4 Jamal Anderson 2.50 6.00
ST5 Eddie George 2.50 6.00
ST6 Keyshawn Johnson 2.50 6.00
ST7 Kordell Stewart 1.50 4.00
ST8 Barry Sanders 8.00 20.00
ST9 Tim Brown 2.50 6.00
ST10 Mark Brunell 2.50 6.00
ST11 Fred Taylor 2.50 6.00
ST12 Randy Moss 6.00 15.00
ST13 Peyton Manning 8.00 20.00
ST14 Emmitt Smith 5.00 12.00
ST15 Deion Sanders 2.00 5.00
ST16 Troy Aikman 5.00 12.00
ST17 Brett Favre 8.00 20.00
ST18 Dan Marino 8.00 20.00
ST19 Terrell Davis 2.50 6.00
ST20 John Elway 8.00 20.00

1999 Playoff Prestige EXP Terrell Davis Salute

Inserted at a rate of one in 289, these five cards feature Terrell Davis. The first 150 of these cards were all autographed by Terrell Davis and the cards all have a "TD" prefix.
COMPLETE SET (5) 20.00 40.00
COMMON CARD (TD1-TD5) 4.00 10.00
STATED ODDS 1:289
COMMON AUTO (TD1-TD5) 15.00 40.00
FIRST 150-CARDS WERE AUTOGRAPHED

1999 Playoff Prestige SSD

This 200 card set was issued in five card packs. The last 50 cards, which feature either the best 1998 rookies (151-160) or 40 key rookies entering the 1999 season (161-200) were inserted at a rate of one every two packs. Notable Rookie Cards include Tim Couch, Edgerrin James and Ricky Williams.
COMPLETE SET (200) 75.00 150.00
COMP.SET w/o SP's (150) 25.00 50.00
1 Jake Plummer .25 .60
2 Adrian Murrell .25 .60
3 Frank Sanders .25 .60
4 Rob Moore .25 .60
5 Jamal Anderson .30 .75
6 Chris Chandler .30 .75
7 Terance Mathis .25 .60
8 Tim Dwight .30 .75
9 O.J. Santiago .25 .60
10 Priest Holmes .25 .60
11 Jermaine Lewis .25 .60
12 Doug Flutie .40 1.00
13 Antowain Smith .25 .60
14 Eric Moulds .25 .60
15 Thurman Thomas .30 .75
16 Andre Reed .40 1.00
17 Bruce Smith .30 .75
18 Tim Biakabutuka .30 .75
19 Steve Beuerlein .30 .75
20 Muhsin Muhammad .25 .60
21 Curtis Enis .25 .60
22 Curtis Conway .30 .75
23 Bobby Engram .25 .60
24 Corey Dillon .25 .60
25 Carl Pickens .30 .75
26 Jeff Blake .30 .75
27 Darnay Scott .25 .60
28 Leslie Shepherd .25 .60
29 Ty Detmer .25 .60
30 Terry Kirby .25 .60
31 Chris Spielman .30 .75
32 Troy Aikman .50 1.25
33 Emmitt Smith .60 1.50
34 Deion Sanders .30 .75
35 Michael Irvin .40 1.00
36 Ernie Mills .25 .60
37 John Elway .60 1.50
38 Terrell Davis .30 .75
39 Ed McCaffrey .30 .75
40 Rod Smith .30 .75
41 Shannon Sharpe .30 .75
42 Marcus Nash .25 .60
43 Charlie Batch .25 .60
44 Herman Moore .30 .75
45 Barry Sanders .60 1.50
46 Germane Crowell .25 .60
47 Johnnie Morton .30 .75
48 Brett Favre .75 2.00
49 Dorsey Levens .30 .75
50 Antonio Freeman .30 .75
51 Mark Chmura .25 .60
52 Robert Brooks .30 .75
53 Peyton Manning 1.25 3.00
54 Marvin Harrison .30 .75
55 Jerome Pathon .25 .60
56 Mark Brunell .30 .75
57 Fred Taylor .25 .60
58 Jimmy Smith .30 .75
59 Keenan McCardell .30 .75
60 Tavian Banks .25 .60
61 Elvis Grbac .25 .60
62 Andre Rison .30 .75
63 Byron Bam Morris .25 .60
64 Derrick Alexander WR .25 .60
65 Rashaan Shehee .25 .60
66 Karim Abdul-Jabbar .25 .60
67 Dan Marino .75 2.00
68 O.J. McDuffie .30 .75
69 John Avery .25 .60
70 Lamar Thomas .25 .60
71 Randall Cunningham .30 .75
72 Robert Smith .25 .60
73 Cris Carter .40 1.00
74 Randy Moss .30 .75
75 Jake Reed .30 .75
76 Leroy Hoard .25 .60
77 Drew Bledsoe .30 .75
78 Terry Glenn .30 .75
79 Darick Holmes .25 .60
80 Ben Coates .30 .75
81 Tony Simmons .25 .60
82 Cam Cleeland .25 .60
83 Eddie Kennison .30 .75
84 Lamar Smith .25 .60
85 Gary Brown .25 .60
86 Kent Graham .25 .60
87 Ike Hilliard .25 .60
88 Tiki Barber .30 .75
89 Joe Jurevicius .25 .60
90 Curtis Martin .30 .75
91 Vinny Testaverde .25 .60
92 Keyshawn Johnson .30 .75
93 Wayne Chrebet .25 .60
94 Napoleon Kaufman .25 .60
95 Tim Brown .40 1.00
96 Rickey Dudley .25 .60
97 James Jett .25 .60
98 Charles Woodson .40 1.00
99 Duce Staley .25 .60
100 Charlie Garner .30 .75
101 Bobby Hoying .25 .60
102 Kordell Stewart .25 .60
103 Jerome Bettis .40 1.00
104 Chris Fuamatu-Ma'afala .25 .60
105 Courtney Hawkins .25 .60
106 Ryan Leaf .30 .75
107 Natrone Means .30 .75
108 Mikhael Ricks .25 .60
109 Junior Seau .30 .75
110 Steve Young .50 1.25
111 Garrison Hearst .25 .60
112 Jerry Rice 1.00 2.50
113 Terrell Owens .30 .75
114 J.J. Stokes .25 .60
115 Trent Green .25 .60
116 Marshall Faulk .30 .75
117 Greg Hill .25 .60
118 Robert Holcombe .25 .60
119 Isaac Bruce .40 1.00
120 Amp Lee .25 .60
121 Jon Kitna .25 .60
122 Ricky Watters .30 .75
123 Joey Galloway .30 .75
124 Ahman Green .30 .75
125 Trent Dilfer .25 .60
126 Warrick Dunn .25 .60
127 Mike Alstott .25 .60
128 Warren Sapp .30 .75
129 Reidel Anthony .25 .60
130 Jacquez Green .25 .60
131 Eric Zeier .25 .60
132 Eddie George .30 .75
133 Steve McNair .30 .75
134 Yancey Thigpen .25 .60
135 Frank Wycheck .30 .75
136 Kevin Dyson .25 .60
137 Albert Connell .25 .60
138 Terry Allen .30 .75
139 Skip Hicks .25 .60
140 Michael Westbrook .25 .60
141 Tyrone Wheatley .30 .75
142 Chris Calloway .25 .60
143 Charles Johnson .25 .60
144 Brad Johnson .30 .75
145 Kerry Collins .25 .60
146 Scott Mitchell .25 .60
147 Rich Gannon .30 .75
148 Jeff George .25 .60
149 Warren Moon .40 1.00
150 Jim Harbaugh .30 .75
151 Randy Moss RP .60 1.50
152 Peyton Manning RP 2.50 6.00
153 Fred Taylor RP .50 1.25
154 Charlie Batch RP .50 1.25
155 Curtis Enis RP .50 1.25
156 Ryan Leaf RP .60 1.50
157 Tim Dwight RP .60 1.50
158 Brian Griese RP .50 1.25
159 Skip Hicks RP .50 1.25
160 Charles Woodson RP .75 2.00
161 Tim Couch RC 1.25 3.00
162 Ricky Williams RC 1.50 4.00
163 Donovan McNabb RC 3.00 8.00
164 Edgerrin James RC 1.50 4.00
165 Champ Bailey RC 2.00 5.00
166 Torry Holt RC 2.00 5.00
167 Chris Claiborne RC 1.00 2.50
168 David Boston RC 1.00 2.50
169 Akili Smith RC 1.00 2.50
170 Daunte Culpepper RC 1.50 4.00
171 Peerless Price RC 1.00 2.50
172 Troy Edwards RC 1.00 2.50
173 Rob Konrad RC 1.00 2.50
174 Kevin Johnson RC 1.25 3.00
175 D'Wayne Bates RC 1.00 2.50
176 Dameane Douglas RC 1.00 2.50
177 Amos Zereoue RC 1.00 2.50
178 Shaun King RC 1.00 2.50
179 Cade McNown RC 1.00 2.50
180 Brock Huard RC 1.00 2.50
181 Sedrick Irvin RC 1.00 2.50
182 Chris McAlister RC 1.00 2.50
183 Kevin Faulk RC 1.00 2.50
184 Andy Katzenmoyer RC 1.25 3.00
185 Joe Germaine RC 1.25 3.00
186 Craig Yeast RC 1.00 2.50
187 Joe Montgomery RC 1.00 2.50
188 Ebenezer Ekuban RC 1.00 2.50
189 Jermaine Fazande RC 1.00 2.50
190 Tai Streets RC 1.25 3.00
191 James Johnson RC 1.00 2.50
192 Mike Cloud RC 1.00 2.50
193 Karsten Bailey RC 1.00 2.50
194 Shawn Bryson RC 1.00 2.50
195 Jeff Paulk RC 1.00 2.50
196 Travis McGriff RC 1.00 2.50
197 Aaron Brooks RC 1.25 3.00
198 Jevon Kearse RC 1.25 3.00
199 Al Wilson RC 1.50 4.00
200 Anthony McFarland RC 1.25 3.00

1999 Playoff Prestige SSD Spectrum Blue

*STARS: 1.2X TO 3X BASIC CARDS
*RCs: .6X TO 1.5X BASIC CARDS
STATED PRINT RUN 500 SETS

1999 Playoff Prestige SSD Spectrum Gold

*GOLDS: .4X TO 1X SPECTRUM BLUES
STATED PRINT RUN 500 SETS

1999 Playoff Prestige SSD Spectrum Green

*GREENS: .4X TO 1X SPECTRUM BLUES
STATED PRINT RUN 500 SETS

1999 Playoff Prestige SSD Spectrum Purple

*PURPLES: .4X TO 1X SPECTRUM BLUES
STATED PRINT RUN 500 SETS

1999 Playoff Prestige SSD Spectrum Red

*REDS: .4X TO 1X SPECTRUM BLUES
STATED PRINT RUN 500 SETS

1999 Playoff Prestige SSD Alma Maters

Inserted at a rate of one in 17 packs, these 30 cards feature two players from the same college featured on mirror board with gold foil stamping.
COMPLETE SET (30) 100.00 200.00
STATED ODDS 1:17
*JUMBOS: .3X TO .8X HI COL.
JUMBOS ONE PER SSD HOBBY BOX
AM1 R.Williams 2.00 5.00
P.Holmes
AM2 T.Couch 1.00 2.50
D.Dawson
AM3 T.Davis 3.00 8.00
G.Hearst
AM4 R.Moss 8.00 20.00
T.Brown
AM5 B.Sanders 10.00 25.00
T.Thomas
AM6 F.Taylor 6.00 15.00
E.Smith
AM7 D.Flutie 3.00 8.00
B.Romanowski
AM8 B.Favre 10.00 25.00
M.Jackson
AM9 C.Batch 3.00 8.00
R.Rice
AM10 M.Brunell 3.00 8.00
C.Chandler
AM11 W.Dunn 3.00 8.00
D.Sanders
AM12 E.George 3.00 8.00
C.Carter
AM13 D.Bledsoe 4.00 10.00
R.Leaf
AM14 C.Dillon 3.00 8.00
N.Kaufman
AM15 J.Bettis 3.00 8.00
T.Brown
AM16 M.Faulk 4.00 10.00
D.Scott
AM17 H.Moore 2.00 5.00
T.Barber
AM18 J.Anderson 3.00 8.00
C.Fua.Ma
AM19 T.Aikman 6.00 15.00
C.McNown
AM20 B.Griese 3.00 8.00
C.Woodson
AM21 K.Stewart 2.00 5.00
C.Johnson
AM22 K.Faulk 1.00 2.50
E.Kennison
AM23 D.McNabb 5.00 12.00
R.Moore
AM24 S.McNair 3.00 8.00
J.Thierry
AM25 V.Testaverde 2.00 5.00
M.Irvin
AM26 Cunningham 3.00 8.00
McCard.
AM27 Key.Johnson 3.00 8.00
J.Seau
AM28 S.Hicks 2.00 5.00
K.Abdul-Jabbar
AM29 C.Enis 2.00 5.00
O.J. McDuffie
AM30 J.Galloway 2.00 5.00
R.Smith

1999 Playoff Prestige SSD Checklists

Inserted one every 17 packs, these mirror-board cards with foil stamping are sequenced in alphabetical order by team and feature a star from each team on the front and photos of other players from that team featured in the base set on the back. The cards have a "CL" prefix.
COMPLETE SET (31) 100.00 200.00
STATED ODDS 1:17
CL1 Jake Plummer 1.25 3.00
CL2 Chris Chandler 1.25 3.00
CL3 Priest Holmes 3.00 8.00
CL4 Doug Flutie 2.00 5.00
CL5 Wesley Walls 1.25 3.00
CL6 Curtis Enis .75 2.00
CL7 Corey Dillon 2.00 5.00
CL8 Kevin Johnson 1.50 4.00
CL9 Troy Aikman 5.00 12.00
CL10 Terrell Davis 2.00 5.00
CL11 Barry Sanders 8.00 20.00
CL12 Antonio Freeman 2.00 5.00
CL13 Peyton Manning 8.00 20.00
CL14 Fred Taylor 2.00 5.00
CL15 Byron Bam Morris .75 2.00
CL16 Dan Marino 8.00 20.00
CL17 Randy Moss 6.00 15.00
CL18 Kevin Faulk 1.50 4.00
CL19 Ricky Williams 2.50 6.00
CL20 Joe Montgomery 1.25 3.00
CL21 Vinny Testaverde 1.25 3.00
CL22 Tim Brown 2.00 5.00
CL23 Duce Staley 2.00 5.00
CL24 Jerome Bettis 2.00 5.00
CL25 Natrone Means 1.25 3.00
CL26 Terrell Owens 2.00 5.00
CL27 Joey Galloway 1.25 3.00
CL28 Isaac Bruce 2.00 5.00
CL29 Mike Alstott 2.00 5.00
CL30 Eddie George 2.00 5.00
CL31 Skip Hicks .75 2.00

1999 Playoff Prestige SSD Checklists Autographs

Randomly inserted into packs, this is a parallel to the Checklist insert set. Each card had a stated print run of 250-cards. Not all cards were packed out and a few were only available through a mail exchange. Those cards had an expiration date of May 1, 2000. According to a spokeman at Playoff, Skip Hicks and Curtis Enis never signed cards for this set. Hicks redemption card #CL31 was exchanged for a variety of other signed Playoff cards while Enis' redemption card was exchanged for Cade McNown signed cards #CL6.
STATED PRINT RUN 250 SERIAL #'d SETS
CL1 Jake Plummer 12.50 30.00
CL2 Chris Chandler 12.50 30.00
CL3 Priest Holmes 15.00 40.00
CL4 Doug Flutie 15.00 40.00
CL5 Wesley Walls 7.50 20.00
CL6 Cade McNown 7.50 20.00
CL7 Corey Dillon 15.00 40.00
CL8 Kevin Johnson 7.50 20.00
CL9 Troy Aikman 40.00 80.00
CL10 Terrell Davis 15.00 40.00
CL11 Barry Sanders 50.00 100.00
CL12 Antonio Freeman 12.50 30.00
CL13 Peyton Manning 60.00 120.00
CL14 Fred Taylor 15.00 40.00
CL15 Byron Bam Morris SP 7.50 20.00
CL16 Dan Marino 75.00 150.00
CL17 Randy Moss 40.00 80.00
CL18 Kevin Faulk 12.50 30.00
CL19 Ricky Williams 12.00 30.00
CL20 Joe Montgomery 7.50 20.00
CL21 Vinny Testaverde 12.50 30.00
CL22 Tim Brown 15.00 40.00
CL23 Duce Staley 15.00 40.00
CL24 Jerome Bettis 40.00 80.00
CL25 Natrone Means 12.50 30.00
CL26 Terrell Owens 15.00 40.00
CL27 Joey Galloway 12.50 30.00
CL28 Isaac Bruce 10.00 25.00
CL29 Mike Alstott 15.00 40.00
CL30 Eddie George 15.00 40.00

1999 Playoff Prestige SSD Draft Picks

Issued one every nine packs, these micro-etched mirror board cards feature top rookies from the 1999 NFL draft.
COMPLETE SET (30) 75.00 150.00
STATED ODDS 1:9
DP1 Tim Couch 1.50 4.00
DP2 Ricky Williams 2.50 6.00
DP3 Donovan McNabb 6.00 15.00
DP4 Edgerrin James 5.00 12.00
DP5 Champ Bailey 2.00 5.00
DP6 Torry Holt 3.00 8.00
DP7 Chris Claiborne .75 2.00
DP8 David Boston 1.50 4.00
DP9 Akili Smith .60 1.50
DP10 Daunte Culpepper 5.00 12.00
DP11 Peerless Price 1.50 4.00
DP12 Troy Edwards 1.25 3.00
DP13 Rob Konrad 1.50 4.00
DP14 Kevin Johnson 1.50 4.00
DP15 D'Wayne Bates 1.25 3.00
DP16 Cecil Collins .75 2.00
DP17 Amos Zereoue 1.50 4.00
DP18 Shaun King 1.25 3.00
DP19 Cade McNown 1.25 3.00
DP20 Brock Huard 1.50 4.00
DP21 Sedrick Irvin .75 2.00
DP22 Chris McAlister 1.25 3.00
DP23 Kevin Faulk 1.50 4.00
DP24 Jevon Kearse 2.00 5.00
DP25 Joe Germaine 1.25 3.00
DP26 Andy Katzenmoyer 1.25 3.00
DP27 Joe Montgomery 1.25 3.00
DP28 Al Wilson 1.25 3.00
DP29 Jermaine Fazande 1.25 3.00
DP30 Ebenezer Ekuban 1.25 3.00

1999 Playoff Prestige SSD For the Record

Issued at a rate of one in 161 packs, these 30 holographic foil cards with micro-etching and foil stamping feature players who have set NFL records.
COMPLETE SET (30) 300.00 600.00
STATED ODDS 1:161
FR1 Mark Brunell 6.00 15.00
FR2 Jerry Rice 15.00 40.00
FR3 Peyton Manning 25.00 60.00
FR4 Barry Sanders 25.00 60.00
FR5 Deion Sanders 6.00 15.00
FR6 Eddie George 6.00 15.00
FR7 Corey Dillon 6.00 15.00
FR8 Jerome Bettis 6.00 15.00
FR9 Curtis Martin 6.00 15.00
FR10 Ricky Williams 8.00 20.00
FR11 Jake Plummer 4.00 10.00
FR12 Emmitt Smith 15.00 40.00
FR13 Dan Marino 25.00 60.00
FR14 Terrell Davis 6.00 15.00
FR15 Fred Taylor 6.00 15.00
FR16 Warrick Dunn 6.00 15.00
FR17 Steve McNair 6.00 15.00
FR18 Cris Carter 6.00 15.00
FR19 Mike Alstott 6.00 15.00
FR20 Steve Young 10.00 25.00
FR21 Charlie Batch 6.00 15.00
FR22 Tim Couch 5.00 12.00
FR23 Jamal Anderson 6.00 15.00
FR24 Randy Moss 20.00 50.00
FR25 Brett Favre 25.00 60.00
FR26 Drew Bledsoe 10.00 25.00
FR27 Troy Aikman 15.00 40.00
FR28 John Elway 25.00 60.00
FR29 Kordell Stewart 4.00 10.00
FR30 Keyshawn Johnson 6.00 15.00

1999 Playoff Prestige SSD Gridiron Heritage

Issued one every 33 packs, these 24 cards printed on leather trace each player's career from high school all the way to the NFL.
COMPLETE SET (24) 125.00 300.00
STATED ODDS 1:33
GH1 Randy Moss 10.00 25.00
GH2 Terrell Davis 3.00 8.00
GH3 Brett Favre 12.50 30.00
GH4 Barry Sanders 12.50 30.00
GH5 Peyton Manning 12.50 30.00
GH6 John Elway 12.50 30.00
CH7 Fred Taylor 3.00 8.00
GH8 Cris Carter 3.00 8.00
GH9 Jamal Anderson 3.00 8.00
GH10 Jake Plummer 2.00 5.00
GH11 Steve Young 5.00 12.00
GH12 Mark Brunell 3.00 8.00
GH13 Dan Marino 12.50 30.00
GH14 Emmitt Smith 8.00 20.00
GH15 Deion Sanders 3.00 8.00
GH16 Troy Aikman 8.00 20.00
GH17 Drew Bledsoe 5.00 12.00
GH18 Jerry Rice 8.00 20.00
GH19 Ricky Williams 5.00 12.00
GH20 Tim Couch 3.00 8.00
GH21 Jerome Bettis 3.00 8.00
GH22 Eddie George 3.00 8.00
GH23 Marshall Faulk 4.00 10.00
GH24 Terrell Owens 3.00 8.00

1999 Playoff Prestige SSD Inside the Numbers

Issued at a overall rate of one in 49, these die-cut clear plastic cards showcase the player against a number marked in black flocking and silver foil. That number is important to the player's career and since each player has a different number of cards issued, we have put that print run next to the player's name.
COMPLETE SET (20) 100.00 250.00
OVERALL STATED ODDS 1:49
IN1 Tim Brown/1012* 3.00 8.00
IN2 Charlie Batch/2178* 4.00 10.00
IN3 Deion Sanders/226* 5.00 12.00
IN4 Eddie George/1294* 4.00 10.00
IN5 Keyshawn Johnson/1131* 4.00 10.00
IN6 Jamal Anderson/1846* 4.00 10.00
IN7 Steve Young/4170* 4.00 10.00
IN8 Tim Couch/4275* 4.00 10.00
IN9 Ricky Williams/6279* 4.00 10.00
IN10 Jerry Rice/1157* 10.00 25.00
IN11 Randy Moss/1313* 10.00 25.00
IN12 Edgerrin James/1416* 15.00 40.00
IN13 Peyton Manning/3739* 7.50 20.00
IN14 John Elway/2806* 12.50 30.00
IN15 Terrell Davis/2008* 4.00 10.00
IN16 Fred Taylor/1213* 4.00 10.00
IN17 Brett Favre/4212* 10.00 25.00
IN18 Jake Plummer/3737* 4.00 10.00
IN19 Mark Brunell/2601* 4.00 10.00
IN20 Barry Sanders/1491* 15.00 40.00

1999 Playoff Prestige SSD Barry Sanders

These 10 cards, inserted at an overall rate of one in 161, feature sequentially numbered cards of Barry Sanders featuring each year in his career. These cards all have a "RFTR" (Run for the Record) prefix.
COMPLETE SET (10) 350.00 700.00
OVERALL STATED ODDS 1:161
1 Barry Sanders/89 30.00 80.00
2 Barry Sanders/90 30.00 80.00
3 Barry Sanders/91 30.00 80.00
4 Barry Sanders/92 30.00 80.00
5 Barry Sanders/93 30.00 80.00
6 Barry Sanders/94 30.00 80.00
7 Barry Sanders/95 30.00 80.00
8 Barry Sanders/96 30.00 80.00
9 Barry Sanders/97 30.00 80.00
10 Barry Sanders/98 30.00 80.00

2000 Playoff Prestige

Released in late July of 2000, Prestige features a 300-card base set comprised of 200 base veteran cards, 50 Performer cards sequentially numbered to 2500, and 50 Rookie cards sequentially numbered to 2500. Base cards are on foil board card stock. Prestige was packaged in 16-pack boxes with packs containing six cards.
COMPLETE SET (300) 175.00 350.00
COMP.SET w/o SP's (200) 10.00 25.00
251-300 ROOKIE PRINT RUN 2500
1 Frank Sanders .15 .40
2 Rob Moore .15 .40
3 Michael Pittman .15 .40
4 Jake Plummer .15 .40
5 David Boston .15 .40
6 Chris Chandler .20 .50
7 Tim Dwight .20 .50
8 Shawn Jefferson .15 .40
9 Terance Mathis .15 .40
10 Jamal Anderson .20 .50
11 Byron Hanspard .15 .40
12 Ken Oxendine .15 .40
13 Priest Holmes .15 .40
14 Tony Banks .15 .40
15 Shannon Sharpe .20 .50
16 Rod Woodson .25 .60
17 Jermaine Lewis .15 .40
18 Qadry Ismail .15 .40
19 Eric Moulds .15 .40
20 Doug Flutie .20 .50
21 Jay Riemersma .15 .40
22 Antowain Smith .20 .50
23 Jonathan Linton .15 .40
24 Peerless Price .20 .50
25 Rob Johnson .20 .50
26 Muhsin Muhammad .15 .40
27 Wesley Walls .15 .40
28 Tim Biakabutuka .20 .50
29 Steve Beuerlein .20 .50
30 Patrick Jeffers .15 .40
31 Natrone Means .20 .50
32 Curtis Enis .15 .40
33 Bobby Engram .15 .40
34 Marcus Robinson .20 .50
35 Marty Booker .15 .40
36 Cade McNown .15 .40
37 Darnay Scott .20 .50
38 Carl Pickens .20 .50
39 Corey Dillon .15 .40
40 Akili Smith .15 .40
41 Michael Basnight .15 .40
42 Karim Abdul-Jabbar .15 .40
43 Tim Couch .20 .50
44 Kevin Johnson .15 .40
45 Darrin Chiaverini .15 .40
46 Errict Rhett .20 .50
47 Emmitt Smith .40 1.00
48 Deion Sanders .20 .50
49 Michael Irvin .25 .60
50 Rocket Ismail .20 .50
51 Troy Aikman .30 .75
52 Jason Tucker .15 .40
53 Joey Galloway .20 .50
54 David LaFleur .15 .40
55 Wane McGarity .15 .40
56 Ed McCaffrey .20 .50
57 Rod Smith .20 .50
58 Brian Griese .15 .40
59 John Elway .40 1.00
60 Gus Frerotte .15 .40
61 Neil Smith .15 .40
62 Terrell Davis .20 .50
63 Olandis Gary .20 .50
64 Johnnie Morton .20 .50
65 Charlie Batch .15 .40
66 Barry Sanders .40 1.00
67 James Stewart .15 .40
68 Germane Crowell .15 .40
69 Sedrick Irvin .15 .40
70 Herman Moore .15 .40
71 Corey Bradford .15 .40
72 Dorsey Levens .20 .50
73 Antonio Freeman .20 .50
74 Brett Favre .50 1.25
75 De'Mond Parker .15 .40
76 Bill Schroeder .20 .50
77 Donald Driver .30 .75
78 E.G. Green .15 .40
79 Marvin Harrison .20 .50
80 Peyton Manning .60 1.50
81 Terrence Wilkins .15 .40
82 Edgerrin James .20 .50
83 Keenan McCardell .20 .50
84 Mark Brunell .20 .50
85 Fred Taylor .15 .40
86 Jimmy Smith .20 .50
87 Derrick Alexander .15 .40
88 Andre Rison .20 .50
89 Elvis Grbac .15 .40
90 Tony Gonzalez .20 .50
91 Donnell Bennett .15 .40
92 Warren Moon .25 .60
93 Kimble Anders .15 .40
94 Tony Richardson RC .15 .40
95 Jay Fiedler .20 .50
96 Zach Thomas .20 .50
97 Oronde Gadsden .20 .50
98 Dan Marino .50 1.25
99 O.J. McDuffie .20 .50
100 Tony Martin .20 .50
101 James Johnson .15 .40
102 Rob Konrad .15 .40
103 Damon Huard .15 .40
104 Thurman Thomas .20 .50
105 Randy Moss .20 .50
106 Cris Carter .25 .60
107 Robert Smith .15 .40
108 Randall Cunningham .20 .50
109 John Randle .25 .60
110 Leroy Hoard .15 .40
111 Daunte Culpepper .20 .50
112 Matthew Hatchette .15 .40
113 Troy Brown .15 .40
114 Tony Simmons .15 .40
115 Terry Glenn .20 .50
116 Ben Coates .15 .40
117 Drew Bledsoe .20 .50
118 Terry Allen .20 .50
119 Kevin Faulk .15 .40
120 Ricky Williams .20 .50
121 Jake Delhomme RC .20 .50
122 Jake Reed .20 .50
123 Jeff Blake .20 .50
124 Amani Toomer .15 .40
125 Kerry Collins .15 .40
126 Tiki Barber .20 .50
127 Ike Hilliard .15 .40
128 Joe Montgomery .15 .40
129 Sean Bennett .15 .40
130 Curtis Martin .20 .50
131 Vinny Testaverde .15 .40
132 Wayne Chrebet .15 .40
133 Ray Lucas .15 .40
134 Tyrone Wheatley .15 .40
135 Napoleon Kaufman .20 .50
136 Tim Brown .25 .60
137 Rickey Dudley .15 .40
138 James Jett .20 .50
139 Rich Gannon .20 .50
140 Charles Woodson .25 .60
141 Duce Staley .15 .40
142 Donovan McNabb .20 .50
143 Na Brown .15 .40
144 Kordell Stewart .15 .40
145 Jerome Bettis .25 .60
146 Hines Ward .20 .50
147 Troy Edwards .15 .40
148 Curtis Conway .20 .50
149 Junior Seau .20 .50
150 Jim Harbaugh .20 .50
151 Jermaine Fazande .15 .40
152 Terrell Owens .20 .50
153 J.J. Stokes .20 .50
154 Charlie Garner .20 .50
155 Jerry Rice .60 1.50
156 Garrison Hearst .15 .40
157 Steve Young .30 .75
158 Jeff Garcia .15 .40
159 Derrick Mayes .15 .40
160 Ahman Green .20 .50
161 Ricky Watters .20 .50
162 Jon Kitna .15 .40
163 Karsten Bailey .15 .40
164 Sean Dawkins .15 .40
165 Az-Zahir Hakim .15 .40
166 Isaac Bruce .25 .60
167 Marshall Faulk .20 .50
168 Trent Green .15 .40
169 Kurt Warner .40 1.00
170 Torry Holt .20 .50
171 Robert Holcombe .15 .40
172 Kevin Carter .15 .40
173 Keyshawn Johnson .20 .50
174 Jacquez Green .15 .40
175 Reidel Anthony .15 .40
176 Warren Sapp .20 .50
177 Mike Alstott .20 .50
178 Warrick Dunn .15 .40
179 Trent Dilfer .15 .40
180 Shaun King .15 .40
181 Neil O'Donnell .15 .40
182 Eddie George .20 .50
183 Yancey Thigpen .15 .40
184 Steve McNair .20 .50
185 Kevin Dyson .20 .50
186 Frank Wycheck .15 .40
187 Jevon Kearse .20 .50
188 Adrian Murrell .15 .40
189 Jeff George .20 .50
190 Stephen Davis .20 .50
191 Stephen Alexander .15 .40
192 Darrell Green .15 .40
193 Skip Hicks .15 .40
194 Brad Johnson .20 .50
195 Michael Westbrook .15 .40
196 Albert Connell .15 .40
197 Irving Fryar .20 .50
198 Bruce Smith .20 .50
199 Champ Bailey .20 .50
200 Larry Centers .15 .40
201 Jake Plummer PP .30 .75
202 Doug Flutie PP .40 1.00
203 Eric Moulds PP .40 1.00
204 Muhsin Muhammad PP .30 .75
205 Marcus Robinson PP .40 1.00
206 Cade McNown PP .30 .75
207 Corey Dillon PP .30 .75
208 Tim Couch PP .40 1.00
209 Kevin Johnson PP .30 .75
210 Emmitt Smith PP .75 2.00
211 Troy Aikman PP .60 1.50
212 Brian Griese PP .30 .75
213 Olandis Gary PP .40 1.00
214 Germane Crowell PP .30 .75
215 Brett Favre PP 1.00 2.50
216 Charlie Batch PP .30 .75
217 Antonio Freeman PP .40 1.00
218 Dorsey Levens PP .40 1.00
219 Peyton Manning PP 1.25 3.00
220 Edgerrin James PP .40 1.00
221 Marvin Harrison PP .40 1.00
222 Fred Taylor PP .30 .75
223 Mark Brunell PP .40 1.00
224 Jimmy Smith PP .40 1.00
225 Dan Marino PP 1.00 2.50
226 Randy Moss PP .40 1.00
227 Cris Carter PP .50 1.25
228 Robert Smith PP .30 .75
229 Drew Bledsoe PP .40 1.00
230 Terry Glenn PP .40 1.00
231 Ricky Williams PP .40 1.00
232 Amani Toomer PP .30 .75
233 Keyshawn Johnson PP .40 1.00
234 Curtis Martin PP .40 1.00
235 Ray Lucas PP .30 .75
236 Tim Brown PP .50 1.25
237 Duce Staley PP .30 .75
238 Donovan McNabb PP .40 1.00
239 Jerry Rice PP 1.25 3.00
240 Jon Kitna PP .30 .75
241 Isaac Bruce PP .50 1.25
242 Kurt Warner PP .75 2.00
243 Torry Holt PP .40 1.00
244 Mike Alstott PP .30 .75
245 Marshall Faulk PP .40 1.00
246 Shaun King PP .30 .75
247 Eddie George PP .40 1.00
248 Steve McNair PP .40 1.00
249 Stephen Davis PP .30 .75
250 Brad Johnson PP .40 1.00
251 Rondell Mealey RC 1.00 2.50
252 Peter Warrick RC 1.00 2.50
253 Courtney Brown RC 1.25 3.00
254 Plaxico Burress RC 1.25 3.00
255 Corey Simon RC 1.25 3.00
256 Thomas Jones RC 1.25 3.00
257 Travis Taylor RC 1.00 2.50
258 Shaun Alexander RC 1.50 4.00
259 Chris Redman RC 1.00 2.50
260 Chad Pennington RC 1.25 3.00
261 Jamal Lewis RC 1.50 4.00
262 Bubba Franks RC 1.00 2.50
263 Dez White RC 1.00 2.50
264 Ron Dayne RC 1.50 4.00
265 Sylvester Morris RC 1.00 2.50
266 R.Jay Soward RC 1.00 2.50
267 Sherrod Gideon RC 1.00 2.50
268 Travis Prentice RC 1.00 2.50
269 Darrell Jackson RC 1.00 2.50
270 Giovanni Carmazzi RC 1.00 2.50
271 Anthony Lucas RC 1.00 2.50
272 Danny Farmer RC 1.00 2.50
273 Dennis Northcutt RC 1.00 2.50
274 Troy Walters RC 1.00 2.50
275 Laveranues Coles RC 1.25 3.00
276 Tee Martin RC 1.00 2.50
277 J.R. Redmond RC 1.00 2.50
278 Jerry Porter RC 1.50 4.00
279 Sebastian Janikowski RC 1.50 4.00
280 Michael Wiley RC 1.00 2.50
281 Reuben Droughns RC 1.00 2.50
282 Trung Canidate RC 1.00 2.50
283 Shyrone Stith RC 1.00 2.50
284 Trevor Gaylor RC 1.00 2.50
285 Marc Bulger RC 1.25 3.00
286 Tom Brady RC 125.00 250.00
287 Todd Husak RC 1.00 2.50
288 Jarious Jackson RC 1.25 3.00
289 Terrelle Smith RC 1.00 2.50
290 Chad Morton RC 1.25 3.00
291 Chris Cole RC 1.25 3.00
292 Kwame Cavil RC 1.00 2.50
293 JaJuan Dawson RC 1.00 2.50
294 Curtis Keaton RC 1.00 2.50
295 Tim Rattay RC 1.25 3.00
296 Joe Hamilton RC 1.00 2.50
297 Gari Scott RC 1.00 2.50
298 Mike Anderson RC 1.00 2.50
299 Ron Dugans RC 1.00 2.50
300 Todd Pinkston RC 1.00 2.50

2000 Playoff Prestige Spectrum Green

*VETS 1-200: 20X TO 50X BASIC CARDS
*VET PP 201-250: 10X TO 25X
*ROOKIES 251-300: 3X TO 8X
GREEN PRINT RUN 25 SER.#'d SETS
GREEN/RED OVERALL ODDS 1:28
286 Tom Brady 600.00 1000.00

2000 Playoff Prestige Spectrum Red

*VETS 1-200: 8X TO 20X BASIC CARDS
*VET PP 201-250: 4X TO 10X
*ROOKIES 251-300: 1.2X TO 3X
RED PRINT RUN 100 SER.#'d SETS
GREEN/RED OVERALL ODDS 1:28
286 Tom Brady 700.00 1200.00

2000 Playoff Prestige Alma Mater Materials

Randomly inserted in packs at the rate of one in 335, this 10-card set features swatches of game worn college jerseys along with player action shots.
STATED ODDS 1:335
*PATCHES: .6X TO 1.5X BASIC JSY
PATCH STATED ODDS 1:2005
AM1 John Elway 12.00 30.00
AM2 Drew Bledsoe 6.00 15.00
AM3 Ricky Williams 6.00 15.00
AM4 Edgerrin James 6.00 15.00
AM5 Fred Taylor 5.00 12.00
AM6 J.J. Stokes 6.00 15.00
AM7 Eddie George 6.00 15.00
AM8 Frank Wycheck 6.00 15.00
AM9 Tim Biakabutuka 6.00 15.00
AM10 Ryan Leaf 6.00 15.00

2000 Playoff Prestige Award Winning Materials

Randomly inserted in Hobby packs, this 23-card set features swatches of game-used jerseys. Each player has an individual card and also appears on a triple jersey swatch card. Single jerseys are numbered out of 75 and triple jerseys are numbered out of 25.
SINGLE JERSEY PRINT RUN 75
TRIPLE JERSEY PRINT RUN 25
OVERALL STATED ODDS 1:429
AW1 Brett Favre 20.00 50.00
AW2 Barry Sanders 15.00 40.00
AW3 Thurman Thomas 8.00 20.00
AW4 T.Thom/B.Sand/Favre 30.00 80.00
AW5 Dan Marino 20.00 50.00
AW6 Steve Young 12.00 30.00
AW7 Kurt Warner 15.00 40.00
AW8 Marino/Young/Warner 30.00 80.00
AW9 John Elway 15.00 40.00
AW10 Terrell Davis 8.00 20.00
AW11 Phil Simms 10.00 25.00
AW12 Elway/T.Davis/Simms 25.00 60.00
AW13 Troy Aikman 12.00 30.00
AW14 Emmitt Smith 15.00 40.00
AW15 Jerry Rice 25.00 60.00
AW16 Aikman/E.Smith/Rice 40.00 100.00
AW17 Randy Moss 8.00 20.00
AW18 Eddie George 8.00 20.00
AW19 Jerome Bettis 10.00 25.00
AW20 Moss/E.George/Bettis 15.00 40.00
AW21 Edgerrin James 8.00 20.00
AW22 Curtis Martin 8.00 20.00
AW23 Marshall Faulk 8.00 20.00
AW24 James/Martin/M.Faulk 12.00 30.00

2000 Playoff Prestige Award Winning Performers

Randomly inserted in Hobby packs at the rate of one in 31, this 24-card set features both single and triple player cards of MVP's, Rookies of the Year, and Super Bowl MVP's from the last 15 years.
COMPLETE SET (24) 25.00 60.00
STATED ODDS 1:31 HOBBY
AW1 Brett Favre 1.50 4.00
AW2 Barry Sanders 1.25 3.00
AW3 Thurman Thomas .60 1.50
AW4 T.Thomas 1.50 4.00
B.Sand
Favre
AW5 Dan Marino 1.50 4.00
AW6 Steve Young 1.00 2.50
AW7 Kurt Warner 1.25 3.00
AW8 Marino 1.50 4.00
Young
Warner
AW9 John Elway 1.25 3.00
AW10 Terrell Davis .60 1.50
AW11 Phil Simms .75 2.00
AW12 Elway 1.25 3.00
T.Davis
Simms
AW13 Troy Aikman 1.00 2.50
AW14 Emmitt Smith 1.25 3.00
AW15 Jerry Rice 2.00 5.00
AW16 Aikman 2.00 5.00
E.Smith
Rice
AW17 Randy Moss .60 1.50
AW18 Eddie George .60 1.50
AW19 Jerome Bettis .75 2.00
AW20 Moss .75 2.00
E.George
Bettis
AW21 Edgerrin James .60 1.50
AW22 Curtis Martin .60 1.50
AW23 Marshall Faulk .60 1.50
AW24 James .60 1.50
C.Mart
M.Faulk

2000 Playoff Prestige Award Winning Signatures

Randomly inserted in Hobby packs, this 24-card set parallels the base Award Winning Performers insert set in an autographed version. Single autograph cards are numbered out of 100 and double autograph cards are numbered out of 25. Some cards were issued via redemption cards which carried an expiration date of 4/30/2001.
SINGLE AUTO PRINT RUN 100
TRIPLE AUTO PRINT RUN 25
OVERALL STATED ODDS 1:330
AW1 Brett Favre 125.00 200.00
AW2 Barry Sanders 60.00 120.00
AW3 Thurman Thomas 12.00 30.00
AW4 T.Thom/B.Sand/Favre 250.00 400.00
AW5 Dan Marino 100.00 200.00
AW6 Steve Young 30.00 60.00
AW7 Kurt Warner 40.00 80.00
AW8 Marino/Young/Warner 250.00 400.00
AW9 John Elway 60.00 120.00
AW10 Terrell Davis 12.00 30.00
AW11 Phil Simms 15.00 40.00
AW12 Elway/T.Davis/Simms 125.00 250.00
AW13 Troy Aikman 40.00 100.00
AW14 Emmitt Smith 125.00 250.00
AW15 Jerry Rice 60.00 120.00
AW16 Aikman/E.Smith/Rice 300.00 450.00
AW17 Randy Moss 40.00 80.00
AW18 Eddie George 12.00 30.00
AW19 Jerome Bettis 50.00 80.00
AW20 R.Moss/George/Bettis 125.00 250.00
AW21 Edgerrin James 12.00 30.00
AW23 Marshall Faulk 12.00 30.00
AW24 James/C.Mart/M.Faulk 125.00 250.00

2000 Playoff Prestige Draft Picks

These cards were randomly seeded in 2000 Prestige hobby only packs at the rate of 1:8. Each features a top pick from the 2000 NFL Draft.
COMPLETE SET (10) 15.00 40.00
STATED ODDS 1:8 HOBBY
DP1 Joe Hamilton .40 1.00
DP2 Peter Warrick .40 1.00
DP3 Courtney Brown .50 1.25
DP4 Plaxico Burress .50 1.25
DP5 Thomas Jones .50 1.25
DP6 Travis Taylor .40 1.00

DP7 Shaun Alexander .60 1.50
DP8 Chris Redman .40 1.00
DP9 Chad Pennington .50 1.25
DP10 Jamal Lewis .60 1.50
DP11 Bubba Franks .40 1.00
DP12 Dez White .40 1.00
DP13 Ron Dayne .60 1.50
DP14 Sylvester Morris .40 1.00
DP15 R.Jay Soward .40 1.00
DP16 Travis Prentice .40 1.00
DP17 Darrell Jackson .40 1.00
DP18 Giovanni Carmazzi .40 1.00
DP19 Danny Farmer .40 1.00
DP20 Dennis Northcutt .40 1.00
DP21 Laveranues Coles .50 1.25
DP22 J.R. Redmond .40 1.00
DP23 Jerry Porter .60 1.50
DP24 Reuben Droughns .40 1.00
DP25 Trung Canidate .40 1.00
DP26 Trevor Gaylor .40 1.00
DP27 Chris Cole .50 1.25
DP28 Tim Rattay .50 1.25
DP29 Ron Dugans .40 1.00
DP30 Todd Pinkston .40 1.00

2000 Playoff Prestige Human Highlight Film

Randomly inserted in Hobby packs at the rate of one in 15 and Retail packs at the rate of one in 30, this 70-card set is printed on holographic silver foil board and features player action shots against a "film strip" background. A Gold parallel version was produced and randomly inserted in packs. Each Gold card was sequentially numbered of 50-sets produced.

COMPLETE SET (70) 75.00 150.00
STATED ODDS 1:15H, 1:30R
*GOLD/50: 2X TO 5X BASIC INSERTS
GOLD PRINT RUN 50 SER.#'d SETS
HH1 Randy Moss .60 1.50
HH2 Brett Favre 1.50 4.00
HH3 Dan Marino 1.50 4.00
HH4 Barry Sanders 1.25 3.00
HH5 John Elway 1.25 3.00
HH6 Peyton Manning 2.00 5.00
HH7 Terrell Davis .60 1.50
HH8 Emmitt Smith 1.25 3.00
HH9 Troy Aikman 1.00 2.50
HH10 Jerry Rice 2.00 5.00
HH11 Fred Taylor .50 1.25
HH12 Jake Plummer .50 1.25
HH13 Charlie Batch .50 1.25
HH14 Drew Bledsoe .60 1.50
HH15 Mark Brunell .60 1.50
HH16 Steve Young 1.00 2.50
HH17 Eddie George .60 1.50
HH18 Mike Alstott .50 1.25
HH19 Jamal Anderson .60 1.50
HH20 Jerome Bettis .75 2.00
HH21 Tim Brown .75 2.00
HH22 Cris Carter .75 2.00
HH23 Stephen Davis .50 1.25
HH24 Corey Dillon .50 1.25
HH25 Warrick Dunn .50 1.25
HH26 Curtis Enis .50 1.25
HH27 Marshall Faulk .60 1.50
HH28 Doug Flutie .60 1.50
HH29 Antonio Freeman .60 1.50
HH30 Joey Galloway .60 1.50
HH31 Terry Glenn .60 1.50
HH32 Marvin Harrison .60 1.50
HH33 Brad Johnson .60 1.50
HH34 Keyshawn Johnson .60 1.50
HH35 Jon Kitna .50 1.25
HH36 Dorsey Levens .60 1.50
HH37 Curtis Martin .60 1.50
HH38 Steve McNair .60 1.50
HH39 Eric Moulds .50 1.25
HH40 Terrell Owens .60 1.50
HH41 Deion Sanders .60 1.50
HH42 Antowain Smith .60 1.50
HH43 Robert Smith .50 1.25
HH44 Duce Staley .50 1.25
HH45 Kordell Stewart .50 1.25
HH46 Isaac Bruce .75 2.00
HH47 Germane Crowell .50 1.25
HH48 Michael Irvin .75 2.00
HH49 Ed McCaffrey .60 1.50
HH50 Muhsin Muhammad .50 1.25
HH51 Jimmy Smith .60 1.50
HH52 James Stewart .50 1.25
HH53 Amani Toomer .50 1.25
HH54 Ricky Watters .60 1.50
HH55 Michael Westbrook .50 1.25
HH56 Brian Griese .50 1.25
HH57 Marcus Robinson .60 1.50
HH58 Kurt Warner 1.25 3.00
HH59 Edgerrin James .60 1.50
HH60 Tim Couch .60 1.50
HH61 Ricky Williams .60 1.50
HH62 Donovan McNabb .60 1.50
HH63 Cade McNown .50 1.25
HH64 Daunte Culpepper .60 1.50
HH65 Akili Smith .50 1.25
HH66 Torry Holt .60 1.50
HH67 Peerless Price .60 1.50
HH68 Kevin Johnson .50 1.25
HH69 Shaun King .50 1.25
HH70 Olandis Gary .60 1.50

2000 Playoff Prestige Inside the Numbers

Randomly inserted in Hobby packs at the rate of one in 15 and Retail packs at the rate of one in 30, this 100-card set features action player shots coupled with a number of significance to each particular player.

COMPLETE SET (100) 75.00 150.00
STATED ODDS 1:15 HOB, 1:30 RET
IN1 Ricky Williams .75 2.00
IN2 Edgerrin James .75 2.00
IN3 Brett Favre 2.00 5.00
IN4 Donovan McNabb .75 2.00
IN5 James Stewart .60 1.50
IN6 Corey Dillon .60 1.50
IN7 Tim Couch .75 2.00
IN8 Doug Flutie .75 2.00
IN9 Jake Plummer .60 1.50
IN10 Akili Smith .60 1.50
IN11 Jerry Rice 2.50 6.00
IN12 Brian Griese .60 1.50
IN13 Peyton Manning 2.50 6.00
IN14 Fred Taylor .60 1.50
IN15 Brad Johnson .75 2.00
IN16 Courtney Brown .75 2.00
IN17 Randy Moss .75 2.00
IN18 Deion Sanders .75 2.00
IN19 Bruce Smith .75 2.00
IN20 Natrone Means .75 2.00
IN21 Dez White .60 1.50
IN22 Robert Smith .60 1.50
IN23 Jon Kitna .60 1.50
IN24 Duce Staley .60 1.50
IN25 Emmitt Smith 1.50 4.00
IN26 Dennis Northcutt .60 1.50
IN27 Antowain Smith .75 2.00
IN28 Mike Alstott .60 1.50
IN29 Ike Hilliard .60 1.50
IN30 Ed McCaffrey .75 2.00
IN31 Cade McNown .60 1.50
IN32 Jamal Lewis 1.00 2.50
IN33 Ron Dayne 1.00 2.50
IN34 Isaac Bruce 1.00 2.50
IN35 Tim Brown 1.00 2.50
IN36 Steve Beuerlein .75 2.00
IN37 Olandis Gary .75 2.00
IN38 Shyrone Stith .60 1.50
IN39 Jerome Bettis 1.00 2.50
IN40 Todd Pinkston .60 1.50
IN41 Kurt Warner 1.50 4.00
IN42 Peter Warrick .60 1.50
IN43 Steve Young 1.25 3.00
IN44 Corey Simon .75 2.00
IN45 Drew Bledsoe .75 2.00
IN46 Ron Dugans .60 1.50
IN47 Germane Crowell .60 1.50
IN48 Dan Marino 2.00 5.00
IN49 Eric Moulds .60 1.50
IN50 Peerless Price .75 2.00
IN51 Travis Taylor .60 1.50
IN52 Torry Holt .75 2.00
IN53 Charlie Batch .60 1.50
IN54 Shaun Alexander 1.00 2.50
IN55 John Elway 1.50 4.00
IN56 Amani Toomer .60 1.50
IN57 Thomas Jones .75 2.00
IN58 David Boston .60 1.50
IN59 Terrell Davis .75 2.00
IN60 Marvin Harrison .75 2.00
IN61 Priest Holmes .60 1.50
IN62 Troy Aikman 1.25 3.00
IN63 Chris Redman .60 1.50
IN64 Eddie George .75 2.00
IN65 Plaxico Burress .75 2.00
IN66 Kevin Johnson .60 1.50
IN67 Chad Pennington .75 2.00
IN68 Marshall Faulk .75 2.00
IN69 Sylvester Morris .60 1.50
IN70 Jimmy Smith .75 2.00
IN71 Dorsey Levens .75 2.00
IN72 Joey Galloway .75 2.00
IN73 Daunte Culpepper .75 2.00
IN74 Curtis Martin .75 2.00
IN75 Shaun King .60 1.50
IN76 Stephen Davis .60 1.50
IN77 Danny Farmer .60 1.50
IN78 Travis Prentice .60 1.50
IN79 Terrell Owens .75 2.00
IN80 Jamal Anderson .75 2.00
IN81 Antonio Freeman .75 2.00
IN82 Mark Brunell .75 2.00
IN83 Steve McNair .75 2.00
IN84 Marcus Robinson .75 2.00
IN85 Keenan McCardell .75 2.00
IN86 Jevon Kearse .60 1.50
IN87 Thurman Thomas .75 2.00
IN88 Patrick Jeffers .60 1.50
IN89 Keyshawn Johnson .75 2.00
IN90 Terry Glenn .75 2.00
IN91 Jerry Porter 1.00 2.50
IN92 J.R. Redmond .60 1.50
IN93 Yancey Thigpen .60 1.50
IN94 Troy Edwards .60 1.50
IN95 Cris Carter 1.00 2.50
IN96 Muhsin Muhammad .60 1.50
IN97 Ricky Watters .75 2.00
IN98 R.Jay Soward .60 1.50
IN99 Barry Sanders 1.50 4.00
IN100 James Johnson .60 1.50

2000 Playoff Prestige League Leader Quads

Randomly inserted in Hobby packs at the rate of one in 159, this 12-card set features four league leaders in the categories of Passing, Rushing, or Receiving leaders on each card. Player action photos are set on a foil micro-etched card enhanced with gold foil stamping.

COMPLETE SET (12) 25.00 60.00
STATED ODDS 1:159 HOBBY
1 Mann/Gann/Lucas/Brunell 6.00 15.00
2 Grbac/Banks/McNair/Kitna 2.00 5.00
3 Warner/Beurl/JGeor/B.John 4.00 10.00
4 Batch/Frerott/Chand/Aikmn 3.00 8.00
5 James/Martn/EGrge/Watt 2.00 5.00
6 Dillon/OGary/Bettis/Wheatly 2.50 6.00
7 SDav/ESmth/MFaulk/Staley 4.00 10.00
8 CGarn/Levens/RSmth/Alstot 2.00 5.00
9 Harris/JSmth/TBrwn/Kev.J 2.50 6.00
10 Glenn/Ismail/TMartn/D.Scot 2.00 5.00
11 Moss/Robns/Crowel/Muhm 2.00 5.00
12 Toomr/CCrter/Westb/Bruce 2.50 6.00

2000 Playoff Prestige League Leader Tandems

Randomly inserted in Retail packs at the rate of one in 95, this 24-card set pairs league leaders in passing, receiving, or rushing on a dual-sided mirror board with micro-etching and gold foil highlights.

COMPLETE SET (24) 30.00 60.00
STATED ODDS 1:95 RETAIL
1 P.Manning/R.Gannon 2.00 5.00
2 R.Lucas/M.Brunell .60 1.50
3 E.Grbac/T.Banks .50 1.25
4 S.McNair/J.Kitna .60 1.50
5 K.Warner/S.Beuerlein 1.25 3.00
6 J.George/B.Johnson .60 1.50
7 C.Batch/G.Frerotte .50 1.25
8 C.Chandler/T.Aikman 1.00 2.50
9 E.James/C.Martin .60 1.50
10 E.George/R.Watters .60 1.50
11 C.Dillon/O.Gary .60 1.50
12 J.Bettis/T.Wheatley .75 2.00
13 S.Davis/E.Smith 1.25 3.00
14 M.Faulk/D.Staley .60 1.50
15 C.Garner/D.Levens .60 1.50
16 R.Smith/M.Alstott .50 1.25
17 M.Harrison/J.Smith .60 1.50
18 T.Brown/K.Johnson .75 2.00
19 T.Glenn/Q.Ismail .60 1.50
20 T.Martin/D.Scott .60 1.50
21 R.Moss/M.Robinson .60 1.50
22 G.Crowell/M.Muhammad .50 1.25
23 C.Carter/A.Toomer .75 2.00
24 I.Bruce/M.Westbrook .75 2.00

2000 Playoff Prestige Stars of the NFL

Randomly inserted in Retail packs at the rate of one in 47, this 30-card set showcases top NFL stars on a die cut foil card stock. Each card is sequentially numbered to 500.

COMPLETE SET (30) 40.00 100.00
STATED ODDS 1:47 RETAIL
STATED PRINT RUN 500 SER.#'d SETS
1 Randy Moss 1.25 3.00
2 Brett Favre 3.00 8.00
3 Dan Marino 3.00 8.00
4 Barry Sanders 2.50 6.00
5 John Elway 2.50 6.00
6 Peyton Manning 4.00 10.00
7 Terrell Davis 1.25 3.00
8 Emmitt Smith 2.50 6.00
9 Troy Aikman 2.00 5.00
10 Jerry Rice 4.00 10.00
11 Fred Taylor 1.00 2.50
12 Jake Plummer 1.00 2.50
13 Drew Bledsoe 1.25 3.00
14 Mark Brunell 1.25 3.00
15 Steve Young 2.00 5.00
16 Eddie George 1.25 3.00
17 Cris Carter 1.50 4.00
18 Marshall Faulk 1.25 3.00
19 Marvin Harrison 1.25 3.00
20 Brad Johnson 1.25 3.00
21 Keyshawn Johnson 1.25 3.00
22 Jon Kitna 1.00 2.50
23 Dorsey Levens 1.25 3.00
24 Steve McNair 1.25 3.00
25 Eric Moulds 1.00 2.50
26 Brian Griese 1.00 2.50
27 Kurt Warner 2.50 6.00
28 Edgerrin James 1.25 3.00
29 Tim Couch 1.25 3.00
30 Ricky Williams 1.25 3.00

2000 Playoff Prestige Team Checklist

This set is divided into three different subsets: #1-31 "bronze foil base checklist" can be found in hobby packs at the rate of 1:15 and retail packs at 1:18, #32-62 "silver foil insert checklist" can be found 1:31 hobby or 1:62 retail, #63-93 "gold foil overall checklist" were seeded 1:63 hobby or 1:126 retail. All cards #63-93 were autographed by the featured player. Some cards were issued via redemption cards which carried an expiration date of 4/30/2001.

CL1-CL31 ODDS 1:15H, 1:18R
CL32-CL62 ODDS 1:31H, 1:62R
CL63-CL93 ODDS 1:63H, 1:126R
CL1 Jake Plummer .40 1.00
CL2 Jamal Anderson .50 1.25
CL3 Jamal Lewis .60 1.50
CL4 Rob Johnson .50 1.25
CL5 Muhsin Muhammad .40 1.00
CL6 Marcus Robinson .50 1.25
CL7 Peter Warrick .40 1.00
CL8 Tim Couch .50 1.25
CL9 Emmitt Smith 1.00 2.50
CL10 Terrell Davis .50 1.25
CL11 Charlie Batch .40 1.00
CL12 Brett Favre 1.25 3.00
CL13 Peyton Manning 1.50 4.00
CL14 Mark Brunell .50 1.25
CL15 Sylvester Morris .40 1.00
CL16 Dan Marino 1.25 3.00
CL17 Randy Moss .50 1.25
CL18 Drew Bledsoe .50 1.25
CL19 Jeff Blake .50 1.25
CL20 Kerry Collins .40 1.00
CL21 Chad Pennington .50 1.25
CL22 Tim Brown .60 1.50
CL23 Duce Staley .40 1.00
CL24 Jerome Bettis .60 1.50
CL25 Jim Harbaugh .50 1.25
CL26 Jerry Rice 1.50 4.00
CL27 Jon Kitna .40 1.00
CL28 Kurt Warner 1.00 2.50
CL29 Keyshawn Johnson .50 1.25
CL30 Eddie George .50 1.25
CL31 Stephen Davis .40 1.00
CL32 Thomas Jones .60 1.50
CL33 Chris Chandler .60 1.50
CL34 Tony Banks .50 1.25
CL35 Eric Moulds .50 1.25
CL36 Tim Biakabutuka .60 1.50
CL37 Curtis Enis .50 1.25
CL38 Corey Dillon .50 1.25
CL39 Courtney Brown .60 1.50
CL40 Troy Aikman 1.00 2.50
CL41 Brian Griese .50 1.25
CL42 Herman Moore .50 1.25
CL43 Antonio Freeman .60 1.50
CL44 Edgerrin James .60 1.50
CL45 Fred Taylor .50 1.25
CL46 Derrick Alexander .50 1.25
CL47 James Johnson .50 1.25
CL48 Cris Carter .75 2.00
CL49 Terry Glenn .60 1.50
CL50 Sherrod Gideon .50 1.25
CL51 Ron Dayne .75 2.00
CL52 Curtis Martin .60 1.50
CL53 Rich Gannon .60 1.50
CL54 Todd Pinkston .50 1.25
CL55 Kordell Stewart .50 1.25
CL56 Junior Seau .60 1.50
CL57 Steve Young 1.00 2.50
CL58 Shaun Alexander .75 2.00
CL59 Marshall Faulk .60 1.50
CL60 Shaun King .50 1.25
CL61 Jevon Kearse .50 1.25
CL62 Brad Johnson .60 1.50
CL63 Frank Sanders AU 3.00 8.00
CL64 Tim Dwight AU 4.00 10.00
CL65 Qadry Ismail AU 3.00 8.00
CL66 Antowain Smith AU 4.00 10.00
CL67 Patrick Jeffers AU 3.00 8.00
CL68 Cade McNown AU 3.00 8.00
CL69 Akili Smith AU 3.00 8.00
CL70 Kevin Johnson AU 3.00 8.00
CL71 Joey Galloway AU 4.00 10.00
CL72 Olandis Gary AU 4.00 10.00
CL73 Germane Crowell AU 3.00 8.00
CL74 Dorsey Levens AU 4.00 10.00
CL75 Marvin Harrison AU 4.00 10.00
CL76 Jimmy Smith AU 4.00 10.00
CL77 Elvis Grbac AU 3.00 8.00
CL78 Tony Martin AU 4.00 10.00
CL79 D.Culpepper AU 4.00 10.00
CL80 Kevin Faulk AU 3.00 8.00
CL81 Ricky Williams AU 4.00 10.00
CL82 Amani Toomer AU 3.00 8.00
CL83 Ray Lucas AU 3.00 8.00
CL84 Tyrone Wheatley AU 3.00 8.00
CL85 Donovan McNabb AU 10.00 25.00
CL86 Troy Edwards AU 3.00 8.00
CL87 Jermaine Fazande AU 3.00 8.00
CL88 Charlie Garner AU 4.00 10.00
CL89 Derrick Mayes AU 3.00 8.00
CL90 Isaac Bruce AU 5.00 12.00
CL91 Mike Alstott AU 3.00 8.00
CL92 Steve McNair AU 4.00 10.00
CL93 Albert Connell AU 3.00 8.00

2000 Playoff Prestige Team Checklist Inaugural Years

OVERALL STATED ODDS 1:216
STATED PRINT RUN 20-99
CL1 Jake Plummer/20 5.00 12.00
CL2 Jamal Anderson/66 4.00 10.00
CL3 Jamal Lewis/50 5.00 12.00
CL4 Rob Johnson/60 4.00 10.00
CL5 Muhsin Muhammad/95 2.50 6.00
CL6 Marcus Robinson/20 6.00 15.00
CL7 Peter Warrick/68 3.00 8.00
CL8 Tim Couch/99 3.00 8.00
CL9 Emmitt Smith/60 8.00 20.00
CL10 Terrell Davis/60 4.00 10.00
CL11 Charlie Batch/30 4.00 10.00
CL12 Brett Favre/21 60.00 150.00
CL13 Peyton Manning/53 12.00 30.00
CL14 Mark Brunell/95 3.00 8.00
CL15 Sylvester Morris/60 3.00 8.00
CL16 Dan Marino/66 10.00 25.00
CL17 Randy Moss/61 4.00 10.00
CL18 Drew Bledsoe/60 4.00 10.00
CL19 Jeff Blake/67 4.00 10.00
CL20 Kerry Collins/25 5.00 12.00
CL21 Chad Pennington/60 4.00 10.00
CL22 Tim Brown/60 5.00 12.00
CL23 Duce Staley/33 4.00 10.00
CL24 Jerome Bettis/33 6.00 15.00
CL25 Jim Harbaugh/60 4.00 10.00
CL26 Jerry Rice/50 12.00 30.00
CL27 Jon Kitna/76 3.00 8.00
CL28 Kurt Warner/37 10.00 25.00
CL29 Keyshawn Johnson/76 4.00 10.00
CL30 Eddie George/60 4.00 10.00
CL31 Stephen Davis/32 4.00 10.00
CL32 Thomas Jones/20 6.00 15.00
CL33 Chris Chandler/66 4.00 10.00
CL34 Tony Banks/50 3.00 8.00
CL35 Eric Moulds/60 3.00 8.00
CL36 Tim Biakabutuka/95 3.00 8.00
CL37 Curtis Enis/20 5.00 12.00
CL38 Corey Dillon/68 3.00 8.00
CL39 Courtney Brown/99 3.00 8.00
CL40 Troy Aikman/60 6.00 15.00
CL41 Brian Griese/60 3.00 8.00
CL42 Herman Moore/30 4.00 10.00
CL43 Antonio Freeman/21 6.00 15.00
CL44 Edgerrin James/53 4.00 10.00
CL45 Fred Taylor/95 2.50 6.00
CL46 Derrick Alexander/60 3.00 8.00
CL47 James Johnson/66 3.00 8.00
CL48 Cris Carter/61 5.00 12.00
CL49 Terry Glenn/60 4.00 10.00
CL50 Sherrod Gideon/67 3.00 8.00
CL51 Ron Dayne/25 8.00 20.00
CL52 Curtis Martin/60 4.00 10.00
CL53 Rich Gannon/60 4.00 10.00
CL54 Todd Pinkston/33 4.00 10.00
CL55 Kordell Stewart/33 4.00 10.00
CL56 Junior Seau/60 4.00 10.00
CL57 Steve Young/50 6.00 15.00
CL58 Shaun Alexander/76 5.00 12.00
CL59 Marshall Faulk/37 5.00 12.00
CL60 Shaun King/76 3.00 8.00
CL61 Jevon Kearse/60 3.00 8.00
CL62 Brad Johnson/32 5.00 12.00
CL63 Frank Sanders/20* 5.00 12.00
CL64 Tim Dwight/66* 4.00 10.00
CL65 Qadry Ismail/50* 3.00 8.00
CL66 Antowain Smith/60* 4.00 10.00
CL67 Patrick Jeffers/95* 2.50 6.00
CL68 Cade McNown/20* 5.00 12.00
CL69 Akili Smith/68* 3.00 8.00
CL70 Kevin Johnson/99* 2.50 6.00
CL71 Joey Galloway/60* 4.00 10.00
CL72 Olandis Gary/60* 4.00 10.00
CL73 Germane Crowell/30* 4.00 10.00
CL74 Dorsey Levens/21* 6.00 15.00
CL75 Marvin Harrison/53* 4.00 10.00
CL76 Jimmy Smith/95* 4.00 10.00
CL77 Elvis Grbac/60* 3.00 8.00
CL78 Tony Martin/66* 4.00 10.00
CL79 Daunte Culpepper/61* 4.00 10.00
CL80 Kevin Faulk/60* 3.00 8.00
CL81 Ricky Williams/67* 4.00 10.00
CL82 Amani Toomer/25* 5.00 12.00
CL83 Ray Lucas/60* 3.00 8.00
CL84 Tyrone Wheatley/60* 3.00 8.00
CL85 Donovan McNabb/33* 5.00 12.00
CL86 Troy Edwards/33* 4.00 10.00
CL87 Jermaine Fazande/60* 3.00 8.00
CL88 Charlie Garner/50* 4.00 10.00
CL89 Derrick Mayes/76* 3.00 8.00
CL90 Isaac Bruce/37* 6.00 15.00
CL91 Mike Alstott/76* 3.00 8.00
CL92 Steve McNair/60* 4.00 10.00
CL93 Albert Connell/32* 4.00 10.00

2000 Playoff Prestige Xtra Points

Randomly inserted in Hobby packs at the rate of one in 47, this 40-card set showcases the 1999 season's record breakers on an all foil card stock with holographic foil highlights.

COMPLETE SET (40) 60.00 120.00
STATED ODDS 1:47 HOBBY
XP1 Randy Moss 1.25 3.00
XP2 Brett Favre 3.00 8.00
XP3 Dan Marino 3.00 8.00
XP4 Peyton Manning 4.00 10.00
XP5 Emmitt Smith 2.50 6.00
XP6 Troy Aikman 2.00 5.00
XP7 Jerry Rice 4.00 10.00
XP8 Fred Taylor 1.00 2.50
XP9 Jake Plummer 1.00 2.50
XP10 Drew Bledsoe 1.25 3.00
XP11 Mark Brunell 1.25 3.00
XP12 Eddie George 1.25 3.00
XP13 Cris Carter 1.50 4.00
XP14 Stephen Davis 1.00 2.50
XP15 Corey Dillon 1.00 2.50
XP16 Marshall Faulk 1.25 3.00
XP17 Doug Flutie 1.25 3.00
XP18 Antonio Freeman 1.25 3.00
XP19 Terry Glenn 1.25 3.00
XP20 Marvin Harrison 1.25 3.00
XP21 Brad Johnson 1.25 3.00
XP22 Keyshawn Johnson 1.25 3.00
XP23 Jon Kitna 1.00 2.50
XP24 Dorsey Levens 1.25 3.00
XP25 Curtis Martin 1.25 3.00
XP26 Steve McNair 1.25 3.00
XP27 Isaac Bruce 1.50 4.00
XP28 Germane Crowell 1.00 2.50
XP29 Muhsin Muhammad 1.00 2.50
XP30 Jimmy Smith 1.25 3.00
XP31 Brian Griese 1.00 2.50
XP32 Marcus Robinson 1.25 3.00
XP33 Kurt Warner 2.50 6.00
XP34 Edgerrin James 1.25 3.00
XP35 Tim Couch 1.25 3.00
XP36 Ricky Williams 1.25 3.00
XP37 Torry Holt 1.25 3.00
XP38 Kevin Johnson 1.00 2.50
XP39 Shaun King 1.00 2.50
XP40 Olandis Gary 1.25 3.00

2002 Playoff Prestige Samples

*SAMPLE SILVER: .6X TO 1.5X BASE CARDS
*SAMPLE GOLD: 1.2X TO 2.5X BASE CARDS

2002 Playoff Prestige

This 216-card set includes 150-veterans and 66-short printed rookies. The product was released in early May 2002 with boxes containing 20-packs of 5 cards each. The SRP was $4 per pack.

COMP.SET w/o SP's (150) 15.00 40.00
1 David Boston .25 .60
2 MarTay Jenkins .25 .60
3 Jake Plummer .25 .60
4 Chris Chandler .30 .75
5 Jamal Anderson .30 .75
6 Michael Vick .30 .75
7 Maurice Smith .25 .60
8 Elvis Grbac .25 .60
9 Jamal Lewis .30 .75
10 Todd Heap .25 .60
11 Qadry Ismail .25 .60
12 Shannon Sharpe .30 .75
13 Ray Lewis .40 1.00
14 Rod Woodson .40 1.00
15 Travis Henry .25 .60
16 Rob Johnson .30 .75
17 Eric Moulds .25 .60
18 Nate Clements .25 .60
19 Donald Hayes .25 .60
20 Muhsin Muhammad .25 .60
21 Steve Smith .40 1.00
22 Wesley Walls .30 .75
23 Chris Weinke .25 .60
24 James Allen .25 .60
25 David Terrell .25 .60
26 Anthony Thomas .30 .75
27 Dez White .25 .60
28 Brian Urlacher .40 1.00
29 Mike Brown .25 .60
30 Corey Dillon .25 .60
31 Chad Johnson .25 .60
32 Peter Warrick .25 .60
33 Justin Smith .30 .75
34 Tim Couch .25 .60
35 James Jackson .25 .60
36 Quincy Morgan .25 .60
37 Kevin Johnson .25 .60
38 Gerard Warren .25 .60
39 Anthony Henry .25 .60
40 Quincy Carter .25 .60
41 Joey Galloway .30 .75
42 Rocket Ismail .30 .75
43 Ryan Leaf .25 .60
44 Emmitt Smith .60 1.50
45 Troy Hambrick .25 .60
46 Mike Anderson .25 .60
47 Terrell Davis .30 .75
48 Brian Griese .25 .60
49 Rod Smith .30 .75
50 Ed McCaffrey .30 .75
51 Charlie Batch .25 .60
52 Johnnie Morton .30 .75
53 Germane Crowell .25 .60
54 James Stewart .25 .60
55 Shaun Rogers .25 .60
56 Brett Favre .75 2.00
57 Antonio Freeman .40 1.00
58 Ahman Green .30 .75
59 Bill Schroeder .25 .60
60 Kabeer Gbaja-Biamila .25 .60
61 Marvin Harrison .30 .75
62 Terrence Wilkins .25 .60
63 Dominic Rhodes .25 .60
64 Reggie Wayne .30 .75
65 Edgerrin James .30 .75
66 Mark Brunell .30 .75
67 Keenan McCardell .30 .75
68 Jimmy Smith .30 .75
69 Fred Taylor .25 .60
70 Derrick Alexander .25 .60
71 Tony Gonzalez .30 .75
72 Trent Green .25 .60
73 Priest Holmes .25 .60
74 Snoop Minnis .25 .60
75 Chris Chambers .25 .60
76 Jay Fiedler .30 .75
77 Travis Minor .25 .60
78 Lamar Smith .25 .60
79 Zach Thomas .30 .75
80 Michael Bennett .25 .60
81 Cris Carter .40 1.00
82 Daunte Culpepper .30 .75
83 Randy Moss .30 .75
84 Drew Bledsoe .30 .75
85 Tom Brady 2.00 5.00
86 Troy Brown .25 .60
87 Antowain Smith .30 .75
88 Aaron Brooks .25 .60
89 Joe Horn .25 .60
90 Deuce McAllister .30 .75
91 Ricky Williams .30 .75
92 Kerry Collins .25 .60
93 Ron Dayne .30 .75
94 Michael Strahan .30 .75
95 Jason Sehorn .30 .75
96 Wayne Chrebet .25 .60
97 Laveranues Coles .30 .75
98 LaMont Jordan .30 .75
99 Curtis Martin .30 .75
100 Santana Moss .30 .75
101 Vinny Testaverde .25 .60
102 Tim Brown .40 1.00
103 Jerry Porter .25 .60
104 Jerry Rice .75 2.00
105 Charlie Garner .30 .75
106 Tyrone Wheatley .30 .75
107 Charles Woodson .40 1.00
108 Correll Buckhalter .25 .60
109 Todd Pinkston .25 .60
110 Freddie Mitchell .25 .60
111 James Thrash .30 .75
112 Duce Staley .25 .60
113 Jerome Bettis .40 1.00
114 Plaxico Burress .25 .60
115 Kordell Stewart .25 .60
116 Hines Ward .30 .75
117 Kendrell Bell .25 .60
118 Drew Brees .75 2.00
119 Curtis Conway .30 .75
120 Doug Flutie .30 .75
121 LaDainian Tomlinson .40 1.00
122 Junior Seau .30 .75
123 Kevan Barlow .25 .60
124 Jeff Garcia .25 .60
125 Garrison Hearst .25 .60
126 Terrell Owens .30 .75
127 Andre Carter .25 .60
128 Shaun Alexander .25 .60
129 Matt Hasselbeck .25 .60
130 Koren Robinson .25 .60
131 Ricky Watters .30 .75
132 Isaac Bruce .40 1.00
133 Trung Canidate .25 .60
134 Marshall Faulk .30 .75
135 Torry Holt .30 .75
136 Kurt Warner .30 .75
137 Mike Alstott .25 .60
138 Warrick Dunn .25 .60
139 Brad Johnson .30 .75
140 Keyshawn Johnson .30 .75
141 Warren Sapp .30 .75
142 Eddie George .30 .75
143 Derrick Mason .25 .60
144 Steve McNair .30 .75
145 Jevon Kearse .25 .60
146 Stephen Davis .25 .60
147 Rod Gardner .25 .60
148 Champ Bailey .30 .75
149 Bruce Smith .30 .75
150 Houston Texans .40 1.00
151 David Carr RC .75 2.00
152 Julius Peppers RC 2.00 5.00
153 Joey Harrington RC .75 2.00
154 Quentin Jammer RC 1.25 3.00
155 Ryan Sims RC 1.25 3.00
156 Bryant McKinnie RC .75 2.00
157 Roy Williams RC .75 2.00
158 John Henderson RC 1.00 2.50
159 Dwight Freeney RC 1.50 4.00
160 Wendell Bryant RC .75 2.00
161 Donte Stallworth RC 1.25 3.00
162 Jeremy Shockey RC 1.25 3.00
163 Albert Haynesworth RC 1.25 3.00
164 William Green RC 1.00 2.50
165 Phillip Buchanon RC 1.25 3.00
166 T.J. Duckett RC .75 2.00
167 Ashley Lelie RC .75 2.00
168 Javon Walker RC 1.25 3.00
169 Daniel Graham RC 1.00 2.50
170 Napoleon Harris RC 1.00 2.50
171 Lito Sheppard RC 1.25 3.00
172 Robert Thomas RC .75 2.00
173 Patrick Ramsey RC 1.00 2.50
174 Jabar Gaffney RC .75 2.00
175 DeShaun Foster RC 1.25 3.00
176 Kalimba Edwards RC 1.00 2.50
177 Josh Reed RC 1.00 2.50
178 Larry Tripplett RC .75 2.00
179 Andre Davis RC .75 2.00
180 Reche Caldwell RC 1.00 2.50
181 Levar Fisher RC .75 2.00
182 Clinton Portis RC 1.25 3.00
183 Anthony Weaver RC .75 2.00
184 Maurice Morris RC 1.00 2.50
185 Ladell Betts RC 1.25 3.00
186 Antwaan Randle El RC 1.00 2.50
187 Antonio Bryant RC 1.25 3.00
188 Rocky Calmus RC 1.00 2.50
189 Josh McCown RC 1.25 3.00
190 Lamar Gordon RC 1.00 2.50
191 Marquise Walker RC .75 2.00
192 Cliff Russell RC .75 2.00
193 Eric Crouch RC 1.25 3.00
194 Dennis Johnson RC .75 2.00
195 Alex Brown RC 1.25 3.00
196 David Garrard RC 1.00 2.50
197 Rohan Davey RC 1.25 3.00
198 Alan Harper RC .75 2.00
199 Ron Johnson RC 1.00 2.50
200 Andra Davis RC .75 2.00
201 Kurt Kittner RC .75 2.00
202 Freddie Milons RC .75 2.00
203 Adrian Peterson RC 1.00 2.50
204 Luke Staley RC .75 2.00
205 Tracey Wistrom RC 1.00 2.50
206 Woody Dantzler RC 1.00 2.50
207 Chad Hutchinson RC .75 2.00
208 Zak Kustok RC .75 2.00
209 Damien Anderson RC .75 2.00
210 James Mungro RC 1.25 3.00
211 Cortlen Johnson RC .75 2.00
212 Demontray Carter RC .75 2.00
213 Kelly Campbell RC 1.00 2.50
214 Brian Poli-Dixon RC .75 2.00
215 Mike Rumph RC .75 2.00
216 Najeh Davenport RC .75 2.00

2002 Playoff Prestige Xtra Points Green

*1-150 VETS: 2.5X TO 6X BASIC CARDS
1-150 VETERAN PRINT RUN 150
*151-216 ROOKIES: 3X TO 8X
151-216 ROOKIE PRINT RUN 25

2002 Playoff Prestige Xtra Points Purple

*1-150 VETS: 2.5X TO 6X BASIC CARDS
1-150 VETERAN PRINT RUN 150
*151-216 ROOKIES: 3X TO 8X
151-216 ROOKIE PRINT RUN 25

2002 Playoff Prestige Banner Season

This 40-card insert set resembles that of a banner spotlighting landmark seasons from retired legends. The set is sequentially numbered to the standout year. A signed verision called "Ink" was also produced with each card serial numbered to 25.

STATED PRINT RUN 1947-1991
BS1 Archie Griffin/1979 1.00 2.50
BS2 Archie Manning/1980 1.25 3.00
BS3 Art Monk/1984 1.50 4.00
BS4 Charley Taylor/1966 1.00 2.50
BS5 Cris Collinsworth/1986 1.25 3.00
BS6 Craig Morton/1981 1.25 3.00
BS7 Dick Butkus/1965 2.00 5.00
BS8 Don Maynard/1967 1.25 3.00
BS9 Drew Pearson/1979 1.25 3.00
BS10 Dwight Clark/1981 1.25 3.00
BS11 Eric Dickerson/1984 1.25 3.00
BS12 Fran Tarkenton/1975 1.50 4.00
BS13 Franco Harris/1975 1.50 4.00
BS14 Frank Gifford/1956 1.50 4.00
BS15 Fred Biletnikoff/1969 1.50 4.00
BS16 John Fuqua/1970 1.00 2.50
BS17 Gale Sayers/1966 1.50 4.00
BS18 Henry Ellard/1988 1.00 2.50
BS19 James Lofton/1991 1.00 2.50
BS20 Jim Plunkett/1983 1.25 3.00
BS21 Joe Greene/1972 1.50 4.00
BS22 Joe Theismann/1983 1.50 4.00
BS23 John Hadl/1968 1.00 2.50
BS24 John Stallworth/1984 1.25 3.00
BS25 Kellen Winslow/1980 1.25 3.00
BS26 Ken Anderson/1981 1.25 3.00
BS27 Lance Alworth/1965 1.50 4.00
BS28 Mike Singletary/1985 1.50 4.00
BS29 Otto Graham/1953 1.25 3.00
BS30 Paul Hornung/1960 1.50 4.00
BS31 Paul Warfield/1971 1.25 3.00
BS32 Raymond Berry/1960 1.25 3.00
BS33 Rocky Bleier/1976 1.25 3.00
BS34 Ronnie Lott/1986 1.25 3.00
BS35 Sammy Baugh/1947 1.50 4.00
BS36 Sonny Jurgensen/1967 1.50 4.00
BS37 Steve Largent/1979 1.50 4.00
BS38 Terry Bradshaw/1978 2.00 5.00
BS39 Todd Christensen/1983 1.00 2.50
BS40 Y.A. Tittle/1963 1.50 4.00

2002 Playoff Prestige Banner Season Ink Autographs

This 40-card retail only parallel set features the same design as the Banner Season set with the inclusion of an authentic autograph. Each card is serial #'d to 25.

STATED PRINT RUN 25 SER.#'d SETS
BS1 Archie Griffin 12.00 30.00
BS2 Archie Manning 15.00 40.00
BS3 Art Monk
BS4 Charley Taylor 12.00 30.00
BS5 Cris Collinsworth 15.00 40.00
BS6 Craig Morton 15.00 40.00
BS7 Dick Butkus 60.00 100.00
BS8 Don Maynard 15.00 40.00
BS9 Drew Pearson 15.00 40.00
BS10 Dwight Clark 15.00 40.00
BS11 Eric Dickerson 15.00 40.00
BS12 Fran Tarkenton 30.00 60.00
BS13 Franco Harris 60.00 100.00
BS14 Frank Gifford 20.00 50.00
BS15 Fred Biletnikoff
BS16 John Fuqua 20.00 50.00
BS17 Gale Sayers 20.00 50.00
BS18 Henry Ellard
BS19 James Lofton 12.00 30.00
BS20 Jim Plunkett 15.00 40.00
BS21 Joe Greene 25.00 60.00
BS22 Joe Theismann 20.00 50.00
BS23 John Hadl
BS24 John Stallworth 30.00 60.00
BS25 Kellen Winslow 15.00 40.00
BS26 Ken Anderson 15.00 40.00
BS27 Lance Alworth 25.00 60.00
BS28 Mike Singletary 25.00 60.00
BS29 Otto Graham 40.00 80.00
BS30 Paul Hornung 20.00 50.00
BS31 Paul Warfield 20.00 50.00
BS32 Raymond Berry 20.00 50.00
BS33 Rocky Bleier 20.00 50.00
BS34 Ronnie Lott 40.00 80.00
BS35 Sammy Baugh 75.00 150.00
BS36 Sonny Jurgensen 20.00 50.00
BS37 Steve Largent 20.00 50.00
BS38 Terry Bradshaw 75.00 150.00
BS39 Todd Christensen 12.00 30.00
BS40 Y.A. Tittle 20.00 50.00

2002 Playoff Prestige Connections Jerseys

This 30-card insert set features two players, along with jersey swatches from each player. Cards are serial #'d to 500.

STATED PRINT RUN 500 SER.#'d SETS
C1 K.Warner/I.Bruce 4.00 10.00
C2 D.Culpepper/C.Carter 4.00 10.00
C3 J.Fiedler/C.Chambers 3.00 8.00
C4 T.Brady/T.Brown 20.00 50.00
C5 B.Griese/E.McCaffrey 3.00 8.00
C6 J.Garcia/T.Owens 3.00 8.00
C7 C.Weinke/M.Muhammed 2.50 6.00
C8 J.Plummer/D.Boston 2.50 6.00
C9 V.Testaverde/L.Coles 3.00 8.00
C10 B.Favre/A.Freeman 8.00 20.00
C11 M.Brunell/J.Smith 3.00 8.00
C12 R.Johnson/E.Moulds 3.00 8.00
C13 T.Couch/Q.Morgan 2.50 6.00
C14 K.Collins/A.Toomer 2.50 6.00
C15 R.Gannon/T.Brown 4.00 10.00
C16 D.McNabb/T.Pinkston 3.00 8.00
C17 C.Batch/G.Crowell 2.50 6.00
C18 K.Warner/A.Hakim 3.00 8.00
C19 B.Johnson/K.Johnson 3.00 8.00
C20 M.Brunell/K.McCardell 3.00 8.00
C21 P.Manning/M.Harrison 10.00 25.00
C22 B.Griese/R.Smith 3.00 8.00
C23 S.McNair/K.Dyson 3.00 8.00
C24 K.Warner/T.Holt 3.00 8.00
C25 T.Couch/K.Johnson 2.50 6.00
C26 J.Plummer/F.Sanders 2.50 6.00
C27 K.Stewart/P.Burress 2.50 6.00
C28 D.Culpepper/R.Moss 3.00 8.00
C29 V.Testaverde/W.Chrebet 2.50 6.00
C30 R.Gannon/J.Rice 8.00 20.00

2002 Playoff Prestige Draft Picks

This 25-card insert set features top rookies from the 2002 draft class. Each card is serial #'d to 2002.

STATED PRINT RUN 2002 SER.#'d SETS
DP1 David Carr .75 2.00
DP2 Joey Harrington .75 2.00
DP3 Kurt Kittner .75 2.00
DP4 Rohan Davey 1.25 3.00
DP5 Eric Crouch 1.25 3.00
DP6 William Green 1.00 2.50
DP7 T.J. Duckett .75 2.00
DP8 DeShaun Foster 1.25 3.00
DP9 Travis Stephens .75 2.00
DP10 Luke Staley .75 2.00
DP11 Clinton Portis 1.25 3.00
DP12 Antonio Bryant 1.25 3.00
DP13 Josh Reed 1.00 2.50
DP14 Marquise Walker .75 2.00
DP15 Andre Davis .75 2.00
DP16 Ashley Lelie .75 2.00
DP17 Jabar Gaffney .75 2.00
DP18 Reche Caldwell 1.00 2.50
DP19 Daniel Graham 1.00 2.50
DP20 Jeremy Shockey 1.25 3.00
DP21 Julius Peppers 2.00 5.00
DP22 John Henderson 1.00 2.50
DP23 Ed Reed 5.00 12.00
DP24 Roy Williams .75 2.00
DP25 Bryant McKinnie .75 2.00

2002 Playoff Prestige Draft Picks Autographs

This set is a parallel of the Draft Picks set, with each card being signed by the respective player. All cards were available via redemption only, with an expiration date of 11/8/2003. Each card once redeemed was serial numbered of 50.

STATED PRINT RUN 50 SER.#'d SETS
1 David Carr 8.00 20.00
2 Joey Harrington 8.00 20.00
3 Kurt Kittner 8.00 20.00
4 Rohan Davey 12.00 30.00
5 Eric Crouch 12.00 30.00
6 William Green 10.00 25.00
7 T.J. Duckett 8.00 20.00
8 DeShaun Foster 12.00 30.00
10 Luke Staley 8.00 20.00
11 Clinton Portis 12.00 30.00
12 Antonio Bryant 12.00 30.00
13 Josh Reed 10.00 25.00
14 Marquise Walker 8.00 20.00
15 Andre Davis 8.00 20.00
16 Ashley Lelie 8.00 20.00
17 Jabar Gaffney 8.00 20.00
19 Daniel Graham 10.00 25.00
20 Jeremy Shockey 12.00 30.00
21 Julius Peppers 60.00 120.00
22 John Henderson 10.00 25.00
23 Ed Reed 50.00 100.00
24 Roy Williams 8.00 20.00
25 Bryant McKinnie 8.00 20.00

2002 Playoff Prestige Gridiron Heritage Helmets

This 20-card insert set features game-worn helmet swatches. Each card was serial #'d to 100.

STATED PRINT RUN 100 SER.#'d SETS
GH1 Mike Anderson 3.00 8.00
GH2 Stephen Davis 3.00 8.00
GH3 Mark Brunell 4.00 10.00
GH4 Rich Gannon 4.00 10.00
GH5 Kordell Stewart 3.00 8.00
GH6 Curtis Martin 4.00 10.00
GH7 Michael Vick 4.00 10.00
GH8 Duce Staley 3.00 8.00
GH9 Troy Aikman 6.00 15.00
GH10 Warren Moon 5.00 12.00
GH11 Daunte Culpepper 4.00 10.00
GH12 Jerome Bettis 5.00 12.00
GH13 Junior Seau 4.00 10.00
GH14 Cris Carter 5.00 12.00
GH15 John Elway 8.00 20.00
GH16 Lamar Smith 3.00 8.00
GH17 Doug Flutie 4.00 10.00
GH18 Keyshawn Johnson 4.00 10.00
GH19 LaDainian Tomlinson 5.00 12.00
GH20 Aaron Brooks 3.00 8.00

2002 Playoff Prestige Inside the Numbers

Inserted at a rate of 1:18, this set examines the stats of some of the NFL's best offensive and defensive weapons.

STATED ODDS 1:18
*GOLD/52-89: 1.2X TO 3X BASIC INSERTS
*GOLD/32-37: 2X TO 5X BASIC INSERTS
*GOLD/21-28: 2.5X TO 6X BASIC INSERTS
GOLD STATED PRINT RUN 2-89
SERIAL #'d UNDER 20 NOT PRICED
IN1 Aaron Brooks .60 1.50
IN2 Mark Brunell .75 2.00
IN3 Daunte Culpepper .75 2.00
IN4 Brad Johnson .75 2.00
IN5 Steve McNair .75 2.00
IN6 Kurt Warner .75 2.00
IN7 Donovan McNabb .75 2.00
IN8 Brian Griese .60 1.50
IN9 Tom Brady 5.00 12.00
IN10 Marshall Faulk .75 2.00
IN11 Edgerrin James .75 2.00
IN12 LaDainian Tomlinson 1.00 2.50
IN13 Eddie George .75 2.00
IN14 Curtis Martin .75 2.00
IN15 Jerome Bettis 1.00 2.50
IN16 Shaun Alexander .60 1.50
IN17 Ricky Williams .75 2.00
IN18 Emmitt Smith 1.50 4.00
IN19 Randy Moss .75 2.00
IN20 Jimmy Smith .75 2.00
IN21 Troy Brown .60 1.50
IN22 Rod Smith .75 2.00
IN23 Chris Chambers .60 1.50
IN24 Terrell Owens .75 2.00
IN25 Marvin Harrison .75 2.00
IN26 Tim Brown 1.00 2.50
IN27 David Boston .60 1.50
IN28 Ray Lewis 1.00 2.50
IN29 Brian Urlacher 1.00 2.50
IN30 Zach Thomas .75 2.00

2002 Playoff Prestige League Leader Tandems

Inserted at a rate of 1:18, this set features league leading tandems on a horizontal card design.

STATED ODDS 1:18
LL1 B.Griese/K.Warner 1.00 2.50
LL2 P.Manning/B.Favre 3.00 8.00
LL3 R.Gannon/D.Culpepper 1.00 2.50
LL4 D.Flutie/K.Collins 1.00 2.50
LL5 J.Fiedler/J.Plummer 1.00 2.50
LL6 M.Brunell/J.Garcia 1.00 2.50
LL7 K.Stewart/B.Johnson 1.00 2.50
LL8 J.Bettis/R.Williams 1.25 3.00
LL9 S.Alexander/A.Green 1.00 2.50
LL10 C.Martin/M.Faulk 1.00 2.50
LL11 L.Tomlinson/S.Davis 1.25 3.00
LL12 C.Dillon/T.Barber 1.00 2.50
LL13 L.Smith/E.Smith 2.00 5.00
LL14 R.Smith/D.Boston 1.00 2.50

LL15 M.Harrison/T.Owens 1.00 2.50
LL16 Tr.Brown/Key.Johnson 1.00 2.50
LL17 Tim.Brown/I.Bruce 1.25 3.00
LL18 J.Smith/J.Morton 1.00 2.50
LL19 Kev.Johnson/T.Holt 1.00 2.50
LL20 J.Kearse/M.Strahan 1.00 2.50

2002 Playoff Prestige League Leader Tandems Materials

This set is a parallel of the League Leader Tandems set, with the inclusion of game jersey swatches. Each card was #'d to 250.
STATED PRINT RUN 250 SER.#'d SETS
LL1 B.Griese/K.Warner 3.00 8.00
LL2 P.Manning/B.Favre 10.00 25.00
LL3 R.Gannon/D.Culpepper 3.00 8.00
LL4 D.Flutie/K.Collins 3.00 8.00
LL5 J.Fiedler/J.Plummer 3.00 8.00
LL6 M.Brunell/J.Garcia 3.00 8.00
LL7 K.Stewart/B.Johnson 3.00 8.00
LL8 J.Bettis/R.Williams 4.00 10.00
LL9 S.Alexander/A.Green 3.00 8.00
LL10 C.Martin/M.Faulk 3.00 8.00
LL11 L.Tomlinson/S.Davis 4.00 10.00
LL12 C.Dillon/T.Barber 3.00 8.00
LL13 L.Smith/E.Smith 6.00 15.00
LL14 R.Smith/D.Boston 3.00 8.00
LL15 M.Harrison/T.Owens 3.00 8.00
LL16 Tr.Brown/Key.Johnson 3.00 8.00
LL17 Tim.Brown/I.Bruce 4.00 10.00
LL18 J.Smith/J.Morton 3.00 8.00
LL19 Kev.Johnson/T.Holt 3.00 8.00
LL20 J.Kearse/M.Strahan 3.00 8.00

2002 Playoff Prestige Sophomore Signatures

This 40-card set contains autographs of standout performers from the 2001 rookie class. Several cards were available via redemption only, with an expiration date of 11/8/2003. Of those cards, a few players ultimately did not sign for the set and their cards were issued with "No Autograph" printed on the fronts as noted below.
SS1 Mike McMahon SP 5.00 12.00
SS2 Alge Crumpler SP 6.00 15.00
SS3 Anthony Thomas 5.00 12.00
SS4 Carlos Polk 4.00 10.00
SS5 Cedric Scott 4.00 10.00
SS6 Cedrick Wilson 5.00 12.00
SS7 Chad Johnson 4.00 10.00
SS8 Chris Weinke 4.00 10.00
SS9 David Terrell 4.00 10.00
SS10 Deuce McAllister 5.00 12.00
SS11 Drew Brees 40.00 80.00
SS12 Ennis Davis 4.00 10.00
SS13 Hakim Akbar 4.00 10.00
SS14 Heath Evans 5.00 12.00
SS15 Jamal Reynolds 4.00 10.00
SS16 Jesse Palmer 4.00 10.00
SS17 Justin Smith 5.00 12.00
SS18 Karon Riley 4.00 10.00
SS19 Kendrell Bell SP 5.00 12.00
SS20 Kenny Smith 4.00 10.00
SS21 Kenyatta Walker 4.00 10.00
SS22 Ken-Yon Rambo 4.00 10.00
SS23 Kevan Barlow 4.00 10.00
SS24 Koren Robinson 4.00 10.00
SS25 Marcus Stroud 4.00 10.00
SS26 Snoop Minnis No Auto/100 4.00 10.00
SS27 Michael Bennett 4.00 10.00
SS28 Moran Norris SP 5.00 12.00
SS29 Morlon Greenwood SP 5.00 12.00
SS30 N.Clements No Auto/100 4.00 10.00
SS31 Quincy Carter 4.00 10.00
SS32 Quincy Morgan 4.00 10.00
SS33 Reggie Germany 4.00 10.00
SS34 Robert Ferguson 5.00 12.00
SS35 Rudi Johnson 4.00 10.00
SS36 Santana Moss 5.00 12.00
SS37 T.J. Houshmandzadeh 4.00 10.00
SS38 Todd Heap 4.00 10.00
SS39 Travis Henry No Auto/100 4.00 10.00
SS40 Travis Minor 4.00 10.00

2002 Playoff Prestige Stars of the NFL Jerseys

This set features jersey swatches from several of the best players the NFL has to offer. Each card was serial #'d to 300. Autographed versions were also available.
STATED PRINT RUN 300 SER.#'d SETS
SN1 Edgerrin James 3.00 8.00
SN2 Jerome Bettis 4.00 10.00
SN3 Shaun Alexander 2.50 6.00
SN4 Brett Favre 8.00 20.00
SN5 Donovan McNabb 3.00 8.00
SN6 Marshall Faulk 3.00 8.00
SN7 John Elway 6.00 15.00
SN8 Troy Aikman 5.00 12.00
SN9 Jeff Garcia 2.50 6.00
SN10 Randy Moss 3.00 8.00
SN11 Stephen Davis 2.50 6.00
SN12 Emmitt Smith 6.00 15.00
SN13 Dan Marino 8.00 20.00
SN14 Brian Urlacher 4.00 10.00
SN15 Mike Anderson 2.50 6.00
SN16 Jevon Kearse 2.50 6.00
SN17 Terrell Owens 3.00 8.00
SN18 Peyton Manning 10.00 25.00
SN19 Ricky Williams 3.00 8.00
SN20 Warren Sapp 3.00 8.00

2002 Playoff Prestige Stars of the NFL Autographs

This 10-card set features jersey swatches and authentic autographs from the best of the best in the NFL. Each card is numbered to the player's jersey number.
STATED PRINT RUN 4-90
SERIAL #'d UNDER 34 NOT PRICED
SN11 Stephen Davis/48 15.00 40.00
SN14 Brian Urlacher/54 40.00 100.00
SN15 Mike Anderson/38 15.00 40.00
SN16 Jevon Kearse/90 15.00 40.00
SN17 Terrell Owens/81 25.00 60.00
SN19 Ricky Williams/34 25.00 50.00

2003 Playoff Prestige Atlantic City National Promos

UNPRICED PROMO PRINT RUN 5

2003 Playoff Prestige Samples

*VETS 1-150: .8X TO 2X BASE CARDS

2003 Playoff Prestige Samples Gold

*VETS 1-150: 2.5X TO 6X BASE CARDS

2003 Playoff Prestige

This 229-card set was released in May, 2003. The set was issued in six-card packs with a $3 SRP which came 24 to a box. Cards numbered 1-150 feature veterans while cards numbered 151-230 featured rookies. The rookies were issued at a stated rate of one in two packs. Please note that card number 169 was never released.
COMP.SET w/o RC's (150) 12.50 30.00
151-230 ROOKIE STATED ODDS 1:2
1 David Boston .25 .60
2 Thomas Jones .25 .60
3 Jake Plummer .25 .60
4 Marcel Shipp .25 .60
5 T.J. Duckett .25 .60
6 Warrick Dunn .25 .60
7 Michael Vick .30 .75
8 Jeff Blake .30 .75
9 Todd Heap .25 .60
10 Jamal Lewis .30 .75
11 Ray Lewis .40 1.00
12 Drew Bledsoe .30 .75
13 Travis Henry .25 .60
14 Eric Moulds .25 .60
15 Peerless Price .25 .60
16 Josh Reed .25 .60
17 DeShaun Foster .30 .75
18 Muhsin Muhammad .25 .60
19 Steve Smith .40 1.00
20 Julius Peppers .40 1.00
21 Marty Booker .25 .60
22 David Terrell .25 .60
23 Anthony Thomas .30 .75
24 Brian Urlacher .40 1.00
25 Corey Dillon .25 .60
26 Chad Johnson .25 .60
27 Jon Kitna .25 .60
28 Peter Warrick .25 .60
29 Tim Couch .25 .60
30 Andre Davis .25 .60
31 William Green .25 .60
32 Quincy Morgan .25 .60
33 Dennis Northcutt .25 .60
34 Antonio Bryant .25 .60
35 Quincy Carter .25 .60
36 Troy Hambrick .25 .60
37 Chad Hutchinson .25 .60
38 Emmitt Smith .60 1.50
39 Roy Williams .25 .60
40 Brian Griese .25 .60
41 Ashley Lelie .25 .60
42 Ed McCaffrey .30 .75
43 Clinton Portis .25 .60
44 Rod Smith .30 .75
45 Germane Crowell .25 .60
46 Az-Zahir Hakim .25 .60
47 Joey Harrington .25 .60
48 James Stewart .25 .60
49 Donald Driver .30 .75
50 Brett Favre .75 2.00
51 Terry Glenn .30 .75
52 Ahman Green .30 .75
53 Javon Walker .30 .75
54 Corey Bradford .25 .60
55 David Carr .25 .60
56 Jabar Gaffney .25 .60
57 Jonathan Wells .25 .60
58 Marvin Harrison .30 .75
59 Edgerrin James .30 .75
60 Peyton Manning 1.00 2.50
61 James Mungro .25 .60
62 Reggie Wayne .30 .75
63 Mark Brunell .30 .75
64 David Garrard .25 .60
65 Stacey Mack .25 .60
66 Jimmy Smith .30 .75
67 Fred Taylor .25 .60
68 Marc Boerigter .25 .60
69 Tony Gonzalez .30 .75
70 Trent Green .25 .60
71 Priest Holmes .25 .60
72 Eddie Kennison .25 .60
73 Cris Carter .40 1.00
74 Chris Chambers .25 .60
75 Jay Fiedler .25 .60
76 Randy McMichael .25 .60
77 Zach Thomas .30 .75
78 Ricky Williams .30 .75
79 Michael Bennett .25 .60
80 Todd Bouman .25 .60
81 Daunte Culpepper .30 .75
82 Randy Moss .30 .75
83 Tom Brady 1.50 4.00
84 Deion Branch .25 .60
85 Troy Brown .25 .60
86 Kevin Faulk .25 .60
87 Antowain Smith .30 .75
88 Aaron Brooks .25 .60
89 Joe Horn .25 .60
90 Deuce McAllister .30 .75
91 Donte Stallworth .25 .60
92 Tiki Barber .30 .75
93 Kerry Collins .25 .60
94 Jeremy Shockey .25 .60
95 Michael Strahan .30 .75
96 Amani Toomer .25 .60
97 Laveranues Coles .25 .60
98 LaMont Jordan .30 .75
99 Curtis Martin .30 .75
100 Santana Moss .30 .75
101 Chad Pennington .25 .60
102 Tim Brown .40 1.00
103 Rich Gannon .30 .75
104 Charlie Garner .30 .75
105 Jerry Rice .75 2.00
106 Charles Woodson .40 1.00
107 Antonio Freeman .30 .75
108 Dorsey Levens .30 .75
109 Donovan McNabb .30 .75
110 Duce Staley .25 .60
111 James Thrash .25 .60
112 Jerome Bettis .40 1.00
113 Plaxico Burress .25 .60
114 Tommy Maddox .25 .60
115 Antwaan Randle El .25 .60
116 Kordell Stewart .25 .60
117 Hines Ward .30 .75
118 Drew Brees .40 1.00
119 Curtis Conway .25 .60
120 Junior Seau .30 .75
121 LaDainian Tomlinson .40 1.00
122 Kevan Barlow .25 .60
123 Jeff Garcia .25 .60
124 Garrison Hearst .25 .60
125 Terrell Owens .30 .75
126 Shaun Alexander .25 .60
127 Trent Dilfer .25 .60
128 Darrell Jackson .30 .75
129 Maurice Morris .25 .60
130 Koren Robinson .30 .75
131 Isaac Bruce .40 1.00
132 Marc Bulger .25 .60
133 Marshall Faulk .30 .75
134 Torry Holt .30 .75
135 Kurt Warner .30 .75
136 Mike Alstott .25 .60
137 Brad Johnson .30 .75
138 Keyshawn Johnson .40 1.00
139 Dexter Jackson RC .40 1.00
140 Warren Sapp .30 .75
141 Kevin Dyson .25 .60
142 Eddie George .30 .75
143 Jevon Kearse .25 .60
144 Derrick Mason .25 .60
145 Steve McNair .30 .75
146 Stephen Davis .25 .60
147 Rod Gardner .25 .60
148 Shane Matthews .25 .60
149 Patrick Ramsey .30 .75
150 Derrius Thompson .25 .60
151 Byron Leftwich RC 1.00 2.50
152 Carson Palmer RC 1.50 4.00
153 Chris Simms RC .75 2.00
154 Kliff Kingsbury RC 1.25 3.00
155 Dave Ragone RC .75 2.00
156 Jason Gesser RC 1.00 2.50
157 Ken Dorsey RC 1.00 2.50
158 Kyle Boller RC .75 2.00
159 Brad Banks RC 1.00 2.50
160 Rex Grossman RC 1.00 2.50
161 Seneca Wallace RC 1.00 2.50
162 Brian St.Pierre RC .75 2.00
163 Larry Johnson RC 1.00 2.50
164 Earnest Graham RC 1.25 3.00
165 Musa Smith RC .75 2.00
166 Lee Suggs RC .75 2.00
167 Willis McGahee RC 1.00 2.50
168 Onterrio Smith RC .75 2.00
170 Sultan McCullough RC .75 2.00
171 Chris Brown RC .75 2.00
172 Justin Fargas RC 1.25 3.00
173 Avon Cobourne RC .75 2.00
174 Dahrran Diedrick RC .75 2.00
175 LaBrandon Toefield RC .75 2.00
176 Artose Pinner RC .75 2.00
177 Quentin Griffin RC 1.00 2.50
178 ReShard Lee RC 1.25 3.00
179 Andrew Pinnock RC 1.00 2.50
180 B.J. Askew RC 1.00 2.50
181 Andre Johnson RC 2.00 5.00
182 Brandon Lloyd RC 1.25 3.00
183 Bryant Johnson RC 1.25 3.00
184 Charles Rogers RC 1.00 2.50
185 Doug Gabriel RC 1.00 2.50
186 Justin Gage RC 1.00 2.50
187 Kareem Kelly RC .75 2.00
188 Kelley Washington RC .75 2.00
189 Taylor Jacobs RC .75 2.00
190 Terrence Edwards RC .75 2.00
191 Anquan Boldin RC 1.25 3.00
192 Billy McMullen RC .75 2.00
193 Talman Gardner RC .75 2.00
194 Arnaz Battle RC 1.25 3.00
195 Sam Aiken RC 1.00 2.50
196 Bobby Wade RC 1.00 2.50
197 Mike Bush RC .75 2.00
198 Keenan Howry RC .75 2.00
199 Jerel Myers RC .75 2.00
200 Dallas Clark RC 1.25 3.00
201 Mike Pinkard RC .75 2.00
202 Teyo Johnson RC 1.00 2.50
203 Trent Smith RC 1.00 2.50
204 George Wrighster RC .75 2.00
205 Jason Witten RC 3.00 8.00
206 Cory Redding RC 1.00 2.50
207 DeWayne White RC .75 2.00
208 Jerome McDougle RC .75 2.00
209 Michael Haynes RC .75 2.00
210 Chris Kelsay RC 1.00 2.50
211 Calvin Pace RC .75 2.00
212 Kenny King RC 1.00 2.50
213 Jimmy Kennedy RC 1.00 2.50
214 William Joseph RC .75 2.00
215 DeWayne Robertson RC 1.00 2.50
216 Jarret Johnson RC 1.00 2.50
217 Rien Long RC .75 2.00
218 Boss Bailey RC 1.00 2.50
219 Terrell Suggs RC 1.00 2.50
220 Terry Pierce RC .75 2.00
221 Bradie James RC 1.25 3.00
222 Angelo Crowell RC 1.00 2.50
223 Andre Woolfolk RC .75 2.00
224 Dennis Weathersby RC .75 2.00
225 Marcus Trufant RC 1.00 2.50
226 Terence Newman RC 1.25 3.00
227 Ricky Manning RC 1.00 2.50
228 Mike Doss RC 1.25 3.00
229 Julian Battle RC 1.00 2.50
230 Rashean Mathis RC .75 2.00
LH1 Lester Hayes Promo 1.50 4.00

2003 Playoff Prestige Xtra Points Green

*VETS 1-150: 3X TO 8X BASIC CARDS
1-250 VETERAN PRINT RUN 100
*ROOKIES 151-230: 2.5X TO 6X
151-230 ROOKIE PRINT RUN 25
ISSUED ONLY IN RETAIL PACKS

2003 Playoff Prestige Xtra Points Purple

*VETS 1-150: 3X TO 8X BASIC CARDS
1-150 VETERAN PRINT RUN 100
*ROOKIES 151-230: 2.5X TO 6X
151-230 ROOKIE PRINT RUN 25

2003 Playoff Prestige 2002 Reunion

Randomly inserted into packs, this 30-card set features some of the leading rookies of the 2002 season. Each of these cards were issued to a stated print run of 2002 serial numbered sets.
COMPLETE SET (30) 20.00 50.00
STATED PRINT RUN 2002 SER.#'d SETS
R1 David Carr .60 1.50
R2 Joey Harrington .60 1.50
R3 Patrick Ramsey .75 2.00
R4 William Green .60 1.50
R5 T.J. Duckett .60 1.50
R6 DeShaun Foster .75 2.00
R7 Jonathan Wells .60 1.50
R8 Clinton Portis .60 1.50
R9 Brian Westbrook .60 1.50
R10 Donte Stallworth .60 1.50
R11 Ashley Lelie .60 1.50
R12 Javon Walker .75 2.00
R13 Jabar Gaffney .60 1.50
R14 Josh Reed .60 1.50
R15 Andre Davis .60 1.50
R16 Antwaan Randle El .60 1.50
R17 Antonio Bryant .60 1.50
R18 Deion Branch .60 1.50
R19 Jeremy Shockey .60 1.50
R20 Daniel Graham .60 1.50
R21 Randy McMichael .60 1.50
R22 Julius Peppers 1.00 2.50
R23 Dwight Freeney .60 1.50
R24 John Henderson .75 2.00
R25 Quentin Jammer .60 1.50
R26 Phillip Buchanon .60 1.50
R27 Roy Williams .60 1.50
R28 Ed Reed .75 2.00
R29 Coy Wire .60 1.50
R30 Napoleon Harris .60 1.50

2003 Playoff Prestige 2002 Reunion Materials

Randomly inserted into packs, this is a partial parallel to the 2002 Reunion set. Each of these cards feature a game-used memorabila piece and were issued to a stated print run of 150 serial numbered sets.
STATED PRINT RUN 150 SER.#'d SETS
R1 David Carr 2.50 6.00
R2 Joey Harrington 2.50 6.00
R4 William Green 2.50 6.00
R5 T.J. Duckett 2.50 6.00
R8 Clinton Portis 2.50 6.00
R10 Donte Stallworth 2.50 6.00
R14 Josh Reed 2.50 6.00
R19 Jeremy Shockey 2.50 6.00
R22 Julius Peppers 4.00 10.00
R27 Roy Williams 2.50 6.00

2003 Playoff Prestige Backfield Tandems

Randomly inserted in packs, these 20 cards feature two players from the same NFL backfield. Each of these cards feature two-swatches of game-used jerseys and are issued to a stated print run of 400 serial numbered sets.
STATED PRINT RUN 400 SER.#'d SETS
BT1 J.Plummer/M.Shipp 3.00 8.00
BT2 D.Bledsoe/T.Henry 4.00 10.00
BT3 T.Couch/W.Green 3.00 8.00
BT4 B.Griese/C.Portis 3.00 8.00
BT5 B.Favre/A.Green 10.00 25.00
BT6 J.Stewart/J.Harrington 3.00 8.00
BT7 P.Manning/E.James 12.00 30.00
BT8 M.Brunell/F.Taylor 4.00 10.00
BT9 T.Green/P.Holmes 3.00 8.00
BT10 J.Fiedler/R.Williams 4.00 10.00
BT11 D.Culpepper/M.Bennett 4.00 10.00
BT12 T.Brady/A.Smith 20.00 50.00
BT13 A.Brooks/D.McAllister 4.00 10.00
BT14 C.Pennington/C.Martin 4.00 10.00
BT15 D.McNabb/D.Staley 4.00 10.00
BT16 K.Stewart/J.Bettis 5.00 12.00
BT17 D.Brees/L.Tomlinson 5.00 12.00
BT18 J.Garcia/G.Hearst 3.00 8.00
BT19 K.Warner/M.Faulk 4.00 10.00
DT20 S.McNair/E.George 4.00 10.00

2003 Playoff Prestige Game Day Jerseys

This forty-card set was issued in both hobby and retail packs. Cards numbered 1 through 20 were issued in hobby packs and were inserted at a stated rate of one in 34, while cards 21 through 40 were inserted inserted in retail packs at a stated rate of one in 28. Five cards were also issued in a signed version with each card serial numbered to 25.
1-20 STATED ODDS 1:34 HOBBY
21-40 STATED ODDS 1:28 RETAIL
GDJ1 Aaron Brooks 2.50 6.00
GDJ2 Brett Favre 8.00 20.00
GDJ3 Brian Griese 2.50 6.00
GDJ4 Daunte Culpepper 3.00 8.00
GDJ5 Emmitt Smith 6.00 15.00
GDJ6 Isaac Bruce 4.00 10.00
GDJ7 Jevon Kearse 2.50 6.00
GDJ8 Joe Horn 2.50 6.00
GDJ9 Kordell Stewart 2.50 6.00
GDJ10 Kurt Warner 3.00 8.00
GDJ11 Marshall Faulk 3.00 8.00
GDJ12 Marvin Harrison 3.00 8.00
GDJ13 Mike Alstott 2.50 6.00
GDJ14 Peyton Manning 10.00 25.00
GDJ15 Randy Moss 3.00 8.00
GDJ16 Rod Smith 3.00 8.00
GDJ17 Terry Glenn 3.00 8.00
GDJ18 Tiki Barber 3.00 8.00
GDJ19 Tim Brown 4.00 10.00
GDJ20 Torry Holt 3.00 8.00
GDJ21 Akili Smith 3.00 8.00
GDJ22 Amani Toomer 2.50 6.00
GDJ23 Corey Simon 3.00 8.00
GDJ24 Curtis Martin 3.00 8.00
GDJ25 Dennis Northcutt 2.50 6.00
GDJ26 Duce Staley 2.50 6.00
GDJ27 Frank Sanders 2.50 6.00
GDJ28 Freddie Mitchell 3.00 8.00
GDJ29 Ike Hilliard 2.50 6.00
GDJ30 Jamel White 2.50 6.00
GDJ31 Jason Sehorn 3.00 8.00
GDJ32 Jimmy Smith 3.00 8.00
GDJ33 J.J. Stokes 2.50 6.00
GDJ34 Junior Seau 3.00 8.00
GDJ35 Kevin Johnson 2.50 6.00
GDJ36 Marcel Shipp 2.50 6.00
GDJ37 Mark Brunell 3.00 8.00
GDJ38 Samari Rolle 3.00 8.00
GDJ39 Shaun King 2.50 6.00
GDJ40 Stephen Davis 2.50 6.00

2003 Playoff Prestige Game Day Jerseys Autographs

Randomly inserted in packs, these five-cards are a partial parallel to the Game Day Jersey insert set. Each of these cards feature an authentic autograph of the player and were issued to a stated print run of 25 serial numbered sets. Marvin Harrison did not return his cards in time for pack-out and the exchange cards could be redeemed until October 14, 2004.
STATED PRINT RUN 25 SER.#'d SETS
GDJ8 Joe Horn 20.00 50.00
GDJ10 Kurt Warner 40.00 80.00
GDJ15 Randy Moss 50.00 100.00
GDJ16 Rod Smith 20.00 50.00

2003 Playoff Prestige Gridiron Heritage

Issued at a stated rate of one in 17, these 25-cards feature players who would have fit in at any time in football history.
COMPLETE SET (25) 15.00 40.00
STATED ODDS 1:17
GH1 Randy Moss .60 1.50
GH2 Ray Lewis .75 2.00
GH3 Cris Carter .75 2.00
GH4 Corey Dillon .50 1.25
GH5 Marvin Harrison .75 2.00
GH6 Jake Plummer .50 1.25
GH7 Tim Couch .50 1.25
GH8 Hines Ward .60 1.50
GH9 Edgerrin James .60 1.50
GH10 Jevon Kearse .50 1.25
GH11 Garrison Hearst .50 1.25
GH12 Anthony Thomas .60 1.50
GH13 Brett Favre 1.50 4.00
GH14 Junior Seau .60 1.50
GH15 Emmitt Smith 1.25 3.00
GH16 Kurt Warner .60 1.50
GH17 Donovan McNabb .60 1.50
GH18 Terrell Owens .60 1.50
GH19 Chad Pennington .50 1.25
GH20 Eric Moulds .50 1.25
GH21 Jeff Garcia .50 1.25
GH22 David Boston .50 1.25
GH23 Derrick Mason .50 1.25
GH24 Fred Taylor .50 1.25
GH25 Thomas Jones .50 1.25

2003 Playoff Prestige Gridiron Heritage Jerseys

Randomly inserted in packs, this set parallels the Heritage insert set. Each of these cards feature either a game-used helmet or a game-used jersey swatch. Cards number 1 through 10 feature helmet swatches and were issued to a stated print run of 100 serial numbered sets while cards 11 through 25 feature jersey swatches and were issued to a stated print run of 250 serial numbered sets.
1-10 HELMET SWATCH PRINT RUN 100
11-25 JSY SWATCH PRINT RUN 250
GH1 Randy Moss HEL 6.00 15.00
GH2 Ray Lewis HEL 8.00 20.00
GH3 Cris Carter HEL 8.00 20.00
GH4 Corey Dillon HEL 5.00 12.00
GH5 Marvin Harrison HEL 6.00 15.00
GH6 Jake Plummer HEL 5.00 12.00
GH7 Tim Couch HEL 5.00 12.00
GH8 Hines Ward HEL 6.00 15.00
GH9 Edgerrin James HEL 6.00 15.00
GH10 Jevon Kearse HEL 5.00 12.00
GH11 Garrison Hearst JSY 3.00 8.00
GH12 Anthony Thomas JSY 4.00 10.00
GH13 Brett Favre JSY 10.00 25.00
GH14 Junior Seau JSY 4.00 10.00
GH15 Emmitt Smith JSY 8.00 20.00
GH16 Kurt Warner JSY 4.00 10.00
GH17 Donovan McNabb JSY 4.00 10.00
GH18 Terrell Owens JSY 4.00 10.00
GH19 Chad Pennington JSY 3.00 8.00
GH20 Eric Moulds JSY 3.00 8.00
GH21 Jeff Garcia JSY 3.00 8.00
GH22 David Boston JSY 3.00 8.00
GH23 Derrick Mason JSY 3.00 8.00
GH24 Fred Taylor JSY 3.00 8.00
GH25 Thomas Jones JSY 3.00 8.00

2003 Playoff Prestige Inside the Numbers

Randomly inserted in packs, these 25 cards feature players who put up big numbers during the 2002 season. Each of these cards were issued to a stated print run of 2002 serial numbered sets.
COMPLETE SET (25) 15.00 40.00
STATED PRINT RUN 2002 SER.#'d SETS
*DIE CUT/80-96: 2X TO 5X BASE INSERT
*DIE CUT/31-34: 3X TO 8X BASE INSERT
*DIE CUT/20-28: 4X TO 10X BASE INSERT
DIE CUT PRINT RUN 2-96
IN1 Brett Favre 2.00 5.00
IN2 Rich Gannon .75 2.00
IN3 Tommy Maddox .60 1.50
IN4 Drew Bledsoe .75 2.00
IN5 Chad Pennington .60 1.50
IN6 Jeff Garcia .60 1.50
IN7 Aaron Brooks .60 1.50
IN8 Michael Vick .75 2.00
IN9 LaDainian Tomlinson 1.00 2.50
IN10 Priest Holmes .60 1.50
IN11 Deuce McAllister .75 2.00
IN12 Marshall Faulk .75 2.00
IN13 Ricky Williams .75 2.00
IN14 Jamal Lewis .75 2.00
IN15 Travis Henry .60 1.50
IN16 Michael Bennett .60 1.50
IN17 Marvin Harrison .75 2.00
IN18 Eric Moulds .60 1.50
IN19 Peerless Price .60 1.50
IN20 Jerry Rice 2.00 5.00
IN21 Donald Driver .75 2.00
IN22 Plaxico Burress .60 1.50
IN23 Terrell Owens .75 2.00
IN24 Julius Peppers 1.00 2.50
IN25 Andre Carter .60 1.50

2003 Playoff Prestige Signature Impressions

Randomly inserted into packs, these cards feature authentic autographs of the featured player. Each of these cards were issued to a stated print run of 50 serial numbered sets. Some of the players did not return their cards in time for pack out and those exchange cards could be redeemed until October 14, 2004.
STATED PRINT RUN 50 SER.#'d SETS
SI1 Antowain Smith 15.00 40.00
SI2 Brian Urlacher 40.00 100.00
SI3 Deion Branch 12.00 30.00
SI5 Donald Driver 30.00 60.00
SI6 Drew Bledsoe 15.00 40.00
SI7 Eddie George 15.00 40.00
SI8 Garrison Hearst 12.00 30.00
SI9 Jeff Garcia 12.00 30.00
SI10 Jerome Bettis 40.00 80.00
SI11 LaDainian Tomlinson 40.00 80.00
SI12 Mike Alstott 12.00 30.00
SI13 Priest Holmes 12.00 30.00
SI16 Hines Ward 35.00 60.00
SI19 Ed McCaffrey 15.00 40.00
SI22 Terrell Owens 15.00 40.00
SI24 Kurt Warner 15.00 40.00
SI25 Michael Vick 40.00 80.00

2003 Playoff Prestige Stars of the NFL Jerseys

Randomly inserted in packs, these 20-cards feature not only some of the leading NFL players but also game-used memorabilia swatches featuring those players. Each of these cards were issued to a stated print run of 250 serial numbered sets. Please note that a patch version was also issued, with each card being serial numbered to 50. Five cards were also issued in a signed version with each card serial numbered to 25.
STATED PRINT RUN 250 SER.#'d SETS
*PATCH/50: 1X TO 2.5X JSY/250
PATCHES PRINT RUN 50 SER.#'d SETS
SN1 Anthony Thomas 3.00 8.00
SN2 Chris Chambers 2.50 6.00
SN3 Donte Stallworth 2.50 6.00
SN4 Eddie George 3.00 8.00
SN5 Eric Moulds 2.50 6.00
SN6 Isaac Bruce 4.00 10.00
SN7 Jeff Garcia 2.50 6.00
SN8 Jerome Bettis 4.00 10.00
SN9 Jerry Rice 8.00 20.00
SN10 Joey Harrington 2.50 6.00
SN11 Koren Robinson 3.00 8.00
SN12 Kurt Warner 3.00 8.00
SN13 Mark Brunell 3.00 8.00
SN14 Michael Bennett 2.50 6.00
SN15 Michael Strahan 3.00 8.00
SN16 Plaxico Burress 2.50 6.00
SN17 Rich Gannon 3.00 8.00
SN18 Rod Smith 3.00 8.00
SN19 Steve McNair 3.00 8.00
SN20 Terrell Owens 3.00 8.00

2003 Playoff Prestige Stars of the NFL Patches Autographs

Randomly inserted into packs, these cards feature authentic autographs of the featured players. Each of these players signed 25 cards.
STATED PRINT RUN 25 SETS
5 Eric Moulds 20.00 50.00
12 Kurt Warner 25.00 60.00
17 Rich Gannon 25.00 60.00
19 Steve McNair 25.00 60.00

2003 Playoff Prestige Turning Pro Jerseys

Randomly inserted into packs, these cards feature two-pieces of game-used jersey from the featured player. Each of these cards were issued to a stated print run of 250 serial numbered sets.
STATED PRINT RUN 250 SER.#'d SETS
TP1 Drew Bledsoe 3.00 8.00
TP2 Curtis Martin 3.00 8.00
TP3 Fred Taylor 2.50 6.00
TP4 Jevon Kearse 2.50 6.00
TP5 Ahman Green 3.00 8.00
TP6 Eddie George 3.00 8.00
TP7 Shaun Alexander 2.50 6.00
TP8 Edgerrin James 3.00 8.00
TP9 Keyshawn Johnson 4.00 10.00
TP10 Ricky Williams 3.00 8.00

2003 Playoff Prestige Draft Picks

Randomly inserted in packs, this set honors some of the most popular players selected in the 2003 NFL Draft. Each of these cards were issued to a stated print run of 2003 serial numbered sets. Please note that card DP22 was not issued.
COMPLETE SET (24) 25.00 60.00
STATED PRINT RUN 2003 SER.#'d SETS
DP1 Byron Leftwich .75 2.00
DP2 Carson Palmer 1.25 3.00
DP3 Dave Ragone .60 1.50
DP4 Larry Johnson .75 2.00
DP5 Musa Smith .60 1.50
DP6 Lee Suggs .60 1.50
DP7 Onterrio Smith .60 1.50
DP8 Chris Brown .60 1.50
DP9 Andre Johnson 1.50 4.00
DP10 Brandon Lloyd 1.00 2.50
DP11 Bryant Johnson 1.00 2.50
DP12 Charles Rogers .75 2.00
DP13 Kelley Washington .60 1.50
DP14 Taylor Jacobs .60 1.50
DP15 Terrence Edwards .60 1.50
DP16 Mike Pinkard .60 1.50
DP17 Teyo Johnson .75 2.00
DP18 DeWayne White .60 1.50
DP19 Jerome McDougle .60 1.50
DP20 Jimmy Kennedy .75 2.00
DP21 William Joseph .60 1.50
DP23 Terrell Suggs .75 2.00
DP24 Terence Newman 1.00 2.50
DP25 Mike Doss 1.00 2.50

2003 Playoff Prestige Draft Picks Autographs

Randomly inserted in packs, this is a parallel to the Draft Pick insert set. Each of these cards feature authentic autographs of the featured player. These cards were issued to a stated print run of 50 serial numbered sets. Many of the players in the set did not return their cards in time for inclusion in pack-out. Those exchange cards could be redeemed until October 14, 2004.
STATED PRINT RUN 50 SER.#'d SETS
DP1 Byron Leftwich 12.00 30.00
DP2 Carson Palmer 20.00 50.00
DP4 Larry Johnson 20.00 50.00
DP5 Musa Smith
DP6 Lee Suggs 10.00 25.00
DP7 Onterrio Smith 10.00 25.00
DP8 Chris Brown 10.00 25.00
DP9 Andre Johnson 50.00 100.00
DP12 Charles Rogers 12.00 30.00
DP13 Kelley Washington 10.00 25.00
DP15 Terrence Edwards 10.00 25.00
DP18 DeWayne White
DP19 Jerome McDougal 10.00 25.00
DP20 Jimmy Kennedy 12.00 30.00
DP21 William Joseph 10.00 25.00
DP23 Terrell Suggs 25.00 50.00
DP24 Terence Newman 15.00 40.00

2003 Playoff Prestige League Leader Quads

Randomly inserted into packs, this 10-card set features four leaders at a key position. Each of these cards were issued to a stated print run of 500 serial numbered sets. A Materials version of each card was also issued with each serial numbered of 25.
COMPLETE SET (10) 30.00 80.00
STATED PRINT RUN 500 SER.#'d SETS
LLQ1 Garcia/Gann/Favre/Penn 5.00 12.00
LLQ2 McNa/Johnson/Bled/Brooks 2.00 5.00
LLQ3 Mann/Vick/Brady/Coll 10.00 25.00
LLQ4 Toml/Faulk/Holmes/McAll 2.50 6.00
LLQ5 Willi/Green/Dillon/Benn 2.00 5.00
LLQ6 Port/Stew/Taylor/E.Smith 4.00 10.00
LLQ7 Harr/Horn/Moulds/Johns 2.50 6.00
LLQ8 Price 5.00 12.00
Holt
Rice
Owens
LLQ9 Burress/Driver/Ward/Moss 2.00 5.00
LLQ10 Pepp/Thomas/Sapp/Bullu 2.50 6.00

2003 Playoff Prestige League Leader Quads Materials

Randomly inserted into packs, this is a parallel to the League Leader Quad set. Each of these cards feature four pieces of game-used memorabilia and were issued to a stated print run of 25 serial numbered sets.
STATED PRINT RUN 25 SER.#'d SETS
LLQ1 Garc/Gann/Favre/Penn 30.00 80.00
LLQ2 McNair/Jhnsn/Bldso/Brks 12.00 30.00
LLQ3 Mann/Vick/Brady/Collins 60.00 150.00
LLQ4 Tomlin/Faulk/Hlms/McAll 15.00 40.00
LLQ5 Williams/Green/Dillon/Benn 12.00 30.00
LLQ6 Portis/Stewrt/Taylor/Smith 25.00 60.00
LLQ7 Hrrisn/Horn/Mlds/Jhnsn 15.00 40.00
LLQ8 Price/Holt/Rice/Owens 30.00 80.00
LLQ9 Burress/Driver/Ward/Moss 12.00 30.00
LLQ10 Pepprs/Thms/Sapp/Bullck 15.00 40.00

2003 Playoff Prestige League Leader Tandems

Randomly inserted into packs, this 20-card set features two players at the same position who are among the league leaders. Each of these cards were issued to a stated print run of 2002 serial numbered sets.
COMPLETE SET (20) 20.00 50.00
STATED PRINT RUN 2002 SER.#'d SETS
LLT1 J.Garcia/R.Gannon .75 2.00
LLT2 B.Favre/C.Pennington 2.00 5.00
LLT3 S.McNair/B.Johnson .75 2.00
LLT4 D.Bledsoe/A.Brooks .75 2.00
LLT5 P.Manning/M.Vick 2.50 6.00
LLT6 T.Brady/K.Collins 4.00 10.00
LLT7 L.Tomlinson/M.Faulk 1.00 2.50
LLT8 P.Holmes/D.McAllister .75 2.00
LLT9 R.Williams/A.Green .75 2.00
LLT10 C.Dillon/M.Bennett .60 1.50
LLT11 C.Portis/J.Stewart .60 1.50
LLT12 F.Taylor/E.Smith 1.50 4.00
LLT13 M.Harrison/J.Horn .75 2.00
LLT14 E.Moulds/Key.Johnson 1.00 2.50
LLT15 P.Price/T.Holt .75 2.00
LLT16 J.Rice/T.Owens 2.00 5.00
LLT17 P.Burress/D.Driver .75 2.00
LLT18 H.Ward/R.Moss .75 2.00
LLT19 J.Peppers/Z.Thomas 1.00 2.50
LLT20 W.Sapp/K.Bulluck .75 2.00

2003 Playoff Prestige League Leader Tandems Materials

Randomly inserted into packs, these cards parallel the League Leader Tandem insert set. Each of these cards feature two game-used memorabilia pieces and were issued to a stated print run of 250 serial numbered sets.
STATED PRINT RUN 250 SER.#'d SETS
LLT1 J.Garcia/R.Gannon 5.00 12.00
LLT2 B.Favre/C.Pennington 12.00 30.00
LLT3 S.McNair/B.Johnson 5.00 12.00
LLT4 D.Bledsoe/A.Brooks 5.00 12.00
LLT5 P.Manning/M.Vick 15.00 40.00
LLT6 T.Brady/K.Collins 25.00 60.00
LLT7 L.Tomlinson/M.Faulk 6.00 15.00
LLT8 P.Holmes/D.McAllister 5.00 12.00
LLT9 R.Williams/A.Green 5.00 12.00
LLT10 C.Dillon/M.Bennett 4.00 10.00
LLT11 C.Portis/J.Stewart 4.00 10.00
LLT12 F.Taylor/E.Smith 10.00 25.00
LLT13 M.Harrison/J.Horn 5.00 12.00
LLT14 E.Moulds/Key.Johnson 6.00 15.00
LLT15 P.Price/T.Holt 5.00 12.00
LLT16 J.Rice/T.Owens 12.00 30.00
LLT17 P.Burress/D.Driver 5.00 12.00
LLT18 H.Ward/R.Moss 8.00 20.00
LLT19 J.Peppers/Z.Thomas 6.00 15.00
LLT20 W.Sapp/K.Bulluck 5.00 12.00

2004 Playoff Prestige

Playoff Prestige released in May of 2004 and was the first full NFL product of the year. The base set consists of 227 cards including 150 veterans and 77 rookies. Within the rookie subset, ten cards were short-printed and seeded at a ratio of 1:6 boxes. Note that Mike Williams and Maurice Clarett both made an apearance in this product although they were declared ineligible for the NFL Draft. Hobby boxes contained 24-packs of 6-cards along with an extensive selection of insert and game-used sets highlighted by the Draft Picks Rights Autograph set and the very first LaVar Arrington game-used memorabilia card.
COMP.SET w/o RC's (150) 10.00 25.00
SP RC ANNOUNCED ODDS 1:6 BOXES
1 Anquan Boldin .25 .60
2 Emmitt Smith .60 1.50
3 Jeff Blake .30 .75
4 Marcel Shipp .25 .60
5 Michael Vick .30 .75
6 Peerless Price .25 .60
7 T.J. Duckett .25 .60
8 Warrick Dunn .25 .60
9 Ed Reed .30 .75
10 Jamal Lewis .30 .75
11 Kyle Boller .25 .60
12 Ray Lewis .40 1.00
13 Todd Heap .25 .60
14 Drew Bledsoe .30 .75
15 Eric Moulds .25 .60
16 Josh Reed .25 .60
17 Travis Henry .25 .60
18 DeShaun Foster .30 .75
19 Stephen Davis .25 .60
20 Jake Delhomme .25 .60
21 Julius Peppers .30 .75
22 Steve Smith .40 1.00
23 Anthony Thomas .30 .75
24 Brian Urlacher .40 1.00
25 Marty Booker .25 .60
26 Rex Grossman .25 .60
27 Chad Johnson .25 .60
28 Corey Dillon .25 .60
29 Carson Palmer .30 .75
30 Peter Warrick .25 .60
31 Rudi Johnson .25 .60
32 Andre Davis .25 .60
33 Quincy Morgan .25 .60
34 William Green .25 .60
35 Kelly Holcomb .25 .60
36 Antonio Bryant .30 .75
37 Quincy Carter .25 .60
38 Roy Williams S .25 .60
39 Terence Newman .30 .75
40 Terry Glenn .30 .75
41 Troy Hambrick .25 .60
42 Ashley Lelie .25 .60
43 Clinton Portis .25 .60
44 Rod Smith .30 .75
45 Shannon Sharpe .30 .75
46 Mike Anderson .25 .60
47 Jake Plummer .25 .60
48 Charles Rogers .25 .60
49 Joey Harrington .25 .60
50 Ahman Green .30 .75
51 Brett Favre .75 2.00
52 Donald Driver .30 .75
53 Javon Walker .25 .60
54 Robert Ferguson .25 .60
55 Andre Johnson .30 .75
56 David Carr .25 .60
57 Domanick Davis .25 .60
58 Jabar Gaffney .25 .60
59 Dwight Freeney .25 .60
60 Dallas Clark .25 .60
61 Edgerrin James .30 .75
62 Marvin Harrison .30 .75
63 Peyton Manning 1.00 2.50
64 Reggie Wayne .30 .75
65 Byron Leftwich .25 .60
66 Fred Taylor .25 .60
67 Jimmy Smith .30 .75
68 Johnnie Morton .30 .75
69 Priest Holmes .25 .60
70 Tony Gonzalez .30 .75
71 Trent Green .25 .60
72 Chris Chambers .25 .60
73 Jay Fiedler .25 .60
74 Randy McMichael .25 .60
75 Ricky Williams .30 .75
76 Zach Thomas .30 .75
77 Daunte Culpepper .30 .75
78 Kelly Campbell .25 .60
79 Michael Bennett .25 .60
80 Moe Williams .25 .60
81 Nate Burleson .30 .75
82 Randy Moss .30 .75
83 Deion Branch .25 .60
84 Kevin Faulk .25 .60
85 Tom Brady 1.50 4.00
86 Troy Brown .25 .60
87 Tedy Bruschi .30 .75
88 Aaron Brooks .25 .60
89 Deuce McAllister .30 .75
90 Donte Stallworth .25 .60
91 Joe Horn .25 .60
92 Amani Toomer .25 .60
93 Ike Hilliard .25 .60
94 Jeremy Shockey .25 .60
95 Kerry Collins .25 .60
96 Michael Strahan .30 .75
97 Tiki Barber .30 .75
98 Chad Pennington .25 .60
99 Curtis Martin .30 .75
100 LaMont Jordan .30 .75
101 Santana Moss .30 .75
102 Charlie Garner .30 .75
103 Jerry Porter .25 .60
104 Jerry Rice .75 2.00
105 Justin Fargas .30 .75
106 Rich Gannon .30 .75
107 Rod Woodson .30 .75
108 Tim Brown .40 1.00
109 Brian Westbrook .25 .60
110 Correll Buckhalter .25 .60
111 Donovan McNabb .30 .75
112 Freddie Mitchell .25 .60
113 James Thrash .25 .60
114 Amos Zereoue .25 .60
115 Antwaan Randle El .25 .60
116 Hines Ward .30 .75
117 Joey Porter .30 .75
118 Kendrell Bell .25 .60
119 Plaxico Burress .25 .60
120 David Boston .25 .60
121 Drew Brees .40 1.00
122 LaDainian Tomlinson .40 1.00
123 Jeff Garcia .25 .60
124 Kevan Barlow .25 .60
125 Tai Streets .25 .60
126 Terrell Owens .30 .75
127 Tim Rattay .25 .60
128 Darrell Jackson .30 .75
129 Koren Robinson .25 .60
130 Matt Hasselbeck .25 .60
131 Shaun Alexander .25 .60
132 Isaac Bruce .40 1.00
133 Marc Bulger .25 .60
134 Marshall Faulk .30 .75
135 Torry Holt .30 .75
136 Brad Johnson .30 .75
137 Derrick Brooks .25 .60
138 Keenan McCardell .25 .60
139 Keyshawn Johnson .30 .75
140 Mike Alstott .25 .60
141 Derrick Mason .25 .60
142 Drew Bennett .30 .75
143 Jevon Kearse .25 .60
144 Justin McCareins .25 .60
145 Steve McNair .30 .75
146 Tyrone Calico .30 .75
147 Bruce Smith .30 .75
148 Laveranues Coles .25 .60
149 Patrick Ramsey .30 .75
150 LaVar Arrington .25 .60
151 Eli Manning RC 5.00 12.00
152 Larry Fitzgerald RC 2.50 6.00
153 Philip Rivers RC 2.00 5.00
154 Sean Taylor RC 4.00 10.00
155 Kellen Winslow RC .60 1.50
156 Roy Williams RC .60 1.50
157 DeAngelo Hall RC 1.00 2.50
158 Reggie Williams RC .60 1.50
159 Ben Roethlisberger RC 5.00 12.00
160 Jonathan Vilma RC .75 2.00
161 Lee Evans RC 1.00 2.50
162 Tommie Harris RC .75 2.00
163 Michael Clayton RC .75 2.00
164 D.J. Williams SP RC 10.00 25.00
165 Will Smith RC .75 2.00
166 Kenechi Udeze RC .75 2.00
167 Vince Wilfork SP RC 10.00 25.00
168 J.P. Losman RC .60 1.50
169 Steven Jackson SP RC 4.00 10.00
170 Ahmad Carroll RC .60 1.50
171 Chris Perry RC .60 1.50
172 Jason Babin SP RC 10.00 25.00
173 Chris Gamble RC .60 1.50
174 Michael Jenkins RC .60 1.50
175 Kevin Jones RC .75 2.00
176 Rashaun Woods RC .60 1.50
177 Ben Watson RC .75 2.00
178 Karlos Dansby RC .75 2.00
179 Teddy Lehman RC .60 1.50

180 Ricardo Colclough SP RC 6.00 15.00
181 Daryl Smith RC .60 1.50
182 Ben Troupe RC .60 1.50
183 Tatum Bell RC .60 1.50
184 Julius Jones RC .60 1.50
185 Bob Sanders RC 1.25 3.00
186 Devery Henderson RC .60 1.50
187 Dwan Edwards RC .60 1.50
188 Michael Boulware RC 1.00 2.50
189 Darius Watts RC .60 1.50
190 Greg Jones RC .60 1.50
191 Antwan Odom RC .60 1.50
192 Sean Jones SP RC 6.00 15.00
193 Courtney Watson RC .60 1.50
194 Keary Colbert RC .60 1.50
195 Keith Smith RC .60 1.50
196 Derrick Strait RC .60 1.50
197 Bernard Berrian RC .60 1.50
198 Devard Darling RC .60 1.50
199 Matt Schaub RC .60 1.50
200 Will Poole RC 1.00 2.50
201 Samie Parker RC .60 1.50
202 Luke McCown SP RC 6.00 15.00
203 Jerricho Cotchery RC .75 2.00
204 Mewelde Moore RC .75 2.00
205 Ernest Wilford RC .75 2.00
206 Cedric Cobbs SP RC 6.00 15.00
207 Johnnie Morant RC .60 1.50
208 Craig Krenzel RC .60 1.50
209 Michael Turner RC .60 1.50
210 D.J. Hackett RC .60 1.50
211 P.K. Sam RC .60 1.50
212 Josh Harris RC .60 1.50
213 Drew Henson RC .60 1.50
214 Jeff Smoker RC .75 2.00
215 John Navarre RC .60 1.50
216 Cody Pickett RC .60 1.50
217 Quincy Wilson RC .60 1.50
218 Derek Abney RC .60 1.50
219 Maurice Clarett SP RC 8.00 20.00
220 Mike Williams SP RC 8.00 20.00
221 B.J. Johnson RC .60 1.50
222 Brandon Everage RC .60 1.50
223 Derek McCoy RC .60 1.50
224 Jared Lorenzen RC .75 2.00
225 Jarrett Payton RC .75 2.00
226 Jason Fife RC .60 1.50
227 Robert Kent RC .60 1.50

2004 Playoff Prestige Xtra Points Black

*VETS: 10X TO 25X BASIC CARDS
*ROOKIES: 5X TO 12X BASIC RC
*ROOKIES: .5X TO 1.2X BASIC SP RC
HOBBY INSERT PRINT RUN 25
19 Stephen Davis AU 12.00 30.00
38 Roy Williams S AU 12.00 30.00
57 Domanick Davis AU 12.00 30.00
67 Jimmy Smith AU 15.00 40.00
72 Chris Chambers AU 12.00 30.00
88 Aaron Brooks AU 12.00 30.00
91 Joe Horn AU 12.00 30.00
97 Tiki Barber AU 15.00 40.00
116 Hines Ward AU 50.00 100.00
141 Derrick Mason AU 12.00 30.00
213 Drew Henson AU 12.00 30.00

2004 Playoff Prestige Xtra Points Green

*VETS: 10X TO 25X BASIC CARDS
*ROOKIES: 5X TO 12X BASIC RC
*ROOKIES: .5X TO 1.2X BASIC SP RC
PRINT RUN 25 SER.#'d SETS RETAIL ONLY

2004 Playoff Prestige Xtra Points Purple

*VETS: 4X TO 10X BASIC CARDS
*ROOKIES: 1.5X TO 4X BASIC RC
*ROOKIES: .15X TO .4X BASIC SP RC
HOBBY INSERT PRINT RUN 75

2004 Playoff Prestige Xtra Points Red

*VETS: 3X TO 8X BASE CARD HI
*ROOKIES: 1.5X TO 4X BASIC RC
*ROOKIES: .15X TO .4X BASIC SP RC
RETAIL INSERT PRINT RUN 100

2004 Playoff Prestige Achievements

COMPLETE SET (15) 12.50 30.00
A1 Brian Urlacher 1.00 2.50
A2 Emmitt Smith 1.50 4.00
A3 Clinton Portis .60 1.50
A4 Brett Favre 2.00 5.00
A5 Peyton Manning 2.50 6.00
A6 Ricky Williams .75 2.00
A7 Randy Moss .75 2.00
A8 Tom Brady 4.00 10.00
A9 LaDainian Tomlinson 1.00 2.50
A10 Marshall Faulk .75 2.00
A11 Jamal Lewis .75 2.00
A12 Steve McNair .75 2.00
A13 Rich Gannon .75 2.00
A14 Kurt Warner .75 2.00
A15 Torry Holt .75 2.00

2004 Playoff Prestige Achievements Materials

STATED PRINT RUN 93-103
A1 Brian Urlacher/100 4.00 10.00
A2 Emmitt Smith/93 6.00 15.00
A3 Clinton Portis/102 2.50 6.00
A4 Brett Favre/97 8.00 20.00
A5 Peyton Manning/103 10.00 25.00
A6 Ricky Williams/102 3.00 8.00
A7 Randy Moss/98 3.00 8.00
A8 Tom Brady/101 12.00 30.00
A9 LaDainian Tomlinson/102 4.00 10.00
A10 Marshall Faulk/100 3.00 8.00
A11 Jamal Lewis/103 3.00 8.00
A12 Steve McNair/103 3.00 8.00
A13 Rich Gannon/102 3.00 8.00
A14 Kurt Warner/99 3.00 8.00
A15 Torry Holt/103 3.00 8.00

2004 Playoff Prestige Changing Stripes

STATED PRINT RUN 225 SER.#'d SETS
*PRIME/25: 1X TO 2.5X BASIC DUAL/225
PRIME PRINT RUN 25 SER.#'d SETS
CS1 David Boston 2.00 5.00
CS2 Priest Holmes 2.00 5.00
CS3 Trent Green 2.00 5.00
CS4 Jerry Rice 6.00 15.00
CS5 Jake Plummer 2.00 5.00
CS6 Emmitt Smith 5.00 12.00
CS7 Laveranues Coles 2.00 5.00
CS8 Brad Johnson 2.50 6.00
CS9 Junior Seau 3.00 8.00
CS10 Stephen Davis 2.00 5.00

2004 Playoff Prestige Draft Picks

COMPLETE SET (25) 30.00 80.00
DP1 Ben Roethlisberger 5.00 12.00
DP2 Eli Manning 5.00 12.00
DP3 J.P. Losman .60 1.50
DP4 Philip Rivers 2.00 5.00
DP5 Steven Jackson 1.00 2.50
DP6 Kevin Jones .75 2.00
DP7 Chris Perry .60 1.50
DP8 Greg Jones .60 1.50
DP9 Michael Turner .60 1.50
DP10 Roy Williams WR .60 1.50
DP11 Rashaun Woods .60 1.50
DP12 Reggie Williams .60 1.50
DP13 Michael Clayton .75 2.00
DP14 Lee Evans 1.00 2.50
DP15 Kellen Winslow Jr. .60 1.50
DP16 Matt Schaub .60 1.50
DP17 Quincy Wilson .60 1.50
DP18 Julius Jones .60 1.50
DP19 Larry Fitzgerald 2.50 6.00
DP20 Ernest Wilford .75 2.00
DP21 Keary Colbert .60 1.50
DP22 Tommie Harris .75 2.00
DP23 Jonathan Vilma .75 2.00
DP24 Chris Gamble .60 1.50
DP25 Sean Taylor 4.00 10.00

2004 Playoff Prestige Draft Picks Autographs

STATED PRINT RUN 50 SER.#'d SETS
DP1 Ben Roethlisberger 60.00 150.00
DP2 Eli Manning 75.00 150.00
DP3 J.P. Losman 10.00 25.00
DP4 Philip Rivers 30.00 80.00
DP5 Steven Jackson 15.00 40.00
DP6 Kevin Jones 12.00 30.00
DP7 Chris Perry 10.00 25.00
DP8 Greg Jones 10.00 25.00
DP9 Michael Turner 10.00 25.00
DP10 Roy Williams WR 10.00 25.00
DP12 Reggie Williams 10.00 25.00
DP13 Michael Clayton 12.00 30.00
DP14 Lee Evans 15.00 40.00
DP15 Kellen Winslow Jr. 10.00 25.00
DP16 Matt Schaub 10.00 25.00
DP17 Quincy Wilson 10.00 25.00
DP18 Julius Jones 10.00 25.00
DP19 Larry Fitzgerald 50.00 100.00
DP20 Ernest Wilford 12.00 30.00
DP21 Keary Colbert 10.00 25.00
DP23 Jonathan Vilma 12.00 30.00
DP24 Chris Gamble 10.00 25.00

2004 Playoff Prestige Game Day Jerseys

GJ1-GJ20 INSERTED IN HOBBY PACKS
GJ21-GJ40 INSERTED IN RETAIL PACKS
GJ1 Anquan Boldin 2.00 5.00
GJ2 Marcel Shipp 2.00 5.00
GJ3 Peerless Price 2.00 5.00
GJ4 Travis Henry 2.00 5.00
GJ5 Jimmy Smith 2.50 6.00
GJ6 Amani Toomer 2.00 5.00
GJ7 Tim Brown 3.00 8.00
GJ8 Correll Buckhalter 2.00 5.00
GJ9 Donovan McNabb 2.50 6.00
GJ10 Jerome Bettis 3.00 8.00
GJ11 Jeff Garcia 2.00 5.00
GJ12 Isaac Bruce 3.00 8.00
GJ13 Warren Sapp 2.50 6.00
GJ14 Steve McNair 2.50 6.00
GJ15 Jamal Lewis 2.50 6.00
GJ16 Roy Williams S 2.00 5.00
GJ17 David Carr 2.00 5.00
GJ18 Peyton Manning 8.00 20.00
GJ19 Chris Chambers 2.00 5.00
GJ20 Michael Bennett 2.00 5.00
GJ21 Jason McAddley 2.00 5.00
GJ22 Muhsin Muhammad 2.00 5.00
GJ23 David Terrell 2.00 5.00
GJ24 Dennis Northcutt 2.00 5.00
GJ25 William Green 2.00 5.00
GJ26 Tim Couch 2.50 6.00
GJ27 Rod Smith 2.50 6.00
GJ28 Scotty Anderson 2.00 5.00
GJ29 Antonio Freeman 2.50 6.00
GJ30 Fred Taylor 2.00 5.00
GJ31 Mark Brunell 2.50 6.00
GJ32 Byron Chamberlain 2.00 5.00
GJ33 Antowain Smith 2.50 6.00
GJ34 Tedy Bruschi 2.50 6.00
GJ35 Ike Hilliard 2.00 5.00
GJ36 Ron Dayne 2.50 6.00
GJ37 Wayne Chrebet 2.00 5.00
GJ38 Josh McCown 2.50 6.00
GJ39 Duce Staley 2.00 5.00
GJ40 Jeremy Shockey 2.00 5.00

2004 Playoff Prestige Gamers

STATED PRINT RUN 750 SER.#'d SETS
G1 Michael Vick .75 2.00
G2 Jamal Lewis .75 2.00
G3 Ray Lewis 1.00 2.50
G4 Travis Henry .60 1.50
G5 Brian Urlacher 1.00 2.50
G6 Clinton Portis .60 1.50
G7 Brett Favre 2.00 5.00
G8 Ahman Green .75 2.00
G9 David Carr .60 1.50
G10 Marvin Harrison .75 2.00
G11 Peyton Manning 2.50 6.00
G12 Priest Holmes .60 1.50
G13 Ricky Williams .75 2.00
G14 Daunte Culpepper .75 2.00
G15 Randy Moss .75 2.00
G16 Tom Brady 4.00 10.00
G17 Deuce McAllister .75 2.00
G18 Jeremy Shockey .60 1.50
G19 Chad Pennington .60 1.50
G20 Jerry Rice 2.00 5.00
G21 Donovan McNabb .75 2.00
G22 LaDainian Tomlinson 1.00 2.50
G23 Terrell Owens .75 2.00
G24 Torry Holt .75 2.00
G25 Steve McNair .75 2.00

2004 Playoff Prestige Gamers Jerseys

STATED PRINT RUN 100 SER.#'d SETS
G1 Michael Vick 3.00 8.00
G2 Jamal Lewis 3.00 8.00
G3 Ray Lewis 4.00 10.00
G4 Travis Henry 2.50 6.00
G5 Brian Urlacher 4.00 10.00
G6 Clinton Portis 2.50 6.00
G7 Brett Favre 8.00 20.00
G8 Ahman Green 3.00 8.00
G9 David Carr 2.50 6.00
G10 Marvin Harrison 3.00 8.00
G11 Peyton Manning 10.00 25.00
G12 Priest Holmes 2.50 6.00
G13 Ricky Williams 3.00 8.00
G14 Daunte Culpepper 3.00 8.00
G15 Randy Moss 3.00 8.00
G16 Tom Brady 15.00 40.00
G17 Deuce McAllister 3.00 8.00
G18 Jeremy Shockey 2.50 6.00
G19 Chad Pennington 2.50 6.00
G20 Jerry Rice 8.00 20.00
G21 Donovan McNabb 3.00 8.00
G22 LaDainian Tomlinson 4.00 10.00
G23 Terrell Owens 3.00 8.00
G24 Torry Holt 3.00 8.00
G25 Steve McNair 3.00 8.00

2004 Playoff Prestige Gridiron Heritage

COMPLETE SET (20) 15.00 40.00
GH1 Marcel Shipp .60 1.50
GH2 Eric Moulds .60 1.50
GH3 Anthony Thomas .75 2.00
GH4 Corey Dillon .60 1.50
GH5 Kelly Holcomb .60 1.50
GH6 Rod Smith .75 2.00
GH7 Joey Harrington .60 1.50
GH8 Brett Favre 2.00 5.00
GH9 Edgerrin James .75 2.00
GH10 Fred Taylor .60 1.50
GH11 Zach Thomas .75 2.00
GH12 Aaron Brooks .60 1.50
GH13 Tiki Barber .75 2.00
GH14 Curtis Martin .75 2.00
GH15 Tim Brown 1.00 2.50
GH16 Correll Buckhalter .60 1.50
GH17 Hines Ward .75 2.00
GH18 Jeff Garcia .60 1.50
GH19 Mike Alstott .60 1.50
GH20 Eddie George .75 2.00

2004 Playoff Prestige Gridiron Heritage Jerseys

GH1 Marcel Shipp 2.00 5.00
GH2 Eric Moulds 2.00 5.00
GH3 Anthony Thomas 2.50 6.00
GH4 Corey Dillon 2.00 5.00
GH5 Kelly Holcomb 2.00 5.00
GH6 Rod Smith 2.50 6.00
GH7 Joey Harrington 2.00 5.00
GH8 Brett Favre 6.00 15.00
GH9 Edgerrin James 2.50 6.00
GH10 Fred Taylor 2.00 5.00
GH11 Zach Thomas 2.50 6.00
GH12 Aaron Brooks 2.00 5.00
GH13 Tiki Barber 2.50 6.00
GH14 Curtis Martin 2.50 6.00
GH15 Tim Brown 3.00 8.00
GH16 Correll Buckhalter 2.00 5.00
GH17 Hines Ward 2.50 6.00
GH18 Jeff Garcia 2.00 5.00
GH19 Mike Alstott 2.00 5.00
GH20 Eddie George 2.50 6.00

2004 Playoff Prestige League Leaders

COMPLETE SET (20) 20.00 50.00
LL1 P.Manning/T.Green 2.50 6.00
LL2 A.Brooks/D.Culpepper .75 2.00
LL3 B.Favre/Q.Carter 2.00 5.00
LL4 D.McNabb/K.Collins .75 2.00
LL5 B.Johnson/M.Bulger .75 2.00
LL6 S.McNair/T.Brady 4.00 10.00
LL7 J.Lewis/Ri.Williams .75 2.00
LL8 D.McAllister/S.Davis .75 2.00
LL9 C.Portis/C.Martin .75 2.00
LL10 F.Taylor/P.Holmes .60 1.50
LL11 A.Green/S.Alexander .75 2.00
LL12 L.Tomlinson/T.Henry 1.00 2.50
LL13 E.George/E.James .75 2.00
LL14 A.Thomas/T.Barber .75 2.00
LL15 L.Coles/T.Holt .75 2.00
LL16 A.Boldin/R.Moss .75 2.00
LL17 Ch.Johnson/D.Mason .60 1.50
LL18 H.Ward/M.Harrison .75 2.00
LL19 A.Johnson/S.Moss .75 2.00
LL20 A.Toomer/T.Owens .75 2.00

2004 Playoff Prestige League Leaders Jerseys

LL1 P.Manning/T.Green 8.00 20.00
LL2 A.Brooks/D.Culpepper 2.50 6.00
LL3 B.Favre/Q.Carter 6.00 15.00
LL4 D.McNabb/K.Collins 2.50 6.00
LL5 B.Johnson/M.Bulger 2.50 6.00
LL6 S.McNair/T.Brady 12.00 30.00
LL7 J.Lewis/R.Williams 2.50 6.00
LL8 D.McAllister/S.Davis 2.50 6.00
LL9 C.Portis/C.Martin 2.50 6.00
LL10 F.Taylor/P.Holmes 2.00 5.00
LL11 A.Green/S.Alexander 2.50 6.00
LL12 L.Tomlinson/T.Henry 3.00 8.00
LL13 E.George/E.James 2.50 6.00
LL14 A.Thomas/T.Barber 2.50 6.00
LL15 L.Coles/T.Holt 2.50 6.00
LL16 A.Boldin/R.Moss 2.50 6.00
LL17 C.Johnson/D.Mason 2.00 5.00
LL18 H.Ward/M.Harrison 2.50 6.00
LL19 A.Johnson/S.Moss 2.50 6.00
LL20 A.Toomer/T.Owens 2.50 6.00

2004 Playoff Prestige Stars of the NFL Jerseys

STATED PRINT RUN 150 SER.#'d SETS
*PATCH/25: .8X TO 2X BASIC JSY/150
PATCH STATED PRINT RUN 25
NFL1 Michael Vick 3.00 8.00
NFL2 Jamal Lewis 3.00 8.00
NFL3 Drew Bledsoe 3.00 8.00
NFL4 Brian Urlacher 4.00 10.00
NFL5 Clinton Portis 2.50 6.00
NFL6 Emmitt Smith 6.00 15.00
NFL7 Ahman Green 3.00 8.00
NFL8 Brett Favre 8.00 20.00
NFL9 David Carr 2.50 6.00
NFL10 Edgerrin James 3.00 8.00
NFL11 Peyton Manning 10.00 25.00
NFL12 Priest Holmes 2.50 6.00
NFL13 Ricky Williams 3.00 8.00
NFL14 Randy Moss 3.00 8.00
NFL15 Tom Brady 15.00 40.00
NFL16 Deuce McAllister 3.00 8.00
NFL17 Jeremy Shockey 2.50 6.00
NFL18 Chad Pennington 2.50 6.00
NFL19 Jerry Rice 8.00 20.00
NFL20 Donovan McNabb 3.00 8.00
NFL21 LaDainian Tomlinson 4.00 10.00
NFL22 Jeff Garcia 2.50 6.00
NFL23 LaVar Arrington 2.50 6.00
NFL24 Marshall Faulk 3.00 8.00
NFL25 Steve McNair 3.00 8.00

2004 Playoff Prestige Stars of the NFL Patches Autographs

STATED PRINT RUN 25 SER.#'d SETS
NFL7 Ahman Green 40.00 80.00
NFL15 Tom Brady 200.00 350.00
NFL16 Deuce McAllister 40.00 80.00

2004 Playoff Prestige Super Bowl Heroes

COMPLETE SET (10) 12.50 30.00
SB1 Tom Brady 8.00 20.00
SB2 Deion Branch 1.25 3.00
SB3 Adam Vinatieri 1.25 3.00
SB4 Mike Vrabel 2.00 5.00
SB5 Antowain Smith 1.50 4.00
SB6 David Givens 1.25 3.00
SB7 Troy Brown 1.25 3.00
SB8 Kevin Faulk 1.25 3.00
SB9 Jake Delhomme 1.25 3.00
SB10 Muhsin Muhammad 1.25 3.00

2004 Playoff Prestige Turning Pro Jerseys

STATED PRINT RUN 225 SER.#'d SETS
*PRIME/25: .8X TO 2X DUAL JSY/225
PRIME PRINT RUN 25 SER.#'d SETS
TP1 Anquan Boldin 2.00 5.00
TP2 Doug Flutie 2.50 6.00
TP3 Clinton Portis 2.00 5.00
TP4 Ahman Green 2.50 6.00
TP5 Edgerrin James 2.50 6.00
TP6 Reggie Wayne 2.50 6.00
TP7 Jeremy Shockey 2.00 5.00
TP8 Marshall Faulk 2.50 6.00
TP9 Tyrone Calico 2.50 6.00
TP10 Andre Johnson 2.50 6.00

2005 Playoff Prestige

Playoff Prestige was initially released in mid-May 2005. The base set consists of 244-cards including 94-rookies issued one per pack. Ten of those rookie cards were short-printed. Hobby boxes contained 24-packs of 8-cards and carried an S.R.P. of $3 per pack. Four parallel sets and a variety of inserts can be found seeded in packs highlighted by the Draft Picks Right Autograph inserts.

COMP.SET w/o SP's (234) 50.00 100.00
COMP.SET w/o RC's (150) 10.00 25.00
ONE 151-244 DRAFT PICK PER PACK
1 Anquan Boldin .25 .60
2 Emmitt Smith .75 2.00
3 Josh McCown .30 .75
4 Larry Fitzgerald .40 1.00
5 Michael Vick .30 .75
6 Peerless Price .25 .60
7 Alge Crumpler .30 .75
8 T.J. Duckett .25 .60
9 Warrick Dunn .25 .60
10 Ed Reed .30 .75
11 Jamal Lewis .30 .75
12 Kyle Boller .25 .60
13 Ray Lewis .40 1.00
14 Todd Heap .25 .60
15 Drew Bledsoe .30 .75
16 Eric Moulds .25 .60
17 Lee Evans .30 .75
18 Travis Henry .25 .60
19 Willis McGahee .25 .60
20 Anthony Thomas .25 .60
21 Brian Urlacher .40 1.00
22 Rex Grossman .25 .60
23 David Terrell .25 .60
24 Thomas Jones .25 .60
25 Carson Palmer .30 .75
26 Chad Johnson .25 .60
27 Peter Warrick .25 .60
28 Rudi Johnson .25 .60
29 Antonio Bryant .25 .60
30 William Green .25 .60
31 Jeff Garcia .25 .60
32 Kellen Winslow .25 .60
33 Lee Suggs .25 .60
34 Drew Henson .25 .60
35 Julius Jones .25 .60
36 Jason Witten .30 .75
37 Keyshawn Johnson .30 .75
38 Roy Williams S .25 .60
39 Ashley Lelie .25 .60
40 Champ Bailey .30 .75
41 Jake Plummer .25 .60
42 Reuben Droughns .25 .60
43 Rod Smith .30 .75
44 Charles Rogers .25 .60
45 Joey Harrington .25 .60
46 Kevin Jones .25 .60
47 Roy Williams WR .25 .60
48 Ahman Green .30 .75
49 Donald Driver .30 .75
50 Javon Walker .25 .60
51 Brett Favre .75 2.00
52 Andre Johnson .30 .75
53 David Carr .25 .60
54 Domanick Davis .25 .60
55 Jabar Gaffney .25 .60
56 Edgerrin James .30 .75
57 Marvin Harrison .30 .75
58 Brandon Stokley .25 .60
59 Peyton Manning 1.00 2.50
60 Reggie Wayne .30 .75
61 Byron Leftwich .25 .60
62 Fred Taylor .25 .60
63 Jimmy Smith .30 .75
64 Priest Holmes .25 .60
65 Tony Gonzalez .30 .75
66 Johnnie Morton .30 .75
67 Trent Green .25 .60
68 Chris Chambers .25 .60
69 Randy McMichael .25 .60
70 A.J. Feeley .25 .60
71 Zach Thomas .30 .75
72 Daunte Culpepper .30 .75
73 Marcus Robinson .25 .60
74 Mewelde Moore .25 .60
75 Nate Burleson .25 .60
76 Onterrio Smith .25 .60
77 Randy Moss .30 .75
78 Corey Dillon .25 .60
79 Tom Brady 1.50 4.00
80 Deion Branch .25 .60
81 Tedy Bruschi .30 .75
82 David Givens .25 .60
83 David Patten .25 .60
84 Aaron Brooks .25 .60
85 Deuce McAllister .30 .75
86 Donte Stallworth .25 .60
87 Joe Horn .25 .60
88 Eli Manning .60 1.50
89 Jeremy Shockey .25 .60
90 Kurt Warner .30 .75
91 Michael Strahan .30 .75
92 Tiki Barber .30 .75
93 Amani Toomer .25 .60
94 Chad Pennington .25 .60
95 Curtis Martin .30 .75
96 Santana Moss .30 .75
97 Justin McCareins .25 .60
98 Charles Woodson .40 1.00
99 Kerry Collins .25 .60
100 Warren Sapp .30 .75
101 Jerry Porter .25 .60
102 Donovan McNabb .30 .75
103 Jevon Kearse .25 .60
104 Terrell Owens .30 .75
105 Brian Westbrook .25 .60
106 Todd Pinkston .25 .60
107 Duce Staley .25 .60
108 Hines Ward .30 .75
109 Jerome Bettis .40 1.00
110 Joey Porter .25 .60
111 Plaxico Burress .25 .60
112 Ben Roethlisberger .60 1.50
113 Drew Brees .40 1.00
114 LaDainian Tomlinson .40 1.00
115 Keenan McCardell .30 .75
116 Philip Rivers .40 1.00
117 Antonio Gates .40 1.00
118 Eric Johnson .25 .60
119 Kevan Barlow .25 .60
120 Brandon Lloyd .25 .60
121 Tim Rattay .25 .60
122 Darrell Jackson .25 .60
123 Koren Robinson .25 .60
124 Jerry Rice .75 2.00
125 Matt Hasselbeck .25 .60
126 Shaun Alexander .25 .60
127 Isaac Bruce .40 1.00
128 Marc Bulger .25 .60
129 Marshall Faulk .30 .75
130 Steven Jackson .25 .60
131 Torry Holt .30 .75
132 Derrick Brooks .25 .60
133 Michael Clayton .25 .60
134 Michael Pittman .25 .60
135 Chris Simms .25 .60
136 Chris Brown .25 .60
137 Derrick Mason .25 .60
138 Drew Bennett .30 .75
139 Steve McNair .30 .75
140 Clinton Portis .25 .60
141 LaVar Arrington .25 .60
142 Laveranues Coles .25 .60
143 Patrick Ramsey .30 .75
144 Rod Gardner .25 .60
145 DeShaun Foster .30 .75
146 Stephen Davis .25 .60
147 Jake Delhomme .25 .60
148 Muhsin Muhammad .25 .60
149 Steve Smith .40 1.00
150 Keary Colbert .25 .60
151 Aaron Rodgers SP RC 20.00 40.00
152 Adrian McPherson SP RC 6.00 15.00
153 Alex Smith QB RC 2.50 6.00
154 Andrew Walter RC .60 1.50
155 Brock Berlin RC .60 1.50
156 Charlie Frye SP RC 6.00 15.00
157 Chris Rix RC .75 2.00
158 Dan Orlovsky RC .60 1.50
159 Darian Durant RC .60 1.50
160 David Greene RC .60 1.50
161 Derek Anderson RC .75 2.00
162 Gino Guidugli RC .60 1.50
163 Jason Campbell RC .60 1.50
164 Jason White RC 1.00 2.50
165 Kyle Orton RC .60 1.50
166 Matt Jones SP RC 10.00 25.00
167 Ryan Fitzpatrick RC 1.00 2.50
168 Stefan LeFors RC .60 1.50
169 Timmy Chang RC .60 1.50
170 Alvin Pearman RC .60 1.50
171 Anthony Davis RC .60 1.50
172 Brandon Jacobs RC .75 2.00
173 Cadillac Williams RC .60 1.50
174 Cedric Benson RC .60 1.50
175 Cedric Houston RC 1.00 2.50
176 Ciatrick Fason RC .60 1.50
177 Damien Nash RC .75 2.00
178 Darren Sproles RC 1.00 2.50
179 Eric Shelton SP RC 6.00 15.00
180 Frank Gore SP RC 15.00 40.00
181 J.J. Arrington SP RC 8.00 20.00
182 Kay-Jay Harris RC .60 1.50
183 Marion Barber RC .60 1.50
184 Ronnie Brown RC .75 2.00
185 Ryan Moats RC .60 1.50
186 T.A. McLendon RC .60 1.50
187 Vernand Morency RC .60 1.50
188 Walter Reyes RC .60 1.50
189 Braylon Edwards RC .60 1.50
190 Charles Frederick RC .60 1.50
191 Chris Henry RC .75 2.00
192 Courtney Roby RC .60 1.50
193 Craig Bragg RC .60 1.50
194 Craphonso Thorpe SP RC 6.00 15.00
195 Dante Ridgeway RC .60 1.50
196 Fred Amey RC .60 1.50
197 Fred Gibson RC .60 1.50
198 J.R. Russell RC .60 1.50
199 Jerome Mathis SP RC 10.00 25.00
200 Josh Davis RC .60 1.50
201 Larry Brackins RC .60 1.50
202 Mark Bradley RC .60 1.50
203 Mark Clayton SP RC 6.00 15.00
204 Mike Williams .75 2.00
205 Reggie Brown RC .60 1.50
206 Roddy White RC 1.00 2.50
207 Roscoe Parrish RC .60 1.50
208 Roydell Williams RC .75 2.00
209 Steve Savoy RC .60 1.50
210 Tab Perry RC .60 1.50
211 Taylor Stubblefield RC .60 1.50
212 Terrence Murphy RC .60 1.50
213 Troy Williamson RC .60 1.50
214 Vincent Jackson RC 1.00 2.50
215 Alex Smith TE RC .60 1.50
216 Heath Miller RC 1.25 3.00
217 Dan Cody RC .60 1.50
218 David Pollack RC .60 1.50
219 Erasmus James RC .60 1.50
220 Justin Tuck RC .75 2.00
221 Marcus Spears RC .60 1.50
222 Matt Roth RC .60 1.50
223 Anttaj Hawthorne RC .60 1.50
224 Mike Patterson RC .60 1.50
225 Shaun Cody RC .75 2.00
226 Travis Johnson RC .60 1.50
227 Channing Crowder RC .75 2.00
228 Darryl Blackstock RC .60 1.50
229 DeMarcus Ware RC 2.00 5.00
230 Derrick Johnson RC .75 2.00
231 Kevin Burnett RC .75 2.00
232 Shawne Merriman RC 1.00 2.50
233 Adam Jones RC .75 2.00
234 Antrel Rolle RC 1.00 2.50
235 Brandon Browner RC 1.00 2.50
236 Bryant McFadden RC .75 2.00
237 Carlos Rogers RC 1.00 2.50
238 Corey Webster RC .75 2.00
239 Fabian Washington RC .60 1.50
240 Justin Miller RC .60 1.50
241 Marlin Jackson RC .60 1.50
242 Ernest Shazor RC .75 2.00
243 Josh Bullocks RC .75 2.00
244 Thomas Davis RC .60 1.50

2005 Playoff Prestige Xtra Points Black

*VETERANS: 8X TO 20X BASIC CARDS
*ROOKIES: 4X TO 10X BASIC CARDS
*ROOKIES: .5X TO 1.2X BASIC SP RC
STATED PRINT RUN 25 SER.#'d SETS
151 Aaron Rodgers 100.00 200.00

2005 Playoff Prestige Xtra Points Green

*VETERANS: 5X TO 12X BASIC CARDS
*ROOKIES: 2.5X TO 6X BASIC CARDS
*ROOKIES: .3X TO .8X BASIC RC SP
STATED PRINT RUN 50 SER.#'d SETS
151 Aaron Rodgers 50.00 120.00

2005 Playoff Prestige Xtra Points Purple

*VETERANS: 3X TO 8X BASIC CARDS
*ROOKIES: 1.5X TO 4X BASIC CARDS
*ROOKIES: ..25X TO .6X BASIC SP RC
STATED PRINT RUN 100 SER.#'d SETS
151 Aaron Rodgers 30.00 80.00

2005 Playoff Prestige Xtra Points Red

*VETERANS: 3X TO 8X BASIC CARDS
*ROOKIES: 1.5X TO 4X BASIC CARDS
*ROOKIES: .25X TO .6X BASIC SP RC
VETERAN PRINT RUN 125 SER.#'d SETS
ROOKIE PRINT RUN 150 SER.#'d SETS
151 Aaron Rodgers 30.00 80.00

2005 Playoff Prestige Changing Stripes

*PRIME/25: .8X TO 2X BASIC JSY/250
CS1 Ahman Green 4.00 10.00
CS2 Clinton Portis 3.00 8.00
CS3 Duce Staley 3.00 8.00
CS4 Jevon Kearse 3.00 8.00
CS5 Terrell Owens 4.00 10.00
CS6 Jeff Garcia 3.00 8.00
CS7 Keyshawn Johnson 4.00 10.00
CS8 Drew Bledsoe 4.00 10.00
CS9 Jake Plummer 3.00 8.00
CS10 Marshall Faulk 4.00 10.00

2005 Playoff Prestige Draft Picks

COMPLETE SET (10) 15.00 40.00
STATED ODDS 1:24
*FOIL: 1X TO 2.5X BASIC INSERTS
FOIL PRINT RUN 100 SER.#'d SETS
*HOLOFOIL: 2.5X TO 6X BASIC INSERTS
HOLOFOIL PRINT RUN 25 SER.#'d SETS
DP1 Alex Smith QB 2.50 6.00
DP2 Aaron Rodgers 8.00 20.00
DP3 Charlie Frye .60 1.50
DP4 Cedric Benson .60 1.50
DP5 Ronnie Brown .75 2.00
DP6 Cadillac Williams .60 1.50
DP7 Vernand Morency .60 1.50
DP8 Braylon Edwards .60 1.50
DP9 Troy Williamson .60 1.50
DP10 Roddy White 1.00 2.50

2005 Playoff Prestige Draft Picks Rights Autographs

STATED PRINT RUN 50 SER.#'d SETS
DP1 Alex Smith QB 50.00 100.00
DP2 Aaron Rodgers 250.00 400.00
DP3 Charlie Frye 10.00 25.00
DP4 Cedric Benson 20.00 50.00
DP5 Ronnie Brown 12.00 30.00
DP6 Cadillac Williams 10.00 25.00
DP7 Vernand Morency 10.00 25.00
DP8 Braylon Edwards 10.00 25.00
DP9 Troy Williamson 10.00 25.00
DP10 Roddy White 15.00 40.00

2005 Playoff Prestige Fans of the Game

COMPLETE SET (4) 4.00 10.00
STATED ODDS 1:24
FG1 Rick Reilly 1.00 2.50
FG2 Heather Mitts 1.25 3.00
FG3 Rulon Gardner .75 2.00
FG4 Sue Bird 1.25 3.00

2005 Playoff Prestige Fans of the Game Autographs

STATED ODDS 1:625
FG1 Rick Reilly 12.00 30.00
FG2 Heather Mitts 20.00 50.00
FG3 Rulon Gardner 12.00 30.00
FG4 Sue Bird 20.00 50.00

2005 Playoff Prestige Game Day Jerseys

GJ1 David Carr 2.00 5.00
GJ2 Peyton Manning 8.00 20.00
GJ3 Randy Moss 2.50 6.00
GJ4 Donovan McNabb 2.50 6.00
GJ5 Tom Brady 12.00 30.00
GJ6 Larry Fitzgerald 3.00 8.00
GJ7 Shaun Alexander 2.00 5.00
GJ8 Anquan Boldin 2.00 5.00
GJ9 Daunte Culpepper 2.50 6.00
GJ10 Chris Brown 2.00 5.00
GJ11 Isaac Bruce 3.00 8.00
GJ12 Rod Smith 2.50 6.00
GJ13 Roy Williams S 2.00 5.00
GJ14 Tony Gonzalez 2.50 6.00
GJ15 Torry Holt 2.50 6.00
GJ16 John Abraham 2.00 5.00
GJ17 Ike Hilliard 2.00 5.00
GJ18 Jimmy Smith 2.50 6.00
GJ19 Byron Leftwich 2.00 5.00
GJ20 Stephen Davis 2.00 5.00
GJ21 T.J. Duckett 2.00 5.00
GJ22 Travis Henry 2.00 5.00
GJ23 Julius Peppers 2.50 6.00
GJ24 Charles Rogers 2.00 5.00
GJ25 Eric Moulds 2.00 5.00
GJ26 Freddie Mitchell 2.00 5.00
GJ27 Anthony Thomas 2.00 5.00
GJ28 Steve McNair 2.50 6.00
GJ29 Brian Urlacher 3.00 8.00
GJ30 Donte Stallworth 2.00 5.00

2005 Playoff Prestige Gridiron Heritage

STATED ODDS 1:24
*FOIL: .6X TO 1.5X BASIC INSERTS
FOIL PRINT RUN 100 SER.#'d SETS
*HOLOFOIL: 2X TO 5X BASIC INSERTS
HOLOFOIL PRINT RUN 25 SER.#'d SETS
GH1 Brett Favre 2.50 6.00
GH2 Edgerrin James 1.00 2.50
GH3 Byron Leftwich .75 2.00
GH4 Peyton Manning 3.00 8.00
GH5 Larry Fitzgerald 1.25 3.00
GH6 Shaun Alexander .75 2.00
GH7 Daunte Culpepper 1.00 2.50
GH8 Marshall Faulk 1.00 2.50
GH9 Steve McNair 1.00 2.50
GH10 Zach Thomas 1.00 2.50
GH11 Mike Alstott .75 2.00
GH12 Jeremiah Trotter .75 2.00
GH13 Drew Brees 1.25 3.00
GH14 Isaac Bruce 1.25 3.00
GH15 Chris Chambers .75 2.00
GH16 Santana Moss 1.00 2.50
GH17 Peerless Price .75 2.00
GH18 Donald Driver 1.00 2.50
GH19 Amani Toomer .75 2.00
GH20 Todd Pinkston .75 2.00
GH21 Derrick Mason .75 2.00
GH22 Jimmy Smith 1.00 2.50
GH23 Michael Vick 1.00 2.50
GH24 Andre Johnson 1.00 2.50
GH25 Josh McCown 1.00 2.50

2005 Playoff Prestige Gridiron Heritage Jerseys

STATED ODDS 1:60
GH1 Brett Favre 8.00 20.00
GH2 Edgerrin James 3.00 8.00
GH3 Byron Leftwich 2.50 6.00
GH4 Peyton Manning 10.00 25.00
GH5 Larry Fitzgerald 4.00 10.00
GH6 Shaun Alexander 2.50 6.00
GH7 Daunte Culpepper 3.00 8.00
GH8 Marshall Faulk 3.00 8.00
GH9 Steve McNair 3.00 8.00
GH10 Zach Thomas 3.00 8.00
GH11 Mike Alstott 2.50 6.00
GH12 Jeremiah Trotter 2.50 6.00
GH13 Drew Brees 4.00 10.00
GH14 Isaac Bruce 4.00 10.00
GH15 Chris Chambers 2.50 6.00
GH16 Santana Moss 3.00 8.00
GH17 Peerless Price 2.50 6.00
GH18 Donald Driver 3.00 8.00
GH19 Amani Toomer 2.50 6.00
GH20 Todd Pinkston 2.50 6.00
GH21 Derrick Mason 2.50 6.00
GH22 Jimmy Smith 3.00 8.00
GH23 Michael Vick 3.00 8.00
GH24 Andre Johnson 3.00 8.00
GH25 Josh McCown 3.00 8.00

2005 Playoff Prestige League Leaders

STATED ODDS 1:24
*FOIL: .6X TO 1.5X BASIC INSERTS
FOIL PRINT RUN 100 SER.#'d SETS
*HOLOFOIL: 2X TO 5X BASIC INSERTS
HOLOFOIL PRINT RUN 25 SER.#'d SETS
LL1 P.Manning/T.Green 3.00 8.00
LL2 D.Culpepper/B.Favre 2.50 6.00
LL3 D.McNabb/A.Brooks 1.00 2.50
LL4 J.Plummer/D.Bledsoe 1.00 2.50
LL5 T.Brady/D.Carr 5.00 12.00
LL6 M.Bulger/M.Hasselbeck .75 2.00
LL7 C.Palmer/B.Leftwich 1.00 2.50
LL8 S.Alexander/C.Portis .75 2.00
LL9 E.James/C.Dillon 1.00 2.50
LL10 C.Martin/L.Tomlinson 1.25 3.00
LL11 T.Barber/A.Green 1.00 2.50
LL12 Ru.Johnson/F.Taylor .75 2.00
LL13 W.McGahee/D.Davis .75 2.00
LL14 Kev.Jones/McAllister 1.00 2.50
LL15 Key.Johnson/L.Coles 1.00 2.50
LL16 J.Walker/T.Holt 1.00 2.50
LL17 Ch.Johnson/D.Bennett 1.00 2.50
LL18 I.Bruce/T.Owens 1.25 3.00
LL19 R.Smith/P.Burress 1.00 2.50
LL20 M.Clayton/D.Jackson .75 2.00
LL21 Mart/Dill/Alex/Barb 1.00 2.50
LL22 James/Toml/Port/A.Grn 1.50 4.00
LL23 Ru.Jhn/Tay/K.Jns/McAllis 1.25 3.00
LL24 T.Grn/P.Mnn/Fvre/Culp 4.00 10.00
LL25 Plum/Brdy/Dlhm/McNbb 6.00 15.00
LL26 Carr/Plmer/Blger/Brooks 1.25 3.00
LL27 C.Jhn/Ben/Ky.Jhn/Cles 1.25 3.00
LL28 Gonz/Burress/Walk/Holt 1.25 3.00
LL29 J.Smth/R.Smth/Brce/Driv 1.50 4.00
LL30 Masn/An.Jhn/TO/Mi.Clyt 1.25 3.00

2005 Playoff Prestige League Leaders Jerseys

STATED PRINT RUN 250 SER.#'d SETS
*PRIME: 1X TO 2.5X BASIC JERSEYS
PRIME PRINT RUN 25 SER.#'d SETS
LL1 P.Manning/T.Green 12.00 30.00
LL2 D.Culpepper/B.Favre 10.00 25.00
LL3 D.McNabb/A.Brooks 4.00 10.00
LL4 J.Plummer/D.Bledsoe 4.00 10.00
LL5 T.Brady/D.Carr 10.00 25.00
LL6 M.Bulger/M.Hasselbeck 3.00 8.00
LL7 C.Palmer/B.Leftwich 4.00 10.00
LL8 S.Alexander/C.Portis 3.00 8.00
LL9 E.James/C.Dillon 4.00 10.00
LL10 C.Martin/L.Tomlinson 5.00 12.00
LL11 T.Barber/A.Green 4.00 10.00
LL12 Ru.Johnson/F.Taylor 3.00 8.00
LL13 W.McGahee/D.Davis 3.00 8.00
LL14 Kev.Jones/McAllister 4.00 10.00
LL15 Key.Johnson/L.Coles 4.00 10.00
LL16 J.Walker/T.Holt 4.00 10.00
LL17 Ch.Johnson/D.Bennett 4.00 10.00
LL18 I.Bruce/T.Owens 5.00 12.00
LL19 R.Smith/P.Burress 4.00 10.00
LL20 M.Clayton/D.Jackson 3.00 8.00
LL21 Mart/Dill/Alex/Barb 6.00 15.00
LL22 James/Toml/Port/A.Grn 8.00 20.00
LL23 Ru.Jhn/Tay/K.Jns/McAllis 6.00 15.00
LL24 T.Grn/P.Mnn/Fvre/Culp 20.00 50.00
LL25 Plum/Brdy/Dlhm/McNbb 15.00 40.00
LL26 Carr/Plmer/Blger/Brooks 6.00 15.00
LL27 C.Jhn/Ben/Ky.Jhn/Cles 6.00 15.00
LL28 Gonz/Burress/Walk/Holt 6.00 15.00
LL29 J.Smth/R.Smth/Brce/Driv 8.00 20.00
LL30 Masn/An.Jhn/TO/Mi.Clyt 6.00 15.00

2005 Playoff Prestige Prestigious Pros Orange

ORANGE PRINT RUN 500 SER.#'d SETS
*BLUE/250: .6X TO 1.5X ORANGE
BLUE PRINT RUN 250 SER.#'d SETS
*GOLD/25: 2X TO 5X BASIC INSERTS
GOLD PRINT RUN 25 SER.#'d SETS
*GREEN/75: 1X TO 2.5X BASIC INSERTS
GREEN PRINT RUN 75 SER.#'d SETS
*PLATINUM/10: 3X TO 8X ORANGE
UNPRICED PLATINUM PRINT RUN 10 SETS
*PURPLE/100: 1X TO 2.5X BASIC INSERTS
PURPLE PRINT RUN 100 SER.#'d SETS
*RED/150: .8X TO 2X BASIC INSERTS
RED PRINT RUN 150 SER.#'d SETS
*SILVER/50: 1.2X TO 3X BASIC INSERTS
SILVER PRINT RUN 50 SER.#'d SETS
PP1 Aaron Brooks .60 1.50
PP2 Andre Johnson .75 2.00
PP3 Ben Roethlisberger 1.50 4.00
PP4 Brett Favre 2.00 5.00
PP5 Brian Urlacher 1.00 2.50
PP6 Byron Leftwich .60 1.50
PP7 Carson Palmer .75 2.00
PP8 Chad Pennington .60 1.50
PP9 Corey Dillon .60 1.50
PP10 Daunte Culpepper .75 2.00
PP11 David Carr .60 1.50
PP12 Deuce McAllister .75 2.00
PP13 Donovan McNabb .75 2.00
PP14 Drew Bledsoe .75 2.00
PP15 Drew Brees 1.00 2.50
PP16 Duce Staley .60 1.50
PP17 Edgerrin James .75 2.00
PP18 Hines Ward .75 2.00
PP19 Isaac Bruce 1.00 2.50
PP20 Jake Plummer .60 1.50
PP21 Jamal Lewis .75 2.00
PP22 Javon Walker .60 1.50
PP23 Jeff Garcia .60 1.50
PP24 Jeremy Shockey .60 1.50
PP25 Jevon Kearse .60 1.50
PP26 Joey Harrington .60 1.50
PP27 Keyshawn Johnson .75 2.00
PP28 LaDainian Tomlinson 1.00 2.50
PP29 LaVar Arrington .60 1.50
PP30 Lee Suggs .60 1.50
PP31 Marc Bulger .60 1.50
PP32 Marshall Faulk .75 2.00
PP33 Marvin Harrison .75 2.00
PP34 Matt Hasselbeck .60 1.50
PP35 Michael Vick .75 2.00
PP36 Peyton Manning 2.50 6.00
PP37 Plaxico Burress .60 1.50
PP38 Priest Holmes .60 1.50
PP39 Randy Moss .75 2.00
PP40 Ray Lewis 1.00 2.50
PP41 Rex Grossman .60 1.50
PP42 Rudi Johnson .60 1.50
PP43 Shaun Alexander .60 1.50
PP44 Steve McNair .75 2.00
PP45 Terrell Owens .75 2.00
PP46 Tiki Barber .75 2.00
PP47 Tom Brady 4.00 10.00
PP48 Tony Gonzalez .75 2.00
PP49 Torry Holt .75 2.00
PP50 Trent Green .60 1.50

2005 Playoff Prestige Prestigious Pros Jerseys Gold

GOLD PRINT RUN 100 SER.#'d SETS
UNPRICED PLAT.PATCH PRINT RUN 10
PP1 Aaron Brooks 3.00 8.00
PP2 Andre Johnson 4.00 10.00
PP3 Ben Roethlisberger 8.00 20.00
PP4 Brett Favre 10.00 25.00
PP5 Brian Urlacher 5.00 12.00
PP6 Byron Leftwich 3.00 8.00
PP7 Carson Palmer 4.00 10.00
PP8 Chad Pennington 3.00 8.00
PP9 Corey Dillon 3.00 8.00
PP10 Daunte Culpepper 4.00 10.00
PP11 David Carr 3.00 8.00
PP12 Deuce McAllister 4.00 10.00
PP13 Donovan McNabb 4.00 10.00
PP14 Drew Bledsoe 4.00 10.00
PP15 Drew Brees 5.00 12.00
PP16 Duce Staley 3.00 8.00
PP17 Edgerrin James 4.00 10.00
PP18 Hines Ward 4.00 10.00
PP19 Isaac Bruce 5.00 12.00
PP20 Jake Plummer 3.00 8.00
PP21 Jamal Lewis 4.00 10.00
PP22 Javon Walker 3.00 8.00
PP23 Jeff Garcia 3.00 8.00
PP24 Jeremy Shockey 3.00 8.00
PP25 Jevon Kearse 3.00 8.00
PP26 Joey Harrington 3.00 8.00
PP27 Keyshawn Johnson 4.00 10.00
PP28 LaDainian Tomlinson 5.00 12.00
PP29 LaVar Arrington 3.00 8.00
PP30 Lee Suggs 3.00 8.00
PP31 Marc Bulger 3.00 8.00
PP32 Marshall Faulk 4.00 10.00
PP33 Marvin Harrison 4.00 10.00
PP34 Matt Hasselbeck 3.00 8.00
PP35 Michael Vick 4.00 10.00
PP36 Peyton Manning 12.00 30.00
PP37 Plaxico Burress 3.00 8.00
PP38 Priest Holmes 3.00 8.00
PP39 Randy Moss 4.00 10.00
PP40 Ray Lewis 5.00 12.00
PP41 Rex Grossman 3.00 8.00
PP42 Rudi Johnson 3.00 8.00
PP43 Shaun Alexander 3.00 8.00
PP44 Steve McNair 4.00 10.00
PP45 Terrell Owens 4.00 10.00
PP46 Tiki Barber 4.00 10.00
PP47 Tom Brady 20.00 50.00
PP48 Tony Gonzalez 4.00 10.00
PP49 Torry Holt 4.00 10.00
PP50 Trent Green 3.00 8.00

2005 Playoff Prestige Stars of the NFL

STATED ODDS 1:24
*FOIL: .8X TO 2X BASIC INSERTS
FOIL PRINT RUN 100 SER.#'d SETS
*HOLOFOIL: 2X TO 5X BASIC INSERTS
HOLOFOIL PRINT RUN 25 SER.#'d SETS
1 Aaron Brooks .75 2.00

2 Andre Johnson 1.00 2.50
3 Brett Favre 2.50 6.00
4 Brian Urlacher 1.25 3.00
5 Byron Leftwich .75 2.00
6 Chad Johnson .75 2.00
7 Chad Pennington .75 2.00
8 Chris Brown .75 2.00
9 Daunte Culpepper 1.00 2.50
10 David Carr .75 2.00
11 Donovan McNabb 1.00 2.50
12 Drew Bledsoe 1.00 2.50
13 Edgerrin James 1.00 2.50
14 Isaac Bruce 1.25 3.00
15 Jake Delhomme .75 2.00
16 Javon Walker .75 2.00
17 Jeremy Shockey .75 2.00
18 LaDainian Tomlinson 1.25 3.00
19 Marvin Harrison 1.00 2.50
20 Matt Hasselbeck .75 2.00
21 Michael Vick 1.00 2.50
22 Peyton Manning 3.00 8.00
23 Randy Moss 1.00 2.50
24 Priest Holmes .75 2.00
25 Tom Brady 5.00 12.00

2005 Playoff Prestige Stars of the NFL Jersey

STATED ODDS 1:104
*PRIME: 1X TO 2.5X BASIC INSERTS
PRIME PRINT RUN 25 SER.#'d SETS
1 Aaron Brooks 2.50 6.00
2 Andre Johnson 3.00 8.00
3 Brett Favre 8.00 20.00
4 Brian Urlacher 4.00 10.00
5 Byron Leftwich 2.50 6.00
6 Chad Johnson 2.50 6.00
7 Chad Pennington 2.50 6.00
8 Chris Brown 2.50 6.00
9 Daunte Culpepper 3.00 8.00
10 David Carr 2.50 6.00
11 Donovan McNabb 3.00 8.00
12 Drew Bledsoe 3.00 8.00
13 Edgerrin James 3.00 8.00
14 Isaac Bruce 4.00 10.00
15 Jake Delhomme 2.50 6.00
16 Javon Walker 2.50 6.00
17 Jeremy Shockey 2.50 6.00
18 LaDainian Tomlinson 4.00 10.00
19 Marvin Harrison 3.00 8.00
20 Matt Hasselbeck 2.50 6.00
21 Michael Vick 3.00 8.00
22 Peyton Manning 10.00 25.00
23 Randy Moss 3.00 8.00
24 Priest Holmes 2.50 6.00
25 Tom Brady 15.00 40.00

2005 Playoff Prestige Super Bowl Heroes

COMPLETE SET (10) 7.50 20.00
STATED ODDS 1:24
*FOIL: .8X TO 2X BASIC INSERTS
FOIL PRINT RUN 100 SER.#'d SETS
SH1 Tom Brady 5.00 12.00
SH2 Deion Branch .75 2.00
SH3 Corey Dillon .75 2.00
SH4 David Givens .75 2.00
SH5 Mike Vrabel 1.25 3.00
SH6 Tedy Bruschi 1.00 2.50
SH7 Rodney Harrison .75 2.00
SH8 Adam Vinatieri .75 2.00
SH9 Donovan McNabb 1.00 2.50
SH10 Terrell Owens 1.00 2.50

2005 Playoff Prestige Super Bowl Heroes Holofoil

HOLOFOIL PRINT RUN 25 SER.#'d SETS
SH1 Tom Brady SP 40.00 100.00
SH1AU Tom Brady AU 175.00 300.00
SH2 Deion Branch 4.00 10.00
SH3 Corey Dillon AU 40.00 80.00
SH4 David Givens 4.00 10.00
SH5 Mike Vrabel 6.00 15.00
SH6 Tedy Bruschi SP 10.00 25.00
SH6AU Tedy Bruschi AU SP 90.00 150.00
SH7 Rodney Harrison 4.00 10.00
SH8 Adam Vinatieri SP 15.00 40.00
SH8AU Adam Vinatieri AU SP 60.00 100.00
SH9 Donovan McNabb AU 50.00 100.00
SH10 Terrell Owens

2005 Playoff Prestige Turning Pro Jerseys

*PRIME/25: .8X TO 2X BASIC JSY/250
TP1 Lee Suggs 3.00 8.00
TP2 Barry Sanders 8.00 20.00
TP3 Andre Johnson 4.00 10.00
TP4 Kyle Boller 3.00 8.00
TP5 Carson Palmer 4.00 10.00
TP6 Michael Vick 4.00 10.00
TP7 Laveranues Coles 3.00 8.00
TP8 Clinton Portis 3.00 8.00
TP9 Edgerrin James 4.00 10.00
TP10 Marshall Faulk 4.00 10.00

2006 Playoff Prestige

This 250-card set was released in May, 2006. The set was issued in both hobby and retail form. The hobby packs had five-cards in them with an $3 SRP and those packs came 24 to a box while the retail packs had eight cards, with a $2.99 SRP, and those packs also came 24 to a box. Cards numbered 1-150 featured players in first name alphabetical order sequenced in alphabetical team order while cards numbered 151-250 featured 2006 rookies in first name alphabetical order. The rookies were inserted into the packs at a stated rate of oner per. A few rookies were printed in shorter quantity and we have notated those cards in our checklist.

COMP.SET w/o SP's (239) 50.00 100.00
COMP.SET w/o RC's (150) 10.00 25.00
ONE ROOKIE PER HOBBY PACK
1 Anquan Boldin .25 .60
2 J.J. Arrington .25 .60
3 Josh McCown .25 .60
4 Larry Fitzgerald .30 .75
5 Marcel Shipp .25 .60
6 Alge Crumpler .30 .75
7 Michael Vick .30 .75
8 T.J. Duckett .25 .60
9 Warrick Dunn .25 .60
10 Michael Jenkins .25 .60
11 Derrick Mason .25 .60
12 Jamal Lewis .30 .75
13 Kyle Boller .25 .60
14 Mark Clayton .25 .60
15 Ray Lewis .40 1.00
16 Eric Moulds .25 .60
17 J.P. Losman .30 .75
18 Lee Evans .30 .75
19 Willis McGahee .25 .60
20 Jake Delhomme .25 .60
21 Julius Peppers .30 .75
22 Keary Colbert .25 .60
23 Stephen Davis .25 .60
24 Steve Smith .40 1.00
25 Brian Urlacher .40 1.00
26 Cedric Benson .25 .60
27 Kyle Orton .25 .60
28 Mark Bradley .25 .60
29 Muhsin Muhammad .25 .60
30 Thomas Jones .25 .60
31 Carson Palmer .30 .75
32 Chad Johnson .25 .60
33 Rudi Johnson .25 .60
34 T.J. Houshmandzadeh .25 .60
35 Braylon Edwards .25 .60
36 Dennis Northcutt .25 .60
37 Antonio Bryant .25 .60
38 Reuben Droughns .30 .75
39 Trent Dilfer .25 .60
40 Drew Bledsoe .30 .75
41 Jason Witten .30 .75
42 Julius Jones .25 .60
43 Keyshawn Johnson .30 .75
44 Roy Williams S .25 .60
45 Terry Glenn .30 .75
46 Ashley Lelie .25 .60
47 Jake Plummer .25 .60
48 Mike Anderson .25 .60
49 Rod Smith .30 .75
50 Tatum Bell .25 .60
51 Joey Harrington .25 .60
52 Kevin Jones .25 .60
53 Mike Williams .25 .60
54 Roy Williams WR .25 .60
55 Aaron Rodgers 1.00 2.50
56 Brett Favre .75 2.00
57 Donald Driver .30 .75
58 Javon Walker .30 .75
59 Ahman Green .30 .75
60 Andre Johnson .30 .75
61 Corey Bradford .25 .60
62 David Carr .25 .60
63 Domanick Davis .25 .60
64 Jabar Gaffney .25 .60
65 Brandon Stokley .25 .60
66 Dallas Clark .25 .60
67 Edgerrin James .30 .75
68 Marvin Harrison .30 .75
69 Peyton Manning 1.00 2.50
70 Reggie Wayne .30 .75
71 Byron Leftwich .25 .60
72 Fred Taylor .25 .60
73 Jimmy Smith .30 .75
74 Matt Jones .25 .60
75 Reggie Williams .30 .75
76 Eddie Kennison .25 .60
77 Larry Johnson .25 .60
78 Priest Holmes .25 .60
79 Tony Gonzalez .30 .75
80 Trent Green .25 .60
81 Chris Chambers .25 .60
82 Marty Booker .25 .60
83 Randy McMichael .25 .60
84 Ricky Williams .25 .60
85 Ronnie Brown .30 .75
86 Zach Thomas .30 .75
87 Daunte Culpepper .30 .75
88 Mewelde Moore .25 .60
89 Nate Burleson .25 .60
90 Jim Kleinsasser .25 .60
91 Corey Dillon .25 .60
92 David Givens .30 .75
93 Deion Branch .25 .60
94 Tedy Bruschi .30 .75
95 Tom Brady 1.25 3.00
96 Aaron Brooks .25 .60
97 Deuce McAllister .30 .75
98 Donte Stallworth .25 .60
99 Joe Horn .25 .60
100 Amani Toomer .25 .60
101 Eli Manning .30 .75
102 Jeremy Shockey .25 .60
103 Plaxico Burress .25 .60
104 Tiki Barber .30 .75
105 Chad Pennington .25 .60
106 Curtis Martin .30 .75
107 Justin McCareins .25 .60
108 Laveranues Coles .25 .60
109 Jerry Porter .25 .60
110 Kerry Collins .25 .60
111 LaMont Jordan .30 .75
112 Randy Moss .30 .75
113 Brian Westbrook .25 .60
114 Donovan McNabb .30 .75
115 Terrell Owens .30 .75
116 L.J. Smith .25 .60
117 Ben Roethlisberger .50 1.25
118 Hines Ward .30 .75
119 Heath Miller .25 .60
120 Willie Parker .30 .75
121 Jerome Bettis .40 1.00
122 Antonio Gates .40 1.00
123 Drew Brees .40 1.00
124 Keenan McCardell .30 .75
125 LaDainian Tomlinson .40 1.00
126 Alex Smith QB .30 .75
127 Brandon Lloyd .25 .60
128 Frank Gore .30 .75
129 Kevan Barlow .25 .60
130 Darrell Jackson .30 .75
131 Joe Jurevicius .25 .60
132 Matt Hasselbeck .25 .60
133 Shaun Alexander .25 .60
134 Isaac Bruce .40 1.00
135 Marc Bulger .25 .60
136 Marshall Faulk .30 .75
137 Steven Jackson .25 .60
138 Torry Holt .30 .75
139 Cadillac Williams .30 .75
140 Derrick Brooks .25 .60
141 Joey Galloway .30 .75
142 Michael Clayton .25 .60
143 Brandon Jones .25 .60
144 Chris Brown .25 .60
145 Steve McNair .30 .75
146 Tyrone Calico .25 .60
147 Clinton Portis .25 .60
148 Mark Brunell .30 .75
149 Santana Moss .30 .75
150 David Patten .25 .60
151 A.J. Hawk SP RC 15.00 40.00
152 Abdul Hodge RC .75 2.00
153 Alan Zemaitis RC .75 2.00
154 Andre Hall RC 1.00 2.50
155 Anthony Fasano RC .75 2.00
156 Ashton Youboty RC .75 2.00
157 Erik Meyer RC .75 2.00
158 Bobby Carpenter RC .75 2.00
159 Brad Smith RC 1.00 2.50
160 Brandon Kirsch RC 1.00 2.50
161 Brandon Marshall SP RC 8.00 20.00
162 Brandon Williams RC .75 2.00
163 Brian Calhoun SP RC 6.00 15.00
164 Brodie Croyle SP RC 10.00 25.00
165 Brodrick Bunkley RC 1.00 2.50
166 Bruce Gradkowski RC 1.00 2.50
167 Cedric Griffin RC 1.00 2.50
168 Cedric Humes RC .75 2.00
169 Chad Greenway RC 1.25 3.00
170 Chad Jackson RC .75 2.00
171 Charlie Whitehurst RC .75 2.00
172 Cory Rodgers RC .75 2.00
173 D.J. Shockley RC 1.00 2.50
174 Darnell Bing RC 1.00 2.50
175 Darrell Hackney RC 1.00 2.50
176 David Thomas SP RC 6.00 15.00
177 D'Brickashaw Ferguson RC .75 2.00
178 DeAngelo Williams RC 1.00 2.50
179 Dee Webb RC 1.00 2.50
180 Delanie Walker RC 1.50 4.00
181 DeMeco Ryans RC 1.00 2.50
182 Demetrius Williams RC .75 2.00
183 Derek Hagan RC 1.00 2.50
184 Devin Aromashodu RC .75 2.00
185 Dominique Byrd RC .75 2.00
186 DonTrell Moore RC 1.00 2.50
187 D'Qwell Jackson RC .75 2.00
188 Drew Olson RC .75 2.00
189 Eric Winston RC .75 2.00
190 Ernie Sims RC .75 2.00
191 Gerald Riggs RC 1.00 2.50
192 Greg Jennings RC 1.25 3.00
193 Greg Lee RC .75 2.00
194 Haloti Ngata RC 1.00 2.50
195 Hank Baskett RC .75 2.00
196 Jason Avant RC .75 2.00
197 Jason Carter RC 1.00 2.50
198 Jay Cutler RC 1.00 2.50
199 Jeff Webb RC 1.00 2.50
200 Jeremy Bloom RC .75 2.00
201 Jerious Norwood RC .75 2.00
202 Jerome Harrison RC .75 2.00
203 Jimmy Williams RC .75 2.00
204 Joe Klopfenstein RC .75 2.00
205 Johnathan Joseph RC 1.00 2.50
206 Jonathan Orr RC 1.00 2.50
207 Joseph Addai RC .75 2.00
208 Kai Parham RC 1.25 3.00
209 Kamerion Wimbley RC 1.00 2.50
210 Kellen Clemens RC .75 2.00
211 Kelly Jennings RC 1.00 2.50
212 Ko Simpson RC 1.00 2.50
213 Laurence Maroney RC .75 2.00
214 Lawrence Vickers RC 1.00 2.50
215 LenDale White RC .75 2.00
216 Leon Washington RC .75 2.00
217 Leonard Pope RC 1.25 3.00
218 Marcedes Lewis RC .75 2.00
219 Marcus Vick SP RC 8.00 20.00
220 Mario Williams RC 1.25 3.00
221 Martin Nance RC .75 2.00
222 Mathias Kiwanuka RC 1.25 3.00
223 Matt Leinart RC .75 2.00
224 Maurice Drew SP RC 15.00 30.00
225 Maurice Stovall SP RC 6.00 15.00
226 Michael Huff RC 1.00 2.50
227 Michael Robinson SP RC 6.00 15.00
228 Mike Hass RC .75 2.00
229 Omar Jacobs RC .75 2.00
230 Paul Pinegar RC .75 2.00
231 Reggie Bush RC 1.25 3.00
232 Reggie McNeal RC .75 2.00
233 Rodrique Wright RC .75 2.00
234 Santonio Holmes RC 1.00 2.50
235 Sinorice Moss RC .75 2.00
236 Skyler Green RC .75 2.00
237 Tamba Hali RC 1.25 3.00
238 Tarvaris Jackson RC .75 2.00
239 Taurean Henderson RC .75 2.00
240 Terrence Whitehead RC 1.00 2.50
241 Tim Day SP RC 6.00 15.00
242 Todd Watkins RC .75 2.00
243 Travis Wilson RC .75 2.00
244 Tye Hill RC .75 2.00
245 Vernon Davis RC 1.00 2.50
246 Vince Young RC .75 2.00
247 Wali Lundy RC .75 2.00
248 Wendell Mathis RC 1.00 2.50
249 Willie Reid SP RC 6.00 15.00
250 Winston Justice RC 1.00 2.50

2006 Playoff Prestige Xtra Points Black

*VETERANS: 8X TO 20X BASIC CARDS
*ROOKIES: 3X TO 8X BASIC CARDS
*ROOKIE SPs: .5X TO 1.2X BASIC CARDS
STATED PRINT RUN 25 SER.#'d SETS

2006 Playoff Prestige Xtra Points Blue

*VETERANS: 1.5X TO 4X BASIC CARDS
*ROOKIES: .8X TO 2X BASIC CARDS
*ROOKIE SPs: .1X TO .25X BASIC CARDS
RANDOM INSERTS IN RETAIL PACKS

2006 Playoff Prestige Xtra Points Brown Retail

*VETS: 2X TO 5X BASIC CARDS
*ROOKIES: 1X TO 2.5X BASIC CARDS
*ROOKIE SPs: .25X TO .6X BASIC CARDS
RANDOM INSERTS IN RETAIL PACKS

2006 Playoff Prestige Xtra Points Gold

*VETS: 2X TO 5X BASIC CARDS
*ROOKIES: 1X TO 2.5X BASIC CARDS
*ROOKIE SPs: .25X TO .6X BASIC CARDS

2006 Playoff Prestige Xtra Points Green

*VETERANS: 5X TO 12X BASIC CARDS
*ROOKIES: 2X TO 5X BASIC CARDS
*ROOKIE SPs: .4X TO 1X BASIC CARDS
STATED PRINT RUN 50 SER.#'d SETS

2006 Playoff Prestige Xtra Points Purple

*VETERANS: 4X TO 10X BASIC CARDS
*ROOKIES: 1.5X TO 4X BASIC CARDS
*ROOKIE SPs: .3X TO .8X BASIC CARDS
STATED PRINT RUN 75 SER.#'d SETS

2006 Playoff Prestige Xtra Points Red

*VETERANS: 3X TO 8X BASIC CARDS
*ROOKIES: 1.2X TO 3X BASIC CARDS
*ROOKIE SPs: .3X TO .8X BASIC CARDS
STATED PRINT RUN 100 SER.#'d SETS

2006 Playoff Prestige Changing Stripes

*PRIME/25: .8X TO 2X BASIC JSY/250
1 Randy Moss 3.00 8.00
2 Drew Bledsoe 3.00 8.00
3 Laveranues Coles 2.50 6.00
4 Corey Dillon 2.50 6.00
5 Curtis Martin 3.00 8.00
6 Justin McCareins 2.50 6.00
7 Ricky Williams 2.50 6.00
8 Thomas Jones 2.50 6.00
9 Trent Green 2.50 6.00
10 Warrick Dunn 2.50 6.00

2006 Playoff Prestige Draft Picks

STATED ODDS 1:14
*FOIL: 1X TO 2.5X BASIC INSERTS
FOIL PRINT RUN 100 SER.#'d SETS
*HOLOFOIL: 2X TO 5X BASIC INSERTS
HOLOFOIL PRINT RUN 25 SER.#'d SETS
1 Reggie Bush .75 2.00
2 Matt Leinart .50 1.25
3 Vince Young .50 1.25
4 Jay Cutler .60 1.50
5 DeAngelo Williams .60 1.50
6 Joseph Addai .50 1.25
7 Santonio Holmes .60 1.50
8 Demetrius Williams .50 1.25
9 Jason Avant .50 1.25
10 D'Brickashaw Ferguson .50 1.25
11 Mario Williams .75 2.00
12 A.J. Hawk .60 1.50
13 Tye Hill .50 1.25
14 Michael Huff .60 1.50
15 Joe Klopfenstein .50 1.25
16 Sinorice Moss .50 1.25
17 Maurice Stovall .50 1.25
18 Michael Robinson .50 1.25
19 Travis Wilson .50 1.25
20 LenDale White .50 1.25

2006 Playoff Prestige Draft Picks Rights Autographs

STATED PRINT RUN 50 SER.#'d SETS
DP1 Reggie Bush 15.00 40.00
DP2 Matt Leinart 10.00 25.00
DP3 Vince Young 10.00 25.00
DP4 Jay Cutler 12.00 30.00
DP5 DeAngelo Williams 12.00 30.00
DP6 Joseph Addai 10.00 25.00
DP7 Santonio Holmes 12.00 30.00
DP8 Demetrius Williams 10.00 25.00
DP9 Jason Avant 10.00 25.00
DP10 D'Brickashaw Ferguson 10.00 25.00
DP11 Mario Williams 15.00 40.00
DP12 A.J. Hawk 12.00 30.00
DP13 Tye Hill 10.00 25.00
DP14 Michael Huff 12.00 30.00
DP15 Joe Klopfenstein 10.00 25.00
DP16 Sinorice Moss 10.00 25.00
DP17 Maurice Stovall 10.00 25.00
DP18 Michael Robinson 10.00 25.00
DP19 Travis Wilson 10.00 25.00
DP20 LenDale White 10.00 25.00

2006 Playoff Prestige Gridiron Heritage

STATED ODDS 1:17 HOB, 1:10 RET
*FOIL: .8X TO 2X BASIC INSERTS
FOIL PRINT RUN 100 SER.#'d SETS
*HOLOFOIL: 2X TO 5X BASIC INSERTS
HOLOFOIL PRINT RUN 25 SER.#'d SETS
1 Aaron Brooks .60 1.50
2 Ahman Green .75 2.00
3 Alge Crumpler .75 2.00
4 Antonio Gates 1.00 2.50
5 Byron Leftwich .60 1.50
6 Jonathan Vilma .60 1.50
7 Julius Peppers .75 2.00
8 Darrell Jackson .75 2.00
9 Daunte Culpepper .75 2.00
10 David Carr .60 1.50
11 David Givens .75 2.00
12 Brett Favre 2.00 5.00
13 Chad Pennington .60 1.50
14 Deuce McAllister .75 2.00
15 Domanick Davis .60 1.50
16 Terrell Suggs .60 1.50
17 Drew Brees 1.00 2.50
18 Eric Moulds .60 1.50
19 Jerome Bettis 1.00 2.50
20 Kyle Brady .60 1.50
21 Kevin Jones .60 1.50
22 Keyshawn Johnson .75 2.00
23 Marc Bulger .60 1.50
24 Marcel Shipp .60 1.50
25 Marvin Harrison .75 2.00
26 Matt Hasselbeck .60 1.50
27 Michael Vick .75 2.00
28 Richard Seymour .60 1.50
29 Peyton Manning 2.50 6.00
30 Randy Moss .75 2.00
31 Ricky Williams .60 1.50
32 Shaun Alexander .60 1.50
33 Michael Bennett .60 1.50
34 Tony Gonzalez .75 2.00
35 Trent Green .60 1.50

2006 Playoff Prestige Gridiron Heritage Jerseys

*PRIME/50: .6X TO 1.5X BASIC INSERTS
*PRIME/20: 1X TO 2.5X BASIC INSERTS
1 Aaron Brooks 2.00 5.00
2 Ahman Green 2.50 6.00
3 Alge Crumpler 2.50 6.00
4 Antonio Gates 3.00 8.00
5 Byron Leftwich 2.00 5.00
6 Jonathan Vilma 2.00 5.00
7 Julius Peppers 2.50 6.00
8 Darrell Jackson 2.50 6.00
9 Daunte Culpepper 2.50 6.00
10 David Carr 2.00 5.00
11 David Givens 2.50 6.00
12 Brett Favre 6.00 15.00
13 Chad Pennington 2.00 5.00
14 Deuce McAllister 2.50 6.00
15 Domanick Davis 2.00 5.00
16 Terrell Suggs 2.00 5.00
17 Drew Brees 3.00 8.00
18 Eric Moulds 2.00 5.00
19 Jerome Bettis 3.00 8.00
20 Kyle Brady 2.00 5.00
21 Kevin Jones 2.00 5.00
22 Keyshawn Johnson 2.50 6.00
23 Marc Bulger 2.00 5.00
24 Marcel Shipp 2.00 5.00
25 Marvin Harrison 2.50 6.00
26 Matt Hasselbeck 2.00 5.00
27 Michael Vick 2.50 6.00
28 Richard Seymour 2.00 5.00
29 Peyton Manning 8.00 20.00
30 Randy Moss 2.50 6.00
31 Ricky Williams 2.00 5.00
32 Shaun Alexander 2.00 5.00
33 Michael Bennett 2.00 5.00
34 Tony Gonzalez 2.50 6.00
35 Trent Green 2.00 5.00

2006 Playoff Prestige League Leaders

STATED ODDS 1:11
*FOIL: 1X TO 2.5X BASIC INSERTS
FOIL PRINT RUN 100 SER.#'d SETS
*HOLOFOIL: 2.5X TO 6X BASIC INSERTS
HOLOFOIL PRINT RUN 25 SER.#'d SETS
1 B.Favre/E.Manning 1.50 4.00
2 T.Brady/T.Green 2.50 6.00
3 D.Bledsoe/C.Palmer .60 1.50
4 M.Hasselbeck/K.Collins .50 1.25
5 S.Alexander/T.Barber .60 1.50
6 L.Johnson/E.James .60 1.50
7 C.Portis/L.Tomlinson .75 2.00
8 W.Dunn/R.Johnson .50 1.25
9 S.Smith/S.Moss .75 2.00
10 C.Johnson/M.Harrison .60 1.50
11 L.Fitzgerald/C.Chambers .60 1.50
12 A.Boldin/R.Smith .60 1.50
13 S.Alexander/S.Smith .75 2.00
14 L.Johnson/L.Tomlinson .75 2.00
15 S.Davis/E.James .60 1.50
16 T.Barber/C.Dillon .60 1.50
17 S.Smith/L.Fitzgerald .75 2.00
18 M.Harrison/C.Chambers .60 1.50
19 S.Alexander/S.Davis .50 1.25
20 L.Johnson/L.Tomlinson .75 2.00
21 Favre/Brady/Eli/Green 3.00 8.00
22 Bledsoe/Palmer/Hass/Collins .75 2.00
23 Alex/Johnson/Tiki/James .75 2.00
24 Portis/LT/Dunn/Rudi 1.00 2.50
25 S.Smith/Chad/Sntna/Marvin 1.00 2.50
26 Fitz/Chambers/Boldin/Rod .75 2.00
27 Alex/Johnson/Smith/LT 1.00 2.50
28 Davis/James/Tiki/Dillon .75 2.00
29 S.Smith/Marvin/Fitz/Chmb 1.00 2.50
30 Alexand/LJ/S.Davis/LT 1.00 2.50

2006 Playoff Prestige League Leaders Jerseys

STATED PRINT RUN 250 SER.#'d SETS
*PRIME/25: .8X TO 2X BASIC JSYs
1 B.Favre/E.Manning 8.00 20.00
2 T.Brady/T.Green 12.00 30.00
3 D.Bledsoe/C.Palmer 3.00 8.00
4 M.Hasselbeck/K.Collins 2.50 6.00
5 S.Alexander/T.Barber 3.00 8.00
6 L.Johnson/E.James 3.00 8.00
7 C.Portis/L.Tomlinson 4.00 10.00
8 W.Dunn/R.Johnson 2.50 6.00
9 S.Smith/S.Moss 4.00 10.00
10 C.Johnson/M.Harrison 3.00 8.00
11 L.Fitzgerald/C.Chambers 3.00 8.00
12 A.Boldin/R.Smith 3.00 8.00
13 S.Alexander/S.Smith 4.00 10.00
14 L.Johnson/L.Tomlinson 4.00 10.00
15 S.Davis/E.James 3.00 8.00
16 T.Barber/C.Dillon 3.00 8.00
17 S.Smith/L.Fitzgerald 4.00 10.00
18 M.Harrison/C.Chambers 3.00 8.00
19 S.Alexander/S.Davis 2.50 6.00
20 L.Johnson/L.Tomlinson 4.00 10.00
21 Favre/Brady/Eli/Green 12.00 30.00
22 Bledsoe/Palmer/Hass/Collins 3.00 8.00
23 Alex/Johnson/Tiki/James 3.00 8.00
24 Portis/LT/Dunn/Rudi 4.00 10.00
25 S.Smith/Chad/Sntna/Marvin 4.00 10.00
26 Fitz/Chambers/Boldin/Rod 3.00 8.00
27 Alex/Johnson/Smith/LT 4.00 10.00
28 Davis/James/Tiki/Dillon 3.00 8.00
29 S.Smith/Marvin/Fitz/Chmb 4.00 10.00
30 Alex/Johnson/Davis/LT 4.00 10.00

2006 Playoff Prestige Prestigious Pros Bronze

*BLACK: 1X TO 2.5X BRONZE
BLACK PRINT RUN 125 SER.#'d SETS
*BLUE: .8X TO 2X BRONZE
BLUE PRINT RUN 250 SER.#'d SETS
*GOLD: 2.5X TO 6X BRONZE
GOLD PRINT RUN 25 SER.#'d SETS
*GREEN: 1.2X TO 3X BRONZE
GREEN PRINT RUN 75 SER.#'d SETS
*ORANGE: .5X TO 1.2X BRONZE
ORANGE PRINT RUN 500 SER.#'d SETS
UNPRICED PLATINUM SER.#'d TO 10
*PURPLE: 1.2X TO 3X BRONZE
PURPLE PRINT RUN 100 SER.#'d SETS
*RED: 1X TO 2.5X BRONZE
RED PRINT RUN 150 SER.#'d SETS
*SILVER: 1.5X TO 4X BRONZE
SILVER PRINT RUN 50 SER.#'d SETS
UNPRICED AUTO PRINT RUN 1-10 SETS
1 Amani Toomer .60 1.50
2 Andre Johnson .75 2.00
3 Antwaan Randle El .60 1.50
4 Ashley Lelie .60 1.50
5 Anquan Boldin .60 1.50
6 Ben Roethlisberger 1.25 3.00
7 Bethel Johnson .60 1.50
8 Brandon Lloyd .60 1.50
9 Brian Urlacher 1.00 2.50
10 Bryant Johnson .60 1.50
11 Chad Johnson .60 1.50
12 Carson Palmer .75 2.00
13 Darrell Jackson .75 2.00
14 Domanick Davis .60 1.50
15 Donovan McNabb .75 2.00
16 Isaac Bruce 1.00 2.50
17 J.P. Losman .75 2.00
18 Jake Delhomme .60 1.50
19 Jevon Kearse .60 1.50
20 Jeff Garcia .60 1.50
21 Jimmy Smith .75 2.00
22 Corey Dillon .60 1.50
23 Josh McCown .60 1.50
24 Josh Reed .60 1.50
25 Curtis Martin .75 2.00
26 Julius Jones .60 1.50
27 Randy McMichael .60 1.50
28 Keary Colbert .60 1.50
29 Joey Harrington .60 1.50
30 LaMont Jordan .75 2.00
31 Marshall Faulk .75 2.00
32 Tom Brady 3.00 8.00
33 Michael Strahan .75 2.00
34 Nate Clements .60 1.50
35 Mike Anderson .60 1.50
36 Nick Barnett .60 1.50
37 Randy Moss .75 2.00
38 Reggie Wayne .75 2.00
39 Rex Grossman .60 1.50
40 Priest Holmes .60 1.50
41 Ricky Williams .60 1.50
42 Rudi Johnson .60 1.50
43 T.J. Duckett .60 1.50
44 Steve Smith 1.00 2.50
45 Tatum Bell .60 1.50
46 Donte Stallworth .60 1.50
47 Thomas Jones .60 1.50
48 Torry Holt .75 2.00
49 Wayne Chrebet .60 1.50
50 Robert Ferguson .60 1.50

2006 Playoff Prestige Prestigious Pros Jerseys Green

GREEN PRINT RUN 100 SER.#'d SETS
*BLACK/15: .8X TO 2X GREEN JSYs
*BRONZE/122-250: .3X TO .8X GREEN JSYs
*BRONZE/35-50: .5X TO 1.2X GREEN JSYs
*GOLD/25: .6X TO 1.5X GREEN JSYs
*PLATINUM/25: .8X TO 2X GREEN JSYs
*ORANGE: .3X TO .8X GREEN JSYs
1 Amani Toomer 4.00 10.00
2 Andre Johnson 5.00 12.00
3 Antwaan Randle El 4.00 10.00
4 Ashley Lelie 4.00 10.00
5 Anquan Boldin 4.00 10.00
6 Ben Roethlisberger 10.00 25.00
7 Bethel Johnson 4.00 10.00
8 Brandon Lloyd 4.00 10.00
9 Brian Urlacher 6.00 15.00
10 Bryant Johnson 4.00 10.00
11 Chad Johnson 4.00 10.00
12 Carson Palmer 5.00 12.00
13 Darrell Jackson 5.00 12.00
14 Domanick Davis 4.00 10.00
15 Donovan McNabb 5.00 12.00
16 Isaac Bruce 6.00 15.00
17 J.P. Losman 5.00 12.00
18 Jake Delhomme 4.00 10.00
19 Jevon Kearse 4.00 10.00
20 Jeff Garcia 4.00 10.00
21 Jimmy Smith 5.00 12.00
22 Corey Dillon 4.00 10.00
23 Josh McCown 4.00 10.00
24 Josh Reed 4.00 10.00
25 Curtis Martin 5.00 12.00
26 Julius Jones 4.00 10.00
27 Randy McMichael 4.00 10.00
28 Keary Colbert 4.00 10.00
29 Joey Harrington 4.00 10.00
30 LaMont Jordan 5.00 12.00
31 Marshall Faulk 5.00 12.00
32 Tom Brady 12.50 30.00
33 Michael Strahan 5.00 12.00
34 Nate Clements 4.00 10.00
35 Mike Anderson 4.00 10.00
36 Nick Barnett 4.00 10.00
37 Randy Moss 5.00 12.00
38 Reggie Wayne 5.00 12.00
39 Rex Grossman 4.00 10.00
40 Priest Holmes 4.00 10.00
41 Ricky Williams 4.00 10.00
42 Rudi Johnson 4.00 10.00
43 T.J. Duckett 4.00 10.00
44 Steve Smith 6.00 15.00
45 Tatum Bell 4.00 10.00
46 Donte Stallworth 4.00 10.00
47 Thomas Jones 4.00 10.00
48 Torry Holt 5.00 12.00
49 Wayne Chrebet 4.00 10.00
50 Robert Ferguson 4.00 10.00

2006 Playoff Prestige Prestigious Pros Autographs

UNPRICED AUTO PRINT RUN 1-10 SETS

2006 Playoff Prestige Stars of the NFL

STATED ODDS 1:17 HOB, 1:10 RET
*FOIL/100: .8X TO 2X BASIC INSERTS
FOIL PRINT RUN 100 SER.#'d SETS
*HOLO/25: 2X TO 5X BASIC INSERTS
HOLOFOIL PRINT RUN 25 SER.#'d SETS
1 LaDainian Tomlinson 1.00 2.50
2 Michael Vick .75 2.00
3 Peyton Manning 2.50 6.00
4 Tom Brady 3.00 8.00
5 Steven Jackson .60 1.50
6 Shaun Alexander .60 1.50
7 Julius Jones .60 1.50
8 Priest Holmes .60 1.50
9 Randy Moss .75 2.00
10 Steve Smith 1.00 2.50
11 Terrell Owens .75 2.00
12 Donovan McNabb .75 2.00
13 Brett Favre 2.00 5.00
14 Clinton Portis .60 1.50
15 Carson Palmer .75 2.00
16 Chad Johnson .60 1.50
17 Drew Bledsoe .75 2.00
18 Edgerrin James .75 2.00
19 Eli Manning .75 2.00
20 Larry Fitzgerald .75 2.00
21 Ben Roethlisberger 1.25 3.00
22 Thomas Jones .60 1.50
23 Willis McGahee .60 1.50
24 Ronnie Brown .75 2.00
25 Cadillac Williams .75 2.00
26 Laveranues Coles .60 1.50
27 Matt Hasselbeck .60 1.50
28 Torry Holt .75 2.00
29 Trent Green .60 1.50
30 Tiki Barber .75 2.00
31 Jake Delhomme .60 1.50
32 Jake Plummer .60 1.50
33 Warrick Dunn .60 1.50
34 Steve McNair .75 2.00
35 Keyshawn Johnson .75 2.00

2006 Playoff Prestige Stars of the NFL Jerseys

*PRIME/25: .8X TO 2X BASIC JSY
1 LaDainian Tomlinson 3.00 8.00
2 Michael Vick 2.50 6.00
3 Peyton Manning 8.00 20.00
4 Tom Brady 10.00 25.00
5 Steven Jackson 2.00 5.00
6 Shaun Alexander 2.00 5.00
7 Julius Jones 2.00 5.00
8 Priest Holmes 2.00 5.00
9 Randy Moss 2.50 6.00
10 Steve Smith 3.00 8.00
11 Terrell Owens 2.50 6.00
12 Donovan McNabb 2.50 6.00
13 Brett Favre 6.00 15.00
14 Clinton Portis 2.00 5.00
15 Carson Palmer 2.50 6.00
16 Chad Johnson 2.00 5.00
17 Drew Bledsoe 2.50 6.00
18 Edgerrin James 2.50 6.00
19 Eli Manning 2.50 6.00
20 Larry Fitzgerald 2.50 6.00
21 Ben Roethlisberger 4.00 10.00
22 Thomas Jones 2.00 5.00
23 Willis McGahee 2.00 5.00
24 Ronnie Brown 2.50 6.00
25 Cadillac Williams 2.50 6.00
26 Laveranues Coles 2.00 5.00
27 Matt Hasselbeck 2.00 5.00
28 Torry Holt 2.50 6.00
29 Trent Green 2.00 5.00
30 Tiki Barber 2.50 6.00
31 Jake Delhomme 2.00 5.00
32 Jake Plummer 2.00 5.00
33 Warrick Dunn 2.00 5.00
34 Steve McNair 2.50 6.00
35 Keyshawn Johnson 2.50 6.00

2006 Playoff Prestige Super Bowl Heroes

STATED ODDS 1:29 HOB, 1:152 RET
*FOIL: .8X TO 2X BASIC INSERTS
FOIL PRINT RUN 100 SER.#'d SETS
*HOLOFOIL: 2X TO 5X BASIC INSERTS
HOLOFOIL PRINT RUN 25 SER.#'d SETS
UNPRICED AUTO PRINT RUN 10 SETS
1 Hines Ward 1.00 2.50
2 Willie Parker 1.00 2.50
3 Ben Roethlisberger 1.50 4.00
4 Antwaan Randle El .75 2.00
5 Jerome Bettis 1.25 3.00
6 Troy Polamalu 1.25 3.00
7 Matt Hasselbeck .75 2.00
8 Shaun Alexander .75 2.00
9 Jerramy Stevens 1.00 2.50
10 Darrell Jackson 1.00 2.50

2006 Playoff Prestige Super Bowl Heroes Holofoil Autographs

UNPRICED AUTO PRINT RUN 10 SETS

2006 Playoff Prestige Turning Pro

STATED ODDS 1:29 HOB, 1:152 RET
*FOIL: .6X TO 1.5X BASIC INSERTS
FOIL PRINT RUN 100 SER.#'d SETS
*HOLOFOIL: 1.5X TO 4X BASIC INSERTS
HOLOFOIL PRINT RUN 25 SER.#'d SETS
1 Cadillac Williams 1.25 3.00
2 Cedric Benson 1.00 2.50
3 Julius Jones 1.00 2.50
4 Michael Clayton 1.00 2.50
5 Roy Williams S 1.00 2.50
6 Steven Jackson 1.00 2.50
7 Hines Ward 1.25 3.00
8 Ronnie Brown 1.25 3.00
9 Willis McGahee 1.00 2.50
10 Braylon Edwards 1.00 2.50

2006 Playoff Prestige Turning Pro Jerseys

STATED PRINT RUN 250 SER.#'d SETS
1 Cadillac Williams 6.00 15.00
2 Cedric Benson 6.00 15.00
3 Julius Jones 6.00 15.00
4 Michael Clayton 5.00 12.00
5 Roy Williams S 5.00 12.00
6 Steven Jackson 6.00 15.00
7 Hines Ward 6.00 15.00
8 Ronnie Brown 6.00 15.00
9 Willis McGahee 5.00 12.00
10 Braylon Edwards 6.00 15.00

2007 Playoff Prestige

This 252-card set was released in May, 2007. The set was issued into the hobby in eight-card packs, with a $3 SRP, which came 24 packs to a box. Cards numbered 1-150 feature veterans in their 2006 team alphabetical order while cards numbered 151-252 feature 2007 NFL rookies. A few rookies were printed in lesser quantities and we have notated that information in our checklist and cards numbered 251 and 252 were issued to a stated print run of 100 copies.

COMP.SET w/o SP's (240) 75.00 150.00
COMP.SET w/o RC's (150) 10.00 25.00
1 Anquan Boldin .25 .60
2 Edgerrin James .30 .75
3 Larry Fitzgerald .30 .75
4 Matt Leinart .25 .60
5 Alge Crumpler .30 .75
6 Michael Vick .30 .75
7 Jerious Norwood .25 .60
8 Michael Jenkins .25 .60
9 Warrick Dunn .25 .60
10 Todd Heap .25 .60
11 Jamal Lewis .30 .75
12 Mark Clayton .25 .60
13 Demetrius Williams .25 .60
14 Steve McNair .30 .75
15 Ray Lewis .40 1.00
16 J.P. Losman .25 .60
17 Josh Reed .25 .60
18 Lee Evans .30 .75
19 Willis McGahee .25 .60
20 DeAngelo Williams .25 .60
21 DeShaun Foster .30 .75
22 Jake Delhomme .25 .60
23 Keyshawn Johnson .30 .75
24 Steve Smith .30 .75
25 Bernard Berrian .25 .60
26 Brian Urlacher .40 1.00
27 Cedric Benson .25 .60
28 Muhsin Muhammad .25 .60
29 Rex Grossman .25 .60
30 Thomas Jones .25 .60
31 Carson Palmer .30 .75
32 Chad Johnson .25 .60
33 Rudi Johnson .25 .60
34 T.J. Houshmandzadeh .25 .60
35 Braylon Edwards .25 .60
36 Kellen Winslow .25 .60
37 Charlie Frye .30 .75
38 Reuben Droughns .30 .75
39 Terry Glenn .30 .75
40 Julius Jones .25 .60
41 Roy Williams S .25 .60
42 Marion Barber .30 .75
43 Terrell Owens .30 .75
44 Tony Romo .50 1.25
45 Javon Walker .30 .75
46 Jay Cutler .25 .60
47 Mike Bell .30 .75
48 Brandon Marshall .30 .75
49 Tatum Bell .25 .60
50 Jon Kitna .25 .60
51 Kevin Jones .25 .60
52 Roy Williams WR .25 .60
53 Mike Furrey .30 .75
54 A.J. Hawk .25 .60
55 Brett Favre .75 2.00
56 Donald Driver .30 .75
57 Greg Jennings .25 .60
58 Ahman Green .30 .75
59 Andre Johnson .30 .75
60 David Carr .25 .60
61 Eric Moulds .25 .60
62 Owen Daniels .25 .60
63 Wali Lundy .25 .60
64 Joseph Addai .25 .60
65 Marvin Harrison .30 .75
66 Peyton Manning 1.00 2.50
67 Reggie Wayne .30 .75
68 Dallas Clark .30 .75
69 Byron Leftwich .25 .60
70 Fred Taylor .25 .60
71 Marcedes Lewis .25 .60
72 Maurice Jones-Drew .25 .60
73 Reggie Williams .30 .75
74 Eddie Kennison .25 .60
75 Larry Johnson .25 .60
76 Tony Gonzalez .30 .75
77 Trent Green .25 .60
78 Chris Chambers .25 .60
79 Daunte Culpepper .30 .75
80 Marty Booker .25 .60
81 Ronnie Brown .25 .60
82 Chester Taylor .25 .60
83 Tarvaris Jackson .25 .60
84 Troy Williamson .25 .60
85 Travis Taylor .25 .60
86 Ben Watson .25 .60
87 Tom Brady 1.25 3.00
88 Corey Dillon .25 .60
89 Laurence Maroney .30 .75
90 Deuce McAllister .30 .75
91 Drew Brees .40 1.00
92 Marques Colston .25 .60
93 Reggie Bush .25 .60
94 Joe Horn .25 .60
95 Brandon Jacobs .25 .60
96 Eli Manning .30 .75
97 Jeremy Shockey .25 .60
98 Plaxico Burress .25 .60
99 Chad Pennington .25 .60
100 Jerricho Cotchery .25 .60
101 Laveranues Coles .25 .60
102 Leon Washington .25 .60
103 Kevan Barlow .30 .75
104 Ronald Curry .25 .60
105 LaMont Jordan .30 .75
106 John Madsen .25 .60
107 Michael Huff .30 .75
108 Randy Moss .30 .75
109 Brian Westbrook .25 .60
110 Donovan McNabb .30 .75
111 Hank Baskett .30 .75
112 Donte Stallworth .30 .75
113 Reggie Brown .25 .60
114 Ben Roethlisberger .40 1.00
115 Hines Ward .30 .75
116 Troy Polamalu .40 1.00
117 Willie Parker .30 .75
118 Santonio Holmes .25 .60
119 Antonio Gates .40 1.00
120 LaDainian Tomlinson .40 1.00
121 Vincent Jackson .25 .60
122 Philip Rivers .40 1.00
123 Shawne Merriman .25 .60
124 Alex Smith QB .30 .75
125 Antonio Bryant .25 .60
126 Frank Gore .30 .75
127 Vernon Davis .25 .60
128 Darrell Jackson .25 .60
129 Deion Branch .25 .60
130 Matt Hasselbeck .25 .60
131 Shaun Alexander .25 .60
132 Isaac Bruce .40 1.00
133 Marc Bulger .25 .60
134 Steven Jackson .25 .60
135 Joe Klopfenstein .25 .60
136 Torry Holt .30 .75
137 Bruce Gradkowski .25 .60
138 Cadillac Williams .30 .75
139 Joey Galloway .30 .75
140 Mike Alstott .25 .60
141 Adam Jones .25 .60
142 Drew Bennett .25 .60
143 LenDale White .30 .75
144 Vince Young .25 .60
145 Travis Henry .30 .75
146 Clinton Portis .25 .60
147 Jason Campbell .25 .60
148 Ladell Betts .25 .60
149 Santana Moss .30 .75
150 Chris Cooley .25 .60
151 Brady Quinn RC .75 2.00
152 JaMarcus Russell RC .75 2.00
153 Troy Smith RC .75 2.00
154 Drew Stanton RC .75 2.00
155 Adrian Peterson RC 2.50 6.00
156 Marshawn Lynch RC 1.50 4.00
157 Michael Bush RC .75 2.00
158 Kenny Irons SP RC 6.00 15.00
159 Antonio Pittman RC .75 2.00
160 Tony Hunt RC .75 2.00
161 Darius Walker SP RC 6.00 15.00
162 DeShawn Wynn RC .75 2.00
163 Calvin Johnson RC 2.50 6.00
164 Ted Ginn Jr. RC 1.00 2.50

165 Dwayne Jarrett RC 1.00 2.50
166 Sidney Rice RC 1.00 2.50
167 Dwayne Bowe RC .75 2.00
168 Robert Meachem RC 1.00 2.50
169 Anthony Gonzalez SP RC 6.00 15.00
170 Craig Buster Davis RC .75 2.00
171 Johnnie Lee Higgins RC .75 2.00
172 Steve Smith USC RC .75 2.00
173 Chansi Stuckey RC 1.00 2.50
174 David Clowney RC .75 2.00
175 Aundrae Allison RC .75 2.00
176 Jason Hill SP RC 6.00 15.00
177 Zach Miller RC .75 2.00
178 Greg Olsen RC 1.25 3.00
179 Gaines Adams RC 1.00 2.50
180 Jamaal Anderson RC 1.00 2.50
181 Victor Abiamiri RC .75 2.00
182 Adam Carriker RC .75 2.00
183 LaMarr Woodley RC 1.50 4.00
184 Quentin Moses RC .75 2.00
185 Charles Johnson RC .75 2.00
186 Alan Branch RC .75 2.00
187 Amobi Okoye RC 1.00 2.50
188 DeMarcus Tank Tyler RC .75 2.00
189 Patrick Willis SP RC 12.00 30.00
190 Paul Posluszny RC .75 2.00
191 Lawrence Timmons RC 1.25 3.00
192 Darrelle Revis RC 1.00 2.50
193 Leon Hall RC .75 2.00
194 Daymeion Hughes RC .75 2.00
195 Chris Houston RC .75 2.00
196 A.J. Davis RC .75 2.00
197 Aaron Ross RC .75 2.00
198 LaRon Landry RC 1.25 3.00
199 Reggie Nelson RC .75 2.00
200 Michael Griffin RC .75 2.00
201 Trent Edwards RC .75 2.00
202 Kevin Kolb RC 1.00 2.50
203 John Beck RC .75 2.00
204 Kenneth Darby RC .75 2.00
205 Lorenzo Booker RC 1.00 2.50
206 Jason Snelling RC .75 2.00
207 Selvin Young RC .75 2.00
208 Ahmad Bradshaw RC 1.25 3.00
209 Brandon Jackson RC .75 2.00
210 Courtney Taylor RC .75 2.00
211 Paul Williams SP RC 6.00 15.00
212 Rhema McKnight RC .75 2.00
213 David Ball RC .75 2.00
214 Syvelle Newton RC 1.00 2.50
215 Joel Filani RC .75 2.00
216 Chris Davis RC .75 2.00
217 Laurent Robinson RC 1.25 3.00
218 Jarrett Hicks RC 1.00 2.50
219 Dallas Baker RC .75 2.00
220 Matt Trannon RC .75 2.00
221 Mike Walker RC 1.25 3.00
222 Anthony Spencer RC 1.00 2.50
223 Jarvis Moss RC .75 2.00
224 Tim Crowder RC 1.00 2.50
225 Brandon Siler RC .75 2.00
226 David Harris RC .75 2.00
227 Buster Davis RC 1.00 2.50
228 Jon Abbate RC .75 2.00
229 Rufus Alexander RC .75 2.00
230 Jon Beason RC .75 2.00
231 Jonathan Wade RC .75 2.00
232 Marcus McCauley RC .75 2.00
233 Tanard Jackson RC .75 2.00
234 Kenny Scott RC .75 2.00
235 Brandon Meriweather RC 1.00 2.50
236 Aaron Rouse RC .75 2.00
237 Eric Weddle RC 1.00 2.50
238 Brian Leonard RC .75 2.00
239 Jared Zabransky SP RC 6.00 15.00
240 Chris Leak SP RC 6.00 15.00
241 Jordan Palmer SP RC 8.00 20.00
242 Garrett Wolfe SP RC 6.00 15.00
243 Gary Russell RC 1.00 2.50
244 Isaiah Stanback RC .75 2.00
245 Tyler Palko RC 1.25 3.00
246 Jeff Rowe RC .75 2.00
247 Kolby Smith RC .75 2.00
248 Dwayne Wright RC .75 2.00
249 Nate Ilaoa RC 1.00 2.50
250 Steve Breaston RC .75 2.00
251 Chris Henry RC/100*
252 Joe Thomas RC/100*

2007 Playoff Prestige Draft Picks Light Blue

*ROOKIES: .8X TO 2X BASIC CARDS
*ROOKIES: .08X TO .2X BASIC SPs
STATED PRINT RUN 999 SER.#'d SETS

2007 Playoff Prestige Xtra Points Black

UNPRICED BLACK PRINT RUN 10

2007 Playoff Prestige Xtra Points Gold

*VETS 1-150: 2X TO 5X BASIC CARDS
*ROOKIES 151-250: .8X TO 2X BASIC CARDS
*ROOKIE SPs: .08X TO .2X BASIC CARDS
STATED ODDS 1:14

2007 Playoff Prestige Xtra Points Green

*VETS 1-150: 6X TO 15X BASIC CARDS
*ROOKIES 151-250: 3X TO 8X BASIC CARDS
*ROOKIE SPs: .3X TO .8X BASIC CARDS
GREEN PRINT RUN 25 SER.#'d SETS

2007 Playoff Prestige Xtra Points Purple

*VETS 1-150: 5X TO 1X BASIC CARDS
*ROOKIES 151-250: 2X TO 5X BASIC CARDS
*ROOKIE SPs: .2X TO .5X BASIC CARDS
PURPLE PRINT RUN 50 SER.#'d SETS

2007 Playoff Prestige Xtra Points Red

*VET 1-150: 3X TO 8X BASIC CARDS
*ROOKIES 151-250: 1.2X TO 3X BASIC CARDS
*ROOKIE SPs: .1X TO .3X BASIC CARDS
RED PRINT RUN 100 SER.#'d SETS

2007 Playoff Prestige Changing Stripes Materials

STATED PRINT RUN 250 SER.#'d SETS
*PRIME/25: 1X TO 2.5X BASIC JSYs
PRIME PRINT RUN 25 SER.#'d SETS
1 Drew Brees 4.00 10.00
2 Terrell Owens 3.00 8.00
3 Edgerrin James 3.00 8.00
4 Donte Stallworth 3.00 8.00
5 Deion Branch 2.50 6.00
6 Javon Walker 3.00 8.00
7 Steve McNair 3.00 8.00
8 Daunte Culpepper 3.00 8.00
9 Keyshawn Johnson 3.00 8.00
10 Chester Taylor 2.50 6.00

2007 Playoff Prestige Draft Picks Rights Autographs

STATED PRINT RUN 5-150
SERIAL #'d UNDER 25 NOT PRICED
151 Brady Quinn/25 25.00 60.00
152 JaMarcus Russell/25 20.00 50.00
154 Drew Stanton/50 10.00 25.00
155 Adrian Peterson/25 150.00 300.00
156 Marshawn Lynch/50 20.00 50.00
161 Darius Walker/50 10.00 25.00
163 Calvin Johnson/25 100.00 200.00
164 Ted Ginn Jr./50 12.00 30.00
165 Dwayne Jarrett/50 12.00 30.00
166 Sidney Rice/50 12.00 30.00
167 Dwayne Bowe/50 10.00 25.00
168 Robert Meachem/50 12.00 30.00
172 Steve Smith USC/50 10.00 25.00
173 Chansi Stuckey/50 12.00 30.00
174 David Clowney/50 10.00 25.00
176 Jason Hill/50 10.00 25.00
178 Greg Olsen/50 15.00 40.00
179 Gaines Adams/50 12.00 30.00
181 Victor Abiamiri/150 5.00 12.00
182 Adam Carriker/50 10.00 25.00
183 LaMarr Woodley/150 12.00 30.00
184 Quentin Moses/150 5.00 12.00
191 Lawrence Timmons/25 20.00 50.00
193 Leon Hall/100 6.00 15.00
196 A.J. Davis/150 5.00 12.00
198 LaRon Landry/50 15.00 40.00
199 Reggie Nelson/25 12.00 30.00
204 Kenneth Darby/25 12.00 30.00
205 Lorenzo Booker/25 15.00 40.00
208 Ahmad Bradshaw/100 10.00 25.00
211 Paul Williams/50 10.00 25.00
213 David Ball/150 5.00 12.00
215 Joel Filani/100 6.00 15.00
219 Dallas Baker/100 6.00 15.00
221 Mike Walker/100 10.00 25.00
225 Brandon Siler/150 5.00 12.00
226 David Harris/150 5.00 12.00
229 Rufus Alexander/150 5.00 12.00
230 Jon Beason/150 5.00 12.00
232 Marcus McCauley/150 5.00 12.00
234 Kenny Scott/150 5.00 12.00
236 Aaron Rouse/150 5.00 12.00
239 Jared Zabransky/50 10.00 25.00
245 Tyler Palko/150 8.00 20.00
246 Jeff Rowe/150 5.00 12.00
247 Kolby Smith/25 12.00 30.00

2007 Playoff Prestige Gridiron Heritage

STATED ODDS 1:35 HOB, 1:19 RET
*FOIL/100: .5X TO 1.2X BASIC INSERTS
FOIL PRINT RUN 100 SER.#'d SETS
*HOLOFOIL/25: 1.2X TO 3X BASIC INSERTS
HOLOFOIL PRINT RUN 25 SER.#'d SETS
1 Tony Gonzalez .75 2.00
2 Trent Green .60 1.50
3 Larry Johnson .60 1.50
4 Aaron Rodgers 2.50 6.00
5 Ahman Green .75 2.00
6 Alge Crumpler .75 2.00
7 Andre Johnson .75 2.00
8 Anquan Boldin .60 1.50
9 Bernard Berrian .60 1.50
10 Braylon Edwards .60 1.50
11 Brian Westbrook .60 1.50
12 Brian Urlacher 1.00 2.50
13 Cadillac Williams .75 2.00
14 Chris Chambers .60 1.50
15 Clinton Portis .60 1.50
16 Curtis Martin .75 2.00
17 Darrell Jackson .60 1.50
18 Deuce McAllister .75 2.00
19 Donald Driver .75 2.00
20 Fred Taylor .60 1.50
21 Hines Ward .75 2.00
22 Isaac Bruce 1.00 2.50
23 J.P. Losman .60 1.50
24 Jake Delhomme .60 1.50
25 Jamal Lewis .75 2.00
26 Jason Campbell .60 1.50
27 Jason Witten .75 2.00
28 Jeremy Shockey .60 1.50
29 Joe Horn .60 1.50
30 Joey Galloway .75 2.00
31 Julius Jones .60 1.50
32 Kevin Jones .60 1.50
33 LaMont Jordan .75 2.00
34 Larry Fitzgerald .75 2.00
35 Laveranues Coles .60 1.50
36 Lee Evans .75 2.00
37 Mark Clayton .60 1.50
38 Matt Hasselbeck .60 1.50
39 Matt Jones .75 2.00
40 Michael Strahan .75 2.00
41 Muhsin Muhammad .60 1.50
42 Randy McMichael .60 1.50
43 Randy Moss .75 2.00
44 Reggie Brown .60 1.50
45 Reggie Wayne .75 2.00
46 Rudi Johnson .60 1.50
47 T.J. Houshmandzadeh .60 1.50
48 Thomas Jones .60 1.50
49 Todd Heap .60 1.50
50 Willis McGahee .60 1.50

2007 Playoff Prestige Gridiron Heritage Materials

STATED ODDS 1:46 HOB, 1:88 RET
*PRIME/50: .8X TO 2X BASIC JSY
PRIME PRINT RUN 50 SER.#'d SETS
1 Tony Gonzalez 2.50 6.00
2 Trent Green 2.00 5.00
3 Larry Johnson 2.00 5.00
4 Aaron Rodgers 8.00 20.00
5 Ahman Green 2.50 6.00
6 Alge Crumpler 2.50 6.00
7 Andre Johnson 2.50 6.00
8 Anquan Boldin 2.00 5.00
9 Bernard Berrian 2.00 5.00
10 Braylon Edwards 2.00 5.00
11 Brian Westbrook 2.00 5.00
12 Brian Urlacher 3.00 8.00
13 Cadillac Williams 2.50 6.00
14 Chris Chambers 2.00 5.00
15 Clinton Portis 2.00 5.00
16 Curtis Martin 2.50 6.00
17 Darrell Jackson 2.00 5.00
18 Deuce McAllister 2.50 6.00
19 Donald Driver 2.50 6.00
20 Fred Taylor 2.00 5.00
21 Hines Ward 2.50 6.00
22 Isaac Bruce 3.00 8.00
23 J.P. Losman 2.00 5.00
24 Jake Delhomme 2.00 5.00
25 Jamal Lewis 2.50 6.00
26 Jason Campbell 2.00 5.00
27 Jason Witten 2.50 6.00
28 Jeremy Shockey 2.00 5.00
29 Joe Horn 2.00 5.00
30 Joey Galloway 2.50 6.00
31 Julius Jones 2.00 5.00
32 Kevin Jones 2.00 5.00
33 LaMont Jordan 2.50 6.00
34 Larry Fitzgerald 2.50 6.00
35 Laveranues Coles 2.00 5.00
36 Lee Evans 2.50 6.00
37 Mark Clayton 2.00 5.00
38 Matt Hasselbeck 2.00 5.00
39 Matt Jones 2.50 6.00
40 Michael Strahan 2.50 6.00
41 Muhsin Muhammad 2.00 5.00
42 Randy McMichael 2.00 5.00
43 Randy Moss 2.50 6.00
44 Reggie Brown 2.00 5.00
45 Reggie Wayne 2.50 6.00
46 Rudi Johnson 2.00 5.00
47 T.J. Houshmandzadeh 2.00 5.00
48 Thomas Jones 2.00 5.00
49 Todd Heap 2.00 5.00
50 Willis McGahee 2.00 5.00

2007 Playoff Prestige League Leaders

STATED ODDS 1:35 HOB, 1:19 RET
*FOIL/100: .8X TO 2X BASIC INSERTS
FOIL PRINT RUN 100 SER.#'d SETS
*HOLOFOIL/25: 2X TO 5X BASIC INSERTS
HOLOFOIL PRINT RUN 25 SER.#'d SETS
1 D.Brees/P.Manning 2.50 6.00
2 M.Bulger/J.Kitna .60 1.50
3 C.Palmer/B.Favre 2.00 5.00
4 T.Brady/B.Roethlisberger 3.00 8.00
5 P.Rivers/C.Pennington 1.00 2.50
6 E.Manning/R.Grossman .75 2.00
7 L.Tomlinson/L.Johnson 1.00 2.50
8 F.Gore/T.Barber .75 2.00
9 S.Jackson/W.Parker .75 2.00
10 R.Johnson/B.Westbrook .60 1.50
11 C.Johnson/M.Harrison .75 2.00
12 R.Wayne/R.Williams WR .75 2.00
13 D.Driver/L.Evans .75 2.00
14 A.Boldin/T.Holt .75 2.00
15 T.Owens/S.Smith WR .75 2.00
16 M.Leinart/V.Young .60 1.50
17 J.Addai/Jones-Drew .60 1.50
18 T.Owens/M.Harrison .75 2.00
19 D.Jackson/P.Burress .60 1.50
20 L.Tomlinson/L.Johnson 1.00 2.50
21 Brees/Tomlin/P.Mann/LJ 3.00 8.00
22 Bulger/Gore/Kitna/Barber 1.00 2.50
23 C.Jhn/Hrsn/Wayne/Roy Will. 1.00 2.50
24 Tomlin/Owens/LJ/Harrison 1.25 3.00
25 Leinart/Addai/Young/J-Drew .75 2.00

2007 Playoff Prestige League Leaders Materials

LEAGUE LDR JERSEY PRINT RUN 50-250
*PRIME/25: 1X TO 2.5X BASIC JSY/250
*PRIME/25: .8X TO 2X BASIC JSY/100
PRIME PRINT RUN 10-25
1 D.Brees/P.Manning/100 20.00 50.00
2 M.Bulger/J.Kitna/250 4.00 10.00
3 C.Palmer/B.Favre/250 12.00 30.00
4 Brady/Roethlisbrgr/100 25.00 60.00
5 Rivers/Pennington/250 6.00 15.00
6 Eli/R.Grossman/250 5.00 12.00
7 Tomlinson/L.Jhnsn/100 8.00 20.00
8 F.Gore/T.Barber/250 5.00 12.00
9 S.Jackson/W.Parker/250 5.00 12.00
10 R.Johnsn/Westbrook/250 4.00 10.00
11 C.Johnson/M.Harrison/250 5.00 12.00
12 Wayne/Roy Will WR/250 5.00 12.00
13 D.Driver/L.Evans/250 5.00 12.00
14 A.Boldin/T.Holt/250 5.00 12.00
15 T.Owens/S.Smith WR/100 6.00 15.00
16 M.Leinart/V.Young/50 8.00 20.00
17 J.Addai/Jones-Drew/250 4.00 10.00
18 T.Owens/M.Harrison/250 5.00 12.00
19 D.Jackson/P.Burress/250 4.00 10.00
20 Tomlinson/L.Johnsn/100 8.00 20.00
21 Brees/Tomlin/P.Mnn/LJ/50 40.00 100.00
22 Bulger/Gore/Kitna/Brbr/50 12.00 30.00
23 C.Jhn/Hrsn/Wyn/Ro.Will/50 12.00 30.00
24 Tomlin/Owens/LJ/Hrrisn/50 15.00 40.00
25 Leinrt/Addai/Yng/J-Drew/50 10.00 25.00

2007 Playoff Prestige NFL Draft

STATED ODDS 1:20 HOB, 1:12 RET
*RED: .4X TO 1X BASIC INSERTS
RED INSERTS IN SPECIAL RETAIL BOXES
*FOIL/100: .8X TO 2X BASIC INSERTS
FOIL PRINT RUN 100 SER.#'d SETS
*HOLOFOIL/25: 2X TO 5X BASIC INSERTS
HOLOFOIL PRINT RUN 25 SER.#'d SETS
1 Brady Quinn .50 1.25
2 JaMarcus Russell .50 1.25
3 Troy Smith .50 1.25
4 Drew Stanton .50 1.25
5 Adrian Peterson 1.50 4.00
6 Marshawn Lynch 1.00 2.50
7 Michael Bush .50 1.25
8 Kenny Irons .50 1.25
9 Antonio Pittman .50 1.25
10 Tony Hunt .50 1.25
11 Darius Walker .50 1.25
12 DeShawn Wynn .50 1.25
13 Calvin Johnson 1.50 4.00
14 Ted Ginn Jr. .60 1.50
15 Dwayne Jarrett .60 1.50
16 Sidney Rice .60 1.50
17 Dwayne Bowe .50 1.25
18 Robert Meachem .60 1.50
19 Anthony Gonzalez .50 1.25
20 Craig Buster Davis .50 1.25
21 Johnnie Lee Higgins .50 1.25
22 Steve Smith USC .50 1.25
23 Chansi Stuckey .60 1.50
24 David Clowney .50 1.25
25 Aundrae Allison .50 1.25
26 Jason Hill .50 1.25
27 Zach Miller .50 1.25
28 Greg Olsen .75 2.00
29 Gaines Adams .60 1.50
30 Jamaal Anderson .60 1.50
31 Alan Branch .50 1.25
32 Amobi Okoye .60 1.50
33 DeMarcus Tank Tyler .50 1.25
34 Patrick Willis .75 2.00
35 Paul Posluszny .50 1.25
36 Darrelle Revis .60 1.50
37 Aaron Ross .50 1.25
38 LaRon Landry .75 2.00
39 Paul Williams .50 1.25
40 Jordan Palmer .60 1.50

2007 Playoff Prestige NFL Draft Autographs

STATED PRINT RUN 5-50
SERIAL #'d UNDER 25 NOT PRICED
1 Brady Quinn/25 30.00 80.00
2 JaMarcus Russell/25 12.00 30.00
4 Drew Stanton/50 10.00 25.00
5 Adrian Peterson/25 150.00 300.00
6 Marshawn Lynch/50 20.00 50.00
11 Darius Walker/50 10.00 25.00
13 Calvin Johnson/25 100.00 200.00
14 Ted Ginn Jr./50 12.00 30.00
15 Dwayne Jarrett/50 12.00 30.00
16 Sidney Rice/50 12.00 30.00
17 Dwayne Bowe/50 10.00 25.00
18 Robert Meachem/50 12.00 30.00
22 Steve Smith USC/50 10.00 25.00
23 Chansi Stuckey/50 12.00 30.00
24 David Clowney/50 10.00 25.00
26 Jason Hill/50 10.00 25.00
28 Greg Olsen/50 15.00 40.00
29 Gaines Adams/50 12.00 30.00
38 LaRon Landry/50 15.00 40.00
39 Paul Williams/50 10.00 25.00

2007 Playoff Prestige Prestigious Picks Blue

BLUE PRINT RUN 1000 SER.#'d SETS
*RED/750: .4X TO 1X BLUE/1000
RED PRINT RUN 750 SER.#'d SETS
*BLACK/500: .5X TO 1.2X BLUE/1000
BLACK PRINT RUN 500 SER.#'d SETS
*PURPLE/250: .6X TO 1.5X BLUE/1000
PURPLE PRINT RUN 250 SER.#'d SETS
*GREEN/100: .8X TO 2X BLUE/1000
GREEN PRINT RUN 100 SER.#'d SETS
*SILVER/50: 1.2X TO 3X BLUE/1000
SILVER PRINT RUN 50 SER.#'d SETS
*GOLD/25: 2X TO 5X BLUE/1000
GOLD PRINT RUN 25 SER.#'d SETS
*PLATINUM/10: 3X TO 8X BLUE/1000
PLATINUM PRINT RUN 10 SER.#'d SETS
1 Kenny Irons .50 1.25
2 JaMarcus Russell .50 1.25
3 Robert Meachem .60 1.50
4 Dwayne Bowe .50 1.25
5 Craig Buster Davis .50 1.25
6 Adrian Peterson 1.50 4.00
7 Dwayne Jarrett .60 1.50
8 Steve Smith USC .50 1.25
9 Brady Quinn .50 1.25
10 Zach Miller .50 1.25

2007 Playoff Prestige Prestigious Picks Materials Gold

GOLD PRINT RUN 50 SER.#'d SETS
*BLACK/25: .8X TO 2X GOLD/50
BLACK PRINT RUN 25 SER.#'d SETS
UNPRICED PLATINUM PATCH PRINT RUN 10
1 Kenny Irons 3.00 8.00
2 JaMarcus Russell 3.00 8.00
3 Robert Meachem 4.00 10.00
4 Dwayne Bowe 3.00 8.00
5 Craig Buster Davis 3.00 8.00
6 Adrian Peterson 10.00 25.00
7 Dwayne Jarrett 4.00 10.00
8 Steve Smith USC 3.00 8.00
9 Brady Quinn 3.00 8.00
10 Zach Miller 3.00 8.00

2007 Playoff Prestige Prestigious Pros Blue

BLUE PRINT RUN 1000 SER.#'d SETS
*RED/750: .4X TO 1X BLUE/1000
RED PRINT RUN 750 SER.#'d SETS
*BLACK/500: .5X TO 1.2X BLUE/1000
BLACK PRINT RUN 500 SER.#'d SETS
*PURPLE/250: .6X TO 1.5X BLUE/1000
PURPLE PRINT RUN 250 SER.#'d SETS
*GREEN/100: .8X TO 2X BLUE/1000
GREEN PRINT RUN 100 SER.#'d SETS
*SILVER/50: 1X TO 2.5X BLUE/1000
SILVER PRINT RUN 50 SER.#'d SETS
*GOLD/25: 1.5X TO 4X BLUE/1000
GOLD PRINT RUN 25 SER.#'d SETS
*PLATINUM/10: 3X TO 8X BLUE/1000
PLATINUM PRINT RUN 10 SER.#'d SETS
1 Ahman Green 1.00 2.50
2 Brian Westbrook .75 2.00
3 Clinton Portis .75 2.00
4 Jake Delhomme .75 2.00
5 Kevin Jones .75 2.00
6 Reggie Brown .75 2.00
7 Rudi Johnson .75 2.00
8 Tony Gonzalez 1.00 2.50
9 Alex Smith QB 1.00 2.50
10 Ben Roethlisberger 1.25 3.00
11 Tom Brady 4.00 10.00
12 Willie Parker 1.00 2.50
13 Frank Gore 1.00 2.50
14 Ronnie Brown .75 2.00
15 LaDainian Tomlinson 1.25 3.00
16 Tiki Barber 1.00 2.50
17 Roy Williams WR .75 2.00
18 Brett Favre 2.50 6.00
19 Steven Jackson .75 2.00
20 Torry Holt 1.00 2.50
21 Larry Johnson .75 2.00
22 Anquan Boldin .75 2.00
23 Cadillac Williams 1.00 2.50
24 Hines Ward 1.00 2.50
25 Julius Jones .75 2.00
26 Matt Hasselbeck .75 2.00
27 Reggie Wayne 1.00 2.50
28 Thomas Jones .75 2.00
29 Willis McGahee .75 2.00
30 Antonio Gates 1.25 3.00
31 Tony Romo 1.50 4.00
32 Peyton Manning 3.00 8.00
33 Shaun Alexander .75 2.00
34 Carson Palmer 1.00 2.50
35 Michael Vick 1.00 2.50
36 Philip Rivers 1.25 3.00
37 Chad Johnson .75 2.00
38 Drew Brees 1.25 3.00
39 Eli Manning 1.00 2.50
40 Steve Smith 1.00 2.50

2007 Playoff Prestige Prestigious Pros Autographs

STATED PRINT RUN 1-25
SERIAL #'d UNDER 20 NOT PRICED
6 Reggie Brown/20 20.00 40.00
7 Rudi Johnson/25 10.00 25.00
13 Frank Gore/25 12.00 30.00
26 Matt Hasselbeck/25 20.00 50.00
28 Thomas Jones/25 10.00 25.00

2007 Playoff Prestige Prestigious Pros Materials Red

RED STATED ODDS 1:68 RETAIL
*PURPLE/250: .4X TO 1X RED JSYs
PURPLE PRINT RUN 250 SER.#'d SETS
*GREEN/100: .5X TO 1.2X RED JSYs
GREEN PRINT RUN 100 SER.#'d SETS
*GOLD/50: .6X TO 1.5X RED JSYs
GOLD PRINT RUN 50 SER.#'d SETS
*BLACK/25: 1X TO 2.5X RED JSYs
BLACK PRINT RUN 25 SER.#'d SETS
UNPRICED PLATINUM PATCH PRINT RUN 10
1 Ahman Green 3.00 8.00
2 Brian Westbrook 2.50 6.00
3 Clinton Portis 2.50 6.00
4 Jake Delhomme 2.50 6.00
5 Kevin Jones 2.50 6.00
6 Reggie Brown 2.50 6.00
7 Rudi Johnson 2.50 6.00
8 Tony Gonzalez 3.00 8.00
9 Alex Smith QB 3.00 8.00
10 Ben Roethlisberger 4.00 10.00
11 Tom Brady 12.00 30.00
12 Willie Parker 3.00 8.00
13 Frank Gore 3.00 8.00
14 Ronnie Brown 2.50 6.00
15 LaDainian Tomlinson 4.00 10.00
16 Tiki Barber 3.00 8.00
17 Roy Williams WR 2.50 6.00
18 Brett Favre 8.00 20.00
19 Steven Jackson 2.50 6.00
20 Torry Holt 3.00 8.00
21 Larry Johnson 2.50 6.00
22 Anquan Boldin 2.50 6.00
23 Cadillac Williams 3.00 8.00
24 Hines Ward 3.00 8.00
25 Julius Jones 2.50 6.00
26 Matt Hasselbeck 2.50 6.00
27 Reggie Wayne 3.00 8.00
28 Thomas Jones 2.50 6.00
29 Willis McGahee 2.50 6.00
30 Antonio Gates 4.00 10.00
31 Tony Romo 5.00 12.00
32 Peyton Manning 10.00 25.00
33 Shaun Alexander 2.50 6.00
34 Carson Palmer 3.00 8.00
35 Michael Vick 3.00 8.00
36 Philip Rivers 4.00 10.00
37 Chad Johnson 2.50 6.00
38 Drew Brees 4.00 10.00
39 Eli Manning 3.00 8.00
40 Steve Smith 3.00 8.00

2007 Playoff Prestige Stars of the NFL

STATED ODDS 1:35 HOB, 1:19 RET
*FOIL/100: .8X TO 2X BASIC INSERTS
FOIL PRINT RUN 100 SER.#'d SETS
*HOLOFOIL/25: 2X TO 5X BASIC INSERTS
HOLOFOIL PRINT RUN 25 SER.#'d SETS
1 Alex Smith QB .50 1.25
2 Antonio Gates .60 1.50
3 Ben Roethlisberger .60 1.50
4 Tony Romo .75 2.00
5 Tom Brady 2.00 5.00
6 Peyton Manning 1.50 4.00
7 Willie Parker .50 1.25
8 Shaun Alexander .40 1.00
9 Frank Gore .50 1.25
10 Carson Palmer .50 1.25
11 Ronnie Brown .40 1.00
12 Michael Vick .50 1.25
13 LaDainian Tomlinson .60 1.50
14 Philip Rivers .60 1.50
15 Marvin Harrison .50 1.25
16 Larry Johnson .40 1.00
17 Tiki Barber .50 1.25
18 Chad Johnson .40 1.00
19 Roy Williams WR .40 1.00
20 Drew Brees .60 1.50
21 Brett Favre 1.25 3.00
22 Eli Manning .50 1.25
23 Steven Jackson .40 1.00
24 Steve Smith .50 1.25
25 Torry Holt .50 1.25

2007 Playoff Prestige Stars of the NFL Materials

STATED ODDS 1:46 HOB, 1:90 RET
*PRIME/25: 1X TO 2.5X BASIC INSERTS
PRIME PRINT RUN 25
UNPRICED AUTOs SER.#'d TO 10
1 Alex Smith QB 2.00 5.00
2 Antonio Gates 2.50 6.00
3 Ben Roethlisberger 2.50 6.00
4 Tony Romo 3.00 8.00
5 Tom Brady 8.00 20.00
6 Peyton Manning 6.00 15.00
7 Willie Parker 2.00 5.00
8 Shaun Alexander 1.50 4.00
9 Frank Gore 2.00 5.00
10 Carson Palmer 2.00 5.00
11 Ronnie Brown 1.50 4.00
12 Michael Vick 2.00 5.00
13 LaDainian Tomlinson 2.50 6.00
14 Philip Rivers 2.50 6.00
15 Marvin Harrison 2.00 5.00
16 Larry Johnson 1.50 4.00
17 Tiki Barber 2.00 5.00
18 Chad Johnson 1.50 4.00
19 Roy Williams WR 1.50 4.00
20 Drew Brees 2.50 6.00
21 Brett Favre 5.00 12.00
22 Eli Manning 2.00 5.00
23 Steven Jackson 1.50 4.00
24 Steve Smith 2.00 5.00
25 Torry Holt 2.00 5.00

2007 Playoff Prestige Stars of the NFL Materials Prime Autographs

STATED PRINT RUN 10 SER.#'d SETS

2007 Playoff Prestige Super Bowl Heroes

STATED ODDS 1:46 HOB, 1:80 RET
*FOIL/100: 1X TO 2.5X BASIC INSERTS
FOIL PRINT RUN 100 SER.#'d SETS
*HOLOFOIL/25: 2.5X TO 6X BASIC INSERTS
HOLOFOIL PRINT RUN 25 SER.#'d SETS
1 Peyton Manning 5.00 12.00
2 Reggie Wayne 1.50 4.00
3 Dominic Rhodes 1.25 3.00
4 Joseph Addai 1.25 3.00
5 Marvin Harrison 1.50 4.00
6 Adam Vinatieri 1.25 3.00
7 Kelvin Hayden 1.25 3.00
8 Devin Hester 1.50 4.00
9 Thomas Jones 1.25 3.00
10 Brian Urlacher 2.00 5.00

2007 Playoff Prestige Super Bowl Heroes Holofoil Autographs

STATED PRINT RUN 1-25
SERIAL #'d UNDER 25 NOT PRICED
9 Thomas Jones/25 15.00 30.00

2007 Playoff Prestige Turning Pro

STATED ODDS 1:46 HOBBY
STATED ODDS 1:80 RETAIL
*FOIL/100: .8X TO 2X BASIC INSERTS
FOIL PRINT RUN 100 SER.#'d SETS
*HOLOFOIL/25: 1.5X TO 4X BASIC INSERTS
HOLOFOIL PRINT RUN 25 SER.#'d SETS
1 Jay Cutler .60 1.50
2 Matt Leinart .60 1.50
3 Joseph Addai .60 1.50
4 Maurice Jones-Drew .60 1.50
5 Reggie Bush .60 1.50
6 Laurence Maroney .75 2.00
7 Mario Williams .75 2.00
8 Sinorice Moss .75 2.00
9 LenDale White .75 2.00
10 Demetrius Williams .60 1.50

2007 Playoff Prestige Turning Pro Materials

STATED PRINT RUN 250 SER.#'d SETS
*PRIME/25: .8X TO 2X BASIC JSYs
PRIME PRINT RUN 25 SER.#'d SETS
1 Jay Cutler 4.00 10.00
2 Matt Leinart 4.00 10.00
3 Joseph Addai 4.00 10.00
4 Maurice Jones-Drew 4.00 10.00
5 Reggie Bush 4.00 10.00
6 Laurence Maroney 5.00 12.00
7 Mario Williams 5.00 12.00
8 Sinorice Moss 5.00 12.00
9 LenDale White 5.00 12.00
10 Demetrius Williams 4.00 10.00

2008 Playoff Prestige

This set was released on May 14, 2008. The base set consists of 200 cards. Cards 1-100 feature veterans, and cards 101-200 are rookies. Card #201 Jake Long was issued only in Target and Wal-Mart retail blaster boxes.

COMP.SET w/o SP's (190) 40.00 80.00
COMP.SET w/o RC's (100) 8.00 20.00
ONE ROOKIE CARD PER PACK
1 Anquan Boldin .20 .50
2 Larry Fitzgerald .25 .60
3 Edgerrin James .25 .60
4 Matt Leinart .20 .50
5 Warrick Dunn .20 .50
6 Roddy White .20 .50
7 Derrick Mason .20 .50
8 Todd Heap .20 .50
9 Willis McGahee .20 .50
10 J.P. Losman .20 .50
11 Lee Evans .25 .60
12 Marshawn Lynch .25 .60
13 Steve Smith .25 .60
14 Keary Colbert .20 .50
15 DeShaun Foster .20 .50
16 Bernard Berrian .20 .50
17 Cedric Benson .20 .50
18 Devin Hester .25 .60
19 Carson Palmer .25 .60
20 Rudi Johnson .20 .50
21 T.J. Houshmandzadeh .20 .50
22 Chad Johnson .20 .50
23 Derek Anderson .20 .50
24 Kellen Winslow .20 .50
25 Braylon Edwards .20 .50
26 Tony Romo .25 .60
27 Terrell Owens .25 .60
28 Marion Barber .20 .50
29 Jay Cutler .20 .50
30 Javon Walker .25 .60
31 Brandon Marshall .25 .60
32 Jon Kitna .20 .50
33 Calvin Johnson .30 .75
34 Roy Williams WR .20 .50
35 Brett Favre .60 1.50
36 Donald Driver .25 .60
37 Greg Jennings .20 .50
38 Matt Schaub .20 .50
39 Andre Johnson .25 .60
40 Ahman Green .25 .60
41 Peyton Manning .75 2.00
42 Joseph Addai .20 .50
43 Reggie Wayne .25 .60
44 Marvin Harrison .25 .60
45 David Garrard .20 .50
46 Fred Taylor .20 .50
47 Maurice Jones-Drew .20 .50
48 Tony Gonzalez .25 .60
49 Dwayne Bowe .25 .60
50 Larry Johnson .20 .50
51 Ted Ginn Jr. .20 .50
52 Ronnie Brown .20 .50
53 Tarvaris Jackson .20 .50
54 Adrian Peterson .30 .75
55 Chester Taylor .20 .50
56 Tom Brady 1.00 2.50
57 Randy Moss .25 .60
58 Wes Welker .25 .60
59 Laurence Maroney .25 .60
60 Drew Brees .30 .75
61 Reggie Bush .20 .50
62 Deuce McAllister .25 .60
63 Marques Colston .20 .50
64 Eli Manning .25 .60
65 Brandon Jacobs .20 .50
66 Plaxico Burress .20 .50
67 Jeremy Shockey .20 .50
68 Jerricho Cotchery .20 .50
69 Laveranues Coles .20 .50
70 Thomas Jones .20 .50
71 JaMarcus Russell .20 .50
72 Jerry Porter .20 .50
73 Ronald Curry .20 .50
74 Donovan McNabb .25 .60
75 Brian Westbrook .20 .50
76 Kevin Curtis .20 .50
77 Ben Roethlisberger .30 .75
78 Willie Parker .25 .60
79 Hines Ward .25 .60
80 Philip Rivers .30 .75
81 Antonio Gates .25 .60
82 LaDainian Tomlinson .30 .75
83 Alex Smith QB .25 .60
84 Frank Gore .25 .60
85 Vernon Davis .20 .50
86 Matt Hasselbeck .20 .50
87 Shaun Alexander .20 .50
88 Deion Branch .20 .50
89 Marc Bulger .20 .50
90 Steven Jackson .25 .60
91 Torry Holt .25 .60
92 Jeff Garcia .20 .50
93 Joey Galloway .25 .60
94 Cadillac Williams .25 .60
95 Vince Young .20 .50
96 LenDale White .20 .50
97 Brandon Jones .20 .50
98 Jason Campbell .20 .50
99 Clinton Portis .20 .50
100 Chris Cooley .20 .50
101 Adarius Bowman RC .75 2.00
102 Adrian Arrington RC .60 1.50
103 Ali Highsmith RC .60 1.50
104 Allen Patrick RC .60 1.50
105 Andre Caldwell RC .60 1.50
106 Andre Woodson RC .60 1.50
107 Anthony Alridge RC .60 1.50
108 Antoine Cason RC .75 2.00
109 Aqib Talib RC 1.00 2.50
110 C.Washington SP RC 10.00 25.00
111 Bernard Morris RC .75 2.00
112 Brad Cottam RC .60 1.50
113 Brian Brohm RC .60 1.50
114 Chad Henne RC .75 2.00
115 Chris Johnson RC .75 2.00
116 Chris Long SP RC 8.00 20.00
117 Colt Brennan RC .75 2.00
118 Cory Boyd RC .60 1.50
119 Curtis Lofton RC .75 2.00
120 DJ Hall RC .60 1.50
121 Dan Connor SP RC 12.00 30.00
122 Dantrell Savage RC .75 2.00
123 Darius Reynaud RC .60 1.50
124A Darren McFadden Red RC .60 1.50
124B Darren McFadden Wht RC 5.00 12.00
125 Davone Bess RC .75 2.00
126 Dennis Dixon RC .60 1.50
127 Derrick Harvey RC .60 1.50
128 DeSean Jackson RC 1.25 3.00
129 Devin Thomas RC .60 1.50
130 Dexter Jackson RC 1.00 2.50
131 D.Rodgers-Cromartie RC .75 2.00
132 Donnie Avery RC .75 2.00
133 Dorien Bryant RC .75 2.00
134 Earl Bennett RC 1.00 2.50
135 Early Doucet RC .60 1.50
136 Eddie Royal RC .60 1.50
137 Erik Ainge RC .60 1.50
138 Erin Henderson RC .75 2.00
139 Felix Jones SP RC 6.00 15.00
140 Fred Davis RC .60 1.50
141 Glenn Dorsey RC .60 1.50
142 Harry Douglas SP RC 8.00 20.00
143 Jacob Hester RC .60 1.50
144 Jacob Tamme RC .75 2.00
145 Jamaal Charles RC 1.00 2.50
146 James Hardy RC .60 1.50
147 Jason Rivers RC .60 1.50
148 Jed Collins SP RC 8.00 20.00
149 Jermichael Finley RC .60 1.50
150 Jerome Simpson RC .75 2.00
151 Joe Flacco RC 1.25 3.00
152 John Carlson RC .60 1.50
153 John David Booty RC .60 1.50
154 Jonathan Stewart RC 1.00 2.50
155 Jordy Nelson SP RC 12.00 30.00
156 Josh Johnson RC .60 1.50
157 Josh Morgan RC .60 1.50
158 Justin Forsett RC .75 2.00
159 Kalvin McRae RC .60 1.50
160 Keenan Burton RC .60 1.50
161 Keith Rivers RC .60 1.50
162 Kellen Davis RC .60 1.50
163 Kenny Phillips RC .60 1.50
164 Kevin O'Connell RC .60 1.50
165 Kevin Robinson RC .60 1.50
166 Kevin Smith SP RC 10.00 25.00
167 Lavelle Hawkins RC .75 2.00
168 Leodis McKelvin RC .75 2.00
169 Limas Sweed RC .60 1.50
170 Malcolm Kelly RC .60 1.50
171 Marcus Monk RC .75 2.00
172 Marcus Smith RC .75 2.00
173 Mario Manningham RC .60 1.50
174 Mark Bradford RC .60 1.50
175 Martellus Bennett RC .75 2.00
176 Martin Rucker RC .60 1.50
177 Matt Flynn SP RC 6.00 15.00
178 Matt Forte RC 1.00 2.50
179 Matt Ryan RC 2.00 5.00
180 Mike Hart RC .60 1.50
181 Mike Jenkins RC .60 1.50
182 Owen Schmitt RC .60 1.50
183 Paul Hubbard RC .60 1.50
184 Paul Smith RC .60 1.50
185 Peyton Hillis RC 1.00 2.50
186 Quentin Groves RC .75 2.00
187 Rashard Mendenhall RC .60 1.50
188 Ray Rice RC .60 1.50
189 Reggie Smith SP RC 8.00 20.00
190 Ryan Grice-Mullen RC .60 1.50
191 Sam Keller RC .60 1.50
192 Sedrick Ellis RC .60 1.50
193 Steve Slaton RC .60 1.50
194 Tashard Choice RC .60 1.50
195 Terrell Thomas RC .60 1.50
196 Thomas Brown RC .60 1.50
197 Tracy Porter RC .75 2.00
198 Vernon Gholston RC .60 1.50
199 Will Franklin RC .75 2.00
200 Xavier Adibi RC .60 1.50
201 Jake Long SP RC 75.00 150.00

2008 Playoff Prestige 10th Anniversary

*VETS 1-100: 12X TO 30X BASIC CARDS
*ROOKIES: 5X TO 12X BASIC RC
*ROOKIES: .6X TO 1.5X BASIC RC SP
10TH ANNIVERSARY PRINT RUN 10

2008 Playoff Prestige Draft Picks Light Blue

*ROOKIES: .6X TO 1.5X BASIC RC
*ROOKIES: .1X TO .25X BASIC SP RC
STATED PRINT RUN 999 SER.#'d SETS

2008 Playoff Prestige Xtra Points

*VETS 1-100: 2X TO 5X BASIC CARDS
*ROOKIES 101-200: .8X TO 2X BASIC RC
*ROOKIES: .1X TO .3X BASIC SP RC
STATED PRINT RUN 300 SER.#'d SETS

2008 Playoff Prestige Xtra Points Black

*VETS 1-100: 12X TO 30X BASIC CARDS
*ROOKIES: 5X TO 12X BASIC RC
*ROOKIES: .6X TO 1.5X BASIC SP RC
XTRA POINTS BLACK PRINT RUN 10
124 Darren McFadden 8.00 20.00

2008 Playoff Prestige Xtra Points Gold

*VETS 1-100: 2X TO 5X BASIC CARDS
*ROOKIES: .8X TO 2X BASIC RC
*ROOKIES: .1X TO .3X BASIC SP RC
STATED PRINT RUN 250 SER.#'d SETS

2008 Playoff Prestige Xtra Points Green

*VETS 1-100: 6X TO 15X BASIC CARDS
*ROOKIES: 2.5X TO 6X BASIC RC
*ROOKIES: .4X TO 1X BASIC SP RC
STATED PRINT RUN 25 SER.#'d SETS

2008 Playoff Prestige Xtra Points Purple

*VETS 1-100: 4X TO 10X BASIC CARDS
*ROOKIES: 1.5X TO 4X BASIC RC
*ROOKIES: .25X TO .6X BASIC SP RC
STATED PRINT RUN 50 SER.#'d SETS

2008 Playoff Prestige Xtra Points Red

*VET 1-100: 2.5X TO 6X BASIC CARDS
*ROOKIES: 1X TO 2.5X BASIC RC
*ROOKIES: .15X TO .4X BASIC SP RC
STATED PRINT RUN 100 SER.#'d SETS

2008 Playoff Prestige Award Winners

*FOIL/100: .5X TO 1.2X BASIC INSERTS
FOIL PRINT RUN 100 SER.#'d SETS
*HOLOFOIL/25: 1.2X TO 3X BASIC INSERTS
HOLOFOIL PRINT RUN 25 SER.#'d SETS
UNPRICED AUTO PRINT RUN 4-10
1 Adrian Peterson .75 2.00
2 Patrick Willis .60 1.50
3 Bob Sanders .60 1.50
4 Tom Brady 2.50 6.00
5 Greg Ellis .50 1.25
6 Tom Brady 2.50 6.00
7 Brett Favre 1.50 4.00
8 Brett Favre 1.50 4.00
9 Eli Manning .60 1.50
10 Adrian Peterson .75 2.00

2008 Playoff Prestige Award Winners Autographs

UNPRICED AUTO PRINT RUN 4-10

2008 Playoff Prestige Award Winners Materials

STATED PRINT RUN 100 SER.#'d SETS
*PRIME/25: .8X TO 2X BASIC JSY
PRIME PRINT RUN 25 SER.#'d SETS
1 Adrian Peterson 4.00 10.00
2 Patrick Willis 3.00 8.00
4 Tom Brady 12.00 30.00
6 Tom Brady 12.00 30.00
7 Brett Favre 8.00 20.00
8 Brett Favre 8.00 20.00
9 Eli Manning 3.00 8.00
10 Adrian Peterson 4.00 10.00

2008 Playoff Prestige Connections

*FOIL/100: .6X TO 1.5X BASIC INSERTS
FOIL PRINT RUN 100 SER.#'d SETS
*HOLOFOIL/25: 1.2X TO 3X BASIC INSERTS
HOLOFOIL PRINT RUN 25 SER.#'d SETS
1 T.Romo/T.Owens .60 1.50
2 T.Brady/R.Moss 2.50 6.00
3 Roeth/S.Holmes .75 2.00
4 C.Palmer/C.Johnson .60 1.50
5 Anderson/Edwards .50 1.25
6 Palmer/Housh .60 1.50
7 P.Manning/D.Clark 2.00 5.00
8 P.Rivers/A.Gates .75 2.00
9 D.Brees/M.Colston .75 2.00
10 E.Manning/P.Burress .60 1.50
11 P.Manning/R.Wayne 2.00 5.00
12 J.Kitna/R.Williams WR .50 1.25
13 B.Favre/G.Jennings 1.50 4.00
14 J.Garcia/J.Galloway .60 1.50
15 K.Warner/L.Fitzgerald .60 1.50
16 M.Schaub/A.Johnson .60 1.50
17 T.Brady/W.Welker 2.50 6.00
18 J.Cutler/B.Marshall .60 1.50
19 M.Bulger/T.Holt .60 1.50
20 J.Campbell/C.Cooley .50 1.25

2008 Playoff Prestige Connections Materials

STATED PRINT RUN 250 SER.#'d SETS
*PRIME/25: 1X TO 2.5X BASIC JSYs
PRIME PRINT RUN 25 SER.#'d SETS
1 T.Romo/T.Owens 3.00 8.00
2 T.Brady/R.Moss 20.00 50.00

3 B.Roeth/S.Holmes 4.00 10.00
4 C.Palmer/C.Johnson 3.00 8.00
5 Anderson/Edwards 2.50 6.00
6 C.Palmer/T.Housh 3.00 8.00
7 P.Manning/D.Clark 10.00 25.00
8 P.Rivers/A.Gates 4.00 10.00
9 D.Brees/M.Colston 4.00 10.00
10 E.Manning/P.Burress 3.00 8.00
11 P.Manning/R.Wayne 10.00 25.00
12 J.Kitna/R.Williams WR 2.50 6.00
13 B.Favre/G.Jennings 8.00 20.00
14 J.Garcia/J.Galloway 3.00 8.00
15 K.Warner/L.Fitzgerald 3.00 8.00
16 M.Schaub/A.Johnson 3.00 8.00
17 T.Brady/W.Welker 12.00 30.00
18 J.Cutler/B.Marshall 3.00 8.00
19 M.Bulger/T.Holt 3.00 8.00
20 J.Campbell/C.Cooley 2.50 6.00

2008 Playoff Prestige Draft Picks Rights Autographs

AUTO PRINT RUN 50-250
101 Adarius Bowman/250 5.00 12.00
104 Allen Patrick/250 4.00 10.00
105 Andre Caldwell/250 4.00 10.00
106 Andre Woodson/100 5.00 12.00
107 Anthony Alridge/250 4.00 10.00
108 Antoine Cason/250 5.00 12.00
110 C.Washington/250 5.00 12.00
111 Bernard Morris/250 5.00 12.00
112 Brad Cottam/250 4.00 10.00
113 Brian Brohm/50 6.00 15.00
114 Chad Henne/100 6.00 15.00
115 Chris Johnson/250 5.00 12.00
116 Chris Long/100 6.00 15.00
117 Colt Brennan/100 6.00 15.00
118 Cory Boyd/250 4.00 10.00
119 Curtis Lofton/250 5.00 12.00
120 DJ Hall/250 4.00 10.00
121 Dan Connor/250 4.00 10.00
122 Dantrell Savage/250 5.00 12.00
123 Darius Reynaud/250 4.00 10.00
124 Darren McFadden/100 5.00 12.00
125 Davone Bess/250 5.00 12.00
126 Dennis Dixon/100 5.00 12.00
128 DeSean Jackson/50 12.00 30.00
129 Devin Thomas/100 5.00 12.00
130 Dexter Jackson/250 6.00 15.00
131 D.Rodgers-Cromartie/250 5.00 12.00
132 Donnie Avery/100 6.00 15.00
133 Dorien Bryant/250 5.00 12.00
134 Earl Bennett/100 8.00 20.00
137 Erik Ainge/100 5.00 12.00
138 Erin Henderson/250 5.00 12.00
139 Felix Jones/100 5.00 12.00
143 Jacob Hester/250 4.00 10.00
144 Jacob Tamme/250 5.00 12.00
145 Jamaal Charles/250 6.00 15.00
146 James Hardy/100 5.00 12.00
148 Jed Collins/250 5.00 12.00
151 Joe Flacco/250 15.00 40.00
152 John Carlson/250 4.00 10.00
153 John David Booty/100 5.00 12.00
154 Jonathan Stewart/100 20.00 50.00
156 Josh Johnson/250 4.00 10.00
157 Josh Morgan/250 4.00 10.00
158 Justin Forsett/250 5.00 12.00
159 Kalvin McRae/250 4.00 10.00
161 Keith Rivers/250 4.00 10.00
162 Kellen Davis/250 4.00 10.00
164 Kevin O'Connell/100 5.00 12.00
167 Lavelle Hawkins/250 5.00 12.00
168 Leodis McKelvin/250 5.00 12.00
169 Limas Sweed/100 5.00 12.00
170 Malcolm Kelly/100 5.00 12.00
171 Marcus Monk/250 5.00 12.00
173 Mario Manningham/250 8.00 20.00
174 Mark Bradford/250 4.00 10.00
175 Martellus Bennett/250 8.00 20.00
177 Matt Flynn/250 4.00 10.00
178 Matt Forte/250 15.00 40.00
179 Matt Ryan/100 40.00 100.00
180 Mike Hart/250 4.00 10.00
182 Owen Schmitt/250 4.00 10.00
183 Paul Hubbard/250 4.00 10.00
184 Paul Smith/250 4.00 10.00
185 Peyton Hillis/250 6.00 15.00
186 Quentin Groves/250 5.00 12.00
187 Rashard Mendenhall/100 5.00 12.00
188 Ray Rice/250 4.00 10.00
191 Sam Keller/250 4.00 10.00
194 Tashard Choice/100 5.00 12.00
195 Terrell Thomas/250 4.00 10.00
197 Tracy Porter/250 5.00 12.00
198 Vernon Gholston/250 4.00 10.00
199 Will Franklin/250 5.00 12.00

2008 Playoff Prestige League Leaders

*FOIL/100: .8X TO 2X BASIC INSERTS
FOIL PRINT RUN 100 SER.#'d SETS
*HOLOFOIL/25: 1.5X TO 4X BASIC INSERTS
HOLOFOIL PRINT RUN 25 SER.#'d SETS
1 T.Brady/D.Brees 2.00 5.00
2 T.Romo/B.Favre 1.25 3.00
3 C.Palmer/J.Kitna .50 1.25
4 P.Mann/Hasselbeck 1.50 4.00
5 D.Anderson/J.Cutler .40 1.00
6 Tomlinson/Peterson .60 1.50
7 Westbrook/W.Parker .50 1.25
8 J.Lewis/C.Portis .50 1.25
9 E.James/W.McGahee .50 1.25
10 F.Taylor/T.Jones .40 1.00
11 R.Wayne/R.Moss .50 1.25
12 C.Johnson/L.Fitzgerald .50 1.25
13 T.Owens/B.Marshall .50 1.25
14 B.Edwards/M.Colston .40 1.00
15 R.White/T.Holt .50 1.25
16 Brady/Brees/Romo/Favre 2.50 6.00
17 Toml/Ptrsn/Wstbrk/Prkr .75 2.00
18 Wyn/Mos/Jnsn/Fitz .60 1.50
19 Plmr/Kit/P.Mnn/Hsslb 2.00 5.00
20 Lws/Prts/Jms/McGa .60 1.50
21 Owns/Mrshll/Edw/Clstn .60 1.50
22 Mos/Edwrds/Owns/Burr .60 1.50
23 Toml/Adda/Ptrsn/Prts .75 2.00
24 Brdy/Rom/Roeth/P.Man 2.50 6.00
25 Moss/Toml/Edwrds/Add .75 2.00

2008 Playoff Prestige League Leaders Materials

STATED PRINT RUN 250 SER.#'d SETS
*PRIME: .8X TO 2X BASIC INSERTS
PRIME PRINT RUN 25 SER.#'d SETS
1 T.Brady/D.Brees 8.00 20.00
2 T.Romo/B.Favre 8.00 20.00
3 C.Palmer/J.Kitna 3.00 8.00
4 P.Manning/M.Hasselbeck 10.00 25.00
5 D.Anderson/J.Cutler 2.50 6.00
6 L.Tomlinson/A.Peterson 4.00 10.00
7 B.Westbrook/W.Parker 3.00 8.00
8 J.Lewis/C.Portis 3.00 8.00
9 E.James/W.McGahee 3.00 8.00
10 F.Taylor/T.Jones 2.50 6.00
11 R.Wayne/R.Moss 3.00 8.00
12 C.Johnson/L.Fitzgerald 3.00 8.00
13 T.Owens/B.Marshall 3.00 8.00
14 B.Edwards/M.Colston 2.50 6.00
15 R.White/T.Holt 3.00 8.00
16 Brady/Brees/Romo/Favre 20.00 40.00
17 Toml/Ptrsn/Wstbrk/Prkr 5.00 12.00
18 Wyn/Mos/Jnsn/Fitz 4.00 10.00
19 Plmr/Kit/P.Mnn/Hsslb 12.00 30.00
20 Lws/Prts/Jms/McGa 4.00 10.00
21 Owns/Mrshll/Edw/Clstn 4.00 10.00
22 Mos/Edwrds/Owns/Burr 4.00 10.00
23 Toml/Adda/Ptrsn/Prts 10.00 25.00
24 Brdy/Rom/Roeth/P.Man 20.00 40.00
25 Moss/Toml/Edwrds/Add 5.00 12.00

2008 Playoff Prestige NFL Draft

26-35 ISSUED IN RETAIL PACKS
*FOIL/100: .6X TO 1.5X BASIC INSERTS
FOIL PRINT RUN 100 SER.#'d SETS
*HOLOFOIL/25: 1.2X TO 3X BASIC INSERTS
HOLOFOIL PRINT RUN 25 SER.#'d SETS
1 Darren McFadden .40 1.00
2 Matt Ryan 1.25 3.00
3 Keith Rivers .40 1.00
4 Mike Jenkins .40 1.00
5 DeSean Jackson .75 2.00
6 Kenny Phillips .40 1.00
7 Jonathan Stewart .60 1.50
8 Brian Brohm .40 1.00
9 Leodis McKelvin .50 1.25
10 Rashard Mendenhall .40 1.00
11 Dan Connor .40 1.00
12 Fred Davis .40 1.00
13 Felix Jones .40 1.00
14 James Hardy .40 1.00
15 Dominique Rodgers-Cromartie .50 1.25
16 Antoine Cason .50 1.25
17 Malcolm Kelly .40 1.00
18 Early Doucet .40 1.00
19 Mario Manningham .40 1.00
20 Chad Henne .50 1.25
21 Jamaal Charles .60 1.50
22 Chris Johnson .50 1.25
23 Andre Woodson .40 1.00
24 Martellus Bennett .50 1.25
25 Andre Caldwell .40 1.00
26 Chris Long .50 1.25
27 John David Booty .40 1.00
28 Mike Hart .40 1.00
29 Colt Brennan .50 1.25
30 Ray Rice .40 1.00
31 Limas Sweed .40 1.00
32 Devin Thomas .40 1.00
33 Kevin Smith .40 1.00
34 Steve Slaton .40 1.00
35 Joe Flacco .75 2.00

2008 Playoff Prestige NFL Draft Autographs

STATED PRINT RUN 25-100
1 Darren McFadden/50 6.00 15.00
2 Matt Ryan/50 50.00 120.00
3 Keith Rivers/25 12.00 30.00
5 DeSean Jackson/25 20.00 50.00
7 Jonathan Stewart/50 10.00 25.00
8 Brian Brohm/25
9 Leodis McKelvin/100 6.00 15.00
10 Rashard Mendenhall/25 10.00 25.00
11 Dan Connor/25 10.00 25.00
13 Felix Jones/25 10.00 25.00
14 James Hardy/50 15.00 40.00
15 Dominique Rodgers-Cromartie/100 6.00 15.00
16 Antoine Cason/100 6.00 15.00
17 Malcolm Kelly/25 30.00 60.00
19 Mario Manningham/50 6.00 15.00
20 Chad Henne/25 12.00 30.00
21 Jamaal Charles/25 25.00 60.00
22 Chris Johnson/25 12.00 30.00
23 Andre Woodson/50 6.00 15.00
24 Martellus Bennett/100 6.00 15.00
25 Andre Caldwell/50 6.00 15.00

2008 Playoff Prestige NFL Draft Autographed Patch College Logo

STATED PRINT RUN 50-100
1 Matt Ryan/50 60.00 120.00
2 Chad Henne/50 8.00 20.00
3 Erik Ainge/100 30.00 50.00
4 Darren McFadden/50 6.00 15.00
5 Jonathan Stewart/50 40.00 80.00
6 Rashard Mendenhall/50 6.00 15.00
7 Tashard Choice/100 5.00 12.00
8 Malcolm Kelly/50 30.00 60.00
9 Limas Sweed/50 6.00 15.00
10 Devin Thomas/100 20.00 40.00

2008 Playoff Prestige NFL Draft Autographed Patch Draft Logo

STATED PRINT RUN 100-250
1 Matt Ryan/100 40.00 100.00
2 Chad Henne/100 6.00 15.00
3 Erik Ainge/250 15.00 30.00
4 Darren McFadden/100 5.00 12.00
5 Jonathan Stewart/100 30.00 60.00
6 Rashard Mendenhall/100 5.00 12.00
7 Tashard Choice/250 4.00 10.00
8 Malcolm Kelly/100 20.00 50.00
9 Limas Sweed/100 5.00 12.00
10 Devin Thomas/250 12.00 30.00

2008 Playoff Prestige NFL Draft Autographed Patch NFL Logo

STATED PRINT RUN 25 SER.#'d SETS
1 Matt Ryan 75.00 150.00
2 Chad Henne 12.00 30.00
3 Erik Ainge 30.00 60.00
4 Darren McFadden 10.00 25.00
5 Jonathan Stewart 25.00 60.00
6 Rashard Mendenhall 10.00 25.00
7 Tashard Choice 10.00 25.00
8 Malcolm Kelly 50.00 100.00
9 Limas Sweed 10.00 25.00

2008 Playoff Prestige Preferred Materials

STATED PRINT RUN 100 SER.#'d SETS
*PRIME/25: .8X TO 2X BASIC JSYs
PRIME PRINT RUN 25 SER.#'d SETS
UNPRICED AUTO PRINT RUN 7-24
1 Peyton Manning 10.00 25.00
2 Marion Barber 2.50 6.00
3 T.J. Houshmandzadeh 2.50 6.00
4 Joseph Addai 2.50 6.00
5 Tony Romo 3.00 8.00
6 Adrian Peterson 4.00 10.00
7 Willie Parker 3.00 8.00
8 LaDainian Tomlinson 4.00 10.00
9 Eli Manning 3.00 8.00
10 Willis McGahee 2.50 6.00

2008 Playoff Prestige Preferred Materials Signatures Prime

PATCH AUTO PRINT RUN 5-25
SERIAL #'d UNDER 25 NOT PRICED
2 Marion Barber/25 30.00 60.00
10 Willis McGahee/25 25.00 50.00

2008 Playoff Prestige Preferred Materials Signatures

UNPRICED AUTO PRINT RUN 7-24
SERIAL #'d UNDER 24 NOT PRICED
2 Marion Barber/24 25.00 50.00

2008 Playoff Prestige Preferred Signatures

STATED PRINT RUN 10-25
SERIAL #'d UNDER 25 NOT PRICED
2 Marion Barber/25 20.00 40.00
10 Willis McGahee/25 15.00 30.00

2008 Playoff Prestige Prestigious Picks Blue

BLUE PRINT RUN 1000 SER.#'d SETS
*RED/750: .4X TO 1X BLUE/1000
RED PRINT RUN 750 SER.#'d SETS
*BLACK/500: .4X TO 1X BLUE/1000
BLACK PRINT RUN 500 SER.#'d SETS
*PURPLE/250: .5X TO 1.2X BLUE/1000
PURPLE PRINT RUN 250 SER.#'d SETS
*GREEN/100: .6X TO 1.5X BLUE/1000
GREEN PRINT RUN 100 SER.#'d SETS
*SILVER/50: .8X TO 2X BLUE/1000
SILVER PRINT RUN 50 SER.#'d SETS
*GOLD/25: 1X TO 2.5X BLUE/1000
GOLD PRINT RUN 25 SER.#'d SETS
*PLATINUM/10: 2X TO 5X BLUE/1000
PLATINUM PRINT RUN 10 SER.#'d SETS
1 Simeon Castille .60 1.50
2 Shawn Crable .60 1.50
3 Chris Long .75 2.00
4 DJ Hall .60 1.50
5 Antoine Cason .75 2.00
6 Felix Jones .60 1.50
7 Darren McFadden .60 1.50
8 Marcus Monk .75 2.00
9 Quentin Groves .75 2.00
10 Matt Ryan 2.00 5.00
11 DeSean Jackson 1.25 3.00
12 Colt Brennan .75 2.00
13 Rashard Mendenhall .60 1.50
14 Aqib Talib 1.00 2.50
15 Harry Douglas .75 2.00
16 Brian Brohm .60 1.50
17 Glenn Dorsey .60 1.50
18 Early Doucet .60 1.50
19 Ali Highsmith .60 1.50
20 Chevis Jackson .60 1.50
21 Matt Flynn .60 1.50
22 Craig Steltz .60 1.50
23 Kenny Phillips .60 1.50
24 Calais Campbell .75 2.00
25 Mike Hart .60 1.50
26 Chad Henne .75 2.00
27 Jamar Adams .60 1.50
28 Mario Manningham .60 1.50
29 Adrian Arrington .60 1.50
30 Ernie Wheelwright .75 2.00
31 Vernon Gholston .60 1.50
32 Malcolm Kelly .60 1.50
33 Allen Patrick .60 1.50
34 Jonathan Stewart 1.00 2.50
35 Dennis Dixon .60 1.50
36 Dan Connor .60 1.50
37 Erik Ainge .60 1.50
38 Jonathan Hefney .60 1.50
39 Jamaal Charles 1.00 2.50
40 Limas Sweed .60 1.50
41 Robert Killebrew .75 2.00
42 Sedrick Ellis .60 1.50
43 Keith Rivers .60 1.50
44 Fred Davis .60 1.50
45 John David Booty .60 1.50
46 Terrell Thomas .60 1.50
47 Xavier Adibi .60 1.50
48 Brandon Flowers .75 2.00
49 Eddie Royal .60 1.50
50 Steve Slaton .60 1.50

2008 Playoff Prestige Prestigious Picks Autographs

STATED PRINT RUN 25-100
1 Simeon Castille/25 10.00 25.00
2 Shawn Crable/100 5.00 12.00
3 Chris Long/50 8.00 20.00
4 DJ Hall/25 10.00 25.00
5 Antoine Cason/100 6.00 15.00
6 Felix Jones/25 10.00 25.00
7 Darren McFadden/25 10.00 25.00
8 Marcus Monk/100 6.00 15.00
9 Quentin Groves/25 12.00 30.00
10 Matt Ryan/25 60.00 120.00
11 DeSean Jackson/25 20.00 50.00
12 Colt Brennan/25 12.00 30.00
13 Rashard Mendenhall/25 10.00 25.00
16 Brian Brohm/25
20 Chevis Jackson/100 5.00 12.00
21 Matt Flynn/25 10.00 25.00
22 Craig Steltz/25 10.00 25.00
24 Calais Campbell/25 12.00 30.00
25 Mike Hart/25 10.00 25.00
26 Chad Henne/25 12.00 30.00
27 Jamar Adams/100 5.00 12.00
28 Mario Manningham/50 6.00 15.00
30 Ernie Wheelwright/100 6.00 15.00
31 Vernon Gholston/100 5.00 12.00
32 Malcolm Kelly/25 10.00 25.00
33 Allen Patrick/25 10.00 25.00
34 Jonathan Stewart/25 15.00 40.00
35 Dennis Dixon/50 10.00 25.00
36 Dan Connor/25 10.00 25.00
37 Erik Ainge /25 10.00 25.00
39 Jamaal Charles/25 15.00 40.00
40 Limas Sweed/25 10.00 25.00
43 Keith Rivers/25 10.00 25.00
45 John David Booty/25 10.00 25.00
46 Terrell Thomas/100 5.00 12.00
48 Brandon Flowers/100 6.00 15.00

2008 Playoff Prestige Prestigious Picks Materials Red

RED PRINT RUN 250 SER.#'d SETS
*PURPLE/100: .5X TO 1.2X RED/250
PURPLE PRINT RUN 100 SER.#'d SETS
*GREEN/75: .6X TO 1.5X RED/250
GREEN PRINT RUN 75 SER.#'d SETS
*GOLD/50: .6X TO 1.5X RED/250
GOLD PRINT RUN 50 SER.#'d SETS
*BLACK/25: .8X TO 2X RED/250
BLACK PRINT RUN 25 SER.#'d SETS
*PLAT.PATCH/25: 1X TO 2.5X RED/250
PLATINUM PATCHES PRINT RUN 25 SER.#'d SETS
1 Simeon Castille 1.50 4.00
2 Shawn Crable 1.50 4.00
3 Chris Long 2.00 5.00
4 DJ Hall 1.50 4.00
5 Antoine Cason 2.50 6.00
6 Felix Jones 1.50 4.00
7 Darren McFadden 1.50 4.00
8 Marcus Monk 2.00 5.00
9 Quentin Groves 2.00 5.00
10 Matt Ryan 5.00 12.00
11 DeSean Jackson 3.00 8.00
12 Colt Brennan 2.00 5.00
13 Rashard Mendenhall 1.50 4.00
14 Aqib Talib 2.50 6.00
15 Harry Douglas 2.50 6.00
16 Brian Brohm 1.50 4.00
17 Glenn Dorsey 1.50 4.00
18 Early Doucet 1.50 4.00
19 Ali Highsmith 2.50 6.00
20 Chevis Jackson 1.50 4.00
21 Matt Flynn 1.50 4.00
22 Craig Steltz 1.50 4.00
23 Kenny Phillips 1.50 4.00
24 Calais Campbell 2.50 6.00
25 Mike Hart 1.50 4.00
26 Chad Henne 2.00 5.00
27 Jamar Adams 2.50 6.00
28 Mario Manningham 1.50 4.00
29 Adrian Arrington 1.50 4.00
30 Ernie Wheelwright 2.50 6.00
31 Vernon Gholston 1.50 4.00
32 Malcolm Kelly 1.50 4.00
33 Allen Patrick 1.50 4.00
34 Jonathan Stewart 2.50 6.00
35 Dennis Dixon 1.50 4.00
36 Dan Connor 1.50 4.00
37 Erik Ainge 4.00 10.00
38 Jonathan Hefney 2.50 6.00
39 Jamaal Charles 2.50 6.00
40 Limas Sweed 1.50 4.00
41 Robert Killebrew 2.50 6.00
42 Sedrick Ellis 1.50 4.00
43 Keith Rivers 1.50 4.00
44 Fred Davis 1.50 4.00
45 John David Booty 1.50 4.00
46 Terrell Thomas 2.50 6.00
47 Xavier Adibi 2.50 6.00
48 Brandon Flowers 2.50 6.00
49 Eddie Royal 1.50 4.00
50 Steve Slaton 1.50 4.00

2008 Playoff Prestige Prestigious Pros Blue

BLUE PRINT RUN 1000 SER.#'d SETS
*RED/750: .4X TO 1X BLUE/1000
RED PRINT RUN 750 SER.#'d SETS
*BLACK/500: .5X TO 1.2X BLUE/1000
BLACK PRINT RUN 500 SER.#'d SETS
*PURPLE/250: .6X TO 1.5X BLUE/1000
PURPLE PRINT RUN 250 SER.#'d SETS
*GREEN/100: .8X TO 2X BLUE/1000
GREEN PRINT RUN 100 SER.#'d SETS
*SILVER/50: 1X TO 2.5X BLUE/1000
SILVER PRINT RUN 50 SER.#'d SETS
*GOLD/25: 1.2X TO 3X BLUE/1000
GOLD PRINT RUN 25 SER.#'d SETS
*PLATINUM/10: 2.5X TO 6X BLUE/1000
PLATINUM PRINT RUN 10 SER.#'d SETS
1 Matt Hasselbeck .75 2.00
2 Derek Anderson .75 2.00
3 Jeff Garcia .75 2.00
4 Philip Rivers 1.25 3.00
5 Alex Smith QB 1.00 2.50
6 Thomas Jones .75 2.00
7 Ronnie Brown .75 2.00
8 DeShaun Foster .75 2.00
9 Larry Johnson .75 2.00
10 Brandon Jacobs .75 2.00
11 Cedric Benson .75 2.00
12 Frank Gore 1.00 2.50
13 Shaun Alexander .75 2.00
14 Warrick Dunn .75 2.00
15 Laurence Maroney 1.00 2.50
16 Steven Jackson .75 2.00
17 Rudi Johnson .75 2.00
18 Anquan Boldin .75 2.00
19 Torry Holt 1.00 2.50
20 Brandon Marshall 1.00 2.50
21 Antonio Gates 1.00 2.50
22 Roy Williams WR .75 2.00
23 Donald Driver 1.00 2.50
24 Dwayne Bowe 1.00 2.50
25 Steve Smith 1.00 2.50
26 Marvin Harrison 1.00 2.50
27 Andre Johnson 1.00 2.50
28 Marion Barber .75 2.00
29 Tony Gonzalez 1.00 2.50
30 Jerricho Cotchery .75 2.00
31 Peyton Manning 3.00 8.00
32 Tom Brady 4.00 10.00
33 Tony Romo 1.00 2.50
34 Brett Favre 2.50 6.00
35 Adrian Peterson 1.25 3.00
36 Willie Parker 1.00 2.50
37 Marshawn Lynch 1.00 2.50
38 LaDainian Tomlinson 1.25 3.00
39 Brian Westbrook .75 2.00
40 Randy Moss 1.00 2.50
41 Reggie Wayne 1.00 2.50
42 Terrell Owens 1.00 2.50
43 Larry Fitzgerald 1.00 2.50
44 Marques Colston .75 2.00
45 Reggie Bush .75 2.00
46 Maurice Jones-Drew .75 2.00
47 Ben Roethlisberger 1.25 3.00
48 Jay Cutler .75 2.00
49 Plaxico Burress .75 2.00
50 Edgerrin James 1.00 2.50

2008 Playoff Prestige Prestigious Pros Autographs

STATED PRINT RUN 1-100
SERIAL #'d UNDER 15 NOT PRICED
7 Ronnie Brown/35 6.00 15.00
9 Larry Johnson/50 5.00 12.00
10 Brandon Jacobs/30 6.00 15.00
11 Cedric Benson/50 5.00 12.00
12 Frank Gore/35 8.00 20.00
15 Laurence Maroney/15 10.00 25.00
16 Steven Jackson/25 8.00 20.00
17 Rudi Johnson/50 5.00 12.00
18 Anquan Boldin/25 8.00 20.00
19 Torry Holt/16 12.00 30.00
20 Brandon Marshall/100 6.00 15.00
22 Roy Williams WR/15 8.00 20.00
23 Donald Driver/25 10.00 25.00
25 Steve Smith/15 12.00 30.00
30 Jerricho Cotchery/75 5.00 12.00
39 Brian Westbrook/15 8.00 20.00
44 Marques Colston/100 6.00 15.00
46 Maurice Jones-Drew/25 8.00 20.00

2008 Playoff Prestige Prestigious Pros Materials Green

GREEN PRINT RUN 50-100
*GOLD/50: .5X TO 1.2X GREEN
GOLD PRINT RUN 50 SER.#'d SETS
*BLACK/25: .8X TO 2X GREEN
BLACK PRINT RUN 25 SER.#'d SETS
*PLAT.PATCH/25: 1X TO 2.5X GREEN
PLATINUM PATCH PRINT RUN 25
1 Matt Hasselbeck 3.00 8.00
2 Derek Anderson 3.00 8.00
3 Jeff Garcia 3.00 8.00
4 Philip Rivers 5.00 12.00
5 Alex Smith QB 4.00 10.00
6 Thomas Jones 3.00 8.00
7 Ronnie Brown 3.00 8.00
9 Larry Johnson 3.00 8.00
10 Brandon Jacobs 3.00 8.00
11 Cedric Benson 3.00 8.00
12 Frank Gore 4.00 10.00
13 Shaun Alexander 3.00 8.00
14 Warrick Dunn 3.00 8.00
15 Laurence Maroney 4.00 10.00
16 Steven Jackson 3.00 8.00
17 Rudi Johnson 3.00 8.00
18 Anquan Boldin 3.00 8.00
19 Torry Holt 4.00 10.00
20 Brandon Marshall 4.00 10.00
21 Antonio Gates 4.00 10.00
22 Roy Williams WR 3.00 8.00
23 Donald Driver 4.00 10.00
24 Dwayne Bowe 4.00 10.00
25 Steve Smith 4.00 10.00
26 Marvin Harrison 4.00 10.00
27 Andre Johnson 4.00 10.00
28 Marion Barber 3.00 8.00
29 Tony Gonzalez 4.00 10.00
30 Jerricho Cotchery 3.00 8.00
31 Peyton Manning/75 12.00 30.00
32 Tom Brady/50 15.00 40.00
33 Tony Romo 4.00 10.00
34 Brett Favre 10.00 25.00
35 Adrian Peterson 5.00 12.00
36 Willie Parker 4.00 10.00
37 Marshawn Lynch 4.00 10.00
38 LaDainian Tomlinson 5.00 12.00
39 Brian Westbrook 3.00 8.00
40 Randy Moss 4.00 10.00
41 Reggie Wayne 4.00 10.00
42 Terrell Owens 4.00 10.00
43 Larry Fitzgerald 4.00 10.00
44 Marques Colston 3.00 8.00
45 Reggie Bush 3.00 8.00
46 Maurice Jones-Drew 3.00 8.00
47 Ben Roethlisberger 5.00 12.00
48 Jay Cutler 3.00 8.00
49 Plaxico Burress 3.00 8.00
50 Edgerrin James 4.00 10.00

2008 Playoff Prestige Rookie Review

151A A.J. Hawk 1.00 2.50
151B Brady Quinn 1.00 2.50
152 JaMarcus Russell 1.00 2.50
153 Troy Smith 1.25 3.00
155 Adrian Peterson 5.00 12.00
156 Marshawn Lynch 1.25 3.00
157 Michael Bush 1.00 2.50
158 Kenny Irons 1.00 2.50
161 Brandon Marshall 1.25 3.00
162 Brandon Williams 1.00 2.50
163 Calvin Johnson 1.50 4.00
164 Ted Ginn Jr. 1.00 2.50
165 Dwayne Jarrett 1.25 3.00
166 Sidney Rice 1.00 2.50
167 Dwayne Bowe 1.25 3.00
168 Robert Meachem 1.00 2.50
169 Anthony Gonzalez 1.00 2.50
170 Chad Jackson 1.25 3.00
172 Steve Smith USC 1.25 3.00
176 Jason Hill 1.00 2.50
178A Greg Olsen 1.25 3.00
178B DeAngelo Williams 1.00 2.50
183 Derek Hagan 1.00 2.50
189 Patrick Willis 1.25 3.00
196 Jason Avant 1.00 2.50
201A Jerious Norwood 1.00 2.50
201B Trent Edwards 1.00 2.50
202 Kevin Kolb 1.00 2.50
203 John Beck 1.00 2.50
209 Brandon Jackson 1.25 3.00
210 Kellen Clemens 1.00 2.50
211 Paul Williams 1.00 2.50
213 Laurence Maroney 1.25 3.00
215 LenDale White 1.00 2.50
216 Leon Washington 1.00 2.50
223 Matt Leinart 1.00 2.50
224 Maurice Jones-Drew 1.00 2.50
227 Michael Robinson 1.00 2.50
231 Reggie Bush 1.00 2.50
234 Santonio Holmes 1.00 2.50
235 Sinorice Moss 1.25 3.00
238A Tarvaris Jackson 1.00 2.50
238B Brian Leonard 1.00 2.50
242 Garrett Wolfe 1.25 3.00
245 Vernon Davis 1.00 2.50
246 Vince Young 1.00 2.50
251 Chris Henry RB 1.25 3.00
252 Joe Thomas 1.25 3.00
253 Yamon Figurs 1.00 2.50
254 Marques Colston 1.00 2.50

2008 Playoff Prestige Rookie Review Autographs

STATED PRINT RUN 1-50
SERIAL #'d UNDER 25 NOT PRICED
151 A.J. Hawk/50 12.00 30.00
161 Brandon Marshall/25 12.00 30.00
178 DeAngelo Williams/25 12.00 30.00
201 Jerious Norwood/35 8.00 20.00
215 LenDale White/25 10.00 25.00
224 Maurice Jones-Drew/32 12.00 30.00
242 Garrett Wolfe/25 10.00 25.00
252 Joe Thomas/42 8.00 20.00
254 Marques Colston/50 8.00 20.00

2008 Playoff Prestige Rookie Review Materials

*PRIME/50-100: .8X TO 2X BASIC JSYs
PRIME PRINT RUN 1-100
151 A.J. Hawk 3.00 8.00
151 Brady Quinn 3.00 8.00
152 JaMarcus Russell 3.00 8.00
153 Troy Smith 4.00 10.00
155 Adrian Peterson 5.00 12.00
156 Marshawn Lynch 4.00 10.00
157 Michael Bush 3.00 8.00
158 Kenny Irons 3.00 8.00
161 Brandon Marshall 4.00 10.00
162 Brandon Williams 3.00 8.00
163 Calvin Johnson 5.00 12.00
164 Ted Ginn Jr. 3.00 8.00
165 Dwayne Jarrett 4.00 10.00
166 Sidney Rice 3.00 8.00
167 Dwayne Bowe 4.00 10.00
168 Robert Meachem 3.00 8.00
169 Anthony Gonzalez 3.00 8.00
170 Chad Jackson 4.00 10.00
172 Steve Smith USC 4.00 10.00
176 Jason Hill 3.00 8.00
178 Greg Olsen 4.00 10.00
178 DeAngelo Williams 3.00 8.00
183 Derek Hagan 3.00 8.00
189 Patrick Willis 4.00 10.00
196 Jason Avant 3.00 8.00
201 Jerious Norwood 3.00 8.00
201 Trent Edwards 3.00 8.00
202 Kevin Kolb 3.00 8.00
203 John Beck 3.00 8.00
209 Brandon Jackson 4.00 10.00
210 Kellen Clemens 3.00 8.00
211 Paul Williams 3.00 8.00
213 Laurence Maroney 4.00 10.00
215 LenDale White 3.00 8.00
216 Leon Washington 3.00 8.00
223 Matt Leinart 3.00 8.00
224 Maurice Jones-Drew 3.00 8.00
227 Michael Robinson 3.00 8.00
231 Reggie Bush 3.00 8.00
234 Santonio Holmes 3.00 8.00
235 Sinorice Moss 4.00 10.00
238 Tarvaris Jackson 3.00 8.00
238 Brian Leonard 3.00 8.00
242 Garrett Wolfe 4.00 10.00
245 Vernon Davis 3.00 8.00
246 Vince Young 3.00 8.00
251 Chris Henry RB 4.00 10.00
252 Joe Thomas 4.00 10.00
253 Yamon Figurs 3.00 8.00

2008 Playoff Prestige Stars of the NFL

*FOIL/100: .8X TO 2X BASIC INSERTS
FOIL PRINT RUN 100 SER.#'d SETS
*HOLOFOIL/25: 1.5X TO 4X BASIC INSERTS
HOLOFOIL PRINT RUN 25 SER.#'d SETS
1 Tom Brady 2.50 6.00
2 Tony Romo .60 1.50
3 Ben Roethlisberger .75 2.00
4 Peyton Manning 2.00 5.00
5 Chad Johnson .50 1.25
6 Terrell Owens .60 1.50
7 Randy Moss .60 1.50
8 LaDainian Tomlinson .75 2.00
9 Reggie Bush .50 1.25
10 Vince Young .50 1.25
11 Willie Parker .60 1.50
12 Reggie Wayne .60 1.50
13 Marshawn Lynch .60 1.50
14 Calvin Johnson .75 2.00
15 Adrian Peterson .75 2.00
16 Brett Favre 1.50 4.00
17 Steve Smith .60 1.50
18 Joseph Addai .50 1.25
19 Eli Manning .60 1.50
20 Brian Westbrook .50 1.25

2008 Playoff Prestige Stars of the NFL Materials

STATED PRINT RUN 100 SER.#'d SETS
*PRIME/25: .8X TO 2X BASIC JSYs
PRIME PRINT RUN 25 SER.#'d SETS
1 Tom Brady 10.00 25.00
2 Tony Romo 2.50 6.00
3 Ben Roethlisberger 3.00 8.00
4 Peyton Manning 8.00 20.00
5 Chad Johnson 2.00 5.00
6 Terrell Owens 2.50 6.00
7 Randy Moss 2.50 6.00
8 LaDainian Tomlinson 3.00 8.00
9 Reggie Bush 2.00 5.00
10 Vince Young 2.00 5.00
11 Willie Parker 2.50 6.00
12 Reggie Wayne 2.50 6.00
13 Marshawn Lynch 2.50 6.00
14 Calvin Johnson 3.00 8.00
15 Adrian Peterson 3.00 8.00
16 Brett Favre 6.00 15.00
17 Steve Smith 2.50 6.00
18 Joseph Addai 2.00 5.00
19 Eli Manning 2.50 6.00
20 Brian Westbrook 2.00 5.00

2008 Playoff Prestige TD Sensations

*FOIL/100: .6X TO 1.5X BASIC INSERTS
FOIL PRINT RUN 100 SER.#'d SETS
*HOLOFOIL/25: 1.2X TO 3X BASIC INSERTS
HOLOFOIL PRINT RUN 25 SER.#'d SETS
1 Randy Moss .60 1.50
2 Braylon Edwards .50 1.25
3 T.J. Houshmandzadeh .50 1.25
4 Plaxico Burress .50 1.25
5 Terrell Owens .60 1.50
6 Wes Welker .60 1.50
7 Dallas Clark .50 1.25
8 Laveranues Coles .50 1.25
9 Santonio Holmes .50 1.25
10 Greg Jennings .50 1.25
11 Adrian Peterson .75 2.00
12 LaDainian Tomlinson .75 2.00
13 Joseph Addai .50 1.25
14 Marion Barber .50 1.25
15 Marshawn Lynch .60 1.50
16 Clinton Portis .50 1.25
17 Edgerrin James .60 1.50
18 Maurice Jones-Drew .50 1.25
19 Brian Westbrook .50 1.25
20 Devin Hester .60 1.50

2008 Playoff Prestige TD Sensations Materials

STATED PRINT RUN 100 SER.#'d SETS
*PRIME/25: .8X TO 2X BASIC JSYs
PRIME PRINT RUN 25 SER.#'d SETS
1 Randy Moss 2.50 6.00
2 Braylon Edwards 2.00 5.00
3 T.J. Houshmandzadeh 2.00 5.00
4 Plaxico Burress 2.00 5.00
5 Terrell Owens 2.50 6.00
6 Wes Welker 2.50 6.00
7 Dallas Clark 2.00 5.00
8 Laveranues Coles 2.00 5.00
9 Santonio Holmes 2.00 5.00
10 Greg Jennings 2.00 5.00
11 Adrian Peterson 3.00 8.00
12 LaDainian Tomlinson 3.00 8.00
13 Joseph Addai 2.00 5.00
14 Marion Barber 2.00 5.00
15 Marshawn Lynch 2.50 6.00
16 Clinton Portis 2.00 5.00
17 Edgerrin James 2.50 6.00
18 Maurice Jones-Drew 2.00 5.00
19 Brian Westbrook 2.00 5.00
20 Devin Hester 2.50 6.00

2008 Playoff Prestige True Colors

*FOIL/100: .6X TO 1.5X BASIC INSERTS
FOIL PRINT RUN 100 SER.#'d SETS
*HOLOFOIL/25: 1.2X TO 3X BASIC INSERTS
HOLOFOIL PRINT RUN 25 SER.#'d SETS
UNPRICED AUTO PRINT RUN 4-10
1 Carson Palmer .60 1.50
2 Tom Brady 2.50 6.00
3 Terrell Owens .60 1.50
4 Clinton Portis .50 1.25
5 Vince Young .50 1.25
6 Jay Cutler .50 1.25
7 Brett Favre 1.50 4.00
8 Reggie Bush .50 1.25
9 Ben Roethlisberger .75 2.00
10 LaDainian Tomlinson .75 2.00

2008 Playoff Prestige True Colors Autographs

UNPRICED AUTO PRINT RUN 4-10

2008 Playoff Prestige True Colors Materials

STATED PRINT RUN 100 SER.#'d SETS
*PRIME/25: .8X TO 2X BASIC JSYs
PRIME PRINT RUN 25 SER.#'d SETS
1 Carson Palmer 2.50 6.00
2 Tom Brady 10.00 25.00
3 Terrell Owens 2.50 6.00
4 Clinton Portis 2.00 5.00
5 Vince Young 2.00 5.00
6 Jay Cutler 2.00 5.00
7 Brett Favre 6.00 15.00
8 Reggie Bush 2.00 5.00
9 Ben Roethlisberger 3.00 8.00
10 LaDainian Tomlinson 3.00 8.00

2008 Playoff Prestige Hawaii Trade Conference

COMPLETE SET (6) 6.00 12.00
1 Adrian Peterson .50 1.25
2 Tom Brady 1.50 4.00
3 Eli Manning .40 1.00
4 Darren McFadden .25 .60
5 Matt Ryan .75 2.00
6 Devin Hester .40 1.00

2009 Playoff Prestige

COMP.SET w/o RC's (100) 8.00 20.00
ONE ROOKIE PER PACK
1 Kurt Warner .25 .60
2 Larry Fitzgerald .25 .60
3 Anquan Boldin .20 .50
4 Tim Hightower .20 .50
5 Roddy White .20 .50
6 Michael Turner .20 .50
7 Matt Ryan .25 .60
8 Willis McGahee .20 .50
9 Joe Flacco .25 .60
10 Trent Edwards .20 .50
11 Marshawn Lynch .25 .60
12 Lee Evans .25 .60
13 Steve Smith .25 .60
14 DeAngelo Williams .20 .50
15 Jake Delhomme .20 .50
16 Jonathan Stewart .20 .50
17 Greg Olsen .25 .60
18 Kyle Orton .20 .50
19 Matt Forte .20 .50
20 Carson Palmer .25 .60
21 Chad Ocho Cinco .20 .50
22 T.J. Houshmandzadeh .20 .50
23 Brady Quinn .20 .50
24 Jamal Lewis .25 .60
25 Kellen Winslow .20 .50
26 Braylon Edwards .20 .50
27 Tony Romo .25 .60
28 Terrell Owens .25 .60
29 Marion Barber .25 .60
30 Roy Williams WR .20 .50
31 Jay Cutler .20 .50
32 Brandon Marshall .25 .60
33 Eddie Royal .20 .50
34 Calvin Johnson .30 .75
35 Kevin Smith .20 .50
36 Aaron Rodgers .60 1.50
37 Ryan Grant .25 .60
38 Greg Jennings .20 .50
39 Matt Schaub .20 .50
40 Andre Johnson .25 .60
41 Steve Slaton .20 .50
42 Peyton Manning .75 2.00
43 Joseph Addai .20 .50
44 Reggie Wayne .25 .60
45 Anthony Gonzalez .20 .50
46 David Garrard .20 .50
47 Matt Jones .25 .60
48 Maurice Jones-Drew .20 .50
49 Larry Johnson .20 .50
50 Dwayne Bowe .25 .60
51 Chad Pennington .20 .50
52 Ronnie Brown .20 .50
53 Ted Ginn .20 .50
54 Bernard Berrian .20 .50
55 Adrian Peterson .30 .75
56 Chester Taylor .20 .50
57 Tom Brady 1.00 2.50
58 Randy Moss .25 .60
59 Wes Welker .25 .60
60 Drew Brees .30 .75
61 Reggie Bush .20 .50
62 Marques Colston .20 .50
63 Eli Manning .25 .60
64 Steve Smith USC .25 .60
65 Brandon Jacobs .20 .50
66 Kellen Clemens .20 .50
67 Jerricho Cotchery .20 .50
68 Leon Washington .20 .50
69 Thomas Jones .20 .50
70 JaMarcus Russell .20 .50
71 Justin Fargas .20 .50
72 Darren McFadden .30 .75
73 Donovan McNabb .25 .60
74 Brian Westbrook .20 .50
75 DeSean Jackson .25 .60
76 Ben Roethlisberger .30 .75
77 Willie Parker .20 .50
78 Hines Ward .25 .60
79 Santonio Holmes .20 .50
80 Philip Rivers .30 .75
81 LaDainian Tomlinson .30 .75
82 Antonio Gates .25 .60
83 Frank Gore .25 .60
84 Vernon Davis .20 .50
85 Matt Hasselbeck .20 .50
86 Deion Branch .20 .50
87 Julius Jones .20 .50
88 Marc Bulger .20 .50
89 Steven Jackson .20 .50
90 Torry Holt .25 .60
91 Antonio Bryant .20 .50
92 Earnest Graham .20 .50
93 Michael Clayton .20 .50
94 Kerry Collins .20 .50
95 LenDale White .20 .50
96 Chris Johnson .20 .50
97 Jason Campbell .20 .50
98 Clinton Portis .20 .50
99 Santana Moss .25 .60
100 Chris Cooley .20 .50
101A Aaron Curry RC 1.00 2.50
101B Aaron Curry SP Draft 6.00 15.00
102 Aaron Kelly RC .60 1.50
103 Aaron Maybin RC .75 2.00
104 Alphonso Smith RC .60 1.50
105 Andre Brown RC .75 2.00
106 Andre Smith RC .60 1.50
107 Arian Foster RC 1.50 4.00
108 Asher Allen RC .60 1.50
109 Austin Collie RC .60 1.50
110 B.J. Raji SP RC 10.00 25.00
111 Brandon Gibson RC .75 2.00
112A Brandon Pettigrew RC .60 1.50
112B B.Pettigrew SP Orng pants 2.50 6.00
113 Brandon Tate RC .75 2.00
114A Brian Cushing SP RC 10.00 25.00
114B Brian Cushing SP Draft 10.00 25.00
115A Brian Orakpo RC .75 2.00
115B Brian Orakpo SP Draft 8.00 20.00
116A Brian Robiskie RC .60 1.50
116B Brian Robiskie SP Red 6.00 15.00
117 Brooks Foster RC .60 1.50
118 Cedric Peerman RC .60 1.50
119A Chase Coffman RC .60 1.50
119B Chase Coffman SP Yellow 4.00 10.00
120 Chase Daniel SP RC 10.00 25.00
121 Chip Vaughn RC .60 1.50
122A Chris Wells RC .60 1.50
122B Chris Wells SP White 8.00 20.00
123 Clay Matthews RC 2.50 6.00
124A Clint Sintim RC .60 1.50
124B Clint Sintim SP White 4.00 10.00
125 Cornelius Ingram RC .60 1.50
126 Tony Fiammetta RC .60 1.50
127A D.J. Moore RC .75 2.00
127B D.J. Moore SP Gold 3.00 8.00
128 Darius Butler RC .75 2.00
129 Darius Passmore RC .60 1.50
130A Darrius Heyward-Bey RC 1.00 2.50
130B D.Heyward-Bey SP White 8.00 20.00
131 Travis Beckum RC .60 1.50
132 Deon Butler RC .60 1.50
133 Victor Harris RC .75 2.00
134A Derrick Williams RC .60 1.50
134B Derrick Williams SP Blue 4.00 10.00
135A Donald Brown RC .60 1.50
135B Donald Brown SP Blue 10.00 25.00
136 Eugene Monroe RC .60 1.50
137 Everette Brown RC .60 1.50
138 Duke Robinson RC .60 1.50
139 Glen Coffee RC .60 1.50
140A Graham Harrell SP RC 10.00 25.00
140B Graham Harrell SP Red 10.00 25.00
141 Demetrius Byrd RC .75 2.00
142A Hakeem Nicks SP RC 3.00 8.00
142B Hakeem Nicks SP 3.00 8.00
143 Hunter Cantwell RC .60 1.50
144 Ian Johnson SP RC 10.00 25.00
145 Jairus Byrd RC 1.00 2.50
146A James Casey RC .75 2.00
146B James Casey SP White 3.00 8.00
147 James Davis RC .60 1.50
148A James Laurinaitis RC .60 1.50
148B James Laurinaitis SP 2.50 6.00
149 Jared Cook SP RC 6.00 15.00
150 Jarett Dillard RC .60 1.50
151 Jason Smith RC .60 1.50
152A Javon Ringer RC .60 1.50
152B J.Ringer SP Ball in left arm 4.00 10.00
153A Jeremiah Johnson RC .60 1.50
153B Jeremiah Johnson SP Yellow 2.50 6.00
154 Vontae Davis RC .60 1.50
155A Jeremy Maclin RC .75 2.00
155B Jeremy Maclin SP Yellow 3.00 8.00
156 John Parker Wilson RC .60 1.50
157 John Phillips RC 1.00 2.50
158A Josh Freeman RC .60 1.50
158B Josh Freeman SP Draft 2.50 6.00
159A Juaquin Iglesias SP RC 12.00 30.00
159B Juaquin Iglesias SP White 10.00 25.00
160 Keenan Lewis RC 1.00 2.50
161A Kenny Britt RC 1.00 2.50

161B Kenny Britt SP Red 4.00 10.00
162 Kenny McKinley RC .60 1.50
163 Kevin Ogletree RC .75 2.00
164A Knowshon Moreno RC .60 1.50
164B K.Moreno SP White 2.50 6.00
165 Larry English RC .75 2.00
166A LeSean McCoy RC 1.50 4.00
166B LeSean McCoy SP Blue 6.00 15.00
167 William Moore RC .60 1.50
168 Louis Delmas RC .75 2.00
169A Louis Murphy RC .60 1.50
169B Louis Murphy SP White 2.50 6.00
170A Malcolm Jenkins RC .60 1.50
170B Malcolm Jenkins SP Red 2.50 6.00
171A Mark Sanchez RC .60 1.50
171B Mark Sanchez SP White 15.00 30.00
172A Matthew Stafford RC 3.00 8.00
172B Matthew Stafford SP Draft 15.00 30.00
173 Tom Brandstater RC .75 2.00
174A Michael Crabtree RC 1.00 2.50
174B Michael Crabtree SP Draft 4.00 10.00
175 Michael Hamlin RC .60 1.50
176 Michael Johnson RC .60 1.50
177 Michael Oher RC 1.00 2.50
178 Mike Mickens RC .60 1.50
179 Mike Thomas RC .60 1.50
180 Mohamed Massaquoi SP RC 6.00 15.00
181A Nate Davis RC .60 1.50
181B Nate Davis SP White 2.50 6.00
182 Nic Harris RC .75 2.00
183 P.J. Hill RC .60 1.50
184A Pat White RC .75 2.00
184B Pat White SP White 10.00 25.00
185 Patrick Chung RC .60 1.50
186 Patrick Turner RC .60 1.50
187A Percy Harvin RC .60 1.50
187B Percy Harvin SP White 2.50 6.00
188 Peria Jerry RC .60 1.50
189 Quan Cosby RC .60 1.50
190 Quinn Johnson RC .60 1.50
191A Ramses Barden RC .60 1.50
191B Ramses Barden SP w
o FB 4.00 10.00
192A Rashad Jennings RC .75 2.00
192B R.Jennings SP Bowl visible 3.00 8.00
193 Rashad Johnson RC .60 1.50
194A Rey Maualuga RC 1.00 2.50
194B Rey Maualuga SP White 8.00 20.00
195 Rhett Bomar RC .60 1.50
196 Sean Smith RC .60 1.50
197 Shawn Nelson RC .60 1.50
198 Sherrod Martin RC .60 1.50
199A Shonn Greene SP RC 10.00 25.00
199B Shonn Greene SP White 12.50 25.00
200 Stephen McGee RC .60 1.50

2009 Playoff Prestige Draft Picks Light Blue

*LIGHT BLUE/999: .6X TO 1.5X BASIC RC
*LIGHT BLUE/999: .1X TO .25X BASIC SP RC
STATED PRINT RUN 999 SER.#'d SETS

2009 Playoff Prestige Xtra Points Black

*VETS: 10X TO 25X BASIC CARDS
*ROOKIES: 4X TO 10X BASIC RC
*ROOKIES: .5X TO 1.2X BASIC SP RC
STATED PRINT RUN 10 SER.#'d SETS

2009 Playoff Prestige Xtra Points Gold

*VETS: 2X TO 5X BASIC CARDS
*ROOKIES: .8X TO 2X BASIC RC
*ROOKIES: .1X TO .3X BASIC SP RC
STATED PRINT RUN 250 SER.#'d SETS

2009 Playoff Prestige Xtra Points Green

*VETS: 6X TO 15X BASIC CARDS
*ROOKIES: 2.5X TO 6X BASIC RC
*ROOKIES: .4X TO 1X BASIC SP RC
STATED PRINT RUN 25 SER.#'d SETS

2009 Playoff Prestige Xtra Points Orange

*VETS: 2X TO 5X BASIC CARDS
*ROOKIES: .8X TO 2X BASIC RC
*ROOKIES: .1X TO .3X BASIC SP RC
STATED PRINT RUN 300 SER.#'d SETS

2009 Playoff Prestige Xtra Points Purple

*VETS: 4X TO 10X BASIC CARDS
*ROOKIES: 1.5X TO 4X BASIC SP RC
*ROOKIES: .25X TO .6X BASIC SP RC
STATED PRINT RUN 50 SER.#'d SETS

2009 Playoff Prestige Xtra Points Red

*VETS: 3X TO 8X BASIC CARDS
*ROOKIES: 1.2X TO 3X BASIC RC
*ROOKIES: .2X TO .5X BASIC SP RC
STATED PRINT RUN 100 SER.#'d SETS

2009 Playoff Prestige Connections

1 K.Warner/A.Boldin .75 2.00
2 A.Rodgers/G.Jennings 2.00 5.00
3 K.Clemens/L.Coles .60 1.50
4 Roethlisberger/H.Ward 1.00 2.50
5 M.Ryan/R.White .75 2.00
6 P.Rivers/V.Jackson 1.00 2.50
7 J.Cutler/E.Royal .60 1.50
8 Delhomme/Muhammad .60 1.50
9 P.Manning/M.Harrison 2.50 6.00
10 J.Delhomme/S.Smith .75 2.00
11 K.Warner/Fitzgerald .75 2.00
12 T.Romo/T.Owens .75 2.00
13 J.Campbell/S.Moss .75 2.00
14 D.McNabb/Westbrook .75 2.00
15 P.Manning/R.Wayne 2.50 6.00
16 P.Rivers/A.Gates 1.00 2.50
17 A.Rodgers/D.Driver 2.00 5.00
18 K.Clemens/J.Cotchery .60 1.50
19 J.Garcia/I.Hilliard .60 1.50
20 E.Manning/A.Toomer .75 2.00

2009 Playoff Prestige Connections Materials

STATED PRINT RUN 29-250
*PRIME/25: .8X TO 2X BASIC JSY/250
*PRIME/25: .6X TO 1.5X BASIC JSY/59
*PRIME/25: .6X TO 1.5X BASIC JSY/29
PRIME PRINT RUN 9-25
3 K.Clemens/L.Coles/250 2.50 6.00
4 Roeth/H.Ward/250 4.00 10.00
5 M.Ryan/R.White/250 3.00 8.00
6 P.Rivers/V.Jackson/250 4.00 10.00
7 J.Cutler/E.Royal/250 2.50 6.00
9 P.Mann/M.Harrison/29 20.00 50.00
10 J.Delhomme/S.Smith/95 4.00 10.00
12 T.Romo/T.Owens/250 3.00 8.00
13 J.Campbell/S.Moss/250 3.00 8.00
14 McNabb/Westbrook/250 3.00 8.00
15 P.Manning/R.Wayne/250 8.00 20.00
16 P.Rivers/A.Gates/250 4.00 10.00
17 A.Rodgers/D.Driver/59 12.00 30.00
18 Clemens/Cotchery/250 2.50 6.00
19 J.Garcia/I.Hilliard/250 2.50 6.00
20 E.Mann/A.Toomer/250 3.00 8.00

2009 Playoff Prestige Draft Picks Autographs

STATED PRINT RUN 99-499
102 Aaron Kelly/499 4.00 10.00
109 Austin Collie/499 4.00 10.00
110 B.J. Raji/499 8.00 20.00
111 Brandon Gibson/300 5.00 12.00
113 Brandon Tate/299 12.50 25.00
114 Brian Cushing/399 4.00 10.00
115 Brian Orakpo/399 6.00 15.00
117 Brooks Foster/499 4.00 10.00
118 Cedric Peerman/299 4.00 10.00
119 Chase Coffman/499 4.00 10.00
122 Chris Wells/199 4.00 10.00
123 Clay Matthews/399 20.00 50.00
124 Clint Sintim/499 4.00 10.00
125 Cornelius Ingram/499 4.00 10.00
130 Darrius Heyward-Bey/199 6.00 15.00
132 Deon Butler/499 4.00 10.00
135 Donald Brown/199 4.00 10.00
140 Graham Harrell/499 10.00 25.00
142 Hakeem Nicks/399 5.00 12.00
146 James Casey/299 5.00 12.00
149 Jared Cook/399 5.00 12.00
155 Jeremy Maclin/199 5.00 12.00
156 John Parker Wilson/299 4.00 10.00
158 Josh Freeman/199 4.00 10.00
159 Juaquin Iglesias/199 4.00 10.00
162 Kenny McKinley/499 4.00 10.00
163 Kevin Ogletree/499 5.00 12.00
164 Knowshon Moreno/199 4.00 10.00
165 Larry English/499 5.00 12.00
166 LeSean McCoy/99 20.00 50.00
170 Malcolm Jenkins/199 4.00 10.00
171 Mark Sanchez/299 25.00 60.00
172 Matthew Stafford/199 30.00 80.00
173 Tom Brandstater/299 5.00 12.00
174 Michael Crabtree/299 6.00 15.00
179 Mike Thomas/299 4.00 10.00
180 Mohamed Massaquoi/299 4.00 10.00
183 P.J. Hill/499 4.00 10.00
184 Pat White/199 5.00 12.00
186 Patrick Turner/499 4.00 10.00
187 Percy Harvin/99 4.00 10.00
189 Quan Cosby/499 4.00 10.00
190 Quinn Johnson/499 4.00 10.00
191 Ramses Barden/299 4.00 10.00
192 Rashad Jennings/399 5.00 12.00
194 Rey Maualuga/399 6.00 15.00
197 Shawn Nelson/499 4.00 10.00

2009 Playoff Prestige Inside the Numbers

1 Michael Turner .60 1.50
2 Brandon Jacobs .60 1.50
3 Thomas Jones .60 1.50
4 Larry Fitzgerald .75 2.00
5 Roddy White .60 1.50
6 Calvin Johnson 1.00 2.50
7 Adrian Peterson 1.00 2.50
8 Clinton Portis .60 1.50
9 Andre Johnson .75 2.00
10 Marion Barber .75 2.00

2009 Playoff Prestige Inside the Numbers Autographs

STATED PRINT RUN 15-25
1 Michael Turner/25 8.00 20.00
2 Brandon Jacobs/25 8.00 20.00
5 Roddy White/25 8.00 20.00
6 Calvin Johnson/15 12.00 30.00
7 Adrian Peterson/15 50.00 100.00
10 Marion Barber/15 15.00 40.00

2009 Playoff Prestige Inside the Numbers Materials

STATED PRINT RUN 43-100
*PRIME/50: .6X TO 1.5X BASIC JSY/100
*PRIME/50: .8X TO 2X BASIC JSY/100
PRIME PRINT RUN 25-50
1 Michael Turner/43 4.00 10.00
2 Brandon Jacobs/100 3.00 8.00
3 Thomas Jones/100 3.00 8.00
4 Larry Fitzgerald/100 4.00 10.00
5 Roddy White/100 3.00 8.00
6 Calvin Johnson/100 5.00 12.00
7 Adrian Peterson/100 5.00 12.00
8 Clinton Portis/100 3.00 8.00
9 Andre Johnson/100 4.00 10.00
10 Marion Barber/100 4.00 10.00

2009 Playoff Prestige League Leaders

1 D.Brees/K.Warner 1.25 3.00
2 J.Cutler/A.Rodgers 2.50 6.00
3 P.Rivers/P.Manning 1.25 3.00
4 A.Peterson/M.Turner 1.25 3.00
5 De.Williams/C.Portis .75 2.00
6 T.Jones/S.Slaton .75 2.00
7 M.Forte/C.Johnson .75 2.00
8 R.Grant/L.Tomlinson 1.25 3.00
9 B.Jacobs/S.Jackson .75 2.00
10 A.Johnson/L.Fitzgerald 1.00 2.50
11 S.Smith/R.White 1.00 2.50
12 C.Johnson/G.Jennings 1.25 3.00
13 B.Marshall/W.Welker 1.00 2.50
14 R.Wayne/V.Jackson 1.00 2.50
15 T.Gonzalez/T.Owens 1.00 2.50
16 S.Moss/H.Ward 1.00 2.50
17 M.Ryan/J.Flacco 1.00 2.50
18 Slaton/Forte/Jnsn/Stwrt .75 2.00
19 Ptrsn/Trnr/A.Jhns/Fitz 1.25 3.00
20 D.Will/Trnr/Jacbs/T.Jns .75 2.00
21 Fitz/C.Jhnsn/oldin/Moss 1.25 3.00
22 D.Will/Trnr/Jacbs/White .75 2.00
23 Ptrsn/Trnr/D.Will/Prtis 1.25 3.00
24 A.Jhnsn/Fitz/S.Smt/R.Wht 1.00 2.50
25 Ryan/Slaton/Royal/Forte 1.00 2.50

2009 Playoff Prestige League Leaders Materials

3-17 DUAL PRINT RUN 250
18-25 QUAD PRINT RUN 150
*PRIME/25: .8X TO 2X BASIC DUAL
*PRIME/25: .6X TO 1.5X BASIC QUAD
PRIME PRINT RUN 25 SER.#'d SETS
3 P.Rivers/P.Manning 5.00 12.00
4 A.Peterson/M.Turner 5.00 12.00
5 De.Williams/C.Portis 3.00 8.00
6 T.Jones/S.Slaton 3.00 8.00
7 M.Forte/C.Johnson 3.00 8.00
8 R.Grant/L.Tomlinson 5.00 12.00
9 B.Jacobs/S.Jackson 3.00 8.00
10 A.Johnson/L.Fitzgerald 4.00 10.00
11 S.Smith/R.White 4.00 10.00
12 C.Johnson/G.Jennings 5.00 12.00
13 B.Marshall/W.Welker 4.00 10.00
14 R.Wayne/V.Jackson 4.00 10.00
15 T.Gonzalez/T.Owens 4.00 10.00
16 S.Moss/H.Ward 4.00 10.00
17 M.Ryan/J.Flacco 4.00 10.00
18 Slaton/Forte/Jnsn/Stwrt 5.00 12.00
19 Ptrsn/Trnr/A.Jhns/Fitz 8.00 20.00
20 D.Will/Trnr/Jacbs/T.Jns 5.00 12.00
21 Fitz/C.Jhnsn/oldin/Moss 8.00 20.00
22 D.Will/Trnr/Jacbs/White 5.00 12.00
23 Ptrsn/Trnr/D.Will/Prtis 8.00 20.00
24 A.Jhnsn/Fitz/S.Smt/R.Wht 6.00 15.00
25 Ryan/Slaton/Royal/Forte 6.00 15.00

2009 Playoff Prestige NFL Draft

1 Aaron Curry 1.00 2.50
2 Andre Brown .75 2.00
3 Brandon Pettigrew .60 1.50
4 Brian Robiskie .60 1.50
5 Chris Wells .60 1.50
6 Darrius Heyward-Bey 1.00 2.50
7 Donald Brown .60 1.50
8 Graham Harrell .60 1.50
9 Hakeem Nicks .75 2.00
10 James Casey .75 2.00
11 Jared Cook .75 2.00
12 Jeremy Maclin .75 2.00
13 Josh Freeman .60 1.50
14 Knowshon Moreno .60 1.50
15 LeSean McCoy 1.50 4.00
16 Malcolm Jenkins .60 1.50
17 Mark Sanchez .60 1.50
18 Matthew Stafford 3.00 8.00
19 Michael Crabtree 1.00 2.50
20 Nate Davis .60 1.50
21 Pat White .75 2.00
22 Percy Harvin .60 1.50
23 Rashad Jennings .75 2.00
24 Rey Maualuga 1.00 2.50
25 Shonn Greene .60 1.50
26 Brian Cushing .60 1.50
27 Brian Orakpo .75 2.00
28 Cedric Peerman .60 1.50
29 D.J. Moore .75 2.00
30 James Laurinaitis .60 1.50
31 Javon Ringer .60 1.50
32 Juaquin Iglesias .60 1.50
33 Kenny Britt 1.00 2.50
34 Rhett Bomar .60 1.50
35 Vontae Davis .60 1.50

2009 Playoff Prestige NFL Draft Autographed Patch College Logo

STATED PRINT RUN 35-50
6 Darrius Heyward-Bey/50 12.00 30.00
7 Donald Brown/50 8.00 20.00
8 Graham Harrell/50 15.00 40.00
9 Hakeem Nicks/50 10.00 25.00
10 James Casey/50 10.00 25.00
11 Jared Cook/50 10.00 25.00
12 Jeremy Maclin/50 10.00 25.00
14 Knowshon Moreno/50 8.00 20.00
17 Mark Sanchez/35 40.00 100.00
18 Matthew Stafford/50 75.00 150.00
19 Michael Crabtree/50 12.00 30.00
21 Pat White/35 10.00 25.00
27 Brian Orakpo/50 10.00 25.00
28 Cedric Peerman/50 8.00 20.00
32 Juaquin Iglesias/50 8.00 20.00

2009 Playoff Prestige NFL Draft Autographed Patch Draft Logo

DRAFT LOGO PATCH PRINT RUN 100
*NFL EQUIP/25: .6X TO 1.5X DRAFT/100
NFL EQUIPMENT PRINT RUN 25
6 Darrius Heyward-Bey 10.00 25.00
7 Donald Brown 6.00 15.00
8 Graham Harrell 15.00 40.00
9 Hakeem Nicks 8.00 20.00
10 James Casey 8.00 20.00
11 Jared Cook 8.00 20.00
12 Jeremy Maclin 8.00 20.00
14 Knowshon Moreno 6.00 15.00
18 Matthew Stafford 30.00 80.00
19 Michael Crabtree 10.00 25.00
23 Rashad Jennings 8.00 20.00
27 Brian Orakpo 8.00 20.00
28 Cedric Peerman 6.00 15.00
32 Juaquin Iglesias 6.00 15.00

2009 Playoff Prestige NFL Draft Autographs

STATED PRINT RUN 50-100
5 Chris Wells/100 15.00 40.00
6 Darrius Heyward-Bey/100 8.00 20.00
7 Donald Brown/50 6.00 15.00
8 Graham Harrell/100 12.00 30.00
9 Hakeem Nicks/50 8.00 20.00
10 James Casey/100 6.00 15.00
11 Jared Cook/50 8.00 20.00
12 Jeremy Maclin/100 6.00 15.00
13 Josh Freeman/100 5.00 12.00
14 Knowshon Moreno/50 6.00 15.00
15 LeSean McCoy/100 12.00 30.00
16 Malcolm Jenkins/100 5.00 12.00
17 Mark Sanchez/100 25.00 60.00
18 Matthew Stafford/50 40.00 100.00
19 Michael Crabtree/50 10.00 25.00
21 Pat White/100 6.00 15.00
22 Percy Harvin/100 5.00 12.00
23 Rashad Jennings/50 8.00 20.00
24 Rey Maualuga/100 8.00 20.00
26 Brian Cushing/100 5.00 12.00
27 Brian Orakpo/50 8.00 20.00
28 Cedric Peerman/50 6.00 15.00
32 Juaquin Iglesias/50 6.00 15.00

2009 Playoff Prestige Preferred Materials

STATED PRINT RUN 100 SER.#'d SETS
*PATCH/25: .8X TO 2X BASIC JSY
PATCH PRINT RUN 25 SER.#'d SETS
1 Frank Gore 4.00 10.00
2 Joseph Addai 3.00 8.00
3 DeAngelo Williams 3.00 8.00
4 Drew Brees 5.00 12.00
5 Jason Witten 4.00 10.00
6 Matt Forte 3.00 8.00
7 Steve Slaton 3.00 8.00
8 Chris Johnson 3.00 8.00
9 Eddie Royal 3.00 8.00
10 Wes Welker 4.00 10.00

2009 Playoff Prestige Preferred Signatures

STATED PRINT RUN 25-50
1 Frank Gore/25 10.00 25.00
2 Joseph Addai/50 6.00 15.00
3 DeAngelo Williams/50 6.00 15.00
4 Drew Brees/50 30.00 60.00
5 Jason Witten/50 12.00 30.00
6 Matt Forte/25 15.00 40.00
7 Steve Slaton/50 6.00 15.00
9 Eddie Royal/50 6.00 15.00
10 Wes Welker/25 25.00 50.00

2009 Playoff Prestige Prestigious Picks Blue

BLUE PRINT RUN 1000 SER.#'d SETS
*BLACK/25: 1X TO 2.5X BLUE/1000
BLACK PRINT RUN 25 SER.#'d SETS
*GOLD/100: .6X TO 1.5X BLUE/1000
GOLD PRINT RUN 100 SER.#'d SETS
*GREEN/500: .5X TO 1.2X BLUE/1000
GREEN PRINT RUN 500 SER.#'d SETS
*PLATINUM/10: 2X TO 5X BLUE/1000
PLATINUM PRINT RUN 10 SER.#'d SETS
1 Aaron Curry 1.00 2.50
2 Andre Smith .60 1.50
3 B.J. Raji .75 2.00
4 Brandon Pettigrew .60 1.50
5 Brandon Tate .75 2.00
6 Brandon Gibson .75 2.00
7 Brian Orakpo .75 2.00
8 Brian Cushing .60 1.50
9 Brian Robiskie .60 1.50
10 Brooks Foster .60 1.50
11 Chase Coffman .60 1.50
12 Chris Wells .60 1.50
13 Clint Sintim .60 1.50
14 Cornelius Ingram .60 1.50
15 D.J. Moore .75 2.00
16 Darrius Heyward-Bey 1.00 2.50
17 Derrick Williams .60 1.50
18 Donald Brown .60 1.50
19 Eugene Monroe .60 1.50
20 Everette Brown .60 1.50
21 Graham Harrell .60 1.50
22 Hakeem Nicks .75 2.00
23 James Laurinaitis .60 1.50
24 James Casey .75 2.00
25 Jared Cook .75 2.00
26 Jarett Dillard .60 1.60
27 Javon Ringer .60 1.50
28 Jeremiah Johnson .60 1.50
29 Jeremy Maclin .75 2.00
30 Josh Freeman .60 1.50
31 Juaquin Iglesias .60 1.50
32 Kenny Britt 1.00 2.50
33 Knowshon Moreno .60 1.50
34 Larry English .75 2.00
35 LeSean McCoy 1.50 4.00
36 Louis Murphy .60 1.50
37 Malcolm Jenkins .60 1.50
38 Mark Sanchez .60 1.50
39 Matthew Stafford 3.00 8.00
40 Michael Crabtree 1.00 2.50
41 Michael Johnson .60 1.50
42 Mohamed Massaquoi .60 1.50
43 Nate Davis .60 1.50
44 Pat White .75 2.00
45 Percy Harvin .60 1.50
46 Quan Cosby .60 1.50
47 Ramses Barden .60 1.50
48 Rashad Jennings .75 2.00
49 Rey Maualuga 1.00 2.50
50 Shonn Greene .60 1.50

2009 Playoff Prestige Prestigious Picks Autographs

STATED PRINT RUN 100 SER.#'d SETS
3 B.J. Raji 5.00 12.00
5 Brandon Tate 5.00 12.00
6 Brandon Gibson 5.00 12.00
7 Brian Orakpo 5.00 12.00
8 Brian Cushing 4.00 10.00
10 Brooks Foster 4.00 10.00
11 Chase Coffman 4.00 10.00
12 Chris Wells 15.00 40.00
13 Clint Sintim 4.00 10.00
14 Cornelius Ingram 4.00 10.00
16 Darrius Heyward-Bey 6.00 15.00
18 Donald Brown 4.00 10.00
21 Graham Harrell 10.00 25.00
22 Hakeem Nicks 5.00 12.00
24 James Casey 5.00 12.00
25 Jared Cook 5.00 12.00
29 Jeremy Maclin 5.00 12.00
30 Josh Freeman 4.00 10.00
31 Juaquin Iglesias 4.00 10.00
33 Knowshon Moreno 4.00 10.00
34 Larry English 5.00 12.00
35 LeSean McCoy 10.00 25.00
37 Malcolm Jenkins 4.00 10.00
38 Mark Sanchez 25.00 60.00
39 Matthew Stafford 40.00 100.00
40 Michael Crabtree 6.00 15.00
42 Mohamed Massaquoi 4.00 10.00
44 Pat White 5.00 12.00
45 Percy Harvin 4.00 10.00
46 Quan Cosby 4.00 10.00
47 Ramses Barden 4.00 10.00
48 Rashad Jennings 5.00 12.00
49 Rey Maualuga 6.00 15.00

2009 Playoff Prestige Prestigious Picks Materials Blue

BLUE PRINT RUN 250 SER.#'d SETS
*BLACK/25: .8X TO 2X BLUE/250
BLACK PRINT RUN 25 SER.#'d SETS
*GOLD/50: .6X TO 1.5X BLUE/250
GOLD PRINT RUN 50 SER.#'d SETS
*GREEN/100: .5X TO 1.2X BLUE/250
GREEN PRINT RUN 100 SER.#'d SETS
*PLAT.PATCH/25: 1X TO 2.5X BLUE/250
PLATINUM PATCH PRINT RUN 25
5 Brandon Tate 2.00 5.00
6 Brandon Gibson 3.00 8.00
7 Brian Orakpo 3.00 8.00
8 Brian Cushing 1.50 4.00
17 Derrick Williams 3.00 8.00
18 Donald Brown 1.50 4.00
21 Graham Harrell 3.00 8.00
23 James Laurinaitis 5.00 12.00
28 Jeremiah Johnson 4.00 10.00
30 Josh Freeman 1.50 4.00
31 Juaquin Iglesias 1.50 4.00
35 LeSean McCoy 5.00 12.00
38 Mark Sanchez 1.50 4.00
39 Matthew Stafford 8.00 20.00
42 Mohamed Massaquoi 3.00 8.00
46 Quan Cosby 3.00 8.00
47 Ramses Barden 3.00 8.00
49 Rey Maualuga 2.50 6.00

2009 Playoff Prestige Prestigious Pros Blue

BLUE PRINT RUN 1000 SER.#'d SETS
*BLACK/25: 1.2X TO 3X BLUE/1000
BLACK PRINT RUN 25 SER.#'d SETS
*GOLD/100: .6X TO 1.5X BLUE/1000
GOLD PRINT RUN 100 SER.#'d SETS
*GREEN/500: .5X TO 1.2X BLUE/1000
GREEN PRINT RUN 500 SER.#'d SETS
*PLATINUM/10: 2.5X TO 6X BLUE/1000
PLATINUM PRINT RUN 10 SER.#'d SETS
1 Aaron Rodgers 2.50 6.00
2 Adrian Peterson 1.25 3.00
3 Andre Johnson 1.00 2.50
4 Anthony Gonzalez .75 2.00
5 Ben Roethlisberger 1.25 3.00
6 Brandon Jacobs .75 2.00
7 Brandon Marshall 1.00 2.50
8 Braylon Edwards .75 2.00
9 Brian Westbrook .75 2.00
10 Chad Ocho Cinco .75 2.00
11 Chris Cooley .75 2.00
12 Clinton Portis .75 2.00
13 Selvin Young .75 2.00
14 DeAngelo Williams .75 2.00
15 Donovan McNabb 1.00 2.50
16 Drew Brees 1.25 3.00
17 Eli Manning 1.00 2.50
18 Frank Gore 1.00 2.50
19 Jake Delhomme .75 2.00
20 Jason Campbell .75 2.00
21 Jason Witten 1.00 2.50
22 Jay Cutler .75 2.00
23 Jerricho Cotchery .75 2.00
24 Kellen Winslow .75 2.00
25 Kevin Curtis .75 2.00
26 Kurt Warner 1.00 2.50
27 LaDainian Tomlinson 1.25 3.00
28 Larry Fitzgerald 1.00 2.50
29 Larry Johnson .75 2.00
30 Lee Evans 1.00 2.50
31 Marion Barber 1.00 2.50
32 Marques Colston .75 2.00
33 Marshawn Lynch 1.00 2.50
34 Michael Turner .75 2.00
35 Peyton Manning 3.00 8.00
36 Philip Rivers 1.25 3.00
37 Reggie Bush .75 2.00
38 Reggie Wayne 1.00 2.50
39 Roddy White .75 2.00
40 Ronnie Brown .75 2.00
41 Ryan Grant 1.00 2.50
42 Steven Jackson .75 2.00
43 Terrell Owens 1.00 2.50
44 Thomas Jones .75 2.00
45 T.J. Houshmandzadeh .75 2.00
46 Tom Brady 4.00 10.00
47 Tony Romo 1.00 2.50
48 Trent Edwards .75 2.00
49 Willie Parker .75 2.00
50 Willis McGahee .75 2.00

2009 Playoff Prestige Prestigious Pros Autographs

STATED PRINT RUN 5-100
SERIAL #'d UNDER 15 NOT PRICED
2 Adrian Peterson/15 40.00 100.00
4 Anthony Gonzalez/100 6.00 15.00
6 Brandon Jacobs/25 8.00 20.00
7 Brandon Marshall/25 10.00 25.00
8 Braylon Edwards/25 8.00 20.00
10 Chad Ocho Cinco/50 6.00 15.00
13 Selvin Young/50 6.00 15.00
14 DeAngelo Williams/50 6.00 15.00
16 Drew Brees/50 30.00 60.00
18 Frank Gore/25 10.00 25.00
21 Jason Witten/25 15.00 30.00
25 Kevin Curtis/100 6.00 15.00
29 Larry Johnson/50 6.00 15.00
32 Marques Colston/100 6.00 15.00
38 Reggie Wayne/25 10.00 25.00
39 Roddy White/25 8.00 20.00
40 Ronnie Brown/50 6.00 15.00
45 T.J. Houshmandzadeh/25 8.00 20.00
47 Tony Romo/25 30.00 60.00
48 Trent Edwards/100 6.00 15.00
49 Willie Parker/25 15.00 30.00

2009 Playoff Prestige Prestigious Pros Materials Blue

BLUE PRINT RUN 250 SER.#'d SETS
*BLACK/25: .8X TO 2X BLUE/250
BLACK PRINT RUN 25 SER.#'d SETS
*GOLD/50: .6X TO 1.5X BLUE/250
GOLD PRINT RUN 50 SER.#'d SETS
*GREEN/100: .5X TO 1.2X BLUE/250
GREEN PRINT RUN 100 SER.#'d SETS
*PLAT.PATCH/25: 1X TO 2.5X BLUE/250
PLATINUM PATCH PRINT RUN 25
2 Adrian Peterson 4.00 10.00
3 Andre Johnson 3.00 8.00
4 Anthony Gonzalez 2.50 6.00
5 Ben Roethlisberger 4.00 10.00
6 Brandon Jacobs 2.50 6.00
7 Brandon Marshall 3.00 8.00
8 Braylon Edwards 2.50 6.00
9 Brian Westbrook 2.50 6.00
10 Chad Ocho Cinco 2.50 6.00
11 Chris Cooley 2.50 6.00
12 Clinton Portis 2.50 6.00
13 Selvin Young 2.50 6.00
14 DeAngelo Williams 2.50 6.00
15 Donovan McNabb 3.00 8.00
16 Drew Brees 4.00 10.00
17 Eli Manning 3.00 8.00
18 Frank Gore 3.00 8.00
20 Jason Campbell 2.50 6.00
21 Jason Witten 3.00 8.00
22 Jay Cutler 2.50 6.00
23 Jerricho Cotchery 2.50 6.00
24 Kellen Winslow 2.50 6.00
25 Kevin Curtis 2.50 6.00
27 LaDainian Tomlinson 4.00 10.00
28 Larry Fitzgerald 3.00 8.00
29 Larry Johnson 2.50 6.00
30 Lee Evans 3.00 8.00
31 Marion Barber 3.00 8.00
32 Marques Colston 2.50 6.00
33 Marshawn Lynch 3.00 8.00
34 Michael Turner 2.50 6.00
35 Peyton Manning 10.00 25.00
36 Philip Rivers 4.00 10.00
37 Reggie Bush 2.50 6.00
38 Reggie Wayne 3.00 8.00
39 Roddy White 2.50 6.00
40 Ronnie Brown 2.50 6.00
41 Ryan Grant 3.00 8.00
42 Steven Jackson 2.50 6.00
43 Terrell Owens 3.00 8.00
44 Thomas Jones 2.50 6.00
45 T.J. Houshmandzadeh 2.50 6.00
46 Tom Brady 12.00 30.00
47 Tony Romo 3.00 8.00
48 Trent Edwards 2.50 6.00
49 Willie Parker 2.50 6.00
50 Willis McGahee 2.50 6.00

2009 Playoff Prestige Rookie Review

1 Andre Caldwell 1.00 2.50
2 Aqib Talib 1.00 2.50
3 Brandon Flowers 1.00 2.50
4 Brian Brohm 1.00 2.50
5 Chad Henne 1.25 3.00
6 Chris Horton 1.25 3.00
7 Chris Johnson 1.00 2.50
8 Chris Long 1.25 3.00
9 Curtis Lofton 1.00 2.50
10 Darren McFadden 1.50 4.00
11 Davone Bess 1.00 2.50
12 DeSean Jackson 1.25 3.00
13 Devin Thomas 1.00 2.50
14 Dexter Jackson 1.00 2.50
15 Donnie Avery 1.00 2.50
16 Dustin Keller 1.00 2.50
17 Earl Bennett 1.25 3.00
18 Early Doucet 1.25 3.00
19 Eddie Royal 1.00 2.50
20 Felix Jones 1.00 2.50
21 Glenn Dorsey 1.00 2.50
22 Harry Douglas 1.00 2.50
23 Jake Long 1.00 2.50
24 Jamaal Charles 1.25 3.00
25 James Hardy 1.25 3.00
26 Jerod Mayo 1.25 3.00
27 Jerome Simpson 1.00 2.50
28 Joe Flacco 1.25 3.00
29 John Carlson 1.25 3.00
30 John David Booty 1.25 3.00
31 Jonathan Stewart 1.00 2.50
32 Jordy Nelson 1.25 3.00
33 Josh Morgan 1.00 2.50
34 Kenny Phillips 1.00 2.50
35 Kevin O'Connell 1.00 2.50
36 Kevin Smith 1.00 2.50
37 Leodis McKelvin 1.00 2.50
38 Limas Sweed 1.25 3.00
39 Malcolm Kelly 1.00 2.50
40 Mario Manningham 1.00 2.50
41 Martellus Bennett 1.00 2.50
42 Matt Forte 1.00 2.50
43 Matt Ryan 1.25 3.00
44 Peyton Hillis 1.25 3.00
45 Quintin Demps 1.00 2.50
46 Rashard Mendenhall 1.00 2.50
47 Ray Rice 1.00 2.50
48 Steve Slaton 1.00 2.50
49 Tashard Choice 1.00 2.50
50 Tim Hightower 1.00 2.50

2009 Playoff Prestige Rookie Review Autographs

STATED PRINT RUN 13-250
SERIAL #'d UNDER 20 NOT PRICED
1 Andre Caldwell/250 5.00 12.00
2 Aqib Talib/250 5.00 12.00
3 Brandon Flowers/100 6.00 15.00
4 Brian Brohm/100 6.00 15.00
5 Chad Henne/100 8.00 20.00
6 Chris Horton/250 6.00 15.00
8 Chris Long/250 6.00 15.00
9 Curtis Lofton/250 5.00 12.00
11 Davone Bess/250 5.00 12.00
12 DeSean Jackson/100 8.00 20.00
13 Devin Thomas/250 5.00 12.00
14 Dexter Jackson/250 5.00 12.00
15 Donnie Avery/250 5.00 12.00
16 Dustin Keller/100 6.00 15.00
17 Earl Bennett/250 6.00 15.00
18 Early Doucet/50 8.00 20.00
19 Eddie Royal/100 6.00 15.00
20 Felix Jones/50 20.00 40.00
22 Harry Douglas/250 5.00 12.00
23 Jake Long/250 5.00 12.00
24 Jamaal Charles/250 6.00 15.00
25 James Hardy/250 6.00 15.00
26 Jerod Mayo/50 10.00 25.00
27 Jerome Simpson/250 5.00 12.00
28 Joe Flacco/50 20.00 40.00
29 John Carlson/100 8.00 20.00
30 John David Booty/250 6.00 15.00
31 Jonathan Stewart/50 6.00 15.00
32 Jordy Nelson/50 8.00 20.00
33 Josh Morgan/250 5.00 12.00
34 Kenny Phillips/250 5.00 12.00
35 Kevin O'Connell/250 5.00 12.00
36 Kevin Smith/250 5.00 12.00
37 Leodis McKelvin/250 5.00 12.00
38 Limas Sweed/250 6.00 15.00
40 Mario Manningham/100 6.00 15.00
41 Martellus Bennett/100 6.00 15.00
42 Matt Forte/50 20.00 40.00
43 Matt Ryan/50 30.00 60.00
44 Peyton Hillis/250 20.00 40.00
45 Quintin Demps/250 5.00 12.00
46 Rashard Mendenhall/100 6.00 15.00
47 Ray Rice/250 5.00 12.00
48 Steve Slaton/250 5.00 12.00
49 Tashard Choice/50 6.00 15.00
50 Tim Hightower/50 6.00 15.00

2009 Playoff Prestige Rookie Review Materials

*PRIME/50: .8X TO 2X BASIC JSY
*PRIME/25-35: 1X TO 2.5X BASIC JSY
PRIME PRINT RUN 25-50
1 Andre Caldwell 2.00 5.00
4 Brian Brohm 2.00 5.00
5 Chad Henne 2.50 6.00
7 Chris Johnson 2.00 5.00
10 Darren McFadden 3.00 8.00
12 DeSean Jackson 2.50 6.00
13 Devin Thomas 2.00 5.00
14 Dexter Jackson 2.00 5.00
15 Donnie Avery 2.00 5.00
16 Dustin Keller 2.00 5.00
17 Earl Bennett 2.50 6.00
18 Early Doucet 2.50 6.00
19 Eddie Royal 2.00 5.00
20 Felix Jones 2.00 5.00
21 Glenn Dorsey 2.00 5.00
22 Harry Douglas 2.00 5.00
23 Jake Long 2.00 5.00
24 Jamaal Charles 2.50 6.00
25 James Hardy 2.50 6.00
27 Jerome Simpson 2.00 5.00
28 Joe Flacco 2.50 6.00
30 John David Booty 2.50 6.00
31 Jonathan Stewart 2.00 5.00
32 Jordy Nelson 2.50 6.00
35 Kevin O'Connell 2.00 5.00
36 Kevin Smith 2.00 5.00
38 Limas Sweed 2.50 6.00
39 Malcolm Kelly 2.00 5.00
40 Mario Manningham 2.00 5.00
42 Matt Forte 2.00 5.00
43 Matt Ryan 2.50 6.00
46 Rashard Mendenhall 2.00 5.00
47 Ray Rice 2.00 5.00
48 Steve Slaton 2.00 5.00

2009 Playoff Prestige Stars of the NFL

1 Tom Brady 3.00 8.00
2 Matt Ryan .75 2.00
3 Tony Romo .75 2.00
4 Eli Manning .75 2.00
5 Eddie Royal .60 1.50
6 Matt Forte .60 1.50
7 Andre Johnson .75 2.00
8 Torry Holt .75 2.00
9 Maurice Jones-Drew .60 1.50
10 Adrian Peterson 1.00 2.50
11 Brian Westbrook .60 1.50
12 Philip Rivers 1.00 2.50
13 Clinton Portis .60 1.50
14 Randy Moss .75 2.00
15 Hines Ward .75 2.00
16 Anquan Boldin .60 1.50
17 Reggie Wayne .75 2.00
18 Fred Taylor .60 1.50
19 Antonio Gates .75 2.00
20 Chris Johnson .60 1.50

2009 Playoff Prestige Stars of the NFL Materials

STATED PRINT RUN 100 SER.#'d SETS
*PRIME/50: .6X TO 1.5X BASIC JSY/100
*PRIME/25: .8X TO 2X BASIC JSY/100
PRIME PRINT RUN 25-50
1 Tom Brady 12.00 30.00
2 Matt Ryan 3.00 8.00
3 Tony Romo 3.00 8.00
4 Eli Manning 3.00 8.00
5 Eddie Royal 2.50 6.00
6 Matt Forte 2.50 6.00
7 Andre Johnson 3.00 8.00
8 Torry Holt 3.00 8.00
9 Maurice Jones-Drew 2.50 6.00
10 Adrian Peterson 4.00 10.00
11 Brian Westbrook 2.50 6.00
12 Philip Rivers 4.00 10.00
13 Clinton Portis 2.50 6.00
14 Randy Moss 3.00 8.00
15 Hines Ward 3.00 8.00
16 Anquan Boldin 2.50 6.00
17 Reggie Wayne 3.00 8.00
18 Fred Taylor 2.50 6.00
19 Antonio Gates 3.00 8.00
20 Chris Johnson 2.50 6.00

2009 Playoff Prestige TD Sensations

1 Thomas Jones .60 1.50
2 Michael Turner .60 1.50
3 LenDale White .60 1.50
4 DeAngelo Williams .60 1.50
5 Brandon Jacobs .60 1.50
6 Brian Westbrook .60 1.50
7 Anquan Boldin .60 1.50
8 Maurice Jones-Drew .60 1.50
9 Ronnie Brown .60 1.50
10 Matt Forte .60 1.50
11 Marion Barber .75 2.00
12 Adrian Peterson 1.00 2.50
13 Steve Slaton .60 1.50
14 Reggie Bush .60 1.50
15 Calvin Johnson 1.00 2.50
16 Marshawn Lynch .75 2.00
17 Randy Moss .75 2.00
18 Terrell Owens .75 2.00
19 Frank Gore .75 2.00
20 Greg Jennings .60 1.50

2009 Playoff Prestige TD Sensations Materials

STATED PRINT RUN 100 SER.#'d SETS
*PRIME/45-50: .6X TO 1.5X BASIC JSY/100
*PRIME/25: .8X TO 2X BASIC JSY/100
PRIME PRINT RUN 25-50
1 Thomas Jones 2.50 6.00
2 Michael Turner 2.50 6.00
3 LenDale White 2.50 6.00
4 DeAngelo Williams 2.50 6.00
5 Brandon Jacobs 2.50 6.00
6 Brian Westbrook 2.50 6.00
7 Anquan Boldin 2.50 6.00
8 Maurice Jones-Drew 2.50 6.00
9 Ronnie Brown 2.50 6.00
10 Matt Forte 2.50 6.00
11 Marion Barber 3.00 8.00
12 Adrian Peterson 4.00 10.00
13 Steve Slaton 2.50 6.00
14 Reggie Bush 2.50 6.00
15 Calvin Johnson 4.00 10.00
16 Marshawn Lynch 3.00 8.00
17 Randy Moss 3.00 8.00
18 Terrell Owens 3.00 8.00
19 Frank Gore 3.00 8.00
20 Greg Jennings 2.50 6.00

2009 Playoff Prestige True Colors

1 Greg Jennings .60 1.50
2 Vincent Jackson .60 1.50
3 Dallas Clark .60 1.50
4 Randy Moss .75 2.00
5 T.J. Houshmandzadeh .60 1.50
6 Santonio Holmes .60 1.50
7 Derrick Ward .60 1.50
8 Dwayne Bowe .75 2.00
9 Brian Westbrook .60 1.50
10 Brandon Marshall .75 2.00

2009 Playoff Prestige True Colors Autographs

STATED PRINT RUN 15-50
1 Greg Jennings/50 6.00 15.00
2 Vincent Jackson/50 6.00 15.00
3 Dallas Clark/50 6.00 15.00
5 T.J. Houshmandzadeh/25 8.00 20.00
6 Santonio Holmes/25 8.00 20.00
7 Derrick Ward/25 8.00 20.00
10 Brandon Marshall/25 15.00 40.00

2009 Playoff Prestige True Colors Materials

STATED PRINT RUN 100 SER.#'d SETS
*PRIMARY COLOR/50: .6X TO 1.5X BASIC JSY
PRIMARY COLORS PRINT RUN 50
1 Greg Jennings 2.50 6.00
2 Vincent Jackson 2.50 6.00
3 Dallas Clark 2.50 6.00
4 Randy Moss 3.00 8.00
5 T.J. Houshmandzadeh 2.50 6.00
6 Santonio Holmes 2.50 6.00
7 Derrick Ward 2.50 6.00
8 Dwayne Bowe 3.00 8.00
9 Brian Westbrook 2.50 6.00
10 Brandon Marshall 3.00 8.00

2009 Playoff Prestige Xtra Points Black Autographs

STATED PRINT RUN 5-100
SERIAL #'d UNDER 23 NOT PRICED
4 Tim Hightower/50 6.00 15.00
5 Roddy White/50 6.00 15.00
6 Michael Turner/50 6.00 15.00
7 Matt Ryan/50 25.00 60.00
8 Willis McGahee/25 8.00 20.00
9 Joe Flacco/50 15.00 40.00
10 Trent Edwards/100 6.00 15.00
11 Marshawn Lynch/25 10.00 25.00
14 DeAngelo Williams/100 6.00 15.00
16 Jonathan Stewart/50 6.00 15.00
19 Matt Forte/25 20.00 40.00
21 Chad Ocho Cinco/25 8.00 20.00
22 T.J. Houshmandzadeh/25 8.00 20.00
26 Braylon Edwards/25 8.00 20.00
27 Tony Romo/25 30.00 60.00
29 Marion Barber/25 20.00 40.00
30 Roy Williams WR/44 6.00 15.00
32 Brandon Marshall/25 10.00 25.00
33 Eddie Royal/100 6.00 15.00
34 Calvin Johnson/25 25.00 50.00
35 Kevin Smith/100 6.00 15.00
38 Greg Jennings/100 10.00 25.00
41 Steve Slaton/100 6.00 15.00
43 Joseph Addai/25 8.00 20.00
44 Reggie Wayne/25 12.00 30.00
45 Anthony Gonzalez/100 6.00 15.00
48 Maurice Jones-Drew/25 8.00 20.00
49 Larry Johnson/50 6.00 15.00
52 Ronnie Brown/50 6.00 15.00
54 Bernard Berrian/50 6.00 15.00
55 Adrian Peterson/25 60.00 120.00
56 Chester Taylor/50 6.00 15.00
60 Drew Brees/25 40.00 80.00
62 Marques Colston/100 6.00 15.00
65 Brandon Jacobs/25 8.00 20.00
67 Jerricho Cotchery/23 8.00 20.00
71 Justin Fargas/100 6.00 15.00
77 Willie Parker/25 12.00 30.00
79 Santonio Holmes/100 10.00 25.00
83 Frank Gore/25 10.00 25.00
84 Vernon Davis/100 6.00 15.00
89 Steven Jackson/25 8.00 20.00
95 LenDale White/50 6.00 15.00

2009 Playoff Prestige Promos

Cards from this promo set were issued at either the 2009 Hawai Trade Conference Mainland Editon or the actual NFL Draft in April 2009.
MC Michael Crabtree/500* 5.00 12.00
MS Matthew Stafford/1000* 5.00 12.00

1995 Playoff Prime

COMPLETE SET (200) 5.00 12.00
*PRIME CARDS: .3X TO .8X ABSOLUTE

1995 Playoff Prime Fantasy Team

This 20-card standard-size set was randomly inserted into "Prime" packs. The players featured are often taken early in "rotisserie" drafts and were printed on clear plastic with the letters from the set name "Fantasy Team" in foil jumbled in the background. The player's name is in gold foil above the shot of the player. Card backs are numbered with an "FT" prefix.
COMPLETE SET (20) 20.00 50.00
STATED ODDS 1:25 PRIME
FT1 Jerome Bettis 1.00 2.50
FT2 Shannon Sharpe .50 1.25
FT3 Fuad Reveiz .25 .60
FT4 John Carney .25 .60
FT5 Steve Young 2.00 5.00
FT6 Brett Favre 5.00 12.00
FT7 Tim Brown 1.00 2.50
FT8 Ben Coates .50 1.25
FT9 Marshall Faulk 3.00 8.00
FT10 Stan Humphries .50 1.25
FT11 Dan Marino 5.00 12.00
FT12 Jerry Rice 2.50 6.00
FT13 Errict Rhett .50 1.25
FT14 Chris Warren .50 1.25
FT15 Barry Sanders 4.00 10.00
FT16 Cris Carter 1.00 2.50
FT17 Michael Irvin 1.00 2.50
FT18 Emmitt Smith 4.00 10.00
FT19 Terance Mathis .50 1.25
FT20 Herman Moore 1.00 2.50

1995 Playoff Prime Minis

COMPLETE SET (200) 60.00 150.00
*STARS: 3X TO 8X BASE ABSOLUTES
*ROOKIES: 1.2X TO 3X BASE ABSOLUTES
STATED ODDS 1:7 PRIME

1996 Playoff Prime Samples

These promo cards were issued to preview the 1996 Playoff Prime release. Each is very similar to its base brand card in design, except for the word "sample" where the card number otherwise would be.
COMPLETE SET (3) 2.50 6.00
1 Zack Crockett .30 .75
2 Terrell Davis 1.20 3.00
3 Antonio Freeman .50 1.25
4 Rashaan Salaam .40 1.00
5 J.J. Stokes .30 .75
6 Tamarick Vanover .30 .75

1996 Playoff Prime

The 1996 Playoff Prime set was issued in one series totalling 200 cards. The five-card packs retail for $3.75 each and were distributed in three color-coded pack types: bronze (#1-100), silver (#101-150), and gold (#151-200). The fronts feature color player photos with player statistics on the backs.

COMPLETE SET (200) 40.00 100.00
COMP. BRONZE SET (100) 6.00 15.00
1 Brett Favre 1.00 2.50
2 Jerry Rice .60 1.50
3 Troy Aikman .60 1.50
4 Bruce Smith .08 .25
5 Marshall Faulk .25 .60
6 Erik Kramer .02 .10
7 Carl Pickens .08 .25
8 Anthony Miller .08 .25
9 Cris Carter .20 .50
10 Todd Kinchen .02 .10
11 Stoney Case .02 .10
12 Chris Calloway .02 .10
13 Andre Rison .08 .25
14 Bill Brooks .02 .10
15 Shawn Jefferson .02 .10
16 Eric Zeier .02 .10
17 Yancey Thigpen .08 .25
18 Edgar Bennett .08 .25
19 Garrison Hearst .08 .25
20 Daryl Johnston .08 .25
21 Tyrone Wheatley .08 .25
22 Darick Holmes .02 .10
23 Dave Brown .02 .10
24 Leeland McElroy RC .08 .25
25 Craig Heyward .02 .10
26 Kevin Hardy RC .20 .50
27 Scott Mitchell .08 .25
28 Willie Green .02 .10
29 Vincent Brisby .02 .10
30 Mike Tomczak .02 .10
31 Luther Elliss .02 .10
32 Mike Pritchard .02 .10
33 Robert Green .02 .10
34 Jeff Graham .02 .10
35 Tamarick Vanover .08 .25
36 William Floyd .08 .25
37 Alvin Harper .02 .10
38 Stan Humphries .08 .25
39 Herman Moore .08 .25
40 Tony Martin .08 .25
41 Jonathan Ogden RC .50 1.25
42 Randall Cunningham .20 .50
43 Chris Warren .08 .25
44 Bobby Hebert .02 .10
45 Jerome Bettis .20 .50
46 Joey Galloway .20 .50
47 Ernie Mills .02 .10
48 Steve McNair .40 1.00
49 Karim Abdul-Jabbar RC .20 .50
50 Chad May .02 .10
51 Jim Everett .02 .10
52 Robert Smith .08 .25
53 Tony Boselli .02 .10
54 William Henderson .20 .50
55 Terry Glenn UER RC .60 1.50
56 Neil O'Donnell .08 .25
57 Chris Chandler .08 .25
58 Michael Jackson .08 .25
59 Jason Dunn RC .08 .25
60 James O. Stewart .08 .25
61 Greg Hill .08 .25
62 Mark Carrier WR .02 .10
63 Bernie Parmalee .02 .10
64 Chris Sanders .08 .25
65 Jeff Hostetler .02 .10
66 Eric Moulds RC .75 2.00
67 James Jett .08 .25
68 Henry Ellard .02 .10
69 Mario Bates .08 .25
70 Natrone Means .08 .25
71 Bobby Engram RC .20 .50
72 Christian Fauria .02 .10
73 Gus Frerotte .08 .25
74 Aaron Hayden .02 .10
75 Reggie White .20 .50
76 Dave Meggett .02 .10
77 Harvey Williams .02 .10
78 Terance Mathis .02 .10
79 Byron Bam Morris .02 .10
80 Trent Dilfer .20 .50
81 Irving Fryar .08 .25
82 Quinn Early .02 .10
83 Lake Dawson .02 .10
84 Todd Collins .08 .25
85 Eric Metcalf .02 .10
86 Tim Biakabutuka RC .20 .50
87 Rob Johnson .20 .50
88 Charlie Garner .08 .25
89 Mike Mamula .02 .10
90 Steve Walsh .02 .10
91 Charles Haley .08 .25
92 Mike Alstott RC .60 1.50
93 Wayne Chrebet .30 .75
94 Vinny Testaverde .08 .25
95 Fred Barnett .02 .10
96 Boomer Esiason .08 .25
97 Zack Crockett .02 .10
98 Kevin Williams .02 .10
99 Eric Bieniemy .02 .10
100 Bryan Cox .02 .10
101 Larry Centers .40 1.00
102 Jeff George .40 1.00
103 Bryce Paup .40 1.00
104 Kerry Collins .75 2.00
105 Derrick Moore .20 .50
106 Adrian Murrell .40 1.00
107 Harold Green .20 .50
108 Ki-Jana Carter .40 1.00
109 Sherman Williams .20 .50
110 Deion Sanders 2.00 4.00
111 Emmitt Smith 3.00 8.00
112 Shannon Sharpe .40 1.00
113 Johnnie Morton .40 1.00
114 Eddie Kennison RC .75 2.00
115 Marvin Harrison RC 4.00 10.00
116 Amani Toomer RC .75 2.00
117 Rickey Dudley RC .75 2.00
118 Alex Van Dyke RC .40 1.00
119 Dorsey Levens .75 2.00
120 Antonio Freeman .75 2.00
121 Willie Davis WR .40 1.00
122 Lamont Warren .20 .50
123 Sean Dawkins .20 .50
124 Willie Jackson .40 1.00
125 Kimble Anders .20 .50
126 Dan Marino 4.00 10.00
127 Terry Kirby .40 1.00
128 Amp Lee .20 .50
129 Jake Reed .40 1.00
130 Curtis Martin 1.50 4.00
131 Ray Zellars .20 .50
132 Herschel Walker .40 1.00
133 Mike Sherrard .20 .50
134 Kyle Brady .40 1.00
135 Rocket Ismail .40 1.00
136 Ricky Watters .40 1.00
137 Kordell Stewart .75 2.00
138 Andre Hastings .02 .10
139 Ronnie Harmon .20 .50
140 Terrell Fletcher .20 .50
141 J.J. Stokes .75 2.00
142 Brent Jones .20 .50
143 Tony McGee .20 .50
144 Brian Blades .40 1.00
145 Isaac Bruce .75 2.00
146 Errict Rhett .40 1.00
147 Warren Sapp .20 .50
148 Horace Copeland .20 .50
149 Heath Shuler .40 1.00
150 Michael Westbrook .75 2.00
151 Frank Sanders .60 1.50
152 Rob Moore .60 1.50
153 Bert Emanuel .60 1.50
154 J.J. Birden .30 .75
155 Thurman Thomas 1.00 2.50
156 Jim Kelly 1.00 2.50
157 Curtis Conway .60 1.50
158 Darnay Scott .60 1.50
159 Jeff Blake 1.00 2.50
160 Jay Novacek .60 1.50
161 Michael Irvin 1.00 2.50
162 John Elway 5.00 12.00
163 Terrell Davis 2.50 6.00
164 Barry Sanders 3.00 8.00
165 Brett Perriman .60 1.50
166 Keyshawn Johnson RC 2.00 5.00
167 Eddie George RC 2.50 6.00
168 Derrick Mayes RC 1.00 2.50
169 Simeon Rice RC 2.50 6.00
170 Lawrence Phillips RC .60 1.50
171 Robert Brooks .60 1.50
172 Mark Chmura .60 1.50
173 Rodney Thomas .30 .75
174 Jim Harbaugh .60 1.50
175 Ken Dilger .60 1.50
176 Mark Brunell 2.00 5.00
177 Steve Bono .60 1.50
178 Marcus Allen 1.00 2.50
179 O.J. McDuffie .60 1.50
180 Eric Green .30 .75
181 Warren Moon 1.00 2.50
182 Drew Bledsoe 2.00 5.00
183 Ben Coates .60 1.50
184 Michael Haynes .60 1.50
185 Rodney Hampton .60 1.50
186 Rashaan Salaam .60 1.50
187 Napoleon Kaufman 1.00 2.50
188 Tim Brown 1.00 2.50
189 Rodney Peete .30 .75
190 Calvin Williams .30 .75
191 Erric Pegram .60 1.50
192 Mark Bruener .30 .75
193 Junior Seau 1.00 2.50
194 Steve Young 2.50 6.00
195 Derek Loville .30 .75
196 Rick Mirer .60 1.50
197 Mark Rypien .30 .75
198 Jackie Harris .30 .75
199 Terry Allen .60 1.50
200 Brian Mitchell .30 .75

1996 Playoff Prime X's and O's

*1-100 STARS: 4X TO 10X BASE CARD HI
*1-100 ROOKIES: 1.5X TO 4X BASE CARD HI
*101-150 STARS: 1.2X TO 3X BASE CARD HI
*101-150 ROOKIES: .6X TO 1.5X BASE CARD HI
*151-200 STARS: .8X TO 2X BASE CARD HI
*151-200 ROOKIES: .5X TO 1.2X BASE CARDS
STATED ODDS 1:7.2

1996 Playoff Prime Boss Hogs

Randomly inserted in silver inner packs of the regular Playoff Prime set at a rate of one in 96, this 18-card set features color player photos of some of the NFL's best players on all-leather fronts with black and gold foil stamping. The closely cropped back photos show full-color action printed on acetate.

COMPLETE SET (18) 40.00 80.00
STATED ODDS 1:96
1 Curtis Martin 3.00 8.00
2 Chris Warren 1.25 3.00
3 Emmitt Smith 6.00 15.00
4 Barry Sanders 6.00 15.00
5 Rashaan Salaam 2.00 5.00
6 Marshall Faulk 2.50 6.00
7 Errict Rhett 1.25 3.00
8 Thurman Thomas 2.00 5.00
9 Kerry Collins 2.00 5.00
10 Dan Marino 7.50 20.00
11 Jerry Rice 4.00 10.00
12 Troy Aikman 4.00 10.00
13 Jeff George 1.25 3.00
14 Brett Favre 7.50 20.00
15 Robert Brooks 2.00 5.00
16 John Elway 7.50 20.00
17 Deion Sanders 2.50 6.00
18 Kordell Stewart 2.00 5.00

1996 Playoff Prime Honors

Randomly inserted in packs at a rate of one in 7200, this three-card set features color player images on a leather-like embossed background. The backs carry a borderless color player action photo.

COMPLETE SET (3) 30.00 80.00
STATED ODDS 1:7200
PH1 Emmitt Smith 15.00 40.00
PH2 Curtis Martin 7.50 20.00
PH3 Brett Favre 20.00 50.00

1996 Playoff Prime Surprise

Randomly inserted in packs at a rate of one in 288, this 14-card set features color player images on colorful foil backgrounds. The backs carry another image of the same player on a different colored foil background.

COMPLETE SET (14) 25.00 60.00
STATED ODDS 1:288
1 Dan Marino 5.00 12.00
2 Brett Favre 5.00 12.00
3 Emmitt Smith 5.00 12.00
4 Kordell Stewart .75 2.00
5 Jerry Rice 2.50 6.00
6 Troy Aikman 2.50 6.00
7 Barry Sanders 4.00 10.00
8 Curtis Martin 1.00 2.50
9 Marshall Faulk 1.00 2.50
10 Joey Galloway .50 1.25
11 Robert Brooks .50 1.25
12 Deion Sanders 1.00 2.50
13 Reggie White .75 2.00
14 Marcus Allen .75 2.00

2002 Playoff Prime Signatures Samples

*1-64 SILVER VETS: .4X TO 1X BASE CARDS
*65-110 SLVR ROOKIES: .1X TO .25X
*1-64 GOLD VETS: .8X TO 2X BASE CARDS
*65-110 GOLD ROOKIES: .2X TO .5X

2002 Playoff Prime Signatures

Released in early January 2003, this set consists of 64 veterans, and 46 rookies. The rookies were serial #'d to 250. SRP for each tin was $40. Each tin contained one autograph, one rookie, and two base cards. Each tin was also serial numbered, and limited to 10,000 produced.

ROOKIE PRINT RUN 250 SER.#'d SETS
1 Aaron Brooks .75 2.00
2 Brett Favre 2.50 6.00
3 Drew Bledsoe 1.00 2.50
4 Jake Plummer .75 2.00
5 Jeff Blake 1.00 2.50
6 Jevon Kearse .75 2.00
7 Ricky Williams 1.00 2.50
8 Terrell Davis 1.00 2.50
9 Chris Chambers .75 2.00
10 Cris Carter 1.25 3.00
11 Emmitt Smith 2.00 5.00
12 Randall Cunningham 1.00 2.50
13 Corey Dillon .75 2.00
14 Brian Griese .75 2.00
15 Isaac Bruce 1.25 3.00
16 Koren Robinson .75 2.00
17 David Terrell .75 2.00
18 Mark Brunell 1.00 2.50
19 Eric Moulds .75 2.00
20 Kevan Barlow .75 2.00
21 David Boston .75 2.00
22 LaMont Jordan 1.00 2.50
23 Jimmy Smith 1.00 2.50
24 Marvin Harrison 1.00 2.50
25 Marcus Robinson 1.00 2.50
26 Ray Lewis 1.25 3.00
27 Mike Anderson .75 2.00
28 Randy Moss 1.00 2.50
29 Michael Bennett .75 2.00
30 Quincy Carter .75 2.00
31 Tim Brown 1.25 3.00
32 Michael Strahan 1.00 2.50
33 Tony Gonzalez 1.00 2.50
34 Santana Moss 1.00 2.50
35 Torry Holt 1.00 2.50
36 Anthony Thomas 1.00 2.50
37 Chris Weinke .75 2.00
38 Deuce McAllister 1.00 2.50
39 Drew Brees 2.50 6.00
40 Edgerrin James 1.00 2.50
41 Freddie Mitchell .75 2.00
42 James Jackson .75 2.00
43 Kendrell Bell .75 2.00
44 LaDainian Tomlinson 1.25 3.00
45 Mike McMahon .75 2.00
46 Quincy Morgan .75 2.00
47 Robert Ferguson 1.00 2.50
48 Steve Smith 1.25 3.00
49 Terrell Owens 1.00 2.50
50 Eddie George 1.00 2.50
51 Kurt Warner 1.00 2.50
52 Chad Johnson .75 2.00
53 Dan Marino 4.00 10.00
54 Jim Kelly 2.00 5.00
55 John Elway 3.00 8.00
56 Michael Irvin 2.00 5.00
57 Phil Simms 1.50 4.00
58 Steve Young 2.50 6.00
59 Troy Aikman 2.50 6.00
60 Warren Moon 2.00 5.00
61 Barry Sanders 3.00 8.00
62 Joe Montana 6.00 15.00
63 Joe Namath 3.00 8.00
64 Thurman Thomas 1.50 4.00
65 T.J. Duckett RC 2.00 5.00
66 William Green RC 2.50 6.00
67 Travis Stephens RC 2.00 5.00
68 Tim Carter RC 2.50 6.00
69 Terry Charles RC 2.00 5.00
70 Roy Williams RC 2.00 5.00
71 Marquise Walker RC 2.00 5.00
72 Rohan Davey RC 3.00 8.00
73 Quentin Jammer RC 3.00 8.00
74 Reche Caldwell RC 2.50 6.00
75 Maurice Morris RC 2.50 6.00
76 Woody Dantzler RC 2.50 6.00
77 Patrick Ramsey RC 2.50 6.00
78 Tavon Mason RC 2.00 5.00
79 Ladell Betts RC 3.00 8.00
80 Kahlil Hill RC 2.00 5.00
81 Josh Scobey RC 2.50 6.00
82 Brian Westbrook RC 4.00 10.00
83 Javon Walker RC 3.00 8.00
84 DeShaun Foster RC 3.00 8.00
85 Kelly Campbell RC 2.50 6.00
86 Ashley Lelie RC 2.00 5.00
87 Donte Stallworth RC 3.00 8.00
88 David Carr RC 2.00 5.00
89 Kurt Kittner RC 2.00 5.00
90 Clinton Portis RC 3.00 8.00
91 Josh Reed RC 2.50 6.00
92 Joey Harrington RC 2.00 5.00
93 Antwaan Randle El RC 2.50 6.00
94 Randy Fasani RC 2.00 5.00
95 Cliff Russell RC 2.00 5.00
96 John Henderson RC 2.50 6.00
97 Luke Staley RC 2.00 5.00
98 Antonio Bryant RC 3.00 8.00
99 Jonathan Wells RC 2.50 6.00
100 Chester Taylor RC 3.00 8.00
101 Lamar Gordon RC 2.50 6.00
102 Deion Branch RC 3.00 8.00
103 Josh McCown RC 3.00 8.00
104 Andre Davis RC 2.00 5.00
105 Freddie Milons RC 2.00 5.00
106 David Garrard RC 2.50 6.00
107 Chad Hutchinson RC 2.00 5.00
108 Jabar Gaffney RC 2.00 5.00
109 Eric Crouch RC 3.00 8.00
110 Albert Haynesworth RC 3.00 8.00
NNO Jeff Garcia TIN 1.25 3.00

2002 Playoff Prime Signatures Proofs

*1-52 VETS: 1.5X TO 4X BASIC CARDS
*53-64 RETIRED: 1.2X TO 3X BASIC CARDS
1-64 STATED PRINT RUN 50
*ROOKIES: 1X TO 2.5X BASIC CARDS
65-110 ROOKIE PRINT RUN 25

2002 Playoff Prime Signatures Honor Roll Autographs

Randomly inserted into packs, this set consists of 119 cards that were signed by the player, and serial numbered to varying quantities. Each card features the Honor Roll logo.

STATED PRINT RUN 1-48
SERIAL #'d UNDER 24 NOT PRICED
50 D.Flutie 00ConHaw/33 12.00 30.00
51 D.Flutie 00Pre/36 12.00 30.00
59 D.Flutie 99Con/48 12.00 30.00
62 D.Flutie 99ConPlayoffTix/24 15.00 40.00
65 D.Flutie 99Mom/25 15.00 40.00
114 R.Williams 99AbsGreen/20

2002 Playoff Prime Signatures Autographs

Inserted one per tin, this set features 105-cards including authentic autographs. Each cards was serial numbered as noted below.

AUTO/5-250 ODDS ONE PER PACK
SERIAL #'d UNDER 20 NOT PRICED
UNPRICED PRIME CUTS SER.#'d OF 5
1 Aaron Brooks/58 10.00 25.00
2 Brett Favre/62 75.00 150.00
4 Jake Plummer/20 15.00 40.00
7 Ricky Williams/116 10.00 25.00
8 Terrell Davis/21 20.00 50.00
9 Chris Chambers/223 8.00 20.00
10 Cris Carter/38 20.00 50.00
11 Emmitt Smith/40 100.00 200.00
13 Corey Dillon/102 8.00 20.00
14 Brian Griese/81 8.00 20.00
15 Isaac Bruce/53 15.00 40.00
16 Koren Robinson/147 8.00 20.00
17 David Terrell/233 8.00 20.00
19 Eric Moulds/30 12.00 30.00
20 Kevan Barlow/210 8.00 20.00
22 LaMont Jordan/115 10.00 25.00
23 Jimmy Smith/30 15.00 40.00
24 Marvin Harrison/94 10.00 25.00
25 Marcus Robinson/20 20.00 50.00
28 Randy Moss/195 30.00 60.00
29 Michael Bennett/250 8.00 20.00
30 Quincy Carter/95 8.00 20.00
31 Tim Brown/57 30.00 60.00
32 Michael Strahan/20 20.00 50.00
33 Tony Gonzalez/87 10.00 25.00
34 Santana Moss/115 10.00 25.00
35 Torry Holt/174 10.00 25.00
36 Anthony Thomas/131 10.00 25.00
37 Chris Weinke/99 8.00 20.00
38 Deuce McAllister/113 10.00 25.00
39 Drew Brees/57 40.00 80.00
40 Edgerrin James/28 20.00 50.00
41 Freddie Mitchell/126 8.00 20.00
42 James Jackson/126 8.00 20.00
43 Kendrell Bell/145 8.00 20.00
44 LaDainian Tomlinson/59 30.00 80.00
45 Mike McMahon/192 8.00 20.00
46 Quincy Morgan/160 8.00 20.00
47 Robert Ferguson/225 10.00 25.00
48 Steve Smith/209 12.00 30.00
49 Terrell Owens/98 20.00 50.00
50 Eddie George/22 20.00 50.00
51 Kurt Warner/176 15.00 40.00
52 Chad Johnson/216 8.00 20.00
53 Dan Marino/40 100.00 200.00
54 Jim Kelly/39 40.00 80.00
55 John Elway/68 60.00 150.00
56 Michael Irvin/143 20.00 50.00
57 Phil Simms/62 20.00 50.00
58 Steve Young/101 30.00 80.00
59 Troy Aikman/64 50.00 100.00
61 Barry Sanders/38 75.00 150.00
62 Joe Montana/98 75.00 150.00
63 Joe Namath/216 40.00 80.00
64 Thurman Thomas/40 12.00 30.00
67 Travis Stephens/20 15.00 40.00
68 Tim Carter/120 10.00 25.00
69 Terry Charles/145 8.00 20.00
70 Roy Williams/70 10.00 25.00
71 Marquise Walker/95 8.00 20.00
72 Rohan Davey/20 25.00 60.00
73 Quentin Jammer/95 12.00 30.00
74 Reche Caldwell/45 12.00 30.00
75 Maurice Morris/20 20.00 50.00
76 Woody Dantzler/20 20.00 50.00
77 Patrick Ramsey/120 10.00 25.00
78 Tavon Mason/95 8.00 20.00
79 Ladell Betts/95 12.00 30.00
80 Kahlil Hill/45 10.00 25.00
81 Josh Scobey/145 10.00 25.00
82 Brian Westbrook/145 25.00 60.00
84 DeShaun Foster/70 15.00 40.00
85 Kelly Campbell/45 12.00 30.00
86 Ashley Lelie/120 8.00 20.00
87 Donte Stallworth/95 12.00 30.00
88 David Carr/70 10.00 25.00
89 Kurt Kittner/45 10.00 25.00
90 Clinton Portis/95 12.00 30.00
91 Josh Reed/120 10.00 25.00
92 Joey Harrington/95 8.00 20.00
93 Antwaan Randle El/45 12.00 30.00
94 Randy Fasani/120 8.00 20.00
95 Cliff Russell/95 8.00 20.00
96 John Henderson/95 10.00 25.00
97 Luke Staley/95 8.00 20.00
98 Antonio Bryant/45 15.00 40.00
100 Chester Taylor/95 12.00 30.00
101 Lamar Gordon/45 12.00 30.00
102 Deion Branch/95 15.00 40.00
103 Josh McCown/95 12.00 30.00
104 Andre Davis/95 8.00 20.00
105 Freddie Milons/75 10.00 25.00
106 David Garrard/120 10.00 25.00
107 Chad Hutchinson/145 8.00 20.00
108 Jabar Gaffney/95 8.00 20.00
109 Eric Crouch/95 12.00 30.00

2004 Playoff Prime Signatures

Playoff Prime Signatures initially released in mid-December 2004. The base set consists of 158-cards including 100-veteran or retired player cards serial numbered of 999, 25-dual rookie autographed cards numbered of 199 and 33-autographed rookie cards numbered of 99 signed on replica jersey material. Hobby boxes contained 1-pack of 4-cards and carried an S.R.P. of $60 per pack. Four parallel sets and a variety of autograph inserts can be found seeded in packs making it a hot product for autographed card collectors.

126-158 ROOKIE AU PRINT RUN 99
UNPRICED PLATINUM PRINT RUN 1
UNPRICED PRIME CUT PRINT RUN 1
1 Anquan Boldin 1.00 2.50
2 Josh McCown 1.25 3.00
3 Alge Crumpler 1.25 3.00
4 Michael Vick 1.25 3.00
5 Jamal Lewis 1.25 3.00
6 Todd Heap 1.00 2.50
7 Jim Kelly 2.00 5.00
8 Thurman Thomas 1.50 4.00
9 Travis Henry 1.00 2.50
10 Jake Delhomme 1.00 2.50
11 Stephen Davis 1.00 2.50
12 Steve Smith 1.50 4.00
13 Brian Urlacher 1.50 4.00
14 Dick Butkus 2.50 6.00
15 Gale Sayers 2.00 5.00
16 Mike Ditka 2.00 5.00
17 Mike Singletary 2.00 5.00
18 Rex Grossman 1.00 2.50
19 Richard Dent 1.25 3.00
20 Chad Johnson 1.00 2.50
21 Rudi Johnson 1.00 2.50
22 Jim Brown 2.50 6.00
23 Lee Suggs 1.25 3.00
24 Ozzie Newsome 1.50 4.00
25 Paul Warfield 1.50 4.00
26 Quincy Morgan 1.00 2.50
27 William Green 1.00 2.50
28 Antonio Bryant 1.25 3.00
29 Herschel Walker 2.00 5.00
30 Jimmy Johnson 1.50 4.00
31 Keyshawn Johnson 1.25 3.00
32 Roger Staubach 2.50 6.00
33 Terence Newman 1.25 3.00
34 Tony Dorsett 2.00 5.00
35 Terrell Davis 1.50 4.00
36 Joey Harrington 1.00 2.50
37 Ahman Green 1.25 3.00
38 Javon Walker 1.00 2.50
39 Paul Hornung 2.00 5.00
40 Reggie White 2.00 5.00
41 Robert Ferguson 1.00 2.50
42 Sterling Sharpe 1.50 4.00
43 David Carr 1.00 2.50
44 Domanick Davis 1.00 2.50
45 Earl Campbell 2.00 5.00
46 Peyton Manning 4.00 10.00
47 Reggie Wayne 1.25 3.00
48 Dante Hall 1.00 2.50
49 Priest Holmes 1.00 2.50
50 Trent Green 1.00 2.50
51 A.J. Feeley 1.00 2.50
52 Don Shula 2.00 5.00
53 Chris Chambers 1.00 2.50
54 Travis Minor 1.00 2.50
55 Fran Tarkenton 2.00 5.00
56 Bill Belichick 2.00 5.00
57 Tom Brady 6.00 15.00
58 Aaron Brooks 1.00 2.50
59 Deuce McAllister 1.25 3.00
60 Boo Williams 1.00 2.50
61 Joe Horn 1.00 2.50
62 Lawrence Taylor 2.00 5.00
63 Mark Bavaro 1.25 3.00
64 Michael Strahan 1.25 3.00
65 Tiki Barber 1.25 3.00
66 Herman Edwards 1.50 4.00
67 Joe Namath 3.00 8.00
68 Justin McCareins 1.00 2.50
69 LaMont Jordan 1.25 3.00
70 Santana Moss 1.25 3.00
71 Bo Jackson 2.50 6.00
72 Fred Biletnikoff 2.00 5.00
73 George Blanda 2.00 5.00
74 Jim Plunkett 1.50 4.00
75 Marcus Allen 2.00 5.00
76 Barry Switzer 2.50 6.00
77 Correll Buckhalter 1.00 2.50
78 Donovan McNabb 1.25 3.00
79 Antwaan Randle El 1.00 2.50
80 Bill Cowher 1.50 4.00
81 Franco Harris 2.50 6.00
82 Jack Lambert 2.50 6.00
83 Joe Greene 2.00 5.00
84 Kendrell Bell 1.00 2.50
85 L.C. Greenwood 1.25 3.00
86 Mel Blount 1.50 4.00
87 Terry Bradshaw 2.50 6.00
88 LaDainian Tomlinson 1.50 4.00
89 Andre Carter 1.00 2.50
90 Bill Walsh 2.00 5.00
91 Shaun Alexander 1.00 2.50
92 Steve Largent 2.00 5.00
93 Matt Hasselbeck 1.00 2.50
94 Torry Holt 1.25 3.00
95 Clinton Portis 1.00 2.50
96 Laveranues Coles 1.00 2.50
97 Mark Brunell 1.25 3.00
98 Patrick Ramsey 1.25 3.00
99 Reuben Droughns 1.25 3.00
100 Sonny Jurgensen 1.50 4.00
101 Mauck AU RC/Luke AU RC 6.00 15.00
102 D.Wll AU RC/Miree AU RC 10.00 25.00
103 Frncs AU RC/Mrnt AU RC 6.00 15.00
104 Vilma AU RC/Ward AU RC 10.00 25.00
105 Wlfrk AU RC/Sam AU RC 10.00 25.00
106 Srgi AU RC/Crthn AU RC 8.00 20.00
107 Flmng AU RC/Pytn AU RC 8.00 20.00
108 Bbin AU RC/Symns AU RC 10.00 25.00
109 J.Hrrs AU RC/Mre AU RC 6.00 15.00
110 M.Mnn AU RC/Brmlt AU RC 6.00 15.00
111 S.Jns AU RC/Eche.AU RC 8.00 20.00
112 A.Hll AU RC/B.Pry AU RC 6.00 15.00
113 J.Tylr AU RC/Lmzn AU RC 8.00 20.00
114 Gmble AU RC/Crtr AU RC 8.00 20.00
115 Hnsn AU RC/Kmzl AU RC 6.00 15.00
116 T.Hrrs AU RC/Crrll AU RC 8.00 20.00
117 Smkr AU RC/Hcktt AU RC 8.00 20.00
118 Wlfrd AU RC/Ctchry AU RC 8.00 20.00
119 W.Smth AU RC/Ude.AU RC 8.00 20.00
120 Prkr AU RC/Turner AU RC 6.00 15.00
121 Thom.AU RC/B.Jhn.AU RC 8.00 20.00
122 Nava.AU RC/Pick.AU RC 6.00 15.00
123 Colcl.AU RC/Q.Wil.AU RC 6.00 15.00
124 S.Taylor RC/Cooley AU RC 20.00 40.00
125 M.Boul.AU RC/Lehman RC 10.00 25.00
126 J.P. Losman AU RC 8.00 20.00
127 Lee Evans AU RC 12.00 30.00
128 Ben Watson AU RC 10.00 25.00
129 Cedric Cobbs AU RC 8.00 20.00
130 Devard Darling AU RC 8.00 20.00
131 Chris Perry AU RC 8.00 20.00
132 Kellen Winslow AU RC 8.00 20.00
133 Luke McCown AU RC 8.00 20.00
134 B.Roethlisberger AU RC 125.00 250.00
135 Dunta Robinson AU RC 8.00 20.00
136 Greg Jones AU RC 8.00 20.00
137 Reggie Williams AU RC 8.00 20.00
138 Ben Troupe AU RC 8.00 20.00
139 Tatum Bell AU RC 8.00 20.00
140 Darius Watts AU RC 8.00 20.00
141 Robert Gallery AU RC 10.00 25.00
142 Philip Rivers AU RC 50.00 100.00
143 Julius Jones AU RC 8.00 20.00
144 Eli Manning AU RC 75.00 150.00
145 Bernard Berrian AU RC 10.00 25.00
146 Roy Williams AU RC 8.00 20.00
147 Kevin Jones AU RC 10.00 25.00
148 Mewelde Moore AU RC 10.00 25.00
149 DeAngelo Hall AU RC 12.00 30.00
150 Michael Jenkins AU RC 8.00 20.00
151 Matt Schaub AU RC 8.00 20.00
152 Keary Colbert AU RC 8.00 20.00
153 Devery Henderson AU RC 8.00 20.00
154 Michael Clayton AU RC 10.00 25.00
155 Larry Fitzgerald AU RC 50.00 100.00
156 Rashaun Woods AU RC 8.00 20.00
157 Derrick Hamilton AU RC 8.00 20.00
158 Steven Jackson AU RC 12.00 30.00

2004 Playoff Prime Signatures Bronze Proofs

*VETS: 1.2X TO 3X BASIC CARDS
*RETIRED: 1X TO 2.5X BASIC CARDS
STATED PRINT RUN 50 SER.#'d SETS

2004 Playoff Prime Signatures Gold Proofs

UNPRICED 1-100 PRINT RUN 5
*GOLD DUAL AUTO/50: .5X TO 1.2X
101-125 AU PRINT RUN 50
UNPRICED 126-158 AU PRINT RUN 5

2004 Playoff Prime Signatures Silver Proofs

*VETS: 2X TO 5X BASIC CARDS
*RETIRED: 1.5X TO 4X BASIC CARDS
SILVER PRINT RUN 25 SER.#'d SETS

2004 Playoff Prime Signatures Prime Cuts Autographs

UNPRICED PRIME CUT PRINT RUN 1

2004 Playoff Prime Signatures Prime Pairings Autographs

STATED PRINT RUN 1-50
CARDS SER.#'d UNDER 20 NOT PRICED
PP1 Favre/Culp/Boller/42 100.00 200.00
PP2 Lftwch/Pennin/Dlhme/50 25.00 60.00
PP4 Mont/Stblr/Plmr/Grca/28 125.00 250.00
PP5 B.Snd/Prry/Flk/Brlw/31 100.00 200.00
PP6 Rce/Clyt/Hrsn/A.Jhn/31 125.00 250.00
PP7 R.Lw/K.Bll/Mrgn/Vlm/24 40.00 100.00
PP8 Gonz/Clrk/Crmplr/Heap/26 25.00 60.00
PP9 Aik/Irvn/Hnsn/J.Jns/26 100.00 200.00
PP10 Lsmn/McG/Lftn/Evns/39 40.00 100.00
PP11 Mrn/Grs/Csnk/Ri.Wl/28 175.00 300.00
PP13 McAl/Dck/Grg/D.Dv/50 25.00 60.00
PP17 BS/SB/AM/TA/RC/DB/33 200.00 400.00
PP18 JR/SJ/IW/QG/TB/OS/49 50.00 100.00
PP20 DJ/DS/ER/JP/AV/DM/33 125.00 200.00
PP21 RW/SS/JS/RW/KW/BL/50 30.00 80.00
PP22 EJ/CD/TH/JJ/BW/MB/20 30.00 80.00
PP23 DB/PW/BJ/KC/RG/BB/41 30.00 80.00
PP25 MI/CR/LC/DM/AL/DM/24 50.00 120.00

2004 Playoff Prime Signatures Signature Proofs Bronze

BRONZE STATED PRINT RUN 3-150
BRONZE SER.#'d UNDER 20 NOT PRICED
1 Anquan Boldin/125 6.00 15.00
2 Josh McCown/65 10.00 25.00
3 Alge Crumpler/150 8.00 20.00
4 Michael Vick/85 25.00 50.00
5 Jamal Lewis/31 15.00 40.00
6 Todd Heap/150 6.00 15.00
7 Jim Kelly/44 25.00 50.00
8 Thurman Thomas/46 15.00 40.00
9 Travis Henry/81 8.00 20.00
10 Jake Delhomme/150 6.00 15.00
11 Stephen Davis/125 6.00 15.00
12 Steve Smith/150 10.00 25.00
14 Dick Butkus/51 40.00 80.00
15 Gale Sayers/51 30.00 60.00
16 Mike Ditka/89 20.00 40.00
17 Mike Singletary/110 12.00 30.00
18 Rex Grossman/150 6.00 15.00
19 Richard Dent/50 10.00 25.00
20 Chad Johnson/85 8.00 20.00
21 Rudi Johnson/150 6.00 15.00
22 Jim Brown/150 30.00 60.00
23 Lee Suggs/20 12.00 30.00
24 Ozzie Newsome/82 10.00 25.00
25 Paul Warfield/125 10.00 25.00
26 Quincy Morgan/109 6.00 15.00
27 William Green/87 8.00 20.00
28 Antonio Bryant/59 10.00 25.00
29 Herschel Walker/134 10.00 25.00
30 Jimmy Johnson/45 15.00 40.00
31 Keyshawn Johnson/64 10.00 25.00
32 Roger Staubach/75 40.00 80.00
33 Terence Newman/83 10.00 25.00
34 Tony Dorsett/75 15.00 40.00
35 Terrell Davis/68 10.00 25.00
36 Joey Harrington/83 8.00 20.00
38 Javon Walker/133 6.00 15.00
39 Paul Hornung/99 15.00 40.00
40 Reggie White/92 200.00 300.00
41 Robert Ferguson/112 6.00 15.00
42 Sterling Sharpe/125 8.00 20.00
43 David Carr/65 8.00 20.00
44 Domanick Davis/150 6.00 15.00
45 Earl Campbell/65 15.00 40.00
46 Peyton Manning/75 60.00 100.00
47 Reggie Wayne/87 10.00 25.00
48 Dante Hall/82 8.00 20.00
49 Priest Holmes/57 8.00 20.00
50 Trent Green/89 8.00 20.00
51 A.J. Feeley/94 8.00 20.00
52 Don Shula/40 20.00 50.00
53 Chris Chambers/63 8.00 20.00
55 Fran Tarkenton/86 15.00 40.00
56 Bill Belichick/125 60.00 120.00
57 Tom Brady/86 125.00 250.00
58 Aaron Brooks/99 8.00 20.00
59 Deuce McAllister/125 8.00 20.00
61 Joe Horn/49 8.00 20.00
62 Lawrence Taylor/65 20.00 40.00
64 Michael Strahan/125 8.00 20.00
65 Tiki Barber/139 8.00 20.00
66 Herman Edwards/65 12.00 30.00
67 Joe Namath/99 40.00 80.00
68 Justin McCareins/49 8.00 20.00
69 LaMont Jordan/96 10.00 25.00
70 Santana Moss/81 10.00 25.00
71 Bo Jackson/49 30.00 80.00
72 Fred Biletnikoff/75 12.00 30.00
73 George Blanda/150 20.00 40.00
74 Jim Plunkett/143 10.00 25.00
75 Marcus Allen/150 12.00 30.00
76 Barry Switzer/125 30.00 60.00
78 Donovan McNabb/50 40.00 80.00
79 Antwaan Randle El/82 8.00 20.00
80 Bill Cowher/125 50.00 100.00
81 Franco Harris/60 30.00 50.00
82 Jack Lambert/58 40.00 80.00
83 Joe Greene/75 15.00 40.00
84 Kendrell Bell/150 6.00 15.00
85 L.C. Greenwood/96 10.00 25.00
86 Mel Blount/87 15.00 40.00
87 Terry Bradshaw/94 40.00 80.00
88 LaDainian Tomlinson/68 15.00 40.00
90 Bill Walsh/125 75.00 125.00
91 Shaun Alexander/99 8.00 20.00
92 Steve Largent/150 12.00 30.00
93 Matt Hasselbeck/108 6.00 15.00
94 Torry Holt/69 10.00 25.00
95 Clinton Portis/65 8.00 20.00
96 Laveranues Coles/150 5.00 12.00
97 Mark Brunell/49 12.00 30.00
98 Patrick Ramsey/99 10.00 25.00
99 Reuben Droughns/150 8.00 20.00
100 Sonny Jurgensen/150 10.00 25.00

2004 Playoff Prime Signatures Signature Proofs Gold

*GOLD/21-50: .8X TO 2X BRONZE
GOLD SER.#'d UNDER 20 NOT PRICED
40 Reggie White/25 200.00 350.00
54 Travis Minor/50 12.00 30.00
56 Bill Belichick/45 125.00 200.00
60 Boo Williams/23 15.00 40.00
69 LaMont Jordan/34 20.00 50.00
77 Correll Buckhalter/50 12.00 30.00
89 Andre Carter/21 15.00 40.00
90 Bill Walsh/49 75.00 150.00

2004 Playoff Prime Signatures Signature Proofs Silver

*SILVER: .5X TO 1.2X BRONZE
SILVER SER.#'d UNDER 20 NOT PRICED
40 Reggie White/38 200.00 350.00
54 Travis Minor/100 8.00 20.00
56 Bill Belichick/99 100.00 175.00
57 Tom Brady/55 150.00 300.00
77 Correll Buckhalter/100 8.00 20.00
90 Bill Walsh/83 75.00 125.00

1996 Playoff Trophy Contenders Samples

These "sample" cards were issued before the rest of the product to promote the release of the 1996 Playoff Trophy Contenders set. Each card is nearly identical to the corresponding base set issue except for very slight differences in print style as noted below. There are likely more cards that belong to this listing, therefore any additions are welcomed.

40 Sherman Williams .40 1.00
79 Zack Crockett .40 1.00
118 Mark Chmura .40 1.00

1996 Playoff Trophy Contenders

The 1996 Playoff Trophy Contenders set was issued in one series totalling 120 cards. The six-card packs retail for $3.75 each. The only Rookie Card of note in this set is Aaron Hayden.

COMPLETE SET (120) 7.50 20.00
1 Brett Favre .75 2.00
2 Troy Aikman .40 1.00
3 Dan Marino .75 2.00
4 Emmitt Smith .60 1.50
5 Marshall Faulk .20 .50
6 Jeff Blake .15 .40
7 John Elway .75 2.00
8 Steve Young .30 .75
9 Curtis Martin .30 .75
10 Kordell Stewart .15 .40
11 Drew Bledsoe .25 .60
12 Jim Kelly .15 .40
13 Steve Bono .02 .10
14 Neil O'Donnell .07 .20
15 Jeff Hostetler .02 .10
16 Jim Harbaugh .07 .20
17 Jim Everett .02 .10
18 Erric Pegram .02 .10
19 Tyrone Wheatley .07 .20
20 Barry Sanders .60 1.50
21 Deion Sanders .25 .60
22 Harvey Williams .02 .10
23 Garrison Hearst .07 .20
24 Aaron Hayden RC .02 .10
25 Dorsey Levens .15 .40
26 Napoleon Kaufman .15 .40
27 Rodney Hampton .07 .20
28 Scott Mitchell .07 .20
29 Greg Hill .07 .20
30 Charlie Garner .07 .20
31 Rashaan Salaam .07 .20
32 Errict Rhett .07 .20
33 Byron Bam Morris .02 .10
34 Edgar Bennett .07 .20
35 Jeff George .07 .20
36 Rodney Peete .02 .10
37 Stan Humphries .07 .20
38 Kimble Anders .07 .20
39 Natrone Means .07 .20
40 Sherman Williams .02 .10
41 Eric Metcalf .02 .10
42 Chris Warren .07 .20
43 Marcus Allen .15 .40
44 Bill Brooks .02 .10
45 Wayne Chrebet .25 .60
46 Irving Fryar .07 .20
47 Tony Martin .07 .20
48 Daryl Johnston .07 .20
49 O.J. McDuffie .07 .20
50 Frank Sanders .07 .20
51 Ken Norton .02 .10
52 Jake Reed .07 .20
53 Bert Emanuel .07 .20
54 Floyd Turner .02 .10
55 Junior Seau .15 .40
56 Ernie Mills .02 .10
57 Mark Pike .02 .10
58 Warren Moon .07 .20
59 Mike Mamula .02 .10
60 Kerry Collins .15 .40
61 Nate Newton .02 .10
62 Terry Allen .07 .20
63 Bernie Parmalee .02 .10
64 James O.Stewart .07 .20
65 Isaac Bruce .15 .40
66 Lake Dawson .02 .10
67 Terance Mathis .02 .10
68 Chris Sanders .07 .20
69 Anthony Miller .07 .20
70 Jay Novacek .02 .10
71 Sean Dawkins .02 .10
72 J.J. Birden .02 .10
73 Calvin Williams .02 .10
74 Rick Mirer .07 .20
75 Steve McNair .30 .75
76 Lamont Warren .02 .10
77 Rod Woodson .07 .20
78 Larry Brown .02 .10
79 Zack Crockett .02 .10
80 Jerry Rice .40 1.00
81 Tim Brown .15 .40
82 Yancey Thigpen .07 .20
83 J.J. Stokes .15 .40
84 Herman Moore .07 .20
85 Kevin Williams .02 .10
86 Gus Frerotte .07 .20
87 Robert Brooks .15 .40
88 Michael Irvin .15 .40
89 Steve Tasker .02 .10
90 Joey Galloway .15 .40
91 Kevin Greene .07 .20
92 Reggie White .15 .40
93 Cris Carter .15 .40
94 Charles Haley .07 .20
95 Bryce Paup .02 .10
96 Heath Shuler .07 .20
97 Eric Zeier .02 .10
98 Antonio Freeman .15 .40
99 Erik Kramer .02 .10
100 Derek Loville .02 .10
101 Rodney Thomas .02 .10
102 Terrell Davis .30 .75
103 Ricky Watters .07 .20
104 Craig Heyward .02 .10
105 Terry Kirby .07 .20
106 Bruce Smith .07 .20
107 Curtis Conway .15 .40
108 Charles Johnson .02 .10
109 Brett Perriman .02 .10
110 Carl Pickens .07 .20
111 Michael Westbrook .15 .40
112 Brent Jones .02 .10
113 Ken Dilger .07 .20
114 Fred Barnett .02 .10
115 Mark Bruener .02 .10
116 Tamarick Vanover .07 .20
117 Quinn Early .02 .10
118 Mark Chmura .07 .20
119 Andre Hastings .02 .10
120 Craig Newsome .02 .10

1996 Playoff Trophy Contenders Mini Back-To-Backs

Randomly inserted in packs at a rate of one in 17, this 60-card measure 2 1/4" by 3". These cards were inserted approximately one every 17 packs. The first 11 cards in the set feature Super Bowl XXX opponents: Dallas and Pittsburgh on each side.

COMPLETE SET (60) 200.00 400.00
STATED ODDS 1:17
1 T.Aikman 7.50 20.00
O'Donnell
2 K.Stewart 5.00 12.00
S.Williams
3 D.Sanders 6.00 15.00
A.Hastings
4 E.Smith 10.00 25.00
B.Morris
5 D.Johnston 2.00 5.00
E.Pegram
6 N.Newton 2.00 5.00
K.Greene
7 L.Brown 2.00 5.00
C.Johnson
8 J.Novacek 3.00 8.00
M.Bruener
9 Thigpen 3.00 8.00
K.Williams
10 M.Irvin 5.00 12.00
E.Mills
11 C.Haley 3.00 8.00
R.Woodson
12 B.Favre 15.00 40.00
S.Young
13 E.Bennett 3.00 8.00
D.Loville
14 R.White 5.00 12.00
K.Norton
15 J.Rice 7.50 20.00
R.Brooks
16 J.J.Stokes 5.00 12.00
D.Levens
17 M.Chmura 3.00 8.00
B.Jones
18 C.Newsome 5.00 12.00
A.Freeman
19 D.Marino 12.50 30.00
J.Kelly
20 B.Parmalee 3.00 8.00
B.Smith
21 I.Fryar 2.00 5.00
B.Brooks
22 McDuffie 3.00 8.00
S.Tasker
23 T.Kirby 3.00 8.00
B.Paup
24 J.Harbaugh 3.00 8.00
S.Bono
25 M.Faulk 6.00 15.00
G.Hill
26 L.Warren 5.00 12.00
M.Allen
27 F.Turner 2.00 5.00
K.Anders
28 S.Dawkins 3.00 8.00
L.Dawson
29 T.Vanover 5.00 12.00
Z.Crockett
30 S.Mitchell 2.00 5.00
R.Peete
31 B.Sanders 12.50 30.00
R.Watters

32 B.Perriman 3.00 8.00
C.Williams
33 H.Moore 3.00 8.00
F.Barnett
34 S.Humphries 3.00 8.00
J.George
35 N.Means 3.00 8.00
C.Heyward
36 A.Hayden 2.00 5.00
T.Mathis
37 J.Seau 5.00 12.00
B.Emanuel
38 T.Martin 2.00 5.00
J.J.Birden
39 J.Blake 3.00 8.00
C.Pickens
40 E.Kramer 3.00 8.00
C.Conway
41 F.Sanders 5.00 12.00
G.Hearst
42 J.Elway 12.50 30.00
A.Miller
43 S.McNair 6.00 15.00
C.Sanders
44 W.Moon 3.00 8.00
C.Carter
45 C.Martin 6.00 15.00
D.Bledsoe
46 J.Everett 3.00 8.00
Q.Early
47 R.Hampton 3.00 8.00
T.Wheatley
48 J.Hostetler 5.00 12.00
T.Brown
49 J.Galloway 5.00 12.00
R.Mirer
50 M.Westbrook 3.00 8.00
Frerotte
51 H.Shuler 3.00 8.00
T.Allen
52 C.Garner 3.00 8.00
M.Mamula
53 N.Kaufman 3.00 8.00
H.Williams
54 E.Rhett 3.00 8.00
R.Salaam
55 K.Collins 5.00 12.00
M.Pike
56 K.Dilger 3.00 8.00
E.Zeier
57 T.Davis 6.00 15.00
C.Warren
58 I.Bruce 5.00 12.00
J.Reed
59 W.Chrebet 6.00 15.00
E.Metcalf
60 R.Thomas 3.00 8.00
J.O.Stewart

1996 Playoff Trophy Contenders Playoff Zone

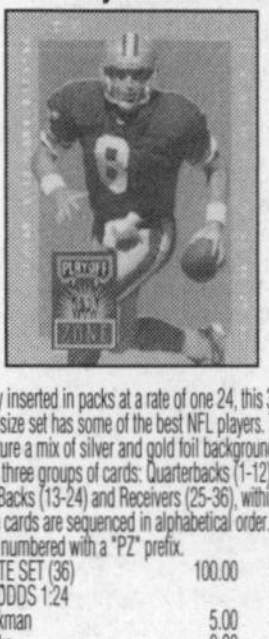

Randomly inserted in packs at a rate of one 24, this 36-card standard-size set has some of the best NFL players. The cards feature a mix of silver and gold foil backgrounds. There are three groups of cards: Quarterbacks (1-12), Running Backs (13-24) and Receivers (25-36), within each group the cards are sequenced in alphabetical order. The cards are numbered with a "PZ" prefix.

COMPLETE SET (36) 100.00 200.00
STATED ODDS 1:24
1 Troy Aikman 5.00 12.00
2 Jeff Blake 2.00 5.00
3 John Elway 10.00 25.00
4 Brett Favre 10.00 25.00
5 Jeff George 1.00 2.50
6 Jim Harbaugh 1.00 2.50
7 Erik Kramer .50 1.25
8 Dan Marino 10.00 25.00
9 Scott Mitchell 1.00 2.50
10 Warren Moon 1.00 2.50
11 Neil O'Donnell 1.00 2.50
12 Steve Young 4.00 10.00
13 Marcus Allen 2.00 5.00
14 Terry Allen 1.00 2.50
15 Edgar Bennett 1.00 2.50
16 Marshall Faulk 2.50 6.00
17 Rodney Hampton 1.00 2.50
18 Craig Heyward .50 1.25
19 Errict Rhett 1.00 2.50
20 Barry Sanders 8.00 20.00
21 Emmitt Smith 8.00 20.00
22 Chris Warren 1.00 2.50
23 Ricky Watters 1.00 2.50
24 Harvey Williams .50 1.25
25 Robert Brooks 2.00 5.00
26 Isaac Bruce 2.00 5.00
27 Cris Carter 2.00 5.00
28 Curtis Conway 2.00 5.00
29 Michael Irvin 2.00 5.00
30 Anthony Miller 1.00 2.50
31 Herman Moore 1.00 2.50
32 Brett Perriman .50 1.25
33 Carl Pickens 1.00 2.50
34 Jerry Rice 5.00 12.00
35 Deion Sanders 3.00 8.00
36 Yancey Thigpen 1.00 2.50

1996 Playoff Trophy Contenders Rookie Stallions

Randomly inserted in packs at a rate of one in 24, this 20-card standard-size set featured leading 1995 NFL rookies. The player's photo is etched into a gold foil background of stallions. The cards are numbered with an "RS" prefix and are sequenced in alphabetical order.

COMPLETE SET (20) 40.00 100.00
STATED ODDS 1:24
1 Mark Bruener .50 1.25
2 Wayne Chrebet 3.00 8.00
3 Kerry Collins 2.00 5.00
4 Zack Crockett .50 1.25
5 Terrell Davis 4.00 10.00
6 Antonio Freeman 2.00 5.00
7 Joey Galloway 2.00 5.00
8 Napoleon Kaufman 2.00 5.00
9 Curtis Martin 4.00 10.00
10 Steve McNair 4.00 10.00
11 Rashaan Salaam 1.00 2.50
12 Chris Sanders 1.00 2.50
13 Frank Sanders 1.00 2.50
14 Kordell Stewart 2.00 5.00
15 J.J. Stokes 2.00 5.00
16 Rodney Thomas .50 1.25
17 Tamarick Vanover 1.00 2.50
18 Michael Westbrook 2.00 5.00
19 Tyrone Wheatley 1.00 2.50
20 Eric Zeier .50 1.25

1997 Playoff Zone

The 1997 Playoff Zone set was issued in one series totalling 150 cards and was distributed in five-card packs with a suggested retail price of $2.99. The fronts feature color action player photos printed on 24 pt. Tekchrome card stock. The backs carry player information and complete career stats. Gold foil parallel cards of the base set as well as every insert set were produced and numbered of 5-sets made.

COMPLETE SET (150) 10.00 25.00
1 Brett Favre .75 2.00
2 Dorsey Levens .20 .50
3 William Henderson .10 .30
4 Derrick Mayes .10 .30
5 Antonio Freeman .20 .50
6 Robert Brooks .10 .30
7 Mark Chmura .10 .30
8 Reggie White .20 .50
9 Randall Cunningham .20 .50
10 Brad Johnson .20 .50
11 Robert Smith .10 .30
12 Cris Carter .20 .50
13 Jake Reed .10 .30
14 Trent Dilfer .20 .50
15 Errict Rhett .07 .20
16 Mike Alstott .20 .50
17 Scott Mitchell .10 .30
18 Barry Sanders .60 1.50
19 Herman Moore .10 .30
20 Erik Kramer .07 .20
21 Rick Mirer .07 .20
22 Rashaan Salaam .07 .20
23 Troy Aikman .40 1.00
24 Deion Sanders .20 .50
25 Emmitt Smith .60 1.50
26 Daryl Johnston .10 .30
27 Anthony Miller .07 .20
28 Eric Bjornson .07 .20
29 Michael Irvin .20 .50
30 Chris T. Jones .07 .20
31 Ty Detmer .10 .30
32 Ricky Watters .10 .30
33 Irving Fryar .10 .30
34 Rodney Peete .07 .20
35 Jeff Hostetler .07 .20
36 Terry Allen .20 .50
37 Michael Westbrook .10 .30
38 Gus Frerotte .07 .20
39 Frank Sanders .10 .30
40 Larry Centers .10 .30
41 Kent Graham .07 .20
42 Dave Brown .07 .20
43 Rodney Hampton .10 .30
44 Tyrone Wheatley .10 .30
45 Chris Calloway .07 .20
46 Ernie Mills .07 .20
47 Tim Biakabutuka .10 .30
48 Anthony Johnson .07 .20
49 Wesley Walls .10 .30
50 Muhsin Muhammad .10 .30
51 Kerry Collins .20 .50
52 Terrell Owens .25 .60
53 Garrison Hearst .10 .30
54 Jerry Rice .40 1.00
55 Steve Young .25 .60
56 Lawrence Phillips .07 .20
57 Isaac Bruce .20 .50
58 Eddie Kennison .10 .30
59 Tony Banks .10 .30
60 Heath Shuler .07 .20
61 Andre Hastings .07 .20
62 Mario Bates .07 .20
63 Chris Chandler .10 .30
64 Jamal Anderson .20 .50
65 Bert Emanuel .10 .30
66 Drew Bledsoe .25 .60
67 Curtis Martin .25 .60
68 Ben Coates .10 .30
69 Terry Glenn .20 .50
70 Dan Marino .75 2.00
71 Karim Abdul-Jabbar .20 .50
72 Fred Barnett .07 .20
73 O.J. McDuffie .10 .30
74 Jim Harbaugh .10 .30
75 Marshall Faulk .25 .60
76 Zack Crockett .07 .20
77 Ken Dilger .07 .20
78 Marvin Harrison .20 .50
79 Keyshawn Johnson .20 .50
80 Neil O'Donnell .10 .30
81 Adrian Murrell .10 .30
82 Wayne Chrebet .20 .50
83 Todd Collins .07 .20
84 Thurman Thomas .20 .50
85 Bruce Smith .10 .30
86 Eric Moulds .20 .50
87 Rob Johnson .20 .50
88 Mark Brunell .25 .60
89 Natrone Means .10 .30
90 Jimmy Smith .10 .30
91 Keenan McCardell .10 .30
92 Kordell Stewart .20 .50
93 Jerome Bettis .20 .50
94 Charles Johnson .10 .30
95 Courtney Hawkins .07 .20
96 Greg Lloyd .07 .20
97 Ki-Jana Carter .07 .20
98 Carl Pickens .10 .30
99 Jeff Blake .10 .30
100 Steve McNair .25 .60
101 Chris Sanders .07 .20
102 Eddie George .20 .50
103 Vinny Testaverde .10 .30
104 Michael Jackson .10 .30
105 Derrick Alexander WR .10 .30
106 Willie Green .07 .20
107 Shannon Sharpe .10 .30
108 Rod Smith WR .20 .50
109 Terrell Davis .25 .60
110 John Elway .75 2.00
111 Elvis Grbac .10 .30
112 Greg Hill .07 .20
113 Marcus Allen .20 .50
114 Derrick Thomas .20 .50
115 Brett Perriman .07 .20
116 Andre Rison .10 .30
117 Rickey Dudley .10 .30
118 Tim Brown .20 .50
119 Desmond Howard .10 .30
120 Napoleon Kaufman .20 .50
121 Jeff George .10 .30
122 Warren Moon .20 .50
123 John Friesz .07 .20
124 Chris Warren .10 .30
125 Joey Galloway .10 .30
126 Stan Humphries .10 .30
127 Tony Martin .10 .30
128 Eric Metcalf .10 .30
129 Jim Everett .07 .20
130 Warrick Dunn RC .60 1.50
131 Reidel Anthony RC .20 .50
132 Derrick Mason RC .40 1.00
133 Joey Kent RC .20 .50
134 Will Blackwell UER RC .10 .30
135 Jim Druckenmiller RC .10 .30
136 Byron Hanspard RC .10 .30
137 John Allred RC .07 .20
138 David LaFleur RC .07 .20
139 Danny Wuerffel RC .20 .50
140 Tiki Barber RC 1.25 3.00
141 Ike Hilliard RC .30 .75
142 Troy Davis RC .10 .30
143 Leon Johnson RC .10 .30
144 Tony Gonzalez RC .75 2.00
145 Jake Plummer RC .75 2.00
146 Antowain Smith RC .50 1.25
147 Rae Carruth RC .07 .20
148 Darnell Autry RC .10 .30
149 Corey Dillon RC .75 2.00
150 Orlando Pace RC .20 .50

1997 Playoff Zone Close-Ups

Randomly inserted in packs at the rate of one in six, this 32-card set features black-and-white close-up photos of top NFL stars printed with silver foil stock. The backs display full-color action player photos. A Gold foil version was produced as well, but only 5 of each card were made and randomly inserted.

COMPLETE SET (32) 50.00 100.00
STATED ODDS 1:6
1 Brett Favre 4.00 10.00
2 Mark Brunell 1.25 3.00
3 Dan Marino 4.00 10.00
4 Kerry Collins 1.00 2.50
5 Troy Aikman 2.00 5.00
6 Drew Bledsoe 1.25 3.00
7 John Elway 4.00 10.00
8 Kordell Stewart 1.00 2.50
9 Steve Young 1.25 3.00
10 Steve McNair 1.25 3.00
11 Tony Banks .60 1.50
12 Emmitt Smith 3.00 8.00
13 Barry Sanders 3.00 8.00
14 Jerry Rice 2.00 5.00
15 Deion Sanders 1.00 2.50
16 Terrell Davis 1.25 3.00
17 Curtis Martin 1.25 3.00
18 Karim Abdul-Jabbar 1.00 2.50
19 Terry Glenn 1.00 2.50
20 Eddie George 1.00 2.50
21 Keyshawn Johnson 1.00 2.50
22 Marvin Harrison 1.00 2.50
23 Muhsin Muhammad .60 1.50
24 Joey Galloway .60 1.50
25 Terrell Owens 1.25 3.00
26 Antonio Freeman 1.00 2.50
27 Ricky Watters .60 1.50
28 Jeff Blake .60 1.50
29 Reggie White 1.00 2.50
30 Michael Irvin 1.00 2.50
31 Eddie Kennison .60 1.50
32 Robert Brooks .60 1.50

1997 Playoff Zone Frenzy

Randomly inserted in packs at the rate of one in 12, this 26-card set features color player images printed on brightly colored, etched foil cards. A Gold foil version was made as well and randomly inserted. Only five of each gold card was produced.

COMPLETE SET (26) 75.00 150.00
STATED ODDS 1:12
1 Brett Favre 8.00 20.00
2 Dan Marino 8.00 20.00
3 Troy Aikman 4.00 10.00
4 Drew Bledsoe 2.50 6.00
5 John Elway 8.00 20.00
6 Kordell Stewart 2.00 5.00
7 Steve Young 2.50 6.00
8 Steve McNair 2.50 6.00
9 Tony Banks 1.25 3.00
10 Emmitt Smith 6.00 15.00
11 Barry Sanders 6.00 15.00
12 Deion Sanders 2.00 5.00
13 Terrell Davis 2.50 6.00
14 Curtis Martin 2.50 6.00
15 Karim Abdul-Jabbar 2.00 5.00
16 Terry Glenn 2.00 5.00
17 Eddie George 2.00 5.00
18 Keyshawn Johnson 2.00 5.00
19 Marvin Harrison 2.00 5.00
20 Joey Galloway 1.25 3.00
21 Antonio Freeman 2.00 5.00
22 Jeff Blake 1.25 3.00
23 Michael Irvin 2.00 5.00
24 Eddie Kennison 1.25 3.00
25 Reggie White 2.00 5.00
26 Robert Brooks 1.25 3.00

1997 Playoff Zone Prime Target

Randomly inserted in packs at the rate of one in 24, this 20-card set features color action player images of top pass catching wide receivers and running backs printed on a metallic blue and silver die-cut design. A Red version was randomly inserted at the rate of 1:96 packs and a Purple version was inserted in special retail packs. Finally, a Gold version was made and randomly inserted. Only five of each gold card was produced.

COMPLETE SET (20) 60.00 120.00
STATED ODDS 1:24
*RED: .8X TO 2X BASIC INSERTS
RED STATED ODDS 1:96
*PURPLE: .4X TO 1X BASIC INSERTS
PURPLES INSERTED IN SPECIAL RETAIL
1 Emmitt Smith 10.00 25.00
2 Barry Sanders 10.00 25.00
3 Jerry Rice 6.00 15.00
4 Terrell Davis 4.00 10.00
5 Curtis Martin 4.00 10.00
6 Karim Abdul-Jabbar 3.00 8.00
7 Terry Glenn 3.00 8.00
8 Eddie George 3.00 8.00
9 Keyshawn Johnson 3.00 8.00
10 Joey Galloway 2.00 5.00
11 Antonio Freeman 3.00 8.00
12 Herman Moore 2.00 5.00
13 Tim Brown 3.00 8.00
14 Michael Irvin 3.00 8.00
15 Isaac Bruce 3.00 8.00
16 Eddie Kennison 2.00 5.00
17 Shannon Sharpe 2.00 5.00
18 Cris Carter 3.00 8.00
19 Napoleon Kaufman 3.00 8.00
20 Carl Pickens 2.00 5.00

1997 Playoff Zone Rookies

Randomly inserted in packs at the rate of 1:8, this 24-card set features color photos of future star players printed on shining etched silver foil. A Gold foil version was made as well and randomly inserted. Only 5 of each gold card was produced.

COMPLETE SET (24) 15.00 40.00
STATED ODDS 1:8
1 Jake Plummer 2.50 6.00
2 George Jones .25 .60
3 Pat Barnes .40 1.00
4 Brian Manning .25 .60
5 O.J. Santiago .40 1.00
6 Byron Hanspard .40 1.00
7 Antowain Smith 1.50 4.00
8 Rae Carruth .25 .60
9 Darnell Autry .40 1.00
10 Corey Dillon 2.50 6.00
11 David LaFleur .25 .60
12 Tony Gonzalez 2.50 6.00
13 Leon Johnson .40 1.00
14 Danny Wuerffel .60 1.50
15 Troy Davis .40 1.00
16 Jay Graham .25 .60
17 Tiki Barber 4.00 10.00
18 Will Blackwell .40 1.00
19 Jim Druckenmiller .40 1.00
20 Orlando Pace .60 1.50
21 Warrick Dunn 2.00 5.00
22 Reidel Anthony .60 1.50
23 Derrick Mason 1.25 3.00
24 Joey Kent .60 1.50

1997 Playoff Zone Sharpshooters

Randomly inserted at the rate of one in 24, this 18-card set features color photos of top quarterbacks highlighted with blue flaming graphics. A Red parallel was inserted at the rate of 1:72 packs. Finally, a Gold foil version was made and randomly inserted. Only five of each gold card was produced.

COMPLETE SET (18) 60.00 150.00
STATED ODDS 1:24
*REDS: .6X TO 1.5X BASIC INSERTS
RED STATED ODDS 1:72
1 Brett Favre 8.00 20.00
2 Dan Marino 8.00 20.00
3 John Elway 8.00 20.00
4 Troy Aikman 4.00 10.00
5 Drew Bledsoe 2.50 6.00
6 Todd Collins .75 2.00
7 Brad Johnson 2.00 5.00
8 Stan Humphries 1.25 3.00
9 John Friesz .75 2.00
10 Tony Banks 1.25 3.00
11 Ty Detmer 1.25 3.00
12 Steve McNair 2.50 6.00
13 Rob Johnson 2.00 5.00
14 Kordell Stewart 2.00 5.00
15 Danny Wuerffel 2.00 5.00
16 Jim Druckenmiller 1.25 3.00
17 Jake Plummer 10.00 25.00
18 Kerry Collins 2.00 5.00

1997 Playoff Zone Treasures

Randomly inserted in packs at the rate of one in 196, this 12-card set features color player images printed on etched copper foil on one side and brightly inked mirror board on the flip side. A Gold foil version was made as well and randomly inserted. Only 5 of each gold card was produced..

COMPLETE SET (12) 75.00 200.00
STATED ODDS 1:196
1 Brett Favre 15.00 40.00
2 Dan Marino 15.00 40.00
3 Troy Aikman 8.00 20.00
4 Drew Bledsoe 5.00 12.00
5 Emmitt Smith 12.50 30.00
6 Barry Sanders 12.50 30.00
7 Warrick Dunn 6.00 15.00
8 Deion Sanders 4.00 10.00
9 Terrell Davis 5.00 12.00
10 Curtis Martin 5.00 12.00
11 Tiki Barber 12.50 30.00
12 Eddie George 4.00 10.00

1985 Police Raiders/Rams

This 30-card set is actually two subsets, 15 cards featuring Los Angeles Rams and 15 cards featuring Los Angeles Raiders. The set was actually sponsored by the Sheriff's Department of Los Angeles County, KIIS Radio, and the Rams/Raiders, so technically it is a safety set but not a "police" set. The cards are unnumbered except for the uniform number listed on the card back. The list below is organized alphabetically within each team. Card backs are printed in black ink on white card stock. Cards measure approximately 2 13/16" by 4 1/8".

COMPLETE SET (30) 10.00 25.00
1 Marcus Allen 3.00 8.00
2 Lyle Alzado .50 1.25
3 Todd Christensen .50 1.25
4 Dave Dalby .40 1.00
5 Mike Davis .40 1.00
6 Ray Guy .50 1.25
7 Frank Hawkins .40 1.00
8 Lester Hayes .50 1.25
9 Mike Haynes .50 1.25
10 Howie Long .75 2.00
11 Rod Martin .40 1.00
12 Mickey Marvin .40 1.00
13 Jim Plunkett .50 1.25
14 Brad Van Pelt .40 1.00
15 Dokie Williams .40 1.00
16 Bill Bain .30 .75
17 Mike Barber .30 .75
18 Dieter Brock .40 1.00
19 Nolan Cromwell .40 1.00
20 Eric Dickerson .75 2.00
21 Reggie Doss .30 .75
22 Carl Ekern .30 .75
23 Kent Hill .30 .75
24 LeRoy Irvin .40 1.00
25 Johnnie Johnson .30 .75
26 Jeff Kemp .40 1.00
27 Mike Lansford .30 .75
28 Mel Owens .30 .75
29 Barry Redden .30 .75
30 Mike Wilcher .30 .75

1986 Police Bears/Patriots

This set was supposedly not an authorized police issue as it is unclear which police department(s) truly sponsored the set. The 17 cards feature members of the Chicago Bears and New England Patriots who were in the Super Bowl in early 1986. The cards measure approximately 2 5/8" by 4 1/4". The card fronts give the player's name and uniform number under his red/blue bordered color photo. The card backs are printed in black ink on white card stock. Cards are numbered on the back in the lower right corner: the Bears (2-9) and the Patriots (10-17).

COMPLETE SET (17) .75 2.00
1 Title Card .04 .10
2 Richard Dent .12 .30
3 Walter Payton .40 1.00
4 William Perry .08 .20
5 Jim McMahon .08 .20
6 Dave Duerson .04 .10
7 Gary Fencik .04 .10
8 Otis Wilson .04 .10
9 Willie Gault .04 .10
10 Craig James .08 .20
11 Fred Marion .04 .10
12 Ronnie Lippett .04 .10
13 Stanley Morgan .08 .20
14 John Hannah .08 .20
15 Andre Tippett .04 .10
16 Tony Franklin .04 .10
17 Tony Eason .04 .10

2013 Pop Century

COMMON CARD 3.00 8.00
*SILVER/25: .5X TO 1.2X BASIC CARDS
*BLUE/10: UNPRICED DUE TO SCARCITY
*RED/5: UNPRICED DUE TO SCARCITY
*GOLD/1: UNPRICED DUE TO SCARCITY
*P.P.BLACK/1: UNPRICED DUE TO SCARCITY
*P.P.CYAN/1: UNPRICED DUE TO SCARCITY
*P.P.MAGENTA/1: UNPRICED DUE TO SCARCITY
*P.P.YELLOW/1: UNPRICED DUE TO SCARCITY
BAYAT Y.A. Tittle 8.00 20.00

2013 Pop Century Co-Stars Autographs

COMMON CARD 6.00 15.00
*SILVER/25: .5X TO 1.2X BASIC CARDS
*BLUE/10: UNPRICED DUE TO SCARCITY
*RED/5: UNPRICED DUE TO SCARCITY
*GOLD/1: UNPRICED DUE TO SCARCITY
*P.P.BLACK/1: UNPRICED DUE TO SCARCITY
*P.P.CYAN/1: UNPRICED DUE TO SCARCITY
*P.P.MAGENTA/1: UNPRICED DUE TO SCARCITY
*P.P.YELLOW/1: UNPRICED DUE TO SCARCITY
CS19 M.Oher/Q.Aaron 12.00 30.00

1976 Popsicle Teams

This set of 28 teams is printed on plastic material similar to that found on thin credit cards. There is a variation on the New York Giants card; one version shows the helmet logo as Giants and the other shows it as New York. The title card appears to be short-printed and reads, "Pro Quarterback, Pro Football's Leading Magazine". The cards measure approximately 3 3/8" by 2 1/8", have rounded corners, and are slightly thinner than a credit card. Below the NFL logo and the team, the front features a color helmet shot and a color action photo. We've noted below prominent players that can be identified in the photos. The backs contais a brief team history. Some consider the new expansion teams, Tampa Bay and Seattle, to be somewhat tougher to find. The cards are unnumbered and are ordered below alphabetically by team location name. The set is considered complete with just the 28 team cards.

COMPLETE SET (28) 40.00 80.00
1 Atlanta Falcons 1.50 3.00
2 Baltimore Colts 1.50 3.00
3 Buffalo Bills 1.50 3.00
4 Chicago Bears 1.50 3.00
5 Cincinnati Bengals 1.50 3.00
6 Cleveland Browns 1.50 3.00
7 Dallas Cowboys 2.00 4.00
8 Denver Broncos 1.50 3.00
9 Detroit Lions 1.50 3.00
10 Green Bay Packers 1.50 3.00
11 Houston Oilers 1.50 3.00
12 Kansas City Chiefs 1.50 3.00
13 Los Angeles Rams 1.50 3.00
14 Miami Dolphins 2.00 4.00
15 Minnesota Vikings 1.50 3.00
16 New England Patriots 1.50 3.00
17 New Orleans Saints 1.50 3.00
18A New York Giants 1.50 3.00
18B New York Giants 1.50 3.00
19 New York Jets 1.50 3.00
20 Oakland Raiders 2.00 4.00
21 Philadelphia Eagles 1.50 3.00
22 Pittsburgh Steelers 2.00 4.00
23 St. Louis Cardinals 1.50 3.00
24 San Diego Chargers 1.50 3.00
25 San Francisco 49ers 2.00 4.00
26 Seattle Seahawks 1.50 3.00
27 Tampa Bay Buccaneers 1.50 3.00
28 Washington Redskins 2.00 4.00
NNO Title Card SP 15.00 30.00

1974 Portland Storm WFL Team Issue 5X7

The photos measure roughly 5" x 7 1/2" and feature black and white images with the player's name in the lower left below the photo, his position (initials) centered, and the team name on the right side below the photo. The backs are blank.

1 Dick Coury CO 6.00 12.00
2 Marv Kendricks 6.00 12.00
3 Mike Taylor 6.00 12.00
4 Tony Terry 6.00 12.00

1960 Post Cereal

These large cards measure approximately 7" by 8 3/4". The 1960 Post Cereal Sports Stars set contains nine cards depicting current baseball, football and basketball players. Each card comprised the entire back of a Grape Nuts Flakes Box and is blank backed. The color player photos are set on a colored background surrounded by a wooden frame design, and they are unnumbered (assigned numbers below for reference according to sport). The catalog designation is F278-26.

COMPLETE SET (9) 3000.00 5000.00
FB1 Frank Gifford 200.00 400.00
FB2 John Unitas 350.00 600.00

1962 Post Cereal

The 1962 Post Cereal set of 200 cards is Post's only American football issue. The cards were distributed on the back panels of various flavors of Post Cereals. As is typical of the Post package-back issues, the cards are blank-backed and are typically found poorly cut from the cereal box. The cards (when properly trimmed) measure 2 1/2" by 3 1/2". The cards are grouped in order of the team's 1961 season finish. The players within each team are also grouped in alphabetical order with the exception of 135 Frank Clarke of the Cowboys. Certain cards printed only on unpopular types of cereal are relatively difficult to obtain. Thirty-one such cards are known and are indicated by an SP (short printed) in the checklist. Some players who had been traded had asterisks after their positions. Jim Ninowski (57) and Sam Baker (74) can be found with either a red or black (traded) asterisk. The set price below does not include both variations. The cards of Jim Johnson, Bob Lilly, and Larry Wilson predate their Rookie Cards. Also noteworthy is the card of Fran Tarkenton, whose rookie year for cards is 1962.

COMPLETE SET (200) 2700.00 4500.00
1 Dan Currie 3.50 7.00
2 Boyd Dowler 3.50 7.00
3 Bill Forester 2.50 5.00
4 Forrest Gregg 4.00 8.00
5 Dave Hanner 2.50 5.00
6 Paul Hornung 10.00 20.00
7 Hank Jordan 4.00 8.00
8 Jerry Kramer SP 25.00 40.00
9 Max McGee SP 15.00 25.00
10 Tom Moore SP 125.00 200.00
11 Jim Ringo 4.00 8.00
12 Bart Starr 15.00 25.00
13 Jim Taylor 7.50 15.00
14 Fuzzy Thurston 3.50 7.00
15 Jesse Whittenton 2.00 4.00
16 Erich Barnes 2.50 5.00
17 Roosevelt Brown 3.50 7.00
18 Bob Gaiters 2.00 4.00
19 Roosevelt Grier 3.50 7.00
20 Sam Huff 5.00 10.00
21 Jim Katcavage 2.50 5.00
22 Cliff Livingston 2.00 4.00
23 Dick Lynch 2.00 4.00
24 Joe Morrison SP 35.00 60.00
25 Dick Nolan SP 30.00 50.00
26 Andy Robustelli 4.00 8.00
27 Kyle Rote 3.50 7.00
28 Del Shofner SP 60.00 100.00
29 Y.A. Tittle SP 75.00 125.00
30 Alex Webster 2.50 5.00
31 Bill Barnes 2.00 4.00
32 Maxie Baughan 2.50 5.00
33 Chuck Bednarik 5.00 10.00
34 Tom Brookshier 3.50 7.00
35 Jimmy Carr 2.00 4.00
36 Ted Dean SP 30.00 50.00
37 Sonny Jurgensen 7.50 15.00
38 Tommy McDonald 3.50 7.00
39 Clarence Peaks 2.00 4.00
40 Pete Retzlaff 2.50 5.00
41 Jesse Richardson SP 50.00 100.00
42 Leo Sugar 2.00 4.00
43 Bobby Walston SP 35.00 70.00
44 Chuck Weber 5.00 10.00
45 Ed Khayat 2.00 4.00
46 Howard Cassady 2.50 5.00
47 Gail Cogdill 2.00 4.00
48 Jim Gibbons SP 25.00 50.00
49 Bill Glass 2.00 4.00
50 Alex Karras 5.00 10.00
51 Dick Lane 3.50 7.00
52 Yale Lary 3.50 7.00
53 Dan Lewis 2.00 4.00
54 Darris McCord SP 40.00 80.00
55 Jim Martin 2.00 4.00
56 Earl Morrall 2.50 5.00
57A Jim Ninowski (red*) 2.50 5.00
57B Jim Ninowski (blk*) 2.50 5.00
58 Nick Pietrosante 2.50 5.00
59 Joe Schmidt SP 60.00 100.00
60 Harley Sewell 2.00 4.00
61 Jim Brown 40.00 75.00
62 Galen Fiss SP 35.00 60.00
63 Bob Gain 2.00 4.00
64 Jim Houston 2.00 4.00
65 Mike McCormack 3.50 7.00
66 Gene Hickerson 5.00 10.00
67 Bobby Mitchell 4.00 8.00
68 John Morrow 2.00 4.00
69 Bernie Parrish 2.00 4.00
70 Milt Plum 2.50 5.00
71 Ray Renfro 2.50 5.00
72 Dick Schafrath 2.50 5.00
73 Jim Ray Smith 2.00 4.00
74A Sam Baker SP red* 200.00 350.00
74B Sam Baker SP blk* 175.00 300.00
75 Paul Wiggin SP 15.00 30.00
76 Raymond Berry 5.00 10.00
77 Bob Boyd DB 2.00 4.00
78 Ordell Braase 2.00 4.00
79 Art Donovan 5.00 10.00
80 Dee Mackey 2.00 4.00
81 Gino Marchetti 4.00 8.00
82 Lenny Moore 5.00 10.00
83 Jim Mutscheller 2.00 4.00
84 Steve Myhra 2.00 4.00
85 Jimmy Orr 2.50 5.00
86 Jim Parker 4.00 8.00
87 Bill Pellington 2.00 4.00
88 Alex Sandusky 2.00 4.00
89 Dick Szymanski 2.00 4.00
90 Johnny Unitas 15.00 30.00
91 Bruce Bosley 2.00 4.00
92 John Brodie 6.00 12.00
93 Dave Baker SP 250.00 450.00
94 Tommy Davis 2.00 4.00
95 Bob Harrison 2.00 4.00
96 Matt Hazeltine 2.00 4.00
97 Jim Johnson SP 35.00 70.00
98 Billy Kilmer 3.50 7.00
99 Jerry Mertens 2.00 4.00
100 Frank Morze 2.00 4.00
101 R.C. Owens 2.50 5.00
102 J.D. Smith 2.00 4.00
103 Bob St. Clair SP 45.00 80.00
104 Monty Stickles 2.00 4.00
105 Abe Woodson 2.00 4.00
106 Doug Atkins 4.00 8.00
107 Ed Brown 2.50 5.00
108 J.C. Caroline 2.00 4.00
109 Rick Casares 2.50 5.00
110 Angelo Coia SP 150.00 250.00
111 Mike Ditka SP 75.00 125.00
112 Joe Fortunato 2.00 4.00
113 Willie Galimore 2.50 5.00
114 Bill George 3.50 7.00
115 Stan Jones 3.50 7.00
116 Johnny Morris 2.50 5.00
117 Larry Morris SP 35.00 60.00
118 Richie Petitbon 2.50 5.00
119 Bill Wade 2.50 5.00
120 Maury Youmans 2.00 4.00
121 Preston Carpenter 2.00 4.00
122 Buddy Dial 2.50 5.00
123 Bobby Joe Green 2.00 4.00
124 Mike Henry 2.00 4.00
125 John Henry Johnson 4.00 8.00
126 Bobby Layne 10.00 20.00
127 Gene Lipscomb 3.50 7.00
128 Lou Michaels 2.50 5.00
129 John Nisby 2.00 4.00
130 John Reger 2.00 4.00
131 Mike Sandusky 2.00 4.00
132 George Tarasovic 2.00 4.00
133 Tom Tracy SP 70.00 110.00
134 Glynn Gregory 2.00 4.00
135 Frank Clarke SP 45.00 80.00
136 Mike Connelly SP 35.00 70.00
137 L.G. Dupre 2.00 4.00
138 Bob Fry 2.00 4.00
139 Allen Green SP 75.00 125.00
140 Billy Howton 2.50 5.00
141 Bob Lilly 25.00 40.00
142 Don Meredith 20.00 35.00
143 Dick Moegle 2.00 4.00
144 Don Perkins 3.50 7.00
145 Jerry Tubbs SP 75.00 125.00
146 J.W. Lockett 2.00 4.00
147 Ed Cook 2.00 4.00
148 John David Crow 2.50 5.00
149 Sam Etcheverry 2.00 4.00
150 Frank Fuller 2.00 4.00
151 Prentice Gautt 2.00 4.00
152 Jimmy Hill 2.00 4.00
153 Bill Koman SP 30.00 50.00
154 Larry Wilson 7.50 15.00
155 Dale Meinert 2.00 4.00
156 Ed Henke 2.00 4.00
157 Sonny Randle 2.00 4.00
158 Ralph Guglielmi SP 30.00 50.00
159 Joe Childress 2.00 4.00
160 Jon Arnett 2.50 5.00
161 Dick Bass 2.00 4.00
162 Zeke Bratkowski 2.50 5.00
163 Carroll Dale SP 25.00 40.00
164 Art Hunter 2.00 4.00
165 John Lovetere 2.00 4.00
166 Lamar Lundy 2.50 5.00
167 Ollie Matson 5.00 10.00
168 Ed Meador 2.00 4.00
169 Jack Pardee SP 45.00 80.00
170 Jim Phillips 2.00 4.00
171 Les Richter 2.50 5.00
172 Frank Ryan 2.50 5.00
173 Frank Varrichione 2.00 4.00
174 Grady Alderman 2.50 5.00
175 Rip Hawkins 2.00 4.00
176 Don Joyce SP 75.00 125.00
177 Bill Lapham 2.00 4.00
178 Tommy Mason 2.50 5.00
179 Hugh McElhenny 5.00 10.00
180 Dave Middleton 2.00 4.00
181 Dick Pesonen SP 20.00 35.00
182 Karl Rubke 2.00 4.00
183 George Shaw 2.00 4.00
184 Fran Tarkenton 30.00 50.00
185 Mel Triplett 2.00 4.00
186 Frank Youso SP 60.00 100.00
187 Bill Bishop 2.50 5.00
188 Bill Anderson SP 40.00 75.00
189 Don Bosseler 2.00 4.00
190 Fred Hageman 2.00 4.00
191 Sam Horner 2.00 4.00
192 Jim Kerr 2.00 4.00
193 Joe Krakoski SP 150.00 250.00
194 Fred Dugan 2.00 4.00
195 John Paluck 2.00 4.00
196 Vince Promuto 2.00 4.00
197 Joe Rutgens 2.00 4.00
198 Norm Snead 3.50 7.00
199 Andy Stynchula 2.00 4.00
200 Bob Toneff 2.00 4.00

1962 Post Booklets

Each of these booklets measures approximately 5" by 3" and contained fifteen pages. The front cover carries the title of each booklet and a color cartoon headshot of the player inside a circle. While the first page presents biography and career summary, the remainder of each booklet consists of various tips, diagrams of basic formations and plays, officials' signals, football lingo, statistics, or team standings. The booklets are illustrated throughout by crude color drawings. These booklets are numbered on the front page in the upper right corner.

COMPLETE SET (4) 75.00 150.00
1 Jon Arnett 15.00 30.00
2 Paul Hornung 25.00 50.00
3 Sonny Jurgensen 20.00 40.00
4 Sam Huff 20.00 40.00

2002 Post Cereal

These cards were issued in specially marked boxes of Post Brand cereals in 2002. Each measures 2 5/8" by 3 3/4" and was produced with lenticular (magic motion) technology and rounded corners. Two players per card are included and the helmet logos have been removed since the cards were only licensed through Players Inc.

1 Mark Clayton 3.00 8.00
Dan Marino
2 Joe Montana 3.00 8.00
Jerry Rice
4 Johnny Unitas 2.50 6.00
Raymond Berry

1926 Pottsville Maroons Postcards

1 Heinie Benkert 600.00 1000.00
2 Charlie Berry 1250.00 2000.00
3 Jesse Brown 600.00 1000.00
4 Frank Bucher 600.00 1000.00
5 Jack Ernst 800.00 1200.00
6 Hoot Flanagan 800.00 1200.00
7 Russ Hathaway 600.00 1000.00
8 Heinie Jawish 600.00 1000.00
9 George Kenneally 600.00 1000.00
10 Tony Latone 900.00 1500.00
11 Bob Millman 600.00 1000.00
12 Duke Osborn 800.00 1200.00
13 Frank Racis 600.00 1000.00
14 Herb Stein 800.00 1200.00
15 Jim Welsh 600.00 1000.00
16 Barney Wentz 800.00 1200.00
17 Zeke Wissinger 600.00 1000.00
18 Frank Youngfleish 600.00 1000.00

1977 Pottsville Maroons 1925

Reportedly issued in 1977, this standard-size 17-card set features helmetless player photos of the disputed 1925 NFL champion Pottsville Maroons on the card fronts. The pictures are white-bordered and red-screened, with the player's name, card number, and team name in red beneath each photo. The player's name, team, and card number appear again at the top of the card back, along with the name of the college (if any) attended previous to playing for the Maroons and brief biographical information, all in red. The set producer's name, Joseph C. Zacko Sr., appears at the bottom, along with the copyright date, 1977.

COMPLETE SET (17) 10.00 20.00
1 Team History .75 2.00
2 The Symbolic Shoe .75 1.50
3 Jack Ernst .75 2.00
4 Tony Latone .75 1.50
5 Duke Osborn .75 1.50
6 Frank Bucher .75 1.50
7 Frankie Racis .75 1.50
8 Russ Hathaway .75 1.50
9 W.H.(Hoot) Flanagan .75 1.50
10 Charlie Berry 1.00 2.00
11 Russ Stein .75 1.50
12 Howard Lebengood .75 1.50
13 Denny Hughes .75 1.50
14 Barney Wentz .75 1.50
15 Eddie Doyle UER .75 1.50
16 Walter French .75 1.50
17 Dick Rauch .75 2.00

1992 Power

The 1992 Power set produced by Pro Set consists of 330 standard-size cards that were issued in 12-card packs. Rookie Cards include Edgar Bennett, Steve Bono, Quentin Coryatt, Steve Emtman, Amp Lee, Johnny Mitchell, Carl Pickens and Tommy Vardell.

COMPLETE SET (330) 5.00 12.00
1 Warren Moon .08 .25
2 Mike Horan .01 .05
3 Bobby Hebert .01 .05
4 Jim Harbaugh .08 .25
5 Sean Landeta .01 .05
6 Bubby Brister .02 .10
7 John Elway .50 1.25
8 Troy Aikman .30 .75
9 Rodney Peete .02 .10
10 Dan McGwire .01 .05
11 Mark Rypien .01 .05
12 Randall Cunningham .08 .25
13 Dan Marino .50 1.25
14 Vinny Testaverde .02 .10
15 Jeff Hostetler .02 .10
16 Joe Montana .50 1.25
17 Dave Krieg .02 .10
18 Jeff Jaeger .01 .05
19 Bernie Kosar .02 .10
20 Barry Sanders .50 1.25
21 Deion Sanders .20 .50
22 Emmitt Smith .60 1.50
23 Mel Gray .02 .10
24 Stanley Richard .01 .05
25 Brad Muster .01 .05
26 Rod Woodson .08 .25
27 Rodney Hampton .02 .10
28 Darrell Green .01 .05
29 Barry Foster .02 .10
30 Dave Meggett .02 .10
31 Lonnie Young .01 .05
32 Marcus Allen .08 .25
33 Merril Hoge .01 .05
34 Thurman Thomas .08 .25
35 Neal Anderson .01 .05
36 Bennie Blades .01 .05
37 Pat Terrell .01 .05
38 Nick Bell .01 .05
39 Johnny Johnson .01 .05
40 Bill Bates .01 .05
41 Keith Byars .01 .05
42 Ronnie Lott .02 .10
43 Elvis Patterson .01 .05
44 Lorenzo White .01 .05
45 Tony Stargell .01 .05
46 Tim McDonald .01 .05
47 Kirby Jackson .01 .05
48 Lionel Washington .01 .05
49 Dennis Smith .01 .05
50 Mike Singletary .02 .10
51 Mike Croel .01 .05
52 Pepper Johnson .01 .05
53 Vaughan Johnson .01 .05
54 Chris Spielman .02 .10
55 Junior Seau .08 .25
56 Lawrence Taylor .08 .25
57 Clay Matthews .02 .10
58 Derrick Thomas .08 .25
59 Seth Joyner .01 .05
60 Stan Thomas .01 .05
61 Nate Newton .01 .05
62 Matt Brock .01 .05
63 Gene Chilton RC .01 .05
64 Randall McDaniel .02 .10
65 Max Montoya .01 .05
66 Joe Jacoby .01 .05
67 Russell Maryland .01 .05
68 Ed King .01 .05
69 Mark Schlereth RC .01 .05
70 Charles McRae .01 .05
71 Charles Mann .01 .05
72 William Perry .02 .10
73 Simon Fletcher .01 .05
74 Paul Gruber .01 .05
75 Howie Long .08 .25
76 Steve McMichael .02 .10
77 Karl Mecklenburg .01 .05
78 Anthony Munoz .02 .10
79 Ray Childress .01 .05
80 Jerry Rice .30 .75
81 Art Monk .02 .10
82 John Taylor .02 .10
83 Andre Reed .02 .10
84 Haywood Jeffires .02 .10
85 Mark Duper .01 .05
86 Fred Barnett .02 .10
87 Tom Waddle .01 .05
88 Michael Irvin .08 .25
89 Brian Blades .02 .10
90 Neil Smith .08 .25
91 Kevin Greene .02 .10
92 Reggie White .08 .25
93 Jerry Ball .01 .05
94 Charles Haley .02 .10
95 Richard Dent .02 .10
96 Clyde Simmons .01 .05
97 Cornelius Bennett .02 .10
98 Eric Swann .02 .10
99 Doug Smith .01 .05
100 Jim Kelly .08 .25
101 Michael Jackson .02 .10
102 Steve Christie .01 .05
103 Timm Rosenbach .01 .05
104 Brett Favre 1.00 2.50

105 Jeff Feagles .01 .05
106 Kevin Butler .01 .05
107 Boomer Esiason .02 .10
108 Steve Young .25 .60
109 Norm Johnson .01 .05
110 Jay Schroeder .01 .05
111 Jeff George .08 .25
112 Chris Miller .02 .10
113 Steve Bono RC .08 .25
114 Neil O'Donnell .02 .10
115 David Klingler RC .01 .05
116 Rich Gannon .08 .25
117 Chris Chandler .08 .25
118 Stan Gelbaugh .01 .05
119 Scott Mitchell .02 .10
120 Mark Carrier DB .01 .05
121 Terry Allen .08 .25
122 Tim McKyer .01 .05
123 Barry Word .01 .05
124 Freeman McNeil .02 .10
125 Louis Oliver .01 .05
126 Jarvis Williams .01 .05
127 Steve Atwater .01 .05
128 Cris Dishman .01 .05
129 Eric Dickerson .02 .10
130 Brad Baxter .01 .05
131 Frank Minnifield .01 .05
132 Ricky Watters .08 .25
133 David Fulcher .01 .05
134 Herschel Walker .02 .10
135 Christian Okoye .01 .05
136 Jerome Henderson .01 .05
137 Nate Odomes .01 .05
138 Todd Scott .01 .05
139 Robert Delpino .01 .05
140 Gary Anderson RB .01 .05
141 Todd Lyght .01 .05
142 Chris Warren .02 .10
143 Mike Brim RC .01 .05
144 Tom Rathman .01 .05
145 Dexter McNabb RC .01 .05
146 Vince Workman .01 .05
147 Anthony Johnson .02 .10
148 Brian Washington .01 .05
149 David Tate .01 .05
150 Johnny Holland .01 .05
151 Monte Coleman .01 .05
152 Keith McCants .01 .05
153 Eugene Seale RC .01 .05
154 Al Smith .01 .05
155 Andre Collins .01 .05
156 Pat Swilling .01 .05
157 Rickey Jackson .01 .05
158 Wilber Marshall .01 .05
159 Kyle Clifton .01 .05
160 Fred Stokes .01 .05
161 Lance Smith .01 .05
162 Guy McIntyre .01 .05
163 Bill Maas .01 .05
164 Gerald Perry .01 .05
165 Bart Oates .01 .05
166 Tony Jones T .01 .05
167 Moe Gardner .01 .05
168 Joe Wolf .01 .05
169 Tim Krumrie .01 .05
170 Leonard Marshall .01 .05
171 Kevin Call .01 .05
172 Keith Kartz .01 .05
173 Ron Heller .01 .05
174 Steve Wallace .01 .05
175 Tony Casillas .01 .05
176 Tim Irwin .01 .05
177 Pat Harlow .01 .05
178 Bruce Smith .08 .25
179 Jim Lachey .01 .05
180 Andre Rison .02 .10
181 Michael Haynes .02 .10
182 Rod Bernstine .01 .05
183 Mark Clayton .02 .10
184 Jay Novacek .02 .10
185 Rob Moore .02 .10
186 Willie Green .01 .05
187 Ricky Proehl .01 .05
188 Al Toon .02 .10
189 Webster Slaughter .01 .05
190 Tony Bennett .01 .05
191 Jeff Cross .01 .05
192 Michael Dean Perry .02 .10
193 Greg Townsend .01 .05
194 Alfred Williams .01 .05
195 William Fuller .01 .05
196 Cortez Kennedy .02 .10
197 Henry Thomas .01 .05
198 Esera Tuaolo .01 .05
199 Tim Green .01 .05
200 Keith Jackson .02 .10
201 Don Majkowski .01 .05
202 Steve Beuerlein .02 .10
203 Hugh Millen .01 .05
204 Browning Nagle .01 .05
205 Chip Lohmiller .01 .05
206 Phil Simms .02 .10
207 Jim Everett .02 .10
208 Erik Kramer .02 .10
209 Todd Marinovich .01 .05
210 Henry Jones .01 .05
211 Dwight Stone .01 .05
212 Andre Waters .01 .05
213 Darryl Henley .01 .05
214 Mark Higgs .01 .05
215 Dalton Hilliard .01 .05
216 Earnest Byner .01 .05
217 Eric Metcalf .02 .10
218 Gill Byrd .01 .05
219 Robert Williams RC .01 .05
220 Kenneth Davis .01 .05
221 Larry Brown DB .01 .05
222 Mark Collins .01 .05
223 Vinnie Clark .01 .05
224 Patrick Hunter .01 .05
225 Gaston Green .01 .05
226 Everson Walls .01 .05
227 Harold Green .01 .05
228 Albert Lewis .01 .05
229 Don Griffin .01 .05
230 Lorenzo Lynch .01 .05
231 Brian Mitchell .02 .10
232 Thomas Everett .01 .05
233 Leonard Russell .02 .10
234 Eric Bieniemy .01 .05
235 John L. Williams .01 .05
236 Leroy Hoard .02 .10
237 Darren Lewis .01 .05
238 Reggie Cobb .01 .05
239 Steve Broussard .01 .05
240 Marion Butts .01 .05
241 Mike Pritchard .02 .10
242 Dexter Carter .01 .05
243 Aeneas Williams .02 .10
244 Bruce Pickens .01 .05
245 Harvey Williams .02 .10
246 Bobby Humphrey .01 .05
247 Duane Bickett .01 .05
248 James Francis .01 .05
249 Broderick Thomas .01 .05
250 Chip Banks .01 .05
251 Bryan Cox .02 .10
252 Sam Mills .01 .05
253 Ken Norton Jr. .02 .10
254 Jeff Herrod .01 .05
255 John Roper .01 .05
256 Darryl Talley .01 .05
257 Andre Tippett .01 .05
258 Jeff Lageman .01 .05
259 Chris Doleman .01 .05
260 Shane Conlan .01 .05
261 Jessie Tuggle .01 .05
262 Eric Hill .01 .05
263 Bruce Armstrong .01 .05
264 Bill Fralic .01 .05
265 Alvin Harper .02 .10
266 Bill Brooks .01 .05
267 Henry Ellard .02 .10
268 Cris Carter .20 .50
269 Irving Fryar .02 .10
270 Lawrence Dawsey .02 .10
271 James Lofton .02 .10
272 Ernest Givins .02 .10
273 Terance Mathis .02 .10
274 Randal Hill .01 .05
275 Eddie Brown .01 .05
276 Tim Brown .08 .25
277 Anthony Carter .02 .10
278 Wendell Davis .01 .05
279 Mark Ingram .01 .05
280 Anthony Miller .02 .10
281 Clarence Verdin .01 .05
282 Flipper Anderson .01 .05
283 Ricky Sanders .01 .05
284 Steve Jordan .01 .05
285 Gary Clark .02 .10
286 Sterling Sharpe .08 .25
287 Herman Moore .08 .25
288 Stephen Baker .01 .05
289 Marv Cook .01 .05
290 Ernie Jones .01 .05
291 Eric Green .01 .05
292 Mervyn Fernandez .01 .05
293 Greg McMurtry .01 .05
294 Quinn Early .02 .10
295 Tim Harris .01 .05
296 Will Furrer RC .01 .05
297 Jason Hanson RC .02 .10
298 Chris Hakel RC .01 .05
299 Ty Detmer .08 .25
300 David Klingler .01 .05
301 Amp Lee RC .01 .05
302 Troy Vincent RC .01 .05
303 Kevin Smith RC .01 .05
304 Terrell Buckley RC .01 .05
305 Dana Hall RC .01 .05
306 Tony Smith RC .01 .05
307 Steve Israel RC .01 .05
308 Vaughn Dunbar RC .01 .05
309 Ashley Ambrose RC .08 .25
310 Edgar Bennett RC .08 .25
311 Dale Carter RC .02 .10
312 Rodney Culver RC .01 .05
313 Matt Darby RC .01 .05
314 Tommy Vardell RC .01 .05
315 Quentin Coryatt RC .01 .05
316 Robert Jones RC .01 .05
317 Joe Bowden RC .01 .05
318 Eugene Chung RC .01 .05
319 Troy Auzenne RC .01 .05
320 Santana Dotson RC .02 .10
321 Greg Skrepenak RC .01 .05
322 Steve Emtman RC .01 .05
323 Carl Pickens RC .08 .25
324 Johnny Mitchell RC .01 .05
325 Patrick Rowe RC .01 .05
326 Alonzo Spellman RC .02 .10
327 Robert Porcher RC .08 .25
328 Chris Mims RC .01 .05
329 Marc Boutte RC .01 .05
330 Shane Dronett RC .01 .05

1992 Power Combos

Randomly inserted into foil packs, this ten-card, standard-size set spotlights powerful offensive and defensive player combinations.

COMPLETE SET (10) 10.00 25.00
RANDOM INSERTS IN FOIL PACKS
1 S.Emtman 1.25 3.00
Q.Coryatt
2 B.Word/C.Okoye .75 2.00
3 S.Mills/V.Johnson .75 2.00
4 B.Thomas/K.McCants .75 2.00
5 E.Smith/M.Irvin 5.00 12.00
6 J.Ball/C.Spielman .75 2.00
7 R.Sand/Clark/Monk 1.50 4.00
8 D.Johnson/R.Woodson 1.25 3.00
9 B.Fralic/C.Hinton .75 2.00
10 I.Fryar/M.Cook 1.25 3.00

1992-93 Power Emmitt Smith

This ten-card standard size set features Emmitt Smith's career highlights. The production run was 25,000 sets. The offer for this set was found on the back of a Pro Set Emmitt Smith special card, which was randomly inserted in second series foil packs. To order the ten-card set, the collector had to mail in ten 1992 NFL Pro Set (first or second series) wrappers and ten 1992 Pro Set Power wrappers along with 7.50 for each set ordered (limit four sets per person). For an additional 20.00, the first 7500 orders received a personally autographed uncut sheet hand numbered. The signed sheet had a limit of one per person. The cards are numbered on the back and have a "PS" prefix.

COMPLETE SET (10) 10.00 25.00
COMMON CARD (1-10) 1.20 3.00
S1 Emmitt Smith Sheet AU/7500 75.00 125.00

1993 Power Prototypes

This nine-card standard-size set was issued to preview the style of the 1993 Pro Set Power football series. Pro Set sent one of these prototype cards to each dealer or wholesaler. The cards were also packaged in a cello pack with an ad card and given away at the 1993 National Sports Collectors Convention. The full-bleed color action photos on the fronts have a shadow-border effect that gives the appearance of depth to the pictures. The player's name and team name are printed in a red, gray, and blue-striped box at the lower left corner. The Pro Set Power logo is silver foil stamped on the fronts. The horizontal backs carry a color close-up photo, career summary, and a rating of players (from 1 to 10).

COMPLETE SET (10) 4.00 10.00
20 Barry Sanders .80 2.00
22 Emmitt Smith .80 2.00
26 Rod Woodson .10 .30
32 Ricky Watters .10 .30
37 Larry Centers .10 .30
71 Santana Dotson .10 .30
80 Jerry Rice .40 1.00
138 Reggie Rivers .10 .30
193 Trace Armstrong .10 .30
NNO Title .10 .30
Ad Card

1993 Power

The 1993 Power set produced by Pro Set consists of 200 standard-size cards. Including foil and jumbo cases, a total of 8,000 cases were produced. Cards were issued in 12 and 25-card packs. Randomly inserted in 1993 Power foil packs were two redemption cards entitling the collector to receive an Emmitt Smith hologram (HOLO) card through a mail-in offer. Randomly inserted in jumbo packs were seven update cards depicting traded players in their new uniforms. Except for the new player photos and "UD" suffixes on the back, the design is identical to the regular Power cards. Also one parallel gold Power card was inserted in every pack. These are distinguished by gold within the Power logo on front. Larry Centers is the only Rookie Card of note in this set.

COMPLETE SET (200) 4.00 10.00
1 Warren Moon .08 .25
2 Steve Christie .01 .05
3 Jim Breech .01 .05
4 Brett Favre .75 2.00
5 Sean Landeta .01 .05
6 Jim Arnold .01 .05
7 John Elway .60 1.50
8 Troy Aikman .30 .75
9 Rodney Peete .01 .05
10 Pete Stoyanovich .01 .05
11 Mark Rypien .01 .05
12 Jim Kelly .08 .25
13 Dan Marino .60 1.50
14 Neil O'Donnell .08 .25
15 David Klingler .01 .05
16 Rich Gannon .08 .25
16UD Rich Gannon .08 .25
17 Dave Krieg .02 .10
18 Jeff Jaeger .01 .05
19 Bernie Kosar .02 .10
20 Barry Sanders .50 1.25
21 Deion Sanders .20 .50
22 Emmitt Smith .60 1.50
23 Barry Word .01 .05
23UD Barry Word .02 .10
24 Stanley Richard .01 .05
25 Louis Oliver .01 .05
26 Rod Woodson .08 .25
27 Rodney Hampton .02 .10
28 Cris Dishman .01 .05
29 Barry Foster .02 .10
30 Dave Meggett .01 .05
31 Kevin Ross .01 .05
32 Ricky Watters .08 .25
33 Darren Lewis .01 .05
34 Thurman Thomas .08 .25
35 Rodney Culver .01 .05
36 Bennie Blades .01 .05
37 Larry Centers RC .08 .25
38 Todd Scott .01 .05
39 Darren Perry .01 .05
40 Robert Massey .01 .05
41 Keith Byars .01 .05
41UD Keith Byars UER .02 .10
42 Chris Warren .02 .10
43 Cleveland Gary .01 .05
44 Lorenzo White .01 .05
45 Tony Stargell .01 .05
46 Bennie Thompson .01 .05
47 A.J. Johnson .01 .05
48 Daryl Johnston .08 .25
49 Dennis Smith .01 .05
50 Johnny Holland .01 .05
51 Ken Norton Jr. .02 .10
52 Pepper Johnson .01 .05
52UD Pepper Johnson .02 .10
53 Vaughan Johnson .01 .05
54 Chris Spielman .02 .10
55 Junior Seau .08 .25
56 Chris Doleman .01 .05
57 Rickey Jackson .01 .05
58 Derrick Thomas .08 .25
59 Seth Joyner .01 .05
60 Stan Thomas .01 .05
61 Nate Newton .02 .10
62 Matt Brock .01 .05
63 Mike Munchak .02 .10
64 Randall McDaniel .02 .10
65 Ron Hallstrom .01 .05
66 Andy Heck .01 .05
67 Russell Maryland .01 .05
68 Bruce Wilkerson .01 .05
69 Mark Schlereth .01 .05
70 John Fina .01 .05
71 Santana Dotson .02 .10
72 Don Mosebar UER .01 .05
73 Simon Fletcher .01 .05
74 Paul Gruber .01 .05
75 Howard Ballard .01 .05
76 John Alt .01 .05
77 Carlton Haselrig .01 .05
78 Bruce Smith .08 .25
79 Ray Childress .01 .05
80 Jerry Rice .40 1.00
01 Art Monk .02 .10
82 John Taylor .02 .10
83 Andre Reed .02 .10
84 Sterling Sharpe .08 .25
85 Sam Graddy .01 .05
86 Fred Barnett .02 .10
87 Ricky Proehl .01 .05
88 Michael Irvin .08 .25
89 Webster Slaughter .01 .05
90 Tony Bennett .01 .05
91 Leslie O'Neal .02 .10
92 Michael Dean Perry .02 .10
93 Greg Townsend .01 .05
94 Anthony Smith .01 .05
95 Richard Dent .02 .10
96 Clyde Simmons .01 .05
97 Cornelius Bennett .02 .10
98 Eric Swann .01 .05
99 Cortez Kennedy .02 .10
100 Emmitt Smith HL .40 1.00
101 Michael Jackson .02 .10
102 Lin Elliott .01 .05
103 Rohn Stark .01 .05
104 Jim Harbaugh .08 .25
105 Greg Davis .01 .05
106 Mike Cofer .01 .05
107 Morten Andersen .01 .05
108 Steve Young .30 .75
109 Norm Johnson .01 .05
110 Dan McGwire .01 .05
111 Jim Everett .02 .10
112 Randall Cunningham .08 .25
113 Steve Bono .02 .10
114 Cody Carlson .01 .05
115 Jeff Hostetler .02 .10
116 Rich Camarillo .01 .05
117 Chris Chandler .02 .10
118 Stan Gelbaugh .01 .05
119 Tony Sacca .01 .05
120 Henry Jones .01 .05
121 Terry Allen .08 .25
122 Amp Lee .01 .05
123 Mel Gray .02 .10
124 Jon Vaughn .01 .05
124UD Jon Vaughn UER .02 .10
125 Bubba McDowell .01 .05
126 Audray McMillian .01 .05
127 Terrell Buckley .01 .05
128 Dana Hall .01 .05
129 Eric Dickerson .02 .10
130 Martin Bayless .01 .05
131 Steve Israel .01 .05
132 Vaughn Dunbar .01 .05
133 Ronnie Harmon .01 .05
134 Dale Carter .01 .05
135 Neal Anderson .01 .05
136 Merton Hanks .01 .05
137 James Washington .01 .05
138 Reggie Rivers RC .01 .05
139 Bruce Pickens .01 .05
140 Gary Anderson RB .01 .05
141 Eugene Robinson .01 .05
142 Charles Mincy RC .01 .05
143 Matt Darby .01 .05
144 Tom Rathman .01 .05
145 Mike Prior .01 .05
146 Sean Lumpkin .01 .05
147 Greg Jackson .01 .05
148 Wes Hopkins .01 .05
149 David Tate UER .01 .05
150 James Francis .01 .05
151 Bryan Cox .01 .05
152 Keith McCants .01 .05
152UD Keith McCants .02 .10
153 Mark Stepnoski .01 .05
154 Al Smith .01 .05
155 Robert Jones .01 .05
156 Lawrence Taylor .08 .25
157 Clay Matthews .02 .10
158 Wilber Marshall .01 .05
158UD Wilbor Marshall UER .02 .10
159 Mike Johnson .01 .05
160 Adam Schreiber RC .01 .05
161 Tim Grunhard .01 .05
162 Mark Bortz .01 .05
163 Gene Chilton .01 .05
164 Jamie Dukes .01 .05
165 Bart Oates .01 .05
166 Kevin Gogan .01 .05
167 Kent Hull .01 .05
168 Ed King .01 .05
169 Eugene Chung .01 .05
170 Troy Auzenne .01 .05
171 Charles Mann .01 .05
172 William Perry .02 .10
173 Mike Lodish .01 .05
174 Bruce Matthews .01 .05
175 Tony Casillas .01 .05
176 Steve Wisniewski .01 .05
177 Karl Mecklenburg .01 .05
178 Richmond Webb .01 .05
179 Erik Williams .01 .05
180 Andre Rison .02 .10
181 Michael Haynes .02 .10
182 Don Beebe .01 .05
183 Anthony Miller .02 .10
184 Jay Novacek .02 .10
185 Rob Moore .02 .10
186 Willie Green .01 .05
187 Tom Waddle .01 .05
188 Keith Jackson .02 .10
189 Steve Tasker .02 .10
190 Marco Coleman .01 .05
191 Jeff Wright .01 .05
192 Burt Grossman .01 .05
193 Trace Armstrong .01 .05
194 Charles Haley .02 .10
195 Greg Lloyd .02 .10
196 Marc Boutte .01 .05
197 Rufus Porter .01 .05
198 Dennis Gibson .01 .05
199 Shane Dronett .01 .05
200 Joe Montana .60 1.50
H1 Emmitt Smith HOLO 7.50 20.00
H2 Emmitt Smith HOLO 7.50 20.00

1993 Power Gold

COMPLETE SET (200) 15.00 40.00
*GOLD CARDS: .8X TO 2X BASIC CARDS
ONE GOLD PER PACK

1993 Power All-Power Defense

Randomly inserted at a rate of two per jumbo pack, these 25 standard-size cards feature on their fronts borderless color player photos with textured brown backgrounds. The cards are numbered on the back with an "APD" prefix. Parallel gold cards were also randomly inserted in packs.

COMPLETE SET (25) 2.00 5.00
*GOLDS: .8X to 2X BASIC INSERTS
TWO PER JUMBO PACK
1 Clyde Simmons .05 .15
2 Anthony Smith .05 .15
3 Ray Childress .05 .15
4 Michael Dean Perry .10 .30
5 Bruce Smith .30 .75
6 Cortez Kennedy .10 .30
7 Charles Haley .10 .30
8 Marco Coleman .05 .15
9 Alonzo Spellman .05 .15
10 Junior Seau .30 .75
11 Ken Norton Jr. .10 .30
12 Derrick Thomas .30 .75
13 Wilber Marshall .05 .15
14 Chris Doleman .05 .15
15 Seth Joyner .05 .15
16 Al Smith .05 .15
17 Deion Sanders .60 1.50
18 Rod Woodson .30 .75
19 Audray McMillian .05 .15
20 Dale Carter .05 .15
21 Terrell Buckley .05 .15
22 Bennie Thompson .05 .15
23 Chris Spielman .10 .30
24 Lawrence Taylor .30 .75
25 Tony Bennett .05 .15

1993 Power Combos

Randomly inserted in foil packs, these ten standard-size cards feature on their horizontal fronts two-player photos that are bordered in black, blue, and purple. Gold Combos parallel cards were also randomly inserted in packs and cards from the 10-card Prism Combos parallel set were randomly inserted in Power Update jumbo packs.

COMPLETE SET (10) 2.00 5.00
RANDOM INSERTS IN FOIL PACKS
*GOLDS: .8X to 2X BASIC INSERTS
ONE GOLD PER PACK
TWO GOLDS PER JUMBO PACK
*PRISMS: 1.2X to 3X BASIC INSERTS
RANDOM INSERTS IN UPDATE JUMBOS
1 E.Smith 1.25 3.00
B.Sanders
2 St.Sharpe/T.Buckley .20 .50
3 J.Seau/G.Plummer .30 .75
4 D.Sanders/T.McKyer .40 1.00
5 B.Smith/D.Talley .30 .75
6 W.Moon/W.Slaughter .30 .75
7 C.Doleman/H.Thomas .10 .30
8 Mecklenburg/M.Brooks .10 .30
9 K.Norton/R.Jones .20 .50
10 M.Coleman/B.Cox .20 .50

1993 Power Draft Picks

Randomly inserted in 1993 Power packs, these 30 standard-size cards feature on their fronts borderless color player photos with black-and-white backgrounds. The cards are numbered on the back with a "PDP" prefix. Gold parallel cards were also randomly inserted.

COMPLETE SET (30) 2.50 6.00
*GOLDS: .8X TO 2X BASIC INSERTS
ONE GOLD PER PACK
TWO GOLDS PER JUMBO PACK
PDP1 Lincoln Kennedy UER .05 .15
PDP2 Thomas Smith UER .05 .15
PDP3 Robert Smith UER .50 1.25
PDP4 John Copeland UER .05 .15
PDP5 Dan Footman UER .05 .15
PDP6 Darrin Smith UER .05 .15
PDP7 Qadry Ismail UER .20 .50
PDP8 Ryan McNeil UER .20 .50
PDP9 George Teague UER .05 .15
PDP10 Brad Hopkins .05 .15
PDP11 Ernest Dye .05 .15
PDP12 Jaime Fields .05 .15
PDP13 Patrick Bates .05 .15
PDP14 Jerome Bettis 2.00 5.00
PDP15 O.J.McDuffie .20 .50
PDP16 Gino Torretta .08 .25
PDP17 Drew Bledsoe 1.25 3.00
PDP18 Irv Smith .05 .15
PDP19 Marcus Buckley .05 .15
PDP20 Coleman Rudolph .05 .15
PDP21 Leonard Renfro .05 .15
PDP22 Garrison Hearst .30 .75
PDP23 Deon Figures .05 .15
PDP24 Natrone Means .20 .50
PDP25 Todd Kelly .05 .15
PDP26 Carlton Gray .05 .15
PDP27 Eric Curry .05 .15
PDP28 Tom Carter .05 .15
PDP29 AFC Logo CL .05 .15
PDP30 NFC Logo CL .05 .15

1993 Power Moves

The first 30 cards of this 40-card standard-size set were randomly inserted in 1993 Power packs, the last ten were random inserts in 1993 Power jumbo packs. The cards are numbered on the back with a "PM" prefix. Gold parallel cards were randomly inserted in packs.

COMPLETE SET (40) 2.00 5.00
COMPLETE SERIES 1 (30) 1.25 3.00
COMPLETE SERIES 2 (10) .75 2.00
PM1-PM30 RANDOM INS.IN FOIL PACKS
PM31-PM40 RANDOM INS.IN JUMBO PACKS
*GOLDS: .8X TO 2X BASIC INSERTS
ONE GOLD PER PACK
TWO GOLDS PER JUMBO PACK
PM1 Bobby Hebert .05 .15
PM2 Bill Brooks .08 .25
PM3 Vinny Testaverde .08 .25
PM4 Hugh Millen .05 .15
PM5 Rod Bernstine .05 .15
PM6 Robert Delpino .05 .15
PM7 Pat Swilling .08 .25
PM8 Reggie White .20 .50
PM9 Aaron Cox .05 .15
PM10 Joe Montana 1.00 2.50
PM11 Gaston Green .05 .15
PM12 Jeff Hostetler .08 .25
PM13 Shane Conlan .05 .15
PM14 Irv Eatman .05 .15
PM15 Mark Ingram .05 .15
PM16 Irving Fryar .08 .25
PM17 Don Majkowski .05 .15
PM18 Will Wolford .05 .15
PM19 Boomer Esiason .08 .25
PM20 Ronnie Lott .08 .25
PM21 Johnny Johnson .05 .15
PM22 Steve Beuerlein .08 .25
PM23 Chuck Cecil .05 .15
PM24 Gary Clark .08 .25
PM25 Kevin Greene .08 .25
PM26 Jerrol Williams .05 .15
PM27 Tim McDonald .05 .15
PM28 Ferrell Edmunds .05 .15
PM29 Kelvin Martin .05 .15
PM30 Hardy Nickerson .05 .15
PM31 Jerry Ball .05 .15
PM32 Jim McMahon .08 .25
PM33 Marcus Allen .20 .50
PM34 John Stephens .05 .15
PM35 John Booty .05 .15
PM36 Wade Wilson .05 .15
PM37 Mark Bavaro .05 .15
PM38 Bill Fralic .05 .15
PM39 Mark Clayton .05 .15
PM40 Mike Sherrard .05 .15

1993 Power Update Moves

These 50 standard-size cards shared nine-card packs with 1993 Power Update Prospects cards. The cards are numbered on the back with a "PMUD" prefix. Gold parallel versions were also inserted in packs.

COMPLETE SET (50) 2.00 5.00
PMUD PREFIX ON CARD NUMBERS
*GOLDS: .8X to 2X BASIC INSERTS
1 Bobby Hebert .02 .10
2 Bill Brooks .05 .15
3 Vinny Testaverde .05 .15
4 Hugh Millen .02 .10
5 Rod Bernstine .02 .10
6 Robert Delpino .02 .10
7 Pat Swilling .05 .15
8 Reggie White .08 .25
9 Aaron Cox .02 .10
10 Joe Montana 1.00 2.50
11 Vinnie Clark UER .02 .10
12 Jeff Hostetler .05 .15
13 Shane Conlan .02 .10
14 Irv Eatman .02 .10
15 Mark Ingram .05 .15
16 Irving Fryar .05 .15
17 Don Majkowski .02 .10
18 Will Wolford .02 .10
19 Boomer Esiason .05 .15
20 Ronnie Lott .05 .15
21 Johnny Johnson .02 .10
22 Steve Beuerlein .05 .15
23 Chuck Cecil .02 .10
24 Gary Clark .05 .15
25 Kevin Greene .05 .15
26 Jerrol Williams .02 .10
27 Tim McDonald .02 .10
28 Ferrell Edmunds .02 .10
29 Kelvin Martin .02 .10
30 Hardy Nickerson .02 .10
31 Jumpy Geathers .02 .10
32 Craig Heyward .05 .15
33 Tim McKyer .02 .10
34 Mark Carrier WR .08 .25
35 Gary Zimmerman .02 .10
36 Jay Schroeder .02 .10
37 Keith Millard UER .02 .10
38 Vince Workman .02 .10
39 Kirk Lowdermilk .02 .10
40 Fred Stokes .02 .10
41 Ernie Jones UER .02 .10
42 Keith Byars .02 .10
43 Carlton Bailey .02 .10
44 Michael Brooks .02 .10
45 Tim McGee .02 .10
46 Leonard Marshall .02 .10
47 Bubby Brister .02 .10
48 Mike Tomczak .05 .15
49 Mark Jackson .02 .10
50 Wade Wilson .02 .10

1993 Power Update Prospects

These 60 standard-size cards were issued in nine-card retail packs with the Power Update Moves cards. The cards are numbered on the back with a "PP" prefix. Rookie Cards include Jerome Bettis, Drew Bledsoe, Reggie Brooks , Curtis Conway, Garrison Hearst, Rick Mirer, Ronald Moore and Kevin Williams. Gold Parallel cards were also inserted in packs.

COMPLETE SET (60) 7.50 15.00
1 Drew Bledsoe RC 1.00 2.50
2 Rick Mirer RC .08 .25
3 Trent Green RC 2.00 5.00
4 Mark Brunell RC .60 1.50
5 Billy Joe Hobert RC .08 .25
6 Ronald Moore RC .02 .10
7 Elvis Grbac RC .60 1.50
8 Garrison Hearst RC .30 .75
9 Jerome Bettis RC 1.50 4.00
10 Reggie Brooks RC .02 .10
11 Robert Smith RC .50 1.25
12 Vaughn Hebron RC .01 .05
13 Derek Brown RBK RC .02 .10
14 Roosevelt Potts RC .02 .10
15 Terry Kirby RC .02 .10
16 Glyn Milburn RC .02 .10
17 Greg Robinson RC .01 .05
18 Natrone Means RC .08 .25
19 Curtis Conway RC .15 .40
20 James Jett RC .08 .25
21 O.J.McDuffie RC .08 .25
22 Rocket Ismail .08 .25
23 Qadry Ismail RC .08 .25
24 Kevin Williams RC WR .02 .10
25 Victor Bailey UER RC .01 .05
26 Vincent Brisby RC .08 .25
27 Irv Smith RC .01 .05
28 Troy Drayton RC .01 .05
29 Wayne Simmons RC .01 .05
30 Marvin Jones RC .01 .05
31 Demetrius DuBose RC .01 .05
32 Chad Brown RC LB .02 .10
33 Micheal Barrow RC .08 .25
34 Darrin Smith RC .01 .05
35 Deon Figures RC .01 .05
36 Darrien Gordon RC .01 .05
37 Patrick Bates RC .01 .05
38 George Teague RC .01 .05
39 Lance Gunn RC .01 .05
40 Tom Carter RC .01 .05
41 Carlton Gray RC .01 .05
42 John Copeland RC .01 .05
43 Eric Curry RC .01 .05
44 Dana Stubblefield RC .08 .25
45 Leonard Renfro RC .01 .05
46 Dan Williams RC .01 .05
47 Todd Kelly RC .01 .05
48 Chris Slade RC .01 .05
49 Carl Simpson RC .01 .05
50 Coleman Rudolph RC .01 .05
51 Michael Strahan RC .60 1.50
52 Dan Footman RC .01 .05
53 Steve Everitt RC .01 .05
54 Will Shields RC .08 .25
55 Ben Coleman RC .01 .05
56 Willie Roaf RC .10 .30
57 Lincoln Kennedy RC .01 .05
58 Brad Hopkins RC .01 .05
59 Ernest Dye RC .01 .05
60 Jason Elam RC .08 .25

1993 Power Update Prospects Gold

COMPLETE SET (60) 12.50 25.00
*GOLDS: .8X TO 2X BASIC CARDS
ONE GOLD PER UPDATE PACK
TWO GOLDS PER UPDATE JUMBO PACK

1993 Power Update Combos

Randomly inserted in 1993 Power Update packs, these 10 standard-size multiplayer cards feature on their horizontal fronts multicolor-bordered color player action shots. The cards are numbered on the back with a "PC" prefix. Gold parallel cards were randomly inserted in Update packs. Parallel Prism cards were also random inserts in Update packs.

COMPLETE SET (10) 3.00 8.00
RANDOM INS.IN POWER UPDATE PACKS
*GOLDS: .6X to 1.5X BASIC INSERTS
RANDOM INS.IN POWER UPDATE PACKS
*PRISMS: 1X to 2.5X BASIC INSERTS
RANDOM INS.IN UPDATE JUMBOS
PC1 Rison/Haynes/Prit/Hill .30 .75
PC2 J.Rice/Young UER 1.50 3.00
PC3 J.Kelly/F.Reich .40 1.00
PC4 M.Irvin/A.Harper .40 1.00
PC5 R.Woodson/D.Figures .20 .50
PC6 B.Smith/C.Bennett .30 .75
PC7 B.Cox/M.Coleman .20 .50
PC8 T.Aikman/E.Smith 2.50 3.00
PC9 T.Brown/R.Ismail .40 1.00
PC10 Monk/How./R.Sanders .30 .75

1993 Power Update Impact Rookies

Randomly inserted in 1993 Power Update packs, these 15 standard-size cards feature gray-bordered color player action shots on their fronts. The cards are numbered on the back with an "IR" prefix.

COMPLETE SET (15) 3.00 8.00
RANDOM INS.IN POWER UPDATE PACKS
*GOLDS: .8X TO 2X BASIC INSERTS
RANDOM INS.IN POWER UPDATE PACKS
IR1 Rick Mirer .30 .75
IR2 Drew Bledsoe 1.50 4.00
IR3 Jerome Bettis 2.50 6.00
IR4 Derek Brown RBK .10 .30
IR5 Roosevelt Potts .10 .30
IR6 Glyn Milburn .20 .50
IR7 Adrian Murrell .30 .75
IR8 Victor Bailey .10 .30
IR9 Vincent Brisby .20 .50
IR10 O.J.McDuffie .30 .75
IR11 James Jett .10 .30
IR12 Eric Curry .10 .30
IR13 Dana Stubblefield .20 .50
IR14 Willie Roaf .50 1.25
IR15 Patrick Bates .10 .30

1997-98 Premier Replays

This set of cards was produced by Premier Replays and initially released in 1997. The cards were released throughout 1998 as well with the addition of Randy Moss to the list. Each card is a lenticular designed motion card mounted on a black plastic backing. The player's name and NFL logos are also included on the cardfronts and the cardbacks are blank. The Randy Moss card was issued, after the initial 8-cards, primarily to dealers and features two photos of Moss' first touchdown reception.

COMPLETE SET (9) 12.00 30.00
1 Troy Aikman 1.20 3.00
2 Drew Bledsoe 1.20 3.00
3 Kerry Collins .80 2.00
4 Terrell Davis 2.40 6.00
5 Brett Favre 2.40 6.00
6 Curtis Martin 1.20 3.00
7 Emmitt Smith 2.00 5.00
8 Reggie White 1.00 2.50
9 Randy Moss 4.80 12.00

1994 Press Pass SB Photo Board

Press Pass shipped 50,000 individually numbered (approximately) 10" by 14" Photo Boards to hobby and retail outlets Jan. 24, the day after both Buffalo and Dallas earned their Super Bowl berths. The front describes each team's road to the Super Bowl with color photos from NFL playoff action. The back carries color action photos of AFC and NFC statistical leaders and an outstanding 1993 rookie from each conference as well as accompanying statistics. The sheet is unnumbered, and the AFC and NFC statistical leaders honored on its back are listed below.

1 SB XXVIII Photo Board 3.20 8.00

2010 Prestige

COMP.SET w/o RC's (200) 10.00 25.00
ONE ROOKIE PER HOBBY PACK
1 Anquan Boldin .20 .50
2 Chris Wells .20 .50
3 Dominique Rodgers-Cromartie .20 .50
4 Matt Leinart .20 .50
5 Larry Fitzgerald .25 .60
6 Adrian Wilson .20 .50
7 Tim Hightower .20 .50
8 Jason Snelling .25 .60
9 Matt Ryan .25 .60
10 Michael Jenkins .20 .50
11 Michael Turner .20 .50
12 Roddy White .20 .50
13 Tony Gonzalez .25 .60
14 Derrick Mason .20 .50
15 Joe Flacco .25 .60
16 Mark Clayton .20 .50
17 Ray Lewis .30 .75
18 Ray Rice .20 .50
19 Todd Heap .20 .50
20 Willis McGahee .20 .50
21 Fred Jackson .25 .60
22 Jairus Byrd .25 .60
23 Lee Evans .25 .60
24 Marshawn Lynch .25 .60
25 Ryan Fitzpatrick .20 .50
26 Aaron Schobel .20 .50
27 DeAngelo Williams .20 .50
28 Jon Beason .20 .50
29 Jonathan Stewart .20 .50
30 Julius Peppers .25 .60
31 Muhsin Muhammad .20 .50
32 Steve Smith .25 .60
33 Brian Urlacher .30 .75
34 Devin Hester .25 .60
35 Earl Bennett .25 .60
36 Greg Olsen .25 .60
37 Jay Cutler .20 .50
38 Johnny Knox .20 .50
39 Matt Forte .20 .50
40 Andre Caldwell .20 .50
41 Carson Palmer .25 .60
42 Cedric Benson .20 .50
43 Chad Ochocinco .20 .50
44 Dhani Jones .20 .50
45 Johnathan Joseph .20 .50
46 Abram Elam RC .30 .75
47 Jake Delhomme .20 .50
48 Jerome Harrison .20 .50
49 Josh Cribbs .20 .50
50 Kamerion Wimbley .20 .50
51 Mohamed Massaquoi .25 .60
52 DeMarcus Ware .25 .60
53 Felix Jones .20 .50
54 Jason Witten .25 .60
55 Jay Ratliff .25 .60
56 Marion Barber .25 .60
57 Miles Austin .20 .50
58 Tony Romo .25 .60
59 Brandon Marshall .25 .60
60 Elvis Dumervil .20 .50
61 Jabar Gaffney .20 .50
62 Knowshon Moreno .20 .50
63 Kyle Orton .20 .50
64 Tony Scheffler .20 .50
65 Brandon Pettigrew .20 .50
66 Bryant Johnson .20 .50
67 Calvin Johnson .30 .75
68 Kevin Smith .20 .50
69 Matthew Stafford .25 .60
70 Aaron Rodgers .60 1.50
71 Charles Woodson .30 .75
72 Donald Driver .25 .60
73 Greg Jennings .20 .50
74 Jermichael Finley .20 .50
75 Ryan Grant .25 .60
76 Andre Johnson .25 .60
77 Brian Cushing .20 .50
78 Kevin Walter .25 .60
79 Matt Schaub .20 .50
80 Owen Daniels .20 .50
81 Steve Slaton .20 .50
82 Anthony Gonzalez .20 .50
83 Dallas Clark .20 .50
84 Dwight Freeney .20 .50
85 Joseph Addai .20 .50
86 Peyton Manning .75 2.00
87 Pierre Garcon .25 .60
88 Reggie Wayne .25 .60
89 David Garrard .20 .50
90 Marcedes Lewis .20 .50
91 Maurice Jones-Drew .20 .50
92 Mike Sims-Walker .20 .50
93 Mike Thomas .25 .60
94 Torry Holt .25 .60
95 Brandon Flowers .20 .50
96 Chris Chambers .20 .50
97 Dwayne Bowe .25 .60
98 Jamaal Charles .25 .60
99 Matt Cassel .20 .50
100 Brian Hartline .25 .60
101 Chad Henne .25 .60
102 Davone Bess .20 .50
103 Greg Camarillo .20 .50
104 Ricky Williams .25 .60
105 Ronnie Brown .20 .50
106 Ted Ginn .20 .50
107 Adrian Peterson .30 .75
108 Bernard Berrian .20 .50
109 Brett Favre .60 1.50
110 Jared Allen .20 .50
111 Percy Harvin .20 .50
112 Sidney Rice .20 .50
113 Visanthe Shiancoe .25 .60
114 Ben Watson .20 .50
115 Julian Edelman .30 .75
116 Laurence Maroney .20 .50
117 Randy Moss .25 .60
118 Tom Brady .75 2.00
119 Wes Welker .25 .60
120 Devery Henderson .20 .50
121 Drew Brees .30 .75
122 Jeremy Shockey .20 .50
123 Marques Colston .20 .50
124 Pierre Thomas .20 .50
125 Reggie Bush .20 .50
126 Robert Meachem .20 .50
127 Ahmad Bradshaw .20 .50
128 Brandon Jacobs .20 .50
129 Eli Manning .25 .60
130 Hakeem Nicks .20 .50
131 Kevin Boss .20 .50
132 Mario Manningham .20 .50
133 Steve Smith USC .20 .50
134 Braylon Edwards .20 .50
135 Darrelle Revis .20 .50
136 Jerricho Cotchery .20 .50
137 Leon Washington .20 .50
138 Mark Sanchez .20 .50
139 Shonn Greene .20 .50
140 Thomas Jones .20 .50
141 Chaz Schilens .20 .50
142 Darren McFadden .20 .50
143 Louis Murphy .20 .50
144 Michael Bush .20 .50
145 Nnamdi Asomugha .20 .50
146 Zach Miller .20 .50
147 Asante Samuel .20 .50
148 Brent Celek .20 .50
149 Brian Westbrook .20 .50
150 DeSean Jackson .25 .60
151 Donovan McNabb .25 .60
152 Jeremy Maclin .20 .50
153 LeSean McCoy .30 .75
154 Ben Roethlisberger .30 .75
155 Heath Miller .20 .50
156 Hines Ward .25 .60
157 Mike Wallace .20 .50
158 Rashard Mendenhall .20 .50
159 Santonio Holmes .20 .50
160 Troy Polamalu .30 .75
161 Antonio Gates .25 .60
162 Darren Sproles .25 .60
163 LaDainian Tomlinson .30 .75
164 Malcom Floyd .20 .50
165 Philip Rivers .30 .75
166 Vincent Jackson .20 .50
167 Shawne Merriman .20 .50
168 Alex Smith QB .25 .60
169 Frank Gore .25 .60
170 Josh Morgan .25 .60
171 Michael Crabtree .20 .50
172 Patrick Willis .25 .60
173 Vernon Davis .20 .50
174 John Carlson .20 .50
175 Julius Jones .20 .50
176 Justin Forsett .25 .60
177 Matt Hasselbeck .20 .50
178 Nate Burleson .20 .50
179 T.J. Houshmandzadeh .20 .50
180 Brandon Gibson .20 .50
181 Donnie Avery .20 .50
182 James Laurinaitis .25 .60
183 Kyle Boller .20 .50
184 Steven Jackson .20 .50
185 Antonio Bryant .20 .50
186 Aqib Talib .20 .50
187 Cadillac Williams .20 .50

188 Derrick Ward .20 .50
189 Josh Freeman .25 .60
190 Kellen Winslow .20 .50
191 Bo Scaife .20 .50
192 Chris Johnson .20 .50
193 Kenny Britt .20 .50
194 Nate Washington .20 .50
195 Vince Young .20 .50
196 Antwaan Randle El .20 .50
197 Chris Cooley .20 .50
198 Clinton Portis .20 .50
199 Devin Thomas .20 .50
200 Santana Moss .25 .60
201 Aaron Hernandez SP RC 4.00 10.00
202 Andre Anderson RC .50 1.25
203 Andre Dixon RC .75 2.00
204 Andre Roberts RC .60 1.50
205 Anthony Dixon RC .50 1.25
206 Anthony McCoy RC .50 1.25
207 Antonio Brown RC 4.00 10.00
208 Arrelious Benn SP RC 8.00 20.00
209 Ben Tate RC .50 1.25
210 Blair White RC .50 1.25
211 Brandon Graham RC .60 1.50
212 Brandon LaFell RC .75 2.00
213 Brandon Spikes RC .50 1.25
214A Bryan Bulaga RC .50 1.25
214B Bryan Bulaga Draft SP 8.00 20.00
215A C.J. Spiller RC .50 1.25
215B C.J. Spiller Draft SP 8.00 20.00
216 Carlos Dunlap RC .50 1.25
217 Carlton Mitchell RC .50 1.25
218 Chad Jones RC .50 1.25
219 Charles Scott RC .50 1.25
220 Chris Brown RC .75 2.00
221 Chris Cook RC .50 1.25
222 Chris McGaha RC .50 1.25
223 Colt McCoy RC .60 1.50
224 Corey Wootton RC .50 1.25
225 Damian Williams RC .50 1.25
226 Dan LeFevour SP RC 10.00 25.00
227 Danario Alexander RC .50 1.25
228 Daryl Washington RC .50 1.25
229 David Gettis RC .50 1.25
230A Demaryius Thomas RC 1.25 3.00
230B D.Thomas Draft SP 10.00 25.00
231A Derrick Morgan RC .50 1.25
231B Derrick Morgan Draft SP 8.00 20.00
232 Devin McCourty RC .60 1.50
233 Dexter McCluster SP RC 5.00 12.00
234 Dez Bryant RC 1.25 3.00
235 Dezmon Briscoe RC .50 1.25
236 Dominique Franks RC .50 1.25
237 Earl Thomas RC 1.25 3.00
238 Ed Dickson RC .50 1.25
239A Eric Berry RC .75 2.00
239B Eric Berry Draft SP 10.00 25.00
240 Eric Decker RC .60 1.50
241 Everson Griffen RC .50 1.25
242 Freddie Barnes RC .50 1.25
243 Garrett Graham RC .50 1.25
244A Gerald McCoy SP RC 8.00 20.00
244B Gerald McCoy Draft SP 8.00 20.00
245 Golden Tate RC .60 1.50
246 Jacoby Ford RC .50 1.25
247A Jahvid Best RC .50 1.25
247B Jahvid Best Draft SP 8.00 20.00
248 James Starks RC .60 1.50
249 Jarrett Brown RC .50 1.25
250 Jason Pierre-Paul RC .75 2.00
251 Jason Worilds RC .50 1.25
252 Jeremy Williams RC .50 1.25
253 Jermaine Gresham RC .50 1.25
254 Jerry Hughes RC .50 1.25
255 Jevan Snead RC .50 1.25
256 Jimmy Clausen RC .50 1.25
257 Jimmy Graham RC 1.25 3.00
258A Joe Haden RC .75 2.00
258B Joe Haden Draft SP 8.00 20.00
259 Joe McKnight RC .50 1.25
260 John Skelton RC .60 1.50
261 Joique Bell RC .50 1.25
262 Jonathan Crompton RC .50 1.25
263 Jonathan Dwyer RC .50 1.25
264 Jordan Shipley SP RC 8.00 20.00
265 Kareem Jackson RC .50 1.25
266 Kyle Wilson RC .50 1.25
267 LeGarrette Blount RC 1.00 2.50
268 Lonyae Miller RC .60 1.50
269 Marcus Easley RC .50 1.25
270 Mardy Gilyard RC .50 1.25
271 Mike Kafka RC .60 1.50
272 Mike Williams SP RC 8.00 20.00
273 Montario Hardesty RC .50 1.25
274 Morgan Burnett RC .60 1.50
275 Nate Allen RC .75 2.00
276 NaVorro Bowman RC 1.00 2.50
277A Ndamukong Suh RC 1.00 2.50
277B Ndamukong Suh Draft SP 20.00 40.00
278 Pat Paschall RC .50 1.25
279 Patrick Robinson RC .60 1.50
280 Perrish Cox RC .60 1.50
281 Ricky Sapp RC .50 1.25
282 Riley Cooper RC .50 1.25
283A Rob Gronkowski RC 1.50 4.00
283B Rob Gronkowski Draft SP 12.00 30.00
284 Rolando McClain SP RC 4.00 10.00
285A Russell Okung SP RC 10.00 25.00
285B Russell Okung Draft SP 10.00 25.00
286 Ryan Mathews RC .50 1.25
287A Sam Bradford RC .60 1.50
287B Sam Bradford Draft SP 20.00 40.00
288 Sean Canfield SP RC 6.00 15.00
289 Sean Lee RC 1.00 2.50
290 Sean Weatherspoon RC .50 1.25
291 Sergio Kindle RC .50 1.25
292 Seyi Ajirotutu RC .50 1.25
293 Shay Hodge RC .50 1.25
294 Taylor Mays RC .50 1.25
295 Taylor Price RC .50 1.25
296A Tim Tebow RC 1.50 4.00
296B Tim Tebow Draft SP 12.00 30.00
297 Toby Gerhart RC .50 1.25
298 Tony Pike RC .50 1.25
299A Trent Williams RC .60 1.50
299B Trent Williams Draft SP 5.00 12.00
300 Zac Robinson RC .60 1.50
301 Ed Wang SP RC 30.00 60.00
302 L.Houston Draft SP RC 20.00 40.00
303 Jared Odrick Draft SP RC 25.00 50.00
304 Dan Williams Draft SP RC 20.00 40.00

2010 Prestige Draft Picks Light Blue

*ROOKIES: .5X TO 1.2X BASIC RC
*ROOKIES: .05X TO .15X BASIC SP RC
STATED PRINT RUN 999 SER.#'d SETS

2010 Prestige Xtra Points Black

*1-200 VETS: 10X TO 25X BASIC CARDS
*201-300 ROOKIES: 4X TO 10X BASIC RC
*201-300 ROOKIES: .5X TO 1.2X BASIC SP RC
STATED PRINT RUN 10 SER.#'d SETS

2010 Prestige Xtra Points Gold

*1-200 VETS: 2X TO 5X BASIC CARDS
*201-300 ROOKIES: .8X TO 2X BASIC RC
*201-300 ROOKIES: .1X TO .25X BASIC SP RC
STATED PRINT RUN 250 SER.#'d SETS

2010 Prestige Xtra Points Green

*VETS: 8X TO 20X BASIC CARDS
*ROOKIES: 3X TO 8X BASIC RC
*ROOKIES: .4X TO 1X BASIC SP RC
STATED PRINT RUN 25 SER.#'d SETS

2010 Prestige Xtra Points Orange

*1-200 VETS: 3X TO 8X BASIC CARDS
*201-300 ROOKIES: 1.2X TO 3X BASIC RC
*201-300 ROOKIES: .15X TO .4X BASIC SP RC
RANDOM INSERTS IN RETAIL PACKS

2010 Prestige Xtra Points Purple

*1-200 VETS: 4X TO 10X BASIC CARDS
*201-300 ROOKIES: 1.5X TO 4X BASIC RC
*201-300 ROOKIES: .2X TO .5X BASIC SP RC
STATED PRINT RUN 50 SER.#'d SETS

2010 Prestige Xtra Points Red

*1-200 VETS: 3X TO 8X BASIC CARDS
*201-300 ROOKIES: 1.2X TO 3X BASIC RC
*201-300 ROOKIES: 1.5X TO .4X BASIC SP RC
STATED PRINT RUN 100 SER.#'d SETS

2010 Prestige Collegiate Lettermen Autographs

1 Jimmy Clausen 12.00 30.00
2 Sam Bradford 30.00 60.00
3 Colt McCoy 12.00 30.00
4 Tim Tebow 40.00 80.00
5 C.J. Spiller 12.00 30.00
6 Toby Gerhart 15.00 40.00
7 Dez Bryant 20.00 50.00
8 Golden Tate 12.00 30.00
10 Jordan Shipley 12.00 30.00
11 Jermaine Gresham 12.00 30.00

2010 Prestige Connections

1 B.Favre/S.Rice 3.00 8.00
2 T.Brady/W.Welker 4.00 10.00
3 M.Schaub/A.Johnson 1.25 3.00
4 P.Manning/R.Wayne 4.00 10.00
5 B.Roethlisberger/S.Holmes 1.50 4.00
6 E.Manning/S.Smith USC 1.25 3.00
7 P.Rivers/A.Gates 1.50 4.00
8 D.McNabb/D.Jackson 1.25 3.00
9 D.Brees/M.Colston 1.50 4.00
10 M.Hasselbeck/N.Burleson 1.00 2.50
11 K.Orton/B.Marshall 1.25 3.00
12 T.Romo/M.Austin 1.25 3.00
13 K.Warner/L.Fitzgerald 1.25 3.00
14 C.Palmer/C.Ochocinco 1.25 3.00
15 M.Ryan/R.White 1.25 3.00
16 J.Flacco/D.Mason 1.25 3.00
17 A.Rodgers/D.Driver 3.00 8.00
18 J.Cutler/G.Olsen 1.25 3.00
19 D.Garrard/M.Sims-Walker 1.00 2.50
20 A.Smith/V.Davis 1.25 3.00

2010 Prestige Connections Materials

STATED PRINT RUN 250 SER.#'d SETS
1 B.Favre/S.Rice 10.00 25.00
3 M.Schaub/A.Johnson 4.00 10.00
4 P.Manning/R.Wayne 6.00 15.00
5 B.Roethlisberger/S.Holmes 5.00 12.00
7 P.Rivers/A.Gates 5.00 12.00
9 D.Brees/M.Colston 5.00 12.00
10 M.Hasselbeck/N.Burleson 3.00 8.00
12 T.Romo/M.Austin 4.00 10.00
14 C.Palmer/C.Ochocinco 4.00 10.00
15 M.Ryan/R.White 6.00 15.00
16 J.Flacco/D.Mason 4.00 10.00
17 A.Rodgers/D.Driver 6.00 15.00
18 J.Cutler/G.Olsen 4.00 10.00
20 A.Smith/V.Davis 4.00 10.00

2010 Prestige Connections Materials Prime

*PRIME/50: .6X TO 1.5X BASIC DUAL JSY
PRIME PRINT RUN 5-50
2 T.Brady/W.Welker/50 20.00 50.00

2010 Prestige Draft Picks Rights Autographs

STATED PRINT RUN 99-999
201 Aaron Hernandez/399 4.00 10.00
202 Andre Anderson/999 3.00 8.00
204 Andre Roberts/399 5.00 12.00
206 Anthony McCoy/999 3.00 8.00
207 Antonio Brown/999 30.00 60.00
208 Arrelious Benn/299 4.00 10.00
209 Ben Tate/399 4.00 10.00
210 Blair White/999 3.00 8.00
211 Brandon Graham/399 5.00 12.00
212 Brandon LaFell/299 6.00 15.00
214 Bryan Bulaga/399 4.00 10.00
215 C.J. Spiller/199 5.00 12.00
218 Chad Jones/399 4.00 10.00
221 Chris Cook/399 4.00 10.00
222 Chris McGaha/999
223 Colt McCoy/199 6.00 15.00
224 Corey Wootton/799 3.00 8.00
225 Damian Williams/299 4.00 10.00
226 Dan LeFevour/599 3.00 8.00
227 Danario Alexander/999 3.00 8.00
229 David Gettis/999 3.00 8.00
230 Demaryius Thomas/299 10.00 25.00
231 Derrick Morgan/399 4.00 10.00
232 Devin McCourty/399 5.00 12.00
233 Dexter McCluster/199 6.00 15.00
234 Dez Bryant/199 12.00 30.00
235 Dezmon Briscoe/599 3.00 8.00
236 Dominique Franks/799 3.00 8.00
237 Earl Thomas/399 10.00 25.00
238 Ed Dickson/399 4.00 10.00
240 Eric Decker/199 6.00 15.00
242 Freddie Barnes/999 3.00 8.00
243 Garrett Graham/799 3.00 8.00
245 Golden Tate/99 10.00 25.00
246 Jacoby Ford/399 4.00 10.00
247 Jahvid Best/199 5.00 12.00
248 James Starks/599 4.00 10.00
249 Jarrett Brown/999 3.00 8.00
250 Jason Pierre-Paul/399 6.00 15.00
251 Jason Worilds/399 4.00 10.00
252 Jeremy Williams/999 3.00 8.00
253 Jermaine Gresham/399 4.00 10.00
254 Jerry Hughes/399 4.00 10.00
255 Jevan Snead/999 3.00 8.00
256 Jimmy Clausen/99 8.00 20.00
261 Joique Bell/999 3.00 8.00
262 Jonathan Crompton/399 4.00 10.00
263 Jonathan Dwyer/399 4.00 10.00
264 Jordan Shipley/399 4.00 10.00
267 LeGarrette Blount/999 6.00 15.00
268 Lonyae Miller/999 4.00 10.00
271 Mike Kafka/599 4.00 10.00
273 Montario Hardesty/399 4.00 10.00
274 Morgan Burnett/399 5.00 12.00
275 Nate Allen/399 6.00 15.00
278 Pat Paschall/999
279 Patrick Robinson/399 5.00 12.00
283 Rob Gronkowski/399 25.00 50.00
284 Rolando McClain/399 4.00 10.00
286 Ryan Mathews/199 5.00 12.00
287 Sam Bradford/199 15.00 40.00
288 Sean Canfield/999 3.00 8.00
289 Sean Lee/399 8.00 20.00
290 Sean Weatherspoon/399 4.00 10.00
292 Seyi Ajirotutu/999 3.00 8.00
293 Shay Hodge/999 3.00 8.00
295 Taylor Price/399 4.00 10.00
296 Tim Tebow/99 25.00 60.00
297 Toby Gerhart/299 4.00 10.00
298 Tony Pike/499 4.00 10.00
300 Zac Robinson/799 4.00 10.00

2010 Prestige Inside The Numbers

1 Chris Johnson 1.00 2.50
2 Miles Austin 1.00 2.50
3 Percy Harvin 1.00 2.50
4 Reggie Wayne 1.25 3.00
5 Josh Cribbs 1.00 2.50
6 Drew Brees 1.50 4.00
7 Adrian Peterson 1.50 4.00
8 Andre Johnson 1.25 3.00
9 Wes Welker 1.25 3.00
10 Maurice Jones-Drew 1.00 2.50

2010 Prestige Inside The Numbers Autographs

STATED PRINT RUN 5-25
1 Chris Johnson/10
5 Josh Cribbs/25 25.00 50.00
6 Drew Brees/5

2010 Prestige Inside The Numbers Materials

STATED PRINT RUN 220-250
*PRIME/50: .8X TO 2X BASIC JSY
*PRIME/20: 1X TO 2.5X BASIC JSY
PRIME PRINT RUN 20-50
1 Chris Johnson/250 2.50 6.00
2 Miles Austin/220 2.50 6.00
3 Percy Harvin/250 2.50 6.00
4 Reggie Wayne/250 3.00 8.00
5 Josh Cribbs/250 4.00 10.00
6 Drew Brees/250 4.00 10.00
7 Adrian Peterson/250 4.00 10.00
8 Andre Johnson/250 3.00 8.00
9 Wes Welker/250 3.00 8.00
10 Maurice Jones-Drew/250 2.50 6.00

2010 Prestige League Leaders

1 M.Schaub/P.Manning 3.00 8.00
2 T.Romo/A.Rodgers 2.50 6.00
3 T.Brady/D.Brees 3.00 8.00
4 B.Roethlisberger/P.Rivers 1.25 3.00
5 B.Favre/E.Manning 2.50 6.00
6 C.Johnson/S.Jackson .75 2.00
7 T.Jones/M.Jones-Drew .75 2.00
8 A.Peterson/R.Rice 1.25 3.00
9 R.Grant/C.Benson 1.00 2.50
10 J.Stewart/R.Williams 1.00 2.50
11 A.Johnson/W.Welker 1.00 2.50
12 M.Austin/S.Rice .75 2.00
13 R.Moss/R.Wayne 1.00 2.50
14 S.Holmes/S.Smith USC .75 2.00
15 V.Jackson/D.Jackson 1.00 2.50
16 Brees/Favre/P.Mann/Rodgers 4.00 10.00
17 Ptrsn/Jns-Drw/Jhnson/Jones 1.50 4.00
18 Davis/Fitzgerald/Moss/Austin 1.25 3.00
19 Schb/P.Mann/Romo/Rodgrs 4.00 10.00
20 Jhnsn/Jcksn/Jnes/Jnes-Drw 1.00 2.50
21 Johnson/Welker/Austin/Rice 1.25 3.00
22 Brees/Peterson/Davis/Cribbs 1.50 4.00
23 Ptrsn/Jnes-Drw/Davis/Fitz 1.50 4.00
24 Dumervil/Allen/Frney/Wdley 1.00 2.50
25 Byrd/Saml/Sharpr/Wdson 1.50 4.00

2010 Prestige League Leaders Materials

1-13 DUAL JSY PRINT RUN 145-250
16-23 QUAD JSY PRINT RUN 100
*PRIME DUAL/50: .6X TO 1.5X BASIC DUAL
*PRIME QUAD/25: .6X TO 1.5X BASIC QUAD
STATED PRINT RUN 1-50
1 M.Schaub/P.Manning/250 12.00 30.00
2 T.Romo/A.Rodgers/250 10.00 25.00
3 T.Brady/D.Brees/230 12.00 30.00
4 B.Roethlisberger/P.Rivers/250 5.00 12.00
5 B.Favre/E.Manning/250 10.00 25.00
6 C.Johnson/S.Jackson/250 3.00 8.00
7 T.Jones/M.Jones-Drew/250 3.00 8.00
9 R.Grant/C.Benson/145 4.00 10.00
10 J.Stewart/R.Williams/250 4.00 10.00
11 A.Johnson/W.Welker/250 4.00 10.00
12 M.Austin/S.Rice/250 3.00 8.00
13 R.Moss/R.Wayne/250 4.00 10.00
16 Brs/Fvre/Mnnng/Rdgrs/100 20.00 50.00
17 Ptrsn/Drw/Jhnsn/Jnes/100 8.00 20.00
18 Dvs/Ftzgrd/Mss/Astn/100 6.00 15.00
19 Schb/Mnnng/Rmo/Rdgrs/100 20.00 50.00
20 Jhnsn/Jcksn/Jns/Drw/100 5.00 12.00
21 Jhnsn/Wlkr/Astn/Rce/100 6.00 15.00
22 Brs/Ptrsn/Dvs/Crbbs/100 8.00 20.00
23 Ptrsn/Drw/Davis/Fitz/100 8.00 20.00

2010 Prestige NFL Draft

1 Ndamukong Suh 1.25 3.00
2 Eric Berry 1.00 2.50
3 Gerald McCoy .60 1.50
4 Russell Okung .60 1.50
5 Joe Haden 1.00 2.50
6 C.J. Spiller .60 1.50
7 Jimmy Clausen .60 1.50
8 Derrick Morgan .60 1.50
9 Sam Bradford .75 2.00
10 Rolando McClain .60 1.50
11 Dez Bryant 1.50 4.00
12 Taylor Mays .60 1.50
13 Carlos Dunlap .60 1.50
14 Trent Williams .75 2.00
15 Golden Tate .75 2.00
16 Ricky Sapp .60 1.50
17 Jonathan Dwyer .60 1.50
18 Earl Thomas 1.50 4.00
19 Sergio Kindle .60 1.50
20 Colt McCoy .75 2.00
21 Tim Tebow 2.00 5.00
22 Jahvid Best .60 1.50
23 Ryan Mathews .60 1.50
24 Brandon LaFell 1.00 2.50
25 Jermaine Gresham .60 1.50
26 Damian Williams .60 1.50
27 Brandon Spikes .60 1.50
28 Jordan Shipley .60 1.50
29 Demaryius Thomas 1.50 4.00
30 Arrelious Benn .60 1.50
31 Anthony Dixon .60 1.50
32 Carlton Mitchell .60 1.50
33 Dezmon Briscoe .60 1.50
34 Joe McKnight .60 1.50
35 Toby Gerhart .60 1.50

2010 Prestige NFL Draft Autographed Patch Draft Logo

3 Gerald McCoy 8.00 20.00
5 Joe Haden 12.00 30.00
6 C.J. Spiller 8.00 20.00
7 Jimmy Clausen 8.00 20.00
8 Derrick Morgan 8.00 20.00
9 Sam Bradford 15.00 40.00
10 Rolando McClain 8.00 20.00
11 Dez Bryant 20.00 50.00
15 Golden Tate 10.00 25.00
17 Jonathan Dwyer 8.00 20.00
18 Earl Thomas 20.00 50.00
20 Colt McCoy 10.00 25.00
21 Tim Tebow 30.00 60.00
22 Jahvid Best 8.00 20.00
23 Ryan Mathews 8.00 20.00
24 Brandon LaFell 12.00 30.00
25 Jermaine Gresham 8.00 20.00
26 Damian Williams 8.00 20.00
28 Jordan Shipley 8.00 20.00
29 Demaryius Thomas 20.00 50.00
30 Arrelious Benn 8.00 20.00
33 Dezmon Briscoe 8.00 20.00
35 Toby Gerhart 8.00 20.00

2010 Prestige NFL Draft Autographed Patch NFL Equipment Logo

*NFL EQUIP LOGO: .5X TO 1.2X DRAFT LOGO
9 Sam Bradford 20.00 50.00
21 Tim Tebow 40.00 100.00

2010 Prestige NFL Draft Autographed Patch NFL Shield Logo

*NFL SHIELD LOGO: .6X TO 1.5X DRAFT LOGO
9 Sam Bradford 25.00 60.00
21 Tim Tebow 40.00 100.00

2010 Prestige NFL Draft Autographs

3 Gerald McCoy 4.00 10.00
5 Joe Haden 6.00 15.00
6 C.J. Spiller 4.00 10.00
7 Jimmy Clausen 4.00 10.00
8 Derrick Morgan 4.00 10.00
9 Sam Bradford 15.00 40.00
10 Rolando McClain 4.00 10.00
11 Dez Bryant 25.00 60.00
15 Golden Tate 5.00 12.00
17 Jonathan Dwyer 4.00 10.00
18 Earl Thomas 10.00 25.00
20 Colt McCoy 5.00 12.00
21 Tim Tebow 30.00 80.00
22 Jahvid Best 4.00 10.00
23 Ryan Mathews 4.00 10.00
24 Brandon LaFell 6.00 15.00
25 Jermaine Gresham 4.00 10.00
26 Damian Williams 4.00 10.00
28 Jordan Shipley 4.00 10.00
29 Demaryius Thomas 10.00 25.00
30 Arrelious Benn 4.00 10.00
33 Dezmon Briscoe 4.00 10.00
35 Toby Gerhart 12.00 30.00

2010 Prestige Preferred Materials

STATED PRINT RUN 250 SER.#'d SETS
1 Brandon Marshall 3.00 8.00
3 Drew Brees 4.00 10.00
4 Jamaal Charles 3.00 8.00
7 Sidney Rice 4.00 10.00
8 Brett Favre 15.00 40.00
9 Roddy White 2.50 6.00

2010 Prestige Preferred Materials Patch

*PATCH/25: 1X TO 2.5X BASIC JSY/250
PATCH PRINT RUN 25 SER.#'d SETS
10 Ryan Grant 8.00 20.00

2010 Prestige Preferred Materials Signatures

STATED PRINT RUN 10-25
1 Brandon Marshall/15 12.00 30.00
3 Drew Brees/10
4 Jamaal Charles/15 12.00 30.00
7 Sidney Rice/20 20.00 40.00
8 Brett Favre/10
9 Roddy White/10
10 Ryan Grant/25 12.00 30.00

2010 Prestige Preferred Signatures

STATED PRINT RUN 4-30
1 Brandon Marshall/5
2 DeSean Jackson/5
3 Drew Brees/5
4 Jamaal Charles/8
5 Rashard Mendenhall/13
6 Ray Rice/30 8.00 20.00
8 Brett Favre/4

2010 Prestige Prestigious Pros Blue

*BLACK/25: 1.2X TO 3X BLUE
*GOLD/100: .6X TO 1.5X BLUE
*GREEN/250: .5X TO 1.2X BLUE
*PLATINUM/10: 2.5X TO 6X BLUE
1 Anquan Boldin .75 2.00
2 Bernard Berrian .75 2.00
3 Brandon Jacobs .75 2.00
4 Brian Westbrook .75 2.00
5 Cadillac Williams .75 2.00
6 Chester Taylor .75 2.00
7 Chris Cooley .75 2.00
8 Dallas Clark .75 2.00
9 Jerricho Cotchery .75 2.00
10 Darren McFadden .75 2.00
11 Darren Sproles 1.00 2.50
12 David Garrard .75 2.00
13 Davone Bess .75 2.00
14 Devery Henderson .75 2.00
15 Devin Hester 1.00 2.50
16 Donald Driver 1.00 2.50
17 Dustin Keller .75 2.00
18 Eddie Royal .75 2.00
19 Felix Jones .75 2.00
20 Greg Jennings .75 2.00
21 Greg Olsen 1.00 2.50
22 Heath Miller .75 2.00
23 James Jones .75 2.00
24 Jeremy Maclin .75 2.00
25 Jermichael Finley .75 2.00
26 Jonathan Stewart .75 2.00
27 Joseph Addai .75 2.00
28 Ladell Betts .75 2.00
29 Laurence Maroney .75 2.00
30 Lee Evans 1.00 2.50
31 Mario Manningham .75 2.00
32 Marion Barber 1.00 2.50
33 Marques Colston .75 2.00
34 Matt Forte .75 2.00
35 Matt Ryan 1.00 2.50
36 Matthew Stafford 1.00 2.50
37 Michael Crabtree .75 2.00
38 Michael Turner .75 2.00
39 Steven Jackson .75 2.00
40 Patrick Crayton .75 2.00
41 Pierre Garcon 1.00 2.50
42 Rashard Mendenhall .75 2.00
43 Ray Rice .75 2.00
44 Ronnie Brown .75 2.00
45 Santana Moss 1.00 2.50
46 Steve Smith 1.00 2.50
47 Tony Romo 1.00 2.50
48 Vince Young .75 2.00
49 Visanthe Shiancoe 1.00 2.50
50 Zach Miller .75 2.00

2010 Prestige Prestigious Pros Autographs

STATED PRINT RUN 7-100
2 Bernard Berrian/7
6 Chester Taylor/25 10.00 25.00
13 Davone Bess/50 6.00 15.00
14 Devery Henderson/100 6.00 15.00
17 Dustin Keller/75 6.00 15.00
18 Eddie Royal/75 6.00 15.00
23 James Jones/75
24 Jeremy Maclin/14
25 Jermichael Finley/100 6.00 15.00
26 Jonathan Stewart/20 10.00 25.00
28 Ladell Betts/53 6.00 15.00
31 Mario Manningham/100 6.00 15.00
33 Marques Colston/23 10.00 25.00
34 Matt Forte/50 6.00 15.00
36 Matthew Stafford/15 30.00 60.00
37 Michael Crabtree/15 25.00 50.00
40 Patrick Crayton/87 6.00 15.00
41 Pierre Garcon/100 10.00 25.00
42 Rashard Mendenhall/10
43 Ray Rice/34 8.00 20.00

2010 Prestige Prestigious Pros Materials Gold

GOLD PRINT RUN 50 SER.#'d SETS
*BLACK/10: .8X TO 2X GOLD/50
BLACK PRINT RUN 10 SER.#'d SETS
*BLUE/240-250: .25X TO .6X GOLD/50
*BLUE/35: .4X TO 1X GOLD/50
BLUE PRINT RUN 35-250
*GREEN/100: .3X TO .8X GOLD/50
*GREEN/25: .5X TO 1.2X GOLD/50
GREEN PRINT RUN 25-100
*PLAT.PATCH/25: .6X TO 1.5X GOLD/50
PLATINUM PATCH PRINT RUN 25
1 Anquan Boldin 4.00 10.00
2 Bernard Berrian 4.00 10.00
3 Brandon Jacobs 4.00 10.00
4 Brian Westbrook 4.00 10.00
5 Cadillac Williams 4.00 10.00
6 Chester Taylor 4.00 10.00
7 Chris Cooley 4.00 10.00
8 Dallas Clark 4.00 10.00
9 Jerricho Cotchery 4.00 10.00
10 Darren McFadden 4.00 10.00
11 Darren Sproles 5.00 12.00
12 David Garrard 4.00 10.00
14 Devery Henderson 4.00 10.00
15 Devin Hester 5.00 12.00
16 Donald Driver 5.00 12.00
17 Dustin Keller 4.00 10.00
18 Eddie Royal 4.00 10.00
19 Felix Jones 4.00 10.00
20 Greg Jennings 4.00 10.00
21 Greg Olsen 5.00 12.00
22 Heath Miller 4.00 10.00
23 James Jones 4.00 10.00
24 Jeremy Maclin 4.00 10.00
26 Jonathan Stewart 4.00 10.00
27 Joseph Addai 4.00 10.00
28 Ladell Betts 4.00 10.00
29 Laurence Maroney 4.00 10.00
30 Lee Evans 5.00 12.00
32 Marion Barber 5.00 12.00
33 Marques Colston 4.00 10.00
34 Matt Forte 4.00 10.00
35 Matt Ryan 5.00 12.00
36 Matthew Stafford 5.00 12.00
37 Michael Crabtree 4.00 10.00
38 Michael Turner 4.00 10.00
39 Steven Jackson 4.00 10.00
40 Patrick Crayton 4.00 10.00
44 Ronnie Brown 4.00 10.00
45 Santana Moss 5.00 12.00
46 Steve Smith 5.00 12.00
47 Tony Romo 5.00 12.00
48 Vince Young 4.00 10.00
49 Visanthe Shiancoe 5.00 12.00
50 Zach Miller 4.00 10.00

2010 Prestige Pro Helmets Autographs

AB Arrelious Benn 6.00 15.00
AH Aaron Hernandez 6.00 15.00
AM Anthony McCoy 6.00 15.00
BL Brandon LaFell 10.00 25.00
CM Colt McCoy 8.00 20.00
CS C.J. Spiller 6.00 15.00
DB Dez Bryant 40.00 80.00
DBR Dezmon Briscoe 6.00 15.00
DM Derrick Morgan 6.00 15.00
DMC Dexter McCluster 8.00 20.00
DT Demaryius Thomas 15.00 40.00
DW Damian Williams 6.00 15.00
ED Eric Decker 8.00 20.00
ET Earl Thomas 12.00 30.00
GM Gerald McCoy 6.00 15.00
GT Golden Tate 8.00 20.00
JB Jahvid Best 6.00 15.00
JBR Jarrett Brown 6.00 15.00
JC Jimmy Clausen 6.00 15.00
JD Jonathan Dwyer 6.00 15.00
JG Jermaine Gresham 6.00 15.00
JH Joe Haden 10.00 25.00
JS Jevan Snead 6.00 15.00
JSH Jordan Shipley 6.00 15.00
JW Jeremy Williams 6.00 15.00
RG Rob Gronkowski 25.00 50.00
RM Ryan Mathews 6.00 15.00
RMC Rolando McClain 6.00 15.00
SB Sam Bradford 15.00 40.00
SC Sean Canfield 6.00 15.00
TG Toby Gerhart 6.00 15.00
TP Tony Pike 6.00 15.00
TT Tim Tebow 30.00 80.00

2010 Prestige Rookie Review

1 Mark Sanchez .75 2.00
2 Matthew Stafford 1.00 2.50
3 Josh Freeman 1.00 2.50
4 Chris Wells .75 2.00
5 Knowshon Moreno .75 2.00
6 LeSean McCoy 1.25 3.00
7 Shonn Greene .75 2.00
8 Percy Harvin .75 2.00
9 Jeremy Maclin .75 2.00
10 Kenny Britt .75 2.00
11 Hakeem Nicks .75 2.00
12 Michael Crabtree .75 2.00
13 Mike Thomas 1.00 2.50
14 Mike Wallace .75 2.00
15 Mohamed Massaquoi 1.00 2.50
16 Brandon Pettigrew .75 2.00
17 Darrius Heyward-Bey 1.00 2.50
18 Aaron Curry 1.00 2.50
19 Glen Coffee .75 2.00
20 Donald Brown .75 2.00
21 Tyson Jackson .75 2.00
22 Jason Smith .75 2.00
23 Brandon Gibson .75 2.00
24 Sammie Stroughter .75 2.00
25 Julian Edelman 1.25 3.00
26 Louis Murphy .75 2.00
27 Brian Hartline 1.00 2.50
28 James Laurinaitis 1.00 2.50
29 Brian Cushing .75 2.00
30 Jairus Byrd 1.00 2.50
31 Brian Orakpo .75 2.00
32 Clay Matthews 1.25 3.00
33 LaRod Stephens-Howling 1.00 2.50
34 Johnny Knox .75 2.00
35 Austin Collie .75 2.00

2010 Prestige Rookie Review Autographs

2 Matthew Stafford 25.00 50.00
3 Josh Freeman 10.00 25.00
4 Chris Wells 8.00 20.00
5 Knowshon Moreno 12.00 30.00
7 Shonn Greene
9 Jeremy Maclin 8.00 20.00
12 Michael Crabtree 12.00 30.00
14 Mike Wallace 8.00 20.00
16 Brandon Pettigrew 8.00 20.00
22 Jason Smith 8.00 20.00
26 Louis Murphy 8.00 20.00

2010 Prestige Rookie Review Materials

1 Mark Sanchez DP 6.00 15.00
2 Matthew Stafford DP 5.00 12.00
3 Josh Freeman 4.00 10.00
4 Chris Wells 3.00 8.00
5 Knowshon Moreno 3.00 8.00
6 LeSean McCoy 6.00 15.00
7 Shonn Greene 3.00 8.00
8 Percy Harvin DP 5.00 12.00
9 Jeremy Maclin 3.00 8.00
10 Kenny Britt 3.00 8.00
11 Hakeem Nicks 3.00 8.00
13 Mike Thomas 4.00 10.00
14 Mike Wallace 3.00 8.00
15 Mohamed Massaquoi 4.00 10.00
16 Brandon Pettigrew 3.00 8.00
17 Darrius Heyward-Bey 4.00 10.00
18 Aaron Curry 4.00 10.00
19 Glen Coffee 3.00 8.00
20 Donald Brown 3.00 8.00
21 Tyson Jackson 3.00 8.00
22 Jason Smith 3.00 8.00

2010 Prestige Rookie Review Materials Prime

*PRIME/50: .8X TO 2X BASIC JSY
PRIME PRINT RUN 50 SER.#'d SETS
12 Michael Crabtree 6.00 15.00

2010 Prestige Stars of the NFL

1 Aaron Rodgers 2.50 6.00
2 Adrian Peterson 1.25 3.00
3 Andre Johnson 1.00 2.50
4 Calvin Johnson 1.25 3.00
5 Chris Johnson .75 2.00
6 Donovan McNabb 1.00 2.50
7 Maurice Jones-Drew .75 2.00
8 Peyton Manning 3.00 8.00
9 Santonio Holmes .75 2.00
10 Tom Brady 3.00 8.00
11 Tony Romo 1.00 2.50
12 Vincent Jackson .75 2.00
13 Chad Ochocinco .75 2.00
14 Drew Brees 1.25 3.00
15 Frank Gore 1.00 2.50
16 Wes Welker 1.00 2.50
17 Philip Rivers 1.25 3.00
18 DeAngelo Williams .75 2.00
19 Eli Manning 1.00 2.50
20 Thomas Jones .75 2.00

2010 Prestige Stars of the NFL Materials

STATED PRINT RUN 100-250
1 Aaron Rodgers/180 6.00 15.00
2 Adrian Peterson/250 4.00 10.00
3 Andre Johnson/250 3.00 8.00
4 Calvin Johnson/250 4.00 10.00
5 Chris Johnson/250 2.50 6.00
6 Donovan McNabb/250 3.00 8.00
7 Maurice Jones-Drew/250 2.50 6.00
8 Peyton Manning/250 10.00 25.00
9 Santonio Holmes/250 2.50 6.00
10 Tom Brady/170 10.00 25.00
11 Tony Romo/250 5.00 12.00
12 Vincent Jackson/250 2.50 6.00
13 Chad Ochocinco/250 2.50 6.00
14 Drew Brees/250 4.00 10.00
15 Frank Gore/250 3.00 8.00
17 Philip Rivers/250 4.00 10.00
18 DeAngelo Williams/250 2.50 6.00
19 Eli Manning/250 3.00 8.00
20 Thomas Jones/100 3.00 8.00

2010 Prestige Stars of the NFL Materials Prime

*PRIME/40-50: .8X TO 2X BASIC JSY/170-250
*PRIME/24: 1X TO 2.5X BASIC JSY/250
*PRIME/20: .8X TO 2X BASIC JSY/100
PRIME PRINT RUN 20-50
16 Wes Welker/50 6.00 15.00

2010 Prestige Touchdown Sensations

1 Adrian Peterson 1.25 3.00
2 Brandon Marshall 1.00 2.50
3 Chris Johnson .75 2.00
4 DeSean Jackson 1.00 2.50
5 Frank Gore 1.00 2.50
6 Joseph Addai .75 2.00
7 LaDainian Tomlinson 1.25 3.00
8 Larry Fitzgerald 1.00 2.50
9 Marques Colston .75 2.00
10 Maurice Jones-Drew .75 2.00
11 Michael Turner .75 2.00
12 Miles Austin .75 2.00
13 Percy Harvin .75 2.00
14 Randy Moss 1.00 2.50
15 Reggie Wayne 1.00 2.50
16 Ricky Williams 1.00 2.50
17 Thomas Jones .75 2.00
18 Vernon Davis .75 2.00
19 Visanthe Shiancoe 1.00 2.50
20 Willis McGahee .75 2.00

2010 Prestige Touchdown Sensations Materials

STATED PRINT RUN 50-250
*PRIME/50: .8X TO 2X BASIC JSY/250
*PRIME/25: .6X TO 1.5X BASIC JSY/50
PRIME PRINT RUN 25-50
1 Adrian Peterson/250 4.00 10.00
2 Brandon Marshall/250 3.00 8.00
3 Chris Johnson/250 2.50 6.00
5 Frank Gore/250 3.00 8.00
6 Joseph Addai/250 2.50 6.00
7 LaDainian Tomlinson/250 4.00 10.00
8 Larry Fitzgerald/250 3.00 8.00
9 Marques Colston/250 2.50 6.00
10 Maurice Jones-Drew/250 2.50 6.00
11 Michael Turner/250 2.50 6.00
12 Miles Austin/250 2.50 6.00
13 Percy Harvin/250 2.50 6.00
14 Randy Moss/250 3.00 8.00
15 Reggie Wayne/250 3.00 8.00
16 Ricky Williams/250 3.00 8.00
17 Thomas Jones/50 4.00 10.00
18 Vernon Davis/250 2.50 6.00
19 Visanthe Shiancoe/250 3.00 8.00
20 Willis McGahee/250 2.50 6.00

2010 Prestige True Colors

1 Jason Witten 1.00 2.50
2 Larry Fitzgerald 1.00 2.50
3 Brett Favre 2.50 6.00
4 LaDainian Tomlinson 1.25 3.00
5 Marshawn Lynch 1.00 2.50
6 Chad Ochocinco .75 2.00
7 Frank Gore 1.00 2.50
8 Drew Brees 1.25 3.00
9 Andre Johnson 1.00 2.50
10 Ryan Grant 1.00 2.50

2010 Prestige True Colors Autographs

3 Brett Favre/4
8 Drew Brees/5

2010 Prestige True Colors Materials

STATED PRINT RUN 200-250
*PRIMARY CLR/50: .8X TO 2X BASIC JSY/250
*PRIMARY CLR/15-25: 1X TO 2.5X JSY/200-250
PRIMARY COLOR PRINT RUN 15-50
1 Jason Witten 3.00 8.00
2 Larry Fitzgerald 3.00 8.00
3 Brett Favre 10.00 25.00
4 LaDainian Tomlinson 4.00 10.00
5 Marshawn Lynch 3.00 8.00
6 Chad Ochocinco 2.50 6.00
7 Frank Gore 3.00 8.00
8 Drew Brees 4.00 10.00
9 Andre Johnson 3.00 8.00
10 Ryan Grant 3.00 8.00

2010 Prestige Xtra Points Black Autographs

STATED PRINT RUN 4-250
2 Chris Wells/12
3 D.Rodgers-Cromartie/134
8 Jason Snelling/44 10.00 25.00
9 Matt Ryan/26 25.00 50.00
15 Joe Flacco/25 25.00 50.00
27 DeAngelo Williams/10
29 Jonathan Stewart/19 10.00 25.00
35 Earl Bennett/50 8.00 20.00
39 Matt Forte/97 6.00 15.00
49 Josh Cribbs/15 25.00 50.00
59 Brandon Marshall/25 12.00 30.00
68 Kevin Smith/41 8.00 20.00
69 Matthew Stafford/42 30.00 60.00
74 Jermichael Finley/97 10.00 25.00
81 Steve Slaton/12
87 Pierre Garcon/125 10.00 25.00
92 Mike Sims-Walker/5
95 Brandon Flowers/96 6.00 15.00
102 Davone Bess/63 6.00 15.00
109 Brett Favre/10
120 Devery Henderson/250 5.00 12.00
121 Drew Brees/4
132 Mario Manningham/113 6.00 15.00
135 Darrelle Revis/100 10.00 25.00
141 Chaz Schilens/250 5.00 12.00
150 DeSean Jackson/30 10.00 25.00
157 Mike Wallace/150 8.00 20.00
167 Shawne Merriman/5
171 Michael Crabtree/50 15.00 40.00
172 Patrick Willis/17 15.00 40.00
176 Justin Forsett/250 6.00 15.00

2011 Prestige

COMP.SET w/o RCs (200) 10.00 25.00
ONE ROOKIE PER PACK
1 Chris Wells .20 .50
2 Early Doucet .20 .50
3 Larry Fitzgerald .25 .60
4 Steve Breaston .20 .50
5 Tim Hightower .20 .50
6 Curtis Lofton .20 .50
7 Jason Snelling .20 .50
8 Matt Ryan .25 .60
9 Michael Turner .20 .50
10 Roddy White .20 .50
11 Tony Gonzalez .25 .60
12 Anquan Boldin .20 .50
13 Ed Reed .25 .60
14 Haloti Ngata .20 .50
15 Joe Flacco .25 .60
16 Ray Lewis .30 .75
17 Ray Rice .20 .50
18 T.J. Houshmandzadeh .20 .50
19 Todd Heap .20 .50
20 C.J. Spiller .20 .50
21 Fred Jackson .20 .50
22 Lee Evans .25 .60
23 Roscoe Parrish .20 .50
24 Ryan Fitzpatrick .20 .50
25 Steve Johnson .20 .50
26 DeAngelo Williams .20 .50
27 Mike Goodson .20 .50
28 Jimmy Clausen .20 .50
29 Jon Beason .20 .50
30 Jonathan Stewart .20 .50
31 Steve Smith .25 .60
32 Brian Urlacher .30 .75
33 Devin Hester .25 .60
34 Earl Bennett .20 .50
35 Greg Olsen .25 .60
36 Jay Cutler .20 .50
37 Johnny Knox .20 .50
38 Julius Peppers .25 .60
39 Matt Forte .20 .50
40 Carson Palmer .25 .60
41 Cedric Benson .20 .50
42 Chad Johnson .20 .50
43 Jermaine Gresham .20 .50
44 Jordan Shipley .20 .50
45 Terrell Owens .25 .60
46 Ben Watson .20 .50
47 Colt McCoy .20 .50
48 Josh Cribbs .20 .50
49 Mohamed Massaquoi .20 .50
50 Peyton Hillis .20 .50
51 DeMarcus Ware .25 .60
52 Dez Bryant .30 .75
53 Felix Jones .20 .50
54 Jason Witten .25 .60
55 Miles Austin .20 .50
56 Roy Williams WR .20 .50
57 Tony Romo .25 .60
58 Brandon Lloyd .20 .50
59 Eddie Royal .20 .50
60 Jabar Gaffney .20 .50
61 Knowshon Moreno .20 .50
62 Champ Bailey .25 .60
63 Tim Tebow .30 .75
64 Brandon Pettigrew .20 .50
65 Calvin Johnson .30 .75
66 Jahvid Best .20 .50
67 Matthew Stafford .25 .60
68 Nate Burleson .20 .50
69 Ndamukong Suh .25 .60
70 Aaron Rodgers .50 1.25
71 Charles Woodson .30 .75
72 Clay Matthews .30 .75
73 Donald Driver .25 .60
74 Greg Jennings .20 .50
75 Jordy Nelson .25 .60
76 Ryan Grant .20 .50
77 Andre Johnson .25 .60
78 Arian Foster .20 .50
79 Brian Cushing .20 .50
80 Jacoby Jones .20 .50
81 Kevin Walter .20 .50
82 Matt Schaub .20 .50
83 Austin Collie .20 .50
84 Dallas Clark .20 .50
85 Dwight Freeney .20 .50
86 Jacob Tamme .20 .50
87 Joseph Addai .20 .50
88 Peyton Manning .60 1.50
89 Reggie Wayne .25 .60
90 David Garrard .20 .50
91 Marcedes Lewis .20 .50
92 Maurice Jones-Drew .25 .60
93 Mike Sims-Walker .20 .50
94 Mike Thomas .20 .50
95 Brandon Flowers .20 .50
96 Dexter McCluster .20 .50
97 Dwayne Bowe .20 .50
98 Jamaal Charles .25 .60
99 Matt Cassel .20 .50
100 Thomas Jones .20 .50
101 Tony Moeaki .20 .50
102 Anthony Fasano .20 .50
103 Brandon Marshall .20 .50
104 Brian Hartline .20 .50
105 Chad Henne .20 .50
106 Davone Bess .20 .50
107 Ronnie Brown .20 .50
108 Adrian Peterson .50 1.25
109 Jared Allen .20 .50
110 Percy Harvin .25 .60
111 Sidney Rice .20 .50
112 Tarvaris Jackson .20 .50
113 Visanthe Shiancoe .20 .50
114 Aaron Hernandez .20 .50
115 BenJarvus Green-Ellis .20 .50
116 Brandon Meriweather .20 .50
117 Danny Woodhead .25 .60
118 Deion Branch .20 .50
119 Rob Gronkowski .25 .60
120 Tom Brady .75 2.00
121 Wes Welker .25 .60
122 Drew Brees .30 .75
123 Lance Moore .20 .50
124 Marques Colston .20 .50
125 Pierre Thomas .20 .50
126 Reggie Bush .25 .60
127 Robert Meachem .20 .50
128 Ahmad Bradshaw .20 .50
129 Brandon Jacobs .20 .50
130 Eli Manning .25 .60
131 Hakeem Nicks .25 .60
132 Kevin Boss .20 .50
133 Mario Manningham .20 .50
134 Steve Smith USC .20 .50
135 Braylon Edwards .20 .50

136 Darrelle Revis .20 .50
137 Dustin Keller .25 .60
138 LaDainian Tomlinson .30 .75
139 Mark Sanchez .20 .50
140 Santonio Holmes .20 .50
141 Shonn Greene .20 .50
142 Darren McFadden .20 .50
143 Darrius Heyward-Bey .20 .50
144 Louis Murphy .20 .50
145 Jacoby Ford .25 .60
146 Michael Huff .20 .50
147 Zach Miller .20 .50
148 Asante Samuel .20 .50
149 Brent Celek .20 .50
150 DeSean Jackson .25 .60
151 Jeremy Maclin .20 .50
152 LeSean McCoy .30 .75
153 Michael Vick .25 .60
154 Ben Roethlisberger .30 .75
155 Heath Miller .20 .50
156 Hines Ward .25 .60
157 James Harrison .25 .60
158 Mike Wallace .20 .50
159 Rashard Mendenhall .20 .50
160 Troy Polamalu .30 .75
161 Antonio Gates .20 .50
162 Darren Sproles .25 .60
163 Malcom Floyd .20 .50
164 Mike Tolbert .20 .50
165 Philip Rivers .30 .75
166 Ryan Mathews .25 .60
167 Frank Gore .25 .60
168 Josh Morgan .20 .50
169 Michael Crabtree .20 .50
170 Patrick Willis .25 .60
171 Alex Smith .25 .60
172 Vernon Davis .20 .50
173 John Carlson .20 .50
174 Justin Forsett .25 .60
175 Marshawn Lynch .25 .60
176 Matt Hasselbeck .20 .50
177 Mike Williams USC .20 .50
178 Brandon Gibson .20 .50
179 Danny Amendola .25 .60
180 Donnie Avery .20 .50
181 James Laurinaitis .20 .50
182 Sam Bradford .20 .50
183 Steven Jackson .20 .50
184 Barrett Ruud .20 .50
185 Cadillac Williams .20 .50
186 Josh Freeman .25 .60
187 Kellen Winslow Jr. .20 .50
188 LeGarrette Blount .25 .60
189 Mike Williams .25 .60
190 Bo Scaife .20 .50
191 Chris Johnson .20 .50
192 Kenny Britt .20 .50
193 Nate Washington .20 .50
194 Randy Moss .25 .60
195 Vince Young .20 .50
196 Chris Cooley .20 .50
197 Ryan Torain .20 .50
198 Donovan McNabb .25 .60
199 LaRon Landry .20 .50
200 Santana Moss .25 .60
201A A.J. Green RC 1.25 3.00
201B A.J. Green Draft SP 6.00 15.00
202 Aaron Williams RC .50 1.25
203A Adrian Clayborn SP RC 12.00 30.00
203B A.Clayborn SP Draft 6.00 15.00
204 Ahmad Black SP RC 6.00 15.00
205 Akeem Ayers RC .50 1.25
206A Aldon Smith RC .50 1.25
206B Aldon Smith Draft SP 2.00 5.00
207 Andy Dalton RC 1.00 2.50
208 Austin Pettis RC .50 1.25
209 Bilal Powell RC .60 1.50
210A Blaine Gabbert RC .50 1.25
210B Blaine Gabbert Draft SP 2.00 5.00
211 Brandon Harris RC .50 1.25
212 Brooks Reed RC .60 1.50
213 Bruce Carter SP RC 10.00 25.00
214A Cam Newton RC 2.50 6.00
214B Cam Newton Draft SP 8.00 20.00
214C C.Newton SP Blu Nme 6.00 15.00
215 Cameron Heyward RC .60 1.50
216A Cameron Jordan RC .60 1.50
216B C.Jordan SP Draft 2.50 6.00
217 Cecil Shorts RC .50 1.25
218 Christian Ballard RC .50 1.25
219 Christian Ponder RC .50 1.25
220 Colin Kaepernick RC .75 2.00
221 Colin McCarthy RC .60 1.50
222 Corey Liuget RC .50 1.25
223 Courtney Smith RC .50 1.25
224 Curtis Brown SP RC 10.00 25.00
225 D.J. Williams RC .50 1.25
226 Daniel Thomas RC .50 1.25
227 Da'Quan Bowers RC .50 1.25
228 Darvin Adams RC .50 1.25
229 Davon House RC .50 1.25
230 DeAndre Brown RC .75 2.00
231 DeAndre McDaniel RC .50 1.25
232 Delone Carter RC .50 1.25
233 DeMarco Murray RC 1.00 2.50
234 Denarius Moore RC .50 1.25
235 Derrick Locke RC .60 1.50
236 Dion Lewis RC .60 1.50
237 Drake Nevis RC .50 1.25
238 Dwayne Harris RC .50 1.25
239 Edmond Gates SP RC 10.00 25.00
240 Evan Royster RC .50 1.25
241 Greg Jones RC .60 1.50
242 Greg Little RC .60 1.50
243 Greg Salas RC .50 1.25
244A J.J. Watt RC 2.50 6.00
244B J.J. Watt SP Draft 10.00 25.00
245 Jabaal Sheard RC .50 1.25
246 Jacquizz Rodgers RC .50 1.25
247 Jake Locker RC .50 1.25
248 Jamie Harper RC .50 1.25
249 Jeremy Kerley RC .75 2.00
250 Jerrel Jernigan RC .50 1.25
251 Jimmy Smith RC .50 1.25
252 John Clay RC .75 2.00
253 Jonathan Baldwin RC .50 1.25
254 Jordan Todman RC .50 1.25
255 Tyron Smith SP RC 12.00 30.00
256A Julio Jones RC 1.50 4.00
256B Julio Jones SP Draft 6.00 15.00
257 Justin Houston RC .60 1.50
258 Kendall Hunter RC .50 1.25
259 Kyle Rudolph RC .50 1.25
260 Lance Kendricks RC .50 1.25
261 Leonard Hankerson RC .50 1.25
262 Luke Stocker RC .50 1.25
263A Marcell Dareus RC .50 1.25
263B M.Dareus SP Draft 2.00 5.00
264 Mark Herzlich RC .50 1.25
265A Mark Ingram SP RC 8.00 20.00
265B Mark Ingram Draft SP 3.00 8.00
266 Martez Wilson RC .50 1.25
267 Mike McNeill SP RC 12.00 30.00
268 Mikel Leshoure RC .50 1.25
269A Nick Fairley SP RC 12.00 30.00
269B Nick Fairley Draft SP 6.00 15.00
270 Niles Paul RC .50 1.25
271 Noel Devine RC .75 2.00
272 Owen Marecic RC .50 1.25
273 Pat Devlin RC .75 2.00
274A Patrick Peterson RC 1.00 2.50
274B P.Peterson SP Draft 4.00 10.00
275A Phil Taylor RC .50 1.25
275B Phil Taylor Draft SP 3.00 8.00
276A Prince Amukamara RC .50 1.25
276B P.Amukamara SP Draft 2.00 5.00
277 Quan Sturdivant RC .60 1.50
278 Quinton Carter RC .50 1.25
279 Rahim Moore RC .50 1.25
280 Randall Cobb RC .75 2.00
281 Ricky Stanzi SP RC 5.00 12.00
282 Rob Housler RC .50 1.25
283 Robert Quinn RC .50 1.25
284 Ronald Johnson RC .50 1.25
285A Ryan Kerrigan RC .60 1.50
285B R.Kerrigan SP Draft 4.00 10.00
286 Ryan Mallett RC .50 1.25
287 Ryan Whalen RC .50 1.25
288 Ryan Williams RC .50 1.25
289 Shane Vereen RC .60 1.50
290 Stanley Havili RC .50 1.25
291 Stephen Paea RC .50 1.25
292 Stevan Ridley RC .50 1.25
293 Taiwan Jones RC .50 1.25
294 Tandon Doss RC .50 1.25
295 Terrence Toliver RC .60 1.50
296 Titus Young RC .50 1.25
297 Torrey Smith RC .50 1.25
298 Tyler Sash RC .50 1.25
299 Vincent Brown RC .50 1.25
300A Von Miller RC .75 2.00
300B Von Miller Draft SP 3.00 8.00
301 Mike Pouncey Drft SP RC 4.00 10.00

2011 Prestige Draft Picks Light Blue

*ROOKIES/999: .5X TO 1.2X BASIC RC
*ROOKIES/999: .05X TO .15X BASIC SP RC
STATED PRINT RUN 999 SER.#'d SETS

2011 Prestige Xtra Points Black

*1-200 VETS: 10X TO 25X BASIC CARDS
*201-300 ROOKIES: .4X TO 10X BASIC RC
*201-300 ROOKIES: .5X TO 1.2X BASIC SP RC
STATED PRINT RUN 10 SER.#'d SETS

2011 Prestige Xtra Points Gold

*1-200 VETS: 2X TO 5X BASIC CARDS
*201-300 ROOKIES: .8X TO 2X BASIC RC
*201-300 ROOKIES: .1X TO .25X BASIC SP RC
STATED PRINT RUN 250 SER.#'d SETS

2011 Prestige Xtra Points Green

*1-200 VETS: 8X TO 20X BASIC CARDS
*201-300 ROOKIES: 3X TO 8X BASIC RC
*201-300 ROOKIES: .4X TO 1X BASIC SP RC
STATED PRINT RUN 25 SER.#'d SETS

2011 Prestige Xtra Points Orange

*1-200 VETS: 3X TO 8X BASIC CARDS
*201-300 ROOKIES: 1.2X TO 3X BASIC RC
*201-300 ROOKIES: .15X TO .4X BASIC SP RC
RANDOM INSERTS IN RETAIL PACKS

2011 Prestige Xtra Points Purple

*1-200 VETS: 4X TO 10X BASIC CARDS
*201-300 ROOKIES: 1.5X TO 4X BASIC RC
*201-300 ROOKIES: .2X TO .5X BASIC SP RC
STATED PRINT RUN 50 SER.#'d SETS

2011 Prestige Xtra Points Red

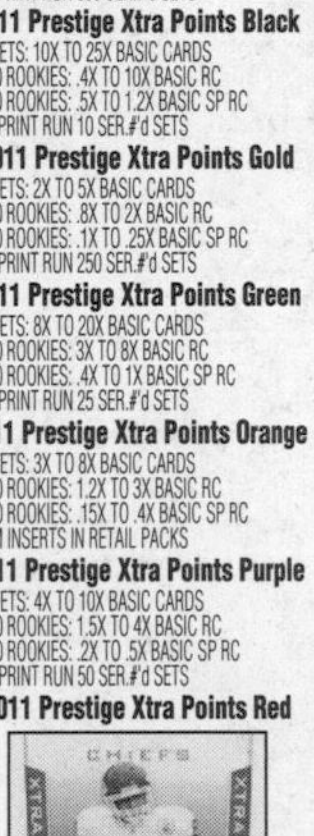

*1-200 VETS: 3X TO 8X BASIC CARDS
*201-300 ROOKIES: 1.2X TO 3X BASIC RC
*201-300 ROOKIES: .15X TO .4X BASIC SP RC
STATED PRINT RUN 100 SER.#'d SETS

2011 Prestige Collegiate Lettermen Autographs

RANDOM INSERTS IN PACKS
1 A.J. Green 15.00 40.00
2 Blaine Gabbert 6.00 15.00
4 D.J. Williams 10.00 25.00
5 Daniel Thomas 6.00 15.00
6 DeMarco Murray 12.00 30.00
7 Jake Locker 6.00 15.00
8 Jerrel Jernigan 8.00 20.00
9 Jonathan Baldwin 6.00 15.00
10 Jordan Todman 8.00 20.00
11 Julio Jones 25.00 60.00
12 Kyle Rudolph 6.00 15.00
13 Leonard Hankerson 6.00 15.00
15 Mikel Leshoure 6.00 15.00
16 Randall Cobb 10.00 25.00
17 Ronald Johnson 6.00 15.00
18 Ryan Mallett 6.00 15.00
19 Ryan Williams 6.00 15.00
20 Torrey Smith 6.00 15.00

2011 Prestige Connections

RANDOM INSERTS IN PACKS
1 M.Cassel/D.Bowe 1.00 2.50
2 C.Johnson/J.Best 1.25 3.00
3 A.Rodgers/G.Jennings 2.00 5.00
4 P.Rivers/A.Gates 1.25 3.00
5 E.Manning/H.Nicks 1.00 2.50
6 M.Vick/J.Maclin 1.00 2.50
7 D.Bryant/M.Austin 1.25 3.00
8 B.Roethlisberger/M.Wallace 1.25 3.00
9 M.Ryan/R.White 1.00 2.50
10 D.Brees/M.Colston 1.25 3.00
11 M.Crabtree/V.Davis .75 2.00
12 M.Schaub/A.Johnson 1.00 2.50
13 M.Sanchez/B.Edwards .75 2.00
14 J.Flacco/A.Boldin 1.00 2.50
15 P.Manning/R.Wayne 2.50 6.00
16 J.Cutler/G.Olsen 1.00 2.50
17 J.Stewart/S.Smith 1.00 2.50
18 B.Jacobs/S.Smith USC .75 2.00
19 D.McNabb/S.Moss 1.00 2.50
20 A.Peterson/P.Harvin 1.25 3.00
21 C.Henne/B.Marshall 1.00 2.50
22 S.Greene/S.Holmes .75 2.00
23 T.Brady/W.Welker 3.00 8.00
24 J.Campbell/D.McFadden .75 2.00
25 D.Garrard/M.Jones-Drew .75 2.00

2011 Prestige Connections Materials

STATED PRINT RUN 249-250
*PRIME/50: .6X TO 1.5X BASIC DUAL
*PRIME/25: .8X TO 2X BASIC DUAL
1 M.Cassel/D.Bowe/250 4.00 10.00
3 A.Rodgers/Jennings/250 8.00 20.00
4 P.Rivers/A.Gates/250 5.00 12.00
5 E.Manning/H.Nicks/250 4.00 10.00
6 M.Vick/J.Maclin/250 4.00 10.00
7 D.Bryant/M.Austin/250 5.00 12.00
8 Roeth/M.Wallace/249 5.00 12.00
9 M.Ryan/R.White/250 4.00 10.00
10 D.Brees/M.Colston/250 5.00 12.00
11 M.Crabtree/V.Davis/250 3.00 8.00
12 Schaub/A.Johnson/250 4.00 10.00
13 Sanchez/B.Edwards/250 3.00 8.00
14 J.Flacco/A.Boldin/250 4.00 10.00
15 P.Manning/R.Wayne/250 10.00 25.00
16 J.Cutler/G.Olsen/250 4.00 10.00
17 J.Stewart/S.Smith/250 4.00 10.00
18 Jacobs/S.Smith USC/250 3.00 8.00
19 D.McNabb/S.Moss/250 4.00 10.00
20 A.Peterson/P.Harvin/250 5.00 12.00
22 S.Greene/S.Holmes/250 3.00 8.00
23 T.Brady/W.Welker/250 12.00 30.00
24 Campbell/McFadden/250 3.00 8.00
25 Garrard/Jones-Drew/250 3.00 8.00

2011 Prestige Draft Picks Rights Autographs

STATED PRINT RUN 50-1499
EXCH EXPIRATION: 11/25/2012
201 A.J. Green/99 20.00 40.00
202 Aaron Williams/599 3.00 8.00
203 Adrian Clayborn/599 8.00 20.00
204 Ahmad Black/699 4.00 10.00
205 Akeem Ayers/99 5.00 12.00
206 Aldon Smith/99 5.00 12.00
207 Andy Dalton/499 6.00 15.00
208 Austin Pettis/199 4.00 10.00
209 Bilal Powell/599 4.00 10.00
210 Blaine Gabbert/99 5.00 12.00
211 Brandon Harris/599 3.00 8.00
215 Cameron Heyward/599 4.00 10.00
216 Cameron Jordan/599 4.00 10.00
217 Cecil Shorts/699 3.00 8.00
219 Christian Ponder/199 4.00 10.00
220 Colin Kaepernick/299 12.00 30.00
222 Corey Liuget/599 3.00 8.00
223 Courtney Smith/1499 2.50 6.00
225 D.J. Williams/299 4.00 10.00
226 Daniel Thomas/99 5.00 12.00
227 Da'Quan Bowers/99 5.00 12.00
228 Darvin Adams/99 5.00 12.00
231 DeAndre McDaniel/1499 2.50 6.00
232 Delone Carter/599 3.00 8.00
233 DeMarco Murray/99 10.00 25.00
234 Denarius Moore/99 20.00 40.00
235 Derrick Locke/1499 3.00 8.00
236 Dion Lewis/599 4.00 10.00
238 Dwayne Harris/99 5.00 12.00
239 Edmond Gates/599 3.00 8.00
240 Evan Royster/599 3.00 8.00
241 Greg Jones/99 6.00 15.00
242 Greg Little/499 4.00 10.00
243 Greg Salas/499 3.00 8.00
244 J.J. Watt/699 30.00 60.00
246 Jacquizz Rodgers/99 5.00 12.00
247 Jake Locker/99 5.00 12.00
248 Jamie Harper/199 4.00 10.00
249 Jeremy Kerley/799 5.00 12.00
250 Jerrel Jernigan/499 3.00 8.00
251 Jimmy Smith/599 6.00 15.00
252 John Clay/1499 4.00 10.00
253 Jonathan Baldwin/99 5.00 12.00
254 Jordan Todman/50 10.00 25.00
256 Julio Jones/99 25.00 50.00
257 Justin Houston/99 6.00 15.00
258 Kendall Hunter/499 3.00 8.00
259 Kyle Rudolph/99 5.00 12.00
260 Lance Kendricks/99 5.00 12.00
261 Leonard Hankerson/99 5.00 12.00
262 Luke Stocker/599 3.00 8.00
263 Marcell Dareus/299 4.00 10.00
266 Martez Wilson/99 5.00 12.00
268 Mikel Leshoure/99 5.00 12.00
270 Niles Paul/499 3.00 8.00
271 Noel Devine/99 EXCH 8.00 20.00
273 Pat Devlin/1499 4.00 10.00
276 Prince Amukamara/299 4.00 10.00
278 Quinton Carter/99 8.00 20.00
279 Rahim Moore/99 5.00 12.00
280 Randall Cobb/99 8.00 20.00
281 Ricky Stanzi/99 5.00 12.00
284 Ronald Johnson/99 5.00 12.00
285 Ryan Kerrigan/599 4.00 10.00
286 Ryan Mallett/299 4.00 10.00
287 Ryan Whalen/99 5.00 12.00
288 Ryan Williams/99 5.00 12.00
289 Shane Vereen/199 5.00 12.00
290 Stanley Havili/699 3.00 8.00
291 Stephen Paea/99 5.00 12.00
292 Stevan Ridley/599 3.00 8.00
293 Taiwan Jones/699 3.00 8.00
294 Tandon Doss/99 5.00 12.00
295 Terrence Toliver/1499 3.00 8.00
296 Titus Young/99 5.00 12.00
297 Torrey Smith/99 5.00 12.00
298 Tyler Sash/699 3.00 8.00
299 Vincent Brown/99 5.00 12.00
300 Von Miller/499 8.00 20.00

2011 Prestige Inside The Numbers

RANDOM INSERTS IN PACKS
1 Aaron Rodgers 2.00 5.00
2 Adrian Peterson 1.25 3.00
3 Andre Johnson 1.00 2.50
4 Arian Foster .75 2.00
5 Drew Brees 1.25 3.00
6 Jamaal Charles 1.00 2.50
7 Maurice Jones-Drew .75 2.00
8 Philip Rivers 1.25 3.00
9 Reggie Wayne 1.00 2.50
10 Roddy White .75 2.00

2011 Prestige Inside The Numbers Autographs

STATED PRINT RUN 25 SER.#'d SETS
8 Philip Rivers 25.00 50.00

2011 Prestige Inside The Numbers Materials

STATED PRINT RUN 100-250
*PRIME/35-50: .8X TO 2X BASIC JSY/250
*PRIME/35-50: .6X TO 1.5X BASIC JSY/100
1 Aaron Rodgers/250 6.00 15.00
2 Adrian Peterson/250 4.00 10.00
3 Andre Johnson/250 3.00 8.00
4 Arian Foster/250 2.50 6.00
5 Drew Brees/250 4.00 10.00
6 Jamaal Charles/200 3.00 8.00
7 Maurice Jones-Drew/100 3.00 8.00
8 Philip Rivers/250 4.00 10.00
9 Reggie Wayne/250 3.00 8.00
10 Roddy White/250 2.50 6.00

2011 Prestige League Leaders

RANDOM INSERTS IN PACKS
1 P.Rivers/P.Manning 2.00 5.00
2 D.Brees/M.Schaub 1.00 2.50
3 E.Manning/C.Palmer .75 2.00
4 A.Rodgers/T.Brady 2.50 6.00
5 A.Foster/J.Charles .75 2.00
6 M.Turner/C.Johnson .60 1.50
7 Jones-Drew/A.Peterson 1.00 2.50
8 R.Mendenhall/S.Jackson .60 1.50
9 B.Lloyd/R.White .60 1.50
10 R.Wayne/G.Jennings .75 2.00
11 M.Wallace/A.Johnson .75 2.00
12 D.Bowe/L.Fitzgerald .75 2.00
13 A.Foster/D.Bowe .75 2.00
14 T.Brady/D.Brees 2.50 6.00
15 E.Reed/D.McCourty .75 2.00
16 Rivrs/P.Mann/Brs/Schb 2.50 6.00
17 Eli/Palmr/Rodgers/Brdy 3.00 8.00
18 Foster/Charles/Trnr/Jhnsn 1.00 2.50
19 Jns-Drw/Ptrs/Mendl/Jcksn 1.25 3.00
20 Lloyd/White/Wayne/Jenn 1.00 2.50
21 Wall/Jhnsn/Bowe/Fitz 1.00 2.50
22 Bowe/Jenn/Fstr/Grn-El 1.00 2.50
23 Brdy/Brees/P.Mann/Eli 3.00 8.00
24 Reed/McCrty/Plmlu/Sml 1.25 3.00
25 Ware/Hali/Wake/Matthews 1.25 3.00

2011 Prestige League Leaders Materials

1-14 STATED PRINT RUN 130-200
16-23 STATED PRINT RUN 100
*1-14 PRIME/50: .6X TO 1.5X DUAL/130-200
*16-23 PRIME/50: .5X TO 1.2X TRPL/100
1 P.Rivers/P.Manning/200 10.00 25.00
2 D.Brees/M.Schaub/200 5.00 12.00
3 E.Manning/C.Palmer/200 4.00 10.00
4 A.Rodgers/T.Brady/200 12.00 30.00
5 A.Foster/J.Charles/200 6.00 15.00
6 M.Turner/C.Johnson/200 3.00 8.00
7 Jones-Drew/A.Peterson/200 5.00 12.00
8 R.Mendenhall/S.Jackson/200 3.00 8.00
9 B.Lloyd/R.White/200 3.00 8.00
10 R.Wayne/G.Jennings/130 4.00 10.00
11 M.Wallace/A.Johnson/200 4.00 10.00
12 D.Bowe/L.Fitzgerald/200 4.00 10.00
13 A.Foster/D.Bowe/200 4.00 10.00
14 T.Brady/D.Brees/200 12.00 30.00
16 Rivrs/P.Mann/Brs/Schb/100 12.00 30.00
17 Eli/Palmr/Rodgers/Brdy/100 20.00 50.00
18 Foster/Charles/Trnr/Jhnsn/100 6.00 15.00
19 Jns-Drw/Ptrs/Mendl/Jcksn/100 8.00 20.00
20 Lloyd/White/Wayne/Jenn/100 6.00 15.00
21 Wall/Jhnsn/Bowe/Fitz/100 6.00 15.00
23 Brdy/Brees/P.Mann/Eli/100 20.00 50.00

2011 Prestige NFL Draft

RANDOM INSERTS IN PACKS
1 A.J. Green 1.00 2.50
2 Aldon Smith .40 1.00
3 Austin Pettis .40 1.00
4 Blaine Gabbert .40 1.00
5 Cam Newton 2.00 5.00
6 Christian Ponder .40 1.00
7 D.J. Williams .40 1.00
8 Daniel Thomas .40 1.00
9 Da'Quan Bowers .40 1.00
10 DeAndre McDaniel .40 1.00
11 Delone Carter .40 1.00
12 DeMarco Murray .75 2.00
13 Jacquizz Rodgers .40 1.00
14 Jake Locker .40 1.00
15 Jamie Harper .40 1.00
16 Jerrel Jernigan .40 1.00
17 Jonathan Baldwin .40 1.00
18 Jordan Todman .40 1.00
19 Julio Jones 1.25 3.00
20 Kendall Hunter .40 1.00
21 Kyle Rudolph .40 1.00
22 Leonard Hankerson .40 1.00
23 Mark Ingram .60 1.50
24 Martez Wilson .40 1.00
25 Mikel Leshoure .40 1.00
26 Nick Fairley .40 1.00
27 Niles Paul .40 1.00
28 Pat Devlin .60 1.50
29 Patrick Peterson .75 2.00
30 Prince Amukamara .40 1.00
31 Quinton Carter .40 1.00
32 Randall Cobb .60 1.50
33 Ronald Johnson .40 1.00
34 Ryan Mallett .40 1.00
35 Ryan Williams .40 1.00
36 Shane Vereen .50 1.25
37 Tandon Doss .40 1.00
38 Titus Young .40 1.00
39 Torrey Smith .40 1.00
40 Von Miller .60 1.50
BF1 Mark Ingram BF .50 1.25
BF2 Cam Newton BF 1.50 4.00
BF3 Terrelle Pryor BF .50 1.25

2011 Prestige NFL Draft Autographed Patch Draft Logo

RANDOM INSERTS IN PACKS
EXCH EXPIRATION: 11/25/2012
*NFL EQUIP: .5X TO 1.2X DRFT PATCH AU
*NFL SHIELD: .6X TO 1.5X DRFT PTCH AU
1 A.J. Green 15.00 40.00
2 Aldon Smith 6.00 15.00
3 Austin Pettis 6.00 15.00
4 Blaine Gabbert 6.00 15.00
6 Christian Ponder 6.00 15.00
7 D.J. Williams 6.00 15.00
8 Daniel Thomas 6.00 15.00
9 Da'Quan Bowers 6.00 15.00
10 DeAndre McDaniel 6.00 15.00
11 Delone Carter 6.00 15.00
12 DeMarco Murray 12.00 30.00
13 Jacquizz Rodgers 6.00 15.00
14 Jake Locker 6.00 15.00
15 Jamie Harper 6.00 15.00
16 Jerrel Jernigan 6.00 15.00
17 Jonathan Baldwin 6.00 15.00
18 Jordan Todman 6.00 15.00
19 Julio Jones 25.00 50.00
20 Kendall Hunter 6.00 15.00
21 Kyle Rudolph 6.00 15.00
22 Leonard Hankerson 6.00 15.00
24 Martez Wilson 6.00 15.00
25 Mikel Leshoure 6.00 15.00
27 Niles Paul 6.00 15.00
28 Pat Devlin 10.00 25.00
30 Prince Amukamara 6.00 15.00
31 Quinton Carter 6.00 15.00
32 Randall Cobb 10.00 25.00
33 Ronald Johnson 6.00 15.00
34 Ryan Mallett 6.00 15.00
35 Ryan Williams 20.00 40.00
36 Shane Vereen 8.00 20.00
37 Tandon Doss 6.00 15.00
38 Titus Young 6.00 15.00
39 Torrey Smith 6.00 15.00
40 Von Miller 15.00 40.00

2011 Prestige NFL Draft Autographs

RANDOM INSERTS IN PACKS
EXCH EXPIRATION: 11/25/2012
1 A.J. Green 10.00 25.00
2 Aldon Smith 4.00 10.00
3 Austin Pettis 4.00 10.00
4 Blaine Gabbert 4.00 10.00
6 Christian Ponder 4.00 10.00
7 D.J. Williams 4.00 10.00
8 Daniel Thomas 4.00 10.00
9 Da'Quan Bowers 4.00 10.00
10 DeAndre McDaniel 4.00 10.00
11 Delone Carter 4.00 10.00
12 DeMarco Murray 8.00 20.00
13 Jacquizz Rodgers 4.00 10.00
14 Jake Locker 4.00 10.00
15 Jamie Harper 4.00 10.00
16 Jerrel Jernigan 4.00 10.00
17 Jonathan Baldwin 4.00 10.00
18 Jordan Todman 4.00 10.00
19 Julio Jones 12.00 30.00
20 Kendall Hunter 4.00 10.00
21 Kyle Rudolph 4.00 10.00
22 Leonard Hankerson 4.00 10.00
24 Martez Wilson 8.00 20.00
25 Mikel Leshoure 4.00 10.00
27 Niles Paul 4.00 10.00
28 Pat Devlin 5.00 12.00
30 Prince Amukamara 4.00 10.00
31 Quinton Carter 8.00 20.00
32 Randall Cobb 6.00 15.00
33 Ronald Johnson 5.00 12.00
34 Ryan Mallett 4.00 10.00
35 Ryan Williams
36 Shane Vereen 5.00 12.00
37 Tandon Doss 4.00 10.00
38 Titus Young 4.00 10.00
39 Torrey Smith 4.00 10.00
40 Von Miller 10.00 25.00
BFAU Terrelle Pryor AU/22 BF 12.00 30.00

2011 Prestige NFL Passport

RANDOM INSERTS IN PACKS
*HOLOKOTE/100: .6X TO 1.5X BASIC INSERTS
1 A.J. Green 1.50 4.00
2 Aaron Williams .60 1.50
3 Adrian Clayborn .60 1.50
4 Ahmad Black .75 2.00
5 Aldon Smith .60 1.50
6 Blaine Gabbert .60 1.50
7 Brandon Harris .60 1.50
8 Cam Newton 3.00 8.00
9 Christian Ponder .60 1.50
10 D.J. Williams .60 1.50
11 Daniel Thomas .60 1.50
12 Da'Quan Bowers .60 1.50
13 DeAndre McDaniel .60 1.50
14 Delone Carter .60 1.50
15 DeMarco Murray 1.25 3.00
16 Jake Locker .60 1.50
17 Jerrel Jernigan .60 1.50
18 Jonathan Baldwin .60 1.50
19 Jordan Todman .60 1.50
20 Julio Jones 2.00 5.00
21 Kyle Rudolph .60 1.50
22 Leonard Hankerson .60 1.50
23 Marcell Dareus .60 1.50
24 Mark Ingram 1.00 2.50
25 Martez Wilson .60 1.50
26 Mikel Leshoure .60 1.50
27 Nick Fairley .60 1.50
28 Owen Marecic .60 1.50
29 Patrick Peterson 1.25 3.00
30 Prince Amukamara .60 1.50
31 Quinton Carter .60 1.50
32 Rahim Moore .60 1.50
33 Randall Cobb 1.00 2.50
34 Robert Quinn .60 1.50
35 Ronald Johnson .60 1.50
36 Ryan Mallett .60 1.50
37 Ryan Williams .60 1.50
38 Stephen Paea .60 1.50
39 Torrey Smith .60 1.50
40 Von Miller 1.00 2.50

2011 Prestige NFL Passport Autographs

STATED PRINT RUN 25 SER.#'d SETS
EXCH EXPIRATION: 11/25/2012
1 A.J. Green 30.00 60.00
2 Aaron Williams 6.00 15.00
3 Adrian Clayborn 20.00 50.00
4 Ahmad Black 15.00 40.00
5 Aldon Smith
6 Blaine Gabbert 6.00 15.00
7 Brandon Harris 6.00 15.00
9 Christian Ponder 6.00 15.00
10 D.J. Williams 6.00 15.00
11 Daniel Thomas 6.00 15.00
12 Da'Quan Bowers 6.00 15.00
13 DeAndre McDaniel 6.00 15.00
14 Delone Carter 6.00 15.00
15 DeMarco Murray 12.00 30.00
16 Jake Locker 6.00 15.00
17 Jerrel Jernigan 6.00 15.00
18 Jonathan Baldwin 12.00 30.00
19 Jordan Todman 12.00 30.00
20 Julio Jones 20.00 50.00
21 Kyle Rudolph 6.00 15.00
22 Leonard Hankerson 6.00 15.00
23 Marcell Dareus 6.00 15.00
25 Martez Wilson 12.00 30.00
26 Mikel Leshoure 6.00 15.00
30 Prince Amukamara 6.00 15.00
31 Quinton Carter 12.00 30.00
32 Rahim Moore 6.00 15.00
33 Randall Cobb 10.00 25.00
35 Ronald Johnson 8.00 20.00
36 Ryan Mallett 6.00 15.00
37 Ryan Williams 20.00 40.00
38 Stephen Paea 6.00 15.00
39 Torrey Smith 6.00 15.00
40 Von Miller 15.00 40.00

2011 Prestige Platinum Patches

RANDOM INSERTS IN PACKS
8 Matt Ryan 8.00 20.00
9 Michael Turner 4.00 10.00
10 Roddy White 4.00 10.00
11 Tony Gonzalez 5.00 12.00
12 Anquan Boldin 4.00 10.00
16 Ray Lewis 8.00 20.00
19 Todd Heap 4.00 10.00
20 C.J. Spiller 4.00 10.00
22 Lee Evans 5.00 12.00
24 Ryan Fitzpatrick 4.00 10.00
26 DeAngelo Williams 4.00 10.00
31 Steve Smith 5.00 12.00
32 Brian Urlacher 6.00 15.00
33 Devin Hester 6.00 15.00
35 Greg Olsen 5.00 12.00
36 Jay Cutler 4.00 10.00
39 Matt Forte 4.00 10.00
40 Carson Palmer 5.00 12.00
41 Cedric Benson 4.00 10.00
42 Chad Johnson 4.00 10.00
49 Mohamed Massaquoi 4.00 10.00
51 DeMarcus Ware 5.00 12.00
52 Dez Bryant 6.00 15.00
53 Felix Jones 4.00 10.00
54 Jason Witten 5.00 12.00
55 Miles Austin 4.00 10.00
56 Roy Williams WR 4.00 10.00
57 Tony Romo 5.00 12.00
59 Eddie Royal 4.00 10.00
63 Tim Tebow 6.00 15.00
65 Calvin Johnson 6.00 15.00
77 Andre Johnson 5.00 12.00
84 Dallas Clark 4.00 10.00
87 Joseph Addai 4.00 10.00
92 Maurice Jones-Drew 4.00 10.00
93 Mike Sims-Walker 5.00 12.00
97 Dwayne Bowe 5.00 12.00
98 Jamaal Charles 5.00 12.00
99 Matt Cassel 4.00 10.00
108 Adrian Peterson 6.00 15.00
109 Jared Allen 6.00 15.00
110 Percy Harvin 4.00 10.00
111 Sidney Rice 4.00 10.00
112 Tarvaris Jackson 4.00 10.00
113 Visanthe Shiancoe 5.00 12.00
120 Tom Brady 15.00 40.00
121 Wes Welker 5.00 12.00
122 Drew Brees 6.00 15.00
124 Marques Colston 4.00 10.00
125 Pierre Thomas 4.00 10.00
126 Reggie Bush 4.00 10.00
127 Robert Meachem 4.00 10.00
128 Ahmad Bradshaw 4.00 10.00
129 Brandon Jacobs 4.00 10.00
130 Eli Manning 5.00 12.00
131 Hakeem Nicks 4.00 10.00
132 Kevin Boss 4.00 10.00
134 Steve Smith USC 4.00 10.00
136 Darrelle Revis 4.00 10.00
141 Shonn Greene 4.00 10.00
144 Louis Murphy 4.00 10.00
150 DeSean Jackson 5.00 12.00
151 Jeremy Maclin 4.00 10.00
152 LeSean McCoy 6.00 15.00
153 Michael Vick 5.00 12.00
155 Heath Miller 4.00 10.00
156 Hines Ward 5.00 12.00
158 Mike Wallace 4.00 10.00
160 Troy Polamalu 6.00 15.00
161 Antonio Gates 4.00 10.00
162 Darren Sproles 5.00 12.00
163 Malcom Floyd 4.00 10.00
165 Philip Rivers 6.00 15.00
166 Ryan Mathews 5.00 12.00
169 Michael Crabtree 4.00 10.00
170 Patrick Willis 5.00 12.00
171 Alex Smith 5.00 12.00
172 Vernon Davis 4.00 10.00
176 Matt Hasselbeck 4.00 10.00
183 Steven Jackson 4.00 10.00
190 Bo Scaife 4.00 10.00
191 Chris Johnson 4.00 10.00
192 Kenny Britt 4.00 10.00
194 Randy Moss 5.00 12.00
195 Vince Young 4.00 10.00
196 Chris Cooley 4.00 10.00
199 LaRon Landry 4.00 10.00
200 Santana Moss 5.00 12.00

2011 Prestige Preferred Materials

RANDOM INSERTS IN PACKS
*PATCH/50: .6X TO 1.5X BASIC JSY/250
UNPRICED JSY AU PRINT RUN 10
UNPRICED PATCH AU PRINT RUN 5
1 Calvin Johnson 4.00 10.00
2 Dwayne Bowe 3.00 8.00
3 LeSean McCoy 4.00 10.00
4 Mark Sanchez 2.50 6.00
5 Matt Ryan 3.00 8.00
6 Michael Turner 2.50 6.00
7 Peyton Manning 8.00 20.00
8 Rashard Mendenhall 2.50 6.00
9 Sam Bradford 2.50 6.00
10 Tom Brady 10.00 25.00

2011 Prestige Preferred Signatures

STATED PRINT RUN 5-15
3 LeSean McCoy/15 15.00 40.00
4 Mark Sanchez/15 15.00 40.00
6 Michael Turner/15 10.00 25.00
8 Rashard Mendenhall/15 10.00 25.00
9 Sam Bradford/15 10.00 25.00

2011 Prestige Prestigious Pros Autographs

STATED PRINT RUN 5-25
3 Chris Wells 10.00 25.00
5 Brent Celek 10.00 25.00
7 C.J. Spiller 10.00 25.00
14 Darren Sproles 12.00 30.00
18 DeMarcus Ware 12.00 30.00
22 Donald Driver 15.00 40.00
24 Frank Gore 12.00 30.00
30 Jeremy Maclin 10.00 25.00
40 Rashard Mendenhall 10.00 25.00
42 Ronnie Brown 12.00 30.00
43 Ryan Grant 10.00 25.00
44 Ryan Mathews 12.00 30.00
45 Santonio Holmes 10.00 25.00
46 Sidney Rice 10.00 25.00

2011 Prestige Prestigious Pros Red

RANDOM INSERTS IN PACKS
*BLACK/25: 1.2X TO 3X BASIC RED
*GREEN/250: .5X TO 1.2X BASIC RED
*GOLD/100: .6X TO 1.5X BASIC RED
*PLATINUM/10: 2.5X TO 6X BASIC RED
1 Adrian Peterson 1.25 3.00
2 Anquan Boldin .75 2.00
3 Chris Wells .75 2.00
4 Brandon Marshall 1.00 2.50
5 Brent Celek .75 2.00
6 Braylon Edwards .75 2.00
7 C.J. Spiller .75 2.00
8 Cadillac Williams .75 2.00
9 Cedric Benson .75 2.00
10 Chad Greenway 1.00 2.50
11 Chad Henne 1.00 2.50
12 Clinton Portis .75 2.00
13 Dallas Clark .75 2.00
14 Darren Sproles 1.00 2.50
15 David Garrard .75 2.00
16 DeAngelo Hall .75 2.00
17 DeAngelo Williams .75 2.00
18 DeMarcus Ware 1.00 2.50
19 Devery Henderson .75 2.00
20 Devin Hester 1.00 2.50
21 Dez Bryant 1.25 3.00
22 Donald Driver 1.00 2.50
23 Dustin Keller 1.00 2.50
24 Frank Gore 1.00 2.50
25 Greg Olsen 1.00 2.50
26 Hakeem Nicks .75 2.00
27 Heath Miller .75 2.00
28 Jamaal Charles 1.00 2.50
29 Jared Allen .75 2.00
30 Jeremy Maclin .75 2.00
31 Johnny Knox .75 2.00
32 Josh Freeman 1.00 2.50
33 Julius Peppers 1.00 2.50
34 Kenny Britt .75 2.00
35 LaDainian Tomlinson 1.25 3.00
36 Lee Evans 1.00 2.50
37 Marques Colston .75 2.00
38 Nate Washington .75 2.00
39 Randy Moss 1.00 2.50
40 Rashard Mendenhall .75 2.00
41 Reggie Bush .75 2.00
42 Ronnie Brown 1.00 2.50
43 Ryan Grant .75 2.00
44 Ryan Mathews 1.00 2.50
45 Santonio Holmes .75 2.00
46 Sidney Rice .75 2.00
47 Terrell Suggs .75 2.00
48 Tim Tebow 1.25 3.00
49 Tony Romo 1.00 2.50
50 Visanthe Shiancoe 1.00 2.50

2011 Prestige Prestigious Pros Materials Green

GREEN STATED PRINT RUN 90-100
*BLACK/10: 1X TO 2.5X GREEN/90-100
*GOLD/50: .5X TO 1.2X GREEN/90-100
*PLATINUM/45-50: .6X TO 1.5X GRN/90-100
*RED/170-250: .3X TO .8X GREEN/90-100
1 Adrian Peterson/100 5.00 12.00
2 Anquan Boldin/100 3.00 8.00
3 Chris Wells/100 3.00 8.00
5 Brent Celek/100 3.00 8.00
6 Braylon Edwards/100 3.00 8.00
7 C.J. Spiller/100 3.00 8.00
8 Cadillac Williams/100 3.00 8.00
9 Cedric Benson/100 3.00 8.00
10 Chad Greenway/100 5.00 12.00
12 Clinton Portis/100 3.00 8.00
13 Dallas Clark/100 3.00 8.00
14 Darren Sproles/100 4.00 10.00
15 David Garrard/100 3.00 8.00
16 DeAngelo Hall/100 3.00 8.00
17 DeAngelo Williams/100 3.00 8.00
18 DeMarcus Ware/100 4.00 10.00
19 Devery Henderson/100 3.00 8.00
20 Devin Hester/100 4.00 10.00
21 Dez Bryant/90 5.00 12.00
22 Donald Driver/100 4.00 10.00
23 Dustin Keller/100 4.00 10.00
24 Frank Gore/100 4.00 10.00
25 Greg Olsen/100 4.00 10.00
26 Hakeem Nicks/100 3.00 8.00
27 Heath Miller/100 3.00 8.00
28 Jamaal Charles/100 4.00 10.00
29 Jared Allen/100 3.00 8.00
30 Jeremy Maclin/100 3.00 8.00
31 Johnny Knox/100 3.00 8.00
32 Josh Freeman/100 4.00 10.00
34 Kenny Britt/100 3.00 8.00
35 LaDainian Tomlinson/100 5.00 12.00
36 Lee Evans/100 4.00 10.00
37 Marques Colston/100 3.00 8.00
38 Nate Washington/100 3.00 8.00
39 Randy Moss/100 4.00 10.00
40 Rashard Mendenhall/100 3.00 8.00
41 Reggie Bush/100 3.00 8.00
42 Ronnie Brown/100 4.00 10.00
43 Ryan Grant/100 3.00 8.00
44 Ryan Mathews/100 4.00 10.00
45 Santonio Holmes/100 3.00 8.00
46 Sidney Rice/100 3.00 8.00
47 Terrell Suggs/100 3.00 8.00
48 Tim Tebow/100 8.00 20.00
49 Tony Romo/100 4.00 10.00
50 Visanthe Shiancoe/100 4.00 10.00

2011 Prestige Pro Helmets Autographs

RANDOM INSERTS IN PACKS
2 Da'Quan Bowers 8.00 20.00
3 Jake Locker 8.00 20.00
4 Ryan Williams 25.00 50.00
5 Von Miller 20.00 50.00
6 Aldon Smith 8.00 20.00
7 Delone Carter 8.00 20.00
8 Leonard Hankerson 8.00 20.00
9 Tandon Doss 8.00 20.00
11 D.J. Williams 8.00 20.00
12 A.J. Green 20.00 50.00
13 Mikel Leshoure 8.00 20.00
14 Julio Jones 20.00 50.00
15 Ronald Johnson 8.00 20.00
17 Titus Young 8.00 20.00
18 Prince Amukamara 8.00 20.00
19 DeMarco Murray 15.00 40.00
20 Jonathan Baldwin 8.00 20.00
21 Blaine Gabbert 8.00 20.00
22 Kyle Rudolph 8.00 20.00
23 Niles Paul 8.00 20.00
24 Ryan Mallett 8.00 20.00
26 Jacquizz Rodgers 8.00 20.00
27 Austin Pettis 8.00 20.00
28 Shane Vereen 10.00 25.00
29 Quinton Carter 8.00 20.00
30 Kendall Hunter 8.00 20.00
31 Jamie Harper 10.00 25.00
32 Daniel Thomas 8.00 20.00
33 Torrey Smith 8.00 20.00
34 Christian Ponder 8.00 20.00
35 Jerrel Jernigan 8.00 20.00
36 Randall Cobb 12.00 30.00
37 Jordan Todman 10.00 25.00
38 Martez Wilson 8.00 20.00

2011 Prestige Rookie Debut Autographed Patch

RANDOM INSERTS IN PACKS
1 Prince Amukamara 8.00 20.00
2 Randall Cobb 12.00 30.00
3 Blaine Gabbert 8.00 20.00
4 Mark Ingram 12.00 30.00
5 Julio Jones 25.00 60.00
6 Von Miller 20.00 50.00
7 Patrick Peterson 15.00 40.00
8 Aldon Smith 8.00 20.00

2011 Prestige Rookie Review

RANDOM INSERTS IN PACKS
1 Aaron Hernandez 1.00 2.50
2 Arrelious Benn .75 2.00
3 Blair White .75 2.00
4 Brandon LaFell .75 2.00
5 C.J. Spiller .75 2.00
6 Chris Ivory 1.00 2.50
7 Colt McCoy .75 2.00
8 Damian Williams .75 2.00
9 Danario Alexander .75 2.00
10 David Gettis .75 2.00
11 Demaryius Thomas 1.25 3.00
12 Devin McCourty .75 2.00
13 Dexter McCluster .75 2.00
14 Dez Bryant 1.25 3.00
15 Eric Berry 1.00 2.50
16 Eric Decker .75 2.00
17 Gerald McCoy .75 2.00
18 Golden Tate .75 2.00
19 Jacoby Ford 1.00 2.50
20 Jahvid Best .75 2.00
21 Jason Pierre-Paul .75 2.00
22 Jermaine Gresham .75 2.00
23 Jimmy Clausen .75 2.00
24 Jimmy Graham 1.25 3.00
25 Joe Haden .75 2.00
26 Jordan Shipley .75 2.00
27 Keiland Williams .75 2.00
28 LeGarrette Blount 1.00 2.50
29 Mardy Gilyard .75 2.00
30 Mike Williams 1.00 2.50
31 Ndamukong Suh 1.00 2.50
32 Marc Mariani 1.00 2.50
33 Rob Gronkowski 1.25 3.00
34 Rolando McClain .75 2.00
35 Ryan Mathews 1.00 2.50
36 Sam Bradford .75 2.00
37 Seyi Ajirotutu .75 2.00
38 Tim Tebow 1.25 3.00
39 T.J. Ward .75 2.00
40 Toby Gerhart 1.00 2.50

2011 Prestige Rookie Review Autographs

RANDOM INSERTS IN PACKS
2 Arrelious Benn 5.00 12.00
4 Brandon LaFell 5.00 12.00
5 C.J. Spiller 5.00 12.00
7 Colt McCoy 20.00 40.00
8 Damian Williams 5.00 12.00
16 Eric Decker 8.00 20.00
18 Golden Tate 5.00 12.00
23 Jimmy Clausen 5.00 12.00
34 Rolando McClain 5.00 12.00
35 Ryan Mathews 15.00 30.00
36 Sam Bradford 5.00 12.00
38 Tim Tebow 30.00 80.00
40 Toby Gerhart

2011 Prestige Rookie Review Materials Prime

*BASE JSY: .25X TO .6X PRIME JSY
RANDOM INSERTS IN PACKS
2 Arrelious Benn 4.00 10.00
4 Brandon LaFell 4.00 10.00
5 C.J. Spiller 4.00 10.00
7 Colt McCoy 4.00 10.00
8 Damian Williams 4.00 10.00
11 Demaryius Thomas 6.00 15.00
13 Dexter McCluster 4.00 10.00
14 Dez Bryant 6.00 15.00
15 Eric Berry 5.00 12.00
16 Eric Decker 4.00 10.00
17 Gerald McCoy 4.00 10.00
18 Golden Tate 4.00 10.00
20 Jahvid Best 4.00 10.00
22 Jermaine Gresham 4.00 10.00
23 Jimmy Clausen 4.00 10.00
26 Jordan Shipley 4.00 10.00
29 Mardy Gilyard 4.00 10.00
30 Mike Williams 5.00 12.00
31 Ndamukong Suh 8.00 20.00
33 Rob Gronkowski 6.00 15.00
34 Rolando McClain 4.00 10.00
35 Ryan Mathews 5.00 12.00
36 Sam Bradford 4.00 10.00
38 Tim Tebow 6.00 15.00
40 Toby Gerhart 5.00 12.00

2011 Prestige Stars of the NFL

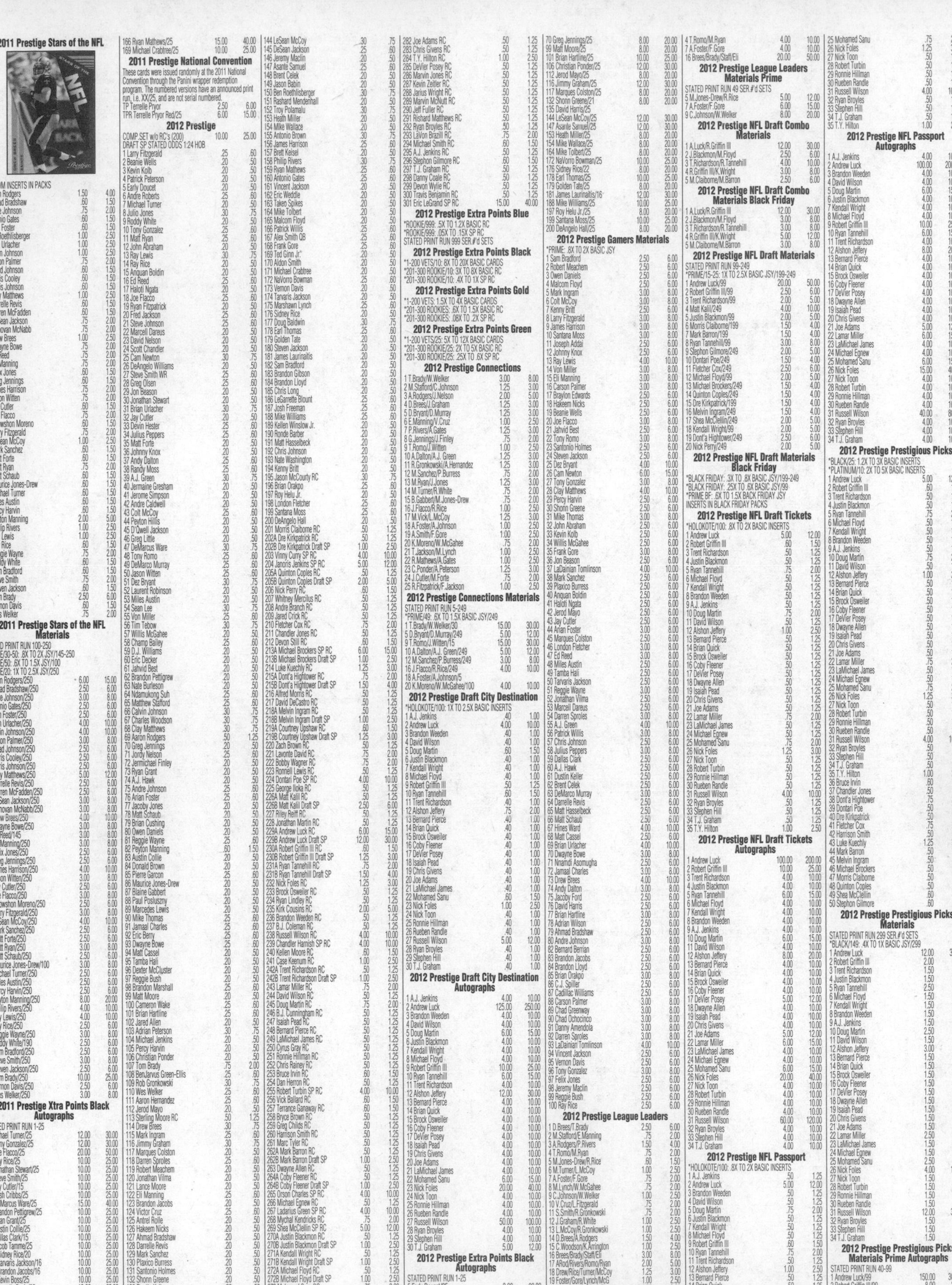

RANDOM INSERTS IN PACKS
1 Aaron Rodgers 1.50 4.00
2 Ahmad Bradshaw .60 1.50
3 Andre Johnson .75 2.00
4 Antonio Gates .60 1.50
5 Arian Foster .60 1.50
6 Ben Roethlisberger 1.00 2.50
7 Brian Urlacher 1.00 2.50
8 Calvin Johnson 1.00 2.50
9 Carson Palmer .75 2.00
10 Chad Johnson .60 1.50
11 Chris Cooley .60 1.50
12 Chris Johnson .60 1.50
13 Clay Matthews 1.00 2.50
14 Darrelle Revis .60 1.50
15 Darren McFadden .60 1.50
16 DeSean Jackson .75 2.00
17 Donovan McNabb .75 2.00
18 Drew Brees 1.00 2.50
19 Dwayne Bowe .75 2.00
20 Ed Reed .75 2.00
21 Eli Manning .75 2.00
22 Felix Jones .60 1.50
23 Greg Jennings .60 1.50
24 James Harrison .75 2.00
25 Jason Witten .75 2.00
26 Jay Cutler .60 1.50
27 Joe Flacco .75 2.00
28 Knowshon Moreno .60 1.50
29 Larry Fitzgerald .75 2.00
30 LeSean McCoy 1.00 2.50
31 Mark Sanchez .60 1.50
32 Matt Forte .60 1.50
33 Matt Ryan .75 2.00
34 Matt Schaub .60 1.50
35 Maurice Jones-Drew .60 1.50
36 Michael Turner .60 1.50
37 Miles Austin .60 1.50
38 Percy Harvin .60 1.50
39 Peyton Manning 2.00 5.00
40 Philip Rivers 1.00 2.50
41 Ray Lewis 1.00 2.50
42 Ray Rice .60 1.50
43 Reggie Wayne .75 2.00
44 Roddy White .60 1.50
45 Sam Bradford .60 1.50
46 Steve Smith .75 2.00
47 Steven Jackson .60 1.50
48 Tom Brady 2.50 6.00
49 Vernon Davis .60 1.50
50 Wes Welker .75 2.00

2011 Prestige Stars of the NFL Materials

STATED PRINT RUN 100-250
*PRIME/30-50: .8X TO 2X JSY/145-250
*PRIME/50: .6X TO 1.5X JSY/100
*PRIME/20: 1X TO 2.5X JSY/250
1 Aaron Rodgers/250 6.00 15.00
2 Ahmad Bradshaw/250 2.50 6.00
3 Andre Johnson/250 3.00 8.00
4 Antonio Gates/250 2.50 6.00
5 Arian Foster/250 2.50 6.00
7 Brian Urlacher/250 4.00 10.00
8 Calvin Johnson/250 4.00 10.00
9 Carson Palmer/250 3.00 8.00
10 Chad Johnson/250 2.50 6.00
11 Chris Cooley/250 2.50 6.00
12 Chris Johnson/250 2.50 6.00
13 Clay Matthews/250 5.00 12.00
14 Darrelle Revis/250 2.50 6.00
15 Darren McFadden/250 2.50 6.00
16 DeSean Jackson/250 3.00 8.00
17 Donovan McNabb/250 3.00 8.00
18 Drew Brees/250 4.00 10.00
19 Dwayne Bowe/250 3.00 8.00
20 Ed Reed/145 3.00 8.00
21 Eli Manning/250 3.00 8.00
22 Felix Jones/250 2.50 6.00
23 Greg Jennings/250 2.50 6.00
24 James Harrison/250 4.00 10.00
25 Jason Witten/250 3.00 8.00
26 Jay Cutler/250 2.50 6.00
27 Joe Flacco/250 3.00 8.00
28 Knowshon Moreno/250 2.50 6.00
29 Larry Fitzgerald/250 3.00 8.00
30 LeSean McCoy/250 4.00 10.00
31 Mark Sanchez/250 2.50 6.00
32 Matt Forte/250 2.50 6.00
33 Matt Ryan/250 3.00 8.00
34 Matt Schaub/250 2.50 6.00
35 Maurice Jones-Drew/100 3.00 8.00
36 Michael Turner/250 2.50 6.00
37 Miles Austin/250 2.50 6.00
38 Percy Harvin/250 2.50 6.00
39 Peyton Manning/250 8.00 20.00
40 Philip Rivers/250 4.00 10.00
41 Ray Lewis/250 4.00 10.00
42 Ray Rice/250 2.50 6.00
43 Reggie Wayne/250 3.00 8.00
44 Roddy White/190 2.50 6.00
45 Sam Bradford/250 2.50 6.00
46 Steve Smith/250 3.00 8.00
47 Steven Jackson/250 2.50 6.00
48 Tom Brady/250 10.00 25.00
49 Vernon Davis/250 2.50 6.00
50 Wes Welker/250 3.00 8.00

2011 Prestige Xtra Points Black Autographs

STATED PRINT RUN 1-25
9 Michael Turner/25 12.00 30.00
11 Tony Gonzalez/25 12.00 30.00
15 Joe Flacco/25 20.00 50.00
17 Ray Rice/25 10.00 25.00
30 Jonathan Stewart/25 10.00 25.00
31 Steve Smith/25 10.00 25.00
36 Jay Cutler/15 10.00 25.00
48 Josh Cribbs/25 10.00 25.00
51 DeMarcus Ware/25 15.00 40.00
64 Brandon Pettigrew/25 10.00 25.00
76 Ryan Grant/25 10.00 25.00
83 Austin Collie/25 10.00 25.00
84 Dallas Clark/15 10.00 25.00
86 Jacob Tamme/25 10.00 25.00
111 Sidney Rice/20 10.00 25.00
112 Tarvaris Jackson/16 10.00 25.00
129 Brandon Jacobs/16 10.00 25.00
132 Kevin Boss/25 10.00 25.00
136 Darrelle Revis/25 10.00 25.00
139 Mark Sanchez/15 15.00 40.00
140 Santonio Holmes/25 10.00 25.00
144 Louis Murphy/25 10.00 25.00
140 Bront Colok/17 10.00 25.00
150 DeSean Jackson/15 12.00 30.00
151 Jeremy Maclin/25 10.00 25.00
153 Michael Vick/25 15.00 40.00
159 Rashard Mendenhall/15 10.00 25.00
164 Mike Tolbert/25 10.00 25.00
165 Philip Rivers/15 25.00 50.00
166 Ryan Mathews/25 15.00 40.00
169 Michael Crabtree/25 10.00 25.00

2011 Prestige National Convention

These cards were issued randomly at the 2011 National Convention through the Panini wrapper redemption program. The numbered versions have an announced print run, i.e. XX/25, and are not serial numbered.
TP Terrelle Pryor 2.50 6.00
TPR Terrelle Pryor Red/25 6.00 15.00

2012 Prestige

COMP.SET w/o RC's (200) 10.00 25.00
DRAFT SP STATED ODDS 1:24 HOB
1 Larry Fitzgerald .25 .60
2 Beanie Wells .20 .50
3 Kevin Kolb .20 .50
4 Patrick Peterson .20 .50
5 Early Doucet .20 .50
6 Andre Roberts .25 .60
7 Michael Turner .20 .50
8 Julio Jones .30 .75
9 Roddy White .20 .50
10 Tony Gonzalez .25 .60
11 Matt Ryan .25 .60
12 John Abraham .20 .50
13 Ray Lewis .30 .75
14 Ray Rice .20 .50
15 Anquan Boldin .20 .50
16 Ed Reed .25 .60
17 Haloti Ngata .20 .50
18 Joe Flacco .25 .60
19 Ryan Fitzpatrick .20 .50
20 Fred Jackson .25 .60
21 Steve Johnson .25 .60
22 Marcell Dareus .20 .50
23 David Nelson .20 .50
24 Scott Chandler .20 .50
25 Cam Newton .30 .75
26 DeAngelo Williams .20 .50
27 Steve Smith WR .25 .60
28 Greg Olsen .25 .60
29 Jon Beason .20 .50
30 Jonathan Stewart .20 .50
31 Brian Urlacher .30 .75
32 Jay Cutler .20 .50
33 Devin Hester .25 .60
34 Julius Peppers .25 .60
35 Matt Forte .20 .50
36 Johnny Knox .20 .50
37 Andy Dalton .25 .60
38 Randy Moss .25 .60
39 A.J. Green .30 .75
40 Jermaine Gresham .20 .50
41 Jerome Simpson .20 .50
42 Andre Caldwell .20 .50
43 Colt McCoy .25 .60
44 Peyton Hillis .20 .50
45 D'Qwell Jackson .20 .50
46 Greg Little .20 .50
47 DeMarcus Ware .30 .75
48 Tony Romo .25 .60
49 DeMarco Murray .25 .60
50 Jason Witten .25 .60
51 Dez Bryant .30 .75
52 Laurent Robinson .20 .50
53 Miles Austin .20 .50
54 Sean Lee .30 .75
55 Von Miller .25 .60
56 Tim Tebow .30 .75
57 Willis McGahee .20 .50
58 Champ Bailey .25 .60
59 D.J. Williams .20 .50
60 Eric Decker .20 .50
61 Jahvid Best .20 .50
62 Brandon Pettigrew .20 .50
63 Nate Burleson .20 .50
64 Ndamukong Suh .25 .60
65 Matthew Stafford .25 .60
66 Calvin Johnson .30 .75
67 Charles Woodson .30 .75
68 Clay Matthews .30 .75
69 Aaron Rodgers .50 1.25
70 Greg Jennings .20 .50
71 Jordy Nelson .25 .60
72 Jermichael Finley .20 .50
73 Ryan Grant .20 .50
74 A.J. Hawk .20 .50
75 Andre Johnson .25 .60
76 Arian Foster .25 .60
77 Jacoby Jones .20 .50
78 Matt Schaub .20 .50
79 Brian Cushing .20 .50
80 Owen Daniels .20 .50
81 Reggie Wayne .25 .60
82 Peyton Manning .60 1.50
83 Austin Collie .20 .50
84 Donald Brown .20 .50
85 Pierre Garcon .25 .60
86 Maurice Jones-Drew .20 .50
87 Blaine Gabbert .20 .50
88 Paul Posluszny .20 .50
89 Marcedes Lewis .20 .50
90 Mike Thomas .25 .60
91 Jamaal Charles .25 .60
92 Eric Berry .25 .60
93 Dwayne Bowe .25 .60
94 Matt Cassel .20 .50
95 Tamba Hali .20 .50
96 Dexter McCluster .20 .50
97 Reggie Bush .20 .50
98 Brandon Marshall .25 .60
99 Matt Moore .20 .50
100 Cameron Wake .25 .60
101 Brian Hartline .25 .60
102 Jared Allen .20 .50
103 Adrian Peterson .30 .75
104 Michael Jenkins .20 .50
105 Percy Harvin .20 .50
106 Christian Ponder .20 .50
107 Tom Brady .75 2.00
108 BenJarvus Green-Ellis .25 .60
109 Rob Gronkowski .30 .75
110 Wes Welker .25 .60
111 Aaron Hernandez .25 .60
112 Jerod Mayo .20 .50
113 Sterling Moore RC .50 1.25
114 Drew Brees .30 .75
115 Mark Ingram .25 .60
116 Jimmy Graham .30 .75
117 Marques Colston .20 .50
118 Darren Sproles .25 .60
119 Robert Meachem .20 .50
120 Jonathan Vilma .20 .50
121 Lance Moore .20 .50
122 Eli Manning .25 .60
123 Brandon Jacobs .20 .50
124 Victor Cruz .25 .60
125 Antrel Rolle .20 .50
126 Hakeem Nicks .20 .50
127 Ahmad Bradshaw .20 .50
128 Darrelle Revis .20 .50
129 Mark Sanchez .20 .50
130 Plaxico Burress .20 .50
131 Santonio Holmes .20 .50
132 Shonn Greene .20 .50
133 Dustin Keller .20 .50
134 LaDainian Tomlinson .30 .75
135 David Harris .20 .50
136 Darren McFadden .20 .50
137 Terrelle Pryor .25 .60
138 Richard Seymour .20 .50
139 Carson Palmer .25 .60
140 Jacoby Ford .20 .50
141 Darrius Heyward-Bey .20 .50
142 Nnamdi Asomugha .20 .50
143 Michael Vick .25 .60
144 LeSean McCoy .30 .75
145 DeSean Jackson .25 .60
146 Jeremy Maclin .20 .50
147 Asante Samuel .25 .60
148 Brent Celek .20 .50
149 Jason Babin .20 .50
150 Ben Roethlisberger .30 .75
151 Rashard Mendenhall .20 .50
152 Troy Polamalu .30 .75
153 Heath Miller .20 .50
154 Mike Wallace .20 .50
155 Antonio Brown .30 .75
156 James Harrison .25 .60
157 Brett Keisel .20 .50
158 Philip Rivers .30 .75
159 Ryan Mathews .25 .60
160 Antonio Gates .25 .60
161 Vincent Jackson .20 .50
162 Eric Weddle .20 .50
163 Takeo Spikes .20 .50
164 Mike Tolbert .20 .50
165 Malcom Floyd .20 .50
166 Patrick Willis .25 .60
167 Alex Smith QB .25 .60
168 Frank Gore .25 .60
169 Ted Ginn Jr.* .20 .50
170 Aldon Smith .20 .50
171 Michael Crabtree .20 .50
172 NaVorro Bowman .25 .60
173 Vernon Davis .20 .50
174 Tarvaris Jackson .20 .50
175 Marshawn Lynch .25 .60
176 Sidney Rice .20 .50
177 Doug Baldwin .30 .75
178 Earl Thomas .25 .60
179 Golden Tate .20 .50
180 Steven Jackson .20 .50
181 James Laurinaitis .20 .50
182 Sam Bradford .20 .50
183 Brandon Gibson .20 .50
184 Brandon Lloyd .20 .50
185 Chris Long .20 .50
186 LeGarrette Blount .25 .60
187 Josh Freeman .25 .60
188 Mike Williams .25 .60
189 Kellen Winslow Jr. .20 .50
190 Ronde Barber .20 .50
191 Matt Hasselbeck .20 .50
192 Chris Johnson .20 .50
193 Nate Washington .20 .50
194 Kenny Britt .20 .50
195 Jason McCourty RC .30 .75
196 Brian Orakpo .25 .60
197 Roy Helu Jr. .20 .50
198 London Fletcher .25 .60
199 Santana Moss .25 .60
200 DeAngelo Hall .20 .50
201 Morris Claiborne RC .50 1.25
202A Dre Kirkpatrick RC .50 1.25
202B Dre Kirkpatrick Draft SP 1.00 2.50
203 Vinny Curry SP RC 4.00 10.00
204 Janoris Jenkins SP RC 5.00 12.00
205A Quinton Coples RC .50 1.25
205B Quinton Coples Draft SP 2.00 5.00
206 Nick Perry RC .60 1.50
207 Whitney Mercilus RC .50 1.25
208 Andre Branch RC .50 1.25
209 Jared Crick RC .50 1.25
210 Fletcher Cox RC .75 2.00
211 Chandler Jones RC .50 1.25
212 Devon Still RC .60 1.50
213A Michael Brockers SP RC 6.00 15.00
213B Michael Brockers Draft SP 1.00 2.50
214 Luke Kuechly RC 1.25 3.00
215A Dont'a Hightower RC .75 2.00
215B Dont'a Hightower Draft SP 1.50 4.00
216 Alfred Morris RC .50 1.25
217 David DeCastro RC .50 1.25
218A Melvin Ingram RC .50 1.25
218B Melvin Ingram Draft SP 1.00 2.50
219A Courtney Upshaw RC .60 1.50
219B Courtney Upshaw Draft SP 1.25 3.00
220 Zach Brown RC .50 1.25
221 Lavonte David RC .75 2.00
222 Bobby Wagner RC .75 2.00
223 Ronnell Lewis RC .50 1.25
224 Dontari Poe SP RC 4.00 10.00
225 George Iloka RC .50 1.25
226A Matt Kalil RC .50 1.25
226B Matt Kalil Draft SP 2.50 6.00
227 Riley Reiff RC .50 1.25
228 Jonathan Martin RC .50 1.25
229A Andrew Luck RC 6.00 15.00
229B Andrew Luck Draft SP 12.00 30.00
230A Robert Griffin III RC .60 1.50
230B Robert Griffin III Draft SP 1.25 3.00
231A Ryan Tannehill RC .75 2.00
231B Ryan Tannehill Draft SP 1.50 4.00
232 Nick Foles RC 1.25 3.00
233 Brock Osweiler RC .50 1.25
234 Ryan Lindley RC .50 1.25
235 Kirk Cousins RC 2.00 5.00
236 Brandon Weeden RC .50 1.25
237 B.J. Coleman RC .50 1.25
238 Russell Wilson RC 4.00 10.00
239 Chandler Harnish SP RC 4.00 10.00
240 Kellen Moore RC .60 1.50
241 Case Keenum RC 1.00 2.50
242A Trent Richardson RC .50 1.25
242B Trent Richardson Draft SP 1.00 2.50
243 Lamar Miller RC .75 2.00
244 David Wilson RC .50 1.25
245 Doug Martin RC .75 2.00
246 B.J. Cunningham RC .50 1.25
247 Isaiah Pead RC .50 1.25
248 Bernard Pierce RC .50 1.25
249 LaMichael James RC .50 1.25
250 Cyrus Gray RC .50 1.25
251 Ronnie Hillman RC .50 1.25
252 Chris Rainey RC .50 1.25
253 Bruce Irvin RC .60 1.50
254 Dan Herron RC .50 1.25
255 Robert Turbin SP RC 4.00 10.00
256 Vick Ballard RC .60 1.50
257 Terrance Ganaway RC .60 1.50
258 Bryce Brown RC .50 1.25
259 Greg Childs RC .50 1.25
260 Harrison Smith RC .50 1.25
261 Marc Tyler RC .50 1.25
262A Mark Barron RC .50 1.25
262B Mark Barron Draft SP 1.00 2.50
263 Dwayne Allen RC .50 1.25
264A Coby Fleener RC .50 1.25
264B Coby Fleener Draft SP 1.00 2.50
265 Orson Charles SP RC 4.00 10.00
266 Michael Egnew RC .50 1.25
267 Ladarius Green SP RC 4.00 10.00
268 Mychal Kendricks RC .75 2.00
269 Shea McClellin SP RC 5.00 12.00
270A Justin Blackmon RC .50 1.25
270B Justin Blackmon Draft SP 1.00 2.50
271A Kendall Wright RC .50 1.25
271B Kendall Wright Draft SP 1.00 2.50
272A Michael Floyd RC .50 1.25
272B Michael Floyd Draft SP 1.00 2.50
273 Mohamed Sanu RC .75 2.00
274 Alshon Jeffery RC 1.00 2.50
275A Rueben Randle RC .50 1.25
275B Rueben Randle Draft SP 2.00 5.00
276A Stephen Hill RC .50 1.25
276B Stephen Hill Draft SP 1.00 2.50
277 Nick Toon RC .50 1.25
278 Juron Criner RC .50 1.25
279 Keshawn Martin RC .60 1.50
280 Brian Quick RC .50 1.25
281 Tommy Streeter SP RC 4.00 10.00
282 Joe Adams RC .50 1.25
283 Chris Givens RC .50 1.25
284 T.Y. Hilton RC 1.00 2.50
285 DeVier Posey RC .50 1.25
286 Marvin Jones RC .50 1.25
287 Kevin Zeitler RC .50 1.25
288 Jarius Wright RC .50 1.25
289 Marvin McNutt RC .50 1.25
290 Jeff Fuller RC .50 1.25
291 Rishard Matthews RC .50 1.25
292 Ryan Broyles RC .50 1.25
293 LaVon Brazill RC .75 2.00
294 Michael Smith RC .60 1.50
295 A.J. Jenkins RC .50 1.25
296 Stephon Gilmore RC .60 1.50
297 T.J. Graham RC .50 1.25
298 Danny Coale RC .50 1.25
299 Devon Wylie RC .50 1.25
300 Travis Benjamin RC .50 1.25
301 Eric LeGrand SP RC 15.00 40.00

2012 Prestige Extra Points Blue

*ROOKIE/999: .5X TO 1.2X BASIC RC
*ROOKIE/999: .05X TO .15X SP RC
STATED PRINT RUN 999 SER.#'d SETS

2012 Prestige Extra Points Black

*1-200 VETS/10: 8X TO 20X BASIC CARDS
*201-300 ROOKIE/10: 3X TO 8X BASIC RC
*201-300 ROOKIE/10: .4X TO 1X SP RC

2012 Prestige Extra Points Gold

*1-200 VETS: 1.5X TO 4X BASIC CARDS
*201-300 ROOKIES: .6X TO 1.5X BASIC RC
*201-300 ROOKIES: .08X TO .2X SP RC

2012 Prestige Extra Points Green

*1-200 VETS/25: 5X TO 12X BASIC CARDS
*201-300 ROOKIE/25: 2X TO 5X BASIC RC
*201-300 ROOKIE/25: .25X TO .6X SP RC

2012 Prestige Connections

1 T.Brady/W.Welker 3.00 8.00
2 M.Stafford/C.Johnson 1.25 3.00
3 A.Rodgers/J.Nelson 2.00 5.00
4 D.Brees/J.Graham 1.25 3.00
5 D.Bryant/D.Murray 1.25 3.00
6 E.Manning/V.Cruz 1.00 2.50
7 P.Rivers/A.Gates 1.25 3.00
8 G.Jennings/J.Finley .75 2.00
9 T.Romo/J.Witten 1.00 2.50
10 A.Dalton/A.J. Green 1.25 3.00
11 R.Gronkowski/A.Hernandez 1.25 3.00
12 M.Sanchez/P.Burress .75 2.00
13 M.Ryan/J.Jones 1.25 3.00
14 M.Turner/R.White .75 2.00
15 B.Gabbert/M.Jones-Drew .75 2.00
16 J.Flacco/R.Rice 1.00 2.50
17 M.Vick/L.McCoy 1.25 3.00
18 A.Foster/A.Johnson 1.00 2.50
19 A.Smith/F.Gore 1.00 2.50
20 K.Moreno/W.McGahee .75 2.00
21 T.Jackson/M.Lynch 1.00 2.50
22 R.Mathews/A.Gates 1.00 2.50
23 C.Ponder/A.Peterson 1.25 3.00
24 J.Cutler/M.Forte .75 2.00
25 R.Fitzpatrick/F.Jackson 1.00 2.50

2012 Prestige Connections Materials

STATED PRINT RUN 5-249
*PRIME/49: .6X TO 1.5X BASIC JSY/249
1 T.Brady/W.Welker/30 15.00 30.00
5 D.Bryant/D.Murray/249 5.00 12.00
9 T.Romo/J.Witten/15 15.00 30.00
10 A.Dalton/A.J. Green/249 5.00 12.00
12 M.Sanchez/P.Burress/249 3.00 8.00
16 J.Flacco/R.Rice/249 4.00 10.00
18 A.Foster/A.Johnson/5
20 K.Moreno/W.McGahee/100 4.00 10.00

2012 Prestige Draft City Destination

*HOLOKOTE/100: 1X TO 2.5X BASIC INSERTS
1 A.J. Jenkins .40 1.00
2 Andrew Luck 4.00 10.00
3 Brandon Weeden .40 1.00
4 David Wilson .40 1.00
5 Doug Martin .60 1.50
6 Justin Blackmon .40 1.00
7 Kendall Wright .40 1.00
8 Michael Floyd .40 1.00
9 Robert Griffin III .50 1.25
10 Ryan Tannehill .60 1.50
11 Trent Richardson .40 1.00
12 Alshon Jeffery .75 2.00
13 Bernard Pierce .40 1.00
14 Brian Quick .40 1.00
15 Brock Osweiler .40 1.00
16 Coby Fleener .40 1.00
17 DeVier Posey .40 1.00
18 Isaiah Pead .40 1.00
19 Chris Givens .40 1.00
20 Joe Adams .40 1.00
21 LaMichael James .40 1.00
22 Mohamed Sanu .60 1.50
23 Nick Foles 1.00 2.50
24 Nick Toon .40 1.00
25 Ronnie Hillman .40 1.00
26 Rueben Randle .40 1.00
27 Russell Wilson 5.00 12.00
28 Ryan Broyles .40 1.00
29 Stephen Hill .40 1.00
30 T.J. Graham .40 1.00

2012 Prestige Draft City Destination Autographs

1 A.J. Jenkins 4.00 10.00
2 Andrew Luck 125.00 250.00
3 Brandon Weeden 4.00 10.00
4 David Wilson 4.00 10.00
5 Doug Martin 6.00 15.00
6 Justin Blackmon 4.00 10.00
7 Kendall Wright 4.00 10.00
8 Michael Floyd 4.00 10.00
9 Robert Griffin III 10.00 25.00
10 Ryan Tannehill 6.00 15.00
11 Trent Richardson 4.00 10.00
12 Alshon Jeffery 12.00 30.00
13 Bernard Pierce 4.00 10.00
14 Brian Quick 4.00 10.00
15 Brock Osweiler 4.00 10.00
16 Coby Fleener 4.00 10.00
17 DeVier Posey 4.00 10.00
18 Isaiah Pead 4.00 10.00
19 Chris Givens 4.00 10.00
20 Joe Adams 4.00 10.00
21 LaMichael James 4.00 10.00
22 Mohamed Sanu 6.00 15.00
23 Nick Foles 20.00 40.00
24 Nick Toon 4.00 10.00
25 Ronnie Hillman 4.00 10.00
26 Rueben Randle 4.00 10.00
27 Russell Wilson 50.00 100.00
28 Ryan Broyles 4.00 10.00
29 Stephen Hill 4.00 10.00
30 T.J. Graham 5.00 12.00

2012 Prestige Extra Points Black Autographs

STATED PRINT RUN 1-25
5 Early Doucet/25 8.00 20.00
6 Andre Roberts/25 10.00 25.00
8 Julio Jones/16 12.00 30.00
23 David Nelson/25 8.00 20.00
27 Steve Smith WR/25 10.00 25.00
28 Greg Olsen/25 10.00 25.00
30 Jonathan Stewart/25 8.00 20.00
33 Devin Hester/15
37 Andy Dalton/25 15.00 40.00
39 A.J. Green/25 15.00 40.00
44 Peyton Hillis/23 8.00 20.00
70 Greg Jennings/25 8.00 20.00
99 Matt Moore/25 8.00 20.00
101 Brian Hartline/25 10.00 25.00
106 Christian Ponder/25 12.00 30.00
112 Jerod Mayo/25 8.00 20.00
116 Jimmy Graham/25 12.00 30.00
117 Marques Colston/25 8.00 20.00
132 Shonn Greene/21 8.00 20.00
135 David Harris/25
144 LeSean McCoy/25 12.00 30.00
147 Asante Samuel/25 12.00 30.00
153 Heath Miller/25 8.00 20.00
154 Mike Wallace/25 8.00 20.00
164 Mike Tolbert/25 8.00 20.00
172 NaVorro Bowman/25 10.00 25.00
176 Sidney Rice/22 8.00 20.00
178 Earl Thomas/25 10.00 25.00
179 Golden Tate/25 8.00 20.00
181 James Laurinaitis/16 12.00 30.00
188 Mike Williams/25 10.00 25.00
197 Roy Helu Jr./25 8.00 20.00
199 Santana Moss/25 10.00 25.00
200 DeAngelo Hall/25 8.00 20.00

2012 Prestige Gamers Materials

*PRIME: .8X TO 2X BASIC JSY
1 Sam Bradford 2.50 6.00
2 Robert Meachem 2.50 6.00
3 Owen Daniels 2.50 6.00
4 Malcom Floyd 2.50 6.00
5 Mark Ingram 3.00 8.00
6 Colt McCoy 3.00 8.00
7 Kenny Britt 2.50 6.00
8 Larry Fitzgerald 3.00 8.00
9 James Harrison 3.00 8.00
10 Santana Moss 3.00 8.00
11 Joseph Addai 2.50 6.00
12 Johnny Knox 2.50 6.00
13 Ray Lewis 4.00 10.00
14 Von Miller 3.00 8.00
15 Eli Manning 3.00 8.00
16 Carson Palmer 3.00 8.00
17 Braylon Edwards 2.50 6.00
18 Hakeem Nicks 2.50 6.00
19 Beanie Wells 2.50 6.00
20 Joe Flacco 3.00 8.00
21 Jahvid Best 2.50 6.00
22 Tony Romo 3.00 8.00
23 Santonio Holmes 2.50 6.00
24 Steven Jackson 2.50 6.00
25 Dez Bryant 4.00 10.00
26 Cam Newton 6.00 15.00
27 Tony Gonzalez 3.00 8.00
28 Clay Matthews 4.00 10.00
29 Percy Harvin 2.50 6.00
30 Shonn Greene 2.50 6.00
31 Mike Thomas 3.00 8.00
32 John Abraham 2.50 6.00
33 Kevin Kolb 2.50 6.00
34 Willis McGahee 2.50 6.00
35 Frank Gore 3.00 8.00
36 Jon Beason 2.50 6.00
37 LaDainian Tomlinson 4.00 10.00
38 Mark Sanchez 2.50 6.00
39 Plaxico Burress 2.50 6.00
40 Anquan Boldin 2.50 6.00
41 Haloti Ngata 2.50 6.00
42 Jerod Mayo 2.50 6.00
43 Jay Cutler 2.50 6.00
44 Arian Foster 3.00 8.00
45 Marques Colston 2.50 6.00
46 London Fletcher 3.00 8.00
47 Ed Reed 3.00 8.00
48 Miles Austin 2.50 6.00
49 Tamba Hali 2.50 6.00
50 Tarvaris Jackson 2.50 6.00
51 Reggie Wayne 3.00 8.00
52 Jonathan Vilma 2.50 6.00
53 Marcell Dareus 2.50 6.00
54 Darren Sproles 3.00 8.00
55 A.J. Green 4.00 10.00
56 Patrick Willis 3.00 8.00
57 Chris Johnson 2.50 6.00
58 Julius Peppers 3.00 8.00
59 Dallas Clark 2.50 6.00
60 A.J. Hawk 2.50 6.00
61 Dustin Keller 2.50 6.00
62 Brent Celek 2.50 6.00
63 DeMarco Murray 3.00 8.00
64 Darrelle Revis 2.50 6.00
65 Matt Hasselbeck 2.50 6.00
66 Matt Schaub 2.50 6.00
67 Hines Ward 4.00 10.00
68 Matt Cassel 2.50 6.00
69 Brian Urlacher 4.00 10.00
70 Dwayne Bowe 3.00 8.00
71 Nnamdi Asomugha 2.50 6.00
72 Jamaal Charles 3.00 8.00
73 Drew Brees 4.00 10.00
74 Andy Dalton 3.00 8.00
75 Jacoby Ford 2.50 6.00
76 David Harris 2.50 6.00
77 Brian Hartline 3.00 8.00
78 Adrian Wilson 2.50 6.00
79 Ahmad Bradshaw 2.50 6.00
80 Andre Johnson 3.00 8.00
82 Bernard Berrian 2.50 6.00
83 Brandon Jacobs 2.50 6.00
84 Brandon Lloyd 2.50 6.00
85 Brian Orakpo 3.00 8.00
86 C.J. Spiller 2.50 6.00
87 Cadillac Williams 2.50 6.00
88 Carson Palmer 3.00 8.00
89 Chad Greenway 3.00 8.00
90 Chad Ochocinco 3.00 8.00
91 Danny Amendola 3.00 8.00
92 Darren Sproles 3.00 8.00
93 LaDainian Tomlinson 4.00 10.00
94 Vincent Jackson 2.50 6.00
95 Vernon Davis 2.50 6.00
96 Tony Gonzalez 3.00 8.00
97 Felix Jones 2.50 6.00
98 Jeremy Maclin 2.50 6.00
99 Reggie Bush 2.50 6.00
100 Ray Rice 2.50 6.00

2012 Prestige League Leaders

1 D.Brees/T.Brady 2.50 6.00
2 M.Stafford/E.Manning .75 2.00
3 A.Rodgers/P.Rivers 1.50 4.00
4 T.Romo/M.Ryan .75 2.00
5 M.Jones-Drew/R.Rice .60 1.50
6 M.Turner/L.McCoy 1.00 2.50
7 A.Foster/F.Gore .75 2.00
8 M.Lynch/W.McGahee .75 2.00
9 C.Johnson/W.Welker 1.00 2.50
10 V.Cruz/L.Fitzgerald .75 2.00
11 S.Smith/R.Gronkowski .75 2.00
12 J.Graham/R.White 1.00 2.50
13 L.McCoy/R.Gronkowski 1.00 2.50
14 D.Brees/A.Rodgers 1.50 4.00
15 C.Woodson/K.Arrington 1.00 2.50
16 Brees/Brady/Staff/Eli 3.00 8.00
17 ARod/Rivers/Romo/Ryan 2.00 5.00
18 Drew/Rice/Turner/McCoy 1.25 3.00
19 Foster/Gore/Lynch/McG 1.00 2.50
20 CJohn/Welker/Cruz/Fitz 1.25 3.00
21 Smith/Gronk/Graham/White 1.00 2.50
22 Gronk/CJohn/McCoy/Cam 1.25 3.00
23 Brees/ARod/Staff/Brady 3.00 8.00
24 Weddle/Wood/Arrgtn/Wbstr 1.25 3.00
25 Allen/Ware/Babin/JPP 1.25 3.00

2012 Prestige League Leaders Materials

STATED PRINT RUN 249 SER.#'d SETS
1 D.Brees/T.Brady 12.00 30.00
4 T.Romo/M.Ryan 4.00 10.00
7 A.Foster/F.Gore 4.00 10.00
16 Brees/Brady/Staff/Eli 20.00 50.00

2012 Prestige League Leaders Materials Prime

STATED PRINT RUN 49 SER.#'d SETS
5 M.Jones-Drew/R.Rice 5.00 12.00
7 A.Foster/F.Gore 6.00 15.00
9 C.Johnson/W.Welker 8.00 20.00

2012 Prestige NFL Draft Combo Materials

1 A.Luck/R.Griffin III 12.00 30.00
2 J.Blackmon/M.Floyd 2.50 6.00
3 T.Richardson/R.Tannehill 4.00 10.00
4 R.Griffin III/K.Wright 3.00 8.00
5 M.Claiborne/M.Barron 2.50 6.00

2012 Prestige NFL Draft Combo Materials Black Friday

1 A.Luck/R.Griffin III 12.00 30.00
2 J.Blackmon/M.Floyd 3.00 8.00
3 T.Richardson/R.Tannehill 3.00 8.00
4 R.Griffin III/K.Wright 5.00 12.00
5 M.Claiborne/M.Barron 3.00 8.00

2012 Prestige NFL Draft Materials

STATED PRINT RUN 99-249
*PRIME/15-25: 1X TO 2.5X BASIC JSY/199-249
1 Andrew Luck/99 20.00 50.00
2 Robert Griffin III/99 2.50 6.00
3 Trent Richardson/99 2.00 5.00
4 Matt Kalil/249 4.00 10.00
5 Justin Blackmon/99 2.00 5.00
6 Morris Claiborne/199 1.50 4.00
7 Mark Barron/199 1.50 4.00
8 Ryan Tannehill/99 3.00 8.00
9 Stephon Gilmore/249 2.00 5.00
10 Dontari Poe/249 1.50 4.00
11 Fletcher Cox/249 2.50 6.00
12 Michael Floyd/99 2.00 5.00
13 Michael Brockers/249 1.50 4.00
14 Quinton Coples/249 1.50 4.00
15 Dre Kirkpatrick/199 1.50 4.00
16 Melvin Ingram/249 1.50 4.00
17 Shea McClellin/249 2.00 5.00
18 Kendall Wright/99 2.00 5.00
19 Dont'a Hightower/249 2.50 6.00
20 Nick Perry/249 2.00 5.00

2012 Prestige NFL Draft Materials Black Friday

*BLACK FRIDAY: .3X TO .8X BASIC JSY/199-249
*BLACK FRIDAY: .25X TO .6X BASIC JSY/99
*PRIME BF: .6X TO 1.5X BACK FRIDAY JSY
INSERTS IN BLACK FRIDAY PACKS

2012 Prestige NFL Draft Tickets

*HOLOKOTE/100: .8X TO 2X BASIC INSERTS
1 Andrew Luck 5.00 12.00
2 Robert Griffin III .60 1.50
3 Trent Richardson .50 1.25
4 Justin Blackmon .50 1.25
5 Ryan Tannehill .75 2.00
6 Michael Floyd .50 1.25
7 Kendall Wright .50 1.25
8 Brandon Weeden .50 1.25
9 A.J. Jenkins .50 1.25
10 Doug Martin .75 2.00
11 David Wilson .50 1.25
12 Alshon Jeffery 1.00 2.50
13 Bernard Pierce .50 1.25
14 Brian Quick .50 1.25
15 Brock Osweiler .50 1.25
16 Coby Fleener .50 1.25
17 DeVier Posey .50 1.25
18 Dwayne Allen .50 1.25
19 Isaiah Pead .50 1.25
20 Chris Givens .50 1.25
21 Joe Adams .50 1.25
22 Lamar Miller .75 2.00
23 LaMichael James .50 1.25
24 Michael Egnew .50 1.25
25 Mohamed Sanu .75 2.00
26 Nick Foles 1.25 3.00
27 Nick Toon .50 1.25
28 Robert Turbin .50 1.25
29 Ronnie Hillman .50 1.25
30 Rueben Randle .50 1.25
31 Russell Wilson 4.00 10.00
32 Ryan Broyles .50 1.25
33 Stephen Hill .50 1.25
34 T.J. Graham .50 1.25
35 T.Y. Hilton 1.00 2.50

2012 Prestige NFL Draft Tickets Autographs

1 Andrew Luck 100.00 200.00
2 Robert Griffin III 10.00 25.00
3 Trent Richardson 4.00 10.00
4 Justin Blackmon 4.00 10.00
5 Ryan Tannehill 6.00 15.00
6 Michael Floyd 4.00 10.00
7 Kendall Wright 4.00 10.00
8 Brandon Weeden 4.00 10.00
9 A.J. Jenkins 4.00 10.00
10 Doug Martin 6.00 15.00
11 David Wilson 4.00 10.00
12 Alshon Jeffery 8.00 20.00
13 Bernard Pierce 4.00 10.00
14 Brian Quick 4.00 10.00
15 Brock Osweiler 4.00 10.00
16 Coby Fleener 4.00 10.00
17 DeVier Posey 5.00 12.00
18 Dwayne Allen 4.00 10.00
19 Isaiah Pead 4.00 10.00
20 Chris Givens 4.00 10.00
21 Joe Adams 5.00 12.00
22 Lamar Miller 6.00 15.00
23 LaMichael James 4.00 10.00
24 Michael Egnew 4.00 10.00
25 Mohamed Sanu 6.00 15.00
26 Nick Foles 20.00 40.00
27 Nick Toon 4.00 10.00
28 Robert Turbin 4.00 10.00
29 Ronnie Hillman 4.00 10.00
30 Rueben Randle 4.00 10.00
31 Russell Wilson 60.00 120.00
32 Ryan Broyles 4.00 10.00
33 Stephen Hill 4.00 10.00
34 T.J. Graham 4.00 10.00

2012 Prestige NFL Passport

*HOLOKOTE/100: .8X TO 2X BASIC INSERTS
1 A.J. Jenkins .50 1.25
2 Andrew Luck 5.00 12.00
3 Brandon Weeden .50 1.25
4 David Wilson .50 1.25
5 Doug Martin .75 2.00
6 Justin Blackmon .50 1.25
7 Kendall Wright .50 1.25
8 Michael Floyd .50 1.25
9 Robert Griffin III .60 1.50
10 Ryan Tannehill .75 2.00
11 Trent Richardson .50 1.25
12 Alshon Jeffery 1.00 2.50
13 Bernard Pierce .50 1.25
14 Brian Quick .50 1.25
15 Brock Osweiler .50 1.25
16 Coby Fleener .50 1.25
17 DeVier Posey .50 1.25
18 Dwayne Allen .50 1.25
19 Isaiah Pead .50 1.25
20 Chris Givens .50 1.25
21 Joe Adams .50 1.25
22 Lamar Miller .75 2.00
23 LaMichael James .50 1.25
24 Michael Egnew .50 1.25
25 Mohamed Sanu .75 2.00
26 Nick Foles 1.25 3.00
27 Nick Toon .50 1.25
28 Robert Turbin .50 1.25
29 Ronnie Hillman .50 1.25
30 Rueben Randle .50 1.25
31 Russell Wilson 4.00 10.00
32 Ryan Broyles .50 1.25
33 Stephen Hill .50 1.25
34 T.J. Graham .50 1.25
35 T.Y. Hilton 1.00 2.50

2012 Prestige NFL Passport Autographs

1 A.J. Jenkins 4.00 10.00
2 Andrew Luck 100.00 200.00
3 Brandon Weeden 4.00 10.00
4 David Wilson 4.00 10.00
5 Doug Martin 6.00 15.00
6 Justin Blackmon 4.00 10.00
7 Kendall Wright 4.00 10.00
8 Michael Floyd 4.00 10.00
9 Robert Griffin III 10.00 25.00
10 Ryan Tannehill 6.00 15.00
11 Trent Richardson 4.00 10.00
12 Alshon Jeffery 8.00 20.00
13 Bernard Pierce 4.00 10.00
14 Brian Quick 4.00 10.00
15 Brock Osweiler 4.00 10.00
16 Coby Fleener 4.00 10.00
17 DeVier Posey 4.00 10.00
18 Dwayne Allen 4.00 10.00
19 Isaiah Pead 4.00 10.00
20 Chris Givens 4.00 10.00
21 Joe Adams 5.00 12.00
22 Lamar Miller 6.00 15.00
23 LaMichael James 4.00 10.00
24 Michael Egnew 4.00 10.00
25 Mohamed Sanu 6.00 15.00
26 Nick Foles 15.00 40.00
27 Nick Toon 4.00 10.00
28 Robert Turbin 4.00 10.00
29 Ronnie Hillman 4.00 10.00
30 Rueben Randle 4.00 10.00
31 Russell Wilson 40.00 80.00
32 Ryan Broyles 4.00 10.00
33 Stephen Hill 4.00 10.00
34 T.J. Graham 4.00 10.00

2012 Prestige Prestigious Picks

*BLACK/25: 1.2X TO 3X BASIC INSERTS
*PLATINUM/10: 2X TO 5X BASIC INSERTS
1 Andrew Luck 5.00 12.00
2 Robert Griffin III .60 1.50
3 Trent Richardson .50 1.25
4 Justin Blackmon .50 1.25
5 Ryan Tannehill .75 2.00
6 Michael Floyd .50 1.25
7 Kendall Wright .50 1.25
8 Brandon Weeden .50 1.25
9 A.J. Jenkins .50 1.25
10 Doug Martin .75 2.00
11 David Wilson .50 1.25
12 Alshon Jeffery 1.00 2.50
13 Bernard Pierce .50 1.25
14 Brian Quick .50 1.25
15 Brock Osweiler .50 1.25
16 Coby Fleener .50 1.25
17 DeVier Posey .50 1.25
18 Dwayne Allen .50 1.25
19 Isaiah Pead .50 1.25
20 Chris Givens .50 1.25
21 Joe Adams .50 1.25
22 Lamar Miller .75 2.00
23 LaMichael James .50 1.25
24 Michael Egnew .50 1.25
25 Mohamed Sanu .75 2.00
26 Nick Foles 1.25 3.00
27 Nick Toon .50 1.25
28 Robert Turbin .50 1.25
29 Ronnie Hillman .50 1.25
30 Rueben Randle .50 1.25
31 Russell Wilson 4.00 10.00
32 Ryan Broyles .50 1.25
33 Stephen Hill .50 1.25
34 T.J. Graham .50 1.25
35 T.Y. Hilton 1.00 2.50
36 Bruce Irvin .60 1.50
37 Chandler Jones .50 1.25
38 Dont'a Hightower .75 2.00
39 Dontari Poe .50 1.25
40 Dre Kirkpatrick .50 1.25
41 Fletcher Cox .75 2.00
42 Harrison Smith .50 1.25
43 Luke Kuechly 1.25 3.00
44 Mark Barron .50 1.25
45 Melvin Ingram .50 1.25
46 Michael Brockers .50 1.25
47 Morris Claiborne .50 1.25
48 Quinton Coples .50 1.25
49 Shea McClellin .60 1.50
50 Stephon Gilmore .60 1.50

2012 Prestige Prestigious Picks Materials

STATED PRINT RUN 299 SER.#'d SETS
*BLACK/149: .4X TO 1X BASIC JSY/299
1 Andrew Luck 12.00 30.00
2 Robert Griffin III 2.00 5.00
3 Trent Richardson 1.50 4.00
4 Justin Blackmon 1.50 4.00
5 Ryan Tannehill 2.50 6.00
6 Michael Floyd 1.50 4.00
7 Kendall Wright 1.50 4.00
8 Brandon Weeden 1.50 4.00
9 A.J. Jenkins 1.50 4.00
10 Doug Martin 2.50 6.00
11 David Wilson 1.50 4.00
12 Alshon Jeffery 3.00 8.00
13 Bernard Pierce 1.50 4.00
14 Brian Quick 1.50 4.00
15 Brock Osweiler 1.50 4.00
16 Coby Fleener 1.50 4.00
17 DeVier Posey 1.50 4.00
18 Dwayne Allen 1.50 4.00
19 Isaiah Pead 1.50 4.00
20 Chris Givens 1.50 4.00
21 Joe Adams 1.50 4.00
22 Lamar Miller 2.50 6.00
23 LaMichael James 1.50 4.00
24 Michael Egnew 1.50 4.00
25 Mohamed Sanu 2.50 6.00
26 Nick Foles 4.00 10.00
27 Nick Toon 1.50 4.00
28 Robert Turbin 1.50 4.00
29 Ronnie Hillman 1.50 4.00
30 Rueben Randle 1.50 4.00
31 Russell Wilson 12.00 30.00
32 Ryan Broyles 1.50 4.00
33 Stephen Hill 1.50 4.00
34 T.J. Graham 1.50 4.00

2012 Prestige Prestigious Picks Materials Prime Autographs

STATED PRINT RUN 40-99
1 Andrew Luck/99 150.00 300.00
2 Robert Griffin III/99 8.00 20.00
3 Trent Richardson/99 6.00 15.00
4 Justin Blackmon/99 6.00 15.00
5 Ryan Tannehill/99 10.00 25.00
6 Michael Floyd/99 10.00 25.00
7 Kendall Wright/99 6.00 15.00
8 Brandon Weeden/99 6.00 15.00
9 A.J. Jenkins/99 6.00 15.00
10 Doug Martin/99 10.00 25.00
11 David Wilson/99 6.00 15.00
12 Alshon Jeffery/99 15.00 40.00

13 Bernard Pierce/99 6.00 15.00
14 Brian Quick/99 6.00 15.00
15 Brock Osweiler/99 6.00 15.00
16 Coby Fleener/99 6.00 15.00
17 DeVier Posey/99 6.00 15.00
18 Dwayne Allen/99 6.00 15.00
19 Isaiah Pead/99 6.00 15.00
20 Chris Givens/99 6.00 15.00
21 Joe Adams/99 6.00 15.00
22 Lamar Miller/99 10.00 25.00
23 LaMichael James/99 6.00 15.00
24 Michael Egnew/99 6.00 15.00
25 Mohamed Sanu/99 12.00 30.00
26 Nick Foles/99 30.00 60.00
27 Nick Toon/99 15.00 40.00
28 Robert Turbin/99 6.00 15.00
29 Ronnie Hillman/99 6.00 15.00
30 Rueben Randle/99 15.00 40.00
31 Russell Wilson/99 75.00 150.00
32 Ryan Broyles/99 6.00 15.00
33 Stephen Hill/99 6.00 15.00
34 T.J. Graham/40 6.00 15.00

2012 Prestige Rookie Autographs

STATED PRINT RUN 183-999
EXCH EXPIRATION: 12/27/2013
201 Morris Claiborne/249 4.00 10.00
202 Dre Kirkpatrick/499 EXCH 3.00 8.00
205A Quinton Coples/799 3.00 8.00
205B Quinton Coples Draft 5.00 12.00
206 Nick Perry/499 4.00 10.00
207 Whitney Mercilus/899 3.00 8.00
208 Andre Branch/899 3.00 8.00
209 Jared Crick/899 5.00 12.00
210 Fletcher Cox/799 5.00 12.00
212 Devon Still/899 4.00 10.00
213A Michael Brockers/899 3.00 8.00
213B Michael Brockers Draft 5.00 12.00
214 Luke Kuechly/799 10.00 25.00
215A Dont'a Hightower/499 6.00 15.00
215B Dont'a Hightower Draft 10.00 25.00
216 Alfred Morris/899 3.00 8.00
217 David DeCastro/899 3.00 8.00
218 Melvin Ingram/499 3.00 8.00
219A Courtney Upshaw/599 4.00 10.00
219B Courtney Upshaw Draft 6.00 15.00
222 Bobby Wagner/799 5.00 12.00
224 Dontari Poe/899 3.00 8.00
225 George Iloka/899 3.00 8.00
226A Matt Kalil/899 3.00 8.00
226B Matt Kalil Draft 5.00 12.00
227 Riley Reiff/899 6.00 15.00
228 Jonathan Martin/899 3.00 8.00
229A Andrew Luck/299 75.00 150.00
229B Andrew Luck Draft 100.00 200.00
230A Robert Griffin III/299 12.00 30.00
230B Robert Griffin III Draft 20.00 50.00
231A Ryan Tannehill/299 6.00 15.00
231B Ryan Tannehill Draft 10.00 25.00
232 Nick Foles/499 12.00 30.00
233 Brock Osweiler/299 4.00 10.00
235 Kirk Cousins/299 15.00 40.00
236 Brandon Weeden/299 4.00 10.00
238 Russell Wilson/499 50.00 100.00
240 Kellen Moore/499 4.00 10.00
242A Trent Richardson/299 4.00 10.00
242B Trent Richardson Draft 5.00 12.00
243 Lamar Miller/499 5.00 12.00
244 David Wilson/499 3.00 8.00
245 Doug Martin/499 5.00 12.00
247 Isaiah Pead/499 3.00 8.00
248 Bernard Pierce/286 4.00 10.00
249 LaMichael James/499 3.00 8.00
250 Cyrus Gray/499 3.00 8.00
254 Dan Herron/799 3.00 8.00
255 Robert Turbin/349 4.00 10.00
256 Vick Ballard/699 4.00 10.00
257 Terrance Ganaway/645 4.00 10.00
260 Harrison Smith/999 6.00 15.00
261 Marc Tyler/899 3.00 8.00
262 Mark Barron/499 3.00 8.00
263 Dwayne Allen/899 3.00 8.00
264A Coby Fleener/899 3.00 8.00
264B Coby Fleener Draft 5.00 12.00
265 Orson Charles/840 3.00 8.00
266 Michael Egnew/899 3.00 8.00
267 Ladarius Green/899 3.00 8.00
268 Mychal Kendricks/899 5.00 12.00
270A Justin Blackmon/299 4.00 10.00
270B Justin Blackmon Draft 5.00 12.00
271A Kendall Wright/499 3.00 8.00
271B Kendall Wright Draft 5.00 12.00
272A Michael Floyd/499 3.00 8.00
272B Michael Floyd Draft 5.00 12.00
273 Mohamed Sanu/499 5.00 12.00
274 Alshon Jeffery/299 15.00 40.00
275 Rueben Randle/499 6.00 15.00
276A Stephen Hill/183 8.00 20.00
276B Stephen Hill Draft 12.00 30.00
277 Nick Toon/799 3.00 8.00
278 Juron Criner/799 3.00 8.00
280 Brian Quick/799 3.00 8.00
282 Joe Adams/799 3.00 8.00
283 Chris Givens/799 3.00 8.00
284 T.Y. Hilton/799 6.00 15.00
285 DeVier Posey/499 3.00 8.00
286 Marvin Jones/799 3.00 8.00
288 Jarius Wright/499 3.00 8.00
289 Marvin McNutt/899 3.00 8.00
290 Jeff Fuller/799 3.00 8.00
291 Rishard Matthews/799 3.00 8.00
292 Ryan Broyles/799 3.00 8.00
295 A.J. Jenkins/499 3.00 8.00
296 Stephon Gilmore/499 4.00 10.00
298 Danny Coale/599 3.00 8.00

2012 Prestige Stars of the NFL

1 Larry Fitzgerald .60 1.50
2 Michael Turner .50 1.25
3 Ray Lewis .75 2.00
4 Fred Jackson .60 1.50
5 Cam Newton .75 2.00
6 Brian Urlacher .75 2.00
7 Cedric Benson .50 1.25
8 Peyton Hillis .50 1.25
9 DeMarcus Ware .75 2.00
10 Tim Tebow .75 2.00
11 Ndamukong Suh .60 1.50
12 Calvin Johnson .75 2.00
13 Aaron Rodgers 1.25 3.00
14 Clay Matthews .75 2.00
15 Andre Johnson .60 1.50
16 Peyton Manning 1.50 4.00
17 Maurice Jones-Drew .50 1.25
18 Jamaal Charles .60 1.50
19 Reggie Bush .50 1.25
20 Adrian Peterson .75 2.00
21 Tom Brady 2.00 5.00
22 Drew Brees .75 2.00
23 Ahmad Bradshaw .50 1.25
24 Mark Sanchez .50 1.25
25 Darren McFadden .50 1.25
26 Michael Vick .60 1.50
27 Ben Roethlisberger .75 2.00
28 Antonio Gates .60 1.50
29 Philip Rivers .75 2.00
30 Frank Gore .60 1.50
31 Marshawn Lynch .60 1.50
32 James Laurinaitis .50 1.25
33 LeGarrette Blount .60 1.50
34 Chris Johnson .50 1.25
35 Brian Orakpo .60 1.50
36 Jason Witten .60 1.50
37 Jared Allen .50 1.25
38 Rob Gronkowski .75 2.00
39 Eric Berry .60 1.50
40 LeSean McCoy .75 2.00
41 DeSean Jackson .60 1.50
42 Tony Romo .60 1.50
43 Darrelle Revis .50 1.25
44 Devin Hester .60 1.50
45 Ray Rice .50 1.25
46 Marques Colston .50 1.25
47 Greg Jennings .50 1.25
48 Reggie Wayne .60 1.50
49 Ryan Mathews .60 1.50
50 Dez Bryant .75 2.00

2012 Prestige Stars of the NFL Materials

STATED PRINT RUN 2-249
1 Larry Fitzgerald/249 3.00 8.00
2 Michael Turner/249 2.50 6.00
3 Ray Lewis/249 4.00 10.00
5 Cam Newton/249 6.00 15.00
6 Brian Urlacher/249 4.00 10.00
7 Cedric Benson/115 2.50 6.00
8 Peyton Hillis/5
9 DeMarcus Ware/249 4.00 10.00
10 Tim Tebow/55 5.00 12.00
12 Calvin Johnson/2
13 Aaron Rodgers/185 10.00 25.00
14 Clay Matthews/249 5.00 12.00
15 Andre Johnson/175 3.00 8.00
16 Peyton Manning/40 10.00 25.00
17 Maurice Jones-Drew/185 2.50 6.00
18 Jamaal Charles/249 3.00 8.00
19 Reggie Bush/185 2.50 6.00
20 Adrian Peterson/35 6.00 15.00
21 Tom Brady/249 10.00 25.00
22 Drew Brees/249 4.00 10.00
23 Ahmad Bradshaw/120 2.50 6.00
24 Mark Sanchez/249 2.50 6.00
25 Darren McFadden/95 3.00 8.00
26 Michael Vick/249 3.00 8.00
28 Antonio Gates/120 3.00 8.00
30 Frank Gore/249 3.00 8.00
32 James Laurinaitis/125 2.50 6.00
34 Chris Johnson/249 2.50 6.00
35 Brian Orakpo/140 3.00 8.00
37 Jared Allen/220 2.50 6.00
42 Tony Romo/249 3.00 8.00
43 Darrelle Revis/249 2.50 6.00
44 Devin Hester/50 4.00 10.00
45 Ray Rice/249 2.50 6.00
46 Marques Colston/249 2.50 6.00
48 Reggie Wayne/249 3.00 8.00
50 Dez Bryant/249 4.00 10.00

2012 Prestige Stars of the NFL Materials Prime

PRIME STATED PRINT RUN 5-49
3 Ray Lewis/20 8.00 20.00
5 Cam Newton/49 10.00 25.00
6 Brian Urlacher/49 6.00 15.00
7 Cedric Benson/49 4.00 10.00
9 DeMarcus Ware/49 6.00 15.00
10 Tim Tebow/49 6.00 15.00
14 Clay Matthews/15 10.00 25.00
17 Maurice Jones-Drew/49 4.00 10.00
18 Jamaal Charles/49 5.00 12.00
22 Drew Brees/35 6.00 15.00
23 Ahmad Bradshaw/49 4.00 10.00
25 Darren McFadden/30 4.00 10.00
28 Antonio Gates/49 5.00 12.00
30 Frank Gore/49 5.00 12.00
34 Chris Johnson/49 4.00 10.00
35 Brian Orakpo/49 5.00 12.00
42 Tony Romo/49 5.00 12.00
43 Darrelle Revis/49 4.00 10.00
44 Devin Hester/49 5.00 12.00
45 Ray Rice/49 4.00 10.00
46 Marques Colston/49 4.00 10.00
49 Ryan Mathews/49 5.00 12.00
50 Dez Bryant/49 6.00 15.00

2012 Prestige Team Foundations Combo Materials

STATED PRINT RUN 249 SER.#'d SETS
*PRIME/49: .8X TO 2X BASIC COMBO/249
1 J.Maclin/L.McCoy 5.00 12.00
2 F.Gore/V.Davis 4.00 10.00
3 R.White/M.Ryan 4.00 10.00
4 C.Johnson/M.Stafford 6.00 15.00
5 B.Roethlisberger/R.Mendenhall 5.00 12.00

2012 Prestige Team Foundations Materials

STATED PRINT RUN 1-249
*PRIME/49: .8X TO 2X BASIC JSY/249
1 Adrian Peterson/249 4.00 10.00
2 Beanie Wells/249 2.50 6.00
3 Ben Roethlisberger/249 4.00 10.00
4 Calvin Johnson/249 4.00 10.00
5 Cam Newton/249 6.00 15.00
6 Chris Johnson/249 2.50 6.00
7 Darren McFadden/249 2.50 6.00
8 Darrius Heyward-Bey/249 2.50 6.00
9 Dez Bryant/249 4.00 10.00
10 Dwayne Bowe/249 3.00 8.00
11 Eli Manning/249 3.00 8.00
12 Felix Jones/249 2.50 6.00
13 Frank Gore/249 3.00 8.00
14 Hakeem Nicks/249 2.50 6.00
15 Jeremy Maclin/249 2.50 6.00
16 Joe Flacco/249 3.00 8.00
17 Kenny Britt/249 2.50 6.00
18 Knowshon Moreno/249 2.50 6.00
19 Larry Fitzgerald/249 3.00 8.00
20 LeSean McCoy/249 4.00 10.00
22 Matthew Stafford/249 3.00 8.00
23 Maurice Jones-Drew/249 2.50 6.00
24 Michael Crabtree/249 2.50 6.00
25 Mike Williams/249 3.00 8.00
26 Ndamukong Suh/249 3.00 8.00
27 Philip Rivers/249 4.00 10.00
28 Rashard Mendenhall/249 2.50 6.00
29 Ray Rice/249 2.50 6.00
30 Roddy White/249 2.50 6.00
31 Rob Gronkowski/249 4.00 10.00
32 Sam Bradford/249 2.50 6.00
33 Von Miller/249 3.00 8.00
34 Vernon Davis/249 2.50 6.00
35 A.J. Green/1

2012 Prestige Team Foundations Quad Materials

STATED PRINT RUN 149-249
*PRIME/49: 1X TO 2.5X BASIC QUAD/249
1 Gore/Davis/Willis/Crab/249 10.00 25.00
2 Gresh/Shipley/Dalton/Green/249 6.00 15.00
3 Reed/Flacco/Boldin/Lewis/149 12.00 30.00
4 Fitz/Doucet/Wells/Rob/249 5.00 12.00
5 John/Stafford/Best/Suh/249 12.00 30.00

2012 Prestige Team Foundations Trios Materials

STATED PRINT RUN 99-249
*PRIME/49: .8X TO 2X BASIC TRIO/249
1 Reed/Flacco/Boldin/99 12.00 30.00
2 Gore/Davis/Willis/249 5.00 12.00
3 Bowe/McCluster/Baldwin/249 5.00 12.00
4 Jones/Dez/Murray/249 6.00 15.00
5 White/Ryan/Jones/249 6.00 15.00

2012 Prestige Tim Tebow

COMMON TEBOW (1-14) 1.25 3.00
15 Tim Tebow AU/15

2013 Prestige

COMP.SET w/o RC's (200) 10.00 25.00
ONE ROOKIE PER PACK
1 Carson Palmer .25 .60
2 Larry Fitzgerald .25 .60
3 Michael Floyd .20 .50
4 Ryan Williams .20 .50
5 Rashard Mendenhall .20 .50
6 Patrick Peterson .20 .50
7 Matt Ryan .25 .60
8 Roddy White .20 .50
9 Julio Jones .30 .75
10 Steven Jackson .20 .50
11 Jacquizz Rodgers .25 .60
12 Sean Weatherspoon .20 .50
13 Joe Flacco .25 .60
14 Haloti Ngata .20 .50
15 Torrey Smith .20 .50
16 Ray Rice .20 .50
17 Dennis Pitta .20 .50
18 Jacoby Jones .20 .50
19 Terrell Suggs .20 .50
20 Tarvaris Jackson .20 .50
21 Steve Johnson .25 .60
22 Kevin Kolb .20 .50
23 C.J. Spiller .20 .50
24 Fred Jackson .25 .60
25 Scott Chandler .20 .50
26 Cam Newton .30 .75
27 Steve Smith .25 .60
28 Brandon LaFell .20 .50
29 DeAngelo Williams .20 .50
30 Jonathan Stewart .20 .50
31 Greg Olsen .25 .60
32 Jay Cutler .20 .50
33 Brandon Marshall .25 .60
34 Devin Hester .25 .60
35 Matt Forte .20 .50
36 Michael Bush .20 .50
37 Charles Tillman .25 .60
38 Lance Briggs .25 .60
39 Andy Dalton .25 .60
40 A.J. Green .30 .75
41 Andrew Hawkins .20 .50
42 BenJarvus Green-Ellis .25 .60
43 Jermaine Gresham .25 .60
44 Rey Maualuga .20 .50
45 Brandon Weeden .20 .50
46 Greg Little .20 .50
47 Josh Gordon .20 .50
48 Josh Cribbs .20 .50
49 Trent Richardson .20 .50
50 Joe Haden .20 .50
51 Tony Romo .25 .60
52 Dez Bryant .30 .75
53 Miles Austin .20 .50
54 DeMarco Murray .25 .60
55 Jason Witten .25 .60
56 DeMarcus Ware .30 .75
57 Sean Lee .25 .60
58 Peyton Manning .60 1.50
59 Demaryius Thomas .25 .60
60 Eric Decker .20 .50
61 Willis McGahee .20 .50
62 Wes Welker .25 .60
63 Von Miller .25 .60
64 Matthew Stafford .25 .60
65 Calvin Johnson .30 .75
66 Ryan Broyles .25 .60
67 Mikel Leshoure .20 .50
68 Brandon Pettigrew .20 .50
69 Ndamukong Suh .25 .60
70 Reggie Bush .20 .50
71 Aaron Rodgers .50 1.25
72 James Jones .20 .50
73 Jordy Nelson .25 .60
74 Randall Cobb .25 .60
75 Jermichael Finley .20 .50
76 Clay Matthews .30 .75
77 Matt Schaub .20 .50
78 Andre Johnson .20 .50
79 DeVier Posey .20 .50
80 Arian Foster .25 .60
81 Owen Daniels .20 .50
82 J.J. Watt .25 .60
83 Andrew Luck .50 1.25
84 Reggie Wayne .25 .60
85 T.Y. Hilton .25 .60
86 Vick Ballard .20 .50
87 Donald Brown .20 .50
88 Jerrell Freeman RC .30 .75
89 Blaine Gabbert .20 .50
90 Cecil Shorts .20 .50
91 Justin Blackmon .20 .50
92 Maurice Jones-Drew .20 .50
93 Rashad Jennings .20 .50
94 Marcedes Lewis .20 .50
95 Dwayne Bowe .25 .60
96 Jonathan Baldwin .20 .50
97 Jamaal Charles .25 .60
98 Alex Smith .25 .60
99 Tony Moeaki .20 .50
100 Tamba Hali .20 .50
101 Ryan Tannehill .25 .60
102 Brian Hartline .20 .50
103 Mike Wallace .20 .50
104 Daniel Thomas .20 .50
105 Dustin Keller .20 .50
106 Cameron Wake .20 .50
107 Christian Ponder .20 .50
108 Greg Jennings .20 .50
109 Jarius Wright .20 .50
110 Adrian Peterson .30 .75
111 Kyle Rudolph .20 .50
112 Jared Allen .20 .50
113 Tom Brady .75 2.00
114 Danny Amendola .25 .60
115 Shane Vereen .25 .60
116 Stevan Ridley .20 .50
117 Rob Gronkowski .30 .75
118 Aaron Hernandez .25 .60
119 Vince Wilfork .20 .50
120 Drew Brees .30 .75
121 Marques Colston .20 .50
122 Lance Moore .20 .50
123 Darren Sproles .25 .60
124 Mark Ingram .25 .60
125 Jimmy Graham .30 .75
126 Eli Manning .25 .60
127 Hakeem Nicks .20 .50
128 Victor Cruz .25 .60
129 Andre Brown .25 .60
130 David Wilson .20 .50
131 Brandon Myers .25 .60
132 Mark Sanchez .20 .50
133 Santonio Holmes .20 .50
134 Joe McKnight .20 .50
135 Bilal Powell .20 .50
136 Jeremy Kerley .20 .50
137 Darrelle Revis .20 .50
138 Matt Flynn .20 .50
139 Jacoby Ford .20 .50
140 Denarius Moore .20 .50
141 Darren McFadden .25 .60
142 Richard Seymour .20 .50
143 Marcel Reece .20 .50
144 Nick Foles .25 .60
145 DeSean Jackson .25 .60
146 Jeremy Maclin .20 .50
147 LeSean McCoy .30 .75
148 Brent Celek .20 .50
149 Bryce Brown .20 .50
150 Michael Vick .25 .60
151 Ben Roethlisberger .30 .75
152 Plaxico Burress .20 .50
153 Antonio Brown .30 .75
154 Jonathan Dwyer .20 .50
155 Isaac Redman .30 .75
156 Heath Miller .20 .50
157 Troy Polamalu .30 .75
158 Sam Bradford .20 .50
159 Jared Cook .20 .50
160 Chris Givens .20 .50
161 Isaiah Pead .20 .50
162 Daryl Richardson .20 .50
163 James Laurinaitis .25 .60
164 Philip Rivers .30 .75
165 Malcom Floyd .20 .50
166 Robert Meachem .20 .50
167 Vincent Brown .20 .50
168 Ryan Mathews .25 .60
169 Antonio Gates .25 .60
170 Colin Kaepernick .25 .60
171 Michael Crabtree .20 .50
172 Frank Gore .25 .60
173 Vernon Davis .20 .50
174 Patrick Willis .25 .60
175 Anquan Boldin .20 .50
176 Russell Wilson .60 1.50
177 Sidney Rice .20 .50
178 Golden Tate .20 .50
179 Marshawn Lynch .25 .60
180 Percy Harvin .20 .50
181 Richard Sherman .30 .75
182 Josh Freeman .25 .60
183 Vincent Jackson .20 .50
184 Mike Williams .25 .60
185 Doug Martin .25 .60
186 Dallas Clark .20 .50
187 Lavonte David .20 .50
188 Jake Locker .25 .60
189 Kenny Britt .20 .50
190 Kendall Wright .20 .50
191 Nate Washington .20 .50
192 Chris Johnson .20 .50
193 Shonn Greene .20 .50
194 Robert Griffin III .20 .50
195 Pierre Garcon .25 .60
196 Santana Moss .25 .60
197 Alfred Morris .20 .50
198 Fred Davis .20 .50
199 Brian Orakpo .25 .60
200 Ryan Kerrigan .20 .50
201 Aaron Dobson RC .40 1.00
202 Aaron Mellette RC .40 1.00
203 Ace Sanders RC .40 1.00
204 Alec Lemon RC .50 1.25
205 Alec Ogletree RC .40 1.00
206 Alex Okafor RC .40 1.00
207 Andre Ellington RC .40 1.00
208 Barkevious Mingo RC .40 1.00
209 Bjoern Werner RC .40 1.00
210 Darius Slay RC .40 1.00
211 Eric Fisher RC .40 1.00
212 Chris Gragg RC .40 1.00
213 Chris Harper RC .40 1.00
214 Christine Michael RC .40 1.00
215 Cierre Wood RC .40 1.00
216 Cobi Hamilton RC .40 1.00
217A Knile Davis RC .40 1.00
wearing gloves
217B K.Davis SP no gloves 1.25 3.00
218 Chance Warmack RC .40 1.00
219 Conner Vernon RC .40 1.00
220A Cordarrelle Patterson RC .40 1.00
220B C.Patterson Draft SP 1.25 3.00
221 Corey Fuller RC .40 1.00
222 Damontre Moore RC .40 1.00
223 Da'Rick Rogers RC .40 1.00
224 Datone Jones RC .40 1.00
225A DeAndre Hopkins RC 1.00 2.50
225B D.Hopkins SP wht 3.00 8.00
226 Dee Milliner RC .40 1.00
227 Denard Robinson RC .40 1.00
228 Dion Jordan RC .40 1.00
229 Dion Sims RC .40 1.00
230A Eddie Lacy RC .40 1.00
230B Eddie Lacy SP 00 3.00 8.00
231A EJ Manuel RC .40 1.00
231B EJ Manuel Draft SP 4.00 10.00
232 Eric Reid RC .50 1.25
233 Gavin Escobar RC .40 1.00
234A Geno Smith RC .40 1.00
234B Geno Smith Draft SP 1.25 3.00
235 Giovani Bernard RC .40 1.00
236 Jamar Taylor RC .40 1.00
237 Jarvis Jones RC .40 1.00
238 Jawan Jamison RC .40 1.00
239 Ezekiel Ansah RC .40 1.00
240 Johnthan Banks RC .40 1.00
241 Johnathan Hankins RC .40 1.00
242 Johnathan Franklin RC .40 1.00
243 Jordan Poyer RC .40 1.00
244 Jordan Reed RC .60 1.50
245 Joseph Randle RC .40 1.00
246 Josh Boyce RC .40 1.00
247 Justin Hunter RC .40 1.00
248 Keenan Allen RC .75 2.00
249 Kenjon Barner RC .40 1.00
250 Kenny Stills RC .40 1.00
251 Kenny Vaccaro RC .40 1.00
252 Kerwynn Williams RC .40 1.00
253 Kevin Minter RC .40 1.00
254 Landry Jones RC .40 1.00
255 Le'Veon Bell RC 1.25 3.00
256 Logan Ryan RC .50 1.25
257 Luke Joeckel RC .40 1.00
258A Manti Te'o RC blue .50 1.25
258B Manti Te'o SP white 1.50 4.00
259 Marcus Davis RC .40 1.00
260 Marcus Lattimore RC .40 1.00
261 Margus Hunt RC .40 1.00
262 Desmond Trufant RC .40 1.00
263 Vance McDonald RC .50 1.25
264 Markus Wheaton RC .40 1.00
265 Marquess Wilson RC .60 1.50
266 Marquise Goodwin RC .40 1.00
267 Matt Barkley RC .40 1.00
268 Matt Elam RC .40 1.00
269 Matt Scott RC .40 1.00
270 Mike Gillislee RC .40 1.00
271 Mike Glennon RC .40 1.00
272 Montee Ball RC .40 1.00
273 Nick Kasa RC .40 1.00
274 Phillip Thomas RC .40 1.00
275 Quinton Patton RC .40 1.00
276 Ray Graham RC .40 1.00
277 Ryan Otten RC .40 1.00
278 Rex Burkhead RC .50 1.25
279 Tyrann Mathieu RC .60 1.50
280 Robert Woods RC .60 1.50
281 Rodney Smith RC .40 1.00
282 Ryan Nassib RC .40 1.00
283 Ryan Swope RC .40 1.00
284 Sam Montgomery RC .40 1.00
285 Sheldon Richardson RC .40 1.00
286 Star Lotulelei RC .50 1.25
287 Stedman Bailey RC .40 1.00
288 Stepfan Taylor RC .40 1.00
289 Tavarres King RC .40 1.00
290A Tavon Austin RC .50 1.25
290B Tavon Austin SP 1.50 4.00
291 Terrance Williams RC .40 1.00
292 Theo Riddick RC .40 1.00
293 Travis Kelce RC 1.00 2.50
294 Tyler Bray RC .40 1.00
295 Tyler Eifert RC .40 1.00
296 Tyler Wilson RC .40 1.00
297 Arthur Brown RC .40 1.00
298 Xavier Rhodes RC .40 1.00
299 Zac Dysert RC .40 1.00
300 Zach Ertz RC .75 2.00
301 Leon Sandcastle (Deion) SP 6.00 15.00

2013 Prestige Extra Points Black

*ROOKIES/10: 3X TO 8X BASIC RC

2013 Prestige Extra Points Blue

*BLUE: .6X TO 1.5X BASIC RC

2013 Prestige Extra Points Gold

*GOLD/50: 1.2X TO 3X BASIC RC

2013 Prestige Extra Points Green

*1-200 VETS/25: 5X TO 12X BASIC CARDS
*201-300 ROOKIE/25: 2.5X TO 6X BASIC RC

2013 Prestige Extra Points Purple

*1-200 VETS/100: 2X TO 5X BASIC CARDS
*201-300 ROOKIE/100: 1X TO 2.5X BASIC RC

2013 Prestige Extra Points Red

*ROOKIES: .5X TO 1.2X BASIC RC

2013 Prestige Connections Materials

1 T.Brady/W.Welker/299 8.00 20.00
2 J.Flacco/T.Smith/199 3.00 8.00
3 M.Sanchez/S.Holmes/299
4 C.Palmer/D.Heyward-Bey/299
5 P.Rivers/A.Gates/199 4.00 10.00
6 J.Cutler/B.Marshall/99 8.00 20.00
7 C.Ponder/P.Harvin/299
8 M.Ryan/J.Jones/199 4.00 10.00
9 T.Romo/D.Bryant/299 6.00 15.00
10 D.Brees/M.Colston/299 4.00 10.00
11 E.Manning/H.Nicks/199 3.00 8.00
12 M.Vick/D.Jackson/299 3.00 8.00
13 A.Foster/A.Johnson/25 5.00 12.00
14 R.Bush/D.Thomas/299
15 D.Thomas/E.Decker/299 3.00 8.00
16 F.Davis/S.Moss/299
17 L.Fitzgerald/B.Wells/299 3.00 8.00
18 V.Davis/M.Crabtree/199 2.50 6.00
19 A.Luck/C.Fleener/299 6.00 15.00
20 D.Williams/J.Stewart/199

2013 Prestige Draft City Destinations

*HOLOKOTE/100: 1X TO 2.5X BASIC INSERTS
1 Cordarrelle Patterson .40 1.00
2 Tavon Austin .50 1.25
3 DeAndre Hopkins 1.00 2.50
4 EJ Manuel .40 1.00
5 Tyler Eifert .40 1.00
6 Geno Smith .40 1.00
7 Keenan Allen .75 2.00
8 Eddie Lacy .40 1.00
9 Mike Glennon .40 1.00
10 Robert Woods .60 1.50
11 Giovani Bernard .40 1.00
12 Justin Hunter .40 1.00
13 Terrance Williams .40 1.00
14 Markus Wheaton .40 1.00
15 Montee Ball .40 1.00
16 Zach Ertz .75 2.00
17 Aaron Dobson .40 1.00
18 Le'Veon Bell 1.25 3.00
19 Stedman Bailey .40 1.00
20 Christine Michael .40 1.00

2013 Prestige Draft City Destinations Autographs

1 Cordarrelle Patterson 3.00 8.00
2 Tavon Austin 4.00 10.00
3 DeAndre Hopkins 8.00 20.00
4 EJ Manuel 3.00 8.00
5 Tyler Eifert 4.00 10.00
6 Geno Smith 3.00 8.00
7 Keenan Allen 6.00 15.00
8 Eddie Lacy 3.00 8.00
9 Mike Glennon 4.00 10.00
10 Robert Woods 5.00 12.00
11 Giovani Bernard 3.00 8.00
12 Justin Hunter 3.00 8.00
13 Terrance Williams 3.00 8.00
14 Markus Wheaton 3.00 8.00
15 Montee Ball 3.00 8.00
16 Zach Ertz 6.00 15.00
17 Aaron Dobson 3.00 8.00
18 Le'Veon Bell 10.00 25.00
19 Stedman Bailey 3.00 8.00
20 Christine Michael 3.00 8.00

2013 Prestige Draft Picks Gold

*GOLD/25: 1.5X TO 4X BASIC INSERTS
*PLATINUM/10: 2.5X TO 6X BASIC INSERTS
1 Cordarrelle Patterson .40 1.00
2 Tavon Austin .50 1.25
3 DeAndre Hopkins 1.00 2.50
4 EJ Manuel .40 1.00
5 Tyler Eifert .40 1.00
6 Geno Smith .40 1.00
7 Keenan Allen .75 2.00
8 Eddie Lacy .40 1.00
9 Mike Glennon .40 1.00
10 Robert Woods .60 1.50
11 Giovani Bernard .40 1.00
12 Justin Hunter .40 1.00
13 Terrance Williams .40 1.00
14 Markus Wheaton .40 1.00
15 Montee Ball .40 1.00
16 Zach Ertz .75 2.00
17 Aaron Dobson .40 1.00
18 Le'Veon Bell 1.25 3.00
19 Stedman Bailey .40 1.00
20 Christine Michael .40 1.00

2013 Prestige Draft Picks Rights Autographs

1 Tavon Austin/25 6.00 15.00
2 EJ Manuel/25 5.00 12.00
3 Tyler Eifert/25 5.00 12.00
4 DeAndre Hopkins/25 12.00 30.00
5 Cordarrelle Patterson/25 5.00 12.00
7 Eddie Lacy/25 30.00 60.00
8 Montee Ball/25
9 Robert Woods/25 8.00 20.00
10 Zach Ertz/25 10.00 25.00
11 Manti Te'o/25 6.00 15.00
12 Justin Hunter/25 5.00 12.00
13 Giovani Bernard/25 5.00 12.00
14 Gavin Escobar/25 12.00 30.00
15 Le'Veon Bell/25 25.00 50.00

2013 Prestige Extra Points Black Autographs

1-50 VETERAN PRINT RUN 1-99
201-300 UNPRICED ROOKIE PRINT RUN 10
1 Aaron Hernandez/49 10.00 25.00
5 Antoine Bethea/49 5.00 12.00
8 Ben Roethlisberger/20 40.00 80.00
11 Brandon Pettigrew/25 8.00 20.00
12 Brent Celek/99 5.00 12.00
15 Champ Bailey/99 8.00 20.00
16 David Nelson/49 5.00 12.00
18 Demaryius Thomas/25 10.00 25.00
19 Denarius Moore/99 5.00 12.00
20 Derrick Johnson/99 6.00 15.00
21 DeSean Jackson/25
22 Dexter McCluster/99 6.00 15.00
24 Dustin Keller/99 5.00 12.00
25 Greg Olsen/49 8.00 20.00
26 Jared Allen/25 8.00 20.00
27 Jared Cook/49 5.00 12.00
29 Jeremy Maclin/49 5.00 12.00
32 Jerod Mayo/49 6.00 15.00
33 J.J. Watt/25 40.00 80.00
34 Jonathan Baldwin/99 5.00 12.00
35 Jonathan Stewart/49 5.00 12.00
36 Josh Freeman/25 10.00 25.00
37 Kenny Britt/99 5.00 12.00
38 Kevin Walter/49 5.00 12.00
39 Knowshon Moreno/49 5.00 12.00
40 Kyle Rudolph/99 5.00 12.00
42 Mike Wallace/25
43 Owen Daniels/49 5.00 12.00
44 Patrick Peterson/49 15.00 40.00
46 Randall Cobb/49
47 Sean Lee/49 20.00 40.00
50 Christian Ponder/25 8.00 20.00

2013 Prestige Extra Points Blue Autographs

*BLUE: .3X TO .8X GOLD AU/50
217B Knile Davis no glv/25 6.00 15.00
220B C.Patterson Draft/25 6.00 15.00
225B D.Hopkins wht/25 15.00 40.00
230B Eddie Lacy 00 jer#/25 6.00 15.00
231B EJ Manuel Draft/25 6.00 15.00
258B Manti Te'o white/25 8.00 20.00
290B Tavon Austin Draft/25 8.00 20.00
301 L.Sandcastle/21 (Deion) 150.00 250.00

2013 Prestige Extra Points Gold Autographs

*GREEN/25: .5X TO 1.2X GOLD/50
*PURPLE/100: .3X TO .8X GOLD/50
*RED: .25X TO .6X GOLD/50
201 Aaron Dobson 5.00 12.00
202 Aaron Mellette 5.00 12.00
203 Ace Sanders 8.00 20.00
205 Alec Ogletree 5.00 12.00
206 Alex Okafor 5.00 12.00
207 Andre Ellington 5.00 12.00
208 Barkevious Mingo 5.00 12.00
209 Bjoern Werner 5.00 12.00
210 Darius Slay 5.00 12.00
211 Eric Fisher 8.00 20.00
212 Chris Gragg 5.00 12.00
213 Chris Harper 5.00 12.00
214 Christine Michael 5.00 12.00
217 Knile Davis 5.00 12.00
218 Chance Warmack 5.00 12.00
219 Conner Vernon 5.00 12.00
220 Cordarrelle Patterson 5.00 12.00
221 Corey Fuller 5.00 12.00
222 Damontre Moore 5.00 12.00
223 Da'Rick Rogers 5.00 12.00
224 Datone Jones 5.00 12.00
225 DeAndre Hopkins 12.00 30.00
226 Dee Milliner 5.00 12.00
227 Denard Robinson 5.00 12.00
228 Dion Jordan 5.00 12.00
229 Dion Sims 5.00 12.00
230 Eddie Lacy 5.00 12.00
231 EJ Manuel 5.00 12.00
232 Eric Reid 10.00 25.00
233 Gavin Escobar 5.00 12.00
234 Geno Smith 5.00 12.00
235 Giovani Bernard 5.00 12.00
237 Jarvis Jones 5.00 12.00
242 Johnathan Franklin 5.00 12.00
243 Jordan Poyer 5.00 12.00
245 Joseph Randle 5.00 12.00
246 Josh Boyce 5.00 12.00
247 Justin Hunter 5.00 12.00
248 Keenan Allen 10.00 25.00
249 Kenjon Barner 5.00 12.00
250 Kenny Stills 5.00 12.00
251 Kenny Vaccaro 10.00 25.00
253 Kevin Minter 5.00 12.00
254 Landry Jones 5.00 12.00
255 Le'Veon Bell 15.00 40.00
257 Luke Joeckel 5.00 12.00
258 Manti Te'o 6.00 15.00
259 Marcus Davis 5.00 12.00
260 Marcus Lattimore 5.00 12.00
261 Margus Hunt 5.00 12.00
262 Desmond Trufant 5.00 12.00
263 Vance McDonald 6.00 15.00
264 Markus Wheaton 5.00 12.00
266 Marquise Goodwin 5.00 12.00
267 Matt Barkley 5.00 12.00
268 Matt Elam 5.00 12.00
269 Matt Scott 5.00 12.00
271 Mike Glennon 5.00 12.00
272 Montee Ball 5.00 12.00
273 Nick Kasa 5.00 12.00
274 Phillip Thomas 5.00 12.00
275 Quinton Patton 5.00 12.00
277 Ryan Otten 5.00 12.00
278 Rex Burkhead 6.00 15.00
279 Tyrann Mathieu 10.00 25.00
280 Robert Woods 8.00 20.00
281 Rodney Smith 5.00 12.00
282 Ryan Nassib 5.00 12.00
283 Ryan Swope 5.00 12.00
284 Sam Montgomery 5.00 12.00
287 Stedman Bailey 5.00 12.00
288 Stepfan Taylor 5.00 12.00
289 Tavarres King 5.00 12.00
290 Tavon Austin 6.00 15.00
291 Terrance Williams 5.00 12.00
293 Travis Kelce 20.00 50.00
294 Tyler Bray 5.00 12.00
295 Tyler Eifert 5.00 12.00
296 Tyler Wilson 5.00 12.00
297 Arthur Brown 5.00 12.00
298 Xavier Rhodes 5.00 12.00
299 Zac Dysert 5.00 12.00
300 Zach Ertz 10.00 25.00

2013 Prestige Fantasy Team

1 Drew Brees 1.50 4.00
2 Aaron Rodgers 2.50 6.00
3 Tom Brady 4.00 10.00
4 Cam Newton 1.50 4.00
5 Robert Griffin III 1.00 2.50
6 Peyton Manning 3.00 8.00
7 Matt Ryan 1.25 3.00
8 Tony Romo 1.25 3.00
9 Andrew Luck 2.50 6.00
10 Russell Wilson 3.00 8.00
11 Adrian Peterson 1.50 4.00
12 Doug Martin 1.25 3.00
13 Arian Foster 1.25 3.00
14 Marshawn Lynch 1.25 3.00
15 Alfred Morris 1.00 2.50
16 Calvin Johnson 1.50 4.00
17 Brandon Marshall 1.25 3.00
18 Dez Bryant 1.50 4.00
19 A.J. Green 1.50 4.00
20 Demaryius Thomas 1.25 3.00
21 Jimmy Graham 1.50 4.00
22 Rob Gronkowski 1.50 4.00
23 Tony Gonzalez 1.25 3.00
24 Heath Miller 1.00 2.50
25 Jason Witten 1.25 3.00

2013 Prestige First Impressions Autographs

1 Robert Griffin III/25 40.00 80.00
5 Doug Martin/99 6.00 15.00
6 Alfred Morris/99 5.00 12.00
7 Ryan Tannehill/49 12.00 30.00
8 Nick Foles/99 12.00 30.00
10 Justin Blackmon/49 6.00 15.00
11 David Wilson/99 5.00 12.00
12 Bryce Brown/99 6.00 15.00
14 T.Y. Hilton/99 6.00 15.00
15 Lavonte David/25 8.00 20.00
16 Luke Kuechly/99 10.00 25.00

2013 Prestige Gamers Materials

*PRIME: .8X TO 2X BASIC JSY
1 A.J. Green 4.00 10.00
2 Adrian Peterson 4.00 10.00
3 Ahmad Bradshaw 2.50 6.00
4 Andy Dalton 3.00 8.00
5 Anquan Boldin 2.50 6.00
6 Anthony Fasano 2.50 6.00
7 Antonio Gates 3.00 8.00
8 Arian Foster 3.00 8.00
9 Beanie Wells 2.50 6.00
10 BenJarvus Green-Ellis 3.00 8.00
11 Brian Orakpo 3.00 8.00
12 Brian Urlacher 4.00 10.00
13 C.J. Spiller 2.50 6.00
14 Carson Palmer 3.00 8.00
15 Champ Bailey 3.00 8.00
16 Chris Long 2.50 6.00
17 Christian Ponder 2.50 6.00
18 Darrelle Revis 2.50 6.00
19 Darren McFadden 3.00 8.00
20 Darren Sproles 3.00 8.00
21 Darrius Heyward-Bey 2.50 6.00
22 Davone Bess 2.50 6.00
23 DeAngelo Hall 2.50 6.00
24 DeAngelo Williams 2.50 6.00
25 DeMarco Murray 3.00 8.00
26 DeMarcus Ware 4.00 10.00
27 Demaryius Thomas 3.00 8.00
28 Denarius Moore 2.50 6.00
29 DeSean Jackson 3.00 8.00
30 Devin Hester 3.00 8.00
31 Dez Bryant 4.00 10.00
32 Drew Brees 4.00 10.00
33 Dustin Keller 2.50 6.00
34 Dwayne Bowe 3.00 8.00
35 Earl Bennett 2.50 6.00
36 Eli Manning 3.00 8.00
37 Eric Decker 2.50 6.00
38 Fred Davis 2.50 6.00
39 Fred Jackson 3.00 8.00
40 Hakeem Nicks 2.50 6.00
41 Jamaal Charles 3.00 8.00
42 James Laurinaitis 3.00 8.00
43 Jared Allen 2.50 6.00
44 Jason Witten 3.00 8.00
45 Jay Cutler 4.00 10.00
46 Jeremy Maclin 2.50 6.00
47 Jermaine Gresham 3.00 8.00
48 Jimmy Graham 4.00 10.00
49 Joe Flacco 3.00 8.00
50 Jonathan Stewart 2.50 6.00
51 Josh Freeman 3.00 8.00
52 Julio Jones 4.00 10.00
53 Julius Peppers 3.00 8.00
54 Justin Tuck 3.00 8.00
55 Karlos Dansby 2.50 6.00
56 Kenny Britt 2.50 6.00
57 Knowshon Moreno 2.50 6.00
58 Kyle Rudolph 2.50 6.00
59 Lance Briggs 3.00 8.00
60 Larry Fitzgerald 3.00 8.00
61 London Fletcher 3.00 8.00
62 Malcom Floyd 2.50 6.00
63 Marcedes Lewis 2.50 6.00
64 Mark Sanchez 2.50 6.00
65 Marques Colston 2.50 6.00
66 Matt Forte 2.50 6.00
67 Matt Ryan 3.00 8.00
68 Maurice Jones-Drew 2.50 6.00
69 Michael Crabtree 2.50 6.00
70 Michael Turner 2.50 6.00
71 Michael Vick 3.00 8.00
72 Mike Wallace 2.50 6.00
73 Miles Austin 2.50 6.00
74 Osi Umenyiora 2.50 6.00
75 Percy Harvin 2.50 6.00
76 Philip Rivers 4.00 10.00
77 Ray Lewis 4.00 10.00
78 Ray Rice 2.50 6.00
79 Reggie Bush 2.50 6.00
80 Richard Seymour 2.50 6.00
81 Roddy White 2.50 6.00
82 Ryan Fitzpatrick 2.50 6.00
83 Ryan Mathews 3.00 8.00
84 Sam Bradford 2.50 6.00
85 Santana Moss 3.00 8.00
86 Santonio Holmes 2.50 6.00
87 Shonn Greene 2.50 6.00
88 Sidney Rice 2.50 6.00
89 Steve Johnson 3.00 8.00
90 Steve Smith 3.00 8.00
91 Steven Jackson 2.50 6.00
92 Tamba Hali 2.50 6.00
93 Tom Brady 10.00 25.00
94 Tony Gonzalez 3.00 8.00
95 Torrey Smith 2.50 6.00
96 Vernon Davis 2.50 6.00
97 Von Miller 3.00 8.00
98 Wes Welker 3.00 8.00
99 Willis McGahee 2.50 6.00
100 Zach Miller 2.50 6.00

2013 Prestige Inside the Numbers

1 Aaron Rodgers 2.50 6.00
2 Eli Manning 1.25 3.00
3 Matt Schaub 1.00 2.50
4 Matthew Stafford 1.25 3.00
5 Drew Brees 1.50 4.00
6 Peyton Manning 3.00 8.00
7 Andy Dalton 1.25 3.00
8 Cam Newton 1.50 4.00
9 Tom Brady 4.00 10.00
10 Tony Romo 1.25 3.00
11 Adrian Peterson 1.50 4.00
12 DeMarco Murray 1.25 3.00
13 Ray Rice 1.00 2.50
14 C.J. Spiller 1.00 2.50
15 LeSean McCoy 1.50 4.00
16 Calvin Johnson 1.50 4.00
17 Andre Johnson 1.00 2.50
18 Julio Jones 1.50 4.00
19 Eric Decker 1.00 2.50
20 Michael Crabtree 1.00 2.50
21 Jimmy Graham 1.50 4.00
22 Antonio Gates 1.25 3.00
23 Aaron Hernandez 1.25 3.00
24 Frank Gore 1.25 3.00
25 Chris Johnson 1.00 2.50

2013 Prestige League Leaders Combo Materials

*PRIME/25: .8X TO 2X COMBO JSY/199-299
*PRIME/25: .6X TO 1.5X COMBO JSY/49
1 J.Witten/T.Gonzalez/49 4.00 10.00
2 R.Rice/B.Green-Ellis/199 3.00 8.00
3 C.Spiller/D.Murray/299 3.00 8.00
4 M.Crabtree/M.Wallace/199 2.50 6.00
5 T.Romo/J.Cutler/299 3.00 8.00

2013 Prestige League Leaders Materials

*PRIME/25: .8X TO 2X BASIC JSY/199-299
*PRIME/25: .6X TO 1.5X BASIC JSY/99
1 Adrian Peterson/299 4.00 10.00
2 Alfred Morris/299 2.50 6.00
3 Jamaal Charles/299 3.00 8.00
4 Doug Martin/299 3.00 8.00
5 Drew Brees/299 4.00 10.00
6 Tom Brady/199 10.00 25.00
7 Matt Ryan/299 3.00 8.00
8 Eli Manning/299 3.00 8.00
9 Andy Dalton/299 3.00 8.00
10 Demaryius Thomas/299 3.00 8.00
11 Dez Bryant/199 4.00 10.00
12 Wes Welker/299 3.00 8.00
13 Roddy White/99 3.00 8.00
14 A.J. Green/299 4.00 10.00
15 Von Miller/299 3.00 8.00
16 Cameron Wake/299 2.50 6.00
18 James Laurinaitis/299 3.00 8.00
19 Ed Reed/299 3.00 8.00
20 Jimmy Graham/199 4.00 10.00

2013 Prestige League Leaders Quad Materials

*PRIME/25: 1X TO 2.5X QUAD JSY/199-299
1 Brs/Brdy/Ryn/Flco/299 12.00 30.00
2 Frte/Grne/Brdsh/Bsh/299 3.00 8.00
3 Dckr/Clstn/Jnes/Smith/299 5.00 12.00
4 Grhm/Grshm/Dvls/Rdp/199 5.00 12.00
5 Eli/Ncks/Pndr/Hrvin/299 4.00 10.00

2013 Prestige NFL Draft Combo Materials

*PRIME/25: .8X TO 2X COMBO/299
1 EJ Manuel/T.Austin 1.50 4.00
2 C.Patterson/T.Austin 1.50 4.00
3 E.Fisher/L.Joeckel 4.00 10.00
4 D.Jordan/E.Ansah 1.25 3.00
5 J.Cooper/C.Warmack
6 K.Vaccaro/Eric Reid 3.00 8.00
7 D.Milliner/X.Rhodes 1.25 3.00
8 S.Floyd/S.Richardson 4.00 10.00
9 D.Milliner/S.Richardson 1.25 3.00
10 D.Fluker/L.Johnson

2013 Prestige NFL Draft Materials

*PRIME/25: .8X TO 2X BASIC JSY/299
1 Eric Fisher 4.00 10.00
2 Luke Joeckel 1.25 3.00
3 Dion Jordan 1.25 3.00
4 Lane Johnson
5 Ezekiel Ansah
6 Barkevious Mingo
7 Jonathan Cooper
8 Tavon Austin 1.50 4.00
9 Dee Milliner 1.25 3.00
10 Chance Warmack
11 D.J. Fluker
12 Sheldon Richardson
13 Kenny Vaccaro
14 EJ Manuel 1.25 3.00
15 Eric Reid
16 Sharrif Floyd
17 Bjoern Werner
18 Xavier Rhodes
19 Cordarrelle Patterson 1.25 3.00

2013 Prestige NFL Draft Tickets

*HOLOKOTE/100: .8X TO 2X BASIC INSERTS
1 Cordarrelle Patterson .40 1.00
2 Tavon Austin .50 1.25
3 DeAndre Hopkins 1.00 2.50
4 EJ Manuel .40 1.00
5 Tyler Eifert .40 1.00
6 Geno Smith .40 1.00
7 Keenan Allen .75 2.00
8 Eddie Lacy .40 1.00
9 Mike Glennon .40 1.00
10 Robert Woods .60 1.50
11 Giovani Bernard .40 1.00
12 Justin Hunter .40 1.00
13 Terrance Williams .40 1.00
14 Markus Wheaton .40 1.00
15 Montee Ball .40 1.00
16 Zach Ertz .75 2.00
17 Aaron Dobson .40 1.00
18 Le'Veon Bell 1.25 3.00
19 Steptan Taylor .40 1.00
20 Christine Michael .40 1.00
21 Marquise Goodwin .40 1.00
22 Matt Barkley .40 1.00
23 Tyler Wilson .40 1.00
24 Quinton Patton .40 1.00
25 Ryan Nassib .40 1.00
26 Johnathan Franklin .40 1.00
27 Marcus Lattimore .40 1.00
28 Landry Jones .40 1.00
29 Joseph Randle .40 1.00
30 Stedman Bailey .40 1.00
31 Manti Te'o .50 1.25
32 Vance McDonald .50 1.25
33 Denard Robinson .40 1.00
34 Andre Ellington .40 1.00
35 Kenny Stills .40 1.00
36 Knile Davis .40 1.00
37 Jordan Reed .60 1.50
38 Mike Gillislee .40 1.00
39 Gavin Escobar .40 1.00
40 Dion Jordan .40 1.00

2013 Prestige NFL Draft Tickets Autographs

1 Cordarrelle Patterson 3.00 8.00
2 Tavon Austin 4.00 10.00
3 DeAndre Hopkins 8.00 20.00
4 EJ Manuel 3.00 8.00
5 Tyler Eifert 3.00 8.00
6 Geno Smith 3.00 8.00
7 Keenan Allen 6.00 15.00
8 Eddie Lacy 3.00 8.00
9 Mike Glennon 3.00 8.00
10 Robert Woods 5.00 12.00
11 Giovani Bernard 3.00 8.00
12 Justin Hunter 3.00 8.00
13 Terrance Williams 6.00 15.00
14 Markus Wheaton 3.00 8.00
15 Montee Ball 3.00 8.00
16 Zach Ertz 6.00 15.00
17 Aaron Dobson 3.00 8.00
18 Le'Veon Bell 10.00 25.00
19 Stepfan Taylor 3.00 8.00
20 Christine Michael 3.00 8.00
21 Marquise Goodwin 3.00 8.00
22 Matt Barkley 3.00 8.00
23 Tyler Wilson 3.00 8.00
24 Quinton Patton 3.00 8.00
25 Ryan Nassib 3.00 8.00
26 Johnathan Franklin 3.00 8.00
27 Marcus Lattimore 3.00 8.00
28 Landry Jones 3.00 8.00
29 Joseph Randle 3.00 8.00
30 Stedman Bailey 3.00 8.00
31 Manti Te'o 4.00 10.00
32 Vance McDonald 6.00 15.00
33 Denard Robinson 3.00 8.00
34 Andre Ellington 3.00 8.00
35 Kenny Stills 3.00 8.00
36 Knile Davis 3.00 8.00
37 Jordan Reed 5.00 12.00
38 Mike Gillislee 3.00 8.00
39 Gavin Escobar 8.00 20.00
40 Dion Jordan 3.00 8.00

2013 Prestige NFL Passport

*HOLOKOTE/100: .8X TO 2X BASIC INSERTS
1 Cordarrelle Patterson .40 1.00
2 Tavon Austin .50 1.25
3 DeAndre Hopkins 1.00 2.50
4 EJ Manuel .40 1.00
5 Tyler Eifert .40 1.00
6 Geno Smith .40 1.00
7 Keenan Allen .75 2.00
8 Eddie Lacy .40 1.00
9 Mike Glennon .40 1.00
10 Robert Woods .60 1.50
11 Giovani Bernard .40 1.00
12 Justin Hunter .40 1.00
13 Terrance Williams .40 1.00
14 Markus Wheaton .40 1.00
15 Montee Ball .40 1.00
16 Zach Ertz .75 2.00
17 Aaron Dobson .40 1.00
18 Le'Veon Bell 1.25 3.00
19 Stepfan Taylor .40 1.00
20 Christine Michael .40 1.00
21 Marquise Goodwin .40 1.00
22 Matt Barkley .40 1.00
23 Tyler Wilson .40 1.00
24 Quinton Patton .40 1.00
25 Ryan Nassib .40 1.00
26 Johnathan Franklin .40 1.00
27 Marcus Lattimore .40 1.00
28 Landry Jones .40 1.00
29 Joseph Randle .40 1.00
30 Stedman Bailey .40 1.00
31 Manti Te'o .50 1.25
32 Vance McDonald .50 1.25
33 Denard Robinson .40 1.00
34 Andre Ellington .40 1.00
35 Kenny Stills .40 1.00
36 Knile Davis .40 1.00
37 Jordan Reed .60 1.50
38 Mike Gillislee .40 1.00
39 Gavin Escobar .40 1.00
40 Dion Jordan .40 1.00

2013 Prestige NFL Passport Autographs

1 Cordarrelle Patterson 3.00 8.00
2 Tavon Austin 4.00 10.00
3 DeAndre Hopkins 8.00 20.00
4 EJ Manuel 3.00 8.00
5 Tyler Eifert 3.00 8.00
6 Geno Smith 3.00 8.00
7 Keenan Allen 6.00 15.00
8 Eddie Lacy 3.00 8.00
9 Mike Glennon 3.00 8.00
10 Robert Woods 5.00 12.00
11 Giovani Bernard 3.00 8.00
12 Justin Hunter 3.00 8.00
13 Terrance Williams 3.00 8.00
14 Markus Wheaton 3.00 8.00
15 Montee Ball 3.00 8.00
16 Zach Ertz 6.00 15.00
17 Aaron Dobson 3.00 8.00
18 Le'Veon Bell 10.00 25.00
19 Steptan Taylor 3.00 8.00
20 Christine Michael 3.00 8.00
21 Marquise Goodwin 3.00 8.00
22 Matt Barkley 3.00 8.00
23 Tyler Wilson 3.00 8.00
24 Quinton Patton 3.00 8.00
25 Ryan Nassib 3.00 8.00
26 Johnathan Franklin 3.00 8.00
27 Marcus Lattimore 3.00 8.00
28 Landry Jones 3.00 8.00
29 Joseph Randle 3.00 8.00
30 Stedman Bailey 3.00 8.00
31 Manti Te'o 4.00 10.00
32 Vance McDonald 5.00 12.00
33 Denard Robinson 3.00 8.00
34 Andre Ellington 3.00 8.00
35 Kenny Stills 3.00 8.00
36 Knile Davis 3.00 8.00
37 Jordan Reed 5.00 12.00
38 Mike Gillislee 3.00 8.00
39 Gavin Escobar 6.00 15.00
40 Dion Jordan 3.00 8.00

2013 Prestige NFL Shield

1 Peyton Manning 5.00 12.00
2 Larry Fitzgerald 2.00 5.00
3 Roddy White 1.50 4.00
4 Ray Rice 1.50 4.00
5 C.J. Spiller 1.50 4.00
6 Cam Newton 2.50 6.00
7 Jay Cutler 1.50 4.00
8 A.J. Green 2.50 6.00
9 Dez Bryant 2.50 6.00
10 Calvin Johnson 2.50 6.00
11 Aaron Rodgers 5.00 12.00
12 Arian Foster 2.00 5.00
13 Andrew Luck 4.00 10.00
14 Adrian Peterson 2.50 6.00
15 Rob Gronkowski 2.50 6.00
16 Drew Brees 2.50 6.00
17 Victor Cruz 2.00 5.00
18 LeSean McCoy 2.50 6.00
19 Ben Roethlisberger 2.50 6.00
20 Colin Kaepernick 2.00 5.00
21 Marshawn Lynch 2.00 5.00
22 Doug Martin 2.00 5.00
23 Chris Johnson 1.50 4.00
24 Robert Griffin III 1.50 4.00
25 Darren McFadden 2.00 5.00

2013 Prestige Prestigious Picks Gold

*BLACK/25: 1.5X TO 4X BASIC INSERTS
*PLATINUM/10: 2.5X TO 6X BASIC INSERTS
1 Cordarrelle Patterson .40 1.00
2 Tavon Austin .50 1.25
3 DeAndre Hopkins 1.00 2.50
4 EJ Manuel .40 1.00
5 Tyler Eifert .40 1.00
6 Geno Smith .40 1.00
7 Keenan Allen .75 2.00
8 Eddie Lacy .50 1.25
9 Mike Glennon .40 1.00
10 Robert Woods .60 1.50
11 Giovani Bernard .40 1.00
12 Justin Hunter .40 1.00
13 Terrance Williams .40 1.00
14 Markus Wheaton .40 1.00
15 Montee Ball .40 1.00
16 Zach Ertz .75 2.00
17 Aaron Dobson .40 1.00
18 Le'Veon Bell 1.25 3.00
19 Stepfan Taylor .40 1.00
20 Christine Michael .40 1.00
21 Marquise Goodwin .40 1.00
22 Matt Barkley .40 1.00
23 Tyler Wilson .40 1.00
24 Quinton Patton .40 1.00
25 Ryan Nassib .40 1.00
26 Johnathan Franklin .40 1.00
27 Marcus Lattimore .40 1.00
28 Landry Jones .40 1.00
29 Joseph Randle .40 1.00
30 Stedman Bailey .40 1.00
31 Manti Te'o .60 1.50
32 Vance McDonald .50 1.25
33 Denard Robinson .40 1.00
34 Andre Ellington .40 1.00
35 Kenny Stills .40 1.00
36 Knile Davis .40 1.00
37 Jordan Reed .60 1.50
38 Mike Gillislee .40 1.00
39 Gavin Escobar .40 1.00
40 Dion Jordan .40 1.00

2013 Prestige Prestigious Picks Materials Gold

*BLACK/199: .5X TO 1.2X GOLD JSY/399
*PLATINUM/49: .8X TO 2X GOLD JSY/399
1 Cordarrelle Patterson 1.25 3.00
2 Tavon Austin 1.50 4.00
3 DeAndre Hopkins 3.00 8.00
4 EJ Manuel 1.25 3.00
5 Tyler Eifert 1.25 3.00
6 Geno Smith 1.25 3.00
7 Keenan Allen 2.50 6.00
8 Eddie Lacy 1.25 3.00
9 Mike Glennon 1.25 3.00
10 Robert Woods 2.00 5.00
11 Giovani Bernard 1.25 3.00
12 Justin Hunter 1.25 3.00
13 Terrance Williams 1.25 3.00
14 Markus Wheaton 1.25 3.00
15 Montee Ball 1.25 3.00
16 Zach Ertz 2.50 6.00
17 Aaron Dobson 1.25 3.00
18 Le'Veon Bell 4.00 10.00
19 Stepfan Taylor 1.25 3.00
20 Christine Michael 1.25 3.00
21 Marquise Goodwin 1.25 3.00
22 Matt Barkley 1.25 3.00
23 Tyler Wilson 1.25 3.00
24 Quinton Patton 1.25 3.00
25 Ryan Nassib 1.25 3.00
26 Johnathan Franklin 1.25 3.00
27 Marcus Lattimore 1.25 3.00
28 Landry Jones 1.25 3.00
29 Joseph Randle 1.25 3.00
30 Stedman Bailey 1.25 3.00
31 Manti Te'o 4.00 10.00
32 Vance McDonald 2.50 6.00
33 Denard Robinson 1.25 3.00
34 Andre Ellington 1.25 3.00
35 Kenny Stills 1.25 3.00
36 Knile Davis 1.25 3.00
37 Jordan Reed 3.00 8.00
38 Mike Gillislee 1.25 3.00
39 Gavin Escobar 2.50 6.00
40 Dion Jordan 1.25 3.00

2013 Prestige Rookie League Leaders Combo Materials

PRIME/24-25: .8X TO 2X BASIC DUAL/299
1 Justin Blackmon/Kendall Wright 2.50 6.00
2 Russell Wilson/Andrew Luck 8.00 20.00
3 Doug Martin/Trent Richardson 3.00 8.00
4 Justin Blackmon/Mohamed Sanu 2.50 6.00
5 Andrew Luck/Nick Foles 5.00 12.00

2013 Prestige Rookie League Leaders Materials

*PRIME/25: .6X TO 1.5X BASIC JSY/299
1 Andrew Luck 8.00 20.00
2 Brandon Weeden
3 Ryan Tannehill 3.00 8.00
4 Robert Griffin III 2.50 6.00
5 Russell Wilson 8.00 20.00
6 Doug Martin 3.00 8.00
7 Trent Richardson 2.50 6.00
8 Justin Blackmon 2.50 6.00
9 Kendall Wright 2.50 6.00
10 David Wilson 2.50 6.00

2013 Prestige Rookie League Leaders Quad Materials

*PRIME/20-25: .8X TO 2X BASIC QUAD/299
1 Luck/Weeden/Tannehill/Griffin 8.00 20.00
2 Wilson/Luck/Griffin/Weeden 10.00 25.00
3 Blackmon/ Wright/Richardson/Martin 4.00 10.00
4 Blackmon/Givens/Wright/Floyd 3.00 8.00
5 Luck/Martin/Blackmon/Wilson 8.00 20.00

2013 Prestige Stars of the NFL

1 Tony Romo 1.50 4.00
2 Ray Rice 1.25 3.00
3 A.J. Green 2.00 5.00
4 Trent Richardson 1.25 3.00
5 Mike Wallace 1.25 3.00
6 Arian Foster 2.00 5.00
7 Reggie Wayne 1.50 4.00
8 C.J. Spiller 1.25 3.00
9 Tom Brady 5.00 12.00
10 Peyton Manning 4.00 10.00
11 Robert Griffin III 1.25 3.00
12 Brandon Marshall 1.50 4.00
13 Calvin Johnson 2.00 5.00
14 Aaron Rodgers 3.00 8.00
15 Adrian Peterson 2.00 5.00
16 Julio Jones 2.00 5.00
17 Cam Newton 2.00 5.00
18 Drew Brees 2.00 5.00
19 Victor Cruz 1.50 4.00
20 LeSean McCoy 2.00 5.00
21 Andrew Luck 3.00 8.00
22 Larry Fitzgerald 1.50 4.00
23 Colin Kaepernick 1.50 4.00
24 Marshawn Lynch 1.50 4.00
25 Chris Johnson 1.25 3.00

2013 Prestige Turning Pro Autographs

1 Tavon Austin/25 6.00 15.00
2 EJ Manuel/25 5.00 12.00
3 Tyler Eifert/25
4 Cordarrelle Patterson/25 5.00 12.00
5 Eric Fisher/25 5.00 12.00
6 Dion Jordan/25 5.00 12.00
8 Chance Warmack/25 5.00 12.00
9 Kenny Vaccaro/25 5.00 12.00
10 Dee Milliner/25 5.00 12.00
11 Jarvis Jones/25
12 Eric Reid/25 6.00 15.00
14 Xavier Rhodes/25 5.00 12.00
15 Bjoern Werner/25 5.00 12.00

2014 Prestige

COMP.SET w/o RC's (200) 10.00 25.00
ONE ROOKIE PER PACK
1 EJ Manuel .20 .50
2 Steve Johnson .25 .60
3 Robert Woods .25 .60
4 C.J. Spiller .20 .50
5 Scott Chandler .20 .50
6 Kiko Alonso .20 .50
7 Ryan Tannehill .25 .60
8 Mike Wallace .20 .50
9 Brian Hartline .20 .50
10 Lamar Miller .20 .50
11 Cameron Wake .20 .50
12 Knowshon Moreno .20 .50
13 Tom Brady .75 2.00
14 Danny Amendola .25 .60
15 Julian Edelman .30 .75
16 Stevan Ridley .20 .50
17 Darrelle Revis .20 .50
18 Rob Gronkowski .30 .75
19 Shane Vereen .25 .60
20 Geno Smith .20 .50
21 Michael Vick .25 .60
22 Jeremy Kerley .20 .50
23 Eric Decker .20 .50
24 Chris Johnson .20 .50
25 Sheldon Richardson .20 .50
26 Joe Flacco .25 .60
27 Torrey Smith .20 .50
28 Marlon Brown .20 .50
29 Ray Rice .20 .50
30 Dennis Pitta .20 .50
31 Steve Smith .25 .60
32 Andy Dalton .25 .60
33 A.J. Green .30 .75
34 Marvin Jones .20 .50
35 Giovani Bernard .20 .50
36 Jermaine Gresham .20 .50
37 Vontaze Burfict .20 .50
38 Geno Atkins .20 .50
39 Brian Hoyer .20 .50
40 Josh Gordon .20 .50
41 Ben Tate .20 .50
42 Jordan Cameron .20 .50
43 Joe Haden .20 .50
44 Barkevious Mingo .20 .50
45 Ben Roethlisberger .30 .75
46 Antonio Brown .30 .75
47 Lance Moore .20 .50
48 Le'Veon Bell .25 .60
49 Heath Miller .20 .50
50 Markus Wheaton .20 .50
51 Garrett Graham .20 .50
52 Andre Johnson .25 .60
53 DeAndre Hopkins .25 .60
54 Arian Foster .25 .60
55 Keshawn Martin .20 .50
56 J.J. Watt .30 .75
57 Andrew Luck .40 1.00
58 Reggie Wayne .25 .60
59 T.Y. Hilton .25 .60
60 Hakeem Nicks .20 .50
61 Da'Rick Rogers .20 .50
62 Vick Ballard .20 .50
63 Trent Richardson .20 .50
64 Robert Mathis .20 .50
65 Chad Henne .20 .50
66 Ace Sanders .20 .50
67 Cecil Shorts .20 .50
68 Jordan Todman .20 .50
69 Marcedes Lewis .20 .50
70 Paul Posluszny .20 .50
71 Jake Locker .25 .60
72 Dexter McCluster .25 .60
73 Justin Hunter .20 .50
74 Kendall Wright .20 .50
75 Delanie Walker .20 .50
76 Shonn Greene .20 .50
77 Peyton Manning .60 1.50
78 Demaryius Thomas .25 .60
79 Wes Welker .25 .60
80 Emmanuel Sanders .25 .60
81 DeMarcus Ware .25 .60
82 Montee Ball .20 .50
83 Julius Thomas .20 .50
84 Danny Trevathan .20 .50
85 Alex Smith .25 .60
86 Dwayne Bowe .25 .60
87 Donnie Avery .20 .50
88 Jamaal Charles .25 .60
89 Brandon Flowers .20 .50
90 Justin Houston .20 .50
91 Eric Berry .25 .60
92 Matt Schaub .20 .50
93 Andre Holmes RC .30 .75
94 Denarius Moore .20 .50
95 Darren McFadden .20 .50
96 Maurice Jones-Drew .20 .50
97 Philip Rivers .30 .75
98 Keenan Allen .25 .60
99 Vincent Brown .25 .60
100 Antonio Gates .20 .50
101 Ryan Mathews .25 .60
102 Danny Woodhead .25 .60
103 Tony Romo .25 .60
104 Dez Bryant .30 .75
105 Terrance Williams .20 .50
106 DeMarco Murray .25 .60
107 Jason Witten .25 .60
108 Sean Lee .25 .60
109 Eli Manning .25 .60
110 Victor Cruz .25 .60
111 Rueben Randle .20 .50
112 David Wilson .20 .50
113 Rashad Jennings .20 .50
114 Jason Pierre-Paul .20 .50
115 Nick Foles .25 .60
116 Darren Sproles .25 .60
117 Jeremy Maclin .20 .50
118 LeSean McCoy .30 .75
119 Brent Celek .20 .50
120 Riley Cooper .25 .60
121 Robert Griffin III .25 .60
122 Pierre Garcon .25 .60
123 Alfred Morris .20 .50
124 Jordan Reed .20 .50
125 DeSean Jackson .25 .60
126 Jay Cutler .20 .50
127 Brandon Marshall .20 .50
128 Alshon Jeffery .25 .60
129 Matt Forte .20 .50
130 Martellus Bennett .20 .50
131 Tim Jennings .20 .50
132 Matthew Stafford .25 .60
133 Calvin Johnson .30 .75
134 Kris Durham .20 .50
135 Reggie Bush .20 .50
136 Brandon Pettigrew .20 .50
137 Ndamukong Suh .25 .60
138 Aaron Rodgers .60 1.50
139 Jordy Nelson .25 .60
140 Randall Cobb .25 .60
141 Julius Peppers .25 .60
142 Eddie Lacy .20 .50
143 Clay Matthews .30 .75
144 Adrian Peterson .30 .75
145 Matt Cassel .20 .50
146 Greg Jennings .20 .50
147 Cordarrelle Patterson .20 .50
148 Kyle Rudolph .20 .50
149 Chad Greenway .25 .60
150 Matt Ryan .25 .60
151 Julio Jones .30 .75
152 Roddy White .20 .50
153 Steven Jackson .20 .50
154 Harry Douglas .20 .50
155 Sean Weatherspoon .20 .50
156 Cam Newton .30 .75
157 Jerricho Cotchery .20 .50
158 Luke Kuechly .25 .60
159 DeAngelo Williams .20 .50
160 Jonathan Stewart .20 .50
161 Greg Olsen .25 .60
162 Drew Brees .30 .75
163 Marques Colston .20 .50
164 Mark Ingram .25 .60
165 Jimmy Graham .30 .75
166 Pierre Thomas .20 .50
167 Kenny Stills .20 .50
168 Cameron Jordan .20 .50
169 Mike Glennon .25 .60
170 Vincent Jackson .20 .50
171 Mike Williams .25 .60
172 Doug Martin .25 .60
173 Timothy Wright .20 .50
174 Lavonte David .20 .50
175 Carson Palmer .25 .60
176 Larry Fitzgerald .25 .60
177 Michael Floyd .20 .50
178 Ted Ginn Jr. .20 .50
179 Andre Ellington .20 .50
180 Patrick Peterson .20 .50
181 Tyrann Mathieu .25 .60
182 Sam Bradford .20 .50
183 Kenny Britt .20 .50
184 Tavon Austin .20 .50
185 Zac Stacy .20 .50
186 Robert Quinn .25 .60
187 Colin Kaepernick .25 .60
188 Anquan Boldin .20 .50
189 Michael Crabtree .20 .50
190 Frank Gore .25 .60
191 Vernon Davis .20 .50
192 NaVorro Bowman .25 .60
193 Aldon Smith .20 .50
194 Russell Wilson .50 1.25
195 Jermaine Kearse .20 .50
196 Percy Harvin .20 .50
197 Marshawn Lynch .25 .60
198 Richard Sherman .30 .75
199 Earl Thomas .25 .60
200 Malcolm Smith RC .30 .75
201 A.J. McCarron RC .30 .75
202 Aaron Donald RC .75 2.00
203 Aaron Murray RC .30 .75
204 Cody Latimer RC .40 1.00
205 Allen Robinson RC .50 1.25
206 Andre Williams RC .30 .75
207 Anthony Barr RC .30 .75
208 Austin Seferian-Jenkins RC .30 .75
209 Bishop Sankey RC .30 .75
210A Blake Bortles RC .40 1.00
210B Blake Bortles SP 1.25 3.00
211 Bradley Roby RC .30 .75
212 Brandin Cooks RC .50 1.25
213 Brandon Coleman RC .30 .75
214 Brett Smith RC .30 .75
215 Bruce Ellington RC .30 .75
216 C.J. Mosley RC .40 1.00
217 Calvin Pryor RC .30 .75
218 Carlos Hyde RC .40 1.00
219 Charles Sims RC .30 .75
220 Chris Borland RC .30 .75
221 Chris Smith RC .30 .75
222 Connor Shaw RC .30 .75
223 Justin Gilbert RC .30 .75
224 Cyrus Kouandjio RC .40 1.00
225 Darqueze Dennard RC .40 1.00
226 Davante Adams RC .50 1.25
227 David Fales RC .30 .75
228 De'Anthony Thomas RC .30 .75
229 Dee Ford RC .30 .75
230 Deone Bucannon RC .30 .75
231A Derek Carr RC 2.00 5.00
231B Derek Carr SP 6.00 15.00
232 Devonta Freeman RC .50 1.25
233 Donte Moncrief RC .30 .75
234 Dri Archer RC .30 .75
235 Ryan Grant RC .30 .75
236A Eric Ebron RC .40 1.00
236B Eric Ebron SP 1.25 3.00
237 Greg Robinson RC .30 .75
238 Ha Ha Clinton-Dix RC .40 1.00
239 Jace Amaro RC .30 .75
240 Kevin Norwood RC .30 .75
241A Jadeveon Clowney RC .40 1.00
241B Jadeveon Clowney SP 1.25 3.00
242 Jake Matthews RC .30 .75
243 Jalen Saunders RC .30 .75
244 James White RC .60 1.50
245 Lorenzo Taliaferro RC .30 .75
246 Jared Abbrederis RC .30 .75
247 Jarvis Landry RC .60 1.50
248 Jason Verrett RC .30 .75
249 Jeremy Hill RC .40 1.00
250 Jerick McKinnon RC .40 1.00
251 Tom Savage RC .30 .75
252 Jimmy Garoppolo RC 2.50 6.00
253A Johnny Manziel RC .50 1.25
253B Johnny Manziel SP 1.50 4.00
254 Jordan Matthews RC .50 1.25
255 Josh Huff RC .40 1.00
256 Ka'Deem Carey RC .30 .75
257 Kelvin Benjamin RC .50 1.25
258 Khalil Mack RC 1.25 3.00
259 Kony Ealy RC .40 1.00
260 Kyle Fuller RC .30 .75
261 Kyle Van Noy RC .40 1.00
262 Devin Street RC .30 .75
263 Lache Seastrunk RC .30 .75
264 Lamarcus Joyner RC .40 1.00
265 Logan Thomas RC .30 .75
266 Louis Nix III RC .30 .75
267 Richard Rodgers RC .50 1.25
268 Marcus Smith RC .30 .75
269 Marion Grice RC .30 .75
270A Marqise Lee RC .40 1.00
270B Marqise Lee SP 1.25 3.00
271 Martavis Bryant RC .40 1.00
272 Michael Sam RC .30 .75
273 C.J. Fiedorowicz RC .30 .75
274A Mike Evans RC .75 2.00
274B Mike Evans SP 2.50 6.00
275 Odell Beckham Jr. RC .75 2.00
276 Paul Richardson RC .40 1.00
277 Demarcus Lawrence RC .40 1.00
278 Ra'Shede Hageman RC .30 .75
279 Ryan Shazier RC .50 1.25
280A Sammy Watkins RC .50 1.25
280B S.Watkins SP NFL JSY 1.50 4.00
281 Scott Crichton RC .30 .75
282 Shaq Evans RC .30 .75
283 John Brown RC .50 1.25
284 Stephon Tuitt RC .50 1.25
285 Dominique Easley RC .30 .75
286 Tajh Boyd RC .30 .75
287 Taylor Lewan RC .30 .75
288A Teddy Bridgewater RC .50 1.25
288B Teddy Bridgewater SP 1.50 4.00
289 Telvin Smith RC .30 .75
290 Terrance West RC .30 .75
291 Tevin Reese RC .30 .75
292 Timmy Jernigan RC .30 .75
293 Michael Campanaro RC .30 .75
294A Tre Mason RC .30 .75
294B Tre Mason SP 1.00 2.50
295 Trent Murphy RC .30 .75
296 Troy Niklas RC .30 .75
297 Ja'Wuan James RC .30 .75
298 Jimmie Ward RC .40 1.00
299 Zach Mettenberger RC .30 .75
300 Zack Martin RC .40 1.00

2014 Prestige Extra Points Black

*1-200 VETS/10: 6X TO 15X BASIC CARDS
*201-300 ROOK/10: 4X TO 10X BASIC RC

2014 Prestige Extra Points Blue

*BLUE ROOK: .6X TO 1.5X BASIC RC

2014 Prestige Extra Points Gold

*GOLD ROOK/50: 1.2X TO 3X BASIC RC

2014 Prestige Extra Points Purple

*1-200 VETS/100: 1.2X TO 3X BASIC CARDS
*201-300 ROOK/100: .8X TO 2X BASIC RC

2014 Prestige Extra Points Red

*ROOKIES: .5X TO 1.2X BASIC CARDS

2014 Prestige Extra Points Silver Holofoil

*1-200 VETS/25: 4X TO 10X BASIC
*201-300 ROOK/25: 2.5X TO 6X BASIC RC

2014 Prestige All Fantasy Team

1 Peyton Manning 3.00 8.00
2 Aaron Rodgers 3.00 8.00
3 Jamaal Charles 1.25 3.00
4 LeSean McCoy 1.50 4.00
5 Adrian Peterson 1.50 4.00
6 Calvin Johnson 1.50 4.00
7 Josh Gordon 1.00 2.50
8 Demaryius Thomas 1.25 3.00
9 Jimmy Graham 1.50 4.00
10 Julius Thomas 1.00 2.50
11 Rob Gronkowski 1.50 4.00
12 Stephen Gostkowski 1.25 3.00
13 Drew Brees 1.50 4.00
14 Matt Forte 1.00 2.50
15 Brandon Marshall 1.00 2.50

2014 Prestige Autographs

1 Zac Stacy/199 6.00 15.00
2 Tyrann Mathieu/199 4.00 10.00
4 Tavon Austin/116 3.00 8.00
5 Da'Rick Rogers/99
6 Jeremy Kerley/199 3.00 8.00
7 Andrew Luck/5
8 Chris Ivory/125
9 Jarrett Boykin/199 8.00 20.00
10 Marlon Brown/199 3.00 8.00
11 Aaron Rodgers/5
12 Frank Gore/49 8.00 20.00
13 Andre Brown/125 3.00 8.00
14 Victor Cruz/199 8.00 20.00
15 Trindon Holliday/199 4.00 10.00
16 Richard Sherman/5
17 Bernard Pierce/13
19 Nick Foles/5
20 Kendall Wright/68 6.00 15.00
21 Shonn Greene/39
23 Peyton Manning/5
24 Ryan Broyles/46 6.00 15.00
25 Doug Martin/125 6.00 15.00
26 Pat Angerer/18
27 Fletcher Cox/22
28 T.Y. Hilton/199 4.00 10.00
31 Daryl Richardson/15
32 Jake Ballard/99 4.00 10.00
33 Dennis Pitta/99 4.00 10.00
37 Eli Manning/5
38 Jordan Cameron/48 6.00 15.00
41 Kirk Cousins/199 5.00 12.00
43 Matthew Stafford/5
44 Michael Floyd/14
45 Sam Bradford/5
46 Tony Romo/5
47 C.J. Spiller/99 4.00 10.00
48 Brandon LaFell/15
49 Brian Cushing/20
50 Reggie Wayne/99 6.00 15.00
51 Bruce Smith/5
52 Bill Romanowski/99 8.00 20.00
53 Chuck Foreman/99
54 Cris Collinsworth/99 5.00 12.00
55 Daryle Lamonica/73 10.00 25.00
56 Eddie George/27
57 Ed McCaffrey/40 10.00 25.00
58 Jim Kiick/199 3.00 8.00
59 L.C. Greenwood/99
60 Rocket Ismail/99 5.00 12.00

2014 Prestige Behind The Jersey Numbers

1 Marshawn Lynch 1.25 3.00
2 Vernon Davis 1.00 2.50
3 Zac Stacy 1.00 2.50
4 Russell Wilson 2.50 6.00
5 Jimmy Graham 1.50 4.00
6 Cam Newton 1.50 4.00
7 Harry Douglas 1.00 2.50
8 Patrick Peterson 1.00 2.50
9 Jordy Nelson 1.25 3.00
10 Matthew Stafford 1.25 3.00
11 Brandon Marshall 1.00 2.50
12 Alfred Morris 1.00 2.50
13 DeSean Jackson 1.25 3.00
14 Dez Bryant 1.50 4.00
15 Antonio Gates 1.00 2.50
16 Von Miller 1.25 3.00
17 Chris Johnson 1.00 2.50
18 Trent Richardson 1.00 2.50
19 J.J. Watt 1.50 4.00
20 Antonio Brown 1.50 4.00
21 A.J. Green 1.50 4.00
22 Terrell Suggs 1.00 2.50
23 Danny Amendola 1.25 3.00
24 Mike Wallace 1.00 2.50
25 C.J. Spiller 1.00 2.50

2014 Prestige Big Four Jerseys

*PRIME/25: .6X TO 1.5X BASIC QUAD
1 Dvs/Gre/Smth/Wlls/49 8.00 20.00
2 Wlsn/Mllr/Irvn/Smth/49 12.00 30.00
3 Astn/Brdfrd/Lng/Qunn/99 5.00 12.00
4 Plmr/Flyd/Ftzgrld/Ptrsn/49 5.00 12.00
5 Clstn/Thms/Grhm/Brs/99 6.00 15.00
6 Wllms/Nwtn/Stwrt/Olsn/49 6.00 15.00
7 Ryn/Jns/Whte/Dgls/99 6.00 15.00
9 Wlkr/Bll/Mllr/Wbstr/49 5.00 12.00
10 Mngo/Hdn/Bnjmn/Grdn/49 4.00 10.00

2014 Prestige Big Three Jerseys

*PRIME/25: .6X TO 1.5X BASIC TRIO/49-99
1 Woods/Manuel/Spiller/25 5.00 12.00
2 Flacco/Rice/Smith/49 4.00 10.00
3 Dalton/Green/Bernard/49 5.00 12.00
4 Manning/Thomas/Thomas/49 10.00 25.00
5 Smith/Bowe/Charles/99 4.00 10.00
6 Rivers/Allen/Te'o/75 5.00 12.00
7 Romo/Bryant/Murray/49 5.00 12.00
8 Maclin/McCoy/Ryans/49 5.00 12.00
9 Griffin/Garcon/Morris/49 4.00 10.00
10 Sherman/Thomas/Chancellor/49 12.00 30.00

2014 Prestige Captains

1 Carson Palmer 1.25 3.00
2 Fred Jackson 1.25 3.00
3 Luke Kuechly 1.25 3.00
4 Jay Cutler 1.00 2.50
5 Andy Dalton 1.25 3.00
6 Jason Witten 1.25 3.00
7 Peyton Manning 3.00 8.00
8 Matthew Stafford 1.25 3.00
9 Andre Johnson 1.25 3.00
10 Andrew Luck 2.00 5.00
11 Alex Smith 1.25 3.00
12 James Laurinaitis 1.25 3.00
13 Drew Brees 1.50 4.00
14 Eli Manning 1.25 3.00
15 Vincent Jackson 1.00 2.50
16 Gerald McCoy 1.00 2.50
17 Eric Weddle 1.00 2.50
18 Bernard Pollard 1.00 2.50
19 Robert Griffin III 1.00 2.50
20 Russell Wilson 2.50 6.00

2014 Prestige Connections Dual Jerseys

*PRIME/25: .6X TO 1.5X BASIC DUAL/49-99
1 R.Wilson/M.Lynch/49 8.00 20.00
2 C.Palmer/L.Fitzgerald/49 4.00 10.00
3 P.Manning/W.Welker/49 10.00 25.00
4 J.Cutler/M.Forte/99 3.00 8.00
5 C.Kaepernick/A.Boldin/49 4.00 10.00
6 P.Rivers/K.Allen/49 5.00 12.00
7 G.Smith/C.Ivory/99 4.00 10.00
8 J.Charles/K.Davis/99 4.00 10.00
9 R.Griffin/J.Reed/49 3.00 8.00

2014 Prestige Draft Big Board

*SILVER/25: 1.5X TO 4X BASIC INSERTS
1 Johnny Manziel .50 1.25
2 Teddy Bridgewater .50 1.25
3 Blake Bortles .40 1.00
4 Sammy Watkins .50 1.25
5 Mike Evans .75 2.00
6 Marqise Lee .40 1.00
8 Brandin Cooks .50 1.25
9 Kelvin Benjamin .50 1.25
10 Derek Carr 2.00 5.00
11 A.J. McCarron .30 .75
12 Jordan Matthews .50 1.25
13 Eric Ebron .40 1.00
14 Lache Seastrunk .30 .75
15 Zach Mettenberger .30 .75
16 Aaron Murray .30 .75
17 Jadeveon Clowney .40 1.00
18 Jace Amaro .30 .75
19 Donte Moncrief .30 .75
20 Tre Mason .30 .75

2014 Prestige Draft Big Board Signatures

1 Johnny Manziel 5.00 12.00
2 Teddy Bridgewater 5.00 12.00
3 Blake Bortles 4.00 10.00
4 Sammy Watkins 40.00 80.00
5 Mike Evans 8.00 20.00
6 Jeremy Hill 4.00 10.00
7 Odell Beckham Jr. 20.00 50.00
8 Brandin Cooks 5.00 12.00
10 Derek Carr 25.00 50.00
11 Jimmy Garoppolo 30.00 60.00
12 A.J. McCarron 3.00 8.00
13 Carlos Hyde 4.00 10.00
14 Ka'Deem Carey 8.00 20.00
15 Bishop Sankey 3.00 8.00
16 Allen Robinson 5.00 12.00
17 Davante Adams 10.00 25.00
18 Jordan Matthews 5.00 12.00
19 Paul Richardson 6.00 15.00
20 Tajh Boyd 3.00 8.00
21 Charles Sims 3.00 8.00
22 Cody Latimer 4.00 10.00
23 Andre Williams 3.00 8.00
24 Terrance West 3.00 8.00
25 Devonta Freeman 5.00 12.00
26 Tom Savage 3.00 8.00
27 Aaron Murray 3.00 8.00
29 Jadeveon Clowney 4.00 10.00
30 Jace Amaro 3.00 8.00
31 Austin Seferian-Jenkins 3.00 8.00
33 Donte Moncrief 3.00 8.00
34 Dri Archer 3.00 8.00
35 De'Anthony Thomas 3.00 8.00

2014 Prestige Draft Day Standouts

*SILVER/25: 1X TO 2.5X BASIC INSERTS
1 Patrick Peterson .75 2.00
2 Colin Kaepernick 1.00 2.50
3 Marques Colston .75 2.00
4 Russell Wilson 2.00 5.00
5 Tom Brady 3.00 8.00
6 Richard Sherman 1.25 3.00
7 Maurice Jones-Drew .75 2.00
8 Steve Johnson 1.00 2.50
9 Robert Mathis .75 2.00
10 Zac Stacy .75 2.00
11 Brandon Marshall .75 2.00
12 Frank Gore 1.00 2.50
13 Andre Ellington .75 2.00
14 Tyrann Mathieu 1.00 2.50
15 Keenan Allen 1.00 2.50

2014 Prestige Draft Pick Rights Autographs

STATED PRINT RUN 25-99
1 A.J. McCarron/75 5.00 12.00
2 Aaron Murray/99 5.00 12.00
3 Blake Bortles/25 10.00 25.00
4 Derek Carr/75 25.00 60.00
5 Eric Ebron/99 6.00 15.00
6 Jadeveon Clowney/75 6.00 15.00
7 Johnny Manziel/25 8.00 20.00
8 Khalil Mack/99 20.00 50.00
9 Marqise Lee/99 6.00 15.00
10 Mike Evans/50 12.00 30.00
11 Sammy Watkins/99 15.00 40.00
12 Teddy Bridgewater/25 12.00 30.00
13 Odell Beckham Jr./75 30.00 80.00

2014 Prestige Draft Picks

*GREEN/25: 1.5X TO 4X BASIC INSERTS
DP1 A.J. McCarron .40 1.00
DP2 Aaron Murray .40 1.00
DP3 Blake Bortles .50 1.25
DP4 Derek Carr 2.50 6.00
DP5 Eric Ebron .50 1.25
DP6 Jadeveon Clowney .50 1.25
DP7 Johnny Manziel .60 1.50
DP8 Jordan Matthews .60 1.50
DP9 Khalil Mack 1.50 4.00
DP10 Marqise Lee .50 1.25
DP11 Mike Evans 1.00 2.50
DP12 Sammy Watkins .60 1.50
DP13 Teddy Bridgewater .60 1.50
DP14 Tre Mason .40 1.00
DP15 Odell Beckham Jr. 1.00 2.50

2014 Prestige Draft Picks Retail

JUMBO RED: .8X TO 2X BASIC INSERTS
DP1 A.J. McCarron .40 1.00
DP2 Aaron Murray .40 1.00
DP3 Blake Bortles .50 1.25
DP4 Derek Carr 2.50 6.00
DP5 Eric Ebron .50 1.25
DP6 Jadeveon Clowney .50 1.25
DP7 Johnny Manziel .60 1.50
DP8 Jordan Matthews .60 1.50
DP9 Lache Seastrunk .40 1.00
DP10 Marqise Lee .50 1.25
DP11 Mike Evans 1.00 2.50
DP12 Sammy Watkins .60 1.50
DP13 Teddy Bridgewater .60 1.50
DP14 Tre Mason .40 1.00
DP15 Zach Mettenberger .40 1.00

2014 Prestige Draft Picks Jumbo Blue

1 A.J. McCarron .50 1.25
2 Aaron Murray .50 1.25
3 Blake Bortles .60 1.50
4 Derek Carr 3.00 8.00
5 Eric Ebron .60 1.50
6 Jadeveon Clowney .60 1.50
7 Johnny Manziel .75 2.00
8 Jordan Matthews .75 2.00
9 Lache Seastrunk .50 1.25
10 Marqise Lee .60 1.50
11 Mike Evans 1.25 3.00
12 Sammy Watkins .75 2.00
13 Teddy Bridgewater .75 2.00
14 Tre Mason .50 1.25
15 Zach Mettenberger .50 1.25

2014 Prestige Dual NFL Jerseys

1 A.Morris/K.Cousins 8.00 20.00
2 K.Allen/P.Rivers 8.00 20.00
3 A.Boldin/C.Kaepernick 6.00 15.00
4 A.Smith/D.Bowe 6.00 15.00
5 T.Brady/S.Ridley 20.00 50.00

2014 Prestige Dual Rookie Draft Jerseys

*PRIME/25: .8X TO 2X BASIC DUAL/99
1 T.Bridgewater/B.Bortles 4.00 10.00
2 B.Cooks/S.Watkins 4.00 10.00
3 G.Robinson/J.Matthews 2.50 6.00
4 H.Clinton-Dix/C.Pryor 3.00 8.00
5 J.Verrett/O.Beckham 6.00 15.00
6 J.Clowney/K.Mack 10.00 25.00
7 J.Manziel/M.Evans 6.00 15.00
8 E.Ebron/T.Lewan 3.00 8.00
9 K.Fuller/J.Gilbert 2.50 6.00
10 R.Shazier/C.Mosley 4.00 10.00

2014 Prestige Dual Rookie League Leaders Jerseys

*PRIME/25: .8X TO 2X BASIC DUAL/49-99
*PRIME/25: .5X TO 1.2X BASIC DUAL/49-99
1 M.Glennon/M.Barkley/49 3.00 8.00
2 G.Smith/E.Manuel/25 4.00 10.00
3 E.Lacy/L.Bell/15 5.00 12.00
4 Z.Stacy/G.Bernard/25 4.00 10.00
5 A.Ellington/M.Ball/99 2.50 6.00
8 J.Hunter/T.Austin/25 4.00 10.00
10 D.Milliner/T.Mathieu/25 5.00 12.00

2014 Prestige Extra Points Blue Autographs

*RED: .4X TO 1X BLUE AU
*SILVER/10-25: .8X TO 2X BLUE
201 A.J. McCarron 2.50 6.00
202 Aaron Donald 8.00 20.00
203 Aaron Murray 2.50 6.00
204 Cody Latimer 3.00 8.00
205 Allen Robinson 4.00 10.00
206 Andre Williams 2.50 6.00
207 Anthony Barr 2.50 6.00
208 Austin Seferian-Jenkins 2.50 6.00
209 Bishop Sankey 2.50 6.00
210 Blake Bortles 3.00 8.00
211 Bradley Roby 2.50 6.00
212 Brandin Cooks 4.00 10.00
213 Brandon Coleman 2.50 6.00
214 Brett Smith 2.50 6.00
215 Bruce Ellington 2.50 6.00
217 Calvin Pryor 2.50 6.00
218 Carlos Hyde 3.00 8.00
219 Charles Sims 2.50 6.00
220 Chris Borland 2.50 6.00
221 Chris Smith 2.50 6.00
222 Connor Shaw 2.50 6.00
225 Darqueze Dennard 3.00 8.00
227 David Fales 2.50 6.00
228 De'Anthony Thomas 2.50 6.00
229 Dee Ford 2.50 6.00
230 Deone Bucannon 2.50 6.00
231 Derek Carr 25.00 50.00
232 Devonta Freeman 4.00 10.00
233 Donte Moncrief 2.50 6.00
234 Dri Archer 2.50 6.00
235 Ed Reynolds 2.50 6.00
236 Eric Ebron 3.00 8.00
237 Greg Robinson 2.50 6.00
238 Ha Ha Clinton-Dix 3.00 8.00

239 Jace Amaro 2.50 6.00
240 Kevin Norwood 2.50 6.00
241 Jadeveon Clowney 3.00 8.00
242 Jake Matthews 2.50 6.00
244 James White
245 James Wilder Jr. 3.00 8.00
246 Jared Abbrederis 2.50 6.00
248 Jason Verrett 2.50 6.00
249 Jeremy Hill 3.00 8.00
250 Jerick McKinnon 3.00 8.00
252 Jimmy Garoppolo 25.00 50.00
253 Johnny Manziel 4.00 10.00
255 Josh Huff 3.00 8.00
256 Ka'Deem Carey 2.50 6.00
257 Kelvin Benjamin 4.00 10.00
258 Khalil Mack 10.00 25.00
259 Kony Ealy 3.00 8.00
260 Kyle Fuller 2.50 6.00
261 Kyle Van Noy 3.00 8.00
262 L'Damian Washington 3.00 8.00
263 Lache Seastrunk 2.50 6.00
264 Lamarcus Joyner 3.00 8.00
265 Logan Thomas 2.50 6.00
266 Louis Nix III 2.50 6.00
268 Marcus Smith 2.50 6.00
269 Marion Grice 2.50 6.00
270 Marqise Lee 3.00 8.00
271 Martavis Bryant 3.00 8.00
272 Michael Sam 2.50 6.00
273 C.J. Fiedorowicz 2.50 6.00
274 Mike Evans 6.00 15.00
275 Odell Beckham Jr. 25.00 50.00
276 Paul Richardson 5.00 12.00
277 Isaiah Crowell 3.00 8.00
278 Ra'Shede Hageman 2.50 6.00
279 Ryan Shazier 4.00 10.00
280 Sammy Watkins 4.00 10.00
281 Scott Crichton 2.50 6.00
282 Shaq Evans 2.50 6.00
283 Shayne Skov 2.50 6.00
285 Dominique Easley 2.50 6.00
286 Tajh Boyd 2.50 6.00
287 Taylor Lewan 2.50 6.00
288 Teddy Bridgewater 4.00 10.00
289 Telvin Smith 2.50 6.00
290 Terrance West 2.50 6.00
291 Tevin Reese 2.50 6.00
292 Timmy Jernigan 2.50 6.00
293 Michael Campanaro 2.50 6.00
295 Trent Murphy 2.50 6.00
296 Troy Niklas 2.50 6.00
298 Jimmie Ward 3.00 8.00
300 Zack Martin 5.00 12.00

2014 Prestige Extra Points Gold Autographs

*GOLD/35-50: .6X TO 1.5X BLUE
*GOLD/20: .8X TO 2X BLUE
210 Blake Bortles/15 6.00 15.00
228 De'Anthony Thomas/50 4.00 10.00

2014 Prestige Extra Points Purple Autographs

*PURPLE/75-100: .5X TO 1.2X BLUE
210 Blake Bortles/25 6.00 15.00

2014 Prestige First Impressions Autographs

1 A.J. McCarron/75 5.00 12.00
2 Aaron Murray/99 5.00 12.00
3 Andre Williams/99 5.00 12.00
4 Bishop Sankey/99 5.00 12.00
5 Blake Bortles/25 10.00 25.00
6 Carlos Hyde/99 6.00 15.00
7 Derek Carr/75 30.00 80.00
8 Devonta Freeman/99 8.00 20.00
9 Donte Moncrief/99 5.00 12.00
10 Eric Ebron/99 10.00 25.00
11 Jadeveon Clowney/75 6.00 15.00
12 Jeremy Hill/99 6.00 15.00
13 Jimmy Garoppolo/75 30.00 80.00
14 Johnny Manziel/25 12.00 30.00
15 Ka'Deem Carey/99 5.00 12.00
16 Kelvin Benjamin/99 8.00 20.00
17 Terrance West/99 8.00 20.00
18 Marqise Lee/99 8.00 20.00
19 Mike Evans/50 12.00 30.00
20 Odell Beckham Jr./99 40.00 100.00
21 Sammy Watkins/75 8.00 20.00
22 Teddy Bridgewater/25 12.00 30.00
23 Brandin Cooks/75 8.00 20.00

2014 Prestige First Rounders

*SILVER/25: 1.2X TO 3X BASIC INSERTS
1 EJ Manuel .75 2.00
2 Robert Griffin III .75 2.00
3 Doug Martin 1.00 2.50
4 Patrick Peterson .75 2.00
5 J.J. Watt 1.25 3.00
6 Dez Bryant 1.25 3.00
7 Demaryius Thomas 1.00 2.50
8 Michael Crabtree .75 2.00
9 Percy Harvin .75 2.00
10 Joe Flacco 1.00 2.50
11 Calvin Johnson 1.25 3.00
12 Adrian Peterson 1.25 3.00
13 Reggie Bush .75 2.00
14 Aaron Rodgers 2.50 6.00
15 Troy Polamalu 1.25 3.00

2014 Prestige League Leaders Jerseys

*PRIME/25: .6X TO 1.5X BASIC JSY/49-99
1 Peyton Manning/99 8.00 20.00
2 Drew Brees/99 4.00 10.00
3 Matt Ryan/99 3.00 8.00
4 Philip Rivers/99 4.00 10.00
5 LeSean McCoy/99 4.00 10.00
6 Eddie Lacy/15 4.00 10.00
7 Josh Gordon/99 2.50 6.00
8 Antonio Brown/99 4.00 10.00
9 Robert Quinn/99 3.00 8.00
10 Richard Sherman/49 10.00 25.00

2014 Prestige NFL Jerseys

*PRIME: .8X TO 2X BASIC JSY
1 Adrian Peterson 4.00 10.00
2 Andrew Luck 5.00 12.00
3 Russell Wilson 6.00 15.00
4 Geno Smith 2.50 6.00
5 Cordarrelle Patterson 2.50 6.00
6 EJ Manuel 2.50 6.00
7 Malcolm Smith 4.00 10.00
8 Le'Veon Bell 3.00 8.00
9 Marshawn Lynch 3.00 8.00
10 Chris Ivory 3.00 8.00
11 Eddie Lacy 2.50 6.00
12 Andre Johnson 3.00 8.00
13 Vincent Jackson 2.50 6.00
14 Manti Te'o 3.00 8.00
15 Shonn Greene 2.50 6.00

2014 Prestige NFL Shield

1 Drew Brees 2.00 5.00
2 Jordan Cameron 1.25 3.00
3 Victor Cruz 1.50 4.00
4 Larry Fitzgerald 1.50 4.00
5 Nick Foles 1.50 4.00
6 Arian Foster 1.50 4.00
7 Robert Griffin III 1.25 3.00
8 Rob Gronkowski 2.00 5.00
9 Alshon Jeffery 1.50 4.00
10 Calvin Johnson 2.00 5.00
11 Eddie Lacy 1.25 3.00
12 Colin Kaepernick 1.50 4.00
13 Andrew Luck 2.50 6.00
14 Peyton Manning 4.00 10.00
15 Adrian Peterson 2.00 5.00
16 Keenan Allen 1.50 4.00
17 Philip Rivers 2.00 5.00
18 Aaron Rodgers 4.00 10.00
19 Ben Roethlisberger 2.00 5.00
20 Tony Romo 1.50 4.00
21 Alex Smith 1.50 4.00
22 Geno Smith 1.25 3.00
23 Russell Wilson 3.00 8.00
24 Robert Woods 1.50 4.00
25 Steve Smith 1.50 4.00

2014 Prestige NFL Passport Signatures

1 Johnny Manziel 8.00 20.00
2 Teddy Bridgewater 8.00 20.00
3 Blake Bortles 6.00 15.00
4 Sammy Watkins 8.00 20.00
5 Mike Evans 12.00 30.00
6 Marqise Lee 8.00 20.00
7 Odell Beckham Jr. 30.00 60.00
8 Brandin Cooks 8.00 20.00
9 Kelvin Benjamin 8.00 20.00
10 Derek Carr 30.00 80.00
11 Jimmy Garoppolo 30.00 60.00
12 A.J. McCarron 5.00 12.00
13 Tre Mason 5.00 12.00
14 Jeremy Hill 6.00 15.00
15 Tajh Boyd 5.00 12.00
16 De'Anthony Thomas 5.00 12.00
17 Dri Archer 5.00 12.00
18 Paul Richardson 8.00 20.00
19 Eric Ebron 6.00 15.00
20 Cody Latimer 6.00 15.00
21 Andre Williams 6.00 15.00
22 Terrance West 8.00 20.00
23 Devonta Freeman 8.00 20.00
24 Tom Savage 10.00 25.00
25 Austin Seferian-Jenkins 5.00 12.00
26 Logan Thomas 5.00 12.00
27 Jadeveon Clowney 6.00 15.00
28 Jace Amaro 5.00 12.00

2014 Prestige Number Ones

1 Andrew Luck 1.25 3.00
2 Cam Newton 1.00 2.50
3 Matthew Stafford .75 2.00
4 Mario Williams .60 1.50
5 Alex Smith .75 2.00
6 Michael Vick .75 2.00
7 Peyton Manning 2.00 5.00
8 Troy Aikman 1.25 3.00
9 Bruce Smith .75 2.00
10 John Elway 1.50 4.00

2014 Prestige Prestigious Picks Jerseys

*PRIME/25: .8X TO 2X BASIC JSY/99
1 A.J. McCarron 2.00 5.00
2 Aaron Murray 2.00 5.00
3 Allen Robinson 3.00 8.00
4 Andre Williams 2.00 5.00
5 Bishop Sankey 2.00 5.00
6 Blake Bortles 2.50 6.00
7 Brandin Cooks 3.00 8.00
8 Austin Seferian-Jenkins 2.00 5.00
9 Carlos Hyde 2.50 6.00
10 Charles Sims 2.00 5.00
11 Cody Latimer 2.50 6.00
12 Devonta Freeman 3.00 8.00
13 Donte Moncrief 2.00 5.00
14 Eric Ebron 2.50 6.00
15 Jadeveon Clowney 2.50 6.00
16 Jeremy Hill 2.50 6.00
17 Jimmy Garoppolo 15.00 40.00
18 Johnny Manziel 3.00 8.00
19 Jordan Matthews 3.00 8.00
20 Ka'Deem Carey 2.00 5.00
21 Kelvin Benjamin 3.00 8.00
22 Davante Adams 3.00 8.00
23 Marqise Lee 2.50 6.00
24 Mike Evans 5.00 12.00
25 Odell Beckham Jr. 5.00 12.00
26 Paul Richardson 2.50 6.00
27 Sammy Watkins 3.00 8.00
28 Teddy Bridgewater 3.00 8.00
29 Tre Mason 2.00 5.00
30 Dri Archer 2.00 5.00

2014 Prestige Road to the NFL

*SILVER/25: 1.5X TO 4X BASIC INSERTS
1 Johnny Manziel .50 1.25
2 Teddy Bridgewater .50 1.25
3 Blake Bortles .40 1.00
4 Sammy Watkins .50 1.25
5 Mike Evans .75 2.00
6 Marqise Lee .40 1.00
7 Odell Beckham Jr. .75 2.00
8 Brandin Cooks .50 1.25
9 Kelvin Benjamin .50 1.25
10 Derek Carr 2.00 5.00
11 Jimmy Garoppolo 2.50 6.00
12 A.J. McCarron .30 .75
13 Carlos Hyde .40 1.00
14 Ka'Deem Carey .30 .75
15 Bishop Sankey .30 .75
16 Allen Robinson .50 1.25
17 Davante Adams .50 1.25
18 Jordan Matthews .50 1.25
19 Paul Richardson .40 1.00
20 Eric Ebron .40 1.00
21 Charles Sims .30 .75
22 Cody Latimer .40 1.00
23 Andre Williams .30 .75
24 Terrance West .30 .75
25 Devonta Freeman .50 1.25
26 Tom Savage .30 .75
27 Aaron Murray .30 .75
28 Logan Thomas .30 .75
29 Jadeveon Clowney .40 1.00
30 Jace Amaro .30 .75
31 Austin Seferian-Jenkins .30 .75
33 Donte Moncrief .30 .75
34 Dri Archer .30 .75
35 De'Anthony Thomas .30 .75
36 Khalil Mack 1.25 3.00
37 Tajh Boyd .30 .75
38 Michael Sam .30 .75
39 Jeremy Hill .40 1.00
40 Tre Mason .30 .75

2014 Prestige Road to the NFL Signatures

1 Johnny Manziel 8.00 20.00
2 Teddy Bridgewater 8.00 20.00
3 Blake Bortles 6.00 15.00
4 Sammy Watkins 8.00 20.00
5 Mike Evans 12.00 30.00
6 Marqise Lee 6.00 15.00
7 Odell Beckham Jr. 30.00 60.00
8 Tre Mason 5.00 12.00
9 Derek Carr 30.00 80.00
10 Jimmy Garoppolo 30.00 80.00
11 A.J. McCarron 5.00 12.00
12 Carlos Hyde 6.00 15.00
13 Kelvin Benjamin 8.00 20.00
14 Ka'Deem Carey 5.00 12.00
15 Bishop Sankey 5.00 12.00
16 Allen Robinson 8.00 20.00
17 Davante Adams 8.00 20.00
18 Jordan Matthews 8.00 20.00
19 Eric Ebron 6.00 15.00
20 Charles Sims 5.00 12.00
21 Cody Latimer 6.00 15.00
22 Tajh Boyd 5.00 12.00
23 Terrance West 6.00 15.00
24 Tom Savage 8.00 20.00
25 Aaron Murray 5.00 12.00
26 Logan Thomas
27 Jadeveon Clowney 6.00 15.00
28 Jace Amaro 5.00 12.00
29 Austin Seferian-Jenkins 5.00 12.00
30 Jarvis Landry 10.00 25.00
31 Donte Moncrief 5.00 12.00
32 Dri Archer 5.00 12.00
33 De'Anthony Thomas 5.00 12.00

2014 Prestige Rookie Autographs

201 A.J. McCarron 2.50 6.00
202 Aaron Donald 6.00 15.00
203 Aaron Murray 2.50 6.00
204 Cody Latimer 3.00 8.00
205 Allen Robinson 4.00 10.00
206 Andre Williams 2.50 6.00
207 Anthony Barr 2.50 6.00
208 Austin Seferian-Jenkins 2.50 6.00
209 Bishop Sankey 2.50 6.00
210 Blake Bortles 3.00 8.00
211 Bradley Roby 2.50 6.00
212 Brandin Cooks 4.00 10.00
213 Brandon Coleman 2.50 6.00
214 Brett Smith 2.50 6.00
215 Bruce Ellington 2.50 6.00
217 Calvin Pryor 2.50 6.00
218 Carlos Hyde 3.00 8.00
219 Charles Sims 2.50 6.00
220 Chris Borland 2.50 6.00
221 Chris Smith 2.50 6.00
222 Connor Shaw 2.50 6.00
225 Darqueze Dennard 3.00 8.00
227 David Fales 2.50 6.00
228 De'Anthony Thomas 2.50 6.00
229 Dee Ford 2.50 6.00
230 Deone Bucannon 2.50 6.00
231 Derek Carr 15.00 40.00
232 Devonta Freeman 4.00 10.00
233 Donte Moncrief 2.50 6.00
234 Dri Archer 2.50 6.00
235 Ed Reynolds 2.50 6.00
236 Eric Ebron 3.00 8.00
237 Greg Robinson 2.50 6.00
238 Ha Ha Clinton-Dix 3.00 8.00
239 Jace Amaro 2.50 6.00
240 Kevin Norwood 2.50 6.00
241 Jadeveon Clowney 3.00 8.00
242 Jake Matthews 2.50 6.00
245 James Wilder Jr. 3.00 8.00
246 Jared Abbrederis 2.50 6.00
248 Jason Verrett 2.50 6.00
249 Jeremy Hill 3.00 8.00
250 Jerick McKinnon 3.00 8.00
252 Jimmy Garoppolo 25.00 50.00
253 Johnny Manziel 4.00 10.00
255 Josh Huff 3.00 8.00
256 Ka'Deem Carey 2.50 6.00
257 Kelvin Benjamin 4.00 10.00
258 Khalil Mack 10.00 25.00
259 Kony Ealy 3.00 8.00
260 Kyle Fuller 2.50 6.00
261 Kyle Van Noy 3.00 8.00
262 L'Damian Washington 3.00 8.00
263 Lache Seastrunk 2.50 6.00
264 Lamarcus Joyner 3.00 8.00
265 Logan Thomas 2.50 6.00
266 Louis Nix III 2.50 6.00
268 Marcus Smith 2.50 6.00
269 Marion Grice 2.50 6.00
270 Marqise Lee 3.00 8.00
271 Martavis Bryant 3.00 8.00
272 Michael Sam 2.50 6.00
273 C.J. Fiedorowicz 2.50 6.00
274 Mike Evans 6.00 15.00
275 Odell Beckham Jr. 30.00 60.00
276 Paul Richardson 5.00 12.00
277 Isaiah Crowell 3.00 8.00
278 Ra'Shede Hageman 2.50 6.00
279 Ryan Shazier 4.00 10.00
280 Sammy Watkins 4.00 10.00
281 Scott Crichton 2.50 6.00
282 Shaq Evans 2.50 6.00
283 Shayne Skov 5.00 12.00
285 Dominique Easley 2.50 6.00
286 Tajh Boyd 2.50 6.00
287 Taylor Lewan 2.50 6.00
288 Teddy Bridgewater 4.00 10.00
289 Telvin Smith 2.50 6.00
290 Terrance West 2.50 6.00
291 Tevin Reese 2.50 6.00
292 Timmy Jernigan 2.50 6.00
293 Michael Campanaro 2.50 6.00
295 Trent Murphy 2.50 6.00
296 Troy Niklas 2.50 6.00
298 Jimmie Ward 3.00 8.00
300 Zack Martin 5.00 12.00

2014 Prestige Rookie Draft Jerseys

*PRIME/17-25: .8X TO 2X BASIC JSY/99
1 Jadeveon Clowney 2.50 6.00
2 Greg Robinson 2.00 5.00
3 Khalil Mack 8.00 20.00
4 Jake Matthews 2.00 5.00
5 Mike Evans 5.00 12.00
6 Blake Bortles 2.50 6.00
7 Justin Gilbert 2.00 5.00
8 Eric Ebron 2.50 6.00
9 Taylor Lewan 2.00 5.00
10 Odell Beckham Jr. 5.00 12.00
11 Kyle Fuller 2.00 5.00
12 Ryan Shazier 3.00 8.00
13 C.J. Mosley 2.50 6.00
14 Johnny Manziel 3.00 8.00
15 Calvin Pryor 2.00 5.00
16 Brandin Cooks 3.00 8.00
17 Ha Ha Clinton-Dix 2.50 6.00
18 Jason Verrett 2.00 5.00
19 Sammy Watkins 3.00 8.00
20 Teddy Bridgewater 3.00 8.00

2014 Prestige Rookie Jumbo Jerseys Patch

*BASE JUMBO/250: .3X TO .8X BASIC PATCH
*PURPLE/100: .5X TO 1.2X BASIC PATCH
*GOLD/50: .6X TO 1.5X BASIC PATCH
*SILVER/25: 1X TO 2.5X BASIC PATCH
AA Asa Watson 2.00 5.00
AJ A.J. McCarron 2.00 5.00
AM Aaron Murray 2.00 5.00
AR Allen Robinson 3.00 8.00
AS Austin Seferian-Jenkins 2.00 5.00
AW Andre Williams 2.00 5.00
BB Blake Bortles 2.50 6.00
BC Brandin Cooks 3.00 8.00
BS Bishop Sankey 2.00 5.00
CH Carlos Hyde 2.50 6.00
CL Cody Latimer 2.50 6.00
CS1 Connor Shaw 2.00 5.00
CS2 Charles Sims 2.00 5.00
DA1 Davante Adams 3.00 8.00
DA2 Dri Archer 2.00 5.00
DF Devonta Freeman 3.00 8.00
DM Donte Moncrief 2.00 5.00
DT De'Anthony Thomas 2.00 5.00
EE Eric Ebron 2.50 6.00
JC Jadeveon Clowney 2.50 6.00
JG Jimmy Garoppolo 15.00 40.00
JH Jeremy Hill 2.50 6.00
JL Jarvis Landry 4.00 10.00
JM Jordan Matthews 3.00 8.00
JM1 Johnny Manziel 3.00 8.00
KB Kelvin Benjamin 3.00 8.00
KC Ka'Deem Carey 2.00 5.00
KM Khalil Mack 8.00 20.00
LT Logan Thomas 2.00 5.00
ME Mike Evans 5.00 12.00
ML Marqise Lee 2.50 6.00
OB Odell Beckham Jr. 5.00 12.00
PR Paul Richardson 2.50 6.00
SW Sammy Watkins 3.00 8.00
TB1 Tajh Boyd 2.00 5.00
TB2 Teddy Bridgewater 3.00 8.00
TM Tre Mason 2.00 5.00
TS Tom Savage 2.00 5.00
TW Terrance West 2.00 5.00

2014 Prestige Rookie League Leader Jerseys

*PRIME/25: .6X TO 1.5X BASIC JSY/49-99
1 Geno Smith/25 4.00 10.00
2 Mike Glennon/49 4.00 10.00
3 EJ Manuel/25 4.00 10.00
4 Eddie Lacy/15 4.00 10.00
5 Zac Stacy/25 4.00 10.00
6 Le'Veon Bell/49 4.00 10.00
7 Andre Ellington/99 3.00 8.00
8 Giovani Bernard/99 3.00 8.00
9 Montee Ball/99 3.00 8.00
10 Keenan Allen/49 4.00 10.00
11 DeAndre Hopkins/25 5.00 12.00
12 Kenny Stills/99 3.00 8.00
13 Cordarrelle Patterson/99 3.00 8.00
14 Robert Woods/99 4.00 10.00
15 Jordan Reed/49 3.00 8.00
16 Tyler Eifert/99 4.00 10.00
17 Sheldon Richardson/99 3.00 8.00
18 Ezekiel Ansah/99 3.00 8.00
19 Kiko Alonso/25 4.00 10.00
20 Eric Reid/25 5.00 12.00

2014 Prestige Top of the Class

1 Andre Ellington 1.25 3.00
2 Cordarrelle Patterson 1.25 3.00
3 DeAndre Hopkins 1.50 4.00
4 Eddie Lacy 1.25 3.00
5 EJ Manuel 1.25 3.00
6 Geno Smith 1.25 3.00
7 Giovani Bernard 1.25 3.00
8 Keenan Allen 1.50 4.00
9 Mike Glennon 1.50 4.00
10 Terrance Williams 1.25 3.00

2014 Prestige Black Friday Draft Picks

DP1 Aaron Murray .50 1.25
DP2 A.J. McCarron .50 1.25
DP3 Andre Williams .50 1.25
DP4 Bishop Sankey .50 1.25
DP5 Blake Bortles .60 1.50
DP6 Brandin Cooks .75 2.00
DP7 Carlos Hyde .60 1.50
DP8 Cody Latimer .60 1.50
DP9 Derek Carr 3.00 8.00
DP10 Dri Archer .50 1.25
DP11 Jadeveon Clowney .60 1.50
DP12 Jeremy Hill .60 1.50
DP13 Sammy Watkins .75 2.00
DP13 Jimmy Garoppolo 4.00 10.00
DP14 Johnny Manziel .75 2.00
DP15 Jordan Matthews .75 2.00
DP16 Kelvin Benjamin .75 2.00
DP17 Logan Thomas .50 1.25
DP18 Marqise Lee .60 1.50
DP19 Mike Evans 1.25 3.00
DP20 Odell Beckham Jr. 1.25 3.00
DP21 Paul Richardson .60 1.50
DP23 Teddy Bridgewater .75 2.00
DP24 Tom Savage .50 1.25
DP25 Tre Mason .50 1.25

2015 Prestige

COMP.SET w/o SP's (300) 50.00 80.00
COMP.SET w/o RC's (200) 10.00 25.00
BASE ROOKIES FEATURE COLLEGE UNIFORM
SP ROOKIES FEATURE PRO UNIFORM
ONE ROOKIE PER PACK OVERALL
1 Tom Brady .75 2.00
2 Julian Edelman .30 .75
3 Rob Gronkowski .30 .75
4 Brandon Bolden .20 .50
5 LeGarrette Blount .25 .60
6 Danny Amendola .25 .60
7 Malcolm Butler .30 .75
8 Russell Wilson .40 1.00
9 Marshawn Lynch .25 .60
10 Doug Baldwin .25 .60
11 Jermaine Kearse .20 .50
12 Richard Sherman .30 .75
13 Kam Chancellor .30 .75
14 Jimmy Graham .30 .75
15 EJ Manuel .20 .50
16 Sammy Watkins .25 .60
17 Robert Woods .25 .60
18 Fred Jackson .25 .60
19 LeSean McCoy .30 .75
20 Percy Harvin .20 .50
21 Ryan Tannehill .25 .60
22 Kenny Stills .20 .50
23 Jordan Cameron .20 .50
24 Jarvis Landry .25 .60
25 Lamar Miller .20 .50
26 Ndamukong Suh .25 .60
27 Geno Smith .20 .50
28 Eric Decker .20 .50
29 Brandon Marshall .20 .50
30 Jeremy Kerley .20 .50
31 Chris Ivory .25 .60
32 Darrelle Revis .20 .50
33 Tony Romo .25 .60
34 Cole Beasley .30 .75
35 Dez Bryant .30 .75
36 Jason Witten .25 .60
37 Terrance Williams .20 .50
38 Darren McFadden .20 .50
39 Eli Manning .25 .60
40 Victor Cruz .25 .60
41 Odell Beckham Jr. .30 .75
42 Rashad Jennings .20 .50
43 Larry Donnell .20 .50
44 Jason Pierre-Paul .20 .50
45 Sam Bradford .20 .50
46 DeMarco Murray .25 .60
47 Riley Cooper .25 .60
48 Jordan Matthews .25 .60
49 Darren Sproles .25 .60
50 Zach Ertz .25 .60
51 Robert Griffin III .20 .50
52 Alfred Morris .20 .50
53 DeSean Jackson .25 .60
54 Pierre Garcon .25 .60
55 Jordan Reed .20 .50
56 Ryan Kerrigan .20 .50
57 Joe Flacco .25 .60
58 Dennis Pitta .20 .50
59 Steve Smith .25 .60
60 Justin Forsett .25 .60
61 Lorenzo Taliaferro .20 .50
62 C.J. Mosley .30 .75
63 Andy Dalton .25 .60
64 A.J. Green .30 .75
65 Mohamed Sanu .20 .50
66 Giovani Bernard .20 .50
67 Jeremy Hill .20 .50
68 Geno Atkins .20 .50
69 Josh McCown .25 .60
70 Johnny Manziel .25 .60
71 Brian Hartline .25 .60
72 Isaiah Crowell .20 .50
73 Andrew Hawkins .20 .50
74 Dwayne Bowe .25 .60
75 Ben Roethlisberger .30 .75
76 Le'Veon Bell .25 .60
77 Antonio Brown .30 .75
78 Martavis Bryant .20 .50
79 Heath Miller .20 .50
80 DeAngelo Williams .20 .50
81 Jay Cutler .20 .50
82 Marquess Wilson .20 .50
83 Alshon Jeffery .25 .60
84 Matt Forte .20 .50
85 Martellus Bennett .20 .50
86 Eddie Royal .20 .50
87 Matthew Stafford .25 .60
88 Calvin Johnson .30 .75
89 Golden Tate .20 .50
90 Brandon Pettigrew .20 .50
91 Joique Bell .20 .50
92 Ezekiel Ansah .20 .50
93 Aaron Rodgers .60 1.50
94 Eddie Lacy .20 .50
95 Jordy Nelson .25 .60
96 Randall Cobb .25 .60
97 Julius Peppers .25 .60
98 Clay Matthews .30 .75
99 Teddy Bridgewater .25 .60
100 Mike Wallace .20 .50
101 Cordarrelle Patterson .20 .50
102 Kyle Rudolph .20 .50
103 Matt Asiata .20 .50
104 Harrison Smith .20 .50
105 Brian Hoyer .20 .50
106 Arian Foster .25 .60
107 Alfred Blue .20 .50
108 DeAndre Hopkins .25 .60
109 Garrett Graham .20 .50
110 J.J. Watt .30 .75
111 Andrew Luck .40 1.00
112 Donte Moncrief .25 .60
113 T.Y. Hilton .25 .60
114 Frank Gore .25 .60
115 Dwayne Allen .20 .50
116 Andre Johnson .25 .60
117 Blake Bortles .20 .50
118 Julius Thomas .20 .50
119 Marqise Lee .20 .50
120 Marcedes Lewis .20 .50
121 Denard Robinson .20 .50
122 Paul Posluszny .20 .50
123 Zach Mettenberger .20 .50
124 Justin Hunter .20 .50
125 Kendall Wright .20 .50
126 Bishop Sankey .20 .50
127 Delanie Walker .20 .50
128 Shonn Greene .20 .50
129 Matt Ryan .25 .60
130 Julio Jones .30 .75
131 Roddy White .20 .50
132 Devin Hester .25 .60
133 Devonta Freeman .25 .60
134 Levine Toilolo .20 .50
135 Cam Newton .30 .75
136 Kelvin Benjamin .25 .60
137 Jerricho Cotchery .20 .50
138 Greg Olsen .25 .60
139 Jonathan Stewart .20 .50
140 Ted Ginn Jr. .20 .50
141 Luke Kuechly .25 .60
142 Drew Brees .30 .75
143 Jairus Byrd .20 .50
144 Marques Colston .20 .50
145 C.J. Spiller .20 .50
146 Mark Ingram .25 .60
147 Khiry Robinson .25 .60
148 Brandin Cooks .25 .60
149 Lavonte David .20 .50
150 Vincent Jackson .20 .50
151 Mike Evans .25 .60
152 Doug Martin .25 .60
153 Bobby Rainey .20 .50
154 Gerald McCoy .20 .50
155 Peyton Manning .60 1.50
156 Demaryius Thomas .25 .60
157 Emmanuel Sanders .25 .60
158 Cody Latimer .20 .50
159 Montee Ball .20 .50
160 C.J. Anderson .25 .60
161 Owen Daniels .20 .50
162 Von Miller .25 .60
163 DeMarcus Ware .25 .60
164 Alex Smith .25 .60
165 Jeremy Maclin .20 .50
166 Knile Davis .20 .50
167 Jamaal Charles .25 .60
168 Travis Kelce .30 .75
169 Tamba Hali .20 .50
170 Derek Carr .30 .75
171 Latavius Murray .20 .50
172 Rod Streater .20 .50
173 Trent Richardson .20 .50
174 James Jones .20 .50
175 Philip Rivers .30 .75
176 Keenan Allen .25 .60
177 Malcom Floyd .20 .50
178 Antonio Gates .20 .50
179 Branden Oliver .25 .60
180 Danny Woodhead .25 .60
181 Eric Weddle .20 .50
182 Carson Palmer .25 .60
183 Larry Fitzgerald .25 .60
184 Michael Floyd .20 .50
185 John Carlson .20 .50
186 Andre Ellington .20 .50
187 Patrick Peterson .20 .50
188 Nick Foles .25 .60
189 Kenny Britt .20 .50
190 Tavon Austin .20 .50
191 Jared Cook .20 .50
192 Tre Mason .25 .60
193 Aaron Donald .30 .75
194 Colin Kaepernick .25 .60
195 Torrey Smith .20 .50
196 Anquan Boldin .20 .50
197 Vernon Davis .20 .50
198 Carlos Hyde .20 .50
199 Reggie Bush .20 .50
200 Aldon Smith .20 .50
201 Bud Dupree RC .40 1.00
202A Amari Cooper RC 1.00 2.50
202B Amari Cooper SP 2.00 5.00
203A Ameer Abdullah RC .50 1.25
203B Ameer Abdullah SP 1.00 2.50
204 Antwan Goodley RC .30 .75
205 Arik Armstead RC .30 .75
206 Austin Hill RC .30 .75
207 Ben Koyack RC .50 1.25
208 Benardrick McKinney RC .30 .75
209 Blake Sims RC .30 .75
210 Byron Jones RC .50 1.25
211A Breshad Perriman RC .30 .75
211B Breshad Perriman SP .75 2.00
212A Brett Hundley RC .30 .75
212B Brett Hundley SP .60 1.50
213 Bryan Bennett RC .30 .75
214A Bryce Petty RC .30 .75
214B Bryce Petty SP .60 1.50
215 Cameron Artis-Payne RC .30 .75
216 Carl Davis RC .40 1.00
217A Chris Conley RC .30 .75
217B Chris Conley SP .60 1.50
218 Clive Walford RC .30 .75
219 Danielle Hunter RC .40 1.00
220 Danny Shelton RC .30 .75
221 Dante Fowler Jr. RC .50 1.25
222 Darren Waller RC .40 1.00
223 DaVaris Daniels RC .30 .75
224A David Cobb RC .30 .75
224B David Cobb SP .60 1.50
225A David Johnson RC .75 2.00
225B David Johnson SP 1.50 4.00
226 DeAndrew White RC .50 1.25
227 Denzel Perryman RC .30 .75
228 Deontay Greenberry RC .30 .75
229A DeVante Parker RC .50 1.25
229B DeVante Parker SP 1.00 2.50
230A Devin Funchess RC .50 1.25
230B Devin Funchess SP 1.00 2.50
231A Devin Smith RC .30 .75
231B Devin Smith SP .60 1.50
232 Dezmin Lewis RC .30 .75
233A Dorial Green-Beckham RC .30 .75
233B Dorial Green-Beckham SP .60 1.50
234 Dres Anderson RC .30 .75
235A Duke Johnson RC .50 1.25
235B Duke Johnson SP 1.00 2.50
236 Eddie Goldman RC .30 .75
237 Eli Harold RC .30 .75
238 Eric Kendricks RC .30 .75
239 Eric Rowe RC .30 .75
240A Garrett Grayson RC .30 .75
240B Garrett Grayson SP .60 1.50
241 Ifo Ekpre-Olomu RC .30 .75
242A Jaelen Strong RC .40 1.00
242B Jaelen Strong SP .75 2.00
243 Jalen Collins RC .30 .75
244A Jameis Winston RC .75 2.00
244B Jameis Winston SP 1.50 4.00
245A Jamison Crowder RC .40 1.00
245B Jamison Crowder SP .75 2.00
246A Buck Allen RC .40 1.00
246B Buck Allen SP .75 2.00
247A Jay Ajayi RC .50 1.25
247B Jay Ajayi SP 1.00 2.50
248A Jeremy Langford RC .30 .75
248B Jeremy Langford SP .60 1.50
249 Jesse James RC .40 1.00
250 J.J. Nelson RC .30 .75
251 Josh Harper RC .30 .75
252 Josh Robinson RC .30 .75
253 Josh Shaw RC .50 1.25
254A Justin Hardy RC .30 .75
254B Justin Hardy SP .60 1.50
255 Karlos Williams RC .30 .75
256 Kenny Bell RC .50 1.25
257 Kevin Johnson RC .30 .75
258A Kevin White RC .40 1.00
258B Kevin White SP .75 2.00
259 Kwon Alexander RC .40 1.00
260 Landon Collins RC .40 1.00
261A Leonard Williams RC .30 .75
261B Leonard Williams SP .60 1.50
262 Malcolm Brown RC .40 1.00
263 Malcom Brown RC .30 .75
264A Marcus Mariota RC 1.25 3.00
264B Marcus Mariota SP 2.50 6.00
265 Marcus Peters RC .50 1.25
266 Mario Alford RC .30 .75
267A Matt Jones RC .30 .75
267B Matt Jones SP .60 1.50
268A Maxx Williams RC .30 .75
268B Maxx Williams SP .60 1.50
269A Melvin Gordon RC .75 2.00
269B Melvin Gordon SP 1.50 4.00
270 Michael Dyer RC .50 1.25
271A Mike Davis RC .30 .75
271B Mike Davis SP .60 1.50
272A Nelson Agholor RC .40 1.00
272B Nelson Agholor SP .75 2.00
273 Nick O'Leary RC .30 .75
274 Owamagbe Odighizuwa RC .40 1.00
275 P.J. Williams RC .40 1.00
276A Phillip Dorsett RC .30 .75
276B Phillip Dorsett SP .60 1.50
277 Randy Gregory RC .30 .75
278A Rashad Greene RC .30 .75
278B Rashad Greene SP .60 1.50
279 Ronald Darby RC .30 .75
280A Sammie Coates RC .40 1.00
280B Sammie Coates SP .75 2.00
281A Sean Mannion RC .30 .75
281B Sean Mannion SP .60 1.50
282 Shane Carden RC .30 .75
283 Shane Ray RC .30 .75
284 Shaq Thompson RC .40 1.00
285A Stefon Diggs RC .75 2.00
285B Stefon Diggs SP 1.50 4.00
286 Stephone Anthony RC .30 .75
287A T.J. Yeldon RC .30 .75
287B T.J. Yeldon SP .60 1.50
288 Taylor Heinicke RC .50 1.25
289A Tevin Coleman RC .40 1.00
289B Tevin Coleman SP .75 2.00
290 Titus Davis RC .40 1.00
291A Todd Gurley RC 1.25 3.00
291B Todd Gurley SP 2.50 6.00
292 Tony Lippett RC .30 .75
293 Trae Waynes RC .30 .75
294 Tre McBride RC .30 .75
295 Trey Flowers RC .50 1.25
296 Trey Williams RC .40 1.00
297A Ty Montgomery RC .30 .75
297B Ty Montgomery SP .60 1.50
298A Tyler Lockett RC .50 1.25
298B Tyler Lockett SP 1.00 2.50
299 Vic Beasley Jr. RC .40 1.00
300A Vince Mayle RC .40 1.00
300B Vince Mayle SP .75 2.00

2015 Prestige Extra Points Black

*1-200 VETS/10: 6X TO 15X BASIC CARDS
*201-300 ROOKIES/10: 4X TO 10X BASIC RC
244 Jameis Winston 50.00 100.00
264 Marcus Mariota 40.00 80.00

2015 Prestige Extra Points Blue

*1-200 VETS: 1.2X TO 3X BASIC CARDS
*201-300 ROOKIES: .8X TO 2X BASIC RC

2015 Prestige Extra Points Gold

*1-200 VETS/50: 2X TO 5X BASIC CARDS
*201-300 ROOKIES/50: 1.2X TO 3X BASIC RC
244 Jameis Winston 10.00 25.00
264 Marcus Mariota 20.00 40.00

2015 Prestige Extra Points Green

*1-200 VETS: 1X TO 2.5X BASIC CARDS
*201-300 ROOKIES: .6X TO 1.5X BASIC RC

2015 Prestige Extra Points Platinum

*1-200 VETS/25: 4X TO 10X BASIC CARDS
*201-300 ROOKIES/25: 2.5X TO 6X BASIC RC
244 Jameis Winston 25.00 50.00
264 Marcus Mariota 60.00 100.00

2015 Prestige Extra Points Purple

*1-200 VETS/100: 1.2X TO 3X BASIC CARDS
*201-300 ROOKIES/100: .8X TO 2X BASIC RC

2015 Prestige Extra Points Red

*1-200 VETS: 1X TO 2.5X BASIC CARDS
*201-300 ROOKIES: .6X TO 1.5X BASIC RC
264 Marcus Mariota 6.00 15.00

2015 Prestige All Americans

1 Marcus Mariota 1.50 4.00
2 Brandon Scherff .60 1.50
3 Melvin Gordon 1.00 2.50
4 Landon Collins .50 1.25
5 Jaelen Strong .50 1.25
6 Gerod Holliman .60 1.50
7 Nick O'Leary .40 1.00
8 Senquez Golson .40 1.00
9 Tevin Coleman .50 1.25
10 Amari Cooper 1.25 3.00
11 Hau'oli Kikaha .50 1.25
12 Shane Ray .40 1.00
13 Maxx Williams .40 1.00
14 Kevin White .50 1.25
15 Tre Jackson .60 1.50

2015 Prestige Autographs

1 Latavius Murray/99 8.00 20.00
2 Jimmy Garoppolo/79 30.00 60.00
4 Micah Hyde/99 10.00 25.00
5 Lorenzo Taliaferro/99 5.00 12.00
7 Teddy Bridgewater/20
8 Brandin Cooks/99 6.00 15.00
9 Kony Ealy/99 5.00 12.00
10 Randall Cobb/49 20.00 40.00
11 Jadeveon Clowney/49 6.00 15.00
12 Luke Kuechly/79 12.00 30.00
13 DeSean Jackson/49 8.00 20.00
14 Earl Thomas/99 10.00 25.00
15 Isaiah Crowell/99 5.00 12.00
16 Martavis Bryant/99 5.00 12.00
17 Jamaal Charles/49 10.00 25.00
18 Michael Floyd/99 5.00 12.00
19 Rob Gronkowski/49 20.00 40.00
21 David Fales/99 5.00 12.00
22 Paul Posluszny/99 5.00 12.00
24 Sio Moore/99 5.00 12.00
25 Danny Lansanah/99 5.00 12.00
26 Jason Witten/49 25.00 50.00
27 Blake Bortles/20 10.00 25.00
28 Andy Dalton/20 12.00 30.00
29 Anquan Boldin/49 6.00 15.00
31 Carson Palmer/20 12.00 30.00
32 Devonta Freeman/99 6.00 15.00
33 Coby Fleener/99 5.00 12.00
34 Aaron Donald/99 8.00 20.00
35 Demaryius Thomas/49 8.00 20.00
36 EJ Manuel/79 5.00 12.00
37 Jarvis Landry/99 6.00 15.00
38 Bishop Sankey/99 5.00 12.00
39 Danny Woodhead/79 6.00 15.00
40 Geno Smith/49 6.00 15.00
41 Anthony Barr/99 5.00 12.00
42 Andre Williams/99 5.00 12.00
44 Jordan Matthews/99 6.00 15.00
45 Connor Shaw/99 5.00 12.00
46 Giovani Bernard/79 5.00 12.00
47 Terrance Williams/99 5.00 12.00
48 Austin Seferian-Jenkins/99 5.00 12.00
49 Justin Houston/99 6.00 15.00
50 Joe Flacco/20 12.00 30.00

2015 Prestige Big Four Jerseys

*PRIME/10: 1X TO 1.5X BASIC JSY/25
1 Dltn/Brnrd/Grshm/Snu 6.00 15.00
2 Alnso/McKlvn/Drs/Wllms 6.00 15.00
3 Tlb/Rby/Wre/Mllr 6.00 15.00
4 Mrry/Brynt/Wttn/Rmo 10.00 25.00
5 Cly/Lndry/Mllr/Tnnhll 6.00 15.00

2015 Prestige Big Three Jerseys

*PRIME/10: .6X TO 1.5X BASIC JSY/25
1 Krkptrck/Mlga/Brfct 5.00 12.00
2 Gdwn/Wds/Chndlr 6.00 15.00
3 Thms/Thms/Wlkr 6.00 15.00
4 Jhnsn/Brry/Hstn 6.00 15.00
5 Wttn/Wllms/Rmo 6.00 15.00
6 Lndry/Wllce/Tnnhll 6.00 15.00
7 Rbnsn/Shrts/Lee 6.00 15.00
8 Amndla/Edlmn/Gronk 8.00 20.00
9 Flcco/Dnls/Smth 6.00 15.00
10 Flyd/Rvrs/Mthws 8.00 20.00

2015 Prestige Blue Chip Recruits

1 DeVante Parker .50 1.25
2 Amari Cooper 1.00 2.50
3 Jameis Winston .75 2.00
4 Dorial Green-Beckham .30 .75
5 Todd Gurley 1.25 3.00
6 Dante Fowler Jr. .50 1.25
7 T.J. Yeldon .30 .75
8 Jay Ajayi .50 1.25
9 Vic Beasley Jr. .40 1.00
10 Ameer Abdullah .50 1.25
11 Jaelen Strong .50 1.25
12 Marcus Mariota 1.25 3.00
13 Sammie Coates .40 1.00
14 Melvin Gordon .75 2.00
15 Brett Hundley .30 .75
16 Kevin White .40 1.00
17 Maxx Williams .30 .75
18 Leonard Williams .30 .75
19 Breshad Perriman .30 .75
20 Bryce Petty .30 .75

2015 Prestige Campus Legends

1 John Elway 3.00 8.00
2 Barry Sanders 3.00 8.00
3 Bo Jackson 2.50 6.00
4 Deion Sanders 1.50 4.00
5 Tony Dorsett 2.00 5.00

2015 Prestige Captain Collection

1 Matt Ryan 1.00 2.50
2 Mario Williams .75 2.00
3 Cam Newton 1.25 3.00
4 Carson Palmer 1.00 2.50
5 Tony Romo 1.00 2.50
6 Demaryius Thomas 1.00 2.50
7 Luke Kuechly 1.00 2.50
8 Aaron Rodgers 3.00 8.00
9 Eli Manning 1.00 2.50
10 Andrew Luck 1.50 4.00
11 Andy Dalton 1.00 2.50
12 Russell Wilson 1.50 4.00
13 Drew Brees 1.25 3.00
14 Victor Cruz 1.00 2.50
15 Vincent Jackson .75 2.00
16 Philip Rivers 1.25 3.00
17 Ryan Tannehill 1.00 2.50
18 Kam Chancellor 1.25 3.00

2015 Prestige Collegiate Jerseys

*PRIME/10: .6X TO 1.5X BASIC JSY/25
1 Amari Cooper 10.00 25.00
2 T.J. Yeldon 3.00 8.00
3 Jaelen Strong 4.00 10.00
4 Bryce Petty 3.00 8.00
5 Jay Ajayi 5.00 12.00
6 Breshad Perriman 3.00 8.00
7 Jameis Winston 8.00 20.00
8 Todd Gurley 12.00 30.00
9 Tevin Coleman 4.00 10.00
10 DeVante Parker 5.00 12.00
11 Phillip Dorsett 3.00 8.00
12 Duke Johnson 5.00 12.00
13 Devin Funchess 5.00 12.00
14 Ameer Abdullah 5.00 12.00
15 Maxx Williams 3.00 8.00
16 Marcus Mariota 12.00 30.00
17 Brett Hundley 3.00 8.00
18 Nelson Agholor 4.00 10.00
19 Kevin White 4.00 10.00
20 Melvin Gordon 8.00 20.00

2015 Prestige Connections Jerseys

*PRIME/10: .6X TO 1.5X BASIC JSY/15-25
1 M.Wallace/Tannehill/25 5.00 12.00
2 D.Bryant/T.Romo/25 6.00 15.00
3 J.Maclin/N.Foles/25 5.00 12.00
4 E.Manning/V.Cruz/15 5.00 12.00
5 A.Green/A.Dalton/25 6.00 15.00
6 J.Flacco/S.Smith/15 5.00 12.00
7 B.Bortles/M.Lee/25 4.00 10.00
8 M.Ryan/R.White/15 5.00 12.00
9 P.Manning/W.Welker/15 12.00 30.00
10 M.Floyd/P.Rivers/25 6.00 15.00
11 C.Palmer/L.Fitzgerald/25 5.00 12.00
12 S.Vereen/S.Ridley/25 5.00 12.00
13 K.Moreno/L.Miller/25 4.00 10.00
14 D.Murray/J.Randle/25 5.00 12.00
15 D.Sproles/L.McCoy/25 6.00 15.00
16 G.Bernard/J.Hill/25 4.00 10.00
17 D.Robinson/T.Gerhart/25 4.00 10.00
18 D.Williams/J.Stewart/25 4.00 10.00
19 Woodhead/R.Mathews/25 5.00 12.00
20 M.Ball/R.Hillman/25 4.00 10.00

2015 Prestige Draft Big Board
1 Jameis Winston .75 2.00
2 Todd Gurley 1.25 3.00
3 Maxx Williams .30 .75
4 Kevin White .40 1.00
5 Jay Ajayi .50 1.25
6 Marcus Mariota 1.25 3.00
7 DeVante Parker .50 1.25
8 Ameer Abdullah .50 1.25
9 Jaelen Strong .40 1.00
10 Sean Mannion .30 .75
11 Breshad Perriman .30 .75
12 Melvin Gordon .75 2.00
13 Dorial Green-Beckham .30 .75
14 Brett Hundley .30 .75
15 Duke Johnson .50 1.25
16 Sammie Coates .40 1.00
17 Clive Walford .30 .75
18 Tevin Coleman .40 1.00
19 Bryce Petty .30 .75
20 Amari Cooper 1.00 2.50

2015 Prestige Draft Day Jerseys
PRIME/10: .6X TO 1.5X BASIC JSY/25
1 Dante Fowler Jr. 5.00 12.00
2 Brandon Scherff 5.00 12.00
3 Leonard Williams 3.00 8.00
4 Kevin White 4.00 10.00
5 Vic Beasley Jr. 4.00 10.00
6 Todd Gurley 12.00 30.00
7 Trae Waynes 3.00 8.00
8 Danny Shelton 3.00 8.00
9 Andrus Peat 3.00 8.00
10 DeVante Parker 5.00 12.00
11 Melvin Gordon 8.00 20.00
12 Kevin Johnson 3.00 8.00
13 Cameron Erving 4.00 10.00
14 Cedric Ogbuehi 3.00 8.00
15 Bud Dupree 4.00 10.00
16 Shane Ray 3.00 8.00
17 D.J. Humphries 3.00 8.00
18 Breshad Perriman 3.00 8.00
19 Byron Jones 5.00 12.00
20 Laken Tomlinson 3.00 8.00

2015 Prestige Draft Picks
1 Jameis Winston .75 2.00
2 Marcus Mariota 1.25 3.00
3 Amari Cooper 1.00 2.50
4 Kevin White .40 1.00
5 Todd Gurley 1.25 3.00
6 Leonard Williams .30 .75
7 DeVante Parker .50 1.25
8 Melvin Gordon .75 2.00
9 Sammie Coates .40 1.00
10 Dorial Green-Beckham .30 .75
11 Devin Funchess .50 1.25
12 Ameer Abdullah .50 1.25
13 Jaelen Strong .40 1.00
14 Sean Mannion .30 .75
15 Bryce Petty .30 .75

2015 Prestige Draft Picks Autographs
DPSAA Ameer Abdullah/99 5.00 12.00
DPSBH Brett Hundley/25 5.00 12.00
DPSBP Breshad Perriman/99 3.00 8.00
DPSBPE Bryce Petty/50 4.00 10.00
DPSCW Clive Walford/99 3.00 8.00
DPSDF Dante Fowler Jr./99 5.00 12.00
DPSDG Dorial Green-Beckham/99 3.00 8.00
DPSDJ David Johnson/99 12.00 30.00
DPSDJO Duke Johnson/99 5.00 12.00
DPSDP DeVante Parker/99 5.00 12.00
DPSJA Jay Ajayi/99 5.00 12.00
DPSJS Jaelen Strong/99 4.00 10.00
DPSJW Jameis Winston/25 60.00 120.00
DPSKW Kevin White/25 15.00 40.00
DPSLW Leonard Williams/99 3.00 8.00
DPSMM Marcus Mariota/25 50.00 100.00
DPSMW Maxx Williams/99 3.00 8.00
DPSNA Nelson Agholor/25 6.00 15.00
DPSSC Sammie Coates/99 4.00 10.00
DPSTC Tevin Coleman/99 4.00 10.00
DPSTG Todd Gurley/25 20.00 50.00
DPSTW Trae Waynes/99 3.00 8.00
DPSVB Vic Beasley Jr./99 4.00 10.00

2015 Prestige Draft Picks Jumbo Blue
*JUMBO BLACK/10: X TO X JUMBO BLUE
1 Jameis Winston 1.50 4.00
2 Marcus Mariota 2.50 6.00
3 Amari Cooper 2.00 5.00
4 Kevin White .75 2.00
5 Todd Gurley 2.50 6.00
6 Dante Fowler Jr. 1.00 2.50
7 DeVante Parker 1.00 2.50
8 Melvin Gordon 1.50 4.00
9 Nelson Agholor .75 2.00
10 Breshad Perriman .60 1.50
11 Phillip Dorsett .60 1.50
12 Ameer Abdullah 1.00 2.50
13 Garrett Grayson .60 1.50
14 Brett Hundley .60 1.50
15 Devin Smith .60 1.50

2015 Prestige Draft Picks Retail
1 Jameis Winston .75 2.00
2 Marcus Mariota 1.25 3.00
3 Amari Cooper 1.00 2.50
4 Kevin White .40 1.00
5 Todd Gurley 1.25 3.00
6 Dante Fowler Jr. .50 1.25
7 DeVante Parker .50 1.25
8 Melvin Gordon .75 2.00
9 Nelson Agholor .40 1.00
10 Breshad Perriman .30 .75
11 Phillip Dorsett .30 .75
12 Ameer Abdullah .50 1.25
13 Garrett Grayson .30 .75
14 Brett Hundley .30 .75
15 Devin Smith .30 .75

2015 Prestige Draft Picks Retail Jumbo Red
*JUMBO BLACK/10: X TO X JUMBO RED
1 Jameis Winston 1.50 4.00
2 Marcus Mariota 2.50 6.00
3 Amari Cooper 2.00 5.00
4 Kevin White .75 2.00
5 Todd Gurley 2.50 6.00
6 Leonard Williams .60 1.50
7 DeVante Parker 1.00 2.50
8 Melvin Gordon 1.50 4.00
9 Sammie Coates .75 2.00
10 Dorial Green-Beckham .60 1.50
11 Devin Funchess 1.00 2.50
12 Ameer Abdullah 1.00 2.50
13 Jaelen Strong .75 2.00
14 Sean Mannion .60 1.50
15 Bryce Petty .60 1.50
16 Brett Hundley .60 1.50
17 Nelson Agholor .75 2.00
18 T.J. Yeldon .60 1.50
19 Breshad Perriman .60 1.50
20 Phillip Dorsett .60 1.50
21 Tyler Lockett 1.00 2.50

2015 Prestige First Impressions Autographs
FIAA Ameer Abdullah/99 5.00 12.00
FIBH Brett Hundley/25 5.00 12.00
FIBP Breshad Perriman/99 3.00 8.00
FIBPE Bryce Petty/50 20.00 40.00
FICW Clive Walford/99 3.00 8.00
FIDF Dante Fowler Jr./99 5.00 12.00
FIDG Dorial Green-Beckham/99 3.00 8.00
FIDJ David Johnson/99 10.00 25.00
FIDJO Duke Johnson/99 5.00 12.00
FIDP [illegible]
FIJA Jay Ajayi/99 5.00 12.00
FIJS Jaelen Strong/99 4.00 10.00
FIJW Jameis Winston/25 75.00 150.00
FIKW Kevin White/25 15.00 40.00
FILW Leonard Williams/99 3.00 8.00
FIMM Marcus Mariota/25 50.00 100.00
FIMW Maxx Williams/99 3.00 8.00
FINA Nelson Agholor/25
FISC Sammie Coates/99 4.00 10.00
FITC Tevin Coleman/99 4.00 10.00
FITG Todd Gurley/25 20.00 50.00
FITW Trae Waynes/99 3.00 8.00
FIVB Vic Beasley Jr./99 4.00 10.00

2015 Prestige Franchise Favorites
1 Eddie Lacy 1.00 2.50
2 Alshon Jeffery 1.25 3.00
3 Antonio Brown 1.50 4.00
4 Joe Flacco 1.25 3.00
5 Rob Gronkowski 1.50 4.00
6 Calvin Johnson 1.50 4.00
7 Cameron Wake 1.00 2.50
8 Matt Ryan 1.25 3.00
9 Charles Woodson 1.50 4.00
10 Arian Foster 1.25 3.00
11 Cordarrelle Patterson 1.00 2.50
12 Robert Quinn 1.25 3.00
13 Larry Fitzgerald 1.25 3.00
14 Muhammad Wilkerson 1.00 2.50
15 Jason Witten 1.25 3.00
16 Marques Colston 1.00 2.50
17 Russell Wilson 2.00 5.00
18 Luke Kuechly 1.25 3.00
19 Anquan Boldin 1.00 2.50
20 Peyton Manning 3.00 8.00
21 Keenan Allen 1.25 3.00
22 Fred Jackson 1.25 3.00
23 Odell Beckham Jr. 1.50 4.00
24 Andrew Luck 2.00 5.00
25 Alfred Morris 1.00 2.50
26 Andy Dalton 1.25 3.00
27 Brent Celek 1.00 2.50
28 Blake Bortles 1.00 2.50
29 Bishop Sankey 1.00 2.50
30 Joe Haden 1.00 2.50
31 Doug Martin 1.25 3.00
32 Jamaal Charles 1.25 3.00

2015 Prestige Franchise Favorites Materials
*PRIME/10: .6X TO 1.5X BASIC JSY/15-20
1 Matt Forte/15 4.00 10.00
2 Joe Haden/20 4.00 10.00
3 Colin Kaepernick/15 5.00 12.00
4 A.J. Green/15 6.00 15.00
5 Julian Edelman/20 6.00 15.00
6 Calvin Johnson/15 6.00 15.00
7 Larry Fitzgerald/15 5.00 12.00
8 Vincent Jackson/20 4.00 10.00
9 Aaron Rodgers/15 12.00 30.00
10 Demaryius Thomas/15 5.00 12.00
11 Jonathan Stewart/20 4.00 10.00
12 Fred Jackson/20 5.00 12.00
13 Marshawn Lynch/15 5.00 12.00
14 Alfred Morris/20 4.00 10.00
15 James Laurinaitis/20 5.00 12.00
16 Jason Witten/15 5.00 12.00
17 Roddy White/20 4.00 10.00
18 Antonio Brown/15 6.00 15.00
19 Marques Colston/15 4.00 10.00
20 Jamaal Charles/20 5.00 12.00
21 Antonio Gates/20 4.00 10.00
22 T.Y. Hilton/20 5.00 12.00
23 Denard Robinson/20 4.00 10.00
24 Eric Decker/15 4.00 10.00
25 Andy Dalton/20 5.00 12.00

2015 Panini Next Day Autographs
RANDOM INSERTS IN PRESTIGE PACKS
NDAA Ameer Abdullah 5.00 12.00
NDAC Amari Cooper 30.00 60.00
NDBA Buck Allen 4.00 10.00
NDBH Brett Hundley 3.00 8.00
NDBP Breshad Perriman 3.00 8.00
NDBPE Bryce Petty 3.00 8.00
NDCC Chris Conley 3.00 8.00
NDDC David Cobb 3.00 8.00
NDDF Devin Funchess 5.00 12.00
NDDGB Dorial Green-Beckham 3.00 8.00
NDDJ David Johnson 8.00 20.00
NDDJO Duke Johnson 5.00 12.00
NDDP DeVante Parker 5.00 12.00
NDDS Devin Smith 3.00 8.00
NDGG Garrett Grayson 3.00 8.00
NDJA Jay Ajayi 5.00 12.00
NDJC Jamison Crowder 4.00 10.00
NDJH Justin Hardy 3.00 8.00
NDJL Jeremy Langford 3.00 8.00
NDJS Jaelen Strong 4.00 10.00
NDJW Jameis Winston 30.00 60.00
NDKW Kevin White 4.00 10.00
NDKWI Karlos Williams 3.00 8.00
NDLW Leonard Williams 3.00 8.00
NDMD Mike Davis 3.00 8.00
NDMG Melvin Gordon 40.00 80.00
NDMJ Matt Jones 3.00 8.00
NDMM Marcus Mariota 40.00 80.00
NDMW Maxx Williams 3.00 8.00
NDNA Nelson Agholor 4.00 10.00
NDPD Phillip Dorsett 3.00 8.00
NDRG Rashad Greene 3.00 8.00
NDSC Sammie Coates 4.00 10.00
NDSD Stefon Diggs 8.00 20.00
NDSM Sean Mannion 3.00 8.00
NDTC Tevin Coleman 4.00 10.00
NDTG Todd Gurley 40.00 80.00
NDTL Tyler Lockett 5.00 12.00
NDTM Ty Montgomery 3.00 8.00
NDTY T.J. Yeldon 3.00 8.00
NDVM Vince Mayle 4.00 10.00

2015 Prestige NFL Shield
1 Andre Ellington 1.00 2.50
2 Julio Jones 1.50 4.00
3 Steve Smith 1.25 3.00
4 Sammy Watkins 1.25 3.00
5 Cam Newton 1.50 4.00
6 Matt Forte 1.00 2.50
7 A.J. Green 1.50 4.00
8 Johnny Manziel 1.25 3.00
9 Dez Bryant 1.50 4.00
10 Peyton Manning 3.00 8.00
11 Matthew Stafford 1.25 3.00
12 Jordy Nelson 1.25 3.00
13 DeAndre Hopkins 1.25 3.00
14 T.Y. Hilton 1.25 3.00
15 Travis Kelce 1.50 4.00
16 Lamar Miller 1.00 2.50
17 Teddy Bridgewater 1.25 3.00
18 Julian Edelman 1.50 4.00
19 Mark Ingram 1.25 3.00
20 Eli Manning 1.25 3.00
21 Eric Decker 1.00 2.50
22 Derek Carr 1.50 4.00
23 Darren Sproles 1.25 3.00
24 Le'Veon Bell 1.25 3.00
25 Antonio Gates 1.00 2.50
26 Vernon Davis 1.00 2.50
27 Richard Sherman 1.50 4.00
28 James Laurinaitis 1.25 3.00
29 Mike Evans 1.25 3.00
30 DeSean Jackson 1.25 3.00

2015 Prestige Past and Present Jerseys
*GOLD/15-25: .6X TO 1.5X BASIC JSY/149
*PURPLE/49: .5X TO 1.2X BASIC JSY/149
*PLATINUM/49: [illegible]
PPAS Alex Smith 3.00 8.00
PPBC Brandin Cooks 3.00 8.00
PPDJ DeSean Jackson 3.00 8.00
PPDR Darrelle Revis 2.50 6.00
PPDS Darren Sproles 3.00 8.00
PPDW DeMarcus Ware 3.00 8.00
PPEE Eric Ebron 2.50 6.00
PPES Emmanuel Sanders 3.00 8.00
PPJA Jared Allen 2.50 6.00
PPJH Jeremy Hill 2.50 6.00
PPJM Johnny Manziel 3.00 8.00
PPJP Julius Peppers 3.00 8.00
PPKB Kelvin Benjamin 3.00 8.00
PPKM Khalil Mack 4.00 10.00
PPME Mike Evans 3.00 8.00
PPOB Odell Beckham Jr. 4.00 10.00
PPSW Sammy Watkins 3.00 8.00
PPTB Teddy Bridgewater 3.00 8.00
PPTG Toby Gerhart 2.50 6.00
PPVJ Vincent Jackson 2.50 6.00

2015 Prestige Prestigious Picks
1 Jameis Winston .75 2.00
2 Marcus Mariota 1.25 3.00
3 Amari Cooper 1.00 2.50
4 Kevin White .40 1.00
5 Todd Gurley 1.25 3.00
6 Dante Fowler Jr. .50 1.25
7 DeVante Parker .50 1.25
8 Melvin Gordon .75 2.00
9 Nelson Agholor .40 1.00
10 Breshad Perriman .30 .75
11 Phillip Dorsett .30 .75
12 Ameer Abdullah .50 1.25
13 Garrett Grayson .30 .75
14 Brett Hundley .30 .75
15 Devin Smith .30 .75
16 Leonard Williams .30 .75
17 T.J. Yeldon .30 .75
18 Dorial Green-Beckham .30 .75
19 Devin Funchess .50 1.25
20 Tyler Lockett .50 1.25

2015 Prestige Prestigious Picks Jerseys
*PRIME/10: .6X TO 1.5X BASIC JSY/25
1 Jameis Winston 8.00 20.00
2 Marcus Mariota 12.00 30.00
3 Amari Cooper 10.00 25.00
4 Kevin White 4.00 10.00
5 Todd Gurley 12.00 30.00
6 Dante Fowler Jr. 5.00 12.00
7 DeVante Parker 5.00 12.00
8 Melvin Gordon 8.00 20.00
9 Nelson Agholor 4.00 10.00
10 Breshad Perriman 3.00 8.00
11 Phillip Dorsett 3.00 8.00
12 Ameer Abdullah 5.00 12.00
13 Garrett Grayson 3.00 8.00
14 Brett Hundley 3.00 8.00
15 Devin Smith 3.00 8.00
16 Leonard Williams 3.00 8.00
17 T.J. Yeldon 3.00 8.00
18 Dorial Green-Beckham 3.00 8.00
19 Devin Funchess 5.00 12.00
20 Tyler Lockett 5.00 12.00
21 Jaelen Strong 4.00 10.00
22 Tevin Coleman 4.00 10.00
23 Maxx Williams 3.00 8.00
24 Chris Conley 3.00 8.00
25 Duke Johnson 5.00 12.00
26 Sammie Coates 4.00 10.00
27 Sean Mannion 3.00 8.00
28 Bryce Petty 3.00 8.00
29 David Johnson 8.00 20.00
30 Ty Montgomery 3.00 8.00

2015 Prestige Road to the NFL
1 Jameis Winston .75 2.00
2 Todd Gurley 1.25 3.00
3 Maxx Williams .30 .75
4 Kevin White .40 1.00
5 Jay Ajayi .50 1.25
6 Marcus Mariota 1.25 3.00
7 DeVante Parker .50 1.25
8 Ameer Abdullah .50 1.25
9 Jaelen Strong .40 1.00
10 Sean Mannion .30 .75
11 Breshad Perriman .30 .75
12 Melvin Gordon .75 2.00
13 Dorial Green-Beckham .30 .75
14 Brett Hundley .30 .75
15 Duke Johnson .50 1.25
16 Sammie Coates .40 1.00
17 Clive Walford .30 .75
18 Tevin Coleman .40 1.00
19 Bryce Petty .30 .75
20 Amari Cooper 1.00 2.50

2015 Prestige Rookie Autographs
201 Bud Dupree 3.00 8.00
202 Amari Cooper SP 40.00 80.00
203 Ameer Abdullah 4.00 10.00
204 Antwan Goodley 2.50 6.00
205 Arik Armstead 2.50 6.00
206 Austin Hill 2.50 6.00
207 Ben Koyack 4.00 10.00
208 Benardrick McKinney 2.50 6.00
209 Blake Sims 2.50 6.00
210 Byron Jones 8.00 20.00
211 Breshad Perriman 2.50 6.00
212 Brett Hundley 2.50 6.00
213 Bryan Bennett 2.50 6.00
214 Bryce Petty 2.50 6.00
215 Cameron Artis-Payne 2.50 6.00
216 Carl Davis 3.00 8.00
217 Chris Conley 2.50 6.00
218 Clive Walford 2.50 6.00
219 Danielle Hunter 3.00 8.00
220 Danny Shelton 2.50 6.00
221 Dante Fowler Jr. 4.00 10.00
222 Darren Waller 3.00 8.00
223 DaVaris Daniels 2.50 6.00
224 David Cobb 2.50 6.00
225 David Johnson 6.00 15.00
226 DeAndrew White 4.00 10.00
227 Denzel Perryman 2.50 6.00
228 Deontay Greenberry 2.50 6.00
229 DeVante Parker 4.00 10.00
230 Devin Funchess 4.00 10.00
231 Devin Smith 2.50 6.00
232 Dezmin Lewis 2.50 6.00
233 Dorial Green-Beckham 2.50 6.00
234 Dres Anderson 2.50 6.00
235 Duke Johnson 4.00 10.00
237 Eli Harold 2.50 6.00
238 Eric Kendricks 2.50 6.00
239 Eric Rowe 2.50 6.00
241 Ifo Ekpre-Olomu 2.50 6.00
242 Jaelen Strong 3.00 8.00
244 Jameis Winston SP 25.00 50.00
245 Jamison Crowder 3.00 8.00
247 Jay Ajayi 4.00 10.00
248 Jeremy Langford 2.50 6.00
249 Jesse James 3.00 8.00
250 J.J. Nelson 2.50 6.00
251 Josh Harper 2.50 6.00
252 Josh Robinson 2.50 6.00
253 Josh Shaw 4.00 10.00
254 Justin Hardy 2.50 6.00
255 Karlos Williams 2.50 6.00
256 Kenny Bell 4.00 10.00
257 Kevin Johnson 2.50 6.00
258 Kevin White SP 3.00 8.00
259 Kwon Alexander 3.00 8.00
260 Landon Collins 3.00 8.00
261 Leonard Williams 2.50 6.00
262 [illegible]
263 Malcom Brown 2.50 6.00
264 Marcus Mariota SP 30.00 80.00
265 Marcus Peters 4.00 10.00
266 Mario Alford 2.50 6.00
267 Matt Jones 2.50 6.00
268 Maxx Williams 2.50 6.00
269 Melvin Gordon SP
270 Michael Dyer 4.00 10.00
271 Mike Davis 2.50 6.00
272 Nelson Agholor 3.00 8.00
273 Nick O'Leary 2.50 6.00
274 Owamagbe Odighizuwa 3.00 8.00
275 P.J. Williams 3.00 8.00
276 Phillip Dorsett 2.50 6.00
277 Randy Gregory 2.50 6.00
278 Rashad Greene 2.50 6.00
279 Ronald Darby 2.50 6.00
280 Sammie Coates 3.00 8.00
281 Sean Mannion 2.50 6.00
282 Shane Carden 2.50 6.00
283 Shane Ray 2.50 6.00
284 Shaq Thompson 3.00 8.00
285 Stefon Diggs 6.00 15.00
286 Stephone Anthony 2.50 6.00
287 T.J. Yeldon 2.50 6.00
288 Taylor Heinicke 4.00 10.00
289 Tevin Coleman 3.00 8.00
290 Titus Davis 3.00 8.00
291 Todd Gurley SP 15.00 40.00
292 Tony Lippett 2.50 6.00
293 Trae Waynes 2.50 6.00
294 Tre McBride 2.50 6.00
295 Trey Flowers 4.00 10.00
296 Trey Williams 3.00 8.00
298 Tyler Lockett 4.00 10.00
299 Vic Beasley Jr. 3.00 8.00
300 Vince Mayle 3.00 8.00

2015 Prestige Rookie Autographs Blue
*BLUE: X TO X BASIC AUTO
269 Melvin Gordon

2015 Prestige Rookie Autographs Gold
*GOLD/50: .6X TO 1.5X BASIC AUTO
269 Melvin Gordon/15
291 Todd Gurley/50 20.00 50.00

2015 Prestige Rookie Autographs Platinum
*PLATINUM/25: .8X TO 2X BASIC AUTO
258 Kevin White/25 6.00 15.00
291 Todd Gurley/25 25.00 60.00

2015 Prestige Rookie Autographs Purple
*PURPLE/100: .5X TO 1.2X BASIC AUTO
264 Marcus Mariota/100 40.00 100.00
269 Melvin Gordon/20
291 Todd Gurley/100 15.00 40.00

2015 Prestige Rookie Autographs Red
*RED: .4X TO 1X BASIC AUTO
264 Marcus Mariota SP 30.00 80.00
269 Melvin Gordon SP

2015 Prestige Rookie Jumbo Jerseys Patch Red
*JUMBO JSY/75: .4X TO 1X PATCH RED
*PATCH BLACK/10: 1X TO 2.5X PATCH RED
*PATCH GOLD/50: .6X TO 1.5X PATCH RED
*PATCH PLAT/25: .8X TO 2X PATCH RED
*PATCH PURPLE/100: .5X TO 1.2X PATCH RED
RJJAA Ameer Abdullah 3.00 8.00
RJJAC Amari Cooper 6.00 15.00
RJJBA Buck Allen 2.50 6.00
RJJBH Brett Hundley 2.00 5.00
RJJBP Breshad Perriman 2.00 5.00
RJJBPE Bryce Petty 2.00 5.00
RJJCC Chris Conley 2.00 5.00
RJJDC David Cobb 2.00 5.00
RJJDF Devin Funchess 3.00 8.00
RJJDG Dorial Green-Beckham 2.00 5.00
RJJDJ David Johnson 5.00 12.00
RJJDJO Duke Johnson 3.00 8.00
RJJDP DeVante Parker 3.00 8.00
RJJDS Devin Smith 2.00 5.00
RJJGG Garrett Grayson 2.00 5.00
RJJJA Jay Ajayi 3.00 8.00
RJJJC Jamison Crowder 2.50 6.00
RJJJH Justin Hardy 2.00 5.00
RJJJL Jeremy Langford 2.00 5.00
RJJJS Jaelen Strong 2.50 6.00
RJJJW Jameis Winston 12.00 30.00
RJJKW Kevin White 2.50 6.00
RJJLW Leonard Williams 2.00 5.00
RJJMD Mike Davis 2.00 5.00
RJJMG Melvin Gordon 5.00 12.00
RJJMJ Matt Jones 2.00 5.00
RJJMM Marcus Mariota 8.00 20.00
RJJMW Maxx Williams 2.00 5.00
RJJNA Nelson Agholor 2.50 6.00
RJJPD Phillip Dorsett 2.00 5.00
RJJRG Rashad Greene 2.00 5.00
RJJSC Sammie Coates 2.50 6.00
RJJSD Stefon Diggs 5.00 12.00
RJJSM Sean Mannion 2.00 5.00
RJJTC Tevin Coleman 2.50 6.00
RJJTG Todd Gurley 8.00 20.00
RJJTL Tyler Lockett 3.00 8.00
RJJTM Ty Montgomery 2.00 5.00
RJJTY T.J. Yeldon 2.00 5.00
RJJVM Vince Mayle 2.50 6.00

2015 Prestige Super Bowl Heroes
1 Bart Starr 2.00 5.00
2 Joe Namath 1.50 4.00
3 Roger Staubach 1.50 4.00
4 Larry Csonka 1.00 2.50
5 Franco Harris 1.25 3.00
6 Terry Bradshaw 1.50 4.00
7 John Riggins 1.00 2.50
8 Marcus Allen 1.25 3.00
9 Jerry Rice 2.00 5.00
10 Joe Montana 3.00 8.00
11 Troy Aikman 1.50 4.00
12 Emmitt Smith 2.00 5.00
13 Steve Young 1.50 4.00
14 John Elway 2.00 5.00
15 Tom Brady 2.50 6.00
16 Peyton Manning 2.00 5.00
17 Eli Manning .75 2.00
18 Drew Brees 1.00 2.50
19 Aaron Rodgers 2.00 5.00
20 Malcolm Butler 1.00 2.50

2016 Prestige
1 Carson Palmer .25 .60
2 Chris Johnson .20 .50
3 David Johnson .30 .75
4 John Brown .25 .60
5 Larry Fitzgerald .25 .60
6 Michael Floyd .20 .50
7 Patrick Peterson .20 .50
8 Matt Ryan .25 .60
9 Devonta Freeman .25 .60
10 Tevin Coleman .25 .60
11 Julio Jones .30 .75
12 Jacob Tamme .20 .50
13 Joe Flacco .25 .60
14 Justin Forsett .25 .60
15 Buck Allen .20 .50
16 Kamar Aiken .20 .50
17 Steve Smith .25 .60
18 C.J. Mosley .25 .60
19 Tyrod Taylor .25 .60
20 LeSean McCoy .30 .75
21 Karlos Williams [illegible]
22 Sammy Watkins .30 .75
23 Charles Clay .20 .50
24 Jerry Hughes .20 .50
25 Cam Newton .30 .75
26 Jonathan Stewart .20 .50
27 Greg Olsen .25 .60
28 Ted Ginn Jr. .20 .50
29 Devin Funchess .20 .50
30 Kelvin Benjamin .25 .60
31 Luke Kuechly .25 .60
32 Jay Cutler .20 .50
33 Matt Forte .20 .50
34 Jeremy Langford .25 .60
35 Alshon Jeffery .25 .60
36 Kevin White .20 .50
37 Pernell McPhee .20 .50
38 Andy Dalton .25 .60
39 Giovani Bernard .20 .50
40 Jeremy Hill .20 .50
41 A.J. Green .30 .75
42 Tyler Eifert .25 .60
43 A.J. McCarron .20 .50
44 Reggie Nelson .20 .50
45 Josh McCown .20 .50
46 Duke Johnson .20 .50
47 Isaiah Crowell .20 .50
48 Travis Benjamin .20 .50
49 Gary Barnidge .20 .50
50 Karlos Dansby .20 .50
51 Tony Romo .25 .60
52 Darren McFadden .20 .50
53 Jason Witten .25 .60
54 Dez Bryant .30 .75
55 Terrance Williams .20 .50
56 Sean Lee .25 .60
57 Peyton Manning .60 1.50
58 Brock Osweiler .20 .50
59 C.J. Anderson .25 .60
60 Ronnie Hillman .20 .50
61 Demaryius Thomas .25 .60
62 Emmanuel Sanders .30 .75
63 Von Miller .25 .60
64 Matthew Stafford .25 .60
65 Ameer Abdullah .20 .50
66 Calvin Johnson .30 .75
67 Golden Tate .20 .50
68 Theo Riddick .20 .50
69 Ezekiel Ansah .20 .50
70 Aaron Rodgers .60 1.50
71 Eddie Lacy .20 .50
72 Randall Cobb .25 .60
73 Jordy Nelson .25 .60
74 Richard Rodgers .25 .60
75 James Jones .20 .50
76 Clay Matthews .30 .75
77 Brian Hoyer .20 .50
78 Alfred Blue .20 .50
79 Arian Foster .25 .60
80 DeAndre Hopkins .25 .60
81 J.J. Watt .30 .75
82 Whitney Mercilus .20 .50
83 Andrew Luck .40 1.00
84 Frank Gore .25 .60
85 T.Y. Hilton .25 .60
86 Donte Moncrief .25 .60
87 Andre Johnson .25 .60
88 Coby Fleener .20 .50
89 Adam Vinatieri .25 .60
90 Blake Bortles .20 .50
91 T.J. Yeldon .20 .50
92 Denard Robinson .20 .50
93 Allen Robinson .25 .60
94 Allen Hurns .20 .50
95 Julius Thomas .20 .50
96 Alex Smith .25 .60
97 Charcandrick West .20 .50
98 Jamaal Charles .25 .60
99 Jeremy Maclin .20 .50
100 Travis Kelce .30 .75
101 Eric Berry .25 .60
102 Justin Houston .20 .50
103 Ryan Tannehill .25 .60
104 Lamar Miller .20 .50
105 Jay Ajayi .25 .60
106 Jarvis Landry .25 .60
107 DeVante Parker .25 .60
108 Rishard Matthews .20 .50
109 Ndamukong Suh .25 .60
110 Teddy Bridgewater .25 .60
111 Adrian Peterson .30 .75
112 Stefon Diggs .25 .60
113 Mike Wallace .20 .50
114 Kyle Rudolph .20 .50
115 Harrison Smith .20 .50
116 Tom Brady .75 2.00
117 LeGarrette Blount .25 .60
118 Dion Lewis .20 .50
119 Rob Gronkowski .30 .75
120 Julian Edelman .30 .75
121 Chandler Jones .20 .50
122 Danny Amendola .25 .60
123 Drew Brees .30 .75
124 Mark Ingram .25 .60
125 Brandin Cooks .25 .60
126 Willie Snead .25 .60
127 Cameron Jordan .20 .50
128 Eli Manning .25 .60
129 Rashad Jennings .20 .50
130 Odell Beckham Jr. .30 .75
131 Rueben Randle .20 .50
132 Robert Ayers .20 .50
133 Landon Collins .20 .50
134 Ryan Fitzpatrick .20 .50
135 Chris Ivory .25 .60
136 Brandon Marshall .20 .50
137 Eric Decker .20 .50
138 Darrelle Revis .20 .50
139 Muhammad Wilkerson .20 .50
140 Derek Carr .30 .75
141 Latavius Murray .20 .50
142 Amari Cooper .30 .75
143 Michael Crabtree .20 .50
144 Khalil Mack .30 .75
145 Charles Woodson .30 .75
146 Sam Bradford .20 .50
147 DeMarco Murray .25 .60
148 Ryan Mathews .25 .60
149 Darren Sproles .25 .60
150 Jordan Matthews .25 .60
151 Zach Ertz .25 .60
152 Ben Roethlisberger .30 .75
153 Le'Veon Bell .25 .60
154 DeAngelo Williams .20 .50
155 Antonio Brown .30 .75
156 Heath Miller .20 .50
157 Markus Wheaton .20 .50
158 Martavis Bryant .20 .50
159 Philip Rivers .30 .75
160 Melvin Gordon .25 .60
161 Danny Woodhead .25 .60
162 Keenan Allen .25 .60
163 Antonio Gates .20 .50
164 Melvin Ingram .20 .50
165 Blaine Gabbert .20 .50
166 Colin Kaepernick .25 .60
167 Carlos Hyde .20 .50
168 Anquan Boldin .20 .50
169 Torrey Smith .20 .50
170 NaVorro Bowman .25 .60
171 Russell Wilson .40 1.00
172 Marshawn Lynch .25 .60
173 Thomas Rawls .20 .50
174 Jimmy Graham .30 .75
175 Doug Baldwin .25 .60
176 Tyler Lockett .25 .60
177 Richard Sherman .30 .75
178 Nick Foles .25 .60
179 Case Keenum .25 .60
180 Todd Gurley II .30 .75
181 Tavon Austin .20 .50
182 Mark Barron .20 .50
183 James Laurinaitis .25 .60
184 Jameis Winston .30 .75
185 Doug Martin .25 .60
186 Mike Evans .25 .60
187 Vincent Jackson .20 .50
188 Gerald McCoy .20 .50
189 Marcus Mariota .30 .75
190 David Cobb .20 .50
191 Delanie Walker .20 .50
192 Kendall Wright .20 .50
193 Dorial Green-Beckham .20 .50
194 Jurrell Casey .20 .50
195 Kirk Cousins .30 .75
196 Robert Griffin III .20 .50
197 Alfred Morris .20 .50
198 DeSean Jackson .25 .60
199 Jamison Crowder .20 .50
200 Jordan Reed .20 .50
201 Jared Goff RC 2.00 5.00
202 Carson Wentz RC 3.00 8.00
203 Paxton Lynch RC .30 .75
204 Connor Cook RC SP 12.00 30.00
205 Christian Hackenberg RC .30 .75
206 Dak Prescott RC 1.50 4.00
207 Cardale Jones RC SP 12.00 30.00
208 Charone Peake RC .30 .75
209 Kevin Hogan RC .40 1.00
210 Nate Sudfeld RC .30 .75
211 Brandon Doughty RC .30 .75
212 Cody Kessler RC .30 .75
213 Brandon Allen RC .30 .75
214 Jacoby Brissett RC .40 1.00
215 Jeff Driskel RC .30 .75
216 Malcolm Mitchell RC .30 .75
217 Ezekiel Elliott RC 1.50 4.00
218 Derrick Henry RC .75 2.00
219 C.J. Prosise RC .30 .75
220 Devontae Booker RC SP 25.00 50.00
221 Alex Collins RC .40 1.00
222 Kenneth Dixon RC .30 .75
223 Jordan Howard RC .75 2.00
224 Paul Perkins RC .30 .75
225 Kenyan Drake RC SP 10.00 25.00
226 Jonathan Williams RC .40 1.00
227 Kelvin Taylor RC .30 .75
228 Aaron Green RC .30 .75
229 D.J. Foster RC .40 1.00
230 Josh Ferguson RC .30 .75
231 Tre Madden RC .30 .75
232 Demarcus Ayers RC .30 .75
233 Wendell Smallwood RC .30 .75
234 Tyler Ervin RC .30 .75
235 Keith Marshall RC .30 .75
236 Glenn Gronkowski RC SP 10.00 25.00
237 Laquon Treadwell RC .40 1.00
238 Corey Coleman RC .50 1.25
239 Michael Thomas RC .60 1.50
240 Josh Doctson RC .40 1.00
241 Will Fuller RC .50 1.25
242 Tyler Boyd RC .40 1.00
243 Pharoh Cooper RC .30 .75
244 Sterling Shepard RC .40 1.00
245 Kenny Lawler RC .50 1.25
246 Leonte Carroo RC .30 .75
247 De'Runnya Wilson RC .30 .75
248 Braxton Miller RC .30 .75
249 Demarcus Robinson RC .30 .75
250 Rashard Higgins RC SP 10.00 25.00
251 Jordan Williams RC .30 .75
252 Tajae Sharpe RC .40 1.00
253 Bralon Addison RC .30 .75
254 Aaron Burbridge RC .30 .75
255 Jordan Payton RC .30 .75
256 Jalin Marshall RC .50 1.25
257 Thomas Duarte RC .30 .75
258 Daniel Braverman RC .30 .75
259 Kolby Listenbee RC .30 .75
260 Nelson Spruce RC .30 .75
261 Cayleb Jones RC .30 .75
262 Byron Marshall RC .30 .75
263 Hunter Henry RC .40 1.00
264 Austin Hooper RC .30 .75
265 Nick Vannett RC .30 .75
266 Jerell Adams RC SP 12.00 30.00
267 Laremy Tunsil RC .30 .75
268 Ronnie Stanley RC .40 1.00
269 Taylor Decker RC .40 1.00
270 A'Shawn Robinson RC .30 .75
271 Robert Nkemdiche RC .40 1.00
272 Jarran Reed RC .30 .75
273 Kenny Clark RC .30 .75
274 Austin Johnson RC .30 .75
275 Adolphus Washington RC .30 .75
276 Andrew Billings RC .40 1.00
277 Sheldon Rankins RC .40 1.00
278 Joey Bosa RC .60 1.50
279 DeForest Buckner RC .30 .75
280 Shaq Lawson RC .30 .75
281 Emmanuel Ogbah RC .40 1.00
282 Jonathan Bullard RC .30 .75
283 Shilique Calhoun RC .30 .75
284 Kevin Dodd RC .30 .75
285 Reggie Ragland RC .30 .75
286 Myles Jack RC SP 10.00 25.00
287 Jaylon Smith RC SP 10.00 25.00
288 Scooby Wright III RC .30 .75
289 Darron Lee RC .30 .75
290 Leonard Floyd RC .40 1.00
291 Noah Spence RC .30 .75
292 Su'a Cravens RC .30 .75
293 Kamalei Correa RC .30 .75
294 Mackensie Alexander RC .30 .75
295 Vernon Hargreaves III RC .50 1.25
296 Eli Apple RC .40 1.00
297 Jalen Ramsey RC .50 1.25
298 Jayron Kearse RC .30 .75
299 Vonn Bell RC .40 1.00
300 Jeremy Cash RC .40 1.00

2016 Prestige Xtra Points Blue
*1-200 VETS: 1.2X TO 3X BASIC CARDS
*201-300 ROOKIES: .8X TO 2X BASIC RC
RANDOM INSERTS IN RETAIL PACKS

2016 Prestige Xtra Points Gold
*1-200 VETS/50: 2X TO 5X BASIC CARDS
*201-300 ROOKIES/50: 1.2X TO 3X BASIC RC

2016 Prestige Xtra Points Green
*1-200 VETS: 1X TO 2.5X BASIC CARDS
*201-300 ROOKIES: .6X TO 1.5X BASIC RC
RANDOM INSERTS IN HOBBY PACKS

2016 Prestige Xtra Points Platinum
*VETS/25: 2.5X TO 6X BASIC CARDS
*ROOKIES/25: 1.5X TO 4X BASIC CARDS

2016 Prestige Xtra Points Purple
*1-200 VETS/100: 1.2X TO 3X BASIC CARDS
*201-300 ROOKIES/100: .8X TO 2X BASIC RC

2016 Prestige Xtra Points Red
*1-200 VETS: 1X TO 2.5X BASIC CARDS
*201-300 ROOKIES: .6X TO 1.5X BASIC RC

2016 Prestige All Americans
1 Derrick Henry 1.00 2.50
2 Ezekiel Elliott 2.00 5.00
3 Corey Coleman .60 1.50
4 Josh Doctson .50 1.25
5 Laquon Treadwell .50 1.25
6 Hunter Henry .50 1.25
7 Shaq Lawson .40 1.00
8 Reggie Ragland .40 1.00
9 Vernon Hargreaves III .60 1.50
10 Vonn Bell .50 1.25
11 Joey Bosa .75 2.00
12 DeForest Buckner .40 1.00
13 Robert Nkemdiche .50 1.25
14 Jalen Ramsey .60 1.50
15 Jayron Kearse .40 1.00

2016 Prestige Alma Maters
1 Aaron Rodgers 2.00 5.00
2 Amari Cooper 1.00 2.50
3 Bishop Sankey .60 1.50
4 Bryce Petty .60 1.50
5 Derek Carr 1.00 2.50
6 Jameis Winston 1.00 2.50
7 Jarvis Landry .75 2.00
8 Jeremy Langford .75 2.00
9 Johnny Manziel .75 2.00
10 Kevin White .60 1.50
11 Marcus Mariota 1.00 2.50
12 Marshall Faulk .75 2.00
13 Melvin Gordon .75 2.00
14 Odell Beckham Jr. 1.00 2.50
15 Rob Gronkowski 1.00 2.50
16 Rod Woodson .75 2.00
17 Sammy Watkins 1.00 2.50
18 Sebastian Janikowski .60 1.50
19 Stefon Diggs .75 2.00
20 T.J. Yeldon .60 1.50
21 Teddy Bridgewater .75 2.00
22 Todd Gurley II 1.00 2.50
23 Troy Aikman 1.25 3.00
24 Brian Cushing .60 1.50
25 Chandler Jones .60 1.50

2016 Prestige Alma Maters Jerseys
1 Aaron Rodgers 8.00 20.00
2 Amari Cooper 4.00 10.00
3 Bishop Sankey 2.50 6.00
4 Bryce Petty 2.50 6.00
5 Derek Carr 4.00 10.00
6 Jameis Winston 4.00 10.00
7 Jarvis Landry 3.00 8.00
8 Jeremy Langford 3.00 8.00
9 Johnny Manziel 3.00 8.00
10 Kevin White 2.50 6.00
11 Marcus Mariota 4.00 10.00
12 Marshall Faulk 3.00 8.00
13 Melvin Gordon 3.00 8.00
14 Odell Beckham Jr. 4.00 10.00
15 Rob Gronkowski 4.00 10.00
16 Rod Woodson 6.00 15.00
17 Sammy Watkins 4.00 10.00
18 Sebastian Janikowski 2.50 6.00
19 Stefon Diggs 3.00 8.00
20 T.J. Yeldon 2.50 6.00
21 Teddy Bridgewater 3.00 8.00
22 Todd Gurley II 4.00 10.00
23 Troy Aikman 5.00 12.00
24 Brian Cushing 2.50 6.00
25 Chandler Jones 2.50 6.00

2016 Prestige Autographs
*PURPLE/70-100: .5X TO 1.2X BASIC AU
*PURPLE/30-50: .6X TO 1.5X BASIC AU
*PURPLE/25: .8X TO 2X BASIC AU
*PURPLE/15: 1X TO 2.5X BASIC AU
*GOLD/43-50: .6X TO 1.5X BASIC AU
*GOLD/25: .8X TO 2X BASIC AU
*GOLD/15: 1X TO 2.5X BASIC AU
1 A.J. Green 8.00 20.00
2 Aaron Donald 5.00 12.00
3 Amari Cooper 12.00 30.00
4 Ameer Abdullah 3.00 8.00
5 Andrew Luck 30.00 60.00
6 Andy Dalton 8.00 20.00
7 Anthony Barr 3.00 8.00
8 Antonio Brown 12.00 30.00
9 Antonio Gates 3.00 8.00
10 Arian Foster 4.00 10.00
11 Austin Seferian-Jenkins 3.00 8.00
12 Ben Roethlisberger 40.00 80.00
13 Blake Bortles 8.00 20.00
14 Brandon Coleman 3.00 8.00
15 Breshad Perriman 3.00 8.00
16 Brock Osweiler 3.00 8.00
17 Bryce Petty 3.00 8.00
18 Cameron Artis-Payne 3.00 8.00
19 Carson Palmer 6.00 15.00
20 Case Keenum 4.00 10.00
21 Charcandrick West 3.00 8.00
22 Charles Woodson 40.00 80.00
23 Chris Conley 3.00 8.00
24 Clay Matthews 12.00 30.00
25 Clive Walford 3.00 8.00
26 Colin Kaepernick 6.00 15.00
27 Crockett Gillmore 3.00 8.00
28 Danielle Hunter 3.00 8.00
30 Darrelle Revis 3.00 8.00
31 Darren McFadden 3.00 8.00
32 Darren Sproles 8.00 20.00
33 David Johnson
34 DeAngelo Williams 3.00 8.00
35 DeMarcus Ware 4.00 10.00
36 Derek Carr 15.00 40.00
37 DeSean Jackson 6.00 15.00
38 DeVante Parker 4.00 10.00
39 Devin Funchess 3.00 8.00
40 Devonta Freeman 4.00 10.00
41 Dez Bryant 20.00 40.00
42 Doug Martin 4.00 10.00
43 Drew Brees 25.00 50.00
44 Duke Johnson 3.00 8.00
45 Eddie Lacy 8.00 20.00
46 Eli Manning 20.00 40.00
47 Eric Decker 3.00 8.00
48 Frank Gore 4.00 10.00
49 Giovani Bernard 3.00 8.00
50 Greg Olsen 4.00 10.00
51 Heath Miller 10.00 25.00
52 Isaiah Crowell 3.00 8.00
53 Jameis Winston 25.00 50.00
54 James Harrison 25.00 50.00
55 Jason Witten
56 Jeremy Maclin 3.00 8.00
57 Jimmy Garoppolo 6.00 15.00
58 John Brown 4.00 10.00
59 Joique Bell 3.00 8.00
60 Jordy Nelson 8.00 20.00
61 Julius Thomas 3.00 8.00
62 Kelvin Benjamin 4.00 10.00
63 Kevin White 3.00 8.00
64 Kirk Cousins
65 Lamar Miller
66 Landon Collins 3.00 8.00
67 Latavius Murray 3.00 8.00
68 Manti Te'o 3.00 8.00
69 Marcus Mariota 40.00 80.00
70 Matt Forte
71 Matt Jones 4.00 10.00
72 Matt Ryan 10.00 25.00
73 Matthew Stafford
74 Maxx Williams 4.00 10.00
75 Melvin Gordon 4.00 10.00
76 Michael Floyd 3.00 8.00
77 Peyton Manning
78 Philip Rivers 10.00 25.00
79 Preston Smith 4.00 10.00
80 Rashad Greene 3.00 8.00
81 Rob Gronkowski 20.00 40.00
82 Robert Griffin III 3.00 8.00
83 Russell Wilson 40.00 80.00
84 Sam Bradford 10.00 25.00
85 Sammie Coates 3.00 8.00
86 Scott Chandler 3.00 8.00
87 Jeremy Langford 4.00 10.00
88 Stefon Diggs 4.00 10.00

89 Steve Smith 4.00 10.00
90 Teddy Bridgewater 12.00 30.00
91 Theo Riddick 3.00 8.00
92 Thomas Rawls 12.00 30.00
93 Todd Gurley II 25.00 50.00
94 Tony Romo 25.00 50.00
95 Torrey Smith 3.00 8.00
96 Tyler Eifert 4.00 10.00
97 Tyler Lockett 10.00 25.00
98 Tyrod Taylor
99 Vic Beasley Jr. 3.00 8.00
100 Von Miller 10.00 25.00

2016 Prestige Banner Season

1 Ameer Abdullah .40 1.00
2 Anthony Barr .40 1.00
3 Bill Parcells .60 1.50
4 Blake Bortles .40 1.00
5 Bo Jackson .75 2.00
6 Carl Eller .40 1.00
7 Case Keenum .50 1.25
8 Champ Bailey .50 1.25
9 Charlie Joiner .40 1.00
10 Clinton Portis .40 1.00
11 Dan Hampton .40 1.00
12 Derek Carr .60 1.50
13 Devin Funchess .40 1.00
14 Devonta Freeman .50 1.25
15 Doug Martin .50 1.25
16 Duke Johnson .40 1.00
17 Fred Biletnikoff .60 1.50
18 Ickey Woods .40 1.00
19 Jamal Lewis .50 1.25
20 Jerome Bettis .60 1.50
21 Joique Bell .40 1.00
22 Latavius Murray .40 1.00
23 Michael Strahan .50 1.25
24 Ricky Williams .50 1.25
25 Stefon Diggs .50 1.25
26 Teddy Bridgewater .50 1.25
27 Thomas Rawls .40 1.00
28 Tim Brown .60 1.50
29 Torry Holt .50 1.25
30 Trent Dilfer .40 1.00
31 Tyler Lockett .50 1.25
32 Vic Beasley Jr. .40 1.00
33 Vincent Jackson .40 1.00
34 Warren Moon .60 1.50
35 Zach Ertz .50 1.25
36 Andre Rison .50 1.25
37 Dermontti Dawson .50 1.25
38 Giovani Bernard .40 1.00
39 Isaiah Crowell .40 1.00
40 Kurt Warner .50 1.25

2016 Prestige Banner Season Ink

1 Ameer Abdullah 6.00 15.00
2 Anthony Barr 6.00 15.00
3 Bill Parcells 15.00 40.00
4 Blake Bortles 12.00 30.00
5 Bo Jackson 40.00 80.00
6 Carl Eller 6.00 15.00
7 Case Keenum 8.00 20.00
8 Champ Bailey 8.00 20.00
9 Charlie Joiner 6.00 15.00
10 Clinton Portis 6.00 15.00
11 Dan Hampton 6.00 15.00
12 Derek Carr 12.00 30.00
13 Devin Funchess 6.00 15.00
14 Devonta Freeman 8.00 20.00
15 Doug Martin 8.00 20.00
16 Duke Johnson 6.00 15.00
17 Fred Biletnikoff 10.00 25.00
18 Ickey Woods 6.00 15.00
19 Jamal Lewis 8.00 20.00
20 Jerome Bettis 30.00 60.00
21 Joique Bell 6.00 15.00
22 Latavius Murray 6.00 15.00
23 Michael Strahan 25.00 50.00
24 Ricky Williams 15.00 30.00
25 Stefon Diggs 8.00 20.00
26 Teddy Bridgewater 25.00 50.00
27 Thomas Rawls 25.00 50.00
28 Tim Brown 12.00 30.00
29 Torry Holt 8.00 20.00
30 Trent Dilfer 6.00 15.00
31 Tyler Lockett 8.00 20.00
32 Vic Beasley Jr. 6.00 15.00
33 Vincent Jackson 6.00 15.00
34 Warren Moon 10.00 25.00
35 Zach Ertz 8.00 20.00
36 Andre Rison 8.00 20.00
37 Dermontti Dawson 8.00 20.00
38 Giovani Bernard 6.00 15.00
39 Isaiah Crowell 6.00 15.00
40 Kurt Warner 40.00 80.00

2016 Prestige Blue Chip Recruits

1 Alex Collins .50 1.25
2 Andrew Billings .50 1.25
3 Austin Hooper .40 1.00
4 Carson Wentz 4.00 10.00
5 Corey Coleman .60 1.50
6 DeForest Buckner .40 1.00
7 Derrick Henry 1.00 2.50
8 Devontae Booker .50 1.25
9 Eli Apple .50 1.25
10 Jalen Ramsey .60 1.50
11 Jared Goff 2.50 6.00
12 Laremy Tunsil .40 1.00
13 Leonard Floyd .50 1.25
14 Michael Thomas .75 2.00
15 Myles Jack .50 1.25
16 Paxton Lynch .40 1.00
17 Reggie Ragland .40 1.00
18 Robert Nkemdiche .50 1.25
19 Shaq Lawson .40 1.00
20 Vernon Hargreaves III .60 1.50

2016 Prestige Blue Chip Recruits Ink

1 Alex Collins 5.00 12.00
2 Andrew Billings 5.00 12.00
3 Austin Hooper 4.00 10.00
4 Carson Wentz 60.00 125.00
5 Corey Coleman 6.00 15.00
6 DeForest Buckner 4.00 10.00
7 Derrick Henry 10.00 25.00
8 Devontae Booker 5.00 12.00
9 Eli Apple 5.00 12.00
10 Jalen Ramsey 6.00 15.00
11 Jared Goff 50.00 100.00
12 Laremy Tunsil 4.00 10.00
13 Leonard Floyd 5.00 12.00
14 Michael Thomas 8.00 20.00
15 Myles Jack 5.00 12.00
16 Paxton Lynch 4.00 10.00
17 Reggie Ragland 4.00 10.00
18 Robert Nkemdiche 5.00 12.00
19 Shaq Lawson 4.00 10.00
20 Vernon Hargreaves III 6.00 15.00

2016 Prestige Connections

1 C.Palmer/M.Floyd .75 2.00
2 J.Jones/M.Ryan 1.00 2.50
3 B.Perriman/J.Flacco .75 2.00
4 C.Newton/D.Funchess 1.00 2.50
5 J.Cutler/K.White .60 1.50
6 A.Dalton/T.Eifert .75 2.00
7 J.Witten/T.Romo .75 2.00
8 E.Sanders/P.Manning 2.00 5.00
9 E.Ebron/M.Stafford .75 2.00
10 B.Hundley/D.Adams .60 1.50
11 A.Robinson/B.Bortles .75 2.00
12 J.Landry/R.Tannehill .75 2.00
13 S.Diggs/T.Bridgewater .75 2.00
14 E.Manning/O.Beckham Jr. 1.00 2.50
15 B.Petty/D.Smith .60 1.50
16 A.Cooper/D.Carr 1.00 2.50
17 A.Gates/P.Rivers 1.00 2.50
18 C.Hyde/C.Kaepernick .75 2.00
19 R.Wilson/T.Lockett 1.25 3.00
20 J.Winston/M.Evans 1.00 2.50
21 D.Walker/M.Mariota 1.00 2.50
22 B.Osweiler/D.Thomas .75 2.00
23 A.Green/A.Dalton 1.00 2.50
24 J.Cutler/J.Langford .75 2.00
25 S.Watkins/T.Taylor 1.00 2.50

2016 Prestige Connections Jerseys

1 C.Palmer/M.Floyd 4.00 10.00
2 J.Jones/M.Ryan 5.00 12.00
3 B.Perriman/J.Flacco 4.00 10.00
4 C.Newton/D.Funchess 5.00 12.00
5 J.Cutler/K.White 3.00 8.00
6 A.Dalton/T.Eifert 4.00 10.00
7 J.Witten/T.Romo 4.00 10.00
8 E.Sanders/P.Manning 10.00 25.00
9 E.Ebron/M.Stafford 4.00 10.00
10 B.Hundley/D.Adams 3.00 8.00
11 A.Robinson/B.Bortles 4.00 10.00
12 J.Landry/R.Tannehill 4.00 10.00
13 S.Diggs/T.Bridgewater 4.00 10.00
14 E.Manning/O.Beckham Jr. 5.00 12.00
15 B.Petty/D.Smith 3.00 8.00
16 A.Cooper/D.Carr 5.00 12.00
17 A.Gates/P.Rivers 5.00 12.00
18 C.Hyde/C.Kaepernick 4.00 10.00
19 R.Wilson/T.Lockett 6.00 15.00
20 J.Winston/M.Evans 5.00 12.00
21 D.Walker/M.Mariota 5.00 12.00
22 B.Osweiler/D.Thomas 4.00 10.00
23 A.Green/A.Dalton 5.00 12.00
24 J.Cutler/J.Langford 4.00 10.00
25 S.Watkins/T.Taylor 5.00 12.00

2016 Prestige Draft Big Board

1 Jared Goff 2.00 5.00
2 Carson Wentz 3.00 8.00
3 Ezekiel Elliott 1.50 4.00
4 Derrick Henry .75 2.00
5 Laquon Treadwell .40 1.00
6 Corey Coleman .50 1.25
7 Hunter Henry .40 1.00
8 Laremy Tunsil .30 .75
9 Jack Conklin .50 1.25
10 A'Shawn Robinson .30 .75
11 Jarran Reed .30 .75
12 Joey Bosa .60 1.50
13 DeForest Buckner .30 .75
14 Reggie Ragland .30 .75
15 Myles Jack .40 1.00
16 Mackensie Alexander .30 .75
17 Vernon Hargreaves III .50 1.25
18 Jalen Ramsey .50 1.25
19 Vonn Bell .40 1.00
20 Jeremy Cash .40 1.00

2016 Prestige Draft Big Board Ink

1 Jared Goff 30.00 60.00
2 Carson Wentz 50.00 100.00
3 Ezekiel Elliott 75.00 150.00
4 Derrick Henry 10.00 25.00
5 Laquon Treadwell 5.00 12.00
6 Corey Coleman 6.00 15.00
7 Hunter Henry 5.00 12.00
8 Laremy Tunsil 4.00 10.00
9 Jack Conklin 6.00 15.00
10 A'Shawn Robinson 4.00 10.00
11 Jarran Reed 4.00 10.00
12 Joey Bosa 8.00 20.00
13 DeForest Buckner 4.00 10.00
14 Reggie Ragland 4.00 10.00
15 Myles Jack 5.00 12.00
16 Mackensie Alexander 4.00 10.00
17 Vernon Hargreaves III 6.00 15.00
18 Jalen Ramsey 6.00 15.00
19 Vonn Bell 5.00 12.00
20 Jeremy Cash 5.00 12.00

2016 Prestige Draft Day Signatures

AC Alex Collins/40* 10.00 25.00
BM Braxton Miller/75* 6.00 15.00
CC Connor Cook/30* 12.00 30.00
CCL Corey Coleman/40* 12.00 30.00
CH Christian Hackenberg/30* 10.00 25.00
CJ Cardale Jones/30* 10.00 25.00
CJP C.J. Prosise/40* 8.00 20.00
CK Cody Kessler/40* 8.00 20.00
CM Chris Moore/60* 8.00 20.00
CW Carson Wentz/30*
DB Devontae Booker/60* 8.00 20.00
DH Derrick Henry/34* 20.00 50.00
DP Dak Prescott/40* 40.00 80.00
DR Demarcus Robinson/75* 6.00 15.00
DW DeAndre Washington/75* 6.00 15.00
EE Ezekiel Elliott/35* 100.00 200.00
HH Hunter Henry/75* 8.00 20.00
JB Joey Bosa/30* 20.00 50.00
JD Josh Doctson/50* 10.00 25.00
JG Jared Goff/30* 60.00 150.00
JH Jordan Howard/40* 20.00 50.00
JW Jonathan Williams/60* 8.00 20.00
KD Kenneth Dixon/60* 6.00 15.00
KDR Kenyan Drake/60* 10.00 25.00
KH Kevin Hogan/75* 8.00 20.00
KR Keenan Reynolds/75* 8.00 20.00
LC Leonte Carroo/75* 6.00 15.00
LT Laquon Treadwell/40* 10.00 25.00
MT Michael Thomas/50* 15.00 40.00
PC Pharoh Cooper/75* 6.00 15.00
PL Paxton Lynch/30* 10.00 25.00
PP Paul Perkins/40* 8.00 20.00
RL Ricardo Louis/75* 6.00 15.00
SS Sterling Shepard/75* 8.00 20.00
TB Tyler Boyd/75* 8.00 20.00
TD Trevor Davis/75* 6.00 15.00
TE Tyler Ervin/75* 6.00 15.00
WF Will Fuller/50* 12.00 30.00
WS Wendell Smallwood/70* 6.00 15.00

2016 Prestige Draft Picks Blue

1 Connor Cook .50 1.25
2 Christian Hackenberg .40 1.00
3 Dak Prescott 2.00 5.00
4 Cardale Jones .40 1.00
5 Kenneth Dixon .40 1.00
6 Devontae Booker .50 1.25
7 Jordan Howard 1.00 2.50
8 Jonathan Williams .50 1.25
9 Josh Doctson .50 1.25
10 Tyler Boyd .50 1.25
11 Pharoh Cooper .40 1.00
12 Sterling Shepard .50 1.25
13 Braxton Miller .40 1.00
14 De'Runnya Wilson .40 1.00
15 Leonte Carroo .40 1.00
16 Jordan Payton .40 1.00
17 Nick Vannett .40 1.00
18 Taylor Decker .50 1.25
19 Cody Whitehair .60 1.50
20 Kevin Dodd .40 1.00
21 Emmanuel Ogbah .50 1.25
22 Jonathan Bullard .40 1.00
23 Andrew Billings .50 1.25
24 Kenny Clark .40 1.00
25 Austin Johnson .40 1.00
26 Su'a Cravens .40 1.00
27 Noah Spence .40 1.00
28 Leonard Floyd .50 1.25
29 Scooby Wright III .40 1.00
30 Kendall Fuller .50 1.25
31 Will Redmond .60 1.50
32 William Jackson III .50 1.25
33 Vonn Bell .50 1.25
34 Darian Thompson .40 1.00
35 Kevin Byard .40 1.00

2016 Prestige Hardwear

1 Allen Robinson .75 2.00
2 Amari Cooper 1.00 2.50
3 Ameer Abdullah .60 1.50
4 Breshad Perriman .60 1.50
5 Buck Allen .60 1.50
6 David Cobb .60 1.50
7 David Johnson 1.00 2.50
8 Devin Funchess .60 1.50
9 Devonta Freeman .75 2.00
10 Dorial Green-Beckham .60 1.50
11 Duke Johnson .60 1.50
12 Eric Ebron .60 1.50
13 Jaelen Strong .60 1.50
14 Jameis Winston 1.00 2.50
15 Jeremy Langford .75 2.00
16 Jordan Matthews .75 2.00
17 Karlos Williams .60 1.50
18 Marcus Mariota 1.00 2.50
19 Matt Jones .75 2.00
20 Phillip Dorsett .60 1.50
21 Stefon Diggs .75 2.00
22 T.J. Yeldon .60 1.50
23 Teddy Bridgewater .75 2.00
24 Todd Gurley II 1.00 2.50
25 Ty Montgomery .75 2.00

2016 Prestige Hardwear Jerseys

1 Allen Robinson 6.00 15.00
2 Amari Cooper 8.00 20.00
3 Ameer Abdullah 5.00 12.00
4 Breshad Perriman 5.00 12.00
5 Buck Allen 5.00 12.00
6 David Cobb 5.00 12.00
7 David Johnson 8.00 20.00
8 Devin Funchess 5.00 12.00
9 Devonta Freeman 6.00 15.00
10 Dorial Green-Beckham 5.00 12.00
11 Duke Johnson 5.00 12.00
12 Eric Ebron 5.00 12.00
13 Jaelen Strong 5.00 12.00
14 Jameis Winston 8.00 20.00
15 Jeremy Langford 6.00 15.00
16 Jordan Matthews 6.00 15.00
17 Karlos Williams 5.00 12.00
18 Marcus Mariota 8.00 20.00
19 Matt Jones 6.00 15.00
20 Phillip Dorsett 5.00 12.00
21 Stefon Diggs 6.00 15.00
22 T.J. Yeldon 5.00 12.00
23 Teddy Bridgewater 6.00 15.00
24 Todd Gurley II 8.00 20.00
25 Ty Montgomery 6.00 15.00

2016 Prestige Inside the Numbers

1 Ben Roethlisberger .60 1.50
2 Tom Brady 1.50 4.00
3 Carson Palmer .50 1.25
4 Blake Bortles .40 1.00
5 Derek Carr .60 1.50
6 Russell Wilson .75 2.00
7 Aaron Rodgers 1.25 3.00
8 Cam Newton .60 1.50
9 Marcus Mariota .60 1.50
10 Adrian Peterson .60 1.50
11 Todd Gurley II .60 1.50
12 Thomas Rawls .40 1.00
13 LeSean McCoy .60 1.50
14 Darren McFadden .40 1.00
15 Ronnie Hillman .40 1.00
16 Le'Veon Bell .50 1.25
17 Chris Ivory .50 1.25
18 Antonio Brown .60 1.50
19 DeAndre Hopkins .50 1.25
20 Julio Jones .60 1.50
21 Rob Gronkowski .60 1.50
22 Larry Fitzgerald .50 1.25
23 Odell Beckham Jr. .60 1.50
24 Eric Decker .40 1.00
25 Stefon Diggs .50 1.25
26 J.J. Watt .60 1.50
27 Chandler Jones .40 1.00
28 Von Miller .50 1.25
29 Charles Woodson .60 1.50
30 Josh Norman .40 1.00

2016 Prestige NFL Passport

1 Christian Hackenberg .30 .75
2 Connor Cook .40 1.00
3 Dak Prescott 1.50 4.00
4 Cardale Jones .30 .75
5 Devontae Booker .40 1.00
6 Jonathan Williams .40 1.00
7 Jordan Howard .75 2.00
8 Kenneth Dixon .30 .75
9 Braxton Miller .30 .75
10 Josh Doctson .40 1.00
11 Kenny Lawler .50 1.25
12 Pharoh Cooper .30 .75
13 Sterling Shepard .40 1.00
14 Glenn Gronkowski .30 .75
15 Jerell Adams .30 .75
16 Joey Bosa .60 1.50
17 Kevin Dodd .30 .75
18 Noah Spence .30 .75
19 Kendall Fuller .40 1.00
20 Jayron Kearse .30 .75

2016 Prestige NFL Passport Ink

1 Christian Hackenberg 4.00 10.00
2 Connor Cook 5.00 12.00
3 Dak Prescott 30.00 60.00
4 Cardale Jones 4.00 10.00
5 Devontae Booker 5.00 12.00
6 Jonathan Williams 5.00 12.00
7 Jordan Howard 10.00 25.00
8 Kenneth Dixon 4.00 10.00
9 Braxton Miller 4.00 10.00
10 Josh Doctson 5.00 12.00
11 Kenny Lawler 6.00 15.00
12 Pharoh Cooper 4.00 10.00
13 Sterling Shepard 5.00 12.00
14 Glenn Gronkowski 4.00 10.00
15 Jerell Adams 4.00 10.00
16 Joey Bosa 8.00 20.00
17 Kevin Dodd 4.00 10.00
18 Noah Spence 4.00 10.00
19 Kendall Fuller 5.00 12.00
20 Jayron Kearse 4.00 10.00

2016 Prestige NFL Shield

1 Tony Romo .50 1.25
2 Eli Manning .50 1.25
3 Jeremy Langford .50 1.25
4 Matthew Stafford .50 1.25
5 Clay Matthews .60 1.50
6 Teddy Bridgewater .50 1.25
7 Devonta Freeman .50 1.25
8 Cam Newton .60 1.50
9 Doug Martin .50 1.25
10 Larry Fitzgerald .50 1.25
11 Richard Sherman .60 1.50
12 Tyrod Taylor .50 1.25
13 Rob Gronkowski .60 1.50
14 Ryan Fitzpatrick .40 1.00
15 Andy Dalton .50 1.25
16 Le'Veon Bell .50 1.25
17 J.J. Watt .60 1.50
18 Allen Robinson .50 1.25
19 Marcus Mariota .60 1.50
20 Demaryius Thomas .50 1.25
21 Jamaal Charles .50 1.25
22 Derek Carr .60 1.50
23 Keenan Allen .50 1.25

2016 Prestige Rising Stars Jerseys

1 David Johnson 3.00 8.00
2 Devonta Freeman 2.50 6.00
3 Justin Hardy 2.00 5.00
4 Tevin Coleman 2.50 6.00
5 Breshad Perriman 2.00 5.00
6 Buck Allen 2.00 5.00
7 Karlos Williams 2.00 5.00
8 Devin Funchess 2.00 5.00
9 Kelvin Benjamin 2.50 6.00
10 Jeremy Langford 2.50 6.00
11 Kevin White 2.00 5.00
12 Giovani Bernard 2.00 5.00
13 Duke Johnson 2.00 5.00
14 Travis Benjamin 2.00 5.00
15 Ameer Abdullah 2.00 5.00
16 Davante Adams 2.00 5.00
17 Donte Moncrief 2.50 6.00
18 Phillip Dorsett 2.00 5.00
19 Allen Robinson 2.50 6.00
20 Blake Bortles 2.00 5.00
21 T.J. Yeldon 2.00 5.00
22 Jarvis Landry 2.50 6.00
23 Jay Ajayi 2.50 6.00
24 Stefon Diggs 2.50 6.00
25 Teddy Bridgewater 2.50 6.00
26 Jimmy Garoppolo 4.00 10.00
27 Brandin Cooks 2.50 6.00
28 Garrett Grayson 2.00 5.00
29 Odell Beckham Jr. 3.00 8.00
30 Bryce Petty 2.00 5.00
31 Devin Smith 2.00 5.00
32 Amari Cooper 3.00 8.00
33 Derek Carr 3.00 8.00
34 Khalil Mack 3.00 8.00
35 Jordan Matthews 2.50 6.00
36 Nelson Agholor 2.00 5.00
37 Melvin Gordon 2.50 6.00
38 Carlos Hyde 2.00 5.00
39 Tyler Lockett 2.50 6.00
40 Sean Mannion 2.00 5.00
41 Todd Gurley II 3.00 8.00
42 Austin Seferian-Jenkins 2.00 5.00
43 Jameis Winston 3.00 8.00
44 Mike Evans 2.50 6.00
45 David Cobb 2.00 5.00
46 Dorial Green-Beckham 2.00 5.00
47 Marcus Mariota 3.00 8.00
48 Jamison Crowder 2.00 5.00
49 Matt Jones 2.50 6.00
50 Andre Ellington 2.00 5.00

2016 Prestige Rookie Autographs

1 Aaron Burbridge 2.50 6.00
2 Aaron Green 2.50 6.00
3 Adolphus Washington 2.50 6.00
4 Alex Collins 3.00 8.00
5 Andrew Billings 3.00 8.00
6 Xavien Howard 3.00 8.00
7 A'Shawn Robinson 2.50 6.00
8 Austin Hooper 2.50 6.00
9 Austin Johnson 2.50 6.00
10 Bralon Addison 2.50 6.00
11 Brandon Allen 2.50 6.00
12 Brandon Doughty 2.50 6.00
13 Braxton Miller 2.50 6.00
14 Byron Marshall 2.50 6.00
15 C.J. Prosise 2.50 6.00
16 Cardale Jones 6.00 15.00
17 Carson Wentz 60.00 120.00
18 Cayleb Jones 2.50 6.00
19 Christian Hackenberg 8.00 20.00
20 Cody Kessler 2.50 6.00
21 Connor Cook 3.00 8.00
22 Corey Coleman 4.00 10.00
23 Dak Prescott 40.00 80.00
24 Darron Lee 2.50 6.00
25 DeForest Buckner 2.50 6.00
26 Demarcus Robinson 2.50 6.00
27 Derrick Henry 6.00 15.00
28 De'Runnya Wilson 2.50 6.00
29 Devontae Booker 8.00 20.00
30 Eli Apple 3.00 8.00
31 Emmanuel Ogbah 3.00 8.00
32 Ezekiel Elliott 75.00 150.00
33 Glenn Gronkowski 2.50 6.00
34 Hunter Henry 3.00 8.00
35 Jacoby Brissett 12.00 30.00
36 Charone Peake 2.50 6.00
37 Jalen Ramsey 4.00 10.00
38 Jalin Marshall 4.00 10.00
39 Jared Goff 25.00 50.00
40 Jarran Reed 2.50 6.00
41 Jaylon Smith 2.50 6.00
42 Jayron Kearse 2.50 6.00
43 Jeff Driskel 2.50 6.00
44 Jerell Adams 2.50 6.00
45 Jeremy Cash 3.00 8.00
46 Joey Bosa 5.00 12.00
47 Jonathan Bullard 2.50 6.00
48 Jonathan Williams 3.00 8.00
49 Jordan Howard 6.00 15.00
50 Jordan Payton 2.50 6.00
51 Jordan Williams 2.50 6.00
52 Josh Doctson 3.00 8.00
53 Josh Ferguson 2.50 6.00
54 Kamalei Correa 2.50 6.00
55 KeiVarae Russell 2.50 6.00
56 Kelvin Taylor 2.50 6.00
57 Kendall Fuller 8.00 20.00
58 Kenneth Dixon 2.50 6.00
59 Kenny Clark 2.50 6.00
60 Kenny Lawler 4.00 10.00
61 Kenyan Drake 4.00 10.00
62 Kevin Dodd 2.50 6.00
63 Kevin Hogan 3.00 8.00
64 Laquon Treadwell 12.00 30.00
65 Leonard Floyd 3.00 8.00
66 Leonte Carroo 2.50 6.00
67 Mackensie Alexander 2.50 6.00
68 Michael Thomas 5.00 12.00
69 Myles Jack 3.00 8.00
70 Nate Sudfeld 2.50 6.00
71 Nelson Spruce 2.50 6.00
72 Nick Vannett 2.50 6.00
73 Noah Spence 2.50 6.00
74 Paul Perkins 2.50 6.00
75 Paxton Lynch 40.00 80.00
76 Pharoh Cooper 2.50 6.00
77 Rashard Higgins 2.50 6.00
78 Reggie Ragland 2.50 6.00
79 Robert Nkemdiche 3.00 8.00
81 Scooby Wright III 2.50 6.00
82 Shaq Lawson 2.50 6.00
83 Sheldon Rankins 3.00 8.00
84 Shilique Calhoun 2.50 6.00
85 D.J. Foster 3.00 8.00
86 Sterling Shepard 3.00 8.00
87 Su'a Cravens 2.50 6.00
88 Tajae Sharpe 3.00 8.00
89 Taylor Decker 3.00 8.00
90 Thomas Duarte 2.50 6.00
91 Keith Marshall 2.50 6.00
92 Tre Madden 2.50 6.00
93 Malcolm Mitchell 2.50 6.00
94 Kolby Listenbee 2.50 6.00
95 Tyler Ervin 2.50 6.00
96 Vernon Hargreaves III 4.00 10.00
97 Vonn Bell 3.00 8.00
98 Will Fuller 4.00 10.00
99 Will Redmond 4.00 10.00
100 Jay Lee 2.50 6.00

2016 Prestige Rookie Autographs Xtra Points Gold

*GOLD/50: .75X TO 2X BASIC AU
17 Carson Wentz 100.00 200.00

2016 Prestige Rookie Autographs Xtra Points Platinum

*PLATINUM/25: 1X TO 2.5X BASIC AU
32 Ezekiel Elliott 100.00 200.00

2016 Prestige Rookie Autographs Xtra Points Purple

*PURPLE/100: .6X TO 1.5X BASIC AU
17 Carson Wentz 75.00 150.00
32 Ezekiel Elliott 75.00 150.00

2016 Prestige Rookie Autographs Xtra Points Red

*RED: .5X TO 1.2X BASIC AU
32 Ezekiel Elliott 75.00 150.00

2016 Prestige Shirt Off My Back Jerseys

1 Allen Hurns 2.00 5.00
2 Allen Robinson 2.50 6.00
3 Andy Dalton 2.50 6.00
4 Antonio Cromartie 2.00 5.00
5 Barry Church 2.00 5.00
6 Bradley Roby 2.00 5.00
7 C.J. Anderson 2.50 6.00
8 Cameron Wake 2.00 5.00
9 Cole Beasley 3.00 8.00
10 De'Anthony Thomas 2.00 5.00
11 DeMarcus Ware 2.50 6.00
12 Denard Robinson 2.00 5.00
13 Dontari Poe 2.00 5.00
14 Doug Martin 2.50 6.00
15 EJ Manuel 2.00 5.00
16 Eric Berry 2.50 6.00
17 Geno Atkins 2.00 5.00
18 Hakeem Nicks 2.00 5.00
19 Jadeveon Clowney 2.00 5.00
20 Jarvis Landry 2.50 6.00
21 Jay Cutler 2.00 5.00
22 Jeremy Hill 2.00 5.00
23 Joe Haden 2.00 5.00
24 Kirk Cousins 3.00 8.00
25 Julius Thomas 2.00 5.00
26 Khalil Mack 3.00 8.00
27 Lamar Miller 2.00 5.00
28 Larry Fitzgerald 2.50 6.00
29 LeSean McCoy 3.00 8.00
30 Manti Te'o 2.00 5.00
31 Marcell Dareus 2.00 5.00
32 Mario Williams 2.00 5.00
33 Matt Kalil 2.00 5.00
34 Matt Ryan 2.50 6.00
35 Michael Griffin 2.00 5.00
36 Percy Harvin 2.00 5.00
37 Peyton Manning 6.00 15.00
38 Philip Rivers 3.00 8.00
39 Robert Woods 2.50 6.00
40 Roddy White 2.00 5.00
41 Ronnie Hillman 2.00 5.00
42 Ryan Kerrigan 2.00 5.00
43 Ryan Tannehill 2.50 6.00
44 Sammy Watkins 3.00 8.00
45 Tamba Hali 2.00 5.00
46 Telvin Smith 2.00 5.00
47 Terrance Williams 2.00 5.00
48 Tyler Eifert 2.50 6.00
49 Tyron Smith 2.00 5.00
50 Von Miller 2.50 6.00

2016 Prestige Stars of the NFL

1 Tom Brady 1.50 4.00
2 Peyton Manning 1.25 3.00
3 Blake Bortles .40 1.00
4 Aaron Rodgers 1.25 3.00
5 Andrew Luck .75 2.00
6 Devonta Freeman .50 1.25
7 Todd Gurley II .60 1.50
8 Danny Woodhead .50 1.25
9 Adrian Peterson .60 1.50
10 Doug Martin .50 1.25
11 Julio Jones .60 1.50
12 DeAndre Hopkins .50 1.25
13 Antonio Brown .60 1.50
14 Odell Beckham Jr. .60 1.50
15 Larry Fitzgerald .50 1.25
16 Demaryius Thomas .50 1.25
17 Amari Cooper .60 1.50
18 Mike Evans .50 1.25
19 Sammy Watkins .60 1.50
20 Tyler Eifert .50 1.25
21 J.J. Watt .60 1.50
22 Kam Chancellor .60 1.50
23 DeMarcus Ware .50 1.25
24 Ezekiel Ansah .40 1.00
25 Darrelle Revis .40 1.00

2016 Prestige Stars of the NFL Jerseys

1 Tom Brady 12.00 30.00
2 Peyton Manning 10.00 25.00
3 Blake Bortles 3.00 8.00
4 Aaron Rodgers 10.00 25.00
5 Andrew Luck 6.00 15.00
6 Devonta Freeman 4.00 10.00
7 Todd Gurley II 5.00 12.00
8 Danny Woodhead 4.00 10.00
9 Adrian Peterson 5.00 12.00
10 Doug Martin 4.00 10.00
11 Julio Jones 5.00 12.00
12 DeAndre Hopkins 4.00 10.00
13 Antonio Brown 5.00 12.00
14 Odell Beckham Jr. 5.00 12.00
15 Larry Fitzgerald 4.00 10.00
16 Demaryius Thomas 4.00 10.00
17 Amari Cooper 5.00 12.00
18 Mike Evans 4.00 10.00
19 Sammy Watkins 5.00 12.00
20 Tyler Eifert 4.00 10.00
21 J.J. Watt 5.00 12.00
22 Kam Chancellor 5.00 12.00
23 DeMarcus Ware 4.00 10.00
24 Ezekiel Ansah 3.00 8.00
25 Darrelle Revis 3.00 8.00

2016 Prestige Super Bowl Heroes

1 Franco Harris .60 1.50
2 Jim McMahon .50 1.25
3 Charles Haley .60 1.50
4 Joe Montana 1.50 4.00
5 Emmitt Smith 1.00 2.50
6 Adam Vinatieri .50 1.25
7 Tom Brady 1.50 4.00
8 Hines Ward .50 1.25
9 Peyton Manning 1.25 3.00
10 Devin Hester .50 1.25
11 Eli Manning .50 1.25
12 Ben Roethlisberger .60 1.50
13 James Harrison .50 1.25
14 Larry Fitzgerald .50 1.25
15 Drew Brees .60 1.50
16 Tracy Porter .40 1.00
17 Aaron Rodgers 1.25 3.00
18 Jordy Nelson .50 1.25
19 Eli Manning .50 1.25
20 Hakeem Nicks .40 1.00
21 Joe Flacco .50 1.25
22 Jacoby Jones .40 1.00
23 Colin Kaepernick .50 1.25
24 Russell Wilson .75 2.00
25 Malcolm Smith .60 1.50
26 Demaryius Thomas .50 1.25
27 Tom Brady 1.50 4.00
28 Malcolm Butler .60 1.50
29 Von Miller .50 1.25
30 DeMarcus Ware .50 1.25

2016 Prestige Team Logos

1 Dez Bryant .60 1.50
2 Odell Beckham Jr. .60 1.50
3 Sam Bradford .40 1.00
4 Kirk Cousins .60 1.50
5 Alshon Jeffery .50 1.25
6 Calvin Johnson .60 1.50
7 Aaron Rodgers 1.25 3.00
8 Adrian Peterson .60 1.50
9 Julio Jones .60 1.50
10 Luke Kuechly .50 1.25
11 Drew Brees .60 1.50
12 Jameis Winston .60 1.50
13 Carson Palmer .50 1.25
14 Carlos Hyde .40 1.00
15 Russell Wilson .75 2.00
16 Todd Gurley II .60 1.50
17 LeSean McCoy .60 1.50
18 Ryan Tannehill .50 1.25
19 Tom Brady 1.50 4.00
20 Brandon Marshall .40 1.00
21 Kamar Aiken .40 1.00
22 A.J. Green .60 1.50
23 Duke Johnson .40 1.00
24 Ben Roethlisberger .60 1.50
25 DeAndre Hopkins .50 1.25
26 Andrew Luck .75 2.00
27 Blake Bortles .40 1.00
28 Marcus Mariota .60 1.50
29 Peyton Manning 1.25 3.00
30 Jeremy Maclin .40 1.00
31 Amari Cooper .60 1.50
32 Philip Rivers .60 1.50

2017 Prestige

1 Jason Witten .25 .60
2 Terrance West .20 .50
3 Phillip Dorsett .20 .50
4 Ben Roethlisberger .30 .75
5 Virgil Green .20 .50
6 Jeremy Kerley .20 .50
7 DeAndre Washington .20 .50
8 Taylor Gabriel .20 .50
9 Cameron Brate .20 .50
10 Chris Conley .20 .50
11 Jimmy Graham .30 .75
12 Carlos Hyde .20 .50
13 John Brown .25 .60
14 Jacquizz Rodgers .20 .50
15 Dwayne Allen .20 .50
16 Adam Humphries .20 .50
17 Brandon Marshall .20 .50
18 Jordan Matthews .20 .50
19 Danny Woodhead .25 .60
20 LeGarrette Blount .25 .60
21 Andy Dalton .25 .60
22 Will Tye .20 .50
23 Brandin Cooks .25 .60
24 Quincy Enunwa .20 .50
25 Randall Cobb .25 .60
26 Joe Flacco .25 .60
27 Latavius Murray .20 .50
28 Jordan Reed .20 .50
29 Chris Ivory .25 .60
30 Ryan Tannehill .25 .60
31 Khalil Mack .30 .75
32 Tyreek Hill .30 .75
33 Brock Osweiler .20 .50
34 Spencer Ware .20 .50
35 Matt Forte .20 .50
36 Dennis Pitta .20 .50
37 Doug Baldwin .25 .60
38 Chris Hogan .20 .50
39 Ezekiel Elliott .40 1.00
40 Devonta Freeman .25 .60
41 Jack Doyle .20 .50
42 Rishard Matthews .20 .50
43 Golden Tate III .20 .50
44 Jason Pierre-Paul .20 .50
45 Dak Prescott .30 .75
46 Cole Beasley .30 .75
47 Derrick Henry .25 .60
48 Ted Ginn Jr. .20 .50
49 Andrew Luck .40 1.00
50 Jamison Crowder .20 .50
51 Kyle Rudolph .20 .50
52 Joey Bosa .30 .75
53 J.J. Nelson .20 .50
54 Larry Fitzgerald .25 .60
55 Tyler Lockett .25 .60
56 LeSean McCoy .30 .75
57 Mike Wallace .20 .50
58 Tony Romo .25 .60
59 Tom Brady .75 2.00
60 Marcus Mariota .30 .75
61 Julius Thomas .20 .50
62 C.J. Anderson .25 .60
63 Tom Savage .20 .50
64 Coby Fleener .20 .50
65 Mohamed Sanu .20 .50
66 Martellus Bennett .20 .50
67 Carson Wentz .40 1.00
68 Matthew Stafford .25 .60
69 Ryan Mathews .25 .60
70 Zach Miller .20 .50
71 Colin Kaepernick .25 .60
72 Dez Bryant .30 .75
73 DeMarco Murray .25 .60
74 Ameer Abdullah .20 .50
75 Antonio Brown .30 .75
76 Doug Martin .25 .60
77 Carson Palmer .25 .60
78 Lamar Miller .20 .50
79 Eric Decker .20 .50
80 Darrius Heyward-Bey .20 .50
81 Jeremy Maclin .20 .50
82 Jameis Winston .25 .60
83 Brian Quick .20 .50
84 Duke Johnson .20 .50
85 Kenny Stills .20 .50
86 Casey Hayward .20 .50
87 T.J. Yeldon .20 .50
88 Blake Bortles .20 .50
89 Tyrell Williams .20 .50
90 Torrey Smith .20 .50
91 DeVante Parker .25 .60
92 Odell Beckham Jr. .30 .75
93 Robert Kelley .20 .50
94 Le'Veon Bell .25 .60
95 Marvin Jones Jr. .20 .50
96 Brandon LaFell .20 .50
97 Mark Ingram .25 .60
98 Amari Cooper .30 .75
99 Alex Smith .25 .60
100 Todd Gurley II .30 .75
101 Will Fuller V .20 .50
102 Lorenzo Taliaferro .20 .50
103 Charles Clay .20 .50
104 Jarvis Landry .25 .60
105 Greg Olsen .25 .60
106 Kelvin Benjamin .25 .60
107 Paul Perkins .20 .50
108 Allen Robinson .25 .60
109 Lance Kendricks .20 .50
110 Gary Barnidge .20 .50
111 David Johnson .30 .75
112 Davante Adams .25 .60
113 Marqise Lee .20 .50
114 Delanie Walker .20 .50
115 Zach Ertz .25 .60
116 Mike Gillislee .20 .50
117 Julio Jones .30 .75
118 Jeremy Langford .25 .60
119 Michael Crabtree .20 .50
120 Kirk Cousins .30 .75
121 Robert Woods .25 .60
122 Pierre Garcon .25 .60
123 Tevin Coleman .25 .60
124 Cam Newton .30 .75
125 A.J. Green .30 .75
126 Tajae Sharpe .20 .50
127 Eric Ebron .20 .50
128 Isaiah Crowell .20 .50
129 Adrian Peterson .30 .75
130 Jeremy Hill .20 .50
131 Philip Rivers .30 .75
132 Aaron Rodgers .60 1.50
133 T.Y. Hilton .25 .60
134 Eddie Lacy .20 .50
135 Cameron Meredith .20 .50
136 Russell Wilson .40 1.00
137 Jermaine Gresham .25 .60
138 Antonio Gates .20 .50
139 Eli Rogers .20 .50
140 Melvin Gordon .25 .60
141 Kenny Britt .20 .50
142 Adam Thielen .30 .75
143 Devin Funchess .20 .50
144 Vance McDonald .20 .50
145 Sterling Shepard .25 .60
146 DeSean Jackson .25 .60
147 Tyrod Taylor .25 .60
148 C.J. Fiedorowicz .20 .50
149 Drew Brees .30 .75
150 Keenan Allen .25 .60
151 Eli Manning .25 .60
152 Landon Collins .20 .50
153 J.J. Watt .30 .75
154 Corey Coleman .20 .50
155 Giovani Bernard .20 .50
156 Mike Glennon .25 .60
157 Stefon Diggs .25 .60
158 Vic Beasley Jr. .20 .50
159 Allen Hurns .20 .50
160 Travis Kelce .30 .75
161 Theo Riddick .20 .50
162 Jalen Richard .20 .50
163 Emmanuel Sanders .30 .75
164 Jerick McKinnon .20 .50
165 Jared Goff .30 .75
166 Frank Gore .25 .60
167 Ndamukong Suh .25 .60
168 Sammy Watkins .30 .75
169 Demaryius Thomas .25 .60
170 Alshon Jeffery .25 .60
171 Willie Snead .25 .60
172 Cody Kessler .20 .50
173 Matt Ryan .25 .60
174 Quinton Patton .20 .50
175 Tavon Austin .20 .50
176 Derek Carr .30 .75
177 Mike Evans .25 .60
178 Julian Edelman .30 .75
179 Wendell Smallwood .20 .50
180 DeAndre Hopkins .25 .60
181 Jordan Howard .30 .75
182 Bilal Powell .20 .50
183 Trevor Siemian .20 .50
184 Josh McCown .20 .50
185 Jonathan Stewart .20 .50
186 Jermaine Kearse .20 .50
187 Michael Thomas .30 .75
188 Terrelle Pryor Sr. .20 .50
189 Jay Ajayi .25 .60
190 Devontae Booker .20 .50
191 Von Miller .25 .60
192 Tyler Boyd .20 .50
193 Richard Sherman .30 .75
194 Jordy Nelson .25 .60
195 DeAngelo Williams .20 .50
196 Ty Montgomery .20 .50
197 Rob Gronkowski .30 .75
198 Darren Sproles .25 .60
199 Thomas Rawls .20 .50
200 Sam Bradford .20 .50
201 Carlos Henderson RC .30 .75
202 Malik McDowell RC .30 .75
203 ArDarius Stewart RC .30 .75
204 Mitchell Trubisky RC 1.50 4.00
205 Dalvin Cook RC .75 2.00
206 Elijah Hood RC .30 .75
207 Marlon Humphrey RC .30 .75
208 Jordan Leggett RC .30 .75
209 Cameron Sutton RC .30 .75
210 Malachi Dupre RC .30 .75
211 Elijah Qualls RC .30 .75
212 Stacy Coley RC .30 .75
213 Deshaun Watson RC 2.00 5.00
214 Eddie Jackson RC .40 1.00
215 Christian McCaffrey RC .75 2.00
216 Cam Robinson RC .30 .75
217 Marshon Lattimore RC .40 1.00
218 Evan Engram RC .40 1.00
219 Gareon Conley RC .30 .75
220 Cooper Kupp RC .50 1.25
221 Caleb Brantley RC .30 .75
222 Chris Godwin RC .40 1.00
223 DeShone Kizer RC .30 .75
224 D'Onta Foreman RC .40 1.00
225 Donnel Pumphrey RC .40 1.00
226 Quincy Wilson RC .30 .75
227 Mike Williams RC .50 1.25
228 Jonathan Allen RC .40 1.00
229 R. Joshua Dobbs RC .40 1.00
230 Reuben Foster RC .30 .75
231 Zay Jones RC .40 1.00
232 Patrick Mahomes II RC 4.00 10.00
233 Teez Tabor RC .40 1.00
234 James Conner RC .60 1.50
235 Adoree' Jackson RC .40 1.00
236 John Ross RC .40 1.00
237 Derek Barnett RC .40 1.00
238 KD Cannon RC .30 .75
239 Zach Cunningham RC .40 1.00
240 Greg Ward Jr. RC .30 .75
241 Raekwon McMillan RC .30 .75
242 Jarrad Davis RC .40 1.00
243 Travis Rudolph RC .30 .75
244 Sidney Jones RC .30 .75
245 JuJu Smith-Schuster RC .75 2.00
246 Carl Lawson RC .30 .75
247 Josh Malone RC .30 .75
248 Jabrill Peppers RC .50 1.25
249 Kevin King RC .40 1.00
250 Jerod Evans RC .40 1.00
251 Alvin Kamara RC 1.25 3.00
252 Jamaal Williams RC .30 .75
253 Desmond King RC .40 1.00
254 Corey Davis RC .50 1.25
255 Charles Harris RC .30 .75
256 Artavis Scott RC .30 .75
257 Tim Williams RC .40 1.00
258 Cole Hikutini RC .30 .75
259 Davis Webb RC .30 .75
260 Matthew Dayes RC .30 .75
261 Joe Mixon RC .60 1.50
262 Jourdan Lewis RC .30 .75
263 Dede Westbrook RC .30 .75
264 Taco Charlton RC .30 .75
265 Chad Hansen RC .30 .75
266 Takkarist McKinley RC .30 .75
267 Jeremy Sprinkle RC .30 .75
268 Chad Kelly RC .30 .75
269 Wayne Gallman RC .40 1.00
270 O.J. Howard RC .40 1.00
271 Cordrea Tankersley RC .40 1.00
272 Curtis Samuel RC .40 1.00
273 Jordan Willis RC .30 .75
274 Noah Brown RC .40 1.00
275 Jamal Adams RC .30 .75
276 Marquez White RC .30 .75
277 Nathan Peterman RC .40 1.00

278 Brian Hill RC .30 .75
279 Jake Butt RC .40 1.00
280 Tre'Davious White RC .30 .75
281 Amara Darboh RC .30 .75
282 DeMarcus Walker RC .30 .75
283 Shelton Gibson RC .30 .75
284 Malik Hooker RC .30 .75
285 Dawuane Smoot RC .30 .75
286 Leonard Fournette RC 1.00 2.50
287 Corey Clement RC .40 1.00
288 Bucky Hodges RC .30 .75
289 Isaiah Ford RC .30 .75
290 Solomon Thomas RC .30 .75
291 Marlon Mack RC SP 8.00 20.00
292 Josh Reynolds RC SP 15.00 40.00
293 T.J. Watt RC SP 20.00 50.00
294 Myles Garrett RC SP 25.00 60.00
295 David Njoku RC SP 12.00 30.00
296 Samaje Perine RC SP 12.00 30.00
297 Brad Kaaya RC SP 12.00 30.00
298 Ryan Switzer RC SP 12.00 30.00
299 Jeremy McNichols RC SP 6.00 15.00
300 Kareem Hunt RC SP 15.00 40.00

2017 Prestige Xtra Points Blue

*VETS: .8X TO 2X BASIC CARDS
*ROOKIES: .6X TO 1.2X BASIC CARDS

2017 Prestige Xtra Points Gold

*VETS/50: 2X TO 5X BASIC CARDS
*ROOKIES/50: 1.2X TO 3X BASIC CARDS

2017 Prestige Xtra Points Green

*VETS/150: 1X TO 2.5X BASIC CARDS
*ROOKIES/150: .6X TO 1.5X BASIC CARDS

2017 Prestige Xtra Points Platinum

*VETS/25: 2.5X TO 6X BASIC CARDS
*ROOKIES/25: 1.5X TO 4X BASIC CARDS

2017 Prestige Xtra Points Purple

*VETS/100: 1.2X TO 3X BASIC CARDS
*ROOKIES/100: .8X TO 2X BASIC CARDS
*SP ROOKIES/100: .2X TO .5X BASIC CARDS

2017 Prestige Xtra Points Red

*VETS: .8X TO 2X BASIC CARDS
*ROOKIES: .5X TO 1.2X BASIC CARDS

2017 Prestige All Panini Team

*RED: .8X TO 2X BASIC INSERTS
*PLATINUM/25: 2X TO 5X BASIC INSERTS
1 Le'Veon Bell .40 1.00
2 Tom Brady 1.25 3.00
3 Ezekiel Elliott .60 1.50
4 Aaron Rodgers 1.00 2.50
5 Odell Beckham Jr. .50 1.25
6 Andrew Luck .60 1.50
7 Antonio Brown .50 1.25
8 Drew Brees .50 1.25
9 Julio Jones .50 1.25
10 Ben Roethlisberger .50 1.25

2017 Prestige Alma Maters

1 Sterling Shepard .40 1.00
2 Ezekiel Elliott .60 1.50
3 Jay Ajayi .40 1.00
4 Amari Cooper .50 1.25
5 Jordan Howard .50 1.25
6 Cody Kessler .30 .75
7 Marcus Mariota .50 1.25
8 Dak Prescott .50 1.25
9 Michael Thomas .50 1.25
10 Derrick Henry .40 1.00
11 Todd Gurley II .50 1.25
12 Jameis Winston .40 1.00
13 Jeremy Langford .40 1.00
14 Carson Wentz .60 1.50
15 Josh Doctson .30 .75
16 Corey Coleman .30 .75
17 Melvin Gordon .40 1.00
18 David Johnson .50 1.25
19 Stefon Diggs .40 1.00
20 Devontae Booker .30 .75
21 Braxton Miller .30 .75
22 Jared Goff .50 1.25
23 Joey Bosa .50 1.25
24 Christian Hackenberg .30 .75
25 Laquon Treadwell .30 .75

2017 Prestige Banner Season

1 Dak Prescott .40 1.00
2 Don Maynard .30 .75
3 Sterling Shepard .30 .75
4 Earl Campbell .40 1.00
5 Reggie Wayne .30 .75
6 Christian Okoye .25 .60
7 Richard Sherman .40 1.00
8 Mark Brunell .30 .75
9 Jerry Rice .60 1.50
10 Devonta Freeman .30 .75
11 Ezekiel Elliott .50 1.25
12 Dallas Clark .25 .60
13 Jalen Ramsey .25 .60
14 Len Dawson .40 1.00
15 Terrell Davis .30 .75
16 Kordell Stewart .25 .60
17 J.J. Watt .40 1.00
18 Mark Gastineau .25 .60
19 Peyton Manning .75 2.00
20 Antonio Freeman .30 .75
21 Carson Wentz .50 1.25
22 Ahman Green .30 .75
23 Randy Moss .30 .75
24 Victor Cruz .30 .75
25 Eddie George .30 .75
26 Steve Bartkowski .30 .75
27 Matt Ryan .30 .75
28 Lenny Moore .25 .60
29 Joe Namath .50 1.25
30 Edgerrin James .30 .75
31 Tyreek Hill .40 1.00
32 Ricky Williams .30 .75
33 Landon Collins .25 .60
34 LaDainian Tomlinson .30 .75
35 Joe Greene .40 1.00
36 Robert Brooks .30 .75
37 Terry Bradshaw .60 1.50
38 Kellen Winslow .30 .75
39 Wes Welker .30 .75
40 Torry Holt .30 .75

2017 Prestige Blue Chip Prospects

1 Mitchell Trubisky 2.00 5.00
2 Myles Garrett 1.25 3.00
3 Dalvin Cook 1.00 2.50
4 Alvin Kamara 1.50 4.00
5 Brad Kaaya .40 1.00
6 David Njoku .50 1.25
7 Corey Davis .60 1.50
8 Patrick Mahomes II 5.00 12.00
9 Leonard Fournette 1.25 3.00
10 Dede Westbrook .40 1.00
11 DeShone Kizer .40 1.00
12 Curtis Samuel .50 1.25
13 Mike Williams .60 1.50
14 Cooper Kupp .60 1.50
15 Christian McCaffrey 1.00 2.50
16 O.J. Howard .50 1.25
17 Malachi Dupre .40 1.00
18 D'Onta Foreman .50 1.25
19 Deshaun Watson 2.50 6.00
20 John Ross .50 1.25

2017 Prestige Blue Chip Prospects Ink

1 Mitchell Trubisky 30.00 80.00
3 Dalvin Cook 15.00 40.00
4 Alvin Kamara 25.00 60.00
5 Brad Kaaya 6.00 15.00
[illegible]
8 Patrick Mahomes II 125.00 250.00
9 Leonard Fournette 20.00 50.00
10 Dede Westbrook 6.00 15.00
11 DeShone Kizer 6.00 15.00
12 Curtis Samuel 8.00 20.00
13 Mike Williams 10.00 25.00
14 Cooper Kupp 10.00 25.00
15 Christian McCaffrey 15.00 40.00
16 O.J. Howard 8.00 20.00
17 Malachi Dupre 6.00 15.00
18 D'Onta Foreman 8.00 20.00
19 Deshaun Watson
20 John Ross 8.00 20.00

2017 Prestige Connections

1 D.Prescott/E.Elliott 1.25 3.00
2 C.Newton/K.Benjamin 1.00 2.50
3 J.Elway/V.Johnson 1.50 4.00
4 O.Beckham/E.Manning 1.00 2.50
5 K.Wright/M.Mariota 1.00 2.50
6 A.Rodgers/D.Adams 2.00 5.00
7 D.Thomas/P.Manning 2.00 5.00
8 A.Luck/T.Hilton 1.25 3.00
9 C.Wentz/J.Matthews 1.25 3.00
10 B.Bortles/A.Robinson .75 2.00
11 T.Taylor/S.Watkins 1.00 2.50
12 L.Fitzgerald/C.Palmer .75 2.00
13 D.Baldwin/R.Wilson 1.25 3.00
14 B.Favre/S.Sharpe 2.00 5.00
15 J.Jones/M.Ryan 1.00 2.50
16 A.Green/A.Dalton 1.00 2.50
17 A.Gates/P.Rivers 1.00 2.50
18 A.Brown/B.Rthlsbrgr 1.00 2.50
19 R.Grnkwski/T.Brady 2.50 6.00
20 A.Peterson/B.Favre 2.00 5.00
21 J.Montana/J.Rice 2.50 6.00
22 M.Evans/J.Winston .75 2.00
23 J.Landry/R.Tannehill .75 2.00
24 B.Perriman/J.Flacco .75 2.00
25 G.Tate/M.Stafford .75 2.00

2017 Prestige Connections Jerseys

1 D.Prescott/E.Elliott 5.00 12.00
2 C.Newton/K.Benjamin 4.00 10.00
3 J.Elway/V.Johnson 6.00 15.00
4 O.Beckham/E.Manning 4.00 10.00
5 K.Wright/M.Mariota 4.00 10.00
6 A.Rodgers/D.Adams 8.00 20.00
7 D.Thomas/P.Manning 8.00 20.00
8 A.Luck/T.Hilton 5.00 12.00
9 C.Wentz/J.Matthews 5.00 12.00
10 B.Bortles/A.Robinson 3.00 8.00
11 T.Taylor/S.Watkins 4.00 10.00
12 L.Fitzgerald/C.Palmer 3.00 8.00
13 D.Baldwin/R.Wilson 5.00 12.00
14 B.Favre/S.Sharpe 8.00 20.00
15 J.Jones/M.Ryan 4.00 10.00
16 A.Green/A.Dalton 4.00 10.00
17 A.Gates/P.Rivers 4.00 10.00
18 A.Brown/B.Rthlsbrgr 4.00 10.00
19 R.Grnkwski/T.Brady 10.00 25.00
20 A.Peterson/B.Favre 8.00 20.00
21 J.Montana/J.Rice 10.00 25.00
22 M.Evans/J.Winston 3.00 8.00
23 J.Landry/R.Tannehill 3.00 8.00
24 B.Perriman/J.Flacco 3.00 8.00
25 G.Tate/M.Stafford 3.00 8.00

2017 Prestige Draft Big Board

1 Patrick Mahomes II 5.00 12.00
2 Leonard Fournette 1.25 3.00
3 Dede Westbrook .40 1.00
4 Mitchell Trubisky 2.00 5.00
5 Myles Garrett 1.25 3.00
6 Dalvin Cook 1.00 2.50
7 Alvin Kamara 1.50 4.00
8 Brad Kaaya .40 1.00
9 Curtis Samuel .50 1.25
10 Corey Davis .60 1.50
11 D'Onta Foreman .50 1.25
12 Deshaun Watson 2.50 6.00
13 John Ross .50 1.25
14 DeShone Kizer .40 1.00
15 Jonathan Allen .50 1.25
16 Mike Williams .60 1.50
17 Cooper Kupp .60 1.50
18 Christian McCaffrey 1.00 2.50
19 David Njoku .50 1.25
20 Malachi Dupre .40 1.00

2017 Prestige Draft Big Board Ink

1 Patrick Mahomes II 125.00 250.00
2 Leonard Fournette 20.00 50.00
3 Dede Westbrook 6.00 15.00
4 Mitchell Trubisky 30.00 80.00
6 Dalvin Cook 15.00 40.00
7 Alvin Kamara 25.00 60.00
8 Brad Kaaya 6.00 15.00
9 Curtis Samuel 8.00 20.00
10 Corey Davis 10.00 25.00
11 D'Onta Foreman 8.00 20.00
12 Deshaun Watson
13 John Ross 8.00 20.00
14 DeShone Kizer 6.00 15.00
15 Jonathan Allen 8.00 20.00
16 Mike Williams 10.00 25.00
17 Cooper Kupp 10.00 25.00
18 Christian McCaffrey 15.00 40.00
20 Malachi Dupre 6.00 15.00

2017 Prestige Hardwear

1 Tevin Coleman .40 1.00
2 Hunter Henry .30 .75
3 Jay Ajayi .40 1.00
4 Braxton Miller .30 .75
5 Jordan Howard .50 1.25
6 Christian Hackenberg .30 .75
7 Melvin Gordon .40 1.00
8 Corey Coleman .30 .75
9 Paxton Lynch .30 .75
10 Derrick Henry .40 1.00
11 Tyler Lockett .40 1.00
12 Jamison Crowder .30 .75
13 Jeremy Langford .40 1.00
14 C.J. Prosise .30 .75
15 Josh Doctson .30 .75
16 Connor Cook .30 .75
17 Michael Thomas .50 1.25
18 Dak Prescott .50 1.25
19 Phillip Dorsett .30 .75
20 Ezekiel Elliott .60 1.50
21 Will Fuller V .30 .75
22 Jared Goff .50 1.25
23 Joey Bosa .50 1.25
24 Carson Wentz .60 1.50
25 Laquon Treadwell .30 .75

2017 Prestige Hardwear Jerseys

1 Tevin Coleman 2.50 6.00
2 Hunter Henry 2.00 5.00
3 Jay Ajayi 2.50 6.00
4 Braxton Miller 2.00 5.00
5 Jordan Howard 3.00 8.00
6 Christian Hackenberg 2.00 5.00
7 Melvin Gordon 2.50 6.00
8 Corey Coleman 2.00 5.00
9 Paxton Lynch 2.00 5.00
10 Derrick Henry 2.50 6.00
11 Tyler Lockett 2.50 6.00
12 Jamison Crowder 2.00 5.00
13 Jeremy Langford 2.50 6.00
14 C.J. Prosise 2.00 5.00
15 Josh Doctson 2.00 5.00
16 Connor Cook 2.00 5.00
17 Michael Thomas 3.00 8.00
18 Dak Prescott 3.00 8.00
19 Phillip Dorsett 2.00 5.00
20 Ezekiel Elliott 4.00 10.00
21 Will Fuller V 2.00 5.00
22 Jared Goff 3.00 8.00
23 Joey Bosa 3.00 8.00
24 Carson Wentz 4.00 10.00
25 Laquon Treadwell 2.00 5.00

2017 Prestige Legendary Signatures

*PLATINUM/25: .6X TO 1.5X BASIC AU/100
*PLATINUM/25: .5X TO 1.2X BASIC AU/50
*PLATINUM/15: .5X TO 1.2X BASIC AU/25
1 Fran Tarkenton/25 15.00 40.00
2 Kellen Winslow/50 6.00 15.00
3 Donald Driver/25 8.00 20.00
4 Ray Guy/50 5.00 12.00
5 Dave Wilcox/100 4.00 10.00
6 Ernest Givins/100 4.00 10.00
7 Edgerrin James/50 6.00 15.00
8 Bob Griese/25 10.00 25.00
9 Ted Hendricks/25 6.00 15.00
10 Chris Cooley/25 8.00 20.00
11 Eddie George/25 15.00 40.00
12 Jim Zorn/100 8.00 20.00
13 Ahmad Rashad/100 10.00 25.00
14 Harold Carmichael/100 4.00 10.00
15 Rocky Bleier/50 6.00 15.00
16 Ottis Anderson/100 4.00 10.00
17 Larry Csonka/25 12.00 30.00
18 Vance Johnson/100 4.00 10.00
19 Neil Smith/100 4.00 10.00
20 Mark Brunell/50 10.00 25.00
21 Michael Strahan/25 8.00 20.00
22 Phil McConkey/100 5.00 12.00
23 Deion Sanders/25
24 Dallas Clark/50 5.00 12.00
25 Morten Andersen/100 4.00 10.00
26 Jimmy Johnson/100 4.00 10.00
27 Dermontti Dawson/100 5.00 12.00
28 Greg Jennings/25
29 Steve Atwater/50 12.00 30.00
30 Harry Carson/50 5.00 12.00

2017 Prestige Living Legends

*BLUE: .8X TO 2X BASIC INSERTS
*PLATINUM/25: 2X TO 5X BASIC INSERTS
1 Jerome Bettis .50 1.25
2 Jim Brown .60 1.50
3 Joe Namath .60 1.50
4 Deion Sanders .40 1.00
5 John Riggins .40 1.00
6 Terry Bradshaw .75 2.00
7 Marshall Faulk .40 1.00
8 Brett Favre 1.00 2.50
9 Roger Staubach .60 1.50
10 Jerry Rice .75 2.00
11 Troy Aikman .60 1.50
12 Barry Sanders .75 2.00
13 Franco Harris .50 1.25
14 Marcus Allen .40 1.00
15 Steve Young .60 1.50
16 Emmitt Smith .75 2.00
17 Brian Urlacher .50 1.25
18 John Elway .75 2.00
19 Ray Lewis .50 1.25
20 Peyton Manning 1.00 2.50

2017 Prestige NFL Passport

1 O.J. Howard .40 1.00
2 Brad Kaaya .30 .75
3 Davis Webb .30 .75
4 Corey Davis .50 1.25
5 Patrick Mahomes II 4.00 10.00
6 Leonard Fournette 1.00 2.50
7 Dede Westbrook .30 .75
8 Mitchell Trubisky 1.50 4.00
9 Myles Garrett 1.00 2.50
10 Dalvin Cook .75 2.00
11 Alvin Kamara 1.25 3.00
12 Christian McCaffrey .75 2.00
13 David Njoku .40 1.00
14 Malachi Dupre .30 .75
15 D'Onta Foreman .40 1.00
16 Deshaun Watson 2.00 5.00
17 John Ross .40 1.00
18 DeShone Kizer .30 .75
19 Curtis Samuel .40 1.00
20 Mike Williams .50 1.25

2017 Prestige NFL Passport Ink

1 O.J. Howard 8.00 20.00
2 Brad Kaaya 6.00 15.00
3 Davis Webb 6.00 15.00
4 Corey Davis 10.00 25.00
5 Patrick Mahomes II 125.00 250.00
6 Leonard Fournette 20.00 50.00
7 Dede Westbrook 6.00 15.00
8 Mitchell Trubisky 30.00 80.00
10 Dalvin Cook 15.00 40.00
11 Alvin Kamara 25.00 60.00
12 Christian McCaffrey 15.00 40.00
14 Malachi Dupre 6.00 15.00
15 D'Onta Foreman 8.00 20.00
16 Deshaun Watson
17 John Ross 8.00 20.00
18 DeShone Kizer 6.00 15.00
19 Curtis Samuel 8.00 20.00
20 Mike Williams 10.00 25.00

2017 Prestige Phenomenal Athletes

*BLUE: .6X TO 1.5X BASIC INSERTS
*RED: .8X TO 2X BASIC INSERTS
*PLATINUM/25: 2X TO 5X BASIC INSERTS
1 Deion Sanders .40 1.00
2 Antonio Brown .50 1.25
3 Darrell Green .50 1.25
4 Marcus Mariota .50 1.25
5 Andrew Luck .60 1.50
6 Terrelle Pryor Sr. .30 .75
7 Jalen Ramsey .30 .75
8 Von Miller .40 1.00
9 Corey Coleman .30 .75
10 Julio Jones .50 1.25
11 Jim Brown .60 1.50
12 Aaron Rodgers 1.00 2.50
13 Gale Sayers .50 1.25
14 Russell Wilson .60 1.50
15 David Johnson .50 1.25
16 Demaryius Thomas .40 1.00
17 Le'Veon Bell .40 1.00
18 J.J. Watt .50 1.25
19 Joey Bosa .50 1.25
20 Adrian Peterson .50 1.25
21 Bo Jackson .60 1.50
22 Tyrod Taylor .40 1.00
23 Vernon Davis .30 .75
24 Jamaal Charles .40 1.00
25 Eric Berry .40 1.00
26 Jason Pierre-Paul .30 .75
27 Odell Beckham Jr. .50 1.25
28 Antonio Gates .30 .75
29 Ezekiel Elliott .60 1.50
30 Jimmy Graham .50 1.25
31 Barry Sanders .75 2.00
32 Rob Gronkowski .50 1.25
33 Roger Staubach .60 1.50
34 Brandin Cooks .40 1.00
35 Randy Moss .40 1.00
36 Cam Newton .50 1.25
37 Julius Peppers .40 1.00
38 Darrius Heyward-Bey .30 .75
39 Dak Prescott .50 1.25
40 Patrick Peterson .30 .75
41 Lawrence Taylor .50 1.25
42 Will Fuller V .30 .75

2017 Prestige Rising Stars Jerseys

1 Sammie Coates 2.00 5.00
2 Dak Prescott 3.00 8.00
3 Todd Gurley II 3.00 8.00
4 Braxton Miller 2.00 5.00
5 Jay Ajayi 2.50 6.00
6 David Johnson 3.00 8.00
7 Brandin Cooks 2.50 6.00
8 Cardale Jones 2.00 5.00
9 Bryce Petty 2.00 5.00
10 Jeremy Hill 2.00 5.00
11 Hunter Henry 2.00 5.00
12 Devontae Booker 2.00 5.00
13 Derrick Henry 2.50 6.00
14 Jadeveon Clowney 2.00 5.00
15 Kenyan Drake 2.00 5.00
16 Devonta Freeman 2.50 6.00
17 Michael Thomas 3.00 8.00
18 Devin Funchess 2.00 5.00
19 Leonard Williams 2.00 5.00
20 Tyler Boyd 2.00 5.00
21 Joey Bosa 3.00 8.00
22 Paxton Lynch 2.00 5.00
23 Marcus Mariota 3.00 8.00
24 Will Fuller V 2.00 5.00
25 Laquon Treadwell 2.00 5.00
26 Tevin Coleman 2.50 6.00
27 Odell Beckham Jr. 3.00 8.00
28 Kelvin Benjamin 2.50 6.00
29 Amari Cooper 3.00 8.00
30 Cody Kessler 2.00 5.00
31 C.J. Prosise 2.00 5.00
32 Davante Adams 2.50 6.00
33 Tajae Sharpe 2.00 5.00
34 Jared Goff 3.00 8.00
35 Stefon Diggs 2.50 6.00
36 Breshad Perriman 2.00 5.00
37 Paul Perkins 2.00 5.00
38 Jeremy Langford 2.50 6.00
39 DeAndre Washington 2.00 5.00
40 Corey Coleman 2.00 5.00
41 Tyler Lockett 2.50 6.00
42 Ty Montgomery 2.00 5.00
43 Josh Doctson 2.00 5.00
44 Jarvis Landry 2.50 6.00
45 Jimmy Garoppolo 4.00 10.00
46 Kenneth Dixon 2.00 5.00
47 Sterling Shepard 2.50 6.00
48 Jordan Howard 3.00 8.00
49 Carson Wentz 4.00 10.00
50 Duke Johnson 2.00 5.00

2017 Prestige Rookie Autographs

201 Carlos Henderson 2.50 6.00
202 Malik McDowell 2.50 6.00
203 ArDarius Stewart 2.50 6.00
204 Mitchell Trubisky 12.00 30.00
205 Dalvin Cook 6.00 15.00
206 Elijah Hood 2.50 6.00
207 Marlon Humphrey 2.50 6.00
208 Jordan Leggett 2.50 6.00
209 Cameron Sutton 2.50 6.00
210 Malachi Dupre 2.50 6.00
211 Elijah Qualls 2.50 6.00
212 Stacy Coley 2.50 6.00
213 Deshaun Watson 15.00 40.00
214 Eddie Jackson 3.00 8.00
215 Christian McCaffrey 6.00 15.00
217 Marshon Lattimore 3.00 8.00
218 Evan Engram 3.00 8.00
220 Cooper Kupp 4.00 10.00
221 Caleb Brantley 2.50 6.00
222 Chris Godwin 3.00 8.00
223 DeShone Kizer 2.50 6.00
224 D'Onta Foreman 3.00 8.00
225 Donnel Pumphrey 3.00 8.00
226 Quincy Wilson 2.50 6.00
227 Mike Williams 4.00 10.00
228 Jonathan Allen 3.00 8.00
229 R. Joshua Dobbs 12.00 30.00
231 Zay Jones 3.00 8.00
232 Patrick Mahomes II 125.00 250.00
234 James Conner 5.00 12.00
235 Adoree' Jackson 3.00 8.00
236 John Ross 3.00 8.00
238 KD Cannon 2.50 6.00
239 Zach Cunningham 3.00 8.00
241 Raekwon McMillan 2.50 6.00
242 Jarrad Davis 3.00 8.00
243 Travis Rudolph 2.50 6.00
244 Sidney Jones 2.50 6.00
245 JuJu Smith-Schuster 6.00 15.00
246 Carl Lawson 2.50 6.00
247 Josh Malone 2.50 6.00
248 Jabrill Peppers 4.00 10.00
249 Kevin King 3.00 8.00
250 Jerod Evans 3.00 8.00
251 Alvin Kamara 10.00 25.00
252 Jamaal Williams 2.50 6.00
253 Desmond King 3.00 8.00
254 Corey Davis 4.00 10.00
255 Charles Harris 2.50 6.00
256 Artavis Scott 2.50 6.00
257 Tim Williams 3.00 8.00
258 Cole Hikutini 2.50 6.00
259 Davis Webb 2.50 6.00
260 Matthew Dayes 2.50 6.00
261 Joe Mixon 5.00 12.00
263 Dede Westbrook 2.50 6.00
264 Taco Charlton 2.50 6.00
265 Chad Hansen 2.50 6.00
268 Chad Kelly 2.50 6.00
269 Wayne Gallman 3.00 8.00
270 O.J. Howard 3.00 8.00
271 Cordrea Tankersley 3.00 8.00
272 Curtis Samuel 3.00 8.00
273 Jordan Willis 2.50 6.00
274 Noah Brown 3.00 8.00
275 Jamal Adams 2.50 6.00
276 Marquez White 2.50 6.00
278 Brian Hill 2.50 6.00
279 Jake Butt 3.00 8.00
280 Tre'Davious White 2.50 6.00
281 Amara Darboh 2.50 6.00
282 DeMarcus Walker 2.50 6.00
283 Shelton Gibson 2.50 6.00
284 Malik Hooker 2.50 6.00
285 Dawuane Smoot 2.50 6.00
286 Leonard Fournette 8.00 20.00
287 Corey Clement 3.00 8.00
288 Bucky Hodges 2.50 6.00
289 Isaiah Ford 2.50 6.00
290 Solomon Thomas 2.50 6.00
291 Marlon Mack 4.00 10.00
292 Josh Reynolds 2.50 6.00
293 T.J. Watt 8.00 20.00
296 Samaje Perine 2.50 6.00
297 Brad Kaaya 2.50 6.00
298 Ryan Switzer 3.00 8.00
299 Jeremy McNichols 2.50 6.00
300 Kareem Hunt 5.00 12.00

2017 Prestige Rookie Autographs Xtra Points Gold

*GOLD/50: .8X TO 2X BASIC AU

2017 Prestige Rookie Autographs Xtra Points Green

*GREEN/150: .6X TO 1.5X BASIC AU
213 Deshaun Watson 25.00 60.00

2017 Prestige Rookie Autographs Xtra Points Platinum

*PLATINUM/25: 1X TO 2.5X BASIC AU

2017 Prestige Rookie Autographs Xtra Points Purple

*PURPLE/100: .6X TO 1.5X BASIC AU
213 Deshaun Watson 25.00 60.00

2017 Prestige Shirt Off My Back Jerseys

1 Maliek Collins 2.00 5.00
2 Michael Floyd 2.00 5.00
3 Demaryius Thomas 2.50 6.00
4 Sammy Watkins 3.00 8.00
5 Devontae Booker 2.00 5.00
6 Tyler Boyd 2.00 5.00
7 Ryan Tannehill 2.50 6.00
8 Cody Core 2.00 5.00
9 Zack Martin 2.00 5.00
10 Mario Williams 2.00 5.00
11 Terrance Williams 2.00 5.00
12 Devonta Freeman 2.50 6.00
13 Chris Harris 2.00 5.00
14 LeSean McCoy 3.00 8.00
15 Blake Bortles 2.00 5.00
16 Jeremy Hill 2.00 5.00
17 Jarvis Landry 2.50 6.00
18 Darqueze Dennard 2.00 5.00
19 Tony Romo 2.50 6.00
20 Reshad Jones 2.00 5.00
21 Barry Church 2.00 5.00
22 Marcell Dareus 2.00 5.00
23 Bradley Roby 2.00 5.00
24 Charles Clay 2.00 5.00
25 Myles Jack 2.00 5.00
26 A.J. Green 3.00 8.00
27 Cameron Wake 2.00 5.00
28 Giovani Bernard 2.00 5.00
29 Byron Jones 2.00 5.00
30 Kenyan Drake 2.00 5.00
31 Alfred Morris 2.00 5.00
32 Tyrod Taylor 2.50 6.00
33 Paxton Lynch 2.00 5.00
34 Andy Dalton 2.50 6.00
35 Allen Robinson 2.50 6.00
36 Geno Atkins 2.00 5.00
37 Ndamukong Suh 2.50 6.00
38 Travis Frederick 2.00 5.00
39 Ezekiel Elliott 4.00 10.00
40 Xavien Howard 2.00 5.00
41 Emmanuel Sanders 3.00 8.00
42 Robert Woods 2.50 6.00
43 T.J. Ward 2.00 5.00
44 Vontaze Burfict 2.00 5.00
45 Marqise Lee 2.00 5.00
46 Tyler Eifert 2.50 6.00
47 Leonte Carroo 2.00 5.00
48 Tyron Smith 2.00 5.00
49 Cole Beasley 3.00 8.00
50 Mike Gillislee 2.00 5.00

2017 Prestige Sophomore Signatures

*PLATINUM/25: .6X TO 1.5X BASIC AU/100
1 Juston Burris 4.00 10.00
2 Javon Hargrave 4.00 10.00
3 T.J. Green 4.00 10.00
4 Kenneth Farrow 4.00 10.00
5 Justin Simmons 4.00 10.00
6 Peyton Barber 4.00 10.00
7 Sheldon Day 4.00 10.00
8 Robert Nkemdiche 4.00 10.00
9 Devin Fuller 4.00 10.00
10 Cole Wick 4.00 10.00
11 Roger Lewis 4.00 10.00
12 Temarrick Hemingway 4.00 10.00
13 Robby Anderson 4.00 10.00
14 Chester Rogers 4.00 10.00
15 Jakeem Grant 4.00 10.00
16 Brandon Williams 4.00 10.00
17 Jeff Driskel 4.00 10.00
18 Maliek Collins 4.00 10.00
19 Tyler Matakevich 4.00 10.00
20 Andy Janovich 4.00 10.00

2017 Prestige Spectacular Catch

*BLUE: .8X TO 2X BASIC INSERTS
*RED: .8X TO 2X BASIC INSERTS
*PLATINUM/25: 2X TO 5X BASIC INSERTS
1 Curtis Martin .40 1.00
2 Randy Moss .40 1.00
3 Tony Romo .40 1.00
4 Jim Plunkett .40 1.00
5 Jerome Bettis .50 1.25
6 John Elway .75 2.00
7 Joe Montana 1.25 3.00
8 Marshall Faulk .40 1.00
9 Matt Forte .30 .75
10 Marcus Allen .40 1.00
11 James Harrison .40 1.00
12 Rod Woodson .40 1.00
13 Kevin Greene .40 1.00
14 Drew Brees .50 1.25
15 Steve Largent .50 1.25
16 Steve Young .60 1.50
17 Brett Favre 1.00 2.50
18 Charles Woodson .50 1.25
19 Josh Norman .30 .75
20 Mike Vrabel .30 .75
21 Antonio Gates .30 .75
22 Peyton Manning 1.00 2.50
23 Shannon Sharpe .40 1.00
24 Kurt Warner .40 1.00
25 Eric Dickerson .50 1.25
26 Warren Moon .50 1.25
27 Jerry Rice .75 2.00
28 Deion Sanders .40 1.00

2017 Prestige Stars of the NFL

1 Larry Csonka .40 1.00
2 Aaron Rodgers 1.00 2.50
3 Matt Ryan .40 1.00
4 Barry Sanders .75 2.00
5 Russell Wilson .60 1.50
6 Cam Newton .50 1.25
7 Peyton Manning 1.00 2.50
8 Eli Manning .40 1.00
9 Tony Romo .40 1.00
10 Joe Namath .60 1.50
11 Le'Veon Bell .40 1.00
12 Adrian Peterson .50 1.25
13 Matthew Stafford .40 1.00
14 Ben Roethlisberger .50 1.25
15 Steve Young .60 1.50
16 Drew Brees .50 1.25
17 Tony Dorsett .50 1.25
18 Joe Flacco .40 1.00
19 Troy Aikman .60 1.50
20 Julio Jones .50 1.25
21 Marcus Mariota .50 1.25
22 Antonio Brown .50 1.25
23 Roger Staubach .60 1.50
24 Bob Griese .50 1.25
25 Tom Brady 1.25 3.00

2017 Prestige Stars of the NFL Jerseys

1 Larry Csonka 2.50 6.00
2 Aaron Rodgers 6.00 15.00
3 Matt Ryan 2.50 6.00
4 Barry Sanders 5.00 12.00
5 Russell Wilson 4.00 10.00
6 Cam Newton 3.00 8.00
7 Peyton Manning 6.00 15.00
8 Eli Manning 2.50 6.00
9 Tony Romo 2.50 6.00
10 Joe Namath 4.00 10.00
11 Le'Veon Bell 2.50 6.00
12 Adrian Peterson 3.00 8.00
13 Matthew Stafford 2.50 6.00
14 Ben Roethlisberger 3.00 8.00
15 Steve Young 4.00 10.00
16 Drew Brees 3.00 8.00
17 Tony Dorsett 3.00 8.00
18 Joe Flacco 2.50 6.00
19 Troy Aikman 4.00 10.00
20 Julio Jones 3.00 8.00
21 Marcus Mariota 3.00 8.00
22 Antonio Brown 3.00 8.00
23 Roger Staubach 4.00 10.00
24 Bob Griese 3.00 8.00
25 Tom Brady 8.00 20.00

2017 Prestige Veteran Signatures

*PLATINUM/25: .6X TO 1.5X BASIC AU/100
*PLATINUM/25: .5X TO 1.2X BASIC AU/35-65
*PLATINUM/15: .5X TO 1.2X BASIC AU/25
1 Aaron Donald/50 8.00 20.00
2 Adam Vinatieri/35 5.00 12.00
3 Allen Hurns/50 5.00 12.00
4 Alshon Jeffery/35 6.00 15.00
5 Andrew Luck/25 25.00 50.00
6 Blake Bortles/25
7 Brandin Cooks/50 6.00 15.00
8 Brian Cushing/50 5.00 12.00
9 Byron Jones/100 4.00 10.00
10 Carlos Hyde/65 5.00 12.00
11 Charcandrick West/100 4.00 10.00
12 Chris Ivory/50 6.00 15.00
13 Christian Hackenberg/50 5.00 12.00
14 Jerick McKinnon/65 5.00 12.00
15 Jaelen Strong/65 5.00 12.00
16 DeAngelo Williams/35 5.00 12.00
17 Derek Carr/35 15.00 40.00
18 DeSean Jackson/35 6.00 15.00
19 Doug Baldwin/50 10.00 25.00
20 Eric Berry/65 12.00 30.00
21 Frank Gore/35 6.00 15.00
22 Haloti Ngata/50 5.00 12.00
23 J.J. Watt/25 25.00 50.00
24 James White/100 5.00 12.00
25 Jay Cutler/25 6.00 15.00
26 Jeremy Maclin/35 5.00 12.00
27 Joe Haden/50 5.00 12.00
28 Joe Thomas/50 5.00 12.00
29 Joey Bosa/65 8.00 20.00
30 John Kuhn/100 10.00 25.00
31 Julius Thomas/50 5.00 12.00
32 Keenan Allen/50 6.00 15.00
33 Latavius Murray/65 10.00 25.00
34 Mason Crosby/100 4.00 10.00
35 Matt Jones/50 6.00 15.00
36 Matt Ryan/25
37 Mike Tolbert/100 4.00 10.00
38 Mohamed Sanu/65 5.00 12.00
39 Muhammad Wilkerson/50 5.00 12.00
40 Philip Rivers/25
41 Richard Sherman/25 25.00 50.00
42 Ryan Shazier/65 5.00 12.00
43 Sebastian Janikowski/50 5.00 12.00
44 Thomas Davis/65 10.00 25.00
45 Travis Benjamin/100 4.00 10.00
46 Trevor Siemian/50 5.00 12.00
47 Victor Cruz/35 6.00 15.00
48 Vincent Jackson/35 5.00 12.00
49 Kony Ealy/100 4.00 10.00
50 Hunter Henry/100 4.00 10.00

2018 Prestige

1 Carlos Hyde .20 .50
2 Marquise Goodwin .20 .50
3 Reuben Foster .20 .50
4 Solomon Thomas .20 .50
5 Matt Breida .25 .60
6 Dontrelle Inman .20 .50
7 Andy Dalton .25 .60
8 A.J. Green .30 .75
9 Geno Atkins .20 .50
10 Tyrod Taylor .25 .60
11 Darron Lee .20 .50
12 Charles Clay .20 .50
13 A.J. McCarron .20 .50
14 Brandon McManus .20 .50
15 Chris Harris Jr. .20 .50
16 Demaryius Thomas .25 .60
17 Emmanuel Sanders .30 .75
18 Von Miller .25 .60
19 Brandon Marshall .20 .50
20 DeShone Kizer .25 .60
21 Duke Johnson .20 .50
22 Patrick Mahomes II .75 2.00
23 Cameron Brate .20 .50
24 Kendell Beckwith .20 .50
25 Lavonte David .20 .50
26 Kwon Alexander .20 .50
27 Sam Bradford .20 .50
28 Larry Fitzgerald .25 .60
29 Patrick Peterson .20 .50
30 Melvin Gordon .25 .60
31 Keenan Allen .25 .60
32 Tyrell Williams .20 .50
33 Joey Bosa .30 .75
34 Alex Smith .25 .60
35 Travis Kelce .30 .75
36 Eric Berry .25 .60
37 T.Y. Hilton .25 .60
38 Quincy Wilson .20 .50
39 Malik Hooker .20 .50
40 Jason Witten .25 .60
41 DeMarcus Lawrence .20 .50
42 Sean Lee .25 .60
43 Dez Bryant .30 .75
44 Ryan Tannehill .25 .60
45 Kenyan Drake .20 .50
46 Danny Amendola .25 .60
47 DeVante Parker .25 .60
48 Reshad Jones .20 .50
49 Zach Ertz .25 .60
50 Nelson Agholor .20 .50
51 Malcolm Jenkins .20 .50
52 Julio Jones .30 .75
53 Deion Jones .20 .50
54 Keanu Neal .20 .50
55 Landon Collins .20 .50
56 Odell Beckham Jr. .30 .75
57 Blake Bortles .20 .50
58 Allen Robinson .25 .60
59 Jalen Ramsey .25 .60
60 A.J. Bouye .20 .50
61 Josh McCown .20 .50
62 Jermaine Kearse .20 .50
63 Teddy Bridgewater .25 .60
64 Jamal Adams .25 .60
65 Marcus Maye .20 .50
66 Marvin Jones Jr. .20 .50
67 Golden Tate III .20 .50
68 Tahir Whitehead .20 .50
69 Ezekiel Ansah .20 .50
70 Davante Adams .25 .60
71 Clay Matthews .25 .60
72 Cam Newton .30 .75
73 Devin Funchess .20 .50
74 Luke Kuechly .25 .60
75 Tom Brady .75 2.00
76 Brandin Cooks .25 .60
77 Julian Edelman .30 .75
78 Zach Cunningham .20 .50
79 Dion Lewis .20 .50
80 Marshawn Lynch .25 .60
81 Amari Cooper .30 .75
82 Khalil Mack .30 .75
83 Jared Goff .30 .75
84 Le'Veon Bell .25 .60
85 Robert Woods .25 .60
86 Sammy Watkins .30 .75
87 Joe Flacco .25 .60
88 Alex Collins .20 .50
89 Terrell Suggs .20 .50
90 Eric Weddle .20 .50
91 Jamison Crowder .20 .50
92 Josh Doctson .20 .50
[illegible]
94 Josh Norman .20 .50
95 Mark Ingram .25 .60
96 Michael Thomas .30 .75
97 Marshon Lattimore .20 .50
98 Vonn Bell .20 .50
99 Doug Baldwin .25 .60
100 Paul Richardson .20 .50
101 Jerick McKinnon .20 .50
102 Earl Thomas III .25 .60
103 Ryan Hewitt .20 .50
104 Ryan Shazier .20 .50
105 DeAndre Hopkins .25 .60
106 Will Fuller V .20 .50
107 Marcus Mariota .30 .75
108 Derrick Henry .30 .75
109 Delanie Walker .20 .50
110 Corey Davis .25 .60
111 Brian Orakpo .20 .50
112 Case Keenum .25 .60
113 Dalvin Cook .25 .60
114 Adam Thielen .30 .75
115 Harrison Smith .30 .75
116 Kyle Rudolph .20 .50
117 Kelvin Benjamin .25 .60
118 Dan Vitale .20 .50
119 Corey Coleman .20 .50
120 Isaiah Crowell .20 .50
121 Robert Nkemdiche .20 .50
122 Budda Baker .20 .50
123 Desmond King .20 .50
124 Spencer Ware .20 .50
125 Cameron Erving .20 .50
126 Jack Doyle .20 .50
127 Antonio Morrison .20 .50
128 Jacoby Brissett .20 .50
129 Charles Tapper .20 .50
130 La'el Collins .20 .50
131 Jerrell Freeman .20 .50
132 Mike Thomas .20 .50
133 Nick Kwiatkoski .20 .50
134 Taylor Gabriel .20 .50
135 Sterling Shepard .25 .60
136 Akeem Ayers .20 .50
137 Chris Ivory .25 .60
138 Chad Williams .20 .50
139 Miles Killebrew .20 .50
140 Aaron Jones .25 .60
141 Aaron Ripkowski .20 .50
142 Kenny Clark .20 .50
143 Shaq Thompson .20 .50
144 Kyle Van Noy .20 .50
145 Karl Joseph .20 .50
146 Jordy Nelson .25 .60
147 Temarrick Hemingway .20 .50
148 Brandon Williams .20 .50
149 Tavon Young .20 .50
150 Tyler Lockett .25 .60
151 Arthur Moats .20 .50
152 Nick Vigil .20 .50
153 Khalfani Muhammad .20 .50
154 Tajae Sharpe .20 .50
155 Eric Kendricks .20 .50
156 Jameis Winston .25 .60
157 Mike Evans .25 .60
158 David Johnson .30 .75
159 Philip Rivers .30 .75
160 Kareem Hunt .25 .60
161 Tyreek Hill .30 .75
162 Andrew Luck .40 1.00
163 Dak Prescott .30 .75
164 Ezekiel Elliott .40 1.00
165 Carson Wentz .40 1.00
166 Jay Ajayi .25 .60
167 Alshon Jeffery .25 .60
168 Matt Ryan .25 .60
169 Devonta Freeman .25 .60
170 Eli Manning .25 .60
171 Evan Engram .20 .50
172 Mitchell Trubisky .30 .75
173 Leonard Fournette .30 .75
174 Jordan Howard .30 .75
175 Matthew Stafford .25 .60
176 Aaron Rodgers .60 1.50
177 Jimmy Graham .30 .75
178 Tarik Cohen .25 .60
179 Christian McCaffrey .30 .75
180 Greg Olsen .25 .60
181 Rob Gronkowski .30 .75
182 Derek Carr .30 .75
183 Todd Gurley II .30 .75
184 Cooper Kupp .25 .60
185 Aaron Donald .30 .75
186 Kirk Cousins .30 .75
187 Chris Thompson .20 .50
188 Joe Mixon .25 .60
189 Drew Brees .30 .75
190 Alvin Kamara .25 .60
191 Russell Wilson .40 1.00
192 Ben Roethlisberger .30 .75
193 Antonio Brown .30 .75
194 JuJu Smith-Schuster .30 .75
195 Deshaun Watson .40 1.00
196 D'Onta Foreman .20 .50
197 J.J. Watt .30 .75
198 LeSean McCoy .30 .75
199 Jimmy Garoppolo .40 1.00
200 Josh Gordon .20 .50
201 Akrum Wadley RC .30 .75
202 Arden Key RC .30 .75
203 Baker Mayfield RC 3.00 8.00
204 Bradley Chubb RC .50 1.25
205 Cedrick Wilson Jr. RC .30 .75
206 Courtland Sutton RC .50 1.25
207 DaeSean Hamilton RC .40 1.00
208 Vita Vea RC .50 1.25
209 Darren Carrington II RC .40 1.00
210 Deon Cain RC 1.50 4.00
211 Duke Dawson RC .30 .75
212 James Washington RC .60 1.50
213 Jordan Lasley RC .30 .75
214 Josh Rosen RC 4.00 10.00
215 Kenny Hill RC .40 1.00
216 Lavon Coleman RC .40 1.00
217 Marcus Baugh RC .30 .75
218 Maurice Hurst RC .40 1.00
219 Nick Chubb RC 1.00 2.50
220 Tre'Quan Smith RC .50 1.25
221 Robert Foster RC .30 .75
222 Royce Freeman RC .40 1.00
223 Sony Michel RC 1.00 2.50
224 Trey Quinn RC .30 .75
225 Allen Lazard RC .30 .75
226 Austin Allen RC .40 1.00
227 Calvin Ridley RC 3.00 8.00
228 Marcus Davenport RC 2.50 6.00
229 Dalton Schultz RC .40 1.00
230 DeAndre Goolsby RC .30 .75
231 Derrius Guice RC .60 1.50
232 Harold Landry RC .30 .75
233 Jaylen Samuels RC .40 1.00
234 Josh Allen RC 1.25 3.00
235 Kerryon Johnson RC .50 1.25
236 Mason Rudolph RC .75 2.00
237 Ogbonnia Okoronkwo RC .50 1.25
238 Ronnie Harrison RC .40 1.00
239 Sam Darnold RC 8.00 20.00
240 Tanner Lee RC .40 1.00
241 Troy Fumagalli RC .40 1.00
242 Anthony Miller RC .50 1.25
243 Bo Scarbrough RC .40 1.00
244 D.J. Moore RC .60 1.50
245 Deontay Burnett RC .40 1.00
246 Jerome Baker RC .40 1.00
247 Justin Jackson RC .40 1.00
248 Logan Woodside RC .50 1.25
[illegible]
250 Mark Andrews RC .50 1.25

251 Max Browne RC .40 1.00
252 Orlando Brown RC .50 1.25
253 Roquan Smith RC 4.00 10.00
254 Tarvarus McFadden RC .40 1.00
255 Auden Tate RC .30 .75
256 Billy Price RC .40 1.00
257 Dallas Goedert RC 1.50 4.00
258 Dorance Armstrong Jr. RC .30 .75
259 Kamryn Pettway RC .50 1.25
260 Mike Gesicki RC .40 1.00
261 Saquon Barkley RC 4.00 10.00
262 Sam Hubbard RC .40 1.00
263 Marquis Haynes RC .30 .75
264 Daron Payne RC .50 1.25
265 J.T. Barrett RC .50 1.25
266 Josh Adams RC .60 1.50
267 Mark Walton RC .40 1.00
268 Ray-Ray McCloud RC 1.25 3.00
269 Tremaine Edmunds RC .60 1.50
270 Minkah Fitzpatrick RC 2.50 6.00
271 Kurt Benkert RC .40 1.00
272 Hayden Hurst RC .40 1.00
273 D.J. Chark RC .40 1.00
274 Carlton Davis RC .40 1.00
275 Denzel Ward RC .75 2.00
276 Dylan Cantrell RC .30 .75
277 Leighton Vander Esch RC 1.00 2.50
278 J'Mon Moore RC .30 .75
279 Lamar Jackson RC 2.00 5.00
280 Rashaad Penny RC .50 1.25
281 Simmie Cobbs Jr. RC .50 1.25
282 Christian Kirk RC 2.00 5.00
283 Isaiah Oliver RC .30 .75
284 Derwin James RC .60 1.50
285 John Kelly RC .40 1.00
286 Luke Falk RC .40 1.00
287 Michael Gallup RC .60 1.50
288 Riley Ferguson RC .50 1.25
289 Ronald Jones II RC .30 .75
290 Ryan Izzo RC .30 .75
291 Dante Pettis RC .50 1.25
292 Equanimeous St. Brown RC .50 1.25
293 Joshua Jackson RC .60 1.50
294 Malik Jefferson RC .40 1.00
295 Nyheim Hines RC .40 1.00
296 Kalen Ballage RC .40 1.00
297 Kyle Lauletta RC .50 1.25
298 Marquez Valdes-Scantling RC .40 1.00
299 Kyzir White RC .50 1.25
300 Trey Marshall RC .40 1.00

2018 Prestige Highlight Reel

*BLUE: .6X TO 1.5X BASIC INSERTS
*RED: .6X TO 1.5X BASIC INSERTS
*PLATINUM/25: 1.5X TO 4X BASIC INSERTS
1 Cam Newton .60 1.50
2 Russell Wilson .75 2.00
3 Kareem Hunt .50 1.25
4 Todd Gurley II .60 1.50
5 Le'Veon Bell .50 1.25
6 LeSean McCoy .60 1.50
7 Leonard Fournette .60 1.50
8 Ezekiel Elliott .75 2.00
9 Alvin Kamara .50 1.25
10 Tyreek Hill .60 1.50
11 Stefon Diggs .50 1.25
12 DeAndre Hopkins .50 1.25
13 Keenan Allen .50 1.25
14 Antonio Brown .60 1.50
15 Julio Jones .60 1.50

2018 Prestige Highlight Reel Jerseys

*PRIME/25: .8X TO 2X BASIC JSY
1 Cam Newton 2.50 6.00
2 Russell Wilson 3.00 8.00
3 Kareem Hunt 2.00 5.00
4 Todd Gurley II 2.50 6.00
5 Le'Veon Bell 2.00 5.00
6 LeSean McCoy 2.50 6.00
7 Leonard Fournette 2.50 6.00
8 Ezekiel Elliott 3.00 8.00
9 Alvin Kamara 2.00 5.00
10 Tyreek Hill 2.50 6.00
11 Stefon Diggs 2.00 5.00
12 DeAndre Hopkins 2.00 5.00
13 Keenan Allen 2.00 5.00
14 Antonio Brown 2.50 6.00
15 Julio Jones 2.50 6.00

2018 Prestige NFL Passport

*BLUE: .6X TO 1.5X BASIC INSERTS
*RED: .6X TO 1.5X BASIC INSERTS
*PLATINUM/25: 1.5X TO 4X BASIC INSERTS
1 Sam Darnold 2.50 6.00
2 Josh Rosen 1.25 3.00
3 Sony Michel 1.25 3.00
4 J'Mon Moore .40 1.00
5 Josh Allen 1.50 4.00
6 Baker Mayfield 4.00 10.00
7 Auden Tate .40 1.00
8 Christian Kirk .60 1.50
9 Saquon Barkley 3.00 8.00
10 Deontay Burnett .50 1.25
11 Ronald Jones II .40 1.00
12 J.T. Barrett .60 1.50
13 Calvin Ridley 1.00 2.50
14 Derrius Guice .75 2.00
15 Bo Scarbrough .50 1.25
16 James Washington .75 2.00
17 D.J. Chark .50 1.25
18 Mason Rudolph 1.00 2.50
19 Courtland Sutton .60 1.50
20 John Kelly .50 1.25

2018 Prestige NFL Passport Jerseys

*GOLD/25: .8X TO 2X BASIC JSY
1 Sam Darnold 10.00 25.00
2 Josh Rosen 5.00 12.00
3 Sony Michel 5.00 12.00
4 J'Mon Moore 1.50 4.00
5 Josh Allen 6.00 15.00
6 Baker Mayfield 15.00 40.00
7 Auden Tate 1.50 4.00
8 Christian Kirk 2.50 6.00
10 Deontay Burnett 2.00 5.00
11 Ronald Jones II 1.50 4.00
12 J.T. Barrett 2.50 6.00
13 Calvin Ridley 4.00 10.00
14 Derrius Guice 3.00 8.00
15 Bo Scarbrough 2.00 5.00
16 James Washington 3.00 8.00
17 D.J. Chark 2.00 5.00
18 Mason Rudolph 4.00 10.00
19 Courtland Sutton 2.50 6.00
20 John Kelly 2.00 5.00

2018 Prestige Power House

*BLUE: .6X TO 1.5X BASIC INSERTS
*RED: .6X TO 1.5X BASIC INSERTS
*PLATINUM/25: 1.5X TO 4X BASIC INSERTS
1 Derrick Henry .60 1.50
2 Jared Goff .60 1.50
3 Deshaun Watson .75 2.00
4 Saquon Barkley 3.00 8.00
5 Dalvin Cook .50 1.25
6 Jameis Winston .50 1.25
7 Todd Gurley II .60 1.50
8 Leonard Fournette .60 1.50
9 Jabrill Peppers .40 1.00
10 Devin Funchess .40 1.00
11 Dak Prescott .60 1.50
12 Sam Darnold 2.50 6.00
13 Ryan Switzer .40 1.00
14 Michael Thomas .60 1.50
15 Baker Mayfield 4.00 10.00
16 Joe Mixon .50 1.25
17 Calvin Ridley 1.00 2.50
18 James Conner .60 1.50
19 Christian McCaffrey .60 1.50
20 D'Onta Foreman .40 1.00

2018 Prestige Power House Jerseys

*GOLD/25: .8X TO 2X BASIC JSY
1 Derrick Henry 2.50 6.00
2 Jared Goff 2.50 6.00
3 Deshaun Watson 3.00 8.00
5 Dalvin Cook 2.00 5.00
6 Jameis Winston 2.00 5.00
7 Todd Gurley II 2.50 6.00
8 Leonard Fournette 2.50 6.00
9 Jabrill Peppers 1.50 4.00
10 Devin Funchess 1.50 4.00
11 Dak Prescott 2.50 6.00
12 Sam Darnold 6.00 15.00
13 Ryan Switzer 1.50 4.00
14 Michael Thomas 2.50 6.00
15 Baker Mayfield 6.00 15.00
16 Joe Mixon 2.00 5.00
17 Calvin Ridley 4.00 10.00
18 James Conner 2.50 6.00
19 Christian McCaffrey 2.50 6.00
20 D'Onta Foreman 1.50 4.00

2018 Prestige Rising Stars

*BLUE: .6X TO 1.5X BASIC INSERTS
*RED: .6X TO 1.5X BASIC INSERTS
*PLATINUM/25: 1.5X TO 4X BASIC INSERTS
1 Alvin Kamara .50 1.25
2 Christian McCaffrey .60 1.50
3 Cooper Kupp .50 1.25
4 Dalvin Cook .50 1.25
5 Corey Davis .50 1.25
6 Deshaun Watson .75 2.00
7 Joe Mixon .50 1.25
8 JuJu Smith-Schuster .60 1.50
9 Kareem Hunt .50 1.25
10 Leonard Fournette .60 1.50
11 Jalen Ramsey .50 1.25
12 D'Onta Foreman .40 1.00
13 T.J. Watt .50 1.25
14 Marshon Lattimore .40 1.00
15 Jamal Adams .50 1.25
16 Carson Wentz .75 2.00
17 Joey Bosa .60 1.50
18 Ezekiel Elliott .75 2.00
19 Tyreek Hill .60 1.50
20 Derek Barnett .40 1.00

2018 Prestige Rookie Signatures

201 Akrum Wadley 2.50 6.00
202 Arden Key 2.50 6.00
203 Baker Mayfield
204 Bradley Chubb
205 Cedrick Wilson Jr. 2.50 6.00
206 Courtland Sutton
207 DaeSean Hamilton 3.00 8.00
208 Vita Vea 4.00 10.00
209 Darren Carrington II 3.00 8.00
211 Duke Dawson 2.50 6.00
212 James Washington
213 Jordan Lasley 2.50 6.00
214 Josh Rosen
215 Kenny Hill 3.00 8.00
216 Lavon Coleman 3.00 8.00
217 Marcus Baugh 2.50 6.00
218 Maurice Hurst 3.00 8.00
219 Nick Chubb
220 Tre'Quan Smith 4.00 10.00
221 Robert Foster 2.50 6.00
222 Royce Freeman
223 Sony Michel
224 Trey Quinn 2.50 6.00
225 Allen Lazard 2.50 6.00
226 Austin Allen 3.00 8.00
227 Calvin Ridley
228 Marcus Davenport
229 Dalton Schultz 3.00 8.00
230 DeAndre Goolsby 2.50 6.00
231 Derrius Guice
232 Harold Landry 2.50 6.00
233 Jaylen Samuels 3.00 8.00
234 Josh Allen
235 Kerryon Johnson 4.00 10.00
236 Mason Rudolph
237 Ogbonnia Okoronkwo 4.00 10.00
238 Ronnie Harrison 3.00 8.00
239 Sam Darnold
240 Tanner Lee 3.00 8.00
241 Troy Fumagalli 3.00 8.00
242 Anthony Miller 4.00 10.00
243 Bo Scarbrough 3.00 8.00
244 D.J. Moore 5.00 12.00
245 Deontay Burnett 3.00 8.00
246 Jerome Baker 3.00 8.00
247 Justin Jackson 3.00 8.00
248 Logan Woodside 4.00 10.00
249 Marcell Ateman 3.00 8.00
250 Mark Andrews 4.00 10.00
251 Max Browne 3.00 8.00
252 Orlando Brown 4.00 10.00
253 Roquan Smith
254 Tarvarus McFadden 3.00 8.00
255 Auden Tate 2.50 6.00
256 Billy Price 3.00 8.00
257 Dallas Goedert 3.00 8.00
258 Dorance Armstrong Jr. 2.50 6.00
259 Kamryn Pettway 4.00 10.00
260 Mike Gesicki 3.00 8.00
261 Saquon Barkley
262 Sam Hubbard 3.00 8.00
263 Marquis Haynes 2.50 6.00
264 Daron Payne
265 J.T. Barrett
266 Josh Adams 5.00 12.00
267 Mark Walton 3.00 8.00
268 Ray-Ray McCloud 2.50 6.00
269 Tremaine Edmunds
270 Minkah Fitzpatrick
271 Kurt Benkert 3.00 8.00
272 Hayden Hurst 3.00 8.00
273 D.J. Chark 3.00 8.00
274 Carlton Davis 3.00 8.00
275 Denzel Ward
276 Dylan Cantrell 2.50 6.00
277 Leighton Vander Esch
278 J'Mon Moore 2.50 6.00
280 Rashaad Penny
281 Simmie Cobbs Jr. 4.00 10.00
282 Christian Kirk 4.00 10.00
283 Isaiah Oliver 2.50 6.00
284 Derwin James
285 John Kelly
286 Luke Falk
287 Michael Gallup 5.00 12.00
288 Riley Ferguson 4.00 10.00
289 Ronald Jones II
290 Ryan Izzo 2.50 6.00
291 Dante Pettis 4.00 10.00
293 Joshua Jackson
294 Malik Jefferson 3.00 8.00
295 Nyheim Hines 3.00 8.00
296 Kalen Ballage 3.00 8.00
297 Kyle Lauletta
298 Marquez Valdes-Scantling 3.00 8.00
299 Kyzir White 4.00 10.00
300 Trey Marshall 3.00 8.00

2018 Prestige Stars of the NFL

*BLUE: .6X TO 1.5X BASIC INSERTS
*RED: .6X TO 1.5X BASIC INSERTS
*PLATINUM/25: 1.5X TO 4X BASIC INSERTS
1 Dak Prescott .60 1.50
2 Doug Baldwin .50 1.25
3 Jadeveon Clowney .40 1.00
4 Matthew Stafford .50 1.25
5 Matt Ryan .50 1.25
6 Sterling Shepard .50 1.25
7 DeVante Parker .50 1.25
8 Russell Wilson .75 2.00
9 Stefon Diggs .50 1.25
10 Tom Brady 1.50 4.00
11 Melvin Gordon .50 1.25
12 Amari Cooper .60 1.50
13 Ty Montgomery .40 1.00
14 Jordan Howard .60 1.50
15 Joey Bosa .60 1.50
16 David Johnson .60 1.50
17 Nelson Agholor .40 1.00
18 Jared Goff .60 1.50
19 Devin Funchess .40 1.00
20 Derrick Henry .60 1.50
21 Alvin Kamara .50 1.25
22 Leonard Fournette .60 1.50
23 JuJu Smith-Schuster .60 1.50
24 Aaron Rodgers 1.25 3.00
25 Carson Wentz .75 2.00

2018 Prestige Stars of the NFL Jerseys

*GOLD/25: .8X TO 2X BASIC JSY
1 Dak Prescott 2.50 6.00
2 Doug Baldwin 2.00 5.00
3 Jadeveon Clowney 1.50 4.00
4 Matthew Stafford 2.00 5.00
5 Matt Ryan 2.00 5.00
6 Sterling Shepard 2.00 5.00
7 DeVante Parker 2.00 5.00
8 Russell Wilson 3.00 8.00
9 Stefon Diggs 2.00 5.00
10 Tom Brady 6.00 15.00
11 Melvin Gordon 2.00 5.00
12 Amari Cooper 2.50 6.00
13 Ty Montgomery 1.50 4.00
14 Jordan Howard 2.50 6.00
15 Joey Bosa 2.50 6.00
16 David Johnson 2.50 6.00
17 Nelson Agholor 1.50 4.00
18 Jared Goff 2.50 6.00
19 Devin Funchess 1.50 4.00
20 Derrick Henry 2.50 6.00
21 Alvin Kamara 2.00 5.00
22 Leonard Fournette 2.50 6.00
23 JuJu Smith-Schuster 2.50 6.00
24 Aaron Rodgers 5.00 12.00
25 Carson Wentz 3.00 8.00

2018 Prestige Veteran Signatures

101 Jerick McKinnon 3.00 8.00
102 Earl Thomas III
103 Ryan Hewitt 3.00 8.00
104 Ryan Shazier 3.00 8.00
106 Will Fuller V 3.00 8.00
108 Derrick Henry 5.00 12.00
109 Delanie Walker 3.00 8.00
111 Brian Orakpo 3.00 8.00
112 Case Keenum 4.00 10.00
118 Dan Vitale 3.00 8.00
119 Corey Coleman 3.00 8.00
120 Isaiah Crowell 3.00 8.00
121 Robert Nkemdiche 3.00 8.00
122 Budda Baker 3.00 8.00
123 Desmond King 3.00 8.00
124 Spencer Ware 3.00 8.00
125 Cameron Erving 3.00 8.00
126 Jack Doyle 3.00 8.00
127 Antonio Morrison 3.00 8.00
128 Jacoby Brissett 3.00 8.00
129 Charles Tapper 3.00 8.00
130 La'el Collins 3.00 8.00
131 Jerrell Freeman 3.00 8.00
132 Mike Thomas 3.00 8.00
133 Nick Kwiatkoski 3.00 8.00
134 Taylor Gabriel 3.00 8.00
135 Sterling Shepard 4.00 10.00
136 Akeem Ayers 3.00 8.00
137 Chris Ivory 4.00 10.00
138 Chad Williams 3.00 8.00
139 Miles Killebrew 3.00 8.00
140 Aaron Jones 4.00 10.00
141 Aaron Ripkowski 3.00 8.00
142 Kenny Clark 3.00 8.00
143 Shaq Thompson 3.00 8.00
144 Kyle Van Noy 3.00 8.00
145 Karl Joseph 3.00 8.00
147 Temarrick Hemingway 3.00 8.00
148 Brandon Williams 3.00 8.00
149 Tavon Young 3.00 8.00
150 Tyler Lockett 4.00 10.00
151 Arthur Moats 3.00 8.00
152 Nick Vigil 3.00 8.00
153 Khalfani Muhammad 3.00 8.00
154 Tajae Sharpe 3.00 8.00
155 Eric Kendricks 3.00 8.00
156 Jameis Winston
157 Mike Evans 4.00 10.00
158 David Johnson 5.00 12.00
159 Philip Rivers 5.00 12.00
162 Andrew Luck 15.00
164 Ezekiel Elliott
165 Carson Wentz
169 Devonta Freeman 4.00 10.00
170 Eli Manning 12.00
172 Mitchell Trubisky
173 Leonard Fournette
176 Aaron Rodgers
178 Tarik Cohen 4.00 10.00
179 Christian McCaffrey
180 Greg Olsen 4.00 10.00
182 Derek Carr
185 Aaron Donald 5.00 12.00
186 Kirk Cousins 5.00 12.00
188 Joe Mixon 4.00 10.00
189 Drew Brees
190 Alvin Kamara
191 Russell Wilson
192 Ben Roethlisberger
193 Antonio Brown
195 Deshaun Watson
196 D'Onta Foreman 3.00 8.00
199 Jimmy Garoppolo
200 Josh Gordon 3.00 8.00

2019 Prestige

1 Saquon Barkley .40 1.00
2 Travis Kelce .30 .75
3 Ezekiel Elliott .40 1.00
4 Chandler Jones .20 .50
5 Xavien Howard .20 .50
6 Marcus Mariota .30 .75
7 Aaron Rodgers .60 1.50
8 Doug Baldwin .25 .60
9 Michael Thomas .30 .75
10 Harrison Smith .20 .50
11 Andrew Luck .40 1.00
12 Chris Carson .25 .60
13 Deshaun Watson .40 1.00
14 Cam Newton .30 .75
15 Julio Jones .30 .75
16 Jared Goff .30 .75
17 Sam Darnold .30 .75
18 Adam Thielen .30 .75
19 Patrick Mahomes II .75 2.00
20 Darius Slay .20 .50
21 Von Miller .25 .60
22 A.J. Green .30 .75
23 Sean Lee .25 .60
24 Drew Brees .30 .75
25 Dalvin Cook .25 .60
26 Robert Woods .25 .60
27 Tahir Whitehead .20 .50
28 Josh Allen .30 .75
29 Jason Pierre-Paul .20 .50
30 Dak Prescott .30 .75
31 Mason Crosby .20 .50
32 Bradley McDougald .20 .50
33 Christian McCaffrey .30 .75
34 Cole Beasley .30 .75
35 Baker Mayfield .50 1.25
36 Justin Houston .20 .50
37 Tyler Boyd .20 .50
38 Luke Kuechly .25 .60
39 Allen Robinson II .25 .60
40 David Johnson .30 .75
41 A.J. Bouye .20 .50
42 Sterling Shepard .25 .60
43 Evan Engram .20 .50
44 Jameis Winston .25 .60
45 Damien Williams .20 .50
46 Kyle Fuller .20 .50
47 Bobby Wagner .20 .50
48 Nyheim Hines .25 .60
49 Geno Atkins .20 .50
50 James White .25 .60
51 Denzel Ward .25 .60
52 Anthony Miller .25 .60
53 Stefon Diggs .25 .60
54 Nick Chubb .30 .75
55 Ryan Kerrigan .20 .50
56 Kenny Golladay .20 .50
57 Amari Cooper .30 .75
58 Gerald McCoy .20 .50
59 Calais Campbell .20 .50
60 Vance McDonald .20 .50
61 Julian Edelman .30 .75
62 Tyron Smith .20 .50
63 Kyle Rudolph .20 .50
64 Jordan Thomas .20 .50
65 Courtland Sutton .25 .60
66 Anthony Hitchens .20 .50
67 Eddie Jackson .20 .50
68 Derek Wolfe .20 .50
69 Keke Coutee .20 .50
70 Josh Rosen .30 .75
71 Rex Burkhead .20 .50
72 Josh Doctson .20 .50
73 Aqib Talib .20 .50
74 Olivier Vernon .20 .50
75 Cameron Brate .20 .50
76 Marquez Valdes-Scantling .25 .60
77 Keenan Allen .25 .60
78 Quandre Diggs .20 .50
79 JuJu Smith-Schuster .30 .75
80 Aaron Jones .25 .60
81 Rob Gronkowski .30 .75
82 Kirk Cousins .30 .75
83 DeAndre Washington .20 .50
84 Dede Westbrook .20 .50
85 Jordan Howard .30 .75
86 Trenton Cannon .20 .50
87 Austin Ekeler .20 .50
88 Larry Fitzgerald .25 .60
89 Khalil Mack .30 .75
90 Jordan Reed .20 .50
91 Robbie Gould .20 .50
92 Jon Bostic .20 .50
93 Derek Carr .30 .75
94 Adam Vinatieri .20 .50
95 Andy Dalton .25 .60
96 Melvin Gordon III .25 .60
97 Patrick Peterson .20 .50
98 DeAndre Hopkins .25 .60
99 Jalen Ramsey .25 .60
100 Mitchell Trubisky .30 .75
101 Derrius Guice .25 .60
102 Phillip Lindsay .30 .75
103 Matt Breida .20 .50
104 Alvin Kamara .25 .60
105 Will Fuller V .20 .50
106 Leighton Vander Esch .25 .60
107 Davante Adams .25 .60
108 Greg Zuerlein .20 .50
109 Matthew Stafford .25 .60
110 Odell Beckham Jr. .30 .75
111 Darius Leonard .25 .60
112 James Conner .30 .75
113 Demarcus Robinson .20 .50
114 Leonard Fournette .30 .75
115 David Njoku .20 .50
116 Leonard Williams .20 .50
117 Chris Thompson .20 .50
118 Tyler Higbee .20 .50
119 Marquise Goodwin .20 .50
120 Stephon Gilmore .20 .50
121 Royce Freeman .20 .50
122 Cameron Heyward .20 .50
123 Tarik Cohen .25 .60
124 Matt Ryan .30 .75
125 Minkah Fitzpatrick .20 .50
126 Marlon Mack .20 .50
127 Kerryon Johnson .25 .60
128 Jimmy Graham .30 .75
129 Eli Manning .25 .60
130 LeSean McCoy .30 .75
131 Chris Herndon IV .20 .50
132 Marcell Ateman .20 .50
133 Myles Jack .20 .50
134 Taylor Lewan .20 .50
135 Calvin Ridley .25 .60
136 Jimmy Garoppolo .30 .75
137 Jarvis Landry .25 .60
138 Marshon Lattimore .20 .50
139 Kenyan Drake .20 .50
140 D.J. Moore .25 .60
141 Austin Hooper .20 .50
142 Ben Roethlisberger .25 .60
143 Cameron Jordan .20 .50
144 Kenny Stills .20 .50
145 Vic Beasley Jr. .20 .50
146 Joe Mixon .25 .60
147 Zach Ertz .25 .60
148 Malcolm Butler .20 .50
149 George Kittle .20 .50
150 Antonio Brown .30 .75
151 Mark Andrews .20 .50
152 James Develin .20 .50
153 Uchenna Nwosu .20 .50
154 Kalen Ballage .25 .60
155 Myles Garrett .20 .50
156 Marcus Peters .20 .50
157 Eric Ebron .20 .50
158 Shaq Lawson .20 .50
159 Mark Ingram II .25 .60
160 Michael Gallup .30 .75
161 Karl Joseph .20 .50
162 Alshon Jeffery .25 .60
163 Taysom Hill .20 .50
164 John Brown .25 .60
165 Dion Lewis .20 .50
166 Dante Pettis .25 .60
167 Todd Gurley II .30 .75
168 Harrison Butker .20 .50
169 Le'Veon Bell .25 .60
170 Gus Edwards .20 .50
171 Curtis Samuel .20 .50
172 Joe Flacco .25 .60
173 Joey Bosa .25 .60
174 Carson Wentz .40 1.00
175 Derrick Henry .30 .75
176 Tyler Lockett .25 .60
177 J.J. Watt .30 .75
178 Nick Foles .25 .60
179 Philip Rivers .30 .75
180 Zay Jones .20 .50
181 Lamar Jackson .30 .75
182 Sony Michel .30 .75
183 Derwin James .25 .60
184 Blake Jarwin .20 .50
185 Fletcher Cox .20 .50
186 Quincy Enunwa .20 .50
187 Corey Davis .25 .60
188 Russell Wilson .40 1.00
189 T.Y. Hilton .25 .60
190 Aaron Donald .30 .75
191 Terrell Suggs .20 .50
192 Greg Olsen .25 .60
193 DeSean Jackson .25 .60
194 Devonta Freeman .25 .60
195 Devin McCourty .20 .50
196 Blake Martinez .20 .50
197 Willie Snead IV .20 .50
198 Golden Tate III .25 .60
199 Mike Evans .25 .60
200 Tom Brady .75 2.00
201 Kyler Murray RC 3.00 8.00
202 Drew Lock RC 1.50 4.00
203 Jerry Tillery RC .40 1.00
204 Daniel Jones RC 1.50 4.00
205 Devin Bush II RC 1.25 3.00
206 Byron Murphy RC .30 .75
207 Devin Singletary RC .40 1.00
208 Noah Fant RC .60 1.50
209 Darrell Henderson RC .75 2.00
210 Dexter Lawrence RC .50 1.25
211 Nick Bosa RC 1.00 2.50
212 Zach Allen RC .50 1.25
213 Brian Burns RC .40 1.00
214 Amani Oruwariye RC .40 1.00
215 Taylor Rapp RC .30 .75
216 Darius Slayton RC .50 1.25
217 Deebo Samuel RC .75 2.00
218 Deionte Thompson RC .40 1.00
219 Will Grier RC SP 15.00 40.00
220 T.J. Hockenson RC .75 2.00
221 Christian Wilkins RC 1.25 3.00
222 Quinnen Williams RC SP 15.00 40.00
223 D.K. Metcalf RC 1.00 2.50
224 Andy Isabella RC .50 1.25
225 Jordan Scarlett RC .30 .75
226 Travis Fulgham RC .30 .75
227 Myles Gaskin RC .60 1.50
228 Trayvon Mullen Jr. RC .50 1.25
229 Gary Jennings Jr. RC .50 1.25
230 Hakeem Butler RC .60 1.50
231 Terry Godwin II RC .40 1.00
232 Rashan Gary RC .60 1.50
233 Irv Smith Jr. RC .60 1.50
234 Clelin Ferrell RC .50 1.25
235 Travis Homer RC .30 .75
236 Caleb Wilson RC .30 .75
237 David Montgomery RC 1.25 3.00
238 Jace Sternberger RC .40 1.00
239 Dillon Mitchell RC SP 25.00 50.00
240 Josh Jacobs RC 1.50 4.00
241 Devin White RC 1.00 2.50
242 Qadree Ollison RC .40 1.00
243 Riley Ridley RC .50 1.25
244 Dexter Williams RC .40 1.00
245 Chase Winovich RC 1.00 2.50
246 Johnathan Abram RC .30 .75
247 Jeffery Simmons RC SP 12.00 30.00
248 Jaylon Ferguson RC .30 .75
249 Ryan Finley RC .60 1.50
250 Rock Ya-Sin RC .40 1.00
251 Jarrett Stidham RC 1.00 2.50
252 Hunter Renfrow RC .60 1.50
253 A.J. Brown RC .75 2.00
254 Justice Hill RC SP 15.00 40.00
255 Rodney Anderson RC SP 15.00 40.00
256 Parris Campbell RC .75 2.00
257 Damien Harris RC SP 15.00 40.00
258 Miles Sanders RC .75 2.00
259 Montez Sweat RC 1.00 2.50
260 Marquise Brown RC 1.00 2.50
261 Trayveon Williams RC .40 1.00
262 Josh Allen RC 1.25 3.00
263 N'Keal Harry RC 1.00 2.50
264 J.J. Arcega-Whiteside RC .50 1.25
265 Dwayne Haskins RC 1.50 4.00
266 Miles Boykin RC .40 1.00
267 Greedy Williams RC 1.00 2.50
268 Gardner Minshew II RC .50 1.25
269 Deandre Baker RC .75 2.00
270 Clayton Thorson RC SP 15.00 40.00
271 Bryce Love RC SP 25.00 50.00
272 Trace McSorley RC .75 2.00
273 Mack Wilson RC SP 25.00 50.00
274 Mecole Hardman Jr. RC .75 2.00
275 Oshane Ximines RC .30 .75
276 Justin Layne RC .60 1.50
277 Terry McLaurin RC .40 1.00
278 Ed Oliver RC .50 1.25
279 Mike Weber RC .50 1.25
280 Kelvin Harmon RC .50 1.25
281 Alexander Mattison RC .60 1.50
282 Tony Pollard RC .75 2.00
283 Tyree Jackson RC .75 2.00
284 Alex Barnes RC .40 1.00
285 Elijah Holyfield RC .50 1.25
286 Karan Higdon RC .40 1.00
287 Anthony Johnson RC .40 1.00
288 Antoine Wesley RC .30 .75
289 David Sills V RC 1.00 2.50
290 Emanuel Hall RC .30 .75
291 Lil'Jordan Humphrey RC .40 1.00
292 Penny Hart RC .40 1.00
293 Preston Williams RC .30 .75
294 Stanley Morgan Jr. RC .50 1.25
295 Emmanuel Butler RC .50 1.25
296 Julian Love RC .40 1.00
297 Easton Stick RC .50 1.25
298 Diontae Johnson RC .40 1.00
299 Ryquell Armstead RC .30 .75
300 Blessuan Austin RC .40 1.00

2019 Prestige Xtra Points Blue

*VETS: .8X TO 2X BASIC CARDS
*ROOKIES: .6X TO 1.2X BASIC CARDS
*SP ROOKIES: .12X TO .3X BASIC CARDS

2019 Prestige Xtra Points Bronze

*VETS/25: 2.5X TO 6X BASIC CARDS
*ROOKIES/25: 1.5X TO 4X BASIC CARDS
*SP ROOK/25: .4X TO 1X BASIC CARDS

2019 Prestige Xtra Points Gold

*VETS/50: 2X TO 5X BASIC CARDS
*ROOKIES/50: 1.2X TO 3X BASIC CARDS
*SP ROOKIES: .3X TO .8X BASIC CARDS

2019 Prestige Xtra Points Green

*VETS: .8X TO 2X BASIC CARDS
*ROOKIES: .6X TO 1.2X BASIC CARDS
*SP ROOKIES: .12X TO .3X BASIC CARDS

2019 Prestige Xtra Points Purple

*VETS/100: 1.2X TO 3X BASIC CARDS
*ROOKIES/100: .8X TO 2X BASIC CARDS
*SP ROOKIES/100: .2X TO .5X BASIC CARDS

2019 Prestige Xtra Points Red

2017 Prestige Xtra Points Red
2017 Prestige Xtra Points Red
2017 Prestige Xtra Points Red

2019 Prestige Alma Mater Jerseys

*BLUE: .5X TO 1.2X BASIC JSY
*PRIME/50: .6X TO 1.5X BASIC JSY
*PRIME/25: .8X TO 2X BASIC JSY
1 Patrick Mahomes II 6.00 15.00
2 Ezekiel Elliott 3.00 8.00
3 Saquon Barkley 3.00 8.00
4 James Conner 2.50 6.00
5 Lamar Jackson 2.50 6.00
6 Baker Mayfield 4.00 10.00
8 Jordan Howard 2.50 6.00
9 Melvin Gordon III 2.00 5.00
10 Davante Adams 2.00 5.00
11 Jared Goff 2.50 6.00
12 Calvin Ridley 2.00 5.00
13 Sony Michel 2.50 6.00
14 Josh Allen 6.00 15.00
15 JuJu Smith-Schuster 2.50 6.00

2019 Prestige Banner Season

*BLUE: .6X TO 1.5X BASIC INSERTS
*GREEN/199: .8X TO 2X BASIC INSERTS
*GOLD/50: 1.2X TO 3X BASIC INSERTS
*BRONZE/25: 1.5X TO 4X BASIC INSERTS
1 Jerry Rice .60 1.50
2 Aaron Rodgers .75 2.00
3 Isaac Bruce .40 1.00
4 Dan Marino .75 2.00
5 Devin Hester .30 .75
6 Ray Lewis .40 1.00
7 Chris Doleman .25 .60
8 Marshall Faulk .30 .75
9 Tom Brady 1.00 2.50
10 Peyton Manning .75 2.00
11 Lawrence Taylor .40 1.00
12 Patrick Mahomes II 1.00 2.50
13 Matt Ryan .40 1.00
14 Terrell Davis .30 .75
15 LaDainian Tomlinson .30 .75
16 Kurt Warner .30 .75
17 Barry Sanders .60 1.50
18 Adrian Peterson .40 1.00
19 Cam Newton .40 1.00
20 Steve Young .50 1.25

2019 Prestige Blue Chip Recruits

*BLUE/299: .5X TO 1.2X BASIC INSERTS
*GREEN/99: .8X TO 2X BASIC INSERTS
*GOLD/50: 1X TO 2.5X BASIC INSERTS
*BRONZE/25: 1X TO 2.5X BASIC INSERTS
1 Nick Bosa 1.25 3.00
2 Kyler Murray 4.00 10.00
3 Dwayne Haskins 2.00 5.00
4 Josh Allen 1.50 4.00
5 Montez Sweat 1.25 3.00
6 Brian Burns .50 1.25
7 Marquise Brown 1.25 3.00
8 T.J. Hockenson 1.00 2.50
9 Byron Murphy .40 1.00
10 Rashan Gary .75 2.00
11 Clelin Ferrell .60 1.50
12 Drew Lock 2.00 5.00
13 Daniel Jones 2.00 5.00
14 D.K. Metcalf 1.25 3.00
15 Devin White 1.25 3.00

2019 Prestige Changing Stripes Jerseys

1 Alshon Jeffery 2.00 5.00
3 Frank Gore 2.00 5.00
4 Jerick McKinnon 1.50 4.00
5 Richard Sherman 2.00 5.00
6 Jarvis Landry 2.00 5.00
7 Kiko Alonso 1.50 4.00
8 Amari Cooper 2.50 6.00
9 Jay Ajayi 2.00 5.00
10 LeSean McCoy 2.50 6.00

2019 Prestige Highlight Reel

*BLUE: .6X TO 1.5X BASIC INSERTS
*GREEN/199: .8X TO 2X BASIC INSERTS
*GOLD/50: 1.2X TO 3X BASIC INSERTS
*BRONZE/25: 1.5X TO 4X BASIC INSERTS
1 Baker Mayfield .60 1.50
2 DeAndre Hopkins .30 .75
3 Ezekiel Elliott .50 1.25
4 Todd Gurley II .40 1.00
5 JuJu Smith-Schuster .40 1.00
6 A.J. Green .40 1.00
7 David Johnson .40 1.00
8 Julio Jones .40 1.00
9 Patrick Mahomes II 1.00 2.50
10 Russell Wilson .50 1.25
11 Melvin Gordon III .30 .75
12 Tom Brady 1.00 2.50
13 Davante Adams .30 .75
14 Carson Wentz .50 1.25
15 Drew Brees .40 1.00
16 Aaron Rodgers .75 2.00
17 Saquon Barkley .50 1.25
18 Cam Newton .40 1.00
19 Adam Thielen .40 1.00
20 Alvin Kamara .30 .75

2019 Prestige History Makers

*BLUE: .8X TO 2X BASIC INSERTS
*GREEN/199: .8X TO 2X BASIC INSERTS
*GOLD/50: 1.2X TO 3X BASIC INSERTS
*BRONZE/25: 1.5X TO 4X BASIC INSERTS
1 Dan Marino .75 2.00
2 Emmitt Smith .60 1.50
3 Jerry Rice .60 1.50
4 Isaac Bruce .40 1.00
5 Dan Fouts .30 .75
6 Calvin Johnson .30 .75
7 Donald Driver .30 .75
8 Ed Reed .30 .75
9 Howie Long .30 .75
10 John Elway .60 1.50
11 Paul Krause .25 .60
12 Dante Hall .25 .60
13 John Lynch .25 .60
14 Joe Greene .30 .75
15 LaVar Arrington .25 .60

2019 Prestige Honor Roll

*BLUE/299: .8X TO 2X BASIC INSERTS
*GREEN/99: 1X TO 2.5X BASIC INSERTS
*GOLD/50: 1.2X TO 3X BASIC INSERTS
*BRONZE/25: 1.5X TO 4X BASIC INSERTS
1 Baker Mayfield .60 1.50
2 Saquon Barkley .50 1.25
3 Tom Brady 1.00 2.50
4 Ezekiel Elliott .50 1.25
5 Christian McCaffrey .40 1.00
6 James Conner .40 1.00
7 LeSean McCoy .40 1.00
8 Rob Gronkowski .40 1.00
9 Nick Chubb .40 1.00
10 Melvin Gordon III .30 .75
11 Davante Adams .30 .75
12 Calvin Ridley .30 .75
13 JuJu Smith-Schuster .40 1.00
14 Devonta Freeman .30 .75
15 Patrick Mahomes II 1.00 2.50
16 Phillip Lindsay .40 1.00
17 Keenan Allen .30 .75
18 Todd Gurley II .40 1.00
19 Michael Thomas .40 1.00
20 Andrew Luck .50 1.25

2019 Prestige Impressions

*BLUE/299: .8X TO 2X BASIC INSERTS
*GREEN/99: 1X TO 2.5X BASIC INSERTS
*GOLD/50: 1.2X TO 3X BASIC INSERTS
*BRONZE/25: 1.5X TO 4X BASIC INSERTS
1 Nick Chubb .40 1.00
2 Saquon Barkley .50 1.25
3 Mitchell Trubisky .40 1.00
4 Amari Cooper .40 1.00
5 Mike Williams .25 .60
6 Stefon Diggs .30 .75
7 Sony Michel .40 1.00
8 Tarik Cohen .30 .75
9 Ezekiel Elliott .50 1.25
10 Josh Allen 1.00 2.50
11 Alvin Kamara .30 .75
12 Chris Carson .30 .75
13 Jared Goff .40 1.00
14 Zach Ertz .30 .75
15 Dante Pettis .30 .75
16 Mike Evans .30 .75
17 Patrick Mahomes II 1.00 2.50
18 James Washington .30 .75
19 Evan Engram .25 .60
20 Melvin Gordon III .30 .75
21 Deshaun Watson .50 1.25
22 Baker Mayfield .60 1.50
23 James Conner .40 1.00
24 Dak Prescott .40 1.00
25 Lamar Jackson .40 1.00
26 Christian McCaffrey .40 1.00
27 D.J. Moore .30 .75
28 Todd Gurley II .40 1.00
29 Sam Darnold .40 1.00
30 Davante Adams .30 .75

2019 Prestige League Leaders Jerseys

*BLUE: .5X TO 1.2X BASIC JSY
*PRIME/50: .6X TO 1.5X BASIC JSY
*PRIME/25: .8X TO 2X BASIC JSY
1 Todd Gurley II 2.50 6.00
2 Drew Brees 2.50 6.00
3 Patrick Mahomes II 6.00 15.00
4 JuJu Smith-Schuster 2.50 6.00
5 Saquon Barkley 3.00 8.00
6 Aaron Donald 2.50 6.00
7 Sony Michel 2.50 6.00
8 Tarik Cohen 2.00 5.00
9 Jakeem Grant 1.50 4.00
10 Julio Jones 2.50 6.00
11 Michael Thomas 2.50 6.00
12 Derrick Henry 2.50 6.00
13 Ben Roethlisberger 2.00 5.00
14 J.J. Watt 2.50 6.00
15 Ezekiel Elliott 3.00 8.00

2019 Prestige Old School

*BLUE/299: .8X TO 2X BASIC INSERTS
*GREEN/199: .8X TO 2X BASIC INSERTS
*GOLD/50: 1.2X TO 3X BASIC INSERTS
*BRONZE/25: 1.5X TO 4X BASIC INSERTS
1 Dan Hampton .25 .60
2 Ed Too Tall Jones .25 .60
3 Randall McDaniel .30 .75
4 Ron Yary .25 .60
5 Elvin Bethea .25 .60
6 Mel Renfro .25 .60
7 Christian Okoye .25 .60
8 Steve Bartkowski .30 .75
9 Jack Ham .30 .75
10 Jack Youngblood .25 .60
11 Brent Jones .25 .60
12 Mark Gastineau .25 .60
13 Chris Doleman .25 .60
14 Curley Culp .30 .75
15 Andre Rison .30 .75
16 Brett Favre .75 2.00
17 Ted Hendricks .25 .60
18 James Lofton .25 .60
19 Mike Wagner .25 .60
20 Boomer Esiason .30 .75

2019 Prestige Power House

*BLUE: .6X TO 1.5X BASIC INSERTS
*GREEN/199: .8X TO 2X BASIC INSERTS
*GOLD/50: 1.2X TO 3X BASIC INSERTS
*BRONZE/25: 1.5X TO 4X BASIC INSERTS
1 Todd Gurley II .40 1.00
2 Ezekiel Elliott .50 1.25
3 David Johnson .40 1.00
4 Saquon Barkley .50 1.25
5 Leonard Fournette .40 1.00
6 Alvin Kamara .30 .75
7 Christian McCaffrey .40 1.00
8 Devonta Freeman .30 .75
9 Khalil Mack .40 1.00
10 J.J. Watt .40 1.00
11 Aaron Donald .40 1.00
12 Phillip Lindsay .40 1.00
13 DeMarcus Lawrence .25 .60
14 Sony Michel .40 1.00
15 Von Miller .30 .75
16 Derrick Henry .40 1.00
17 Nick Chubb .40 1.00
18 LeSean McCoy .40 1.00
19 Luke Kuechly .30 .75
20 Melvin Gordon III .30 .75

2019 Prestige Prestigious Pros

*BLUE: .6X TO 1.5X BASIC INSERTS
*GREEN/199: .8X TO 2X BASIC INSERTS
*GOLD/50: 1.2X TO 3X BASIC INSERTS
*BRONZE/25: 1.5X TO 4X BASIC INSERTS
1 Tom Brady 1.00 2.50
2 Jimmy Garoppolo .40 1.00
3 Ezekiel Elliott .50 1.25
4 Alvin Kamara .30 .75
5 Todd Gurley II .40 1.00
6 Russell Wilson .50 1.25
7 Aaron Rodgers .75 2.00
8 DeAndre Hopkins .30 .75
9 Khalil Mack .40 1.00
10 Drew Brees .40 1.00
11 Julio Jones .40 1.00
12 Carson Wentz .50 1.25
13 Christian McCaffrey .40 1.00
14 A.J. Green .40 1.00
15 Patrick Mahomes II 1.00 2.50
16 Jared Goff .40 1.00
17 Keenan Allen .30 .75
18 Davante Adams .30 .75
19 Deshaun Watson .50 1.25
20 Adam Thielen .40 1.00

2019 Prestige Rising Stars

*BLUE: .6X TO 1.5X BASIC INSERTS
*GREEN/199: .8X TO 2X BASIC INSERTS
*GOLD/50: 1.2X TO 3X BASIC INSERTS
*BRONZE/25: 1.5X TO 4X BASIC INSERTS
1 Phillip Lindsay .40 1.00
2 Calvin Ridley .30 .75
3 D.J. Moore .30 .75
4 Baker Mayfield .60 1.50
5 Sony Michel .40 1.00
6 Darius Leonard .30 .75
7 Saquon Barkley .50 1.25
8 Roquan Smith .40 1.00
9 Tremaine Edmunds .30 .75
10 Nick Chubb .40 1.00
11 Leighton Vander Esch .30 .75
12 Patrick Mahomes II 1.00 2.50
13 Sam Darnold .40 1.00
14 JuJu Smith-Schuster .40 1.00
15 Christian Kirk .25 .60
16 Josh Allen .40 1.00
17 Tarik Cohen .30 .75
18 Dante Pettis .30 .75
19 Josh Rosen .40 1.00
20 Derwin James .30 .75

2019 Prestige Stars of the NFL Jerseys

*BLUE: .5X TO 1.2X BASIC JSY
*PRIME/50: .6X TO 1.5X BASIC JSY
*PRIME/25: .8X TO 2X BASIC JSY
*PRIME/20-21: 1X TO 2.5X BASIC JSY
1 Alvin Kamara 2.00 5.00
2 Ezekiel Elliott 3.00 8.00
3 Patrick Mahomes II 6.00 15.00
4 JuJu Smith-Schuster 2.50 6.00
5 Melvin Gordon III 2.00 5.00
6 James Washington 2.00 5.00
7 D.J. Moore 2.00 5.00
8 Calvin Ridley 2.00 5.00
9 Marlon Mack 1.50 4.00
10 Saquon Barkley 3.00 8.00
11 Sony Michel 2.50 6.00
12 Lamar Jackson 2.50 6.00
13 Sam Darnold 2.50 6.00
14 Nick Chubb 2.50 6.00
15 Deshaun Watson 3.00 8.00

16 Mitchell Trubisky 2.50 6.00
17 Dak Prescott 2.50 6.00
18 Leonard Fournette 2.50 6.00
19 Christian McCaffrey 2.50 6.00
20 James Conner 2.50 6.00
21 Evan Engram 1.50 4.00
22 Baker Mayfield 4.00 10.00
23 Cooper Kupp 2.00 5.00
24 Carson Wentz 3.00 8.00
25 Josh Allen 2.50 6.00
26 Hunter Henry 1.50 4.00
27 Michael Thomas 2.50 6.00
28 Dalvin Cook 2.00 5.00
29 Jared Goff 2.50 6.00
30 Mike Williams 1.50 4.00

2019 Prestige Xtra Points Signatures

3 Ezekiel Elliott
5 Xavien Howard 3.00 8.00
6 Marcus Mariota
7 Aaron Rodgers
10 Harrison Smith 25.00 50.00
11 Andrew Luck
13 Deshaun Watson 6.00 15.00
16 Jared Goff
18 Adam Thielen
19 Patrick Mahomes II 150.00 300.00
20 Darius Slay 3.00 8.00
22 A.J. Green
24 Drew Brees 30.00 60.00
25 Dalvin Cook
26 Robert Woods 4.00 10.00
28 Josh Allen
33 Christian McCaffrey
34 Cole Beasley 5.00 12.00
40 David Johnson 5.00 12.00
44 Jameis Winston
48 Nyheim Hines 4.00 10.00
51 Denzel Ward 4.00 10.00
54 Nick Chubb 5.00 12.00
55 Ryan Kerrigan 3.00 8.00
63 Kyle Rudolph
64 Jordan Thomas 3.00 8.00
65 Courtland Sutton 4.00 10.00
66 Anthony Hitchens 6.00 15.00
67 Eddie Jackson 3.00 8.00
70 Josh Rosen
72 Josh Doctson 3.00 8.00
77 Keenan Allen 4.00 10.00
78 Quandre Diggs 3.00 8.00
81 Rob Gronkowski 15.00 40.00
82 Kirk Cousins 8.00 20.00
84 Dede Westbrook 3.00 8.00
85 Jordan Howard 5.00 12.00
86 Trenton Cannon 3.00 8.00
90 Jordan Reed 3.00 8.00
93 Derek Carr 5.00 12.00
95 Andy Dalton 4.00 10.00
96 Melvin Gordon III 4.00 10.00
98 DeAndre Hopkins 4.00 10.00
100 Mitchell Trubisky 15.00 40.00
101 Derrius Guice 4.00 10.00
102 Phillip Lindsay 5.00 12.00
103 Matt Breida
106 Leighton Vander Esch 8.00 20.00
108 Greg Zuerlein
109 Matthew Stafford 12.00 30.00
111 Darius Leonard 4.00 10.00
114 Leonard Fournette
115 David Njoku 3.00 8.00
119 Marquise Goodwin 3.00 8.00
122 Cameron Heyward 3.00 8.00
124 Matt Ryan
127 Kerryon Johnson 4.00 10.00
129 Eli Manning
135 Calvin Ridley 4.00 10.00
136 Jimmy Garoppolo 50.00 100.00
138 Marshon Lattimore 3.00 8.00
140 D.J. Moore 4.00 10.00
142 Ben Roethlisberger
143 Cameron Jordan 3.00 8.00
150 Antonio Brown
151 Mark Andrews 3.00 8.00
158 Shaq Lawson
159 Mark Ingram II 4.00 10.00
160 Michael Gallup 5.00 12.00
162 Alshon Jeffery 10.00 25.00
172 Joe Flacco
175 Derrick Henry 5.00 12.00
177 J.J. Watt
179 Philip Rivers
181 Lamar Jackson 5.00 12.00
185 Fletcher Cox
186 Quincy Enunwa 3.00 8.00
187 Corey Davis 4.00 10.00
192 Greg Olsen
193 DeSean Jackson 4.00 10.00
194 Devonta Freeman 4.00 10.00
200 Tom Brady 300.00 600.00
201 Kyler Murray 60.00 125.00
202 Drew Lock 12.00 30.00
203 Jerry Tillery 3.00 8.00
204 Daniel Jones 25.00 50.00
206 Byron Murphy 2.50 6.00
207 Devin Singletary 3.00 8.00
208 Noah Fant 5.00 12.00
209 Darrell Henderson 6.00 15.00
210 Dexter Lawrence 4.00 10.00
211 Nick Bosa 8.00 20.00
212 Zach Allen 4.00 10.00
213 Brian Burns 3.00 8.00
214 Amani Oruwariye 3.00 8.00
215 Taylor Rapp 2.50 6.00
216 Darius Slayton 4.00 10.00
217 Deebo Samuel 6.00 15.00
218 Deionte Thompson 3.00 8.00
219 Will Grier 8.00 20.00
220 T.J. Hockenson 6.00 15.00
221 Christian Wilkins 10.00 25.00
223 D.K. Metcalf 8.00 20.00
224 Andy Isabella 4.00 10.00
225 Jordan Scarlett 2.50 6.00
226 Travis Fulgham 2.50 6.00
227 Myles Gaskin 5.00 12.00
228 Trayvon Mullen Jr. 4.00 10.00
229 Gary Jennings Jr. 4.00 10.00
232 Rashan Gary 5.00 12.00
233 Irv Smith Jr. 5.00 12.00
234 Clelin Ferrell 4.00 10.00
235 Travis Homer 2.50 6.00
236 Caleb Wilson 2.50 6.00
237 David Montgomery 10.00 25.00
238 Jace Sternberger 5.00 12.00
239 Dillon Mitchell 3.00 8.00
240 Josh Jacobs 15.00 40.00
241 Devin White 8.00 20.00
242 Qadree Ollison 3.00 8.00
243 Riley Ridley 4.00 10.00
244 Dexter Williams 3.00 8.00
246 Johnathan Abram 2.50 6.00
247 Jeffery Simmons 2.50 6.00
248 Jaylon Ferguson 2.50 6.00
249 Ryan Finley 5.00 12.00
250 Rock Ya-Sin 3.00 8.00
251 Jarrett Stidham 8.00 20.00
252 Hunter Renfrow 5.00 12.00
253 A.J. Brown 6.00 15.00
254 Justice Hill 4.00 10.00
255 Rodney Anderson 3.00 8.00
256 Parris Campbell 6.00 15.00
257 Damien Harris 6.00 15.00
258 Miles Sanders 6.00 15.00
260 Marquise Brown 8.00 20.00
261 Trayveon Williams 3.00 8.00
263 N'Keal Harry 8.00 20.00
264 J.J. Arcega-Whiteside 4.00 10.00
265 Dwayne Haskins 50.00 100.00
266 Miles Boykin 3.00 8.00
267 Greedy Williams 8.00 20.00
268 Gardner Minshew II 4.00 10.00
269 Deandre Baker 6.00 15.00
270 Clayton Thorson 4.00 10.00
271 Bryce Love 4.00 10.00
272 Trace McSorley 6.00 15.00
273 Mack Wilson 3.00 8.00
274 Mecole Hardman Jr. 6.00 15.00
275 Oshane Ximines 2.50 6.00
277 Terry McLaurin 3.00 8.00
278 Ed Oliver 4.00 10.00
279 Mike Weber 4.00 10.00
280 Kelvin Harmon 4.00 10.00
281 Alexander Mattison
282 Tony Pollard 6.00 15.00
283 Tyree Jackson 6.00 15.00
284 Alex Barnes 3.00 8.00
285 Elijah Holyfield 4.00 10.00
286 Karan Higdon 3.00 8.00
287 Anthony Johnson
288 Antoine Wesley 2.50 6.00
289 David Sills V 8.00 20.00
290 Emanuel Hall 2.50 6.00
291 Lil'Jordan Humphrey 3.00 8.00
292 Penny Hart 3.00 8.00
293 Preston Williams 2.50 6.00
294 Stanley Morgan Jr. 4.00 10.00
295 Emmanuel Butler 4.00 10.00
296 Julian Love 3.00 8.00
297 Easton Stick 4.00 10.00
298 Diontae Johnson 3.00 8.00
299 Ryquell Armstead 2.50 6.00
300 Blessuan Austin 3.00 8.00

2012 Prestige Father's Day NFL Equipment Autographs

1 Robert Griffin III 20.00 50.00
2 Andrew Luck 300.00 600.00

2012 Prestige National Wrapper Redemption

ISSUED AT 2012 NATIONAL CONVENTION
CRACKED ICE/25: 2.5X TO 6X
56 Tim Tebow 1.50 4.00
82 Peyton Manning 1.50 4.00

1950 Prest-o-Lite Postcards

These postcards were issued to promote the "Prest-O-Lite" batteries. The front contains an action photo of the star while the back has a promotion for those batteries. There might be more photos so any additions are appreciated.
1 Leon Hart 12.50 25.00

2011 Prime Signatures

ROOKIE AUTO PRINT RUN 99-249
EXCH EXPIRATION: 9/28/2013
1 Aaron Rodgers 3.00 8.00
2 Adrian Peterson 1.50 4.00
3 Alex Karras 1.25 3.00
4 Andre Reed 1.25 3.00
5 Anquan Boldin 1.00 2.50
6 Antonio Gates 1.00 2.50
7 Arian Foster 1.00 2.50
8 Arrelious Benn 1.00 2.50
9 Austin Collie 1.00 2.50
10 Barry Sanders 2.50 6.00
11 Bart Starr 2.50 6.00
12 Beanie Wells 1.00 2.50
13 Ben Roethlisberger 1.50 4.00
14 Ben Tate 1.00 2.50
15 BenJarvus Green-Ellis 1.00 2.50
16 Billy Howton 1.00 2.50
17 Bo Jackson 2.00 5.00
18 Bo Scaife 1.00 2.50
19 Brandon Lloyd 1.00 2.50
20 Brandon Meriweather 1.00 2.50
21 Brandon Spikes 1.00 2.50
22 Brett Favre 3.00 8.00
23 Brian Cushing 1.00 2.50
24 Brian Hartline 1.25 3.00
25 C.J. Spiller 1.00 2.50
26 Chad Greenway 1.25 3.00
27 Chad Henne 1.25 3.00
28 Chad Ochocinco 1.00 2.50
29 Charley Taylor 1.00 2.50
30 Charley Trippi 1.00 2.50
31 Charlie Joiner 1.00 2.50
32 Chris Cooley 1.00 2.50
33 Clay Matthews 1.50 4.00
34 Colt McCoy 1.00 2.50
35 Craig James 1.00 2.50
36 Cris Carter 1.50 4.00
37 Curtis Martin 1.25 3.00
38 Dallas Clark 1.00 2.50
39 Dan Marino 3.00 8.00
40 Danny Amendola 1.25 3.00
41 Darrelle Revis 1.25 3.00
42 Darren McFadden 1.00 2.50
43 Darren Woodson 1.00 2.50
44 Daryle Lamonica 1.00 2.50
45 Dave Casper 1.00 2.50
46 David Harris 1.00 2.50
47 DeAngelo Hall 1.00 2.50
48 DeAngelo Williams 1.25 3.00
49 Deion Sanders 1.25 3.00
50 Demaryius Thomas 1.50 4.00
51 DeSean Jackson 1.25 3.00
52 Dez Bryant 1.50 4.00
53 Don Perkins 1.25 3.00
54 Donald Driver 1.25 3.00
55 Drew Brees 1.50 4.00
56 Dub Jones 1.00 2.50
57 Dwayne Bowe 1.25 3.00
58 Ed Too Tall Jones 1.00 2.50
59 Eddie George 1.25 3.00
60 Eli Manning 1.25 3.00
61 Emmanuel Sanders 1.50 4.00
62 Emmitt Smith 2.50 6.00
63 Eric Dickerson 1.25 3.00
64 Everson Walls 1.00 2.50
65 Felix Jones 1.00 2.50
66 Franco Harris 1.50 4.00
67 Frank Gore 1.25 3.00
68 Gale Sayers 1.50 4.00
69 Gary Collins 1.00 2.50
70 Greg Jennings 1.00 2.50
71 Greg Olsen 1.25 3.00
72 Hakeem Nicks 1.00 2.50
73 Harlon Hill 1.00 2.50
74 Heath Miller 1.00 2.50
75 Hines Ward 1.25 3.00
76 Irving Fryar 1.00 2.50
77 Jack Youngblood 1.00 2.50
78 Jacoby Ford 1.25 3.00
79 Jahvid Best 1.00 2.50
80 Jamaal Charles 1.00 2.50
81 James Laurinaitis 1.00 2.50
82 Jan Stenerud 1.00 2.50
83 Jared Allen 1.00 2.50
84 Jason Witten 1.25 3.00
85 Jay Cutler 1.00 2.50
86 Jermaine Gresham 1.00 2.50
87 Jerod Mayo 1.00 2.50
88 Jerome Bettis 1.50 4.00
89 Jerome Simpson 1.00 2.50
90 Jerry Rice 2.50 6.00
91 Jim Kelly 1.50 4.00
92 Jim Plunkett 1.25 3.00
93 Jimmy Graham 1.50 4.00
94 Jimmy Orr 1.00 2.50
95 Joe Flacco 1.25 3.00
96 Joe Greene 1.50 4.00
97 Joe Klecko 1.00 2.50
98 Joe Montana 4.00 10.00
99 Joe Namath 2.00 5.00
100 John Brodie 1.00 2.50
101 John Elway 2.50 6.00
102 Jonathan Stewart 1.00 2.50
103 Josh Freeman 1.25 3.00
104 Kevin Walter 1.00 2.50
105 Knowshon Moreno 1.00 2.50
106 LaDainian Tomlinson 1.50 4.00
107 Larry Fitzgerald 1.25 3.00
108 Laurent Robinson 1.00 2.50
109 Lem Barney 1.00 2.50
110 Lenny Moore 1.00 2.50
111 Leroy Kelly 1.25 3.00
112 LeSean McCoy 1.50 4.00
113 Lydell Mitchell 1.00 2.50
114 Malcom Floyd 1.00 2.50
115 Mark Carrier 1.00 2.50
116 Mark Duper 1.00 2.50
117 Mark Sanchez 1.00 2.50
118 Matt Cassel 1.00 2.50
119 Matt Forte 1.00 2.50
120 Matt Ryan 1.25 3.00
121 Matt Schaub 1.00 2.50
122 Matthew Stafford 1.25 3.00
123 Maurice Jones-Drew 1.00 2.50
124 Michael Crabtree 1.00 2.50
125 Michael Turner 1.00 2.50
126 Michael Vick 1.25 3.00
127 Mike Tolbert 1.00 2.50
128 Mike Wallace 1.00 2.50
129 Mike Williams 1.25 3.00
130 Miles Austin 1.00 2.50
131 Nnamdi Asomugha 1.00 2.50
132 Ottis Anderson 1.00 2.50
133 Ozzie Newsome 1.25 3.00
134 Percy Harvin 1.00 2.50
135 Pete Retzlaff 1.00 2.50
136 Peyton Hillis 1.00 2.50
137 Peyton Manning 3.00 8.00
138 Philip Rivers 1.50 4.00
139 Pierre Thomas 1.00 2.50
140 Randy Moss 1.25 3.00
141 Rashard Mendenhall 1.00 2.50
142 Ray Rice 1.00 2.50
143 Reggie Bush 1.00 2.50
144 Reggie Wayne 1.25 3.00
145 Rick Casares 1.00 2.50
146 Rod Woodson 1.25 3.00
147 Roddy White 1.00 2.50
148 Roger Craig 1.25 3.00
149 Ron Mix 1.00 2.50
150 Rosey Grier 1.25 3.00
151 Russ Grimm 1.00 2.50
152 Ryan Mathews 1.25 3.00
153 Ryan Torain 1.00 2.50
154 Sam Bradford 1.00 2.50
155 Santana Moss 1.25 3.00
156 Santonio Holmes 1.00 2.50
157 Sidney Rice 1.00 2.50
158 Steve Bartkowski 1.25 3.00
159 Steve Johnson 1.00 2.50
160 Steve Smith 1.25 3.00
161 Steve Young 2.00 5.00
162 Terrell Davis 1.25 3.00
163 Thurman Thomas 1.25 3.00
164 Tim Tebow 1.50 4.00
165 Todd Christensen 1.00 2.50
166 Tom Brady 4.00 10.00
167 Tony Moeaki 1.00 2.50
168 Tony Romo 1.25 3.00
169 Troy Aikman 2.00 5.00
170 Troy Polamalu 1.50 4.00
171 Vernon Davis 1.00 2.50
172 Warren Moon 1.50 4.00
173 Warren Sapp 1.25 3.00
174 William Perry 1.00 2.50
175 Willie Davis 1.00 2.50
176 Aaron Williams AU/199 RC 4.00 10.00
177 Adrian Clayborn AU/199 RC 4.00 10.00
178 Akeem Ayers AU/199 RC EXCH 4.00 10.00
179 Aldon Smith AU/199 RC EXCH
180 Allen Bradford AU/199 RC 4.00 10.00
181 Brandon Harris AU/199 RC 4.00 10.00
182 Cameron Heyward AU/199 RC 5.00 12.00
183 Cameron Jordan AU/199 RC 5.00 12.00
184 Cecil Shorts AU/199 RC 4.00 10.00
185 Corey Liuget AU/199 RC 4.00 10.00
186 D.J. Williams AU/199 RC 4.00 10.00
187 Da'Quan Bowers AU/199 RC 4.00 10.00
188 Da'Rel Scott AU/199 RC 4.00 10.00
189 Denarius Moore AU/199 RC 4.00 10.00
190 Dion Lewis AU/199 RC 5.00 12.00
191 Greg Jones AU/199 RC 5.00 12.00
192 Greg Salas AU/199 RC 4.00 10.00
193 J.J. Watt AU/199 RC 40.00 80.00
194 Jacquizz Rodgers AU/199 RC 4.00 10.00
195 Jeremy Kerley AU/199 RC 6.00 15.00
196 Jimmy Smith AU/199 RC 4.00 10.00
197 Johnny White AU/199 RC 4.00 10.00
198 Julius Thomas AU/199 RC 5.00 12.00
199 Justin Houston AU/199 RC 5.00 12.00
200 Kris Durham AU/199 RC 4.00 10.00
201 Lance Kendricks AU/199 RC 4.00 10.00
202 Luke Stocker AU/199 RC 4.00 10.00
203 Nathan Enderle AU/199 RC EXCH 4.00 10.00
204 Niles Paul AU/199 RC 4.00 10.00
205 Phil Taylor AU/199 RC 4.00 10.00
206 Prince Amukamara AU/199 RC 4.00 10.00
207 Rahim Moore AU/199 RC 4.00 10.00
208 Ricky Stanzi AU/199 RC 4.00 10.00
209 Roy Helu AU/199 RC 4.00 10.00
210 Ryan Kerrigan AU/199 RC 5.00 12.00
211 T.J. Yates AU/199 RC 4.00 10.00
212 Tandon Doss AU/199 RC 4.00 10.00
213 Terrelle Pryor AU/199 RC 6.00 15.00
214 Tyrod Taylor AU/199 RC 8.00 20.00
215 Joe Lefeged AU/199 RC 5.00 12.00
216 Jacquian Williams AU/199 RC EXCH 6.00 15.00
217 K.J. Wright AU/199 RC 6.00 15.00
218 Mason Foster AU/199 RC 4.00 10.00
219 Casey Matthews AU/199 RC 4.00 10.00
220 Anthony Allen AU/199 RC 4.00 10.00
221 Armond Smith AU/199 RC 5.00 12.00
222 Dane Sanzenbacher AU/199 RC 4.00 10.00
223 Doug Baldwin AU/199 RC 10.00 25.00
224 LaQuan Williams AU/199 RC 5.00 12.00
225 Mark Herzlich AU/199 RC 4.00 10.00
226 A.J. Green AU/199 RC 20.00 40.00
227 Alex Green AU/249 RC 4.00 10.00
228 Andy Dalton AU/249 RC 10.00 25.00
229 Austin Pettis AU/249 RC 4.00 10.00
230 Bilal Powell AU/99 RC 6.00 15.00
231 Blaine Gabbert AU/199 RC 4.00 10.00
232 Cam Newton AU/199 RC 75.00 150.00
233 Christian Ponder AU/199 RC 4.00 10.00
234 Clyde Gates AU/249 RC 4.00 10.00
235 Colin Kaepernick AU/249 RC 6.00 15.00
236 Daniel Thomas AU/249 RC 4.00 10.00
237 Delone Carter AU/249 RC 4.00 10.00
238 DeMarco Murray AU/99 RC 10.00 25.00
239 Greg Little AU/249 RC 5.00 12.00
240 Jake Locker AU/199 RC 4.00 10.00
241 Jamie Harper AU/249 RC 4.00 10.00
242 Jerrel Jernigan AU/249 RC 4.00 10.00
243 Jonathan Baldwin AU/249 RC 4.00 10.00
244 Jordan Todman AU/249 RC 4.00 10.00
245 Julio Jones AU/249 RC EXCH 20.00 40.00
246 Kendall Hunter AU/249 RC 4.00 10.00
247 Kyle Rudolph AU/249 RC 8.00 20.00
248 Leonard Hankerson AU/249 RC 4.00 10.00
249 Marcell Dareus AU/249 RC 4.00 10.00
250 Mark Ingram AU/199 RC 6.00 15.00
251 Mikel Leshoure AU/249 RC 4.00 10.00
252 Randall Cobb AU/99 RC 8.00 20.00
253 Ryan Mallett AU/199 RC 4.00 10.00
254 Ryan Williams AU/249 RC 4.00 10.00
255 Shane Vereen AU/249 RC 5.00 12.00
256 Stevan Ridley AU/249 RC 4.00 10.00
257 Taiwan Jones AU/249 RC 4.00 10.00
258 Titus Young AU/249 RC 4.00 10.00
259 Torrey Smith AU/249 RC 4.00 10.00
260 Vincent Brown AU/249 RC 4.00 10.00
261 Von Miller AU/249 RC 10.00 25.00

2011 Prime Signatures Prime Proof Blue

*BLUE/49: 1.2X TO 3X BASIC CARDS
BLUE STATED PRINT RUN 49

2011 Prime Signatures Prime Proof Green

*GREEN/25: 2X TO 5X BASIC CARDS
GREEN STATED PRINT RUN 25

2011 Prime Signatures Prime Proof Red

*RED/99: .8X TO 2X BASIC CARDS
RED STATED PRINT RUN 99

2011 Prime Signatures Autographs Bronze

*BRONZE/59-75: .25X TO .6X GOLD/20-25
*BRONZE/39-49: .3X TO .8X GOLD/20-25
*BRONZE/33-50: .25X TO .6X GOLD/10-15
BRONZE PRINT RUN 33-75

2011 Prime Signatures Autographs Gold

1-175 VETS/RET PRINT RUN 10-25
*ROOKIES/49: .5X TO 1.2X BASIC AU RC
176-261 ROOKIE AU PRINT RUN 49
EXCH EXPIRATION: 9/28/2013
1 Aaron Rodgers/20 125.00 200.00
3 Alex Karras/25 12.00 30.00
4 Andre Reed/25 12.00 30.00
5 Anquan Boldin/25 8.00 20.00
6 Antonio Gates/25 8.00 20.00
7 Arian Foster/25 25.00 50.00
8 Arrelious Benn/25 8.00 20.00
9 Austin Collie/15 10.00 25.00
10 Barry Sanders/20 60.00 120.00
11 Bart Starr/20 75.00 135.00
12 Beanie Wells/10 10.00 25.00
13 Ben Roethlisberger/20 50.00 100.00
14 Ben Tate/25 8.00 20.00
15 BenJarvus Green-Ellis/25 8.00 20.00
16 Billy Howton/25 10.00 25.00
17 Bo Jackson/25 30.00 60.00
18 Bo Scaife/25 8.00 20.00
19 Brandon Lloyd/25 8.00 20.00
20 Brandon Meriweather/25 8.00 20.00
21 Brandon Spikes/25 10.00 25.00
22 Brett Favre/20 100.00 175.00
23 Brian Cushing/25 8.00 20.00
24 Brian Hartline/25 10.00 25.00
25 C.J. Spiller/25 8.00 20.00
26 Chad Greenway/25 10.00 25.00
27 Chad Henne/25 10.00 25.00
28 Chad Ochocinco/25 8.00 20.00
29 Charley Taylor/25 12.00 30.00
30 Charley Trippi/20
32 Chris Cooley/25 8.00 20.00
33 Clay Matthews/25 40.00 80.00
34 Colt McCoy/25 8.00 20.00
35 Craig James/25
36 Cris Carter/25 40.00 80.00
37 Curtis Martin/25 25.00 60.00
38 Dallas Clark/25 20.00 40.00
40 Danny Amendola/25 15.00 40.00
42 Darren McFadden/10
43 Darren Woodson/25 25.00 50.00
44 Daryle Lamonica/25 10.00 25.00
45 Dave Casper/25
46 David Harris/25 8.00 20.00
47 DeAngelo Hall/15
48 DeAngelo Williams/25 8.00 20.00
49 Deion Sanders/20 40.00 80.00
50 Demaryius Thomas/25 15.00 30.00
52 Dez Bryant/25 20.00 50.00
53 Don Perkins/25 12.00 30.00
54 Donald Driver/25 15.00 40.00
55 Drew Brees/20
56 Dub Jones/25 10.00 25.00
57 Dwayne Bowe/15 12.00 30.00
58 Ed Too Tall Jones/25 15.00 40.00
59 Eddie George/25 25.00 50.00
60 Eli Manning/25 50.00 100.00
61 Emmanuel Sanders/25 12.00 30.00
62 Emmitt Smith/20 100.00 175.00
63 Eric Dickerson/25 20.00 40.00
64 Everson Walls/10 25.00 50.00
65 Felix Jones/25
66 Franco Harris/25 15.00 40.00
67 Frank Gore/25 10.00 25.00
68 Gale Sayers/25 30.00 60.00
69 Gary Collins/15
70 Greg Jennings/25 8.00 20.00
71 Greg Olsen/20 10.00 25.00
72 Hakeem Nicks/25 8.00 20.00
73 Harlon Hill/25 12.00 30.00
74 Heath Miller/25 8.00 20.00
75 Hines Ward/25 40.00 80.00
76 Irving Fryar/20 12.00 30.00
77 Jack Youngblood/15
78 Jacoby Ford/25 10.00 25.00
79 Jahvid Best/25 8.00 20.00
80 Jamaal Charles/25 12.00 30.00
81 James Laurinaitis/15 10.00 25.00
82 Jan Stenerud/10 12.00 30.00
83 Jared Allen/25 20.00 40.00
84 Jason Witten/25 20.00 40.00
85 Jay Cutler/25 30.00 60.00
86 Jermaine Gresham/25 8.00 20.00
87 Jerod Mayo/20 8.00 20.00
88 Jerome Bettis/25
89 Jerome Simpson/15 10.00 25.00
90 Jerry Rice/20 100.00 175.00
91 Jim Kelly/15 30.00 60.00
92 Jim Plunkett/25 12.00 30.00
93 Jimmy Graham/25 12.00 30.00
94 Jimmy Orr/25 10.00 25.00
96 Joe Greene/25 30.00 60.00
97 Joe Klecko/25 12.00 30.00
98 Joe Montana/20 90.00 150.00
99 Joe Namath/20 40.00 80.00
100 John Brodie/25 15.00 40.00
101 John Elway/20 75.00 135.00
102 Jonathan Stewart/25 8.00 20.00
103 Josh Freeman/25 10.00 25.00
104 Kevin Walter/25 8.00 20.00
105 Knowshon Moreno/25 8.00 20.00
106 LaDainian Tomlinson/25 15.00 40.00
107 Larry Fitzgerald/15
108 Laurent Robinson/20
109 Lem Barney/25 10.00 25.00
110 Lenny Moore/25 15.00 40.00
111 Leroy Kelly/25 12.00 30.00
112 LeSean McCoy/25 12.00 30.00
113 Lydell Mitchell/25 10.00 25.00
114 Malcom Floyd/25 8.00 20.00
115 Mark Carrier/25 12.00 30.00
116 Mark Duper/25 10.00 25.00
117 Mark Sanchez/25 15.00 40.00
118 Matt Cassel/20 8.00 20.00
119 Matt Forte/10 10.00 25.00
120 Matt Ryan/15 25.00 50.00
121 Matt Schaub/25 8.00 20.00
122 Matthew Stafford/25 25.00 50.00
123 Maurice Jones-Drew/20 8.00 20.00
124 Michael Crabtree/20 8.00 20.00
125 Michael Turner/20 8.00 20.00
127 Mike Tolbert/25 8.00 20.00
128 Mike Wallace/20 8.00 20.00
129 Mike Williams/25
130 Miles Austin/25 15.00 40.00
131 Nnamdi Asomugha/10 15.00 40.00
132 Ottis Anderson/15 12.00 30.00
133 Ozzie Newsome/25 12.00 30.00
134 Percy Harvin/25 8.00 20.00
135 Pete Retzlaff/25 10.00 25.00
136 Peyton Hillis/25 12.00 30.00
137 Peyton Manning/18 75.00 150.00
138 Philip Rivers/25 15.00 40.00
139 Pierre Thomas/25 8.00 20.00
140 Randy Moss/25 EXCH 12.00 30.00
141 Rashard Mendenhall/25 8.00 20.00
142 Ray Rice/25 15.00 40.00
143 Reggie Bush/25
144 Reggie Wayne/25 10.00 25.00
145 Rick Casares/25 12.00 30.00
146 Rod Woodson/15
148 Roger Craig/15
149 Ron Mix/25 10.00 25.00
150 Rosey Grier/15 15.00 40.00
151 Russ Grimm/25 12.00 30.00
152 Ryan Mathews/25 10.00 25.00
153 Ryan Torain/25 8.00 20.00
154 Sam Bradford/25 8.00 20.00
155 Santana Moss/25 10.00 25.00
156 Santonio Holmes/25 8.00 20.00
157 Sidney Rice/15 10.00 25.00
158 Steve Bartkowski/25
159 Steve Johnson/25 8.00 20.00
160 Steve Smith/25 10.00 25.00
161 Steve Young/20 30.00 60.00
162 Terrell Davis/25 25.00 50.00
163 Thurman Thomas/25 12.00 30.00
164 Tim Tebow/20 40.00 100.00
165 Todd Christensen/15 12.00 30.00
167 Tony Moeaki/25 8.00 20.00
168 Tony Romo/20 60.00 120.00
169 Troy Aikman/20 EXCH 50.00 80.00
170 Troy Polamalu/25 50.00 100.00
171 Vernon Davis/15 10.00 25.00
172 Warren Moon/25 25.00 50.00
173 Warren Sapp/25 12.00 30.00
175 Willie Davis/15 15.00 40.00
228 Andy Dalton/49 10.00 25.00
232 Cam Newton/49 75.00 150.00
235 Colin Kaepernick/49 8.00 20.00
240 Jake Locker/49 5.00 12.00

2011 Prime Signatures Autographs Platinum

*ROOKIES/25: .6X TO 1.5X BASIC AU RC
1-175 UNPRICED PLATINUM PRINT RUN 5
EXCH EXPIRATION: 9/28/2013
226 A.J. Green 40.00 80.00
228 Andy Dalton 12.00 30.00
232 Cam Newton 100.00 200.00
240 Jake Locker 6.00 15.00

2011 Prime Signatures Autographs Silver

*SILVER/30-49: .3X TO .8X GOLD/20-25
*SILVER/31-49: .25X TO .6X GOLD/15
*SILVER/20-29: .3X TO .8X GOLD/10-15
*SILVER/30-39: .25X TO .6X GOLD/10
*SILVER/15-19: .4X TO 1X GOLD/10
SILVER PRINT RUN 15-49

2012 Prime Signatures

1-175 STATED PRINT RUN 499
176-275 ROOKIE AU PRINT RUN 99-199
276-310 DUAL/TRIPLE AU PRINT RUN 25
EXCH EXPIRATION: 5/7/2014
1 Tom Brady 3.00 8.00
2 Peyton Manning 3.00 8.00
3 Charles Woodson 1.50 4.00
4 Adrian Peterson 1.50 4.00
5 Aaron Rodgers 4.00 10.00
6 Ben Roethlisberger 1.50 4.00
7 Eli Manning 1.25 3.00
8 Tony Romo 1.25 3.00
9 Drew Brees 1.50 4.00
10 Cam Newton 1.50 4.00
11 Tim Tebow 1.50 4.00
12 Matt Ryan 1.25 3.00
13 Philip Rivers 1.50 4.00
14 Larry Fitzgerald 1.25 3.00
15 Matthew Stafford 1.25 3.00
16 Michael Vick 1.25 3.00
17 Sam Bradford 1.00 2.50
18 Jay Cutler 1.00 2.50
19 Joe Flacco 1.25 3.00
20 Troy Polamalu 1.50 4.00
21 Steven Jackson 1.00 2.50
22 Donald Driver 1.25 3.00
23 Miles Austin 1.00 2.50
24 Jake Locker 1.50 4.00
25 Alex Smith 1.25 3.00
26 Anquan Boldin 1.00 2.50
27 Arian Foster 1.25 3.00
28 Kevin Kolb 1.00 2.50
29 Mark Ingram 1.25 3.00
30 Reggie Wayne 1.25 3.00
31 Tony Gonzalez 1.25 3.00
32 Santonio Holmes 1.00 2.50
33 Andy Dalton 1.25 3.00
34 Blaine Gabbert 1.00 2.50
35 DeAngelo Williams 1.00 2.50
36 Dallas Clark 1.00 2.50
37 Dez Bryant 1.50 4.00
38 Frank Gore 1.25 3.00
39 Jason Witten 1.25 3.00
40 Jonathan Stewart 1.00 2.50
41 Matt Cassel 1.00 2.50
42 Matt Schaub 1.00 2.50
43 Michael Turner 1.00 2.50
44 Mike Wallace 1.00 2.50
45 Percy Harvin 1.00 2.50
46 Rashard Mendenhall 1.00 2.50
47 Roddy White 1.00 2.50
48 Ryan Fitzpatrick 1.00 2.50
49 Steve Smith 1.25 3.00
50 Reggie Bush 1.00 2.50
51 Christian Ponder 1.00 2.50
52 A.J. Green 1.50 4.00
53 Antonio Gates 1.25 3.00
54 Brandon Lloyd 1.00 2.50
55 C.J. Spiller 1.00 2.50
56 Darren McFadden 1.00 2.50
57 Darren Sproles 1.25 3.00
58 DeSean Jackson 1.25 3.00
59 Greg Jennings 1.00 2.50
60 Jeremy Maclin 1.00 2.50
61 Knowshon Moreno 1.00 2.50
62 LeSean McCoy 1.25 3.00
63 Matt Forte 1.00 2.50
64 Michael Crabtree 1.00 2.50
65 Santana Moss 1.25 3.00
66 Jamaal Charles 1.25 3.00
67 Vernon Davis 1.00 2.50
68 Rob Gronkowski 1.50 4.00
69 Vincent Jackson 1.00 2.50
70 DeMarco Murray 1.25 3.00
71 Patrick Willis 1.25 3.00
72 Brandon Pettigrew 1.00 2.50
73 Pierre Thomas 1.00 2.50
74 Brandon Jacobs 1.00 2.50
75 DeMarcus Ware 1.50 4.00
76 Hakeem Nicks 1.00 2.50
77 Heath Miller 1.00 2.50
78 Jordy Nelson 1.25 3.00
79 Marshawn Lynch 1.25 3.00
80 Lance Briggs 1.25 3.00
81 Plaxico Burress 1.00 2.50
82 Ray Rice 1.00 2.50
83 Ronde Barber 1.00 2.50
84 Shonn Greene 1.00 2.50
85 Victor Cruz 1.25 3.00
86 Josh Cribbs 1.00 2.50
87 Nate Washington 1.00 2.50
88 BenJarvus Green-Ellis 1.25 3.00
89 Jermichael Finley 1.00 2.50
90 Mario Williams 1.00 2.50
91 Brian Cushing 1.00 2.50
92 Jermaine Gresham 1.00 2.50
93 Nnamdi Asomugha 1.00 2.50
94 Pierre Garcon 1.25 3.00
95 Steve Johnson 1.25 3.00
96 Von Miller 1.25 3.00
97 Antonio Brown 1.50 4.00
98 Brian Hartline 1.25 3.00
99 Darrius Heyward-Bey 1.00 2.50
100 Denarius Moore 1.00 2.50
101 Fred Jackson 1.25 3.00
102 Greg Olsen 1.25 3.00
103 James Laurinaitis 1.00 2.50
104 Jared Allen 1.00 2.50
105 Jason Pierre-Paul 1.00 2.50
106 J.J. Watt 1.50 4.00
107 LeGarrette Blount 1.25 3.00
108 London Fletcher 1.25 3.00
109 Randall Cobb 1.25 3.00
110 Tony Moeaki 1.00 2.50
111 Torrey Smith 1.00 2.50
112 Mike Williams 1.25 3.00
113 Ryan Williams 1.00 2.50
114 Jerod Mayo 1.00 2.50
115 Fred Davis 1.00 2.50
116 Jabar Gaffney 1.00 2.50
117 Greg Little 1.00 2.50
118 Paul Posluszny 1.00 2.50
119 Matt Flynn 1.00 2.50
120 Jon Beason 1.00 2.50
121 Robert Mathis 1.00 2.50
122 Titus Young 1.00 2.50
123 Brandon LaFell 1.00 2.50
124 David Nelson 1.00 2.50
125 Derrick Johnson 1.00 2.50
126 James Starks 1.00 2.50
127 Tamba Hali 1.00 2.50
128 Kevin Walter 1.00 2.50
129 Delone Carter 1.00 2.50
130 Taiwan Jones 1.00 2.50
131 Danario Alexander 1.00 2.50
132 Brian Orakpo 1.25 3.00
133 Chris Cooley 1.00 2.50
134 Ronnie Lott 1.25 3.00
135 Deion Sanders 1.25 3.00
136 Rod Woodson 1.25 3.00
137 Warren Sapp 1.25 3.00
138 Joe Greene 1.50 4.00
139 Jack Lambert 1.50 4.00
140 Joe Montana 4.00 10.00
141 Boomer Esiason 1.25 3.00
142 Doug Flutie 1.25 3.00
143 John Elway 2.50 6.00
144 Bernie Kosar 1.25 3.00
145 Dan Marino 3.00 8.00
146 Randall Cunningham 1.25 3.00
147 Phil Simms 1.25 3.00
148 Joe Namath 2.50 6.00
149 Bart Starr 2.50 6.00
150 Brett Favre 3.00 8.00
151 Jim Plunkett 1.25 3.00
152 Archie Manning 1.25 3.00
153 Fran Tarkenton 1.50 4.00
154 Earl Campbell 1.50 4.00
155 Thurman Thomas 1.25 3.00
156 Priest Holmes 1.00 2.50
157 Emmitt Smith 2.50 6.00
158 Fred Taylor 1.00 2.50
159 Curtis Martin 1.25 3.00
160 Barry Sanders 2.50 6.00
161 Paul Hornung 1.50 4.00
162 Bo Jackson 2.00 5.00
163 Marcus Allen 1.50 4.00
164 Eric Dickerson 1.25 3.00
165 Jerome Bettis 1.50 4.00
166 Jerry Rice 2.50 6.00
167 Andre Reed 1.25 3.00
168 Ed McCaffrey 1.00 2.50
169 Keyshawn Johnson 1.25 3.00
170 Michael Irvin 1.50 4.00
171 Paul Warfield 1.25 3.00
172 Sterling Sharpe 1.25 3.00
173 Hines Ward 1.25 3.00
174 Steve Largent 1.50 4.00
175 Cris Carter 1.50 4.00
176 Bobby Wagner AU/199 RC 5.00 12.00
177 Case Keenum AU/199 RC 15.00 40.00
178 Chandler Harnish AU/199 RC 3.00 8.00
179 Chris Polk AU/199 RC 3.00 8.00
180 Chris Rainey AU/199 RC 6.00 15.00
181 Cory Harkey AU/199 RC 4.00 10.00
182 Courtney Upshaw AU/199 RC 4.00 10.00
183 Cyrus Gray AU/199 RC 3.00 8.00
184 Dan Herron AU/199 RC 3.00 8.00
185 Danny Coale AU/199 RC 3.00 8.00
186 David DeCastro AU/199 RC 3.00 8.00
187 Davin Meggett AU/199 RC 3.00 8.00
188 Devon Still AU/199 RC 4.00 10.00
189 Dont'a Hightower AU/199 RC 5.00 12.00
190 Dontari Poe AU/199 RC 3.00 8.00
191 Dre Kirkpatrick AU/199 RC 3.00 8.00
192 Dwight Jones AU/199 RC 3.00 8.00
193 Fletcher Cox AU/199 RC 5.00 12.00
194 George Iloka AU/199 RC 3.00 8.00
195 Gerell Robinson AU/199 RC 3.00 8.00
196 Janoris Jenkins AU/199 RC 4.00 10.00
197 Jared Crick AU/199 RC 3.00 8.00
198 Jeff Fuller AU/199 RC 3.00 8.00
199 Jonathan Martin AU/199 RC 3.00 8.00
200 Juron Criner AU/199 RC 3.00 8.00
201 Kellen Moore AU/199 RC 4.00 10.00
202 Kirk Cousins AU/199 RC 15.00 40.00
203 Ladarius Green AU/199 RC 3.00 8.00
204 Lavonte David AU/199 RC 5.00 12.00
205 Luke Kuechly AU/199 RC 8.00 20.00
206 Marc Tyler AU/199 RC 3.00 8.00
207 Mark Barron AU/199 RC 3.00 8.00
208 Marquis Maze AU/199 RC 3.00 8.00
209 Marvin Jones AU/199 RC 3.00 8.00
210 Marvin McNutt AU/199 RC 3.00 8.00
211 Matt Kalil AU/199 RC 3.00 8.00
212 Melvin Ingram AU/199 RC 3.00 8.00
213 Michael Brockers AU/199 RC 3.00 8.00
214 Mychal Kendricks AU/199 RC 5.00 12.00
215 Orson Charles AU/199 RC 3.00 8.00
216 Quinton Coples AU/199 RC 3.00 8.00
217 Riley Reiff AU/199 RC 3.00 8.00
218 Rishard Matthews AU/199 RC 3.00 8.00
219 Ronnell Lewis AU/199 RC 3.00 8.00
220 Stephon Gilmore AU/199 RC 4.00 10.00
221 T.Y. Hilton AU/199 RC 6.00 15.00
222 Tauren Poole AU/199 RC 3.00 8.00
223 Terrance Ganaway AU/199 RC 4.00 10.00
224 Tim Benford AU/199 RC 3.00 8.00
225 Tommy Streeter AU/199 RC 3.00 8.00
226 Travis Benjamin AU/199 RC 3.00 8.00
227 Vick Ballard AU/199 RC 6.00 15.00
228 Whitney Mercilus AU/199 RC 3.00 8.00
229 Derek Wolfe AU/199 RC 4.00 10.00
230 Andre Branch AU/199 RC 3.00 8.00
231 B.J. Coleman AU/199 RC 3.00 8.00
232 B.J. Cunningham AU/199 RC 3.00 8.00
233 Morris Claiborne AU/99 RC 3.00 8.00
234 Shea McClellin AU/199 RC 4.00 10.00
235 Casey Hayward AU/199 RC 3.00 8.00
236 Bruce Irvin AU/199 RC 4.00 10.00
237 Kendall Reyes AU/199 RC 3.00 8.00
238 Jerel Worthy AU/199 RC 3.00 8.00
239 Tyrone Crawford AU/199 RC 3.00 8.00
240 Brandon Taylor AU/199 RC 3.00 8.00
241 A.J. Jenkins AU/199 RC 3.00 8.00
242 Alshon Jeffery AU/199 RC 12.00 30.00
243 Andrew Luck AU/149 RC 125.00 250.00
244 Bernard Pierce AU/199 RC 3.00 8.00
245 Brandon Weeden AU/149 RC 3.00 8.00
246 Brian Quick AU/199 RC 3.00 8.00
247 Brock Osweiler AU/199 RC 3.00 8.00
248 Coby Fleener AU/199 RC 3.00 8.00
249 David Wilson AU/199 RC 3.00 8.00
250 DeVier Posey AU/199 RC 3.00 8.00
251 Doug Martin AU/199 RC 5.00 12.00
252 Dwayne Allen AU/199 RC 3.00 8.00
253 Isaiah Pead AU/199 RC 3.00 8.00
254 Jarius Wright AU/199 RC 3.00 8.00
255 Joe Adams AU/199 RC 3.00 8.00
256 Justin Blackmon AU/149 RC 3.00 8.00
257 Kendall Wright AU/199 RC 3.00 8.00
258 Lamar Miller AU/199 RC 5.00 12.00
259 LaMichael James AU/199 RC 3.00 8.00
260 Michael Egnew AU/199 RC 3.00 8.00
261 Michael Floyd AU/199 RC 3.00 8.00
262 Mohamed Sanu AU/199 RC 5.00 12.00
263 Nick Foles AU/199 RC 25.00 50.00
264 Nick Toon AU/199 RC 3.00 8.00
265 Robert Griffin III AU/149 RC 8.00 20.00
266 Robert Turbin AU/199 RC 3.00 8.00
267 Ronnie Hillman AU/199 RC 3.00 8.00
268 Rueben Randle AU/199 RC 3.00 8.00
269 Russell Wilson AU/199 RC 100.00 175.00
270 Ryan Broyles AU/199 RC 6.00 15.00
271 Ryan Tannehill AU/149 RC 5.00 12.00
272 Stephen Hill AU/199 RC 3.00 8.00
273 T.J. Graham AU/199 RC 3.00 8.00
274 Chris Givens AU/199 RC 3.00 8.00
275 Trent Richardson AU/149 RC 3.00 8.00
276 J.Fleming/R.Lindley
277 K.Zeitler/V.Burfict 15.00 40.00
278 B.Osweiler/O.Bolden 10.00 25.00
279 B.Brown/Curry 10.00 25.00
280 C.Givens/T.Johnson 8.00 20.00
281 M.Smith/N.Goode 12.00 30.00
282 B.Hardin/S.McClellin 12.00 30.00
283 B.Bentley/R.Lewis
284 J.Worthy/N.Perry
285 K.Martin/W.Mercilus 10.00 25.00
286 D.Wylie/D.Poe 8.00 20.00
287 J.Martin/O.Vernon 10.00 25.00
288 H.Smith/M.Kalil
289 D.Coale/J.Hanna
290 A.Morris/K.Cousins 12.00 30.00
291 D.DeCastro/S.Spence
292 B.Wagner/B.Irvin 12.00 30.00
293 L.Brazill/T.Hilton 30.00 60.00
294 L.Kuechly/T.Poole 20.00 50.00
295 D.Kirkpatrick/G.Iloka 15.00 40.00
296 Claiborne/Crawford 8.00 20.00
297 B.Coleman/M.Tyler 8.00 20.00
298 F.Cox/M.Kendricks 12.00 30.00
299 K.Reyes/M.Ingram
300 J.Jenkins/Brockers EXCH 10.00 25.00
301 Still/Kirkpatrick/Iloka 12.00 30.00
302 Rainey/Upshw/Streetr
303 Rainey/DeCastro/Maze 12.00 30.00
304 David/Barron/Goode 12.00 30.00
305 Reyes/Green/Ingram
306 Cox/McNutt/Kendricks
307 Davis/Coples/Hill
308 Sensabh/Martin/Brown 10.00 25.00
309 Bolden/Jones/Wilson 10.00 25.00
310 Childs/Robinson/Ellison 12.00 30.00

2012 Prime Signatures Prime Proof Blue

*1-133 VETS/49: 1X TO 2.5X BASIC CARDS
*134-175 LEGENDS/49: 1X TO 2.5X BASIC CARDS

2012 Prime Signatures Prime Proof Green

*1-133 VETS/25: 1.5X TO 4X BASIC CARDS
*134-175 LEGENDS/25: 1.5X TO 4X BASIC CARDS

2012 Prime Signatures Prime Proof Red

*1-133 VETS/99: .8X TO 2X BASIC CARDS
*134-175 LEGENDS/99: .8X TO 2X BASIC CARDS
STATED PRINT RUN 99 SER.#'d SETS

2012 Prime Signatures Autographs Gold

*176-275 GOLD/25: .8X TO 2X AU/149-199
*176-275 GOLD/25: .6X TO 1.5X AU/99
EXCH EXPIRATION: 5/7/2014
1 Tom Brady/20 125.00 200.00
2 Peyton Manning/20 125.00 250.00
3 Charles Woodson/20 75.00 135.00
4 Adrian Peterson/20 75.00 150.00
5 Aaron Rodgers/20 125.00 200.00
6 Ben Roethlisberger/20 40.00 100.00
7 Eli Manning/20 40.00 80.00
8 Tony Romo/20 40.00 80.00
9 Drew Brees/20 40.00 80.00
10 Cam Newton/20 30.00 80.00
11 Tim Tebow/20 15.00 40.00
12 Matt Ryan/20 25.00 50.00
13 Philip Rivers/20 12.00 30.00
14 Larry Fitzgerald/20 12.00 30.00
15 Matthew Stafford/20 25.00 50.00
16 Michael Vick/20
17 Sam Bradford/20 8.00 20.00
18 Jay Cutler/20
19 Joe Flacco/20 10.00 25.00
20 Troy Polamalu/20 60.00 120.00
22 Donald Driver/20 12.00 30.00
23 Miles Austin/20
24 Jake Locker/20
25 Alex Smith/20
26 Anquan Boldin/20 8.00 20.00
27 Arian Foster/20 20.00 40.00
28 Kevin Kolb/20
29 Mark Ingram/20 10.00 25.00
30 Reggie Wayne/20 12.00 30.00
66 Jamaal Charles/15
67 Vernon Davis/15 12.00 30.00
68 Rob Gronkowski/15
69 Vincent Jackson/15 8.00 20.00
70 DeMarco Murray/15 EXCH 10.00 25.00
71 Patrick Willis/15
72 Brandon Pettigrew/15
73 Pierre Thomas/15 8.00 20.00
74 Brandon Jacobs/15 8.00 20.00
75 DeMarcus Ware/15 20.00 40.00
76 Hakeem Nicks/15 8.00 20.00
77 Heath Miller/15
78 Jordy Nelson/15 30.00 60.00
79 Marshawn Lynch/15
81 Plaxico Burress/15
82 Ray Rice/15
83 Ronde Barber/15 12.00 30.00
84 Shonn Greene/15 8.00 20.00
85 Victor Cruz/15
86 Josh Cribbs/15
87 Nate Washington/15
88 BenJarvus Green-Ellis/15
89 Jermichael Finley/15 8.00 20.00
90 Mario Williams/15
91 Brian Cushing/15
92 Jermaine Gresham/15 8.00 20.00
93 Nnamdi Asomugha/15
94 Pierre Garcon/15
95 Steve Johnson/15
96 Von Miller/15 12.00 30.00
97 Antonio Brown/15 20.00 40.00
98 Brian Hartline/15 10.00 25.00
99 Darrius Heyward-Bey/15
100 Denarius Moore/15 8.00 20.00
101 Fred Jackson/15 12.00 30.00
102 Greg Olsen/15 10.00 25.00
103 James Laurinaitis/15 8.00 20.00
104 Jared Allen/15 20.00 40.00
105 Jason Pierre-Paul/15
106 J.J. Watt/15 25.00 50.00

107 LeGarrette Blount/15 10.00 25.00
108 London Fletcher/15 12.00 30.00
109 Randall Cobb/15
110 Tony Moeaki/15
111 Torrey Smith/15
112 Mike Williams/15
113 Ryan Williams/15 8.00 20.00
114 Jerod Mayo/25 8.00 20.00
115 Fred Davis/25 8.00 20.00
116 Jabar Gaffney/25
117 Greg Little/25 8.00 20.00
118 Paul Posluszny/25
119 Matt Flynn/25
120 Jon Beason/25
121 Robert Mathis/25 15.00 40.00
122 Titus Young/25
123 Brandon LaFell/25
124 David Nelson/25 8.00 20.00
125 Derrick Johnson/25
126 James Starks/25 8.00 20.00
127 Tamba Hali/25 8.00 20.00
128 Kevin Walter/25 8.00 20.00
129 Delone Carter/25
130 Taiwan Jones/25
131 Danario Alexander/25
132 Brian Orakpo/25 8.00 20.00
133 Chris Cooley/25
134 Ronnie Lott/15 30.00 60.00
135 Deion Sanders/15
136 Rod Woodson/15 50.00 100.00
137 Warren Sapp/15
138 Joe Greene/15 20.00 40.00
139 Jack Lambert/25 30.00 60.00
140 Joe Montana/15 100.00 200.00
141 Boomer Esiason/25 12.00 30.00
142 Doug Flutie/25 15.00 40.00
143 John Elway/15 75.00 150.00
144 Bernie Kosar/25 15.00 40.00
146 Randall Cunningham/25
147 Phil Simms/15
148 Joe Namath/15 50.00 100.00
150 Brett Favre/15 100.00 200.00
151 Jim Plunkett/15 12.00 30.00
152 Archie Manning/25 15.00 40.00
155 Thurman Thomas/15 12.00 30.00
156 Priest Holmes/25 10.00 25.00
158 Fred Taylor/25
159 Curtis Martin/25 12.00 30.00
161 Paul Hornung/15
162 Bo Jackson/25 30.00 80.00
163 Marcus Allen/25 15.00 40.00
164 Eric Dickerson/25 15.00 40.00
165 Jerome Bettis/25 30.00 80.00
166 Jerry Rice/15 75.00 150.00
167 Andre Reed/25
169 Keyshawn Johnson/25 12.00 30.00
170 Michael Irvin/15 25.00 50.00
171 Paul Warfield/25
172 Sterling Sharpe/25 12.00 30.00
173 Hines Ward/15 60.00 120.00
174 Steve Largent/15 15.00 40.00
175 Cris Carter/25 15.00 40.00
243 Andrew Luck/25 250.00 500.00
263 Nick Foles/25 40.00 100.00
265 Robert Griffin III/25 15.00 40.00
269 Russell Wilson/25 150.00 250.00

2012 Prime Signatures Autographs Silver

*176-275 SILVER/49: .6X TO 1.5X AU/149-199
*176-275 SILVER/49: .5X TO 1.2X AU/99
EXCH EXPIRATION: 5/7/2014
31 Tony Gonzalez/20 10.00 25.00
32 Santonio Holmes/20
33 Andy Dalton/20 15.00 40.00
34 Blaine Gabbert/20 8.00 20.00
35 DeAngelo Williams/20 8.00 20.00
36 Dallas Clark/20 15.00 40.00
37 Dez Bryant/20 20.00 50.00
38 Frank Gore/20 10.00 25.00
39 Jason Witten/20 25.00 50.00
40 Jonathan Stewart/20 8.00 20.00
41 Matt Cassel/20 8.00 20.00
42 Matt Schaub/20 12.00 30.00
43 Michael Turner/20 8.00 20.00
44 Mike Wallace/20 12.00 30.00
45 Percy Harvin/20 8.00 20.00
46 Rashard Mendenhall/20 8.00 20.00
47 Roddy White/20 15.00 40.00
48 Ryan Fitzpatrick/20 8.00 20.00
49 Steve Smith/20 10.00 25.00
50 Reggie Bush/20 15.00 40.00
51 Christian Ponder/20 8.00 20.00
52 A.J. Green/20 12.00 30.00
53 Antonio Gates/20 10.00 25.00
54 Brandon Lloyd/20 8.00 20.00
55 C.J. Spiller/20 8.00 20.00
56 Darren McFadden/20 12.00 30.00
57 Darren Sproles/20 10.00 25.00
58 DeSean Jackson/20 10.00 25.00
59 Greg Jennings/20 8.00 20.00
60 Jeremy Maclin/20 8.00 20.00
61 Knowshon Moreno/20 8.00 20.00
62 LeSean McCoy/20 20.00 50.00
63 Matt Forte/20 8.00 20.00
64 Michael Crabtree/20 8.00 20.00
65 Santana Moss/20 10.00 25.00
66 Jamaal Charles/25 10.00 25.00
67 Vernon Davis/25
68 Rob Gronkowski/25 25.00 50.00
69 Vincent Jackson/25 8.00 20.00
70 DeMarco Murray/25
71 Patrick Willis/25 20.00 50.00
72 Brandon Pettigrew/25 8.00 20.00
73 Pierre Thomas/25 8.00 20.00
74 Brandon Jacobs/25 8.00 20.00
75 DeMarcus Ware/25 15.00 40.00
76 Hakeem Nicks/25 8.00 20.00
77 Heath Miller/25 10.00 25.00
78 Jordy Nelson/25 25.00 50.00
79 Marshawn Lynch/25 20.00 40.00
81 Plaxico Burress/25 8.00 20.00
82 Ray Rice/25 8.00 20.00
83 Ronde Barber/25 8.00 20.00
84 Shonn Greene/25 8.00 20.00
85 Victor Cruz/25 15.00 40.00
86 Josh Cribbs/25 8.00 20.00
87 Nate Washington/25 8.00 20.00
88 BenJarvus Green-Ellis/25 10.00 25.00
89 Jermichael Finley/25 8.00 20.00
90 Mario Williams/25 8.00 20.00
91 Brian Cushing/25 10.00 25.00
92 Jermaine Gresham/25 8.00 20.00
93 Nnamdi Asomugha/25 8.00 20.00
94 Pierre Garcon/25 10.00 25.00
95 Steve Johnson/25 10.00 25.00
96 Von Miller/25 15.00 40.00
97 Antonio Brown/25 60.00 125.00
98 Brian Hartline/25 8.00 20.00
99 Darrius Heyward-Bey/25
100 Denarius Moore/25 8.00 20.00
101 Fred Jackson/25 10.00 25.00
102 Greg Olsen/25 10.00 25.00
103 James Laurinaitis/25 8.00 20.00
104 Jared Allen/25 15.00 40.00
105 Jason Pierre-Paul/25 12.00 30.00
106 J.J. Watt/25 25.00 60.00
107 LeGarrette Blount/25
108 London Fletcher/25 15.00 40.00
109 Randall Cobb/25 12.00 30.00
110 Tony Moeaki/25 8.00 20.00
111 Torrey Smith/25 8.00 20.00
112 Mike Williams/25 10.00 25.00
113 Ryan Williams/25 8.00 20.00
114 Jerod Mayo/49 6.00 15.00
115 Fred Davis/49 6.00 15.00
116 Jabar Gaffney/49 6.00 15.00
117 Greg Little/49
118 Paul Posluszny/49 6.00 15.00
119 Matt Flynn/49 6.00 15.00
120 Jon Beason/49 6.00 15.00
121 Robert Mathis/49 8.00 20.00
122 Titus Young/49 6.00 15.00
123 Brandon LaFell/49
124 David Nelson/49 6.00 15.00
125 Derrick Johnson/49 6.00 15.00
126 James Starks/49
127 Tamba Hali/49 6.00 15.00
128 Kevin Walter/49 6.00 15.00
129 Delone Carter/49 6.00 15.00
130 Taiwan Jones/49 6.00 15.00
131 Danario Alexander/49 6.00 15.00
132 Brian Orakpo/49 8.00 20.00
133 Chris Cooley/49 10.00 25.00
243 Andrew Luck/49 200.00 400.00
265 Robert Griffin III/49 10.00 25.00
269 Russell Wilson/49 90.00 150.00

2012 Prime Signatures Pen Pals

1 B.Osweiler/N.Foles 12.00 30.00
2 B.Osweiler/R.Hillman 8.00 20.00
3 D.Wilson/R.Randle 12.00 30.00
4 A.Luck/R.Griffin III 150.00 300.00
5 B.Quick/I.Pead 12.00 30.00
6 Miller/Egnew/Tannehill 12.00 30.00
7 Jenkins/Posey/Toon
8 Luck/Griffin III/Richardson 150.00 300.00
9 Luck/Blackmon/Richardson 125.00 250.00
10 Luck/Fleener/Allen/Hilton 125.00 250.00
11 Weedn/Blckmn/Wright/RG3 50.00 100.00
12 Wilson/Miller/Hill/Graham 12.00 30.00
13 Jenkns/James/Trbin/Wilsn 60.00 120.00
14 Flnr/Mrtn/Aln/Blk/Flyd/Rcsn 30.00 80.00
15 Lk/Wdn/Osw/RG3/Wls/Tnh 150.00 300.00
16 Wls/Mrn/Pd/Jms/Hlm/Rch 20.00 50.00
17 Offensive Rookies 100.00 200.00
18 Rookie Receivers

2012 Prime Signatures Rookie Jumbo Materials Prime Signatures

STATED PRINT RUN 25 SER.#'d SETS
EXCH EXPIRATION: 5/7/2014
1 Jarius Wright 10.00 25.00
2 Russell Wilson 175.00 300.00
3 Brandon Weeden 10.00 25.00
4 T.J. Graham 10.00 25.00
5 Joe Adams 10.00 25.00
6 Brock Osweiler 10.00 25.00
7 A.J. Jenkins 10.00 25.00
8 Alshon Jeffery 20.00 50.00
9 Nick Foles 50.00 125.00
10 Robert Griffin III 40.00 100.00
11 DeVier Posey 10.00 25.00
12 Andrew Luck 250.00 500.00
13 Kendall Wright 10.00 25.00
14 Justin Blackmon 10.00 25.00
15 Michael Floyd 10.00 25.00
16 Robert Turbin 10.00 25.00
17 Ryan Tannehill 15.00 40.00
18 Trent Richardson 15.00 40.00
19 Ronnie Hillman EXCH 10.00 25.00
20 David Wilson 10.00 25.00
21 Lamar Miller 15.00 40.00
22 Doug Martin 15.00 40.00
23 LaMichael James 10.00 25.00
24 Isaiah Pead 10.00 25.00
25 Coby Fleener 10.00 25.00
26 Rueben Randle 10.00 25.00
27 Brian Quick 10.00 25.00
28 Ryan Broyles 10.00 25.00
29 Nick Toon 10.00 25.00
30 Bernard Pierce 10.00 25.00

2012 Prime Signatures Rookie Prime Materials Signatures

1 Andrew Luck/49 200.00 400.00
2 Brandon Weeden/49 8.00 20.00
3 Brock Osweiler/49 8.00 20.00
4 Nick Foles/99 30.00 80.00
5 Robert Griffin III/49 10.00 25.00
6 Russell Wilson/99 75.00 150.00
7 Ryan Tannehill/49 12.00 30.00
8 David Wilson/99 6.00 15.00
9 Doug Martin/49 12.00 30.00
10 Bernard Pierce/99 6.00 15.00
11 Isaiah Pead/99 6.00 15.00
12 Lamar Miller/49 12.00 30.00
13 LaMichael James/99 6.00 15.00
14 Robert Turbin/99 6.00 15.00
15 Ronnie Hillman/99 6.00 15.00
16 Trent Richardson/49 8.00 20.00
17 A.J. Jenkins/99 6.00 15.00
18 Alshon Jeffery/99 15.00 40.00
19 Brian Quick/99 6.00 15.00
20 Chris Givens/99 6.00 15.00
21 DeVier Posey/99 6.00 15.00
22 Jarius Wright/99 6.00 15.00
23 Joe Adams/99 6.00 15.00
24 Justin Blackmon/49 8.00 20.00
25 Kendall Wright/49 8.00 20.00
26 Michael Floyd/49 10.00 25.00
27 Mohamed Sanu/99 10.00 25.00
28 Nick Toon/99 6.00 15.00
29 Rueben Randle/99 6.00 15.00
30 Ryan Broyles/99 6.00 15.00
31 Stephen Hill/99 6.00 15.00
32 T.J. Graham/99 6.00 15.00
33 Coby Fleener/99 6.00 15.00
34 Dwayne Allen/99 6.00 15.00
35 Michael Egnew/99 6.00 15.00

2016 Prime Signatures

1 LeSean McCoy 1.50 4.00
2 Dorial Green-Beckham 1.00 2.50
3 Charcandrick West 1.00 2.50
4 Chris Johnson 1.00 2.50
5 Darren McFadden 1.00 2.50
6 T.J. Yeldon 1.00 2.50
7 Nick Foles 1.25 3.00
8 Joe Theismann 1.50 4.00
9 Khalil Mack 1.50 4.00
10 Marqise Lee 1.00 2.50
11 Kendall Wright 1.00 2.50
12 Greg Olsen 1.25 3.00
13 DeAngelo Williams 1.00 2.50
14 Arian Foster 1.25 3.00
15 Shane Vereen 1.25 3.00
16 Fran Tarkenton 1.50 4.00
17 LaDainian Tomlinson 1.25 3.00
18 Antonio Gates 1.00 2.50
19 Steve Smith 1.25 3.00
20 Jay Cutler 1.00 2.50
21 Lamar Miller 1.00 2.50
22 Jamaal Charles 1.25 3.00
23 Melvin Gordon 1.25 3.00
24 Jerry Rice 2.50 6.00
25 Terry Bradshaw 2.00 5.00
26 Von Miller 1.25 3.00
27 Tevin Coleman 1.25 3.00
28 Rob Gronkowski 1.50 4.00
29 Joe Haden 1.00 2.50
30 Drew Brees 1.50 4.00
31 Jimmy Graham 1.50 4.00
32 Peyton Manning 3.00 8.00
33 Allen Robinson 1.25 3.00
34 Eddie Lacy 1.00 2.50
35 Ronnie Hillman 1.00 2.50
36 Matt Jones 1.25 3.00
37 Derek Carr 1.50 4.00
38 Mike Wallace 1.00 2.50
39 Kelvin Benjamin 1.25 3.00
40 Ryan Tannehill 1.25 3.00
41 Clay Matthews 1.50 4.00
42 Ryan Mathews 1.25 3.00
43 Ben Roethlisberger 1.50 4.00
44 Sam Bradford 1.00 2.50
45 Jason Witten 1.25 3.00
46 Justin Hardy 1.00 2.50
47 Albert Wilson 1.00 2.50
48 Brandon Marshall 1.00 2.50
49 Mike Evans 1.25 3.00
50 Tyler Eifert 1.25 3.00
51 Ryan Fitzpatrick 1.00 2.50
52 Ndamukong Suh 1.25 3.00
53 Eddie Royal 1.00 2.50
54 Nelson Agholor 1.00 2.50
55 Josh Norman 1.00 2.50
56 Tony Romo 1.25 3.00
57 Aaron Rodgers 3.00 8.00
58 Tim Hightower 1.00 2.50
59 Julius Thomas 1.00 2.50
60 Julio Jones 1.50 4.00
61 Torrey Smith 1.00 2.50
62 Curtis Martin 1.25 3.00
63 Justin Forsett 1.25 3.00
64 Randall Cobb 1.25 3.00
65 Gary Barnidge 1.00 2.50
66 John Elway 2.50 6.00
67 Alshon Jeffery 1.25 3.00
68 Mark Ingram 1.25 3.00
69 Alfred Blue 1.00 2.50
70 Brian Hoyer 1.00 2.50
71 Jim Kelly 1.50 4.00
72 Michael Floyd 1.00 2.50
73 DeVante Parker 1.25 3.00
74 Stefon Diggs 1.25 3.00
75 Anquan Boldin 1.00 2.50
76 Markus Wheaton 1.00 2.50
77 Jeremy Maclin 1.00 2.50
78 Kurt Warner 1.25 3.00
79 Calvin Johnson 1.50 4.00
80 Rueben Randle 1.00 2.50
81 Joe Flacco 1.25 3.00
82 Michael Strahan 1.25 3.00
83 Alfred Morris 1.00 2.50
84 Willie Snead 1.25 3.00
85 John Brown 1.25 3.00
86 Danny Woodhead 1.25 3.00
87 Giovani Bernard 1.00 2.50
88 Carlos Hyde 1.00 2.50
89 Emmanuel Sanders 1.50 4.00
90 Jordan Reed 1.00 2.50
91 Antonio Brown 1.50 4.00
92 Doug Martin 1.25 3.00
93 Tyrod Taylor 1.25 3.00
94 Danny Amendola 1.25 3.00
95 Brandin Cooks 1.25 3.00
96 Andy Dalton 1.25 3.00
97 Jermaine Kearse 1.00 2.50
98 Jordy Nelson 1.25 3.00
99 Dez Bryant 1.50 4.00
100 Carson Palmer 1.25 3.00
101 Latavius Murray 1.00 2.50
102 Andrew Luck 2.00 5.00
103 Duke Johnson 1.00 2.50
104 Emmitt Smith 2.50 6.00
105 Matthew Stafford 1.25 3.00
106 Jordan Matthews 1.25 3.00
107 Brett Favre 3.00 8.00
108 Derrick Brooks 1.00 2.50
109 DeAndre Hopkins 1.25 3.00
110 Thomas Rawls 1.00 2.50
111 Brian Urlacher 1.50 4.00
112 Allen Hurns 1.00 2.50
113 David Cobb 1.00 2.50
114 Russell Wilson 2.00 5.00
115 T.Y. Hilton 1.25 3.00
116 Tavon Austin 1.00 2.50
117 Kirk Cousins 1.50 4.00
118 Delanie Walker 1.00 2.50
119 Odell Beckham Jr. 1.50 4.00
120 Coby Fleener 1.00 2.50
121 Tim Brown 1.50 4.00
122 David Johnson 1.50 4.00
123 Teddy Bridgewater 1.25 3.00
124 Blake Bortles 1.00 2.50
125 Ameer Abdullah 1.00 2.50
126 Rashad Jennings 1.00 2.50
127 Jeremy Hill 1.00 2.50
128 Austin Davis 1.25 3.00
129 Joe Montana 4.00 10.00
130 DeMarco Murray 1.25 3.00
131 Isaiah Crowell 1.00 2.50
132 Kyle Rudolph 1.00 2.50
133 Golden Tate 1.00 2.50
134 Michael Crabtree 1.00 2.50
135 Todd Gurley 1.50 4.00
136 C.J. Anderson 1.25 3.00
137 Luke Kuechly 1.25 3.00
138 DeSean Jackson 1.25 3.00
139 Zach Ertz 1.25 3.00
140 Doug Baldwin 1.25 3.00
141 Barry Sanders 2.50 6.00
142 Eli Manning 1.25 3.00
143 Roddy White 1.00 2.50
144 Jeremy Langford 1.25 3.00
145 Nate Washington 1.00 2.50
146 Devin Funchess 1.00 2.50
147 Adrian Peterson 1.50 4.00
148 Marques Colston 1.00 2.50
149 Travis Kelce 1.50 4.00
150 Jarvis Landry 1.25 3.00
151 Gale Sayers 1.50 4.00
152 Matt Ryan 1.25 3.00
153 Thurman Thomas 1.25 3.00
154 Larry Fitzgerald 1.25 3.00
155 Michael Irvin 1.50 4.00
156 Travis Benjamin 1.00 2.50
157 Keenan Allen 1.25 3.00
158 Ronnie Lott 1.25 3.00
159 Alex Smith 1.25 3.00
160 Darrelle Revis 1.00 2.50
161 Vincent Jackson 1.00 2.50
162 James White 1.25 3.00
163 Marcus Mariota 1.50 4.00
164 Le'Veon Bell 1.25 3.00
165 Kamar Aiken 1.00 2.50
166 Jameis Winston 1.50 4.00
167 Troy Aikman 2.00 5.00
168 A.J. Green 1.50 4.00
169 Richard Sherman 1.50 4.00
170 Joe Namath 2.00 5.00
171 Bo Jackson 2.00 5.00
172 Marcell Dareus 1.00 2.50
173 Pierre Garcon 1.25 3.00
174 Demaryius Thomas 1.25 3.00
175 Philip Rivers 1.50 4.00
176 J.J. Watt 1.50 4.00
177 Kenny Britt 1.00 2.50
178 Julian Edelman 1.50 4.00
179 Colin Kaepernick 1.25 3.00
180 Tyler Lockett 1.25 3.00
181 Sammy Watkins 1.50 4.00
182 Tom Brady 4.00 10.00
183 Eric Decker 1.00 2.50
184 Devonta Freeman 1.25 3.00
185 Donte Moncrief 1.25 3.00
186 Terrell Suggs 1.00 2.50
187 Frank Gore 1.25 3.00
188 Jonathan Stewart 1.00 2.50
189 Dan Marino 3.00 8.00
190 Ted Ginn Jr. 1.00 2.50
191 Eric Ebron 1.00 2.50
192 Amari Cooper 1.50 4.00
193 James Starks 1.00 2.50
194 Cam Newton 1.50 4.00
195 Martavis Bryant 1.00 2.50
196 Marvin Jones 1.00 2.50
197 Buck Allen 1.00 2.50
198 Austin Seferian-Jenkins 1.00 2.50
199 Matt Forte 1.00 2.50
200 Eric Dickerson 1.25 3.00
201 Kolby Listenbee AU RC 3.00 8.00
202 A'Shawn Robinson AU RC 3.00 8.00
203 Josh Ferguson AU RC 3.00 8.00
205 Joshua Perry AU RC 3.00 8.00
206 Keith Marshall AU RC 3.00 8.00
207 Kenny Lawler AU RC 5.00 12.00
208 Jeremy Cash AU RC 4.00 10.00
209 Daniel Braverman AU RC 3.00 8.00
210 Shaq Lawson AU RC 3.00 8.00
211 Karl Joseph AU RC 3.00 8.00
212 Tyler Ervin AU RC 3.00 8.00
214 Eli Apple AU RC 4.00 10.00
215 Hunter Henry AU RC 4.00 10.00
216 Andrew Billings AU RC 4.00 10.00
217 Jordan Payton AU RC 3.00 8.00
218 DeForest Buckner AU RC 3.00 8.00
219 Bralon Addison AU RC 3.00 8.00
220 Su'a Cravens AU RC 3.00 8.00
221 Robert Nkemdiche AU RC 12.00 30.00
222 Byron Marshall AU RC 3.00 8.00
223 Darron Lee AU RC 3.00 8.00
224 Kevin Dodd AU RC 3.00 8.00
225 Jeff Driskel AU RC 3.00 8.00
227 Nelson Spruce AU RC 3.00 8.00
228 Reggie Ragland AU RC 3.00 8.00
229 Adolphus Washington AU RC 3.00 8.00
230 Austin Hooper AU RC 3.00 8.00
231 Charles Tapper AU RC 4.00 10.00
232 Emmanuel Ogbah AU RC 4.00 10.00
233 Tre Madden AU RC 3.00 8.00
234 Mackensie Alexander AU RC 3.00 8.00
236 Jerell Adams AU RC 3.00 8.00
237 Maliek Collins AU RC 3.00 8.00
238 Jordan Williams AU RC 3.00 8.00
239 Jarran Reed AU RC 3.00 8.00
240 Wendell Smallwood AU RC 3.00 8.00
241 Jonathan Bullard AU RC 3.00 8.00
242 Malcolm Mitchell AU RC 3.00 8.00
243 Vonn Bell AU RC 4.00 10.00
244 Glenn Gronkowski AU RC 3.00 8.00
245 Noah Spence AU RC 3.00 8.00
246 Tajae Sharpe AU RC 4.00 10.00
247 Daniel Lasco AU RC 3.00 8.00
248 DeAndre Washington AU RC 3.00 8.00
249 Myles Jack AU RC 4.00 10.00
250 Kenny Clark AU RC 3.00 8.00
251 Demarcus Robinson AU RC 3.00 8.00
252 Kendall Fuller AU RC 4.00 10.00
253 Austin Johnson AU RC 3.00 8.00
254 Nick Vannett AU RC 3.00 8.00
255 Kamalei Correa AU RC 3.00 8.00
256 Thomas Duarte AU RC 3.00 8.00
257 Xavien Howard AU RC 4.00 10.00
258 Aaron Green AU RC 3.00 8.00
259 Shilique Calhoun AU RC 3.00 8.00
260 Scooby Wright III AU RC 3.00 8.00
261 Josh Doctson JSY AU RC 6.00 15.00
262 Brandon Doughty JSY AU RC 5.00 12.00
263 Jonathan Williams JSY AU RC 6.00 15.00
264 Jacoby Brissett JSY AU RC 6.00 15.00
265 Kenneth Dixon JSY AU RC 5.00 12.00
266 Corey Coleman JSY AU RC 8.00 20.00
267 Jared Goff JSY AU RC 30.00 80.00
268 Sterling Shepard JSY AU RC 6.00 15.00
269 Nate Sudfeld JSY AU RC 5.00 12.00
271 Devontae Booker JSY AU RC 6.00 15.00
272 Connor Cook JSY AU RC 6.00 15.00
273 Kelvin Taylor JSY AU RC 5.00 12.00
274 Joey Bosa JSY AU RC 10.00 25.00
275 Kenyan Drake JSY AU RC 8.00 20.00
276 Cardale Jones JSY AU RC 5.00 12.00
277 Aaron Burbridge JSY AU RC 5.00 12.00
278 Derrick Henry JSY AU RC 12.00 30.00
279 Leonte Carroo JSY AU RC 5.00 12.00
280 Paxton Lynch JSY AU RC 5.00 12.00
281 Will Fuller JSY AU RC 8.00 20.00
282 Ezekiel Elliott JSY AU RC 50.00 100.00
283 Michael Thomas JSY AU RC 10.00 25.00
284 Dak Prescott JSY AU RC 30.00 60.00
285 Laquon Treadwell JSY AU RC 30.00 80.00
286 Cody Kessler JSY AU RC 5.00 12.00
287 Paul Perkins JSY AU RC 5.00 12.00
288 Pharoh Cooper JSY AU RC 5.00 12.00
289 Carson Wentz JSY AU RC 50.00 100.00
290 Brandon Allen JSY AU RC 5.00 12.00
291 Jalen Ramsey JSY AU RC 8.00 20.00
292 Jordan Howard JSY AU RC 12.00 30.00
293 De'Runnya Wilson JSY AU RC 5.00 12.00
294 Christian Hackenberg JSY AU RC 5.00 12.00
295 Rashard Higgins JSY AU RC 5.00 12.00
296 Vernon Hargreaves III JSY AU RC 8.00 20.00
297 Braxton Miller JSY AU RC 5.00 12.00
298 Kevin Hogan JSY AU RC 6.00 15.00
299 C.J. Prosise JSY AU RC 5.00 12.00
300 Alex Collins JSY AU RC 6.00 15.00

2016 Prime Signatures Prime Proof Blue

*VETS/49: .8X TO 2X BASIC CARDS
282 Ezekiel Elliott JSY AU 75.00 150.00
289 Carson Wentz JSY AU 100.00 200.00

2016 Prime Signatures Prime Proof Red

*VETS/149: .5X TO 1.2X BASIC CARDS
282 Ezekiel Elliott JSY AU 60.00 125.00
289 Carson Wentz JSY AU 90.00 150.00

2016 Prime Signatures Autographs Red

*RED/49: .5X TO 1.2X BASIC AU/99
*RED/49: .4X TO 1X BASIC AU/60
*RED/25: .6X TO 1.5X BASIC AU/99
*RED/25: .5X TO 1.2X BASIC AU/49

2016 Prime Signatures Dual Autographs

1 T.Dorsett/R.White/25 30.00 60.00
2 D.Fouts/K.Winslow/15 75.00 150.00
3 L.Murray/M.Allen/49 10.00 25.00
4 J.Landry/D.Parker/99 12.00 30.00
5 A.Dalton/A.Green/25 20.00 40.00
6 T.Brdgwtr/S.Diggs/49 10.00 25.00
7 D.Wdhead/M.Gordon/25 12.00 30.00
8 A.Smith/L.Dawson/25 25.00 50.00
9 J.Goff/K.Lawler/99 40.00 100.00
10 A.Abdllh/J.Lngfrd/99 8.00 20.00
12 K.Bnjmn/D.Fnchss/99 8.00 20.00
13 T.Smith/A.Bldin/25 10.00 25.00
14 I.Crowell/D.Johnson/99 6.00 15.00
15 S.Watkins/A.Reed/25 15.00 40.00
16 K.Wright/D.GrnBckhm/99 6.00 15.00
17 E.Elliott/D.Henry/99 30.00 80.00
18 S.Largent/T.Lockett/25 40.00 80.00
19 J.Goff/C.Wentz/99 100.00 200.00
20 V.Hrgrves/J.Ramsey/99 10.00 25.00
21 C.Joiner/K.Allen/99 8.00 20.00
22 D.Martin/C.Sims/99 8.00 20.00
24 L.Trdwll/C.Clemn/99 10.00 25.00
26 V.Cruz/H.Nicks/49 10.00 25.00
27 H.Henry/A.Collins/99 8.00 20.00
28 I.Woods/C.Clinswrth/25 30.00 60.00
30 D.Carr/L.Murray/75 20.00 50.00
31 M.Thomas/B.Miller/99 12.00 30.00
32 D.McFadden/A.Collins/49 10.00 25.00
34 F.Taylor/T.Yeldon/49 8.00 20.00
35 C.Cook/A.Burbridge/99 8.00 20.00
36 R.Craig/D.Clark/49 20.00 50.00
37 D.Driver/B.Franks/49 10.00 25.00
39 D.Henry/K.Drake/99 15.00 40.00
41 H.Crmchl/W.Mntgmry/99 6.00 15.00
42 J.Lofton/T.Montgomery/99 8.00 20.00
43 D.Prsctt/D.Wilson/99 30.00 80.00
44 A.Cooper/T.Drown/25 40.00 100.00
45 C.Portis/M.Jones/99 8.00 20.00

2016 Prime Signatures Icons

*COSMIC/100: .6X TO 1.5X BASIC INSERTS
1 Joe Montana 5.00 12.00
2 Brett Favre 4.00 10.00
3 Emmitt Smith 3.00 8.00
4 Jerry Rice 3.00 8.00
5 Barry Sanders 3.00 8.00

2016 Prime Signatures New Wave

*COSMIC: .6X TO 1.5X BASIC INSERTS
1 Amari Cooper 2.00 5.00
2 David Johnson 2.00 5.00
3 Tyler Lockett 1.50 4.00
4 Ameer Abdullah 1.25 3.00
5 DeVante Parker 1.50 4.00
6 Teddy Bridgewater 1.50 4.00
7 Jameis Winston 2.00 5.00
8 Marcus Mariota 2.00 5.00
9 Sammy Watkins 2.00 5.00
10 Mike Evans 1.50 4.00
11 Odell Beckham Jr. 2.00 5.00
12 Brandin Cooks 1.50 4.00
13 Stefon Diggs 1.50 4.00
14 Kelvin Benjamin 1.50 4.00
15 Todd Gurley 2.00 5.00

2016 Prime Signatures Prime Signature Swatches

1 Derek Carr/15 15.00 40.00
2 T.J. Yeldon/49 6.00 15.00
3 Brandin Cooks/15 12.00 30.00
5 Ameer Abdullah/25 8.00 20.00
6 Kelvin Benjamin/49 8.00 20.00
8 Jeremy Langford/99 6.00 15.00
9 Doug Martin/15
10 Allen Robinson/25 10.00 25.00
12 Nelson Agholor/49 6.00 15.00
13 Julius Thomas/25 8.00 20.00
14 Matt Jones/99 6.00 15.00
15 David Johnson/99 8.00 20.00
17 Danny Woodhead/25 10.00 25.00
18 Stefon Diggs/99 10.00 25.00
20 Blake Bortles/15
21 Mike Evans/25 10.00 25.00
22 DeVante Parker/49 8.00 20.00
23 Teddy Bridgewater/25 10.00 25.00
24 Chris Conley/99 5.00 12.00
26 Karlos Williams/99 5.00 12.00
28 Lamar Miller/25 8.00 20.00
29 Kevin White/49 6.00 15.00
30 Devin Funchess/99 5.00 12.00
32 Eddie Lacy/25 8.00 20.00
33 Tyler Lockett/99 6.00 15.00
34 DeMarcus Ware/15 25.00 50.00
35 Jamison Crowder/99 5.00 12.00
36 Dorial Green-Beckham/99 5.00 12.00
38 Melvin Gordon/25 10.00 25.00
39 Sammy Watkins /25 12.00 30.00
40 Duke Johnson/99 5.00 12.00

2016 Prime Signatures Prime Timers

*COSMIC/100: .6X TO 1.5X BASIC INSERTS
1 Drew Brees 2.00 5.00
2 Adrian Peterson 2.00 5.00
3 Tom Brady 5.00 12.00
4 Julio Jones 2.00 5.00
5 Ben Roethlisberger 2.00 5.00
6 Odell Beckham Jr. 2.00 5.00
7 Aaron Rodgers 4.00 10.00
8 Dez Bryant 2.00 5.00
9 Peyton Manning 4.00 10.00
10 Todd Gurley 2.00 5.00
11 Cam Newton 2.00 5.00
12 Demaryius Thomas 1.50 4.00
13 Russell Wilson 2.50 6.00
14 Antonio Brown 2.00 5.00
15 Carson Palmer 1.50 4.00

2016 Prime Signatures Proteges

*COSMIC/100: .6X TO 1.5X BASIC INSERTS
1 E.Dickerson/T.Gurley 3.00 8.00
2 T.Brady/J.Garoppolo 8.00 20.00
3 T.Brown/A.Cooper 3.00 8.00
4 A.Reed/S.Watkins 3.00 8.00
5 M.Irvin/D.Bryant 3.00 8.00
6 V.Cruz/O.Beckham 3.00 8.00
7 V.Jackson/M.Evans 2.50 6.00
8 C.Carter/S.Diggs 3.00 8.00
9 B.Sanders/A.Abdullah 5.00 12.00
10 S.Largent/T.Lockett 3.00 8.00
11 P.Manning/A.Luck 6.00 15.00
12 M.Colston/B.Cooks 2.50 6.00
13 B.Favre/A.Rodgers 6.00 15.00
14 L.Tmlnsn/M.Gordon 2.50 6.00
15 L.Ftzgrld/J.Brown 2.50 6.00

2016 Prime Signatures Ring Bearers

*COSMIC/100: .6X TO 1.5X BASIC INSERTS
1 Tom Brady 5.00 12.00
2 Terry Bradshaw 2.50 6.00
3 Joe Montana 5.00 12.00
4 Troy Aikman 2.50 6.00
5 John Elway 3.00 8.00

2016 Prime Signatures Rookie Revolution

*COSMIC/100: .6X TO 1.5X BASIC INSERTS
1 Joey Bosa 1.50 4.00
2 Jared Goff 5.00 12.00
3 Laquon Treadwell 1.00 2.50
4 Paxton Lynch .75 2.00
5 Ezekiel Elliott 4.00 10.00
6 Carson Wentz 8.00 20.00
7 Corey Coleman 1.25 3.00
8 Michael Thomas 1.50 4.00
9 Josh Doctson 1.00 2.50
10 Derrick Henry 2.00 5.00
11 Tyler Boyd 1.00 2.50
12 Pharoh Cooper .75 2.00
13 Christian Hackenberg .75 2.00
14 Alex Collins 1.00 2.50
15 Connor Cook 1.00 2.50

2016 Prime Signatures Showstoppers

*COSMIC/100: .6X TO 1.5X BASIC INSERTS
1 Lawrence Taylor 2.00 5.00
2 J.J. Watt 2.00 5.00
3 Luke Kuechly 1.50 4.00
4 Darrelle Revis 1.25 3.00
5 Richard Sherman 2.00 5.00
6 Josh Norman 1.25 3.00
7 Charles Woodson 2.00 5.00
8 Clay Matthews 2.00 5.00
9 Bruce Smith 1.50 4.00
10 Rod Woodson 1.50 4.00
11 Patrick Peterson 1.25 3.00
12 Joe Haden 1.25 3.00
13 Ndamukong Suh 1.50 4.00
14 Von Miller 1.50 4.00
15 Khalil Mack 2.00 5.00

2016 Prime Signatures Sight Lines

*COSMIC/100: .6X TO 1.5X BASIC INSERTS
1 Marshawn Lynch 1.50 4.00
2 Tyrod Taylor 1.50 4.00
3 Antonio Brown 2.00 5.00
4 Cam Newton 2.00 5.00
5 Devonta Freeman 1.50 4.00
6 Marcus Mariota 2.00 5.00
7 Dez Bryant 2.00 5.00
8 Clinton Portis 1.25 3.00
9 Jarvis Landry 1.50 4.00
10 LaDainian Tomlinson 1.50 4.00
11 Julio Jones 2.00 5.00
12 Ricky Williams 1.50 4.00
13 Odell Beckham Jr. 2.00 5.00
14 Le'Veon Bell 1.50 4.00
15 Calvin Johnson 2.00 5.00

2000 Private Stock

Released as a 150-card base set, Private Stock is comprised of 100 veteran cards and 50 rookie cards which are sequentially numbered to 278. Base cards feature a player image that appears to have been sketched on the card which is printed to look like canvas. Cards are enhanced with gold foil highlights. Private Stock packs contained five cards.

COMP.SET w/o SP's (100) 10.00 25.00
1 Rob Moore .25 .60
2 Jake Plummer .25 .60
3 Frank Sanders .25 .60
4 Jamal Anderson .30 .75
5 Chris Chandler .30 .75
6 Tim Dwight .30 .75
7 Tony Banks .25 .60
8 Priest Holmes .25 .60
9 Doug Flutie .30 .75
10 Rob Johnson .30 .75
11 Eric Moulds .25 .60
12 Antowain Smith .30 .75
13 Steve Beuerlein .30 .75
14 Tim Biakabutuka .30 .75
15 Patrick Jeffers .25 .60
16 Muhsin Muhammad .25 .60
17 Curtis Enis .25 .60
18 Cade McNown .25 .60
19 Marcus Robinson .30 .75
20 Corey Dillon .25 .60
21 Akili Smith .25 .60
22 Tim Couch .30 .75
23 Kevin Johnson .25 .60
24 Troy Aikman .50 1.25
25 Rocket Ismail .30 .75
26 Emmitt Smith .60 1.50
27 Terrell Davis .30 .75
28 Olandis Gary .30 .75
29 Brian Griese .25 .60
30 Ed McCaffrey .30 .75
31 Charlie Batch .25 .60
32 Germane Crowell .25 .60
33 Herman Moore .25 .60
34 Barry Sanders .60 1.50
35 Brett Favre .75 2.00
36 Antonio Freeman .30 .75
37 Dorsey Levens .30 .75
38 Marvin Harrison .30 .75
39 Edgerrin James .30 .75
40 Peyton Manning 1.00 2.50
41 Terrence Wilkins .25 .60
42 Mark Brunell .30 .75
43 Keenan McCardell .30 .75
44 Jimmy Smith .30 .75
45 Fred Taylor .25 .60
46 Derrick Alexander .25 .60
47 Donnell Bennett .25 .60
48 Tony Gonzalez .30 .75
49 Elvis Grbac .25 .60
50 Damon Huard .25 .60
51 James Johnson .25 .60
52 Dan Marino .75 2.00
53 O.J. McDuffie .30 .75
54 Cris Carter .40 1.00
55 Daunte Culpepper .30 .75
56 Randy Moss .30 .75
57 Robert Smith .25 .60
58 Drew Bledsoe .30 .75
59 Kevin Faulk .25 .60
60 Terry Glenn .30 .75
61 Keith Poole .25 .60
62 Ricky Williams .30 .75
63 Kerry Collins .25 .60
64 Ike Hilliard .25 .60
65 Amani Toomer .25 .60
66 Wayne Chrebet .25 .60
67 Ray Lucas .25 .60
68 Curtis Martin .30 .75
69 Tim Brown .40 1.00
70 Rich Gannon .30 .75
71 Napoleon Kaufman .30 .75
72 Donovan McNabb .30 .75
73 Duce Staley .25 .60
74 Jerome Bettis .40 1.00
75 Troy Edwards .25 .60
76 Kordell Stewart .25 .60
77 Isaac Bruce .40 1.00
78 Marshall Faulk .30 .75
79 Torry Holt .30 .75
80 Kurt Warner .60 1.50
81 Jermaine Fazande .25 .60
82 Jim Harbaugh .30 .75
83 Junior Seau .30 .75
84 Charlie Garner .30 .75
85 Terrell Owens .30 .75
86 Jerry Rice 1.00 2.50
87 Jon Kitna .25 .60
88 Derrick Mayes .25 .60
89 Ricky Watters .30 .75
90 Mike Alstott .25 .60
91 Warrick Dunn .25 .60
92 Jacquez Green .25 .60
93 Shaun King .25 .60
94 Eddie George .30 .75
95 Jevon Kearse .25 .60
96 Steve McNair .30 .75
97 Yancey Thigpen .25 .60
98 Stephen Davis .25 .60
99 Brad Johnson .30 .75
100 Michael Westbrook .25 .60
101 Thomas Jones RC 5.00 12.00
102 Doug Johnson RC 4.00 10.00
103 Mareno Philyaw RC 4.00 10.00
104 Jamal Lewis RC 6.00 15.00
105 Chris Redman RC 4.00 10.00
106 Travis Taylor RC 4.00 10.00
107 Frank Murphy RC 4.00 10.00
108 Dez White RC 4.00 10.00
109 Ron Dugans RC 4.00 10.00
110 Curtis Keaton RC 4.00 10.00
111 Peter Warrick RC 4.00 10.00
112 Courtney Brown RC 5.00 12.00
113 JaJuan Dawson RC 4.00 10.00
114 Dennis Northcutt RC 4.00 10.00
115 Travis Prentice RC 4.00 10.00
116 Michael Wiley RC 4.00 10.00
117 Chris Cole RC 5.00 12.00
118 Jarious Jackson RC 5.00 12.00
119 Reuben Droughns RC 4.00 10.00
120 Bubba Franks RC 4.00 10.00
121 Anthony Lucas RC 4.00 10.00
122 Rondell Mealey RC 4.00 10.00
123 R.Jay Soward RC 4.00 10.00
124 Shyrone Stith RC 4.00 10.00
125 Sylvester Morris RC 4.00 10.00
126 Quinton Spotwood RC 4.00 10.00
127 Troy Walters RC 4.00 10.00
128 Tom Brady RC 150.00 300.00
129 J.R. Redmond RC 4.00 10.00
130 Marc Bulger RC 5.00 12.00
131 Sherrod Gideon RC 4.00 10.00
132 Ron Dayne RC 6.00 15.00
133 Anthony Becht RC 4.00 10.00
134 Laveranues Coles RC 5.00 12.00
135 Chad Pennington RC 5.00 12.00
136 Sebastian Janikowski RC 8.00 20.00
137 Jerry Porter RC 6.00 15.00
138 Todd Pinkston RC 4.00 10.00
139 Gari Scott RC 4.00 10.00
140 Plaxico Burress RC 5.00 12.00
141 Danny Farmer RC 4.00 10.00
142 Tee Martin RC 4.00 10.00
143 Trung Canidate RC 4.00 10.00
144 Trevor Gaylor RC 4.00 10.00
145 Giovanni Carmazzi RC 4.00 10.00
146 Tim Rattay RC 5.00 12.00
147 Shaun Alexander RC 6.00 15.00
148 Darrell Jackson RC 4.00 10.00
149 Joe Hamilton RC 4.00 10.00
150 Todd Husak RC 4.00 10.00
S1 Jon Kitna Sample .40 1.00

2000 Private Stock Retail

COMP.SET w/o RCs (100) 10.00 25.00
*VETS 1-100: .4X TO 1X HOBBY
*ROOKIES 101-150: .2X TO .5X HOBBY
101-150 ROOKIE PRINT RUN 650
128 Tom Brady RC 150.00 300.00

2000 Private Stock Gold

*VETS 1-100: 3X TO 8X BASIC CARDS
*ROOKIES 101-150: .2X TO .5X
GOLD PRINT RUN 181 SER.#'d SETS
128 Tom Brady 200.00 400.00

2000 Private Stock Premiere Date

*VETS 1-100: 5X TO 12X BASIC CARDS
*ROOKIES 101-150: .3X TO .8X
PREM.DATE PRINT RUN 95 SER.#'d SETS
128 Tom Brady 250.00 500.00

2000 Private Stock Silver

*VETS 1-100: 2.5X TO 6X BASIC CARDS
*ROOKIES 101-150: .15X TO .4X
SILVER/330 STATED ODDS 3:25
SILVER STAT.PRINT RUN 330 SER.#'d SETS
128 Tom Brady 150.00 300.00

2000 Private Stock Artist's Canvas

Randomly inserted in packs at the rate of one in 45, this 20-card set is printed on canvas. It contains black and white "drawings" of players and gold foil highlights. Card backs are blank except for the Pacific logo and the card number.

COMPLETE SET (20) 30.00 80.00
STATED ODDS 1:45
UNPRICED PROOF PRINT RUN 1
1 Jamal Lewis 1.50 4.00
2 Peter Warrick 1.00 2.50
3 Tim Couch 1.50 4.00
4 Emmitt Smith 3.00 8.00
5 Olandis Gary 1.50 4.00
6 Marvin Harrison 1.50 4.00
7 Edgerrin James 1.50 4.00
8 Mark Brunell 1.50 4.00
9 Fred Taylor 1.25 3.00
10 Randy Moss 1.50 4.00
11 Ron Dayne 1.50 4.00
12 Chad Pennington 1.25 3.00
13 Jerome Bettis 2.00 5.00
14 Plaxico Burress 1.25 3.00
15 Marshall Faulk 1.50 4.00
16 Kurt Warner 3.00 8.00
17 Jon Kitna 1.25 3.00
18 Shaun King 1.25 3.00
19 Eddie George 1.50 4.00
20 Stephen Davis 1.25 3.00

2000 Private Stock Extreme Action

Randomly inserted in hobby or retail packs at the rate of one in 23, this 20-card set features full color wide angle action photography. Each card is framed by a blue and tan border and features blue and gold foil highlights.

COMPLETE SET (20) 15.00 40.00
STATED ODDS 2:23
1 Jake Plummer .75 2.00
2 Tim Couch 1.00 2.50
3 Emmitt Smith 2.00 5.00
4 Olandis Gary 1.00 2.50
5 Marvin Harrison 1.00 2.50
6 Edgerrin James 1.00 2.50
7 Mark Brunell 1.00 2.50
8 Fred Taylor .75 2.00
9 Randy Moss 1.00 2.50
10 Drew Bledsoe 1.00 2.50
11 Ricky Williams 1.00 2.50
12 Ron Dayne 1.25 3.00
13 Donovan McNabb 1.00 2.50
14 Isaac Bruce 1.25 3.00
15 Marshall Faulk 1.00 2.50
16 Kurt Warner 2.00 5.00
17 Jon Kitna .75 2.00
18 Shaun King .75 2.00
19 Steve McNair 1.00 2.50
20 Stephen Davis .75 2.00

2000 Private Stock Private Signings

Randomly inserted in Retail packs and inserted at 2 per box for Hobby, this set was printed on die cut card stock with the shape of a football along the right edge. Each card contains an authentic player autograph. Some cards were later released in 2001 Crown Royale packs as well.

TWO PER HOBBY BOX
1 Thomas Jones 6.00 15.00
2 Jamal Lewis 8.00 20.00
3 Chris Redman 5.00 12.00
4 Travis Taylor 5.00 12.00
5 Dez White 5.00 12.00
6 Peter Warrick 5.00 12.00
8 JaJuan Dawson 5.00 12.00
9 Dennis Northcutt 5.00 12.00
11 Michael Wiley 5.00 12.00
12 Chris Cole 6.00 15.00
13 Reuben Droughns 5.00 12.00
14 Anthony Lucas 5.00 12.00
15 Rondell Mealey 5.00 12.00
16 R.Jay Soward 5.00 12.00
17 Shyrone Stith 5.00 12.00
18 Sylvester Morris 5.00 12.00
19 Quinton Spotwood 5.00 12.00
20 Troy Walters 5.00 12.00
21 J.R. Redmond 5.00 12.00
22 Marc Bulger 6.00 15.00
23 Ron Dayne 8.00 20.00
24 Laveranues Coles 6.00 15.00
25 Chad Pennington 6.00 15.00
28 Plaxico Burress 6.00 15.00
29 Danny Farmer 5.00 12.00
30 Tee Martin 5.00 12.00
31 Chafie Fields 5.00 12.00
32 Tim Rattay 6.00 15.00
33 Shaun Alexander 8.00 20.00
36 Todd Husak 5.00 12.00

2000 Private Stock PS2000 Action

Randomly inserted in packs at the rate of two in one, this 60-card set measures 1 1/2" x 2 3/4". Player action photos are set inside the white borders and cards are accented with gold foil highlights.

COMPLETE SET (60) 10.00 25.00
STATED ODDS 2:1
1 Thomas Jones .20 .50
2 Jake Plummer .15 .40
3 Jamal Lewis .25 .60
4 Chris Redman .15 .40
5 Travis Taylor .15 .40
6 Doug Flutie .20 .50
7 Cade McNown .15 .40
8 Marcus Robinson .20 .50
9 Dez White .15 .40
10 Akili Smith .15 .40
11 Peter Warrick .15 .40
12 Tim Couch .20 .50

13 Dennis Northcutt .15 .40
14 Travis Prentice .15 .40
15 Troy Aikman .30 .75
16 Emmitt Smith .40 1.00
17 Terrell Davis .20 .50
18 Olandis Gary .20 .50
19 Brian Griese .15 .40
20 Reuben Droughns .15 .40
21 Barry Sanders .40 1.00
22 Brett Favre .50 1.25
23 Antonio Freeman .20 .50
24 Marvin Harrison .20 .50
25 Edgerrin James .20 .50
26 Peyton Manning .60 1.50
27 Mark Brunell .20 .50
28 R.Jay Soward .15 .40
29 Fred Taylor .15 .40
30 Sylvester Morris .15 .40
31 Dan Marino .50 1.25
32 Cris Carter .25 .60
33 Randy Moss .20 .50
34 Drew Bledsoe .20 .50
35 J.R. Redmond .15 .40
36 Ricky Williams .20 .50
37 Ron Dayne .25 .60
38 Laveranues Coles .20 .50
39 Curtis Martin .20 .50
40 Chad Pennington .20 .50
41 Napoleon Kaufman .20 .50
42 Donovan McNabb .20 .50
43 Jerome Bettis .25 .60
44 Plaxico Burress .20 .50
45 Tee Martin .15 .40
46 Isaac Bruce .25 .60
47 Marshall Faulk .20 .50
48 Kurt Warner .40 1.00
49 Giovanni Carmazzi .15 .40
50 Terrell Owens .20 .50
51 Jerry Rice .60 1.50
52 Shaun Alexander .25 .60
53 Jon Kitna .15 .40
54 Warrick Dunn .15 .40
55 Joe Hamilton .15 .40
56 Shaun King .15 .40
57 Eddie George .20 .50
58 Steve McNair .20 .50
59 Stephen Davis .15 .40
60 Brad Johnson .20 .50

2000 Private Stock PS2000 New Wave

Randomly inserted in packs, this 25-card set measures 1 1/2" x 2 3/4". Each card features young stars in action with white borders and contains red foil highlights. Cards are sequentially numbered to 202.

COMPLETE SET (25) 30.00 80.00
STATED PRINT RUN 202 SER.#'d SETS
1 Jake Plummer 1.00 2.50
2 Eric Moulds 1.00 2.50
3 Cade McNown 1.00 2.50
4 Marcus Robinson 1.25 3.00
5 Akili Smith 1.00 2.50
6 Tim Couch 1.25 3.00
7 Kevin Johnson 1.00 2.50
8 Olandis Gary 1.25 3.00
9 Brian Griese 1.00 2.50
10 Marvin Harrison 1.25 3.00
11 Edgerrin James 1.25 3.00
12 Peyton Manning 4.00 10.00
13 Fred Taylor 1.00 2.50
14 Tony Gonzalez 1.25 3.00
15 Damon Huard 1.00 2.50
16 Randy Moss 1.25 3.00
17 Ricky Williams 1.25 3.00
18 Donovan McNabb 1.25 3.00
19 Duce Staley 1.00 2.50
20 Kurt Warner 2.50 6.00
21 Terrell Owens 1.25 3.00
22 Jon Kitna 1.00 2.50
23 Shaun King 1.00 2.50
24 Steve McNair 1.25 3.00
25 Stephen Davis 1.00 2.50

2000 Private Stock PS2000 Rookies

Randomly inserted in packs, this 25-card set measures 1 1/2" x 2 3/4". Each card is white bordered and contains blue foil highlights. Cards are sequentially numbered to 106.

COMPLETE SET (25) 60.00 150.00
STATED PRINT RUN 106 SER.#'d SETS
1 Thomas Jones 1.25 3.00
2 Jamal Lewis 1.50 4.00
3 Chris Redman 1.00 2.50
4 Travis Taylor 1.00 2.50
5 Dez White 1.00 2.50
6 Ron Dugans 1.00 2.50
7 Peter Warrick 1.00 2.50
8 Dennis Northcutt 1.00 2.50
9 Travis Prentice 1.00 2.50
10 Reuben Droughns 1.00 2.50
11 R.Jay Soward 1.00 2.50
12 Sylvester Morris 1.00 2.50
13 Troy Walters 1.00 2.50
14 J.R. Redmond 1.00 2.50
15 Ron Dayne 1.50 4.00
16 Laveranues Coles 1.25 3.00
17 Chad Pennington 1.25 3.00
18 Jerry Porter 1.50 4.00
19 Todd Pinkston 1.00 2.50
20 Plaxico Burress 1.25 3.00
21 Tee Martin 1.00 2.50
22 Giovanni Carmazzi 1.00 2.50
23 Shaun Alexander 1.50 4.00
24 Joe Hamilton 1.00 2.50
25 Todd Husak 1.00 2.50

2000 Private Stock PS2000 Stars

Randomly inserted in packs, this 25-card set measures 1 1/2" x 2 3/4". Each card is white bordered and contains bronze foil highlights. Each card is sequentially numbered to 298.

COMPLETE SET (25) 25.00 60.00
STATED PRINT RUN 298 SER.#'d SETS
1 Jamal Anderson 1.25 3.00
2 Doug Flutie 1.25 3.00
3 Troy Aikman 2.00 5.00
4 Emmitt Smith 2.50 6.00
5 Terrell Davis 1.25 3.00
6 Herman Moore 1.00 2.50
7 Barry Sanders 2.50 6.00
8 Brett Favre 3.00 8.00
9 Antonio Freeman 1.25 3.00
10 Dorsey Levens 1.25 3.00
11 Mark Brunell 1.25 3.00
12 Dan Marino 3.00 8.00
13 Cris Carter 1.50 4.00
14 Robert Smith 1.00 2.50
15 Drew Bledsoe 1.25 3.00
16 Curtis Martin 1.25 3.00
17 Tim Brown 1.50 4.00
18 Napoleon Kaufman 1.25 3.00
19 Jerome Bettis 1.50 4.00
20 Isaac Bruce 1.50 4.00
21 Marshall Faulk 1.25 3.00
22 Jerry Rice 4.00 10.00
23 Warrick Dunn 1.00 2.50
24 Eddie George 1.25 3.00
25 Brad Johnson 1.25 3.00

2000 Private Stock Reserve

Randomly inserted in Hobby packs at the rate of one in 23, this 20-card set features top NFL players framed by a tan border with gold foil highlights. Cards are printed on a paper card stock with backs featuring no more than the card number.

COMPLETE SET (20) 30.00 80.00
STATED ODDS 1:23 HOBBY
1 Cade McNown 1.00 2.50
2 Peter Warrick 1.00 2.50
4 Troy Aikman 2.00 5.00
5 Emmitt Smith 2.50 6.00
6 Terrell Davis 1.25 3.00
7 Barry Sanders 2.50 6.00
8 Brett Favre 3.00 8.00
9 Edgerrin James 1.25 3.00
10 Peyton Manning 4.00 10.00
11 Mark Brunell 1.25 3.00
12 Fred Taylor 1.00 2.50
13 Randy Moss 1.25 3.00
14 Ron Dayne 1.50 4.00
15 Chad Pennington 1.25 3.00
16 Marshall Faulk 1.25 3.00
17 Kurt Warner 2.50 6.00
18 Jerry Rice 4.00 10.00
19 Shaun Alexander 1.50 4.00
20 Eddie George 1.25 3.00

2001 Private Stock

Pacific released its Private Stock set in August of 2001. The set was made up of 175 cards, 75 of those were short printed rookies (serial numbered of 200). The hobby packs carried an SRP of $14.99, due to the jersey card in every pack. The cards were highlighted with gold-foil lettering and a gold-foil Private Stock logo.

COMP.SET w/o RC's (100) 30.00 60.00
1 David Boston .25 .60
2 Thomas Jones .25 .60
3 Jake Plummer .25 .60
4 Jamal Anderson .30 .75
5 Chris Chandler .30 .75
6 Eric Zeier .25 .60
7 Elvis Grbac .30 .75
8 Jamal Lewis .40 1.00
9 Shannon Sharpe .30 .75
10 Rob Johnson .30 .75
11 Eric Moulds .25 .60
12 Peerless Price .25 .60
13 Tim Biakabutuka .25 .60
14 Jeff Lewis .25 .60
15 Muhsin Muhammad .25 .60
16 James Allen .25 .60
17 Cade McNown .30 .75
18 Marcus Robinson .30 .75
19 Brian Urlacher .50 1.25
20 Corey Dillon .25 .60
21 Jon Kitna .25 .60
22 Akili Smith .25 .60
23 Peter Warrick .25 .60
24 Tim Couch .25 .60
25 Kevin Johnson .25 .60
26 Travis Prentice .25 .60
27 Rocket Ismail .30 .75
28 Emmitt Smith .60 1.50
29 Mike Anderson .25 .60
30 Terrell Davis .30 .75
31 Brian Griese .25 .60
32 Ed McCaffrey .30 .75
33 Charlie Batch .25 .60
34 Germane Crowell .25 .60
35 James Stewart .25 .60
36 Brett Favre .75 2.00
37 Antonio Freeman .40 1.00
38 Ahman Green .30 .75
39 Marvin Harrison .30 .75
40 Edgerrin James .30 .75
41 Peyton Manning 1.00 2.50
42 Mark Brunell .30 .75
43 Jimmy Smith .30 .75
44 Fred Taylor .25 .60
45 Derrick Alexander .25 .60
46 Tony Gonzalez .30 .75
47 Trent Green .25 .60
48 Priest Holmes .25 .60
49 Jay Fiedler .30 .75
50 Oronde Gadsden .25 .60
51 Lamar Smith .30 .75
52 Cris Carter .40 1.00
53 Daunte Culpepper .30 .75
54 Randy Moss .30 .75
55 Drew Bledsoe .30 .75
56 Kevin Faulk .25 .60
57 Terry Glenn .30 .75
58 Jeff Blake .30 .75
59 Aaron Brooks .25 .60
60 Joe Horn .25 .60
61 Ricky Williams .30 .75
62 Tiki Barber .30 .75
63 Kerry Collins .25 .60
64 Ron Dayne .30 .75
65 Amani Toomer .25 .60
66 Wayne Chrebet .25 .60
67 Curtis Martin .30 .75
68 Vinny Testaverde .25 .60
69 Tim Brown .40 1.00
70 Rich Gannon .30 .75
71 Charlie Garner .30 .75
72 Jerry Rice .75 2.00
73 Tyrone Wheatley .30 .75
74 Donovan McNabb .30 .75
75 Duce Staley .25 .60
76 Jerome Bettis .40 1.00
77 Kordell Stewart .25 .60
78 Hines Ward .30 .75
79 Isaac Bruce .40 1.00
80 Marshall Faulk .30 .75
81 Torry Holt .30 .75
82 Kurt Warner .60 1.50
83 Curtis Conway .30 .75
84 Doug Flutie .30 .75
85 Jeff Garcia .25 .60
86 Terrell Owens .30 .75
87 Shaun Alexander .25 .60
88 Matt Hasselbeck .25 .60
89 Darrell Jackson .30 .75
90 Ricky Watters .30 .75
91 Mike Alstott .25 .60
92 Warrick Dunn .25 .60
93 Keyshawn Johnson .30 .75
94 Brad Johnson .30 .75
95 Eddie George .40 1.00
96 Derrick Mason .25 .60
97 Steve McNair .30 .75
98 Stephen Davis .25 .60
99 Jeff George .30 .75
100 Michael Westbrook .25 .60
101 Bobby Newcombe RC 2.50 6.00
102 Corey Brown RC 2.00 5.00
103 Alge Crumpler RC 3.00 8.00
104 Vinny Sutherland RC 2.00 5.00
105 Michael Vick RC 5.00 12.00
106 Chris Barnes RC 2.00 5.00
107 Todd Heap RC 2.50 6.00
108 Nate Clements RC 2.50 6.00
109 Tim Hasselbeck RC 2.50 6.00
110 Travis Henry RC 2.50 6.00
111 Dee Brown RC 2.00 5.00
112 Dan Morgan RC 2.50 6.00
113 Steve Smith RC 6.00 15.00
114 Chris Weinke RC 2.50 6.00
115 John Capel RC 2.00 5.00
116 David Terrell RC 2.50 6.00
117 Anthony Thomas RC 3.00 8.00
118 T.J. Houshmandzadeh RC 2.50 6.00
119 Chad Johnson RC 3.00 8.00
120 Rudi Johnson RC 3.00 8.00
121 James Jackson RC 2.00 5.00
122 Quincy Morgan RC 2.50 6.00
123 Quincy Carter RC 2.50 6.00
124 Kevin Kasper RC 2.00 5.00
125 Scotty Anderson RC 2.00 5.00
126 Mike McMahon RC 2.50 6.00
127 Robert Ferguson RC 3.00 8.00
128 David Martin RC 2.00 5.00
129 Jamal Reynolds RC 2.00 5.00
130 Reggie Wayne RC 4.00 10.00
132 Marcus Stroud RC 2.50 6.00
133 Derrick Blaylock RC 2.50 6.00
134 Snoop Minnis RC 2.00 5.00
135 Chris Chambers RC 2.00 5.00
136 Jamar Fletcher RC 2.00 5.00
137 Josh Heupel RC 3.00 8.00
138 Travis Minor RC 2.50 6.00
139 Michael Bennett RC 2.50 6.00
140 Deuce McAllister RC 3.00 8.00
141 Moran Norris RC 2.00 5.00
142 Onomo Ojo RC 2.00 5.00
143 Will Allen RC 3.00 8.00
144 Jonathan Carter RC 2.00 5.00
145 Jesse Palmer RC 2.50 6.00
146 LaMont Jordan RC 3.00 8.00
147 Santana Moss RC 3.00 8.00
148 Derek Combs RC 2.00 5.00
149 Derrick Gibson RC 2.00 5.00
150 Javon Green RC 2.00 5.00
151 Ken-Yon Rambo RC 2.00 5.00
152 Marques Tuiasosopo RC 2.50 6.00
153 Correll Buckhalter RC 2.00 5.00
154 Freddie Mitchell RC 2.00 5.00
155 Joey Getherall RC 2.00 5.00
156 Chris Taylor RC 2.00 5.00
157 Adam Archuleta RC 2.50 6.00
158 David Rivers RC 2.00 5.00
159 Francis St. Paul RC 2.00 5.00
160 Drew Brees RC 40.00 80.00
161 LaDainian Tomlinson RC 10.00 25.00
162 David Allen RC 2.00 5.00
163 Kevan Barlow RC 2.50 6.00
164 Andre Carter RC 2.50 6.00
165 Cedrick Wilson RC 2.50 6.00
166 Alex Bannister RC 2.00 5.00
167 Josh Booty RC 2.50 6.00
168 Heath Evans RC 2.50 6.00
169 Koren Robinson RC 2.50 6.00
170 Margin Hooks RC 2.00 5.00
171 Dan Alexander RC 2.50 6.00
172 Eddie Berlin RC 2.00 5.00
173 Rod Gardner RC 2.50 6.00
174 Damerien McCants RC 2.50 6.00
175 Sage Rosenfels RC 2.50 6.00

2001 Private Stock Blue Framed

*VETS 1-100: 5X TO 12X BASIC CARDS
*ROOKIES 101-175: .5X TO 1.2X
STATED PRINT RUN 75 SER. #'d SETS

2001 Private Stock Gold Framed

*VETS 1-100: 6X TO 15X BASIC CARDS
*ROOKIES 101-175: .6X TO 1.5X
STATED PRINT RUN 49 SER. #'d SETS

2001 Private Stock Premiere Date

*VETS 1-100: 3X TO 8X BASIC CARDS
*ROOKIES 101-175: .3X TO .8X
STATED PRINT RUN 95 SER. #'d SETS

2001 Private Stock Retail

COMP.SET w/o RCs (100) 30.00 60.00
*VETS 1-100: .4X TO 1X HOBBY
*ROOKIES 101-175: .25X TO .6X HOBBY
101-175 ROOKIES PRINT RUN 500

2001 Private Stock Silver Framed

*VETS 1-100: 3X TO 8X BASIC CARDS
*ROOKIES 101-175: .3X TO .8X
STATED PRINT RUN 99 SER. #'d SETS

2001 Private Stock Artists Reserve

Artists Reserve were inserted in packs of 2001 Pacific Private Stock. This 10-card set featured some of the top rookies from the 2001 NFL Draft. Each card was serial numbered to 99.

COMPLETE SET (10) 50.00 120.00
STATED PRINT RUN 99 SER.#'d SETS
1 Michael Vick 5.00 12.00
2 Chris Weinke 2.50 6.00
3 David Terrell 2.50 6.00
4 Quincy Carter 2.50 6.00
5 Michael Bennett 2.50 6.00
6 Deuce McAllister 3.00 8.00
7 Marques Tuiasosopo 2.50 6.00
8 Drew Brees 60.00 125.00
9 LaDainian Tomlinson 10.00 25.00
10 Koren Robinson 2.50 6.00

2001 Private Stock Game Worn Gear

Game Worn Gear was randomly inserted in packs of 2001 Pacific Private Stock at a rate of 1:1 hobby and 1:49 retail. The 150-card set featured a swatch from a game uniform of the featured player. The set was broken into 140 jersey cards and 10 pants cards.

STATED ODDS 1:1 HOB, 1:49 RET
*PATCH/175-375: .6X TO 1.5X BASIC JSY
*PATCH/75-150: .8X TO 2X BASIC JSY
*PATCH/50: 1X TO 2.5X BASIC JSY
*PATCH/25: 1.5X TO 4X BASIC JSY
PATCH PRINT RUN 25-375
1 Thomas Jones JSY 2.00 5.00
2 Rob Moore 2.00 5.00
3 Jake Plummer JSY 2.00 5.00
4 Frank Sanders 2.00 5.00
5 Chris Chandler 2.50 6.00
6 Doug Johnson 2.00 5.00
7 Terance Mathis 2.00 5.00
8 Randall Cunningham 2.50 6.00
9 Elvis Grbac 2.50 6.00
10 Jamal Lewis 3.00 8.00
12 Shawn Bryson 2.00 5.00
13 Kwame Cavil 2.00 5.00
14 Jonathan Linton 2.00 5.00
15 Jeremy McDaniel 2.00 5.00
16 Eric Moulds 2.00 5.00
17 Thurman Thomas 2.50 6.00
18 Michael Bates 2.00 5.00
19 Dameyune Craig 2.00 5.00
20 William Floyd 2.00 5.00
21 Patrick Jeffers 2.00 5.00
22 Wesley Walls 2.00 5.00
23 Chris Weinke 2.50 6.00
24 Marlon Barnes 2.00 5.00
25 D'Wayne Bates 2.00 5.00
26 Marty Booker 2.00 5.00
27 Cade McNown 2.50 6.00
28 Anthony Thomas 3.00 8.00
29 Brian Urlacher 4.00 10.00
30 Brandon Bennett 2.00 5.00
31 Curtis Keaton 2.00 5.00
32 Jon Kitna 2.00 5.00
33 Peter Warrick JSY 2.00 5.00
34 Darrin Chiaverini 2.00 5.00
35 Tim Couch 2.00 5.00
36 Rickey Dudley 2.00 5.00
37 Curtis Enis 2.00 5.00
38 Kevin Johnson 2.00 5.00
39 Dennis Northcutt 2.00 5.00
40 Troy Aikman 4.00 10.00
41 Wane McGarity 2.00 5.00
42 Carl Pickens 2.50 6.00
43 Emmitt Smith 5.00 12.00
44 Michael Wiley 2.00 5.00
45 Anthony Wright 2.00 5.00
46 Mike Anderson 2.00 5.00
47 Steve Beuerlein 2.50 6.00
48 Terrell Davis 2.50 6.00
49 Olandis Gary 2.00 5.00
50 Brian Griese 2.00 5.00
51 Eddie Kennison 2.50 6.00
52 Deltha O'Neal 2.00 5.00
53 Keith Poole 2.00 5.00
54 Bill Romanowski 2.50 6.00
55 Charlie Batch 2.00 5.00
56 Desmond Howard 2.50 6.00
57 Sedrick Irvin 2.00 5.00
58 Tyrone Davis 2.00 5.00
60 Brett Favre 6.00 15.00
61 Ahman Green 2.50 6.00
62 Charles Lee 2.00 5.00
63 Bill Schroeder 2.50 6.00
64 E.G. Green 2.00 5.00
65 Edgerrin James 2.50 6.00
66 Peyton Manning 8.00 20.00
67 Jerome Pathon 2.00 5.00
68 Marcus Pollard 2.00 5.00
69 Kyle Brady 2.00 5.00
70 Mark Brunell 2.50 6.00
71 Jamie Martin 2.00 5.00
72 Keenan McCardell 2.50 6.00
73 Shyrone Stith 2.00 5.00
74 Fred Taylor 2.00 5.00
75 Alvis Whitted 2.00 5.00
76 Derrick Alexander 2.00 5.00
77 Kimble Anders 2.00 5.00
78 Mike Cloud 2.00 5.00
79 Trent Green 2.00 5.00
80 Tony Horne 2.00 5.00
81 Warren Moon 3.00 8.00
82 Rob Konrad 2.00 5.00
83 Ray Lucas 2.00 5.00
84 Tony Martin 2.50 6.00
85 O.J. McDuffie 2.00 5.00
86 James McKnight 2.00 5.00
87 Leslie Shepherd 2.00 5.00
88 Dedric Ward 2.00 5.00
89 Cris Carter 3.00 8.00
90 Daunte Culpepper 2.50 6.00
91 Randy Moss 2.50 6.00
92 Jake Reed 2.50 6.00
93 Robert Smith 2.00 5.00
94 Moe Williams 2.00 5.00
95 Michael Bishop 2.50 6.00
96 Drew Bledsoe 2.50 6.00
97 Troy Brown 2.00 5.00
98 Bert Emanuel 2.00 5.00
99 David Patten 2.00 5.00
100 J.R. Redmond 2.00 5.00
101 Albert Connell 2.00 5.00
102 Willie Jackson 2.00 5.00
103 Chad Morton 2.00 5.00
104 Ricky Williams 2.50 6.00
105 Ron Dayne 2.50 6.00
106 Ron Dixon 2.00 5.00
107 Joe Jurevicius 2.00 5.00
108 Richie Anderson 2.00 5.00
109 Matthew Hatchette 2.00 5.00
110 Chad Pennington 2.00 5.00
111 Reggie Barlow 2.00 5.00
112 Napoleon Kaufman 2.00 5.00
113 Jerry Rice 6.00 15.00
114 Andre Rison 2.50 6.00
115 Marques Tuiasosopo 2.50 6.00
116 Charles Woodson 3.00 8.00
118 Freddie Mitchell 2.00 5.00
119 Trung Canidate 2.00 5.00
120 Marshall Faulk JSY 2.50 6.00
121 Kurt Warner JSY 5.00 12.00
122 Drew Brees 12.00 30.00
124 Jermaine Fazande 2.00 5.00
125 Doug Flutie 2.50 6.00
126 LaDainian Tomlinson 10.00 25.00
127 Jeff Garcia 2.00 5.00
128 Tai Streets 2.00 5.00
129 Shaun Alexander 2.00 5.00
130 Matt Hasselbeck 2.00 5.00
131 Warrick Dunn 2.00 5.00
132 Shaun King 2.00 5.00
133 Ryan Leaf 2.00 5.00
134 Eddie George 3.00 8.00
135 Jevon Kearse 2.00 5.00
136 Steve McNair 2.50 6.00
137 Chris Sanders 2.00 5.00
138 Donnell Bennett 2.00 5.00
139 Kevin Lockett 2.00 5.00
140 David Boston Pants 2.00 5.00
141 Thomas Jones Pants 2.00 5.00
142 Jake Plummer Pants 2.00 5.00
143 Corey Dillon Pants 2.00 5.00
144 Akili Smith Pants 2.00 5.00
145 Peter Warrick Pants 2.00 5.00
146 Isaac Bruce Pants 3.00 8.00
147 Marshall Faulk Pants 2.50 6.00
148 Az-Zahir Hakim Pants 2.00 5.00
149 Torry Holt Pants 2.50 6.00
150 Kurt Warner Pants 5.00 12.00

2001 Private Stock Moments In Time

Moments In Time were randomly inserted into packs of 2001 Pacific Private Stock. This 15-card set featured some of the top players from the 2001 NFL Draft. Each of these cards were serial numbered to 499.

COMPLETE SET (15) 25.00 60.00
STATED PRINT RUN 499 SER.#'d SETS
1 Michael Vick 1.25 3.00
2 Travis Henry .60 1.50
3 Chris Weinke .60 1.50
4 David Terrell .60 1.50
5 Anthony Thomas .75 2.00
6 Quincy Carter .60 1.50
7 Michael Bennett .60 1.50
8 Deuce McAllister .75 2.00
9 Santana Moss .75 2.00
10 Marques Tuiasosopo .60 1.50
11 Freddie Mitchell .50 1.25
12 Drew Brees 15.00 40.00
13 LaDainian Tomlinson 2.50 6.00
14 Koren Robinson .60 1.50
15 Rod Gardner .60 1.50

2001 Private Stock PS-2001

PS-2001 cards were randomly inserted into packs of 2001 Pacific Private Stock at a rate of 2 per pack. This 162-card set featured 10 short printed cards with blue backs. The cards were unintentionally printed with two versions having different sized card numbers on the back.

COMP.SET w/o SP's (152) 40.00 80.00
OVERALL STATED ODDS TWO PER PACK
*SMALL CARD #: .4X TO 1X BASIC CARD
1 David Boston .30 .75
2 Thomas Jones .30 .75
3 Jake Plummer .30 .75
4 Jamal Anderson .40 1.00
5 Terance Mathis .30 .75
6 Elvis Grbac .40 1.00
7 Jamal Lewis .50 1.25
8 Chris Redman .50 1.25
9 Shannon Sharpe .40 1.00
10 Travis Taylor .30 .75
11 Rob Johnson .40 1.00
12 Eric Moulds .30 .75
13 Peerless Price .30 .75
14 Tim Biakabutuka .30 .75
15 Patrick Jeffers .30 .75
16 Muhsin Muhammad .30 .75
17 James Allen .30 .75
18 Cade McNown .40 1.00
19 Marcus Robinson .40 1.00
20 Brian Urlacher .60 1.50
21 Corey Dillon .30 .75
22 Peter Warrick .30 .75
23 Tim Couch .30 .75
24 Kevin Johnson .30 .75
25 Dennis Northcutt .30 .75
26 Travis Prentice .30 .75
27 Rocket Ismail .40 1.00
28 Emmitt Smith .75 2.00
29 Mike Anderson .30 .75
30 Terrell Davis .40 1.00
31 Brian Griese .30 .75
32 Ed McCaffrey .40 1.00
33 Charlie Batch .30 .75
34 Johnnie Morton .40 1.00
35 James Stewart .30 .75
36 Brett Favre 1.00 2.50
37 Antonio Freeman .50 1.25
38 Ahman Green .40 1.00
39 Marvin Harrison .40 1.00
40 Jerome Pathon .30 .75
41 Terrence Wilkins .30 .75
42 Mark Brunell .40 1.00
43 Keenan McCardell .40 1.00
44 Jimmy Smith .40 1.00
45 Fred Taylor .30 .75
46 Derrick Alexander .30 .75
47 Tony Gonzalez .40 1.00
48 Trent Green .30 .75
49 Sylvester Morris .30 .75
50 Jay Fiedler .40 1.00
51 Oronde Gadsden .30 .75
52 Lamar Smith .40 1.00
53 Cris Carter .50 1.25
54 Doug Chapman .30 .75
55 Daunte Culpepper .40 1.00
56 Drew Bledsoe .40 1.00
57 Kevin Faulk .30 .75
58 Terry Glenn .40 1.00
59 J.R. Redmond .30 .75
60 Jeff Blake .40 1.00
61 Aaron Brooks .30 .75
62 Joe Horn .30 .75
63 Ricky Williams .40 1.00
64 Tiki Barber .40 1.00
65 Kerry Collins .30 .75
66 Ron Dayne .40 1.00
67 Amani Toomer .30 .75
68 Curtis Martin .40 1.00
69 Chad Pennington .30 .75
70 Vinny Testaverde .30 .75
71 Tim Brown .50 1.25
72 Rich Gannon .40 1.00
73 Jerry Rice 1.00 2.50
74 Tyrone Wheatley .40 1.00
75 Donovan McNabb .40 1.00
76 Duce Staley .30 .75
77 Jerome Bettis .50 1.25
78 Kordell Stewart .30 .75
79 Isaac Bruce .50 1.25
80 Marshall Faulk .40 1.00
81 Az-Zahir Hakim .30 .75
82 Torry Holt .40 1.00
83 Tim Dwight .40 1.00
84 Doug Flutie .40 1.00
85 Jeff Garcia .30 .75
86 Terrell Owens .40 1.00
87 Shaun Alexander .30 .75
88 Matt Hasselbeck .30 .75
89 Darrell Jackson .40 1.00
90 Ricky Watters .40 1.00
91 Mike Alstott .30 .75
92 Warrick Dunn .30 .75
93 Brad Johnson .40 1.00
94 Keyshawn Johnson .40 1.00
95 Eddie George .50 1.25
96 Derrick Mason .30 .75
97 Steve McNair .40 1.00
98 Stephen Davis .30 .75
99 Jeff George .40 1.00
100 Michael Westbrook .30 .75
101 Bobby Newcombe .40 1.00
102 Alge Crumpler .50 1.25
103 Vinny Sutherland .30 .75
104 Todd Heap .40 1.00
105 Tim Hasselbeck .40 1.00
106 Travis Henry .40 1.00
107 Dee Brown .30 .75
108 Dan Morgan .40 1.00
109 Steve Smith 1.00 2.50
110 Chris Weinke .40 1.00
111 Anthony Thomas .50 1.25
112 T.J. Houshmandzadeh .40 1.00
113 Chad Johnson .50 1.25
114 Rudi Johnson .50 1.25
115 James Jackson .30 .75
116 Quincy Morgan .40 1.00
117 Quincy Carter .40 1.00
118 Kevin Kasper .30 .75
119 Scotty Anderson .30 .75
120 Mike McMahon .40 1.00
121 Robert Ferguson .50 1.25
122 Reggie Wayne .60 1.50
123 Derrick Blaylock .40 1.00
124 Snoop Minnis .30 .75
125 Chris Chambers .30 .75
126 Jamar Fletcher .30 .75
127 Josh Heupel .50 1.25
128 Travis Minor .40 1.00
129 Michael Bennett .40 1.00
130 Deuce McAllister .50 1.25
131 Moran Norris .30 .75
132 Will Allen .50 1.25
133 Jonathan Carter .30 .75
134 Jesse Palmer .40 1.00
135 LaMont Jordan .50 1.25
136 Ken-Yon Rambo .30 .75
137 Marques Tuiasosopo .40 1.00
138 Correll Buckhalter .30 .75
139 Freddie Mitchell .30 .75
140 Chris Taylor .30 .75
141 Adam Archuleta .40 1.00
142 Francis St. Paul .30 .75
143 Kevan Barlow .40 1.00
144 Cedrick Wilson .40 1.00
145 Alex Bannister .30 .75
146 Josh Booty .40 1.00
147 Heath Evans .40 1.00
148 Dan Alexander .40 1.00
149 Eddie Berlin .30 .75
150 Rod Gardner .40 1.00
151 Damerien McCants .40 1.00
152 Sage Rosenfels .40 1.00
153 Michael Vick SP
154 David Terrell SP
155 Edgerrin James SP
156 Peyton Manning SP
157 Randy Moss SP
158 Santana Moss SP
159 Kurt Warner SP
160 Drew Brees SP
161 LaDainian Tomlinson SP
162 Koren Robinson SP

2001 Private Stock Reserve

Reserve was inserted into hobby packs of 2001 Pacific Private Stock at a rate of 1:21. This 20-card set featured top players from the NFL. The cards were printed on a lightweight paper stock similar to that of a business card. The cards were highlighted with gold-foil markings.

COMPLETE SET (20) 40.00 80.00
STATED ODDS 1:21 HOBBY
1 Jamal Lewis 2.00 5.00
2 Peter Warrick 1.25 3.00
3 Emmitt Smith 3.00 8.00
4 Mike Anderson 1.25 3.00
5 Terrell Davis 1.50 4.00
6 Brian Griese 1.50 4.00
7 Brett Favre 5.00 12.00
8 Edgerrin James 2.00 5.00
9 Peyton Manning 4.00 10.00
10 Mark Brunell 1.50 4.00
11 Daunte Culpepper 1.50 4.00
12 Randy Moss 3.00 8.00
13 Drew Bledsoe 2.00 5.00
14 Ricky Williams 1.50 4.00
15 Ron Dayne 1.25 3.00
16 Donovan McNabb 2.00 5.00
17 Marshall Faulk 2.00 5.00
18 Kurt Warner 3.00 8.00
19 Eddie George 1.50 4.00
20 Steve McNair 1.50 4.00

2002 Private Stock

This 150-card set includes 100 veterans and 50 rookie year players. The rookie year player cards were serial numbered to their jersey number and feature a swatch of a game-used football on the front.

COMP.SET w/o SP's (100) 15.00 40.00
1 David Boston .30 .75
2 Thomas Jones .30 .75
3 Jake Plummer .30 .75
4 Jamal Anderson .40 1.00
5 Warrick Dunn .30 .75
6 Shawn Jefferson .30 .75
7 Michael Vick .40 1.00
8 Jamal Lewis .40 1.00
9 Chris Redman .30 .75
10 Travis Taylor .30 .75
11 Travis Henry .30 .75
12 Eric Moulds .30 .75
13 Peerless Price .30 .75
14 Muhsin Muhammad .30 .75
15 Lamar Smith .30 .75
16 Chris Weinke .30 .75
17 Marty Booker .30 .75
18 Jim Miller .30 .75
19 Anthony Thomas .40 1.00
20 Corey Dillon .30 .75
21 Darnay Scott .40 1.00
22 Peter Warrick .30 .75
23 Tim Couch .30 .75
24 James Jackson .30 .75
25 Kevin Johnson .30 .75
26 Quincy Carter .30 .75
27 Rocket Ismail .40 1.00
28 Emmitt Smith .75 2.00
29 Mike Anderson .30 .75
30 Terrell Davis .40 1.00
31 Brian Griese .30 .75
32 Rod Smith .40 1.00
33 Mike McMahon .30 .75
34 Johnnie Morton .40 1.00
35 Brett Favre 1.00 2.50
36 Antonio Freeman .50 1.25
37 Ahman Green .40 1.00
38 Corey Bradford .30 .75
39 Jermaine Lewis .30 .75
40 Jamie Sharper .40 1.00
41 Marvin Harrison .40 1.00
42 Edgerrin James .40 1.00
43 Mark Brunell .40 1.00
44 Jimmy Smith .40 1.00
45 Fred Taylor .30 .75
46 Tony Gonzalez .40 1.00
47 Trent Green .30 .75
48 Priest Holmes .30 .75
49 Chris Chambers .30 .75
50 Jay Fiedler .40 1.00
51 James McKnight .30 .75
52 Ricky Williams .40 1.00
53 Michael Bennett .30 .75
54 Cris Carter .50 1.25
55 Daunte Culpepper .40 1.00
56 Randy Moss .40 1.00
57 Drew Bledsoe .40 1.00
58 Tom Brady 2.50 6.00
59 Troy Brown .30 .75
60 Antowain Smith .40 1.00
61 Aaron Brooks .30 .75
62 Joe Horn .30 .75
63 Deuce McAllister .40 1.00
64 Tiki Barber .40 1.00
65 Kerry Collins .30 .75
66 Ron Dayne .40 1.00
67 Laveranues Coles .40 1.00
68 Curtis Martin .40 1.00
69 Vinny Testaverde .30 .75
70 Tim Brown .50 1.25
71 Rich Gannon .40 1.00
72 Jerry Rice 1.00 2.50
73 Correll Buckhalter .30 .75
74 Duce Staley .30 .75
75 James Thrash .40 1.00
76 Jerome Bettis .50 1.25
77 Plaxico Burress .30 .75
78 Kordell Stewart .30 .75
79 Hines Ward .40 1.00
80 Isaac Bruce .50 1.25
81 Marshall Faulk .40 1.00
82 Torry Holt .40 1.00
83 Kurt Warner .40 1.00
84 Drew Brees 1.00 2.50
85 Doug Flutie .40 1.00
86 LaDainian Tomlinson .50 1.25
87 Jeff Garcia .30 .75
88 Garrison Hearst .30 .75
89 Terrell Owens .40 1.00
90 Shaun Alexander .30 .75
91 Trent Dilfer .30 .75
92 Darrell Jackson .40 1.00
93 Ricky Watters .40 1.00
94 Brad Johnson .40 1.00
95 Keyshawn Johnson .40 1.00
96 Eddie George .40 1.00
97 Derrick Mason .30 .75
98 Steve McNair .40 1.00
99 Stephen Davis .30 .75
100 Rod Gardner .30 .75
101 Damien Anderson FB/20 10.00 25.00
102 Ladell Betts FB/46 15.00 40.00
103 Antonio Bryant FB/80 12.00 30.00
104 Wendell Bryant FB/77 8.00 20.00
111 Andre Davis FB/88 8.00 20.00
113 DeShaun Foster FB/26 15.00 40.00
116 Lamar Gordon FB/28 12.00 30.00
117 Daniel Graham FB/89 10.00 25.00
121 Verron Haynes FB/35 10.00 25.00
122 John Henderson FB/98 10.00 25.00
132 James Mungro FB/23 15.00 40.00
135 Brian Poli-Dixon FB/82 8.00 20.00
136 Clinton Portis FB/28 15.00 40.00
139 Josh Reed FB/25 12.00 30.00
143 Jeremy Shockey FB/88 12.00 30.00
147 Javon Walker FB/80 12.00 30.00
149 Brian Westbrook FB/20 20.00 50.00
150 Roy Williams FB/38 10.00 25.00

2002 Private Stock Retail

*RETAIL VETS 1-100: .25X TO .6X HOBBY
101 Damien Anderson RC .60 1.50
102 Ladell Betts RC 1.00 2.50
103 Antonio Bryant RC 1.00 2.50
104 Wendell Bryant RC .60 1.50
105 Reche Caldwell RC .75 2.00
106 Kelly Campbell RC .75 2.00
107 David Carr RC .60 1.50
108 Eric Crouch RC 1.00 2.50
109 Ronald Curry RC .60 1.50
110 Rohan Davey RC 1.00 2.50
111 Andre Davis RC .60 1.50
112 T.J. Duckett RC .60 1.50
113 DeShaun Foster RC 1.00 2.50
114 Jabar Gaffney RC .60 1.50
115 David Garrard RC .75 2.00
116 Lamar Gordon RC .75 2.00
117 Daniel Graham RC .75 2.00
118 William Green RC .75 2.00
119 Joey Harrington RC .60 1.50
120 Napoleon Harris RC .75 2.00
121 Verron Haynes RC .60 1.50
122 John Henderson RC .75 2.00
123 Kahlil Hill RC .60 1.50
124 Quentin Jammer RC 1.00 2.50
125 Ron Johnson RC .75 2.00
126 Kurt Kittner RC .60 1.50
127 Zak Kustok RC .60 1.50
128 Ashley Lelie RC .60 1.50
129 Josh McCown RC 1.00 2.50
130 Freddie Milons RC .60 1.50
131 Maurice Morris RC .75 2.00
132 James Mungro RC 1.00 2.50
133 David Neill RC .60 1.50
134 Adrian Peterson RC .75 2.00
135 Brian Poli-Dixon RC .60 1.50
136 Clinton Portis RC 1.00 2.50
137 Patrick Ramsey RC .75 2.00
138 Antwaan Randle El RC .75 2.00
139 Josh Reed RC .75 2.00
140 Cliff Russell RC .60 1.50
141 Josh Scobey RC .75 2.00
142 Lito Sheppard RC 1.00 2.50
143 Jeremy Shockey RC 1.00 2.50
144 Luke Staley RC .60 1.50
145 Donte Stallworth RC 1.00 2.50
146 Lamont Thompson RC .75 2.00
147 Javon Walker RC 1.00 2.50
148 Marquise Walker RC .60 1.50
149 Brian Westbrook RC 1.25 3.00
150 Roy Williams RC .60 1.50

2002 Private Stock Atomic Previews

This 25-card insert was inserted in packs at a rate of 1:9. These cards were meant to preview the 2002 Pacific Atomic brand.

STATED ODDS 1:9
101 Damien Anderson 1.00 2.50
102 Ladell Betts 1.50 4.00
103 Antonio Bryant 1.50 4.00
104 Reche Caldwell 1.25 3.00
105 Kelly Campbell 1.25 3.00
106 David Carr 1.00 2.50
107 Rohan Davey 1.50 4.00
108 Andre Davis 1.00 2.50
109 T.J. Duckett 1.00 2.50
110 DeShaun Foster 1.50 4.00
111 David Garrard 1.25 3.00
112 Lamar Gordon 1.25 3.00
113 William Green 1.25 3.00
114 Joey Harrington 1.00 2.50
115 Kurt Kittner 1.00 2.50
116 Ashley Lelie 1.00 2.50
117 Josh McCown 1.50 4.00
118 Clinton Portis 1.50 4.00
119 Patrick Ramsey 1.25 3.00
120 Antwaan Randle El 1.25 3.00
121 Josh Reed 1.25 3.00
122 Luke Staley 1.00 2.50
123 Donte Stallworth 1.50 4.00
124 Marquise Walker 1.00 2.50
125 Brian Westbrook 2.00 5.00

2002 Private Stock Banner Year

This 10-card set was inserted in packs at a rate of 1:17. The set is standard sized and is designed to resemble that of a hanging banner.

COMPLETE SET (10) 15.00 40.00
STATED ODDS 1:17
1 Michael Vick 1.00 2.50
2 Anthony Thomas 1.00 2.50
3 Emmitt Smith 2.00 5.00
4 Brett Favre 2.50 6.00
5 Randy Moss 1.00 2.50
6 Tom Brady 6.00 15.00
7 Jerry Rice 2.50 6.00
8 Marshall Faulk 1.00 2.50
9 Kurt Warner 1.00 2.50
10 LaDainian Tomlinson 1.25 3.00

2002 Private Stock Class Act

Inserted in packs at a rate of 2:9, this 20-card insert set includes cards from many of the best 2002 rookies.

COMPLETE SET (20) 12.00 30.00
STATED ODDS 2:9
1 Antonio Bryant .75 2.00
2 Reche Caldwell .60 1.50
3 David Carr .50 1.25
4 Eric Crouch .75 2.00
5 Rohan Davey .75 2.00
6 Andre Davis .50 1.25
7 T.J. Duckett .50 1.25
8 DeShaun Foster .75 2.00
9 Lamar Gordon .60 1.50
10 William Green .60 1.50
11 Joey Harrington .50 1.25
12 Kurt Kittner .50 1.25
13 Ashley Lelie .50 1.25
14 Josh McCown .75 2.00
15 Clinton Portis .75 2.00
16 Patrick Ramsey .60 1.50
17 Antwaan Randle El .60 1.50
18 Josh Reed .60 1.50
19 Luke Staley .50 1.25
20 Donte Stallworth .75 2.00

2002 Private Stock Divisional Realignment

Inserted in packs at a rate of 1:9, this 32-card insert set highlights players from teams involved in the divisional realignment for 2002.

STATED ODDS 1:9
1 David Boston .75 2.00
2 Michael Vick 1.00 2.50
3 Jamal Lewis 1.00 2.50
4 Travis Henry .75 2.00
5 Chris Weinke .75 2.00
6 Anthony Thomas 1.00 2.50
7 Corey Dillon .75 2.00
8 Tim Couch .75 2.00
9 Emmitt Smith 2.00 5.00
10 Terrell Davis 1.00 2.50
11 Mike McMahon .75 2.00
12 Brett Favre 2.50 6.00
13 Jermaine Lewis .75 2.00
14 Edgerrin James 1.00 2.50
15 Mark Brunell 1.00 2.50
16 Priest Holmes .75 2.00
17 Chris Chambers .75 2.00
18 Randy Moss 1.00 2.50
19 Tom Brady 6.00 15.00
20 Aaron Brooks .75 2.00
21 Ron Dayne 1.00 2.50
22 Curtis Martin 1.00 2.50
23 Jerry Rice 2.50 6.00
24 Duce Staley .75 2.00
25 Jerome Bettis 1.25 3.00
26 Kurt Warner 1.00 2.50
27 LaDainian Tomlinson 1.25 3.00
28 Jeff Garcia .75 2.00
29 Shaun Alexander .75 2.00
30 Mike Alstott .75 2.00
31 Eddie George 1.00 2.50
32 Rod Gardner .75 2.00

2002 Private Stock Game Worn Jerseys

This 125 card insert set was inserted in packs at a rate of one per. The announced print runs vary from 500 to 1000 and were provided by Pacific on some cards as noted below. Each card contains a swatch of game worn jersey.

OVERALL ODDS ONE PER PACK
ANNOUNCED PRINT RUNS 56-1000

1 David Boston 2.50 6.00
2 Steve Bush 2.50 6.00
3 Arnold Jackson 2.50 6.00
4 Thomas Jones/398* 2.50 6.00
5 Rob Moore/400* 2.50 6.00
6 Jake Plummer 2.50 6.00
7 Jamal Anderson/395* 3.00 8.00
8 Maurice Smith 2.50 6.00
9 Michael Vick/510* 3.00 8.00
10 Todd Heap 2.50 6.00
11 Travis Taylor/511* 2.50 6.00
12 Randall Cunningham/250* 3.00 8.00
13 Elvis Grbac 2.50 6.00
14 Jamal Lewis/100* 4.00 10.00
15 Ray Lewis 4.00 10.00
16 Shannon Sharpe/560* 3.00 8.00
17 Moe Williams 2.50 6.00
18 Larry Centers 2.50 6.00
19 Travis Henry/387* 2.50 6.00
20 Isaac Byrd/112* 3.00 8.00
21 Jim Harbaugh 3.00 8.00
22 Richard Huntley 2.50 6.00
23 Chris Weinke/410* 2.50 6.00
24 Autry Denson 2.50 6.00
25 David Terrell/259* 2.50 6.00
26 Anthony Thomas/111* 4.00 10.00
27 Brian Urlacher/512* 4.00 10.00
28 Corey Dillon/500* 2.50 6.00
29 T.J. Houshmandzadeh/313* 2.50 6.00
30 Chad Johnson/264* 2.50 6.00
31 Rudi Johnson 2.50 6.00
32 Jon Kitna 2.50 6.00
33 Peter Warrick/276* 2.50 6.00
34 Tim Couch/510* 2.50 6.00
35 Darrin Chiaverini/111* 3.00 8.00
36 Richmond Flowers 2.50 6.00
37 Joey Galloway 3.00 8.00
38 La'Roi Glover/506* 2.50 6.00
39 Troy Hambrick/260* 2.50 6.00
40 Emmitt Smith 12.00 30.00
41 Mike Anderson/197* 2.50 6.00
42 Tony Carter 2.50 6.00
43 Terrell Davis 3.00 8.00
44 Brian Griese 2.50 6.00
45 Todd Husak 3.00 8.00
46 Kevin Kasper/313* 2.50 6.00
47 Scotty Anderson/260* 2.50 6.00
48 Karsten Bailey/302* 2.50 6.00
49 Reggie Brown 3.00 8.00
50 Brett Favre 12.00 30.00
51 Robert Ferguson/262* 3.00 8.00
52 Antonio Freeman 4.00 10.00
53 Ahman Green/490* 3.00 8.00
54 David Martin/508* 2.50 6.00
55 Jermaine Lewis 2.50 6.00
56 Frank Moreau 2.50 6.00
57 Marvin Harrison 3.00 8.00
58 Edgerrin James/411* 3.00 8.00
59 Tony Simmons 2.50 6.00
60 Mark Brunell 3.00 8.00
61 Sean Dawkins 3.00 8.00
62 Jimmy Smith 3.00 8.00
63 Fred Taylor 2.50 6.00
64 Tony Gonzalez 3.00 8.00
65 Trent Green 2.50 6.00
66 Mikhael Ricks 2.50 6.00
67 Cade McNown/259* 3.00 8.00
68 Ricky Williams 3.00 8.00
69 Michael Bennett/159* 2.50 6.00
70 Cris Carter 4.00 10.00
71 Corey Chavous 2.50 6.00
72 Daunte Culpepper/510* 3.00 8.00
73 Randy Moss/509* 6.00 15.00
74 Travis Prentice 2.50 6.00
75 Drew Bledsoe 3.00 8.00
76 Tom Brady/505* 12.00 30.00
77 Marc Edwards 2.50 6.00
78 Kevin Faulk 2.50 6.00
79 Antowain Smith 3.00 8.00
80 Aaron Brooks/261* 2.50 6.00
81 Albert Connell/503* 2.50 6.00
82 Deuce McAllister/162* 3.00 8.00
83 Wane McGarity/170* 2.50 6.00
84 Jake Reed 3.00 8.00
85 Ron Dayne/504* 3.00 8.00
86 Curtis Martin/442* 3.00 8.00
87 Chad Morton 2.50 6.00
88 Craig Yeast/67* 3.00 8.00
89 Tim Brown 4.00 10.00
90 Rich Gannon 3.00 8.00
91 Charlie Garner 3.00 8.00
92 Jerry Rice 8.00 20.00
93 Freddie Mitchell/309* 2.50 6.00
94 Todd Pinkston 2.50 6.00
95 James Thrash 3.00 8.00
96 Jerome Bettis 8.00 20.00
97 Kordell Stewart 2.50 6.00
98 Hines Ward 3.00 8.00
99 Isaac Bruce/511* 4.00 10.00
100 Marshall Faulk 3.00 8.00
101 Damon Griffin 2.50 6.00
102 Kurt Warner/509* 5.00 12.00
103 Drew Brees/497* 8.00 20.00
104 Doug Flutie 3.00 8.00
105 LaDainian Tomlinson/405* 4.00 10.00
106 Jeff Garcia/435* 2.50 6.00
107 Terrell Owens 3.00 8.00
108 Tim Rattay 3.00 8.00
109 Shockmain Davis 2.50 6.00
110 Bobby Engram/56* 3.00 8.00
111 Matt Hasselbeck 2.50 6.00
112 Koren Robinson/314* 2.50 6.00
113 Ricky Watters/403* 3.00 8.00
114 Mike Alstott/500* 2.50 6.00
115 Marco Battaglia 2.50 6.00
116 Rob Johnson 3.00 8.00
117 Brad Johnson 3.00 8.00
118 Michael Pittman 3.00 8.00
119 Dan Alexander 2.50 6.00
120 Eddie Berlin 2.50 6.00
121 Eddie George 3.00 8.00
122 Skip Hicks 2.50 6.00
123 Derrick Mason 2.50 6.00
124 Steve McNair 3.00 8.00
125 Rod Gardner/260* 2.50 6.00

2002 Private Stock Game Worn Jerseys Logos

This set is a parallel of the Game Worn Jerseys set, with each card featuring a team logo die-cut and a swatch of game worn jersey.

COMMON CARD/104-194 3.00 8.00
SEMISTARS/104-194 4.00 10.00
UNL.STARS/104-194 5.00 12.00
COMMON CARD/60-92 4.00 10.00
SEMISTARS/60-92 5.00 12.00
UNL.STARS/60-92 6.00 15.00
COMMON CARD/30-56 5.00 12.00
SEMISTARS/30-56 6.00 15.00
UNL.STARS/30-56 8.00 20.00
COMMON CARD/20-28 8.00 20.00
UNL.STARS/20-28 10.00 25.00
STATED PRINT RUN 2-194
SERIAL #'d UNDER 20 NOT PRICED
27 Brian Urlacher/108 5.00 12.00
40 Emmitt Smith/44 12.00 30.00
76 Tom Brady/24 50.00 125.00
92 Jerry Rice/160 10.00 25.00
105 LaDainian Tomlinson/42 8.00 20.00

2002 Private Stock Game Worn Jerseys Numbers

This set is a parallel of the Game Worn Jerseys set, with each card featuring a number die-cut and a swatch of game worn jersey. Cards are numbered to the players jersey number.

COMMON CARD/80-97 4.00 10.00
SEMISTARS/80-97 5.00 12.00
UNL.STARS/80-97 6.00 15.00
COMMON CARD/30-54 5.00 12.00
SEMISTARS/30-54 6.00 15.00
UNL.STARS/30-54 8.00 20.00
COMMON CARD/20-29 6.00 15.00
SEMISTARS/20-29 8.00 20.00
UNL.STARS/20-29 10.00 25.00
STATED PRINT RUN 1-97
SERIAL #'d UNDER 20 NOT PRICED
27 Brian Urlacher/54 8.00 20.00
40 Emmitt Smith/22 15.00 40.00
73 Randy Moss/84 8.00 20.00
92 Jerry Rice/80 12.00 30.00
105 LaDainian Tomlinson/21 10.00 25.00

2002 Private Stock Game Worn Jerseys Patches

This set is a parallel of the Game Worn Jerseys set, with each serial numbered card featuring a patch swatch from a game worn jersey.

COMMON CARD (1-122) 3.00 8.00
SEMISTARS 4.00 10.00
UNLISTED STARS 5.00 12.00
COMMON CARD/76-102 4.00 10.00
SEMISTARS/76-102 5.00 12.00
COMMON CARD/31-55 5.00 12.00
SEMISTARS/31-55 6.00 15.00
COMMON CARD/20-25 6.00 15.00
SEMISTARS/20-25 8.00 20.00
STATED PRINT RUN 4-252
27 Brian Urlacher/126 5.00 12.00
40 Emmitt Smith/199 8.00 20.00
50 Brett Favre/50 15.00 40.00
73 Randy Moss/201 6.00 15.00
76 Tom Brady/101 30.00 80.00
92 Jerry Rice/201 10.00 25.00

2002 Private Stock Moments in Time

Inserted at a rate of 1:193, this set highlights 10 of the top rookies from the 2002 draft class. Cards were serial #'d to 90.

STATED ODDS 1:193
STATED PRINT RUN 90 SER.#'d SETS
1 Antonio Bryant 3.00 8.00
2 David Carr 2.00 5.00
3 T.J. Duckett 2.00 5.00
4 DeShaun Foster 3.00 8.00
5 William Green 2.50 6.00
6 Joey Harrington 2.00 5.00
7 Kurt Kittner 2.00 5.00
8 Clinton Portis 3.00 8.00
9 Patrick Ramsey 2.50 6.00
10 Donte Stallworth 3.00 8.00

1993-94 Pro Athletes Outreach

This 12-card set was issued by Pro Athletes Outreach, a Christian leadership training ministry for pro athletes and their families. The tri-fold cards measure approximately 7 1/8" by 4 1/8". The right portion of the tri-fold carries a color player photo bordered in white on a light gray background. Below the picture are the player's name, position, and the PAO logo. The remainder of the card front and back contains the player's personal Christian testimony followed by an invitation to write them in care of the PAO address, for more information. With the exception of the Gill Byrd card, a second black-and-white player photo appears on the left portion of the tri-fold card. A brief career summary rounds out the card. The cards are unnumbered and checklisted below in alphabetical order.

COMPLETE SET (13) 4.00 10.00
1 Mark Boyer .20 .50
2 Gill Byrd .30 .75
3 Darren Carrington .20 .50
4 Ron Coder .20 .50
5 Paul Coffman .20 .50
6 Burnell Dent .20 .50
7 Johnny Holland .20 .50
8 Jeff Kemp .30 .75
9 Steve Largent 1.60 4.00
10 John Offerdahl .20 .50
11 Stephone Paige .20 .50
12 Doug Smith .20 .50
13 Rob Taylor .20 .50

1993 Pro Bowl POGs

These POGs measure approximately 1 5/8" in diameter and feature members selected to the 1993 Pro Bowl team.

COMPLETE SET (24) 6.00 15.00
1 Gill Byrd .20 .50
2 Barry Foster .30 .75
3 Mel Gray .20 .50
4 Harold Green .20 .50
5 Rodney Hampton .30 .75
6 Joel Hilgenberg .20 .50
7 Pierce Holt .20 .50
8 Haywood Jeffires .30 .75
9 Brent Jones .30 .75
10 Nick Lowery .20 .50
11 Tim McDonald .20 .50
12 Guy McIntyre .20 .50
13 Jay Novacek .40 1.00
14 Richmond Webb .30 .75
15 Todd Scott .20 .50
16 Elbert Shelley .20 .50
17 Clyde Simmons .30 .75
18 Emmitt Smith 2.00 5.00
19 Mark Stepnoski .20 .50
20 Jessie Tuggle .20 .50
21 Will Wolford .20 .50
22 NFL Players .20 .50
23 1993 Pro Bowlers Show Blaisdell Arena .20 .50
24 1993 Pro Bowlers Show .20 .50

1996 Pro Cube

Pro Cubes feature one player and measure roughly 3 1/8" square. Each includes numerous photos of the player and can be folded and twisted to form the different pictures. They were distributed primarily through major retail outlets with one cube per package.

COMPLETE SET (10) 14.00 35.00
1 Troy Aikman 1.60 4.00
2 Terrell Davis 1.60 4.00
3 John Elway 2.00 5.00
4 Brett Favre 2.00 5.00
5 Dan Marino 2.00 5.00
6 Jerry Rice 1.60 4.00
7 Barry Sanders 2.00 5.00
8 Emmitt Smith 2.00 5.00
9 Kordell Stewart 1.20 3.00
10 Steve Young 1.20 3.00

1990-91 Pro Line Samples

Unlike the borderless regular set, the fronts of these standard-size cards have silver borders. Many photos (both front and back) are different or are cropped differently than the corresponding regular-issue cards, and many of the quotes on the back also are different from the regular issue cards. The word "SAMPLE" is printed in small type next to the mugshots on the backs. The cards are skipnumbered on the back by odd numbers except that sample card number 15 was apparently not issued.

COMPLETE SET (18) 48.00 120.00
1 Charles Mann 2.00 5.00
3 Troy Aikman 6.00 15.00
5 Boomer Esiason 2.80 7.00
7 Warren Moon 4.00 10.00
9 Bill Fralic 2.00 5.00
11 Lawrence Taylor 4.00 10.00
13 George Seifert CO 2.00 5.00
17 Dan Marino 12.00 30.00
19 Jim Everett 2.80 7.00
21 John Elway 12.00 30.00
23 Jeff George 2.80 7.00
25 Lindy Infante CO 2.00 5.00
27 Dan Reeves CO 2.80 7.00
29 Steve Largent 4.00 10.00
31 Roger Craig 2.80 7.00
33 Marty Schottenheimer CO 2.00 5.00
35 Mike Ditka CO 4.00 10.00
37 Sam Wyche CO 2.00 5.00

1991 Pro Line Portraits

This 300-card standard-size set features some of the NFL's most popular players in non-game shots. The players and coaches are posed wearing their team's colors. The fronts are full-color borderless shots of the players, while the backs feature a quote from the player and a portrait pose of the player. The cards were available in wax packs. Essentially the whole set was available individually autographed; these certified autographed cards were randomly seeded into packs and feature no card numbers. An Emmitt Smith card was printed for inclusion in the Autographs set, but was never released in packs. A very small number of signed copies of the card were released at the 1992 Super Bowl Card Show with the majority of the Smith cards remaining unsigned. However, all of the Emmitt cards produced carried the certified stamp or crimp on the lower right hand corner of the card. The Santa Claus card could be obtained through a mail-in offer in exchange for ten 1991 ProLine Portraits foil pack wrappers. Complete sets featuring "National 1991" embossed logos were produced and distributed to guests of an event at The National Sports Collector's Convention in Anaheim. Reportedly, 250-complete sets were produced with the special logo.

COMPLETE SET (300) 3.00 6.00
1 Jim Kelly .07 .20
2 Carl Banks .01 .05
3 Neal Anderson .02 .10
4 James Brooks .01 .05
5 Reggie Langhorne .01 .05
6 Robert Awalt .01 .05
7 Greg Kragen .01 .05
8 Steve Young .25 .60
9 Nick Bell RC .01 .05
10 Ray Childress .02 .10
11 Albert Bentley .01 .05
12 Albert Lewis .01 .05
13 Howie Long .02 .10
14 Flipper Anderson .01 .05
15 Mark Clayton .02 .10
16 Jarrod Bunch RC .01 .05
17 Bruce Armstrong .01 .05
18 Vinnie Clark RC .01 .05
19 Rob Moore .02 .10
20 Eric Allen .01 .05
21 Timm Rosenbach .01 .05
22 Gary Anderson K .01 .05
23 Martin Bayless .01 .05
24 Kevin Fagan .01 .05
25 Brian Blades .02 .10
26 Gary Anderson RB .01 .05
27 Earnest Byner .02 .10
28 O.J.Simpson RET .07 .20
29 Dan Henning CO .01 .05
30 Sean Landeta .01 .05
31 James Lofton .02 .10
32 Mike Singletary .02 .10
33 David Fulcher .01 .05
34 Mark Murphy .01 .05
35 Issiac Holt .01 .05
36 Dennis Smith .01 .05
37 Lomas Brown .01 .05
38 Ernest Givins .02 .10
39 Duane Bickett .01 .05
40 Barry Word .01 .05
41 Tony Mandarich .01 .05
42 Cleveland Gary .01 .05
43 Ferrell Edmunds .01 .05
44 Randal Hill RC .02 .10
45 Irving Fryar .02 .10
46 Henry Jones RC .02 .10
47 Blair Thomas .01 .05
48 Andre Waters .01 .05
49 J.T. Smith .01 .05
50 Thomas Everett .01 .05
51 Marion Butts .02 .10
52 Tom Rathman .01 .05
53 Vann McElroy .01 .05
54 Mark Carrier WR .02 .10
55 Jim Lachey .01 .05
56 Joe Theismann RET .02 .10
57 Jerry Glanville CO .01 .05
58 Doug Riesenberg .01 .05
59 Cornelius Bennett .02 .10
60 Mark Carrier DB .02 .10
61 Rodney Holman .01 .05
62 Leroy Hoard .02 .10
63 Michael Irvin .07 .20
64 Bobby Humphrey .01 .05
65 Mel Gray .02 .10
66 Brian Noble .01 .05
67 Al Smith .01 .05
68 Eric Dickerson .02 .10
69 Steve DeBerg .02 .10
70 Jay Schroeder .01 .05
71 Irv Pankey .01 .05
72 Reggie Roby .01 .05
73 Wade Wilson .01 .05
74 Johnny Rembert .01 .05
75 Russell Maryland RC .02 .10
76 Al Toon .02 .10
77 Randall Cunningham .07 .20
78 Lonnie Young .01 .05
79 Carnell Lake .01 .05
80 Burt Grossman .01 .05
81 Jim Mora CO .01 .05
82 Dave Krieg .01 .05
83 Bruce Hill .01 .05
84 Ricky Sanders .01 .05
85 Roger Staubach RET .07 .20
86 Richard Williamson CO .01 .05
87 Everson Walls .01 .05
88 Shane Conlan .01 .05
89 Mike Ditka CO .07 .20
90 Mark Bortz .01 .05
91 Tim McGee .01 .05
92 Michael Dean Perry .02 .10
93 Danny Noonan .01 .05
94 Mark Jackson .01 .05
95 Chris Miller .02 .10
96 Ed McCaffrey RC .30 .75
97 Lorenzo White .02 .10
98 Ray Donaldson .01 .05
99 Nick Lowery .01 .05
100 Steve Smith .01 .05
101 Jackie Slater .01 .05
102 Louis Oliver .01 .05
103 Kanavis McGhee RC .01 .05
104 Ray Agnew .01 .05
105 Sam Mills .02 .10
106 Bill Pickel .01 .05
107 Keith Byars .02 .10
108 Ricky Proehl .01 .05
109 Merril Hoge .01 .05
110 Rod Bernstine .01 .05
111 Andy Heck .01 .05
112 Broderick Thomas .01 .05
113 Andre Collins .01 .05
114 Paul Warfield RET .02 .10
115 Bill Belichick CO RC .60 1.50
116 Ottis Anderson .02 .10
117 Andre Reed .02 .10
118 Andre Rison .02 .10
119 Dexter Carter .01 .05
120 Anthony Munoz .02 .10
121 Bernie Kosar .02 .10
122 Alonzo Highsmith .01 .05
123 David Treadwell .01 .05
124 Rodney Peete .02 .10
125 Haywood Jeffires .02 .10
126 Clarence Verdin .01 .05
127 Christian Okoye .01 .05
128 Greg Townsend .01 .05
129 Tom Newberry .01 .05
130 Keith Sims .01 .05
131 Myron Guyton .01 .05
132 Andre Tippett .01 .05
133 Steve Walsh .01 .05
134 Erik McMillan .01 .05
135 Jim McMahon .02 .10
136 Derek Hill .01 .05
137 D.J. Johnson .01 .05
138 Leslie O'Neal .02 .10
139 Pierce Holt .01 .05
140 Cortez Kennedy .02 .10
141 Danny Peebles .01 .05
142 Alvin Walton .01 .05
143 Drew Pearson RET .01 .05
144 Dick MacPherson CO .01 .05
145 Erik Howard .01 .05
146 Steve Tasker .02 .10
147 Bill Fralic .01 .05
148 Don Warren .01 .05
149 Eric Thomas .01 .05
150 Jack Pardee CO .01 .05
151 Gary Zimmerman .02 .10
152 Leonard Marshall .01 .05
153 Chris Spielman .02 .10
154 Sam Wyche CO .01 .05
155 Rohn Stark .01 .05
156 Stephone Paige .01 .05
157 Lionel Washington .01 .05
158 Henry Ellard .02 .10
159 Dan Marino .60 1.50
160 Lindy Infante CO .01 .05
161 Dan McGwire RC .01 .05
162 Ken O'Brien .01 .05
163 Tim McDonald .01 .05
164 Louis Lipps .01 .05
165 Billy Joe Tolliver .01 .05
166 Harris Barton .01 .05
167 Tony Woods .01 .05
168 Matt Millen .02 .10
169 Gale Sayers RET .07 .20
170 Ron Meyer CO .01 .05
171 William Roberts .01 .05
172 Thurman Thomas .07 .20
173 Steve McMichael .01 .05
174 Ickey Woods .01 .05
175 Eugene Lockhart .01 .05
176 George Seifert CO .02 .10
177 Keith Jones .01 .05
178 Jack Trudeau .01 .05
179 Kevin Porter .01 .05
180 Ronnie Lott .02 .10
181 M. Schottenheimer CO .01 .05
182 Morten Andersen .01 .05
183 Anthony Thompson .01 .05
184 Tim Worley .01 .05
185 Billy Ray Smith .01 .05
186 David Whitmore RC .01 .05
187 Jacob Green .01 .05
188 Browning Nagle RC .01 .05
189 Franco Harris RET .02 .10
190 Art Shell CO .02 .10
191 Bart Oates .01 .05
192 William Perry .02 .10
193 Chuck Noll CO .02 .10
194 Troy Aikman .30 .75
195 Jeff George .02 .10
196 Derrick Thomas .07 .20
197 Roger Craig .02 .10
198 John Fourcade .01 .05
199 Rod Woodson .07 .20
200 Anthony Miller .02 .10
201 Jerry Rice .30 .75
202 Eugene Robinson .01 .05
203 Charles Mann .01 .05
204 Mel Blount RET .02 .10
205 Don Shula CO .02 .10
206 Jumbo Elliott .01 .05
207 Jay Hilgenberg .01 .05
208 Deron Cherry .01 .05
209 Dan Reeves CO .02 .10
210 Roman Phifer RC .01 .05
211 David Little .01 .05
212 Lee Williams .01 .05
213 John Taylor .02 .10
214 Monte Coleman .01 .05
215 Walter Payton RET .20 .50
216 John Robinson CO .01 .05
217 Pepper Johnson .01 .05
218 Tom Thayer .01 .05
219 Dan Saleaumua .01 .05
220 Ernest Spears RC .01 .05
221 Bubby Brister .01 .05
222 Junior Seau .07 .20
223 Brent Jones .02 .10
224 Rufus Porter .01 .05
225 Jack Kemp RET .07 .20
226 Wayne Fontes CO .01 .05
227 Phil Simms .02 .10
228 Shaun Gayle .01 .05
229 Bill Maas .01 .05
230 Renaldo Turnbull .01 .05
231 Bryan Hinkle .01 .05
232 Gary Plummer .01 .05
233 Jerry Burns CO .01 .05
234 Lawrence Taylor .02 .10
235 Joe Gibbs CO .02 .10
236 Neil Smith .07 .20
237 Rich Kotite CO .01 .05
238 Jim Covert .01 .05
239 Tim Grunhard .01 .05
240 Joe Bugel CO .01 .05
241 David Wyman .01 .05
242 Maury Buford .01 .05
243 Kevin Ross .01 .05
244 Jimmy Johnson CO .02 .10
245 Jim Morrissey RC .01 .05
246 Jeff Hostetler .02 .10
247 Andre Ware .02 .10
248 Steve Largent RET .07 .20
249 Chuck Knox CO .01 .05
250 Boomer Esiason .02 .10
251 Kevin Butler .01 .05
252 Bruce Smith .07 .20
253 Webster Slaughter .02 .10
254 Mike Sherrard .01 .05
255 Steve Broussard .01 .05
256 Warren Moon .07 .20
257 John Elway .60 1.50
258 Bob Golic .01 .05
259 Jim Everett .02 .10
260 Bruce Coslet CO .01 .05
261 James Francis .01 .05
262 Eric Dorsey .01 .05
263 Marcus Dupree .08 .25
264 Hart Lee Dykes .01 .05
265 Vinny Testaverde .02 .10
266 Chip Lohmiller .01 .05
267 John Riggins RET .02 .10
268 Mike Schad .01 .05
269 Kevin Greene .02 .10
270 Dean Biasucci .01 .05
271 Mike Pritchard RC .02 .10
272 Ted Washington RC .01 .05
273 Alfred Williams RC .01 .05
274 Chris Zorich RC .02 .10
275 Reggie Barrett .01 .05
276 Chris Hinton .01 .05
277 Tracy Johnson RC .01 .05
278 Jim Harbaugh .02 .10
279 John Roper .01 .05
280 Mike Dumas RC .01 .05
281 Herman Moore RC .07 .20
282 Eric Turner RC .02 .10
283 Steve Atwater .01 .05
284 Michael Cofer .01 .05
285 Darion Conner .01 .05
286 Darryl Talley .01 .05
287 Donnell Woolford .01 .05
288 Keith McCants .01 .05
289 Ray Handley CO .01 .05
290 Ahmad Rashad RET .02 .10
291 Eric Swann RC .02 .10
292 Dalton Hilliard .01 .05
293 Rickey Jackson .02 .10
294 Vaughan Johnson .01 .05
295 Eric Martin .01 .05
296 Pat Swilling .02 .10
297 Anthony Carter .02 .10
298 Guy McIntyre .01 .05
299 Bennie Blades .01 .05
300 Paul Farren .01 .05
P1 Derrick Thomas Promo .20 .50
PLC1 Ahmad Rashad Family .30 .75
PLC2 Payne Stewart .30 .75
NNO Emmitt Smith 6.00 15.00
NNO Santa '91 Sendaway SP .30 .75

1991 Pro Line Portraits Autographs

This standard-size set features some of the NFL's most popular players in non-game shots. These certified autographed cards were randomly included into packs as unnumbered cards. They are listed below in alphabetical order. It has been reported by collectors that an autographed card is found with a frequency of about one per three boxes of 1991 Pro Line. All cards were signed in varying numbers with no prints being announced, therefore some are considered much more difficult to find. Other cards were returned late by the featured player and did not make the pack-out for the 1991 product. These cards were distributed later on through one or more of the following means: at the 1992 Super Bowl Card Show, a mail order contest through Impel Marketing, or in packs of 1992 Pro Line. We've noted below the most common method of distribution according to NFL Properties. Reportedly, an Emmitt Smith card was produced and just a few were actually signed and released at the Super Bowl Card Show. This and the Tim McDonald card are not included in the set price since only a handful are known to exist. Cards with signatures cut short are considered to have major defects. The autographed Santa cards are also not considered part of the set.

1 Ray Agnew 6.00 15.00
2 Troy Aikman 30.00 80.00
3 Eric Allen 6.00 15.00
4 Morten Andersen 6.00 15.00
5 Flipper Anderson 6.00 15.00
6 Gary Anderson K 12.50 25.00
7 Gary Anderson RB 6.00 15.00
8 Neal Anderson 8.00 20.00
9 Ottis Anderson 8.00 20.00
10 Bruce Armstrong 8.00 20.00
11 Steve Atwater 10.00 25.00
12 Robert Awalt 5.00 12.00
13 Carl Banks 8.00 20.00
14 Reggie Barrett 5.00 12.00
15 Harris Barton 5.00 12.00
16 Martin Bayless 5.00 12.00
17 Bill Belichick CO 60.00 120.00
18 Nick Bell 5.00 12.00
19 Cornelius Bennett 8.00 20.00
20 Albert Bentley 5.00 12.00
21 Rod Bernstine 5.00 12.00
22 Dean Biasucci 5.00 12.00
23 Duane Bickett 6.00 15.00
24 Bennie Blades 5.00 12.00
25 Brian Blades 8.00 20.00
26 Mel Blount RET 10.00 25.00
27 Mark Bortz 5.00 12.00
28 Bubby Brister 6.00 15.00
29 James Brooks 6.00 15.00
30 Steve Broussard 5.00 12.00
31 Lomas Brown 5.00 12.00
32 Maury Buford 5.00 12.00
33 Joe Bugel CO 5.00 12.00
34 Jarrod Bunch 5.00 12.00
35 Jerry Burns CO 5.00 12.00
36 Kevin Butler 8.00 20.00
37 Marion Butts 6.00 15.00
38 Keith Byars 6.00 15.00
39 Earnest Byner 6.00 15.00
40 Mark Carrier DB SP 50.00 100.00
41 Mark Carrier WR 6.00 15.00
42 Anthony Carter 8.00 20.00
43 Dexter Carter 5.00 12.00
44 Deron Cherry 5.00 12.00
45 Ray Childress 6.00 15.00
46 Vinnie Clark 5.00 12.00
47 Mark Clayton 8.00 20.00
48 Michael Cofer 5.00 12.00
49 Monte Coleman 6.00 15.00
50 Andre Collins 5.00 12.00
51 Shane Conlan 5.00 12.00
52 Darion Conner 5.00 12.00
53 Bruce Coslet CO 5.00 12.00
54 Jim Covert 6.00 15.00
55 Roger Craig 10.00 25.00
56 Randall Cunningham 12.50 25.00
57 Steve DeBerg 6.00 15.00
58 Eric Dickerson 15.00 40.00
59 Mike Ditka CO 15.00 30.00
60 Ray Donaldson 8.00 20.00
61 Eric Dorsey 5.00 12.00
62 Mike Dumas 5.00 12.00
63 Marcus Dupree 12.00 30.00
64 Hart Lee Dykes 5.00 12.00
65 Ferrell Edmunds 5.00 12.00
66 Henry Ellard 6.00 15.00
67 Jumbo Elliott 6.00 15.00
68 John Elway 40.00 100.00
69 Boomer Esiason 10.00 25.00
70 Jim Everett 6.00 15.00
71 Thomas Everett 5.00 12.00
72 Kevin Fagan 5.00 12.00
73 Paul Farren 5.00 12.00
74 Wayne Fontes CO 5.00 12.00
75 John Fourcade 5.00 12.00
76 Bill Fralic 5.00 12.00
77 James Francis SP 175.00 300.00
78 Irving Fryar 8.00 20.00
79 David Fulcher 5.00 12.00
80 Cleveland Gary 6.00 20.00
81 Shaun Gayle 5.00 12.00
82 Jeff George 8.00 20.00
83 Joe Gibbs CO 15.00 30.00
84 Ernest Givins 6.00 15.00
85 Jerry Glanville CO 6.00 15.00
86 Bob Golic 6.00 15.00
87 Mel Gray 6.00 15.00
88 Jacob Green 5.00 12.00
89 Kevin Greene 8.00 20.00
90 Burt Grossman 5.00 12.00
91 Tim Grunhard 5.00 12.00
92 Myron Guyton 5.00 12.00
93 Ray Handley CO 8.00 20.00
94 Jim Harbaugh 15.00 30.00
95 Franco Harris RET 25.00 50.00
96 Andy Heck 5.00 12.00
97 Dan Henning CO 5.00 12.00
98 Alonzo Highsmith SP 90.00 150.00
99 Jay Hilgenberg 8.00 20.00
100 Bruce Hill 5.00 12.00
101 Derek Hill 5.00 12.00
102 Randal Hill 6.00 15.00
103 Dalton Hilliard 6.00 15.00
104 Bryan Hinkle 5.00 12.00
105 Chris Hinton 5.00 12.00
106 Leroy Hoard 8.00 20.00
107 Merril Hoge 8.00 20.00
108 Rodney Holman SP 150.00 300.00
109 Issiac Holt 5.00 12.00
110 Pierce Holt 5.00 12.00
111 Jeff Hostetler 6.00 15.00
112 Erik Howard 5.00 12.00
113 Bobby Humphrey 5.00 12.00
114 Lindy Infante CO 5.00 12.00
115 Michael Irvin 20.00 35.00
116 Mark Jackson 6.00 15.00
117 Rickey Jackson 25.00 50.00
118 Haywood Jeffires 6.00 15.00
119 D.J. Johnson 5.00 12.00
120 Jimmy Johnson CO 15.00 40.00
121 Pepper Johnson 6.00 15.00
122 Tracy Johnson 5.00 12.00
123 Vaughan Johnson 5.00 12.00
124 Brent Jones 6.00 15.00
125 Henry Jones 5.00 12.00
126 Keith Jones 5.00 12.00
127A Jim Kelly Autopen 8.00 20.00
127B Jim Kelly Real 125.00 250.00
128 Jack Kemp Autopen 12.50 30.00
129 Cortez Kennedy 20.00 40.00
130 Chuck Knox CO 6.00 15.00
131 Bernie Kosar 10.00 25.00
132 Rich Kotite CO 5.00 12.00
133 Greg Kragen 6.00 15.00
134 Dave Krieg 6.00 15.00
135 Jim Lachey 6.00 15.00
136 Carnell Lake 6.00 15.00
137 Sean Landeta 5.00 12.00
138 Reggie Langhorne SP 125.00 250.00
139 Steve Largent RET 10.00 25.00
140 Albert Lewis SP 40.00 80.00
141 Louis Lipps 6.00 15.00
142 David Little 8.00 20.00
143 Eugene Lockhart 5.00 12.00
144 James Lofton 8.00 20.00
145 Chip Lohmiller 5.00 12.00
146 Howie Long 20.00 40.00
147 Ronnie Lott 10.00 25.00
148 Nick Lowery 5.00 12.00
149 Dick MacPherson CO 5.00 12.00
150 Ed McCaffrey 8.00 20.00
151 Keith McCants 5.00 12.00
152 Vann McElroy 5.00 12.00
153 Tim McGee 5.00 12.00
154 Kanavis McGhee 5.00 12.00
155 Dan McGwire 5.00 12.00
156 Guy McIntyre SP 30.00 80.00
157 Jim McMahon SP 150.00 300.00
158 Steve McMichael 6.00 15.00
159 Erik McMillan 5.00 12.00
160 Bill Maas 5.00 12.00
161 Tony Mandarich 6.00 15.00
162 Charles Mann 6.00 15.00
163 Dan Marino 40.00 100.00
164 Leonard Marshall 8.00 20.00
165 Eric Martin 6.00 15.00
166 Russell Maryland 6.00 15.00
167 Tim McDonald SP
168 Ron Meyer CO 5.00 12.00
169 Matt Millen 6.00 15.00
170 Anthony Miller 6.00 15.00
171 Chris Miller 6.00 15.00
172 Sam Mills 15.00 40.00
173 Warren Moon 15.00 30.00
174 Herman Moore 10.00 25.00
175 Rob Moore 8.00 20.00
176 Jim Mora CO 5.00 12.00
177 Jim Morrissey 5.00 12.00
178 Anthony Munoz 8.00 20.00
179 Mark Murphy 5.00 12.00
180 Browning Nagle 5.00 12.00
181 Tom Newberry 5.00 12.00
182 Brian Noble 5.00 12.00
183 Chuck Noll CO 25.00 50.00
184 Danny Noonan 5.00 12.00
185 Ken O'Brien 6.00 15.00
186 Leslie O'Neal 6.00 15.00
187 Bart Oates 5.00 12.00
188 Christian Okoye 6.00 15.00
189 Louis Oliver 5.00 12.00
190 Stephone Paige 5.00 12.00
191 Irv Pankey 5.00 12.00
192 Jack Pardee CO 5.00 12.00
193 Walter Payton RET 125.00 250.00
194 Drew Pearson RET 8.00 20.00
195 Danny Peebles 5.00 12.00
196 Rodney Peete 6.00 15.00
197 Michael Dean Perry 6.00 15.00
198 William Perry 15.00 30.00
199 Roman Phifer 5.00 12.00
200 Bill Pickel 5.00 12.00
201 Gary Plummer 5.00 12.00
202 Kevin Porter 5.00 12.00
203 Rufus Porter 5.00 12.00
204 Mike Pritchard 5.00 12.00
205 Ricky Proehl 6.00 15.00
206 Ahmad Rashad RET SP 125.00 200.00
207 Tom Rathman 8.00 20.00
208 Andre Reed 8.00 20.00
209 Dan Reeves CO 8.00 20.00
210 Johnny Rembert 5.00 12.00
211 Jerry Rice 40.00 100.00
212 Doug Riesenberg 5.00 12.00
213 John Riggins RET 20.00 50.00
214 Andre Rison Pen 6.00 15.00
215 Andre Rison Sharpie 15.00 30.00
216 William Roberts 5.00 12.00
217 Eugene Robinson 6.00 15.00
218 John Robinson CO 6.00 15.00
219 Reggie Roby 15.00 30.00
220 John Roper 5.00 12.00
221 Timm Rosenbach 5.00 12.00
222 Kevin Ross 5.00 12.00
223 Ricky Sanders 6.00 15.00
224 Dan Saleaumua 5.00 12.00
225 Gale Sayers RET 15.00 30.00
226 Mike Schad 5.00 12.00
227 M.Schottenheimer CO 12.00 30.00
228 Jay Schroeder 5.00 12.00
229 Junior Seau 20.00 40.00
230 George Seifert CO 8.00 20.00
231 Art Shell CO 10.00 25.00
232 Mike Sherrard 5.00 12.00
233 Don Shula CO ! 15.00 40.00
234 O.J. Simpson RET 40.00 100.00
235 Phil Simms 12.50 30.00
236 Keith Sims 5.00 12.00
237 Mike Singletary 20.00 50.00
238 Jackie Slater 8.00 20.00
239 Webster Slaughter 6.00 15.00
240 Al Smith 5.00 12.00
241 Billy Ray Smith 5.00 12.00
242 Bruce Smith 15.00 30.00
243 Dennis Smith 8.00 20.00
244 J.T. Smith 5.00 12.00
245 Emmitt Smith SP 75.00 150.00
246 Neil Smith 20.00 50.00
247 Steve Smith 5.00 12.00
248 Ernest Spears 5.00 12.00
249 Chris Spielman 8.00 20.00
250 Rohn Stark 5.00 12.00
251 Roger Staubach RET 60.00 120.00
252 Eric Swann 6.00 15.00
253 Pat Swilling 6.00 15.00
254 Darryl Talley 6.00 15.00
255 Steve Tasker 8.00 20.00
256 John Taylor 8.00 20.00
257 Lawrence Taylor 12.50 30.00
258 Vinny Testaverde 6.00 15.00
259 Tom Thayer 5.00 12.00
260 Joe Theismann RET 15.00 30.00
261 Blair Thomas 5.00 12.00
262 Broderick Thomas 5.00 12.00
263 Derrick Thomas 20.00 50.00
264 Eric Thomas 5.00 12.00
265 Thurman Thomas 12.50 30.00
266 Anthony Thompson 5.00 12.00
267 Andre Tippett 8.00 20.00
268 Billy Joe Tolliver 5.00 12.00
269 Al Toon 6.00 15.00
270 Greg Townsend SP 90.00 175.00
271 David Treadwell 5.00 12.00
272 Jack Trudeau 5.00 12.00
273 Renaldo Turnbull 6.00 15.00
274 Eric Turner 8.00 20.00
275 Clarence Verdin 5.00 12.00
276 Everson Walls 6.00 15.00
277 Steve Walsh 5.00 12.00
278 Alvin Walton 5.00 12.00
279 Andre Ware 8.00 20.00
280 Paul Warfield RET 8.00 20.00
281 Don Warren 8.00 20.00
282 Lionel Washington SP 75.00 150.00
283 Ted Washington 6.00 15.00
284 Andre Waters 6.00 15.00
285 Lorenzo White 5.00 12.00
286 David Whitmore 5.00 12.00
287 Alfred Williams 5.00 12.00
288 Lee Williams 5.00 12.00
289 Richard Williamson CO 5.00 12.00
290 Wade Wilson 6.00 15.00
291 Ickey Woods 6.00 15.00
292 Tony Woods 5.00 12.00
293 Rod Woodson 30.00 60.00
294 Donnell Woolford 5.00 12.00
295 Barry Word 5.00 12.00
296 Tim Worley 6.00 15.00
297 Sam Wyche CO 6.00 15.00
298 David Wyman 5.00 12.00
299 Lonnie Young 5.00 12.00
300 Steve Young 15.00 40.00
301 Gary Zimmerman 15.00 40.00
302 Chris Zorich 6.00 15.00
PLC2 Payne Stewart 100.00 200.00
NNO Santa Claus Unnumbered 12.50 30.00
NNO Santa Claus/200 25.00 60.00

1991 Pro Line Portraits Wives

This seven-card standard size set was issued with the 1991 Pro Line Portraits set as inserts in the regular foil packs. These seven cards feature wives of some of the NFL's most popular personalities, including former television actress Jennifer Montana and star of the Cosby show, Phylicia Rashad. The cards are numbered on the back with an "SC" prefix.

COMPLETE SET (7) .30 .75
SC1 Jennifer Montana .10 .30
SC2 Babette Kosar .02 .10
SC3 Janet Elway .02 .10
SC4 Michelle Oates .02 .10
SC5 Toni Lipps .02 .10
SC6 Stacey O'Brien .02 .10
SC7 Phylicia Rashad .05 .15

1991 Pro Line Portraits Wives Autographs

This seven-card standard-size set was included in the 1991 Pro Line Portraits set as inserts in the regular foil packs. These cards feature wives of some of the NFL's most popular personalities, including former television actress Jennifer Montana and star of the Cosby show, Phylicia Rashad. Less than 15 of Rashad's cards are currently known to exist. The cards are unnumbered and checklisted below in alphabetical order.

1 Janet Elway 20.00 50.00
2 Babette Kosar 6.00 15.00
3 Toni Lipps 6.00 15.00
4 Jennifer Montana 50.00 100.00
5 Michelle Oates 6.00 15.00
6 Stacey O'Brien 6.00 15.00
7 Phylicia Rashad 350.00 600.00

1991 Pro Line Portraits National Convention

COMP.FACTORY SET (309) 150.00 300.00
*PLAYER NATIONAL CARDS: 15X TO 40X
*WIVES NATIONAL CARDS: 8X TO 20X

1991 Pro Line Punt, Pass and Kick

This 12-card standard-size set was issued to honor 1991 NFL quarterbacks in conjunction with the long-standing Punt, Pass, and Kick program. Cards 1-11 show each quarterback in various still-life poses. Card fronts also feature an embossed Punt, Pass, and Kick logo in the lower right corner and the NFL Pro Line Portraits logo at the bottom center.

COMPLETE SET (12) 40.00 100.00
PPK1 Troy Aikman 8.00 20.00
PPK2 Bubby Brister 1.60 4.00
PPK3 Randall Cunningham 2.40 6.00
PPK4 John Elway 12.00 30.00
PPK5 Boomer Esiason 1.60 4.00
PPK6 Jim Everett 1.60 4.00
PPK7 Jim Kelly 2.40 6.00
PPK8 Bernie Kosar 1.20 3.00
PPK9 Dan Marino 12.00 30.00
PPK10 Warren Moon 2.40 6.00
PPK11 Phil Simms 1.60 4.00
SC3 Punt& Pass& and Kick 1.20 3.00

1991-92 Pro Line Profiles Anthony Munoz

This nine-card standard-size set was inserted into the Super Bowl XXVI game program. The slick four-color cards depict different phases of the career of Munoz, and the Pro Line Profile logo is centered at the bottom of each perforated card.

COMPLETE SET (9) 1.60 4.00
COMMON CARD (1-9) .20 .50

1992 Pro Line Draft Day

Each of these draft day collectible cards measures the standard size. The fronts feature full-bleed color photos, while the horizontally oriented backs have an head shot surrounded by an extended quote. Emtman is pictured sitting on a boat holding a fishing rod, with a "stringer" of NFL helmets dangling from the bow. The other card features a group picture of NFL coaches on the front, while the head shot and extended quote on the back are by Chris Berman, an ESPN commentator.

1 Steve Emtman 1.00 2.50
2 Coaches Photo 1.00 2.50

1992 Pro Line Mobil

Produced by NFL Properties, this 72-card regionally distributed standard-size set consists of 1991 Portraits (1-9) and 1992 Profiles (10-72) cards. The set was part of an eight-week promotion in Southern California. Each week a nine-card pack could be obtained by purchasing at least eight gallons of Mobil Super Unleaded Plus. The nine cards available the first week were a title card, a checklist, and seven Portrait cards which have printed on their fronts the dates that nine-card packs of that player would be available. During the following seven weeks, one player was featured per week in the packs. The cards carry full-bleed posed and action color player/family photos. The Pro Line logo is at the bottom. The backs feature player information with the Mobil logo at the bottom. Card number 9 picturing Eric Dickerson in a Raiders' uniform is exclusive to the set. The cards are numbered on the back "X of 9" and arranged below chronologically according to the eight-week promotion. The week the cards were available is listed under the first card of the nine-card subsets. Each nine-card cello pack included an unperforated sheet with four coupon offers.

COMPLETE SET (72)	3.20	8.00
1 Title Card	.02	.10
2 Checklist	.02	.10
3 Ronnie Lott	.05	.15
4 Junior Seau	.08	.25
5 Jim Everett	.02	.10
6 Howie Long	.05	.15
7 Jerry Rice	.30	.75
8 Art Shell CO	.05	.15
9 Eric Dickerson	.05	.15
10 Ronnie Lott	.05	.15
11 Ronnie Lott	.05	.15
12 Ronnie Lott	.05	.15
13 Ronnie Lott	.05	.15
14 Ronnie Lott	.05	.15
15 Ronnie Lott	.05	.15
16 Ronnie Lott	.05	.15
17 Ronnie Lott	.05	.15
18 Ronnie Lott	.05	.15
19 Junior Seau	.08	.25
20 Junior Seau	.08	.25
21 Junior Seau	.08	.25
22 Junior Seau	.08	.25
23 Junior Seau	.08	.25
24 Junior Seau	.08	.25
25 Junior Seau	.08	.25
26 Junior Seau	.08	.25
27 Junior Seau	.08	.25
28 Jim Everett	.02	.10
29 Jim Everett	.02	.10
30 Jim Everett	.02	.10
31 Jim Everett	.02	.10
32 Jim Everett	.02	.10
33 Jim Everett	.02	.10
34 Jim Everett	.02	.10
35 Jim Everett	.02	.10
36 Jim Everett	.02	.10
37 Howie Long	.05	.15
38 Howie Long	.05	.15
39 Howie Long	.05	.15
40 Howie Long	.05	.15
41 Howie Long	.05	.15
42 Howie Long	.05	.15
43 Howie Long	.05	.15
44 Howie Long	.05	.15
45 Howie Long	.05	.15
46 Jerry Rice	.30	.75
47 Jerry Rice	.30	.75
48 Jerry Rice	.30	.75
49 Jerry Rice	.30	.75
50 Jerry Rice	.30	.75
51 Jerry Rice	.30	.75
52 Jerry Rice	.30	.75
53 Jerry Rice	.30	.75
54 Jerry Rice	.30	.75
55 Art Shell CO	.05	.15
56 Art Shell CO	.05	.15
57 Art Shell CO	.05	.15
58 Art Shell CO	.05	.15
59 Art Shell CO	.05	.15
60 Art Shell CO	.05	.15
61 Art Shell CO	.05	.15
62 Art Shell CO	.05	.15
63 Art Shell CO	.05	.15
64 Eric Dickerson	.05	.15
65 Eric Dickerson	.05	.15
66 Eric Dickerson	.05	.15
67 Eric Dickerson	.05	.15
68 Eric Dickerson	.05	.15
69 Eric Dickerson	.05	.15
70 Eric Dickerson	.05	.15
71 Eric Dickerson	.05	.15
72 Eric Dickerson	.05	.15

1992 Pro Line Prototypes

This 13-card sample standard-size set was distributed by Pro Line to show the design of their 1992 Pro Line football card series. The cards were distributed as a complete set in a cello pack. The fronts feature full-bleed color photos, while the backs carry a color close-up photo, extended quote, or statistics. The set includes samples of the following Pro Line series: Profiles (28-36), Spirit (12), and Portraits (379, 386). The cards are numbered on the back, and their numbering is the same as in the regular series. These cards were also distributed by Classic at major card and trade shows. These prototypes can be distinguished from the regular issue cards in that they are vertically marked "prototype" in the lower left corner of the Profiles reverse and or "sample" next to the picture on the Portraits reverse.

COMPLETE SET (13)	3.20	8.00
12 Kathie Lee Gifford	.30	.75
28 Thurman Thomas	.30	.75
29 Thurman Thomas	.30	.75
30 Thurman Thomas	.30	.75
31 Thurman Thomas	.30	.75
32 Thurman Thomas	.30	.75
33 Thurman Thomas	.30	.75
34 Thurman Thomas	.30	.75
35 Thurman Thomas	.30	.75
36 Thurman Thomas	.30	.75
379 Jessie Tuggle	.20	.50
386 Neil O'Donnell	.30	.75
NNO Advertisement Card	.20	.50

1992 Pro Line Portraits

This 167-card standard-size set is numbered in continuation of the 1991 ProLine Portraits set. Each Pro Line Collection pack contained nine Profiles and three Portraits cards. Pro Line's goal was to have an autographed card in each box and, as a bonus, some 1991 ProLine Portrait autographed cards were included. Also autograph cards could be obtained through a mail-in offer in exchange for 12 1991 ProLine Portraits wrappers (black) and 12 1992 ProLine wrappers (white). The fronts display full-bleed color photos in non-game shots while the backs carry personal information. A special boxed set, with the cards displayed in two notebooks, was distributed at the National. The promo cards differ from the regular series in two respects: the cards are unnumbered and are stamped with a "The National, 1992" seal. The key Rookie Cards in this set are Edgar Bennett, Terrell Buckley, Dale Carter, Marco Coleman, Quentin Coryatt, Steve Emtman, Johnny Mitchell and Tommy Vardell. The 1992 ProLine Santa Claus card could be obtained through a mail-in offer in exchange for ten 1991 Pro Line Portraits wrappers (black) and ten 1992 Pro Line Collection wrappers (white). The first 10,000 to respond to the offer received Mrs. Claus card.through a mail-in offer in exchange for ten 1991 Pro Line Portraits wrappers (black) and ten 1992 Pro Line Collection wrappers (white). The first 10,000 to respond to the offer received a Mrs. Claus card.

COMPLETE SET (167)	2.50	6.00
301 Steve Emtman RC	.01	.05
302 Al Edwards	.01	.05
303 Wendell Davis	.01	.05
304 Lewis Billups	.01	.05
305 Brian Brennan	.01	.05
306 John Gesek	.01	.05
307 Terrell Buckley RC	.01	.05
308 Johnny Mitchell RC	.01	.05
309 LeRoy Butler	.01	.05
310 William Fuller	.01	.05
311 Bill Brooks	.02	.10
312 Dino Hackett	.01	.05
313 Willie Gault	.02	.10
314 Aaron Cox	.01	.05
315 Jeff Cross	.01	.05
316 Emmitt Smith	.75	2.00
317 Marv Cook	.01	.05
318 Gill Fenerty	.01	.05
319 Jeff Carlson RC	.01	.05
320 Brad Baxter	.01	.05
321 Fred Barnett	.02	.10
322 Kurt Barber RC	.01	.05
323 Eric Green	.02	.10
324 Greg Clark RC	.01	.05
325 Keith DeLong	.01	.05
326 Patrick Hunter	.01	.05
327 Troy Vincent RC	.01	.05
328 Gary Clark	.02	.10
329 Joe Montana	1.00	2.50
330 Michael Haynes	.02	.10
331 Edgar Bennett RC	.07	.20
332 Darren Lewis	.01	.05
333 Derrick Fenner	.01	.05
334 Rob Burnett	.01	.05
335 Alvin Harper	.02	.10
336 Vance Johnson	.01	.05
337 William White	.01	.05
338 Sterling Sharpe	.07	.20
339 Sean Jones	.01	.05
340 Jeff Herrod	.01	.05
341 Chris Martin	.01	.05
342 Ethan Horton	.01	.05
343 Robert Delpino	.01	.05
344 Mark Higgs	.01	.05
345 Chris Doleman	.02	.10
346 Tommy Hodson	.01	.05
347 Craig Heyward	.02	.10
348 Cary Conklin	.01	.05
349 James Hasty	.01	.05
350 Antone Davis	.01	.05
351 Ernie Jones	.01	.05
352 Greg Lloyd	.02	.10
353 John Friesz	.02	.10
354 Charles Haley	.02	.10
355 Tracy Scroggins RC	.01	.05
356 Paul Gruber	.01	.05
357 Ricky Ervins	.01	.05
358 Brad Muster	.01	.05
359 Deion Sanders	.20	.50
360 Mitch Frerotte RC	.01	.05
361 Stan Thomas	.01	.05
362 Harold Green	.02	.10
363 Eric Metcalf	.07	.20
364 Ken Norton Jr.	.02	.10
365 Dave Widell	.01	.05
366 Mike Tomczak	.01	.05
367 Bubba McDowell	.01	.05
368 Jessie Hester	.01	.05
369 Ervin Randle	.01	.05
370 Anthony Smith DT	.01	.05
371 Pat Terrell	.01	.05
372 Jim C. Jensen	.01	.05
373 Mike Merriweather	.01	.05
374 Chris Singleton	.01	.05
375 Floyd Turner	.01	.05
376 Jim Sweeney	.01	.05
377 Keith Jackson	.02	.10
378 Walter Reeves	.01	.05
379 Neil O'Donnell	.02	.10
380 Nate Lewis	.01	.05
381 Keith Henderson	.01	.05
382 Kelly Stouffer	.01	.05
383 Ricky Reynolds	.01	.05
384 Joe Jacoby	.01	.05
385 Fred Biletnikoff RET	.02	.10
386 Jessie Tuggle	.01	.05
387 Tom Waddle	.01	.05
388 David Shula CO RC	.01	.05
389 Van Waiters RC	.01	.05
390 Jay Novacek	.02	.10
391 Michael Young	.01	.05
392 Mike Holmgren CO RC	.07	.20
393 Doug Smith	.01	.05
394 Mike Prior	.01	.05
395 Harvey Williams	.02	.10
396 Aaron Wallace	.01	.05
397 Tony Zendejas	.01	.05
398 Sammie Smith	.01	.05
399 Henry Thomas	.01	.05
400 Jon Vaughn	.01	.05
401 Brian Washington	.01	.05
402 Leon Searcy RC	.01	.05
403 Lance Smith	.01	.05
404 Warren Williams	.01	.05
405 Bobby Ross CO RC	.01	.05
406 Harry Sydney	.01	.05
407 John L. Williams	.01	.05
408 Ken Willis	.01	.05
409 Brian Mitchell	.02	.10
410 Dick Butkus RET	.02	.10
411 Chuck Knox CO	.01	.05
412 Robert Porcher RC	.07	.20
413 Calvin Williams	.02	.10
414 Bill Cowher CO RC	.30	.75
415 Eric Moore	.01	.05
416 Derek Brown TE RC	.01	.05
417 Dennis Green CO RC	.02	.10
418 Tom Flores CO	.01	.05
419 Dale Carter RC	.02	.10
420 Tony Dorsett RET	.02	.10
421 Marco Coleman RC	.01	.05
422 Sam Wyche CO	.01	.05
423 Ray Crockett	.01	.05
424 Dan Fouts RET	.02	.10
425 Hugh Millen	.01	.05
426 Quentin Coryatt RC	.01	.05
427 Brian Jordan	.02	.10
428 Frank Gifford RET	.02	.10
429 Toby Caston RC	.01	.05
430 Ted Marchibroda CO	.01	.05
431 Cris Carter	.07	.20
432 Tim Krumrie	.01	.05
433 Otto Graham RET	.02	.10
434 Vaughn Dunbar RC	.01	.05
435 John Fina RC	.01	.05
436 Sonny Jurgensen RET	.02	.10
437 Robert Jones RC	.01	.05
438 Steve DeOssie	.01	.05
439 Eddie LeBaron RET	.01	.05
440 Chester McGlockton RC	.02	.10
441 Ken Stabler RET	.02	.10
442 Joe DeLamielleure RET	.02	.10
443 Charley Taylor RET	.01	.05
444 Greg Skrepenak RC	.01	.05
445 Y.A.Tittle RET	.02	.10
446 Chuck Smith RC	.01	.05
447 Kellen Winslow RET	.01	.05
448 Kevin Smith RC	.01	.05
449 Phillippi Sparks RC	.01	.05
450 Alonzo Spellman RC	.02	.10
451 Mark Rypien	.01	.05
452 Darryl Williams RC	.01	.05
453 Tommy Vardell RC	.01	.05
454 Tommy Maddox RC	.60	1.50
455 Steve Israel RC	.01	.05
456 Marquez Pope RC	.01	.05
457 Eugene Chung RC	.01	.05
458 Lynn Swann RET	.02	.10
459 Sean Gilbert RC	.02	.10
460 Chris Mims RC	.01	.05
461 Al Davis OWN	.02	.10
462 Richard Todd RET	.01	.05
463 Mike Fox	.01	.05
464 David Klingler RC	.01	.05
465 Darren Woodson RC	.07	.20
466 Jason Hanson RC	.02	.10
467 Lem Barney RET	.01	.05
NNO Santa Sendaway	.40	1.00
NNO Mrs.Claus Sendaway	.40	1.00

1992 Pro Line Portraits Autographs

This 167-card standard-size set features actual autographs on the cardfronts. All of the cards were issued without card numbers while some have also been found with the standard card number on the back. Pro Line's goal was to have an autographed card in each box. Also autograph cards could be obtained through a mail-in offer in exchange for 12 1991 Pro Line Portraits wrappers (black) and 12 1992 Pro Line Collection wrappers (white). The fronts display full-bleed color photos in non-game shots while the backs carry personal information. The cards are unnumbered and checklisted below in alphabetical order. The following player cards were not signed: James Hasty, Anthony Smith, Dennis Green, Frank Gifford, Richard Todd.

1 Kurt Barber	4.00	10.00
2 Fred Barnett	5.00	12.00
3 Lem Barney RET	6.00	15.00
4 Brad Baxter	4.00	10.00
5 Edgar Bennett	6.00	15.00
6 Fred Biletnikoff RET	25.00	60.00
7 Lewis Billups	4.00	10.00
8 Brian Brennan	4.00	10.00
9 Bill Brooks	5.00	12.00
10 Derek Brown TE	4.00	10.00
11 Terrell Buckley	6.00	15.00
12 Rob Burnett	4.00	10.00
13 Dick Butkus RET	15.00	30.00
14 LeRoy Butler	15.00	30.00
15 Jeff Carlson	4.00	10.00
16 Cris Carter	10.00	25.00
17 Dale Carter	5.00	12.00
18 Toby Caston	4.00	10.00
19 Eugene Chung	4.00	10.00
20 Gary Clark	6.00	15.00
21 Greg Clark	4.00	10.00
22 Marco Coleman	5.00	12.00
23 Cary Conklin	4.00	10.00
24 Marv Cook	4.00	10.00
25 Quentin Coryatt	5.00	12.00
26 Bill Cowher CO	30.00	50.00
27 Aaron Cox	4.00	10.00
28 Ray Crockett	4.00	10.00
29 Jeff Cross	4.00	10.00
30 Joe DeLamielleure RET	6.00	15.00
31 Keith DeLong	4.00	10.00
32 Steve DeOssie	4.00	10.00
33 Al Davis OWN	250.00	350.00
34 Antone Davis	4.00	10.00
35 Wendell Davis	4.00	10.00
36 Robert Delpino	4.00	10.00
37 Chris Doleman	8.00	20.00
38 Tony Dorsett RET	12.00	30.00
39 Vaughn Dunbar	4.00	10.00
40 Al Edwards	4.00	10.00
41 Steve Emtman	4.00	10.00
42 Ricky Ervins	4.00	10.00
43 Gill Fenerty	4.00	10.00
44 Derrick Fenner	4.00	10.00
45 John Fina	4.00	10.00
46 Tom Flores CO	5.00	12.00
47 Dan Fouts RET	8.00	20.00
48 Mike Fox	4.00	10.00
49 Mitch Frerotte	4.00	10.00
50 John Friesz	4.00	10.00
51 William Fuller	5.00	12.00
52 Willie Gault	6.00	15.00
53 John Gesek	4.00	10.00
54 Sean Gilbert	4.00	10.00
55 Otto Graham RET	15.00	30.00
56 Eric Green	4.00	10.00
57 Harold Green	4.00	10.00
58 Paul Gruber	4.00	10.00
59 Dino Hackett	4.00	10.00
60 Charles Haley	6.00	15.00
61 Jason Hanson	8.00	20.00
62 Alvin Harper	6.00	15.00
63 Michael Haynes	5.00	12.00
64 Keith Henderson	4.00	10.00
65 Jeff Herrod	4.00	10.00
66 Jessie Hester	4.00	10.00
67 Craig Heyward	15.00	30.00
68 Mark Higgs	4.00	10.00
69 Tommy Hodson	4.00	10.00
70 Mike Holmgren CO	15.00	30.00
71 Ethan Horton	4.00	10.00
72 Patrick Hunter	4.00	10.00
73 Steve Israel	4.00	10.00
74 Keith Jackson	6.00	15.00
75 Joe Jacoby	6.00	15.00
76 Jim C. Jensen	4.00	10.00
77 Vance Johnson	4.00	10.00
78 Ernie Jones	4.00	10.00
79 Robert Jones	4.00	10.00
80 Sean Jones	5.00	12.00
81 Brian Jordan	6.00	15.00
82 Sonny Jurgensen RET	12.00	30.00
83 David Klingler	4.00	10.00
84 Chuck Knox CO	4.00	10.00
85 Tim Krumrie	4.00	10.00
86 Eddie LeBaron RET	6.00	15.00
87 Darren Lewis	4.00	10.00
88 Nate Lewis	4.00	10.00
89 Greg Lloyd	15.00	30.00
90 Bubba McDowell	4.00	10.00
91 Chester McGlockton	5.00	12.00
92 Tommy Maddox	8.00	20.00
93 Ted Marchibroda CO	6.00	15.00
94 Chris Martin	4.00	10.00
95 Mike Merriweather	4.00	10.00
96 Eric Metcalf	5.00	12.00
97 Chris Mims	4.00	10.00
98 Hugh Millen	4.00	10.00
99 Brian Mitchell	6.00	15.00
100 Johnny Mitchell	4.00	10.00
101 Joe Montana	40.00	100.00
102 Eric Moore	4.00	10.00
103 Brad Muster	4.00	10.00
104 Ken Norton Jr.	5.00	12.00
105 Jay Novacek	8.00	20.00
106 Neil O'Donnell	6.00	15.00
107 Marquez Pope	4.00	10.00
108 Robert Porcher	5.00	12.00
109 Mike Prior	4.00	10.00
110 Ervin Randle	4.00	10.00
111 Walter Reeves	4.00	10.00
112 Ricky Reynolds	4.00	10.00
113 Bobby Ross CO	5.00	12.00
114 Mark Rypien	25.00	50.00
115 Deion Sanders	20.00	50.00
116 Tracy Scroggins	4.00	10.00
117 Leon Searcy	4.00	10.00
118 Sterling Sharpe	6.00	15.00
119 David Shula CO	4.00	10.00
120 Chris Singleton	4.00	10.00
121 Greg Skrepenak	4.00	10.00
122 Chuck Smith	4.00	10.00
123 Doug Smith	4.00	10.00
124 Emmitt Smith	50.00	100.00
125 Kevin Smith	4.00	10.00
126 Lance Smith	4.00	10.00
127 Sammie Smith	4.00	10.00
128 Phillippi Sparks	4.00	10.00
129 Alonzo Spellman	4.00	10.00
130 Ken Stabler RET	15.00	30.00
131 Kelly Stouffer	4.00	10.00
132 Lynn Swann RET	60.00	150.00
133 Jim Sweeney	4.00	10.00
134 Harry Sydney	4.00	10.00
135 Charley Taylor RET	6.00	15.00
136 Pat Terrell	4.00	10.00
137 Henry Thomas	4.00	10.00
138 Stan Thomas	4.00	10.00
139 Y.A. Tittle RET	12.50	25.00
140 Mike Tomczak	4.00	10.00
141 Jessie Tuggle	4.00	10.00
142 Floyd Turner	4.00	10.00
143 Tommy Vardell	5.00	12.00
144 Jon Vaughn	4.00	10.00
145 Troy Vincent	6.00	15.00
146 Tom Waddle	4.00	10.00
147 Van Waiters	4.00	10.00
148 Aaron Wallace	4.00	10.00
149 Brian Washington	4.00	10.00
150 William White	4.00	10.00
151 Dave Widell	4.00	10.00
152 Calvin Williams	5.00	12.00
153 Darryl Williams	4.00	10.00
154 Harvey Williams	4.00	10.00
155 John L. Williams	5.00	12.00
156 Warren Williams	4.00	10.00
157 Ken Willis	4.00	10.00
158 Kellen Winslow RET	8.00	20.00
159 Darren Woodson	8.00	20.00
160 Sam Wyche CO	5.00	12.00
161 Michael Young	4.00	10.00
162 Tony Zendejas	4.00	10.00
NNO Santa Claus	6.00	15.00
NNO Mrs. Santa	10.00	25.00
NNO Santa Mrs. Claus Dual	8.00	20.00

1992 Pro Line Portraits Collectibles

These standard-size cards were inserted in 1992 Pro Line foil packs. Their numbering picks up after the two special collectible cards issued the previous year. The fronts display full-bleed color photos, while the backs carry extended quotes on a silver panel.

COMPLETE SET (6)	1.50	4.00
PLC3 Chris Berman Coaches	.20	.50
PLC4 Joe Gibbs Racing	.20	.50
PLC5 Gifford Family	.20	.50
PLC6 Dale Jarrett	.40	1.00
PLC7 Paul Tagliabue	.20	.50
PLC8 Don David Shula	.40	1.00

1992 Pro Line Portraits Collectibles Autographs

These standard-size cards were inserted in 1992 Pro Line foil packs. The fronts display full-bleed color photos, while the backs carry extended quotes on a silver panel. The cards are unnumbered and checklisted below in alphabetical order.

1 C.Berman Coaches	15.00	30.00
2 Dale Jarrett	20.00	50.00
3 Don David Shula	25.00	50.00
4 Paul Tagliabue COM	15.00	30.00

1992 Pro Line Portraits QB Gold

Featuring the top NFL quarterbacks, this 18-card set was randomly inserted into 1992 Pro Line foil packs at a rate of three per box. A complete set was also packed with each hobby case. Special retail packs that were later produced included a QB Gold card in each pack. The cards measure the standard size and feature posed color player photos of NFL quarterbacks of the fronts. The pictures are bordered on two sides by gold foil stripes that run the length of the card. The player's name and the words "Quarterback Gold" are printed in black on the stripes. The backs are bordered by gold stripes at the top and bottom. The background is off-white and displays passing and rushing statistics in black print. The cards are arranged in alphabetical order.

COMPLETE SET (18)	3.00	8.00
RANDOM INSERTS IN FOIL PACKS		
ONE PER SPECIAL RETAIL PACK		
ONE SET PER HOBBY CASE		
1 Troy Aikman	.40	1.00
2 Bubby Brister	.10	.30
3 Randall Cunningham	.20	.50
4 John Elway	.75	2.00
5 Boomer Esiason	.10	.30
6 Jim Everett	.07	.20
7 Jeff George	.10	.30
8 Jim Harbaugh	.10	.30
9 Jeff Hostetler	.10	.30
10 Jim Kelly	.20	.50
11 Bernie Kosar	.07	.20
12 Dan Marino	.75	2.00
13 Chris Miller	.07	.20
14 Joe Montana	.75	2.00
15 Warren Moon	.20	.50
16 Mark Rypien	.07	.20
17 Phil Simms	.10	.30
18 Steve Young	.30	.75
5AU Boomer Esiason AU/1992	5.00	12.00

1992 Pro Line Portraits Rookie Gold

Featuring the top NFL rookies, one card of this 28-card standard-size set was inserted into each 1992 Pro Line jumbo pack. The cards feature posed color player photos on the fronts. The pictures are bordered on two sides by gold foil stripes that run the length of the card. The player's name and the words "Rookie Gold" are printed in black on the stripes. The backs are bordered by gold stripes at the top and bottom. The background is white and displays complete college statistics in black print. Production was limited to 4,000 cases of the jumbo packs. The cards are arranged in alphabetical order by team.

COMPLETE SET (28)	2.50	6.00
ONE PER JUMBO PACK		
1 Tony Smith RB	.08	.25
2 John Fina	.08	.25
3 Alonzo Spellman	.08	.25
4 David Klingler	.15	.40
5 Tommy Vardell	.15	.40
6 Kevin Smith DB	.08	.25
7 Tommy Maddox	.50	1.25
8 Robert Porcher	.08	.25
9 Terrell Buckley	.15	.40
10 Eddie Robinson	.08	.25
11 Steve Emtman	.15	.40
12 Quentin Coryatt	.15	.40
13 Dale Carter	.15	.40
14 Chester McGlockton	.15	.40
15 Sean Gilbert	.15	.40
16 Troy Vincent	.08	.25
17 Robert Harris	.08	.25
18 Eugene Chung	.08	.25
19 Vaughn Dunbar	.08	.25
20 Derek Brown TE	.08	.25
21 Johnny Mitchell	.15	.40
22 Siran Stacy	.08	.25
23 Tony Sacca	.08	.25
24 Leon Searcy	.08	.25
25 Chris Mims	.08	.25
26 Dana Hall	.08	.25
27 Courtney Hawkins	.15	.40
28 Shane Collins	.08	.25

1992 Pro Line Portraits Team NFL

This five-card standard-size set marks the debut of Pro Line's Team NFL cards, which features stars from other sports as well as celebrities from the entertainment world. The cards were randomly inserted in 1992 Pro Line Portraits packs. On the fronts, each personality is pictured wearing attire of their favorite NFL team. The horizontal backs have team color-coded stripes at the top and an extended quote on a silver panel. In small print to the left of the card number, it reads "Team NFL."

COMPLETE SET (5)	2.50	6.00
TNC1 Muhammad Ali	1.25	3.00
TNC2 Milton Berle	.40	1.00
TNC3 Don Mattingly	.60	1.50
TNC4 Martin Mull	.40	1.00
TNC5 Isiah Thomas	.40	1.00

1992 Pro Line Portraits Team NFL Autographs

This five-card standard-size set marks the debut of Pro Line's Team NFL Collectible cards, which features stars from other sports as well as celebrities from the entertainment world. On the fronts, each personality is pictured wearing attire of their favorite NFL team. The horizontal backs have team color-coded stripes at the top and an extended quote on a silver panel. The cards are unnumbered and checklisted below in alphabetical order. Muhammad Ali signed cards in two different forms: Muhammad Ali or Cassius Clay. Both versions were initially signed only on the card backs with no autograph on the front. It is commonly thought that only 50 cards were signed as Cassius Clay. Dual signed cards (Ali on the front and Clay on the back) surfaced much later and are largely thought to be the result of an aftermarket signing.

1A Muhammad Ali back AU	250.00	500.00
1B Cassius Clay back AU	300.00	600.00
2 Milton Berle	15.00	40.00
3 Don Mattingly	20.00	50.00
4 Martin Mull	6.00	15.00
5 Isiah Thomas	10.00	25.00

1992 Pro Line Portraits Wives

This 16-card standard-size set was issued with the 1992 Pro Line Portraits set as foil pack inserts. Its numbering is in continuation of the 1991 Pro Line Wives set. The set features full-bleed photos of wives of star NFL players and coaches. The cards are numbered on the back with an "SC" prefix.

COMPLETE SET (16)	.40	1.00
SC8 Ortancis Carter	.02	.10
SC9 Faith Cherry	.02	.10
SC10 Kaye Cowher	.02	.10
SC11 Dainnese Gault	.02	.10
SC12 Kathie Lee Gifford	.07	.20
SC13 Carole Hinton	.02	.10
SC14 Diane Long	.02	.10
SC15 Karen Lott	.02	.10
SC16 Felicia Moon	.02	.10
SC17 Cindy Noble	.02	.10
SC18 Linda Seifert	.02	.10
SC19 Mitzi Testaverde	.02	.10
SC20 Robin Swilling	.02	.10
SC21 Lesley Visser	.07	.20
SC22 Toni Doleman	.02	.10
SC23 Diana Ditka	.15	.40

1992 Pro Line Portraits Wives Autographs

This 16-card standard-size set was included in the 1992 Pro Line Portraits set, and is a continuation of the 1991 Pro Line Wives set. The set features full-bleed photos of wives of star NFL players and coaches. The cards are unnumbered and checklisted below in alphabetical order. Kathie Lee Gifford did not sign her cards.

COMPLETE SET (16)	75.00	125.00
1 Ortancis Carter	4.00	10.00
2 Faith Cherry	4.00	10.00
3 Kaye Cowher	8.00	20.00
4 Diana Ditka	6.00	15.00
5 Toni Doleman	4.00	10.00
6 Dainnese Gault	4.00	10.00
7 Carole Hinton	4.00	10.00
8 Diane Long	8.00	20.00
9 Karen Lott	8.00	20.00
10 Felicia Moon	4.00	10.00
11 Cindy Noble	4.00	10.00
12 Linda Seifert	4.00	10.00
13 Mitzi Testaverde	4.00	10.00
14 Robin Swilling	4.00	10.00
15 Lesley Visser ANN	5.00	12.00

1992 Pro Line Portraits National Convention

COMP.FACT.SET (194)	300.00	600.00
*PLAYER NATIONAL CARDS: 15X TO 40X		
*WIVES NATIONAL CARDS: 10X TO 25X		
*PLC NATIONAL CARDS: 6X TO 15X		
*TEAM NFL NATIONAL CARDS: 3X TO 8X		

1992 Pro Line Profiles

Together with the 1992 Pro Line Portraits, this 495-card standard-size set constitutes the bulk of the 1992 ProLine issue. This Profiles set consists of nine-card mini-biographies on 55 of the NFL's most well-known personalities. Each set chronicles the player's career from his days in college to the present day, including his life off of the football field. Each Pro Line pack contained nine Profiles and three Portraits cards, and Quarterback Gold cards were randomly inserted throughout the packs. The fronts display full-bleed color photos, and the fifth card in each subset features a color portrait by a noted sports artist. The text on the backs captures moments from the player's career or life, including quotes from the player himself. The set concludes with a ten-card Art Monk bonus set, which was available through a mail-in offer in exchange for ten 1991 ProLine Portraits wrappers (black) and ten 1992 ProLine wrappers (white). The cards in each subset are numbered "X of 9." A special boxed set, with the cards displayed in two notebooks, was distributed at the National. These cards differ from the regular series in two respects, the cards are unnumbered (except within nine-card subsets) and are stamped with a "The National, 1992" seal.

COMPLETE SET (495)	4.00	10.00
COMMON RONNIE LOTT	.02	.10
COMMON RODNEY PEETE	.01	.05
COMMON CARL BANKS	.01	.05
COMMON THURMAN THOMAS	.07	.20
COMMON ROGER STAUBACH	.07	.20
COMMON JERRY RICE	.20	.50
COMMON VINNY TESTAVERDE	.02	.10
COMMON ANTHONY CARTER	.02	.10
COMMON STERLING SHARPE	.02	.10
COMMON ANTHONY MUNOZ	.01	.05
COMMON BUDDY BRISTER	.01	.05
COMMON BERNIE KOSAR	.01	.05
COMMON ART SHELL	.02	.10
COMMON DON SHULA	.02	.10
COMMON JOE GIBBS	.02	.10
COMMON JUNIOR SEAU	.07	.20
COMMON AL TOON	.01	.05
COMMON JACK KEMP	.07	.20
COMMON JIM HARBAUGH	.02	.10
COMMON DAN MCGWIRE	.01	.05
COMMON TROY AIKMAN	.20	.50
COMMON KEITH BYARS	.01	.05
COMMON TIMM ROSENBACH	.01	.05
COMMON GARY CLARK	.02	.10
COMMON CHRIS DOLEMAN	.01	.05
COMMON JOHN ELWAY	.40	1.00
COMMON BOOMER ESIASON	.02	.10
COMMON JIM EVERETT	.02	.10
COMMON ERIC GREEN	.01	.05
COMMON JERRY GLANVILLE	.01	.05
COMMON JEFF HOSTLETER	.01	.05
COMMON HAYWOOD JEFFIRES	.02	.10
COMMON MICHAEL IRVIN	.07	.20
COMMON STEVE LARGENT	.07	.20
COMMON KEN O'BRIEN	.01	.05
COMMON CHRISTIAN OKOYE	.01	.05
COMMON MICHAEL DEAN PERRY	.02	.10
COMMON CHRIS MILLER	.01	.05
COMMON PHIL SIMMS	.07	.20
COMMON BRUCE SMITH	.02	.10
COMMON DERRICK THOMAS	.07	.20
COMMON PAT SWILLING	.01	.05
COMMON ERIC DICKERSON	.02	.10
COMMON HOWIE LONG	.02	.10
COMMON MIKE SINGLETARY	.02	.10
COMMON JOHN TAYLOR	.01	.05
COMMON ANDRE TIPPETT	.01	.05
COMMON JIM KELLY	.07	.20
COMMON MARK RYPIEN	.01	.05
COMMON WARREN MOON	.02	.10
COMMON DEION SANDERS	.07	.20
COMMON LAWRENCE TAYLOR	.07	.20
COMMON RANDALL CUNNINGHAM	.02	.10
COMMON EARNEST BYNER	.01	.05
COMMON MIKE DITKA	.02	.10
MONK SENDAWAY (496-504)	.15	.40

1992 Pro Line Profiles Autographs

TROY AIKMAN (181-189)	20.00	50.00
CARL BANKS (19-27	3.00	8.00
BUBBY BRISTER (91-99)	3.00	8.00
KEITH BYARS (190-198)	3.00	8.00
EARNEST BYNER (478-486)	5.00	12.00
ANTHONY CARTER (64-72)	3.00	8.00
GARY CLARK (208-216)	3.00	8.00
R.CUNNINGHAM (469-477)	10.00	25.00
ERIC DICKERSON (379-387)	15.00	40.00
MIKE DITKA (487-495)	12.50	25.00
CHRIS DOLEMAN (217-225)	6.00	15.00
JOHN ELWAY (226-234)	40.00	80.00
BOOMER ESIASON (235-243)	6.00	15.00
JIM EVERETT (244-252)	5.00	12.00
JOE GIBBS (127-135)	20.00	40.00
JERRY GLANVILLE (262-270)	2.50	6.00
ERIC GREEN (253-261)	2.50	6.00
JIM HARBAUGH (163-171)	8.00	20.00
JEFF HOSTETLER (271-279)	3.00	8.00
MICHAEL IRVIN (289-297)	15.00	30.00
HAYWOOD JEFFIRES (280-288)	3.00	8.00
JIM KELLY (424-432)	20.00	35.00
JACK KEMP (154-162)	15.00	30.00
BERNIE KOSAR (100-108)	10.00	25.00
STEVE LARGENT (298-306)	12.50	30.00
HOWIE LONG (388-396)	15.00	40.00
RONNIE LOTT (1-9)	8.00	20.00
DAN MCGWIRE (172-180)	2.50	6.00
ART MONK (496-504)	20.00	40.00
WARREN MOON (442-450)	10.00	25.00
ANTHONY MUNOZ (82-90)	5.00	12.00
KEN O'BRIEN (307-315)	2.50	6.00
CHRISTIAN OKOYE (316-324)	6.00	15.00
RODNEY PEETE (10-18)	2.50	6.00
MICHAEL D. PERRY (325-333)	2.50	6.00
JERRY RICE (46-54)	40.00	100.00
TIMM ROSENBACH (199-207)	3.00	8.00
DEION SANDERS (451-459)	20.00	40.00
JUNIOR SEAU (136-144)	20.00	50.00
STERLING SHARPE (73-81)	10.00	25.00
ART SHELL (109-117)	10.00	25.00
DON SHULA (118-126)	12.50	30.00
PHIL SIMMS (343-351)	8.00	20.00
MIKE SINGLETARY (397-405)	6.00	15.00
BRUCE SMITH (352-360)	15.00	40.00
ROGER STAUBACH (37-45)	20.00	50.00
PAT SWILLING (370-378)	3.00	8.00
JOHN TAYLOR (406-414)	5.00	12.00
LAW.TAYLOR (460-468)	15.00	30.00
VINNY TESTAVERDE (55-63)	5.00	12.00
DERRICK THOMAS (361-369)	25.00	50.00
THURMAN THOMAS (28-36)	8.00	20.00
ANDRE TIPPETT (415-423)	6.00	15.00
AL TOON (145-153)	3.00	8.00
46 Jerry Rice SP	40.00	100.00
47 Jerry Rice SP	40.00	100.00
48 Jerry Rice SP	40.00	100.00
49 Jerry Rice SP	40.00	100.00
56 Vinny Testaverde SP	8.00	20.00
58 Vinny Testaverde SP	8.00	20.00
102 Bernie Kosar SP	25.00	50.00
111 Art Shell CO SP	25.00	50.00
426 Jim Kelly SP	75.00	135.00

1992 Pro Line Profiles National Convention

COMPLETE SET (495)	150.00	300.00
*NATIONAL CARDS: 15X TO 40X		

1992-93 Pro Line SB Program

This nine-card standard-size set features Steve Young. One Steve Young promo card was inserted in each copy of the 1993 Super Bowl program. The fronts display full-bleed glossy color photos that capture Young both on and off the field. In text printed around a small color picture, the backs discuss chapters in Young's career and life and carry Young's comments as well. The cards are numbered on the back "X of 9."

COMPLETE SET (9)	3.20	8.00
COMMON CARD (1-9)	.40	1.00

1993 Pro Line Live Draft Day NYC

Packaged in a cello pack, this set of ten standard-size cards was passed out at the NFL Draft held April 25th in New York. The cards were created in anticipation of the draft, thus portraying the featured players with several possible teams, and to preview the 1993 Classic NFL Pro Line card design. The full-bleed color player photos on the fronts are accented on the right by a team color-coded stripe that carries the player's name and team name. The "Classic ProLine Live" and "NFL Draft 1993" logos at the lower corners round out the card face. Above a team color-coded panel presenting biography, statistics, and career highlights, the backs display a full-bleed color close-up photo. All the cards are numbered "1" on the back and are checklisted below alphabetically according to player's last name. Suffixes have been added in order to differentiate specific cards. Reportedly about 1,000 sets were distributed at the NFL Draft in New York City.

COMPLETE SET (10)	12.00	30.00
COMMON DREW BLEDSOE	3.00	8.00
COMMON ERIC CURRY	.40	1.00
COMMON MARVIN JONES	.40	1.00
COMMON RICK MIRER	.75	2.00

1993 Pro Line Live Draft Day QVC

Packaged in a cello pack, this set of ten standard-size cards has the same fronts as the set passed out at the NFL Draft held April 25th in New York. The cards were created in anticipation of the draft, thus portraying the featured players with several possible teams, and to preview the 1993 Classic NFL Pro Line card design. The full-bleed color player photos on the fronts are accented on the right by a team color-coded stripe that carries the player's name and team name. The "Classic ProLine Live" and "NFL Draft 1993" logos at the lower corners round out the card face. On a white, screened back with "1993 Draft Day" in gray lettering, the QVC-version's back has an oversized version of the Classic ProLine Live logo with black lettering immediately below. Reportedly only 9,300 sets with this special back were produced for sale through QVC.

COMPLETE SET (10)	6.00	15.00
COMMON DREW BLEDSOE	2.00	5.00
COMMON ERIC CURRY	.20	.50
COMMON MARVIN JONES	.20	.50
COMMON RICK MIRER	.40	1.00

1993 Pro Line Previews

Featuring the last five number one NFL Draft Picks, these five standard-size cards were randomly inserted in 1993 Classic Football Draft Pick foil packs. Twelve Thousand of each card were produced. The fronts from the Classic Pro Line Live, Profiles and Portraits sets appear in this preview of Pro Line's main sets. The backs, however, are more or less the same, featuring the set logo, year and player who was selected the number one draft pick, all printed on a gray background of diagonal Team NFL logos. The NFL and Classic logos appear in the bottom corners. The production number is shown at the bottom.

COMPLETE SET (5)	25.00	35.00
PL1 Troy Aikman Live	10.00	12.00
PL2 Jeff George Profile	3.00	5.00
PL3 Russell Maryland Live	2.00	3.00
PL4 Steve Emtman	2.00	3.00
PL5 Drew Bledsoe Portrait	10.00	15.00

1993 Pro Line Live

The 1993 edition of Pro Line consists of 286 Pro Line Live cards, 48 Portraits and thirteen nine-card (117) Profiles. All three sets were distributed by Classic through 12 and 23-card packs. The fronts feature full-bleed color action photos that are bordered on the right by a team color-coded stripe that carries the player's name and team name. The top portion of the back has a second color action photo, while the bottom portion consists of a team color-coded panel overprinted with player information. A collector could also have ordered a 100-card uncut sheet - featuring better players - from Classic for $39.95 plus shipping and handling. The cards are numbered on the back and checklisted below alphabetically according to teams. Rookie Cards include Jerome Bettis, Drew Bledsoe, Reggie Brooks, Curtis Conway, Garrison Hearst, Billy Joe Hobert, Terry Kirby, O.J. McDuffie, Natrone Means, Glyn Milburn, Rick Mirer, Robert Smith and Kevin Williams. Troy Aikman promo cards were produced and are listed below.

COMPLETE SET (285)	7.00	15.00
1 Michael Haynes	.02	.10
2 Chris Hinton	.01	.05
3 Pierce Holt	.01	.05
4 Chris Miller	.02	.10
5 Mike Pritchard	.02	.10
6 Andre Rison	.02	.10
7 Deion Sanders	.20	.50
8 Jessie Tuggle	.01	.05
9 Lincoln Kennedy RC	.01	.05
10 Roger Harper RC	.01	.05
11 Cornelius Bennett	.02	.10
12 Henry Jones	.01	.05
13 Jim Kelly	.08	.25
14 Bill Brooks	.01	.05
15 Nate Odomes	.01	.05
16 Andre Reed	.02	.10
17 Frank Reich	.02	.10
18 Bruce Smith	.08	.25
19 Steve Tasker	.02	.10
20 Thurman Thomas	.08	.25
21 Thomas Smith RC	.02	.10
22 John Parrella RC	.01	.05
23 Neal Anderson	.01	.05
24 Mark Carrier DB	.01	.05
25 Jim Harbaugh	.08	.25
26 Darren Lewis	.01	.05
27 Steve McMichael	.02	.10
28 Alonzo Spellman	.01	.05
29 Tom Waddle	.01	.05
30 Curtis Conway RC	.15	.40
31 Carl Simpson RC	.01	.05
32 David Fulcher	.01	.05
33 Harold Green	.01	.05
34 David Klingler	.01	.05
35 Tim Krumrie	.01	.05
36 Carl Pickens	.02	.10
37 Alfred Williams	.01	.05
38 Darryl Williams	.01	.05
39 John Copeland RC	.02	.10
40 Tony McGee RC	.02	.10
41 Bernie Kosar	.02	.10
42 Kevin Mack	.01	.05
43 Clay Matthews	.02	.10
44 Eric Metcalf	.02	.10
45 Michael Dean Perry	.02	.10
46 Vinny Testaverde	.02	.10
47 Jerry Ball	.01	.05
48 Tommy Vardell	.01	.05
49 Steve Everitt RC	.01	.05
50 Dan Footman RC	.01	.05
51 Troy Aikman	.30	.75
52 Daryl Johnston	.08	.25
53 Tony Casillas	.01	.05
54 Charles Haley	.02	.10
55 Alvin Harper	.02	.10
56 Michael Irvin	.08	.25
57 Robert Jones	.01	.05
58 Russell Maryland	.01	.05
59 Nate Newton	.02	.10
60 Ken Norton Jr.	.02	.10
61 Jay Novacek	.02	.10
62 Emmitt Smith	.60	1.50
63 Kevin Smith	.02	.10
64 Kevin Williams RC WR	.01	.05
65 Darrin Smith RC	.02	.10
66 Steve Atwater	.01	.05
67 Rod Bernstine	.01	.05
68 Mike Croel	.01	.05
69 John Elway	.60	1.50
70 Tommy Maddox	.08	.25
71 Karl Mecklenburg	.01	.05
72 Shannon Sharpe	.08	.25
73 Dennis Smith	.01	.05
74 Dan Williams RC	.01	.05
75 Glyn Milburn RC	.08	.25
76 Pat Swilling	.01	.05
77 Bennie Blades	.01	.05
78 Herman Moore	.08	.25
79 Rodney Peete	.01	.05
80 Brett Perriman	.08	.25
81 Barry Sanders	.50	1.25
82 Chris Spielman	.02	.10
83 Andre Ware	.01	.05
84 Ryan McNeil RC	.08	.25
85 Antonio London RC	.01	.05
86 Tony Bennett	.01	.05
87 Terrell Buckley	.01	.05
88 Brett Favre	.75	2.00
89 Brian Noble	.01	.05
90 Ken O'Brien	.01	.05
91 Sterling Sharpe	.08	.25
92 Reggie White	.08	.25
93 John Stephens	.01	.05
94 Wayne Simmons RC	.01	.05
95 George Teague RC	.02	.10
96 Ray Childress	.01	.05
97 Curtis Duncan	.01	.05
98 Ernest Givins	.02	.10
99 Haywood Jeffires	.02	.10
100 Bubba McDowell	.01	.05
101 Warren Moon	.08	.25
102 Al Smith	.01	.05
103 Lorenzo White	.01	.05
104 Brad Hopkins RC	.01	.05
105 Micheal Barrow RC	.08	.25
106 Duane Bickett	.01	.05
107 Quentin Coryatt	.02	.10
108 Steve Emtman	.01	.05
109 Jeff George	.08	.25
110 Anthony Johnson	.02	.10
111 Reggie Langhorne	.01	.05
112 Jack Trudeau	.01	.05
113 Clarence Verdin	.01	.05
114 Jessie Hester	.01	.05
115 Roosevelt Potts RC	.01	.05
116 Dale Carter	.01	.05
117 Dave Krieg	.02	.10
118 Nick Lowery	.01	.05
119 Christian Okoye	.01	.05
120 Neil Smith	.08	.25
121 Derrick Thomas	.08	.25
122 Harvey Williams	.02	.10
123 Barry Word	.01	.05
124 Joe Montana	.60	1.50
125 Marcus Allen	.08	.25
126 James Lofton	.02	.10
127 Nick Bell	.01	.05
128 Tim Brown	.08	.25
129 Eric Dickerson	.02	.10
130 Jeff Hostetler	.02	.10
131 Howie Long	.08	.25
132 Todd Marinovich	.01	.05
133 Greg Townsend	.01	.05
134 Patrick Bates RC	.01	.05
135 Billy Joe Hobert RC	.08	.25
136 Flipper Anderson	.01	.05
137 Shane Conlan	.01	.05
138 Henry Ellard	.02	.10
139 Jim Everett	.02	.10
140 Cleveland Gary	.01	.05
141 Sean Gilbert	.02	.10
142 Todd Lyght	.01	.05
143 Jerome Bettis RC	1.50	4.00
144 Troy Drayton RC	.02	.10

145 Louis Oliver .01 .05
146 Marco Coleman .01 .05
147 Bryan Cox .01 .05
148 Mark Duper .01 .05
149 Irving Fryar .02 .10
150 Mark Higgs .01 .05
151 Keith Jackson .02 .10
152 Dan Marino .60 1.50
153 Troy Vincent .01 .05
154 Richmond Webb .01 .05
155 O.J.McDuffie RC .08 .25
156 Terry Kirby RC .08 .25
157 Terry Allen .08 .25
158 Anthony Carter .02 .10
159 Cris Carter .08 .25
160 Chris Doleman .01 .05
161 Randall McDaniel .02 .10
162 Audray McMillian .01 .05
163 Henry Thomas .01 .05
164 Gary Zimmerman .01 .05
165 Robert Smith RC .50 1.25
166 Qadry Ismail RC .08 .25
167 Vincent Brown .01 .05
168 Marv Cook .01 .05
169 Greg McMurtry .01 .05
170 Jon Vaughn .01 .05
171 Leonard Russell .02 .10
172 Andre Tippett .01 .05
173 Scott Zolak .01 .05
174 Drew Bledsoe RC 1.00 2.50
175 Chris Slade RC .02 .10
176 Morten Andersen .01 .05
177 Vaughn Dunbar .01 .05
178 Rickey Jackson .01 .05
179 Vaughan Johnson .01 .05
180 Eric Martin .01 .05
181 Sam Mills .01 .05
182 Brad Muster .01 .05
183 Willie Roaf RC .10 .30
184 Irv Smith RC .01 .05
185 Reggie Freeman RC .01 .05
186 Michael Brooks .01 .05
187 Dave Brown RC .08 .25
188 Rodney Hampton .02 .10
189 Pepper Johnson .01 .05
190 Ed McCaffrey .08 .25
191 Dave Meggett .01 .05
192 Bart Oates .01 .05
193 Phil Simms .02 .10
194 Lawrence Taylor .08 .25
195 Michael Strahan RC .60 1.50
196 Brad Baxter .01 .05
197 Johnny Johnson .01 .05
198 Boomer Esiason .02 .10
199 Ronnie Lott .02 .10
200 Johnny Mitchell .01 .05
201 Rob Moore .02 .10
202 Browning Nagle .01 .05
203 Blair Thomas .01 .05
204 Marvin Jones RC .01 .05
205 Coleman Rudolph RC .01 .05
206 Eric Allen .01 .05
207 Fred Barnett .02 .10
208 Tim Harris .01 .05
209 Randall Cunningham .08 .25
210 Seth Joyner .01 .05
211 Clyde Simmons .01 .05
212 Herschel Walker .02 .10
213 Calvin Williams .02 .10
214 Lester Holmes RC .01 .05
215 Leonard Renfro RC .01 .05
216 Chris Chandler .02 .10
217 Gary Clark .02 .10
218 Ken Harvey .01 .05
219 Randal Hill .01 .05
220 Steve Beuerlein .02 .10
221 Ricky Proehl .01 .05
222 Timm Rosenbach .01 .05
223 Garrison Hearst RC .30 .75
224 Ernest Dye RC .01 .05
225 Bubby Brister .01 .05
226 Dermontti Dawson .02 .10
227 Barry Foster .02 .10
228 Kevin Greene .02 .10
229 Merril Hoge .01 .05
230 Greg Lloyd .02 .10
231 Neil O'Donnell .08 .25
232 Rod Woodson .08 .25
233 Deon Figures RC .01 .05
234 Chad Brown RC LB .02 .10
235 Marion Butts .01 .05
236 Gill Byrd .01 .05
237 Ronnie Harmon .01 .05
238 Stan Humphries .02 .10
239 Anthony Miller .02 .10
240 Leslie O'Neal .02 .10
241 Stanley Richard .01 .05
242 Junior Seau .08 .25
243 Darrien Gordon RC .01 .05
244 Natrone Means RC .08 .25
245 Dana Hall .01 .05
246 Brent Jones .02 .10
247 Tim McDonald .01 .05
248 Steve Bono .02 .10
249 Jerry Rice .40 1.00
250 John Taylor .02 .10
251 Ricky Watters .08 .25
252 Steve Young .30 .75
253 Dana Stubblefield RC .08 .25
254 Todd Kelly RC .01 .05
255 Brian Blades .02 .10
256 Ferrell Edmunds .01 .05
257 Stan Gelbaugh .01 .05
258 Cortez Kennedy .02 .10
259 Dan McGwire .01 .05
260 Chris Warren .02 .10
261 John L. Williams .01 .05
262 David Wyman .01 .05
263 Rick Mirer RC .08 .25
264 Carlton Gray RC .01 .05
265 Marty Carter .01 .05
266 Reggie Cobb .01 .05
267 Lawrence Dawsey .01 .05
268 Santana Dotson .02 .10
269 Craig Erickson .02 .10
270 Paul Gruber .01 .05
271 Keith McCants .01 .05
272 Broderick Thomas .01 .05
273 Eric Curry RC .01 .05
274 Demetrius DuBose RC .01 .05
275 Earnest Byner UER .01 .05
276 Ricky Ervins .01 .05
277 Brad Edwards .01 .05
278 Jim Lachey .01 .05
279 Charles Mann .01 .05
280 Carl Banks .01 .05
281 Art Monk .02 .10
282 Mark Rypien .01 .05
283 Ricky Sanders .01 .05
284 Tom Carter RC .02 .10
285 Reggie Brooks RC .02 .10
P1 Troy Aikman Promo .50 1.25
P2 Troy Aikman Promo .40 1.00

1993 Pro Line Live Autographs

The 1993 Pro Line Live Autographs set comprises standard-size cards. Randomly inserted at an average of two per 1993 Pro Line Live 10 box case, the cards are similar in design to that issue. The fronts sport color player action photos that are bordered on the right by a team color-coded stripe that carries the player's name and team name. The player's autograph across the photo and the hand written serial number round out the card front. The white backs carry a congratulatory message. The cards are unnumbered and checklisted below in alphabetical order. There has been speculation that Troy Aikman's cards may have been autopenned. Also note that the Marco Coleman cards were signed on the card back. Finally, an Emmitt Smith signed card appeared on the market after Score Board ceased card operations and liquidated its inventory. The cards are serial numbered to 700, but it is though that fewer than that number were actually released.

STATED PRINT RUN 400-1200
1 Troy Aikman/700 25.00 50.00
2 Neal Anderson/1050 6.00 15.00
3 Rod Bernstine/1000 5.00 12.00
4 Terrell Buckley/1050 5.00 12.00
5 Earnest Byner/750 UER 6.00 15.00
6 Anthony Carter/950 6.00 15.00
7 Ray Childress/950 6.00 15.00
8 Gary Clark/1050 6.00 15.00
9 Marco Coleman/1000 5.00 12.00
10 Quentin Coryatt/900 6.00 15.00
11 Eric Dickerson/900 12.50 30.00
12 Chris Doleman/1000 5.00 12.00
13 Steve Emtman/800 6.00 15.00
14 Brett Favre/650 75.00 150.00
15 Barry Foster/750 6.00 15.00
16 Jeff George/1050 6.00 15.00
17 Rodney Hampton/650 6.00 15.00
18 Keith Jackson/650 8.00 20.00
19 Haywood Jeffires/950 6.00 15.00
20 David Klingler/1200 5.00 12.00
21 Howie Long/950 20.00 40.00
22 Ronnie Lott/1050 10.00 25.00
23 Tommy Maddox/1050 6.00 15.00
24 Art Monk/750 15.00 30.00
25 Joe Montana/600 40.00 100.00
26 Rob Moore/900 6.00 15.00
27 Neil O'Donnell/1050 6.00 15.00
28 Christian Okoye/900 6.00 15.00
29 Rodney Peete/1000 6.00 15.00
30 Andre Reed/1050 8.00 20.00
31 Deion Sanders/900 20.00 40.00
32 Junior Seau/900 30.00 60.00
33 Sterling Sharpe/1050 8.00 20.00
34 Emmitt Smith/700 75.00 150.00
35 Neil Smith/1050 8.00 20.00
36 Pat Swilling/950 12.00 30.00
37 Vinny Testaverde/900 6.00 15.00
38 Derrick Thomas/550 50.00 100.00
39 Herschel Walker/400 8.00 20.00

1993 Pro Line Live Future Stars

The 1993 Pro Line Live Future Stars set comprises 28 standard-size cards. The insertion rate was one per 1993 Pro Line Live jumbo pack. The fronts sport color player action shots with black-and-white backgrounds that are borderless, except on the right, where a gold foil-stamped stripe carries the player's name and team name. The gold foil-stamped production number, "1 of 22,000," also appears along the right side. Above a team color-coded panel presenting biography, statistics, and career highlights, the backs carry a full-bleed color action player shot. The cards are numbered on the back with an "FS" prefix.

COMPLETE SET (28) 5.00 12.00
ONE PER JUMBO PACK
1 Patrick Bates .05 .15
2 Jerome Bettis 4.00 10.00
3 Drew Bledsoe 2.50 6.00
4 Tom Carter .08 .25
5 Curtis Conway .40 1.00
6 Steve Everitt .05 .15
7 Deon Figures .05 .15
8 Darrien Gordon .05 .15
9 Lester Holmes .05 .15
10 Brad Hopkins .05 .15
11 Marvin Jones .05 .15
12 Lincoln Kennedy .05 .15
13 O.J.McDuffie .25 .60
14 Rick Mirer .25 .60
15 Willie Roaf .30 .75
16 Will Shields .05 .15
17 Wayne Simmons .05 .15
18 Robert Smith 1.25 3.00
19 Thomas Smith .08 .25
20 Michael Strahan 1.50 4.00
21 Dana Stubblefield .25 .60
22 Dan Williams .05 .15
23 Kevin Williams WR .05 .15
24 Garrison Hearst .75 2.00
25 John Copeland .08 .25
26 Ryan McNeil .25 .60
27 Eric Curry .05 .15
28 Roosevelt Potts .05 .15

1993 Pro Line Live Illustrated

Illustrated by comic artist Neal Adams, this six-card standard size set was randomly inserted on an average of three per case in 1993 Classic Pro Line packs. Reportedly 10,000 of each card were produced. The front of each card features Adams' colorful player action illustration, which is borderless on three sides. The right side is edged by a team-colored stripe that carries the player's name and team name. In its top half, the back carries a portion of the same player action drawing, followed below by career highlights in a team-colored area at the bottom. The cards are numbered on the back with an "SP" prefix.

COMPLETE SET (6) 6.00 15.00
SP1 Troy Aikman 2.00 5.00
SP2 Jerry Rice 2.50 6.00
SP3 Michael Irvin .60 1.50
SP4 Thurman Thomas .60 1.50
SP5 Lawrence Taylor .60 1.50
SP6 Deion Sanders 1.25 3.00

1993 Pro Line Live LPs

These 20 limited-print, foil-stamped standard-size cards spotlight top young NFL talent along with three top NBA draft picks. The cards were randomly inserted throughout 1993 Classic Pro Line packs on an average of four per point of purchase box. Each card front features a color player action shot that is borderless on three sides. The right side is edged by a team-colored stripe that carries the player's name in gold foil. The gold-foil limited print seal, which carries the words "One of 40,000," appears at the lower right. In its top half, the back carries another player action shot, followed below by career highlights in a team-colored area at the bottom. The cards are numbered on the back with an "LP" prefix.

COMPLETE SET (20) 6.00 15.00
LP1 Chris Webber .75 2.00
LP2 Shaquille O'Neal 1.50 4.00
LP3 Jamal Mashburn .10 .30
LP4 Marcus Allen .30 .75
LP5 Neal Anderson .05 .15
LP6 Reggie Cobb .05 .15
LP7 Rod Bernstine .05 .15
LP8 Barry Word .05 .15
LP9 Troy Aikman 1.00 2.50
LP10 Brett Favre 2.50 6.00
LP11 Ricky Watters .30 .75
LP12 Terry Allen .30 .75
LP13 Rodney Hampton .10 .30
LP14 Garrison Hearst 1.00 2.50
LP15 Jerome Bettis 5.00 12.00
LP16 Barry Foster .10 .30
LP17 Harold Green .05 .15
LP18 Tommy Vardell .05 .15
LP19 Lorenzo White .05 .15
LP20 Marion Butts .05 .15

1993 Pro Line Live Tonx

Issued to herald the release of 1993 Classic NFL Tonx in the fall, these six "milk cap" game cards were random inserts in packs of 1993 Pro Line Live. The cards included a circular piece that measures about 1 5/8" in diameter and could be popped out of its standard-size card. The front of each disc features a borderless color player action shot. The black back carries the player's team helmet at the top, followed below by his position, and name within a blue stripe. The cards are unnumbered and checklisted below in alphabetical order.

COMPLETE SET (6) 1.60 4.00
1 Troy Aikman .60 1.50
2 Michael Irvin .15 .40
3 Jerry Rice .60 1.50
4 Deion Sanders .25 .60
5 Lawrence Taylor .08 .25
6 Thurman Thomas .15 .40

1993 Pro Line Portraits

As part of the 1993 Classic Pro Line issue, this 44-card standard-size set features full-bleed non-game photos on the front. The bottom center of the back has a color head shot, and a player quote on a silver panel wraps around the picture. The set closes with a Throwbacks (507-511) subset. The cards are numbered on the back in continuation of the 1992 Pro Line Portraits set. This set was the last of the Portraits series ('91-'93). Rookie Cards include Jerome Bettis, Drew Bledsoe, Garrison Hearst and Rick Mirer.

COMPLETE SET (44) 2.50 6.00
468 Willie Roaf RC .10 .30
469 Terry Allen .07 .20
470 Jerry Ball .01 .05
471 Patrick Bates RC .01 .05
472 Ray Bentley .01 .05
473 Jerome Bettis RC 1.50 4.00
474 Steve Beuerlein .02 .10
475 Drew Bledsoe RC 1.00 2.50
476 Dave Brown RC .07 .20
477 Gill Byrd .01 .05
478 Tony Casillas .01 .05
479 Chuck Cecil .01 .05
480 Reggie Cobb .01 .05
481 Pat Harlow .01 .05
482 John Copeland RC .02 .10
483 Bryan Cox .01 .05
484 Eric Curry RC .01 .05
485 Jeff Lageman .01 .05
486 Brett Favre UER .75 2.00
487 Barry Foster .02 .10
488 Gaston Green .01 .05
489 Rodney Hampton .02 .10
490 Tim Harris .01 .05
491 Garrison Hearst RC .30 .75
492 Tony Smith RB .01 .05
493 Marvin Jones RC .01 .05
494 Lincoln Kennedy RC .01 .05
495 Wilber Marshall .01 .05
496 Terry McDaniel .01 .05
497 Rick Mirer RC .07 .20
498 Art Monk .02 .10
499 Mike Munchak .02 .10
500 Frank Reich .02 .10
501 Barry Sanders .60 1.50
502 Shannon Sharpe .07 .20
503 Gino Torretta RC .01 .05
504 Ricky Watters .07 .20
505 Richmond Webb .01 .05
506 Reggie White .07 .20
507 Bert Jones TB .01 .05
508 Billy Kilmer TB .01 .05
509 John Mackey TB .01 .05
510 Archie Manning TB .02 .10
511 Harvey Martin TB .01 .05

1993 Pro Line Portraits Autographs

Randomly inserted in packs, the 1993 Pro Line Portraits Autographs set features 27-standard-size signed cards. These cards are identical to the 1993 Pro Line Portraits set except for the additional of the signature, the Pro Line Certified embossing and the lack of a card number. Out of the 44 players featured in the basic set, only 27-signed cards. The cards are unnumbered and checklisted below in alphabetical order.

COMPLETE SET (27) 400.00 750.00
1 Patrick Bates 7.50 20.00
2 Jerome Bettis 60.00 120.00
3 Steve Beuerlein 10.00 25.00
4 Drew Bledsoe 50.00 80.00
5 Tony Casillas 7.50 20.00
6 Chuck Cecil 7.50 20.00
7 Reggie Cobb 7.50 20.00
8 John Copeland 7.50 20.00
9 Eric Curry 7.50 20.00
10 Brett Favre 175.00 300.00
11 Gaston Green 7.50 20.00
12 Rodney Hampton 10.00 25.00
13 Pat Harlow 7.50 20.00
14 Bert Jones TB 10.00 25.00
15 Marvin Jones 7.50 20.00
16 Lincoln Kennedy 7.50 20.00
17 Billy Kilmer TB 10.00 25.00
18 Jeff Lageman 7.50 20.00
19 Archie Manning TB 12.50 30.00
20 Harvey Martin TB 15.00 40.00
21 Terry McDaniel 7.50 20.00
22 Mike Munchak 20.00 40.00
23 Frank Reich 7.50 20.00
24 Willie Roaf 10.00 25.00
25 Shannon Sharpe 25.00 50.00
26 Tony Smith RB 7.50 20.00
27 Gino Torretta 12.50 30.00

1993 Pro Line Portraits Wives

Randomly inserted in 1993 Pro Line packs, this four-card standard-size set features wives of NFL stars. The fronts feature full-bleed color action photos, while the horizontal backs carry a quote and a color close-up shot. The cards are numbered on the back in continuation of the 1992 Pro Line Wives ("Spirit") insert. Card SC24 was never produced.

COMPLETE SET (4) .20 .50
SC25 Annette Rypien .05 .15
SC26 Ann Stark .05 .15
SC27 Cindy Walker .05 .15
SC28 Cindy Reed .05 .15

1993 Pro Line Portraits Wives Autographs

Randomly inserted in packs, the 1993 Pro Line Portraits Wives features three standard-size signed cards. These cards are identical to the 1993 Pro Line Portraits Wives sets except for the signatures and the Pro Line certified stamp. Out of the four wives featured in the basic set, three signed cards. The cares are unnumbered and checklisted below in alphabetical order.

COMPLETE SET (3) 20.00 50.00
1 Cindy Reed 7.50 20.00
2 Annette Rypien 6.00 15.00
3 Ann Stark 7.50 20.00

1993 Pro Line Profiles

As part of the 1993 Classic Pro Line issue, this 117-card standard-size set features thirteen nine-card subsets devoted to outstanding NFL players. The fronts display full-bleed color action player photos. The lettering and the stripe carrying the player's name are team color-coded. The backs have a second color action shot, career highlights in the form of an expanded caption, and a player quote. The cards are individually numbered on the back as an extension of the 1992 Profiles issue. Each subset ("X of 9") is also numbered.

COMPLETE SET (117) 2.50 6.00
COMMON RAY CHILDRESS .01 .04
COMMON JEFF GEORGE .01 .04
COMMON FRANCO HARRIS .02 .08
COMMON KEITH JACKSON .01 .04
COMMON JIMMY JOHNSON .03 .15
COMMON JAMES LOFTON .02 .08
COMMON DAN MARINO .25 .60
COMMON JOE MONTANA .30 .75
COMMON JAY NOVACEK .01 .04
COMMON GALE SAYERS .02 .08
COMMON EMMITT SMITH .25 .60
COMMON HERSCHEL WALKER .02 .08
COMMON STEVE YOUNG .10 .30

1993 Pro Line Profiles Autographs

Cards from this set are identical to the 1993 Pro Line Profiles except for the signatures and the Pro Line certified stamp. The prices below refer to all autograph cards that are known to exist. However, the list is likely incomplete. The signed cards were issued randomly in various 1993 Pro Line packaging types, including hobby, jumbo, and retail packs. Additional cards made their way onto the market following the sale of Classic Inc. assets.

RAY CHILDRESS (496-504) 4.00 10.00
JEFF GEORGE (505-513) 6.00 15.00
FRANCO HARRIS (514-521) 15.00 40.00
KEITH JACKSON (523-531) 4.00 10.00
J.JOHNSON (533/535/538-540) 8.00 20.00
J.JOHNSON (532/534/536/537) 25.00 50.00
JAY NOVACEK (568-576) 10.00 25.00
GALE SAYERS (577-585) 15.00 40.00
EMMITT SMITH (586-594) 60.00 150.00

1994 Pro Line Live Draft Day NYC

This 13-card standard-size set previews the 1994 NFL Draft by portraying the featured players with several possible teams (with the exception of Troy Aikman) and were distributed in part at the NFL Draft in New York. The fronts feature full-bleed color action player photos. At the bottom the player's name is printed in team color-coded letters, which in turn are underscored by a team color-coded stripe. The backs have a full-bleed ghosted photo except for a square at the player's head. The set name, draft date (April 24, 1994), and production figures (1 of 19,940) are stenciled over the ghosted photo. Note that the cards follow the 1994 Pro Line Live card design, but contain the Classic logo on the cardfronts not the Pro Line Live logo.

COMPLETE SET (13) 10.00 25.00
FD1 Dan Wilkinson .40 1.00
FD2 Dan Wilkinson .40 1.00
FD3 Marshall Faulk 2.00 5.00
FD4 Marshall Faulk 2.00 5.00
FD5 Marshall Faulk 2.00 5.00
FD6 Troy Aikman 1.50 4.00
FD7 Trent Dilfer .75 2.00
FD8 Trent Dilfer .75 2.00
FD9 Heath Shuler .50 1.25
FD10 Heath Shuler .50 1.25
FD11 Aaron Glenn .40 1.00
FD12 Aaron Glenn .40 1.00
FD13 Dan Wilkinson .40 1.00

1994 Pro Line Live Draft Day QVC

This set of standard-size cards has the same fronts as the set passed out at the NFL Draft held in New York but different backs. The cards were initially created in anticipation of the draft, thus portraying the featured players with several possible teams, and to preview the 1994 Pro Line card design. The "Classic ProLine Live" and "NFL Draft 1994" logos are featured on the cardfronts. Each card was numbered of 9,400 sets and were sold in set form through QVC.

COMPLETE SET (12) 6.00 15.00
DD1 Troy Aikman 1.50 4.00
DD2 Trent Dilfer .75 2.00
DD3 Trent Dilfer .75 2.00
DD4 Marshall Faulk 1.50 4.00
DD5 Marshall Faulk 1.50 4.00
DD6 Heath Shuler .50 1.25
DD7 Heath Shuler .50 1.25
DD8 Antonio Langham .40 1.00
DD9 Antonio Langham .40 1.00
DD10 Marshall Faulk 1.50 4.00
DD11 Dan Wilkinson .40 1.00
DD12 Dan Wilkinson .40 1.00

1994 Pro Line Live Previews

Randomly inserted in 1994 Classic NFL Draft Picks packs, the five standard-size cards comprising this set feature borderless color player action shots on their fronts. The player's name in upper case lettering, along with his team's name in a colored stripe, appears at the bottom. The back carries a color player action shot with colored borders above and on one side. The player's name and position appear in the margin above the photo; career highlights and a brief biography appear in the margin alongside. Player statistics appear within a ghosted band near the bottom of the photo. A message in black lettering states that production was limited to 12,000 of each card. The cards are numbered on the back with a "PL" prefix.

COMPLETE SET (5) 25.00 50.00
PL1 Troy Aikman 6.00 12.00
PL2 Jerry Rice 6.00 12.00
PL3 Steve Young 5.00 10.00
PL4 Rick Mirer 4.00 8.00
PL5 Drew Bledsoe 4.00 10.00

1994 Pro Line Live

Produced by Classic, these 405 standard-size cards were issued in 10 and 16-card packs. Cards feature borderless fronts and color action shots. The player's name appears in uppercase lettering at the bottom along with his team name within a team color-coded stripe. The backs carry another color player action shot with statistics appearing within a ghosted stripe near the bottom of the photo. Career highlights and biography appear within a team color-coded band down the left side. Rookie Cards include Derrick Alexander, Isaac Bruce, Lake Dawson, Marshall Faulk, William Floyd, Greg Hill, Charles Johnson, Bam Morris, Errict Rhett, Darnay Scott and Heath Shuler.

COMPLETE SET (405) 7.50 20.00
1 Emmitt Smith .50 1.25
2 Andre Rison .02 .10
3 Deion Sanders .15 .40
4 Jeff George .08 .25
5 Cornelius Bennett .02 .10
6 Jim Kelly .08 .25
7 Andre Reed .02 .10
8 Bruce Smith .08 .25
9 Thurman Thomas .08 .25
10 Mark Carrier DB .01 .05
11 Curtis Conway .08 .25
12 Donnell Woolford .01 .05
13 Chris Zorich .01 .05
14 Erik Kramer .02 .10
15 John Copeland .01 .05
16 Harold Green .01 .05
17 David Klingler .01 .05
18 Tony McGee .01 .05
19 Carl Pickens .02 .10
20 Michael Jackson .02 .10
21 Eric Metcalf .02 .10
22 Michael Dean Perry .02 .10
23 Vinny Testaverde .02 .10
24 Eric Turner .01 .05
25 Tommy Vardell .01 .05
26 Troy Aikman .30 .75
27 Charles Haley .02 .10
28 Michael Irvin .08 .25
29 Pierce Holt .01 .05
30 Russell Maryland .01 .05
31 Erik Williams .01 .05
32 Thomas Everett .01 .05
33 Steve Atwater .01 .05
34 John Elway .60 1.50
35 Glyn Milburn .02 .10
36 Shannon Sharpe .02 .10
37 Anthony Miller .02 .10
38 Barry Sanders .50 1.25
39 Chris Spielman .02 .10
40 Pat Swilling .01 .05
41 Brett Perriman .02 .10
42 Herman Moore .08 .25
43 Scott Mitchell .02 .10
44 Edgar Bennett .08 .25
45 Terrell Buckley .01 .05
46 LeRoy Butler .01 .05
47 Brett Favre .60 1.50
48 Jackie Harris .01 .05
49 Sterling Sharpe .02 .10
50 Reggie White .08 .25
51 Gary Brown .01 .05
52 Cody Carlson .01 .05
53 Ray Childress .01 .05
54 Ernest Givins .02 .10
55 Bruce Matthews .01 .05
56 Quentin Coryatt .01 .05
57 Steve Emtman .01 .05
58 Roosevelt Potts .01 .05
59 Tony Bennett .01 .05
60 Marcus Allen .08 .25
61 Joe Montana .60 1.50
62 Neil Smith .02 .10
63 Derrick Thomas .08 .25
64 Dale Carter .01 .05
65 Tim Brown .08 .25
66 Jeff Hostetler .02 .10
67 Terry McDaniel .01 .05
68 Chester McGlockton .01 .05
69 Anthony Smith .01 .05
70 Albert Lewis .01 .05
71 Jerome Bettis .20 .50
72 Shane Conlan .01 .05
73 Troy Drayton .01 .05
74 Sean Gilbert .01 .05
75 Chris Miller .01 .05
76 Bryan Cox .01 .05
77 Irving Fryar .02 .10
78 Keith Jackson .01 .05
79 Terry Kirby .08 .25
80 Dan Marino .60 1.50
81 O.J.McDuffie .08 .25
82 Terry Allen .02 .10
83 Cris Carter .15 .40
84 Chris Doleman .01 .05
85 Randall McDaniel .02 .10
86 John Randle .02 .10
87 Robert Smith .08 .25
88 Jason Belser .01 .05
89 Jack Del Rio .01 .05
90 Vincent Brown .01 .05
91 Ben Coates .02 .10
92 Chris Slade .01 .05
93 Derek Brown RBK .01 .05
94 Morten Andersen .01 .05
95 Willie Roaf .01 .05
96 Irv Smith .01 .05
97 Tyrone Hughes .02 .10
98 Michael Haynes .02 .10
99 Jim Everett .02 .10
100 Michael Brooks .01 .05
101 Leroy Thompson .01 .05
102 Rodney Hampton .02 .10
103 Dave Meggett .01 .05
104 Phil Simms .02 .10
105 Boomer Esiason .02 .10
106 Johnny Johnson .01 .05
107 Gary Anderson K .01 .05
108 Mo Lewis .01 .05
109 Ronnie Lott .02 .10
110 Johnny Mitchell .01 .05
111 Howard Cross .01 .05
112 Victor Bailey .01 .05
113 Fred Barnett .02 .10
114 Randall Cunningham .08 .25
115 Calvin Williams .02 .10
116 Steve Beuerlein .02 .10
117 Gary Clark .02 .10
118 Ronald Moore .01 .05
119 Ricky Proehl .01 .05
120 Eric Swann .02 .10
121 Barry Foster .01 .05
122 Kevin Greene .02 .10
123 Greg Lloyd .02 .10
124 Neil O'Donnell .08 .25
125 Rod Woodson .02 .10
126 Ronnie Harmon .01 .05
127 Mark Higgs .01 .05
128 Stan Humphries .02 .10
129 Leslie O'Neal .01 .05
130 Chris Mims .01 .05
131 Stanley Richard .01 .05
132 Junior Seau .08 .25
133 Brent Jones .02 .10
134 Tim McDonald .01 .05
135 Jerry Rice .30 .75
136 Dana Stubblefield .02 .10
137 Ricky Watters .02 .10
138 Steve Young .25 .60
139 Cortez Kennedy .02 .10
140 Rick Mirer .08 .25
141 Eugene Robinson .01 .05
142 Chris Warren .02 .10
143 Nate Odomes .01 .05
144 Howard Ballard .01 .05
145 Flipper Anderson .01 .05
146 Chris Jacke .01 .05
147 Santana Dotson .02 .10
148 Craig Erickson .01 .05
149 Hardy Nickerson .02 .10
150 Lawrence Dawsey .01 .05
151 Terry Wooden .01 .05
152 Ethan Horton .01 .05
153 John Kasay .01 .05
154 Desmond Howard .02 .10
155 Ken Harvey .01 .05
156 William Fuller .01 .05
157 Clyde Simmons .01 .05
158 Randal Hill .01 .05
159 Garrison Hearst .08 .25
160 Mike Pritchard .01 .05
161 Jessie Tuggle .01 .05
162 Erric Pegram .01 .05
163 Kevin Ross .01 .05
164 Bill Brooks .01 .05
165 Darryl Talley .01 .05
166 Steve Tasker .02 .10
167 Pete Stoyanovich .01 .05
168 Dante Jones .01 .05
169 Vencie Glenn .01 .05
170 Tom Waddle .01 .05
171 Harlon Barnett .01 .05
172 Trace Armstrong .01 .05
173 Tim Worley .01 .05
174 Alfred Williams .01 .05
175 Louis Oliver .01 .05
176 Darryl Williams .01 .05
177 Clay Matthews .01 .05
178 Kyle Clifton .01 .05
179 Alvin Harper .02 .10
180 Jay Novacek .02 .10
181 Ken Norton Jr. .02 .10
182 Kevin Williams WR .02 .10
183 Daryl Johnston .02 .10
184 Rod Bernstine .01 .05
185 Karl Mecklenburg .01 .05
186 Dennis Smith .01 .05
187 Robert Delpino .01 .05
188 Bennie Blades .01 .05
189 Jason Hanson .01 .05
190 Derrick Moore .01 .05
191 Mark Clayton .01 .05
192 Webster Slaughter .01 .05
193 Haywood Jeffires .02 .10
194 Bubba McDowell .01 .05
195 Warren Moon .08 .25
196 Al Smith .01 .05
197 Bill Romanowski .01 .05
198 John Carney .01 .05
199 Kerry Cash .01 .05
200 Darren Carrington .01 .05
201 Jeff Lageman .01 .05
202 Tracy Simien .01 .05
203 Willie Davis .02 .10
204 Dan Saleaumua .01 .05
205 Rocket Ismail .02 .10
206 James Jett .01 .05
207 Todd Lyght .01 .05
208 Roman Phifer .01 .05
209 Jimmie Jones .01 .05
210 Jeff Cross .01 .05
211 Eric Davis .01 .05
212 Keith Byars .01 .05
213 Richmond Webb .01 .05
214 Anthony Carter .02 .10
215 Henry Thomas .01 .05
216 Andre Tippett .01 .05
217 Rickey Jackson .01 .05
218 Vaughan Johnson .01 .05
219 Eric Martin .01 .05
220 Sam Mills .01 .05
221 Renaldo Turnbull .01 .05
222 Mark Collins .01 .05
223 Mike Johnson .01 .05
224 Rob Moore .02 .10
225 Seth Joyner .01 .05
226 Herschel Walker .02 .10
227 Eric Green .01 .05
228 Marion Butts .01 .05
229 John Friesz .02 .10
230 John Taylor .02 .10
231 Dexter Carter .01 .05
232 Brian Blades .02 .10
233 Reggie Cobb .01 .05
234 Paul Gruber .01 .05
235 Ricky Reynolds .01 .05
236 Vince Workman .01 .05
237 Darrell Green .01 .05
238 Jim Lachey .01 .05
239 James Hasty .01 .05
240 Howie Long .08 .25
241 Aeneas Williams .01 .05
242 Mike Kenn .01 .05
243 Henry Jones .01 .05
244 Kenneth Davis .01 .05
245 Tim Krumrie .01 .05
246 Derrick Fenner .01 .05
247 Mark Carrier WR .02 .10
248 Robert Porcher .01 .05
249 Darren Woodson .02 .10
250 Kevin Smith .01 .05
251 Mark Stepnoski .01 .05
252 Simon Fletcher .01 .05
253 Derek Russell .01 .05
254 Mike Croel .01 .05
255 Johnny Holland .01 .05
256 Bryce Paup .02 .10
257 Cris Dishman .01 .05
258 Sean Jones .01 .05
259 Marcus Robertson .01 .05
260 Steve Jackson .01 .05
261 Jeff Herrod .01 .05
262 John Alt .01 .05
263 Nick Lowery .01 .05
264 Greg Robinson .01 .05
265 Alexander Wright .01 .05
266 Steve Wisniewski .01 .05
267 Henry Ellard .02 .10
268 Tracy Scroggins .01 .05
269 Jackie Slater .01 .05
270 Troy Vincent .01 .05
271 Qadry Ismail .08 .25
272 Steve Jordan .01 .05
273 Leonard Russell .01 .05
274 Maurice Hurst .01 .05
275 Scottie Graham RC .02 .10
276 Carlton Bailey .01 .05
277 John Elliott .01 .05
278 Corey Miller .01 .05
279 Brad Baxter .01 .05
280 Brian Washington .01 .05
281 Tim Harris .01 .05
282 Byron Evans .01 .05
283 Dermontti Dawson .02 .10
284 Carnell Lake .01 .05
285 Jeff Graham .01 .05
286 Merton Hanks .02 .10
287 Harris Barton .01 .05
288 Guy McIntyre .01 .05
289 Kelvin Martin .01 .05
290 John L. Williams .01 .05
291 Courtney Hawkins .01 .05
292 Vaughn Hebron .01 .05
293 Brian Mitchell .01 .05
294 Andre Collins .01 .05
295 Art Monk .02 .10
296 Mark Rypien .01 .05
297 Ricky Sanders .01 .05
298 Eric Hill .01 .05
299 Larry Centers .08 .25
300 Norm Johnson .01 .05
301 Pete Metzelaars .01 .05
302 Ricardo McDonald .01 .05
303 Stevon Moore .01 .05
304 Mike Sherrard .01 .05
305 Andy Harmon .01 .05
306 Anthony Johnson .02 .10
307 J.J. Birden .01 .05
308 Neal Anderson .01 .05
309 Lewis Tillman .01 .05
310 Richard Dent .02 .10
311 Nate Newton .01 .05
312 Sean Dawkins RC .08 .25
313 Lawrence Taylor .08 .25
314 Wilber Marshall .01 .05
315 Tom Carter .01 .05
316 Reggie Brooks .02 .10
317 Eric Curry .01 .05
318 Horace Copeland .01 .05
319 Natrone Means .08 .25
320 Eric Allen .01 .05
321 Marvin Jones .01 .05
322 Keith Hamilton .01 .05
323 Vincent Brisby .02 .10
324 Drew Bledsoe .30 .75
325 Tom Rathman .01 .05
326 Ed McCaffrey .08 .25
327 Steve Israel .01 .05
328 Dan Wilkinson RC .02 .10
329 Marshall Faulk RC 2.00 5.00
330 Heath Shuler RC .08 .25
331 Willie McGinest RC .08 .25
332 Trev Alberts RC .02 .10
333 Trent Dilfer RC .50 1.25
334 Bryant Young RC .15 .40
335 Sam Adams RC .02 .10
336 Antonio Langham RC .02 .10
337 Jamir Miller RC .02 .10
338 John Thierry RC .01 .05
339 Aaron Glenn RC .08 .25
340 Joe Johnson RC .01 .05
341 Bernard Williams RC .01 .05
342 Wayne Gandy RC .01 .05
343 Aaron Taylor RC .01 .05
344 Charles Johnson RC .08 .25
345 Dewayne Washington RC .02 .10
346 Todd Steussie RC .02 .10
347 Tim Bowens RC .02 .10
348 Johnnie Morton RC .20 .50
349 Rob Fredrickson RC .02 .10
350 Shante Carver RC .01 .05
351 Thomas Lewis RC .02 .10
352 Greg Hill RC .08 .25
353 Henry Ford RC .01 .05
354 Jeff Burris RC .02 .10
355 William Floyd RC .08 .25
356 Derrick Alexander WR RC .08 .25
357 Darnay Scott RC .20 .50
358 Isaac Bruce RC 2.00 4.00
359 Errict Rhett RC .08 .25
360 Kevin Lee RC .01 .05
361 Chuck Levy RC .01 .05
362 David Palmer RC .08 .25
363 Ryan Yarborough RC .01 .05
364 Charlie Garner RC .50 1.25
365 Isaac Davis RC .01 .05
366 Mario Bates RC .08 .25
367 Bert Emanuel RC .08 .25
388 Thomas Randolph RC .01 .05
369 Bucky Brooks RC .01 .05
370 Allen Aldridge RC .01 .05
371 Charlie Ward RC .08 .25
372 Aubrey Beavers RC .01 .05
373 Donnell Bennett RC .08 .25
374 Jason Sehorn RC .15 .40
375 Lonnie Johnson RC .01 .05
376 Tyronne Drakeford RC .01 .05
377 Andre Coleman RC .01 .05
378 Lamar Smith RC .50 1.25
379 Calvin Jones RC .01 .05
380 LeShon Johnson RC .02 .10
381 Byron Bam Morris RC .02 .10
382 Lake Dawson RC .02 .10
383 Corey Sawyer RC .02 .10
384 Willie Jackson RC .08 .25
385 Perry Klein RC .01 .05
386 Ronnie Woolfork RC .01 .05
387 Doug Nussmeier RC .01 .05
388 Rob Waldrop RC .01 .05
389 Glenn Foley RC .08 .25
390 Troy Aikman Irvin CC .15 .40
391 Jerry Rice S.Young CC .15 .40
392 Brett Favre St.Sharpe CC .30 .75
393 Jim Kelly A.Reed CC .08 .25
394 John Elway Sh.Sharpe CC .30 .75
395 Carolina Panthers .05 .15
396 Jacksonville Jaguars .05 .15
397 Checklist 1 .01 .05
398 Checklist 2 .01 .05
399 Checklist 3 .01 .05
400 Checklist 4 .01 .05
401 Sterling Sharpe ILL .02 .10
402 Derrick Thomas ILL .02 .10
403 Joe Montana ILL .25 .60
404 Emmitt Smith ILL .20 .50
405 Barry Sanders ILL .25 .60
ES1 E.Smith MVP/15000 6.00 15.00
JB1 Jerome Bettis ROY 5.00 12.00
P1 Troy Aikman Promo .50 1.25
PR1 Emmitt Smith Promo .75 2.00

1994 Pro Line Live Autographs

Issued one per Pro Line Live box, the standard-size cards that make up this set are identical in design on front to the basic card. The individually numbered autograph appears on the front and the back offers a congratulatory message. The cards are unnumbered and checklisted below in alphabetical order. Additional cards of some players were released later after the Score Board bankruptcy.

STATED ODDS 1:36
1 Troy Aikman/340 50.00 100.00
2 Derrick Alexander WR/950 5.00 12.00
3 Eric Allen/1980 5.00 12.00
4 Steve Atwater/1040 5.00 12.00
5 Victor Bailey/450 4.00 10.00
6 Harris Barton/2120 6.00 15.00
7 Mario Bates/1145 4.00 10.00
8 Brad Baxter/1070 4.00 10.00
9 Aubrey Beavers/1150 4.00 10.00
10 Donnell Bennett/1130 4.00 10.00
11 Rod Bernstine/1010 20.00 50.00
12 Steve Beuerlein/970 5.00 12.00
13 Drew Bledsoe/1150 12.00 30.00
14 Bill Brooks/1030 4.00 10.00
15 Bucky Brooks/1090 4.00 10.00
16 Reggie Brooks/460 5.00 12.00
17 Derek Brown RBK/449 4.00 10.00
18 Gary Brown/950 4.00 10.00
19 Tim Brown/1920 12.50 30.00
20 Jeff Burris/1140 4.00 10.00
21 Marion Butts/2040 4.00 10.00
22 Keith Byars/1020 5.00 12.00
23 Anthony Carter/1020 5.00 12.00
24 Dale Carter/1031 5.00 12.00
25 Tom Carter/460 4.00 10.00
26 Shante Carver/1160 4.00 10.00
27 Ray Childress/2240 5.00 12.00
28 Andre Coleman/1000 4.00 10.00
29 Andre Collins/1100 4.00 10.00
30 Shane Conlan/1110 4.00 10.00
31 Horace Copeland/450 4.00 10.00
32 Quentin Coryatt/970 5.00 12.00
33 Isaac Davis/1150 4.00 10.00
34 Kenneth Davis/1170 5.00 12.00
35 Lake Dawson/1100 5.00 12.00
36 Robert Delpino/1030 4.00 10.00
37 Trent Dilfer/2680 6.00 15.00
38 Troy Drayton/450 4.00 10.00
39 John Elliott/2150 4.00 10.00
40 John Elway/1000 50.00 100.00
41 Steve Emtman/1900 4.00 10.00
42 Boomer Esiason/920 6.00 15.00
43 Jim Everett/1265 5.00 12.00
44 Marshall Faulk/2230 25.00 50.00
45 Brett Favre/1130 60.00 120.00
46 William Floyd/950 5.00 12.00
47 Glenn Foley/890 4.00 10.00
48 Henry Ford/1110 4.00 10.00
49 Barry Foster/1080 5.00 12.00
50 Rob Fredrickson/1160 4.00 10.00
51 John Friesz/2150 4.00 10.00
52 Irving Fryar/1040 6.00 15.00
53 Wayne Gandy/1040 4.00 10.00
54 Charlie Garner/1130 5.00 12.00
55 Jeff George/2140 5.00 12.00
56 Aaron Glenn/1140 5.00 12.00
57 Rodney Hampton/1090 5.00 12.00
58 Garrison Hearst/1435 5.00 12.00
59 Mark Higgs/980 4.00 10.00
60 Greg Hill/1145 5.00 12.00
61 Pierce Holt/2020 4.00 10.00
62 Jeff Hostetler/955 5.00 12.00
63 Tyrone Hughes/470 15.00 30.00
64 Michael Irvin/450 15.00 30.00
65 Qadry Ismail/450 5.00 12.00
66 Steve Israel/2020 4.00 10.00
67 Keith Jackson/1020 5.00 12.00
68 Michael Jackson/1490 5.00 12.00
69 Willie Jackson/1140 5.00 12.00
70 Charles Johnson/950 5.00 12.00
71 Brent Jones/1880 5.00 12.00
72 Calvin Jones/960 12.00 30.00
73 Perry Klein/1000 4.00 10.00
74 David Klingler/2140 4.00 10.00
75 Erik Kramer/1020 5.00 12.00
76 Jim Lachey/1850 4.00 10.00
77 Carnell Lake/1985 4.00 10.00
78 Antonio Langham/1240 5.00 12.00
79 Kevin Lee/1190 4.00 10.00
80 Chuck Levy/950 5.00 12.00
81 Thomas Lewis/1140 4.00 10.00
82 Ronnie Lott/910 12.00 30.00
83 Ed McCaffrey/2030 6.00 15.00
84 Terry McDaniel/1980 4.00 10.00
85 Tim McDonald/2040 4.00 10.00
86 Willie McGinest/3520 5.00 12.00
87 Russell Maryland/1945 5.00 12.00
88 Clay Matthews/2000 6.00 15.00
89 Natrone Means/445 6.00 15.00
90 Glyn Milburn/440 4.00 10.00
91 Anthony Miller/2070 5.00 12.00
92 Sam Mills/1115 20.00 50.00
93 Joe Montana/920 50.00 100.00
94 Rob Moore/1025 5.00 12.00
95 Byron Bam Morris/1130 4.00 10.00
96 Johnnie Morton/2945 6.00 15.00
97 Hardy Nickerson/1175 4.00 10.00
98 Doug Nussmeier/1150 4.00 10.00
99 Leslie O'Neal/2050 4.00 10.00
100 David Palmer/950 4.00 10.00
101 Erric Pegram/1020 4.00 10.00
102 Roman Phifer/2140 4.00 10.00

103 Ricky Proehl/1020 5.00 12.00
104 Thomas Randolph/1100 4.00 10.00
105 Tom Rathman/2230 12.50 30.00
106 Errict Rhett/1120 5.00 12.00
107 Darnay Scott/1400 5.00 12.00
108 Jason Sehorn/950 5.00 12.00
109 Shannon Sharpe/1020 10.00 25.00
110 Sterling Sharpe/450 12.50 30.00
111 Heath Shuler/2020 5.00 12.00
112 Jackie Slater/1110 6.00 15.00
113 Emmitt Smith/925 60.00 120.00
114 Irv Smith/470 4.00 10.00
115 Lamar Smith/1130 5.00 12.00
116 Neil Smith/1000 6.00 15.00
117 Todd Steussie/2100 5.00 12.00
118 Aaron Taylor/950 4.00 10.00
119 John Taylor/1030 6.00 15.00
120 John Thierry/1150 4.00 10.00
121 Derrick Thomas/1087 50.00 80.00
122 Andre Tippett/1090 20.00 40.00
123 Renaldo Turnbull/945 4.00 10.00
124 Eric Turner/1030 6.00 15.00
125 Tommy Vardell/1000 4.00 10.00
126 Dewayne Washington/1040 5.00 12.00
127 Richmond Webb/1020 5.00 12.00
128 Dan Wilkinson/1960 5.00 12.00
129 Steve Wisniewski/2150 4.00 10.00
130 Donnell Woolford/1000 4.00 10.00
131 Ronnie Woolfork/360 4.00 10.00
132 Steve Young/925 15.00 40.00
133 Aikman/Irv.Combo/345 50.00 120.00
134 Young/Rice Combo/450 60.00 150.00

1994 Pro Line Live MVP Sweepstakes

Issued in packs at a rate of five per case, collectors who also obtained one of 2,083 cards of the eventual 1994 Associated Press NFL MVP could have redeemed the card for an exclusive limited-edition uncut sheet of this set. The offer expired on 3/31/1995. The winner was San Francisco's Steve Young. The attractive fronts feature four color photos with the player's name at the top and the Classic Pro Line Live logo in gold in the middle. The backs offer a complete checklist and contest information. The cards are numbered with an "MVP" prefix.

COMPLETE SET (45) 50.00 120.00
STATED ODDS 1:72
1 Jeff George 1.00 2.50
2 Andre Rison .40 1.00
3 Jim Kelly 1.00 2.50
4 Thurman Thomas 1.00 2.50
5 Troy Aikman 3.00 8.00
6 Emmitt Smith 5.00 12.00
7 Michael Irvin 1.00 2.50
8 John Elway 6.00 15.00
9 Brett Favre 6.00 15.00
10 Sterling Sharpe .40 1.00
11 Barry Sanders 5.00 12.00
12 Scott Mitchell .40 1.00
13 Gary Brown .20 .50
14 Warren Moon 1.00 2.50
15 Marcus Allen 1.00 2.50
16 Joe Montana 6.00 15.00
17 Tim Brown 1.00 2.50
18 Jeff Hostetler .40 1.00
19 Dan Marino 6.00 15.00
20 Terry Kirby 1.00 2.50
21 Terry Allen .40 1.00
22 Drew Bledsoe 3.00 8.00
23 Chris Miller .20 .50
24 Jerome Bettis 2.00 5.00
25 Derek Brown RBK .20 .50
26 Rodney Hampton .40 1.00
27 Phil Simms .40 1.00
28 Randall Cunningham 1.00 2.50
29 Barry Foster .20 .50
30 Neil O'Donnell 1.00 2.50
31 Boomer Esiason .40 1.00
32 Johnny Johnson .20 .50
33 Garrison Hearst 1.00 2.50
34 Ronald Moore .20 .50
35 Natrone Means 1.00 2.50
36 Steve Young WIN Exp. 2.50 6.00
37 Ricky Watters .40 1.00
38 Jerry Rice 3.00 8.00
39 Rick Mirer 1.00 2.50
40 Chris Warren .40 1.00
41 Reggie Brooks .40 1.00
42 Marshall Faulk 6.00 15.00
43 Heath Shuler .40 1.00
44 Trent Dilfer 1.50 4.00
45 Field Card .20 .50

1994 Pro Line Live Spotlight

Issued one per 16-card pack, the 25-card Spotlight standard-size set showcases top players. Metallic, full-bleed fronts feature an action photo with the player's name in a stripe up the right side. The backs contain a photo, 1993 and career statistics. The cards are numbered with a "PB" prefix.

COMPLETE SET (25) 6.00 15.00
ONE PER 16-CARD PACK
PB1 Trent Dilfer .25 .60
PB2 Heath Shuler .07 .20
PB3 Marshall Faulk 1.00 2.50
PB4 Troy Aikman .50 1.25
PB5 Emmitt Smith .75 2.00
PB6 Thurman Thomas .15 .40
PB7 Andre Rison .07 .20
PB8 Jerry Rice .50 1.25
PB9 Sterling Sharpe .07 .20
PB10 Brett Favre 1.00 2.50
PB11 Steve Young .40 1.00
PB12 Drew Bledsoe .50 1.25
PB13 Rick Mirer .15 .40
PB14 Barry Sanders .75 2.00
PB15 Joe Montana 1.00 2.50
PB16 Jerome Bettis .30 .75
PB17 Ricky Watters .07 .20
PB18 Rodney Hampton .07 .20
PB19 Tim Brown .15 .40
PB20 Reggie Brooks .07 .20
PB21 Natrone Means .15 .40
PB22 Marcus Allen .15 .40
PB23 Gary Brown .02 .10
PB24 Barry Foster .02 .10
PB25 Dan Marino 1.00 2.50

1995 Pro Line GameBreakers Previews

This five-card standard-size set was inserted in Classic Draft NFL Rookie packs at the rate of 1:36. The cards preview the 1995 ProLine GameBreakers design and feature five leading NFL players.

COMPLETE SET (5) 10.00 25.00
STATED ODDS 1:36 CLASSIC NFL ROOKIES
GP1 Dan Marino 4.00 10.00
GP2 Natrone Means .25 .60
GP3 Joe Montana 4.00 10.00
GP4 Barry Sanders 3.00 8.00
GP5 Deion Sanders 1.00 2.50

1995 Pro Line Previews Phone Cards $2

Both 5 card sets were randomly inserted into packs of 1995 Classic Basketball Rookies. These cards previewed the $2 and $5 phone cards that were inserted into packs of 1995 ProLine. The phone time expired on Sept.1, 1996.

COMPLETE $2 SET (5) 2.50 6.00
RANDOM INS IN CLASSIC BK ROOKIES
*$5 PHONE CARDS: .8X TO 2X $2 CARDS
1 Troy Aikman .75 2.00
2 Drew Bledsoe .50 1.25
3 Ki-Jana Carter .25 .60
4 Marshall Faulk 1.00 2.50
5 Steve Young .60 1.50

1995 Pro Line

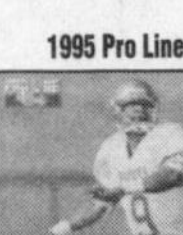

The set was produced by Classic. This 400-card standard-size set was issued in 10-card packs. These packs are in 36 count boxes with 12 boxes per case. Each box was guaranteed by the manufacturer to contain a signed card. Hot boxes (containing mostly insert cards) are inserted one in ten cases for retail and one in five for hobby. The hobby "Hot Boxes" are identified while the retail "Hot Boxes" are not explicitly identified. The full-bleed fronts feature color action photos. The player's name, position and team name are printed in white lettering near the bottom. The backs feature another color photo, biographical information, player information as well as recent and career statistics. Rookie Cards in this set include Jeff Blake, Ki-Jana Carter, Kerry Collins, Joey Galloway, Steve McNair, Kordell Stewart, J.J. Stokes, Yancey Thigpen, Tamarick Vanover and Michael Westbrook. The basic set includes three parallels: a Silver set inserted one per hobby and retail pack, a Printer's Proof set inserted two per hobby box and a Printer's Proof Silver set inserted one per hobby box. A Marshall Faulk GameBreakers Promo card was produced for distribution at the 1995 St.Louis National Card Collectors Convention. It carries the card number NA1.

COMPLETE SET (400) 8.00 20.00
1 Garrison Hearst .08 .25
2 Anthony Miller .02 .10
3 Brett Favre .60 1.50
4 Jessie Hester .01 .05
5 Mike Fox .01 .05
6 Jeff Blake RC .25 .60
7 J.J. Birden .01 .05
8 Greg Jackson .01 .05
9 Leon Lett .01 .05
10 Bruce Matthews .01 .05
11 Andre Reed .02 .10
12 Joe Montana .60 1.50
13 Craig Heyward .02 .10
14 Henry Ellard UER .02 .10
15 Chris Spielman .02 .10
16 Tony Woods .01 .05
17 Carl Banks .01 .05
18 Eric Zeier RC .08 .25
19 Michael Brooks .01 .05
20 Kevin Ross .01 .05
21 Qadry Ismail .02 .10
22 Mel Gray .01 .05
23 Ty Law RC .50 1.25
24 Mark Collins .01 .05
25 Neil O'Donnell .02 .10
26 Ellis Johnson RC .01 .05
27 Rick Mirer .02 .10
28 Fred Barnett .02 .10
29 Mike Mamula RC .01 .05
30 Jim Jeffcoat .01 .05
31 Reggie Cobb .01 .05
32 Mark Carrier WR UER .02 .10
33 Darnay Scott .02 .10
34 Michael Jackson .02 .10
35 Terrell Buckley .01 .05
36 Nolan Harrison .01 .05
37 Thurman Thomas .08 .25
38 Anthony Smith .01 .05
39 Phillippi Sparks .01 .05
40 Cornelius Bennett .02 .10
41 Robert Young .01 .05
42 Pierce Holt .01 .05
43 Greg Lloyd .02 .10
44 Chad May RC .01 .05
45 Darrien Gordon .01 .05
46 Bryan Cox .01 .05
47 Junior Seau .08 .25
48 Al Smith .01 .05
49 Chris Slade .01 .05
50 Hardy Nickerson .01 .05
51 Brad Baxter .01 .05
52 Darryll Lewis .01 .05
53 Bryant Young .02 .10
54 Chris Warren .02 .10
55 Darion Conner .01 .05
56 Thomas Everett .01 .05
57 Charles Haley .02 .10
58 Chris Mims .01 .05
59 Sean Jones .01 .05
60 Tamarick Vanover RC .08 .25
61 Daryl Johnston .02 .10
62 Rashaan Salaam RC .02 .10
63 James Hasty .01 .05
64 Dante Jones .01 .05
65 Darren Perry UER .01 .05
66 Troy Drayton .01 .05
67 Mark Fields RC .08 .25
68 Brian Williams LB RC .01 .05
69 Steve Bono UER .02 .10
70 Eric Allen .01 .05
71 Chris Zorich .01 .05
72 Dave Brown .02 .10
73 Ken Norton Jr. .02 .10
74 Wayne Martin .01 .05
75 Mo Lewis .01 .05
76 Johnny Mitchell .01 .05
77 Todd Lyght .01 .05
78 Erric Pegram .02 .10
79 Kevin Greene .02 .10
80 Randal Hill .01 .05
81 Brett Perriman .02 .10
82 Mike Sherrard .01 .05
83 Curtis Conway .08 .25
84 Mark Tuinei .01 .05
85 Mark Seay .02 .10
86 Randy Baldwin .01 .05
87 Ricky Ervins .01 .05
88 Chester McGlockton .02 .10
89 Tyrone Wheatley RC .40 1.00
90 Micheal Barrow UER .01 .05
91 Kenneth Davis .01 .05
92 Napoleon Kaufman RC .40 1.00
93 Webster Slaughter .01 .05
94 Darren Woodson .02 .10
95 Pete Stoyanovich .01 .05
96 Jimmie Jones .01 .05
97 Craig Erickson .01 .05
98 Michael Westbrook RC .08 .25
99 Steve McNair RC 1.00 2.50
100 Errict Rhett .02 .10
101 Devin Bush RC .01 .05
102 Dewayne Washington .02 .10
103 Bart Oates .01 .05
104 Aaron Pierce .01 .05
105 Warren Sapp RC .50 1.25
106 Eric Green .01 .05
107 Glyn Milburn .01 .05
108 Johnny Johnson .01 .05
109 Marshall Faulk .40 1.00
110 William Thomas .01 .05
111 George Koonce .01 .05
112 Dana Stubblefield .02 .10
113 Steve Tovar .01 .05
114 Steve Israel .01 .05
115 Brent Williams .01 .05
116 Shane Conlan .01 .05
117 Winston Moss .01 .05
118 Nate Newton .02 .10
119 Michael Irvin .08 .25
120 Jeff Lageman .01 .05
121 Ki-Jana Carter RC .08 .25
122 Dan Marino .60 1.50
123 Tony Casillas .01 .05
124 Kevin Carter RC .08 .25
125 Warren Moon .02 .10
126 Byron Bam Morris .01 .05
127 Ben Coates .02 .10
128 Michael Bankston .01 .05
129 Anthony Parker .01 .05
130 LeRoy Butler .01 .05
131 Tony Bennett .01 .05
132 Alvin Harper .01 .05
133 Tim Brown .08 .25
134 Tom Carter .01 .05
135 Lorenzo White .01 .05
136 Shane Dronett .01 .05
137 John Elliott UER .01 .05
138 Korey Stringer RC .07 .20
139 Jerry Rice .30 .75
140 Sherman Williams RC .01 .05
141 Kevin Turner .01 .05
142 Randall Cunningham .08 .25
143 Vinny Testaverde .02 .10
144 Tim Bowens .01 .05
145 Russell Maryland .01 .05
146 Chris Miller .01 .05
147 Vince Buck .01 .05
148 Willie Clay .01 .05
149 Jeff Graham .01 .05
150 Shannon Sharpe .02 .10
151 Carnell Lake .01 .05
152 Mark Bruener RC .02 .10
153 James Washington .01 .05
154 Pepper Johnson .01 .05
155 Bert Emanuel .08 .25
156 Mark Stepnoski .01 .05
157 Robert Jones .01 .05
158 Cris Dishman .01 .05
159 Henry Jones .01 .05
160 Henry Thomas .01 .05
161 John L. Williams .01 .05
162 Joe Cain .01 .05
163 Mike Johnson .01 .05
164 Merton Hanks .01 .05
165 Deion Sanders .15 .40
166 William Floyd .02 .10
167 Leroy Thompson .01 .05
168 Ray Childress .01 .05
169 Donnell Woolford .01 .05
170 Tony Siragusa .01 .05
171 Chad Brown .02 .10
172 Stanley Richard .01 .05
173 Rob Johnson RC .30 .75
174 Derrick Brooks RC .50 1.25
175 Drew Bledsoe .20 .50
176 Maurice Hurst .01 .05
177 Ricky Watters .02 .10
178 Myron Guyton .01 .05
179 Ricky Proehl .01 .05
180 Haywood Jeffires .01 .05
181 Michael Strahan .08 .25
182 Charles Wilson .01 .05
183 Mark Carrier DB .01 .05
184 James O. Stewart RC .40 1.00
185 Andy Harmon .01 .05
186 Ronnie Lott .02 .10
187 Clay Matthews .02 .10
188 John Carney .01 .05
189 Andre Rison .02 .10
190 Aeneas Williams .01 .05
191 Alexander Wright .01 .05
192 Desmond Howard .02 .10
193 Herman Moore .08 .25
194 Alfred Williams .01 .05
195 Tyrone Poole RC .08 .25
196 Darren Mickell RC .01 .05
197 Steve Young .25 .60
198 Roman Phifer .01 .05
199 Darrell Green .01 .05
200 Terry Wooden .01 .05
201 Chris Calloway .01 .05
202 Lewis Tillman .01 .05
203 Cris Carter .08 .25
204 Jim Everett .01 .05
205 Adrian Murrell .02 .10
206 Barry Sanders .50 1.25
207 Mario Bates .02 .10
208 Shawn Lee .01 .05
209 Charles Mincy .01 .05
210 Kerry Collins RC .75 2.00
211 Steve Walsh .01 .05
212 Chris Chandler .02 .10
213 Bennie Blades .01 .05
214 Kevin Williams WR .02 .10
215 Jim Kelly .08 .25
216 Marion Butts .01 .05
217 Jay Novacek .02 .10
218 Shawn Jefferson .01 .05
219 O.J. McDuffie .08 .25
220 Ray Seals .01 .05
221 Arthur Marshall .01 .05
222 Karl Mecklenburg .01 .05
223 Terance Mathis .02 .10
224 David Klingler .02 .10
225 Rod Woodson .02 .10
226 Quentin Coryatt .02 .10
227 Leroy Hoard .01 .05
228 Brian Blades .02 .10
229 Rob Moore .02 .10
230 Boomer Esiason .02 .10
231 Dave Krieg .01 .05
232 Sterling Sharpe .02 .10
233 Marcus Allen .08 .25
234 John Randle .02 .10
235 Craig Powell RC .01 .05
236 John Elway .60 1.50
237 Mark Ingram .01 .05
238 Cortez Kennedy .02 .10
239 Brent Jones .01 .05
240 Ken Harvey .01 .05
241 Keenan McCardell .08 .25
242 Dan Wilkinson .02 .10
243 Don Beebe .01 .05
244 Jack Del Rio .01 .05
245 Byron Evans .01 .05
246 Ronald Moore .01 .05
247 Edgar Bennett .02 .10
248 William Fuller .01 .05
249 James Williams LB .01 .05
250 Neil Smith .02 .10
251 Sam Mills .02 .10
252 Willie McGinest .02 .10
253 Howard Cross .01 .05
254 Troy Aikman .30 .75
255 Herschel Walker .02 .10
256 Dale Carter .02 .10
257 Sean Dawkins .02 .10
258 Greg Hill .02 .10
259 Stan Humphries .02 .10
260 Erik Kramer .01 .05
261 Leslie O'Neal .02 .10
262 Trezelle Jenkins RC .01 .05
263 Antonio Langham .01 .05
264 Bryce Paup .02 .10
265 Jake Reed .02 .10
266 Richmond Webb .01 .05
267 Eric Davis .01 .05
268 Mark McMillian .01 .05
269 John Walsh RC .01 .05
270 Irving Fryar .02 .10
271 Rocket Ismail .02 .10
272 Phil Hansen .01 .05
273 J.J. Stokes RC .08 .25
274 Craig Newsome RC .01 .05
275 Leonard Russell .01 .05
276 Derrick Deese RC .01 .05
277 Broderick Thomas .01 .05
278 Bobby Houston .01 .05
279 Lamar Lathon .01 .05
280 Eugene Robinson .01 .05
281 Dan Saleaumua .01 .05
282 Kyle Brady RC .08 .25
283 John Taylor .01 .05
284 Tony Boselli RC .08 .25
285 Seth Joyner .01 .05
286 Steve Beuerlein .02 .10
287 Sam Adams .01 .05
288 Frank Reich .01 .05
289 Patrick Hunter .01 .05
290 Sean Gilbert .02 .10
291 Dermontti Dawson UER .08 .20
292 Shaun Gayle .01 .05
293 Vincent Brown .01 .05
294 Terry Kirby .02 .10
295 Courtney Hawkins .01 .05
296 Carl Pickens .02 .10
297 Luther Elliss RC .01 .05
298 Steve Atwater .01 .05
299 James Francis .01 .05
300 Rob Burnett .01 .05
301 Keith Hamilton .01 .05
302 Rob Fredrickson .01 .05
303 Jerome Bettis .08 .25
304 Emmitt Smith .50 1.25
305 Clyde Simmons .01 .05
306 Reggie White .08 .25
307 Rodney Hampton .02 .10
308 Steve Emtman .01 .05
309 Hugh Douglas RC .08 .25
310 Bernie Parmalee .02 .10
311 Trent Dilfer .08 .25
312 Flipper Anderson .01 .05
313 Heath Shuler .02 .10
314 Rod Smith DB .02 .10
315 Ray Zellars RC .02 .10
316 Robert Brooks .08 .25
317 Lee Woodall .01 .05
318 Robert Porcher .01 .05
319 Todd Collins RC .30 .75
320 Willie Roaf .01 .05
321 Erik Williams .01 .05
322 Steve Wisniewski .01 .05
323 Derrick Alexander DE RC .01 .05
324 Frank Warren .01 .05
325 Kelvin Pritchett .01 .05
326 Dennis Gibson .01 .05
327 Jason Belser .01 .05
328 Vincent Brisby .01 .05
329 Calvin Williams .02 .10
330 Derek Brown RBK .01 .05
331 Blake Brockermeyer .01 .05
332 Jeff Herrod .01 .05
333 Darryl Williams .01 .05
334 Aaron Glenn .01 .05
335 Eric Metcalf .02 .10
336 Billy Milner RC .01 .05
337 Terry McDaniel .01 .05
338 Trace Armstrong .01 .05
339 Yancey Thigpen RC .02 .10
340 Jackie Harris .01 .05
341 Jeff George .02 .10
342 Darryl Talley .01 .05
343 Marcus Robertson .01 .05
344 Robert Massey .01 .05
345 Jessie Tuggle .01 .05
346 Scott Mitchell .02 .10
347 Harvey Williams .01 .05
348 Jack Jackson RC .01 .05
349 Brian Mitchell .01 .05
350 Lawrence Dawsey .01 .05
351 Erik Howard .01 .05
352 Quinn Early .02 .10
353 Terry Allen .02 .10
354 Simon Fletcher .01 .05
355 Eric Turner .01 .05
356 Natrone Means .02 .10
357 Frank Sanders RC .08 .25
358 Michael Timpson .01 .05
359 Michael Haynes .02 .10
360 Ruben Brown RC .08 .25
361 Troy Vincent UER .01 .05
362 Floyd Turner .01 .05
363 Larry Centers .02 .10
364 Eric Swann .02 .10
365 Albert Lewis .01 .05
366 Barry Foster .02 .10
367 Michael Dean Perry .01 .05
368 Jumpy Geathers UER .01 .05
369 Kordell Stewart RC .50 1.25
370 Chuck Smith .01 .05
371 Lake Dawson .02 .10
372 Terry Hoage .01 .05
373 Jeff Cross .01 .05
374 Tony McGee .01 .05
375 Eric Curry .01 .05
376 Harold Green .01 .05
377 Eric Hill .01 .05
378 Ray Buchanan .01 .05
379 Willie Davis .02 .10
380 Chris T.Jones RC .01 .05
381 Martin Mayhew .01 .05
382 Anthony Pleasant .01 .05
383 Joey Galloway RC .50 1.25
384 Anthony Morgan .01 .05
385 Harlon Barnett .01 .05
386 Bruce Smith .08 .25
387 Jeff Hostetler .02 .10
388 Randall McDaniel .02 .10
389 Dave Meggett .01 .05
390 Bill Romanowski .01 .05
391 Gary Brown .01 .05
392 Charles Johnson .02 .10
393 Chris Doleman .01 .05
394 Tony Martin .02 .10
395 Raymont Harris .01 .05
396 John Copeland .01 .05
397 Emmitt Smith CL .08 .25
398 Steve Young CL .02 .10
399 Marshall Faulk CL .20 .50
400 Ki-Jana Carter CL .02 .10
HP1 Marshall Faulk Sample .60 1.50
P1 Marshall Faulk Promo .60 1.50
P2 Jerome Bettis Natl. Promo .60 1.50

1995 Pro Line National Silver

COMPLETE SET (400) 100.00 200.00
*STARS: 4X TO 10X BASIC CARDS
*RCs: 2X TO 5X BASIC CARDS
ONE PER NATIONAL PACK

1995 Pro Line Printer's Proofs

COMP.PRINT.PROOF (400) 100.00 200.00
*STARS: 4X TO 10X HI COL.
*RCS: 2X TO 5X HI COL.
TWO PER HOBBY BOX

1995 Pro Line Printer's Proofs Silver

COMPLETE SET (400) 150.00 300.00
*PP SILVER STARS: 6X TO 15X BASIC CARDS
*PP SILVER RC's: 3X TO 8X BASIC CARDS
ONE PER HOBBY BOX
ANNOUNCE PRINT RUN 175 SETS

1995 Pro Line Silver

COMPLETE SET (400) 20.00 40.00
*STARS: .8X TO 2X BASIC CARDS
*RCs: .6X TO 1.5X BASIC CARDS
ONE PER PACK

1995 Pro Line Autographs

This standard-size set was inserted into packs. Classic, the producers of the set, guaranteed an autograph card in each box. The cards were inserted in either hobby or retail packs and are similar in design to the base Pro Line issue. The backs carry a congratulatory message. The cards are unnumbered and checklisted below in alphabetical order. The tough John Elway card and many of the numbering variation cards are not considered part of the complete set price. Elway signed 50 cards for each major card manufacturer to be inserted in one the company's card brands for 1995. Many players have two or more signed cards with a different numbering scheme as noted below. Although the "AP" designation is printed with the serial number right on the cardfront, it's not known exactly what the letters represent.

STATED ODDS 1:36H,1:24J,1:90R SER.1
1 Troy Aikman/500 25.00 60.00
2A Eric Allen/1225 5.00 12.00
2B Eric Allen/2398AP 5.00 12.00
2C Eric Allen/745AP 5.00 12.00
3 Flipper Anderson/1140 4.00 10.00
4A Randy Baldwin/1435 4.00 10.00
4B Randy Baldwin/2405AP 4.00 10.00
4C Randy Baldwin/760AP 4.00 10.00
5 Mario Bates/1480 4.00 10.00
6A Don Beebe/1200 5.00 12.00
6B Don Beebe/275AP 5.00 12.00
7A Cornelius Bennett/1200 6.00 15.00
7B Cornelius Bennett/255AP 6.00 15.00
8 Edgar Bennett/1475 6.00 15.00
9 Tony Bennett/1475 4.00 10.00
10 Steve Beuerlein/1465 5.00 12.00
11 J.J. Birden/775 4.00 10.00
12 Brian Blades/1465 5.00 12.00
13 Jeff Blake/1200 6.00 15.00
14 Drew Bledsoe/515 15.00 40.00
15A B.Brockermeyer/1445 4.00 10.00
15B B.Brockermeyer/2315AP 4.00 10.00
16 Derrick Brooks/1470 8.00 20.00
17 Tim Brown/2410 12.50 30.00
18 Dale Carter/1400 5.00 12.00
19A Ray Childress/1200 4.00 10.00
19B Ray Childress/235AP 4.00 10.00
20 Ben Coates/1175 6.00 15.00
21 Mark Collins/1430 4.00 10.00
22 Kerry Collins/3300 6.00 15.00
23 Curtis Conway/1200 5.00 12.00
24 Quentin Coryatt/1400 5.00 12.00
25 Randall Cunningham/470 12.50 30.00
26A Jack Del Rio/1480 8.00 20.00
26B Jack Del Rio/930AP 8.00 20.00
27 Willie Davis/1500 5.00 12.00
28A Derrick Deese/1200 4.00 10.00
28B Derrick Deese/2375AP 4.00 10.00
28C Derrick Deese/735AP 4.00 10.00
29A Trent Dilfer/2010 6.00 15.00
29B Trent Dilfer/306AP 6.00 15.00
30 Troy Drayton/1375 4.00 10.00
31 Quinn Early/1200 5.00 12.00
32 Henry Ellard/1440 8.00 20.00
33 John Elliott/2380 4.00 10.00
34 Luther Elliss/1470 4.00 10.00
35 John Elway/50 125.00 250.00
36 Bert Emanuel/1445 5.00 12.00
37 Steve Emtman/2365 4.00 10.00
38A Craig Erickson/630 4.00 10.00
38B Craig Erickson/890AP 4.00 10.00
39 Boomer Esiason/1700 6.00 15.00
40 Marshall Faulk/1030 20.00 40.00
41 Barry Foster/1455 5.00 12.00
42 Mike Fox/1445 4.00 10.00
43 Irving Fryar/1500 6.00 15.00
44 Joey Galloway/1445 6.00 15.00
45A Shaun Gayle/1200 4.00 10.00
45B Shaun Gayle/265AP 4.00 10.00
46 Jeff George/1295 5.00 12.00
47 Darrien Gordon/2400 4.00 10.00
48 Jeff Graham/1465 4.00 10.00
49 Eric Green/1460 4.00 10.00
50 Charles Haley/1420 8.00 20.00
51 Rodney Hampton/1120 5.00 12.00
52 Andy Harmon/1200 4.00 10.00
53 Courtney Hawkins/1445 4.00 10.00
54 Michael Haynes/1180 4.00 10.00
55 Garrison Hearst/1460 6.00 15.00
56A Craig Heyward/1200 10.00 25.00
56B Craig Heyward/265AP 10.00 25.00
57 Greg Hill/1455 5.00 12.00
58 Pierce Holt/1440 4.00 10.00
59 Patrick Hunter/2375 4.00 10.00
60 Michael Irvin/1490 20.00 40.00
61 Sean Jones/2385 4.00 10.00
62 Qadry Ismail/1170 5.00 12.00
63A Steve Israel/1200 4.00 10.00
63B Steve Israel/2413AP 4.00 10.00
63C Steve Israel/750AP 4.00 10.00
64 Jack Jackson/1475 4.00 10.00
65 Michael Jackson/1200 5.00 12.00
66A Shawn Jefferson/1200 4.00 10.00
66B Shawn Jefferson/240AP 5.00 12.00
67 Haywood Jeffires/1470 5.00 12.00
68 Trezelle Jenkins/1470 4.00 10.00
69A Rob Johnson/2815 5.00 12.00
69B Rob Johnson/500 5.00 12.00
70 Seth Joyner/1480 6.00 15.00
71 Jim Kelly/470 15.00 40.00
72 Cortez Kennedy/1380 6.00 15.00
73 Terry Kirby/1450 4.00 10.00
74 Dave Krieg/1470 5.00 12.00
75A Ant.Langham/1200 4.00 10.00
75B Ant.Langham/260AP 4.00 10.00
76 Ty Law/1460 12.00 30.00
77 Leon Lett/1550 4.00 10.00
78 Ronnie Lott/1900 8.00 20.00
79A Keenan McCardell/1235 5.00 12.00
79B Keenan McCardell/2403AP 5.00 12.00
79C Keenan McCardell/754AP 5.00 12.00
80 Terry McDaniel/2340 4.00 10.00
81 Tony McGee/1385 5.00 12.00
82A Willie McGinest/1160 6.00 15.00
82B Willie McGinest/2407AP 6.00 15.00
82C Willie McGinest/754AP 6.00 15.00
83 Chester McGlockton/1280 4.00 10.00
84A Mark McMillian/1175 4.00 10.00
84B Mark McMillian/2400AP 4.00 10.00
84C Mark McMillian/825AP 4.00 10.00
85 Steve McNair/3490 10.00 25.00
86 Mike Mamula/1250 4.00 10.00
87A Arthur Marshall/1165 4.00 10.00
87B Arthur Marshall/2400AP 4.00 10.00
87C Arthur Marshall/870AP 4.00 10.00
88 Russell Maryland/1250 5.00 12.00
89 Clay Matthews/2385 10.00 25.00
90A Chad May/1180 4.00 10.00
90B Chad May/2410AP 4.00 10.00
91 Natrone Means/1058 5.00 12.00
92 Anthony Miller/2385 5.00 12.00
93 Sam Mills/1470 25.00 60.00
94 Herman Moore/2070 5.00 12.00
95 Byron Bam Morris/1430 4.00 10.00
96 Jay Novacek/1195 15.00 30.00
97A Brett Perriman/1380 4.00 10.00
97B Brett Perriman/935 4.00 10.00
98A Michael D.Perry/1200 6.00 15.00
98B Michael D.Perry/295AP 6.00 15.00
99 Roman Phifer/2395 4.00 10.00
100 Ricky Proehl/1475 5.00 12.00
101A John Randle/1170 8.00 20.00
101B John Randle/2400AP 8.00 20.00
101C John Randle/757AP 8.00 20.00
102 Andre Reed/1440 8.00 20.00
103 Jake Reed/1470 5.00 12.00
104 Errict Rhett/1400 5.00 12.00
105A Willie Roaf/1200 5.00 12.00
105B Willie Roaf/245AP 5.00 12.00
106 Bill Romanowski/1450 6.00 15.00
107 Rashaan Salaam/1320 5.00 12.00
108 Mike Sherrard/1450 4.00 10.00
109A Heath Shuler/2000 6.00 15.00
109B Heath Shuler/366AP 6.00 15.00
110 Clyde Simmons/735 6.00 15.00
111A Chris Slade/1100 4.00 10.00
111B Chris Slade/2417AP 4.00 10.00
111C Chris Slade/750AP 4.00 10.00
112 Al Smith/1360 4.00 10.00
113 Emmitt Smith/500 75.00 135.00
114 Neil Smith/1465 6.00 15.00
115 Mark Stepnoski/1500 4.00 10.00
116 J.J. Stokes/1435 5.00 12.00
117 Vinny Testaverde/1020 6.00 15.00
118 Henry Thomas/1420 4.00 10.00
119 Lewis Tillman/1170 4.00 10.00
120A Jessie Tuggle/1200 5.00 12.00
120B Jessie Tuggle/195AP 5.00 12.00
121 Tamarick Vanover/1155 5.00 12.00
122 Troy Vincent/1490 4.00 10.00
123 John Walsh/3340 4.00 10.00
124A Steve Walsh/1185 4.00 10.00
124B Steve Walsh/1015AP 4.00 10.00
125A Brian Williams LB/1175 4.00 10.00
125B Brian Williams LB/2670AP 4.00 10.00
125C Brian Williams LB/865AP 4.00 10.00
126 Calvin Williams/1200 5.00 12.00
127 Sherman Williams/1460 4.00 10.00
128 Steve Young/500 20.00 40.00
129 Eric Zeier/500 5.00 12.00

1995 Pro Line Autograph Printer's Proofs

Eight players signed 50-each of their 1995 Pro Line Printer's Proof cards which were randomly inserted into packs. Each signed card was numbered of 50 signed and contains the Classic corporate seal. Reportedly, approximately 80 percent of the 400 total autographs were inserted into 1995 Pro Line Hot Box packs. The signed cards are virtually identical to the Printer's Proof version, on both front and back, except that the UV coating was left off so that the autograph would adhere to the card.

STATED PRINT RUN 50 NUMBERED SETS
99 Steve McNair 30.00 80.00
175 Drew Bledsoe 40.00 100.00
197 Steve Young 50.00 120.00
210 Kerry Collins 25.00 60.00
230 Boomer Esiason 15.00 40.00
254 Troy Aikman 75.00 150.00
304 Emmitt Smith 125.00 250.00
311 Trent Dilfer 15.00 40.00

1995 Pro Line Bonus Card Jumbos

This 14 card jumbo-sized (2 1/2" by 4 3/4") set was distributed in four different modes. The first three cards, featuring top picks, were issued one per Classic NFL Rookies Hobby case. Cards 4-8 were issued one per ProLine Series 1 Hobby case. Cards 9-11 were issued one per ProLine Series 2 Hobby case. Cards 13-15 were issued one per 1996 Classic NFL Experience case. Card number 12 was never issued. There was 1,250 of each card made for cards 1-11. The fronts feature a full-color action photo with the player's name and position at the bottom. The background is silver and has the team's name or logo on it numerous times and the middle has a multi-color cloudiness to it. The backs have a small player photo in the middle with his name above it and information below or beside it. The background is gray, tan or green with the team's name or logo shown many times. Cards 13-15 have a colorful foil background with the player's name in gold script. Card backs contain an action shot of the player with information underneath.

COMPLETE SET (14) 20.00 50.00
1-3: INSERTED IN CLASSIC NFL ROOKIES
4-8: INSERTED IN PROLINE SERIES 1
9-11: INSERTED IN PROLINE SERIES 2
13-15: INSERTED IN 96 NFL EXPERIENCE
1 Ki-Jana Carter .30 .75
2 Steve McNair 3.00 8.00
3 Kerry Collins 1.50 4.00
4 Deion Sanders 1.25 3.00
5 Steve Young 2.00 5.00
6 Emmitt Smith 4.00 10.00
7 Natrone Means .30 .75
8 Drew Bledsoe 1.50 4.00
9 Troy Aikman 2.50 6.00
10 Marshall Faulk 3.00 8.00
11 J.J.Stokes .30 .75
13 Emmitt Smith 4.00 10.00
14 Rashaan Salaam .10 .30
15 Reggie White .75 2.00

1995 Pro Line Field Generals

Inserted at a rate of one in 60 Series 2 packs, this 10 card set features a clear plastic stock in the background. Card fronts contain a shot of the player with his name and the "Field General" logo at the bottom of the card. Card backs contain a small shot of the player with a brief statistical summary. Cards are numbered out of 1,700 and have a "G" prefix.

COMPLETE SET (10) 30.00 80.00
STATED ODDS 1:60 SER.2
G1 Marshall Faulk 6.00 15.00
G2 Emmitt Smith 8.00 20.00
G3 Steve Young 4.00 10.00
G4 Ki-Jana Carter .75 2.00
G5 Rashaan Salaam .30 .75
G6 Dan Marino 10.00 25.00
G7 J.J. Stokes .75 2.00
G8 Drew Bledsoe 3.00 8.00
G9 Brett Favre 10.00 25.00
G10 Barry Sanders 8.00 20.00

1995 Pro Line Game of the Week Home

This 30-card interactive set was randomly inserted one per special retail packs and features a match-up of teams for different weeks of the season. Cards either contain a "H" or "V" prefix on the back to denote the potential winning team as home or visitor. Reportedly, the first 1000 participants who submitted 21-30 different game cards with the actual winner of the game received the first prize which was a complete set of 30 NFL Pro Line winner cards printed on silver foil board with the final score of the game foil stamped on the front. The first 2500 participants who submitted 10-20 different game cards with the actual winner of the game received the second prize which was a complete set of 30 NFL Pro Line winner cards with the final score of the game foil stamped on the card. Each participant who sent in all 30 winning cards were eligible for the grand prize drawing, which was either a Steve Young or Jerry Rice game-used jersey from the 1995 season. The redemption cards expired on 3/10/1996.

COMPLETE SET (60) 8.00 20.00
*VISITOR: .4X TO 1X HOME
ONE PER SPECIAL RETAIL PACK
*PRIZES: .6X TO 1.5X HOME
*PRIZES FOIL: 1X TO 2.5X HOME
H1 B.Sanders R.White .60 1.50
H2 J.Elway J.Hostetler .75 2.00
H3 M.Westbrook R.Watters .10 .30
H4 J.Kelly M.Lewis .30 .75
H5 M.Faulk J.Bettis .50 1.25
H6 N.Means B.Morris .10 .30
H7 E.Smith E.Joyner .60 1.50
H8 E.Rhett H.Shuler .20 .50
H9 J.Seau Cunningham .20 .50
H10 D.Bledsoe S.Young .30 .75
H11 K.Collins D.Krieg .40 1.00
H12 S.Beuerlein A.Harper .20 .50
H13 B.Coates T.Vincent .10 .30
H14 J.Rice M.Irvin .50 1.25
H15 R.Hampton C.Kennedy .10 .30
H16 S.McNair L.Hoard .60 1.50
H17 T.Thomas I.Fryar .20 .50
H18 Ki.Carter A.Rison .10 .30
H19 D.Marino B.Esiason .75 2.00
H20 B.Favre W.Moon 1.00 2.50
H21 A.Miller T.Brown .20 .50
H22 C.Warren S.Bono .10 .30
H23 Sh.Sharpe N.Smith .20 .50
H24 J.Randle D.Stubblefield .10 .30
H25 J.Everett T.Mathis .10 .30
H26 T.Aikman M.Mamula .40 1.00
H27 T.Dilfer C.Carter .20 .50
H28 S.Walsh S.Mitchell .08 .25
H29 G.Lloyd V.Testaverde .10 .30
H30 J.George G.Hearst .10 .30

1995 Pro Line GameBreakers

This 30-card standard-size set was randomly inserted into both retail and hobby packs. They were inserted at a ratio of one card per box. The fronts feature an action photo against a metallic background. The title "GameBreakers" as well as the player's name is located at the bottom. The backs have a full-bleed photo and player information. 175 Printer's proofs of each card were also produced and randomly inserted at a rate of one per case. Card backs are numbered with a "GB" prefix.

COMPLETE SET (30) 25.00 60.00
STATED ODDS 1:36HOB,1:30JUM SER.1
*GB PRINT.PROOF: 1.2X TO 3X BASE INSERT
STATED ODDS 1:432 SER.1 HOBBY
GB1 Troy Aikman 2.00 5.00
GB2 Drew Bledsoe 1.25 3.00
GB3 Tim Brown .60 1.50
GB4 Cris Carter .60 1.50
GB5 Ki-Jana Carter .30 .75
GB6 Kerry Collins 1.50 4.00
GB7 John Elway 4.00 10.00
GB8 Marshall Faulk 2.50 6.00
GB9 Brett Favre 4.00 10.00
GB10 Garrison Hearst .60 1.50
GB11 Michael Irvin .60 1.50
GB12 Jim Kelly .60 1.50
GB13 Dan Marino 4.00 10.00
GB14 Natrone Means .25 .60
GB15 Eric Metcalf .25 .60
GB16 J.J.Stokes .30 .75
GB17 Carl Pickens .25 .60
GB18 Jerry Rice 2.00 5.00
GB19 Andre Rison .25 .60
GB20 Barry Sanders 3.00 8.00
GB21 Deion Sanders 1.00 2.50
GB22 Junior Seau .60 1.50
GB23 Emmitt Smith 3.00 8.00
GB24 Thurman Thomas .60 1.50
GB25 Ricky Watters .25 .60
GB26 Reggie White .60 1.50
GB27 Rod Woodson .25 .60
GB28 Steve Young 1.50 4.00
GB29 Rashaan Salaam .10 .30
GB30 Michael Westbrook .30 .75

1995 Pro Line Grand Gainers

Inserted in retail packs at a rate of one per pack, this 30 card set features a white mesh card front on one half, with game action in the background on the other half. The player's name and position are located in the bottom right corner. Card backs include a particular statistic on the right side of the card with a brief commentary. Cards are numbered with a "G" prefix.

COMPLETE SET (30) 7.50 20.00
ONE PER SPECIAL RETAIL PACK
G1 Barry Sanders 1.00 2.50
G2 Emmitt Smith 1.00 2.50
G3 Natrone Means .07 .20
G4 Marshall Faulk .75 2.00
G5 Errict Rhett .07 .20
G6 Jerry Rice .60 1.50
G7 Tim Brown .20 .50
G8 Cris Carter .20 .50
G9 Irving Fryar .07 .20
G10 Ben Coates .07 .20
G11 Fred Barnett .07 .20
G12 Andre Rison .07 .20
G13 Drew Bledsoe .40 1.00
G14 Dan Marino 1.25 3.00
G15 Warren Moon .07 .20
G16 Steve Young .50 1.25
G17 Brett Favre 1.25 3.00
G18 John Elway 1.25 3.00
G19 Randall Cunningham .20 .50
G20 Stan Humphries .07 .20
G21 Jim Kelly .20 .50
G22 Ki-Jana Carter .08 .25
G23 Rodney Hampton .07 .20
G24 Tyrone Wheatley .40 1.00
G25 J.J. Stokes .08 .25
G26 Michael Irvin .20 .50
G27 Herman Moore .20 .50
G28 Kerry Collins .60 1.50
G29 Steve McNair 1.00 2.50
G30 Rob Johnson .30 .75

1995 Pro Line Images Previews

Randomly inserted into Series 2 packs at a rate of one in 18 packs, this set previewed the 1995 Images release.

COMPLETE SET (5) 6.00 15.00
STATED ODDS 1:18 SERIES 2
1 Emmitt Smith 2.50 6.00
2 Steve Young 1.25 3.00
3 Drew Bledsoe 1.00 2.50
4 Kerry Collins 1.25 3.00
5 Marshall Faulk 2.00 5.00

1995 Pro Line Impact

Sequentially numbered out of 4,500, these 30 standard-size cards were randomly inserted into retail packs. These cards were available at a rate of one per box. Horizontally designed, the card fronts feature a full-bleed metallic finish. The player stands out from the rest of the photo which is lightly shaded. The backs present career highlights, a small photo and are numbered with an "I" prefix. A gold parallel set, numbered out of 1,750, was also produced and randomly inserted at a rate of one in 90 retail packs.

COMPLETE SET (30) 15.00 40.00
SILVER/4500 ODDS 1:1 SER.1 RETAIL BOX
*GOLD/1750: .8X TO 2X SILVER/4500
GOLD/1750 ODDS 1:90 SER.1 RETAIL
1 Jim Kelly .40 1.00
2 Thurman Thomas .40 1.00
3 Troy Aikman 1.25 3.00
4 Michael Irvin .40 1.00
5 Emmitt Smith 2.00 5.00
6 John Elway 2.50 6.00

7 Barry Sanders 2.00 5.00
8 Brett Favre 2.50 6.00
9 Reggie White .40 1.00
10 Marshall Faulk 1.50 4.00
11 Ki-Jana Carter .20 .50
12 Tim Brown .40 1.00
13 Jeff Hostetler .15 .40
14 Dan Marino 2.50 6.00
15 Drew Bledsoe .75 2.00
16 Ben Coates .15 .40
17 Rodney Hampton .15 .40
18 Randall Cunningham .40 1.00
19 Ricky Watters .15 .40
20 Byron Bam Morris .07 .20
21 Natrone Means .15 .40
22 Junior Seau .40 1.00
23 Jerry Rice 1.25 3.00
24 Steve Young 1.00 2.50
25 William Floyd .15 .40
26 Rick Mirer .15 .40
27 Chris Warren .15 .40
28 Jerome Bettis .40 1.00
29 Alvin Harper .07 .20
30 Heath Shuler .15 .40

1995 Pro Line MVP Redemption

This 35-card horizontal standard-size set was randomly inserted into packs. These cards were inserted one every two boxes (Hobby or Retail). Thirty-four players as well as one field card was issued. If the player featured on the card won the 1995 Associated Press Offensive MVP award, a special Favre card would be awarded along with on the following: if the card was stamped one of 4,000 the bearer received a prepaid $50 phone card of that player. For a card hand-numbered to 200, the owner received a $100 prepaid phone card of that player. If a collector had the #1 card that was hand-numbered, he would receive not only the $100 prepaid phone card but also a complete 1995 Pro Line Live Autographed set. The redemption expiration date was 3/31/96.

COMPLETE SET (35) 50.00 120.00
STATED ODDS 1:72H,1:60J,1:48SR SER.1
*NUMB.OF 200: 1.2X to 3X BASIC INSERTS
1 Garrison Hearst 1.00 2.50
2 Terance Mathis .40 1.00
3 Jim Kelly 1.00 2.50
4 Thurman Thomas 1.00 2.50
5 Kerry Collins 2.00 5.00
6 Rashaan Salaam .15 .40
7 Ki-Jana Carter .40 1.00
8 Andre Rison .40 1.00
9 Troy Aikman 3.00 8.00
10 Michael Irvin 1.00 2.50
11 Emmitt Smith 5.00 12.00
12 John Elway 6.00 15.00
13 Barry Sanders 5.00 12.00
14 Brett Favre WIN 6.00 15.00
15 Marshall Faulk 4.00 10.00
16 Marcus Allen 1.00 2.50
17 Jeff Hostetler .40 1.00
18 Dan Marino 6.00 15.00
19 Cris Carter 1.00 2.50
20 Warren Moon .40 1.00
21 Drew Bledsoe 2.00 5.00
22 Ben Coates .40 1.00
23 Rodney Hampton .40 1.00
24 Boomer Esiason .40 1.00
25 Ricky Watters .40 1.00
26 Barry Foster .40 1.00
27 Natrone Means .40 1.00
28 Rick Mirer .40 1.00
29 Chris Warren .40 1.00
30 Jerry Rice 3.00 8.00
31 Steve Young 2.50 6.00
32 Jerome Bettis 1.00 2.50
33 Errict Rhett .40 1.00
34 Heath Shuler .40 1.00
35 Field Card .20 .50
MVP Brett Favre MVP/2500 3.00 8.00

1995 Pro Line National Attention

This 10 card set was inserted in 1995 Pro Line National boxes that were only available to dealers who participated in the National Sports Collectors Convention show held in St. Louis, MO. Due to the relocation of the NFL Rams franchise to St. Louis, this set contains several players from the 1995 Rams team, as well as other major stars. Reportedly, 1250 of each card were produced.

COMPLETE SET (10) 10.00 25.00
STATED ODDS 1:18 NATIONAL
NA1 Jerome Bettis .75 2.00
NA2 Sean Gilbert .30 .75
NA3 Chris Miller .15 .40
NA4 Troy Aikman 2.50 6.00
NA5 Kevin Carter .75 2.00
NA6 Marshall Faulk 3.00 8.00
NA7 Drew Bledsoe 1.50 4.00
NA8 Shane Conlan .15 .40
NA9 Emmitt Smith 4.00 10.00
NA10 Steve Young 2.00 5.00

1995 Pro Line Phone Cards $1

Randomly inserted at a rate of at least one per series 2 pack (unless another denomination was pulled), this 30 card set is phone card sized with a full bleed shot of the player on the front. Information about using the phone card is contained on the back. The phone time expiration date is 12/31/96. A parallel Printer's Proof set was also randomly inserted at a rate of one in 44 packs.

COMPLETE SET (30) 4.00 10.00
ONE PER SERIES 2 PACK
*PRINT.PROOFS: 1.5X TO 4X BASIC INSERTS
PRINT.PROOF ODDS 1:44 SERIES 2
1 Kerry Collins .40 1.00
2 Barry Foster .05 .15
3 Jeff Blake .20 .50
4 Troy Aikman .50 1.25
5 Reggie White .15 .40
6 Marshall Faulk .60 1.50
7 Steve Bono .05 .15
8 Drew Bledsoe .30 .75
9 Byron Bam Morris .02 .10
10 Rodney Hampton .05 .15
11 Trent Dilfer .15 .40
12 Errict Rhett .05 .15
13 Heath Shuler .05 .15
14 Mike Mamula .02 .10
15 Ricky Watters .05 .15
16 Stan Humphries .05 .15
17 Natrone Means .05 .15
18 William Floyd .05 .15
19 Joey Galloway .40 1.00
20 Ki-Jana Carter .07 .20
21 Andre Rison .05 .15
22 Steve McNair .75 2.00
23 Napoleon Kaufman .30 .75
24 Kyle Brady .15 .40
25 Steve Beuerlein .05 .15
26 Ben Coates .05 .15
27 Eric Metcalf .05 .15
28 Desmond Howard .05 .15
29 Deion Sanders .25 .60
30 J.J. Stokes .07 .20
1P Kerry Collins Promo .60 1.50

1995 Pro Line Phone Cards $2

Randomly inserted at a rate of one in six Series 2 packs, this 25 card set is phone card sized with a full bleed shot of the player on the front. Information about using the phone card is contained on the back. The phone time expiration date is 12/31/96. A parallel Printer's Proof set was also randomly inserted at a rate of one in 75 packs.

COMPLETE SET (25) 6.00 15.00
STATED ODDS 1:6 SER.2
*PRINT.PROOFS: 1.5X TO 4X BASIC INSERTS
PRINT.PROOF ODDS 1:75 SERIES 2
1 Kerry Collins .50 1.25
2 Barry Foster .10 .30
3 Andre Rison .10 .30
4 Troy Aikman 1.00 2.50
5 Steve McNair 1.00 2.50
6 Marshall Faulk 1.25 3.00
7 J.J. Stokes .08 .25
8 Drew Bledsoe .60 1.50
9 Byron Bam Morris .05 .15
10 Rodney Hampton .10 .30
11 Deion Sanders .50 1.25
12 Errict Rhett .10 .30
13 Heath Shuler .10 .30
14 Mike Mamula .05 .15
15 Ricky Watters .10 .30
16 Stan Humphries .10 .30
17 Natrone Means .10 .30
18 William Floyd .10 .30
19 Kyle Brady .30 .75
20 Ki-Jana Carter .08 .25
21 Jeff Blake .75 2.00
22 Eric Metcalf .10 .30
23 Steve Bono .10 .30
24 Steve Beuerlein .10 .30
25 Eric Green .05 .15

1995 Pro Line Phone Cards $5

Randomly inserted at a rate of one in 18 Series 2 packs, this 15 card set is phone card sized with a full bleed shot of the player on the front. Information about using the phone card is contained on the back. The phone time expiration date was 12/31/96. A parallel Printer's Proof set was also randomly inserted at a rate of one in 210 packs.

COMPLETE SET (15) 25.00 50.00
STATED ODDS 1:18 SER.2
*PRINT.PROOFS: 1.5X TO 4X BASIC INSERTS
PRINT.PROOF ODDS 1:210 SERIES 2
1 Marshall Faulk 2.50 6.00
2 Troy Aikman 2.00 5.00
3 J.J. Stokes .20 .50
4 Kyle Brady .60 1.50
5 Steve McNair 2.00 5.00
6 Deion Sanders 1.00 2.50
7 Ki-Jana Carter .20 .50
8 Kerry Collins 1.00 2.50
9 Drew Bledsoe 1.25 3.00
10 Emmitt Smith 3.00 8.00
11 William Floyd .25 .60
12 Ricky Watters .25 .60
13 Reggie White .60 1.50
14 Steve Young 1.50 4.00
15 Warren Sapp 1.00 2.50

1995 Pro Line Phone Cards $20

Randomly inserted at a rate of one in 144 Series 2 packs, this 5 card set is phone card sized with a full bleed shot of the player on the front. Information about using the phone card is contained on the back. The phone time expiration date is 12/31/96.

COMPLETE SET (5) 25.00 60.00
STATED ODDS 1:144 SER.2
1 Steve Young 6.00 15.00
2 Drew Bledsoe 5.00 12.00
3 Marshall Faulk 10.00 25.00
4 Ki-Jana Carter 2.50 6.00
5 Kerry Collins 5.00 12.00

1995 Pro Line Phone Cards $100

Randomly inserted at a rate of one in 266 Series 2 packs, this 5 card set is phone card sized with a full bleed shot of the player on the front. Information about using the phone card is contained on the back. The phone time expiration date is 12/31/96.

COMPLETE SET (5) 50.00 120.00
STATED ODDS 1:266 SER.2
1 Emmitt Smith 20.00 50.00
2 Steve Young 10.00 25.00
3 Drew Bledsoe 8.00 20.00
4 Ki-Jana Carter 4.00 10.00
5 Troy Aikman 12.50 30.00

1995 Pro Line Phone Cards $1000/$1500

Randomly inserted at a rate of one in 2,995 Series 2 packs for the $1000 cards and one in 11,980 for the $1500 card, this 5 card set is phone card sized with a full bleed shot of the player on the front. The Emmitt Smith is the only card that has a $1500 denomination and is not included in the complete set price. Information about using the phone card is contained on the back. The phone time expiration date was 12/31/96.

$1000 STATE ODDS 1:2995 SER.2 PACKS
$1500 STATE ODDS 1:11980 SER.2 PACKS
1 Steve Young 60.00 150.00
1B Emmitt Smith 1500 125.00 300.00
2 Drew Bledsoe 60.00 150.00
3 Ki-Jana Carter 40.00 80.00
4 Troy Aikman 75.00 200.00

1995 Pro Line Pogs

Randomly inserted in retail packs, this 30-card set contains a dual player Pogs. Card fronts contain action shots with the two Pogs in the middle. Card backs are brown with each player's name on their Pog and some brief statistical summary below. Cards are numbered with a "C" prefix.

COMPLETE SET (30) 2.50 6.00
RANDOM INS.IN SPECIAL RETAIL PACKS
C1 G.Hearst S.Joyner .05 .15
C2 T.Mathis J.George .01 .05
C3 J.Kelly T.Thomas .05 .15
C4 K.Collins B.Foster .30 .75
C5 S.Walsh R.Salaam .01 .05
C6 B.Sanders H.Moore .30 .75
C7 J.Elway Sh.Sharpe .40 1.00
C8 T.Aikman E.Smith .30 .75
C9 L.Hoard A.Rison .01 .05
C10 J.Blake K.Carter .15 .40
C11 B.Favre R.White .40 1.00
C12 S.McNair G.Brown .40 1.00
C13 M.Faulk Q.Coryatt .25 .60
C14 T.Boselli S.Beuerlein .01 .05
C15 M.Allen S.Bono .05 .15
C16 J.Everett M.Bates .01 .05
C17 D.Bledsoe B.Coates .10 .30
C18 W.Moon C.Carter .05 .15
C19 D.Marino I.Fryar .40 1.00
C20 J.Hostetler T.Brown .05 .15
C21 K.Greene B.Morris .01 .05
C22 D.Brown R.Hampton .01 .05
C23 B.Esiason M.Lewis .01 .05
C24 R.Cunningham R.Watters .05 .15
C25 N.Means J.Seau .05 .15
C26 H.Shuler M.Westbrook .02 .10
C27 T.Dilfer E.Rhett .05 .15
C28 J.Bettis K.Carter .05 .15
C29 S.Young J.Rice .20 .50
C30 R.Mirer C.Warren .01 .05

1995 Pro Line Precision Cuts

Inserted at a rate of one in 45 packs, this 20 card set was randomly inserted into Series 2 packs. Card fronts contain a blue background with a diamond-shape die cut design at the top. Card backs contain a shot of the player with a brief commentary. Card backs are numbered with a "P" prefix.

COMPLETE SET (20) 50.00 120.00
STATED ODDS 1:45 SER.2
*SAMPLES: .2X TO .5X BASIC INSERTS
P1 Jim Kelly 2.50 6.00
P2 John Elway 8.00 20.00
P3 Kerry Collins 3.00 8.00
P4 Ki-Jana Carter .75 2.00
P5 Andre Rison 1.25 3.00
P6 Troy Aikman 5.00 12.00
P7 Emmitt Smith 8.00 20.00
P8 Barry Sanders 6.00 15.00
P9 Warren Moon 1.50 4.00
P10 Jeff Hostetler .75 2.00
P11 Dan Marino 8.00 20.00
P12 Drew Bledsoe 2.00 5.00
P13 Rodney Hampton 1.25 3.00
P14 Ricky Watters 1.25 3.00
P15 Byron Bam Morris .75 2.00
P16 Natrone Means 1.25 3.00
P17 Steve Young 4.00 10.00
P18 Jerry Rice 5.00 12.00
P19 J.J. Stokes .75 2.00
P20 Errict Rhett 1.25 3.00

1995 Pro Line Pro Bowl

Randomly inserted in pre-priced ($1.99) retail packs at a rate of one per box, this 30-card set highlights players named to past and present Pro Bowls. Card fronts are die cut in the shape of a ticket stub with an all foil silver background. Each card contains the number "250392" on the top and bottom. Card backs show a game action shot with a brief commentary on the player. Cards are numbered with a "PB" prefix.

COMPLETE SET (30) 7.50 20.00
ONE PER SPECIAL RETAIL PACK
PB1 Seth Joyner .02 .10
PB2 Andre Reed .07 .20
PB3 Bruce Smith .20 .50
PB4 Michael Irvin .20 .50
PB5 Troy Aikman .60 1.50
PB6 Emmitt Smith 1.00 2.50
PB7 Charles Haley .07 .20
PB8 Shannon Sharpe .07 .20
PB9 John Elway 1.25 3.00
PB10 Barry Sanders 1.00 2.50
PB11 Reggie White .20 .50
PB12 Marshall Faulk .75 2.00
PB13 Tim Brown .20 .50
PB14 Chester McGlockton .07 .20
PB15 Dan Marino 1.25 3.00
PB16 Cris Carter .20 .50
PB17 Warren Moon .07 .20
PB18 Ben Coates .07 .20
PB19 Drew Bledsoe .40 1.00
PB20 Rod Woodson .07 .20
PB21 Natrone Means .07 .20
PB22 Leslie O'Neal .07 .20
PB23 Junior Seau .20 .50
PB24 Jerry Rice .60 1.50
PB25 Chris Warren .07 .20
PB26 Brent Jones .02 .10
PB27 Steve Young .50 1.25
PB28 Dana Stubblefield .07 .20
PB29 Deion Sanders .30 .75
PB30 Jerome Bettis .20 .50

1995 Pro Line Record Breakers

This ten card standard-size set was randomly inserted only in the "Hot Boxes" and split five in the hobby series and five in the retail. The first five cards are from hobby packs and commemorate a new NFL record. The last five are from retail packs and commemorate a new team record. The fronts of these acetate cards, have a color photo of the player on a solid orange background in the middle of the card. Surrounding that is a see through purple border. The player's name is at the bottom and is also see through. The backs have a head shot, player information and the player's name backwards, due to the see through front. The background is the same as the front. Cards numbered with a "HB" prefix were randomly inserted into Series 1 hobby hot boxes and are hand numbered out of 425. Cards numbered with a "RB" prefix were randomly inserted into Series 1 retail hot boxes and are numbered out of 350.

COMPLETE SET (10) 50.00 120.00
HB1-HB5 INS.IN SER.1 HOBBY HOT BOXES
HB1-HB5 PRINT RUN 425 SERIAL #'d SETS
RB1-RB5 INS.IN SER.1 RETAIL HOT BOXES
RB1-RB5 PRINT RUN 350 SERIAL #'d SETS
HB1 Drew Bledsoe 5.00 12.00
HB2 Cris Carter 2.50 6.00
HB3 Jerry Rice 8.00 20.00
HB4 Steve Young 6.00 15.00
HB5 Marshall Faulk 10.00 25.00
RB1 Emmitt Smith 8.00 20.00
RB2 Barry Sanders 12.50 30.00
RB3 Natrone Means 1.00 2.50
RB4 Ben Coates 1.00 2.50
RB5 Bruce Smith 2.50 6.00

1995 Pro Line Series 2

Issued by Classic, this 75 card set came in 6 card packs and included one prepaid phone card per pack. Card fronts are similar to series one, but the player's name and team are against a blue holographic background at the bottom of the card. The "ProLine" emblem at the top left also shows the card as being a series 2 card. Terrell Fletcher is the only Rookie Card of note in this set. Card backs are numbered with a "II" prefix.

COMPLETE SET (75) 6.00 15.00
1 Jim Kelly .08 .25
2 Steve Walsh .01 .05
3 Jeff Blake .08 .25
4 Vinny Testaverde .02 .10
5 Jeff Hostetler .02 .10
6 Dan Marino .60 1.50
7 Cris Carter .08 .25
8 Drew Bledsoe .20 .50
9 Jim Everett .01 .05
10 Neil O'Donnell .02 .10
11 Rodney Hampton .02 .10
12 Troy Aikman .30 .75
13 John Elway .60 1.50
14 Barry Sanders .50 1.25
15 Reggie White .08 .25
16 Marshall Faulk .40 1.00
17 Marcus Allen .08 .25
18 James O. Stewart .08 .25
19 Randall Cunningham .08 .25
20 Natrone Means .02 .10
21 Rick Mirer .02 .10
22 Jerry Rice .30 .75
23 Errict Rhett .02 .10
24 Heath Shuler .02 .10
25 Jerome Bettis .08 .25
26 Garrison Hearst .08 .25
27 Jeff George .02 .10
28 Andre Reed .02 .10
29 Warren Moon .02 .10
30 Ben Coates .02 .10
31 Mario Bates .02 .10
32 Byron Bam Morris .01 .05
33 Dave Brown .02 .10
34 Emmitt Smith .50 1.25
35 Anthony Miller .02 .10
36 Herman Moore .08 .25
37 Brett Favre .60 1.50
38 Steve Bono .02 .10
39 Stan Humphries .02 .10
40 Steve Young .25 .60
41 Trent Dilfer .08 .25
42 Chris Miller .01 .05
43 Herschel Walker .02 .10
44 Michael Irvin .08 .25
45 Junior Seau .08 .25
46 Deion Sanders .15 .40
47 William Floyd .02 .10
48 Ki-Jana Carter .02 .10
49 Kerry Collins .30 .75
50 Steve McNair .30 .75
51 Tony Boselli .02 .10
52 Kyle Brady .08 .25
53 Mike Mamula .01 .05
54 Warren Sapp .08 .25
55 J.J. Stokes .02 .10
56 Joey Galloway .15 .40
57 Hugh Douglas .02 .10
58 Michael Westbrook .08 .25
59 Napoleon Kaufman .08 .25
60 Rashaan Salaam .02 .10
61 Tyrone Wheatley .08 .25
62 Terrell Fletcher RC .01 .05
63 Eric Metcalf .02 .10
64 Kevin Carter .08 .25
65 Andre Rison .02 .10
66 Eric Green .01 .05
67 Dave Meggett .01 .05
68 Ricky Watters .02 .10
69 Steve Beuerlein .02 .10
70 Craig Erickson .01 .05
71 Michael Dean Perry .01 .05
72 Alvin Harper .01 .05
73 Rob Moore .02 .10
74 Frank Reich .01 .05
75 Checklist .01 .05

1995 Pro Line Series 2 Printer's Proofs

COMPLETE SET (75) 100.00 200.00
*PRINTER'S PROOFS: 5X TO 12X BASIC CARDS
STATED ODDS 1:18

1995 Pro Line 5000

COMPLETE SET (5) 6.00 15.00
1 Emmitt Smith 2.50 6.00
2 Drew Bledsoe 1.25 3.00
3 Marshall Faulk 1.25 3.00
4 Kerry Collins 1.00 2.50
5 Steve Young 1.50 4.00

1996 Pro Line

The 1996 Pro Line set was issued in one series totalling 350 standard-size cards. The set was issued in 10 card packs (suggested retail price of $1.79) with 28 packs in a box and 12 boxes in a case. There is a Rookies subset as well as checklists that feature players on the front. An unnumbered Emmitt Smith Promo card was produced and priced below.

COMPLETE SET (350) 10.00 25.00
1 Troy Aikman .40 1.00
2 Steve Young .30 .75
3 John Elway .75 2.00
4 Jim Kelly .15 .40
5 Dan Marino .75 2.00
6 Brett Favre .75 2.00
7 Kerry Collins .15 .40
8 Jeff Blake .15 .40
9 Stan Humphries .07 .20
10 Steve Bono .02 .10
11 Jeff George .07 .20
12 Mark Brunell .25 .60
13 Scott Mitchell .07 .20
14 Steve McNair .30 .75
15 Jeff Hostetler .02 .10
16 Jim Everett .02 .10
17 Rick Mirer .07 .20
18 Boomer Esiason .07 .20
19 Neil O'Donnell .07 .20
20 Dave Brown .02 .10
21 Erik Kramer .02 .10
22 Trent Dilfer .15 .40
23 Jim Harbaugh .07 .20
24 Vinny Testaverde .07 .20
25 Thurman Thomas .15 .40
26 Rodney Peete .02 .10
27 Gus Frerotte .07 .20
28 Warren Moon .07 .20
29 Eric Zeier .02 .10
30 Randall Cunningham .15 .40
31 Heath Shuler .07 .20
32 John Friesz .02 .10
33 Tommy Maddox .15 .40
34 Glenn Foley .07 .20
35 Drew Bledsoe .25 .60
36 Kordell Stewart .15 .40
37 Natrone Means .07 .20
38 Errict Rhett .07 .20
39 Rashaan Salaam .07 .20
40 Emmitt Smith .60 1.50
41 Larry Centers .07 .20
42 Terrell Davis .30 .75
43 Marshall Faulk .20 .50
44 Rodney Hampton .07 .20
45 Byron Bam Morris .02 .10
46 Chris Warren .07 .20
47 Curtis Martin .30 .75
48 Ricky Watters .07 .20
49 Marcus Allen .15 .40
50 Barry Sanders .60 1.50
51 Edgar Bennett .07 .20
52 Adrian Murrell .07 .20
53 James O. Stewart .07 .20
54 Leroy Hoard .02 .10
55 Jerome Bettis .15 .40
56 Craig Heyward .02 .10
57 Harvey Williams .02 .10
58 Bernie Parmalee .02 .10
59 Garrison Hearst .07 .20
60 Terry Allen .07 .20
61 Charlie Garner .07 .20
62 Dorsey Levens .15 .40
63 Derek Loville .02 .10
64 Greg Hill .07 .20
65 Derrick Moore .02 .10
66 Rodney Thomas .02 .10
67 Daryl Johnston .07 .20
68 Mario Bates .07 .20
69 Aaron Hayden RC .02 .10
70 Napoleon Kaufman .15 .40
71 Terry Kirby .07 .20
72 Glyn Milburn .02 .10
73 Robert Smith .07 .20
74 Ki-Jana Carter .07 .20
75 Tyrone Wheatley .07 .20
76 Erric Pegram .02 .10
77 Brian Mitchell .02 .10
78 Vaughn Dunbar .02 .10
79 Dave Meggett .02 .10
80 Scottie Graham .02 .10
81 Darick Holmes .02 .10
82 Marion Butts .02 .10
83 Harold Green .02 .10
84 Zack Crockett .02 .10
85 Amp Lee .02 .10
86 Lamont Warren .02 .10
87 Mark Chmura .07 .20
88 Irving Fryar .07 .20
89 Tim Brown .15 .40
90 Michael Irvin .15 .40
91 Tony Martin .07 .20
92 Alvin Harper .02 .10
93 Darnay Scott .07 .20
94 Eric Metcalf .02 .10
95 Michael Timpson .02 .10
96 Sean Dawkins .02 .10
97 Qadry Ismail .07 .20
98 Yancey Thigpen .07 .20
99 Joey Galloway .15 .40
100 Herman Moore .07 .20
101 J.J. Stokes .15 .40
102 Wayne Chrebet .25 .60
103 Ernest Givins .02 .10
104 Michael Jackson .07 .20
105 Henry Ellard .02 .10
106 Thomas Lewis .02 .10
107 Anthony Miller .07 .20
108 Terance Mathis .02 .10
109 Horace Copeland .02 .10
110 Rocket Ismail .02 .10
111 Quinn Early .02 .10
112 Haywood Jeffires .02 .10
113 Mark Carrier WR .02 .10
114 Brent Jones .02 .10
115 Ben Coates .07 .20
116 Ken Dilger .07 .20
117 Irv Smith .02 .10
118 Jay Novacek .02 .10
119 Tony McGee .02 .10
120 Troy Drayton .02 .10
121 Johnny Mitchell .02 .10
122 Rob Moore .07 .20
123 Kevin Williams WR .02 .10
124 O.J. McDuffie .07 .20
125 Carl Pickens .07 .20
126 Curtis Conway .15 .40
127 Ed McCaffrey .07 .20
128 Arthur Marshall .02 .10
129 Ernie Mills .02 .10
130 Cris Carter .15 .40
131 Isaac Bruce .15 .40
132 Brian Blades .02 .10
133 Michael Westbrook .15 .40
134 Andre Reed .07 .20
135 Andre Rison .07 .20
136 Brett Perriman .02 .10
137 Willie Jackson .07 .20
138 Ryan Yarborough .02 .10
139 Chris T. Jones .07 .20
140 Jerry Rice .40 1.00
141 Lake Dawson .02 .10
142 Robert Brooks .15 .40
143 Vincent Brisby .02 .10
144 Desmond Howard .07 .20
145 Johnnie Morton .07 .20
146 Steve Tasker .02 .10
147 Ty Detmer .07 .20
148 Todd Kinchen .02 .10
149 Mike Sherrard .02 .10
150 Eric Green .02 .10
151 Mark Bruener .02 .10
152 Kyle Brady .02 .10
153 Frank Sanders .07 .20
154 Willie Green .02 .10
155 Jeff Graham .02 .10
156 Bert Emanuel .07 .20
157 Courtney Hawkins .02 .10
158 Mark Seay .02 .10
159 Chris Calloway .02 .10
160 John Taylor .02 .10
161 Fred Barnett .02 .10
162 Tamarick Vanover .07 .20
163 Keenan McCardell .15 .40
164 Bill Brooks .02 .10
165 Alexander Wright .02 .10
166 Jake Reed .07 .20
167 Floyd Turner .02 .10
168 Mike Pritchard .02 .10
169 Lawrence Dawsey .02 .10
170 Shawn Jefferson .02 .10
171 Michael Haynes .02 .10
172 Shannon Sharpe .07 .20
173 Jackie Harris .02 .10
174 Daryl Hobbs RC .02 .10
175 Chris Sanders .07 .20
176 Willie Davis .02 .10
177 Marco Coleman .02 .10
178 Pat Swilling .02 .10
179 Alonzo Spellman .02 .10
180 Simon Fletcher .02 .10
181 Sean Gilbert .02 .10
182 Tracy Scroggins .02 .10
183 Hugh Douglas .07 .20
184 Eric Swann .02 .10
185 Russell Maryland .02 .10
186 Warren Sapp .02 .10
187 Jim Flanigan .02 .10
188 Cortez Kennedy .02 .10
189 Andy Harmon .02 .10
190 Dan Saleaumua .02 .10
191 Kelvin Pritchett .02 .10
192 John Randle .07 .20
193 Dan Wilkinson .02 .10
194 Chester McGlockton .02 .10
195 Leon Lett .02 .10
196 Neil Smith .07 .20
197 Mike Mamula .02 .10
198 Mike Jones .02 .10
199 Reggie White .15 .40
200 Anthony Pleasant .02 .10
201 Phil Hansen .02 .10
202 Ray Seals .02 .10
203 Tony Bennett .02 .10
204 Leslie O'Neal .02 .10
205 Jeff Cross .02 .10
206 Anthony Cook .02 .10
207 Clyde Simmons .02 .10
208 Renaldo Turnbull .02 .10
209 Charles Haley .07 .20
210 John Copeland .02 .10
211 John Thierry .02 .10
212 Michael Strahan .07 .20
213 Jeff Lageman .02 .10
214 William Fuller .02 .10
215 Rickey Jackson .02 .10
216 Wayne Martin .02 .10
217 Steve Emtman .02 .10
218 Shawn Lee .02 .10
219 Chris Zorich .02 .10
220 Henry Thomas .02 .10
221 Dana Stubblefield .07 .20
222 D'Marco Farr .02 .10
223 Pierce Holt .02 .10
224 Sean Jones .02 .10
225 Robert Porcher .02 .10
226 Kevin Carter .02 .10
227 Chris Doleman .02 .10
228 Tony Tolbert .02 .10
229 Bruce Smith .07 .20
230 Marvin Washington .02 .10
231 Blaine Bishop .02 .10
232 Bryant Young .07 .20
233 Rob Burnett .02 .10
234 Lawrence Phillips RC .15 .40
235 Trev Alberts .02 .10
236 Eric Curry .02 .10
237 Anthony Smith .02 .10
238 Sam Mills .02 .10
239 Seth Joyner .02 .10
240 Quentin Coryatt .02 .10
241 Levon Kirkland .02 .10
242 Cornelius Bennett .02 .10
243 Chris Spielman .02 .10
244 Mo Lewis .02 .10
245 Lee Woodall .02 .10
246 Derrick Thomas .15 .40
247 Willie McGinest .02 .10
248 Terry Wooden .02 .10
249 Greg Lloyd .07 .20
250 Jack Del Rio .02 .10
251 Hardy Nickerson .02 .10
252 Micheal Barrow .02 .10
253 Lamar Lathon .02 .10
254 Bryan Cox .02 .10
255 Randy Kirk .02 .10
256 Jessie Tuggle .02 .10
257 Roman Phifer .02 .10
258 Ken Harvey .02 .10
259 Junior Seau .15 .40
260 Pepper Johnson .02 .10
261 Chris Slade .02 .10
262 Gary Plummer .02 .10
263 Wayne Simmons .02 .10
264 Bryce Paup .02 .10
265 William Thomas .02 .10
266 Kevin Greene .07 .20
267 Bobby Engram RC .15 .40
268 Ken Norton .02 .10
269 Eric Hill .02 .10
270 Darion Conner .02 .10
271 Tyrone Poole .02 .10
272 Cris Dishman .02 .10
273 Marcus Jones RC .02 .10
274 Rod Woodson .07 .20
275 Mark McMillian .02 .10
276 Dale Carter .02 .10
277 Darrell Green .02 .10
278 Donnell Woolford .02 .10
279 Troy Vincent .02 .10
280 Larry Brown .02 .10
281 Aeneas Williams .02 .10
282 Eric Allen .02 .10
283 Ray Buchanan .02 .10
284 Ty Law .15 .40
285 Eric Davis .02 .10
286 Todd Lyght .02 .10
287 Terry McDaniel .02 .10
288 Darryll Lewis .02 .10
289 Deion Sanders .25 .60
290 Phillippi Sparks .02 .10
291 Bobby Taylor .02 .10
292 Mark Collins .02 .10
293 Steve Atwater .02 .10
294 Stanley Richard .07 .20
295 Stevon Moore .02 .10
296 Bennie Blades .02 .10
297 Tim McDonald .02 .10
298 Shaun Gayle .02 .10
299 Darren Woodson .07 .20
300 Mark Carrier DB .02 .10
301 Carnell Lake .02 .10
302 James Washington .02 .10
303 LeRoy Butler .02 .10
304 Henry Jones .02 .10
305 Darryl Williams .02 .10
306 Darron Porry .02 .10
307 Merton Hanks .02 .10
308 Orlando Thomas .02 .10
309 Eric Turner .02 .10
310 Nate Newton .02 .10
311 Steve Wisniewski .02 .10
312 Derrick Deese .02 .10
313 Larry Allen .02 .10
314 Aaron Taylor .02 .10
315 Blake Brockermeyer .02 .10
316 William Roaf .02 .10
317 Jumbo Elliott .02 .10
318 Keyshawn Johnson RC .40 1.00
319 Karim Abdul-Jabbar RC .15 .40
320 Kevin Hardy RC .15 .40
321 Duane Clemons RC .02 .10
322 Jevon Langford RC .02 .10
323 Mike Alstott RC .40 1.00
324 Scott Greene RC .02 .10
325 Derrick Mayes RC .15 .40
326 Chris Doering RC .02 .10
327 Amani Toomer RC .40 1.00
328 Eric Moulds RC .50 1.25
329 Alex Molden RC .02 .10
330 Lawyer Milloy RC .20 .50
331 Daryl Gardener RC .02 .10
332 Randall Godfrey RC .02 .10
333 Willie Anderson RC .02 .10
334 Tony Banks RC .15 .40
335 Jeff Lewis RC .07 .20
336 Roman Oben RC .02 .10
337 Andre Johnson RC .02 .10
338 Brian Roche RC .02 .10
339 Johnny McWilliams RC .07 .20
340 Alex Van Dyke RC .07 .20
341 Ray Mickens RC .02 .10
342 Marvin Harrison RC 1.00 2.50
343 Terry Glenn RC .40 1.00
344 Tim Biakabutuka RC .15 .40
345 Simeon Rice RC .40 1.00
346 Cedric Jones RC .02 .10
347 Eddie George RC .50 1.25
348 Drew Bledsoe CL .15 .40
349 Emmitt Smith CL .20 .50
350 Keyshawn Johnson CL .15 .40

1996 Pro Line Headliners

COMPLETE SET (350) 150.00 300.00
*STARS: 3X TO 8X BASIC CARDS
*RCs: 1.5X TO 4X BASIC CARDS
ONE PER JUMBO PACK

1996 Pro Line National

COMPLETE SET (350) 150.00 300.00
*NATIONAL STARS: 3X TO 8X BASIC CARDS
*NATIONAL RCs: 1.5X TO 4X BASIC CARDS
ONE PER NATIONAL PACK

1996 Pro Line Printer's Proofs

COMPLETE SET (350) 250.00 500.00
*PP STARS: 5X TO 12X BASIC CARDS
*PP RCs: 2.5X TO 6X BASIC CARDS
STATED ODDS 1:10 SPECIAL RETAIL

1996 Pro Line Autographs Gold

This set features borderless color action player photos with a gold foil player autograph. We have priced the gold foil versions which were inserted at a rate of every 170 packs in hobby and retail packs and one every 200 in jumbo packs. The blue foil varieties were inserted more frequently. Blue foil versions were inserted one ever 25 hobby and retail packs and one every 90 jumbo packs. There are five cards that were only included in the Gold foil version: Troy Aikman/Smith, Keyshawn Johnson/Neil O'Donnell, Neil O'Donnell, Emmitt Smith, and Steve Young. Since the cards are not numbered we have sequenced them alphabetically.

GOLD STAT.ODDS 1:170 HOB/RET, 1:200 JUM
1 Aikman E.Smith 150.00 300.00
2 Eric Allen 5.00 12.00
3 Mike Alstott 12.50 30.00
4 Tony Banks 8.00 20.00
5 Blaine Bishop 5.00 12.00
6 Drew Bledsoe 30.00 80.00
7 Tim Brown 15.00 40.00
8 Marion Butts 5.00 12.00
10 Sedric Clark 5.00 12.00
11 Duane Clemons 5.00 12.00
12 Marcus Coleman 5.00 12.00
13 Kerry Collins 12.50 30.00
14 Eric Davis 5.00 12.00
15 Derrick Deese 5.00 12.00
16 Jack Del Rio 5.00 12.00
17 Ty Detmer 8.00 20.00
18 Chris Doering 5.00 12.00
19 Jumbo Elliott 5.00 12.00
20 Marshall Faulk 25.00 50.00
21 Glenn Foley 5.00 12.00
22 John Friesz 5.00 12.00
23 Daryl Gardener 5.00 12.00
24 Randall Godfrey 5.00 12.00
25 Scott Greene 5.00 12.00
26 Rhett Hall 5.00 12.00
27 Merton Hanks 5.00 12.00
28 Kevin Hardy 5.00 12.00
29 Richard Huntley 5.00 12.00
30 Michael Jackson 5.00 12.00
31 Ron Jaworski 12.50 30.00
32 Andre Johnson 5.00 12.00
33 Keyshawn Johnson 12.50 30.00
34 K.Johnson O'Donnell 25.00 50.00
35 Mike Jones 5.00 12.00
36 Jim Kiick 12.50 30.00
37 Carnell Lake 5.00 12.00
38 Jeff Lewis 5.00 12.00
39 Tommy Maddox 12.50 30.00
40 Arthur Marshall 5.00 12.00
41 Russell Maryland 5.00 12.00
42 Derrick Mayes 5.00 12.00
43 Ed McCaffrey 8.00 20.00
44 Keenan McCardell 8.00 20.00
45 Terry McDaniel 5.00 12.00
46 Tim McDonald 5.00 12.00
47 Willie McGinest 12.50 30.00
48 Mark McMillian 5.00 12.00
49 Johnny McWilliams 5.00 12.00
50 Ray Mickens 5.00 12.00
51 Anthony Miller 5.00 12.00
52 Rick Mirer 8.00 20.00
53 Alex Molden 5.00 12.00
54 Johnnie Morton 8.00 20.00
55 Eric Moulds 8.00 20.00
56 Roman Oben 5.00 12.00
57 Neil O'Donnell 12.50 30.00
58 Leslie O'Neal 5.00 12.00
59 Roman Phifer 5.00 12.00
60 Gary Plummer 5.00 12.00
61 Jim Plunkett 12.50 30.00
62 Stanley Pritchett 5.00 12.00
63 John Randle 10.00 25.00
64 Brian Roche 5.00 12.00
65 Orpheus Roye 5.00 12.00
66 Mark Seay 5.00 12.00
67 Mike Sherrard 5.00 12.00
68 Chris Slade 5.00 12.00
69 Scott Slutzker 5.00 12.00
70 Emmitt Smith 100.00 250.00
71 Steve Taneyhill 5.00 12.00
72 Robb Thomas 5.00 12.00
73 William Thomas 5.00 12.00
75 Alex Van Dyke 5.00 12.00
76 Randy White 12.50 30.00
77 Steve Young 40.00 100.00

1996 Pro Line Autographs Blue

*BLUE CARDS: .25X TO .6X GOLDS
74 Amani Toomer 15.00 30.00

1996 Pro Line Cels

These 20 standard-size all-acetate cards are inserted approximately one every 75 hobby packs. There are two player photos on the front as well as the words "ProLine Cels 96" in the upper right corner. The backs have some text and are numbered with a "PC" prefix.

COMPLETE SET (20) 60.00 150.00
STATED ODDS 1:75 HOBBY
PC1 Bryce Paup .60 1.50
PC2 Kerry Collins 2.50 6.00
PC3 Troy Aikman 6.00 15.00
PC4 Deion Sanders 4.00 10.00
PC5 Emmitt Smith 10.00 25.00
PC6 Steve McNair 3.00 8.00
PC7 Drew Bledsoe 4.00 10.00
PC8 Kordell Stewart 2.50 6.00
PC9 Ricky Watters 1.25 3.00
PC10 Jerry Rice 6.00 15.00
PC11 Steve Young 5.00 12.00
PC12 Errict Rhett 1.25 3.00
PC13 Brett Favre 12.50 30.00
PC14 Jeff Blake 2.50 6.00
PC15 Joey Galloway 2.50 6.00
PC16 Herman Moore 1.25 3.00
PC17 Curtis Martin 5.00 12.00
PC18 Keyshawn Johnson 2.50 6.00
PC19 Eddie George 3.00 8.00
PC20 Simeon Rice 1.25 3.00

1996 Pro Line Cover Story

These 20 standard-size cards are randomly inserted into one of every 30 periodical packs. They feature some leading NFL players of 1995 as well as some 1996 rookies and are numbered with a "CS" prefix.

COMPLETE SET (20) 20.00 50.00
STATED ODDS 1:30 JUMBO
CS1 Bryce Paup .30 .75
CS2 Kerry Collins 1.25 3.00
CS3 Rashaan Salaam .60 1.50
CS4 Troy Aikman 3.00 8.00
CS5 Emmitt Smith 5.00 12.00
CS6 Herman Moore .60 1.50
CS7 Curtis Martin 2.50 6.00
CS8 Kordell Stewart 1.25 3.00
CS9 Ricky Watters .60 1.50
CS10 Carl Pickens .60 1.50
CS11 Joey Galloway 1.25 3.00
CS12 Errict Rhett .60 1.50
CS13 Deion Sanders 2.00 5.00
CS14 Reggie White 1.25 3.00
CS15 Hugh Douglas .60 1.50
CS16 Tamarick Vanover .60 1.50
CS17 Derrick Mayes .60 1.50
CS18 Marvin Harrison 4.00 10.00
CS19 Tim Biakabutuka .60 1.50
CS20 Terry Glenn 1.50 4.00

1996 Pro Line Rivalries

These 20 standard-size double-sided cards feature two players from the same division. Each side has a player photo, a team logo and a "Pro Line 1996 Rivalries" line on the bottom. The cards are numbered with an "R" prefix and were randomly inserted into both hobby and national packs at the rate of 1:15.

COMPLETE SET (20) 25.00 60.00
STATED ODDS 1:15
R1 D.Bledsoe J.Kelly 1.25 3.00
R2 D.Marino G.Lloyd 4.00 10.00

R3 K.Stewart 1.00 2.50
M.Brunell
R4 T.Vanover .75 2.00
N.Kaufman
R5 J.Elway 4.00 10.00
J.Blake
R6 E.Smith 3.00 8.00
R.Watters
R7 T.Aikman 2.00 5.00
S.Young
R8 D.Sanders 1.25 3.00
G.Frerotte
R9 B.Favre 4.00 10.00
E.Rhett
R10 R.Salaam .40 1.00
W.Moon
R11 K.Collins .75 2.00
K.Norton Jr.
R12 J.George .75 2.00
I.Bruce
R13 R.Woodson .40 1.00
R.Thomas
R14 H.Moore .40 1.00
R.White
R15 M.Faulk 1.00 2.50
C.Marlin
R16 K.Johnson 2.50 6.00
M.Harrison
R17 K.Hardy .40 1.00
A.Molden
R18 T.Glenn 1.00 2.50
S.Rice
R19 E.George 1.00 2.50
T.Biakabutuka
R20 K.Abdul-Jabbar .40 1.00
C.Jones

1996 Pro Line Touchdown Performers

These 20 standard-size cards are randomly inserted into retail packs. They feature leading NFL players as well as some rookies and are numbered with a "TD" prefix.

COMPLETE SET (20) 25.00 60.00
STATED ODDS 1:75 RETAIL
TD1 Kerry Collins 1.50 4.00
TD2 Troy Aikman 4.00 10.00
TD3 Deion Sanders 2.50 6.00
TD4 Emmitt Smith 6.00 15.00
TD5 Mark Brunell 1.50 4.00
TD6 Steve McNair 3.00 8.00
TD7 Marshall Faulk 2.00 5.00
TD8 Dan Marino 8.00 20.00
TD9 Cris Carter 1.50 4.00
TD10 Drew Bledsoe 2.50 6.00
TD11 Yancey Thigpen .75 2.00
TD12 Jerry Rice 4.00 10.00
TD13 J.J. Stokes 1.50 4.00
TD14 Terrell Davis 3.00 8.00
TD15 Carl Pickens .75 2.00
TD16 Joey Galloway 1.50 4.00
TD17 Kordell Stewart 1.50 4.00
TD18 Isaac Bruce 1.50 4.00
TD19 Keyshawn Johnson 1.50 4.00
TD20 Amani Toomer 1.50 4.00

1996 Pro Line National Laser Promos

These five promo cards were distributed at the 1996 National Card Collector's Convention in Anaheim. Each card was distributed during the show at the Classic booth. Complete sets framed in a lucite holder were also produced and individually numbered of 300.

COMPLETE SET (5) 8.00 20.00
COMP.FRAMED SET (5) 10.00 25.00
1 Kordell Stewart 1.60 4.00
2 Troy Aikman 2.00 5.00
3 Emmitt Smith 3.20 8.00
4 Lawrence Phillips 1.20 3.00
5 Keyshawn Johnson 1.60 4.00

1997 Pro Line

The 1997 Pro Line set was issued in one series totaling 300 cards and was distributed in eight-card packs with a suggested retail price of $2.79. The set features color player photos of the top NFL veterans, traded players, free agents, and rookies for 1997. Each box of 28 packs also contained at least one autographed card and a chance to win autographed memorabilia from two-time MVP Brett Favre.

COMPLETE SET (300) 10.00 25.00
1 Larry Centers .10 .30
2 Kent Graham .07 .20
3 LeShon Johnson .07 .20
4 Leeland McElroy .07 .20
5 Rob Moore .10 .30
6 Simeon Rice .10 .30
7 Frank Sanders .10 .30
8 Eric Swann .07 .20
9 Aeneas Williams .07 .20
10 Jamal Anderson .20 .50
11 Cornelius Bennett .07 .20
12 Ray Buchanan .07 .20
13 Bert Emanuel .10 .30
14 Terance Mathis .10 .30
15 Eric Metcalf .10 .30
16 Jessie Tuggle .07 .20
17 Derrick Alexander WR .10 .30
18 Earnest Byner .07 .20
19 Michael Jackson .10 .30
20 Antonio Langham .07 .20
21 Ray Lewis .30 .75
22 Byron Bam Morris .07 .20
23 Jonathan Ogden .07 .20
24 Vinny Testaverde .10 .30
25 Eric Moulds .20 .50
26 Todd Collins .07 .20
27 Quinn Early .07 .20
28 Phil Hansen .07 .20
29 Darick Holmes .07 .20
30 Bryce Paup .07 .20
31 Andre Reed .10 .30
32 Bruce Smith .10 .30
33 Chris Spielman .07 .20
34 Matt Stevens .07 .20
35 Steve Tasker .07 .20
36 Thurman Thomas .20 .50
37 Mark Carrier WR .07 .20
38 Kerry Collins .20 .50
39 Tim Biakabutuka .10 .30
40 Eric Davis .07 .20
41 Kevin Greene .10 .30
42 Anthony Johnson .07 .20
43 Lamar Lathon .07 .20
44 Sam Mills .07 .20
45 Wesley Walls .10 .30
46 Muhsin Muhammad .10 .30
47 Mark Carrier DB .07 .20
48 Curtis Conway .10 .30
49 Bryan Cox .07 .20
50 Bobby Engram .10 .30
51 Raymont Harris .07 .20
52 Walt Harris .07 .20
53 Rick Mirer .07 .20
54 Rashaan Salaam .10 .30
55 Alonzo Spellman .07 .20
56 Ashley Ambrose .07 .20
57 Jeff Blake .10 .30
58 Ki-Jana Carter .07 .20
59 John Copeland .07 .20
60 James Francis .07 .20
61 Tony McGee .07 .20
62 Carl Pickens .10 .30
63 Darnay Scott .10 .30
64 Steve Tovar .07 .20
65 Dan Wilkinson .07 .20
66 Troy Aikman .40 1.00
67 Eric Bjornson .07 .20
68 Michael Irvin .20 .50
69 Daryl Johnston .10 .30
70 Nate Newton .07 .20
71 Deion Sanders .20 .50
72 Emmitt Smith .60 1.50
73 Kevin Smith .07 .20
74 Kevin Williams .07 .20
75 Darren Woodson .07 .20
76 Mark Tuinei .07 .20
77 Steve Atwater .07 .20
78 Terrell Davis .25 .60
79 John Elway .75 2.00
80 Ed McCaffrey .10 .30
81 Anthony Miller .07 .20
82 John Mobley .07 .20
83 Michael Dean Perry .07 .20
84 Shannon Sharpe .10 .30
85 Alfred Williams .07 .20
86 Reggie Brown LB .10 .30
87 Luther Elliss .07 .20
88 Scott Mitchell .10 .30
89 Herman Moore .10 .30
90 Johnnie Morton .10 .30
91 Brett Perriman .07 .20
92 Robert Porcher .07 .20
93 Barry Sanders .60 1.50
94 Henry Thomas .07 .20
95 Edgar Bennett .10 .30
96 Robert Brooks .10 .30
97 Gilbert Brown .10 .30
98 LeRoy Butler .07 .20
99 Mark Chmura .10 .30
100 Brett Favre .75 2.00
101 Santana Dotson .07 .20
102 Antonio Freeman .20 .50
103 Dorsey Levens .20 .50
104 Wayne Simmons .07 .20
105 Reggie White .20 .50
106 Willie Davis .07 .20
107 Eddie George .20 .50
108 Darryll Lewis .07 .20
109 Steve McNair .25 .60
110 Marcus Robertson .07 .20
111 Chris Sanders .07 .20
112 Al Smith .07 .20
113 Tony Bennett .07 .20
114 Quentin Coryatt .07 .20
115 Ken Dilger .07 .20
116 Sean Dawkins .07 .20
117 Marshall Faulk .25 .60
118 Jim Harbaugh .10 .30
119 Marvin Harrison .20 .50
120 Jeff Herrod .07 .20
121 Tony Boselli .07 .20
122 Tony Brackens .07 .20
123 Mark Brunell .25 .60
124 Kevin Hardy .07 .20
125 Jeff Lageman .07 .20
126 Keenan McCardell .10 .30
127 Natrone Means .10 .30
128 Eddie Robinson .07 .20
129 Jimmy Smith .10 .30
130 James O.Stewart .10 .30
131 Marcus Allen .20 .50
132 Dale Carter .07 .20
133 Mark Collins .07 .20
134 Lake Dawson .07 .20
135 Greg Hill .07 .20
136 Sean LaChapelle .07 .20
137 Chris Penn .07 .20
138 Derrick Thomas .20 .50
139 Tamarick Vanover .10 .30
140 Elvis Grbac .10 .30
141 Karim Abdul-Jabbar .20 .50
142 Fred Barnett .07 .20
143 Terrell Buckley .07 .20
144 Daryl Gardener .07 .20
145 Randal Hill .07 .20
146 Dan Marino .75 2.00
147 O.J. McDuffie .10 .30
148 Jerris McPhail .07 .20
149 Zach Thomas .20 .50
150 Cris Carter .20 .50
151 Dixon Edwards .07 .20
152 Leroy Hoard .07 .20
153 Qadry Ismail .10 .30
154 Brad Johnson .20 .50
155 John Randle .10 .30
156 Jake Reed .10 .30
157 Robert Smith .10 .30
158 Orlando Thomas .07 .20
159 Dewayne Washington .07 .20
160 Drew Bledsoe .25 .60
161 Tedy Bruschi .40 1.00
162 Willie Clay .07 .20
163 Ben Coates .10 .30
164 Terry Glenn .20 .50
165 Shawn Jefferson .07 .20
166 Ty Law .10 .30
167 Curtis Martin .25 .60
168 Willie McGinest .07 .20
169 Chris Slade .07 .20
170 Eric Allen .07 .20
171 Mario Bates .07 .20
172 Heath Shuler .07 .20
173 Michael Haynes .07 .20
174 Wayne Martin .07 .20
175 Torrance Small .07 .20
176 Dave Brown .07 .20
177 Chris Calloway .07 .20
178 Rodney Hampton .10 .30
179 Danny Kanell .10 .30
180 Thomas Lewis .07 .20
181 Jason Sehorn .10 .30
182 Amani Toomer .10 .30
183 Charles Way .10 .30
184 Tyrone Wheatley .10 .30
185 Wayne Chrebet .20 .50
186 Hugh Douglas .07 .20
187 Aaron Glenn .07 .20
188 Jeff Graham .07 .20
189 Keyshawn Johnson .20 .50
190 Mo Lewis .07 .20
191 Adrian Murrell .10 .30
192 Neil O'Donnell .10 .30
193 Tim Brown .20 .50
194 Rickey Dudley .10 .30
195 Jeff George .10 .30
196 Napoleon Kaufman .20 .50
197 Russell Maryland .07 .20
198 Terry McDaniel .07 .20
199 Chester McGlockton .07 .20
200 Desmond Howard .10 .30
201 Pat Swilling .07 .20
202 Ty Detmer .10 .30
203 Jason Dunn .07 .20
204 Ray Farmer .07 .20
205 Irving Fryar .10 .30
206 Chris T. Jones .07 .20
207 Bobby Taylor .07 .20
208 William Thomas .07 .20
209 Hollis Thomas RC .07 .20
210 Kevin Turner .07 .20
211 Ricky Watters .10 .30
212 Jerome Bettis .20 .50
213 Andre Hastings .07 .20
214 Charles Johnson .10 .30
215 Levon Kirkland .07 .20
216 Carnell Lake .07 .20
217 Greg Lloyd .07 .20
218 Darren Perry .07 .20
219 Kordell Stewart .20 .50
220 Rod Woodson .10 .30
221 Andre Coleman .07 .20
222 Marco Coleman .07 .20
223 Leonard Russell .07 .20
224 Stan Humphries .10 .30
225 Shawn Lee .07 .20
226 Tony Martin .10 .30
227 Chris Mims .07 .20
228 Junior Seau .20 .50
229 Chris Doleman .07 .20
230 William Floyd .10 .30
231 Merton Hanks .07 .20
232 Brent Jones .10 .30
233 Terry Kirby .10 .30
234 Ken Norton .07 .20
235 Terrell Owens .25 .60
236 Jerry Rice .40 1.00
237 Bryant Young .07 .20
238 Steve Young .25 .60
239 Garrison Hearst .10 .30
240 Brian Blades .07 .20
241 Chad Brown .07 .20
242 John Friesz .07 .20
243 Joey Galloway .10 .30
244 Cortez Kennedy .07 .20
245 Chris Warren .10 .30
246 Darryl Williams .07 .20
247 Tony Banks .10 .30
248 Isaac Bruce .20 .50
249 Kevin Carter .07 .20
250 Eddie Kennison .10 .30
251 Todd Lyght .07 .20
252 Leslie O'Neal .07 .20
253 Anthony Parker .07 .20
254 Roman Phifer .07 .20
255 Lawrence Phillips .07 .20
256 Mike Alstott .20 .50
257 Derrick Brooks .20 .50
258 Trent Dilfer .20 .50
259 Jackie Harris .07 .20
260 Hardy Nickerson .07 .20
261 Errict Rhett .07 .20
262 Warren Sapp .10 .30
263 Terry Allen .20 .50
264 Jamie Asher .07 .20
265 Henry Ellard .07 .20
266 Gus Frerotte .07 .20
267 Sean Gilbert .07 .20
268 Darrell Green .10 .30
269 Ken Harvey .07 .20
270 Brian Mitchell .07 .20
271 Michael Westbrook .10 .30
272 Koy Detmer RC .40 1.00
273 Yatil Green RC .10 .30
274 Troy Davis RC .10 .30
275 Darrell Russell RC .07 .20
276 Warrick Dunn RC .60 1.50
277 David LaFleur RC .07 .20
278 Tony Gonzalez RC .75 2.00
279 Jake Plummer RC .75 2.00
280 Antowain Smith RC .50 1.25
281 Peter Boulware RC .20 .50
282 Shawn Springs RC .10 .30
283 Bryant Westbrook RC .07 .20
284 Rae Carruth RC .07 .20
285 Corey Dillon RC .75 2.00
286 Byron Hanspard RC .10 .30
287 Greg Jones RC .07 .20
288 Trevor Pryce RC .20 .50
289 Michael Booker RC .07 .20
290 Orlando Pace RC .20 .50
291 James Farrior RC .20 .50
292 Walter Jones RC .30 .75
293 Reinard Wilson RC .10 .30
294 Ike Hilliard RC .30 .75
295 Kenard Lang RC .10 .30
296 Reidel Anthony RC .20 .50
297 Brett Favre CL .20 .50
298 Kerry Collins CL .10 .30
299 Drew Bledsoe CL .10 .30
300 Terrell Davis CL .20 .50

1997 Pro Line Autographs

Signed cards of top NFL players were randomly inserted at the rate of 1:28 packs. Unlike previous issues, each card is not a parallel of the base set but has been completely re-designed. A white box appears on the cardfront containing the signature. Cardbacks are unnumbered and contain a congratulatory message. The cards are checklisted below alphabetically. Troy Davis was hand serial numbered to 5000 and his card and the Michael Booker card both surfaced after the product was released.

STATED ODDS 1:28
1 Karim Abdul-Jabbar 8.00 20.00
2 Troy Aikman 50.00 100.00
3 Eric Allen 6.00 15.00
4 Mike Alstott 8.00 20.00
5 Marco Battaglia 4.00 10.00
6 Eric Bjornson 4.00 10.00
8 Peter Boulware 6.00 15.00
9 Ray Buchanon 8.00 20.00
10 Rae Carruth 4.00 10.00
11 Kerry Collins 8.00 20.00
12 Stephen Davis 8.00 20.00
13 Terrell Davis 15.00 40.00
14 Troy Davis/5000 4.00 10.00
15 Derrick Deese 4.00 10.00
16 Koy Detmer 6.00 15.00
17 Ken Dilger 6.00 15.00
18 Corey Dillon 8.00 20.00
19 Hugh Douglas 6.00 15.00
20 Jason Dunn 4.00 10.00
21 Warrick Dunn 8.00 20.00
22 Ray Farmer 4.00 10.00
23 Brett Favre 75.00 150.00
24 Joey Galloway 6.00 15.00
25 Norberto Garrido 4.00 10.00
26 Terry Glenn 8.00 20.00
27 Tony Gonzalez 20.00 40.00
28 Byron Hanspard 4.00 10.00
29 Kevin Hardy 6.00 15.00
30 Steve Israel 4.00 10.00
31 Brad Johnson 8.00 20.00
32 Keyshawn Johnson 8.00 20.00
33 Lance Johnstone 4.00 10.00
34 Greg Jones 4.00 10.00
35 Mike Jones 6.00 15.00
36 Danny Kanell 6.00 15.00
37 David LaFleur 4.00 10.00
38 Keenan McCardell 6.00 15.00
39 Leeland McElroy 4.00 10.00
40 Willie McGinest 8.00 20.00
41 Mark McMillian 4.00 10.00
42 Nate Newton 8.00 20.00
43 Jake Plummer 8.00 20.00
44 Trevor Pryce 8.00 20.00
45 John Randle 12.00 30.00
46 Simeon Rice 6.00 15.00
47 Jon Runyan 6.00 15.00
48 Chris Slade 4.00 10.00
49 Antowain Smith 8.00 20.00
50 Emmitt Smith 60.00 120.00
51 Jimmy Smith 8.00 20.00
52 Matt Stevens 4.00 10.00
53 Kordell Stewart 8.00 20.00
54 Mark Tuinei 15.00 30.00
55 Bryant Westbrook 4.00 10.00
56 Brian Williams LB 4.00 10.00
57 Dusty Zeigler 4.00 10.00

1997 Pro Line Autographs Emerald

Score Board produced a parallel set to its 1997 Pro Line Autograph series. Each card includes Emerald colored foil on the front along with the player's autograph. All Autographs were randomly inserted at the rate of 1:28 packs. Each of the Emerald cards was also individually numbered, unlike the base Autograph set. We've numbered the cards below alphabetically according to the base autograph card numbers.

STATED PRINT RUN 40-530
1 Karim Abdul-Jabbar/190 12.00 30.00
2 Troy Aikman/40 125.00 250.00
3 Eric Allen/250 10.00 25.00
5 Marco Battaglia/500 8.00 20.00
6 Eric Bjornson/390 8.00 20.00
7A Peter Boulware/430 10.00 25.00
7B Peter Boulware/400 10.00 25.00
8 Ray Buchanon/390 12.00 30.00
9 Rae Carruth/525 8.00 20.00
10 Kerry Collins/170 20.00 40.00
11 Stephen Davis/530 12.00 30.00
12 Terrell Davis/100 30.00 60.00
13 Troy Davis/525 8.00 20.00
16 Ken Dilger/525 8.00 20.00
17 Corey Dillon/470 10.00 25.00
18 Hugh Douglas/400 8.00 20.00
19 Jason Dunn/525 8.00 20.00
20 Warrick Dunn/430 12.00 30.00
21 Ray Farmer/340 8.00 20.00
22 Brett Favre/100 125.00 250.00
23 Joey Galloway/300 10.00 25.00
25 Terry Glenn/380 12.00 30.00
27 Byron Hanspard/500 8.00 20.00
28 Kevin Hardy/500 8.00 20.00
30 Brad Johnson/410 12.00 30.00
31 Keyshawn Johnson/100 25.00 50.00
33 Greg Jones/470 8.00 20.00
35 Danny Kanell/450 10.00 25.00
36 David LaFleur/500 8.00 20.00
37 Keenan McCardell/220 10.00 25.00
38 Leeland McElroy/440 8.00 20.00
39 Willie McGinest/210 12.00 30.00
41 Nate Newton/340 10.00 25.00
42 Jake Plummer/440 12.00 30.00
44 John Randle/400 20.00 50.00
45 Simeon Rice/375 10.00 25.00
46 Jon Runyan/500 8.00 20.00
47 Chris Slade/260 8.00 20.00
49 Emmitt Smith/200 75.00 150.00
50 Jimmy Smith/280 10.00 25.00
51 Matt Stevens/450 8.00 20.00
52 Kordell Stewart/130 20.00 50.00
53 Mark Tuinei/400 12.00 30.00
54 Bryant Westbrook/525 10.00 25.00
56 Dusty Zeigler/480 8.00 20.00

1997 Pro Line Board Members

Randomly inserted in packs at a rate of one in 112, this 15-card set features color photos of players Score Board signed to contracts.

COMPLETE SET (15) 40.00 100.00
STATED ODDS 1:112
BM1 Troy Aikman 6.00 15.00
BM2 Kerry Collins 3.00 8.00
BM3 Terrell Davis 4.00 10.00
BM4 Brett Favre 12.50 30.00
BM5 Gus Frerotte 1.25 3.00
BM6 Emmitt Smith 10.00 25.00
BM7 Kordell Stewart 3.00 8.00
BM8 Steve Young 4.00 10.00
BM9 Eddie George 3.00 8.00
BM10 Terry Glenn 3.00 8.00
BM11 Troy Davis 1.00 2.50
BM12 Darrell Russell .60 1.50
BM13 Peter Boulware 1.50 4.00
BM14 Warrick Dunn 5.00 12.00
BM15 Rae Carruth .60 1.50

1997 Pro Line Brett Favre

This 10-card set was randomly inserted in packs. The first nine cards were inserted at the rate of one in 28 or roughly one per box of 1997 Pro Line. Card #10 was inserted at the rate of 1:3024 packs. The set traces the career of Brett Favre from his early NFL days with the Atlanta Falcons to his becoming the Super Bowl XXXI champion quarterback. Collectors could redeem the complete set for either a Brett Favre autographed jersey or a Super Bowl XXXI autographed plaque. A drawing was held to distribute all the prizes. The contest expired on 7/1/1998.

COMPLETE SET (9) 15.00 40.00
COMMON CARD (BF1-BF9) 2.00 5.00
1-9: STATED ODDS 1:28
10: STATED ODDS 1:3024
BF10 Brett Favre 50.00 120.00

1997 Pro Line Rivalries

Randomly inserted in packs at a rate of one in 35, this 20-card set features double-sided cards with color photos of two players who are nemeses on rival teams.

COMPLETE SET (20) 25.00 60.00
STATED ODDS 1:35
RV1 J.Elway 6.00 15.00
D.Thomas
RV2 J.Blake .75 2.00
V.Testaverde
RV3 E.Smith 5.00 12.00
R.Watters
RV4 J.Harbaugh .75 2.00
T.Thomas
RV5 B.Sanders 5.00 12.00
R.White
RV6 D.Howard 1.25 3.00
J.Seau
RV7 D.Marino 4.00 10.00
H.Douglas
RV8 J.Bettis 1.25 3.00
C.Pickens
RV9 M.Brunell 1.25 3.00
K.Stewart
RV10 K.Abdul-Jabbar .75 2.00
B.Smith
RV11 R.Salaam 1.25 3.00
B.Johnson
RV12 S.Young 3.00 8.00
K.Collins
RV13 B.Favre 6.00 15.00
T.Aikman
RV14 D.Bledsoe 1.25 3.00
M.Faulk
RV15 S.McNair 1.25 3.00
K.Carter
RV16 J.Rice 4.00 10.00
T.Davis
RV17 D.Sanders 1.25 3.00
D.Brown
RV18 D.Russell .75 2.00
O.Pace
RV19 R.Anthony .60 1.50
B.Westbrook
RV20 Y.Green 3.00 8.00
W.Dunn

1996 Pro Line DC3

The 1996 ProLine DC3 set was issued in one series totalling 100 cards. The first all-die cut series from Classic features the top 1995 NFL veterans and rookies. There are no Rookie Cards in this set. The set was issued in five-card packs. An Emmitt Smith Sample card was produced and priced below.

COMPLETE SET (100) 7.50 20.00
1 Emmitt Smith .60 1.50
2 Larry Centers .07 .20
3 Jeff George .07 .20
4 Jim Kelly .15 .40
5 Kerry Collins .15 .40
6 Erik Kramer .02 .10
7 Jeff Blake .15 .40
8 Andre Rison .07 .20
9 John Elway .75 2.00
10 Herman Moore .07 .20
11 Robert Brooks .15 .40
12 Steve McNair .30 .75
13 Jim Harbaugh .07 .20
14 Mark Brunell .25 .60
15 Steve Bono .02 .10
16 Dan Marino .75 2.00
17 Warren Moon .07 .20
18 Drew Bledsoe .25 .60
19 Jim Everett .02 .10
20 Rodney Hampton .07 .20
21 Kyle Brady .02 .10
22 Jeff Hostetler .02 .10
23 Neil O'Donnell .07 .20
24 Ricky Watters .07 .20
25 Isaac Bruce .15 .40
26 Steve Young .30 .75
27 Stan Humphries .07 .20
28 Joey Galloway .15 .40
29 Errict Rhett .07 .20
30 Terry Allen .07 .20
31 Eric Swann .02 .10
32 Craig Heyward .02 .10
33 Bryce Paup .02 .10
34 Sam Mills .02 .10
35 Jim Flanigan .02 .10
36 Carl Pickens .07 .20
37 Pepper Johnson .02 .10
38 Troy Aikman .40 1.00
39 Terrell Davis .30 .75
40 Scott Mitchell .07 .20
41 Brett Favre .75 2.00
42 Chris Sanders .07 .20
43 Marshall Faulk .20 .50
44 James O. Stewart .07 .20
45 Marcus Allen .15 .40
46 Bernie Parmalee .02 .10
47 Cris Carter .15 .40
48 Ben Coates .07 .20
49 Quinn Early .02 .10
50 Tyrone Wheatley .07 .20
51 Adrian Murrell .07 .20
52 Tim Brown .15 .40
53 Yancey Thigpen .07 .20
54 Andy Harmon .02 .10
55 Jerome Bettis .15 .40
56 Jerry Rice .40 1.00
57 Natrone Means .07 .20
58 Chris Warren .07 .20
59 Warren Sapp .02 .10
60 Michael Westbrook .15 .40
61 Aeneas Williams .02 .10
62 Eric Metcalf .02 .10
63 Bruce Smith .07 .20
64 Rashaan Salaam .07 .20
65 Michael Irvin .15 .40
66 Anthony Miller .07 .20
67 Barry Sanders .60 1.50
68 Reggie White .15 .40
69 Rodney Thomas .02 .10
70 Zack Crockett .02 .10
71 Neil Smith .07 .20
72 Bryan Cox .02 .10
73 Curtis Martin .30 .75
74 Eric Allen .02 .10
75 Hugh Douglas .07 .20
76 Napoleon Kaufman .15 .40
77 Greg Lloyd .07 .20
78 Charlie Garner .07 .20
79 Lee Woodall .02 .10
80 Tony Martin .07 .20
81 Cortez Kennedy .02 .10
82 Gus Frerotte .07 .20
83 Darick Holmes .02 .10
84 Jay Novacek .02 .10
85 Brett Perriman .02 .10
86 Mark Chmura .07 .20
87 Chester McGlockton .02 .10
88 Dave Brown .02 .10
89 William Thomas .02 .10
90 Ken Norton .02 .10
91 Junior Seau .15 .40
92 Deion Sanders .25 .60
93 J.J. Stokes .15 .40
94 Kordell Stewart .15 .40
95 Tamarick Vanover .07 .20
96 Ken Harvey .02 .10
97 John Randle .07 .20
98 Lamont Warren .02 .10
99 Dorsey Levens .15 .40
100 Frank Sanders .07 .20
S1 Emmitt Smith Sample .80 2.00

1996 Pro Line DC3 All-Pros

Randomly inserted in packs at a rate of one in 100, this 20-card set includes Pro Bowl and Pro Bowl-caliber players. The cards were printed on 24-point textured card stock and were die cut at the top.

COMPLETE SET (20) 30.00 80.00
STATED ODDS 1:100
AP1 Bryce Paup .60 1.50
AP2 Kerry Collins 1.25 3.00
AP3 Rashaan Salaam .75 2.00
AP4 Emmitt Smith 5.00 12.00
AP5 Terrell Davis 2.00 5.00
AP6 Herman Moore .75 2.00
AP7 Barry Sanders 4.00 10.00
AP8 Brett Favre 6.00 15.00
AP9 Marshall Faulk 1.50 4.00
AP10 Dan Marino 6.00 15.00
AP11 Cris Carter 1.25 3.00
AP12 Curtis Martin 2.50 6.00
AP13 Hugh Douglas .75 2.00
AP14 Kordell Stewart 1.25 3.00
AP15 Jerry Rice 3.00 8.00
AP16 J.J. Stokes 1.25 3.00
AP17 Joey Galloway 1.25 3.00
AP18 Isaac Bruce 1.25 3.00
AP19 Steve McNair 2.00 5.00
AP20 Tim Brown 1.25 3.00

1996 Pro Line DC3 Road to the Super Bowl

Randomly inserted in packs at a rate of one in 15, this 30-card set printed on 24-point micro-lined silver foil board includes key moments from the 1995 season. Every card back features statistics or a brief "box score" from the game, allowing collectors to relive the highlights of the game featured.

COMPLETE SET (30) 30.00 80.00
STATED ODDS 1:15
1 Larry Centers .50 1.25
2 Eric Metcalf .25 .60
3 Jim Kelly 1.00 2.50
4 Bryce Paup .25 .60
5 Kerry Collins 1.00 2.50
6 Carl Pickens .50 1.25
7 Emmitt Smith 4.00 10.00
8 Michael Irvin 1.00 2.50
9 Troy Aikman 2.50 6.00
10 Terrell Davis 2.00 5.00
11 Barry Sanders 4.00 10.00
12 Herman Moore .50 1.25
13 Brett Favre 5.00 12.00
14 Robert Brooks 1.00 2.50
15 Jim Harbaugh .50 1.25
16 Tony Bennett .25 .60
17 Steve Bono .25 .60
18 Dan Marino 5.00 12.00
19 Cris Carter 1.00 2.50
20 Curtis Martin 2.00 5.00
21 Tim Brown 1.00 2.50
22 Ricky Watters .50 1.25
23 Yancey Thigpen .50 1.25
24 Neil O'Donnell .50 1.25
25 Kordell Stewart 1.00 2.50
26 Isaac Bruce 1.00 2.50
27 Tony Martin .50 1.25
28 Steve Young 2.00 5.00
29 Jerry Rice 2.50 6.00
30 Chris Warren .50 1.25

1997 Pro Line DC3

The 1997 Pro Line DC3 set was issued in one series totaling 100 cards and was distributed in four card packs with a suggested retail price of $3.99. The set features top NFL stars from the previous season on a unique die-cut design with detailed copy and statistical information that recaps the 1996 NFL season and allows the collector to accurately judge and compare the performances of offensive and defensive players. The set contains the topical subsets: DC Rewind (68-89) and DC Top Ten (90-100).

COMPLETE SET (100) 6.00 15.00
1 Emmitt Smith .60 1.50
2 Rod Woodson .10 .30
3 Eddie George .20 .50
4 Ty Detmer .10 .30
5 Zach Thomas .20 .50
6 Kevin Greene .10 .30
7 Michael Jackson .10 .30
8 Isaac Bruce .20 .50
9 Joey Galloway .10 .30
10 Bryant Young .07 .20
11 Terrell Davis .25 .60
12 Mark Brunell .25 .60
13 Marvin Harrison .20 .50
14 Jake Reed .10 .30
15 Terry Allen .20 .50
16 Kordell Stewart .20 .50
17 Reggie White .20 .50
18 Michael Irvin .20 .50
19 Tony Martin .10 .30
20 Barry Sanders .60 1.50
21 Tony Boselli .07 .20
22 Carl Pickens .10 .30
23 Simeon Rice .10 .30
24 Adrian Murrell .10 .30
25 Lamar Lathon .07 .20
26 Thurman Thomas .20 .50
27 Tim Brown .20 .50
28 Karim Abdul-Jabbar .20 .50
29 Brad Johnson .20 .50
30 Keenan McCardell .10 .30
31 Keyshawn Johnson .20 .50
32 Ricky Watters .10 .30
33 Michael McCrary .07 .20
34 Brett Favre .75 2.00
35 Steve McNair .25 .60
36 Herman Moore .10 .30
37 Tony Banks .10 .30
38 Deion Sanders .20 .50
39 Kerry Collins .20 .50
40 Shannon Sharpe .10 .30
41 Drew Bledsoe .25 .60
42 Jim Everett .07 .20
43 Jamal Anderson .20 .50
44 Irving Fryar .10 .30
45 Terry Glenn .20 .50
46 Jerry Rice .40 1.00
47 Curtis Martin .25 .60
48 Curtis Conway .10 .30
49 Jerome Bettis .20 .50
50 Vinny Testaverde .10 .30
51 Mike Alstott .20 .50
52 Anthony Johnson .07 .20
53 Dan Marino .75 2.00
54 Junior Seau .20 .50
55 Steve Young .25 .60
56 Troy Aikman .40 1.00
57 Jimmy Smith .10 .30
58 Cris Carter .20 .50
59 Gus Frerotte .07 .20
60 Marcus Allen .20 .50
61 Rodney Hampton .10 .30
62 Bruce Smith .10 .30
63 LeRoy Butler .07 .20
64 Jeff Blake .10 .30
65 Antonio Freeman .20 .50
66 John Elway .75 2.00
67 B.Favre .20 .50
Rison CL
68 Barry Sanders REW .30 .75
69 Troy Aikman REW .20 .50
70 Jerome Bettis REW .10 .30
71 Mark Brunell REW .20 .50
72 Junior Seau REW .10 .30
73 John Elway REW .40 1.00
74 Chad Brown REW .07 .20
75 Irving Fryar REW .07 .20
76 Drew Bledsoe REW .20 .50
77 Jerry Rice REW .20 .50
78 Larry Centers REW .07 .20
79 Terrell Davis REW .20 .50
80 Carl Pickens REW .07 .20
81 Emmitt Smith REW .30 .75
82 Kerry Collins REW .10 .30
83 Eddie Kennison REW .10 .30
84 Kordell Stewart REW .10 .30
85 Natrone Means REW .10 .30
86 Curtis Martin REW UER .20 .50
87 Dorsey Levens REW .20 .50
88 Desmond Howard REW .10 .30
89 Brett Favre REW CL .20 .50
90 Brett Favre T10 .40 1.00
91 Terrell Davis T10 .20 .50
92 Kevin Greene T10 .07 .20
93 Terry Allen T10 .07 .20
94 Barry Sanders T10 .30 .75
95 John Elway T10 .40 1.00
96 Ricky Watters T10 .07 .20
97 Reggie White T10 .10 .30
98 Jerome Bettis T10 .10 .30
99 Jerry Rice T10 .20 .50
100 Brett Favre T10 CL .20 .50

1997 Pro Line DC3 Autographs

Randomly inserted at the rate of only one per case, this six-card insert set features color player photos of six hot, up-and-coming NFL stars. Only a maximum of 300 cards were signed by each player.

STATED ODDS 1:240
STATED PRINT RUN 300 SER.#'d SETS
1 Kordell Stewart 12.00 30.00
2 Kerry Collins 7.50 20.00
3 Terrell Davis 25.00 50.00
4 Eddie George 25.00 50.00
5 Karim Abdul-Jabbar 6.00 15.00
6 Keyshawn Johnson 12.00 30.00

1997 Pro Line DC3 All-Pros

Randomly inserted in packs at a rate of one in 22, this 20-card set features color photos of perennial all-pros and future all-pro players with a unique die-cut card design with bronze foil layering.

COMPLETE SET (20) 40.00 100.00
STATED ODDS 1:24
1 Emmitt Smith 5.00 12.00
2 Brett Favre 6.00 15.00
3 Jerry Rice 3.00 8.00
4 Steve Young 2.00 5.00
5 Barry Sanders 5.00 12.00
6 Reggie White 1.50 4.00
7 Ricky Watters 1.00 2.50
8 Lawrence Phillips 1.00 2.50
9 Kerry Collins 1.50 4.00
10 Mark Brunell 2.00 5.00
11 John Elway 6.00 15.00
12 Dan Marino 6.00 15.00
13 Drew Bledsoe 2.00 5.00
14 Curtis Martin 2.00 5.00
15 Terrell Davis 2.00 5.00
16 Karim Abdul-Jabbar 1.50 4.00
17 Marvin Harrison 1.50 4.00
18 Keyshawn Johnson 1.50 4.00
19 Terry Glenn 1.50 4.00
20 Eddie George 1.50 4.00

1997 Pro Line DC3 Draftnix Redemption

The Draftnix redemption cards were randomly seeded in 1997 Pro Line DC3 packs. The cards expired on 3/4/1998. The common silver version was inserted at the rate of 1:24 packs and was redeemable for a foil card of the featured player. The more difficult foil redemption card versions (bronze and gold) were redeemable for signed jerseys or complete uniforms of the featured player.

COMPLETE SET (3) 6.00 15.00
SILVER BASE STATED ODDS 1:24
1 Darrell Russell .75 2.00
2 Warrick Dunn 4.00 10.00
3 Tony Gonzalez 5.00 12.00

1997 Pro Line DC3 Road to the Super Bowl

Randomly inserted in packs at a rate of one in 12, this 30-card set features color photos on a die-cut design of NFL players who excelled throughout the regular season and playoffs. The cards are numbered with an "SB" prefix.

COMPLETE SET (30) 40.00 100.00
STATED ODDS 1:12
SB1 Ricky Watters .75 2.00
SB2 Ty Detmer .75 2.00
SB3 Emmitt Smith 4.00 10.00
SB4 Troy Aikman 2.50 6.00
SB5 Kerry Collins 1.25 3.00
SB6 Kevin Greene .75 2.00
SB7 Steve Young 1.50 4.00
SB8 Jerry Rice 2.50 6.00
SB9 Brett Favre 5.00 12.00
SB10 Reggie White 1.25 3.00
SB11 Cris Carter 1.25 3.00
SB12 Brad Johnson 1.25 3.00
SB13 Drew Bledsoe 1.50 4.00
SB14 Curtis Martin 1.50 4.00
SB15 Bruce Smith .75 2.00
SB16 Thurman Thomas 1.25 3.00
SB17 Jim Harbaugh .75 2.00
SB18 Marshall Faulk 1.25 3.00
SB19 Mark Brunell 1.50 4.00
SB20 Natrone Means .75 2.00
SB21 John Elway 5.00 12.00
SB22 Terrell Davis 1.50 4.00
SB23 Kordell Stewart 1.25 3.00
SB24 Jerome Bettis 1.25 3.00
SB25 Eddie George 1.25 3.00
SB26 Dan Marino 5.00 12.00
SB27 Terry Glenn 1.25 3.00
SB28 Antonio Freeman 1.25 3.00
SB29 Anthony Johnson .50 1.25
SB30 Kevin Hardy .50 1.25

1998 Pro Line DC3

The 1998 Pro Line DC3 set was issued in one series totalling 100-cards and distributed in four-card hobby packs with a suggested retail price of $3.99. Retail blister 3-card packs were offered at $2.99 suggested retail. The fronts features color player photos on die-cut cards. The backs carry player information. Hobby packs contained cards printed with Gold foil fronts, while retail packs featured cardfronts with no foil layering. The set contains the topical subsets: DC Rewind (69-89), and Rookie Uprising (90-100).

COMPLETE SET (100) 10.00 25.00
1 Drew Bledsoe .50 1.25
2 Emmitt Smith 1.00 2.50
3 Dana Stubblefield .10 .30
4 Brett Favre 1.25 3.00
5 Derrick Alexander WR .20 .50
6 Bert Emanuel .20 .50
7 Joey Galloway .20 .50
8 Terrell Davis .30 .75
9 Mark Brunell .30 .75
10 Marshall Faulk .40 1.00
11 Jake Reed .20 .50
12 Terry Allen .30 .75
13 Kordell Stewart .30 .75
14 Reggie White .30 .75
15 Michael Irvin .30 .75
16 Tony Martin .20 .50
17 Barry Sanders 1.00 2.50
18 Carl Pickens .20 .50
19 Bobby Hoying .20 .50
20 Adrian Murrell .20 .50
21 Jeff George .20 .50
22 Tim Brown .30 .75
23 Karim Abdul-Jabbar .30 .75
24 Robert Smith .30 .75
25 Eddie George .30 .75
26 Corey Dillon .30 .75
27 Keyshawn Johnson .30 .75
28 Ricky Watters .20 .50
29 Robert Brooks .20 .50
30 Antonio Freeman .30 .75
31 Danny Kanell .20 .50
32 Steve McNair .30 .75
33 Antowain Smith .30 .75
34 Warrick Dunn .30 .75
35 Napoleon Kaufman .30 .75
36 Trent Dilfer .30 .75
37 Herman Moore .20 .50
38 Brad Johnson .30 .75
39 Deion Sanders .30 .75
40 Kerry Collins .20 .50
41 Shannon Sharpe .20 .50
42 Irving Fryar .20 .50
43 Dorsey Levens .30 .75
44 Jerry Rice .60 1.50
45 Curtis Martin .30 .75
46 Jerome Bettis .30 .75
47 Raymont Harris .10 .30
48 Vinny Testaverde .20 .50
49 Dan Marino 1.25 3.00
50 Junior Seau .30 .75
51 Steve Young .30 .75
52 Troy Aikman .60 1.50
53 Jimmy Smith .20 .50
54 Ben Coates .20 .50
55 Gus Frerotte .10 .30
56 Marcus Allen .30 .75
57 Bruce Smith .20 .50
58 Jeff Blake .20 .50
59 John Elway 1.25 3.00
60 Rod Smith WR .20 .50
61 Andre Rison .20 .50
62 Isaac Bruce .30 .75
63 Cris Carter .30 .75
64 Danny Wuerffel .20 .50
65 Rob Moore .20 .50
66 Garrison Hearst .30 .75
67 Warren Moon .30 .75
68 Jerome Bettis CL .10 .30
69A Marcus Allen DCR .20 .50
69B Darrien Gordon DCR .10 .30
70 James O.Stewart DCR .20 .50
71 Karim Abdul-Jabbar DCR .20 .50
72 Joey Galloway DCR .20 .50
73 Corey Dillon DCR .20 .50
74 Andre Rison DCR .10 .30
75 Napoleon Kaufman DCR .20 .50
76 Dorsey Levens DCR .20 .50
77 Irving Fryar DCR .10 .30
78 Eric Metcalf DCR .10 .30
80 Neil O'Donnell DCR .20 .50
81 Rod Woodson DCR .20 .50
82 Rob Johnson DCR .20 .50
83 Michael Westbrook DCR .20 .50
84 Jake Plummer DCR .20 .50
85 Bobby Hoying DCR .10 .30
86 Adrian Murrell DCR .10 .30
87 Jim Druckenmiller DCR .10 .30
88 Warren Moon DCR .20 .50
89 Dorsey Levens DCR CL .10 .30
90 Tony Gonzalez RU .30 .75
91 Jim Druckenmiller RU .10 .30
92 Corey Dillon RU .20 .50
93 Darrell Russell RU .10 .30
94 Byron Hanspard RU .10 .30
95 Rae Carruth RU .10 .30
96 Peter Boulware RU .10 .30
97 Troy Davis RU .10 .30
98 Reidel Anthony RU .20 .50
99 Tiki Barber RU .30 .75
100 Jake Plummer RU CL .20 .50

1998 Pro Line DC3 Gold

COMPLETE SET (100) 10.00 25.00
*GOLD FOIL HOBBY CARDS: SAME PRICE

1998 Pro Line DC3 Perfect Cut

STATED ODDS 1:2033

1998 Pro Line DC3 Choice Cuts

This 10 card insert set featuring leading NFL players was randomly inserted approximately one every 24 retail packs.

COMPLETE SET (10) 15.00 40.00
STATED ODDS 1:24 RETAIL
CHC1 Deion Sanders 1.50 4.00
CHC2 Jerome Bettis 1.50 4.00
CHC3 Troy Aikman 3.00 8.00
CHC4 Jerry Rice 3.00 8.00
CHC5 Mark Brunell 1.50 4.00
CHC6 Curtis Martin 1.50 4.00
CHC7 Cris Carter 1.50 4.00
CHC8 Steve Young 1.50 4.00
CHC9 Reggie White 1.50 4.00
CHC10 Dan Marino 6.00 15.00

1998 Pro Line DC3 Clear Cuts

Randomly inserted in hobby packs only at the rate of one in 95, this 10-card set features photos of some of the NFL's best players silhouetted on acetate cards with holographic foil highlights. Only 500 of this set were produced and are sequentially numbered.

COMPLETE SET (10) 60.00 150.00
STATED ODDS 1:95 HOBBY
STATED PRINT RUN 500 SERIAL #'d SETS
CLC1 John Elway 12.50 30.00
CLC2 Drew Bledsoe 5.00 12.00
CLC3 Terrell Davis 3.00 8.00
CLC4 Brett Favre 12.50 30.00
CLC5 Cris Carter 3.00 8.00
CLC6 Eddie George 3.00 8.00
CLC7 Kordell Stewart 3.00 8.00
CLC8 Warrick Dunn 3.00 8.00
CLC9 Tim Brown 3.00 8.00
CLC10 Barry Sanders 10.00 25.00

1998 Pro Line DC3 Decade Draft

Randomly inserted in packs at the rate of one in 24, this 10-card set features a look at the NFL Draft since 1989 with redemption cards for the first NFL cards of the players from the 1998 draft. The cards carry a portrait photo of the first player selected in the draft along with an action photo of a top impact player from that same rookie class.

COMPLETE SET (10) 25.00 60.00
STATED ODDS 1:24
DD1 T.Aikman B.Sanders 5.00 12.00
DD2 J.George E.Smith 5.00 12.00
DD3 R.Maryland B.Favre 6.00 15.00
DD4 S.Emtman C.Pickens 1.00 2.50
DD5 D.Bledsoe D.Bledsoe 2.50 6.00
DD6 D.Wilkinson M.Faulk 2.00 5.00
DD7 K.Carter T.Davis 1.50 4.00
DD8 K.Johnson E.George 1.50 4.00
DD9 O.Pace W.Dunn 1.50 4.00
DD10 1998 Top Pick Redemp. .20 .50

1998 Pro Line DC3 Team Totals

Randomly inserted in packs at the rate of one in eight, this 30-card set features color player photos recapping the 1997 regular season for each NFL team including a brand new DC Team Rating for offense and defense. Note that the cards carry a 1997 copyright date but were released in 1998.

COMPLETE SET (30) 20.00 50.00
STATED ODDS 1:8
TT1 B.Coates W.McGinest 1.00 2.50
TT2 M.Irvin D.Sanders 1.50 4.00
TT3 C.Pickens D.Wilkinson 1.00 2.50
TT4 L.Butler A.Freeman 1.50 4.00
TT5 A.Murrell H.Douglas 1.00 2.50
TT6 R.Harris B.Cox .60 1.50
TT7 R.Watters W.Thomas 1.00 2.50
TT8 N.Smith Sh.Sharpe 1.00 2.50
TT9 D.Stubblefield G.Hearst 1.50 4.00
TT10 K.McCardell J.Lageman 1.00 2.50
TT11 R.Carruth L.Lathon .60 1.50
TT12 Y.Thigpen G.Lloyd .60 1.50
TT13 C.Calloway M.Strahan 1.00 2.50
TT14 Tr.Davis W.Martin .60 1.50
TT15 W.Moon C.Kennedy 1.50 4.00
TT16 R.Moore S.Rice 1.00 2.50
TT17 O.J.McDuffie Z.Thomas 1.50 4.00
TT18 J.Randle Rob.Smith 1.50 4.00
TT19 D.Thomas E.Grbac 1.50 4.00
TT20 Ant.Smith B.Smith 1.50 4.00
TT21 J.George D.Russell 1.00 2.50
TT22 S.McNair D.Lewis 1.50 4.00
TT23 I.Bruce L.O'Neal 1.50 4.00
TT24 J.Seau T.Martin 1.50 4.00
TT25 W.Sapp M.Alstott 1.50 4.00
TT26 J.Tuggle J.Anderson 1.50 4.00
TT27 M.Jackson P.Boulware .60 1.50
TT28 Q.Coryatt M.Harrison 1.50 4.00
TT29 B.Westbrook S.Mitchell 1.00 2.50
TT30 M.Westbrook D.Green 1.00 2.50

1998 Pro Line DC3 X-Tra Effort

Randomly inserted in hobby packs at the rate of one in 24, this 20-card set features color player images of superstars on a die-cut, lightening design background. Each card features gold foil on the front and was serial numbered on the back of 1000-sets made.

COMPLETE SET (20) 60.00 150.00
STATED ODDS 1:24 HOBBY
STATED PRINT RUN 1000 SER.#'d SETS
XE1 Reggie White 2.50 6.00
XE2 Emmitt Smith 8.00 20.00
XE3 Junior Seau 2.50 6.00
XE4 Brett Favre 10.00 25.00
XE5 Warrick Dunn 2.50 6.00
XE6 Keyshawn Johnson 2.50 6.00
XE7 Dan Marino 10.00 25.00
XE8 Thurman Thomas 2.50 6.00
XE9 Steve Young 2.50 6.00
XE10 Curtis Martin 2.50 6.00
XE11 Karim Abdul-Jabbar 2.50 6.00
XE12 John Elway 10.00 25.00
XE13 Marcus Allen 2.50 6.00
XE14 Napoleon Kaufman 2.50 6.00
XE15 Irving Fryar 1.50 4.00
XE16 Mark Brunell 2.50 6.00
XE17 Andre Rison 1.50 4.00
XE18 Herman Moore 1.50 4.00
XE19 Jerry Rice 5.00 12.00
XE20 Kordell Stewart 2.50 6.00

1997 Pro Line Gems

The 1997 ProLine Gems set was issued in one series totalling 100 cards and distributed in four-card packs. This limited edition three tiered set features color action photos printed on 18 pt. card stock of 60 of the top rated veteran players, 30 of the league's highest profile rookies, and 10 potential leaders. Each card in the three subsets carry an exclusive foil stamp design and color. A Brett Favre championship ring card was randomly inserted in packs at the rate of one in 240. It features a color photo of Brett Favre wearing his championship ring with an actual diamond embedded in the card. Only 1997 of these cards were produced.

COMPLETE SET (100) 10.00 20.00
1 Brett Favre .75 2.00
2 Robert Brooks .10 .30
3 Reggie White .20 .50
4 Drew Bledsoe .25 .60
5 Curtis Martin .25 .60
6 Terry Glenn .20 .50
7 Kerry Collins .20 .50
8 Kevin Greene .10 .30
9 Troy Aikman .40 1.00
10 Emmitt Smith .60 1.50
11 Deion Sanders .20 .50
12 John Elway .75 2.00
13 Terrell Davis .25 .60
14 Kordell Stewart .20 .50
15 Jerome Bettis .20 .50
16 Steve Young .25 .60
17 Jerry Rice .40 1.00
18 Bruce Smith .10 .30
19 Thurman Thomas .20 .50
20 Jim Harbaugh .10 .30
21 Marshall Faulk .25 .60
22 Marvin Harrison .20 .50
23 Ricky Watters .10 .30
24 Seth Joyner .07 .20
25 Mark Brunell .25 .60
26 Natrone Means .10 .30
27 Dan Marino .75 2.00
28 Zach Thomas .20 .50
29 Karim Abdul-Jabbar .20 .50
30 Isaac Bruce .20 .50
31 Eddie Kennison .10 .30
32 Tony Banks .10 .30
33 Tony Martin .10 .30
34 Junior Seau .20 .50
35 Barry Sanders .60 1.50
36 Herman Moore .10 .30
37 Leeland McElroy .07 .20
38 Jamal Anderson .20 .50
39 Rick Mirer .07 .20
40 Rashaan Salaam .07 .20
41 Vinny Testaverde .10 .30
42 Elvis Grbac .10 .30
43 Cris Carter .20 .50
44 Brad Johnson .20 .50
45 Keyshawn Johnson .20 .50
46 Adrian Murrell .10 .30
47 Joey Galloway .10 .30
48 Trent Dilfer .20 .50
49 Gus Frerotte .07 .20
50 Terry Allen .20 .50
51 Tim Brown .20 .50
52 Desmond Howard .10 .30
53 Jeff George .10 .30
54 Heath Shuler .07 .20
55 Steve McNair .25 .60
56 Eddie George .20 .50
57 Jeff Blake .10 .30
58 Carl Pickens .10 .30
59 Dave Brown .07 .20
60 Brett Favre CL .20 .50
61 Antowain Smith PL .20 .50
62 Emmitt Smith PL .30 .75
63 Terry Glenn PL .10 .30
64 Herman Moore PL .10 .30
65 Barry Sanders PL .30 .75
66 Derrick Thomas PL .20 .50
67 Brett Favre PL .40 1.00
68 Warrick Dunn PL .25 .60
69 Emmitt Smith PL .30 .75
70 Brett Favre CL .20 .50
71 Orlando Pace RC .20 .50
72 Darrell Russell RC .07 .20
73 Shawn Springs RC .10 .30
74 Warrick Dunn RC .60 1.50
75 Tiki Barber RC 1.25 3.00
76 Tom Knight RC .07 .20
77 Peter Boulware RC .20 .50
78 David LaFleur RC .07 .20
79 Tony Gonzalez RC .75 2.00
80 Yatil Green RC .10 .30
81 Ike Hilliard RC .30 .75
82 James Farrior RC .20 .50
83 Jim Druckenmiller RC .10 .30
84 Jon Harris RC .07 .20
85 Walter Jones RC .30 .75
86 Reidel Anthony RC .20 .50
87 Jake Plummer RC .75 2.00
88 Reinard Wilson RC .10 .30
89 Kevin Lockett RC .10 .30
90 Rae Carruth RC .07 .20
91 Byron Hanspard RC .10 .30
92 Renaldo Wynn RC .07 .20
93 Troy Davis RC .10 .30
94 Duce Staley RC 1.50 4.00
95 Kenard Lang RC .10 .30
96 Freddie Jones RC .10 .30
97 Corey Dillon RC .75 2.00
98 Antowain Smith RC .50 1.25
99 Dwayne Rudd RC .20 .50
100 Warrick Dunn CL .25 .60
CR1 Brett Favre Ring/1997 20.00 50.00

1997 Pro Line Gems Gems of the NFL 23K Gold

Redemption cards were randomly inserted in packs at the rate of one in 24. These redemptions were exchangeable for a 23K Gold version with an actual gemstone embedded in each card. The odd numbered cards carried actual emeralds while the even numbered cards carried real sapphires. The prize cards featuring the embedded stone are priced below. The redemption expired September 18, 1998.

COMPLETE SET (15) 80.00 200.00
STATED ODDS 1:24
G1 Kerry Collins 3.00 8.00
G2 Troy Aikman 6.00 15.00
G3 Emmitt Smith 10.00 25.00
G4 Terrell Davis 4.00 10.00
G5 Barry Sanders 10.00 25.00
G6 Brett Favre 12.50 30.00
G7 Eddie George 3.00 8.00
G8 Mark Brunell 4.00 10.00
G9 Dan Marino 12.50 30.00
G10 Curtis Martin 4.00 10.00
G11 Terry Glenn 3.00 8.00
G12 Jerome Bettis 3.00 8.00
G13 Steve Young 4.00 10.00
G14 Jerry Rice 6.00 15.00
G15 Warrick Dunn 5.00 12.00
G16 John Elway 1999 Retirement 8.00 20.00

1997 Pro Line Gems Through the Years

Randomly inserted in packs at the rate of one in 12, this 20-card set features color action photos of ten top veterans superstars and ten top young stars printed on foil stamped cards and made to be matched one veteran and one young star together to form an oversized trading card.

COMPLETE SET (20) 20.00 50.00
STATED ODDS 1:12
TY1 Emmitt Smith 3.00 8.00
TY2 Brett Favre 4.00 10.00
TY3 Deion Sanders 1.00 2.50
TY4 Dan Marino 4.00 10.00
TY5 Barry Sanders 3.00 8.00
TY6 Herman Moore .60 1.50
TY7 Curtis Martin 1.25 3.00
TY8 Jerome Bettis 1.00 2.50
TY9 Mark Brunell 1.00 2.50
TY10 Jerry Rice 2.00 5.00
TY11 Warrick Dunn 1.50 4.00
TY12 Jim Druckenmiller .30 .75
TY13 Shawn Springs .30 .75
TY14 Tony Banks .60 1.50
TY15 Byron Hanspard .30 .75
TY16 Ike Hilliard .60 1.50
TY17 Antowain Smith 1.00 2.50
TY18 Eddie George 1.00 2.50
TY19 Jake Plummer 2.00 5.00
TY20 Terry Glenn 1.00 2.50

1996 Pro Line Intense

The 1996 Pro Line Intense set was issued in one series totalling 100-cards and was distributed in five-card packs. The fronts feature borderless color action player photos with the player's name and team helmet at the bottom. The backs carry player information and career statistics.

COMPLETE SET (100) 6.00 15.00
1 Kerry Collins .08 .25
2 Jeff George .02 .10
3 Mark Brunell .20 .50
4 Steve McNair .25 .60
5 Rick Mirer .02 .10
6 Dave Brown .01 .05
7 Rashaan Salaam .01 .05
8 Marshall Faulk .10 .30
9 Erric Pegram .01 .05
10 Cris Carter .08 .25
11 Eric Allen .01 .05
12 Jim Kelly .08 .25
13 Jeff Blake .08 .25
14 Stan Humphries .02 .10
15 Scott Mitchell .02 .10
16 Jeff Hostetler .01 .05
17 Rodney Peete .01 .05
18 Warren Moon .02 .10
19 Errict Rhett .02 .10
20 Terrell Davis .25 .60
21 J.J. Stokes .08 .25
22 Marco Coleman .01 .05
23 Heath Shuler .02 .10
24 Duane Clemons RC .01 .05
25 Amani Toomer RC .30 .75
26 Leslie O'Neal .01 .05
27 Tamarick Vanover .02 .10
28 Steve Bono .01 .05
29 Jim Everett .01 .05
30 Erik Kramer .01 .05
31 Trent Dilfer .08 .25
32 Jim Harbaugh .02 .10
33 Vinny Testaverde .02 .10
34 Rodney Hampton .02 .10
35 Chris Warren .02 .10
36 Curtis Martin .25 .60
37 Eddie Kennison RC .08 .25
38 Herman Moore .02 .10
39 Terance Mathis .01 .05
40 Carl Pickens .02 .10
41 Isaac Bruce .08 .25
42 Reggie White .08 .25
43 Junior Seau .08 .25
44 Bryce Paup .01 .05
45 Deion Sanders .10 .30
46 Thurman Thomas .08 .25
47 Gus Frerotte .02 .10
48 Tony Mandarich .01 .05
49 Michael Irvin .08 .25
50 Wayne Chrebet .10 .30
51 Bobby Engram RC .08 .25
52 Marcus Jones RC .01 .05
53 Daryl Gardener RC .01 .05
54 Alex Van Dyke RC .02 .10
55 Andre Rison .02 .10
56 Regan Upshaw RC .01 .05
57 Jason Dunn RC .02 .10
58 Mark Chmura .02 .10
59 Ray Lewis RC 1.50 4.00
60 Rickey Dudley RC .08 .25
61 Leeland McElroy RC .02 .10
62 Derrick Thomas .08 .25
63 Bobby Hoying RC .08 .25
64 Robert Brooks .02 .10
65 Tim Brown .08 .25
66 Michael Westbrook .08 .25
67 Jim Miller .08 .25
68 Aaron Hayden .01 .05
69 Marcus Allen .08 .25
70 Troy Aikman .30 .75
71 Steve Young .20 .50
72 Neil O'Donnell .02 .10
73 Drew Bledsoe .20 .50
74 Emmitt Smith .50 1.25
75 Ki-Jana Carter .02 .10
76 Irving Fryar .02 .10
77 Joey Galloway .08 .25
78 Russell Maryland .01 .05
79 Kordell Stewart .08 .25
80 Barry Sanders .50 1.25
81 Bryan Cox .01 .05
82 Keyshawn Johnson RC .30 .75
83 Karim Abdul-Jabbar RC .08 .25
84 Kevin Hardy RC .08 .25
85 Rodney Thomas .01 .05
86 John Elway .40 1.50
87 Dan Marino .60 1.50
88 Brett Favre .60 1.50
89 Eric Metcalf .01 .05
90 Jonathan Ogden RC .40 1.00
91 Eddie George RC .40 1.00
92 Simeon Rice RC .25 .60
93 Tim Biakabutuka RC .08 .25
94 Terry Glenn RC .30 .75
95 Marvin Harrison RC .75 2.00
96 Lawrence Phillips RC .08 .25
97 Natrone Means .02 .10
98 Jerry Rice .30 .75
99 Ricky Watters .02 .10
100 Emmitt Smith CL .08 .25

1996 Pro Line Intense Double Intensity

COMPLETE SET (100) 40.00 100.00
*STARS: 2X TO 5X BASIC CARDS
*RCs: .8X TO 2X BASIC CARDS
STATED ODDS 1:5

1996 Pro Line Intense Determined

Randomly inserted in packs at a rate of one in 50, this 20-card set features color player images on a silver metallic-look background of a large head photo of the player. The backs feature another player image with a paragraph about the player.

COMPLETE SET (20) 15.00 40.00
STATED ODDS 1:50
1 Kerry Collins .60 1.50
2 Troy Aikman 2.00 5.00
3 Herman Moore .25 .60
4 Mark Brunell 1.25 3.00
5 Dan Marino 4.00 10.00
6 Kordell Stewart .60 1.50
7 Junior Seau .60 1.50
8 Steve Young 1.25 3.00
9 John Elway 4.00 10.00
10 Emmitt Smith 3.00 8.00
11 Steve McNair 1.50 4.00
12 Drew Bledsoe 1.25 3.00
13 Joey Galloway .60 1.50
14 Deion Sanders .75 2.00
15 Kevin Hardy .30 .75
16 Keyshawn Johnson 1.00 2.50
17 Marvin Harrison 2.50 6.00
18 Tim Biakabutuka .30 .75
19 Eddie George 1.25 3.00
20 Terry Glenn 1.00 2.50

1996 Pro Line Intense Phone Cards $3

Randomly inserted in 1996 Pro Line Intense packs at a rate of one in 18, this 50-card set includes $3.00 worth of Sprint long distance per card. Two parallel sets of the $3.00 cards were also included in the Phone Card pack release. Proof cards were inserted at the rate of 1:29 and Test cards were inserted at the rate of 1:55 packs.

COMPLETE SET (50) 30.00 50.00
*PROOF CARDS: .6X TO 1.5X BASIC INSERTS
*TEST CARDS: 1.2X TO 3X BASIC INSERTS
1 Jim Kelly .40 1.00
2 Kerry Collins .40 1.00
3 Jeff George .20 .50
4 Troy Aikman .60 1.50
5 John Elway 1.25 3.00
6 Herman Moore .40 1.00
7 Barry Sanders 1.25 3.00
8 Brett Favre 1.25 3.00
9 Jim Harbaugh .20 .50
10 Steve Bono .20 .50
11 Dan Marino 1.25 3.00
12 Drew Bledsoe .60 1.50
13 Jim Everett .20 .50
14 Neil O'Donnell .20 .50
15 Ricky Watters .40 1.00
16 Junior Seau .40 1.00
17 Jerry Rice .60 1.50
18 Errict Rhett .20 .50
19 Joey Galloway .60 1.50
20 Steve Young .50 1.25
21 Kordell Stewart .60 1.50
22 Rodney Hampton .20 .50
23 Curtis Martin .60 1.50
24 Mark Brunell .60 1.50
25 Steve McNair .60 1.50
26 Deion Sanders .40 1.00
27 Carl Pickens .20 .50
28 Michael Irvin .40 1.00
29 Tamarick Vanover .20 .50
30 Trent Dilfer .40 1.00
31 Chris Warren .20 .50
32 Stan Humphries .20 .50
33 J.J. Stokes .40 1.00
34 Tim Biakabutuka .20 .50
35 Keyshawn Johnson .60 1.50
36 Simeon Rice .20 .50
37 Jonathan Ogden .40 1.00
38 Rashaan Salaam .40 1.00
39 Bobby Engram .20 .50
40 Reggie White .40 1.00
41 Isaac Bruce .40 1.00
42 Eddie George 1.25 3.00
43 Marvin Harrison .50 1.25
44 Kevin Hardy .20 .50
45 Karim Abdul-Jabbar .40 1.00
46 Duane Clemons .20 .50
47 Terry Glenn .50 1.25
48 Marcus Allen .40 1.00
49 Rickey Dudley .20 .50
50 Lawrence Phillips .20 .50

1996 Pro Line Intense Phone Cards $5

Randomly inserted in 1996 Pro Line Intense packs at a rate of one in 35, this 20-card set includes $5 worth of Sprint long distance phone calls per card. The expiration date for calling is March 26, 1998. The cards were released as well in 1996 Score Board NFL Phone Card packs. Two parallel sets of the $5 cards were included in the Phone Card pack release. Proof cards were inserted at the rate of 1:65 (numbered of 108 made) and Test cards were inserted at the rate of 1:130 packs (numbered of 52 made).

COMPLETE SET (20) 30.00 60.00
*PROOFS: .6X TO 1.5X BASIC INSERTS
*TEST CARDS: 1.2X TO 3X BASIC INSERTS
1 Kerry Collins .30 .75
2 Troy Aikman 1.00 2.50
3 Reggie White .40 1.00
4 Mark Brunell 1.00 2.50
5 Dan Marino 2.00 5.00
6 Kordell Stewart .75 2.00
7 Junior Seau .30 .75
8 Steve Young .75 2.00
9 John Elway 2.00 5.00
10 Emmitt Smith 2.00 5.00
11 Steve McNair .75 2.00
12 Drew Bledsoe 1.00 2.50
13 Joey Galloway .50 1.25
14 Deion Sanders .40 1.00
15 Kevin Hardy .30 .75
16 Keyshawn Johnson .75 2.00
17 Marvin Harrison .75 2.00
18 Tim Biakabutuka .40 1.00
19 Eddie George 1.50 4.00
20 Terry Glenn .75 2.00

1996 Pro Line Intense Phone Cards $10

Randomly inserted in Score Board Phone Card packs at a rate of one in 12, this 10-card set features color action player photos with the Sprint calling value of the card printed on the front. The backs carry the instructions on how to use the phone cards. Only 1130 of each card was produced and each is sequentially numbered. Two parallel sets were also included in the Phone Card pack release. Proof cards were inserted at the rate of 1:400 and Test cards were inserted at the rate of 1:800 packs. The expiration date is March 26, 1998.

COMPLETE SET (10) 30.00 50.00
*PROOF CARDS: .6X TO 1.5X BASIC INSERTS
*TEST CARDS: 1.2X TO 3X BASIC INSERTS
1 Dan Marino 4.00 10.00
2 Jim Harbaugh 1.00 2.50
3 Troy Aikman 2.00 5.00
4 Curtis Martin 2.00 5.00
5 Kordell Stewart 2.00 5.00
6 Steve Young 1.50 4.00
7 Barry Sanders 4.00 10.00
8 Keyshawn Johnson 2.00 5.00
9 Lawrence Phillips .60 1.50
10 Eddie George 3.00 8.00

1996 Pro Line Intense Phone Cards $25 Die Cuts

Randomly inserted in 1996 Score Board Phone Card packs at a rate of one in 36, this 10-card set features color action player photos with the calling value of the card printed on the die-cut front. The backs carry the instructions on how to use the phone cards. Only 377 of each card was produced and are sequentially numbered. Two parallel sets were also included in the Phone Card pack release. Proof cards were inserted at the rate of 1:550 and Test cards were inserted at the rate of 1:1100 packs. The expiration date is March 26, 1998.

COMPLETE SET (10) 60.00 100.00
*PROOFS: .6X TO 1.5X BASIC INSERTS
*TEST CARDS: 1X TO 2.5X BASIC INSERTS
1 Jim Kelly 1.50 4.00
2 Troy Aikman 4.00 10.00
3 John Elway 8.00 20.00
4 Kerry Collins 1.50 4.00
5 Barry Sanders 8.00 20.00
6 Drew Bledsoe 4.00 10.00
7 Keyshawn Johnson 4.00 10.00
8 Deion Sanders .30 8.00
9 Dan Marino 8.00 20.00
10 Brett Favre 8.00 20.00

1996 Pro Line Intense Phone Cards $1000

Randomly inserted in packs at a rate of one in 3700, this five-card set features color action player photos with the calling value of the card printed on the front. The backs carry the instructions on how to use the phone cards. Only seven of each card was produced, sequentially numbered, and randomly inserted in Phone Card packs at the rate of 1:3750. Proof and Test parallels were also created for each card.

NOT PRICED DUE TO SCARCITY
1 John Elway
2 Keyshawn Johnson
3 Troy Aikman
4 Dan Marino
5 Brett Favre

1996 Pro Line Memorabilia

COMPLETE SET (100) 10.00 25.00
*MEMOR.CARDS: .6X to 1.5X INTENSE

1996 Pro Line Memorabilia Producers

Randomly inserted in packs at a rate of one in six, this 10-card set features color player image with a silver foil shadow on a copper metallic-look background. The backs carry another player image and a paragraph about the player.

COMPLETE SET (10) 12.50 30.00
STATED ODDS 1:6
*SILVER SIGS: 1.5X TO 4X BASIC INSERTS
SILVER STATED ODDS 1:100
P1 Keyshawn Johnson .75 2.00
P2 Barry Sanders 2.50 6.00
P3 Eddie George 1.00 2.50
P4 Emmitt Smith 2.50 6.00
P5 Jerry Rice 1.50 4.00
P6 Brett Favre 3.00 8.00
P7 Ricky Watters .20 .50
P8 Dan Marino 2.50 6.00
P9 Deion Sanders .60 1.50
P10 Marshall Faulk .60 1.50

1996 Pro Line Memorabilia Rookie Autographs

Randomly inserted in packs at the rate of one in 12, this 16-card set features borderless color action player photos of NFL rookies with the player's autograph on the front. A limited number of each card was signed by the pictured player and are sequentially numbered. The cards are unnumbered and checklisted below alphabetically.

COMPLETE SET (16) 200.00 400.00
STATED ODDS 1:12
1 Tim Biakabutuka/210 12.50 30.00
2 T.Biakab E.George/600 12.00 30.00
3 Duane Clemons/1255 6.00 15.00
4 Daryl Gardener/1390 6.00 15.00
5 Eddie George/395 20.00 40.00
6 T.Glenn K.Johnson/600 15.00 40.00
7 Kevin Hardy/940 7.50 20.00
8 Jeff Hartings/1370 10.00 25.00
9 Andre Johnson/1370 6.00 15.00
10 Keyshawn Johnson/195 25.00 50.00
11 Pete Kendall/1495 6.00 15.00
12 Alex Molden/1320 6.00 15.00
13 Eric Moulds/1010 12.50 30.00
14 Jamain Stephens/795 6.00 15.00
15 Regan Upshaw 6.00 15.00
16 Jerome Woods/1375 6.00 15.00

1996 Pro Line Memorabilia Stretch Drive

Randomly inserted in packs at a rate of one in three, this 30-card set features color player photos with a three-sided silver-tone border. The backs carry another player photo and a paragraph about the player.

COMPLETE SET (30) 15.00 40.00
STATED ODDS 1:3
*SILVER SIGS: .8X TO 2X BASIC INSERTS
SILVER STATED ODDS 1:25
DS1 Jim Kelly .30 .75
DS2 Kerry Collins .30 .75
DS3 Rashaan Salaam .10 .30
DS4 Jeff Blake .30 .75
DS5 Deion Sanders .40 1.00
DS6 Troy Aikman 1.00 2.50
DS7 Emmitt Smith 1.50 4.00
DS8 John Elway 2.00 5.00
DS9 Terrell Davis .75 2.00
DS10 Barry Sanders 1.50 4.00
DS11 Brett Favre 2.00 5.00
DS12 Steve McNair .75 2.00
DS13 Eddie George .60 1.50
DS14 Marshall Faulk .40 1.00
DS15 Marvin Harrison 1.25 3.00
DS16 Herman Moore .10 .30
DS17 Dan Marino 2.00 5.00
DS18 Curtis Martin .75 2.00
DS19 Drew Bledsoe .60 1.50
DS20 Terry Glenn .30 .75
DS21 Lawrence Phillips .10 .30
DS22 Neil O'Donnell .10 .30
DS23 Keyshawn Johnson .30 .75
DS24 Isaac Bruce .30 .75
DS25 Ricky Watters .10 .30
DS26 Kordell Stewart .30 .75
DS27 J.J. Stokes .30 .75
DS28 Steve Young .60 1.50
DS29 Joey Galloway .30 .75
DS30 Errict Rhett .10 .30

1997 Pro Line Memorabilia

Distributed in five-card packs, this 50-card set features color action photos of top players as selected by Score Board. The backs carry player information. A blue foil Signature Series parallel set was also produced and randomly inserted in 1:5 packs.

COMPLETE SET (50) 15.00 30.00
1 Jake Plummer RC .60 1.50
2 Byron Hanspard RC .10 .30
3 Vinny Testaverde .10 .30
4 Thurman Thomas .20 .50
5 Antowain Smith RC .50 1.25
6 Rae Carruth RC .07 .20
7 Kerry Collins .20 .50
8 Rashaan Salaam .10 .30
9 Rick Mirer .07 .20
10 Jeff Blake .10 .30
11 Troy Aikman .40 1.00
12 Emmitt Smith .60 1.50
13 John Elway .75 2.00
14 Terrell Davis .25 .60
15 Barry Sanders .60 1.50
16 Herman Moore .10 .30
17 Brett Favre .75 2.00
18 Reggie White .20 .50
19 Dorsey Levens .20 .50
20 Eddie George .20 .50
21 Jim Harbaugh .10 .30
22 Mark Brunell .25 .60
23 Tony Gonzalez RC .60 1.50
24 Elvis Grbac .10 .30
25 Dan Marino .75 2.00
26 Karim Abdul-Jabbar .20 .50
27 Brad Johnson .20 .50
28 Drew Bledsoe .25 .60
29 Curtis Martin .25 .60
30 Terry Glenn .20 .50
31 Heath Shuler .07 .20
32 Danny Wuerffel RC .20 .50
33 Ike Hilliard RC .30 .75
34 Keyshawn Johnson .20 .50
35 Darrell Russell RC .07 .20
36 Jeff George .10 .30
37 Ricky Watters .10 .30
38 Bobby Hoying .10 .30
39 Jerome Bettis .20 .50
40 Kordell Stewart .20 .50
41 Junior Seau .20 .50
42 Shawn Springs RC .10 .30
43 Jim Druckenmiller RC .10 .30
44 Steve Young .25 .60
45 Jerry Rice .40 1.00
46 Orlando Pace RC .20 .50
47 Isaac Bruce .20 .50
48 Warrick Dunn RC .50 1.25
49 Gus Frerotte .07 .20
50 Brett Favre CL .20 .50

1997 Pro Line Memorabilia Signature Series

COMPLETE SET (50) 25.00 60.00
*SIG.SERIES STARS: 1.5X TO 4X BASIC CARDS
*SIG.SERIES RCs: .8X TO 2X BASIC CARDS
STATED ODDS 1:5

1997 Pro Line Memorabilia Bustin' Out

Bustin' Out cards were randomly seeded at the rate of 1:20 Pro Line Memorabilia packs. A Gold foil parallel set was also produced and seeded at the rate of 1:65 packs.

COMPLETE SET (20) 40.00 100.00
STATED ODDS 1:20
*GOLD CARDS: .8X TO 2X SILVERS
GOLD STATED ODDS 1:65
B1 Antowain Smith 2.00 5.00
B2 Kerry Collins 1.50 4.00
B3 Jeff Blake 1.00 2.50
B4 Emmitt Smith 5.00 12.00
B5 Troy Aikman 3.00 8.00
B6 Terrell Davis 2.00 5.00
B7 Barry Sanders 5.00 12.00
B8 Brett Favre 6.00 15.00
B9 Mark Brunell 2.00 5.00
B10 Dan Marino 6.00 15.00
B11 Brad Johnson 1.50 4.00
B12 Curtis Martin 2.00 5.00
B13 Keyshawn Johnson 1.50 4.00
B14 Darrell Russell .60 1.50
B15 Reggie White 1.50 4.00
B16 Kordell Stewart 1.50 4.00
B17 Jerry Rice 3.00 8.00
B18 Isaac Bruce 1.50 4.00
B19 Warrick Dunn 2.50 6.00
B20 Eddie George 1.50 4.00

1997 Pro Line Memorabilia Rookie Autographs

Randomly inserted at the rate of 1:10 Pro Line Memorabilia packs, each card was signed by the featured player. The autograph appears within a football design on the cardfront. Cardbacks contain only a congratulatory message.

COMPLETE SET (26) 125.00 250.00
STATED ODDS 1:10
1 John Allred 2.50 6.00
2 Darnell Autry 2.50 6.00
3 Pat Barnes 2.50 6.00
4 Michael Booker 2.50 6.00
5 Peter Boulware 4.00 10.00
6 Rae Carruth 2.50 6.00
7 Troy Davis 4.00 10.00
8 Jim Druckenmiller 4.00 10.00
9 Warrick Dunn 10.00 25.00
10 James Farrior 6.00 15.00
11 Tony Gonzalez 10.00 25.00
12 Yatil Green 6.00 15.00
13 Byron Hanspard 4.00 10.00
14 Ike Hilliard 4.00 10.00
15 David LaFleur 2.50 6.00
16 Kevin Lockett 4.00 10.00
17 Jake Plummer 10.00 25.00
18 Trevor Pryce 6.00 15.00
19 Derrick Rodgers 2.50 6.00
20 Dwayne Rudd 2.50 6.00
21 Darrell Russell 2.50 6.00
22 Matt Russell 2.50 6.00
23 Sedrick Shaw 4.00 10.00
24 Antowain Smith 8.00 20.00
25 Reinard Wilson 2.50 6.00
26 Bryant Westbrook 4.00 10.00

1997 Pro Line Memorabilia Veteran Autographs

Cards in this set were produced with the same basic design as the Rookie Autographs inserts, however, it appears that none of the cards were inserted into Pro Line Memorabilia packs They seem to have appeared on the secondary market after Score Board liquidated its inventory. Each card was signed by the featured player and the autograph appears within a football design on the cardfront. Most were created with the Pro Line Memorabilia logo on the front but a few have a very basic "SB" or Score Board logo. The cardbacks contain only a congratulatory message.

1 Eric Allen 6.00 15.00
2 Lamont Hollinquest SB 5.00 12.00
2 Randy Baldwin SB 5.00 12.00
3 Keenan McCardell 6.00 15.00
4 Willie McGinest 5.00 12.00
5 Chris Slade 5.00 12.00
6 Jimmy Smith 8.00 20.00

1994 Pro Mags

These magnets measure approximately 2 1/8" by 3 3/8" and have rounded corners. They were sold in five-magnet packs that included a free team magnet, measuring 2 1/8" by 3/4" and a checklist of all 140 players. Collectors could receive a special Warren Moon magnet by mailing in a redemption card that was included in every pack, three proofs of purchase, and 6.00. The fronts display borderless color action player photos. The player's last name in big letters appears along the right side. His first name in team color-coded letters is printed on the bottom, with the team logo next to it. The magnets are numbered on the front, grouped alphabetically within teams, and checklisted below according to teams. The team magnets are unnumbered and are checklisted below in alphabetical order with a "T" prefix. Troy Aikman and Chris Martin promo magnets were produced and are listed below. An oversized Warren Moon artist's rendering magnet was randomly inserted in boxes.

COMPLETE SET (168) 50.00 125.00
1 Rod Bernstine .25 .60
2 John Elway 3.20 8.00
3 Glyn Milburn .40 1.00
4 Shannon Sharpe .40 1.00
5 Dennis Smith .25 .60
6 Cody Carlson .25 .60
7 Ernest Givins .40 1.00
8 Haywood Jeffires .40 1.00
9 Bruce Matthews .25 .60
10 Webster Slaughter .25 .60
11 O.J. McDuffie .40 1.00
12 Keith Byars .25 .60
13 Bryan Cox .25 .60
14 Irving Fryar .40 1.00
15 Dan Marino 3.20 8.00
16 Barry Foster .25 .60
17 Kevin Greene .14 .35
18 Greg Lloyd .14 .35
19 Neil O'Donnell .40 1.00
20 Rod Woodson .14 .35
21 Steve Beuerlein .14 .35
22 Chuck Cecil .25 .60
23 Randal Hill .25 .60
24 Ricky Proehl .25 .60
25 Eric Swann .40 1.00
26 Troy Aikman 1.60 4.00
27 Emmitt Smith 2.40 6.00
28 Michael Irvin .60 1.50
29 Russell Maryland .25 .60
30 Jay Novacek .40 1.00
31 Jerome Bettis .80 2.00
32 Sean Gilbert .25 .60
33 Todd Lyght .25 .60
34 Chris Martin .25 .60
35 Roman Phifer .25 .60
36 Neal Anderson .25 .60
37 Quinn Early .25 .60
38 Rickey Jackson .25 .60
39 Sam Mills .25 .60
40 Willie Roaf .25 .60
41 Cornelius Bennett .25 .60
42 Jim Kelly .60 1.50
43 Kenneth Davis .25 .60
44 Darryl Talley .25 .60
45 Andre Reed .40 1.00
46 Cris Carter .60 1.50
47 Warren Moon .60 1.50
48 Terry Allen .40 1.00
49 Qadry Ismail .40 1.00
50 Robert Smith .60 1.50
51 Erric Pegram .40 1.00
52 Andre Rison .60 1.50
53 Deion Sanders .80 2.00
54 Jessie Tuggle .25 .60
55 Jeff George .60 1.50
56 Brian Blades .40 1.00
57 Rick Mirer .40 1.00
58 Cortez Kennedy .40 1.00
59 Chris Warren .60 1.50
60 Eugene Robinson .25 .60
61 Reggie Brooks .25 .60
62 Ricky Ervins .25 .60
63 Brian Mitchell .25 .60
64 Ricky Sanders .25 .60
65 Sterling Palmer .25 .60
66 Tim Brown .60 1.50
67 Jeff Hostetler .40 1.00
68 Rocket Ismail .40 1.00
69 Terry McDaniel .25 .60
70 James Jett .25 .60
71 Sterling Sharpe .40 1.00
72 Brett Favre 3.20 8.00
73 Reggie White .60 1.50
74 Terrell Buckley .25 .60
75 Edgar Bennett .40 1.00
76 Jerry Rice 1.60 4.00
77 Steve Young 1.20 3.00
78 Ricky Watters .14 .35
79 Dana Stubblefield .14 .35
80 John Taylor .40 1.00
81 Ronnie Harmon .25 .60
82 Stan Humphries .14 .35
83 Natrone Means .60 1.50
84 Junior Seau .60 1.50
85 Eric Bieniemy .25 .60
86 Dean Biasucci .25 .60
87 Jim Harbaugh .60 1.50
88 Roosevelt Potts .25 .60
89 Scott Radecic .25 .60
90 Rohn Stark .25 .60
91 Eric Metcalf .40 1.00
92 Michael Dean Perry .25 .60
93 Vinny Testaverde .40 1.00
94 Mark Carrier WR .25 .60
95 Michael Jackson .25 .60
96 Marcus Allen .60 1.50
97 Dale Carter .25 .60
98 Neil Smith .25 .60
99 J.J. Birden .25 .60
100 Willie Davis .40 1.00
101 Rodney Hampton .14 .35
102 Mark Jackson .25 .60
103 Dave Meggett .25 .60
104 Jumbo Elliott .25 .60
105 Kenyon Rasheed .25 .60
106 Boomer Esiason .40 1.00
107 Johnny Johnson .25 .60
108 Johnny Mitchell .25 .60
109 Brad Baxter .25 .60
110 Ronnie Lott .40 1.00
111 Derrick Fenner .25 .60
112 David Klingler .25 .60
113 Bruce Pickens .25 .60
114 Harold Green .25 .60
115 Jeff Query .25 .60
116 Leonard Russell .25 .60
117 Drew Bledsoe 1.60 4.00
118 Marv Cook .25 .60
119 Vincent Brisby .14 .35
120 Vincent Brown .25 .60
121 Trace Armstrong .25 .60
122 Curtis Conway .60 1.50
123 Dante Jones .25 .60
124 Tim Worley .25 .60
125 Chris Zorich .25 .60
126 Ronald Moore .25 .60
127 Barry Sanders 3.20 8.00
128 Pat Swilling .25 .60
129 Brett Perriman .25 .60
130 Chris Spielman .25 .60
131 Mark Bavaro .25 .60
132 Fred Barnett .40 1.00
133 Randall Cunningham .60 1.50
134 Herschel Walker .40 1.00
135 Bubby Brister .25 .60
136 Craig Erickson .25 .60
137 Hardy Nickerson .25 .60
138 Demetrius DuBose .25 .60
139 Dan Stryzinski .25 .60
140 Charles Wilson .25 .60
T1 Arizona Cardinals .14 .35
T2 Atlanta Falcons .14 .35
T3 Buffalo Bills .20 .50
T4 Chicago Bears .20 .50
T5 Cincinnati Bengals .14 .35
T6 Cleveland Browns .20 .50
T7 Dallas Cowboys .20 .50
T8 Denver Broncos .20 .50
T9 Detroit Lions .14 .35
T10 Green Bay Packers .20 .50
T11 Houston Oilers .14 .35
T12 Indianapolis Colts .14 .35
T13 Kansas City Chiefs .20 .50
T14 Los Angeles Raiders .20 .50
T15 Los Angeles Rams .14 .35
T16 Miami Dolphins .20 .50
T17 Minnesota Vikings .20 .50
T18 New England Patriots .14 .35
T19 New Orleans Saints .14 .35
T20 New York Giants .20 .50
T21 New York Jets .20 .50
T22 Philadelphia Eagles .14 .35
T23 Pittsburgh Steelers .20 .50
T24 San Diego Chargers .14 .35
T25 San Francisco 49ers .20 .50
T26 Seattle Seahawks .14 .35
T27 Tampa Bay Buccaneers .14 .35
T28 Washington Redskins .20 .50
P3 Jim Kelly Promo 1.00 2.50
P1 Chris Martin Promo .40 1.00
P2 Troy Aikman Promo 1.25 3.00
NNO Warren Moon 3.20 8.00

1995 Pro Mags

Sold in packs of five and produced by Chris Martin Enterprises, this 150-magnet set features borderless color player photos with rounded corners. The magnets, measuring approximately 2 1/8" by 3 3/8," are grouped alphabetically within teams and checklisted below according to team. Some packs also contained a random assortment of insert magnets.

COMPLETE SET (150) 50.00 125.00
1 Larry Centers .20 .50
2 Garrison Hearst .40 1.00
3 Seth Joyner .20 .50
4 Ronald Moore .20 .50
5 Eric Swann .20 .50
6 Chris Doleman .20 .50
7 Jeff George .40 1.00
8 Craig Heyward .20 .50
9 Terance Mathis .40 1.00
10 Jessie Tuggle .20 .50
11 Cornelius Bennett .40 1.00
12 Jim Kelly .50 1.25
13 Andre Reed .40 1.00
14 Bruce Smith .50 1.25
15 Darryl Talley .20 .50
16 Trace Armstrong .20 .50
17 Dante Jones .20 .50
18 Steve Walsh .20 .50
19 Donnell Woolford .20 .50
20 Tim Worley .20 .50
21 Jeff Blake .50 1.25
22 Harold Green .20 .50
23 Carl Pickens .40 1.00
24 Darnay Scott .40 1.00
25 Dan Wilkinson .20 .50
26 Derrick Alexander WR .40 1.00
27 Leroy Hoard .20 .50
28 Antonio Langham .20 .50
29 Vinny Testaverde .40 1.00
30 Eric Turner .40 1.00
31 Troy Aikman 1.20 3.00
32 Michael Irvin .50 1.25
33 Daryl Johnston .40 1.00
34 Russell Maryland .20 .50
35 Emmitt Smith 2.00 5.00
36 Rod Bernstine .20 .50
37 John Elway 2.40 6.00
38 Glyn Milburn .40 1.00
39 Anthony Miller .40 1.00
40 Shannon Sharpe .50 1.25
41 Scott Mitchell .40 1.00
42 Herman Moore .50 1.25
43 Brett Perriman .40 1.00
44 Barry Sanders 2.40 6.00
45 Chris Spielman .20 .50
46 Edgar Bennett .40 1.00
47 Robert Brooks .50 1.25
48 Brett Favre 2.40 6.00
49 Sean Jones .40 1.00
50 Reggie White .50 1.25
51 Gary Brown .20 .50
52 Cody Carlson .20 .50
53 Ernest Givins .20 .50
54 Haywood Jeffires .20 .50
55 Bruce Matthews .20 .50
56 Quentin Coryatt .20 .50
57 Steve Emtman .20 .50
58 Marshall Faulk 1.00 2.50
59 Jim Harbaugh .40 1.00
60 Roosevelt Potts .20 .50
61 Marcus Allen .50 1.25
62 Steve Bono .40 1.00
63 Willie Davis .40 1.00
64 Lake Dawson .20 .50
65 Neil Smith .40 1.00
66 Tim Brown .50 1.25
67 Jeff Hostetler .40 1.00
68 Rocket Ismail .40 1.00
69 James Jett .40 1.00
70 Harvey Williams .40 1.00
71 Jerome Bettis .50 1.25
72 Troy Drayton .20 .50
73 Wayne Gandy .20 .50
74 Sean Gilbert .20 .50
75 Todd Lyght .20 .50
76 Tim Bowens .20 .50
77 Bryan Cox .20 .50
78 Irving Fryar .40 1.00
79 Dan Marino 2.40 6.00
80 Bernie Parmalee .20 .50
81 Terry Allen .50 1.25
82 Cris Carter .50 1.25
83 Qadry Ismail .40 1.00
84 Warren Moon .50 1.25
85 John Randle .40 1.00
86 Bruce Armstrong .20 .50
87 Drew Bledsoe 1.20 3.00
88 Vincent Brisby .20 .50
89 Marion Butts .20 .50
90 Ben Coates .40 1.00
91 Morten Andersen .20 .50
92 Quinn Early .20 .50
93 Jim Everett .20 .50
94 Tyrone Hughes .20 .50
95 Renaldo Turnbull .20 .50
96 Michael Brooks .20 .50
97 Dave Brown .20 .50
98 Jumbo Elliott .20 .50
99 Rodney Hampton .40 1.00
100 Mike Sherrard .20 .50
101 Boomer Esiason .40 1.00
102 Johnny Johnson .20 .50
103 Nick Lowery .20 .50
104 Johnny Mitchell .20 .50
105 Aaron Glenn .20 .50
106 Fred Barnett .40 1.00
107 Bubby Brister .40 1.00
108 Randall Cunningham .50 1.25
109 Charlie Garner .50 1.25
110 Calvin Williams .20 .50
111 Byron Bam Morris .20 .50
112 Barry Foster .20 .50
113 Kevin Greene .40 1.00
114 Neil O'Donnell .40 1.00
115 Rod Woodson .40 1.00
116 Ronnie Harmon .20 .50
117 Stan Humphries .40 1.00
118 Tony Martin .40 1.00
119 Natrone Means .40 1.00
120 Junior Seau .40 1.00
121 William Floyd .40 1.00
122 Jerry Rice 1.20 3.00
123 Deion Sanders .80 2.00
124 Dana Stubblefield .40 1.00
125 Steve Young 1.00 2.50
126 Brian Blades .20 .50
127 Cortez Kennedy .40 1.00
128 Rick Mirer .40 1.00
129 Eugene Robinson .20 .50
130 Chris Warren .40 1.00
131 Trent Dilfer .50 1.25
132 Santana Dotson .20 .50
133 Craig Erickson .40 1.00
134 Thomas Everett .20 .50
135 Errict Rhett .40 1.00
136 Reggie Brooks .20 .50
137 Ricky Ervins .20 .50
138 Darrell Green .20 .50
139 Brian Mitchell .20 .50
140 Heath Shuler .40 1.00
141 Randy Baldwin .20 .50
142 Bob Christian .20 .50
143 Kerry Collins .50 1.25
144 Tyrone Poole .50 1.25
145 Sam Mills .20 .50
146 Steve Beuerlein .40 1.00
147 Cedric Tillman .20 .50
148 Reggie Cobb .20 .50
149 Eugene Chung .20 .50
150 Desmond Howard .40 1.00
NNO Steve Young MVP 1.20 3.00
NNO Emmitt Smith Promo 1.60 4.00

1995 Pro Mags Classics

This 12-card set was produced by Chris Martin Enterpises and features color action player photos over a background of columns with the team logo on a flexible magnet. The magnets were randomly inserted in packs of 1995 Pro Mags at the average rate of one per three packs.

COMPLETE SET (12) 10.00 25.00
CL1 Barry Sanders 2.00 5.00
CL2 Deion Sanders .60 1.50
CL3 Dan Marino 2.00 5.00
CL4 Drew Bledsoe 1.00 2.50
CL5 Marcus Allen .40 1.00
CL6 Jerome Bettis .40 1.00
CL7 John Elway 2.00 5.00
CL8 Jerry Rice 1.00 2.50
CL9 Emmitt Smith 1.60 4.00
CL10 Steve Young .80 2.00
CL11 Marshall Faulk .40 1.00
CL12 Troy Aikman 1.00 2.50

1995 Pro Mags In The Zone

This 12-card In The Zone set features borderless color action player photos on a flexible magnet. The magnets were randomly inserted in packs of 1995 Pro Mags at the rate of 1:3 packs.

COMPLETE SET (12) 8.00 20.00
1 Troy Aikman 1.00 2.50
2 Drew Bledsoe 1.00 2.50
3 John Elway 2.00 5.00
4 Brett Favre 2.00 5.00
5 Jeff Hostetler .30 .75
6 Stan Humphries .30 .75
7 Dan Marino 2.00 5.00
8 Jim Kelly .50 1.25
9 Warren Moon .50 1.25
10 Neil O'Donnell .30 .75
11 Rick Mirer .40 1.00
12 Steve Young .80 2.00

1995 Pro Mags Rookies

This 12-magnet set features top rookies from the 1994 NFL Draft. Each measures approximately 2-1/8" by 3-3/8" and includes a color player photo with the player's name printed in gold foil near the bottom of the card.

COMPLETE SET (12) 4.00 10.00
1 Trent Dilfer .60 1.50
2 Heath Shuler .40 1.00
3 John Thierry .30 .75
4 Wayne Gandy .30 .75
5 Errict Rhett .50 1.25
6 David Palmer .40 1.00
7 Andre Coleman .30 .75
8 Lake Dawson .40 1.00
9 Marshall Faulk 1.60 4.00
10 Dan Wilkinson .30 .75
11 Greg Hill .40 1.00
12 Willie McGinest .40 1.00

1995 Pro Mags Superhero Jumbos

These three jumbo Pro Magnets were released one per box, as well as via mail order for $6 each directly from Chris Martin Enterprises, Inc. The offer could be found in packs of the 1995 Pro Magnets product. The jumbos feature an artist's rendering of the player, measure approximately 3-3/4" by 7" and have rounded corners.

COMPLETE SET (3) 8.00 20.00
1 Jerome Bettis 2.00 5.00
2 John Elway 4.80 12.00
3 Warren Moon 2.00 5.00

1995 Pro Mags Teams

This set of magnets was released as a 5-card promotional set. Each unnumbered magnet features color photos of three top players from one team along with an embossed team logo.

COMPLETE SET (5) 8.00 20.00
1 Chargers 1.00 2.50
2 Cowboys 2.40 6.00
3 Dolphins 3.20 8.00
4 49ers 2.00 5.00
5 Steelers 1.00 2.50

1996 Pro Mags

Chris Martin Enterprises issued this set through five-magnet packs with 24-packs per box. Each magnet featured a borderless color player photo with rounded corners. The magnets, measuring approximately 2 1/8" by 3 3/8," are grouped alphabetically within teams below. Some hobby packs contained randomly inserted Draft Day Future Stars magnets, while retail packs had randomly inserted Destination All-Pro magnets.

COMPLETE SET (100) 40.00 100.00
1 Troy Aikman 1.00 2.50
2 Michael Irvin .50 1.25
3 Emmitt Smith 1.60 4.00
4 Deion Sanders .60 1.50
5 Jay Novacek .40 1.00
6 Jerry Rice 1.00 2.50
7 Steve Young .80 2.00
8 J.J. Stokes .50 1.25
9 William Floyd .40 1.00
10 Merton Hanks .25 .60
11 Greg Lloyd .40 1.00
12 Rod Woodson .50 1.25
13 Kordell Stewart .80 2.00
14 Yancey Thigpen .50 1.25
15 Charles Johnson .40 1.00
16 Richmond Webb .25 .60
17 Eric Green .25 .60
18 Bernie Parmalee .25 .60
19 Dan Marino 2.00 5.00
20 O.J. McDuffie .40 1.00
21 Brett Favre 2.00 5.00
22 Reggie White .50 1.25
23 Robert Brooks .50 1.25
24 Edgar Bennett .40 1.00
25 Marcus Allen .50 1.25
26 Tamarick Vanover .40 1.00
27 Lake Dawson .40 1.00
28 Neil Smith .40 1.00
29 Steve Bono .40 1.00
30 Harvey Williams .40 1.00
31 Tim Brown .50 1.25
32 Jeff Hostetler .40 1.00
33 Drew Bledsoe 1.00 2.50
34 Vincent Brisby .40 1.00
35 Curtis Martin .80 2.00
36 Rashaan Salaam .40 1.00
37 Erik Kramer .40 1.00
38 Curtis Conway .40 1.00
39 Kerry Collins .50 1.25
40 Sam Mills .25 .60
41 Mark Carrier WR .25 .60
42 Dave Brown .25 .60
43 Rodney Hampton .40 1.00
44 Tyrone Wheatley .50 1.25
45 Vinny Testaverde .40 1.00
46 Andre Rison .50 1.25
47 Eric Turner .25 .60
48 Michael Jackson .40 1.00
49 Mark Brunell 1.00 2.50
50 Jeff Lageman .25 .60
51 Roman Phifer .25 .60
52 Isaac Bruce .50 1.25
53 Rodney Peete .25 .60
54 Ricky Watters .50 1.25
55 Calvin Williams .25 .60
56 Warren Moon .50 1.25
57 Cris Carter .50 1.25
58 David Palmer .25 .60
59 Scott Mitchell .40 1.00
60 Barry Sanders 2.00 5.00
61 Herman Moore .40 1.00
62 Brett Perriman .40 1.00
63 Jim Kelly .50 1.25
64 Bruce Smith .40 1.00
65 Bryce Paup .40 1.00
66 Junior Seau .50 1.25
67 Stan Humphries .40 1.00
68 Andre Coleman .25 .60
69 Tony Martin .50 1.25
70 Terry Allen .50 1.25
71 Heath Shuler .40 1.00
72 John Elway 2.00 5.00
73 Terrell Davis 2.00 5.00
74 Mike Pritchard .25 .60
75 Neil O'Donnell .40 1.00
76 Kyle Brady .25 .60
77 Jim Harbaugh .50 1.25
78 Marshall Faulk .50 1.25
79 Zack Crockett .25 .60
80 Quentin Coryatt .25 .60
81 Jeff George .50 1.25
82 Morten Andersen .25 .60
83 Eric Metcalf .40 1.00
84 Joey Galloway .60 1.50
85 Rick Mirer .40 1.00
86 Chris Warren .40 1.00
87 Ray Zellars .25 .60
88 Eric Allen .25 .60
89 Jim Everett .25 .60
90 Jeff Blake .50 1.25
91 Carl Pickens .40 1.00
92 Ki-Jana Carter .40 1.00
93 Larry Centers .40 1.00
94 Garrison Hearst .50 1.25
95 Trent Dilfer .50 1.25
96 Errict Rhett .40 1.00
97 Hardy Nickerson .25 .60
98 Alvin Harper .25 .60
99 Steve McNair .80 2.00
100 Haywood Jeffires .25 .60

1996 Pro Mags Destination All-Pro

These magnets were randomly inserted in 1996 Chris Martin Enterprises Pro Mags retail packs. The odds of pulling one of the inserts was 1:4 packs.

COMPLETE SET (6) 10.00 25.00
PB1 Jim Harbaugh 1.20 3.00
PB2 Curtis Martin 1.60 4.00
PB3 Yancey Thigpen .80 2.00
PB4 Brett Favre 3.20 8.00
PB5 Jerry Rice 2.00 5.00
PB6 Barry Sanders 3.20 8.00

1996 Pro Mags Die-Cut Magnets

Chris Martin Enterprises produced these fifteen Die-Cut Magnets packaged one per cello pack. Each measures roughly 3 1/2" by 3 1/2." The magnets are unnumbered and listed below alphabetically.

COMPLETE SET (15) 10.00 25.00
1 Troy Aikman .75 2.00
2 Deion Sanders .60 1.50
3 Emmitt Smith 1.25 3.00
4 Jerry Rice 1.00 2.50
5 Steve Young .75 2.00
6 Kordell Stewart .50 1.25
7 Dan Marino 1.50 4.00
8 Brett Favre 1.50 4.00
9 Marcus Allen .60 1.50
10 Drew Bledsoe .60 1.50
11 Barry Sanders 1.00 2.50
12 Marshall Faulk .60 1.50
13 John Elway 1.25 3.00
14 Rashaan Salaam .40 1.00
15 Jeff Hostetler .40 1.00
16 Keyshawn Johnson .40 1.00

1996 Pro Mags Draft Day Future Stars

These magnets were randomly inserted in 1996 Chris Martin Enterprises Pro Mags hobby packs. The odds of pulling one of the inserts was 1:4 packs.

COMPLETE SET (6) 6.00 15.00
1 Kevin Hardy .60 1.50
2 Eddie George 3.20 8.00
3 Keyshawn Johnson 2.00 5.00
4 Tim Biakabutuka 1.00 2.50
5 Lawrence Phillips .60 1.50
6 Alex Molden .60 1.50

1996 Pro Mags 12

Produced by Chris Martin Enterprises, these 12-magnets contain a player photo against a metallic foil background. They were issued one per cello pack and measure approximately 3 1/2" by 2 1/4."

COMPLETE SET (12) 4.00 10.00
1 Tim Brown .20 .50
2 John Elway .80 2.00
3 Marshall Faulk .30 .75
4 Dan Marino .80 2.00
5 Curtis Martin .40 1.00
6 Rashaan Salaam .10 .30
7 Barry Sanders .80 2.00
8 Emmitt Smith .80 2.00
9 Neil Smith .10 .30
10 Reggie White .20 .50
11 Rod Woodson .10 .30
12 Steve Young .30 .75

1997 Pro Magnets

This set of magnets was produced by Crown Pro and distributed through retail chains. Each magnet features a color player photo on the front printed on silver foil stock. The cards measure roughly 2 1/2" by 3 1/2" and feature rounded corners and blankbacks. The original retail price was $1.49 per magnet.

S1 Troy Aikman 1.50 4.00
S2 Emmitt Smith 2.50 6.00
S3 Brett Favre 2.50 6.00
S4 Barry Sanders 2.00 5.00
S6 Dan Marino 2.50 6.00

1997 Pro Magnets 4x5

This set of magnets was produced by Crown Pro and distributed through retail chains. Each magnet features a larger color player photo on the front along with a smaller photo and a team logo. The magnets measure roughly 3 1/2" by 4" and feature rounded corners and blankbacks. The original retail price was $1.99 per magnet.

PF1 Brett Favre 2.00 5.00
PF2 Barry Sanders 1.50 4.00
PF3 Emmitt Smith 2.00 5.00
PF4 Dan Marino 2.00 5.00
PF7 Mark Brunell .75 2.00

1998 Pro Magnets

This set of magnets was produced by Crown Pro and distributed through retail chains. Each magnet features a color player photo on the front and a colorful team name and logo on the back. The cards measure roughly 2 1/2" by 3 1/2" and feature rounded corners.

COMPLETE SET (7) 10.00 25.00
1 Brett Favre 2.50 6.00
2 Dan Marino 2.50 6.00
3 Troy Aikman 1.25 3.00
4 Emmitt Smith 2.00 5.00
7 Barry Sanders 1.50 4.00
8 John Elway 2.00 5.00
9 Terrell Davis 1.00 2.50

1995 ProMint Marino Promo

ProMint released this Dan Marino Promo "gold" card. It was printed on front and back fully in gold foil with a 22 Karat Gold notation at the bottom of the cardfront. The back includes a write-up, the card number 1, and the Promo designation.

1 Dan Marino 6.00 15.00

1988 Pro Set Test

This eight-card standard-size set was reportedly produced as a give-away to show interested parties what the new "Pro Set" cards were going to be like. They were produced in limited quantities and merely given away primarily at the National Candy show in Phoenix. The only front photo that was the same in the actual set was Jerry Rice. This set is also distinguishable in that the backs are oriented vertically rather than horizontally as the regular set.

COMPLETE SET (8) 175.00 350.00
1 Dan Marino 75.00 150.00
2 Jerry Rice 30.00 80.00
3 Eric Dickerson 8.00 20.00
4 Reggie White 15.00 40.00
5 Mike Singletary 8.00 20.00
6 Frank Minnifield 6.00 15.00
7 Phil Simms 8.00 20.00
8 Jim Kelly 15.00 40.00

1989 Pro Set Promos

Cards 445, 455; and 463 were planned for inclusion in the Pro Set second series but were withdrawn before mass production began. Note, however, that Thomas Sanders was included in the set but as number 446. The Santa Claus card was mailed out to dealers and NFL dignitaries in December 1989. The Super Bowl Show card was given out to attendees at the show in New Orleans in late January 1990. All of these cards are standard size and utilize the 1989 Pro Set design.

COMPLETE SET (5) 40.00 100.00
445 Thomas Sanders 8.00 20.00
455 Blair Bush 8.00 20.00
463 James Lofton 10.00 25.00
1989 Santa Claus 15.00 40.00
NNO Super Bowl Show I .75 2.00

1989 Pro Set Test Designs

These five Randall Cunningham standard-size cards are the test designs for the 1990 Pro Set football cards. As tests, they were produced in very small quantities. It seems that all cards in this five-card set were printed at the same time and in the same (small) quantities. The five variations are basically experiments with and without borders and different color combinations. Horizontally oriented backs have a close-up photograph of player, statistical and biographical information, card number, and the Pro Set logo in a box enclosed in a white border. Player's name and personal statistics appear in reverse-out lettering in a colored band across the top of the card.

COMPLETE SET (5) 100.00 250.00
315A Randall Cunningham (No name or team designated on card front; borderless; vertical logo) 20.00 50.00
315B Randall Cunningham (No name or team designated on card front; silver border; vertical logo) 20.00 50.00
315C Randall Cunningham (Name and team designated on card front; borderless; horizontal logo) 20.00 50.00
315D Randall Cunningham (Name and team designated on card front; black border; horizontal logo) 20.00 50.00
315E Randall Cunningham (Name and team designated on card front; gray border; horizontal logo) 20.00 50.00

1989 Pro Set

Pro Set entered the football card market with a three series offering for 1989. A first series consisted of 440 cards followed by a 100-card second series offering. A Final Update set consisted of 21 cards for a total of 561 standard-size full-color cards. The backs are horizontal with a small photo, statistics and highlights. The first series is ordered numerically by teams and alphabetically within teams. The second series, issued five cards per Series II pack, includes first-round draft picks (485-515) from the previous spring's college draft and cards numbered 516-540 are "Pro Set Prospects". The second series cards differ in design by having a red border. The Final Update set includes Pro Set Prospects (542-549) and several cards (550-561) of players that were traded since the start of the season. These cards were also part of the second series offering. Complete Final Update sets were offered direct from Pro Set for $2.00 plus 50 Pro Set Play Book points. Rookie Cards include Troy Aikman, Flipper Anderson, Don Beebe, Brian Blades, Tim Brown, Cris Carter, Michael Irvin, Keith Jackson, Dave Meggett, Eric Metcalf, Anthony Miller, Jay Novacek, Rodney Peete, Andre Rison, Mark Rypien, Barry Sanders, Deion Sanders, Sterling Sharpe, Neil Smith, Chris Spielman, John Taylor, Derrick Thomas, Thurman Thomas and Rod Woodson. Card No. 47A William Perry, was pulled early in the initial production run creating a short print. He was replaced by Ron Morris (47B). A single print by design, the Pete Rozelle commemorative card was randomly inserted in one out of every 200 first series packs. The set is considered complete without either the Perry or the Rozelle cards.

COMPLETE SET (561) 10.00 25.00
COMP.SERIES 1 (440) 3.00 6.00
COMP.SERIES 2 (100) 10.00 20.00
COMP.FINAL FACT.SET (21) .75 2.00
1 Stacey Bailey .04 .10
2 Aundray Bruce RC .06 .15
3 Rick Bryan .04 .10
4 Bobby Butler .04 .10
5 Scott Case RC .04 .10
6 Tony Casillas .06 .15
7 Floyd Dixon .04 .10
8 Rick Donnelly .04 .10
9 Bill Fralic .06 .15
10 Mike Gann .04 .10
11 Mike Kenn .04 .10
12 Chris Miller RC .10 .25
13 John Rade .04 .10
14 Gerald Riggs UER .06 .15
15 John Settle RC .04 .10
16 Marion Campbell CO .04 .10
17 Cornelius Bennett .06 .15
18 Derrick Burroughs .04 .10
19 Shane Conlan .04 .10
20 Ronnie Harmon .06 .15
21 Kent Hull RC .06 .15
22 Jim Kelly .20 .50
23 Mark Kelso .06 .15
24 Pete Metzelaars .06 .15
25 Scott Norwood RC .06 .15
26 Andre Reed .10 .25
27 Fred Smerlas .04 .10
28 Bruce Smith .10 .25
29 Leonard Smith .04 .10
30 Art Still .04 .10
31 Darryl Talley .06 .15
32 Thurman Thomas RC .50 1.25
33 Will Wolford RC .06 .15
34 Marv Levy CO .06 .15
35 Neal Anderson .06 .15
36 Kevin Butler .04 .10
37 Jim Covert .06 .15
38 Richard Dent .06 .15
39 Dave Duerson .04 .10
40 Dennis Gentry .04 .10
41 Dan Hampton .06 .15
42 Jay Hilgenberg .04 .10
43 Dennis McKinnon UER .04 .10
44 Jim McMahon .06 .15
45 Steve McMichael .06 .15
46 Brad Muster RC .06 .15
47A William Perry SP 6.00 15.00
47B Ron Morris RC .04 .10
48 Ron Rivera .04 .10
49 Vestee Jackson RC .04 .10
50 Mike Singletary .06 .15
51 Mike Tomczak .06 .15
52 Keith Van Horne RC .04 .10
53A Mike Ditka CO .10 .25
53B Mike Ditka CO HOF .10 .25
54 Lewis Billups .04 .10
55 James Brooks .06 .15
56 Eddie Brown .04 .10
57 Jason Buck RC .04 .10
58 Boomer Esiason .06 .15
59 David Fulcher .06 .15
60A Rodney Holman ERR RC .06 .15
60B Rodney Holman COR RC .10 .25
61 Reggie Williams .06 .15
62 Joe Kelly RC .04 .10
63 Tim Krumrie .04 .10
64 Tim McGee .06 .15
65 Max Montoya .04 .10
66 Anthony Munoz .06 .15
67 Jim Skow RC .04 .10
68 Eric Thomas RC .04 .10
69 Leon White RC .04 .10
70 Ickey Woods RC .20 .50
71 Carl Zander .04 .10
72 Sam Wyche CO .04 .10
73 Brian Brennan .04 .10
74 Earnest Byner .06 .15
75 Hanford Dixon .04 .10
76 Mike Pagel .04 .10
77 Bernie Kosar .06 .15
78 Reggie Langhorne RC .06 .15
79 Kevin Mack .06 .15
80 Clay Matthews .06 .15
81 Gerald McNeil .04 .10
82 Frank Minnifield .04 .10
83 Cody Risien .04 .10
84 Webster Slaughter .06 .15
85 Felix Wright .04 .10
86 Bud Carson CO UER .04 .10
87 Bill Bates .06 .15
88 Kevin Brooks .04 .10
89 Michael Irvin RC .60 1.50
90 Jim Jeffcoat .04 .10
91 Ed Too Tall Jones .06 .15
92 Eugene Lockhart RC .04 .10
93 Nate Newton RC .06 .15
94 Danny Noonan RC .04 .10
95 Steve Pelluer .04 .10
96 Herschel Walker .06 .15
97 Everson Walls .04 .10
98 Jimmy Johnson CO RC .10 .25
99 Keith Bishop .04 .10
100A John Elway DRAFT 2.50 6.00
100B John Elway TRADE .75 2.00
101 Simon Fletcher RC .06 .15
102 Mike Harden .04 .10
103 Mike Horan .04 .10
104 Mark Jackson .06 .15
105 Vance Johnson .06 .15
106 Rulon Jones .04 .10
107 Clarence Kay .04 .10
108 Karl Mecklenburg .06 .15
109 Ricky Nattiel .04 .10
110 Steve Sewell RC .04 .10
111 Dennis Smith .06 .15
112 Gerald Willhite .04 .10
113 Sammy Winder .04 .10
114 Dan Reeves CO .06 .15
115 Jim Arnold .04 .10
116 Jerry Ball RC .06 .15
117 Bennie Blades RC .04 .10
118 Lomas Brown .06 .15
119 Mike Cofer .04 .10
120 Garry James .04 .10
121 James Jones FB .04 .10
122 Chuck Long .04 .10
123 Pete Mandley .04 .10
124 Eddie Murray .04 .10
125 Chris Spielman RC .10 .25
126 Dennis Gibson .04 .10
127 Wayne Fontes CO .04 .10
128 John Anderson .04 .10
129 Brent Fullwood RC .04 .10
130 Mark Cannon RC .04 .10
131 Tim Harris .04 .10
132 Mark Lee .04 .10
133 Don Majkowski RC .06 .15
134 Mark Murphy .04 .10
135 Brian Noble .04 .10
136 Ken Ruettgers RC .04 .10
137 Johnny Holland .04 .10
138 Randy Wright .04 .10
139 Lindy Infante CO .04 .10
140 Steve Brown .04 .10
141 Ray Childress .06 .15
142 Jeff Donaldson .04 .10
143 Ernest Givins .06 .15
144 John Grimsley .04 .10
145 Alonzo Highsmith .06 .15
146 Drew Hill .06 .15
147 Robert Lyles RC .04 .10
148 Bruce Matthews RC .30 .75
149 Warren Moon .10 .25
150 Mike Munchak .06 .15
151 Allen Pinkett RC .06 .15
152 Mike Rozier .06 .15
153 Tony Zendejas .04 .10
154 Jerry Glanville CO .04 .10
155 Albert Bentley .04 .10
156 Dean Biasucci .04 .10
157 Duane Bickett .04 .10
158 Bill Brooks .06 .15
159 Chris Chandler RC .40 1.00
160 Pat Beach .04 .10
161 Ray Donaldson .04 .10
162 Jon Hand .04 .10
163 Chris Hinton .04 .10
164 Rohn Stark .04 .10
165 Fredd Young .04 .10
166 Ron Meyer CO .04 .10
167 Lloyd Burruss .04 .10
168 Carlos Carson .04 .10
169 Deron Cherry .06 .15
170 Irv Eatman .04 .10
171 Dino Hackett .04 .10
172 Steve DeBerg .06 .15
173 Albert Lewis .04 .10
174 Nick Lowery .04 .10
175 Bill Maas .04 .10
176 Christian Okoye .06 .15
177 Stephone Paige .06 .15
178 Mark Adickes RC .04 .10
179 Kevin Ross RC .06 .15
180 Neil Smith RC .20 .50
181 M. Schottenheimer CO .04 .10
182 Marcus Allen .10 .25
183 Tim Brown RC .60 1.50
184 Willie Gault .06 .15
185 Bo Jackson .12 .30
186 Howie Long .10 .25
187 Vann McElroy .04 .10
188 Matt Millen .06 .15
189 Don Mosebar RC .04 .10
190 Bill Pickel .04 .10
191 Jerry Robinson UER .04 .10
192 Jay Schroeder .04 .10
193A Stacey Toran .04 .10
193B Stacey Toran .40 1.00
193C Stacey Toran 1.25 3.00
194 Mike Shanahan CO RC .06 .15
195 Greg Bell .04 .10
196 Ron Brown .04 .10
197 Aaron Cox RC .04 .10
198 Henry Ellard .10 .25
199 Jim Everett .06 .15
200 Jerry Gray .04 .10
201 Kevin Greene .10 .25
202 Pete Holohan .04 .10
203 LeRoy Irvin .06 .15
204 Mike Lansford .04 .10
205 Tom Newberry RC .04 .10
206 Mel Owens .04 .10
207 Jackie Slater .06 .15
208 Doug Smith .04 .10
209 Mike Wilcher .04 .10
210 John Robinson CO .04 .10
211 John Bosa .04 .10
212 Mark Brown .04 .10
213 Mark Clayton .06 .15
214A Ferrell Edmonds ERR RC .20 .50
214B Ferrell Edmonds COR RC .04 .10
215 Roy Foster .04 .10
216 Lorenzo Hampton .04 .10
217 Jim C.Jensen UER RC .04 .10
218 William Judson .04 .10
219 Eric Kumerow RC .04 .10
220 Dan Marino .75 2.00
221 John Offerdahl .04 .10
222 Fuad Reveiz .04 .10
223 Reggie Roby .04 .10
224 Brian Sochia .04 .10
225 Don Shula CO RC .10 .25
226 Alfred Anderson .04 .10
227 Joey Browner .04 .10
228 Anthony Carter .06 .15
229 Chris Doleman .06 .15
230 Hassan Jones RC .04 .10
231 Steve Jordan .04 .10
232 Tommy Kramer .06 .15
233 Carl Lee RC .04 .10
234 Kirk Lowdermilk RC .04 .10
235 Randall McDaniel RC .50 1.25
236 Doug Martin .04 .10
237 Keith Millard .04 .10
238 Darrin Nelson .04 .10
239 Jesse Solomon .04 .10
240 Scott Studwell .04 .10
241 Wade Wilson .06 .15
242 Gary Zimmerman .10 .25
243 Jerry Burns CO .04 .10
244 Bruce Armstrong RC .06 .15
245 Raymond Clayborn .04 .10
246 Reggie Dupard .04 .10
247 Tony Eason .04 .10
248 Sean Farrell .04 .10
249 Doug Flutie .30 .75
250 Brent Williams RC .04 .10
251 Roland James .04 .10
252 Ronnie Lippett .04 .10
253 Fred Marion .04 .10
254 Larry McGrew RC .04 .10
255 Stanley Morgan .06 .15
256 Johnny Rembert RC .04 .10
257 John Stephens RC .04 .10
258 Andre Tippett .10 .25
259 Garin Veris .04 .10
260A Raymond Berry CO .06 .15
260B Raymond Berry CO HOF .06 .15
261 Morten Andersen .06 .15
262 Hoby Brenner .04 .10
263 Stan Brock .04 .10
264 Brad Edelman .04 .10
265 Jumpy Geathers .04 .10
266A Bobby Hebert Passers .20 .50
266B Bobby Hebert Passes .06 .15
267 Craig Heyward RC .10 .25
268 Lonzell Hill .04 .10
269 Dalton Hilliard .04 .10
270 Rickey Jackson .06 .15
271 Steve Korte RC .04 .10
272 Eric Martin .04 .10
273 Rueben Mayes .04 .10
274 Sam Mills .06 .15
275 Brett Perriman RC .10 .25
276 Pat Swilling .06 .15
277 John Tice .04 .10
278 Jim Mora CO .04 .10
279 Eric Moore RC .04 .10
280 Carl Banks .06 .15
281 Mark Bavaro .06 .15
282 Maurice Carthon .04 .10
283 Mark Collins RC .06 .15
284 Erik Howard .04 .10
285 Terry Kinard .04 .10
286 Sean Landeta .04 .10
287 Lionel Manuel .06 .15
288 Leonard Marshall .06 .15
289 Joe Morris .06 .15
290 Bart Oates .04 .10
291 Phil Simms .06 .15
292 Lawrence Taylor .10 .25
293 Bill Parcells CO RC .06 .15
294 Dave Cadigan RC .04 .10
295 Kyle Clifton RC .04 .10
296 Alex Gordon .04 .10
297 James Hasty RC .04 .10
298 Johnny Hector .04 .10
299 Bobby Humphery .06 .15
300 Pat Leahy .04 .10
301 Marty Lyons .04 .10
302 Reggie McElroy RC .06 .15
303 Erik McMillan RC .04 .10
304 Freeman McNeil .06 .15
305 Ken O'Brien .06 .15
306 Pat Ryan .04 .10
307 Mickey Shuler .04 .10
308 Al Toon .06 .15
309 Jo Jo Townsell .04 .10
310 Roger Vick .04 .10
311 Joe Walton CO .04 .10
312 Jerome Brown .06 .15
313 Keith Byars .06 .15
314 Cris Carter RC .60 1.50
315 Randall Cunningham .15 .40
316 Terry Hoage .04 .10
317 Wes Hopkins .04 .10
318 Keith Jackson RC .10 .25
319 Mike Quick .06 .15
320 Mike Reichenbach .04 .10
321 Dave Rimington .04 .10
322 John Teltschik .04 .10
323 Anthony Toney .04 .10
324 Andre Waters .06 .15
325 Reggie White .10 .25
326 Luis Zendejas .04 .10
327 Buddy Ryan CO .06 .15
328 Robert Awalt .04 .10
329 Tim McDonald RC .06 .15
330 Roy Green .06 .15
331 Neil Lomax .06 .15
332 Cedric Mack .04 .10
333 Stump Mitchell .04 .10
334 Niko Noga RC .04 .10
335 Jay Novacek RC .10 .25
336 Freddie Joe Nunn .04 .10
337 Luis Sharpe .04 .10
338 Val Sikahema .04 .10
339 J.T. Smith .04 .10
340 Ron Wolfley .04 .10
341 Gene Stallings CO RC .06 .15
342 Gary Anderson K .04 .10
343 Bubby Brister RC .10 .25
344 Dermontti Dawson RC .20 .50
345 Thomas Everett RC .04 .10
346 Delton Hall RC .04 .10
347 Bryan Hinkle RC .04 .10
348 Merril Hoge RC .06 .15
349 Tunch Ilkin RC .04 .10
350 Aaron Jones RC .04 .10
351 Louis Lipps .06 .15
352 David Little .04 .10
353 Hardy Nickerson RC .10 .25
354 Rod Woodson RC .40 1.00
355A Chuck Noll CO ERR RC .06 .15
355B Chuck Noll CO COR RC .06 .15
356 Gary Anderson RB .06 .15
357 Rod Bernstine RC .06 .15
358 Gill Byrd .04 .10
359 Vencie Glenn .04 .10
360 Dennis McKnight .04 .10
361 Lionel James .04 .10
362 Mark Malone .04 .10
363A Anthony Miller RC .10 .25
363B Anthony Miller RC .10 .25
364 Ralf Mojsiejenko .04 .10
365 Leslie O'Neal .06 .15
366 Jamie Holland RC .04 .10
367 Lee Williams .04 .10
368 Dan Henning CO .04 .10
369 Harris Barton RC .04 .10
370 Michael Carter .04 .10
371 Mike Cofer RC .04 .10
372 Roger Craig .10 .25
373 Riki Ellison RC .04 .10
374 Jim Fahnhorst .04 .10
375 John Frank .04 .10
376 Jeff Fuller .04 .10
377 Don Griffin .04 .10
378 Charles Haley .10 .25
379 Ronnie Lott .06 .15
380 Tim McKyer .04 .10
381 Joe Montana .75 2.00
382 Tom Rathman .06 .15
383 Jerry Rice .60 1.50
384 John Taylor RC .20 .50
385 Keena Turner .04 .10
386 Michael Walter .04 .10
387 Bubba Paris RC .04 .10
388 Steve Young .40 1.00
389 George Seifert CO RC .06 .15
390 Brian Blades RC .10 .25
391A B.Bosworth Seattle .12 .30
391B B.Bosworth Seahawks .06 .15
392 Jeff Bryant .04 .10
393 Jacob Green .06 .15
394 Norm Johnson .04 .10
395 Dave Krieg .06 .15
396 Steve Largent .10 .25
397 Bryan Millard RC .04 .10
398 Paul Moyer .04 .10
399 Joe Nash .04 .10
400 Rufus Porter RC .04 .10
401 Eugene Robinson RC .10 .25
402 Bruce Scholtz .04 .10
403 Kelly Stouffer RC .04 .10
404A Curt Warner 1455 .50 1.25
404B Curt Warner 6074 .06 .15
405 John L. Williams .04 .10
406 Tony Woods RC .06 .15
407 David Wyman RC .04 .10
408 Chuck Knox CO .06 .15
409 Mark Carrier RC .10 .25
410 Randy Grimes RC .04 .10
411 Paul Gruber RC .06 .15
412 Harry Hamilton .04 .10
413 Ron Holmes .04 .10
414 Donald Igwebuike .04 .10
415 Dan Turk .04 .10
416 Ricky Reynolds .04 .10
417 Bruce Hill RC .04 .10
418 Lars Tate .04 .10
419 Vinny Testaverde .12 .30
420 James Wilder .04 .10
421 Ray Perkins CO .04 .10
422 Jeff Bostic .04 .10
423 Kelvin Bryant .04 .10
424 Gary Clark .10 .25
425 Monte Coleman .04 .10
426 Darrell Green .06 .15
427 Joe Jacoby .06 .15
428 Jim Lachey .06 .15
429 Charles Mann .04 .10
430 Dexter Manley .06 .15
431 Darryl Grant .04 .10
432 Mark May RC .06 .15
433 Art Monk .06 .15
434 Mark Rypien RC .10 .25
435 Ricky Sanders .06 .15
436 Alvin Walton RC .04 .10
437 Don Warren .04 .10
438 Jamie Morris .04 .10
439 Doug Williams .06 .15
440 Joe Gibbs CO RC .10 .25
441 Marcus Cotton RC .04 .10
442 Joel Williams .04 .10
443 Joe Devlin .04 .10
444 Robb Riddick .04 .10
445 William Perry .06 .15
446 Thomas Sanders RC .04 .10
447 Brian Blados .04 .10
448 Cris Collinsworth .06 .15
449 Stanford Jennings .04 .10
450 Barry Krauss UER .04 .10
451 Ozzie Newsome .06 .15
452 Mike Oliphant RC .04 .10
453 Tony Dorsett .10 .25
454 Bruce McNorton .04 .10
455 Eric Dickerson .06 .15
456 Keith Bostic .04 .10
457 Sam Clancy RC .04 .10
458 Jack Del Rio RC .10 .25
459 Mike Webster .06 .15
460 Bob Golic .04 .10
461 Otis Wilson .04 .10
462 Mike Haynes .06 .15
463 Greg Townsend .06 .15
464 Mark Duper .06 .15
465 E.J. Junior .06 .15
466 Troy Stradford .04 .10
467 Mike Merriweather .06 .15
468 Irving Fryar .10 .25
469 Vaughan Johnson RC .06 .15
470 Pepper Johnson .06 .15
471 Gary Reasons RC .04 .10
472 Perry Williams RC .04 .10
473 Wesley Walker .06 .15
474 Anthony Bell RC .06 .15
475 Earl Ferrell .04 .10
476 Craig Wolfley .04 .10
477 Billy Ray Smith .04 .10
478A Jim McMahon NOTR .12 .30

478B Jim McMahon TR .06 .15
478C Jim McMahon TR 15.00 40.00
479 Eric Wright .04 .10
480A Earnest Byner NOTR .06 .15
480B Earnest Byner TR .12 .30
480C Earnest Byner TR 15.00 40.00
480D Earnest Byner NOTR 75.00 150.00
481 Russ Grimm .06 .15
482 Wilber Marshall .06 .15
483A Gerald Riggs NOTR .06 .15
483B Gerald Riggs TR .12 .30
483C Gerald Riggs TR 15.00 40.00
483D Gerald Riggs NOTR 75.00 150.00
484 Brian Davis RC .04 .10
485 Shawn Collins RC .04 .10
486 Deion Sanders RC .60 1.50
487 Trace Armstrong RC .06 .15
488 Donnell Woolford RC .06 .15
489 Eric Metcalf RC .10 .25
490 Troy Aikman RC 4.00 10.00
491 Steve Walsh RC .06 .15
492 Steve Atwater RC .10 .25
493 Bobby Humphrey RC .06 .15
494 Barry Sanders RC 3.00 8.00
495 Tony Mandarich RC .06 .15
496 David Williams RC .04 .10
497 Andre Rison UER RC .40 1.00
498 Derrick Thomas RC .60 1.50
499 Cleveland Gary RC .04 .10
500 Bill Hawkins RC .04 .10
501 Louis Oliver RC .06 .15
502 Sammie Smith RC .04 .10
503 Hart Lee Dykes RC .04 .10
504 Wayne Martin RC .04 .10
505 Brian Williams OL RC .04 .10
506 Jeff Lageman RC .06 .15
507 Eric Hill RC .06 .15
508 Joe Wolf RC .04 .10
509 Timm Rosenbach RC .06 .15
510 Tom Ricketts RC .04 .10
511 Tim Worley RC .04 .10
512 Burt Grossman RC .06 .15
513 Keith DeLong RC .04 .10
514 Andy Heck RC .04 .10
515 Broderick Thomas RC .10 .25
516 Don Beebe RC .10 .25
517 James Thornton RC .04 .10
518 Eric Kattus .04 .10
519 Bruce Kozerski RC .04 .10
520 Brian Washington RC .04 .10
521 Rodney Peete RC .20 .50
522 Erik Affholter RC .04 .10
523 Anthony Dilweg RC .04 .10
524 O'Brien Alston .04 .10
525 Mike Elkins RC .04 .10
526 Jonathan Hayes RC .04 .10
527 Terry McDaniel RC .04 .10
528 Frank Stams RC .04 .10
529 Darryl Ingram RC .04 .10
530 Henry Thomas .04 .10
531 Eric Coleman DB RC .04 .10
532 Sheldon White RC .04 .10
533 Eric Allen RC .10 .25
534 Robert Drummond .04 .10
535A Gizmo Williams RC bal 15.00 40.00
535B Gizmo Williams RC .10 .25
535C Gizmo Williams RC .06 .15
536 Billy Joe Tolliver RC .06 .15
537 Daniel Stubbs RC .04 .10
538 Wesley Walls RC .15 .40
539A James Jefferson ERR RC .12 .30
539B James Jefferson COR RC .04 .10
540 Tracy Rocker .04 .10
541 Art Shell CO .06 .15
542 Lemuel Stinson RC .04 .10
543 Tyrone Braxton UER RC .04 .10
544 David Treadwell RC .04 .10
545 Flipper Anderson RC .10 .25
546 Dave Meggett RC .10 .25
547 Lewis Tillman RC .04 .10
548 Carnell Lake RC .10 .25
549 Marion Butts RC .06 .15
550 Sterling Sharpe RC .40 1.00
551 Ezra Johnson .04 .10
552 Clarence Verdin RC .04 .10
553 Mervyn Fernandez RC .04 .10
554 Ottis Anderson .06 .15
555 Gary Hogeboom .04 .10
556 Paul Palmer TR .04 .10
557 Jesse Solomon TR .04 .10
558 Chip Banks TR .06 .15
559 Steve Pelluer TR .04 .10
560 Darrin Nelson TR .04 .10
561 Herschel Walker TR .06 .15
CC1 Pete Rozelle COMM SP .20 .50

1989 Pro Set Announcers

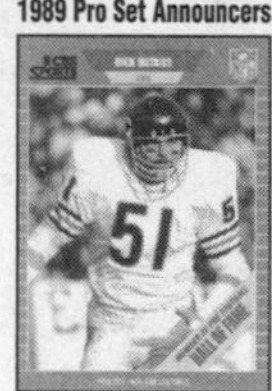

The 1989 Pro Set Announcers set contains 30 standard-size cards. The fronts have color photos bordered in red with TV network logos; otherwise, they are similar in appearance to the regular 1989 Pro Set cards. One announcer card was included in each Series II pack. Although Dan Jiggetts was listed as card number 21 on early checklists, he was replaced by Verne Lundquist when the cards were actually released. Those announcers who had previously played in the NFL were depicted with a photo from their active playing career.

COMPLETE SET (30) 1.25 3.00
1 Dan Dierdorf .08 .20
2 Frank Gifford .15 .40
3 Al Michaels .04 .10
4 Pete Axthelm .04 .10
5 Chris Berman .08 .20
6 Tom Jackson .08 .20
7 Mike Patrick .08 .20
8 John Saunders .04 .10
9 Joe Theismann .08 .20
10 Steve Sabol .04 .10
11 Jack Buck .04 .10
12 Terry Bradshaw .30 .75
13 James Brown ANN .08 .20
14 Dan Fouts .08 .20
15 Dick Butkus .15 .40
16 Irv Cross .04 .10
17 Brent Musburger .04 .10
18 Ken Stabler .15 .40
19 Dick Stockton .04 .10
20 Hank Stram .08 .20
21 Verne Lundquist .04 .10
22 Will McDonough .04 .10
23 Bob Costas .04 .10
24 Dick Enberg .04 .10
25 Joe Namath .30 .75
26 Bob Trumpy .04 .10
27 Merlin Olsen .08 .20
28 Ahmad Rashad .08 .20
29 O.J. Simpson .08 .20
30 Bill Walsh .08 .20

1989 Pro Set Super Bowl Logos

This 23-card standard-size set contains a card for each Super Bowl played up through the production of the 1989 Pro Set regular set. These cards were inserted with the regular player cards in the wax packs of the 1989 Pro Set. The cards are unnumbered.

COMPLETE SET (23) 1.25 3.00
COMMON CARD (1-23) .07 .20

1989-90 Pro Set Super Bowl XXIV Binder

This set was produced by Pro Set for GTE and issued in a special folder inside plastic sheets. Each ticket holder at the Super Bowl game in New Orleans received a set. Later Pro Set offered their surplus of these sets to the public at 20.00 per set, one to a customer; they apparently ran out quickly. The cards are standard size and feature solely members of the San Francisco 49ers and Denver Broncos. The cards are distinguished from the regular issue Pro Set cards (even though they have the same card numbers) by their silver and gold top and bottom borders on each card front.

COMPLETE SET (40) 6.00 15.00
99 Keith Bishop .07 .20
100 John Elway 2.00 5.00
101 Simon Fletcher .07 .20
103 Mike Horan .07 .20
104 Mark Jackson .10 .30
105 Vance Johnson .10 .30
107 Clarence Kay .07 .20
108 Karl Mecklenburg .10 .30
109 Ricky Nattiel .07 .20
110 Steve Sewell .07 .20
111 Dennis Smith .07 .20
113 Sammy Winder .07 .20
114 Dan Reeves CO .10 .30
369 Harris Barton .07 .20
370 Michael Carter .07 .20
371 Mike Cofer .07 .20
372 Roger Craig .10 .30
374 Jim Fahnhorst .07 .20
377 Don Griffin .07 .20
378 Charles Haley .10 .30
379 Ronnie Lott .20 .50
380 Tim McKyer .07 .20
381 Joe Montana 2.50 6.00
382 Tom Rathman .10 .30
383 Jerry Rice 1.25 3.00
384 John Taylor .10 .30
385 Keena Turner .07 .20
386 Michael Walter .07 .20
387 Bubba Paris .07 .20
388 Steve Young .75 2.00
389 George Seifert CO .10 .30
479 Eric Wright .07 .20
492 Steve Atwater .07 .20
493 Bobby Humphrey .07 .20
537 Daniel Stubbs .07 .20
543 Tyrone Braxton .07 .20
544 David Treadwell .07 .20
NNO AFC Logo .07 .20
NNO NFC Logo .07 .20
NNO Superdome .07 .20

1990 Pro Set Draft Day

This four-card standard-size set was issued by Pro Set on the date of the 1990 NFL draft. The cards feature action shots in the 1990 Pro Set design of potential number one draft picks with a yellow triangular shaped area in the lower right that reads "Number 1 Pick." The backs of the cards have a typical Pro Set format with one half of the card being a full-color portrait of the player and the other half consisting of biographical information. The fourth card in the set (Jeff George Colts) is not listed below but featured in the 1990 Pro Set regular issue checklist since it was also inserted into 1990 Pro Set first series packs. An additional blank backed version of each of the four cards surfaced much later that included a bronze colored top and bottom border and was printed without the yellow triangular area.

COMPLETE SET (3) 5.00 12.00
669A Jeff George Falcons 2.00 5.00
669B Jeff George Patriots 2.00 5.00
669C Keith McCants 1.25 3.00

1990 Pro Set

This set consists of 801 standard-size cards issued in three series. The first series contains 377 cards, the second series 392 and a 32-card Final Update. The set was issued in 14-card packs. The fronts have striking color action photos and team colored borders on the top and bottom edges. Cards 1-29 are special selections from Pro Set commemorating events or leaders from the previous year. Pro Set also produced and randomly inserted 10,000 Lombardi Trophy hologram cards, creating quite a hobby sensation. Speculation is that one special Lombardi card was inserted in every tenth case. These attractive cards were hand serial numbered out of 10,000 (printed as 10M) and feature the words "Collector Edition" on the back. An "Owner Edition" version, as printed on the cardback (not serial numbered), exists but surfaced long after Pro Set closed the business. Additional blanback, blankfront and even panels and strips of the Lomdardi trophy card have surfaced, but we've chosen to catalog just the original version. Due to a contractual dispute, the Pro Bowl card of Eric Dickerson (No. 338) was withdrawn early creating a short print, but quantities of this card were released after Pro Set closed and sold off old inventory. The set price below does not include any of the tougher variation cards: 1A Barry Sanders, 72A Dexter Manley and 75A Cody Risien. The 1990 Pro Set Final Update series was issued in a special mail-away offer. The series included a special Ronnie Lott Stay in School card and the 1990 Pro Set Rookie of the Year card which introduced the 1991 Pro Set design.

COMPLETE SET (801) 15.00 40.00
COMP.SERIES 1 (377) 8.00 20.00
COMP.SERIES 2 (392) 8.00 20.00
COMP.FINAL SERIES (32) 2.00 5.00
COMP.FINAL FACT. (32) 2.00 5.00
1A Ba.Sanders ROY Hawaii 60.00 150.00
1B Barry Sanders ROY .25 .60
2A Joe Montana POY 3521 ERR .20 .50
2B Joe Montana POY 3130 COR .20 .50
3 Lindy Infante COY UER .02 .05
4 Warren Moon MOY UER .08 .25
5 Keith Millard D-POY .02 .05
6 Derrick Thomas D-ROY .08 .25
7 Ottis Anderson CB POY .04 .10
8 Joe Montana LL UER .20 .50
9 Christian Okoye LL .02 .05
10 Thurman Thomas LL .08 .25
11 Mike Cofer LL .02 .05
12 Dalton Hilliard LL UER .02 .05
13 Sterling Sharpe LL .08 .25
14 Rich Camarillo LL .02 .05
15A Walter Stanley LL ERR 8 .20 .50
15B Walter Stanley LL COR 86 .02 .05
16 Rod Woodson LL .08 .25
17 Felix Wright LL .02 .05
18A Chris Doleman LL ERR .20 .50
18B Chris Doleman LL COR .20 .50
19A Andre Ware RC no draft .04 .10
19B Andre Ware RC draft .04 .10
20A Mo Elewonibi RC .02 .05
20B Mo Elewonibi RC .02 .05
21A Percy Snow no draft .20 .50
21B Percy Snow draft .02 .05
22A Anthony Thompson RC .02 .05
22B A.Thompson RC draft .02 .05
23 Buck Buchanan HOF .02 .05
24 Bob Griese HOF .04 .10
25A Franco Harris HOF ERR .20 .50
25B Franco Harris HOF COR .04 .10
26 Ted Hendricks HOF .02 .05
27A Jack Lambert HOF ERR .20 .50
27B Jack Lambert HOF COR .20 .50
28 Tom Landry HOF .04 .10
29 Bub St.Clair HOF .02 .05
30 Aundray Bruce UER .02 .05
31 Tony Casillas UER .02 .05
32 Shawn Collins .02 .05
33 Marcus Cotton .02 .05
34 Bill Fralic .02 .05
35 Chris Miller .04 .10
36 Deion Sanders UER .20 .50
37 John Settle .02 .05
38 Jerry Glanville CO .02 .05
39 Cornelius Bennett .04 .10
40 Jim Kelly .08 .25
41 Mark Kelso UER .02 .05
42 Scott Norwood .02 .05
43 Nate Odomes RC .04 .10
44 Scott Radecic .02 .05
45 Jim Ritcher RC .02 .05
46 Leonard Smith .02 .05
47 Darryl Talley .02 .05
48 Marv Levy CO .02 .05
49 Neal Anderson .04 .10
50 Kevin Butler .02 .05
51 Jim Covert .02 .05
52 Richard Dent .04 .10
53 Jay Hilgenberg .02 .05
54 Steve McMichael .04 .10
55 Ron Morris .02 .05
56 John Roper .02 .05
57 Mike Singletary .04 .10
58 Keith Van Horne .02 .05
59A Mike Ditka CO LL 10.00 20.00
59B Mike Ditka CO SL .30 .75
60 Lewis Billups .02 .05
61 Eddie Brown .02 .05
62 Jason Buck .02 .05
63A Rickey Dixon ERR RC .20 .50
63B Rickey Dixon COR RC .20 .50
64 Tim McGee .02 .05
65 Eric Thomas .02 .05
66 Ickey Woods .02 .05
67 Carl Zander .02 .05
68A Sam Wyche CO ERR .20 .50
68B Sam Wyche CO COR .20 .50
69 Paul Farren RC .02 .05
70 Thane Gash RC .02 .05
71 David Grayson .02 .05
72 Bernie Kosar .04 .10
73 Reggie Langhorne .02 .05
74 Eric Metcalf .08 .25
75A Ozzie Newsome ERR .20 .50
75B Ozzie Newsome COR .20 .50
75C Cody Risien SP .20 .50
76 Felix Wright .02 .05
77 Bud Carson CO .02 .05
78 Troy Aikman .30 .75
79 Michael Irvin .08 .25
80 Jim Jeffcoat .02 .05
81 Crawford Ker .02 .05
82 Eugene Lockhart .02 .05
83 Kelvin Martin RC .02 .05
84 Ken Norton RC .08 .25
85 Jimmy Johnson CO .04 .10
86 Steve Atwater .02 .05
87 Tyrone Braxton .02 .05
88 John Elway .50 1.25
89 Simon Fletcher .02 .05
90 Ron Holmes .02 .05
91 Bobby Humphrey .02 .05
92 Vance Johnson .02 .05
93 Ricky Nattiel .02 .05
94 Dan Reeves CO .02 .05
95 Jim Arnold .02 .05
96 Jerry Ball .02 .05
97 Bennie Blades .02 .05
98 Lomas Brown .02 .05
99 Michael Cofer .02 .05
100 Richard Johnson .02 .05
101 Eddie Murray .02 .05
102 Barry Sanders .50 1.25
103 Chris Spielman .08 .25
104 William White RC .02 .05
105 Eric Williams RC .02 .05
106 Wayne Fontes CO UER .02 .05
107 Brent Fullwood .02 .05
108 Ron Hallstrom RC .02 .05
109 Tim Harris .02 .05
110A Johnny Holland ERR NN .20 .50
110B Johnny Holland COR .20 .50
111A Perry Kemp ERR .20 .50
111B Perry Kemp COR .20 .50
112 Don Majkowski .02 .05
113 Mark Murphy .02 .05
114A Sterling Sharpe ERR Gle .08 .25
114B Sterling Sharpe COR Chi .20 .50
115 Ed West RC .02 .05
116 Lindy Infante CO .02 .05
117 Steve Brown .02 .05
118 Ray Childress .02 .05
119 Ernest Givins .04 .10
120 John Grimsley .02 .05
121 Alonzo Highsmith .02 .05
122 Drew Hill .02 .05
123 Bubba McDowell .02 .05
124 Dean Steinkuhler .02 .05
125 Lorenzo White .04 .10
126 Tony Zendejas .02 .05
127 Jack Pardee CO .02 .05
128 Albert Bentley .02 .05
129 Dean Biasucci .02 .05
130 Duane Bickett .02 .05
131 Bill Brooks .02 .05
132 Jon Hand .02 .05
133 Mike Prior .02 .05
134A Andre Rison NOTR .08 .25
134B Andre Rison TR .08 .25
134C Andre Rison TR Lud/back .08 .25
135 Rohn Stark .02 .05
136 Donnell Thompson .02 .05
137 Clarence Verdin .02 .05
138 Fredd Young .02 .05
139 Ron Meyer CO .02 .05
140 John Alt RC .02 .05
141 Steve DeBerg .02 .05
142 Irv Eatman .02 .05
143 Dino Hackett .02 .05
144 Nick Lowery .02 .05
145 Bill Maas .02 .05
146 Stephone Paige .02 .05
147 Neil Smith .08 .25
148 Marty Schottenheimer CO .02 .05
149 Steve Beuerlein .04 .10
150 Tim Brown .08 .25
151 Mike Dyal RC .02 .05
152A Mervyn Fernandez ERR .30 .75
152B Mervyn Fernandez COR .30 .75
153 Willie Gault .04 .10
154 Bob Golic .02 .05
155 Bo Jackson .10 .30
156 Don Mosebar .02 .05
157 Steve Smith .02 .05
158 Greg Townsend .02 .05
159 Bruce Wilkerson RC .02 .05
160 Steve Wisniewski .04 .10
161A Art Shell CO ERR .20 .50
161B Art Shell CO COR 3.00 8.00
161C Art Shell CO COR 4.00 10.00
162 Flipper Anderson .02 .05
163 Greg Bell UER .02 .05
164 Henry Ellard .04 .10
165 Jim Everett .04 .10
166 Jerry Gray .02 .05
167 Kevin Greene .04 .10
168 Pete Holohan .02 .05
169 Larry Kelm RC .02 .05
170 Tom Newberry .02 .05
171 Vince Newsome RC .02 .05
172 Irv Pankey .02 .05
173 Jackie Slater .02 .05
174 Fred Strickland RC .02 .05
175 Mike Wilcher UER .02 .05
176 John Robinson CO UER .02 .05
177 Mark Clayton .04 .10
178 Roy Foster .02 .05
179 Harry Galbreath RC .02 .05
180 Jim C. Jensen .02 .05
181 Dan Marino .50 1.25
182 Louis Oliver .02 .05
183 Sammie Smith .02 .05
184 Brian Sochia .02 .05
185 Don Shula CO .04 .10
186 Joey Browner .02 .05
187 Anthony Carter .04 .10
188 Chris Doleman .02 .05
189 Steve Jordan .02 .05
190 Carl Lee .02 .05
191 Randall McDaniel .05 .15
192 Mike Merriweather .02 .05
193 Keith Millard .02 .05
194 Al Noga .02 .05
195 Scott Studwell .02 .05
196 Henry Thomas .02 .05
197 Herschel Walker .04 .10
198 Wade Wilson .04 .10
199 Gary Zimmerman .04 .10
200 Jerry Burns CO .02 .05
201 Vincent Brown RC .02 .05
202 Hart Lee Dykes .02 .05
203 Sean Farrell .02 .05
204A Fred Marion belt 40.00 100.00
204B Fred Marion no belt .02 .05
205 Stanley Morgan UER .02 .05
206 Eric Sievers RC .02 .05
207 John Stephens .02 .05
208 Andre Tippett .02 .05
209 Rod Rust CO .02 .05
210A Morten Andersen wht .20 .50
210B Morten Andersen blk .20 .50
211 Brad Edelman .02 .05
212 John Fourcade .02 .05
213 Dalton Hilliard .02 .05
214 Rickey Jackson .04 .10
215 Vaughan Johnson .02 .05
216A Eric Martin wht .20 .50
216B Eric Martin blk .20 .50
217 Sam Mills .04 .10
218 Pat Swilling UER .04 .10
219 Frank Warren RC .02 .05
220 Jim Wilks .02 .05
221A Jim Mora CO wht .20 .50
221B Jim Mora CO blk .20 .50
222 Raul Allegre .02 .05
223 Carl Banks .02 .05
224 John Elliott .02 .05
225 Erik Howard .02 .05
226 Pepper Johnson .02 .05
227 Leonard Marshall UER .02 .05
228 Dave Meggett .04 .10
229 Bart Oates .02 .05
230 Phil Simms .04 .10
231 Lawrence Taylor .08 .25
232 Bill Parcells CO .04 .10
233 Troy Benson .02 .05
234 Kyle Clifton UER .02 .05
235 Johnny Hector .02 .05
236 Jeff Lageman .02 .05
237 Pat Leahy .02 .05
238 Freeman McNeil .02 .05
239 Ken O'Brien .02 .05
240 Al Toon .04 .10
241 Jo Jo Townsell .02 .05
242 Bruce Coslet CO .02 .05
243 Eric Allen .02 .05
244 Jerome Brown .02 .05
245 Keith Byars .02 .05
246 Cris Carter .20 .50
247 Randall Cunningham .08 .25
248 Keith Jackson .04 .10
249 Mike Quick .02 .05
250 Clyde Simmons .02 .05
251 Andre Waters .02 .05
252 Reggie White .08 .25
253 Buddy Ryan CO .02 .05
254 Rich Camarillo .02 .05
255 Earl Ferrell .02 .05
256 Roy Green .04 .10
257 Ken Harvey RC .08 .25
258 Ernie Jones RC .02 .05
259 Tim McDonald .02 .05
260 Timm Rosenbach UER .02 .05
261 Luis Sharpe .02 .05
262 Vai Sikahema .02 .05
263 J.T. Smith .02 .05
264 Ron Wolfley UER .02 .05
265 Joe Bugel CO .02 .05
266 Gary Anderson K .02 .05
267 Bubby Brister .02 .05
268 Merril Hoge .02 .05
269 Carnell Lake .02 .05
270 Louis Lipps .04 .10
271 David Little .02 .05
272 Greg Lloyd .08 .25
273 Keith Willis .02 .05
274 Tim Worley .02 .05
275 Chuck Noll CO .04 .10
276 Marion Butts .04 .10
277 Gill Byrd .02 .05
278 Vencie Glenn UER .02 .05
279 Burt Grossman .02 .05
280 Gary Plummer .02 .05
281 Billy Ray Smith .02 .05
282 Billy Joe Tolliver .02 .05
283 Dan Henning CO .02 .05
284 Harris Barton .02 .05
285 Michael Carter .02 .05
286 Mike Cofer .02 .05
287 Roger Craig .04 .10
288 Don Griffin .02 .05
289A Charles Haley ERR 4 fum 4.00 10.00
289B Charles Haley COR 5 fum .30 .75
290 Pierce Holt RC .02 .05
291 Ronnie Lott .04 .10
292 Guy McIntyre .02 .05
293 Joe Montana .50 1.25
294 Tom Rathman .02 .05
295 Jerry Rice .30 .75
296 Jesse Sapolu RC .02 .05
297 John Taylor .04 .10
298 Michael Walter .02 .05
299 George Seifert CO .04 .10
300 Jeff Bryant .02 .05
301 Jacob Green .02 .05
302 Norm Johnson UER .02 .05
303 Bryan Millard .02 .05
304 Joe Nash .02 .05
305 Eugene Robinson .02 .05
306 John L. Williams .02 .05
307 David Wyman .02 .05
308 Chuck Knox CO .02 .05
309 Mark Carrier WR .08 .25
310 Paul Gruber .02 .05
311 Harry Hamilton .02 .05
312 Bruce Hill .02 .05
313 Donald Igwebuike .02 .05
314 Kevin Murphy .02 .05
315 Ervin Randle .02 .05
316 Mark Robinson .02 .05
317 Lars Tate .02 .05
318 Vinny Testaverde .04 .10
319A Ray Perkins CO ERR NN .30 .75
319B Ray Perkins CO COR .02 .05
320 Earnest Byner .02 .05
321 Gary Clark .08 .25
322 Darryl Grant .02 .05
323 Darrell Green .04 .10
324 Jim Lachey .02 .05
325 Charles Mann .02 .05
326 Wilber Marshall .02 .05
327 Ralf Mojsiejenko .02 .05
328 Art Monk .04 .10
329 Gerald Riggs .04 .10
330 Mark Rypien .04 .10
331 Ricky Sanders .02 .05
332 Alvin Walton .02 .05
333 Joe Gibbs CO .04 .10
334 Aloha Stadium .02 .05
335 Brian Blades PB .02 .05
336 James Brooks PB .02 .05
337 Shane Conlan PB .02 .05
338A Eric Dickerson PB SP 2.00 5.00
338B Lud Denny Promo 125.00 250.00
339 Ray Donaldson PB .02 .05
340 Ferrell Edmunds PB .02 .05
341 Boomer Esiason PB .02 .05
342 David Fulcher PB .02 .05
343A Chris Hinton PB No Trad 3.00 8.00
343B Chris Hinton PB Trade .02 .05
343C Chris Hinton PB Trade
344 Rodney Holman PB .02 .05
345 Kent Hull PB .02 .05
346 Tunch Ilkin PB .02 .05
347 Mike Johnson PB .02 .05
348 Greg Kragen PB .02 .05
349 Dave Krieg PB .04 .10
350 Albert Lewis PB .02 .05
351 Howie Long PB .04 .10
352 Bruce Matthews PB .02 .05
353 Clay Matthews PB .02 .05
354 Erik McMillan PB .02 .05
355 Karl Mecklenburg PB .02 .05
356 Anthony Miller PB .02 .05
357 Frank Minnifield PB .02 .05
358 Max Montoya PB .02 .05
359 Warren Moon PB .08 .25
360 Mike Munchak PB .02 .05
361 Anthony Munoz PB .02 .05
362 John Offerdahl PB .02 .05
363 Christian Okoye PB .02 .05
364 Leslie O'Neal PB .02 .05
365 Rufus Porter PB UER .02 .05
366 Andre Reed PB .04 .10
367 Johnny Rembert PB .02 .05
368 Reggie Roby PB .02 .05
369 Kevin Ross PB .02 .05
370 Webster Slaughter PB .02 .05
371 Bruce Smith PB .04 .10
372 Dennis Smith PB .02 .05
373 Derrick Thomas PB .04 .10
374 Thurman Thomas PB .08 .25
375 David Treadwell PB .02 .05
376 Lee Williams PB .02 .05
377 Rod Woodson PB .04 .10
378 Bud Carson CO PB .02 .05
379 Eric Allen PB .02 .05
380 Neal Anderson PB .04 .10
381 Jerry Ball PB .02 .05
382 Joey Browner PB .02 .05
383 Rich Camarillo PB .02 .05
384 Mark Carrier WR PB .02 .05
385 Roger Craig PB .04 .10
386A R.Cunningham PB small .20 .50
386B R.Cunningham PB large .20 .50
387 Chris Doleman PB .02 .05
388 Henry Ellard PB .02 .05
389 Bill Fralic PB .02 .05
390 Brent Fullwood PB .02 .05
391 Jerry Gray PB .02 .05
392 Kevin Greene PB .04 .10
393 Tim Harris PB .02 .05
394 Jay Hilgenberg PB .02 .05
395 Dalton Hilliard PB .02 .05
396 Keith Jackson PB .04 .10
397 Vaughan Johnson PB .02 .05
398 Steve Jordan PB .02 .05
399 Carl Lee PB .02 .05
400 Ronnie Lott PB .04 .10
401 Don Majkowski PB .02 .05
402 Charles Mann PB .02 .05
403 Randall McDaniel PB .04 .10
404 Tim McDonald PB .02 .05
405 Guy McIntyre PB .02 .05
406 Dave Meggett PB .02 .05
407 Keith Millard PB .02 .05
408 Joe Montana PB .20 .50
409 Eddie Murray PB .02 .05
410 Tom Newberry PB .02 .05
411 Jerry Rice PB .20 .50
412 Mark Rypien PB .02 .05
413 Barry Sanders PB .25 .60
414 Luis Sharpe PB .02 .05
415 Sterling Sharpe PB .02 .05
416 Mike Singletary PB .04 .10
417 Jackie Slater PB .02 .05
418 Doug Smith PB .02 .05
419 Chris Spielman PB .02 .05
420 Pat Swilling PB .02 .05
421 John Taylor PB .02 .05
422 Lawrence Taylor PB .04 .10
423 Reggie White PB .04 .10
424 Ron Wolfley PB .02 .05
425 Gary Zimmerman PB .04 .10
426 John Robinson CO PB .02 .05
427 Scott Case UER .02 .05
428 Mike Kenn .02 .05
429 Mike Gann .02 .05
430 Tim Green RC .02 .05
431 Michael Haynes RC .08 .25
432 Jessie Tuggle UER RC .02 .05
433 John Rade .02 .05
434 Andre Rison .08 .25
435 Don Beebe .04 .10
436 Ray Bentley .02 .05
437 Shane Conlan .02 .05
438 Kent Hull .02 .05
439 Pete Metzelaars .02 .05
440 Andre Reed UER .08 .25
441 Frank Reich .08 .25
442 Leon Seals RC .02 .05
443 Bruce Smith .08 .25
444 Thurman Thomas .08 .25
445 Will Wolford .02 .05
446 Trace Armstrong .02 .05
447 Mark Bortz RC .02 .05
448 Tom Thayer RC .02 .05
449A Dan Hampton DE .20 .50
449B Dan Hampton DT 4.00 10.00
450 Shaun Gayle RC .02 .05
451 Dennis Gentry .02 .05
452 Jim Harbaugh .08 .25
453 Vestee Jackson .02 .05
454 Brad Muster .02 .05
455 William Perry .04 .10
456 Ron Rivera .02 .05
457 James Thornton .02 .05
458 Mike Tomczak .04 .10
459 Donnell Woolford .02 .05
460 Eric Ball .02 .05
461 James Brooks .04 .10
462 David Fulcher .02 .05
463 Boomer Esiason .04 .10
464 Rodney Holman .02 .05
465 Bruce Kozerski .02 .05
466 Tim Krumrie .02 .05
467 Anthony Munoz .04 .10
468 Brian Blados .02 .05
469 Mike Baab .02 .05
470 Brian Brennan .02 .05
471 Raymond Clayborn .02 .05
472 Mike Johnson .02 .05
473 Kevin Mack .02 .05
474 Clay Matthews .04 .10
475 Frank Minnifield .02 .05
476 Gregg Rakoczy RC .02 .05
477 Webster Slaughter .04 .10
478 James Dixon .02 .05
479 Robert Awalt .02 .05
480 Dennis McKinnon UER .02 .05
481 Danny Noonan .02 .05
482 Jesse Solomon .02 .05
483 Daniel Stubbs UER .02 .05
484 Steve Walsh .04 .10
485 Michael Brooks RC .02 .05
486 Mark Jackson .02 .05
487 Greg Kragen .02 .05
488 Ken Lanier RC .02 .05
489 Karl Mecklenburg .02 .05
490 Steve Sewell .02 .05
491 Dennis Smith .02 .05
492 David Treadwell .02 .05
493 Michael Young RC .02 .05
494 Robert Clark RC .02 .05
495 Dennis Gibson .02 .05
496A Kevin Glover RC C/G .20 .50
496B Kevin Glover RC C .02 .05
497 Mel Gray .04 .10
498 Rodney Peete .04 .10
499 Dave Brown DB .02 .05
500 Jerry Holmes .02 .05
501 Chris Jacke .02 .05
502 Alan Veingrad .02 .05
503 Mark Lee .02 .05
504 Tony Mandarich .02 .05
505 Brian Noble .02 .05
506 Jeff Query .02 .05
507 Ken Ruettgers .02 .05
508 Patrick Allen .02 .05
509 Curtis Duncan .02 .05
510 William Fuller .04 .10
511 Haywood Jeffires RC .08 .25
512 Sean Jones .04 .10
513 Terry Kinard .02 .05
514 Bruce Matthews .04 .10
515 Gerald McNeil .02 .05
516 Greg Montgomery RC .02 .05
517 Warren Moon .08 .25
518 Mike Munchak .04 .10
519 Allen Pinkett .02 .05
520 Pat Beach .02 .05
521 Eugene Daniel .02 .05
522 Kevin Call .02 .05
523 Ray Donaldson .02 .05
524 Jeff Herrod RC .02 .05
525 Keith Taylor .02 .05
526 Jack Trudeau .02 .05
527 Deron Cherry .02 .05
528 Jeff Donaldson .02 .05
529 Albert Lewis .02 .05
530 Pete Mandley .02 .05
531 Chris Martin RC .02 .05
532 Christian Okoye .02 .05
533 Steve Pelluer .02 .05
534 Kevin Ross .02 .05
535 Dan Saleaumua .02 .05
536 Derrick Thomas .08 .25
537 Mike Webster .04 .10
538 Marcus Allen .08 .25
539 Greg Bell .02 .05
540 Thomas Benson RC .02 .05
541 Ron Brown .02 .05
542 Scott Davis .02 .05
543 Rikl Ellison .02 .05
544 Jamie Holland .02 .05
545 Howie Long .08 .25
546 Terry McDaniel .02 .05
547 Max Montoya .02 .05
548 Jay Schroeder .02 .05
549 Lionel Washington .02 .05
550 Robert Delpino .02 .05
551 Bobby Humphery .02 .05
552 Mike Lansford .02 .05
553 Michael Stewart RC .02 .05
554 Doug Smith .02 .05
555 Curt Warner .02 .05
556 Alvin Wright RC .02 .05
557 Jeff Cross .02 .05
558 Jeff Dellenbach RC .02 .05
559 Mark Duper .04 .10
560 Ferrell Edmunds .02 .05
561 Tim McKyer .02 .05
562 John Offerdahl .02 .05
563 Reggie Roby .02 .05
564 Pete Stoyanovich .02 .05
565 Alfred Anderson .02 .05
566 Ray Berry .02 .05
567 Rick Fenney .02 .05
568 Rich Gannon RC .60 1.50
569 Tim Irwin .02 .05
570 Hassan Jones .02 .05
571 Cris Carter .20 .50
572 Kirk Lowdermilk .02 .05
573 Reggie Rutland RC .02 .05
574 Ken Stills .02 .05
575 Bruce Armstrong .02 .05
576 Irving Fryar .04 .10
577 Roland James .02 .05
578 Robert Perryman .02 .05
579 Cedric Jones RC .02 .05
580 Steve Grogan .04 .10
581 Johnny Rembert .02 .05
582 Ed Reynolds .02 .05
583 Brent Williams .02 .05
584 Marc Wilson .02 .05
585 Hoby Brenner .02 .05
586 Stan Brock .02 .05
587 Jim Dombrowski RC .02 .05
588 Joel Hilgenberg RC .02 .05
589 Robert Massey .02 .05
590 Floyd Turner .02 .05
591 Ottis Anderson .04 .10
592 Mark Bavaro .02 .05
593 Maurice Carthon .02 .05
594 Eric Dorsey RC .02 .05
595 Myron Guyton .02 .05
596 Jeff Hostetler RC .08 .25
597 Sean Landeta .02 .05
598 Lionel Manuel .02 .05
599 Odessa Turner RC .02 .05
600 Perry Williams .02 .05
601 James Hasty .02 .05
602 Erik McMillan .02 .05
603 Alex Gordon UER .02 .05
604 Ron Stallworth .02 .05
605 Byron Evans RC .02 .05
606 Ron Heller RC .02 .05
607 Wes Hopkins .02 .05
608 Mickey Shuler UER .02 .05
609 Seth Joyner .04 .10
610 Jim McMahon .04 .10
611 Mike Pitts .02 .05
612 Izel Jenkins RC .02 .05
613 Anthony Bell .02 .05
614 David Galloway .02 .05
615 Eric Hill .02 .05
616 Cedric Mack .02 .05
617 Freddie Joe Nunn .02 .05
618 Tootie Robbins .02 .05
619 Tom Tupa RC .02 .05
620 Joe Wolf .02 .05
621 Dermontti Dawson .08 .20
622 Thomas Everett .02 .05
623 Tunch Ilkin .02 .05
624 Hardy Nickerson .04 .10
625 Gerald Williams RC .02 .05
626 Rod Woodson .08 .25
627A Rod Bernstine TE .20 .50
627B Rod Bernstine RB .02 .05
628 Courtney Hall .02 .05
629 Ronnie Harmon .04 .10
630A Anthony Miller WR .08 .25
630B Anthony Miller WR-KR .04 .10
631 Joe Phillips RC .02 .05
632A Leslie O'Neal LB-DE .05 .15
632B Leslie O'Neal LB .04 .10
633A David Richards ERR RC .05 .15
633B David Richards G RC .05 .15
634 Mark Vlasic .02 .05
635 Lee Williams .02 .05
636 Chet Brooks .02 .05
637 Keena Turner .02 .05
638 Kevin Fagan RC .02 .05
639 Brent Jones RC .08 .25
640 Matt Millen .04 .10
641 Bubba Paris .02 .05
642 Bill Romanowski RC .40 1.00
643 Fred Smerlas UER .02 .05
644 Dave Waymer .02 .05
645 Steve Young .20 .50
646 Brian Blades .04 .10
647 Andy Heck .02 .05
648 Dave Krieg .04 .10
649 Rufus Porter .02 .05
650 Kelly Stouffer .02 .05
651 Tony Woods .02 .05
652 Gary Anderson RB .02 .05
653 Reuben Davis .02 .05
654 Randy Grimes .02 .05
655 Ron Hall .02 .05
656 Eugene Marve .02 .05
657A Curt Jarvis ERR .20 .50
657B Curt Jarvis COR 4.00 10.00
658 Ricky Reynolds .02 .05
659 Broderick Thomas .02 .05
660 Jeff Bostic .02 .05
661 Todd Bowles RC .40 1.00
662 Ravin Caldwell .02 .05
663 Russ Grimm UER .04 .10
664 Joe Jacoby .02 .05
665 Mark May .02 .05
666A Walter Stanley .02 .05
666B Steven Young VP Promo 2.00 5.00
667 Don Warren .02 .05
668 Stan Humphries RC .08 .25
669A Jeff George Illinois SP .40 1.00
669B Jeff George RC .20 .50
670 Blair Thomas RC .04 .10
671 Cortez Kennedy UER RC .20 .50
672 Keith McCants RC .02 .05
673 Junior Seau RC .50 1.25
674 Mark Carrier DB RC .08 .25
675 Andre Ware .04 .10
676 Chris Singleton UER RC .02 .05
677 Richmond Webb RC .02 .05
678 Ray Agnew RC .02 .05
679 Anthony Smith RC .02 .05
680 James Francis RC .02 .05
681 Percy Snow RC .02 .05
682 Renaldo Turnbull RC .02 .05
683 Lamar Lathon RC .04 .10
684 James Williams DB RC .02 .05
685 Emmitt Smith RC 2.00 5.00
686 Tony Bennett RC .08 .25
687 Darrell Thompson RC .02 .05
688 Steve Broussard RC .02 .05
689 Eric Green RC .04 .10
690 Ben Smith RC .02 .05
691 Bern Brostek UER RC .02 .05
692 Rodney Hampton RC .08 .25
693 Dexter Carter RC .02 .05
694 Rob Moore RC .20 .50
695 Alexander Wright RC .02 .05
696 Darion Conner RC .04 .10
697 Reggie Rembert UER RC .02 .05
698A Terry Wooden ERR RC .20 .50
698B Terry Wooden COR RC .02 .05
699 Reggie Cobb RC .02 .05
700 Anthony Thompson .02 .05
701 Fred Washington RC .02 .05
702 Ron Cox RC .02 .05
703 Robert Blackmon RC .02 .05
704 Dan Owens RC .02 .05
705 Anthony Johnson RC .08 .25
706 Aaron Wallace RC .02 .05
707 Harold Green RC .08 .25
708 Keith Sims RC .02 .05
709 Tim Grunhard RC .02 .05
710 Jeff Alm RC .02 .05
711 Carwell Gardner RC .02 .05
712 Kenny Davidson RC .02 .05
713 Vince Buck RC .02 .05
714 Leroy Hoard RC .08 .25
715 Andre Collins RC .02 .05
716 Dennis Brown RC .02 .05
717 LeRoy Butler RC .08 .25
718A Pat Terrell 41 ERR RC .20 .50
718B Pat Terrell 37 COR RC .02 .05
719 Mike Bellamy RC .02 .05
720 Mike Fox RC .02 .05
721 Alton Montgomery RC .02 .05
722 Eric Davis RC .04 .10
723A Oliver Barnett DT RC .20 .50
723B Oliver Barnett NT RC .02 .05
724 Houston Hoover RC .02 .05
725 Howard Ballard RC .02 .05
726 Keith McKeller RC .02 .05
727 Wendell Davis RC .02 .05
728 Peter Tom Willis RC .02 .05
729 Bernard Clark .02 .05
730 Doug Widell RC .02 .05
731 Eric Andolsek RC .02 .05
732 Jeff Campbell RC .02 .05
733 Marc Spindler RC .02 .05
734 Keith Woodside .02 .05
735 Willis Peguese RC .02 .05
736 Frank Stams .02 .05
737 Jeff Uhlenhake .02 .05
738 Todd Kalis .02 .05
739 Tommy Hodson UER RC .02 .05
740 Greg McMurtry RC .02 .05
741 Mike Buck RC .02 .05
742 Kevin Haverdink RC .02 .05
743A Johnny Bailey RC .04 .10
743B Johnny Bailey RC .04 .10
744A Eric Moore NPSP .05 .15
744B Eric Moore PSP 4.00 10.00
745 Tony Stargell RC .02 .05
746 Fred Barnett RC .08 .25
747 Walter Reeves .02 .05
748 Derek Hill RC .02 .05
749 Quinn Early .08 .25
750 Ronald Lewis .02 .05
751 Ken Clark RC .02 .05
752 Garry Lewis RC .02 .05
753 James Lofton .04 .10
754 Steve Tasker UER .08 .25
755 Jim Shofner CO .02 .05
756 Jimmie Jones RC .02 .05
757 Jay Novacek .08 .25
758 Jessie Hester RC .02 .05
759 Barry Word RC .02 .05
760 Eddie Anderson RC .02 .05
761 Cleveland Gary .02 .05
762 Marcus Dupree RC .30 .75
763 David Griggs RC .02 .05
764 Rueben Mayes .02 .05
765 Stephen Baker .02 .05
766 Reyna Thompson UER RC .02 .05
767 Everson Walls .02 .05
768 Brad Baxter RC .02 .05
709 Steve Walsh .04 .10
770 Heath Sherman RC .02 .05

771 Johnny Johnson RC .04 .10
772A Dexter Manley Subst 200.00 400.00
772B Dexter Manley No Subst .02 .05
773 Ricky Proehl RC .08 .25
774 Frank Cornish .02 .05
775 Tommy Kane RC .02 .05
776 Derrick Fenner RC .02 .05
777 Steve Christie RC .02 .05
778 Wayne Haddix RC .02 .05
779 Richard Williamson UER .02 .05
780 Brian Mitchell RC .08 .25
781 American Bowl: London .02 .05
782 American Bowl: Berlin .01 .04
783 American Bowl: Tokyo .01 .04
784 American Bowl: Montreal .01 .04
785A Paul Tagliabue peered .30 .75
785B Paul Tagliabue poses .30 .75
786 Al Davis NEWS .01 .04
787 Jerry Glanville .01 .04
788 NFL Goes International .01 .04
789 Overseas Appeal .01 .04
790 Mike Mularkey PHOTO .01 .04
791 G.Reasons/Humphrey PHOTO .01 .04
792 M.Hurst/D.Hill PHOTO .01 .04
793 Ronnie Lott PHOTO .01 .04
794 Barry Sanders PHOTO .20 .50
795 George Seifert PHOTO .01 .04
796 Doug Smith PHOTO .01 .04
797 Doug Widell PHOTO .01 .04
798 Cris Carter PHOTO .08 .25
799 Ronnie Lott School .04 .10
800D Mark Carrier DB D-ROY .04 .10
800O Emmitt Smith O-ROY .60 1.50
1990 Santa Claus SP .20 .50
CC2 Paul Tagliabue SP .15 .40
CC3 Joe Robbie Mem SP .20 .50
SC Super Pro SP .20 .50
SC4 Fred Washington UER .01 .04
SP1 Payne Stewart SP .40 1.00
NNO Lombardi HOLO/10000 50.00 100.00
NNO Super Bowl XXIV Logo .02 .05

1990 Pro Set Super Bowl MVP's

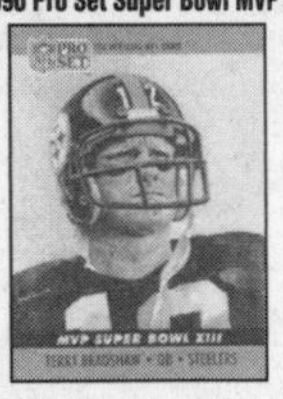

This 24-card standard size set displays color portraits of Super Bowl MVP's by noted sports artist Merv Corning. The cards are numbered on the back; the set numbering is in chronolgical order by Super Bowl number. These cards were included as an insert with Pro Set's second series football card packs.

COMPLETE SET (24) 1.50 4.00
1 Bart Starr .15 .40
2 Bart Starr .15 .40
3 Joe Namath .15 .40
4 Len Dawson .08 .25
5 Chuck Howley .05 .15
6 Roger Staubach .15 .40
7 Jake Scott .05 .15
8 Larry Csonka .08 .25
9 Franco Harris .08 .25
10 Lynn Swann .08 .25
11 Fred Biletnikoff .08 .25
12 Harvey Martin .05 .15
13 Terry Bradshaw .15 .40
14 Terry Bradshaw .15 .40
15 Jim Plunkett .05 .15
16 Joe Montana .30 .75
17 John Riggins .08 .25
18 Marcus Allen .08 .25
19 Joe Montana .30 .75
20 Richard Dent .05 .15
21 Phil Simms .08 .25
22 Doug Williams .05 .15
23 Jerry Rice .30 .75
24 Joe Montana .30 .75

1990 Pro Set Theme Art

The 1990 Pro Set Super Bowl Theme Art set contains 25 standard-size cards. The fronts have full color theme art from the Super Bowls; both sides have attractive silver borders. The horizontally-oriented backs have photos of the winning teams' rings and miscellaneous info about the games. These cards were distributed one per 1990 Pro Set Series I pack.

COMPLETE SET (24) 1.20 3.00
COMMON CARD (1-24) .06 .15

1990 Pro Set Collect-A-Books

This 36-card (booklet) set, which measures the standard size, features some of the leading stars of the National Football League. The set features action photos of the players on the front of the card along with their name on the top of the front and the NFL Pro Set logo on the lower left hand corner. The cards have six pages including the outer cover photos and is interesting in that both Michael Dean Perry and Eric Dickerson have cards in this set but do not have cards in the regular Pro Set series. The set was released in three series of 12 cards each, with there being one rookie in each of the subsets. Not included in the complete set price below is a 1990-91 Pro Set Collect-A-Book Super Bowl XXV, numbered "SB" in the checklist below which presents color pictures with captions summarizing Super Bowls I-XXIV. The front and back cover form one painting of a wall and table covered with football memorabilia. This single item was apparently only available as part of the Super Bowl XXV Commemorative Tin.

COMPLETE SET (36) 3.20 8.00
1 Jim Kelly .15 .40
2 Andre Ware .05 .15
3 Phil Simms .08 .25
4 Bubby Brister .05 .15
5 Bernie Kosar .08 .25
6 Eric Dickerson .08 .25
7 Barry Sanders 1.00 2.50
8 Jerry Rice .40 1.00
9 Keith Millard .05 .15
10 Erik McMillan .05 .15
11 Ickey Woods .05 .15
12 Mike Singletary .15 .40
13 Randall Cunningham .15 .40
14 Boomer Esiason .08 .25
15 John Elway .80 2.00
16 Wade Wilson .05 .15
17 Troy Aikman .40 1.00
18 Dan Marino .80 2.00
19 Lawrence Taylor .08 .25
20 Roger Craig .08 .25
21 Merril Hoge .05 .15
22 Christian Okoye .05 .15
23 Blair Thomas .05 .15
24 William Perry .05 .15
25 Bill Fralic .05 .15
26 Warren Moon .15 .40
27 Jim Everett .08 .25
28 Jeff George .08 .25
29 Shane Conlan .05 .15
30 Carl Banks .05 .15
31 Charles Mann .05 .15
32 Anthony Munoz .08 .25
33 Dan Hampton .05 .15
34 Michael Dean Perry .05 .15
35 Joey Browner .05 .15
36 Ken O'Brien .05 .15
SB Super Bowl Story .08 .25

1990-91 Pro Set Pro Bowl 106

This 106 standard-size set honored the Pro Bowl squad members. The set features regular cards already issued by Pro Set with no indication that these cards were specially issued for the Pro Bowl. There are no differences on most of these cards. The cards in the set are 39, 40, 49, 52, 53, 57, 86, 91, 96, 98, 102, 114, 118, 119, 122, 135, 137, 144, 155, 156, 158, 160, 173, 186, 188, 189, 190, 191, 210, 215, 218, 226, 229, 231, 244, 247, 248, 252, 271, 276, 289, 291, 292, 293, 295, 320, 321, 323, 324, 334, 434, 438, 440, 443, 444, 447, 462, 464, 467, 491, 497, 514, 517, 529, 534, 536, 557, 560, 562, 575, 597, 626, 630, 632, 677, 800D. The only exception are the four players who were in Pro Set's Final Update. These Pro Bowl cards show "1990 Final Update" on the front; this notation was not used on the regular issue Final Update cards. These are obviously the key cards in the set as they are distinguishable from regular Pro Set's issue whereas the other Pro Bowl cards are not. Therefore, we are only explicitly listing these four cards. In addition to the player cards, the 1990 Super Bowl Theme Art insert set was also issued. This set is housed in an attractive white binder with the identification of the Pro Bowl game on the front of the binder.

COMPLETE SET (106) 30.00 60.00
754 Steve Tasker 8.00 20.00
766 Reyna Thompson 6.00 15.00
771 Johnny Johnson 6.00 15.00
778 Wayne Haddix 6.00 15.00

1990-91 Pro Set Super Bowl 160

This 160-card standard-size set was issued by Pro Set as a complete set in a special commemorative box. Cards were also issued in eight-card wax packs along with six pieces of gum. The cards were introduced at the first Dallas Cowboys Pro Set Sports Collectors Show at Texas Stadium. The set features the highlights of the first 24 Super Bowls with the set being divided into the following sub-sets: Super Bowl Tickets (1-24), Super Bowl Supermen (25-135), Super Bowl Super Moments (136-151), and nine puzzle cards depicting the twenty-fifth Super Bowl Art (152-160).

COMP.FACT SET (160) 1.50 4.00
1 SB I Ticket .01 .03
2 SB II Ticket .01 .03
3 SB III Ticket .01 .03
4 SB IV Ticket .01 .03
5 SB V Ticket .01 .03
6 SB VI Ticket .01 .03
7 SB VII Ticket .01 .03
8 SB VIII Ticket .01 .03
9 SB IX Ticket .01 .03
10 SB X Ticket .01 .03
11 SB XI Ticket .01 .03
12 SB XII Ticket .01 .03
13 SB XIII Ticket .01 .03
14 SB XIV Ticket .01 .03
15 SB XV Ticket .01 .03
16 SB XVI Ticket .01 .03
17 SB XVII Ticket .01 .03
18 SB XVIII Ticket .01 .03
19 SB XIX Ticket .01 .03
20 SB XX Ticket .01 .03
21 SB XXI Ticket .01 .03
22 SB XXII Ticket .01 .03
23 SB XXIII Ticket .01 .03
24 SB XXIV Ticket .01 .03
25 Tom Flores CO .01 .05
26 Joe Gibbs CO .02 .10
27 Tom Landry CO .08 .25
28 Vince Lombardi CO .10 .30
29 Chuck Noll CO .05 .15
30 Don Shula CO .05 .15
31 Bill Walsh CO .05 .15
32 Terry Bradshaw .08 .25
33 Joe Montana .40 1.00
34 Joe Namath .20 .50
35 Jim Plunkett .02 .10
36 Bart Starr .10 .30
37 Roger Staubach .10 .30
38 Marcus Allen .07 .20
39 Roger Craig .02 .10
40 Larry Csonka .05 .15
41 Franco Harris .02 .10
42 John Riggins .02 .10
43 Timmy Smith .01 .05
44 Matt Snell .01 .05
45 Fred Biletnikoff .05 .15
46 Cliff Branch .02 .10
47 Max McGee .01 .05
48 Jerry Rice .20 .50
49 Ricky Sanders .01 .05
50 George Sauer Jr. .01 .05
51 John Stallworth .02 .10
52 Lynn Swann .05 .15
53 Dave Casper .01 .05
54 Marv Fleming .01 .05
55 Dan Ross .01 .05
56 Forrest Gregg .02 .10
57 Winston Hill .01 .05
58 Joe Jacoby .01 .05
59 Anthony Munoz .02 .10
60 Art Shell .02 .10
61 Rayfield Wright .01 .05
62 Ron Yary .02 .10
63 Randy Cross .01 .05
64 Jerry Kramer .02 .10
65 Bob Kuechenberg .01 .05
66 Larry Little .02 .10
67 Gerry Mullins .01 .05
68 John Niland .01 .05
69 Gene Upshaw .02 .10
70 Dave Dalby .01 .05
71 Jim Langer .01 .05
72 Dwight Stephenson .02 .10
73 Mike Webster .02 .10
74 Ross Browner .01 .05
75 Willie Davis .02 .10
76 Richard Dent .02 .10
77 L.C. Greenwood .02 .10
78 Ed Too Tall Jones .02 .10
79 Harvey Martin .02 .10
80 Dwight White .02 .10
81 Buck Buchanan .02 .10
82 Curley Culp .01 .05
83 Manny Fernandez .01 .05
84 Joe Greene .05 .15
85 Bob Lilly .05 .15
86 Alan Page .02 .10
87 Randy White .05 .15
88 Nick Buoniconti .02 .10
89 Lee Roy Jordan .02 .10
90 Jack Lambert .05 .15
91 Willie Lanier .02 .10
92 Ray Nitschke .02 .10
93 Mike Singletary .02 .10
94 Carl Banks .02 .10
95 Charles Haley .02 .10
96 Jack Ham .02 .10
97 Ted Hendricks .02 .10
98 Chuck Howley .01 .05
99 Rod Martin .01 .05
100 Herb Adderley .02 .10
101 Mel Blount .02 .10
102 Willie Brown .02 .10
103 Lester Hayes .01 .05
104 Mike Haynes .01 .05
105 Ronnie Lott .02 .10
106 Mel Renfro .02 .10
107 Eric Wright .01 .05
108 Dick Anderson .01 .05
109 David Fulcher .01 .05
110 Cliff Harris .02 .10
111 Johnny Robinson .01 .05
112 Jake Scott .01 .05
113 Donnie Shell .02 .10
114 Mike Wagner .01 .05
115 Willie Wood .02 .10
116 Ray Guy .02 .10
117 Lee Johnson .01 .05
118 Larry Seiple .01 .05
119 Jerrel Wilson .01 .05
120 Kevin Butler .01 .05
121 Don Chandler .01 .05
122 Jan Stenerud .02 .10
123 Jim Turner .01 .05
124 Ray Wersching .01 .05
125 Larry Anderson .01 .05
126 Stanford Jennings .01 .05
127 Mike Nelms .01 .05
128 John Taylor .02 .10
129 Fulton Walker .01 .05
130 E.J. Holub .01 .05
131 George Seifert CO .02 .10
132 Jim Taylor .05 .15
133 Joe Theismann .05 .15
134 Johnny Unitas .10 .30
135 Reggie Williams .01 .05
136 Two Networks .02 .10
137 First Fly-Over .01 .05
138 Weeb Ewbank .01 .05
139 Otis Taylor .02 .10
140 Jim O'Brien .01 .05
141 Garo Yepremian .01 .05
142 Pete Rozelle .01 .05
143 Percy Howard .01 .05
144 Jackie Smith .02 .10
145 Record Crowd .01 .05
146 Yellow Ribbon UER .01 .05
147 Dan Bunz and .01 .05
148 Smurfs (Redskins) .01 .05
149 The Fridge .02 .10
150 Phil McConkey .01 .05
151 Doug Williams .02 .10
P1 Top row left .01 .03
P2 Top row middle .01 .03
P3 Top row right .01 .03
P4 Center row left .01 .03
P5 Center row middle .01 .03
P6 Center row right .01 .03
P7 Bottom row left .01 .03
P8 Bottom row middle .01 .03
P9 Bottom row right .01 .05
NNO Special Offer Card .01 .05

1990-91 Pro Set Super Bowl XXV Binder

This set of 56 standard-size cards features members of the all-time Super Bowl team and members of the teams which competed in the 25th Super Bowl: the New York Giants and Buffalo Bills. This set also included card number 799 from the 1990 Pro Set Football set: the Ronnie Lott Stay in School Card. Published reports indicated that Pro Set made 125,000 of these sets, 90,000 for distribution at the Super Bowl and 35,000 for a special mail-away offer at $30.00 per set. The set is housed in an attractive binder with special plastic pages holding four cards per. The cards of the players playing in the Super Bowl have the same number on the back as their regular issue set but the fronts acknowledge their teams as champions of their conferences. Cards for players from the two losing teams in the Conference Championship games (49ers and Raiders) were also printed, but apparently where not destroyed as commonly thought since many of them surfaced some twenty years later.

COMPLETE SET (56) 8.00 20.00
1 Vince Lombardi CO .20 .50
2 Joe Montana 3.20 8.00
3 Larry Csonka .20 .50
4 Franco Harris .20 .50
5 Jerry Rice 1.60 4.00
6 Lynn Swann .20 .50
7 Forrest Gregg .10 .30
8 Art Shell .10 .30
9 Jerry Kramer .07 .20
10 Gene Upshaw .07 .20
11 Mike Webster .07 .20
12 Dave Casper .07 .20
13 Jan Stenerud .07 .20
14 John Taylor .07 .20
15 L.C. Greenwood .07 .20
16 Ed Too Tall Jones .10 .30
17 Joe Greene .20 .50
18 Randy White .20 .50
19 Jack Lambert .20 .50
20 Mike Singletary .10 .30
21 Jack Ham .10 .30
22 Ted Hendricks .10 .30
23 Mel Blount .10 .30
24 Ronnie Lott .10 .30
25 Donnie Shell .07 .20
26 Willie Wood .10 .30
27 Ray Guy .07 .20
39 Cornelius Bennett .10 .30
40 Jim Kelly .40 1.00
47 Darryl Talley .07 .20
48 Marv Levy CO .07 .20
223 Carl Banks .07 .20
226 Pepper Johnson .07 .20
228 Dave Meggett .10 .30
230 Phil Simms .10 .30
231 Lawrence Taylor .15 .40
232 Bill Parcells CO .07 .20
437 Shane Conlan .07 .20
438 Kent Hull .07 .20
440 Andre Reed .10 .30
443 Bruce Smith .10 .30
444 Thurman Thomas .40 1.00
591 Ottis Anderson .07 .20
592 Mark Bavaro .07 .20
596 Jeff Hostetler .10 .30
692 Rodney Hampton .20 .50
725 Howard Ballard .07 .20
753 James Lofton .10 .30
754 Steve Tasker .07 .20
765 Stephen Baker .07 .20
766 Reyna Thompson .07 .20
799 Ronnie Lott Education .10 .30
SC1 2&000&000th Fan .07 .20
SC2 Buick Checklist Card .07 .20
SC3 Lamar Hunt Trophy .07 .20
SC4 George Halas Trophy .07 .20

1990-91 Pro Set Super Bowl XXV 49ers

COMPLETE SET (12) 100.00 200.00
287 Roger Craig 6.00 15.00
289 Charles Haley 8.00 20.00
290 Pierce Holt 4.00 10.00
291 Ronnie Lott 10.00 25.00
292 Guy McIntyre 4.00 10.00
293 Joe Montana 40.00 80.00
295 Jerry Rice 30.00 60.00
297 John Taylor 6.00 15.00
299 George Seifert CO 5.00 12.00
639 Brent Jones 5.00 12.00
640 Matt Millen 5.00 12.00
644 Dave Waymer 4.00 10.00

1990-91 Pro Set Super Bowl XXV Raiders

COMPLETE SET (12) 60.00 120.00
152 Mervyn Fernandez 4.00 10.00
153 Willie Gault 5.00 12.00
155 Bo Jackson 8.00 20.00
156 Don Mosebar 4.00 10.00
158 Greg Townsend 4.00 10.00
160 Steve Wisniewski 5.00 12.00
161 Art Shell 5.00 12.00
538 Marcus Allen 6.00 15.00
545 Howie Long 6.00 15.00
546 Terry McDaniel 4.00 10.00
547 Max Montoya 4.00 10.00
548 Jay Schroeder 4.00 10.00

1991 Pro Set Draft Day

This eight-card standard-size set was issued by Pro Set on April 21, 1991 the date of the NFL draft. The cards, which are all numbered 694, feature action shots in the 1991 Pro Set design of all the potential number one draft picks. The backs of the cards have a horizontal format, with one half of the card boing a full color portrait of the playor and the other half consisting of biographical information. The set is checklisted below in alphabetical order. The Russell Maryland card was eventually released (on a somewhat limited basis) with the first series of 1991 Pro Set cards and is listed there rather than here.

COMPLETE SET (7) 125.00 250.00
694A Nick Bell 15.00 30.00
694B Mike Croel 20.00 40.00
694C Rocket Ismail 15.00 30.00
694D Rocket Ismail 25.00 60.00
694E Rocket Ismail 15.00 40.00
694F Todd Lyght 15.00 30.00
694G Dan McGwire 15.00 30.00

1991 Pro Set Promos

The Tele-Clinic card was given away as a promotion at Super Bowl XXV and was co-sponsored by NFL Pro Set, The Learning Channel, and Sports Illustrated for Kids. The card features a color photo on the front of an NFL player giving some football tips to a young kid. This card promotes the annual Super Bowl football clinic, in which current and former NFL stars talk to kids about football and life. The Super Bowl Card Show II card was issued in conjunction with the second annual Super Bowl show which was held in Tampa, Florida across the street from Tampa Stadium. The card is in the design on the Pro Set Super Bowl insert set from 1989 with a little inset on the bottom right hand corner of the card which states "Super Bowl Card Show II, January 24-27, 1991". The back of the card has information about the show and the other promotional activities which accompanied Super Bowl week. The Perry and Roberts cards were apparently planned but pulled from the Pro Bowl albums just prior to distribution. All of the above cards measure the standard size.

NNO1 Michael Dean Perry 8.00 20.00
NNO2 Michael Dean Perry 8.00 20.00
NNO3 William Roberts 12.00 30.00
NNO4 NFL Kids on the Block .20 .50
NNO5 Super Bowl XXV .20 .50
NNO6 Dan Marino 8.00 20.00
School's the Ticket
City of Dallas Public
Service Announcement back
PSG1 Emmitt Smith Gazette 1.00 2.50

1991 Pro Set

This set contains 850 standard-size cards issued in three series of 405, 407 and a 38-card Final Update set. The front design features full-bleed glossy color action photos with player, position and team name at the bottom in two stripes reflecting the team's colors. The horizontally oriented backs have a color head shot on the right side, with player profile highlights and statistics on the left. The set starts with NFL leaders (3-19), 1990 milestones (20-26), 1991 Hall of Fame inductees (27-31), college award winners (32-36), past Heisman trophy winners (37-45) and Super Bowl XXV highlights (46-54). Cards 55-324 and 433-684 are in team order. Further subsets include special games of the 1990 season (325-342), NFL officals (352-369), Stay in School (370-378) and 54 All-NFC (379-405) and All-AFC (406-432) drawings by artist Merv Corning, NFL Newsreel (685-693/813-815), Legends (694-702), World League Leaders (703-711), Hall of Fame Photo Contest (712-720), Think About It (721-729), first through third round Draft Choices (730-772) and a Super Bowl XXV Theme Art card. Since two #1 cards were issued, no #2 card exists.

COMPLETE SET (850) 15.00 40.00
COMP.SERIES 1 (405) 6.00 15.00
COMP.SERIES 2 (407) 6.00 15.00
COMP.FINAL FACT. (38) 4.00 10.00
1D Mark Carrier DB D-ROY .02 .10
1O Emmitt Smith O-ROY .50 1.25
3 Joe Montana POY .20 .50
4 Art Shell COY .02 .10
5 Mike Singletary .02 .10
6 Bruce Smith POY .02 .10
7 Barry Word POY .01 .05
8A Jim Kelly LL w/LOGO .08 .25
8B Jim Kelly LL NO LOGO .08 .25
8C Jim Kelly LL Reg NO LOGO 3.00 6.00
9 Warren Moon LL .02 .10
10 Barry Sanders LL .20 .50
11 Jerry Rice LL .15 .40
12 Jay Novacek .02 .10
13 Thurman Thomas LL .02 .10
14 Nick Lowery .01 .05
15 Mike Horan LL .01 .05
16 Clarence Verdin .01 .05
17 Kevin Clark LL RC .01 .05
18 Mark Carrier DB LL .02 .10
19A Derrick Thomas LL Bills 7.50 20.00
19B Derrick Thomas LL COR .02 .10
20 Ottis Anderson ML .02 .10
21 Roger Craig ML .02 .10
22 Art Monk ML .02 .10
23 Chuck Noll ML .02 .10
24 Randall Cunningham ML .02 .10
25 Dan Marino ML .20 .50
26 49ers Road Record ML .01 .05
27 Earl Campbell HOF .01 .05
28 John Hannah HOF .01 .05
29 Stan Jones HOF .01 .05
30 Tex Schramm HOF .01 .05
31 Jan Stenerud HOF .01 .05
32 Russell Maryland RC .02 .10
33 Chris Zorich RC .02 .10
34 Darryll Lewis UER RC .02 .10
35 Alfred Williams RC .01 .05
36 Rocket Ismail TW RC .40 1.00
37 Ty Detmer HH RC .15 .40
38 Andre Ware HH .02 .10
39 Barry Sanders HH .20 .50
40 Tim Brown HH .02 .10
41 Vinny Testaverde HH .02 .10
42 Bo Jackson HH .10 .30
43 Mike Rozier HH .01 .05
44 Herschel Walker HH .02 .10
45 Marcus Allen HH .02 .10
46A James Lofton SB .02 .10
46B James Lofton SB .02 .10
47A Bruce Smith SB black ink .02 .10
47B Bruce Smith SB white ink .02 .10
48 Myron Guyton SB .01 .05
49 Stephen Baker SB .01 .05
50 Mark Ingram SB UER .01 .05
51 Ottis Anderson SB .02 .10
52 Thurman Thomas SB .08 .25
53 Matt Bahr SB .01 .05
54 Scott Norwood SB .01 .05
55 Stephen Baker .01 .05
56 Carl Banks .01 .05
57 Mark Collins .01 .05
58 Steve DeOssie .01 .05
59 Eric Dorsey .01 .05
60 John Elliott .01 .05
61 Myron Guyton .01 .05
62 Rodney Hampton .08 .25
63 Jeff Hostetler .02 .10
64 Erik Howard .01 .05
65 Mark Ingram .02 .10
66 Greg Jackson RC .01 .05
67 Leonard Marshall .01 .05
68 Dave Meggett .02 .10
69 Eric Moore .01 .05
70 Bart Oates .01 .05
71 Gary Reasons .01 .05
72 Bill Parcells CO .02 .10
73 Howard Ballard .01 .05
74A Corn.Bennett w/LOGO .08 .25
74B Corn.Bennett NO LOGO .01 .05
75 Shane Conlan .01 .05
76 Kent Hull .01 .05
77 Kirby Jackson RC .01 .05
78A Jim Kelly w/LOGO .25 .60
78B Jim Kelly NO LOGO .08 .25
79 Mark Kelso .01 .05
80 Nate Odomes .01 .05
81 Andre Reed .02 .10
82 Jim Ritcher .01 .05
83 Bruce Smith .08 .25
84 Darryl Talley .01 .05
85 Steve Tasker .02 .10
86 Thurman Thomas .08 .25
87 James Williams .01 .05
88 Will Wolford .01 .05
89 Jeff Wright UER RC .01 .05
90 Marv Levy CO .01 .05
91 Steve Broussard .01 .05
92A Darion Conner ERR '99 4.00 10.00
92B Darion Conner COR .08 .25
93 Bill Fralic .01 .05
94 Tim Green .01 .05
95 Michael Haynes .08 .25
96 Chris Hinton .01 .05
97 Chris Miller UER .02 .10
98 Deion Sanders UER .15 .40
99 Jerry Glanville CO .01 .05
100 Kevin Butler .01 .05
101 Mark Carrier DB .02 .10
102 Jim Covert .01 .05
103 Richard Dent .02 .10
104 Jim Harbaugh .08 .25
105 Brad Muster .01 .05
106 Lemuel Stinson .01 .05
107 Keith Van Horne .01 .05
108 Mike Ditka CO UER .08 .25
109 Lewis Billups .01 .05
110 James Brooks .02 .10
111 Boomer Esiason .02 .10
112 James Francis .01 .05
113 David Fulcher .01 .05
114 Rodney Holman .01 .05
115 Tim McGee .01 .05
116 Anthony Munoz .02 .10
117 Sam Wyche CO .01 .05
118 Paul Farren .01 .05
119 Thane Gash .01 .05
120 Mike Johnson .01 .05
121A Bernie Kosar w/Logo .02 .10
121B Bernie Kosar No Logo .02 .10
122 Clay Matthews .02 .10
123 Eric Metcalf .02 .10
124 Frank Minnifield .01 .05
125A Webster Slaughter w/Logo .02 .10
125B Webster Slaughter No Logo .02 .10
126 Bill Belichick CO RC 1.50 4.00
127 Tommie Agee .01 .05
128 Troy Aikman .30 .75
129 Jack Del Rio .02 .10
130 John Gesek RC .01 .05
131 Issiac Holt .01 .05
132 Michael Irvin .08 .25
133 Ken Norton .02 .10
134 Daniel Stubbs .01 .05
135 Jimmy Johnson CO .02 .10
136 Steve Atwater .01 .05
137 Michael Brooks .01 .05
138 John Elway .50 1.25
139 Wymon Henderson .01 .05
140 Bobby Humphrey .01 .05
141 Mark Jackson .01 .05
142 Karl Mecklenburg .01 .05
143 Doug Widell .01 .05
144 Dan Reeves CO .01 .05
145 Eric Andolsek .01 .05
146 Jerry Ball .01 .05
147 Bennie Blades .01 .05
148 Lomas Brown .01 .05
149 Robert Clark .01 .05
150 Michael Cofer .01 .05
151 Dan Owens .01 .05
152 Rodney Peete .02 .10
153 Wayne Fontes CO .01 .05
154 Tim Harris .01 .05
155 Johnny Holland .01 .05
156 Don Majkowski .01 .05
157 Tony Mandarich .01 .05
158 Mark Murphy .01 .05
159 Brian Noble .01 .05
160 Jeff Query .01 .05
161 Sterling Sharpe .08 .25
162 Lindy Infante CO .01 .05
163 Ray Childress .01 .05
164 Ernest Givins .02 .10
165 Richard Johnson CB .01 .05
166 Bruce Matthews .02 .10
167 Warren Moon .08 .25
168 Mike Munchak .02 .10
169 Al Smith .01 .05
170 Lorenzo White .01 .05
171 Jack Pardee CO .01 .05
172 Albert Bentley .01 .05
173 Duane Bickett .01 .05
174 Bill Brooks .01 .05
175A E.Dickerson w/LOGO .15 .40
175B E.Dickerson NO LOGO 667 .50 1.25
175C E.Dickerson NO LOGO 677 .08 .25
176 Ray Donaldson .01 .05
177 Jeff George .08 .25
178 Jeff Herrod .01 .05
179 Clarence Verdin .01 .05
180 Ron Meyer CO .01 .05
181 John Alt .01 .05
182 Steve DeBerg .01 .05
183 Albert Lewis .01 .05
184 Nick Lowery UER .01 .05
185 Christian Okoye .01 .05
186 Stephone Paige .01 .05
187 Kevin Porter .01 .05
188 Derrick Thomas .08 .25
189 Marty Schottenheimer CO .01 .05
190 Willie Gault .02 .10
191 Howie Long .08 .25
192 Terry McDaniel .01 .05
193 Jay Schroeder UER .01 .05
194 Steve Smith .01 .05
195 Greg Townsend .01 .05
196 Lionel Washington .01 .05
197 Steve Wisniewski UER .01 .05
198 Art Shell CO .02 .10
199 Henry Ellard .02 .10
200 Jim Everett .02 .10
201 Jerry Gray .01 .05
202 Kevin Greene .02 .10
203 Buford McGee .01 .05
204 Tom Newberry .01 .05
205 Frank Stams .01 .05
206 Alvin Wright .01 .05
207 John Robinson CO .01 .05
208 Jeff Cross .01 .05
209 Mark Duper .02 .10
210 Dan Marino .50 1.25
211A Tim McKyer .02 .10
211B Tim McKyer TR .08 .25
212 John Offerdahl .01 .05
213 Sammie Smith .01 .05
214 Richmond Webb .01 .05
215 Jarvis Williams .01 .05
216 Don Shula CO .02 .10
217A D.Fullington ERR .02 .10
217B D.Fullington COR .02 .10
218 Tim Irwin .01 .05
219 Mike Merriweather .01 .05
220 Keith Millard .01 .05
221 Al Noga .01 .05
222 Henry Thomas .01 .05
223 Wade Wilson .02 .10
224 Gary Zimmerman .02 .10
225 Jerry Burns CO .01 .05
226 Bruce Armstrong .01 .05
227 Marv Cook .01 .05
228 Hart Lee Dykes .01 .05
229 Tommy Hodson .01 .05
230 Ronnie Lippett .01 .05
231 Ed Reynolds .01 .05
232 Chris Singleton .01 .05
233 John Stephens .01 .05
234 Dick MacPherson CO .01 .05
235 Stan Brock .01 .05
236 Craig Heyward .02 .10
237 Vaughan Johnson .01 .05
238 Robert Massey .01 .05
239 Brett Maxie .01 .05
240 Rueben Mayes .01 .05
241 Pat Swilling .02 .10
242 Renaldo Turnbull .01 .05
243 Jim Mora CO .01 .05
244 Kyle Clifton .01 .05
245 Jeff Criswell .01 .05
246 James Hasty .01 .05
247 Erik McMillan .01 .05
248 Scott Mersereau RC .01 .05
249 Ken O'Brien .01 .05
250A Blair Thomas w/LOGO .08 .25
250B Blair Thomas NO LOGO .02 .10
251 Al Toon .02 .10
252 Bruce Coslet CO .01 .05
253 Eric Allen .01 .05
254 Fred Barnett .08 .25
255 Keith Byars .01 .05
256 Randall Cunningham .08 .25
257 Seth Joyner .02 .10
258 Clyde Simmons .01 .05
259 Jessie Small .01 .05
260 Andre Waters .01 .05
261 Rich Kotite CO .01 .05
262 Roy Green .01 .05
263 Ernie Jones .01 .05
264 Tim McDonald .01 .05
265 Timm Rosenbach .01 .05
266 Rod Saddler .01 .05
267 Luis Sharpe .01 .05
268 Anthony Thompson UER .01 .05
269 Marcus Turner RC .01 .05
270 Joe Bugel CO .01 .05
271 Gary Anderson K .01 .05
272 Dermontti Dawson .02 .10
273 Eric Green .01 .05
274 Merril Hoge .01 .05
275 Tunch Ilkin .01 .05
276 D.J. Johnson .01 .05
277 Louis Lipps .01 .05
278 Rod Woodson .08 .25
279 Chuck Noll CO .02 .10
280 Martin Bayless .01 .05
281 Marion Butts UER .02 .10
282 Gill Byrd .01 .05
283 Burt Grossman .01 .05
284 Courtney Hall .01 .05
285 Anthony Miller .02 .10
286 Leslie O'Neal .02 .10
287 Billy Joe Tolliver .01 .05
288 Dan Henning CO .01 .05
289 Dexter Carter .01 .05
290 Michael Carter .01 .05
291 Kevin Fagan .01 .05
292 Pierce Holt .01 .05
293 Guy McIntyre/Montana .01 .05
294 Tom Rathman .01 .05
295 John Taylor .02 .10
296 Steve Young .30 .75
297 George Seifert CO .02 .10
298 Brian Blades .02 .10
299 Jeff Bryant .01 .05
300 Norm Johnson .01 .05
301 Tommy Kane .01 .05
302 Cortez Kennedy UER .08 .25
303 Bryan Millard .01 .05
304 John L. Williams .01 .05
305 David Wyman .01 .05
306A Chuck Knox CO w/LOGO .01 .05
306B Chuck Knox CO NO LOGO .20 .50
307 Gary Anderson RB .01 .05
308 Reggie Cobb .01 .05
309 Randy Grimes .01 .05
310 Harry Hamilton .01 .05
311 Bruce Hill .01 .05
312 Eugene Marve .01 .05
313 Ervin Randle .01 .05
314 Vinny Testaverde .02 .10
315 Richard Williamson CO .01 .05
316 Earnest Byner .01 .05
317 Gary Clark .08 .25
318A Andre Collins w/Logo .02 .10
318B Andre Collins No Logo .02 .10
319 Darryl Grant .01 .05
320 Chip Lohmiller .01 .05
321 Martin Mayhew .01 .05
322 Mark Rypien .02 .10
323 Alvin Walton .01 .05
324 Joe Gibbs CO UER .02 .10
325 Jerry Glanville REP .01 .05
326A J.Elway REP LOGO 2.00 4.00
326B J.Elway REP NO LOGO .75 2.00
327 Boomer Esiason REP .01 .05
328A Steve Tasker REP 2.00 4.00
328B Steve Tasker REP .75 2.00
329 J.Montana/Rice REP .15 .40
330 Jeff Rutledge REP .01 .05
331 K.C. Defense REP .01 .05
332 Cleveland Gary REP .01 .05
333 John Taylor REP .01 .05
334A R.Cunningham w/LOGO .01 .05
334B R.Cunningham NO LOGO .01 .05
335A Bo .20 .50
Barry REP w
LOGO
335B Bo .20 .50
Barry REP NO LOGO
336 Lawrence Taylor REP .08 .25
337 Warren Moon REP .08 .25
338 Alan Grant REP .01 .05
339 Todd McNair REP .01 .05
340A Miami Dolphins REP .01 .05
340B Miami Dolphins REP .01 .05
341A Highest Scoring REP 2.00 4.00
341B Highest Scoring REP .75 2.00
342 Matt Bahr REP .01 .05
343 R.Tisch/W.Mara NEW .01 .05
344 Sam Jankovich NEW .01 .05
345 John Elway NEW .01 .05
346 Bo Jackson NEW .02 .10
347 Teacher of Year/Tagliabue .01 .05
348 Ronnie Lott NEW .02 .10
349 Super Bowl XXV .02 .10
350 Whitney Houston .30 .75
351 U.S. Troops in SA .01 .05
352 Art McNally OFF .01 .05
353 Dick Jorgenson OFF .01 .05
354 Jerry Seeman OFF .01 .05
355 Jim Tunney OFF .01 .05
356 Gerry Austin OFF .01 .05
357 Gene Barth OFF .01 .05
358 Red Cashion OFF .01 .05
359 Tom Dooley OFF .01 .05
360 Johnny Grier OFF .01 .05
361 Pat Haggerty OFF .01 .05
362 Dale Hamer OFF .01 .05
363 Dick Hantak OFF .01 .05
364 Jerry Markbreit OFF .01 .05
365 Gordon McCarter OFF .01 .05
366 Bob McElwee OFF .01 .05
367 Howard Roe OFF .01 .05
368 Tom White OFF .01 .05
369 Norm Schachter OFF .01 .05
370A Warren Moon Crck sml .08 .25
370B Warren Moon Crck lrg .08 .25
371A B.Esiason uppr lowr .20 .50
371B B.Esiason all caps .02 .10
372A Troy Aikman sml .15 .40
372B Troy Aikman lrg .15 .40
373A Carl Banks sml .20 .50
373B Carl Banks lrg .01 .05
374A Jim Everett sml .20 .50
374B Jim Everett lrg .02 .10
375A Anth.Munoz dificul .02 .10
375B Anth.Munoz dificil .02 .10
375C Anth.Munoz large type .02 .10
375D Anth.Munoz Quedate .02 .10
376A Ray Childress sml .50 1.25
376B Ray Childress lrg .01 .05
377A Charles Mann sml .50 1.25
377B Charles Mann lrg .01 .05
378A Jackie Slater sml .50 1.25
378B Jackie Slater lrg .01 .05
379 Jerry Rice NFC .15 .40
380 Andre Rison NFC .02 .10
381 Jim Lachey NFC .01 .05
382 Jackie Slater NFC .01 .05
383 Randall McDaniel NFC .02 .10
384 Mark Bortz NFC .01 .05
385 Jay Hilgenberg NFC .01 .05
386 Keith Jackson NFC .01 .05
387 Joe Montana NFC .20 .50
388 Barry Sanders NFC .20 .50
389 Neal Anderson NFC .01 .05
390 Reggie White NFC .08 .25
391 Chris Doleman NFC .01 .05
392 Jerome Brown NFC .01 .05
393 Charles Haley NFC .01 .05
394 Lawrence Taylor NFC .08 .25
395 Pepper Johnson NFC .01 .05
396 Mike Singletary NFC .02 .10
397 Darrell Green NFC .01 .05
398 Carl Lee NFC .01 .05
399 Joey Browner NFC .01 .05
400 Ronnie Lott NFC .02 .10
401 Sean Landeta NFC .01 .05
402 Morten Andersen NFC .01 .05
403 Mel Gray NFC .01 .05
404 Reyna Thompson NFC .01 .05
405 Jimmy Johnson CO NFC .02 .10
406 Andre Reed AFC .02 .10
407 Anthony Miller AFC .02 .10
408 Anthony Munoz AFC .02 .10
409 Bruce Armstrong AFC .01 .05
410 Bruce Matthews AFC .01 .05
411 Mike Munchak AFC .01 .05
412 Kent Hull AFC .01 .05
413 Rodney Holman AFC .01 .05
414 Warren Moon AFC .08 .25
415 Thurman Thomas AFC .08 .25
416 Marion Butts AFC .02 .10
417 Bruce Smith AFC .02 .10
418 Greg Townsend AFC .01 .05
419 Ray Childress AFC .01 .05
420 Derrick Thomas AFC .08 .25
421 Leslie O'Neal AFC .02 .10
422 John Offerdahl AFC .01 .05
423 Shane Conlan AFC .01 .05
424 Rod Woodson AFC .08 .25
425 Albert Lewis AFC .01 .05
426 Steve Atwater AFC .01 .05
427 David Fulcher AFC .01 .05
428 Rohn Stark AFC .01 .05
429 Nick Lowery AFC .01 .05
430 Clarence Verdin AFC .01 .05
431 Steve Tasker AFC .01 .05
432 Art Shell CO AFC .02 .10
433 Scott Case .01 .05
434 Tory Epps UER .01 .05
435 Mike Gann UER .01 .05
436 Brian Jordan UER .02 .10
437 Mike Kenn .01 .05
438 John Rade .01 .05
439 Andre Rison .02 .10
440 Mike Rozier .01 .05
441 Jessie Tuggle .01 .05
442 Don Beebe .01 .05
443 John Davis RC .01 .05
444 James Lofton .02 .10
445 Keith McKeller .01 .05
446 Jamie Mueller .01 .05
447 Scott Norwood .01 .05
448 Frank Reich .02 .10
449 Leon Seals .01 .05
450 Leonard Smith .01 .05
451 Neal Anderson .02 .10
452 Trace Armstrong .01 .05
453 Mark Bortz .01 .05
454 Wendell Davis .01 .05
455 Shaun Gayle .01 .05
456 Jay Hilgenberg .01 .05
457 Steve McMichael .02 .10
458 Mike Singletary .02 .10
459 Donnell Woolford .01 .05
460 Jim Breech .01 .05
461 Eddie Brown .01 .05
462 Barney Bussey RC .01 .05
463 Bruce Kozerski .01 .05
464 Tim Krumrie .01 .05
465 Bruce Reimers .01 .05
466 Kevin Walker RC .01 .05
467 Ickey Woods .01 .05
468 Carl Zander UER .01 .05
469 Mike Baab .01 .05
470 Brian Brennan .01 .05
471 Rob Burnett RC .02 .10
472 Raymond Clayborn .01 .05
473 Reggie Langhorne .01 .05
474 Kevin Mack .01 .05
475 Anthony Pleasant .01 .05
476 Joe Morris .01 .05
477 Dan Fike .01 .05
478 Ray Horton .01 .05
479 Jim Jeffcoat .01 .05
480 Jimmie Jones .01 .05
481 Kelvin Martin .01 .05
482 Nate Newton .02 .10
483 Danny Noonan .01 .05
484 Jay Novacek .08 .25
485 Emmitt Smith 1.00 2.50
486 James Washington RC .01 .05
487 Simon Fletcher .01 .05
488 Ron Holmes .01 .05
489 Mike Horan .01 .05
490 Vance Johnson .01 .05
491 Keith Kartz .01 .05
492 Greg Kragen .01 .05
493 Ken Lanier .01 .05
494 Warren Powers .01 .05
495 Dennis Smith .01 .05
496 Jeff Campbell .01 .05
497 Ken Dallafior .01 .05
498 Dennis Gibson .01 .05
499 Kevin Glover .01 .05
500 Mel Gray .02 .10
501 Eddie Murray .01 .05
502 Barry Sanders .50 1.25
503 Chris Spielman .02 .10

504 William White .01 .05
505 Matt Brock RC .01 .05
506 Robert Brown .01 .05
507 LeRoy Butler .02 .10
508 James Campen RC .01 .05
509 Jerry Holmes .01 .05
510 Perry Kemp .01 .05
511 Ken Ruettgers .01 .05
512 Scott Stephen RC .01 .05
513 Ed West .01 .05
514 Cris Dishman RC .01 .05
515 Curtis Duncan .01 .05
516 Drew Hill UER .01 .05
517 Haywood Jeffires .02 .10
518 Sean Jones .02 .10
519 Lamar Lathon .01 .05
520 Don Maggs .01 .05
521 Bubba McDowell .01 .05
522 Johnny Meads .01 .05
523A Chip Banks ERR No Text 1.25 3.00
523B Chip Banks COR with text .01 .05
524 Pat Beach .01 .05
525 Sam Clancy .01 .05
526 Eugene Daniel .01 .05
527 Jon Hand .01 .05
528 Jessie Hester .01 .05
529A Mike Prior ERR No Text 1.25 3.00
529B Mike Prior COR w/Text .01 .05
530 Keith Taylor .01 .05
531 Donnell Thompson .01 .05
532 Dino Hackett .01 .05
533 David Lutz RC .01 .05
534 Chris Martin .01 .05
535 Kevin Ross .01 .05
536 Dan Saleaumua .01 .05
537 Neil Smith .08 .25
538 Percy Snow .01 .05
539 Robb Thomas .01 .05
540 Barry Word .01 .05
541 Marcus Allen .08 .25
542 Eddie Anderson .01 .05
543 Scott Davis .01 .05
544 Mervyn Fernandez .01 .05
545 Ethan Horton .01 .05
546 Ronnie Lott .02 .10
547 Don Mosebar .01 .05
548 Jerry Robinson .01 .05
549 Aaron Wallace .01 .05
550 Flipper Anderson .01 .05
551 Cleveland Gary .01 .05
552 Damone Johnson RC .01 .05
553 Duval Love RC .01 .05
554 Irv Pankey .01 .05
555 Mike Piel .01 .05
556 Jackie Slater .01 .05
557 Michael Stewart .01 .05
558 Pat Terrell .01 .05
559 J.B. Brown .01 .05
560 Mark Clayton .02 .10
561 Ferrell Edmunds .01 .05
562 Harry Galbreath .01 .05
563 David Griggs .01 .05
564 Jim C. Jensen .01 .05
565 Louis Oliver .01 .05
566 Tony Paige .01 .05
567 Keith Sims .01 .05
568 Joey Browner .01 .05
569 Anthony Carter .02 .10
570 Chris Doleman .01 .05
571 Rich Gannon UER .08 .25
572 Hassan Jones .01 .05
573 Steve Jordan .01 .05
574 Carl Lee .01 .05
575 Randall McDaniel .02 .10
576 Herschel Walker .02 .10
577 Ray Agnew .01 .05
578 Vincent Brown .01 .05
579 Irving Fryar .02 .10
580 Tim Goad .01 .05
581 Maurice Hurst .01 .05
582 Fred Marion .01 .05
583 Johnny Rembert .01 .05
584 Andre Tippett .01 .05
585 Brent Williams .01 .05
586 Morten Andersen .01 .05
587 Toi Cook RC .01 .05
588 Jim Dombrowski .01 .05
589 Dalton Hilliard .01 .05
590 Rickey Jackson .01 .05
591 Eric Martin .01 .05
592 Sam Mills .01 .05
593 Bobby Hebert .01 .05
594 Steve Walsh .01 .05
595 Ottis Anderson .02 .10
596 Pepper Johnson .01 .05
597 Bob Kratch RC .01 .05
598 Sean Landeta .01 .05
599 Doug Riesenberg .01 .05
600 William Roberts .01 .05
601 Phil Simms .02 .10
602 Lawrence Taylor .08 .25
603 Everson Walls .01 .05
604 Brad Baxter .01 .05
605 Dennis Byrd .01 .05
606 Jeff Lageman .01 .05
607 Pat Leahy .01 .05
608 Rob Moore .08 .25
609 Joe Mott .01 .05
610 Tony Stargell .01 .05
611 Brian Washington .01 .05
612 Marvin Washington RC .01 .05
613 David Alexander .01 .05
614 Jerome Brown .01 .05
615 Byron Evans .01 .05
616 Ron Heller .01 .05
617 Wes Hopkins .01 .05
618 Keith Jackson .02 .10
619 Heath Sherman .01 .05
620 Reggie White .08 .25
621 Calvin Williams .02 .10
622 Ken Harvey .02 .10
623 Eric Hill .01 .05
624 Johnny Johnson .01 .05
625 Freddie Joe Nunn .01 .05
626 Ricky Proehl .01 .05
627 Tootie Robbins .01 .05
628 Jay Taylor RC .01 .05
629 Tom Tupa .01 .05
630 Jim Wahler RC .01 .05
631 Bubby Brister .01 .05
632 Thomas Everett .01 .05
633 Bryan Hinkle .01 .05
634 Carnell Lake .01 .05
635 David Little .01 .05
636 Hardy Nickerson .02 .10
637 Gerald Williams .01 .05
638 Keith Willis .01 .05
639 Tim Worley .01 .05
640 Rod Bernstine .01 .05
641 Frank Cornish .01 .05
642 Gary Plummer .01 .05
643 Henry Rolling RC .01 .05
644 Sam Seale .01 .05
645 Junior Seau .08 .25
646 Billy Ray Smith .01 .05
647 Broderick Thompson .01 .05
648 Derrick Walker RC .01 .05
649 Todd Bowles .08 .25
650 Don Griffin .01 .05
651 Charles Haley .02 .10
652 Brent Jones UER .02 .10
653 Joe Montana .50 1.25
654 Jerry Rice .30 .75
655 Bill Romanowski .01 .05
656 Michael Walter .01 .05
657 Dave Waymer .01 .05
658 Jeff Chadwick .01 .05
659 Derrick Fenner .01 .05
660 Nesby Glasgow .01 .05
661 Jacob Green .01 .05
662 Dwayne Harper RC .01 .05
663 Andy Heck .01 .05
664 Dave Krieg .02 .10
665 Rufus Porter .01 .05
666 Eugene Robinson .01 .05
667 Mark Carrier WR .08 .25
668 Steve Christie .01 .05
669 Reuben Davis .01 .05
670 Paul Gruber .01 .05
671 Wayne Haddix .01 .05
672 Ron Hall .01 .05
673 Keith McCants UER .01 .05
674 Ricky Reynolds .01 .05
675 Mark Robinson .01 .05
676 Jeff Bostic .01 .05
677 Darrell Green .01 .05
678 Markus Koch .01 .05
679 Jim Lachey .01 .05
680 Charles Mann .01 .05
681 Wilber Marshall .01 .05
682 Art Monk .02 .10
683 Gerald Riggs .01 .05
684 Ricky Sanders .01 .05
685 Ray Handley NEW .01 .05
686 NFL expansion NEW .01 .05
687 Super Bowl XXIX NEW .01 .05
688 George Young GM NEW .01 .05
689 HOF Five-millionth fan NEW .01 .05
690 Sports Illustrated NEW .01 .05
691 American Bowl NEW .01 .05
692 American Bowl NEW .01 .05
693 American Bowl NEW .01 .05
694A Russell Maryland .08 .25
694B Joe Ferguson LEG .01 .05
695 Carl Hairston LEG .02 .10
696 Dan Hampton LEG .02 .10
697 Mike Haynes LEG .01 .05
698 Marty Lyons LEG .01 .05
699 Ozzie Newsome LEG .02 .10
700 Scott Studwell LEG .01 .05
701 Mike Webster LEG .01 .05
702 Dwayne Woodruff LEG .01 .05
703 Larry Kennan CO .01 .05
704 Stan Gelbaugh RC LL .02 .10
705 John Brantley LL .01 .05
706 Danny Lockett LL .01 .05
707 Anthony Parker RC LL .02 .10
708 Dan Crossman LL .01 .05
709 Eric Wilkerson LL .01 .05
710 Judd Garrett LL RC .01 .05
711 Tony Baker LL .01 .05
712 Ran.Cunningham PHOTO .01 .05
713 2nd Place BW PHOTO .01 .05
714 3rd Place BW PHOTO .01 .05
715 1st Place Color PHOTO .01 .05
716 2nd Place Color PHOTO .01 .05
717 3rd Place Color PHOTO .01 .05
718 1st Place Color PHOTO .01 .05
719 2nd Place Color PHOTO .01 .05
720 3rd Place Color PHOTO .01 .05
721 Ray Bentley .01 .05
722 Earnest Byner .01 .05
723 Bill Fralic .01 .05
724 Joe Jacoby .01 .05
725 Howie Long .08 .25
726 Dan Marino THINK .20 .50
727 Ron Rivera .01 .05
728 Mike Singletary .02 .10
729 Cornelius Bennett .02 .10
730 Russell Maryland .08 .25
731 Eric Turner RC .02 .10
732 Bruce Pickens UER RC .01 .05
733 Mike Croel RC .01 .05
734 Todd Lyght RC .01 .05
735 Eric Swann RC .08 .25
736 Charles McRae RC .01 .05
737 Antone Davis RC .01 .05
738 Stanley Richard RC .01 .05
739 Herman Moore RC .08 .25
740 Pat Harlow RC .01 .05
741 Alvin Harper RC .08 .25
742 Mike Pritchard RC .08 .25
743 Leonard Russell RC .08 .25
744 Huey Richardson RC .01 .05
745 Dan McGwire RC .01 .05
746 Bobby Wilson RC .01 .05
747 Alfred Williams .01 .05
748 Vinnie Clark RC .01 .05
749 Kelvin Pritchett RC .02 .10
750 Harvey Williams RC .08 .25
751 Stan Thomas .01 .05
752 Randal Hill RC .02 .10
753 Todd Marinovich RC .01 .05
754 Ted Washington RC .01 .05
755 Henry Jones RC .02 .10
756 Jarrod Bunch RC .01 .05
757 Mike Dumas RC .01 .05
758 Ed King RC .01 .05
759 Reggie Johnson RC .01 .05
760 Roman Phifer RC .01 .05
761 Mike Jones DE RC .01 .05
762 Brett Favre RC 3.00 8.00
763 Browning Nagle RC .01 .05
764 Esera Tuaolo RC .01 .05
765 George Thornton RC .01 .05
766 Dixon Edwards RC .01 .05
767 Darryll Lewis .02 .10
768 Eric Bieniemy RC .01 .05
769 Shane Curry .01 .05
770 Jerome Henderson RC .01 .05
771 Wesley Carroll RC .01 .05
772 Nick Bell RC .01 .05
773 John Flannery RC .01 .05
774 Ricky Watters RC .60 1.50
775 Jeff Graham RC .08 .25
776 Eric Moten RC .01 .05
777 Jesse Campbell RC .01 .05
778 Chris Zorich .02 .10
779 Joe Valerio RC .01 .05
780 Doug Thomas RC .01 .05
781 Lamar Rogers UER RC .01 .05
782 John Johnson RC .01 .05
783 Phil Hansen RC .01 .05
784 Kanavis McGhee RC .01 .05
785 Calvin Stephens UER RC .01 .05
786 James Jones RC .01 .05
787 Reggie Barrett .01 .05
788 Aeneas Williams RC .50 1.25
789 Aaron Craver RC .01 .05
790 Keith Traylor RC .01 .05
791 Godfrey Myles RC .01 .05
792 Mo Lewis RC .02 .10
793 James Richard RC .01 .05
794 Carlos Jenkins RC .01 .05
795 Lawrence Dawsey RC .02 .10
796 Don Davey .01 .05
797 Jake Reed RC .20 .50
798 Dave McCloughan .01 .05
799 Erik Williams RC .02 .10
800 Steve Jackson RC .01 .05
801 Bob Dahl .01 .05
802 Ernie Mills RC .02 .10
803 David Daniels RC .01 .05
804 Rob Selby RC .01 .05
805 Ricky Ervins RC .02 .10
806 Tim Barnett RC .01 .05
807 Chris Gardocki RC .08 .25
808 Kevin Donnalley RC .01 .05
809 Robert Wilson RC .01 .05
810 Chuck Webb RC .01 .05
811 Darryl Wren RC .01 .05
812 Ed McCaffrey RC .75 2.00
813 Shula's 300th NEW .01 .05
814 Raiders-49ers sell out NEW .01 .05
815 NFL International NEW .01 .05
816 Moe Gardner RC .01 .05
817 Tim McKyer .01 .05
818 Tom Waddle RC .01 .05
819 Michael Jackson WR RC .08 .25
820 Tony Casillas .01 .05
821 Gaston Green .01 .05
822 Kenny Walker RC .01 .05
823 Willie Green RC .01 .05
824 Erik Kramer RC .08 .25
825 William Fuller .02 .10
826 Allen Pinkett .01 .05
827 Rick Venturi CO .01 .05
828 Bill Maas .01 .05
829 Jeff Jaeger .01 .05
830 Robert Delpino .01 .05
831 Mark Higgs RC .01 .05
832 Reggie Roby .01 .05
833 Terry Allen RC .60 1.50
834 Cris Carter .20 .50
835 John Randle RC 3.00 8.00
836 Hugh Millen RC .01 .05
837 Jon Vaughn RC .01 .05
838 Gill Fenerty .01 .05
839 Floyd Turner .01 .05
840 Irv Eatman .01 .05
841 Lonnie Young .01 .05
842 Jim McMahon .02 .10
843 Randal Hill .01 .05
844 Barry Foster .02 .10
845 Neil O'Donnell RC .08 .25
846 John Friesz UER .08 .25
847 Broderick Thomas .01 .05
848 Brian Mitchell .02 .10
849 Mike Utley RC .02 .10
850 Mike Croel ROY .01 .05
SC1 SB XXVI Theme Art .08 .25
SC3 Jim Thorpe Pioneer .30 .75
SC4 Otto Graham Pioneer .30 .75
SC5 Paul Brown Pioneer .30 .75
PSS1 Walter Payton .20 .50
PSS2 Red Grange .20 .50
MVPC25 Ottis Anderson .08 .25
AU336 L.Taylor REP AU/500 100.00 175.00
AU394 L.Taylor PB AU/500 100.00 175.00
AU699 Ozzie Newsome AU 25.00 50.00
AU824 Erik Kramer AU 25.00 50.00
NNO Mini Pro Set Gazette .08 .25
NNO Pro Set Gazette .08 .25
NNO Santa Claus .20 .50
NNO Super Bowl XXV Art .08 .25
NNO Super Bowl XXV Logo .08 .25

1991 Pro Set WLAF Helmets

This set of ten standard size cards features (on the front of each card) a helmet of the teams of the WLAF's first season. These cards were included in the 1991 Pro Set first series wax packs. The back has information about the teams.

COMPLETE SET (10) .80 2.00
1 Barcelona Dragons .08 .25
2 Birmingham Fire .08 .25
3 Frankfurt Galaxy .08 .25
4 London Monarchs .08 .25
5 Montreal Machine .08 .25
6 NY-NJ Knights .08 .25
7 Orlando Thunder .08 .25
8 Ral.-Durham Skyhawks .08 .25
9 Sacramento Surge .08 .25
10 San Antonio Riders .08 .25

1991 Pro Set WLAF Inserts

This 32-card standard size set was issued by Pro Set as an insert to the 1991 Pro Set Football first series. This set features the leading players from the WLAF. All ten WLAF teams are represented, and each team's head coach and quarterback are depicted on a card.

COMPLETE SET (32) 1.60 4.00
1 Mike Lynn .02 .10
2 London vs. Frankfurt .02 .10
3 Jack Bicknell CO .02 .10
4 Scott Erney .02 .10
5 A.J. Green .02 .10
6 Chan Gailey CO .10 .30
7 Paul McGowan .02 .10
8 Brent Pease .02 .10
9 Jack Elway CO .10 .30
10 Mike Perez .02 .10
11 Mike Teeter .02 .10
12 Larry Kennan CO UER .02 .10
13 Corris Ervin .02 .10
14 John Witkowski .02 .10
15 Jacques Dussault CO .02 .10
16 Ray Savage .02 .10
17 Kevin Sweeney .02 .10
18 Mouse Davis CO .10 .30
19 Todd Hammel UER .02 .10
20 Anthony Parker .10 .30
21 Don Matthews CO .02 .10
22 Kerwin Bell .10 .30
23 Wayne Davis LB .02 .10
24 Roman Gabriel CO .15 .40
25 Jon Carter .02 .10
26 Mark Maye .02 .10
27 Kay Stephenson CO .02 .10
28 Ben Bennett .02 .10
29 Shawn Knight .02 .10
30 Mike Riley CO .02 .10
31 Jason Garrett 1.25 3.00
32 Greg Gilbert .02 .10

1991 Pro Set Cinderella Story

This nine-card set was issued as a perforated insert sheet in The Official NFL Pro Set Card Book, which chronicles the history of NFL Pro Set cards. The unifying theme of this set is summed up by the words "Cinderella Story" on the card fronts. The set highlights players or teams who overcame formidable obstacles to become winners. After perforation, the cards measure the standard size. The front design is similar to the 1991 regular issue, with full-bleed player photos and player (or team) identification in colored stripes traversing the bottom of the card. All the cards feature color photos, with the exception of card numbers 4-6. The back has an extended caption for the card on the left portion, and a different photo on the right portion.

COMPLETE SET (9) 25.00 50.00
1 Rocky Bleier 3.00 6.00
2 Tom Dempsey 1.50 3.00
3 Dan Hampton 2.00 4.00
4 Charlie Hennigan 1.50 3.00
5 Dante Lavelli 2.00 4.00
6 Jim Plunkett 2.00 4.00
7 1968 New York Jets 4.00 10.00
8 1981 San Francisco 10.00 20.00
9 1979 Tampa Bay Bucs 1.50 3.00

1991 Pro Set National Banquet

This five-card standard-size set was given away by Pro Set, one of the sponsors of the 1991 12th National Sports Collectors Convention in Anaheim, California. The cards have full-bleed color photos on the fronts. The horizontally oriented backs have other color photos and career summaries. The back of the ProFiles card has a picture of TV announcers Tim Brant and Craig James.

COMPLETE SET (5) 2.00 5.00
1 Ronnie Lott .50 1.25
2 Roy Firestone .40 1.00
3 Roger Craig .50 1.25
4 ProFiles .40 1.00
5 Title card .40 1.00

1991 Pro Set Pro Files

These cards measure the standard size. The fronts have full-bleed color photos, with facsimile autographs inscribed across the bottom of the pictures. Reportedly only 150 of each were produced and approximately 100 of each were handed out as part of a contest on the Pro Files TV show. Each week viewers were invited to send in their names and addresses to a Pro Set post office box. All subjects in the set made appearances on the TV show. The show was hosted by Craig James and Tim Brant and was aired on Saturday nights in Dallas and sponsored by Pro Set. The cards were subtitled "Signature Series". The cards are unnumbered and are listed in alphabetical order by subject in the checklist below. All of the cards were facsimile autographed except for Anne Smith who signed all of her cards personally.

COMPLETE SET (13) 120.00 300.00
1 Troy Aikman 75.00 150.00

1991 Pro Set Super Bowl Tickets

This set was produced by Pro Set and distributed by Commemorative Sports Fragrances in factory set form. Each card features a replica Super Bowl ticket on the front and game stats on the back.

COMP.FACT SET (25) 20.00 50.00
COMMON CARD (1-25) 1.00 2.50

1991 Pro Set Spanish

The 1991 Pro Set Spanish football card set contains 300 standard-size cards selected from 1991 Pro Set Series I and II along with five special collectibles cards. Though the cards display the same player photos, the terminology has been translated into Spanish. The cards are numbered on the back and checklisted alphabetically according to teams.

COMPLETE SET (305) 25.00 50.00
1 Steve Broussard .05 .15
2 Darion Conner .05 .15
3 Tory Epps .05 .15
4 Bill Fralic .05 .15
5 Mike Gann .05 .15
6 Chris Miller .08 .25
7 Andre Rison .20 .50
8 Deion Sanders .50 1.25
9 Jessie Tuggle .05 .15
10 Cornelius Bennett .08 .25
11 Shane Conlan .05 .15
12 Kent Hull .05 .15
13 Kirby Jackson .05 .15
14 James Lofton .08 .25
15 Andre Reed .08 .25
16 Bruce Smith .20 .50
17 Darryl Talley .05 .15
18 Thurman Thomas .20 .50
19 Neal Anderson .08 .25
20 Trace Armstrong .05 .15
21 Mark Carrier DB .08 .25
22 Wendell Davis .05 .15
23 Richard Dent .05 .15
24 Jim Harbaugh .20 .50
25 Ron Rivera .05 .15
26 Mike Singletary .08 .25
27 Lemuel Stinson .05 .15
28 James Brooks .05 .15
29 Eddie Brown .05 .15
30 Boomer Esiason .08 .25
31 James Francis .05 .15
32 David Fulcher .05 .15
33 Rodney Holman .05 .15
34 Anthony Munoz .08 .25
35 Bruce Reimers .05 .15
36 Ickey Woods .05 .15
37 Mike Baab .05 .15
38 Brian Brennan .05 .15
39 Raymond Clayborn .05 .15
40 Mike Johnson .05 .15
41 Clay Matthews .08 .25
42 Eric Metcalf .20 .50
43 Frank Minnifield .05 .15
44 Joe Morris .05 .15
45 Anthony Pleasant .05 .15
46 Troy Aikman 1.00 2.50
47 Jack Del Rio .08 .25
48 Issiac Holt .05 .15
49 Michael Irvin .20 .50
50 Jimmie Jones .05 .15
51 Nate Newton .08 .25
52 Danny Noonan .05 .15
53 Jay Novacek .20 .50
54 Emmitt Smith 2.50 6.00
55 Steve Atwater .05 .15
56 Michael Brooks .05 .15
57 John Elway 3.00 6.00
58 Mike Horan .05 .15
59 Mark Jackson .05 .15
60 Karl Mecklenburg .05 .15
61 Warren Powers .05 .15
62 Dennis Smith .05 .15
63 Doug Widell .05 .15
64 Jerry Ball .05 .15
65 Bennie Blades .05 .15
66 Robert Clark .05 .15
67 Ken Dallafior .05 .15
68 Mel Gray .08 .25
69 Eddie Murray .05 .15
70 Rodney Peete .08 .25
71 Barry Sanders 2.00 5.00
72 Chris Spielman .08 .25
73 Robert Brown .05 .15
74 LeRoy Butler .08 .25
75 Perry Kemp .05 .15
76 Don Majkowski .05 .15
77 Tony Mandarich .05 .15
78 Mark Murphy .05 .15
79 Brian Noble .05 .15
80 Sterling Sharpe .20 .50
81 Ed West .05 .15
82 Ray Childress .08 .25
83 Cris Dishman .05 .15
84 Ernest Givins .08 .25
85 Drew Hill .08 .25
86 Haywood Jeffires .08 .25
87 Lamar Lathon .05 .15
88 Bruce Matthews .08 .25
89 Bubba McDowell .05 .15
90 Warren Moon .08 .25
91 Chip Banks .05 .15
92 Albert Bentley .05 .15
93 Duane Bickett .05 .15
94 Bill Brooks .05 .15
95 Sam Clancy .05 .15
96 Ray Donaldson .05 .15
97 Jeff George .20 .50
98 Mike Prior .05 .15
99 Clarence Verdin .05 .15
100 Steve DeBerg .08 .25
101 Albert Lewis .05 .15
102 Christian Okoye .05 .15
103 Kevin Ross .05 .15
104 Stephone Paige .05 .15
105 Kevin Porter .05 .15
106 Percy Snow .05 .15
107 Derrick Thomas .20 .50
108 Barry Word .05 .15
109 Marcus Allen .20 .50
110 Mervyn Fernandez .05 .15
111 Howie Long .20 .50
112 Ronnie Lott .08 .25
113 Terry McDaniel .08 .25
114 Max Montoya .05 .15
115 Don Mosebar .05 .15
116 Jay Schroeder .06 .16
117 Greg Townsend .05 .15
118 Flipper Anderson .05 .15
119 Henry Ellard .08 .25
120 Jim Everett .08 .25
121 Kevin Greene .08 .25
122 Damone Johnson .05 .15
123 Buford McGee .05 .15
124 Tom Newberry .05 .15
125 Michael Stewart .05 .15
126 Alvin Wright .05 .15
127 Mark Clayton .08 .25
128 Jeff Cross .05 .15
129 Mark Duper .08 .25
130 Ferrell Edmunds .05 .15
131 Dan Marino 3.00 6.00
132 Tim McKyer .05 .15
133 John Offerdahl .05 .15
134 Louis Oliver .05 .15
135 Sammie Smith .05 .15
136 Joey Browner .05 .15
137 Anthony Carter .08 .25
138 Chris Doleman .08 .25
139 Hassan Jones .05 .15
140 Steve Jordan .05 .15
141 Carl Lee .05 .15
142 Al Noga .05 .15
143 Henry Thomas .08 .25
144 Herschel Walker .08 .25
145 Ray Agnew .05 .15
146 Bruce Armstrong .05 .15
147 Marv Cook .05 .15
148 Irving Fryar .08 .25
149 Tommy Hodson .05 .15
150 Fred Marion .05 .15
151 Johnny Rembert .05 .15
152 Chris Singleton .05 .15
153 Andre Tippett .05 .15
154 Morten Andersen .05 .15
155 Toi Cook .05 .15
156 Craig Heyward .08 .25
157 Dalton Hilliard .05 .15
158 Rickey Jackson .08 .25
159 Vaughan Johnson .05 .15
160 Rueben Mayes .05 .15
161 Pat Swilling .08 .25
162 Bobby Hebert .08 .25
163 Ottis Anderson .08 .25
164 Carl Banks .05 .15
165 Rodney Hampton .20 .50
166 Jeff Hostetler .08 .25
167 Mark Ingram .05 .15
168 Leonard Marshall .05 .15
169 Dave Meggett .08 .25
170 Lawrence Taylor .20 .50
171 Everson Walls .05 .15
172 Brad Baxter .05 .15
173 Jeff Lageman .05 .15
174 Pat Leahy .05 .15
175 Erik McMillan .05 .15
176 Scott Mersereau .05 .15
177 Rob Moore .08 .25
178 Ken O'Brien .05 .15
179 Blair Thomas .05 .15
180 Al Toon .05 .15
181 Eric Allen .05 .15
182 Jerome Brown .08 .25
183 Keith Byars .08 .25
184 Randall Cunningham .20 .50
185 Byron Evans .05 .15
186 Keith Jackson .08 .25
187 Heath Sherman .05 .15
188 Clyde Simmons .08 .25
189 Reggie White .20 .50
190 Rich Camarillo .05 .15
191 Johnny Johnson .05 .15
192 Ernie Jones .05 .15
193 Tim McDonald .05 .15
194 Freddie Joe Nunn .05 .15
195 Luis Sharpe .05 .15
196 Jay Taylor .05 .15
197 Anthony Thompson .05 .15
198 Tom Tupa .05 .15
199 Gary Anderson K .05 .15
200 Bubby Brister .08 .25
201 Eric Green .08 .25
202 Bryan Hinkle .05 .15
203 Merril Hoge .05 .15
204 Carnell Lake .08 .25
205 Louis Lipps .05 .15
206 Keith Willis .05 .15
207 Rod Woodson .20 .50
208 Rod Bernstine .05 .15
209 Marion Butts .05 .15
210 Anthony Miller .08 .25
211 Leslie O'Neal .08 .25
212 Henry Rolling .05 .15
213 Junior Seau .20 .50
214 Billy Ray Smith .05 .15
215 Broderick Thompson .05 .15
216 Derrick Walker .05 .15
217 Dexter Carter .05 .15
218 Don Griffin .05 .15
219 Charles Haley .08 .25
220 Pierce Holt .05 .15
221 Joe Montana 4.00 8.00
222 Jerry Rice 1.00 2.50
223 John Taylor .08 .25
224 Michael Walter .05 .15
225 Steve Young .80 2.00
226 Brian Blades .08 .25
227 Jeff Bryant .05 .15
228 Jacob Green .05 .15
229 Tommy Kane .05 .15
230 Dave Krieg .08 .25
231 Bryan Millard .05 .15
232 Rufus Porter .05 .15
233 Eugene Robinson .05 .15
234 John L. Williams .05 .15
235 Gary Anderson RB .05 .15
236 Mark Carrier WR .08 .25
237 Reggie Cobb .05 .15
238 Reuben Davis .05 .15
239 Paul Gruber .05 .15
240 Harry Hamilton .05 .15
241 Keith McCants .05 .15
242 Ricky Reynolds .05 .15
243 Vinny Testaverde .08 .25
244 Earnest Byner .06 .15
245 Gary Clark .08 .25
246 Andre Collins .06 .15
247 Darrell Green .08 .25
248 Jim Lachey .05 .15
249 Charles Mann .05 .15
250 Wilber Marshall .05 .15
251 Art Monk .08 .25
252 Mark Rypien .08 .25
253 Russell Maryland .05 .15
254 Mike Croel .05 .15
255 Stanley Richard .08 .25
256 Leonard Russell .20 .50
257 Dan McGwire .05 .15
258 Todd Marinovich .05 .15
259 Eric Swann .20 .50
260 Mike Pritchard .20 .50
261 Alfred Williams .05 .15
262 Brett Favre 6.00 15.00
263 Browning Nagle .05 .15
264 Darryll Lewis .08 .25
265 Nick Bell .05 .15
266 Jeff Graham .20 .50
267 Eric Moten .05 .15
268 Roman Phifer .05 .15
269 Eric Bieniemy .08 .25
270 Phil Hansen .05 .15
271 Reggie Barrett .05 .15
272 Aeneas Williams .50 1.25
273 Aaron Craver .05 .15
274 Lawrence Dawsey .08 .25
275 Ricky Ervins .05 .15
276 Jake Reed .20 .50
277 Erik Williams .08 .25
278 Tim Barnett .05 .15
279 Keith Traylor .05 .15
280 Jerry Rice PB UER .50 1.25
281 Jim Lachey .05 .15
282 Barry Sanders PB 1.00 2.50
283 Neal Anderson .08 .25
284 Reggie White .20 .50
285 Lawrence Taylor .20 .50
286 Mike Singletary .08 .25
287 Joey Browner .05 .15
288 Morten Andersen SS .05 .15
289 Andre Reed SS .08 .25
290 Anthony Munoz SS .08 .25
291 Warren Moon SS .20 .50
292 Thurman Thomas SS .20 .50
293 Ray Childress SS .05 .15
294 Derrick Thomas SS .20 .50
295 Rod Woodson SS .20 .50
296 Steve Atwater SS .05 .15
297 David Fulcher SS .05 .15
298 Anthony Munoz Think .08 .25
299 Ron Rivera Think .05 .15
300 Cornelius Bennett .08 .25
E1 Tom Flores .40 1.00
E2 Anthony Munoz .40 1.00
E3 Tony Casillas .40 1.00
E4 Super Bowl XXVI Logo .40 1.00
E5 Felicidades .40 1.00

1991 Pro Set UK Sheets

This set of five (approximately) 5 1/8" by 11 3/4" six-card strips was issued by Pro Set in England as an advertisement in Today, a newspaper in Middlesex, England. The unperforated strips are numbered 1-5, and each presents a "collection" of six player cards that measure the standard size. The sheets were issued one per week in consecutive Sunday editions of the paper during the Fall of 1991. The cards and their numbering are identical to the 1991 regular issues. They are checklisted below by strips, and within strips listed beginning from the top left card and moving to the bottom right card.

COMPLETE SET (5) 25.00 60.00
1 Quarterbacks 8.00 20.00
2 Running Backs 6.00 15.00
3 Receivers 4.00 10.00
4 Kickers 2.00 5.00
5 Defensive 4.00 10.00

1991 Pro Set WLAF 150

The premier edition of the 1991 Pro Set World League of American Football set contains 150 standard-size cards. The first 29 cards of the set are subdivided as follows: League Overview (1-3), World Bowl (4-9), Helmet Collectibles (10-19), and 1991 Statistical Leaders (20-29). The player cards are numbered 30-150, and they are checklisted below alphabetically within and according to teams.

COMPLETE SET (150) 1.60 4.00
1 World League Logo .01 .05
2 Mike Lynn PRES .01 .05
3 First Weekend .01 .05
4 World Bowl Trophy .01 .05
5 Jon Horton .01 .05
6 Stan Gelbaugh .07 .20
7 Dan Crossman .01 .05
8 Marlon Brown .01 .05
9 Judd Garrett .02 .10
10 Barcelona Dragons .02 .10
11 Birmingham Fire .02 .10
12 Frankfurt Galaxy .02 .10
13 London Monarchs .02 .10
14 Montreal Machine .02 .10
15 NY-NJ Knights .02 .10
16 Orlando Thunder .02 .10
17 Raleigh-Durham .02 .10
18 Sacramento Surge .02 .10
19 San Antonio Riders .02 .10
20 Eric Wilkerson SL .01 .05
21 Stan Gelbaugh SL .07 .20
22 Judd Garrett SL .01 .05
23 Tony Baker SL .07 .20
24 Byron Williams SL .01 .05
25 Chris Mohr SL .01 .05
26 Errol Tucker SL .01 .05
27 Carl Painter SL .01 .05
28 Anthony Parker SL .02 .10
29 Danny Lockett SL .01 .05
30 Scott Adams .01 .05
31 Jim Bell .01 .05
32 Lydell Carr .02 .10
33 Bruce Clark .01 .05
34 Demetrius Davis .02 .10
35 Scott Erney .01 .05
36 Ron Goetz .01 .05
37 Xisco Marcos .01 .05
38 Paul Palmer .01 .05
39 Tony Rice .07 .20
40 Bobby Sign .01 .05
41 Gene Taylor .01 .05
42 Barry Voorhees .01 .05
43 Jack Bicknell CO .01 .05
44 Ken Bell .01 .05
45 Willie Bouyer .01 .05
46 John Brantley .01 .05
47 Elroy Harris .01 .05
48 James Henry .01 .05
49 John Holland .01 .05
50 Arthur Hunter .01 .05
51 Eric Jones QB .01 .05
52 Kirk Maggio .01 .05
53 Paul McGowan .01 .05
54 John Miller .01 .05
55 Maurice Oliver .01 .05
56 Darrell Phillips .01 .05
57 Chan Gailey CO .20 .50
58 Tony Baker .07 .20
59 Tim Broady .01 .05
60 Garry Frank .01 .05
61 Jason Johnson .01 .05
62 Stefan Maslo .01 .05
63 Mark Mraz .01 .05
64 Yepi Pau'u .01 .05
65 Mike Perez .01 .05
66 Mike Teeter .01 .05
67 Chris Williams DT .01 .05
68 Jack Elway CO .02 .10
69 Theo Adams .01 .05
70 Jeff Alexander .01 .05
71 Phil Alexander .01 .05
72 Paul Berardelli .01 .05
73 Dana Brinson .01 .05
74 Marlon Brown .01 .05
75 Dedrick Dodge .01 .05
76 Victor Ebubedike .01 .05
77 Corris Ervin .01 .05
78 Steve Gabbard .01 .05
79 Judd Garrett .02 .10
80 Stan Gelbaugh .07 .20
81 Roy Hart .01 .05
82 Jon Horton .01 .05
83 Danny Lockett .01 .05
84 Doug Marrone .40 1.00
85 Ken Sale .01 .05
86 Larry Kennan CO .01 .05
87 Mike Cadore .01 .05
88 K.D. Dunn .02 .05
89 Ricky Johnson .01 .05
90 Chris Mohr .02 .10
91 Bjorn Nittmo .01 .05
92 Michael Proctor .01 .05
93 Richard Shelton .01 .05
94 Tracy Simien .07 .20
95 Jacques Dussault CO .01 .05
96 Cornell Burbage .01 .05
97 Joe Campbell LB .01 .05
98 Monty Gilbreath .01 .05
99 Jeff Graham QB .20 .50
100 Kip Lewis .01 .05
101 Bobby Lilljedahl .01 .05
102 Falanda Newton .01 .05
103 Anthony Parker .07 .20
104 Caesar Rentie .01 .05
105 Ron Sancho .01 .05
106 Craig Schlicting .01 .05
107 Lonnie Turner .01 .05
108 Eric Wilkerson .01 .05
109 Tony Woods Okl. .02 .10
110 Darrell(Mouse) Davis .02 .10
111 Kerwin Bell .07 .20
112 Wayne Davis LB .01 .05
113 John Guerrero .01 .05
114 Myron Jones .01 .05
115 Eric Mitchel .01 .05
116 Billy Owens .01 .05
117 Carl Painter .01 .05
118 Rob Sterling .01 .05
119 Errol Tucker .01 .05
120 Byron Williams .01 .05
121 Mike Withycombe .01 .05
122 Don Matthews CO .01 .05
123 Jon Carter .01 .05
124 Marvin Hargrove .01 .05
125 Clarkston Hines .01 .05
126 Ray Jackson .01 .05
127 Bobby McAllister .01 .05
128 Darryl McGill .01 .05
129 Pat McGuirk .01 .05
130 Shawn Woodson .01 .05
131 Roman Gabriel CO .07 .20
132 Greg Coauette .01 .05
133 Mike Elkins .01 .05
134 Victor Floyd .01 .05
135 Shawn Knight .01 .05
136 Pete Najarian .01 .05
137 Carl Parker .01 .05
138 Richard Stephens .01 .05
139 Curtis Wilson .01 .05
140 Kay Stephenson CO .01 .05
141 Ricky Blake .02 .10
142 Donnie Gardner .01 .05
143 Jason Garrett 1.25 3.00
144 Mike Johnson QB .01 .05
145 Undra Johnson .01 .05
146 John Layfield .60 1.50
147 Mark Ledbetter .01 .05
148 Gary Richard .01 .05
149 Tim Walton LB .01 .05
150 Mike Riley CO .01 .05

1991 Pro Set WLAF World Bowl Combo

With a few subtle changes, this 43-card standard-size set is a reissue of the 1991 Pro Set WLAF Helmet and 1991 Pro Set WLAF insert sets. The first 32-cards are identical to the 1991 Pro Set WLAF Inserts set, except for cards #26 and #28, so those have not been listed below. However, the helmet cards have been re-numbered and can also be distinguished on the back by the presence of a team narrative instead of a team schedule so those are priced below. Finally a newly created World Bowl Trophy card was added to round out the 43-card set. The set was passed out to attendees of the World Bowl Game in Wembley Stadium, London, England.

COMPLETE SET (43) 6.00 12.00
26 Bobby McAllister .75 2.00
28 Mike Elkins .75 2.00
33 World Bowl Trophy .40 1.00
34 Barcelona Dragons .40 1.00
35 Birmingham Fire .40 1.00
36 Frankfurt Galaxy .40 1.00
37 London Monarchs .40 1.00
38 Montreal Machine .40 1.00
39 NY-NJ Knights .40 1.00
40 Orlando Thunder .40 1.00
41 Ral.-Durham Skyhawks .40 1.00
42 Sacramento Surge .40 1.00
43 San Antonio Riders .40 1.00

1991-92 Pro Set Super Bowl XXVI Binder

This 49-card standard-size set was sponsored by American Express and produced by Pro Set to commemorate Super Bowl XXVI. The set was sold in a white binder that housed four cards per page. It includes five new cards (1-5), four Think About It cards (300, 370, 725-726), as well as player cards for the Buffalo Bills (73-77, 79-84, 86, 88-90, 444-445, 449-450) and Washington Redskins (316-318, 320-324, 676-684, 746, 805, 848). The player cards are the same as the regular issue (including numbering), except that the Bills' cards have a "1991 AFC Champs" logo on the front, while the Redskins' cards carry a "1991 NFC Champs" logo on their fronts. A Jim Kelly card was apparently produced separately (individually cellophane wrapped and unnumbered) and was only available at the Super Bowl with the seat-cushion sets. Kelly was not included in sets sent out as as part of the mail-away offer advertised after the Super Bowl. The Kelly card does not include the Pro Set logo on the back.

COMPLETE SET (49) 8.00 20.00
1 The NFL Experience .20 .50
2 Super Bowl XXVI .07 .20
3 AFC Standings .07 .20
4 NFC Standings .07 .20
5 The Metrodome .07 .20
73 Howard Ballard .07 .20
74 Cornelius Bennett .20 .50
75 Shane Conlan .07 .20
76 Kent Hull .07 .20
77 Kirby Jackson .07 .20
79 Mark Kelso .07 .20
80 Nate Odomes .10 .30
81 Andre Reed .20 .50
82 Jim Ritcher .07 .20
83 Bruce Smith .20 .50
84 Darryl Talley .07 .20
86 Thurman Thomas .30 .75
88 Will Wolford .07 .20
89 Jeff Wright .07 .20
90 Marv Levy CO .07 .20
300 Cornelius Bennett .10 .30
316 Earnest Byner .10 .30
317 Gary Clark .20 .50
318 Andre Collins .10 .30
320 Chip Lohmiller .07 .20
321 Martin Mayhew .07 .20
322 Mark Rypien .10 .30
323 Alvin Walton .07 .20
324 Joe Gibbs CO .20 .50
370 Warren Moon .15 .40
444 James Lofton .20 .50
445 Keith McKeller .07 .20
449 Leon Seals .07 .20
450 Leonard Smith .07 .20
676 Jeff Bostic .07 .20
677 Darrell Green .10 .30
678 Markus Koch .07 .20
679 Jim Lachey .10 .30
680 Charles Mann .10 .30
681 Wilber Marshall .10 .30
682 Art Monk .15 .40
683 Gerald Riggs .07 .20
684 Ricky Sanders .10 .30
725 Howie Long .20 .50
726 Dan Marino .80 2.00
746 Bobby Wilson .07 .20
805 Ricky Ervins .10 .30
848 Brian Mitchell .20 .50
NNU Jim Kelly SP 6.00 15.00

1992 Pro Set

This standard-size set contains 700 cards issued in two differently designed series of 400 and 300. Cards for either series were issued in 15-card packs. First series fronts feature full-bleed color player photos with the player's name in a stripe at the bottom. The NFL Pro Set logo in the lower right corner. In a horizontal format, the backs have a close-up color player photo, biography, career highlights and complete statistical information. Second series cards are full-bleed on the right side with the players name running up the left border. A team logo is at the bottom left. Vertical backs have stats from the last three years, highlights and a small photo. Gray backgrounds contain all NFL team logos in white. The set opens with the following subsets: League Leaders (1-18), Milestones (19-27), Draft Day (28-33), Innovators (34-36), 1991 Replays (37-63), and Super Bowl XXVI Replays (64-72). Other than Washington and Buffalo leading off the first series, player cards are in team order by series. A number of subsets include Pro Set Newsreel (343-346), Magic Numbers (347-351), Play Smart (352-360), NFC Spirit of the Game (361-374), AFC Pro Bowl Stars (375-400), NFC Pro Bowl (401-427), Spirit of the Game (680-693) cards and some miscellaneous special cards (694-700). The key Rookie Cards in the set are Edgar Bennett, Steve Bono, Quentin Coryatt, Amp Lee and Carl Pickens. Randomly inserted in packs and listed at the end of the checklist below were Emmitt Smith and Erik Kramer autograph cards. Each player signed 1,000 cards that are individually numbered. Also inserted were a Smith Power Preview card, a Santa Claus card and Super Bowl XXVI logo card.

COMPLETE SET (700) 8.00 20.00
COMP.SERIES 1 (400) 4.00 10.00
COMP.SERIES 2 (300) 4.00 10.00
1 Mike Croel ROY .01 .05
2 Thurman Thomas POY .08 .25
3 Wayne Fontes COY .01 .05
4 Anthony Munoz MOY .02 .10
5 Steve Young LL .10 .30
6 Warren Moon LL .02 .10
7 Emmitt Smith LL .25 .60
8 Haywood Jeffires LL .01 .05
9 Marv Cook LL .01 .05
10 Michael Irvin LL .08 .25
11 Thurman Thomas LL .08 .25
12 Chip Lohmiller LL UER .01 .05
13 Barry Sanders LL .20 .50
14 Reggie Roby LL .01 .05
15 Mel Gray LL .01 .05
16 Ronnie Lott LL .02 .10
17 Pat Swilling LL .01 .05
18 Reggie White MVP .02 .10
19 Haywood Jeffires ML .01 .05
20 Pat Leahy MILE .01 .05
21 James Lofton MILE .02 .10
22 Art Monk MILE .02 .10
23 Don Shula MILE .02 .10
24A Nick Lowery MILE ERR .01 .05
24B Nick Lowery MILE COR .01 .05
25 John Elway ML .20 .50
26 Chicago Bears MILE .01 .05
27 Marcus Allen MILE .02 .10
28 Terrell Buckley RC .01 .05
29 Amp Lee RC .01 .05
30 Chris Mims RC .01 .05
31 Leon Searcy RC .01 .05
32 Jimmy Smith RC 1.25 3.00
33 Siran Stacy RC .01 .05
34 Pete Gogolak INN .01 .05
35 Cheerleaders INN .01 .05
36 Houston Astrodome INN .01 .05
37 Christian Okoye REP .01 .05
38 Don Beebe REP .01 .05
39 Wendell Davis REP .01 .05
40 Don Shula REP .01 .05
41 Ronnie Lott EP .01 .05
42 Art Monk REP .01 .05
43 Thurman Thomas REP .02 .10
44 John Stephens REP .01 .05
45 Herschel Walker REP .01 .05
46 Chris Burkett REP .01 .05
47 Week 11 REPLAY .01 .05
48 Andre Rison REP .01 .05
49 M.Irvin/Beuerlein REP .02 .10
50 Irving Fryar REP .01 .05
51 Bills REP .01 .05
52 Kelvin Martin REP .01 .05
53 Bruce Coslet REP .01 .05
54 Fred Jones REP .01 .05
55 Oilers REP .01 .05
56 Bill Bates REP .01 .05
57 Michael Haynes REP .01 .05
58 Broncos REP .01 .05
59 Thurman Thomas REP .02 .10
60 Erik Kramer REP .01 .05
61 Darrelll Green REP .01 .05
62 Carlton Bailey REP .01 .05
63 Mark Rypien REP .01 .05
64 Super Bowl XXVI REP .01 .05
65 Brad Edwards SB REP .01 .05
66 Mark Rypien SB REP .01 .05
67 Gerlad Riggs SB REP .01 .05
68 Kurt Gouveia SB REP .01 .05
69 Thurman Thomas SB REP .02 .10
70 Gary Clark SB REP .01 .05
71 Bills SB REP .01 .05
72 Redskins SB REP .01 .05
73 Jeff Bostic .01 .05
74 Earnest Byner .01 .05
75 Gary Clark .08 .25
76 Andre Collins .01 .05
77 Darrell Green .01 .05
78 Joe Jacoby .01 .05
79 Jim Lachey .01 .05
80 Chip Lohmiller .01 .05
81 Charles Mann .01 .05
82 Martin Mayhew .01 .05
83 Matt Millen .02 .10
84 Brian Mitchell .02 .10
85 Art Monk .02 .10
86 Gerald Riggs .01 .05
87 Mark Rypien .01 .05
88 Fred Stokes .01 .05
89 Bobby Wilson .01 .05
90 Joe Gibbs CO .02 .10
91 Howard Ballard .01 .05
92 Cornelius Bennett UER .02 .10
93 Kenneth Davis .01 .05
94 Al Edwards .01 .05
95 Kent Hull .01 .05
96 Kirby Jackson .01 .05
97 Mark Kelso .01 .05
98 James Lofton .02 .10
99 Keith McKeller .01 .05
100 Nate Odomes .01 .05
101 Jim Ritcher .01 .05
102 Leon Seals .01 .05
103 Steve Tasker .02 .10
104 Darryl Talley .01 .05
105 Thurman Thomas .08 .25
106 Will Wolford .01 .05
107 Jeff Wright .01 .05
108 Marv Levy CO .01 .05
109 Darion Conner .01 .05
110 Bill Fralic .01 .05
111 Moe Gardner .01 .05
112 Michael Haynes .02 .10
113 Chris Miller .02 .10
114 Erric Pegram .02 .10
115 Bruce Pickens .01 .05
116 Andre Rison .02 .10
117 Jerry Glanville CO .01 .05
118 Neal Anderson .01 .05
119 Trace Armstrong .01 .05
120 Wendell Davis .01 .05
121 Richard Dent .02 .10
122 Jay Hilgenberg .01 .05
123 Lemuel Stinson .01 .05
124 Stan Thomas .01 .05
125 Tom Waddle .01 .05
126 Mike Ditka CO .08 .25
127 James Brooks .02 .10
128 Eddie Brown .01 .05
129 David Fulcher .01 .05
130 Harold Green .01 .05
131 Tim Krumrie UER .01 .05
132 Anthony Munoz .02 .10
133 Craig Taylor .01 .05
134 Eric Thomas .01 .05
135 David Shula CO RC .01 .05
136 Mike Baab .01 .05
137 Brian Brennan .01 .05
138 Michael Jackson .02 .10
139 James Jones DT UER .01 .05
140 Ed King .01 .05
141 Clay Matthews .02 .10
142 Eric Metcalf .02 .10
143 Joe Morris .01 .05
144A Bill Belichick CO NPO .08 .25
144B Bill Belichick CO .08 .25
145 Steve Beuerlein .02 .10
146 Larry Brown DB .01 .05
147 Ray Horton .01 .05
148 Ken Norton .02 .10
149 Mike Saxon .01 .05
150 Emmitt Smith .60 1.50
151 Mark Stepnoski .02 .10
152 Alexander Wright .01 .05
153 Jimmy Johnson CO .02 .10
154 Mike Croel .01 .05
155 John Elway .50 1.25
156 Gaston Green UER .01 .05
157 Wymon Henderson .01 .05
158 Karl Mecklenburg UER .01 .05
159 Warren Powers .01 .05
160 Steve Sewell UER .01 .05
161 Doug Widell .01 .05
162 Dan Reeves CO .01 .05
163 Eric Andolsek .01 .05
164 Jerry Ball .01 .05
165 Bennie Blades .01 .05
166 Ray Crockett .01 .05
167 Willie Green UER .01 .05
168 Erik Kramer .02 .10
169 Barry Sanders .50 1.25
170 Chris Spielman UER .01 .05
171 Wayne Fontes CO .01 .05
172 Vinnie Clark .01 .05
173 Tony Mandarich .01 .05
174 Brian Noble .01 .05
175 Bryce Paup .08 .25
176 Sterling Sharpe .08 .25
177 Darrell Thompson .01 .05
178 Esera Tuaolo UER .01 .05
179 Ed West .01 .05
180 Mike Holmgren CO RC .08 .25
181 Ray Childress .01 .05
182 Cris Dishman .01 .05
183 Curtis Duncan .01 .05
184 William Fuller .01 .05
185 Lamar Lathon .01 .05
186 Warren Moon .08 .25
187 Bo Orlando RC .01 .05
188 Lorenzo White .01 .05
189 Jack Pardee CO .01 .05
190 Chip Banks .01 .05
191 Dean Biasucci UER .01 .05
192 Bill Brooks .01 .05
193 Ray Donaldson .01 .05
194 Jeff Herrod .01 .05
195 Mike Prior .01 .05
196 Mark Vander Poel .01 .05
197 Clarence Verdin .01 .05
198 Ted Marchibroda CO .01 .05
199 John Alt .01 .05
200 Deron Cherry .01 .05
201 Steve DeBerg .01 .05
202 Nick Lowery .01 .05
203 Neil Smith .08 .25
204 Derrick Thomas .08 .25
205 Joe Valerio .01 .05
206 Barry Word .01 .05
207 M. Schottenheimer CO .01 .05
208 Marcus Allen .08 .25
209 Nick Bell .01 .05
210 Tim Brown .08 .25
211 Howie Long .08 .25
212 Ronnie Lott .02 .10
213 Todd Marinovich .01 .05
214 Greg Townsend .01 .05
215 Steve Wright .01 .05
216 Art Shell CO .02 .10
217 Flipper Anderson .01 .05
218 Robert Delpino .01 .05
219 Henry Ellard .02 .10
220 Kevin Greene .02 .10
221 Todd Lyght .01 .05
222 Tom Newberry .01 .05
223 Roman Phifer .01 .05
224 Michael Stewart .01 .05
225 Chuck Knox CO .01 .05
226 Aaron Craver .01 .05
227 Jeff Cross .01 .05
228 Mark Duper .01 .05
229 Ferrell Edmunds .01 .05
230 Jim C. Jensen .01 .05
231 Louis Oliver UER .01 .05
232 Reggie Roby .01 .05
233 Sammie Smith .01 .05
234 Don Shula CO .02 .10
235 Joey Browner .01 .05
236 Anthony Carter .02 .10
237 Chris Doleman .01 .05
238 Steve Jordan .01 .05
239 Kirk Lowdermilk .01 .05
240 Henry Thomas .01 .05
241 Herschel Walker .02 .10
242 Felix Wright .01 .05
243 Dennis Green CO RC .02 .10
244 Ray Agnew .01 .05
245 Marv Cook .01 .05
246 Irving Fryar UER .02 .10
247 Pat Harlow .01 .05
248 Hugh Millen .01 .05
249 Leonard Russell .02 .10
250 Andre Tippett .01 .05
251 Jon Vaughn .01 .05
252 Dick MacPherson CO .01 .05
253 Morten Andersen .01 .05
254 Bobby Hebert .01 .05
255 Joel Hilgenberg .01 .05
256 Vaughan Johnson .01 .05
257 Sam Mills .01 .05
258 Pat Swilling .01 .05
259 Floyd Turner .01 .05
260 Steve Walsh .01 .05
261 Jim Mora CO UER .01 .05
262 Stephen Baker .01 .05
263 Mark Collins .01 .05
264 Rodney Hampton .02 .10
265 Jeff Hostetler .02 .10
266 Erik Howard .01 .05
267 Sean Landeta .01 .05
268 Gary Reasons UER .01 .05
269 Everson Walls .01 .05
270 Ray Handley CO .01 .05
271 Louie Aguiar RC .01 .05
272 Brad Baxter .01 .05
273 Chris Burkett .01 .05
274 Irv Eatman .01 .05
275 Jeff Lageman .01 .05
276 Freeman McNeil .01 .05
277 Rob Moore .02 .10
278 Lonnie Young .01 .05
279 Bruce Coslet CO .01 .05
280 Jerome Brown .01 .05
281 Keith Byars .01 .05
282 Bruce Collie UER .01 .05
283 Keith Jackson .02 .10
284 James Joseph .01 .05
285 Seth Joyner .01 .05
286 Andre Waters .01 .05
287 Reggie White .08 .25
288 Rich Kotite CO .01 .05
289 Rich Camarillo .01 .05
290 Garth Jax .01 .05
291 Ernie Jones .01 .05
292 Tim McDonald .01 .05
293 Rod Saddler .01 .05
294 Anthony Thompson UER .01 .05
295 Tom Tupa UER .01 .05
296 Ron Wolfley .01 .05
297 Joe Bugel CO .01 .05
298 Gary Anderson K .01 .05
299 Jeff Graham .08 .25
300 Eric Green .01 .05
301 Bryan Hinkle .01 .05
302 Tunch Ilkin .01 .05
303 Louis Lipps .01 .05
304 Neil O'Donnell .02 .10
305 Rod Woodson .08 .25
306 Bill Cowher CO RC .30 .75
307 Eric Bieniemy .01 .05
308 Marion Butts .01 .05
309 John Friesz .02 .10
310 Courtney Hall .01 .05
311 Ronnie Harmon .01 .05
312 Henry Rolling .01 .05
313 Billy Ray Smith .01 .05
314 George Thornton .01 .05
315 Bobby Ross CO RC .01 .05
316 Todd Bowles .08 .25
317 Michael Carter .01 .05
318 Don Griffin .01 .05
319 Charles Haley .02 .10
320 Brent Jones .02 .10
321 John Taylor .02 .10
322 Ted Washington .01 .05
323 Steve Young .25 .60
324 George Seifert CO .02 .10
325 Brian Blades .02 .10
326 Jacob Green .01 .05
327 Patrick Hunter .01 .05
328 Tommy Kane .01 .05
329 Cortez Kennedy .02 .10
330 Dave Krieg .02 .10
331 Rufus Porter .01 .05
332 John L. Williams .01 .05
333 Tom Flores CO .01 .05
334 Gary Anderson RB .01 .05
335 Mark Carrier WR .02 .10
336 Reuben Davis .01 .05
337 Lawrence Dawsey .02 .10
338 Keith McCants UER .01 .05
339 Vinny Testaverde .02 .10
340 Broderick Thomas .01 .05
341 Robert Wilson .01 .05
342 Sam Wyche CO .01 .05
343 Teacher of Year .01 .05
344 Owners Reject Replay .01 .05
345 NFL Experience .01 .05
346 Chuck Noll Retires .02 .10
347 Curtis/McGee MN UER .01 .05
348 D.Pearson/Irvin MN .02 .10
349 B.Sanders/Sims MN .20 .50
350 Marinovich/Stabler MN .01 .05
351 C.James/Russell MN .02 .10
352 Bob Golic .01 .05
353 Pat Harlow .01 .05
354 Esera Tuaolo .01 .05
355 Mark Schlereth RC .01 .05
356 Trace Armstrong .01 .05
357 Eric Bieniemy .01 .05
358 Bill Romanowski .01 .05
359 Irv Eatman .01 .05
360 Jonathan Hayes .01 .05
361 Atlanta Falcons .01 .05
362 Chicago Bears .01 .05
363 Dallas Cowboys .01 .05
364 Detroit Lions .01 .05
365 Green Bay Packers .01 .05
366 Los Angeles Rams .01 .05
367 Minnesota Vikings .01 .05
368 New Orleans Saints UER .01 .05
369 New York Giants .01 .05
370 Philadelphia Eagles .01 .05
371 Phoenix Cardinals .01 .05
372 San Francisco 49ers .01 .05
373 Tampa Bay Buccaneers .01 .05
374 Washington Redskins .01 .05
375 Steve Atwater PB UER .01 .05
376 Cornelius Bennett PB .02 .10
377 Tim Brown PB .02 .10
378 Marion Butts PB .01 .05
379 Ray Childress PB .01 .05
380 Mark Clayton PB .01 .05
381 Marv Cook PB .01 .05
382 Cris Dishman PB .01 .05
383 William Fuller PB .01 .05
384 Gaston Green PB .01 .05
385 Jeff Jaeger PB .01 .05
386 Haywood Jeffires PB .02 .10
387 James Lofton PB .02 .10
388 Ronnie Lott PB .02 .10
389 Karl Mecklenburg PB UER .01 .05
390 Warren Moon PB .02 .10
391 Anthony Munoz PB .01 .05
392 Dennis Smith PB .01 .05
393 Neil Smith PB .02 .10
394 Darryl Talley PB .01 .05
395 Derrick Thomas PB .02 .10
396 Thurman Thomas PB .02 .10
397 Greg Townsend PB .01 .05
398 Richmond Webb PB .01 .05
399 Rod Woodson PB .02 .10
400 Dan Reeves CO PB .01 .05
401 Troy Aikman PB .15 .40
402 Eric Allen PB .01 .05
403 Bennie Blades PB .01 .05
404 Lomas Brown PB .01 .05
405 Mark Carrier DB PB .01 .05
406 Gary Clark PB .02 .10
407 Mel Gray PB .01 .05
408 Darrell Green PB .01 .05
409 Michael Irvin PB .08 .25
410 Vaughan Johnson PB .01 .05
411 Seth Joyner PB .01 .05
412 Jim Lachey PB .01 .05
413 Chip Lohmiller PB .01 .05
414 Charles Mann PB .01 .05
415 Chris Miller PB .02 .10
416 Sam Mills PB .01 .05
417 Bart Oates PB .01 .05
418 Jerry Rice PB .15 .40
419 Andre Rison PB .02 .10
420 Mark Rypien PB .01 .05
421 Barry Sanders PB .20 .50
422 Deion Sanders PB .08 .25
423 Mark Schlereth PB .01 .05
424 Mike Singletary PD .01 .05
425 Emmitt Smith PB .25 .60
426 Pat Swilling PB .01 .05
427 Reggie White PB .02 .10
428 Rick Bryan .01 .05
429 Tim Green .01 .05
430 Drew Hill .01 .05
431 Norm Johnson .01 .05
432 Keith Jones .01 .05
433 Mike Pritchard .02 .10
434 Deion Sanders .20 .50
435 Tony Smith RC .01 .05
436 Jessie Tuggle .01 .05
437 Steve Christie .01 .05
438 Shane Conlan .01 .05
439 Matt Darby RC .01 .05
440 John Fina RC .01 .05
441 Henry Jones .01 .05
442 Jim Kelly .08 .25
443 Pete Metzelaars .01 .05
444 Andre Reed .02 .10
445 Bruce Smith .08 .25
446 Troy Auzenne RC .01 .05
447 Mark Carrier DB .01 .05
448 Will Furrer RC .01 .05
449 Jim Harbaugh .08 .25
450 Brad Muster .01 .05
451 Darren Lewis .01 .05
452 Mike Singletary .02 .10
453 Alonzo Spellman RC .02 .10
454 Chris Zorich .02 .10
455 Jim Breech .01 .05
456 Boomer Esiason .02 .10
457 Derrick Fenner .01 .05
458 James Francis .01 .05
459 David Klingler RC .01 .05
460 Tim McGee .01 .05
461 Carl Pickens RC .08 .25
462 Alfred Williams .01 .05
463 Darryl Williams RC .01 .05
464 Mark Bavaro .01 .05
465 Jay Hilgenberg .01 .05
466 Leroy Hoard .02 .10
467 Bernie Kosar .02 .10
468 Michael Dean Perry .02 .10
469 Todd Philcox RC .01 .05
470 Patrick Rowe RC .01 .05
471 Tommy Vardell RC .01 .05
472 Everson Walls .01 .05
473 Troy Aikman .30 .75
474 Kenneth Gant RC .01 .05
475 Charles Haley .02 .10
476 Michael Irvin .08 .25
477 Robert Jones RC .01 .05
478 Russell Maryland .01 .05
479 Jay Novacek .02 .10
480 Kevin Smith RC .01 .05
481 Tony Tolbert .01 .05
482 Steve Atwater .01 .05
483 Shane Dronett RC .01 .05
484 Simon Fletcher .01 .05
485 Greg Lewis .01 .05
486 Tommy Maddox RC .75 2.00
487 Shannon Sharpe .08 .25
488 Dennis Smith .01 .05
489 Sammie Smith .01 .05
490 Kenny Walker .01 .05
491 Lomas Brown .01 .05
492 Mike Farr .01 .05
493 Mel Gray .02 .10
494 Jason Hanson RC .02 .10
495 Herman Moore .08 .25
496 Rodney Peete .02 .10
497 Robert Porcher RC .08 .25
498 Kelvin Pritchett .01 .05
499 Andre Ware .01 .05
500 Sanjay Beach RC .01 .05
501 Edgar Bennett RC .08 .25
502 Lewis Billups .01 .05
503 Terrell Buckley .01 .05
504 Ty Detmer .08 .25
505 Brett Favre 1.25 2.50
506 Johnny Holland .01 .05
507 Dexter McNabb RC .01 .05
508 Vince Workman .01 .05
509 Cody Carlson .01 .05
510 Ernest Givins .02 .10
511 Jerry Gray .01 .05
512 Haywood Jeffires .02 .10
513 Bruce Matthews .01 .05
514 Bubba McDowell .01 .05
515 Bucky Richardson RC .01 .05
516 Webster Slaughter .01 .05
517 Al Smith .01 .05
518 Mel Agee .01 .05
519 Ashley Ambrose RC .08 .25
520 Kevin Call .01 .05
521 Ken Clark .01 .05
522 Quentin Coryatt RC .01 .05
523 Steve Emtman RC .01 .05
524 Jeff George .08 .25
525 Jessie Hester .01 .05
526 Anthony Johnson .02 .10
527 Tim Barnett .01 .05
528 Martin Bayless .01 .05
529 J.J. Birden .01 .05
530 Dale Carter RC .02 .10
531 Dave Krieg .02 .10
532 Albert Lewis .01 .05
533 Nick Lowery .01 .05
534 Christian Okoye .01 .05
535 Harvey Williams .08 .25
536 Aundray Bruce .01 .05
537 Eric Dickerson .02 .10
538 Willie Gault .02 .10
539 Ethan Horton .01 .05
540 Jeff Jaeger .01 .05
541 Napoleon McCallum .01 .05
542 Chester McGlockton RC .02 .10
543 Steve Smith .01 .05
544 Steve Wisniewski .01 .05
545 Marc Boutte RC .01 .05
546 Pat Carter .01 .05
547 Jim Everett .02 .10
548 Cleveland Gary .01 .05
549 Sean Gilbert RC .02 .10
550 Steve Israel RC .01 .05
551 Todd Kinchen RC .01 .05
552 Jackie Slater .01 .05
553 Tony Zendejas .01 .05
554 Robert Clark .01 .05
555 Mark Clayton .02 .10
556 Marco Coleman RC .01 .05
557 Bryan Cox .02 .10
558 Keith Jackson .02 .10
559 Dan Marino .50 1.25
560 John Offerdahl .01 .05
561 Troy Vincent RC .01 .05
562 Richmond Webb .01 .05
563 Terry Allen .08 .25
564 Cris Carter .20 .50
565 Roger Craig .02 .10
566 Rich Gannon .08 .25
567 Hassan Jones .01 .05
568 Randall McDaniel .01 .05
569 Al Noga .01 .05
570 Todd Scott .01 .05
571 Van Waiters RC .01 .05
572 Bruce Armstrong .01 .05
573 Gene Chilton RC .01 .05
574 Eugene Chung RC .01 .05
575 Todd Collins RC .01 .05
576 Hart Lee Dykes .01 .05
577 David Howard RC .01 .05
578 Eugene Lockhart .01 .05
579 Greg McMurtry .01 .05
580 Rod Smith DB RC .01 .05
581 Gene Atkins .01 .05
582 Vince Buck .01 .05
583 Wesley Carroll .01 .05
584 Jim Dombrowski .01 .05
585 Vaughn Dunbar RC .01 .05
586 Craig Heyward .02 .10
587 Dalton Hilliard .01 .05
588 Wayne Martin .01 .05
589 Renaldo Turnbull .01 .05
590 Carl Banks .01 .05
591 Derek Brown TE RC .01 .05
592 Jarrod Bunch .01 .05
593 Mark Ingram .01 .05
594 Ed McCaffrey .10 .30
595 Phil Simms .02 .10
596 Phillippi Sparks RC .01 .05
597 Lawrence Taylor .08 .25
598 Lewis Tillman .01 .05
599 Kyle Clifton .01 .05
600 Mo Lewis .01 .05
601 Terance Mathis .02 .10
602 Scott Mersereau .01 .05
603 Johnny Mitchell RC .01 .05
604 Browning Nagle .01 .05
605 Ken O'Brien .01 .05
606 Al Toon .02 .10
607 Marvin Washington .01 .05
608 Eric Allen .01 .05
609 Fred Barnett .08 .25
610 John Booty .01 .05
611 Randall Cunningham .08 .25
612 Rich Miano .01 .05
613 Clyde Simmons .01 .05
614 Siran Stacy .01 .05
615 Herschel Walker .02 .10
616 Calvin Williams .02 .10
617 Chris Chandler .08 .25
618 Randal Hill .01 .05
619 Johnny Johnson .01 .05
620 Lorenzo Lynch .01 .05
621 Robert Massey .01 .05
622 Ricky Proehl .01 .05
623 Timm Rosenbach .01 .05
624 Tony Sacca RC .01 .05
625 Aeneas Williams UER .02 .10
626 Bubby Brister .01 .05
627 Barry Foster .02 .10
628 Merril Hoge .01 .05
629 D.J. Johnson .01 .05
630 David Little .01 .05
631 Greg Lloyd .02 .10
632 Ernie Mills .01 .05
633 Leon Searcy RC .01 .05
634 Dwight Stone .01 .05
635 Sam Anno RC .01 .05
636 Burt Grossman .01 .05
637 Stan Humphries .08 .25
638 Nate Lewis .01 .05
639 Anthony Miller .02 .10
640 Chris Mims .08 .25
641 Marquez Pope RC .01 .05
642 Stanley Richard .01 .05
643 Junior Seau .08 .25
644 Brian Bollinger RC .01 .05
645 Steve Bono RC .08 .25
646 Dexter Carter .01 .05
647 Dana Hall RC .01 .05
648 Amp Lee .01 .05
649 Joe Montana .50 1.25
650 Tom Rathman .01 .05
651 Jerry Rice .30 .75
652 Ricky Watters .08 .25
653 Robert Blackmon .01 .05
654 John Kasay .01 .05
655 Ronnie Lee RC .01 .05
656 Dan McGwire .01 .05
657 Ray Roberts RC .01 .05
658 Kelly Stouffer .01 .05
659 Chris Warren .08 .25
660 Tony Woods .01 .05
661 David Wyman .01 .05
662 Reggie Cobb .01 .05
663A Steve DeBerg ERR .02 .10
663B Steve DeBerg COR .02 .10
664 Santana Dotson RC .02 .10
665 Willie Drewery .01 .05
666 Paul Gruber .01 .05
667 Ron Hall .01 .05
668 Courtney Hawkins RC .02 .10
669 Charles McRae .01 .05
670 Ricky Reynolds .01 .05
671 Monte Coleman .01 .05
672 Brad Edwards .01 .05
673 Jumpy Geathers UER .01 .05
674 Kelly Goodburn .01 .05
675 Kurt Gouveia .01 .05
676 Chris Hakel RC .01 .05
677 Wilber Marshall .01 .05
678 Ricky Sanders .01 .05
679 Mark Schlereth .01 .05
680 Buffalo Bills .01 .05
681 Cincinnati Bengals .01 .05
682 Cleveland Browns .01 .05
683 Denver Broncos .01 .05
684 Houston Oilers .01 .05
685 Indianapolis Colts .01 .05
686 Tracy Simien SG .01 .05
687 Los Angeles Raiders .01 .05
688 Miami Dolphins .01 .05
689 New England Patriots .01 .05
690 New York Jets .01 .05
691 Pittsburgh Steelers .01 .05
692 San Diego Chargers .01 .05
693 Seattle Seahawks .01 .05
694 Play Smart .01 .05
695 Hank Williams Jr. NEW .01 .05
696 3 Brothers in NFL NEWS .01 .05
697 Japan Bowl NEWS .01 .05
698 Georgia Dome NEWS .01 .05
699 Theme Art NEWS .01 .05
700 Mark Rypien SB MVP NEW .01 .05
AU150 Emmitt Smith AU/1000 50.00 100.00
AU168 Erik Kramer AU/1000 12.50 30.00
NNO E.Smith Power Preview .30 .75
NNO Santa Claus .20 .50
SC5 Super Bowl XXVI Logo .10 .30
P1 Cover Card Promo .40 1.00

1992 Pro Set Emmitt Smith Holograms

This four-card hologram set was randomly inserted into 1992 Pro Set I foil packs. The ES1 card was the least difficult to find, while the ES4 card was the most difficult. The holograms on the fronts capture different moments in Smith's career, while the red, white, and blue backs present player profile, statistics (1991 and projected), or career summary.

COMPLETE SET (4) 20.00 50.00
RANDOM INSERTS IN SER.1 PACKS
ES1 Statistics 1990-1999 2.50 6.00
ES2 Drafted by Cowboys 4.00 10.00
ES3 Rookie of the Year 7.50 20.00
ES4 NFL Rushing Leader 10.00 25.00

1992 Pro Set Gold MVPs

This 30-card standard-size insert set features the most valuable player for each of the 28 NFL teams plus two outstanding coaches. Card numbers 1-15 were offered one per series I jumbo pack, while card numbers 16-30 were inserted one per series II jumbo pack. Series II jumbo pack production was limited to 4,000 numbered cases. The cards differ in design according to series. Series I inserts have full-bleed color action player photos. A diamond-shaped "92 MVP" emblem appears at the upper right corner, while a gold-foil stamped bar (carrying the player's name) and NFL/Pro Set logo cuts across the bottom. The horizontal backs have career summary, statistics, biography, and a color head shot. Series II inserts have full-bleed color action photos edged on the left by a two-toned stripe. A gray block at the lower left corner carries "MVP" in gold foil. On a screened background, the backs have a color close-up shot and career summary. The set is arranged as follows: AFC "Team MVPs" (1-14), a coach card of Don Shula (15), 14 NFC "Team MVPs" (16-29), and a coach card of Jimmy Johnson (30). All cards are numbered on the back with an "MVP" prefix.

COMPLETE SET (30) 6.00 15.00
ONE PER JUMBO PACK
MVP1 Thurman Thomas .20 .50
MVP2 Anthony Munoz .07 .20
MVP3 Clay Matthews .07 .20
MVP4 John Elway 1.25 2.50
MVP5 Warren Moon .20 .50
MVP6 Bill Brooks .02 .10
MVP7 Derrick Thomas .20 .50
MVP8 Todd Marinovich .02 .10
MVP9 Mark Higgs .02 .10
MVP10 Leonard Russell .07 .20
MVP11 Rob Moore .07 .20
MVP12 Rod Woodson .20 .50
MVP13 Marion Butts .02 .10
MVP14 Brian Blades .07 .20
MVP15 Don Shula CO .07 .20
MVP16 Deion Sanders .40 1.00
MVP17 Neal Anderson .02 .10
MVP18 Emmitt Smith 1.50 3.00
MVP19 Barry Sanders 1.25 2.50
MVP20 Brett Favre 2.50 5.00
MVP21 Kevin Greene .07 .20
MVP22 Terry Allen .20 .50
MVP23 Pat Swilling .02 .10
MVP24 Rodney Hampton .07 .20
MVP25 Randall Cunningham .20 .50
MVP26 Randal Hill .02 .10
MVP27 Jerry Rice .75 1.50
MVP28 Vinny Testaverde .10 .20
MVP29 Mark Rypien .02 .10
MVP30 Jimmy Johnson CO .07 .20

1992 Pro Set Ground Force

These six standard-size cards were randomly inserted only in foil packs of numbered hobby cases. They are identical in design and numbering to their regular issue counterparts, except that these insert cards are stamped with a gold foil "Ground Force" logo.

COMPLETE SET (6) 10.00 25.00
RANDOM INSERTS IN SER.1 PACKS
86 Gerald Riggs 2.00 5.00
105 Thurman Thomas 4.00 10.00
118 Neal Anderson 2.50 6.00
150 Emmitt Smith 6.00 15.00
206 Barry Word 2.00 5.00
249 Leonard Russell 2.00 5.00

1992 Pro Set HOF Inductees

This "Special Collectibles" subset was issued as a random insert with 1992 Pro Set first series packs. These standard-size cards are numbered with an "SC" prefix and feature the 1992 Pro Football Hall of Fame induction class.

COMPLETE SET (4) .40 1.00
RANDOM INSERTS IN SER.1 PACKS
SC1 Lem Barney HOF .10 .30
SC2 Al Davis HOF .10 .30
SC3 John Mackey HOF .10 .30
SC4 John Riggins HOF .20 .50

1992 Pro Set HOF 2000

This ten-card standard size set features ten of the NFL's all-time top players whom Pro Set predicts are worthy candidates for the Hall of Fame in the beginning of the next century. The cards were randomly inserted in series II foil packs. The fronts are like the regular issue Pro Set series, with full-bleed color action photos edged on the left a two-toned stripe, except that "HOF-2000" is gold-foil stamped on two horizontal bars at the lower left corner. On the backs, a purple panel on a screened background summarizes the player's career. The cards are numbered on the back "X/10."

COMPLETE SET (10) 10.00 20.00
RANDOM INSERTS IN SER.2 FOIL PACKS
1 Marcus Allen 1.00 2.00
2 Richard Dent .30 .75
3 Eric Dickerson .30 .75
4 Ronnie Lott .30 .75
5 Art Monk .30 .75
6 Joe Montana 5.00 10.00
7 Warren Moon 1.00 2.00
8 Anthony Munoz .30 .75
9 Mike Singletary .30 .75
10 Lawrence Taylor 1.00 2.00

1992 Pro Set Club

The theme of the 1992 Pro Set Club set is "Football Practice." Each of the nine cards measures the standard-size. The full-bleed color photos on the fronts illustrate various aspects of the game. The card subtitle appears in a pastel purple bar superimposed over the picture toward the bottom. At the left end of the bar is the Pro Set Club logo. On a yellow panel inside a turquoise bordered speckled with green, the backs discuss how to play football and challenge the reader to "do it yourself," "think about it," "check it out," or "take a look."

COMPLETE SET (9) 2.00 5.00
1 Quarterback Throwing .40 1.00
2 Coach Reviewing Play .30 .75
3 Team Stretching .30 .75
4 Offensive Play .30 .75
5 Kickoff .30 .75
6 Player's Stance .30 .75
7 Football Is a .30 .75
8 Defensive Practice .30 .75
9 Play in Motion .30 .75

1992 Pro Set Emmitt Smith Promo Sheet

Pro Set produced this five-card sheet to announce Emmitt Smith as the company spokesman for Pro Set. The sheet features reprints of Smith's past Pro Set cards up to that time: 1990, 1991, 1991 Platinum, 1991 Platinum Game Breaker, and 1992 with a checklist back. Each sheet is numbered of 2000 produced and measures approximately 7" by 13."

NNO Emmitt Smith Sheet 4.00 10.00

1992-93 Pro Set Super Bowl XXVII

Produced by Pro Set to commemorate Super Bowl XXVII, this 38-card standard-size set was packaged in two cello packs. For those who paid admission to Super Bowl XXVII, January 31, 1993, in Pasadena, a set was inserted into the GTE seat cushion. The set was also available through mail-order for 22.00 plus either a Dallas Cowboys or Buffalo Bills mini-binder. Just 7,000 sets were produced for the mail-away offer. The cards have the same design as the regular issue except for the following differences: 1) all cards have a Super Bowl XXVII emblem on their fronts; 2) the Bills' and the Cowboys' cards have AFC Champion and NFC Champion respectively printed beneath the player's name; and 3) all the backs have a screened background of Super Bowl XXVII emblems. The set includes an AFL Conference logo card (1), Buffalo Bills (2-18), an NFL Conference logo card (19), Dallas Cowboys (20-36), a Newsreel card (37), and a card of Marco Coleman (701), the 1992 Pro Set Rookie of the Year. With the exception of the Coleman, all the cards are numbered on the back "XXVII" and checklisted below in alphabetical order within teams.

COMPLETE SET (38) 4.80 12.00
1 AFC Logo .07 .20
2 Cornelius Bennett .10 .30
3 Steve Christie .07 .20
4 Shane Conlan .07 .20
5 Matt Darby .07 .20
6 Kenneth Davis .07 .20
7 John Fina .07 .20
8 Henry Jones .07 .20
9 Jim Kelly .30 .75
10 Marv Levy CO .07 .20
11 James Lofton .10 .30
12 Pete Metzelaars .07 .20
13 Nate Odomes .07 .20
14 Andre Reed .20 .50
15 Bruce Smith .20 .50
16 Darryl Talley .07 .20
17 Steve Tasker .07 .20
18 Thurman Thomas .30 .75
19 NFC Logo .07 .20
20 Troy Aikman 1.00 2.50
21 Steve Beuerlein .10 .30
22 Tony Casillas .07 .20
23 Kenneth Gant .07 .20
24 Charles Haley .10 .30
25 Alvin Harper .07 .20
26 Michael Irvin .30 .75
27 Jimmy Johnson CO .10 .30
28 Robert Jones .07 .20
29 Russell Maryland .07 .20
30 Nate Newton .07 .20
31 Ken Norton Jr. .10 .30
32 Jay Novacek .10 .30
33 Emmitt Smith 2.00 5.00
34 Kevin Smith .07 .20
35 Mark Stepnoski .07 .20
36 Tony Tolbert .07 .20
37 Newsreel Art .07 .20
701 Marco Coleman PS-ROY .07 .20

1993 Pro Set Promos

These six standard-size cards were distributed to dealers, promoters, and card show attendees to promote the release of the 1993 Pro Set issue. The six cards were also issued in an uncut ten-card 8" by 13 1/2" sheet, the bottom row of which consisted of five copies of the Emmitt Smith card. The fronts feature color player action shots that are borderless, except at the bottom, where the photo appears to be torn away, revealing an irregular gray stripe that carries the player's name in team color-coded lettering. On the regular series cards, the color of this stripe varies, reflecting the team's primary color. The back appears to be torn away on the left edge, revealing a gray stripe that carries the player's name in vertical team color-coded lettering, and his position and team in black lettering. A color player action photo is displayed at the top, which blends into a grayish background that carries the player's biography, career highlights, and stats. On the regular cards, the stat box has a white background rather than a grayish one. The cards are unnumbered and checklisted below in alphabetical order.

COMPLETE SET (6) 2.40 6.00
1 Jerome Bettis .60 1.50
2 Reggie Brooks .40 1.00
3 Cortez Kennedy .30 .75
4 Junior Seau .40 1.00
5 Emmitt Smith 1.20 3.00
6 Wade Wilson .30 .75

1993 Pro Set

The 1993 Pro Set football set was issued in one series of 449 standard-size cards. Including foil and jumbo cases, a total of 15,000 cases were reportedly produced. Cards were issued in 15-card foil packs and 32-card jumbo packs. After an 18-card Stat Leader subset (1-18) and an 11-card Replay 1992 subset (19-29), the cards are checklisted below according to teams. Rookie Cards include Jerome Bettis, Drew Bledsoe, Vincent Brisby, Reggie Brooks, Derek Brown, Mark Brunell, Curtis Conway, Garrison Hearst, Billy Joe Hobert, Qadry Ismail, Terry Kirby, O.J. McDuffie, Rick Mirer, Natrone Means, Glyn Milburn, Ronald Moore, Robert Smith, Dana Stubblefield and Kevin Williams.

COMPLETE SET (449) 8.00 20.00
1 Marco Coleman .01 .05
2 Steve Young LL .10 .30
3 Mike Holmgren .02 .10
4 John Elway LL .30 .75
5 Steve Young LL .10 .30
6 Dan Marino LL .30 .75
7 Emmitt Smith LL .30 .75
8 Sterling Sharpe LL .02 .10
9 Jay Novacek .02 .10
10 Sterling Sharpe LL .02 .10
11 Thurman Thomas LL .02 .10
12 Pete Stoyanovich .01 .05
13 Greg Montgomery .01 .05
14 Johnny Bailey .01 .05
15 Jon Vaughn .01 .05
16 Audray McMillian .01 .05
17 Clyde Simmons .01 .05
18 Cortez Kennedy .01 .05
19 AFC Wildcard .01 .05
20 AFC Wildcard .01 .05
21 NFC Wildcard .01 .05
22 NFC Wildcard .01 .05
23 AFC Divisional .01 .05
24 Dan Marino REP .30 .75
25 Troy Aikman REP .20 .50
26 Ricky Watters REP .02 .10
27 AFC Championship .01 .05
28 NFC Championship .01 .05
29 Super Bowl XXVIII Logo .01 .05
30 Troy Aikman .30 .75
31 Thomas Everett .01 .05
32 Charles Haley .02 .10
33 Alvin Harper .02 .10
34 Michael Irvin .08 .25
35 Robert Jones .01 .05
36 Russell Maryland .01 .05
37 Ken Norton .02 .10
38 Jay Novacek .02 .10
39 Emmitt Smith .50 1.50
40 Darrin Smith RC .02 .10
41 Mark Stepnoski .01 .05
42 Kevin Williams RC WR .08 .25
43 Daryl Johnston .08 .25
44 Derrick Lassic RC .01 .05
45 Don Beebe .01 .05
46 Cornelius Bennett .02 .10
47 Bill Brooks .01 .05
48 Kenneth Davis .01 .05
49 Jim Kelly .08 .25
50 Andre Reed .02 .10
51 Bruce Smith .08 .25
52 Thomas Smith RC .02 .10
53 Darryl Talley .01 .05
54 Thurman Thomas .08 .25
55 Russell Copeland RC .02 .10
56 Steve Christie .01 .05

1992 Pro Set

57 Pete Metzelaars .01 .05
58 Frank Reich .02 .10
59 Henry Jones .01 .05
60 Vinnie Clark .01 .05
61 Eric Dickerson .02 .10
62 Jumpy Geathers .01 .05
63 Roger Harper RC .01 .05
64 Michael Haynes .02 .10
65 Bobby Hebert .01 .05
66 Lincoln Kennedy RC .01 .05
67 Chris Miller .02 .10
68 Andre Rison .02 .10
69 Deion Sanders .20 .50
70 Jessie Tuggle .01 .05
71 Ron George .01 .05
72 Erric Pegram .02 .10
73 Melvin Jenkins .01 .05
74 Pierce Holt .01 .05
75 Neal Anderson .01 .05
76 Mark Carrier DB .01 .05
77 Curtis Conway RC .15 .40
78 Richard Dent .02 .10
79 Jim Harbaugh .08 .25
80 Craig Heyward .02 .10
81 Darren Lewis .01 .05
82 Alonzo Spellman .01 .05
83 Tom Waddle .01 .05
84 Wendell Davis .01 .05
85 Chris Zorich .01 .05
86 Carl Simpson RC .01 .05
87 Chris Gedney RC .01 .05
88 Trace Armstrong .01 .05
89 Peter Tom Willis .01 .05
90 John Copeland RC .02 .10
91 Derrick Fenner .01 .05
92 James Francis .01 .05
93 Harold Green .01 .05
94 David Klingler .01 .05
95 Tim Krumrie .01 .05
96 Tony McGee RC .02 .10
97 Carl Pickens .02 .10
98 Alfred Williams .01 .05
99 Doug Pelfrey RC .01 .05
100 Lance Gunn RC .01 .05
101 Jay Schroeder .01 .05
102 Steve Tovar RC .01 .05
103 Jeff Query .01 .05
104 Ty Parten RC .01 .05
105 Jerry Ball .01 .05
106 Mark Carrier WR .02 .10
107 Rob Burnett .01 .05
108 Michael Jackson .02 .10
109 Mike Johnson .01 .05
110 Bernie Kosar .02 .10
111 Clay Matthews .02 .10
112 Eric Metcalf .02 .10
113 Michael Dean Perry .02 .10
114 Vinny Testaverde .02 .10
115 Eric Turner .01 .05
116 Tommy Vardell .01 .05
117 Leroy Hoard .02 .10
118 Steve Everitt RC .01 .05
119 Everson Walls .01 .05
120 Steve Atwater .01 .05
121 Rod Bernstine .01 .05
122 Mike Croel .01 .05
123 John Elway .60 1.50
124 Simon Fletcher .01 .05
125 Glyn Milburn RC .08 .25
126 Reggie Rivers RC .01 .05
127 Shannon Sharpe .08 .25
128 Dennis Smith .01 .05
129 Dan Williams RC .01 .05
130 Rondell Jones RC .01 .05
131 Jason Elam RC .08 .25
132 Arthur Marshall RC .01 .05
133 Gary Zimmerman .01 .05
134 Karl Mecklenburg .01 .05
135 Bennie Blades .01 .05
136 Lomas Brown .01 .05
137 Bill Fralic .01 .05
138 Mel Gray .02 .10
139 Willie Green .01 .05
140 Ryan McNeil RC .08 .25
141 Rodney Peete .01 .05
142 Barry Sanders .50 1.25
143 Chris Spielman .02 .10
144 Pat Swilling .01 .05
145 Andre Ware .01 .05
146 Herman Moore .08 .25
147 Tim McKyer .01 .05
148 Brett Perriman .08 .25
149 Antonio London RC .01 .05
150 Edgar Bennett .08 .25
151 Terrell Buckley .01 .05
152 Brett Favre .75 2.00
153 Jackie Harris .01 .05
154 Johnny Holland .01 .05
155 Sterling Sharpe .08 .25
156 Tim Hauck .01 .05
157 George Teague RC .02 .10
158 Reggie White .08 .25
159 Mark Clayton .01 .05
160 Ty Detmer .08 .25
161 Wayne Simmons RC .01 .05
162 Mark Brunell RC .60 1.50
163 Tony Bennett .01 .05
164 Brian Noble .01 .05
165 Cody Carlson .01 .05
166 Ray Childress .01 .05
167 Cris Dishman .01 .05
168 Curtis Duncan .01 .05
169 Brad Hopkins RC .01 .05
170 Haywood Jeffires .02 .10
171 Wilber Marshall .01 .05
172 Micheal Barrow UER RC .08 .25
173 Bubba McDowell .01 .05
174 Warren Moon .08 .25
175 Webster Slaughter .01 .05
176 Travis Hannah RC .01 .05
177 Lorenzo White .01 .05
178 Ernest Givins UER .02 .10
179 Keith McCants .01 .05
180 Kerry Cash .01 .05
181 Quentin Coryatt .02 .10
182 Kirk Lowdermilk .01 .05
183 Rodney Culver .01 .05
184 Rohn Stark .01 .05
185 Steve Emtman .01 .05
186 Jeff George .08 .25
187 Jeff Herrod .01 .05
188 Reggie Langhorne .01 .05
189 Roosevelt Potts RC .01 .05
190 Jack Trudeau .01 .05
191 Will Wolford .01 .05
192 Jessie Hester .01 .05
193 Anthony Johnson .02 .10
194 Ray Buchanan RC .08 .25
195 Dale Carter .01 .05
196 Willie Davis .08 .25
197 John Alt .01 .05
198 Joe Montana .60 1.50
199 Will Shields RC .08 .25
200 Neil Smith .08 .25
201 Derrick Thomas .08 .25
202 Harvey Williams .02 .10
203 Marcus Allen .08 .25
204 J.J. Birden .01 .05
205 Tim Barnett .01 .05
206 Albert Lewis .01 .05
207 Nick Lowery .01 .05
208 Dave Krieg .02 .10
209 Keith Cash .01 .05
210 Patrick Dates RC .01 .05
211 Nick Bell .01 .05
212 Tim Brown .08 .25
213 Willie Gault .01 .05
214 Ethan Horton .01 .05
215 Jeff Hostetler .02 .10
216 Howie Long .08 .25
217 Greg Townsend .01 .05
218 Rocket Ismail .02 .10
219 Alexander Wright .01 .05
220 Greg Robinson RC .01 .05
221 Billy Joe Hobert RC .08 .25
222 Steve Wisniewski .01 .05
223 Steve Smith .01 .05
224 Vince Evans .01 .05
225 Flipper Anderson .01 .05
226 Jerome Bettis RC 1.50 4.00
227 Troy Drayton RC .02 .10
228 Henry Ellard .02 .10
229 Jim Everett .02 .10
230 Tony Zendejas .01 .05
231 Todd Lyght .01 .05
232 Todd Kinchen .01 .05
233 Jackie Slater .01 .05
234 Fred Stokes .01 .05
235 Russell White RC .02 .10
236 Cleveland Gary .01 .05
237 Sean LaChapelle RC .01 .05
238 Steve Israel .01 .05
239 Shane Conlan .01 .05
240 Keith Byars .01 .05
241 Marco Coleman .01 .05
242 Bryan Cox .01 .05
243 Irving Fryar .02 .10
244 Richmond Webb .01 .05
245 Mark Higgs .01 .05
246 Terry Kirby RC .08 .25
247 Mark Ingram .01 .05
248 John Offerdahl .01 .05
249 Keith Jackson .02 .10
250 Dan Marino .60 1.50
251 O.J.McDuffie RC .08 .25
252 Louis Oliver .01 .05
253 Pete Stoyanovich .01 .05
254 Troy Vincent .01 .05
255 Anthony Carter .02 .10
256 Cris Carter .08 .25
257 Roger Craig .02 .10
258 Jack Del Rio .01 .05
259 Chris Doleman .01 .05
260 Barry Word .01 .05
261 Qadry Ismail RC .08 .25
262 Jim McMahon .02 .10
263 Robert Smith RC .50 1.25
264 Fred Strickland .01 .05
265 Randall McDaniel .02 .10
266 Carl Lee .01 .05
267 Olanda Truitt UER RC .01 .05
268 Terry Allen .08 .25
269 Audray McMillian .01 .05
270 Drew Bledsoe RC 1.00 2.50
271 Eugene Chung .01 .05
272 Marv Cook .01 .05
273 Pat Harlow .01 .05
274 Greg McMurtry .01 .05
275 Leonard Russell .02 .10
276 Chris Slade RC .02 .10
277 Andre Tippett .01 .05
278 Vincent Brisby RC .08 .25
279 Ben Coates .20 .50
280 Sam Gash RC .08 .25
281 Bruce Armstrong .01 .05
282 Rod Smith DB .01 .05
283 Michael Timpson .01 .05
284 Scott Sisson RC .01 .05
285 Morten Andersen .01 .05
286 Reggie Freeman RC .01 .05
287 Dalton Hilliard .01 .05
288 Rickey Jackson .01 .05
289 Vaughan Johnson .01 .05
290 Eric Martin .01 .05
291 Sam Mills .01 .05
292 Brad Muster .01 .05
293 Willie Roaf RC .10 .30
294 Irv Smith RC .01 .05
295 Wade Wilson .01 .05
296 Derek Brown RBK RC .02 .10
297 Quinn Early .02 .10
298 Steve Walsh .01 .05
299 Renaldo Turnbull .01 .05
300 Jessie Armstead RC .02 .10
301 Carlton Bailey .01 .05
302 Michael Brooks .01 .05
303 Rodney Hampton .02 .10
304 Ed McCaffrey .08 .25
305 Dave Meggett .01 .05
306 Bart Oates .01 .05
307 Mike Sherrard .01 .05
308 Phil Simms .02 .10
309 Lawrence Taylor .08 .25
310 Mark Jackson .01 .05
311 Jarrod Bunch .01 .05
312 Howard Cross .01 .05
313 Michael Strahan RC .60 1.50
314 Marcus Buckley RC .01 .05
315 Brad Baxter .01 .05
316 Adrian Murrell RC .08 .25
317 Boomer Esiason .02 .10
318 Johnny Johnson .01 .05
319 Marvin Jones RC .01 .05
320 Jeff Lageman .01 .05
321 Ronnie Lott .02 .10
322 Leonard Marshall .01 .05
323 Johnny Mitchell .01 .05
324 Rob Moore .02 .10
325 Browning Nagle .01 .05
326 Blair Thomas .01 .05
327 Brian Washington .01 .05
328 Terance Mathis .02 .10
329 Kyle Clifton .01 .05
330 Eric Allen .01 .05
331 Victor Bailey RC .01 .05
332 Fred Barnett .02 .10
333 Mark Bavaro .01 .05
334 Randall Cunningham .08 .25
335 Ken O'Brien .01 .05
336 Seth Joyner .01 .05
337 Leonard Renfro RC .01 .05
338 Heath Sherman .01 .05
339 Clyde Simmons .01 .05
340 Herschel Walker .02 .10
341 Calvin Williams .02 .10
342 Bubby Brister .01 .05
343 Vaughn Hebron RC .01 .05
344 Keith Millard .01 .05
345 Johnny Bailey .01 .05
346 Steve Beuerlein .02 .10
347 Chuck Cecil .01 .05
348 Larry Centers RC .08 .25
349 Chris Chandler .02 .10
350 Ernest Dye RC .01 .05
351 Garrison Hearst RC .30 .75
352 Randal Hill .01 .05
353 John Booty .01 .05
354 Gary Clark .02 .10
355 Ronald Moore RC .02 .10
356 Ricky Proehl .01 .05
357 Eric Swann .02 .10
358 Ken Harvey .01 .05
359 Ben Coleman RC .01 .05
360 Deon Figures RC .01 .05
361 Barry Foster .02 .10
362 Jeff Graham .02 .10
363 Eric Green .01 .05
364 Kevin Greene .02 .10
365 Andre Hastings RC .02 .10
366 Greg Lloyd .02 .10
367 Neil O'Donnell .08 .25
368 Dwight Stone .01 .05
369 Mike Tomczak .01 .05
370 Rod Woodson .08 .25
371 Chad Brown RC LB .02 .10
372 Ernie Mills .01 .05
373 Darren Perry .01 .05
374 Leon Searcy .01 .05
375 Marion Butts .01 .05
376 John Carney .01 .05
377 Ronnie Harmon .01 .05
378 Stan Humphries .02 .10
379 Nate Lewis .01 .05
380 Natrone Means RC .08 .25
381 Anthony Miller .02 .10
382 Chris Mims .01 .05
383 Leslie O'Neal .02 .10
384 Joe Cocozzo RC .01 .05
385 Junior Seau .08 .25
386 Jerrol Williams .01 .05
387 John Friesz .02 .10
388 Darrien Gordon RC .01 .05
389 Derrick Walker .01 .05
390 Dana Hall .01 .05
391 Brent Jones .02 .10
392 Todd Kelly RC .01 .05
393 Amp Lee .01 .05
394 Tim McDonald .01 .05
395 Jerry Rice .40 1.00
396 Dana Stubblefield RC .08 .25
397 John Taylor .02 .10
398 Ricky Watters .08 .25
399 Steve Young .30 .75
400 Steve Bono .02 .10
401 Adrian Hardy .01 .05
402 Tom Rathman .01 .05
403 Elvis Grbac RC .60 1.50
404 Bill Romanowski .01 .05
405 Brian Blades .02 .10
406 Ferrell Edmunds .01 .05
407 Carlton Gray RC .01 .05
408 Cortez Kennedy .02 .10
409 Kelvin Martin .01 .05
410 Dan McGwire .01 .05
411 Rick Mirer RC .08 .25
412 Rufus Porter .01 .05
413 Chris Warren .02 .10
414 Jon Vaughn .01 .05
415 John L. Williams .01 .05
416 Eugene Robinson .01 .05
417 Michael McCrary RC .02 .10
418 Michael Bates RC .01 .05
419 Stan Gelbaugh .01 .05
420 Reggie Cobb .01 .05
421 Eric Curry RC .01 .05
422 Lawrence Dawsey .01 .05
423 Santana Dotson .02 .10
424 Craig Erickson .02 .10
425 Ron Hall .01 .05
426 Courtney Hawkins .01 .05
427 Broderick Thomas .01 .05
428 Vince Workman .01 .05
429 Demetrius DuBose RC .01 .05
430 Lamar Thomas RC .01 .05
431 John Lynch RC .25 .60
432 Hardy Nickerson .02 .10
433 Horace Copeland RC .02 .10
434 Steve DeBerg .01 .05
435 Joe Jacoby .01 .05
436 Tom Carter RC .02 .10
437 Andre Collins .01 .05
438 Darrell Green .01 .05
439 Desmond Howard .02 .10
440 Chip Lohmillor .01 .05
441 Charles Mann .01 .05
442 Tim McGee .01 .05
443 Art Monk .02 .10
444 Mark Rypien .01 .05
445 Ricky Sanders .01 .05
446 Brian Mitchell .02 .10
447 Reggie Brooks RC .02 .10
448 Carl Banks .01 .05
449 Cary Conklin .01 .05
NNO Santa Claus .60 1.50

1993 Pro Set All-Rookies

The 1993 Pro Set All-Rookies set comprises 27 standard-size cards, randomly inserted in 1993 Pro Set foil packs.

COMPLETE SET (27) 3.00 8.00
RANDOM INSERTS IN FOIL PACKS
1 Rick Mirer .15 .40
2 Garrison Hearst .60 1.25
3 Jerome Bettis 2.00 5.00
4 Vincent Brisby .15 .40
5 O.J.McDuffie .15 .40
6 Curtis Conway .25 .60
7 Rocket Ismail .10 .15
8 Steve Everitt .02 .10
9 Ernest Dye .02 .10
10 Todd Rucci .02 .10
11 Willie Roaf .20 .50
12 Lincoln Kennedy .02 .10
13 Irv Smith .02 .10
14 Jason Elam .15 .40
15 Harold Alexander .02 .10
16 John Copeland .05 .15
17 Eric Curry .02 .10
18 Dana Stubblefield .15 .40
19 Leonard Renfro .02 .10
20 Marvin Jones .02 .10
21 Demetrius DuBose .02 .10
22 Chris Slade .05 .15
23 Darrin Smith .05 .15
24 Deon Figures .02 .10
25 Darrien Gordon .02 .10
26 Patrick Bates .02 .10
27 George Teague .05 .15

1993 Pro Set College Connections

Randomly inserted in 32-card jumbo packs, this 10-card, standard size set spotlights NFL stars who came from the same college. The cards are numbered with a "CC" prefix.

COMPLETE SET (10) 8.00 20.00
RANDOM INSERTS IN JUMBO PACKS
CC1 B.Sanders 3.00 6.00
T.Thomas
CC2 J.Bettis 1.00 2.50
R.Brooks
CC3 E.Smith 3.00 6.00
N.Anderson
CC4 R.Ismail .60 1.50
T.Brown
CC5 G.Hearst .40 1.00
R.Hampton
CC6 D.Thomas .50 1.25
C.Bennett
CC7 S.Young 1.50 3.00
J.McMahon
CC8 R.Mirer 2.50 5.00
J.Montana UER
CC9 D.Sanders 1.50 3.00
T.Buckley
CC10 D.Bledsoe 2.00 5.00
M.Rypien

1993 Pro Set Rookie Quarterbacks

The 1993 Pro Set Rookie Quarterbacks set comprises six standard-size cards, randomly inserted in 1993 Pro Set jumbo packs. The cards are numbered on the back with an "RQ" prefix.

COMPLETE SET (6) 4.00 10.00
RANDOM INSERTS IN JUMBO PACKS
RQ1 Drew Bledsoe 1.25 3.00
RQ2 Rick Mirer .20 .50
RQ3 Mark Brunell 1.00 2.50
RQ4 Billy Joe Hobert .08 .25
RQ5 Trent Green 2.50 6.00
RQ6 Elvis Grbac .75 2.00

1993 Pro Set Rookie Running Backs

The 1993 Pro Set Rookie Running Backs set comprises 14 standard-size cards, randomly inserted in 1993 Pro Set foil packs. The cards are numbered on the back with an "RRB" prefix.

COMPLETE SET (14) 3.00 8.00
RANDOM INSERTS IN FOIL PACKS
1 Derrick Lassic .02 .10
2 Reggie Brooks .05 .15
3 Garrison Hearst .60 1.25
4 Ronald Moore .05 .15
5 Robert Smith 1.00 2.00
6 Jerome Bettis 2.00 5.00
7 Russell White .05 .15
8 Derek Brown RBK .05 .15
9 Roosevelt Potts .02 .10
10 Terry Kirby .15 .40
11 Glyn Milburn .15 .40
12 Greg Robinson .02 .10
13 Natrone Means .15 .40
14 Vaughn Hebron .02 .10

1994 Pro Set National Promos

Distributed during the 1994 National Sports Collectors Convention, cards 1-5 and the letter-numbered card are prototypes from Pro Set football, Power football, and Power racing. Cards 6-8 were inserted in Tuff Stuff and bear a gold foil "Tuff Stuff" emblem; they are part of a 5-card set made for that magazine and inserted one per month. The cards of Darrien Gordon and Joe Montana/Marcus Allen were released after Pro Set closed operations. The cardbacks feature a black diagonal "proto" stripe cutting across the lower right corner. The front of the title card has the convention logo on a blue screened background with the words Pro Set faintly detectible. The title card also carries the serial number "X" out of 10,000. The football cards are unnumbered and checklisted below in alphabetical order.

COMPLETE SET (10) 10.00 25.00
1 Jerome Bettis .75 2.00
Power Fire Power
2 Drew Bledsoe .75 2.00
Power
3 Brett Favre 2.50 6.00
Sterling Sharpe
Power Air Power
4 Ronald Moore .30 .75
5 Willie Roaf .30 .75
Power Line
6 Garrison Hearst .40 1.00
Power, Oct. Tuff Stuff
7 Natrone Means .50 1.25
Power, Nov. Tuff Stuff
8 Richmond Webb .30 .75
Power, Sept. Tuff Stuff
9 Darrien Gordon .30 .75
10 J.Montana/M.Allen 2.50 6.00
NNO Title Card .30 .75

1991 Pro Set Platinum

This set contains 315 standard-size cards. The cards were issued in series of 150 and 165. Cards were issued in 12-card packs for both series. The cards are checklisted below alphabetically according to teams. Special Collectibles (PC1-PC10) cards were randomly distributed in 12-card second series foil packs. Also randomly inserted in the packs were 2,150 bonus card certificates. One thousand five hundred could be redeemed for limited edition platinum cards of Paul Brown (first series) and 650 for Emmitt Smith (second series). Rookie Cards include Ricky Ervins, Brett Favre, Mike Pritchard, Leonard Russell and Harvey Williams.

COMPLETE SET (315) 5.00 10.00
COMP.SERIES 1 (150) 2.00 4.00
COMP.SERIES 2 (165) 3.00 6.00
1 Chris Miller .02 .10
2 Andre Rison .08 .25
3 Tim Green .01 .05
4 Jessie Tuggle .01 .05
5 Thurman Thomas .08 .25
6 Darryl Talley .01 .05
7 Kent Hull .01 .05
8 Bruce Smith .08 .25
9 Shane Conlan .01 .05
10 Jim Harbaugh .08 .25
11 Neal Anderson .02 .10
12 Mark Bortz .01 .05
13 Richard Dent .02 .10
14 Steve McMichael .01 .05
15 James Brooks .01 .05
16 Boomer Esiason .02 .10
17 Tim Krumrie .01 .05
18 James Francis .01 .05
19 Lewis Billups .01 .05
20 Eric Metcalf .08 .25
21 Kevin Mack .01 .05
22 Clay Matthews .02 .10
23 Mike Johnson .01 .05
24 Troy Aikman .30 .75
25 Emmitt Smith 1.00 2.50
26 Daniel Stubbs .01 .05
27 Ken Norton .02 .10
28 John Elway .50 1.25
29 Bobby Humphrey .01 .05
30 Simon Fletcher .01 .05
31 Karl Mecklenburg .01 .05
32 Rodney Peete .02 .10
33 Barry Sanders .50 1.25
34 Michael Cofer .01 .05
35 Jerry Ball .01 .05
36 Sterling Sharpe .08 .25
37 Tony Mandarich .01 .05
38 Brian Noble .01 .05
39 Tim Harris .01 .05
40 Warren Moon .02 .10
41 Ernest Givins UER .02 .10
42 Mike Munchak .02 .10
43 Sean Jones .02 .10
44 Ray Childress .02 .10
45 Jeff George .08 .25
46 Albert Bentley .01 .05
47 Duane Bickett .01 .05
48 Steve DeBerg .02 .10
49 Christian Okoye .02 .10
50 Neil Smith .08 .25
51 Derrick Thomas .08 .25
52 Willie Gault .02 .10
53 Don Mosebar .01 .05
54 Howie Long .08 .25
55 Greg Townsend .01 .05
56 Terry McDaniel .02 .10
57 Jackie Slater .01 .05
58 Jim Everett .02 .10
59 Cleveland Gary .01 .05
60 Mike Piel .01 .05
61 Jerry Gray .01 .05
62 Dan Marino .50 1.25
63 Sammie Smith .01 .05
64 Richmond Webb .01 .05
65 Louis Oliver .01 .05
66 Ferrell Edmunds .01 .05
67 Jeff Cross .01 .05
68 Wade Wilson .01 .05
69 Chris Doleman .02 .10
70 Joey Browner .01 .05
71 Keith Millard .01 .05
72 John Stephens .01 .05
73 Andre Tippett .01 .05
74 Brent Williams .01 .05
75 Craig Heyward .02 .10
76 Eric Martin .01 .05
77 Pat Swilling .02 .10
78 Sam Mills .02 .10
79 Jeff Hostetler .02 .10
80 Ottis Anderson .02 .10
81 Lawrence Taylor .08 .25
82 Pepper Johnson .01 .05
83 Blair Thomas .01 .05
84 Al Toon .02 .10
85 Ken O'Brien .01 .05
86 Erik McMillan .01 .05
87 Dennis Byrd .02 .10
88 Randall Cunningham .08 .25
89 Fred Barnett .08 .25
90 Seth Joyner .02 .10
91 Reggie White .08 .25
92 Timm Rosenbach .01 .05
93 Johnny Johnson .01 .05
94 Tim McDonald .01 .05
95 Freddie Joe Nunn .01 .05
96 Bubby Brister .02 .10
97 Gary Anderson K UER .01 .05
98 Merril Hoge .01 .05
99 Keith Willis .01 .05
100 Rod Woodson .08 .25
101 Billy Joe Tolliver .01 .05
102 Marion Butts .02 .10
103 Rod Bernstine .01 .05
104 Lee Williams .01 .05
105 Burt Grossman UER .01 .05
106 Tom Rathman .01 .05
107 John Taylor .02 .10
108 Michael Carter .01 .05
109 Guy McIntyre .01 .05
110 Pierce Holt .01 .05
111 John L. Williams .01 .05
112 Dave Krieg .02 .10
113 Bryan Millard .01 .05
114 Cortez Kennedy .08 .25
115 Derrick Fenner .01 .05
116 Vinny Testaverde .02 .10
117 Reggie Cobb .01 .05
118 Gary Anderson RB .01 .05
119 Bruce Hill .01 .05
120 Wayne Haddix .01 .05
121 Broderick Thomas .01 .05
122 Keith McCants .01 .05
123 Andre Collins .02 .10
124 Earnest Byner .01 .05
125 Jim Lachey .01 .05
126 Mark Rypien .02 .10
127 Charles Mann .01 .05
128 Nick Lowery .01 .05
129 Chip Lohmiller .01 .05
130 Mike Horan .01 .05
131 Rohn Stark .01 .05
132 Sean Landeta .01 .05
133 Clarence Verdin .01 .05
134 Johnny Bailey .01 .05
135 Herschel Walker .02 .10
136 Bo Jackson PP .10 .30
137 Dexter Carter PP .01 .05
138 Warren Moon PP .02 .10
139 Joe Montana PP .50 1.25
140 Jerry Rice PP .30 .75
141 Deion Sanders PP .15 .40
142 Ronnie Lippett PP .01 .05
143 Terance Mathis .08 .25
144 Gaston Green PP .01 .05
145 Dean Biasucci PP .01 .05
146 Charles Haley PP .02 .10
147 Derrick Thomas PP .08 .25
148 Lawrence Taylor PP .02 .10
149 Art Shell CO PP .02 .10
150 Bill Parcells CO PP .02 .10
151 Steve Broussard .01 .05
152 Darion Conner .01 .05
153 Bill Fralic .01 .05
154 Mike Cann .01 .05
155 Tim McKyer .01 .05
156 Don Beebe UER .01 .05
157 Cornelius Bennett .02 .10
158 Andre Reed .08 .25
159 Leonard Smith .01 .05
160 Will Wolford .01 .05
161 Mark Carrier DB .02 .10
162 Wendell Davis .01 .05
163 Jay Hilgenberg .01 .05
164 Brad Muster .01 .05
165 Mike Singletary .02 .10
166 Eddie Brown .01 .05
167 David Fulcher .01 .05
168 Rodney Holman .01 .05
169 Anthony Munoz .02 .10
170 Craig Taylor RC .01 .05
171 Mike Baab .01 .05
172 David Grayson .01 .05
173 Reggie Langhorne .01 .05
174 Joe Morris .01 .05
175 Kevin Gogan RC .01 .05
176 Jack Del Rio .02 .10
177 Issiac Holt .01 .05
178 Michael Irvin .08 .25
179 Jay Novacek .08 .25
180 Steve Atwater .01 .05
181 Mark Jackson .01 .05
182 Ricky Nattiel .01 .05
183 Warren Powers .01 .05
184 Dennis Smith .01 .05
185 Bennie Blades .01 .05
186 Lomas Brown UER .01 .05
187 Robert Clark UER .01 .05
188 Mel Gray .02 .10
189 Chris Spielman .02 .10
190 Johnny Holland .01 .05
191 Don Majkowski .01 .05
192 Bryce Paup RC .08 .25
193 Darrell Thompson .01 .05
194 Ed West UER .01 .05
195 Cris Dishman RC .02 .10
196 Drew Hill .02 .10
197 Bruce Matthews .02 .10
198 Bubba McDowell .01 .05
199 Allen Pinkett .01 .05
200 Bill Brooks .02 .10
201 Jeff Herrod .01 .05
202 Anthony Johnson .02 .10
203 Mike Prior .01 .05
204 John Alt .01 .05
205 Stephone Paige .01 .05
206 Kevin Ross .01 .05
207 Dan Saleaumua .01 .05
208 Barry Word .01 .05
209 Marcus Allen .08 .25
210 Roger Craig .02 .10
211 Ronnie Lott .02 .10
212 Winston Moss .01 .05
213 Jay Schroeder .01 .05
214 Robert Delpino .01 .05
215 Henry Ellard .02 .10
216 Kevin Greene .02 .10
217 Tom Newberry .01 .05
218 Michael Stewart .01 .05
219 Mark Duper .02 .10
220 Mark Higgs RC .01 .05
221 John Offerdahl UER .01 .05
222 Keith Sims .01 .05
223 Anthony Carter .02 .10
224 Cris Carter .20 .50
225 Steve Jordan .01 .05
226 Randall McDaniel .02 .10
227 Al Noga .01 .05
228 Ray Agnew .01 .05
229 Bruce Armstrong .01 .05
230 Irving Fryar .02 .10
231 Greg McMurtry .01 .05
232 Chris Singleton .01 .05
233 Morten Andersen .01 .05
234 Vince Buck .01 .05
235 Gill Fenerty .01 .05
236 Rickey Jackson .02 .10
237 Vaughan Johnson .01 .05
238 Carl Banks .01 .05
239 Mark Collins .01 .05
240 Rodney Hampton .08 .25
241 Dave Meggett .02 .10
242 Bart Oates .01 .05
243 Kyle Clifton .01 .05
244 Jeff Lageman .02 .10
245 Freeman McNeil UER .02 .10
246 Rob Moore .08 .25
247 Eric Allen .01 .05
248 Keith Byars .02 .10
249 Keith Jackson .02 .10
250 Jim McMahon .02 .10
251 Andre Waters .01 .05
252 Ken Harvey .02 .10
253 Ernie Jones .01 .05
254 Luis Sharpe .01 .05
255 Anthony Thompson .01 .05
256 Tom Tupa .01 .05
257 Eric Green .02 .10
258 Barry Foster .02 .10
259 Bryan Hinkle .01 .05
260 Tunch Ilkin .01 .05
261 Louis Lipps .01 .05
262 Gill Byrd .01 .05
263 John Friesz .02 .10
264 Anthony Miller .02 .10
265 Junior Seau .08 .25
266 Ronnie Harmon .02 .10
267 Harris Barton .01 .05
268 Todd Bowles .08 .25
269 Don Griffin .01 .05
270 Bill Romanowski .01 .05
271 Steve Young .30 .75
272 Brian Blades .02 .10
273 Jacob Green .01 .05
274 Rufus Porter .01 .05
275 Eugene Robinson .01 .05
276 Mark Carrier WR .02 .10
277 Reuben Davis .01 .05
278 Paul Gruber .01 .05
279 Gary Clark .08 .25
280 Darrell Green .02 .10
281 Wilber Marshall .01 .05
282 Matt Millen .02 .10
283 Alvin Walton .01 .05
284 Joe Gibbs CO UER .02 .10
285 Don Shula CO UER .02 .10
286 Larry Brown DB RC .02 .10
287 Mike Croel RC .01 .05
288 Antone Davis RC .01 .05
289 Ricky Ervins UER RC .02 .10
290 Brett Favre RC 3.00 8.00
291 Pat Harlow RC .01 .05
292 Michael Jackson WR RC .08 .25
293 Henry Jones RC .02 .10
294 Aaron Craver RC .01 .05
295 Nick Bell RC .01 .05
296 Todd Lyght RC .02 .10
297 Todd Marinovich RC .01 .05
298 Russell Maryland RC .02 .10
299 Kanavis McGhee RC .01 .05
300 Dan McGwire RC .02 .10
301 Charles McRae RC .01 .05
302 Eric Moten RC .01 .05
303 Jerome Henderson RC .01 .05
304 Browning Nagle RC .01 .05
305 Mike Pritchard RC .08 .25
306 Stanley Richard RC .02 .10
307 Randal Hill RC .02 .10
308 Leonard Russell RC .02 .10
309 Eric Swann RC .02 .10
310 Phil Hansen RC .01 .05
311 Moe Gardner RC .01 .05
312 Jon Vaughn RC .01 .05
313 Aeneas Williams RC .50 1.25
314 Alfred Williams RC .01 .05
315 Harvey Williams RC .08 .25
PM1 Emmitt Smith Plat. 125.00 250.00
PM2 Paul Brown Plat. 25.00 60.00

1991 Pro Set Platinum PC

These ten Pro Set Platinum Collectible PC cards were randomly inserted in 1991 Pro Set Platinum second series foil packs. The set is subdivided as follows: Platinum Profile (1-3), Platinum Photo (4-5), and Platinum Game Breaker (6-10). The Platinum Game Breaker cards present in alphabetical order five standout NFL running backs. The cards are numbered on the back with a "PC" prefix.

COMPLETE SET (10) 4.00 10.00
RANDOM INSERTS IN SER.2 PACKS
PC1 Bobby Hebert .05 .15
PC2 Art Monk .08 .25
PC3 Kenny Walker .05 .15
PC4 Low Fives .05 .15
PC5 Touchdown .05 .15
PC6 Neal Anderson .08 .25
PC7 Gaston Green .05 .15
PC8 Barry Sanders 1.25 3.00
PC9 Emmitt Smith 2.00 5.00
PC10 Thurman Thomas .25 .60

1991-92 Pro Set Platinum

The 1991-92 Pro Set Platinum hockey set was released in two series of 150 standard-size cards. The front design features full-bleed glossy color action player photos, with the Pro Set Platinum icon superimposed at the lower right corner. Player names do not appear on the front.

COMPLETE SET (300) 3.00 8.00
COMP.SERIES 1 (150) 1.50 4.00
COMP.SERIES 2 (150) 1.50 4.00
293 Jim Kelly CAP .07 .20

1995 Pro Stamps

Chris Martin Enterprises produced this stamp set with distribution in sheets of 12 stamps. Each stamp measures approximately 1 1/2" by 2." The first 140-stamps were included as part of the 12-stamp sheets with four stamps being double-printed.

COMPLETE SET (140) 16.00 40.00
1 Steve Young DP .30 .75
2 Jerry Rice .60 1.50
3 Deion Sanders .30 .75
4 Dana Stubblefield .05 .15
5 William Floyd .08 .25
6 Troy Aikman DP .50 1.25
7 Michael Irvin .20 .50
8 Emmitt Smith DP .80 2.00
9 Russell Maryland .05 .15
10 Daryl Johnston .08 .25
11 Dan Marino DP .80 2.00
12 Bernie Parmalee .05 .15
13 Tim Bowens .05 .15
14 Irving Fryar .08 .25
15 Bryan Cox .05 .15
16 Drew Bledsoe .60 1.50
17 Bruce Armstrong .05 .15
18 Vincent Brisby .05 .15
19 Marion Butts .05 .15
20 Ben Coates .08 .25
21 Dave Brown .05 .15
22 Michael Brooks .05 .15
23 Jumbo Elliott .05 .15
24 Rodney Hampton .08 .25
25 Mike Sherrard .05 .15
26 Jeff Hostetler .05 .15
27 Tim Brown .20 .50
28 Rocket Ismail .08 .25
29 James Jett .08 .25
30 Harvey Williams .05 .15
31 Heath Shuler .08 .25
32 Reggie Brooks .05 .15
33 Ricky Ervins .05 .15
34 Darrell Green UER .05 .15
35 Brian Mitchell .05 .15
36 Trace Armstrong .05 .15
37 Dante Jones .05 .15
38 Steve Walsh .05 .15
39 Donnell Woolford .05 .15
40 Tim Worley .05 .15
41 Boomer Esiason .08 .25
42 Aaron Glenn .05 .15
43 Johnny Johnson .05 .15
44 Nick Lowery .05 .15
45 Johnny Mitchell .05 .15
46 Neil O'Donnell .08 .25
47 Barry Foster .05 .15
48 Byron Bam Morris .05 .15
49 Rod Woodson .08 .25
50 Kevin Greene .08 .25
51 Randall Cunningham .20 .50
52 Bubby Brister .05 .15
53 Fred Barnett .05 .15
54 Charlie Garner .05 .15
55 Calvin Williams .05 .15
56 Brett Favre 1.20 3.00
57 Reggie White .20 .50
58 Edgar Bennett .05 .15
59 Robert Brooks .08 .25
60 Sean Jones .05 .15
61 Ronnie Harmon .05 .15
62 Stan Humphries .08 .25
63 Natrone Means .08 .25
64 Tony Martin .20 .50
65 Junior Seau .20 .50
66 John Elway 1.20 3.00
67 Glyn Milburn .05 .15
68 Rod Bernstine .05 .15
69 Anthony Miller .08 .25
70 Shannon Sharpe .20 .50
71 Barry Sanders 1.20 3.00
72 Scott Mitchell .08 .25
73 Herman Moore .20 .50
74 Brett Perriman .08 .25
75 Chris Spielman .08 .25
76 Marcus Allen .20 .50
77 Steve Bono .08 .25
78 Willie Davis .08 .25
79 Lake Dawson .08 .25
80 Neil Smith .08 .25
81 Vinny Testaverde .08 .25
82 Eric Turner .05 .15
83 Antonio Langham .05 .15
84 Leroy Hoard .05 .15
85 Derrick Alexander WR .08 .25
86 Jim Kelly .20 .50
87 Cornelius Bennett .08 .25
88 Andre Reed .08 .25
89 Bruce Smith .20 .50
90 Darryl Talley .05 .15
91 Warren Moon .20 .50
92 Qadry Ismail .05 .15
93 Terry Allen .20 .50
94 Cris Carter .20 .50
95 John Randle .08 .25
96 Jeff George .20 .50
97 Chris Doleman .05 .15
98 Craig Heyward .08 .25
99 Terance Mathis .08 .25
100 Jessie Tuggle .05 .15
101 Jerome Bettis .20 .50
102 Sean Gilbert .05 .15
103 Troy Drayton .05 .15
104 Wayne Gandy .05 .15
105 Todd Lyght .05 .15
106 Jeff Blake .20 .50
107 Harold Green .05 .15
108 Carl Pickens .08 .25
109 Dan Wilkinson .05 .15
110 Darnay Scott .08 .25
111 Cody Carlson .05 .15
112 Gary Brown .05 .15
113 Ernest Givins .05 .15
114 Haywood Jeffires .05 .15
115 Bruce Matthews .05 .15
116 Jim Everett .05 .15
117 Morten Andersen .05 .15
118 Quinn Early .05 .15
119 Tyrone Hughes .05 .15
120 Renaldo Turnbull .05 .15
121 Larry Centers .08 .25
122 Garrison Hearst .20 .50
123 Seth Joyner .05 .15
124 Ronald Moore .05 .15
125 Eric Swann .05 .15
126 Rick Mirer .08 .25
127 Chris Warren .08 .25
128 Brian Blades .05 .15
129 Cortez Kennedy .05 .15
130 Eugene Robinson .05 .15
131 Marshall Faulk .20 .50
132 Quentin Coryatt .05 .15
133 Jim Harbaugh .20 .50
134 Roosevelt Potts .05 .15
135 Steve Emtman .05 .15
136 Trent Dilfer .08 .25
137 Santana Dotson .05 .15
138 Errict Rhett .08 .25
139 Thomas Everett .05 .15
140 Craig Erickson .05 .15

1996 Pro Stamps

Chris Martin Enterprises released two different Pro Stamps sets in 1996. This set was sold in 12-stamp packages. They were essentially a re-make of the 1995 issue with the same stamp design and many of the same player photos. Some new players, however, were added for 1996 as were stamps for the two expansion teams. Each stamp measures approximately 1 1/2" by 2." Unlike the team set stamps, these are numbered in gold foil above the player's name.

COMPLETE SET (144) 14.00 35.00
1 Steve Young .30 .75
2 Jerry Rice .40 1.00
3 Merton Hanks .05 .15
4 J.J.Stokes .15 .40
5 William Floyd .08 .25
6 Troy Aikman .40 1.00
7 Michael Irvin .15 .40
8 Emmitt Smith .80 2.00
9 Deion Sanders .25 .60
10 Daryl Johnston .08 .25
11 Dan Marino 1.00 2.50
12 Bernie Parmalee .05 .15
13 O.J. McDuffie .08 .25
14 Richmond Webb .05 .15
15 Eric Green .05 .15
16 Drew Bledsoe .30 .75
17 Bruce Armstrong .05 .15
18 Dave Meggett .05 .15
19 Curtis Martin .30 .75
20 Ben Coates .08 .25
21 Dave Brown .05 .15
22 Michael Brooks .05 .15
23 Tyrone Wheatley .08 .25
24 Rodney Hampton .08 .25
25 Jeff Hostetler .05 .15
26 Tim Brown .15 .40
27 Rocket Ismail .08 .25
28 James Jett .08 .25
29 Harvey Williams .08 .25
30 Heath Shuler .08 .25
31 Michael Westbrook .15 .40
32 Terry Allen .15 .40
33 Darrell Green .08 .25
34 Brian Mitchell .05 .15
35 Rashaan Salaam .08 .25
36 Erik Kramer UER 37 .05 .15
37 Donnell Woolford .05 .15
38 Alonzo Spellman .05 .15

1996 Pro Stamps

39 Kyle Brady .08 .25
40 Aaron Glenn .05 .15
41 Adrian Murrell .08 .25
42 Nick Lowery .05 .15
43 Charles Johnson .08 .25
44 Kordell Stewart .30 .75
45 Yancey Thigpen .08 .25
46 Rod Woodson .08 .25
47 Greg Lloyd .15 .40
48 Randall Cunningham .15 .40
49 Rodney Peete .05 .15
50 Ricky Watters .15 .40
51 Charlie Garner .08 .25
52 Calvin Williams .05 .15
53 Brett Favre 1.00 2.50
54 Reggie White .15 .40
55 Edgar Bennett .08 .25
56 Robert Brooks .15 .40
57 Sean Jones .05 .15
58 Ronnie Harmon .05 .15
59 Stan Humphries .08 .25
60 Andre Coleman .05 .15
61 Tony Martin .08 .25
62 Junior Seau .15 .40
63 John Elway 1.00 2.50
64 Mike Pritchard .05 .15
65 Terrell Davis 1.00 2.50
66 Anthony Miller .08 .25
67 Shannon Sharpe .15 .40
68 Barry Sanders 1.00 2.50
69 Scott Mitchell .08 .25
70 Herman Moore .08 .25
71 Brett Perriman .08 .25
72 Johnnie Morton .08 .25
73 Marcus Allen .15 .40
74 Steve Bono .08 .25
75 Tamarick Vanover .08 .25
76 Lake Dawson .08 .25
77 Neil Smith .08 .25
78 Vinny Testaverde .08 .25
79 Eric Turner .05 .15
80 Michael Jackson .08 .25
81 Leroy Hoard .05 .15
82 Andre Rison .15 .40
83 Jim Kelly .15 .40
84 Carwell Gardner .05 .15
85 Andre Reed .08 .25
86 Bruce Smith .15 .40
87 Bryce Paup .08 .25
88 Warren Moon .15 .40
89 Qadry Ismail .08 .25
90 Robert Smith .08 .25
91 Cris Carter .15 .40
92 David Palmer .05 .15
93 Jeff George .15 .40
94 Morten Andersen .05 .15
95 Craig Heyward .05 .15
96 Eric Metcalf .08 .25
97 Jessie Tuggle .05 .15
98 Roman Phifer .05 .15
99 Todd Lyght .05 .15
100 Troy Drayton .05 .15
101 Isaac Bruce .15 .40
102 Sean Gilbert .05 .15
103 Jeff Blake .15 .40
104 Harold Green .05 .15
105 Carl Pickens .08 .25
106 Dan Wilkinson .05 .15
107 Ki-Jana Carter .08 .25
108 Steve McNair .40 1.00
109 Gary Brown .05 .15
110 Haywood Jeffires .05 .15
111 Bruce Matthews .05 .15
112 Jim Everett .05 .15
113 Mario Bates .08 .25
114 Ray Zellars .05 .15
115 Tyrone Hughes .05 .15
116 Eric Allen .05 .15
117 Larry Centers .08 .25
118 Garrison Hearst .15 .40
119 Aeneas Williams .05 .15
120 Rob Moore .08 .25
121 Neil O'Donnell .08 .25
122 Rick Mirer .08 .25
123 Chris Warren .08 .25
124 Eric Swann .05 .15
125 Cortez Kennedy .08 .25
126 Joey Galloway .25 .60
127 Marshall Faulk .15 .40
128 Quentin Coryatt .05 .15
129 Jim Harbaugh .15 .40
130 Trev Alberts .05 .15
131 Zack Crockett .05 .15
132 Trent Dilfer .15 .40
133 Hardy Nickerson .05 .15
134 Errict Rhett .15 .40
135 Alvin Harper .05 .15
136 Sam Mills .05 .15
137 Tyrone Poole .08 .25
138 Kerry Collins .15 .40
139 Bob Christian .05 .15
140 Randy Baldwin .05 .15
141 Steve Beuerlein .08 .25
142 Mark Brunell .40 1.00
143 Tony Boselli .08 .25
144 Jeff Lageman .05 .15

1996 Pro Stamps Team Sets

Chris Martin Enterprises released a second version of some of its Pro Stamps from 1996. This set was sold as four different 6-stamp team sets. Five player stamps and one team logo stamp was included in each pack. They were essentially a re-make of the 1995 issue with the same stamp design and many of the same player photos. Some new players, however, were added for 1996 as were stamps for the two expansion teams. Each stamp measures approximately 1 1/2" by 2." These team set stamps are unnumbered, but have been assigned numbers below according to the alphabetical player list by team. The team logos were added to the end of the player listings.

COMPLETE SET (24) 6.00 15.00
CP1 Randy Baldwin .14 .35
CP2 Bob Christian .14 .35
CP3 Kerry Collins .20 .50
CP4 Sam Mills .14 .35
CP5 Tyrone Poole .14 .35
CP6 Panthers Logo .20 .50
DC1 Troy Aikman .50 1.25
DC2 Michael Irvin .20 .50
DC3 Daryl Johnston .20 .50
DC4 Deion Sanders .30 .75
DC5 Emmitt Smith .80 2.00
DC6 Cowboys Logo .20 .50
JJ1 Steve Beuerlein .20 .50
JJ2 Tony Boselli .20 .50
JJ3 Mark Brunell .50 1.25
JJ4 Desmond Howard .14 .35
JJ5 Jeff Lageman .14 .35
JJ6 Jaguars Logo .14 .35
SF1 William Floyd .20 .50
SF2 Merton Hanks .14 .35
SF3 Jerry Rice .50 1.25
SF4 Dana Stubblefield .20 .50
SF5 Steve Young .40 1.00
SF6 49ers Logo .20 .50

1998 Pro Stamps

These stamps were issued by Crown Pro in sheets of six with each sheet representing a category, such as NFC Quarterbacks. We've listed and priced them below in panels as this is the form in which they are most commonly traded. Each stamp measures roughly 1 13/16" by 1 3/8" while the entire panel along with the backer board measures 4 1/2" by 7 1/2."

COMPLETE SET (7) 5.60 14.00
1 Plummer 1.20 3.00
Aikman
Favre
Kanell
Hoying
Syoung
2 Elway 1.20 3.00
Marino
Kstewart
Brunell
Jgeorge
Rleds
3 Emmitt 1.20 3.00
Barry
Dunn
Tallen
Janderson
Alstott
4 Bettis .80 2.00
Idavis
Mallen
Asmith
Egeorge
Dillon
5 Jrice .80 2.00
Rbrooks
Ccarter
Conway
Bruce
Hmoore
6 Rison 1.20 3.00
Tbrown
Gallo.
Tglenn
Mharr.
Kjohnson
7 Jrandle .80 2.00
Wmartin
Lathon
Seau
Dthomas
Boul.

1994 Pro Tags

This set of 168 Pro Tags marks the third consecutive year that Chris Martin Enterprises, Inc. has issued this line of sports collectibles. This first two sets were called Dog Tags. Measuring approximately 2 1/8" by 3 3/8", the plastic tags were sold six to a blister pack. A checklist card (printed on glossy paper) and a free team tag were included in each blister pack. Pro tags autographed by Jerome Bettis, J.J. Birden, Dale Carter, Keith Cash, Willie Davis, Sean Gilbert, Todd Lyght, Chris Martin, Roman Phifer, and Neil Smith were randomly seeded in packs. The set included an offer to receive 6 AFC or 6 NFC Super Rookie Pro Tags for $10.99 and 3 Proofs-of-Purchase for each set, or all 12 Super Rookies for $15.99 and 5 Proofs-of-Purchase. The factory set included three autographed cards, all 168 base cards, 12 Super Rookies, and a Super Bowl XXIX logo card.

COMPLETE SET (168) 35.00 80.00
*SUPER BOWL XXIX: .4X TO 1X BASIC CARDS
1 Steve Beuerlein .40 1.00
2 Chuck Cecil .20 .50
3 Randal Hill .20 .50
4 Garrison Hearst .20 .50
5 Ricky Proehl .20 .50
6 Eric Swann .40 1.00
7 Jeff George .50 1.25
8 Drew Hill .20 .50
9 Erric Pegram .40 1.00
10 Andre Rison .50 1.25
11 Deion Sanders .80 2.00
12 Jessie Tuggle .20 .50
13 Cornelius Bennett .40 1.00
14 Kenneth Davis .20 .50
15 Jim Kelly .50 1.25
16 Andre Reed .40 1.00
17 Darryl Talley .20 .50
18 Steve Tasker .40 1.00
19 Trace Armstrong .20 .50
20 Curtis Conway UER 22 .50 1.25
21 Dante Jones .20 .50
22 Donnell Woolford .20 .50
23 Tim Worley .20 .50
24 Chris Zorich .40 1.00
25 Derrick Fenner .20 .50
26 Harold Green .20 .50
27 David Klingler .20 .50
28 Tony McGee .20 .50
29 Carl Pickens .40 1.00
30 Jeff Query .20 .50
31 Mark Carrier WR .40 1.00
32 Michael Jackson .40 1.00
33 Eric Metcalf .40 1.00
34 Michael Dean Perry .40 1.00
35 Vinny Testaverde .40 1.00
36 Tommy Vardell .20 .50
37 Troy Aikman 1.20 3.00
38 Alvin Harper .20 .50
39 Michael Irvin .50 1.25
40 Russell Maryland .40 1.00
41 Jay Novacek .40 1.00
42 Emmitt Smith 2.00 5.00
43 Rod Bernstine .20 .50
44 Mike Croel .20 .50
45 John Elway 2.40 6.00
46 Glyn Milburn .40 1.00
47 Shannon Sharpe .50 1.25
48 Dennis Smith .20 .50
49 Jason Hanson .20 .50
50 Herman Moore .50 1.25
51 Brett Perriman .40 1.00
52 Barry Sanders 2.40 6.00
53 Chris Spielman .40 1.00
54 Pat Swilling .40 1.00
55 Edgar Bennett .40 1.00
56 Terrell Buckley .20 .50
57 Brett Favre 2.40 6.00
58 Chris Jacke .20 .50
59 Sterling Sharpe .40 1.00
60 Reggie White .50 1.25
61 Gary Brown .20 .50
62 Cody Carlson .20 .50
63 Ernest Givins .20 .50
64 Haywood Jeffires .40 1.00
65 Bruce Matthews .20 .50
66 Webster Slaughter .20 .50
67 Jason Belser .20 .50
68 Kerry Cash .20 .50
69 Rodney Culver .20 .50
70 Jim Harbaugh .50 1.25
71 Scott Radecic .20 .50
72 Roosevelt Potts .20 .50
73 Marcus Allen .50 1.25
74 J.J. Birden .20 .50
75 Dale Carter .20 .50
76 Keith Cash .20 .50
77 Willie Davis .40 1.00
78 Neil Smith .40 1.00
79 Eddie Anderson .20 .50
80 Tim Brown .50 1.25
81 Jeff Hostetler .40 1.00
82 Rocket Ismail .50 1.25
83 James Jett .20 .50
84 Terry McDaniel .20 .50
85 Flipper Anderson .20 .50
86 Jerome Bettis .80 2.00
87 Troy Drayton .40 1.00
88 Sean Gilbert UER 87 .20 .50
89 Todd Lyght .20 .50
90 Chris Martin .20 .50
91 Keith Byars .20 .50
92 Bryan Cox .20 .50
93 Irving Fryar .40 1.00
94 Terry Kirby .40 1.00
95 Dan Marino 2.40 6.00
96 O.J. McDuffie .50 1.25
97 Terry Allen .50 1.25
98 Cris Carter .50 1.25
99 Qadry Ismail .40 1.00
100 Randall McDaniel .20 .50
101 Warren Moon .50 1.25
102 Robert Smith .50 1.25
103 Drew Bledsoe 1.20 3.00
104 Vincent Brisby .40 1.00
105 Vincent Brown .20 .50
106 Marv Cook .20 .50
107 Leonard Russell .20 .50
108 Reyna Thompson .20 .50
109 Morten Andersen .20 .50
110 Quinn Early .20 .50
111 Tyrone Hughes .20 .50
112 Sam Mills .20 .50
113 Willie Roaf .20 .50
114 Renaldo Turnbull .20 .50
115 Phil Simms .40 1.00
116 John Elliott .20 .50
117 Rodney Hampton .40 1.00
118 Mark Jackson .20 .50
119 Dave Meggett .20 .50
120 Kenyon Rasheed .20 .50
121 Brad Baxter .20 .50
122 Boomer Esiason .40 1.00
123 Johnny Johnson .20 .50
124 Ronnie Lott .40 1.00
125 Johnny Mitchell .20 .50
126 Rob Moore .40 1.00
127 Fred Barnett .40 1.00
128 Mark Bavaro .20 .50
129 Bubby Brister .40 1.00
130 Randall Cunningham .50 1.25
131 Tim Harris .20 .50
132 Herschel Walker .40 1.00
133 Gary Anderson K .20 .50
134 Barry Foster .20 .50
135 Kevin Greene .40 1.00
136 Greg Lloyd .40 1.00
137 Neil O'Donnell .40 1.00
138 Rod Woodson .40 1.00
139 Eric Bieniemy UER 189 .20 .50
140 Ronnie Harmon UER 190 .40 1.00
141 Stan Humphries UER 191 .40 1.00
142 Natrone Means UER 192 .50 1.25
143 Leslie O'Neal UER 193 .40 1.00
144 Junior Seau UER 194 .50 1.25
145 Tim McDonald .20 .50
146 Jerry Rice 1.20 3.00
147 Dana Stubblefield .40 1.00
148 John Taylor .40 1.00
149 Ricky Watters UER 147 .40 1.00
150 Steve Young 1.00 2.50
151 Brian Blades .40 1.00
152 Cortez Kennedy .40 1.00
153 Rick Mirer .40 1.00
154 Rufus Porter .20 .50
155 Eugene Robinson .20 .50
156 Chris Warren .40 1.00
157 Santana Dotson .40 1.00
158 Craig Erickson .20 .50
159 Hardy Nickerson .40 1.00
160 Dan Stryzinski .20 .50
161 Charles Wilson .20 .50
162 Thomas Everett UER 147 .20 .50
163 Reggie Brooks .20 .50
164 Darrell Green .20 .50
165 Ricky Ervins .20 .50
166 John Friesz .40 1.00
167 Brian Mitchell .40 1.00
168 Sterling Palmer .20 .50
CL Chris Martin CL .08 .25

1994 Pro Tags Super Rookies

COMPLETE SET (12) 4.00 10.00
*SUPER BOWL XXIX: .4X TO 1X
1 Dan Wilkinson .30 .75
2 Marshall Faulk 2.00 5.00
3 Johnnie Morton .40 1.00
4 Trent Dilfer .75 2.00
5A Greg Hill .40 1.00
5B Errict Rhett .40 1.00
6 Lake Dawson .30 .75
7 Willie McGinest .40 1.00
8 Andre Coleman .20 .50
9 Heath Shuler .50 1.25
10 Wayne Gandy .20 .50
11 John Thierry .20 .50

2000 Quad City Steamwheelers AF2

COMPLETE SET (35) 10.00 20.00
1 Corey Brown .30 .75
2 Chad Buntin .30 .75
3 Frank Carter .30 .75
4 Cornelius Coe .30 .75
5 Billy Dicken .30 .75
6 Jesse Eaton .30 .75
7 Jay Ellers .30 .75
8 Josh Fourdyce .30 .75
9 Eddie Gibson .30 .75
10 Mike Gluski .30 .75
11 Frank Haege CO .30 .75
12 Brion Hurley .30 .75
13 Scott Hvistendahl .30 .75
14 Shon King .30 .75
15 Sean McNamara .30 .75
16 Xavier Patterson .30 .75
17 Hiawatha Phifer .30 .75
18 Spencer Stevens .30 .75
19 Clarence Thompson .30 .75
20 Russ Van Wetzinga .30 .75
21 Jamarr Ward .30 .75
22 Jeremy Wilkinson .30 .75
23 Damon Williams .30 .75
24 Jim Foster OWN .30 .75
25 Asst Coaches .30 .75
26 Staemwheeler (Mascot) .30 .75
27 Broadcasters .30 .75
28 Office Staff .30 .75
29 Deckmates .30 .75
Joanne Landis
Kristina Lindquist
30 Deckmates .30 .75
Carolina Espinoza
Deanna Ludin
31 Deckmates .30 .75
Jae Lynne McClellan
Wendy Taets
32 Deckmates .30 .75
Shelly Engler
Nicky Hyneck
33 Deckmates .30 .75
Jennifer Hopkins
Julie Adams
34 Deckmates .30 .75
Sarah Widick
Megan Linke
35 Deckmates .30 .75
Tennesha McCannon
Allison Samson

2002 Quad City Steamwheelers AF2

This set was sponsored by Sprint PCS and features members of the Quad City Steamrollers of the Arena Football League 2. Each card includes the team name and year running vertically on the left hand side of the front along with a color player photo. The cardbacks are also printed in color and feature another player photo and a player bio.

COMPLETE SET (40) 6.00 15.00
1 Chris Anthony .30 .75
2 LaVance Banks .20 .50
3 Cory Bern .20 .50
4 Corey Brown .20 .50
5 Brent Browner .20 .50
6 Lamon Caldwell .20 .50
7 Mike Cawley .30 .75
8 Trent Clemen .20 .50
9 Derrick Davison .20 .50
10 Jay Eilers .20 .50
11 Jim Foster OWN .20 .50
12 Josh Fourdyce .20 .50
13 Ira Gooch .20 .50
14 Phil Hayek MGR .20 .50
Phil Roehlk ASST CO
15 Brian Hegnauer .20 .50
16 Jeff Hewitt .30 .75
17 Rich Ingold CO .20 .50
18 Reggie Mathis ASST CO .20 .50
19 Tim McGill .20 .50
20 Dan McMullen .20 .50
21 Shawn Orr .20 .50
22 Hiawatha Phifer .20 .50
23 Jon Roehlk ASST CO .20 .50
24 Mike Schaefer .20 .50
25 T.J. Schneckloth .20 .50
26 Justin Thies .20 .50
27 Eric Thigpen .20 .50
28 Brett Thompson .20 .50
29 Frank Trentadue .30 .75
30 Damon Williams .20 .50
31 Pee-Wee Woods .20 .50
32 Tony Zimmerman .40 1.00
33 Jim Albracht .20 .50
John Furlong
(Broadcast Team)
34 DeckMates - First Year .20 .50
35 DeckMates - Veterans .20 .50
36 Front Office Staff .20 .50
37 Physical Therapy .20 .50
Training Staff
38 Steamwheeler Willie/ MASCOT .20 .50
39 Team Physicians .20 .50
40 Cover Card .20 .50

2003 Quad City Steamwheelers AF2

This set was sponsored by US Celular and features members of the Quad City Steamwheelers of the Arena Football League 2. Each card includes the team name below the player photo and the player's name above. The cardbacks are also feature a player photo as well as a player bio.

COMPLETE SET (39) 6.00 15.00
1 Brian Berg .20 .50
2 Cory Bern .20 .50
3 Corey Brown .20 .50
4 Tony Burrier .20 .50
5 Jamaal Cherry .20 .50
6 LaRico Cole .20 .50
7 Tim Dodge .30 .75
8 Leo FenceRoy .20 .50
9 Jim Foster AFL Founder .20 .50
10 Matt Forbes .20 .50
11 Josh Fourdyce .20 .50
12 Asa Francis .20 .50
13 Ira Gooch .20 .50
14 Ronnie Gordon .20 .50
15 Jeff Hewitt .30 .75
16 James Houston .20 .50
17 Rich Ingold CO .20 .50
18 Randall Lane .20 .50
19 Ed Lanford .20 .50
Jon Roehlk Asst.CO
20 Shawn Orr .20 .50
21 O.J. Payne .20 .50
22 Paul Savich .20 .50
23 Michael Schaefer .20 .50
24 T.J. Schneckloth .20 .50
25 Justin Thies .20 .50
26 Danny Thomas .20 .50
27 Pete Traynor .20 .50
28 Lee Wiggins .20 .50
29 Damon Williams .20 .50
30 Tony Zimmerman .40 1.00
31 DeckMates .20 .50
Janette Duhm
Allie Toolate
Ashley Wadsworth
32 DeckMates .20 .50
Steph Hillyer
Kim Pierce
Jen Hopkins-Tarchinski
33 DeckMates .20 .50
Julie Ziegenhorn
Ashley Rubino
AnMarie McCrery
Brittany Corbett
34 Quad Cities Arena .20 .50
Cover Card
35 Radio Broadcast Team .20 .50
Jim Albracht
John Furlong
36 Senior Management .20 .50
37 Steamwheelers Mascot .20 .50
Jill Bartlett-Hill
Cheerleading Coach
38 Steamwheelers Staff .20 .50
39 Craig Wainwright .20 .50
Trainer
Phil Hayek
Equipment Manager

2005 Quad City Steamwheelers AF2

COMPLETE SET (40) 7.50 15.00
1 Fred Barr .20 .50
2 Nate Bell .20 .50
3 Corey Brown .20 .50
4 Travis Burns .20 .50
5 Larry Bush Asst.CO .20 .50
6 Jason Cedeno .20 .50
7 Sam Clemons .20 .50
8 John Culp .20 .50
9 Giovanni Deloatch .20 .50
10 Tim Dodge .20 .50
11 Steve Fickert Ast.CO .20 .50
12 Matt Forbes .20 .50
13 Jim Foster OWN .20 .50
14 Mike Fox Asst.CO .20 .50
15 Rick Frazier CO .20 .50
16 Nick Gatto .20 .50
17 Jeff Hewitt .20 .50
18 Pat Hughes .20 .50
19 Johnathan Katona Asst.CO .20 .50
20 Ed Langford Asst.CO .20 .50
21 Torey Morris .20 .50
22 A.J. Novak .20 .50
23 Matt Pike .20 .50
24 Scott Power .20 .50
25 Jon Roehlk Asst.CO .20 .50
26 Kofi Smith .20 .50
27 DeOnte' Taylor .20 .50
28 Mark Taylor Asst.CO .20 .50
29 Pete Traynor .20 .50
30 Jack Walker Jr. .20 .50
31 Broadcasters .20 .50
32 DeckMates .20 .50
33 DeckMates .20 .50
34 Steamwheeler (Mascot) .20 .50
35 Trainers .20 .50
36 Veteran Staff .20 .50
37 First Year Staff .20 .50
38 Intern Staff .20 .50
39 Valley Bank Sponsor Coupon .20 .50
40 Valley Bank Sponsor Locations .20 .50

2006 Quad City Steamwheelers AF2

COMPLETE SET (29) 4.00 8.00
1 Shonn Bell .20 .50
2 Larry Bush OWN .20 .50
3 Chris Chandler .20 .50
4 Mike Custer CO .20 .50
5 Tim Dodge .30 .75
6 Rick Frazier CO .20 .50
7 Troy Graham .20 .50
8 Tim Hicks .30 .75
9 Patrick Horne .20 .50
10 David Hurst .20 .50
11 Chris Jahnke .20 .50
12 Kika Kaululaau .20 .50
13 Sidney Lewis .20 .50
14 William Lobendahn .20 .50
15 Jeff Macrea .20 .50
16 Matt Manuma .20 .50
17 Kimo Naehu .20 .50
18 A.J. Novak .20 .50
19 James Parham .20 .50
20 Kris Peters .20 .50
21 Matt Pike .30 .75
22 Sean Ponder CO .20 .50
23 Alfonso Pugh .20 .50
24 Jon Roehlk CO .20 .50
25 Mataese Togafau .20 .50
26 Jack Walker .20 .50
27 Adrian Wilson .20 .50
28 Steamwheeler Willie .20 .50
(Mascot)
29 Deck Mates .40 1.00
Cheerleaders; measures 3 1/2 x 5)

1954 Quaker Sports Oddities

This 27-card set features strange moments in sports and was issued as an insert inside Quaker Puffed Rice cereal boxes. Fronts of the cards are drawings depicting the person or the event. In a stripe at the top of the card face appear the words "Sports Oddities." Two colorful drawings fill the remaining space: the left half is a portrait, while the right half is action-oriented. A variety of sports are included. The cards measure approximately 2 1/4" by 3 1/2" and have rounded corners. The last line on the back of each card declares, "It's Odd but True." A person could also buy the complete set for fifteen cents and two box tops from Quaker Puffed Wheat or Quaker Rice. If a collector did send in their material to Quaker Oats the set came back in a specially marked box with the cards in cellophane wrapping. Sets in original wrapping are valued at 1.25x to 1.5X the high column listings in our checklist.

COMPLETE SET (27) 125.00 250.00
1 Johnny Miller 3.00 6.00
6 Wake Forest College 3.00 6.00
7 Amos Alonzo Stagg 12.50 25.00
19 George Halas 15.00 30.00
25 Texas University 3.00 6.00
Northwestern
26 Bronko Nagurski 30.00 60.00

2000 Quantum Leaf Previews

Randomly inserted in 1999 Score Supplemental packs, this 18-card set previews the 2000 Quantum Leaf set which was slated as the first 2000 football release for the Playoff Company. The cards were printed in dot-matrix hologram form.

COMPLETE SET (18) 60.00 120.00
QLP1 Barry Sanders 5.00 12.00
QLP2 Ricky Williams 2.00 5.00
QLP3 Terrell Davis 2.50 6.00
QLP4 John Elway 6.00 15.00
QLP5 Edgerrin James 2.50 6.00
QLP6 Tim Couch 1.50 4.00
QLP7 Peyton Manning 6.00 15.00
QLP8 Kurt Warner 5.00 12.00
QLP9 Randy Moss 2.50 6.00
QLP10 Dan Marino 6.00 15.00
QLP11 Brett Favre 6.00 15.00
QLP12 Eddie George 2.00 5.00
QLP13 Marvin Harrison 2.50 6.00
QLP14 Jerry Rice 4.00 10.00
QLP15 Emmitt Smith 5.00 12.00
QLP16 Keyshawn Johnson 2.00 5.00
QLP17 Drew Bledsoe 2.50 6.00
QLP18 Marshall Faulk 2.50 6.00

2000 Quantum Leaf

2000 Quantum Leaf was released as a 350-card base set containing 300 regular-issue veteran cards and 50 rookie subset cards seeded at one in two packs. Base cards feature full color player photos set a against a silver holographic fractal background, and rookie subset cards with the same format but enhanced with a gold stamp of the draft team and round drafted. Later in the season, card numbers 351-381 were issued as part of a wrapper redemption (24-wrappers plus $5.99) upon the initial release. Quantum Leaf was packaged in boxes containing 24-packs of four cards per pack which carried a suggested retail price of $2.99.

COMPLETE SET (350) 60.00 150.00
COMP.SET w/o SP's (300) 10.00 25.00
COMP.ROOKIE UPDATE (31) 10.00 20.00
ROOKIE SUBSET ODDS 1:2
1 Frank Sanders .25 .60
2 Adrian Murrell .25 .60
3 Rob Moore .25 .60
4 Simeon Rice .30 .75
5 Michael Pittman .25 .60
6 Jake Plummer .25 .60
7 David Boston .25 .60
8 Mario Bates .25 .60
9 Chris Chandler .30 .75
10 Tim Dwight .30 .75
11 Chris Calloway .25 .60
12 Terance Mathis .25 .60
13 Jamal Anderson .30 .75
14 Byron Hanspard .25 .60
15 Ken Oxendine .25 .60
16 Tony Graziani .30 .75
17 Bob Christian .25 .60
18 Priest Holmes .25 .60
19 Tony Banks .25 .60
20 Patrick Johnson .25 .60
21 Rod Woodson .40 1.00
22 Jermaine Lewis .25 .60
23 Errict Rhett .30 .75
24 Stoney Case .25 .60
25 Peter Boulware .25 .60
26 Qadry Ismail .25 .60
27 Brandon Stokley .25 .60
28 Andre Reed .40 1.00
29 Eric Moulds .25 .60
30 Doug Flutie .30 .75
31 Bruce Smith .30 .75
32 Jay Riemersma .25 .60
33 Antowain Smith .30 .75
34 Thurman Thomas .30 .75
35 Jonathan Linton .25 .60
36 Peerless Price .30 .75
37 Rob Johnson .30 .75
38 Sam Gash .25 .60
39 Muhsin Muhammad .25 .60
40 Wesley Walls .25 .60
41 Fred Lane .25 .60
42 Kevin Greene .40 1.00
43 Tim Biakabutuka .30 .75
44 Steve Beuerlein .30 .75
45 Donald Hayes .25 .60
46 Patrick Jeffers .25 .60
47 Curtis Enis .25 .60
48 Bobby Engram .25 .60
49 Curtis Conway .30 .75
50 Marcus Robinson .30 .75
51 Marty Booker .25 .60
52 Cade McNown .25 .60
53 Shane Matthews .25 .60
54 Jim Miller .25 .60
55 Darnay Scott .30 .75
56 Carl Pickens .30 .75
57 Corey Dillon .25 .60
58 Jeff Blake .30 .75
59 Akili Smith .25 .60
60 Michael Basnight .25 .60
61 Karim Abdul-Jabbar .25 .60
62 Tim Couch .30 .75
63 Kevin Johnson .25 .60
64 Terry Kirby .25 .60
65 Ty Detmer .25 .60
66 Leslie Shepherd .25 .60
67 Darrin Chiaverini .25 .60
68 Emmitt Smith .60 1.50
69 Deion Sanders .30 .75
70 Michael Irvin .40 1.00
71 Rocket Ismail .30 .75
72 Troy Aikman .50 1.25
73 Daryl Johnston .30 .75
74 Chris Warren .25 .60
75 Jason Garrett .40 1.00
76 Jason Tucker .25 .60
77 Lawyer Milloy .25 .60
78 Dexter Coakley .25 .60
79 Greg Ellis .25 .60
80 David LaFleur .25 .60
81 Todd Lyght .25 .60
82 Ernie Mills .25 .60
83 Wane McGarity .25 .60
84 Chris Brazzell RC .25 .60
85 Ed McCaffrey .30 .75
86 Rod Smith .30 .75
87 Shannon Sharpe .30 .75
88 Brian Griese .25 .60
89 John Elway .60 1.50
90 Neil Smith .25 .60
91 Terrell Davis .30 .75
92 Olandis Gary .30 .75
93 Derek Loville .25 .60
94 John Avery .25 .60
95 Bubby Brister .25 .60
96 Byron Chamberlain .25 .60
97 Dale Carter .25 .60
98 Johnnie Morton .30 .75
99 Charlie Batch .25 .60
100 Barry Sanders .60 1.50
101 Germane Crowell .25 .60
102 Gus Frerotte .25 .60
103 Desmond Howard .30 .75
104 Terry Fair .25 .60
105 Ron Rivers .25 .60
106 Greg Hill .25 .60
107 Sedrick Irvin .25 .60
108 David Sloan .25 .60
109 Herman Moore .25 .60
110 Robert Porcher .25 .60
111 Corey Bradford .25 .60
112 Dorsey Levens .30 .75
113 Antonio Freeman .30 .75
114 Brett Favre .75 2.00
115 De'Mond Parker .25 .60
116 Bill Schroeder .30 .75
117 Matt Hasselbeck .25 .60
118 Donald Driver .50 1.25
119 Basil Mitchell .25 .60
120 E.G. Green .25 .60
121 Ken Dilger .25 .60
122 Marvin Harrison .30 .75
123 Peyton Manning 1.00 2.50
124 Terrence Wilkins .25 .60
125 Edgerrin James .30 .75
126 Jerome Pathon .25 .60
127 Marcus Pollard .25 .60
128 Keenan McCardell .30 .75
129 Mark Brunell .30 .75
130 Fred Taylor .25 .60
131 Jimmy Smith .30 .75
132 James Stewart .25 .60
133 Kyle Brady .25 .60
134 Tony Brackens .25 .60
135 Derrick Thomas .40 1.00
136 Rashaan Shehee .25 .60
137 Derrick Alexander .25 .60
138 Bam Morris .25 .60
139 Andre Rison .30 .75
140 Elvis Grbac .25 .60
141 Tony Gonzalez .30 .75
142 Donnell Bennett .25 .60
143 Warren Moon .40 1.00
144 Tamarick Vanover .25 .60
145 Kimble Anders .25 .60
146 Tony Richardson RC .25 .60
147 Zach Thomas .30 .75
148 Oronde Gadsden .30 .75
149 Dan Marino .75 2.00
150 O.J. McDuffie .30 .75
151 Tony Martin .30 .75
152 Cecil Collins .25 .60
153 James Johnson .25 .60
154 Rob Konrad .25 .60
155 Yatil Green .25 .60
156 Damon Huard .25 .60
157 Nate Jacquet .25 .60
158 Stanley Pritchett .25 .60
159 Sam Madison .25 .60
160 Randy Moss .30 .75
161 Cris Carter .40 1.00
162 Robert Smith .25 .60
163 Randall Cunningham .30 .75
164 Jake Reed .30 .75
165 John Randle .40 1.00
166 Leroy Hoard .25 .60
167 Jeff George .30 .75
168 Daunte Culpepper .30 .75
169 Matthew Hatchette .25 .60
170 Robert Tate .25 .60
171 Ty Law .40 1.00
172 Troy Brown .25 .60
173 Tony Simmons .25 .60
174 Terry Glenn .30 .75
175 Ben Coates .25 .60
176 Drew Bledsoe .30 .75
177 Terry Allen .30 .75
178 Kevin Faulk .25 .60
179 Shawn Jefferson .25 .60
180 Andy Katzenmoyer .25 .60
181 Willie McGinest .30 .75
182 Cameron Cleeland .25 .60
183 Eddie Kennison .25 .60
184 Ricky Williams .30 .75
185 Danny Wuerffel .40 1.00
186 Brett Bech .25 .60
187 Billy Joe Hobert .25 .60
188 Jake Delhomme RC .30 .75
189 Wilmont Perry .25 .60
190 Keith Poole .25 .60
191 Ashley Ambrose .25 .60
192 Amani Toomer .25 .60
193 Kerry Collins .25 .60
194 Tiki Barber .30 .75
195 Ike Hilliard .25 .60
196 Jason Sehorn .25 .60
197 Joe Montgomery .25 .60
198 Joe Jurevicius .25 .60
199 Michael Strahan .30 .75
200 Sean Bennett .25 .60
201 Jessie Armstead .25 .60
202 Pete Mitchell .25 .60
203 Curtis Martin .30 .75
204 Vinny Testaverde .25 .60
205 Keyshawn Johnson .30 .75
206 Wayne Chrebet .25 .60
207 Ray Lucas .25 .60
208 Tyrone Wheatley .25 .60
209 Napoleon Kaufman .30 .75
210 Tim Brown .40 1.00
211 Rickey Dudley .25 .60
212 James Jett .30 .75
213 Rich Gannon .30 .75
214 Charles Woodson .40 1.00
215 Zack Crockett .25 .60
216 Darrell Russell .25 .60
217 Duce Staley .25 .60
218 Donovan McNabb .30 .75
219 Charles Johnson .25 .60
220 Dameane Douglas .25 .60
221 Doug Pederson .25 .60
222 Torrance Small .25 .60
223 Troy Vincent .25 .60
224 Na Brown .25 .60
225 Kordell Stewart .25 .60
226 Jerome Bettis .40 1.00
227 Hines Ward .30 .75
228 Troy Edwards .25 .60
229 Richard Huntley .25 .60
230 Mark Bruener .30 .75
231 Pete Gonzalez .25 .60
232 Levon Kirkland .25 .60
233 Bobby Shaw RC .25 .60
234 Amos Zereoue .25 .60
235 Natrone Means .30 .75
236 Junior Seau .30 .75
237 Jim Harbaugh .30 .75
238 Ryan Leaf .30 .75
239 Mikhael Ricks .25 .60
240 Jermaine Fazande .25 .60
241 Jeff Graham .25 .60
242 Tremayne Stephens .25 .60
243 Terrell Owens .30 .75
244 J.J. Stokes .30 .75
245 Charlie Garner .30 .75
246 Jerry Rice 1.00 2.50
247 Garrison Hearst .25 .60
248 Steve Young .50 1.25
249 Jeff Garcia .25 .60
250 Fred Beasley .25 .60
251 Bryant Young .25 .60
252 Derrick Mayes .25 .60
253 Ahman Green .30 .75
254 Joey Galloway .30 .75
255 Ricky Watters .30 .75
256 Jon Kitna .25 .60
257 Sean Dawkins .25 .60
258 Sam Adams .25 .60
259 Christian Fauria .25 .60
260 Shawn Springs .25 .60
261 Az-Zahir Hakim .25 .60
262 Isaac Bruce .40 1.00
263 Marshall Faulk .30 .75
264 Trent Green .25 .60
265 Kurt Warner .60 1.50
266 Torry Holt .30 .75
267 Robert Holcombe .25 .60
268 Kevin Carter .25 .60
269 Amp Lee .25 .60
270 Roland Williams .25 .60
271 Jacquez Green .25 .60
272 Reidel Anthony .25 .60
273 Warren Sapp .30 .75
274 Mike Alstott .25 .60
275 Warrick Dunn .25 .60
276 Trent Dilfer .25 .60
277 Shaun King .25 .60
278 Bert Emanuel .25 .60
279 Eric Zeier .25 .60
280 Neil O'Donnell .25 .60
281 Eddie George .30 .75
282 Yancey Thigpen .25 .60
283 Steve McNair .30 .75
284 Kevin Dyson .30 .75
285 Frank Wycheck .30 .75
286 Jevon Kearse .25 .60
287 Bruce Matthews .25 .60
288 Lorenzo Neal .25 .60
289 Stephen Davis .25 .60
290 Stephen Alexander .25 .60
291 Darrell Green .30 .75
292 Skip Hicks .25 .60
293 Brad Johnson .30 .75
294 Michael Westbrook .25 .60
295 Albert Connell .25 .60
296 Irving Fryar .30 .75
297 Champ Bailey .30 .75
298 Larry Centers .25 .60
299 Brian Mitchell .25 .60
300 James Thrash .30 .75
301 LaVar Arrington RC 1.25 3.00
302 Peter Warrick RC .60 1.50
303 Courtney Brown RC .75 2.00
304 Plaxico Burress RC .75 2.00
305 Corey Simon RC .75 2.00
306 Thomas Jones RC .75 2.00
307 Travis Taylor RC .60 1.50
308 Shaun Alexander RC 1.00 2.50
309 Chris Redman RC .60 1.50
310 Chad Pennington RC .75 2.00
311 Jamal Lewis RC 1.00 2.50
312 Brian Urlacher RC 3.00 8.00
313 Keith Bulluck RC .75 2.00
314 Bubba Franks RC .60 1.50
315 Dez White RC .60 1.50
316 Ahmed Plummer RC .60 1.50
317 Ron Dayne RC 1.00 2.50
318 Shaun Ellis RC .75 2.00
319 Sylvester Morris RC .60 1.50
320 Deltha O'Neal RC .60 1.50
321 R.Jay Soward RC .60 1.50
322 Sherrod Gideon RC .60 1.50
323 John Abraham RC 1.00 2.50
324 Travis Prentice RC .60 1.50
325 Darrell Jackson RC .60 1.50
326 Giovanni Carmazzi RC .60 1.50
327 Anthony Lucas RC .60 1.50
328 Danny Farmer RC .60 1.50
329 Dennis Northcutt RC .60 1.50
330 Troy Walters RC .60 1.50
331 Laveranues Coles RC .75 2.00
332 Tee Martin RC .60 1.50
333 J.R. Redmond RC .60 1.50
334 Jerry Porter RC 1.00 2.50
335 Sebastian Janikowski RC 1.00 2.50
336 Michael Wiley RC .60 1.50
337 Reuben Droughns RC .60 1.50
338 Trung Canidate RC .60 1.50
339 Shyrone Stith RC .60 1.50
340 Trevor Gaylor RC .60 1.50
341 Rob Morris RC .75 2.00
342 Marc Bulger RC .75 2.00
343 Tom Brady RC 50.00 100.00
344 Todd Husak RC .60 1.50
345 Gari Scott RC .60 1.50
346 Erron Kinney RC .60 1.50
347 Julian Peterson RC 1.00 2.50
348 Doug Chapman RC .60 1.50
349 Ron Dugans RC .60 1.50
350 Todd Pinkston RC .60 1.50
351 Deon Grant RC .40 1.00
352 Na'il Diggs RC .40 1.00
353 Raynoch Thompson RC .40 1.00
354 Mario Edwards RC .40 1.00
355 John Engelberger RC .40 1.00

356 Dwayne Goodrich RC .40 1.00
357 Ben Kelly RC .40 1.00
358 Sekou Sanyika RC .40 1.00
359 Brandon Short RC .40 1.00
360 Jabari Issa RC .40 1.00
361 Darwin Walker RC .40 1.00
362 Jerry Johnson RC .40 1.00
363 Robaire Smith RC .40 1.00
364 Mark Roman RC .40 1.00
365 Leonardo Carson RC .40 1.00
366 Mark Simoneau RC .40 1.00
367 Hank Poteat RC .40 1.00
368 Darren Howard RC .40 1.00
369 David Macklin RC .40 1.00
370 Adalius Thomas RC 1.25 3.00
371 Ralph Brown RC .40 1.00
372 Mondriel Fulcher RC .40 1.00
373 Sammy Morris RC .40 1.00
374 Rondell Mealey RC .40 1.00
375 Deon Dyer RC .40 1.00
376 Mareno Philyaw RC .40 1.00
377 Thomas Hamner RC .40 1.00
378 Jarious Jackson RC .50 1.25
379 Joe Hamilton RC .40 1.00
380 Tim Rattay RC .50 1.25
381 Chris Hovan RC .50 1.25
SB1 Kurt Warner MVP/1000 3.00 8.00
SB1A Kurt Warner MVP AU/100 40.00 80.00
NFL1 Kurt Warner MVP/1000 3.00 8.00
NFL1A Kurt Warner MVP AU/100 40.00 80.00

2000 Quantum Leaf All-Millennium Team

Randomly inserted in packs, this 28-card set assembles some of the NFL's best players spanning over 40 years to comprise Quantum Leaf's All-Millennium Team. Each card is enhanced with a gold holographic foil border and is sequentially numbered to 1000. Card's serial numbered 0001/1000 to 0100/1000 are autographed.
COMPLETE SET (28) 60.00 120.00
STATED PRINT RUN 1000 SER.#'d SETS
FIRST 100 SER.#'d CARDS SIGNED
BS Barry Sanders 2.50 6.00
CC Cris Carter 1.50 4.00
DM Dan Marino 3.00 8.00
EC Earl Campbell 1.50 4.00
ED Eric Dickerson 1.25 3.00
ES Emmitt Smith 2.50 6.00
FB Fred Biletnikoff 1.50 4.00
GS Gale Sayers 1.50 4.00
JB Jim Brown 2.00 5.00
JE John Elway 2.50 6.00
JL James Lofton 1.00 2.50
JM Joe Montana 5.00 12.00
JR Jerry Rice 4.00 10.00
JU Johnny Unitas 4.00 10.00
KW Kellen Winslow 1.25 3.00
LA Lance Alworth 1.50 4.00
MA Marcus Allen 1.50 4.00
PH Paul Hornung 1.50 4.00
PW Paul Warfield 1.50 4.00
RB Raymond Berry 1.25 3.00
RM Randy Moss 1.25 3.00
RS Roger Staubach 2.00 5.00
SB Sammy Baugh 1.50 4.00
SL Steve Largent 1.50 4.00
TB Terry Bradshaw 4.00 10.00
TD Terrell Davis 1.25 3.00
BST Bart Starr 4.00 10.00
TDO Tony Dorsett 1.50 4.00

2000 Quantum Leaf All-Millennium Team Autographs

Randomly inserted in packs, this 28-card set parallels the base All-Millennium Team set but are autographed by each respective player. These cards are included in the original print run so they are numbered 0001/1000 to 0100/1000.
FIRST 100 SER.#'d CARDS SIGNED
BS Barry Sanders 75.00 150.00
CC Cris Carter 25.00 60.00
DM Dan Marino 125.00 200.00
EC Earl Campbell 25.00 60.00
ED Eric Dickerson 25.00 60.00
ES Emmitt Smith 125.00 200.00
FB Fred Biletnikoff 25.00 60.00
GS Gale Sayers 25.00 60.00
JB Jim Brown 40.00 100.00
JE John Elway 100.00 200.00
JL James Lofton 15.00 40.00
JM Joe Montana 100.00 200.00
JR Jerry Rice 75.00 150.00
JU Johnny Unitas 200.00 350.00
KW Kellen Winslow 20.00 50.00
LA Lance Alworth 25.00 60.00
MA Marcus Allen 40.00 80.00
PH Paul Hornung 40.00 80.00
PW Paul Warfield 25.00 60.00
RB Raymond Berry 20.00 50.00
RM Randy Moss 50.00 100.00
RS Roger Staubach 75.00 150.00
SB Sammy Baugh 100.00 175.00
SL Steve Largent 25.00 60.00
TB Terry Bradshaw 75.00 150.00
TD Terrell Davis 40.00 80.00
BST Bart Starr 125.00 200.00
TDO Tony Dorsett 40.00 80.00

2000 Quantum Leaf Banner Season

Randomly inserted in packs, this 40-card set showcases the best statistical performers of the 1999 season. Base cards are die-cut in the form of a banner and are highlighted with silver foil borders and stamping. Each card is serial numbered to the respective stat the card features.
COMPLETE SET (40) 50.00 100.00
STATED PRINT RUN 1-4857
CARDS SER.#'d TO 1999 SEASON STAT
*CENT/99: 1.5X TO 4X BAN SEAS/2111-4857
*CENT/99: 1.2X TO 3X BAN SEAS/732-1663
*CENT/99: 1X TO 2.5X BAN SEASON/334
CENTURY PRINT RUN 99 SER.#'d SETS
BS1 Brett Favre/4091 2.00 5.00
BS2 Marvin Harrison/1663 1.00 2.50
BS3 Tim Brown/1344 1.25 3.00
BS4 Randy Moss/1413 1.00 2.50
BS5 Edgerrin James/2139 .75 2.00
BS6 Kurt Warner/4353 1.50 4.00
BS7 Marshall Faulk/2429 .75 2.00
BS8 Dan Marino/2448 2.00 5.00
BS9 Tim Couch/2447 .75 2.00
BS10 Ricky Williams/884 1.00 2.50
BS11 Eddie George/1304 1.00 2.50
BS12 Jerry Rice/830 3.00 8.00
BS13 Troy Aikman/2964 1.25 3.00
BS14 Emmitt Smith/1397 2.00 5.00
BS15 Antonio Freeman/1074 1.00 2.50
BS16 Jimmy Smith/1636 1.00 2.50
BS17 Charlie Batch/4857 .60 1.50
BS18 Jake Plummer/2111 .60 1.50
BS19 Drew Bledsoe/3985 .75 2.00
BS20 Germane Crowell/1338 .75 2.00
BS21 Cris Carter/1241 1.25 3.00
BS22 Deion Sanders/334 1.25 3.00
BS23 Donovan McNabb/948 1.00 2.50
BS24 Mark Brunell/3060 .75 2.00
BS25 Fred Taylor/732 .75 2.00
BS26 Stephen Davis/1405 .75 2.00
BS27 Brad Johnson/4005 .75 2.00
BS28 Jon Kitna/3346 .60 1.50
BS29 Curtis Martin/1464 1.00 2.50
BS30 Keyshawn Johnson/1170 1.00 2.50
BS31 Shaun King/875 .75 2.00
BS32 Isaac Bruce/1165 1.25 3.00
BS33 Kevin Johnson/986 .75 2.00
BS34 Steve McNair/2179 .75 2.00
BS35 Eric Moulds/994 .75 2.00
BS36 Peyton Manning/4130 2.50 6.00
BS37 Dorsey Levens/1607 1.00 2.50
BS38 Olandis Gary/1159 1.00 2.50
BS39 James Stewart/931 .75 2.00
BS40 Terry Glenn/1147 1.00 2.50

2000 Quantum Leaf Double Team

Randomly seeded in packs, this 60-card set features top ground gainers paired with passing performers. On this double-sided player card, each side is enhanced with holographic foil, and cards are numbered to 1000. Card Backs carry a "DT" prefix.
COMPLETE SET (30) 30.00 60.00
STATED PRINT RUN 1500 SER.#'d SETS
DT1 J.Johnson D.Marino 2.50 6.00
DT2 E.James P.Manning 3.00 8.00
DT3 K.Faulk D.Bledsoe 1.00 2.50
DT4 A.Smith D.Flutie 1.00 2.50
DT5 C.Martin V.Testaverde 1.00 2.50
DT6 J.Bettis K.Stewart 1.25 3.00
DT7 E.George S.McNair 1.00 2.50
DT8 F.Taylor M.Brunell 1.00 2.50
DT9 E.Rhett T.Banks 1.00 2.50
DT10 K.Abdul-Jabbar T.Couch 1.00 2.50
DT11 C.Dillon A.Smith 1.00 2.50
DT12 T.Davis B.Griese 1.00 2.50
DT13 D.Bennett E.Grbac .75 2.00
DT14 R.Watters J.Kitna 1.00 2.50
DT15 T.Wheatley R.Gannon 1.00 2.50
DT16 N.Means J.Harbaugh 1.00 2.50
DT17 E.Smith T.Aikman 2.00 5.00
DT18 S.Davis B.Johnson 1.00 2.50
DT19 D.Staley D.McNabb 1.00 2.50
DT20 M.Pittman J.Plummer .75 2.00
DT21 D.Levens B.Favre 2.50 6.00
DT22 R.Smith J.George 1.00 2.50
DT23 M.Alstott S.King .75 2.00
DT24 C.Enis C.McNown .75 2.00
DT25 B.Sanders C.Batch 2.00 5.00
DT26 M.Faulk K.Warner 2.00 5.00
DT27 R.Williams J.Blake 1.00 2.50
DT28 C.Garner S.Young 1.50 4.00
DT29 T.Biakabutuka S.Beuerlein 1.00 2.50
DT30 J.Anderson C.Chandler 1.00 2.50

2000 Quantum Leaf Gamers

Randomly inserted in hobby packs, this 20-card set features premium swatches of authentic jerseys that include portions of the pictured player's jersey number and team logos. Each card is serial numbered out of 25.
STATED PRINT RUN 25 SER.#'d SETS
G1 Brett Favre 40.00 100.00
G2 Dan Marino 40.00 100.00
G3 Barry Sanders 30.00 80.00
G4 John Elway 30.00 80.00
G5 Peyton Manning 50.00 120.00
G6 Terrell Davis 15.00 40.00
G7 Fred Taylor 12.00 30.00
G8 Drew Bledsoe 15.00 40.00
G9 Mark Brunell 15.00 40.00
G10 Eddie George 15.00 40.00
G11 Isaac Bruce 20.00 50.00
G12 Jerry Rice 50.00 120.00
G13 Ray Lucas 12.00 30.00
G14 Olandis Gary 15.00 40.00
G15 Emmitt Smith 30.00 80.00
G16 Shaun King 12.00 30.00
G17 Edgerrin James 15.00 40.00
G18 Cris Carter 20.00 50.00
G19 Jimmy Smith 15.00 40.00
G20 Brian Griese 12.00 30.00

2000 Quantum Leaf Hardwear

Randomly inserted in hobby packs, this 15-card set featuers swatches of authentic game-used helmets. Each card is sequentially numbered to 125.
STATED PRINT RUN 125 SER.#'d SETS
HW1 Brett Favre 20.00 50.00
HW2 Dan Marino 20.00 50.00
HW3 Barry Sanders 15.00 40.00
HW4 John Elway 15.00 40.00
HW5 Terrell Davis 8.00 20.00
HW6 Troy Aikman 12.00 30.00
HW7 Steve Young 12.00 30.00
HW8 Eddie George 8.00 20.00
HW9 Brad Johnson 8.00 20.00
HW10 Herman Moore 6.00 15.00
HW11 Antowain Smith 8.00 20.00
HW12 Kordell Stewart 6.00 15.00
HW13 Dorsey Levens 8.00 20.00
HW14 Peyton Manning 25.00 60.00
HW15 Jerry Rice 25.00 60.00

2000 Quantum Leaf Infinity Green

*VETS 1-100: 6X TO 15X BASIC CARDS
1-100 VETERAN PRINT RUN 100
*VETS 101-200: 12X TO 30X BASIC CARDS
101-200 VETERAN PRINT RUN 25
*VETS 201-300: 8X TO 20X BASIC CARDS
201-300 VETERAN PRINT RUN 50
*ROOKIES 301-350: 2X TO 5X
*ROOKIES 351-381: 3X TO 8X
301-381 ROOKIE PRINT RUN 75
343 Tom Brady 300.00 500.00

2000 Quantum Leaf Infinity Purple

*VETS 1-100: 12X TO 30X BASIC CARDS
1-100 VETERAN PRINT RUN 25
*VETS 101-200: 8X TO 20X BASIC CARDS
101-200 VETERAN PRINT RUN 50
*VETS 201-300: 6X TO 15X BASIC CARDS
201-300 VETERAN PRINT RUN 100
*ROOKIES 301-330: 3X TO 12X
*ROOKIES 351-381: 8X TO 20X
301-381 ROOKIE PRINT RUN 15
343 Tom Brady 600.00 1000.00

2000 Quantum Leaf Infinity Red

*VETS 1-100: 8X TO 20X BASIC CARDS
1-100 VETERAN PRINT RUN 50
*VETS 101-200: 6X TO 15X BASIC CARDS
101-200 VETERAN PRINT RUN 100
*VETS 201-300: 12X TO 30X BASIC CARDS
201-300 VETERAN PRINT RUN 25
*ROOKIES 301-350: 3X TO 8X
*ROOKIES 351-381: 5X TO 12X
301-381 ROOKIE PRINT RUN 35
343 Tom Brady 500.00 1000.00

2000 Quantum Leaf Millennium Moments

Randomly inserted in packs, this set features some of football's most defining moments over the past decade. Each card is printed on embossed canvas stock with platinum holographic foil stamping. Cards are sequentially numbered to 1000. Card backs carry an "MM" prefix.
COMPLETE SET (20) 40.00 80.00
STATED PRINT RUN 1000 SER.#'d SETS
MM1 Drew Bledsoe 1.00 2.50
MM2 Emmitt Smith 2.00 5.00
MM3 Mark Brunell 1.00 2.50
MM4 Brett Favre 2.50 6.00
MM5 Randy Moss 1.00 2.50
MM6 Kurt Warner 2.00 5.00
MM7 John Elway 2.00 5.00
MM8 Steve Young 1.50 4.00
MM9 Eddie George 1.00 2.50
MM10 Marshall Faulk 1.00 2.50
MM11 Edgerrin James 1.00 2.50
MM12 Antonio Freeman 1.00 2.50
MM13 Dan Marino 2.50 6.00
MM14 Terrell Davis 1.00 2.50
MM15 Doug Flutie 1.00 2.50
MM16 Jerry Rice 3.00 8.00
MM17 Fred Taylor .75 2.00
MM18 Peyton Manning 3.00 8.00
MM19 Troy Aikman 1.50 4.00
MM20 Barry Sanders 2.00 5.00

2000 Quantum Leaf Rookie Revolution

Randomly seeded in packs, this 20-card set pictures the top 20 rookies from the 2000 NFL draft on a 3D plastic card with silver foil stamping. Each card is sequentially numbered to 5000. Card backs carry an "RR" prefix.
COMPLETE SET (20) 25.00 50.00
STATED PRINT RUN 5000 SER.#'d SETS
*FIRST STRIKE: 3X TO 8X BASIC INSERTS
FIRST STRIKE RANDOM INSERTS IN RETAIL
FIRST STRIKE PRINT RUN 50 SER.#'d SETS
RR1 Peter Warrick .50 1.25
RR2 J.R. Redmond .50 1.25
RR3 Chris Redman .50 1.25
RR4 R.Jay Soward .50 1.25
RR5 Ron Dayne .75 2.00
RR6 Chad Pennington .60 1.50
RR7 Anthony Lucas .50 1.25
RR8 Tim Rattay .60 1.50
RR9 Shaun Alexander .75 2.00
RR10 Dez White .50 1.25
RR11 Tee Martin .50 1.25
RR12 Travis Taylor .50 1.25
RR13 Travis Prentice .50 1.25
RR14 Sylvester Morris .50 1.25
RR15 Jamal Lewis .75 2.00
RR16 Plaxico Burress .60 1.50
RR17 Sherrod Gideon .50 1.25
RR18 Shyrone Stith .50 1.25
RR19 Thomas Jones .60 1.50
RR20 Kwame Cavil .50 1.25

2000 Quantum Leaf Shirt Off My Back

Randomly inserted in packs, this 20-card set showcases top NFL players pictured next to a swatch of a game used jersey. Each card is sequentially numbered to 100.
STATED PRINT RUN 100 SER.#'d SETS
SB1 Brett Favre 20.00 50.00
SB2 Dan Marino 20.00 50.00
SB3 Barry Sanders 15.00 40.00
SB4 John Elway 15.00 40.00
SB5 Peyton Manning 25.00 60.00
SB6 Terrell Davis 8.00 20.00
SB7 Fred Taylor 6.00 15.00
SB8 Drew Bledsoe 8.00 20.00
SB9 Mark Brunell 8.00 20.00
SB10 Eddie George 8.00 20.00
SB11 Isaac Bruce 10.00 25.00
SB12 Jerry Rice 25.00 60.00
SB13 Ray Lucas 6.00 15.00
SB14 Olandis Gary 8.00 20.00
SB15 Emmitt Smith 15.00 40.00
SB16 Shaun King 6.00 15.00
SB17 Edgerrin James 8.00 20.00
SB18 Cris Carter 10.00 25.00
SB19 Jimmy Smith 8.00 20.00
SB20 Brian Griese 6.00 15.00

2000 Quantum Leaf Star Factor

Randomly inserted in packs, this 40-card set showcases 40 of the NFL's top athletes on a 3D plastic card stock enhanced with gold foil stamping. Each card is sequentially numbered to 2500 and each card appears to have been printed on two slightly different paper stocks: one a silver background behind the player image and the other a cream colored background. A Quasar parallel was also produced with each card serial numbered of 50.
COMPLETE SET (40) 40.00 80.00
STATED PRINT RUN 2500 SER.#'d SETS
*QUASAR/50: 3X TO 8X BASIC INSERTS
*CREAM STOCK: .4X TO 1X BASIC INSERTS
SF1 Edgerrin James .60 1.50
SF2 Cris Carter .75 2.00
SF3 Terrell Owens .60 1.50
SF4 Brett Favre 1.50 4.00
SF5 Tim Couch .60 1.50
SF6 Terry Glenn .60 1.50
SF7 John Elway 1.25 3.00
SF8 Troy Aikman 1.00 2.50
SF9 Charlie Batch .50 1.25
SF10 Steve McNair .60 1.50
SF11 Drew Bledsoe .60 1.50
SF12 Joey Galloway .60 1.50
SF13 Dan Marino 1.50 4.00
SF14 Marshall Faulk .60 1.50
SF15 Jamal Anderson .60 1.50
SF16 Jake Plummer .50 1.25
SF17 Curtis Martin .60 1.50
SF18 Peyton Manning 2.00 5.00
SF19 Keyshawn Johnson .60 1.50
SF20 Barry Sanders 1.25 3.00
SF21 Jerry Rice 2.00 5.00
SF22 Emmitt Smith 1.25 3.00
SF23 Daunte Culpepper .60 1.50
SF24 Brad Johnson .60 1.50
SF25 Kurt Warner 1.25 3.00
SF26 Steve Young 1.00 2.50
SF27 Eddie George .60 1.50
SF28 Fred Taylor .50 1.25
SF29 Randy Moss .60 1.50
SF30 Terrell Davis .60 1.50
SF31 Eric Moulds .50 1.25
SF32 Antonio Freeman .60 1.50
SF33 Isaac Bruce .75 2.00
SF34 Ricky Williams .60 1.50
SF35 Donovan McNabb .60 1.50
SF36 Stephen Davis .50 1.25
SF37 Jon Kitna .50 1.25
SF38 Marvin Harrison .60 1.50
SF39 Doug Flutie .60 1.50
SF40 Mark Brunell .60 1.50

2001 Quantum Leaf

2001 Quantum Leaf was initially released as a 260-card base set containing 200 veteran cards and 60 rookie subset cards seeded at one in two packs with an assortment of short-printed rookies seeded at 1:720 packs. The base veteran cards feature full color player photos set a against a blue background with silver glitter highlights. Some collectors have reported that the veterans can sometimes be found missing this silver glitter. The rookie subset cards follow the same basic format but are enhanced with gold foil of the draft team and round drafted, and a silver holographic fractal background. Later in the season, card numbers 261-290 were issued as part of a wrapper redemption (24-wrappers plus $6.99). Quantum Leaf was packaged in boxes containing 24-packs of five cards per pack which carried a suggested retail price of $2.99. While a large number of "promos" can be found on the secondary market, with the word "promo" stamped in foil on the backs, it is not yet confirmed if these cards were actually produced by Donruss/Playoff.
COMP.SET w/o SP's (200) 10.00 25.00
COMP.ROOKIE UPDATE (36) 6.00 15.00
201-260 ROOKIE ODDS 1:2
201-260 ROOKIE SP ODDS 1:720
1 David Boston .20 .50
2 Frank Sanders .20 .50
3 Jake Plummer .20 .50
4 Michael Pittman .25 .60
5 Rob Moore .20 .50
6 Thomas Jones .20 .50
7 Chris Chandler .25 .60
8 Doug Johnson .20 .50
9 Jamal Anderson .25 .60
10 Tim Dwight .25 .60
11 Chris Redman .30 .75
12 Jamal Lewis .30 .75
13 Qadry Ismail .20 .50
14 Ray Lewis .30 .75
15 Rod Woodson .30 .75
16 Shannon Sharpe .25 .60
17 Travis Taylor .20 .50
18 Trent Dilfer .20 .50
19 Doug Flutie .25 .60
20 Eric Moulds .20 .50
21 Jay Riemersma .20 .50
22 Peerless Price .20 .50
23 Rob Johnson .25 .60
24 Sammy Morris .20 .50
25 Shawn Bryson .20 .50
26 Donald Hayes .20 .50
27 Muhsin Muhammad .20 .50
28 Patrick Jeffers .20 .50
29 Reggie White DE .30 .75
30 Steve Beuerlein .25 .60
31 Tim Biakabutuka .20 .50
32 Wesley Walls .20 .50
33 Brian Urlacher .40 1.00
34 Cade McNown .25 .60
35 Dez White .25 .60
36 James Allen .20 .50
37 Marcus Robinson .25 .60
38 Marty Booker .20 .50
39 Akili Smith .20 .50
40 Corey Dillon .20 .50
41 Danny Farmer .20 .50
42 Peter Warrick .20 .50
43 Ron Dugans .20 .50
44 Courtney Brown .20 .50
45 Dennis Northcutt .20 .50
46 JaJuan Dawson .20 .50
47 Kevin Johnson .20 .50
48 Tim Couch .20 .50
49 Travis Prentice .20 .50
50 Anthony Wright .20 .50
51 Emmitt Smith .50 1.25
52 James McKnight .20 .50
53 Joey Galloway .25 .60
54 Rocket Ismail .25 .60
55 Randall Cunningham .25 .60
56 Troy Aikman .40 1.00
57 Brian Griese .20 .50
58 Ed McCaffrey .25 .60
59 Gus Frerotte .20 .50
60 John Elway .50 1.25
61 Mike Anderson .20 .50
62 Olandis Gary .20 .50
63 Rod Smith .25 .60
64 Terrell Davis .25 .60
65 Barry Sanders .50 1.25
66 Charlie Batch .20 .50
67 Germane Crowell .20 .50
68 Herman Moore .20 .50
69 James Stewart .20 .50
70 Johnnie Morton .25 .60
71 Ahman Green .25 .60
72 Antonio Freeman .30 .75
73 Bill Schroeder .25 .60
74 Brett Favre .60 1.50
75 Dorsey Levens .25 .60
76 Matt Hasselbeck .20 .50
77 Edgerrin James .25 .60
78 Jerome Pathon .20 .50
79 Ken Dilger .20 .50
80 Marvin Harrison .25 .60
81 Peyton Manning .75 2.00
82 Fred Taylor .20 .50
83 Hardy Nickerson .20 .50
84 Jimmy Smith .25 .60
85 Keenan McCardell .25 .60
86 Mark Brunell .25 .60
87 Tony Brackens .20 .50
88 Derrick Alexander .20 .50
89 Elvis Grbac .25 .60
90 Sylvester Morris .20 .50
91 Tony Gonzalez .25 .60
92 Tony Richardson .20 .50
93 Warren Moon .30 .75
94 Dan Marino .60 1.50
95 Jay Fiedler .25 .60
96 Lamar Smith .25 .60
97 Oronde Gadsden .20 .50
98 Sam Madison .20 .50
99 Thurman Thomas .25 .60
100 Tony Martin .25 .60
101 Zach Thomas .25 .60
102 Cris Carter .30 .75
103 Daunte Culpepper .25 .60
104 John Randle .25 .60
105 Randy Moss .25 .60
106 Robert Smith .20 .50
107 Drew Bledsoe .25 .60
108 J.R. Redmond .20 .50
109 Kevin Faulk .20 .50
110 Michael Bishop .25 .60
111 Terry Glenn .25 .60
112 Troy Brown .20 .50
113 Aaron Brooks .20 .50
114 Jake Reed .25 .60
115 Jeff Blake .25 .60
116 Joe Horn .20 .50
117 La'Roi Glover .20 .50
118 Ricky Williams .25 .60
119 Willie Jackson .20 .50
120 Amani Toomer .20 .50
121 Ike Hilliard .20 .50
122 Jason Sehorn .25 .60
123 Kerry Collins .20 .50
124 Michael Strahan .25 .60
125 Ron Dayne .25 .60
126 Ron Dixon .20 .50
127 Tiki Barber .25 .60
128 Chad Pennington .20 .50
129 Curtis Martin .25 .60
130 Dedric Ward .20 .50
131 Laveranues Coles .25 .60
132 Vinny Testaverde .20 .50
133 Wayne Chrebet .20 .50
134 Charles Woodson .30 .75
135 Napoleon Kaufman .20 .50
136 Rich Gannon .25 .60
137 Tim Brown .30 .75
138 Tyrone Wheatley .25 .60
139 Charles Johnson .20 .50
140 Donovan McNabb .25 .60
141 Duce Staley .20 .50
142 Hugh Douglas .20 .50
143 Na Brown .20 .50
144 Todd Pinkston .20 .50
145 Bobby Shaw .20 .50
146 Hines Ward .25 .60
147 Jerome Bettis .30 .75
148 Kordell Stewart .20 .50
149 Levon Kirkland .20 .50
150 Plaxico Burress .20 .50
151 Richard Huntley .20 .50
152 Troy Edwards .20 .50
153 Jim Harbaugh .25 .60
154 Junior Seau .25 .60
155 Ryan Leaf .20 .50
156 Charlie Garner .25 .60
157 Jeff Garcia .20 .50
158 Jerry Rice .60 1.50
159 Steve Young .40 1.00
160 Terrell Owens .25 .60
161 Brock Huard .20 .50
162 Darrell Jackson .25 .60
163 Derrick Mayes .20 .50
164 Ricky Watters .25 .60
165 Shaun Alexander .20 .50
166 Az-Zahir Hakim .20 .50
167 Isaac Bruce .30 .75
168 Kurt Warner .50 1.25
169 Marshall Faulk .25 .60
170 Torry Holt .25 .60
171 Trent Green .20 .50
172 Derrick Brooks .20 .50
173 Jacquez Green .20 .50
174 John Lynch .20 .50
175 Keyshawn Johnson .25 .60
176 Mike Alstott .25 .60
177 Reidel Anthony .20 .50
178 Shaun King .20 .50
179 Warren Sapp .20 .50
180 Warrick Dunn .25 .60
181 Carl Pickens .20 .50
182 Derrick Mason .20 .50
183 Eddie George .30 .75
184 Frank Wycheck .20 .50
185 Jevon Kearse .25 .60
186 Neil O'Donnell .20 .50
187 Steve McNair .25 .60
188 Yancey Thigpen .20 .50
189 Albert Connell .20 .50
190 Andre Reed .30 .75
191 Brad Johnson .25 .60
192 Bruce Smith .25 .60
193 Champ Bailey .30 .75
194 Darrell Green .25 .60
195 Deion Sanders .25 .60
196 Irving Fryar .25 .60
197 James Thrash .25 .60
198 Jeff George .25 .60
199 Michael Westbrook .20 .50
200 Stephen Davis .20 .50
201 Michael Vick RC 1.25 3.00
202 Drew Brees RC 15.00 40.00
203 Chris Weinke RC .60 1.50
204 Sage Rosenfels RC .60 1.50
205 Josh Heupel RC .75 2.00
206 Marques Tuiasosopo RC .60 1.50
207 Mike McMahon SP RC 12.00 30.00
208 Deuce McAllister SP RC 15.00 40.00
209 LaMont Jordan RC .75 2.00
210 LaDainian Tomlinson RC 2.50 6.00
211 James Jackson RC .50 1.25
212 Anthony Thomas RC .75 2.00
213 Travis Henry RC .60 1.50
214 Travis Minor RC .60 1.50
215 Rudi Johnson RC .75 2.00
216 Michael Bennett RC .60 1.50
217 Kevan Barlow RC .60 1.50
218 Dan Alexander RC .60 1.50
219 Correll Buckhalter SP RC 10.00 25.00
220 Moran Norris RC .50 1.25
221 Jesse Palmer RC .60 1.50
222 Heath Evans RC .60 1.50
223 David Terrell SP RC 12.00 30.00
224 Santana Moss RC .75 2.00
225 Rod Gardner RC .60 1.50
226 Quincy Morgan SP RC 12.00 30.00
227 Freddie Mitchell RC .50 1.25
228 Reggie Wayne RC 1.00 2.50
229 Bobby Newcombe RC .60 1.50
230 Casey Hampton RC .75 2.00
231 Robert Ferguson RC .75 2.00
232 Ken-Yon Rambo RC .50 1.25
233 Alex Bannister RC .50 1.25
234 Koren Robinson RC .60 1.50
235 Chad Johnson RC .75 2.00
236 Chris Chambers RC .50 1.25
237 Snoop Minnis RC .50 1.25
238 Vinny Sutherland RC .50 1.25
239 Cedrick Wilson RC .60 1.50
240 T.J. Houshmandzadeh RC .60 1.50
241 Todd Heap RC .60 1.50
242 Alge Crumpler RC .75 2.00
243 Jabari Holloway RC .60 1.50
244 Tony Stewart RC .50 1.25
245 Jamal Reynolds RC .50 1.25
246 Andre Carter SP RC 12.00 30.00
247 Justin Smith SP RC 20.00 50.00
248 Richard Seymour RC .75 2.00
249 Marcus Stroud RC .60 1.50
250 Damione Lewis RC .60 1.50
251 Gerard Warren SP RC 12.00 30.00
252 Tommy Polley SP RC 10.00 25.00
253 Dan Morgan RC .60 1.50
254 Jamar Fletcher RC .50 1.25
255 Ken Lucas RC .60 1.50
256 Fred Smoot SP RC 12.00 30.00
257 Nate Clements RC .60 1.50
258 Will Allen RC .75 2.00
259 Derrick Gibson RC .50 1.25
260 Adam Archuleta RC .60 1.50
261 Karon Riley RC .25 .60
262 Cedric Scott RC .25 .60
263 Kenny Smith RC .25 .60
264 Willie Howard RC .25 .60
265 Shaun Rogers RC .40 1.00
266 Ennis Davis RC .25 .60
267 Morlon Greenwood RC .25 .60
268 Gary Baxter RC .25 .60
269 Keith Adams RC .25 .60
270 Brian Allen RC .25 .60
271 Carlos Polk RC .25 .60
272 Torrance Marshall RC .30 .75
273 Jamie Winborn RC .25 .60
274 Hakim Akbar RC .25 .60
275 David Rivers RC .25 .60
276 Ben Leard RC .25 .60
277 Tim Hasselbeck RC .30 .75
278 DeAngelo Evans RC .30 .75
279 David Allen RC .25 .60
280 Reggie White RC .25 .60
281 Ja'Mar Toombs RC .25 .60
282 Dustin McClintock RC .30 .75
283 Boo Williams RC .25 .60
284 Ronney Daniels RC .25 .60
285 Daniel Guy RC .25 .60
286 Javon Green RC .25 .60
287 Marcellus Rivers RC .25 .60
288 Rashon Burns RC .25 .60
289 Jevaris Johnson RC .25 .60
290 David Warren RC .25 .60
291 John Capel RC .25 .60
292 Kendrell Bell RC .40 1.00
294 Willie Middlebrooks RC .30 .75
295 Reggie Germany RC .25 .60
296 Quincy Carter RC .30 .75

2001 Quantum Leaf Autographs

Available only through Playoff, these cards were used as replacements for redemption cards they were unable to fulfull. Cards are crimped with the Playoff logo and serial numbered out of 20.
202 Drew Brees/20 250.00 500.00

2001 Quantum Leaf Infinity Green

*VETS 1-100: 5X TO 12X BASIC CARDS
1-100 VETERAN PRINT RUN 100
*VETS 101-200: 12X TO 30X BASIC CARDS
101-200 VETERAN PRINT RUN 25
*ROOKIES 201-260: 3X TO 8X BASIC RC
*ROOKIES 201-260: .2X TO .5X RC SP
*ROOKIES 261-296: 6X TO 15X
201-296 ROOKIE PRINT RUN 75
202 Drew Brees 50.00 100.00

2001 Quantum Leaf Infinity Purple

*VETS 1-100: 12X TO 30X BASIC CARDS
1-100 VETERAN PRINT RUN 25
*VETS 101-200: 8X TO 20X BASIC CARDS
101-200 VETERAN PRINT RUN 50
*ROOKIES 201-260: 8X TO 20X BASE RC
*ROOKIES 201-260: .4X TO 1X RC SP
*ROOKIES 261-296: 15X TO 40X
201-296 ROOKIE PRINT RUN 15
202 Drew Brees 150.00 300.00

2001 Quantum Leaf Infinity Red

*VETS 1-100: 8X TO 20X BASIC CARDS
1-100 VETERAN PRINT RUN 50
*VETS 101-200: 5X TO 12X BASIC CARDS
101-200 VETERAN PRINT RUN 100
*ROOKIE 201-260: 5X TO 12X BASE RC
*ROOKIE 201-260: .25X TO .6X RC SP
*ROOKIES 261-296: 10X TO 25X
201-296 ROOKIE PRINT RUN 35
202 Drew Brees 75.00 150.00

2001 Quantum Leaf All-Millennium Marks

Randomly inserted this 29-card set features career highlights for some of the greatest football players of all time. The set was serial numbered to 1000 sets. Note there is no card AMAR10.
COMPLETE SET (29) 50.00 100.00
STATED PRINT RUN 1000 SER.#'d SETS
AMAR1 Walter Payton 6.00 15.00
AMAR2 Barry Sanders 2.50 6.00
AMAR3 Emmitt Smith 2.50 6.00
AMAR4 Eric Dickerson 1.50 4.00
AMAR5 Ricky Watters 1.25 3.00
AMAR6 Jim Brown 2.50 6.00
AMAR7 Marcus Allen 2.00 5.00
AMAR8 Jerome Bettis 1.50 4.00
AMAR9 Thurman Thomas 1.25 3.00
AMAR11 Jerry Rice 3.00 8.00
AMAR12 Ozzie Newsome 1.50 4.00
AMAR13 Henry Ellard 1.25 3.00
AMAR14 Charley Taylor 1.25 3.00
AMAR15 Steve Largent 2.00 5.00
AMAR16 Cris Carter 1.50 4.00
AMAR17 Art Monk 2.00 5.00
AMAR18 Irving Fryar 1.50 4.00
AMAR19 Michael Irvin 1.50 4.00
AMAR20 Tim Brown 1.50 4.00
AMAR21 Dan Marino 3.00 8.00
AMAR22 John Elway 2.50 6.00
AMAR23 Warren Moon 2.00 5.00
AMAR24 Fran Tarkenton 2.00 5.00
AMAR25 Dan Fouts 1.50 4.00
AMAR26 Joe Montana 5.00 12.00
AMAR27 Johnny Unitas 4.00 10.00
AMAR28 Boomer Esiason 1.25 3.00
AMAR29 Jim Kelly 1.50 4.00
AMAR30 Vinny Testaverde 1.00 2.50

2001 Quantum Leaf All-Millennium Marks Autographs

Randomly inserted this 28-card set features career highlights for some of the greatest football players of all time. The set was serial numbered to 100 sets, and was issued as redemption cards for most of the set. There were no AMAR1 Walter Payton or AMAR10 autographs, but the Payton was included in packs without a signature on them. Some cards were issued redemption cards which carried an expiration date of 5/31/2003.
STATED PRINT RUN 100 SER.#'d SETS
AMAR1 Walter Payton No AU 15.00 30.00
AMAR2 Barry Sanders 75.00 150.00
AMAR3 Emmitt Smith 125.00 200.00
AMAR4 Eric Dickerson 35.00 65.00
AMAR5 Ricky Watters 12.00 30.00
AMAR6 Jim Brown 50.00 100.00
AMAR7 Marcus Allen 25.00 60.00
AMAR8 Jerome Bettis 60.00 120.00
AMAR9 Thurman Thomas 12.00 30.00
AMAR11 Jerry Rice 75.00 150.00
AMAR12 Ozzie Newsome 15.00 40.00
AMAR13 Henry Ellard 10.00 25.00
AMAR14 Charley Taylor 10.00 25.00
AMAR15 Steve Largent 15.00 40.00
AMAR16 Cris Carter 15.00 40.00
AMAR17 Art Monk 15.00 40.00
AMAR18 Irving Fryar 12.00 30.00
AMAR19 Michael Irvin 20.00 50.00
AMAR20 Tim Brown 15.00 40.00
AMAR21 Dan Marino 60.00 120.00
AMAR22 John Elway 75.00 150.00
AMAR23 Warren Moon 15.00 40.00
AMAR24 Fran Tarkenton 20.00 50.00
AMAR25 Dan Fouts 30.00 60.00
AMAR26 Joe Montana 75.00 150.00
AMAR27 Johnny Unitas 175.00 300.00
AMAR28 Boomer Esiason 15.00 40.00
AMAR29 Jim Kelly 30.00 80.00
AMAR30 Vinny Testaverde 10.00 25.00

2001 Quantum Leaf All-Millennium Materials

Randomly inserted into packs, this 29-card set features a swatch of game-worn jersey and was serial numbered to 100 sets. Each card was printed with silver foil highlights and the first 25-serial numbered cards for most players were autographed. Note that card AMAT10 does not exist.
STATED PRINT RUN 100 SERIAL #'d SETS
AMAT1 Walter Payton 20.00 50.00
AMAT2 Barry Sanders 15.00 40.00
AMAT3 Emmitt Smith 15.00 40.00
AMAT4 Eric Dickerson 4.00 10.00
AMAT5 Ricky Watters 4.00 10.00
AMAT6 Jim Brown 10.00 25.00
AMAT7 Marcus Allen 5.00 12.00
AMAT8 Jerome Bettis 5.00 12.00
AMAT9 Thurman Thomas 4.00 10.00
AMAT11 Jerry Rice 15.00 40.00
AMAT12 Ozzie Newsome 4.00 10.00
AMAT13 Henry Ellard 3.00 8.00
AMAT14 Charley Taylor 3.00 8.00
AMAT15 Steve Largent 5.00 12.00
AMAT16 Cris Carter 5.00 12.00
AMAT17 Art Monk 5.00 12.00
AMAT18 Irving Fryar 4.00 10.00
AMAT19 Michael Irvin 5.00 12.00
AMAT20 Tim Brown 5.00 12.00
AMAT21 Dan Marino 10.00 25.00
AMAT22 John Elway 8.00 20.00
AMAT23 Warren Moon 5.00 12.00
AMAT24 Fran Tarkenton 5.00 12.00
AMAT25 Dan Fouts 4.00 10.00
AMAT26 Joe Montana 15.00 40.00
AMAT27 Johnny Unitas 10.00 25.00
AMAT28 Boomer Esiason 4.00 10.00
AMAT29 Jim Kelly 5.00 12.00
AMAT30 Vinny Testaverde 3.00 8.00

2001 Quantum Leaf All-Millennium Materials Autographs

Randomly inserted into packs, this 28-card set features a swatch of game-worn jersey and was serial numbered to 100 sets. The first 25 serial numbered cards were autographed and each card was printed with holographic foil highlights on the front. Card AMAT10 does not exist. The Exchange card expiration date was 5/31/2003.
FIRST 25 CARDS WERE SIGNED
AMAT2 Barry Sanders 200.00 350.00
AMAT3 Emmitt Smith 250.00 400.00
AMAT4 Eric Dickerson 75.00 150.00
AMAT5 Ricky Watters 40.00 80.00
AMAT6 Jim Brown 150.00 300.00
AMAT7 Marcus Allen 75.00 150.00
AMAT8 Jerome Bettis 150.00 300.00
AMAT9 Thurman Thomas 50.00 100.00
AMAT11 Jerry Rice 200.00 350.00
AMAT12 Ozzie Newsome 40.00 100.00
AMAT14 Charley Taylor 40.00 80.00
AMAT15 Steve Largent 125.00 200.00
AMAT16 Cris Carter 125.00 200.00
AMAT17 Art Monk 100.00 200.00
AMAT18 Irving Fryar 40.00 80.00
AMAT19 Michael Irvin 100.00 175.00
AMAT20 Tim Brown 125.00 200.00
AMAT21 Dan Marino 250.00 400.00
AMAT22 John Elway 200.00 350.00
AMAT23 Warren Moon 75.00 150.00
AMAT24 Fran Tarkenton 75.00 150.00
AMAT25 Dan Fouts 75.00 150.00
AMAT26 Joe Montana 250.00 400.00
AMAT27 Johnny Unitas 250.00 400.00
AMAT28 Boomer Esiason 40.00 80.00
AMAT29 Jim Kelly 125.00 200.00
AMAT30 Vinny Testaverde 20.00 50.00

2001 Quantum Leaf All-Millennium Milestones

Randomly inserted into packs, this 4-card set was serial numbered to 1000 sets. The set was highlighted with silver foil stamping, and featured some sure fire HOF's. The first 25-cards were signed by one or more players. Note that card AMILE4 does not exist.
STATED PRINT RUN 1000 SERIAL #'d SETS
AMILE1 J.Elway/D.Marino 7.50 20.00
AMILE2 C.Carter/J.Rice 5.00 12.00
AMILE3 E.Smith/B.Sndrs/Payton 7.50 20.00
AMILE5 Marino/Rice/E.Smith 7.50 20.00

2001 Quantum Leaf All-Millennium Milestones Autographs

Randomly inserted into packs, this 4-card set was serial numbered to 25 sets. The set was highlighted with silver foil stamping, and featured some sure fire HOF's. Note that AMILE4 was not included in this set and some cards were not signed by all of the players featured. Some cards were issued via mail redemption cards that carried an expiration date of 5/31/2003.
STATED PRINT RUN 25 SERIAL #'d SETS
1 J.Elway AU/D.Marino AU 200.00 350.00
2 C.Carter/J.Rice AU 200.00 350.00
3 Smith AU/B.Sand AU/Payt 300.00 450.00
5 Mari.AU/Rice AU/E.Smt.AU 500.00 750.00

2001 Quantum Leaf Century Season

Randomly inserted into packs, this 61-card set was serial numbered to 1000, and featured silver foil stamping. This set highlighted some of the NFL's elite players and their greatest seasons. Most cards were also issued in a signed version serial numbered of 21. Note that CS19, CS30, CS35, and CS42 do not exist.
COMPLETE SET (61) 100.00 200.00
STATED PRINT RUN 1000 SER.#'d SETS
UNPRICED AUTO PRINT RUN 21
CS1 Eric Dickerson 1.50 4.00
CS2 Barry Sanders 2.50 6.00
CS3 John Elway 2.50 6.00
CS4 Jim Brown 2.50 6.00
CS5 Sammy Baugh 2.00 5.00
CS6 Marcus Allen 2.00 5.00
CS7 Tony Gonzalez 1.25 3.00
CS8 Franco Harris 2.00 5.00
CS9 Dan Marino 3.00 8.00
CS10 Mike Singletary 2.00 5.00
CS11 Fred Biletnikoff 2.00 5.00
CS12 Warren Moon 2.00 5.00
CS13 Steve Largent 2.00 5.00
CS14 Fran Tarkenton 2.00 5.00
CS15 Lawrence Taylor 2.00 5.00
CS16 Roger Staubach 2.50 6.00
CS17 Roger Craig 1.50 4.00
CS18 Bart Starr 4.00 10.00
CS20 Steve Young 2.00 5.00
CS21 Don Maynard 1.50 4.00
CS22 Joe Montana 6.00 15.00
CS23 Tony Dorsett 2.00 5.00
CS24 Joe Namath 3.00 8.00
CS25 Johnny Unitas 4.00 10.00
CS26 Paul Hornung 2.00 5.00
CS27 Bob Griese 2.00 5.00
CS28 Isaac Bruce 1.50 4.00
CS29 Dan Fouts 1.50 4.00
CS31 Terry Bradshaw 2.50 6.00
CS32 Larry Csonka 2.00 5.00
CS33 Jim Kelly 1.50 4.00
CS34 Lance Alworth 1.50 4.00
CS36 Sonny Jurgensen 2.00 5.00
CS37 Ozzie Newsome 1.50 4.00
CS38 Kellen Winslow 1.50 4.00
CS39 Stephen Davis 1.00 2.50
CS40 Frank Gifford 2.00 5.00
CS41 Terrell Davis 1.25 3.00
CS43 Edgerrin James 1.25 3.00
CS44 Jerry Rice 3.00 8.00
CS45 Marshall Faulk 1.25 3.00
CS46 Kurt Warner 2.50 6.00
CS47 Cris Carter 1.50 4.00
CS48 Bruce Smith 1.25 3.00
CS49 Emmitt Smith 2.50 6.00
CS50 Ray Lewis 1.50 4.00
CS51 Jamal Lewis 1.50 4.00
CS52 Marvin Harrison 1.25 3.00
CS53 Eric Moulds 1.00 2.50
CS54 Eddie George 1.50 4.00
CS55 Ricky Williams 1.25 3.00
CS56 Mark Brunell 1.25 3.00
CS57 Brian Griese 1.00 2.50
CS58 Brett Favre 3.00 8.00
CS59 Daunte Culpepper 1.25 3.00
CS60 Mike Anderson 1.00 2.50
CS61 Donovan McNabb 1.25 3.00
CS62 Randall Cunningham 1.25 3.00
CS63 Drew Bledsoe 1.25 3.00
CS64 Troy Aikman 2.00 5.00
CS65 Randy Moss 1.25 3.00

2001 Quantum Leaf Century Season Autographs

Randomly inserted into packs, this 61-card set was serial numbered to 21, and featured silver foil stamping. This set highlighted some of the NFL's elite players and their greatest seasons. Note that CS19,CS30,CS35, and CS42 are not included as autographs. Some cards were issued via mail redemption cards that carried an expiration date of 5/31/2003.
STATED PRINT RUN 21 SER.#'d SETS

CS1 Eric Dickerson 25.00 60.00
CS2 Barry Sanders 100.00 175.00
CS3 John Elway 100.00 175.00
CS4 Jim Brown 60.00 120.00
CS5 Sammy Baugh 60.00 120.00
CS6 Marcus Allen 25.00 60.00
CS7 Tony Gonzalez 40.00 80.00
CS8 Franco Harris 40.00 80.00
CS9 Dan Marino 125.00 200.00
CS10 Mike Singletary 30.00 80.00
CS11 Fred Biletnikoff 25.00 60.00
CS12 Warren Moon 25.00 60.00
CS13 Steve Largent 30.00 80.00
CS14 Fran Tarkenton 25.00 60.00
CS15 Lawrence Taylor 25.00 60.00
CS16 Roger Staubach 30.00 80.00
CS17 Roger Craig 20.00 50.00
CS18 Bart Starr 100.00 200.00
CS20 Steve Young 30.00 80.00
CS21 Don Maynard 20.00 50.00
CS22 Joe Montana 125.00 200.00
CS23 Tony Dorsett 25.00 60.00
CS24 Joe Namath 50.00 100.00
CS25 Johnny Unitas 250.00 400.00
CS26 Paul Hornung 30.00 80.00
CS27 Bob Griese 25.00 60.00
CS28 Isaac Bruce 20.00 50.00
CS29 Dan Fouts 30.00 80.00
CS31 Terry Bradshaw 75.00 150.00
CS32 Larry Csonka 30.00 80.00
CS33 Jim Kelly 25.00 60.00
CS34 Lance Alworth 25.00 60.00
CS36 Sonny Jurgensen 25.00 60.00
CS37 Ozzie Newsome 20.00 50.00
CS38 Kellen Winslow 25.00 60.00
CS39 Stephen Davis 12.00 30.00
CS40 Frank Gifford 40.00 80.00
CS41 Terrell Davis 15.00 40.00
CS43 Edgerrin James 15.00 40.00
CS44 Jerry Rice 125.00 200.00
CS45 Marshall Faulk 30.00 60.00
CS46 Kurt Warner 50.00 100.00
CS47 Cris Carter 50.00 100.00
CS49 Emmitt Smith 125.00 200.00
CS50 Ray Lewis 125.00 200.00
CS51 Jamal Lewis 20.00 50.00
CS52 Marvin Harrison 15.00 40.00
CS53 Eric Moulds 12.00 30.00
CS54 Eddie George 20.00 50.00
CS55 Ricky Williams 15.00 40.00
CS56 Mark Brunell 15.00 40.00
CS57 Brian Griese 12.00 30.00
CS58 Brett Favre 125.00 200.00
CS59 Daunte Culpepper 20.00 50.00
CS60 Mike Anderson 12.00 30.00
CS61 Donovan McNabb 15.00 40.00
CS62 Randall Cunningham 15.00 40.00
CS63 Drew Bledsoe 30.00 60.00
CS64 Troy Aikman 40.00 80.00
CS65 Randy Moss 40.00 80.00

2001 Quantum Leaf Gamers

Randomly inserted in hobby packs, this 10-card set features premium swatches of authentic jerseys that include portions of the pictured player's jersey number and team logos. Each card is serial numbered out of 25.

STATED PRINT RUN 25 SER.#'d SETS
G1 Akili Smith 15.00 40.00
G2 Corey Dillon 15.00 40.00
G3 Donovan McNabb 20.00 50.00
G4 Edgerrin James 20.00 50.00
G5 Fred Taylor 15.00 40.00
G6 Isaac Bruce 25.00 60.00
G7 Shaun King 15.00 40.00
G8 Tim Couch 15.00 40.00
G9 J.Kelly/J.Elway/D.Marino 150.00 300.00
G10 Six 1999 Quarterbacks 100.00 250.00

2001 Quantum Leaf Hardwear

Randomly inserted in hobby packs, this 30-card set featuers swatches of authentic game-used helmets. Each card is sequentially numbered to 100. The first 25-cards of some players were autographed.

STATED PRINT RUN 100 SER.#'d SETS
HW1 Akili Smith 6.00 15.00
HW2 Charlie Garner 8.00 20.00
HW3 Corey Dillon 6.00 15.00
HW4 Dan Marino 20.00 50.00
HW5 Donovan McNabb 8.00 20.00
HW6 Duce Staley 6.00 15.00
HW7 Edgerrin James 8.00 20.00
HW8 Fred Taylor 6.00 15.00
HW9 Isaac Bruce 10.00 25.00
HW10 Jamal Anderson 8.00 20.00
HW11 Jason Sehorn 8.00 20.00
HW12 Jay Fiedler 8.00 20.00
HW13 Jerome Bettis 10.00 25.00
HW14 Jerry Rice 20.00 50.00
HW15 John Elway 15.00 40.00
HW16 Junior Seau 8.00 20.00
HW17 Ray Lewis 10.00 25.00
HW18 Reggie White DE 25.00 50.00
HW19 Ricky Watters 8.00 20.00
HW20 Ryan Leaf 6.00 15.00
HW21 Shaun King 6.00 15.00
HW22 Steve Young 12.00 30.00
HW23 Terrell Davis 8.00 20.00
HW24 Terry Glenn 8.00 20.00
HW25 Tim Couch 6.00 15.00
HW26 Torry Holt 8.00 20.00
HW27 Vinny Testaverde 6.00 15.00
HW28 Warren Sapp 8.00 20.00
HW29 Wayne Chrebet 6.00 15.00
HW30 Zach Thomas 8.00 20.00

2001 Quantum Leaf Hardwear Autographs

Randomly inserted in hobby packs, this 10-card set featuers swatches of authentic game-used helmets. Each card is sequentially numbered to 100, but there were only the first 25 of the serial numbers that were autographed. Some cards were issued via mail redemption cards that carried an expiration date of 5/31/2003.

FIRST 25 CARDS WERE SIGNED
HW4 Dan Marino 150.00 300.00
HW5 Donovan McNabb 60.00 120.00
HW7 Edgerrin James 40.00 80.00
HW9 Isaac Bruce 40.00 80.00
HW13 Jerome Bettis 75.00 150.00
HW14 Jerry Rice 125.00 250.00
HW15 John Elway 125.00 250.00
HW17 Ray Lewis 60.00 120.00
HW22 Steve Young 75.00 150.00

2001 Quantum Leaf Rookie Revolution

Randomly seeded in packs, this 20-card set pictures the top 20 rookies from the 2001 NFL draft with silver foil stamping. Each card is sequentially numbered to 4000. Card backs carry an "RR" prefix.

COMPLETE SET (20) 15.00 40.00
STATED PRINT RUN 4000 SER.#'d SETS
RR1 Michael Vick 1.00 2.50
RR2 David Terrell .50 1.25
RR3 Deuce McAllister .60 1.50
RR4 Drew Brees 2.50 6.00
RR5 Santana Moss .60 1.50
RR6 Anthony Thomas .60 1.50
RR7 Chris Weinke .50 1.25
RR8 Rod Gardner .50 1.25
RR9 LaDainian Tomlinson 2.00 5.00
RR10 Quincy Carter .50 1.25
RR11 Koren Robinson .50 1.25
RR12 Travis Henry .50 1.25
RR13 Quincy Morgan .50 1.25
RR14 LaMont Jordan .60 1.50
RR15 Rudi Johnson .60 1.50
RR16 Reggie Wayne .75 2.00
RR17 Michael Bennett .50 1.25
RR18 Freddie Mitchell .40 1.00
RR19 Chris Chambers .40 1.00
RR20 Chad Johnson .60 1.50

2001 Quantum Leaf Rookie Revolution Autographs

Randomly seeded in packs, this 20-card set pictures the top 20 rookies from the 2000 NFL draft with silver foil stamping. Each card is sequentially numbered to 50. Card backs carry an "RR" prefix and are die-cut. Some cards were issued via mail redemption cards that carried an expiration date of 5/31/2003.

STATED PRINT RUN 50 SER.#'d SETS
RR1 Michael Vick 30.00 80.00
RR2 David Terrell 20.00 50.00
RR3 Deuce McAllister 20.00 50.00
RR4 Drew Brees 400.00 800.00
RR5 Santana Moss 20.00 50.00
RR6 Anthony Thomas 20.00 50.00
RR7 Chris Weinke 15.00 40.00
RR8 Rod Gardner 20.00 50.00
RR9 LaDainian Tomlinson 100.00 200.00
RR11 Koren Robinson 15.00 40.00
RR12 Travis Henry 15.00 40.00
RR13 Quincy Morgan 15.00 40.00
RR14 LaMont Jordan 20.00 50.00
RR15 Rudi Johnson 20.00 50.00
RR16 Reggie Wayne 50.00 80.00
RR17 Michael Bennett 15.00 40.00
RR18 Freddie Mitchell 12.00 30.00
RR19 Chris Chambers 12.00 30.00
RR20 Chad Johnson 30.00 80.00

2001 Quantum Leaf Shirt Off My Back

Randomly inserted in packs, this 30-card set showcases top NFL players pictured next to a swatch of a game used jersey. Each card is sequentially numbered to 100. Ten players signed the first 25-copies of their cards. Some cards were issued via mail redemptions that carried an expiration date of May 31, 2003.

STATED PRINT RUN 100 SER.#'d SETS
SB1 Jamal Lewis 10.00 25.00
SB2 Mike Anderson 6.00 15.00
SB3 Ron Dayne 8.00 20.00
SB4 Peter Warrick 6.00 15.00
SB5 Shaun Alexander 6.00 15.00
SB6 Warrick Dunn 6.00 15.00
SB7 Shaun King 6.00 15.00
SB8 Tim Couch 6.00 15.00
SB9 Cade McNown 8.00 20.00
SB10 Akili Smith 6.00 15.00
SB11 Rich Gannon 8.00 20.00
SB12 Daunte Culpepper 8.00 20.00
SB13 Randy Moss 8.00 20.00
SB14 Cris Carter 10.00 25.00
SB15 Robert Smith 6.00 15.00
SB16 Kurt Warner 15.00 40.00
SB17 Marshall Faulk 8.00 20.00
SB18 Ricky Williams 8.00 20.00
SB19 Terrell Owens 8.00 20.00
SB20 Corey Dillon 6.00 15.00
SB21 Fred Taylor 6.00 15.00
SB22 Edgerrin James 8.00 20.00
SB23 Curtis Martin 8.00 20.00
SB24 Donovan McNabb 8.00 20.00
SB25 Steve McNair 8.00 20.00
SB26 Peyton Manning 25.00 60.00
SB27 Eric Moulds 6.00 15.00
SB28 Stephen Davis 6.00 15.00
SB29 Brian Griese 6.00 15.00
SB30 Isaac Bruce 10.00 25.00

2001 Quantum Leaf Shirt Off My Back Autographs

Randomly inserted in packs, this 10-card autograph set showcases top NFL players pictured next to a swatch of a game used jersey. Some cards were issued via mail redemption cards that carried an expiration date of 5/31/2003.

STATED PRINT RUN 25 SER.#'d SETS
SB1 Jamal Lewis 30.00 80.00
SB2 Mike Anderson EXCH
SB11 Rich Gannon 25.00 60.00
SB12 Daunte Culpepper 30.00 80.00
SB16 Kurt Warner 40.00 100.00
SB18 Ricky Williams 30.00 80.00
SB22 Edgerrin James 30.00 80.00
SB24 Donovan McNabb 75.00 150.00
SB28 Stephen Davis 25.00 60.00
SB30 Isaac Bruce 40.00 100.00

2001 Quantum Leaf Star Factor

Randomly inserted in packs, this 40-card set showcases 40 of the NFL's top athletes on card stock enhanced with gold foil stamping. Each card is sequentially numbered to 2000. Card backs carry an "SF" prefix. A die-cut parallel called X-Factor was also produced with each card serial numbered of 25.

COMPLETE SET (40) 25.00 60.00
STATED PRINT RUN 2000 SER.#'d SETS
*X-FACTOR/25: 5X TO 12X BASIC INSERTS
X-FACTOR PRINT RUN 25 SER.#'d SETS
SF1 Peyton Manning 2.00 5.00
SF2 Edgerrin James .60 1.50
SF3 Marvin Harrison .60 1.50
SF4 Curtis Martin .60 1.50
SF5 Eric Moulds .50 1.25
SF6 Dan Marino 1.50 4.00
SF7 Jake Plummer .50 1.25
SF8 Troy Aikman 1.00 2.50
SF9 Jamal Lewis .75 2.00
SF10 Eddie George .75 2.00
SF11 Steve McNair .60 1.50
SF12 Steve Young 1.00 2.50
SF13 Jerome Bettis .75 2.00
SF14 Tim Couch .50 1.25
SF15 Mark Brunell .60 1.50
SF16 Fred Taylor .50 1.25
SF17 Corey Dillon .50 1.25
SF18 Chad Pennington .50 1.25
SF19 Brian Griese .50 1.25
SF20 Mike Anderson .50 1.25
SF21 John Elway 1.25 3.00
SF22 Terrell Owens .60 1.50
SF23 Rich Gannon .60 1.50
SF24 Jerry Rice 1.50 4.00
SF25 Ricky Williams .60 1.50
SF26 Aaron Brooks .50 1.25
SF27 Kurt Warner 1.25 3.00
SF28 Marshall Faulk .60 1.50
SF29 Isaac Bruce .75 2.00
SF30 Brett Favre 1.50 4.00
SF31 Antonio Freeman .75 2.00
SF32 Daunte Culpepper .60 1.50
SF33 Randy Moss .60 1.50
SF34 Cris Carter .75 2.00
SF35 Barry Sanders 1.25 3.00
SF36 Emmitt Smith 1.25 3.00
SF37 Stephen Davis .50 1.25
SF38 Ron Dayne .60 1.50
SF39 Donovan McNabb .60 1.50
SF40 Peter Warrick .50 1.25

2001 Quantum Leaf Touchdown Club

Randomly inserted into packs, this 40-card set features the hottest stars of the NFL, who visit the endzone most frequently. These cards were serial numbered to 2000. These cards were found in hobby and retail packs with the odd numbers being distributed only in hobby packs and the evens only in retail packs.

COMPLETE SET (40) 25.00 60.00
ODD #'s FOUND IN HOBBY PACKS
EVEN #'s FOUND IN RETAIL PACKS
STATED PRINT RUN 2000 SER.#'d SETS
*TOTAL/266-429: 1X TO 2.5X BASIC INSERTS
*TOTAL/109-187: 1.2X TO 3X BASIC INSERTS
*TOTAL/62-90: 1.5X TO 4X BASIC INSERTS
*TOTAL/40-50: 2X TO 5X BASIC INSERTS
*TOTAL/35-38: 2.5X TO 6X BASIC INSERTS
*TOTAL/24: 3X TO 8X BASIC INSERTS
*TOTAL/11-15: 4X TO 10X BASIC INSERTS
TOTALS PRINT RUN 5-429
TC1 Marshall Faulk .60 1.50
TC2 Edgerrin James .60 1.50
TC3 Randy Moss .60 1.50
TC4 Eddie George .75 2.00
TC5 Terrell Owens .60 1.50
TC6 Mike Anderson .50 1.25
TC7 Stephen Davis .50 1.25
TC8 Marvin Harrison .60 1.50
TC9 Robert Smith .50 1.25
TC10 Fred Taylor .50 1.25
TC11 Daunte Culpepper .60 1.50
TC12 Curtis Martin .60 1.50
TC13 Emmitt Smith 1.25 3.00
TC14 Jamal Lewis .75 2.00
TC15 Ricky Williams .60 1.50
TC16 John Elway 1.25 3.00
TC17 Jerry Rice 1.50 4.00
TC18 Peyton Manning 2.00 5.00
TC19 Kurt Warner 1.25 3.00
TC20 Tim Brown .75 2.00
TC21 Brett Favre 1.50 4.00
TC22 Jimmy Smith .60 1.50
TC23 Cris Carter .75 2.00
TC24 Terrell Davis .60 1.50
TC25 Jeff Garcia .50 1.25
TC26 Peter Warrick .50 1.25
TC27 Ron Dayne .60 1.50
TC28 Tony Gonzalez .60 1.50
TC29 Isaac Bruce .75 2.00
TC30 Drew Bledsoe .60 1.50
TC31 Marcus Robinson .60 1.50
TC32 Ricky Watters .60 1.50
TC33 Ahman Green .60 1.50
TC34 Dan Marino 1.50 4.00
TC35 Donovan McNabb .60 1.50
TC36 Eric Moulds .50 1.25
TC37 Aaron Brooks .50 1.25
TC38 Steve McNair .60 1.50
TC39 Barry Sanders 1.25 3.00
TC40 Brian Griese .50 1.25

2001 Quantum Leaf X-ponential Power

Randomly inserted into packs, this 10-card set features the hottest stars of the NFL. The cards were serial numbered to 1000. The cards were found in hobby and retail packs with the odd numbers being distributed only in retail packs and the evens only in hobby packs.

COMPLETE SET (10) 20.00 40.00
EVEN #'d CARD HOBBY ONLY
ODD #'d CARDS RETAIL ONLY
STATED PRINT RUN 1000 SER.#'d SETS
*X-FTR GREEN/75: 1.2X TO 3X BASIC INSERTS
X-FACTOR GREEN PRINT RUN 75
*X-FTR PRPL/15: 5X TO 12X BASIC INSERTS
X-FACTOR PURPLE PRINT RUN 15
*X-FCTR RED/35: 2.5X TO 6X BASIC INSERTS
X-FACTOR RED PRINT RUN 35
XP1 Kurt Warner 2.00 5.00
XP2 Peyton Manning 3.00 8.00
XP3 Steve Young 1.50 4.00
XP4 Dan Marino 2.50 6.00
XP5 Jerry Rice 2.50 6.00
XP6 John Elway 2.00 5.00
XP7 Barry Sanders 2.00 5.00
XP8 Steve McNair 1.00 2.50
XP9 Brett Favre 2.50 6.00
XP10 Terrell Davis 1.00 2.50

1991 Quarterback Legends

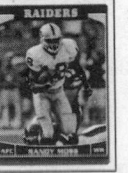

This 50-card set, measuring the standard size was produced by NFL Quarterback Legends and issued on high-quality card stock. The set is packaged in a red, white, and blue box. Card fronts feature a color action shot of the player. At the bottom of the card appears a red stripe and a blue and white checker board stripe, with the words "Quarterback Legends" reversed out in white and blue lettering. Card backs, printed horizontally, feature a full-bleed red stripe at the top with player's name in blue, another action photo, and statistical and biographical information. Sponsors' (QB Legends and Team NFL) logos and card number appear to the bottom right of card. The cards are numbered on the back. The first 46 cards in the set are ordered alphabetically by name. The last four cards depict legendary feats. The team name listed in the checklist below corresponds to uniform on front of cards; the photo on back of cards sometimes has player in a different team uniform. This set was introduced and distributed at the Quarterback Legends Show in Nashville, Tennessee in January, 1992.

COMPLETE SET (50) 12.50 25.00
1 Ken Anderson .30 .75
2 Steve Bartkowski .20 .50
3 George Blanda .30 .75
4 Terry Bradshaw .75 2.00
5 Zeke Bratkowski .15 .40
6 John Brodie .30 .75
7 Charley Conerly .20 .50
8 Len Dawson .30 .75
9 Lynn Dickey .15 .40
10 Joe Ferguson .15 .40
11 Vince Ferragamo .15 .40
12 Tom Flores .20 .50
13 Dan Fouts .30 .75
14 Roman Gabriel .20 .50
15 Otto Graham .30 .75
16 Bob Griese .40 1.00
17 Steve Grogan .20 .50
18 John Hadl .20 .50
19 James Harris .15 .40
20 Jim Hart .15 .40
21 Ron Jaworski .15 .40
22 Charley Johnson .15 .40
23 Bert Jones .20 .50
24 Sonny Jurgensen .30 .75
25 Joe Kapp .15 .40
26 Billy Kilmer .20 .50
27 Daryle Lamonica .20 .50
28 Greg Landry .15 .40
29 Neil Lomax .15 .40
30 Archie Manning .20 .50
31 Earl Morrall .15 .40
32 Craig Morton .20 .50
33 Gifford Nielsen .15 .40
34 Dan Pastorini .15 .40
35 Jim Plunkett .20 .50
36 Norm Snead .15 .40
37 Ken Stabler .40 1.00
38 Bart Starr .75 2.00
39 Roger Staubach .75 2.00
40 Joe Theismann .30 .75
41 Y.A. Tittle .30 .75
42 Johnny Unitas .75 2.00
43 Bill Wade .15 .40
44 Danny White .20 .50
45 Doug Williams .20 .50
46 Jim Zorn .20 .50
47 Otto Graham .30 .75
48 Johnny Unitas .75 2.00
49 Bart Starr .75 2.00
50 Terry Bradshaw .75 2.00

1992 Quarterback Greats GE

Produced by NFL Properties, this 12-card standard-size set was prepared for General Electric Silicones and features members of the Quarterback Club. The cards could be obtained by sending in proofs of purchase. The fronts carry action color player photos on a red face. The player's name is printed in white lettering above the picture. A blue and red bar icon containing the words "Quarterback Greats" runs horizontally from the top right and overlaps the picture. The backs carry statistics and career highlights. The GE logo and NFL Team Players logo appear at the bottom. The Quarterback Club icon (a black box with a brightly colored football player outline) is in the upper left corner.

COMPLETE SET (12) 12.00 30.00
1 Troy Aikman 1.60 4.00
2 Bubby Brister .30 .75
3 Randall Cunningham .40 1.00
4 John Elway 3.20 8.00
5 Boomer Esiason .40 1.00
6 Jim Everett .30 .75
7 Jim Kelly .60 1.50
8 Bernie Kosar .30 .75
9 Dan Marino 3.20 8.00
10 Warren Moon .40 1.00
11 Phil Simms .40 1.00
NNO Title Card .30 .75

1993 Quarterback Legends

This 50-card standard-size set showcases outstanding quarterbacks throughout NFL history. The fronts feature action player photos in which the player appears in color against a sepia-toned background. The borders shade from white to pastel yellow as one moves from left to right, and the set title "Quarterback Legends" is printed vertically on the left edge in bronze lettering. The horizontal backs carry a close-up color player photo and career summary. The set closes with a Legendary Feats (48-50) subset.

COMPLETE SET (50) 6.00 15.00
1 Checklist Card .14 .35
2 Ken Anderson .25 .60
3 Steve Bartkowski .14 .35
4 George Blanda .25 .60
5 Terry Bradshaw 1.00 2.50
6 Zeke Bratkowski .08 .25
7 John Brodie .20 .50
8 Charley Conerly .14 .35
9 Len Dawson .20 .50
10 Lynn Dickey .08 .25
11 Joe Ferguson .08 .25
12 Vince Ferragamo .08 .25
13 Tom Flores .14 .35
14 Dan Fouts .30 .75
15 Roman Gabriel .14 .35
16 Otto Graham .40 1.00
17 Bob Griese .40 1.00
18 Steve Grogan .14 .35
19 John Hadl .14 .35
20 James Harris .08 .25
21 Jim Hart .08 .25
22 Ron Jaworski .08 .25
23 Charley Johnson .08 .25
24 Bert Jones .14 .35
25 Sonny Jurgensen .20 .50
26 Joe Kapp .08 .25
27 Billy Kilmer .14 .35
28 Daryle Lamonica .14 .35
29 Greg Landry .08 .25
30 Neil Lomax .08 .25
31 Archie Manning .20 .50
32 Earl Morrall .08 .25
33 Craig Morton .14 .35
34 Gifford Nielsen .08 .25
35 Dan Pastorini .08 .25
36 Jim Plunkett .14 .35
37 Norm Snead .08 .25
38 Ken Stabler .40 1.00
39 Bart Starr .60 1.50
40 Roger Staubach 1.00 2.50
41 Joe Theismann .25 .60
42 Y.A. Tittle .30 .75
43 Johnny Unitas .60 1.50
44 Bill Wade .08 .25
45 Danny White .14 .35
46 Doug Williams .08 .25
47 Jim Zorn .08 .25
48 George Blanda .25 .60
49 Bob Griese .20 .50
50 Doug Williams .08 .25

1935 R311-2 National Chicle Premiums

The R311-2 (as referenced in the American Card Catalog) Football Stars and Scenes set consists of 17 glossy, unnumbered, 6" by 8" photos. Both professional and collegiate players are pictured on these photos. These blank-back photos have been numbered in the checklist below alphabetically by the player's name or title. These premium photos were available from National Chicle with one premium given for every 20 wrappers turned in to the retailer.

COMPLETE SET (17) 3000.00 4500.00
1 Joe Bach SP 350.00 500.00
2 Eddie Casey 150.00 250.00
3 George Christensen SP 350.00 500.00
4 Red Grange 400.00 750.00
5 Stan Kostka 125.00 200.00
6 Joe Maniaci SP 200.00 350.00
7 Harry Newman 125.00 200.00
8 Walter Switzer 125.00 200.00
9 Chicago Bears Team 250.00 400.00
10 New York Giants Team 200.00 350.00
11 Bill Shakespeare punting 175.00 300.00
12 Pittsburgh U. in Rough 125.00 200.00
13 Pittsburgh Pirates 175.00 300.00
14 S.L. Morton 125.00 200.00
15 Dixie Howell 150.00 250.00
16 Cotton Warburton 150.00 250.00
17 A.Gutowsky/S.Hokuf 150.00 250.00

1962 Raiders Team Issue

The Raiders likely released these photos over a number of seasons. Each measures approximately 8" by 10" and includes a black and white photo on the cardfront with a blank cardback. The team name, player's name, and position (abbreviated) appear below the photo from left to right. The checklist is thought to be incomplete. Any additions to this list are appreciated.

COMPLETE SET (4) 35.00 60.00
1 Clem Daniels 10.00 20.00
2 Wayne Hawkins 10.00 20.00
3 Jon Jelacic 7.50 15.00
4 Chuck McMurtry 7.50 15.00
5 Pete Nicklas 7.50 15.00

1964 Raiders Team Issue

The Raiders likely released these photos over a number of seasons. Each measures approximately 8" by 10" and includes a black and white photo on the front with a blank back. The player's name, position (spelled out in full) and team name appear below the photo. The text style and size varies slightly from photo to photo and the checklist is thought to be incomplete. Any additions to this list are appreciated.

COMPLETE SET (19) 150.00 250.00
1 Bill Budness 7.50 15.00
2 Billy Cannon 12.50 25.00
3 Clem Daniels 10.00 20.00
4 Ben Davidson 12.50 25.00
5 Cotton Davidson 10.00 20.00
6 Claude Gibson 7.50 15.00
7 Wayne Hawkins 10.00 20.00
8 Ken Herock 7.50 15.00
9 Jon Jelacic 7.50 15.00
10 Dick Klein 7.50 15.00
11 Joe Krakoski 7.50 15.00
12 Mike Mercer 7.50 15.00
13 Tommy Morrow 7.50 15.00
14 Clancy Osborne 7.50 15.00
15 Jim Otto 20.00 35.00
16 Art Powell 10.00 20.00
17 Ken Rice 7.50 15.00
18 Bo Roberson 7.50 15.00
19 Howie Williams 7.50 15.00

1968 Raiders Team Issue

The Raiders likely released these photos over a number of seasons. Each measures approximately 8" by 10 1/4" to 8 1/2" by 10 1/2" in size and includes a black and white photo on the cardfront with a blank cardback. All of the photos were taken outdoors with a rolling hillside in the far background. The player's name, position initials and team name appear below the photo. The text style and size varies slightly from photo to photo. The 1969 issue looks very similar to this set, but it was printed on slightly thicker, larger, and slightly less glossy paper stock than this 1968 release. Any additions to this list are appreciated.

COMPLETE SET (34) 200.00 400.00
1 Fred Biletnikoff 12.50 25.00
2 Dan Birdwell 6.00 12.00
3 Bill Budness 6.00 12.00
4 Billy Cannon 7.50 15.00
5 Dan Conners 6.00 12.00
6 Ben Davidson 7.50 15.00
(portrait holding helmet)
7 Cotton Davidson 6.00 12.00
8 Eldridge Dickey 6.00 12.00
9A Hewritt Dixon 6.00 12.00
9B Hewritt Dixon 6.00 12.00
(position omitted)
10 John Eason 6.00 12.00
11 Mike Eischeid 6.00 12.00
12 Dave Grayson 6.00 12.00
13 Roger Hagberg 6.00 12.00
14 James Harvey 6.00 12.00
15 Wayne Hawkins 6.00 12.00
16 Tom Keating 6.00 12.00
17 Bob Kruse 6.00 12.00
18A Daryle Lamonica 10.00 20.00
18B Daryle Lamonica 10.00 20.00
(passing pose)
19 Ike Lassiter 6.00 12.00
20 Marv Marinovich 6.00 12.00
(portrait)
21 Kent McCloughan 6.00 12.00
22 Bill Miller 6.00 12.00
23 Carleton Oats 6.00 12.00
24 Gus Otto 6.00 12.00
25 Jim Otto 10.00 20.00
26 Warren Powers 6.00 12.00
27 John Rauch CO 6.00 12.00
28A Harry Schuh 6.00 12.00
(position is OT)
28B Harry Schuh 6.00 12.00
(position omitted)
29 Art Shell 15.00 30.00
30 Charlie Smith 6.00 12.00
31 Bob Svihus 6.00 12.00
32 Larry Todd 6.00 12.00
33 Warren Wells 6.00 12.00
34 Howie Williams 6.00 12.00

1969 Raiders Team Issue

The Raiders issued these photos shrink wrapped in a package of 8 defensive or offensive players along with a small paper checklist. Each measures approximately 8 1/2" by 10 3/8" and includes a black and white photo on the cardfront with a blank cardback. The player's name, position initials (except Dave Grayson) and team name appear below the photo. The text style and size and some of the photos are nearly identical to the 1968 listing. This issue was printed on thicker, slightly less glossy, paper stock than the 1968 photos along with difference in size.

COMPLETE SET (8) 100.00 200.00
1 George Atkinson 6.00 12.00
2 Fred Biletnikoff 12.50 25.00
3 Willie Brown 10.00 20.00
4 Dan Conners 6.00 12.00
5 Ben Davidson 7.50 15.00
6 Hewritt Dixon 7.50 15.00
7 Dave Grayson 6.00 12.00
8 Tom Keating 6.00 12.00
9 Daryle Lamonica 10.00 20.00
10 Carleton Oats 6.00 12.00
11 Gus Otto 6.00 12.00
12 Jim Otto 10.00 20.00
13 Harry Schuh 6.00 12.00
14 Charlie Smith 6.00 12.00
15 Gene Upshaw 10.00 20.00
16 Warren Wells 6.00 12.00

1985 Raiders Shell Oil Posters

Available only at participating Southern California Shell stations during the 1985 season, these five posters measure approximately 11 5/8" by 18" and feature an artist's color renderings of the Raiders in action. The unnumbered posters are blank-backed, except for number 1 below, the back of which carries the Raiders and Shell logos along with the month in which each subsequent poster was released. The posters are listed below accordingly.

COMPLETE SET (5) 10.00 25.00
1 Pro Bowl 3.00 8.00
2 Defensive Front 2.00 5.00
3 Deep Secondary 2.00 5.00
4 Big Offensive Line 2.00 5.00
5 Scores 2.00 5.00

1985 Raiders Fire Safety

This four-card set of Los Angeles Raiders was also sponsored by Kodak. The cards measure approximately 2 5/8" by 4 1/8". The cards are numbered (and dated) on the back. The fire safety tip on the back is in the form of a cartoon. There are also two or three paragraphs of biographical information about the player on the card backs. The card fronts show a full-color photo inside a white border. The player's name, team, position, height, and weight are given at the bottom of the card front.

COMPLETE SET (4) 1.50 4.00
1 Marcus Allen .75 2.00
2 Tom Flores CO .15 .40
3 Howie Long .60 1.50
4 Rod Martin .15 .40

1985 Raiders Police

This set of cards was distributed by Police Officers in the Los Angeles area and sponsored by KIIIS Radio. The unnumbered cards are listed alphabetically below. Uncut sheets of both the 1985 Rams and Raiders Police sets together are also on the market.

COMPLETE SET (15) 7.50 20.00
1 Marcus Allen 2.50 6.00
2 Lyle Alzado 1.25 3.00
3 Todd Christensen .60 1.50
4 Dave Dalby .40 1.00
5 Mike Davis .40 1.00
6 Ray Guy .60 1.50
7 Frank Hawkins .40 1.00
8 Lester Hayes .60 1.50
9 Mike Haynes .60 1.50
10 Howie Long 2.50 6.00
11 Rod Martin .40 1.00
12 Mickey Marvin .40 1.00
13 Jim Plunkett 1.25 3.00
14 Brad Van Pelt .40 1.00
15 Dukie Williams .40 1.00

1987 Raiders Smokey Color-Grams

This set is actually a 14-page booklet featuring 13 player caricatures (all from the Los Angeles Raiders) and one of Smokey and Huddles. Each page includes a 5 5/8" by 3 11/16" postcard perforated with a card measuring 2 1/2" by 3 11/16". The booklet itself is approximately 8 1/8" by 3 11/16". The set is headlined as "Arsonbusters" in white over a black frame. The backs offer a fire prevention tip from Smokey. The cards are unnumbered, but are listed below according to booklet page number.

COMPLETE SET (14) 20.00 40.00
1 Smokey and Huddles .60 1.50
2 Matt Millen .75 2.00
3 Rod Martin .75 2.00
4 Sean Jones 1.00 2.50
5 Dokie Williams .60 1.50
6 Don Mosebar .75 2.00
7 Todd Christensen .75 2.00
8 Bill Pickel .60 1.50
9 Marcus Allen 5.00 12.00
10 Charley Hannah .60 1.50
11 Howie Long 3.00 8.00
12 Vann McElroy .60 1.50
13 Reggie McKenzie .60 1.50
14 Mike Haynes 1.25 3.00

1988 Raiders Ace Fact Pack

Cards from this 33-card set measure approximately 2 1/4" by 3 5/8". This set consists of 22-player cards and 11-additional informational cards about the Raiders team. We've checklisted the cards alphabetically beginning with the 22-players. The cards have square corners (as opposed to rounded like the 1987 sets) and a playing card design on the back printed in blue. These cards were manufactured in West Germany (by Ace Fact Pack) and released primarily in Great Britain.

COMPLETE SET (33) 200.00 350.00
1 Marcus Allen 40.00 80.00
2 Chris Bahr 2.00 5.00
3 Bob Buczkowski 2.00 5.00
4 Todd Christensen 4.00 10.00
5 John Clay 2.00 5.00
6 Vince Evans 2.50 6.00
7 Mervyn Fernandez 2.00 5.00
8 Mike Haynes 10.00 25.00
9 Jessie Hester 2.00 5.00
10 Brian Holloway 2.00 5.00
11 Bo Jackson 40.00 80.00
12 James Lofton 10.00 25.00
13 Howie Long 15.00 40.00
14 Rod Martin 2.50 6.00
15 Vann McElroy 2.00 5.00
16 Reggie McKenzie 2.00 5.00
17 Matt Millen 4.00 10.00
18 Don Mosebar 2.00 5.00
19 Bill Pickel 2.00 5.00
20 Jerry Robinson 2.50 6.00
21 Stacey Toran UER 2.00 5.00
22 Greg Townsend 2.00 5.00
23 1987 Team Statistics 2.00 5.00
24 All-Time Greats 2.00 5.00
25 Career Record Holders 2.00 5.00
26 Coaching History 2.00 5.00
27 Game Record Holders 2.00 5.00
28 Memorial Coliseum 2.00 5.00
29 Record 1968-87 2.00 5.00
30 Raiders Helmet Cover 2.00 5.00
31 Raiders Helmet Info 2.00 5.00
32 Raiders Uniform 2.00 5.00
33 Season Record Holders 2.00 5.00

1988 Raiders Police

The 1988 Police Los Angeles Raiders set contains 12 numbered cards measuring approximately 2 3/4" by 4 1/8". There are 11 player cards and one coach card. The backs have biographical information and safety tips. The set was sponsored by Texaco and the Los Angeles Raiders.

COMPLETE SET (12) 5.00 10.00
1 Vann McElroy .25 .60
2 Bill Pickel .25 .60
3 Marcus Allen 1.25 3.00
4 Rod Martin .30 .75
5 Lionel Washington .25 .60
6 Don Mosebar .25 .60
7 Reggie McKenzie .25 .60
8 Todd Christensen .30 .75
9 Bo Jackson .75 2.00
10 James Lofton .40 1.00
11 Howie Long .60 1.50
12 Mike Shanahan CO .40 1.00

1988 Raiders Smokey

This 14-card set is distinguished by its thick black border on the front of every card as well as the presence of "Arsonbusters" in orange as a subtitle. The cards measure approximately 3" by 5". The set is not numbered although the players' uniform numbers are in small print on the back; the list below has been ordered alphabetically. Each card back features a different fire safety cartoon starring Smokey.

COMPLETE SET (14) 10.00 20.00
1 Marcus Allen 2.00 5.00
2 Todd Christensen .60 1.50
3 Bo Jackson 1.25 3.00
4 James Lofton .75 2.00
5 Howie Long 1.25 3.00
6 Rod Martin .60 1.50
7 Vann McElroy .50 1.25
8 Don Mosebar .50 1.25
9 Bill Pickel .50 1.25
10 Jerry Robinson .50 1.25
11 Mike Shanahan CO .60 1.50
12 Smokey Bear .50 1.25
13 Stacey Toran .50 1.25
14 Greg Townsend .50 1.25

1989 Raiders Knudsen Bookmarks

This unnumbered 12-card set (of bookmarks) issued by Knudsen's Dairy in California measures approximately 2" by 8" and features members of the 1989 Los Angeles Raiders. These sets were distributed during the football season to those youngsters who checked out a book a week during the 1989 season from the Los Angeles Public Library. The backs of these bookmarks feature various reading tips for the youth to follow. The set is checklisted below by player's uniform number. The Shanahan card was apparently undistributed or withdrawn after he left the team.

COMPLETE SET (14) 20.00 50.00
6 Jeff Gossett 1.25 3.00
13 Jay Schroeder 1.50 4.00
26 Vann McElroy 1.25 3.00
35 Steve Smith 1.50 4.00
36 Terry McDaniel 1.50 4.00
70 Scott Davis 1.25 3.00
72 Don Mosebar 1.25 3.00
75 Howie Long 2.00 5.00
76 Steve Wisniewski 1.50 4.00
81 Tim Brown 5.00 12.00
83 Willie Gault 1.50 4.00
NNO Mike Shanahan SP CO 6.00 15.00
NNO Raiders 1.25 3.00
Super Bowl
NNO Raiderettes SP 1.50 4.00

1989 Raiders Swanson

This three-card set was issued in a perforated strip containing five card slots; after perforation, the cards measure approximately 2 1/2" by 3 3/4". The first two slots consist of manufacturer's coupons to save 25 cents on the purchase of any variety of Swanson Hungry-Man dinners. The player cards feature an oval-shamped black and white player photo on a silver card face. A red diagonal with the words "Hungry-Man" cuts across the upper left corner, and the player's name appears in black lettering below the picture. The horizontal backs present biographical information and player profile. The cards are unnumbered and checklisted below in alphabetical order.

COMPLETE SET (3) 5.00 12.00
1 Marcus Allen 3.00 8.00
2 Howie Long 1.25 3.00
3 Jim Plunkett 1.00 2.50

1990 Raiders Smokey

This 16-card standard size set was issued by the USDA Forest Service in conjuction with the USDI Bureau of Land Management, USDI National Park Service, California Department of Forestry and Fire Prevention, and BDA. The set features solid black borders framing a full-color action shot with the Los Angeles Raiders team name in white. The player's name and uniform number is directly underneath the photo and there is a photo of the Smokey the Bear mascot in the lower left hand corner of the card. The back of the card has only the basic biographical information, as well as a fire safety tip. Surprisingly, there is no card of either Bo Jackson or Marcus Allen in this set. The set has been checklisted below in alphabetical order.

COMPLETE SET (16) 12.50 25.00
1 Eddie Anderson .60 1.50
2 Thomas Benson .60 1.50
3 Mervyn Fernandez .75 2.00
4 Bob Golic .60 1.50
5 Jeff Gossett .60 1.50
6 Rory Graves .60 1.50
7 Jeff Jaeger .60 1.50
8 Howie Long 1.50 4.00
9 Don Mosebar .60 1.50
10 Jay Schroeder .75 2.00
11 Art Shell CO 1.00 2.50
12 Greg Townsend .75 2.00
13 Lionel Washington .60 1.50
14 Steve Wisniewski .75 2.00
15 Commitment to .60 1.50
16 Denise Franzen .60 1.50

1990-91 Raiders Main Street Dairy Mile Cartons

This set of six half-pint milk cartons features the Raiders' team patch, a head shot of a player, and a safety tip to youngsters on one of its panels. When collapsed, the cartons measure approximately 4 1/2" by 6". The cartons were issued in the Los Angeles area and were printed in three colors, brown (chocolate lowfat), red (vitamin D), and blue (2 percent low fat). The primary color of the carton is given on the continuation line below.

COMPLETE SET (6) 12.00 30.00
1 Bob Golic 2.40 6.00
2 Terry McDaniel 2.00 5.00
3 Don Mosebar 2.00 5.00
4 Jay Schroeder 2.40 6.00
5 Art Shell CO 3.20 8.00
6 Steve Wisniewski 2.00 5.00

1991 Raiders Police

This 12-card standard-size set was sponsored by Clovis Police Department, REHCO Heating and Air Conditioning, and the Los Angeles Raiders. Five thousand sets were distributed throughout the Fresno/Clovis area as part of a sixth grade DARE (Drug Awareness Resistance Education) program. Card fronts feature color action player photos with white borders. The player's name appears in a gray stripe above the picture, while sponsor logos overlay another gray stripe at the bottom of the card face. The backs have biographical information and a safety tip printed in black lettering on a white background.

COMPLETE SET (12) 10.00 20.00
1 Art Shell CO 1.00 2.50
2 Marcus Allen 2.00 5.00
3 Mervyn Fernandez .50 1.25
4 Willie Gault .60 1.50
5 Howie Long 1.50 3.00
6 Don Mosebar .50 1.25
7 Winston Moss .50 1.25
8 Jay Schroeder .60 1.50
9 Steve Wisniewski .50 1.25
10 Ethan Horton .50 1.25
11 Lionel Washington .50 1.25
12 Greg Townsend .50 1.25

1991-92 Raiders Adohr Farms Dairy

This set of ten half-pint milk cartons features the Raiders' team patch, a head shot of a player, and a safety message on one of its panels. When collapsed, the cartons measure approximately 4 1/2" by 6". The cartons were issued in the Los Angeles area and were printed in red (vitamin D) and blue (2 percent lowfat). Apparently only the Greg Townsend carton was issued in two varieties. The primary color of the carton is given on the continuation line. The cartons are unnumbered and checklisted below in alphabetical order. Apparently Adohr Farms Dairy bought out Main Street Dairy and with the buyout, obtained the rights to produce the selected Raiders.

COMPLETE SET (10) 20.00 40.00
1 Jeff Gossett 2.00 5.00
2 Ethan Horton 2.00 5.00
3 Jeff Jaeger 2.00 5.00
4 Ronnie Lott 3.00 8.00
5 Terry McDaniel 2.00 5.00
6 Don Mosebar 2.00 5.00
7 Jay Schroeder 2.00 5.00
8 Art Shell CO 2.50 6.00
9 Greg Townsend 2.00 5.00
10 Steve Wisniewski 2.00 5.00

1993-94 Raiders Adohr Farms Dairy

This set of six half-pint vitamin D milk cartons features the Raiders team patch, a head shot of a player, and a message about education or crime prevention, all printed in red. When collapsed, the cartons measure approximately 4 1/2" by 6". Two million milk cartons were distributed only to Los Angeles area schools and hospitals in a two-week period during the season. Reportedly only 1,400 were produced flat and undistributed. The cartons are unnumbered and checklisted below in alphabetical order.

COMPLETE SET (6) 15.00 30.00
1 Jeff Gossett 2.00 5.00
2 Ethan Horton 2.00 5.00
3 Terry McDaniel 2.00 5.00
4 Don Mosebar 2.00 5.00
5 Art Shell CO 2.50 6.00
6 Steve Wisniewski 2.00 5.00

1994-95 Raiders Adohr Farms Dairy

This set of four half-pint Vitamin D milk cartons features the Raiders' team patch, a head shot of the player, and a safety tip on one of its panels. When collapsed, the cartons measure approximately 4 1/2" by 6". All cartons are printed in red with some black lettering. It was reported that 20,000,000 cartons (or five million sets) were issued in a three-week period. Ninety percent were distributed to hospitals, schools, and airlines, while ten percent were sold to the general public. Reportedly, 800 cartons (or 200 sets) were left flat and undistributed. The cartons are unnumbered and checklisted below in alphabetical order.

COMPLETE SET (4) 10.00 20.00
1 Jeff Jaeger 2.00 5.00
2 Terry McDaniel 2.00 5.00
3 Art Shell CO 2.50 6.00
4 Steve Wisniewski 2.00 5.00

2006 Raiders Topps

COMPLETE SET (12) 3.00 6.00
OAK1 LaMont Jordan .30 .75
OAK2 Warren Sapp .30 .75
OAK3 Kirk Morrison .25 .60

OAK4 Jerry Porter .25 .60
OAK5 Robert Gallery .25 .60
OAK6 Ronald Curry .25 .60
OAK7 Doug Gabriel .25 .60
OAK8 Randy Moss .30 .75
OAK9 Fabian Washington .25 .60
OAK10 Derrick Burgess .25 .60
OAK11 Aaron Brooks .25 .60
OAK12 Michael Huff .30 .75

2006 Raiders Topps Pepsi

These 6-cards were produced by Topps and inserted one card per 24-pack of Pepsi Cola product in the Oakland area. Each unnumbered card is completely redesigned compared to basic issue 2006 Topps football.

COMPLETE SET (6) 5.00 10.00
1 Aaron Brooks .60 1.50
2 Derrick Gibson .60 1.50
3 Michael Huff .75 2.00
4 Randy Moss .75 2.00
5 Jerry Porter .60 1.50
6 Warren Sapp .75 2.00

2007 Raiders Topps

COMPLETE SET (12) 3.00 6.00
1 Andrew Walter .40 1.00
2 Nnamdi Asomugha .40 1.00
3 Kirk Morrison .40 1.00
4 Michael Huff .50 1.25
5 Ronald Curry .40 1.00
6 Derrick Burgess .40 1.00
7 Dominic Rhodes .40 1.00
8 LaMont Jordan .50 1.25
9 Warren Sapp .50 1.25
10 JaMarcus Russell .40 1.00
11 Zach Miller .40 1.00
12 Michael Bush .40 1.00

2008 Raiders Topps

COMPLETE SET (12) 2.50 5.00
1 DeAngelo Hall .40 1.00
2 Justin Fargas .40 1.00
3 Zach Miller .40 1.00
4 JaMarcus Russell .40 1.00
5 Ronald Curry .40 1.00
6 Daunte Culpepper .50 1.25
7 LaMont Jordan .50 1.25
8 Thomas Howard .40 1.00
9 Kirk Morrison .40 1.00
10 Derrick Burgess .40 1.00
11 Darren McFadden .40 1.00
12 Nnamdi Asomugha .40 1.00

1950 Rams Admiral

This 35-card set was sponsored by Admiral Televisions and features cards measuring approximately 3 1/2" by 5 1/2" (#1-25) and 3 1/8" by 5 3/8" (#26-35). The front design has a black and white action pose of the player, without borders on the sides of the picture. The words "Your Admiral dealer presents" followed by the player's name and position appear in the black stripe at the top of each card. A black border separates the bottom of the picture from the biographical information below. In a horizontal format, the backs are blank on the right half, and have a season schedule as well as Admiral advertisements on the left half (#1-25) or are blankbacked (#26-35). The cards are numbered on the front underneath the photos. Norm Van Brocklin appears in his Rookie Card year.

COMPLETE SET (35) 4000.00 7000.00
1 Joe Stydahar CO 125.00 200.00
2 Hampton Pool CO 100.00 175.00
3 Fred Naumetz 100.00 175.00
4 Jack Finlay 100.00 175.00
5 Gil Bouley 100.00 175.00
6 Bob Reinhard 100.00 175.00
7 Dob Doyd 100.00 175.00
8 Bob Waterfield 300.00 500.00
9 Mel Hein CO 125.00 200.00
10 Howard(Red) Hickey CO 100.00 175.00
11 Ralph Pasquariello 100.00 175.00
12 Jack Zilly 100.00 175.00
13 Tom Kalmanir 100.00 175.00
14 Norm Van Brocklin 400.00 750.00
15 Woodley Lewis 100.00 175.00
16 Glenn Davis 150.00 250.00
17 Dick Hoerner 100.00 175.00
18 Bob Kelley ANN 100.00 175.00
19 Paul (Tank) Younger 125.00 200.00
20 George Sims 100.00 175.00
21 Dick Huffman 100.00 175.00
22 Tom Fears 175.00 300.00
23 Vitamin T. Smith 100.00 175.00
24 Elroy Hirsch 350.00 600.00
25 Don Paul 100.00 175.00
26 Bill Lange 100.00 175.00
27 Paul Barry 100.00 175.00
28 Deacon Dan Towler 125.00 200.00
29 Vic Vasicek 100.00 175.00
30 Bill Smyth 100.00 175.00
31 Larry Brink 100.00 175.00
32 Jerry Williams 100.00 175.00
33 Stan West 100.00 175.00
34 Art Statuto 100.00 175.00
35 Ed Champagne 100.00 175.00

1950 Rams Matchbooks

These matchbook covers were produced by Universal Match Corporation around 1950 and feature members of the Los Angeles Rams. Each cover features a blue border and yellow-tinted player photo along with the Rams team logo. The inside or "back" of the covers is blank. Any additions to the list below are appreciated.

1 Bob Waterfield 20.00 40.00

1953 Rams Team Issue

This 36-card unnumbered set measures approximately 4 1/4" by 6 3/8" and was issued by the Los Angeles Rams for their fans. This set has black borders on the front framing posed action shots with the player's signature across the bottom portion of the picture. Biographical information on the back relating to the player pictured listing the player's name, height, weight, age, and college is also included. Among the interesting cards in this set are early cards of Dick "Night-Train" Lane and Andy Robustelli. The cards were available directly from the team as a complete set. We have checklisted this set in alphabetical order. Many cards from the 1953-1955 and 1957 Rams Team Issue Black Border sets are identical except for text differences on the card backs. Player stat lines are also helpful in identifying year of issue; the year of issue is typically the next year after the last year on the stats. The first few words of the first line of text is listed for players without stat lines.

COMPLETE SET (36) 250.00 400.00
1 Ben Agajanian 5.00 8.00
2 Bob Boyd 5.00 8.00
3 Larry Brink 5.00 8.00
4 Rudy Bukich 5.00 8.00
5 Tom Dahms 5.00 8.00
6 Dick Daugherty 5.00 8.00
7 Jack Dwyer 5.00 8.00
8 Tom Fears 15.00 30.00
9 Bob Fry 5.00 8.00
10 Frank Fuller 5.00 8.00
11 Norbert Hecker 5.00 8.00
12 Elroy Hirsch 25.00 40.00
13 John Hock 5.00 8.00
14 Bob Kelley ANN 5.00 8.00
15 Dick Lane 15.00 30.00
16 Woodley Lewis 5.00 8.00
17 Tom McCormick 5.00 8.00
18 Lewis(Bud) McFadin 5.00 8.00
19 Leon McLaughlin 5.00 8.00
20 Brad Myers 5.00 8.00
21 Don Paul LB 5.00 8.00
22 Hampton Pool CO 5.00 8.00
23 Duane Putnam 5.00 8.00
24 Volney Quinlan 5.00 8.00
25 Herb Rich 5.00 8.00
26 Andy Robustelli 20.00 35.00
27 Vitamin T. Smith 5.00 8.00
28 Harland Svare 5.00 8.00
29 Len Teeuws 5.00 8.00
30 Harry Thompson 5.00 8.00
31 Charley Toogood 5.00 8.00
32 Deacon Dan Towler 6.00 10.00
33 Norm Van Brocklin 35.00 60.00
34 Stan West 5.00 8.00
35 Paul(Tank) Younger 6.00 10.00
36 Coaches: John Sauer& 5.00 8.00

1953-54 Rams Burgermeister Beer Team Photos

These oversized (roughly 6 1/4" by 9") color team photos were sponsored by Burgermeister Beer and distributed in the Los Angeles area. Each were printed on card stock and included advertising messages on the back.

1953 Los Angeles Rams 35.00 60.00
1954 Los Angeles Rams 35.00 60.00

1954 Rams Team Issue

This 36-card set measures approximately 4 1/4" by 6 3/8". The front features a black and white posed action photo enclosed by a black border, with the player's signature across the bottom portion of the picture. The back lists the player's name, height, weight, age, and college, along with basic biographical information. The set was available direct from the team as part of a package for their fans. The cards are listed alphabetically below since they are unnumbered. Many cards from the 1953-1955 and 1957 Rams Team Issue Black Border sets are identical except for text differences on the card backs. Player stat lines are also helpful in identifying year of issue; the year of issue is typically the next year after the last year on the stats. The first few words of the first line of text is listed for players without stat lines. The set features the first card appearance of Gene "Big Daddy" Lipscomb.

COMPLETE SET (36) 200.00 400.00
1 Bob Boyd 4.00 8.00
2 Bob Carey 4.00 8.00
3 Bobby Cross 4.00 8.00
4 Tom Dahms 4.00 8.00
5 Don Doll 4.00 8.00
6 Jack Dwyer 4.00 8.00
7 Tom Fears 12.50 25.00
8 Bob Griffin 4.00 8.00
9 Art Hauser 4.00 8.00
10 Hall Haynes 4.00 8.00
11 Elroy Hirsch 20.00 35.00
12 Ed Hughes 4.00 8.00
13 Bob Kelley ANN 4.00 8.00
14 Woodley Lewis 4.00 8.00
15 Gene Lipscomb 10.00 20.00
16 Tom McCormick 4.00 8.00
17 Bud McFadin 4.00 8.00
18 Leon McLaughlin 4.00 8.00
19 Paul Miller 4.00 8.00
20 Don Paul LB 4.00 8.00
21 Hampton Pool CO 4.00 8.00
22 Duane Putnam 4.00 8.00
23 Volney Quinlan 4.00 8.00
24 Les Richter 4.00 8.00
25 Andy Robustelli 12.50 25.00
26 Willard Sherman 4.00 8.00
27 Harland Svare 4.00 8.00
28 Harry Thompson 4.00 8.00
29 Charley Toogood 4.00 8.00
30 Deacon Dan Towler 5.00 10.00
31 Norm Van Brocklin 25.00 50.00
32 Bill Wade 7.50 15.00
33 Duane Wardlow 4.00 8.00
34 Stan West 4.00 8.00
35 Paul(Tank) Younger 5.00 10.00
36 Coaches Card 4.00 8.00

1955 Rams Team Issue

This 37-card set measures approximately 4 1/4" by 6 3/8". The front features a black and white posed action photo enclosed by a black border, with the player's signature across the bottom portion of the picture. The back lists the player's name, height, weight, age, and college, along with basic biographical information. The set was available direct from the team as part of a package for their fans. The cards are listed alphabetically below since they are unnumbered. Many cards from the 1953-1955 and 1957 Rams Team Issue Black Border sets are identical except for text differences on the card backs. Player stat lines are also helpful in identifying year of issue; the year of issue is typically the next year after the last year on the stats. The first few words of the first line of text is listed for players without stat lines.

COMPLETE SET (37) 200.00 325.00
1 Jack Bighead 4.00 8.00
2 Bob Boyd 4.00 8.00
3 Don Burroughs 4.00 8.00
4 Jim Cason 4.00 8.00
5 Bobby Cross 4.00 8.00
6 Jack Ellena 4.00 8.00
7 Tom Fears 7.50 15.00
8 Sid Fournet 4.00 8.00
9 Frank Fuller 4.00 8.00
10 Sid Gillman and staff 6.00 12.00
11 Bob Griffin 4.00 8.00
12 Art Hauser 4.00 8.00
13 Hall Haynes 4.00 8.00
14 Elroy Hirsch 15.00 30.00
15 John Hock 4.00 8.00
16 Glenn Holtzman 4.00 8.00
17 Ed Hughes 4.00 8.00
18 Woodley Lewis 4.00 8.00
19 Gene Lipscomb 7.50 15.00
20 Tom McCormick 4.00 8.00
21 Bud McFadin 4.00 8.00
22 Leon McLaughlin 4.00 8.00
23 Paul Miller 4.00 8.00
24 Larry Morris 4.00 8.00
25 Don Paul LB 4.00 8.00
26 Duane Putnam 4.00 8.00
27 Volney Quinlan 4.00 8.00
28 Les Richter 4.00 8.00
29 Andy Robustelli 7.50 15.00
30 Willard Sherman 4.00 8.00
31 Corky Taylor 4.00 8.00
32 Charley Toogood 4.00 8.00
33 Deacon Dan Towler 5.00 10.00
34 Norm Van Brocklin 20.00 40.00
35 Bill Wade 6.00 12.00
36 Ron Waller 4.00 8.00
37 Paul(Tank) Younger 5.00 10.00

1956 Rams Team Issue

This 37-card team-issued set measures approximately 4 1/4" by 6 3/8" and features members of the Los Angeles Rams. The set has posed action shots on the front framed by a white border with the player's signature across the picture, while the back has biographical information about the player listing the player's name, height, weight, age, number of years in NFL, and college. We have checklisted this (unnumbered) set in alphabetical order. The set was initially available for fans direct from the team for $1.

COMPLETE SET (37) 150.00 300.00
1 Bob Boyd 4.00 8.00
2 Rudy Bukich 4.00 8.00
3 Don Burroughs 4.00 8.00
4 Jim Cason 4.00 8.00
5 Leon Clarke 4.00 8.00
6 Dick Daugherty 4.00 8.00
7 Jack Ellena 4.00 8.00
8 Tom Fears 7.50 15.00
9 Sid Fournet 4.00 8.00
10 Bob Fry 4.00 8.00
11 Coaches 6.00 12.00
12 Bob Griffin 4.00 8.00
13 Art Hauser 4.00 8.00
14 Elroy Hirsch 12.50 25.00
15 John Hock 4.00 8.00
16 Bob Holladay 4.00 8.00
17 Glenn Holtzman 4.00 8.00
18 Bob Kelley ANN 4.00 8.00
19 Joe Marconi 4.00 8.00
20 Bud McFadin 4.00 8.00
21 Paul Miller 4.00 8.00
22 Ron Miller DE 4.00 8.00
23 Larry Morris 4.00 8.00
24 John Morrow 4.00 8.00
25 Brad Myers 4.00 8.00
26 Hugh Pitts 4.00 8.00
27 Duane Putnam 4.00 8.00
28 Les Richter 4.00 8.00
29 Willard Sherman 4.00 8.00
30 Charley Toogood 4.00 8.00
31 Norm Van Brocklin 17.50 35.00
32 Bill Wade 6.00 12.00
33 Ron Waller 4.00 8.00
34 Duane Wardlow 4.00 8.00
35 Jesse Whittenton 4.00 8.00
36 Tom Wilson 4.00 8.00
37 Paul(Tank) Younger 5.00 10.00

1957-61 Rams Falstaff Beer Team Photos

These oversized (roughly 6 1/4" by 9") color team photos were sponsored by Falstaff Beer and distributed in the Los Angeles area. Each was printed on card stock and included advertising and/or photos of the team's coaching staff on the back.

1957 Rams Team 30.00 50.00
1958 Rams Team 30.00 50.00
1959 Rams Team 30.00 50.00
1960 Rams Team 25.00 40.00
1961 Rams Team 25.00 40.00

1957 Rams Team Issue

This 38-card team-issued set measures approximately 4 1/4" by 6 3/8" and features posed action shots on the front surrounded by black borders with the player's signature across the picture. The card backs contain biographical information about the player listing the player's name, height, weight, age, number of years in NFL, and college. We have checklisted this (unnumbered) set in alphabetical order. The set was available direct from the team as part of a package for their fans. Many cards from the 1953-1955 and 1957 Rams Team Issue Black Border sets are identical except for text differences on the card backs. Player stat lines are also helpful in identifying year of issue; the year of issue is typically the next year after the last year on the stats. The first few words of the first line of text is listed for players without stat lines. The set features the first card appearance of Jack Pardee.

COMPLETE SET (38) 150.00 300.00
1 Jon Arnett 5.00 10.00
2 Bob Boyd 4.00 8.00
3 Alex Bravo 4.00 8.00
4 Bill Brundige ANN 4.00 8.00
5 Don Burroughs 4.00 8.00
6 Jerry Castete 4.00 8.00
7 Leon Clarke 4.00 8.00
8 Paige Cothren 4.00 8.00
9 Dick Daugherty 4.00 8.00
10 Bob Dougherty 4.00 8.00
11 Bob Fry 4.00 8.00
12 Frank Fuller 4.00 8.00
13 Coaches: Sid Gillman 12.50 25.00
14 Bob Griffin 4.00 8.00
15 Art Hauser 4.00 8.00
16 Elroy Hirsch 12.50 25.00
17 John Hock 4.00 8.00
18 Glenn Holtzman 4.00 8.00
19 John Houser 4.00 8.00
20 Bob Kelley ANN 4.00 8.00
21 Lamar Lundy 5.00 10.00
22 Joe Marconi 4.00 8.00
23 Paul Miller 4.00 8.00
24 Larry Morris 4.00 8.00
25 Ken Panfil 4.00 8.00
26 Jack Pardee 6.00 12.00
27 Duane Putnam 4.00 8.00
28 Les Richter 4.00 8.00
29 Willard Sherman 4.00 8.00
30 Del Shofner 5.00 10.00
31 Billy Ray Smith 4.00 8.00
32 George Strugar 4.00 8.00
33 Norm Van Brocklin 15.00 30.00
34 Bill Wade 6.00 12.00
35 Ron Waller 4.00 8.00
36 Jesse Whittenton 4.00 8.00
37 Tom Wilson 4.00 8.00
38 Paul(Tank) Younger 5.00 10.00

1959 Rams Bell Brand

The 1959 Bell Brand Los Angeles Rams set contains 40-regular issue standard-size cards. The catalog designation for this set is F387-1. The obverses contain white-bordered color photos of the player with a facsimile autograph. The backs contain the card number, a short biography and vital statistics of the player, a Bell Brand ad, and advertisements for Los Angeles Rams' merchandise. These cards were issued as inserts in potato chip and corn chip bags in the Los Angeles area and are frequently found with oil stains from the chips. Cards #41 Bill Jobko and #43 Tom Franckhauer were recently discovered. Much like the 1960 Gene Selawski card #2, it is thought that the Jobko and Franckhauser cards were withdrawn early in production and available only upon request from the company. It is not considered part of the complete set price below.

COMPLETE SET (40) 1200.00 2000.00
1 Bill Wade 40.00 75.00
2 Buddy Humphrey 30.00 50.00
3 Frank Ryan 35.00 60.00
4 Ed Meador 30.00 50.00
5 Tom Wilson 30.00 50.00
6 Don Burroughs 30.00 50.00
7 Jon Arnett 35.00 60.00
8 Del Shofner 35.00 60.00
9 Jack Pardee 35.00 60.00
10 Ollie Matson 60.00 100.00
11 Joe Marconi 30.00 50.00
12 Jim Jones 30.00 50.00
13 Jack Morris 30.00 50.00
14 Willard Sherman 30.00 50.00
15 Clendon Thomas 30.00 50.00
16 Les Richter 35.00 60.00
17 John Morrow 30.00 50.00
18 Lou Michaels 35.00 60.00
19 Bob Reifsnyder 30.00 50.00
20 John Guzik 30.00 50.00
21 Duane Putnam 30.00 50.00
22 John Houser 30.00 50.00
23 Buck Lansford 30.00 50.00
24 Gene Selawski 30.00 50.00
25 John Baker 30.00 50.00
26 Bob Fry 30.00 50.00
27 John Lovetere 30.00 50.00
28 George Strugar 30.00 50.00
29 Roy Wilkins 30.00 50.00
30 Charley Bradshaw 30.00 50.00
31 Gene Brito 30.00 50.00
32 Jim Phillips 35.00 60.00
33 Leon Clarke 30.00 50.00
34 Lamar Lundy 40.00 75.00
35 Sam Williams 30.00 50.00
36 Sid Gillman CO 50.00 80.00
37 Jack Faulkner CO 30.00 50.00
38 Joe Madro CO 30.00 50.00
39 Don Paul LB CO 30.00 50.00
40 Lou Rymkus CO 35.00 60.00
41 Bill Jobko SP 1200.00 2000.00
43 Tom Franckhauser SP 1200.00 2000.00

1960 Rams Bell Brand

The 1960 Bell Brand Los Angeles Rams Football set contains 39 standard-size cards in a format similar to the 1959 Bell Brand set. The fronts of the cards have distinctive yellow borders. The catalog designation for this set is F387-2. Card numbers 1-18, except number 2, are repeated photos from the 1959 set and were available throughout the season. Numbers 19-39 were available later in the 1960 season. These cards were issued as inserts in potato chip and corn chip bags in the Los Angeles area and are frequently found with oil stains from the chips. Card number 2 Selawski was withdrawn early in the year (after he was cut from the team) and was reportedly available only upon request from the company. It is not considered part of the complete set price below.

COMPLETE SET (38) 1500.00 2500.00
COMMON CARD (1-18) 30.00 50.00
COMMON CARD (19-39) 50.00 80.00
1 Joe Marconi 30.00 50.00
2 Gene Selawski SP 1200.00 2000.00
3 Frank Ryan 30.00 50.00
4 Ed Meador 35.00 60.00
5 Tom Wilson 30.00 50.00
6 Gene Brito 35.00 60.00
7 Jon Arnett 30.00 50.00
8 Buck Lansford 30.00 50.00
9 Jack Pardee 30.00 50.00
10 Ollie Matson 50.00 80.00
11 John Lovetere 30.00 50.00
12 Bill Jolko 30.00 50.00
13 Jim Phillips 35.00 60.00
14 Lamar Lundy 30.00 50.00
15 Del Shofner 30.00 50.00
16 Les Richter 35.00 60.00
17 Bill Wade 30.00 50.00
18 Lou Michaels 35.00 60.00
19 Dick Bass 60.00 100.00
20 Charley Britt 50.00 80.00
21 Willard Sherman 50.00 80.00
22 George Strugar 50.00 80.00
23 Bob Long LB 50.00 80.00
24 Danny Villanueva 50.00 80.00
25 Jim Boeke 50.00 80.00
26 Clendon Thomas 50.00 80.00
27 Art Hunter 50.00 80.00
28 Carl Karilivacz 50.00 80.00
29 John Baker 50.00 80.00
30 Charley Bradshaw 50.00 80.00
31 John Guzik 50.00 80.00
32 Buddy Humphrey 50.00 80.00
33 Carroll Dale 50.00 80.00
34 Don Ellersick 50.00 80.00
35 Roy Hord 50.00 80.00
36 Charlie Janerette 50.00 80.00
37 John Kennerson 50.00 80.00
38 Jerry Stalcup 50.00 80.00
39 Bob Waterfield CO 125.00 200.00

1967 Rams Team Issue

The Los Angeles Rams issued these black and white player photos around 1967. Each includes the player's name and team name below the photo, measures roughly 5 1/4" by 7" and is blankbacked.

COMPLETE SET (27) 125.00 250.00
1 Maxie Baughan 6.00 12.00
2 Joe Carollo 6.00 12.00
3 Bernie Casey 6.00 12.00
4 Don Chuy 6.00 12.00
5 Charlie Cowan 6.00 12.00
6 Irv Cross 6.00 12.00
7 Dan Currie 6.00 12.00
8 Willie Daniel 6.00 12.00
9 Willie Ellison 6.00 12.00
10 Roman Gabriel 7.50 15.00
11 Bruce Gossett 6.00 12.00
12 Roosevelt Grier 7.50 15.00
13 Anthony Guillory 6.00 12.00
14 Ken Iman 6.00 12.00
15 Deacon Jones 7.50 15.00
16 Les Josephson 6.00 12.00
17 Chuck Lamson 6.00 12.00
18 Tom Mack 7.50 15.00
19 Tommy Mason 6.00 12.00
20 Marlin McKeever 6.00 12.00
21 Bill Munson 6.00 12.00
22 Jack Pardee 6.00 12.00
23 Myron Pottios 6.00 12.00
24 Joe Scibelli 6.00 12.00
25 Jack Snow 6.00 12.00
26 Clancy Williams 6.00 12.00
27 Doug Woodlief 6.00 12.00

1968 Rams Team Issue

The Los Angeles Rams issued these black and white player photos. Each measures roughly 8" by 10" and is blank backed. The checklist below is thought to be incomplete.

COMPLETE SET (9) 50.00 100.00
1 George Allen CO 10.00 20.00
2 Dick Bass 5.00 10.00
3 Bernie Casey 5.00 10.00
4 Lamar Lundy 6.00 12.00
5 Deacon Jones 7.50 15.00
6 Les Josephson 5.00 10.00
7 Merlin Olsen 7.50 15.00
8 Jack Snow 5.00 10.00
9 Team Photo 5.00 10.00

1968 Rams Volpe Tumblers

These Rams artist's renderings were part of a plastic cup tumbler product produced in 1968 and distributed by White Front Stroes. The noted sports artist Volpe created the artwork which includes an action scene and a player portrait. The "cards" are unnumbered, each measures approximately 5" by 8 1/2" and is curved in the shape required to fit inside a plastic cup. The manufacturer notation PGC (programs General Corp) is printed on each piece as well. There are thought to be 6-cups included in this set. Any additions to this list are appreciated.

COMPLETE SET (6) 100.00 200.00
1 Dick Bass 15.00 30.00
2 Roger Brown 15.00 30.00
3 Roman Gabriel 25.00 50.00
4 Deacon Jones 25.00 50.00
5 Lamar Lundy 15.00 30.00
6 Merlin Olsen 30.00 60.00

1973 Rams Team Issue Color

The NFLPA worked with many teams in 1973 to issued photo packs to be sold at stadium concession stands. Each measures approximately 7" by 8-5/8" and features a color player photo with a blank back. A small sheet with a player checklist was included in each 6-photo pack.

COMPLETE SET (6) 25.00 50.00
1 Jim Bertelsen 4.00 8.00
2 John Hadl 6.00 12.00
3 Harold Jackson 5.00 10.00
4 Merlin Olsen 6.00 12.00
5 Isiah Robertson 4.00 8.00
6 Jack Snow 4.00 8.00

1974 Rams Team Issue

The Rams issued this group of photos around 1974. Each measures roughly 5" by 7 1/4" and features a black and white player photo on blankbacked paper stock. There is a thin white border on three sides with roughly a 1" border below the photo. The team's helmet logo, player's name and position (initials) are included in the border below the photo. The Rams' helmet logo has a single bar facemask, is oriented to the left on all the photos unless noted below, and measures roughly 5/8" high. The photos are identical in format to the 1978 team issue. Any additions to the list below are appreciated.

COMPLETE SET (30) 100.00 200.00
1 Larry Brooks 4.00 8.00
2 Mike Burke 4.00 8.00
3 Bud Carson CO 5.00 10.00
4 Al Clark 4.00 8.00
5 Bill Curry 4.00 8.00
6 Dave Elmendorf 4.00 8.00
7 Clyde Evans ASST 4.00 8.00
8 Jack Faulkner ASST 4.00 8.00
9 Chuck Knox CO 5.00 10.00
10 Paul Lanham CO 4.00 8.00
11 Frank Lauterbur CO 4.00 8.00
12 Tom Mack 6.00 12.00
13 Lawrence McCutcheon 5.00 10.00
14 Willie McGee 4.00 8.00
15 Eddie McMillan 4.00 8.00
16 Phil Olsen 4.00 8.00
17 Jim Peterson 4.00 8.00
18 Tony Plummer 4.00 8.00
19 Steve Preece 4.00 8.00
20 David Ray 4.00 8.00
21 Jack Reynolds 5.00 10.00
22 Isiah Robertson 5.00 10.00
23 Rich Saul 4.00 8.00
24 Rob Scribner 4.00 8.00
25 Bob Stein 4.00 8.00
26 Tim Stokes 4.00 8.00
27 Charlie Stukes 4.00 8.00
28 Lionel Taylor CO 5.00 10.00
29 LaVern Torgeson CO 4.00 8.00
30 John Williams G 4.00 8.00

1978 Rams Team Issue

The Rams issued this group of photos around 1978. Each measures roughly 5" by 7 1/4" and features a black and white player photo on blankbacked paper stock. There is a thin white border on three sides with roughly a 1" border below the photo. The team's helmet logo, player's name and position (initials) are included in the border below the photo. The Rams' helmet logo has a single bar facemask, is oriented to the left on all the photos unless noted below, and measures roughly 5/8" high. The photos are identical in format to the 1974 team issue. Any additions to the list below are appreciated.

COMPLETE SET (37) 100.00 200.00
1 Bob Brudzinski 3.00 6.00
2 Frank Corral 3.00 6.00
3 Nolan Cromwell 3.00 6.00
4 Reggie Doss 3.00 6.00
5 Fred Dryer 4.00 8.00
6 Carl Ekern 3.00 6.00
7 Mike Fanning 3.00 6.00
8 Vince Ferragamo 4.00 8.00
9 Doug France 3.00 6.00
10 Ed Fulton 3.00 6.00
11 Pat Haden 4.00 8.00
12 Dennis Harrah 3.00 6.00
13 Greg Horton 3.00 6.00
14 Ron Jaworski 5.00 10.00
15 Ron Jessie 3.00 6.00
16 Jim Jodat 3.00 6.00
17 Cody Jones 3.00 6.00
18 Lawrence McCutcheon 3.00 6.00
19 Kevin McLain 3.00 6.00
20 Willie Miller 3.00 6.00
21 Joe Namath 12.50 25.00
22 Terry Nelson 3.00 6.00
23 Rod Perry 3.00 6.00
24 Rod Phillips 3.00 6.00
25 Jack Reynolds 4.00 8.00
26 Dan Ryczek 3.00 6.00
27 Bill Simpson 3.00 6.00
28 Jackie Slater 6.00 12.00
29 Doug Smith C 3.00 6.00
30 Ron Smith WR 3.00 6.00
31 Pat Thomas 3.00 6.00
32 Wendell Tyler 3.00 6.00
33 Billy Waddy 3.00 6.00
34 Glen Walker 3.00 6.00
35 Charle Young 3.00 6.00
36 Jack Youngblood 5.00 10.00
37 Jim Youngblood 3.00 6.00

1979 Rams Team Issue

The Rams issued this group of photos around 1979. Each measures roughly 5" by 7 1/4" and features a black and white player photo on blankbacked paper stock. There is a thin white border on three sides with roughly a 1" border below the photo. The team's helmet logo, player's name and position (initials) are included in the border below the photo. The Rams' helmet logo has a double bar facemask that is oriented to the left on all of the photos and measures roughly 5/8" high. The photos are identical in format to the 1978 team issue except for the double bar facemask instead of single. Any additions to the list below are appreciated.

COMPLETE SET (34) 75.00 150.00
1 George Andrews 3.00 6.00
2 Larry Brooks 3.00 6.00
3 Dave Elmendorf 3.00 6.00
4 Doug France 3.00 6.00
5 Dennis Harrah 3.00 6.00
6 Drew Hill 5.00 10.00
7 Eddie Hill 3.00 6.00
8 Bill Hickman ASST 3.00 6.00
9 Kent Hill 3.00 6.00
10 Ron Jessie 4.00 8.00
11 Jim Jodat 3.00 6.00
12 Cody Jones 3.00 6.00
13 Sid Justin 3.00 6.00
14 Lawrence McCutcheon 4.00 8.00
15 Kevin McLain 3.00 6.00
16 Terry Nelson 3.00 6.00
17 Dwayne O'Steen 3.00 6.00
18 Elvis Peacock 3.00 6.00
19 Rod Perry 3.00 6.00
20 Dan Radakovich CO 3.00 6.00
21 Jack Reynolds 4.00 8.00
22 Jeff Rutledge 3.00 6.00
23 Dan Ryczek 3.00 6.00
24 Rich Saul 3.00 6.00
25 Jackie Slater 6.00 12.00
26 Doug Smith 3.00 6.00
27 Ron Smith WR 3.00 6.00
28 Pat Thomas 3.00 6.00
29 Wendell Tyler 4.00 8.00
30 Billy Waddy 4.00 8.00
31 Jerry Wilkinson 3.00 6.00
32 Charle Young 4.00 8.00
33 Jack Youngblood 6.00 12.00
34 Jim Youngblood 3.00 6.00

1980 Rams Police

This unnumbered, 14-card set has been listed in the checklist below by uniform number, which appears on the fronts of the cards. The cards measure approximately 2 5/8" by 4 1/8". The Kiwanis Club, who sponsored this set along with the local law enforcement agency and the Rams, has their logo on the fronts of the cards. These cards, which contain "Rams Tips" on the backs, were distributed by police officers, one per week over a 14-week period.

COMPLETE SET (14) 10.00 20.00
11 Pat Haden 1.50 4.00
15 Vince Ferragamo 1.00 2.50
21 Nolan Cromwell 1.00 2.50
26 Wendell Tyler .75 2.00
32 Cullen Bryant .50 1.25
53 Jim Youngblood .50 1.25
59 Bob Brudzinski .40 1.00
61 Rich Saul .40 1.00
77 Doug France .40 1.00
82 Willie Miller .40 1.00
85 Jack Youngblood 2.00 5.00
88 Preston Dennard .40 1.00
90 Larry Brooks .40 1.00
NNO Ray Malavasi CO .40 1.00

1980 Rams Team Issue

The Rams issued this group of photos around 1980. Each measures roughly 5" by 7" or 5" by 7 1/4" and features a black and white player photo on blankbacked paper stock. There is a thin white border on three sides with roughly a 1" border below the photo. The team's helmet logo, player's name and position (spelled out) are included in the border below the photo. The Rams' helmet logo has a double bar facemask that is oriented to the left on all of the photos and measures roughly 1" high. The photos are identical in format to the 1979 team issue except for the larger (1") helmet logo. Any additions to the list below are appreciated.

COMPLETE SET (52) 100.00 200.00
1 George Andrews 2.00 5.00
2 Walt Arnold 2.00 5.00
3 Bill Bain 2.00 5.00
4 Larry Brooks 2.00 5.00
5 Bob Brudzinski 2.00 5.00
6 Cullen Bryant 2.00 5.00
7 Howard Carson 2.00 5.00
8 Frank Corral 2.00 5.00
9 Nolan Cromwell 2.00 5.00
10 Nolan Cromwell 2.00 5.00
11 Jeff Delaney 2.00 5.00
12 Preston Dennard 2.00 5.00
13 Reggie Doss 2.00 5.00
14 Fred Dryer 2.50 6.00
15 Carl Ekern 2.00 5.00
16 Mike Fanning 2.00 5.00
17 Doug France 2.00 5.00
18 Mike Guman 2.00 5.00
19 Pat Haden 2.50 6.00
20 Dennis Harrah 2.00 5.00
21 Joe Harris 2.00 5.00
22 Victor Hicks 2.00 5.00
23 Drew Hill 3.00 8.00
24 Eddie Hill 2.00 5.00
25 Kent Hill 2.00 5.00
26 LeRoy Irvin 2.00 5.00
27 Johnnie Johnson 2.00 5.00
28 Cody Jones 2.00 5.00
29 Jeff Kemp 2.00 5.00
30 Bob Lee 2.00 5.00
31 Ray Malavasi CO 2.00 5.00
32 Willie Miller 2.00 5.00
33 Jeff Moore 2.00 5.00
34 Phil Murphy 2.00 5.00
35 Terry Nelson 2.00 5.00
36 Irv Pankey 2.00 5.00
37 Herb Paterra CO 2.00 5.00
38 Elvis Peacock 2.00 5.00
39 Rod Perry 2.00 5.00
40 Jack Reynolds 2.50 6.00
41 Jeff Rutledge 2.00 5.00
42 Rich Saul 2.00 5.00
43 Jackie Slater 3.00 8.00
44 Doug Smith C 2.00 5.00
45 Lucious Smith 2.00 5.00
46 Ivory Sully 2.00 5.00
47 Jewerl Thomas 2.00 5.00
48 Pat Thomas 2.00 5.00
49 Wendell Tyler 2.50 6.00
50 Billy Waddy 2.50 6.00
51 Jack Youngblood 3.00 8.00
52 Jim Youngblood 2.00 5.00

1981 Rams Team Issue

The Rams issued this group of photos around 1980. Each measures roughly 5" by 7" or 5" by 7 1/4" and features a black and white player photo on blankbacked paper stock. There is a thin white border on three sides with roughly a 1" border below the photo. The team's helmet logo, player's name and position (spelled out) are included in the border below the photo. The Rams' helmet logo has a double bar facemask that is oriented to the left on all of the photos and measures roughly 1 1/8" high. The photos are nearly identical in format to the 1980 team issue except for the larger (1 1/8") helmet logo and the much thinner white border that surrounds three sides of the photo. Any additions to the list below are appreciated.

COMPLETE SET (10) 20.00 40.00
1 Henry Childs 2.00 5.00
2 Kirk Collins 2.00 5.00
3 Nolan Cromwell 2.00 5.00
4 Johnnie Johnson 2.00 5.00
5 Jeff Kemp 2.00 5.00
6 Willie Miller 2.00 5.00
7 Mel Owens 2.00 5.00
8 Jairo Penaranda 2.00 5.00
9 Rod Perry 2.00 5.00
10 Lucious Smith 2.00 5.00

1984 Rams Team Issue

The Rams issued this group of photos around 1984. Each measures roughly 5" by 7" and features a black and white player photo on blankbacked paper stock. There is a thin white border on three sides with roughly a 1" border below the photo. The team's helmet logo, player's name and position (spelled out) are included in the border below the photo. The Rams' helmet logo has a double bar facemask that is oriented to the left on all of the photos and measures roughly 1" high. The photos are identical in format to the 1980 team issue except that each player was photographed in their training camp mesh jerseys. Any additions to the list below are appreciated.

COMPLETE SET (16) 30.00 50.00
1 Dieter Brock 2.00 5.00
2 Jim Collins 1.25 3.00
3 Nolan Cromwell 1.25 3.00
4 Steve Dils 1.25 3.00
5 Reggie Doss 1.25 3.00
6 Carl Ekern 1.25 3.00
7 Henry Ellard 2.00 5.00
8 Dennis Harrah 1.25 3.00
9 Drew Hill 1.50 4.00
10 Kent Hill 1.25 3.00
11 Johnnie Johnson 1.25 3.00
12A Mike Lansford 1.25 3.00
12B Mike Lansford 1.25 3.00
13 Vince Newsome 1.25 3.00
14 Joe Shearin 1.25 3.00
15 Doug Smith C 1.25 3.00

1985 Rams Police

This set of cards was distributed by Police Officers in the Los Angeles area and sponsored by KIIS Radio. The unnumbered cards are listed alphabetically below. Uncut sheets of both the 1985 Rams and Raiders Police sets together are also on the market.

COMPLETE SET (15) 3.00 8.00
1 Bill Bain .20 .50
2 Mike Barber .30 .75
3 Dieter Brock .50 1.25
4 Nolan Cromwell .30 .75
5 Eric Dickerson 1.00 2.50
6 Reggie Doss .20 .50
7 Carl Ekern .20 .50
8 Kent Hill .20 .50
9 LeRoy Irvin .30 .75
10 Johnnie Johnson .20 .50
11 Jeff Kemp .50 1.25
12 Mike Lansford .20 .50
13 Mel Owens .20 .50
14 Barry Redden .20 .50
15 Mike Wilcher .20 .50

1985 Rams Smokey

This set of 24 cards was issued in the Summer of 1985 and features players of the Los Angeles Rams. The cards measure approximately 4" by 6". Each card photo also features Smokey Bear. The cards are numbered on the back essentially in alphabetical order; there are a few exceptions and two Smokey cards are unnumbered (listed at the end of the checklist below). Supposedly, LeRoy Irvin is more difficult to find than the other cards in the set.

COMPLETE SET (24) 15.00 30.00
1 George Andrews .40 1.00
2 Bill Bain .40 1.00
3 Russ Bolinger .40 1.00
4 Jim Collins .40 1.00
5 Nolan Cromwell .50 1.25
6 Reggie Doss .40 1.00
7 Carl Ekern .40 1.00
8 Vince Ferragamo .60 1.50
9 Gary Green .40 1.00
10 Mike Guman .40 1.00
11 David Hill .40 1.00
12 LeRoy Irvin SP 2.50 6.00
13 Mark Jerue .40 1.00
14 Johnnie Johnson .40 1.00
15 Jeff Kemp .50 1.25
16 Mel Owens .40 1.00
17 Irv Pankey .40 1.00
18 Doug Smith .40 1.00
19 Ivory Sully .40 1.00
20 Jack Youngblood .75 2.00
21 Mike McDonald .40 1.00
22 Norwood Vann .40 1.00
23 Smokey Bear .40 1.00
24 Smokey Bear .40 1.00

1986 Rams Smokey Flipbooks

In conjunction with California Fire Prevention, the Rams issued these flipbooks in 1986. The books contain a black and white flip movie of the player on one side and a movie of Smokey on the other side, along with fire prevention tips. The books measure approximately 2 3/4" by 4 1/2" and are unnumbered. We have assigned card numbers to them alphabetically.

COMPLETE SET (2) 3.00 8.00
1 Steve Dils 1.50 4.00
2 Mike Lansford 1.50 4.00

1987 Rams Ace Fact Pack

This 33-card set measures approximately 2 1/4" by 3 5/8" and has rounded corners. This set was manufactured in West Germany (by Ace Fact Pack) for release in Great Britain. There are 22 player cards in the set, checklisted below in alphabetical order. The backs of the cards feature a playing card design. The set contains members of the Los Angeles Rams.

COMPLETE SET (33) 40.00 100.00
1 Nolan Cromwell 2.00 5.00
2 Eric Dickerson 8.00 20.00
3 Reggie Doss 1.25 3.00
4 Carl Ekern 1.25 3.00
5 Henry Ellard 4.00 10.00
6 Jim Everett 2.50 6.00
7 Jerry Gray 2.00 5.00
8 Dennis Harrah 1.25 3.00
9 David Hill 1.25 3.00
10 Kevin House 2.00 5.00
11 LeRoy Irvin 2.00 5.00
12 Mark Jerue 1.25 3.00
13 Shawn Miller 1.25 3.00
14 Tom Newberry 2.00 5.00
15 Vince Newsome 1.25 3.00
16 Mel Owens 1.25 3.00
17 Irv Pankey 1.25 3.00
18 Doug Reed 1.25 3.00
19 Doug Smith 2.00 5.00
20 Jackie Slater 3.00 8.00
21 Charles White 2.00 5.00
22 Mike Wilcher 1.25 3.00
23 Rams Helmet 1.25 3.00
24 Rams Information 1.25 3.00
25 Rams Uniform 1.25 3.00
26 Game Record Holders 1.25 3.00
27 Season Record Holders 1.25 3.00
28 Career Record Holders 1.25 3.00
29 Record 1967-86 1.25 3.00
30 1986 Team Statistics 1.25 3.00
31 All-Time Greats 1.25 3.00
32 Roll of Honour 1.25 3.00
33 Anaheim Stadium 1.25 3.00

1987 Rams Jello/General Foods

This ten-card standard-size set was sponsored by Jello and Birds Eye and features players of the Los Angeles Rams. The cards are numbered on the back; card backs are printed in black ink on heavy white card stock. The set comes as a perforated sheet including a coupon each for Birds Eye Cob Corn and any Jello product. This unnumbered set is listed below alphabetically.

COMPLETE SET (10) 6.00 12.00
1 Ron Brown .40 1.00
2 Nolan Cromwell .40 1.00
3 Eric Dickerson 1.25 3.00
4 Carl Ekern .40 1.00
5 Jim Everett .75 2.00
6 Dennis Harrah .40 1.00
7 LeRoy Irvin .40 1.00
8 Mike Lansford .40 1.00
9 Jackie Slater .50 1.25
10 Doug Smith .40 1.00

1987 Rams Oscar Mayer

This 19-card standard-size set was sponsored by Oscar Mayer to honor the Special Teams Player of the Week. On a light blue background, the front features a color head shot inside a bullet hole design, with the jagged edges of the paper turned out. The team helmet and sponsor logo appear below the head shot. In dark blue print on white, the backs have biographical information as well as the Rams' helmet and the sponsor logo. The cards are unnumbered and checklisted below in alphabetical order.

COMPLETE SET (19) 25.00 50.00
1 Sam Anno 1.25 3.00
2 Ron Brown 1.50 4.00
3 Nolan Cromwell 1.50 4.00
4 Henry Ellard 2.00 5.00
5 Jerry Gray 1.50 4.00
6 Kevin Greene 2.50 6.00
7 Mike Guman 1.25 3.00
8 Dale Hatcher 1.25 3.00
9 Clifford Hicks 1.25 3.00
10 Mark Jerue 1.25 3.00
11 Johnnie Johnson 1.25 3.00
12 Larry Kelm 1.25 3.00
13 Mike Lansford 1.25 3.00
14 Vince Newsome 1.25 3.00
15 Michael Stewart 1.25 3.00
16 Mickey Sutton DB 1.25 3.00
17 Tim Tyrrell 1.25 3.00
18 Norwood Vann 1.25 3.00
19 Charles White 1.50 4.00

1989 Rams Police

This 16-card standard size set was issued in an uncut (perforated) sheet of 16 numbered cards which feature an action photo of various members of the 1989 Rams on the front and a football tip along with a safety tip on the back of the card. The safety tip features the popular anti-crime mascot McGruff. There was also a coupon for Frito-Lay products on the bottom of the sheet. The set was also sponsored by 7-Eleven stores.

COMPLETE SET (16) 5.00 12.00
1 John Robinson CO .60 1.50
2 Jim Everett .75 2.00
3 Doug Smith .50 1.25
4 Duval Love .40 1.00
5 Henry Ellard 1.00 2.50
6 Mel Owens .40 1.00
7 Jerry Gray .50 1.25
8 Kevin Greene 1.25 3.00
9 Vince Newsome .40 1.00
10 Irv Pankey .40 1.00
11 Tom Newberry .50 1.25
12 Pete Holohan .40 1.00
13 Mike Lansford .40 1.00
14 Greg Bell .50 1.25
15 Jackie Slater .50 1.25
16 Dale Hatcher .40 1.00

1990 Rams Knudsen

This six-card set (of bookmarks) which measures approximately 2" by 8" was produced by Knudsen's to help promote readership by people under 15 years old in the Los Angeles area. Between the Knudsen company name, the front features a color action photo of the player superimposed on a football stadium. The field is green, the bleachers are yellow with gray print, and the scoreboard above the player reads "The Reading Team". The box below the player gives brief biographical information and player highlights. The back has logos of the sponsors and describes two books that are available at the public library.

We have checklisted this set in alphabetical order because they are otherwise unnumbered except for the player's uniform number displayed on the card front.

COMPLETE SET (6)	10.00	25.00
1 Henry Ellard	2.40	6.00
2 Jim Everett	2.40	6.00
3 Jerry Gray	2.00	5.00
4 Pete Holohan	2.00	5.00
5 Mike Lansford	2.00	5.00
6 Irv Pankey	2.00	5.00

1990 Rams Smokey

This 12-card set features members of the 1990 Rams and was sponsored by local Fire Departments. Borderless cardfronts feature a color player photo with backs including a small black and white photo and player bio. The cards measure approximately 3 3/4" by 5 3/4" and are unnumbered.

COMPLETE SET (12)	8.00	20.00
1 Aaron Cox	.60	1.50
2 Henry Ellard	1.20	3.00
3 Jim Everett	.80	2.00
4 Jerry Gray	.60	1.50
5 Kevin Greene	1.20	3.00
6 Pete Holohan	.60	1.50
7 Mike Lansford	.60	1.50
8 Vince Newsome	.60	1.50
9 Doug Reed	.60	1.50
10 Jackie Slater	.80	2.00
11 Fred Strickland	.60	1.50
12 Mike Wilcher	.60	1.50

1992 Rams Carl's Jr.

This 21-card safety standard-size set was sponsored by Carl's Jr. restaurants and distributed by the Orange County Sheriff's Department. It was reported that 80,000 sets were produced. Eleven Rams players participated in the program with autograph sessions at six Carl's Junior restaurants in Southern California. The fronts feature color action player photos inside a blue picture frame on a white card face. Player information appears below the photo between a Rams' helmet and a "Drug Use is Life Abuse" warning. Printed in black on white, the horizontal backs have a black-and-white headshot, biography, player profile, and an anti-drug or alcohol slogan.

COMPLETE SET (21)	10.00	20.00
1 Carl Karcher	.40	1.00
2 Happy Star	.40	1.00
3 Tony Zendejas	.40	1.00
4 Henry Ellard	.60	1.50
5 Jackie Slater	.50	1.25
6 Bern Brostek	.40	1.00
7 Cleveland Gary	.40	1.00
8 Larry Kelm	.40	1.00
9 Roman Phifer	.40	1.00
10 Jim Everett	.50	1.25
11 Anthony Newman	.40	1.00
12 Steve Israel	.40	1.00
13 Marc Boutte	.40	1.00
14 Darryl Henley	.40	1.00
15 Michael Stewart	.40	1.00
16 Flipper Anderson	.50	1.25
17 Kevin Greene	.75	2.00
18 Sean Gilbert	.50	1.25
NNO Skippy	.40	1.00
NNO Spike	.40	1.00
NNO Wise Owl Mike	.40	1.00

1994 Rams L.A. Times

These 32 collector sheets were issued by the Los Angeles Times, were printed on semi-gloss paper, and measure approximately 5 1/2" by 8 1/2". The fronts feature color player action shots that are borderless, except at the bottom, where a yellow border carries the team name and helmet logo. The player's last name appears in large white vertical lettering near the right edge. The white back carries the player's name at the top, followed below by his uniform number, position, biography, head shot, career highlights and Rams 1994 game schedule. The sheets are numbered on the front as "X of 32." These sheets were distributed as inserts in weekend issues of the paper. Cleveland Gary and Marc Boutte were pulled from the set and not distributed since they were no longer with the Rams at the inception of the promotion.

COMPLETE SET (32)	4.80	12.00
1 Toby Wright	.15	.40
2 Tim Lester	.15	.40
3 Shane Conlan	.20	.50
4 Troy Drayton	.20	.50
5 Fred Stokes	.15	.40
6 Jerome Bettis	1.00	2.50
7 Jimmie Jones	.15	.40
8 Henry Rolling	.15	.40
9 Anthony Newman	.15	.40
10 Flipper Anderson	.30	.75
11 Steve Israel	.15	.40
12 Johnny Bailey	.15	.40
13 Jackie Slater	.20	.50
14 Chris Chandler	.20	.50
15 Sean Landeta	.15	.40
16 Bern Brostek	.15	.40
17 Roman Phifer	.15	.40
18 Robert Young	.20	.50
19 Leo Goeas	.15	.40
20 Chris Miller	.30	.75
21 Darryl Ashmore	.15	.40
22 Joe Kelly	.15	.40
23 Wayne Gandy	.20	.50
24 Tony Zendejas	.15	.40
25 Tom Newberry	.15	.40
26 David Lang	.15	.40
27 Sean Gilbert	.20	.50
28 Chris Martin	.15	.40
29 Thomas Homco	.15	.40
30 Chuck Knox CO	.20	.50
31 Todd Lyght	.20	.50
32 Jerome Bettis	.50	1.25

1995 Rams Upper Deck McDonald's

Upper Deck produced this set for distribution through McDonald's restaurants in the St.Louis area. The cards were sold in five-card packs for 79 cents per pack with the purchase of any McDonald's Value Meal. The cards were primarily available in the month of October and all royalties for the promotion were donated to Ronald McDonald Children's Charities. The phrases "Special Edition" and "Premiere Season" are printed in gold lettering running up the edge of the front, and the McDonald's logo appears in the upper right corner. The backs present biography, a second color photo, and a table displaying season-by-season statistics.

COMPLETE SET (26)	3.20	8.00
MCD1 Johnny Bailey	.08	.25
MCD2 Jerome Bettis	.50	1.25
MCD3 Isaac Bruce	1.20	3.00
MCD4 Kevin Carter	.50	1.25
MCD5 Shane Conlan	.08	.25
MCD6 Troy Drayton	.15	.40
MCD7 Wayne Gandy	.15	.40
MCD8 Sean Gilbert	.15	.40
MCD9 Jessie Hester	.08	.25
MCD10 Bern Brostek	.08	.25
MCD11 Jimmie Jones	.08	.25
MCD12 Todd Kinchen	.15	.40
MCD13 Sean Landeta	.08	.25
MCD14 Thomas Homco	.08	.25
MCD15 Todd Lyght	.08	.25
MCD16 Keith Lyle	.08	.25
MCD17 Chris Miller	.15	.40
MCD18 Toby Wright	.08	.25
MCD19 Anthony Parker	.08	.25
MCD20 Roman Phifer	.08	.25
MCD21 Leonard Russell	.08	.25
MCD22 Jackie Slater	.15	.40
MCD23 Fred Stokes	.08	.25
MCD24 Alexander Wright	.08	.25
MCD25 Robert Young	.15	.40
NNO Checklist Card	.15	.40

1996 Rams Team Issue

This 50-card set of the Los Angeles Rams features black-and-white player portaits in white borders measuring approximately 5" by 7" and sponsored by Northwest Plaza Mall. The team and sponsor logo is printed in the wide bottom margin. The backs carry player information and a large sponsor logo. The cards are unnumbered and checklisted below in alphabetical order.

COMPLETE SET (50)	20.00	50.00
1 Tony Banks	2.40	6.00
2 Chuck Belin	.40	1.00
3 Bern Brostek	.40	1.00
4 Isaac Bruce	2.40	6.00
5 Kevin Carter	.60	1.50
6 Hayward Clay	.40	1.00
7 Ernie Conwell	.40	1.00
8 Keith Crawford	.40	1.00
9 Torin Dorn	.40	1.00
10 D'Marco Farr	.40	1.00
11 Cedric Figaro	.40	1.00
12 Wayne Gandy	.40	1.00
13 Percell Gaskins	.40	1.00
14 Leo Goeas	.40	1.00
15 Harold Green	.40	1.00
16 Mike Gruttadauria	.40	1.00
17 Derrick Harris	.40	1.00
18 James Harris	.40	1.00
19 Tom Homco	.40	1.00
20 Carlos Jenkins	.40	1.00
21 Jimmie Jones	.40	1.00
22 Robert Jones	.40	1.00
23 Eddie Kennison	1.60	4.00
24 Jon Kirksey	.40	1.00
25 Aaron Laing	.40	1.00
26 Sean Landeta	.40	1.00
27 Jeremy Lincoln	.40	1.00
28 Chip Lohmiller	.40	1.00
29 Todd Lyght	.40	1.00
30 Keith Lyle	.40	1.00
31 Jamie Martin	1.25	3.00
32 Gerald McBurrows	.40	1.00
33 Fred Miller	.40	1.00
34 Jerald Moore	.60	1.50
35 Leslie O'Neal	.60	1.50
36 Chuck Osborne	.40	1.00
37 Anthony Parker	.40	1.00
38 Roman Phifer	.40	1.00
39 Lawrence Phillips	1.00	2.50
40 Greg Robinson	.40	1.00
41 Jermaine Ross	.40	1.00
42 Mike Scurlock	.40	1.00
43 J.T. Thomas	.40	1.00
44 Steve Walsh	.60	1.50
45 Alberto White	.40	1.00
46 Dwayne White	.40	1.00
47 Zach Wiegert	.40	1.00
48 Billy Williams	.40	1.00
49 Alexander Wright	.40	1.00
50 Toby Wright	.40	1.00

1997 Rams Team Issue

This 53-card set was released by the team for fans and player appearances. Each measures roughly 5" by 7" and features a black and white player photo on the front. The cardbacks include player information and the Northwest Plaza Mall sponsor logo. The unnumbered cards are listed below alphabetically.

COMPLETE SET (53)	20.00	50.00
1 Taje Allen	.40	1.00
2 Tony Banks	1.60	4.00
3 Will Brice	.40	1.00
4 Bern Brostek	.40	1.00
5 Isaac Bruce	2.40	6.00
6 Kevin Carter	.60	1.50
7 Charlie Clemons	.60	1.50
8 Ernie Conwell	.40	1.00
9 Keith Crawford	.40	1.00
10 Nate Dingle	.40	1.00
11 Ernest Dye	.40	1.00
12 D'Marco Farr	.40	1.00
13 Will Furrer	.40	1.00
14 Wayne Gandy	.40	1.00
15 John Gerak	.40	1.00
16 Mike Gruttadauria	.40	1.00
17 Britt Hager	.40	1.00
18 Derrick Harris	.40	1.00
19 Craig Heyward	.60	1.50
20 Mitch Jacoby	.40	1.00
21 Billy Jenkins Jr.	.40	1.00
22 Bill Johnson	.40	1.00
23 Mike Jones	.40	1.00
24 Robert Jones	.40	1.00
25 Muadianvita Kazadi	.40	1.00
26 Eddie Kennison	1.00	2.50
27 Aaron Laing	.40	1.00
28 Amp Lee	.40	1.00
29 Todd Lyght	.40	1.00
30 Keith Lyle	.40	1.00
31 Gerald McBurrows	.40	1.00
32 Dexter McCleon	1.00	2.50
33 Ryan McNeil	.40	1.00
34 Fred Miller	.40	1.00
35 Jerald Moore	.60	1.50
36 Ron Moore	.60	1.50
37 Leslie O'Neal	.40	1.00
38 Orlando Pace	1.00	2.50
39 Roman Phifer	.40	1.00
40 Lawrence Phillips	.60	1.50
41 Bryan Robinson	.40	1.00
42 Jeff Robinson	.40	1.00
43 Jermaine Ross	.40	1.00
44 Mark Rypien	.60	1.50
45 Torrance Small	.40	1.00
46 Vernice Smith	.40	1.00
47 J.T. Thomas	.40	1.00
48 Marquis Walker	.40	1.00
49 Zach Wiegert	.40	1.00
50 Jay Williams	.40	1.00
51 Jeff Wilkins	.40	1.00
52 Toby Wright	.40	1.00
53 Jeff Zgonina	.40	1.00

1998 Rams Team Issue

This set was released by the team for fans and player appearances. Each measures roughly 5" by 7" and features a black and white player photo on the front along with the title sponsor's logo - Sprint. The cardbacks include player information and additional sponsor logos. The unnumbered cards are listed below alphabetically.

COMPLETE SET (52)	60.00	100.00
1 Ray Agnew	.40	1.00
2 Taje Allen	.40	1.00
3 Tyji Armstrong	.40	1.00
4 Tony Banks	1.00	2.50
5 Steve Bono	.60	1.50
6 Ethan Brooks	.40	1.00
7 Issac Bruce	1.00	2.50
8 Kevin Carter	.60	1.50
9 Charlie Clemons	.60	1.50
10 Ernie Conwell	.40	1.00
11 D'Marco Farr	.40	1.00
12 John Flannery	.40	1.00
13 London Fletcher	1.25	3.00
14 Wayne Gandy	.40	1.00
15 Mike Gruttadauria	.40	1.00
16 Derrick Harris	.40	1.00
17 Az-Zahir Hakim	2.50	5.00
18 June Henley	.40	1.00
19 Eric Hill	.40	1.00
20 Greg Hill	.60	1.50
21 Robert Holcombe	1.25	3.00
22 Tony Horne	1.00	2.50
23 Billy Jenkins	.40	1.00
24 Mike Jones LB	.40	1.00
25 Mike Jones DE	.40	1.00
26 Eddie Kennison	1.00	2.50
27 Leonard Little	1.00	2.50
28 Todd Lyght	.40	1.00
29 Keith Lyle	.40	1.00
30 Gerald McBurrows	.40	1.00
31 Dexter McCleon	.60	1.50
32 Ryan McNeil	.40	1.00
33 Fred Miller	.40	1.00
34 Jerald Moore	.60	1.50
35 Tom Nutten	.40	1.00
36 Orlando Pace	.60	1.50
37 Roman Phifer	.40	1.00
38 Joe Phillips	.40	1.00
39 Ricky Proehl	.60	1.50
40 Jeff Robinson	.40	1.00
41 Mike Scurlock	.40	1.00
42 Lorenzo Styles	.40	1.00
43 J.T. Thomas	.40	1.00
44 Ryan Tucker	.40	1.00
45 Rick Tuten	.40	1.00
46 Kurt Warner	30.00	60.00
47 Zach Wiegert	.40	1.00
48 Jeff Wilkins	.40	1.00
49 Jay Williams	.40	1.00
50 Roland Williams	.40	1.00
51 Grant Wistrom	.60	1.50
52 Toby Wright	.40	1.00

1999 Rams Reader Team

These cards were produced by the Rams and distributed to school students as part of the Rams Reader Team program. Each unnumbered card features a color photo of the player on the cardfront with a brief bio on the back.

COMPLETE SET (5)	4.00	10.00
1 Tony Banks	1.20	3.00
2 Isaac Bruce	1.60	4.00
3 Kevin Carter	.60	1.50
4 Keith Lyle	.40	1.00
5 Jeff Wilkins	.40	1.00

1999 Rams Team Issue

These cards were released by the team for fans and player autograph appearances. Each measures roughly 5" by 7" and features a black and white player photo on the front. The cardbacks include player information and sponsor logos. The unnumbered cards are listed below alphabetically.

COMPLETE SET (53)	50.00	80.00
1 Ray Agnew	.40	1.00
2 Taje Allen	.40	1.00
3 Lionel Barnes	.40	1.00
4 Dre Bly	1.00	2.50
5 Isaac Bruce	2.00	4.00
6 Devin Bush	.40	1.00
7 Ron Carpenter DB	.40	1.00
8 Kevin Carter	.60	1.50
9 Charlie Clemons	.60	1.50
10 Rich Coady	.40	1.00
11 Todd Collins	.40	1.00
12 Ernie Conwell	.40	1.00
13 D'Marco Farr	.40	1.00
14 Marshall Faulk	4.00	8.00
15 London Fletcher	1.00	2.50
16 Joe Germaine	1.50	4.00
17 Trent Green	1.00	2.50
18 Mike Gruttadauria	.40	1.00
19 Az-Zahir Hakim	1.00	2.50
20 James Hodgins	.40	1.00
21 Robert Holcombe	.60	1.50
22 Torry Holt	5.00	10.00
23 Tony Horne	1.00	2.50
24 Gaylon Hyder	.40	1.00
25 Billy Jenkins	.40	1.00
26 Willie Jones	.40	1.00
27 Paul Justin	.40	1.00
28 Amp Lee	.40	1.00
29 Chad Lewis	.40	1.00
30 Chad Levitt	.40	1.00
31 Todd Lyght	.40	1.00
32 Keith Lyle	.40	1.00
33 Dexter McCleon	.60	1.50
34 Andy McCollum	.40	1.00
35 Fred Miller	.40	1.00
36 Mike Morton	.40	1.00
37 Tom Nutten	.40	1.00
38 Orlando Pace	.60	1.50
39 Troy Pelshak	.40	1.00
40 Ricky Proehl	.60	1.50
41 Jeff Robinson	.40	1.00
42 Cameron Spikes	.40	1.00
43 Lorenzo Styles	.40	1.00
44 Adam Timmerman	.40	1.00
45 Ryan Tucker	.40	1.00
46 Rick Tuten	.40	1.00
47 Kurt Warner	12.50	25.00
48 Justin Watson	.40	1.00
49 Jeff Wilkins	.40	1.00
50 Jay Williams	.40	1.00
51 Roland Williams	.40	1.00
52 Grant Wistrom	.60	1.50
53 Jeff Zgonina	.40	1.00

2000 Rams Bank of America

This card was released in the seat cushions at Super Bowl XXXIV. It features 3-Rams players and was produced on a thick plastic stock with the "magic motion" style printing process.

1 K.Warner I.Bruce M.Faulk	24.00	60.00

2000 Rams Future and Hope

These three cards were produced and distributed by the religious organization www.futureandhope.org. Each card features a Rams player on the front along with the team name, year, and a short religious message. The unnumbered cardbacks include some brief player biographical information as well as a number of additional religious messages.

COMPLETE SET (3)	2.50	5.00
1 Isaac Bruce	.75	2.00
2 Ernie Conwell	.60	1.50
3 Kurt Warner	1.25	3.00

2000 Rams Team Issue

The Rams continued their oversized card program in 2000. These cards were released by the team to fulfill fan requests and for player appearances. Each measures roughly 5" by 7" and features a black and white player photo on the front along with the title sponsor's logo - Sega Sports. The cardbacks include player information and additional sponsor logos. The unnumbered cards are listed below alphabetically.

COMPLETE SET (54)	50.00	80.00
1 Ray Agnew	.40	1.00
2 Taje Allen	.40	1.00
3 John Baker	.40	1.00
4 Lionel Barnes	.40	1.00
5 Dre Bly	.40	1.00
6 Matt Bowen	.40	1.00
7 Isaac Bruce	2.00	4.00
8 Devin Bush	.40	1.00
9 Trung Canidate	2.00	5.00
10 Kevin Carter	.60	1.50
11 Rich Coady	.40	1.00
12 Todd Collins	.40	1.00
13 Ernie Conwell	.40	1.00
14 Steve Everitt	.40	1.00
15 D'Marco Farr	.40	1.00
16 Marshall Faulk	4.00	8.00
17 London Fletcher	.75	2.00
18 Joe Germaine	.60	1.50
19 Trent Green	1.00	2.50
20 Az-Zahir Hakim	.60	1.50
21 Nate Hobgood-Chittick	.40	1.00
22 James Hodgins	.40	1.00
23 Robert Holcombe	.60	1.50
24 Torry Holt	2.00	5.00
25 Tony Horne	.60	1.50
26 Mike Jones LB	.40	1.00
27 Leonard Little	1.00	2.50
28 Todd Lyght	.40	1.00
29 Keith Lyle	.40	1.00
30 Dexter McCleon	.40	1.00
31 Andy McCollum	.40	1.00
32 Keith Miller	.40	1.00
33 Sean Moran	.40	1.00
34 Kaulana Noa	.40	1.00
35 Tom Nutten	.40	1.00
36 Orlando Pace	.60	1.50
37 Ricky Proehl	.60	1.50
38 Jeff Robinson	.40	1.00
39 Jacoby Shepherd	.40	1.00
40 Jamel Smith	.40	1.00
41 Cameron Spikes	.40	1.00
42 John St.Clair	.40	1.00
43 Lorenzo Styles	.40	1.00
44 Pete Swanson	.40	1.00
45 Chris Thomas	.40	1.00
46 Adam Timmerman	.40	1.00
47 Ryan Tucker	.40	1.00
48 Kurt Warner	10.00	20.00
49 Justin Watson	.40	1.00
50 Jeff Wilkins	.40	1.00
51 Roland Williams	.40	1.00
52 Grant Wistrom	.60	1.50
53 Brian Young	.40	1.00
54 Jeff Zgonina	.40	1.00

2001 Rams Future and Hope

These three cards were produced and distributed by the religious organization www.futureandhope.org. Each card features a Rams player on the front along with the year printed in a small red box. The unnumbered cardbacks include some brief player biographical information as well as a number of religious messages.

COMPLETE SET (3)	2.50	5.00
1 Ray Agnew	.60	1.50
2 Trung Canidate	.75	2.00
3 Kurt Warner	1.25	3.00

2001 Rams Team Issue

Cards from this set were issued by the team for fan mail requests and player autograph appearances. Each measures roughly 5" by 7" and features a black and white player photo on the front along with the Rams helmet and Reebok logo. The cardbacks include player information and sponsor logos with Reebok being the main sponsor. The unnumbered cards are listed below alphabetically.

COMPLETE SET (54)	50.00	80.00
1 Chidi Ahanotu	.40	1.00
2 Brian Allen	.60	1.50
3 Adam Archuleta	1.00	2.50
4 Kole Ayi	.40	1.00
5 John Baker	.40	1.00
6 Dre Bly	.40	1.00
7 Matt Bowen	.40	1.00
8 Isaac Bruce	2.00	4.00
9 Marc Bulger	6.00	12.00
10 Jerametrius Butler	.40	1.00
11 Trung Canidate	.60	1.50
12 Rich Coady	.40	1.00
13 Dustin Cohen	.40	1.00
14 Ernie Conwell	.40	1.00
15 Don Davis	.40	1.00
16 Marshall Faulk	4.00	8.00
17 Mark Fields	.40	1.00
18 London Fletcher	.40	1.00
19 Frank Garcia	.40	1.00
20 Az-Zahir Hakim	.60	1.50
21 Kim Herring	.40	1.00
22 James Hodgins	.40	1.00
23 Robert Holcombe	.60	1.50
24 Torry Holt	1.50	4.00
25 Tyoka Jackson	.40	1.00
26 Rod Jones	.40	1.00
27 Paul Justin	.40	1.00
28 Damione Lewis	.40	1.00
29 Leonard Little	.60	1.50
30 Brandon Manumaleuna	.40	1.00
31 Jamie Martin	1.00	2.50
32 Dexter McCleon	.40	1.00
33 Andy McCollum	.40	1.00
34 Sean Moran	.40	1.00
35 Yo Murphy	.60	1.50
36 Kaulana Noa	.40	1.00
37 Tom Nutten	.40	1.00
38 Orlando Pace	.60	1.50
39 Ryan Pickett	.40	1.00
40 Tommy Polley	.60	1.50
41 Ricky Proehl	.60	1.50
42 Jeff Robinson	.40	1.00
43 Jacoby Shepherd	.40	1.00
44 John St.Clair	.40	1.00
45 Cameron Spikes	.40	1.00
46 Adam Timmerman	.40	1.00
47 Ryan Tucker	.40	1.00
48 Kurt Warner	6.00	15.00
49 Justin Watson	.40	1.00
50 Jeff Wilkins	.40	1.00
51 Aeneas Williams	.60	1.50
52 Grant Wistrom	.60	1.50
53 Brian Young	.40	1.00
54 Jeff Zgonina	.40	1.00

2002 Rams Team Issue

Cards from this set were issued by the team for fan mail requests and player autograph appearances. Each measures roughly 5" by 7" and features a color player photo on the front along with the Rams helmet and a Gatorade sponsorship logo. The cardbacks include a player bio and small black and white photo. The unnumbered cards are listed below alphabetically.

COMPLETE SET (53)	50.00	80.00
1 Adam Archuleta	.60	1.50
2 Kole Ayi	.40	1.00
3 Steve Bellisari	1.00	2.50
4 Mitch Berger	.40	1.00
5 Dre Bly	.40	1.00
6 Isaac Bruce	2.00	4.00
7 Marc Bulger	2.50	6.00
8 Courtland Bullard	.40	1.00
9 Jerametrius Butler	.40	1.00
10 Trung Canidate	1.00	2.50
11 Ernie Conwell	.40	1.00
12 Chad Cota	.40	1.00
13 Don Davis	.40	1.00
14 Jamie Duncan	.40	1.00
15 Troy Edwards	.40	1.00
16 Marshall Faulk	2.50	6.00
17 Bryce Fisher	1.00	2.50
18 Travis Fisher	.40	1.00
19 Frank Garcia	.40	1.00
20 Lamar Gordon	.50	1.25
21 Chris Hetherington	.40	1.00
22 Kim Herring	.40	1.00
23 James Hodgins	.40	1.00
24 Torry Holt	1.50	4.00
25 Heath Irwin	.40	1.00
26 Tyoka Jackson	.40	1.00
27 Damione Lewis	.40	1.00
28 Leonard Little	.40	1.00
29 Brandon Manumaleuna	.40	1.00
30 Chris Massey	.40	1.00
31 Jamie Martin	.60	1.50
32 Dexter McCleon	.40	1.00
33 Andy McCollum	.40	1.00
34 Yo Murphy	.40	1.00
35 Tom Nutten	.40	1.00
36 Orlando Pace	.60	1.50
37 Ryan Pickett	.40	1.00
38 Tommy Polley	.40	1.00
39 Ricky Proehl	.60	1.50
40 Travis Scott	.40	1.00
41 Nick Sorensen	.40	1.00
42 John St. Clair	.40	1.00
43 Robert Thomas	.60	1.50
44 Adam Timmerman	.40	1.00
45 Kurt Warner	6.00	12.00
46 James Whitley	.40	1.00
47 Jeff Wilkins	.40	1.00
48 Terrence Wilkins	.40	1.00
49 Aeneas Williams	.60	1.50
50 Grant Williams	.40	1.00
51 Grant Wistrom	.60	1.50
52 Brian Young	.40	1.00
53 Jeff Zgonina	.40	1.00

2006 Rams Topps

COMPLETE SET (12)	3.00	5.00
STL1 Marc Bulger	.25	.60
STL2 Isaac Bruce	.40	1.00
STL3 Shaun McDonald	.25	.60
STL4 Kevin Curtis	.30	.75
STL5 Steven Jackson	.25	.60
STL6 Torry Holt	.30	.75
STL7 Marshall Faulk	.30	.75
STL8 Ryan Fitzpatrick	.40	1.00
STL9 Jeff Wilkins	.25	.60
STL10 Orlando Pace	.25	.60
STL11 Tye Hill	.25	.60
STL12 Joe Klopfenstein	.25	.60

2007 Rams Topps

COMPLETE SET (12)	2.50	5.00
1 Marc Bulger	.40	1.00
2 Torry Holt	.50	1.25
3 Steven Jackson	.40	1.00
4 Isaac Bruce	.60	1.50
5 Leonard Little	.40	1.00
6 Randy McMichael	.40	1.00
7 Jeff Wilkins	.40	1.00
8 Will Witherspoon	.40	1.00
9 Joe Klopfenstein	.40	1.00
10 Drew Bennett	.40	1.00
11 Brian Leonard	.40	1.00
12 Adam Carriker	.40	1.00

2008 Rams Topps

COMPLETE SET (12)	2.50	5.00
1 Steven Jackson	.40	1.00
2 Torry Holt	.50	1.25
3 Marc Bulger	.40	1.00
4 Trent Green	.40	1.00
5 Randy McMichael	.40	1.00
6 Corey Chavous	.40	1.00
7 Brian Leonard	.40	1.00
8 O.J. Atogwe	.40	1.00
9 Drew Bennett	.40	1.00
10 Will Witherspoon	.40	1.00
11 Chris Long	.50	1.25
12 Donnie Avery	.50	1.25

1961 Random House Football Portfolio

These color photos were issued as a set in the early 1960s by Random House. They were distributed in a colorful folder that featured the title "Football Portfolio" at the top and the Random House identification at the bottom. The body of the folder included the image of the Giants and Packers with Y.A. Tittle in the foreground. Each photo features a color image of a player or game action with only the photographer's notation on the front to use as identification. The backs are blank and the photos are borderless and measure roughly 7 7/8" by 11".

COMPLETE SET (6)	75.00	150.00
1 Bart Starr	15.00	40.00
2 Jim Taylor	12.50	30.00
3 Bart Starr Jerry Kramer	12.50	30.00
4 Jim Taylor being tackled	10.00	25.00
5 Giants vs. Packers game action	12.50	30.00
6 Don Chandler Phil King	7.50	20.00

1996 Ravens Score Board/Exxon

Score Board produced this team set for distribution by the Baltimore area Exxon stations. Each card appears similar to a 1996 Pro Line card, but contains the Score Board logo at the top. The Exxon sponsor logo appears only on the checklist card. Packs could be obtained, with the appropriate gasoline purchase, for 49-cents each and contained three-player cards and a checklist card.

COMPLETE SET (9)	1.50	4.00
BR1 Vinny Testaverde	.15	.40
BR2 Eric Zeier	.15	.40
BR3 Earnest Byner	.08	.25
BR4 Derrick Alexander WR	.30	.75
BR5 Michael Jackson	.15	.40
BR6 Jonathan Ogden	.60	1.50
BR7 Ray Lewis	1.00	2.50
BR8 Eric Turner	.08	.25
BR9 Ravens Checklist	.08	.25

2005 Ravens Activa Medallions

COMPLETE SET (22)	30.00	60.00
1 Kyle Boller	1.25	3.00
2 Orlando Brown	1.25	3.00
3 Mark Clayton	1.00	2.50
4 Will Demps	1.25	3.00
5 Mike Flynn	1.25	3.00
6 Kelly Gregg	1.25	3.00
7 Todd Heap	1.25	3.00
8 Jamal Lewis	1.50	4.00
9 Ray Lewis	1.50	4.00
10 Derrick Mason	1.25	3.00
11 Chris McCallister	1.25	3.00
12 Edwin Mulatalo	1.25	3.00
13 Jonathan Ogden	1.25	3.00
14 Ed Reed	1.25	3.00
15 Samari Rolle	1.25	3.00
16 Deion Sanders	1.50	4.00
17 Matt Stover	1.25	3.00
18 Terrell Suggs	1.25	3.00
19 Chester Taylor	1.25	3.00
20 Adalius Thomas	1.25	3.00
21 Anthony Weaver	1.25	3.00
22 Ravens Logo	1.00	2.50

2006 Ravens Topps

COMPLETE SET (12)	3.00	6.00
BAL1 Mike Anderson	.25	.60
BAL2 Ray Lewis	.40	1.00
BAL3 Jonathan Ogden	.30	.75
BAL4 Kyle Boller	.25	.60
BAL5 Derrick Mason	.25	.60
BAL6 Mark Clayton	.25	.60
BAL7 Ed Reed	.30	.75
BAL8 Chris McAlister	.25	.60
BAL9 Jamal Lewis	.30	.75
BAL10 Todd Heap	.25	.60
BAL11 Haloti Ngata	.30	.75
BAL12 Demetrius Williams	.25	.60

2007 Ravens Topps

COMPLETE SET (12)	2.50	5.00
1 Willis McGahee	.40	1.00
2 Todd Heap	.40	1.00
3 Steve McNair	.50	1.25
4 Mark Clayton	.40	1.00
5 Ray Lewis	.60	1.50
6 Ed Reed	.50	1.25
7 Trevor Pryce	.40	1.00
8 Terrell Suggs	.40	1.00
9 Derrick Mason	.40	1.00
10 Jonathan Ogden	.50	1.25
11 Chris McAlister	.40	1.00
12 Troy Smith	.40	1.00

2008 Ravens Topps

COMPLETE SET (12)	3.00	6.00
1 Kyle Boller	.40	1.00
2 Willis McGahee	.40	1.00
3 Derrick Mason	.40	1.00
4 Ray Lewis	.60	1.50
5 Ed Reed	.50	1.25
6 Todd Heap	.40	1.00
7 Jonathan Ogden	.50	1.25
8 Troy Smith	.50	1.25
9 Mark Clayton	.40	1.00
10 Terrell Suggs	.40	1.00
11 Joe Flacco	.75	2.00
12 Ray Rice	.40	1.00

2009 Ravens Breast Cancer Awareness

This three card set was issued at a home game in 2009. Each unnumbered card was created by one of the three NFL licensed manufacturers and features the pink ribbon breast cancer awareness logo on the fronts.

COMPLETE SET (3)	2.50	5.00
1 Joe Flacco Upper Deck	.75	2.00
2 Ray Lewis Topps	1.00	2.50
3 Derrick Mason Panini	.60	1.50

2012 Ravens Topps Super Bowl XLVII

COMPLETE SET (5)	3.00	6.00
ER Ed Reed	.50	1.25
JF Joe Flacco	.50	1.25
RL Ray Lewis	.60	1.50
RR Ray Rice	.40	1.00
TS Torrey Smith	.40	1.00

1962-66 Rawlings Advisory Staff Photos

These photos were likely issued over a period of years in the early to mid-1960s. Each is unnumbered and checklisted below in alphabetical order. The cards measure roughly 8 1/8" by 10 1/8" and include a white box containing the player's facsimile autograph and Rawlings Advisory Staff identification lines. Any additions to the list below are appreciated.

COMMON CARD (1-13)	7.50	15.00
1 Jim Bakken	7.50	15.00
2 Billy Cannon	10.00	20.00
3 Roman Gabriel	15.00	25.00
4 John Hadl	15.00	25.00
5 Jim Hart	15.00	25.00
6 Harlon Hill	7.50	15.00
7 Bobby Layne	20.00	40.00
8 Don Meredith	20.00	40.00
9 Sonny Randle	7.50	15.00
10 Kyle Rote	10.00	20.00
11 Tobin Rote	7.50	15.00
12 John Stofa	7.50	15.00
13 Alex Webster	7.50	15.00

1976 RC Cola Colts Cans

This set of RC Cola cans was release in the Baltimore area and featured members of the Colts. The cans are blue and feature a black and white player photo. They are similar in design to the nationally issued 1977 set but include a red banner below the player's photo as well as different statistics for each player versus the 1977 release. Prices below reflect that of opened empty cans.

COMPLETE SET (43)	50.00	100.00
1 Mike Barnes	1.50	3.00
2 Tim Baylor	1.50	3.00
3 Forrest Blue	2.00	4.00
4 Roger Carr	1.50	3.00
5 Raymond Chester	2.00	4.00
6 Jim Cheyunski	1.50	3.00
7 Elmer Collett	1.50	3.00
8 Fred Cook	1.50	3.00
9 Dan Dickel	1.50	3.00
10 John Dutton	1.50	3.00
11 Joe Ehrmann	2.00	4.00
12 Ron Fernandes	1.50	3.00
13 Glenn Doughty	1.50	3.00
14 Randy Hall	1.50	3.00
15 Ken Huff	1.50	3.00
16 Bert Jones	3.00	6.00
17 Jimmie Kennedy	1.50	3.00
18 Mike Kirkland	1.50	3.00
19 George Kunz	1.50	3.00
20 Bruce Laird	1.50	3.00
21 Roosevelt Leaks	2.00	4.00
22 David Lee	2.00	4.00
23 Ron Lee	1.50	3.00
24 Toni Linhart	1.50	3.00
25 Derrel Luce	1.50	3.00
26 Don McCauley	2.00	4.00
27 Ken Mendenhall	1.50	3.00
28 Lydell Mitchell	3.00	6.00
29 Lloyd Mumphord	2.00	4.00
30 Nelson Munsey	1.50	3.00
31 Ken Novak	1.50	3.00
32 Ray Oldham	1.50	3.00
33 Robert Pratt	1.50	3.00
34 Sanders Shiver	1.50	3.00
35 Freddie Scott	1.50	3.00
36 Ed Simonini	1.50	3.00
37 Howard Stevens	1.50	3.00
38 David Taylor	1.50	3.00
39 Ricky Thompson	1.50	3.00
40 Bill Troup	1.50	3.00
41 Jackie Wallace	1.50	3.00
42 Bob Van Duyne	1.50	3.00
43 Stan White	2.00	4.00

1977 RC Cola Cans

RC Cola distributed this set of cans regionally in NFL team areas. Each can features a black and white NFL player photo along with a brief player summary and a football trivia question. Quite a few variations exist with regards to the trivia question presented on the can and we've included the first few words of the trivia question for those known variations. Ten players were issued for each NFL team, except for the Washington Redskins which featured over 40. We've catalogued the set below according to team (alphabetized). Prices below reflect opened empty cans.

COMPLETE SET (298)	500.00	1000.00
1 Steve Bartkowski	3.00	6.00
2 Bubba Bean	2.00	4.00
3 Ray Brown	2.00	4.00
4A John Gilliam (Jake Scott holds...)	2.00	4.00
4B John Gilliam (Ken Anderson completed...)	2.00	4.00
5 Claude Humphrey	3.00	6.00
6A Alfred Jenkins (Jackie Smith holds...)	2.00	4.00
6B Alfred Jenkins (Don Cockroft is...)	2.00	4.00
7A Nick Mike-Mayer (Bert Jones holds...)	2.00	4.00
7B Nick Mike-Mayer (Walter Payton had...)	2.00	4.00
8 Jim Mitchell	2.00	4.00
9 Ralph Ortega	2.00	4.00
10A Jeff Van Note (Bert Jones holds...)	2.00	4.00
10B Jeff Van Note (Don Woods set...)	2.00	4.00
11 Forrest Blue	2.00	4.00
12 Raymond Chester	2.00	4.00
13 Joe Ehrmann	2.00	4.00
14 Bert Jones	3.00	6.00
15 Roosevelt Leaks	2.00	4.00
16 David Lee	2.00	4.00
17 Don McCauley	2.00	4.00
18 Lydell Mitchell	2.00	4.00
19 Lloyd Mumphord	2.00	4.00
20 Stan White	2.00	4.00
21 Marv Bateman	2.00	4.00
22 Bob Chandler	3.00	6.00
23 Joe DeLamielleure	3.00	6.00
24 Joe Ferguson	3.00	6.00
25 Dave Foley	2.00	4.00
26 Steve Freeman	2.00	4.00
27 Mike Kadish	2.00	4.00
28 Jeff Lloyd	2.00	4.00
29 Reggie McKenzie	3.00	6.00
30 Bob Nelson	2.00	4.00
31 Lionel Antoine	2.00	4.00
32 Bob Avellini	2.00	4.00
33 Brian Baschnagel	2.00	4.00
34 Waymond Bryant	2.00	4.00
35 Doug Buffone	2.00	4.00
36A Wally Chambers (Jackie Smith holds...)	2.00	4.00
36B Wally Chambers (Don Cockroft is...)	2.00	4.00
37A Virgil Livers (Walter Payton had...)	2.00	4.00
37B Virgil Livers (Jake Scott holds...)	2.00	4.00
38 Johnny Musso	2.00	4.00
39 Walter Payton	20.00	40.00
40 Bo Rather	2.00	4.00
41 Ken Anderson	3.00	6.00
42 Coy Bacon	2.00	4.00
43A Tommy Casanova (Lydell Mitchell hadâ¦)	2.00	4.00
43B Tommy Casanova (Fred Dryer holdsâ¦)	2.00	4.00
44A Boobie Clark (Lydell Mitchell hadâ¦)	2.00	4.00
44B Boobie Clark (MacArthur Lane caughtâ¦)	2.00	4.00
45A Archie Griffin (Dan Pastorini holds...)	3.00	6.00
45B Archie Griffin (Rocky Bleier rushed...)	3.00	6.00
46A Jim LeClair Ken Houston holds...)	2.00	4.00
46B Jim LeClair Steve Grogan ran...)	2.00	4.00
47A Rufus Mayes (John Hicks offensive...)	2.00	4.00
47B Rufus Mayes (Fred Dryer holds...)	2.00	4.00
48A Chip Myers (Jackie Smith holds...)	2.00	4.00
48B Chip Myers (Lydell Mitchell had...)	2.00	4.00
49A Ken Riley (MacArthur Lane caught...)	2.00	4.00
49B Ken Riley (Don Woods set...)	2.00	4.00
50A Bob Trumpy (Dan Pastorini holds...)	2.00	4.00
50B Bob Trumpy (Ken Houston holds...)	2.00	4.00
51 Don Cockroft	2.00	4.00
52A Thom Darden (Dan Pastorini holds...)	2.00	4.00
52B Thom Darden (Dick Anderson tied...)	2.00	4.00
53A Tom DeLeone (Jim Turner holds...)	2.00	4.00
53B Tom DeLeone (Roger Wehrli attended...)	2.00	4.00
54A John Garlington (Jack Youngblood a...)	2.00	4.00
54B John Garlington (Dick Anderson tied...)	2.00	4.00
55A Walter Johnson (Bert Jones holdsâ¦)	2.00	4.00
55B Walter Johnson (Ed To Tall Jonesâ¦)	2.00	4.00
56A Joe Jones (Jim Turner holds...)	2.00	4.00
56B Joe Jones (Ken Anderson completed...)	2.00	4.00
57 Cleo Miller	2.00	4.00
58 Greg Pruitt	3.00	6.00
59A Reggie Rucker (Jack Youngblood a...)	2.00	4.00
59B Reggie Rucker (MacArthur Lane...)	2.00	4.00
60 Paul Warfield	5.00	10.00
61A Cliff Harris (Ken Houston holds...)	3.00	6.00
61B Cliff Harris (Dan Pastorini holds...)	3.00	6.00
62 Ed Too Tall Jones	5.00	10.00
63A Ralph Neely (Lydell Mitchell had...)	2.00	4.00
63B Ralph Neely (Fred Dryer holds...)	2.00	4.00
64 Robert Newhouse	2.00	4.00
65 Drew Pearson	4.00	8.00
66A Jethro Pugh (Fred Dryer holds...)	2.00	4.00
66B Jethro Pugh (John Hicks offensive...)	2.00	4.00
67 Mel Renfro	4.00	8.00
68A Golden Richards (MacArthur Lane...)	2.00	4.00
68B Golden Richards (Don Woods set...)	2.00	4.00
69 Charlie Waters	3.00	6.00
70 Randy White	6.00	12.00
71A Otis Armstrong (Jake Scott holds...)	2.00	4.00
71B Otis Armstrong (Jackie Smith holds...)	2.00	4.00
72 Jon Keyworth	2.00	4.00
73 Jim Kiick	3.00	6.00
74 Craig Morton	3.00	6.00
75A Haven Moses (Don Woods set...)	2.00	4.00
75B Haven Moses (Levi Johnson had...)	2.00	4.00
76 Riley Odoms	2.00	4.00
77 Bill Thompson	2.00	4.00
78 Jim Turner	2.00	4.00
79 Rick Upchurch	3.00	6.00
80 Louis Wright	3.00	6.00
81 Lem Barney	2.00	4.00
82A Larry Hand (Fred Cox holds...)	2.00	4.00
82B Larry Hand (Cliff Harris attended...)	2.00	4.00
83A J.D. Hill (Pat Haden is...)	2.00	4.00
83B J.D. Hill (Ed Too Tall Jones...)	2.00	4.00
84A Levi Johnson (Fred Cox holds...)	2.00	4.00
84B Levi Johnson (Terry Metcalf set...)	2.00	4.00
85A Greg Landry (Fred Cox holds...)	2.00	4.00
85B Greg Landry	2.00	4.00

Card	Low	High
(Fred Dryer holds...)		
86 Jon Morris	2.00	4.00
87 Paul Naumoff	2.00	4.00
88 Charlie Sanders	2.00	4.00
89 Charlie West	2.00	4.00
90 Jim Yarbrough	2.00	4.00
91 John Brockington	2.00	4.00
92 Willie Buchanon	2.00	4.00
93 Fred Carr	2.00	4.00
94 Lynn Dickey	2.00	4.00
95A Bob Hyland	2.00	4.00
(Mike Curtis linebacker...)		
95B Bob Hyland	2.00	4.00
(Dan Pastorini holds...)		
96A Chester Marcol	2.00	4.00
(Roman Gabriel recovered...)		
96B Chester Marcol	2.00	4.00
(Jim Turner holds...)		
97 Mike McCoy	2.00	4.00
98 Rich McGeorge	2.00	4.00
99A Steve Odom	2.00	4.00
(Cliff Harris attended...)		
99B Steve Odom	2.00	4.00
(Ken Stabler threw...)		
100A Clarence Williams	2.00	4.00
(Pat Haden is...)		
100B Clarence Williams	2.00	4.00
(Mike Curtis linebacker...)		
101A Willie Alexander	2.00	4.00
(Ken Anderson completed...)		
101B Willie Alexander	2.00	4.00
(Jim Turner holds...)		
102A Duane Benson	2.00	4.00
(Dick Anderson tied...)		
102B Duane Benson	2.00	4.00
(Jake Scott holds...)		
103A Elvin Bethea	3.00	6.00
(Roger Wehrli attended...)		
103B Elvin Bethea	3.00	6.00
(Don Woods set...)		
104A Ken Burrough	2.50	5.00
(MacArthur Lane...)		
104B Ken Burrough	2.50	5.00
(Jack Youngblood a...)		
105A Skip Butler	2.00	4.00
(Dan Pastorini holds...)		
105B Skip Butler	2.00	4.00
(Ed Too Tall Jones...)		
106A Curley Culp	3.00	6.00
(Jim Turner holds...)		
106B Curley Culp	3.00	6.00
(MacArthur lane caught...)		
107A Elbert Drungo	2.00	4.00
(Dick Anderson tied...)		
107B Elbert Drungo	2.00	4.00
(Dan Pastorini holds...)		
108A Billy Johnson	2.50	5.00
(Dick Anderson tied...)		
108B Billy Johnson	2.50	5.00
(Roger Wehrli attended...)		
109A Carl Mauck	2.00	4.00
(Jack Youngblood a...)		
109B Carl Mauck	2.00	4.00
(Dick Anderson tied...)		
110A Dan Pastorini	2.50	5.00
(Ed Too Tall Jones...)		
110B Dan Pastorini	2.50	5.00
(Jim Turner holds...)		
111 Tom Condon	2.00	4.00
112 MacArthur Lane	2.00	4.00
113 Willie Lee	2.00	4.00
114 Mike Livingston	2.00	4.00
115 Jim Nicholson	2.00	4.00
116A Jim Lynch	2.00	4.00
(Dan Pastorini holds...)		
116B Jim Lynch	2.00	4.00
(Rocky Bleier rushed...)		
117 Barry Pearson	2.00	4.00
118 Ed Podolak	2.00	4.00
119A Jan Stenerud	3.00	6.00
(MacArthur Lane caught...)		
119B Jan Stenerud	3.00	6.00
(Don Woods set...)		
120 Walter White	2.00	4.00
121 Jim Bertelsen	2.00	4.00
122 John Cappelletti	3.00	6.00
123 Fred Dryer	3.00	6.00
124 Pat Haden	3.00	6.00
125 Harold Jackson	3.00	6.00
126 Ron Jessie	2.00	4.00
127 Lawrence McCutcheon	2.00	4.00
128 Isiah Robertson	2.00	4.00
129 Bucky Scribner	2.00	4.00
130 Jack Youngblood	3.00	6.00
131 Dick Anderson	6.00	12.00
132 Norm Bulaich	5.00	10.00
133 Dave Foley	5.00	10.00
134 Vern Den Herder	5.00	10.00
135A Bob Kuechenberg	5.00	10.00
(Alfred Jenkins caught...)		
135B Bob Kuechenberg	5.00	10.00
(Ken Houston holds...)		
136A Larry Little	6.00	12.00
(Fred Cox holds...)		
136B Larry Little	6.00	12.00
(Fred Dryer holds...)		
137A Jim Mandich	5.00	10.00
(Cliff Harris attended...)		
137B Jim Mandich	5.00	10.00
(Lydell Mitchell had...)		
138 Don Nottingham	5.00	10.00
139 Larry Seiple	5.00	10.00
140 Howard Twilley	5.00	10.00
141 Bobby Bryant	2.00	4.00
142 Fred Cox	2.00	4.00
143 Carl Eller	3.00	6.00
144 Chuck Foreman	2.00	4.00
145 Paul Krause	3.00	6.00
146 Jeff Siemon	2.00	4.00
147 Mick Tingelhoff	2.00	4.00
148 Ed White	2.00	4.00
149 Nate Wright	2.00	4.00
150 Ron Yary	3.00	6.00
151 Marlin Briscoe	2.00	4.00
152 Sam Cunningham	2.00	4.00
153 Steve Grogan	3.00	6.00
154 John Hannah	4.00	8.00
155 Andy Johnson	2.00	4.00
156 Tony McGee DE	2.00	4.00
157 John Sanders	2.00	4.00
158 Randy Vataha	2.00	4.00
159 George Webster	2.00	4.00
160 Steve Zabel	2.00	4.00
161 Larry Burton	2.00	4.00
162 Tony Galbreath	2.00	4.00
163 Don Herrmann	2.00	4.00
164 Archie Manning	5.00	10.00
165 Alvin Maxson	2.00	4.00
166 Jim Merlo	2.00	4.00
167 Derland Moore	2.00	4.00
168 Chuck Muncie	3.00	6.00
169 Tom Myers	2.00	4.00
170 Bob Pollard	2.00	4.00
171 Rich Dvorak	2.00	4.00
172 Walker Gillette	2.00	4.00
173 Jack Gregory	2.00	4.00
174 John Hicks	2.00	4.00
175 Brian Kelley	2.00	4.00
176 John Mendenhall	2.00	4.00
177 Clyde Powers	2.00	4.00
178 Bob Tucker	3.00	6.00
179 Doug Van Horn	2.00	4.00
180 Brad Van Pelt	3.00	6.00
181 Jerome Barkum	2.00	4.00
182 Richard Caster	2.00	4.00
183 Clark Gaines	2.00	4.00
184 Pat Leahy	2.00	4.00
185 Ed Marinaro	3.00	6.00
186 Richard Neal	2.00	4.00
187 Lou Piccone	2.00	4.00
188 Walt Suggs	2.00	4.00
189 Richard Todd	3.00	6.00
190 Phil Wise	2.00	4.00
191 Fred Biletnikoff	6.00	12.00
192A Dave Casper	3.00	6.00
(Pat Haden is...)		
192B Dave Casper	3.00	6.00
(Ed Too Tall Jones...)		
193 Ted Hendricks	4.00	8.00
194 Marv Hubbard	2.00	4.00
195 Ted Kwalick	2.00	4.00
196 Otis Sistrunk	3.00	6.00
197 Ken Stabler	10.00	20.00
198 Gene Upshaw	4.00	8.00
199 Mark Van Eeghen	3.00	6.00
200 Phil Villapiano	3.00	6.00
201 Bill Bergey	3.00	6.00
202 Harold Carmichael	3.00	6.00
203 Roman Gabriel	3.00	6.00
204 Art Malone	2.00	4.00
205 James McAlister	2.00	4.00
206 John Outlaw	2.00	4.00
207 Jerry Sisemore	2.00	4.00
208 Manny Sistrunk	2.00	4.00
209 Tom Sullivan	2.00	4.00
210 Will Wynn	2.00	4.00
211 Rocky Bleier	3.00	6.00
212 Mel Blount	4.00	8.00
213 Terry Bradshaw	12.50	25.00
214 Roy Gerela	2.00	4.00
215 Joe Greene	5.00	10.00
216 Jack Ham	4.00	8.00
217 Ernie Holmes	2.00	4.00
218 Jack Lambert	6.00	12.00
219 Ray Mansfield	2.00	4.00
220 Dwight White	2.00	4.00
221A Tom Banks	2.00	4.00
(In 1970 Bruce Taylor...)		
221B Tom Banks	2.00	4.00
(Roman Gabriel recovered...)		
222A Dan Dierdorf	4.00	8.00
(Clark Gaines led...)		
222B Dan Dierdorf	4.00	8.00
(Ken Stone intercepted...)		
223A Conrad Dobler	2.00	4.00
(Archie Manning QB...)		
223B Conrad Dobler	2.00	4.00
(Marv Bateman punter...)		
224 Mel Gray	3.00	6.00
225A Terry Metcalf	3.00	6.00
(Ken Stabler threw...)		
225B Terry Metcalf	3.00	6.00
(Don Cockroft is...)		
226A Jackie Smith	4.00	8.00
(Levi Johnson had...)		
226B Jackie Smith	4.00	8.00
(1970 Bruce Taylor...)		
227 Roger Wehrli	3.00	6.00
228 Ron Yankowski	2.00	4.00
229 Bob Young	2.00	4.00
230A John Zook	2.00	4.00
(Don Cockroft is...)		
230B John Zook	2.00	4.00
(Clark Gaines led...)		
231 Pat Curran	2.00	4.00
232 Fred Dean	2.00	4.00
233A Ed Flanagan	2.00	4.00
(Marv Bateman punter...)		
233B Ed Flanagan	2.00	4.00
(Terry Metcalf set...)		
234A Mike Fuller	2.00	4.00
(Ken Stabler threw...)		
234B Mike Fuller	2.00	4.00
(Alfred Jenkins caught...)		
235 Don Goode	2.00	4.00
236 Charlie Joiner	5.00	10.00
237 Louie Kelcher	3.00	6.00
238 Bo Matthews	2.00	4.00
239 Hal Stringert	2.00	4.00
240 Don Woods	2.00	4.00
241A Cas Banaszek	2.00	4.00
(In 1970 Bruce Taylor...)		
241B Cas Banaszek	2.00	4.00
(Roman Gabriel recovered...)		
242 Cedrick Hardman	2.00	4.00
243 Tommy Hart	2.00	4.00
244 Wilbur Jackson	2.00	4.00
245 Mel Phillips	2.00	4.00
246 Jim Plunkett	4.00	8.00
247A Bruce Taylor	2.00	4.00
(Walter Payton had...)		
247B Bruce Taylor	2.00	4.00
(Archie Manning QB...)		
248 Gene Washington 49er	3.00	6.00
249 Delvin Williams	2.00	4.00
250 Skip Vanderbundt	2.00	4.00
251 Mike Curtis	3.00	6.00
252 Norm Evans	2.00	4.00
253 Don Hansen	2.00	4.00
254 Fred Hoaglin	2.00	4.00
255 Ron Howard	2.00	4.00
256 Al Matthews	2.00	4.00
257 Sam McCullum	2.00	4.00
258 Eddie McMillan	2.00	4.00
259 Steve Niehaus	2.00	4.00
260 Jim Zorn	3.00	6.00
261A Mike Boryla	2.00	4.00
(Chester Marcol...)		
261B Mike Boryla	2.00	4.00
(In 1970 Bruce Taylor...)		
262A Anthony Davis	3.00	6.00
(Archie Manning QB...)		
262B Anthony Davis	3.00	6.00
(Walter Payton had...)		
263A Jimmy DuBose	2.00	4.00
(John Hicks offensive...)		
263B Jimmy DuBose	2.00	4.00
(in 1970 Bruce Taylor...)		
264 Jimmy Gunn	2.00	4.00
265A Essex Johnson	2.00	4.00
(Steve Grogan ran...)		
265B Essex Johnson	2.00	4.00
(Ken Stone intercepted...)		
266A Bob Moore TE	2.00	4.00
(John Hicks offensive...)		
266B Bob Moore TE	2.00	4.00
(Chester Marcol in...)		
267 Jim Peterson	2.00	4.00
268 Dan Ryczek	2.00	4.00
269A Barry Smith	2.00	4.00
(Rocky Bleier rushed...)		
269B Barry Smith	2.00	4.00
(John Hicks offensive...)		
270A Ken Stone	2.00	4.00
(Mike Curtis linebacker...)		
270B Ken Stone	2.00	4.00
(Steve Grogan ran...)		
271 Mike Bragg	2.00	4.00
272 Eddie Brown	2.00	4.00
273 Bill Brundige	2.00	4.00
274 Dave Butz	2.00	4.00
275 Brad Dusek	2.00	4.00
276 Pat Fischer	3.00	6.00
277 Jean Fugett	2.00	4.00
278 Frank Grant	2.00	4.00
279 Chris Hanburger	3.00	6.00
280 Len Hauss	2.00	4.00
281 Terry Hermeling	2.00	4.00
282 Calvin Hill	2.00	4.00
283 Ken Houston	3.00	6.00
284 Bob Kuziel	2.00	4.00
285 Joe Lavender	2.00	4.00
286 Mark Moseley	2.00	4.00
287 Dan Nugent	2.00	4.00
288 Brig Owens	2.00	4.00
289 John Riggins	6.00	12.00
290 Ron Saul	2.00	4.00
291 Jake Scott	3.00	6.00
292 George Starke	2.00	4.00
293 Tim Stokes	2.00	4.00
294 Diron Talbert	2.00	4.00
295 Charley Taylor	3.00	6.00
296 Joe Theismann	6.00	12.00
297 Mike Thomas	2.00	4.00
298 Pete Wysocki	2.00	4.00

2006 Reading Express AIFL

Card	Low	High
COMPLETE SET (2)	2.50	6.00
1 Sheet 1	1.25	3.00
2 Sheet 2	1.25	3.00

2008 Reading Express AIFL

Card	Low	High
COMPLETE SET (30)	6.00	12.00
1 Michael Baldwin	.20	.50
2 Scott Blum	.20	.50
3 Tardon Brantley	.20	.50
4 Chad Clark	.20	.50
5 Ian Cooper	.20	.50
6 Robert Flowers	.20	.50
7 Shawn Foxworth	.20	.50
8 Corey Gipe	.20	.50
9 Jason Henley	.20	.50
10 Adam Hoffman	.20	.50
11 Trent Jones	.20	.50
12 Dan Kelly	.20	.50
13 Brett Kolk	.20	.50
14 Sean McKnight CO	.20	.50
15 Preston McKnight CO	.20	.50
16 Kenny Miller CO	.20	.50
17 Ronnie Montgomery	.20	.50
18 Bernie Nowotarski CO	.20	.50
19 Chris Nunn	.20	.50
20 Carmelo Ocasio	.20	.50
21 Mike Robinson CO	.20	.50
22 Erik Rockhold	.20	.50
23 Marcus Sargeant	.20	.50
24 Mike Schwebel	.20	.50
25 David Smith	.20	.50
26 Matt Sola	.20	.50
27 Mark Steinmeyer	.20	.50
28 Mark Stout	.20	.50
29 Chris Thompson GM	.20	.50
30 Jeff Willis	.20	.50

1995 Real Action Pop-Ups

Card	Low	High
COMPLETE SET (7)	2.50	6.00
2 John Elway	.60	1.50

1939 Redskins Matchbooks

Sponsored by Ross Jewelers, these 20 matchbooks measure approximately 1 1/2" by 4 1/2" (when completely folded out) and feature black-and-white photos of the 1939 Washington Redskins, with simulated autographs on the inside panel. The player's position and college, along with his height and weight, appear below the photo. The bottom half of the inside panel reads "This is one of 20 autographed pictures of the Washington Redskins compliments of the Ross Jewelry Co." In maroon lettering upon a gold background, the top half of the outside of the matchbook carries on its front the Ross Company name and address within a drawing of a football. the Redskins 1939 home game schedule is shown on the bottom half. This is the only distinguishing characteristic between the 1939 and 1940 issues. The covers of Jim Barber and Steve Slivinski are considered scarce. The matchbooks are unnumbered and checklisted below in alphabetical order. The prices given are for full covers (with strikers) missing the actual matches. This is the form in which the matchbooks are most commonly found. Complete books with matches typically carry a 50% premium. Books missing the striker are considered VG at best.

Card	Low	High
COMPLETE SET (20)	1000.00	1500.00
1 Jim Barber SP	250.00	400.00
2 Sammy Baugh	90.00	150.00
3 Hal Bradley	20.00	35.00
4 Vic Carroll	20.00	35.00
5 Bud Erickson	20.00	35.00
6 Andy Farkas	20.00	35.00
7 Frank Filchock	20.00	35.00
8 Ray Flaherty CO	25.00	40.00
9 Don Irwin	20.00	35.00
10 Ed Justice	20.00	35.00
11 Jim Karcher	20.00	35.00
12 Max Krause	20.00	35.00
13 Charley Malone	20.00	35.00
14 Bob Masterson	20.00	35.00
15 Wayne Millner	25.00	40.00
16 Mickey Parks	20.00	35.00
17 Erny Pinckert	20.00	35.00
18 Steve Slivinski SP	250.00	400.00
19 Clem Stralka	20.00	35.00
20 Jay Turner	20.00	35.00

1939 Redskins Postcards

This series of postcards was produced for and issued by the team in 1939. Each card measures roughly 3 1/2" by 5 1/2" and features a typically postcard style back with a black and white player photo on the front. The player's name, position, and team name is included within the player photo.

Card	Low	High
COMPLETE SET (15)	1200.00	1800.00
1 Jim Barber	75.00	125.00
2 Sammy Baugh	300.00	500.00
3 Andy Farkas	75.00	125.00
4 Jimmy German	75.00	125.00
5 Don Irwin	75.00	125.00
6 Jimmy Johnston	75.00	125.00
7 Ed Justice	75.00	125.00
8 Jim Karcher	75.00	125.00
9 Charley Malone	75.00	125.00
10 Bob McChesney	75.00	125.00
11 Jim Meade	75.00	125.00
12 Boyd Morgan	75.00	125.00
13 Bo Russell	75.00	125.00
14 Clyde Shugart	75.00	125.00
15 Bill Young	75.00	125.00

1940 Redskins Matchbooks

Made for Ross Jewelers by the Universal Match Corp. of Philadelphia, these 20 matchbooks measure approximately 1 1/2" by 4 1/2" (when completely folded out) and feature black-and-white photos of the 1940 Washington Redskins, with simulated autographs, on the inside panel. The player's position and college, along with his height and weight, appear below the photo. The bottom half of the inside panel reads "This is one of 20 autographed pictures of the Washington Redskins compliments of Ross Jewelry Co." In maroon lettering upon a gold background, the top half of the outside of the matchbook carries on its front the Ross Company name and address within a drawing of a football. On the bottom half is shown the Redskins 1940 home game schedule. This is the only distinguishing characteristic between the 1939 and 1940 issues. The matchbooks are unnumbered and checklisted below in alphabetical order. The prices given are for full covers (with strikers) missing the actual matches. This is the form in which the matchbooks are most commonly found. Complete books with matches typically carry a 50% premium. Books missing the striker are considered VG at best.

Card	Low	High
COMPLETE SET (20)	200.00	350.00
1 Jim Barber	10.00	18.00
2 Sammy Baugh	50.00	80.00
3 Vic Carroll	10.00	18.00
4 Turk Edwards	18.00	30.00
5 Andy Farkas	10.00	18.00
6 Dick Farman	10.00	18.00
7 Bob Hoffman	10.00	18.00
8 Don Irwin	10.00	18.00
9 Charley Malone	10.00	18.00
10 Bob Masterson	10.00	18.00
11 Wayne Millner	12.00	20.00
12 Mickey Parks	10.00	18.00
13 Erny Pinckert	10.00	18.00
14 Bo Russell	10.00	18.00
15 Clyde Shugart	10.00	18.00
16 Steve Slivinski	10.00	18.00
17 Clem Stralka	10.00	18.00
18 Dick Todd	10.00	18.00
19 Bill Young	10.00	18.00
20 Roy Zimmerman	10.00	18.00

1941 Redskins Matchbooks

Made for Home Laundry by the Maryland Match Co. of Baltimore, these 20 matchbooks measure approximately 1 1/2" by 4 1/2" (when completely folded out) and feature black-and-white photos of the 1941 Washington Redskins, with simulated autographs on the inside panel. The player's position and college, along with his height and weight, appear below the photo. The bottom half of the inside panel reads "This is one of 20 autographed pictures of the Washington Redskins compliments of Home Laundry," followed by the business's 1941 six-digit phone number, ATlantic 2400. In gold lettering upon a maroon background, the outside of the matchbook carries on its front the Home Laundry name and telephone number within a drawing of a football. On the back is shown the Redskins 1941 home game schedule, which ended with a game against Philadelphia, on Sunday, Dec. 7, 1941. The matchbooks are unnumbered and checklisted below in alphabetical order. The prices given are for full covers (with strikers) missing the actual matches. This is the form in which the matchbooks are most commonly found. Complete books with matches typically carry a 50% premium. Books missing the striker are considered VG at best.

Card	Low	High
COMPLETE SET (20)	150.00	250.00
1 Ki Aldrich	7.00	12.00
2 Jim Barber	7.00	12.00
3 Sammy Baugh	35.00	60.00
4 Vic Carroll	7.00	12.00
5 Fred Davis	7.00	12.00
6 Andy Farkas	7.00	12.00
7 Dick Farman	7.00	12.00
8 Frank Filchock	7.00	12.00
9 Ray Flaherty CO	9.00	15.00
10 Bob Masterson	7.00	12.00
11 Bob McChesney	7.00	12.00
12 Wayne Millner	9.00	15.00
13 Wilbur Moore	7.00	12.00
14 Bob Seymour	7.00	12.00
15 Clyde Shugart	7.00	12.00
16 Clem Stralka	7.00	12.00
17 Robert Titchenal	7.00	12.00
18 Dick Todd	7.00	12.00
19 Bill Young	7.00	12.00
20 Roy Zimmerman	7.00	12.00

1942 Redskins Matchbooks

Made for Home Laundry by the Maryland Match Co. of Baltimore, these 20 matchbooks measure approximately 1 1/2" by 4 1/2" (when completely folded out) and feature black-and-white photos of the 1942 Washington Redskins, with simulated autographs, on the inside panel. The player's position and college, along with his height and weight, appear below the photo. The bottom half of the inside panel reads "This is one of 20 autographed pictures of the Washington Redskins compliments of Home Laundry," followed by the business's 1942 six-digit phone number, ATlantic 2400. In maroon lettering upon a yellow-orange background, the outside of the matchbook carries on its front the Home Laundry name and telephone number within a drawing of a football. On the back is shown the Redskins 1942 home game schedule. The matchbooks are unnumbered and checklisted below in alphabetical order. The prices given are for full covers (with strikers) missing the actual matches. This is the form in which the matchbooks are most commonly found. Complete books with matches typically carry a 50% premium. Books missing the striker are considered VG at best.

Card	Low	High
COMPLETE SET (20)	150.00	250.00
1 Ki Aldrich	7.00	12.00
2 Sammy Baugh	35.00	60.00
3 Joe Beinor	7.00	12.00
4 Vic Carroll	7.00	12.00
5 Ed Cifers	7.00	12.00
6 Fred Davis	7.00	12.00
7 Turk Edwards	12.00	20.00
8 Andy Farkas	7.00	12.00
9 Dick Farman	7.00	12.00
10 Ray Flaherty CO	9.00	15.00
11 Al Krueger	7.00	12.00
12 Bob Masterson	7.00	12.00
13 Bob McChesney	7.00	12.00
14 Wilbur Moore	7.00	12.00
15 Bob Seymour	7.00	12.00
16 Clyde Shugart	7.00	12.00
17 Clem Stralka	7.00	12.00
18 Dick Todd	7.00	12.00
19 Willie Wilkin	7.00	12.00
20 Bill Young	7.00	12.00

1951-52 Redskins Matchbooks

Sponsored by Arcade Pontiac and produced by the Universal Match Corp.,Washington D.C., these matchbooks measure approximately 1 1/2" by 4 1/2" (when completely folded out) and feature small black-and-white photos of Washington Redskins with simulated autographs on the inside panel. The player's position and college, along with his height and weight, appear below the photo. The bottom half of the inside panel reads "This is one of 20 autographed pictures of the Washington Redskins compliments of Jack Blank, President Arcade Pontiac Co.," followed by the business' 1950s six-digit phone number, ADams 8500. The outside of the matchbook carries on its top half the Arcade Pontiac name along with a logo on a black and gold background. On the bottom half is shown the Redskins logo on a gold background. The matchbooks are unnumbered and checklisted below in alphabetical order. Although the covers read "20" to the set, it is thought that only 17-matchbooks were released in 1951 and 19 in 1952. Many of the matchbooks were released in both 1951 and 1952 with a few containing only very minor differences in the photo cropping. Otherwise, the two sets are indistinguishable. Thus, we've listed the two sets together for ease in cataloging. Major variations between the two years (only the Herman Ball cover) and covers reportedly issued only one year are listed below as such. The prices given are for full covers (with strikers) missing the actual matches. This is the form in which the matchbooks are most commonly found. Complete books with matches typically carry a 50% premium. Books missing the striker are considered VG at best.

Card	Low	High
COMPLETE SET (25)	250.00	400.00
1 John Badaczewski	5.00	10.00
2A Herman Ball CO	6.00	12.00
2B Herman Ball CO	6.00	12.00
3 Sammy Baugh	25.00	50.00
4 Ed Berrang 1951	6.00	12.00
5 Dan Brown 1951	6.00	12.00
6 Al DeMao	5.00	10.00
7 Harry Dowda 1952	10.00	20.00
8 Chuck Drazenovich	5.00	10.00
9 Bill Dudley 1951	10.00	20.00
10 Harry Gilmer	7.50	15.00
11 Bob Goode 1951	6.00	12.00
12 Leon Heath 1952	10.00	20.00
13 Charlie Justice 1952	12.50	25.00
14 Lou Karras	5.00	10.00
15 Eddie LeBaron 1952	15.00	30.00
16 Paul Lipscomb	5.00	10.00
17 Laurie Niemi	5.00	10.00
18 Johnny Papit 1952	10.00	20.00
19 James Peebles 1951	6.00	12.00
20 Ed Quirk	5.00	10.00
21 Jim Ricca 1952	10.00	20.00
22 James Staton 1951	6.00	12.00
23 Hugh Taylor	6.00	12.00
24 Joe Tereshinski	5.00	10.00
25 Dick Todd CO 1952	10.00	20.00

1952 Redskins Postcards

Card	Low	High
1 Dick Alban	30.00	50.00
2 Don Boll	30.00	50.00
3 Gene Brito	30.00	50.00
4 Jack Cloud	30.00	50.00
5 Al Demao	30.00	50.00
6 Chuck Drazenovich	30.00	50.00
7 Harry Gilmer	35.00	60.00
8 Jerry Hennessy	30.00	50.00
9 Paul Lipscomb	30.00	50.00
10 Laurie Niemi	30.00	50.00
11 Knox Ramsey	30.00	50.00
12 Julie Rykovich	30.00	50.00
13 Jack Scarbath	30.00	50.00
14 Joe Tereshinski	30.00	50.00
15 Johnny Williams	30.00	50.00

1957 Redskins Team Issue 5x7

This set of 5x7 photos was issued by the team to fulfill fan requests and for player appearances. Each includes a black and white photo of a Redskins player with just his name below the image. The backs are blank and unnumbered.

Card	Low	High
COMPLETE SET (12)	75.00	150.00
1 Sam Baker	7.50	15.00
2 Don Bosseler	7.50	15.00
3 Gene Brito	7.50	15.00
4 John Carson	7.50	15.00
5 Chuck Drazenovich	7.50	15.00
6 Ralph Guglielmi	7.50	15.00
7 Dick James	7.50	15.00
8 Eddie LeBaron	12.50	25.00
9 Jim Podoley	7.50	15.00
10 Jim Schrader	7.50	15.00
11 Ed Sutton	7.50	15.00
12 Albert Zagers	7.50	15.00

1957 Redskins Team Issue 8x10

This set of black and white photos was issued by the team for fan requests and public appearances. Each measures roughly 8" by 10 1/4" with a 1/4" white border around all four sides. The team name and player name appear below the photo and the backs are blank and unnumbered.

Card	Low	High
COMPLETE SET (14)	125.00	250.00
1 Sam Baker	10.00	20.00
2 Gene Brito	10.00	20.00
3 John Carson	10.00	20.00
4 Bob Dee	10.00	20.00
5 Chuck Drazenovich	10.00	20.00
6 Ralph Felton	10.00	20.00
7 Norb Hecker	10.00	20.00
8 Dick James	10.00	20.00
9 Eddie LeBaron	15.00	30.00
10 Ray Lemek	10.00	20.00
11 Volney Peters	10.00	20.00
12 Joe Scudero	10.00	20.00
13 Dick Stanfel	12.50	25.00
14 Lavern Torgeson	10.00	20.00

1958-59 Redskins Matchbooks

Sponsored by First Federal Savings and produced by Universal Match Corp., Washington D.C., these 20 matchcovers measure approximately 1 1/2" by 4 1/2" (when completely folded out). Each front cover features a small black-and-white photo of a popular Washington Redskins player with the Redskins logo and the title "Famous Redskins" on the bottom half and a First Federal Savings advertisement on the top half. A player profile is given at the top of the matchcover back along with the words "This is one of twenty famous Redskins presented for you by your 1st Federal Savings and Loan Association of Washington& Bethesda Branch," followed by the address. The matchbooks are unnumbered and checklisted below in alphabetical order. It is most commonly thought that the set was issued in two ten-cover series over a two-year period. We've included the presumed year of issue after each cover. The matchbooks are very similar to the 1960-61 issue, but can be distinguished by their light gray colored paper stock instead of off-white. The prices given are for full covers (with strikers) missing the actual matches. This is the form in which the matchbooks are most commonly found. Complete books with matches typically carry a 50% premium. Books missing the striker are considered VG at best.

Card	Low	High
COMPLETE SET (20)	125.00	250.00
1 Steve Bagarus 58	5.00	10.00
2 Cliff Battles 58	10.00	20.00
3 Sammy Baugh 58	20.00	40.00
4 Gene Brito 58	5.00	10.00
5 Jim Castiglia 58	5.00	10.00
6 Al DeMao 58	5.00	10.00
7 Chuck Drazenovich 59	5.00	10.00
8 Bill Dudley 59	10.00	20.00
9 Al Fiorentino 59	5.00	10.00
10 Don Irwin 59	5.00	10.00
11 Eddie LeBaron 58	7.50	15.00
12 Wayne Millner 58	7.50	15.00
13 Wilbur Moore 58	5.00	10.00
14 Jim Schrader 59	5.00	10.00
15 Riley Smith 59	5.00	10.00
16 Mike Sommer 59	5.00	10.00
17 Joe Tereshinski 58	5.00	10.00
18 Dick Todd 59	6.00	12.00
19 Willie Wilkin 59	5.00	10.00
20 Casimir Witucki 59	5.00	10.00

1959 Redskins San Giorgio Flipbooks

This set features members of the Washington Redskins printed on velum type paper stock created in a multi-image action sequence. The set is commonly referenced as the San Giorgio Macaroni Football Flipbooks. Members of the Philadelphia Eagles, Pittsburgh Steelers, and Washington Redskins were produced regionally with 15-players, reportedly, issued per team. Some players were produced in more than one sequence of poses with different captions and/or slightly different photos used. When the flipbooks are still in uncut form (which is most desirable), they measure approximately 5 3/4" by 3 9/16". The sheets are blank backed, in black and white, and provide 14-small numbered pages when cut apart. Collectors were encouraged to cut out each photo and stack them in such a way as to create a moving image of the player when flipped with the fingers. Any additions to this list are appreciated.

Card	Low	High
1 Sam Baker	100.00	175.00
2 Don Bosseler	90.00	150.00
3 Eddei LeBaron	150.00	250.00
4 Mike Sommer	90.00	150.00

1960-61 Redskins Matchbooks

Sponsored by First Federal Savings and produced by Universal Match Corp., Washington D.C., these 20 matchcovers measure approximately 1 1/2" by 4 1/2" (when completely folded out). Each front cover features a small black-and-white photo of a popular Washington Redskins player with the Redskins logo and the title "Famous Redskins" on the bottom half and a First Federal Savings advertisement on the top half. A player profile is given at the top of the matchcover back along with the words "This is one of twenty famous Redskins presented for you by your 1st Federal Savings and Loan Association of Washington, Bethesda Branch," followed by the address and a Universal Match Corporation company logo. The matchbooks are unnumbered and checklisted below in alphabetical order. It is most commonly thought that the set was issued in two ten-cover series over a two-year period. We've included the presumed year of issue after each cover. The matchbooks are very similar to the 1958-59 issue& but can be distinguished by their off-white colored paper stock instead of light gray. The prices given are for full covers (with strikers) missing the actual matches. This is the form in which the matchbooks are most commonly found. Complete books with matches typically carry a 50% premium. Books missing the striker are considered VG at best.

Card	Low	High
COMPLETE SET (20)	100.00	200.00
1 Bill Anderson 61	6.00	12.00
2 Don Bosseler 60	6.00	12.00
3 Turk Edwards 60	12.50	25.00
4 Ralph Guglielmi 61	6.00	12.00
5 Bill Hartman 60	5.00	10.00
6 Norb Hecker 61	5.00	10.00
7 Dick James 61	6.00	12.00
8 Charlie Justice 60	10.00	20.00
9 Ray Krouse 61	5.00	10.00
10 Ray Lemek 61	5.00	10.00
11 Tommy Mont 60	5.00	10.00
12 John Olszewski 61	6.00	12.00
13 John Paluck 61	5.00	10.00
14 Jim Peebles 60	5.00	10.00
15 Bo Russell 60	5.00	10.00
16 Jim Schrader 61	5.00	10.00
17 Louis Stephens 61	5.00	10.00
18 Ed Sutton 60	5.00	10.00
19 Bob Toneff 60	6.00	12.00
20 Lavern Torgeson 60	6.00	12.00

1960 Redskins Jay Publishing

This 12-card set features (approximately) 5" by 7" black-and-white player photos. The photos show players in traditional poses with the quarterback preparing to throw, the runner heading downfield, and the defenseman ready for the tackle. These cards were packaged 12 to a packet and originally sold for 25 cents. The backs are blank. The cards are unnumbered and checklisted below in alphabetical order.

Card	Low	High
COMPLETE SET (12)	40.00	80.00
1 Sam Baker	4.00	8.00
2 Don Bosseler	4.00	8.00
3 Gene Brito	4.00	8.00
4 Johnny Carson	4.00	8.00
5 Chuck Drazenovich	4.00	8.00
6 Ralph Guglielmi	4.00	8.00
7 Dick James	4.00	8.00
8 Eddie LeBaron	6.00	12.00
9 Jim Podoley	4.00	8.00
10 Jim Schrader	4.00	8.00
11 Ed Sutton	4.00	8.00
12 Albert Zagers	4.00	8.00

1961 Redskins Jay Publishing

This 12-card set features 5" by 7" black-and-white player photos. The photos show players in traditional poses with the quarterback preparing to throw, the runner heading downfield, and the defenseman ready for the tackle. These cards were packaged 12 to a packet and originally sold for 25 cents through Jay Publishing's annual football magazine. The backs are blank. The cards are unnumbered and checklisted below in alphabetical order.

Card	Low	High
COMPLETE SET (12)	50.00	100.00
1 Don Bosseler	5.00	10.00
2 Eagle Day	4.00	8.00
3 Fred Dugan	4.00	8.00
4 Gary Glick	4.00	8.00
5 Sam Horner	4.00	8.00
6 Dick James	5.00	10.00
7 Bob Khayat	4.00	8.00
8 Bill McPeak CO	4.00	8.00
9 Jim Schrader	4.00	8.00
10 Norm Snead	7.50	15.00
11 Bob Toneff	4.00	8.00
12 Ed Vereb	4.00	8.00

1965 Redskins Team Issue

These black and white photos were issued by the Redskins in the mid-1960s. Each was printed on high gloss stock with a blankback and no identifying marks on the fronts. The Redskins often stamped the name of the player on the photo backs.

Card	Low	High
COMPLETE SET (10)	50.00	100.00
1 Willie Adams	6.00	12.00
2 Len Hauss	6.00	12.00
3 Bob Jencks	6.00	12.00
4 Bob Pellegrini	6.00	12.00
5 Jim Steffen	6.00	12.00
6 Pat Richter	6.00	12.00
7 Fred Williams	6.00	12.00
8 Unidentified Player #24	6.00	12.00
9 Unidentified Player #27	6.00	12.00
10 Unidentified Player #71	6.00	12.00

1965 Redskins Volpe Tumblers

These Redskins artist's renderings were inserted into a plastic cup tumbler produced in 1965. The noted sports artist Volpe created the artwork which includes an action scene and a player portrait. The paper inserts are unnumbered, each measures approximately 5" by 8 1/2" and are curved in the shape required to fit inside the plastic cup. This set is believed to contain up to 12-cups. Any additions to this list are welcomed.

Card	Low	High
1 Sam Huff	50.00	80.00
2 Sonny Jurgensen	60.00	100.00
3 Paul Krause	30.00	50.00
4 Bobby Mitchell	35.00	60.00
5 John Paluck	25.00	40.00
6 Joe Rutgens	25.00	40.00
7 Charley Taylor	35.00	60.00

1966 Redskins Team Issue

This set of photos was issued in the mid-1960s and features a black and white photo of a Redskins player on each. The photos measure roughly 5" by 7" and include the player's name, his position (spelled out), and the team name below the each player image. The backs are blank. A complete set is thought to include 12-photos, therefore any additions to this list are appreciated.

Card	Low	High
COMPLETE SET (6)	40.00	80.00
1 Chris Hanburger	7.50	15.00
2 Sonny Jurgensen	12.50	25.00
3 Bobby Mitchell	10.00	20.00
4 Brig Owens	6.00	12.00
5 Joe Rutgens	6.00	12.00
6 Ron Snidow	6.00	12.00

1969 Redskins High's Dairy

This eight-card set was sponsored by High's Dairy Stores and measures approximately 8" by 10". The front has white borders and a full color painting of the player by Alex Fournier, with the player's signature near the bottom of the portrait. The plain white back gives biographical and statistical information on the player on its left side, and information about Fournier on the right. Reportedly 70,000 of each photo was produced. Collectors could receive a free card for each two half gallons of milk they purchased or could buy them from High's Dairy Stores for ten cents each. The cards are unnumbered and checklisted below in alphabetical order. Reportedly, Bobby Mitchell was drawn for this set but never printed as he retired before the 1969 season began.

Card	Low	High
COMPLETE SET (8)	75.00	125.00
1 Chris Hanburger	7.50	15.00
2 Len Hauss	6.00	12.00
3 Sam Huff	10.00	20.00
4 Sonny Jurgensen	20.00	35.00
5 Carl Kammerer	6.00	12.00
6 Brig Owens	6.00	12.00
7 Pat Richter	6.00	12.00
8 Charley Taylor	10.00	20.00

1971 Redskins Team Issue

This set of black and white player photos was released around 1971. Each measures roughly 8" by 10 1/8" and features the player in the yellow Redskins helmet. No player names are identified on the fronts but either a stamped or written name was often included on the, otherwise blank, cardbacks. They look very similar to the 1973 set but can be identified by the yellow player helmets.

Card	Low	High
COMPLETE SET (20)	100.00	200.00
1 Verlon Biggs	5.00	10.00
2 Larry Brown	6.00	12.00
3 George Burman	5.00	10.00
4 Boyd Dowler	6.00	12.00
5 Pat Fischer	5.00	10.00
6 Chris Hanburger	6.00	12.00
7 Charlie Harraway	5.00	10.00
8 Jon Jaqua	5.00	10.00
9 Sonny Jurgensen	10.00	20.00
10 Billy Kilmer	7.50	15.00
11 Curt Knight	5.00	10.00
12 Tommy Mason	5.00	10.00
13 Clifton McNeil	5.00	10.00
14 Brig Owens	5.00	10.00
15 Jack Pardee	6.00	12.00
16 Jerry Smith	5.00	10.00
17 Diron Talbert	5.00	10.00
18 Charley Taylor	7.50	15.00
19 Ted Vactor	5.00	10.00
20 John Wilbur	5.00	10.00

1972 Redskins Characatures

This set was produced by Dick Shuman and Compu-Set, Inc. in 1972 and features players of the Washington Redskins. Each card measures approxiamtely 8" by 10" and features a characature drawing of the player with his name printed below. The cards are unnumbered and blankbacked.

Card	Low	High
COMPLETE SET (31)	200.00	350.00
1 Mack Alston	6.00	12.00
2 Mike Bass	7.50	15.00
3 Verlon Biggs	6.00	12.00
4 Mike Bragg	6.00	12.00
5 Larry Brown	10.00	20.00
6 Speedy Duncan	7.50	15.00
7 Pat Fischer	7.50	15.00
8 Chris Hanburger	7.50	15.00
9 Charlie Harraway	6.00	12.00
10 Len Hauss	6.00	12.00
11 Roy Jefferson	7.50	15.00
12 Sonny Jurgensen	12.50	25.00
13 Billy Kilmer	10.00	20.00
14 Curt Knight	6.00	12.00
15 Ron McDole	6.00	12.00
16 Clifton McNeil	6.00	12.00
17 George Nock	6.00	12.00
18 Brig Owens	6.00	12.00
19 Jack Pardee	7.50	15.00
20 Richie Petitbon	7.50	15.00
21 Myron Pottios	6.00	12.00
22 Walter Rock	6.00	12.00
23 Ray Schoenke	6.00	12.00
24 Manny Sistrunk	6.00	12.00
25 Jerry Smith	6.00	12.00
26 Jim Snowden	6.00	12.00
27 Diron Talbert	6.00	12.00
28 Charley Taylor	10.00	20.00
29 Ted Vactor	6.00	12.00
30 John Wilbur	6.00	12.00
31 Cover Card	7.50	15.00
Pardee		
M.Bass		
M.Sistrunk		
Hanburger		

1972 Redskins Picture Pack

This set of 8 1/2" by 11" photos was distributed in two separate "picture packs" with 14-defensive players in one and 16-offensive players in the other envelope. The fronts feature a player photo with his jersey number and name below the photo and the team name below that. The backs are blank and unnumbered.

Card	Low	High
COMPLETE SET (30)	75.00	150.00
1 Mack Alston	2.50	5.00
2 Mike Bass	2.50	5.00
3 Verlon Biggs	2.50	5.00
4 Larry Brown	4.00	8.00
5 Bill Brundige	2.50	5.00
6 Bob Brunet	2.50	5.00
7 Pat Fischer	2.50	5.00
8 Chris Hanburger	3.00	6.00
9 Charlie Harraway	2.50	5.00
10 Len Hauss	2.50	5.00
11 Terry Hermeling	2.50	5.00
12 Jon Jaqua	2.50	5.00
13 Roy Jefferson	3.00	6.00
14 Sonny Jurgensen	6.00	12.00
15 Billy Kilmer	5.00	10.00
16 Paul Laaveg	2.50	5.00
17 Harold McLinton	2.50	5.00
18 Ron McDole	2.50	5.00
19 Clifton McNeil	2.50	5.00
20 Brig Owens	2.50	5.00
21 Jack Pardee	3.00	6.00
22 Myron Pottios	2.50	5.00
23 Walter Rock	2.50	5.00
24 Manny Sistrunk	2.50	5.00
25 Jerry Smith	2.50	5.00
26 Diron Talbert	2.50	5.00
27 Charley Taylor	5.00	10.00
28 Roosevelt Taylor	3.00	6.00
29 Ted Vactor	2.50	5.00
30 John Wilbur	2.50	5.00

1973 Redskins McDonald's

These 11" by 14" color posters were sponsored by and distributed through McDonald's stores. Each includes an artist's rendering of one Redskins player along with the year and the "McDonald's Superstars Collector's Series" notation below the picture. Reprints can often be found of these prints but can be identified by the new white flat finish paper stock. The originals were printed on glossy cream colored stock.

Card	Low	High
COMPLETE SET (4)	60.00	100.00
1 Chris Hanburger	12.00	20.00
2 Sonny Jurgensen	25.00	40.00
3 Billy Kilmer	15.00	25.00
4 Charley Taylor	15.00	25.00

1973 Redskins Newspaper Posters

These oversized (roughly 14 1/4" by 21 1/2") posters were inserted into issues of The Sunday Star and The Washington Daily News throughout the 1973 season. Each poster features an artist's rendering of a player with just his name printed inside the image. Within the border below the image are the names of the two newspapers. The backs feature newsprint from another page of the paper. There were thought to have been 26-different posters produced. Any additions to this list are appreciated.

Card	Low	High
COMPLETE SET (24)	175.00	300.00
1 George Allen CO	12.50	25.00
2 Mike Bass	6.00	12.00
3 Verlon Biggs	6.00	12.00
4 Mike Bragg	6.00	12.00
5 Larry Brown	10.00	20.00
6 Speedy Duncan	7.50	15.00
7 Pat Fischer	7.50	15.00
8 Chris Hanburger	7.50	15.00
9 Charlie Harraway	6.00	12.00
10 Len Hauss	6.00	12.00
11 Roy Jefferson	6.00	12.00
12 Sonny Jurgensen	12.50	25.00
13 Billy Kilmer	10.00	20.00
14 Curt Knight	6.00	12.00
15 Paul Laaveg	6.00	12.00
16 Ron McDole	6.00	12.00
17 Brig Owens	6.00	12.00
18 Walter Rock	6.00	12.00
19 Ray Schoenke	6.00	12.00

20 Manny Sistrunk 6.00 12.00
21 Jerry Smith 6.00 12.00
22 Diron Talbert 6.00 12.00
23 Charley Taylor 10.00 20.00
24 Roosevelt Taylor 7.50 15.00

1973 Redskins Team Issue

This set of black and white player photos was released around 1973. Each measures roughly 8" by 10 1/8" and features the player in the red Redskins helmet in a kneeling pose. No player names are identified on the fronts but either a stamped or written name was often included on the, otherwise blank, cardbacks. They look very similar to the 1971 set but can be identified by the red player helmets.

COMPLETE SET (43) 175.00 300.00
1 George Allen CO 10.00 20.00
2 Mike Bass 5.00 10.00
3 Verlon Biggs 5.00 10.00
4 Mike Bragg 5.00 10.00
5 Larry Brown 6.00 12.00
6 Bill Brundige 5.00 10.00
7 Bob Brunet 5.00 10.00
8 Speedy Duncan 5.00 10.00
9 Brad Dusek 5.00 10.00
10 Pat Fischer 5.00 10.00
11 Frank Grant 5.00 10.00
12 Charlie Harraway 5.00 10.00
13 Chris Hanburger 6.00 12.00
14 Mike Hancock 5.00 10.00
15 Len Hauss 5.00 10.00
16 Terry Hermeling 5.00 10.00
17 Mike Hull 5.00 10.00
18 Dennis Johnson 5.00 10.00
19 Jimmie Jones 5.00 10.00
20 Sonny Jurgensen 10.00 20.00
21 Billy Kilmer 7.50 15.00
22 Curt Knight 5.00 10.00
23 Paul Laaveg 5.00 10.00
24 Bill Malinchak 5.00 10.00
25 Ron McDole 5.00 10.00
26 Harold McLinton 5.00 10.00
27 Herb Mul-Key 5.00 10.00
28 Brig Owens 5.00 10.00
29 Richie Petitbon 5.00 10.00
30 Myron Pottios 5.00 10.00
31 Walter Rock 5.00 10.00
32 Dan Ryczek 5.00 10.00
33 Ray Schoenke 5.00 10.00
34 Manny Sistrunk 5.00 10.00
35 Jerry Smith 5.00 10.00
36 Diron Talbert 5.00 10.00
37 Charley Taylor 7.50 15.00
38 Roosevelt Taylor 6.00 12.00
39 Duane Thomas 5.00 10.00
40 Russell Tillman 5.00 10.00
41 Ted Vactor 5.00 10.00
42 John Wilbur 5.00 10.00
43 Sam Wyche 6.00 12.00

1973 Redskins Team Issue Color

The NFLPA worked with many teams in 1973 to issued photo packs to be sold at stadium concession stands. Each measures approximately 7" by 8-5/8" and features a color player photo with a blank back. A small sheet with a player checklist was included in each 6-photo pack.

COMPLETE SET (6) 25.00 40.00
1 Larry Brown 4.00 8.00
2 Chris Hanburger 4.00 8.00
3 Sonny Jurgensen 6.00 12.00
4 Billy Kilmer 5.00 10.00
5 Charley Taylor 5.00 10.00
6 Duane Thomas 4.00 8.00

1974 Redskins McDonald's

For the second year, these 11" by 14" color posters were sponsored by and distributed through McDonald's stores. Each includes an artist's rendering of a Redskins player along with the year and the "McDonald's Superstars Collector's Series" notation below the picture. Reprints can often be found of these prints but can be identified by the new white flat finish paper stock. The originals were printed on glossy cream colored stock.

COMPLETE SET (4) 35.00 60.00
1 Larry Brown 12.00 20.00
2 Roy Jefferson 12.00 20.00
3 Herb Mul-Key 10.00 15.00
4 Diron Talbert 10.00 15.00

1977 Redskins Team Issue

This set of photos was released by the Washington Redskins. Each measures roughly 5" by 7" and includes a player photo on the front with a 1/2" white border on the top and bottom and a 3/8" border on the left and right. There is no player identification except for the facsimile autograph that appears on some of the photos. The backs are blank and unnumbered. The photos are similar in appearance to the 1979 issue. Any additions to this list are appreciated.

COMPLETE SET (7) 30.00 60.00
1 Eddie Brown 4.00 8.00
2 Chris Hanburger 5.00 10.00
3 Terry Hermeling 4.00 8.00
4 Billy Kilmer 6.00 12.00
5 Joe Theismann 10.00 20.00
6 Jersey #50 4.00 8.00
7 Jersey #57 4.00 8.00

1979 Redskins Team Issue

This set of photos was released by the Washington Redskins. Each measures roughly 5" by 7" and includes a player photo on the front with a 1/4" white border on all four sides. There is no player identification except for the facsimile autograph that appears on the photo. The backs are blank and unnumbered. The photos are similar in appearance to the 1977 issue.

COMPLETE SET (14) 50.00 100.00
1 Coy Bacon 4.00 8.00
2 Mike Curtis 5.00 10.00
3 Fred Dean 5.00 10.00
4 Greg Dubinetz 4.00 8.00
5 Phil DuBois 4.00 8.00
6 Ted Fritsch 4.00 8.00
7 Don Harris 4.00 8.00
8 Don Hover 4.00 8.00
9 Benny Malone 4.00 8.00
10 Kim McQuilken 4.00 8.00
11 Jack Pardee CO 5.00 10.00
12 Paul Smith 4.00 8.00
13 Diron Talbert 4.00 8.00
14 Joe Theismann 10.00 20.00

1981 Redskins Frito Lay Schedules

This 30-card bi-fold schedule set sponsored by Frito Lay measures approximately standard card size when folded and opens to measure 3-1/2" by 7-1/2." Each schedule features a color action shot of a Washington Redskins player inside with sponsor logos on the back. When completely opened, the left panel contains the 1981 schedule. The center panel features a color action player shot with the player's name, biography, and profile appearing on another fold. The regular season schedule is printed on the right inside panel. The schedules are unnumbered and checklisted below in alphabetical order.

COMPLETE SET (30) 50.00 100.00
1 Coy Bacon 2.00 5.00
2 Perry Brooks 1.50 4.00
3 Dave Butz 2.00 5.00
4 Rickey Claitt 1.50 4.00
5 Monte Coleman 2.00 5.00
6 Mike Connell 1.50 4.00
7 Brad Dusek 2.00 5.00
8 Ike Forte 1.50 4.00
9 Clarence Harmon 1.50 4.00
10 Terry Hermeling 1.50 4.00
11 Wilbur Jackson 1.50 4.00
12 Mike Kruczek 1.50 4.00
13 Bob Kuziel 1.50 4.00
14 Joe Lavender 2.00 5.00
15 Karl Lorch 1.50 4.00
16 John McDaniel 1.50 4.00
17 Rich Milot 1.50 4.00
18 Art Monk 2.50 6.00
19 Mark Moseley 2.00 5.00
20 Mark Murphy 2.00 5.00
21 Mike Nelms 1.50 4.00
22 Neal Olkewicz 1.50 4.00
23 Lemar Parrish 2.00 5.00
24 Tony Peters 1.50 4.00
25 Ron Saul 1.50 4.00
26 George Starke 1.50 4.00
27 Joe Theismann 2.50 6.00
28 Ricky Thompson 1.50 4.00
29 Don Warren 2.00 5.00
30 Jeris White 1.50 4.00

1982 Redskins Frito Lay Schedules

This 15-card bi-fold schedule set measures the standard card size when folded and opens to measure 3-1/2" by 7-1/2." Each schedule features a color action shot of a Washington Redskins player inside with sponsor logos on the back. When completely opened, the left panel contains the preseason and postseason schedules. The center panel features a color action player shot with the player's name, biography, and profile appearing on another fold. The regular season schedule is printed on the right inside panel. The schedules are unnumbered and checklisted below in alphabetical order.

COMPLETE SET (15) 20.00 40.00
1 Dave Butz 1.50 4.00
2 Monte Coleman 1.50 4.00
3 Brad Dusek 1.25 3.00
4 Joe Lavender 1.50 4.00
5 Art Monk 2.00 5.00
6 Mark Moseley 1.50 4.00
7 Mark Murphy 1.50 4.00
8 Mike Nelms 1.25 3.00
9 Neal Olkewicz 1.25 3.00
10 Tony Peters 1.25 3.00
11 John Riggins 2.50 6.00
12 George Starke 1.25 3.00
13 Joe Theismann 2.00 5.00
14 Don Warren 1.25 3.00
15 Joe Washington 1.50 4.00

1982 Redskins Police

The 1982 Washington Redskins set contains 15 numbered (in very small print on the card backs) full-color cards. The cards measure approximately 2 5/8" by 4 1/8". The set was sponsored by Frito-Lay, the local law enforcement agency, the Washington Redskins, and an organization known as PACT (Police and Citizens Together). Logos of Frito-Lay and PACT appear on the backs of the cards as do "Redskins PACT Tips". A Redskins helmet appears on the fronts of the cards.

COMPLETE SET (15) 4.00 10.00
1 Dave Butz .30 .75
2 Art Monk .75 2.00
3 Mark Murphy .20 .50
4 Monte Coleman .30 .75
5 Mark Moseley .30 .75
6 George Starke .20 .50
7 Perry Brooks .20 .50
8 Joe Washington .30 .75
9 Don Warren .30 .75
10 Joe Lavender .20 .50
11 Joe Theismann .75 2.00
12 Tony Peters .20 .50
13 Neal Olkewicz .20 .50
14 Mike Nelms .20 .50
15 John Riggins .75 2.00

1983 Redskins Frito Lay Schedules

This 15-card bi-fold schedule set measures 2 1/2" by 3 1/2" when folded and features the Super Bowl trophy and a Redskins helmet on front with sponsor logos on the back. When completely opened, the left panel contains the preseason and post season schedules. The center panel features a color action player shot with the player's name, biography, and profile appearing on another fold. The regular season schedule is printed on the right inside panel. The schedules are unnumbered and checklisted below in alphabetical order.

COMPLETE SET (15) 20.00 40.00
1 Charlie Brown 1.50 4.00
2 Dave Butz 1.50 4.00
3 The Hogs 1.50 4.00
4 Dexter Manley 1.50 4.00
5 Rich Milot 1.25 3.00
6 Art Monk 2.00 5.00
7 Mark Moseley 1.50 4.00
8 Mark Murphy 1.25 3.00
9 Mike Nelms 1.25 3.00
10 Neal Olkewicz 1.25 3.00
11 Tony Peters 1.25 3.00
12 John Riggins 2.50 6.00
13 Joe Theismann 2.00 5.00
14 Joe Washington 1.50 4.00
15 Jeris White 1.25 3.00

1983 Redskins Police

The 1983 Washington Redskins Police set consists of 16 numbered cards sponsored by Frito-Lay, the local law enforcement agency, PACT, and the Redskins. The cards measure 2 5/8" by 4 1/8" and were given out one per week (and are numbered according to that order) by the police department, except for week number 10, whose card featured Jeris White. White sat out the season and his card was not distributed; hence, it is available in lesser quantity than other cards in the set. Interestingly enough, the seventh week featured the issuance of Joe Theisman's card, who coincidentally, wears uniform number 7. The final card in this set, issued the 16th week, featured John Riggins. Logos of Frito-Lay and PACT appear on the back along with "Redskins/PACT Tips." The backs are printed in black with red accent on white card stock. There were some cards produced with a maroon color back. Although these maroon backs are more difficult to find, they are valued essentially the same.

COMPLETE SET (16) 4.00 10.00
1 Joe Washington .40 1.00
2 The Hogs .30 .75
3 Mark Moseley .40 1.00
4 Monte Coleman .20 .50
5 Mike Nelms .20 .50
6 Neal Olkewicz .20 .50
7 Joe Theismann 1.00 2.50
8 Charlie Brown .30 .75
9 Dave Butz .30 .75
10 Jeris White SP .60 1.50
11 Mark Murphy .20 .50
12 Dexter Manley .30 .75
13 Art Monk 1.00 2.50
14 Rich Milot .20 .50
15 Vernon Dean .20 .50
16 John Riggins 1.00 2.50

1984 Redskins Frito Lay Schedules

This 15-card bi-fold schedule set measures the standard card size when folded and opens to measure 3-1/2" by 7-1/2." Each schedule features a color action shot of a Washington Redskins player inside with sponsor logos on the back. When completely opened, the left panel contains the preseason and postseason schedules. The center panel features a color action player shot with the player's name, biography, and profile appearing on another fold. The regular season schedule is printed on the right inside panel. The schedules are unnumbered and checklisted below in alphabetical order.

COMPLETE SET (15) 20.00 40.00
1 Charlie Brown 1.50 4.00
2 Dave Butz 1.50 4.00
3 Ken Coffey 1.25 3.00
4 Clint Didier 1.25 3.00
5 Darryl Grant 1.25 3.00
6 Darrell Green 2.00 5.00
7 Jeff Hayes 1.25 3.00
8 The Hogs 1.50 4.00
9 Rich Milot 1.25 3.00
10 Art Monk 2.00 5.00
11 Mark Murphy 1.25 3.00
12 John Riggins 2.50 6.00
13 Joe Theismann 2.00 5.00
14 Don Warren 1.50 4.00
15 Joe Washington 1.50 4.00

1984 Redskins Police

This numbered (on back) set of 16 cards features the Washington Redskins. Cards measure approximately 2 5/8" by 4 1/8". Backs are printed in black ink with a maroon accent. The set was sponsored by Frito-Lay, the local law enforcement agency, and the Washington Redskins.

COMPLETE SET (16) 3.00 8.00
1 John Riggins .60 1.50
2 Darryl Grant .15 .40
3 Art Monk .60 1.50
4 Neal Olkewicz .15 .40
5 The Hogs .20 .50
6 Jeff Hayes .15 .40
7 Joe Theismann .50 1.25
8 Clint Didier .15 .40
9 Mark Murphy .15 .40
10 Don Warren .20 .50
11 Darrell Green .40 1.00
12 Dave Butz .20 .50
13 Ken Coffey .15 .40
14 Rich Milot .15 .40
15 Charlie Brown .20 .50
16 Joe Washington .20 .50

1985 Redskins Police

This 16-card set of Washington Redskins is numbered on the back. Cards measure approximately 2 5/8" by 4 1/8" and the backs contain a "McGruff Says". Each player's uniform number is given on the card front. The set was sponsored by Frito-Lay, the Redskins, and local law enforcement agencies. Card backs are written in maroon and black on white card stock.

COMPLETE SET (16) 2.50 6.00
1 Darrell Green .30 .75
2 Clint Didier .15 .40
3 Neal Olkewicz .15 .40
4 Darryl Grant .15 .40
5 Joe Jacoby .20 .50
6 Vernon Dean .15 .40
7 Joe Theismann .40 1.00
8 Mel Kaufman .15 .40
9 Calvin Muhammad .15 .40
10 Dexter Manley .20 .50
11 John Riggins .40 1.00
12 Mark May .20 .50
13 Dave Butz .20 .50
14 Art Monk .50 1.25
15 Russ Grimm .20 .50
16 Charles Mann .20 .50

1986 Redskins Frito Lay Schedules

These schedules feature all-time great members of the Redskins in celebration of the team's 50th anniversary in Washington. They are standard schedule size and were sponsored by Frito Lay. The schedules measure 2 1/2" by 3 1/2" when folded and opens to approximately 3 1/2" by 7 1/2." The schedules feature the Redskins' 50th Anniversary logo against a yellow background on the front with Frito-Lay's sponsor logos on the back. When completely opened the left panel contains the preseason and post season schedules with the center panel featuring the player's photo. The regular season schedule is printed on the right inside panel with the player's profile featured on the other side. Each schedule is unnumbered and checklisted below in alphabetical order.

COMPLETE SET (16) 15.00 30.00
1 Cliff Battles 1.25 3.00
2 Sammy Baugh 1.50 4.00
3 Larry Brown 1.00 2.50
4 Bill Dudley 1.25 3.00
5 Turk Edwards 1.00 2.50
6 Pat Fischer 1.00 2.50
7 Chris Hanburger 1.00 2.50
8 Wayne Millner 1.00 2.50
9 Sam Huff 1.50 4.00
10 Ken Houston 1.25 3.00
11 Sonny Jurgensen 1.50 4.00
12 Wayne Millner 1.25 3.00
13 Wayne Millner 1.25 3.00
14 Bobby Mitchell 1.50 4.00
15 Brig Owens 1.00 2.50
16 Charley Taylor .75 2.00

1986 Redskins Police

This 16-card set of Washington Redskins is numbered on the back. Cards measure approximately 2 5/8" by 4 1/8" and the backs contain a "Crime Prevention Tip". Each player's uniform number is given on the card front. The set was sponsored by Frito Lay, the Redskins, WMAL-AM63, and local law enforcement agencies. Card backs are printed in maroon and black on white card stock. The set commemorates the Redskins 50th Anniversary as a team.

COMPLETE SET (16) 2.50 6.00
1 Darrell Green .30 .75
2 Joe Jacoby .20 .50
3 Charles Mann .20 .50
4 Jay Schroeder .20 .50
5 Raphel Cherry .15 .40
6 Russ Grimm .20 .50
7 Mel Kaufman .15 .40
8 Gary Clark .50 1.25
9 Vernon Dean .15 .40
10 Mark May .20 .50
11 Dave Butz .20 .50
12 Jeff Bostic .20 .50
13 Dean Hamel .15 .40
14 Dexter Manley .20 .50
15 George Rogers .20 .50
16 Art Monk .40 1.00

1987 Redskins Ace Fact Pack

This 33-card set measures approximately 2 1/4" by 3 5/8" and features members of the Washington Redskins. This set was made in West Germany (by Ace Fact Pack) and the card design features rounded corners. We have checklisted the players portrayed in the set in alphabetical order.

COMPLETE SET (33) 100.00 200.00
1 Jeff Bostic 2.50 6.00
2 Dave Butz 2.50 6.00
3 Gary Clark 8.00 20.00
4 Monte Coleman 2.50 6.00
5 Vernon Dean 1.25 3.00
6 Clint Didier 1.25 3.00
7 Darryl Grant 2.50 6.00
8 Darrell Green 10.00 25.00
9 Russ Grimm 2.50 6.00
10 Joe Jacoby 2.50 6.00
11 Curtis Jordan 1.25 3.00
12 Dexter Manley 2.50 6.00
13 Charles Mann 2.50 6.00
14 Mark May 2.50 6.00
15 Rich Milot 1.25 3.00
16 Art Monk 20.00 50.00
17 Neal Olkewicz 1.25 3.00
18 George Rogers 2.50 6.00
19 Jay Schroeder 2.50 6.00
20 R.C. Thielemann 1.25 3.00
21 Alvin Walton 1.25 3.00
22 Don Warren 2.50 6.00
23 Redskins Helmet 1.25 3.00
24 Redskins Information 1.25 3.00
25 Redskins Uniform 1.25 3.00
26 Game Record Holders 1.25 3.00
27 Season Record Holders 1.25 3.00
28 Career Record Holders 1.25 3.00
29 Record 1967-86 1.25 3.00
30 1986 Team Statistics 1.25 3.00
31 All-Time Greats 1.25 3.00
32 Roll of Honour 1.25 3.00
33 Robert F. Kennedy 1.25 3.00

1987 Redskins Frito Lay Schedules

This 16-card bi-fold schedule set measures the standard card size when folded and opens to measure 3-1/2" by 7-1/2." Each schedule features a color action shot of a Washington Redskins player on the inside with sponsor logos on the back and Jay Schroeder on the front. When completely opened, the inside contains the season schedule. The schedules are unnumbered and checklisted below in alphabetical order.

COMPLETE SET (16) 15.00 30.00
1 Jeff Bostic 1.25 3.00
2 Kelvin Bryant 1.25 3.00
3 Dave Butz 1.25 3.00
4 Gary Clark 1.25 3.00
5 Steve Cox 1.00 2.50
6 Clint Didier 1.00 2.50
7 Darryl Grant 1.00 2.50
8 Darrell Green 1.25 3.00
9 Joe Jacoby 1.25 3.00
10 Dexter Manley 1.25 3.00
11 Charles Mann 1.25 3.00
12 Mark May 1.00 2.50
13 Art Monk 1.50 4.00
14 Jay Schroeder 1.00 2.50
15 Alvin Walton 1.00 2.50
16 Don Warren 1.00 2.50

1987 Redskins Police

This 16-card set of Washington Redskins is numbered on the back. The cards measure approximately 2 5/8" by 4 1/8" and the backs contain a "McGruff Says" crime prevention tip. The set was sponsored by Frito Lay and PACT (Police and Citizens Together). Card backs are written in red and black on white card stock. The cards were given out one per week in the greater Washington metropolitan area.

COMPLETE SET (16) 2.00 5.00
1 Joe Jacoby .15 .40
2 Gary Clark .30 .75
3 Dexter Manley .15 .40
4 Darrell Green .15 .40
5 Alvin Walton .12 .30
6 Clint Didier .12 .30
7 Art Monk .40 1.00
8 Darryl Grant .12 .30
9 Kelvin Bryant .15 .40
10 Jay Schroeder .15 .40
11 Don Warren .15 .40
12 Steve Cox .12 .30
13 Mark May .15 .40
14 Jeff Bostic .15 .40
15 Charles Mann .15 .40
16 Dave Butz .15 .40

1988 Redskins Frito Lay Schedules

This 16-card bi-fold schedule set measures 2 1/2" by 3 1/2" when folded and opens to approximately 3 1/2" by 7 1/2." The schedules feature the Super Bowl trophy on front against a maroon background with Frito-Lay sponsor logos on the back. When completely opened the left panel contains the preseason schedule and the center panel features a color action player shot with the player's name, biography, and profile appearing on another fold. The regular season schedule is printed on the right inside panel. Each schedule is unnumbered and checklisted below in alphabetical order.

COMPLETE SET (16) 15.00 30.00
1 Jeff Bostic 1.00 2.50
2 Dave Butz 1.00 2.50
3 Gary Clark 1.25 3.00
4 Brian Davis 1.00 2.50
5 Joe Jacoby 1.00 2.50
6 Markus Koch 1.00 2.50
7 Charles Mann 1.25 3.00
8 Wilber Marshall 1.25 3.00
9 Mark May 1.00 2.50
10 Raleigh McKenzie 1.00 2.50
11 Art Monk 1.50 4.00
12 Ricky Sanders 1.25 3.00
13 Alvin Walton 1.00 2.50
14 Don Warren 1.00 2.50
15 Barry Wilburn 1.00 2.50
16 Doug Williams .60 1.50

1988 Redskins Police

The 1988 Police Washington Redskins set contains 16 player cards measuring approximately 2 5/8" by 4 1/8". The fronts feature color action photos. The backs feature career highlights and safety tips. The Redskins team name appearing above the photo on the card front differentiates this set from other similar-looking Police Redskins sets.

COMPLETE SET (16) 2.00 5.00
1 Jeff Bostic .15 .40
2 Dave Butz .15 .40
3 Gary Clark .30 .75
4 Brian Davis .12 .30
5 Joe Jacoby .15 .40
6 Markus Koch .12 .30
7 Charles Mann .15 .40
8 Wilber Marshall .15 .40
9 Mark May .15 .40
10 Raleigh McKenzie .12 .30
11 Art Monk .40 1.00
12 Ricky Sanders .30 .75
13 Alvin Walton .12 .30
14 Don Warren .15 .40
15 Barry Wilburn .12 .30
16 Doug Williams .30 .75

1989 Redskins Mobil Schedules

This 16-card bi-fold schedule set sponsored by Mobil Oil measures the standard card size when folded and opens to measure 3-1/2" by 7-1/2." Each schedule features a color action shot of a Washington Redskins player with sponsor logos on the back. When completely opened, the inside contains the season schedule. The schedules are unnumbered and checklisted below in alphabetical order.

COMPLETE SET (16) 5.00 12.00
1 Ravin Caldwell .30 .75
2 Gary Clark .40 1.00
3 Monte Coleman .30 .75
4 Brian Davis .30 .75
5 Joe Jacoby .40 1.00
6 Jim Lachey .40 1.00
7 Chip Lohmiller .30 .75
8 Charles Mann .40 1.00
9 Wilber Marshall .40 1.00
10 Mark May .40 1.00
11 Raleigh McKenzie .30 .75
12 Art Monk .60 1.50
13 Mark Rypien .40 1.00
14 Ricky Sanders .30 .75
15 Don Warren .30 .75
16 Doug Williams .40 1.00

1989 Redskins Police

The 1989 Police Washington Redskins set contains 16 cards measuring approximately 2 5/8" by 4 1/8". The fronts have maroon borders and color action photos; the vertically oriented backs have safety tips, bios, and career highlights. These cards were printed on very thin stock. The cards are unnumbered, so therefore are listed below according to uniform number.

COMPLETE SET (16) 2.00 5.00
11 Mark Rypien .25 .60
17 Doug Williams .25 .60
21 Earnest Byner .15 .40
22 Jamie Morris .12 .30
28 Darrell Green .15 .40
34 Brian Davis .12 .30
37 Gerald Riggs .15 .40
50 Ravin Caldwell .12 .30
52 Neal Olkewicz .12 .30
58 Wilber Marshall .15 .40
73 Mark May .15 .40
74 Markus Koch .12 .30
81 Art Monk .40 1.00
83 Ricky Sanders .25 .60
84 Gary Clark .30 .75
85 Don Warren .15 .40

1990 Redskins Mobil Schedules

This 16-card bi-fold schedule set sponsored by Mobil Oil measures the standard card size when folded and opens to measure 3-1/2" by 7-1/2." Each schedule features a color action shot of a Washington Redskins player with sponsor logos on the back. When completely opened, the inside contains the season schedule. The schedules are unnumbered and checklisted below in alphabetical order.

COMPLETE SET (16) 4.80 12.00
1 Jeff Bostic .30 .75
2 Earnest Byner .40 1.00
3 Gary Clark .40 1.00
4 Darryl Grant .30 .75
5 Darrell Green .40 1.00
6 Jim Lachey .30 .75
7 Chip Lohmiller .40 1.00
8 Charles Mann .40 1.00
9 Wilber Marshall .40 1.00
10 Ralf Mojsiejenko .30 .75
11 Art Monk .60 1.50
12 Gerald Riggs .40 1.00
13 Mark Rypien .40 1.00
14 Ricky Sanders .40 1.00
15 Alvin Walton .30 .75
16 Don Warren .30 .75

1990 Redskins Police

This 16-card set, which measures approximately 2 5/8" by 4 1/8", features members of the 1990 Washington Redskins. This set features white borders surrounding full-color photos on the front and biographical information on the back along with a safety tip. The set was sponsored by Mobil Oil, PACT (Police and Citizens Together), and Fox-5 of Washington WTIC. We have checklisted this set alphabetically.

COMPLETE SET (16) 2.00 5.00
1 Todd Bowles .30 .75
2 Earnest Byner .14 .35
3 Ravin Caldwell .08 .25
4 Gary Clark .25 .60
5 Darrell Green .14 .35
6 Jimmie Johnson .08 .25
7 Jim Lachey .14 .35
8 Chip Lohmiller .14 .35
9 Charles Mann .14 .35
10 Greg Manusky .08 .25
11 Wilber Marshall .14 .35
12 Art Monk .30 .75
13 Gerald Riggs .14 .35
14 Mark Rypien .14 .35
15 Alvin Walton .08 .25
16 Don Warren .14 .35

1991 Redskins Mobil Schedules

Distributed at area Mobil stations, this 16-piece tri-fold paper schedule set measures 2 1/2" by 3 1/2" when folded and features a color action shot of Art Monk on the front with the Mobil logo on the back. When completely opened, the left panel contains the preseason and postseason schedule while the right panel presents the regular season schedule. The center panel features a full color action player shot. The player's name, biography, and profile appear on the following fold. The schedules are unnumbered and checklisted below in alphabetical order.

COMPLETE SET (16) 4.80 12.00
1 Earnest Byner .40 1.00
2 Gary Clark .30 .75
3 Andre Collins .30 .75
4 Kurt Gouveia .30 .75
5 Darrell Green .40 1.00
6 Jimmie Johnson .30 .75
7 Markus Koch .30 .75
8 Jim Lachey .40 1.00
9 Chip Lohmiller .30 .75
10 Charles Mann .40 1.00
11 Martin Mayhew .30 .75
12 Art Monk .60 1.50
13 Mark Rypien .40 1.00
14 Mark Schlereth .30 .75
15 Ed Simmons .30 .75
16 Eric Williams .30 .75

1991 Redskins Police

This 16-card set was jointly sponsored by Mobil, PACT (Police and Citizens Together), and WTTG Channel 5 TV. The set was released in the Washington area during the 1991 season. The cards measure approximately 2 5/8" by 4 1/8" and are printed on thin card stock. Card fronts carry a full-color player action shot on a white background. The word "Washington" is printed in black in a gold bar at top of card while the team name appears in large red print up the left side. Player's name is reversed out in a black stripe at bottom, while player's number appears in a gold circle to the left. Vertically printed backs present biographical information, player profile, an anti-drug message, and trivia question. Sponsors' logos appear at bottom. The cards are unnumbered and checklisted below in alphabetical order.

COMPLETE SET (16) 2.00 5.00
1 John Brandes .08 .25
2 Earnest Byner .14 .35
3 Gary Clark .25 .60
4 Andre Collins .14 .35
5 Darrell Green .14 .35
6 Joe Howard .08 .25
7 Tim Johnson .08 .25
8 Jim Lachey .14 .35
9 Chip Lohmiller .08 .25
10 Charles Mann .14 .35
11 Art Monk .30 .75
12 Mark Rypien .14 .35
13 Mark Schlereth .08 .25
14 Fred Stokes .08 .25
15 Don Warren .14 .35
16 Eric Williams .08 .25

1992 Redskins Mobil Schedules

Distributed at area Mobil stations, this 16-piece bi-fold paper schedule set measures 2 1/2" by 3 1/2" when folded and features a color action shot of Fred Stokes sacking Jim Kelly on the front with the Mobil logo on the back. When completely opened, the left panel contains the preseason and postseason schedule while the right panel contains the regular season schedule. The center panel features a full color action player shot. The player's name, biography, and profile appear on the following fold. The schedules are unnumbered and checklisted below in alphabetical order.

COMPLETE SET (16) 4.00 10.00
1 Gary Clark .30 .75
2 Brad Edwards .25 .60
3 Ricky Ervins .30 .75
4 Jumpy Geathers .25 .60
5 Darrell Green .30 .75
6 Joe Jacoby .25 .60
7 Tim Johnson .25 .60
8 Charles Mann .30 .75
9 Wilber Marshall .30 .75
10 Ron Middleton .25 .60
11 Brian Mitchell .30 .75
12 Art Monk .40 1.00
13 Jim Lachey .25 .60
14 Chip Lohmiller .25 .60
15 Mark Rypien .30 .75
16 Fred Stokes .25 .60

1992 Redskins Police

This 16-card set was jointly sponsored by Mobil, PACT (Police and Citizens Together), and Fox WTTG Channel 5. The cards measure approximately 2 1/2" by 4 1/8" and features action color player photos on a brick-red background. The pictures are offset, bleeding off the right edge of the card, and are framed on the other three sides in white. At the upper left corner of the picture is the Vince Lombardi trophy, and at the lower left corner is the uniform number in a circle. The team name appears at the top in mustard. The white backs feature biographical information, career highlights, and anti-drug and crime prevention tips in the form of player quotes. The cards are unnumbered and checklisted below in alphabetical order.

COMPLETE SET (16) 2.00 5.00
1 Jeff Bostic .15 .40
2 Earnest Byner .15 .40
3 Gary Clark .25 .60
4 Monte Coleman .15 .40
5 Andre Collins .15 .40
6 Danny Copeland .10 .30
7 Kurt Gouvela .10 .30
8 Darrell Green .15 .40
9 Jim Lachey .15 .40
10 Charles Mann .15 .40
11 Wilber Marshall .15 .40
12 Raleigh McKenzie .10 .30
13 Art Monk .40 1.00
14 Mark Rypien .15 .40
15 Mark Schlereth .10 .30
16 Eric Williams .10 .30

1993 Redskins Mobil Schedules

Distributed at area Mobil stations, this 16-piece tri-fold paper schedule set measures 2 1/2" by 3 1/2" when folded and features a color action shot of Andre Collins tackling Emmitt Smith on the front with the Mobil logo on the back. When completely opened, the left panel contains the preseason and postseason schedule while the right panel contains the regular season schedule. The center panel features a full color action player shot. The player's name, biography, and profile appear on the following fold. The schedules are unnumbered and checklisted below in alphabetical order.

COMPLETE SET (16) 4.00 10.00
1 Todd Bowles .40 1.00
2 Earnest Byner .30 .75
3 Monte Coleman .30 .75
4 Andre Collins .30 .75
5 Shane Collins .25 .60
6 Danny Copeland .25 .60
7 Kurt Gouveia .25 .60
8 Darrell Green .30 .75
9 A.J. Johnson .25 .60
10 Jim Lachey .25 .60
11 Ron Middleton .25 .60
12 Brian Mitchell .40 1.00
13 Mark Rypien .30 .75
14 Ricky Sanders .30 .75
15 Mark Schlereth .25 .60
16 Ed Simmons .25 .60

1993 Redskins Police

These 16 cards measure approximately 2 3/4" by 4 1/8" and feature on their fronts yellow-bordered color player action shots. The player's name, team helmet, and uniform number rest within the bottom yellow margin. The white back carries the player's name and uniform number at the top, followed below by biography, career highlights, and safety message. The logos for Mobil, Cellular One, and Police and Citizens Together (PACT) at the bottom round out the card. The cards are unnumbered and checklisted below in alphabetical order.

COMPLETE SET (16) 2.00 5.00
1 Ray Brown OL .10 .30
2 Andre Collins .15 .40
3 Brad Edwards .10 .30
4 Matt Elliott .10 .30
5 Ricky Ervins .15 .40
6 Darrell Green .15 .40
7 Desmond Howard .30 .75
8 Joe Jacoby .15 .40
9 Tim Johnson .10 .30
10 Jim Lachey .15 .40
11 Chip Lohmiller .10 .30
12 Charles Mann .15 .40
13 Raleigh McKenzie .10 .30
14 Brian Mitchell .20 .50
15 Terry Orr .10 .30
16 Mark Rypien .15 .40

1994 Redskins Mobil Schedules

Distributed at area Mobil stations, this 16-piece bi-fold paper schedule set measures 2 1/2" by 3 1/2" when folded and features a color action shot on the front with the Mobil logo on the back. When completely opened, the left panel contains the preseason and postseason schedule while the right panel contains the regular season schedule. The center panel features a full color action player shot. The player's name, biography, and profile appear on the following fold. The schedules are unnumbered and checklisted below in alphabetical order.

COMPLETE SET (16) 3.20 8.00
1 Reggie Brooks .30 .75
2 Ray Brown .25 .60
3 Tom Carter .30 .75
4 Shane Collins .25 .60
5 Darrell Green .30 .75
6 Ken Harvey .30 .75
7 Lamont Hollinquest .25 .60
8 Desmond Howard .40 1.00
9 Tim Johnson .25 .60
10 Jim Lachey .25 .60
11 Chip Lohmiller .25 .60
12 Brian Mitchell .30 .75
13 Sterling Palmer .25 .60
14 Heath Shuler .50 1.25
15 Bobby Wilson .25 .60
16 Frank Wycheck .25 .60

1994 Redskins Police

These 16 cards measure approximately 2 3/4" by 4 1/8" and feature on their fronts maroon-bordered color player action shots. The player's name, team helmet, and uniform number rest within the bottom margin. The white back carries the player's name and uniform number at the top, followed below by biography, career highlights, and safety message. The cards are unnumbered and checklisted below in alphabetical order.

COMPLETE SET (16) 2.40 6.00
1 Tom Carter .15 .40
2 Monte Coleman .15 .40
3 Andre Collins .10 .30
4 Pat Eilers .10 .30
5 Henry Ellard .30 .75
6 Ricky Ervins .15 .40
7 Darrell Green .30 .75
8 Ethan Horton .10 .30
9 Desmond Howard .30 .75
10 Jim Lachey .15 .40
11 Alvoid Mays .10 .30
12 Ron Middleton .10 .30
13 Brian Mitchell .15 .40
14 Raleigh McKenzie .10 .30
15 Reggie Roby .10 .30
16 Ed Simmons .10 .30

1995 Redskins Program Sheets

These eight sheets measure approximately 8" by 10" and appeared in regular-season issues of the Redskins' GameDay program. The set features panoramic stadium photographs at which championship games involving the Washington Redskins were played. The sheets are listed below in chronological order.

COMPLETE SET (8) 10.00 25.00
1 Wrigley Field 1.40 3.50
Redskins vs Bears 1937, 1943
2 Griffith Stadium 1.40 3.50
Redskins vs Bears, 1940, 1942
3 Cleveland Stadium 1.40 3.50
Redskins vs Rams, 1945
4 L.A. Coliseum 1.40 3.50
Redskins vs Dolphins, S.B. VII
5 Rose Bowl 1.40 3.50
Redskins vs Dolphins, S.B. XVII
6 Tampa Stadium 1.40 3.50
Redskins vs Raiders, S.B. XVIII
7 Jack Murphy Stadium 1.40 3.50
Skins vs Broncos, S.B. XXII
8 H.H.H. Metrodome 1.40 3.50
Redskins vs Bills, S.B. XXVI

1996 Redskins Score Board/Exxon

Score Board produced this team set for distribution by the Washington D.C. area Exxon stations. Each card appears similar to a 1996 Pro Line card, but contains the Score Board logo at the top. The Exxon sponsor logo appears only on the checklist card. Packs could be obtained, with the appropriate gasoline purchase, for 49-cents each and contained three-player cards and a checklist card.

COMPLETE SET (9) 1.40 3.50
WR1 Gus Frerotte .30 .75
WR2 Terry Allen .30 .75
WR3 Henry Ellard .15 .40
WR4 Michael Westbrook .60 1.50
WR5 Brian Mitchell .08 .25
WR6 Sean Gilbert .08 .25
WR7 Ken Harvey .08 .25
WR8 Darrell Green .15 .40
WR9 Redskins Checklist .08 .25

2001 Redskins Read Bookmarks

1 Jeff George .75 2.00
2 Chris Samuels .75 2.00

2006 Redskins Topps

COMPLETE SET (12) 3.00 6.00
WAS1 Clinton Portis .25 .60
WAS2 Jason Campbell .25 .60
WAS3 Carlos Rogers .25 .60
WAS4 Shawn Springs .25 .60
WAS5 Santana Moss .30 .75
WAS6 Chris Cooley .25 .60
WAS7 Antwaan Randle El .25 .60
WAS8 Mark Brunell .30 .75
WAS9 Brandon Lloyd .25 .60
WAS10 Adam Archuleta .25 .60
WAS11 Rocky McIntosh .25 .60
WAS12 Sean Taylor .40 1.00

2007 Redskins Activa Medallions

COMPLETE SET (22) 30.00 60.00
1 George Allen 1.50 4.00
2 Sammy Baugh 1.50 4.00
3 Dave Butz 1.50 3.50
4 Gary Clark 1.50 3.50
5 Monte Coleman 1.50 3.50
6 Joe Gibbs 1.50 4.00
7 Russ Grimm 1.50 3.50
8 Joe Jacoby 1.50 3.50
9 Ken Houston 1.50 3.50
10 Sam Huff 1.50 4.00
11 Sonny Jurgensen 1.50 4.00
12 Billy Kilmer 1.50 3.50
13 Dexter Manley 1.50 3.50
14 Bobby Mitchell 1.50 4.00
15 Mark Moseley 1.50 3.50
16 John Riggins 1.50 4.00
17 Mark Rypien 1.50 3.50
18 Charley Taylor 1.50 3.50
19 Joe Theismann 1.50 4.00
20 Don Warren 1.50 3.50
21 Doug Williams 1.50 3.50
22 Super Bowl Wins 1.50 3.50

2007 Redskins Topps

COMPLETE SET (12) 2.50 5.00
1 London Fletcher .50 1.25
2 Antwaan Randle El .40 1.00
3 Jason Campbell .40 1.00
4 Sean Taylor .60 1.50
5 Clinton Portis .40 1.00
6 Santana Moss .50 1.25
7 Chris Cooley .40 1.00
8 Ladell Betts .40 1.00
9 Mark Brunell .50 1.25
10 Lemar Marshall .40 1.00
11 Carlos Rogers .40 1.00
12 LaRon Landry .60 1.50

2008 Redskins Topps

COMPLETE SET (12) 2.50 5.00
1 Jason Campbell .40 1.00
2 Clinton Portis .40 1.00
3 Chris Cooley .40 1.00
4 Santana Moss .40 1.00
5 Todd Collins .40 1.00
6 Ladell Betts .40 1.00
7 Antwaan Randle El .40 1.00
8 Andre Carter .40 1.00
9 London Fletcher .50 1.25
10 LaRon Landry .50 1.25
11 Devin Thomas .40 1.00
12 Malcolm Kelly .40 1.00

2004 Reflections

Reflections initially released in mid-August 2004. The base set consists of -294cards including 194-rookies numbered between 450 and 1150. Hobby boxes contained 8-packs of 4-cards and carried an S.R.P. of $14.99 per pack. Four parallel sets and a variety of inserts can be found seeded in hobby packs highlighted by the Signature Reflections and Signature Threads autograph inserts.

COMP.SET w/o SP's (100) 15.00 40.00
201-294 RC PRINT RUN 1150 SER.#'d SETS
OVERALL RC STATED ODDS 1:1
1 Emmitt Smith 1.00 2.50
2 Anquan Boldin .40 1.00
3 Josh McCown .50 1.25
4 Michael Vick .50 1.25
5 Peerless Price .40 1.00
6 T.J. Duckett .40 1.00
7 Todd Heap .40 1.00
8 Jamal Lewis .50 1.25
9 Kyle Boller .40 1.00
10 Drew Bledsoe .50 1.25
11 Travis Henry .40 1.00
12 Eric Moulds .40 1.00
13 Jake Delhomme .40 1.00
14 Steve Smith .60 1.50
15 Stephen Davis .40 1.00
16 Rex Grossman .40 1.00
17 Brian Urlacher .60 1.50
18 Anthony Thomas .50 1.25
19 Rudi Johnson .40 1.00
20 Carson Palmer .50 1.25
21 Chad Johnson .40 1.00
22 Jeff Garcia .40 1.00
23 Andre Davis .40 1.00
24 Quincy Morgan .40 1.00
25 Keyshawn Johnson .50 1.25
26 Roy Williams S .40 1.00
27 Quincy Carter .40 1.00
28 Ashley Lelie .40 1.00
29 Champ Bailey .50 1.25
30 Jake Plummer .40 1.00
31 Az-Zahir Hakim .40 1.00
32 Joey Harrington .40 1.00
33 Charles Rogers .40 1.00
34 Javon Walker .40 1.00
35 Ahman Green .50 1.25

36 Brett Favre 1.25 3.00
37 Domanick Davis .40 1.00
38 David Carr .40 1.00
39 Andre Johnson .50 1.25
40 Edgerrin James .50 1.25
41 Marvin Harrison .50 1.25
42 Dwight Freeney .40 1.00
43 Peyton Manning 1.50 4.00
44 Fred Taylor .40 1.00
45 Jimmy Smith .50 1.25
46 Byron Leftwich .40 1.00
47 Dante Hall .40 1.00
48 Tony Gonzalez .50 1.25
49 Trent Green .40 1.00
50 Priest Holmes .40 1.00
51 Zach Thomas .50 1.25
52 A.J. Feeley .40 1.00
53 Chris Chambers .40 1.00
54 Ricky Williams .50 1.25
55 Randy Moss .50 1.25
56 Onterrio Smith .40 1.00
57 Daunte Culpepper .50 1.25
58 Tom Brady 2.50 6.00
59 Troy Brown .40 1.00
60 Corey Dillon .40 1.00
61 Donte Stallworth .40 1.00
62 Deuce McAllister .50 1.25
63 Aaron Brooks .40 1.00
64 Amani Toomer .40 1.00
65 Jeremy Shockey .40 1.00
66 Michael Strahan .50 1.25
67 Curtis Martin .50 1.25
68 Chad Pennington .40 1.00
69 Santana Moss .50 1.25
70 Jerry Porter .40 1.00
71 Jerry Rice 1.25 3.00
72 Rich Gannon .50 1.25
73 Tim Brown .60 1.50
74 Terrell Owens .50 1.25
75 Brian Westbrook .40 1.00
76 Donovan McNabb .50 1.25
77 Tommy Maddox .40 1.00
78 Hines Ward .50 1.25
79 Duce Staley .40 1.00
80 Donnie Edwards .50 1.25
81 LaDainian Tomlinson .60 1.50
82 Drew Brees .60 1.50
83 Brandon Lloyd .50 1.25
84 Tim Rattay .40 1.00
85 Kevan Barlow .40 1.00
86 Koren Robinson .40 1.00
87 Shaun Alexander .40 1.00
88 Matt Hasselbeck .40 1.00
89 Torry Holt .50 1.25
90 Marc Bulger .40 1.00
91 Marshall Faulk .50 1.25
92 Brad Johnson .50 1.25
93 Keenan McCardell .40 1.00
94 Charlie Garner .50 1.25
95 Steve McNair .50 1.25
96 Chris Brown .40 1.00
97 Eddie George .50 1.25
98 Mark Brunell .50 1.25
99 Laveranues Coles .40 1.00
100 Clinton Portis .40 1.00
101 Kris Wilson/750 RC 1.50 4.00
102 Carlos Francis/750 RC 1.25 3.00
103 D.J. Williams/750 RC 2.00 5.00
104 Devery Henderson/450 RC 1.50 4.00
105 Craig Krenzel/750 RC 1.25 3.00
106 Jonathan Vilma/750 RC 1.50 4.00
107 Luke McCown/750 RC 1.25 3.00
108 Michael Turner/750 RC 1.25 3.00
109 Richard Seigler/750 RC 1.25 3.00
110 Stuart Schweigert/750 RC 1.50 4.00
111 Ben Watson/750 RC 1.50 4.00
112 Chris Perry/450 RC 1.50 4.00
113 Jason Fife/750 RC 1.25 3.00
114 Eli Manning/450 RC 12.00 30.00
115 Matt Kegel/750 RC 2.00 5.00
116 Kellen Winslow/450 RC 1.50 4.00
117 Chris Cooley/750 RC 1.50 4.00
118 Quincy Wilson/750 RC 1.25 3.00
119 Samie Parker/750 RC 1.25 3.00
120 Vince Wilfork/750 RC 2.00 5.00
121 Bernard Berrian/750 RC 1.25 3.00
122 Ahmad Carroll/750 RC 1.25 3.00
123 Derrick Hamilton/750 RC 1.25 3.00
124 Rich Gardner/750 RC 1.50 4.00
125 Jeff Smoker/750 RC 1.50 4.00
126 Kenechi Udeze/750 RC 1.50 4.00
127 Mewelde Moore/750 RC 1.50 4.00
128 Keyaron Fox/750 RC 1.50 4.00
129 Sean Jones/750 RC 1.25 3.00
130 Will Poole/750 RC 2.00 5.00
131 Travelle Wharton/750 RC 1.25 3.00
132 Demorrio Williams/750 RC 2.00 5.00
133 Jason Babin/750 RC 2.00 5.00
134 Ernest Wilford/750 RC 1.50 4.00
135 Jerricho Cotchery/750 RC 1.50 4.00
136 Kevin Jones/450 RC 2.00 5.00
137 Michael Boulware/750 RC 2.00 5.00
138 D.J. Hackett/750 RC 1.25 3.00
139 Sean Taylor/450 RC 10.00 25.00
140 Will Smith/750 RC 1.50 4.00
141 John Standeford/750 RC 1.25 3.00
142 Max Starks/750 RC 1.50 4.00
143 Cody Pickett/750 RC 1.25 3.00
144 Derrick Strait/750 RC 1.25 3.00
145 Greg Jones/450 RC 1.50 4.00
146 John Navarre/750 RC 1.25 3.00
147 Larry Fitzgerald/450 RC 6.00 15.00
148 Michael Clayton/450 RC 2.00 5.00
149 Rashaun Woods/450 RC 1.50 4.00
150 Shawn Andrews/750 RC 1.50 4.00
151 B.J. Symons/750 RC 1.25 3.00
152 Cedric Cobbs/450 RC 1.50 4.00
153 Darius Watts/750 RC 1.25 3.00
154 B.J. Johnson/750 RC 1.25 3.00
155 Ricardo Colclough/750 RC 1.25 3.00
156 Josh Harris/750 RC 1.25 3.00
157 Derek Abney/750 RC 1.25 3.00
158 Kendrick Starling/750 RC 1.25 3.00
159 Robert Gallery/450 RC 2.00 5.00
160 Tatum Bell/450 RC 1.50 4.00
161 Ben Hartsock/750 RC 1.25 3.00
162 Dwan Edwards/750 RC 1.25 3.00
163 Darnell Dockett/750 RC 2.00 5.00
164 Igor Olshansky/750 RC 1.50 4.00
165 Justin Smiley/750 RC 1.50 4.00
166 Julius Jones/450 RC 1.50 4.00
167 Matt Mauck/750 RC 1.25 3.00
168 Derek McCoy/750 RC 1.25 3.00
169 Chris Pittman/750 RC 1.25 3.00
170 Teddy Lehman/750 RC 1.25 3.00
171 Ben Troupe/450 RC 1.50 4.00
172 Chris Gamble/750 RC 1.25 3.00
173 DeAngelo Hall/750 RC 2.00 5.00
174 Dunta Robinson/750 RC 1.25 3.00
175 Jason Shivers/750 RC 1.25 3.00
176 Keary Colbert/450 RC 1.50 4.00
177 Jared Lorenzen/750 RC 1.50 4.00
178 Philip Rivers/450 RC 5.00 12.00
179 Roy Williams/450 RC 1.50 4.00
180 Bob Sanders/750 RC 2.50 6.00
181 Antwan Odom/750 RC 1.25 3.00
182 Josh Davis/750 RC 1.50 4.00
183 Courtney Watson/750 RC 1.25 3.00
184 Devard Darling/750 RC 1.25 3.00
185 J.P. Losman/450 RC 1.50 4.00
186 Johnnie Morant/750 RC 1.25 3.00
187 Lee Evans/450 RC 2.50 6.00
188 Michael Jenkins/450 RC 1.50 4.00
189 Reggie Williams/450 RC 1.50 4.00
190 Steven Jackson/450 RC 2.50 6.00
191 Roethlisberger/450 RC 12.00 30.00
192 P.K. Sam/750 RC 1.25 3.00
193 Derrick Knight/750 RC 1.25 3.00
194 Drew Henson/450 RC 1.50 4.00
195 Marquise Hill/750 RC 1.25 3.00
196 Karlos Dansby/750 RC 1.50 4.00
197 Matt Schaub/750 RC 1.25 3.00
198 Ben Utecht/750 RC 1.50 4.00
199 Darrion Scott/750 RC 1.50 4.00
200 Tommie Harris/750 RC 1.50 4.00
201 Andrae Thurman RC 1.00 2.50
202 Matt Kranchick RC 1.25 3.00
203 Shaun Phillips RC 1.25 3.00
204 Landon Johnson RC 1.00 2.50
205 Jeff Dugan RC 1.00 2.50
206 Wes Welker RC 5.00 12.00
207 Michael Gaines RC 1.00 2.50
208 Jamaar Taylor RC 1.00 2.50
209 Brandon Chillar RC 1.25 3.00
210 Jermaine Green RC 1.00 2.50
211 Triandos Luke RC 1.00 2.50
212 Brandon Miree RC 1.00 2.50
213 Dexter Reid RC 1.00 2.50
214 Isaac Hilton RC 1.25 3.00
215 Adrian Jones RC 1.00 2.50
216 Grant Wiley RC 1.00 2.50
217 Matt Cherry RC 1.00 2.50
218 Courtney Anderson RC 1.00 2.50
219 Antonio Smith RC 1.25 3.00
220 Sean Tufts RC 1.00 2.50
221 Johnny Lamar RC 1.00 2.50
222 Shawn Johnson RC 1.00 2.50
223 Jason Peters RC 1.25 3.00
224 Rodney Leisle RC 1.00 2.50
225 Lane Danielsen RC 1.00 2.50
226 Zack Abron RC 1.00 2.50
227 Romar Crenshaw RC 1.00 2.50
228 Keiwan Ratliff RC 1.00 2.50
229 Chad Lavalais RC 1.00 2.50
230 Jason Wright RC 1.00 2.50
231 Rayshun Reed RC 1.00 2.50
232 Patrick Crayton RC 1.50 4.00
233 Casey Bramlet RC 1.00 2.50
234 Nathaniel Adibi RC 1.00 2.50
235 Dontarrious Thomas RC 1.25 3.00
236 B.J. Sander RC 1.25 3.00
237 Ryan McGuffey RC 1.00 2.50
238 Shawntae Spencer RC 1.00 2.50
239 Amon Gordon RC 1.00 2.50
240 Vernon Carey RC 1.00 2.50
241 Stanford Samuels RC 1.00 2.50
242 Thomas Tapeh RC 1.25 3.00
243 Keith Smith RC 1.00 2.50
244 Casey Clausen RC 1.25 3.00
245 Jake Grove RC 1.00 2.50
246 Omar Nazel RC 1.00 2.50
247 Jammal Lord RC 1.00 2.50
248 Jeremy LeSueur RC 1.00 2.50
249 Daryl Smith RC 1.00 2.50
250 Nat Dorsey RC 1.00 2.50
251 Tim Anderson RC 1.25 3.00
252 Chris Snee RC 2.00 5.00
253 Sean Ryan RC 1.00 2.50
254 Tank Johnson RC 1.00 2.50
255 Marquis Cooper RC 1.00 2.50
256 Josh Scobee RC 1.25 3.00
257 Justin Jenkins RC 1.00 2.50
258 Nate Lawrie RC 1.00 2.50
259 Randy Starks RC 1.00 2.50
260 Caleb Miller RC 1.00 2.50
261 A.J. Ricker RC 1.00 2.50
262 Andy Hall RC 1.00 2.50
263 Troy Fleming RC 1.00 2.50
264 Matt Ware RC 1.50 4.00
265 Christian Ferrara RC 1.00 2.50
266 Stacy Andrews RC 1.00 2.50
267 Reggie Torbor RC 1.00 2.50
268 Jeris McIntyre RC 1.00 2.50
269 Jarrett Payton RC 1.25 3.00
270 Ronald Jones RC 1.00 2.50
271 Kelly Butler RC 1.00 2.50
272 Bryan Hickman RC 1.00 2.50
273 Chris Collins RC 1.00 2.50
274 Ryan Dinwiddie RC 1.00 2.50
275 Robert Geathers RC 1.00 2.50
276 Niko Koutouvides RC 1.00 2.50
277 Clarence Farmer RC 1.00 2.50
278 Jim Sorgi RC 1.25 3.00
279 Ran Carthon RC 1.00 2.50
280 Michael Waddell RC 1.00 2.50
281 Andrew Strojny RC 1.00 2.50
282 Sloan Thomas RC 1.25 3.00
283 Tim Euhus RC 1.00 2.50
284 Lawrence Richardson RC 1.00 2.50
285 Nate Kaeding RC 1.25 3.00
286 Ryan Krause RC 1.00 2.50
287 Derrick Ward RC 1.50 4.00
288 Nathan Vasher RC 1.50 4.00
289 Bobby McCray RC 1.00 2.50
290 Scott Rislov RC 1.00 2.50
291 Ryan Boschetti RC 1.00 2.50
292 Fred Russell RC 1.25 3.00
293 Von Hutchins RC 1.00 2.50
294 Derrick Crawford RC 1.00 2.50

2004 Reflections Black

UNPRICED BLACK PRINT RUN 1
NOT PRICED DUE TO SCARCITY

2004 Reflections Blue

*VETS: 6X TO 15X BASIC CARDS
*ROOKIES: 2X TO 5X ROOKIE/450
*ROOKIES: 2.5X TO 6X ROOKIE/750
*ROOKIES: 3X TO 8X ROOKIE/1150
BLUE STATED PRINT RUN 10

2004 Reflections Green

*VETS: 3X TO 8X BASIC CARDS
*ROOKIES: 1X TO 2.5X ROOKIE/450
*ROOKIES: 1.2X TO 3X ROOKIE/750
*ROOKIES: 1.5X TO 4X ROOKIE/1150
STATED PRINT RUN 50 SER.#'d SETS

2004 Reflections Red

*VETS: 2X TO 5X BASIC CARDS
*ROOKIES: .6X TO 1.5X ROOKIE/450
*ROOKIES: .8X TO 2X ROOKIE/750
*ROOKIES: 1X TO 2.5X ROOKIE/1150
STATED PRINT RUN 100 SER.#'d SETS

2004 Reflections Fantasy Fabrics

STATED PRINT RUN 99 SER.#'d SETS
*LTD PATCH/21: 1X TO 2.5X BASIC JSY
LTD PATCH PRINT RUN 21 SETS
*RAINBOW/15: 1.2X TO 3X BASIC JSY
RAINBOW PRINT RUN 15 SETS
FFAB Anquan Boldin 2.00 5.00
FFAG Ahman Green 2.50 6.00
FFAR Antwaan Randle El 2.00 5.00
FFBF Brett Favre 6.00 15.00
FFCC Chris Chambers 2.00 5.00
FFCH Chad Pennington 2.00 5.00
FFCJ Chad Johnson 2.00 5.00
FFCM Curtis Martin 2.50 6.00
FFCP Clinton Portis 2.00 5.00
FFDA David Carr 2.00 5.00
FFDC Daunte Culpepper 2.50 6.00
FFDD Domanick Davis 2.00 5.00
FFDE Deuce McAllister 2.50 6.00
FFDM Donovan McNabb 2.50 6.00
FFEJ Edgerrin James 2.50 6.00
FFGR Trent Green 2.00 5.00
FFHW Hines Ward 2.50 6.00
FFJB Jerome Bettis 3.00 8.00
FFJL Jamal Lewis 2.50 6.00
FFJW Javon Walker 2.00 5.00
FFKR Koren Robinson 2.00 5.00
FFLC Laveranues Coles 2.00 5.00
FFLT LaDainian Tomlinson 3.00 8.00
FFMA Derrick Mason 2.00 5.00
FFMF Marshall Faulk 2.50 6.00
FFMH Marvin Harrison 2.50 6.00
FFMO Santana Moss 2.50 6.00
FFMV Michael Vick 2.50 6.00
FFPH Priest Holmes 2.00 5.00
FFPM Peyton Manning 8.00 20.00
FFPP Peerless Price 2.00 5.00
FFPR Patrick Ramsey 2.50 6.00
FFRJ Rudi Johnson 2.00 5.00
FFRM Randy Moss 2.50 6.00
FFRW Ricky Williams 2.50 6.00
FFSA Shaun Alexander 2.00 5.00
FFSD Stephen Davis 2.00 5.00
FFSM Steve McNair 2.50 6.00
FFTB Tom Brady 12.00 30.00
FFTG Tony Gonzalez 2.50 6.00
FFTH Torry Holt 2.50 6.00
FFTR Travis Henry 2.00 5.00

2004 Reflections Focus on the Future Jerseys Gold

GOLD STATED ODDS 1:3
*RAINBOW/85: .6X TO 1.5X GOLD
RAINBOW PRINT RUN 85
FOAB Anquan Boldin 2.00 5.00
FOAJ Andre Johnson 2.50 6.00
FOAL Ashley Lelie 2.00 5.00
FOBJ Bethel Johnson 2.00 5.00
FOBL Byron Leftwich 2.00 5.00
FOBR Ben Roethlisberger 10.00 25.00
FOCB Chris Brown 2.00 5.00
FOCC Chris Chambers 2.00 5.00
FOCH Chris Perry 2.00 5.00
FOCP Carson Palmer 2.50 6.00
FOCR Charles Rogers 2.00 5.00
FODC David Carr 2.00 5.00
FODD Domanick Davis 2.00 5.00
FODH Dante Hall 2.00 5.00
FODS Donte Stallworth 2.00 5.00
FOEM Eli Manning 10.00 25.00
FOJH Joey Harrington 2.00 5.00
FOJJ Julius Jones 1.25 3.00
FOJP J.P. Losman 1.25 3.00
FOJS Jeremy Shockey 2.00 5.00
FOKB Kyle Boller 2.00 5.00
FOKJ Kevin Jones 2.50 6.00
FOKR Koren Robinson 2.00 5.00
FOKW Kellen Winslow Jr. 1.25 3.00
FOLC Laveranues Coles SP 2.00 5.00
FOLF Larry Fitzgerald 5.00 12.00
FOLS Lee Suggs SP 2.50 6.00
FOMB Marc Bulger 2.00 5.00
FOOS Onterrio Smith 2.00 5.00
FOPA Patrick Ramsey SP 2.50 6.00
FOPB Plaxico Burress 2.00 5.00
FOPR Philip Rivers 4.00 10.00
FORE Reggie Williams 2.00 5.00
FORG Rex Grossman 2.00 5.00
FORJ Rudi Johnson 2.00 5.00
FORO Roy Williams WR 1.25 3.00
FORW Roy Williams S 2.00 5.00
FOSJ Steven Jackson 2.00 5.00
FOTB Tatum Bell 2.00 5.00
FOTC Tyrone Calico 2.50 6.00
FOTH Todd Heap 2.00 5.00
FOTS Terrell Suggs 2.00 5.00

2004 Reflections Offensive Threads

STATED PRINT RUN 99 SER.#'d SETS
*LTD PATCH/21: 1X TO 2.5X BASIC JSY
LTD PATCH PRINT RUN 21 SETS
*RAINBOW/15: 1.2X TO 3X BASIC JSY
RAINBOW PRINT RUN 15 SETS
OTAB Aaron Brooks 2.50 6.00
OTAG Ahman Green 3.00 8.00
OTAJ Andre Johnson 3.00 8.00
OTBF Brett Favre 8.00 20.00
OTBJ Brad Johnson 3.00 8.00
OTBL Byron Leftwich 2.50 6.00
OTCD Corey Dillon 2.50 6.00
OTCL Clinton Portis 2.50 6.00
OTCP Chad Pennington 2.50 6.00
OTCR Charles Rogers 2.50 6.00
OTDB David Boston 2.50 6.00
OTDC Daunte Culpepper 3.00 8.00
OTDE Deuce McAllister 3.00 8.00
OTDH Dante Hall 2.50 6.00
OTDM Donovan McNabb 3.00 8.00
OTDR Drew Bledsoe 3.00 8.00
OTEJ Edgerrin James 3.00 8.00
OTHA Matt Hasselbeck 2.50 6.00
OTJH Joey Harrington 2.50 6.00
OTJL Jamal Lewis 3.00 8.00
OTJP Jake Plummer 2.50 6.00
OTJR Jerry Rice 8.00 20.00
OTJS Jeremy Shockey 2.50 6.00
OTLT LaDainian Tomlinson 4.00 10.00
OTMA Derrick Mason 2.50 6.00
OTMB Marc Bulger 2.50 6.00
OTMF Marshall Faulk 3.00 8.00
OTMH Marvin Harrison 3.00 8.00
OTMV Michael Vick 3.00 8.00
OTPB Plaxico Burress 2.50 6.00
OTPH Priest Holmes 2.50 6.00
OTPM Peyton Manning 10.00 25.00
OTQC Quincy Carter 2.50 6.00
OTRM Randy Moss 3.00 8.00
OTRW Ricky Williams 3.00 8.00
OTSA Shaun Alexander 2.50 6.00
OTSD Stephen Davis 2.50 6.00
OTSM Steve McNair 3.00 8.00
OTTB Tom Brady 15.00 40.00
OTTH Torry Holt 3.00 8.00
OTTO Terrell Owens 3.00 8.00
OTTR Troy Brown 2.50 6.00

2004 Reflections Pro Cuts Jerseys Gold

OVERALL PRO CUTS ODDS 1:6
*SILVER/85: .6X TO 1.5X GOLD
SILVER PRINT RUN 85 SER.#'d SETS
PCAB Aaron Brooks 2.00 5.00
PCAG Ahman Green 2.50 6.00
PCBF Brett Favre 6.00 15.00
PCBR Tim Brown 3.00 8.00
PCBU Brian Urlacher 3.00 8.00
PCCH Chad Pennington 2.00 5.00
PCCJ Chad Johnson 2.00 5.00
PCCM Curtis Martin 2.50 6.00
PCCP Clinton Portis 2.00 5.00
PCDC Daunte Culpepper 2.50 6.00
PCDM Deuce McAllister 2.50 6.00
PCDO Donovan McNabb 2.50 6.00
PCEG Eddie George 2.50 6.00
PCEJ Edgerrin James 2.50 6.00
PCES Emmitt Smith 5.00 12.00
PCJD Jake Delhomme SP 2.00 5.00
PCJH Joe Horn 2.00 5.00
PCJL Jamal Lewis 2.50 6.00
PCJR Jerry Rice 6.00 15.00
PCJS Junior Seau 3.00 8.00
PCKJ Keyshawn Johnson 2.50 6.00
PCLA LaVar Arrington SP 2.00 5.00
PCLT LaDainian Tomlinson 3.00 8.00
PCMF Marshall Faulk SP 2.50 6.00
PCMH Marvin Harrison 2.50 6.00
PCMS Michael Strahan 2.50 6.00
PCMV Michael Vick 2.50 6.00
PCPH Priest Holmes 2.00 5.00
PCPM Peyton Manning 8.00 20.00
PCRI Ricky Williams 2.50 6.00
PCRL Ray Lewis 3.00 8.00
PCRM Randy Moss 2.50 6.00
PCRW Roy Williams S 2.00 5.00
PCSM Santana Moss 2.50 6.00
PCST Steve McNair 2.50 6.00
PCTB Tom Brady 12.00 30.00
PCTG Tony Gonzalez 2.50 6.00
PCTH Torry Holt 2.50 6.00
PCTI Tiki Barber 2.50 6.00
PCTO Terrell Owens 2.50 6.00
PCWS Warren Sapp 2.50 6.00

2004 Reflections Select Swatch

STATED PRINT RUN 99 SER.#'d SETS
*LTD PATCH/21: 1X TO 2.5X BASIC JSY
LTD PATCH PRINT RUN 21 SETS
*RAINBOW/15: 1.2X TO 3X BASIC JSY
RAINBOW PRINT RUN 15 SETS
SSAB Aaron Brooks 2.50 6.00
SSAG Ahman Green 3.00 8.00
SSAN Anquan Boldin 2.50 6.00
SSBF Brett Favre 8.00 20.00
SSBU Brian Urlacher 4.00 10.00
SSCJ Chad Johnson 2.50 6.00
SSCL Clinton Portis 2.50 6.00
SSCP Chad Pennington 2.50 6.00
SSDA David Carr 2.50 6.00
SSDC Daunte Culpepper 3.00 8.00
SSDD Domanick Davis 2.50 6.00
SSDE Deuce McAllister 3.00 8.00
SSDH Dante Hall 2.50 6.00
SSDM Donovan McNabb 3.00 8.00
SSEJ Edgerrin James 3.00 8.00
SSHW Hines Ward 3.00 8.00
SSJL Jamal Lewis 3.00 8.00
SSJR Jerry Rice 8.00 20.00
SSJS Jeremy Shockey 2.50 6.00
SSKR Koren Robinson 2.50 6.00
SSLA LaVar Arrington 2.50 6.00
SSLC Laveranues Coles 2.50 6.00
SSLT LaDainian Tomlinson 4.00 10.00
SSMA Matt Hasselbeck 2.50 6.00
SSMB Marc Bulger 2.50 6.00
SSMF Marshall Faulk 3.00 8.00
SSMH Marvin Harrison 3.00 8.00
SSMS Michael Strahan 3.00 8.00
SSMV Michael Vick 3.00 8.00
SSPH Priest Holmes 2.50 6.00
SSPM Peyton Manning 10.00 25.00
SSRL Ray Lewis 4.00 10.00
SSRM Randy Moss 3.00 8.00
SSRW Ricky Williams 3.00 8.00
SSSA Shaun Alexander 2.50 6.00
SSSM Steve McNair 3.00 8.00
SSTB Tom Brady 15.00 40.00
SSTG Tony Gonzalez 3.00 8.00
SSTH Torry Holt 3.00 8.00
SSTO Terrell Owens 3.00 8.00
SSWI Roy Williams S 2.50 6.00
SSZT Zach Thomas 3.00 8.00

2004 Reflections Signature Reflections

STATED ODDS 1:28
SRAR Andy Reid 10.00 25.00
SRBB Bernard Berrian 6.00 15.00
SRBF Brett Favre 100.00 200.00
SRBP Bill Parcells 20.00 40.00
SRBR Ben Roethlisberger SP 100.00 200.00
SRBT Ben Troupe 6.00 15.00
SRCP Chris Perry 6.00 15.00
SRDC Daunte Culpepper 10.00 25.00
SRDE DeAngelo Hall 10.00 25.00
SRDH Drew Henson 6.00 15.00
SRDM Donovan McNabb SP 15.00 40.00
SRDV Devery Henderson 6.00 15.00
SRDW Darius Watts 6.00 15.00
SREM Eli Manning 75.00 150.00
SRGJ Greg Jones 6.00 15.00
SRGR Jon Gruden SP 20.00 35.00
SRJF John Fox 8.00 20.00
SRJO Joe Montana SP 150.00 250.00
SRJP J.P. Losman 6.00 15.00
SRKC Keary Colbert 6.00 15.00
SRKJ Kevin Jones 8.00 20.00
SRKW Kellen Winslow Jr. 6.00 15.00
SRLE Lee Evans 10.00 25.00
SRLF Larry Fitzgerald SP 75.00 150.00
SRLM Luke McCown 6.00 15.00
SRMC Michael Clayton 8.00 20.00
SRMJ Michael Jenkins 6.00 15.00
SRMS Matt Schaub 6.00 15.00
SRMV Michael Vick 20.00 50.00
SRPM Peyton Manning 50.00 100.00
SRPR Philip Rivers 25.00 60.00
SRRE Reggie Williams 6.00 15.00
SRRG Rex Grossman 8.00 20.00
SRRO Robert Gallery 8.00 20.00
SRRW Ricky Williams 10.00 25.00
SRSJ Steven Jackson 10.00 25.00
SRTB Tom Brady SP 150.00 250.00
SRTH Travis Henry SP 8.00 20.00
SRTR Troy Aikman SP 40.00 80.00
SRWI Roy Williams WR 6.00 15.00
SRWO Rashaun Woods 6.00 15.00

2004 Reflections Signature Threads

STATED PRINT RUN 99 SER.#'d SETS
STBF Brett Favre 100.00 200.00
STBL Byron Leftwich 10.00 25.00
STBR Ben Roethlisberger 100.00 200.00
STCB Chris Brown 8.00 20.00
STCH Chris Perry 8.00 20.00
STCJ Chad Johnson 10.00 25.00
STCPO Chad Pennington 10.00 25.00
STDB Drew Bledsoe 12.00 30.00
STDC David Carr 10.00 25.00
STDD Domanick Davis 10.00 25.00
STDH Dante Hall 10.00 25.00
STDM Donovan McNabb 10.00 25.00
STEM Eli Manning 100.00 200.00
STGA Robert Gallery 10.00 25.00
STJG Joey Galloway 12.00 30.00
STJM Josh McCown 10.00 25.00
STJP Jesse Palmer 10.00 25.00
STJT Joe Theismann 15.00 40.00
STKB Kyle Boller 10.00 25.00
STKE Kellen Winslow 12.00 30.00
STKJ Kevin Jones 10.00 25.00
STKW Kelley Washington 10.00 25.00
STLE Lee Evans 12.00 30.00
STLO J.P. Losman 8.00 20.00
STLT LaDainian Tomlinson 15.00 40.00
STMA Mark Brunell 12.00 30.00
STMC Deuce McAllister 12.00 30.00
STMV Michael Vick 30.00 60.00
STPM Peyton Manning 75.00 135.00
STPR Philip Rivers 50.00 120.00
STRG Rex Grossman 10.00 25.00
STRJ Rudi Johnson 10.00 25.00
STRO Roy Williams S 10.00 25.00
STRW Ricky Williams 12.00 30.00
STSM Steve McNair 25.00 50.00
STTB Tom Brady 400.00 800.00
STTG Tony Gonzalez 12.00 30.00
STTH Todd Heap 10.00 25.00
STTR Travis Henry 10.00 25.00
STWI Roy Williams WR 8.00 20.00
STWM Willis McGahee 10.00 25.00
STZT Zach Thomas 12.00 30.00

2004 Reflections Signature Threads LTD Patch

*LTD PATCH: .6X TO 1.5X BASIC INSERTS
STATED PRINT RUN 21 SER.#'d SETS
STPBF Brett Favre 150.00 300.00
STPBR Ben Roethlisberger 150.00 300.00
STPEM Eli Manning 125.00 250.00
STPPM Peyton Manning 125.00 250.00
STPPR Philip Rivers 75.00 200.00
STPTB Tom Brady 150.00 300.00

2004 Reflections Signature Threads Rainbow

*RAINBOW: 1.2X TO 3X BASIC INSERTS
RAINBOW STATED PRINT RUN 15
STBF Brett Favre 200.00 350.00
STBR Ben Roethlisberger 200.00 350.00
STEM Eli Manning 200.00 350.00
STPM Peyton Manning 150.00 300.00
STTB Tom Brady 200.00 350.00

2005 Reflections

This 300-card set was released in October, 2005. The set was issued in the hobby through four-card packs with a $9.99 SRP which came 12 packs to a box. Cards numbered 1-100 were veterans in team alphabetical order while cards numbered 101-300 featured 2005 NFL rookies. Cards numbered 101-175 were printed to a stated print run of 899 serial numbered sets, cards numbered 176-225 were printed to a stated print run of 699 serial numbered sets, cards numbered 226-275 wewre printed to a stated print run of 499 and the final cards in the set (276-300) were printed to a stated print run of 299 serial numbered sets. The rookie cardxs were inserted into packs at an overall stated rate of one in three.

COMP.SET w/o SP's (100) 12.50 30.00
101-175 PRINT RUN 899 SER.#'d SETS
176-225 PRINT RUN 699 SER.#'d SETS
226-275 PRINT RUN 499 SER.#'d SETS
276-300 PRINT RUN 299 SER.#'d SETS
OVERALL DRAFT PICK ODDS 1:3
UNPRICED RAINBOW PRINT RUN 1 SET
1 Larry Fitzgerald .50 1.25
2 Anquan Boldin .30 .75
3 Josh McCown .40 1.00
4 Michael Vick .40 1.00
5 Warrick Dunn .30 .75
6 Peerless Price .30 .75
7 Ray Lewis .50 1.25
8 Jamal Lewis .40 1.00
9 Kyle Boller .30 .75
10 Derrick Mason .30 .75
11 J.P. Losman .30 .75
12 Willis McGahee .30 .75
13 Lee Evans .40 1.00
14 Eric Moulds .30 .75
15 Jake Delhomme .30 .75
16 Keary Colbert .30 .75
17 DeShaun Foster .40 1.00
18 Brian Urlacher .50 1.25
19 Rex Grossman .30 .75
20 Muhsin Muhammad .30 .75
21 Carson Palmer .40 1.00
22 Rudi Johnson .30 .75
23 Chad Johnson .30 .75
24 Julius Jones .30 .75
25 Keyshawn Johnson .40 1.00
26 Drew Bledsoe .40 1.00
27 Tatum Bell .30 .75
28 Jake Plummer .30 .75
29 Ashley Lelie .30 .75
30 Roy Williams WR .30 .75
31 Kevin Jones .30 .75
32 Jeff Garcia .30 .75
33 Brett Favre 1.00 2.50
34 Ahman Green .40 1.00
35 Javon Walker .30 .75
36 David Carr .30 .75
37 Andre Johnson .40 1.00
38 Domanick Davis .30 .75
39 Peyton Manning 1.25 3.00
40 Reggie Wayne .40 1.00
41 Edgerrin James .40 1.00
42 Marvin Harrison .40 1.00
43 Byron Leftwich .30 .75
44 Fred Taylor .30 .75
45 Jimmy Smith .40 1.00
46 Priest Holmes .30 .75
47 Larry Johnson .30 .75
48 Trent Green .30 .75
49 A.J. Feeley .30 .75
50 Chris Chambers .30 .75
51 Randy McMichael .30 .75
52 Daunte Culpepper .40 1.00
53 Onterrio Smith .30 .75
54 Nate Burleson .30 .75
55 Tom Brady 2.00 5.00
56 Corey Dillon .30 .75
57 Deion Branch .30 .75
58 David Givens .30 .75
59 Aaron Brooks .30 .75
60 Deuce McAllister .40 1.00
61 Joe Horn .30 .75
62 Eli Manning .75 2.00
63 Jeremy Shockey .30 .75
64 Tiki Barber .40 1.00
65 Chad Pennington .30 .75
66 Curtis Martin .40 1.00
67 Laveranues Coles .30 .75
68 Kerry Collins .30 .75
69 Jerry Porter .30 .75
70 Randy Moss .40 1.00
71 Donovan McNabb .40 1.00
72 Terrell Owens .40 1.00
73 Brian Dawkins .50 1.25
74 Brian Westbrook .30 .75
75 Ben Roethlisberger .75 2.00
76 Jerome Bettis .50 1.25
77 Hines Ward .40 1.00
78 Duce Staley .30 .75
79 Drew Brees .50 1.25
80 LaDainian Tomlinson .50 1.25
81 Antonio Gates .50 1.25
82 Tim Rattay .30 .75
83 Kevan Barlow .30 .75
84 Eric Johnson .30 .75
85 Shaun Alexander .30 .75
86 Darrell Jackson .30 .75
87 Matt Hasselbeck .30 .75
88 Marc Bulger .30 .75
89 Steven Jackson .30 .75
90 Marshall Faulk .40 1.00
91 Torry Holt .40 1.00
92 Michael Pittman .30 .75
93 Brian Griese .30 .75
94 Michael Clayton .30 .75
95 Steve McNair .40 1.00
96 Billy Volek .30 .75
97 Chris Brown .30 .75
98 Clinton Portis .30 .75
99 Patrick Ramsey .40 1.00
100 Santana Moss .40 1.00
101 James Kilian RC 1.25 3.00
102 Matt Cassel RC 1.25 3.00
103 Keron Henry RC 1.25 3.00
104 Adrian McPherson RC 1.25 3.00
105 Marcus Randall RC 1.50 4.00
106 Roydel Williams RC 1.50 4.00
107 Dante Ridgeway RC 1.25 3.00
108 Marcus Maxwell RC 1.25 3.00
109 Paris Warren RC 1.50 4.00
110 Courtney Roby RC 1.25 3.00
111 Mark Bradley RC 1.25 3.00
112 Brandon Jones RC 1.50 4.00
113 Chase Lyman RC 1.25 3.00
114 LeRon McCoy RC 1.25 3.00
115 Adam Bergen RC 1.25 3.00
116 Harry Williams RC 1.50 4.00
117 Lance Moore RC 15.00 30.00
118 Jason Anderson RC 1.25 3.00
119 Lionel Gates RC 1.25 3.00
120 Darrell Shropshire RC 1.25 3.00
121 Will Matthews RC 1.25 3.00
122 Noah Herron RC 1.25 3.00
123 Jerome Collins RC 1.50 4.00
124 Stanford Routt RC 1.50 4.00
125 Nick Collins RC 2.00 5.00
126 Maurice Clarett 1.25 3.00
127 Kelvin Hayden RC 1.50 4.00
128 Bo Scaife RC 1.50 4.00
129 Eric King RC 1.25 3.00
130 Kerry Rhodes RC 1.50 4.00
131 Darrent Williams RC 2.00 5.00
132 Stanley Wilson RC 1.50 4.00
133 Nick Speegle RC 1.25 3.00
134 Brodney Pool RC 1.50 4.00
135 Ellis Hobbs RC 2.00 5.00
136 Sean Considine RC 1.25 3.00
137 Josh Bullocks RC 1.50 4.00
138 Jovan Haye RC 1.25 3.00
139 Jimmy Verdon RC 1.25 3.00
140 Ryan Riddle RC 1.25 3.00
141 Luis Castillo RC 1.50 4.00
142 Jesse Lumsden RC 1.25 3.00
143 David Baas RC 1.25 3.00
144 Chris Spencer RC 2.00 5.00
145 Jamaal Brown RC 2.00 5.00
146 Marcus Lawrence RC 1.25 3.00
147 Todd Mortensen RC 1.25 3.00
148 Shane Boyd RC 1.25 3.00
149 Darian Durant RC 1.25 3.00
150 Chance Mock RC 1.50 4.00
151 Damien Nash RC 1.50 4.00
152 Deandra Cobb RC 1.25 3.00
153 Jamaica Rector RC 1.25 3.00
154 Carlyle Holiday RC 1.50 4.00
155 Nehemiah Broughton RC 1.50 4.00
156 Efrem Hill RC 1.25 3.00
157 Dominic Robinson RC 1.25 3.00
158 Rick Razzano RC 1.25 3.00
159 Rasheed Marshall RC 1.50 4.00
160 Lofa Tatupu RC 1.50 4.00
161 Robert McCune RC 1.50 4.00
162 Channing Crowder RC 1.50 4.00
163 Ryan Claridge RC 1.25 3.00
164 Fred Amey RC 1.25 3.00
165 Jordan Beck RC 1.50 4.00
166 Leroy Hill RC 2.00 5.00
167 Travis Daniels RC 1.50 4.00
168 Jerome Carter RC 1.25 3.00
169 Chad Friehauf RC 1.50 4.00
170 Scott Starks RC 1.50 4.00
171 Marviel Underwood RC 1.50 4.00
172 Domonique Foxworth RC 1.50 4.00
173 Jon Goldsberry RC 2.00 5.00
174 Jonathan Babineaux RC 1.25 3.00
175 Sione Pouha RC 1.25 3.00
176 Kerry Wright RC 1.50 4.00
177 Jason White RC 2.00 5.00
178 Matt Jones RC 1.25 3.00
179 Gino Guidugli RC 1.25 3.00
180 Timmy Chang RC 1.25 3.00
181 Chris Rix RC 1.50 4.00
182 Ryan Fitzpatrick RC 2.00 5.00
183 Brock Berlin RC 1.25 3.00
184 Bryan Randall RC 1.50 4.00
185 Stefan LeFors RC 1.25 3.00
186 Larry Brackins RC 1.25 3.00
187 Charles Frederick RC 1.25 3.00
188 J.R. Russell RC 1.25 3.00
189 Vincent Jackson RC 2.00 5.00
190 Josh Davis RC 1.25 3.00
191 Chad Owens RC 1.25 3.00
192 Airese Currie RC 1.25 3.00
193 Chauncey Stovall RC 1.25 3.00
194 Jovan Witherspoon RC 1.25 3.00
195 Trent Cole RC 2.00 5.00
196 Tab Perry RC 1.25 3.00
197 Cedric Houston RC 2.00 5.00
198 Brandon Jacobs RC 1.50 4.00
199 Bobby Purify RC 1.50 4.00
200 Marion Barber RC 1.25 3.00
201 Alvin Pearman RC 1.25 3.00
202 Madison Hedgecock RC 2.00 5.00
203 Justin Green RC 2.00 5.00
204 Manuel White RC 1.50 4.00
205 Kevin Everett RC 2.00 5.00
206 Matthew Tant RC 1.25 3.00
207 Bryant McFadden RC 1.50 4.00
208 Ryan Moats RC 1.25 3.00
209 Fabian Washington RC 1.25 3.00
210 Oshiomogho Atogwe RC 1.50 4.00
211 Dustin Fox RC 1.50 4.00
212 Shaun Cody RC 1.50 4.00
213 Matt Roth RC 1.25 3.00
214 Vincent Burns RC 1.25 3.00
215 Bill Swancutt RC 1.25 3.00
216 Brady Poppinga RC 2.00 5.00
217 Logan Mankins RC 2.00 5.00
218 Michael Roos RC 1.25 3.00
219 Alfred Fincher RC 1.50 4.00
220 Darryl Blackstock RC 1.25 3.00
221 Jared Newberry RC 1.50 4.00
222 Khalif Barnes RC 1.25 3.00
223 Alex Barron RC 1.25 3.00
224 Patrick Estes RC 1.25 3.00
225 Elton Brown RC 1.25 3.00
226 David Greene RC 1.50 4.00
227 Dan Orlovsky RC 1.50 4.00
228 Derek Anderson RC 2.00 5.00
229 Kyle Orton RC 1.50 4.00
230 Chris Henry RC 2.00 5.00
231 Fred Gibson RC 1.50 4.00
232 Craphonso Thorpe RC 1.50 4.00
233 Terrence Murphy RC 1.50 4.00
234 Steve Savoy RC 1.50 4.00
235 Roscoe Parrish RC 1.50 4.00
236 Reggie Brown RC 1.50 4.00
237 Craig Bragg RC 1.50 4.00
238 Eric Shelton RC 1.50 4.00
239 T.A. McLendon RC 1.50 4.00
240 Walter Reyes RC 1.50 4.00
241 Anthony Davis RC 1.50 4.00
242 J.J. Arrington RC 2.00 5.00
243 Frank Gore RC 3.00 8.00
244 Alex Smith TE RC 1.50 4.00
245 Jeb Huckeba RC 2.00 5.00
246 Adam Jones RC 1.50 4.00
247 Brandon Browner RC 2.50 6.00
248 Carlos Rogers RC 2.50 6.00
249 Corey Webster RC 2.00 5.00
250 Justin Miller RC 1.50 4.00
251 Eric Green RC 1.50 4.00
252 Kurt Campbell RC 1.50 4.00
253 Ronald Bartell RC 2.00 5.00
254 Billy Bajema RC 1.50 4.00
255 Vincent Fuller RC 2.00 5.00
256 Donte Nicholson RC 1.50 4.00
257 Derrick Johnson RC 2.00 5.00
258 Mike Patterson RC 1.50 4.00
259 Anttaj Hawthorne RC 1.50 4.00
260 Erasmus James RC 1.50 4.00
261 David Pollack RC 1.50 4.00
262 Garrett Cross RC 1.50 4.00
263 Justin Tuck RC 2.00 5.00
264 DeMarcus Ware RC 5.00 12.00
265 Odell Thurman RC 2.50 6.00
266 Barrett Ruud RC 2.00 5.00
267 Lance Mitchell RC 2.00 5.00
268 Kevin Burnett RC 2.00 5.00
269 Daven Holly RC 1.50 4.00
270 James Butler RC 2.00 5.00
271 Kirk Morrison RC 2.50 6.00
272 Mike Nugent RC 2.00 5.00
273 Zach Tuiasosopo RC 1.50 4.00
274 Kay-Jay Harris RC 1.50 4.00
275 Darren Sproles RC 2.50 6.00
276 Ciatrick Fason RC 2.00 5.00
277 Charlie Frye RC 2.00 5.00
278 Vernand Morency RC 2.00 5.00
279 Jason Campbell RC 2.00 5.00
280 Antrel Rolle RC 3.00 8.00
281 Derrick Johnson RC 2.50 6.00
282 Shawne Merriman RC 3.00 8.00
283 Marlin Jackson RC 2.00 5.00
284 Jerome Mathis RC 3.00 8.00
285 Mike Williams 2.50 6.00
286 Dan Cody RC 2.00 5.00
287 Travis Johnson RC 2.00 5.00
288 Thomas Davis RC 2.00 5.00
289 Marcus Spears RC 2.00 5.00
290 Andrew Walter RC 2.00 5.00
291 Heath Miller RC 4.00 10.00
292 Mark Clayton RC 2.00 5.00
293 Troy Williamson RC 2.00 5.00
294 Roddy White RC 3.00 8.00
295 Braylon Edwards RC 2.00 5.00
296 Cedric Benson RC 2.00 5.00
297 Cadillac Williams RC 2.00 5.00
298 Ronnie Brown RC 2.50 6.00
299 Alex Smith QB RC 8.00 20.00
300 Aaron Rodgers RC 40.00 80.00

2005 Reflections Black

*VETERANS 1-100: 6X TO 15X BASIC CARDS
*ROOKIES 101-175: 1.5X TO 4X BASIC CARDS
*ROOKIES 176-225: 1.5X TO 4X BASIC CARDS
*ROOKIES 226-275: 1.2X TO 3X BASIC CARDS
*ROOKIES 276-300: 1X TO 2.5X BASIC CARDS
STATED PRINT RUN 25 SER.#'d SETS
OVERALL PARALLEL ODDS 1:6
300 Aaron Rodgers 175.00 300.00

2005 Reflections Blue

*VETERANS 1-100: 2.5X TO 6X BASIC CARDS
*ROOKIES 101-175: .6X TO 1.5X
*ROOKIES 176-225: .6X TO 1.5X
*ROOKIES 226-275: .5X TO 1.2X
*ROOKIES 276-300: .4X TO 1X
STATED PRINT RUN 99 SER.#'d SETS
300 Aaron Rodgers 60.00 120.00

2005 Reflections Gold

*VETERANS 1-100: 4X TO 10X BASIC CARDS
*ROOKIES 101-175: 1X TO 2.5X BASIC CARDS
*ROOKIES 176-225: 1X TO 2.5X BASIC CARDS
*ROOKIES 226-275: .8X TO 2X BASIC CARDS
*ROOKIES 276-300: .6X TO 1.5X
STATED PRINT RUN 50 SER.#'d SETS
300 Aaron Rodgers 100.00 200.00

2005 Reflections Green

*VETERANS: 3X TO 8 BASIC CARDS
*ROOKIES 101-175: .8X TO 2X BASIC CARDS
*ROOKIES 176-225: .8X TO 2X BASIC CARDS
*ROOKIES 226-275: .6X TO 1.5X
*ROOKIES 276-300: .5X TO 1.2X
STATED PRINT RUN 75 SER.#'d SETS
300 Aaron Rodgers 125.00 200.00

2005 Reflections Cut From the Same Cloth Red

RED STATED ODDS 1:12
*BLUE/50: .6X TO 1.5X RED
CCBJ M.Bulger/S.Jackson 2.50 6.00
CCBR M.Bradley/Re.Brown 2.50 6.00
CCBT T.Barber/F.Taylor SP 3.00 8.00
CCBW Ro.Brown/C.Williams 3.00 8.00
CCCJ Ma.Clayton/J.Lewis 3.00 8.00
CCCP K.Colbert/C.Palmer 3.00 8.00
CCDM D.Davis/V.Morency 2.50 6.00
CCEP L.Evans/R.Parrish 3.00 8.00
CCET B.Edwards/T.Williamson 2.50 6.00
CCEW B.Edwards/Ro.Will.WR 2.50 6.00
CCFC C.Frye/J.Campbell 2.50 6.00
CCFL C.Frye/B.Leftwich 2.50 6.00
CCGB A.Gates/D.Brees 4.00 10.00
CCGF A.Green/B.Favre SP 12.00 30.00
CCGJ A.Gates/V.Jackson 4.00 10.00
CCGS F.Gore/A.Smith QB 10.00 25.00
CCJB Ru.Johnson/Ro.Brown 3.00 8.00
CCJD J.Jones/T.Dorsett 5.00 12.00
CCJG S.Jackson/A.Green 3.00 8.00
CCJH Ch.Johnson/J.Horn 2.50 6.00
CCJM J.Jones/D.McAllister 3.00 8.00
CCJR A.Jones/A.Rolle 4.00 10.00
CCJW Ru.Johnson/Ca.Williams 2.50 6.00
CCMB D.McNabb/Re.Brown 3.00 8.00
CCME D.Marino/J.Elway 12.00 30.00
CCMF P.Manning/B.Favre 12.00 30.00
CCMG T.Murphy/A.Green 3.00 8.00
CCML J.Montana/E.Manning 12.00 30.00
CCMM P.Manning/E.Manning 10.00 25.00
CCMP E.Manning/C.Palmer 6.00 15.00
CCMR D.Marino/Roethlisberger 12.00 30.00
CCMS P.Manning/A.Smith QB 10.00 25.00
CCPW A.Walter/C.Palmer 3.00 8.00
CCRF B.Roethlisbeger/C.Frye 10.00 25.00
CCSA B.Sanders/T.Aikman 12.00 30.00
CCSC A.Smith QB/D.Carr 7.50 20.00
CCSM B.Sanders/V.Morency 7.50 20.00
CCSR D.Sanders/A.Rolle 4.00 10.00
CCTF F.Taylor/C.Fason 2.50 6.00
CCVM M.Vick SP/D.McNabb 4.00 10.00
CCWJ Williamson/Ch.Johnson 2.50 6.00
CCWP R.Wayne/R.Parrish 3.00 8.00

2005 Reflections Dual Signature Reflections Red

STATED PRINT RUN 70 SER.#'d SETS
UNPRICED GOLD PRINT RUN 1 SET
DSAC De.Ander/Ma.Clayton 15.00 40.00
DSAR J.Arrington/A.Rodgers 100.00 200.00
DSBB N.Burleson/D.Bennett 10.00 25.00
DSBC B.Edwards/Ma.Clayton 30.00 80.00
DSBG M.Bradley/F.Gibson 10.00 25.00
DSBJ D.Bledsoe/J.Jones 25.00 60.00
DSBK M.Barber/K.Burnett 15.00 40.00
DSBM Re.Brown/R.Moats 12.00 30.00
DSBS M.Barber/E.Shelton 15.00 40.00
DSBT A.Boldin/C.Thorpe 15.00 40.00
DSBW N.Burleson/R.Wayne 15.00 40.00
DSCB Ma.Clayton/M.Bradley 10.00 25.00
DSCM M.Clarett/R.Moats 10.00 25.00
DSDC Do.Davis/Mi.Clayton 10.00 25.00
DSDP Th.Davis/D.Pollack 10.00 25.00
DSEA E.Manning/A.Smith QB 90.00 150.00
DSEC L.Evans/K.Colbert 10.00 25.00
DSEF B.Edwards/C.Frye 30.00 80.00
DSET B.Edwards/Williamson 30.00 80.00
DSFG C.Frye/D.Greene 10.00 25.00
DSFM B.Favre/T.Murphy 100.00 200.00
DSGG D.Greene/F.Gibson 10.00 25.00
DSGS A.Gates/D.Sproles 25.00 50.00
DSGT T.Green/C.Thorpe 10.00 25.00
DSHG C.Henry/F.Gibson 10.00 25.00
DSJB B.Jacobs/T.Barber 30.00 60.00
DSJC Ru.Johnson/C.Henry 15.00 40.00
DSJE M.Jackson/B.Edwards 25.00 60.00
DSJH A.Jones/C.Henry 15.00 40.00

DSKJ K.Burnett/Ju.Jones 15.00 40.00
DSMA H.Miller/A.Crumpler 15.00 40.00
DSMD D.McAllister/D.Davis 15.00 40.00
DSMM M.Bradley/Muhammad 12.00 30.00
DSMP M.Bulger/P.Manning 60.00 120.00
DSOF D.Orlovsky/C.Frye 10.00 25.00
DSOW Orlovsky/Ro.Will.WR 15.00 40.00
DSPG D.Pollack/D.Greene 12.00 30.00
DSRA A.Rolle/J.J.Arrington 10.00 25.00
DSRC C.Rogers/J.Campbell 25.00 50.00
DSRG A.Rolle/F.Gore 15.00 40.00
DSRJ A.Rolle/A.Jones 12.00 30.00
DSRS J.Russell/E.Shelton 10.00 25.00
DSRW B.Ruud/J.White 15.00 40.00
DSSD D.Sproles/An.Davis 15.00 40.00
DSTR C.Thorpe/J.Russell 10.00 25.00
DSVB M.Vick/G.Blanda 40.00 80.00
DSWC J.White/Ma.Clayton 10.00 25.00
DSWF Williamson/C.Fason 10.00 25.00
DSWH J.White/P.Hornung 20.00 50.00
DSWO A.Walter/Orlovsky 10.00 25.00

2005 Reflections Fabrics

STATED ODDS 1:12
FRBF Brett Favre SP 8.00 20.00
FRBL Byron Leftwich 2.00 5.00
FRBR Ben Roethlisberger 5.00 12.00
FRBU Brian Urlacher 3.00 8.00
FRCH Chad Pennington 2.00 5.00
FRCL Clinton Portis 2.00 5.00
FRCM Curtis Martin 2.50 6.00
FRCP Carson Palmer 2.50 6.00
FRDA Daunte Culpepper 2.50 6.00
FRDB Drew Bledsoe 2.50 6.00
FRDC David Carr 2.00 5.00
FRDM Donovan McNabb 2.50 6.00
FRDR Drew Brees 3.00 8.00
FREJ Edgerrin James 2.50 6.00
FREM Eli Manning 5.00 12.00
FRJH Joey Harrington 2.00 5.00
FRJJ Julius Jones 2.00 5.00
FRJR Jerry Rice 6.00 15.00
FRLS Lee Suggs 2.00 5.00
FRLT LaDainian Tomlinson 3.00 8.00
FRMH Marvin Harrison 2.50 6.00
FRPH Priest Holmes 2.00 5.00
FRPM Peyton Manning 8.00 20.00
FRRM Randy Moss 2.50 6.00
FRSA Shaun Alexander 2.00 5.00
FRSM Steve McNair 2.50 6.00
FRTB Tom Brady 12.00 30.00
FRTO Terrell Owens 2.50 6.00

2005 Reflections Fabrics Gold

*GOLD: 1X TO 2.5X BASIC INSERTS
GOLD PRINT RUN 25 SER.#'d SETS
FRMV Michael Vick 6.00 15.00

2005 Reflections Fabrics Patches

*PATCH: 1.2X TO 3X BASIC JSYs
PATCH PRINT RUN 30 SER.#'d SETS
FRPAJ Andre Johnson 8.00 20.00
FRPMV Michael Vick 8.00 20.00

2005 Reflections Future Fabrics

STATED ODDS 1:12
*GOLD/25: 1.2X TO 3X BASIC JSYs
*PATCH/30: 1.2X TO 3X BASIC JSYs
FFRAN Antrel Rolle 3.00 8.00
FFRAS Alex Smith QB 8.00 20.00
FFRAW Andrew Walter 2.00 5.00
FFRBE Braylon Edwards 2.00 5.00
FFRCA Carlos Rogers 3.00 8.00
FFRCF Charlie Frye 2.00 5.00
FFRCI Ciatrick Fason 2.00 5.00
FFRCR Courtney Roby 2.00 5.00
FFRCW Cadillac Williams 2.00 5.00
FFRES Eric Shelton 2.00 5.00
FFRFG Frank Gore 4.00 10.00
FFRJC Jason Campbell 2.00 5.00
FFRJJ J.J. Arrington 2.50 6.00
FFRKO Kyle Orton 2.00 5.00
FFRMB Mark Bradley 2.00 5.00
FFRMC Mark Clayton 2.00 5.00
FFRMO Maurice Clarett 2.00 5.00
FFRRB Ronnie Brown 2.50 6.00
FFRRE Reggie Brown 2.00 5.00
FFRRM Ryan Moats 2.00 5.00
FFRRP Roscoe Parrish 2.00 5.00
FFRRW Roddy White 3.00 8.00
FFRSL Stefan LeFors 2.00 5.00
FFRTM Terrence Murphy 2.00 5.00
FFRTW Troy Williamson SP 2.00 5.00
FFRVJ Vincent Jackson 3.00 8.00
FFRVM Vernand Morency 2.00 5.00

2005 Reflections Rookie Exclusives Autographs Red

STATED PRINT RUN 100 SER.#'d SETS
UNPRICED GOLD PRINT RUN 1 SET
READ Anthony Davis 8.00 20.00
REAH Anttaj Hawthorne 8.00 20.00
REAJ Adam Jones 8.00 20.00
REAN Antrel Rolle 12.00 30.00
REAR Aaron Rodgers 175.00 300.00
REAS Alex Smith QB 40.00 80.00
REAW Andrew Walter 8.00 20.00
REBE Braylon Edwards 12.00 30.00
REBR Barrett Ruud 10.00 25.00
RECB Cedric Benson 8.00 20.00
RECF Charlie Frye 8.00 20.00
RECH Chris Henry 10.00 25.00
RECI Ciatrick Fason 8.00 20.00
RECR Carlos Rogers 12.00 30.00
RECT Craphonso Thorpe 8.00 20.00
RECW Cadillac Williams 25.00 60.00
REDA Derek Anderson 10.00 25.00
REDG David Greene 8.00 20.00
REDO Dan Orlovsky 8.00 20.00
REDP David Pollack 8.00 20.00
REDS Darren Sproles 15.00 40.00
REEJ Erasmus James 8.00 20.00
REES Eric Shelton 8.00 20.00
REFG Fred Gibson 8.00 20.00
REFR Frank Gore 20.00 50.00
REHM Heath Miller 25.00 50.00
REJC Jason Campbell 15.00 40.00
REJJ J.J. Arrington 10.00 25.00
REKH Kay-Jay Harris 8.00 20.00
REKO Kyle Orton 8.00 20.00
REMA Marion Barber 8.00 20.00
REMB Mark Bradley 8.00 20.00
REMC Mark Clayton 8.00 20.00
REMJ Marlin Jackson 8.00 20.00
REMO Maurice Clarett 8.00 20.00
RERB Ronnie Brown 10.00 25.00
RERE Reggie Brown 8.00 20.00
RERM Ryan Moats 8.00 20.00
RERP Roscoe Parrish 8.00 20.00
RERW Roddy White 12.00 30.00
RESL Stefan LeFors 8.00 20.00
RESM Shawne Merriman 12.00 30.00
RETD Thomas Davis 8.00 20.00
RETJ Travis Johnson 8.00 20.00
RETM Terrence Murphy 8.00 20.00
RETW Troy Williamson 8.00 20.00
REVJ Vincent Jackson 12.00 30.00
REVM Vernand Morency 8.00 20.00
REWE Corey Webster 10.00 25.00

2005 Reflections Signature Reflections Red

RED STATED ODDS 1:12
UNPRICED BLUE PRINT RUN 15 SETS
*GOLD: .5X TO 1.2X BASIC REDS
*GOLD: .4X TO 1X RED SP's
GOLD PRINT RUN 89 SER.#'d SETS
SRAB Aaron Brooks 5.00 12.00
SRAC Alge Crumpler 6.00 15.00
SRAD Anthony Davis 5.00 12.00
SRAF A.J. Feeley 5.00 12.00
SRAG Ahman Green 6.00 15.00
SRAH Anttaj Hawthorne 5.00 12.00
SRAJ Adam Jones 5.00 12.00
SRAN Antrel Rolle 8.00 20.00
SRAQ Anquan Boldin SP 6.00 15.00
SRAR Aaron Rodgers 175.00 300.00
SRAS Alex Smith QB SP 20.00 50.00
SRAT Antonio Gates SP 10.00 25.00
SRAW Andrew Walter 5.00 12.00
SRBD Brian Dawkins 8.00 20.00
SRBE Braylon Edwards 12.00 30.00
SRBF Brett Favre SP 60.00 120.00
SRBJ Brandon Jacobs 6.00 15.00
SRBL Byron Leftwich SP 6.00 15.00
SRBR Barrett Ruud 6.00 15.00
SRCB Chris Brown 5.00 12.00
SRCC Cris Collinsworth 8.00 20.00
SRCF Charlie Frye 5.00 12.00
SRCH Chris Henry 6.00 15.00
SRCI Ciatrick Fason SP 6.00 15.00
SRCJ Chad Johnson 5.00 12.00
SRCN Chuck Noll 15.00 40.00
SRCO Corey Webster 6.00 15.00
SRCT Craphonso Thorpe 5.00 12.00
SRCW Cadillac Williams SP 20.00 50.00
SRDA Derek Anderson 6.00 15.00
SRDB Drew Bennett 6.00 15.00
SRDC Dan Cody 5.00 12.00
SRDD Domanick Davis 5.00 12.00
SRDE Deuce McAllister SP 8.00 20.00
SRDG David Greene 5.00 12.00
SRDJ Deacon Jones 10.00 25.00
SRDO Dan Orlovsky 5.00 12.00
SRDP David Pollack 5.00 12.00
SRDR Drew Bledsoe SP 12.00 30.00
SRDS Darren Sproles 10.00 25.00
SREJ Edgerrin James SP 15.00 40.00
SREM Eli Manning SP 50.00 100.00
SRER Erasmus James 5.00 12.00
SRES Eric Shelton 5.00 12.00
SRFG Frank Gore 12.00 30.00
SRFR Charles Frederick 5.00 12.00
SRFR Fred Gibson 5.00 12.00
SRFT Fred Taylor 5.00 12.00
SRHM Heath Miller 10.00 25.00
SRJA James Butler 6.00 15.00
SRJB Jim Brown SP 50.00 120.00
SRJC Jason Campbell 5.00 12.00
SRJE John Elway SP 100.00 175.00
SRJH Joe Horn SP 6.00 15.00
SRJJ Julius Jones SP 6.00 15.00
SRJM Joe Montana SP 125.00 200.00
SRJP J.P. Losman SP 6.00 15.00
SRJR J.R. Russell 5.00 12.00
SRJW Jason White 8.00 20.00
SRKB Kevin Burnett 6.00 15.00
SRKC Keary Colbert 5.00 12.00
SRKH Kay-Jay Harris 5.00 12.00
SRKO Kyle Orton 5.00 12.00
SRLE Lee Evans SP 8.00 20.00
SRLJ LaMont Jordan 6.00 15.00
SRLY Larry Johnson 5.00 12.00
SRMB Marion Barber 6.00 15.00
SRMC Michael Clayton SP 6.00 15.00
SRMJ Marlin Jackson 5.00 12.00
SRMM Muhsin Muhhamad 5.00 12.00
SRMO Maurice Clarett 5.00 12.00
SRMU Marc Bulger SP 6.00 15.00
SRMW Mike Williams SP 8.00 20.00
SRNB Nate Burleson SP 6.00 15.00
SRPM Peyton Manning SP 60.00 100.00
SRRA Reggie Wayne SP 12.00 30.00
SRRB Ronnie Brown SP 20.00 50.00
SRRJ Rudi Johnson SP 6.00 15.00
SRRO Roy Williams WR 5.00 12.00
SRSM Shawne Merriman 8.00 20.00
SRTD Thomas Davis 5.00 12.00
SRTE Terrence Murphy 5.00 12.00
SRTG Trent Green SP 6.00 15.00
SRTJ Travis Johnson 5.00 12.00
SRTM T.A. McLendon 5.00 12.00
SRTS Taylor Stubblefield 5.00 12.00
SRTW Troy Williamson 5.00 12.00
SRVM Vernand Morency 5.00 12.00
SRWR Walter Reyes 5.00 12.00

2005 Reflections Super Swatch

SSAG Ahman Green 10.00 25.00
SSAN Antrel Rolle 10.00 25.00
SSAO Antonio Gates 12.00 30.00
SSAS Alex Smith QB 20.00 50.00
SSBE Braylon Edwards 8.00 20.00
SSBF Brett Favre 25.00 60.00
SSBL Byron Leftwich 8.00 20.00
SSBR Ben Roethlisberger 25.00 60.00
SSBS Barry Sanders 30.00 60.00
SSCA Carlos Rogers 10.00 25.00
SSCF Charlie Frye 6.00 15.00
SSCI Ciatrick Fason 6.00 15.00
SSCJ Chad Johnson 8.00 20.00
SSCP Carson Palmer 10.00 25.00
SSCW Cadillac Williams 6.00 15.00
SSDD Domanick Davis 8.00 20.00
SSDM Deuce McAllister 10.00 25.00
SSEM Eli Manning 20.00 50.00
SSES Eric Shelton 6.00 15.00
SSFT Fran Tarkenton 15.00 40.00
SSJC Jason Campbell 6.00 15.00
SSJH Joe Horn 8.00 20.00
SSJJ Julius Jones 15.00 40.00
SSJM Joe Montana 30.00 60.00
SSLE Lee Evans 10.00 25.00
SSLJ Larry Johnson 8.00 20.00
SSMA Mark Clayton 6.00 15.00
SSMB Marc Bulger 8.00 20.00
SSMC Michael Clayton 6.00 15.00
SSMO Maurice Clarett 6.00 15.00
SSNB Nate Burleson 8.00 20.00
SSPM Peyton Manning 20.00 50.00
SSRB Ronnie Brown 8.00 20.00
SSRJ Rudi Johnson 8.00 20.00
SSRP Roscoe Parrish 6.00 15.00
SSSJ Steven Jackson 8.00 20.00
SSSL Stefan LeFors 6.00 15.00
SSTW Troy Williamson 6.00 15.00

1997 Revolution

The 1997 Pacific Revolution set was issued in one series totalling 150 cards and distributed in three-card packs. The fronts feature color photos of prominent players with holographic foil, etching and embossing. The backs carry a small player head photo and career highlights.

COMPLETE SET (150) 40.00 80.00
1 Larry Centers .30 .75
2 Kent Graham .20 .50
3 Leeland McElroy .20 .50
4 Rob Moore .30 .75
5 Jake Plummer RC 2.50 6.00
6 Jamal Anderson .50 1.25
7 Bert Emanuel .30 .75
8 Byron Hanspard RC .30 .75
9 Terance Mathis .30 .75
10 O.J. Santiago RC .30 .75
11 Derrick Alexander WR .30 .75
12 Peter Boulware RC .50 1.25
13 Jay Graham RC .30 .75
14 Michael Jackson .30 .75
15 Vinny Testaverde .30 .75
16 Todd Collins .20 .50
17 Andre Reed .30 .75
18 Jay Riemersma .20 .50
19 Antowain Smith RC 1.50 4.00
20 Bruce Smith .30 .75
21 Thurman Thomas .50 1.25
22 Rae Carruth RC .20 .50
23 Kerry Collins .50 1.25
24 Anthony Johnson .20 .50
25 Muhsin Muhammad .30 .75
26 Wesley Walls .30 .75
27 Curtis Conway .30 .75
28 Bobby Engram .30 .75
29 Raymont Harris .20 .50
30 Rick Mirer .20 .50
31 Rashaan Salaam .20 .50
32 Jeff Blake .30 .75
33 Corey Dillon RC 2.50 6.00
34 Carl Pickens .30 .75
35 Darnay Scott .30 .75
36 Troy Aikman 1.00 2.50
37 Michael Irvin .50 1.25
38 Daryl Johnston .30 .75
39 Deion Sanders .50 1.25
40 Emmitt Smith 1.50 4.00
41 Terrell Davis .60 1.50
42 John Elway 2.00 5.00
43 Ed McCaffrey .30 .75
44 Shannon Sharpe .30 .75
45 Neil Smith .30 .75
46 Scott Mitchell .30 .75
47 Herman Moore .30 .75
48 Johnnie Morton .30 .75
49 Barry Sanders 1.50 4.00
50 Robert Brooks .30 .75
51 LeRoy Butler .20 .50
52 Brett Favre 2.00 5.00
53 Antonio Freeman .50 1.25
54 Dorsey Levens .50 1.25
55 Reggie White .50 1.25
56 Sean Dawkins .20 .50
57 Ken Dilger .20 .50
58 Marshall Faulk .60 1.50
59 Jim Harbaugh .30 .75
60 Marvin Harrison .50 1.25
61 Mark Brunell .60 1.50
62 Keenan McCardell .30 .75
63 Natrone Means .30 .75
64 Jimmy Smith .30 .75
65 James O.Stewart .30 .75
66 Marcus Allen .50 1.25
67 Tony Gonzalez RC 2.50 6.00
68 Elvis Grbac .30 .75
69 Greg Hill .20 .50
70 Andre Rison .30 .75
71 Karim Abdul-Jabbar .50 1.25
72 Fred Barnett .20 .50
73 Dan Marino 2.00 5.00
74 O.J. McDuffie .30 .75
75 Irving Spikes .20 .50
76 Cris Carter .50 1.25
77 Matthew Hatchette RC .30 .75
78 Brad Johnson .50 1.25
79 Jake Reed .30 .75
80 Robert Smith .30 .75
81 Drew Bledsoe .60 1.50
82 Ben Coates .30 .75
83 Terry Glenn .50 1.25
84 Curtis Martin .60 1.50
85 Dave Meggett .20 .50
86 Troy Davis RC .30 .75
87 Andre Hastings .20 .50
88 Heath Shuler .20 .50
89 Irv Smith .20 .50
90 Danny Wuerffel RC .50 1.25
91 Ray Zellars .20 .50
92 Tiki Barber RC 4.00 10.00
93 Dave Brown .20 .50
94 Chris Calloway .20 .50
95 Rodney Hampton .30 .75
96 Amani Toomer .30 .75
97 Wayne Chrebet .50 1.25
98 Keyshawn Johnson .50 1.25
99 Adrian Murrell .30 .75
100 Neil O'Donnell .30 .75
101 Dedric Ward RC .30 .75
102 Tim Brown .50 1.25
103 Rickey Dudley .30 .75
104 Jeff George .30 .75
105 Desmond Howard .30 .75
106 Napoleon Kaufman .50 1.25
107 Ty Detmer .30 .75
108 Jason Dunn .20 .50
109 Irving Fryar .30 .75
110 Rodney Peete .20 .50
111 Ricky Watters .30 .75
112 Jerome Bettis .50 1.25
113 Will Blackwell RC .30 .75
114 Charles Johnson .30 .75
115 Kordell Stewart .50 1.25
116 Tony Banks .30 .75
117 Isaac Bruce .50 1.25
118 Ernie Conwell .20 .50
119 Eddie Kennison .30 .75
120 Lawrence Phillips .20 .50
121 Stan Humphries .30 .75
122 Tony Martin .30 .75
123 Eric Metcalf .30 .75
124 Junior Seau .50 1.25
125 Jim Druckenmiller RC .30 .75
126 Kevin Greene .30 .75
127 Garrison Hearst .30 .75
128 Terrell Owens .60 1.50
129 Jerry Rice 1.00 2.50
130 J.J. Stokes .30 .75
131 Rod Woodson .30 .75
132 Steve Young .60 1.50
133 Joey Galloway .30 .75
134 Cortez Kennedy .20 .50
135 Jon Kitna RC 5.00 10.00
136 Warren Moon .50 1.25
137 Chris Warren .30 .75
138 Mike Alstott .50 1.25
139 Reidel Anthony RC .50 1.25
140 Trent Dilfer .50 1.25
141 Warrick Dunn RC 2.00 5.00
142 Willie Davis .20 .50
143 Eddie George .50 1.25
144 Steve McNair .60 1.50
145 Chris Sanders .20 .50
146 Terry Allen .50 1.25
147 Jamie Asher .20 .50
148 Henry Ellard .20 .50
149 Gus Frerotte .20 .50
150 Leslie Shepherd .20 .50
S1 Mark Brunell Sample .40 1.00

1997 Revolution Copper

COMPLETE SET (150) 150.00 300.00
*COPPER STARS: 1.5X TO 4X BASIC CARDS
*COPPER RCs: .6X TO 1.5X BASIC CARDS
STATED ODDS 2:25 HOBBY

1997 Revolution Platinum Blue

*PLAT.BLUE VETS: 2X TO 5X BASIC CARDS
*PLAT.BLUE RCs: 1X TO 2.5X
PLAT.BLUE STATED ODDS 1:49

1997 Revolution Red

COMPLETE SET (150) 125.00 250.00
*RED STARS: 1.2X TO 3X BASIC CARDS
*RED RCs: .6X TO 1.5X BASIC CARDS
STATED ODDS 2:25 SPECIAL RETAIL

1997 Revolution Silver

COMPLETE SET (150) 150.00 300.00
*SILVER STARS: 1.5X TO 4X BASIC CARDS
*SILVER RCs: .6X TO 1.5X BASIC CARDS
STATED ODDS 2:25 RETAIL

1997 Revolution Air Mail Die Cuts

Randomly inserted in packs at the rate of one in 25, this 36-card set features color player images printed on a die-cut, stamp-like design card.

COMPLETE SET (36) 50.00 120.00
STATED ODDS 1:25
1 Vinny Testaverde .75 2.00
2 Andre Reed .75 2.00
3 Kerry Collins 1.25 3.00
4 Jeff Blake .75 2.00
5 Troy Aikman 2.50 6.00
6 Deion Sanders 1.25 3.00
7 Emmitt Smith 4.00 10.00
8 Michael Irvin 1.25 3.00
9 Terrell Davis 1.50 4.00
10 John Elway 5.00 12.00
11 Barry Sanders 4.00 10.00
12 Brett Favre 5.00 12.00
13 Antonio Freeman 1.25 3.00
14 Mark Brunell 1.25 3.00
15 Marcus Allen 1.25 3.00
16 Elvis Grbac .75 2.00
17 Dan Marino 5.00 12.00
18 Brad Johnson 1.25 3.00
19 Drew Bledsoe 1.50 4.00
20 Terry Glenn 1.25 3.00
21 Curtis Martin 1.50 4.00
22 Danny Wuerffel .40 1.00
23 Jeff George .75 2.00
24 Napoleon Kaufman 1.25 3.00
25 Kordell Stewart 1.25 3.00
26 Tony Banks .75 2.00
27 Isaac Bruce 1.25 3.00
28 Jim Druckenmiller .40 1.00
29 Jerry Rice 2.50 6.00
30 Steve Young 1.50 4.00
31 Warren Moon 1.25 3.00
32 Trent Dilfer 1.25 3.00
33 Warrick Dunn 2.50 6.00
34 Eddie George 1.25 3.00
35 Steve McNair 1.50 4.00
36 Gus Frerotte .40 1.00

1997 Revolution Proteges

Randomly inserted in packs at the rate of two in 25, this 20-card set features color images of top NFL veterans pictured side-by-side with their proteges on an elaborate red, blue, and gold foiled design background. A Silver parallel version was produced as well and distributed one per special retail box as a chiptopper.

COMPLETE SET (20) 20.00 50.00
GOLD STATED ODDS 2:25
*SILVER CARDS: .25X TO .5X GOLDS
SILVERS ONE PER SPECIAL RETAIL BOX
1 K.Graham J.Plummer 1.50 4.00
2 J.Anderson B.Hanspard .60 1.50
3 T.Thomas A.Smith 1.25 3.00
4 T.Aikman J.Garrett 2.50 6.00
5 E.Smith S.Williams 4.00 10.00
6 J.Elway J.Lewis 5.00 12.00
7 B.Sanders R.Rivers 4.00 10.00
8 B.Favre D.Pederson 5.00 12.00
9 M.Brunell R.Johnson 2.00 5.00
10 M.Allen G.Hill 1.00 2.50
11 D.Marino D.Huard 5.00 12.00
12 C.Martin M.Grier 1.50 4.00
13 H.Shuler D.Wuerffel 1.00 2.50
14 R.Hampton T.Barber 2.00 5.00
15 J.Bettis G.Jones 1.00 2.50
16 J.Rice T.Owens 4.00 10.00
17 S.Young J.Druckenmiller 2.00 5.00
18 W.Moon J.Kitna 2.00 5.00
19 E.Rhett W.Dunn 1.50 4.00
20 T.Allen S.Davis 1.00 2.50

1997 Revolution Ring Bearers

Randomly inserted in packs at the rate of one in 121, this 12-card set features color images of top NFL players printed on a fully foiled and embossed, die-cut and laser-cut card in the shape of a championship ring.

COMPLETE SET (12) 50.00 120.00
STATED ODDS 1:121
1 Emmitt Smith 8.00 20.00
2 John Elway 6.00 15.00
3 Barry Sanders 6.00 15.00
4 Brett Favre 8.00 20.00
5 Mark Brunell 2.50 6.00
6 Dan Marino 8.00 20.00
7 Drew Bledsoe 3.00 8.00
8 Steve Young 4.00 10.00
9 Warrick Dunn 4.00 10.00
10 Eddie George 2.50 6.00
11 Troy Aikman 5.00 12.00
12 Jerry Rice 5.00 12.00

1997 Revolution Silks

Randomly inserted in packs at the rate of one in 49, this 3 1/2" by 5" 18-card set features color player images printed on a silk-like material. These Silks are often found with fold creases since they were inserted into 2 1/2" by 3 1/2" packs but a large number of unfolded cards did make their way onto the market after Pacific ceased card operations.

COMPLETE SET (18) 15.00 40.00
STATED ODDS 1:49
1 Kerry Collins 1.00 2.50
2 Troy Aikman 2.00 5.00
3 Deion Sanders 1.50 4.00
4 Emmitt Smith 3.00 8.00
5 Terrell Davis 1.25 3.00
6 John Elway 2.50 6.00
7 Barry Sanders 2.50 6.00
8 Brett Favre 3.00 8.00
9 Mark Brunell 1.00 2.50
10 Marcus Allen 1.25 3.00
11 Dan Marino 3.00 8.00
12 Drew Bledsoe 1.25 3.00
13 Curtis Martin 1.25 3.00
14 Jerome Bettis 1.25 3.00
15 Jim Druckenmiller .75 2.00
16 Jerry Rice 2.00 5.00
17 Warrick Dunn 1.25 3.00
18 Eddie George 1.00 2.50
P1 Mark Brunell Promo 2.00 5.00

1998 Revolution

The 1998 Pacific Revolution set was issued in one series with a total of 150 cards. The fronts feature action player images printed using dual foiling, etching and embossing. The backs display full year-by-year career statistics for the pictured player.

COMPLETE SET (150) 40.00 100.00
1 Larry Centers .30 .75
2 Leeland McElroy .30 .75
3 Rob Moore .50 1.25
4 Jake Plummer .75 2.00
5 Frank Sanders .50 1.25
6 Jamal Anderson .75 2.00
7 Chris Chandler .50 1.25
8 Byron Hanspard .30 .75
9 Jay Graham .30 .75
10 Michael Jackson .30 .75
11 Vinny Testaverde .50 1.25
12 Eric Zeier .50 1.25
13 Todd Collins .30 .75
14 Quinn Early .30 .75
15 Andre Reed .50 1.25
16 Antowain Smith .75 2.00
17 Bruce Smith .50 1.25
18 Thurman Thomas .75 2.00
19 Rae Carruth .30 .75
20 Kerry Collins .50 1.25
21 Wesley Walls .50 1.25
22 Darnell Autry .30 .75
23 Curtis Conway .50 1.25
24 Bobby Engram .50 1.25
25 Curtis Enis RC .50 1.25
26 Raymont Harris .30 .75
27 Jeff Blake .50 1.25
28 Corey Dillon .75 2.00
29 Carl Pickens .50 1.25
30 Darnay Scott .50 1.25
31 Troy Aikman 1.50 4.00
32 Michael Irvin .75 2.00
33 Deion Sanders .75 2.00
34 Emmitt Smith 1.50 4.00
35 Steve Atwater .30 .75
36 Terrell Davis .75 2.00
37 John Elway 3.00 8.00
38 Brian Griese RC 2.00 5.00
39 Ed McCaffrey .50 1.25
40 Marcus Nash RC .50 1.25
41 Shannon Sharpe .50 1.25
42 Neil Smith .50 1.25
43 Rod Smith .50 1.25
44 Charlie Batch RC 1.00 2.50
45 Germane Crowell RC .75 2.00
46 Scott Mitchell .50 1.25
47 Herman Moore .50 1.25
48 Barry Sanders 2.50 6.00
49 Robert Brooks .50 1.25
50 Mark Chmura .50 1.25
51 Brett Favre 3.00 8.00
52 Antonio Freeman .75 2.00
53 Dorsey Levens .75 2.00
54 Aaron Bailey .30 .75
55 Ken Dilger .30 .75
56 Marshall Faulk 1.00 2.50
57 Marvin Harrison .75 2.00
58 Peyton Manning RC 10.00 25.00
59 Tavian Banks RC .75 2.00
60 Tony Brackens .30 .75
61 Mark Brunell .75 2.00
62 Keenan McCardell .50 1.25
63 Natrone Means .50 1.25
64 Jimmy Smith .50 1.25
65 James Stewart .50 1.25
66 Fred Taylor RC 1.50 4.00
67 Tony Gonzalez .75 2.00
68 Elvis Grbac .50 1.25
69 Greg Hill .30 .75
70 Andre Rison .50 1.25
71 Derrick Thomas .75 2.00
72 Karim Abdul-Jabbar .75 2.00
73 John Avery RC .75 2.00
74 Troy Drayton .30 .75
75 Dan Marino 3.00 8.00
76 O.J. McDuffie .50 1.25
77 Cris Carter .75 2.00
78 Brad Johnson .75 2.00
79 John Randle .50 1.25
80 Jake Reed .50 1.25
81 Robert Smith .75 2.00
82 Drew Bledsoe 1.25 3.00
83 Ben Coates .50 1.25
84 Robert Edwards RC .75 2.00
85 Terry Glenn .75 2.00
86 Tony Simmons RC .75 2.00
87 Troy Davis .30 .75
88 Heath Shuler .30 .75
89 Danny Wuerffel .50 1.25
90 Ray Zellars .30 .75
91 Tiki Barber .75 2.00
92 Joe Jurevicius RC 1.00 2.50
93 Danny Kanell .50 1.25
94 Charles Way .30 .75
95 Tyrone Wheatley .50 1.25
96 Wayne Chrebet .75 2.00
97 Glenn Foley .50 1.25
98 Keyshawn Johnson .75 2.00
99 Curtis Martin .75 2.00
100 Tim Brown .75 2.00
101 Rickey Dudley .30 .75
102 Jeff George .50 1.25
103 Desmond Howard .50 1.25
104 Napoleon Kaufman .75 2.00
105 Charles Woodson RC 2.00 5.00
106 Jason Dunn .30 .75
107 Irving Fryar .50 1.25
108 Charlie Garner .50 1.25
109 Bobby Hoying .50 1.25
110 Jerome Bettis .75 2.00
111 Mark Bruener .30 .75
112 Charles Johnson .30 .75
113 Levon Kirkland .30 .75
114 Kordell Stewart .75 2.00
115 Hines Ward RC 5.00 10.00
116 Tony Banks .50 1.25
117 Isaac Bruce .75 2.00
118 Robert Holcombe RC .75 2.00
119 Eddie Kennison .50 1.25
120 Freddie Jones .30 .75
121 Ryan Leaf RC 1.00 2.50
122 Tony Martin .50 1.25
123 Junior Seau .75 2.00
124 Jim Druckenmiller .30 .75
125 Garrison Hearst .75 2.00
126 Terrell Owens .75 2.00
127 Jerry Rice 1.50 4.00
128 J.J. Stokes .50 1.25
129 Steve Young 1.00 2.50
130 Joey Galloway .50 1.25
131 Ahman Green RC 2.00 5.00
132 Cortez Kennedy .30 .75
133 Jon Kitna .75 2.00
134 James McKnight .75 2.00
135 Warren Moon .75 2.00
136 Mike Alstott .75 2.00
137 Reidel Anthony .50 1.25
138 Trent Dilfer .75 2.00
139 Warrick Dunn .75 2.00
140 Warren Sapp .50 1.25
141 Kevin Dyson RC 1.00 2.50
142 Eddie George .75 2.00
143 Steve McNair .75 2.00
144 Chris Sanders .30 .75
145 Frank Wycheck .30 .75
146 Stephen Alexander RC .75 2.00
147 Terry Allen .75 2.00
148 Gus Frerotte .30 .75
149 Skip Hicks RC .75 2.00
150 Michael Westbrook .50 1.25
S1 Warrick Dunn Sample .40 1.00

1998 Revolution Shadows

*SHADOW STARS: 4X TO 10X HI COL.
*SHADOW RCs: 1.5X TO 4X BASIC CARDS
SHADOW PRINT RUN 99 SERIAL #'d SETS

1998 Revolution Icons

Randomly inserted in packs at the rate of one in 121, this 10-card set features color action photos of all-time football greats printed in full foil and etching with a die-cut design.

COMPLETE SET (10) 125.00 250.00
STATED ODDS 1:121
1 Emmitt Smith 10.00 25.00
2 Terrell Davis 3.00 8.00
3 John Elway 12.50 30.00
4 Barry Sanders 10.00 25.00
5 Brett Favre 12.50 30.00
6 Mark Brunell 3.00 8.00
7 Dan Marino 12.50 30.00
8 Jerry Rice 6.00 15.00
9 Warrick Dunn 3.00 8.00
10 Eddie George 3.00 8.00

1998 Revolution Prime Time Performers

Randomly inserted in packs at the rate of one in 25, this 20-card set features color action player photos printed with advanced laser-cutting technology.

COMPLETE SET (20) 60.00 150.00
STATED ODDS 1:25
1 Jake Plummer 2.00 5.00
2 Corey Dillon 2.00 5.00
3 Troy Aikman 4.00 10.00
4 Deion Sanders 2.00 5.00
5 Emmitt Smith 6.00 15.00
6 Terrell Davis 2.00 5.00
7 John Elway 8.00 20.00
8 Barry Sanders 6.00 15.00
9 Brett Favre 8.00 20.00
10 Peyton Manning 15.00 40.00
11 Mark Brunell 2.00 5.00
12 Dan Marino 8.00 20.00
13 Drew Bledsoe 3.00 8.00
14 Jerome Bettis 2.00 5.00
15 Kordell Stewart 2.00 5.00
16 Jerry Rice 4.00 10.00
17 Steve Young 2.50 6.00
18 Warrick Dunn 2.00 5.00
19 Eddie George 2.00 5.00
20 Steve McNair 2.00 5.00

1998 Revolution Rookies and Stars

Randomly inserted in packs at the rate of four in 25, this set features color photos of outstanding rookies and stars. The backs carry player information. A gold version of this set was also produced with only 50 of each card made and serially numbered.

COMPLETE SET (30) 75.00 150.00
STATED ODDS 4:25
*GOLD/50: 6X TO 15X BASIC INSERTS
1 Michael Pittman .50 1.25
2 Curtis Enis .50 1.25
3 Takeo Spikes .50 1.25
4 Greg Ellis .50 1.25
5 Emmitt Smith 5.00 12.00
6 Terrell Davis 1.50 4.00
7 John Elway 6.00 15.00
8 Brian Griese 1.50 4.00
9 Marcus Nash .50 1.25
10 Charlie Batch 1.00 2.50
11 Barry Sanders 5.00 12.00
12 Brett Favre 6.00 15.00
13 Vonnie Holliday .50 1.25
14 E.G. Green .50 1.25
15 Peyton Manning 12.00 30.00
16 Fred Taylor 1.50 4.00
17 John Avery .50 1.25
18 Dan Marino 6.00 15.00
19 Drew Bledsoe 2.50 6.00
20 Robert Edwards .50 1.25
21 Joe Jurevicius 1.00 2.50
22 Charles Woodson 2.50 6.00
23 Kordell Stewart 1.50 4.00
24 Robert Holcombe .50 1.25
25 Ryan Leaf 1.00 2.50
26 Warrick Dunn 1.50 4.00
27 Jacquez Green 1.00 2.50
28 Kevin Dyson 1.00 2.50
29 Eddie George 1.50 4.00
30 Stephen Alexander .50 1.25

1998 Revolution Showstoppers

Randomly inserted in packs at the rate of two in 25, this 36-card set features photos of some of the NFL's most exciting players printed with holographic silver foil and etching. A red foil parallel set was later issued in special 5-pack retail boxes at the rate of one card per box.

COMPLETE SET (36) 50.00 120.00
STATED ODDS 2:25
*RED: .4X TO 1X SILVER
1 Jake Plummer 1.50 4.00
2 Antowain Smith 1.50 4.00
3 Kerry Collins 1.00 2.50
4 Corey Dillon 1.50 4.00
5 Troy Aikman 3.00 8.00
6 Deion Sanders 1.50 4.00
7 Emmitt Smith 5.00 12.00
8 Terrell Davis 1.50 4.00
9 John Elway 6.00 15.00
10 Shannon Sharpe 1.00 2.50
11 Herman Moore 1.00 2.50
12 Barry Sanders 5.00 12.00
13 Brett Favre 6.00 15.00
14 Antonio Freeman 1.50 4.00
15 Dorsey Levens 1.50 4.00
16 Peyton Manning 10.00 25.00
17 Mark Brunell 1.50 4.00
18 Dan Marino 6.00 15.00
19 Robert Smith 1.50 4.00
20 Drew Bledsoe 2.50 6.00
21 Danny Kanell 1.00 2.50
22 Curtis Martin 1.50 4.00
23 Tim Brown 1.50 4.00
24 Napoleon Kaufman 1.50 4.00
25 Jerome Bettis 1.50 4.00
26 Kordell Stewart 1.50 4.00
27 Ryan Leaf 1.00 2.50
28 Terrell Owens 1.50 4.00
29 Jerry Rice 3.00 8.00
30 Steve Young 2.00 6.00
31 Ricky Watters 1.00 2.50
32 Mike Alstott 1.50 4.00
33 Trent Dilfer 1.50 4.00
34 Warrick Dunn 1.50 4.00
35 Eddie George 1.50 4.00
36 Steve McNair 1.50 4.00

1998 Revolution Touchdown

Randomly inserted in packs at the rate of one in 49, this 20-card set features action photos of football's top scorers printed on an intricate laser-cut card design.

COMPLETE SET (20) 100.00 200.00
STATED ODDS 1:49
1 Jake Plummer 2.50 6.00
2 Corey Dillon 2.50 6.00
3 Troy Aikman 5.00 12.00
4 Emmitt Smith 8.00 20.00
5 Terrell Davis 2.50 6.00
6 John Elway 10.00 25.00
7 Barry Sanders 8.00 20.00
8 Brett Favre 10.00 25.00
9 Dorsey Levens 2.50 6.00
10 Peyton Manning 20.00 50.00
11 Mark Brunell 2.50 6.00
12 Marcus Allen 2.50 6.00
13 Dan Marino 10.00 25.00
14 Drew Bledsoe 4.00 10.00
15 Jerome Bettis 2.50 6.00
16 Kordell Stewart 2.50 6.00
17 Jerry Rice 5.00 12.00
18 Steve Young 3.00 8.00
19 Warrick Dunn 2.50 6.00
20 Eddie George 2.50 6.00

1999 Revolution

This 175 card set was issued by Pacific in three card packs and was released in July, 1999. Many of the Rookie Cards (45) in this set were shortprinted and released at a rate of one in four packs. Since the Rookie Cards were scattered throughout the set, we have identfied them with a SP next to their name.

COMPLETE SET (175) 50.00 100.00
1 David Boston RC .50 1.25
2 Joel Makovicka SP RC .75 2.00
3 Rob Moore .25 .60
4 Adrian Murrell .25 .60
5 Jake Plummer .25 .60
6 Frank Sanders .25 .60
7 Jamal Anderson .30 .75
8 Chris Chandler .30 .75
9 Tim Dwight .30 .75
10 Terance Mathis .25 .60
11 Jeff Paulk SP RC .75 2.00
12 O.J. Santiago .25 .60
13 Peter Boulware .25 .60
14 Priest Holmes .25 .60
15 Michael Jackson .25 .60
16 Jermaine Lewis .25 .60
17 Doug Flutie .40 1.00
18 Eric Moulds .25 .60
19 Peerless Price SP RC .75 2.00
20 Andre Reed .40 1.00
21 Antowain Smith .25 .60
22 Bruce Smith .30 .75
23 Steve Beuerlein .30 .75
24 Kevin Greene .40 1.00
25 Fred Lane .25 .60
26 Muhsin Muhammad .25 .60
27 Wesley Walls .30 .75
28 Marty Booker SP RC .75 2.00
29 Curtis Conway .30 .75
30 Bobby Engram .25 .60
31 Curtis Enis .25 .60
32 Erik Kramer .30 .75
33 Cade McNown RC .50 1.25
34 Scott Covington RC .50 1.25
35 Corey Dillon .25 .60
36 Carl Pickens .30 .75
37 Darnay Scott .25 .60
38 Akili Smith RC .50 1.25
39 Craig Yeast SP RC .75 2.00
40 Darrin Chiaverini SP RC .75 2.00
41 Tim Couch RC .60 1.50
42 Ty Detmer .25 .60
43 Kevin Johnson RC .60 1.50
44 Terry Kirby .25 .60
45 Daylon McCutcheon SP RC .75 2.00
46 Irv Smith .25 .60
47 Troy Aikman .50 1.25
48 Michael Irvin .40 1.00
49 Wane McGarity SP RC .75 2.00
50 Dat Nguyen SP RC 1.25 3.00
51 Deion Sanders .30 .75
52 Emmitt Smith .60 1.50
53 Terrell Davis .30 .75
54 John Elway .60 1.50
55 Brian Griese .25 .60
56 Ed McCaffrey .30 .75
57 Travis McGriff SP RC .75 2.00
58 Shannon Sharpe .30 .75
59 Rod Smith WR .30 .75
60 Charlie Batch .25 .60
61 Chris Claiborne RC .50 1.25
62 Sedrick Irvin RC .50 1.25
63 Herman Moore .30 .75
64 Johnnie Morton .30 .75
65 Barry Sanders .60 1.50
66 Aaron Brooks SP RC 1.00 2.50
67 Mark Chmura .25 .60
68 Brett Favre .75 2.00
69 Antonio Freeman .30 .75
70 Dorsey Levens .30 .75
71 De'Mond Parker SP RC .75 2.00
72 Marvin Harrison .30 .75
73 Edgerrin James RC .75 2.00
74 Peyton Manning 1.25 3.00
75 Jerome Pathon .25 .60
76 Mike Peterson SP RC .75 2.00
77 Reggie Barlow .25 .60
78 Mark Brunell .30 .75
79 Keenan McCardell .30 .75
80 Jimmy Smith .30 .75
81 Fred Taylor .25 .60
82 Mike Cloud RC .50 1.25
83 Tony Gonzalez .30 .75
84 Elvis Grbac .25 .60
85 Larry Parker RC SP 1.00 2.50
86 Andre Rison .30 .75
87 Brian Shay SP RC .75 2.00
88 Karim Abdul-Jabbar .25 .60
89 Oronde Gadsden .25 .60
90 James Johnson RC .50 1.25
91 Rob Konrad RC .50 1.25
92 Dan Marino .75 2.00
93 O.J. McDuffie .30 .75
94 Cris Carter .40 1.00
95 Daunte Culpepper RC .75 2.00
96 Randall Cunningham .30 .75
97 Jim Kleinsasser SP RC 1.25 3.00
98 Randy Moss .30 .75
99 Jake Reed .30 .75
100 Robert Smith .25 .60
101 Drew Bledsoe .30 .75
102 Ben Coates .30 .75
103 Kevin Faulk RC .50 1.25
104 Terry Glenn .30 .75
105 Shawn Jefferson .25 .60
106 Andy Katzenmoyer SP RC 1.00 2.50
107 Cameron Cleeland .25 .60
108 Andre Hastings .25 .60
109 Billy Joe Tolliver .25 .60
110 Ricky Williams RC .75 2.00
111 Gary Brown .25 .60
112 Kent Graham .25 .60
113 Ike Hilliard .25 .60
114 Joe Montgomery SP RC .75 2.00
115 Amani Toomer .25 .60
116 Wayne Chrebet .25 .60
117 Keyshawn Johnson .30 .75
118 Leon Johnson .25 .60
119 Curtis Martin .30 .75
120 Vinny Testaverde .25 .60

121 Dedric Ward .25 .60
122 Tim Brown .40 1.00
123 Dameane Douglas SP RC .75 2.00
124 Rickey Dudley .25 .60
125 James Jett .25 .60
126 Napoleon Kaufman .25 .60
127 Charles Woodson .40 1.00
128 Na Brown SP RC .75 2.00
129 Cecil Martin SP RC .75 2.00
130 Donovan McNabb RC 3.00 8.00
131 Duce Staley .25 .60
132 Kevin Turner .25 .60
133 Jerome Bettis .40 1.00
134 Troy Edwards RC .50 1.25
135 Courtney Hawkins .25 .60
136 Malcolm Johnson SP RC .75 2.00
137 Kordell Stewart .25 .60
138 Jerame Tuman SP RC .75 2.00
139 Amos Zereoue RC .50 1.25
140 Isaac Bruce .40 1.00
141 Joe Germaine RC .60 1.50
142 Torry Holt SP RC 1.50 4.00
143 Amp Lee .25 .60
144 Ricky Proehl .25 .60
145 Freddie Jones .25 .60
146 Ryan Leaf .30 .75
147 Natrone Means .30 .75
148 Mikhael Ricks .25 .60
149 Garrison Hearst .25 .60
150 Terry Jackson SP RC .75 2.00
151 Terrell Owens .30 .75
152 Jerry Rice 1.00 2.50
153 J.J. Stokes .25 .60
154 Steve Young .50 1.25
155 Karsten Bailey RC .50 1.25
156 Joey Galloway .30 .75
157 Ahman Green .30 .75
158 Brock Huard RC .50 1.25
159 Jon Kitna .25 .60
160 Ricky Watters .30 .75
161 Mike Alstott .25 .60
162 Reidel Anthony .25 .60
163 Trent Dilfer .25 .60
164 Warrick Dunn .25 .60
165 Shaun King RC .50 1.25
166 Anthony McFarland RC .60 1.50
167 Kevin Dyson .25 .60
168 Eddie George .30 .75
169 Darran Hall RC .50 1.25
170 Steve McNair .30 .75
171 Frank Wycheck .30 .75
172 Stephen Alexander .25 .60
173 Champ Bailey RC 1.00 2.50
174 Skip Hicks .25 .60
175 Michael Westbrook .25 .60

1999 Revolution Opening Day

*STARS: 8X TO 20X BASIC CARDS
*RCs: 1.5X TO 4X BASIC CARDS
*RC SPs: 1.2X TO 3X BASIC CARDS
OPEN.DAY PRINT RUN 68 SER.#'d SETS

1999 Revolution Red

COMPLETE SET (175) 125.00 250.00
*STARS: 1.5X TO 4X BASIC CARDS
*RCs: .6X TO 1.5X BASIC CARDS
*RC SPs: .5X TO 1.2X BASIC CARDS
RED STATED PRINT RUN 299 SER.#'d SETS

1999 Revolution Shadows

*STARS: 5X TO 12X BASIC CARDS
*RCs: 1X TO &72.5X BASIC CARDS
*RC SPs: .8X TO 2X BASIC CARDS
SHADOWS PRINT RUN 99 SER.#'d SETS

1999 Revolution Chalk Talk

Inserted one every 49 packs, these 20 horizontal cards feature Pacfic's laser cutting process and show how various plays are diagrammed on one side with the player's photo on the other side.
COMPLETE SET (20) 40.00 100.00
STATED ODDS 1:49
1 Jake Plummer 1.25 3.00
2 Jamal Anderson 2.00 5.00
3 Doug Flutie 2.00 5.00
4 Tim Couch 1.25 3.00
5 Troy Aikman 4.00 10.00
6 Emmitt Smith 4.00 10.00
7 Terrell Davis 2.00 5.00
8 John Elway 6.00 15.00
9 Barry Sanders 6.00 15.00
10 Brett Favre 6.00 15.00
11 Peyton Manning 6.00 15.00
12 Mark Brunell 2.00 5.00
13 Fred Taylor 2.00 5.00
14 Dan Marino 6.00 15.00
15 Randy Moss 5.00 12.00
16 Drew Bledsoe 2.50 6.00
17 Ricky Williams 2.00 5.00
18 Jerry Rice 4.00 10.00
19 Jon Kitna 2.00 5.00
20 Eddie George 2.00 5.00

1999 Revolution Icons

Inserted one every 121 packs, these 10 cards feature players who have done great things on the field. These cards are designed like a shield and the cards are fully silver foiled.
COMPLETE SET (10) 75.00 150.00
STATED ODDS 1:121
1 Emmitt Smith 6.00 15.00
2 Terrell Davis 3.00 8.00
3 John Elway 10.00 25.00
4 Barry Sanders 10.00 25.00
5 Brett Favre 10.00 25.00
6 Peyton Manning 10.00 25.00
7 Dan Marino 10.00 25.00
8 Randy Moss 8.00 20.00
9 Jerry Rice 6.00 15.00
10 Jon Kitna 3.00 8.00

1999 Revolution Showstoppers

Inserted at a rate of two in 25, these 36 etched and full holographic silver-foil cards feature leading offensive threats in football.
COMPLETE SET (36) 75.00 150.00
STATED ODDS 2:25
1 Jake Plummer 1.00 2.50
2 Jamal Anderson 1.50 4.00
3 Priest Holmes 2.50 6.00
4 Doug Flutie 1.50 4.00
5 Antowain Smith 1.50 4.00
6 Cade McNown 1.00 2.50
7 Tim Couch 1.25 3.00
8 Corey Dillon 1.50 4.00
9 Akili Smith 1.00 2.50
10 Troy Aikman 3.00 8.00
11 Emmitt Smith 3.00 8.00
12 Terrell Davis 1.50 4.00
13 John Elway 5.00 12.00
14 Charlie Batch 1.50 4.00
15 Barry Sanders 5.00 12.00
16 Brett Favre 5.00 12.00
17 Antonio Freeman 1.50 4.00
18 Edgerrin James 4.00 10.00
19 Peyton Manning 5.00 12.00
20 Mark Brunell 1.50 4.00
21 Fred Taylor 1.50 4.00
22 Dan Marino 5.00 12.00
23 Randall Cunningham 1.50 4.00
24 Randy Moss 4.00 10.00
25 Drew Bledsoe 2.00 5.00
26 Ricky Williams 2.00 5.00
27 Curtis Martin 1.50 4.00
28 Napoleon Kaufman 1.50 4.00
29 Donovan McNabb 5.00 12.00
30 Kordell Stewart 1.00 2.50
31 Terrell Owens 1.50 4.00
32 Jerry Rice 3.00 8.00
33 Steve Young 2.00 5.00
34 Jon Kitna 1.50 4.00
35 Warrick Dunn 1.50 4.00
36 Eddie George 1.50 4.00

1999 Revolution Thorn in the Side

Inserted at a rate on one in 25, these die-cut cards feature players who torment other teams. The cards are die-cut, feature full holographic foil and are designed to look like they have thorns.
COMPLETE SET (20) 30.00 80.00
STATED ODDS 1:25
1 Jake Plummer .75 2.00
2 Jamal Anderson 1.25 3.00
3 Doug Flutie 1.25 3.00
4 Tim Couch 1.00 2.50
5 Troy Aikman 2.50 6.00
6 Emmitt Smith 2.50 6.00
7 Terrell Davis 1.25 3.00
8 John Elway 4.00 10.00
9 Barry Sanders 4.00 10.00
10 Brett Favre 4.00 10.00
11 Peyton Manning 4.00 10.00
12 Fred Taylor 1.25 3.00
13 Dan Marino 4.00 10.00
14 Randy Moss 3.00 8.00
15 Drew Bledsoe 1.50 4.00
16 Ricky Williams 1.50 4.00
17 Curtis Martin 1.25 3.00
18 Jerome Bettis 1.25 3.00
19 Jerry Rice 2.50 6.00
20 Jon Kitna 1.25 3.00

1999 Revolution Three-Deep Zone

Inserted four per 25 packs, these 30 cards feature some of the leading players in football.There is also a parallel of the three-deep zone insert set is seperated into three tiers. Cards numbered from 1 to 10 are serial numbered to 99, while cards numbered from 11 to 20 are serial numbered to 199 and cards numbered from 212 through 30 are serial numbered to 299. These cards are considered to be "gold".
COMPLETE SET (30) 25.00 60.00
GOLD STATED ODDS 4:25
*SILVERS 1-10: 5X TO 12X GOLDS
SILVER 1-10 PRINT RUN 99 SER.#'d SETS
*SILVERS 11-20: 1.25X TO 3X GOLDS
SILVER 11-20 PRINT RUN 199 SER.#'d SETS
*SILVERS 21-30: .6X TO 1.5X GOLDS
SILVER 21-30 PRINT RUN 299 SER.#'d SETS
1 Troy Aikman 1.25 3.00
2 Emmitt Smith 1.25 3.00
3 Terrell Davis .60 1.50
4 John Elway 2.00 5.00
5 Barry Sanders 2.00 5.00
6 Brett Favre 2.00 5.00
7 Peyton Manning 2.00 5.00
8 Dan Marino 2.00 5.00
9 Randy Moss 1.50 4.00
10 Drew Bledsoe .75 2.00
11 Jake Plummer .40 1.00
12 Jamal Anderson .60 1.50
13 Doug Flutie .60 1.50
14 Mark Brunell .60 1.50
15 Fred Taylor .60 1.50
16 Randall Cunningham .60 1.50
17 Terrell Owens .60 1.50
18 Jerry Rice 1.25 3.00
19 Steve Young .75 2.00
20 Jon Kitna .60 1.50
21 Antowain Smith .60 1.50
22 Antonio Freeman .60 1.50
23 Curtis Martin .60 1.50
24 Eddie George .60 1.50
25 Cade McNown .50 1.25
26 Tim Couch .60 1.50
27 Akili Smith .50 1.25
28 Edgerrin James 2.00 5.00
29 Ricky Williams 1.00 2.50
30 Donovan McNabb 2.50 6.00

2000 Revolution

Released in late November 2000, Revolution features a 150-card base set divided up into 100 veteran cards and 50 rookie cards sequentially numbered to 300. Base cards have a stadium backdrop colored to match each specific player's team and a team gold foil overlay behind full color player action photography. Revolution was offered in both Hobby and Retial versions. Hobby was packaged in a two card pack with one Beckett Grading Services graded card and carried a suggested retail price of $34.99. Hobby boxes also contained one BGS graded rookie card. Retail packs were released as a two card pack and carried a suggested retail price of $2.99.
COMP.SET w/o RC's (100) 20.00 40.00
1 David Boston .30 .75
2 Jake Plummer .30 .75
3 Frank Sanders .30 .75
4 Jamal Anderson .40 1.00
5 Chris Chandler .40 1.00
6 Tim Dwight .40 1.00
7 Terance Mathis .30 .75
8 Tony Banks .30 .75
9 Qadry Ismail .30 .75
10 Shannon Sharpe .40 1.00
11 Rob Johnson .40 1.00
12 Eric Moulds .30 .75
13 Peerless Price .40 1.00
14 Antowain Smith .40 1.00
15 Steve Beuerlein .40 1.00
16 Tim Biakabutuka .40 1.00
17 Muhsin Muhammad .30 .75
18 Curtis Enis .30 .75
19 Cade McNown .30 .75
20 Marcus Robinson .40 1.00
21 Corey Dillon .30 .75
22 Akili Smith .30 .75
23 Tim Couch .40 1.00
24 Kevin Johnson .30 .75
25 Troy Aikman .60 1.50
26 Rocket Ismail .40 1.00
27 Emmitt Smith .75 2.00
28 Terrell Davis .40 1.00
29 Brian Griese .30 .75
30 Ed McCaffrey .40 1.00
31 Charlie Batch .30 .75
32 Herman Moore .30 .75
33 James Stewart .30 .75
34 Brett Favre 1.00 2.50
35 Antonio Freeman .40 1.00
36 Dorsey Levens .40 1.00
37 Marvin Harrison .40 1.00
38 Edgerrin James .40 1.00
39 Peyton Manning 1.25 3.00
40 Terrence Wilkins .30 .75
41 Mark Brunell .40 1.00
42 Keenan McCardell .40 1.00
43 Jimmy Smith .40 1.00
44 Fred Taylor .30 .75
45 Derrick Alexander .30 .75
46 Tony Gonzalez .40 1.00
47 Elvis Grbac .30 .75
48 Damon Huard .30 .75
49 James Johnson .30 .75
50 O.J. McDuffie .40 1.00
51 Cris Carter .50 1.25
52 Daunte Culpepper .40 1.00
53 Randy Moss .40 1.00
54 Robert Smith .30 .75
55 Drew Bledsoe .40 1.00
56 Terry Glenn .40 1.00
57 Jeff Blake .40 1.00
58 Ricky Williams .40 1.00
59 Tiki Barber .40 1.00
60 Kerry Collins .30 .75
61 Ike Hilliard .30 .75
62 Amani Toomer .30 .75
63 Wayne Chrebet .30 .75
64 Curtis Martin .40 1.00
65 Vinny Testaverde .30 .75
66 Dedric Ward .30 .75
67 Tim Brown .50 1.25
68 Napoleon Kaufman .40 1.00
69 Tyrone Wheatley .30 .75
70 Charles Johnson .30 .75
71 Donovan McNabb .40 1.00
72 Duce Staley .30 .75
73 Jerome Bettis .50 1.25
74 Troy Edwards .30 .75
75 Kordell Stewart .30 .75
76 Isaac Bruce .50 1.25
77 Marshall Faulk .40 1.00
78 Az-Zahir Hakim .30 .75
79 Torry Holt .40 1.00
80 Kurt Warner .75 2.00
81 Curtis Conway .40 1.00
82 Jermaine Fazande .30 .75
83 Ryan Leaf .40 1.00
84 Junior Seau .40 1.00
85 Jeff Garcia .30 .75
86 Charlie Garner .40 1.00
87 Terrell Owens .40 1.00
88 Jerry Rice 1.25 3.00
89 Jon Kitna .30 .75
90 Derrick Mayes .30 .75
91 Ricky Watters .40 1.00
92 Mike Alstott .30 .75
93 Warrick Dunn .30 .75
94 Keyshawn Johnson .40 1.00
95 Shaun King .30 .75
96 Eddie George .40 1.00
97 Jevon Kearse .30 .75
98 Steve McNair .40 1.00
99 Stephen Davis .30 .75
100 Brad Johnson .40 1.00
101 Thomas Jones RC 3.00 8.00
102 Doug Johnson RC 2.50 6.00
103 Jamal Lewis RC 4.00 10.00
104 Chris Redman RC 2.50 6.00
105 Travis Taylor RC 2.50 6.00
106 Troy Walters RC 2.50 6.00
107 Kwame Cavil RC 2.50 6.00
108 Sammy Morris RC 2.50 6.00
109 Dez White RC 2.50 6.00
110 Ron Dugans RC 2.50 6.00
111 Danny Farmer RC 2.50 6.00
112 Curtis Keaton RC 2.50 6.00
113 Peter Warrick RC 2.50 6.00
114 Dennis Northcutt RC 2.50 6.00
115 Travis Prentice RC 2.50 6.00
116 Kevin Thompson RC 2.50 6.00
117 Spergon Wynn RC 2.50 6.00
118 Michael Wiley RC 2.50 6.00
119 Mike Anderson RC 2.50 6.00
120 Chris Cole RC 3.00 8.00
121 Jarious Jackson RC 3.00 8.00
122 Charles Lee RC 2.50 6.00
123 Anthony Lucas RC 2.50 6.00
124 R.Jay Soward RC 2.50 6.00
125 Shyrone Stith RC 2.50 6.00
126 Sylvester Morris RC 3.00 8.00
127 Doug Chapman RC 2.50 6.00
128 Tom Brady RC 400.00 800.00
129 Gari Scott RC 2.50 6.00
130 J.R. Redmond RC 2.50 6.00
131 Ron Dayne RC 4.00 10.00
132 Ron Dixon RC 2.50 6.00
133 Laveranues Coles RC 3.00 8.00
134 Ronney Jenkins RC 2.50 6.00
135 Chad Pennington RC 3.00 8.00
136 Jerry Porter RC 4.00 10.00
137 Todd Pinkston RC 2.50 6.00
138 Plaxico Burress RC 3.00 8.00
139 Trung Canidate RC 2.50 6.00
140 Troy Walters RC 2.50 6.00
141 Giovanni Carmazzi RC 2.50 6.00
142 Tim Rattay RC 3.00 8.00
143 Shaun Alexander RC 4.00 10.00
144 Darrell Jackson RC 2.50 6.00
145 James Williams RC 2.50 6.00
146 Joe Hamilton RC 2.50 6.00
147 Aaron Stecker RC 2.50 6.00
148 Erron Kinney RC 2.50 6.00
149 Billy Volek RC 4.00 10.00
150 Todd Husak RC 2.50 6.00

2000 Revolution Premiere Date

*VETS: 5X TO 12X BASIC CARDS
PREMIERE DATE/85 ODDS 1:7 HOB
STATED PRINT RUN 85 SER.#'d SETS

2000 Revolution Red

*VETS 1-100: 5X TO 12X BASIC CARDS
RED/99 INSERTS IN RETAIL PACKS

2000 Revolution Silver

*VETS 1-100: 5X TO 12X BASIC CARDS
SILVER/80 INSERTS IN HOBBY PACKS

2000 Revolution First Look

Randomly inserted in packs at the rate of four in 25, this 36-card set features some of this year's top rookies on a card with a circular background that frames the color action photo of the featured player. Cards are accented with gold foil highlights.
COMPLETE SET (36) 40.00 80.00
STATED ODDS 4:25
1 Thomas Jones .30 .75
2 Doug Johnson .25 .60
3 Jamal Lewis .40 1.00
4 Chris Redman .25 .60
5 Travis Taylor .25 .60
6 Sammy Morris .25 .60
7 Dez White .25 .60
8 Ron Dugans .25 .60
9 Curtis Keaton .25 .60
10 Peter Warrick .25 .60
11 Courtney Brown .30 .75
12 Dennis Northcutt .25 .60
13 Travis Prentice .25 .60
14 Mike Anderson .25 .60
15 Jarious Jackson .30 .75
16 Bubba Franks .25 .60
17 R.Jay Soward .25 .60
18 Frank Moreau .25 .60
19 Sylvester Morris .25 .60
20 Deon Dyer .25 .60
21 Doug Chapman .25 .60
22 Tom Brady 40.00 80.00
23 Ron Dayne .40 1.00
24 Laveranues Coles .30 .75
25 Chad Pennington .30 .75
26 Jerry Porter .40 1.00
27 Todd Pinkston .25 .60
28 Plaxico Burress .30 .75
29 Tee Martin .25 .60
30 Trung Canidate .25 .60
31 JaJuan Seider .25 .60
32 Giovanni Carmazzi .25 .60
33 Tim Rattay .30 .75
34 Darrell Jackson .25 .60
35 Shaun Alexander .40 1.00
36 Joe Hamilton .25 .60

2000 Revolution First Look Super Bowl XXXV

22 Tom Brady 300.00 500.00

2000 Revolution Game Worn Jerseys

Randomly inserted in packs, this 20-card set features player action photography coupled with a swatch of a game worn jersey. Player action photography appears on the right side of the card, while a circular swatch of game worn jersey appears on the left. Announced print runs are listed below.
PACIFIC ANNOUNCED PRINT RUNS
1 Rod Woodson/1145* 6.00 15.00
2 Jamir Miller/1295* 4.00 10.00
3 Olandis Gary/75* 8.00 20.00
4 Brett Favre/15* 100.00 200.00
5 Mark Brunell/735* 5.00 12.00
6 Keenan McCardell/679* 5.00 12.00
7 Fred Taylor/380* 4.00 10.00
8 Dan Marino/777* 12.00 30.00
9 Cris Carter/235* 15.00 40.00
10 Randy Moss/85* 15.00 40.00
11 Drew Bledsoe/645* 5.00 12.00
12 Ricky Williams/35* 8.00 20.00
13 Koy Detmer/726* 4.00 10.00
14 Torrance Small/481* 4.00 10.00
15 Duce Staley/35* 6.00 15.00
16 Jerome Bettis/65* 15.00 40.00
17 Junior Seau/60* 8.00 20.00
18 Jerry Rice/828* 15.00 40.00
19 Brock Huard/706* 4.00 10.00
20 Steve McNair/52* 8.00 20.00

2000 Revolution Making the Grade Black

Randomly inserted in Hobby Packs at the rate of four in 13 and retail packs at the rate of two in 25, this 20-card set features player action shots and a black one point box in the lower right hand corner. Once ten points are gathered, a collector may redeem them for a coupon to have one Pacific trading card graded by Beckett Grading Services. A five point red version and a 10 point gold version were issued also.
COMPLETE SET (20) 15.00 40.00
BLACK 1-POINT ODDS 4:13 H, 2:25 R
*RED: 1.2X TO 3X BLACK
RED 5-POINT ODDS 1:49 H, 2:481 R
*GOLD: 2X TO 5X BLACK
GOLD 10-POINT ODDS 1:97 H, 1:481 R
1 Peter Warrick .40 1.00
2 Tim Couch .50 1.25
3 Troy Aikman .75 2.00
4 Emmitt Smith 1.00 2.50
5 Terrell Davis .50 1.25
6 Brian Griese .40 1.00
7 Brett Favre 1.25 3.00
8 Peyton Manning 1.50 4.00
9 Edgerrin James .50 1.25
10 Mark Brunell .50 1.25
11 Fred Taylor .40 1.00
12 Randy Moss .50 1.25
13 Ricky Williams .50 1.25
14 Ron Dayne .60 1.50
15 Chad Pennington .50 1.25
16 Marshall Faulk .50 1.25
17 Kurt Warner 1.00 2.50
18 Jerry Rice 1.50 4.00
19 Eddie George .50 1.25
20 Steve McNair .50 1.25

2000 Revolution Ornaments

Randomly inserted in packs at the rate of one in 25, this 20-card set features full color player action photography set on a die cut Christmas ornament. Each ornamant comes with a hole punched in the top for hanging.
COMPLETE SET (20) 25.00 60.00
STATED ODDS 1:25
1 Thomas Jones 1.00 2.50
2 Jake Plummer 1.25 3.00
3 Jamal Anderson 1.50 4.00
4 Jamal Lewis 1.25 3.00
5 Cade McNown 1.25 3.00
6 Corey Dillon 1.25 3.00
7 Peter Warrick .75 2.00
8 Troy Aikman 2.50 6.00
9 Emmitt Smith 3.00 8.00
10 Mike Anderson .75 2.00
11 Marvin Harrison 1.50 4.00
12 Edgerrin James 1.50 4.00
13 Peyton Manning 5.00 12.00
14 Mark Brunell 1.50 4.00
15 Daunte Culpepper 1.50 4.00
16 Ron Dayne 2.00 5.00
17 Plaxico Burress 1.00 2.50
18 Marshall Faulk 1.50 4.00
19 Kurt Warner 3.00 8.00
20 Shaun King 1.25 3.00

2000 Revolution Shields

Randomly inserted in packs at the rate of one in 97, this 20-card set features a die cut card stock in the shape of the NFL logo shield with a silver border and full color player action photography.
COMPLETE SET (20) 30.00 80.00
STATED ODDS 1:97
1 Peter Warrick 1.00 2.50
2 Tim Couch 1.25 3.00
3 Troy Aikman 2.00 5.00
4 Emmitt Smith 2.50 6.00
5 Terrell Davis 1.25 3.00
6 Brett Favre 3.00 8.00
7 Edgerrin James 1.25 3.00
8 Peyton Manning 4.00 10.00
9 Mark Brunell 1.25 3.00
10 Daunte Culpepper 1.25 3.00
11 Randy Moss 1.25 3.00
12 Drew Bledsoe 1.25 3.00
13 Ricky Williams 1.25 3.00
14 Chad Pennington 1.00 2.50
15 Marshall Faulk 1.25 3.00
16 Kurt Warner 2.50 6.00
17 Eddie George 1.25 3.00
18 Steve McNair 1.25 3.00
19 Stephen Davis 1.00 2.50
20 Brad Johnson 1.25 3.00

1993 Rice Council

Sponsored by the USA Rice Council (Houston, Texas), this ten-card standard-size set of recipe trading cards was issued to promote the consumption of rice. These sets were originally available from the Rice Council for 2.00. The fronts feature color photos with either blue or red borders. The player's name appears in black lettering in an orange stripe beneath the picture. The backs present biographical information, career summary, a favorite rice recipe, an up-close trivia fact, and the athlete's favorite charity to which the profits generated from the sale of the cards will be donated. The sports represented in this set are baseball (1, 3, 7), football (2, 5), tennis (4), swimming (6), and bobsledding (8).
COMPLETE SET (10) 4.00 10.00
2 Troy Aikman FB .75 2.00
5 Warren Moon FB .40 1.00

2007 Rochester Raiders CIFL

COMPLETE SET (17) 7.50 15.00
1 Omar Baker .40 1.00
2 Jeff Bruckman .40 1.00
3 Jason Coley .40 1.00
4 Mike Condello .40 1.00
5 Matt Cottengim .40 1.00
6 Reggie Cox .40 1.00
7 Gerald Dias .40 1.00
8 Noah Fehrenbach .40 1.00
9 Dennis Greco CO .40 1.00
10 Maurice Jackson .40 1.00
11 Mike Kalfelz .40 1.00
12 Dave McCarthy OWN .40 1.00
13 Jeff Richardson .40 1.00
14 Darius Smith .40 1.00
15 Mark Tisdale .40 1.00
16 The 8th Man .40 1.00
17 The Raiderrettes .40 1.00

2006 Rock River Raptors UIF

COMPLETE SET (31) 6.00 12.00
1 Ade Adeyemo .20 .50
2 Brian Akins .20 .50
3 Todd Allen Asst.CO .20 .50
4 Ryan Aulenbacher .20 .50
5 Randy Bell .20 .50
6 Tyus Boyd .20 .50
7 Tyrece Butler .20 .50
8 Brian Ceaser .20 .50
9 Billy Cook .20 .50
10 Mike Davis .20 .50
11 Roger Farrar Jr. Asst.CO .20 .50
12 Keith Glover .20 .50
13 Jermaine Hampton .20 .50
14 Anthony Harris .20 .50
15 Sean Hilliard .20 .50
16 John Hollins .20 .50
17 Craig Howard .20 .50
18 Dave Jones Asst.CO .20 .50
19 Markus Lewis .20 .50
20 Luke McArdle .20 .50
21 Ty Myers .20 .50
22 Jack Phillips Jr. Asst.CO .20 .50
23 Dillon Piefer .20 .50
24 Rik Richards CO .20 .50
25 Lance Samuseva .20 .50
26 Billy Sanders Asst.CO .20 .50
27 Ben Sankey .20 .50
28 Fernandez Shaw .20 .50
29 Anthony Stone .20 .50
30 Jeremiah Thompson .20 .50
31 Checklist Card .20 .50

1930 Rogers Peet

The Rogers Peet Department Store in New York released this set in early 1930. The cards were given out four at time to employees at the store for enrolling boys in Ropeco (the store's magazine club). Employees who completed the set, and pasted them in the album designed to house the cards, were eligible to win prizes. The blankbacked cards measure roughly 1 3/4" by 2 1/2" and feature a black and white photo of the famous athlete with his name and card number below the picture. Additions to this list are appreciated.
31 Red Grange 800.00 1200.00
Football
33 Ken Strong 250.00 400.00
Football
37 Ed Wittmer 100.00 175.00
Football
41 Chris Cagle 125.00 200.00
Football

2006 Rome Renegade AIFL

COMPLETE SET (34) 10.00 20.00
1 Danny Marshall .30 .75
2 Courtney Stanley .30 .75
3 Jason Colts .30 .75
4 Lew Thomas .30 .75
5 Gerald Gales .30 .75
6 Gerald Gales .30 .75
7 Bo Bartik .30 .75
8 Reggie Jiles .30 .75
9 T.J. Anderson .30 .75
10 Bart Gloyd .30 .75
11 Andrew Amerson .30 .75
12 John Bowman .30 .75
13 Marcus Brady .30 .75
14 Marcus Brady .30 .75
15 Joe Clark .30 .75
16 Jermaine Collins .30 .75
17 Jamaal Greer .30 .75
18 Charles Jones .30 .75
19 Lemar Parrish .30 .75
20 Harold Lindsey .30 .75
21 Leon Moore .30 .75
22 Russell Green .30 .75
23 Reggie Poole .30 .75
24 Dwayne Morgan .30 .75
25 Terel Toomer .30 .75
26 Harry Pierce OWN .30 .75
27 Renegade Race Car .30 .75
28 Cheer Team .30 .75
29 Richie The Renegade .30 .75
30 David Humphrey CO .30 .75
31 Scott Chandler CO .30 .75
32 J.J. Owens CO .30 .75
33 Greg Carter CO .30 .75
34 Scott Hines CO .30 .75

1998 Ron Mix HOF Platinum Autographs

NFL Hall of Famer Ron Mix produced this set in 1998 but released it in 1999. Each card features an artist's rendering of a Hall of Fame football player. These attractive, full color 4" by 6" cards were signed by the players and issued in factory set form only. Production was limited to 2500 sets with each card hand-numbered. Of the 116 cards, two players only signed their first name -- Sid Gillman and Doak Walker. The Doak Walker signature was apparantly done after his tragic skiing accident.
COMPLETE SET (116) 1500.00 2000.00
1 Herb Adderley 7.50 15.00
2 Lance Alworth 10.00 20.00
3 Doug Atkins 7.50 15.00
4 Lem Barney 8.00 20.00
5 Sammy Baugh 50.00 100.00
6 Chuck Bednarik 10.00 20.00
7 Bobby Bell 7.50 15.00
8 Raymond Berry 8.00 20.00
9 Fred Biletnikoff 12.50 25.00
10 George Blanda 25.00 50.00
11 Mel Blount 10.00 20.00
12 Roosevelt Brown 10.00 20.00
13 Willie Brown 7.50 15.00
14 Dick Butkus 20.00 40.00
15 Tony Canadeo 10.00 20.00
16 George Connor 12.50 25.00
17 Lou Creekmur 10.00 20.00
18 Larry Csonka 20.00 35.00
19 Willie Davis 7.50 15.00
20 Len Dawson 12.50 25.00
21 Dan Dierdorf 7.50 15.00
22 Mike Ditka 15.00 30.00
23 Art Donovan 10.00 20.00
24 Tony Dorsett 20.00 35.00
25 Bill Dudley 8.00 20.00
26 Weeb Ewbank 15.00 30.00
27 Tom Fears 20.00 35.00
28 Dan Fouts 12.50 30.00
29 Frank Gatski 10.00 20.00
30 Joe Gibbs 15.00 30.00
31 Sid Gillman (signed Sid) 12.50 25.00
32 Otto Graham 15.00 30.00
33 Bud Grant 20.00 40.00
34 Bob Griese 12.50 30.00
35 Lou Groza 15.00 30.00
36 Jack Ham 10.00 20.00
37 John Hannah 8.00 20.00
38 Franco Harris 20.00 40.00
39 Mike Haynes 8.00 20.00
40 Ted Hendricks 8.00 20.00
41 Crazylegs Hirsch 15.00 30.00
42 Paul Hornung 12.50 25.00
43 Ken Houston 7.50 15.00
44 Sam Huff 10.00 20.00
45 John Henry Johnson 12.50 25.00
46 Jimmy Johnson DB 7.50 15.00
47 Charlie Joiner 8.00 20.00
48 Deacon Jones 7.50 15.00
49 Stan Jones 10.00 20.00
50 Sonny Jurgensen 20.00 40.00
51 Leroy Kelly 8.00 20.00
52 Paul Krause 7.50 15.00
53 Tom Landry 50.00 80.00
54 Dick Lane 12.50 25.00
55 Jim Langer 7.50 15.00
56 Willie Lanier 7.50 15.00
57 Steve Largent 8.00 20.00
58 Yale Lary 7.50 15.00
59 Dante Lavelli 12.50 25.00
60 Bob Lilly 10.00 20.00
61 Larry Little 7.50 15.00
62 John Mackey 10.00 20.00
63 Gino Marchetti 10.00 20.00
64 Don Maynard 7.50 15.00
65 Mike McCormack 10.00 20.00
66 Tommy McDonald 7.50 15.00
67 Hugh McElhenny 10.00 20.00
68 Bobby Mitchell 12.50 25.00
69 Ron Mix 8.00 20.00
70 Lenny Moore 10.00 20.00
71 Marion Motley 25.00 50.00
72 Anthony Munoz 7.50 15.00
73 George Musso 12.50 25.00
74 Joe Namath 40.00 80.00
75 Chuck Noll CO 15.00 30.00
76 Leo Nomellini 12.50 25.00
77 Merlin Olsen 8.00 20.00
78 Jim Otto 7.50 15.00
79 Alan Page 8.00 20.00
80 Ace Parker 7.50 15.00
81 Jim Parker 12.50 25.00
82 Joe Perry 10.00 20.00
83 Pete Pihos 12.50 25.00
84 Mel Renfro 7.50 15.00
85 Jim Ringo 12.50 25.00
86 Andy Robustelli 7.50 15.00
87 Gale Sayers 20.00 40.00
88 Joe Schmidt 7.50 15.00
89 Tex Schramm 15.00 30.00
90 Lee Roy Selmon 7.50 15.00
91 Art Shell 8.00 20.00
92 Don Shula CO 25.00 50.00
93 Mike Singletary 10.00 20.00
94 O.J. Simpson 20.00 40.00
95 Jackie Smith 7.50 15.00
96 Bob St. Clair 7.50 15.00
97 Roger Staubach 30.00 60.00
98 Ernie Stautner 15.00 30.00
99 Jan Stenerud 7.50 15.00
100 Dwight Stephenson 7.50 15.00
101 Charley Taylor 7.50 15.00
102 Jim Taylor 10.00 20.00
103 Y.A. Tittle 10.00 25.00
104 Charley Trippi 7.50 15.00
105 Gene Upshaw 12.50 25.00
106 Steve Van Buren 10.00 20.00
107 Bill Walsh CO 30.00 50.00
108 Doak Walker 20.00 40.00
Post Accident-only signed Doak
109 Paul Warfield 7.50 15.00
110 Mike Webster 25.00 50.00
111 Arnie Weinmeister 12.50 25.00
112 Randy White 12.50 25.00
113 Bill Willis 10.00 20.00
114 Larry Wilson 8.00 20.00
115 Kellen Winslow 8.00 20.00
116 Willie Wood 7.50 15.00

2003 Ron Mix HOF Gold

The Gold version of the Ron Mix art card set was issued in 2003 as a follow up to the 1998 Platinum release. Each card was printed with a gold colored stripe along the left edge instead of Platinum. Factory sets included all 115-cards with just one of those signed by a player. Two additional Platinum autographed cards were also included in each Gold factory set. Initial retail price for the factory set was $149.
COMPLETE SET (115) 75.00 150.00
1 Herb Adderley .60 1.50
2 Lance Alworth .75 2.00
3 Doug Atkins .50 1.25
4 Red Badgro .50 1.25
5 Lem Barney .50 1.25
6 Sammy Baugh 1.50 4.00
7 Chuck Bednarik .60 1.50
8 Bobby Dell .60 1.50
9 Raymond Berry .75 2.00
10 Fred Biletnikoff .75 2.00
11 Mel Blount .75 2.00
12 Roosevelt Brown .50 1.25
13 Willie Brown .60 1.50
14 Dick Butkus 1.50 4.00
15 Tony Canadeo .60 1.50
16 George Connor .60 1.50
17 Lou Creekmur .50 1.25
18 Larry Csonka .75 2.00
19 Willie Davis .60 1.50
20 Len Dawson 1.00 2.50
21 Dan Dierdorf .60 1.50
22 Mike Ditka 1.25 3.00
23 Art Donovan .60 1.50
24 Tony Dorsett 1.25 3.00
25 Bill Dudley .60 1.50
26 Weeb Ewbank .50 1.25
27 Tom Fears .60 1.50
28 Dan Fouts .75 2.00
29 Frank Gatski .50 1.25
30 Sid Gillman .50 1.25
31 Otto Graham 1.00 2.50
32 Bud Grant .50 1.25
33 Lou Groza .75 2.00
34 Jack Ham .75 2.00
35 John Hannah .60 1.50
36 Franco Harris 1.25 3.00
37 Mike Haynes .50 1.25
38 Ted Hendricks .60 1.50
39 Elroy Hirsch .75 2.00
40 Paul Hornung 1.00 2.50
41 Ken Houston .50 1.25
42 Sam Huff .75 2.00
43 John Henry Johnson .75 2.00
44 Jimmy Johnson DB .50 1.25
45 Charlie Joiner .75 2.00
46 Stan Jones .50 1.25
47 Sonny Jurgensen .75 2.00
48 Leroy Kelly .60 1.50
49 Paul Krause .50 1.25
50 Tom Landry 1.00 2.50
51 Dick Lane .60 1.50
52 Jim Langer .50 1.25
53 Willie Lanier .50 1.25
54 Steve Largent .75 2.00
55 Yale Lary .50 1.25
56 Dante Lavelli .60 1.50
57 Bob Lilly .75 2.00
58 Larry Little .60 1.50
59 Sid Luckman .75 2.00
60 John Mackey .60 1.50
61 Gino Marchetti .60 1.50
62 Ollie Matson .75 2.00
63 Don Maynard .75 2.00
64 George McAfee .50 1.25
65 Mike McCormack .50 1.25
66 Tommy McDonald .50 1.25
67 Hugh McElhenny .75 2.00
68 Bobby Mitchell .75 2.00
69 Ron Mix .60 1.50
70 Lenny Moore .75 2.00
71 Marion Motley .75 2.00
72 Anthony Munoz .60 1.50
73 George Musso .50 1.25
74 Chuck Noll CO .75 2.00
75 Leo Nomellini .60 1.50
76 Merlin Olsen .75 2.00
77 Jim Otto .75 2.00
78 Alan Page .60 1.50
79 Ace Parker .50 1.25
80 Jim Parker .60 1.50
81 Joe Perry .75 2.00
82 Pete Pihos .60 1.50
83 Mel Renfro .60 1.50
84 Jim Ringo .60 1.50
85 Andy Robustelli .60 1.50
86 Gale Sayers 1.50 4.00
87 Joe Schmidt .60 1.50
88 Tex Schramm .50 1.25
89 Lee Roy Selmon .60 1.50
90 Art Shell .75 2.00
91 Don Shula CO .75 2.00
92 Mike Singletary .75 2.00
93 O.J. Simpson .75 2.00
94 Jackie Smith .60 1.50
95 Bob St. Clair .50 1.25
96 Roger Staubach 2.00 5.00
97 Ernie Stautner .60 1.50
98 Jan Stenerud .50 1.25
99 Dwight Stephenson .50 1.25
100 Charley Taylor .60 1.50
101 Jim Taylor .75 2.00
102 Y.A. Tittle .75 2.00
103 Charley Trippi .60 1.50
104 Bulldog Turner .60 1.50
105 Steve Van Buren .75 2.00
106 Bill Walsh CO .60 1.50
107 Doak Walker .75 2.00
108 Paul Warfield .75 2.00
109 Mike Webster .60 1.50
110 Arnie Weinmeister .60 1.50
111 Randy White .75 2.00
112 Bill Willis .50 1.25
113 Larry Wilson .50 1.25
114 Kellen Winslow .60 1.50
115 Willie Wood .60 1.50

2010 Rookies and Stars

COMP.SET w/o RC's (150) 8.00 20.00
ROOKIE AUTO PRINT RUN 71-299
EXCH EXPIRATION: 2/18/2012
1 Chris Wells .20 .50
2 Larry Fitzgerald .25 .60
3 Matt Leinart .20 .50
4 Steve Breaston .20 .50
5 Matt Ryan .25 .60
6 Michael Turner .20 .50
7 Roddy White .20 .50
8 Tony Gonzalez .25 .60
9 Anquan Boldin .20 .50
10 Derrick Mason .20 .50
11 Joe Flacco .25 .60
12 Ray Rice .20 .50
13 Todd Heap .20 .50
14 Fred Jackson .25 .60
15 Lee Evans .25 .60
16 Marshawn Lynch .25 .60
17 Ryan Fitzpatrick .20 .50
18 DeAngelo Williams .20 .50
19 Jonathan Stewart .20 .50
20 Matt Moore .20 .50
21 Steve Smith .25 .60
22 Brian Urlacher .30 .75
23 Devin Hester .25 .60
24 Greg Olsen .25 .60
25 Jay Cutler .25 .60
26 Matt Forte .20 .50
27 Andre Caldwell .20 .50
28 Antonio Bryant .20 .50
29 Carson Palmer .25 .60
30 Cedric Benson .20 .50
31 Chad Ochocinco .20 .50
32 Ben Watson .20 .50
33 Jake Delhomme .20 .50
34 Jerome Harrison .20 .50
35 Josh Cribbs .20 .50
36 Mohamed Massaquoi .25 .60
37 Felix Jones .20 .50
38 Jason Witten .25 .60
39 Marion Barber .25 .60
40 Miles Austin .20 .50
41 Tony Romo .25 .60
42 Brandon Marshall .25 .60
43 Eddie Royal .25 .60
44 Jabar Gaffney .20 .50
45 Knowshon Moreno .20 .50
46 Kyle Orton .20 .50
47 Brandon Pettigrew .20 .50
48 Calvin Johnson .30 .75
49 Matthew Stafford .25 .60
50 Nate Burleson .20 .50
51 Aaron Rodgers .60 1.50
52 Donald Driver .25 .60
53 Greg Jennings .20 .50
54 Jermichael Finley .20 .50
55 Ryan Grant .25 .60
56 Andre Johnson .25 .60
57 Kevin Walter .25 .60
58 Matt Schaub .20 .50
59 Owen Daniels .20 .50
60 Steve Slaton .20 .50
61 Pierre Garcon .25 .60
62 Dallas Clark .20 .50
63 Joseph Addai .20 .50
64 Peyton Manning .75 2.00
65 Reggie Wayne .25 .60
66 David Garrard .20 .50
67 Maurice Jones-Drew .20 .50
68 Mike Sims-Walker .25 .60
69 Mike Thomas .20 .50
70 Torry Holt .25 .60
71 Chris Chambers .20 .50
72 Dwayne Bowe .25 .60
73 Jamaal Charles .25 .60
74 Matt Cassel .20 .50
75 Thomas Jones .20 .50
76 Brian Hartline .25 .60
77 Chad Henne .25 .60
78 Davone Bess .20 .50
79 Greg Camarillo .20 .50
80 Ronnie Brown .20 .50
81 Adrian Peterson .30 .75
82 Brett Favre .60 1.50
83 Percy Harvin .20 .50
84 Sidney Rice .20 .50
85 Visanthe Shiancoe .25 .60
86 Laurence Maroney .20 .50
87 Randy Moss .20 .50
88 Tom Brady .75 2.00
89 Wes Welker .25 .60
90 Devery Henderson .20 .50
91 Drew Brees .30 .75
92 Jeremy Shockey .20 .50
93 Marques Colston .20 .50
94 Pierre Thomas .20 .50
95 Brandon Jacobs .20 .50
96 Eli Manning .25 .60
97 Hakeem Nicks .20 .50
98 Kevin Boss .20 .50
99 Steve Smith USC .20 .50
100 Braylon Edwards .20 .50
101 Jerricho Cotchery .20 .50
102 LaDainian Tomlinson .30 .75
103 Mark Sanchez .20 .50
104 Shonn Greene .20 .50
105 Chaz Schilens .20 .50
106 Darren McFadden .20 .50
107 Jason Campbell .20 .50

108 Louis Murphy .20 .50
109 Zach Miller .20 .50
110 Brent Celek .20 .50
111 DeSean Jackson .25 .60
112 Jeremy Maclin .20 .50
113 Kevin Kolb .20 .50
114 LeSean McCoy .30 .75
115 Ben Roethlisberger .30 .75
116 Heath Miller .20 .50
117 Rashard Mendenhall .20 .50
118 Santonio Holmes .20 .50
119 Troy Polamalu .30 .75
120 Antonio Gates .25 .60
121 Darren Sproles .25 .60
122 Philip Rivers .30 .75
123 Vincent Jackson .20 .50
124 Alex Smith QB .25 .60
125 Frank Gore .25 .60
126 Josh Morgan .25 .60
127 Michael Crabtree .20 .50
128 Vernon Davis .20 .50
129 Deion Branch .20 .50
130 John Carlson .20 .50
131 Julius Jones .20 .50
132 Matt Hasselbeck .20 .50
133 T.J. Houshmandzadeh .20 .50
134 Danny Amendola .30 .75
135 Donnie Avery .20 .50
136 James Laurinaitis .25 .60
137 Steven Jackson .20 .50
138 Cadillac Williams .20 .50
139 Josh Freeman .25 .60
140 Kellen Winslow Jr. .20 .50
141 Sammie Stroughter .20 .50
142 Bo Scaife .20 .50
143 Chris Johnson .20 .50
144 Kenny Britt .20 .50
145 Vince Young .20 .50
146 Chris Cooley .20 .50
147 Clinton Portis .20 .50
148 Donovan McNabb .25 .60
149 Larry Johnson .20 .50
150 Santana Moss .25 .60
151 Dallas Clark ELE .75 2.00
152 Peyton Manning ELE 3.00 8.00
153 Lee Evans ELE 1.00 2.50
154 David Garrard ELE .75 2.00
155 Derrick Mason ELE .75 2.00
156 Calvin Johnson ELE 1.25 3.00
157 Joe Flacco ELE 1.00 2.50
158 Vince Young ELE .75 2.00
159 Chris Johnson ELE .75 2.00
160 Tom Brady ELE 3.00 8.00
161 Wes Welker ELE 1.00 2.50
162 Ryan Fitzpatrick ELE .75 2.00
163 Fred Jackson ELE 1.00 2.50
164 Laurence Maroney ELE .75 2.00
165 Randy Moss ELE 1.00 2.50
166 A.J. Edds RC 1.25 3.00
167 Alterraun Verner RC 1.25 3.00
168 Amari Spievey RC 1.00 2.50
169 Andre Anderson RC 1.00 2.50
170 Andre Dixon RC 1.50 4.00
171 Anthony Davis RC 1.25 3.00
172 Anthony Dixon RC 1.00 2.50
173 Antonio Brown RC 8.00 20.00
174 Blair White RC 1.00 2.50
175 Brandon Ghee RC 1.00 2.50
176 Brandon Graham RC 1.25 3.00
177 Brian Price RC 1.00 2.50
178 Bryan Bulaga RC 1.00 2.50
179 Chad Jones RC 1.00 2.50
180 Charles Scott RC 1.00 2.50
181 Chris Cook RC 1.00 2.50
182 Chris McGaha RC 1.00 2.50
183 Corey Wootton RC 1.00 2.50
184 Dan Williams RC 1.00 2.50
185 Darrell Stuckey RC 1.00 2.50
186 Darryl Sharpton RC 1.00 2.50
187 Daryl Washington RC 1.00 2.50
188 David Gettis RC 1.00 2.50
189 Dennis Pitta RC 1.00 2.50
190 Devin McCourty RC 1.25 3.00
191 Dominique Franks RC 1.00 2.50
192 Donald Butler RC 1.00 2.50
193 Ed Dickson RC 1.00 2.50
194 Eric Norwood RC 1.25 3.00
195 Everson Griffen RC 1.00 2.50
196 Freddie Barnes RC 1.00 2.50
197 Garrett Graham RC 1.00 2.50
198 James Starks RC 1.25 3.00
199 Jared Odrick RC 1.25 3.00
200 Jarrett Brown RC 1.00 2.50
201 Jason Pierre-Paul RC 1.50 4.00
202 Jason Worilds RC 1.00 2.50
203 Javier Arenas RC 1.00 2.50
204 Jeremy Williams RC 1.00 2.50
205 Jermaine Cunningham RC 1.00 2.50
206 Jerome Murphy RC 1.25 3.00
207 Jerry Hughes RC 1.00 2.50
208 Jevan Snead RC 1.00 2.50
209 Jimmy Graham RC 2.50 6.00
210 Joique Bell RC 1.00 2.50
211 Kareem Jackson RC 1.00 2.50
212 Kevin Thomas RC 1.25 3.00
213 Koa Misi RC 1.25 3.00
214 Kyle Wilson RC 1.00 2.50
215 Lamarr Houston RC 1.25 3.00
216 LeGarrette Blount RC 2.00 5.00
217 Linval Joseph RC 1.00 2.50
218 Lonyae Miller RC 1.25 3.00
219 Major Wright RC 1.00 2.50
220 Maurkice Pouncey RC 1.25 3.00
221 Mike Hoomanawanui RC 1.50 4.00
222 Mike Iupati RC 1.50 4.00
223 Morgan Burnett RC 1.25 3.00
224 Myron Lewis RC 1.25 3.00
225 Nate Allen RC 1.50 4.00
226 NaVorro Bowman RC 2.00 5.00
227 Pat Angerer RC 1.00 2.50
228 Pat Paschall RC 1.00 2.50
229 Patrick Robinson RC 1.25 3.00
230 Perrish Cox RC 1.25 3.00
231 Perry Riley RC 1.25 3.00
232 Rennie Curran RC 1.00 2.50
233 Riley Cooper RC 1.00 2.50
234 Roddrick Muckelroy RC 1.00 2.50
235 Russell Okung RC 1.00 2.50
236 Sean Canfield RC 1.00 2.50
237 Sean Lee RC 2.00 5.00
238 Sean Weatherspoon RC 1.00 2.50
239 Sergio Kindle RC 1.00 2.50
240 Seyi Ajirotutu RC 1.00 2.50
241 T.J. Ward RC 1.50 4.00
242 Thaddeus Gibson RC 1.25 3.00
243 Tony Moeaki RC 1.25 3.00
244 Tony Pike RC 1.00 2.50
245 Torell Troup RC 1.00 2.50
246 Trent Williams RC 1.25 3.00
247 Trevard Lindley RC 1.00 2.50
248 Tyson Alualu RC 1.00 2.50
249 Walter Thurmond RC 1.00 2.50
250 Zac Robinson RC 1.25 3.00
251 A.Hernandez AU/299 RC 15.00 30.00
252 Andre Roberts AU/203 RC 6.00 15.00
253 Anthony McCoy AU/299 RC 5.00 12.00
254 Armanti Edwards AU/121 RC 6.00 15.00
255 Arrelious Benn AU/299 RC 5.00 12.00
256 Ben Tate AU/299 RC 5.00 12.00
257 Brandon LaFell AU/201 RC 8.00 20.00
258 Brandon Spikes AU/299 RC 5.00 12.00
259 C.J. Spiller AU/201 RC 5.00 12.00
260 Carlos Dunlap AU/299 RC 5.00 12.00
261 Carlton Mitchell AU/299 RC 5.00 12.00
262 Colt McCoy AU/201 RC 6.00 15.00
263 Damian Williams AU/121 RC 5.00 12.00
264 Dan LeFevour AU/299 RC 5.00 12.00
265 D.Thomas AU/201 RC 12.00 30.00
266 Derrick Morgan AU/299 RC 5.00 12.00
267 Dexter McCluster AU/121 RC 6.00 15.00
268 Dez Bryant AU/200 RC 30.00 60.00
269 Dezmon Briscoe AU/299 RC 5.00 12.00
270 Earl Thomas AU/299 RC 12.00 30.00
271 Emmanuel Sanders AU/251 RC 8.00 20.00
272 Eric Berry AU/251 RC 8.00 20.00
273 Eric Decker AU/251 RC 6.00 15.00
274 Gerald McCoy AU/245 RC 5.00 12.00
275 Golden Tate AU/201 RC 6.00 15.00
276 Jacoby Ford AU/299 RC 5.00 12.00
277 Jahvid Best AU/299 RC 5.00 12.00
278 Jermaine Gresham AU/171 RC 5.00 12.00
279 Jimmy Clausen AU/199 RC 5.00 12.00
280 Joe Haden AU/299 RC 8.00 20.00
281 Joe McKnight AU/171 RC 5.00 12.00
282 John Skelton AU/299 RC 6.00 15.00
283 Jonathan Crompton AU/299 RC 5.00 12.00
284 Jonathan Dwyer AU/299 RC 5.00 12.00
285 Jordan Shipley AU/171 RC 5.00 12.00
286 Marcus Easley AU/251 RC 5.00 12.00
287 Mardy Gilyard AU/201 RC 5.00 12.00
288 Mike Kafka AU/251 RC 6.00 15.00
289 Mike Williams AU/170 RC 5.00 12.00
290 Montario Hardesty AU/121 RC 5.00 12.00
291 Ndamukong Suh AU/297 RC 10.00 25.00
292 Ricky Sapp AU/299 RC 5.00 12.00
293 Rob Gronkowski AU/71 RC 30.00 60.00
294 Rolando McClain AU/201 RC 5.00 12.00
295 Ryan Mathews AU/201 RC 5.00 12.00
296 Sam Bradford AU/202 RC 6.00 15.00
297 Taylor Mays AU/299 RC 5.00 12.00
298 Taylor Price AU/251 RC 5.00 12.00
299 Tim Tebow AU/201 RC 25.00 60.00
300 Toby Gerhart AU/200 RC 5.00 12.00

2010 Rookies and Stars Gold

*VETS 1-150: .8X TO 2X BASIC CARDS
*ELEMENT 151-165: .4X TO 1X BASIC CARDS
*ROOKIES 166-250: .4X TO 1X BASIC CARDS
RANDOM INSERTS IN RETAIL PACKS

2010 Rookies and Stars Longevity Parallel Gold

*VETS 1-150: 4X TO 10X BASIC CARDS
*ELEMENT 151-165: 1X TO 2.5X BASIC CARDS
*ROOKIES 166-250: 1.2X TO 3X BASIC CARDS
STATED PRINT RUN 49 SER.#'d SETS

2010 Rookies and Stars Longevity Parallel Platinum

*VETS 1-150: 5X TO 12X BASIC CARDS
*ELEMENT 151-165: 1.2X TO 3X BASIC CARDS
*ROOKIES 166-250: 1.5X TO 4X BASIC CARDS
STATED PRINT RUN 25 SER.#'d SETS

2010 Rookies and Stars Longevity Parallel Silver

*VETS 1-150: 2X TO 5X BASIC CARDS
*ELEMENT 151-165: .5X TO 1.2X BASIC CARDS
*ROOKIES 166-250: .8X TO 2X BASIC CARDS
STATED PRINT RUN 249 SER.#'d SETS

2010 Rookies and Stars Longevity Parallel Silver Holofoil

*VETS 1-150: 3X TO 8X BASIC CARDS
*ELEMENT 151-165: .8X TO 2X BASIC CARDS
*ROOKIES 166-250: 1X TO 2.5X BASIC CARDS
STATED PRINT RUN 99 SER.#'d SETS

2010 Rookies and Stars Autographs

STATED PRINT RUN 1-25
7 Roddy White/15 8.00 20.00
15 Lee Evans/15 10.00 25.00
37 Felix Jones/15 20.00 40.00
90 Devery Henderson/15 8.00 20.00
98 Kevin Boss/25 8.00 20.00
103 Mark Sanchez/20 30.00 60.00
108 Louis Murphy/20 8.00 20.00
112 Jeremy Maclin/15 8.00 20.00
116 Heath Miller/15 8.00 20.00
118 Santonio Holmes/25 8.00 20.00
127 Michael Crabtree/15 25.00 50.00

2010 Rookies and Stars Crosstraining

*BLACK/100: .6X TO 1.5X BASIC INSERTS
*GOLD/500: .5X TO 1.2X BASIC INSERTS
1 Jahvid Best .50 1.25
2 Jermaine Gresham .50 1.25
3 Jimmy Clausen .50 1.25
4 Joe McKnight .50 1.25
5 Jonathan Dwyer .50 1.25
6 Jordan Shipley .50 1.25
7 Mardy Gilyard .50 1.25
8 Mike Williams .50 1.25
9 Toby Gerhart .50 1.25
10 Tim Tebow 1.50 4.00
11 Sam Bradford .60 1.50
12 Ryan Mathews .50 1.25
13 Rolando McClain .50 1.25
14 Ndamukong Suh 1.00 2.50
15 Mike Kafka .60 1.50
16 Golden Tate .60 1.50
17 Eric Decker .60 1.50
18 Emmanuel Sanders .75 2.00
19 Eric Berry .75 2.00
20 Montario Hardesty .50 1.25
21 Taylor Price .50 1.25
22 Dez Bryant 1.25 3.00
23 Damian Williams .50 1.25
24 Colt McCoy .60 1.50
25 Dexter McCluster .60 1.50
26 Rob Gronkowski 1.50 4.00
27 Andre Roberts .60 1.50
28 Arrelious Benn .50 1.25
29 Armanti Edwards .60 1.50
30 Ben Tate .50 1.25
31 Brandon LaFell .75 2.00
32 C.J. Spiller .50 1.25
33 Demaryius Thomas 1.25 3.00
34 Gerald McCoy .50 1.25
35 Marcus Easley .50 1.25

2010 Rookies and Stars Crosstraining Materials

STATED PRINT RUN 299 SER.#'d SETS
*PRIME/50: .8X TO 2X BASIC JSY/299
*LONG/249: .4X TO 1X BASIC JSY/299
1 Jahvid Best 1.25 3.00
2 Jermaine Gresham 1.25 3.00
3 Jimmy Clausen 1.25 3.00
4 Joe McKnight 1.25 3.00
5 Jonathan Dwyer 1.25 3.00
6 Jordan Shipley 1.25 3.00
7 Mardy Gilyard 1.25 3.00
8 Mike Williams 1.25 3.00
9 Toby Gerhart 1.25 3.00
10 Tim Tebow 4.00 10.00
11 Sam Bradford 1.50 4.00
12 Ryan Mathews 1.25 3.00
13 Rolando McClain 1.25 3.00
14 Ndamukong Suh 2.50 6.00
15 Mike Kafka 1.50 4.00
16 Golden Tate 1.50 4.00
17 Eric Decker 1.50 4.00
18 Emmanuel Sanders 2.00 5.00
19 Eric Berry 2.00 5.00
20 Montario Hardesty 1.25 3.00
21 Taylor Price 1.25 3.00
22 Dez Bryant 3.00 8.00
23 Damian Williams 1.25 3.00
24 Colt McCoy 1.50 4.00
25 Dexter McCluster 1.50 4.00
26 Rob Gronkowski 4.00 10.00
27 Andre Roberts 1.50 4.00
28 Arrelious Benn 1.25 3.00
29 Armanti Edwards 1.50 4.00
30 Ben Tate 1.25 3.00
31 Brandon LaFell 2.00 5.00
32 C.J. Spiller 1.25 3.00
33 Demaryius Thomas 3.00 8.00
34 Gerald McCoy 1.25 3.00
35 Marcus Easley 1.25 3.00

2010 Rookies and Stars Crosstraining Materials Autographs

STATED PRINT RUN 25-100
1 Jahvid Best/25 8.00 20.00
2 Jermaine Gresham/100 4.00 10.00
3 Jimmy Clausen/25 8.00 20.00
4 Joe McKnight/100 4.00 10.00
5 Jonathan Dwyer/100 4.00 10.00
6 Jordan Shipley/50 5.00 12.00
7 Mardy Gilyard/100 4.00 10.00
8 Mike Williams/100 4.00 10.00
9 Toby Gerhart/50 5.00 12.00
10 Tim Tebow/25 40.00 100.00
11 Sam Bradford/25 10.00 25.00
12 Ryan Mathews/25 8.00 20.00
13 Rolando McClain/100 4.00 10.00
14 Ndamukong Suh/25 30.00 60.00
15 Mike Kafka/100 5.00 12.00
16 Golden Tate/25 10.00 25.00
17 Eric Decker/100 5.00 12.00
18 Emmanuel Sanders/100 6.00 15.00
19 Eric Berry/100 6.00 15.00
20 Montario Hardesty/100 4.00 10.00
21 Taylor Price/100 8.00 25.00
22 Dez Bryant/25 40.00 80.00
23 Damian Williams/50 5.00 12.00
24 Colt McCoy/25 10.00 25.00
25 Dexter McCluster/50 6.00 15.00
26 Rob Gronkowski/100 20.00 40.00
27 Andre Roberts/100 5.00 12.00
28 Arrelious Benn/25 8.00 20.00
29 Armanti Edwards/100 5.00 12.00
30 Ben Tate/100 4.00 10.00
31 Brandon LaFell/100 6.00 15.00
32 C.J. Spiller/25 8.00 20.00
33 Demaryius Thomas/25 20.00 50.00
34 Gerald McCoy/100 4.00 10.00
35 Marcus Easley/100 4.00 10.00

2010 Rookies and Stars Dress for Success Jerseys

STATED PRINT RUN 299 SER.#'d SETS
*PRIME/50: .8X TO 2X BASIC JSY/299
*LONG/249: .4X TO 1X BASIC JSY/299
1 Rob Gronkowski 4.00 10.00
2 Brandon LaFell 2.00 5.00
3 Toby Gerhart 1.25 3.00
4 Jermaine Gresham 1.25 3.00
5 Eric Berry 2.00 5.00
6 Ben Tate 1.25 3.00
7 Jimmy Clausen 1.25 3.00
8 Jordan Shipley 1.25 3.00
9 Emmanuel Sanders 2.00 5.00
10 Mike Williams 1.25 3.00
11 Mike Kafka 1.50 4.00
12 C.J. Spiller 1.25 3.00
13 Tim Tebow 4.00 10.00
14 Eric Decker 1.50 4.00
15 Rolando McClain 1.25 3.00
16 Gerald McCoy 1.25 3.00
17 Damian Williams 1.25 3.00
18 Ryan Mathews 1.25 3.00
19 Montario Hardesty 1.25 3.00
20 Taylor Price 1.25 3.00
21 Mardy Gilyard 1.25 3.00
22 Colt McCoy 1.50 4.00
23 Dez Bryant 3.00 8.00
24 Golden Tate 1.50 4.00
25 Jahvid Best 1.25 3.00
26 Armanti Edwards 1.50 4.00
27 Andre Roberts 1.50 4.00
28 Arrelious Benn 1.25 3.00
29 Dexter McCluster 1.50 4.00
30 Joe McKnight 1.25 3.00
31 Jonathan Dwyer 1.25 3.00
32 Demaryius Thomas 3.00 8.00
33 Ndamukong Suh 2.50 6.00
34 Sam Bradford 1.50 4.00
35 Marcus Easley 1.25 3.00

2010 Rookies and Stars Dress for Success Jerseys Autographs

STATED PRINT RUN 25-100
1 Rob Gronkowski/100 20.00 40.00
2 Brandon LaFell/100 6.00 15.00
3 Toby Gerhart/50 5.00 12.00
4 Jermaine Gresham/100 4.00 10.00
5 Eric Berry/100 6.00 15.00
6 Ben Tate/100 4.00 10.00
7 Jimmy Clausen/25 8.00 20.00
8 Jordan Shipley/50 5.00 12.00
9 Emmanuel Sanders/100 6.00 15.00
10 Mike Williams/100 4.00 10.00
11 Mike Kafka/100 5.00 12.00
12 C.J. Spiller/25 8.00 20.00
13 Tim Tebow/25 40.00 100.00
14 Eric Decker/100 5.00 12.00
15 Rolando McClain/100 4.00 10.00
16 Gerald McCoy/100 4.00 10.00
17 Damian Williams/50 5.00 12.00
18 Ryan Mathews/25 8.00 20.00
19 Montario Hardesty/100 4.00 10.00
20 Taylor Price/100 4.00 10.00
21 Mardy Gilyard/100 4.00 10.00
22 Colt McCoy/25 10.00 25.00
23 Dez Bryant/25 40.00 80.00
24 Golden Tate/25 10.00 25.00
25 Jahvid Best/25 8.00 20.00
26 Armanti Edwards/100 5.00 12.00
27 Andre Roberts/100 5.00 12.00
28 Arrelious Benn/25 8.00 20.00
29 Dexter McCluster/50 6.00 15.00
31 Jonathan Dwyer/100 4.00 10.00
32 Demaryius Thomas/25 20.00 50.00
33 Ndamukong Suh/25 15.00 40.00
34 Sam Bradford/25 40.00 80.00
35 Marcus Easley/100 4.00 10.00

2010 Rookies and Stars Elements Materials

STATED PRINT RUN 100-175
*FOIL: .5X TO 1.2X BASIC JSY
152 Peyton Manning/100 12.00 30.00
156 Calvin Johnson/175 4.00 10.00
157 Joe Flacco/100 4.00 10.00
158 Vince Young/175 2.50 6.00
159 Chris Johnson/100 3.00 8.00
160 Tom Brady/175 10.00 25.00
161 Wes Welker/100 4.00 10.00
165 Randy Moss/100 4.00 10.00

2010 Rookies and Stars Elements Materials Holofoil

STATED PRINT RUN 10-50
151 Dallas Clark/50 4.00 10.00
152 Peyton Manning/10
154 David Garrard/25 5.00 12.00
156 Calvin Johnson/50 6.00 15.00
157 Joe Flacco/15 6.00 15.00
158 Vince Young/50 4.00 10.00
159 Chris Johnson/50 4.00 10.00
160 Tom Brady/50 15.00 40.00
161 Wes Welker/50 5.00 12.00
164 Laurence Maroney/50 4.00 10.00
165 Randy Moss/50 5.00 12.00

2010 Rookies and Stars Freshman Orientation Materials Jerseys

STATED PRINT RUN 299 SER.#'d SETS
*PRIME/50: .8X TO 2X BASIC JSY/299
*LONG/249: .4X TO 1X BASIC JSY/299
1 Sam Bradford 1.50 4.00
2 Jonathan Dwyer 1.25 3.00
3 Dexter McCluster 1.50 4.00
4 Armanti Edwards 1.50 4.00
5 Dez Bryant 3.00 8.00
6 Montario Hardesty 1.25 3.00
7 Rolando McClain 1.25 3.00
8 C.J. Spiller 1.25 3.00
9 Jordan Shipley 1.25 3.00
10 Rob Gronkowski 4.00 10.00
11 Jermaine Gresham 1.25 3.00
12 Emmanuel Sanders 2.00 5.00
13 Gerald McCoy 1.25 3.00
14 Taylor Price 1.25 3.00
15 Tim Tebow 4.00 10.00
16 Colt McCoy 1.50 4.00
17 Arrelious Benn 1.25 3.00
18 Demaryius Thomas 3.00 8.00
19 Ndamukong Suh 2.50 6.00
20 Golden Tate 1.50 4.00
21 Jahvid Best 1.25 3.00
22 Toby Gerhart 1.25 3.00
23 Brandon LaFell 2.00 5.00
24 Mike Williams 1.25 3.00
25 Mike Kafka 1.50 4.00
26 Ryan Mathews 1.25 3.00
27 Mardy Gilyard 1.25 3.00
28 Damian Williams 1.25 3.00
29 Andre Roberts 1.50 4.00
30 Joe McKnight 1.25 3.00
31 Ben Tate 1.25 3.00
32 Marcus Easley 1.25 3.00
33 Eric Berry 2.00 5.00
34 Jimmy Clausen 1.25 3.00
35 Eric Decker 1.50 4.00

2010 Rookies and Stars Freshman Orientation Materials Jerseys Autographs

STATED PRINT RUN 25-100
1 Sam Bradford/25 40.00 80.00
2 Jonathan Dwyer/100 4.00 10.00
3 Dexter McCluster/50 6.00 15.00
4 Armanti Edwards/100 5.00 12.00
5 Dez Bryant/25 40.00 80.00
6 Montario Hardesty/100 4.00 10.00
7 Rolando McClain/100 4.00 10.00
8 C.J. Spiller/25 8.00 20.00
9 Jordan Shipley/50 5.00 12.00
10 Rob Gronkowski/100 20.00 40.00
11 Jermaine Gresham/100 4.00 10.00
12 Emmanuel Sanders/100 6.00 15.00
13 Gerald McCoy/100 4.00 10.00
14 Taylor Price/100 4.00 10.00
15 Tim Tebow/25 50.00 100.00
16 Colt McCoy/25 10.00 25.00
17 Arrelious Benn/25 8.00 20.00
18 Demaryius Thomas/25 20.00 50.00
19 Ndamukong Suh/25 15.00 40.00
20 Golden Tate/25 10.00 25.00
21 Jahvid Best/25 8.00 20.00
22 Toby Gerhart/50 5.00 12.00
23 Brandon LaFell/100 6.00 15.00
24 Mike Williams/100 4.00 10.00
25 Mike Kafka/100 5.00 12.00
26 Ryan Mathews/25 8.00 20.00
27 Mardy Gilyard/100 4.00 10.00
28 Damian Williams/50 5.00 12.00
29 Andre Roberts/100 5.00 12.00
30 Joe McKnight/100 4.00 10.00
31 Ben Tate/100 4.00 10.00
32 Marcus Easley/100 4.00 10.00
34 Jimmy Clausen/25 8.00 20.00
35 Eric Decker/100 5.00 12.00

2010 Rookies and Stars Gold Stars

*BLACK/100: .6X TO 1.5X BASIC INSERTS
*GOLD/500: .5X TO 1.2X BASIC INSERTS
1 Brent Celek .60 1.50
2 Carson Palmer .75 2.00
3 Philip Rivers 1.00 2.50
4 Larry Fitzgerald .75 2.00
5 Calvin Johnson 1.00 2.50
6 Drew Brees 1.00 2.50
7 Randy Moss .75 2.00
8 Chris Cooley .60 1.50
9 Troy Polamalu 1.00 2.50
10 Mark Sanchez .60 1.50
11 Jason Witten .75 2.00
12 Vince Young .60 1.50
13 LeSean McCoy 1.00 2.50
14 Ray Rice .60 1.50
15 Ben Roethlisberger 1.00 2.50

2010 Rookies and Stars Gold Stars Materials

STATED PRINT RUN 25-299
*PRIME/50: .8X TO 2X BASIC JSY/299
*PRIME/50: .6X TO 1.5X BASIC JSY/100-150
*PRIME/50: .4X TO 1X BASIC JSY/25
2 Carson Palmer/299 2.50 6.00
3 Philip Rivers/100 4.00 10.00
4 Larry Fitzgerald/100 3.00 8.00
5 Calvin Johnson/100 4.00 10.00
6 Drew Brees/299 3.00 8.00
7 Randy Moss/140 3.00 8.00
8 Chris Cooley/25 4.00 10.00
9 Troy Polamalu/150 4.00 10.00
10 Mark Sanchez/299 2.00 5.00
11 Jason Witten/125 3.00 8.00
12 Vince Young/299 2.00 5.00
13 LeSean McCoy/125 4.00 10.00
15 Ben Roethlisberger/125 4.00 10.00

2010 Rookies and Stars Materials Black Prime Longevity

COMMON CARD/15-25 5.00 12.00
SEMISTARS/15-25 6.00 15.00
UNL.STARS/15-25 8.00 20.00
STATED PRINT RUN 3-25
41 Tony Romo/25 6.00 15.00
81 Adrian Peterson/25 8.00 20.00
88 Tom Brady/25 20.00 50.00

2010 Rookies and Stars Materials Emerald Prime Longevity

COMMON CARD/35-50 4.00 10.00
SEMISTARS/35-50 5.00 12.00
UNL.STARS/35-50 6.00 15.00
COMMON CARD/12-25 8.00 20.00
STATED PRINT RUN 12-50
41 Tony Romo/50 5.00 12.00
64 Peyton Manning/25 20.00 50.00
81 Adrian Peterson/50 6.00 15.00
88 Tom Brady/50 15.00 40.00
103 Mark Sanchez/25 5.00 12.00

2010 Rookies and Stars Materials Gold

RANDOM INSERTS IN RETAIL PACKS
1 Chris Wells 2.00 5.00
2 Larry Fitzgerald 2.50 6.00
3 Matt Leinart 2.00 5.00
5 Matt Ryan 2.50 6.00
7 Roddy White 2.00 5.00
8 Tony Gonzalez 2.50 6.00
10 Derrick Mason 2.00 5.00
11 Joe Flacco 2.50 6.00
13 Todd Heap 2.00 5.00
16 Marshawn Lynch 2.50 6.00
18 DeAngelo Williams 2.00 5.00
23 Devin Hester 2.50 6.00
24 Greg Olsen 2.50 6.00
25 Jay Cutler 2.00 5.00
29 Carson Palmer 2.50 6.00
30 Cedric Benson 2.00 5.00
31 Chad Ochocinco 2.00 5.00
37 Felix Jones 2.00 5.00
38 Jason Witten 2.50 6.00
39 Marion Barber 2.50 6.00
41 Tony Romo 2.50 6.00
43 Eddie Royal 2.00 5.00
45 Knowshon Moreno 2.00 5.00
46 Kyle Orton 2.00 5.00
48 Calvin Johnson 3.00 8.00
49 Matthew Stafford 2.50 6.00
53 Greg Jennings 2.00 5.00
56 Andre Johnson 2.50 6.00
59 Owen Daniels 2.00 5.00
60 Steve Slaton 2.00 5.00
62 Dallas Clark 2.00 5.00
63 Joseph Addai 2.00 5.00
64 Peyton Manning 8.00 20.00
66 David Garrard 2.00 5.00
67 Maurice Jones-Drew 2.00 5.00
72 Dwayne Bowe 2.50 6.00
81 Adrian Peterson 3.00 8.00
82 Brett Favre 6.00 15.00
83 Percy Harvin 2.00 5.00
86 Laurence Maroney 2.00 5.00
87 Randy Moss 2.50 6.00
88 Tom Brady 8.00 20.00
90 Devery Henderson 2.00 5.00
91 Drew Brees 3.00 8.00
93 Marques Colston 2.00 5.00
96 Eli Manning 2.50 6.00
99 Steve Smith USC 2.00 5.00
101 Jerricho Cotchery 2.00 5.00
103 Mark Sanchez 2.00 5.00
104 Shonn Greene 2.00 5.00
106 Darren McFadden 2.00 5.00
108 Louis Murphy 2.00 5.00
109 Zach Miller 2.00 5.00
115 Ben Roethlisberger 3.00 8.00
117 Rashard Mendenhall 2.00 5.00
119 Troy Polamalu 3.00 8.00
120 Antonio Gates 2.50 6.00
121 Darren Sproles 2.50 6.00
122 Philip Rivers 3.00 8.00
123 Vincent Jackson 2.00 5.00
124 Alex Smith QB 2.50 6.00
125 Frank Gore 2.50 6.00
127 Michael Crabtree 2.00 5.00
128 Vernon Davis 2.00 5.00
132 Matt Hasselbeck 2.00 5.00
138 Cadillac Williams 2.00 5.00
139 Josh Freeman 2.50 6.00
144 Kenny Britt 2.00 5.00
145 Vince Young 2.00 5.00
146 Chris Cooley 2.00 5.00
147 Clinton Portis 2.00 5.00
150 Santana Moss 2.50 6.00

2010 Rookies and Stars Prime Cuts

STATED PRINT RUN 50 SER.#'d SETS
*COMBO/25: .5X TO 1.2X BASIC INSERTS
1 Chad Ochocinco 4.00 10.00
2 Dallas Clark 4.00 10.00
4 Michael Turner 4.00 10.00
5 DeAngelo Williams 4.00 10.00
6 Marques Colston 4.00 10.00
7 Eli Manning 5.00 12.00
8 Vernon Davis 4.00 10.00
9 Darren Sproles 5.00 12.00
10 Josh Cribbs 4.00 10.00

2010 Rookies and Stars Rookie Autographs Holofoil

STATED PRINT RUN 299 SER.#'d SETS
*LONGEVITY/249: .4X TO 1X R&S HOLO.AU/299
*LONGEVITY/49: .6X TO 1.5X R&S HOLO.AU/299
LONGEVITY ROOK.AU PRINT RUN 49-249
169 Andre Anderson 2.50 6.00
170 Andre Dixon 4.00 10.00
172 Anthony Dixon 2.50 6.00
173 Antonio Brown 12.00 30.00
174 Blair White 2.50 6.00
176 Brandon Graham 3.00 8.00
178 Bryan Bulaga 6.00 15.00
179 Chad Jones 2.50 6.00
180 Charles Scott 2.50 6.00
181 Chris Cook 2.50 6.00
182 Chris McGaha 2.50 6.00
183 Corey Wootton 2.50 6.00
187 Daryl Washington 2.50 6.00
188 David Gettis 2.50 6.00
190 Devin McCourty 3.00 8.00
191 Dominique Franks 2.50 6.00
193 Ed Dickson 2.50 6.00
195 Everson Griffen 2.50 6.00
196 Freddie Barnes 2.50 6.00
197 Garrett Graham 2.50 6.00
198 James Starks 3.00 8.00
200 Jarrett Brown 2.50 6.00
201 Jason Pierre-Paul 4.00 10.00
202 Jason Worilds 2.50 6.00
204 Jeremy Williams 2.50 6.00
207 Jerry Hughes 2.50 6.00
208 Jevan Snead 2.50 6.00
209 Jimmy Graham 8.00 20.00
210 Joique Bell 2.50 6.00
211 Kareem Jackson 2.50 6.00
216 LeGarrette Blount 6.00 15.00
218 Lonyae Miller 3.00 8.00
223 Morgan Burnett 3.00 8.00
225 Nate Allen 4.00 10.00
226 NaVorro Bowman 5.00 12.00
228 Pat Paschall 2.50 6.00
229 Patrick Robinson 3.00 8.00
230 Perrish Cox 3.00 8.00
233 Riley Cooper 2.50 6.00
235 Russell Okung 6.00 15.00
236 Sean Canfield 2.50 6.00
237 Sean Lee 6.00 15.00
238 Sean Weatherspoon 2.50 6.00
239 Sergio Kindle 2.50 6.00
240 Seyi Ajirotutu 2.50 6.00
244 Tony Pike 2.50 6.00
246 Trent Williams 6.00 15.00
250 Zac Robinson 3.00 8.00

2010 Rookies and Stars Rookie Jersey Jumbo Swatch

STATED PRINT RUN 50 SER.#'d SETS
*EMERALD/10: 1X TO 2.5X BASIC JSY/50
*GOLD/25: .5X TO 1.2X BASIC JSY/50
*LONGEVITY/50: .4X TO 1X BASIC JSY/50
252 Andre Roberts 4.00 10.00
254 Armanti Edwards 4.00 10.00
255 Arrelious Benn 3.00 8.00
256 Ben Tate 3.00 8.00
257 Brandon LaFell 5.00 12.00
259 C.J. Spiller 3.00 8.00
262 Colt McCoy 4.00 10.00
263 Damian Williams 3.00 8.00
265 Demaryius Thomas 8.00 20.00
267 Dexter McCluster 4.00 10.00
268 Dez Bryant 8.00 20.00
271 Emmanuel Sanders 5.00 12.00
272 Eric Berry 5.00 12.00
273 Eric Decker 4.00 10.00
274 Gerald McCoy 3.00 8.00
275 Golden Tate 4.00 10.00
277 Jahvid Best 3.00 8.00
278 Jermaine Gresham 3.00 8.00
279 Jimmy Clausen 3.00 8.00
281 Joe McKnight 3.00 8.00
284 Jonathan Dwyer 3.00 8.00
285 Jordan Shipley 3.00 8.00
286 Marcus Easley 3.00 8.00
287 Mardy Gilyard 3.00 8.00
288 Mike Kafka 4.00 10.00
289 Mike Williams 3.00 8.00
290 Montario Hardesty 3.00 8.00
291 Ndamukong Suh 6.00 15.00
293 Rob Gronkowski 10.00 25.00
294 Rolando McClain 3.00 8.00
295 Ryan Mathews 3.00 8.00
296 Sam Bradford 4.00 10.00
298 Taylor Price 3.00 8.00
299 Tim Tebow 10.00 25.00
300 Toby Gerhart 3.00 8.00

2010 Rookies and Stars Rookie Patch Autographs Blue NFL Logo

*ROOKIE AU: .6X TO 1.5X BASIC AU RC
STATED PRINT RUN 19-42
EXCH EXPIRATION: 2/18/2012
296 Sam Bradford/22 30.00 60.00
299 Tim Tebow/22 60.00 120.00

2010 Rookies and Stars Rookie Patch Autographs Blue Team Logo

*ROOKIE AU: .6X TO 1.5X BASIC AU RC
STATED PRINT RUN 25 SER.#'d SETS
EXCH EXPIRATION: 2/18/2012
296 Sam Bradford 30.00 60.00
299 Tim Tebow 60.00 120.00

2010 Rookies and Stars Statistical Standouts Materials Prime

STATED PRINT RUN 20-50
*BASE JSY/100-150: .25X TO .6X PRIME/50
*BASE JSY/100-150: .2X TO .5X PRIME/20-25
*BASE JSY/25: .4X TO 1X PRIME/50
1 Aaron Rodgers/50 15.00 40.00
2 Adrian Peterson/50 6.00 15.00
3 Andre Johnson/50 5.00 12.00
4 Chris Johnson/50 4.00 10.00
6 Maurice Jones-Drew/50 4.00 10.00
7 Miles Austin/20 5.00 12.00
8 Peyton Manning/15 20.00 50.00
9 Reggie Wayne/25 6.00 15.00
10 Ryan Grant/50 5.00 12.00
11 Sidney Rice/50 4.00 10.00
12 Steven Jackson/50 4.00 10.00
13 Tom Brady/50 15.00 40.00
14 Tony Romo/50 5.00 12.00
15 Wes Welker/50 5.00 12.00

2010 Rookies and Stars Studio Rookies

*BLACK/100: .6X TO 1.5X BASIC INSERTS
*GOLD/500: .5X TO 1.2X BASIC INSERTS
1 Tim Tebow 1.50 4.00
2 Sam Bradford .60 1.50
3 Rolando McClain .50 1.25
4 Ndamukong Suh 1.00 2.50
5 Golden Tate .60 1.50
6 Eric Decker .60 1.50
7 Eric Berry .75 2.00
8 Montario Hardesty .50 1.25
9 Gerald McCoy .50 1.25
10 Demaryius Thomas 1.25 3.00
11 Ben Tate .50 1.25
12 Arrelious Benn .50 1.25
13 Dexter McCluster .60 1.50
14 Damian Williams .50 1.25
15 Colt McCoy .60 1.50
16 Jermaine Gresham .50 1.25
17 Jimmy Clausen .50 1.25
18 Joe McKnight .50 1.25
19 Mike Williams .50 1.25
20 Toby Gerhart .50 1.25
21 Ryan Mathews .50 1.25
22 Armanti Edwards .60 1.50
23 C.J. Spiller .50 1.25
24 Brandon LaFell .75 2.00
25 Marcus Easley .50 1.25
26 Rob Gronkowski 1.50 4.00
27 Andre Roberts .60 1.50
28 Mike Kafka .60 1.50
29 Taylor Price .50 1.25
30 Mardy Gilyard .50 1.25
31 Jordan Shipley .50 1.25
32 Jonathan Dwyer .50 1.25
33 Jahvid Best .50 1.25
34 Emmanuel Sanders .75 2.00
35 Dez Bryant 1.25 3.00

2010 Rookies and Stars Studio Rookies Materials

STATED PRINT RUN 299 SER.#'d SETS
*PRIME/50: .8X TO 2X BASIC JSY/299
1 Tim Tebow 4.00 10.00
2 Sam Bradford 1.50 4.00
3 Rolando McClain 1.25 3.00
4 Ndamukong Suh 2.50 6.00
5 Golden Tate 1.50 4.00
6 Eric Decker 1.50 4.00
7 Eric Berry 2.00 5.00
8 Montario Hardesty 1.25 3.00
9 Gerald McCoy 1.25 3.00
10 Demaryius Thomas 3.00 8.00
11 Ben Tate 1.25 3.00
12 Arrelious Benn 1.25 3.00
13 Dexter McCluster 1.50 4.00
14 Damian Williams 1.25 3.00
15 Colt McCoy 1.50 4.00
16 Jermaine Gresham 1.25 3.00
17 Jimmy Clausen 1.25 3.00
18 Joe McKnight 1.25 3.00
19 Mike Williams 1.25 3.00
20 Toby Gerhart 1.25 3.00
21 Ryan Mathews 1.25 3.00
22 Armanti Edwards 1.50 4.00
23 C.J. Spiller 1.25 3.00
24 Brandon LaFell 2.00 5.00
25 Marcus Easley 1.25 3.00
26 Rob Gronkowski 4.00 10.00
27 Andre Roberts 1.50 4.00
28 Mike Kafka 1.50 4.00
29 Taylor Price 1.25 3.00
30 Mardy Gilyard 1.25 3.00
31 Jordan Shipley 1.25 3.00
32 Jonathan Dwyer 1.25 3.00
33 Jahvid Best 1.25 3.00
34 Emmanuel Sanders 2.00 5.00
35 Dez Bryant 3.00 8.00

2010 Rookies and Stars Studio Rookies Combos

*BLACK/100: .6X TO 1.5X BASIC INSERTS
*GOLD/500: .5X TO 1.2X BASIC INSERTS
1 S.Bradford/M.Gilyard .60 1.50
2 T.Tebow/D.Thomas 1.50 4.00
3 J.Clausen/B.LaFell .75 2.00
4 C.McCoy/M.Hardesty .60 1.50
5 J.Gresham/J.Shipley .50 1.25
6 C.Spiller/M.Easley .50 1.25
7 N.Suh/J.Best 1.00 2.50
8 G.McCoy/M.Williams .50 1.25
9 E.Berry/D.McCluster .60 1.50
10 R.Gronkowski/T.Price 1.50 4.00

2010 Rookies and Stars Studio Rookies Combos Materials

STATED PRINT RUN 299 SER.#'d SETS
*PRIME/50: .6X TO 1.5X BASIC JSY/299
1 S.Bradford/M.Gilyard 2.50 6.00
2 T.Tebow/D.Thomas 10.00 25.00
3 J.Clausen/B.LaFell 3.00 8.00
4 C.McCoy/M.Hardesty 2.50 6.00
5 J.Gresham/J.Shipley 2.00 5.00
6 C.Spiller/M.Easley 2.00 5.00
7 N.Suh/J.Best 4.00 10.00
8 G.McCoy/M.Williams 2.00 5.00
9 E.Berry/D.McCluster 2.50 6.00
10 R.Gronkowski/T.Price 6.00 15.00

2011 Rookies and Stars

151-250 ROOKIES ONE PER PACK
251-300 ROOKIE AU PRINT RUN 299
1 Chris Wells .20 .50
2 Larry Fitzgerald .25 .60
3 Steve Breaston .20 .50
4 Tim Hightower .20 .50
5 Jason Snelling .20 .50
6 Matt Ryan .25 .60
7 Michael Turner .20 .50
8 Roddy White .20 .50
9 Tony Gonzalez .25 .60
10 Anquan Boldin .20 .50
11 Joe Flacco .25 .60
12 Ray Lewis .30 .75
13 Ray Rice .20 .50
14 Todd Heap .20 .50
15 C.J. Spiller .20 .50
16 Fred Jackson .20 .50
17 Lee Evans .25 .60
18 Ryan Fitzpatrick .20 .50
19 Steve Johnson .20 .50
20 DeAngelo Williams .20 .50
21 Jimmy Clausen .20 .50
22 Jonathan Stewart .20 .50
23 Steve Smith .25 .60
24 Brian Urlacher .30 .75
25 Devin Hester .25 .60
26 Jay Cutler .20 .50
27 Johnny Knox .20 .50
28 Matt Forte .20 .50
29 Carson Palmer .25 .60
30 Cedric Benson .20 .50
31 Chad Ochocinco .20 .50
32 Jordan Shipley .20 .50
33 Terrell Owens .25 .60
34 Ben Watson .20 .50
35 Colt McCoy .20 .50
36 Josh Cribbs .20 .50
37 Peyton Hillis .20 .50
38 Dez Bryant .30 .75
39 Felix Jones .20 .50
40 Jason Witten .25 .60
41 Miles Austin .20 .50
42 Tony Romo .25 .60
43 Brandon Lloyd .20 .50
44 Eddie Royal .20 .50
45 Jabar Gaffney .20 .50
46 Knowshon Moreno .20 .50
47 Tim Tebow .30 .75
48 Brandon Pettigrew .20 .50
49 Calvin Johnson .30 .75
50 Jahvid Best .20 .50
51 Matthew Stafford .25 .60
52 Nate Burleson .20 .50
53 Aaron Rodgers .50 1.25
54 Clay Matthews .30 .75
55 Donald Driver .25 .60
56 Greg Jennings .20 .50
57 Jordy Nelson .25 .60
58 Andre Johnson .25 .60
59 Arian Foster .20 .50
60 Brian Cushing .20 .50
61 Kevin Walter .20 .50
62 Matt Schaub .20 .50
63 Austin Collie .20 .50
64 Dallas Clark .20 .50
65 Joseph Addai .20 .50
66 Peyton Manning .60 1.50
67 Reggie Wayne .25 .60
68 David Garrard .20 .50
69 Marcedes Lewis .20 .50
70 Maurice Jones-Drew .20 .50
71 Mike Sims-Walker .25 .60
72 Mike Thomas .25 .60
73 Dwayne Bowe .25 .60
74 Jamaal Charles .25 .60
75 Matt Cassel .20 .50
76 Tony Moeaki .20 .50
77 Brandon Marshall .25 .60
78 Brian Hartline .25 .60
79 Chad Henne .25 .60
80 Davone Bess .20 .50
81 Ronnie Brown .25 .60
82 Adrian Peterson .30 .75
83 Percy Harvin .20 .50
84 Sidney Rice .20 .50
85 Joe Webb .20 .50
86 Visanthe Shiancoe .25 .60
87 BenJarvus Green-Ellis .20 .50
88 Danny Woodhead .25 .60
89 Deion Branch .20 .50
90 Tom Brady .75 2.00
91 Wes Welker .25 .60
92 Drew Brees .30 .75
93 Lance Moore .20 .50
94 Marques Colston .20 .50
95 Pierre Thomas .20 .50
96 Reggie Bush .20 .50
97 Ahmad Bradshaw .20 .50
98 Eli Manning .25 .60
99 Hakeem Nicks .20 .50
100 Mario Manningham .20 .50
101 Steve Smith USC .20 .50
102 Braylon Edwards .20 .50
103 LaDainian Tomlinson .30 .75
104 Mark Sanchez .20 .50
105 Santonio Holmes .20 .50
106 Shonn Greene .20 .50
107 Darren McFadden .20 .50
108 Darrius Heyward-Bey .20 .50
109 Louis Murphy .20 .50
110 Zach Miller .20 .50
111 DeSean Jackson .25 .60
112 Jeremy Maclin .20 .50
113 LeSean McCoy .30 .75
114 Michael Vick .25 .60
115 Ben Roethlisberger .30 .75
116 Hines Ward .25 .60
117 Mike Wallace .20 .50
118 Rashard Mendenhall .20 .50
119 Troy Polamalu .30 .75
120 Antonio Gates .20 .50
121 Malcom Floyd .20 .50
122 Mike Tolbert .20 .50
123 Philip Rivers .30 .75
124 Ryan Mathews .25 .60
125 Frank Gore .25 .60
126 Michael Crabtree .20 .50
127 Patrick Willis .25 .60
128 Vernon Davis .20 .50
129 John Carlson .20 .50
130 Marshawn Lynch .25 .60

131 Matt Hasselbeck .20 .50
132 Mike Williams USC .20 .50
133 Danny Amendola .25 .60
134 Donnie Avery .20 .50
135 Sam Bradford .20 .50
136 Steven Jackson .20 .50
137 Cadillac Williams .20 .50
138 Josh Freeman .25 .60
139 Kellen Winslow Jr. .20 .50
140 LeGarrette Blount .25 .60
141 Mike Williams .25 .60
142 Bo Scaife .20 .50
143 Chris Johnson .20 .50
144 Kenny Britt .20 .50
145 Nate Washington .20 .50
146 Randy Moss .25 .60
147 Chris Cooley .20 .50
148 Donovan McNabb .25 .60
149 Ryan Torain .20 .50
150 Santana Moss .25 .60
151 Aaron Williams RC .60 1.50
152 Adrian Clayborn RC .60 1.50
153 Ahmad Black RC .75 2.00
154 Akeem Ayers RC .60 1.50
155 Akeem Dent RC .75 2.00
156 Aldrick Robinson RC .75 2.00
157 Alex Henery RC .75 2.00
158 Allen Bailey RC .60 1.50
159 Allen Bradford RC .60 1.50
160 Anthony Allen RC .60 1.50
161 Anthony Castonzo RC .60 1.50
162 Anthony Sherman RC .60 1.50
163 Baron Batch RC .75 2.00
164 Brandon Harris RC .60 1.50
165 Brooks Reed RC .75 2.00
166 Bruce Carter RC .60 1.50
167 Cameron Heyward RC .75 2.00
168 Cameron Jordan RC .75 2.00
169 Casey Matthews RC .60 1.50
170 Chimdi Chekwa RC .75 2.00
171 Chris Conte RC .60 1.50
172 Chris Culliver RC .60 1.50
173 Christian Ballard RC .60 1.50
174 Colin McCarthy RC .75 2.00
175 Corey Liuget RC .60 1.50
176 Cortez Allen RC .60 1.50
177 Curtis Brown RC .60 1.50
178 Danny Watkins RC .60 1.50
179 Da'Norris Searcy RC .60 1.50
180 Da'Rel Scott RC .60 1.50
181 David Ausberry RC .60 1.50
182 DeMarco Sampson RC .60 1.50
183 Denarius Moore RC .60 1.50
184 Derek Sherrod RC .60 1.50
185 Dion Lewis RC .75 2.00
186 Dontay Moch RC .60 1.50
187 Drake Nevis RC .60 1.50
188 Dwayne Harris RC .60 1.50
189 Evan Royster RC .60 1.50
190 Gabe Carimi RC .75 2.00
191 Greg Jones RC .75 2.00
192 Greg McElroy RC 1.00 2.50
193 Jabaal Sheard RC .60 1.50
194 Jah Reid RC .60 1.50
195 Jaiquawn Jarrett RC .60 1.50
196 James Carpenter RC .75 2.00
197 Jarvis Jenkins RC .60 1.50
198 Jay Finley RC .75 2.00
199 Jimmy Smith RC .60 1.50
200 Johnny White RC .60 1.50
201 Jonas Mouton RC .75 2.00
202 Jordan Cameron RC .75 2.00
203 Julius Thomas RC .75 2.00
204 Justin Houston RC .75 2.00
205 Kealoha Pilares RC .60 1.50
206 Kelvin Sheppard RC .60 1.50
207 Kris Durham RC .60 1.50
208 Lee Smith RC .75 2.00
209 Luke Stocker RC .60 1.50
210 Marcus Cannon RC .60 1.50
211 Marcus Gilchrist RC .60 1.50
212 Martez Wilson RC .60 1.50
213 Marvin Austin RC .60 1.50
214 Mason Foster RC .60 1.50
215 Cheta Ozougwu RC .60 1.50
216 Mike Pouncey RC 1.00 2.50
217 Muhammad Wilkerson RC .60 1.50
218 Nate Irving RC .75 2.00
219 Nate Solder RC .60 1.50
220 Nathan Enderle RC .60 1.50
221 Nick Fairley RC .60 1.50
222 Owen Marecic RC .60 1.50
223 Patrick Peterson RC 1.25 3.00
224 Pernell McPhee RC 1.00 2.50
225 Phil Taylor RC .60 1.50
226 Prince Amukamara RC .60 1.50
227 Quan Sturdivant RC .75 2.00
228 Quinton Carter RC .60 1.50
229 Rahim Moore RC .60 1.50
230 Ras-I Dowling RC .60 1.50
231 Richard Gordon RC .60 1.50
232 Robert Housler RC .60 1.50
233 Robert Quinn RC .60 1.50
234 Robert Sands RC .60 1.50
235 Ronald Johnson RC .60 1.50
236 Ross Homan RC .75 2.00
237 Ryan Whalen RC .60 1.50
238 Sam Acho RC .60 1.50
239 Scotty McKnight RC .60 1.50
240 Terrelle Pryor RC 1.00 2.50
241 Sione Fua RC .60 1.50
242 Stanley Havili RC .60 1.50
243 Stefen Wisniewski RC 1.00 2.50
244 Stephen Burton RC .60 1.50
245 Stephen Paea RC .60 1.50
246 T.J. Yates RC .60 1.50
247 Tyler Sash RC .60 1.50
248 Tyrod Taylor RC 1.25 3.00
249 Tyron Smith RC .75 2.00
250 Virgil Green RC .60 1.50
251 Cam Newton AU RC 50.00 100.00
252 Blaine Gabbert AU RC 5.00 12.00
253 Jamie Harper AU RC 5.00 12.00
254 Leonard Hankerson AU RC 5.00 12.00
255 Mikel Leshoure AU RC 5.00 12.00
256 Ryan Mallett AU RC 5.00 12.00
257 Shane Vereen AU RC 6.00 15.00
258 Taiwan Jones AU RC 5.00 12.00
259 Mark Ingram AU RC 8.00 20.00
260 Colin Kaepernick AU RC 8.00 20.00
261 Jordan Todman AU RC 5.00 12.00
262 Titus Young AU RC 5.00 12.00
263 Clyde Gates AU RC 5.00 12.00
264 DeMarco Murray AU RC 10.00 25.00
265 Kyle Rudolph AU RC 5.00 12.00
266 Stevan Ridley AU RC 5.00 12.00
267 Von Miller AU RC 12.00 30.00
268 Andy Dalton AU RC 15.00 40.00
269 Jerrel Jernigan AU RC 5.00 12.00
270 Randall Cobb AU RC 8.00 20.00
271 A.J. Green AU RC 20.00 40.00
272 Marcell Dareus AU RC 5.00 12.00
273 Torrey Smith AU RC 5.00 12.00
274 Delone Carter AU RC 5.00 12.00
275 Bilal Powell AU RC 6.00 15.00
276 Jake Locker AU RC 5.00 12.00
277 Ryan Williams AU RC 5.00 12.00
278 Vincent Brown AU RC 5.00 12.00
279 Alex Green AU RC 5.00 12.00
280 Christian Ponder AU RC 5.00 12.00
281 Greg Little AU RC 6.00 15.00
282 Jonathan Baldwin AU RC 5.00 12.00
283 Daniel Thomas AU RC 5.00 12.00
284 Kendall Hunter AU RC 5.00 12.00
285 Austin Pettis AU RC 5.00 12.00
286 Julio Jones AU RC 20.00 40.00
287 Aldon Smith AU RC EXCH
288 Cecil Shorts AU RC 5.00 12.00
289 D.J. Williams AU RC EXCH 5.00 12.00
290 Da'Quan Bowers AU RC 5.00 12.00
291 Greg Salas AU RC 5.00 12.00
292 J.J. Watt AU RC 100.00 175.00
293 Jacquizz Rodgers AU RC 5.00 12.00
294 Jeremy Kerley AU RC 8.00 20.00
295 Lance Kendricks AU RC EXCH 5.00 12.00
296 Niles Paul AU RC 5.00 12.00
297 Ricky Stanzi AU RC 5.00 12.00
298 Roy Helu AU RC 5.00 12.00
299 Ryan Kerrigan AU RC 6.00 15.00
300 Tandon Doss AU RC 5.00 12.00

2011 Rookies and Stars Gold

*VETS 1-150: .8X TO 2X BASIC CARDS
*ROOKIES 151-250: .4X TO 1X BASIC CARDS
RANDOM INSERTS IN RETAIL PACKS

2011 Rookies and Stars Longevity Parallel Gold

*1-150 VETS/49: 4X TO 10X BASIC CARDS
*151-250 ROOKIES/49: 1.5X TO 4X BASIC CARDS
STATED PRINT RUN 49 SER.#'d SETS

2011 Rookies and Stars Longevity Parallel Silver Holofoil

*1-150 VETS/99: 3X TO 8X BASIC CARDS
*151-250 ROOKIES/99: 1.2X TO 3X BASIC CARDS
STATED PRINT RUN 99 SER.#'d SETS

2011 Rookies and Stars Longevity Parallel Platinum

*1-150 VETS/25: 5X TO 12X BASIC CARDS
*151-250 ROOKIES/25: 2X TO 5X BASIC R&S
STATED PRINT RUN 25 SER.#'d SETS

2011 Rookies and Stars Longevity Parallel Silver

*1-150 VETS/249: 2.5X TO 6X BASIC CARDS
*151-250 ROOKIES/249: 1X TO 2.5X BASIC CARDS
STATED PRINT RUN 249 SER.#'d SETS

2011 Rookies and Stars Rookie Patch Autographs Gold NFL Logo

*NFL LOGO/25: .8X TO 2X BASIC AU/299
STATED PRINT RUN 25 SER.#'d SETS
251 Cam Newton 125.00 250.00
260 Colin Kaepernick 15.00 40.00
276 Jake Locker 10.00 25.00

2011 Rookies and Stars All Americans

UNPRICED STATED PRINT RUN 10

2011 Rookies and Stars Dress for Success Jerseys

STATED PRINT RUN 299 SER.#'d SETS
*PRIME/50: .8X TO 2X BASIC JSY/299
*LONGEVITY/249: .4X TO 1X DRESS FOR SUCCESS
1 Jamie Harper 1.50 4.00
2 Stevan Ridley 1.50 4.00
3 Ryan Williams 1.50 4.00
4 Blaine Gabbert 1.50 4.00
5 Von Miller 2.50 6.00
6 Kyle Rudolph 1.50 4.00
7 Titus Young 1.50 4.00
8 Delone Carter 1.50 4.00
9 Randall Cobb 2.50 6.00
10 Bilal Powell 2.00 5.00
11 Alex Green 1.50 4.00
12 Mikel Leshoure 1.50 4.00
13 Colin Kaepernick 2.50 6.00
14 Cam Newton 8.00 20.00
15 Taiwan Jones 1.50 4.00
16 Andy Dalton 3.00 8.00
17 DeMarco Murray 3.00 8.00
18 Kendall Hunter 1.50 4.00
19 Torrey Smith 1.50 4.00
20 Julio Jones 6.00 15.00
21 Leonard Hankerson 1.50 4.00
22 Marcell Dareus 1.50 4.00
23 A.J. Green 4.00 10.00
24 Jake Locker 1.50 4.00
25 Greg Little 2.00 5.00
26 Austin Pettis 1.50 4.00
27 Christian Ponder 1.50 4.00
28 Ryan Mallett 1.50 4.00
29 Jonathan Baldwin 1.50 4.00
30 Jerrel Jernigan 1.50 4.00
31 Jordan Todman 1.50 4.00
32 Daniel Thomas 1.50 4.00
33 Mark Ingram 2.50 6.00
34 Shane Vereen 2.00 5.00
35 Vincent Brown 1.50 4.00
36 Clyde Gates 1.50 4.00

2011 Rookies and Stars Dress for Success Jerseys Autographs

STATED PRINT RUN 25-50
*PRIME/25: .6X TO 1.5X BASIC JSY AU/50
1 Jamie Harper/50 5.00 12.00
2 Stevan Ridley/50 5.00 12.00
3 Ryan Williams/25 8.00 20.00
4 Blaine Gabbert/25 8.00 20.00
5 Von Miller/25 20.00 50.00
6 Kyle Rudolph/50 5.00 12.00
7 Titus Young/25 8.00 20.00
8 Delone Carter/50 5.00 12.00
9 Randall Cobb/50 8.00 20.00
10 Bilal Powell/50 6.00 15.00
11 Alex Green/50 5.00 12.00
12 Mikel Leshoure/25 8.00 20.00
13 Colin Kaepernick/25 12.00 30.00
14 Cam Newton/25 75.00 150.00
15 Taiwan Jones/50 5.00 12.00
16 Andy Dalton/25 40.00 80.00
17 DeMarco Murray/25 15.00 40.00
18 Kendall Hunter/50 5.00 12.00
19 Torrey Smith/25 8.00 20.00
20 Julio Jones/25 40.00 80.00
21 Leonard Hankerson/50 5.00 12.00
22 Marcell Dareus/50 5.00 12.00
23 A.J. Green/25 30.00 80.00
24 Jake Locker/25 8.00 20.00
25 Greg Little/50 6.00 15.00
26 Austin Pettis/50 5.00 12.00
27 Christian Ponder/25 8.00 20.00
28 Ryan Mallett/25 8.00 20.00
29 Jonathan Baldwin/25 15.00 50.00
30 Jerrel Jernigan/50 5.00 12.00
31 Jordan Todman/25 8.00 20.00
32 Daniel Thomas/50 5.00 12.00
33 Mark Ingram/25 12.00 30.00
34 Shane Vereen/50 6.00 15.00
35 Vincent Brown/50 12.00 30.00
36 Clyde Gates/50 5.00 12.00

2011 Rookies and Stars Freshman Orientation Jerseys

*FRESH/299: .4X TO 1X DRESS FOR SUCCESS
STATED PRINT RUN 299 SER.#'d SETS
*PRIME/50: .8X TO 2X BASIC JSY/299
*LONGEVITY/249: .4X TO 1X DRESS FOR SUCCESS

2011 Rookies and Stars Freshman Orientation Jerseys Autographs

*FRESH: .4X TO 1X DRESS FOR SUCCESS
STATED PRINT RUN 25-50
*PRIME/25: .6X TO 1.5X BASIC JSY AU/50

2011 Rookies and Stars Materials Emerald Prime Longevity

STATED PRINT RUN 2-99
*BLACK/36-50: .5X TO 1.2X EMERALD/74-99
*BLACK/50: .4X TO 1X EMERALD/35
*BLACK/25: .6X TO 1.5X EMERALD/75-80
*BLACK/20: .4X TO 1X EMERALD/15
*BLACK/15-25: .5X TO 1.2X EMERALD/40-50
*BLACK/10-15: .4X TO 1X EMERALD/20-25
1 Chris Wells/99 3.00 8.00
2 Larry Fitzgerald/25 6.00 15.00
6 Matt Ryan/15 6.00 15.00
7 Michael Turner/99 3.00 8.00
8 Roddy White/99 3.00 8.00
9 Tony Gonzalez/99 4.00 10.00
10 Anquan Boldin/99 3.00 8.00
11 Joe Flacco/50 5.00 12.00
12 Ray Lewis/99 5.00 12.00
13 Ray Rice/99 3.00 8.00
14 Todd Heap/99 3.00 8.00
15 C.J. Spiller/99 3.00 8.00
16 Fred Jackson/99 6.00 15.00
17 Lee Evans/99 4.00 10.00
18 Ryan Fitzpatrick/99 3.00 8.00
20 DeAngelo Williams/99 3.00 8.00
21 Jimmy Clausen/99 3.00 8.00
22 Jonathan Stewart/99 3.00 8.00
23 Steve Smith/99 4.00 10.00
24 Brian Urlacher/99 5.00 12.00
25 Devin Hester/99 4.00 10.00
26 Jay Cutler/50 4.00 10.00
27 Johnny Knox/99 3.00 8.00
28 Matt Forte/99 3.00 8.00
29 Carson Palmer/50 5.00 12.00
30 Cedric Benson/99 3.00 8.00
31 Chad Ochocinco/99 3.00 8.00
32 Jordan Shipley/99 3.00 8.00
36 Josh Cribbs/99 3.00 8.00
39 Felix Jones/99 3.00 8.00
40 Jason Witten/99 4.00 10.00
41 Miles Austin/99 5.00 12.00
42 Tony Romo/99 4.00 10.00
43 Brandon Lloyd/99 3.00 8.00
44 Eddie Royal/99 3.00 8.00
45 Jabar Gaffney/99 3.00 8.00
46 Knowshon Moreno/99 3.00 8.00
47 Tim Tebow/50 6.00 15.00
49 Calvin Johnson/99 5.00 12.00
50 Jahvid Best/25 5.00 12.00
51 Matthew Stafford/99 4.00 10.00
53 Aaron Rodgers/50 12.00 30.00
54 Clay Matthews/99 8.00 20.00
55 Donald Driver/85 5.00 12.00
58 Andre Johnson/99 4.00 10.00
62 Matt Schaub/50 4.00 10.00
64 Dallas Clark/99 3.00 8.00
65 Joseph Addai/99 3.00 8.00
66 Peyton Manning/99 10.00 25.00
67 Reggie Wayne/25 6.00 15.00
68 David Garrard/75 3.00 8.00
70 Maurice Jones-Drew/99 3.00 8.00
71 Mike Sims-Walker/40 5.00 12.00
73 Dwayne Bowe/99 4.00 10.00
74 Jamaal Charles/99 4.00 10.00
75 Matt Cassel/2
77 Brandon Marshall/99 4.00 10.00
79 Chad Henne/99 4.00 10.00
81 Ronnie Brown/99 4.00 10.00
82 Adrian Peterson/99 5.00 12.00
83 Percy Harvin/99 3.00 8.00
84 Sidney Rice/99 3.00 8.00
86 Visanthe Shiancoe/99 4.00 10.00
90 Tom Brady/99 12.00 30.00
91 Wes Welker/99 4.00 10.00
92 Drew Brees/50 6.00 15.00
94 Marques Colston/99 3.00 8.00
95 Pierre Thomas /99 3.00 8.00
96 Reggie Bush/99 3.00 8.00
97 Ahmad Bradshaw/99 3.00 8.00
98 Eli Manning/95 4.00 10.00
99 Hakeem Nicks/99 3.00 8.00
101 Steve Smith USC/99 3.00 8.00
102 Braylon Edwards/50 4.00 10.00
103 LaDainian Tomlinson/99 5.00 12.00
104 Mark Sanchez/20 10.00 25.00
105 Santonio Holmes/99 3.00 8.00
106 Shonn Greene/99 3.00 8.00
107 Darren McFadden/75 3.00 8.00
111 DeSean Jackson/99 4.00 10.00
112 Jeremy Maclin/99 3.00 8.00
113 LeSean McCoy/99 5.00 12.00
114 Michael Vick/30 10.00 25.00
116 Hines Ward/80 4.00 10.00
117 Mike Wallace/99 5.00 12.00
118 Rashard Mendenhall/50 4.00 10.00
119 Troy Polamalu/99 5.00 12.00
120 Antonio Gates/99 3.00 8.00
121 Malcom Floyd/99 3.00 8.00
123 Philip Rivers/99 5.00 12.00
124 Ryan Mathews/90 4.00 10.00
125 Frank Gore/99 4.00 10.00
126 Michael Crabtree/99 3.00 8.00
127 Patrick Willis/99 5.00 12.00
128 Vernon Davis/74 3.00 8.00
131 Matt Hasselbeck/35 4.00 10.00
135 Sam Bradford/99 3.00 8.00
136 Steven Jackson/99 3.00 8.00
137 Cadillac Williams/99 3.00 8.00
139 Kellen Winslow Jr./99 3.00 8.00
143 Chris Johnson/99 3.00 8.00
145 Nate Washington/99 3.00 8.00
146 Randy Moss/99 4.00 10.00
147 Chris Cooley/99 3.00 8.00
148 Donovan McNabb/99 4.00 10.00
150 Santana Moss/99 4.00 10.00

2011 Rookies and Stars Prime Cuts

STATED PRINT RUN 20-50
*COMBOS/15-25: .5X TO 1.2X PRIME CUT/30-50
1 Aaron Rodgers/50 20.00 50.00
2 Joe Flacco/50 10.00 25.00
3 Rashard Mendenhall/50 6.00 15.00
4 Michael Vick/30 15.00 40.00
5 Mark Sanchez/20 15.00 40.00
6 Matt Ryan/30 8.00 20.00
7 Larry Fitzgerald/25 10.00 25.00
8 Steven Jackson/50 8.00 20.00

2011 Rookies and Stars Prime Cuts Autographs

STATED PRINT RUN 15-20
1 Aaron Rodgers/20 150.00 250.00
2 Joe Flacco/20 50.00 100.00
3 Rashard Mendenhall/20 20.00 50.00
4 Michael Vick/20 30.00 60.00
5 Mark Sanchez/15 20.00 50.00
6 Matt Ryan/20 50.00 100.00
7 Larry Fitzgerald/15 40.00 80.00
8 Steven Jackson/20 20.00 50.00

2011 Rookies and Stars Rookie Autographs Holofoil

STATED PRINT RUN 300-350
151 Aaron Williams/300 5.00 12.00
152 Adrian Clayborn/300 8.00 20.00
153 Ahmad Black/350 5.00 12.00
154 Akeem Ayers/300 2.50 6.00
156 Aldrick Robinson/300 8.00 20.00
161 Anthony Castonzo/350 2.50 6.00
164 Brandon Harris/300 2.50 6.00
167 Cameron Heyward/300 8.00 20.00
168 Cameron Jordan/300 3.00 8.00
175 Corey Liuget/300 4.00 10.00
183 Denarius Moore/350 10.00 25.00
185 Dion Lewis/300 3.00 8.00
189 Evan Royster/350 2.50 6.00
191 Greg Jones/300 3.00 8.00
199 Jimmy Smith/300 2.50 6.00
200 Johnny White/350 2.50 6.00
202 Jordan Cameron/350 3.00 8.00
204 Justin Houston/350 3.00 8.00
207 Kris Durham/350 2.50 6.00
209 Luke Stocker/300 2.50 6.00
210 Marcus Cannon/350 4.00 10.00
212 Martez Wilson/300 5.00 12.00
225 Phil Taylor/300 5.00 12.00
226 P.Amukamara/300 8.00 20.00
228 Quinton Carter/350 2.50 6.00
229 Rahim Moore/350 2.50 6.00
235 Ronald Johnson/300 2.50 6.00
237 Ryan Whalen/350 2.50 6.00
242 Stanley Havili/350 2.50 6.00
244 Stephen Burton/350 3.00 6.00
245 Stephen Paea/300 2.50 6.00
247 Tyler Sash/300 2.50 6.00
248 Tyrod Taylor/350 5.00 12.00

2011 Rookies and Stars Rookie Jersey Jumbo Swatch

*JUMBO/50: .6X TO 1.5X DRESS FOR SUCCESS
STATED PRINT RUN 50 SER.#'d SETS
*EMERALD/10: 1X TO 2.5X BASIC JUMBO/50
*GOLD/25: .5X TO 1.2X BASIC JUMBO/50
*LONGEVITY/50: .4X TO 1X JUMBO/50

2011 Rookies and Stars Rookie Revolution

RANDOM INSERTS IN PACKS
*BLACK/100: .6X TO 1.5X BASIC INSERTS
*GOLD/500: .5X TO 1.2X BASIC INSERTS
UNPRICED AUTO PRINT RUN 10
1 Blaine Gabbert .60 1.50
2 Daniel Thomas .60 1.50
3 Jamie Harper .60 1.50
4 Julio Jones 2.00 5.00
5 Mikel Leshoure .60 1.50
6 Taiwan Jones .60 1.50
7 Mark Ingram 1.00 2.50
8 DeMarco Murray 1.25 3.00
9 Shane Vereen .75 2.00
10 Stevan Ridley .60 1.50
11 Greg Little .75 2.00
12 Bilal Powell .75 2.00
13 A.J. Green 1.50 4.00
14 Jake Locker .60 1.50
15 Titus Young .60 1.50
16 Marcell Dareus .60 1.50
17 Kendall Hunter .60 1.50
18 Jonathan Baldwin .60 1.50
19 Von Miller 1.00 2.50
20 Alex Green .60 1.50
21 Christian Ponder .60 1.50
22 Jerrel Jernigan .60 1.50
23 Vincent Brown .60 1.50
24 Ryan Mallett .60 1.50
25 Austin Pettis .60 1.50
26 Delone Carter .60 1.50
27 Leonard Hankerson .60 1.50
28 Torrey Smith .60 1.50
29 Andy Dalton 1.25 3.00
30 Colin Kaepernick 1.00 2.50
31 Jordan Todman .60 1.50
32 Ryan Williams .60 1.50
33 Randall Cobb 1.00 2.50
34 Kyle Rudolph .60 1.50
35 Cam Newton 3.00 8.00
36 Clyde Gates .60 1.50

2011 Rookies and Stars Rookie Revolution Materials

*JSY/299: .4X TO 1X DRESS FOR SUCCESS
STATED PRINT RUN 299 SER.#'d SETS
*PRIME/50: .8X TO 2X BASIC JSY/299
*LONGEVITY/249: .4X TO 1X DRESS FOR SUCCESS

2011 Rookies and Stars Rookie Revolution Materials Autographs

*REVOLUTION: .4X TO 1X DRESS FOR SUCCESS
STATED PRINT RUN 25-50
*PRIME/25: .6X TO 1.5X BASIC JSY AU/50

2011 Rookies and Stars Statistical Standouts Materials

STATED PRINT RUN 95-299
*PRIME/30-50: .6X TO 1.5X BASIC JSY/200-299
*PRIME/25: .8X TO 2X BASIC JSY/299
1 Philip Rivers/299 4.00 10.00
2 Peyton Manning/299 8.00 20.00
3 Drew Brees/200 4.00 10.00
4 Matt Schaub/299 2.50 6.00
5 Eli Manning/299 3.00 8.00
6 Carson Palmer/299 3.00 8.00
7 Brandon Lloyd/299 2.50 6.00
8 Roddy White/299 2.50 6.00
9 Reggie Wayne/299 3.00 8.00
10 Ed Reed/200 3.00 8.00
11 Mike Wallace/299 4.00 10.00
12 Andre Johnson/299 3.00 8.00
14 Jamaal Charles/299 3.00 8.00
15 Michael Turner/299 2.50 6.00
16 Chris Johnson/299 2.50 6.00
17 Maurice Jones-Drew/299 2.50 6.00
18 Adrian Peterson/299 4.00 10.00
19 Tom Brady/299 10.00 25.00
20 Dwayne Bowe/200 3.00 8.00
21 Calvin Johnson/299 4.00 10.00
22 Arian Foster/95 5.00 12.00
23 DeMarcus Ware/299 3.00 8.00

2011 Rookies and Stars Statistical Standouts Materials Autographs

STATED PRINT RUN 10-20
EXCH EXPIRATION: 1/27/2013
1 Philip Rivers/20
2 Peyton Manning/15 75.00 150.00
3 Drew Brees/15 60.00 120.00
4 Matt Schaub/20 12.00 30.00
5 Eli Manning/20
6 Carson Palmer/20 EXCH
7 Brandon Lloyd/20 12.00 30.00
8 Roddy White/15 25.00 50.00
9 Reggie Wayne/15
11 Mike Wallace/25
12 Andre Johnson/20 25.00 50.00
14 Jamaal Charles/20 15.00 40.00
15 Michael Turner/20 12.00 30.00
17 Maurice Jones-Drew/20
18 Adrian Peterson/20 50.00 100.00
19 Tom Brady/20 150.00 250.00
20 Dwayne Bowe/20 12.00 30.00
21 Calvin Johnson/20 30.00 60.00

2011 Rookies and Stars Studio Rookies

*STUDIO: .4X TO 1X ROOKIE REVOLUTION
RANDOM INSERTS IN PACKS
*BLACK/100: .6X TO 1.5X BASIC INSERTS
*GOLD/500: .5X TO 1.2X BASIC INSERTS
UNPRICED AUTO PRINT RUN 10

2011 Rookies and Stars Studio Rookies Combos

RANDOM INSERTS IN PACKS
*BLACK/100: .6X TO 1.5X BASIC INSERTS
*GOLD/500: .5X TO 1.2X BASIC INSERTS
1 C.Newton/M.Ingram 2.50 6.00
2 R.Cobb/A.Green .75 2.00
3 J.Todman/V.Brown .50 1.25
4 M.Leshoure/T.Young .50 1.25
5 R.Mallett/S.Vereen .60 1.50
6 C.Ponder/K.Rudolph .50 1.25
7 J.Locker/J.Harper .50 1.25
8 A.Green/A.Dalton 1.25 3.00
9 Kaepernick/K.Hunter .75 2.00
10 M.Ingram/J.Jones 1.50 4.00

2011 Rookies and Stars Studio Rookies Combos Materials

STATED PRINT RUN 299 SER.#'d SETS
*PRIME/50 .8X TO 2X BASIC COMBO/299
1 C.Newton/M.Ingram 10.00 25.00
2 R.Cobb/A.Green 3.00 8.00
3 J.Todman/V.Brown 2.00 5.00
4 M.Leshoure/T.Young 2.00 5.00
5 R.Mallett/S.Vereen 2.50 6.00
6 C.Ponder/K.Rudolph 2.00 5.00
7 J.Locker/J.Harper 2.00 5.00
8 A.Green/A.Dalton 5.00 12.00
9 Kaepernick/K.Hunter 3.00 8.00
10 M.Ingram/J.Jones 10.00 25.00

2011 Rookies and Stars Studio Rookies Materials

*JSY/299: .4X TO 1X DRESS FOR SUCCESS
STATED PRINT RUN 299 SER.#'d SETS
*PRIME/50: .8X TO 2X BASIC JSY/299

2012 Rookies and Stars

1 Kevin Kolb .20 .50
2 Beanie Wells .20 .50
3 Larry Fitzgerald .25 .60
4 Patrick Peterson .20 .50
5 Early Doucet .20 .50
6 Matt Ryan .25 .60
7 Michael Turner .20 .50
8 Roddy White .20 .50
9 Julio Jones .30 .75
10 Tony Gonzalez .25 .60
11 Joe Flacco .25 .60
12 Ray Rice .20 .50
13 Torrey Smith .20 .50
14 Ray Lewis .30 .75
15 Ed Reed .25 .60
16 Ryan Fitzpatrick .20 .50
17 Fred Jackson .25 .60
18 Steve Johnson .25 .60
19 Scott Chandler .20 .50
20 Cam Newton .30 .75
21 DeAngelo Williams .20 .50
22 Steve Smith .25 .60
23 Greg Olsen .25 .60
24 Jay Cutler .20 .50
25 Matt Forte .20 .50
26 Lance Briggs .25 .60
27 Devin Hester .25 .60
28 Brian Urlacher .30 .75
29 Andy Dalton .25 .60
30 Robert Meachem .20 .50
31 A.J. Green .30 .75
32 Jermaine Gresham .20 .50
33 Colt McCoy .25 .60
34 Peyton Hillis .20 .50
35 Josh Cribbs .20 .50
36 Greg Little .20 .50
37 Tony Romo .25 .60
38 Felix Jones .20 .50
39 Miles Austin .20 .50
40 Jason Witten .25 .60
41 DeMarcus Ware .30 .75
42 Dez Bryant .30 .75
43 Tim Tebow .30 .75
44 Willis McGahee .20 .50
45 Eric Decker .20 .50
46 Von Miller .25 .60
47 Matthew Stafford .25 .60
48 Titus Young .20 .50
49 Calvin Johnson .30 .75
50 Ndamukong Suh .25 .60
51 Brandon Pettigrew .20 .50
52 Aaron Rodgers .50 1.25
53 Jordy Nelson .25 .60
54 Greg Jennings .20 .50
55 Jermichael Finley .20 .50
56 Charles Woodson .30 .75
57 Matt Schaub .20 .50
58 Arian Foster .25 .60
59 Andre Johnson .25 .60
60 Owen Daniels .20 .50
61 Brian Cushing .20 .50
62 Peyton Manning .60 1.50
63 Donald Brown .20 .50
64 Reggie Wayne .25 .60
65 Pierre Garcon .25 .60
66 Austin Collie .20 .50
67 Blaine Gabbert .20 .50
68 Maurice Jones-Drew .20 .50
69 Mike Thomas .25 .60
70 Marcedes Lewis .20 .50
71 Matt Cassel .20 .50
72 Jamaal Charles .25 .60
73 Dwayne Bowe .25 .60
74 Derrick Johnson .20 .50
75 Karlos Dansby .20 .50
76 Reggie Bush .20 .50
77 Brandon Marshall .25 .60
78 Anthony Fasano .20 .50
79 Christian Ponder .20 .50
80 Adrian Peterson .30 .75
81 Percy Harvin .20 .50
82 Jared Allen .20 .50
83 Tom Brady .75 2.00
84 BenJarvus Green-Ellis .25 .60
85 Wes Welker .25 .60
86 Rob Gronkowski .30 .75
87 Aaron Hernandez .25 .60
88 Drew Brees .30 .75
89 Mark Ingram .25 .60
90 Jimmy Graham .30 .75
91 Darren Sproles .25 .60
92 Marques Colston .20 .50
93 Eli Manning .25 .60
94 Ahmad Bradshaw .20 .50
95 Victor Cruz .25 .60
96 Hakeem Nicks .20 .50
97 Brandon Jacobs .20 .50
98 Jason Pierre-Paul .20 .50
99 Mark Sanchez .20 .50
100 Shonn Greene .20 .50
101 Dustin Keller .20 .50
102 Santonio Holmes .20 .50
103 Plaxico Burress .20 .50
104 Carson Palmer .25 .60
105 Darren McFadden .20 .50
106 Darrius Heyward Bey .20 .50
107 Michael Bush .20 .50
108 Michael Vick .25 .60
109 LeSean McCoy .30 .75
110 DeSean Jackson .25 .60
111 Jeremy Maclin .20 .50
112 Brent Celek .20 .50
113 Ben Roethlisberger .30 .75
114 Rashard Mendenhall .20 .50
115 Mike Wallace .20 .50
116 Troy Polamalu .30 .75
117 Antonio Brown .30 .75
118 Philip Rivers .30 .75
119 Ryan Mathews .25 .60
120 Vincent Jackson .20 .50
121 Antonio Gates .25 .60
122 Mike Tolbert .20 .50
123 Alex Smith .25 .60
124 Frank Gore .25 .60
125 Michael Crabtree .20 .50
126 Vernon Davis .20 .50
127 NaVorro Bowman .25 .60
128 Tarvaris Jackson .20 .50
129 Marshawn Lynch .25 .60
130 Doug Baldwin .30 .75
131 Sidney Rice .20 .50
132 Sam Bradford .20 .50
133 Steven Jackson .20 .50
134 Brandon Lloyd .20 .50
135 James Laurinaitis .20 .50
136 Josh Freeman .25 .60
137 LeGarrette Blount .25 .60
138 Kellen Winslow Jr. .20 .50
139 Mike Williams .25 .60
140 Dezmon Briscoe .20 .50
141 Matt Hasselbeck .20 .50
142 Chris Johnson .20 .50
143 Nate Washington .20 .50
144 Damian Williams .20 .50
145 Jared Cook .20 .50
146 Rex Grossman .20 .50
147 Roy Helu .20 .50
148 Jabar Gaffney .20 .50
149 Fred Davis .20 .50
150 Ryan Kerrigan .20 .50
151 Alfred Morris RC .60 1.50
152 Zach Brown RC .60 1.50
153 Andre Branch RC .60 1.50
154 B.J. Coleman RC .60 1.50
155 B.J. Cunningham RC .60 1.50
156 Bobby Wagner RC 1.00 2.50
157 Bruce Irvin RC .75 2.00
158 Bryce Brown RC .60 1.50
159 Case Keenum RC 1.25 3.00
160 Chandler Harnish RC .60 1.50
161 Chandler Jones RC .60 1.50
162 Chris Rainey RC .60 1.50
163 Courtney Upshaw RC .75 2.00
164 Cyrus Gray RC .60 1.50
165 Dan Herron RC .60 1.50
166 Danny Coale RC .60 1.50
167 David DeCastro RC .60 1.50
168 Davin Meggett RC .60 1.50
169 Devon Still RC .75 2.00
170 Devon Wylie RC .60 1.50
171 Dont'a Hightower RC 1.00 2.50
172 Dontari Poe RC .60 1.50
173 Dre Kirkpatrick RC .60 1.50
174 Fletcher Cox RC 1.00 2.50
175 George Iloka RC .60 1.50
176 Greg Childs RC .60 1.50
177 Harrison Smith RC .60 1.50
178 Janoris Jenkins RC .75 2.00
179 Jared Crick RC .60 1.50
180 Jonathan Martin RC .60 1.50
181 Juron Criner RC .60 1.50
182 Kellen Moore RC .75 2.00
183 Keshawn Martin RC .75 2.00
184 Kevin Zeitler RC .60 1.50
185 Kirk Cousins RC 2.50 6.00
186 Ladarius Green RC .60 1.50
187 LaVon Brazill RC 1.00 2.50
188 Lavonte David RC 1.00 2.50
189 Luke Kuechly RC 1.50 4.00
190 Mark Barron RC .60 1.50
191 Marvin Jones RC .60 1.50
192 Marvin McNutt RC .60 1.50
193 Matt Kalil RC .60 1.50
194 Melvin Ingram RC .60 1.50
195 Michael Brockers RC .60 1.50
196 Michael Smith RC .75 2.00
197 Morris Claiborne RC .60 1.50
198 Mychal Kendricks RC 1.00 2.50
199 Nick Perry RC .75 2.00
200 Orson Charles RC .60 1.50
201 Quinton Coples RC .60 1.50
202 Riley Reiff RC .60 1.50
203 Rishard Matthews RC .60 1.50
204 Ronnell Lewis RC .60 1.50
205 Ryan Lindley RC .60 1.50
206 Shea McClellin RC .75 2.00
207 Stephon Gilmore RC .75 2.00
208 Tauren Poole RC .60 1.50
209 Terrance Ganaway RC .75 2.00
210 Tommy Streeter RC .60 1.50
211 Travis Benjamin RC .60 1.50
212 Vick Ballard RC .75 2.00
213 Vinny Curry RC .75 2.00
214 Whitney Mercilus RC .60 1.50
215 T.Y. Hilton RC 1.25 3.00
216 Andrew Luck JSY AU RC 100.00 200.00
217 Robert Griffin III JSY AU RC 6.00 15.00
218 T.Richardson JSY AU RC 5.00 12.00
219 Justin Blackmon JSY AU RC 5.00 12.00
220 Ryan Tannehill JSY AU RC 8.00 20.00
221 Michael Floyd JSY AU RC 5.00 12.00
222 K.Wright JSY AU RC 5.00 12.00
223 Brandon Weeden JSY AU RC 5.00 12.00
224 A.J. Jenkins JSY AU RC 5.00 12.00
225 Doug Martin JSY AU RC 8.00 20.00
226 David Wilson JSY AU RC 5.00 12.00
227 Alshon Jeffery JSY AU RC 10.00 25.00
228 B.Pierce JSY AU RC 5.00 12.00
229 Brian Quick JSY AU RC 5.00 12.00
230 Brock Osweiler JSY AU RC 5.00 12.00
231 Coby Fleener JSY AU RC 5.00 12.00
232 DeVier Posey JSY AU RC 5.00 12.00
233 D.Allen JSY AU RC EXCH 5.00 12.00
234 Isaiah Pead JSY AU RC 5.00 12.00
235 Chris Givens JSY AU RC 5.00 12.00
236 Joe Adams JSY AU RC 5.00 12.00
237 Lamar Miller JSY AU RC 8.00 20.00
238 L.James JSY AU RC 5.00 12.00
239 Michael Egnew JSY AU RC 5.00 12.00
240 Mohamed Sanu JSY AU RC 8.00 20.00
241 Nick Foles JSY AU RC 20.00 50.00
242 Nick Toon JSY AU RC 5.00 12.00
243 Robert Turbin JSY AU RC 5.00 12.00
244 R.Hillman JSY AU RC EXCH 5.00 12.00
245 Rueben Randle JSY AU RC 5.00 12.00
246 Russell Wilson JSY AU RC 60.00 125.00
247 Ryan Broyles JSY AU RC 5.00 12.00
248 Stephen Hill JSY AU RC 5.00 12.00
249 T.J. Graham JSY AU RC 5.00 12.00
250 Jarius Wright JSY AU RC 5.00 12.00

2012 Rookies and Stars Longevity Parallel

*1-150 VETS/249: 2X TO 5X BASIC CARDS
*151-215 ROOKIE/249: .8X TO 2X BASIC RC

2012 Rookies and Stars True Blue

*1-150 VETS: 2X TO 5X BASIC CARDS
*151-215 ROOKIES: .6X TO 1.5X BASIC RC
216-250 ROOKIE JSY PRINT RUN 399
216 Andrew Luck JSY 12.00 30.00
217 Robert Griffin III JSY 2.00 5.00
218 Trent Richardson JSY 1.50 4.00
219 Justin Blackmon JSY 1.50 4.00
220 Ryan Tannehill JSY 2.50 6.00
221 Michael Floyd JSY 1.50 4.00
222 Kendall Wright JSY 1.50 4.00
223 Brandon Weeden JSY 1.50 4.00
224 A.J. Jenkins JSY 1.50 4.00
225 Doug Martin JSY 2.50 6.00
226 David Wilson JSY 1.50 4.00
227 Alshon Jeffery JSY 3.00 8.00
228 Bernard Pierce JSY 1.50 4.00
229 Brian Quick JSY 1.50 4.00
230 Brock Osweiler JSY 1.50 4.00
231 Coby Fleener JSY 1.50 4.00
232 DeVier Posey JSY 1.50 4.00
233 Dwayne Allen JSY 1.50 4.00
234 Isaiah Pead JSY 1.50 4.00
235 Chris Givens JSY 1.50 4.00
236 Joe Adams JSY 1.50 4.00
237 Lamar Miller JSY 2.50 6.00
238 LaMichael James JSY 1.50 4.00
239 Michael Egnew JSY 1.50 4.00
240 Mohamed Sanu JSY 2.50 6.00
241 Nick Foles JSY 4.00 10.00
242 Nick Toon JSY 1.50 4.00
243 Robert Turbin JSY 1.50 4.00
244 Ronnie Hillman JSY 1.50 4.00
245 Rueben Randle JSY 1.50 4.00
246 Russell Wilson JSY 12.00 30.00
247 Ryan Broyles JSY 1.50 4.00
248 Stephen Hill JSY 1.50 4.00
249 T.J. Graham JSY 1.50 4.00
250 Jarius Wright JSY 1.50 4.00

2012 Rookies and Stars Autographs

1-150 VET PRINT RUN 1-25
151-215 ROOKIE PRINT RUN 99-999
2 Beanie Wells/25 8.00 20.00
5 Early Doucet/25
7 Michael Turner/15
12 Ray Rice/15
16 Ryan Fitzpatrick/15 8.00 20.00
17 Fred Jackson/25 25.00 50.00
18 Steve Johnson/15 10.00 25.00
20 Cam Newton/15 60.00 100.00
21 DeAngelo Williams/15 8.00 20.00
22 Steve Smith/25 10.00 25.00
23 Greg Olsen/15 10.00 25.00
29 Andy Dalton/25 10.00 25.00
32 Jermaine Gresham/15
36 Greg Little/25 8.00 20.00
37 Tony Romo/15 40.00 80.00
38 Felix Jones/25
40 Jason Witten/15 25.00 50.00
46 Von Miller/15 10.00 25.00
48 Titus Young/25
56 Charles Woodson/25 75.00 150.00
61 Brian Cushing/25
62 Peyton Manning/25 100.00 175.00
64 Reggie Wayne/15 10.00 25.00
65 Pierre Garcon/25 10.00 25.00
67 Blaine Gabbert/25 8.00 20.00
79 Christian Ponder/25 8.00 20.00
81 Percy Harvin/25 8.00 20.00
84 BenJarvus Green-Ellis/25
89 Mark Ingram/25 10.00 25.00
90 Jimmy Graham/25 15.00 40.00
91 Darren Sproles/25 10.00 25.00
93 Eli Manning/20 30.00 60.00
94 Ahmad Bradshaw/25 8.00 20.00
103 Plaxico Burress/25 8.00 20.00
106 Darrius Heyward-Bey/15 8.00 20.00
113 Ben Roethlisberger/15 40.00 100.00
116 Troy Polamalu/25 60.00 120.00
120 Vincent Jackson/15 8.00 20.00
122 Mike Tolbert/25 8.00 20.00
124 Frank Gore/25 10.00 25.00
127 NaVorro Bowman/25 10.00 25.00
135 James Laurinaitis/15
139 Mike Williams/25 10.00 25.00
140 Dezmon Briscoe/25
144 Damian Williams/25 8.00 20.00
146 Rex Grossman/25
147 Roy Helu/25 8.00 20.00
148 Jabar Gaffney/25 8.00 20.00
149 Fred Davis/25
151 Alfred Morris/999 2.00 5.00
152 Zach Brown/99 3.00 8.00
153 Andre Branch/999 2.00 5.00
154 B.J. Coleman/99 3.00 8.00
155 B.J. Cunningham/99 3.00 8.00
156 Bobby Wagner/999 3.00 8.00
157 Bruce Irvin/99 8.00 20.00
158 Bryce Brown/99 3.00 8.00
159 Case Keenum/999 4.00 10.00
160 Chandler Harnish/99 3.00 8.00
161 Chandler Jones/999 2.00 5.00
162 Chris Rainey/99 10.00 25.00
163 Courtney Upshaw/99 4.00 10.00
164 Cyrus Gray/499 2.50 6.00
165 Dan Herron/499 2.50 6.00
166 Danny Coale/99 3.00 8.00
167 David DeCastro/999 2.00 5.00
168 Davin Meggett/999 2.00 5.00
169 Devon Still/999 2.50 6.00
170 Devon Wylie/99 3.00 8.00
171 Dont'a Hightower/999 3.00 8.00
172 Dontari Poe/999 2.00 5.00
173 Dre Kirkpatrick/99 EXCH 3.00 8.00
174 Fletcher Cox/999 3.00 8.00
175 George Iloka/499 2.50 6.00
176 Greg Childs/99 3.00 8.00
177 Harrison Smith/499 2.50 6.00
178 Janoris Jenkins/99 4.00 10.00
179 Jared Crick/499 2.50 6.00
180 Jonathan Martin/499 2.50 6.00
181 Juron Criner/499 2.50 6.00
182 Kellen Moore/399 3.00 8.00
183 Keshawn Martin/99 4.00 10.00
184 Kevin Zeitler/99 3.00 8.00
185 Kirk Cousins/399 10.00 25.00
186 Ladarius Green/399 2.50 6.00
187 LaVon Brazill/99 8.00 20.00
188 Lavonte David/99 5.00 12.00
189 Luke Kuechly/499 8.00 20.00
190 Mark Barron/99 10.00 25.00
191 Marvin Jones/999 2.00 5.00
192 Marvin McNutt/299 2.50 6.00
193 Matt Kalil/499 2.50 6.00
194 Melvin Ingram/99 3.00 8.00
195 Michael Brockers/499 2.50 6.00
196 Michael Smith/99 EXCH 4.00 10.00
197 Morris Claiborne/99 3.00 8.00
198 Mychal Kendricks/399 4.00 10.00
199 Nick Perry/999 2.50 6.00
200 Orson Charles/199 3.00 8.00
201 Quinton Coples/999 2.00 5.00
202 Riley Reiff/499 2.50 6.00
203 Rishard Matthews/399 2.50 6.00
204 Ronnell Lewis/99 3.00 8.00
205 Ryan Lindley/99 3.00 8.00
206 Shea McClellin/99 8.00 20.00
207 Stephon Gilmore/99 6.00 15.00
208 Tauren Poole/999 2.00 5.00
209 Terrance Ganaway/199 4.00 10.00
210 Tommy Streeter/99 3.00 8.00
211 Travis Benjamin/99 3.00 8.00
212 Vick Ballard/399 3.00 8.00
213 Vinny Curry/99 8.00 20.00
214 Whitney Mercilus/399 2.50 6.00
215 T.Y. Hilton/399 5.00 12.00

2012 Rookies and Stars Department of Defense Materials

*PRIME/49: .6X TO 1.5X JSY/149-199
*PRIME/15-25: .8X TO 2X JSY/149-199

1 Terrell Suggs/199 3.00 8.00
3 Jonathan Vilma/199 3.00 8.00
4 Ray Lewis/199 5.00 12.00
5 Haloti Ngata /199 3.00 8.00
6 AJ Hawk/199 3.00 8.00
7 Brian Urlacher/199 5.00 12.00
8 Darrelle Revis/199 3.00 8.00
9 Ed Reed/199 4.00 10.00
10 Will Smith/199 3.00 8.00
11 Patrick Willis/199 4.00 10.00
12 Nnamdi Asomugha/199 3.00 8.00
13 London Fletcher/199 4.00 10.00
14 Julius Peppers/149 4.00 10.00
15 Jay Ratliff/199 4.00 10.00

2012 Rookies and Stars Great American Heroes Autographs

STATED PRINT RUN 3-25
4 Asante Samuel/20 8.00 20.00
7 Bo Scaife/25

2012 Rookies and Stars Greatest Hits

*BLACK/100: .6X TO 1.5X BASIC INSERTS
*GOLD/500: .5X TO 1.2X BASIC INSERTS
*LONGEVITY: .4X TO 1X BASIC INSERTS
1 Patrick Peterson .75 2.00
2 Ray Lewis 1.25 3.00
3 Ed Reed 1.00 2.50
4 Brian Urlacher 1.25 3.00
5 DeMarcus Ware 1.25 3.00
6 Von Miller 1.00 2.50
7 Ndamukong Suh 1.00 2.50
8 Charles Woodson 1.25 3.00
9 Clay Matthews 1.25 3.00
10 Brian Cushing .75 2.00
11 Derrick Johnson .75 2.00
12 Karlos Dansby .75 2.00
13 Jared Allen .75 2.00
14 Jason Pierre-Paul .75 2.00
15 Asante Samuel 1.00 2.50
16 NaVorro Bowman 1.00 2.50
17 James Laurinaitis .75 2.00
18 Ryan Kerrigan .75 2.00
19 Troy Polamalu 1.25 3.00
20 Shaun Phillips .75 2.00
21 Patrick Willis 1.00 2.50
22 James Harrison 1.00 2.50
23 Jerod Mayo .75 2.00
24 Tamba Hali .75 2.00
25 Jon Beason .75 2.00
26 Richard Seymour .75 2.00
27 Cameron Wake 1.00 2.50
28 Lance Briggs 1.00 2.50
29 Mario Williams .75 2.00
30 Jason Babin .75 2.00

2012 Rookies and Stars NFL Team Pennant

1 Arizona Cardinals 1.50 4.00
2 Atlanta Falcons 1.50 4.00
3 Baltimore Ravens 1.50 4.00
4 Buffalo Bills 2.00 5.00
5 Carolina Panthers 1.50 4.00
6 Chicago Bears 2.00 5.00
7 Cincinnati Bengals 1.50 4.00
8 Cleveland Browns 1.50 4.00
9 Dallas Cowboys 2.50 6.00
10 Denver Broncos 2.00 5.00
11 Detroit Lions 1.50 4.00
12 Green Bay Packers 2.50 6.00
13 Houston Texans 1.50 4.00
14 Indianapolis Colts 1.50 4.00
15 Jacksonville Jaguars 1.50 4.00
16 Kansas City Chiefs 1.50 4.00
17 Miami Dolphins 2.00 5.00
18 Minnesota Vikings 1.50 4.00
19 New England Patriots 2.00 5.00
20 New Orleans Saints 1.50 4.00
21 New York Giants 2.00 5.00
22 New York Jets 2.00 5.00
23 Oakland Raiders 2.50 6.00
24 Philadelphia Eagles 2.00 5.00
25 Pittsburgh Steelers 2.50 6.00
26 San Diego Chargers 1.50 4.00
27 San Francisco 49ers 2.00 5.00
28 Seattle Seahawks 1.50 4.00
29 St. Louis Rams 1.50 4.00
30 Tampa Bay Buccaneers 1.50 4.00
31 Tennessee Titans 1.50 4.00
32 Washington Redskins 2.00 5.00

2012 Rookies and Stars Player Pennant

1 Eli Manning 1.25 3.00
2 Tom Brady 4.00 10.00
3 Ray Rice 1.00 2.50
4 Vernon Davis 1.00 2.50
5 Drew Brees 1.50 4.00
6 Tim Tebow 1.50 4.00
7 Arian Foster 1.25 3.00
8 Aaron Rodgers 2.50 6.00
9 Ben Roethlisberger 1.50 4.00
10 Michael Turner 1.00 2.50
11 Calvin Johnson 1.50 4.00
12 A.J. Green 1.50 4.00
13 Chris Johnson 1.00 2.50
14 DeMarcus Ware 1.50 4.00
15 LeSean McCoy 1.50 4.00

2012 Rookies and Stars Prime Cuts

2 Ed Reed/25 25.00 50.00
3 Chris Johnson/25 8.00 20.00
4 Maurice Jones-Drew/25 8.00 20.00
5 Miles Austin/25 8.00 20.00
7 Malcom Floyd/25 8.00 20.00
8 Michael Turner/25
9 Dez Bryant/25 12.00 30.00
10 Chris Cooley/25

2012 Rookies and Stars Revolution Materials

*PRIME/30-49: .8X TO 2X JSY/119-199
*PRIME/49: .6X TO 1.5X JSY/75
*PRIME/15: 1.2X TO 3X JSY/199
1 Mario Manningham/30 4.00 10.00
2 Maurice Jones-Drew/199 2.50 6.00
3 Devin Hester/199 3.00 8.00
4 Andy Dalton/75 4.00 10.00
5 Anquan Boldin/199 2.50 6.00
8 Chris Cooley/199 2.50 6.00
9 Adrian Peterson/119 4.00 10.00
10 Steven Jackson/199 2.50 6.00
11 DeMarco Murray/199 3.00 8.00
12 Devery Henderson/199 2.50 6.00
13 Dez Bryant/199 4.00 10.00
14 Eddie Royal/199 2.50 6.00
15 Eli Manning/199 3.00 8.00
16 Felix Jones/199 2.50 6.00
17 Frank Gore/199 3.00 8.00
18 Tony Gonzalez/199 3.00 8.00
19 Tony Romo/199 3.00 8.00
20 Jamaal Charles/199 3.00 8.00
21 Jay Cutler/199 2.50 6.00
22 A.J. Green/15 8.00 20.00
23 Joe Flacco/199 3.00 8.00
24 Anthony Fasano/199 2.50 6.00
25 Chris Johnson/199 2.50 6.00
28 Mark Sanchez/199 2.50 6.00
29 Marques Colston/199 2.50 6.00
30 Matt Cassel/199 2.50 6.00
31 Matt Hasselbeck/199 2.50 6.00
32 Michael Turner/199 2.50 6.00
33 Michael Vick/199 3.00 8.00
34 Miles Austin/199 2.50 6.00
35 Pierre Thomas /199 2.50 6.00
36 Malcom Floyd/120 2.50 6.00
37 Robert Meachem/199 2.50 6.00
38 Sam Bradford/199 2.50 6.00
39 Shonn Greene/199 2.50 6.00
40 Vonta Leach/199 2.50 6.00

2012 Rookies and Stars Rookie Collection Jerseys

*PRIME/49-75: .6X TO 1.5X BASIC JSY
1 Doug Martin 3.00 8.00
2 Chris Givens 2.00 5.00
3 Michael Floyd 2.00 5.00
4 Lamar Miller 3.00 8.00
5 Russell Wilson 10.00 25.00
6 Mohamed Sanu 3.00 8.00
7 Kendall Wright 2.00 5.00
8 A.J. Jenkins 2.00 5.00
9 Trent Richardson 2.00 5.00
10 Robert Griffin III 2.50 6.00
11 Alshon Jeffery 4.00 10.00
12 Andrew Luck 12.00 30.00
13 Ryan Broyles 2.00 5.00
14 Nick Foles 5.00 12.00
15 Coby Fleener 2.00 5.00
16 Ryan Tannehill 3.00 8.00
17 LaMichael James 2.00 5.00
18 Stephen Hill 2.00 5.00
19 Nick Toon 2.00 5.00
20 Brandon Weeden 2.00 5.00
21 Justin Blackmon 2.00 5.00
22 Michael Egnew 2.00 5.00
23 Rueben Randle 2.00 5.00
24 Brock Osweiler 2.00 5.00
25 David Wilson 2.00 5.00
26 Robert Turbin 2.00 5.00
27 DeVier Posey 2.00 5.00
28 Bernard Pierce 2.00 5.00
29 Ronnie Hillman 2.00 5.00
30 Isaiah Pead 2.00 5.00

2012 Rookies and Stars Rookie Crusade Autographs Red

1 Doug Martin/149 6.00 15.00
2 Chris Givens/199 4.00 10.00
3 Michael Floyd/149 4.00 10.00
4 Lamar Miller/149 6.00 15.00
5 Russell Wilson/199 60.00 100.00
6 Mohamed Sanu/199 6.00 15.00
7 Kendall Wright/149 4.00 10.00
8 A.J. Jenkins/199 4.00 10.00
9 Trent Richardson/99 5.00 12.00
10 Robert Griffin III/99 6.00 15.00
11 Alshon Jeffery/199 8.00 20.00
12 Andrew Luck 100.00 175.00
13 Ryan Broyles/199 4.00 10.00
14 Nick Foles/149 20.00 50.00
15 Coby Fleener/199 4.00 10.00
16 Ryan Tannehill/99 8.00 20.00
17 LaMichael James/199 4.00 10.00
18 Stephen Hill/199 4.00 10.00
19 Nick Toon/199 4.00 10.00
20 Brandon Weeden/99 5.00 12.00
21 Justin Blackmon/99 5.00 12.00
22 Michael Egnew/199 4.00 10.00
23 Rueben Randle/199 4.00 10.00
24 Brock Osweiler/149 4.00 10.00
25 David Wilson/149 4.00 10.00
26 Robert Turbin/199 4.00 10.00
27 DeVier Posey/199 4.00 10.00
28 Bernard Pierce/149 4.00 10.00
29 Ronnie Hillman/199 EXCH 4.00 10.00
30 Isaiah Pead/149 4.00 10.00
31 T.J. Graham/199 4.00 10.00
32 Brian Quick/199 4.00 10.00
33 Dwayne Allen/199 4.00 10.00
34 Joe Adams/199 4.00 10.00
35 Jarius Wright/199 4.00 10.00

2012 Rookies and Stars Rookie Crusade Materials Autographs Red

*PRIME/25: .6X TO 1.5X JSY AU/49
1 Doug Martin 10.00 25.00
2 Chris Givens 6.00 15.00
3 Michael Floyd 6.00 15.00
4 Lamar Miller 10.00 25.00
5 Russell Wilson 100.00 200.00
6 Mohamed Sanu 10.00 25.00
8 A.J. Jenkins 6.00 15.00
9 Trent Richardson 6.00 15.00
10 Robert Griffin III 8.00 20.00
11 Alshon Jeffery 12.00 30.00
12 Andrew Luck 150.00 250.00
13 Ryan Broyles 6.00 15.00
14 Nick Foles 30.00 80.00
15 Coby Fleener 6.00 15.00
16 Ryan Tannehill 10.00 25.00
17 LaMichael James 6.00 15.00
19 Nick Toon 6.00 15.00
20 Brandon Weeden 6.00 15.00
21 Justin Blackmon 6.00 15.00
22 Michael Egnew 6.00 15.00
23 Rueben Randle 6.00 15.00
24 Brock Osweiler 6.00 15.00
25 David Wilson 6.00 15.00
27 DeVier Posey 6.00 15.00
30 Isaiah Pead 6.00 15.00
31 T.J. Graham 6.00 15.00
32 Brian Quick 6.00 15.00
33 Dwayne Allen 6.00 15.00
34 Joe Adams 6.00 15.00
35 Jarius Wright 6.00 15.00

2012 Rookies and Stars Rookie Crusade Materials Red

*GREEN/99: .4X TO 1X RED JSY/199
*PURPLE/49: .5X TO 1.2X RED JSY/199
*PRIME GREEN/25: .8X TO 2X RED JSY/199
*PRIME RED/49: .6X TO 1.5X RED JSY/199
1 Doug Martin 3.00 8.00
2 Chris Givens 2.00 5.00
3 Michael Floyd 2.00 5.00
4 Lamar Miller 3.00 8.00
5 Russell Wilson 15.00 40.00
6 Mohamed Sanu 3.00 8.00
7 Kendall Wright 2.00 5.00
8 A.J. Jenkins 2.00 5.00
9 Trent Richardson 2.00 5.00
10 Robert Griffin III 2.50 6.00
11 Alshon Jeffery 4.00 10.00
12 Andrew Luck 15.00 40.00
13 Ryan Broyles 2.00 5.00
14 Nick Foles 5.00 12.00
15 Coby Fleener 2.00 5.00
16 Ryan Tannehill 3.00 8.00
17 LaMichael James 2.00 5.00
18 Stephen Hill 2.00 5.00
19 Nick Toon 2.00 5.00
20 Brandon Weeden 2.00 5.00
21 Justin Blackmon 2.00 5.00
22 Michael Egnew 2.00 5.00
23 Rueben Randle 2.00 5.00
24 Brock Osweiler 2.00 5.00
25 David Wilson 2.00 5.00
26 Robert Turbin 2.00 5.00
27 DeVier Posey 2.00 5.00
28 Bernard Pierce 2.00 5.00
29 Ronnie Hillman 2.00 5.00
30 Isaiah Pead 2.00 5.00
31 T.J. Graham 2.00 5.00
32 Brian Quick 2.00 5.00
33 Dwayne Allen 2.00 5.00
34 Joe Adams 2.00 5.00
35 Jarius Wright 2.00 5.00

2012 Rookies and Stars Rookie Materials Longevity Parallel

216 Andrew Luck 15.00 40.00
217 Robert Griffin III 2.50 6.00
218 Trent Richardson 2.00 5.00
219 Justin Blackmon 2.00 5.00
220 Ryan Tannehill 3.00 8.00
221 Michael Floyd 2.00 5.00
222 Kendall Wright 2.00 5.00
223 Brandon Weeden 2.00 5.00
224 A.J. Jenkins 2.00 5.00
225 Doug Martin 3.00 8.00
226 David Wilson 2.00 5.00
227 Alshon Jeffery 4.00 10.00
228 Bernard Pierce 2.00 5.00
229 Brian Quick 2.00 5.00
230 Brock Osweiler 2.00 5.00
231 Coby Fleener 2.00 5.00
232 DeVier Posey 2.00 5.00
233 Dwayne Allen 2.00 5.00
234 Isaiah Pead 2.00 5.00
235 Chris Givens 2.00 5.00
236 Joe Adams 2.00 5.00
237 Lamar Miller 3.00 8.00
238 LaMichael James 2.00 5.00
239 Michael Egnew 2.00 5.00
240 Mohamed Sanu 3.00 8.00
241 Nick Foles 5.00 12.00
242 Nick Toon 2.00 5.00
243 Robert Turbin 2.00 5.00
244 Ronnie Hillman 2.00 5.00
245 Rueben Randle 2.00 5.00
246 Russell Wilson 15.00 40.00
247 Ryan Broyles 2.00 5.00
248 Stephen Hill 2.00 5.00
249 T.J. Graham 2.00 5.00
250 Jarius Wright 2.00 5.00

2012 Rookies and Stars Rookie Materials Prime Autographs

*PRIME AU/49: .6X TO 1.5X BASE JSY AU/499
216 Andrew Luck 200.00 400.00
217 Robert Griffin III 10.00 25.00
246 Russell Wilson 100.00 200.00

2012 Rookies and Stars Rookie Premiere Slideshow Autographs

1 David Wilson/50 8.00 20.00
2 Brock Osweiler/50 8.00 20.00
3 Robert Turbin/50 8.00 20.00
4 Ryan Broyles/50 8.00 20.00
5 Michael Egnew/50 8.00 20.00
6 Trent Richardson/50 8.00 20.00
7 Michael Floyd/50 8.00 20.00
8 Doug Martin/50 12.00 30.00
9 Chris Givens/50 8.00 20.00
10 Nick Foles/50 40.00 100.00
11 Rueben Randle/50 8.00 20.00
12 Andrew Luck/50 90.00 150.00
13 Brandon Weeden/50 8.00 20.00
14 Dwayne Allen/50 8.00 20.00
15 Lamar Miller/50 12.00 30.00
16 Nick Toon/41 8.00 20.00
17 Robert Griffin III/50 10.00 25.00
18 A.J. Jenkins/50 8.00 20.00
19 Brian Quick/50 8.00 20.00
20 DeVier Posey/50 8.00 20.00
21 LaMichael James/50 8.00 20.00
22 Stephen Hill/50 8.00 20.00
23 Mohamed Sanu/50 12.00 30.00
24 Ryan Tannehill/50 12.00 30.00
25 Coby Fleener/50 8.00 20.00
26 Ronnie Hillman/50 8.00 20.00
27 T.J. Graham/50 8.00 20.00
28 Justin Blackmon/50 8.00 20.00
29 Alshon Jeffery/50 15.00 40.00
30 Joe Adams/50 8.00 20.00
31 Bernard Pierce/50 8.00 20.00
32 Kendall Wright/50 8.00 20.00
33 Isaiah Pead/50 8.00 20.00
34 Russell Wilson/50 75.00 125.00
35 Jarius Wright/47 8.00 20.00

2012 Rookies and Stars Scoring Core Materials Autographs

STATED PRINT RUN 3-49
*PRIME/19-25: .6X TO 1.5X JSY AU/49
*PRIME/25: .5X TO 1.2X JSY AU/15
1 Maurice Jones-Drew/25 12.00 30.00
2 Brent Celek/25 12.00 30.00
3 Pierre Thomas/49 10.00 25.00
4 A.J. Green/49 15.00 40.00
7 Marques Colston/49 10.00 25.00
9 Felix Jones/20 12.00 30.00
10 Anquan Boldin/20 12.00 30.00
11 Hakeem Nicks/25 EXCH 12.00 30.00
12 Joe Flacco/15 20.00 50.00
14 Larry Fitzgerald/15 20.00 50.00
15 Matthew Stafford/25 25.00 60.00
16 Andy Dalton/35 12.00 30.00
17 Dustin Keller/25 EXCH 12.00 30.00
19 Miles Austin/25 EXCH
20 C.J. Spiller/49 10.00 25.00
21 Brian Hartline/15 15.00 40.00
22 Chris Cooley/49 10.00 25.00
25 Shonn Greene/25 EXCH 12.00 30.00

2012 Rookies and Stars Slideshow

2 Warren Sapp/15
4 Fred Taylor/15 8.00 20.00
5 Rod Smith/15 12.00 30.00
7 Shaun Alexander/15 12.00 30.00
8 Tim Brown/15 10.00 25.00
9 Jerome Bettis/15 30.00 60.00
10 Warrick Dunn/15
12 Cris Carter/15
15 Jerry Rice/15 40.00 100.00
17 Drew Bledsoe/15 10.00 25.00
18 Michael Strahan/15
20 Troy Aikman/15 30.00 60.00
21 Brett Favre/15 40.00 80.00
22 Dan Marino/15 50.00 100.00
23 Terrell Davis/15 10.00 25.00
24 Curtis Martin/15
25 Kurt Warner/15

2012 Rookies and Stars Statistical Standouts

*BLACK/100: .6X TO 1.5X BASIC INSERTS
*GOLD/500: .5X TO 1.2X BASIC INSERTS
*LONGEVITY: .4X TO 1X BASIC INSERTS
1 Drew Brees 1.25 3.00
2 Tom Brady 3.00 8.00
3 Matthew Stafford 1.00 2.50
4 Eli Manning 1.00 2.50
5 Aaron Rodgers 2.00 5.00
6 Maurice Jones-Drew .75 2.00
7 Ray Rice .75 2.00
8 Michael Turner .75 2.00
9 Arian Foster 1.00 2.50
10 Calvin Johnson 1.25 3.00
11 London Fletcher 1.00 2.50
12 D'Qwell Jackson .75 2.00
13 Jared Allen .75 2.00
14 DeMarcus Ware 1.25 3.00
15 Jason Babin .75 2.00
16 Kyle Arrington .75 2.00
17 Eric Weddle .75 2.00
18 Charles Woodson 1.25 3.00
19 LeSean McCoy 1.25 3.00
20 Cam Newton 1.25 3.00
21 Marshawn Lynch 1.00 2.50
22 Rob Gronkowski 1.25 3.00
23 Jordy Nelson 1.00 2.50

2013 Rookies and Stars

COMP.SET w/o RC's (100) 8.00 20.00
1 Larry Fitzgerald .25 .60
2 Rashard Mendenhall .20 .50
3 Carson Palmer .25 .60
4 Matt Ryan .25 .60
5 Julio Jones .30 .75
6 Steven Jackson .20 .50
7 Jacquizz Rodgers .25 .60
8 Joe Flacco .25 .60
9 Torrey Smith .20 .50
10 Ray Rice .20 .50
11 Steve Johnson .25 .60
12 C.J. Spiller .20 .50
13 Fred Jackson .25 .60
14 Cam Newton .30 .75
15 Steve Smith .25 .60
16 Jonathan Stewart .20 .50
17 Jay Cutler .20 .50
18 Brandon Marshall .25 .60
19 Matt Forte .20 .50
20 Charles Tillman .25 .60
21 Andy Dalton .25 .60
22 A.J. Green .30 .75
23 BenJarvus Green-Ellis .25 .60
24 Josh Gordon .20 .50
25 Trent Richardson .20 .50
26 D'Qwell Jackson .20 .50
27 Tony Romo .25 .60
28 Dez Bryant .30 .75
29 DeMarco Murray .25 .60
30 Jason Witten .25 .60
31 Peyton Manning .60 1.50
32 Demaryius Thomas .25 .60
33 Wes Welker .25 .60
34 Ronnie Hillman .20 .50
35 Matthew Stafford .25 .60
36 Calvin Johnson .30 .75
37 Mikel Leshoure .20 .50
38 Aaron Rodgers .50 1.25
39 Jordy Nelson .25 .60
40 Randall Cobb .25 .60
41 Matt Schaub .20 .50
42 Andre Johnson .20 .50
43 Arian Foster .25 .60
44 Andrew Luck .50 1.25
45 Reggie Wayne .25 .60
46 T.Y. Hilton .25 .60
47 Justin Blackmon .20 .50
48 Maurice Jones-Drew .20 .50
49 Marcedes Lewis .20 .50
50 Dwayne Bowe .25 .60
51 Jamaal Charles .25 .60
52 Tamba Hali .20 .50
53 Ryan Tannehill .25 .60
54 Mike Wallace .20 .50
55 Cameron Wake .20 .50
56 Christian Ponder .20 .50
57 Adrian Peterson .30 .75
58 Greg Jennings .20 .50
59 Tom Brady .75 2.00
60 Danny Amendola .25 .60
61 Tim Tebow .25 .60
62 Drew Brees .30 .75
63 Marques Colston .20 .50
64 Jimmy Graham .30 .75
65 Eli Manning .25 .60
66 Victor Cruz .25 .60
67 Hakeem Nicks .20 .50
68 Mark Sanchez .20 .50
69 Santonio Holmes .20 .50
70 Bilal Powell .20 .50
71 Matt Flynn .20 .50
72 Denarius Moore .20 .50
73 Darren McFadden .25 .60
74 Michael Vick .25 .60
75 DeSean Jackson .25 .60
76 LeSean McCoy .30 .75
77 Ben Roethlisberger .30 .75
78 Jonathan Dwyer .20 .50
79 Antonio Brown .30 .75
80 Philip Rivers .30 .75
81 Ryan Mathews .25 .60
82 Antonio Gates .25 .60
83 Colin Kaepernick .25 .60
84 Michael Crabtree .20 .50
85 Frank Gore .25 .60
86 Russell Wilson .60 1.50
87 Percy Harvin .20 .50
88 Marshawn Lynch .25 .60
89 Sam Bradford .20 .50
90 Daryl Richardson .20 .50
91 James Laurinaitis .25 .60
92 Josh Freeman .25 .60
93 Vincent Jackson .20 .50
94 Doug Martin .25 .60
95 Jake Locker .25 .60
96 Kenny Britt .20 .50
97 Chris Johnson .20 .50
98 Robert Griffin III .20 .50
99 Pierre Garcon .25 .60
100 Alfred Morris .20 .50
101 Aaron Dobson RC .40 1.00
102 Aaron Mellette RC .40 1.00
103 Ace Sanders RC .40 1.00
104 Alec Ogletree RC .40 1.00
105 Alex Okafor RC .40 1.00
106 Andre Ellington RC .40 1.00
107 Arthur Brown RC .40 1.00
108 Barkevious Mingo RC .40 1.00
109 Bjoern Werner RC .40 1.00
110 Chance Warmack RC .40 1.00
111 Chris Gragg RC .40 1.00
112 Chris Harper RC .40 1.00
113 Christine Michael RC .40 1.00
114 Cobi Hamilton RC .40 1.00
115 Conner Vernon RC .40 1.00
116 Cordarrelle Patterson RC .40 1.00
117 Corey Fuller RC .40 1.00
118 D.J. Hayden RC .40 1.00
119 Damontre Moore RC .40 1.00
120 Da'Rick Rogers RC .40 1.00
121 Darius Slay RC .40 1.00
122 Datone Jones RC .40 1.00
123 DeAndre Hopkins RC 1.00 2.50
124 Dee Milliner RC .40 1.00
125 Denard Robinson RC .40 1.00
126 Desmond Trufant RC .40 1.00
127 Dion Jordan RC .40 1.00
128 Dion Sims RC .40 1.00
129 Eddie Lacy RC .40 1.00
130 EJ Manuel RC .40 1.00
131 Eric Fisher RC .40 1.00
132 Eric Reid RC .50 1.25
133 Ezekiel Ansah RC .40 1.00
134 Gavin Escobar RC .40 1.00
135 Geno Smith RC .40 1.00
136 Giovani Bernard RC .40 1.00
137 Jamar Taylor RC .40 1.00
138 Jarvis Jones RC .40 1.00
139 Jawan Jamison RC .40 1.00
140 Johnathan Cyprien RC .40 1.00
141 Johnathan Franklin RC .40 1.00
142 Dennis Johnson RC .40 1.00
143 Johnthan Banks RC .40 1.00
144 Jordan Poyer RC .40 1.00
145 Jordan Reed RC .60 1.50
146 Joseph Randle RC .40 1.00
147 Josh Boyce RC .40 1.00
148 Justin Hunter RC .40 1.00
149 Keenan Allen RC .75 2.00
150 Kenjon Barner RC .40 1.00
151 Kenny Stills RC .40 1.00
152 Kenny Vaccaro RC .40 1.00
153 Kevin Minter RC .40 1.00
154 Knile Davis RC .40 1.00
155 Landry Jones RC .40 1.00
156 Le'Veon Bell RC 1.25 3.00
157 Jasper Collins RC .40 1.00
158 Luke Joeckel RC .60 1.50
159 Manti Te'o RC .50 1.25
160 Marcus Davis RC .40 1.00
161 Marcus Lattimore RC .60 1.50
162 Margus Hunt RC .40 1.00
163 Markus Wheaton RC .40 1.00
164 Marquess Wilson RC .60 1.50
165 Marquise Goodwin RC .40 1.00
166 Matt Barkley RC .40 1.00
167 Matt Elam RC .40 1.00
168 Matt Scott RC .40 1.00
169 Mike Gillislee RC .40 1.00
170 Mike Glennon RC .40 1.00
171 Montee Ball RC .40 1.00
172 Nick Kasa RC .40 1.00
173 Phillip Thomas RC .40 1.00
174 Quinton Patton RC .40 1.00
175 Rex Burkhead RC .50 1.25
176 Robert Woods RC .60 1.50
177 Rodney Smith RC .40 1.00
178 Ryan Nassib RC .40 1.00
179 Ryan Otten RC .40 1.00
180 Ryan Swope RC .40 1.00
181 Sam Montgomery RC .40 1.00
182 Onterio McCalebb RC .50 1.25
183 Sheldon Richardson RC .40 1.00
184 David Amerson RC .40 1.00
185 Chris Thompson RC .40 1.00
186 Stedman Bailey RC .40 1.00
187 Stepfan Taylor RC .40 1.00
188 Tavarres King RC .40 1.00
189 Tavon Austin RC .50 1.25
190 Terrance Williams RC .40 1.00
191 Theo Riddick RC .40 1.00
192 Travis Kelce RC 1.00 2.50
193 Tyler Bray RC .40 1.00
194 Tyler Eifert RC .40 1.00
195 Tyler Wilson RC .40 1.00
196 Tyrann Mathieu RC .60 1.50
197 Vance McDonald RC .50 1.25
198 Xavier Rhodes RC .40 1.00
199 Zac Dysert RC .40 1.00
200 Zach Ertz RC .75 2.00
201 Aaron Dobson JSY 1.50 4.00
202 Andre Ellington JSY 1.50 4.00
203 Christine Michael JSY 1.50 4.00
204 Cordarrelle Patterson JSY 1.50 4.00
205 DeAndre Hopkins JSY 4.00 10.00
206 Denard Robinson JSY 1.50 4.00
207 Eddie Lacy JSY 1.50 4.00
208 EJ Manuel JSY 1.50 4.00
209 Gavin Escobar JSY 1.50 4.00
210 Geno Smith JSY 1.50 4.00
211 Giovani Bernard JSY 1.50 4.00
212 Johnathan Franklin JSY 1.50 4.00
213 Jordan Reed JSY 2.50 6.00
214 Joseph Randle JSY 1.50 4.00
215 Justin Hunter JSY 1.50 4.00
216 Keenan Allen JSY 3.00 8.00
217 Kenny Stills JSY 1.50 4.00
218 Knile Davis JSY 1.50 4.00
219 Landry Jones JSY 1.50 4.00
220 Le'Veon Bell JSY 5.00 12.00
221 Manti Te'o JSY 2.00 5.00
222 Marcus Lattimore JSY 1.50 4.00
223 Markus Wheaton JSY 1.50 4.00
224 Marquise Goodwin JSY 1.50 4.00
225 Matt Barkley JSY 1.50 4.00
226 Mike Gillislee JSY 1.50 4.00
227 Mike Glennon JSY 1.50 4.00
228 Montee Ball JSY 1.50 4.00
229 Quinton Patton JSY 1.50 4.00
230 Robert Woods JSY 2.50 6.00
231 Ryan Nassib JSY 1.50 4.00
232 Stedman Bailey JSY 1.50 4.00
233 Stepfan Taylor JSY 1.50 4.00
234 Tavon Austin JSY 2.00 5.00
235 Terrance Williams JSY 1.50 4.00
236 Dion Jordan JSY 1.50 4.00
237 Tyler Eifert JSY 1.50 4.00
238 Tyler Wilson JSY 1.50 4.00
239 Vance McDonald JSY 2.00 5.00
240 Zach Ertz JSY 3.00 8.00

2013 Rookies and Stars Longevity Gold Parallel

*1-100 VETS/49: 3X TO 8X BASIC CARDS
*101-200 ROOKIES/49: 1.5X TO 4X BASIC RC
*201-240 ROOK.JSY/49: .8X TO 2X BASIC JSY

2013 Rookies and Stars Longevity Holofoil Parallel

*1-100 VETS/99: 2.5X TO 6X BASIC CARDS
*101-200 ROOKIES/99: 1.2X TO 3X BASIC RC
*201-240 ROOK.JSY/99: .6X TO 1.5X BASIC JSY

2013 Rookies and Stars Longevity Parallel

*1-100 VETS: 1.5X TO 4X BASIC CARDS
*101-200 ROOKIES: .8X TO 2X BASIC RC
*101-200 RK.JSY/299: .5X TO 1.2X BASIC JSY

2013 Rookies and Stars Longevity Platinum Parallel

*1-100 VETS/25: 4X TO 10X BASIC CARDS
*101-200 ROOKIES/25: 2X TO 5X BASIC RC
*201-240 ROOK.JSY/25: 1X TO 2.5X BASIC JSY

2013 Rookies and Stars Team Logo Holofoil

*1-100 VETS/32: 4X TO 10X BASIC CARDS
*101-200 ROOKIES/32: 2X TO 5X BASIC RC
*201-240 ROOK.JSY/32: 1X TO 2.5X BASIC JSY

2013 Rookies and Stars Crosstraining Materials

*PRIME/25: .8X TO 2X BASIC JSY
1 Andre Ellington 2.00 5.00
2 Christine Michael 2.00 5.00
3 Cordarrelle Patterson 2.00 5.00
4 EJ Manuel 2.00 5.00
5 Geno Smith 2.00 5.00
6 Giovani Bernard 2.00 5.00
7 Jordan Reed 3.00 8.00
8 Joseph Randle 2.00 5.00
9 Justin Hunter 2.00 5.00
10 Kenny Stills 2.00 5.00
11 Knile Davis 2.00 5.00
12 Markus Wheaton 2.00 5.00
13 Marquise Goodwin 2.00 5.00
14 Montee Ball 2.00 5.00
15 Quinton Patton 2.00 5.00
16 Ryan Nassib 2.00 5.00
17 Stedman Bailey 2.00 5.00
18 Tavon Austin 2.50 6.00
19 Tyler Eifert 2.00 5.00
20 Vance McDonald 2.50 6.00

2013 Rookies and Stars Dress for Success Jerseys

*PRIME/25: .8X TO 2X DFS JSY
*FRESH.ORIEN: .4X TO 1X DFS JSY
*FO PRIME/25: .8X TO 2X DFS JSY
1 Aaron Dobson 1.50 4.00
2 Andre Ellington 1.50 4.00
3 Christine Michael 1.50 4.00
4 Cordarrelle Patterson 1.50 4.00
5 DeAndre Hopkins 4.00 10.00
6 Denard Robinson 1.50 4.00
7 Eddie Lacy 1.50 4.00
8 EJ Manuel 1.50 4.00
9 Gavin Escobar 1.50 4.00
10 Geno Smith 1.50 4.00
11 Giovani Bernard 1.50 4.00
12 Johnathan Franklin 1.50 4.00
13 Jordan Reed 2.50 6.00
14 Joseph Randle 1.50 4.00
15 Justin Hunter 1.50 4.00
16 Keenan Allen 3.00 8.00
17 Kenny Stills 1.50 4.00
18 Knile Davis 1.50 4.00
19 Landry Jones 1.50 4.00
20 Le'Veon Bell 5.00 12.00
21 Manti Te'o 2.00 5.00
22 Marcus Lattimore 1.50 4.00
23 Markus Wheaton 1.50 4.00
24 Marquise Goodwin 1.50 4.00
25 Matt Barkley 1.50 4.00
26 Mike Gillislee 1.50 4.00
27 Mike Glennon 1.50 4.00
28 Montee Ball 1.50 4.00
29 Quinton Patton 1.50 4.00
30 Robert Woods 2.50 6.00
31 Ryan Nassib 1.50 4.00
32 Stedman Bailey 1.50 4.00
33 Stepfan Taylor 1.50 4.00
34 Tavon Austin 2.00 5.00
35 Terrance Williams 1.50 4.00
36 Dion Jordan 1.50 4.00
37 Tyler Eifert 1.50 4.00
38 Tyler Wilson 1.50 4.00
39 Vance McDonald 2.00 5.00
40 Zach Ertz 3.00 8.00

2013 Rookies and Stars Game Plan

1 Larry Fitzgerald 1.25 3.00
2 Robert Griffin III 1.00 2.50
3 Ray Rice 1.00 2.50
4 C.J. Spiller 1.00 2.50
5 Cam Newton 1.50 4.00
6 Jay Cutler 1.00 2.50
7 A.J. Green 1.50 4.00
8 DeMarco Murray 1.25 3.00
9 Peyton Manning 3.00 8.00
10 Calvin Johnson 1.50 4.00
11 Aaron Rodgers 2.50 6.00
12 Matt Schaub 1.00 2.50
13 Andrew Luck 2.50 6.00
14 Maurice Jones-Drew 1.00 2.50
15 Adrian Peterson 1.50 4.00
16 Tom Brady 4.00 10.00
17 Drew Brees 1.50 4.00
18 Eli Manning 1.25 3.00
19 Darren McFadden 1.25 3.00
20 LeSean McCoy 1.50 4.00
21 Ben Roethlisberger 1.50 4.00
22 Colin Kaepernick 1.25 3.00
23 Russell Wilson 3.00 8.00
24 Josh Freeman 1.25 3.00
25 Chris Johnson 1.00 2.50

2013 Rookies and Stars Materials Autographs Team Logo

*BASE JSY AU/20-25: .4X TO 1X TEAM/32
*LONG.GOLD/49: .3X TO .8X TEAM/32
*LONG.GOLD/15: .5X TO 1.2X TEAM/32
*LONG.PLAT/25: .4X TO 1X TEAM/32
*LONG.RUBY/42-49: .3X TO .8X TEAM/32
*LONG.RUBY/15: .5X TO 1.2X TEAM/32
*LONG.SAPHR/25: .4X TO 1X TEAM/32
1 Jonathan Baldwin 5.00 12.00
2 Brent Celek 5.00 12.00
3 Marcedes Lewis 5.00 12.00
4 Blaine Gabbert 5.00 12.00
5 Alfred Morris 5.00 12.00
6 Christian Ponder 10.00 25.00
7 Daniel Thomas 5.00 12.00
8 Michael Crabtree 8.00 20.00
9 Ryan Tannehill 12.00 30.00
10 Jonathan Stewart 5.00 12.00
11 Champ Bailey 10.00 25.00
12 Derrick Johnson 15.00 40.00
13 Morris Claiborne 5.00 12.00
14 Tamba Hali 5.00 12.00
15 Knowshon Moreno 5.00 12.00
16 Sidney Rice 5.00 12.00
17 Maurice Jones-Drew 5.00 12.00
18 Jacoby Ford 5.00 12.00
19 Dexter McCluster 6.00 15.00
20 Jeremy Kerley 5.00 12.00

2013 Rookies and Stars NFL Nation

1 Rob Gronkowski 1.50 4.00
2 Arian Foster 1.25 3.00
3 Cam Newton 1.50 4.00
4 Victor Cruz 1.25 3.00
5 Jimmy Graham 1.50 4.00
6 Robert Griffin III 1.00 2.50
7 Aaron Rodgers 2.50 6.00
8 Santonio Holmes 1.00 2.50
9 James Jones 1.00 2.50
10 Chris Johnson 1.00 2.50
11 David Wilson 1.00 2.50
12 Alfred Morris 1.00 2.50
13 Dez Bryant 1.50 4.00
14 Andrew Luck 2.50 6.00
15 DeSean Jackson 1.25 3.00
16 Steve Smith 1.25 3.00
17 Trent Richardson 1.00 2.50
18 Eric Decker 1.00 2.50
19 Roddy White 1.00 2.50
20 Russell Wilson 3.00 8.00
21 Golden Tate 1.00 2.50
22 LeSean McCoy 1.50 4.00
23 Steven Jackson 1.00 2.50
24 Colin Kaepernick 1.25 3.00
25 Darren McFadden 1.25 3.00

2013 Rookies and Stars Rookie Autographs Longevity

*101-200 LONG.AU: .25X TO .6X TEAM HOLO/32
242 B.J. Daniels 4.00 10.00
243 Blidi Wreh-Wilson 3.00 8.00
244 Brad Sorensen 2.50 6.00
245 Brice Butler 2.50 6.00
247 Cornellius Carradine 2.50 6.00
248 D.J. Fluker 2.50 6.00
250 Dustin Hopkins 6.00 15.00
252 Jon Bostic 10.00 25.00
253 Justin Brown 6.00 15.00
254 Kerwynn Williams 2.50 6.00
256 Mychal Rivera 2.50 6.00
258 Robert Alford 2.50 6.00

2013 Rookies and Stars Rookie Autographs Team Logo Holofoil

*LNG.GOLD AU/49: .3X TO .8X TEAM HOL/32
*LNG.HOLO AU/99: .3X TO .8X TEAM HOL/32
*LNG.PLAT AU/25: .4X TO 1X TEAM HOL/32
*LONG.RUBY AU/149-199: .25X TO .6X TEAM HOL/32
*LONG.RUBY AU/25: .4X TO 1X TEAM HOL/32
*LONG.SAPP AU/25: .4X TO 1X TEAM HOL/32
101 Aaron Dobson 4.00 10.00
102 Aaron Mellette 4.00 10.00
103 Ace Sanders 4.00 10.00
104 Alec Ogletree 4.00 10.00
106 Andre Ellington 4.00 10.00
107 Arthur Brown 4.00 10.00
108 Barkevious Mingo 4.00 10.00
109 Bjoern Werner 4.00 10.00
110 Chance Warmack 4.00 10.00
111 Chris Gragg 4.00 10.00
113 Christine Michael 4.00 10.00
116 Cordarrelle Patterson 4.00 10.00
118 D.J. Hayden 12.00 30.00
119 Damontre Moore 4.00 10.00
120 Da'Rick Rogers 4.00 10.00
121 Darius Slay 4.00 10.00
122 Datone Jones 4.00 10.00
123 DeAndre Hopkins 10.00 25.00
125 Denard Robinson 4.00 10.00
126 Desmond Trufant 4.00 10.00
127 Dion Jordan 4.00 10.00
128 Dion Sims 4.00 10.00
129 Eddie Lacy 4.00 10.00
130 EJ Manuel 4.00 10.00
131 Eric Fisher 4.00 10.00
132 Eric Reid 5.00 12.00
133 Ezekiel Ansah 4.00 10.00
134 Gavin Escobar 4.00 10.00
135 Geno Smith 4.00 10.00
136 Giovani Bernard 4.00 10.00
137 Jamar Taylor 4.00 10.00
138 Jarvis Jones 4.00 10.00
140 Johnathan Cyprien 4.00 10.00
141 Johnathan Franklin 4.00 10.00
142 Dennis Johnson 4.00 10.00
143 Johnthan Banks 4.00 10.00
145 Jordan Reed 10.00 25.00
146 Joseph Randle 4.00 10.00
147 Josh Boyce 4.00 10.00
148 Justin Hunter 4.00 10.00
149 Keenan Allen 8.00 20.00
150 Kenjon Barner 4.00 10.00
151 Kenny Stills 4.00 10.00
152 Kenny Vaccaro 4.00 10.00
153 Kevin Minter 4.00 10.00
154 Knile Davis 4.00 10.00
155 Landry Jones 4.00 10.00
156 Le'Veon Bell 20.00 50.00
157 Jasper Collins 4.00 10.00
158 Luke Joeckel 4.00 10.00
159 Manti Te'o 5.00 12.00
160 Marcus Davis 4.00 10.00
161 Marcus Lattimore 4.00 10.00
162 Margus Hunt 4.00 10.00
163 Markus Wheaton 4.00 10.00
164 Marquess Wilson 6.00 15.00
165 Marquise Goodwin 4.00 10.00
166 Matt Barkley 4.00 10.00
167 Matt Elam 4.00 10.00
168 Matt Scott 4.00 10.00
169 Mike Gillislee 4.00 10.00
170 Mike Glennon 4.00 10.00
171 Montee Ball 4.00 10.00
172 Nick Kasa 4.00 10.00
173 Phillip Thomas 4.00 10.00
174 Quinton Patton 4.00 10.00
175 Rex Burkhead 5.00 12.00
176 Robert Woods 6.00 15.00
177 Rodney Smith 4.00 10.00
178 Ryan Nassib 4.00 10.00
179 Ryan Otten 4.00 10.00
180 Ryan Swope 4.00 10.00
181 Sam Montgomery 4.00 10.00
185 Chris Thompson 4.00 10.00
186 Stedman Bailey 4.00 10.00
187 Stepfan Taylor 4.00 10.00
188 Tavarres King 4.00 10.00
189 Tavon Austin 5.00 12.00
190 Terrance Williams 4.00 10.00
191 Theo Riddick 4.00 10.00
192 Travis Kelce 15.00 40.00
193 Tyler Bray 4.00 10.00
194 Tyler Eifert 4.00 10.00
195 Tyler Wilson 4.00 10.00
196 Tyrann Mathieu 6.00 15.00
197 Vance McDonald 5.00 12.00
198 Xavier Rhodes 4.00 10.00
199 Zac Dysert 4.00 10.00
200 Zach Ertz 8.00 20.00

2013 Rookies and Stars Rookie Jersey Autographs

STATED PRINT RUN 299 SER.#'d SETS
*LONGEVITY/99: .5X TO 1.2X JSY AU/299
*LONG.GOLD/49: .5X TO 1.2X JSY AU/299
*LONG.PLAT/25: .6X TO 1.5X JSY AU/299
*LONG.RUBY/99: .5X TO 1.2X JSY AU/299
*LONG.SAPP/25: .6X TO 1.5X JSY AU/299
*TEAM LOGO/32: .6X TO 1.5X JSY AU/299
201 Aaron Dobson 3.00 8.00
202 Andre Ellington 3.00 8.00
203 Christine Michael 3.00 8.00
204 Cordarrelle Patterson 3.00 8.00
205 DeAndre Hopkins 8.00 20.00
206 Denard Robinson 3.00 8.00
207 Eddie Lacy 3.00 8.00
208 EJ Manuel 3.00 8.00
209 Gavin Escobar 3.00 8.00
210 Geno Smith 3.00 8.00
211 Giovani Bernard 4.00 10.00
212 Johnathan Franklin 3.00 8.00
213 Jordan Reed 5.00 12.00
214 Joseph Randle 3.00 8.00
215 Justin Hunter 3.00 8.00
216 Keenan Allen 12.00 30.00
217 Kenny Stills 3.00 8.00
218 Knile Davis 3.00 8.00
219 Landry Jones 3.00 8.00
220 Le'Veon Bell 10.00 25.00
221 Manti Te'o 4.00 10.00
222 Marcus Lattimore 3.00 8.00
223 Markus Wheaton 3.00 8.00
224 Marquise Goodwin 3.00 8.00
225 Matt Barkley 3.00 8.00
226 Mike Gillislee 3.00 8.00
227 Mike Glennon 3.00 8.00
228 Montee Ball 3.00 8.00
229 Quinton Patton 3.00 8.00
230 Robert Woods 5.00 12.00
231 Ryan Nassib 3.00 8.00
232 Stedman Bailey 3.00 8.00
233 Stepfan Taylor 3.00 8.00
234 Tavon Austin 4.00 10.00
235 Terrance Williams 3.00 8.00
236 Dion Jordan 3.00 8.00
237 Tyler Eifert 3.00 8.00
238 Tyler Wilson 3.00 8.00
239 Vance McDonald 4.00 10.00
240 Zach Ertz 6.00 15.00

2013 Rookies and Stars Slideshow Autographs

1 Aaron Dobson/100 5.00 12.00
2 Andre Ellington/97 5.00 12.00
3 Christine Michael/98 5.00 12.00
4 Cordarrelle Patterson/96 5.00 12.00
5 DeAndre Hopkins/95 12.00 30.00
6 Denard Robinson/91 5.00 12.00
7 Eddie Lacy/98 5.00 12.00
8 EJ Manuel/100 5.00 12.00
9 Gavin Escobar/100 5.00 12.00
10 Geno Smith/100 5.00 12.00
11 Giovani Bernard/100 5.00 12.00
12 Johnathan Franklin/100 5.00 12.00
13 Jordan Reed/100 8.00 20.00
14 Joseph Randle/100 5.00 12.00
15 Justin Hunter/98 5.00 12.00
16 Keenan Allen/97 10.00 25.00
17 Kenny Stills/100 5.00 12.00
18 Knile Davis/100 5.00 12.00
19 Landry Jones/100 5.00 12.00
20 Le'Veon Bell/97 15.00 40.00
21 Manti Te'o/100 6.00 15.00
22 Marcus Lattimore/100 5.00 12.00
23 Markus Wheaton/100 5.00 12.00
24 Marquise Goodwin/100 5.00 12.00
25 Matt Barkley/100 5.00 12.00
26 Mike Gillislee/99 5.00 12.00
27 Mike Glennon/100 5.00 12.00
28 Montee Ball/100 5.00 12.00
29 Quinton Patton/99 5.00 12.00
30 Robert Woods/100 8.00 20.00
31 Ryan Nassib/99 5.00 12.00
32 Stedman Bailey/99 5.00 12.00
33 Stepfan Taylor/100 5.00 12.00
34 Tavon Austin/99 6.00 15.00
35 Terrance Williams/100 5.00 12.00
36 Dion Jordan/101 5.00 12.00
37 Tyler Eifert/100 5.00 12.00
38 Tyler Wilson/100 5.00 12.00

39 Vance McDonald/101 6.00 15.00
40 Zach Ertz/99 10.00 25.00

2013 Rookies and Stars Slideshow

1 Aaron Dobson/25 3.00 8.00
2 Andre Ellington/21 3.00 8.00
3 Christine Michael/25 3.00 8.00
4 Cordarrelle Patterson/25 3.00 8.00
5 DeAndre Hopkins/25 8.00 20.00
6 Denard Robinson/25 3.00 8.00
7 Eddie Lacy/25 3.00 8.00
8 EJ Manuel/25 3.00 8.00
9 Gavin Escobar/25 3.00 8.00
10 Geno Smith/25 3.00 8.00
11 Giovani Bernard/25 3.00 8.00
12 Johnathan Franklin/25 3.00 8.00
13 Jordan Reed/25 5.00 12.00
14 Joseph Randle/25 3.00 8.00
15 Justin Hunter/25 3.00 8.00
16 Keenan Allen/25 6.00 15.00
17 Kenny Stills/25 3.00 8.00
18 Knile Davis/25 3.00 8.00
19 Landry Jones/25 3.00 8.00
20 Le'Veon Bell/25 10.00 25.00
21 Manti Te'o/25 4.00 10.00
22 Marcus Lattimore/25 3.00 8.00
23 Markus Wheaton/25 3.00 8.00
24 Marquise Goodwin/25 3.00 8.00
25 Matt Barkley/25 3.00 8.00
26 Mike Gillislee/25 3.00 8.00
27 Mike Glennon/25 3.00 8.00
28 Montee Ball/25 3.00 8.00
29 Quinton Patton/25 3.00 8.00
30 Robert Woods/25 5.00 12.00
31 Ryan Nassib/25 3.00 8.00
32 Stedman Bailey/25 3.00 8.00
33 Stepfan Taylor/25 3.00 8.00
34 Tavon Austin/25 4.00 10.00
35 Terrance Williams/25 3.00 8.00
36 Dion Jordan/25 3.00 8.00
37 Tyler Eifert/25 3.00 8.00
38 Tyler Wilson/19 3.00 8.00
39 Vance McDonald/17 4.00 10.00
40 Zach Ertz/25 6.00 15.00

2013 Rookies and Stars Statistical Standouts

1 Drew Brees 1.50 4.00
2 Matthew Stafford 1.25 3.00
3 Tony Romo 1.25 3.00
4 Adrian Peterson 1.50 4.00
5 Alfred Morris 1.00 2.50
6 Marshawn Lynch 1.25 3.00
7 Calvin Johnson 1.50 4.00
8 Andre Johnson 1.00 2.50
9 Brandon Marshall 1.25 3.00
10 Aaron Rodgers 2.50 6.00
11 Peyton Manning 3.00 8.00
12 Tom Brady 4.00 10.00
13 Arian Foster 1.25 3.00
14 Colin Kaepernick 1.25 3.00
15 Trent Richardson 1.00 2.50
16 Eric Decker 1.00 2.50
17 Dez Bryant 1.50 4.00
18 Luke Kuechly 1.25 3.00
19 NaVorro Bowman 1.25 3.00
20 J.J. Watt 1.25 3.00
21 Aldon Smith 1.00 2.50
22 Russell Wilson 3.00 8.00
23 Richard Sherman 1.50 4.00
24 Robert Griffin III 1.00 2.50
25 Andrew Luck 2.50 6.00

2013 Rookies and Stars Team Chemistry Autographs

5 A.Hawkins
M.Sanu/25
7 S.Lee 20.00 40.00
M.Claiborne/25
8 D.Thomas 20.00 40.00
K.Moreno/25
10 R.Cobb 20.00 40.00
J.Finley/25
13 M.Drew 15.00 30.00
C.Shorts/25
14 T.Hali
D.Johnson/25
15 C.Ponder
K.Rudolph/25

2013 Rookies and Stars Touchdown Club

1 Aaron Rodgers 2.50 6.00
2 Drew Brees 1.50 4.00
3 Peyton Manning 3.00 8.00
4 Tom Brady 4.00 10.00
5 Matt Ryan 1.25 3.00
6 Arian Foster 1.25 3.00
7 Alfred Morris 1.00 2.50
8 Adrian Peterson 1.50 4.00
9 Andrew Luck 2.50 6.00
10 Ray Rice 1.00 2.50
11 Colin Kaepernick 1.25 3.00
12 Dez Bryant 1.50 4.00
13 A.J. Green 1.50 4.00
14 Marques Colston 1.00 2.50
15 Victor Cruz 1.25 3.00
16 Julio Jones 1.50 4.00
17 Demaryius Thomas 1.25 3.00
18 Rob Gronkowski 1.50 4.00
19 Jimmy Graham 1.50 4.00
20 Kyle Rudolph 1.00 2.50
21 Russell Wilson 3.00 8.00
22 Antonio Gates 1.25 3.00
23 Frank Gore 1.25 3.00
24 Cam Newton 1.50 4.00
25 Robert Griffin III 1.00 2.50

2014 Rookies and Stars

COMP.SET w/o SP's (200) 15.00 40.00
COMP.SET w/o RC's (100) 12.00 30.00
1 Colin Kaepernick .25 .60
2 Michael Crabtree .20 .50
3 Frank Gore .25 .60
4 Aldon Smith .20 .50
5 Jay Cutler .20 .50
6 Brandon Marshall .20 .50
7 Alshon Jeffery .25 .60
8 Andy Dalton .25 .60
9 A.J. Green .30 .75
10 Giovani Bernard .20 .50
11 EJ Manuel .20 .50
12 Robert Woods .25 .60
13 C.J. Spiller .20 .50
14 Peyton Manning .60 1.50
15 Demaryius Thomas .25 .60
16 Wes Welker .25 .60
17 Julius Thomas .20 .50
18 Josh Gordon .20 .50
19 Jordan Cameron .20 .50
20 Ben Tate .20 .50
21 Josh McCown .20 .50
22 Vincent Jackson .20 .50
23 Doug Martin .25 .60
24 Philip Rivers .30 .75
25 Keenan Allen .25 .60
26 Ryan Mathews .25 .60
27 Alex Smith .25 .60
28 Dwayne Bowe .25 .60
29 Jamaal Charles .25 .60
30 Andrew Luck .40 1.00
31 Hakeem Nicks .20 .50
32 Trent Richardson .20 .50
33 Ryan Tannehill .25 .60
34 Brian Hartline .20 .50
35 Knowshon Moreno .20 .50
36 Tom Brady .75 2.00
37 Rob Gronkowski .30 .75
38 Darrelle Revis .20 .50
39 Geno Smith .20 .50
40 Chris Ivory .25 .60
41 Eric Decker .20 .50
42 Joe Flacco .25 .60
43 Steve Smith .25 .60
44 Dennis Pitta .20 .50
45 Ben Roethlisberger .30 .75
46 Antonio Brown .30 .75
47 Le'Veon Bell .25 .60
48 Arian Foster .25 .60
49 Andre Johnson .25 .60
50 J.J. Watt .30 .75
51 Chad Henne .20 .50
52 Ace Sanders .20 .50
53 Justin Blackmon .20 .50
54 Jake Locker .25 .60
55 Kendall Wright .20 .50
56 Shonn Greene .20 .50
57 Matt Schaub .20 .50
58 Denarius Moore .20 .50
59 Darren McFadden .20 .50
60 Tony Romo .25 .60
61 Dez Bryant .30 .75
62 DeMarco Murray .25 .60
63 Henry Melton .20 .50
64 Eli Manning .25 .60
65 Victor Cruz .25 .60
66 Rashad Jennings .20 .50
67 Nick Foles .25 .60
68 Jeremy Maclin .20 .50
69 LeSean McCoy .30 .75
70 Robert Griffin III .20 .50
71 Pierre Garcon .25 .60
72 Alfred Morris .20 .50
73 Matthew Stafford .25 .60
74 Calvin Johnson .30 .75
75 Golden Tate .25 .60
76 Aaron Rodgers .60 1.50
77 Jordy Nelson .25 .60
78 Eddie Lacy .20 .50
79 Cordarrelle Patterson .20 .50
80 Greg Jennings .20 .50
81 Adrian Peterson .30 .75
82 Matt Ryan .25 .60
83 Julio Jones .30 .75
84 Steven Jackson .20 .50
85 Cam Newton .30 .75
86 DeAngelo Williams .20 .50
87 Luke Kuechly .25 .60
88 Drew Brees .30 .75
89 Jimmy Graham .30 .75
90 Mark Ingram .25 .60
91 Carson Palmer .25 .60
92 Larry Fitzgerald .25 .60
93 Andre Ellington .20 .50
94 Sam Bradford .20 .50
95 Tavon Austin .20 .50
96 Zac Stacy .20 .50
97 Russell Wilson .50 1.25
98 Percy Harvin .20 .50
99 Marshawn Lynch .25 .60
100 Richard Sherman .30 .75
101A A.J. McCarron RC .40 1.00
101B McCarron SP ball cut off lft .60 1.50
102 Aaron Donald RC 1.00 2.50
103 Aaron Murray RC .40 1.00
104 Ahmad Dixon RC .40 1.00
105 Allen Robinson RC .60 1.50
106A Andre Williams RC .40 1.00
106B A.Williams SP ball lft hand .60 1.50
107 Anthony Barr RC .40 1.00
108 Austin Seferian-Jenkins RC .40 1.00
109A Bishop Sankey RC .40 1.00
109B B.Sankey SP facing right .60 1.50
110A Blake Bortles RC .50 1.25
110B B.Bortles SP smiling .75 2.00
111 Bradley Roby RC .40 1.00
112A Brandin Cooks RC .60 1.50
112B B.Cooks SP rght foot up 1.00 2.50
113 Brandon Coleman RC .40 1.00
114 Brett Smith RC .40 1.00
115 Bruce Ellington RC .40 1.00
116 C.J. Mosley RC .50 1.25
117 Calvin Pryor RC .40 1.00
118 Carlos Hyde RC .50 1.25
119 Charles Sims RC .40 1.00
120 Chris Borland RC .40 1.00
121A Cody Latimer RC .50 1.25
121B C.Latimer SP ball at mask .75 2.00
122 Connor Shaw RC .40 1.00
123 Cyril Richardson RC .40 1.00
124 Cyrus Kouandjio RC .50 1.25
125 Darqueze Dennard RC .50 1.25
126 Davante Adams RC .60 1.50
127 David Fales RC .40 1.00
128 De'Anthony Thomas RC .40 1.00
129 Dee Ford RC .40 1.00
130 Deone Bucannon RC .40 1.00
131 Derek Carr RC 2.50 6.00
132 Devonta Freeman RC .60 1.50
133A Donte Moncrief RC .40 1.00
133B D.Moncrief SP ball lft hand .60 1.50
134 Dri Archer RC .40 1.00
135 Ed Reynolds RC .40 1.00
136A Eric Ebron RC .50 1.25
136B E.Ebron SP ball rght hand .75 2.00
137 Greg Robinson RC .40 1.00
138 Ha Ha Clinton-Dix RC .50 1.25
139 Isaiah Crowell RC .50 1.25
140A Jace Amaro RC .40 1.00
140B J.Amaro SP ball lft hand .60 1.50
141 Jackson Jeffcoat RC .50 1.25
142A Jadeveon Clowney RC .50 1.25
142B J.Clowney SP running .75 2.00
143 Jake Matthews RC .40 1.00
144 Jalen Saunders RC .40 1.00
145 James White RC .75 2.00
146 James Wilder Jr. RC .50 1.25
147 Jared Abbrederis RC .40 1.00
148A Jarvis Landry RC .75 2.00
148B J.Landry SP ball by thigh 1.25 3.00
149 Jason Verrett RC .40 1.00
150 Jeremy Hill RC .50 1.25
151 Jerick McKinnon RC .50 1.25
152 Jimmy Garoppolo RC 3.00 8.00
153A Johnny Manziel RC .60 1.50
153B J.Manziel SP step back pose 1.00 2.50
154A Jordan Matthews RC .60 1.50
154B J.Matthews SP catch pose 1.00 2.50
155 Josh Huff RC .50 1.25
156A Ka'Deem Carey RC .40 1.00
156B K.Carey SP rght hand by leg .60 1.50
157A Kelvin Benjamin RC .60 1.50
157B K.Benjamin SP ball by side 1.00 2.50
158A Khalil Mack RC 1.50 4.00
158B K.Mack SP left knee up 2.50 6.00
159 Kony Ealy RC .50 1.25
160 Kyle Fuller RC .40 1.00
161 Kyle Van Noy RC .50 1.25
162 Lache Seastrunk RC .40 1.00
163 Lamarcus Joyner RC .50 1.25
164 L'Damian Washington RC .50 1.25
165A Logan Thomas RC .40 1.00
165B L.Thomas SP throwing pose .60 1.50
166 Louis Nix III RC .40 1.00
167 Marcus Roberson RC .50 1.25
168 Marcus Smith RC .40 1.00
169 Marion Grice RC .40 1.00
170A Marqise Lee RC .50 1.25
170B M.Lee SP ball covers face .75 2.00
171 Martavis Bryant RC .50 1.25
172 Michael Campanaro RC .40 1.00
173 Michael Sam RC .40 1.00
174 Mike Davis RC .40 1.00
175A Mike Evans RC 1.00 2.50
175B M.Evans SP ball not cut off 1.50 4.00
176A Odell Beckham Jr. RC 1.00 2.50
176B Beckham SP one hand catch 1.50 4.00
177A Paul Richardson RC .50 1.25
177B P.Richardson SP catch pose .75 2.00
178 Ra'Shede Hageman RC .40 1.00
179 Ryan Shazier RC .60 1.50
180A Sammy Watkins RC .60 1.50
180B S.Watkins SP catch pose 1.00 2.50
181 Scott Crichton RC .40 1.00
182 Shaq Evans RC .40 1.00
183 Shayne Skov RC .40 1.00
184 Stephon Tuitt RC .60 1.50
185 Storm Johnson RC .40 1.00
186 Tajh Boyd RC .40 1.00
187 Taylor Lewan RC .40 1.00
188A Teddy Bridgewater RC .60 1.50
188B T.Bridgewater SP pass pose) 1.00 2.50
189 Telvin Smith RC .40 1.00
190 Terrance West RC .40 1.00
191 Tevin Reese RC .40 1.00
192 Timmy Jernigan RC .40 1.00
193A Tom Savage RC .40 1.00
193B T.Savage SP step back pose .60 1.50
194A Tre Mason RC .40 1.00
194B T.Mason SP run pose .60 1.50
195 Trent Murphy RC .40 1.00
196 Troy Niklas RC .40 1.00
197 Xavier Su'A-Filo RC .50 1.25
198 Yawin Smallwood RC .40 1.00
199 Zach Mettenberger RC .40 1.00
200 Zack Martin RC .50 1.25

2014 Rookies and Stars Longevity Parallel

*1-100 VETS: 1X TO 2.5X BASIC R&S
*101-200 ROOKIES: .6X TO 1.5X BASIC R&S

2014 Rookies and Stars Longevity Black Parallel

*1-100 VETS/25: 6X TO 15X BASIC R&S
*101-200 ROOKIES/25: 3X TO 8X BASIC R&S
LONGEVITY BLACK PRINT RUN 10

2014 Rookies and Stars Longevity Gold Parallel

*1-100 VETS/49: 3X TO 8X BASIC CARDS
*101-200 ROOKIES/49: 1.5X TO 4X BASIC RC

2014 Rookies and Stars Longevity Holofoil Parallel

*1-100 VETS/99: 2.5X TO 6X BASIC R&S
*101-200 ROOKIES/99: 1.2X TO 3X BASIC R&S

2014 Rookies and Stars Longevity Platinum Parallel

*1-100 VETS/25: 4X TO 10X BASIC R&S
*101-200 ROOKIES/25: 2X TO 5X BASIC R&S

2014 Rookies and Stars AKA Stars

1 Calvin Johnson 10.00 25.00
2 Marshawn Lynch 5.00 12.00
3 Peyton Manning 12.00 30.00
4 Adrian Peterson 6.00 15.00
5 Johnny Manziel 2.50 6.00
6 Ben Roethlisberger 6.00 15.00
7 Drew Brees 6.00 15.00
8 B.J. Raji 4.00 10.00
9 Rob Gronkowski 6.00 15.00
10 De'Anthony Thomas 1.50 4.00
11 Kam Chancellor 6.00 15.00
12 Andre Johnson 5.00 12.00
13 Darrelle Revis 4.00 10.00
14 Robert Griffin III 4.00 10.00
15 Darren McFadden 4.00 10.00
16 Richard Sherman 10.00 25.00
17 Tom Brady 15.00 40.00
18 Matt Ryan 5.00 12.00
19 Tyrann Mathieu 5.00 12.00
20 Doug Martin 5.00 12.00

2014 Rookies and Stars Cross Training Materials

*PRIME/25: .8X TO 2X BASIC JSY
CTAR Allen Robinson 2.50 6.00
CTBC Brandin Cooks 2.50 6.00
CTBS Bishop Sankey 1.50 4.00
CTCL Cody Latimer 2.00 5.00
CTCS Charles Sims 1.50 4.00
CTDA Dri Archer 1.50 4.00
CTDT De'Anthony Thomas 1.50 4.00
CTEE Eric Ebron 2.00 5.00
CTJA Jace Amaro 1.50 4.00
CTJC Jadeveon Clowney 2.00 5.00
CTJH Jeremy Hill 2.00 5.00
CTJM Johnny Manziel 2.50 6.00
CTKC Ka'Deem Carey 1.50 4.00
CTME Mike Evans 4.00 10.00
CTML Marqise Lee 2.00 5.00
CTOB Odell Beckham Jr. 4.00 10.00
CTPR Paul Richardson 2.00 5.00
CTSW Sammy Watkins 2.50 6.00
CTTB Teddy Bridgewater 2.50 6.00
CTTM Tre Mason 1.50 4.00

2014 Rookies and Stars Crusade Blue

*RED/99: .8X TO 2X BLUE
*PURPLE/49: 1X TO 2.5X BLUE
*GOLD/25: 1.2X TO 3X BLUE
1 C.J. Spiller 1.25 3.00
2 EJ Manuel 1.25 3.00
3 Knowshon Moreno 1.25 3.00
4 Ryan Tannehill 1.50 4.00
5 Tom Brady 5.00 12.00
6 Darrelle Revis 1.25 3.00
7 Geno Smith 1.25 3.00
8 Steve Smith 1.50 4.00
9 A.J. Green 2.00 5.00
10 Giovani Bernard 1.25 3.00
11 Josh Gordon 1.25 3.00
12 Joe Haden 1.25 3.00
13 Le'Veon Bell 1.50 4.00
14 Arian Foster 1.50 4.00
15 Andrew Luck 2.50 6.00
16 Justin Blackmon 1.25 3.00
17 Kendall Wright 1.25 3.00
18 Peyton Manning 4.00 10.00
19 Wes Welker 1.50 4.00
20 Jamaal Charles 1.50 4.00
21 Darren McFadden 1.25 3.00
22 Philip Rivers 2.00 5.00
23 Tony Romo 1.50 4.00
24 Dez Bryant 2.00 5.00
25 Victor Cruz 1.50 4.00
26 Eli Manning 1.50 4.00
27 Nick Foles 1.50 4.00
28 LeSean McCoy 2.00 5.00
29 Robert Griffin III 1.25 3.00
30 Alfred Morris 1.25 3.00
31 Brandon Marshall 1.25 3.00
32 Reggie Bush 1.25 3.00
33 Calvin Johnson 2.00 5.00
34 Aaron Rodgers 4.00 10.00
35 Eddie Lacy 1.25 3.00
36 Keenan Allen 1.50 4.00
37 Adrian Peterson 2.00 5.00
38 Julio Jones 2.00 5.00
39 Cam Newton 2.00 5.00
40 Drew Brees 2.00 5.00
41 Jimmy Graham 2.00 5.00
42 Doug Martin 1.50 4.00
43 Josh McCown 1.25 3.00
44 Patrick Peterson 1.25 3.00
45 Zac Stacy 1.25 3.00
46 Colin Kaepernick 1.50 4.00
47 Anquan Boldin 1.25 3.00
48 Russell Wilson 3.00 8.00
49 Richard Sherman 2.00 5.00
50 Trent Richardson 1.25 3.00

2014 Rookies and Stars Draft Class

1 Jadeveon Clowney .60 1.50
2 Greg Robinson .50 1.25
3 Blake Bortles .60 1.50
4 Sammy Watkins .75 2.00
5 Khalil Mack 2.00 5.00
6 Jake Matthews .50 1.25
7 Mike Evans 1.25 3.00
8 Justin Gilbert .50 1.25
9 Anthony Barr .50 1.25
10 Eric Ebron .60 1.50
11 Taylor Lewan .50 1.25
12 Odell Beckham Jr. 1.25 3.00
13 Aaron Donald 1.25 3.00
14 Kyle Fuller .50 1.25
15 Ryan Shazier .75 2.00
16 Zack Martin .60 1.50
17 C.J. Mosley .60 1.50
18 Calvin Pryor .50 1.25
19 Ja'Wuan James .50 1.25
20 Brandin Cooks .75 2.00
21 Ha Ha Clinton-Dix .60 1.50
22 Johnny Manziel .75 2.00
23 Dee Ford .50 1.25
24 Darqueze Dennard .60 1.50
25 Jason Verrett .50 1.25

2014 Rookies and Stars Pro Bowl

1 Drew Brees 1.50 4.00
2 Alex Smith 1.25 3.00
3 Josh Gordon 1.00 2.50
4 Alshon Jeffery 1.25 3.00
5 Brandon Marshall 1.00 2.50
6 Jimmy Graham 1.50 4.00
7 LeSean McCoy 1.50 4.00
8 DeMarco Murray 1.25 3.00
9 Tyron Smith 1.00 2.50
10 Ryan Kalil 1.00 2.50
11 Robert Quinn 1.25 3.00
12 Vontaze Burfict 1.00 2.50
13 Brandon Flowers 1.00 2.50
14 Eric Reid 1.25 3.00
15 Andrew Luck 2.00 5.00
16 Cam Newton 1.50 4.00
17 Dez Bryant 1.50 4.00
18 A.J. Green 1.50 4.00
19 Jordan Cameron 1.00 2.50
20 Eddie Lacy 1.00 2.50
21 Jamaal Charles 1.25 3.00
22 J.J. Watt 1.50 4.00
23 Luke Kuechly 1.25 3.00
24 Patrick Peterson 1.00 2.50
25 Cordarrelle Patterson 1.00 2.50

2014 Rookies and Stars Rookie Crusade Blue

*GOLD/25: 2X TO 5X BASIC INSERTS
*PURPLE/49: 1.2X TO 3X BASIC INSERTS
*RED/99: .8X TO 2X BASIC INSERTS
1 A.J. McCarron .60 1.50
2 Aaron Murray .60 1.50
3 Allen Robinson 1.00 2.50
4 Andre Williams .60 1.50
5 Austin Seferian-Jenkins .60 1.50
6 Bishop Sankey .60 1.50
7 Blake Bortles .75 2.00
8 Brandin Cooks 1.00 2.50
9 De'Anthony Thomas .60 1.50
10 Carlos Hyde .75 2.00
11 Charles Sims .60 1.50
12 Davante Adams 1.00 2.50
13 Logan Thomas .60 1.50
14 Derek Carr 4.00 10.00
15 Devonta Freeman 1.00 2.50
16 Donte Moncrief .60 1.50
17 Eric Ebron .75 2.00
18 Jace Amaro .60 1.50
19 Jadeveon Clowney .75 2.00
20 Jarvis Landry 1.25 3.00
21 Jeremy Hill .75 2.00
22 Michael Sam .60 1.50
23 Jimmy Garoppolo 5.00 12.00
24 Johnny Manziel 1.00 2.50
25 Jordan Matthews 1.00 2.50
26 Ka'Deem Carey .60 1.50
27 Kelvin Benjamin 1.00 2.50
28 Cody Latimer .75 2.00
29 Marqise Lee .75 2.00
30 Dri Archer .60 1.50
31 Mike Evans 1.25 3.00
32 Odell Beckham Jr. 1.50 4.00
33 Paul Richardson .75 2.00
34 Khalil Mack 2.50 6.00
35 Sammy Watkins 1.00 2.50
36 Teddy Bridgewater 1.00 2.50
37 Terrance West .60 1.50
38 Tre Mason .60 1.50
39 Tajh Boyd .60 1.50
40 Tom Savage .60 1.50
41 Lache Seastrunk .60 1.50
42 Zach Mettenberger .60 1.50
43 Bruce Ellington .60 1.50
44 David Fales .60 1.50
45 Jerick McKinnon .75 2.00
46 Martavis Bryant .75 2.00
47 Robert Herron .60 1.50
48 Tyler Gaffney .60 1.50
49 Justin Gilbert .60 1.50
50 Anthony Barr .60 1.50

2014 Rookies and Stars Rookie Jersey Autographs

*HOLOFOIL/99: .5X TO 1.2X BASIC AU/299
*HOLOFOIL/75: .4X TO 1X BASIC AU/99
*HOLOFOIL/49: .6X TO 1.5X BASIC AU/299
*HOLOFOIL/49: .5X TO 1.2X BASIC AU/75-99
*GOLD/49: .6X TO 1.5X BASIC AU/299
*GOLD/49: .5X TO 1.2X BASIC AU/99
*GOLD/25: .8X TO 2X BASIC AU/299
*GOLD/25: .6X TO 1.5X BASIC AU/75-125
*SAPPHIRE/25: .8X TO 2X BASIC AU/299
*SAPPHIRE/25: .6X TO 1.5X BASIC AU/75-125
*RUBY/75-99: .5X TO 1.2X BASIC AU/299
*RUBY/99: .4X TO 1X BASIC AU/75-99
*RUBY/50: .6X TO 1.5X BASIC AU/299
*RUBY/50: .5X TO 1.2X BASIC AU/99-125
*RUBY/15: .6X TO 1.5X BASIC AU/99
*PLAT/15-25: .8X TO 2X BASIC AU/299
*PLAT/15-25: .6X TO 1.5X BASIC AU/75-125
RMAM A.J. McCarron/75 4.00 10.00
RMAMU Aaron Murray/299 3.00 8.00
RMAR Allen Robinson/99 6.00 15.00
RMAS Austin Seferian-Jenkins/99 4.00 10.00
RMAW Andre Williams/99 4.00 10.00
RMBB Blake Bortles/99 5.00 12.00
RMBC Brandin Cooks/99 6.00 15.00
RMBS Bishop Sankey/299 3.00 8.00
RMCH Carlos Hyde/299 4.00 10.00
RMCL Cody Latimer/299 4.00 10.00
RMCS Connor Shaw/299 3.00 8.00
RMCSI Charles Sims/99 4.00 10.00
RMDA Dri Archer/299 3.00 8.00
RMDC Derek Carr/75 25.00 60.00
RMDF Devonta Freeman/99 6.00 15.00
RMDM Donte Moncrief/299 3.00 8.00
RMDT De'Anthony Thomas/299 3.00 8.00
RMEE Eric Ebron/99 5.00 12.00
RMJA Jace Amaro/299 3.00 8.00
RMJC Jadeveon Clowney/75 5.00 12.00
RMJG Jimmy Garoppolo/75 50.00 100.00
RMJH Jeremy Hill/299 4.00 10.00
RMJL Jarvis Landry/299 8.00 20.00
RMJM Johnny Manziel/99 6.00 15.00
RMJMA Jordan Matthews/299 5.00 12.00
RMKB Kelvin Benjamin/99 6.00 15.00
RMKC Ka'Deem Carey/299 3.00 8.00
RMKM Khalil Mack/299 15.00 40.00
RMLT Logan Thomas/299 3.00 8.00
RMME Mike Evans/299 8.00 20.00
RMML Marqise Lee/99 5.00 12.00
RMOB Odell Beckham Jr./299 30.00 60.00
RMPR Paul Richardson/99 8.00 20.00
RMSW Sammy Watkins/299 5.00 12.00
RMTB Tajh Boyd/99 4.00 10.00
RMTBR Teddy Bridgewater/125 6.00 15.00
RMTS Tom Savage/299 3.00 8.00
RMTW Terrance West/299 3.00 8.00

2014 Rookies and Stars Rookie Materials

*LONGEVITY/299: .5X TO 1.2X BASIC INSERTS
*HOLOFOIL/99: .6X TO 1.5X BASIC INSERTS
*GOLD/49: .8X TO 2X BASIC INSERTS
*PLATINUM/25: 1X TO 2.5X BASIC INSERTS
*LOGO/32: 1X TO 2.5X BASIC INSERTS
*LONG.RUBY/299: .5X TO 1.2X BASIC JSY
*LONG.SAPP/25: 1X TO 2.5X BASIC JSY
*LONG.BLACK/10: 1.5X TO 4X BASIC JSY
*TEAM GOLD/10: 1.5X TO 4X BASIC JSY
RMAJM A.J. McCarron 1.25 3.00
RMAM Aaron Murray 1.25 3.00
RMAR Allen Robinson 2.00 5.00
RMASJ Austin Seferian-Jenkins 1.25 3.00
RMAW Andre Williams 1.25 3.00
RMBB Blake Bortles 1.50 4.00
RMBC Brandin Cooks 2.00 5.00
RMBS Bishop Sankey 1.25 3.00
RMCH Carlos Hyde 1.50 4.00
RMCL Cody Latimer 1.50 4.00
RMCS Connor Shaw 1.25 3.00
RMCSI Charles Sims 1.25 3.00
RMDA Davante Adams 2.00 5.00
RMDAR Dri Archer 1.25 3.00
RMDC Derek Carr 8.00 20.00
RMDF Devonta Freeman 2.00 5.00
RMDM Donte Moncrief 1.25 3.00
RMDT De'Anthony Thomas 1.25 3.00
RMEE Eric Ebron 1.50 4.00
RMJA Jace Amaro 1.25 3.00
RMJC Jadeveon Clowney 1.50 4.00
RMJG Jimmy Garoppolo 10.00 25.00
RMJH Jeremy Hill 1.50 4.00
RMJL Jarvis Landry 2.50 6.00
RMJM Johnny Manziel 2.00 5.00
RMJMA Jordan Matthews 2.00 5.00
RMKB Kelvin Benjamin 2.00 5.00
RMKC Ka'Deem Carey 1.25 3.00
RMKM Khalil Mack 5.00 12.00
RMLT Logan Thomas 1.25 3.00
RMME Mike Evans 3.00 8.00
RMML Marqise Lee 1.50 4.00
RMOB Odell Beckham Jr. 3.00 8.00
RMPR Paul Richardson 1.50 4.00
RMSW Sammy Watkins 2.00 5.00
RMTB Tajh Boyd 1.25 3.00
RMTBR Teddy Bridgewater 2.00 5.00
RMTM Tre Mason 1.25 3.00
RMTS Tom Savage 1.25 3.00
RMTW Terrance West 1.25 3.00

2014 Rookies and Stars Rookie Premiere Slideshow Signatures

1 A.J. McCarron/99 6.00 15.00
2 Aaron Murray/100 6.00 15.00
3 Allen Robinson/100 10.00 25.00
4 Andre Williams/100 6.00 15.00
5 Austin Seferian-Jenkins/99 6.00 15.00
6 Bishop Sankey/99 6.00 15.00
7 Blake Bortles/100 8.00 20.00
8 Brandin Cooks/100 10.00 25.00
9 De'Anthony Thomas/99 6.00 15.00
10 Carlos Hyde/100 8.00 20.00
11 Charles Sims/100 6.00 15.00
12 Davante Adams/99 10.00 25.00
13 Logan Thomas/100 6.00 15.00
14 Derek Carr/100 30.00 60.00
15 Devonta Freeman/98 10.00 25.00
16 Donte Moncrief/100 6.00 15.00
17 Eric Ebron/100 8.00 20.00
18 Jace Amaro/100 6.00 15.00
19 Jadeveon Clowney/100 8.00 20.00
20 Jarvis Landry/100 12.00 30.00
21 Jeremy Hill/100 8.00 20.00
23 Jimmy Garoppolo/100 50.00 125.00
24 Johnny Manziel/99 10.00 25.00
25 Jordan Matthews/100 10.00 25.00
26 Ka'Deem Carey/100 6.00 15.00
27 Kelvin Benjamin/100 10.00 25.00
28 Cody Latimer/100 8.00 20.00
29 Marqise Lee/100 8.00 20.00
30 Dri Archer/99 6.00 15.00
31 Mike Evans/100 12.00 30.00
32 Odell Beckham Jr./98 30.00 60.00
33 Paul Richardson/100 12.00 30.00
34 Khalil Mack/100 15.00 40.00
35 Sammy Watkins/100 20.00 50.00
36 Teddy Bridgewater/100 10.00 25.00
37 Terrance West/100 6.00 15.00
38 Tre Mason/100 6.00 15.00
39 Tajh Boyd/93 6.00 15.00
40 Tom Savage/100 6.00 15.00

2014 Rookies and Stars Slideshow

1 A.J. McCarron 3.00 8.00
2 Aaron Murray 3.00 8.00
3 Allen Robinson 5.00 12.00
4 Andre Williams 3.00 8.00
5 Austin Seferian-Jenkins 3.00 8.00
6 Bishop Sankey 3.00 8.00
7 Blake Bortles 4.00 10.00
8 Brandin Cooks 5.00 12.00
9 De'Anthony Thomas 3.00 8.00
10 Carlos Hyde 4.00 10.00
11 Charles Sims 3.00 8.00
12 Davante Adams 5.00 12.00
13 Logan Thomas 3.00 8.00
14 Derek Carr 20.00 50.00
15 Devonta Freeman 5.00 12.00
16 Donte Moncrief 3.00 8.00
17 Eric Ebron 4.00 10.00
18 Jace Amaro 3.00 8.00
19 Jadeveon Clowney 4.00 10.00
20 Jarvis Landry 6.00 15.00
21 Jeremy Hill 4.00 10.00
22 Connor Shaw 3.00 8.00
23 Jimmy Garoppolo 25.00 60.00
24 Johnny Manziel 5.00 12.00
25 Jordan Matthews 5.00 12.00
26 Ka'Deem Carey 3.00 8.00
27 Kelvin Benjamin 5.00 12.00
28 Cody Latimer 4.00 10.00
29 Marqise Lee 4.00 10.00
30 Dri Archer 3.00 8.00
31 Mike Evans 8.00 20.00
32 Odell Beckham Jr. 8.00 20.00
33 Paul Richardson 4.00 10.00
34 Khalil Mack 12.00 30.00
35 Sammy Watkins 5.00 12.00
36 Teddy Bridgewater 5.00 12.00
37 Terrance West 3.00 8.00
38 Tre Mason 3.00 8.00
39 Tajh Boyd 3.00 8.00
40 Tom Savage 3.00 8.00

2014 Rookies and Stars Super Bowl

1 Peyton Manning 3.00 8.00
2 Knowshon Moreno 1.00 2.50
3 Eric Decker 1.00 2.50
4 Demaryius Thomas 1.25 3.00
5 Wes Welker 1.25 3.00
6 Julius Thomas 1.00 2.50
7 Sylvester Williams 1.00 2.50
8 Danny Trevathan 1.00 2.50
9 Champ Bailey 1.25 3.00
10 D.Rodgers-Cromartie 1.00 2.50
11 Montee Ball 1.00 2.50
12 Trindon Holliday 1.00 2.50
13 Russell Wilson 2.50 6.00
14 Marshawn Lynch 1.25 3.00
15 Doug Baldwin 1.25 3.00
16 Percy Harvin 1.00 2.50
17 Golden Tate 1.25 3.00
18 Russell Okung 1.00 2.50
19 Bruce Irvin 1.00 2.50
20 Malcolm Smith 1.50 4.00
21 Byron Maxwell 2.00 5.00
22 Bobby Wagner 1.00 2.50
23 Richard Sherman 1.50 4.00
24 Kam Chancellor 1.50 4.00
25 Earl Thomas 1.25 3.00

2010 Rookies and Stars Longevity

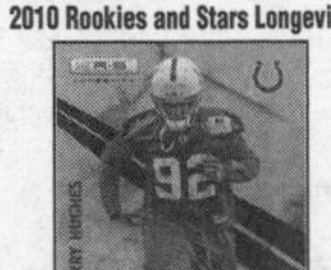

COMP.SET w/o RC's (150) 8.00 20.00
*VETS 1-150: .4X TO 1X BASIC R&S
*ELE 151-165: .25X TO .6X BASIC R&S
*ROOKIES 166-250: .4X TO 1X BASIC R&S
251-300 UNPRICED ROOK.AU PRINT RUN 10
1 Chris Wells .20 .50
2 Larry Fitzgerald .25 .60
3 Matt Leinart .20 .50
4 Steve Breaston .20 .50
5 Matt Ryan .25 .60
6 Michael Turner .20 .50
7 Roddy White .20 .50
8 Tony Gonzalez .25 .60
9 Anquan Boldin .20 .50
10 Derrick Mason .20 .50
11 Joe Flacco .25 .60
12 Ray Rice .20 .50
13 Todd Heap .20 .50
14 Fred Jackson .25 .60
15 Lee Evans .25 .60
16 Marshawn Lynch .25 .60
17 Ryan Fitzpatrick .20 .50
18 DeAngelo Williams .20 .50
19 Jonathan Stewart .20 .50
20 Matt Moore .20 .50
21 Steve Smith .25 .60
22 Brian Urlacher .30 .75
23 Devin Hester .25 .60
24 Greg Olsen .25 .60
25 Jay Cutler .20 .50
26 Matt Forte .20 .50
27 Andre Caldwell .20 .50
28 Antonio Bryant .20 .50
29 Carson Palmer .25 .60
30 Cedric Benson .20 .50
31 Chad Ochocinco .20 .50
32 Ben Watson .20 .50
33 Jake Delhomme .20 .50
34 Jerome Harrison .20 .50
35 Josh Cribbs .20 .50
36 Mohamed Massaquoi .25 .60
37 Felix Jones .20 .50
38 Jason Witten .25 .60
39 Marion Barber .25 .60
40 Miles Austin .20 .50
41 Tony Romo .25 .60
42 Brandon Marshall .25 .60
43 Eddie Royal .20 .50
44 Jabar Gaffney .20 .50
45 Knowshon Moreno .20 .50
46 Kyle Orton .20 .50
47 Brandon Pettigrew .20 .50
48 Calvin Johnson .30 .75
49 Matthew Stafford .25 .60
50 Nate Burleson .20 .50
51 Aaron Rodgers .60 1.50
52 Donald Driver .25 .60
53 Greg Jennings .20 .50
54 Jermichael Finley .20 .50
55 Ryan Grant .25 .60
56 Andre Johnson .25 .60
57 Kevin Walter .25 .60
58 Matt Schaub .20 .50
59 Owen Daniels .20 .50
60 Steve Slaton .20 .50
61 Pierre Garcon .25 .60
62 Dallas Clark .20 .50
63 Joseph Addai .20 .50
64 Peyton Manning .75 2.00
65 Reggie Wayne .25 .60
66 David Garrard .20 .50
67 Maurice Jones-Drew .20 .50
68 Mike Sims-Walker .20 .50
69 Mike Thomas .25 .60
70 Torry Holt .25 .60
71 Chris Chambers .20 .50
72 Dwayne Bowe .25 .60
73 Jamaal Charles .25 .60
74 Matt Cassel .20 .50
75 Thomas Jones .20 .50
76 Brian Hartline .25 .60
77 Chad Henne .25 .60
78 Davone Bess .20 .50
79 Greg Camarillo .20 .50
80 Ronnie Brown .20 .50
81 Adrian Peterson .30 .75
82 Brett Favre .60 1.50
83 Percy Harvin .20 .50
84 Sidney Rice .20 .50
85 Visanthe Shiancoe .25 .60
86 Laurence Maroney .20 .50
87 Randy Moss .25 .60
88 Tom Brady .75 2.00
89 Wes Welker .25 .60
90 Devery Henderson .20 .50
91 Drew Brees .30 .75
92 Jeremy Shockey .20 .50
93 Marques Colston .20 .50
94 Pierre Thomas .20 .50
95 Brandon Jacobs .20 .50
96 Eli Manning .25 .60
97 Hakeem Nicks .20 .50
98 Kevin Boss .20 .50
99 Steve Smith USC .20 .50
100 Braylon Edwards .20 .50
101 Jerricho Cotchery .20 .50
102 LaDainian Tomlinson .30 .75
103 Mark Sanchez .20 .50
104 Shonn Greene .20 .50
105 Chaz Schilens .20 .50
106 Darren McFadden .20 .50
107 Jason Campbell .20 .50
108 Louis Murphy .20 .50
109 Zach Miller .20 .50
110 Brent Celek .20 .50
111 DeSean Jackson .25 .60
112 Jeremy Maclin .20 .50
113 Kevin Kolb .20 .50
114 LeSean McCoy .30 .75
115 Ben Roethlisberger .30 .75
116 Heath Miller .20 .50
117 Rashard Mendenhall .20 .50
118 Santonio Holmes .20 .50
119 Troy Polamalu .30 .75
120 Antonio Gates .25 .60
121 Darren Sproles .25 .60
122 Philip Rivers .30 .75
123 Vincent Jackson .20 .50
124 Alex Smith QB .25 .60
125 Frank Gore .25 .60
126 Josh Morgan .25 .60
127 Michael Crabtree .20 .50
128 Vernon Davis .20 .50
129 Deion Branch .20 .50
130 John Carlson .20 .50
131 Julius Jones .20 .50
132 Matt Hasselbeck .20 .50
133 T.J. Houshmandzadeh .20 .50
134 Danny Amendola .30 .75
135 Donnie Avery .20 .50
136 James Laurinaitis .25 .60
137 Steven Jackson .20 .50
138 Cadillac Williams .20 .50
139 Josh Freeman .25 .60
140 Kellen Winslow Jr. .20 .50
141 Sammie Stroughter .20 .50
142 Bo Scaife .20 .50
143 Chris Johnson .20 .50
144 Kenny Britt .20 .50
145 Vince Young .20 .50
146 Chris Cooley .20 .50
147 Clinton Portis .20 .50
148 Donovan McNabb .25 .60
149 Larry Johnson .20 .50
150 Santana Moss .25 .60
151 Dallas Clark ELE .50 1.25
152 Peyton Manning ELE 2.00 5.00
153 Lee Evans ELE .60 1.50
154 David Garrard ELE .50 1.25
155 Derrick Mason ELE .50 1.25
156 Calvin Johnson ELE .75 2.00
157 Joe Flacco ELE .60 1.50
158 Vince Young ELE .50 1.25
159 Chris Johnson ELE .50 1.25
160 Tom Brady ELE 2.00 5.00
161 Wes Welker ELE .60 1.50
162 Ryan Fitzpatrick ELE .50 1.25
163 Fred Jackson ELE .60 1.50
164 Laurence Maroney ELE .50 1.25
165 Randy Moss ELE .60 1.50
166 A.J. Edds RC 1.25 3.00
167 Alterraun Verner RC 1.25 3.00
168 Amari Spievey RC 1.00 2.50
169 Andre Anderson RC 1.00 2.50
170 Andre Dixon RC 1.50 4.00
171 Anthony Davis RC 1.25 3.00
172 Anthony Dixon RC 1.00 2.50
173 Antonio Brown RC 8.00 20.00
174 Blair White RC 1.00 2.50
175 Brandon Ghee RC 1.00 2.50
176 Brandon Graham RC 1.25 3.00
177 Brian Price RC 1.00 2.50
178 Bryan Bulaga RC 1.00 2.50
179 Chad Jones RC 1.00 2.50
180 Charles Scott RC 1.00 2.50
181 Chris Cook RC 1.00 2.50
182 Chris McGaha RC 1.00 2.50
183 Corey Wootton RC 1.00 2.50
184 Dan Williams RC 1.00 2.50
185 Darrell Stuckey RC 1.00 2.50
186 Darryl Sharpton RC 1.00 2.50
187 Daryl Washington RC 1.00 2.50
188 David Gettis RC 1.00 2.50
189 Dennis Pitta RC 1.00 2.50
190 Devin McCourty RC 1.25 3.00
191 Dominique Franks RC 1.00 2.50
192 Donald Butler RC 1.00 2.50
193 Ed Dickson RC 1.00 2.50
194 Eric Norwood RC 1.25 3.00
195 Everson Griffen RC 1.00 2.50
196 Freddie Barnes RC 1.00 2.50
197 Garrett Graham RC 1.00 2.50
198 James Starks RC 1.25 3.00
199 Jared Odrick RC 1.25 3.00
200 Jarrett Brown RC 1.00 2.50
201 Jason Pierre-Paul RC 1.50 4.00
202 Jason Worilds RC 1.00 2.50
203 Javier Arenas RC 1.00 2.50
204 Jeremy Williams RC 1.00 2.50
205 Jermaine Cunningham RC 1.00 2.50
206 Jerome Murphy RC 1.25 3.00
207 Jerry Hughes RC 1.00 2.50
208 Jevan Snead RC 1.00 2.50
209 Jimmy Graham RC 2.50 6.00
210 Joique Bell RC 1.00 2.50
211 Kareem Jackson RC 1.00 2.50
212 Kevin Thomas RC 1.25 3.00
213 Koa Misi RC 1.25 3.00
214 Kyle Wilson RC 1.00 2.50
215 Lamarr Houston RC 1.25 3.00
216 LeGarrette Blount RC 2.00 5.00
217 Linval Joseph RC 1.00 2.50
218 Lonyae Miller RC 1.25 3.00
219 Major Wright RC 1.00 2.50
220 Maurkice Pouncey RC 1.25 3.00
221 Mike Hoomanawanui RC 1.50 4.00
222 Mike Iupati RC 1.50 4.00
223 Morgan Burnett RC 1.25 3.00
224 Myron Lewis RC 1.25 3.00
225 Nate Allen RC 1.50 4.00
226 NaVorro Bowman RC 2.00 5.00
227 Pat Angerer RC 1.00 2.50
228 Pat Paschall RC 1.00 2.50
229 Patrick Robinson RC 1.25 3.00
230 Perrish Cox RC 1.25 3.00
231 Perry Riley RC 1.25 3.00
232 Rennie Curran RC 1.00 2.50
233 Riley Cooper RC 1.00 2.50
234 Roddrick Muckelroy RC 1.00 2.50
235 Russell Okung RC 1.00 2.50
236 Sean Canfield RC 1.00 2.50
237 Sean Lee RC 2.00 5.00
238 Sean Weatherspoon RC 1.00 2.50
239 Sergio Kindle RC 1.00 2.50
240 Seyi Ajirotutu RC 1.00 2.50
241 T.J. Ward RC 1.50 4.00
242 Thaddeus Gibson RC 1.25 3.00
243 Tony Moeaki RC 1.25 3.00
244 Tony Pike RC 1.00 2.50
245 Torell Troup RC 1.00 2.50
246 Trent Williams RC 1.25 3.00
247 Trevard Lindley RC 1.00 2.50
248 Tyson Alualu RC 1.00 2.50
249 Walter Thurmond RC 1.00 2.50
250 Zac Robinson RC 1.25 3.00

2015 Rookies and Stars

*1-100 VETS: .4X TO 1X LONGEVITY
*101-200 ROOKIES: .4X TO 1X LONGEVITY

2015 Rookies and Stars Gold

*1-100 VETS/25: 4X TO 10X BASIC R&S
*101-200 ROOKIES/25: 2X TO 5X BASIC R&S

2010 Rookies and Stars Longevity Ruby

*VETS 1-150: 3X TO 8X BASIC R&S
*ELE 151-165: .8X TO 2X BASIC R&S

*ROOKIES 166-250: 1X TO 2.5X BASIC R&S
LONGEVITY RUBY PRINT RUN 100

2010 Rookies and Stars Longevity Sapphire

*VETS 1-150: 4X TO 10X BASIC R&S
*ELE 151-165: 1X TO 2.5X BASIC R&S
*ROOKIES 166-250: 1.2X TO 3X BASIC R&S
LONGEVITY SAPPHIRE PRINT RUN 50

2015 Rookies and Stars Purple

*1-100 VETS/99: 2.5X TO 6X BASIC R&S
*101-200 ROOKIES/99: 1.2X TO 3X BASIC R&S

2015 Rookies and Stars Sapphire

*1-100 VETS: .8X TO 2X BASIC R&S
*101-200 ROOKIES: .6X TO 1.5X BASIC R&S

2015 Rookies and Stars Crusade Blue

*RED/99: .8X TO 2X BLUE
*PURPLE/49: 1X TO 2.5X BLUE
*GOLD/25: 1.2X TO 3X BLUE
1 Cam Newton 2.00 5.00
2 Matt Ryan 1.50 4.00
3 Russell Wilson 2.50 6.00
4 Derek Carr 2.00 5.00
5 Teddy Bridgewater 1.50 4.00
6 Jay Cutler 1.25 3.00
7 Colin Kaepernick 1.50 4.00
8 Blake Bortles 1.25 3.00
9 Tony Romo 1.50 4.00
10 Eli Manning 1.50 4.00
11 Larry Fitzgerald 1.50 4.00
12 Andrew Luck 2.50 6.00
13 Odell Beckham Jr. 2.00 5.00
14 Andy Dalton 1.50 4.00
15 Justin Houston 1.25 3.00
16 DeSean Jackson 1.50 4.00
17 Ryan Tannehill 1.50 4.00
18 Peyton Manning 4.00 10.00
19 T.Y. Hilton 1.50 4.00
20 Jordy Nelson 1.50 4.00
21 Tom Brady 5.00 12.00
22 Demaryius Thomas 1.50 4.00
23 Arian Foster 1.50 4.00
24 Marshawn Lynch 1.50 4.00
25 Philip Rivers 2.00 5.00
26 Terry Bradshaw 2.50 6.00
27 Brett Favre 4.00 10.00
28 Adrian Peterson 2.00 5.00
29 Jordan Matthews 1.50 4.00
30 Joe Montana 5.00 12.00
31 Justin Forsett 1.50 4.00
32 Jeremy Hill 1.25 3.00
33 Carson Palmer 1.50 4.00
34 Drew Brees 2.00 5.00
35 Luke Kuechly 1.50 4.00
36 Ben Roethlisberger 2.00 5.00
37 Jamaal Charles 1.50 4.00
38 Rob Gronkowski 2.00 5.00
39 Tashaun Gipson 1.50 4.00
40 Matthew Stafford 1.50 4.00
41 Mark Ingram 1.50 4.00
42 Joe Namath 2.50 6.00
43 Mike Evans 1.50 4.00
44 Tre Mason 1.50 4.00
45 Delanie Walker 1.25 3.00
46 Dez Bryant 2.00 5.00
47 Aaron Rodgers 4.00 10.00
48 Mario Williams 1.25 3.00
49 Calvin Johnson 2.00 5.00
50 J.J. Watt 2.00 5.00

2015 Rookies and Stars Crusade Dual

*RED/99: .6X TO 1.5X BASIC INSERTS
*PURPLE/49: .8X TO 2X BASIC INSERTS
*GOLD/25: 1.2X TO 3X BASIC INSERTS
1 J.Winston/A.Luck 2.00 5.00
2 M.Mariota/R.Griffin 3.00 8.00
3 A.Cooper/D.Carr 2.50 6.00
4 M.Faulk/T.Gurley 3.00 8.00
5 L.Tomlinson/M.Gordon 2.00 5.00
6 T.Yeldon/B.Bortles .75 2.00
7 B.Sanders/A.Abdullah 2.00 5.00
8 A.Jeffery/K.White 1.00 2.50
9 A.Rodgers/B.Hundley 6.00 15.00
10 J.Watt/L.Williams 1.25 3.00

2015 Rookies and Stars Crusade Rookies

*RED/99: .8X TO 2X BASIC INSERTS
*PURPLE/49: 1.2X TO 3X BASIC INSERTS
*GOLD/25: 2X TO 5X BASIC INSERTS
1 Jameis Winston 1.50 4.00
2 Marcus Mariota 2.50 6.00
3 Amari Cooper 2.00 5.00
4 Leonard Williams .60 1.50
5 Kevin White .75 2.00
6 Todd Gurley 2.50 6.00
7 DeVante Parker 1.00 2.50
8 Melvin Gordon 1.50 4.00
9 Nelson Agholor .75 2.00
10 Breshad Perriman .60 1.50
11 Phillip Dorsett .60 1.50
12 T.J. Yeldon .60 1.50
13 Devin Smith .60 1.50
14 Dorial Green-Beckham .60 1.50
15 Devin Funchess 1.00 2.50
16 Ameer Abdullah 1.00 2.50
17 Maxx Williams .60 1.50
18 Tyler Lockett 1.00 2.50
19 Jaelen Strong .75 2.00
20 Tevin Coleman .75 2.00
21 Garrett Grayson .60 1.50
22 Chris Conley .60 1.50
23 Duke Johnson 1.00 2.50
24 David Johnson 1.50 4.00
25 Sammie Coates .75 2.00
26 Sean Mannion .60 1.50
27 Ty Montgomery .60 1.50
28 Matt Jones .60 1.50
29 Bryce Petty .60 1.50
30 Jamison Crowder .75 2.00
31 Jeremy Langford .60 1.50
32 Justin Hardy .60 1.50
33 Vince Mayle .75 2.00
34 Buck Allen .75 2.00
35 Mike Davis .60 1.50
36 David Cobb .60 1.50
37 Rashad Greene .60 1.50
38 Stefon Diggs 1.50 4.00
39 Brett Hundley .60 1.50
40 Jay Ajayi 1.00 2.50

2015 Rookies and Stars Die Cut Rookies

*LONGEVITY: .4X TO 1X R&S INSERTS
*RED/299: .6X TO 1.5X BASIC INSERTS
*LONG RED/99: .8X TO 2X BASIC INSERTS
*PURPLE/99: 1X TO 2.5X BASIC INSERTS
*PURPLE/49: 1.2X TO 3X BASIC INSERTS
*LONG GOLD/25: 1.5X TO 4X BASIC INSERTS
*GOLD/25: 1.5X TO 4X BASIC INSERTS
1 Jameis Winston 1.50 4.00
2 Marcus Mariota 2.50 6.00
3 Melvin Gordon 1.50 4.00
4 Phillip Dorsett .60 1.50
5 Breshad Perriman .60 1.50
6 Devin Funchess 1.00 2.50
7 Todd Gurley 2.50 6.00
8 Sammie Coates .75 2.00
9 Stefon Diggs 1.50 4.00
10 Amari Cooper 2.00 5.00
11 Kevin White .75 2.00
12 Rashad Greene .60 1.50
13 Chris Conley .60 1.50
14 Ameer Abdullah 1.00 2.50
15 Tyler Lockett 1.00 2.50
16 Tevin Coleman .75 2.00
17 Brett Hundley .60 1.50
18 Garrett Grayson .60 1.50
19 Jaelen Strong .75 2.00
20 Leonard Williams .60 1.50

2015 Rookies and Stars Die Cut Stars

*RED/299: .6X TO 1.5X BASIC INSERTS
*PURPLE/99: .8X TO 2X BASIC INSERTS
*GOLD/25: 1.2X TO 3X BASIC INSERTS
*LONGEVITY: .4X TO 1X BASIC INSERTS
*LONG RED/99: .8X TO 2X BASIC INSERTS
*LONG PURPLE/49: 1X TO 2.5X BASIC INSERTS
*LONG GOLD/25: 1.2X TO 3X BASIC INSERTS
1 Mike Evans 1.50 4.00
2 Tom Brady 5.00 12.00
3 Philip Rivers 2.00 5.00
4 Andrew Luck 2.50 6.00
5 Joe Flacco 1.50 4.00
6 Cam Newton 2.00 5.00
7 Nick Foles 1.50 4.00
8 Andy Dalton 1.50 4.00
9 Teddy Bridgewater 1.50 4.00
10 Derek Carr 2.00 5.00
11 Matt Forte 1.25 3.00
12 Blake Bortles 1.25 3.00
13 T.Y. Hilton 1.50 4.00
14 Matthew Stafford 1.50 4.00
15 Russell Wilson 2.50 6.00
16 Julio Jones 2.00 5.00
17 Aaron Rodgers 4.00 10.00
18 Drew Brees 2.00 5.00
19 Tony Romo 1.50 4.00
20 Rob Gronkowski 2.00 5.00

2015 Rookies and Stars Dress for Success Jerseys

*LONG. JSY: .4X TO 1X BASIC JSY
*TEAM NAME/99: .5X TO 1.2X BASIC JSY
*TEAM LOGO/50: .6X TO 1.5X BASIC JSY
*JSY NUMBER/25: .8X TO 2X BASIC JSY
1 Jameis Winston 8.00 20.00
2 Marcus Mariota 6.00 15.00
3 Tevin Coleman 2.00 5.00
4 Maxx Williams 1.50 4.00
5 Matt Jones 1.50 4.00
6 Mike Davis 1.50 4.00
7 Sammie Coates 2.00 5.00
8 Duke Johnson 2.50 6.00
9 Leonard Williams 1.50 4.00
10 Kevin White 5.00 12.00
11 Todd Gurley 5.00 12.00
12 Ty Montgomery 1.50 4.00
13 Stefon Diggs 4.00 10.00
14 Jay Ajayi 2.50 6.00
15 Tyler Lockett 5.00 12.00

2015 Rookies and Stars Embroidered Patches

*LONGEVITY: .4X TO 1X BASIC PATCH
1 A.Rodgers/B.Hundley 4.00 10.00
2 B.Petty/R.Griffin III 1.25 3.00
3 S.Coates/B.Roethlisberger 2.00 5.00
4 A.Abdullah/C.Johnson 2.00 5.00
5 J.Winston/P.Manning 6.00 15.00
6 A.Cooper/O.Beckham Jr. 4.00 10.00
7 M.Mariota/T.Brady 5.00 12.00
8 A.Luck/P.Dorsett 2.50 6.00
9 D.Brees/G.Grayson 2.00 5.00
10 R.Wilson/T.Lockett 2.50 6.00
11 D.Murray/T.Gurley 5.00 12.00
12 M.Gordon/A.Peterson 5.00 12.00
13 M.Ryan/T.Coleman 1.50 4.00
14 K.Williams/M.Williams 1.25 3.00
15 B.Perriman/J.Flacco 1.50 4.00
16 C.Newton/D.Funchess 2.00 5.00
17 D.Johnson/L.Fitzgerald 3.00 8.00
18 J.Cutler/K.White 5.00 12.00
19 T.Yeldon/B.Bortles 1.25 3.00
20 C.Kaepernick/M.Davis 1.50 4.00

2015 Rookies and Stars Progression

*LONGEVITY: .4X TO 1X R&S INSERTS
*RED/299: .6X TO 1.5X BASIC INSERTS
*LONG RED/99: .8X TO 2X BASIC INSERTS
*PURPLE/99: .8X TO 2X BASIC INSERTS
*LONG PURPLE/49: 1.2X TO 3X BASIC INSERTS
*GOLD/25: 2X TO 5X BASIC INSERTS
*LONG GOLD/25: 2X TO 5X BASIC INSERTS
1 David Johnson 1.50 4.00
2 Tevin Coleman .75 2.00
3 Breshad Perriman .60 1.50
4 Maxx Williams .60 1.50
5 Buck Allen .75 2.00
6 Devin Funchess 1.00 2.50
7 Kevin White .75 2.00
8 Duke Johnson 1.00 2.50
9 Ameer Abdullah 1.00 2.50
10 Brett Hundley .60 1.50
11 Jaelen Strong .75 2.00
12 Phillip Dorsett .60 1.50
13 T.J. Yeldon .60 1.50
14 Chris Conley .60 1.50
15 DeVante Parker 1.00 2.50
16 Jay Ajayi 1.00 2.50
17 Stefon Diggs 1.50 4.00
18 Garrett Grayson .60 1.50
19 Bryce Petty .60 1.50
20 Devin Smith .60 1.50
21 Amari Cooper 2.00 5.00
22 Nelson Agholor .75 2.00
23 Sammie Coates .75 2.00
24 Melvin Gordon 1.50 4.00
25 Mike Davis .60 1.50
26 Tyler Lockett 1.00 2.50
27 Todd Gurley 2.50 6.00
28 Dorial Green-Beckham .60 1.50
29 Marcus Mariota 2.50 6.00
30 Jameis Winston 1.50 4.00

2015 Rookies and Stars Rookie Jerseys

*LONGEVITY JSY: .4X TO 1X R&S JSY
*TEAM NAME/99: .5X TO 1.2X BASIC JSY
*TEAM LOGO/50: .6X TO 1.5X BASIC JSY
*PRIME/25: .8X TO 2X BASIC JSY
1 Jameis Winston 8.00 20.00
2 Marcus Mariota 6.00 15.00
3 Breshad Perriman 1.50 4.00
4 Jeremy Langford 1.50 4.00
5 David Cobb 1.50 4.00
6 Devin Funchess 2.50 6.00
7 Justin Hardy 1.50 4.00
8 Duke Johnson 2.50 6.00
9 Ameer Abdullah 2.50 6.00
10 Leonard Williams 1.50 4.00
11 Dorial Green-Beckham 1.50 4.00
12 Jaelen Strong 2.00 5.00
13 Tyler Lockett 5.00 12.00
14 Phillip Dorsett 1.50 4.00
15 Nelson Agholor 2.00 5.00
16 T.J. Yeldon 1.50 4.00
17 Devin Smith 1.50 4.00
18 Chris Conley 1.50 4.00
19 Garrett Grayson 1.50 4.00
20 DeVante Parker 2.50 6.00
21 Stefon Diggs 4.00 10.00
22 Jay Ajayi 2.50 6.00
23 Amari Cooper 6.00 15.00
24 Melvin Gordon 4.00 10.00
25 Bryce Petty 1.50 4.00
26 Sammie Coates 2.00 5.00
27 Mike Davis 1.50 4.00
28 Todd Gurley 5.00 12.00
29 David Johnson 4.00 10.00
30 Tevin Coleman 2.00 5.00
31 Jamison Crowder 2.00 5.00
32 Maxx Williams 1.50 4.00
33 Vince Mayle 2.00 5.00
34 Brett Hundley 1.50 4.00
35 Buck Allen 2.00 5.00
36 Ty Montgomery 1.50 4.00
37 Kevin White 5.00 12.00
38 Rashad Greene 1.50 4.00
39 Matt Jones 1.50 4.00
40 Sean Mannion 1.50 4.00

2015 Rookies and Stars Rookie Jerseys Signatures

1 Jameis Winston 100.00 100.00
2 Marcus Mariota 50.00 100.00
3 Jeremy Langford 3.00 8.00
4 Sammie Coates 4.00 10.00
6 Devin Smith 3.00 8.00
7 Devin Funchess 5.00 12.00
8 Matt Jones 3.00 8.00
9 Tyler Lockett 5.00 12.00
10 Phillip Dorsett 3.00 8.00

2015 Rookies and Stars Star Materials

*LONGEVITY JSY: .4X TO 1X R&S JSY
*TEAM NAME/99: .5X TO 1.2X BASIC JSY
*TEAM NAME/49: .6X TO 1.5X BASIC JSY
*TEAM LOGO/50: .6X TO 1.5X BASIC JSY
*TEAM LOGO/25: .8X TO 2X BASIC JSY
*JSY NUMBER/25: .8X TO 2X BASIC JSY
1 Tony Romo 2.00 5.00
2 J.J. Watt 2.50 6.00
3 DeMarcus Ware 2.00 5.00
4 Sammy Watkins 2.00 5.00
5 Blake Bortles 1.50 4.00
6 Antonio Brown 2.50 6.00
7 Derek Carr 2.50 6.00
8 Mike Evans 2.00 5.00
9 Peyton Manning 5.00 12.00
10 Jeremy Hill 1.50 4.00
11 Brandin Cooks 2.00 5.00
12 Ryan Tannehill 2.00 5.00
13 Odell Beckham Jr. 2.50 6.00
14 Matthew Stafford 2.00 5.00
15 Teddy Bridgewater 2.00 5.00

2016 Rookies and Stars

1 Stefon Diggs .25 .60
2 Michael Crabtree .20 .50
3 Dez Bryant .30 .75
4 Kevin White .20 .50
5 Darren Sproles .25 .60
6 Jeremy Langford .25 .60
7 Ndamukong Suh .25 .60
8 J.J. Watt .30 .75
9 DeSean Jackson .25 .60
10 Charcandrick West .20 .50
11 Jarvis Landry .25 .60
12 Jeremy Maclin .20 .50
13 Ryan Fitzpatrick .20 .50
14 Vincent Jackson .20 .50
15 Julio Jones .30 .75
16 Matt Forte .20 .50
17 Trevor Siemian .20 .50
18 Allen Robinson .25 .60
19 Tavon Austin .20 .50
20 Danny Woodhead .25 .60
21 Richard Sherman .30 .75
22 Janoris Jenkins .20 .50
23 Alshon Jeffery .25 .60
24 Brock Osweiler .20 .50
25 Ryan Tannehill .25 .60
26 Khalil Mack .30 .75
27 Kamar Aiken .20 .50
28 Von Miller .25 .60
29 Odell Beckham Jr. .30 .75
30 Jason Witten .25 .60
31 C.J. Anderson .25 .60
32 Jeremy Hill .20 .50
33 Kirk Cousins .30 .75
34 Aaron Donald .30 .75
35 Victor Cruz .25 .60
36 Blake Bortles .20 .50
37 Willie Snead .25 .60
38 Sam Bradford .20 .50
39 Coby Fleener .20 .50
40 Kyle Rudolph .20 .50
41 Marcus Mariota .30 .75
42 Darren McFadden .20 .50
43 Allen Hurns .20 .50
44 Jordan Matthews .25 .60
45 Antonio Gates .20 .50
46 Jamaal Charles .25 .60
47 Ben Roethlisberger .30 .75
48 Matthew Stafford .25 .60
49 Le'Veon Bell .25 .60
50 Doug Martin .25 .60
51 Dwayne Allen .20 .50
52 Mike Evans .25 .60
53 Frank Gore .25 .60
54 Jameis Winston .30 .75
55 David Johnson .30 .75
56 Harry Douglas .20 .50
57 Jordan Reed .20 .50
58 Andrew Luck .40 1.00
59 Latavius Murray .20 .50
60 LeSean McCoy .30 .75
61 Derek Carr .30 .75
62 Rashad Jennings .20 .50
63 A.J. Green .30 .75
64 Eli Manning .25 .60
65 Duke Johnson .20 .50
66 Todd Gurley .30 .75
67 Aaron Rodgers .60 1.50
68 Travis Kelce .30 .75
69 Brandin Cooks .25 .60
70 Keenan Allen .25 .60
71 T.Y. Hilton .25 .60
72 Doug Baldwin .25 .60
73 Delanie Walker .20 .50
74 Eddie Royal .20 .50
75 Adrian Peterson .30 .75
76 Tyrod Taylor .25 .60
77 Ezekiel Ansah .20 .50
78 Philip Rivers .30 .75
79 Joe Haden .20 .50
80 Vance McDonald .20 .50
81 Jay Ajayi .25 .60
82 DeAngelo Williams .20 .50
83 Navorro Bowman .25 .60
84 Michael Floyd .20 .50
85 Drew Brees .30 .75
86 Lavonte David .20 .50
87 Kenny Britt .20 .50
88 Lamar Miller .20 .50
89 Cam Newton .30 .75
90 Ameer Abdullah .20 .50
91 Carlos Hyde .20 .50
92 Andy Dalton .25 .60
93 Jimmy Graham .30 .75
94 Demaryius Thomas .25 .60
95 Devonta Freeman .25 .60
96 Tony Romo .25 .60
97 Matt Ryan .25 .60
98 Teddy Bridgewater .25 .60
99 Tom Brady .75 2.00
100 Justin Forsett .25 .60
101 DeAndre Hopkins .25 .60
102 Steve Smith Sr. .25 .60
103 Danny Amendola .25 .60
104 Golden Tate III .20 .50
105 Antonio Brown .30 .75
106 Donte Moncrief .25 .60
107 Robert Griffin III .20 .50
108 Julian Edelman .30 .75
109 Jay Cutler .20 .50
110 LeGarrette Blount .25 .60
111 Eddie Lacy .20 .50
112 Jonathan Stewart .20 .50
113 Emmanuel Sanders .30 .75
114 DeMarco Murray .25 .60
115 Russell Wilson .40 1.00
116 Kendall Wright .20 .50
117 Terrance Williams .20 .50
118 Darrelle Revis .20 .50
119 Mohamed Sanu .20 .50
120 Greg Olsen .25 .60
121 Tyler Eifert .25 .60
122 Julius Thomas .20 .50
123 Matt Jones .25 .60
124 Mark Ingram .25 .60
125 Clay Matthews .30 .75
126 Ryan Mathews .25 .60
127 Eric Decker .20 .50
128 Joe Flacco .25 .60
129 Chris Johnson .20 .50
130 Gary Barnidge .20 .50
131 Melvin Gordon .25 .60
132 Rob Gronkowski .30 .75
133 Alex Smith .25 .60
134 Jordy Nelson .25 .60
135 Nelson Agholor .20 .50
136 Luke Kuechly .25 .60
137 Amari Cooper .30 .75
138 Carson Palmer .25 .60
139 Mario Williams .20 .50
140 Jacob Tamme .20 .50
141 Sammy Watkins .30 .75
142 Larry Fitzgerald .25 .60
143 Isaiah Crowell .20 .50
144 Kelvin Benjamin .25 .60
145 Torrey Smith .20 .50
146 Randall Cobb .25 .60
147 Chris Ivory .25 .60
148 Brandon Marshall .20 .50
149 Robert Woods .25 .60
150 Thomas Rawls .20 .50
151 Kenneth Dixon RC 1S .40 1.00
152 Jalen Ramsey RC 1S .60 1.50
153 Tyler Boyd RC 1S .50 1.25
154 Sheldon Rankins RC 1S .50 1.25
155 Cardale Jones RC 1S .40 1.00
156 Christian Hackenberg RC 1S .40 1.00
157 Jonathan Williams RC 1S .50 1.25
158 Leonte Carroo RC 1S .40 1.00
159 Demarcus Robinson RC 1S .40 1.00
160 Jordan Howard RC 1S 1.00 2.50
161 Josh Doctson RC 1S .50 1.25
162 DeForest Buckner RC 1S .40 1.00
163 Laquon Treadwell RC 1S .50 1.25
164 Karl Joseph RC 1S .40 1.00
165 Braxton Miller RC 1S .40 1.00
166 Hunter Henry RC 1S .50 1.25
167 Jared Goff RC 1S 2.50 6.00
168 Kevin Hogan RC 1S .50 1.25
169 C.J. Prosise RC 1S .40 1.00
170 Paul Perkins RC 1S .40 1.00
171 Paxton Lynch RC 1S .40 1.00
172 Leonard Floyd RC 1S .50 1.25
173 Kenyan Drake RC 1S .60 1.50
174 Keanu Neal RC 1S .40 1.00
175 DeAndre Washington RC 1S .40 1.00
176 Carson Wentz RC 1S 4.00 10.00
177 Cody Kessler RC 1S .40 1.00
178 Trevor Davis RC 1S .40 1.00
179 Dak Prescott RC 1S 6.00 15.00
180 Will Fuller RC 1S .60 1.50
181 Moritz Bohringer RC 1S .40 1.00
182 Eli Apple RC 1S .50 1.25
183 Sterling Shepard RC 1S .50 1.25
184 Shaq Lawson RC 1S .40 1.00
185 Corey Coleman RC 1S .60 1.50
186 Ezekiel Elliott RC 1S 6.00 15.00
187 Chris Moore RC 1S .50 1.25
188 Ricardo Louis RC 1S .40 1.00
189 Alex Collins RC 1S .50 1.25
190 Michael Thomas RC 1S .75 2.00
191 Wendell Smallwood RC 1S .40 1.00
192 Vernon Hargreaves III RC 1S .60 1.50
193 Pharoh Cooper RC 1S .40 1.00
194 Darron Lee RC 1S .40 1.00
195 Joey Bosa RC 1S .75 2.00
196 Derrick Henry RC 1S 1.00 2.50
197 Devontae Booker RC 1S .50 1.25
198 Keenan Reynolds RC 1S .50 1.25
199 Connor Cook RC 1S .50 1.25
200 Tyler Ervin RC 1S .40 1.00
201 Andy Janovich RC 2S .60 1.50
202 Temarrick Hemingway RC 2S .50 1.25
203 Kenny Clark RC 2S .50 1.25
204 Cole Wick RC 2S .60 1.50
205 Jaylon Smith RC 2S .50 1.25
206 D.J. Foster RC 2S .60 1.50
207 Brandon Doughty RC 2S .50 1.25
208 Austin Hooper RC 2S .50 1.25
209 Dwayne Washington RC 2S .60 1.50
210 Seth DeValve RC 2S .60 1.50
211 Charles Tapper RC 2S .60 1.50
212 Jerell Adams RC 2S .50 1.25
213 Robert Nkemdiche RC 2S .60 1.50
214 Jhurell Pressley RC 2S .60 1.50
215 Myles Jack RC 2S .60 1.50
216 Joe Callahan RC 2S .60 1.50
217 Nelson Spruce RC 2S .50 1.25
218 Jacoby Brissett RC 2S .60 1.50
219 Daniel Lasco RC 2S .50 1.25
220 Tajae Sharpe RC 2S .60 1.50
221 Robert Kelley RC 2S 4.00 10.00
222 Jakeem Grant RC 2S .50 1.25
223 Vernon Butler RC 2S .50 1.25
224 Cody Core RC 2S .50 1.25
225 Chris Jones RC 2S .50 1.25
226 Aaron Burbridge RC 2S .50 1.25
227 Trevone Boykin RC 2S .50 1.25
228 Malcolm Mitchell RC 2S .50 1.25
229 Chester Rogers RC 2S .60 1.50
230 Jordan Payton RC 2S .50 1.25
231 William Jackson III RC 2S .60 1.50
232 Nate Sudfeld RC 2S .50 1.25
233 Emmanuel Ogbah RC 2S .60 1.50
234 Brandon Allen RC 2S .50 1.25
235 Xavien Howard RC 2S .60 1.50
236 Darius Jackson RC 2S .60 1.50
237 Derek Watt RC 2S .75 2.00
238 Nick Vannett RC 2S .50 1.25
239 Charone Peake RC 2S .50 1.25
240 Tyreek Hill RC 2S 2.00 5.00
241 Artie Burns RC 2S .60 1.50
242 David Morgan RC 2S .75 2.00
243 Kevin Dodd RC 2S .50 1.25
244 Mike Thomas RC 2S .75 2.00
245 Noah Spence RC 2S .50 1.25
246 Jalin Marshall RC 2S .75 2.00
247 Jalen Richard RC 2S .60 1.50
248 Tyler Higbee RC 2S .50 1.25
249 Tommylee Lewis RC 2S .60 1.50
250 Rashard Higgins RC 2S .50 1.25
251 Sean Davis RC 3S .60 1.50
252 B.J. Goodson RC 3S .60 1.50
253 Adam Gotsis RC 3S .60 1.50
254 Deiondre' Hall RC 3S .60 1.50
255 Yannick Ngakoue RC 3S 1.00 2.50
256 Shilique Calhoun RC 3S .60 1.50
257 Reggie Ragland RC 3S .60 1.50
258 Nick Vigil RC 3S .60 1.50
259 Jalran Reed RC 3S .60 1.50
260 Justin Simmons RC 3S .75 2.00
261 Roberto Aguayo RC 3S .60 1.50
262 Joshua Perry RC 3S .60 1.50
263 Kevin Byard RC 3S .60 1.50
264 Derrick Kindred RC 3S .60 1.50
265 Blake Martinez RC 3S .75 2.00
266 Daryl Worley RC 3S .60 1.50
267 Kamalei Correa RC 3S .60 1.50
268 Kyler Fackrell RC 3S .75 2.00
269 Deion Jones RC 3S .60 1.50
270 Joe Schobert RC 3S .75 2.00
271 Cyrus Jones RC 3S .60 1.50
272 Miles Killebrew RC 3S .60 1.50
273 Carl Nassib RC 3S .60 1.50
274 Willie Henry RC 3S .60 1.50
275 Darian Thompson RC 3S .60 1.50
276 Adolphus Washington RC 3S .60 1.50
277 Austin Johnson RC 3S .60 1.50
278 Javon Hargrave RC 3S .60 1.50
279 Su'a Cravens RC 3S .60 1.50
280 Sheldon Day RC 3S .60 1.50
281 Vonn Bell RC 3S .75 2.00
282 Juston Burris RC 3S .60 1.50
283 Maliek Collins RC 3S .60 1.50
284 Rashard Robinson RC 3S .60 1.50
285 Jonathan Bullard RC 3S .60 1.50
286 Jordan Jenkins RC 3S 1.00 2.50
287 Jihad Ward RC 3S .60 1.50
288 Brandon Williams RC 3S .60 1.50
289 Mackensie Alexander RC 3S .60 1.50
290 Tavon Young RC 3S .60 1.50
291 James Bradberry RC 3S .75 2.00
292 Kevon Seymour RC 3S .60 1.50
293 Jatavis Brown RC 3S .60 1.50
294 Tyler Matakevich RC 3S .60 1.50
295 KeiVarae Russell RC 3S .60 1.50
296 Kendall Fuller RC 3S .75 2.00
297 A'Shawn Robinson RC 3S .60 1.50
298 Vincent Valentine RC 3S .60 1.50
299 T.J. Green RC 3S 1.00 2.50
300 Ryan Smith RC 3S .60 1.50

2016 Rookies and Stars Green

*VETS: 1.5X TO 4X BASIC CARDS
*ROOKIES: .8X TO 2X BASIC CARDS

2016 Rookies and Stars Red

*VETS: 1.5X TO 4X BASIC CARDS
*ROOKIES: .8X TO 2X BASIC CARDS

2016 Rookies and Stars True Blue

*VETS: 3X TO 8X BASIC CARDS
*ROOK (151-200): 1.5X TO 4X BASIC CARDS
*ROOK (201-250): 1.2X TO 3X BASIC CARDS
*ROOK (251-300): 1X TO 2.5X BASIC CARDS

2016 Rookies and Stars Action Packed

1 Russell Wilson 1.00 2.50
2 J.J. Watt .75 2.00
3 Adrian Peterson .75 2.00
4 Rob Gronkowski .75 2.00
5 Odell Beckham Jr. .75 2.00
6 Marcus Mariota .75 2.00
7 Todd Gurley .75 2.00
8 Amari Cooper .75 2.00
9 Julio Jones .75 2.00
10 Antonio Brown .75 2.00

2016 Rookies and Stars Century Stars

*BLUE/49: 1.2X TO 3X BASIC INSERTS
1 Russell Wilson 1.00 2.50
2 Rob Gronkowski .75 2.00
3 Odell Beckham Jr. .75 2.00
4 J.J. Watt .75 2.00
5 Richard Sherman .75 2.00
6 Aaron Rodgers 1.50 4.00
7 Julio Jones .75 2.00
8 Tom Brady 2.00 5.00
9 Darrelle Revis .50 1.25
10 Andrew Luck 1.00 2.50

2016 Rookies and Stars Cross Training Jerseys

1 Demarcus Robinson 1.50 4.00
2 Tyler Boyd 2.00 5.00
3 Hunter Henry 2.00 5.00
4 Jordan Howard 3.00 8.00
5 Alex Collins 2.00 5.00
6 Kenyan Drake 2.50 6.00
7 Carson Wentz 6.00 15.00
8 Michael Thomas 3.00 8.00
9 Connor Cook 2.00 5.00
10 Pharoh Cooper 1.50 4.00
11 Derrick Henry 4.00 10.00
12 Tyler Ervin 1.50 4.00
13 Jared Goff 5.00 12.00
14 Josh Doctson 2.00 5.00
15 Braxton Miller 1.50 4.00
16 Kevin Hogan 2.00 5.00
17 Chris Moore 2.00 5.00
18 Moritz Bohringer 1.50 4.00
19 Corey Coleman 2.50 6.00
20 Ricardo Louis 1.50 4.00
21 Devontae Booker 2.00 5.00
22 Wendell Smallwood 1.50 4.00
23 Joey Bosa 3.00 8.00
24 Keenan Reynolds 2.00 5.00
25 C.J. Prosise 1.50 4.00
26 Laquon Treadwell 2.00 5.00
27 Christian Hackenberg 1.50 4.00
28 Paul Perkins 1.50 4.00
29 Dak Prescott 8.00 20.00
30 Sterling Shepard 3.00 8.00
31 Ezekiel Elliott 8.00 20.00
32 Will Fuller 2.50 6.00
33 Jonathan Williams 2.00 5.00
34 Kenneth Dixon 1.50 4.00
35 Cardale Jones 1.50 4.00
36 Leonte Carroo 1.50 4.00
37 Cody Kessler 1.50 4.00
38 Paxton Lynch 4.00 10.00
39 DeAndre Washington 1.50 4.00
40 Trevor Davis 1.50 4.00

2016 Rookies and Stars Crusade

*RED/99: .8X TO 2X BASIC INSERTS
*PURPLE/49: 1X TO 2.5X BASIC INSERTS
*GOLD/25: 1.2X TO 3X BASIC INSERTS
1 Russell Wilson 1.50 4.00
2 Robert Griffin III .75 2.00
3 Derrick Henry 2.00 5.00
4 Aaron Rodgers 2.50 6.00
5 Marcus Mariota 1.25 3.00
6 Ryan Tannehill 1.00 2.50
7 Matt Ryan 1.00 2.50
8 Carson Wentz 8.00 20.00
9 Jamaal Charles 1.00 2.50
10 Eli Manning 1.00 2.50
11 Richard Sherman 1.25 3.00
12 Andy Dalton 1.00 2.50
13 Paxton Lynch .75 2.00
14 Matthew Stafford 1.00 2.50
15 DeMarco Murray 1.00 2.50
16 Matt Forte .75 2.00
17 Julio Jones 1.25 3.00
18 Kirk Cousins 1.25 3.00
19 Von Miller 1.00 2.50
20 Odell Beckham Jr. 1.25 3.00
21 Le'Veon Bell 1.00 2.50
22 A.J. Green 1.25 3.00
23 Corey Coleman 1.25 3.00
24 Andrew Luck 1.50 4.00
25 Jameis Winston 1.25 3.00
26 Tom Brady 3.00 8.00
27 Philip Rivers 1.25 3.00
28 Tony Romo 1.00 2.50
29 Demaryius Thomas 1.00 2.50
30 Joe Flacco 1.00 2.50
31 Carson Palmer 1.00 2.50
32 Jay Cutler .75 2.00
33 Laquon Treadwell 1.00 2.50
34 Blake Bortles .75 2.00
35 Cam Newton 1.25 3.00
36 Rob Gronkowski 1.25 3.00
37 Derek Carr 1.25 3.00
38 Dez Bryant 1.25 3.00
39 Jared Goff 5.00 12.00
40 Ben Roethlisberger 1.25 3.00
41 Larry Fitzgerald 1.00 2.50
42 Adrian Peterson 1.25 3.00
43 Will Fuller 1.25 3.00
44 Drew Brees 1.25 3.00
45 J.J. Watt 1.25 3.00
46 LeSean McCoy 1.25 3.00
47 Amari Cooper 1.25 3.00
48 Ezekiel Elliott 15.00 40.00
49 Todd Gurley 1.25 3.00
50 Antonio Brown 1.25 3.00

2016 Rookies and Stars Dress for Success Jersey Autographs

1 Alex Collins 4.00 10.00
2 Josh Doctson 4.00 10.00
3 Cardale Jones 3.00 8.00
4 Laquon Treadwell 4.00 10.00
5 Christian Hackenberg 3.00 8.00
6 Paul Perkins 3.00 8.00
7 Corey Coleman 5.00 12.00
8 Sterling Shepard 4.00 10.00
9 Devontae Booker 4.00 10.00
10 Jared Goff 20.00 50.00
11 Braxton Miller 3.00 8.00
12 Keenan Reynolds 4.00 10.00
13 Carson Wentz 40.00 80.00
14 Leonte Carroo 3.00 8.00
15 Cody Kessler 3.00 8.00
16 Paxton Lynch 3.00 8.00
17 Dak Prescott 50.00 100.00
18 Tyler Boyd 4.00 10.00
19 Ezekiel Elliott 75.00 150.00
20 Joey Bosa 6.00 15.00
21 C.J. Prosise 3.00 8.00
22 Demarcus Robinson 3.00 8.00
23 Chris Moore 4.00 10.00
24 Michael Thomas 6.00 15.00
25 Connor Cook 4.00 10.00
26 Pharoh Cooper 3.00 8.00
27 Derrick Henry 8.00 20.00
28 Will Fuller 5.00 12.00
29 Hunter Henry 4.00 10.00
30 Jordan Howard 8.00 20.00

2016 Rookies and Stars Dual Jerseys

*PRIME/25: .6X TO 1.5X BASIC JSY/99
1 B.Miller 3.00 8.00
W.Fuller
2 J.Goff 6.00 15.00
T.Davis
3 D.Robinson 2.00 5.00
P.Cooper
4 L.Treadwell 2.50 6.00
M.Bohringer
5 K.Reynolds 2.50 6.00
C.Moore
6 C.Wentz 8.00 20.00
W.Smallwood
7 J.Williams 2.50 6.00
C.Jones
8 C.Wentz 8.00 20.00
J.Goff
9 R.Louis 2.00 5.00
C.Kessler
10 C.Coleman 3.00 8.00
L.Treadwell
11 B.Miller 2.00 5.00
T.Ervin
12 E.Elliott 12.00 30.00
J.Bosa
13 J.Goff 6.00 15.00
P.Cooper
14 P.Perkins 4.00 10.00
S.Shepard
15 K.Reynolds 2.50 6.00
K.Dixon
16 H.Henry 4.00 10.00
J.Bosa
17 C.Kessler 3.00 8.00
C.Coleman
18 P.Lynch 5.00 12.00
C.Hcknbrg
19 D.Prescott 10.00 25.00
E.Elliott
20 J.Doctson 3.00 8.00
W.Fuller
21 T.Ervin 3.00 8.00
W.Fuller
22 B.Miller 2.00 5.00
C.Jones
23 K.Drake 3.00 8.00
L.Carroo
24 D.Washington 2.50 6.00
C.Cook
25 C.Moore 2.50 6.00
K.Dixon
26 A.Collins 2.50 6.00
C.Prosise
27 C.Coleman 3.00 8.00
R.Louis
28 D.Henry 12.00 30.00
E.Elliott
29 D.Booker 5.00 12.00
P.Lynch
30 K.Drake 5.00 12.00
D.Henry

2016 Rookies and Stars Freshman Orientation Jersey Autographs

1 Dak Prescott
2 Sterling Shepard 4.00 10.00
3 Devontae Booker 4.00 10.00
4 Tyler Ervin 3.00 8.00
6 Keenan Reynolds 4.00 10.00
7 Alex Collins 4.00 10.00
8 Kevin Hogan 4.00 10.00
9 Cardale Jones 3.00 8.00
10 Paul Perkins 3.00 8.00
11 DeAndre Washington 3.00 8.00
12 Trevor Davis 3.00 8.00
13 Hunter Henry 4.00 10.00
14 Wendell Smallwood 3.00 8.00
15 Jordan Howard 8.00 20.00
16 Chris Moore 4.00 10.00
17 Braxton Miller 3.00 8.00
18 Leonte Carroo 3.00 8.00
19 Christian Hackenberg 3.00 8.00
20 Pharoh Cooper 3.00 8.00
21 Demarcus Robinson 3.00 8.00
22 Tyler Boyd 4.00 10.00
23 Joey Bosa 6.00 15.00
24 Will Fuller 5.00 12.00
25 Josh Doctson 4.00 10.00
26 Kenyan Drake 5.00 12.00
27 C.J. Prosise 3.00 8.00
28 Cody Kessler 3.00 8.00
29 Moritz Bohringer 3.00 8.00
30 Ricardo Louis 3.00 8.00

2016 Rookies and Stars Great American Heroes

*RED/99: .8X TO 2X BASIC INSERTS
*PURPLE/49: 1X TO 2.5X BASIC INSERTS
*SINGLES: 1.2X TO 3X BASIC INSERTS
1 Y.A. Tittle 1.25 3.00
2 Jim Kelly 1.25 3.00
3 Kurt Warner 1.00 2.50
4 Barry Sanders 2.00 5.00
5 Marvin Harrison 1.00 2.50
6 Brian Urlacher 1.25 3.00
7 Roger Staubach 1.50 4.00
8 Darrell Green 1.00 2.50
9 Gale Sayers 1.25 3.00
10 Terry Bradshaw 1.50 4.00
11 Red Grange 1.50 4.00
12 Larry Csonka 1.00 2.50
13 Jim McMahon 1.00 2.50
14 Bo Jackson 1.50 4.00
15 Michael Irvin 1.25 3.00
16 Bruce Smith 1.00 2.50
17 Shannon Sharpe 1.25 3.00
18 Emmitt Smith 2.00 5.00
19 Tim Brown 1.25 3.00
20 Jerome Bettis 1.25 3.00
21 Clyde "Bulldog" Turner 1.00 2.50
22 Joe Greene 1.25 3.00
23 Bob Griese 1.25 3.00
24 John Stallworth 1.00 2.50
25 Peyton Manning 2.50 6.00
26 Curtis Martin 1.00 2.50
27 Steve Young 1.50 4.00
28 Eric Dickerson 1.00 2.50
29 Tony Dorsett 1.25 3.00
30 Jerry Rice 2.00 5.00
31 Paul Hornung 1.25 3.00
32 Joe Namath 1.50 4.00
33 Marshall Faulk 1.00 2.50
34 Brett Favre 2.50 6.00
35 Ray Lewis 1.25 3.00
36 Dan Marino 2.50 6.00
37 Terrell Davis 1.00 2.50
38 Franco Harris 1.25 3.00
39 Troy Aikman 1.50 4.00
40 Rocky Bleier 1.00 2.50

2016 Rookies and Stars Great American Signatures

*BLUE/25: .6X TO 1.5X BASIC AU/99
*BLUE/25: .5X TO 1.2X BASIC AU/49
*BLUE/24: .8X TO 2X BASIC AU/99
2 Kellen Winslow/99 5.00 12.00
4 Steve Largent/25 10.00 25.00
6 Boomer Esiason/25 8.00 20.00
8 Dwight Clark/49 6.00 15.00
10 Derrick Brooks/99 4.00 10.00
12 Troy Brown/99 4.00 10.00
13 Raymond Berry/25 8.00 20.00
14 James Lofton/25 8.00 20.00
16 Jim Plunkett/49 6.00 15.00
18 Willie McGinest/99 4.00 10.00
20 Mark Chmura/99 4.00 10.00
22 Steve Grogan/99 4.00 10.00
23 Ronnie Lott/25 8.00 20.00
24 Earl Campbell/25 10.00 25.00
26 Herman Edwards/49 6.00 15.00
27 Rocky Bleier/15
28 Jackie Smith/99 4.00 10.00
30 Ickey Woods/99 4.00 10.00

2016 Rookies and Stars Great American Treasures Jerseys

1 Joe Theismann 4.00 10.00
2 Adrian Peterson 4.00 10.00
3 Larry Fitzgerald 3.00 8.00
4 Bo Jackson 5.00 12.00
5 Ozzie Newsome 3.00 8.00
6 Cam Newton 4.00 10.00
7 Ronnie Lott 3.00 8.00
8 Ed "Too Tall" Jones 2.50 6.00
9 Tony Romo 3.00 8.00
10 Jerome Bettis 4.00 10.00
11 John Elway 6.00 15.00
12 Barry Sanders 6.00 15.00
13 Marcus Allen 3.00 8.00
14 Boomer Esiason 3.00 8.00
15 Peyton Manning 8.00 20.00
16 Carl Eller 2.50 6.00
17 Steve Young 5.00 12.00
18 Eli Manning 3.00 8.00
19 Troy Aikman 5.00 12.00
20 Jerry Rice 6.00 15.00
21 Larry Csonka 3.00 8.00
22 Ben Roethlisberger 4.00 10.00
23 Marshall Faulk 3.00 8.00
24 Brett Favre 8.00 20.00
25 Roger Staubach 5.00 12.00
26 Dan Marino 8.00 20.00
27 Tom Brady 15.00 40.00
28 Eric Dickerson 3.00 8.00
29 Warren Moon 4.00 10.00
30 Joe Namath 5.00 12.00

2016 Rookies and Stars NFL Lifestyle Materials

1 Von Miller 2.50 6.00
2 Von Miller 2.50 6.00

2016 Rookies and Stars One Star Materials

1 Stefon Diggs 2.50 6.00
2 Devonta Freeman 2.50 6.00
3 Todd Gurley 3.00 8.00
4 Jarvis Landry 2.50 6.00
5 Jeremy Langford 2.50 6.00
6 Amari Cooper 3.00 8.00
7 Carlos Hyde 2.00 5.00
8 Brandin Cooks 2.50 6.00
9 Kevin White 2.00 5.00
10 Davante Adams 2.00 5.00
11 T.J. Yeldon 2.00 5.00
12 Duke Johnson 2.00 5.00
13 Tyler Lockett 2.50 6.00
14 Jeremy Hill 2.00 5.00
15 Jordan Matthews 2.50 6.00
16 Ameer Abdullah 2.00 5.00
17 Kelvin Benjamin 2.50 6.00
18 Buck Allen 2.00 5.00
19 Khalil Mack 3.00 8.00
20 David Johnson 3.00 8.00

2016 Rookies and Stars Power Tools

*BLUE/49: 1X TO 2.5X BASIC INSERTS
1 Rob Gronkowski 1.00 2.50
2 Julio Jones 1.00 2.50
3 Tom Brady 2.50 6.00
4 Andrew Luck 1.25 3.00
5 Larry Fitzgerald .75 2.00
6 Jameis Winston 1.00 2.50
7 Adrian Peterson 1.00 2.50
8 Russell Wilson 1.25 3.00
9 LeSean McCoy 1.00 2.50
10 Aaron Rodgers 2.00 5.00
11 A.J. Green 1.00 2.50
12 Eli Manning .75 2.00
13 Antonio Brown 1.00 2.50
14 Derek Carr 1.00 2.50
15 J.J. Watt 1.00 2.50
16 Marcus Mariota 1.00 2.50
17 Le'Veon Bell .75 2.00
18 Cam Newton 1.00 2.50
19 Jamaal Charles .75 2.00
20 Drew Brees 1.00 2.50

2016 Rookies and Stars Prime Cuts

1 Jonathan Williams 2.00 5.00
2 Jared Goff 5.00 12.00
3 Cody Kessler 1.50 4.00
4 Chris Moore 2.00 5.00
5 Devontae Booker 2.00 5.00
6 Demarcus Robinson 1.50 4.00
7 C.J. Prosise 1.50 4.00
8 Dak Prescott 8.00 20.00
9 Alex Collins 2.00 5.00
10 Connor Cook 2.00 5.00
11 Kenneth Dixon 1.50 4.00
12 Josh Doctson 2.00 5.00
13 Paxton Lynch 4.00 10.00

14 Moritz Bohringer 1.50 4.00
15 Wendell Smallwood 1.50 4.00
16 Tyler Boyd 2.00 5.00
17 Laquon Treadwell 2.00 5.00
18 Kenyan Drake 2.50 6.00
19 Sterling Shepard 3.00 8.00
20 Pharoh Cooper 1.50 4.00
21 Cardale Jones 1.50 4.00
22 Braxton Miller 1.50 4.00
23 DeAndre Washington 1.50 4.00
24 Corey Coleman 2.50 6.00
25 Joey Bosa 3.00 8.00
26 Christian Hackenberg 1.50 4.00
27 Hunter Henry 2.00 5.00
28 Carson Wentz 6.00 15.00
29 Ezekiel Elliott 8.00 20.00
30 Derrick Henry 4.00 10.00
31 Leonte Carroo 1.50 4.00
32 Kevin Hogan 2.00 5.00
33 Trevor Davis 1.50 4.00
34 Ricardo Louis 1.50 4.00
35 Keenan Reynolds 2.00 5.00
36 Jordan Howard 3.00 8.00
37 Paul Perkins 1.50 4.00
38 Will Fuller 2.50 6.00
39 Michael Thomas 3.00 8.00
40 Tyler Ervin 1.50 4.00

2016 Rookies and Stars Rookie Longevity Signatures

1 Christian Hackenberg/25 4.00 10.00
2 Tyler Ervin/75 2.50 6.00
3 Alex Collins/25 5.00 12.00
4 David Morgan/75 4.00 10.00
5 Hunter Henry/25 5.00 12.00
7 Kenyan Drake/25 6.00 15.00
8 Brandon Doughty/75 2.50 6.00
9 Jared Goff/25 25.00 60.00
10 Moritz Bohringer/75 2.50 6.00
11 Josh Doctson/25 5.00 12.00
12 Xavien Howard/75 3.00 8.00
13 Jordan Howard/25 10.00 25.00
14 Keyarris Garrett/75 2.50 6.00
15 Leonte Carroo/75 2.50 6.00
16 Jalin Marshall/75 4.00 10.00
18 Byron Marshall/75 2.50 6.00
19 Carson Wentz/25
20 Myles Jack/75 3.00 8.00
21 Will Fuller/25 6.00 15.00
24 Maurice Canady/75 2.50 6.00
25 Rashard Higgins/75 2.50 6.00
26 Jordan Jenkins/75 4.00 10.00
27 Jarran Reed/75 2.50 6.00
28 D.J. Foster/75 3.00 8.00
29 Derrick Henry/25 10.00 25.00
30 Nate Sudfeld/75 2.50 6.00
31 C.J. Prosise/16 5.00 12.00
33 Pharoh Cooper/75 2.50 6.00
34 Scooby Wright III/75 2.50 6.00
35 DeForest Buckner/75 2.50 6.00
36 Keith Marshall/75 2.50 6.00
37 Mackensie Alexander/75 2.50 6.00
38 Deion Jones/46 3.00 8.00
39 Paxton Lynch/25 4.00 10.00
40 Nelson Spruce/75 2.50 6.00
41 Paul Perkins/75 2.50 6.00
42 Cody Core/75 2.50 6.00
43 Dak Prescott/25 40.00 80.00
44 Thomas Duarte/75 2.50 6.00
45 Darian Thompson/75 2.50 6.00
47 Malcolm Mitchell/75 2.50 6.00
48 Demarcus Robinson/25 4.00 10.00
49 Ezekiel Elliott/25
50 Nick Vannett/75 2.50 6.00
51 Tyler Boyd/25 5.00 12.00
52 Daniel Braverman/75 2.50 6.00
53 Jacoby Brissett/75 3.00 8.00
55 Aaron Burbridge/75 2.50 6.00
56 Charles Tapper/49 4.00 10.00
57 Ricardo Louis/75 2.50 6.00
58 KeiVarae Russell/75 2.50 6.00
59 Connor Cook/25 5.00 12.00
61 Joey Bosa/31 6.00 15.00
62 DeAndre Washington/25 4.00 10.00
63 Jalen Ramsey/75 4.00 10.00
64 Blake Martinez/75 3.00 8.00
65 Chris Moore/25 5.00 12.00
66 Cyrus Jones/75 2.50 6.00
67 Kyler Fackrell/75 3.00 8.00
68 Jaylon Smith/75 2.50 6.00
69 Laquon Treadwell/25 5.00 12.00
70 Reggie Ragland/49 3.00 8.00
71 Braxton Miller/25 4.00 10.00
72 Glenn Gronkowski/75 2.50 6.00
73 Kenneth Dixon/25 4.00 10.00
75 Jeff Driskel/75 2.50 6.00
76 Jaydon Mickens/75 2.50 6.00
77 Aaron Green/75 2.50 6.00
79 Cardale Jones/25 4.00 10.00
80 Brandon Allen/75 2.50 6.00
81 Cody Kessler/25 4.00 10.00
82 Jeremy Cash/75 3.00 8.00
83 Vernon Hargreaves III/75 4.00 10.00
84 Bronson Kaufusi/75 2.50 6.00
85 Keenan Reynolds/25 5.00 12.00
86 Kevon Seymour/75 2.50 6.00
87 Austin Hooper/75 2.50 6.00
88 Keanu Neal/75 2.50 6.00
89 Corey Coleman/25 6.00 15.00
90 Trevone Boykin/75 2.50 6.00
91 Sterling Shepard/25 5.00 12.00
92 Jordan Payton/75 2.50 6.00
93 Devontae Booker/25 5.00 12.00
94 Charone Peake/75 2.50 6.00
95 Kenny Lawler/75 4.00 10.00
96 Kevin Dodd/75 2.50 6.00
97 Miles Killebrew/75 2.50 6.00
98 Kevin Hogan/23 6.00 15.00
99 Michael Thomas/25 8.00 20.00
100 Trevor Davis/25 4.00 10.00

2016 Rookies and Stars Rookie Longevity Signatures Red

*RED/25: .6X TO 1.5X BASIC AU/75
*RED/25: .5X TO 1.2X BASIC AU/31-49
*RED/25: .4X TO 1X BASIC AU/25
*RED/25: .3X TO .8X BASIC AU/16-23
19 Carson Wentz 50.00 100.00
43 Dak Prescott 40.00 80.00

2016 Rookies and Stars Rookie Longevity Signatures True Blue

*BLUE/49: .5X TO 1.2X BASIC AU/75
*BLUE/49: .4X TO 1X BASIC AU/31-49
*BLUE/49: .3X TO .8X BASIC AU/25
*BLUE/49: .25X TO .6X BASIC AU/16-23
19 Carson Wentz 40.00 80.00
43 Dak Prescott 25.00 60.00
49 Ezekiel Elliott 60.00 125.00

2016 Rookies and Stars Standing Ovation

*BLUE/49: 1X TO 2.5X BASIC INSERTS
1 Peyton Manning 2.00 5.00
2 Eric Dickerson .75 2.00
3 Marvin Harrison .75 2.00
4 LaDainian Tomlinson .75 2.00
5 Aaron Rodgers 2.00 5.00
6 Emmitt Smith 1.50 4.00
7 Jerry Rice 1.50 4.00
8 Bruce Smith .75 2.00
9 Tom Brady 2.50 6.00
10 Michael Strahan .75 2.00

2016 Rookies and Stars Star Search Jerseys

1 Laquon Treadwell 2.50 6.00
2 Cardale Jones 2.00 5.00
3 Joey Bosa 5.00 12.00
4 Jonathan Williams 2.50 6.00
5 Devontae Booker 2.50 6.00
6 Ezekiel Elliott 15.00 40.00
7 Alex Collins 2.50 6.00
8 Trevor Davis 2.00 5.00
9 Paxton Lynch 5.00 12.00
10 Paul Perkins 2.00 5.00
11 Kenyan Drake 3.00 8.00
12 Braxton Miller 2.00 5.00
13 Jared Goff 6.00 15.00
14 Christian Hackenberg 2.00 5.00
15 Demarcus Robinson 2.00 5.00
16 Derrick Henry 5.00 12.00
17 Connor Cook 2.50 6.00
18 Ricardo Louis 2.00 5.00
19 Moritz Bohringer 2.00 5.00
20 Will Fuller 3.00 8.00
21 Sterling Shepard 5.00 12.00
22 DeAndre Washington 2.00 5.00
23 Cody Kessler 2.00 5.00
24 Hunter Henry 2.50 6.00
25 C.J. Prosise 2.00 5.00
26 Leonte Carroo 2.00 5.00
27 Kenneth Dixon 2.00 5.00
28 Wendell Smallwood 2.00 5.00
29 Keenan Reynolds 2.50 6.00
30 Michael Thomas 4.00 10.00
31 Pharoh Cooper 2.00 5.00
32 Corey Coleman 3.00 8.00
33 Chris Moore 2.50 6.00
34 Carson Wentz 8.00 20.00
35 Dak Prescott 8.00 20.00
36 Kevin Hogan 2.50 6.00
37 Josh Doctson 2.50 6.00
38 Jordan Howard 5.00 12.00
39 Tyler Boyd 2.50 6.00
40 Tyler Ervin 2.00 5.00

2016 Rookies and Stars Team Infrastructure

*BLUE/49: 1X TO 2.5X BASIC INSERTS
1 Derrick Johnson .60 1.50
2 Andy Dalton .75 2.00
3 Navorro Bowman .75 2.00
4 Aaron Rodgers 2.00 5.00
5 Marcedes Lewis .60 1.50
6 Ryan Tannehill .75 2.00
7 Doug Martin .75 2.00
8 Brent Celek .60 1.50
9 Matt Ryan .75 2.00
10 Eli Manning .75 2.00
11 Von Miller .75 2.00
12 Jay Cutler .60 1.50
13 Larry Fitzgerald .75 2.00
14 Matthew Stafford .75 2.00
15 J.J. Watt 1.00 2.50
16 Darrelle Revis .60 1.50
17 Cam Newton 1.00 2.50
18 Pierre Garcon .75 2.00
19 Antonio Gates .60 1.50
20 Joe Flacco .75 2.00
21 Richard Sherman 1.00 2.50
22 Adrian Peterson 1.00 2.50
23 Kyle Williams .60 1.50
24 Robert Mathis .60 1.50
25 Delanie Walker .60 1.50
26 Tom Brady 2.50 6.00
27 Drew Brees 1.00 2.50
28 Jason Witten .75 2.00
29 Sebastian Janikowski .60 1.50
30 Ben Roethlisberger 1.00 2.50

2016 Rookies and Stars Ticket Masters

*BLUE/49: 1X TO 2.5X BASIC INSERTS
1 Carson Wentz 8.00 20.00
2 Jameis Winston 1.00 2.50
3 Ezekiel Elliott 3.00 8.00
4 Julio Jones 1.00 2.50
5 Joe Flacco .75 2.00
6 Jared Goff 4.00 10.00
7 A.J. Green 1.00 2.50
8 Adrian Peterson 1.00 2.50
9 Ryan Tannehill .75 2.00
10 Andrew Luck 1.25 3.00
11 Kirk Cousins 1.00 2.50
12 Cam Newton 1.00 2.50
13 Odell Beckham Jr. 1.00 2.50
14 Amari Cooper 1.00 2.50
15 Ben Roethlisberger 1.00 2.50
16 Russell Wilson 1.25 3.00
17 Jay Cutler .60 1.50
18 Aaron Rodgers 2.00 5.00
19 Tom Brady 2.50 6.00
20 Marcus Mariota 1.00 2.50

2017 Rookies and Stars

1 Eddie Lacy .20 .50
2 J.J. Watt .30 .75
3 Devonta Freeman .25 .60
4 Richard Sherman .30 .75
5 Khalil Mack .30 .75
6 Vontae Davis .20 .50
7 Marcus Mariota .30 .75
8 Jared Goff .30 .75
9 Thomas Rawls .20 .50
10 DeAndre Hopkins .25 .60
11 Jimmy Graham .30 .75
12 Pierre Garcon .25 .60
13 Russell Wilson .40 1.00
14 Melvin Gordon .25 .60
15 Jordan Howard .30 .75
16 Philly Brown .20 .50
17 Joe Flacco .25 .60
18 Von Miller .25 .60
19 Josh McCown .20 .50
20 Doug Baldwin .25 .60
21 Darron Lee .20 .50
22 Navorro Bowman .25 .60
23 Duke Johnson .20 .50
24 Tom Savage .20 .50
25 Cam Newton .30 .75
26 Eric Berry .25 .60
27 Kevin White .20 .50
28 Todd Gurley II .30 .75
29 Marqise Lee .20 .50
30 Julio Jones .30 .75
31 Quincy Enunwa .20 .50
32 Jason Pierre-Paul .20 .50
33 Tyler Eifert .25 .60
34 Jameis Winston .25 .60
35 J.J. Nelson .20 .50
36 Rob Gronkowski .30 .75
37 Clay Matthews .25 .60
38 Latavius Murray .20 .50
39 Demaryius Thomas .25 .60
40 Travis Kelce .30 .75
41 Michael Crabtree .20 .50
42 Bilal Powell .20 .50
43 Greg Olsen .25 .60
44 Philip Rivers .30 .75
45 Brian Orakpo .20 .50
46 Larry Fitzgerald .25 .60
47 Will Fuller V .20 .50
48 Jarvis Landry .25 .60
49 Vic Beasley Jr. .20 .50
50 Matt Ryan .25 .60
51 Drew Brees .30 .75
52 Tavon Austin .20 .50
53 Sammy Watkins .30 .75
54 T.Y. Hilton .25 .60
55 Tyreek Hill .30 .75
56 Corey Coleman .20 .50
57 Chris Conley .20 .50
58 Jack Doyle .20 .50
59 Jamaal Charles .25 .60
60 Marvin Jones Jr. .20 .50
61 Mike Evans .25 .60
62 Cameron Wake .20 .50
63 Alex Smith .25 .60
64 Luke Kuechly .25 .60
65 Odell Beckham Jr. .30 .75
66 Rishard Matthews .20 .50
67 Paul Perkins .20 .50
68 Robby Anderson .20 .50
69 Jonathan Stewart .20 .50
70 LeSean McCoy .30 .75
71 Bruce Ellington .20 .50
72 Jalen Ramsey .20 .50
73 Chris Hogan .20 .50
74 Le'Veon Bell .25 .60
75 Dak Prescott .30 .75
76 James Harrison .25 .60
77 Jared Cook .20 .50
78 Devin Funchess .20 .50
79 Matthew Stafford .25 .60
80 Sam Bradford .20 .50
81 Dont'a Hightower .20 .50
82 Antonio Gates .20 .50
83 Brandon LaFell .20 .50
84 Aaron Donald .30 .75
85 Kenny Stills .20 .50
86 Martavis Bryant .20 .50
87 Terrance Williams .20 .50
88 Davante Adams .25 .60
89 Trevor Siemian .20 .50
90 Jeremy Hill .20 .50
91 Charles Sims .20 .50
92 Andrew Luck .40 1.00
93 DeSean Jackson .25 .60
94 Delanie Walker .20 .50
95 Dion Lewis .20 .50
96 Frank Gore .25 .60
97 Eli Manning .25 .60
98 Gerald McCoy .20 .50
99 Brandon Marshall .20 .50
100 Brian Hoyer .20 .50
101 Isaiah Crowell .20 .50
102 Tyrod Taylor .25 .60
103 Dez Bryant .30 .75
104 Allen Hurns .20 .50
105 Kyle Rudolph .20 .50
106 Charles Clay .20 .50
107 Haloti Ngata .20 .50
108 C.J. Fiedorowicz .20 .50
109 Jesse James .20 .50
110 Terrelle Pryor Sr. .20 .50
111 Derek Carr .30 .75
112 Robert Kelley .20 .50
113 Jermaine Kearse .20 .50
114 LeGarrette Blount .25 .60
115 Ted Ginn Jr. .20 .50
116 Nelson Agholor .20 .50
117 Brandin Cooks .25 .60
118 Donte Moncrief .25 .60
119 Marcedes Lewis .20 .50
120 Tevin Coleman .25 .60
121 Tom Brady .75 2.00
122 Stefon Diggs .25 .60
123 DeMarco Murray .25 .60
124 Cordarrelle Patterson .20 .50
125 Tyrann Mathieu .25 .60
126 Zach Ertz .25 .60
127 Andy Dalton .25 .60
128 Ameer Abdullah .20 .50
129 Marshawn Lynch .25 .60
130 Matt Forte .20 .50
131 Kelvin Benjamin .25 .60
132 Ben Roethlisberger .30 .75
133 Geno Atkins .20 .50
134 Lamar Miller .20 .50
135 Fletcher Cox .20 .50
136 Vance McDonald .20 .50
137 Leonard Floyd .20 .50
138 Spencer Ware .20 .50
139 Julius Thomas .20 .50
140 Allen Robinson .25 .60
141 Mike Wallace .20 .50
142 Mike Glennon .25 .60
143 Kenny Britt .20 .50
144 Robert Woods .25 .60
145 Jamie Collins .20 .50
146 C.J. Anderson .25 .60
147 Antonio Brown .30 .75
148 Kirk Cousins .30 .75
149 Jay Cutler .20 .50
150 Sean Lee .25 .60
151 Johnny Hekker .20 .50
152 Aaron Rodgers .60 1.50
153 Doug Martin .25 .60
154 Golden Tate III .20 .50
155 Mark Ingram .25 .60
156 Jeremy Maclin .20 .50
157 Carson Palmer .25 .60
158 Danny Woodhead .25 .60
159 Randall Cobb .25 .60
160 David Johnson .30 .75
161 Jordan Matthews .20 .50
162 Harrison Smith .20 .50
163 Seth DeValve .20 .50
164 A.J. Green .30 .75
165 Michael Thomas .30 .75
166 Zach Brown .20 .50
167 Sterling Shepard .25 .60
168 Eric Ebron .20 .50
169 Blake Bortles .20 .50
170 Martellus Bennett .20 .50
171 Terrell Suggs .20 .50
172 Carlos Hyde .20 .50
173 Travis Benjamin .20 .50
174 Ty Montgomery .20 .50
175 Mohamed Sanu .20 .50
176 Adam Thielen .30 .75
177 Alshon Jeffery .25 .60
178 Adrian Peterson .30 .75
179 Josh Doctson .20 .50
180 Jason Witten .25 .60
181 Eli Rogers .20 .50
182 Ezekiel Elliott .40 1.00
183 Eric Decker .20 .50
184 Jordan Reed .20 .50
185 Lorenzo Alexander .20 .50
186 Cameron Meredith .20 .50
187 Phillip Dorsett .20 .50
188 Jay Ajayi .25 .60
189 Cameron Jordan .20 .50
190 Keenan Allen .25 .60
191 Coby Fleener .20 .50
192 Julian Edelman .30 .75
193 Cole Beasley .30 .75
194 John Brown .25 .60
195 Joey Bosa .30 .75
196 Jordy Nelson .25 .60
197 Emmanuel Sanders .30 .75
198 Carson Wentz .40 1.00
199 Ben Watson .20 .50
200 Amari Cooper .30 .75
201 Patrick Mahomes II RC 8.00 20.00
202 Myles Garrett RC 1.25 3.00
203 R. Joshua Dobbs RC .50 1.25
204 Shelton Gibson RC .40 1.00
205 Adoree' Jackson RC .50 1.25
206 Charles Harris RC .40 1.00
207 Nathan Peterman RC .50 1.25
208 Isaiah Ford RC .40 1.00
209 O.J. Howard RC .50 1.25
210 Sidney Jones RC .40 1.00
211 DeShone Kizer RC .40 1.00
212 David Njoku RC .50 1.25
213 D'Onta Foreman RC .50 1.25
214 Malik Hooker RC .40 1.00
215 Artavis Scott RC .40 1.00
216 Chris Godwin RC .50 1.25
217 Dede Westbrook RC .40 1.00
218 Jabrill Peppers RC .60 1.50
219 Deshaun Watson RC 2.50 6.00
220 Solomon Thomas RC .40 1.00
221 Wayne Gallman RC .50 1.25
222 Haason Reddick RC .40 1.00
223 Zay Jones RC .50 1.25
224 Malik McDowell RC .40 1.00
225 Brad Kaaya RC .40 1.00
226 Cordrea Tankersley RC .50 1.25
227 Samaje Perine RC .40 1.00
228 Jake Butt RC .50 1.25
229 Taywan Taylor RC .40 1.00
230 T.J. Watt RC 1.25 3.00
231 James Conner RC .75 2.00
232 Derek Barnett RC .50 1.25
233 Jeremy McNichols RC .40 1.00
234 Marlon Humphrey RC .40 1.00
235 Brian Hill RC .40 1.00
236 Corey Clement RC .50 1.25
237 Evan Engram RC .50 1.25
238 Jamal Adams RC .40 1.00
239 Jamaal Williams RC .40 1.00
240 Taco Charlton RC .40 1.00
241 John Ross III RC .50 1.25
242 Chad Williams RC .40 1.00
243 Josh Reynolds RC .40 1.00
244 Marshon Lattimore RC .50 1.25
245 Bucky Hodges RC .40 1.00
246 DeMarcus Walker RC .40 1.00
247 Joe Mixon RC .75 2.00
248 Jarrad Davis RC .50 1.25
249 Joe Williams RC .40 1.00
250 Takkarist McKinley RC .40 1.00
251 ArDarius Stewart RC .40 1.00
252 Adam Shaheen RC .40 1.00
253 C.J. Beathard RC .40 1.00
254 Matthew Dayes RC .40 1.00
255 Caleb Brantley RC .40 1.00
256 Desmond King RC .50 1.25
257 Alvin Kamara RC 1.50 4.00
258 Jonathan Allen RC .50 1.25
259 Amara Darboh RC .40 1.00
260 Tim Williams RC .50 1.25
261 Kenny Golladay RC .60 1.50
262 Jonnu Smith RC .40 1.00
263 Leonard Fournette RC 1.25 3.00
264 Noah Brown RC .50 1.25
265 Cameron Sutton RC .40 1.00
266 Donnel Pumphrey RC .50 1.25
267 JuJu Smith-Schuster RC 1.00 2.50
268 Jordan Leggett RC .40 1.00
269 Kareem Hunt RC .75 2.00
270 Travis Rudolph RC .40 1.00
271 Christian McCaffrey RC 1.00 2.50
272 Jehu Chesson RC .50 1.25
273 Cooper Kupp RC .60 1.50
274 Quincy Wilson RC .40 1.00
275 Carl Lawson RC .40 1.00
276 Elijah Hood RC .40 1.00
277 Carlos Henderson RC .40 1.00
278 Jordan Willis RC .40 1.00
279 T.J. Logan RC .60 1.50
280 Tre'Davious White RC .40 1.00
281 Mike Williams RC .60 1.50
282 Khalfani Muhammad RC .40 1.00
283 Mitchell Trubisky RC 2.00 5.00
284 Raekwon McMillan RC .40 1.00
285 Chad Hansen RC .40 1.00
286 Elijah Qualls RC .40 1.00
287 Mack Hollins RC .40 1.00
288 Josh Malone RC .40 1.00
289 Marlon Mack RC .60 1.50
290 Zach Cunningham RC .50 1.25
291 Dalvin Cook RC 1.00 2.50
292 DeAngelo Yancey RC .40 1.00
293 Davis Webb RC .40 1.00
294 Ryan Switzer RC .50 1.25
295 Chad Kelly RC .40 1.00
296 Gareon Conley RC .40 1.00
297 Corey Davis RC .60 1.50
298 Malachi Dupre RC .40 1.00
299 Curtis Samuel RC .50 1.25
300 Tarik Cohen RC .75 2.00

2017 Rookies and Stars Green

*VETS: 1.5X TO 4X BASIC CARDS
*ROOKIES: .8X TO 2X BASIC CARDS

2017 Rookies and Stars Longevity

*VETS: 2.5X TO 6X BASIC CARDS
*ROOKIES: 1.2X TO 3X BASIC CARDS

2017 Rookies and Stars Purple

*VETS: 1.5X TO 4X BASIC CARDS
*ROOKIES: .8X TO 2X BASIC CARDS

2017 Rookies and Stars Red

*VETS: 1.5X TO 4X BASIC CARDS
*ROOKIES: .8X TO 2X BASIC CARDS

2017 Rookies and Stars Red and Blue

*VETS: 4X TO 10X BASIC CARDS
*ROOKIES: 2X TO 5X BASIC CARDS

2017 Rookies and Stars True Blue

*VETS: 3X TO 8X BASIC CARDS
*ROOKIES: 1.5X TO 4X BASIC CARDS

2017 Rookies and Stars Action Packed

*TRUE BLUE/49: 1.2X TO 3X BASIC INSERTS
1 Brett Favre 1.50 4.00
2 Ezekiel Elliott 1.00 2.50
3 Bo Jackson 1.00 2.50
4 Le'Veon Bell .60 1.50
5 Ray Lewis .75 2.00
6 Rob Gronkowski .75 2.00
7 Marshall Faulk .60 1.50
8 Julio Jones .75 2.00
9 Barry Sanders 1.25 3.00
10 Tom Brady 2.00 5.00
11 Randy Moss .60 1.50
12 Odell Beckham Jr. .75 2.00
13 Jerry Rice 1.25 3.00
14 David Johnson .75 2.00
15 John Elway 1.25 3.00
16 J.J. Watt .75 2.00
17 LaDainian Tomlinson .60 1.50
18 Antonio Brown .75 2.00
19 Michael Vick .60 1.50
20 Dak Prescott .75 2.00

2017 Rookies and Stars Airborne

*TRUE BLUE/49: 1.2X TO 3X BASIC INSERTS
1 Tyreek Hill .75 2.00
2 Dez Bryant .75 2.00
3 Marcus Allen .60 1.50
4 Troy Aikman 1.00 2.50
5 Odell Beckham Jr. .75 2.00
6 Marshall Faulk .60 1.50
7 Ezekiel Elliott 1.00 2.50
8 Michael Vick .60 1.50
9 Le'Veon Bell .60 1.50
10 Julio Jones .75 2.00
11 Travis Kelce .75 2.00
12 Todd Gurley II .75 2.00
13 Emmitt Smith 1.25 3.00
14 Curtis Martin .60 1.50
15 Larry Fitzgerald .60 1.50
16 David Johnson .75 2.00
17 LeSean McCoy .75 2.00
18 Antonio Brown .75 2.00
19 Kelvin Benjamin .60 1.50
20 Rob Gronkowski .75 2.00

2017 Rookies and Stars Cross Training Jerseys

*PRIME/25: .6X TO 1.5X BASIC JSY/99
1 Mike Williams 2.50 6.00
2 John Ross III 2.00 5.00
3 ArDarius Stewart 1.50 4.00
4 DeShone Kizer 1.50 4.00
5 Patrick Mahomes II 25.00 50.00
6 Leonard Fournette 5.00 12.00
7 Chris Godwin 2.00 5.00
8 Taywan Taylor 1.50 4.00
9 Jamaal Williams 1.50 4.00
10 Corey Davis 2.50 6.00
11 Davis Webb 1.50 4.00
12 Josh Reynolds 1.50 4.00
13 C.J. Beathard 1.50 4.00
14 D'Onta Foreman 2.00 5.00
15 R. Joshua Dobbs 2.00 5.00
16 Kenny Golladay 2.50 6.00
17 Carlos Henderson 1.50 4.00
18 Evan Engram 2.00 5.00
19 Samaje Perine 1.50 4.00
20 Marlon Mack 2.50 6.00
21 Cooper Kupp 2.50 6.00
22 Zay Jones 2.00 5.00
23 Jeremy McNichols 1.50 4.00
24 Dalvin Cook 3.00 8.00
25 Mack Hollins 1.50 4.00
26 Joe Mixon 3.00 8.00
27 Alvin Kamara 5.00 12.00
28 Dede Westbrook 1.50 4.00
29 Nathan Peterman 2.00 5.00
30 Kareem Hunt 4.00 10.00
31 Christian McCaffrey 5.00 12.00
32 James Conner 3.00 8.00
33 Wayne Gallman 2.00 5.00
34 Mitchell Trubisky 5.00 12.00
35 Curtis Samuel 2.00 5.00
36 Joe Williams 1.50 4.00
37 Amara Darboh 1.50 4.00
38 Deshaun Watson 6.00 15.00
39 O.J. Howard 2.00 5.00
40 JuJu Smith-Schuster 3.00 8.00

2017 Rookies and Stars Crusade

*RED/99: .8X TO 2X BASIC INSERTS
*PURPLE/49: 1X TO 2.5X BASIC INSERTS
*ORANGE/25: 1.2X TO 3X BASIC INSERTS
1 Adrian Peterson 1.25 3.00
2 Evan Engram 1.00 2.50
3 Ben Roethlisberger 1.25 3.00
4 David Johnson 1.25 3.00
5 Cam Newton 1.25 3.00
6 Deshaun Watson 5.00 12.00
7 Aaron Rodgers 2.50 6.00
8 Mike Williams 1.25 3.00
9 Jared Goff 1.25 3.00
10 Kareem Hunt 1.50 4.00
11 Odell Beckham Jr. 1.25 3.00
12 Joe Mixon 1.50 4.00
13 Derek Carr 1.25 3.00
14 Matt Ryan 1.00 2.50
15 Dak Prescott 1.25 3.00
16 Mitchell Trubisky 4.00 10.00
17 Jordy Nelson 1.00 2.50
18 Christian McCaffrey 2.00 5.00
19 Todd Gurley II 1.25 3.00
20 Zay Jones 1.00 2.50
21 Marcus Mariota 1.25 3.00
22 R. Joshua Dobbs 1.00 2.50
23 Amari Cooper 1.25 3.00
24 Julio Jones 1.25 3.00
25 Ezekiel Elliott 1.50 4.00
26 Leonard Fournette 2.50 6.00
27 J.J. Watt 1.25 3.00
28 Dalvin Cook 2.00 5.00
29 Tom Brady 3.00 8.00
30 Dede Westbrook .75 2.00
31 Jameis Winston 1.00 2.50
32 JuJu Smith-Schuster 2.00 5.00
33 Le'Veon Bell 1.00 2.50
34 Joe Flacco 1.00 2.50
35 Von Miller 1.00 2.50
36 DeShone Kizer .75 2.00
37 Tyreek Hill 1.25 3.00
38 Corey Davis 1.25 3.00
39 Rob Gronkowski 1.25 3.00
40 D'Onta Foreman 1.00 2.50
41 Russell Wilson 1.50 4.00
42 Alvin Kamara 3.00 8.00
43 Antonio Brown 1.25 3.00
44 LeSean McCoy 1.25 3.00
45 Matthew Stafford 1.00 2.50
46 Patrick Mahomes II 15.00 40.00
47 Philip Rivers 1.25 3.00
48 John Ross III 1.00 2.50
49 Drew Brees 1.25 3.00
50 O.J. Howard 1.00 2.50

2017 Rookies and Stars Dress for Success Jersey Autographs

1 Nathan Peterman 4.00 10.00
2 Dede Westbrook 3.00 8.00
3 Samaje Perine 3.00 8.00
4 Evan Engram 4.00 10.00
5 Joe Mixon 6.00 15.00
6 Alvin Kamara 25.00 50.00
7 JuJu Smith-Schuster 20.00 50.00
8 Carlos Henderson 3.00 8.00
9 Mack Hollins 3.00 8.00
10 Corey Davis 5.00 12.00
11 O.J. Howard 4.00 10.00
12 Deshaun Watson 50.00 100.00
13 Taywan Taylor 3.00 8.00
14 Jamaal Williams 3.00 8.00
15 Joe Williams 3.00 8.00
16 Amara Darboh 3.00 8.00
17 Kareem Hunt EXCH 6.00 15.00
18 Chris Godwin 4.00 10.00
19 Marlon Mack 5.00 12.00
20 Curtis Samuel 4.00 10.00
21 Patrick Mahomes II 150.00 300.00
22 DeShone Kizer 3.00 8.00
23 Wayne Gallman 4.00 10.00
24 James Conner 6.00 15.00
25 John Ross III 4.00 10.00
26 ArDarius Stewart 3.00 8.00
27 Kenny Golladay 5.00 12.00
28 Christian McCaffrey 8.00 20.00
29 Mike Williams 5.00 12.00
30 Dalvin Cook 8.00 20.00
31 R. Joshua Dobbs 4.00 10.00
32 D'Onta Foreman 4.00 10.00
33 Zay Jones 4.00 10.00
34 Jeremy McNichols 3.00 8.00
35 Josh Reynolds 3.00 8.00
36 C.J. Beathard 3.00 8.00
37 Leonard Fournette 20.00 50.00
38 Cooper Kupp 5.00 12.00
39 Mitchell Trubisky 15.00 40.00
40 Davis Webb 3.00 8.00

2017 Rookies and Stars Freshman Orientation Jersey Autographs

1 Carlos Henderson 3.00 8.00
2 Mack Hollins 3.00 8.00
3 Corey Davis 5.00 12.00
4 Nathan Peterman 4.00 10.00
5 Dede Westbrook 3.00 8.00
6 Samaje Perine 3.00 8.00
7 Evan Engram 4.00 10.00
8 Joe Mixon 6.00 15.00
9 Alvin Kamara 25.00 50.00
10 JuJu Smith-Schuster 20.00 50.00
11 Chris Godwin 4.00 10.00
12 Marlon Mack 5.00 12.00
13 Curtis Samuel 4.00 10.00
14 O.J. Howard 4.00 10.00
15 Deshaun Watson 50.00 100.00
16 Taywan Taylor 3.00 8.00
17 Jamaal Williams 3.00 8.00
18 Joe Williams 3.00 8.00
19 Amara Darboh 3.00 8.00
20 Kareem Hunt EXCH 6.00 15.00
21 Christian McCaffrey 8.00 20.00
22 Mike Williams 5.00 12.00
23 Dalvin Cook 8.00 20.00
24 Patrick Mahomes II 150.00 300.00
25 DeShone Kizer 3.00 8.00
26 Wayne Gallman 4.00 10.00
27 James Conner 6.00 15.00
28 John Ross III 4.00 10.00
29 ArDarius Stewart 3.00 8.00
30 Kenny Golladay 5.00 12.00
31 Cooper Kupp 5.00 12.00
32 Mitchell Trubisky 15.00 40.00
33 Davis Webb 3.00 8.00
34 R. Joshua Dobbs 4.00 10.00
35 D'Onta Foreman 4.00 10.00
36 Zay Jones 4.00 10.00
37 Jeremy McNichols 3.00 8.00
38 Josh Reynolds 3.00 8.00
39 C.J. Beathard 3.00 8.00
40 Leonard Fournette 20.00 50.00

2017 Rookies and Stars Great American Heroes

*RED/99: .8X TO 2X BASIC INSERTS
*PURPLE/49: 1X TO 2.5X BASIC INSERTS
*ORANGE/25: 1.2X TO 3X BASIC INSERTS
1 Howie Long 1.25 3.00
2 Joe Namath 1.50 4.00
3 Alan Page .75 2.00
4 Ken Anderson .75 2.00
5 Dan Fouts 1.00 2.50
6 Marcus Allen 1.00 2.50
7 Doug Flutie 1.00 2.50
8 Mike Ditka 1.25 3.00
9 Edgerrin James 1.00 2.50
10 Randy Moss 1.00 2.50
11 Jerry Rice 2.00 5.00
12 John Elway 2.00 5.00
13 Barry Sanders 2.00 5.00
14 Tom Brady 3.00 8.00
15 Dan Marino 2.50 6.00
16 Mark Brunell 1.00 2.50
17 Ed McCaffrey .75 2.00
18 Peyton Manning 2.50 6.00
19 Emmitt Smith 2.00 5.00
20 Rich Gannon .75 2.00
21 Bo Jackson 1.50 4.00
22 John Riggins 1.00 2.50
23 Brett Favre 2.50 6.00
24 Lance Alworth 1.00 2.50
25 Deion Sanders 1.00 2.50
26 Mark Gastineau .75 2.00
27 Ed Reed 1.00 2.50
28 Phil Simms 1.00 2.50
29 Fran Tarkenton 1.25 3.00
30 Rodney Harrison .75 2.00
31 Jim Plunkett 1.00 2.50
32 Kellen Winslow 1.00 2.50
33 Calvin Johnson 1.25 3.00
34 Len Dawson 1.25 3.00
35 Don Maynard 1.00 2.50
36 Michael Strahan 1.00 2.50
37 Eddie George 1.00 2.50
38 Priest Holmes .75 2.00
39 Fred Taylor 1.00 2.50
40 Terry Bradshaw 2.00 5.00

2017 Rookies and Stars Great American Signatures

1 Len Dawson/49 10.00 25.00
2 Bob Griese/49 8.00 20.00
3 Randall Cunningham/49
4 Earl Campbell/49 10.00 25.00
5 Tedy Bruschi/49
6 Fred Dryer/25 4.00 10.00
7 Jim McMahon/25
8 Bill Parcells/49 10.00 25.00
10 Desmond Howard/49
11 Phil Simms/25
12 Doug Williams/49 4.00 10.00
15 Jimmy Johnson/49 12.00 30.00
16 Fred Taylor/49 4.00 10.00
19 Larry Csonka/25 10.00 25.00

2017 Rookies and Stars Great American Treasures Jerseys

*PRIME/25: .6X TO 1.5X BASIC JSY/99
1 Jim Kelly 3.00 8.00
2 Howie Long 3.00 8.00
3 John Riggins 2.50 6.00
4 Tony Romo 2.50 6.00
5 Hines Ward 2.50 6.00
6 Jim Plunkett 2.50 6.00
7 Andre Reed 2.50 6.00
8 Jerome Bettis 3.00 8.00
9 Thurman Thomas 2.50 6.00
10 Kurt Warner 2.50 6.00
11 Fran Tarkenton 3.00 8.00
12 Mike Ditka 3.00 8.00
13 Earl Campbell 3.00 8.00
14 Troy Aikman 4.00 10.00
15 Joe Theismann 3.00 8.00
16 Lance Alworth 2.50 6.00
17 Brett Favre 6.00 15.00
18 Dwight Clark 2.50 6.00
19 Mark Brunell 2.50 6.00
20 Terrell Davis 2.50 6.00

2017 Rookies and Stars NFL Authentic Jerseys

*PRIME/49: .6X TO 1.5X BASIC JSY
1 Amari Cooper 3.00 8.00
2 Ezekiel Elliott 4.00 10.00
3 Joey Bosa 3.00 8.00
4 Davante Adams 2.50 6.00
5 Todd Gurley II 3.00 8.00
6 David Johnson 3.00 8.00
7 Jameis Winston 2.50 6.00
8 Kelvin Benjamin 2.50 6.00
9 Michael Thomas 3.00 8.00
10 Corey Coleman 2.00 5.00
11 Carson Wentz 4.00 10.00
12 Paxton Lynch 2.00 5.00
13 Derrick Henry 2.50 6.00
14 Jared Goff 3.00 8.00
15 Marcus Mariota 3.00 8.00
16 Devonta Freeman 2.50 6.00
17 Sterling Shepard 2.50 6.00
18 Jordan Howard 3.00 8.00
19 Khalil Mack 3.00 8.00
20 Dak Prescott 3.00 8.00

2017 Rookies and Stars Precision Passers

*TRUE BLUE/49: 1.2X TO 3X BASIC INSERTS
1 Cam Newton .75 2.00
2 Tom Brady 2.00 5.00
3 Aaron Rodgers 1.50 4.00
4 John Elway 1.25 3.00
5 Russell Wilson 1.00 2.50
6 Brett Favre 1.50 4.00
7 Troy Aikman 1.00 2.50
8 Dan Fouts .60 1.50
9 Joe Flacco .60 1.50
10 Dan Marino 1.50 4.00
11 Jeff Garcia .50 1.25
12 Dak Prescott .75 2.00
13 Matt Ryan .60 1.50
14 Steve Young 1.00 2.50
15 Ben Roethlisberger .75 2.00
16 Jim Kelly .75 2.00
17 Derek Carr .75 2.00
18 Peyton Manning 1.50 4.00
19 Andrew Luck 1.00 2.50
20 Drew Brees .75 2.00

2017 Rookies and Stars Prime Cuts

1 John Ross III 3.00 8.00
2 O.J. Howard 3.00 8.00
3 Mike Williams 4.00 10.00
4 Evan Engram 3.00 8.00
5 Taywan Taylor 2.50 6.00
6 D'Onta Foreman 3.00 8.00
7 Dede Westbrook 2.50 6.00
8 Dalvin Cook 5.00 12.00
9 Leonard Fournette 8.00 20.00
10 Mitchell Trubisky 8.00 20.00
11 Joe Mixon 5.00 12.00
12 Curtis Samuel 3.00 8.00
13 Zay Jones 3.00 8.00
14 Christian McCaffrey 8.00 20.00
15 DeShone Kizer 2.50 6.00
16 Deshaun Watson 10.00 25.00
17 Alvin Kamara 8.00 20.00
18 Corey Davis 4.00 10.00
19 Patrick Mahomes II 25.00 50.00
20 R. Joshua Dobbs 3.00 8.00

2017 Rookies and Stars Prowlers

*TRUE BLUE/49: 1.2X TO 3X BASIC INSERTS
1 Aqib Talib .50 1.25
2 Ronnie Lott .60 1.50
3 Steve Atwater .60 1.50
4 Richard Sherman .75 2.00
5 Ed Reed .60 1.50
6 Earl Thomas III .60 1.50
7 Rod Woodson .60 1.50
8 Tyrann Mathieu .60 1.50
9 Charles Woodson .75 2.00
10 Eric Berry .60 1.50

2017 Rookies and Stars Rookies Longevity Signatures

201 Patrick Mahomes II/75 150.00 300.00
203 R. Joshua Dobbs/75 3.00 8.00
204 Shelton Gibson/99 2.50 6.00
206 Charles Harris/99 2.50 6.00
207 Nathan Peterman/99 3.00 8.00
208 Isaiah Ford/99 2.50 6.00
209 O.J. Howard/99 3.00 8.00
210 Sidney Jones/99 2.50 6.00
211 DeShone Kizer/75 2.50 6.00
212 David Njoku/75 3.00 8.00
213 D'Onta Foreman/75 3.00 8.00
214 Malik Hooker/99 2.50 6.00
215 Artavis Scott/99 2.50 6.00
216 Chris Godwin/99 3.00 8.00
217 Dede Westbrook/99 2.50 6.00
218 Jabrill Peppers/75 4.00 10.00
219 Deshaun Watson/75 40.00 80.00
220 Solomon Thomas/99 2.50 6.00
221 Wayne Gallman/99 3.00 8.00
223 Zay Jones/99 3.00 8.00
226 Cordrea Tankersley/99 3.00 8.00
227 Samaje Perine/99 2.50 6.00
228 Jake Butt/99 3.00 8.00
229 Taywan Taylor/75 2.50 6.00
230 T.J. Watt/99 8.00 20.00
231 James Conner/75 5.00 12.00
233 Jeremy McNichols/99 2.50 6.00
234 Marlon Humphrey/99 2.50 6.00
235 Brian Hill/99 2.50 6.00
236 Corey Clement/99 3.00 8.00
237 Evan Engram/75 3.00 8.00
238 Jamal Adams/99 2.50 6.00
239 Jamaal Williams/99 2.50 6.00
240 Taco Charlton/99 2.50 6.00
241 John Ross III/75 3.00 8.00
243 Josh Reynolds/99 2.50 6.00
244 Marshon Lattimore/99 3.00 8.00
246 DeMarcus Walker/99 2.50 6.00
247 Joe Mixon/75 5.00 12.00
249 Joe Williams/99 2.50 6.00
251 ArDarius Stewart/75 2.50 6.00
252 Adam Shaheen/99 2.50 6.00
253 C.J. Beathard/99 2.50 6.00
254 Matthew Dayes/99 2.50 6.00
256 Desmond King/99 3.00 8.00
257 Alvin Kamara/99 25.00 50.00
258 Jonathan Allen/99 3.00 8.00
259 Amara Darboh/99 2.50 6.00
260 Tim Williams/99 3.00 8.00
261 Kenny Golladay/99 4.00 10.00
262 Jonnu Smith/99 2.50 6.00
263 Leonard Fournette/75 20.00 40.00
264 Noah Brown/99 3.00 8.00
265 Cameron Sutton/99 2.50 6.00
267 JuJu Smith-Schuster/75
268 Jordan Leggett/99 2.50 6.00
269 Kareem Hunt/75 5.00 12.00
270 Travis Rudolph/99 2.50 6.00
271 Christian McCaffrey/75 6.00 15.00
272 Jehu Chesson/99 3.00 8.00
273 Cooper Kupp/99 4.00 10.00
274 Quincy Wilson/99 2.50 6.00
275 Carl Lawson/99 2.50 6.00
276 Elijah Hood/99 2.50 6.00
277 Carlos Henderson/75 2.50 6.00
279 T.J. Logan/99 4.00 10.00
280 Tre'Davious White/99 2.50 6.00
281 Mike Williams/75 4.00 10.00
282 Khalfani Muhammad/99 2.50 6.00
283 Mitchell Trubisky/75
284 Raekwon McMillan/99 2.50 6.00
285 Chad Hansen/99 2.50 6.00
286 Elijah Qualls/99 2.50 6.00
287 Mack Hollins/99 2.50 6.00
289 Marlon Mack/75 4.00 10.00
291 Dalvin Cook/75 12.00 30.00
292 DeAngelo Yancey/99 2.50 6.00
293 Davis Webb/99 2.50 6.00
294 Ryan Switzer/99 3.00 8.00
295 Chad Kelly/99 2.50 6.00
296 Gareon Conley/99 2.50 6.00
297 Corey Davis/75 4.00 10.00
298 Malachi Dupre/99 2.50 6.00
299 Curtis Samuel/75 3.00 8.00
300 Tarik Cohen/99 5.00 12.00

2017 Rookies and Stars Rookies Longevity Signatures Blue

*BLUE/49: .5X TO 1.2X BASIC AU/75-99
201 Patrick Mahomes II 175.00 350.00
219 Deshaun Watson 50.00 100.00

2017 Rookies and Stars Rookies Longevity Signatures Purple

*PURPLE/25: .6X TO 1.5X BASIC AU/75-99
201 Patrick Mahomes II 200.00 400.00
219 Deshaun Watson 75.00 150.00
283 Mitchell Trubisky 75.00 150.00

2017 Rookies and Stars Standing Ovation

*TRUE BLUE/49: 1.2X TO 3X BASIC INSERTS
1 Steve Smith Sr. .60 1.50
2 Ickey Woods .50 1.25
3 Von Miller .60 1.50
4 Carson Palmer .60 1.50

5 Odell Beckham Jr. .75 2.00
6 Terrell Davis .60 1.50
7 Ezekiel Elliott 1.00 2.50
8 Randy Moss .60 1.50
9 Antonio Brown .75 2.00
10 Deion Sanders .60 1.50
11 Travis Kelce .75 2.00
12 Dak Prescott .75 2.00
13 T.Y. Hilton .60 1.50
14 Le'Veon Bell .60 1.50
15 Marquette King .50 1.25
16 J.J. Watt .75 2.00
17 Cam Newton .75 2.00
18 Aaron Rodgers 1.50 4.00
19 Rob Gronkowski .75 2.00
20 Mark Gastineau .50 1.25

2017 Rookies and Stars Star Search Jerseys

*PRIME/25: .8X TO 2X BASIC JSY
1 John Ross III 2.00 5.00
2 Josh Reynolds 1.50 4.00
3 Zay Jones 2.00 5.00
4 James Conner 3.00 8.00
5 DeShone Kizer 1.50 4.00
6 D'Onta Foreman 2.00 5.00
7 Dalvin Cook 3.00 8.00
8 Mitchell Trubisky 5.00 12.00
9 Leonard Fournette 5.00 12.00
10 Kenny Golladay 2.50 6.00
11 Joe Mixon 3.00 8.00
12 Joe Williams 1.50 4.00
13 Taywan Taylor 1.50 4.00
14 Evan Engram 2.00 5.00
15 Dede Westbrook 1.50 4.00
16 Deshaun Watson 6.00 15.00
17 Corey Davis 2.50 6.00
18 Marlon Mack 2.50 6.00
19 Kareem Hunt 3.00 8.00
20 JuJu Smith-Schuster 3.00 8.00
21 Mike Williams 2.50 6.00
22 Davis Webb 1.50 4.00
23 Cooper Kupp 2.50 6.00
24 Christian McCaffrey 5.00 12.00
25 ArDarius Stewart 1.50 4.00
26 C.J. Beathard 1.50 4.00
27 Jeremy McNichols 1.50 4.00
28 Wayne Gallman 2.00 5.00
29 Patrick Mahomes II 25.00 50.00
30 R. Joshua Dobbs 2.00 5.00
31 Mack Hollins 1.50 4.00
32 Curtis Samuel 2.00 5.00
33 Chris Godwin 2.00 5.00
34 Carlos Henderson 1.50 4.00
35 Alvin Kamara 5.00 12.00
36 Amara Darboh 1.50 4.00
37 Jamaal Williams 1.50 4.00
38 Samaje Perine 1.50 4.00
39 Nathan Peterman 2.00 5.00
40 O.J. Howard 2.00 5.00

2017 Rookies and Stars Stellar Rookies

*RED/99: .8X TO 2X BASIC INSERTS
*PURPLE/49: 1X TO 2.5X BASIC INSERTS
*ORANGE/25: 1.2X TO 3X BASIC INSERTS
1 Deshaun Watson 5.00 12.00
2 Mitchell Trubisky 4.00 10.00
3 Leonard Fournette 2.50 6.00
4 DeShone Kizer .75 2.00
5 Patrick Mahomes II 25.00 50.00
6 Mike Williams 1.25 3.00
7 Christian McCaffrey 2.00 5.00
8 Dalvin Cook 2.00 5.00
9 Corey Davis 1.25 3.00
10 John Ross III 1.00 2.50

2017 Rookies and Stars Team Duals Jerseys

*PRIME/49: .5X TO 1.2X BASIC JSY/99
1 E.Engram/O.Beckham 3.00 8.00
2 A.Darboh/R.Wilson 4.00 10.00
3 D.Cook/S.Diggs 4.00 10.00
4 J.Mixon/J.Ross 4.00 10.00
5 C.Davis/M.Mariota 3.00 8.00
6 D.Westbrook/L.Fournette 10.00 25.00
7 A.Dalton/J.Ross 2.50 6.00
8 C.Beathard/J.Williams 2.00 5.00
9 D.Watson/D.Hopkins 12.00 30.00
10 T.Taylor/C.Davis 3.00 8.00
11 C.Samuel/C.McCaffrey 10.00 25.00
12 D.Prescott/R.Switzer 3.00 8.00
13 D.Kizer/D.Njoku 2.50 6.00
14 D.Foreman/D.Watson 12.00 30.00
15 M.Williams/P.Rivers 3.00 8.00
16 J.SmthSchstr/J.Dobbs 6.00 15.00
17 P.Mahomes/T.Hill 25.00 50.00
18 O.Howard/C.Godwin 2.50 6.00
19 J.Winston/O.Howard 2.50 6.00
20 N.Peterman/Z.Jones 2.50 6.00

2017 Rookies and Stars Year One Jerseys

*PRIME/25: .8X TO 2X BASIC JSY
1 Leonard Fournette 5.00 12.00
2 Kareem Hunt 3.00 8.00
3 Patrick Mahomes II 25.00 50.00
4 Nathan Peterman 2.00 5.00
5 John Ross III 2.00 5.00
6 Joe Mixon 3.00 8.00
7 Mike Williams 2.50 6.00
8 Mack Hollins 1.50 4.00
9 Zay Jones 2.00 5.00
10 Taywan Taylor 1.50 4.00
11 Cooper Kupp 2.50 6.00
12 Chris Godwin 2.00 5.00
13 DeShone Kizer 1.50 4.00
14 Dede Westbrook 1.50 4.00
15 ArDarius Stewart 1.50 4.00
16 Alvin Kamara 5.00 12.00
17 Dalvin Cook 3.00 8.00
18 Corey Davis 2.50 6.00
19 Jeremy McNichols 1.50 4.00
20 Jamaal Williams 1.50 4.00
21 Mitchell Trubisky 5.00 12.00
22 Marlon Mack 2.50 6.00
23 Wayne Gallman 2.00 5.00
24 Samaje Perine 1.50 4.00
25 Kenny Golladay 2.50 6.00
26 JuJu Smith-Schuster 3.00 8.00
27 R. Joshua Dobbs 2.00 5.00
28 O.J. Howard 2.00 5.00
29 Josh Reynolds 1.50 4.00
30 Joe Williams 1.50 4.00
31 Davis Webb 1.50 4.00
32 Curtis Samuel 2.00 5.00
33 James Conner 3.00 8.00
34 Evan Engram 2.00 5.00
35 Christian McCaffrey 5.00 12.00
36 Carlos Henderson 1.50 4.00
37 D'Onta Foreman 2.00 5.00
38 Deshaun Watson 6.00 15.00
39 C.J. Beathard 1.50 4.00
40 Amara Darboh 1.50 4.00

2018 Rookies and Stars

1 Dak Prescott .30 .75
2 Ezekiel Elliott .40 1.00
3 Allen Hurns .20 .50
4 Eli Manning .25 .60
5 Odell Beckham Jr. .30 .75
6 Landon Collins .20 .50
7 Carson Wentz .40 1.00
8 Jay Ajayi .25 .60
9 Alshon Jeffery .25 .60
10 Alex Smith .25 .60
11 Jordan Reed .20 .50
12 Josh Norman .20 .50
13 Nathan Peterman .20 .50
14 LeSean McCoy .30 .75
15 Kelvin Benjamin .25 .60
16 Ryan Tannehill .25 .60
17 Kenyan Drake .20 .50
18 Cameron Wake .20 .50
19 Tom Brady .75 2.00
20 Rob Gronkowski .30 .75
21 Julian Edelman .30 .75
22 Leonard Williams .20 .50
23 Jamal Adams .25 .60
24 Robby Anderson .20 .50
25 Sam Bradford .20 .50
26 David Johnson .30 .75
27 Larry Fitzgerald .25 .60
28 Jared Goff .30 .75
29 Todd Gurley II .30 .75
30 Aaron Donald .30 .75
31 Brandin Cooks .25 .60
32 Jimmy Garoppolo .40 1.00
33 Marquise Goodwin .20 .50
34 Richard Sherman .30 .75
35 Russell Wilson .40 1.00
36 Doug Baldwin .25 .60
37 Brandon Marshall .20 .50
38 Case Keenum .25 .60
39 Von Miller .25 .60
40 Demaryius Thomas .25 .60
41 Patrick Mahomes II .75 2.00
42 Kareem Hunt .25 .60
43 Tyreek Hill .30 .75
44 Travis Kelce .30 .75
45 Joey Bosa .30 .75
46 Melvin Gordon .25 .60
47 Philip Rivers .30 .75
48 Derek Carr .30 .75
49 Amari Cooper .30 .75
50 Khalil Mack .30 .75
51 Mitchell Trubisky .30 .75
52 Jordan Howard .30 .75
53 Allen Robinson .25 .60
54 Matthew Stafford .25 .60
55 Golden Tate III .20 .50
56 LeGarrette Blount .25 .60
57 Aaron Rodgers .60 1.50
58 Davante Adams .25 .60
59 Clay Matthews .25 .60
60 Adam Thielen .30 .75
61 Kirk Cousins .30 .75
62 Dalvin Cook .25 .60
63 Joe Flacco .25 .60
64 Alex Collins .20 .50
65 Terrell Suggs .20 .50
66 Andy Dalton .25 .60
67 A.J. Green .30 .75
68 Vontaze Burfict .20 .50
69 Tyrod Taylor .25 .60
70 Myles Garrett .30 .75
71 Jarvis Landry .25 .60
72 Ben Roethlisberger .30 .75
73 Le'Veon Bell .25 .60
74 Antonio Brown .30 .75
75 T.J. Watt .25 .60
76 Deshaun Watson .40 1.00
77 Jadeveon Clowney .20 .50
78 DeAndre Hopkins .25 .60
79 Andrew Luck .40 1.00
80 T.Y. Hilton .25 .60
81 Marlon Mack .20 .50
82 Blake Bortles .20 .50
83 Leonard Fournette .30 .75
84 Jalen Ramsey .25 .60
85 Marcus Mariota .30 .75
86 Derrick Henry .30 .75
87 Corey Davis .25 .60
88 Jameis Winston .25 .60
89 Mike Evans .25 .60
90 Drew Brees .30 .75
91 Alvin Kamara .25 .60
92 Michael Thomas .30 .75
93 Cam Newton .30 .75
94 Christian McCaffrey .30 .75
95 Luke Kuechly .25 .60
96 Gerald McCoy .20 .50
97 Matt Ryan .25 .60
98 Julio Jones .30 .75
99 Devonta Freeman .25 .60
100 Vic Beasley Jr. .20 .50
101 Baker Mayfield RC 4.00 10.00
102 Saquon Barkley RC 3.00 8.00
103 Sam Darnold RC 2.50 6.00
104 Bradley Chubb RC .60 1.50
105 Josh Allen RC 1.50 4.00
106 Josh Rosen RC 1.25 3.00
107 D.J. Moore RC .75 2.00
108 Hayden Hurst RC .50 1.25
109 Calvin Ridley RC 1.00 2.50
110 Rashaad Penny RC .60 1.50
111 Sony Michel RC 1.25 3.00
112 Lamar Jackson RC 2.50 6.00
113 Nick Chubb RC 1.25 3.00
114 Ronald Jones II RC .40 1.00
115 Courtland Sutton RC .60 1.50
116 Mike Gesicki RC .50 1.25
117 Kerryon Johnson RC .60 1.50
118 Dante Pettis RC .60 1.50
119 Christian Kirk RC .60 1.50
120 Anthony Miller RC .60 1.50
121 Derrius Guice RC .75 2.00
122 James Washington RC .75 2.00
123 D.J. Chark RC .50 1.25
124 Royce Freeman RC .50 1.25
125 Mason Rudolph RC 1.00 2.50
126 Michael Gallup RC .75 2.00
127 Tre'Quan Smith RC .60 1.50
128 Keke Coutee RC .50 1.25
129 Nyheim Hines RC .50 1.25
130 Kyle Lauletta RC .60 1.50
131 Mark Walton RC .50 1.25
132 DaeSean Hamilton RC .50 1.25
133 Ito Smith RC .50 1.25
134 Kalen Ballage RC .50 1.25
135 Jaleel Scott RC .40 1.00
136 J'Mon Moore RC .40 1.00
137 Daurice Fountain RC .50 1.25
138 Jaylen Samuels RC .50 1.25
139 Mike White RC .50 1.25
140 Marquez Valdes-Scantling RC .50 1.25
141 Denzel Ward RC 1.00 2.50
142 Roquan Smith RC 1.25 3.00
143 Minkah Fitzpatrick RC .75 2.00
144 Will Dissly RC .50 1.25
145 Daron Payne RC .60 1.50
146 Marcus Davenport RC .75 2.00
147 Tremaine Edmunds RC .75 2.00
148 Derwin James RC .75 2.00
149 Jaire Alexander RC .60 1.50
150 Leighton Vander Esch RC 1.25 3.00
151 Rashaan Evans RC .60 1.50
152 Terrell Edmunds RC 1.25 3.00
153 Taven Bryan RC .40 1.00
154 Mike Hughes RC .60 1.50
155 Harold Landry RC .40 1.00
156 Joshua Jackson RC .75 2.00
157 M.J. Stewart RC .40 1.00
158 Deontay Burnett RC .50 1.25
159 Duke Dawson RC .40 1.00
160 Isaiah Oliver RC .40 1.00
161 Carlton Davis RC .50 1.25
162 Lorenzo Carter RC .40 1.00
163 Justin Reid RC .40 1.00
164 Fred Warner RC .40 1.00
165 Jerome Baker RC .50 1.25
166 Derrick Nnadi RC .40 1.00
167 Sam Hubbard RC .50 1.25
168 Malik Jefferson RC .50 1.25
169 Rasheem Green RC .40 1.00
170 Arden Key RC .40 1.00
171 Chukwuma Okorafor RC .40 1.00
172 Ronnie Harrison RC .50 1.25
173 Harrison Phillips RC .40 1.00
174 Mark Andrews RC .60 1.50
175 Dallas Goedert RC .50 1.25
176 Christopher Herndon IV RC .40 1.00
177 Dorian O'Daniel RC .40 1.00
178 Ian Thomas RC .40 1.00
179 Jalyn Holmes RC .60 1.50
180 Antonio Callaway RC .50 1.25
181 Josey Jewell RC .50 1.25
182 Da'Shawn Hand RC .40 1.00
183 Dorance Armstrong Jr. RC .40 1.00
184 Jordan Whitehead RC .40 1.00
185 Anthony Averett RC .50 1.25
186 Kyzir White RC .60 1.50
187 Durham Smythe RC .40 1.00
188 Armani Watts RC .40 1.00
189 Chase Edmonds RC .40 1.00
190 Josh Sweat RC .50 1.25
191 Marquis Haynes RC .40 1.00
192 Dalton Schultz RC .50 1.25
193 Shaquem Griffin RC .60 1.50
194 Maurice Hurst RC .50 1.25
195 D.J. Reed RC .40 1.00
196 Tre Flowers RC .40 1.00
197 Micah Kiser RC .40 1.00
198 Marcus Allen RC .60 1.50
199 Daniel Carlson RC .40 1.00
200 Tyler Conklin RC .40 1.00

2018 Rookies and Stars Green

*VETS: 1.5X TO 4X BASIC CARDS
*ROOKIES: .8X TO 2X BASIC CARDS

2018 Rookies and Stars Longevity

*VETS: 2.5X TO 6X BASIC CARDS
*ROOKIES: 1.2X TO 3X BASIC CARDS

2018 Rookies and Stars Purple

*VETS: 1.5X TO 4X BASIC CARDS

2018 Rookies and Stars Red

*VETS: 1.5X TO 4X BASIC CARDS
*ROOKIES: .8X TO 2X BASIC CARDS

2018 Rookies and Stars Red and Blue

*VETS: 4X TO 10X BASIC CARDS
*ROOKIES: 2X TO 5X BASIC CARDS

2018 Rookies and Stars True Blue

*VETS: 3X TO 8X BASIC CARDS
*ROOKIES: 1.5X TO 4X BASIC CARDS

2018 Rookies and Stars Action Packed

1 Jimmy Garoppolo 1.00 2.50
2 Ben Roethlisberger .75 2.00
3 Russell Wilson 1.00 2.50
4 Marcus Mariota .75 2.00
5 Mike Evans .60 1.50
6 Amari Cooper .75 2.00
7 Robby Anderson .50 1.25
8 Rob Gronkowski .75 2.00
9 Drew Brees .75 2.00
10 Leonard Fournette .75 2.00
11 Todd Gurley II .75 2.00
12 Patrick Mahomes II 2.00 5.00
13 Blake Bortles .50 1.25
14 Dak Prescott .75 2.00
15 Andy Dalton .60 1.50
16 Jordan Howard .75 2.00
17 Matt Ryan .60 1.50
18 Cam Newton .75 2.00
19 Jared Goff .75 2.00
20 Kenyan Drake .50 1.25

2018 Rookies and Stars Airborne Autographs

2 Zach Ertz/25 8.00 20.00
7 Travis Kelce/25 15.00 40.00
15 Robert Woods/25 8.00 20.00
16 Melvin Gordon/25 8.00 20.00
17 Kareem Hunt/25 8.00 20.00
19 Christian McCaffrey/25 10.00 25.00

2018 Rookies and Stars Cross Training Jerseys

*PRIME/25: X TO X BASIC JSY/99
1 Baker Mayfield 12.00 30.00
2 Saquon Barkley 10.00 25.00
3 Sam Darnold 8.00 20.00
4 Bradley Chubb 3.00 8.00
5 Josh Allen 8.00 20.00
6 Josh Rosen 5.00 12.00
7 D.J. Moore 4.00 10.00
8 Hayden Hurst 2.50 6.00
9 Calvin Ridley 4.00 10.00
10 Rashaad Penny 3.00 8.00
11 Sony Michel 4.00 10.00
12 Lamar Jackson 8.00 20.00
13 Nick Chubb 4.00 10.00
14 Ronald Jones II 2.00 5.00
15 Courtland Sutton 3.00 8.00
16 Mike Gesicki 2.50 6.00
17 Kerryon Johnson 3.00 8.00
18 Dante Pettis 3.00 8.00
19 Christian Kirk 3.00 8.00
20 Anthony Miller 3.00 8.00
21 Derrius Guice 4.00 10.00
22 James Washington 4.00 10.00
23 D.J. Chark 2.50 6.00
24 Royce Freeman 2.50 6.00
25 Mason Rudolph 4.00 10.00
26 Michael Gallup 4.00 10.00
27 Tre'Quan Smith 3.00 8.00
28 Keke Coutee 2.50 6.00
29 Nyheim Hines 2.50 6.00
30 Kyle Lauletta 3.00 8.00
31 Mark Walton 2.50 6.00
32 DaeSean Hamilton 2.50 6.00
33 Ito Smith 2.50 6.00
34 Kalen Ballage 2.50 6.00
35 Jaleel Scott 2.00 5.00
36 J'Mon Moore 2.00 5.00
37 Daurice Fountain 2.50 6.00
38 Jaylen Samuels 2.50 6.00
39 Mike White 2.50 6.00
40 Marquez Valdes-Scantling 2.50 6.00

2018 Rookies and Stars Crusade

*ORANGE/35: 1X TO 2.5X BASIC INSERTS
*PINK/85: .8X TO 2X BASIC INSERTS
*PURPLE/65: .8X TO 2X BASIC INSERTS
*RED/99: .8X TO 2X BASIC INSERTS
1 Tom Brady 3.00 8.00
2 Jimmy Garoppolo 1.50 4.00
3 Aaron Rodgers 2.50 6.00
4 Alvin Kamara 1.00 2.50
5 Jordan Howard 1.25 3.00
6 Patrick Mahomes II 3.00 8.00
7 Kareem Hunt 1.00 2.50
8 Ezekiel Elliott 1.50 4.00
9 Dak Prescott 1.25 3.00
10 Cam Newton 1.25 3.00
11 Antonio Brown 1.25 3.00
12 Julio Jones 1.25 3.00
13 A.J. Green 1.25 3.00
14 Jameis Winston 1.00 2.50
15 Kirk Cousins 1.25 3.00
16 Alex Smith 1.00 2.50
17 Jarvis Landry 1.00 2.50
18 Carson Wentz 1.50 4.00
19 J.J. Watt 1.25 3.00
20 Blake Bortles .75 2.00
21 Russell Wilson 1.50 4.00
22 Larry Fitzgerald 1.00 2.50
23 Matthew Stafford 1.00 2.50
24 Jared Goff 1.25 3.00
25 Todd Gurley II 1.25 3.00
26 Joey Bosa 1.25 3.00
27 Marcus Mariota 1.25 3.00
28 Derek Carr 1.25 3.00
29 Odell Beckham Jr. 1.25 3.00
30 Drew Brees 1.25 3.00
31 Josh Rosen 2.50 6.00
32 Saquon Barkley 6.00 15.00
33 Shaquem Griffin 1.25 3.00
34 Josh Allen 3.00 8.00
35 Baker Mayfield 8.00 20.00
36 Calvin Ridley 2.00 5.00
37 Courtland Sutton 1.25 3.00
38 Sony Michel 2.50 6.00
39 Derrius Guice 1.50 4.00
40 Christian Kirk 1.25 3.00
41 Ronald Jones II .75 2.00
42 D.J. Moore 1.50 4.00
43 D.J. Chark 1.00 2.50
44 Mason Rudolph 2.00 5.00
45 Lamar Jackson 5.00 12.00
46 Rashaad Penny 1.25 3.00
47 Nick Chubb 2.50 6.00
48 Anthony Miller 1.25 3.00
49 Bradley Chubb 1.25 3.00
50 Michael Gallup 1.50 4.00

2018 Rookies and Stars Dress for Success Jersey Autographs

*PRIME/25: .6X TO 1.5X BASIC JSY AU/75-99
*PRIME/25: .5X TO 1.2X BASIC JSY AU/49
1 Baker Mayfield/75 EXCH 75.00 150.00
2 Saquon Barkley/75 60.00 125.00
3 Sam Darnold/49 25.00 60.00
4 Bradley Chubb/99 EXCH 5.00 12.00
5 Josh Allen/75 12.00 30.00
6 Josh Rosen/75 10.00 25.00
7 D.J. Moore/99 6.00 15.00
8 Hayden Hurst/49 5.00 12.00
9 Calvin Ridley/49 10.00 25.00
10 Rashaad Penny/99 5.00 12.00
11 Sony Michel/99 10.00 25.00
12 Lamar Jackson/5
13 Nick Chubb/99 10.00 25.00
14 Ronald Jones II/99 3.00 8.00
15 Courtland Sutton/99 5.00 12.00
16 Mike Gesicki/49 5.00 12.00
17 Kerryon Johnson/99 5.00 12.00
18 Dante Pettis/99 5.00 12.00
19 Christian Kirk/25 8.00 20.00
20 Anthony Miller/99 5.00 12.00
21 Derrius Guice/49 8.00 20.00
22 James Washington/99 6.00 15.00
23 D.J. Chark/49 5.00 12.00
24 Royce Freeman/49 5.00 12.00
25 Mason Rudolph/99 8.00 20.00
26 Michael Gallup/49 8.00 20.00
27 Tre'Quan Smith/99 5.00 12.00
28 Keke Coutee/99 4.00 10.00
30 Kyle Lauletta/49 6.00 15.00
31 Mark Walton/99 4.00 10.00
32 DaeSean Hamilton/99 4.00 10.00
33 Ito Smith/99 4.00 10.00
34 Kalen Ballage/99 4.00 10.00
35 Jaleel Scott/99 3.00 8.00
36 J'Mon Moore/99 3.00 8.00
37 Daurice Fountain/99 4.00 10.00
38 Jaylen Samuels/99 4.00 10.00
39 Mike White/49 5.00 12.00
40 Marquez Valdes-Scantling/49 5.00 12.00

2018 Rookies and Stars Freshman Orientation Jersey Autographs Prime

*PRIME/25: .6X TO 1.5X BASIC JSY AU/75-99
*PRIME/25: .5X TO 1.2X BASIC JSY AU/49
1 Baker Mayfield/25 EXCH 125.00 250.00

2018 Rookies and Stars Great American Heroes

*ORANGE/35: 1X TO 2.5X BASIC INSERTS
*PINK/85: .8X TO 2X BASIC INSERTS
*PURPLE/65: .8X TO 2X BASIC INSERTS
*RED/99: .8X TO 2X BASIC INSERTS
1 Alejandro Villanueva 1.00 2.50
2 Roger Staubach 1.50 4.00
3 T.J. Watt 1.00 2.50
4 Drew Brees 1.25 3.00
5 Brian Dawkins 1.25 3.00
6 Randy White 1.00 2.50
7 Brett Keisel .75 2.00
8 Michael Strahan 1.00 2.50
9 Jordan Howard 1.25 3.00
10 Stefon Diggs 1.00 2.50
11 Melvin Gordon 1.00 2.50
12 Luke Kuechly 1.00 2.50
13 Isaac Bruce 1.25 3.00
14 Donald Driver 1.00 2.50
15 John Randle 1.00 2.50
16 J.J. Watt 1.25 3.00
17 Aaron Donald 1.25 3.00
18 Fletcher Cox .75 2.00
19 Tedy Bruschi 1.25 3.00
20 Brian Urlacher 1.25 3.00

2018 Rookies and Stars Great American Heroes Autographs

1 Alejandro Villanueva/25 30.00 60.00
3 T.J. Watt/25 8.00 20.00
5 Brian Dawkins/25 15.00 40.00
6 Randy White/25 8.00 20.00
7 Brett Keisel/15 8.00 20.00
8 Michael Strahan/25 8.00 20.00
9 Jordan Howard/25 10.00 25.00
10 Stefon Diggs/25 8.00 20.00
11 Melvin Gordon/25 8.00 20.00
12 Luke Kuechly/25 12.00 30.00
13 Isaac Bruce/25 10.00 25.00
14 Donald Driver/25 15.00 40.00
15 John Randle/25 8.00 20.00
17 Aaron Donald/25 15.00 40.00
18 Fletcher Cox/25 6.00 15.00
19 Tedy Bruschi/25 10.00 25.00
20 Brian Urlacher/25 10.00 25.00

2018 Rookies and Stars NFL Authentic Jerseys

*PRIME/49: .6X TO 1.5X BASIC JSY
*PRIME/25: .8X TO 2X BASIC JSY
1 Adam Thielen 3.00 8.00
2 David Johnson 3.00 8.00
3 Robby Anderson 2.00 5.00
4 Chris Thompson 2.00 5.00
5 T.J. Watt 2.50 6.00
6 Antonio Gates 2.00 5.00
7 Dak Prescott 3.00 8.00
8 Rob Gronkowski 3.00 8.00
9 Allen Robinson 2.50 6.00
10 Alvin Kamara 2.50 6.00
11 Carson Wentz 4.00 10.00
12 Mitchell Trubisky 3.00 8.00
13 Jared Goff 3.00 8.00
14 Dalvin Cook 2.50 6.00
15 Leonard Fournette 3.00 8.00
16 Patrick Mahomes II 8.00 20.00
17 Derrick Henry 3.00 8.00
18 Christian McCaffrey 3.00 8.00
19 Joe Flacco 2.50 6.00

2018 Rookies and Stars Precision Passers

*TRUE BLUE/49: 1.2X TO 3X BASIC INSERTS
1 Tom Brady 2.00 5.00
2 Aaron Rodgers 1.50 4.00
3 Matt Ryan .60 1.50
4 Russell Wilson 1.00 2.50
5 Jared Goff .75 2.00
6 Carson Wentz 1.00 2.50
7 Ben Roethlisberger .75 2.00
8 Dak Prescott .75 2.00
9 Deshaun Watson 1.00 2.50
10 Cam Newton .75 2.00
11 Andy Dalton .60 1.50
12 Matthew Stafford .60 1.50
13 Blake Bortles .50 1.25
14 Drew Brees .75 2.00
15 Jimmy Garoppolo 1.00 2.50
16 Baker Mayfield 5.00 12.00
17 Josh Allen 2.00 5.00
18 Sam Darnold 3.00 8.00
19 Lamar Jackson 3.00 8.00
20 Josh Rosen 1.50 4.00

2018 Rookies and Stars Prime Cuts

1 Keenan Allen/49 4.00 10.00
2 Aaron Donald/49 5.00 12.00
4 Antonio Brown/25 6.00 15.00
5 Joe Mixon/49 4.00 10.00
6 Chad Williams/49 3.00 8.00
7 Clay Matthews/49 4.00 10.00
8 Marshawn Lynch/49 4.00 10.00
9 Lamar Miller/49 3.00 8.00
10 James Harrison/49 4.00 10.00
11 Jabrill Peppers/49 3.00 8.00
12 Golden Tate III/49 3.00 8.00
13 Earl Thomas III/25 5.00 12.00
14 Sterling Shepard/49 4.00 10.00
15 D'Onta Foreman/49 3.00 8.00
16 Joey Bosa/49 5.00 12.00
17 Kareem Hunt/49 4.00 10.00
18 Travis Kelce/49 5.00 12.00
19 Jordan Howard/49 5.00 12.00
20 Terrell Suggs/49 3.00 8.00

2018 Rookies and Stars Rookie Rush

*TRUE BLUE/49: 1.2X TO 3X BASIC INSERTS
1 Baker Mayfield 5.00 12.00
2 Saquon Barkley 4.00 10.00
3 Sam Darnold 3.00 8.00
4 Bradley Chubb .75 2.00
5 Josh Allen 2.00 5.00
6 Josh Rosen 1.50 4.00
7 D.J. Moore 1.00 2.50
8 Calvin Ridley 1.25 3.00
9 Sony Michel 1.50 4.00
10 Lamar Jackson 3.00 8.00

2018 Rookies and Stars Rookies Longevity Signatures

101 Baker Mayfield/75 EXCH 50.00 100.00
102 Saquon Barkley/75 60.00 125.00
103 Sam Darnold/75 15.00 40.00
104 Bradley Chubb/99 EXCH 4.00 10.00
105 Josh Allen/75 12.00 30.00
106 Josh Rosen/75 8.00 20.00
107 D.J. Moore/99 5.00 12.00
108 Hayden Hurst/75 3.00 8.00
109 Calvin Ridley/75 6.00 15.00
110 Rashaad Penny/99 4.00 10.00
111 Sony Michel/99 8.00 20.00
113 Nick Chubb/99 8.00 20.00
114 Ronald Jones II/99 2.50 6.00
115 Courtland Sutton/99 4.00 10.00
116 Mike Gesicki/75 3.00 8.00
117 Kerryon Johnson/99 EXCH 4.00 10.00
119 Christian Kirk/25 6.00 15.00
120 Anthony Miller/99 4.00 10.00
121 Derrius Guice/75 5.00 12.00
122 James Washington/99 5.00 12.00
124 Royce Freeman/75 3.00 8.00
125 Mason Rudolph/99 6.00 15.00
126 Michael Gallup/75 5.00 12.00
127 Tre'Quan Smith/99 4.00 10.00
128 Keke Coutee/99 3.00 8.00
130 Kyle Lauletta/75 4.00 10.00
131 Mark Walton/99 3.00 8.00
132 DaeSean Hamilton/99 3.00 8.00
133 Ito Smith/99 3.00 8.00
134 Kalen Ballage/99 3.00 8.00
135 Jaleel Scott/99 2.50 6.00
136 J'Mon Moore/99 2.50 6.00
137 Daurice Fountain/99 3.00 8.00
139 Mike White/75 3.00 8.00
140 Marquez Valdes-Scantling/75 3.00 8.00
141 Denzel Ward/99 6.00 15.00
142 Roquan Smith/99 8.00 20.00
143 Minkah Fitzpatrick/99 5.00 12.00
144 Will Dissly/99 3.00 8.00
145 Daron Payne/99 4.00 10.00
146 Marcus Davenport/99 5.00 12.00
147 Tremaine Edmunds/99 5.00 12.00
149 Jaire Alexander/99 4.00 10.00
150 Leighton Vander Esch/99 25.00 50.00
151 Rashaan Evans/99 4.00 10.00
152 Terrell Edmunds/99 8.00 20.00
153 Taven Bryan/99 2.50 6.00
154 Mike Hughes/99 4.00 10.00
155 Harold Landry/99 2.50 6.00
156 Joshua Jackson/99 5.00 12.00
157 M.J. Stewart/99 2.50 6.00
158 Deontay Burnett/99 3.00 8.00
159 Duke Dawson/99 2.50 6.00
160 Isaiah Oliver/99 2.50 6.00
161 Carlton Davis/99 3.00 8.00
163 Justin Reid/99 2.50 6.00
164 Fred Warner/99 2.50 6.00
166 Derrick Nnadi/99 2.50 6.00
167 Sam Hubbard/99 3.00 8.00
168 Malik Jefferson/99 3.00 8.00
169 Rasheem Green/99 2.50 6.00
171 Chukwuma Okorafor/99 2.50 6.00
172 Ronnie Harrison/99 3.00 8.00
173 Harrison Phillips/99 2.50 6.00
174 Mark Andrews/99 4.00 10.00
175 Dallas Goedert/99 3.00 8.00
176 Christopher Herndon IV/99 2.50 6.00
177 Dorian O'Daniel/99 2.50 6.00
181 Josey Jewell/99 10.00 25.00
182 Da'Shawn Hand/99 2.50 6.00
183 Dorance Armstrong Jr./99 2.50 6.00
184 Jordan Whitehead/99 2.50 6.00
185 Anthony Averett/99 3.00 8.00
186 Kyzir White/99 4.00 10.00
187 Durham Smythe/99 2.50 6.00
188 Armani Watts/99 2.50 6.00
189 Chase Edmonds/99 2.50 6.00
190 Josh Sweat/99 3.00 8.00
191 Marquis Haynes/99 2.50 6.00
192 Dalton Schultz/99 3.00 8.00
193 Shaquem Griffin/99 4.00 10.00
194 Maurice Hurst/99 3.00 8.00
195 D.J. Reed/99 2.50 6.00
197 Micah Kiser/99 2.50 6.00
198 Marcus Allen/99 4.00 10.00
199 Daniel Carlson/99 2.50 6.00
200 Tyler Conklin/99 2.50 6.00

2018 Rookies and Stars Standing Ovation

*TRUE BLUE/49: 1.2X TO 3X BASIC INSERTS
1 Tom Brady 2.00 5.00
2 Mitchell Trubisky .75 2.00
3 Alvin Kamara .60 1.50
4 Carson Wentz 1.00 2.50
5 Ezekiel Elliott 1.00 2.50
6 Antonio Brown .75 2.00
7 Julio Jones .75 2.00
8 Deshaun Watson 1.00 2.50
9 Kareem Hunt .60 1.50
10 Larry Fitzgerald .60 1.50
11 Joe Flacco .60 1.50
12 A.J. Green .75 2.00
13 Jarvis Landry .60 1.50
14 Von Miller .60 1.50
15 Matthew Stafford .60 1.50
16 Aaron Rodgers 1.50 4.00
17 Andrew Luck 1.00 2.50
18 Joey Bosa .75 2.00
19 Adam Thielen .75 2.00
20 Eli Manning .60 1.50

2018 Rookies and Stars Star Search Jerseys

*PRIME/25: .8X TO 2X BASIC JSY
1 Baker Mayfield 10.00 25.00
2 Saquon Barkley 8.00 20.00
3 Sam Darnold 6.00 15.00
4 Bradley Chubb 2.50 6.00
5 Josh Allen 4.00 10.00
6 Josh Rosen 4.00 10.00
7 D.J. Moore 3.00 8.00
8 Hayden Hurst 2.00 5.00
9 Calvin Ridley 3.00 8.00
10 Rashaad Penny 2.50 6.00
11 Sony Michel 5.00 12.00
12 Lamar Jackson 6.00 15.00
13 Nick Chubb 3.00 8.00
14 Ronald Jones II 1.50 4.00
15 Courtland Sutton 2.50 6.00
16 Mike Gesicki 2.00 5.00
17 Kerryon Johnson 2.50 6.00
18 Dante Pettis 2.50 6.00
19 Christian Kirk 2.50 6.00
20 Anthony Miller 2.50 6.00
21 Derrius Guice 3.00 8.00
22 James Washington 3.00 8.00
23 D.J. Chark 2.00 5.00
24 Royce Freeman 2.00 5.00
25 Mason Rudolph 3.00 8.00
26 Michael Gallup 3.00 8.00
27 Tre'Quan Smith 2.50 6.00
28 Keke Coutee 2.00 5.00
29 Nyheim Hines 2.00 5.00
30 Kyle Lauletta 2.50 6.00
31 Mark Walton 2.00 5.00
32 DaeSean Hamilton 2.00 5.00
33 Ito Smith 2.00 5.00
34 Kalen Ballage 2.00 5.00
35 Jaleel Scott 1.50 4.00
36 J'Mon Moore 1.50 4.00
37 Daurice Fountain 2.00 5.00
38 Jaylen Samuels 2.00 5.00
39 Mike White 2.00 5.00
40 Marquez Valdes-Scantling 2.00 5.00

2018 Rookies and Stars Star Studded

*TRUE BLUE/49: 1.2X TO 3X BASIC INSERTS
1 Jimmy Garoppolo 1.00 2.50
2 Tom Brady 2.00 5.00
3 Antonio Brown .75 2.00
4 Russell Wilson 1.00 2.50
5 Julio Jones .75 2.00
6 Ezekiel Elliott 1.00 2.50
7 Khalil Mack .75 2.00
8 J.J. Watt .75 2.00
9 Von Miller .60 1.50
10 Drew Brees .75 2.00

2018 Rookies and Stars Statistical Standouts Signatures

*BLUE/25: .6X TO 1.5X BASIC AU/99
*BLUE/25: .5X TO 1.2X BASIC AU/49
6 Kareem Hunt/49 6.00 15.00
9 Jordan Howard/49 8.00 20.00
10 Melvin Gordon/49 6.00 15.00
13 Adam Thielen/49 30.00 60.00
14 Tyreek Hill/49 8.00 20.00
15 Marvin Jones Jr./99 4.00 10.00
17 Chandler Jones/99 4.00 10.00
18 Terrell Suggs/49 5.00 12.00
19 Aaron Donald/49 8.00 20.00
20 Yannick Ngakoue/99 4.00 10.00

2018 Rookies and Stars Stellar Rookies

*ORANGE/35: X TO X BASIC INSERTS
*PINK/85: .8X TO 2X BASIC INSERTS
*PURPLE/65: .8X TO 2X BASIC INSERTS
*RED/99: .8X TO 2X BASIC INSERTS
1 Baker Mayfield 8.00 20.00
2 Saquon Barkley 6.00 15.00
3 Sam Darnold 5.00 12.00
4 Josh Allen 3.00 8.00
5 Josh Rosen 2.50 6.00
6 Calvin Ridley 2.00 5.00
7 Rashaad Penny 1.25 3.00
8 Sony Michel 2.50 6.00
9 Nick Chubb 2.50 6.00
10 Bradley Chubb 1.25 3.00

2018 Rookies and Stars Team Duals Jerseys

*PRIME/49: .5X TO 1.2X BASIC JSY/99
1 D.Johnson/J.Rosen 5.00 12.00
2 M.Ryan/C.Ridley 4.00 10.00
3 L.Jackson/J.Flacco 8.00 20.00
4 J.Allen/Z.Jones 8.00 12.00
5 C.McCaffrey/D.Moore 4.00 10.00
6 A.Miller/M.Trubisky 3.00 8.00
7 J.Mixon/M.Walton 2.50 6.00
8 N.Chubb/B.Mayfield 8.00 20.00
9 D.Prescott/M.Gallup 4.00 10.00
10 B.Chubb/V.Miller 3.00 8.00
11 K.Johnson/A.Abdullah 3.00 8.00
12 J.Moore/M.VldsScntlng 2.50 6.00
13 D.Watson/K.Coutee 4.00 10.00
14 M.Mack/N.Hines 2.50 6.00
15 B.Bortles/D.Chark 2.50 6.00
16 K.Hunt/P.Mahomes 8.00 20.00
17 A.Gates/J.Bosa 3.00 8.00
18 S.Michel/R.Gronkowski 4.00 10.00
19 S.Shepard/S.Barkley 10.00 25.00
20 R.Anderson/S.Darnold 8.00 20.00

2018 Rookies and Stars Touchdown Club

*TRUE BLUE/49: 1.2X TO 3X BASIC INSERTS
1 Russell Wilson 1.00 2.50
2 Carson Wentz 1.00 2.50
3 Tom Brady 2.00 5.00
4 Matthew Stafford .60 1.50
5 Philip Rivers .75 2.00
6 Todd Gurley II .75 2.00
7 Mark Ingram .60 1.50
8 Le'Veon Bell .60 1.50
9 Jordan Howard .75 2.00
10 Leonard Fournette .75 2.00
11 DeAndre Hopkins .60 1.50
12 Davante Adams .60 1.50
13 Antonio Brown .75 2.00
14 Alshon Jeffery .60 1.50
15 Marvin Jones Jr. .50 1.25
16 A.J. Green .75 2.00
17 Rob Gronkowski .75 2.00
18 Kyle Rudolph .50 1.25
19 Travis Kelce .75 2.00
20 Evan Engram .50 1.25

2018 Rookies and Stars Year One Jerseys

*PRIME/25: .8X TO 2X BASIC JSY
1 Baker Mayfield 6.00 15.00
2 Saquon Barkley 8.00 20.00
3 Sam Darnold 6.00 15.00
4 Bradley Chubb 2.50 6.00
5 Josh Allen 4.00 10.00
6 Josh Rosen 4.00 10.00
7 D.J. Moore 3.00 8.00
8 Hayden Hurst 2.00 5.00
9 Calvin Ridley 3.00 8.00
10 Rashaad Penny 2.50 6.00
11 Sony Michel 3.00 8.00
12 Lamar Jackson 6.00 15.00
13 Nick Chubb 5.00 12.00
14 Ronald Jones II 1.50 4.00
15 Courtland Sutton 2.50 6.00
16 Mike Gesicki 2.00 5.00
17 Kerryon Johnson 2.50 6.00
18 Dante Pettis 2.50 6.00
19 Christian Kirk 2.50 6.00
20 Anthony Miller 2.50 6.00
21 Derrius Guice 3.00 8.00
22 James Washington 3.00 8.00
23 D.J. Chark 2.00 5.00
24 Royce Freeman 2.00 5.00
25 Mason Rudolph 4.00 10.00
26 Michael Gallup 3.00 8.00
27 Tre'Quan Smith 2.50 6.00
28 Keke Coutee 2.00 5.00
29 Nyheim Hines 2.00 5.00
30 Kyle Lauletta 2.50 6.00
31 Mark Walton 2.00 5.00
32 DaeSean Hamilton 2.00 5.00
33 Ito Smith 2.00 5.00
34 Kalen Ballage 2.00 5.00
35 Jaleel Scott 1.50 4.00
36 J'Mon Moore 1.50 4.00
37 Daurice Fountain 2.00 5.00
38 Jaylen Samuels 2.00 5.00
39 Mike White 2.00 5.00
40 Marquez Valdes-Scantling 2.00 5.00

2010 Rookies and Stars Longevity Materials Sapphire

LONG.MATER.SAPPHIRE PRINT RUN 5-75
*RUBY JSY/150-175: .3X TO .8X SAPP/75
*RUBY JSY/100-125: .4X TO 1X SAPP/75
*RUBY JSY/100: .3X TO .8X SAPP/50
*RUBY JSY/75: .25X TO .6X SAPP/25
*RUBY JSY/35: .6X TO 1.5X SAPP/75
LONG.MATER.RUBY PRINT RUN 12-175
1 Chris Wells/75 2.50 6.00
2 Larry Fitzgerald/75 3.00 8.00
3 Matt Leinart/75 2.50 6.00
5 Matt Ryan/75 3.00 8.00
7 Roddy White/50 3.00 8.00
8 Tony Gonzalez/75 3.00 8.00
10 Derrick Mason/75 2.50 6.00
11 Joe Flacco/75 3.00 8.00
13 Todd Heap/75 2.50 6.00
16 Marshawn Lynch/75 3.00 8.00
18 DeAngelo Williams/75 2.50 6.00
19 Jonathan Stewart/65 2.50 6.00
21 Steve Smith/75 3.00 8.00
22 Brian Urlacher/75 4.00 10.00
23 Devin Hester/75 3.00 8.00
24 Greg Olsen/75 3.00 8.00
25 Jay Cutler/75 2.50 6.00
29 Carson Palmer/75 3.00 8.00
30 Cedric Benson/75 2.50 6.00
31 Chad Ochocinco/75 2.50 6.00
35 Josh Cribbs/75 2.50 6.00
37 Felix Jones/75 2.50 6.00
38 Jason Witten/50 4.00 10.00
39 Marion Barber/75 3.00 8.00
41 Tony Romo/75 3.00 8.00
43 Eddie Royal/75 2.50 6.00
45 Knowshon Moreno/75 2.50 6.00
46 Kyle Orton/75 2.50 6.00
48 Calvin Johnson/75 4.00 10.00
49 Matthew Stafford/50 4.00 10.00
53 Greg Jennings/75 2.50 6.00
56 Andre Johnson/75 3.00 8.00
59 Owen Daniels/75 2.50 6.00
60 Steve Slaton/75 2.50 6.00
62 Dallas Clark/75 2.50 6.00
63 Joseph Addai/75 2.50 6.00
64 Peyton Manning/75 10.00 25.00
65 Reggie Wayne/75 3.00 8.00
66 David Garrard/75 2.50 6.00
67 Maurice Jones-Drew/75 2.50 6.00
72 Dwayne Bowe/75 3.00 8.00
80 Ronnie Brown/75 2.50 6.00
81 Adrian Peterson/75 8.00 20.00
82 Brett Favre/75 8.00 20.00
83 Percy Harvin/75 2.50 6.00
84 Sidney Rice/75 2.50 6.00
85 Visanthe Shiancoe/45 4.00 10.00
86 Laurence Maroney/75 2.50 6.00
87 Randy Moss/75 3.00 8.00
88 Tom Brady/75 10.00 25.00
90 Devery Henderson/75 2.50 6.00
91 Drew Brees/75 4.00 10.00
93 Marques Colston/75 2.50 6.00
96 Eli Manning/75 3.00 8.00
99 Steve Smith USC/75 2.50 6.00
101 Jerricho Cotchery/75 2.50 6.00
103 Mark Sanchez/75 2.50 6.00
104 Shonn Greene/75 2.50 6.00
106 Darren McFadden/75 2.50 6.00
108 Louis Murphy/75 2.50 6.00
109 Zach Miller/75 2.50 6.00
114 LeSean McCoy/75 4.00 10.00
115 Ben Roethlisberger/75 4.00 10.00
117 Rashard Mendenhall/50 3.00 8.00
119 Troy Polamalu/75 4.00 10.00
120 Antonio Gates/75 3.00 8.00
121 Darren Sproles/75 3.00 8.00
122 Philip Rivers/25 6.00 15.00
123 Vincent Jackson/75 2.50 6.00
124 Alex Smith QB/75 3.00 8.00
125 Frank Gore/75 3.00 8.00
127 Michael Crabtree/75 2.50 6.00
128 Vernon Davis/50 3.00 8.00
129 Deion Branch/75 2.50 6.00
132 Matt Hasselbeck/75 2.50 6.00
137 Steven Jackson/75 2.50 6.00
138 Cadillac Williams/75 2.50 6.00
139 Josh Freeman/75 3.00 8.00
143 Chris Johnson/50 3.00 8.00
144 Kenny Britt/75 2.50 6.00
145 Vince Young/75 2.50 6.00
146 Chris Cooley/75 2.50 6.00
147 Clinton Portis/75 2.50 6.00
148 Donovan McNabb/75 3.00 8.00
150 Santana Moss/75 3.00 8.00

2011 Rookies and Stars Longevity

*1-150 VETS: .4X TO 1X BASIC R&S
*151-250 ROOKIES: .4X TO 1X BASIC R&S
UNPRICED ROOKIE AU PRINT RUN 10
EXCH EXPIRATION: 1/27/2013

2011 Rookies and Stars Longevity Emerald

*1-150 VETS/25: 6X TO 15X BASIC R&S
*151-250 ROOKIES/25: 2X TO 5X BASIC R&S
STATED PRINT RUN 25 SER.#'d SETS

2011 Rookies and Stars Longevity Ruby

*1-150 VETS/150: 2.5X TO 6X BASIC R&S
*151-250 ROOKIES/150: .8X TO 2X BASIC R&S
STATED PRINT RUN 150 SER.#'d SETS

2011 Rookies and Stars Longevity Sapphire

*1-150 VETS/75: 4X TO 10X BASIC R&S
*151-250 ROOKIES/75: 1.2X TO 3X BASIC R&S
STATED PRINT RUN 75 SER.#'d SETS

2011 Rookies and Stars Longevity Rookie Autographs

STATED PRINT RUN 127-175
151 Aaron Williams/150 5.00 12.00
152 Adrian Clayborn/150 6.00 15.00
153 Ahmad Black/175 5.00 12.00
154 Akeem Ayers/150 2.50 6.00
156 Aldrick Robinson/150 6.00 15.00
159 Allen Bradford/150 2.50 6.00
160 Anthony Allen/150 3.00 8.00
161 Anthony Castonzo/175 2.50 6.00
164 Brandon Harris/150 2.50 6.00
167 Cameron Heyward/150 8.00 20.00
168 Cameron Jordan/150 3.00 8.00
175 Corey Liuget/150 4.00 10.00
180 Da'Rel Scott/175 2.50 6.00
183 Denarius Moore/175 10.00 25.00
185 Dion Lewis/150 3.00 8.00
188 Dwayne Harris/150 2.50 6.00
189 Evan Royster/175 2.50 6.00
191 Greg Jones/150 3.00 8.00
192 Greg McElroy/175 4.00 10.00
199 Jimmy Smith/150 2.50 6.00
200 Johnny White/175 2.50 6.00
202 Jordan Cameron/175 3.00 8.00
203 Julius Thomas/175 3.00 8.00
204 Justin Houston/175 3.00 8.00
205 Kealoha Pilares/175 2.50 6.00
207 Kris Durham/175 2.50 6.00
209 Luke Stocker/150 2.50 6.00
210 Marcus Cannon/175 4.00 10.00
212 Martez Wilson/150 5.00 12.00
220 Nathan Enderle/175 2.50 6.00
222 Owen Marecic/175 EXCH 2.50 6.00
225 Phil Taylor/127 5.00 12.00
226 Prince Amukamara/150 8.00 20.00
228 Quinton Carter/175 2.50 6.00
229 Rahim Moore/175 2.50 6.00
232 Robert Housler/175 2.50 6.00
235 Ronald Johnson/150 2.50 6.00
237 Ryan Whalen/175 2.50 6.00
239 Scotty McKnight/175 2.50 6.00
242 Stanley Havili/175 2.50 6.00
244 Stephen Burton/175 3.00 8.00
245 Stephen Paea/150 2.50 6.00
246 T.J. Yates/175 EXCH 2.50 6.00
247 Tyler Sash/150 2.50 6.00
248 Tyrod Taylor/175 5.00 12.00
249 Tyron Smith/175 3.00 8.00

2011 Rookies and Stars Longevity Materials Sapphire

STATED PRINT RUN 50-100
*RUBY/170-299: .3X TO .8X SAPP/75-100
*RUBY/130-145: .4X TO 1X SAPPHIRE/100
*RUBY/99-100: .4X TO 1X SAPP/50-100
*RUBY/49: .5X TO 1.2X SAPPHIRE/100
1 Beanie Wells/100 3.00 8.00
2 Larry Fitzgerald/100 4.00 10.00
6 Matt Ryan/100 4.00 10.00
7 Michael Turner/100 3.00 8.00
8 Roddy White/100 3.00 8.00
9 Tony Gonzalez/100 4.00 10.00
10 Anquan Boldin/100 3.00 8.00
11 Joe Flacco/100 4.00 10.00
12 Ray Lewis/100 5.00 12.00
13 Ray Rice/100 3.00 8.00
14 Todd Heap/100 3.00 8.00
15 C.J. Spiller/100 3.00 8.00
16 Fred Jackson/100 3.00 8.00
17 Lee Evans/100 4.00 10.00
18 Ryan Fitzpatrick/100 3.00 8.00
20 DeAngelo Williams/100 3.00 8.00
21 Jimmy Clausen/100 3.00 8.00
22 Jonathan Stewart/100 3.00 8.00
23 Steve Smith/100 4.00 10.00
24 Brian Urlacher/100 5.00 12.00
25 Devin Hester/100 5.00 12.00
26 Jay Cutler/100 3.00 8.00
27 Johnny Knox/100 3.00 8.00
28 Matt Forte/100 3.00 8.00
29 Carson Palmer/100 4.00 10.00
30 Cedric Benson/100 3.00 8.00
31 Chad Ochocinco/100 3.00 8.00
32 Jordan Shipley/100 3.00 8.00
33 Terrell Owens/80 4.00 10.00
36 Josh Cribbs/100 3.00 8.00
39 Felix Jones/100 3.00 8.00
41 Miles Austin/100 5.00 12.00
42 Tony Romo/100 4.00 10.00
43 Brandon Lloyd/100 3.00 8.00
44 Eddie Royal/100 3.00 8.00
45 Jabar Gaffney/100 3.00 8.00
46 Knowshon Moreno/100 3.00 8.00
47 Tim Tebow/100 5.00 12.00
49 Calvin Johnson/100 5.00 12.00
51 Matthew Stafford/100 4.00 10.00
53 Aaron Rodgers/100 12.00 30.00
54 Clay Matthews/100 5.00 12.00
55 Donald Driver/100 4.00 10.00
58 Andre Johnson/100 4.00 10.00
59 Arian Foster/100 3.00 8.00
62 Matt Schaub/100 3.00 8.00
64 Dallas Clark/100 3.00 8.00
65 Joseph Addai/100 3.00 8.00
66 Peyton Manning/100 10.00 25.00
67 Reggie Wayne/100 4.00 10.00
68 David Garrard/100 3.00 8.00
70 Maurice Jones-Drew/100 3.00 8.00
71 Mike Sims-Walker/75 4.00 10.00
73 Dwayne Bowe/100 4.00 10.00
74 Jamaal Charles/100 4.00 10.00
75 Matt Cassel/100 3.00 8.00
77 Brandon Marshall/100 4.00 10.00
79 Chad Henne/100 4.00 10.00
81 Ronnie Brown/100 4.00 10.00
82 Adrian Peterson/100 5.00 12.00
83 Percy Harvin/100 3.00 8.00
84 Sidney Rice/100 3.00 8.00
86 Visanthe Shiancoe/100 4.00 10.00
90 Tom Brady/100 12.00 30.00
91 Wes Welker/100 4.00 10.00
92 Drew Brees/100 5.00 12.00
94 Marques Colston/100 3.00 8.00
95 Pierre Thomas /100 3.00 8.00
96 Reggie Bush/100 3.00 8.00
97 Ahmad Bradshaw/100 3.00 8.00
98 Eli Manning/100 4.00 10.00
99 Hakeem Nicks/50 3.00 8.00
101 Steve Smith USC/100 3.00 8.00
102 Braylon Edwards/100 3.00 8.00
103 LaDainian Tomlinson/100 5.00 12.00
104 Mark Sanchez/100 3.00 8.00
105 Santonio Holmes/100 3.00 8.00
106 Shonn Greene/100 3.00 8.00
107 Darren McFadden/100 3.00 8.00
109 Louis Murphy/100 3.00 8.00
111 DeSean Jackson/100 4.00 10.00
112 Jeremy Maclin/100 3.00 8.00
113 LeSean McCoy/100 5.00 12.00
114 Michael Vick/100 4.00 10.00
116 Hines Ward/100 5.00 12.00
117 Mike Wallace/100 5.00 12.00
118 Rashard Mendenhall/100 3.00 8.00
119 Troy Polamalu/100 5.00 12.00
120 Antonio Gates/100 3.00 8.00
121 Malcom Floyd/100 3.00 8.00
123 Philip Rivers/100 5.00 12.00
124 Ryan Mathews/100 4.00 10.00
125 Frank Gore/100 4.00 10.00
126 Michael Crabtree/100 3.00 8.00
127 Patrick Willis/100 4.00 10.00
128 Vernon Davis/100 3.00 8.00
131 Matt Hasselbeck/100 3.00 8.00
135 Sam Bradford/100 3.00 8.00
136 Steven Jackson/100 3.00 8.00
137 Cadillac Williams/100 3.00 8.00
139 Kellen Winslow Jr./100 3.00 8.00
142 Bo Scaife/100 3.00 8.00
143 Chris Johnson/100 3.00 8.00
145 Nate Washington/100 3.00 8.00
146 Randy Moss/100 4.00 10.00
147 Chris Cooley/100 3.00 8.00
148 Donovan McNabb/100 4.00 10.00

2012 Rookies and Stars Longevity

*1-150 VETS: .4X TO 1X BASIC R&S
*151-225 ROOKIES: .4X TO 1X BASIC R&S

2012 Rookies and Stars Longevity Holofoil

*1-150 VETS/249: 2X TO 5X BASIC CARDS
*151-215 ROOKIE/249: .8X TO 2X BASIC RC

2012 Rookies and Stars Longevity Ruby

*1-150 VETS: .8X TO 2X BASIC R&S
*151-225 ROOKIES: .6X TO 1.5X BASIC R&S
RANDOM INSERTS IN LONGEVITY PACKS

2012 Rookies and Stars Longevity Dress for Success Jerseys

RANDOM INSERTS IN LONGEVITY PACKS
*PRIME/49: .6X TO 1.5X BASIC JSY
1 Isaiah Pead 1.50 4.00
2 Dwayne Allen 1.50 4.00
3 DeVier Posey 1.50 4.00
4 Coby Fleener 1.50 4.00
5 Brock Osweiler 1.50 4.00
6 Brian Quick 1.50 4.00
7 Bernard Pierce 1.50 4.00
8 Alshon Jeffery 3.00 8.00
9 David Wilson 1.50 4.00
10 Doug Martin 2.50 6.00
11 A.J. Jenkins 1.50 4.00
12 Brandon Weeden 1.50 4.00
13 Kendall Wright 1.50 4.00
14 Michael Floyd 1.50 4.00
15 Ryan Tannehill 2.50 6.00
16 Justin Blackmon 1.50 4.00
17 Trent Richardson 1.50 4.00
18 Robert Griffin III 2.00 5.00
19 Andrew Luck 10.00 25.00
20 Rueben Randle 1.50 4.00
21 Ronnie Hillman 1.50 4.00
22 Robert Turbin 1.50 4.00
23 Nick Toon 1.50 4.00
24 Nick Foles 4.00 10.00
25 Mohamed Sanu 2.50 6.00
26 Michael Egnew 1.50 4.00
27 LaMichael James 1.50 4.00
28 Lamar Miller 2.50 6.00
29 Joe Adams 1.50 4.00
30 Chris Givens 1.50 4.00
31 T.J. Graham 1.50 4.00
32 Stephen Hill 1.50 4.00
33 Ryan Broyles 1.50 4.00
34 Russell Wilson 6.00 15.00
35 Jarius Wright 1.50 4.00

2012 Rookies and Stars Longevity Freshman Orientation Jerseys

*FRESH.JSY: .4X TO 1X DRESS FOR SUCCESS
RANDOM INSERTS IN LONGEVITY PACKS
*PRIME/49: .6X TO 1.5X BASIC JSY

2012 Rookies and Stars Longevity Rookie Autographs Emerald

151 Allred Morris/99 4.00 10.00
152 Zach Brown/99 4.00 10.00
153 Andre Branch/99 4.00 10.00
154 B.J. Coleman/99 4.00 10.00
155 B.J. Cunningham/99 4.00 10.00
156 Bobby Wagner/99 6.00 15.00
157 Bruce Irvin/99 5.00 12.00
158 Bryce Brown/99 4.00 10.00
159 Case Keenum/99 8.00 20.00
160 Chandler Harnish/99 4.00 10.00
161 Chandler Jones/99 4.00 10.00
162 Chris Rainey/99 4.00 10.00
163 Courtney Upshaw/99 5.00 12.00
164 Cyrus Gray/99 4.00 10.00
165 Dan Herron/99 4.00 10.00
166 Danny Coale/25
167 David DeCastro/99 4.00 10.00
168 Davin Meggett/99 4.00 10.00
169 Devon Still/99 5.00 12.00
170 Devon Wylie/99 4.00 10.00
171 Dont'a Hightower/99 6.00 15.00
172 Dontari Poe/99 4.00 10.00
173 Dre Kirkpatrick/99 EXCH 4.00 10.00
174 Fletcher Cox/99 6.00 15.00
175 George Iloka/99 4.00 10.00
176 Greg Childs/99 4.00 10.00
177 Harrison Smith/99 4.00 10.00
178 Janoris Jenkins/99 5.00 12.00
179 Jared Crick/99 4.00 10.00
180 Jonathan Martin/99 4.00 10.00
181 Juron Criner/99 4.00 10.00
182 Kellen Moore/25
183 Keshawn Martin/99 5.00 12.00
184 Kevin Zeitler/99 4.00 10.00
185 Kirk Cousins/25 8.00 20.00
186 Ladarius Green/49
187 LaVon Brazill/99 6.00 15.00
188 Lavonte David/99 6.00 15.00
189 Luke Kuechly/99 10.00 25.00
190 Mark Barron/99 4.00 10.00
191 Marvin Jones/99 4.00 10.00
192 Marvin McNutt/99 4.00 10.00
193 Matt Kalil/99 4.00 10.00
194 Melvin Ingram/99 4.00 10.00
195 Michael Brockers/99 4.00 10.00
196 Michael Smith/99 EXCH 5.00 12.00
197 Morris Claiborne/25
198 Mychal Kendricks/99 6.00 15.00
199 Nick Perry/99 5.00 12.00
200 Orson Charles/99 4.00 10.00
201 Quinton Coples/99 4.00 10.00
202 Riley Reiff/99 4.00 10.00
203 Rishard Matthews/99 4.00 10.00
204 Ronnell Lewis/99 4.00 10.00
205 Ryan Lindley/99 4.00 10.00
206 Shea McClellin/99 5.00 12.00
207 Stephon Gilmore/99 5.00 12.00
208 Tauren Poole/99 4.00 10.00
209 Terrance Ganaway/99 5.00 12.00
210 Tommy Streeter/99 4.00 10.00
211 Travis Benjamin/99 4.00 10.00
212 Vick Ballard/99 5.00 12.00
213 Vinny Curry/99 5.00 12.00
214 Whitney Mercilus/99 4.00 10.00
215 T.Y. Hilton/99 8.00 20.00

2013 Rookies and Stars Longevity

*1-100 VETS: .4X TO 1X BASIC R&S
*101-200 ROOKIES: .4X TO 1X BASIC R&S

2013 Rookies and Stars Longevity Ruby

*1-100 VETS: .8X TO 2X BASIC R&S
*101-200 ROOKIES: .6X TO 1.5X BASIC R&S
*101-200 RK.JSY/299: .5X TO 1.2X BASIC R&S

2013 Rookies and Stars Longevity Sapphire

*1-100 VETS/25: 4X TO 10X BASIC R&S
*101-200 ROOKIES/25: 2X TO 5X BASIC R&S
*201-240 ROOK.JSY/25: .8X TO 2X BASIC R&S

2014 Rookies and Stars Longevity

*1-100 VETS: .4X TO 1X BASIC R&S
*101-200 ROOKIES: .4X TO 1X BASIC R&S
FEATURE GOLD FOIL LONGEVITY ON FRONT

2014 Rookies and Stars Longevity Ruby

*1-100 VETS: .8X TO 2X BASIC R&S
*101-200 ROOKIES: .6X TO 1.5X BASIC R&S
ISSUED IN LONGEVITY PACKS

2014 Rookies and Stars Longevity Sapphire

*1-100 VETS/25: 4X TO 10X BASIC R&S
*101-200 ROOKIES/25: 2X TO 5X BASIC R&S
STATED PRINT RUN 25 SER.#'d SETS

2014 Rookies and Stars Longevity Team Logo Gold

*1-100 VETS/25: 6X TO 15X BASIC R&S
*101-200 ROOKIES/25: 3X TO 8X BASIC R&S

2014 Rookies and Stars Longevity Team Logo Holofoil

*1-100 VETS/32: 4X TO 10X BASIC R&S
*101-200 ROOKIES/32: 2X TO 5X BASIC R&S

2014 Rookies and Stars Longevity Dress 4 Success Materials

*PRIME/25: .8X TO 2X BASIC DFS
*FRESH.ORIENTATION: .4X TO 1X BASIC DFS
*FO PRIME/25: .8X TO 2 BASIC DFS
DSAM A.J. McCarron 1.50 4.00
DSAMU Aaron Murray 1.50 4.00
DSAR Allen Robinson 2.50 6.00
DSAS Austin Seferian-Jenkins 1.50 4.00
DSAW Andre Williams 1.50 4.00
DSBB Blake Bortles 2.00 5.00
DSBC Brandin Cooks 2.50 6.00
DSBS Bishop Sankey 1.50 4.00
DSCH Carlos Hyde 2.00 5.00
DSCL Cody Latimer 2.00 5.00
DSCS Connor Shaw 1.50 4.00
DSCSI Charles Sims 1.50 4.00
DSDA Davante Adams 2.50 6.00
DSDAR Dri Archer 1.50 4.00
DSDC Derek Carr 10.00 25.00
DSDF Devonta Freeman 2.50 6.00
DSDM Donte Moncrief 1.50 4.00
DSDT De'Anthony Thomas 1.50 4.00
DSEE Eric Ebron 2.00 5.00
DSJA Jace Amaro 1.50 4.00
DSJC Jadeveon Clowney 2.00 5.00
DSJG Jimmy Garoppolo 12.00 30.00
DSJH Jeremy Hill 2.00 5.00
DSJL Jarvis Landry 3.00 8.00
DSJM Johnny Manziel 2.50 6.00
DSJMA Jordan Matthews 2.50 6.00
DSKB Kelvin Benjamin 2.50 6.00
DSKC Ka'Deem Carey 1.50 4.00
DSKM Khalil Mack 6.00 15.00
DSLT Logan Thomas 1.50 4.00
DSME Mike Evans 4.00 10.00
DSML Marqise Lee 2.00 5.00
DSOB Odell Beckham Jr. 4.00 10.00
DSPR Paul Richardson 2.00 5.00
DSSW Sammy Watkins 2.50 6.00
DSTB Tajh Boyd 1.50 4.00
DSTBR Teddy Bridgewater 2.50 6.00
DSTM Tre Mason 1.50 4.00
DSTS Tom Savage 1.50 4.00
DSTW Terrance West 1.50 4.00

2014 Rookies and Stars Materials Autographs Longevity Ruby

EXCH EXPIRATION: 2/13/2016
*BASE JSY AU/25: .6X TO 1.5X LNG.RUBY/49
*BASE JSY AU/25: .4X TO 1X LNG.RUBY/15
*LNG.GLD JSY AU/49: .4X TO 1X LNG.RBY/49
*LNG.GLD JSY AU/20-25: .6X TO 1.5X LNG.RBY/49
*LNG.GLD JSY AU/25: .4X TO 1X LNG.RBY/15
*LNG.PLAT.JSY AU/15-25: .6X TO 1.5X LNG.RBY/49
*LNG.PLAT.JSY AU/15: .4X TO 1X LNG.RBY/20
*LNG.SAPP.JSY AU/25: .6X TO 1.5X LNG.RBY/49
*LNG.SAPP.JSY AU/15: .4X TO 1X LNG.RBY/20
*TEAM LOGO JSY AU/32: .5X TO 1.2X LNG.RBY/49
*TEAM LOGO JSY AU/15: .6X TO 1.5X LNG.RBY/49
MSAD Andy Dalton/49 10.00 25.00
MSAL Andrew Luck/20 100.00 175.00
MSCK Colin Kaepernick/15 EXCH 40.00 80.00
MSCP Cordarrelle Patterson/49 8.00 20.00
MSDM Doug Martin/49
MSEL Eddie Lacy/49 8.00 20.00
MSEM EJ Manuel/49 8.00 20.00
MSGB Giovani Bernard/49 8.00 20.00
MSJK Jeremy Kerley/49 8.00 20.00
MSKC Kirk Cousins/49 12.00 30.00
MSLB Le'Veon Bell/49 10.00 25.00
MSRS Richard Sherman/15 75.00 135.00
MSTM Tyrann Mathieu/49 10.00 25.00
MSTR Tony Romo/15 40.00 80.00
MSVC Victor Cruz/49

2014 Rookies and Stars Rookie Autographs Longevity

*HOLOFOIL/75-99: .5X TO 1.2X LONG AU
*HOLOFOIL/49: .6X TO 1.5X LONG.AU
*GOLD/49: .6X TO 1.5X LONG.AU
*GOLD/25: .8X TO 2X LONG AU
*PLATINUM/15-25: .8X TO 2X LONG AU
*RUBY/75-199: .5X TO 1.2X LONG AU
*RUBY/50: .6X TO 1.5X LONG AU
*RUBY/15: .8X TO 2X LONG AU
*SAPPHIRE/25: .8X TO 2X LONG AU
*TM LGO HOLO/32: .6X TO 1.5X LONG AU
*TM LGO HOLO/15: .8X TO 2X LONG AU
101 A.J. McCarron 2.50 6.00
102 Aaron Donald 6.00 15.00
103 Aaron Murray 2.50 6.00
104 Ahmad Dixon 2.50 6.00
105 Allen Robinson 4.00 10.00
106 Andre Williams 2.50 6.00
107 Anthony Barr 2.50 6.00
108 Austin Seferian-Jenkins 2.50 6.00
109 Bishop Sankey 2.50 6.00
110 Blake Bortles 3.00 8.00
111 Bradley Roby 2.50 6.00
112 Brandin Cooks 4.00 10.00
113 Brandon Coleman 2.50 6.00
114 Brett Smith 2.50 6.00
115 Bruce Ellington 2.50 6.00
116 C.J. Mosley 3.00 8.00
117 Calvin Pryor 2.50 6.00
118 Carlos Hyde 3.00 8.00
119 Charles Sims 2.50 6.00
120 Chris Borland 2.50 6.00
121 Cody Latimer 3.00 8.00
122 Connor Shaw 2.50 6.00
123 Cyril Richardson 2.50 6.00
124 Cyrus Kouandjio 3.00 8.00
125 Darqueze Dennard 3.00 8.00
127 David Fales 2.50 6.00
128 De'Anthony Thomas 2.50 6.00
129 Dee Ford 2.50 6.00
130 Deone Bucannon 2.50 6.00
131 Derek Carr 15.00 40.00
132 Devonta Freeman 4.00 10.00
133 Donte Moncrief 2.50 6.00
134 Dri Archer 2.50 6.00
135 Ed Reynolds 2.50 6.00
136 Eric Ebron 3.00 8.00
137 Greg Robinson 2.50 6.00
138 Ha Ha Clinton-Dix 3.00 8.00
139 Isaiah Crowell 4.00 10.00
140 Jace Amaro 2.50 6.00
141 Jackson Jeffcoat 3.00 8.00
142 Jadeveon Clowney 3.00 8.00
143 Jake Matthews 2.50 6.00
146 James Wilder Jr. 3.00 8.00
147 Jared Abbrederis 2.50 6.00
148 Jarvis Landry 5.00 12.00
149 Jason Verrett 2.50 6.00
150 Jeremy Hill 3.00 8.00
151 Jerick McKinnon 3.00 8.00
152 Jimmy Garoppolo 30.00 60.00
153 Johnny Manziel 4.00 10.00
154 Jordan Matthews 4.00 10.00
155 Josh Huff 3.00 8.00
156 Ka'Deem Carey 2.50 6.00
157 Kelvin Benjamin 4.00 10.00
158 Khalil Mack 15.00 40.00
159 Kony Ealy 3.00 8.00
160 Kyle Fuller 2.50 6.00
161 Kyle Van Noy 3.00 8.00
162 Lache Seastrunk 2.50 6.00
163 Lamarcus Joyner 3.00 8.00
164 L'Damian Washington 3.00 8.00
165 Logan Thomas 2.50 6.00
166 Louis Nix III 2.50 6.00
167 Marcus Roberson 3.00 8.00
168 Marcus Smith 2.50 6.00
169 Marion Grice 2.50 6.00
170 Marqise Lee 3.00 8.00
171 Martavis Bryant 3.00 8.00
172 Michael Campanaro 2.50 6.00
173 Michael Sam 2.50 6.00
174 Mike Davis 2.50 6.00
175 Mike Evans 6.00 15.00
176 Odell Beckham Jr. 30.00 60.00
177 Paul Richardson 3.00 8.00
178 Ra'Shede Hageman 2.50 6.00
179 Ryan Shazier 4.00 10.00
180 Sammy Watkins 4.00 10.00
181 Scott Crichton 2.50 6.00
182 Shaq Evans 2.50 6.00
183 Shayne Skov 2.50 6.00
186 Tajh Boyd 2.50 6.00
187 Taylor Lewan 2.50 6.00
188 Teddy Bridgewater 4.00 10.00
189 Telvin Smith 2.50 6.00
190 Terrance West 2.50 6.00
191 Tevin Reese 2.50 6.00
192 Timmy Jernigan 2.50 6.00
193 Tom Savage 2.50 6.00
194 Tre Mason 2.50 6.00
195 Trent Murphy 2.50 6.00
196 Troy Niklas 2.50 6.00
197 Xavier Su'A-Filo 3.00 8.00
198 Yawin Smallwood 2.50 6.00
200 Zack Martin 3.00 8.00

2014 Rookies and Stars Rookie Materials Longevity Team Logo Signatures

RMAJM A.J. McCarron/15 6.00 15.00
RMAM Aaron Murray/32 5.00 12.00
RMAR Allen Robinson/32 8.00 20.00
RMASJ Austin Seferian-Jenkins/32 5.00 12.00
RMAW Andre Williams/32 5.00 12.00
RMBB Blake Bortles/15 8.00 20.00
RMBC Brandin Cooks/32 8.00 20.00
RMBS Bishop Sankey/32 5.00 12.00
RMCH Carlos Hyde/32 6.00 15.00
RMCL Cody Latimer/32 6.00 15.00
RMCS Connor Shaw/32 5.00 12.00
RMCSI Charles Sims/32 5.00 12.00
RMDA Dri Archer/32 5.00 12.00
RMDC Derek Carr/15
RMDF Devonta Freeman/32 8.00 20.00
RMDM Donte Moncrief/32 5.00 12.00
RMDT De'Anthony Thomas/32 5.00 12.00
RMEE Eric Ebron/32 6.00 15.00
RMJA Jace Amaro/32 5.00 12.00
RMJC Jadeveon Clowney/15
RMJG Jimmy Garoppolo/15 50.00 125.00
RMJH Jeremy Hill/32 6.00 15.00
RMJL Jarvis Landry/32 10.00 25.00
RMJM Johnny Manziel/15
RMJMA Jordan Matthews/32 8.00 20.00
RMKB Kelvin Benjamin/15
RMKC Ka'Deem Carey/32 5.00 12.00
RMKM Khalil Mack/32 20.00 50.00
RMLT Logan Thomas/32 5.00 12.00
RMME Mike Evans/32 12.00 30.00
RMML Marqise Lee/32 6.00 15.00
RMOB Odell Beckham Jr./32 20.00 50.00
RMPR Paul Richardson/32 10.00 25.00
RMSW Sammy Watkins/15
RMTB Tajh Boyd/32 5.00 12.00
RMTBR Teddy Bridgewater/15
RMTS Tom Savage/32 5.00 12.00
RMTW Terrance West/32 5.00 12.00

2015 Rookies and Stars Longevity

1 LeSean McCoy .30 .75
2 Sammy Watkins .25 .60
3 Percy Harvin .20 .50
4 Ryan Tannehill .25 .60
5 Jarvis Landry .25 .60
6 Lamar Miller .20 .50
7 Tom Brady .75 2.00
8 Rob Gronkowski .30 .75
9 Julian Edelman .30 .75
10 Geno Smith .20 .50
11 Brandon Marshall .20 .50
12 Eric Decker .20 .50
13 Joe Flacco .25 .60
14 Steve Smith Sr. .25 .60
15 Justin Forsett .25 .60
16 Andy Dalton .25 .60
17 A.J. Green .30 .75
18 Jeremy Hill .20 .50
19 Josh McCown .25 .60
20 Dwayne Bowe .25 .60
21 Terrance West .20 .50
22 Ben Roethlisberger .30 .75
23 Le'Veon Bell .25 .60
24 Antonio Brown .30 .75
25 Brian Hoyer .20 .50
26 Arian Foster .25 .60
27 DeAndre Hopkins .25 .60
28 Andrew Luck .40 1.00
29 T.Y. Hilton .25 .60
30 Frank Gore .25 .60
31 Andre Johnson .25 .60
32 Blake Bortles .20 .50
33 Julius Thomas .20 .50
34 Allen Robinson .25 .60
35 Zach Mettenberger .20 .50
36 Bishop Sankey .20 .50
37 Kendall Wright .20 .50
38 Peyton Manning .60 1.50
39 Demaryius Thomas .25 .60
40 Emmanuel Sanders .25 .60
41 C.J. Anderson .25 .60
42 Alex Smith .25 .60
43 Jamaal Charles .25 .60
44 Jeremy Maclin .20 .50
45 Derek Carr .30 .75
46 Latavius Murray .20 .50
47 James Jones .20 .50
48 Philip Rivers .30 .75
49 Keenan Allen .25 .60
50 Antonio Gates .20 .50
51 Tony Romo .25 .60
52 Dez Bryant .30 .75
53 Jason Witten .25 .60
54 Darren McFadden .20 .50
55 Eli Manning .25 .60
56 Odell Beckham Jr. .30 .75
57 Victor Cruz .25 .60
58 Sam Bradford .20 .50
59 DeMarco Murray .25 .60
60 Jordan Matthews .25 .60
61 Robert Griffin III .20 .50
62 Alfred Morris .20 .50
63 DeSean Jackson .25 .60
64 Jay Cutler .20 .50
65 Matt Forte .20 .50
66 Alshon Jeffery .25 .60
67 Matthew Stafford .25 .60
68 Calvin Johnson .30 .75
69 Golden Tate .20 .50
70 Aaron Rodgers .60 1.50
71 Eddie Lacy .20 .50
72 Jordy Nelson .25 .60
73 Teddy Bridgewater .25 .60
74 Adrian Peterson .30 .75
75 Mike Wallace .20 .50
76 Matt Ryan .25 .60
77 Julio Jones .30 .75
78 Roddy White .20 .50
79 Cam Newton .30 .75
80 Kelvin Benjamin .25 .60
81 Jonathan Stewart .20 .50
82 Drew Brees .30 .75
83 Mark Ingram .25 .60
84 Brandin Cooks .25 .60
85 Mike Glennon .25 .60
86 Doug Martin .25 .60
87 Mike Evans .25 .60
88 Carson Palmer .25 .60
89 Andre Ellington .20 .50
90 Larry Fitzgerald .25 .60
91 Russell Wilson .40 1.00
92 Marshawn Lynch .25 .60
93 Jimmy Graham .30 .75
94 Colin Kaepernick .25 .60
95 Reggie Bush .20 .50
96 Anquan Boldin .20 .50
97 Torrey Smith .20 .50
98 Nick Foles .25 .60
99 Tre Mason .25 .60
100 Tavon Austin .20 .50
101 Bo Wallace RC .40 1.00
102 Rashad Greene RC .40 1.00
103 Jameis Winston RC 1.00 2.50
104 Devin Funchess RC .60 1.50
105 Benardrick McKinney RC .40 1.00
106 Danielle Hunter RC .50 1.25
107 Antwan Goodley RC .40 1.00
108 Marcus Mariota RC 1.50 4.00
109 Jay Ajayi RC .60 1.50
110 Vic Beasley Jr. RC .50 1.25
111 Trey Flowers RC .60 1.50
112 Bryan Bennett RC .40 1.00
113 Jalen Collins RC .40 1.00
114 Kevin White RC .50 1.25
115 T.J. Yeldon RC .40 1.00
116 Trae Waynes RC .40 1.00
117 Brett Hundley RC .40 1.00
118 Ameer Abdullah RC .60 1.50
119 Amari Cooper RC 1.25 3.00
120 Matt Jones RC .40 1.00
121 Eddie Goldman RC .40 1.00
122 DeVante Parker RC .60 1.50
123 Leonard Williams RC .40 1.00
124 Dezmin Lewis RC .40 1.00
125 Mike Davis RC .40 1.00
126 Tevin Coleman RC .50 1.25
127 Taylor Heinicke RC .60 1.50
128 Melvin Gordon RC 1.00 2.50
129 Eric Kendricks RC .40 1.00
130 Todd Gurley RC 1.50 4.00
131 Devin Smith RC .40 1.00
132 Marcus Peters RC .60 1.50
133 Stephone Anthony RC .40 1.00
134 Mario Alford RC .40 1.00
135 Kenny Bell RC .60 1.50
136 Ben Koyack RC .60 1.50
137 Trey Williams RC .50 1.25
138 Ifo Ekpre-Olomu RC .40 1.00
139 Clive Walford RC .40 1.00
140 Tony Lippett RC .40 1.00
141 Malcom Brown RC .40 1.00
142 Josh Shaw RC .60 1.50
143 David Cobb RC .40 1.00
144 Breshad Perriman RC .40 1.00
145 Bryce Petty RC .40 1.00
146 DaVaris Daniels RC .40 1.00
147 Shane Carden RC .40 1.00
148 Garrett Grayson RC .40 1.00
149 David Johnson RC 1.00 2.50
150 Dres Anderson RC .40 1.00
151 Jesse James RC .50 1.25
152 Maxx Williams RC .40 1.00
153 P.J. Williams RC .50 1.25
154 Dorial Green-Beckham RC .40 1.00
155 Titus Davis RC .50 1.25
156 Dante Fowler Jr. RC .60 1.50
157 Ronald Darby RC .40 1.00
158 Eric Rowe RC .40 1.00
159 Josh Robinson RC .40 1.00
160 Josh Harper RC .40 1.00
161 Stefon Diggs RC 1.00 2.50
162 Arik Armstead RC .40 1.00
163 Shaq Thompson RC .50 1.25
164 Justin Hardy RC .40 1.00
165 Jeff Heuerman RC .50 1.25
166 DeAndrew White RC .60 1.50
167 Jeremy Langford RC .40 1.00
168 Nick O'Leary RC .40 1.00
169 Eli Harold RC .40 1.00
170 Karlos Williams RC .40 1.00
171 Kevin Johnson RC .40 1.00
172 Vince Mayle RC .50 1.25
173 Owamagbe Odighizuwa RC .50 1.25
174 Carl Davis RC .50 1.25
175 Tyler Lockett RC .60 1.50
176 Deontay Greenberry RC .40 1.00
177 Duke Johnson RC .60 1.50
178 Cameron Artis-Payne RC .40 1.00
179 Tre McBride RC .40 1.00
180 Blake Bell RC .60 1.50
181 Buck Allen RC .50 1.25
182 Kwon Alexander RC .50 1.25
183 Darren Waller RC .50 1.25
184 Sammie Coates RC .50 1.25
185 Jamison Crowder RC .50 1.25
186 Nelson Agholor RC .50 1.25
187 Landon Collins RC .50 1.25
188 Ty Montgomery RC .40 1.00
189 Phillip Dorsett RC .40 1.00
190 Danny Shelton RC .40 1.00
191 Denzel Perryman RC .40 1.00
192 Bud Dupree RC .50 1.25
193 Sean Mannion RC .40 1.00
194 J.J. Nelson RC .40 1.00
195 Jaelen Strong RC .50 1.25
196 Shane Ray RC .40 1.00
197 Cody Fajardo RC .50 1.25
198 Chris Conley RC .40 1.00
199 Mario Edwards Jr. RC .40 1.00
200 Jordan Phillips RC .40 1.00

2015 Rookies and Stars Longevity Jersey Number

*1-100 VETS/25: 4X TO 10X BASIC R&S
*101-200 ROOKIES/25: 2X TO 5X BASIC R&S

2015 Rookies and Stars Longevity Team Logo

*1-100 VETS/50: 3X TO 8X BASIC R&S
*101-200 ROOKIES/50: 1.5X TO 4X BASIC R&S

2015 Rookies and Stars Longevity Team Name

*VETS/299: 1.5X TO 4X BASIC R&S
*ROOKIES/299: .8X TO 2X BASIC R&S

2015 Rookies and Stars Longevity Star Studded Die Cuts

*R&S INSERT: .4X TO X LONGEVITY INSERTS
*RED/299: .6X TO 1.5X BASIC INSERTS
*PURPLE/49: 1X TO X 2.5BASIC INSERTS
*GOLD/25: 1.2X TO 3X BASIC INSERTS
*LONG RED/299: .6X TO 1.5X BASIC INSERTS
*LONG PURPLE/49: 1X TO X 2.5BASIC INSERTS
*LONG GOLD/25: 1.2X TO 3X BASIC INSERTS

1999 Ruffles QB Club Spanish

These unnumbered cards were sponsored by Ruffles Potato Chips and issued in potato chip bags in Mexico, The cards feature members of the Quarterback Club, both active and retired. Each card measures a small 1 5/16" by 1 15/16" and includes a color photo of the featured player (or team logo) on the front with a Ruffles logo, the QB Club logo, and the NFL logo on the cardfront. The cardbacks feature player stats and are written in Spanish.

COMPLETE SET (30) 25.00 50.00
1 Tony Banks .75 2.00
2 Jeff Blake .75 2.00
3 Drew Bledsoe 1.50 4.00
4 Chris Chandler .75 2.00
5 Kerry Collins 1.00 2.50
6 Randall Cunningham 1.00 2.50
7 Jim Everett .75 2.00
8 Brett Favre 5.00 10.00
9 Gus Frerotte .75 2.00
10 Rich Gannon 1.00 2.50
11 Elvis Grbac .75 2.00
12 Jim Harbaugh .75 2.00
13 Brad Johnson 1.00 2.50
14 Rob Johnson .75 2.00
15 Jim Kelly 2.00 5.00
16 Donovan McNabb 2.00 5.00
17 Steve McNair 1.25 3.00
18 Cade McNown .75 2.00
19 Jake Plummer 1.00 2.50
20 Kordell Stewart 1.00 2.50
21 Vinny Testaverde 1.00 2.50
22 Ricky Williams 1.50 4.00
23 Broncos Logo .75 2.00
24 Cowboys Logo .75 2.00
25 Dolphins Logo .75 2.00
26 49ers Logo .75 2.00
27 Raiders Logo .75 2.00
28 Rams Logo .75 2.00
29 Redskins Logo .75 2.00
30 Steelers Logo .75 2.00

2002 Run With History Emmitt Smith

This set was licensed through Emmitt Smith and the Dallas Cowboys and was issued in box set form through traditional retail outlets. Each card takes an historical look at the career of Emmitt Smith. The stated print run was 16,727 sets.

COMPLETE SET (22) 8.00 12.00
COMMON CARD (1-22) .30 .75

1979 Sacramento Buffaloes Schedules

This set of black and white cards features members of the California Football League Sacramento Buffaloes. Each features a game action photo on the front and the team's schedule on the back with the player identified at the bottom.

COMPLETE SET (6) 12.50 25.00
1 Wayne Dalkse 2.50 5.00
Bill Shiflett
2 Jim Gabriel 2.50 5.00
Rod Lung
3 Earl Green 2.50 5.00
4 Ron Killion 2.50 5.00
5 Rod Lung 2.50 5.00
6 Bob Morris 2.50 5.00

1991 Sacramento Surge Police

This 39-card set was sponsored by American Airlines and presents players of the WLAF Sacramento Surge. The cards measure approximately 2 3/8" by 3 1/2". The fronts feature a color posed photo of the player, with a drawing of the Sacramento helmet inside a triangle at the lower right hand corner. The backs have the Sacramento and WLAF logos at the top, biographical information, and a player quote consisting of an anti-drug message. The set was issued in the Summer of 1991. The cards are unnumbered and hence are listed alphabetically below for convenience.

COMPLETE SET (39) 20.00 40.00
1 Mike Adams .60 1.50
2 Sam Archer .60 1.50
3 John Buddenberg .60 1.50
4 Jon Burman .60 1.50
5 Tony Burse .60 1.50
6 Ricardo Cartwright .60 1.50
7 Greg Coauette .60 1.50
8 Paco Craig .60 1.50
9 John Dominic .60 1.50
10 Mike Elkins .60 1.50
11 Oliver Erhorn .60 1.50
12 Mel Farr Jr. .60 1.50
13 Victor Floyd .60 1.50
14 Byron Forsythe .60 1.50
15 Paul Frazier .60 1.50
16 Tom Gerhart .60 1.50
17 Mike Hall CB .60 1.50
18 Anthony Henton .60 1.50
19 Nate Hill .60 1.50
20 Kubanai Kalombo .60 1.50
21 Shawn Knight .60 1.50
22 Sean Kugler .60 1.50
23 Matti Lindholm .60 1.50
24 Art Malone CB .60 1.50
25 Robert McWright .60 1.50
26 Tim Moore .60 1.50
27 Pete Najarian .60 1.50
28 Mark Nua .60 1.50
29 Carl Parker .60 1.50
30 Leon Perry .60 1.50
31 Juha Salo .60 1.50
32 Saute Sapolu .60 1.50
33 Paul Soltis .60 1.50
34 Richard Stephens .60 1.50
35 Kay Stephenson CO .60 1.50
36 Kendall Trainor .60 1.50
37 Mike Wallace .60 1.50
38 Curtis Wilson .60 1.50
39 Rick Zumwalt .60 1.50

1948-1950 Safe-T-Card

Cards from this set were issued in the Washington D.C. area in the late 1940s and early 1950s. Each card was printed in either black or red and features an artist's rendering of a famous area athlete or personality from a variety of sports. The card backs feature an ad for Jim Gibbons Cartoon-A-Quiz television show along with an ad from a local business. The player's facsimile autograph and team or sport affiliation is included on the fronts.

1 John Adams FB 15.00 30.00
5 Herman Ball FB 15.00 30.00
6 Sammy Baugh FB 50.00 100.00
7 Sammy Baugh QB FB 50.00 100.00
8 Bryan Bell FB 15.00 30.00
14 Billy Conn FB 15.00 30.00
16 Andy Davis FB 15.00 30.00
17 Doug DeGroot CO FB 15.00 30.00
18 Al Demao FB 15.00 30.00
20 Mush Dubofsky CO FB 15.00 30.00
22 Turk Edwards FB 30.00 60.00
24 Tom Farmer FB 15.00 30.00
26 Lou Gambino FB 15.00 30.00
27 Harry Gilmer Hel FB 20.00 40.00
28 Harry Gilmer No Hel FB 20.00 40.00
31 Art Guepe CO FB 15.00 30.00
39 Jan Jankowski CO FB 15.00 30.00
42 Bob Margarita CO FB 15.00 30.00
43 Corrine Griffith Marshall actress 15.00 30.00
44 Dick McCann GM FB 15.00 30.00
47 Wilbur Moore FB 20.00 40.00
51 Dick Poillon FB 15.00 30.00
53 Bo Rowland CO FB 15.00 30.00
54 Dan Sandifer FB 15.00 30.00
55 George Sauer CO FB 15.00 30.00
58 Jim Tatum CO FB 15.00 30.00
59 Joe Tereshinski FB 20.00 40.00
60 Dick Todd FB 15.00 30.00
61 Vic Turyn FB 15.00 30.00
63 Bob Waterfield FB 40.00 80.00
64 John Welchel CO FB 15.00 30.00

1976 Saga Discs

These cards parallel the 1976 Crane Discs set. Instead of the Crane sponsor logo on back, each features the "Saga" logo. The Saga versions are much more difficult to find than their Crane counterparts.

COMPLETE SET (30) 300.00 500.00
1 Ken Anderson 5.00 12.00
2 Otis Armstrong 3.00 8.00
3 Steve Bartkowski 4.00 10.00
4 Terry Bradshaw 25.00 60.00
5 John Brockington 2.50 6.00
6 Doug Buffone 2.50 6.00
7 Wally Chambers 2.50 6.00
8 Isaac Curtis 2.50 6.00
9 Chuck Foreman 3.00 8.00
10 Roman Gabriel 4.00 10.00
11 Mel Gray 3.00 8.00
12 Joe Greene 12.00 30.00
13 James Harris 2.50 6.00
14 Jim Hart 3.00 8.00
15 Billy Kilmer 4.00 10.00
16 Greg Landry 3.00 8.00
17 Ed Marinaro 2.50 6.00
18 Lawrence McCutcheon 3.00 8.00
19 Terry Metcalf 3.00 8.00
20 Lydell Mitchell 2.50 6.00
21 Jim Otis 2.50 6.00
22 Alan Page 4.00 10.00
23 Walter Payton 125.00 250.00
24 Greg Pruitt 3.00 8.00
25 Charlie Sanders 4.00 10.00
26 Ron Shanklin 2.50 6.00
27 Roger Staubach 25.00 60.00
28 Jan Stenerud 4.00 10.00
29 Charley Taylor 5.00 12.00
30 Roger Wehrli 3.00 8.00

2008 Saginaw Sting IFL

COMPLETE SET (9) 5.00 10.00
1 Damon Dowdell .50 1.25
2 Ruben Gay .50 1.25
3 Jeremiah McLaurin .50 1.25
4 Jeff Dembowske .50 1.25
5 Charles Barber .50 1.25
6 Nicholas Body .50 1.25
7 Nate Collins .50 1.25
8 Brandon Genwright .50 1.25
9 Corey Gonzales .50 1.25

1967 Saints Team Doubloons

For a number of years, the New Orleans Saints included one Doubloon (coin) per game day program. The 1967 coins featured on the fronts a player wearing the team helmet for each home game match-up for the Saints season including one pre-season game. The coin backs included an advertisement for Jax Beer. The year of issue is also featured on the coin front and each was produced using a silver colored aluminum metal. We've numbered the set in the order of release.

COMPLETE SET (8) 15.00 30.00
1 Saints vs. Falcons 2.00 4.00
2 Saints vs. Rams 2.00 4.00
3 Saints vs. Redskins 2.50 5.00
4 Saints vs. Browns 2.50 5.00
5 Saints vs. Steelers 2.50 5.00
6 Saints vs. Eagles 2.00 4.00
7 Saints vs. Cowboys 2.50 5.00
8 Saints vs. Falcons 2.00 4.00

1967 Saints Team Issue 5X7 Bordered

The Saints issued several different sets of 5" by 7" photos, presumably over a period of years. Many of the photographs of the same players in either the bordered or borderless sets are identical. The text size and style of each photo in this release are exactly the same. The players full name is to the left, with his position initials in the center, and the full team name printed in all caps to the right. All are head and chest shots instead of action. Each is unnumbered and blankbacked.

COMPLETE SET (20) 75.00 150.00
1 Danny Abramowicz 5.00 10.00
2 Doug Atkins 6.00 12.00
3 Tom Barrington 4.00 8.00
4 Lou Cordileone 4.00 8.00
5 Bruce Cortez 4.00 8.00
6 Gary Cuozzo 5.00 10.00
7 Ted Davis 4.00 8.00
8 Jim Hester 4.00 8.00
9 Les Kelley 4.00 8.00
10 Kent Kramer 4.00 8.00
11 Jake Kupp 4.00 8.00
12 Obert Logan 4.00 8.00
13 Don McCall 4.00 8.00
14 Thomas McNeill 4.00 8.00
15 Ray Ogden 4.00 8.00
16 Ray Rissmiller 4.00 8.00
17 Walter Roberts 4.00 8.00
18 George Rose 4.00 8.00
19 Bill Sandeman 4.00 8.00
20 Phil Vandersea 4.00 8.00
21 Joe Wendryhoski 4.00 8.00
22 Dave Whitsell 4.00 8.00
23 Gary Wood 4.00 8.00

1967-68 Saints Team Issue 5X7 Borderless

The Saints issued two different sets of 5" by 7" photos, presumably over a period of years. The photographs of the same players in both sets are identical except for the white border or lack of a border. The text size and style varies from photo to photo as does the player information below the picture. All are head and chest shots instead of action. The two groups were likely issued together but have been separated for ease in cataloging. Each is unnumbered and blankbacked.

COMPLETE SET (28) 100.00 200.00
1 Charlie Brown RB 4.00 8.00
2 Vern Burke 4.00 8.00
3 Jackie Burkett 4.00 8.00
4 Bill Carr 4.00 8.00
5 Bill Cody 4.00 8.00
6 Ted Davis 4.00 8.00
7 Jim Garcia 4.00 8.00
8 Tom Hall 4.00 8.00
9 Jimmy Heidel 4.00 8.00

10 Les Kelley 4.00 8.00
11 Jake Kupp 4.00 8.00
12 Herman Lee 4.00 8.00
13 John Morrow 4.00 8.00
14 Ray Ogden 4.00 8.00
15 Ray Rissmiller 4.00 8.00
16 Bert Rose GM 4.00 8.00
17 Bill Sandeman 4.00 8.00
18 Roy Schmidt 4.00 8.00
19 Brian Schweda 4.00 8.00
20 Dave Simmons 4.00 8.00
21 Jerry Simmons 4.00 8.00
22 Mike Tilleman 4.00 8.00
23 Joe Wendryhoski 4.00 8.00
24 Ernie Wheelwright UER 4.00 8.00
25 Fred Whittingham 4.00 8.00
26 Del Williams 4.00 8.00
27 Bo Wood 4.00 8.00
28 Gary Wood 4.00 8.00

1967-68 Saints Team Issue 8X10

The Saints released these posed action photos primarily for fans and to fulfill autograph requests. Each measures roughly 8" by 10" and features a black and white player photo with information in the border below the picture. They were likely released over a period of years as the type style and size used varies from photo to photo. There appear to be several distinct types issued with text as follows reading left to right: (1) player's name in all caps, position initials only, and team name in all caps, (2) player's name, position spelled out completely and team in all capital letters, (3) player's name in caps, position spelled out in upper and lower case letters, and team in upper and lower case letters, (4) player's name in all caps (no position) and team name in all caps, (5) player's name in all caps, position spelled out in caps, and team name in all caps, (6) player's name in all caps, no position, team name in upper and lower case letters. Some also appear to have been released through Maison Blanche department stores in New Orleans along with the store's logo stamped on front. These Maison Blanche variations typically sell for a premium as listed below. Any additions to this list and confirmation of Maison Blanche checklist is appreciated.
*MAISON BLANCHE: .75X TO 1.5X
1 Dan Abramowicz 1 6.00 12.00
2 Doug Atkins 1 7.50 15.00
3 Tony Baker 1 5.00 10.00
4A Tom Barrington 1 5.00 10.00
4B Tom Barrington 1 5.00 10.00
5 Jim Boeke 2 5.00 10.00
6 Johnny Brewer 2 5.00 10.00
7 Jackie Burkett 1 5.00 10.00
8 Bo Burris 4 5.00 10.00
9 Bill Cody 4 5.00 10.00
10 Gary Cuozzo 1 6.00 12.00
11 Ted Davis 1 5.00 10.00
12 Tom Dempsey 2 6.00 12.00
13 Al Dodd 1 5.00 10.00
14 John Douglas 1 5.00 10.00
15 Julian Fagan 5.00 10.00
16 Jim Garcia 1 5.00 10.00
17 John Gilliam 4 5.00 10.00
18A Tom Hall 1 5.00 10.00
18B Tom Hall 6 5.00 10.00
19 Kevin Hardy 2 5.00 10.00
20 Edd Hargett 5.00 10.00
21 George Harvey 1 5.00 10.00
22 Jimmy Heidel 1 5.00 10.00
23 Jim Hester 1 5.00 10.00
24 Paul Hornung 6 10.00 20.00
25 Gene Howard 3 5.00 10.00
26 Harry Jacobs 5.00 10.00
27A Les Kelley 1 5.00 10.00
27B Les Kelley 3 5.00 10.00
28 Billy Kilmer 7.50 15.00
29 Elbert Kimbrough 5.00 10.00
30 Kent Kramer 1 5.00 10.00
31 Jake Kupp 1 5.00 10.00
32 Earl Leggett 1 5.00 10.00
33 Andy Livingston 1 5.00 10.00
34 Obert Logan 1 5.00 10.00
35 Tony Lorick 1 5.00 10.00
36 Ray Ogden 1 5.00 10.00
37 Don McCall 1 5.00 10.00
38A Tom McNeill 1 5.00 10.00
38B Tom McNeill 3 5.00 10.00
39 Mike Morgan 5.00 10.00
40 John Morrow 1 5.00 10.00
41 Elijah Nevett 5 5.00 10.00
42 Bob Newland 5.00 10.00
43 Ray Poage 4 5.00 10.00
44 Ray Rissmiller 1 5.00 10.00
45 Walter Roberts 1 5.00 10.00
46 George Rose 1 5.00 10.00
47 David Rowe 4 5.00 10.00
48 Roy Schmidt 4 5.00 10.00
49 Bob Scholtz 6 5.00 10.00
50 Randy Schultz 4 5.00 10.00
51 Brian Schweda 1 5.00 10.00
52 Dave Simmons 1 5.00 10.00
53 Larry Stephens 6 5.00 10.00
54 Monty Stickles 3 5.00 10.00
55 Steve Stonebreaker 1 5.00 10.00
56 Jim Taylor 1 7.50 15.00
57 Mike Tilleman 1 5.00 10.00
58 Willie Townes 5.00 10.00
59 Phil Vandersea 1 5.00 10.00
60 Joe Wendryhoski 1 5.00 10.00
61 Ernie Wheelwright 5.00 10.00
62 Dave Whitsell 1 5.00 10.00
63 Fred Whittingham 1 5.00 10.00
64 Del Williams 1 5.00 10.00
65 Gary Wood 1 5.00 10.00
66 Doug Wyatt 5.00 10.00
67 Team Photo 6.00 12.00

1968 Saints Team Doubloons

For a number of years, the New Orleans Saints included one Doubloon (coin) per game day program. The 1968 coins featured on the fronts the team helmets for each home game match-up for the Saints season including two pre-season games. The coin backs included an advertisement for Jax Beer. The year of issue is also featured on the coin front and each was produced using both a silver colored aluminum and a gold colored metal. We've numbered the set in the order of release.
COMPLETE SET (9) 20.00 40.00
*GOLD COINS: 1X TO 2X SILVERS
1 Saints vs. Patriots 2.00 4.00
2 Saints vs. Browns 2.50 5.00
3 Saints vs. Browns 2.50 5.00
4 Saints vs. Redskins 2.50 5.00
5 Saints vs. Cardinals 2.00 4.00
6 Saints vs. Vikings 2.50 5.00
7 Saints vs. Cowboys 2.50 5.00
8 Saints vs. Bears 2.50 5.00
9 Saints vs. Steelers 2.50 5.00

1968 Saints Team Issue 5X7 Bordered

The Saints issued several different sets of 5" by 7" photos, presumably over a period of years. Many of the photographs of the same players in either the bordered or borderless sets are identical. The text size and style of each photo in this release are different than the 1967 set and differ from each other as noted below. Some photos in this group do not have the player identified at all, as noted below. These photos presumably were issued in haste by the team as several players didn't make the Saints rosters. All are head and chest shots instead of action. This group was not likely issued together but has been combined for ease in cataloging and identification. Each is unnumbered and blankbacked.
COMPLETE SET (17) 60.00 120.00
1 Tom Barrington 4.00 8.00
2 Charlie Brown RB 4.00 8.00
3 Bo Burris 4.00 8.00
4 Bill Cody 4.00 8.00
5 Willie Crittendon 4.00 8.00
6A Charles Durkee 4.00 8.00
6B Charles Durkee 4.00 8.00
7 Jim Hester 4.00 8.00
8 Jerry Jones T 4.00 8.00
9 Elijah Nevett 4.00 8.00
10 Mike Rengel 4.00 8.00
11A Randy Schultz 4.00 8.00
11B Randy Schultz 4.00 8.00
12 Brian Schweda 4.00 8.00
13 Jerry Sturm 4.00 8.00
14 Ernie Wheelwright 4.00 8.00
15 Del Williams G 4.00 8.00

1969 Saints Pro Players Doubloons

These coins were produced by Pro Players Doubloons, Inc. and distributed by the New Orleans Saints at games during the 1969 season. Each coin is unnumbered and measures approximately 1 1/2" in diameter. There were at least three different colored coins (silver, brass, and light gold) with each featuring a player bust on front with a short player bio and copyright information on back.
COMPLETE SET (24) 62.50 125.00
1 Dan Abramowicz 3.00 6.00
2 Doug Atkins 6.00 12.00
3 Tom Barrington 2.50 5.00
4 Johnny Brewer 2.50 5.00
5 Bo Burris 2.50 5.00
6 Ted Davis 2.50 5.00
7 John Douglas 2.50 5.00
8 Charlie Durkee 2.50 5.00
9 Gene Howard 2.50 5.00
10 Billy Kilmer 5.00 10.00
11 Jake Kupp 2.50 5.00
12 Errol Linden 2.50 5.00
13 Tony Lorick 2.50 5.00
14 Don McCall 2.50 5.00
15 Dave Parks 3.00 6.00
16 Dave Rowe 2.50 5.00
17 Brian Schweda 2.50 5.00
18 Monte Stickles 2.50 5.00
19 Jerry Sturm 2.50 5.00
20 Mike Tilleman 2.50 5.00
21 Joe Wendryhoski 2.50 5.00
22 Dave Whitsell 3.00 6.00
23 Fred Whittingham 2.50 5.00
24 Del Williams 2.50 5.00

1969 Saints Team Doubloons

For a number of years, the New Orleans Saints included one Doubloon (coin) per game day program. The 1969 coins featured on the fronts two footballs printed with the team names for each home game match-up for the Saints, as well as the team logos. Seven regular season games and two pre-season games were included. The coin backs included an advertisement for Volkswagon. The year of issue is also featured on the coin front and each was produced using both a silver colored aluminum and a gold colored metal. We've numbered the set in the order of release.
COMPLETE SET (9) 17.50 35.00
1 Saints vs. Falcons 2.00 4.00
2 Saints vs. Oilers 2.00 4.00
3 Saints vs. Redskins 2.50 5.00
4 Saints vs. Cowboys 2.50 5.00
5 Saints vs. Browns 2.50 5.00
6 Saints vs. Colts 2.00 4.00
7 Saints vs. 49ers 2.50 5.00
8 Saints vs. Eagles 2.00 4.00
9 Saints vs. Steelers 2.50 5.00

1970 Saints Team Doubloons

For a number of years, the New Orleans Saints included one Doubloon (coin) per game day program. The 1970 coins featured on the fronts a generic figure of a quarterback with the team names for each home game match-up for the Saints, as well as the team logos. Seven regular season games and two pre-season games were included. The coin backs included the crest of the NFL and the names of both conferences. The year of issue is also featured on the coin front and each was produced using both a silver colored aluminum and a gold colored metal. We've numbered the set in the order of release.
COMPLETE SET (9) 17.50 35.00
1 Saints vs. Lions 2.00 4.00
2 Saints vs. Chargers 2.00 4.00
3 Saints vs. Falcons 2.00 4.00
4 Saints vs. Giants 2.00 4.00
5 Saints vs. Rams 2.00 4.00
6 Saints vs. Lions 2.00 4.00
7 Saints vs. Broncos 2.00 4.00
8 Saints vs. 49ers 2.50 5.00
9 Saints vs. Bears 2.50 5.00

1971-76 Saints Circle Inset

Each of these photos measures approximately 8" by 10." The fronts feature black-and-white action player photos with white borders. Near one of the corners a black-and-white headshot photo appears within a circle. The player's name, position, and team name are typically printed in the lower border in a variety of different type sizes and styles. Some photos are horizontally oriented while others are vertical. The backs are blank. The photos are unnumbered and checklisted below in alphabetical order with some players having more than one type. The year of issue for this set is an estimate with the likelihood of the photos being released over a period of years.
1 Steve Baumgartner 4.00 8.00
2 John Beasley 4.00 8.00
3 Tom Blanchard 4.00 8.00
4 Larry Burton 4.00 8.00
5 Warren Capone 4.00 8.00
6 Rusty Chambers 4.00 8.00
7 Henry Childs 4.00 8.00
8 Larry Cipa 4.00 8.00
9 Don Coleman 4.00 8.00
10 Wayne Colman 4.00 8.00
11 Chuck Crist 4.00 8.00
12 Jack DeGrenier 4.00 8.00
13 Jim Deratt 4.00 8.00
14 John Didion 4.00 8.00
15 Andy Dorris 4.00 8.00
16 Bobby Douglass 5.00 10.00
17 Joe Federspiel 4.00 8.00
18 Jim Flanigan LB 4.00 8.00
19 Johnny Fuller 4.00 8.00
20 Elois Grooms 4.00 8.00
21 Andy Hamilton 4.00 8.00
22 Don Herrmann 4.00 8.00
23 Hugo Hollas 4.00 8.00
24 Ernie Jackson 4.00 8.00
25 Andrew Jones 4.00 8.00
26 Rick Kingrea 4.00 8.00
27 Jake Kupp 4.00 8.00
28 Phil LaPorta 4.00 8.00
29 Odell Lawson 4.00 8.00
30 Archie Manning 12.50 25.00
31 Andy Maurer 4.00 8.00
32 Alvin Maxson 4.00 8.00
33 Bill McClard 4.00 8.00
34 Rod McNeill 4.00 8.00
35 Leon McQuay 4.00 8.00
37 Rick Middleton 4.00 8.00
38 Mark Montgomery 4.00 8.00
39 Derland Moore 4.00 8.00
40 Jerry Moore 4.00 8.00
41 Chuck Muncie 6.00 12.00
43 Joe Owens 4.00 8.00
44 Tinker Owens 4.00 8.00
46 Jess Phillips 4.00 8.00
48 Flex Price 4.00 8.00
49 Ken Reaves 4.00 8.00
50 Steve Rogers 4.00 8.00
51 Terry Schmidt 4.00 8.00
52 Kurt Schumacher 4.00 8.00
53 Bobby Scott 4.00 8.00
54 Paul Seal 4.00 8.00
55 Royce Smith 4.00 8.00
56 Maurice Spencer 4.00 8.00
57 Mike Strachan 4.00 8.00
58 Hank Stram CO 6.00 12.00
59 Rich Szaro 4.00 8.00
60 Jim Thaxton 4.00 8.00
61 Dave Thompson 4.00 8.00
36A Jim Merlo 4.00 8.00
36B Jim Merlo 4.00 8.00
42A Tom Myers 4.00 8.00
42B Tom Myers 4.00 8.00
45A Joel Parker 4.00 8.00
45B Joel Parker 4.00 8.00
47A Bob Pollard 4.00 8.00
47B Bob Pollard 4.00 8.00
62A Greg Westbrooks 4.00 8.00
62B Greg Westbrooks 4.00 8.00
63A Emanuel Zanders 4.00 8.00
63B Emanuel Zanders 4.00 8.00

1971 Saints Team Doubloons

For a number of years, the New Orleans Saints included one Doubloon (coin) per game day program. The 1971 coins featured on the fronts a generic player profile with the team names for each home game match-up for the Saints. Seven regular season games and two pre-season games were included. The coin backs included an advertisement for New Orleans Magazine. The year of issue is also featured on the coin front and each was produced using a silver colored aluminum only. We've numbered the set in the order of release.
COMPLETE SET (9) 17.50 35.00
1 Saints vs. Eagles 2.00 4.00
2 Saints vs. Oilers 2.00 4.00
3 Saints vs. Rams 2.00 4.00
4 Saints vs. 49ers 2.50 5.00
5 Saints vs. Cowboys 2.50 5.00
6 Saints vs. Raiders 2.50 5.00
7 Saints vs. Vikings 2.50 5.00
8 Saints vs. Browns 2.50 5.00
9 Saints vs. Falcons 2.00 4.00

1971-72 Saints Team Issue 4X5

The Saints issued several very similar photo series in the early 1970s. This set was likely issued between 1971 and 1972. Each black and white portrait (no action) photo measures approximately 4" by 5" and carries the player's name and team in the border below the picture. Most include the player's name in large capital letters with the team name abbreviated "N.O. Saints." We've also included a few photos that feature the player's name and team in bold block letters. Any additions to this list are appreciated.
COMPLETE SET (14) 50.00 100.00
1 Carl Cunningham 4.00 8.00
2 Al Dodd 4.00 8.00
3 Julian Fagan 4.00 8.00
4 Edd Hargett 4.00 8.00
5 Glen Ray Hines 4.00 8.00
6 Jake Kupp 4.00 8.00
7 Bivian Lee 4.00 8.00
8 D'Artagnan Martin 4.00 8.00
9 Reynaud Moore 4.00 8.00
10 Don Morrison 4.00 8.00
11 Joe Owens 4.00 8.00
12 Dave Parks 4.00 8.00
13 John Shinners 4.00 8.00
14 Doug Wyatt UER 4.00 8.00

1972 Saints Square Inset

Each of these photos measures approximately 8" by 10." The fronts feature black-and-white action player photos with white borders. Near one of the corners, a black-and-white headshot appears within a square. The player's name, position initials, and team name are printed within one border. The backs are blank and the unnumbered photos are checklisted below in alphabetical order. The list below is thought to be incomplete. Any checklist additions would be appreciated.
COMPLETE SET (9) 30.00 60.00
1 Don Burchfield 4.00 8.00
2 John Didion 4.00 8.00
3 James Ford 4.00 8.00
4 Bob Gresham 4.00 8.00
5 Richard Neal 4.00 8.00
6 Bob Newland 4.00 8.00
7 Dave Parks 4.00 8.00
8 Virgil Robinson 4.00 8.00
9 Jim Strong 4.00 8.00

1972 Saints Team Doubloons

For a number of years, the New Orleans Saints included one Doubloon (coin) per game day program. The 1972 coins featured on the fronts a generic player profile with the team names for each home game match-up for the Saints. Seven regular season games and two pre-season games were included. The coin backs included an advertisement for Burger King. The year of issue is also featured on the coin front and each was produced using a silver colored aluminum only. We've numbered the set in the order of release.
COMPLETE SET (9) 17.50 35.00
1 Saints vs. Cowboys 2.50 5.00
2 Saints vs. Chargers 2.00 4.00
3 Saints vs. Chiefs 2.00 4.00
4 Saints vs. 49ers 2.50 5.00
5 Saints vs. Falcons 2.00 4.00
6 Saints vs. Eagles 2.00 4.00
7 Saints vs. Rams 2.00 4.00
8 Saints vs. Patriots 2.00 4.00
9 Saints vs. Packers 2.50 5.00

1972 Saints Team Issue

The Saints issued several very similar photo series in the early 1970s. This set was most likely released in 1972. Each black and white portrait (no action) photo measures approximately 4" by 5" and carries no pre-printed player identification nor team on the picture at all. Apparently, player names were sometimes written on the photo fronts by a New Orleans Saints employee prior to being shipped out to fans as many are found with this type of written ID.
COMPLETE SET (17) 60.00 120.00
1 Bill Butler 4.00 8.00
2 Al Dodd 4.00 8.00
3 Lawrence Estes 4.00 8.00
4 James Ford 4.00 8.00
5 Edd Hargett 4.00 8.00
6 Glen Ray Hines 4.00 8.00
7 Dave Kopay 4.00 8.00
8 Jake Kupp 4.00 8.00
9 Toni Linhart 4.00 8.00
10 Dave Long 4.00 8.00
11 Don Morrison 4.00 8.00
12 Richard Neal 4.00 8.00
13A Bob Newland 4.00 8.00
13B Bob Newland 4.00 8.00
14 Joe Owens 4.00 8.00
15 Virgil Robinson 4.00 8.00
16 Royce Smith 4.00 8.00

1973 Saints McDonald's

This set of four photos was sponsored by McDonald's. Each photo measures approximately 8" by 10" and features a posed color close-up photo bordered in white. The player's name and team name are printed in black in the bottom white border, and his facsimile autograph is inscribed across the photo. The top portion of the back has biographical information, career summary, and career statistics. The bottom portion includes a list of local McDonald's store addresses and presents the 1973 football schedule for the Saints, Tulane University and LSU. The photos are unnumbered and are checklisted below alphabetically.
COMPLETE SET (4) 17.50 35.00
1 Joe Federspiel 5.00 10.00
2 Jake Kupp 5.00 10.00
3 Joe Owens 5.00 10.00
4 Del Williams 5.00 10.00

1973 Saints Team Doubloons

For a number of years, the New Orleans Saints included one Doubloon (coin) per game day program. The 1973 coins featured on the fronts a generic player profile with the team names for each home game match-up for the Saints. Seven regular season games and two pre-season games were included. The coin backs included an advertisement for Burger King. The year of issue is also featured on the coin front and each was produced using a silver colored aluminum only. We've numbered the set in the order of release.
COMPLETE SET (9) 17.50 35.00
1 Saints vs. Patriots 2.00 4.00
2 Saints vs. Oilers 2.00 4.00
3 Saints vs. Falcons 2.00 4.00
4 Saints vs. Bears 2.50 5.00
5 Saints vs. Lions 2.00 4.00
6 Saints vs. Redskins 2.50 5.00
7 Saints vs. Bills 2.00 4.00
8 Saints vs. Rams 2.00 4.00
9 Saints vs. 49ers 2.50 5.00

1973 Saints Team Issue

The Saints issued several very similar photo series in the early 1970s. This set was most likely issued in 1973. Each black and white portrait (no action) photo measures approximately 4" by 5" and carries the player's name, postion (initials) and team in the border below the picture. The type style used was small (all caps) block lettering with the team name spelled out completely.
COMPLETE SET (17) 60.00 120.00
1 Bill Butler 4.00 8.00
2 Drew Buie 4.00 8.00
3 Bob Davis 4.00 8.00
4 Ernie Jackson 4.00 8.00
5 Ernie Jackson 4.00 8.00
6 Mike Kelly 4.00 8.00
7 Jake Kupp 4.00 8.00
8 Jim Merlo 4.00 8.00
9 Don Morrison 4.00 8.00
10 Bob Newland 4.00 8.00
11 Joe Owens 4.00 8.00
12 Dick Palmer 4.00 8.00
13 Elex Price 4.00 8.00
14 Preston Riley 4.00 8.00
15 Bobby Scott 4.00 8.00
16 Royce Smith 4.00 8.00
17 Howard Stevens 4.00 8.00

1974 Saints Team Doubloons

For a number of years, the New Orleans Saints included one Doubloon (coin) per game day program. The 1974 coins featured on the fronts a generic player profile with the team names for each home game match-up for the Saints. Seven regular season games and two pre-season games were included. The coin backs included an advertisement for Burger King. The year of issue is also featured on the coin front and each was produced using a silver colored aluminum only. We've numbered the set in the order of release.
COMPLETE SET (9) 17.50 35.00
1 Saints vs. Cowboys 2.50 5.00
2 Saints vs. Steelers 2.50 5.00
3 Saints vs. 49ers 2.50 5.00
4 Saints vs. Falcons 2.00 4.00
5 Saints vs. Eagles 2.00 4.00
6 Saints vs. Dolphins 2.50 5.00
7 Saints vs. Rams 2.00 4.00
8 Saints vs. Steelers 2.50 5.00
9 Saints vs. Cardinals 2.00 4.00

1974 Saints Team Issue

The Saints issued several very similar photo series in the early 1970s. This set was most likely issued in 1974. Each black and white portrait (no action) photo measures approximately 4" by 5" and carries the player's name, postion (initials) and team in the border below the picture. The type style used was small italicized block lettering with the team name spelled out completely.
COMPLETE SET (13) 40.00 80.00
1 Andy Dorris 4.00 8.00
2 Paul Fersen 4.00 8.00
3 Len Garrett 4.00 8.00
4 Rick Kingrea 4.00 8.00
5 Odell Lawson 4.00 8.00
6 Jim Merlo 4.00 8.00
7 Jerry Moore 4.00 8.00
8 Don Morrison 4.00 8.00
9 Bob Newland 4.00 8.00
10 Joe Owens 4.00 8.00
11 Elex Price 4.00 8.00
12 Bobby Scott 4.00 8.00
13 Howard Stevens 4.00 8.00

1977 Saints Team Issue

This set of blankbacked photos issued by the Saints was most likely released in 1977. Each black and white action photo measures approximately 8" by 10" and includes the player's name, postion (initials) and team name printed in all upper case letters. The player's facsimile autograph is also printed across the photo.
1 Tony Galbreath 4.00 8.00
2 Archie Manning 7.50 15.00
3 Pollard 4.00 8.00
Fultz
4 Bobby Scott 4.00 8.00
5 K.Schumacher 5.00 10.00
C.Muncie

1979 Saints Coke

The 1979 Coca-Cola New Orleans Saints set contains 45 black and white standard-size cards with red borders. The Coca-Cola logo appears in the upper right hand corner while a New Orleans Saints helmet appears in the lower left. The backs of this gray stock card contain minimal biographical data, the card number and the Coke logo. The cards were produced in conjunction with Topps. There were also unnumbered ad cards for Mr. Pibb and Sprite, one of which was included in each pack of cards.
COMPLETE SET (45) 40.00 80.00
1 Archie Manning 5.00 10.00
2 Ed Burns 1.00 2.00
3 Bobby Scott 1.00 2.00
4 Russell Erxleben 1.00 2.00
5 Eric Felton 1.00 2.00
6 David Gray 1.00 2.00
7 Ricky Ray 1.00 2.00
8 Clarence Chapman 1.00 2.00
9 Kim Jones 1.00 2.00
10 Mike Strachan 1.00 2.00
11 Tony Galbreath 1.25 2.50
12 Tom Myers 1.00 2.00
13 Chuck Muncie 2.50 5.00
14 Jack Holmes 1.00 2.00
15 Don Schwartz 1.00 2.00
16 Ralph McGill 1.00 2.00
17 Ken Bordelon 1.00 2.00
18 Jim Kovach 1.00 2.00
19 Pat Hughes 1.00 2.00
20 Reggie Mathis 1.00 2.00
21 Jim Merlo 1.00 2.00
22 Joe Federspiel 1.00 2.00
23 Don Reese 1.00 2.00
24 Roger Finnie 1.00 2.00
25 John Hill 1.00 2.00
26 Barry Bennett 1.00 2.00
27 Dave Lafary 1.00 2.00
28 Robert Woods 1.00 2.00
29 Conrad Dobler 1.50 3.00
30 John Watson 1.00 2.00
31 Fred Sturt 1.00 2.00
32 J.T. Taylor 1.00 2.00
33 Mike Fultz 1.00 2.00
34 Joe Campbell DT 1.00 2.00
35 Derland Moore 1.00 2.00
36 Elex Price 1.00 2.00
37 Elois Grooms 1.00 2.00
38 Emanuel Zanders 1.00 2.00
39 Ike Harris 1.00 2.00
40 Tinker Owens 1.00 2.00
41 Rich Mauti 1.00 2.00
42 Henry Childs 1.50 3.00
43 Larry Hardy 1.00 2.00
44 Brooks Williams 1.00 2.00
45 Wes Chandler 2.50 5.00
AD1 Mr.Pibb Ad Card .20 .50
AD2 Sprite Ad Card .20 .50

1980 Saints Team Issue

These photos were released by the Saints for fans and for player signing appearances. Each measures roughly 8" by 10" and includes a black and white photo of the player with the player's name (in all caps), his position (intials), and team name (New Orleans Saints stacked) below the picture. The backs are blank and unnumbered.
COMPLETE SET (7) 15.00 30.00
1 Russell Erxleben 2.00 5.00
2 Elois Grooms 2.00 5.00
3 Jack Holmes 2.00 5.00
4 Dave LaFary 2.00 5.00
5 Derland Moore 2.00 5.00
6 Benny Ricardo 2.00 5.00
7 Emanuel Zanders 2.00 5.00

1985 Saints Eckerd Posters

These large (18" by 25") color posters were sponsored by Eckerd Stores. Each was blankbacked and featured a strip of 11-coupons below the player image.
COMPLETE SET (8) 35.00 70.00
1 Hoby Brenner 3.00 8.00
2 Earl Campbell 8.00 20.00
3 Rickey Jackson 4.00 10.00
4 Dave Wilson 3.00 8.00
5 Dave Waymer 3.00 8.00
6 Russell Gary 3.00 8.00
7 Bruce Clark 3.00 8.00
8 Hokie Gajan 3.00 8.00

1992 Saints McDag

This 32-card safety standard-size set was produced by McDag Productions Inc. for the New Orleans Saints and Behavioral Health Inc. The cards feature posed color player photos with white borders. The pictures are studio shots with a blue background. Running horizontally down the left is a wide brown stripe with the team name and year in yellow outline lettering. A mustard stripe at the bottom of the photo intersects the brown stripe and contains the player's name. The backs are white with black print and carry biographical information, career highlights, and "Tips from the Team" in the form of public service messages. There is also an address and phone number for obtaining free cards. The cards are unnumbered and checklisted below in alphabetical order.
COMPLETE SET (32) 4.00 10.00
1 Morten Andersen .20 .50
2 Gene Atkins .15 .40
3 Toi Cook .08 .25
4 Tommy Barnhardt .08 .25
5 Hoby Brenner .08 .25
6 Stan Brock .08 .25
7 Vince Buck .08 .25
8 Wesley Carroll .15 .40
9 Jim Dombrowski .08 .25
10 Vaughn Dunbar .15 .40
11 Quinn Early .30 .75
12 Bobby Hebert .15 .40
13 Craig Heyward .25 .60
14 Joel Hilgenberg .08 .25
15 Dalton Hilliard .08 .25
16 Rickey Jackson .15 .40
17 Vaughan Johnson .15 .40
18 Reginald Jones .08 .25
19 Eric Martin .15 .40
20 Wayne Martin .15 .40
21 Brett Maxie .08 .25
22 Fred McAfee .08 .25
23 Sam Mills .20 .50
24 Jim Mora CO .15 .40
25 Pat Swilling .15 .40
26 John Tice .08 .25
27 Renaldo Turnbull .15 .40
28 Floyd Turner .15 .40
29 Steve Walsh .15 .40
30 Frank Warren .08 .25
31 Jim Wilks .08 .25
32 Saints Cheerleaders .08 .25

1993 Saints Team Issue

These photos were released by the Saints for fans and for player signing appearances. Each measures roughly 4" by 5" and includes a black and white photo of the player with the team helmet and player information below the picture. The backs are blank and unnumbered.
COMPLETE SET (6) 4.80 12.00
1 Derek Brown RBK 1.20 3.00
2 Tyrone Hughes .80 2.00
3 Sean Lumpkin .80 2.00
4 Jim Mora CO .80 2.00
5 Willie Roaf 1.50 4.00
6 James Williams LB .80 2.00

1994 Saints Team Issue

These photos were released by the Saints for fans and for player signing appearances. Each measures roughly 8" by 10" and includes a black and white photo of the player. The backs are blank and unnumbered and no player information is contained on the photos at all. These photos can be identified by the NFL 75th Anniversary patch on the player's sleeves.
COMPLETE SET (10) 8.00 20.00
1 Darion Conner .80 2.00
2 Jim Everett 1.20 3.00
3 Joe Johnson .80 2.00
4 J.J. McCleskey .80 2.00
5 Derrick Ned .80 2.00
6 Doug Nussmeier .80 2.00
7 Chris Port .80 2.00
8 Irv Smith .80 2.00
9 Winfred Tubbs .80 2.00
10 Wesley Walls 1.20 3.00

1996 Saints Team Issue

These photos were released by the Saints for fans and for player signing appearances. Each measures roughly 8" by 10" and includes a black and white photo of the player. The backs are blank and unnumbered and no player information is contained on the photos at all. They can be identified by the Saints 30th Anniversary patch on the player's jersey.
COMPLETE SET (10) 8.00 20.00
1 Mario Bates 1.20 3.00
2 Doug Brien .80 2.00
3 Ernest Dixon .80 2.00
4 Paul Green .80 2.00
5 Richard Harvey .80 2.00
6 Andy McCollum .80 2.00
7 Darren Mickell .80 2.00
8 Alex Molden .80 2.00
9 Willie Roaf 1.20 3.00
10 Brady Smith .80 2.00

2000 Saints Team Issue

This large (roughly 8" by 10") black and white photos were issued by the Saints in 2000. Each includes a player photo with his name, team helmet, and NFL logo below the photo.
COMPLETE SET (11) 15.00 30.00
1 Jeff Blake 2.50 5.00
2 Jerry Fontenot 1.00 2.00
3 La'Roi Glover 1.00 2.00
4 Norman Hand 1.00 2.00
5 Sammy Knight 1.00 2.00
6 Keith Mitchell 1.00 2.00
7 Chad Morton 1.50 3.00
8 William Roaf 1.50 3.00
9 Ricky Williams 5.00 10.00
10 Wally Williams 1.00 2.00
11 Fred Weary 1.00 2.00

2001 Saints Team Issue

These blankbacked photos were issued in 2001 by the Saints for player appearances so they are often found signed. Each is black and white and measures roughly 3 1/2" by 5." Any additions to this list are appreciated.
COMPLETE SET (9) 12.50 25.00
1 Jake Delhomme 2.00 4.00
2 Norman Hand 1.00 2.50
3 Jim Haslett CO 1.50 3.00
4 Joe Horn 2.00 4.00
5 Fred McAfee 1.00 2.50
6 Deuce McAllister 5.00 12.00
7 Randy Mueller GM 1.00 2.50
8 Kenny Smith 1.50 3.00
9 Daryl Terrell 1.00 2.50

2002 Saints Team Issue

This set was issued by the Saints. Each card measures a large 3" by 4" and features a color image of a Saints player on the front with the team name above the photo and his name and position below. Each cardfront also includes a raised gold facsimilie autograph. The cardbacks are black and white.
COMPLETE SET (8) 12.00 20.00
1 Aaron Brooks 1.50 4.00
2 Norman Hand .75 2.00
3 Joe Horn 1.50 4.00
4 Darren Howard .75 2.00
5 Sammy Knight .75 2.00
6 Deuce McAllister 2.50 6.00
7 Terrelle Smith .75 2.00
8 Kyle Turley .75 2.00

2003 Saints Team Issue

This set was issued by the Saints. Each card measures a large 3" by 4" and features a color image of a Saints player on the front with the team name above the photo and his name and position below within a gold broder. Each cardfront also includes a raised gold facsimilie autograph. The cardbacks are black and white.
COMPLETE SET (7) 7.50 15.00
1 Aaron Brooks 1.25 3.00
2 John Carney .75 2.00
3 Charles Grant .75 2.00
4 Joe Horn 1.25 3.00
5 Michael Lewis 1.25 3.00
6 Deuce McAllister 2.00 5.00
7 Donte Stallworth 1.25 3.00

2004 Saints Team Issue

This set was issued by the Saints with each card measuring standard size. The fronts feature a color image of a Saints player with the team name above the photo and his name and position below. Each cardfront also includes a raised gold facsimilie autograph. The cardbacks are black and white and unnumbered.
COMPLETE SET (8) 3.00 6.00
1 Ashley Ambrose .40 1.00
2 LeCharles Bentley .40 1.00
3 Steve Gleason .40 1.00
4 Joe Horn .40 1.00
5 Darren Howard .40 1.00
6 Michael Lewis .50 1.25
7 Deuce McAllister .50 1.25
8 Fred Thomas .40 1.00

2006 Saints Team Issue

This set was issued by the Saints with each card measuring standard size. The fronts feature a color image of a Saints player with the team name above the photo and his name and position below. Each cardfront also includes a raised gold facsimilie autograph. The cardbacks are black and white and unnumbered.
COMPLETE SET (9) 4.00 10.00
1 Drew Brees .60 1.50
2 Reggie Bush .60 1.50
3 Charles Grant .30 .75
4 Joe Horn .40 1.00
5 Mike Karney .40 1.00
6 Deuce McAllister .50 1.25
7 Mike McKenzie .40 1.00
8 Hollis Thomas .40 1.00
9 Brian Young .40 1.00

2006 Saints Topps

COMPLETE SET (12) 5.00 12.00
NO1 Joe Horn .25 .60
NO2 Ernie Conwell .25 .60
NO3 Donte Stallworth .25 .60
NO4 Drew Brees .40 1.00
NO5 Deuce McAllister .30 .75
NO6 Mike McKenzie .25 .60
NO7 Aaron Stecker .25 .60
NO8 Charles Grant .20 .50
NO9 Will Smith .25 .60
NO10 Devery Henderson .25 .60
NO11A Reggie Bush 5 4.00 10.00
NO11B Reggie Bush 25 4.00 10.00
NO12 Mike Hass .30 .75

2007 Saints Team Issue

This set was issued by the Saints with each card measuring standard size. The fronts feature a color image of a Saints player with the team name above the photo and his name and position below. Each cardfront also includes a raised gold facsimilie autograph. The cardbacks are black and white and unnumbered.
COMPLETE SET (9) 4.00 10.00
1 Drew Brees .60 1.50
2 Reggie Bush .40 1.00
3 Marques Colston .40 1.00
4 Scott Fujita .40 1.00
5 Charles Grant .40 1.00
6 Devery Henderson .40 1.00
7 Deuce McAllister .50 1.25
8 Mike McKenzie .40 1.00
9 Will Smith .40 1.00

2007 Saints Topps

COMPLETE SET (12) 2.50 5.00
1 Reggie Bush .40 1.00
2 Devery Henderson .40 1.00
3 Deuce McAllister .50 1.25
4 Marques Colston .40 1.00
5 Drew Brees .60 1.50
6 Eric Johnson .40 1.00
7 Will Smith .40 1.00
8 Mike McKenzie .40 1.00
9 Terrance Copper .50 1.25
10 Mike Karney .40 1.00
11 Charles Grant .40 1.00
12 Robert Meachem .50 1.25

2008 Saints Topps

COMPLETE SET (12) 2.50 5.00
1 Drew Brees .60 1.50
2 Marques Colston .40 1.00
3 Aaron Stecker .40 1.00
4 Reggie Bush .40 1.00
5 David Patten .40 1.00
6 Deuce McAllister .50 1.25
7 Devery Henderson .40 1.00
8 Will Smith .40 1.00
9 Mike McKenzie .40 1.00
10 Scott Fujita .40 1.00
11 Sedrick Ellis .40 1.00
12 Tracy Porter .50 1.25

2009 Saints Team Issue

This set was issued by the Saints with each card measuring standard size. The fronts feature a color image of a Saints player with the team name below the photo and his name and position above. Each cardfront also includes a raised gold facsimilie autograph and a white border. The cardbacks are black and white and unnumbered.
COMPLETE SET (11) 5.00 12.00
1 Drew Brees .60 1.50
2 Reggie Bush .40 1.00
3 Marques Colston .40 1.00
4 Sedrick Ellis .40 1.00
5 Scott Fujita .40 1.00
6 Roman Harper .40 1.00
7 Will Smith .40 1.00
7 Lance Moore .40 1.00
8 Jon Stinchcomb .40 1.00
9 Pierre Thomas .40 1.00
10 Jonathan Vilma .40 1.00

2010 Saints Upper Deck Super Bowl XLIV

COMP.FACT.SET (51) 10.00 20.00
1 Drew Brees .40 1.00
2 Marques Colston .25 .60
3 Reggie Bush .25 .60
4 Pierre Thomas .25 .60
5 Mike Bell .25 .60
6 Jeremy Shockey .25 .60
7 Devery Henderson .25 .60
8 Robert Meachem .25 .60
9 David Thomas .25 .60
10 Lance Moore .25 .60
11 Heath Evans .25 .60
12 Jonathan Vilma .25 .60
13 Roman Harper .25 .60
14 Darren Sharper .25 .60
15 Scott Shanle .25 .60
16 Will Smith .25 .60
17 Malcolm Jenkins .25 .60
18 Charles Grant .25 .60
19 Tracy Porter .25 .60
20 Jabari Greer .25 .60
21 Jahri Evans .25 .60
22 Jonathan Goodwin .25 .60
23 Jon Stinchcomb .25 .60
24 Lynell Hamilton .25 .60
25 John Carney .25 .60
26 Garrett Hartley .25 .60
27 Thomas Morstead .25 .60
28 Courtney Roby .25 .60
29 Scott Fujita .25 .60
30 Anthony Hargrove .25 .60
31 Randall Gay .25 .60
32 Sedrick Ellis .25 .60
33 Remi Ayodele .25 .60
34 Bobby McCray .25 .60
35 Marvin Mitchell .25 .60
36 Pierson Prioleau .25 .60
37 Mark Brunell .25 .60
38 Chase Daniel .25 .60
39 Carl Nicks .25 .60
40 Jermon Bushrod .25 .60
41 Darren Sharper HL .25 .60
42 Drew Brees HL .40 1.00
43 Reggie Bush HL .25 .60
44 Robert Meachem HL .25 .60
45 Jonathan Vilma HL .25 .60
46 Chris Reis HL .25 .60
47 Pierre Thomas HL .25 .60
48 Jeremy Shockey HL .25 .60
49 Tracy Porter HL .25 .60
50 Drew Brees MVP .40 1.00
SBXLIV Super Bowl Champs Jumbo .60 1.50

2012 Saints Topps Super Bowl XLVII

COMPLETE SET (5) 3.00 6.00
DB Drew Brees .60 1.50
DS Darren Sproles .50 1.25
JG Jimmy Graham .60 1.50
MC Marques Colston .40 1.00
MI Mark Ingram .50 1.25

1962-63 Salada Coins

This 154-coin set features popular NFL and AFL players from selected teams. Each team had a specific rim color. The numbering of the coins is essentially by teams, i.e., Colts (1-11 blue), Packers (12-22 green), 49ers (23-33 salmon), Bears (34-44 black), Rams (45-55 yellow), Browns (56-66 black), Steelers (67-77 yellow), Lions (78-88 blue), Redskins (89-99 yellow), Eagles (100-110 green), Giants (111-121 blue), Patriots (122-132 salmon), Titans (133-143 blue), and Bills (144-154 salmon). All players are pictured without their helmets. The coins measure approximately 1 1/2" in diameter. The coin backs give the player's name, position, pro team, college, height, and weight. The coins were originally produced on sheets measuring 31 1/2" by 25"; the 255 coins on the sheet included the complete set as well as duplicates and triplicates. Double prints (DP) and triple prints (TP) are listed below. The double-printed coins are generally from certain teams, i.e., Packers, Bears, Browns, Lions, Eagles, Giants, Patriots, Titans, and Bills. Those coins below not listed explicitly as to the frequency of printing are in fact single printed (SP) and hence more difficult to find. The set is sometimes found intact as a presentation set in its own custom box; such a set would be valued 25 percent higher than the complete set price below.
COMPLETE SET (154) 1250.00 2500.00
1 Johnny Unitas 75.00 150.00
2 Lenny Moore 40.00 80.00
3 Jim Parker 25.00 50.00
4 Gino Marchetti 25.00 50.00
5 Dick Szymanski 15.00 30.00
6 Alex Sandusky 15.00 30.00
7 Raymond Berry 40.00 80.00
8 Jimmy Orr 15.00 30.00
9 Ordell Braase 15.00 30.00
10 Bill Pellington 15.00 30.00
11 Bob Boyd DB 15.00 30.00
12 Paul Hornung DP 20.00 40.00
13 Jim Taylor DP 15.00 30.00
14 Hank Jordan DP 5.00 10.00
15 Dan Currie DP 4.00 8.00
16 Bill Forester DP 4.00 8.00
17 Dave Hanner DP 4.00 8.00
18 Bart Starr DP 25.00 50.00
19 Max McGee DP 5.00 10.00
20 Jerry Kramer DP 6.00 12.00
21 Forrest Gregg DP 6.00 12.00
22 Jim Ringo DP 6.00 12.00
23 Billy Kilmer 25.00 50.00
24 Charlie Krueger 15.00 30.00
25 Bob St. Clair 25.00 50.00
26 Abe Woodson 15.00 30.00
27 Jim Johnson 25.00 50.00
28 Matt Hazeltine 15.00 30.00
29 Bruce Bosley 15.00 30.00
30 Clyde Conner 15.00 30.00
31 John Brodie 30.00 60.00
32 J.D. Smith 15.00 30.00
33 Monty Stickles 15.00 30.00
34 Johnny Morris DP 3.00 6.00
35 Stan Jones DP 5.00 10.00
36 J.C. Caroline DP 2.50 5.00
37 Richie Petitbon DP 3.00 6.00
38 Joe Fortunato DP 3.00 6.00
39 Larry Morris DP 2.50 5.00
40 Doug Atkins DP 6.00 12.00
41 Bill Wade DP 3.00 6.00

42 Rick Casares DP 3.00 6.00
43 Willie Galimore DP 3.00 6.00
44 Angelo Coia DP 2.50 5.00
45 Ollie Matson 30.00 60.00
46 Carroll Dale 15.00 30.00
47 Ed Meador 15.00 30.00
48 Jon Arnett 15.00 30.00
49 Joe Marconi 15.00 30.00
50 John LoVetere 15.00 30.00
51 Red Phillips 15.00 30.00
52 Zeke Bratkowski 20.00 40.00
53 Dick Bass 15.00 30.00
54 Les Richter 15.00 30.00
55 Art Hunter 15.00 30.00
56 Jim Brown TP 25.00 50.00
57 Mike McCormack DP 5.00 10.00
58 Bob Gain DP 2.50 5.00
59 Paul Wiggin DP 2.50 5.00
60 Jim Houston DP 2.50 5.00
61 Ray Renfro DP 3.00 6.00
62 Galen Fiss DP 2.50 5.00
63 J.R. Smith DP 2.50 5.00
64 John Morrow DP 2.50 5.00
65 Gene Hickerson DP 3.00 6.00
66 Jim Ninowski DP 2.50 5.00
67 Tom Tracy 15.00 30.00
68 Buddy Dial 15.00 30.00
69 Mike Sandusky 15.00 30.00
70 Lou Michaels 15.00 30.00
71 Preston Carpenter 15.00 30.00
72 John Reger 15.00 30.00
73 John Henry Johnson 30.00 60.00
74 Gene Lipscomb 20.00 35.00
75 Mike Henry 15.00 30.00
76 George Tarasovic 15.00 30.00
77 Bobby Layne 50.00 100.00
78 Harley Sewell DP 2.50 5.00
79 Darris McCord DP 2.50 5.00
80 Yale Lary DP 5.00 10.00
81 Jim Gibbons DP 3.00 6.00
82 Gail Cogdill DP 2.50 5.00
83 Nick Pietrosante DP 2.50 5.00
84 Alex Karras DP 7.50 15.00
85 Dick Lane DP 5.00 10.00
86 Joe Schmidt DP 6.00 12.00
87 John Gordy DP 2.50 5.00
88 Milt Plum DP 3.00 6.00
89 Andy Stynchula 15.00 30.00
90 Bob Toneff 15.00 30.00
91 Bill Anderson 15.00 30.00
92 Sam Horner 15.00 30.00
93 Norm Snead 20.00 40.00
94 Bobby Mitchell 30.00 60.00
95 Bill Barnes 15.00 30.00
96 Rod Breedlove 15.00 30.00
97 Fred Hageman 15.00 30.00
98 Vince Promuto 15.00 30.00
99 Joe Rutgens 15.00 30.00
100 Maxie Baughan DP 2.50 5.00
101 Pete Retzlaff DP 3.00 6.00
102 Tom Brookshier DP 3.00 6.00
103 Sonny Jurgensen DP 9.00 18.00
104 Ed Khayat DP 2.50 5.00
105 Chuck Bednarik DP 7.50 15.00
106 Tommy McDonald DP 4.00 8.00
107 Bobby Walston DP 2.50 5.00
108 Ted Dean DP 2.50 5.00
109 Clarence Peaks DP 3.00 6.00
110 Jimmy Carr DP 2.50 5.00
111 Sam Huff DP 7.50 15.00
112 Erich Barnes DP 2.50 5.00
113 Del Shofner DP 3.00 6.00
114 Bob Gaiters DP 2.50 5.00
115 Alex Webster DP 3.00 6.00
116 Dick Modzelewski DP 2.50 5.00
117 Jim Katcavage DP 3.00 6.00
118 Roosevelt Brown DP 5.00 10.00
119 Y.A. Tittle DP 12.50 25.00
120 Andy Robustelli DP 6.00 12.00
121 Dick Lynch DP 2.50 5.00
122 Don Webb DP 2.50 5.00
123 Larry Eisenhauer DP 2.50 5.00
124 Babe Parilli DP 3.00 6.00
125 Charles Long DP 2.50 5.00
126 Billy Lott DP 2.50 5.00
127 Harry Jacobs DP 2.50 5.00
128 Bob Dee DP 2.50 5.00
129 Ron Burton DP 3.00 6.00
130 Jim Colclough TP 1.50 3.00
131 Gino Cappelletti DP 3.00 6.00
132 Tommy Addison DP 2.50 5.00
133 Larry Grantham DP 2.50 5.00
134 Dick Christy DP 2.50 5.00
135 Bill Mathis DP 3.00 6.00
136 Butch Songin DP 2.50 5.00
137 Dainard Paulson DP 2.50 5.00
138 Roger Ellis DP 2.50 5.00
139 Mike Hudock DP 2.50 5.00
140 Don Maynard DP 10.00 20.00
141 Al Dorow DP 2.50 5.00
142 Jack Klotz DP 2.50 5.00
143 Lee Riley DP 2.50 5.00
144 Bill Atkins DP 2.50 5.00
145 Art Baker DP 2.50 5.00
146 Stew Barber DP 2.50 5.00
147 Glenn Bass DP 2.50 5.00
148 Al Bemiller DP 2.50 5.00
149 Richie Lucas DP 2.50 5.00
150 Archie Matsos DP 2.50 5.00
151 Warren Rabb DP 2.50 5.00
152 Ken Rice DP 2.50 5.00
153 Billy Shaw DP 3.00 6.00
154 Laverne Torczon DP 2.50 5.00

2005 San Angelo Stampede Express NIFL

COMPLETE SET (34) 7.50 15.00
1 Jeff Anderson .20 .50
2 Ray Brennan .20 .50
3 Demont Burdine .20 .50
4 Andre Cummings .20 .50
5 Barrett Dallmeyer .20 .50
6 Toby Davis .20 .50
7 D'Ambrose Finch .20 .50
8 David Guillen .20 .50
9 Clay Hardt .20 .50
10 Kito Hicks .20 .50
11 Prescott Hill .20 .50
12 Ryan Hunt .20 .50
13 Tyrone Johnson .20 .50
14 Terry Kilpatrick .20 .50
15 Chuck Leonardis .20 .50
16 Gary Love .20 .50
17 Karson Lown .20 .50
18 Marquez Reischl .20 .50
19 Corey Roberson .20 .50
20 Max Schug Asst.CO .20 .50
21 Jessie Shields .20 .50
22 Chris Simpson CO .20 .50
23 Jeff Smith .20 .50
24 Calvin Thomas .20 .50
25 Brian Villanueva .20 .50
26 Kailan Williams .20 .50
27 Demont Burdine .20 .50
Gary Love
Prescott Hill
28 Assistant Coaches .20 .50
Jeff Mann
Randy Matthews
Joe Briley
29 Jeff Smith .20 .50
Clay Hardt
30 Stomper (Mascot) .20 .50
31 Team Card .20 .50
32 Broadcast Team Ad Card .20 .50
33 Gandy Ink Ad Card .20 .50
34 Extreme Imaging Ad Card .20 .50

2006 San Angelo Express IFL

COMPLETE SET (23) 6.00 12.00
1 Johnny Anderson .20 .50
2 David Banks .20 .50
3 Demont Burdine .20 .50
4 James Cardenas .20 .50
5 Barrett Dallmeyer .20 .50
6 Michael Dansby .20 .50
7 Toby Davis .20 .50
8 Paul Francis .20 .50
9 Bruce Hampton .20 .50
10 Terrence Jefferson .20 .50
11 Michael Johnson .20 .50
12 Rashaad Lee .20 .50
13 Quinton Morgan .20 .50
14 Wali Mumin .20 .50
15 Cody Munden (Trainer) .20 .50
16 Sharif Najib .20 .50
17 Jon Nielson .20 .50
18 Larry Newton .20 .50
19 Jaime Salazar .20 .50
20 J.T. Smith CO .20 .50
21 Derik Stotland .20 .50
22 Jackie Warren .20 .50
23 Cody Wilson .20 .50

2007 San Antonio Steers NIFL

COMPLETE SET (4) 2.50 6.00
1 Bo Buescher .60 1.50
2 Garyle Graham .60 1.50
3 Mark Ricker CO .60 1.50
4 Michael Ward .60 1.50

1975 San Antonio Wings WFL Team Issue

This set of black and white photos was issued by the San Antonio Wings to fulfill fan requests and for player appearances. Each measures roughly 5" by 7" and includes the player's name, position, and team name below the photo in varying type styles and sizes. The photo backs are blank.

COMPLETE SET (5) 25.00 50.00
1 Rick Cash 5.00 10.00
2 Luther Palmer 5.00 10.00
3 Dick Pesonen CO 5.00 10.00
4 Lonnie Warwick 5.00 10.00
5 Craig Wiseman 5.00 10.00

2008 San Jose Sabercats AFL

COMPLETE SET (38) 7.50 15.00
1 Darren Arbet CO .20 .50
2 Frank Carter .20 .50
3 Marquis Floyd .20 .50
4 Gene Frederic .20 .50
5 Jason Geathers .20 .50
6 Trestin George .20 .50
7 Mark Grieb .20 .50
8 A.J. Haglund .20 .50
9 Alan Harper .20 .50
10 Brian Johnson .20 .50
11 Ron Jones .20 .50
12 Dan Loney .20 .50
13 Garrett McIntyre .20 .50
14 William Obeng .20 .50
15 Scott Rislov .20 .50
16 James Roe .20 .50
17 Cleannord Saintil .20 .50
18 Omarr Smith .20 .50
19 Clevan Thomas .30 .75
20 Jason Thomas .20 .50
21 Steve Watson .20 .50
22 George Williams .20 .50
23 Rodney Wright .20 .50
24 San Jose Saberkitten: Aimie .20 .50
25 San Jose Saberkitten: Alexis .20 .50
26 San Jose Saberkitten: Amber .20 .50
27 San Jose Saberkitten: Andrea .20 .50
28 San Jose Saberkitten: Charmaine .20 .50
29 San Jose Saberkitten: Christi .20 .50
30 San Jose Saberkitten: Desi .20 .50
31 San Jose Saberkitten: Grecia .20 .50
32 San Jose Saberkitten: Jenna .20 .50
33 San Jose Saberkitten: Jennie .20 .50
34 San Jose Saberkitten: Jennifer .20 .50
35 San Jose Saberkitten: Krystle .20 .50
36 San Jose Saberkitten: Leizl .20 .50
37 San Jose Saberkitten: Meredith .20 .50
38 Title Card .20 .50

1989 Score Promos

This set of six football standard-size full-color cards was intended as a preview of Score's first football set, after two years of baseball card issues. The cards were sent out to prospective dealers along with the ordering forms for Score's debut football set. The cards are distinguishable from the regular issue cards of the same numbers as indicated in the checklist below. One good way to recognize these promos is that the stats on the promo card backs are carried out to only one decimal place instead of two. In addition, the promo cards show a registered symbol (R with circle around it) rather than a trademark (TM) symbol.

COMPLETE SET (6) 80.00 200.00
1 Joe Montana 40.00 100.00
2 Bo Jackson 12.00 30.00
3 Boomer Esiason 8.00 20.00
4 Roger Craig 8.00 20.00
5 Ed Too Tall Jones 6.00 15.00
6 Phil Simms 8.00 20.00

1989 Score

This set of 330 standard-size full-color cards marks Score's entry into the football card market. The set was issued in 15-card packs along with a trivia card. The front has a player photo surrounded by a color border that differs according to team. The player's name and team helmet are at the bottom. The backs contain a photo, statistics and highlights. The first 244 cards in the set are regular player cards. Cards 245-272 are rookie cards of players selected in the '89 NFL draft. Other subsets are post-season action (273-275), combo cards (277-284), All-Pro selections (285-309), Speedburners (310-317), Predators (318-325) and Record Breakers (326-329). The last card in the set is a tribute to Tom Landry. Rookie Cards include Troy Aikman, Steve Atwater, Don Beebe, Steve Beuerlein, Brian Blades, Bubby Brister, Tim Brown, Mark (WR) Carrier, Cris Carter, Gaston Green, Michael Irvin, Keith Jackson, Eric Metcalf, Anthony Miller, Chris Miller, Andre Rison, Mark Rypien, Barry Sanders, Deion Sanders, Chris Spielman, John Taylor, Broderick Thomas, Derrick Thomas, Thurman Thomas, and Rod Woodson.

COMPLETE SET (330) 30.00 80.00
COMP.FACT.SET (330) 30.00 80.00
1 Joe Montana 1.50 4.00
2 Bo Jackson .25 .60
3 Boomer Esiason .08 .20
4 Roger Craig .20 .50
5 Ed Too Tall Jones .08 .20
6 Phil Simms .08 .20
7 Dan Hampton .08 .20
8 John Settle RC .04 .10
9 Bernie Kosar .08 .20
10 Al Toon .08 .20
11 Bubby Brister RC .40 1.00
12 Mark Clayton .08 .20
13 Dan Marino 1.50 4.00
14 Joe Morris .04 .10
15 Warren Moon .20 .50
16 Chuck Long .04 .10
17 Mark Jackson .04 .10
18 Michael Irvin RC 4.00 10.00
19 Bruce Smith .20 .50
20 Anthony Carter .08 .20
21 Charles Haley .20 .50
22 Dave Duerson .04 .10
23 Troy Stradford .04 .10
24 Freeman McNeil .04 .10
25 Jerry Gray .04 .10
26 Bill Maas .04 .10
27 Chris Chandler RC 1.25 3.00
28 Tom Newberry RC .04 .10
29 Albert Lewis .04 .10
30 Jay Schroeder .04 .10
31 Dalton Hilliard .04 .10
32 Tony Eason .04 .10
33 Rick Donnelly UER .04 .10
34 Herschel Walker .08 .20
35 Wesley Walker .04 .10
36 Chris Doleman .08 .20
37 Pat Swilling .08 .20
38 Joey Browner .04 .10
39 Shane Conlan .04 .10
40 Mike Tomczak .08 .20
41 Webster Slaughter .08 .20
42 Ray Donaldson .04 .10
43 Christian Okoye .04 .10
44 John Bosa .04 .10
45 Aaron Cox RC .04 .10
46 Bobby Hebert .08 .20
47 Carl Banks .04 .10
48 Jeff Fuller .04 .10
49 Gerald Willhite .04 .10
50 Mike Singletary .08 .20
51 Stanley Morgan .04 .10
52 Mark Bavaro .08 .20
53 Mickey Shuler .04 .10
54 Keith Millard .04 .10
55 Andre Tippett .04 .10
56 Vance Johnson .08 .20
57 Bennie Blades RC .08 .20
58 Tim Harris .04 .10
59 Hanford Dixon .04 .10
60 Chris Miller RC .40 1.00
61 Cornelius Bennett .20 .50
62 Neal Anderson .08 .20
63 Ickey Woods UER RC .40 1.00
64 Gary Anderson RB .04 .10
65 Vaughan Johnson RC .04 .10
66 Ronnie Lippett .04 .10
67 Mike Quick .04 .10
68 Roy Green .08 .20
69 Tim Krumrie .04 .10
70 Mark Malone .04 .10
71 James Jones FB .04 .10
72 Cris Carter RC 5.00 12.00
73 Ricky Nattiel .04 .10
74 Jim Arnold UER .04 .10
75 Randall Cunningham .40 1.00
76 John L.Williams .04 .10
77 Paul Gruber RC .04 .10
78 Rod Woodson RC 2.00 5.00
79 Ray Childress .04 .10
80 Doug Williams .08 .20
81 Deron Cherry .08 .20
82 John Offerdahl .04 .10
83 Louis Lipps .08 .20
84 Neil Lomax .04 .10
85 Wade Wilson .08 .20
86 Tim Brown RC 4.00 10.00
87 Chris Hinton .04 .10
88 Stump Mitchell .04 .10
89 Tunch Ilkin RC .04 .10
90 Steve Pelluer .04 .10
91 Brian Noble .04 .10
92 Reggie White .20 .50
93 Aundray Bruce RC .04 .10
94 Garry James .04 .10
95 Drew Hill .04 .10
96 Anthony Munoz .08 .20
97 James Wilder .04 .10
98 Dexter Manley .04 .10
99 Lee Williams .04 .10
100 Dave Krieg .08 .20
101A Keith Jackson ERR RC .20 .50
101B Keith Jackson COR RC .20 .50
102 Luis Sharpe .04 .10
103 Kevin Greene .20 .50
104 Duane Bickett .04 .10
105 Mark Rypien RC .20 .50
106 Curt Warner .04 .10
107 Jacob Green .04 .10
108 Gary Clark .20 .50
109 Bruce Matthews RC 1.25 3.00
110 Bill Fralic .04 .10
111 Bill Bates .08 .20
112 Jeff Bryant .04 .10
113 Charles Mann .04 .10
114 Richard Dent .08 .20
115 Bruce Hill RC .04 .10
116 Mark May RC .04 .10
117 Mark Collins RC .04 .10
118 Ron Holmes .04 .10
119 Scott Case RC .04 .10
120 Tom Rathman .04 .10
121 Dennis McKinnon .04 .10
122A Ricky Sanders ERR 46 .10 .25
122B Ricky Sanders COR 83 .20 .50
123 Michael Carter .04 .10
124 Ozzie Newsome .08 .20
125 Irving Fryar UER .08 .20
126A Ron Hall ERR RC .10 .25
126B Ron Hall COR RC .20 .50
127 Clay Matthews .08 .20
128 Leonard Marshall .04 .10
129 Kevin Mack .04 .10
130 Art Monk .08 .20
131 Garin Veris .04 .10
132 Steve Jordan .04 .10
133 Frank Minnifield .04 .10
134 Eddie Brown .04 .10
135 Stacey Bailey .04 .10
136 Rickey Jackson .08 .20
137 Henry Ellard .08 .20
138 Jim Burt .04 .10
139 Jerome Brown .08 .20
140 Rodney Holman RC .04 .10
141 Sammy Winder .04 .10
142 Marcus Cotton RC .04 .10
143 Jim Jeffcoat .04 .10
144 Rueben Mayes .04 .10
145 Jim McMahon .08 .20
146 Reggie Williams .04 .10
147 John Anderson .04 .10
148 Harris Barton RC .04 .10
149 Phillip Epps .04 .10
150 Jay Hilgenberg .04 .10
151 Earl Ferrell .04 .10
152 Andre Reed .20 .50
153 Dennis Gentry .04 .10
154 Max Montoya .04 .10
155 Darrin Nelson .04 .10
156 Jeff Chadwick .04 .10
157 James Brooks .08 .20
158 Keith Bishop .04 .10
159 Robert Awalt .04 .10
160 Marty Lyons .04 .10
161 Johnny Hector .04 .10
162 Tony Casillas .04 .10
163 Kyle Clifton RC .04 .10
164 Cody Risien .04 .10
165 Jamie Holland RC .04 .10
166 Merril Hoge RC .04 .10
167 Chris Spielman RC .40 1.00
168 Carlos Carson .04 .10
169 Jerry Ball RC .04 .10
170 Don Majkowski RC .20 .50
171 Everson Walls .04 .10
172 Mike Rozier .04 .10
173 Matt Millen .08 .20
174 Karl Mecklenburg .04 .10
175 Paul Palmer .04 .10
176 Brian Blades UER RC .20 .50
177 Brent Fullwood RC .04 .10
178 Anthony Miller RC .20 .50
179 Brian Sochia .04 .10
180 Stephen Baker RC .04 .10
181 Jesse Solomon .04 .10
182 John Grimsley .04 .10
183 Timmy Newsome .04 .10
184 Steve Sewell RC .04 .10
185 Dean Biasucci .04 .10
186 Alonzo Highsmith .04 .10
187 Randy Grimes RC .04 .10
188A Mark Carrier ERR RC .40 1.00
188B Mark Carrier COR RC .40 1.00
189 Vann McElroy .04 .10
190 Greg Bell .04 .10
191 Quinn Early RC .40 1.00
192 Lawrence Taylor .20 .50
193 Albert Bentley .04 .10
194 Ernest Givins .08 .20
195 Jackie Slater .04 .10
196 Jim Sweeney .04 .10
197 Freddie Joe Nunn .04 .10
198 Keith Byars .08 .20
199 Hardy Nickerson RC .20 .50
200 Steve Beuerlein RC 1.25 3.00
201 Bruce Armstrong RC .20 .50
202 Lionel Manuel .04 .10
203 J.T. Smith .04 .10
204 Mark Ingram RC .20 .50
205 Fred Smerlas .04 .10
206 Bryan Hinkle RC .04 .10
207 Steve McMichael .08 .20
208 Nick Lowery .04 .10
209 Jack Trudeau .04 .10
210 Lorenzo Hampton .04 .10
211 Thurman Thomas RC 3.00 8.00
212 Steve Young .60 1.50
213 James Lofton .20 .50
214 Jim Covert .04 .10
215 Ronnie Lott .08 .20
216 Stephone Paige .04 .10
217 Mark Duper .08 .20
218A Willie Gault ERR 93 .10 .25
218B Willie Gault COR 83 .20 .50
219 Ken Ruettgers RC .04 .10
220 Kevin Ross RC .04 .10
221 Jerry Rice 1.50 3.00
222 Billy Ray Smith .04 .10
223 Jim Kelly .40 1.00
224 Vinny Testaverde .40 1.00
225 Steve Largent .20 .50
226 Warren Williams RC .04 .10
227 Morten Andersen .04 .10
228 Bill Brooks .08 .20
229 Reggie Langhorne RC .04 .10
230 Pepper Johnson .04 .10
231 Pat Leahy .04 .10
232 Fred Marion .04 .10
233 Gary Zimmerman .08 .20
234 Marcus Allen .20 .50
235 Gaston Green RC .04 .10
236 John Stephens RC .04 .10
237 Terry Kinard .04 .10
238 John Taylor RC .40 1.00
239 Brian Bosworth .08 .20
240 Anthony Toney .04 .10
241 Ken O'Brien .04 .10
242 Howie Long .20 .50
243 Doug Flutie 1.00 2.50
244 Jim Everett .20 .50
245 Broderick Thomas RC .04 .10
246 Deion Sanders RC 4.00 10.00
247 Donnell Woolford RC .04 .10
248 Wayne Martin RC .04 .10
249 David Williams RC .04 .10
250 Bill Hawkins RC .04 .10
251 Eric Hill RC .04 .10
252 Burt Grossman RC .04 .10
253 Tracy Rocker .04 .10
254 Steve Wisniewski RC .20 .50
255 Jessie Small RC .04 .10
256 David Braxton .04 .10
257 Barry Sanders RC 12.00 30.00
258 Derrick Thomas RC 3.00 8.00
259 Eric Metcalf RC .40 1.00
260 Keith DeLong RC .04 .10
261 Hart Lee Dykes RC .04 .10
262 Sammie Smith RC .04 .10
263 Steve Atwater RC .20 .50
264 Eric Ball RC .04 .10
265 Don Beebe RC .20 .50
266 Brian Williams OL RC .04 .10
267 Jeff Lageman RC .04 .10
268 Tim Worley RC .04 .10
269 Tony Mandarich RC .04 .10
270 Troy Aikman RC 10.00 25.00
271 Andy Heck RC .04 .10
272 Andre Rison RC 2.00 5.00
273 AFC Champ .04 .10
Woods
Esiason
274 NFC Champ/J.Montana .40 1.00
275 J.Montana/J.Rice SB .75 2.00
276 Rodney Carter .04 .10
277 M.Jackson/V.Johnson .04 .10
Nattiel
278 John L. Williams .04 .10
Curt Warner
279 J.Montana/J.Rice .75 2.00
280 R.Green/N.Lomax .04 .10
281 R.Cunningham/K.Jackson .04 .10
282 Chris Doleman .04 .10
Keith Millard
283 Mark Duper .04 .10
Mark Clayton
284 Bo Jackson .25 .60
Marcus Allen
285 Frank Minnifield AP .04 .10
286 Bruce Matthews AP .15 .40
287 Joey Browner AP .04 .10
288 Jay Hilgenberg AP .04 .10
289 Carl Lee AP RC .04 .10
290 Scott Norwood RC .04 .10
291 John Taylor AP .20 .50
292 Jerry Rice AP .60 1.50
293A Keith Jackson AP 84 .20 .50
293B Keith Jackson AP 88 .20 .50
294 Gary Zimmerman AP .08 .20
295 Lawrence Taylor AP .20 .50
296 Reggie White AP .20 .50
297 Roger Craig AP .08 .20
298 Boomer Esiason AP .08 .20
299 Cornelius Bennett AP .08 .20
300 Mike Horan AP .04 .10
301 Deron Cherry AP .04 .10
302 Tom Newberry AP .04 .10
303 Mike Singletary AP .08 .20
304 Shane Conlan AP .04 .10
305A Tim Brown AP ERR 80 .75 2.00
305B Tim Brown AP COR 81 .75 2.00
306 Henry Ellard AP .08 .20
307 Bruce Smith AP .08 .20
308 Tim Krumrie AP .04 .10
309 Anthony Munoz AP .08 .20
310 Darrell Green SPEED .04 .10
311 Anthony Miller SPEED .20 .50
312 Wesley Walker SPEED .04 .10
313 Ron Brown SPEED .04 .10
314 Bo Jackson SPEED .25 .60
315 Phillip Epps SPEED .04 .10
316A Eric Thomas RC .10 .25
316B Eric Thomas RC .20 .50
317 Herschel Walker SPEED .08 .20
318 Jacob Green PRED .04 .10
319 Andre Tippett PRED .04 .10
320 Freddie Joe Nunn PRED .04 .10
321 Reggie White PRED .20 .50
322 Lawrence Taylor PRED .20 .50
323 Greg Townsend PRED .04 .10
324 Tim Harris PRED .04 .10
325 Bruce Smith PRED .08 .20
326 Tony Dorsett RB .20 .50
327 Steve Largent RB .20 .50
328 Tim Brown RB .75 2.00
329 Joe Montana RB .60 1.50
330 Tom Landry Tribute .40 1.00

1989 Score Trivia Quiz

COMPLETE SET (28) 1.50 4.00
1 Football Trivia Quiz .10 .25
2 Football Trivia Quiz .10 .25
3 Football Trivia Quiz .10 .25
4 Football Trivia Quiz .10 .25
5 Football Trivia Quiz .10 .25
6 Football Trivia Quiz .10 .25
7 Football Trivia Quiz .10 .25
8 Football Trivia Quiz .10 .25
9 Football Trivia Quiz .10 .25
10 Football Trivia Quiz .10 .25
11 Football Trivia Quiz .10 .25
12 Football Trivia Quiz .10 .25
13 Football Trivia Quiz .10 .25
14 Football Trivia Quiz .10 .25
15 Football Trivia Quiz .10 .25
16 Football Trivia Quiz .10 .25
17 Football Trivia Quiz .10 .25
18 Football Trivia Quiz .10 .25
19 Football Trivia Quiz .10 .25
20 Football Trivia Quiz .10 .25
21 Football Trivia Quiz .10 .25
22 Football Trivia Quiz .10 .25
23 Football Trivia Quiz .10 .25
24 Football Trivia Quiz .10 .25
25 Football Trivia Quiz .10 .25
26 Football Trivia Quiz .10 .25
27 Football Trivia Quiz .10 .25
28 Football Trivia Quiz .10 .25

1989 Score Supplemental

The 1989 Score Supplemental set contains 110 standard-size cards that were issued as a complete set through hobby dealers. The card numbering is a continuation of the basic set except for an "S" suffix. The fronts have purple borders, otherwise, the cards are identical to the regular issue 1989 Score football cards. There is a card of Bo Jackson in baseball regalia. Rookie Cards include Eric Allen, Jack Del Rio, Simon Fletcher, Dave Meggett, Rodney Peete, Frank Reich, Sterling Sharpe, Neil Smith, Steve Walsh and Lorenzo White.

COMP.FACT.SET (110) 6.00 15.00
331S Herschel Walker .15 .40
332S Allen Pinkett RC .04 .10
333S Sterling Sharpe RC 1.25 3.00
334S Alvin Walton RC .04 .10
335S Frank Reich RC .15 .40
336S James Thornton RC .04 .10
337S David Fulcher .08 .20
338S Raul Allegre .04 .10
339S John Elway 2.00 4.00
340S Michael Cofer .04 .10
341S Jim Skow RC .04 .10
342S Steve DeBerg .04 .10
343S Mervyn Fernandez RC .04 .10
344S Mike Lansford .04 .10
345S Reggie Roby .04 .10
346S Raymond Clayborn .04 .10
347S Lonzell Hill .04 .10
348S Ottis Anderson .08 .20
349S Erik McMillan RC .04 .10
350S Al Harris RC .04 .10
351S Jack Del Rio RC .15 .40
352S Gary Anderson K .04 .10
353S Jim McMahon .08 .20
354S Keena Turner .04 .10
355S Tony Woods RC .04 .10
356S Donald Igwebuike .04 .10
357S Gerald Riggs .08 .20
358S Eddie Murray .04 .10
359S Dino Hackett .04 .10
360S Brad Muster RC .04 .10
361S Paul Palmer .04 .10
362S Jerry Robinson .04 .10
363S Simon Fletcher RC .08 .20
364S Tommy Kramer .04 .10
365S Jim C.Jensen RC .04 .10
366S Lorenzo White RC .15 .40
367S Fredd Young .04 .10
368S Ron Jaworski .04 .10
369S Mel Owens .04 .10
370S Dave Waymer .04 .10
371S Sean Landeta .04 .10
372S Sam Mills .08 .20
373S Todd Blackledge .04 .10
374S Jo Jo Townsell .04 .10
375S Ron Wolfley .04 .10
376S Ralf Mojsiejenko .04 .10
377S Eric Wright .04 .10
378S Nesby Glasgow .04 .10
379S Darryl Talley .08 .20
380S Eric Allen RC .15 .40
381S Dennis Smith .08 .20
382S John Tice .04 .10
383S Jesse Solomon .04 .10
384S Bo Jackson FB/BB 1.25 3.00
385S Mike Merriweather .04 .10
386S Maurice Carthon .04 .10
387S David Grayson RC .04 .10
388S Wilber Marshall .04 .10
389S David Wyman RC .04 .10
390S Thomas Everett RC .04 .10
391S Alex Gordon .04 .10
392S D.J. Dozier .04 .10
393S Scott Radecic RC .04 .10
394S Eric Thomas .04 .10
395S Mike Gann .04 .10
396S William Perry .08 .20
397S Carl Hairston .04 .10
398S Billy Ard .04 .10
399S Donnell Thompson .04 .10
400S Mike Webster .08 .20
401S Scott Davis RC .04 .10
402S Sean Farrell .04 .10
403S Mike Golic RC .04 .10
404S Mike Kenn .04 .10
405S Keith Van Horne RC .04 .10
406S Bob Golic .04 .10
407S Neil Smith RC .75 2.00
408S Dermontti Dawson RC .40 1.00
409S Leslie O'Neal .08 .20
410S Matt Bahr .04 .10
411S Guy McIntyre RC .10 .25
412S Bryan Millard .04 .10
413S Joe Jacoby .04 .10
414S Rob Taylor RC .04 .10
415S Tony Zendejas .04 .10
416S Vai Sikahema .04 .10
417S Gary Reasons RC .04 .10
418S Shawn Collins RC .04 .10
419S Mark Green RC .04 .10
420S Courtney Hall RC .04 .10
421S Bobby Humphrey RC .04 .10
422S Myron Guyton RC .04 .10
423S Darryl Ingram RC .04 .10
424S Chris Jacke RC .04 .10
425S Keith Jones RC .04 .10
426S Robert Massey RC .04 .10
427S Bubba McDowell RC .15 .40
428S Dave Meggett RC .15 .40
429S Louis Oliver RC .08 .20
430S Danny Peebles .04 .10
431S Rodney Peete RC .30 .75
432S Jeff Query RC .04 .10
433S Timm Rosenbach UER RC .04 .10
434S Frank Stams RC .04 .10
435S Lawyer Tillman RC .04 .10
436S Billy Joe Tolliver RC .04 .10
437S Floyd Turner RC .08 .20
438S Steve Walsh RC .08 .20
439S Joe Wolf RC .04 .10
440S Trace Armstrong RC .04 .10

1989-90 Score Franco Harris

These standard size cards were given away to all persons at the Super Bowl Show I in New Orleans who acquired Franco Harris' autograph while at the show. However, there were two different backs prepared and distributed since Franco's "Sure-shot" election was announced during the course of the show, after which time the "Hall of Famer" variety was passed out. The card fronts are exactly the same. The only difference in the two varieties on the back is essentially the presence of "Sure-shot" at the beginning of the narrative. The cards are unnumbered. The card fronts are in the style of the popular 1989 Score regular issue football cards. Although both varieties were produced on a limited basis, it is thought that the "Sure-shot" variety is the tougher of the two.

1A Franco Harris 40.00 80.00
(Sure-shot)
1B Franco Harris 30.00 75.00
(Hall of Famer)

1990 Score Promos

This set of standard-size full-color cards was intended as a preview of Score's football set. The cards were sent out to prospective dealers along with the ordering forms for Score's 1990 football set. The cards are distinguishable from the regular issue cards of the same numbers as indicated in the checklist below. The promo cards show a registered symbol (R with circle around it) rather than a trademark (TM) symbol as on the regular cards. In addition, these promos are cropped tighter than the regular issue cards.

COMPLETE SET (4) 4.80 12.00
20 Barry Sanders 4.00 10.00
24 Anthony Miller 2.00 5.00
184 Robert Delpino .80 2.00
256 Cornelius Bennett .80 2.00

1990 Score

The 1990 Score football set consists of 660 standard-size cards issued in two series of 330. The set was issued in 16-card packs along with a trivia card. The fronts have sharp color action photos and multicolored borders. The vertically oriented backs have color photos, stats and highlights. There are numerous subsets including Draft Picks (289-310/618-657), Hot Guns (311-320/563/564), Ground Force (321-330/561/562), Crunch Crew (551-555), Rocket Man (556-560), All-Pros (565-590), Record Breakers (591-594), Hall of Famers (595-601) and Class of '90 (606-617). Rookie Cards include Mark (DB) Carrier, Barry Foster, Barry Foster, Jeff George, Eric Green, Rodney Hampton, Haywood Jeffires, Cortez Kennedy, Scott Mitchell, Junior Seau and Andre Ware. The five-card "Final Five" set was a special insert in factory sets. These cards honor the final five picks of the 1990 National Football League Draft and are numbered with a "B" prefix. These cards have a "Final Five" logo on the front along with the photo of the player, while the back has a brief biographical description of the player.

COMPLETE SET (660) 8.00 20.00
COMP.FACT.SET (665) 10.00 25.00
1 Joe Montana .50 1.25
2 Christian Okoye .04 .10
3 Mike Singletary UER .04 .10
4 Jim Everett UER .04 .10
5 Phil Simms .04 .10
6 Brent Fullwood .02 .05
7 Bill Fralic .02 .05
8 Leslie O'Neal .04 .10
9 John Taylor .08 .25
10 Bo Jackson .10 .30
11 John Stephens .02 .05
12 Art Monk .04 .10
13 Dan Marino .50 1.25
14 John Settle .02 .05
15 Don Majkowski .02 .05
16 Bruce Smith .08 .25
17 Brad Muster .02 .05
18 Jason Buck .02 .05
19 James Brooks .04 .10
20 Barry Sanders .50 1.25
21 Troy Aikman .30 .75
22 Allen Pinkett .02 .05
23 Duane Bickett .02 .05
24 Kevin Ross .02 .05
25 John Elway .50 1.25
26 Jeff Query .02 .05
27 Eddie Murray .02 .05
28 Richard Dent .04 .10
29 Lorenzo White .02 .05
30 Eric Metcalf .08 .25
31 Jeff Dellenbach RC .02 .05
32 Leon White .02 .05
33 Jim Jeffcoat .02 .05
34 Herschel Walker .04 .10
35 Mike Johnson UER .02 .05
36 Joe Phillips RC .02 .05
37 Willie Gault .04 .10
38 Keith Millard .02 .05
39 Fred Marion .02 .05
40 Boomer Esiason .04 .10
41 Dermontti Dawson .08 .20
42 Dino Hackett .02 .05
43 Reggie Roby .02 .05
44 Roger Vick .02 .05
45 Bobby Hebert .02 .05
46 Don Beebe .04 .10
47 Neal Anderson .04 .10
48 Johnny Holland .02 .05
49 Bobby Humphery .02 .05
50 Lawrence Taylor .08 .25
51 Billy Ray Smith .02 .05
52 Robert Perryman .02 .05
53 Gary Anderson K .02 .05
54 Raul Allegre .02 .05
55 Pat Swilling .04 .10
56 Chris Doleman .02 .05
57 Andre Reed .08 .25
58 Seth Joyner .04 .10
59 Bart Oates .02 .05
60 Bernie Kosar .04 .10
61 Dave Krieg .04 .10
62 Lars Tate .02 .05
63 Scott Norwood .02 .05
64 Kyle Clifton .02 .05
65 Alan Veingrad .02 .05
66 Gerald Riggs UER .04 .10
67 Tim Worley .02 .05
68 Rodney Holman .02 .05
69 Tony Zendejas .02 .05
70 Chris Miller .08 .25
71 Wilber Marshall .02 .05
72 Skip McClendon RC .02 .05
73 Jim Covert .02 .05
74 Sam Mills .04 .10
75 Chris Hinton .02 .05
76 Irv Eatman .02 .05
77 Bubba Paris UER .02 .05
78 John Elliott UER .02 .05
79 Thomas Everett .02 .05
80 Steve Smith .02 .05
81 Jackie Slater .02 .05
82 Kelvin Martin RC .02 .05
83 Jo Jo Townsell .02 .05
84 Jim C. Jensen .02 .05
85 Bobby Humphrey .02 .05
86 Mike Dyal RC .02 .05
87 Andre Rison UER .08 .25
88 Brian Sochia .02 .05
89 Greg Bell .02 .05
90 Dalton Hilliard .02 .05
91 Carl Banks .02 .05
92 Dennis Smith .02 .05
93 Bruce Matthews .04 .10
94 Charles Haley .04 .10
95 Deion Sanders .20 .50
96 Stephone Paige .02 .05
97 Marion Butts .04 .10
98 Howie Long .08 .25
99 Donald Igwebuike .02 .05
100 Roger Craig UER .04 .10
101 Charles Mann .02 .05
102 Fredd Young .02 .05
103 Chris Jacke .02 .05
104 Scott Case .02 .05
105 Warren Moon .08 .25
106 Clyde Simmons .02 .05
107 Steve Atwater .02 .05
108 Morten Andersen .02 .05
109 Eugene Marve .02 .05
110 Thurman Thomas .08 .25
111 Carnell Lake .02 .05
112 Jim Kelly .08 .25
113 Stanford Jennings .02 .05
114 Jacob Green .02 .05
115 Karl Mecklenburg .02 .05
116 Ray Childress .02 .05
117 Erik McMillan .02 .05
118 Harry Newsome .02 .05
119 James Dixon .02 .05
120 Hassan Jones .02 .05
121 Eric Allen .02 .05
122 Felix Wright .02 .05
123 Merril Hoge .02 .05
124 Eric Ball .02 .05
125 Flipper Anderson .02 .05
126 James Jefferson .02 .05
127 Tim McDonald .02 .05
128 Larry Kinnebrew .02 .05
129 Mark Collins .02 .05
130 Ickey Woods .02 .05
131 Jeff Donaldson UER .02 .05
132 Rich Camarillo .02 .05
133 Melvin Bratton RC .02 .05
134A Kevin Butler hlmt .12 .35
134B Kevin Butler no hlm .20 .50
135 Albert Bentley .02 .05
136A Vai Sikahema hlmt .12 .35
136B Vai Sikahema no hlm .20 .50
137 Todd McNair RC .02 .05
138 Alonzo Highsmith .02 .05
139 Brian Blades .04 .10
140 Jeff Lageman .02 .05
141 Eric Thomas .02 .05
142 Derek Hill RC .02 .05
143 Rick Fenney .02 .05
144 Herman Heard .02 .05
145 Steve Young .20 .50
146 Kent Hull .02 .05
147A Joey Browner face left .12 .35
147B Joey Browner straight .20 .50
148 Frank Minnifield .02 .05
149 Robert Massey .02 .05
150 Dave Meggett .04 .10
151 Bubba McDowell .02 .05
152 Rickey Dixon RC .02 .05
153 Ray Donaldson .02 .05
154 Alvin Walton .02 .05
155 Mike Cofer .02 .05
156 Darryl Talley .02 .05
157 A.J. Johnson .02 .05
158 Jerry Gray .02 .05
159 Keith Byars .02 .05
160 Andy Heck .02 .05
161 Mike Munchak .04 .10
162 Dennis Gentry .02 .05
163 Timm Rosenbach UER .02 .05
164 Randall McDaniel .05 .15
165 Pat Leahy .02 .05
166 Bubby Brister .02 .05
167 Aundray Bruce .02 .05
168 Bill Brooks .02 .05
169 Eddie Anderson RC .02 .05
170 Ronnie Lott .04 .10
171 Jay Hilgenberg .02 .05
172 Joe Nash .02 .05
173 Simon Fletcher .02 .05
174 Shane Conlan .02 .05
175 Sean Landeta .02 .05
176 John Alt RC .02 .05
177 Clay Matthews .04 .10
178 Anthony Munoz .04 .10
179 Pete Holohan .02 .05
180 Robert Awalt .02 .05
181 Rohn Stark .02 .05
182 Vance Johnson .02 .05
183 David Fulcher .02 .05
184 Robert Delpino .02 .05
185 Drew Hill .02 .05
186 Reggie Langhorne UER .02 .05
187 Lonzell Hill .02 .05
188 Tom Rathman UER .02 .05
189 Greg Montgomery RC .02 .05
190 Leonard Smith .02 .05
191 Chris Spielman .08 .25
192 Tom Newberry .02 .05
193 Cris Carter .20 .50
194 Kevin Porter RC .02 .05
195 Donnell Thompson .02 .05
196 Vaughan Johnson .02 .05
197 Steve McMichael .04 .10
198 Jim Sweeney .02 .05
199 Rich Karlis UER .02 .05
200 Jerry Rice .30 .75
201 Dan Hampton UER .04 .10
202 Jim Lachey .02 .05
203 Reggie White .08 .25
204 Jerry Ball .02 .05
205 Russ Grimm .04 .10
206 Tim Green RC .02 .05
207 Shawn Collins .02 .05
208A R.Mojsiejenko Chargers .05 .15
208B R.Mojsiejenko Redskins .20 .50
209 Trace Armstrong .02 .05
210 Keith Jackson .04 .10
211 Jamie Holland .02 .05
212 Mark Clayton .04 .10
213 Jeff Cross .02 .05
214 Bob Gagliano .02 .05
215 Louis Oliver UER .02 .05
216 Jim Arnold .02 .05
217 Robert Clark RC .02 .05
218 Gill Byrd .02 .05
219 Rodney Peete .04 .10
220 Anthony Miller .08 .25
221 Steve Grogan .04 .10
222 Vince Newsome RC .02 .05
223 Thomas Benson RC .02 .05

224 Kevin Murphy .02 .05
225 Henry Ellard .04 .10
226 Richard Johnson .02 .05
227 Jim Skow .02 .05
228 Keith Jones .02 .05
229 Dave Brown DB .02 .05
230 Marcus Allen .08 .25
231 Steve Walsh .04 .10
232 Jim Harbaugh .08 .25
233 Mel Gray .04 .10
234 David Treadwell .02 .05
235 John Offerdahl .02 .05
236 Gary Reasons .02 .05
237 Tim Krumrie .02 .05
238 Dave Duerson .02 .05
239 Gary Clark UER .08 .25
240 Mark Jackson .02 .05
241 Mark Murphy .02 .05
242 Jerry Holmes .02 .05
243 Tim McGee .02 .05
244 Mike Tomczak .04 .10
245 Sterling Sharpe UER .08 .25
246 Bennie Blades .02 .05
247 Ken Harvey UER RC .08 .25
248 Ron Heller .02 .05
249 Louis Lipps .04 .10
250 Wade Wilson .04 .10
251 Freddie Joe Nunn .02 .05
252 Jerome Brown UER .02 .05
253 Myron Guyton .02 .05
254 Nate Odomes RC .04 .10
255 Rod Woodson .08 .25
256 Cornelius Bennett .04 .10
257 Keith Woodside .02 .05
258 Jeff Uhlenhake UER .02 .05
259 Harry Hamilton .02 .05
260 Mark Bavaro .02 .05
261 Vinny Testaverde .04 .10
262 Steve DeBerg .02 .05
263 Steve Wisniewski UER .04 .10
264 Pete Mandley .02 .05
265 Tim Harris .02 .05
266 Jack Trudeau .02 .05
267 Mark Kelso .02 .05
268 Brian Noble .02 .05
269 Jessie Tuggle RC .02 .05
270 Ken O'Brien .02 .05
271 David Little .02 .05
272 Pete Stoyanovich .02 .05
273 Odessa Turner RC .02 .05
274 Anthony Toney .02 .05
275 Tunch Ilkin .02 .05
276 Carl Lee .02 .05
277 Hart Lee Dykes .02 .05
278 Al Noga .02 .05
279 Greg Lloyd .08 .25
280 Billy Joe Tolliver .02 .05
281 Kirk Lowdermilk .02 .05
282 Earl Ferrell .02 .05
283 Eric Sievers RC .02 .05
284 Steve Jordan .02 .05
285 Burt Grossman .02 .05
286 Johnny Rembert .02 .05
287 Jeff Jaeger RC .02 .05
288 James Hasty .02 .05
289 Tony Mandarich DP .02 .05
290 Chris Singleton RC .02 .05
291 Lynn James RC .02 .05
292 Andre Ware RC .08 .25
293 Ray Agnew RC .02 .05
294 Joel Smeenge RC .02 .05
295 Marc Spindler RC .02 .05
296 Renaldo Turnbull RC .02 .05
297 Reggie Rembert RC .02 .05
298 Jeff Alm RC .02 .05
299 Cortez Kennedy RC .20 .50
300 Blair Thomas RC .04 .10
301 Pat Terrell RC .02 .05
302 Junior Seau RC .50 1.25
303 Mo Elewonibi RC .02 .05
304 Tony Bennett RC .08 .25
305 Percy Snow RC .02 .05
306 Richmond Webb RC .02 .05
307 Rodney Hampton RC .08 .25
308 Barry Foster RC .08 .25
309 John Friesz RC .08 .25
310 Ben Smith RC .02 .05
311 Joe Montana HG .20 .50
312 Jim Everett HG .04 .10
313 Mark Rypien HG .04 .10
314 Phil Simms HG UER .04 .10
315 Don Majkowski HG .02 .05
316 Boomer Esiason HG .02 .05
317 Warren Moon HG Moon .08 .25
318 Jim Kelly HG .08 .25
319 Bernie Kosar HG UER .04 .10
320 Dan Marino HG UER .20 .50
321 Christian Okoye GF .02 .05
322 Thurman Thomas GF .08 .25
323 James Brooks GF .04 .10
324 Bobby Humphrey GF .02 .05
325 Barry Sanders GF .25 .60
326 Neal Anderson GF .02 .05
327 Dalton Hilliard GF .02 .05
328 Greg Bell GF .02 .05
329 Roger Craig GF UER .04 .10
330 Bo Jackson GF .10 .30
331 Don Warren .02 .05
332 Rufus Porter .02 .05
333 Sammie Smith .02 .05
334 Lewis Tillman UER .02 .05
335 Michael Walter .02 .05
336 Marc Logan .02 .05
337 Ron Hallstrom RC .02 .05
338 Stanley Morgan .02 .05
339 Mark Robinson .02 .05
340 Frank Reich .08 .25
341 Chip Lohmiller .02 .05
342 Steve Beuerlein .04 .10
343 John L. Williams .02 .05
344 Irving Fryar .08 .25
345 Anthony Carter .04 .10
346 Al Toon .04 .10
347 J.T. Smith .02 .05
348 Pierce Holt RC .02 .05
349 Ferrell Edmunds .02 .05
350 Mark Rypien .04 .10
351 Paul Gruber .02 .05
352 Ernest Givins .04 .10
353 Ervin Randle .02 .05
354 Guy McIntyre .02 .05
355 Webster Slaughter .04 .10
356 Reuben Davis .02 .05
357 Rickey Jackson .04 .10
358 Earnest Byner .02 .05
359 Eddie Brown .02 .05
360 Troy Stradford .02 .05
361 Pepper Johnson .02 .05
362 Ravin Caldwell .02 .05
363 Chris Mohr RC .02 .05
364 Jeff Bryant .02 .05
365 Bruce Collie RC .02 .05
366 Courtney Hall .02 .05
367 Jerry Olsavsky .02 .05
368 David Galloway .02 .05
369 Wes Hopkins .02 .05
370 Johnny Hector .02 .05
371 Clarence Verdin .02 .05
372 Nick Lowery .02 .05
373 Tim Brown .08 .25
374 Kevin Greene .04 .10
375 Leonard Marshall .02 .05
376 Roland James .02 .05
377 Scott Studwell .02 .05
378 Jarvis Williams .02 .05
379 Mike Saxon .02 .05
380 Kevin Mack .02 .05
381 Joe Kelly .02 .05
382 Tom Thayer RC .02 .05
383 Roy Green .04 .10
384 Michael Brooks RC .02 .05
385 Michael Cofer .02 .05
386 Ken Ruettgers .02 .05
387 Dean Steinkuhler .02 .05
388 Maurice Carthon .02 .05
389 Ricky Sanders .02 .05
390 Winston Moss RC .02 .05
391 Tony Woods .02 .05
392 Keith DeLong .02 .05
393 David Wyman .02 .05
394 Vencie Glenn .02 .05
395 Harris Barton .02 .05
396 Bryan Hinkle .02 .05
397 Derek Kennard .02 .05
398 Heath Sherman RC .02 .05
399 Troy Benson .02 .05
400 Gary Zimmerman .04 .10
401 Mark Duper .04 .10
402 Eugene Lockhart .02 .05
403 Tim Manoa .02 .05
404 Reggie Williams .02 .05
405 Mark Bortz RC .02 .05
406 Mike Kenn .02 .05
407 John Grimsley .02 .05
408 Bill Romanowski RC .40 1.00
409 Perry Kemp .02 .05
410 Norm Johnson .02 .05
411 Broderick Thomas .02 .05
412 Joe Wolf .02 .05
413 Andre Waters .02 .05
414 Jason Staurovsky .02 .05
415 Eric Martin .02 .05
416 Joe Prokop .02 .05
417 Steve Sewell .02 .05
418 Cedric Jones RC .02 .05
419 Alphonso Carreker .02 .05
420 Keith Willis .02 .05
421 Bobby Butler .02 .05
422 John Roper .02 .05
423 Tim Spencer .02 .05
424 Jesse Sapolu RC .02 .05
425 Ron Wolfley .02 .05
426 Doug Smith .02 .05
427 William Howard .02 .05
428 Keith Van Horne .02 .05
429 Tony Jordan .02 .05
430 Mervyn Fernandez .02 .05
431 Shaun Gayle RC .02 .05
432 Ricky Nattiel .02 .05
433 Albert Lewis .02 .05
434 Fred Banks RC .02 .05
435 Henry Thomas .02 .05
436 Chet Brooks .02 .05
437 Mark Ingram .04 .10
438 Jeff Gossett .02 .05
439 Mike Wilcher .02 .05
440 Deron Cherry UER .02 .05
441 Mike Rozier .02 .05
442 Jon Hand .02 .05
443 Ozzie Newsome .04 .10
444 Sammy Martin .02 .05
445 Luis Sharpe .02 .05
446 Lee Williams .02 .05
447 Chris Martin RC .02 .05
448 Kevin Fagan RC .02 .05
449 Gene Lang .02 .05
450 Greg Townsend .02 .05
451 Robert Lyles .02 .05
452 Eric Hill .02 .05
453 John Teltschik .02 .05
454 Vestee Jackson .02 .05
455 Bruce Reimers .02 .05
456 Butch Rolle RC .02 .05
457 Lawyer Tillman .02 .05
458 Andre Tippett .02 .05
459 James Thornton .02 .05
460 Randy Grimes .02 .05
461 Larry Roberts .02 .05
462 Ron Holmes .02 .05
463 Mike Wise DE .02 .05
464 Danny Copeland RC .02 .05
465 Bruce Wilkerson RC .02 .05
466 Mike Quick .02 .05
467 Mickey Shuler .02 .05
468 Mike Prior .02 .05
469 Ron Rivera .02 .05
470 Dean Biasucci .02 .05
471 Perry Williams .02 .05
472 Darren Comeaux UER .02 .05
473 Freeman McNeil .02 .05
474 Tyrone Braxton .02 .05
475 Jay Schroeder .02 .05
476 Naz Worthen RC .02 .05
477 Lionel Washington .02 .05
478 Carl Zander .02 .05
479 Al(Bubba) Baker .04 .10
480 Mike Merriweather .02 .05
481 Mike Gann .02 .05
482 Brent Williams .02 .05
483 Eugene Robinson .02 .05
484 Ray Horton .02 .05
485 Bruce Armstrong .02 .05
486 John Fourcade .02 .05
487 Lewis Billups .02 .05
488 Scott Davis .02 .05
489 Kenneth Sims .02 .05
490 Chris Chandler .08 .25
491 Mark Lee .02 .05
492 Johnny Meads .02 .05
493 Tim Irwin .02 .05
494 E.J. Junior .02 .05
495 Hardy Nickerson .04 .10
496 Rob McGovern RC .02 .05
497 Fred Strickland RC .02 .05
498 Reggie Rutland RC .02 .05
499 Mel Owens .02 .05
500 Derrick Thomas .08 .25
501 Jerrol Williams .02 .05
502 Maurice Hurst RC .02 .05
503 Larry Kelm RC .02 .05
504 Herman Fontenot .02 .05
505 Pat Beach .02 .05
506 Haywood Jeffires RC .08 .25
507 Neil Smith .08 .25
508 Cleveland Gary .02 .05
509 William Perry .04 .10
510 Michael Carter .02 .05
511 Walker Lee Ashley RC .02 .05
512 Bob Golic .02 .05
513 Danny Villa RC .02 .05
514 Matt Millen .04 .10
515 Don Griffin .02 .05
516 Jonathan Hayes .02 .05
517 Gerald Williams RC .02 .05
518 Scott Fulhage .02 .05
519 Irv Pankey .02 .05
520 Randy Dixon RC .02 .05
521 Terry McDaniel .02 .05
522 Dan Saleaumua .02 .05
523 Darrin Nelson .02 .05
524 Leonard Griffin RC .02 .05
525 Michael Ball RC .02 .05
526 Ernie Jones RC .02 .05
527 Tony Eason UER .02 .05
528 Ed Reynolds .02 .05
529 Gary Hogeboom .02 .05
530 Don Mosebar .02 .05
531 Ottis Anderson .04 .10
532 Bucky Scribner .02 .05
533 Aaron Cox .02 .05
534 Sean Jones .04 .10
535 Doug Flutie .20 .50
536 Leo Lewis .02 .05
537 Art Still .02 .05
538 Matt Bahr .02 .05
539 Keena Turner .02 .05
540 Sammy Winder .02 .05
541 Mike Webster .04 .10
542 Doug Riesenberg RC .02 .05
543 Dan Fike .02 .05
544 Clarence Kay .02 .05
545 Jim Burt .02 .05
546 Mike Horan .02 .05
547 Al Harris .02 .05
548 Maury Buford .02 .05
549 Jerry Robinson .02 .05
550 Tracy Rocker .02 .05
551 Karl Mecklenburg CC .02 .05
552 Lawrence Taylor CC .08 .25
553 Derrick Thomas CC .08 .25
554 Mike Singletary CC .04 .10
555 Tim Harris CC .02 .05
556 Jerry Rice RM .20 .50
557 Art Monk RM .04 .10
558 Mark Carrier WR RM .04 .10
559 Andre Reed RM .04 .10
560 Sterling Sharpe RM .08 .25
561 Herschel Walker GF .04 .10
562 Ottis Anderson GF .04 .10
563 Randall Cunningham HG .04 .10
564 John Elway HG .20 .50
565 David Fulcher AP .02 .05
566 Ronnie Lott AP .04 .10
567 Jerry Gray AP .02 .05
568 Albert Lewis AP .02 .05
569 Karl Mecklenburg AP .02 .05
570 Mike Singletary AP .04 .10
571 Lawrence Taylor AP .08 .25
572 Tim Harris AP .02 .05
573 Keith Millard AP .02 .05
574 Reggie White AP .08 .25
575 Chris Doleman AP .02 .05
576 Dave Meggett AP .04 .10
577 Rod Woodson AP .08 .25
578 Sean Landeta AP .02 .05
579 Eddie Murray AP .02 .05
580 Barry Sanders AP .25 .60
581 Christian Okoye AP .02 .05
582 Joe Montana AP .20 .50
583 Jay Hilgenberg AP .02 .05
584 Bruce Matthews AP .04 .10
585 Tom Newberry AP .02 .05
586 Gary Zimmerman AP .04 .10
587 Anthony Munoz AP .04 .10
588 Keith Jackson AP .04 .10
589 Sterling Sharpe AP .08 .25
590 Jerry Rice AP .20 .50
591 Bo Jackson RB .10 .30
592 Steve Largent RB .08 .25
593 Flipper Anderson RB .02 .05
594 Joe Montana RB .20 .50
595 Franco Harris HOF .04 .10
596 Bob St. Clair HOF .02 .05
597 Tom Landry HOF .04 .10
598 Jack Lambert HOF .04 .10
599 Ted Hendricks HOF .02 .05
600A Buck Buchanan HOF ERR 83 .04 .10
600B Buck Buchanan HOF COR 63 .04 .10
601 Bob Griese HOF .04 .10
602 Super Bowl Wrap .02 .05
603A Vince Lombardi w/o logo .07 .20
603B Vince Lombardi Curt.logo .07 .20
604 Mark Carrier WR UER .04 .10
605 Randall Cunningham .08 .25
606 Percy Snow C90 .02 .05
607 Andre Ware C90 .08 .25
608 Blair Thomas C90 .04 .10
609 Eric Green C90 .02 .05
610 Reggie Rembert C90 .02 .05
611 Richmond Webb C90 .02 .05
612 Bern Brostek C90 .02 .05
613 James Williams C90 .02 .05
614 Mark Carrier DB C90 .04 .10
615 Renaldo Turnbull C90 .02 .05
616 Cortez Kennedy C90 .10 .25
617 Keith McCants C90 .02 .05
618 Anthony Thompson RC .02 .05
619 LeRoy Butler RC .08 .25
620 Aaron Wallace RC .02 .05
621 Alexander Wright RC .02 .05
622 Keith McCants RC .02 .05
623 Jimmie Jones RC UER .02 .05
624 Anthony Johnson RC .08 .25
625 Fred Washington RC .02 .05
626 Mike Bellamy RC .02 .05
627 Mark Carrier DB RC .08 .25
628 Harold Green RC .08 .25
629 Eric Green RC .04 .10
630 Andre Collins RC .02 .05
631 Lamar Lathon RC .04 .10
632 Terry Wooden RC .02 .05
633 Jesse Anderson RC .02 .05
634 Jeff George RC .20 .50
635 Carwell Gardner RC .02 .05
636 Darrell Thompson RC .02 .05
637 Vince Buck RC .02 .05
638 Mike Jones TE RC .02 .05
639 Charles Arbuckle RC .02 .05
640 Dennis Brown RC .02 .05
641 James Williams DB RC .02 .05
642 Bern Brostek RC .02 .05
643 Darion Conner RC .04 .10
644 Mike Fox RC .02 .05
645 Cary Conklin RC .02 .05
646 Tim Grunhard RC .02 .05
647 Ron Cox RC .02 .05
648 Keith Sims RC .02 .05
649 Alton Montgomery RC .02 .05
650 Greg McMurtry RC .02 .05
651 Scott Mitchell RC .08 .25
652 Tim Ryan DE RC .02 .05
653 Jeff Mills RC .02 .05
654 Ricky Proehl RC .08 .25
655 Steve Broussard RC .02 .05
656 Peter Tom Willis RC .02 .05
657 Dexter Carter RC .02 .05
658 Tony Casillas .02 .05
659 Joe Morris .02 .05
660 Greg Kragen .02 .05
B1 Matt Stover FF .08 .25
B2 Demetrius Davis FF .02 .05
B3 Ken McMichel FF .02 .05
B4 Judd Garrett FF .02 .05
B5 Elliott Searcy FF .02 .05

1990 Score Hot Cards

This ten-card standard size set was issued by Score as an insert (one per) in their 100-card blister packs, which feature Score cards from both Series 1 and Series 2. The cards have black borders which surround the player's photo set against the sun. The back of the card features a large color photo of the player on the top 2/3 of the card and brief biographical identification on the bottom.

COMPLETE SET (10) 10.00 25.00
ONE PER BLISTER PACK
1 Joe Montana 3.00 6.00
2 Bo Jackson .75 1.50
3 Barry Sanders 3.00 6.00
4 Jerry Rice 2.00 4.00
5 Eric Metcalf .30 .75
6 Don Majkowski .20 .50
7 Christian Okoye .30 .75
8 Bobby Humphrey .20 .50
9 Dan Marino 3.00 6.00
10 Sterling Sharpe .60 1.25

1990 Score Supplemental

This 110-card standard size set was issued in the same design as the regular Score issue, but with blue and purple borders. The set included cards of rookies and cards of players who switched teams during the off-season. The set was released through Score's dealer outlets and was available only in complete set form. The key Rookie Card is Emmitt Smith. Other Rookie Cards include Reggie Cobb, Derrick Fenner, Stan Humphries, Johnny Johnson and Rob Moore. The cards are numbered on the back with a "T" suffix.

COMP.FACT.SET (110) 30.00 60.00
1T Marcus Dupree RC .30 .75
2T Jerry Kauric RC .05 .15
3T Everson Walls .05 .15
4T Elliott Smith .05 .15
5T Donald Evans UER RC .10 .30
6T Jerry Holmes .05 .15
7T Dan Stryzinski RC .05 .15
8T Gerald McNeil .05 .15
9T Rick Tuten RC .05 .15
10T Mickey Shuler .05 .15
11T Jay Novacek .25 .60
12T Eric Williams RC .05 .15
13T Stanley Morgan .05 .15
14T Wayne Haddix RC .05 .15
15T Gary Anderson RB .05 .15
16T Stan Humphries RC .25 .60
17T Raymond Clayborn .05 .15
18T Mark Boyer RC .05 .15
19T Dave Waymer .05 .15
20T Andre Rison .25 .60
21T Daniel Stubbs .05 .15
22T Mike Rozier .05 .15
23T Damian Johnson .05 .15
24T Don Smith RBK RC .05 .15
25T Max Montoya .05 .15
26T Terry Kinard .05 .15
27T Herb Welch .05 .15
28T Cliff Odom .05 .15
29T John Kidd .05 .15
30T Barry Word RC .05 .15
31T Rich Karlis .05 .15
32T Mike Baab .05 .15
33T Ronnie Harmon .10 .30
34T Jeff Donaldson .05 .15
35T Riki Ellison .05 .15
36T Steve Walsh .10 .30
37T Bill Lewis RC .05 .15
38T Tim McKyer .05 .15
39T James Wilder .05 .15
40T Tony Paige .05 .15
41T Derrick Fenner RC .05 .15
42T Thane Gash RC .05 .15
43T Dave Duerson .05 .15
44T Clarence Weathers .05 .15
45T Matt Bahr .05 .15
46T Alonzo Highsmith .05 .15
47T Joe Kelly .05 .15
48T Chris Hinton .05 .15
49T Bobby Humphery .05 .15
50T Greg Bell .05 .15
51T Fred Smerlas .05 .15
52T Walter Stanley .05 .15
53T Jim Skow .05 .15
54T Renaldo Turnbull .05 .15
55T Bern Brostek .05 .15
56T Charles Wilson RC .05 .15
57T Keith McCants .05 .15
58T Alexander Wright .10 .30
59T Ian Beckles RC .05 .15
60T Eric Davis RC .10 .30
61T Chris Singleton .05 .15
62T Rob Moore RC 1.00 2.50
63T Darion Conner .10 .30
64T Tim Grunhard .05 .15
65T Junior Seau 2.50 6.00
66T Tony Stargell RC .05 .15
67T Anthony Thompson .05 .15
68T Cortez Kennedy .50 1.25
69T Darrell Thompson .05 .15
70T Calvin Williams RC .25 .60
71T Rodney Hampton .25 .60
72T Terry Wooden .05 .15
73T Leo Goeas RC .05 .15
74T Ken Willis .05 .15
75T Ricky Proehl .25 .60
76T Steve Christie RC .05 .15
77T Andre Ware .25 .60
78T Jeff George 1.00 2.50
79T Walter Wilson .05 .15
80T Johnny Bailey RC .05 .15
81T Harold Green .10 .30
82T Mark Carrier DB .25 .60
83T Frank Cornish .05 .15
84T James Williams .05 .15
85T James Francis RC .05 .15
86T Percy Snow .05 .15
87T Anthony Johnson .25 .60
88T Tim Ryan DE .05 .15
89T Dan Owens RC .05 .15
90T Aaron Wallace RC .05 .15
91T Steve Broussard .05 .15
92T Eric Green .05 .15
93T Blair Thomas .10 .30
94T Robert Blackmon RC .05 .15
95T Alan Grant RC .05 .15
96T Andre Collins .05 .15
97T Dexter Carter .05 .15
98T Reggie Cobb RC .05 .15
99T Dennis Brown .05 .15
100T Kenny Davidson RC .05 .15
101T Emmitt Smith RC 20.00 40.00
102T Jeff Alm .05 .15
103T Alton Montgomery .05 .15
104T Tony Bennett .25 .60
105T Johnny Johnson RC .10 .30
106T Leroy Hoard RC .25 .60
107T Ray Agnew .05 .15
108T Richmond Webb .05 .15
109T Keith Sims .05 .15
110T Barry Foster .25 .60

1990 Score 100 Hottest

This 100-card standard size set, featuring some of the most popular football stars of 1990, was issued by Score in conjunction with Publications International, which issued an attractive magazine-style publication giving more biographical information about the players featured on the front. These cards have the same photos on the front as the regular issue Score Football cards with the only difference being the numbering on the back of the card.

COMPLETE SET (100) 6.00 15.00
1 Bo Jackson .15 .40
2 Joe Montana 1.60 4.00
3 Deion Sanders .40 1.00
4 Dan Marino 1.20 3.00
5 Barry Sanders 1.60 4.00
6 Neal Anderson .07 .20
7 Phil Simms .07 .20
8 Bobby Humphrey .04 .10
9 Roger Craig .07 .20
10 John Elway 1.20 3.00
11 James Brooks .07 .20
12 Ken O'Brien .04 .10
13 Thurman Thomas .15 .40
14 Troy Aikman .60 1.50
15 Karl Mecklenburg .07 .20
16 Dave Krieg .07 .20
17 Chris Spielman .07 .20
18 Tim Harris .04 .10
19 Tim Worley .04 .10
20 Clay Matthews .07 .20
21 Lars Tate .04 .10
22 Hart Lee Dykes .04 .10
23 Cornelius Bennett .07 .20
24 Anthony Miller .07 .20
25 Lawrence Taylor .07 .20
26 Jay Hilgenberg .04 .10
27 Tom Rathman .07 .20
28 Brian Blades .07 .20
29 David Fulcher .04 .10
30 Cris Carter .50 1.25
31 Marcus Allen .15 .40
32 Eric Metcalf .15 .40
33 Bruce Smith .15 .40
34 Jim Kelly .15 .40
35 Wade Wilson .04 .10
36 Rich Camarillo .04 .10
37 Boomer Esiason .07 .20
38 John Offerdahl .04 .10
39 Vance Johnson .04 .10
40 Ronnie Lott .07 .20
41 Kevin Ross .04 .10
42 Greg Bell .07 .20
43 Erik McMillan .04 .10
44 Mike Singletary .07 .20
45 Roger Vick .04 .10
46 Keith Jackson .15 .40
47 Henry Ellard .07 .20
48 Gary Anderson RB .07 .20
49 Art Monk .07 .20
50 Jim Everett .07 .20
51 Anthony Munoz .07 .20
52 Ray Childress .07 .20
53 Howie Long .15 .40
54 Chris Hinton .04 .10
55 John Stephens .04 .10
56 Reggie White .15 .40
57 Rodney Peete .07 .20
58 Don Majkowski .04 .10
59 Michael Cofer .04 .10
60 Bubby Brister .04 .10
61 Jerry Gray .04 .10
62 Rodney Holman .04 .10
63 Vinny Testaverde .07 .20
64 Sterling Sharpe .15 .40
65 Keith Millard .04 .10
66 Jim Lachey .04 .10
67 Dave Meggett .07 .20
68 Brent Fullwood .04 .10
69 Bobby Hebert .07 .20
70 Joey Browner .04 .10
71 Flipper Anderson .07 .20
72 Tim McGee .04 .10
73 Eric Allen .07 .20
74 Charles Haley .07 .20
75 Christian Okoye .04 .10
76 Herschel Walker .07 .20
77 Kelvin Martin .04 .10
78 Bill Fralic .04 .10
79 Leslie O'Neal .07 .20
80 Bernie Kosar .07 .20
81 Eric Sievers .04 .10
82 Timm Rosenbach .04 .10
83 Steve DeBerg .07 .20
84 Duane Bickett .04 .10
85 Chris Doleman .07 .20
86 Carl Banks .07 .20
87 Vaughan Johnson .04 .10
88 Dennis Smith .04 .10
89 Billy Joe Tolliver .04 .10
90 Dalton Hilliard .04 .10
91 John Taylor .07 .20
92 Mark Rypien .07 .20
93 Chris Miller .07 .20
94 Mark Clayton .07 .20
95 Andre Reed .15 .40
96 Warren Moon .15 .40
97 Bruce Matthews .07 .20
98 Rod Woodson .15 .40
99 Pat Swilling .07 .20
100 Jerry Rice .60 1.50

1990 Score Young Superstars

This 40-card standard size set was issued by Score in 1990 (via a mail-in offer), featuring forty of the leading young football players. This set features a glossy front with the player's photo being surrounded by black borders on the front of the card. The back, meanwhile, features a full color photo of the player along with seasonal and career statistics about the player.

COMPLETE SET (40) 4.00 10.00
1 Barry Sanders 2.40 6.00
2 Bobby Humphrey .05 .15
3 Ickey Woods .05 .15
4 Shawn Collins .05 .15
5 Dave Meggett .05 .15
6 Keith Jackson .10 .30
7 Sterling Sharpe .20 .50
8 Troy Aikman 1.20 3.00
9 Tim McDonald .05 .15
10 Tim Brown .40 1.00
11 Trace Armstrong .05 .15
12 Eric Metcalf UER .10 .30
13 Derrick Thomas .20 .50
14 Eric Hill .05 .15
15 Deion Sanders .60 1.50
16 Steve Atwater .05 .15
17 Carnell Lake .05 .15
18 Andre Reed .10 .30
19 Chris Spielman .10 .30
20 Eric Allen .05 .15
21 Erik McMillan .05 .15
22 Louis Oliver .05 .15
23 Robert Massey .05 .15
24 John Roper .05 .15
25 Burt Grossman .05 .15
26 Chris Jacke .05 .15
27 Steve Wisniewski .05 .15
28 Alonzo Highsmith .05 .15
29 Mark Carrier WR .10 .30
30 Bruce Armstrong .05 .15
31 Jerome Brown .10 .30
32 Cornelius Bennett .10 .30
33 Flipper Anderson .10 .30
34 Brian Blades .10 .30
35 Anthony Miller .10 .30
36 Thurman Thomas .20 .50
37 Chris Miller .10 .30
38 Aundray Bruce .05 .15
39 Robert Clark .05 .15
40 Robert Delpino .05 .15

1990-91 Score Franco Harris

This standard-size card was given away to all persons at the Super Bowl Card Show II in Tampa who acquired Franco Harris' autograph while at the show. It was estimated that between 1500 and 5000 cards were printed. The card features a Leroy Nieman painting of Harris on the front which has the words "All-Time Super Bowl Silver Anniversary Team" on top of the portrait and Franco Harris' name and position underneath the drawing. The back of the card is split horizontally between a shot of Harris celebrating a Super Bowl victory and a brief Super Bowl history of Harris on the back. The card is unnumbered.

1 Franco Harris 15.00 30.00
(Leroy Nieman's artistic rendition)

1991 Score Prototypes

This six-card prototype standard-size set was issued to show the design of the 1991 Score regular series. As with the regular issue, the fronts display color action player photos with borders that shade from white to a solid color, while the horizontal backs carry biographical and statistical information on the left half and a color close up photo on the right. The prototypes may be distinguished from the regular issues by noting the following minor differences: 1) the prototypes omit the tiny trademark symbol next to the Team NFL logo; 2) the shading of the borders on the front has been reversed on the Singletary and Cunningham cards; 3) statistics are printed in bluish-green on the prototypes rather than green as on the regular issues (except for Taylor, whose statistics are printed in red on his regular card); 4) on the Taylor prototype, his name appears in a blue (rather than a black) stripe on the back; and 5) the Montana, Esiason, and Thomas cards are cropped slightly differently. All cards are numbered on the back; the numbering of the prototype cards corresponds to their regular issue counterparts except for the Taylor card, who is card number 529 in the regular issue.

COMPLETE SET (6) 4.00 10.00
1 Joe Montana 3.20 8.00
4 Lawrence Taylor .40 1.00
5 Derrick Thomas .40 1.00
6 Mike Singletary .40 1.00
7 Boomer Esiason .40 1.00
12 Randall Cunningham .60 1.50

1991 Score

The 1991 Score set consists of two series of 345 and 341 for a total of 686 standard size cards. Factory sets include four Super Bowl cards (B1-B4) for a total of 690. Cards were issued in 16-card packs. Subsets include 1991 Rookies (311-319/564-589/591-596/598-612/ 614-616), the players who had plays which resulted in 90 or more yards (320-328), Top Leaders (329-330/662-669), Dream Team (331-345/676-686), Team MVP's (620-647), Crunch Crew (648 654), Sack Attack (655-661), 1991 Hall of Fame (670-674). As part of a promotion, the 11 offensive Dream Team members each signed 500 of their cards. Of this total, 5,478 were randomly inserted in second series packs and 22 were given away in a mail-in sweepstakes. Rookie Cards include Mike Croel, Ricky Ervins, Brett Favre, Alvin Harper, Herman Moore, Mike Pritchard, Jake Reed, Ricky Watters and Harvey Williams.

COMPLETE SET (686) 8.00 20.00
COMP.FACT.SET (690) 12.50 25.00
1 Joe Montana .50 1.25
2 Eric Allen .01 .05
3 Rohn Stark .01 .05
4 Frank Reich .02 .10
5 Derrick Thomas .08 .25
6 Mike Singletary .02 .10
7 Boomer Esiason .02 .10
8 Matt Millen .02 .10
9 Chris Spielman .02 .10
10 Gerald McNeil .01 .05
11 Nick Lowery .01 .05
12 Randall Cunningham .08 .25
13 Marion Butts .02 .10
14 Tim Brown .08 .25
15 Emmitt Smith 1.00 2.50
16 Rich Camarillo .01 .05
17 Mike Merriweather .01 .05
18 Derrick Fenner .01 .05
19 Clay Matthews .02 .10
20 Barry Sanders .50 1.25
21 James Brooks .02 .10
22 Alton Montgomery .01 .05
23 Steve Atwater .01 .05
24 Ron Morris .01 .05
25 Brad Muster .01 .05
26 Andre Rison .02 .10
27 Brian Brennan .01 .05
28 Leonard Smith .01 .05
29 Kevin Butler .01 .05
30 Tim Harris .01 .05
31 Jay Novacek .08 .25
32 Eddie Murray .01 .05
33 Keith Woodside .01 .05
34 Ray Crockett RC .01 .05
35 Eugene Lockhart .01 .05
36 Bill Romanowski .01 .05
37 Eddie Brown .01 .05
38 Eugene Daniel .01 .05
39 Scott Fulhage .01 .05
40 Harold Green .02 .10
41 Mark Jackson .01 .05
42 Sterling Sharpe .08 .25
43 Mel Gray .02 .10
44 Jerry Holmes .01 .05
45 Allen Pinkett .01 .05
46 Warren Powers .01 .05
47 Rodney Peete .02 .10
48 Lorenzo White .01 .05
49 Dan Owens .01 .05
50 James Francis .01 .05
51 Ken Norton .02 .10
52 Ed West .01 .05
53 Andre Reed .02 .10
54 John Grimsley .01 .05
55 Michael Cofer .01 .05
56 Chris Doleman .01 .05
57 Pat Swilling .02 .10
58 Jessie Tuggle .01 .05
59 Mike Johnson .01 .05
60 Steve Walsh .01 .05
61 Sam Mills .01 .05
62 Don Mosebar .01 .05
63 Jay Hilgenberg .01 .05
64 Cleveland Gary .01 .05
65 Andre Tippett .01 .05
66 Tom Newberry .01 .05
67 Maurice Hurst .01 .05
68 Louis Oliver .01 .05
69 Fred Marion .01 .05
70 Christian Okoye .01 .05
71 Marv Cook .01 .05
72 Darryl Talley .01 .05
73 Rick Fenney .01 .05
74 Kelvin Martin .01 .05
75 Howie Long .08 .25
76 Steve Wisniewski .01 .05
77 Karl Mecklenburg .01 .05
78 Dan Saleaumua .01 .05
79 Ray Childress .01 .05
80 Henry Ellard .02 .10
81 Ernest Givins UER .02 .10
82 Ferrell Edmunds .01 .05
83 Steve Jordan .01 .05
84 Tony Mandarich .01 .05
85 Eric Martin .01 .05
86 Rich Gannon .08 .25
87 Irving Fryar .02 .10
88 Tom Rathman .01 .05
89 Dan Hampton .02 .10
90 Barry Word .01 .05
91 Kevin Greene .02 .10
92 Sean Landeta .01 .05
93 Trace Armstrong .01 .05
94 Dennis Byrd .01 .05
95 Timm Rosenbach .01 .05
96 Anthony Toney .01 .05
97 Tim Krumrie .01 .05
98 Jerry Ball .01 .05
99 Tim Green .01 .05
100 Bo Jackson .10 .30
101 Myron Guyton .01 .05
102 Mike Mularkey .01 .05
103 Jerry Gray .01 .05
104 Scott Stephen RC .01 .05
105 Anthony Bell .01 .05
106 Lomas Brown .01 .05
107 David Little .01 .05
108 Brad Baxter .01 .05
109 Freddie Joe Nunn .01 .05
110 Dave Meggett .02 .10
111 Mark Rypien .02 .10
112 Warren Williams .01 .05
113 Ron Rivera .01 .05
114 Torance Mathis .02 .10
115 Anthony Munoz .02 .10
116 Jeff Bryant .01 .05
117 Issiac Holt .01 .05
118 Steve Sewell .01 .05
119 Tim Newton RC .01 .05
120 Emile Harry .01 .05
121 Gary Anderson K .01 .05
122 Mark Lee .01 .05
123 Alfred Anderson .01 .05
124 Anthony Blaylock .01 .05
125 Earnest Byner .01 .05
126 Bill Maas .01 .05
127 Keith Taylor .01 .05
128 Cliff Odom .01 .05
129 Bob Golic .01 .05
130 Bart Oates .01 .05
131 Jim Arnold .01 .05
132 Jeff Herrod .01 .05
133 Bruce Armstrong .01 .05
134 Craig Heyward .02 .10
135 Joey Browner .01 .05
136 Darren Comeaux .01 .05
137 Pat Beach .01 .05
138 Dalton Hilliard .01 .05
139 David Treadwell .01 .05
140 Gary Anderson RB .01 .05
141 Eugene Robinson .01 .05
142 Scott Case .01 .05
143 Paul Farren .01 .05
144 Gill Fenerty .01 .05
145 Tim Irwin .01 .05
146 Norm Johnson .01 .05
147 Willie Gault .02 .10
148 Clarence Verdin .01 .05
149 Jeff Uhlenhake .01 .05
150 Erik McMillan .01 .05
151 Kevin Ross .01 .05
152 Pepper Johnson .01 .05
153 Bryan Hinkle .01 .05
154 Gary Clark .08 .25
155 Robert Delpino .01 .05
156 Doug Smith .01 .05
157 Chris Martin .01 .05
158 Ray Berry .01 .05
159 Steve Christie .01 .05
160 Don Smith RB .01 .05
161 Greg McMurtry .01 .05
162 Jack Del Rio .02 .10
163 Floyd Dixon .01 .05
164 Buford McGee .01 .05
165 Brett Maxie .01 .05
166 Morten Andersen .01 .05
167 Kent Hull .01 .05
168 Skip McClendon .01 .05
169 Keith Sims .01 .05
170 Leonard Marshall .01 .05
171 Tony Woods .01 .05
172 Byron Evans .01 .05
173 Rob Burnett RC .02 .10
174 Tory Epps .01 .05
175 Toi Cook RC .01 .05
176 John Elliott .01 .05
177 Tommie Agee .01 .05
178 Keith Van Horne .01 .05
179 Dennis Smith .01 .05
180 James Lofton .02 .10
181 Art Monk .02 .10
182 Anthony Carter .02 .10
183 Louis Lipps .01 .05
184 Bruce Hill .01 .05
185 Michael Young .01 .05
186 Eric Green .01 .05
187 Barney Bussey RC .01 .05
188 Curtis Duncan .01 .05
189 Robert Awalt .01 .05
190 Johnny Johnson .01 .05
191 Jeff Cross .01 .05
192 Keith McKeller .01 .05
193 Robert Brown .01 .05
194 Vincent Brown .01 .05
195 Calvin Williams .02 .10
196 Sean Jones .02 .10
197 Willie Drewrey .01 .05
198 Bubba McDowell .01 .05
199 Al Noga .01 .05
200 Ronnie Lott .02 .10
201 Warren Moon .08 .25
202 Chris Hinton .01 .05
203 Jim Sweeney .01 .05
204 Wayne Haddix .01 .05
205 Tim Jorden RC .01 .05
206 Marvin Allen .01 .05
207 Jim Morrissey RC .01 .05
208 Ben Smith .01 .05
209 William White .01 .05
210 Jim C. Jensen .01 .05
211 Doug Reed .01 .05
212 Ethan Horton .01 .05
213 Chris Jacke .01 .05
214 Johnny Hector .01 .05
215 Drew Hill UER .01 .05
216 Roy Green .01 .05
217 Dean Steinkuhler .01 .05
218 Cedric Mack .01 .05
219 Chris Miller .02 .10
220 Keith Byars .01 .05
221 Lewis Billups .01 .05
222 Roger Craig .02 .10
223 Shaun Gayle .01 .05
224 Mike Rozier .01 .05
225 Troy Aikman .30 .75
226 Bobby Humphrey .01 .05
227 Eugene Marve .01 .05
228 Michael Carter .01 .05
229 Richard Johnson CB RC .01 .05
230 Billy Joe Tolliver .01 .05
231 Mark Murphy .01 .05
232 John L. Williams .01 .05
233 Ronnie Harmon .01 .05
234 Thurman Thomas .08 .25
235 Martin Mayhew .01 .05
236 Richmond Webb .01 .05
237 Gerald Riggs UER .02 .10
238 Mike Prior .01 .05
239 Mike Gann .01 .05
240 Alvin Walton .01 .05
241 Tim McGee .01 .05
242 Bruce Matthews .02 .10
243 Johnny Holland .01 .05
244 Martin Bayless .01 .05
245 Eric Metcalf .02 .10
246 John Alt .01 .05
247 Max Montoya .01 .05
248 Rod Bernstine .01 .05
249 Paul Gruber .01 .05
250 Charles Haley .02 .10
251 Scott Norwood .01 .05
252 Michael Haddix .01 .05
253 Ricky Sanders .01 .05
254 Ervin Randle .01 .05
255 Duane Bickett .01 .05
256 Mike Munchak .02 .10
257 Keith Jones .01 .05
258 Riki Ellison .01 .05
259 Vince Newsome .01 .05
260 Lee Williams .01 .05
261 Steve Smith .01 .05
262 Sam Clancy .01 .05
263 Pierce Holt .01 .05
264 Jim Harbaugh .08 .25
265 Dino Hackett .01 .05
266 Andy Heck .01 .05
267 Leo Goeas .01 .05
268 Russ Grimm .02 .10
269 Gill Byrd .01 .05
270 Neal Anderson .02 .10
271 Jackie Slater .01 .05
272 Joe Nash .01 .05
273 Todd Bowles .08 .25

Card	Low	High
274 D.J. Dozier	.01	.05
275 Kevin Fagan	.01	.05
276 Don Warren	.01	.05
277 Jim Jeffcoat	.01	.05
278 Bruce Smith	.08	.25
279 Cortez Kennedy	.08	.25
280 Thane Gash	.01	.05
281 Perry Kemp	.01	.05
282 John Taylor	.02	.10
283 Stephone Paige	.01	.05
284 Paul Skansi	.01	.05
285 Shawn Collins	.01	.05
286 Mervyn Fernandez	.01	.05
287 Daniel Stubbs	.01	.05
288 Chip Lohmiller	.01	.05
289 Brian Blades	.02	.10
290 Mark Carrier WR	.08	.25
291 Carl Zander	.01	.05
292 David Wyman	.01	.05
293 Jeff Bostic	.01	.05
294 Irv Pankey	.01	.05
295 Keith Millard	.01	.05
296 Jamie Mueller	.01	.05
297 Bill Fralic	.01	.05
298 Wendell Davis	.01	.05
299 Ken Clarke	.01	.05
300 Wymon Henderson	.01	.05
301 Jeff Campbell	.01	.05
302 Cody Carlson RC	.01	.05
303 Matt Brock RC	.01	.05
304 Maurice Carthon	.01	.05
305 Scott Mersereau RC	.01	.05
306 Steve Wright RC	.01	.05
307 J.B. Brown	.01	.05
308 Ricky Reynolds	.01	.05
309 Darryl Pollard	.01	.05
310 Donald Evans	.01	.05
311 Nick Bell RC	.01	.05
312 Pat Harlow RC	.01	.05
313 Dan McGwire RC	.01	.05
314 Mike Dumas RC	.01	.05
315 Mike Croel RC	.01	.05
316 Chris Smith RC	.01	.05
317 Kenny Walker RC	.01	.05
318 Todd Lyght RC	.01	.05
319 Mike Stonebreaker RC	.01	.05
320 Cunningham/Barnett 90	.02	.10
321 Terance Mathis 90	.08	.25
322 Gaston Green 90	.01	.05
323 Johnny Bailey 90	.01	.05
324 Donnie Elder 90	.01	.05
325 Brister/Stone 90 UER	.01	.05
326 DeBerg/Birden 90	.02	.10
327 Alexander Wright 90	.01	.05
328 Eric Metcalf 90	.02	.10
329 Andre Rison TL	.02	.10
330 Warren Moon TL UER	.02	.10
331 Steve Tasker DT	.01	.05
332 Mel Gray DT	.02	.10
333 Nick Lowery DT	.01	.05
334 Sean Landeta DT	.01	.05
335 David Fulcher DT	.01	.05
336 Joey Browner DT	.01	.05
337 Albert Lewis DT	.01	.05
338 Rod Woodson DT	.02	.10
339 Shane Conlan DT	.01	.05
340 Pepper Johnson DT	.01	.05
341 Chris Spielman DT	.01	.05
342 Derrick Thomas DT	.02	.10
343 Ray Childress DT	.01	.05
344 Reggie White DT	.02	.10
345 Bruce Smith DT	.02	.10
346 Darrell Green	.01	.05
347 Ray Bentley	.01	.05
348 Herschel Walker	.02	.10
349 Rodney Holman	.01	.05
350 Al Toon	.02	.10
351 Harry Hamilton	.01	.05
352 Albert Lewis	.01	.05
353 Renaldo Turnbull	.01	.05
354 Junior Seau	.08	.25
355 Merril Hoge	.01	.05
356 Shane Conlan	.01	.05
357 Jay Schroeder	.01	.05
358 Steve Broussard	.01	.05
359 Mark Bavaro	.01	.05
360 Jim Lachey	.01	.05
361 Greg Townsend	.01	.05
362 Dave Krieg	.02	.10
363 Jessie Hester	.01	.05
364 Steve Tasker	.02	.10
365 Ron Hall	.01	.05
366 Pat Leahy	.01	.05
367 Jim Everett	.02	.10
368 Felix Wright	.01	.05
369 Ricky Proehl	.01	.05
370 Anthony Miller	.02	.10
371 Keith Jackson	.02	.10
372 Pete Stoyanovich	.01	.05
373 Tommy Kane	.01	.05
374 Richard Johnson	.01	.05
375 Randall McDaniel	.02	.10
376 John Stephens	.01	.05
377 Haywood Jeffires	.02	.10
378 Rodney Hampton	.08	.25
379 Tim Grunhard	.01	.05
380 Jerry Rice	.30	.75
381 Ken Harvey	.02	.10
382 Vaughan Johnson	.01	.05
383 J.T. Smith	.01	.05
384 Carnell Lake	.01	.05
385 Dan Marino	.50	1.25
386 Kyle Clifton	.01	.05
387 Wilber Marshall	.01	.05
388 Pete Holohan	.01	.05
389 Gary Plummer	.01	.05
390 William Perry	.02	.10
391 Mark Robinson	.01	.05
392 Nate Odomes	.01	.05
393 Ickey Woods	.01	.05
394 Reyna Thompson	.01	.05
395 Deion Sanders	.15	.40
396 Harris Barton	.01	.05
397 Sammie Smith	.01	.05
398 Vinny Testaverde	.02	.10
399 Ray Donaldson	.01	.05
400 Tim McKyer	.01	.05
401 Nesby Glasgow	.01	.05
402 Brent Williams	.01	.05
403 Rob Moore	.08	.25
404 Bubby Brister	.01	.05
405 David Fulcher	.01	.05
406 Reggie Cobb	.01	.05
407 Jerome Brown	.01	.05
408 Erik Howard	.01	.05
409 Tony Paige	.01	.05
410 John Elway	.50	1.25
411 Charles Mann	.01	.05
412 Luis Sharpe	.01	.05
413 Hassan Jones	.01	.05
414 Frank Minnifield	.01	.05
415 Steve DeBerg	.01	.05
416 Mark Carrier DB	.02	.10
417 Brian Jordan	.02	.10
418 Reggie Langhorne	.01	.05
419 Don Majkowski	.01	.05
420 Marcus Allen	.08	.25
421 Michael Brooks	.01	.05
422 Vai Sikahema	.01	.05
423 Dermontti Dawson	.02	.10
424 Jacob Green	.01	.05
425 Flipper Anderson	.01	.05
426 Bill Brooks	.01	.05
427 Keith McCants	.01	.05
428 Ken O'Brien	.01	.05
429 Fred Barnett	.08	.25
430 Mark Duper	.02	.10
431 Mark Kelso	.01	.05
432 Leslie O'Neal	.02	.10
433 Ottis Anderson	.02	.10
434 Jesse Sapolu	.01	.05
435 Gary Zimmerman	.02	.10
436 Kevin Porter	.01	.05
437 Anthony Thompson	.01	.05
438 Robert Clark	.01	.05
439 Chris Warren	.08	.25
440 Gerald Williams	.01	.05
441 Jim Skow	.01	.05
442 Rick Donnelly	.01	.05
443 Guy McIntyre	.01	.05
444 Jeff Lageman	.01	.05
445 John Offerdahl	.01	.05
446 Clyde Simmons	.01	.05
447 John Kidd	.01	.05
448 Chip Banks	.01	.05
449 Johnny Meads	.01	.05
450 Rickey Jackson	.01	.05
451 Lee Johnson	.01	.05
452 Michael Irvin	.08	.25
453 Leon Seals	.01	.05
454 Darrell Thompson	.01	.05
455 Everson Walls	.01	.05
456 LeRoy Butler	.02	.10
457 Marcus Dupree	.08	.25
458 Kirk Lowdermilk	.01	.05
459 Chris Singleton	.01	.05
460 Seth Joyner	.02	.10
461 Rueben Mayes UER	.01	.05
462 Ernie Jones	.01	.05
463 Greg Kragen	.01	.05
464 Bennie Blades	.01	.05
465 Mark Bortz	.01	.05
466 Tony Stargell	.01	.05
467 Mike Cofer	.01	.05
468 Randy Grimes	.01	.05
469 Tim Worley	.01	.05
470 Kevin Mack	.01	.05
471 Wes Hopkins	.01	.05
472 Will Wolford	.01	.05
473 Sam Seale	.01	.05
474 Jim Ritcher	.01	.05
475 Jeff Hostetler	.08	.25
476 Mitchell Price RC	.01	.05
477 Ken Lanier	.01	.05
478 Naz Worthen	.01	.05
479 Ed Reynolds	.01	.05
480 Mark Clayton	.02	.10
481 Matt Bahr	.01	.05
482 Gary Reasons	.01	.05
483 David Szott RC	.01	.05
484 Barry Foster	.02	.10
485 Bruce Reimers	.01	.05
486 Dean Biasucci	.01	.05
487 Cris Carter	.20	.50
488 Albert Bentley	.01	.05
489 Robert Massey	.01	.05
490 Al Smith	.01	.05
491 Greg Lloyd	.08	.25
492 Steve McMichael UER	.02	.10
493 Jeff Wright RC	.01	.05
494 Scott Davis	.01	.05
495 Freeman McNeil	.01	.05
496 Simon Fletcher	.01	.05
497 Terry McDaniel	.01	.05
498 Heath Sherman	.01	.05
499 Jeff Jaeger	.01	.05
500 Mark Collins	.01	.05
501 Tim Goad	.01	.05
502 Jeff George	.08	.25
503 Jimmie Jones	.01	.05
504 Henry Thomas	.01	.05
505 Steve Young	.30	.75
506 William Roberts	.01	.05
507 Neil Smith	.08	.25
508 Mike Saxon	.01	.05
509 Johnny Bailey	.01	.05
510 Broderick Thomas	.01	.05
511 Wade Wilson	.02	.10
512 Hart Lee Dykes	.01	.05
513 Hardy Nickerson	.02	.10
514 Tim McDonald	.01	.05
515 Frank Cornish	.01	.05
516 Jarvis Williams	.01	.05
517 Carl Lee	.01	.05
518 Carl Banks	.01	.05
519 Mike Golic	.01	.05
520 Brian Noble	.01	.05
521 James Hasty	.01	.05
522 Bubba Paris	.01	.05
523 Kevin Walker RC	.01	.05
524 William Fuller	.02	.10
525 Eddie Anderson	.01	.05
526 Roger Ruzek	.01	.05
527 Robert Blackmon	.01	.05
528 Vince Buck	.01	.05
529 Lawrence Taylor	.08	.25
530 Reggie Roby	.01	.05
531 Doug Riesenberg	.01	.05
532 Joe Jacoby	.01	.05
533 Kirby Jackson RC	.01	.05
534 Robb Thomas	.01	.05
535 Don Griffin	.01	.05
536 Andre Waters	.01	.05
537 Marc Logan	.01	.05
538 James Thornton	.01	.05
539 Ray Agnew	.01	.05
540 Frank Stams	.01	.05
541 Brett Perriman	.08	.25
542 Andre Ware	.02	.10
543 Kevin Haverdink	.01	.05
544 Greg Jackson RC	.01	.05
545 Tunch Ilkin	.01	.05
546 Dexter Carter	.01	.05
547 Rod Woodson	.08	.25
548 Donnell Woolford	.01	.05
549 Mark Boyer	.01	.05
550 Jeff Query	.01	.05
551 Burt Grossman	.01	.05
552 Mike Kenn	.01	.05
553 Richard Dent	.02	.10
554 Gaston Green	.01	.05
555 Phil Simms	.02	.10
556 Brent Jones	.08	.25
557 Ronnie Lippett	.01	.05
558 Mike Horan	.01	.05
559 Danny Noonan	.01	.05
560 Reggie White	.08	.25
561 Rufus Porter	.01	.05
562 Aaron Wallace	.01	.05
563 Vance Johnson	.01	.05
564A Aaron Craver ERR RC	.01	.05
564B Aaron Craver COR RC	.01	.05
565A Russell Maryland ERR RC	.08	.25
565B Russell Maryland COR RC	.08	.25
566 Paul Justin RC	.01	.05
567 Walter Dean	.01	.05
568 Herman Moore RC	.08	.25
569 Bill Musgrave RC	.01	.05
570 Rob Carpenter RC	.01	.05
571 Greg Lewis RC	.01	.05
572 Ed King RC	.01	.05
573 Ernie Mills RC	.02	.10
574 Jake Reed RC	.20	.50
575 Ricky Watters RC	.60	1.50
576 Derek Russell RC	.01	.05
577 Shawn Moore RC	.01	.05
578 Eric Bieniemy RC	.01	.05
579 Chris Zorich RC	.08	.25
580 Scott Miller	.01	.05
581 Jarrod Bunch RC	.01	.05
582 Ricky Ervins RC	.02	.10
583 Browning Nagle RC	.01	.05
584 Eric Turner RC	.02	.10
585 William Thomas RC	.01	.05
586 Stanley Richard RC	.01	.05
587 Adrian Cooper RC	.01	.05
588 Harvey Williams RC	.08	.25
589 Alvin Harper RC	.08	.25
590 John Carney	.01	.05
591 Mark Vander Poel RC	.01	.05
592 Mike Pritchard RC	.08	.25
593 Eric Moten RC	.01	.05
594 Moe Gardner RC	.01	.05
595 Wesley Carroll RC	.01	.05
596 Eric Swann RC	.08	.25
597 Joe Kelly	.01	.05
598 Steve Jackson RC	.01	.05
599 Kelvin Pritchett RC	.02	.10
600 Jesse Campbell RC	.01	.05
601 Darryll Lewis UER RC	.02	.10
602 Howard Griffith	.01	.05
603 Blaise Bryant RC	.01	.05
604 Vinnie Clark RC	.01	.05
605 Mel Agee RC	.01	.05
606 Bobby Wilson RC	.01	.05
607 Kevin Donnalley RC	.01	.05
608 Randal Hill RC	.02	.10
609 Stan Thomas	.01	.05
610 Mike Heldt	.01	.05
611 Brett Favre RC	3.00	8.00
612 Lawrence Dawsey UER RC	.02	.10
613 Dennis Gibson	.01	.05
614 Dean Dingman	.01	.05
615 Bruce Pickens RC	.01	.05
616 Todd Marinovich RC	.01	.05
617 Gene Atkins	.01	.05
618 Marcus Dupree Comeback	.08	.25
619 Warren Moon Man of Year	.02	.10
620 Joe Montana MVP	.20	.50
621 Neal Anderson MVP	.01	.05
622 James Brooks MVP	.02	.10
623 Thurman Thomas MVP	.02	.10
624 Bobby Humphrey MVP	.01	.05
625 Kevin Mack MVP	.01	.05
626 Mark Carrier WR MVP	.01	.05
627 Johnny Johnson MVP	.01	.05
628 Marion Butts MVP	.02	.10
629 Steve DeBerg MVP	.01	.05
630 Jeff George MVP	.02	.10
631 Troy Aikman MVP	.15	.40
632 Dan Marino MVP	.20	.50
633 Randall Cunningham MVP	.02	.10
634 Andre Rison MVP	.02	.10
635 Pepper Johnson MVP	.01	.05
636 Pat Leahy MVP	.01	.05
637 Barry Sanders MVP	.20	.50
638 Warren Moon MVP	.02	.10
639 Sterling Sharpe MVP	.01	.05
640 Bruce Armstrong MVP	.01	.05
641 Bo Jackson MVP	.02	.10
642 Henry Ellard MVP	.02	.10
643 Earnest Byner MVP	.01	.05
644 Pat Swilling MVP	.01	.05
645 John L. Williams MVP	.01	.05
646 Rod Woodson MVP	.02	.10
647 Chris Doleman MVP	.01	.05
648 Joey Browner CC	.01	.05
649 Erik McMillan CC	.01	.05
650 David Fulcher CC	.01	.05
651A Ronnie Lott CC ERR	.02	.10
651B Ronnie Lott CC COR	.02	.10
652 Louis Oliver CC	.01	.05
653 Mark Robinson CC	.01	.05
654 Dennis Smith CC	.01	.05
655 Reggie White SA ERR	.02	.10
656 Charles Haley SA	.01	.05
657 Leslie O'Neal SA	.02	.10
658 Kevin Greene SA	.02	.10
659 Dennis Byrd SA	.01	.05
660 Bruce Smith SA	.02	.10
661 Derrick Thomas SA	.02	.10
662 Steve DeBerg TL	.01	.05
663 Barry Sanders TL	.20	.50
664 Thurman Thomas TL	.02	.10
665 Jerry Rice TL	.15	.40
666 Derrick Thomas TL	.02	.10
667 Bruce Smith TL	.02	.10
668 Mark Carrier DB TL	.01	.05
669 Richard Johnson CB TL	.01	.05
670 Jan Stenerud HOF	.01	.05
671 Stan Jones HOF	.01	.05
672 John Hannah HOF	.01	.05
673 Tex Schramm HOF	.01	.05
674 Earl Campbell HOF	.08	.25
675 Emmitt Smith Carrier ROY	.30	.75
676 Warren Moon DT	.02	.10
677 Barry Sanders DT	.20	.50
678 Thurman Thomas DT	.08	.25
679 Andre Reed DT	.02	.10
680 Andre Rison DT	.02	.10
681 Keith Jackson DT	.01	.05
682 Bruce Armstrong DT	.01	.05
683 Jim Lachey DT	.01	.05
684 Bruce Matthews DT	.01	.05
685 Mike Munchak DT	.01	.05
686 Don Mosebar DT	.01	.05
B1 Jeff Hostetler SB	.08	.25
B2 Matt Bahr SB	.01	.05
B3 Ottis Anderson SB	.02	.10
B4 Ottis Anderson SB	.02	.10

1991 Score Dream Team Autographs

This 11-card standard-size set was randomly inserted in second series packs. The odds of receiving them according to Score is not less than 1 in 5000 packs. The actual signed cards are distinguishable from regular Dream Team cards (which carry facsimile autographs on the backs) because the facsimile autograph has been removed from the cardback. The two versions (signed and facsimile) are easily confused with each other so take care in examining the cards closely. The best approach is to compare a card known to be from the base set (facsimile) to the card in question. Players used a variety of inks and most signed on the cardfronts. According to Score, only 500 of each player's cards were autographed.

Card	Low	High
COMPLETE SET (11)	200.00	400.00
676 Warren Moon	20.00	50.00
677 Barry Sanders	50.00	120.00
678 Thurman Thomas	20.00	50.00
679 Andre Reed	20.00	50.00
680 Andre Rison	15.00	30.00
681 Keith Jackson	10.00	20.00
682 Bruce Armstrong	10.00	20.00
683 Jim Lachey	10.00	20.00
684 Bruce Matthews	25.00	50.00
685 Mike Munchak	15.00	30.00
686 Don Mosebar	10.00	20.00

1991 Score Hot Rookies

The 1991 Score Hot Rookie 10-card standard-size set was inserted in blister packs. The front design has color action shots of the players (in college uniforms) lifted from their real-life background and superimposed on a hot pink and yellow geometric design. The black borders provide a sharp contrast. The back has a color head shot of the player and a brief player profile.

Card	Low	High
COMPLETE SET (10)	1.50	4.00
ONE PER BLISTER PACK		
1 Dan McGwire	.15	.40
2 Todd Lyght	.15	.40
3 Mike Dumas	.15	.40
4 Pat Harlow	.15	.40
5 Nick Bell	.15	.40
6 Chris Smith	.15	.40
7 Mike Stonebreaker	.15	.40
8 Mike Croel	.15	.40
9 Kenny Walker	.15	.40
10 Rob Carpenter WR	.15	.40

1991 Score Supplemental

This 110-card standard size set features rookies and players who switched teams during the off-season. The set was issued only as a complete set. The cards are numbered on the back with a "T" suffix. Rookie Cards include Bryan Cox, Merton Hanks, Michael Jackson, Erric Pegram and Leonard Russell.

Card	Low	High
COMPLETE FACT.SET (110)	1.50	4.00
1T Ronnie Lott	.02	.10
2T Matt Millen	.02	.10
3T Tim McKyer	.01	.05
4T Vince Newsome	.01	.05
5T Gaston Green	.01	.05
6T Brett Perriman	.08	.25
7T Roger Craig	.02	.10
8T Pete Holohan	.01	.05
9T Tony Zendejas	.01	.05
10T Lee Williams	.01	.05
11T Mike Stonebreaker RC	.01	.05
12T Felix Wright	.01	.05
13T Lonnie Young	.01	.05
14T Hugh Millen RC	.01	.05
15T Roy Green	.01	.05
16T Greg Davis RC	.01	.05
17T Dexter Manley	.01	.05
18T Ted Washington RC	.01	.05
19T Norm Johnson	.01	.05
20T Joe Morris	.01	.05
21T Robert Perryman	.01	.05
22T Mike Iaquaniello UER RC	.01	.05
23T Gerald Perry UER RC	.01	.05
24T Zeke Mowatt	.01	.05
25T Rich Miano RC	.01	.05
26T Nick Bell	.01	.05
27T Terry Orr RC	.01	.05
28T Matt Stover RC	.08	.25
29T Bubba Paris	.01	.05
30T Ron Brown	.01	.05
31T Don Davey	.01	.05
32T Lee Rouson	.01	.05
33T Terry Hoage UER	.01	.05
34T Tony Covington	.01	.05
35T John Rienstra	.01	.05
36T Charles Dimry RC	.01	.05
37T Todd Marinovich	.01	.05
38T Winston Moss	.01	.05
39T Vestee Jackson	.01	.05
40T Brian Hansen	.01	.05
41T Irv Eatman	.01	.05
42T Jarrod Bunch	.01	.05
43T Kanavis McGhee RC	.01	.05
44T Vai Sikahema	.01	.05
45T Charles McRae RC	.01	.05
46T Quinn Early	.02	.10
47T Jeff Faulkner RC	.01	.05
48T William Frizzell RC	.01	.05
49T John Booty	.01	.05
50T Tim Harris	.01	.05
51T Derek Russell	.01	.05
52T John Flannery RC	.01	.05
53T Tim Barnett RC	.01	.05
54T Alfred Williams RC	.01	.05
55T Dan McGwire	.01	.05
56T Ernie Mills	.01	.05
57T Stanley Richard	.01	.05
58T Huey Richardson RC	.01	.05
59T Jerome Henderson RC	.01	.05
60T Bryan Cox RC	.08	.25
61T Russell Maryland	.02	.10
62T Reginald Jones RC	.01	.05
63T Mo Lewis RC	.02	.10
64T Moe Gardner	.01	.05
65T Wesley Carroll	.01	.05
66T Michael Jackson WR RC	.08	.25
67T Shawn Jefferson RC	.02	.10
68T Chris Zorich	.02	.10
69T Kenny Walker	.01	.05
70T Erric Pegram RC	.08	.25
71T Alvin Harper	.08	.25
72T Harry Colon RC	.01	.05
73T Scott Miller	.01	.05
74T Lawrence Dawsey	.02	.10
75T Phil Hansen RC	.01	.05
76T Roman Phifer RC	.01	.05
77T Greg Lewis	.01	.05
78T Merton Hanks RC	.08	.25
79T James Jones RC	.01	.05
80T Vinnie Clark	.01	.05
81T R.J. Kors	.01	.05
82T Mike Pritchard	.08	.25
83T Stan Thomas	.01	.05
84T Lamar Rogers RC	.01	.05
85T Erik Williams RC	.02	.10
86T Keith Traylor RC	.01	.05
87T Mike Dumas	.01	.05
88T Mel Agee	.01	.05
89T Harvey Williams	.08	.25
90T Todd Lyght	.01	.05
91T Jake Reed	.15	.40
92T Pat Harlow	.01	.05
93T Antone Davis RC	.01	.05
94T Aeneas Williams RC	.50	1.25
95T Eric Bieniemy	.01	.05
96T John Kasay RC	.02	.10
97T Robert Wilson RC	.01	.05
98T Ricky Ervins	.02	.10
99T Mike Croel	.01	.05
100T David Lang RC	.01	.05
101T Esera Tuaolo RC	.01	.05
102T Randal Hill	.02	.10
103T Jon Vaughn RC	.01	.05
104T Dave McCloughan	.01	.05
105T David Daniels RC	.01	.05
106T Eric Moten	.01	.05
107T Anthony Morgan RC	.01	.05
108T Ed King	.01	.05
109T Leonard Russell RC	.02	.10
110T Aaron Craver	.01	.05

1991 Score National Convention

This set contains ten standard-size cards. The front design is distinctively colorful at the top and bottom of the obverse. In the middle of the back the cards are labeled as 12th National Sports Collectors Convention. The cards were given away as a complete set wrapped in its own cello wrapper.

Card	Low	High
COMPLETE SET (10)	4.00	10.00
*NCWA BACK: .4X TO 1X NATIONAL		
1 Emmitt Smith	2.50	6.00
2 Mark Carrier DB	.30	.75
3 Steve Broussard	.20	.50
4 Johnny Johnson	.20	.50
5 Steve Christie	.20	.50
6 Richmond Webb	.20	.50
7 James Francis	.20	.50
0 Jeff George	.40	1.00
9 Rodney Hampton	.50	1.25
10 Calvin Williams	.30	.75

1991 Score Young Superstars

This 40-card standard-size set features some of the leading young players in football. The key player in the set is Emmitt Smith. This set was available from a mail-away offer on 1991 Score Football wax packs.

Card	Low	High
COMPLETE SET (40)	4.00	10.00
1 Johnny Bailey	.02	.10
2 Johnny Johnson	.02	.10
3 Fred Barnett	.15	.40
4 Keith McCants	.02	.10
5 Brad Baxter	.02	.10
6 Dan Owens	.02	.10
7 Steve Broussard	.02	.10
8 Ricky Proehl	.07	.20
9 Marion Butts	.07	.20
10 Reggie Cobb	.02	.10
11 Dennis Byrd	.07	.20
12 Emmitt Smith	2.50	6.00
13 Mark Carrier DB	.07	.20
14 Keith Sims	.02	.10
15 Dexter Carter	.02	.10
16 Chris Singleton	.02	.10
17 Steve Christie	.07	.20
18 Frank Cornish	.02	.10
19 Timm Rosenbach	.02	.10
20 Sammie Smith	.02	.10
21 Calvin Williams UER	.07	.20
22 Merril Hoge	.02	.10
23 Hart Lee Dykes	.02	.10
24 Darrell Thompson	.02	.10
25 James Francis	.07	.20
26 John Elliott	.02	.10
27 Jeff George	.40	1.00
28 Broderick Thomas	.02	.10
29 Eric Green	.07	.20
30 Steve Walsh	.07	.20
31 Harold Green	.07	.20
32 Andre Ware	.07	.20
33 Richmond Webb	.02	.10
34 Junior Seau	.30	.75
35 Tim Grunhard	.02	.10
36 Tim Worley	.02	.10
37 Haywood Jeffires	.07	.20
38 Rod Woodson	.15	.40
39 Rodney Hampton	.15	.40
40 David Szott	.02	.10

1992 Score

The 1992 Score football set contains 550 standard-size cards. Cards were issued in 16 and 35-card packs. Topical subsets featured include Draft Pick (476-514), Crunch Crew (515-519), Rookie of the Year (520-523), Little Big Men (524-528), Sack Attack (529-533), Hall of Fame (535-537), and 90 Plus Club (538-547). Rookie Cards include Edgar Bennett, Steve Bono, Terrell Buckley, Amp Lee, Derrick Moore, Michael Timpson and Tommy Vardell.

Card	Low	High
COMPLETE SET (550)	12.50	25.00
1 Barry Sanders	.75	2.00
2 Pat Swilling	.01	.05
3 Moe Gardner	.01	.05
4 Steve Young	.40	1.00
5 Chris Spielman	.02	.10
6 Richard Dent	.02	.10
7 Anthony Munoz	.02	.10
8 Martin Mayhew	.01	.05
9 Terry McDaniel	.01	.05
10 Thurman Thomas	.08	.25
11 Ricky Sanders	.01	.05
12 Steve Atwater	.01	.05
13 Tony Tolbert	.01	.05
14 Vince Workman	.01	.05
15 Haywood Jeffires	.02	.10
16 Duane Bickett	.01	.05
17 Jeff Uhlenhake	.01	.05
18 Tim McDonald	.01	.05
19 Cris Carter	.20	.50
20 Derrick Thomas	.08	.25
21 Hugh Millen	.01	.05
22 Bart Oates	.01	.05
23 Eugene Robinson	.01	.05
24 Jerrol Williams	.01	.05
25 Reggie White	.08	.25
26 Marion Butts	.01	.05
27 Jim Sweeney	.01	.05
28 Tom Newberry	.01	.05
29 Pete Stoyanovich	.01	.05
30 Ronnie Lott	.02	.10
31 Simon Fletcher	.01	.05
32 Dino Hackett	.01	.05
33 Morten Andersen	.01	.05
34 Clyde Simmons	.01	.05
35 Mark Rypien	.01	.05
36 Greg Montgomery	.01	.05
37 Nate Lewis	.01	.05
38 Henry Ellard	.02	.10
39 Luis Sharpe	.01	.05
40 Michael Irvin	.08	.25
41 Louis Lipps	.01	.05
42 John L. Williams	.01	.05
43 Broderick Thomas	.01	.05
44 Michael Haynes	.02	.10
45 Don Majkowski	.01	.05
46 William Perry	.02	.10
47 David Fulcher	.01	.05
48 Tony Bennett	.01	.05
49 Clay Matthews	.02	.10
50 Warren Moon	.08	.25
51 Bruce Armstrong	.01	.05
52 Harry Newsome	.01	.05
53 Bill Brooks	.01	.05
54 Greg Townsend	.01	.05
55 Tom Rathman	.01	.05
56 Sean Landeta	.01	.05
57 Kyle Clifton	.01	.05
58 Steve Broussard	.01	.05
59 Mark Carrier WR	.02	.10
60 Mel Gray	.02	.10
61 Tim Krumrie	.01	.05
62 Rufus Porter	.01	.05
63 Kevin Mack	.01	.05
64 Todd Bowles	.08	.25
65 Emmitt Smith	1.25	2.50
66 Mike Croel	.01	.05
67 Brian Mitchell	.02	.10
68 Bennie Blades	.01	.05
69 Carnell Lake	.01	.05
70 Cornelius Bennett	.02	.10
71 Darrell Thompson	.01	.05
72 Wes Hopkins	.01	.05
73 Jessie Hester	.01	.05
74 Irv Eatman	.01	.05
75 Marv Cook	.01	.05
76 Tim Brown	.08	.25
77 Pepper Johnson	.01	.05
78 Mark Duper	.01	.05
79 Robert Delpino	.01	.05
80 Charles Mann	.01	.05
81 Brian Jordan	.02	.10
82 Wendell Davis	.01	.05
83 Lee Johnson	.01	.05
84 Ricky Reynolds	.01	.05
85 Vaughan Johnson	.01	.05
86 Brian Blades	.02	.10
87 Sam Seale	.01	.05
88 Ed King	.01	.05
89 Gaston Green	.01	.05
90 Christian Okoye	.01	.05
91 Chris Jacke	.01	.05
92 Rohn Stark	.01	.05
93 Kevin Greene	.02	.10
94 Jay Novacek	.02	.10
95 Chip Lohmiller	.01	.05
96 Cris Dishman	.01	.05
97 Ethan Horton	.01	.05
98 Pat Harlow	.01	.05
99 Mark Ingram	.01	.05
100 Mark Carrier DB	.01	.05
101 Deron Cherry	.01	.05
102 Sam Mills	.01	.05
103 Mark Higgs	.01	.05
104 Keith Jackson	.02	.10
105 Steve Tasker	.02	.10
106 Ken Harvey	.01	.05
107 Bryan Hinkle	.01	.05
108 Anthony Carter	.02	.10
109 Johnny Hector	.01	.05
110 Randall McDaniel	.02	.10
111 Johnny Johnson	.01	.05
112 Shane Conlan	.01	.05
113 Ray Horton	.01	.05
114 Sterling Sharpe	.08	.25
115 Guy McIntyre	.01	.05
116 Tom Waddle	.01	.05
117 Albert Lewis	.01	.05
118 Riki Ellison	.01	.05
119 Chris Doleman	.01	.05
120 Andre Rison	.02	.10
121 Bobby Hebert	.01	.05
122 Dan Owens	.01	.05
123 Rodney Hampton	.02	.10
124 Ron Holmes	.01	.05
125 Ernie Jones	.01	.05
126 Michael Carter	.01	.05
127 Reggie Cobb	.01	.05
128 Esera Tuaolo	.01	.05
129 Wilber Marshall	.01	.05
130 Mike Munchak	.02	.10
131 Cortez Kennedy	.02	.10
132 Lamar Lathon	.01	.05
133 Todd Lyght	.01	.05
134 Jeff Feagles	.01	.05
135 Burt Grossman	.01	.05
136 Mike Cofer	.01	.05
137 Frank Warren	.01	.05
138 Jarvis Williams	.01	.05
139 Eddie Brown	.01	.05
140 John Elliott	.01	.05
141 Jim Everett	.02	.10
142 Hardy Nickerson	.02	.10
143 Eddie Murray	.01	.05
144 Andre Tippett	.01	.05
145 Heath Sherman	.01	.05
146 Ronnie Harmon	.01	.05
147 Eric Metcalf	.02	.10
148 Tony Martin	.02	.10
149 Chris Burkett	.01	.05
150 Andre Waters	.01	.05
151 Ray Donaldson	.01	.05
152 Paul Gruber	.01	.05
153 Chris Singleton	.01	.05
154 Clarence Kay	.01	.05
155 Ernest Givins	.02	.10
156 Eric Hill	.01	.05
157 Jesse Sapolu	.01	.05
158 Jack Del Rio	.01	.05
159 Erric Pegram	.02	.10
160 Joey Browner	.01	.05
161 Marcus Allen	.08	.25
162 Eric Moten	.01	.05
163 Donnell Thompson	.01	.05
164 Chuck Cecil	.01	.05
165 Matt Millen	.02	.10
166 Barry Foster	.02	.10
167 Kent Hull	.01	.05
168 Tony Jones WR	.01	.05
169 Mike Prior	.01	.05
170 Neal Anderson	.01	.05
171 Roger Craig	.02	.10
172 Felix Wright	.01	.05
173 James Francis	.01	.05
174 Eugene Lockhart	.01	.05
175 Dalton Hilliard	.01	.05
176 Nick Lowery	.01	.05
177 Tim McKyer	.01	.05
178 Lorenzo White	.01	.05
179 Jeff Hostetler	.02	.10
180 Jackie Harris RC	.08	.25
181 Ken Norton	.02	.10
182 Flipper Anderson	.01	.05
183 Don Warren	.01	.05
184 Brad Baxter	.01	.05
185 John Taylor	.02	.10
186 Harold Green	.01	.05
187 James Washington	.01	.05
188 Aaron Craver	.01	.05
189 Mike Merriweather	.01	.05
190 Gary Clark	.08	.25
191 Vince Buck	.01	.05
192 Cleveland Gary	.01	.05
193 Dan Saleaumua	.01	.05
194 Gary Zimmerman	.01	.05
195 Richmond Webb	.01	.05
196 Gary Plummer	.01	.05
197 Willie Green	.01	.05
198 Chris Warren	.08	.25
199 Mike Pritchard	.02	.10
200 Art Monk	.02	.10
201 Matt Stover	.01	.05
202 Tim Grunhard	.01	.05
203 Mervyn Fernandez	.01	.05
204 Mark Jackson	.01	.05
205 Freddie Joe Nunn	.01	.05
206 Stan Thomas	.01	.05
207 Keith McKeller	.01	.05
208 Jeff Lageman	.01	.05
209 Kenny Walker	.01	.05
210 Dave Krieg	.02	.10
211 Dean Biasucci	.01	.05
212 Herman Moore	.08	.25
213 Jon Vaughn	.01	.05
214 Howard Cross	.01	.05
215 Greg Davis	.01	.05
216 Bubby Brister	.01	.05
217 John Kasay	.01	.05
218 Ron Hall	.01	.05
219 Mo Lewis	.01	.05
220 Eric Green	.01	.05
221 Scott Case	.01	.05
222 Sean Jones	.01	.05
223 Winston Moss	.01	.05
224 Reggie Langhorne	.01	.05
225 Greg Lewis	.01	.05
226 Todd McNair	.01	.05
227 Rod Bernstine	.01	.05
228 Joe Jacoby	.01	.05
229 Brad Muster	.01	.05
230 Nick Bell	.01	.05
231 Terry Allen	.08	.25
232 Cliff Odom	.01	.05
233 Brian Hansen	.01	.05
234 William Fuller	.01	.05
235 Issiac Holt	.01	.05
236 Dexter Carter	.01	.05
237 Gene Atkins	.01	.05
238 Pat Beach	.01	.05
239 Tim McGee	.01	.05
240 Dermontti Dawson	.02	.10
241 Dan Fike	.01	.05
242 Don Beebe	.01	.05
243 Jeff Bostic	.01	.05
244 Mark Collins	.01	.05
245 Steve Sewell	.01	.05
246 Steve Walsh	.01	.05
247 Erik Kramer	.02	.10
248 Scott Norwood	.01	.05
249 Jesse Solomon	.01	.05
250 Jerry Ball	.01	.05
251 Eugene Daniel	.01	.05
252 Michael Stewart	.01	.05
253 Fred Barnett	.08	.25
254 Rodney Holman	.01	.05
255 Stephen Baker	.01	.05
256 Don Griffin	.01	.05
257 Will Wolford	.01	.05
258 Perry Kemp	.01	.05
259 Leonard Russell	.02	.10
260 Jeff Gossett	.01	.05
261 Dwayne Harper	.01	.05
262 Vinny Testaverde	.02	.10
263 Maurice Hurst	.01	.05
264 Tony Casillas	.01	.05
265 Louis Oliver	.01	.05
266 Jim Morrissey	.01	.05
267 Kenneth Davis	.01	.05
268 John Alt	.01	.05
269 Michael Zordich RC	.01	.05
270 Brian Brennan	.01	.05
271 Greg Kragen	.01	.05
272 Andre Collins	.01	.05
273 Dave Meggett	.02	.10
274 Scott Fulhage	.01	.05
275 Tony Zendejas	.01	.05
276 Herschel Walker	.02	.10
277 Keith Henderson	.01	.05
278 Johnny Bailey	.01	.05
279 Vince Newsome	.01	.05
280 Chris Hinton	.01	.05
281 Robert Blackmon	.01	.05
282 James Hasty	.01	.05
283 John Offerdahl	.01	.05
284 Wesley Carroll	.01	.05
285 Lomas Brown	.01	.05
286 Neil O'Donnell	.02	.10
287 Kevin Porter	.01	.05
288 Lionel Washington	.01	.05
289 Carlton Bailey RC	.01	.05
290 Leonard Marshall	.01	.05
291 John Carney	.01	.05
292 Bubba McDowell	.01	.05
293 Nate Newton	.01	.05
294 Dave Waymer	.01	.05
295 Rob Moore	.02	.10
296 Earnest Byner	.01	.05
297 Jason Staurovsky	.01	.05
298 Keith McCants	.01	.05
299 Floyd Turner	.01	.05
300 Steve Jordan	.01	.05
301 Nate Odomes	.01	.05
302 Gerald Riggs	.01	.05
303 Marvin Washington	.01	.05
304 Anthony Thompson	.01	.05
305 Steve DeBerg	.01	.05
306 Jim Harbaugh	.08	.25
307 Larry Brown DB	.01	.05
308 Roger Ruzek	.01	.05
309 Jessie Tuggle	.01	.05
310 Al Smith	.01	.05
311 Mark Kelso	.01	.05
312 Lawrence Dawsey	.02	.10
313 Steve Bono RC	.08	.25
314 Greg Lloyd	.02	.10
315 Steve Wisniewski	.01	.05
316 Gill Fenerty	.01	.05
317 Mark Stepnoski	.02	.10
318 Derek Russell	.01	.05
319 Chris Martin	.01	.05
320 Shaun Gayle	.01	.05
321 Bob Golic	.01	.05
322 Larry Kelm	.01	.05
323 Mike Brim RC	.01	.05
324 Tommy Kane	.01	.05
325 Mark Schlereth RC	.01	.05
326 Ray Childress	.01	.05
327 Richard Brown RC	.01	.05
328 Vincent Brown	.01	.05
329 Mike Farr UER	.01	.05
330 Eric Swann	.02	.10
331 Bill Fralic	.01	.05
332 Rodney Peete	.02	.10
333 Jerry Gray	.01	.05
334 Ray Berry	.01	.05
335 Dennis Smith	.01	.05
336 Jeff Herrod	.01	.05
337 Tony Mandarich	.01	.05
338 Matt Bahr	.01	.05
339 Mike Saxon	.01	.05
340 Bruce Matthews	.01	.05
341 Rickey Jackson	.01	.05
342 Eric Allen	.01	.05
343 Lonnie Young	.01	.05
344 Steve McMichael	.02	.10
345 Willie Gault	.02	.10
346 Barry Word	.01	.05
347 Rich Camarillo	.01	.05
348 Bill Romanowski	.01	.05
349 Jim Lachey	.01	.05
350 Jim Ritcher	.01	.05
351 Irving Fryar	.02	.10
352 Gary Anderson K	.01	.05
353 Henry Rolling	.01	.05
354 Mark Bortz	.01	.05
355 Mark Clayton	.02	.10
356 Keith Woodside	.01	.05
357 Jonathan Hayes	.01	.05
358 Derrick Fenner	.01	.05
359 Keith Byars	.01	.05
360 Drew Hill	.01	.05
361 Harris Barton	.01	.05
362 John Kidd	.01	.05
363 Aeneas Williams	.02	.10
364 Brian Washington	.01	.05
365 John Stephens	.01	.05
366 Norm Johnson	.01	.05
367 Darryl Henley	.01	.05
368 William White	.01	.05
369 Mark Murphy	.01	.05
370 Myron Guyton	.01	.05
371 Leon Seals	.01	.05
372 Rich Gannon	.08	.25
373 Toi Cook	.01	.05
374 Anthony Johnson	.02	.10
375 Rod Woodson	.08	.25
376 Alexander Wright	.01	.05
377 Kevin Butler	.01	.05
378 Neil Smith	.08	.25
379 Gary Anderson RB	.01	.05
380 Reggie Roby	.01	.05
381 Jeff Bryant	.01	.05
382 Ray Crockett	.01	.05
383 Richard Johnson CB	.01	.05
384 Hassan Jones	.01	.05
385 Karl Mecklenburg	.01	.05
386 Jeff Jaeger	.01	.05
387 Keith Willis	.01	.05
388 Phil Simms	.02	.10
389 Kevin Ross	.01	.05
390 Chris Miller	.02	.10
391 Brian Noble	.01	.05
392 Jamie Dukes RC	.01	.05
393 George Jamison	.01	.05
394 Rickey Dixon	.01	.05
395 Carl Lee	.01	.05
396 Jon Hand	.01	.05
397 Kirby Jackson	.01	.05
398 Pat Terrell	.01	.05
399 Howie Long	.08	.25
400 Michael Young	.01	.05
401 Keith Sims	.01	.05
402 Tommy Barnhardt	.01	.05
403 Greg McMurtry	.01	.05
404 Keith Van Horne	.01	.05
405 Seth Joyner	.01	.05
406 Jim Jeffcoat	.01	.05

407 Courtney Hall .01 .05
408 Tony Covington .01 .05
409 Jacob Green .01 .05
410 Charles Haley .02 .10
411 Darryl Talley .01 .05
412 Jeff Cross .01 .05
413 John Elway .75 2.00
414 Donald Evans .01 .05
415 Jackie Slater .01 .05
416 John Friesz .02 .10
417 Anthony Smith .01 .05
418 Gill Byrd .01 .05
419 Willie Drewrey .01 .05
420 Jay Hilgenberg .01 .05
421 David Treadwell .01 .05
422 Curtis Duncan .01 .05
423 Sammie Smith .01 .05
424 Henry Thomas .01 .05
425 James Lofton .02 .10
426 Fred Marion .01 .05
427 Bryce Paup .08 .25
428 Michael Timpson RC .01 .05
429 Reyna Thompson .01 .05
430 Mike Kenn .01 .05
431 Bill Maas .01 .05
432 Quinn Early .02 .10
433 Everson Walls .01 .05
434 Jimmie Jones .01 .05
435 Dwight Stone .01 .05
436 Harry Colon .01 .05
437 Don Mosebar .01 .05
438 Calvin Williams .02 .10
439 Tom Tupa .01 .05
440 Darrell Green .01 .05
441 Eric Thomas .01 .05
442 Terry Wooden .01 .05
443 Brett Perriman .08 .25
444 Todd Marinovich .01 .05
445 Jim Breech .01 .05
446 Eddie Anderson .01 .05
447 Jay Schroeder .01 .05
448 William Roberts .01 .05
449 Brad Edwards .01 .05
450 Tunch Ilkin .01 .05
451 Ivy Joe Hunter RC .01 .05
452 Robert Clark .01 .05
453 Tim Barnett .01 .05
454 Jarrod Bunch .01 .05
455 Tim Harris .01 .05
456 James Brooks .02 .10
457 Trace Armstrong .01 .05
458 Michael Brooks .01 .05
459 Andy Heck .01 .05
460 Greg Jackson .01 .05
461 Vance Johnson .01 .05
462 Kirk Lowdermilk .01 .05
463 Erik McMillan .01 .05
464 Scott Mersereau .01 .05
465 Jeff Wright .01 .05
466 Mike Tomczak .01 .05
467 David Alexander .01 .05
468 Bryan Millard .01 .05
469 John Randle .02 .10
470 Joel Hilgenberg .01 .05
471 Bennie Thompson RC .01 .05
472 Freeman McNeil .01 .05
473 Terry Orr RC .01 .05
474 Mike Horan .01 .05
475 Leroy Hoard .02 .10
476 Patrick Rowe RC .01 .05
477 Siran Stacy RC .01 .05
478 Amp Lee RC .01 .05
479 Eddie Blake RC .01 .05
480 Joe Bowden RC .01 .05
481 Rod Milstead RC .01 .05
482 Keith Hamilton RC .02 .10
483 Darryl Williams RC .01 .05
484 Robert Porcher RC .08 .25
485 Ed Cunningham RC .01 .05
486 Chris Mims RC .01 .05
487 Chris Hakel RC .01 .05
488 Jimmy Smith RC 1.50 4.00
489 Todd Harrison RC .01 .05
490 Edgar Bennett RC .08 .25
491 Dexter McNabb RC .01 .05
492 Leon Searcy RC .01 .05
493 Tommy Vardell RC .01 .05
494 Terrell Buckley RC .01 .05
495 Kevin Turner RC .01 .05
496 Russ Campbell RC .01 .05
497 Torrance Small RC .02 .10
498 Nate Turner RC .01 .05
499 Cornelius Benton RC .01 .05
500 Matt Elliott RC .01 .05
501 Robert Stewart RC .01 .05
502 Muhammad Shamsid-Deen RC .01 .05
503 George Williams RC .01 .05
504 Pumpy Tudors RC .01 .05
505 Matt LaBounty RC .01 .05
506 Darryl Hardy RC .01 .05
507 Derrick Moore RC .02 .10
508 Willie Clay RC .01 .05
509 Bob Whitfield RC .01 .05
510 Ricardo McDonald RC .01 .05
511 Carlos Huerta RC .01 .05
512 Selwyn Jones RC .01 .05
513 Steve Gordon RC .01 .05
514 Bob Meeks RC .01 .05
515 Bennie Blades CC .01 .05
516 Andre Waters CC .01 .05
517 Bubba McDowell CC .01 .05
518 Kevin Porter CC .01 .05
519 Carnell Lake CC .01 .05
520 Leonard Russell ROY .02 .10
521 Mike Croel ROY .01 .05
522 Lawrence Dawsey ROY .01 .05
523 Moe Gardner ROY .01 .05
524 Steve Broussard LBM .01 .05
525 Dave Meggett LBM .01 .05
526 Darrell Green LBM .01 .05
527 Tony Jones WR LBM .01 .05
528 Barry Sanders LBM .40 1.00
529 Pat Swilling SA .01 .05
530 Reggie White SA .02 .10
531 William Fuller SA .01 .05
532 Simon Fletcher SA .01 .05
533 Derrick Thomas SA .02 .10
534 Mark Rypien MOY .01 .05
535 John Mackey HOF .01 .05
536 John Riggins HOF .02 .10
537 Lem Barney HOF .01 .05
538 Shawn McCarthy RC 90 .01 .05
539 Al Edwards 90 .01 .05
540 Alexander Wright 90 .01 .05
541 Ray Crockett 90 .01 .05
542 Steve Young .08 .25
J.Taylor 90
543 Nate Lewis 90 .01 .05
544 Dexter Carter 90 .01 .05
545 Reggie Rutland 90 .01 .05
546 Jon Vaughn 90 .01 .05
547 Chris Martin 90 .01 .05
548 Warren Moon HL .02 .10
549 Super Bowl Highlights .01 .05
550 Robb Thomas .01 .05
NNO Dick Butkus Promo 4.00 8.00

1992 Score Dream Team

Randomly inserted in 1992 Score foil packs, this 25-card standard-size set pays tribute to some of the NFL's best offensive and defensive players as chosen by Score. The horizontal fronts are full-bleed and display on the left a close-up color head shot and on the right a color player action photo which stands out against a background shot with a yellowish tint. The Score logo is gold-foil stamped at the lower left corner. On the back, a player profile is printed on a background that shades from tan to purple as one moves down the card face.

COMPLETE SET (25) 30.00 60.00
RANDOM INSERTS IN FOIL PACKS
1 Michael Irvin .75 2.00
2 Haywood Jeffires .30 .75
3 Emmitt Smith 8.00 20.00
4 Barry Sanders 6.00 15.00
5 Marv Cook .15 .40
6 Bart Oates .15 .40
7 Steve Wisniewski .15 .40
8 Randall McDaniel .15 .40
9 Jim Lachey .15 .40
10 Lomas Brown .15 .40
11 Reggie White .75 2.00
12 Clyde Simmons .15 .40
13 Derrick Thomas .75 2.00
14 Seth Joyner .15 .40
15 Darryl Talley .15 .40
16 Karl Mecklenburg .15 .40
17 Sam Mills .15 .40
18 Darrell Green .15 .40
19 Steve Atwater .15 .40
20 Mark Carrier DB .15 .40
21 Jeff Gossett UER .15 .40
22 Chip Lohmiller .15 .40
23 Mel Gray .30 .75
24 Steve Tasker .30 .75
25 Mark Rypien .15 .40

1992 Score Gridiron Stars

Three of these standard-size cards were inserted in each 1992 Score jumbo pack. The fronts feature full-bleed color action player photos. Team color-coded stripes intersect a diamond carrying the team logo in the lower left corner. The vertical stripe has "Gridiron Stars" gold-foil stamped on it, while the player's name and position are printed in the horizontal stripe. On the backs, the team logo and color close-up photo appear on the top half, while on the bottom half a white panel presents biography, statistics, and player profile.

COMPLETE SET (45) 3.00 8.00
1 Barry Sanders .75 2.00
2 Mike Croel .01 .05
3 Thurman Thomas .08 .25
4 Lawrence Dawsey .02 .10
5 Brad Baxter .01 .05
6 Moe Gardner .01 .05
7 Emmitt Smith 1.00 2.50
8 Sammie Smith .01 .05
9 Rodney Hampton .02 .10
10 Mark Carrier DB .01 .05
11 Mo Lewis .01 .05
12 Andre Rison .02 .10
13 Eric Green .01 .05
14 Richmond Webb .01 .05
15 Johnny Bailey .01 .05
16 Mike Pritchard .02 .10
17 John Friesz .02 .10
18 Leonard Russell .02 .10
19 Derrick Thomas .08 .25
20 Ken Harvey .01 .05
21 Fred Barnett .08 .25
22 Aeneas Williams .02 .10
23 Marion Butts .01 .05
24 Harold Green .01 .05
25 Michael Irvin .08 .25
26 Dan Owens .01 .05
27 Curtis Duncan .01 .05
28 Rodney Peete .02 .10
29 Brian Blades .02 .10
30 Marv Cook .01 .05
31 Burt Grossman .01 .05
32 Michael Haynes .02 .10
33 Bennie Blades .01 .05
34 Cornelius Bennett .02 .10
35 Louis Oliver .01 .05
36 Rod Woodson .08 .25
37 Steve Wisniewski .01 .05
38 Neil Smith .08 .25
39 Gaston Green .01 .05
40 Jeff Lageman .01 .05
41 Chip Lohmiller .01 .05
42 Tim McDonald .01 .05
43 John Elliott .01 .05
44 Steve Atwater .01 .05
45 Flipper Anderson .01 .05

1992 Score Follies

1 Franco Harris 4.00 10.00
2 Garo Yepremian 2.00 5.00
3 Jim Marshall 2.50 6.00

1992 Score Young Superstars

This 40-card boxed standard-size set features some of the young stars in the NFL. The fronts feature glossy color action player photos inside a green inner border and a purple outer border speckled with black. The player's name appears in white lettering at the top, while the team name is printed at the lower left corner. On a gradated yellow background, the backs carry a color close-up photo, a scouting report feature, career highlights, biography, and statistics.

COMPLETE SET (40) 2.40 6.00
1 Michael Irvin .40 1.00
2 Cortez Kennedy .07 .20
3 Ken Harvey .02 .10
4 Bubba McDowell .02 .10
5 Mark Higgs .02 .10
6 Andre Rison .15 .40
7 Lamar Lathon .02 .10
8 Bennie Blades .02 .10
9 Anthony Johnson .02 .10
10 Vince Buck .02 .10
11 Pat Harlow .02 .10
12 Mike Croel .02 .10
13 Myron Guyton .02 .10
14 Curtis Duncan .02 .10
15 Michael Haynes .15 .40
16 Alexander Wright .02 .10
17 Greg Lewis .02 .10
18 Chip Lohmiller .02 .10
19 Nate Lewis .02 .10
20 Rodney Peete .07 .20
21 Marv Cook .02 .10
22 Lawrence Dawsey .02 .10
23 Pat Terrell .02 .10
24 John Friesz .07 .20
25 Tony Bennett .02 .10
26 Gaston Green .02 .10
27 Kevin Porter .02 .10
28 Mike Pritchard .15 .40
29 Keith Henderson .02 .10
30 Mo Lewis .02 .10
31 John Randle .07 .20
32 Aeneas Williams .07 .20
33 Floyd Turner .02 .10
34 Neil Smith .07 .20
35 Tom Waddle .02 .10
36 Jeff Lageman .02 .10
37 Cris Carter 1.00 2.50
38 Leonard Russell .02 .10
39 Terry McDaniel .02 .10
40 Moe Gardner .02 .10

1993 Score Samples

This six-card standard-size set was issued to preview the 1993 Score regular series. The fronts feature color action player photos bordered in white. The player's name appears in the bottom white border, while the team name is printed vertically in a team color-coded bar that edges the left side of the picture. On team color-coded and pastel panels, the backs present a color head shot, biography, statistics, and player profile. These cards are also issued as an uncut sheet. In a short yellow bar at the lower right corner, the cards are marked "sample card."

COMPLETE SET (6) 2.40 6.00
1 Barry Sanders 1.60 4.00
2 Moe Gardner .20 .50
3 Ricky Watters .40 1.00
4 Todd Lyght .20 .50
5 Rodney Hampton .30 .75
6 Curtis Duncan .20 .50

1993 Score

The 1993 Score football set consists of 440 standard-size cards. Cards were issued in 16 and 35-card packs. . Subsets featured are Rookies (306-315), Super Bowl Highlights (411-412), Double Trouble (413-416), Rookie of the Year (417-420), 90 Plus Club (421-430), Highlights (431-434), and Hall of Fame (436-439). The set concludes with a Man of the Year card (440), honoring Steve Young. Each 16-card pack included one Pinnacle card from a 55-card "Men of Autumn" set not found in regular Pinnacle packs. Dealers could receive one of 3,000 limited-edition autographed Dick Butkus cards for each order of 20 foil boxes. Rookie Cards include Jerome Bettis, Drew Bledsoe, Curtis Conway and Garrison Hearst.

COMPLETE SET (440) 6.00 15.00
1 Barry Sanders .50 1.25
2 Moe Gardner .01 .05
3 Ricky Watters .08 .25
4 Todd Lyght .01 .05
5 Rodney Hampton .02 .10
6 Curtis Duncan .01 .05
7 Barry Word .01 .05
8 Reggie Cobb .01 .05
9 Mike Kenn .01 .05
10 Michael Irvin .08 .25
11 Bryan Cox .01 .05
12 Chris Doleman .01 .05
13 Rod Woodson .08 .25
14 Emmitt Smith .60 1.50
15 Pete Stoyanovich .01 .05
16 Steve Young .30 .75
17 Randall McDaniel .02 .10
18 Cortez Kennedy .02 .10
19 Mel Gray .02 .10
20 Barry Foster .02 .10
21 Tim Brown .08 .25
22 Todd McNair .01 .05
23 Anthony Johnson .02 .10
24 Nate Odomes .01 .05
25 Brett Favre .75 2.00
26 Jack Del Rio .01 .05
27 Terry McDaniel .01 .05
28 Haywood Jeffires .02 .10
29 Jay Novacek .02 .10
30 Wilber Marshall .01 .05
31 Richmond Webb .01 .05
32 Steve Atwater .01 .05
33 James Lofton .02 .10
34 Harold Green .01 .05
35 Eric Metcalf .02 .10
36 Bruce Matthews .01 .05
37 Albert Lewis .01 .05
38 Jeff Herrod .01 .05
39 Vince Workman .01 .05
40 John Elway .60 1.50
41 Brett Perriman .08 .25
42 Jon Vaughn .01 .05
43 Terry Allen .08 .25
44 Clyde Simmons .01 .05
45 Bennie Thompson .01 .05
46 Wendell Davis .01 .05
47 Bobby Hebert .01 .05
48 John Offerdahl .01 .05
49 Jeff Graham .02 .10
50 Steve Wisniewski .01 .05
51 Louis Oliver .01 .05
52 Rohn Stark .01 .05
53 Cleveland Gary .01 .05
54 John Randle .02 .10
55 Jim Everett .02 .10
56 Donnell Woolford .01 .05
57 Pepper Johnson .01 .05
58 Irving Fryar .02 .10
59 Greg Townsend .01 .05
60 Chris Burkett .01 .05
61 Johnny Johnson .01 .05
62 Ronnie Harmon .01 .05
63 Don Griffin .01 .05
64 Wayne Martin .01 .05
65 John L. Williams .01 .05
66 Brad Edwards .01 .05
67 Toi Cook .01 .05
68 Lawrence Dawsey .01 .05
69 Johnny Bailey .01 .05
70 Mike Brim .01 .05
71 Andre Rison .02 .10
72 Cornelius Bennett .02 .10
73 Brad Muster .01 .05
74 Broderick Thomas .01 .05
75 Tom Waddle .01 .05
76 Paul Gruber .01 .05
77 Jackie Harris .01 .05
78 Kenneth Davis .01 .05
79 Norm Johnson .01 .05
80 Jim Jeffcoat .01 .05
81 Chris Warren .02 .10
82 Greg Kragen .01 .05
83 Ricky Reynolds .01 .05
84 Hardy Nickerson .02 .10
85 Brian Mitchell .02 .10
86 Rufus Porter .01 .05
87 Greg Jackson .01 .05
88 Seth Joyner .01 .05
89 Tim Grunhard .01 .05
90 Tim Harris .01 .05
91 Sterling Sharpe .08 .25
92 Daniel Stubbs .01 .05
93 Rob Burnett .01 .05
94 Rich Camarillo .01 .05
95 Al Smith .01 .05
96 Thurman Thomas .08 .25
97 Morten Andersen .01 .05
98 Reggie White .08 .25
99 Gill Byrd .01 .05
100 Pierce Holt .01 .05
101 Tim McGee .01 .05
102 Rickey Jackson .01 .05
103 Vince Newsome .01 .05
104 Chris Spielman .02 .10
105 Tim McDonald .01 .05
106 James Francis .01 .05
107 Andre Tippett .01 .05
108 Sam Mills .01 .05
109 Hugh Millen .01 .05
110 Brad Baxter .01 .05
111 Ricky Sanders .01 .05
112 Marion Butts .01 .05
113 Fred Barnett .02 .10
114 Wade Wilson .01 .05
115 Dave Meggett .01 .05
116 Kevin Greene .02 .10
117 Reggie Langhorne .01 .05
118 Simon Fletcher .01 .05
119 Tommy Vardell .01 .05
120 Darion Conner .01 .05
121 Darren Lewis .01 .05
122 Charles Mann .01 .05
123 David Fulcher .01 .05
124 Tommy Kane .01 .05
125 Richard Brown .01 .05
126 Nate Lewis .01 .05
127 Tony Tolbert .01 .05
128 Greg Lloyd .02 .10
129 Herman Moore .08 .25
130 Robert Massey .01 .05
131 Chris Jacke .01 .05
132 Keith Byars .01 .05
133 William Fuller .01 .05
134 Rob Moore .02 .10
135 Duane Bickett .01 .05
136 Jarrod Bunch .01 .05
137 Ethan Horton .01 .05
138 Leonard Russell .02 .10
139 Darryl Henley .01 .05
140 Tony Bennett .01 .05
141 Harry Newsome .01 .05
142 Kelvin Martin .01 .05
143 Audray McMillian .01 .05
144 Chip Lohmiller .01 .05
145 Henry Jones .01 .05
146 Rod Bernstine .01 .05
147 Darryl Talley .01 .05
148 Clarence Verdin .01 .05
149 Derrick Thomas .08 .25
150 Raleigh McKenzie .01 .05
151 Phil Hansen .01 .05
152 Lin Elliott RC .01 .05
153 Chip Banks .01 .05
154 Shannon Sharpe .08 .25
155 David Williams .01 .05
156 Gaston Green .01 .05
157 Trace Armstrong .01 .05
158 Todd Scott .01 .05
159 Stan Humphries .02 .10
160 Christian Okoye .01 .05
161 Dennis Smith .01 .05
162 Derek Kennard .01 .05
163 Melvin Jenkins .01 .05
164 Tommy Barnhardt .01 .05
165 Eugene Robinson .01 .05
166 Tom Rathman .01 .05
167 Chris Chandler .02 .10
168 Steve Broussard .01 .05
169 Wymon Henderson .01 .05
170 Bryce Paup .02 .10
171 Kent Hull .01 .05
172 Willie Davis .08 .25
173 Richard Dent .02 .10
174 Rodney Peete .01 .05
175 Clay Matthews .02 .10
176 Erik Williams .01 .05
177 Mike Cofer .01 .05
178 Mark Kelso .01 .05
179 Kurt Gouveia .01 .05
180 Keith McCants .01 .05
181 Jim Arnold .01 .05
182 Sean Jones .01 .05
183 Chuck Cecil .01 .05
184 Mark Rypien .01 .05
185 William Perry .02 .10
186 Mark Jackson .01 .05
187 Jim Dombrowski .01 .05
188 Heath Sherman .01 .05
189 Bubba McDowell .01 .05
190 Fuad Reveiz .01 .05
191 Darren Perry .01 .05
192 Karl Mecklenburg .01 .05
193 Frank Reich .02 .10
194 Tony Casillas .01 .05
195 Jerry Ball .01 .05
196 Jessie Hester .01 .05
197 David Lang .01 .05
198 Sean Landeta .01 .05
199 Jerry Gray .01 .05
200 Mark Higgs .01 .05
201 Bruce Armstrong .01 .05
202 Vaughan Johnson .01 .05
203 Calvin Williams .02 .10
204 Leonard Marshall .01 .05
205 Mike Munchak .02 .10
206 Kevin Ross .01 .05
207 Daryl Johnston .08 .25
208 Jay Schroeder .01 .05
209 Mo Lewis .01 .05
210 Carlton Haselrig .01 .05
211 Cris Carter .08 .25
212 Marv Cook .01 .05
213 Mark Duper .01 .05
214 Jackie Slater .01 .05
215 Mike Prior .01 .05
216 Warren Moon .08 .25
217 Mike Saxon .01 .05
218 Derrick Fenner .01 .05
219 Brian Washington .01 .05
220 Jessie Tuggle .01 .05
221 Jeff Hostetler .02 .10
222 Deion Sanders .20 .50
223 Neal Anderson .01 .05
224 Kevin Mack .01 .05
225 Tommy Maddox .08 .25
226 Neil Smith .08 .25
227 Ronnie Lott .02 .10
228 Flipper Anderson .01 .05
229 Keith Jackson .02 .10
230 Pat Swilling .01 .05
231 Carl Banks .01 .05
232 Eric Allen .01 .05
233 Randal Hill .01 .05
234 Burt Grossman .01 .05
235 Jerry Rice .40 1.00
236 Santana Dotson .02 .10
237 Andre Reed .02 .10
238 Troy Aikman .30 .75
239 Ray Childress .01 .05
240 Phil Simms .02 .10
241 Steve McMichael .02 .10
242 Browning Nagle .01 .05
243 Anthony Miller .02 .10
244 Earnest Byner .01 .05
245 Jay Hilgenberg .01 .05
246 Jeff George .08 .25
247 Marco Coleman .01 .05
248 Mark Carrier DB .01 .05
249 Howie Long .08 .25
250 Ed McCaffrey .08 .25
251 Jim Kelly .08 .25
252 Henry Ellard .02 .10
253 Joe Montana .60 1.50
254 Dale Carter .01 .05
255 Boomer Esiason .02 .10
256 Gary Clark .02 .10
257 Carl Pickens .02 .10
258 Dave Krieg .02 .10
259 Russell Maryland .01 .05
260 Randall Cunningham .08 .25
261 Leslie O'Neal .02 .10
262 Vinny Testaverde .02 .10
263 Ricky Ervins .01 .05
264 Chris Mims .01 .05
265 Dan Marino .60 1.50
266 Eric Martin .01 .05
267 Bruce Smith .08 .25
268 Jim Harbaugh .08 .25
269 Steve Emtman .01 .05
270 Ricky Proehl .01 .05
271 Vaughn Dunbar .01 .05
272 Junior Seau .00 .25
273 Sean Gilbert .02 .10
274 Jim Lachey .01 .05
275 Dalton Hilliard .01 .05
276 David Klingler .01 .05
277 Robert Jones .01 .05
278 David Treadwell .01 .05
279 Tracy Scroggins .01 .05
280 Terrell Buckley .01 .05
281 Quentin Coryatt .02 .10
282 Jason Hanson .01 .05
283 Shane Conlan .01 .05
284 Guy McIntyre .01 .05
285 Gary Zimmerman .01 .05
286 Marty Carter .01 .05
287 Jim Sweeney .01 .05
288 Arthur Marshall RC .01 .05
289 Eugene Chung .01 .05
290 Mike Pritchard .02 .10
291 Jim Ritcher .01 .05
292 Todd Marinovich .01 .05
293 Courtney Hall .01 .05
294 Mark Collins .01 .05
295 Troy Auzenne .01 .05
296 Aeneas Williams .01 .05
297 Andy Heck .01 .05
298 Shaun Gayle .01 .05
299 Kevin Fagan .01 .05
300 Carnell Lake .01 .05
301 Bernie Kosar .02 .10
302 Maurice Hurst .01 .05
303 Mike Merriweather .01 .05
304 Reggie Roby .01 .05
305 Darryl Williams .01 .05
306 Jerome Bettis RC 2.50 5.00
307 Curtis Conway RC .15 .40
308 Drew Bledsoe RC 1.00 2.50
309 John Copeland RC .02 .10
310 Eric Curry RC .01 .05
311 Lincoln Kennedy RC .01 .05
312 Dan Williams RC .01 .05
313 Patrick Bates RC .01 .05
314 Tom Carter RC .02 .10
315 Garrison Hearst RC .30 .75
316 Joel Hilgenberg .01 .05
317 Harris Barton .01 .05
318 Jeff Lageman .01 .05
319 Charles Mincy RC .01 .05
320 Ricardo McDonald .01 .05
321 Lorenzo White .01 .05
322 Troy Vincent .01 .05
323 Bennie Blades .01 .05
324 Dana Hall .01 .05
325 Ken Norton Jr. .02 .10
326 Will Wolford .01 .05
327 Neil O'Donnell .08 .25
328 Tracy Simien .01 .05
329 Darrell Green .01 .05
330 Kyle Clifton .01 .05
331 Elbert Shelley RC .01 .05
332 Jeff Wright .01 .05
333 Mike Johnson .01 .05
334 John Gesek .01 .05
335 Michael Brooks .01 .05
336 George Jamison .01 .05
337 Johnny Holland .01 .05
338 Lamar Lathon .01 .05
339 Bern Brostek .01 .05
340 Steve Jordan .01 .05
341 Gene Atkins .01 .05
342 Aaron Wallace .01 .05
343 Adrian Cooper .01 .05
344 Amp Lee .01 .05
345 Vincent Brown .01 .05
346 James Hasty .01 .05
347 Ron Hall .01 .05
348 Matt Elliott .01 .05
349 Tim Krumrie .01 .05
350 Mark Stepnoski .01 .05
351 Matt Stover .01 .05
352 James Washington .01 .05
353 Marc Spindler .01 .05
354 Frank Warren .01 .05
355 Vai Sikahema .01 .05
356 Dan Saleaumua .01 .05
357 Mark Clayton .01 .05
358 Brent Jones .02 .10
359 Andy Harmon RC .02 .10
360 Anthony Parker .01 .05
361 Chris Hinton .01 .05
362 Greg Montgomery .01 .05
363 Greg McMurtry .01 .05
364 Craig Heyward .02 .10
365 D.J. Johnson .01 .05
366 Bill Romanowski .01 .05
367 Steve Christie .01 .05
368 Art Monk .02 .10
369 Howard Ballard .01 .05
370 Andre Collins .01 .05
371 Alvin Harper .02 .10
372 Blaise Winter RC .01 .05
373 Al Del Greco .01 .05
374 Eric Green .01 .05
375 Chris Mohr .01 .05
376 Tom Newberry .01 .05
377 Cris Dishman .01 .05
378 Jumpy Geathers .01 .05
379 Don Mosebar .01 .05
380 Andre Ware .01 .05
381 Marvin Washington .01 .05
382 Bobby Humphrey .01 .05
383 Marc Logan .01 .05
384 Lomas Brown .01 .05
385 Steve Tasker .02 .10
386 Chris Miller .02 .10
387 Tony Paige .01 .05
388 Charles Haley .02 .10
389 Rich Moran .01 .05
390 Mike Sherrard .01 .05
391 Nick Lowery .01 .05
392 Henry Thomas .01 .05
393 Keith Sims .01 .05
394 Thomas Everett .01 .05
395 Steve Wallace .01 .05
396 John Carney .01 .05
397 Tim Johnson .01 .05
398 Jeff Gossett .01 .05
399 Anthony Smith .01 .05
400 Kelvin Pritchett .01 .05
401 Dermontti Dawson .02 .10
402 Alfred Williams .01 .05
403 Michael Haynes .02 .10
404 Bart Oates .01 .05
405 Ken Lanier .01 .05
406 Vencie Glenn .01 .05
407 John Taylor .02 .10
408 Nate Newton .02 .10
409 Mark Carrier WR .02 .10
410 Ken Harvey .01 .05
411 Troy Aikman SB .15 .40
412 Charles Haley SB .01 .05
413 Warren Moon .02 .10
Jeffires DT
414 Henry Jones DT .01 .05
415 Rickey Jackson DT .01 .05
416 Clyde Simmons DT .01 .05
417 Dale Carter ROY .01 .05
418 Carl Pickens ROY .02 .10
419 Vaughn Dunbar ROY .01 .05
420 Santana Dotson ROY .01 .05
421 Steve Emtman 90 .01 .05
422 Louis Oliver 90 .01 .05
423 Carl Pickens 90 .02 .10
424 Eddie Anderson 90 .01 .05
425 Deion Sanders 90 .08 .25
426 Jon Vaughn 90 .01 .05
427 Darren Lewis 90 .01 .05
428 Kevin Ross 90 .01 .05
429 David Brandon 90 .01 .05
430 Dave Meggett 90 .01 .05
431 Jerry Rice HL .20 .50
432 Sterling Sharpe HL .02 .10
433 Art Monk HL .01 .05
434 James Lofton HL .01 .05
435 Lawrence Taylor .02 .10
436 Bill Walsh HOF RC .02 .10
437 Chuck Noll HOF .02 .10
438 Dan Fouts HOF .01 .05
439 Larry Little HOF .01 .05
440 Steve Young MOY .15 .40
NNO Dick Butkus AU/3000 25.00 50.00

1993 Score Dream Team

Issued one per 1993 Score 35-card jumbo packs, this 26-card standard-size set features the best offensive (1-13) and defensive (14-26) players by position as selected by Score. On a background consisting of a cloudy sky with a dark brown tint, the horizontal fronts have a color player cut-out emerging out of a black stripe on the left portion while the right portion displays a close-up color player cut-out. On the backs, the upper portion displays a larger, fuzzy version of the same player cut-out on the front left portion. The lower portion is a thick black stripe featuring a brief player profile. The team logo in a circle straddles the two portions.

COMPLETE SET (26) 12.50 25.00
ONE PER SUPER PACK
1 Steve Young 2.00 5.00
2 Emmitt Smith 4.00 10.00
3 Barry Foster .25 .60
4 Sterling Sharpe .60 1.50
5 Jerry Rice 2.50 6.00
6 Keith Jackson .25 .60
7 Steve Wallace .10 .30
8 Richmond Webb .10 .30
9 Guy McIntyre .10 .30
10 Carlton Haselrig .10 .30
11 Bruce Matthews .10 .30
12 Morten Andersen .10 .30
13 Rich Camarillo .10 .30
14 Deion Sanders 1.25 3.00
15 Steve Tasker .25 .60
16 Clyde Simmons .10 .30
17 Reggie White .60 1.50
18 Cortez Kennedy .25 .60
19 Rod Woodson .60 1.50
20 Terry McDaniel .10 .30
21 Chuck Cecil .10 .30
22 Steve Atwater .10 .30
23 Bryan Cox .10 .30
24 Derrick Thomas .60 1.50
25 Wilber Marshall .10 .30
26 Sam Mills .10 .30

1993 Score Franchise

Randomly inserted in 1993 Score foil packs at a rate of approximately one in 24, this 28-card standard-size set features a top player from each NFL team. Fronts feature a player photo that stands out from a dark shaded background. The background contain a ghosted player photo. Backs have a small write-up and a close-up shot of the player. The cards are arranged in alphabetical order by team.

COMPLETE SET (28) 30.00 80.00
STATED ODDS 1:24
1 Andre Rison .50 1.25
2 Thurman Thomas 1.25 3.00
3 Richard Dent .50 1.25
4 Harold Green .25 .60
5 Eric Metcalf .50 1.25
6 Emmitt Smith 8.00 20.00
7 John Elway 8.00 20.00
8 Barry Sanders 6.00 15.00
9 Sterling Sharpe 1.25 3.00
10 Warren Moon 1.25 3.00
11 Jeff Herrod .25 .60
12 Derrick Thomas 1.25 3.00
13 Steve Wisniewski .25 .60
14 Cleveland Gary .25 .60
15 Dan Marino 8.00 20.00
16 Chris Doleman .25 .60
17 Marv Cook .25 .60
18 Rickey Jackson .25 .60
19 Rodney Hampton .50 1.25
20 Jeff Lageman .25 .60
21 Clyde Simmons .25 .60
22 Rich Camarillo .25 .60
23 Rod Woodson 1.25 3.00
24 Ronnie Harmon .25 .60
25 Steve Young 4.00 10.00
26 Cortez Kennedy .50 1.25
27 Reggie Cobb .25 .60
28 Mark Rypien .25 .60

1993 Score Ore-Ida QB Club

This set of 18 standard-size cards could be obtained by the purchase of specially marked Ore-Ida products (Bagel Bites, Twice Baked, or Topped Baked Potatoes), filling out the order form on one of the packages, and mailing it plus six proofs-of-purchase and 1.50. Collectors would then receive two nine-card packs. For three proofs-of-purchase and 1.00, collectors could receive one nine-card set. The packs are sequentially numbered, with the first pack containing cards 1-9 and the second containing cards 10-18. Aside from sporting different color player action photos on their fronts (Hostetler and Esiason are pictured in their new Raiders and Jets uniforms, respectively), and the different numbering on the backs, the cards are identical in design to the regular 1993 Score issue.

COMPLETE SET (18) 16.00 40.00
1 John Elway 4.00 10.00
2 Steve Young 1.60 4.00
3 Warren Moon .80 2.00
4 Randall Cunningham .80 2.00
5 Jeff Hostetler .30 .75
6 Phil Simms .40 1.00
7 Jim Everett .30 .75
8 David Klingler .30 .75
9 Brett Favre 4.00 10.00
10 Troy Aikman 2.00 5.00
11 Dan Marino 4.00 10.00
12 Mark Rypien .30 .75
13 Jim Kelly .80 2.00
14 Jim Harbaugh .40 1.00
15 Bernie Kosar .30 .75
16 Boomer Esiason .40 1.00
17 Chris Miller .30 .75
18 Neil O'Donnell .30 .75

1994 Score Samples

These ten sample standard-size cards were issued to herald the August release of the 1994 Score football set. The cards feature on their fronts color player action shots with irregular purple and teal borders, except for the Glyn Milburn card (112), which is a sample foil card from the parallel Gold Zone set. The player's name appears in white lettering below the photo; his position appears in white lettering within a black box at the upper left. The multicolored back carries the player's name and team logo at the top, followed below by his position, biography, profile, and statistics.

COMPLETE SET (10) 1.60 4.00
21 Jerome Bettis .80 2.00
25 Steve Jordan .15 .40
50 Shannon Sharpe .15 .40
112 Glyn Milburn FOIL .15 .40
161 Ronnie Lott .15 .40
257 Derrick Thomas .30 .75
0 Generic Rookie Card .08 .25
NNO Score Ad Card Retail .08 .25
NNO Sample Redemption Card .08 .25
NNO Score Ad Card Hobby .08 .25

1994 Score

The 1994 Score football set consists of 330 standard-size cards. Cards were issued in 14-card foil packs as well as in jumbo packs. Topical subsets featured are Rookies (276-305) and Team Checklists (306-319). Cards of players that were named All-Pro, have an All-Pro (AP) notation on front. Randomly inserted redemption cards gave collectors an opportunity to receive ten cards of top rookie players in their NFL uniforms. Rookie Cards include Derrick Alexander, Marshall Faulk, William Floyd, Greg Hill, Charles Johnson, Errict Rhett, Darnay Scott and Heath Shuler.

COMPLETE SET (330) 6.00 15.00
1 Barry Sanders .50 1.25
2 Troy Aikman .30 .75
3 Sterling Sharpe .02 .10
4 Deion Sanders .20 .50
5 Bruce Smith .08 .25
6 Eric Metcalf .02 .10
7 John Elway .60 1.50
8 Bruce Matthews .01 .05
9 Rickey Jackson .01 .05
10 Cortez Kennedy .02 .10
11 Jerry Rice .30 .75
12 Stanley Richard .01 .05
13 Rod Woodson .02 .10
14 Eric Swann .02 .10
15 Eric Allen .01 .05
16 Richard Dent .02 .10
17 Carl Pickens .02 .10
18 Rohn Stark .01 .05
19 Marcus Allen .08 .25
20 Steve Wisniewski .01 .05
21 Jerome Bettis .20 .50
22 Darrell Green .01 .05
23 Lawrence Dawsey .01 .05
24 Larry Centers .08 .25
25 Steve Jordan .01 .05
26 Johnny Johnson .01 .05
27 Phil Simms .02 .10
28 Bruce Armstrong .01 .05
29 Willie Roaf .01 .05
30 Andre Rison .02 .10
31 Henry Jones .01 .05
32 Warren Moon .08 .25
33 Sean Gilbert .01 .05
34 Ben Coates .02 .10
35 Seth Joyner .01 .05
36 Ronnie Harmon .01 .05
37 Quentin Coryatt .01 .05
38 Ricky Sanders .01 .05
39 Gerald Williams .01 .05
40 Emmitt Smith .40 1.00
41 Jason Hanson .01 .05
42 Kevin Smith .01 .05
43 Irving Fryar .02 .10
44 Boomer Esiason .02 .10
45 Darryl Talley .01 .05
46 Paul Gruber .01 .05
47 Anthony Smith .01 .05
48 John Copeland .01 .05
49 Michael Jackson .02 .10
50 Shannon Sharpe .02 .10
51 Reggie White .08 .25
52 Andre Collins .01 .05
53 Jack Del Rio .01 .05
54 John Elliott .01 .05
55 Kevin Greene .02 .10
56 Steve Young .25 .60
57 Erric Pegram .01 .05
58 Donnell Woolford .01 .05
59 Darryl Williams .01 .05
60 Michael Irvin .08 .25
61 Mel Gray .01 .05
62 Greg Montgomery .01 .05
63 Neil Smith .02 .10
64 Andy Harmon .01 .05
65 Dan Marino .60 1.50
66 Leonard Russell .01 .05
67 Joe Montana .60 1.50
68 John Taylor .02 .10
69 Cris Dishman .01 .05
70 Cornelius Bennett .02 .10
71 Harold Green .01 .05
72 Anthony Pleasant .01 .05
73 Dennis Smith .01 .05
74 Bryce Paup .02 .10
75 Jeff George .08 .25
76 Henry Ellard .02 .10
77 Randall McDaniel .02 .10
78 Derek Brown RBK .01 .05
79 Johnny Mitchell .01 .05
80 Leroy Thompson .01 .05
81 Junior Seau .08 .25
82 Kelvin Martin .01 .05
83 Guy McIntyre .01 .05
84 Elbert Shelley .01 .05
85 Louis Oliver .01 .05
86 Tommy Vardell .01 .05
87 Jeff Herrod .01 .05
88 Edgar Bennett .08 .25
89 Reggie Langhorne .01 .05
90 Terry Kirby .08 .25
91 Marcus Robertson .01 .05
92 Mark Collins .01 .05
93 Calvin Williams .02 .10
94 Barry Foster .01 .05
95 Brent Jones .02 .10
96 Reggie Cobb .01 .05
97 Ray Childress .01 .05
98 Chris Miller .01 .05
99 John Carney .01 .05
100 Ricky Proehl .01 .05
101 Renaldo Turnbull .01 .05
102 John Randle .02 .10
103 Flipper Anderson .01 .05
104 Scottie Graham RC .02 .10
105 Webster Slaughter .01 .05
106 Tyrone Hughes .02 .10
107 Ken Norton Jr. .02 .10
108 Jim Kelly .08 .25
109 Michael Haynes .02 .10
110 Mark Carrier DB .01 .05
111 Eddie Murray .01 .05
112 Glyn Milburn .02 .10
113 Jackie Harris .01 .05
114 Dean Biasucci .01 .05
115 Tim Brown .08 .25
116 Mark Higgs .01 .05
117 Steve Emtman .01 .05
118 Clay Matthews .01 .05
119 Clyde Simmons .01 .05
120 Howard Ballard .01 .05
121 Ricky Watters .02 .10
122 William Fuller .01 .05
123 Robert Brooks .08 .25
124 Brian Blades .02 .10
125 Leslie O'Neal .01 .05
126 Gary Clark .02 .10
127 Jim Sweeney .01 .05
128 Vaughan Johnson .01 .05
129 Gary Brown .01 .05
130 Todd Lyght .01 .05
131 Nick Lowery .01 .05
132 Ernest Givins .02 .10
133 Lomas Brown .01 .05
134 Craig Erickson .01 .05
135 James Francis .01 .05

136 Andre Reed .02 .10
137 Jim Everett .02 .10
138 Nate Odomes .01 .05
139 Tom Waddle .01 .05
140 Stevon Moore .01 .05
141 Rod Bernstine .01 .05
142 Brett Favre .60 1.50
143 Roosevelt Potts .01 .05
144 Chester McGlockton .01 .05
145 LeRoy Butler .01 .05
146 Charles Haley .02 .10
147 Rodney Hampton .02 .10
148 George Teague .01 .05
149 Gary Anderson K .01 .05
150 Mark Stepnoski .01 .05
151 Courtney Hawkins .01 .05
152 Tim Grunhard .01 .05
153 David Klingler .01 .05
154 Erik Williams .01 .05
155 Herman Moore .08 .25
156 Daryl Johnston .02 .10
157 Chris Zorich .01 .05
158 Shane Conlan .01 .05
159 Santana Dotson .02 .10
160 Sam Mills .01 .05
161 Ronnie Lott .02 .10
162 Jesse Sapolu .01 .05
163 Marion Butts .01 .05
164 Eugene Robinson .01 .05
165 Mark Schlereth .01 .05
166 John L. Williams .01 .05
167 Anthony Miller .02 .10
168 Rich Camarillo .01 .05
169 Jeff Lageman .01 .05
170 Michael Brooks .01 .05
171 Scott Mitchell .02 .10
172 Duane Bickett .01 .05
173 Willie Davis .02 .10
174 Maurice Hurst .01 .05
175 Brett Perriman .02 .10
176 Jay Novacek .02 .10
177 Terry Allen .02 .10
178 Pete Metzelaars .01 .05
179 Erik Kramer .02 .10
180 Neal Anderson .01 .05
181 Ethan Horton .01 .05
182 Tony Bennett .01 .05
183 Gary Zimmerman .01 .05
184 Jeff Hostetler .02 .10
185 Jeff Cross .01 .05
186 Vincent Brown .01 .05
187 Herschel Walker .02 .10
188 Courtney Hall .01 .05
189 Norm Johnson .01 .05
190 Hardy Nickerson .02 .10
191 Greg Townsend .01 .05
192 Mike Munchak .02 .10
193 Dante Jones .01 .05
194 Vinny Testaverde .02 .10
195 Vance Johnson .01 .05
196 Chris Jacke .01 .05
197 Will Wolford .01 .05
198 Terry McDaniel .01 .05
199 Bryan Cox .01 .05
200 Nate Newton .01 .05
201 Keith Byars .01 .05
202 Neil O'Donnell .08 .25
203 Harris Barton .01 .05
204 Thurman Thomas .08 .25
205 Jeff Query .01 .05
206 Russell Maryland .01 .05
207 Pat Swilling .01 .05
208 Haywood Jeffires .02 .10
209 John Alt .01 .05
210 O.J. McDuffie .08 .25
211 Keith Sims .01 .05
212 Eric Martin .01 .05
213 Kyle Clifton .01 .05
214 Luis Sharpe .01 .05
215 Thomas Everett .01 .05
216 Chris Warren .02 .10
217 Chris Doleman .01 .05
218 Tony Jones T .01 .05
219 Karl Mecklenburg .01 .05
220 Rob Moore .02 .10
221 Jessie Hester .01 .05
222 Jeff Jaeger .01 .05
223 Keith Jackson .01 .05
224 Mo Lewis .01 .05
225 Mike Horan .01 .05
226 Eric Green .01 .05
227 Jim Ritcher .01 .05
228 Eric Curry .01 .05
229 Stan Humphries .02 .10
230 Mike Johnson .01 .05
231 Alvin Harper .02 .10
232 Bennie Blades .01 .05
233 Cris Carter .20 .50
234 Morten Andersen .01 .05
235 Brian Washington .01 .05
236 Eric Hill .01 .05
237 Natrone Means .08 .25
238 Carlton Bailey .01 .05
239 Anthony Carter .02 .10
240 Jessie Tuggle .01 .05
241 Tim Irwin .01 .05
242 Mark Carrier WR .02 .10
243 Steve Atwater .01 .05
244 Sean Jones .01 .05
245 Bernie Kosar .02 .10
246 Richmond Webb .01 .05
247 Dave Meggett .01 .05
248 Vincent Brisby .02 .10
249 Fred Barnett .02 .10
250 Greg Lloyd .02 .10
251 Tim McDonald .01 .05
252 Mike Pritchard .01 .05
253 Greg Robinson .01 .05
254 Tony McGee .01 .05
255 Chris Spielman .02 .10
256 Keith Loneker RC .01 .05
257 Derrick Thomas .08 .25
258 Wayne Martin .01 .05
259 Art Monk .02 .10
260 Andy Heck .01 .05
261 Chip Lohmiller .01 .05
262 Simon Fletcher .01 .05
263 Ricky Reynolds .01 .05
264 Chris Hinton .01 .05
265 Ronald Moore .01 .05
266 Rocket Ismail .02 .10
267 Pete Stoyanovich .01 .05
268 Mark Jackson .01 .05
269 Randall Cunningham .08 .25
270 Dermontti Dawson .02 .10
271 Bill Romanowski .01 .05
272 Tim Johnson .01 .05
273 Steve Tasker .02 .10
274 Keith Hamilton .01 .05
275 Pierce Holt .01 .05
276 Heath Shuler RC .08 .25
277 Marshall Faulk RC 2.00 5.00
278 Charles Johnson RC .08 .25
279 Sam Adams RC .02 .10
280 Trev Alberts RC .02 .10
281 Derrick Alexander WR RC .08 .25
282 Bryant Young RC .15 .40
283 Greg Hill RC .08 .25
284 Darnay Scott RC .20 .50
285 Willie McGinest RC .08 .25
286 Thomas Randolph RC .01 .05
287 Errict Rhett RC .08 .25
288 Lamar Smith RC .50 1.25
289 William Floyd RC .08 .25
290 Johnnie Morton RC .20 .50
291 Jamir Miller RC .02 .10
292 David Palmer RC .08 .25
293 Dan Wilkinson RC .02 .10
294 Trent Dilfer RC .50 1.25
295 Antonio Langham RC .02 .10
296 Chuck Levy RC .01 .05
297 John Thierry RC .01 .05
298 Kevin Lee RC .01 .05
299 Aaron Glenn RC .08 .25
300 Charlie Garner RC .50 1.25
301 Lonnie Johnson RC .01 .05
302 LeShon Johnson RC .02 .10
303 Thomas Lewis RC .02 .10
304 Ryan Yarborough RC .01 .05
305 Mario Bates RC .08 .25
306 Cardinals/Bills TC .01 .05
307 Falcons/Bengals TC .01 .05
308 Bears/Browns TC .01 .05
309 Cowboys/Broncos TC .01 .05
310 Lions/Oilers TC .01 .05
311 Packers/Colts TC .01 .05
312 Rams/Chiefs TC .01 .05
313 Vikings/Raiders TC .01 .05
314 Saints/Dolphins TC .01 .05
315 Giants/Patriots TC .01 .05
316 Eagles/Jets TC .01 .05
317 49ers/Steelers TC .01 .05
318 Buccaneers/Chargers TC .01 .05
319 Redskins/Seahawks TC .01 .05
320 Garrison Hearst FF .08 .25
321 Drew Bledsoe FF .30 .75
322 Tyrone Hughes FF .02 .10
323 James Jett FF .01 .05
324 Tom Carter FF .01 .05
325 Reggie Brooks FF .01 .05
326 Dana Stubblefield FF .02 .10
327 Jerome Bettis FF .08 .25
328 Chris Slade FF .01 .05
329 Rick Mirer FF .08 .25
330 Emmitt Smith MVP .20 .50

1994 Score Gold Zone

COMPLETE SET (330) 50.00 100.00
*STARS: 3X TO 6X BASIC CARDS
*RCs: 1.5X TO 3X BASIC CARDS
ONE PER PACK

1994 Score Dream Team

Randomly inserted in '94 Score packs, these 18 standard-size cards feature on their horizontal borderless fronts multiple holographic player images. A replica of the player's 1989 Score card appears on a colorful and borderless mottled background on the back. The cards are numbered on the back with a "DT" prefix.

COMPLETE SET (18) 30.00 80.00
STATED ODDS 1:72
DT1 Troy Aikman 6.00 15.00
DT2 Steve Atwater .40 1.00
DT3 Cornelius Bennett .75 2.00
DT4 Tim Brown 2.00 5.00
DT5 Michael Irvin 2.00 5.00
DT6 Bruce Matthews .40 1.00
DT7 Eric Metcalf .75 2.00
DT8 Anthony Miller .75 2.00
DT9 Jerry Rice 6.00 15.00
DT10 Andre Rison .75 2.00
DT11 Barry Sanders 10.00 25.00
DT12 Deion Sanders 4.00 10.00
DT13 Sterling Sharpe .75 2.00
DT14 Neil Smith .75 2.00
DT15 Derrick Thomas 2.00 5.00
DT16 Thurman Thomas 2.00 5.00
DT17 Rod Woodson .75 2.00
DT18 Steve Young 5.00 12.00

1994 Score Rookie Redemption

Randomly inserted in packs at a rate of one in 72, were 10 Rookie Redemption cards that could be exchanged for the player indicated on the card. The player cards feature the rookie in his NFL uniform. Referred to as "Gold Zone" technology, the player photo stands out on a metallic card with gold borders at the top and bottom. The backs have a small up-close photo and highlights from early in the 1994 season.

COMPLETE SET (10) 60.00 120.00
1 Heath Shuler 2.50 6.00
2 Trent Dilfer 12.00 30.00
3 Marshall Faulk 30.00 80.00
4 Charlie Garner 6.00 15.00
5 LeShon Johnson 1.25 3.00
6 Charles Johnson 2.50 6.00
7 Errict Rhett 2.50 6.00
8 Lake Dawson .60 1.50
9 Bert Emanuel 2.50 6.00
10 Greg Hill 2.50 6.00

1994 Score Sophomore Showcase

Randomly inserted in jumbo packs at a rate of one in four, this 18-card standard-size set highlights top second year players. Full-bleed fronts have a player photo over a blurred background. The Sophomore Showcase logo is at bottom left. The backs contain a small photo and a brief write-up. The cards are numbered with an SS prefix.

COMPLETE SET (18) 30.00 60.00
RANDOM INSERTS IN JUMBO PACKS
SS1 Jerome Bettis 4.00 10.00
SS2 Rick Mirer 2.00 5.00
SS3 Reggie Brooks .40 1.00
SS4 Drew Bledsoe 6.00 15.00
SS5 Ronald Moore .40 1.00
SS6 Derek Brown RBK .40 1.00
SS7 Roosevelt Potts .40 1.00
SS8 Terry Kirby 2.00 5.00
SS9 James Jett .40 1.00
SS10 Vincent Brisby .75 2.00
SS11 Tyrone Hughes .75 2.00
SS12 Rocket Ismail .75 2.00
SS13 Tony McGee .40 1.00
SS14 Garrison Hearst 2.00 5.00
SS15 Eric Curry .40 1.00
SS16 Dana Stubblefield .75 2.00
SS17 Tom Carter .40 1.00
SS18 Chris Slade .40 1.00

1995 Score Promos

These cards were issued to preview the 1995 Score series. Four cards were packaged together in a cello wrapper. The Promos can easily be distinguished from their regular issue counterparts by the disclaimer "PROMO" stamped in black across their fronts or the word "Promotional" across the cardbacks.

*PROMO: .8X TO 2X BASIC CARDS
NNO Title Card .20 .50

1995 Score

This 275-card standard-size set is issued in 12 card foil-packs (suggested retail price of 99 cents per pack) and 20-card jumbo packs. Rookie Cards in this set include Jeff Blake, Ki-Jana Carter, Kerry Collins, Joey Galloway, Steve McNair, Rashaan Salaam, Kordell Stewart, J.J Stokes and Michael Westbrook. A foil Steve Young card was distributed to collectors who correctly identified intentional errors from a Pinnacle print ad run throughout the season. The contest was the third part following two baseball ads, thus the AD3 card numbering.

COMPLETE SET (275) 6.00 15.00
1 Steve Young .25 .60
2 Barry Sanders .50 1.25
3 Jerry Rice .30 .75
4 Marshall Faulk .40 1.00
5 Terance Mathis .02 .10
6 Rod Woodson .02 .10
7 Seth Joyner .01 .05
8 Michael Timpson .01 .05
9 Deion Sanders .20 .50
10 Emmitt Smith .50 1.25
11 Cris Carter .08 .25
12 Jake Reed .02 .10
13 Reggie White .08 .25
14 Shannon Sharpe .02 .10
15 Troy Aikman .30 .75
16 Andre Reed .02 .10
17 Tyrone Hughes .02 .10
18 Sterling Sharpe .02 .10
19 Jerome Bettis .08 .25
20 Irving Fryar .02 .10
21 Warren Moon .02 .10
22 Ben Coates .02 .10
23 Frank Reich .01 .05
24 Henry Ellard .02 .10
25 Steve Atwater .01 .05
26 Willie Davis .02 .10
27 Michael Irvin .08 .25
28 Harvey Williams .01 .05
29 Aeneas Williams .01 .05
30 Errict Rhett .02 .10
31 Lorenzo White .01 .05
32 John Elway .60 1.50
33 Rodney Hampton .02 .10
34 Webster Slaughter .01 .05
35 Eric Turner .01 .05
36 Dan Marino .60 1.50
37 Daryl Johnston .02 .10
38 Bruce Smith .08 .25
39 Ronald Moore .01 .05
40 Larry Centers .02 .10
41 Curtis Conway .08 .25
42 Drew Bledsoe .20 .50
43 Quinn Early .02 .10
44 Marcus Allen .08 .25
45 Andre Rison .02 .10
46 Jeff Blake RC .20 .50
47 Barry Foster .02 .10
48 Antonio Langham .01 .05
49 Herman Moore .08 .25
50 Flipper Anderson .01 .05
51 Rick Mirer .02 .10
52 Jay Novacek .02 .10
53 Tim Bowens .01 .05
54 Carl Pickens .02 .10
55 Lewis Tillman .01 .05
56 Lawrence Dawsey .01 .05
57 Leroy Hoard .01 .05
58 Steve Broussard .01 .05
59 Dave Krieg .01 .05
60 John Taylor .01 .05
61 Johnny Mitchell .01 .05
62 Jessie Hester .01 .05
63 Johnny Bailey .01 .05
64 Brett Favre .60 1.50
65 Bryce Paup .02 .10
66 J.J. Birden .01 .05
67 Steve Tasker .02 .10
68 Edgar Bennett .02 .10
69 Ray Buchanan .01 .05
70 Brent Jones .01 .05
71 Dave Meggett .01 .05
72 Jeff Graham .01 .05
73 Michael Brooks .01 .05
74 Ricky Ervins .01 .05
75 Chris Warren .02 .10
76 Natrone Means .02 .10
77 Tim Brown .08 .25
78 Jim Everett .01 .05
79 Chris Calloway .01 .05
80 John L. Williams .01 .05
81 Chris Chandler .02 .10
82 Tim McDonald .01 .05
83 Calvin Williams .02 .10
84 Tony McGee .01 .05
85 Erik Kramer .01 .05
86 Eric Green .01 .05
87 Nate Newton .02 .10
88 Leonard Russell .01 .05
89 Jeff George .02 .10
90 Raymont Harris .01 .05
91 Darnay Scott .02 .10
92 Brian Mitchell .01 .05
93 Craig Erickson .01 .05
94 Cortez Kennedy .02 .10
95 Derrick Alexander WR .08 .25
96 Charles Haley .02 .10
97 Randall Cunningham .08 .25
98 Haywood Jeffires .01 .05
99 Ronnie Harmon .01 .05
100 Dale Carter .02 .10
101 Dave Brown .02 .10
102 Michael Haynes .02 .10
103 Johnny Johnson .01 .05
104 William Floyd .02 .10
105 Jeff Hostetler .02 .10
106 Bernie Parmalee .02 .10
107 Mo Lewis .01 .05
108 Byron Bam Morris .01 .05
109 Vincent Brisby .01 .05
110 John Randle .02 .10
111 Steve Walsh .01 .05
112 Terry Allen .02 .10
113 Greg Lloyd .02 .10
114 Merton Hanks .01 .05
115 Mel Gray .01 .05
116 Jim Kelly .08 .25
117 Don Beebe .01 .05
118 Floyd Turner .01 .05
119 Neil Smith .02 .10
120 Keith Byars .01 .05
121 Rocket Ismail .02 .10
122 Leslie O'Neal .02 .10
123 Mike Sherrard .01 .05
124 Marion Butts .01 .05
125 Andre Coleman .01 .05
126 Charles Johnson .02 .10
127 Derrick Fenner .01 .05
128 Vinny Testaverde .02 .10
129 Chris Spielman .02 .10
130 Bert Emanuel .08 .25
131 Craig Heyward .02 .10
132 Anthony Miller .02 .10
133 Rob Moore .02 .10
134 Gary Brown .01 .05
135 David Klingler .02 .10
136 Sean Dawkins .02 .10
137 Terry McDaniel .01 .05
138 Fred Barnett .02 .10
139 Bryan Cox .01 .05
140 Andrew Jordan .01 .05
141 Leroy Thompson .01 .05
142 Richmond Webb .01 .05
143 Kimble Anders .02 .10
144 Mario Bates .02 .10
145 Irv Smith .01 .05
146 Carnell Lake .01 .05
147 Mark Seay .02 .10
148 Dana Stubblefield .02 .10
149 Kelvin Martin .01 .05
150 Pete Metzelaars .01 .05
151 Roosevelt Potts .01 .05
152 Bubby Brister .01 .05
153 Trent Dilfer .08 .25
154 Ricky Proehl .01 .05
155 Aaron Glenn .01 .05
156 Eric Metcalf .02 .10
157 Kevin Williams WR .02 .10
158 Charlie Garner .08 .25
159 Glyn Milburn .01 .05
160 Fuad Reveiz .01 .05
161 Brett Perriman .02 .10
162 Neil O'Donnell .02 .10
163 Tony Martin .02 .10
164 Sam Adams .01 .05
165 John Friesz .02 .10
166 Bryant Young .02 .10
167 Junior Seau .08 .25
168 Ken Harvey .01 .05
169 Bill Brooks .01 .05
170 Eugene Robinson .01 .05
171 Ricky Sanders .02 .10
172 Rodney Peete .01 .05
173 Boomer Esiason .02 .10
174 Reggie Roby .01 .05
175 Michael Jackson .02 .10
176 Gus Frerotte .02 .10
177 Terry Kirby .02 .10
178 Jessie Tuggle .01 .05
179 Courtney Hawkins .01 .05
180 Heath Shuler .02 .10
181 Jack Del Rio .01 .05
182 O.J. McDuffie .08 .25
183 Ricky Watters .02 .10
184 Willie Roaf .01 .05
185 Glenn Foley .01 .05
186 Blair Thomas .01 .05
187 Darren Woodson .02 .10
188 Kevin Greene .02 .10
189 Jeff Burris .01 .05
190 Jay Schroeder .01 .05
191 Stan Humphries .02 .10
192 Irving Spikes .02 .10
193 Jim Harbaugh .02 .10
194 Robert Brooks .08 .25
195 Greg Hill .02 .10
196 Herschel Walker .02 .10
197 Brian Blades .02 .10
198 Mark Ingram .01 .05
199 Kevin Turner .01 .05
200 Lake Dawson .02 .10
201 Alvin Harper .01 .05
202 Derek Brown RBK .01 .05
203 Qadry Ismail .02 .10
204 Reggie Brooks .02 .10
205 Steve Young SS .10 .30
206 Emmitt Smith SS .25 .60
207 Stan Humphries SS .01 .05
208 Barry Sanders SS .25 .60
209 Marshall Faulk SS .15 .40
210 Drew Bledsoe SS .08 .25
211 Jerry Rice SS .15 .40
212 Tim Brown SS .02 .10
213 Cris Carter SS .08 .25
214 Dan Marino SS .30 .75
215 Troy Aikman SS .15 .40
216 Jerome Bettis SS .02 .10
217 Deion Sanders SS .08 .25
218 Junior Seau SS .02 .10
219 John Elway SS .30 .75
220 Warren Moon SS .01 .05
221 Sterling Sharpe SS .02 .10
222 Marcus Allen SS .08 .25
223 Michael Irvin SS .02 .10
224 Brett Favre SS .30 .75
225 Rodney Hampton SS .01 .05
226 Dave Brown SS .02 .10
227 Ben Coates SS .02 .10
228 Jim Kelly SS .08 .25
229 Heath Shuler SS .02 .10
230 Herman Moore SS .08 .25
231 Jeff Hostetler SS .02 .10
232 Rick Mirer SS .02 .10
233 Byron Bam Morris SS .01 .05
234 Terance Mathis SS .01 .05
235 John Elway .15 .40
B.Sanders CL
236 Troy Aikman CL .08 .25
237 Jerry Rice CL .08 .25
238 Emmitt Smith CL .20 .50
239 Steve Young CL .08 .25
240 Drew Bledsoe CL .08 .25
241 Marshall Faulk CL .08 .25
242 Dan Marino CL .15 .40
243 Junior Seau CL .02 .10
244 Ray Zellars RC .02 .10
245 Rob Johnson RC .30 .75
246 Tony Boselli RC .08 .25
247 Kevin Carter RC .08 .25
248 Steve McNair RC 1.00 2.50
249 Tyrone Wheatley RC .30 .75
250 Steve Stenstrom RC .01 .05
251 Stoney Case RC .01 .05
252 Rodney Thomas RC .02 .10
253 Michael Westbrook RC .08 .25
254 Derrick Alexander DE RC .01 .05
255 Kyle Brady RC .08 .25
256 Kerry Collins RC .75 2.00
257 Rashaan Salaam RC .02 .10
258 Frank Sanders RC .08 .25
259 John Walsh RC .01 .05
260 Sherman Williams RC .01 .05
261 Ki-Jana Carter RC .08 .25
262 Jack Jackson RC .01 .05
263 J.J. Stokes RC .08 .25
264 Kordell Stewart RC .50 1.25
265 Dave Barr RC .01 .05
266 Eddie Goines RC .01 .05
267 Warren Sapp RC .50 1.25
268 James O. Stewart RC .30 .75
269 Joey Galloway RC .50 1.25
270 Tyrone Davis RC .01 .05
271 Napoleon Kaufman RC .40 1.00
272 Mark Bruener RC .02 .10
273 Todd Collins RC .30 .75
274 Billy Williams RC .01 .05
275 James A.Stewart RC .01 .05
AD3 Steve Young 1.25 3.00

1995 Score Red Siege

COMPLETE SET (275) 60.00 120.00
*STARS: 4X TO 8X BASIC CARDS
*RCs: 2X TO 4X BASIC CARDS
STATED ODDS 1:3

1995 Score Red Siege Artist's Proofs

*STARS: 12X TO 30X BASIC CARDS
*RCs: 8X TO 20X BASIC CARDS
STATED ODDS 1:36

1995 Score Dream Team

Randomly inserted into packs at a rate of one in 72, this 10-card standard-size set features some of the leading NFL players. Against a gold metallic background, the fronts feature two photos. One photo is a full color shot while the other is a shaded picture. The horizontal backs feature another photo on the top half with some player information underneath. The cards are numbered in the upper right corner with a "DT" prefix.

COMPLETE SET (10) 15.00 40.00
STATED ODDS 1:72 HOB/RET
DT1 Steve Young 1.50 4.00
DT2 Troy Aikman 2.00 5.00
DT3 Dan Marino 4.00 10.00
DT4 Drew Bledsoe 1.25 3.00
DT5 Emmitt Smith 3.00 8.00
DT6 Barry Sanders 3.00 8.00
DT7 Jerry Rice 2.00 5.00
DT8 Marshall Faulk 2.50 6.00
DT9 Deion Sanders 1.25 3.00
DT10 John Elway 4.00 10.00
DT2P Troy Aikman promo 1.50 4.00

1995 Score Offense Inc.

This 30-card standard-size set was randomly inserted into packs. Odds of finding one of these cards are approximately one in 16 packs. The set features leading NFL offensive players. Card fronts feature two player shots with the player's name and the border on the logo "Offense Inc." in gold foil. The background on the left side of the card is in black. Card backs contain a headshot with a summary to the right. Cards are numbered with an "OF" prefix.

COMPLETE SET (30) 40.00 80.00
STATED ODDS 1:16 HOB, 1:8 JUM, 1:16 RET
1 Steve Young 1.50 4.00
2 Emmitt Smith 3.00 8.00
3 Dan Marino 4.00 10.00
4 Barry Sanders 3.00 8.00
5 Jeff Blake .50 1.25
6 Jerry Rice 2.00 5.00
7 Troy Aikman 2.00 5.00
8 Brett Favre 4.00 10.00
9 Marshall Faulk 2.50 6.00
10 Drew Bledsoe 1.25 3.00
11 Natrone Means .25 .60
12 John Elway 4.00 10.00
13 Chris Warren .25 .60
14 Michael Irvin .60 1.50
15 Mario Bates .25 .60
16 Warren Moon .25 .60
17 Jerome Bettis .60 1.50
18 Herman Moore .60 1.50
19 Barry Foster .25 .60
20 Jeff George .25 .60
21 Cris Carter .60 1.50
22 Sterling Sharpe .25 .60
23 Jim Kelly .60 1.50
24 Heath Shuler .25 .60
25 Marcus Allen .60 1.50
26 Dave Brown .25 .60
27 Rick Mirer .25 .60
28 Rodney Hampton .25 .60
29 Errict Rhett .25 .60
30 Ben Coates .25 .60

1995 Score Pass Time

Randomly inserted into jumbo packs at a rate of one in 18, this 18 card set focuses on the "hottest arms" in the NFL Quarterback Club. Card fronts include two player shots against an all-foil gold background. Card backs have a yellow and white background with two player shots and a brief commentary. Cards are numbered with a "PT" prefix.

COMPLETE SET (18) 75.00 150.00
STATED ODDS 1:18 JUMBO
PT1 Steve Young 5.00 12.00
PT2 Dan Marino 12.50 30.00
PT3 Drew Bledsoe 4.00 10.00
PT4 Troy Aikman 6.00 15.00
PT5 Glenn Foley .40 1.00
PT6 John Elway 12.50 30.00
PT7 Brett Favre 10.00 25.00
PT8 Heath Shuler .75 2.00
PT9 Warren Moon .75 2.00
PT10 Rick Mirer .75 2.00
PT11 Stan Humphries .75 2.00
PT12 Jeff Hostetler .75 2.00
PT13 Jim Kelly 2.00 5.00
PT14 Randall Cunningham 2.00 5.00
PT15 Jeff Blake 2.00 4.00
PT16 Trent Dilfer 2.00 5.00
PT17 Jeff George .75 2.00
PT18 Dave Brown .75 2.00

1995 Score Reflextions

These 10 standard-size cards were randomly inserted into hobby packs at a rate of one in 36. This set features two players at the same position. One of the players is an established star while the other one is a younger player. The cards feature a mirror effect on the front with the "Reflextions" title on the right. Card backs are vertical with "Reflextions" in red at the top and shots of both players with a brief comparison commentary. Cards are numbered with a "RF" prefix.

COMPLETE SET (10) 30.00 60.00
STATED ODDS 1:36 HOBBY
RF1 D.Marino 6.00 15.00
D.Bledsoe
RF2 B.Sanders 5.00 12.00
C.Garner
RF3 R.Mirer 1.50 4.00
W.Moon
RF4 H.Shuler 2.50 6.00
S.Young
RF5 E.Smith 5.00 12.00
M.Faulk
RF6 J.Rice 3.00 8.00
D.Alexander WR
RF7 B.Morris 1.00 2.50
B.Foster
RF8 N.Means 1.50 4.00
C.Warren
RF9 T.Brown 1.50 4.00
L.Dawson
RF10 M.Bates 1.00 2.50
R.Hampton

1995 Score Pin-Cards

Sold in blister packs, each NFL team is represented by either one standard-size card depicting an NFL Quarterback Club member or a team helmet and a pin depicting the team logo. There are also 3 card sets in addition to regular cards for both expansion teams and the relocated St. Louis Rams, as well as a Super Bowl XXX card. The expansion and relocated team cards are black bordered with the team name repeated in the background on the front, and have copy relating to the teams' history, stadium, and logo lore on the back. These cards are also numbered 1-9. The other cards have fronts that feature color action photos of players or team helmets that fade to the surrounding white borders and are unnumbered. The player's or team's name appears on a rusty brown bar at the bottom. On a color panel, the backs present a color closeup photo and a brief player or team history. The cards are listed below by expansion and relocated teams, then alphabetically by player, and alphabetically by helmet. The prices below are for the trading cards only.

COMPLETE SET (40) 14.00 35.00
1 Jacksonville Jaguars-History .30 .75
2 Jacksonville Jaguars-Stadium .30 .75
3 Jacksonville Jaguars-Logo Lore .30 .75
4 Carolina Panthers-History .30 .75
5 Carolina Panthers-Stadium .30 .75
6 Carolina Panthers-Logo Lore .30 .75
7 St. Louis Rams-History .15 .40
8 St. Louis Rams-Stadium .15 .40
9 St. Louis Rams-Logo Lore .15 .40
10 Drew Bledsoe .80 2.00
11 Dave Brown .20 .50
12 Randall Cunningham .40 1.00
13 John Elway 1.60 4.00
14 Jim Everett .20 .50
15 Boomer Esiason .30 .75
16 Brett Favre 1.60 4.00
17 Jeff Hostetler .20 .50
18 Jim Kelly .40 1.00
19 David Klingler .20 .50
20 Dan Marino 1.60 4.00
21 Chris Miller .20 .50
22 Rick Mirer .30 .75
23 Warren Moon .40 1.00
24 Neil O'Donnell .30 .75
25 Jerry Rice .80 2.00
26 Barry Sanders 1.60 4.00
27 Junior Seau .30 .75
28 Heath Shuler .30 .75
29 Emmitt Smith 1.20 3.00
30 Arizona Cardinals .15 .40
31 Atlanta Falcons .15 .40
32 Carolina Panthers .30 .75
33 Chicago Bears .15 .40
34 Cleveland Browns .30 .75
35 Houston Oilers .15 .40
36 Indianapolis Colts .15 .40
37 Jacksonville Jaguars .30 .75
38 Kansas City Chiefs .15 .40
39 Tampa Bay Buccaneers .15 .40
40 Super Bowl XXX logo .15 .40

1995 Score Young Stars

These standard-size cards were available at the 1995 NFL Experience Super Bowl Card Show in exchange for three or five Pinnacle brand wrappers. Each day Pinnacle exchanged a Gold Zone or Platinum card of a different NFL star. Two thousand Gold Zone and one thousand Platinum cards were produced for each of the players listed below. We've included individual prices for the Gold Zone version. The Platinum version is valued using the multiplier line below.

COMPLETE SET (4) 10.00 25.00
*PLATINUM CARDS: 1X TO 2X GOLDS
YSG1 Marshall Faulk 3.20 8.00
YSG2 Jeff Blake 2.40 6.00
YSG3 Drew Bledsoe 4.80 12.00
YSG4 Natrone Means 2.00 5.00

1996 Score

The 1996 Score set was issued in one series totalling 275 standard-size cards. The set was issued in three different pack types: Hobby, Retail and Jumbo. The Hobby and Retail packs had a suggested retail price of .99 per pack and were packed with 10 cards in each pack, 36 packs in a box and 20 boxes in a case. Subsets include: Rookies 214-243, Second Effort 244-268, and Checklists 269-275. A Barry Sanders Dream Team Promo card was produced and priced below.

COMPLETE SET (275) 7.50 20.00
1 Emmitt Smith .50 1.25
2 Flipper Anderson .02 .10
3 Kordell Stewart .15 .40
4 Bruce Smith .07 .20
5 Marshall Faulk .20 .50
6 William Floyd .07 .20
7 Darren Woodson .07 .20
8 Lake Dawson .02 .10
9 Terry Allen .07 .20
10 Ki-Jana Carter .07 .20
11 Tony Boselli .02 .10
12 Christian Fauria .02 .10
13 Jeff George .07 .20
14 Dan Marino .60 1.50
15 Rodney Thomas .02 .10
16 Anthony Miller .07 .20
17 Chris Sanders .07 .20
18 Natrone Means .07 .20
19 Curtis Conway .15 .40
20 Ben Coates .07 .20
21 Alvin Harper .02 .10
22 Frank Sanders .07 .20
23 Boomer Esiason .07 .20
24 Lovell Pinkney .02 .10
25 Troy Aikman .30 .75
26 Quinn Early .02 .10
27 Adrian Murrell .07 .20
28 Chris Spielman .02 .10
29 Tyrone Wheatley .07 .20
30 Tim Brown .15 .40
31 Erik Kramer .02 .10
32 Warren Moon .07 .20
33 Jimmy Oliver .02 .10
34 Herman Moore .07 .20
35 Quentin Coryatt .02 .10
36 Heath Shuler .07 .20
37 Jim Kelly .15 .40
38 Mike Morris .02 .10
39 Harvey Williams .02 .10
40 Vinny Testaverde .07 .20
41 Steve McNair .25 .60
42 Jerry Rice .30 .75
43 Darick Holmes .02 .10
44 Kyle Brady .02 .10
45 Greg Lloyd .07 .20
46 Kerry Collins .15 .40
47 Willie McGinest .02 .10
48 Isaac Bruce .15 .40
49 Carnell Lake .02 .10
50 Charles Haley .07 .20
51 Troy Vincent .02 .10
52 Randall Cunningham .15 .40
53 Rashaan Salaam .07 .20
54 Willie Jackson .07 .20
55 Chris Warren .07 .20
56 Michael Irvin .15 .40
57 Mario Bates .07 .20
58 Warren Sapp .02 .10
59 John Elway .60 1.50
60 Shannon Sharpe .07 .20
61 Cornelius Bennett .02 .10
62 Robert Brooks .15 .40
63 Rodney Hampton .07 .20
64 Ken Norton Jr. .02 .10
65 Bryce Paup .02 .10
66 Eric Swann .02 .10
67 Rodney Peete .02 .10
68 Larry Centers .07 .20
69 Lamont Warren .02 .10
70 Jay Novacek .02 .10
71 Cris Carter .15 .40
72 Terrell Fletcher .02 .10
73 Andre Rison .07 .20
74 Ricky Watters .07 .20
75 Napoleon Kaufman .15 .40
76 Reggie White .15 .40
77 Yancey Thigpen .07 .20
78 Terry Kirby .07 .20
79 Deion Sanders .15 .40
80 Irving Fryar .07 .20
81 Marcus Allen .15 .40
82 Carl Pickens .07 .20
83 Drew Bledsoe .20 .50
84 Eric Metcalf .02 .10
85 Robert Smith .07 .20
86 Tamarick Vanover .07 .20
87 Henry Ellard .02 .10
88 Kevin Greene .07 .20
89 Mark Brunell .20 .50
90 Terrell Davis .25 .60
91 Brian Mitchell .02 .10
92 Aaron Bailey .02 .10
93 Rocket Ismail .02 .10
94 Dave Brown .02 .10
95 Rod Woodson .07 .20
96 Sean Gilbert .02 .10
97 Mark Seay .02 .10
98 Zack Crockett .02 .10
99 Scott Mitchell .07 .20
100 Eric Pegram .02 .10
101 David Palmer .02 .10
102 Vincent Brisby .02 .10
103 Brett Perriman .02 .10
104 Jim Everett .02 .10
105 Tony Martin .07 .20
106 Desmond Howard .07 .20
107 Stan Humphries .07 .20
108 Bill Brooks .02 .10
109 Neil Smith .07 .20
110 Michael Westbrook .15 .40
111 Herschel Walker .07 .20
112 Andre Coleman .02 .10
113 Derrick Alexander WR .07 .20
114 Jeff Blake .15 .40
115 Sherman Williams .02 .10
116 James O.Stewart .07 .20
117 Hardy Nickerson .02 .10
118 Elvis Grbac .07 .20
119 Brett Favre .60 1.50
120 Mike Sherrard .02 .10
121 Edgar Bennett .07 .20
122 Calvin Williams .02 .10
123 Brian Blades .02 .10
124 Jeff Graham .02 .10
125 Gary Brown .02 .10
126 Bernie Parmalee .02 .10
127 Kimble Anders .07 .20
128 Hugh Douglas .07 .20
129 James A.Stewart .02 .10
130 Eric Bjornson .02 .10
131 Ken Dilger .07 .20
132 Jerome Bettis .15 .40
133 Cortez Kennedy .02 .10
134 Bryan Cox .02 .10
135 Darnay Scott .07 .20
136 Bert Emanuel .07 .20
137 Steve Bono .02 .10
138 Charles Johnson .02 .10
139 Glyn Milburn .02 .10
140 Derrick Alexander DE .02 .10
141 Dave Meggett .02 .10
142 Trent Dilfer .15 .40
143 Eric Zeier .02 .10
144 Jim Harbaugh .07 .20
145 Antonio Freeman .15 .40
146 Orlando Thomas .02 .10
147 Russell Maryland .02 .10
148 Chad May .02 .10
149 Craig Heyward .02 .10
150 Aeneas Williams .02 .10
151 Kevin Williams WR .02 .10
152 Charlie Garner .07 .20
153 J.J. Stokes .15 .40
154 Stoney Case .02 .10
155 Mark Chmura .07 .20
156 Mark Bruener .02 .10
157 Derek Loville .02 .10
158 Justin Armour .02 .10
159 Brent Jones .02 .10
160 Aaron Craver .02 .10
161 Terance Mathis .02 .10
162 Chris Zorich .02 .10
163 Glenn Foley .07 .20
164 Johnny Mitchell .02 .10
165 Junior Seau .15 .40
166 Willie Davis .02 .10
167 Rick Mirer .07 .20
168 Mike Jones LB .02 .10
169 Greg Hill .07 .20
170 Steve Tasker .02 .10
171 Tony Bennett .02 .10
172 Jeff Hostetler .02 .10
173 Dave Krieg .02 .10
174 Mark Carrier WR .02 .10
175 Michael Haynes .02 .10
176 Chris Chandler .07 .20
177 Ernie Mills .02 .10
178 Jake Reed .07 .20
179 Errict Rhett .07 .20
180 Garrison Hearst .07 .20
181 Derrick Thomas .15 .40
182 Aaron Hayden RC .02 .10
183 Jackie Harris .02 .10
184 Curtis Martin .25 .60
185 Neil O'Donnell .07 .20
186 Derrick Moore .02 .10
187 Steve Young .25 .60
188 Pat Swilling .02 .10
189 Amp Lee .02 .10
190 Rob Johnson .15 .40
191 Todd Collins .07 .20
192 J.J. Birden .02 .10
193 O.J. McDuffie .07 .20
194 Shawn Jefferson .02 .10
195 Sean Dawkins .02 .10
196 Fred Barnett .02 .10
197 Roosevelt Potts .02 .10
198 Rob Moore .07 .20
199 Kevin Miniefield .02 .10
200 Barry Sanders .50 1.25
201 Floyd Turner .02 .10
202 Wayne Chrebet .25 .60
203 Andre Reed .07 .20
204 Tyrone Hughes .02 .10
205 Keenan McCardell .15 .40
206 Gus Frerotte .07 .20
207 Daryl Johnston .07 .20
208 Steve Broussard .02 .10
209 Steve Atwater .02 .10
210 Thurman Thomas .15 .40
211 Andre Hastings .02 .10
212 Joey Galloway .15 .40
213 Kevin Carter .02 .10
214 Keyshawn Johnson RC .40 1.00
215 Tony Brackens RC .15 .40
216 Stepfret Williams RC .07 .20
217 Mike Alstott RC .40 1.00
218 Terry Glenn RC .40 1.00
219 Tim Biakabutuka RC .15 .40
220 Eric Moulds RC .50 1.25
221 Jeff Lewis RC .07 .20
222 Bobby Engram RC .15 .40
223 Cedric Jones RC .02 .10
224 Stanley Pritchett RC .07 .20
225 Kevin Hardy RC .15 .40
226 Alex Van Dyke RC .07 .20
227 Willie Anderson RC .02 .10
228 Regan Upshaw RC .02 .10
229 Leeland McElroy RC .07 .20
230 Marvin Harrison RC 1.00 2.50
231 Eddie George RC .50 1.25
232 Lawrence Phillips RC .15 .40
233 Daryl Gardener RC .02 .10
234 Alex Molden RC .02 .10
235 Derrick Mayes RC .15 .40
236 John Mobley RC .02 .10
237 Israel Ifeanyi RC .02 .10
238 Pete Kendall RC .02 .10
239 Danny Kanell RC * .15 .40
240 Jonathan Ogden RC .40 1.00
241 Reggie Brown LB RC .02 .10
242 Marcus Jones RC .02 .10
243 Jon Stark RC .02 .10
244 Barry Sanders SE .25 .60
245 Brett Favre SE .30 .75
246 John Elway SE .30 .75
247 Dan Marino SE .30 .75
248 Drew Bledsoe SE .15 .40
249 Michael Irvin SE .07 .20
250 Troy Aikman SE .15 .40
251 Emmitt Smith SE .20 .50
252 Steve Young SE .15 .40
253 Jerry Rice SE .15 .40
254 Jeff Blake SE .07 .20
255 Tim Brown SE .07 .20
256 Eric Metcalf SE .02 .10
257 Rodney Hampton SE .02 .10
258 Scott Mitchell SE .02 .10
259 Garrison Hearst SE .07 .20
260 Larry Centers SE .07 .20
261 Neil O'Donnell SE .07 .20
262 Orlando Thomas SE .02 .10
263 Hugh Douglas SE .02 .10
264 Bill Brooks SE .02 .10
265 Harvey Williams SE .02 .10
266 Charles Haley SE .07 .20
267 Greg Lloyd SE .07 .20
268 Daryl Johnston SE .07 .20
269 Dan Marino CL .15 .40
270 Jeff Blake CL .07 .20
271 John Elway CL .15 .40
272 Emmitt Smith CL .15 .40

273 Brett Favre CL .15 .40
274 Jerry Rice CL .15 .40
275 Six Players CL .15 .40
P1 Barry Sanders DT Promo .75 2.00

1996 Score Artist's Proofs

COMPLETE SET (275) 250.00 500.00
*AP STARS: 5X TO 12X BASIC CARDS
*AP RCs: 2.5X TO 6X BASIC CARDS
STATED ODDS 1:36 H/R, 1:18 JUMBO

1996 Score Field Force

COMPLETE SET (275) 100.00 200.00
*STARS: 2X TO 5X BASIC CARDS
*RCs: 1X TO 2.5X BASIC CARDS
STATED ODDS 1:6 H/R, 1:3 JUMBO

1996 Score Dream Team

Randomly inserted in packs at a rate of one in 72 retail and hobby packs, these 10 standard-size cards feature a full-bleed, rainbow all gold-foil design. The cards are numbered as "X" of 10.

COMPLETE SET (10) 30.00 80.00
STATED ODDS 1:72
1 Troy Aikman 3.00 8.00
2 Michael Irvin 1.50 4.00
3 Emmitt Smith 5.00 12.00
4 John Elway 6.00 15.00
5 Barry Sanders 5.00 12.00
6 Brett Favre 6.00 15.00
7 Dan Marino 6.00 15.00
8 Drew Bledsoe 2.00 5.00
9 Jerry Rice 3.00 8.00
10 Steve Young 2.50 6.00

1996 Score Footsteps

Randomly inserted in hobby packs only at a rate of one in 36, this 15-card horizontal standard-size set features an established player as well as a young player at the same position. The cards are numbered as "X" of 15.

COMPLETE SET (15) 60.00 120.00
STATED ODDS 1:35 HOBBY
1 D.Holmes 1.25 2.50
E.Rhett
2 R.Salaam 2.00 4.00
N.Means
3 B.Sanders 7.50 20.00
Ki.Carter
4 T.Davis 7.50 20.00
M.Faulk
5 R.Thomas 1.25 2.50
C.Warren
6 C.Martin 7.50 20.00
E.Smith
7 K.Collins 6.00 15.00
T.Aikman
8 E.Zeier 3.00 8.00
D.Bledsoe
9 S.McNair 7.50 20.00
B.Favre
10 S.Young 5.00 12.00
K.Stewart
11 J.J.Stokes 6.00 12.00
J.Rice
12 J.Galloway 2.00 4.00
M.Irvin
13 M.Westbrook 2.00 4.00
C.Carter
14 T.Vanover 2.00 4.00
I.Bruce
15 D.Sanders 3.00 6.00
O.Thomas

1996 Score In The Zone

Randomly inserted in retail packs only at a rate of one in 33, this 20-card standard-size set features leading offensive threats. The player's photo is in the middle with his name in the lower left and the words "In the Zone" on the right. The cards are numbered "X" of 20.

COMPLETE SET (20) 50.00 120.00
STATED ODDS 1:33 RETAIL
1 Brett Favre 10.00 25.00
2 Warren Moon 1.25 3.00
3 Erik Kramer .60 1.50
4 Scott Mitchell 1.25 3.00
5 Jeff Blake 2.50 6.00
6 Steve Bono .60 1.50
7 Dan Marino 10.00 25.00
8 Troy Aikman 5.00 12.00
9 Emmitt Smith 8.00 20.00
10 Curtis Martin 4.00 10.00
11 Errict Rhett 1.25 3.00
12 Terrell Davis 4.00 10.00
13 Derek Loville .60 1.50
14 Rodney Hampton 1.25 3.00
15 Cris Carter 2.50 6.00
16 Herman Moore 1.25 3.00
17 Jerry Rice 5.00 12.00
18 Ben Coates 1.25 3.00
19 Michael Irvin 2.50 6.00
20 Carl Pickens 1.25 3.00

1996 Score Numbers Game

Randomly inserted in packs at a rate of one in 17, this 25-card standard-size set features leading players. Jumbo pack ratio was 1:9 packs. The backs have various blurbs which feature player's significant numbers. The cards are numbered "X"of 25 on the back.

COMPLETE SET (25) 40.00 80.00
STATED ODDS 1:17 HOB/RET, 1:9 JUM
1 Barry Sanders 4.00 8.00
2 Drew Bledsoe 2.00 4.00
3 Brett Favre 5.00 10.00
4 John Elway 5.00 10.00
5 Dan Marino 5.00 10.00
6 Michael Irvin 1.50 3.00
7 Troy Aikman 2.50 5.00
8 Emmitt Smith 4.00 8.00
9 Steve Young 2.00 4.00
10 Jerry Rice 2.50 5.00
11 Chris Sanders .75 1.50
12 Herman Moore .75 1.50
13 Frank Sanders .75 1.50
14 Kordell Stewart 1.50 3.00
15 Jeff Blake 1.50 3.00
16 Robert Brooks 1.50 3.00
17 Marshall Faulk 2.00 4.00
18 Carl Pickens .75 1.50
19 Greg Lloyd .75 1.50
20 Curtis Conway 1.50 3.00
21 Chris Warren .75 1.50
22 Natrone Means .75 1.50
23 Deion Sanders 1.50 3.00
24 Neil O'Donnell .75 1.50
25 Ricky Watters .75 1.50

1996 Score Settle the Score

Randomly inserted in packs at a rate of one in 35 jumbo packs, this 30-card standard-size horizontal set features two players who were on opposing teams during 1995 NFL games. The fronts have the players names on the left with each player against a prismatic background. The backs have how the player performed in each game. The cards are numbered as "X" of 30.

COMPLETE SET (30) 150.00 400.00
STATED ODDS 1:36 JUM, 1:72 SPEC.RETAIL
1 F.Sanders 2.50 6.00
C.Garner
2 D.Bledsoe 5.00 12.00
N.O'Donnell
3 J.Rice 6.00 15.00
C.Hoyward
4 E.Smith 10.00 25.00
R.Woodson
5 D.Holmes 8.00 20.00
D.Marino
6 K.Collins 5.00 12.00
S.Young
7 R.Salaam 12.50 30.00
B.Favre
8 C.Conway 12.50 30.00
B.Sanders
9 T.Aikman 15.00 30.00
D.Marino
10 D.Marino 12.50 30.00
N.O'Donnell
11 E.Zeier 4.00 10.00
S.McNair
12 J.Blake 4.00 10.00
K.Stewart
13 T.Aikman 6.00 15.00
H.Shuler
14 M.Irvin 6.00 15.00
J.Rice
15 E.Smith 10.00 25.00
R.Watters
16 J.Elway 12.50 30.00
S.Bono
17 J.Elway 12.50 30.00
R.Mirer
18 J.Elway 12.50 30.00
T.Brown
19 B.Sanders 20.00 40.00
B.Favre
20 B.Sanders 10.00 25.00
W.Moon
21 T.Dilfer 12.50 30.00
B.Favre
22 R.Thomas 1.50 4.00
J.O.Stewart
23 D.Bledsoe 5.00 12.00
J.Harbaugh
24 M.Allen 2.50 6.00
H.Williams
25 T.Vanover 4.00 10.00
J.Galloway
26 D.Marino 12.50 30.00
D.Bledsoe
27 J.Rice 6.00 15.00
M.Bates
28 T.Wheatley 2.50 6.00
M.Westbrook
29 N.Kaufman 4.00 10.00
J.Seau
30 J.J.Stokes 2.50 6.00
I.Bruce

1996 Score WLAF

This 25-card set features players of the World League of American Football. The first six cards were printed using Pinnacle's lenticular technology and titled "Team Leaders." The fronts display color action player photos with the player's name below. The backs carry a head photo along with information about the player. The set was released in its own foil wrapper along with one of six Team Inserts.

COMPLETE SET (25) 15.00 30.00
1 Will Furrer TL .50 1.25
2 Kelly Holcomb TL 6.00 15.00
3 Steve Pelluer TL .40 1.00
4 William Perry TL .80 2.00
5 Manfred Burgsmuller TL .40 1.00
6 Siran Stacy TL .40 1.00
7 T.C. Wright .50 1.25
8 Malcolm Showell .40 1.00
9 Phillip Bobo .40 1.00
10 Marvin Marshall .40 1.00
11 Demetrius Davis .50 1.25
12 Mike Middleton .40 1.00
13 Nathaniel Bolton .40 1.00
14 Mario Bailey .40 1.00
15 George Hegamin .40 1.00
16 Preston Jones .40 1.00
17 Russell White .50 1.25
18 Victor X. Ebubedike .40 1.00
19 Andy Kelly .50 1.25
20 Tommie Boyd .40 1.00
21 Percy Snow .40 1.00
22 Gavin Hastings .40 1.00
23 Steve Matthews .40 1.00
24 George Coghill .40 1.00
NNO Cover Card .40 1.00

1996 Score WLAF Team Inserts

Inserted one per factory set in the 1996 Score WLAF release, each card features four players from one of the six league teams. Two players appear on each side of the card, along with the WLAF logo and the Pinnacle pyramid logo.

COMPLETE SET (6)
1 M.Middleton 1.50 4.00
K.Holcomb
2 Pelluer/Bolton/Bailey/Hegamin 2.00 5.00
5 Boyd 1.50 4.00
Burgsmuller
Kelly
Snow

1997 Score

The 1997 Score set was issued in one series totalling 330 cards. The fronts feature color action player photos in white borders. The backs carry player information and career statistics. The set contains the topical subsets: The Draft Class (273-307), and The Big Play (308-327). Cards were distributed in 20-card retail packs carrying a suggested price of $1.99, as well 27-card blister packs with a suggested retail of $2.99. Blister packs also contained one ad/cover promo card as listed below.

COMPLETE SET (330) 10.00 25.00
1 John Elway .75 2.00
2 Drew Bledsoe .25 .60
3 Brett Favre .75 2.00
4 Emmitt Smith .60 1.50
5 Kerry Collins .20 .50
6 Jerry Rice .40 1.00
7 Kordell Stewart .20 .50
8 Barry Sanders .60 1.50
9 Dan Marino .75 2.00
10 Steve Young .25 .60
11 Erik Kramer .07 .20
12 Warren Moon .20 .50
13 Chris Calloway .07 .20
14 Doug Evans .07 .20
15 Darren Woodson .07 .20
16 Alonzo Spellman .07 .20
17 Greg Hill .07 .20
18 Aaron Craver .07 .20
19 Jeff Hostetler .07 .20
20 William Thomas .07 .20
21 Marco Coleman .07 .20
22 Wayne Simmons .07 .20
23 Donnell Woolford .07 .20
24 Vinny Testaverde .10 .30
25 Ed McCaffrey .10 .30
26 Jim Everett .07 .20
27 Gilbert Brown .10 .30
28 Jason Dunn .07 .20
29 Stanley Pritchett .07 .20
30 Joey Galloway .10 .30
32 Chris Penn .07 .20
33 Aeneas Williams .07 .20
34 Bobby Taylor .07 .20
35 Bryan Still .07 .20
36 Ty Law .10 .30
37 Shannon Sharpe .10 .30
38 Marty Carter .07 .20
39 Sam Mills .07 .20
40 William Floyd .10 .30
41 Brad Johnson .20 .50
42 Sean Dawkins .07 .20
43 Michael Irvin .20 .50
44 Jeff George .10 .30
45 Brent Jones .10 .30
46 Mark Brunell .25 .60
47 Rob Moore .10 .30
48 Hardy Nickerson .07 .20
49 Chris Chandler .10 .30
50 Willie Anderson .07 .20
51 Isaac Bruce .20 .50
52 Natrone Means .10 .30
53 Tony Banks .10 .30
54 Marshall Faulk .25 .60
55 Michael Westbrook .10 .30
56 Bruce Smith .10 .30
57 Jamal Anderson .20 .50
58 Jackie Harris .07 .20
59 Sean Gilbert .07 .20
60 Ki-Jana Carter .07 .20
61 Eric Moulds .20 .50
62 James O.Stewart .10 .30
63 Jeff Blake .10 .30
64 O.J. McDuffie .10 .30
65 Neil Smith .10 .30
66 Kevin Smith .07 .20
67 Terry Allen .20 .50
68 Sean LaChapelle .07 .20
69 Rashaan Salaam .07 .20
70 Jeff Graham .07 .20
71 Mark Carrier WR .07 .20
72 Allen Aldridge .07 .20
73 Keenan McCardell .10 .30
74 Willie McGinest .07 .20
75 Napoleon Kaufman .20 .50
76 Jerris McPhail .07 .20
77 Eric Swann .07 .20
78 Kimble Anders .10 .30
79 Charles Johnson .10 .30
80 Bryan Cox .07 .20
81 Johnnie Morton .10 .30
82 Andre Rison .10 .30
83 Corey Miller .07 .20
84 Troy Drayton .07 .20
85 Jim Harbaugh .10 .30
86 Wesley Walls .10 .30
87 Bryce Paup .07 .20
88 Curtis Martin .25 .60
89 Michael Sinclair .07 .20
90 Chris T. Jones .07 .20
91 Jake Reed .10 .30
92 LeRoy Butler .07 .20
93 Reggie Tongue .07 .20
94 Bert Emanuel .10 .30
95 Stan Humphries .10 .30
96 Neil O'Donnell .10 .30
97 Troy Vincent .07 .20
98 Mike Alstott .20 .50
99 Chad Cota .07 .20
100 Marvin Harrison .20 .50
101 Terrell Owens .25 .60
102 Dave Brown .07 .20
103 Harvey Williams .07 .20
104 Desmond Howard .10 .30
105 Carl Pickens .10 .30
106 Kent Graham .07 .20
107 Michael Bates .07 .20
108 Terrell Davis .25 .60
109 Marcus Allen .20 .50
110 Ray Zellars .07 .20
111 Chris Warren .10 .30
112 Phillippi Sparks .07 .20
113 Craig Erickson .07 .20
114 Eddie George .20 .50
115 Daryl Johnston .10 .30
116 Ricky Watters .10 .30
117 Tedy Bruschi .40 1.00
118 Mike Mamula .07 .20
119 Ken Harvey .07 .20
120 John Randle .10 .30
121 Mark Chmura .10 .30
122 Sam Gash .07 .20
123 John Kasay .07 .20
124 Barry Minter .07 .20
125 Raymont Harris .07 .20
126 Derrick Thomas .20 .50
127 Trent Dilfer .20 .50
128 Carnell Lake .07 .20
129 Brian Dawkins .20 .50
130 Tyronne Drakeford .07 .20
131 Daryl Gardener .07 .20
132 Fred Strickland .07 .20
133 Kevin Hardy .07 .20
134 Winslow Oliver .07 .20
135 Herman Moore .10 .30
136 Keith Byars .07 .20
137 Harold Green .07 .20
138 Ty Detmer .10 .30
139 Lamar Thomas .07 .20
140 Elvis Grbac .10 .30
141 Edgar Bennett .10 .30
142 Cornelius Bennett .07 .20
143 Tony Tolbert .07 .20
144 James Hasty .07 .20
145 Ben Coates .10 .30
146 Errict Rhett .07 .20
147 Jason Sehorn .10 .30
148 Michael Jackson .10 .30
149 John Mobley .07 .20
150 Walt Harris .07 .20
151 Terry Kirby .10 .30
152 Devin Wyman .07 .20
153 Ray Crockett .07 .20
154 Quinn Early .07 .20
155 Rodney Thomas .07 .20
156 Mark Seay .07 .20
157 Derrick Alexander WR .10 .30
158 Lamar Lathon .07 .20
159 Anthony Miller .07 .20
160 Shawn Wooden RC .07 .20
161 Antonio Freeman .20 .50
162 Cortez Kennedy .07 .20
163 Rickey Dudley .10 .30
164 Tony Carter .07 .20
165 Kevin Williams .07 .20
166 Reggie White .20 .50
167 Tim Bowens .07 .20
168 Roy Barker .07 .20
169 Adrian Murrell .10 .30
170 Anthony Johnson .07 .20
171 Terry Glenn .20 .50
172 Jeff Lewis .07 .20
173 Dorsey Levens .20 .50
174 Willie Jackson .07 .20
175 Willie Clay .07 .20
176 Richmond Webb .07 .20
177 Shawn Lee .07 .20
178 Joe Aska .07 .20
179 Rod Woodson .10 .30
180 Jim Schwartz RC .07 .20
181 Alfred Williams .07 .20
182 Ferric Collons .07 .20
183 Ken Norton Jr. .07 .20
184 Rick Mirer .07 .20
185 Leeland McElroy .07 .20
187 Ted Popson RC .07 .20
188 Fred Barnett .07 .20
189 Junior Seau .20 .50
190 Micheal Barrow .07 .20
191 Corey Widmer .07 .20
192 Rodney Peete .07 .20
193 Rod Smith WR .20 .50
194 Muhsin Muhammad .10 .30
195 Keith Jackson .07 .20
196 Jimmy Smith .10 .30
197 Dave Meggett .07 .20
198 Lawrence Phillips .07 .20
199 Chad Brown .07 .20
200 Darrin Smith .07 .20
201 Larry Centers .10 .30
202 Kevin Greene .10 .30
203 Sherman Williams .07 .20
204 Chris Sanders .07 .20
205 Shawn Jefferson .07 .20
206 Thurman Thomas .20 .50
207 Keyshawn Johnson .20 .50
208 Bryant Young .07 .20
209 Tim Biakabutuka .10 .30
210 Troy Aikman .40 1.00
211 Quentin Coryatt .07 .20
212 Karim Abdul-Jabbar .20 .50
213 Brian Blades .07 .20
214 Ray Farmer .07 .20
215 Simeon Rice .10 .30
216 Tyrone Braxton .07 .20
217 Jerome Woods .07 .20
218 Charles Way .10 .30
219 Garrison Hearst .10 .30
220 Bobby Engram .10 .30
221 Billy Davis RC .07 .20
222 Ken Dilger .07 .20
223 Robert Smith .10 .30
224 John Friesz .07 .20
225 Charlie Garner .10 .30
226 Jerome Bettis .20 .50
227 Darnay Scott .10 .30
228 Terance Mathis .10 .30
229 Brian Williams LB .07 .20
230 Cris Carter .20 .50
231 Michael Haynes .07 .20
232 Cedric Jones .07 .20
233 Danny Kanell .10 .30
234 Deion Sanders .20 .50
235 Steve Atwater .07 .20
236 Jonathan Ogden .07 .20
237 Lake Dawson .07 .20
238 Eric Allen .07 .20
239 Eddie Kennison .10 .30
240 Irving Fryar .10 .30
241 Michael Strahan .10 .30
242 Steve McNair .25 .60
243 Terrell Buckley .07 .20
244 Merton Hanks .07 .20
245 Jessie Armstead .07 .20
246 Dana Stubblefield .07 .20
247 Brett Perriman .07 .20
248 Mark Collins .07 .20
249 Willie Roaf .07 .20
250 Gus Frerotte .07 .20
251 William Fuller .07 .20
252 Tamarick Vanover .10 .30
253 Scott Mitchell .10 .30
254 Eric Metcalf .10 .30
255 Herschel Walker .10 .30
256 Robert Brooks .10 .30
257 Zach Thomas .20 .50
258 Alvin Harper .07 .20
259 Wayne Chrebet .20 .50
260 Bill Romanowski .07 .20
261 Willie Green .07 .20
262 Dale Carter .07 .20
263 Chris Slade .07 .20
264 J.J. Stokes .10 .30
265 Tim Brown .20 .50
266 Eric Davis .07 .20
267 Mark Carrier DB .07 .20
268 Tony Martin .10 .30
269 Tyrone Wheatley .10 .30
270 Eugene Robinson .07 .20
271 Curtis Conway .10 .30
272 Michael Timpson .07 .20
273 Orlando Pace RC .20 .50
274 Tiki Barber RC 1.25 3.00
275 Byron Hanspard RC .10 .30
276 Warrick Dunn RC .60 1.50
277 Rae Carruth RC .07 .20
278 Bryant Westbrook RC .07 .20
279 Antowain Smith RC .50 1.25
280 Peter Boulware RC .20 .50
281 Reidel Anthony RC .20 .50
282 Troy Davis RC .10 .30
283 Jake Plummer RC .75 2.00
284 Chris Canty RC .07 .20
285 Dwayne Rudd RC .20 .50
286 Ike Hilliard RC .30 .75
287 Reinard Wilson RC .10 .30
288 Corey Dillon RC .75 2.00
289 Tony Gonzalez RC .75 2.00
290 Darnell Autry RC .10 .30
291 Kevin Lockett RC .10 .30
292 Darrell Russell RC .07 .20
293 Jim Druckenmiller RC .10 .30
294 Shon Mitchell RC .07 .20
295 Joey Kent RC .20 .50
296 Shawn Springs RC .10 .30
297 James Farrior RC .20 .50
298 Sedrick Shaw RC .10 .30
299 Marcus Harris RC .07 .20
300 Danny Wuerffel RC .20 .50
301 Marc Edwards RC .07 .20
302 Michael Booker RC .07 .20
303 David LaFleur RC .07 .20
304 Mike Adams WR RC .07 .20
305 Pat Barnes RC .20 .50
306 George Jones RC .10 .30
307 Yatil Green RC .10 .30
308 Drew Bledsoe TBP .20 .50
309 Troy Aikman TBP .20 .50
310 Terrell Davis TBP .10 .30
311 Jim Everett TBP .07 .20
312 John Elway TBP .40 1.00
313 Barry Sanders TBP .30 .75
314 Jim Harbaugh TBP .10 .30
315 Steve Young TBP .20 .50
316 Dan Marino TBP .40 1.00
317 Michael Irvin TBP .20 .50
318 Emmitt Smith TBP .30 .75
319 Jeff Hostetler TBP .07 .20
320 Mark Brunell TBP .20 .50
321 Jeff Blake TBP .20 .50
322 Scott Mitchell TBP .07 .20
323 Boomer Esiason TBP .10 .30
324 Jerome Bettis TBP .20 .50
325 Warren Moon TBP .10 .30
326 Neil O'Donnell TBP .10 .30
327 Jim Kelly TBP .20 .50
328 Dan Marino CL .20 .50
329 John Elway CL .20 .50
330 Drew Bledsoe CL .10 .30
P1 Troy Aikman Promo .40 1.00
P2 Brett Favre Promo .75 2.00
P3 Dan Marino Promo .75 2.00
P4 Barry Sanders Promo .60 1.50

1997 Score Hobby Reserve

COMPLETE SET (330) 15.00 30.00

1997 Score Reserve Collection

COMPLETE SET (330) 150.00 300.00
*RES.COLLECT.STARS: 6X TO 15X HI COL.
*RES.COLLECT.RCs: 3X TO 8X
STATED ODDS 1:11 HOBBY RESERVE

1997 Score Showcase

COMPLETE SET (330) 60.00 120.00
*SHOWCASE STARS: 2.5X TO 6X BASIC CARDS
*SHOWCASE RCs: 1.2X TO 3X BASIC CARDS
STATED ODDS 1:4 HOB, 1:7 RET

1997 Score Showcase Artist's Proofs

COMPLETE SET (330) 200.00 400.00
*STARS: 8X TO 20X BASIC CARDS
*RCs: 4X TO 10X BASIC CARDS
STATED ODDS 1:17 H,1:35R, 1:23 HOB.RES.

1997 Score Franchise

Franchise cards were randomly inserted in retail packs at the rate of 1:30 and in hobby packs at the rate of 1:47 . Holofoil Enhanced versions were produced and distributed at the rate of 1:166 Hobby Reserve packs and 1:125 retail packs. Each card features a wide white cardfront border trimmed with embossed football lacing.

COMPLETE SET (16) 75.00 150.00
STATED ODDS 1:30 RETAIL
*HOLO.ENHANCED: .6X TO 1.5X BASIC INS.
HOLO.ENHANCED STATED ODDS 1:125
1 Emmitt Smith 8.00 20.00
2 Barry Sanders 8.00 20.00
3 Brett Favre 10.00 25.00
4 Drew Bledsoe 3.00 8.00
5 Jerry Rice 5.00 12.00
6 Troy Aikman 5.00 12.00
7 Dan Marino 10.00 25.00
8 John Elway 10.00 25.00
9 Steve Young 3.00 8.00
10 Eddie George 2.50 6.00
11 Keyshawn Johnson 2.50 6.00
12 Terrell Davis 3.00 8.00
13 Marshall Faulk 3.00 8.00
14 Kerry Collins 2.50 6.00
15 Deion Sanders 2.50 6.00
16 Joey Galloway 1.50 4.00

1997 Score New Breed

New Breed cards were randomly inserted in both Score retail (#1-9, 1:12 packs) and Hobby Reserve (#10-18, 1:15 packs). Each features a young NFL player photo printed on silver foil card stock.

COMPLETE SET (18) 35.00 70.00
COMP.SERIES 1 SET (9) 15.00 30.00
COMP.SERIES 2 SET (9) 20.00 40.00
1-9: STATED ODDS 1:12 RETAIL
10-18: STATED ODDS 1:15 HOBBY RESERVE
1 Eddie George 1.50 4.00
2 Terrell Davis 2.00 5.00
3 Curtis Martin 2.00 5.00
4 Tony Banks 1.00 2.50
5 Lawrence Phillips .60 1.50
6 Terry Glenn 1.50 4.00
7 Jerome Bettis 1.50 4.00
8 Karim Abdul-Jabbar 1.50 4.00
9 Napoleon Kaufman 1.50 4.00
10 Isaac Bruce 1.50 4.00
11 Keyshawn Johnson 1.50 4.00
12 Rickey Dudley 1.00 2.50
13 Eddie Kennison 1.00 2.50
14 Marvin Harrison 1.50 4.00
15 Emmitt Smith 5.00 12.00
16 Barry Sanders 5.00 12.00
17 Kerry Collins 1.50 4.00
18 Brett Favre 6.00 15.00

1997 Score Showdown in Titletown

COMPLETE SET (22) 10.00 25.00
1D Troy Aikman 1.25 3.00
1G Brett Favre 2.50 6.00
2D Emmitt Smith 2.00 5.00
2G Dorsey Levens .60 1.50
3D Daryl Johnston .60 1.50
3G Mark Chmura .50 1.25
4D Michael Irvin .75 2.00
4G Robert Brooks .60 1.50
5D Billy Davis .40 1.00
5G Antonio Freeman .60 1.50
6D Tony Tolbert .40 1.00
6G Reggie White .75 2.00
7D Fred Strickland .40 1.00
7G Brian Williams .40 1.00
8D Deion Sanders .75 2.00
8G LeRoy Butler .50 1.25
9D Kevin Smith .40 1.00
9G Doug Evans .40 1.00
10D Darren Woodson .60 1.50
10G Eugene Robinson .50 1.25
11D Troy Aikman CL .75 2.00
11G Brett Favre CL 1.25 3.00

1997 Score Specialists

Specialists cards were randomly inserted in Score Hobby Reserve packs at the rate of 1:15. Each was printed on silver foil card stock.

COMPLETE SET (18) 50.00 100.00
STATED ODDS 1:15 HOBBY RESERVE
1 Brett Favre 6.00 15.00
2 Drew Bledsoe 2.00 5.00
3 Mark Brunell 2.00 5.00
4 Kerry Collins 1.50 4.00
5 John Elway 6.00 15.00
6 Barry Sanders 5.00 12.00
7 Troy Aikman 3.00 8.00
8 Jerry Rice 3.00 8.00
9 Dan Marino 6.00 15.00
10 Neil O'Donnell 1.00 2.50
11 Scott Mitchell 1.00 2.50
12 Jim Harbaugh 1.00 2.50
13 Emmitt Smith 5.00 12.00
14 Steve Young 2.00 5.00
15 Dave Brown .60 1.50
16 Jeff Blake 1.00 2.50
17 Jim Everett .60 1.50
18 Kordell Stewart 1.50 4.00

1998 Score

The 1998 Score set was issued in one series totalling 270 cards. The fronts feature action color player photos in black-and-white borders. The backs carry player information and career statistics. The set contains the topical subset, Off Season (253-267), and three checklist cards (268-270).

COMPLETE SET (270) 15.00 40.00
1 John Elway .75 2.00
2 Kordell Stewart .20 .50
3 Warrick Dunn .20 .50
4 Brad Johnson .20 .50
5 Kerry Collins .10 .30
6 Danny Kanell .10 .30
7 Emmitt Smith .60 1.50
8 Jamal Anderson .20 .50
9 Jim Harbaugh .10 .30
10 Tony Martin .10 .30
11 Rod Smith .10 .30
12 Dorsey Levens .20 .50
13 Steve McNair .20 .50
14 Derrick Thomas .20 .50
15 Rob Moore .10 .30
16 Peter Boulware .07 .20
17 Terry Allen .20 .50
18 Joey Galloway .10 .30
19 Jerome Bettis .20 .50
20 Carl Pickens .10 .30
21 Napoleon Kaufman .20 .50
22 Troy Aikman .40 1.00
23 Curtis Conway .10 .30
24 Adrian Murrell .10 .30
25 Elvis Grbac .10 .30
27 Chris Sanders .07 .20
28 Scott Mitchell .10 .30
29 Junior Seau .20 .50
30 Chris Chandler .10 .30
31 Kevin Hardy .07 .20
32 Terrell Davis .20 .50
33 Keyshawn Johnson .20 .50
34 Natrone Means .10 .30
35 Antowain Smith .20 .50
36 Jake Plummer .20 .50
37 Isaac Bruce .20 .50
38 Tony Banks .10 .30
39 Reidel Anthony .10 .30
40 Darren Woodson .07 .20
41 Corey Dillon .20 .50
42 Antonio Freeman .20 .50
43 Eddie George .20 .50
44 Yancey Thigpen .07 .20
45 Tim Brown .20 .50
46 Wayne Chrebet .20 .50
47 Andre Rison .10 .30
48 Michael Strahan .10 .30
49 Deion Sanders .20 .50
50 Eric Moulds .20 .50
51 Mark Brunell .20 .50
52 Rae Carruth .07 .20
53 Warren Sapp .10 .30
54 Mark Chmura .10 .30
55 Darrell Green .10 .30
56 Quinn Early .07 .20
57 Barry Sanders .60 1.50
58 Neil O'Donnell .10 .30
59 Tony Brackens .07 .20
60 Willie Davis .07 .20
61 Shannon Sharpe .10 .30
62 Shawn Springs .07 .20
63 Tony Gonzalez .20 .50
64 Rodney Thomas .07 .20
65 Terance Mathis .10 .30
66 Brett Favre .75 2.00
67 Eric Swann .07 .20
68 Kevin Turner .07 .20
69 Tyrone Wheatley .10 .30
70 Trent Dilfer .20 .50
71 Bryan Cox .07 .20
72 Lake Dawson .07 .20
73 Will Blackwell .07 .20
74 Fred Lane .07 .20
75 Ty Detmer .10 .30
76 Eddie Kennison .10 .30
77 Jimmy Smith .10 .30
78 Chris Calloway .07 .20
79 Shawn Jefferson .07 .20
80 Dan Marino .75 2.00
81 LeRoy Butler .07 .20
82 William Roaf .07 .20
83 Rick Mirer .07 .20
84 Dermontti Dawson .15 .40
85 Errict Rhett .10 .30
86 Lamar Thomas .07 .20
87 Lamar Lathon .07 .20
88 John Randle .10 .30
89 Darryl Williams .07 .20
90 Keenan McCardell .10 .30
91 Erik Kramer .07 .20
92 Ken Dilger .07 .20
93 Dave Meggett .07 .20
94 Jeff Blake .10 .30
95 Ed McCaffrey .10 .30
96 Charles Johnson .07 .20
97 Irving Spikes .07 .20
98 Mike Alstott .20 .50
99 Vincent Brisby .07 .20
100 Michael Westbrook .10 .30
101 Rickey Dudley .07 .20
102 Bert Emanuel .10 .30
103 Daryl Johnston .10 .30
104 Lawrence Phillips .07 .20
105 Eric Bieniemy .07 .20
106 Bryant Westbrook .07 .20
107 Rob Johnson .10 .30
108 Ray Zellars .07 .20
109 Anthony Johnson .07 .20
110 Reggie White .20 .50
111 Wesley Walls .10 .30
112 Amani Toomer .10 .30
113 Gary Brown .07 .20
114 Brian Blades .07 .20
115 Alex Van Dyke .07 .20
116 Michael Haynes .07 .20
117 Jessie Armstead .10 .30
118 James Jett .10 .30
119 Troy Drayton .07 .20
120 Craig Heyward .07 .20
121 Steve Atwater .07 .20
122 Tiki Barber .20 .50
123 Karim Abdul-Jabbar .20 .50
124 Kimble Anders .10 .30
125 Frank Sanders .10 .30
126 David Sloan .07 .20
127 Andre Hastings .07 .20
128 Vinny Testaverde .10 .30
129 Robert Smith .20 .50
130 Horace Copeland .07 .20
131 Larry Centers .07 .20
132 J.J. Stokes .10 .30
133 Ike Hilliard .10 .30
134 Muhsin Muhammad .10 .30
135 Sean Dawkins .07 .20
136 Raymont Harris .07 .20
137 Lamar Smith .07 .20
138 David Palmer .07 .20
139 Steve Young .25 .60
140 Bryan Still .07 .20
141 Keith Byars .07 .20
142 Cris Carter .20 .50
143 Charlie Garner .10 .30
144 Drew Bledsoe .30 .75
145 Simeon Rice .10 .30
146 Merton Hanks .07 .20
147 Aeneas Williams .07 .20
148 Rodney Hampton .10 .30
149 Zach Thomas .20 .50
150 Mark Bruener .07 .20
151 Jason Dunn .07 .20
152 Danny Wuerffel .10 .30
153 Jim Druckenmiller .07 .20
154 Greg Hill .07 .20
155 Earnest Byner .07 .20
156 Greg Lloyd .07 .20
157 John Mobley .07 .20
158 Tim Biakabutuka .10 .30
159 Terrell Owens .20 .50
160 O.J. McDuffie .10 .30
161 Glenn Foley .10 .30
162 Derrick Brooks .20 .50
163 Dave Brown .07 .20
164 Ki-Jana Carter .07 .20
165 Bobby Hoying .10 .30
166 Randal Hill .07 .20
167 Michael Irvin .20 .50
168 Bruce Smith .10 .30
169 Troy Davis .07 .20
170 Derrick Mayes .10 .30
171 Henry Ellard .07 .20
172 Dana Stubblefield .07 .20
173 Willie McGinest .07 .20
174 Leeland McElroy .07 .20
175 Edgar Bennett .07 .20
176 Robert Porcher .07 .20
177 Randall Cunningham .20 .50
178 Jim Everett .07 .20
179 Jake Reed .10 .30
180 Quentin Coryatt .07 .20
182 Jason Sehorn .10 .30
183 Carnell Lake .07 .20
184 Dexter Coakley .07 .20
185 Derrick Alexander WR .10 .30
186 Johnnie Morton .10 .30
187 Irving Fryar .10 .30
188 Warren Moon .20 .50
189 Todd Collins .07 .20
190 Ken Norton Jr. .07 .20
191 Terry Glenn .20 .50
192 Rashaan Salaam .07 .20
193 Jerry Rice .40 1.00
194 James O.Stewart .10 .30
195 David LaFleur .07 .20
196 Eric Green .07 .20
197 Gus Frerotte .07 .20
198 Willie Green .07 .20
199 Marshall Faulk .25 .60
200 Brett Perriman .07 .20
201 Darnay Scott .10 .30
202 Marvin Harrison .20 .50
203 Joe Aska .07 .20
204 Darrien Gordon .07 .20
205 Herman Moore .10 .30
206 Curtis Martin .20 .50
207 Derek Loville .07 .20
208 Dale Carter .07 .20
209 Heath Shuler .07 .20
210 Jonathan Ogden .07 .20
211 Leslie Shepherd .07 .20
212 Tony Boselli .07 .20
213 Eric Metcalf .07 .20
214 Neil Smith .10 .30
215 Anthony Miller .07 .20
216 Jeff George .10 .30
217 Charles Way .07 .20
218 Mario Bates .10 .30
219 Ben Coates .10 .30
220 Michael Jackson .07 .20
221 Thurman Thomas .20 .50
222 Kyle Brady .07 .20
223 Marcus Allen .20 .50
224 Robert Brooks .10 .30
225 Yatil Green .07 .20
226 Byron Hanspard .07 .20
227 Andre Reed .10 .30
228 Chris Warren .10 .30
229 Jackie Harris .07 .20
230 Ricky Watters .10 .30
231 Bobby Engram .10 .30
232 Tamarick Vanover .07 .20
233 Peyton Manning RC 6.00 15.00
234 Curtis Enis RC .30 .75
235 Randy Moss RC 4.00 10.00
236 Charles Woodson RC 1.25 3.00
237 Robert Edwards RC .40 1.00
238 Jacquez Green RC .40 1.00
239 Keith Brooking RC .60 1.50
240 Jerome Pathon RC .60 1.50
241 Kevin Dyson RC .60 1.50
242 Fred Taylor RC .75 2.00
243 Tavian Banks RC .40 1.00
244 Marcus Nash RC .30 .75
245 Brian Griese RC 1.00 2.50
246 Andre Wadsworth RC .40 1.00
247 Ahman Green RC 1.25 3.00
248 Joe Jurevicius RC .60 1.50
249 Germane Crowell RC .40 1.00
250 Skip Hicks RC .40 1.00
251 Ryan Leaf RC .60 1.50
252 Hines Ward RC 2.50 6.00
253 John Elway OS .40 1.00
254 Mark Brunell OS .20 .50
255 Brett Favre OS .40 1.00
256 Troy Aikman OS .20 .50
257 Warrick Dunn OS .10 .30
258 Barry Sanders OS .30 .75
259 Eddie George OS .20 .50
260 Kordell Stewart OS .20 .50
261 Emmitt Smith OS .30 .75
262 Steve Young OS .20 .50
263 Terrell Davis OS .20 .50
264 Dorsey Levens OS .10 .30
265 Dan Marino OS .40 1.00
266 Jerry Rice OS .20 .50
267 Drew Bledsoe OS .20 .50
268 Brett Favre CL .25 .60
269 Barry Sanders CL .20 .50
270 Terrell Davis CL .20 .50
251AU Ryan Leaf AUTO 15.00 40.00

1998 Score Showcase

COMPLETE SET (110) 75.00 150.00
*SHOWCASE STARS: 2.5X TO 6X BASIC CARDS
*SHOWCASE RCs: .6X TO 1.5X BASIC CARDS
SHOWCASE STATED ODDS 1:7

1998 Score Showcase One-of-One

STATED PRINT RUN 1 SET

1998 Score Showcase Artist's Proofs

*STARS: 4X TO 10X BASIC CARDS
*ROOKIES: 1.5X TO 4X BASIC CARDS
SHOWCASE STATED ODDS 1:35

1998 Score Complete Players

Randomly inserted in packs at the rate of one in 11, this 30-card set features color action photos of ten top NFL all-around players printed on special cards with holographic foil stamping. Each player has three different cards that highlight three specific attributes.

COMPLETE SET (30) 35.00 80.00
STATED ODDS 1:11
1A Brett Favre 2.00 5.00
1B Brett Favre 2.00 5.00
1C Brett Favre 2.00 5.00
2A John Elway 2.00 5.00
2B John Elway 2.00 5.00
2C John Elway 2.00 5.00
3A Emmitt Smith 1.50 4.00
3B Emmitt Smith 1.50 4.00
3C Emmitt Smith 1.50 4.00
4A Kordell Stewart .50 1.25
4B Kordell Stewart .50 1.25
4C Kordell Stewart .50 1.25
5A Dan Marino 2.00 5.00
5B Dan Marino 2.00 5.00
5C Dan Marino 2.00 5.00
6A Mark Brunell .50 1.25
6B Mark Brunell .50 1.25
6C Mark Brunell .50 1.25
7A Terrell Davis .50 1.25
7B Terrell Davis .50 1.25
7C Terrell Davis .50 1.25
8A Barry Sanders 1.50 4.00
8B Barry Sanders 1.50 4.00
8C Barry Sanders 1.50 4.00
9A Warrick Dunn .50 1.25
9B Warrick Dunn .50 1.25
9C Warrick Dunn .50 1.25
10A Jerry Rice 1.00 2.50
10B Jerry Rice 1.00 2.50
10C Jerry Rice 1.00 2.50

1998 Score Epix

The set was produced as the final installment in the football Pinnacle Epix card sets. Combined with the two 1997 Epix insert sets, each player now has three subsets with three colors of each. Randomly inserted in '98 Score retail packs at the overall rate of one in 61, this set features color action photos that highlight Games, Seasons and Moments related to the featured player. Each subset grouping was produced in varying degress of difficulty with Games being the easiest and Moments the toughest to pull. Additionally, each card was produced in progressively scarce color versions with orange (easiest), purple, and emerald.

OVERALL STATED ODDS 1:61 HOBBY
*PURPLE CARDS: .75X TO 2X ORANGE
*EMERALD CARDS: 2X TO 4X ORANGE
ONLY ORANGE CARDS PRICED BELOW
E1 E.Smith SEASON 7.50 20.00
E2 T.Aikman SEASON 5.00 12.00
E3 T.Davis SEASON 2.50 6.00
E4 D.Bledsoe SEASON 4.00 10.00
E5 J.George SEASON 1.50 4.00
E6 K.Collins SEASON 1.50 4.00
E7 A.Freeman SEA 2.00 5.00
E8 H.Moore SEASON 2.00 5.00
E9 B.Sanders GAME 5.00 12.00
E10 B.Favre GAME 6.00 15.00
E11 M.Irvin GAME 1.25 3.00
E12 S.Young GAME 2.00 5.00
E13 M.Brunell GAME 2.50 6.00
E14 J.Bettis GAME 1.25 3.00
E15 D.Sanders GAME 1.25 3.00
E16 J.Blake GAME 1.25 3.00
E17 D.Marino MOMENT 10.00 25.00
E18 E.George MOMENT 2.00 5.00
E19 J.Rice MOMENT 5.00 12.00
E20 J.Elway MOMENT 10.00 25.00
E21 C.Martin MOMENT 2.50 6.00
E22 K.Stewart MOM 2.00 5.00
E23 J.Seau MOMENT 2.00 5.00
E24 R.White MOMENT 2.00 5.00

1998 Score Epix Hobby

Randomly inserted in packs, this 24-card set features color action player photos printed on high-tech dot matrix hologram cards with red foil highlights. Cards in this set are designated as Image (I1-I6) with only 1500 of these produced , Milestone (M7-M12) with a print run of 500 sets, Journey (J13-J18) with a print run of 3500 sets, and Showdown (S19-S24) with a print run of 2500 sets. A purple foil parallel version with a print run from 200 to 1750 and a green foil parallel version of this set with a print run from 30 to 500 were also produced.

COMPLETE SET (24) 60.00 120.00
RED IMAGE PRINT RUN 1500 SETS
RED MILESTONE PRINT RUN 500 SETS
RED JOURNEY PRINT RUN 3500 SETS
RED SHOWDOWN PRINT RUN 2500 SETS
*PURPLE CARDS: .6X TO 1.5X REDS
PURPLE IMAGE PRINT RUN 750 SETS
PURPLE MILESTONE PRINT RUN 200 SETS
PURPLE JOURNEY PRINT RUN 1750 SETS
PURPLE SHOWDOWN PRINT RUN 1250 SETS
*EMERALD 1-6/13-24: 1.5X TO 4X REDS
EMERALD IMAGE PRINT RUN 250 SETS
EMERALD JOURNEY PRINT RUN 500 SETS
EMERALD SHOWDOWN PRINT RUN 350 SETS
*EMERALD M7-M12: 4X TO 10X REDS
EMERALD MILESTONE PRINT RUN 30 SETS
OVERALL STATED ODDS 1:61
I1 B.Sanders Image 5.00 12.00
I2 C.Martin Image 1.25 3.00
I3 J.Elway Image 6.00 15.00
I4 J.Bettis Image 1.25 3.00
I5 D.Sanders Image 1.25 3.00
I6 C.Dillon Image 1.25 3.00
M7 T.Davis Milestone 4.00 10.00
M8 J.Rice Milestone 7.50 20.00
M9 E.George Milestone 2.00 5.00
M10 M.Brunell Milestone 6.00 15.00
M11 D.Levens Milestone 3.00 8.00
M12 K.Collins Milestone 1.25 3.00
J13 B.Favre Journey 3.00 8.00
J14 K.Stewart Journey 1.25 3.00
J15 S.Young Journey 1.00 2.50
J16 S.McNair Journey .60 1.50
J17 E.Smith Journey 2.50 6.00
J18 T.Glenn Journey .60 1.50
S19 W.Dunn Showdown 1.25 3.00
S20 D.Marino Showdown 4.00 10.00
S21 D.Bledsoe Showdown 1.50 4.00
S22 T.Aikman Showdown 2.00 5.00
S23 A.Freeman SHOW .75 2.00
S24 N.Kaufman SHOW .75 2.00

1998 Score Rookie Autographs

Randomly inserted into packs, this set features color photos of top rookies. Each card is branded to Pinnacle, not Score, and carries an announced print run of 500. Curtis Enis signed cards using either black or blue ink. Finally, an unsigned Peyton Manning card surfaced several years after the product initially was released. It is identical to all other cards in the set except that it does not include the autograph.

STATED PRINT RUN 500 SETS
1 Stephen Alexander 10.00 25.00
2 Tavian Banks 10.00 25.00
3 Charlie Batch 12.50 30.00
4 Keith Brooking 12.50 30.00
5 Thad Busby 10.00 25.00
6 John Dutton 7.50 20.00
7 Tim Dwight 12.50 30.00
8 Kevin Dyson 10.00 25.00
9 Robert Edwards 10.00 25.00
10 Greg Ellis 7.50 20.00
12A Curtis Enis Black Ink 10.00 25.00
12B Curtis Enis Blue Ink 10.00 25.00
13 Chris Fuamatu-Ma'afala 10.00 25.00
14 Ahman Green 20.00 40.00
15 Jacquez Green 10.00 25.00
16 Brian Griese 15.00 40.00
17 Skip Hicks 10.00 25.00
18 Robert Holcombe 10.00 25.00
19 Tebucky Jones 10.00 25.00
20 Joe Jurevicius 12.50 30.00
21 Ryan Leaf 12.50 30.00
22 Leonard Little 12.50 30.00
23 Alonzo Mayes 7.50 20.00
24 Randy Moss 75.00 150.00
25 Michael Myers 7.50 20.00
26 Marcus Nash 7.50 20.00
27 Jerome Pathon 12.50 30.00
28 Jason Peter 7.50 20.00
29 Anthony Simmons 10.00 25.00
30 Tony Simmons 10.00 25.00
31 Takeo Spikes 12.50 30.00
32 Duane Starks 7.50 20.00
33 Fred Taylor 20.00 40.00
34 Hines Ward 50.00 80.00
35 Peyton Manning No Auto 75.00 125.00

1998 Score Star Salute

This 20 card set features leading players from the base Score and Rookie Preview releases. The set was issued one every 35 packs and the cards were printed on textured silver foil stock. A promo version of each card was also issued with the word "promo" printed beneath the card number on the backs.

COMPLETE SET (20) 40.00 100.00
STATED ODDS 1:35
*PROMO: .3X TO .8X BASIC INSERTS
1 Terrell Davis 2.00 5.00
2 Barry Sanders 5.00 12.00
3 Steve Young 2.50 6.00
4 Drew Bledsoe 2.50 6.00
5 Kordell Stewart 1.25 3.00
6 Emmitt Smith 6.00 15.00
7 Dorsey Levens 1.25 3.00
8 Corey Dillon 2.00 5.00
9 Jerome Bettis 2.00 5.00
10 Herman Moore 1.00 2.50
11 Brett Favre 8.00 20.00
12 Antonio Freeman 1.25 3.00
13 Mark Brunell 2.00 5.00
14 John Elway 6.00 15.00
15 Terry Glenn 2.00 5.00
16 Warrick Dunn 2.00 5.00
17 Eddie George 2.00 5.00
18 Troy Aikman 3.00 8.00
19 Deion Sanders 2.00 5.00
20 Jerry Rice 4.00 10.00

1999 Score

This 275 card set, released in June 1999, was issued in 10 card hobby and retail packs. The last 55 cards of the set feature either 1999 Rookies or subsets of popular players and were all short printed. These cards were released in a ratio of one every three hobby packs and one every nine retail packs. Notable Rookie Cards include Tim Couch, Edgerrin James and Ricky Williams.

COMPLETE SET (275) 25.00 60.00
COMP.SET w/o SP's (220) 6.00 15.00
1 Randy Moss .20 .50
2 Randall Cunningham .20 .50
3 Cris Carter .25 .60
4 Robert Smith .15 .40
5 Jake Reed .20 .50
6 Leroy Hoard .15 .40
7 John Randle .25 .60
8 Brett Favre .50 1.25
9 Antonio Freeman .20 .50
10 Dorsey Levens .20 .50
11 Robert Brooks .20 .50
12 Derrick Mayes .15 .40
13 Mark Chmura .15 .40
14 Darick Holmes .15 .40
15 Vonnie Holliday .15 .40
16 Mike Alstott .15 .40
17 Warrick Dunn .15 .40
18 Trent Dilfer .15 .40
19 Jacquez Green .15 .40
20 Reidel Anthony .15 .40
21 Warren Sapp .20 .50
22 Bert Emanuel .20 .50
23 Curtis Enis .15 .40
24 Curtis Conway .20 .50
25 Bobby Engram .15 .40
26 Erik Kramer .20 .50
27 Moses Moreno .20 .50
28 Edgar Bennett .20 .50
29 Barry Sanders .40 1.00
30 Charlie Batch .15 .40
31 Herman Moore .20 .50
32 Johnnie Morton .20 .50
33 Germane Crowell .15 .40
34 Terry Fair .15 .40
35 Gary Brown .15 .40
36 Kent Graham .15 .40
37 Kerry Collins .15 .40
38 Charles Way .15 .40
39 Tiki Barber .20 .50
40 Ike Hilliard .15 .40
41 Joe Jurevicius .15 .40
42 Michael Strahan .20 .50
43 Jason Sehorn .20 .50
44 Brad Johnson .20 .50
45 Terry Allen .20 .50
46 Skip Hicks .15 .40
47 Michael Westbrook .15 .40
48 Leslie Shepherd .15 .40
49 Stephen Alexander .15 .40
50 Albert Connell .15 .40
51 Darrell Green .25 .60
52 Jake Plummer .15 .40
53 Adrian Murrell .15 .40
54 Frank Sanders .15 .40
55 Rob Moore .15 .40
56 Larry Centers .15 .40
57 Simeon Rice .15 .40
58 Andre Wadsworth .15 .40
59 Duce Staley .15 .40
60 Charles Johnson .15 .40
61 Charlie Garner .20 .50
62 Bobby Hoying .15 .40
63 Daryl Johnston .20 .50
64 Emmitt Smith .40 1.00
65 Troy Aikman .30 .75
66 Michael Irvin .25 .60
67 Deion Sanders .20 .50
68 Chris Warren .20 .50
69 Darren Woodson .20 .50
70 Rod Woodson .25 .60
71 Travis Jervey .20 .50
72 Jerry Rice .60 1.50
73 Terrell Owens .20 .50
74 Steve Young .30 .75
75 Garrison Hearst .15 .40
76 J.J. Stokes .15 .40
77 Ken Norton .15 .40
78 R.W. McQuarters .15 .40
79 Bryant Young .20 .50
80 Jamal Anderson .20 .50
81 Chris Chandler .20 .50
82 Terance Mathis .15 .40
83 Tim Dwight .20 .50
84 O.J. Santiago .15 .40
85 Chris Calloway .15 .40
86 Keith Brooking .20 .50
87 Eddie Kennison .20 .50
88 Willie Roaf .15 .40
89 Cam Cleeland .15 .40
90 Lamar Smith .15 .40
91 Sean Dawkins .15 .40
92 Tim Biakabutuka .20 .50
93 Muhsin Muhammad .15 .40
94 Steve Beuerlein .20 .50
95 Rae Carruth .15 .40
96 Wesley Walls .20 .50
97 Kevin Greene .25 .60
98 Trent Green .15 .40
99 Tony Banks .20 .50
100 Greg Hill .15 .40
101 Robert Holcombe .15 .40
102 Isaac Bruce .25 .60
103 Amp Lee .15 .40
104 Az-Zahir Hakim .15 .40
105 Warren Moon .25 .60
106 Jeff George .15 .40
107 Rocket Ismail .20 .50
108 Kordell Stewart .15 .40
109 Jerome Bettis .25 .60
110 Courtney Hawkins .15 .40
111 Chris Fuamatu-Ma'afala .15 .40
112 Levon Kirkland .15 .40
113 Hines Ward .20 .50
114 Will Blackwell .15 .40
115 Corey Dillon .15 .40
116 Carl Pickens .20 .50
117 Neil O'Donnell .20 .50
118 Jeff Blake .20 .50
119 Darnay Scott .15 .40
120 Takeo Spikes .15 .40
121 Steve McNair .20 .50
122 Frank Wycheck .20 .50
123 Eddie George .20 .50
124 Chris Sanders .15 .40
125 Yancey Thigpen .15 .40
126 Kevin Dyson .15 .40
127 Blaine Bishop .15 .40
128 Fred Taylor .15 .40
129 Mark Brunell .20 .50
130 Jimmy Smith .20 .50
131 Keenan McCardell .20 .50
132 Kyle Brady .15 .40
133 Tavian Banks .15 .40
134 James Stewart .15 .40
135 Kevin Hardy .15 .40
136 Jonathan Quinn .15 .40
137 Jermaine Lewis .15 .40
138 Priest Holmes .15 .40
139 Scott Mitchell .15 .40
140 Eric Zeier .15 .40
141 Patrick Johnson .15 .40
142 Ray Lewis .25 .60
143 Terry Kirby .15 .40
144 Ty Detmer .15 .40
145 Irv Smith .15 .40
146 Chris Spielman .20 .50
147 Antonio Langham .15 .40
148 Dan Marino .50 1.25
149 O.J. McDuffie .20 .50
150 Oronde Gadsden .15 .40
151 Karim Abdul-Jabbar .15 .40
152 Yatil Green .15 .40
153 Zach Thomas .20 .50
154 John Avery .15 .40
155 Lamar Thomas .15 .40
156 Drew Bledsoe .20 .50
157 Terry Glenn .20 .50
158 Ben Coates .20 .50
159 Shawn Jefferson .15 .40
160 Sedrick Shaw .15 .40
161 Tony Simmons .15 .40
162 Ty Law .25 .60
163 Robert Edwards .15 .40
164 Curtis Martin .20 .50
165 Keyshawn Johnson .20 .50
166 Vinny Testaverde .15 .40
167 Aaron Glenn .15 .40
168 Wayne Chrebet .15 .40
169 Dedric Ward .15 .40
170 Peyton Manning .75 2.00
171 Marshall Faulk .20 .50
172 Marvin Harrison .20 .50
173 Jerome Pathon .15 .40
174 Ken Dilger .15 .40
175 E.G. Green .15 .40
176 Doug Flutie .25 .60
177 Thurman Thomas .20 .50
178 Andre Reed .25 .60
179 Eric Moulds .15 .40
180 Antowain Smith .15 .40
181 Bruce Smith .20 .50
182 Rob Johnson .20 .50
183 Terrell Davis .20 .50
184 John Elway .40 1.00
185 Ed McCaffrey .20 .50
186 Rod Smith .20 .50
187 Shannon Sharpe .20 .50
188 Marcus Nash .15 .40
189 Brian Griese .15 .40
190 Neil Smith .15 .40
191 Bubby Brister .15 .40
192 Ryan Leaf .20 .50
193 Natrone Means .20 .50
194 Mikhael Ricks .15 .40
195 Junior Seau .20 .50
196 Jim Harbaugh .20 .50
197 Bryan Still .15 .40
198 Freddie Jones .15 .40
199 Andre Rison .20 .50
200 Elvis Grbac .15 .40
201 Byron Bam Morris .15 .40
202 Rashaan Shehee .15 .40
203 Kimble Anders .15 .40
204 Donnell Bennett .15 .40
205 Tony Gonzalez .20 .50
206 Derrick Alexander WR .15 .40
207 Jon Kitna .15 .40
208 Ricky Watters .20 .50
209 Joey Galloway .20 .50
210 Ahman Green .20 .50
211 Shawn Springs .15 .40
212 Michael Sinclair .15 .40
213 Napoleon Kaufman .15 .40
214 Tim Brown .25 .60
215 Charles Woodson .25 .60
216 Harvey Williams .15 .40
217 Jon Ritchie .15 .40
218 Rich Gannon .20 .50
219 Rickey Dudley .15 .40
220 James Jett .15 .40
221 Tim Couch RC .75 2.00
222 Ricky Williams RC 1.00 2.50
223 Donovan McNabb RC 2.00 5.00
224 Edgerrin James RC 1.00 2.50
225 Torry Holt RC 1.25 3.00
226 Daunte Culpepper RC 1.00 2.50
227 Akili Smith RC .60 1.50
228 Champ Bailey RC 1.25 3.00
229 Chris Claiborne RC .60 1.50
230 Chris McAlister RC .60 1.50
231 Troy Edwards RC .60 1.50
232 Jevon Kearse RC .75 2.00
233 Shaun King RC .60 1.50
234 David Boston RC .60 1.50
235 Peerless Price RC .60 1.50
236 Cecil Collins RC .60 1.50
237 Rob Konrad RC .60 1.50
238 Cade McNown UER RC .60 1.50
239 Shawn Bryson RC .60 1.50
240 Kevin Faulk RC .60 1.50
241 Scott Covington RC .60 1.50
242 James Johnson RC .60 1.50
243 Mike Cloud RC .60 1.50
244 Aaron Brooks RC .75 2.00
245 Sedrick Irvin RC .60 1.50
246 Amos Zereoue RC .60 1.50
247 Jermaine Fazande RC .60 1.50
248 Joe Germaine RC .75 2.00
249 Brock Huard RC .60 1.50
250 Craig Yeast RC .60 1.50
251 Travis McGriff RC .60 1.50
252 D'Wayne Bates RC .60 1.50
253 Na Brown RC .60 1.50
254 Tai Streets RC .75 2.00
255 Andy Katzenmoyer RC .75 2.00
256 Kevin Johnson RC .75 2.00
257 Joe Montgomery RC .60 1.50
258 Karsten Bailey RC .60 1.50
259 De'Mond Parker RC .60 1.50
260 Reginald Kelly RC .60 1.50
261 Eddie George AP .50 1.25
262 Jamal Anderson AP .50 1.25
263 Barry Sanders AP 1.00 2.50
264 Fred Taylor AP .40 1.00
265 Keyshawn Johnson AP .50 1.25
266 Jerry Rice AP 1.50 4.00
267 Doug Flutie AP .60 1.50
268 Deion Sanders AP .50 1.25
269 Randall Cunningham AP .50 1.25
270 Steve Young AP .75 2.00
271 J.Elway / T.Davis GC 1.00 2.50
272 P.Manning / M.Faulk GC 2.00 5.00
273 B.Favre / A.Freeman GC 1.25 3.00
274 T.Aikman / E.Smith GC 1.00 2.50
275 C.Carter / R.Moss GC .60 1.50

1999 Score Artist's Proofs

*STARS: 50X TO 120X BASIC CARDS
*RCs: 8X TO 20X BASIC CARDS
*APs/GCs: 15X TO 40X BASIC CARDS
STATED PRINT RUN 10 SERIAL #'d SETS

1999 Score Showcase

COMPLETE SET (275) 200.00 400.00
*STARS: 2.5X TO 6X BASIC CARDS
*RCs: .6X TO 1.5X BASIC CARDS
*APs/GCs: .8X TO 2X BASIC CARDS
STATED PRINT RUN 1989 SERIAL #'d SETS

1999 Score 10th Anniversary Reprints

These 20 cards were randomly inserted into retail packs. These cards were serial numbered to 1989 but only cards numbered above 151 were available in retail packs as they were unsigned.

COMPLETE SET (20) 30.00 60.00
STATED PRINT RUN 1989 SERIAL #'d SETS
FIRST 150-CARDS WERE SIGNED
1 Barry Sanders 5.00 12.00
2 Troy Aikman 3.00 8.00
3 John Elway 5.00 12.00
4 Cris Carter 1.50 4.00
5 Tim Brown 1.50 4.00
6 Doug Flutie 1.50 4.00
7 Chris Chandler 1.00 2.50
8 Thurman Thomas 1.00 2.50
9 Steve Young 2.00 5.00
10 Dan Marino 5.00 12.00
11 Derrick Thomas 1.00 2.50
12 Bubby Brister .60 1.50
13 Jerry Rice 3.00 8.00
14 Andre Rison 1.00 2.50
15 Randall Cunningham 1.50 4.00
16 Vinny Testaverde 1.00 2.50
17 Michael Irvin 1.00 2.50
18 Rod Woodson 1.00 2.50
19 Neil Smith 1.00 2.50
20 Deion Sanders 1.50 4.00

1999 Score 10th Anniversary Reprints Autographs

These 20 cards were randomly inserted into hobby packs. These cards were serial numbered to 150 and are individually autographed. Some cards were issued via mail redemptions that carried an expiration date of 5/1/2000.

STATED PRINT RUN 150 SERIAL #'d SETS
1 Barry Sanders 175.00 300.00
2 Troy Aikman 125.00 250.00
3 John Elway 100.00 200.00
4 Cris Carter 60.00 120.00
5 Tim Brown 60.00 120.00
6 Doug Flutie 30.00 80.00
7 Chris Chandler 30.00 80.00
8 Thurman Thomas 60.00 120.00
9 Steve Young 100.00 200.00
10 Dan Marino 125.00 250.00
11 Derrick Thomas 200.00 350.00
12 Bubby Brister 25.00 60.00
13 Jerry Rice 125.00 250.00
14 Andre Rison 50.00 100.00
15 Randall Cunningham 50.00 100.00
16 Vinny Testaverde 30.00 80.00
17 Michael Irvin 60.00 120.00
18 Rod Woodson 90.00 150.00
19 Neil Smith 25.00 60.00
20 Deion Sanders 100.00 175.00

1999 Score Complete Players

Inserted at a rate of one every 17 hobby packs and one every 25 retail packs, this 30 card set features 30 of the NFL's most versatile players featured on a foil board with foil stamping.

COMPLETE SET (30) 25.00 60.00
STATED ODDS 1:17 HOB, 1:35 RET
1 Antonio Freeman .75 2.00
2 Troy Aikman 1.50 4.00
3 Jerry Rice 1.50 4.00
4 Brett Favre 2.50 6.00
5 Cris Carter .75 2.00
6 Jamal Anderson .75 2.00
7 John Elway 2.50 6.00
8 Mark Brunell .75 2.00
9 Steve McNair .75 2.00
10 Kordell Stewart .50 1.25
11 Drew Bledsoe 1.00 2.50
12 Tim Couch .75 2.00
13 Dan Marino 2.50 6.00
14 Akili Smith .50 1.25
15 Peyton Manning 2.50 6.00
16 Jake Plummer .50 1.25
17 Jerome Bettis .75 2.00
18 Randy Moss 2.00 5.00
19 Keyshawn Johnson .75 2.00
20 Barry Sanders 2.50 6.00
21 Ricky Williams 1.00 2.50
22 Emmitt Smith 1.50 4.00
23 Corey Dillon .75 2.00
24 Dorsey Levens .75 2.00
25 Donovan McNabb 2.50 6.00
26 Curtis Martin .75 2.00
27 Eddie George .75 2.00
28 Fred Taylor .75 2.00
29 Steve Young 1.00 2.50
30 Terrell Davis .75 2.00

1999 Score Franchise

Inserted at a rate of one in 35, these 31 holographic foil cards feature a franchise player from each NFL team.

COMPLETE SET (31) 60.00 120.00
STATED ODDS 1:35
1 Brett Favre 6.00 15.00
2 Randy Moss 5.00 12.00
3 Mike Alstott 2.00 5.00
4 Barry Sanders 6.00 15.00
5 Curtis Enis .75 2.00
6 Ike Hilliard .75 2.00
7 Emmitt Smith 4.00 10.00
8 Jake Plummer 1.25 3.00
9 Brad Johnson 2.00 5.00
10 Duce Staley 2.00 5.00
11 Jamal Anderson 2.00 5.00
12 Steve Young 2.50 6.00
13 Eddie Kennison 1.25 3.00
14 Isaac Bruce 2.00 5.00
15 Muhsin Muhammad 1.25 3.00
16 Dan Marino 6.00 15.00
17 Drew Bledsoe 2.50 6.00
18 Curtis Martin 2.00 5.00
19 Doug Flutie 2.00 5.00
20 Peyton Manning 6.00 15.00
21 Kordell Stewart 1.25 3.00
22 Ty Detmer .75 2.00
23 Corey Dillon 2.00 5.00
24 Mark Brunell 2.00 5.00
25 Priest Holmes 3.00 8.00
26 Eddie George 2.00 5.00
27 John Elway 6.00 15.00
28 Natrone Means 1.25 3.00
29 Tim Brown 2.00 5.00
30 Andre Rison 1.25 3.00
31 Joey Galloway 1.25 3.00

1999 Score Future Franchise

Inserted one every 35 hobby packs, these 31 holographic foil cards feature two players from each team (one player is an established star while the other is a young prospect.

COMPLETE SET (31) 75.00 150.00
STATED ODDS 1:35 HOBBY
1 A.Brooks / B.Favre 5.00 12.00
2 D.Culpepper / R.Moss 4.00 10.00
3 Shaun King / M.Alstott 1.50 4.00
4 Sedrick Irvin / B.Sanders 5.00 12.00
5 Cade McNown / C.Enis 1.50 4.00
6 Joe Montgomery / I.Hilliard 1.25 3.00
7 Wane McGarity / E.Smith 3.00 8.00
8 David Boston / J.Plummer 1.50 4.00
9 Champ Bailey / B.Johnson 1.50 4.00
10 Don.McNabb / D.Staley 5.00 12.00
11 Reginald Kelly / J.Anderson 1.50 4.00
12 Tai Streets / S.Young 2.00 5.00
13 R.Williams / E.Kennison 2.50 6.00
14 Torry Holt / I.Bruce 3.00 8.00
15 Mike Rucker / M.Muhammad 1.50 4.00
16 James Johnson / D.Marino 5.00 12.00
17 Kevin Faulk / D.Bledsoe 1.50 4.00
18 Randy Thomas / C.Martin 1.25 3.00
19 Peerless Price / D.Flutie 2.50 6.00
20 E.James / P.Manning 5.00 12.00
21 Troy Edwards / K.Stewart 1.50 4.00
22 Tim Couch / T.Detmer 1.50 4.00
23 Akili Smith / C.Dillon 1.50 4.00
24 Fernando Bryant / M.Brunell 1.50 4.00
25 Chris McAlister / P.Holmes 2.50 6.00
26 Jevon Kearse / E.George 1.50 4.00
27 Travis McGriff / J.Elway 5.00 12.00
28 Jermaine Fazande / N.Means 1.25 3.00
29 Dameane Douglas / T.Brown 1.50 4.00
30 Mike Cloud / A.Rison 1.25 3.00
31 Brock Huard / J.Galloway 1.50 4.00

1999 Score Millennium Men

Issued exclusively in retail packs, these cards feature Barry Sanders and Ricky Williams. Each card is sequentially numbered to 1000 with the first 100 of each card autographed. Some cards were issued via mail redemptions that carried an expiration date of 5/1/2000.

COMPLETE SET (3) 30.00 60.00
STATED PRINT RUN 1000 SERIAL #'d SETS
FIRST 100-CARDS WERE SIGNED
INSERTED IN RETAIL PACKS ONLY
1 Barry Sanders 10.00 25.00
2 Ricky Williams 4.00 10.00
3 B.Sanders/R.Williams 10.00 25.00
1AU Barry Sanders AU 75.00 150.00
2AU Ricky Williams AU 30.00 80.00
3AU B.Sanders/R.Williams AU 125.00 250.00

1999 Score Numbers Game

Inserted randomly in hobby packs, these 30 holographic foil cards with gold foil stamping feature key yardage numbers for quarterbacks, runners and receivers. Each card is sequentially numbered to the player's specific statistics and that number is listed next to the player's name in the checklist.

COMPLETE SET (30) 25.00 60.00
RANDOM INSERTS IN HOBBY PACKS
1 Brett Favre/4212 2.50 6.00
2 Steve Young/4170 1.00 2.50
3 Jake Plummer/3737 1.00 2.50
4 Drew Bledsoe/3633 1.00 2.50
5 Dan Marino/3497 2.50 6.00
6 Peyton Manning/3739 2.00 5.00
7 Randall Cunningham/3704 .60 1.50
8 John Elway/2806 3.00 8.00
9 Doug Flutie/2711 1.00 2.50
10 Mark Brunell/2601 1.00 2.50
11 Troy Aikman/2330 2.00 5.00
12 Terrell Davis/2008 1.00 2.50
13 Jamal Anderson/1846 .75 2.00
14 Garrison Hearst/1570 .75 2.00
15 Barry Sanders/1491 4.00 10.00
16 Emmitt Smith/1332 2.50 6.00
17 Marshall Faulk/1319 1.50 4.00
18 Eddie George/1294 1.00 2.50
19 Curtis Martin/1287 .75 2.00
20 Fred Taylor/1223 .75 2.00
21 Corey Dillon/1130 .75 2.00
22 Antonio Freeman/1424 .75 2.00
23 Eric Moulds/1368 .75 2.00
24 Randy Moss/1313 2.50 6.00
25 Rod Smith/1222 .60 1.50
26 Jerry Rice/1157 2.50 6.00
27 Keyshawn Johnson/1131 .75 2.00
28 Terrell Owens/1097 1.00 2.50
29 Tim Brown/1012 1.00 2.50
30 Cris Carter/1011 1.00 2.50

1999 Score Rookie Preview Autographs

Randomly inserted into hobby packs, 34-rookies signed 600 cards for this set. Not all the cards were ready to be packed out so a few of them were only available in exchange form. The Shaun King exchange card #22 was later redeemable for an Olandis Gary signed card since King did not sign cards for the set. Some cards were issued via mail redemptions that carried an expiration date of 5/1/2000. The Desmond Clark signed card was released later through the 2001 Score Originals Autograph Graded set, but not issued in packs nor as an ungraded card.

STATED PRINT RUN 600 SIGNED SETS
RANDOM INSERTS IN HOBBY PACKS
1 Champ Bailey 7.50 20.00
2 D'Wayne Bates 4.00 10.00
3 Michael Bishop 6.00 15.00
4 David Boston 6.00 15.00
5 Na Brown 4.00 10.00
6 Shawn Bryson 4.00 10.00
7 Chris Claiborne 4.00 10.00
8 Mike Cloud 4.00 10.00
9 Cecil Collins 3.00 8.00
10 Daunte Culpepper 12.00 30.00
11 Autry Denson 4.00 10.00
12 Troy Edwards 4.00 10.00
13 Kevin Faulk 6.00 15.00
14 Joe Germaine 4.00 10.00
15 Torry Holt 6.00 15.00
16 Sedrick Irvin 3.00 8.00
17 Edgerrin James 20.00 40.00
18 James Johnson 6.00 15.00
19 Kevin Johnson 4.00 10.00
20 Corby Jones 3.00 8.00
21 Jevon Kearse 10.00 25.00
22 Olandis Gary 6.00 15.00
23 Jim Kleinsasser 4.00 10.00
24 Rob Konrad 4.00 10.00
25 Chris McAlister 6.00 15.00
26 Darnell McDonald 4.00 10.00
27 Travis McGriff 3.00 8.00
28 Donovan McNabb 20.00 50.00
29 Cade McNown 4.00 10.00
30 De'Mond Parker 3.00 8.00
31 Peerless Price 6.00 15.00
32 Akili Smith 3.00 8.00
33 Tai Streets 6.00 15.00
34 Ricky Williams 10.00 25.00

1999 Score Scoring Core

Issued at a rate of one in 17 hobby packs and one in 35 retail packs, these 30 holographic foil cards feature players who seem to be able to get the ball in the end zone.

COMPLETE SET (30) 25.00 60.00
STATED ODDS 1:17 HOB, 1:35 RET
1 Antonio Freeman .75 2.00
2 Troy Aikman 1.50 4.00
3 Jerry Rice 1.50 4.00
4 Brett Favre 2.50 6.00
5 Cris Carter .75 2.00
6 Jamal Anderson .75 2.00
7 John Elway 2.50 6.00
8 Tim Brown .75 2.00
9 Mark Brunell .75 2.00
10 Terrell Owens .75 2.00
11 Drew Bledsoe 1.00 2.50
12 Tim Couch .60 1.50
13 Dan Marino 2.50 6.00
14 Marshall Faulk 1.00 2.50
15 Peyton Manning 2.50 6.00
16 Jake Plummer .50 1.25
17 Jerome Bettis .75 2.00
18 Randy Moss 2.00 5.00
19 Charlie Batch .75 2.00
20 Barry Sanders 2.50 6.00
21 Ricky Williams .75 2.00
22 Emmitt Smith 1.50 4.00
23 Joey Galloway .50 1.25
24 Herman Moore .50 1.25
25 Natrone Means .50 1.25
26 Mike Alstott .75 2.00
27 Eddie George .75 2.00
28 Fred Taylor .75 2.00
29 Steve Young 1.00 2.50
30 Terrell Davis .75 2.00

1999 Score Settle the Score

Inserted at a rate on one in 17 retail packs, the dual-sided foil cards matches two players who compete against each other.

COMPLETE SET (30) 30.00 60.00
STATED ODDS 1:17 RETAIL
1 B.Favre / R.Cunningham 2.50 6.00
2 D.Marino / D.Flutie 2.50 6.00
3 E.Smith / T.Allen 1.50 4.00
4 B.Sanders / W.Dunn 2.50 6.00
5 E.George / C.Dillon .75 2.00
6 D.Bledsoe / V.Testaverde 1.00 2.50
7 T.Aikman / J.Plummer 1.50 4.00
8 T.Davis / J.Anderson .75 2.00
9 J.Elway / C.Chandler 2.50 6.00
10 M.Brunell / S.Young .75 2.00
11 C.Carter / H.Moore .75 2.00
12 K.Stewart / S.McNair .75 2.00
13 N.Means / N.Kaufman .75 2.00
14 C.Martin / M.Faulk 1.00 2.50
15 A.Freeman / T.Owens .75 2.00
16 T.Glenn / W.Chrebet .50 1.25
17 G.Hearst / D.Levens .50 1.25
18 R.Leaf / J.Kitna .75 2.00
19 Rob.Smith / M.Alstott .75 2.00
20 J.Rice / R.Moss 2.00 5.00
21 P.Manning / C.Batch 2.50 6.00
22 F.Taylor / J.Bettis .75 2.00
23 K.Johnson / E.Moulds .75 2.00
24 T.Couch / R.Williams 1.50 4.00
25 C.Pickens / I.Bruce .75 2.00
26 D.Sanders / C.Woodson .75 2.00
27 T.Brown / Rod Smith .75 2.00
28 D.Culpepper / D.McNabb 3.00 8.00
29 J.Galloway / E.McCaffrey .50 1.25
30 K.Abdul-Jabbar / Ant.Smith .75 2.00

1999 Score Supplemental

Released in complete set form only, the 1999 Score Supplemental set contains 110-cards intended to update the basic 1999 Score product. The set is broken down into 66 cards labeled 1999 Rookie, 24 Mid-Season update cards (which also included some 1999 rookies previously included in the base Score set), and 20 Star Salute veteran cards. Each sealed factory set also contained two packs of Score Supplemental Cards.

COMPLETE SET (110) 6.00 15.00
COMP.FACT.SET (110) 8.00 20.00
S1 Chris Greisen RC .15 .40
S2 Sherdrick Bonner RC .15 .40
S3 Joel Makovicka RC .15 .40
S4 Andy McCullough RC .15 .40
S5 Jeff Paulk RC .15 .40
S6 Brandon Stokley RC .20 .50
S7 Sheldon Jackson RC .15 .40
S8 Bobby Collins RC .15 .40
S9 Kamil Loud RC .15 .40
S10 Antoine Winfield RC .15 .40
S11 Jerry Azumah RC .15 .40
S12 James Allen RC .15 .40
S13 Nick Williams RC .15 .40
S14 Michael Basnight RC .15 .40
S15 Damon Griffin RC .25 .60
S16 Ronnie Powell RC .15 .40
S17 Darrin Chiaverini RC .15 .40
S18 Mark Campbell RC .15 .40
S19 Mike Lucky RC .15 .40
S20 Wane McGarity RC .15 .40
S21 Jason Tucker RC .20 .50
S22 Ebenezer Ekuban RC .15 .40
S23 Robert Thomas RC .15 .40
S24 Dat Nguyen RC .25 .60
S25 Olandis Gary RC .25 .60
S26 Desmond Clark RC .20 .50
S27 Andre Cooper RC .15 .40
S28 Chris Watson RC .15 .40
S29 Al Wilson RC .25 .60
S30 Cory Sauter RC .15 .40
S31 Brock Olivo RC .15 .40
S32 Basil Mitchell RC .15 .40
S33 Matt Snider RC .15 .40
S34 Antuan Edwards RC .15 .40
S35 Mike McKenzie RC .25 .60
S36 Terrence Wilkins RC .20 .50
S37 Fernando Bryant RC .15 .40
S38 Larry Parker RC .20 .50
S39 Autry Denson RC .15 .40
S40 Jim Kleinsasser RC .25 .60
S41 Michael Bishop RC .20 .50
S42 Andy Katzenmoyer .20 .50
S43 Brett Bech RC .15 .40
S44 Sean Bennett RC .15 .40
S45 Dan Campbell RC .25 .60
S46 Ray Lucas RC .20 .50
S47 Scott Dreisbach RC .15 .40
S48 Cecil Martin RC .15 .40
S49 Dameane Douglas RC .15 .40
S50 Jed Weaver RC .15 .40
S51 Jerame Tuman RC .15 .40
S52 Steve Heiden RC .15 .40
S53 Jeff Garcia RC .75 2.00
S54 Terry Jackson RC .15 .40
S55 Charlie Rogers RC .15 .40
S56 Lamar King RC .15 .40
S57 Kurt Warner RC 2.00 5.00
S58 Dre Bly RC .25 .60
S59 Justin Watson RC .15 .40
S60 Rabih Abdullah RC .15 .40
S61 Martin Gramatica RC .15 .40
S62 Darnell McDonald RC .15 .40
S63 Anthony McFarland RC .20 .50
S64 Larry Brown TE RC .15 .40
S65 Kevin Daft RC .15 .40
S66 Mike Sellers .20 .50
S67 Ken Oxendine MS .15 .40
S68 Errict Rhett MS .15 .40
S69 Stoney Case MS .15 .40
S70 Jonathan Linton MS .15 .40
S71 Marcus Robinson MS .20 .50
S72 Shane Matthews MS .15 .40
S73 Cade McNown MS .15 .40
S74 Akili Smith MS .15 .40
S75 Karim Abdul-Jabbar MS .15 .40
S76 Tim Couch MS .20 .50
S77 Kevin Johnson MS .20 .50
S78 Ron Rivers MS .15 .40
S79 Bill Schroeder MS .20 .50
S80 Edgerrin James MS .25 .60
S81 Cecil Collins MS .15 .40
S82 Matthew Hatchette MS .20 .50
S83 Daunte Culpepper MS .25 .60
S84 Ricky Williams MS .25 .60
S85 Tyrone Wheatley MS .20 .50
S86 Donovan McNabb MS 1.00 2.50
S87 Marshall Faulk MS .20 .50
S88 Torry Holt MS .30 .75
S89 Stephen Davis MS .15 .40
S90 Brad Johnson MS .20 .50
S91 Jake Plummer SS .15 .40
S92 Emmitt Smith SS .40 1.00
S93 Troy Aikman SS .30 .75
S94 John Elway SS .40 1.00
S95 Terrell Davis SS .20 .50
S96 Barry Sanders SS .40 1.00
S97 Brett Favre SS .50 1.25
S98 Antonio Freeman SS .20 .50
S99 Peyton Manning SS .75 2.00
S100 Fred Taylor SS .15 .40
S101 Mark Brunell SS .20 .50
S102 Dan Marino SS .50 1.25
S103 Randy Moss SS .20 .50
S104 Cris Carter SS .25 .60
S105 Drew Bledsoe SS .20 .50
S106 Terry Glenn SS .20 .50
S107 Keyshawn Johnson SS .20 .50
S108 Jerry Rice SS .60 1.50
S109 Steve Young SS .30 .75
S110 Eddie George SS .20 .50

1999 Score Supplemental Behind the Numbers

Randomly inserted in packs, this 30-card set features top players with profiled number statistics on an insert card sequentially numbered to 1000.

COMPLETE SET (30) 60.00 150.00
STATED PRINT RUN 1000 SER.#'d SETS
GOLDS RANDOM INSERTS IN PACKS
BN1 Kurt Warner 7.50 20.00
BN2 Tim Couch 2.50 6.00
BN3 Randy Moss 5.00 12.00
BN4 Brett Favre 6.00 15.00
BN5 Marvin Harrison 2.00 5.00
BN6 Terry Glenn 2.00 5.00
BN7 John Elway 6.00 15.00
BN8 Troy Aikman 4.00 10.00
BN9 Steve McNair 2.00 5.00
BN10 Kordell Stewart 2.00 5.00
BN11 Drew Bledsoe 2.50 6.00
BN12 Jon Kitna 2.00 5.00
BN13 Dan Marino 6.00 15.00
BN14 Jerry Rice 4.00 10.00
BN15 Edgerrin James 4.00 10.00
BN16 Jake Plummer 1.25 3.00
BN17 Antonio Freeman 2.00 5.00
BN18 Peyton Manning 6.00 15.00
BN19 Keyshawn Johnson 2.00 5.00
BN20 Barry Sanders 6.00 15.00
BN21 Cris Carter 2.00 5.00
BN22 Emmitt Smith 4.00 10.00
BN23 Steve Young 2.50 6.00
BN24 Ricky Williams 2.00 5.00
BN25 Doug Flutie 2.00 5.00
BN26 Mark Brunell 2.00 5.00
BN27 Eddie George 2.00 5.00
BN28 Fred Taylor 2.00 5.00
BN29 Donovan McNabb 5.00 12.00
BN30 Terrell Davis 2.00 5.00

1999 Score Supplemental Behind the Numbers Gold

GOLDS SERIAL #'d TO PLAYER'S JERSEY
CARDS SERIAL #'d UNDER 20 NOT PRICED
BN3 Randy Moss/84 20.00 50.00
BN5 Marvin Harrison/88 6.00 15.00
BN6 Terry Glenn/88 6.00 15.00
BN14 Jerry Rice/80 15.00 40.00
BN15 Edgerrin James/32 50.00 120.00
BN17 Antonio Freeman/86 6.00 15.00
BN20 Barry Sanders/20 60.00 150.00
BN21 Cris Carter/80 6.00 15.00
BN22 Emmitt Smith/22 75.00 150.00
BN24 Ricky Williams/34 30.00 60.00
BN27 Eddie George/27 20.00 50.00
BN28 Fred Taylor/28 20.00 50.00
BN30 Terrell Davis/30 30.00 80.00

1999 Score Supplemental Inscriptions

Randomly inserted at one in three sets, this 30-card set features authentic autographs by the pictured player. Some cards were issued in redemption form in packs that carried an expiration date of 5/31/2005.

BG14 Brian Griese 6.00 15.00
BJ14 Brad Johnson 7.50 20.00
BS15 Bart Starr 60.00 100.00
CC12 Chris Chandler 6.00 15.00
CD28 Corey Dillon 7.50 20.00
DL25 Dorsey Levens 7.50 20.00
DS22 Duce Staley 7.50 20.00
EC34 Earl Campbell 20.00 40.00
EM79 Eric Moss 6.00 15.00
EM80 Eric Moulds 7.50 20.00
IB80 Isaac Bruce 7.50 20.00
JB32 Jim Brown 40.00 80.00
JG84 Joey Galloway 7.50 20.00
JK7 Jon Kitna 6.00 15.00
JU19 Johnny Unitas 175.00 300.00
KS10 Kordell Stewart 6.00 15.00
KW13 Kurt Warner 50.00 80.00

MH88 Marvin Harrison 12.50 30.00
NM20 Natrone Means 6.00 15.00
PH33 Priest Holmes 7.50 20.00
RW34 Ricky Williams 12.50 30.00
SD48 Stephen Davis 6.00 15.00
SH20 Skip Hicks 6.00 15.00
SM9 Steve McNair 12.50 30.00
TB21 Tim Biakabutuka 6.00 15.00
TB81 Tim Brown 12.50 30.00
TO81 Terrell Owens 12.50 30.00
TT34 Thurman Thomas 12.50 30.00
VT16 Vinny Testaverde 7.50 20.00
WW85 Wesley Walls 6.00 15.00

1999 Score Supplemental Zenith Z-Team

Randomly inserted in packs, this 20-card set features top NFL players on a clear plastic card stock enhanced with holographic foil stamping. Each card is sequentially numbered to 100.

COMPLETE SET (20) 250.00 500.00
STATED PRINT RUN 100 SER.#'d SETS
1 Steve Young 8.00 20.00
2 Barry Sanders 20.00 50.00
3 Fred Taylor 6.00 15.00
4 Marshall Faulk 8.00 20.00
5 Emmitt Smith 12.50 30.00
6 Brett Favre 20.00 50.00
7 Troy Aikman 12.50 30.00
8 Terrell Davis 6.00 15.00
9 Edgerrin James 40.00 100.00
10 Drew Bledsoe 8.00 20.00
11 Dan Marino 20.00 50.00
12 Randy Moss 15.00 40.00
13 Ricky Williams 20.00 50.00
14 Mark Brunell 6.00 15.00
15 Jake Plummer 4.00 10.00
16 Jerry Rice 12.50 30.00
17 Peyton Manning 20.00 50.00
18 Tim Couch 25.00 60.00
19 Eddie George 6.00 15.00
20 John Elway 20.00 50.00

2000 Score

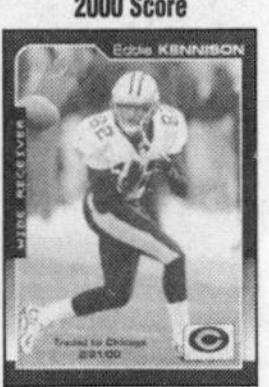

Released as a 330-card set, 2000 Score contained 220 base issue cards and 110 short prints, 55 prospects, 25 All-Pros, 20 League Leaders, and 10 Sophomore Showcase cards. Due to a printing error, in packs, Drew Bledsoe was released both in the base set and parallel sets in twice the quantity of the other cards (no #118 was included in packs). The Playoff Corp. offered a redemption for those that pulled a Bledsoe card in exchange for number 118 Terry Allen which was not issued in packs. Several rookies were issued via redemption cards which carried an expiration date of 7/01/2001.

COMP.SET w/o SP's (220) 7.50 20.00
276-330 ROOKIE ODDS 1:2 HOB, 1:6 RET
ROOKIE SP PRINT RUN 500
1 Michael Pittman .15 .40
2 Jake Plummer .15 .40
3 Rob Moore .15 .40
4 David Boston .15 .40
5 Frank Sanders .15 .40
6 Jamal Anderson .20 .50
7 Chris Chandler .20 .50
8 Tim Dwight .20 .50
9 Terance Mathis .15 .40
10 Shawn Jefferson .15 .40
11 Ashley Ambrose .15 .40
12 Peter Boulware .15 .40
13 Priest Holmes .15 .40
14 Tony Banks .15 .40
15 Qadry Ismail .15 .40
16 Shannon Sharpe .20 .50
17 Rod Woodson .25 .60
18 Matt Stover .15 .40
19 Michael McCrary .15 .40
20 Doug Flutie .20 .50
21 Rob Johnson .20 .50
22 Eric Moulds .15 .40
23 Peerless Price .20 .50
24 Jonathan Linton .15 .40
25 Antowain Smith .20 .50
26 Jay Riemersma .15 .40
27 Muhsin Muhammad .15 .40
28 Tim Biakabutuka .20 .50
29 Patrick Jeffers .15 .40
30 Wesley Walls .15 .40
31 Steve Beuerlein .20 .50
32 John Kasay .15 .40
33 Curtis Enis .15 .40
34 Cade McNown .15 .40
35 Marcus Robinson .20 .50
36 Bobby Engram .15 .40
37 Eddie Kennison .15 .40
38 Akili Smith .15 .40
39 Carl Pickens .20 .50
40 Corey Dillon .15 .40
41 Darnay Scott .20 .50
42 Errict Rhett .20 .50
43 Karim Abdul-Jabbar .15 .40
44 Tim Couch .20 .50
45 Kevin Johnson .15 .40
46 Darrin Chiaverini .15 .40
47 Terry Kirby .15 .40
48 Jason Tucker .15 .40
49 Rocket Ismail .20 .50
50 Joey Galloway .20 .50
51 Michael Irvin .25 .60
52 Troy Aikman .30 .75
53 Emmitt Smith .40 1.00
54 David LaFleur .15 .40
55 Trevor Pryce .15 .40
56 Brian Griese .15 .40
57 Olandis Gary .20 .50
58 Terrell Davis .20 .50
59 Rod Smith .20 .50
60 Ed McCaffrey .20 .50
61 Gus Frerotte .15 .40
62 Jason Elam .15 .40
63 Kavika Pittman .15 .40
64 James Stewart .15 .40
65 Charlie Batch .15 .40
66 Johnnie Morton .20 .50
67 Herman Moore .15 .40
68 Germane Crowell .15 .40
69 Barry Sanders .40 1.00
70 Chris Claiborne .15 .40
71 Brett Favre .50 1.25
72 Antonio Freeman .20 .50
73 Dorsey Levens .20 .50
74 De'Mond Parker .15 .40
75 Corey Bradford .15 .40
76 Basil Mitchell .15 .40
77 Bill Schroeder .20 .50
78 Peyton Manning .60 1.50
79 Marvin Harrison .20 .50
80 Terrence Wilkins .15 .40
81 Edgerrin James .20 .50
82 E.G. Green .15 .40
83 Chad Bratzke .15 .40
84 Mark Brunell .20 .50
85 Fred Taylor .15 .40
86 Jimmy Smith .20 .50
87 Keenan McCardell .20 .50
88 Kevin Hardy .15 .40
89 Aaron Beasley .15 .40
90 Elvis Grbac .15 .40
91 Derrick Alexander .15 .40
92 Tony Gonzalez .20 .50
93 Donnell Bennett .15 .40
94 Warren Moon .25 .60
95 Andre Rison .20 .50
96 James Hasty .15 .40
97 Dan Marino .50 1.25
98 Thurman Thomas .20 .50
99 James Johnson .15 .40
100 O.J. McDuffie .20 .50
101 Tony Martin .20 .50
102 Oronde Gadsden .20 .50
103 Zach Thomas .20 .50
104 Sam Madison .15 .40
105 Jay Fiedler .20 .50
106 Damon Huard .15 .40
107 Robert Smith .15 .40
108 Leroy Hoard .15 .40
109 Randy Moss .20 .50
110 Cris Carter .25 .60
111 Daunte Culpepper .20 .50
112 John Randle .25 .60
113 Randall Cunningham .20 .50
114 Gary Anderson .15 .40
115 Drew Bledsoe DP .20 .50
116 Terry Glenn .20 .50
117 Kevin Faulk .15 .40
118 Terry Allen SP 6.00 15.00
119 Adam Vinatieri .15 .40
120 Ty Law .25 .60
121 Lawyer Milloy .15 .40
122 Troy Brown .15 .40
123 Ben Coates .15 .40
124 Cam Cleeland .15 .40
125 Jeff Blake .20 .50
126 Ricky Williams .20 .50
127 Jake Reed .20 .50
128 Jake Delhomme RC .20 .50
129 Andrew Glover .15 .40
130 Keith Poole .15 .40
131 Joe Horn .20 .50
132 Kerry Collins .15 .40
133 Joe Montgomery .15 .40
134 Sean Bennett .15 .40
135 Amani Toomer .15 .40
136 Ike Hilliard .15 .40
137 Joe Jurevicius .15 .40
138 Tiki Barber .20 .50
139 Victor Green .15 .40
140 Ray Lucas .15 .40
141 Vinny Testaverde .15 .40
142 Curtis Martin .20 .50
143 Wayne Chrebet .15 .40
144 Tyrone Wheatley .15 .40
145 Rich Gannon .20 .50
146 Napoleon Kaufman .20 .50
147 Tim Brown .25 .60
148 Rickey Dudley .15 .40
149 Charles Woodson .25 .60
150 James Jett .20 .50
151 Duce Staley .15 .40
152 Charles Johnson .15 .40
153 Donovan McNabb .20 .50
154 Troy Vincent .15 .40
155 Troy Edwards .15 .40
156 Jerome Bettis .25 .60
157 Kordell Stewart .15 .40
158 Richard Huntley .15 .40
159 Hines Ward .20 .50
160 Levon Kirkland .15 .40
161 Ryan Leaf .20 .50
162 Jim Harbaugh .20 .50
163 Jermaine Fazande .15 .40
164 Natrone Means .20 .50
165 Junior Seau .20 .50
166 Curtis Conway .20 .50
167 Freddie Jones .15 .40
168 Jeff Graham .15 .40
169 Terrell Owens .20 .50
170 Jeff Garcia .15 .40
171 Jerry Rice .60 1.50
172 Steve Young .30 .75
173 Garrison Hearst .15 .40
174 Charlie Garner .20 .50
175 Fred Beasley .15 .40
176 Bryant Young .15 .40
177 Derrick Mayes .15 .40
178 Sean Dawkins .15 .40
179 Jon Kitna .15 .40
180 Ricky Watters .20 .50
181 Charlie Rogers .15 .40
182 Kurt Warner .40 1.00
183 Marshall Faulk .20 .50
184 Isaac Bruce .25 .60
185 Az-Zahir Hakim .15 .40
186 Trent Green .15 .40
187 Jeff Wilkins .15 .40
188 Torry Holt .20 .50
189 London Fletcher RC .40 1.00
190 Robert Holcombe .15 .40
191 Todd Lyght .15 .40
192 Keyshawn Johnson .20 .50
193 Derrick Brooks .15 .40
194 Warren Sapp .20 .50
195 Shaun King .15 .40
196 Warrick Dunn .15 .40
197 Mike Alstott .15 .40
198 Jacquez Green .15 .40
199 Reidel Anthony .15 .40
200 Martin Gramatica .15 .40
201 Donnie Abraham .15 .40
202 Steve McNair .20 .50
203 Eddie George .20 .50
204 Jevon Kearse .15 .40
205 Frank Wycheck .20 .50
206 Kevin Dyson .20 .50
207 Yancey Thigpen .15 .40
208 Al Del Greco .15 .40
209 Jeff George .20 .50
210 Adrian Murrell .15 .40
211 Brad Johnson .20 .50
212 Stephen Davis .15 .40
213 Stephen Alexander .15 .40
214 Michael Westbrook .15 .40
215 Darrell Green .20 .50
216 Champ Bailey .20 .50
217 Albert Connell .15 .40
218 Larry Centers .15 .40
219 Bruce Smith .20 .50
220 Deion Sanders .20 .50
221 Ricky Williams SS .25 .60
222 Edgerrin James SS .25 .60
223 Tim Couch SS .25 .60
224 Cade McNown SS .20 .50
225 Olandis Gary SS .25 .60
226 Torry Holt SS .25 .60
227 Donovan McNabb SS .25 .60
228 Shaun King SS .20 .50
229 Kevin Johnson SS .20 .50
230 Kurt Warner SS .50 1.25
231 Tony Gonzalez AP .25 .60
232 Frank Wycheck AP .25 .60
233 Eddie George AP .25 .60
234 Mark Brunell AP .25 .60
235 Corey Dillon AP .20 .50
236 Peyton Manning AP .75 2.00
237 Keyshawn Johnson AP .25 .60
238 Rich Gannon AP .25 .60
239 Terry Glenn AP .25 .60
240 Tony Brackens AP .20 .50
241 Edgerrin James AP .25 .60
242 Tim Brown AP .30 .75
243 Michael Strahan AP .25 .60
244 Kurt Warner AP .50 1.25
245 Brad Johnson AP .25 .60
246 Aeneas Williams AP .20 .50
247 Marshall Faulk AP .25 .60
248 Dexter Coakley AP .20 .50
249 Warren Sapp AP .25 .60
250 Mike Alstott AP .20 .50
251 David Sloan AP .20 .50
252 Cris Carter AP .30 .75
253 Muhsin Muhammad AP .20 .50
254 Isaac Bruce AP .30 .75
255 Wesley Walls AP .20 .50
256 Steve Beuerlein LL .25 .60
257 Kurt Warner LL .50 1.25
258 Peyton Manning LL .75 2.00
259 Brad Johnson LL .25 .60
260 Edgerrin James LL .25 .60
261 Curtis Martin LL .25 .60
262 Stephen Davis LL .20 .50
263 Emmitt Smith LL .50 1.25
264 Marvin Harrison LL .25 .60
265 Jimmy Smith LL .25 .60
266 Randy Moss LL .25 .60
267 Marcus Robinson LL .25 .60
268 Kevin Carter LL .20 .50
269 Simeon Rice LL .25 .60
270 Robert Porcher LL .20 .50
271 Jevon Kearse LL .20 .50
272 Mike Vanderjagt LL .20 .50
273 Olindo Mare LL .20 .50
274 Todd Peterson LL .20 .50
275 Mike Hollis LL .20 .50
276 Mike Anderson RC/500 5.00 12.00
277 Peter Warrick RC .50 1.25
278 Courtney Brown RC .60 1.50
279 Plaxico Burress RC .60 1.50
280 Corey Simon RC .60 1.50
281 Thomas Jones RC .60 1.50
282 Travis Taylor RC .50 1.25
283 Shaun Alexander RC .75 2.00
284 Patrick Pass RC/500 5.00 12.00
285 Chris Redman RC .50 1.25
286 Chad Pennington RC .60 1.50
287 Jamal Lewis RC .75 2.00
288 Brian Urlacher RC 2.50 6.00
289 Bubba Franks RC .50 1.25
290 Dez White RC .50 1.25
291 Frank Moreau RC/500 5.00 12.00
292 Ron Dayne RC .75 2.00
293 Sylvester Morris RC .50 1.25
294 R.Jay Soward RC .50 1.25
295 Curtis Keaton RC .50 1.25
296 Spergon Wynn RC/500 5.00 12.00
297 Rondell Mealey RC .50 1.25
298 Travis Prentice RC .50 1.25
299 Darrell Jackson RC .50 1.25
300 Giovanni Carmazzi RC .50 1.25
301 Anthony Lucas RC .50 1.25
302 Danny Farmer RC .50 1.25
303 Dennis Northcutt RC .50 1.25
304 Troy Walters RC .50 1.25
305 Laveranues Coles RC .60 1.50
306 Kwame Cavil RC .50 1.25
307 Tee Martin RC .50 1.25
308 J.R. Redmond RC .50 1.25
309 Tim Rattay RC .60 1.50
310 Jerry Porter RC .75 2.00
311 Michael Wiley RC .50 1.25
312 Reuben Droughns RC .50 1.25
313 Trung Canidate RC .50 1.25
314 Shyrone Stith RC .50 1.25
315 Marc Bulger RC .60 1.50
316 Tom Brady RC 60.00 125.00
317 Doug Johnson RC .50 1.25
318 Todd Husak RC .50 1.25
319 Gari Scott RC .50 1.25
320 Windrell Hayes RC/500 5.00 12.00
321 Chris Cole RC .60 1.50
322 Sammy Morris RC .50 1.25
323 Trevor Gaylor RC .50 1.25
324 Jarious Jackson RC .60 1.50
325 Doug Chapman RC/500 5.00 12.00
326 Ron Dugans RC .50 1.25
327 Ron Dixon RC/500 5.00 12.00
328 Joe Hamilton RC .50 1.25
329 Todd Pinkston RC .50 1.25
330 Chad Morton RC .60 1.50

2000 Score Final Score

*1-220 VET/54-66: 10X TO 25X BASIC CARDS
*1-220 VET/40-50: 12X TO 30X BASIC CARD
*1-220 VET/25-35: 15X TO 40X BASIC CARD
*221-275 SUBSET/54-66: 8X TO 20X
*221-275 SUBSET/40-50: 10X TO 25X
*221-275 SUBSET/25-35: 12X TO 30X
*277-330 ROOKIE/54-66: 3X TO 8X
*277-330 ROOKIE/40-50: 4X TO 10X
*277-330 ROOKIE/25-35: 5X TO 12X
*276/284/296/320/327 ROOKIE: .6X TO 1.2X
*291/325 ROOKIE/40-54: .5X TO 1X
CARDS SER.#'d TO A 1999 SEASON STAT
316 Tom Brady/32 400.00 700.00

2000 Score Scorecard

*VETS 1-220: 2X TO 5X BASIC CARDS
*SUBSET 221-275: .8X TO 2X
*ROOKIE 276-330: 1.2X TO 3X BASIC RC
*ROOKIE 276-330: .2X TO .5X BASE RC/500
STATED PRINT RUN 2000 SER.#'d SETS
316 Tom Brady 100.00 200.00

2000 Score Air Mail

Randomly inserted in packs at the rate of one in 70, this 30-card set features top quarterbacks and receivers on a die cut card. In the upper right corner, a "postage stamp" appears with a portrait player photo. Card backs carry an "AM" prefix.

COMPLETE SET (30) 60.00 120.00
STATED ODDS 1:70 HOB/RET
*FIRST CLASS/50: 1.5X TO 4X BASIC INSERTS
FIRST CLASS PRINT RUN 50
AM1 Isaac Bruce 1.00 2.50
AM2 Cris Carter 1.00 2.50
AM3 Tim Dwight .75 2.00
AM4 Joey Galloway .75 2.00
AM5 Marvin Harrison .75 2.00
AM6 Keyshawn Johnson .75 2.00
AM7 Jon Kitna .60 1.50
AM8 Steve McNair .75 2.00
AM9 Eric Moulds .60 1.50
AM10 Drew Bledsoe .75 2.00
AM11 John Elway 1.50 4.00
AM12 Brett Favre 2.00 5.00
AM13 Antonio Freeman .75 2.00
AM14 Peyton Manning 2.50 6.00
AM15 Randy Moss .75 2.00
AM16 Jake Plummer .60 1.50
AM17 Steve Young 1.25 3.00
AM18 Troy Aikman 1.25 3.00
AM19 Mark Brunell .75 2.00
AM20 Tim Couch .75 2.00
AM21 Dan Marino 2.00 5.00
AM22 Jerry Rice 2.50 6.00
AM23 Kevin Johnson .60 1.50
AM24 Michael Westbrook .60 1.50
AM25 Kurt Warner 1.50 4.00
AM26 Doug Flutie .75 2.00
AM27 Jimmy Smith .75 2.00
AM28 Germane Crowell .60 1.50
AM29 Cade McNown .60 1.50
AM30 Muhsin Muhammad .60 1.50

2000 Score Building Blocks

Randomly seeded in packs at the rate of one in 17, this 30-card set highlights young stars who have the potential to be the franchise player of their team. Full color action shots accent the front of the card. Card backs carry a "BB" prefix.

COMPLETE SET (30) 12.50 30.00
STATED ODDS 1:17 HOB, 1:35 RET
BB1 Cade McNown .40 1.00
BB2 Peerless Price .50 1.25
BB3 Akili Smith .40 1.00
BB4 Randy Moss .50 1.25
BB5 Edgerrin James .50 1.25
BB6 Kurt Warner 1.00 2.50
BB7 Ray Lucas .40 1.00
BB8 Jevon Kearse .40 1.00
BB9 Torry Holt .50 1.25
BB10 Ricky Williams .50 1.25
BB11 Daunte Culpepper .50 1.25
BB12 Fred Taylor .40 1.00
BB13 Brian Griese .40 1.00
BB14 Marcus Robinson .50 1.25
BB15 David Boston .40 1.00
BB16 James Johnson .40 1.00
BB17 Charlie Batch .40 1.00
BB18 Jake Plummer .40 1.00
BB19 Duce Staley .40 1.00
BB20 Germane Crowell .40 1.00
BB21 Curtis Enis .40 1.00
BB22 Donovan McNabb .50 1.25
BB23 Tim Couch .50 1.25
BB24 Stephen Davis .40 1.00
BB25 Jon Kitna .40 1.00
BB26 Shaun King .40 1.00
BB27 Kevin Johnson .40 1.00
BB28 Peyton Manning 1.50 4.00
BB29 Olandis Gary .50 1.25
BB30 Muhsin Muhammad .40 1.00

2000 Score Complete Players

Randomly inserted in packs at the rate of one in 17 Hobby and one in 35 Retail, this 40-card set features the NFL's most versatile athletes on red foil board with holographic foil stamping. Card backs carry a "CP" prefix.

COMPLETE SET (40) 25.00 60.00
STATED ODDS 1:17 HOB, 1:35 RET
*BLUE: 2.5X TO 6X BASIC INSERTS
BLUE ODDS 1:359 HOB, 1:718 RET
*GREEN: 4X TO 10X BASIC INSERTS
GREEN ODDS 1:718 HOB,1:1435 RET
CP1 Eric Moulds .40 1.00
CP2 Tim Couch .50 1.25
CP3 Marvin Harrison .50 1.25
CP4 Brett Favre 1.25 3.00
CP5 Steve Young .75 2.00
CP6 Brad Johnson .50 1.25
CP7 Randy Moss .50 1.25
CP8 Mark Brunell .50 1.25
CP9 Steve McNair .50 1.25
CP10 Donovan McNabb .50 1.25
CP11 Drew Bledsoe .50 1.25
CP12 Kurt Warner 1.00 2.50
CP13 Dan Marino 1.25 3.00
CP14 Muhsin Muhammad .40 1.00
CP15 Jimmy Smith .50 1.25
CP16 Fred Taylor .40 1.00
CP17 Corey Dillon .40 1.00
CP18 Peyton Manning 1.50 4.00
CP19 Keyshawn Johnson .50 1.25
CP20 Barry Sanders 1.00 2.50
CP21 Brian Griese .40 1.00
CP22 Emmitt Smith 1.00 2.50
CP23 Jerry Rice 1.50 4.00
CP24 Joey Galloway .50 1.25
CP25 Cris Carter .60 1.50
CP26 Robert Smith .40 1.00
CP27 Eddie George .50 1.25
CP28 Marshall Faulk .50 1.25
CP29 Tim Brown .60 1.50
CP30 Terrell Davis .50 1.25
CP31 Jamal Anderson .50 1.25
CP32 Edgerrin James .50 1.25
CP33 Antowain Smith .50 1.25
CP34 Antonio Freeman .50 1.25
CP35 Isaac Bruce .60 1.50
CP36 Stephen Davis .40 1.00
CP37 Troy Aikman .75 2.00
CP38 Kevin Johnson .40 1.00
CP39 Ricky Watters .50 1.25
CP40 Mike Alstott .40 1.00

2000 Score Franchise

Randomly inserted in Retail packs at the rate of one in 35, this 31-card set features team franchise players on a holographic foil card stock with gold foil highlights.

COMPLETE SET (31) 30.00 60.00
STATED ODDS 1:35 RETAIL
F1 Emmitt Smith 1.50 4.00
F2 Amani Toomer .60 1.50
F3 Jake Plummer .60 1.50
F4 Brad Johnson .75 2.00
F5 Donovan McNabb .75 2.00
F6 Jerry Rice 2.50 6.00
F7 Jamal Anderson .75 2.00
F8 Marshall Faulk .75 2.00
F9 Steve Beuerlein .75 2.00
F10 Ricky Williams .75 2.00
F11 Brett Favre 2.00 5.00
F12 Barry Sanders 1.50 4.00
F13 Randy Moss .75 2.00
F14 Shaun King .60 1.50
F15 Cade McNown .60 1.50
F16 Dan Marino 2.00 5.00
F17 Drew Bledsoe .75 2.00
F18 Curtis Martin .75 2.00
F19 Peyton Manning 2.50 6.00
F20 Eric Moulds .60 1.50
F21 Mark Brunell .75 2.00
F22 Akili Smith .60 1.50
F23 Tim Couch .75 2.00
F24 Jerome Bettis 1.00 2.50
F25 Qadry Ismail .60 1.50
F26 Eddie George .75 2.00
F27 Jim Harbaugh .75 2.00
F28 Terrell Davis .75 2.00
F29 Elvis Grbac .60 1.50
F30 Tim Brown 1.00 2.50
F31 Jon Kitna .60 1.50

2000 Score Future Franchise

Randomly inserted in Hobby packs at the rate of one in 35, this 31-card dual-sided set matches rookies and veterans on an all holographic foil card stock. Card backs carry an "FF" prefix. Some cards were issued via redemption cards which carried an expiration date of 7/01/2001.

COMPLETE SET (30) 25.00 60.00
STATED ODDS 1:35 HOBBY
FF1 M.Wiley E.Smith 1.25 3.00
FF2 R.Dayne A.Toomer .75 2.00
FF3 T.Jones J.Plummer .60 1.50
FF4 T.Husak B.Johnson .60 1.50
FF5 T.Pinkston D.McNabb .60 1.50
FF6 G.Carmazzi J.Rice 2.00 5.00
FF7 M.Philyaw J.Anderson .60 1.50
FF8 T.Canidate M.Faulk .60 1.50
FF9 D.Grant S.Beuerlein .60 1.50
FF10 M.Bulger R.Williams .60 1.50
FF11 B.Franks B.Favre 1.50 4.00
FF12 R.Droughns B.Sanders 1.25 3.00
FF13 D.Chapman R.Moss .60 1.50
FF14 J.Hamilton S.King .50 1.25
FF15 D.White C.McNown .50 1.25
FF16 B.Kelly D.Marino 1.50 4.00
FF17 J.R.Redmond D.Bledsoe .60 1.50
FF18 C.Pennington C.Martin .60 1.50
FF19 R.Morris P.Manning 2.00 5.00
FF20 S.Morris E.Moulds .50 1.25
FF21 R.Soward M.Brunell .60 1.50
FF22 P.Warrick Ak.Smith .50 1.25
FF23 C.Brown T.Couch .60 1.50
FF24 P.Burress J.Bettis .75 2.00
FF25 Jam.Lewis Q.Ismail .75 2.00
FF26 K.Bulluck E.George .60 1.50
FF27 T.Gaylor J.Harbaugh .60 1.50
FF28 C.Cole T.Davis .60 1.50
FF29 Syl.Morris E.Grbac .50 1.25
FF30 J.Porter T.Brown .75 2.00
FF31 S.Alexander J.Kitna .75 2.00

2000 Score Millennium Men

Randomly inserted in Retail packs, this six-card set is a continuation of the 1999 Millennium Men set that contained card numbers 1-3. Cards feature both single player and dual player versions and are sequentially numbered to 1000 with the first 200 serial numbered copies autographed. Card backs carry an "MM" prefix.

COMPLETE SET (6) 40.00 80.00
STATED PRINT RUN 1000 SER.#'d SETS
FIRST 200-CARDS AUTOGRAPHED
MM4 Randy Moss 2.50 6.00
MM5 Chad Pennington 1.50 4.00
MM6 R.Moss C.Pennington 1.50 4.00
MM7 Peyton Manning 8.00 20.00
MM8 Tee Martin 2.00 5.00
MM9 T.Martin P.Manning 8.00 20.00

2000 Score Millennium Men Autographs

Randomly inserted in Retail packs, this 6-card set parallels the base Millennium Men insert set with an autographed variation. The first 200 serial numbered copies were autographed. Card backs carry an "MM" prefix.

FIRST 200-CARDS OF PRINT RUN
MM4 Randy Moss 30.00 60.00
MM5 Chad Pennington 10.00 25.00
MM6 R.Moss C.Pennington 30.00 80.00
MM7 Peyton Manning 40.00 100.00
MM8 Tee Martin 6.00 15.00
MM9 T.Martin P.Manning 40.00 100.00

2000 Score Numbers Game Silver

Randomly inserted in Hobby packs, this 25-card set features 25 of the NFL's top offensive players on a holographic foil card with colors to match each respective player's team. The silver foil version cards are numbered to a total yards rushing, receiving or passing statistic from the 1999 season, while the gold foil cards are numbered to a total attempts, receptions, or completions statistic from the 1999 season.

CARDS SER.#'d TO A 1999 SEASON STAT
STATED PRINT RUN 732-4436
NG1 Kurt Warner/4353 1.00 2.50
NG2 Steve Beuerlein/4436 .50 1.25
NG3 Peyton Manning/4135 1.50 4.00
NG4 Brad Johnson/4005 .50 1.25
NG5 Steve McNair/2179 .60 1.50
NG6 Mark Brunell/3060 .50 1.25
NG7 Marvin Harrison/1663 .60 1.50
NG8 Isaac Bruce/1165 .75 2.00
NG9 Cris Carter/1241 .75 2.00
NG10 Randy Moss/1413 .60 1.50
NG11 Marcus Robinson/1444 .60 1.50
NG12 Terry Glenn/1147 .60 1.50
NG13 Edgerrin James/1553 .60 1.50
NG14 Curtis Martin/1464 .60 1.50
NG15 Stephen Davis/1405 .50 1.25
NG16 Emmitt Smith/1397 1.25 3.00
NG17 Marshall Faulk/1381 .60 1.50
NG18 Eddie George/1304 .60 1.50
NG19 Olandis Gary/1159 .60 1.50
NG20 Dorsey Levens/1034 .60 1.50
NG21 Robert Smith/1015 .50 1.25
NG22 Jerome Bettis/1091 .75 2.00
NG23 Corey Dillon/1200 .50 1.25
NG24 Drew Bledsoe/3985 .50 1.25
NG25 Fred Taylor/732 .50 1.25

2000 Score Numbers Game Gold

STATED PRINT RUN 69-369
CARDS SER.#'d TO A 1999 SEASON STAT
NG1 Kurt Warner/325 2.00 5.00
NG2 Steve Beuerlein/343 1.00 2.50
NG3 Peyton Manning/331 3.00 8.00
NG4 Brad Johnson/316 1.00 2.50
NG5 Steve McNair/187 1.00 2.50
NG6 Mark Brunell/259 1.00 2.50
NG7 Marvin Harrison/115 1.25 3.00
NG8 Isaac Bruce/77 1.50 4.00
NG9 Cris Carter/90 1.50 4.00
NG10 Randy Moss/80 1.25 3.00
NG11 Marcus Robinson/84 1.25 3.00
NG12 Terry Glenn/69 1.25 3.00
NG13 Edgerrin James/369 1.00 2.50
NG14 Curtis Martin/367 1.00 2.50
NG15 Stephen Davis/290 .75 2.00
NG16 Emmitt Smith/329 2.00 5.00
NG17 Marshall Faulk/253 1.00 2.50
NG18 Eddie George/320 1.00 2.50
NG19 Olandis Gary/276 1.00 2.50
NG20 Dorsey Levens/279 1.00 2.50
NG21 Robert Smith/221 .75 2.00
NG22 Jerome Bettis/299 1.25 3.00
NG23 Corey Dillon/263 .75 2.00
NG24 Drew Bledsoe/305 1.00 2.50
NG25 Fred Taylor/159 .75 2.00

2000 Score Rookie Preview Autographs

Randomly inserted in Hobby packs at the rate of one in 70, this set features authentic autographs of top rookies from the 2000 NFL draft. Reportedly, between 300 and 700 of each card were signed. Several cards were issued via redemption cards which carried an expiration date of 7/01/2001. Finally, additional cards appeared on the market after Pinnacle ceased operations including Courtney Brown, Bubba Franks, Ben Kelly, Sekou Sanyika and Brian Urlacher missing the autograph. Neither player apparently signed any certified cards for this set.

STATED ODDS 1:70 HOBBY
ANNOUNCED PRINT RUNS 300-700
SR2 Peter Warrick 6.00 15.00
SR3 Courtney Brown No AU 1.50 4.00
SR4 Plaxico Burress 8.00 20.00
SR5 Corey Simon 8.00 20.00
SR6 Thomas Jones 8.00 20.00
SR7 Travis Taylor 6.00 15.00
SR8 Shaun Alexander 10.00 25.00
SR9 Deon Grant 6.00 15.00
SR10 Chris Redman 6.00 15.00
SR11 Chad Pennington 8.00 20.00
SR12 Jamal Lewis 10.00 25.00
SR13 Brian Urlacher No AU 4.00 10.00
SR14 Bubba Franks No AU 1.25 3.00
SR15 Dez White 6.00 15.00
SR16 Ahmed Plummer 6.00 15.00
SR17 Ron Dayne 10.00 25.00
SR18 Sylvester Morris 6.00 15.00
SR19 R.Jay Soward 6.00 15.00
SR20 Sherrod Gideon 6.00 15.00
SR21 Ben Kelly No AU 1.25 3.00
SR22 Sekou Sanyika No AU 1.25 3.00
SR23 Travis Prentice 6.00 15.00
SR24 Darrell Jackson 6.00 15.00
SR25 Giovanni Carmazzi 6.00 15.00
SR26 Anthony Lucas 6.00 15.00
SR27 Danny Farmer 6.00 15.00
SR28 Dennis Northcutt 6.00 15.00
SR29 Troy Walters 6.00 15.00
SR30 Laveranues Coles 8.00 20.00
SR31 Kwame Cavil 6.00 15.00
SR32 Tee Martin 6.00 15.00
SR33 J.R. Redmond 6.00 15.00
SR34 Tim Rattay 8.00 20.00
SR35 Jerry Porter 10.00 25.00
SR36 Michael Wiley 6.00 15.00
SR37 Reuben Droughns 6.00 15.00
SR38 Trung Canidate 6.00 15.00
SR39 Shyrone Stith 6.00 15.00
SR40 Marc Bulger 8.00 20.00
SR41 Tom Brady 400.00 800.00
SR42 Doug Johnson 6.00 15.00
SR43 Todd Husak 6.00 15.00
SR44 Gari Scott 6.00 15.00
SR45 Chafie Fields 6.00 15.00
SR47 Sammy Morris 6.00 15.00
SR50 Trevor Gaylor 6.00 15.00
SR51 Ron Dugans 6.00 15.00
SR52 Chris Daniels 6.00 15.00
SR53 Joe Hamilton 6.00 15.00
SR54 Todd Pinkston 6.00 15.00

2000 Score Rookie Preview Autographs Roll Call

*AUTO/50: .8X TO 2X BASIC AU
ROLL CALL PRINT RUN 50 SER.#'d SETS
SR41 Tom Brady 2000.00 3000.00

2000 Score Team 2000

Randomly inserted in boxes, this 20-card set features players on their reprinted Score Rookie Card. Card fronts feature a blue foil "Team 2000" stamp and are sequentially numbered to 1500. A Gold foil version was inserted in retail packs with each card serial numbered to the player's rookie year. Green (200-sets) and Red (500-sets) foil parallels were also produced and inserted in hobby packs.

COMPLETE SET (20) 15.00 40.00
BLUE PRINT RUN 1500 SER.#'d SETS
BLUE/1500 HOBBY BOX TOPPER INSERT
*GOLD/1989-1999: .4X TO 1X BLUE/1500
GOLD STATED PRINT RUN 1989-1999
GOLDS RETAIL BOX TOPPER INSERT
*GREEN/200: 1X TO 2.5X BLUE/1500
GREEN PRINT RUN 200 SER.#'d SETS
*RED/500: .6X TO 1.5X BLUE/1500
RED PRINT RUN 500 SER.#'d SETS
TM1 Barry Sanders 1.25 3.00
TM2 Troy Aikman 1.00 2.50
TM3 Cris Carter .75 2.00
TM4 Emmitt Smith 1.25 3.00
TM5 Brett Favre 1.50 4.00
TM6 Jimmy Smith .60 1.50
TM7 Drew Bledsoe .60 1.50
TM8 Marshall Faulk .60 1.50
TM9 Steve McNair .60 1.50
TM10 Marvin Harrison .60 1.50
TM11 Eddie George .60 1.50
TM12 Eric Moulds .50 1.25
TM13 Jake Plummer .50 1.25
TM14 Antowain Smith .60 1.50
TM15 Fred Taylor .50 1.25
TM16 Randy Moss .60 1.50
TM17 Peyton Manning 2.00 5.00
TM18 Ricky Williams .60 1.50
TM19 Edgerrin James .60 1.50
TM20 Kurt Warner 1.25 3.00

2000 Score Team 2000 Autographs

Randomly inserted in Hobby packs, this 18-card skip-numbered set parallels the Retail only Team 2000 insert set. Each card contains an authentic autograph signed on a reprint card of the player's original Score rookie card and is sequentially numbered to 50. Several cards were issued via redemption cards which carried an expiration date of 7/01/2001.

AUTO PRINT RUN 50 SER.#'d SETS
TM1 Barry Sanders 250.00 500.00
TM2 Troy Aikman 100.00 200.00
TM3 Cris Carter 40.00 80.00
TM4 Emmitt Smith 200.00 350.00
TM5 Brett Favre 200.00 350.00
TM6 Jimmy Smith 15.00 40.00
TM7 Drew Bledsoe 15.00 40.00
TM8 Marshall Faulk 30.00 60.00
TM10 Marvin Harrison 40.00 80.00
TM11 Eddie George 100.00 200.00
TM12 Eric Moulds 12.00 30.00
TM13 Jake Plummer 12.00 30.00
TM14 Antowain Smith 15.00 40.00
TM15 Fred Taylor 12.00 30.00
TM16 Randy Moss 40.00 80.00
TM17 Peyton Manning 100.00 200.00
TM18 Ricky Williams 15.00 40.00
TM19 Edgerrin James 15.00 40.00
TM20 Kurt Warner 50.00 100.00

2001 Score

Playoff Inc. released Score as a retail only product on July 2, with a 99-cent per pack SRP. This 330-card set was highlighted by the short-printed rookies which were randomly inserted at a rate of 1:4. The base card design was a basic blue or green border for the standard cards and a red border for the short-printed base cards. The cardbacks featured a Pack Wars character that was assigned a value for playing the popular game. Many cards (possibly all of them) were issued with a tougher parallel variation on the Pack Wars character to include the word "Trump" as a wild card winner during the game. The packs were also distributed in two versions of retail boxes 15 packs for an SRP of $13.99 and 30 packs for $28.99. An exchange card was inserted in packs that was good for an option to purchase a 2001 Score Supplmental factory set. It carried an expiration date of 12/01/2001.

COMPLETE SET (330) 40.00 80.00
COMP.SET w/o SP's (220) 10.00 25.00
271-330 ROOKIE STATED ODDS 1:4
*TRUMP CARD BACKS: .6X TO 1.5X
1 David Boston .10 .25
2 Frank Sanders .10 .25
3 Jake Plummer .10 .25
4 Michael Pittman .12 .30
5 Rob Moore .10 .25
6 Thomas Jones .10 .25
7 Chris Chandler .12 .30
8 Doug Johnson .10 .25
9 Jamal Anderson .12 .30
10 Tim Dwight .12 .30
11 Brandon Stokley .10 .25
12 Chris Redman .15 .40
13 Jamal Lewis .15 .40
14 Qadry Ismail .10 .25
15 Ray Lewis .15 .40
16 Rod Woodson .15 .40
17 Shannon Sharpe .12 .30
18 Travis Taylor .10 .25
19 Trent Dilfer .10 .25
20 Elvis Grbac .12 .30
21 Eric Moulds .10 .25
22 Jay Riemersma .10 .25
23 Peerless Price .10 .25
24 Rob Johnson .12 .30
25 Sam Cowart .10 .25
26 Sammy Morris .10 .25
27 Shawn Bryson .10 .25
28 Donald Hayes .10 .25
29 Muhsin Muhammad .10 .25
30 Patrick Jeffers .10 .25
31 Reggie White DE .15 .40
32 Steve Beuerlein .12 .30
33 Tim Biakabutuka .10 .25
34 Wesley Walls .10 .25
35 Brian Urlacher .20 .50
36 Cade McNown .12 .30
37 Dez White .12 .30
38 James Allen .10 .25
39 Marcus Robinson .12 .30
40 Marty Booker .10 .25
41 Akili Smith .10 .25
42 Corey Dillon .10 .25
43 Danny Farmer .10 .25
44 Peter Warrick .10 .25
45 Ron Dugans .10 .25
46 Takeo Spikes .10 .25
47 Courtney Brown .10 .25
48 Dennis Northcutt .10 .25
49 JaJuan Dawson .10 .25
50 Kevin Johnson .10 .25
51 Tim Couch .10 .25
52 Travis Prentice .10 .25
53 Anthony Wright .10 .25
54 Emmitt Smith .25 .60
55 James McKnight .10 .25
56 Joey Galloway .12 .30
57 Rocket Ismail .12 .30
58 Randall Cunningham .12 .30
59 Troy Aikman .20 .50
60 Brian Griese .10 .25
61 Ed McCaffrey .12 .30
62 Gus Frerotte .10 .25
63 John Elway .25 .60
64 Mike Anderson .10 .25
65 Olandis Gary .10 .25
66 Rod Smith .12 .30
67 Terrell Davis .12 .30
68 Barry Sanders .25 .60
69 Charlie Batch .10 .25
70 Germane Crowell .10 .25
71 Herman Moore .10 .25
72 James Stewart .10 .25
73 Johnnie Morton .12 .30
74 Robert Porcher .10 .25
75 Jim Harbaugh .12 .30
76 Ahman Green .12 .30
77 Antonio Freeman .15 .40
78 Bill Schroeder .12 .30
79 Brett Favre .30 .75
80 Bubba Franks .10 .25
81 Dorsey Levens .12 .30
82 E.G. Green .10 .25
83 Edgerrin James .12 .30
84 Jerome Pathon .10 .25
85 Ken Dilger .10 .25
86 Marcus Pollard .10 .25
87 Marvin Harrison .12 .30
88 Peyton Manning .40 1.00
89 Terrence Wilkins .10 .25
90 Fred Taylor .10 .25
91 Hardy Nickerson .10 .25
92 Jimmy Smith .12 .30
93 Keenan McCardell .12 .30
94 Kyle Brady .10 .25
95 Mark Brunell .12 .30
96 Tony Brackens .10 .25
97 Derrick Alexander .10 .25
98 Sylvester Morris .10 .25
99 Tony Gonzalez .12 .30
100 Tony Richardson .10 .25
101 Kimble Anders .10 .25
102 Warren Moon .15 .40
103 Dan Marino .30 .75
104 Jay Fiedler .12 .30
105 Lamar Smith .12 .30
106 O.J. McDuffie .10 .25
107 Oronde Gadsden .10 .25
108 Sam Madison .10 .25
109 Thurman Thomas .12 .30
110 Tony Martin .12 .30
111 Zach Thomas .12 .30
112 Cris Carter .15 .40
113 Daunte Culpepper .12 .30
114 Matthew Hatchette .10 .25
115 Randy Moss .12 .30
116 Robert Smith .10 .25
117 Drew Bledsoe .12 .30
118 J.R. Redmond .10 .25
119 Kevin Faulk .10 .25
120 Michael Bishop .12 .30
121 Terry Glenn .12 .30
122 Troy Brown .10 .25
123 Ty Law .15 .40
124 Aaron Brooks .10 .25
125 Darren Howard .10 .25
126 Jake Reed .12 .30
127 Jeff Blake .12 .30
128 Joe Horn .10 .25
129 La'Roi Glover .10 .25
130 Ricky Williams .12 .30
131 Willie Jackson .10 .25
132 Albert Connell .10 .25
133 Amani Toomer .10 .25
134 Ike Hilliard .10 .25
135 Jason Sehorn .12 .30
136 Jessie Armstead .10 .25
137 Kerry Collins .10 .25
138 Michael Strahan .12 .30
139 Ron Dayne .12 .30
140 Ron Dixon .10 .25
141 Tiki Barber .12 .30
142 Anthony Becht .10 .25
143 Chad Pennington .10 .25
144 Curtis Martin .12 .30
145 Dedric Ward .10 .25
146 Laveranues Coles .12 .30
147 Vinny Testaverde .10 .25
148 Wayne Chrebet .10 .25
149 Andre Rison .12 .30
150 Charles Woodson .15 .40
151 Darrell Russell .10 .25
152 Napoleon Kaufman .10 .25
153 Rich Gannon .12 .30
154 Tim Brown .15 .40
155 Tyrone Wheatley .12 .30
156 Chad Lewis .10 .25
157 Charles Johnson .10 .25
158 Donovan McNabb .12 .30
159 Duce Staley .10 .25
160 Hugh Douglas .10 .25
161 Na Brown .10 .25
162 Todd Pinkston .10 .25
163 James Thrash .12 .30
164 Bobby Shaw .10 .25
165 Hines Ward .12 .30
166 Jerome Bettis .15 .40

167 Kordell Stewart .10 .25
168 Levon Kirkland .10 .25
169 Plaxico Burress .10 .25
170 Richard Huntley .10 .25
171 Troy Edwards .10 .25
172 Jeff Graham .10 .25
173 Junior Seau .12 .30
174 Doug Flutie .12 .30
175 Charlie Garner .12 .30
176 Jeff Garcia .10 .25
177 Jerry Rice .30 .75
178 Steve Young .20 .50
179 Terrell Owens .12 .30
180 Brock Huard .10 .25
181 Darrell Jackson .12 .30
182 Derrick Mayes .10 .25
183 Ricky Watters .12 .30
184 Shaun Alexander .10 .25
185 Matt Hasselbeck .10 .25
186 John Randle .12 .30
187 Az-Zahir Hakim .10 .25
188 Isaac Bruce .15 .40
189 Kurt Warner .25 .60
190 Marshall Faulk .12 .30
191 Torry Holt .12 .30
192 Trent Green .10 .25
193 Derrick Brooks .10 .25
194 Jacquez Green .10 .25
195 John Lynch .12 .30
196 Keyshawn Johnson .12 .30
197 Mike Alstott .10 .25
198 Reidel Anthony .10 .25
199 Shaun King .10 .25
200 Warren Sapp .12 .30
201 Warrick Dunn .10 .25
202 Ryan Leaf .10 .25
203 Carl Pickens .12 .30
204 Derrick Mason .10 .25
205 Eddie George .15 .40
206 Frank Wycheck .10 .25
207 Jevon Kearse .10 .25
208 Neil O'Donnell .12 .30
209 Steve McNair .12 .30
210 Yancey Thigpen .10 .25
211 Andre Reed .15 .40
212 Brad Johnson .12 .30
213 Bruce Smith .12 .30
214 Champ Bailey .12 .30
215 Darrell Green .15 .40
216 Deion Sanders .12 .30
217 Irving Fryar .12 .30
218 Jeff George .12 .30
219 Michael Westbrook .10 .25
220 Stephen Davis .10 .25
221 Terrell Owens AP .20 .50
222 Peyton Manning AP .60 1.50
223 Stephen Davis AP .15 .40
224 Marvin Harrison AP .20 .50
225 Donovan McNabb AP .20 .50
226 Edgerrin James AP .20 .50
227 Eric Moulds AP .15 .40
228 Daunte Culpepper AP .20 .50
229 Eddie George AP .25 .60
230 Cris Carter AP .25 .60
231 Rich Gannon AP .20 .50
232 Jeff Garcia AP .15 .40
233 Jimmy Smith AP .20 .50
234 Tony Gonzalez AP .20 .50
235 Torry Holt AP .20 .50
236 Jevon Kearse AP .15 .40
237 Ray Lewis AP .25 .60
238 Warren Sapp AP .20 .50
239 Brian Urlacher AP .30 .75
240 Champ Bailey AP .20 .50
241 Peyton Manning LL .60 1.50
242 Jeff Garcia LL .15 .40
243 Elvis Grbac LL .20 .50
244 Daunte Culpepper LL .20 .50
245 Brett Favre LL .50 1.25
246 Edgerrin James LL .20 .50
247 Robert Smith LL .15 .40
248 Eddie George LL .25 .60
249 Mike Anderson LL .15 .40
250 Corey Dillon LL .15 .40
251 Torry Holt LL .20 .50
252 Rod Smith LL .20 .50
253 Isaac Bruce LL .25 .60
254 Terrell Owens LL .20 .50
255 Randy Moss LL .20 .50
256 La'Roi Glover LL .15 .40
257 Trace Armstrong LL .15 .40
258 Warren Sapp LL .20 .50
259 Hugh Douglas LL .15 .40
260 Jason Taylor LL .25 .60
261 Mike Anderson SS .15 .40
262 Jamal Lewis SS .25 .60
263 Sylvester Morris SS .15 .40
264 Darrell Jackson SS .20 .50
265 Peter Warrick SS .15 .40
266 Ron Dayne SS .20 .50
267 Shaun Alexander SS .15 .40
268 Plaxico Burress SS .15 .40
269 Brian Urlacher SS .30 .75
270 Courtney Brown SS .15 .40
271 Michael Vick RC 1.25 3.00
272 Drew Brees RC 10.00 25.00
273 Chris Weinke RC .60 1.50
274 Quincy Carter RC .60 1.50
275 Sage Rosenfels RC .60 1.50
276 Josh Heupel RC .75 2.00
277 David Rivers RC .50 1.25
278 Ben Leard RC .50 1.25
279 Marques Tuiasosopo RC .60 1.50
280 Mike McMahon RC .60 1.50
281 Deuce McAllister RC .75 2.00
282 LaMont Jordan RC .75 2.00
283 LaDainian Tomlinson RC 2.50 6.00
284 James Jackson RC .50 1.25
285 Anthony Thomas RC .75 2.00
286 Travis Henry RC .60 1.50
287 Travis Minor RC .60 1.50
288 Rudi Johnson RC .75 2.00
289 Michael Bennett RC .60 1.50
290 Kevan Barlow RC .60 1.50
291 Reggie White RC .50 1.25
292 Moran Norris RC .50 1.25
293 Ja'Mar Toombs RC .50 1.25
294 Heath Evans RC .60 1.50
295 David Terrell RC .60 1.50
296 Santana Moss RC .75 2.00
297 Rod Gardner RC .60 1.50
298 Quincy Morgan RC .60 1.50
299 Freddie Mitchell RC .50 1.25
300 Boo Williams RC .50 1.25
301 Reggie Wayne RC 1.00 2.50
302 Ronney Daniels RC .50 1.25
303 Bobby Newcombe RC .60 1.50
304 Vinny Sutherland RC .50 1.25
305 Cedrick Wilson RC .60 1.50
306 Robert Ferguson RC .75 2.00
307 Ken-Yon Rambo RC .50 1.25
308 Alex Bannister RC .50 1.25
309 Koren Robinson RC .60 1.50
310 Chad Johnson RC .75 2.00
311 Chris Chambers RC .50 1.25
312 Javon Green RC .50 1.25
313 Snoop Minnis RC .50 1.25
314 Scotty Anderson RC .50 1.25
315 Todd Heap RC .60 1.50
316 Alge Crumpler RC .75 2.00
317 Marcellus Rivers RC .50 1.25
318 Rashon Burns RC .50 1.25
319 Jamal Reynolds RC .50 1.25
320 Andre Carter RC .60 1.50
321 Justin Smith RC 1.00 2.50
322 Gerard Warren RC .60 1.50
323 Tommy Polley RC .50 1.25
324 Dan Morgan RC .60 1.50
325 Torrance Marshall RC .50 1.25
326 Correll Buckhalter RC .50 1.25
327 Derrick Gibson RC .50 1.25
328 Adam Archuleta RC .60 1.50
329 Jamar Fletcher RC .50 1.25
330 Nate Clements RC .60 1.50

2001 Score Scorecard

*VETS/307-540: 4X TO 10X BASIC CARD
*VETS/307-540: 2X TO 5X BASE SP
*ROOKIES/307-540: 1X TO 2.5X
*VETS/161-296: 5X TO 12X BASIC CARD
*VETS/161-296: 2.5X TO 6X BASE SP
*ROOKIES/161-296: 1.2X TO 3X
STATED PRINT RUN 161-540

2001 Score Complete Players

Randomly inserted in retail packs at a rate of 1:35, this 30-card set featured the top players from the NFL. The cardfronts were produced on foilboard and highlighted with a gold-foil header. The cardbacks featured the players acomplishments proving why the player is 'Complete' and carried a "CP" prefix.

COMPLETE SET (30) 30.00 60.00
STATED ODDS 1:35
CP1 Edgerrin James .75 2.00
CP2 Marshall Faulk .75 2.00
CP3 Kurt Warner 1.50 4.00
CP4 Daunte Culpepper .75 2.00
CP5 Donovan McNabb .75 2.00
CP6 Koren Robinson .75 2.00
CP7 Peyton Manning 2.50 6.00
CP8 Eddie George 1.00 2.50
CP9 Fred Taylor .60 1.50
CP10 Drew Brees 6.00 15.00
CP11 Randy Moss .75 2.00
CP12 Cris Carter 1.00 2.50
CP13 Steve Young 1.25 3.00
CP14 Marvin Harrison .75 2.00
CP15 Isaac Bruce 1.00 2.50
CP16 Terrell Owens .75 2.00
CP17 Mike Anderson .60 1.50
CP18 Jamal Lewis 1.00 2.50
CP19 Curtis Martin .75 2.00
CP20 Ricky Williams .75 2.00
CP21 Jerry Rice 2.00 5.00
CP22 Steve McNair .75 2.00
CP23 Michael Vick .75 2.00
CP24 Brett Favre 2.00 5.00
CP25 John Elway 1.50 4.00
CP26 Dan Marino 2.00 5.00
CP27 Barry Sanders 1.50 4.00
CP28 Michael Bennett .75 2.00
CP29 David Terrell .75 2.00
CP30 Emmitt Smith 1.50 4.00

2001 Score Franchise

Randomly inserted in retail packs at a rate of 1:35, this 31-card set featured the top players from the NFL. The cardfronts feature a rainbow holofoil design. The cardbacks feature a piece about why he is The Franchise, and they carried a 'TF' prefix on the card numbering.

COMPLETE SET (31) 25.00 60.00
STATED ODDS 1:35 RETAIL
TF1 Tim Couch .60 1.50
TF2 Peter Warrick .60 1.50
TF3 Jerome Bettis 1.00 2.50
TF4 Fred Taylor .60 1.50
TF5 Eddie George 1.00 2.50
TF6 Jamal Lewis 1.00 2.50
TF7 Peyton Manning 2.50 6.00
TF8 Drew Bledsoe .75 2.00
TF9 Curtis Martin .75 2.00
TF10 Eric Moulds .60 1.50
TF11 Lamar Smith .75 2.00
TF12 Tony Gonzalez .75 2.00
TF13 Rich Gannon .75 2.00
TF14 Ricky Watters .75 2.00
TF15 Junior Seau .75 2.00
TF16 Brian Griese .60 1.50
TF17 Terrell Owens .75 2.00
TF18 Ricky Williams .75 2.00
TF19 Kurt Warner 1.50 4.00
TF20 Muhsin Muhammad .60 1.50
TF21 Jamal Anderson .75 2.00
TF22 Brett Favre 2.00 5.00
TF23 Randy Moss .75 2.00
TF24 Marcus Robinson .75 2.00
TF25 Warrick Dunn .60 1.50
TF26 James Stewart .60 1.50
TF27 Jake Plummer .60 1.50
TF28 Kerry Collins .60 1.50
TF29 Emmitt Smith 1.50 4.00
TF30 Stephen Davis .60 1.50
TF31 Donovan McNabb .75 2.00

2001 Score Franchise Fabrics

Randomly inserted in retail packs at a rate of 1:359, this 31-card set features a swatch of authentic game-worn jersey. The swatch is displayed on the cardfront inside of the 1 inch star shaped cutout, and it features an action photo of the player on the other half of the front. The cardbacks have a photo of the game-worn jersey from which the swatch was taken, and it carried a 'FF' prefix on the card numbering.

STATED ODDS 1:359
FF1 Daunte Culpepper 4.00 10.00
FF2 Stephen Davis 3.00 8.00
FF3 Kurt Warner 8.00 20.00
FF4 Ricky Williams 4.00 10.00
FF5 Terrell Owens 4.00 10.00
FF6 Ricky Watters 4.00 10.00
FF7 Rich Gannon 4.00 10.00
FF8 Mike Anderson 3.00 8.00
FF9 Tony Gonzalez 4.00 10.00
FF10 Jerome Bettis 5.00 12.00
FF11 Peter Warrick 3.00 8.00
FF12 Tim Couch 3.00 8.00
FF13 Mark Brunell 4.00 10.00
FF14 Edgerrin James 4.00 10.00
FF15 Curtis Martin 4.00 10.00
FF16 Brett Favre 10.00 25.00
FF17 Donovan McNabb 4.00 10.00
FF18 Drew Bledsoe 4.00 10.00
FF19 Jake Plummer 3.00 8.00
FF20 Eric Moulds 3.00 8.00
FF21 Lamar Smith 4.00 10.00
FF22 Junior Seau 4.00 10.00
FF23 Wesley Walls 3.00 8.00
FF24 Jamal Anderson 4.00 10.00
FF25 Warren Sapp 4.00 10.00
FF26 Ron Dayne 4.00 10.00
FF27 Jamal Lewis 5.00 12.00
FF28 Cade McNown 4.00 10.00
FF29 Charlie Batch 3.00 8.00
FF30 Eddie George 5.00 12.00
FF31 Troy Aikman 6.00 15.00

2001 Score Millennium Men

Randomly inserted in retail packs this 40-card set was serial numbered to 1000. The cardfronts feature an action pose with silver foil lettering to highlight the words 'Millennium Men'.

COMPLETE SET (40) 30.00 80.00
STATED PRINT RUN 1000 SER.#'d SETS
MM1 Michael Vick 1.25 3.00
MM2 Marvin Harrison .60 1.50
MM3 Curtis Martin .60 1.50
MM4 Eric Moulds .50 1.25
MM5 Dan Marino 1.50 4.00
MM6 Edgerrin James .60 1.50
MM7 Drew Bledsoe .60 1.50
MM8 Drew Brees 10.00 25.00
MM9 Jamal Lewis .75 2.00
MM10 Marshall Faulk .60 1.50
MM11 Eddie George .75 2.00
MM12 Koren Robinson .60 1.50
MM13 Peter Warrick .50 1.25
MM14 Jerome Bettis .75 2.00
MM15 Warren Sapp .60 1.50
MM16 Mark Brunell .60 1.50
MM17 David Terrell .60 1.50
MM18 Steve Young 1.00 2.50
MM19 Ron Dayne .60 1.50
MM20 Michael Bennett .60 1.50
MM21 Brian Griese .50 1.25
MM22 Deuce McAllister .75 2.00
MM23 Kurt Warner 1.25 3.00
MM24 Mike Anderson .50 1.25
MM25 Rudi Johnson .75 2.00
MM26 John Elway 1.25 3.00
MM27 Terrell Owens .60 1.50
MM28 Ricky Williams .60 1.50
MM29 Jerry Rice 1.50 4.00
MM30 Jeff Garcia .50 1.25
MM31 Isaac Bruce .75 2.00
MM32 Aaron Brooks .50 1.25
MM33 Brett Favre 1.50 4.00
MM34 Daunte Culpepper .60 1.50
MM35 Ricky Watters .60 1.50
MM36 Tony Gonzalez .60 1.50
MM37 Stephen Davis .50 1.25
MM38 Santana Moss .75 2.00
MM39 Cris Carter .75 2.00
MM40 Donovan McNabb .60 1.50

2001 Score Millennium Men Autographs

Randomly inserted in retail packs this 40-card autograph set was serial numbered to 25. The cardfronts feature an action pose with silver foil lettering to highlight the words 'Millennium Men'. Many were issued in packs as exchange cards carrying an expiration date of 5/31/2003.

STATED PRINT RUN 25 SERIAL #'d SETS
1 Michael Vick 75.00 150.00
2 Marvin Harrison 25.00 60.00
3 Curtis Martin 30.00 80.00
5 Dan Marino 125.00 250.00
6 Edgerrin James 25.00 60.00
7 Drew Bledsoe 25.00 60.00
8 Drew Brees 175.00 300.00
9 Jamal Lewis 30.00 80.00
10 Marshall Faulk 25.00 60.00
11 Eddie George 20.00 50.00
14 Jerome Bettis 40.00 80.00
16 Mark Brunell 20.00 50.00
17 David Terrell 25.00 60.00
18 Steve Young 50.00 100.00
19 Ron Dayne 20.00 50.00
21 Brian Griese 20.00 50.00
23 Kurt Warner 25.00 60.00
24 Mike Anderson 25.00 60.00
25 Rudi Johnson 40.00 80.00
26 John Elway 75.00 150.00
27 Terrell Owens 30.00 80.00
28 Ricky Williams 25.00 60.00
29 Jerry Rice 125.00 250.00
30 Jeff Garcia 25.00 60.00
32 Aaron Brooks 25.00 60.00
33 Brett Favre 125.00 250.00
34 Daunte Culpepper 30.00 80.00
35 Ricky Watters 20.00 50.00
36 Tony Gonzalez 25.00 60.00
38 Santana Moss 25.00 60.00
39 Cris Carter 30.00 80.00
40 Donovan McNabb 60.00 120.00

2001 Score Numbers Game

Randomly inserted in retail packs this 40-card set was serial numbered to the total yards rushing, receiving, or passing for the featured player in 2000. The cardfronts were on foilboard and featured gold-foil lettering. The cardbacks contained a description of the selected stat used for the serial numbering and carried the prefix 'NG' on the card number.

COMPLETE SET (40) 30.00 80.00
CARDS SER.#'d TO 2000 SEASON STAT
STATED PRINT RUN 582-4413
NG1 Brett Favre/3812 1.25 3.00
NG2 Marshall Faulk/1359 .60 1.50
NG3 Michael Vick/1234 1.25 3.00
NG4 Peyton Manning/4413 1.50 4.00
NG5 David Terrell/994 .60 1.50
NG6 Randy Moss/1437 .60 1.50
NG7 Kurt Warner/3429 1.00 2.50
NG8 Edgerrin James/1709 .60 1.50
NG9 Drew Brees/3666 8.00 20.00
NG10 Daunte Culpepper/3937 .50 1.25
NG11 Jeff Garcia/4278 .40 1.00
NG12 Mike Anderson/1487 .50 1.25
NG13 Jamal Lewis/1364 .75 2.00
NG14 Eddie George/1509 .75 2.00
NG15 Michael Bennett/1681 .60 1.50
NG16 Emmitt Smith/1203 1.25 3.00
NG17 Chris Weinke/4167 .50 1.25
NG18 Tim Brown/1128 .75 2.00
NG19 Eric Moulds/1326 .50 1.25
NG20 Marvin Harrison/1413 .60 1.50
NG21 Deuce McAllister/582 .75 2.00
NG22 Donovan McNabb/3365 .50 1.25
NG23 Fred Taylor/1399 .50 1.25
NG24 Santana Moss/748 .75 2.00
NG25 Cris Carter/1274 .75 2.00
NG26 Robert Smith/1521 .50 1.25
NG27 LaDainian Tomlinson/2158 1.25 3.00
NG28 Isaac Bruce/1471 .75 2.00
NG29 Terrell Owens/1451 .60 1.50
NG30 Torry Holt/1635 .60 1.50
NG31 Ricky Williams/1000 .60 1.50
NG32 Curtis Martin/1204 .60 1.50
NG33 Stephen Davis/1318 .50 1.25
NG34 Corey Dillon/1435 .50 1.25
NG35 Ed McCaffrey/1317 .60 1.50
NG36 Steve McNair/2847 .50 1.25
NG37 Rudi Johnson/1547 .75 2.00
NG38 Antonio Freeman/912 .75 2.00
NG39 Jerry Rice/805 1.50 4.00
NG40 Aaron Brooks/1514 .50 1.25

2001 Score Settle the Score

Randomly inserted in retail packs at a rate of 1:35, this 30-card set featured 2 comparable players going head to head at the same position. The cardfronts were produced on foilboard and featured gold-foil lettering along with the first of the 2 players and the cardbacks featured the second player on a basic glossy card. The card numbering carried 'SS' as the prefix.

COMPLETE SET (30) 25.00 60.00
STATED ODDS 1:35 RETAIL
SS1 K.Warner/S.McNair .75 2.00
SS2 R.Moss/I.Bruce 1.00 2.50
SS3 E.Smith/S.Davis 1.50 4.00
SS4 M.Faulk/R.Smith .75 2.00
SS5 E.George/R.Lewis 1.00 2.50
SS6 F.Taylor/J.Bettis 1.00 2.50
SS7 P.Manning/D.Bledsoe 2.50 6.00
SS8 D.Culpepper/A.Brooks .75 2.00
SS9 M.Harrison/E.Moulds .75 2.00
SS10 J.Rice/C.Carter 2.00 5.00
SS11 C.Martin/E.James .75 2.00
SS12 D.McNabb/R.Dayne .75 2.00
SS13 B.Favre/W.Sapp 2.00 5.00
SS14 T.Gonzalez/S.Sharpe .75 2.00
SS15 W.Chrebet/K.Johnson .75 2.00
SS16 T.Couch/C.McNown .75 2.00
SS17 T.Davis/J.Anderson .75 2.00
SS18 M.Anderson/J.Lewis 1.00 2.50
SS19 T.Owens/A.Freeman 1.00 2.50
SS20 B.Griese/R.Gannon .60 1.50
SS21 R.Watters/C.Garner .75 2.00
SS22 M.Muhammad/R.Williams .75 2.00
SS23 J.Garcia/E.Grbac .75 2.00
SS24 R.Smith/J.Smith .75 2.00
SS25 B.Urlacher/A.Green 1.25 3.00
SS26 D.Jackson/S.Morris .75 2.00
SS27 P.Warrick/T.Taylor .60 1.50
SS28 D.Marino/J.Elway 2.00 5.00
SS29 S.Young/M.Brunell 1.25 3.00
SS30 T.Aikman/J.Plummer .60 1.50

2001 Score Chicago Collection

NOT PRICED DUE TO SCARCITY

2002 Score

This 330-card base set features 250 veterans and 80 rookies. Boxes contained 36 packs, each of which had an $1.99 SRP and contained seven cards.

COMPLETE SET (330) 20.00 50.00
1 David Boston .12 .30
2 Arnold Jackson .12 .30
3 MarTay Jenkins .12 .30
4 Thomas Jones .12 .30
5 Kwamie Lassiter .12 .30
6 Michael Pittman .15 .40
7 Jake Plummer .12 .30
8 Chris Chandler .15 .40
9 Alge Crumpler .15 .40
10 Terance Mathis .12 .30
11 Maurice Smith .12 .30
12 Ray Buchanan .12 .30
13 Jamal Anderson .15 .40
14 Keith Brooking .12 .30
15 Michael Vick .15 .40
16 Obafemi Ayanbadejo .12 .30
17 Jason Brookins .12 .30
18 Randall Cunningham .15 .40
19 Elvis Grbac .12 .30
20 Todd Heap .12 .30
21 Qadry Ismail .12 .30
22 Shannon Sharpe .15 .40
23 Travis Taylor .12 .30
24 Ray Lewis .20 .50
25 Jamal Lewis .15 .40
26 Larry Centers .12 .30
27 Rob Johnson .15 .40
28 Shawn Bryson .12 .30
29 Eric Moulds .12 .30
30 Peerless Price .12 .30
31 Nate Clements .12 .30
32 Travis Henry .12 .30
33 Isaac Byrd .12 .30
34 Nick Goings .12 .30
35 Donald Hayes .12 .30
36 Richard Huntley .12 .30
37 Muhsin Muhammad .12 .30
38 Steve Smith .20 .50
39 Wesley Walls .15 .40
40 Chris Weinke .12 .30
41 James Allen .12 .30
42 Marty Booker .12 .30
43 Jim Miller .12 .30
44 David Terrell .12 .30
45 Dez White .12 .30
46 Brian Urlacher .20 .50
47 Mike Brown .12 .30
48 Anthony Thomas .15 .40
49 T.J. Houshmandzadeh .12 .30
50 Chad Johnson .12 .30
51 Darnay Scott .15 .40
52 Peter Warrick .12 .30
53 Akili Smith .15 .40
54 Jon Kitna .12 .30
55 Justin Smith .15 .40
56 Corey Dillon .12 .30
57 Benjamin Gay .12 .30
58 Kevin Johnson .12 .30
59 Quincy Morgan .12 .30
60 James Jackson .12 .30
61 Anthony Henry .12 .30
62 Gerard Warren .12 .30
63 Jamir Miller .12 .30
64 Tim Couch .12 .30
65 Quincy Carter .12 .30
66 Joey Galloway .15 .40
67 Troy Hambrick .12 .30
68 Rocket Ismail .15 .40
69 Dexter Coakley .12 .30
70 Darren Woodson .15 .40
71 Emmitt Smith .30 .75
72 Mike Anderson .12 .30
73 Terrell Davis .15 .40
74 Kevin Kasper .12 .30
75 Rod Smith .15 .40
76 Ed McCaffrey .15 .40
77 Olandis Gary .15 .40
78 Dwayne Carswell .12 .30
79 Deltha O'Neal .12 .30
80 Brian Griese .12 .30
81 Scotty Anderson .12 .30
82 Johnnie Morton .15 .40
83 Cory Schlesinger .12 .30
84 James Stewart .12 .30
85 Shaun Rogers .12 .30
86 Mike McMahon .12 .30
87 Charlie Batch .12 .30
88 Robert Porcher .12 .30
89 Bubba Franks .12 .30
90 Robert Ferguson .15 .40
91 Antonio Freeman .20 .50
92 Ahman Green .15 .40
93 Bill Schroeder .12 .30
94 Kabeer Gbaja-Biamila .12 .30
95 Jamal Reynolds .12 .30
96 Darren Sharper .12 .30
97 Brett Favre .40 1.00
98 Marvin Harrison .15 .40
99 Dominic Rhodes .12 .30
100 Edgerrin James .15 .40
101 Reggie Wayne .15 .40
102 Terrence Wilkins .12 .30
103 Ken Dilger .12 .30
104 Peyton Manning .50 1.25
105 Elvis Joseph .12 .30
106 Stacey Mack .12 .30
107 Fred Taylor .12 .30
108 Keenan McCardell .15 .40
109 Jimmy Smith .15 .40
110 Mark Brunell .15 .40
111 Derrick Alexander .12 .30
112 Tony Gonzalez .15 .40
113 Trent Green .12 .30
114 Snoop Minnis .12 .30
115 Priest Holmes .12 .30
116 Chris Chambers .12 .30
117 Jay Fiedler .15 .40
118 Oronde Gadsden .12 .30
119 Travis Minor .12 .30
120 Lamar Smith .12 .30
121 Zach Thomas .15 .40
122 Michael Bennett .12 .30
123 Todd Bouman .12 .30
124 Cris Carter .20 .50
125 Byron Chamberlain .12 .30
126 Randy Moss .15 .40
127 Jake Reed .15 .40
128 Daunte Culpepper .15 .40
129 Drew Bledsoe .15 .40
130 Troy Brown .12 .30
131 David Patten .12 .30
132 J.R. Redmond .12 .30
133 Antowain Smith .15 .40
134 Ty Law .20 .50
135 Richard Seymour .15 .40
136 Adam Vinatieri .12 .30
137 Tom Brady 1.00 2.50
138 Joe Horn .12 .30
139 Willie Jackson .12 .30
140 Deuce McAllister .15 .40
141 Boo Williams .12 .30
142 Ricky Williams .15 .40
143 La'Roi Glover .12 .30
144 Sammy Knight .12 .30
145 Aaron Brooks .12 .30
146 Tiki Barber .15 .40
147 Ron Dayne .15 .40
148 Ike Hilliard .12 .30
149 Amani Toomer .12 .30
150 Will Allen .12 .30
151 Michael Strahan .15 .40
152 Jason Sehorn .15 .40
153 Kerry Collins .12 .30
154 Anthony Becht .12 .30
155 Wayne Chrebet .12 .30
156 Laveranues Coles .15 .40
157 LaMont Jordan .15 .40
158 Santana Moss .15 .40
159 Chad Pennington .12 .30
160 John Abraham .15 .40
161 Vinny Testaverde .12 .30
162 Curtis Martin .15 .40
163 Tim Brown .20 .50
164 Rich Gannon .15 .40
165 Charlie Garner .15 .40
166 Jerry Porter .12 .30
167 Marques Tuiasosopo .12 .30
168 Tyrone Wheatley .15 .40
169 Charles Woodson .20 .50
170 Jerry Rice .40 1.00
171 Correll Buckhalter .12 .30
172 Chad Lewis .12 .30
173 Brian Mitchell .15 .40
174 Freddie Mitchell .12 .30
175 Todd Pinkston .12 .30
176 Duce Staley .12 .30
177 Tony Stewart .12 .30
178 James Thrash .15 .40
179 Hugh Douglas .12 .30
180 Donovan McNabb .15 .40
181 Plaxico Burress .12 .30
182 Chris Fuamatu-Ma'afala .12 .30
183 Kordell Stewart .12 .30
184 Hines Ward .15 .40
185 Amos Zereoue .12 .30
186 Kendrell Bell .12 .30
187 Casey Hampton .12 .30
188 Jerome Bettis .20 .50
189 Drew Brees .40 1.00
190 Curtis Conway .15 .40
191 Tim Dwight .12 .30
192 Doug Flutie .15 .40
193 Junior Seau .15 .40
194 Marcellus Wiley .12 .30
195 Ryan McNeil .12 .30
196 Jeff Graham .12 .30
197 LaDainian Tomlinson .20 .50
198 Kevan Barlow .12 .30
199 Garrison Hearst .12 .30
200 Eric Johnson .12 .30
201 Terrell Owens .15 .40
202 J.J. Stokes .12 .30
203 Andre Carter .12 .30
204 Jeff Garcia .12 .30
205 Trent Dilfer .12 .30
206 Matt Hasselbeck .12 .30
207 Darrell Jackson .15 .40
208 Koren Robinson .12 .30
209 Ricky Watters .15 .40
210 John Randle .15 .40
211 Shaun Alexander .12 .30
212 Isaac Bruce .20 .50
213 Trung Canidate .12 .30
214 Marshall Faulk .15 .40
215 Az-Zahir Hakim .12 .30
216 Torry Holt .15 .40
217 Yo Murphy .12 .30
218 Ricky Proehl .15 .40
219 Adam Archuleta .12 .30
220 Dre Bly .12 .30
221 London Fletcher .15 .40
222 Tommy Polley .12 .30
223 Aeneas Williams .12 .30
224 Kurt Warner .15 .40
225 Mike Alstott .12 .30
226 Warrick Dunn .12 .30
227 Jacquez Green .12 .30
228 Derrick Brooks .12 .30
229 John Lynch .15 .40
230 Warren Sapp .15 .40
231 Ronde Barber .12 .30
232 Brad Johnson .15 .40
233 Keyshawn Johnson .15 .40
234 Drew Bennett .15 .40
235 Kevin Dyson .15 .40
236 Eddie George .15 .40
237 Derrick Mason .12 .30
238 Justin McCareins .15 .40
239 Frank Wycheck .12 .30
240 Jevon Kearse .12 .30
241 Samari Rolle .12 .30
242 Steve McNair .15 .40
243 Tony Banks .12 .30
244 Stephen Davis .12 .30
245 Michael Westbrook .12 .30
246 Champ Bailey .15 .40
247 Darrell Green .20 .50
248 Bruce Smith .15 .40
249 Fred Smoot .15 .40
250 Rod Gardner .12 .30
251 David Carr RC .25 .60
252 Joey Harrington RC .25 .60
253 Patrick Ramsey RC .30 .75
254 Kurt Kittner RC .25 .60
255 Eric Crouch RC .40 1.00
256 Josh McCown RC .40 1.00
257 David Garrard RC .30 .75
258 Rohan Davey RC .40 1.00
259 Ronald Curry RC .25 .60
260 Chad Hutchinson RC .25 .60
261 William Green RC .30 .75
262 T.J. Duckett RC .25 .60
263 Clinton Portis RC .40 1.00
264 DeShaun Foster RC .40 1.00
265 Luke Staley RC .25 .60
266 Wes Pate RC .25 .60
267 Travis Stephens RC .25 .60
268 Adrian Peterson RC .30 .75
269 Zak Kustok RC .25 .60
270 Maurice Morris RC .30 .75
271 Lamar Gordon RC .30 .75
272 Chester Taylor RC .40 1.00
273 Najeh Davenport RC .25 .60
274 Ladell Betts RC .40 1.00
275 Ashley Lelie RC .25 .60
276 Josh Reed RC .30 .75
277 Cliff Russell RC .25 .60
278 Javon Walker RC .40 1.00
279 Ron Johnson RC .30 .75
280 Antwaan Randle El RC .30 .75
281 Andre Davis RC .25 .60
282 Marquise Walker RC .25 .60
283 Kelly Campbell RC .30 .75
284 Tavon Mason RC .25 .60
285 Antonio Bryant RC .40 1.00
286 Jabar Gaffney RC .25 .60
287 Donte Stallworth RC .40 1.00
288 Tim Carter RC .30 .75
289 Reche Caldwell RC .30 .75
290 Freddie Milons RC .25 .60
291 Brian Poli-Dixon RC .25 .60
292 Brian Westbrook RC .50 1.25
293 Josh Scobey RC .30 .75
294 Jeremy Shockey RC .40 1.00
295 Daniel Graham RC .30 .75
296 Deion Branch RC .40 1.00
297 Julius Peppers RC .60 1.50
298 Kalimba Edwards RC .30 .75
299 Dwight Freeney RC .50 1.25
300 Terry Charles RC .25 .60
301 Alex Brown RC .40 1.00
302 Jason McAddley RC .30 .75
303 Michael Lewis RC .30 .75
304 Dennis Johnson RC .25 .60
305 Albert Haynesworth RC .40 1.00
306 Ryan Sims RC .40 1.00
307 Larry Tripplett RC .25 .60
308 Anthony Weaver RC .25 .60
309 Wendell Bryant RC .25 .60
310 John Henderson RC .30 .75
311 Alan Harper RC .25 .60
312 Napoleon Harris RC .30 .75
313 Bryan Thomas RC .25 .60
314 Andra Davis RC .25 .60
315 Levar Fisher RC .25 .60
316 Woody Dantzler RC .30 .75
317 Robert Thomas RC .25 .60
318 Quentin Jammer RC .40 1.00
319 Lito Sheppard RC .40 1.00
320 Travis Fisher RC .30 .75
321 Roy Williams RC .25 .60
322 Phillip Buchanon RC .40 1.00
323 Joseph Jefferson RC .25 .60
324 Ed Reed RC 1.50 4.00
325 Lamont Thompson RC .30 .75
326 Raonall Smith RC .25 .60
327 Mike Rumph RC .25 .60
328 Rocky Calmus RC .30 .75
329 Bryant McKinnie RC .25 .60
330 Mike Williams RC .25 .60

2002 Score Final Score

*1-250 VETS: 6X TO 15X BASIC CARDS
*251-330 ROOKIES: 3X TO 8X
STATED PRINT RUN 100 SER.#'d SETS

2002 Score Scorecard

*1-250 VETS: 2.5X TO 6X BASIC CARDS
*251-330 ROOKIES: 1X TO 2.5X
STATED PRINT RUN 400 SER.#'d SETS

2002 Score Changing Stripes

This 14-card insert set was serial numbered to 150, and features two swatches of jersey from two different teams that the player played on.

STATED PRINT RUN 150 SER.#'d SETS
1 Curtis Martin 6.00 15.00
2 Doug Flutie 6.00 15.00
3 Eric Dickerson 6.00 15.00
4 Jerome Bettis 8.00 20.00
5 Jerry Rice 15.00 40.00
7 John Riggins 30.00 80.00
8 Kerry Collins 5.00 12.00
9 Keyshawn Johnson 6.00 15.00
10 Marcus Allen 12.00 30.00
11 Mark Brunell 6.00 15.00
12 Priest Holmes 5.00 12.00
13 Ricky Watters 6.00 15.00
14 Thurman Thomas 10.00 25.00
15 Warren Moon 12.00 30.00
P8 Kerry Collins Sample 6.00 15.00

2002 Score Franchise Fabrics

Inserted in retail packs at a rate of 1:574, this 25-card insert set features some of the NFL's top players along with a swatch of jersey.

STATED ODDS 1:574 RETAIL
1 Ahman Green 5.00 12.00
2 Amani Toomer 4.00 10.00
3 Brad Johnson 5.00 12.00
4 Charles Woodson 6.00 15.00
5 Corey Dillon 4.00 10.00
6 Cris Carter 6.00 15.00
7 David Boston 4.00 10.00
8 Derrick Mason 4.00 10.00
9 Donovan McNabb 5.00 12.00
10 Emmitt Smith 12.00 30.00
11 Hines Ward 5.00 12.00
12 John Elway 12.00 30.00
13 Junior Seau 5.00 12.00
14 Kevin Johnson 4.00 10.00
16 LaDainian Tomlinson 6.00 15.00
17 Marvin Harrison 5.00 12.00
18 Michael Strahan 5.00 12.00
19 Mike Alstott 4.00 10.00
20 Ricky Williams 5.00 12.00
21 Rob Johnson 5.00 12.00
23 Stephen Davis 4.00 10.00
24 Troy Aikman 10.00 25.00
25 Zach Thomas 5.00 12.00

2002 Score In the Zone

Inserted in packs at a rate of 1:35, this 20-card insert set features many of the NFL's top offensive producers.

COMPLETE SET (20) 15.00 40.00
STATED ODDS 1:35 HOB/RET
1 Marshall Faulk 1.00 2.50
2 Terrell Owens 1.00 2.50
3 Shaun Alexander .75 2.00
4 Marvin Harrison 1.00 2.50
5 Antowain Smith 1.00 2.50
6 Corey Dillon .75 2.00
7 Mike Alstott .75 2.00
8 Rod Smith 1.00 2.50
9 Ahman Green 1.00 2.50
10 Derrick Mason .75 2.00
11 Tim Brown 1.25 3.00
12 Curtis Martin 1.00 2.50
13 Priest Holmes .75 2.00
14 Stacey Mack .75 2.00
15 LaDainian Tomlinson 1.25 3.00
16 Dominic Rhodes .75 2.00
17 Randy Moss 1.00 2.50
18 Bill Schroeder .75 2.00
19 Joe Horn .75 2.00
20 Jerry Rice 2.50 6.00

2002 Score Inscriptions

This 40-card autographed insert set was inserted in packs at a rate of 1:347. There is also a parallel version of this set called Inscriptions Personalized, and each card was serial numbered to 25.

STATED ODDS 1:347
*PERSONAL/25: .8X TO 2X BASIC AU
PERSON/25: .6X TO 1.5X BASIC AU/75-125
PERSON/25: .4X TO 1X BASIC AU/25-50
1 Anthony Thomas 8.00 20.00
2 Brian Griese/50* 12.00 30.00
3 Brian Urlacher 15.00 40.00
4 Chad Johnson 6.00 15.00
5 Chad Pennington/100* 8.00 20.00
6 Chris Weinke 6.00 15.00
7 Corey Dillon/75* 8.00 20.00
8 Correll Buckhalter 6.00 15.00
9 Cris Carter/25* 30.00 60.00
10 Daunte Culpepper/75* 10.00 25.00
11 David Terrell/100* 8.00 20.00
12 Deuce McAllister/125* 10.00 25.00
13 Eric Moulds 6.00 15.00
14 Jamal Lewis/100* 10.00 25.00
15 James Jackson 6.00 15.00
16 Jimmy Smith 8.00 20.00
17 Kurt Warner/50* 15.00 40.00
18 Marshall Faulk/50* 15.00 40.00
19 Snoop Minnis/100* No Auto 8.00 20.00
20 Mike McMahon 6.00 15.00
21 Terrell Owens 15.00 40.00
22 Travis Henry/100* No Auto 8.00 20.00
23 Aaron Brooks/100* 8.00 20.00
24 Junior Seau 25.00 50.00
25 Troy Aikman/50* 40.00 80.00
26 Antwaan Randle El 8.00 20.00
27 Jeremy Shockey 10.00 25.00
28 Jabar Gaffney 6.00 15.00
29 Rocky Calmus 8.00 20.00
30 Donte Stallworth 10.00 25.00
31 Ashley Lelie 6.00 15.00
32 Marquise Walker 6.00 15.00
33 Javon Walker No Auto 10.00 25.00
34 Reche Caldwell 8.00 20.00
35 Daniel Graham 8.00 20.00
36 T.J. Duckett 6.00 15.00
37 Antonio Bryant 10.00 25.00
38 William Green 8.00 20.00
39 David Carr/150* 8.00 20.00
40 Ron Johnson 8.00 20.00

2002 Score Monday Matchups

Inserted in packs at a rate of 1:35, this 17-card insert features top players who appeared on Monday Night Football during the 2002 season.

COMPLETE SET (17) 15.00 40.00
ODDS 1:35 HOB/RET, 1:8 JUM
1 Brian Griese .75 2.00
2 Ahman Green 1.00 2.50
3 Garrison Hearst .75 2.00
4 Kurt Warner 1.00 2.50
5 Emmitt Smith 2.00 5.00
6 James Thrash 1.00 2.50
7 Plaxico Burress .75 2.00
8 Tim Brown 1.25 3.00
9 Qadry Ismail .75 2.00
10 Randy Moss 1.00 2.50
11 Mike Alstott .75 2.00
12 Brett Favre 2.50 6.00
13 Jay Fiedler 1.00 2.50
14 Kurt Warner 1.00 2.50
15 Derrick Mason .75 2.00
16 Mike Alstott .75 2.00
17 Terry Allen 1.00 2.50

2002 Score Numbers Game

Inserted in packs at a rate of 1:52, this 30-card insert set features players who has outstanding statistics during the 2001 season.

1-10 PRINT RUN 2843-4830
STATED ODDS 1:52 HOB, 1:13 JUM
11-30 PRINT RUN 729-1598
1 Kurt Warner/4830 1.25 3.00
2 Rich Gannon/3828 1.25 3.00
3 Trent Green/3783 1.00 2.50
4 Kerry Collins/3764 1.00 2.50
5 Jake Plummer/3653 1.00 2.50
6 Steve McNair/3350 1.25 3.00
7 Kordell Stewart/3109 1.00 2.50
8 Tim Couch/3040 1.00 2.50
9 Chris Weinke/2931 1.00 2.50
10 Tom Brady/2843 8.00 20.00
11 Priest Holmes/1555 1.25 3.00
12 Curtis Martin/1513 1.50 4.00
13 Ahman Green/1387 1.50 4.00
14 Marshall Faulk/1382 1.50 4.00
15 Shaun Alexander/1318 1.25 3.00
16 LaDainian Tomlinson/1236 2.00 5.00
17 Garrison Hearst/1206 1.25 3.00
18 Anthony Thomas/1183 1.50 4.00
19 Emmitt Smith/1021 3.00 8.00
20 Travis Henry/729 1.25 3.00
21 David Boston/1598 1.25 3.00
22 Marvin Harrison/1524 1.50 4.00
23 Terrell Owens/1412 1.50 4.00
24 Torry Holt/1363 1.50 4.00
25 Randy Moss/1224 1.50 4.00
26 Troy Brown/1199 1.25 3.00
27 Tim Brown/1165 2.00 5.00
28 Marty Booker/1071 1.25 3.00
29 Plaxico Burress/1008 1.25 3.00
30 Chris Chambers/883 1.25 3.00

2002 Score Originals Autographs

Randomly inserted in hobby packs, this 57-card insert features original Score "bought-back" cards sequentially numbered to varying quantities. Each card features an authentic autograph.

STATED PRINT RUN 1-100
SERIAL #'d UNDER 20 NOT PRICED
3 K.Collins 95Sco/100 15.00 40.00
5 D.Flutie 89Sco/45 15.00 40.00
18 A.Green 98Sco/30 15.00 40.00
19 B.Jackson 89ScoSup/22 40.00 80.00
25 P.Manning 98Sco/31 100.00 175.00
27 W.Moon 89Sco/49 15.00 40.00
38 J.Rice 97Sco/69 50.00 100.00
42 J.Seau 90Sco/30 30.00 60.00
49 S.Young 89Sco/60 40.00 80.00

2002 Score The Franchise

Inserted into packs at a rate of 1:35 hobby packs and 1:8 jumbo packs, this 31-card insert set features the NFL's best franchise players.

STATED ODDS 1:35 HOB, 1:8 JUM
1 David Boston .75 2.00
2 Michael Vick 1.00 2.50
3 Ray Lewis 1.25 3.00
4 Travis Henry .75 2.00
5 Chris Weinke .75 2.00
6 Anthony Thomas 1.00 2.50
7 Corey Dillon .75 2.00
8 Tim Couch .75 2.00
9 Emmitt Smith 2.00 5.00
10 Rod Smith 1.00 2.50
11 Mike McMahon .75 2.00
12 Ahman Green 1.00 2.50
13 Peyton Manning 3.00 8.00
14 Jimmy Smith 1.00 2.50
15 Priest Holmes .75 2.00
16 Chris Chambers .75 2.00
17 Randy Moss 1.00 2.50
18 Tom Brady 6.00 15.00
19 Aaron Brooks .75 2.00
20 Kerry Collins .75 2.00
21 Curtis Martin 1.00 2.50
22 Tim Brown 1.25 3.00
23 Donovan McNabb 1.00 2.50
24 Jerome Bettis 1.25 3.00
25 LaDainian Tomlinson 1.25 3.00
26 Jeff Garcia .75 2.00
27 Shaun Alexander .75 2.00
28 Marshall Faulk 1.00 2.50
29 Keyshawn Johnson 1.00 2.50
30 Steve McNair 1.00 2.50
31 Stephen Davis .75 2.00

2003 Score Atlantic City National Promos

UNPRICED ATLANTIC CITY PRINT RUN 5
UNPRICED AC FINAL SCORE PRINT RUN 1

2003 Score

This set was issued in May, 2003. The cards were distributed in 18-card jumbo hobby packs which carried a $3 SRP and 7-card retail packs. Cards numbered 1-275 feature veterans while cards numbered 276-330 featured rookies. Please note that cards numbers 292, 323 and 328 were intended to have been pulled from packs but a very small number of the cards slipped through and made it onto the secondary market.

COMPLETE SET (327)	20.00	50.00
1 Jeff Blake	.15	.40
2 Todd Heap	.12	.30
3 Ron Johnson	.12	.30
4 Jamal Lewis	.15	.40
5 Ray Lewis	.20	.50
6 Chris Redman	.12	.30
7 Ed Reed	.15	.40
8 Travis Taylor	.12	.30
9 Anthony Weaver	.12	.30
10 Drew Bledsoe	.15	.40
11 Larry Centers	.12	.30
12 Nate Clements	.15	.40
13 Travis Henry	.12	.30
14 Eric Moulds	.12	.30
15 Peerless Price	.12	.30
16 Josh Reed	.12	.30
17 Coy Wire	.12	.30
18 Corey Dillon	.12	.30
19 T.J. Houshmandzadeh	.12	.30
20 Chad Johnson	.12	.30
21 Jon Kitna	.12	.30
22 Lorenzo Neal	.12	.30
23 Peter Warrick	.12	.30
24 Nicolas Luchey RC	.12	.30
25 Tim Couch	.12	.30
26 Andre Davis	.12	.30
27 William Green	.12	.30
28 Kevin Johnson	.12	.30
29 Quincy Morgan	.12	.30
30 Dennis Northcutt	.12	.30
31 Jamel White	.12	.30
32 Mike Anderson	.12	.30
33 Steve Beuerlein	.15	.40
34 Jason Elam	.12	.30
35 Olandis Gary	.12	.30
36 Brian Griese	.12	.30
37 Ashley Lelie	.12	.30
38 Ed McCaffrey	.15	.40
39 Clinton Portis	.12	.30
40 Shannon Sharpe	.15	.40
41 Rod Smith	.15	.40
42 James Allen	.12	.30
43 Corey Bradford	.12	.30
44 David Carr	.12	.30
45 JaJuan Dawson	.12	.30
46 Jabar Gaffney	.12	.30
47 Aaron Glenn	.12	.30
48 Billy Miller	.12	.30
49 Jonathan Wells	.12	.30
50 Dwight Freeney	.12	.30
51 Marvin Harrison	.15	.40
52 Qadry Ismail	.12	.30
53 Edgerrin James	.15	.40
54 Peyton Manning	.50	1.25
55 James Mungro	.12	.30
56 Marcus Pollard	.12	.30
57 Reggie Wayne	.15	.40
58 Kyle Brady	.12	.30
59 Mark Brunell	.15	.40
60 David Garrard	.12	.30
61 John Henderson	.15	.40
62 Stacey Mack	.12	.30
63 Jimmy Smith	.15	.40
64 Fred Taylor	.12	.30
65 Marc Boerigter	.12	.30
66 Tony Gonzalez	.15	.40
67 Trent Green	.12	.30
68 Priest Holmes	.12	.30
69 Eddie Kennison	.12	.30
70 Snoop Minnis	.12	.30
71 Johnnie Morton	.15	.40
72 Cris Carter	.20	.50
73 Chris Chambers	.12	.30
74 Robert Edwards	.15	.40
75 Jay Fiedler	.12	.30
76 Ray Lucas	.12	.30
77 Randy McMichael	.12	.30
78 Travis Minor	.12	.30
79 Zach Thomas	.15	.40
80 Ricky Williams	.15	.40
81 Tom Brady	.75	2.00
82 Deion Branch	.12	.30
83 Troy Brown	.12	.30
84 Tedy Bruschi	.15	.40
85 Kevin Faulk	.12	.30
86 Daniel Graham	.12	.30
87 David Patten	.12	.30
88 Antowain Smith	.15	.40
89 Adam Vinatieri	.12	.30
90 Donnie Abraham	.15	.40
91 Anthony Becht	.12	.30
92 Wayne Chrebet	.12	.30
93 Laveranues Coles	.12	.30
94 LaMont Jordan	.15	.40
95 Curtis Martin	.15	.40
96 Chad Morton	.12	.30
97 Santana Moss	.15	.40
98 Chad Pennington	.12	.30
99 Vinny Testaverde	.12	.30
100 Tim Brown	.20	.50
101 Phillip Buchanon	.12	.30
102 Rich Gannon	.15	.40
103 Charlie Garner	.15	.40
104 Doug Jolley	.12	.30
105 Jerry Porter	.12	.30
106 Jerry Rice	.40	1.00
107 Marques Tuiasosopo	.12	.30
108 Charles Woodson	.20	.50
109 Rod Woodson	.15	.40
110 Kendrell Bell	.12	.30
111 Jerome Bettis	.20	.50
112 Plaxico Burress	.12	.30
113 Tommy Maddox	.12	.30
114 Joey Porter	.20	.50
115 Antwaan Randle El	.12	.30
116 Kordell Stewart	.12	.30
117 Hines Ward	.15	.40
118 Amos Zereoue	.12	.30
119 Drew Brees	.20	.50
120 Reche Caldwell	.12	.30
121 Curtis Conway	.12	.30
122 Tim Dwight	.12	.30
123 Doug Flutie	.15	.40
124 Quentin Jammer	.12	.30
125 Ben Leber	.12	.30
126 Josh Norman	.12	.30
127 Junior Seau	.15	.40
128 LaDainian Tomlinson	.20	.50
129 Keith Bulluck	.12	.30
130 Rocky Calmus	.12	.30
131 Kevin Carter	.12	.30
132 Kevin Dyson	.12	.30
133 Eddie George	.15	.40
134 Albert Haynesworth	.20	.50
135 Jevon Kearse	.12	.30
136 Derrick Mason	.12	.30
137 Justin McCareins	.12	.30
138 Steve McNair	.15	.40
139 Frank Wycheck	.12	.30
140 David Boston	.12	.30
141 MarTay Jenkins	.12	.30
142 Freddie Jones	.12	.30
143 Thomas Jones	.12	.30
144 Jason McAddley	.12	.30
145 Josh McCown	.15	.40
146 Jake Plummer	.12	.30
147 Marcel Shipp	.12	.30
148 Alge Crumpler	.15	.40
149 T.J. Duckett	.12	.30
150 Warrick Dunn	.12	.30
151 Brian Finneran	.12	.30
152 Trevor Gaylor	.12	.30
153 Shawn Jefferson	.12	.30
154 Michael Vick	.15	.40
155 Randy Fasani	.12	.30
156 DeShaun Foster	.15	.40
157 Muhsin Muhammad	.12	.30
158 Rodney Peete	.12	.30
159 Julius Peppers	.20	.50
160 Lamar Smith	.15	.40
161 Steve Smith	.20	.50
162 Chris Weinke	.15	.40
163 Wesley Walls	.15	.40
164 Marty Booker	.12	.30
165 Mike Brown	.12	.30
166 Chris Chandler	.15	.40
167 Jim Miller	.12	.30
168 Marcus Robinson	.15	.40
169 David Terrell	.12	.30
170 Anthony Thomas	.15	.40
171 Brian Urlacher	.20	.50
172 Dez White	.12	.30
173 Antonio Bryant	.12	.30
174 Quincy Carter	.12	.30
175 Dexter Coakley	.15	.40
176 Joey Galloway	.15	.40
177 La'Roi Glover	.12	.30
178 Troy Hambrick	.12	.30
179 Chad Hutchinson	.12	.30
180 Rocket Ismail	.15	.40
181 Emmitt Smith	.30	.75
182 Roy Williams	.12	.30
183 Scotty Anderson	.12	.30
184 Germane Crowell	.12	.30
185 Az-Zahir Hakim	.12	.30
186 Joey Harrington	.12	.30
187 Cory Schlesinger	.12	.30
188 Bill Schroeder	.12	.30
189 James Stewart	.12	.30
190 Marques Anderson	.12	.30
191 Najeh Davenport	.12	.30
192 Donald Driver	.15	.40
193 Brett Favre	.40	1.00
194 Bubba Franks	.15	.40
195 Terry Glenn	.15	.40
196 Ahman Green	.15	.40
197 Darren Sharper	.12	.30
198 Javon Walker	.15	.40
199 D'Wayne Bates	.12	.30
200 Michael Bennett	.12	.30
201 Todd Bouman	.12	.30
202 Byron Chamberlain	.12	.30
203 Daunte Culpepper	.15	.40
204 Randy Moss	.15	.40
205 Kelly Campbell	.12	.30
206 Aaron Brooks	.12	.30
207 Charles Grant	.15	.40
208 Joe Horn	.12	.30
209 Michael Lewis	.12	.30
210 Deuce McAllister	.15	.40
211 Jerome Pathon	.12	.30
212 Donte Stallworth	.12	.30
213 Boo Williams	.12	.30
214 Tiki Barber	.15	.40
215 Tim Carter	.12	.30
216 Kerry Collins	.12	.30
217 Ron Dayne	.15	.40
218 Jesse Palmer	.12	.30
219 Will Peterson	.15	.40
220 Jason Sehorn	.15	.40
221 Jeremy Shockey	.12	.30
222 Michael Strahan	.15	.40
223 Amani Toomer	.12	.30
224 Koy Detmer	.12	.30
225 Antonio Freeman	.15	.40
226 Dorsey Levens	.15	.40
227 Chad Lewis	.15	.40
228 Donovan McNabb	.15	.40
229 Freddie Mitchell	.15	.40
230 Duce Staley	.12	.30
231 James Thrash	.12	.30
232 Brian Westbrook	.12	.30
233 Kevan Barlow	.12	.30
234 Andre Carter	.12	.30
235 Jeff Garcia	.12	.30
236 Garrison Hearst	.12	.30
237 Eric Johnson	.15	.40
238 Terrell Owens	.15	.40
239 Jamal Robertson	.12	.30
240 Tai Streets	.12	.30
241 Shaun Alexander	.12	.30
242 Trent Dilfer	.12	.30
243 Bobby Engram	.12	.30
244 Matt Hasselbeck	.12	.30
245 Darrell Jackson	.15	.40
246 Maurice Morris	.12	.30
247 Koren Robinson	.15	.40
248 Jerramy Stevens	.15	.40
249 Isaac Bruce	.20	.50
250 Marc Bulger	.12	.30
251 Marshall Faulk	.15	.40
252 Lamar Gordon	.12	.30
253 Torry Holt	.15	.40
254 Ricky Proehl	.15	.40
255 Kurt Warner	.15	.40
256 Aeneas Williams	.12	.30
257 Mike Alstott	.12	.30
258 Ken Dilger	.12	.30
259 Brad Johnson	.15	.40
260 Keyshawn Johnson	.20	.50
261 Rob Johnson	.15	.40
262 John Lynch	.15	.40
263 Keenan McCardell	.15	.40
264 Michael Pittman	.12	.30
265 Warren Sapp	.15	.40
266 Marquise Walker	.12	.30
267 Champ Bailey	.15	.40
268 Stephen Davis	.12	.30
269 Rod Gardner	.12	.30
270 Darrell Green	.20	.50
271 Shane Matthews	.12	.30
272 Damerien McCants	.12	.30
273 Patrick Ramsey	.15	.40
274 Bruce Smith	.15	.40
275 Kenny Watson	.12	.30
276 Carson Palmer RC	.60	1.50
277 Byron Leftwich RC	.40	1.00
278 Kyle Boller RC	.30	.75
279 Chris Simms RC	.30	.75
280 Dave Ragone RC	.30	.75
281 Rex Grossman RC	.40	1.00
282 Brian St.Pierre RC	.30	.75
283 Larry Johnson RC	.40	1.00
284 Lee Suggs RC	.30	.75
285 Justin Fargas RC	.50	1.25
286 Onterrio Smith RC	.30	.75
287 Willis McGahee RC	.40	1.00
288 Chris Brown RC	.30	.75
289 Musa Smith RC	.30	.75
290 Artose Pinner RC	.30	.75
291 Cecil Sapp RC	.30	.75
292 Derek Watson SP RC	15.00	40.00
293 LaBrandon Toefield RC	.30	.75
294 Charles Rogers RC	.40	1.00
295 Andre Johnson RC	.75	2.00
296 Taylor Jacobs RC	.30	.75
297 Bryant Johnson RC	.50	1.25
298 Kelley Washington RC	.30	.75
299 Brandon Lloyd RC	.50	1.25
300 Justin Gage RC	.40	1.00
301 Tyrone Calico RC	.30	.75
302 Kevin Curtis RC	.30	.75
303 Sam Aiken RC	.40	1.00
304 Doug Gabriel RC	.40	1.00
305 Talman Gardner RC	.30	.75
306 Jason Witten RC	1.25	3.00
307 Mike Pinkard RC	.30	.75
308 Teyo Johnson RC	.40	1.00
309 Bennie Joppru RC	.30	.75
310 Dallas Clark RC	.50	1.25
311 Terrell Suggs RC	.40	1.00
312 Chris Kelsay RC	.40	1.00
313 Jerome McDougle RC	.30	.75
314 Andrew Williams RC	.30	.75
315 Michael Haynes RC	.30	.75
316 Jimmy Kennedy RC	.40	1.00
317 Kevin Williams RC	.50	1.25
318 Ken Dorsey RC	.40	1.00
319 William Joseph RC	.30	.75
320 Kenny Peterson RC	.40	1.00
321 Rien Long RC	.30	.75
322 Boss Bailey RC	.40	1.00
323 E.J. Henderson SP RC	15.00	40.00
324 Terence Newman RC	.50	1.25
325 Marcus Trufant RC	.40	1.00
326 Andre Woolfolk RC	.30	.75
327 Dennis Weathersby RC	.30	.75
328 Eugene Wilson SP RC	15.00	40.00
329 Mike Doss RC	.50	1.25
330 Rashean Mathis RC	.30	.75

2003 Score Final Score

UNPRICED FINAL SCORE PRINT RUN 2-12

2003 Score Scorecard

*VETS 1-275: 2.5X TO 6X BASIC CARDS
*ROOKIES 276-330: 1X TO 2.5X
STATED PRINT RUN 500 SER.#'d SETS

2003 Score Changing Stripes

Randomly inserted in packs, this 10-card set featured game-used jersey swatches from two different teams the featured player played for in his career. Each of these cards were issued to a stated print run of 250 serial numbered sets.

STATED PRINT RUN 250 SER.#'d SETS

CS1 Drew Bledsoe		
CS2 Ricky Williams	6.00	15.00
CS3 Terry Glenn	6.00	15.00
CS4 Rich Gannon	6.00	15.00
CS5 Brad Johnson	6.00	15.00
CS6 James Stewart	5.00	12.00
CS7 Trent Green	5.00	12.00
CS8 Joe Montana	25.00	60.00
CS9 Art Monk	12.00	30.00
CS10 Warrick Dunn	5.00	12.00

2003 Score Franchise Fabrics

Randomly inserted into packs, these 20-cards feature game-used swatches and were issued to a stated print run of 250 serial numbered sets.

STATED PRINT RUN 250 SER.#'d SETS

FF1 Ahman Green	2.50	6.00
FF2 Corey Dillon	2.00	5.00
FF3 Curtis Martin	2.50	6.00
FF4 Darrell Green	3.00	8.00
FF5 Emmitt Smith	10.00	25.00
FF6 Garrison Hearst	2.00	5.00
FF7 Jake Plummer	2.00	5.00
FF8 Jimmy Smith	2.50	6.00
FF9 Junior Seau	2.50	6.00
FF10 Kevin Johnson	2.00	5.00
FF11 Michael Strahan	2.50	6.00
FF12 Mike Alstott	2.00	5.00
FF13 Plaxico Burress	2.00	5.00
FF14 Ray Lewis	3.00	8.00
FF15 Rod Smith	2.50	6.00
FF16 Stephen Davis	2.00	5.00
FF17 Steve McNair	2.50	6.00
FF18 Tim Brown	3.00	8.00
FF19 Tony Gonzalez	2.50	6.00
FF20 Warren Sapp	2.50	6.00

2003 Score Inscriptions

Inserted in packs at a stated rate of one in 65, these cards feature a mix of rookies, young stars and future greats all of whom signed stickers adhered to these cards. Please note that many were issued in packs as exchange cards with a expiration date of 12/1/2004.

STATED ODDS 1:65
*PERSONALIZED/25: .8X TO 2X BASIC AU
PERSONALIZED SER. #'d TO 25

1 Joe Montana	90.00	150.00
2 Kurt Warner	40.00	80.00
3 Jeff Garcia	8.00	20.00
4 Donald Driver	15.00	40.00
5 Shaun Alexander	8.00	20.00
6 Peerless Price	8.00	20.00
7 Derrick Mason	8.00	20.00
9 Boss Bailey	10.00	25.00
10 Chris Simms	6.00	15.00
11 Jason Witten	25.00	60.00
12 Jimmy Kennedy	10.00	25.00
13 Justin Fargas	10.00	25.00
14 Justin Gage	10.00	25.00
15 Kevin Curtis	8.00	20.00
16 Marcus Trufant	10.00	25.00
17 Mike Pinkard	8.00	20.00
18 Rex Grossman	8.00	20.00
19 Rien Long	8.00	20.00
20 Sam Aiken	10.00	25.00
21 Tyrone Calico	8.00	20.00
22 Willis McGahee	8.00	20.00

2003 Score Monday Night Heroes

Issued at a stated rate of one in nine, these 17-cards feature the leading performers in the 2002 Monday Night football games.

COMPLETE SET (17)	10.00	25.00
STATED ODDS 1:9		
MN1 Tom Brady	3.00	8.00
MN2 Donovan McNabb	.60	1.50
MN3 Derrick Brooks	.50	1.25
MN4 Todd Heap	.50	1.25
MN5 Brett Favre	1.50	4.00
MN6 Terrell Owens	.60	1.50
MN7 Hines Ward	.60	1.50
MN8 Donovan McNabb	.60	1.50
MN9 Ahman Green	.60	1.50
MN10 Rich Gannon	.60	1.50
MN11 Marc Bulger	.50	1.25
MN12 Koy Detmer	.50	1.25
MN13 Tim Brown	.75	2.00
MN14 Ricky Williams	.60	1.50
MN15 Steve McNair	.60	1.50
MN16 Plaxico Burress	.50	1.25
MN17 Dre Bly	.50	1.25

2003 Score Numbers Game

Randomly inserted into packs, this 31-card insert set featured players who amassed some great statistics during the 2002 NFL season. These cards are highlighted with a silver foil stamp and are sequentially numbered to the player's key 2002 stat.

COMPLETE SET (31)	30.00	80.00
STATED PRINT RUN 887-4689		
NG1 Rich Gannon/4689	.75	2.00
NG2 Drew Bledsoe/4359	.75	2.00
NG3 Peyton Manning/4200	2.50	6.00
NG4 Tom Brady/3764	4.00	10.00
NG5 Joey Harrington/2294	.60	1.50
NG6 Brett Favre/3658	2.00	5.00
NG7 Aaron Brooks/3572	.60	1.50
NG8 Michael Vick/2936	.75	2.00
NG9 Steve McNair/3387	.75	2.00
NG10 David Carr/2592	.60	1.50
NG11 Priest Holmes/1615	.75	2.00
NG12 LaDainian Tomlinson/1683	1.25	3.00
NG13 Ricky Williams/1853	1.00	2.50
NG14 Travis Henry/1438	.75	2.00
NG15 Deuce McAllister/1300	1.00	2.50
NG16 Clinton Portis/1508	.75	2.00
NG17 William Green/887	.75	2.00
NG18 Jamal Lewis/1327	1.00	2.50
NG19 Michael Bennett/1296	.75	2.00
NG20 Ahman Green/1240	1.00	2.50
NG21 Eddie George/1165	1.00	2.50
NG22 Marvin Harrison/1722	1.00	2.50
NG23 Hines Ward/1329	1.00	2.50
NG24 Rod Gardner/1006	.75	2.00
NG25 Jerry Rice/1211	2.50	6.00
NG26 Jeremy Shockey/894	.75	2.00
NG27 Peerless Price/1252	.75	2.00
NG28 Eric Moulds/1287	.75	2.00
NG29 Chad Johnson/1166	.75	2.00
NG30 Donald Driver/1064	1.00	2.50
NG31 Koren Robinson/1240	1.00	2.50

2003 Score Reflextions

Issued at a stated rate of one in nine, these 20-cards pair a rising star and an established veteran at the same position.

COMPLETE SET (20)	15.00	40.00
STATED ODDS 1:9		
R1 T.Owens/D.Boston	.75	2.00
R2 E.George/A.Thomas	.75	2.00
R3 E.Smith/L.Tomlinson	1.50	4.00
R4 M.Faulk/P.Holmes	.75	2.00
R5 R.Moss/P.Burress	.75	2.00
R6 B.Favre/K.Warner	2.00	5.00
R7 Z.Thomas/B.Urlacher	1.00	2.50
R8 F.Taylor/M.Bennett	.60	1.50
R9 J.Bettis/T.J.Duckett	1.00	2.50
R10 P.Manning/J.Harrington	2.50	6.00
R11 T.Holt/D.Stallworth	.75	2.00
R12 J.Rice/M.Harrison	2.00	5.00
R13 Key.Johnson/R.Gardner	1.00	2.50
R14 D.Culpepper/A.Brooks	.75	2.00
R15 R.Gannon/J.Garcia	.75	2.00
R16 S.McNair/D.McNabb	.75	2.00
R17 E.James/D.McAllister	.75	2.00
R18 E.Moulds/C.Chambers	.60	1.50
R19 I.Bruce/J.Horn	1.00	2.50
R20 J.Kearse/J.Peppers	1.00	2.50

2003 Score Reflextions Materials

Randomly inserted into packs, these cards parallel the Reflextions insert set. Each of these cards have a game-worn jersey swatch from each player featured on the card and were issued to a stated print run of 250 serial numbered sets.

STATED PRINT RUN 250 SER.#'d SETS

R1 T.Owens/D.Boston	3.00	8.00
R2 E.George/A.Thomas	3.00	8.00
R3 E.Smith/L.Tomlinson	6.00	15.00
R4 M.Faulk/P.Holmes	3.00	8.00
R5 R.Moss/P.Burress	3.00	8.00
R6 B.Favre/K.Warner	8.00	20.00
R7 Z.Thomas/B.Urlacher	4.00	10.00
R8 F.Taylor/M.Bennett	2.50	6.00
R9 J.Bettis/T.J.Duckett	4.00	10.00
R10 P.Manning/J.Harrington	10.00	25.00
R11 T.Holt/D.Stallworth	3.00	8.00
R12 J.Rice/M.Harrison	8.00	20.00
R13 Key.Johnson/R.Gardner	4.00	10.00
R14 D.Culpepper/A.Brooks	3.00	8.00
R15 R.Gannon/J.Garcia	3.00	8.00
R16 S.McNair/D.McNabb	3.00	8.00
R17 E.James/D.McAllister	3.00	8.00
R18 E.Moulds/C.Chambers	2.50	6.00
R19 I.Bruce/J.Horn	4.00	10.00
R20 J.Kearse/J.Peppers	4.00	10.00

2003 Score The Franchise

Issued at a stated rate of one in nine, this 32-card set featured each team's standout star highlighted by a silver foil stamp.

COMPLETE SET (32)	30.00	80.00
STATED ODDS 1:9		
TF1 David Boston	.75	2.00
TF2 Michael Vick	1.00	2.50
TF3 Jamal Lewis	1.00	2.50
TF4 Drew Bledsoe	1.00	2.50
TF5 Julius Peppers	1.25	3.00
TF6 Anthony Thomas	1.00	2.50
TF7 Chad Johnson	.75	2.00
TF8 William Green	.75	2.00
TF9 Emmitt Smith	2.00	5.00
TF10 Clinton Portis	.75	2.00
TF11 Joey Harrington	.75	2.00
TF12 Brett Favre	2.50	6.00
TF13 David Carr	.75	2.00
TF14 Edgerrin James	1.00	2.50
TF15 Fred Taylor	.75	2.00
TF16 Priest Holmes	.75	2.00
TF17 Ricky Williams	1.00	2.50
TF18 Michael Bennett	.75	2.00
TF19 Tom Brady	5.00	12.00
TF20 Deuce McAllister	1.00	2.50
TF21 Tiki Barber	1.00	2.50
TF22 Chad Pennington	.75	2.00
TF23 Jerry Rice	2.50	6.00
TF24 Donovan McNabb	1.00	2.50
TF25 Tommy Maddox	.75	2.00
TF26 Drew Brees	1.25	3.00
TF27 Terrell Owens	1.00	2.50
TF28 Shaun Alexander	.75	2.00
TF29 Marshall Faulk	1.00	2.50
TF30 Warren Sapp	1.00	2.50
TF31 Eddie George	1.00	2.50
TF32 Patrick Ramsey	1.00	2.50

2004 Score

Score initially released in early September 2004. The base set consists of 440-cards including 70-rookies issued one per pack. The retail-only boxes contained 36-packs of 7-cards and carried an S.R.P. of $1 per pack. Three parallel sets and the Inscriptions autographs highlight the inserts.

COMPLETE SET (440)	40.00	80.00
UNPRICED FINAL SCORE #'d TO TEAM WINS		
1 Emmitt Smith	.30	.75
2 Anquan Boldin	.12	.30
3 Bryant Johnson	.12	.30
4 Marcel Shipp	.12	.30
5 Josh McCown	.15	.40
6 Dexter Jackson	.12	.30
7 Bertrand Berry	.15	.40
8 Freddie Jones	.12	.30
9 Duane Starks	.12	.30
10 Michael Vick	.15	.40
11 T.J. Duckett	.12	.30
12 Warrick Dunn	.12	.30
13 Peerless Price	.12	.30
14 Alge Crumpler	.15	.40
15 Brian Finneran	.12	.30
16 Jason Webster	.12	.30
17 Dez White	.15	.40
18 Keith Brooking	.12	.30
19 Rod Coleman	.12	.30
20 Jamal Lewis	.15	.40
21 Kyle Boller	.12	.30
22 Todd Heap	.12	.30
23 Jonathan Ogden	.15	.40
24 Travis Taylor	.12	.30
25 Ray Lewis	.20	.50
26 Peter Boulware	.12	.30
27 Terrell Suggs	.12	.30
28 Chris McAlister	.12	.30
29 Ed Reed	.15	.40
30 Drew Bledsoe	.15	.40
31 Travis Henry	.12	.30
32 Eric Moulds	.12	.30
33 Josh Reed	.12	.30
34 Willis McGahee	.12	.30
35 Takeo Spikes	.12	.30
36 Lawyer Milloy	.12	.30
37 Troy Vincent	.15	.40
38 Sam Adams	.12	.30
39 Nate Clements	.15	.40
40 Jake Delhomme	.12	.30
41 Stephen Davis	.12	.30
42 DeShaun Foster	.15	.40
43 Muhsin Muhammad	.12	.30
44 Steve Smith	.20	.50
45 Ricky Proehl	.15	.40
46 Julius Peppers	.15	.40
47 Kris Jenkins	.15	.40
48 Dan Morgan	.15	.40
49 Ricky Manning	.12	.30
50 Brad Hoover	.15	.40
51 Carson Palmer	.15	.40
52 Rudi Johnson	.12	.30
53 Corey Dillon	.12	.30
54 Chad Johnson	.12	.30
55 Peter Warrick	.12	.30
56 Kelley Washington	.12	.30
57 Kevin Hardy	.15	.40
58 Tory James	.12	.30
59 Ickey Woods	.15	.40
60 Anthony Thomas	.15	.40
61 Thomas Jones	.12	.30
62 Rex Grossman	.12	.30
63 Marty Booker	.12	.30
64 Justin Gage	.15	.40
65 David Terrell	.12	.30
66 Brian Urlacher	.20	.50
67 Mike Brown	.12	.30
68 Charles Tillman	.15	.40
69 Jeff Garcia	.12	.30
70 Lee Suggs	.15	.40
71 William Green	.12	.30
72 Kelly Holcomb	.12	.30
73 Quincy Morgan	.12	.30
74 Andre Davis	.12	.30
75 Dennis Northcutt	.12	.30
76 Gerard Warren	.12	.30
77 Courtney Brown	.15	.40
78 Joey Harrington	.12	.30
79 Shawn Bryson	.12	.30
80 Charles Rogers	.12	.30
81 Mikhael Ricks	.12	.30
82 Artose Pinner	.12	.30
83 Az-Zahir Hakim	.12	.30
84 Dre Bly	.12	.30
85 Fernando Bryant	.12	.30
86 Boss Bailey	.12	.30
87 Tai Streets	.12	.30
88 Jake Plummer	.12	.30
89 Quentin Griffin	.12	.30
90 Mike Anderson	.12	.30
91 Garrison Hearst	.12	.30
92 Rod Smith	.15	.40
93 Ashley Lelie	.12	.30
94 Shannon Sharpe	.15	.40
95 Al Wilson	.12	.30
96 Champ Bailey	.15	.40
97 Jason Elam	.12	.30
98 John Lynch	.15	.40
99 Quincy Carter	.12	.30
100 Antonio Bryant	.15	.40
101 Terry Glenn	.15	.40
102 Keyshawn Johnson	.15	.40
103 Jason Witten	.15	.40
104 La'Roi Glover	.15	.40
105 Dat Nguyen	.12	.30
106 Dexter Coakley	.12	.30
107 Terence Newman	.15	.40
108 Darren Woodson	.15	.40
109 Roy Williams S	.12	.30
110 Brett Favre	.40	1.00
111 Ahman Green	.15	.40
112 Najeh Davenport	.12	.30
113 Donald Driver	.15	.40
114 Robert Ferguson	.12	.30
115 Javon Walker	.12	.30
116 Bubba Franks	.12	.30
117 Kabeer Gbaja-Biamila	.12	.30
118 Darren Sharper	.12	.30
119 Mike McKenzie	.15	.40
120 Nick Barnett	.12	.30
121 David Carr	.12	.30
122 Domanick Davis	.12	.30
123 Andre Johnson	.15	.40
124 Corey Bradford	.12	.30
125 Jabar Gaffney	.12	.30
126 Billy Miller	.12	.30
127 Gary Walker	.12	.30
128 Jamie Sharper	.12	.30
129 Aaron Glenn	.15	.40
130 Robaire Smith	.12	.30
131 Peyton Manning	.50	1.25
132 Edgerrin James	.15	.40
133 Dominic Rhodes	.12	.30
134 Marvin Harrison	.15	.40
135 Reggie Wayne	.15	.40
136 Brandon Stokley	.12	.30
137 Marcus Pollard	.12	.30
138 Dallas Clark	.12	.30
139 Mike Vanderjagt	.12	.30
140 Dwight Freeney	.12	.30
141 Mike Doss	.15	.40
142 Byron Leftwich	.12	.30
143 Fred Taylor	.12	.30
144 LaBrandon Toefield	.12	.30
145 Jimmy Smith	.15	.40
146 Kevin Johnson	.12	.30
147 Marcus Stroud	.12	.30
148 John Henderson	.12	.30
149 Donovin Darius	.12	.30
150 Deon Grant	.12	.30
151 Rashean Mathis	.12	.30
152 Trent Green	.12	.30
153 Priest Holmes	.12	.30
154 Johnnie Morton	.15	.40
155 Eddie Kennison	.15	.40
156 Marc Boerigter	.15	.40
157 Tony Gonzalez	.15	.40
158 Dante Hall	.12	.30
159 Tony Richardson	.12	.30
160 Gary Stills	.12	.30
161 Daunte Culpepper	.15	.40
162 Michael Bennett	.12	.30
163 Moe Williams	.12	.30
164 Onterrio Smith	.12	.30
165 Jim Kleinsasser	.12	.30
166 Antoine Winfield	.15	.40
167 Nate Burleson	.15	.40
168 Randy Moss	.15	.40
169 Marcus Robinson	.12	.30
170 Chris Hovan	.12	.30
171 Brian Russell RC	.12	.30
172 A.J. Feeley	.12	.30
173 Jay Fiedler	.12	.30
174 Ricky Williams	.15	.40
175 Chris Chambers	.12	.30
176 David Boston	.12	.30
177 Randy McMichael	.12	.30
178 Jason Taylor	.15	.40
179 Adewale Ogunleye	.15	.40
180 Zach Thomas	.15	.40
181 Junior Seau	.20	.50
182 Patrick Surtain	.12	.30
183 Tom Brady	.75	2.00
184 Kevin Faulk	.12	.30
185 Troy Brown	.12	.30
186 Deion Branch	.12	.30
187 David Givens	.12	.30
188 Bethel Johnson	.12	.30
189 Richard Seymour	.12	.30
190 Tedy Bruschi	.15	.40
191 Ty Law	.20	.50
192 Rodney Harrison	.12	.30
193 Willie McGinest	.15	.40
194 Adam Vinatieri	.12	.30
195 Aaron Brooks	.12	.30
196 Deuce McAllister	.15	.40
197 Joe Horn	.12	.30
198 Donte Stallworth	.12	.30
199 Jerome Pathon	.12	.30
200 Boo Williams	.12	.30
201 Charles Grant	.12	.30
202 Darren Howard	.12	.30
203 Michael Lewis	.15	.40
204 Johnathan Sullivan	.12	.30
205 LeCharles Bentley RC	.12	.30
206 Kerry Collins	.12	.30
207 Tiki Barber	.15	.40
208 Amani Toomer	.12	.30
209 Ike Hilliard	.12	.30
210 Tim Carter	.12	.30
211 Jeremy Shockey	.12	.30
212 Michael Strahan	.15	.40
213 Will Allen	.12	.30
214 Will Peterson	.12	.30
215 William Joseph	.12	.30
216 Chad Pennington	.12	.30
217 Curtis Martin	.15	.40
218 LaMont Jordan	.15	.40
219 Santana Moss	.15	.40
220 Justin McCareins	.12	.30
221 Wayne Chrebet	.12	.30
222 Anthony Becht	.12	.30
223 Shaun Ellis	.12	.30
224 John Abraham	.12	.30
225 DeWayne Robertson	.12	.30
226 Rich Gannon	.15	.40
227 Justin Fargas	.15	.40
228 Tyrone Wheatley	.15	.40
229 Jerry Rice	.40	1.00
230 Tim Brown	.20	.50
231 Jerry Porter	.12	.30
232 Teyo Johnson	.12	.30
233 Charles Woodson	.20	.50
234 Phillip Buchanon	.15	.40
235 Rod Woodson	.15	.40
236 Warren Sapp	.15	.40
237 Donovan McNabb	.15	.40
238 Brian Westbrook	.12	.30
239 Correll Buckhalter	.12	.30
240 Chad Lewis	.15	.40
241 L.J. Smith	.15	.40
242 Terrell Owens	.15	.40
243 Todd Pinkston	.12	.30
244 Freddie Mitchell	.12	.30
245 Jevon Kearse	.12	.30
246 Brian Dawkins	.12	.30
247 Corey Simon	.15	.40
248 Tommy Maddox	.12	.30
249 Duce Staley	.12	.30
250 Jerome Bettis	.20	.50
251 Hines Ward	.15	.40
252 Plaxico Burress	.12	.30
253 Antwaan Randle El	.12	.30
254 Kendrell Bell	.12	.30
255 Joey Porter	.15	.40
256 Alan Faneca	.20	.50
257 Casey Hampton	.12	.30
258 Drew Brees	.20	.50
259 Doug Flutie	.15	.40
260 LaDainian Tomlinson	.20	.50
261 Reche Caldwell	.15	.40
262 Tim Dwight	.12	.30
263 Eric Parker	.15	.40
264 Kevin Dyson	.12	.30
265 Antonio Gates	.20	.50
266 Quentin Jammer	.12	.30
267 Zeke Moreno	.12	.30
268 Tim Rattay	.12	.30
269 Kevan Barlow	.12	.30
270 Cedrick Wilson	.12	.30
271 Brandon Lloyd	.15	.40
272 Fred Beasley	.12	.30
273 Andre Carter	.12	.30
274 Julian Peterson	.15	.40
275 Ahmed Plummer	.12	.30
276 Tony Parrish	.12	.30
277 Bryant Young	.15	.40
278 Matt Hasselbeck	.12	.30
279 Shaun Alexander	.12	.30
280 Maurice Morris	.15	.40
281 Koren Robinson	.12	.30
282 Darrell Jackson	.15	.40
283 Bobby Engram	.12	.30
284 Grant Wistrom	.15	.40
285 Chad Brown	.12	.30
286 Marcus Trufant	.12	.30
287 Bobby Taylor	.15	.40
288 Marc Bulger	.12	.30
289 Kurt Warner	.15	.40
290 Marshall Faulk	.15	.40
291 Lamar Gordon	.12	.30
292 Torry Holt	.15	.40
293 Isaac Bruce	.20	.50
294 Leonard Little	.12	.30
295 Aeneas Williams	.12	.30
296 Orlando Pace	.12	.30
297 Tommy Polley	.12	.30
298 Pisa Tinoisamoa	.12	.30
299 Brad Johnson	.15	.40
300 Michael Pittman	.15	.40
301 Charlie Garner	.15	.40
302 Mike Alstott	.12	.30
303 Keenan McCardell	.12	.30
304 Joey Galloway	.15	.40
305 Joe Jurevicius	.12	.30
306 Anthony McFarland	.12	.30
307 Derrick Brooks	.12	.30
308 Ronde Barber	.12	.30
309 Shelton Quarles	.12	.30
310 Steve McNair	.15	.40
311 Eddie George	.15	.40
312 Chris Brown	.12	.30
313 Derrick Mason	.12	.30
314 Tyrone Calico	.15	.40
315 Drew Bennett	.15	.40
316 Kevin Carter	.12	.30
317 Keith Bulluck	.12	.30
318 Samari Rolle	.12	.30
319 Albert Haynesworth	.12	.30
320 Erron Kinney	.12	.30
321 Mark Brunell	.15	.40
322 Patrick Ramsey	.15	.40
323 Laveranues Coles	.12	.30
324 Rod Gardner	.12	.30
325 Damerien McCants	.12	.30
326 Clinton Portis	.12	.30
327 LaVar Arrington	.12	.30
328 Shawn Springs	.12	.30
329 Fred Smoot	.12	.30
330 James Thrash	.12	.30
331 Marvin Harrison PB	.10	.25
332 Steve McNair PB	.10	.25
333 Ray Lewis PB	.12	.30
334 Trent Green PB	.07	.20
335 Peyton Manning PB	.30	.75
336 Priest Holmes PB	.07	.20
337 Clinton Portis PB	.07	.20
338 Torry Holt PB	.10	.25
339 Anquan Boldin PB	.07	.20
340 Daunte Culpepper PB	.10	.25
341 Ahman Green PB	.10	.25
342 Brian Urlacher PB	.12	.30
343 Donovan McNabb PB	.10	.25
344 Marc Bulger PB	.07	.20
345 Shaun Alexander PB	.07	.20
346 Peyton Manning LL	.30	.75
347 Daunte Culpepper LL	.10	.25
348 Brett Favre LL	.25	.60
349 Steve McNair LL	.10	.25
350 Tom Brady LL	.50	1.25
351 Jamal Lewis LL	.10	.25
352 Deuce McAllister LL	.10	.25
353 Clinton Portis LL	.07	.20
354 Ahman Green LL	.10	.25
355 LaDainian Tomlinson LL	.12	.30
356 Torry Holt LL	.10	.25
357 Anquan Boldin LL	.07	.20
358 Randy Moss LL	.10	.25
359 Chad Johnson LL	.07	.20
360 Marvin Harrison LL	.10	.25
361 Peyton Manning HL	.30	.75
362 Jamal Lewis HL	.10	.25
363 Ray Lewis HL	.12	.30
364 Anquan Boldin HL	.07	.20
365 Terrell Suggs HL	.07	.20
366 Jamal Lewis HL	.10	.25
367 Priest Holmes HL	.07	.20
368 Tom Brady HL	.50	1.25
369 Marc Bulger HL	.07	.20
370 Steve McNair HL	.10	.25
371 Eli Manning RC	2.50	6.00
372 Robert Gallery RC	.40	1.00
373 Larry Fitzgerald RC	1.25	3.00
374 Philip Rivers RC	1.00	2.50
375 Sean Taylor RC	2.00	5.00
376 Kellen Winslow RC	.30	.75
377 Roy Williams RC	.30	.75
378 DeAngelo Hall RC	.50	1.25
379 Reggie Williams RC	.30	.75
380 Dunta Robinson RC	.30	.75
381 Ben Roethlisberger RC	2.50	6.00
382 Jonathan Vilma RC	.40	1.00
383 Lee Evans RC	.50	1.25
384 Tommie Harris RC	.40	1.00
385 Michael Clayton RC	.40	1.00
386 D.J. Williams RC	.50	1.25
387 Will Smith RC	.40	1.00
388 Kenechi Udeze RC	.40	1.00
389 Vince Wilfork RC	.50	1.25
390 J.P. Losman RC	.30	.75
391 Marcus Tubbs RC	.30	.75
392 Steven Jackson RC	.50	1.25
393 Ahmad Carroll RC	.30	.75
394 Chris Perry RC	.30	.75
395 Jason Babin RC	.50	1.25
396 Chris Gamble RC	.30	.75
397 Michael Jenkins RC	.30	.75
398 Kevin Jones RC	.40	1.00
399 Rashaun Woods RC	.30	.75
400 Ben Watson RC	.40	1.00
401 Karlos Dansby RC	.40	1.00
402 Igor Olshansky RC	.40	1.00
403 Junior Siavii RC	.30	.75
404 Teddy Lehman RC	.30	.75
405 Ricardo Colclough RC	.30	.75
406 Daryl Smith RC	.30	.75
407 Ben Troupe RC	.30	.75
408 Tatum Bell RC	.30	.75
409 Travis LaBoy RC	.40	1.00
410 Julius Jones RC	.30	.75
411 Mewelde Moore RC	.40	1.00
412 Drew Henson RC	.30	.75
413 Dontarrious Thomas RC	.40	1.00
414 Keiwan Ratliff RC	.30	.75
415 Devery Henderson RC	.30	.75
416 Dwan Edwards RC	.30	.75
417 Michael Boulware RC	.50	1.25
418 Darius Watts RC	.30	.75
419 Greg Jones RC	.30	.75
420 Madieu Williams RC	.30	.75
421 Antwan Odom RC	.30	.75
422 Shawntae Spencer RC	.30	.75
423 Sean Jones RC	.30	.75
424 Courtney Watson RC	.30	.75
425 Kris Wilson RC	.40	1.00
426 Keary Colbert RC	.30	.75
427 Marquise Hill RC	.30	.75
428 Darnell Dockett RC	.50	1.25
429 Stuart Schweigert RC	.40	1.00
430 Ben Hartsock RC	.30	.75
431 Joey Thomas RC	.30	.75
432 Randy Starks RC	.30	.75
433 Keith Smith RC	.30	.75
434 Derrick Hamilton RC	.30	.75
435 Bernard Berrian RC	.30	.75
436 Chris Cooley RC	.40	1.00
437 Devard Darling RC	.30	.75
438 Matt Schaub RC	.30	.75
439 Luke McCown RC	.30	.75
440 Cedric Cobbs RC	.30	.75

2004 Score Glossy

*VETS: 1.5X TO 4X BASIC CARDS
*ROOKIES: .6X TO 1.5X BASIC CARDS
ONE GLOSSY PER PACK

2004 Score Inscriptions

6 Dexter Jackson	8.00	20.00
7 Bertrand Berry	6.00	15.00
38 Sam Adams	6.00	15.00
59 Ickey Woods SP	10.00	25.00
147 Marcus Stroud No AU	3.00	8.00
170 Chris Hovan	6.00	15.00
265 Antonio Gates	10.00	25.00
267 Zeke Moreno	6.00	15.00
320 Erron Kinney	6.00	15.00

2004 Score Scorecard

*VETS: 2.5X TO 6X BASIC CARDS
*ROOKIES: 1.2X TO 3X BASIC CARDS
STATED PRINT RUN 625 SER.#'d SETS

2005 Score

This 385-card set was released in August, 2005. The set was issued into the hobby in seven-card packs which came 36 packs to a box. Cards numbered 1-300 feature veteran players sequenced in alphabetical order based on where they played in 2004; cards numbered 301-330 feature players who participated in the 2005 Pro Bowl and the set concludes with 2005 rookies. (Cards #331-385). The rookies were inserted at a stated rate of one per pack.

COMPLETE SET (385)	40.00	80.00
ONE ROOKIE PER PACK		
FINAL SCORE/2-17 TOO SCARCE TO PRICE		
1 Anquan Boldin	.12	.30
2 Bertrand Berry	.12	.30
3 Bryant Johnson	.12	.30
4 Darnell Dockett	.12	.30
5 Freddie Jones	.12	.30
6 Josh McCown	.15	.40
7 Karlos Dansby	.12	.30
8 Larry Fitzgerald	.20	.50
9 Alge Crumpler	.15	.40
10 DeAngelo Hall	.12	.30
11 Keith Brooking	.12	.30
12 Michael Jenkins	.12	.30
13 Michael Vick	.15	.40
14 Peerless Price	.12	.30
15 Rod Coleman	.12	.30
16 T.J. Duckett	.12	.30
17 Warrick Dunn	.12	.30
18 Chris McAlister	.12	.30
19 Clarence Moore	.12	.30
20 Ed Reed	.15	.40
21 Jamal Lewis	.15	.40
22 Jonathan Ogden	.15	.40

23 Kyle Boller .12 .30
24 Peter Boulware .12 .30
25 Ray Lewis .20 .50
26 Terrell Suggs .12 .30
27 Todd Heap .12 .30
28 Drew Bledsoe .15 .40
29 Eric Moulds .12 .30
30 Josh Reed .12 .30
31 Lee Evans .15 .40
32 Nate Clements .15 .40
33 Takeo Spikes .12 .30
34 Travis Henry .12 .30
35 Willis McGahee .12 .30
36 Dan Morgan .12 .30
37 DeShaun Foster .15 .40
38 Jake Delhomme .12 .30
39 Julius Peppers .15 .40
40 Keary Colbert .12 .30
41 Kris Jenkins .12 .30
42 Muhsin Muhammad .12 .30
43 Nick Goings .12 .30
44 Stephen Davis .12 .30
45 Steve Smith .20 .50
46 Anthony Thomas .12 .30
47 Adewale Ogunleye .12 .30
48 Bernard Berrian .12 .30
49 Brian Urlacher .20 .50
50 David Terrell .12 .30
51 Mike Brown .12 .30
52 Rex Grossman .12 .30
53 Thomas Jones .12 .30
54 Tommie Harris .12 .30
55 Carson Palmer .15 .40
56 Chad Johnson .12 .30
57 Chris Perry .12 .30
58 Kelley Washington .12 .30
59 Madieu Williams .12 .30
60 Peter Warrick .12 .30
61 Rudi Johnson .12 .30
62 T.J. Houshmandzadeh .12 .30
63 Tory James .12 .30
64 Andre Davis .12 .30
65 Antonio Bryant .12 .30
66 Dennis Northcutt .12 .30
67 Gerard Warren .12 .30
68 Jeff Garcia .12 .30
69 Kellen Winslow Jr. .12 .30
70 Lee Suggs .12 .30
71 William Green .12 .30
72 Drew Henson .12 .30
73 Jason Witten .15 .40
74 Julius Jones .12 .30
75 Keyshawn Johnson .15 .40
76 La'Roi Glover .12 .30
77 J.P. Losman .12 .30
78 Roy Williams S .12 .30
79 Terence Newman .12 .30
80 Terry Glenn .12 .30
81 Al Wilson .12 .30
82 Ashley Lelie .12 .30
83 Champ Bailey .15 .40
84 D.J. Williams .12 .30
85 Jake Plummer .12 .30
86 Jason Elam .12 .30
87 John Lynch .15 .40
88 Reuben Droughns .12 .30
89 Rod Smith .15 .40
90 Tatum Bell .12 .30
91 Trent Dilfer .12 .30
92 Charles Rogers .12 .30
93 Dre Bly .12 .30
94 Joey Harrington .12 .30
95 Kevin Jones .12 .30
96 Roy Williams WR .12 .30
97 Shawn Bryson .12 .30
98 Tai Streets .12 .30
99 Teddy Lehman .12 .30
100 Ahman Green .15 .40
101 Brett Favre .40 1.00
102 Bubba Franks .12 .30
103 Darren Sharper .12 .30
104 Donald Driver .15 .40
105 Javon Walker .12 .30
106 Najeh Davenport .12 .30
107 Nick Barnett .12 .30
108 Robert Ferguson .12 .30
109 Aaron Glenn .12 .30
110 Andre Johnson .15 .40
111 Corey Bradford .12 .30
112 David Carr .12 .30
113 Domanick Davis .12 .30
114 Dunta Robinson .12 .30
115 Jabar Gaffney .12 .30
116 Jamie Sharper .12 .30
117 Jason Babin .12 .30
118 Brandon Stokley .12 .30
119 Dallas Clark .12 .30
120 Dwight Freeney .12 .30
121 Edgerrin James .15 .40
122 Marcus Pollard .12 .30
123 Marvin Harrison .15 .40
124 Peyton Manning .50 1.25
125 Reggie Wayne .15 .40
126 Robert Mathis RC .60 1.50
127 Byron Leftwich .12 .30
128 Daryl Smith .12 .30
129 Donovan Darius .12 .30
130 Ernest Wilford .12 .30
131 Fred Taylor .12 .30
132 Jimmy Smith .15 .40
133 John Henderson .12 .30
134 Marcus Stroud .12 .30
135 Reggie Williams .12 .30
136 Dante Hall .12 .30
137 Eddie Kennison .12 .30
138 Jared Allen .12 .30
139 Johnnie Morton .15 .40
140 Larry Johnson .12 .30
141 Priest Holmes .12 .30
142 Samie Parker .12 .30
143 Tony Gonzalez .15 .40
144 Trent Green .12 .30
145 A.J. Feeley .12 .30
146 Chris Chambers .12 .30
147 Jason Taylor .15 .40
148 Junior Seau .15 .40
149 Marty Booker .12 .30
150 Patrick Surtain .12 .30
151 Randy McMichael .12 .30
152 Sammy Morris .12 .30
153 Zach Thomas .15 .40
154 Daunte Culpepper .15 .40
155 Jim Kleinsasser .12 .30
156 Kelly Campbell .12 .30
157 Kevin Williams .12 .30
158 Marcus Robinson .12 .30
159 Mewelde Moore .12 .30
160 Michael Bennett .12 .30
161 Nate Burleson .12 .30
162 Onterrio Smith .12 .30
163 Randy Moss .15 .40
164 Adam Vinatieri .12 .30
165 Corey Dillon .12 .30
166 David Givens .12 .30
167 David Patten .12 .30
168 Deion Branch .12 .30
169 Mike Vrabel .20 .50
170 Richard Seymour .12 .30
171 Tedy Bruschi .15 .40
172 Tom Brady .75 2.00
173 Troy Brown .12 .30
174 Ty Law .20 .50
175 Aaron Brooks .12 .30
176 Charles Grant .12 .30
177 Deuce McAllister .15 .40
178 Devery Henderson .12 .30
179 Donte Stallworth .12 .30
180 Jerome Pathon .12 .30
181 Joe Horn .12 .30
182 Will Smith .12 .30
183 Amani Toomer .12 .30
184 Eli Manning .30 .75
185 Gibril Wilson .12 .30
186 Ike Hilliard .12 .30
187 Jeremy Shockey .12 .30
188 Michael Strahan .15 .40
189 Tiki Barber .15 .40
190 Jamaar Taylor .12 .30
191 Tim Carter .12 .30
192 Chad Pennington .12 .30
193 DeWayne Robertson .12 .30
194 Curtis Martin .15 .40
195 John Abraham .12 .30
196 Jonathan Vilma .12 .30
197 Justin McCareins .12 .30
198 LaMont Jordan .15 .40
199 Santana Moss .15 .40
200 Shaun Ellis .12 .30
201 Wayne Chrebet .12 .30
202 Charles Woodson .20 .50
203 Doug Jolley .12 .30
204 Jerry Porter .12 .30
205 Justin Fargas .15 .40
206 Kerry Collins .12 .30
207 Robert Gallery .12 .30
208 Ronald Curry .12 .30
209 Sebastian Janikowski .12 .30
210 Tyrone Wheatley .12 .30
211 Warren Sapp .15 .40
212 Brian Dawkins .20 .50
213 Brian Westbrook .12 .30
214 Chad Lewis .12 .30
215 Corey Simon .12 .30
216 Donovan McNabb .15 .40
217 Freddie Mitchell .12 .30
218 Jevon Kearse .12 .30
219 L.J. Smith .15 .40
220 Lito Sheppard .15 .40
221 Terrell Owens .15 .40
222 Todd Pinkston .12 .30
223 Alan Faneca .30 .75
224 Antwaan Randle El .12 .30
225 Ben Roethlisberger .30 .75
226 Duce Staley .12 .30
227 Hines Ward .15 .40
228 James Farrior .12 .30
229 Jerome Bettis .20 .50
230 Joey Porter .12 .30
231 Kendrell Bell .12 .30
232 Plaxico Burress .12 .30
233 Troy Polamalu .20 .50
234 Antonio Gates .20 .50
235 Reche Caldwell .12 .30
236 Doug Flutie .15 .40
237 Drew Brees .20 .50
238 Eric Parker .12 .30
239 Keenan McCardell .15 .40
240 LaDainian Tomlinson .20 .50
241 Philip Rivers .20 .50
242 Quentin Jammer .12 .30
243 Tim Dwight .12 .30
244 Brandon Lloyd .12 .30
245 Bryant Young .12 .30
246 Cedrick Wilson .12 .30
247 Eric Johnson .12 .30
248 Julian Peterson .12 .30
249 Kevan Barlow .12 .30
250 Rashaun Woods .12 .30
251 Maurice Hicks RC .12 .30
252 Tim Rattay .12 .30
253 Bobby Engram .12 .30
254 Chad Brown .12 .30
255 Darrell Jackson .12 .30
256 Grant Wistrom .12 .30
257 Jerramy Stevens .15 .40
258 Koren Robinson .12 .30
259 Marcus Trufant .12 .30
260 Matt Hasselbeck .12 .30
261 Michael Boulware .12 .30
262 Shaun Alexander .12 .30
263 Isaac Bruce .20 .50
264 Leonard Little .12 .30
265 Marc Bulger .12 .30
266 Marshall Faulk .15 .40
267 Orlando Pace .12 .30
268 Pisa Tinoisamoa .12 .30
269 Shaun McDonald .12 .30
270 Steven Jackson .12 .30
271 Torry Holt .15 .40
272 Anthony McFarland .12 .30
273 Brian Griese .12 .30
274 Charlie Garner .15 .40
275 Derrick Brooks .12 .30
276 Joe Jurevicius .15 .40
277 Joey Galloway .15 .40
278 Michael Clayton .12 .30
279 Michael Pittman .12 .30
280 Mike Alstott .12 .30
281 Ronde Barber .12 .30
282 Albert Haynesworth .12 .30
283 Ben Troupe .12 .30
284 Billy Volek .12 .30
285 Chris Brown .12 .30
286 Derrick Mason .12 .30
287 Drew Bennett .15 .40
288 Keith Bulluck .12 .30
289 Kevin Carter .12 .30
290 Samari Rolle .12 .30
291 Steve McNair .15 .40
292 Tyrone Calico .12 .30
293 Chris Cooley .15 .40
294 Clinton Portis .12 .30
295 Fred Smoot .12 .30
296 LaVar Arrington .12 .30
297 Laveranues Coles .12 .30
298 Patrick Ramsey .15 .40
299 Rod Gardner .12 .30
300 Sean Taylor .20 .50
301 Michael Vick PB .12 .30
302 Daunte Culpepper PB .12 .30
303 Donovan McNabb PB .12 .30
304 Brian Westbrook PB .10 .25
305 Tiki Barber PB .12 .30
306 Ahman Green PB .12 .30
307 Joe Horn PB .10 .25
308 Javon Walker PB .10 .25
309 Torry Holt PB .12 .30
310 Muhsin Muhammad PB .10 .25
311 Jason Witten PB .12 .30
312 Alge Crumpler PB .12 .30
313 Peyton Manning PB .40 1.00
314 Tom Brady PB .60 1.50
315 Drew Brees PB .15 .40
316 LaDainian Tomlinson PB .15 .40
317 Rudi Johnson PB .10 .25
318 Jerome Bettis PB .15 .40
319 Marvin Harrison PB .12 .30
320 Hines Ward PB .12 .30
321 Andre Johnson PB .12 .30
322 Chad Johnson PB .10 .25
323 Tony Gonzalez PB .12 .30
324 Adam Vinatieri PB .10 .25
325 David Akers PB .10 .25
326 Takeo Spikes PB .10 .25
327 Joey Porter PB .10 .25
328 Tedy Bruschi PB .12 .30
329 Ed Reed PB .12 .30
330 Terrell Owens PB .12 .30
331 Alex Smith QB RC 1.00 2.50
332 Ronnie Brown RC .30 .75
333 Braylon Edwards RC .25 .60
334 Cedric Benson RC .25 .60
335 Cadillac Williams RC .25 .60
336 Adam Jones RC .25 .60
337 Troy Williamson RC .25 .60
338 Antrel Rolle RC .40 1.00
339 Carlos Rogers RC .40 1.00
340 Mike Williams .30 .75
341 DeMarcus Ware RC .75 2.00
342 Shawne Merriman RC .40 1.00
343 Thomas Davis RC .25 .60
344 Derrick Johnson RC .30 .75
345 Travis Johnson RC .25 .60
346 David Pollack RC .25 .60
347 Erasmus James RC .25 .60
348 Marcus Spears RC .25 .60
349 Matt Jones RC .25 .60
350 Mark Clayton RC .25 .60
351 Fabian Washington RC .25 .60
352 Aaron Rodgers RC 7.50 15.00
353 Jason Campbell RC .25 .60
354 Roddy White RC .40 1.00
355 Marlin Jackson RC .25 .60
356 Heath Miller RC .50 1.25
357 Mike Patterson RC .25 .60
358 Reggie Brown RC .25 .60
359 Shaun Cody RC .30 .75
360 Mark Bradley RC .25 .60
361 J.J. Arrington RC .30 .75
362 Dan Cody RC .25 .60
363 Eric Shelton RC .25 .60
364 Roscoe Parrish RC .25 .60
365 Terrence Murphy RC .25 .60
366 Vincent Jackson RC .40 1.00
367 Frank Gore RC .50 1.25
368 Charlie Frye RC .25 .60
369 Courtney Roby RC .25 .60
370 Andrew Walter RC .25 .60
371 Vernand Morency RC .25 .60
372 Ryan Moats RC .25 .60
373 Chris Henry RC .30 .75
374 David Greene RC .25 .60
375 Brandon Jones RC .30 .75
376 Maurice Clarett .30 .75
377 Kyle Orton RC .25 .60
378 Marion Barber RC .25 .60
379 Brandon Jacobs RC .30 .75
380 Ciatrick Fason RC .25 .60
381 Jerome Mathis RC .40 1.00
382 Craphonso Thorpe RC .25 .60
383 Stefan LeFors RC .25 .60
384 Darren Sproles RC .40 1.00
385 Fred Gibson RC .25 .60

2005 Score Adrenaline

*VETERANS: 3X TO 8X BASIC CARDS
*ROOKIES: 1.2X TO 3X BASIC CARDS
STATED PRINT RUN 399 SER.#'d SETS

2005 Score Final Score

SERIAL #'d TO TEAM'S 2004 WIN TOTAL
NOT PRICED DUE TO SCARCITY

2005 Score Glossy

*VETERANS: 1.5X TO 4X BASIC CARDS
*ROOKIES: .8X TO 2X BASIC CARDS
ONE GLOSSY PER PACK

2005 Score Revolution

*VETERANS: 5X TO 12X BASIC CARDS
*ROOKIES: 2X TO 5X BASIC CARDS
STATED PRINT RUN 199 SER.#'d SETS

2005 Score Scorecard

*VETS: 5X TO 5X BASIC CARDS
*ROOKIES: 1X TO 2.5X BASIC CARDS
STATED PRINT RUN 599 SER.#'d SETS

2005 Score Inscriptions

ANNOUNCED PRINT RUNS BELOW
13 Michael Vick/25* 40.00 80.00
15 Rod Coleman/1000* 7.50 20.00
43 Nick Goings/1000* 7.50 20.00
138 Jared Allen/1000* 6.00 15.00
203 Doug Jolley/1000* 6.00 15.00
214 Chad Lewis/1000* 6.00 15.00
223 Alan Faneca/1000* 15.00 40.00

2006 Score

This 385-card set was released in July, 2006. This set was issued through retail outlets and those packs contained five packs, with an 99 cent SRP, and those packs came 20 to a box. Cards numbered 331-385 were inserted into packs at a stated rate of one per. Cards numbered 386-440 as well as some variations to cover issues such as switching teams were later issued in the factory set. The variations are priced at the same value as the cards found in packs. Please see our checklist for detailed information about the variations.

COMP.FACT.SET (440) 25.00 50.00
COMPLETE SET (385) 25.00 50.00
331-385 ROOKIE ODDS 1:1
386-440 ROOKIES ISSUED IN FACT.SET
FACTORY SET B VARIATIONS SAME PRICE
1 Kurt Warner .15 .40
2 J.J. Arrington .12 .30
3 Anquan Boldin .12 .30
4 Larry Fitzgerald .15 .40
5 Marcel Shipp .12 .30
6 Bryant Johnson .12 .30
7 Bertrand Berry .12 .30
8 John Navarre .12 .30
9A Michael Vick PB .15 .40
9B Michael Vick Falcons .15 .40
10 Warrick Dunn .12 .30
11 Roddy White .12 .30
12 Alge Crumpler .15 .40
13A T.J. Duckett .12 .30
13B T.J. Duckett Redskins .12 .30
14 Michael Jenkins .12 .30
15 DeAngelo Hall .12 .30
16 Brian Finneran .12 .30
17 Kyle Boller .12 .30
18 Jamal Lewis .15 .40
19A Chester Taylor .15 .40
19B Chester Taylor Vikings .15 .40
20 Derrick Mason .12 .30
21 Mark Clayton .12 .30
22 Todd Heap .12 .30
23 Ray Lewis .20 .50
24 Devard Darling .12 .30
25 J.P. Losman .15 .40
26 Willis McGahee .12 .30
27 Lee Evans .15 .40
28A Eric Moulds .12 .30
28B Eric Moulds Texans .12 .30
29A Lawyer Milloy .12 .30
29B Lawyer Milloy Falcons .12 .30
30 Josh Reed .12 .30
31 Kelly Holcomb .12 .30
32 Jake Delhomme .12 .30
33 DeShaun Foster .15 .40
34 Steve Smith .20 .50
35 Julius Peppers .15 .40
36 Drew Carter .12 .30
37 Chris Gamble .12 .30
38 Stephen Davis .12 .30
39 Keary Colbert .12 .30
40 Nick Goings .12 .30
41 Eric Shelton .12 .30
42 Rex Grossman .12 .30
43 Thomas Jones .12 .30
44 Cedric Benson .12 .30
45 Muhsin Muhammad .12 .30
46 Brian Urlacher .20 .50
47 Mark Bradley .12 .30
48 Kyle Orton .12 .30
49 Tommie Harris .12 .30
50 Adrian Peterson .15 .40
51 Bernard Berrian .12 .30
52 Justin Gage .12 .30
53 Carson Palmer .15 .40
54 Rudi Johnson .12 .30
55 Chad Johnson .12 .30
56 T.J. Houshmandzadeh .12 .30
57 Chris Henry .12 .30
58 Chris Perry .15 .40
59A Jon Kitna .12 .30
59B Jon Kitna Lions .12 .30
60 Deltha O'Neal .12 .30
61 Charlie Frye .15 .40
62 Reuben Droughns .15 .40
63 Braylon Edwards .12 .30
64 Kellen Winslow .12 .30
65A Antonio Bryant .12 .30
65B Antonio Bryant 49ers .12 .30
66A Trent Dilfer .12 .30
66B Trent Dilfer 49ers .12 .30
67 Dennis Northcutt .12 .30
68 Drew Bledsoe .15 .40
69 Julius Jones .12 .30
70 Marion Barber .15 .40
71 Terry Glenn .15 .40
72A Keyshawn Johnson .15 .40
72B Keyshawn Johnson Panthers .15 .40
73 Roy Williams S .12 .30
74 Jason Witten .15 .40
75 Terence Newman .12 .30
76 Drew Henson .12 .30
77 Patrick Crayton .12 .30
78 Jake Plummer .12 .30
79A Mike Anderson .12 .30
79B Mike Anderson Ravens .12 .30
80 Tatum Bell .12 .30
81A Ashley Lelie .12 .30
81B Ashley Lelie Falcons .12 .30
82 Rod Smith .15 .40
83 D.J. Williams .12 .30
84 Darius Watts .12 .30
85 Ron Dayne .15 .40
86A Jeb Putzier .12 .30
86B Jeb Putzier Texans .12 .30
87A Joey Harrington .12 .30
87B Joey Harrington Dolphins .12 .30
88 Kevin Jones .12 .30
89 Roy Williams WR .12 .30
90 Mike Williams .12 .30
91 Charles Rogers .15 .40
92 Teddy Lehman .12 .30
93 Marcus Pollard .12 .30
94 Artose Pinner .12 .30
95 Brett Favre .40 1.00
96 Ahman Green .15 .40
97 Najeh Davenport .12 .30
98 Samkon Gado .12 .30
99A Javon Walker .15 .40
99B Javon Walker Broncos .15 .40
100 Donald Driver .15 .40
101 Aaron Rodgers .50 1.25
102 Robert Ferguson .12 .30
103 David Carr .12 .30
104 Domanick Davis .12 .30
105 Andre Johnson .15 .40
106A Jabar Gaffney .12 .30
106B Jabar Gaffney Eagles .12 .30
107 Jonathan Wells .12 .30
108 Vernand Morency .12 .30
109A Corey Bradford .12 .30
109B Corey Bradford Lions .12 .30
110 Jerome Mathis .12 .30
111A Peyton Manning PB .50 1.25
111B Peyton Manning Colts .50 1.25
112A Edgerrin James .15 .40
112B Edgerrin James Cardinals .15 .40
113 Marvin Harrison .15 .40
114 Reggie Wayne .15 .40
115 Dwight Freeney .12 .30
116 Dallas Clark .12 .30
117 Dominic Rhodes .12 .30
118 Jim Sorgi .12 .30
119 Brandon Stokley .12 .30
120 Bob Sanders .15 .40
121 Mike Doss .12 .30
122 Marlin Jackson .12 .30
123 Byron Leftwich .12 .30
124 Fred Taylor .12 .30
125 Jimmy Smith .15 .40
126 Matt Jones .12 .30
127 Ernest Wilford .12 .30
128 Greg Jones .12 .30
129 Mike Peterson .12 .30
130 Reggie Williams .15 .40
131 Rashean Mathis .12 .30
132 Trent Green .12 .30
133 Larry Johnson .12 .30
134 Priest Holmes .12 .30
135 Eddie Kennison .12 .30
136 Tony Gonzalez .15 .40
137 Kendrell Bell .12 .30
138 Samie Parker .12 .30
139 Dante Hall .12 .30
140A Tony Richardson .12 .30
140B Tony Richardson Vikings .12 .30
141A Gus Frerotte .12 .30
141B Gus Frerotte Rams .12 .30
142 Ronnie Brown .15 .40
143A Neil Rackers .12 .30
143B Neil Rackers Cardinals .12 .30
144 Chris Chambers .12 .30
145 Zach Thomas .15 .40
146 Cliff Russell .12 .30
147A David Boston .12 .30
147B David Boston Bucs .12 .30
148 Wes Welker .15 .40
149 Marty Booker .12 .30
150 Randy McMichael .12 .30
151A Daunte Culpepper .15 .40
151B Daunte Culpepper Dolphins .15 .40
152 Mewelde Moore .12 .30
153A Nate Burleson .12 .30
153B Nate Burleson Seahawks .12 .30
154 Troy Williamson .12 .30
155 Koren Robinson .12 .30
156 Erasmus James .12 .30
157 Marcus Robinson .12 .30
158 E.J. Henderson .12 .30
159 Brad Johnson .15 .40
160A Michael Bennett .12 .30
160B Michael Bennett Chiefs .12 .30
161 Travis Taylor .12 .30
162 Tom Brady .60 1.50
163 Corey Dillon .12 .30
164 Deion Branch .12 .30
165 Tedy Bruschi .15 .40
166 Ben Watson .12 .30
167 Daniel Graham .12 .30
168A Bethel Johnson .12 .30
168B Bethel Johnson Saints .12 .30
169 Kevin Faulk .12 .30
170A David Givens .15 .40
170B David Givens Titans .15 .40
171 Troy Brown .12 .30
172A Aaron Brooks .12 .30
172B Aaron Brooks Raiders .12 .30
173 Deuce McAllister .15 .40
174 Joe Horn .12 .30
175A Donte Stallworth .12 .30
175B Donte Stallworth Eagles .12 .30
176A Antowain Smith .12 .30
176B Antowain Smith Texans .12 .30
177 Devery Henderson .12 .30
178 Eli Manning .15 .40
179 Tiki Barber .15 .40
180 Plaxico Burress .12 .30
181 Jeremy Shockey .12 .30
182A Osi Umenyiora PB .12 .30
182B Osi Umenyiora Giants .12 .30
183 Gibril Wilson .12 .30
184 Brandon Jacobs .12 .30
185 Michael Strahan .15 .40
186A Will Allen .12 .30
186B Will Allen Dolphins .12 .30
187 Amani Toomer .12 .30
188 Chad Pennington .12 .30
189 Curtis Martin .15 .40
190 Laveranues Coles .12 .30
191 Jonathan Vilma .12 .30
192A Ty Law .20 .50
192B Ty Law Chiefs .20 .50
193 Cedric Houston .12 .30
194 Justin McCareins .12 .30
195 Jerald Sowell .12 .30
196 Josh Brown .12 .30
197 LaMont Jordan .15 .40
198 Randy Moss .15 .40
199 Jerry Porter .12 .30
200 Doug Gabriel .12 .30
201 Johnnie Morant .12 .30
202 Zack Crockett .12 .30
203A Derrick Burgess PB .12 .30
203B Derrick Burgess Raiders .12 .30
204 Donovan McNabb .15 .40
205 Brian Westbrook .12 .30
206 Reggie Brown .12 .30
207A Terrell Owens .15 .40
207B Terrell Owens Cowboys .15 .40
208 Ryan Moats .12 .30
209 Correll Buckhalter .12 .30
210 Jevon Kearse .12 .30
211 L.J. Smith .12 .30
212 Lamar Gordon .12 .30
213 Greg Lewis .12 .30
214 Ben Roethlisberger .25 .60
215 Willie Parker .15 .40
216 Jerome Bettis .20 .50
217 Hines Ward .15 .40
218 Troy Polamalu .20 .50
219 Heath Miller .12 .30
220A Antwaan Randle El .12 .30
220B Antwaan Randle El Redskins .12 .30
221 Duce Staley .12 .30
222 Cedrick Wilson .12 .30
223 James Farrior .12 .30
224A Drew Brees .20 .50
224B Drew Brees Saints .20 .50
225 LaDainian Tomlinson .20 .50
226 Keenan McCardell .15 .40
227 Antonio Gates .20 .50
228 Shawne Merriman .15 .40
229 Philip Rivers .20 .50
230 Vincent Jackson .12 .30
231 Donnie Edwards .12 .30
232 Eric Parker .12 .30
233A Reche Caldwell .12 .30
233B Reche Caldwell Patriots .12 .30
234 Alex Smith QB .15 .40
235 Frank Gore .15 .40
236A Brandon Lloyd .12 .30
236B Brandon Lloyd Redskins .12 .30
237A Kevan Barlow .12 .30
237B Kevan Barlow Jets .12 .30
238A Rashaun Woods .12 .30
238B Lorenzo Neal .12 .30
239 Arnaz Battle .12 .30
240 Matt Hasselbeck .12 .30
241 Shaun Alexander .12 .30
242 Darrell Jackson .15 .40
243 Jerramy Stevens .15 .40
244 Lofa Tatupu .12 .30
245 D.J. Hackett .12 .30
246 Bobby Engram .12 .30
247A Joe Jurevicius .12 .30
247B Joe Jurevicius Browns .12 .30
248 Maurice Morris .12 .30
249 Marc Bulger .12 .30
250 Steven Jackson .12 .30
251 Torry Holt .15 .40
252 Isaac Bruce .20 .50
253 Kevin Curtis .15 .40
254 Marshall Faulk .15 .40
255 Shaun McDonald .12 .30
256 Chris Simms .12 .30
257 Cadillac Williams .15 .40
258 Joey Galloway .15 .40
259 Michael Clayton .12 .30
260 Derrick Brooks .12 .30
261 Ronde Barber .12 .30
262 Michael Pittman .12 .30
263 Alex Smith TE .12 .30
264 Simeon Rice .12 .30
265A Steve McNair .15 .40
265B Steve McNair Ravens .15 .40
266 Chris Brown .12 .30
267 Drew Bennett .15 .40
268 Brandon Jones .12 .30
269 Adam Jones .12 .30
270 Keith Bulluck .12 .30
271 Ben Troupe .12 .30
272 Jarrett Payton .12 .30
273 Tyrone Calico .12 .30
274 Bobby Wade .12 .30
275 Troy Fleming .12 .30
276 Mark Brunell .15 .40
277 Clinton Portis .12 .30
278 Santana Moss .15 .40
279 Jason Campbell .12 .30
280 Chris Cooley .12 .30
281 Carlos Rogers .12 .30
282 Ladell Betts .12 .30
283A Patrick Ramsey .15 .40
283B Patrick Ramsey Jets .15 .40
284 Taylor Jacobs .12 .30
285 James Thrash .12 .30
286 Adrian Wilson .12 .30
287 London Fletcher .15 .40
288 Lance Briggs .15 .40
289 Robert Mathis .12 .30
290 Rod Coleman .12 .30
291 Bart Scott RC .60 1.50
292 Brian Moorman RC .20 .50
293 Shayne Graham RC .20 .50
294 Kevin Kaesviharn RC .20 .50
295 Leigh Bodden RC .25 .60
296 Lousaka Polite RC .20 .50
297 Todd Devoe RC .20 .50
298 Scottie Vines .20 .50
299 Cullen Jenkins RC .25 .60
300 Donovan Morgan RC .20 .50
301 C.C. Brown .20 .50
302 Demarcus Faggins RC .20 .50
303 Shantee Orr RC .20 .50
304 Vashon Pearson RC .20 .50
305 Reggie Hayward RC .20 .50
306 Paul Spicer RC .20 .50
307A Kenny Wright Jaguars RC .20 .50
307B Kenny Wright Redskins .20 .50
308 Rich Alexis RC .20 .50
309 Terrence Melton RC .20 .50
310 Willie Whitehead RC .20 .50
311A Kendrick Clancy Giants RC .20 .50
311B Kendrick Clancy Cardinals .20 .50
312 Mark Brown RC .20 .50
313 Tommy Kelly RC .20 .50
314 Josh Parry RC .20 .50
315 Malcom Floyd RC .25 .60
316 Mike Adams RC .30 .75
317 Ben Emanuel RC .20 .50
318 Brandon Moore RC .20 .50
319 Chartric Darby RC .20 .50
320 Bryce Fisher RC .20 .50
321 D.D. Lewis RC .20 .50
322 Jimmy Williams DB RC .30 .75
323A Robert Pollard portrait RC .20 .50
323B Robert Pollard action .20 .50
324A Chris Johnson Rams RC .30 .75
324B Chris Johnson Chiefs .30 .75
325 Edell Shepherd RC .20 .50
326 O.J. Small RC .20 .50
327A Brad Kassell Titans RC .20 .50
327B Brad Kassell Jets .20 .50
328 M.Leinart/R.Bush .30 .75
329 M.Leinart/V.Young .20 .50
330 White/Leinart/Bush .30 .75
331 Matt Leinart RC .30 .75
332A Chad Greenway RC .50 1.25
332B Chad Greenway .50 1.25
333A Devin Aromashodu RC .30 .75
333B Devin Aromashodu .30 .75
334 DeAngelo Williams RC .40 1.00
335 Travis Wilson RC .30 .75
336 Leon Washington RC .30 .75
337 Maurice Stovall RC .30 .75
338 Michael Huff SP RC .40 1.00
339 Charlie Whitehurst RC .30 .75
340 Vince Young RC .30 .75
341 Jerious Norwood RC .30 .75
342A D'Brickashaw Ferguson RC .30 .75
342B D'Brickashaw Ferguson .30 .75
343A Taurean Henderson RC .30 .75
343B Sam Hurd RC .30 .75
344A Dominique Byrd RC .30 .75
344B Dominique Byrd .30 .75
345 Sinorice Moss SP RC .30 .75
346A Martin Nance RC .30 .75
346B Martin Nance .30 .75
347 Vernon Davis RC .40 1.00
348 Ko Simpson RC .40 1.00
349A Jerome Harrison RC .30 .75
349B Jerome Harrison .30 .75
350A Jay Cutler RC .40 1.00
350B Jay Cutler fact .40 1.00
351A Alan Zemaitis RC .30 .75
351B Alan Zemaitis .30 .75
352A Haloti Ngata SP RC .40 1.00
352B Haloti Ngata .40 1.00
353A Greg Lee RC .30 .75
353B Greg Lee .30 .75
354 Laurence Maroney RC .30 .75
355A Bobby Carpenter SP RC .30 .75
355B Bobby Carpenter .30 .75
356A Jonathan Orr RC .40 1.00
356B Jonathan Orr .40 1.00
357 Marcedes Lewis RC .30 .75
358A Brodrick Bunkley SP RC .40 1.00
358B Brodrick Bunkley .40 1.00
359A Todd Watkins RC .30 .75
359B Todd Watkins .30 .75
360 Reggie Bush RC .50 1.25
361A Jimmy Williams RC .30 .75
361B Jimmy Williams .30 .75
362 Maurice Drew RC .50 1.25
363 Mario Williams RC .50 1.25
364 Derek Hagan RC .40 1.00
365 Santonio Holmes RC .40 1.00
366A Tye Hill RC .30 .75
366B Tye Hill .30 .75
367 Jason Avant RC .30 .75
368A Tamba Hali SP RC .50 1.25
368B Tamba Hali .50 1.25
369 Joe Klopfenstein RC .30 .75
370 LenDale White RC .30 .75
371A DeMeco Ryans RC .40 1.00
371B DeMeco Ryans .40 1.00
372A Bruce Gradkowski SP RC .40 1.00
372B Bruce Gradkowski .40 1.00
373 A.J. Hawk RC .40 1.00
374A Gabe Watson RC .30 .75
374B Gabe Watson 1.00 2.50
375A Devin Hester SP RC .60 1.50
375B Devin Hester .60 1.50
376 Demetrius Williams SP RC .30 .75
377A Joseph Addai RC .30 .75
377B Joseph Addai .30 .75
378A Leonard Pope RC .50 1.25
378B Leonard Pope .40 1.00
379 Omar Jacobs RC .30 .75
380A Brad Smith SP RC .40 1.00
380B Brad Smith .40 1.00
381 Michael Robinson RC .30 .75
382A Brodie Croyle RC .30 .75
382B Brodie Croyle .30 .75
383A Anthony Fasano RC .30 .75
383B Anthony Fasano .30 .75
384 Brian Calhoun RC .30 .75
385 Chad Jackson RC .30 .75
386 Drew Olson RC .30 .75
387 Greg Jennings RC .50 1.25
388 Andre Hall RC .40 1.00
389 Mike Espy RC .40 1.00
390 Tim Day RC .40 1.00
391 Brandon Williams RC .30 .75
392 Mark Anderson RC 1.25 3.00
393 DonTrell Moore RC .40 1.00
394 Kellen Clemens RC .30 .75
395 Ernie Sims RC .30 .75
396 Cedric Humes RC .30 .75
397 Brandon Kirsch RC .30 .75
398 Tony Scheffler RC .50 1.25
399 Kelly Jennings RC .40 1.00
400 Manny Lawson RC .40 1.00
401 Terrence Whitehead RC .40 1.00
402 Marcus Vick RC .30 .75
403 De'Arrius Howard RC .50 1.25
404 Wendell Mathis RC .40 1.00
405 Abdul Hodge RC .30 .75
406 Owen Daniels RC .50 1.25
407 Mike Hass RC .30 .75
408 Brett Elliott RC .50 1.25
409 Kamerion Wimbley RC .40 1.00
410 Jeremy Bloom RC .30 .75
411 D.J. Shockley RC .40 1.00
412 Darnell Bing RC .40 1.00
413 Miles Austin RC .40 1.00
414 D'Qwell Jackson RC .30 .75
415 Tarvaris Jackson RC .30 .75
416 Mathias Kiwanuka RC .50 1.25
417 Mike Bell RC .30 .75
418 Paul Pinegar RC .30 .75
419 David Thomas RC .30 .75
420 Hank Baskett RC .30 .75
421 P.J. Daniels RC .30 .75
422 Jon Alston RC .30 .75
423 Reggie McNeal RC .30 .75
424 Brandon Marshall RC .60 1.50
425 Gerald Riggs RC .40 1.00
426 Delanie Walker RC .60 1.50
427 Erik Meyer RC .40 1.00
428 Jeff Webb RC .40 1.00
429 Skyler Green RC .30 .75
430 Thomas Howard RC .30 .75
431 Ashton Youboty RC .30 .75
432 Cedric Griffin RC .40 1.00
433 Donte Whitner RC .40 1.00
434 Jason Allen RC .40 1.00
435 Pat Watkins RC .40 1.00
436 Rocky McIntosh RC .30 .75
437 Ingle Martin RC .40 1.00
438 John David Washington RC .30 .75
439 Cory Rodgers RC .30 .75
440 Willie Reid RC .40 1.00

2006 Score Artist's Proof

*VETS 1-290: 12X TO 30X BASIC CARDS
*VETS 291-327: 6X TO 15X BASIC CARDS
*ROOKIES 328-330: 2X TO 5X BASIC CARDS
*ROOKIES 331-385: 6X TO 15X BASIC CARDS
STATED PRINT RUN 32 SER.#'d SETS

2006 Score Black

UNPRICED BLACK PRINT RUN 6

2006 Score Glossy

*VETS 1-290: 1.5X TO 4X BASIC CARDS
*VETS 291-327: .8X TO 2X BASIC CARDS
*ROOKIES 328-330: .5X TO 1.2X
*ROOKIES 331-385: .5X TO 1.2X
ONE PER PACK

2006 Score Gold

*VETS 1-290: 3X TO 8X BASIC CARDS
*VETS 291-327: 1.5X TO 4X BASIC CARDS
*ROOKIES 328-330: .8X TO 2X BASIC CARDS
*ROOKIES 331-385: 1X TO 2.5X BASIC CARDS
STATED PRINT RUN 600 SER.#'d SETS

2006 Score Green

*ROOKIES 331-385: 1.5X TO 4X BASIC CARDS
INSERTS IN WAL-MART PACKS

2006 Score Red

*VETS 1-290: 5X TO 12X BASIC CARDS
*VETS 291-327: 2.5X TO 6X BASIC CARDS
*ROOKIES 328-330: 1.2X TO 3X BASIC CARDS
*ROOKIES 331-385: 1.5X TO 4X BASIC CARDS
STATED PRINT RUN 120 SER.#'d SETS

2006 Score Scorecard

*VETS 1-290: 2.5X TO 6X BASIC CARDS
*VETS 291-327: 1.2X TO 3X BASIC CARDS
*ROOKIES 328-330: .6X TO 1.5X
*ROOKIES 331-385: .8X TO 2X BASIC CARDS
STATED PRINT RUN 750 SER.#'d SETS

2006 Score Super Bowl XLI Embossed

*VETS/1-290: 4X TO 10X BASIC CARDS
*ROOKIES/328-330: 1X TO 2.5X
*ROOKIES/291-327/331-385: 2X TO 5X
ISSUED AT 2007 SUPER BOWL CARD SHOW

2006 Score Hot Rookies

COMPLETE SET (10) 8.00 20.00
*ART.PROOF/32: 4X TO 10X BASIC INSERTS
ARTIST PROOF PRINT RUN 32 SETS
UNPRICED BLACK PRINT RUN 6 SETS
*GLOSSY: .5X TO 1.2X BASIC INSERTS
*GOLD/600: .6X TO 1.5X BASIC INSERTS
*RED/120: 1.2X TO 3X BASIC INSERTS
*SCORECARD/750: .5X TO 1.2X
1 Matt Leinart .40 1.00
2 Vince Young .40 1.00
3 Jay Cutler .50 1.25
4 Reggie Bush .60 1.50
5 LenDale White .40 1.00
6 DeAngelo Williams .50 1.25
7 Laurence Maroney .40 1.00
8 Santonio Holmes .50 1.25
9 Sinorice Moss .40 1.00
10 Maurice Stovall .40 1.00

2006 Score Hot Rookies National Anaheim Embossed Promos

COMPLETE SET (10) 30.00 60.00
1 Matt Leinart .60 1.50
2 Vince Young .60 1.50
3 Jay Cutler .75 2.00
4 Reggie Bush 1.00 2.50
5 LenDale White .60 1.50
6 DeAngelo Williams .75 2.00
7 Laurence Maroney .60 1.50
8 Santonio Holmes .75 2.00
9 Sinorice Moss .60 1.50
10 Maurice Stovall .60 1.50

2006 Score Hot Rookies Super Bowl XLI Embossed Promos

COMPLETE SET (10) 40.00 80.00
1 Matt Leinart .75 2.00
2 Vince Young .75 2.00
3 Jay Cutler 1.00 2.50
4 Reggie Bush 1.25 3.00
5 LenDale White .75 2.00
6 DeAngelo Williams 1.00 2.50
7 Laurence Maroney .75 2.00
8 Santonio Holmes 1.00 2.50
9 Sinorice Moss .75 2.00
10 Maurice Stovall .75 2.00

2006 Score Inscriptions

ANNOUNCED PRINT RUNS BELOW
PRINT RUNS UNDER 20 NOT PRICED
7 Bertrand Berry/50* 8.00 20.00
8 John Navarre/83*
15 DeAngelo Hall/44* 10.00 25.00
17 Kyle Boller/10*
19 Chester Taylor/20*
22 Todd Heap/100*
24 Devard Darling/47* 5.00 12.00
29 Lawyer Milloy/15*
37 Chris Gamble/30*
49 Tommie Harris/47* 6.00 15.00
50 Adrian Peterson/11*
51 Bernard Berrian/5*
57 Chris Henry/100* 6.00 15.00
58 Chris Perry/9*
62 Reuben Droughns/7*
75 Terence Newman/10*
76 Drew Henson/16*
77 Patrick Crayton/62*
78 Jake Plummer/5*
83 D.J. Williams/116* 6.00 15.00
84 Darius Watts/19*
85 Ron Dayne/2*
100 Donald Driver/2*
102 Robert Ferguson/15*
106 Jabar Gaffney/21*
107 Jonathan Wells/37* 5.00 12.00
116 Dallas Clark/20* 10.00 25.00
117 Dominic Rhodes/12*
118 Jim Sorgi/62* 5.00 12.00
130 Reggie Williams/9*
131 Rashean Mathis/30* 6.00 15.00
137 Kendrell Bell/39* 6.00 15.00
146 Cliff Russell/57* 6.00 15.00
147 David Boston/11*
148 Wes Welker/19* 35.00 60.00
156 Erasmus James/233* 6.00 15.00
157 Marcus Robinson/31*
158 E.J. Henderson/15*
166 Ben Watson/132* 6.00 15.00
167 Daniel Graham/90* 6.00 15.00
168 Bethel Johnson/11*
169 Kevin Faulk/15*
184 Brandon Jacobs/51* 8.00 20.00
186 Will Allen/69* 6.00 15.00
192 Ty Law/15*
200 Doug Gabriel/5*
201 Johnnie Morant/27*
209 Correll Buckhalter/14*
210 Jevon Kearse/25* 6.00 15.00

211 L.J. Smith/59* 10.00 25.00
212 Lamar Gordon/47*
230 Vincent Jackson/1*
231 Donnie Edwards/2*
232 Eric Parker/20*
233 Reche Caldwell/96*
235 Frank Gore/111* 10.00 25.00
238 Rashaun Woods/9*
245 D.J. Hackett/68*
255 Shaun McDonald/43*
256 Chris Simms/21* 20.00 40.00
259 Michael Clayton/64* 10.00 25.00
260 Derrick Brooks/100* 10.00 25.00
261 Ronde Barber/152* 15.00 40.00
271 Ben Troupe/186* 6.00 15.00
272 Jarrett Payton/21* 6.00 15.00
273 Tyrone Calico/57* 6.00 15.00
274 Bobby Wade/34*
275 Troy Fleming/35*
280 Chris Cooley/53* 10.00 25.00
282 Ladell Betts/40* 6.00 15.00
283 Patrick Ramsey/49* 6.00 15.00
325 Edell Shepherd/100*
331 Matt Leinart/5*
332 Chad Greenway/25* 12.50 30.00
333 Devin Aromashodu/50* 10.00 25.00
334 DeAngelo Williams/5*
335 Travis Wilson/10*
336 Leon Washington/10*
337 Maurice Stovall/5*
338 Michael Huff/10*
339 Charlie Whitehurst/10*
340 Vince Young/5*
341 Jerious Norwood/10*
342 D'Brickashaw Ferguson/50* 10.00 25.00
343 Taurean Henderson/50*
344 Dominique Byrd/10*
345 Sinorice Moss/5*
346 Martin Nance/50* 6.00 15.00
347 Vernon Davis/5*
348 Ko Simpson/50* 6.00 15.00
350 Jay Cutler/5*
351 Alan Zemaitis/10*
352 Haloti Ngata/50* 8.00 20.00
353 Greg Lee/50*
354 Laurence Maroney/10*
355 Bobby Carpenter/10*
356 Jonathan Orr/50* 10.00 25.00
357 Marcedes Lewis/25* 12.50 30.00
358 Brodrick Bunkley/10*
359 Todd Watkins/50*
360 Reggie Bush/5*
361 Jimmy Williams/50* 10.00 25.00
362 Maurice Drew/10*
363 Mario Williams/10*
364 Derek Hagan/10*
365 Santonio Holmes/5*
366 Tye Hill/25* 6.00 15.00
367 Jason Avant/10*
368 Tamba Hali/50* 8.00 20.00
369 Joe Klopfenstein/10*
370 LenDale White/5*
371 DeMeco Ryans/50* 12.50 30.00
372 Bruce Gradkowski/10*
373 A.J. Hawk/10*
374 Gabe Watson/10*
375 Devin Hester/10*
376 Demetrius Williams/10*
377 Joseph Addai/10*
378 Leonard Pope/10*
379 Omar Jacobs/10*
380 Brad Smith/50*
381 Michael Robinson/10*
382 Brodie Croyle/10*
383 Anthony Fasano/10*
384 Brian Calhoun/10*
385 Chad Jackson/10*

2006 Score 3-A-Day

COMPLETE SET (5) 6.00 12.00
AR Allen Rossum 1.00 2.50
DF DeShaun Foster 1.00 2.50
EK Erron Kinney 1.00 2.50
RB Ronnie Brown 2.00 5.00
TS Takeo Spikes 1.00 2.50

2006 Score National Anaheim VIP Promos

COMPLETE SET (8) 20.00 40.00
1 Reggie Bush 1.00 2.50
2 Ben Roethlisberger 1.25 3.00
3 Peyton Manning 2.50 6.00
4 Carson Palmer .75 2.00
5 Michael Vick .75 2.00
6 Tom Brady 3.00 8.00
7 Eli Manning .75 2.00
8 Vince Young .60 1.50

2006 Score Pop Warner

COMPLETE SET (6) 6.00 12.00
1 M.Leinart/R.Bush .60 1.50
2 Carson Palmer .50 1.25
3 Donovan McNabb .50 1.25
4 Tony Gonzalez .50 1.25
5 Matt Hasselbeck .40 1.00
6 Torry Holt .50 1.25

2007 Score

This 385-card set was released in July, 2007. The set was issued through retail channels in five-card packs, with a 99 cent SRP, which came 20 packs to a box. Cards numbered 1-288 feature veterans in team alphabetical order by division while cards numbered 289-385 feature 2007 NFL rookies. These Rookie Cards were inserted at a stated rate one per pack and three per jumbo pack. Cards numbered 386-440, which also feature 2007 NFL rookies, were all included in 2007 Score Factory sets.

COMPLETE SET (385) 25.00 50.00
COMP.FACT.SET (440) 15.00 40.00
ROOKIE ODDS 1:1 RET, 3:1 JUM
386-440 INSERTED IN FACTORY SETS
1 Tony Romo .25 .60
2 Julius Jones .12 .30
3 Terry Glenn .15 .40
4 Terrell Owens .15 .40
5 Jason Witten .15 .40
6 Marion Barber .15 .40
7 Patrick Crayton .12 .30
8 Bradie James .12 .30
9 DeMarcus Ware .15 .40
10 Roy Williams S .12 .30
11 Eli Manning .15 .40
12 Plaxico Burress .12 .30
13 Jeremy Shockey .12 .30
14 Brandon Jacobs .12 .30
15 Sinorice Moss .15 .40
16 Antonio Pierce .12 .30
17 David Tyree .12 .30
18 Donovan McNabb .15 .40
19 Brian Westbrook .12 .30
20 Reggie Brown .12 .30
21 L.J. Smith .12 .30
22 Hank Baskett .15 .40
23 Jeremiah Trotter .12 .30
24 Trent Cole .12 .30
25 Lito Sheppard .12 .30
26 Jason Campbell .12 .30
27 Clinton Portis .12 .30
28 Santana Moss .15 .40
29 Drandon Lloyd .12 .30
30 Chris Cooley .12 .30
31 Sean Taylor .20 .50
32 Lemar Marshall .12 .30
33 Ladell Betts .12 .30
34 London Fletcher .15 .40
36 Cedric Benson .12 .30
37 Muhsin Muhammad .12 .30
38 Bernard Berrian .12 .30
39 Desmond Clark .12 .30
40 Lance Briggs .15 .40
41 Robbie Gould .12 .30
42 Devin Hester .15 .40
43 Mark Anderson .15 .40
44 Brian Urlacher .20 .50
45 Jon Kitna .12 .30
46 Kevin Jones .12 .30
47 Roy Williams WR .12 .30
48 Mike Furrey .15 .40
49 Cory Redding .12 .30
50 Ernie Sims .12 .30
51 Tatum Bell .12 .30
52 Brian Calhoun .12 .30
53 Brett Favre .40 1.00
54 Vernand Morency .15 .40
55 Donald Driver .15 .40
56 Greg Jennings .12 .30
57 Aaron Kampman .15 .40
58 Charles Woodson .20 .50
59 A.J. Hawk .12 .30
60 Nick Barnett .12 .30
61 Aaron Rodgers .50 1.25
62 Tarvaris Jackson .12 .30
63 Chester Taylor .12 .30
64 Troy Williamson .12 .30
65 Jim Kleinsasser .12 .30
66 Dwight Smith .12 .30
67 Antoine Winfield .12 .30
68 E.J. Henderson .12 .30
69 Mewelde Moore .12 .30
70 Michael Vick .15 .40
71 Warrick Dunn .12 .30
72 Joe Horn .12 .30
73 Michael Jenkins .12 .30
74 Alge Crumpler .15 .40
75 DeAngelo Hall .12 .30
76 Keith Brooking .12 .30
77 Lawyer Milloy .12 .30
78 Jerious Norwood .12 .30
79 Matt Schaub .12 .30
80 Jake Delhomme .12 .30
81 DeShaun Foster .15 .40
82 Steve Smith .15 .40
83 Keyshawn Johnson .15 .40
84 Julius Peppers .15 .40
85 DeAngelo Williams .12 .30
86 Chris Draft .12 .30
87 Drew Brees .20 .50
88 Deuce McAllister .15 .40
89 Scott Fujita .12 .30
90 Marques Colston .12 .30
91 Terrance Copper .15 .40
92 Will Smith .12 .30
93 Charles Grant .12 .30
94 Devery Henderson .12 .30
95 Reggie Bush .12 .30
96 Jeff Garcia .12 .30
97 Cadillac Williams .15 .40
98 Joey Galloway .15 .40
99 Michael Clayton .12 .30
100 Alex Smith TE .12 .30
101 Ronde Barber .12 .30
102 Jermaine Phillips .12 .30
103 Derrick Brooks .12 .30
104 Matt Leinart .12 .30
105 Edgerrin James .15 .40
106 Anquan Boldin .12 .30
107 Larry Fitzgerald .15 .40
108 Neil Rackers .12 .30
109 Adrian Wilson .12 .30
110 Karlos Dansby .12 .30
111 Chike Okeafor .12 .30
112 Marc Bulger .12 .30
113 Steven Jackson .12 .30
114 Torry Holt .15 .40
115 Isaac Bruce .20 .50
116 Joe Klopfenstein .12 .30
117 Randy McMichael .12 .30
118 Will Witherspoon .12 .30
119 Drew Bennett .12 .30
120 Alex Smith QB .15 .40
121 Frank Gore .15 .40
122 Arnaz Battle .12 .30
123 Ashley Lelie .15 .40
124 Vernon Davis .12 .30
125 Walt Harris .12 .30
126 Brandon Moore .12 .30
127 Nate Clements .12 .30
128 Matt Hasselbeck .12 .30
129 Shaun Alexander .12 .30
130 Deion Branch .12 .30
131 Darrell Jackson .12 .30
132 Nate Burleson .12 .30
133 Julian Peterson .12 .30
134 Lofa Tatupu .12 .30
135 Mack Strong .12 .30
136 Josh Brown .12 .30
137 J.P. Losman .12 .30
138 Anthony Thomas .12 .30
139 Lee Evans .15 .40
140 Josh Reed .12 .30
141 Roscoe Parrish .12 .30
142 Aaron Schobel .12 .30
143 Donte Whitner .12 .30
144 Shaud Williams .12 .30
145 Daunte Culpepper .15 .40
146 Ronnie Brown .12 .30
147 Chris Chambers .12 .30
148 Marty Booker .12 .30
149 Derek Hagan .12 .30
150 Jason Taylor .15 .40
151 Vonnie Holliday .12 .30
152 Zach Thomas .15 .40
153 Channing Crowder .12 .30
154 Joey Porter .12 .30
155 Tom Brady .60 1.50
156 Laurence Maroney .15 .40
157 Chad Jackson .12 .30
158 Wes Welker .15 .40
159 Ben Watson .12 .30
160 Donte Stallworth .15 .40
161 Rosevelt Colvin .12 .30
162 Ty Warren .12 .30
163 Asante Samuel .12 .30
164 Adalius Thomas .12 .30
165 Tedy Bruschi .15 .40
166 Chad Pennington .12 .30
167 Thomas Jones .12 .30
168 Laveranues Coles .12 .30
169 Jerricho Cotchery .12 .30
170 Chris Baker .12 .30
171 Bryan Thomas .12 .30
172 Leon Washington .12 .30
173 Jonathan Vilma .12 .30
174 Eric Barton .12 .30
175 Erik Coleman .12 .30
176 Steve McNair .15 .40
177 Willis McGahee .12 .30
178 Derrick Mason .12 .30
179 Demetrius Williams .12 .30
180 Todd Heap .12 .30
181 Ray Lewis .20 .50
182 Trevor Pryce .12 .30
183 Bart Scott .15 .40
184 Terrell Suggs .12 .30
185 Mark Clayton .12 .30
186 Carson Palmer .15 .40
187 Rudi Johnson .12 .30
188 Chad Johnson .12 .30
189 T.J. Houshmandzadeh .12 .30
191 Justin Smith .12 .30
192 Tory James .12 .30
193 Landon Johnson .12 .30
194 Shayne Graham .12 .30
195 Charlie Frye .15 .40
196 Reuben Droughns .15 .40
197 Braylon Edwards .12 .30
198 Travis Wilson .12 .30
199 Kellen Winslow .12 .30
200 Kamerion Wimbley .12 .30
201 Sean Jones .12 .30
202 Andra Davis .12 .30
203 Jamal Lewis .15 .40
204 Ben Roethlisberger .20 .50
205 Willie Parker .15 .40
206 Hines Ward .15 .40
207 Santonio Holmes .12 .30
208 Heath Miller .12 .30
209 Troy Polamalu .20 .50
210 James Farrior .12 .30
211 Cedrick Wilson .12 .30
212 Dunta Robinson .12 .30
213 Ahman Green .15 .40
214 Andre Johnson .15 .40
215 Jerome Mathis .12 .30
216 Owen Daniels .12 .30
217 DeMeco Ryans .15 .40
218 Wali Lundy .12 .30
219 Mario Williams .15 .40
220 Peyton Manning .50 1.25
221 Joseph Addai .12 .30
222 Marvin Harrison .15 .40
223 Reggie Wayne .15 .40
224 Dallas Clark .15 .40
225 Robert Mathis .12 .30
226 Cato June .12 .30
227 Adam Vinatieri .12 .30
228 Bob Sanders .15 .40
229 Dwight Freeney .12 .30
230 Byron Leftwich .12 .30
231 Fred Taylor .12 .30
232 Matt Jones .15 .40
233 Reggie Williams .15 .40
234 Marcedes Lewis .12 .30
235 Bobby McCray .12 .30
236 Rashean Mathis .12 .30
237 Maurice Jones-Drew .12 .30
238 Ernest Wilford .12 .30
239 Daryl Smith .12 .30
240 Vince Young .12 .30
241 LenDale White .15 .40
242 Brandon Jones .12 .30
243 Bo Scaife .12 .30
244 Keith Bulluck .12 .30
245 Chris Hope .12 .30
246 Kyle Vanden Bosch .12 .30
247 Roydell Williams .12 .30
248 Jay Cutler .12 .30
249 Travis Henry .15 .40
250 Javon Walker .15 .40
251 Rod Smith .15 .40
252 Tony Scheffler .15 .40
253 Elvis Dumervil .12 .30
254 Champ Bailey .15 .40
255 Mike Bell .15 .40
256 Brandon Marshall .15 .40
257 Al Wilson .12 .30
258 Trent Green .12 .30
259 Larry Johnson .12 .30
260 Eddie Kennison .12 .30
261 Samie Parker .12 .30
262 Tony Gonzalez .15 .40
263 Jared Allen .12 .30
264 Kawika Mitchell .12 .30
265 Tamba Hali .12 .30
266 Dante Hall .12 .30
267 Brodie Croyle .15 .40
268 Andrew Walter .12 .30
269 LaMont Jordan .15 .40
270 Dominic Rhodes .12 .30
271 Randy Moss .15 .40
272 Ronald Curry .12 .30
273 Courtney Anderson .12 .30
274 Derrick Burgess .12 .30
275 Warren Sapp .15 .40
276 Michael Huff .15 .40
277 Thomas Howard .12 .30
278 Kirk Morrison .12 .30
279 Philip Rivers .20 .50
280 LaDainian Tomlinson .20 .50
281 Vincent Jackson .12 .30
282 Lorenzo Neal .12 .30
283 Antonio Gates .20 .50
284 Shawne Merriman .12 .30
285 Shaun Phillips .12 .30
286 Michael Turner .12 .30
287 Jamal Williams .12 .30
288 Nate Kaeding .12 .30
289 Michael Okwo RC .40 1.00
290 Gary Russell RC .40 1.00
291 Josh Wilson RC .40 1.00
292 Thomas Clayton RC .40 1.00
293 Jerard Rabb RC .40 1.00
294 Roy Hall RC .50 1.25
295 LaMarr Woodley RC .60 1.50
296 Eric Wright RC .30 .75
297 Dan Bazuin RC .40 1.00
298 A.J. Davis RC .30 .75
299 Buster Davis RC .40 1.00
300 Stewart Bradley RC .30 .75
301 Toby Korrodi RC .40 1.00
302 Marcus McCauley RC .30 .75
303 Demarcus Tank Tyler RC .30 .75
304 Jon Abbate RC .30 .75
305 Ikaika Alama-Francis RC .50 1.25
306 Tim Crowder RC .40 1.00
307 D'Juan Woods RC .30 .75
308 Tim Shaw RC .40 1.00
309 Fred Bennett RC .30 .75
310 Victor Abiamiri RC .30 .75
311 Eric Weddle RC .40 1.00
312 Danny Ware RC .50 1.25
313 Quentin Moses RC .30 .75
314 Ryan McBean RC .50 1.25
315 David Harris RC .30 .75
316 David Irons RC .30 .75
317 Syndric Steptoe RC .40 1.00
318 Eric Frampton RC .40 1.00
319 Jemalle Cornelius RC .40 1.00
320 Earl Everett RC .30 .75
321 Alonzo Coleman RC .40 1.00
322 Josh Gattis RC .30 .75
323 Zak DeOssie RC .40 1.00
324 Jon Beason RC .30 .75
325 Joe Staley RC .40 1.00
326 Aaron Rouse RC .30 .75
327 Reggie Ball RC .40 1.00
328 Rufus Alexander RC .30 .75
329 Daymeion Hughes RC .30 .75
330 Justin Durant RC .50 1.25
331 JaMarcus Russell RC .30 .75
332 Paul Williams RC .30 .75
333 Kenny Irons RC .30 .75
334 Chris Davis RC .30 .75
335 Darius Walker RC .30 .75
336 Dwayne Bowe RC .30 .75
337 Isaiah Stanback RC .30 .75
338 Leon Hall RC .30 .75
339 Sidney Rice RC .40 1.00
340 Amobi Okoye RC .40 1.00
341 Adrian Peterson RC 2.50 6.00
342 LaRon Landry RC .50 1.25
343 Lorenzo Booker RC .40 1.00
344 Craig Buster Davis RC .30 .75
345 Mike Walker RC .50 1.25
347 Levi Brown RC .30 .75
348 Brian Leonard RC .30 .75
349 Aundrae Allison RC .30 .75
350 Brandon Siler RC .30 .75
351 Calvin Johnson RC 1.00 2.50
352 Gaines Adams RC .40 1.00
353 Anthony Gonzalez RC .30 .75
354 John Beck RC .30 .75
355 Joe Thomas RC .50 1.25
356 Michael Bush RC .30 .75
357 Courtney Taylor RC .30 .75
358 Lawrence Timmons RC .50 1.25
359 Drew Stanton RC .30 .75
360 Chansi Stuckey RC .40 1.00
361 Greg Olsen RC .50 1.25
362 Rhema McKnight RC .30 .75
363 Antonio Pittman RC .30 .75
364 Kevin Kolb RC .40 1.00
365 Alan Branch RC .30 .75
366 Robert Meachem RC .40 1.00
367 Troy Smith RC .30 .75
368 Jamaal Anderson RC .40 1.00
369 Tony Hunt RC .30 .75
370 David Clowney RC .30 .75
371 Brady Quinn RC .30 .75
372 Michael Griffin RC .30 .75
373 Jared Zabransky RC .30 .75
374 Jason Hill RC .30 .75
375 Trent Edwards RC .30 .75
376 Dwayne Jarrett RC .40 1.00
377 DeShawn Wynn RC .30 .75
378 Patrick Willis RC .50 1.25
379 Steve Smith USC RC .30 .75
380 David Ball RC .30 .75
381 Marshawn Lynch RC .60 1.50
382 Paul Posluszny RC .30 .75
383 Johnnie Lee Higgins RC .30 .75
384 Kolby Smith RC .30 .75
385 Ted Ginn Jr. RC .40 1.00
386 Adam Carriker RC .30 .75
387 Tyler Palko RC .50 1.25
388 Joel Filani RC .30 .75
389 Garrett Wolfe RC .30 .75
390 Ryne Robinson RC .40 1.00
391 Reggie Nelson RC .30 .75
392 Dallas Baker RC .30 .75
393 Dwayne Wright RC .30 .75
394 Scott Chandler RC .50 1.25
395 Jordan Kent RC .40 1.00
396 Jarvis Moss RC .30 .75
397 Jonathan Wade RC .30 .75
398 Ben Grubbs RC .40 1.00
399 Jason Snelling RC .30 .75
400 Jeff Rowe RC .30 .75
401 Aaron Ross RC .30 .75
402 Daniel Sepulveda RC .40 1.00
403 Chris Henry RC .30 .75
404 James Jones RC .30 .75
405 Matt Spaeth RC .50 1.25
406 Brandon Meriweather RC .40 1.00
407 Nate Ilaoa RC .40 1.00
408 Mason Crosby RC .40 1.00
409 Ray McDonald RC .40 1.00
410 Chris Leak RC .30 .75
411 Darrelle Revis RC .40 1.00
412 Ahmad Bradshaw RC .50 1.25
413 Tyler Thigpen RC .50 1.25
414 Justise Hairston RC .40 1.00
415 Charles Johnson RC .30 .75
416 Anthony Spencer RC .40 1.00
417 Legedu Naanee RC .40 1.00
418 Kenneth Darby RC .30 .75
419 Steve Breaston RC .30 .75
420 Ben Patrick RC .40 1.00
421 Chris Houston RC .30 .75
422 Jordan Palmer RC .40 1.00
423 Laurent Robinson RC .50 1.25
424 Selvin Young RC .30 .75
425 Justin Harrell RC .30 .75
426 Sabby Piscitelli RC .30 .75
427 Yamon Figurs RC .30 .75
428 Brandon Jackson RC .30 .75
429 Jacoby Jones RC .30 .75
430 H.B. Blades RC .30 .75
431 Tanard Jackson RC .30 .75
432 Matt Gutierrez RC .50 1.25
433 Matt Moore RC .50 1.25
434 Clifton Dawson RC .50 1.25
435 Marcus Mason RC .50 1.25
436 Pierre Thomas RC .50 1.25
437 Dante Rosario RC .50 1.25
438 Biren Ealy RC .40 1.00
439 John Broussard RC .40 1.00
440 Kenton Keith RC .40 1.00

2007 Score Artist's Proof

*VETS 1-288: 12X TO 30X BASIC CARDS
*ROOKIES 289-385: 5X TO 12X BASIC CARDS
STATED PRINT RUN 32 SER.#'d SETS

2007 Score Atomic

*VETS 1-288: 2.5X TO 6X BASIC CARDS
*ROOKIES 289-385: 1X TO 2.5X BASIC CARDS
TWO PER JUMBO PACK

2007 Score End Zone Black

UNPRICED BLACK SER.#'d TO 6

2007 Score Factory Set Updates

Cards in this set were inserted exclusively into 2007 Score football factory sets. Each is essentially an updated version of the base card that was inserted into 2007 Score packs with each featuring a new photo. Some veterans were replaced with new players but most of the cards of the veteran players were updated with a photo of the player in his new 2007 team and the rookies generally have a game action photo versus the training camp photo that was used in the pack version.

*VETS: .4X TO 1X BASIC CARDS
*ROOKIES: .4X TO 1X BASIC CARDS

2007 Score Glossy

*VETS 1-288: 1.5X TO 4X BASIC CARDS
*ROOKIES 289-385: .6X TO 1.5X BASIC CARDS
ONE PER RETAIL PACK; THREE PER JUMBO

2007 Score Gold Zone

*VETS 1-288: 3X TO 8X BASIC CARDS
*ROOKIES 289-385: 1.2X TO 3X BASIC CARDS
GOLD PRINT RUN 600 SER.#'d SETS

2007 Score Red Zone

*VETS 1-288: 6X TO 15X BASIC CARDS
*ROOKIES 289-385: 2.5X TO 6X BASIC CARDS
RED PRINT RUN 120 SER.#'d SETS

2007 Score Scorecard

*VETERANS 1-288: 2.5X TO 6X BASIC CARDS
*ROOKIES 289-385: 1X TO 2.5X BASIC CARDS
STATED PRINT RUN 750 SER.#'d SETS

2007 Score Franchise

COMPLETE SET (10) 6.00 15.00
*GLOSSY: .5X TO 1.2X BASIC INSERTS
*SCORECARD/750: .8X TO 2X BASIC INSERTS
SCORECARD PRINT RUN 750 SER.#'d SETS
*GOLD ZONE/600: 1X TO 2.5X BASIC INSERTS
GOLD ZONE PRINT RUN 600 SER.#'d SETS
*RED ZONE/120: 1.5 TO 4X BASIC INSERTS
RED ZONE PRINT RUN 120 SER.#'d SETS
*ARTIST PROOF/32: 3X TO 8X BASIC INSERTS
ARTIST'S PROOF PRINT RUN 32 SER.#'d SETS
UNPRICED BLACK PRINT RUN 6
1 LaDainian Tomlinson .60 1.50
2 Frank Gore .50 1.25
3 Shaun Alexander .40 1.00
4 Brett Favre 1.25 3.00
5 Reggie Bush .40 1.00
6 Jay Cutler .40 1.00
7 Larry Johnson .40 1.00
8 Maurice Jones-Drew .40 1.00
9 Carson Palmer .50 1.25
10 Vince Young .40 1.00

2007 Score Hot Rookies

*ATOMIC: .8X TO 2X BASIC INSERTS
*GLOSSY: .6X TO 1.5X BASIC INSERTS
*SCORECARD/750: .8X TO 2X BASIC INSERTS
SCORECARD PRINT RUN 750 SER.#'d SETS
*GOLD ZONE/600: 1X TO 2.5X BASIC INSERTS
GOLD ZONE PRINT RUN 600 SER.#'d SETS
*RED ZONE/120: 1.5X TO 4X BASIC INSERTS
RED ZONE PRINT RUN 120 SER.#'d SETS
*ARTIST PROOF/32: 3X TO 8X BASIC INSERTS
ARTIST'S PROOF PRINT RUN 32 SER.#'d SETS
UNPRICED BLACK PRINT RUN 6
INSCRIPTIONS TOO SCARCE TO PRICE
1 JaMarcus Russell .40 1.00
2 Brady Quinn .40 1.00
3 Adrian Peterson 1.25 3.00
4 Marshawn Lynch .75 2.00
5 Calvin Johnson 3.00 8.00
6 Ted Ginn Jr. .50 1.25
7 Dwayne Bowe .40 1.00
8 Robert Meachem .50 1.25
9 Dwayne Jarrett .50 1.25
10 Greg Olsen .60 1.50

2007 Score Inscriptions

179 Demetrius Williams 6.00 15.00
255 Mike Bell 8.00 20.00
256 Brandon Marshall 8.00 20.00
289 Michael Okwo 8.00 20.00
290 Gary Russell 8.00 20.00
291 Josh Wilson 8.00 20.00
292 Thomas Clayton 8.00 20.00
293 Jerard Rabb 8.00 20.00
295 LaMarr Woodley 12.00 30.00
297 Dan Bazuin 8.00 20.00
298 A.J. Davis 6.00 15.00
299 Buster Davis 8.00 20.00
300 Stewart Bradley 6.00 15.00
301 Toby Korrodi 8.00 20.00
302 Marcus McCauley 6.00 15.00
306 Tim Crowder 8.00 20.00
307 D'Juan Woods 6.00 15.00
308 Tim Shaw 8.00 20.00
309 Fred Bennett 6.00 15.00
310 Victor Abiamiri 6.00 15.00
312 Danny Ware 10.00 25.00
313 Quentin Moses 6.00 15.00
314 Ryan McBean 10.00 25.00
315 David Harris 6.00 15.00
316 David Irons 6.00 15.00
317 Syndric Steptoe 8.00 20.00
318 Eric Frampton 8.00 20.00
319 Jemalle Cornelius 8.00 20.00
320 Earl Everett 6.00 15.00
321 Alonzo Coleman 8.00 20.00
322 Josh Gattis 6.00 15.00
323 Zak DeOssie 8.00 20.00
324 Jon Beason 6.00 15.00
326 Aaron Rouse 6.00 15.00
327 Reggie Ball 8.00 20.00
328 Rufus Alexander 6.00 15.00
329 Daymeion Hughes 6.00 15.00
331 JaMarcus Russell 6.00 15.00
332 Paul Williams 6.00 15.00
333 Kenny Irons 6.00 15.00
334 Chris Davis 6.00 15.00
335 Darius Walker 6.00 15.00
336 Dwayne Bowe 6.00 15.00
337 Isaiah Stanback 6.00 15.00
338 Leon Hall 6.00 15.00
340 Amobi Okoye 8.00 20.00
341 Adrian Peterson 150.00 250.00
342 LaRon Landry 10.00 25.00
343 Lorenzo Booker 8.00 20.00
345 Mike Walker 10.00 25.00
346 Zach Miller 6.00 15.00
347 Levi Brown 6.00 15.00
348 Brian Leonard 6.00 15.00
349 Aundrae Allison 6.00 15.00
350 Brandon Siler 6.00 15.00
351 Calvin Johnson 50.00 100.00
352 Gaines Adams 8.00 20.00
353 Anthony Gonzalez 6.00 15.00
354 John Beck 6.00 15.00
355 Joe Thomas 10.00 25.00
356 Michael Bush 6.00 15.00
357 Courtney Taylor 6.00 15.00
358 Lawrence Timmons 10.00 25.00
359 Drew Stanton 6.00 15.00
360 Chansi Stuckey 8.00 20.00
361 Greg Olsen 10.00 25.00
362 Rhema McKnight 6.00 15.00
363 Antonio Pittman 6.00 15.00
364 Kevin Kolb 8.00 20.00
366 Robert Meachem 8.00 20.00
367 Troy Smith 6.00 15.00
368 Jamaal Anderson 8.00 20.00
369 Tony Hunt 6.00 15.00
370 David Clowney 6.00 15.00
371 Brady Quinn 6.00 15.00
372 Michael Griffin 6.00 15.00
373 Jared Zabransky 6.00 15.00
374 Jason Hill 6.00 15.00
375 Trent Edwards 6.00 15.00
376 Dwayne Jarrett 8.00 20.00
377 DeShawn Wynn 6.00 15.00
378 Patrick Willis 10.00 25.00
379 Steve Smith USC 6.00 15.00
380 David Ball 6.00 15.00
381 Marshawn Lynch 12.00 30.00
382 Paul Posluszny 6.00 15.00
383 Johnnie Lee Higgins 6.00 15.00
384 Kolby Smith 6.00 15.00
385 Ted Ginn Jr. 8.00 20.00

2008 Score

COMPLETE SET (440) 30.00 60.00
COMP.FACT. SET (440) 30.00 50.00
COMP.SET w/o RC's (330) 15.00 30.00
1 Matt Leinart .12 .30
2 Kurt Warner .15 .40
3 Larry Fitzgerald .15 .40
4 Anquan Boldin .12 .30
5 Edgerrin James .15 .40
6 Neil Rackers .12 .30
7 Steve Breaston .12 .30
8 Antrel Rolle .12 .30
9 Karlos Dansby .12 .30
10 Joey Harrington .12 .30
11 Jerious Norwood .12 .30
12 Roddy White .12 .30
13 Michael Jenkins .12 .30
14 Joe Horn .12 .30
15 Keith Brooking .12 .30
17 John Abraham .12 .30
18 Michael Turner .12 .30
19 Troy Smith .15 .40
20 Willis McGahee .12 .30
21 Musa Smith .12 .30
22 Derrick Mason .12 .30
23 Mark Clayton .12 .30
24 Bart Scott .12 .30
25 Demetrius Williams .12 .30
26 Yamon Figurs .12 .30
27 Ray Lewis .20 .50
28 Terrell Suggs .12 .30
29 Ed Reed .15 .40
30 Trent Edwards .12 .30
31 Marshawn Lynch .15 .40
32 Lee Evans .15 .40
33 Roscoe Parrish .12 .30
34 Paul Posluszny .12 .30
35 John DiGiorgio RC .15 .40
36 Angelo Crowell .12 .30
37 Jabari Greer RC .12 .30
38 Chris Kelsay .12 .30
39 Fred Jackson RC .40 1.00
40 Matt Moore .12 .30
41 Steve Smith .15 .40
42 DeAngelo Williams .12 .30
43 Brad Hoover .12 .30
44 Dante Rosario .12 .30
45 Julius Peppers .15 .40
46 Jon Beason .12 .30
47 Chris Harris .12 .30
48 D.J. Hackett .12 .30
49 Jake Delhomme .12 .30
50 Adrian Peterson .12 .30
51 Mark Anderson .12 .30
52 Desmond Clark .12 .30
53 Greg Olsen .15 .40
54 Devin Hester .15 .40
55 Brian Urlacher .20 .50
56 Jason McKie RC .15 .40
57 Lance Briggs .15 .40
58 Rex Grossman .12 .30
59 Carson Palmer .15 .40
60 Chad Johnson .12 .30
61 T.J. Houshmandzadeh .12 .30
62 Rudi Johnson .12 .30
63 Kenny Watson .12 .30
64 Dhani Jones .12 .30
65 Leon Hall .12 .30
66 Johnathan Joseph .12 .30
67 Derek Anderson .12 .30
68 Brady Quinn .12 .30
69 Jamal Lewis .15 .40
70 Josh Cribbs .12 .30
71 Kellen Winslow .12 .30
72 Braylon Edwards .12 .30
73 Joe Jurevicius .12 .30
74 D'Qwell Jackson .12 .30
75 Leigh Bodden .12 .30
76 Sean Jones .12 .30
77 Tony Romo .15 .40
78 Terrell Owens .15 .40
79 Marion Barber .12 .30
80 Jason Witten .15 .40
81 Patrick Crayton .15 .40
82 Anthony Henry .12 .30
83 DeMarcus Ware .15 .40
84 Terence Newman .12 .30
85 Greg Ellis .12 .30
86 Zach Thomas .15 .40
87 Keary Colbert .12 .30
88 Jay Cutler .12 .30
89 Tony Scheffler .12 .30
90 Selvin Young .12 .30
91 Brandon Marshall .15 .40
92 Brandon Stokley .12 .30
93 Champ Bailey .15 .40
94 John Lynch .15 .40
95 Dre Bly .12 .30
96 Elvis Dumervil .12 .30
97 Jon Kitna .12 .30
98 Tatum Bell .12 .30
99 Shaun McDonald .12 .30
100 Roy Williams WR .12 .30
101 Calvin Johnson .20 .50
102 Mike Furrey .15 .40
103 Ernie Sims .12 .30
104 Aveion Cason .12 .30
105 Aaron Rodgers .40 1.00
106 Brett Favre .40 1.00
107 Ryan Grant .15 .40
108 Greg Jennings .12 .30
109 Donald Driver .15 .40
110 Donald Lee .15 .40
111 James Jones .12 .30
112 Al Harris .12 .30
113 Nick Barnett .12 .30
114 Charles Woodson .20 .50
115 Aaron Kampman .15 .40
116 Mason Crosby .12 .30
117 Matt Schaub .12 .30
118 Ahman Green .15 .40
119 Andre Johnson .15 .40
120 Kevin Walter .15 .40
121 Owen Daniels .12 .30
122 Andre Davis .12 .30
123 DeMeco Ryans .15 .40
124 Mario Williams .15 .40
125 Dunta Robinson .12 .30
126 Chris Brown .12 .30
127 Peyton Manning .50 1.25
128 Joseph Addai .12 .30
129 Marvin Harrison .15 .40
130 Reggie Wayne .15 .40
131 Dallas Clark .12 .30
132 Anthony Gonzalez .12 .30
133 Kenton Keith .12 .30
134 Adam Vinatieri .12 .30
135 Bob Sanders .15 .40
136 Kelvin Hayden .12 .30
137 Freddie Keiaho .12 .30
138 David Garrard .12 .30
139 Fred Taylor .12 .30
140 Maurice Jones-Drew .12 .30
141 Greg Jones .12 .30
142 Dennis Northcutt .12 .30
143 Reggie Williams .15 .40
144 Marcedes Lewis .12 .30
145 Matt Jones .15 .40
146 Reggie Nelson .12 .30
147 Cleo Lemon .12 .30
148 Jerry Porter .12 .30
149 Damon Huard .12 .30
150 Brodie Croyle .15 .40
151 Larry Johnson .12 .30
152 Kolby Smith .12 .30
153 Tony Gonzalez .15 .40
154 Dwayne Bowe .15 .40
155 Donnie Edwards .12 .30
156 Jared Allen .12 .30
157 Patrick Surtain .12 .30
158 Derrick Johnson .12 .30
159 Ernest Wilford .12 .30
160 John Beck .12 .30
161 Ronnie Brown .12 .30
162 Greg Camarillo RC .40 1.00
163 Ted Ginn Jr. .12 .30
164 Derek Hagan .12 .30
165 Channing Crowder .12 .30
166 Joey Porter .12 .30
167 Jason Taylor .15 .40
168 Josh McCown .12 .30
169 Bernard Berrian .12 .30
170 Maurice Hicks .12 .30
172 Adrian Peterson .20 .50
173 Chester Taylor .12 .30
174 Bobby Wade .12 .30
175 Sidney Rice .12 .30
176 Robert Ferguson .12 .30
177 Darren Sharper .12 .30
178 Visanthe Shiancoe .20 .50
179 E.J. Henderson .12 .30
180 Cedric Griffin .12 .30
181 Chad Greenway .12 .30
182 Tom Brady .60 1.50
183 Randy Moss .15 .40
184 Laurence Maroney .15 .40
185 Wes Welker .15 .40
186 Sammy Morris .12 .30
187 Kevin Faulk .12 .30
188 Ben Watson .12 .30
189 Tedy Bruschi .15 .40
190 Rodney Harrison .12 .30
191 Mike Vrabel .12 .30
192 Drew Brees .20 .50
193 Reggie Bush .12 .30
194 Deuce McAllister .15 .40
195 Marques Colston .12 .30
196 David Patten .12 .30
197 Devery Henderson .12 .30
198 Scott Fujita .12 .30
199 Roman Harper .12 .30
200 Mike McKenzie .12 .30
201 Will Smith .12 .30
202 Billy Miller .12 .30
203 Sammy Knight .12 .30
204 Eli Manning .15 .40
205 Plaxico Burress .12 .30
206 Brandon Jacobs .12 .30
207 Ahmad Bradshaw .12 .30
208 David Tyree .12 .30
209 Amani Toomer .12 .30
210 Jeremy Shockey .12 .30
211 Steve Smith USC .15 .40
212 Aaron Ross .12 .30
213 Antonio Pierce .12 .30
214 Michael Strahan .15 .40
215 Jesse Chatman .12 .30
216 Calvin Pace .12 .30
217 Kellen Clemens .12 .30
218 Leon Washington .12 .30
219 Jerricho Cotchery .12 .30
220 Laveranues Coles .12 .30
221 Chris Baker .12 .30
222 Brad Smith .12 .30
223 Thomas Jones .12 .30
224 Darrelle Revis .12 .30
225 David Harris .12 .30
226 DeAngelo Hall .12 .30
227 Drew Carter .12 .30
228 Javon Walker .15 .40
229 JaMarcus Russell .12 .30
230 Justin Fargas .12 .30
231 Michael Bush .12 .30
232 Ronald Curry .12 .30
233 Zach Miller .12 .30
234 Thomas Howard .12 .30
235 Johnnie Lee Higgins .12 .30
236 Kirk Morrison .12 .30
237 Michael Huff .12 .30
238 Asante Samuel .12 .30
239 Donovan McNabb .15 .40
240 Brian Westbrook .12 .30
241 Correll Buckhalter .12 .30
242 Kevin Curtis .12 .30
243 Reggie Brown .12 .30
244 L.J. Smith .12 .30
245 Greg Lewis .12 .30
246 Lito Sheppard .12 .30
247 Omar Gaither .12 .30
248 Ben Roethlisberger .20 .50
249 Willie Parker .15 .40
250 Najeh Davenport .12 .30
251 Hines Ward .15 .40
252 Santonio Holmes .12 .30
253 Heath Miller .12 .30
254 Cedrick Wilson .12 .30
255 James Harrison RC 1.00 2.50
256 Ike Taylor .12 .30
257 James Farrior .12 .30
258 Troy Polamalu .20 .50
259 Philip Rivers .20 .50
260 LaDainian Tomlinson .20 .50
261 Darren Sproles .12 .30
262 Vincent Jackson .12 .30
263 Chris Chambers .12 .30
264 Antonio Gates .15 .40
265 Craig Buster Davis .12 .30
266 Malcom Floyd .12 .30
267 Antonio Cromartie .12 .30
268 Shawne Merriman .12 .30
269 DeShaun Foster .12 .30
270 Alex Smith QB .15 .40
271 Frank Gore .15 .40
272 Michael Robinson .12 .30
273 Vernon Davis .12 .30
274 Arnaz Battle .12 .30
275 Isaac Bruce .20 .50
276 Patrick Willis .15 .40
277 Nate Clements .12 .30
278 Jason Hill .12 .30
279 T.J. Duckett .12 .30
280 Matt Hasselbeck .12 .30
281 Julian Peterson .12 .30
282 Maurice Morris .12 .30
283 Bobby Engram .12 .30
284 Nate Burleson .12 .30
285 Deion Branch .12 .30
286 Lofa Tatupu .12 .30
287 Marcus Trufant .12 .30
288 Darryl Tapp .12 .30
289 Julius Jones .12 .30
290 Marc Bulger .12 .30
291 Steven Jackson .12 .30
292 Brian Leonard .12 .30
293 Torry Holt .15 .40
294 Dante Hall .12 .30
295 Randy McMichael .12 .30
296 Drew Bennett .12 .30
297 Will Witherspoon .12 .30
298 Tye Hill .12 .30
299 Corey Chavous .12 .30
300 Warrick Dunn .12 .30
301 Brian Griese .12 .30
302 Jeff Garcia .12 .30
303 Cadillac Williams .15 .40
304 Earnest Graham .12 .30
305 Joey Galloway .15 .40
306 Ike Hilliard .12 .30
307 Michael Clayton .12 .30
308 Derrick Brooks .12 .30
309 Phillip Buchanon .12 .30
310 Alex Smith TE .20 .50
311 Ronde Barber .12 .30
312 Justin McCareins .12 .30
313 Jevon Kearse .12 .30
314 Vince Young .12 .30
315 LenDale White .12 .30
316 Justin Gage .12 .30
317 Roydell Williams .12 .30
318 Alge Crumpler .12 .30
319 Brandon Jones .12 .30
320 Michael Griffin .12 .30
321 Keith Bulluck .12 .30
322 Jason Campbell .12 .30
323 Clinton Portis .12 .30
324 Ladell Betts .12 .30
325 Santana Moss .12 .30

327 Antwaan Randle El .12 .30
328 London Fletcher .15 .40
329 Shawn Springs .12 .30
330 LaRon Landry .15 .40
331 Jake Long RC .50 1.25
332 Chris Long RC .40 1.00
333 Matt Ryan RC 1.00 2.50
334 Darren McFadden RC .30 .75
335 Glenn Dorsey RC .30 .75
336 Vernon Gholston RC .30 .75
337 Sedrick Ellis RC .30 .75
338 Derrick Harvey RC .30 .75
339 Keith Rivers RC .30 .75
340 Jerod Mayo RC .50 1.25
341 Leodis McKelvin RC .40 1.00
342 Jonathan Stewart RC .50 1.25
343 D.Rodgers-Cromartie RC .40 1.00
344 Joe Flacco RC .60 1.50
345 Aqib Talib RC .50 1.25
346 Felix Jones RC .30 .75
347 Rashard Mendenhall RC .30 .75
348 Chris Johnson RC .40 1.00
349 Mike Jenkins RC .30 .75
350 Antoine Cason RC .40 1.00
351 Lawrence Jackson RC .30 .75
352 Kentwan Balmer RC .30 .75
353 Dustin Keller RC .40 1.00
354 Kenny Phillips RC .30 .75
355 Phillip Merling RC .30 .75
356 Donnie Avery RC .40 1.00
357 Devin Thomas RC .30 .75
358 Brandon Flowers RC .40 1.00
359 Jordy Nelson RC 1.00 2.50
360 Curtis Lofton RC .40 1.00
361 John Carlson RC .30 .75
362 Tracy Porter RC .40 1.00
363 James Hardy RC .30 .75
364 Eddie Royal RC .30 .75
365 Matt Forte RC .50 1.25
366 Jordon Dizon RC .30 .75
367 Jerome Simpson RC .40 1.00
368 Fred Davis RC .30 .75
369 DeSean Jackson RC .60 1.50
370 Calais Campbell RC .40 1.00
371 Malcolm Kelly RC .30 .75
372 Quentin Groves RC .40 1.00
373 Limas Sweed RC .30 .75
374 Ray Rice RC .30 .75
375 Brian Brohm RC .30 .75
376 Chad Henne RC .40 1.00
377 Dexter Jackson RC .50 1.25
378 Martellus Bennett RC .40 1.00
379 Terrell Thomas RC .30 .75
380 Kevin Smith RC .30 .75
381 Anthony Alridge RC .30 .75
382 Jacob Hester RC .30 .75
383 Earl Bennett RC .50 1.25
384 Jamaal Charles RC .50 1.25
385 Dan Connor RC .30 .75
386 Reggie Smith RC .30 .75
387 Brad Cottam RC .30 .75
388 Pat Sims RC .40 1.00
389 Dantrell Savage RC .40 1.00
390 Early Doucet RC .30 .75
391 Harry Douglas RC .40 1.00
392 Steve Slaton RC .30 .75
393 Jermichael Finley RC .30 .75
394 Kevin O'Connell RC .30 .75
395 Mario Manningham RC .30 .75
396 Andre Caldwell RC .30 .75
397 Will Franklin RC .40 1.00
398 Marcus Smith RC .40 1.00
399 Martin Rucker RC .30 .75
400 Xavier Adibi RC .30 .75
401 Craig Steltz RC .30 .75
402 Tashard Choice RC .30 .75
403 Lavelle Hawkins RC .40 1.00
404 Jacob Tamme RC .40 1.00
405 Keenan Burton RC .30 .75
406 John David Booty RC .30 .75
407 Ryan Torain RC .40 1.00
408 Tim Hightower RC .40 1.00
409 Dennis Dixon RC .30 .75
410 Kellen Davis RC .30 .75
411 Josh Johnson RC .30 .75
412 Erik Ainge RC .30 .75
413 Owen Schmitt RC .30 .75
414 Marcus Thomas RC .40 1.00
415 Thomas Brown RC .30 .75
416 Josh Morgan RC .30 .75
417 Kevin Robinson RC .30 .75
418 Colt Brennan RC .40 1.00
419 Paul Hubbard RC .30 .75
420 Andre Woodson RC .30 .75
421 Mike Hart RC .30 .75
422 Matt Flynn RC .30 .75
423 Chauncey Washington RC .40 1.00
424 Caleb Campbell RC .50 1.25
425 Peyton Hillis RC .50 1.25
426 Justin Forsett RC .40 1.00
427 Adrian Arrington RC .30 .75
428 Cory Boyd RC .30 .75
429 Allen Patrick RC .30 .75
430 Marcus Monk RC .40 1.00
431 DJ Hall RC .30 .75
432 Darrell Strong RC .40 1.00
433 Jason Rivers RC .30 .75
434 Jed Collins RC .40 1.00
435 Paul Smith RC .30 .75
436 Darius Reynaud RC .30 .75
437 Ali Highsmith RC .30 .75
438 Davone Bess RC .40 1.00
439 Erin Henderson RC .40 1.00
440 Kalvin McRae RC .30 .75

2008 Score Artist's Proof

*VETS 1-330: 12X TO 30X BASIC CARDS
*ROOKIES 331-440: 5X TO 12X
STATED PRINT RUN 32 SER.#'d SETS

2008 Score End Zone

UNPRICED END ZONE PRINT RUN 6

2008 Score Factory Set Updates

Cards in this set were inserted exclusively into 2008 Score football factory sets. Each is essentially an updated version of the base card that was inserted into 2008 Score packs with each featuring a new updated photo on the front. Most of the cards of the veteran players were updated with a photo of the player's new 2008 team and the rookies generally have a game action photo versus the training camp photo that was used in the pack version. Five new cards/players (#250, 428, 433, 435, 440) replaced other players issued only in packs.
*VETS: .6X TO 1.5X BASIC CARDS
*ROOKIES: .4X TO 1X BASIC CARDS
INSERTED IN FACTORY SETS ONLY
18 Michael Turner .20 .50
21 Musa Smith .20 .50
48 D.J. Hackett .20 .50
75 Leigh Bodden .20 .50
86 Zach Thomas .25 .60
87 Keary Colbert .20 .50
94 John Lynch .25 .60
126 Chris Brown .20 .50
147 Cleo Lemon .20 .50
156 Jared Allen .20 .50
159 Ernest Wilford .20 .50
210 Jeremy Shockey .20 .50
215 Jesse Chatman .20 .50
216 Calvin Pace .20 .50
226 DeAngelo Hall .20 .50
227 Drew Carter .20 .50
228 Javon Walker .25 .60
238 Asante Samuel .20 .50
250 Byron Leftwich .20 .50
254 Ricky Williams .25 .60
269 Deshaun Foster .20 .50
275 Isaac Bruce .30 .75
279 T.J. Duckett .20 .50
289 Julius Jones .20 .50
300 Warrick Dunn .20 .50
301 Brian Griese .20 .50
312 Justin McCareins .20 .50
313 Jevon Kearse .20 .50
318 Alge Crumpler .20 .50
332 Chris Long .40 1.00
336 Vernon Gholston .30 .75
337 Sedrick Ellis .30 .75
338 Derrick Harvey .30 .75
339 Keith Rivers .30 .75
340 Jerod Mayo .50 1.25
341 Leodis McKelvin .40 1.00
343 Dominique Rodgers-Cromartie .40 1.00
345 Aqib Talib .50 1.25
348 Chris Johnson .40 1.00
349 Mike Jenkins .30 .75
350 Antoine Cason .40 1.00
351 Lawrence Jackson .30 .75
354 Kenny Phillips .30 .75
355 Phillip Merling .30 .75
358 Brandon Flowers .40 1.00
360 Curtis Lofton .40 1.00
361 John Carlson .30 .75
362 Tracy Porter .40 1.00
364 Eddie Royal .30 .75
366 Jordon Dizon .30 .75
368 Fred Davis .30 .75
370 Calais Campbell .40 1.00
372 Quentin Groves .40 1.00
374 Ray Rice .30 .75
377 Dexter Jackson .50 1.25
378 Martellus Bennett .40 1.00
379 Terrell Thomas .30 .75
381 Anthony Alridge .30 .75
382 Jacob Hester .30 .75
384 Jamaal Charles .50 1.25
385 Dan Connor .30 .75
386 Reggie Smith .30 .75
387 Brad Cottam .30 .75
388 Pat Sims .40 1.00
389 Dantrell Savage .40 1.00
393 Jermichael Finley .30 .75
397 Will Franklin .40 1.00
398 Marcus Smith .40 1.00
399 Martin Rucker .30 .75
400 Xavier Adibi .30 .75
401 Craig Steltz .30 .75
402 Tashard Choice .30 .75
403 Lavelle Hawkins .40 1.00
404 Jacob Tamme .40 1.00
405 Keenan Burton .30 .75
408 Tim Hightower .40 1.00
409 Dennis Dixon .30 .75
410 Kellen Davis .30 .75
411 Josh Johnson .30 .75
412 Erik Ainge .30 .75
413 Owen Schmitt .30 .75
414 Marcus Thomas .40 1.00
415 Thomas Brown .30 .75
416 Josh Morgan .30 .75
418 Colt Brennan .40 1.00
419 Paul Hubbard .30 .75
420 Andre Woodson .30 .75
421 Mike Hart .30 .75
422 Matt Flynn .30 .75
423 Chauncey Washington .40 1.00
425 Peyton Hillis .50 1.25
426 Justin Forsett .40 1.00
427 Adrian Arrington .30 .75
428 Jalen Parmele RC .40 1.00
429 Allen Patrick .30 .75
430 Marcus Monk .40 1.00
431 DJ Hall .30 .75
432 Darrell Strong .40 1.00
433 Xavier Omon RC .30 .75
434 Jed Collins .40 1.00
435 Marcus Henry RC .30 .75
436 Darius Reynaud .30 .75
437 Ali Highsmith .30 .75
438 Davone Bess .40 1.00
439 Erin Henderson .40 1.00
440 Kenneth Moore RC .30 .75

2008 Score Glossy

*VETS 1-330: 1.2X TO 3X BASIC CARDS
*ROOKIES 331-440: .5X TO 1.2X
ONE PER RETAIL PACK; THREE PER HOBBY
106B Brett Favre Jets 2.50 6.00

2008 Score Gold Zone

*VETS 1-330: 3X TO 8X BASIC CARDS
*ROOKIES 331-440: 1.2X TO 3X
STATED PRINT RUN 400 SER.#'d SETS

2008 Score Red Zone

*VETS 1-330: 5X TO 12X BASIC CARDS
*ROOKIES 331-440: 2X TO 5X
STATED PRINT RUN 100 SER.#'d SETS

2008 Score Scorecard

*VETS 1-330: 2.5X TO 6X BASIC CARDS
*ROOKIES 331-440: 1X TO 2.5X BASIC CARDS
STATED PRINT RUN 649 SER.#'d SETS

2008 Score Player Decals

COMPLETE SET (32) 10.00 25.00
1 Tom Brady 2.00 5.00
2 Reggie Bush .40 1.00
3 Kellen Clemens .40 1.00
4 Jay Cutler .40 1.00
5 Braylon Edwards .40 1.00
6 Joe Flacco .40 1.00
7 Jeff Garcia .40 1.00
8 Frank Gore .50 1.25
9 Matt Hasselbeck .40 1.00
10 Chad Henne .25 .60
11 Devin Hester .50 1.25
12 Torry Holt .50 1.25
13 Andre Johnson .50 1.25
14 Calvin Johnson .60 1.50
15 Larry Johnson .40 1.00
16 Matt Leinart .40 1.00
17 Marshawn Lynch .50 1.25
18 Eli Manning .50 1.25
19 Peyton Manning 1.50 4.00
20 Darren McFadden .20 .50
21 Carson Palmer .50 1.25
22 Adrian Peterson .60 1.50
23 Aaron Rodgers 1.25 3.00
24 Ben Roethlisberger .60 1.50
25 Tony Romo .50 1.25
26 Matt Ryan .60 1.50
27 Jonathan Stewart .30 .75
28 Fred Taylor .40 1.00
29 Devin Thomas .50 1.00
30 LaDainian Tomlinson .60 1.50
31 Brian Westbrook .40 1.00
32 Vince Young .40 1.00

2008 Score Team Logo Decals

COMPLETE SET (32) 5.00 12.00
1 Chicago Bears .40 1.00
2 Cincinnati Bengals .30 .75
3 Buffalo Bills .30 .75
4 Denver Broncos .40 1.00
5 Cleveland Browns .30 .75
6 Tampa Bay Buccaneers .30 .75
7 Arizona Cardinals .30 .75
8 San Diego Chargers .30 .75
9 Kansas City Chiefs .30 .75
10 Indianapolis Colts .40 1.00
11 Dallas Cowboys .50 1.25
12 Miami Dolphins .40 1.00
13 Philadelphia Eagles .30 .75
14 Atlanta Falcons .30 .75
15 San Francisco 49ers .40 1.00
16 New York Giants .40 1.00
17 Jacksonville Jaguars .30 .75
18 New York Jets .40 1.00
19 Detroit Lions .30 .75
20 Green Bay Packers .50 1.25
21 Carolina Panthers .30 .75
22 New England Patriots .40 1.00
23 Oakland Raiders .50 1.25
24 St. Louis Rams .30 .75
25 Baltimore Ravens .30 .75
26 Washington Redskins .40 1.00
27 New Orleans Saints .30 .75
28 Seattle Seahawks .30 .75
29 Pittsburgh Steelers .50 1.25
30 Houston Texans .30 .75
31 Tennessee Titans .30 .75
32 Minnesota Vikings .30 .75

2008 Score Franchise

COMPLETE SET (25) 10.00 25.00
*GLOSSY: .5X TO 1.2X BASIC INSERTS
*SCORECARD/999: .6X TO 1.5X BASIC INSERTS
SCORECARD PRINT RUN 999 SER.#'d SETS
*GOLD ZONE/500: .8X TO 2X BASIC INSERTS
GOLD ZONE PRINT RUN 500 SER.#'d SETS
*RED ZONE/100: 1.5X TO 4X BASIC INSERTS
RED ZONE PRINT RUN 100 SER.#'d SETS
*ARTIST PROOF/32: 3X TO 8X BASIC INSERTS
ARTIST'S PROOF PRINT RUN 32 SER.#'d SETS
UNPRICED END ZONE PRINT RUN 6
1 Tony Romo .50 1.25
2 Tom Brady 2.00 5.00
3 Joseph Addai .40 1.00
4 Randy Moss .50 1.25
5 Terrell Owens .50 1.25
6 Aaron Rodgers 1.25 3.00
7 T.J. Houshmandzadeh .40 1.00
8 Ben Roethlisberger .60 1.50
9 Larry Johnson .40 1.00
10 Drew Brees .60 1.50
11 Jay Cutler .40 1.00
12 Eli Manning .50 1.25
13 Clinton Portis .40 1.00
14 Brian Westbrook .40 1.00
15 Torry Holt .50 1.25
16 Reggie Wayne .50 1.25
17 David Garrard .40 1.00
18 Steve Smith .50 1.25
19 Willie Parker .50 1.25
20 Edgerrin James .50 1.25
21 Andre Johnson .50 1.25
22 LaDainian Tomlinson .60 1.50
23 Donald Driver .50 1.25
24 Fred Taylor .40 1.00
25 Peyton Manning 1.50 4.00

2008 Score Future Franchise

*GLOSSY: .5X TO 1.2X BASIC INSERTS
*SCORECARD/999: .6X TO 1.5X BASIC INSERTS
SCORECARD PRINT RUN 999 SER.#'d SETS
*GOLD ZONE/500: .8X TO 2X BASIC INSERTS
GOLD ZONE PRINT RUN 500 SER.#'d SETS
*RED ZONE: 1.2X TO 3X BASIC INSERTS
RED ZONE PRINT RUN 100 SER.#'d SETS
*ARTIST'S PROOF: 2.5X TO 6X BASIC INSERTS
ARTIST'S PROOF PRINT RUN 32 SER.#'d SETS
UNPRICED END ZONE PRINT RUN 6
1 JaMarcus Russell .40 1.00
2 Brady Quinn .40 1.00
3 Brandon Jacobs .40 1.00
4 Adrian Peterson .60 1.50
5 Dallas Clark .40 1.00
6 Brandon Marshall .50 1.25
7 Santonio Holmes .40 1.00
8 Dwayne Dowe .50 1.25
9 Laurence Maroney .50 1.25
10 Marion Barber .40 1.00
11 Greg Jennings .40 1.00
12 Trent Edwards .40 1.00
13 Wes Welker .50 1.25
14 Michael Turner .40 1.00
15 Derek Anderson .40 1.00
16 Kevin Curtis .40 1.00
17 Reggie Bush .40 1.00
18 Chris Cooley .40 1.00
19 Maurice Jones-Drew .40 1.00
20 Braylon Edwards .40 1.00
21 Willis McGahee .40 1.00
22 Vince Young .40 1.00
23 Frank Gore .50 1.25
24 Roddy White .40 1.00
25 Marques Colston .40 1.00

2008 Score Hot Rookies

COMPLETE SET (25) 12.50 30.00
*GLOSSY: .5X TO 1.2X BASIC INSERTS
*SCORECARD/999: .6X TO 1.5X BASIC INSERTS
SCORECARD PRINT RUN 999 SER.#'d SETS
*GOLD ZONE/500: .8X TO 2X BASIC INSERTS
GOLD ZONE PRINT RUN 500 SER.#'d SETS
*RED ZONE/100: 1.2X TO 3X BASIC INSERTS
RED ZONE PRINT RUN 100 SER.#'d SETS
*ARTIST PROOF/32: 2.5X TO 6X BASIC INSERTS
ARTIST'S PROOF PRINT RUN 32 SER.#'d SETS
UNPRICED END ZONE PRINT RUN 6
1 Brian Brohm .40 1.00
2 Chad Henne .50 1.25
3 Chris Johnson .50 1.25
4 Darren McFadden .40 1.00
5 DeSean Jackson .75 2.00
6 Devin Thomas .40 1.00
7 Dexter Jackson .60 1.50
8 Donnie Avery .50 1.25
9 Eddie Royal .40 1.00
10 Felix Jones .40 1.00
11 Jamaal Charles .60 1.50
12 James Hardy .40 1.00
13 Jerome Simpson .50 1.25
14 Joe Flacco .75 2.00
15 Jonathan Stewart .60 1.50
16 Jordy Nelson 1.25 3.00
17 Kevin Smith .40 1.00
18 Limas Sweed .40 1.00
19 Malcolm Kelly .40 1.00
20 Mario Manningham .40 1.00
21 Matt Forte .60 1.50
22 Matt Ryan 1.25 3.00
23 Rashard Mendenhall .40 1.00
24 Ray Rice .40 1.00
25 Steve Slaton .40 1.00

2008 Score Inscriptions

STATED PRINT RUN 5-250
SERIAL #'d OF 5 NOT PRICED
362 Tracy Porter/100 6.00 15.00
366 Jordon Dizon/100 5.00 12.00
372 Quentin Groves/100 6.00 15.00
381 Anthony Alridge/250 5.00 12.00
387 Brad Cottam/100 5.00 12.00
389 Dantrell Savage/250 6.00 15.00
398 Marcus Smith/250 6.00 15.00
413 Owen Schmitt/242 5.00 12.00
416 Josh Morgan/250 5.00 12.00
419 Paul Hubbard/250 5.00 12.00
423 Chauncey Washington/100 6.00 15.00
424 Caleb Campbell/250 8.00 20.00
425 Peyton Hillis/125 8.00 20.00
426 Justin Forsett/100 6.00 15.00
427 Adrian Arrington/100 5.00 12.00
428 Cory Boyd/100 5.00 12.00
432 Darrell Strong/250 6.00 15.00
433 Jason Rivers/250 5.00 12.00
437 Ali Highsmith/250 5.00 12.00
439 Erin Henderson/250 6.00 15.00

2008 Score Young Stars

COMPLETE SET (25) 8.00 20.00
*GLOSSY: .5X TO 1.2X BASIC INSERTS
*SCORECARD/999: .6X TO 1.5X BASIC INSERTS
SCORECARD PRINT RUN 999 SER.#'d SETS
*GOLD ZONE/500: .8X TO 2X BASIC INSERTS
GOLD ZONE PRINT RUN 500 SER.#'d SETS
*RED ZONE/100: 1.2X TO 3X BASIC INSERTS
RED ZONE PRINT RUN 100 SER.#'d SETS
*ARTIST PROOF/32: 2.5X TO 6X BASIC INSERTS
ARTIST'S PROOF PRINT RUN 32 SER.#'d SETS
UNPRICED END ZONE PRINT RUN 6
1 Earnest Graham .50 1.25
2 Anthony Gonzalez .50 1.25
3 Ted Ginn Jr. .50 1.25
4 Marshawn Lynch .60 1.50
5 Calvin Johnson .75 2.00
6 Steve Smith USC .60 1.50
7 Kenny Watson .50 1.25
8 Vernon Davis .50 1.25
9 LenDale White .50 1.25
10 Vincent Jackson .40 1.00
11 Kolby Smith .50 1.25
12 Selvin Young .50 1.25
13 Patrick Willis .60 1.50
14 Lee Evans .60 1.50
15 Ahmad Bradshaw .50 1.25
16 Justin Fargas .50 1.25
17 Tarvaris Jackson .50 1.25
18 DeMeco Ryans .60 1.50
19 Fred Jackson 1.50 4.00
20 Patrick Crayton .60 1.50
21 James Jones .50 1.25
22 Michael Bush .50 1.25
23 Sidney Rice .50 1.25
24 LaRon Landry .60 1.50
25 Zach Miller .50 1.25

2008 Score Super Bowl XLIII

COMP.FACT.SET (440) 30.00 50.00
*RED: .4X TO 1X BASIC SCORE
BASE SET CARDS HAVE RED BORDER
*BLUE: .5X TO 1.2X RED BORDER
*GOLD: .6X TO 1.5X RED BORDER
*GREEN: .8X TO 2X RED BORDER
*BLACK: 1X TO 2.5X RED BORDER
*GLOSSY/250: 1.2X TO 3X RED

2009 Score

COMPLETE SET (400) 30.00 60.00
1 Adrian Wilson .12 .30
2 Anquan Boldin .12 .30
3 Dominique Rodgers-Cromartie .12 .30
4 Edgerrin James .15 .40
5 Kurt Warner .15 .40
6 Larry Fitzgerald .15 .40
7 Matt Leinart .12 .30
8 Steve Breaston .15 .40
9 Tim Hightower .12 .30
10 Chris Houston .12 .30
11 Curtis Lofton .12 .30
12 Harry Douglas .12 .30
13 Jerious Norwood .12 .30
14 John Abraham .12 .30
15 Matt Ryan .15 .40
16 Michael Jenkins .12 .30
17 Michael Turner .12 .30
18 Roddy White .12 .30
19 Demetrius Williams .12 .30
20 Derrick Mason .12 .30
21 Joe Flacco .15 .40
22 Le'Ron McClain .15 .40
23 Mark Clayton .12 .30
24 Ray Lewis .20 .50
25 Ray Rice .12 .30
26 Terrell Suggs .12 .30
27 Todd Heap .12 .30
28 Willis McGahee .12 .30
29 Derek Fine .12 .30
30 Fred Jackson .15 .40
31 James Hardy .15 .40
32 Lee Evans .15 .40
33 Leodis McKelvin .12 .30
34 Marshawn Lynch .15 .40
35 Paul Posluszny .12 .30
36 Steve Johnson .15 .40
37 Trent Edwards .12 .30
38 Charles Godfrey .12 .30
39 Chris Gamble .12 .30
40 Dante Rosario .12 .30
41 DeAngelo Williams .12 .30
42 Jake Delhomme .12 .30
43 Jon Beason .12 .30
44 Jonathan Stewart .12 .30
45 Muhsin Muhammad .12 .30
46 Steve Smith .15 .40
47 Alex Brown .12 .30
48 Brian Urlacher .20 .50
49 Desmond Clark .12 .30
50 Devin Hester .15 .40
51 Earl Bennett .15 .40
52 Greg Olsen .15 .40
53 Kyle Orton .12 .30
54 Lance Briggs .15 .40
55 Matt Forte .12 .30
56 Andre Caldwell .12 .30
57 Carson Palmer .15 .40
58 Cedric Benson .12 .30
59 Chad Ochocinco .12 .30
60 Dhani Jones .12 .30
61 Jerome Simpson .12 .30
62 Keith Rivers .12 .30
63 Reggie Kelly .12 .30
64 T.J. Houshmandzadeh .12 .30
65 Brady Quinn .12 .30
66 Braylon Edwards .12 .30
67 D'Qwell Jackson .12 .30
68 Jamal Lewis .15 .40
69 Jerome Harrison .12 .30
70 Josh Cribbs .12 .30
71 Kellen Winslow .12 .30
72 Shaun Rogers .12 .30
73 Steve Heiden .12 .30
74 DeMarcus Ware .15 .40
75 Felix Jones .12 .30
76 Jason Witten .15 .40
77 Marion Barber .15 .40
78 Patrick Crayton .12 .30
79 Roy Williams WR .12 .30
80 Tashard Choice .12 .30
81 Terrell Owens .15 .40
82 Terence Newman .12 .30
83 Tony Romo .15 .40
84 Brandon Marshall .15 .40
85 Brandon Stokley .12 .30
86 Champ Bailey .15 .40
87 Daniel Graham .12 .30
88 Eddie Royal .12 .30
89 Jay Cutler .12 .30
90 Peyton Hillis .15 .40
91 D.J. Williams .12 .30
92 Tony Scheffler .12 .30
93 Calvin Johnson .20 .50
94 Daunte Culpepper .15 .40
95 Ernie Sims .12 .30
96 Jerome Felton .12 .30
97 Jordon Dizon .12 .30
98 Kevin Smith .12 .30
99 Paris Lenon .12 .30
100 Rudi Johnson .12 .30
101 Shaun McDonald .12 .30
102 Aaron Rodgers .40 1.00
103 A.J. Hawk .12 .30
104 Brandon Jackson .15 .40
105 Donald Driver .15 .40
106 Donald Lee .12 .30
107 Greg Jennings .12 .30
108 James Jones .12 .30
109 Jermichael Finley .12 .30
110 Jordy Nelson .15 .40
111 Ryan Grant .15 .40
112 Amobi Okoye .12 .30
113 Andre Johnson .15 .40
114 Chester Pitts .12 .30
115 DeMeco Ryans .15 .40
116 Kevin Walter .15 .40
117 Kris Brown .12 .30
118 Mario Williams .15 .40
119 Matt Schaub .12 .30
120 Owen Daniels .12 .30
121 Steve Slaton .12 .30
122 Adam Vinatieri .12 .30
123 Anthony Gonzalez .12 .30
124 Dallas Clark .12 .30
125 Dominic Rhodes .12 .30
126 Dwight Freeney .12 .30
127 Joseph Addai .12 .30
128 Freddie Keiaho .12 .30
129 Mike Hart .15 .40
130 Peyton Manning .50 1.25
131 Reggie Wayne .15 .40
132 David Garrard .12 .30
133 Dennis Northcutt .12 .30
134 Derrick Harvey .12 .30
135 Josh Scobee .12 .30
136 Marcedes Lewis .12 .30
137 Mike Peterson .12 .30
138 Maurice Jones-Drew .12 .30
139 Quentin Groves .12 .30
140 Reggie Nelson .12 .30
141 Brian Williams .12 .30
142 Derrick Johnson .12 .30
143 Matt Cassel .12 .30
144 Dwayne Bowe .15 .40
145 Jamaal Charles .15 .40
146 Kolby Smith .12 .30
147 Larry Johnson .12 .30
148 Mark Bradley .12 .30
149 Tony Gonzalez .15 .40
150 Tyler Thigpen .12 .30
151 Anthony Fasano .12 .30
152 Chad Henne .15 .40
153 Chad Pennington .12 .30
154 Davone Bess .12 .30
155 Joey Porter .15 .40
156 Greg Camarillo .15 .40
157 Jake Long .12 .30
158 Ricky Williams .15 .40
159 Ronnie Brown .12 .30
160 Ted Ginn .12 .30
161 Adrian Peterson .20 .50
162 Bernard Berrian .12 .30
163 Chad Greenway .12 .30
164 Chester Taylor .12 .30
165 Erin Henderson .12 .30
166 Jared Allen .12 .30
167 John David Booty .15 .40
168 Sidney Rice .12 .30
169 Tarvaris Jackson .15 .40
170 Visanthe Shiancoe .15 .40
171 Brandon Meriweather .12 .30
172 Jerod Mayo .15 .40
173 Kevin Faulk .12 .30
174 LaMont Jordan .12 .30
175 Laurence Maroney .15 .40
176 Randy Moss .15 .40
177 Tedy Bruschi .15 .40
178 Terrence Wheatley .12 .30
179 Tom Brady .60 1.50
180 Wes Welker .15 .40
181 Adrian Arrington .12 .30
182 Devery Henderson .12 .30
183 Drew Brees .20 .50
184 Jeremy Shockey .12 .30
185 Jonathan Vilma .12 .30
186 Lance Moore .12 .30
187 Marques Colston .12 .30
188 Pierre Thomas .12 .30
189 Reggie Bush .12 .30
190 Scott Shanle .12 .30
191 Ahmad Bradshaw .12 .30
192 Antonio Pierce .12 .30
193 Brandon Jacobs .12 .30
194 Derrick Ward .12 .30
195 Domenik Hixon .12 .30
196 Eli Manning .15 .40
197 Justin Tuck .12 .30
198 Kenny Phillips .12 .30
199 Kevin Boss .12 .30
200 Steve Smith USC .15 .40
201 Calvin Pace .12 .30
202 Chansi Stuckey .12 .30
203 Dustin Keller .12 .30
204 Jerricho Cotchery .12 .30
205 Kellen Clemens .12 .30
206 Laveranues Coles .12 .30
207 Leon Washington .12 .30
208 Thomas Jones .12 .30
209 Vernon Gholston .12 .30
210 Chaz Schilens .12 .30
211 Darren McFadden .20 .50
212 JaMarcus Russell .12 .30
213 Johnnie Lee Higgins .12 .30
214 Justin Fargas .12 .30
215 Michael Bush .12 .30
216 Nnamdi Asomugha .12 .30
217 Sebastian Janikowski .12 .30
218 Zach Miller .12 .30
219 Brian Westbrook .12 .30
220 Correll Buckhalter .12 .30
221 DeSean Jackson .15 .40
222 Donovan McNabb .15 .40
223 Greg Lewis .12 .30
224 Hank Baskett .12 .30
225 Kevin Curtis .12 .30
226 Reggie Brown .12 .30
227 Stewart Bradley .12 .30
228 Ben Roethlisberger .20 .50
229 Heath Miller .12 .30
230 Hines Ward .15 .40
231 James Harrison .20 .50
232 Troy Polamalu .20 .50
233 Nate Washington .12 .30
234 Rashard Mendenhall .12 .30
235 Santonio Holmes .12 .30
236 Willie Parker .12 .30
237 Antonio Gates .15 .40
238 Chris Chambers .12 .30
239 Darren Sproles .15 .40
240 Eric Weddle .12 .30
241 Jacob Hester .12 .30
242 LaDainian Tomlinson .20 .50
243 Philip Rivers .20 .50
244 Shawne Merriman .12 .30
245 Vincent Jackson .12 .30
246 Brandon Jones .12 .30
247 Frank Gore .15 .40
248 Isaac Bruce .20 .50
249 Josh Morgan .12 .30
250 Michael Robinson .12 .30
251 Patrick Willis .15 .40
252 Reggie Smith .12 .30
253 Shaun Hill .12 .30
254 Vernon Davis .12 .30
255 Deion Branch .12 .30
256 John Carlson .15 .40
257 Julian Peterson .12 .30
258 Julius Jones .12 .30
259 Lofa Tatupu .12 .30
260 Matt Hasselbeck .12 .30
261 Nate Burleson .12 .30
262 Owen Schmitt .12 .30
263 T.J. Duckett .12 .30
264 Antonio Pittman .12 .30
265 Chris Long .15 .40
266 Donnie Avery .12 .30
267 Keenan Burton .12 .30
268 Marc Bulger .12 .30
269 Pisa Tinoisamoa .12 .30
270 Steven Jackson .12 .30
271 Torry Holt .15 .40
272 Antonio Bryant .12 .30
273 Aqib Talib .12 .30
274 Cadillac Williams .15 .40
275 Dexter Jackson .12 .30
276 Earnest Graham .12 .30
277 Gaines Adams .12 .30
278 Michael Clayton .12 .30
279 Ronde Barber .12 .30
280 Barrett Ruud .12 .30
281 Albert Haynesworth .12 .30
282 Bo Scaife .12 .30
283 Chris Johnson .12 .30
284 Justin Gage .12 .30
285 Keith Bulluck .12 .30
286 Kerry Collins .12 .30
287 LenDale White .12 .30
288 Rob Bironas .12 .30
289 Roydell Williams .12 .30
290 Vince Young .12 .30
291 Chris Cooley .12 .30
292 Chris Horton .15 .40
293 Clinton Portis .12 .30
294 Colt Brennan .15 .40
295 Devin Thomas .12 .30
296 Jason Campbell .12 .30
297 Kedric Golston .20 .50
298 Ladell Betts .12 .30
299 Malcolm Kelly .12 .30
300 Santana Moss .15 .40
301 Aaron Brown RC .40 1.00
302 Aaron Curry RC .50 1.25
303 Aaron Kelly RC .30 .75
304 Aaron Maybin RC .40 1.00
305 Alphonso Smith RC .30 .75
306 Andre Brown RC .40 1.00
307 Andre Smith RC .30 .75
308 Anthony Hill RC .30 .75
309 Arian Foster RC .75 2.00
310 Austin Collie RC .30 .75
311 B.J. Raji RC .40 1.00
312 Brandon Gibson RC .40 1.00
313 Brandon Pettigrew RC .30 .75
314 Brandon Tate RC .40 1.00
315 Brian Cushing RC .30 .75
316 Brian Hartline RC .50 1.25
317 Brian Orakpo RC .40 1.00
318 Brian Robiskie RC .30 .75
319 Brooks Foster RC .30 .75
320 Cameron Morrah RC .30 .75
321 Cedric Peerman RC .30 .75
322 Chase Coffman RC .30 .75
323 Chris Wells RC .30 .75
324 Clay Matthews RC 1.25 3.00
325 Clint Sintim RC .30 .75
326 Cornelius Ingram RC .30 .75
327 Curtis Painter RC .30 .75
328 Darius Butler RC .40 1.00
329 Darius Passmore RC .30 .75
330 Darrius Heyward-Bey RC .50 1.25
331 Davon Drew RC .30 .75
332 Demetrius Byrd RC .40 1.00
333 Deon Butler RC .30 .75
334 Derrick Williams RC .30 .75
335 Devin Moore RC .30 .75
336 Dominique Edison RC .30 .75
337 Donald Brown RC .30 .75
338 Eugene Monroe RC .30 .75
339 Everette Brown RC .30 .75
340 Gartrell Johnson RC .30 .75
341 Glen Coffee RC .30 .75
342 Graham Harrell RC .30 .75
343 Hakeem Nicks RC .40 1.00
344 Hunter Cantwell RC .30 .75
345 Jairus Byrd RC .50 1.25
346 James Casey RC .40 1.00
347 James Davis RC .30 .75
348 James Laurinaitis RC .30 .75
349 Jared Cook RC .40 1.00
350 Jarett Dillard RC .30 .75
351 Jason Smith RC .30 .75
352 Javon Ringer RC .30 .75
353 Jeremiah Johnson RC .30 .75
354 Jeremy Childs RC .30 .75
355 Jeremy Maclin RC .40 1.00
356 John Parker Wilson RC .30 .75
357 Johnny Knox RC .40 1.00
358 Josh Freeman RC .30 .75
359 Juaquin Iglesias RC .30 .75
360 Keith Null RC .40 1.00
361 Kenny Britt RC .50 1.25
362 Kenny McKinley RC .30 .75
363 Kevin Ogletree RC .40 1.00
364 Knowshon Moreno RC .30 .75
365 Kory Sheets RC .40 1.00
366 Larry English RC .40 1.00
367 LeSean McCoy RC .75 2.00
368 Louis Murphy RC .30 .75
369 Malcolm Jenkins RC .30 .75
370 Mark Sanchez RC .30 .75
371 Matthew Stafford RC 1.50 4.00
372 Michael Crabtree RC .50 1.25
373 Mike Goodson RC .40 1.00
374 Mike Thomas RC .30 .75
375 Mike Wallace RC .50 1.25
376 Mohamed Massaquoi RC .30 .75
377 Nate Davis RC .30 .75
378 Nathan Brown RC .40 1.00
379 P.J. Hill RC .30 .75
380 Pat White RC .40 1.00
381 Patrick Chung RC .30 .75
382 Patrick Turner RC .30 .75
383 Percy Harvin RC .30 .75
384 Quan Cosby RC .30 .75
385 Quinn Johnson RC .30 .75
386 Quinten Lawrence RC .30 .75
387 Ramses Barden RC .30 .75
388 Rashad Jennings RC .40 1.00
389 Rey Maualuga RC .50 1.25
390 Rhett Bomar RC .30 .75
391 Richard Quinn RC .40 1.00
392 Shawn Nelson RC .30 .75
393 Shonn Greene RC .30 .75
394 Stephen McGee RC .30 .75
395 Tom Brandstater RC .40 1.00
396 Tony Fiammetta RC .30 .75
397 Travis Beckum RC .30 .75
398 Tyrell Sutton RC .30 .75
399 Tyson Jackson RC .30 .75
400 Vontae Davis RC .30 .75

2009 Score Artist's Proof

*VETS 1-300: 12X TO 30X BASIC CARDS
*ROOKIES 301-400: 5X TO 12X BASIC CARDS
STATED PRINT RUN 32 SER.#'d SETS

2009 Score Glossy

*VETS 1-300: 1.2X TO 3X BASIC CARDS
*ROOKIES 301-400: .5X TO 1.2X BASIC CARDS
ONE GLOSSY PER SCORE PACK

2009 Score Gold Zone

*VETS 1-300: 4X TO 10X BASIC CARDS
*ROOKIES 301-400: 1.5X TO 4X BASIC CARDS
STATED PRINT RUN 249 SER.#'d SETS

2009 Score Red Zone

*VETS 1-300: 5X TO 12X BASIC CARDS
*ROOKIES 301-400: 2X TO 5X BASIC CARDS
STATED PRINT RUN 100 SER.#'d SETS

2009 Score Scorecard

*VETS 1-300: 3X TO 8X BASIC CARDS
*ROOKIES 301-400: 1.2X TO 3X BASIC CARDS
STATED PRINT RUN 299 SER.#'d SETS

2009 Score 1989 Score

*GLOSSY: .8X TO 2X BASIC INSERTS
1 Matthew Stafford 3.00 8.00
2 Mark Sanchez .60 1.50
3 Darrius Heyward-Bey 1.00 2.50
4 Michael Crabtree 1.00 2.50
5 Knowshon Moreno .60 1.50
6 Josh Freeman .60 1.50
7 Jeremy Maclin .75 2.00
8 Percy Harvin .60 1.50
9 Hakeem Nicks .75 2.00
10 Chris Wells .60 1.50

2009 Score 1989 Score Autographs

STATED PRINT RUN 20 SER.#'d SETS
1 Matthew Stafford 125.00 250.00
2 Mark Sanchez 15.00 40.00
3 Darrius Heyward-Bey 40.00 80.00
4 Michael Crabtree 15.00 40.00
5 Knowshon Moreno 12.00 30.00
6 Josh Freeman 40.00 80.00
7 Jeremy Maclin 40.00 80.00
8 Percy Harvin 12.00 30.00
9 Hakeem Nicks 30.00 60.00
10 Chris Wells 30.00 60.00

2009 Score Franchise

*ART.PROOF/32: 3X TO 8X BASIC INSERTS
*GLOSSY: .5X TO 1.2X BASIC INSERTS
*GOLD ZONE/299: 1.2X TO 3X BASIC INSERTS
*RED ZONE/100: 1.5X TO 4X BASIC INSERTS
*SCORECARD/499: .8X TO 2X BASIC INSERTS
1 Adrian Peterson .60 1.50
2 Andre Johnson .50 1.25
3 Brady Quinn .40 1.00
4 Brandon Jacobs .40 1.00
5 Brandon Marshall .50 1.25
6 Braylon Edwards .40 1.00
7 Brian Westbrook .40 1.00
8 Calvin Johnson .60 1.50
9 Clinton Portis .40 1.00
10 DeAngelo Williams .40 1.00
11 Frank Gore .50 1.25
12 Greg Jennings .40 1.00
13 Larry Fitzgerald .50 1.25
14 Lee Evans .50 1.25
15 Marion Barber .50 1.25
16 Maurice Jones-Drew .40 1.00
17 Philip Rivers .60 1.50
18 Roddy White .40 1.00
19 Santonio Holmes .40 1.00
20 Dwayne Bowe .50 1.25

2009 Score Future Franchise

*ART.PROOF/32: 2.5X TO 6X BASIC INSERTS
*GLOSSY: .5X TO 1.2X BASIC INSERTS
*GOLD ZONE/299: 1.2X TO 3X BASIC INSERTS
*RED ZONE/100: 1.5X TO 4X BASIC INSERTS
*SCORECARD/499: .8X TO 2X BASIC INSERTS
1 Brian Brohm .40 1.00
2 Chad Henne .50 1.25
3 Chris Johnson .40 1.00
4 Colt Brennan .50 1.25
5 Darren McFadden .60 1.50
6 Derrick Ward .40 1.00
7 DeSean Jackson .50 1.25
8 Eddie Royal .40 1.00
9 Erik Ainge .50 1.25
10 Joe Flacco .50 1.25
11 John David Booty .50 1.25
12 Jonathan Stewart .40 1.00
13 Kevin Smith .40 1.00
14 Matt Cassel .40 1.00
15 Matt Forte .40 1.00
16 Matt Ryan .50 1.25
17 Rashard Mendenhall .40 1.00
18 Ray Rice .40 1.00
19 Steve Slaton .40 1.00
20 Tashard Choice .40 1.00

2009 Score Hot Rookies

*ART.PROOF/32: 2.5X TO 6X BASIC INSERTS
*GLOSSY: .5X TO 1.2X BASIC INSERTS
*GOLD ZONE/299: 1X TO 2.5X BASIC INSERTS
*RED ZONE/100: 1.2X TO 3X BASIC INSERTS
*SCORECARD/499: .8X TO 2X BASIC INSERTS
1 Aaron Curry .60 1.50
2 Brandon Pettigrew .40 1.00
3 Brandon Tate .50 1.25
4 Brian Robiskie .40 1.00
5 Chris Wells .40 1.00
6 Darrius Heyward-Bey .60 1.50
7 Deon Butler .40 1.00
8 Derrick Williams .40 1.00
9 Donald Brown .40 1.00
10 Glen Coffee .40 1.00
11 Hakeem Nicks .50 1.25
12 Jeremy Maclin .50 1.25
13 Josh Freeman .40 1.00
14 Juaquin Iglesias .40 1.00
15 Kenny Britt .60 1.50
16 Knowshon Moreno .40 1.00
17 LeSean McCoy 1.00 2.50
18 Mark Sanchez .40 1.00
19 Matthew Stafford 2.00 5.00
20 Michael Crabtree .60 1.50
21 Mike Thomas .40 1.00
22 Mike Wallace .60 1.50
23 Mohamed Massaquoi .40 1.00
24 Pat White .50 1.25
25 Patrick Turner .40 1.00
26 Percy Harvin .40 1.00
27 Ramses Barden .40 1.00
28 Shonn Greene .40 1.00
29 Stephen McGee .40 1.00
30 Tyson Jackson .40 1.00

2009 Score Inscriptions Autographs Retail

RANDOM INSERTS IN SCORE PACKS
10 Chris Houston 4.00 10.00
11 Curtis Lofton 4.00 10.00
12 Harry Douglas 4.00 10.00
29 Derek Fine 4.00 10.00
30 Fred Jackson 5.00 12.00
36 Steve Johnson 8.00 20.00
38 Charles Godfrey 4.00 10.00
40 Dante Rosario 4.00 10.00
56 Andre Caldwell 4.00 10.00
58 Cedric Benson 4.00 10.00
96 Jerome Felton 4.00 10.00
103 A.J. Hawk 6.00 15.00
104 Brandon Jackson 5.00 12.00
112 Amobi Okoye 4.00 10.00

124 Dallas Clark 4.00 10.00
134 Derrick Harvey 4.00 10.00
139 Quentin Groves 4.00 10.00
165 Erin Henderson 4.00 10.00
171 Brandon Meriweather 4.00 10.00
178 Terrence Wheatley 4.00 10.00
181 Adrian Arrington 4.00 10.00
182 Devery Henderson 4.00 10.00
210 Chaz Schilens 4.00 10.00
223 Greg Lewis 4.00 10.00
262 Owen Schmitt 4.00 10.00
273 Aqib Talib 4.00 10.00
277 Gaines Adams 4.00 10.00
292 Chris Horton 5.00 12.00
303 Aaron Kelly 4.00 10.00
335 Devin Moore 4.00 10.00
363 Kevin Ogletree 5.00 12.00
365 Kory Sheets 5.00 12.00
379 P.J. Hill 4.00 10.00
384 Quan Cosby 4.00 10.00
398 Tyrell Sutton 4.00 10.00

2009 Score Young Stars

*ART.PRROF/32: 2.5X TO 6X BASIC INSERTS
*GLOSSY: .5X TO 1.2X BASIC INSERTS
*GOLD ZONE/299: 1X TO 2.5X BASIC INSERTS
*RED ZONE/100: 1.2X TO 3X BASIC INSERTS
*SCORECARD/499: .8X TO 2X BASIC INSERTS
1 Antoine Cason .50 1.25
2 Aqib Talib .50 1.25
3 Brandon Flowers .50 1.25
4 Chris Horton .60 1.50
5 Dan Connor .50 1.25
6 Davone Bess .50 1.25
7 Donnie Avery .50 1.25
8 Dustin Keller .50 1.25
9 Dwight Lowery .50 1.25
10 Felix Jones .50 1.25
11 Jerod Mayo .60 1.50
12 John Carlson .60 1.50
13 Josh Morgan .50 1.25
14 Leodis McKelvin .50 1.25
15 Le'Ron McClain .60 1.50
16 Malcolm Kelly .50 1.25
17 Martellus Bennett .50 1.25
18 Ryan Torain .50 1.25
19 Steve Johnson .60 1.50
20 Tim Hightower .50 1.25

2009 Score Atomic National Convention

COMPLETE SET (6) 8.00 20.00
*BLUE/50: .6X TO 1.5X
*GOLD/25: .8X TO 2X
*RED/50: .6X TO 1.5X
161 Adrian Peterson 1.00 2.50
323 Chris Wells .40 1.00
364 Knowshon Moreno .40 1.00
370 Mark Sanchez .40 1.00
371 Matthew Stafford 2.00 5.00
372 Michael Crabtree .60 1.50

2010 Score

COMPLETE SET (400) 25.00 50.00
COMP.FACT.HOBBY (400) 25.00 40.00
COMP.FACT.RETAIL (400) 25.00 40.00
COMP.FACT.w/JSYs (402) 35.00 50.00
1 Adrian Wilson .12 .30
2 Anquan Boldin .12 .30
3 Chris Wells .12 .30
4 Dominique Rodgers-Cromartie .12 .30
5 Karlos Dansby .12 .30
6 Larry Fitzgerald .15 .40
7 Matt Leinart .12 .30
8 Steve Breaston .12 .30
9 Tim Hightower .12 .30
10 Curtis Lofton .12 .30
11 Jason Snelling .15 .40
12 Jerious Norwood .12 .30
13 Jonathan Babineaux .12 .30
14 Matt Ryan .15 .40
15 Michael Jenkins .12 .30
16 Michael Turner .12 .30
17 Roddy White .12 .30
18 Tony Gonzalez .15 .40
19 Derrick Mason .12 .30
20 Ed Reed .15 .40
21 Joe Flacco .15 .40
22 Mark Clayton .12 .30
23 Michael Oher .15 .40
24 Ray Lewis .20 .50
25 Ray Rice .12 .30
26 Terrell Suggs .12 .30
27 Todd Heap .12 .30
28 Willis McGahee .12 .30
29 Donte Whitner .12 .30
30 Fred Jackson .15 .40
31 Jairus Byrd .15 .40
32 Josh Reed .12 .30
33 Lee Evans .15 .40
34 Marshawn Lynch .15 .40
35 Paul Posluszny .12 .30
36 Ryan Fitzpatrick .12 .30
37 Aaron Schobel .12 .30
38 Chris Gamble .12 .30
39 DeAngelo Williams .12 .30
40 Matt Moore .12 .30
41 Jon Beason .12 .30
42 Jonathan Stewart .12 .30
43 Julius Peppers .15 .40
44 Richard Marshall .12 .30
45 Muhsin Muhammad .12 .30
46 Steve Smith .15 .40
47 Brian Urlacher .20 .50
48 Devin Hester .15 .40
49 Earl Bennett .15 .40
50 Garrett Wolfe .12 .30
51 Greg Olsen .15 .40
52 Jay Cutler .12 .30
53 Johnny Knox .12 .30
54 Lance Briggs .15 .40
55 Matt Forte .12 .30
56 Andre Caldwell .12 .30
57 Bernard Scott .12 .30
58 Carson Palmer .15 .40
59 Cedric Benson .12 .30
60 Chad Ochocinco .12 .30
61 Dhani Jones .12 .30
62 Johnathan Joseph .12 .30
63 Matt Jones .12 .30
64 Leon Hall .12 .30
65 Abram Elam RC .20 .50
66 Jake Delhomme .12 .30
67 James Davis .12 .30
68 Jerome Harrison .12 .30
69 Joe Thomas .12 .30
70 Josh Cribbs .12 .30
71 Kamerion Wimbley .12 .30
72 Mike Furrey .12 .30
73 Mohamed Massaquoi .15 .40
74 Bradie James .12 .30
75 DeMarcus Ware .15 .40
76 Felix Jones .12 .30
77 Jason Witten .15 .40
78 Jay Ratliff .15 .40
79 Marion Barber .15 .40
80 Mike Jenkins .12 .30
81 Miles Austin .12 .30
82 Roy Williams WR .12 .30
83 Tony Romo .15 .40
84 Brandon Marshall .15 .40
85 Champ Bailey .15 .40
86 Brian Dawkins .12 .30
87 Eddie Royal .12 .30
88 Elvis Dumervil .12 .30
89 Jabar Gaffney .12 .30
90 Knowshon Moreno .12 .30
91 Kyle Orton .12 .30
92 Tony Scheffler .12 .30
93 Brandon Pettigrew .12 .30
94 Bryant Johnson .12 .30
95 Calvin Johnson .20 .50
96 Dennis Northcutt .12 .30
97 Julian Peterson .12 .30
98 Kevin Smith .12 .30
99 Larry Foote .12 .30
100 Louis Delmas .12 .30
101 Matthew Stafford .15 .40
102 Aaron Rodgers .40 1.00
103 A.J. Hawk .12 .30
104 Charles Woodson .20 .50
105 Donald Driver .15 .40
106 Greg Jennings .12 .30
107 James Jones .12 .30
108 Jermichael Finley .12 .30
109 Jordy Nelson .15 .40
110 Ryan Grant .15 .40
111 Clay Matthews .20 .50
112 Andre Johnson .15 .40
113 Brian Cushing .12 .30
114 DeMeco Ryans .12 .30
115 Jacoby Jones .12 .30
116 Kevin Walter .15 .40
117 Mario Williams .15 .40
118 Matt Schaub .12 .30
119 Owen Daniels .12 .30
120 Steve Slaton .12 .30
121 Bob Sanders .15 .40
122 Austin Collie .12 .30
123 Clint Session .12 .30
124 Dallas Clark .12 .30
125 Donald Brown .12 .30
126 Dwight Freeney .12 .30
127 Joseph Addai .12 .30
128 Peyton Manning .50 1.25
129 Pierre Garcon .15 .40
130 Reggie Wayne .15 .40
131 David Garrard .12 .30
132 Marcedes Lewis .12 .30
133 Maurice Jones-Drew .12 .30
134 Mike Sims-Walker .12 .30
135 Mike Thomas .15 .40
136 Rashean Mathis .12 .30
137 Aaron Kampman .15 .40
138 Torry Holt .15 .40
139 Zach Miller Jac .12 .30
140 Thomas Jones .12 .30
141 Brandon Flowers .12 .30
142 Chris Chambers .12 .30
143 Derrick Johnson .12 .30
144 Dwayne Bowe .15 .40
145 Jamaal Charles .15 .40
146 Matt Cassel .12 .30
147 Ryan Succop RC .12 .30
148 Tamba Hali .12 .30
149 Anthony Fasano .12 .30
150 Brian Hartline .15 .40
151 Chad Henne .15 .40
152 Davone Bess .12 .30
153 Greg Camarillo .12 .30
154 Chad Pennington .12 .30
155 Pat White .12 .30
156 Ricky Williams .15 .40
157 Ronnie Brown .12 .30
158 Ted Ginn .12 .30
159 Adrian Peterson .20 .50
160 Bernard Berrian .12 .30
161 Brett Favre .75 2.00
162 Cedric Griffin .12 .30
163 Chad Greenway .12 .30
164 Chester Taylor .12 .30
165 Jared Allen .12 .30
166 Percy Harvin .12 .30
167 Sidney Rice .12 .30
168 Visanthe Shiancoe .15 .40
169 Ben Watson .12 .30
170 Brandon Meriweather .12 .30
171 Vince Wilfork .12 .30
172 Julian Edelman .20 .50
173 Laurence Maroney .12 .30
174 Pierre Woods .12 .30
175 Randy Moss .15 .40
176 Tom Brady .50 1.25
177 Wes Welker .15 .40
178 Darren Sharper .12 .30
179 Devery Henderson .12 .30
180 Drew Brees .20 .50
181 Garrett Hartley RC .12 .30
182 Jeremy Shockey .12 .30
183 Marques Colston .12 .30
184 Pierre Thomas .12 .30
185 Reggie Bush .12 .30
186 Robert Meachem .12 .30
187 Jonathan Vilma .12 .30
188 Ahmad Bradshaw .12 .30
189 Brandon Jacobs .12 .30
190 Eli Manning .15 .40
191 Hakeem Nicks .12 .30
192 Kenny Phillips .12 .30
193 Kevin Boss .12 .30
194 Justin Tuck .12 .30
195 Mario Manningham .12 .30
196 Steve Smith USC .12 .30
197 Terrell Thomas .12 .30
198 Brad Smith .12 .30
199 Braylon Edwards .12 .30
200 Darrelle Revis .12 .30
201 Dustin Keller .12 .30
202 Jerricho Cotchery .12 .30
203 Leon Washington .12 .30
204 Mark Sanchez .12 .30
205 Shonn Greene .12 .30
206 Antonio Cromartie .12 .30
207 Chaz Schilens .12 .30
208 Darren McFadden .12 .30
209 Jason Campbell .12 .30
210 Bruce Gradkowski .12 .30
211 Kirk Morrison .12 .30
212 Louis Murphy .12 .30
213 Michael Bush .12 .30
214 Nnamdi Asomugha .12 .30
215 Sebastian Janikowski .12 .30
216 Zach Miller .12 .30
217 Asante Samuel .12 .30
218 Brent Celek .12 .30
219 Kevin Kolb .12 .30
220 DeSean Jackson .15 .40
221 Donovan McNabb .15 .40
222 Jeremy Maclin .12 .30
223 Leonard Weaver .12 .30
224 LeSean McCoy .20 .50
225 Michael Vick .15 .40
226 Trent Cole .12 .30
227 Ben Roethlisberger .20 .50
228 Heath Miller .12 .30
229 Hines Ward .15 .40
230 James Harrison .20 .50
231 LaMarr Woodley .12 .30
232 Lawrence Timmons .12 .30
233 Mike Wallace .12 .30
234 Rashard Mendenhall .12 .30
235 Santonio Holmes .12 .30
236 Troy Polamalu .20 .50
237 Antonio Gates .15 .40
238 Darren Sproles .15 .40
239 Eric Weddle .12 .30
240 LaDainian Tomlinson .20 .50
241 Legedu Naanee .12 .30
242 Malcom Floyd .12 .30
243 Philip Rivers .20 .50
244 Shawne Merriman .12 .30
245 Vincent Jackson .12 .30
246 Alex Smith QB .15 .40
247 Dre Bly .12 .30
248 Frank Gore .15 .40
249 Glen Coffee .12 .30
250 Josh Morgan .15 .40
251 Manny Lawson .12 .30
252 Michael Crabtree .12 .30
253 Patrick Willis .15 .40
254 Vernon Davis .12 .30
255 Aaron Curry .15 .40
256 Deion Branch .12 .30
257 John Carlson .12 .30
258 Josh Wilson .12 .30
259 Julius Jones .12 .30
260 Justin Forsett .15 .40
261 Matt Hasselbeck .12 .30
262 Nate Burleson .12 .30
263 T.J. Houshmandzadeh .12 .30
264 Brandon Gibson .12 .30
265 Craig Dahl RC .15 .40
266 Danny Amendola .20 .50
267 Donnie Avery .12 .30
268 James Butler .12 .30
269 James Laurinaitis .15 .40
270 Chris Long .12 .30
271 Leonard Little .12 .30
272 Steven Jackson .12 .30
273 Antonio Bryant .12 .30
274 Aqib Talib .12 .30
275 Barrett Ruud .12 .30
276 Cadillac Williams .12 .30
277 Derrick Ward .12 .30
278 Josh Freeman .15 .40
279 Kellen Winslow Jr. .12 .30
280 Ronde Barber .12 .30
281 Sammie Stroughter .12 .30
282 Tanard Jackson .12 .30
283 Bo Scaife .12 .30
284 Chris Johnson .12 .30
285 Cortland Finnegan .12 .30
286 Justin Gage .12 .30
287 Kenny Britt .12 .30
288 LenDale White .12 .30
289 Nate Washington .12 .30
290 Rob Bironas .12 .30
291 Vince Young .12 .30
292 Antwaan Randle El .12 .30
293 Chris Cooley .12 .30
294 Chris Horton .12 .30
295 Clinton Portis .12 .30
296 Devin Thomas .12 .30
297 London Fletcher .15 .40
298 LaRon Landry .12 .30
299 Albert Haynesworth .12 .30
300 Santana Moss .15 .40
301 Aaron Hernandez RC .30 .75
302 Andre Anderson RC .30 .75
303 Andre Dixon RC .50 1.25
304 Andre Roberts RC .40 1.00
305 Anthony Dixon RC .30 .75
306 Anthony McCoy RC .30 .75
307 Antonio Brown RC 2.50 6.00
308 Arrelious Benn RC .30 .75
309 Ben Tate RC .30 .75
310 Blair White RC .30 .75
311 Brandon Graham RC .40 1.00
312 Brandon LaFell RC .50 1.25
313 Brandon Spikes RC .30 .75
314 Bryan Bulaga RC .30 .75
315 C.J. Spiller RC .30 .75
316 Carlos Dunlap RC .30 .75
317 Carlton Mitchell RC .30 .75
318 Chad Jones RC .30 .75
319 Charles Scott RC .30 .75
320 Armanti Edwards RC .40 1.00
321 Chris Cook RC .30 .75
322 Chris McGaha RC .30 .75
323 Colt McCoy RC .40 1.00
324 Corey Wootton RC .30 .75
325 Damian Williams RC .30 .75
326 Dan LeFevour RC .30 .75
327 Tyson Alualu RC .30 .75
328 Daryl Washington RC .30 .75
329 David Gettis RC .30 .75
330 Demaryius Thomas RC .75 2.00
331 Derrick Morgan RC .30 .75
332 Devin McCourty RC .40 1.00
333 Dexter McCluster RC .40 1.00
334 Dez Bryant RC .75 2.00
335 Dezmon Briscoe RC .30 .75
336 Dominique Franks RC .30 .75
337 Earl Thomas RC .75 2.00
338 Ed Dickson RC .30 .75
339 Eric Berry RC .50 1.25
340 Eric Decker RC .40 1.00
341 Everson Griffen RC .30 .75
342 Freddie Barnes RC .30 .75
343 Garrett Graham RC .30 .75
344 Gerald McCoy RC .30 .75
345 Golden Tate RC .40 1.00
346 Jacoby Ford RC .30 .75
347 Jahvid Best RC .30 .75
348 James Starks RC .40 1.00
349 Jarrett Brown RC .30 .75
350 Jason Pierre-Paul RC .50 1.25
351 Jason Worilds RC .30 .75
352 Jeremy Williams RC .30 .75
353 Jermaine Gresham RC .30 .75
354 Jerry Hughes RC .30 .75
355 Jevan Snead RC .30 .75
356 Jimmy Clausen RC .30 .75
357 Jimmy Graham RC .75 2.00
358 Joe Haden RC .50 1.25
359 Joe McKnight RC .30 .75
360 John Skelton RC .40 1.00
361 Emmanuel Sanders RC .50 1.25
362 Jonathan Crompton RC .30 .75
363 Jonathan Dwyer RC .30 .75
364 Jordan Shipley RC .30 .75
365 Kareem Jackson RC .30 .75
366 Kyle Wilson RC .30 .75
367 LeGarrette Blount RC .60 1.50
368 Lonyae Miller RC .40 1.00
369 Marcus Easley RC .30 .75
370 Mardy Gilyard RC .30 .75
371 Mike Kafka RC .40 1.00
372 Mike Williams RC .30 .75
373 Montario Hardesty RC .30 .75
374 Morgan Burnett RC .40 1.00
375 Nate Allen RC .50 1.25
376 NaVorro Bowman RC .60 1.50
377 Ndamukong Suh RC .60 1.50
378 Pat Paschall RC .30 .75
379 Patrick Robinson RC .40 1.00
380 Perrish Cox RC .40 1.00
381 Ricky Sapp RC .30 .75
382 Riley Cooper RC .30 .75
383 Rob Gronkowski RC 1.00 2.50
384 Rolando McClain RC .30 .75
385 Russell Okung RC .30 .75
386 Ryan Mathews RC .30 .75
387 Sam Bradford RC .40 1.00
388 Sean Canfield RC .30 .75
389 Sean Lee RC .60 1.50
390 Sean Weatherspoon RC .30 .75
391 Sergio Kindle RC .30 .75
392 Seyi Ajirotutu RC .30 .75
393 Shay Hodge RC .30 .75
394 Taylor Mays RC .30 .75
395 Taylor Price RC .30 .75
396 Tim Tebow RC 1.00 2.50
397 Toby Gerhart RC .30 .75
398 Tony Pike RC .30 .75
399 Trent Williams RC .40 1.00
400 Zac Robinson RC .40 1.00

2010 Score Artist's Proof

*VETS 1-300: 12X TO 30X BASIC CARDS
*ROOKIES 301-400: 5X TO 12X BASIC CARDS
STATED PRINT RUN 32 SER.#'d SETS

2010 Score Glossy

*VETS 1-300: 1.2X TO 3X BASIC CARDS
*ROOKIES 301-400: .6X TO 1.5X BASIC CARDS
ONE PER PACK, SIX PER RACK PACK

2010 Score Gold Zone

*VETS 1-300: 3X TO 8X BASIC CARDS
*ROOKIES 301-400: 1.2X TO 3X BASIC CARDS
STATED PRINT RUN 299 SER.#'d SETS

2010 Score Red Zone

*VETS 1-300: 5X TO 12X BASIC CARDS
*ROOKIES 301-400: 1X TO 5X BASIC CARDS
STATED PRINT RUN 100 SER.#'d SETS

2010 Score Scorecard

*VETS 1-300: 2.5X TO 6X BASIC CARDS
*ROOKIES 301-400: 1X TO 2.5X BASIC CARDS
STATED PRINT RUN 499 SER.#'d SETS

2010 Score All Pro

COMPLETE SET (30) 8.00 20.00
*ARTIST PROOF/32: 3X TO 8X BASIC INSERT
*GLOSSY: .5X TO 1.2X BASIC INSERT
*GOLD ZONE/299: 1.2X TO 3X BASIC INSERT
*RED ZONE/100: 1.5X TO 4X BASIC INSERT
*SCORECARD/499: .8X TO 2X BASIC INSERT
1 Peyton Manning 1.50 4.00
2 Chris Johnson .40 1.00
3 Adrian Peterson .60 1.50
4 Leonard Weaver .40 1.00
5 Andre Johnson .50 1.25
6 Wes Welker .50 1.25
7 Dallas Clark .40 1.00
8 Jared Allen .40 1.00
9 Dwight Freeney .40 1.00
10 Jay Ratliff .50 1.25
11 Kevin Williams .40 1.00
12 Patrick Willis .50 1.25
13 Ray Lewis .60 1.50
14 Elvis Dumervil .40 1.00
15 DeMarcus Ware .50 1.25
16 Charles Woodson .60 1.50
17 Darrelle Revis .40 1.00
18 Darren Sharper .40 1.00
19 Adrian Wilson .40 1.00
20 Shane Lechler .40 1.00
21 Nate Kaeding .40 1.00
22 Josh Cribbs .40 1.00
23 Drew Brees .60 1.50
24 Ray Rice .40 1.00
25 Steven Jackson .40 1.00
26 Reggie Wayne .50 1.25
27 Larry Fitzgerald .50 1.25
28 Antonio Gates .50 1.25
29 DeSean Jackson .50 1.25
30 Brian Cushing .40 1.00

2010 Score All Pro Signatures

STATED PRINT RUN 10-25
EXCH EXPIRATION: 1/9/2012
15 DeMarcus Ware/25 15.00 40.00
17 Darrelle Revis/25 12.00 30.00
29 DeSean Jackson/15 12.00 30.00

2010 Score Franchise

COMPLETE SET (20) 8.00 20.00
*ARTIST PROOF/32: 3X TO 8X BASIC INSERT
*GLOSSY: .5X TO 1.2X BASIC INSERT
*GOLD ZONE/299: 1.2X TO 3X BASIC INSERT
*RED ZONE/100: 1.5X TO 4X BASIC INSERT
*SCORECARD/499: .8X TO 2X BASIC INSERT
1 Mark Sanchez .40 1.00
2 Matthew Stafford .50 1.25
3 Sidney Rice .40 1.00
4 Drew Brees .60 1.50
5 Michael Turner .40 1.00
6 DeAngelo Williams .40 1.00
7 LeSean McCoy .60 1.50
8 Steven Jackson .40 1.00
9 Peyton Manning 1.50 4.00
10 Jay Cutler .40 1.00
11 Chris Johnson .40 1.00
12 Miles Austin .40 1.00
13 Michael Crabtree .40 1.00
14 Aaron Rodgers 1.25 3.00
15 Josh Freeman .50 1.25
16 Knowshon Moreno .40 1.00
17 Tom Brady 1.50 4.00
18 Jamaal Charles .50 1.25
19 Chad Ochocinco .40 1.00
20 Eli Manning .50 1.25

2010 Score Franchise Signatures

STATED PRINT RUN 1-25
EXCH EXPIRATION: 1/9/2012
1 Mark Sanchez/25 30.00 60.00
13 Michael Crabtree/25 15.00 30.00
20 Eli Manning/15 40.00 80.00

2010 Score Hot Rookies

COMPLETE SET (30) 25.00 50.00
*ARTIST PROOF/32: 2.5X TO 6X BASIC INSERT
*GLOSSY: .5X TO 1.2X BASIC INSERT
*GOLD ZONE/299: 1X TO 2.5X BASIC INSERT
*RED ZONE/100: 1.2X TO 3X BASIC INSERT
*SCORECARD/499: .8X TO 2X BASIC INSERT
1 Armanti Edwards .50 1.25
2 Tim Tebow 1.25 3.00
3 Sam Bradford .50 1.25
4 Rolando McClain .40 1.00
5 Ndamukong Suh .75 2.00
6 Mardy Gilyard .40 1.00
7 Jimmy Clausen .40 1.00
8 Jahvid Best .40 1.00
9 Gerald McCoy .40 1.00
10 Eric Berry .60 1.50
11 Dexter McCluster .50 1.25
12 Damian Williams .40 1.00
13 C.J. Spiller .40 1.00
14 Ben Tate .40 1.00
15 Andre Roberts .50 1.25
16 Arrelious Benn .40 1.00
17 Brandon LaFell .60 1.50
18 Colt McCoy .50 1.25
19 Demaryius Thomas 1.00 2.50
20 Dez Bryant 1.00 2.50
21 Eric Decker .50 1.25
22 Golden Tate .50 1.25
23 Jermaine Gresham .40 1.00
24 Jordan Shipley .40 1.00
25 Montario Hardesty .40 1.00
26 Rob Gronkowski 1.25 3.00
27 Ryan Mathews .40 1.00
28 Taylor Price .40 1.00
29 Toby Gerhart .40 1.00
30 Emmanuel Sanders .60 1.50

2010 Score Hot Rookies Signatures

STATED PRINT RUN 25 SER.#'d SETS
EXCH EXPIRATION: 1/9/2012
1 Armanti Edwards 8.00 20.00
2 Tim Tebow 60.00 120.00
3 Sam Bradford 50.00 100.00
4 Rolando McClain 6.00 15.00
5 Ndamukong Suh 12.00 30.00
6 Mardy Gilyard 6.00 15.00
7 Jimmy Clausen 6.00 15.00
8 Jahvid Best 6.00 15.00
9 Gerald McCoy 6.00 15.00
10 Eric Berry 10.00 25.00
11 Dexter McCluster 8.00 20.00
12 Damian Williams 6.00 15.00
13 C.J. Spiller 6.00 15.00
14 Ben Tate 6.00 15.00
15 Andre Roberts 8.00 20.00
16 Arrelious Benn 6.00 15.00
17 Brandon LaFell 10.00 25.00
18 Colt McCoy 8.00 20.00
19 Demaryius Thomas 15.00 40.00
20 Dez Bryant 50.00 100.00
21 Eric Decker 8.00 20.00
22 Golden Tate 8.00 20.00
23 Jermaine Gresham 6.00 15.00
24 Jordan Shipley 6.00 15.00
25 Montario Hardesty 6.00 15.00
26 Rob Gronkowski 30.00 60.00
27 Ryan Mathews 6.00 15.00
28 Taylor Price 6.00 15.00
29 Toby Gerhart 6.00 15.00
30 Emmanuel Sanders 10.00 25.00

2010 Score NFL Players

COMPLETE SET (19) 8.00 20.00
*ARTIST PROOF/32: 3X TO 8X BASIC INSERT
*GLOSSY: .5X TO 1.2X BASIC INSERT
*GOLD ZONE/299: 1.2X TO 3X BASIC INSERT
*RED ZONE/100: 1.5X TO 4X BASIC INSERT
*SCORECARD/499: .8X TO 2X BASIC INSERT
1 Aaron Rodgers 1.25 3.00
2 Adrian Peterson .60 1.50
3 Andre Johnson .50 1.25
4 Ben Roethlisberger .60 1.50
5 Brandon Jacobs .40 1.00
6 Brett Favre 1.25 3.00
7 Brian Urlacher .60 1.50
8 Carson Palmer .50 1.25
9 Chad Ochocinco .40 1.00
10 Chad Pennington .40 1.00
11 Drew Brees .60 1.50
12 Jay Cutler .40 1.00
13 Larry Fitzgerald .50 1.25
14 Mark Sanchez .40 1.00
15 Matt Ryan .50 1.25
16 Peyton Manning 1.50 4.00
17 Ronde Barber .40 1.00
18 Tom Brady 1.50 4.00
19 Tony Romo .50 1.25

2010 Score NFL Players Signatures

STATED PRINT RUN 1-25
EXCH EXPIRATION: 1/9/2012
14 Mark Sanchez/25 30.00 60.00
19 Tony Romo/15 40.00 80.00

2010 Score Retail Factory Set Jerseys

ONE JSY PER RETAIL FACTORY SET
1 Michael Crabtree 2.00 5.00
2 LeSean McCoy 3.00 8.00
3 Percy Harvin 2.00 5.00
4 Chris Wells 2.00 5.00
5 Mark Sanchez 2.00 5.00
6 Shonn Greene 2.00 5.00
7 Knowshon Moreno 2.00 5.00
8 Matt Forte 2.00 5.00
9 Rashard Mendenhall 2.00 5.00
10 Chris Johnson 2.00 5.00
11 Felix Jones 2.00 5.00
12 Ray Rice 2.00 5.00
13 Sidney Rice 2.00 5.00
14 Adrian Peterson 5.00 12.00
15 Calvin Johnson 3.00 8.00
16 Maurice Jones-Drew 2.00 5.00
17 Kevin Kolb 2.00 5.00
18 Reggie Bush 2.00 5.00
19 Vernon Davis 2.00 5.00
20 DeAngelo Williams 2.00 5.00
21 Matt Ryan 2.50 6.00

2010 Score Retail Factory Set Rookie Jerseys

ONE JSY PER RETAIL FACTORY SET
1 Sam Bradford 1.25 3.00
2 Tim Tebow 3.00 8.00
3 Jimmy Clausen 1.00 2.50
4 Colt McCoy 1.25 3.00
5 Ndamukong Suh 2.00 5.00
6 Dez Bryant 2.50 6.00
7 Ryan Mathews 1.25 3.00
8 C.J. Spiller 1.00 2.50
9 Demaryius Thomas 2.50 6.00
10 Jahvid Best 1.00 2.50

2010 Score Select Factory Set Rookie Bonus

COMPLETE SET (10) 6.00 15.00
INSERTED IN SCORE FACTORY SET
1 Sam Bradford .30 .75
2 Tim Tebow .75 2.00
3 Jimmy Clausen .25 .60
4 Colt McCoy .30 .75
5 Ndamukong Suh .50 1.25
6 Dez Bryant .60 1.50
7 Ryan Mathews .25 .60
8 C.J. Spiller .25 .60
9 Demaryius Thomas .60 1.50
10 Jahvid Best .25 .60

2010 Score Signatures

EXCH EXPIRATION: 1/9/2012
3 Chris Wells 6.00 15.00
10 Curtis Lofton 4.00 10.00
12 Jerious Norwood 4.00 10.00
17 Roddy White 4.00 10.00
21 Joe Flacco
23 Michael Oher 15.00 30.00
39 DeAngelo Williams 6.00 15.00
46 Steve Smith 5.00 12.00
50 Garrett Wolfe 4.00 10.00
55 Matt Forte 6.00 15.00
57 Bernard Scott 4.00 10.00
58 Carson Palmer
64 Leon Hall 4.00 10.00
67 James Davis 4.00 10.00
80 Mike Jenkins 4.00 10.00
83 Tony Romo
87 Eddie Royal 4.00 10.00
91 Kyle Orton 4.00 10.00
93 Brandon Pettigrew 4.00 10.00
101 Matthew Stafford
103 A.J. Hawk 6.00 15.00
107 James Jones 4.00 10.00
109 Jordy Nelson 5.00 12.00
114 DeMeco Ryans 4.00 10.00
118 Matt Schaub 6.00 15.00
122 Austin Collie 6.00 15.00
129 Pierre Garcon 6.00 15.00
144 Dwayne Bowe 5.00 12.00
155 Pat White 4.00 10.00
157 Ronnie Brown 6.00 15.00
161 Brett Favre SP 75.00 150.00
164 Chester Taylor 4.00 10.00
176 Tom Brady
179 Devery Henderson 4.00 10.00
190 Eli Manning 25.00 50.00
192 Kenny Phillips 4.00 10.00
193 Kevin Boss 4.00 10.00
197 Terrell Thomas 4.00 10.00
200 Darrelle Revis 4.00 10.00
201 Dustin Keller 4.00 10.00
204 Mark Sanchez 15.00 40.00
207 Chaz Schilens 4.00 10.00
212 Louis Murphy 4.00 10.00
220 DeSean Jackson 6.00 15.00
221 Donovan McNabb
222 Jeremy Maclin 6.00 15.00
225 Michael Vick 15.00 40.00
227 Ben Roethlisberger
232 Lawrence Timmons 4.00 10.00
233 Mike Wallace 4.00 10.00
237 Antonio Gates 5.00 12.00
239 Eric Weddle 4.00 10.00
241 Legedu Naanee 4.00 10.00
245 Vincent Jackson 4.00 10.00
249 Glen Coffee 6.00 15.00
252 Michael Crabtree 12.50 25.00
258 Josh Wilson 4.00 10.00
260 Justin Forsett 5.00 12.00
291 Vince Young
294 Chris Horton 4.00 10.00
298 LaRon Landry 6.00 15.00
301 Aaron Hernandez 3.00 8.00
302 Andre Anderson 3.00 8.00
303 Andre Dixon 5.00 12.00
304 Andre Roberts 4.00 10.00
305 Anthony Dixon 3.00 8.00
306 Anthony McCoy 3.00 8.00
307 Antonio Brown 25.00 60.00
308 Arrelious Benn 3.00 8.00
309 Ben Tate 3.00 8.00
310 Blair White 3.00 8.00
311 Brandon Graham 4.00 10.00
312 Brandon LaFell 5.00 12.00
313 Brandon Spikes 3.00 8.00
314 Bryan Bulaga 3.00 8.00
315 C.J. Spiller 3.00 8.00
316 Carlos Dunlap 3.00 8.00
317 Carlton Mitchell 3.00 8.00
318 Chad Jones 3.00 8.00
319 Charles Scott 3.00 8.00
320 Armanti Edwards 4.00 10.00
321 Chris Cook 3.00 8.00
322 Chris McGaha 3.00 8.00
323 Colt McCoy 4.00 10.00
324 Corey Wootton 3.00 8.00
325 Damian Williams 3.00 8.00
326 Dan LeFevour 3.00 8.00
328 Daryl Washington No AU 1.00 2.50
329 David Gettis 3.00 8.00
330 Demaryius Thomas 8.00 20.00
331 Derrick Morgan 3.00 8.00
332 Devin McCourty 4.00 10.00
333 Dexter McCluster 4.00 10.00
334 Dez Bryant 30.00 60.00
335 Dezmon Briscoe 3.00 8.00
336 Dominique Franks 3.00 8.00
337 Earl Thomas 8.00 20.00
338 Ed Dickson 3.00 8.00
339 Eric Berry 6.00 15.00
340 Eric Decker 4.00 10.00
341 Everson Griffen 3.00 8.00
342 Freddie Barnes 3.00 8.00
343 Garrett Graham 3.00 8.00
344 Gerald McCoy 3.00 8.00
345 Golden Tate 4.00 10.00
346 Jacoby Ford 3.00 8.00
347 Jahvid Best 3.00 8.00
348 James Starks 4.00 10.00
349 Jarrett Brown 3.00 8.00
350 Jason Pierre-Paul 5.00 12.00
351 Jason Worilds 3.00 8.00
352 Jeremy Williams 3.00 8.00
353 Jermaine Gresham 3.00 8.00
354 Jerry Hughes 3.00 8.00
355 Jevan Snead 3.00 8.00
356 Jimmy Clausen 3.00 8.00
357 Jimmy Graham 15.00 30.00
358 Joe Haden 5.00 12.00
359 Joe McKnight 3.00 8.00
360 John Skelton 4.00 10.00
361 Emmanuel Sanders 5.00 12.00
362 Jonathan Crompton 3.00 8.00
363 Jonathan Dwyer 3.00 8.00
364 Jordan Shipley 3.00 8.00
365 Kareem Jackson 3.00 8.00
366 Kyle Wilson 3.00 8.00
367 LeGarrette Blount 6.00 15.00
368 Lonyae Miller 4.00 10.00
369 Marcus Easley 3.00 8.00
370 Mardy Gilyard 3.00 8.00
371 Mike Kafka 4.00 10.00
372 Mike Williams 3.00 8.00
373 Montario Hardesty 3.00 8.00
374 Morgan Burnett 4.00 10.00
375 Nate Allen 5.00 12.00
376 NaVorro Bowman 6.00 15.00
377 Ndamukong Suh 12.00 30.00
378 Pat Paschall 3.00 8.00
379 Patrick Robinson 4.00 10.00
380 Perrish Cox 4.00 10.00
381 Ricky Sapp 3.00 8.00
382 Riley Cooper 3.00 8.00
383 Rob Gronkowski 15.00 40.00
384 Rolando McClain 3.00 8.00
385 Russell Okung 3.00 8.00
386 Ryan Mathews 3.00 8.00
387 Sam Bradford 4.00 10.00
388 Sean Canfield 3.00 8.00
389 Sean Lee 6.00 15.00
390 Sean Weatherspoon 3.00 8.00
391 Sergio Kindle 3.00 8.00
392 Seyi Ajirotutu 3.00 8.00
393 Shay Hodge 3.00 8.00
394 Taylor Mays 3.00 8.00
395 Taylor Price 3.00 8.00
396 Tim Tebow 30.00 60.00
397 Toby Gerhart 3.00 8.00
398 Tony Pike 3.00 8.00
399 Trent Williams 4.00 10.00
400 Zac Robinson 4.00 10.00

2011 Score

COMP.SET w/o SP's (400) 25.00 50.00
COMP.RETAIL FACT.SET (402) 20.00 50.00
*ROOKIE VARIATION SP: 1.5X TO 4X
ONE ROOKIE PER PACK
1 Adrian Wilson .12 .30
2 Chris Wells .12 .30
3 Darnell Dockett .12 .30
4 Dominique Rodgers-Cromartie .12 .30
5 Jay Feely .12 .30
6 LaRod Stephens-Howling .12 .30
7 Larry Fitzgerald .15 .40
8 Steve Breaston .12 .30
9 Tim Hightower .12 .30
10 Brent Grimes RC .12 .30
11 Curtis Lofton .12 .30
12 Eric Weems RC .12 .30
13 Jason Snelling .12 .30
14 John Abraham .12 .30
15 Matt Ryan .15 .40
16 Michael Jenkins .12 .30
17 Michael Turner .12 .30
18 Roddy White .12 .30
19 Tony Gonzalez .15 .40
20 Anquan Boldin .12 .30
21 Derrick Mason .12 .30
22 Ed Reed .15 .40
23 Haloti Ngata .12 .30
24 Joe Flacco .15 .40
25 Michael Oher .12 .30
26 Ray Lewis .20 .50
27 Ray Rice .12 .30
28 Terrell Suggs .12 .30
29 Todd Heap .12 .30
30 C.J. Spiller .12 .30
31 Fred Jackson .12 .30
32 Jairus Byrd .12 .30
33 Kyle Williams .12 .30
34 Lee Evans .15 .40
35 Paul Posluszny .12 .30
36 Roscoe Parrish .12 .30
37 Ryan Fitzpatrick .12 .30
38 Steve Johnson .12 .30
39 Chris Gamble .12 .30
40 David Gettis .12 .30
41 DeAngelo Williams .12 .30
42 Brandon LaFell .12 .30
43 Jimmy Clausen .12 .30
44 Jon Beason .12 .30
45 Jonathan Stewart .12 .30
46 Mike Goodson .12 .30
47 Steve Smith .15 .40
48 Brian Urlacher .20 .50
49 Devin Hester .15 .40
50 Earl Bennett .12 .30
51 Greg Olsen .15 .40
52 Jay Cutler .12 .30
53 Johnny Knox .12 .30
54 Julius Peppers .15 .40
55 Lance Briggs .15 .40
56 Matt Forte .12 .30
57 Bernard Scott .12 .30
58 Carson Palmer .15 .40
59 Cedric Benson .12 .30
60 Chad Johnson .12 .30
61 Dhani Jones .12 .30
62 Jermaine Gresham .12 .30
63 Jordan Shipley .12 .30
64 Leon Hall .12 .30
65 Terrell Owens .15 .40
66 Abram Elam .12 .30
67 Ben Watson .12 .30
68 Colt McCoy .12 .30
69 Joe Haden .12 .30
70 Joe Thomas .12 .30
71 Josh Cribbs .12 .30
72 Mohamed Massaquoi .12 .30
73 Peyton Hillis .12 .30
74 T.J. Ward .12 .30
75 Bradie James .12 .30
76 DeMarcus Ware .15 .40
77 Dez Bryant .20 .50
78 Felix Jones .12 .30
79 Jason Witten .15 .40
80 Jay Ratliff .15 .40
81 Marion Barber .12 .30
82 Miles Austin .12 .30
83 Tony Romo .15 .40
84 Brandon Lloyd .12 .30
85 Champ Bailey .15 .40
86 D.J. Williams .12 .30
87 Eddie Royal .12 .30
88 Elvis Dumervil .12 .30
89 Jabar Gaffney .12 .30
90 Knowshon Moreno .12 .30
91 Kyle Orton .12 .30
92 Tim Tebow .20 .50
93 Brandon Pettigrew .12 .30
94 Calvin Johnson .20 .50
95 Jahvid Best .12 .30
96 Alphonso Smith .12 .30
97 Louis Delmas .12 .30
98 Matthew Stafford .15 .40
99 Nate Burleson .12 .30
100 Ndamukong Suh .15 .40
101 Shaun Hill .12 .30
102 A.J. Hawk .12 .30
103 Aaron Rodgers .30 .75
104 Charles Woodson .20 .50
105 Clay Matthews .20 .50
106 Donald Driver .15 .40
107 Greg Jennings .12 .30
108 James Starks .12 .30
109 Jermichael Finley .12 .30
110 Nick Collins .12 .30
111 Ryan Grant .12 .30
112 Tramon Williams .12 .30
113 Andre Johnson .15 .40
114 Arian Foster .12 .30
115 Brian Cushing .12 .30
116 DeMeco Ryans .12 .30
117 Jacoby Jones .12 .30
118 Kevin Walter .12 .30
119 Mario Williams .12 .30
120 Matt Schaub .12 .30
121 Owen Daniels .12 .30
122 Austin Collie .12 .30
123 Dallas Clark .12 .30
124 Donald Brown .12 .30
125 Dwight Freeney .12 .30
126 Jacob Tamme .12 .30
127 Joseph Addai .12 .30
128 Peyton Manning .40 1.00
129 Pierre Garcon .15 .40
130 Reggie Wayne .15 .40
131 Robert Mathis .12 .30
132 Daryl Smith .12 .30
133 David Garrard .12 .30
134 Kirk Morrison .12 .30
135 Marcedes Lewis .12 .30
136 Maurice Jones-Drew .12 .30
137 Mike Sims-Walker .15 .40
138 Mike Thomas .15 .40
139 Rashad Jennings .12 .30
140 Rashean Mathis .12 .30
141 Derrick Johnson .12 .30
142 Dexter McCluster .12 .30
143 Dwayne Bowe .15 .40
144 Eric Berry .15 .40
145 Jamaal Charles .15 .40
146 Matt Cassel .12 .30
147 Tamba Hali .12 .30
148 Thomas Jones .12 .30
149 Tony Moeaki .12 .30
150 Anthony Fasano .12 .30
151 Brandon Marshall .15 .40
152 Cameron Wake .15 .40
153 Chad Henne .15 .40
154 Davone Bess .12 .30
155 Jake Long .12 .30
156 Karlos Dansby .12 .30
157 Ricky Williams .15 .40
158 Ronnie Brown .15 .40
159 Adrian Peterson .20 .50
160 Chad Greenway .15 .40
161 E.J. Henderson .12 .30
162 Jared Allen .12 .30
163 Percy Harvin .12 .30
164 Sidney Rice .12 .30
165 Joe Webb .12 .30
166 Toby Gerhart .15 .40
167 Visanthe Shiancoe .15 .40
168 Aaron Hernandez .15 .40
169 Benjarvus Green-Ellis .12 .30
170 Brandon Tate .12 .30
171 Danny Woodhead .15 .40
172 Deion Branch .12 .30
173 Devin McCourty .12 .30
174 Jerod Mayo .12 .30
175 Rob Gronkowski .20 .50
176 Tom Brady .50 1.25
177 Wes Welker .15 .40

178 Chris Ivory .15 .40
179 Drew Brees .20 .50
180 Jimmy Graham .20 .50
181 Jonathan Vilma .12 .30
182 Lance Moore .12 .30
183 Marques Colston .12 .30
184 Reggie Bush .12 .30
185 Robert Meachem .12 .30
186 Roman Harper .12 .30
187 Tracy Porter .12 .30
188 Ahmad Bradshaw .12 .30
189 Brandon Jacobs .12 .30
190 Eli Manning .15 .40
191 Hakeem Nicks .12 .30
192 Justin Tuck .12 .30
193 Kevin Boss .12 .30
194 Mario Manningham .12 .30
195 Osi Umenyiora .12 .30
196 Steve Smith USC .12 .30
197 Terrell Thomas .12 .30
198 Brad Smith .12 .30
199 Braylon Edwards .12 .30
200 Darrelle Revis .12 .30
201 David Harris .12 .30
202 Dustin Keller .15 .40
203 Jerricho Cotchery .12 .30
204 LaDainian Tomlinson .20 .50
205 Mark Sanchez .12 .30
206 Santonio Holmes .12 .30
207 Shonn Greene .12 .30
208 Darren McFadden .12 .30
209 Jacoby Ford .15 .40
210 Jason Campbell .12 .30
211 Louis Murphy .12 .30
212 Michael Bush .12 .30
213 Michael Huff .12 .30
214 Nnamdi Asomugha .12 .30
215 Rolando McClain .12 .30
216 Tyvon Branch .12 .30
217 Zach Miller .12 .30
218 Asante Samuel .12 .30
219 Brent Celek .12 .30
220 DeSean Jackson .15 .40
221 Jeremy Maclin .12 .30
222 Kevin Kolb .12 .30
223 LeSean McCoy .20 .50
224 Michael Vick .15 .40
225 Nate Allen .12 .30
226 Trent Cole .12 .30
227 Ben Roethlisberger .20 .50
228 Brett Keisel .15 .40
229 Heath Miller .12 .30
230 Hines Ward .15 .40
231 James Harrison .15 .40
232 LaMarr Woodley .12 .30
233 Lawrence Timmons .12 .30
234 Mike Wallace .12 .30
235 Rashard Mendenhall .12 .30
236 Troy Polamalu .20 .50
237 Antoine Cason .12 .30
238 Antonio Gates .12 .30
239 Darren Sproles .15 .40
240 Malcom Floyd .12 .30
241 Mike Tolbert .12 .30
242 Philip Rivers .20 .50
243 Ryan Mathews .15 .40
244 Shaun Phillips .12 .30
245 Vincent Jackson .12 .30
246 Alex Smith QB .15 .40
247 Frank Gore .15 .40
248 Josh Morgan .12 .30
249 Justin Smith .12 .30
250 Michael Crabtree .12 .30
251 Patrick Willis .15 .40
252 Takeo Spikes .12 .30
253 Troy Smith .12 .30
254 Vernon Davis .12 .30
255 Aaron Curry .12 .30
256 Chris Clemons .12 .30
257 Earl Thomas .15 .40
258 John Carlson .12 .30
259 Justin Forsett .15 .40
260 Leon Washington .12 .30
261 Marshawn Lynch .15 .40
262 Matt Hasselbeck .12 .30
263 Mike Williams USC .12 .30
264 Brandon Gibson .12 .30
265 Chris Long .12 .30
266 Danny Amendola .15 .40
267 Donnie Avery .12 .30
268 James Hall .12 .30
269 James Laurinaitis .12 .30
270 Mark Clayton .12 .30
271 Sam Bradford .12 .30
272 Steven Jackson .12 .30
273 Arrelious Benn .12 .30
274 Barrett Ruud .12 .30
275 Cadillac Williams .12 .30
276 Gerald McCoy .12 .30
277 Josh Freeman .15 .40
278 Kellen Winslow .12 .30
279 LeGarrette Blount .15 .40
280 Mike Williams .15 .40
281 Ronde Barber .12 .30
282 Chris Johnson .12 .30
283 Cortland Finnegan .12 .30
284 Jason Babin .12 .30
285 Kenny Britt .12 .30
286 Marc Mariani .15 .40
287 Michael Griffin .12 .30
288 Nate Washington .12 .30
289 Randy Moss .15 .40
290 Stephen Tulloch .12 .30
291 Rob Bironas .12 .30
292 Anthony Armstrong .15 .40
293 Brian Orakpo .15 .40
294 Chris Cooley .12 .30
295 DeAngelo Hall .12 .30
296 Donovan McNabb .15 .40
297 Keiland Williams .12 .30
298 LaRon Landry .12 .30
299 London Fletcher .15 .40
300 Santana Moss .15 .40
301A A.J. Green RC .60 1.50
301B A.J. Green SP stnds 2.50 6.00
301C A.J. Green SP stairs 2.50 6.00
302 Aaron Williams RC .25 .60
303 Adrian Clayborn RC .25 .60
304 Ahmad Black RC .30 .75
305 Akeem Ayers RC .25 .60
306 Aldon Smith RC .25 .60
307A Alex Green RC .25 .60
307B Alex Green SP stands 1.00 2.50
308A Andy Dalton RC .50 1.25
308B A.Dalton SP stands 2.00 5.00
308C A.Dalton SP stands 2.00 5.00
309A Austin Pettis RC .25 .60
309B A.Pettis SP stands 1.00 2.50
310A Bilal Powell RC .30 .75
310B Bilal Powell SP 1.25 3.00
311A Blaine Gabbert RC .25 .60
311B B.Gabbert SP stnds 1.00 2.50
311C B.Gabbert SP stnds 1.00 2.50
312 Brandon Harris RC .25 .60
313 Brooks Reed RC .30 .75
314 Bruce Carter RC .25 .60
315A Cam Newton RC 1.25 3.00
315B Newton SP red stnds 5.00 12.00
315C C.Newton SP steps 5.00 12.00
316 Cameron Heyward RC .30 .75
317 Cameron Jordan RC .30 .75
318 Cecil Shorts RC .25 .60
319A Christian Ponder RC .25 .60
319B C.Ponder SP stands 1.00 2.50
319C C.Ponder SP standing 1.00 2.50
320A Colin Kaepernick RC .40 1.00
320B Kaepernick SP stands 1.50 4.00
320C Kaepernick SP no hash 1.50 4.00
321 Colin McCarthy RC .30 .75
322 Corey Liuget RC .25 .60
323 Curtis Brown RC .25 .60
324 D.J. Williams RC .25 .60
325A Daniel Thomas RC .25 .60
325B D.Thomas SP running 1.00 2.50
326 Da'Quan Bowers RC .25 .60
327 Davon House RC .25 .60
328A Delone Carter RC .25 .60
328B D.Carter SP stands 1.00 2.50
329A DeMarco Murray RC .50 1.25
329B D.Murray SP stands 2.00 5.00
330 Denarius Moore RC .25 .60
331 Dion Lewis RC .30 .75
332 Drake Nevis RC .25 .60
333 Dwayne Harris RC .25 .60
334A Clyde Gates RC .25 .60
334B Clyde Gates SP 1.00 2.50
335 Evan Royster RC .25 .60
336 Greg Jones RC .30 .75
337A Greg Little RC .30 .75
337B Greg Little SP 1.25 3.00
338 Greg McElroy RC .40 1.00
339 Greg Salas RC .25 .60
340 J.J. Watt RC 1.25 3.00
341 Jabaal Sheard RC .25 .60
342 Jacquizz Rodgers RC .25 .60
343A Jake Locker RC .25 .60
343B Locker SP both hnds 1.00 2.50
343C J.Locker SP stands 1.00 2.50
344A Jamie Harper RC .25 .60
344B Jamie Harper SP 1.00 2.50
345 Jeremy Kerley RC .40 1.00
346A Jerrel Jernigan RC .25 .60
346B Jerrel Jernigan SP 1.00 2.50
347 Jimmy Smith RC .25 .60
348A Jonathan Baldwin RC .25 .60
348B Jonathan Baldwin SP 1.00 2.50
349 Jordan Cameron RC .30 .75
350A Jordan Todman RC .25 .60
350B J.Todman SP cutting 1.00 2.50
351A Julio Jones RC .75 2.00
351B J.Jones SP stnds left 3.00 8.00
351C J.Jones SP stnds rght 3.00 8.00
352 Justin Houston RC .30 .75
353 Kealoha Pilares RC .25 .60
354A Kendall Hunter RC .25 .60
354B K.Hunter SP down 1.00 2.50
355 Kris Durham RC .25 .60
356A Kyle Rudolph RC .25 .60
356B Kyle Rudolph SP 1.00 2.50
356C K.Rudolph SP stands 1.00 2.50
357 Lance Kendricks RC .25 .60
358A Leonard Hankerson RC .25 .60
358B Leonard Hankerson SP 1.00 2.50
359 Luke Stocker RC .25 .60
360A Marcell Dareus RC .25 .60
360B M.Dareus SP field 1.00 2.50
361A Mark Ingram RC .40 1.00
361B Ingram SP dark stnds 1.50 4.00
361C M.Ingram SP red stnd 1.50 4.00
362 Martez Wilson RC .25 .60
363 Mike Pouncey RC .40 1.00
364A Mikel Leshoure RC .25 .60
364B M.Leshoure SP field 1.00 2.50
364C M.Leshoure SP stnds 1.00 2.50
365 Muhammad Wilkerson RC .25 .60
366 Nate Solder RC .25 .60
367 Nathan Enderle RC .25 .60
368 Nick Fairley RC .25 .60
369 Niles Paul RC .25 .60
370 Owen Marecic RC .25 .60
371 Patrick Peterson RC .50 1.25
372 Phil Taylor RC .25 .60
373 Prince Amukamara RC .25 .60
374 Quan Sturdivant RC .30 .75
375 Quinton Carter RC .25 .60
376 Rahim Moore RC .25 .60
377A Randall Cobb RC .40 1.00
377B R.Cobb SP left 1.50 4.00
377C R.Cobb SP side 1.50 4.00
378 Ras-I Dowling RC .25 .60
379 Ricky Stanzi RC .25 .60
380 Robert Housler RC .25 .60
381 Robert Quinn RC .25 .60
382 Ronald Johnson RC .25 .60
383 Roy Helu RC .25 .60
384 Ryan Kerrigan RC .30 .75
385A Ryan Mallett RC .25 .60
385B Mallett SP red stnds 1.00 2.50
385C R.Mallett SP field 1.00 2.50
386 Ryan Whalen RC .25 .60
387A Ryan Williams RC .25 .60
387B Ryan Williams SP 1.00 2.50
388A Shane Vereen RC .30 .75
388B S.Vereen SP left 1.25 3.00
389 Stanley Havili RC .25 .60
390 Stephen Paea RC .25 .60
391A Stevan Ridley RC .25 .60
391B S.Ridley SP both 1.00 2.50
392 T.J. Yates RC .25 .60
393A Taiwan Jones RC .25 .60
393B Taiwan Jones SP 1.00 2.50
394 Tandon Doss RC .25 .60
395A Titus Young RC .25 .60
395B T.Young SP right 1.00 2.50
396A Torrey Smith RC .25 .60
396B T.Smith SP right 1.00 2.50
397 Tyler Sash RC .25 .60
398 Tyron Smith RC .30 .75
399A Vincent Brown RC .25 .60
399B V.Brown SP both 1.00 2.50
400A Von Miller RC .40 1.00
400B Von Miller SP stnds 1.50 4.00
400C Von Miller SP left 1.50 4.00

2011 Score Artist's Proof

*VETS 1-300: 10X TO 25X BASIC CARDS
*ROOKIES 301-400: 5X TO 12X BASIC CARDS
RANDOM INSERTS IN PACKS

2011 Score End Zone

NOT PRICED DUE TO SCARCITY

2011 Score Factory Set Updates

*FACT.SET: .4X TO 1X BASIC CARDS

2011 Score Glossy

*VETS 1-300: 1X TO 2.5X BASIC CARDS
*ROOKIES 301-400: .6X TO 1.5X BASIC CARDS
ONE GLOSSY PER PACK

2011 Score Gold Zone

*VETS 1-300: 3X TO 8X BASIC CARDS
*ROOKIES 301-400: 1.5X TO 4X BASIC CARDS
RANDOM INSERTS IN PACKS

2011 Score Red Zone

*VETS 1-300: 4X TO 10X BASIC CARDS
*ROOKIES 301-400: 2X TO 5X BASIC CARDS
RANDOM INSERTS IN PACKS

2011 Score Scorecard

*VETS 1-300: 2.5X TO 6X BASIC CARDS
*ROOKIES 301-400: 1.2X TO 3X BASIC CARDS
RANDOM INSERTS IN PACKS

2011 Score Complete Players

COMPLETE SET (20) 5.00 12.00
*ARTIST PROOF: 4X TO 10X BASIC INSERT
*GLOSSY: .6X TO 1.5X BASIC INSERT
*GOLD ZONE: 1.5X TO 4X BASIC INSERT
*RED ZONE: 2X TO 5X BASIC INSERT
*SCORECARD: 1X TO 2.5X BASIC INSERT
END ZONE TOO SCARCE TO PRICE
SIGNATURES TOO SCARCE TO PRICE
1 Carson Palmer .40 1.00
2 Clay Matthews .50 1.25
3 Dallas Clark .30 .75
4 Darrelle Revis .30 .75
5 David Harris .30 .75
6 DeAngelo Williams .30 .75
7 DeSean Jackson .40 1.00
8 Devin Hester .40 1.00
9 Felix Jones .30 .75
10 Jason Witten .40 1.00
11 Knowshon Moreno .30 .75
12 Michael Turner .30 .75
13 Michael Vick .40 1.00
14 Patrick Willis .40 1.00
15 Reggie Bush .30 .75
16 Reggie Wayne .40 1.00
17 Tim Tebow .50 1.25
18 Vernon Davis .30 .75
19 Visanthe Shiancoe .40 1.00
20 Wes Welker .40 1.00

2011 Score Retail Factory Set Jerseys Prime

TWO PER RETAIL FACTORY SET
CM Colt McCoy 2.00 5.00
CS C.J. Spiller 2.00 5.00
DJ DeSean Jackson 2.50 6.00
JF Josh Freeman 2.50 6.00
JF Joe Flacco 2.50 6.00
JM Jeremy Maclin 2.00 5.00
MS Mark Sanchez 2.00 5.00
NS Ndamukong Suh 2.50 6.00
RG Rob Gronkowski 3.00 8.00
RM Rashard Mendenhall 2.00 5.00
RM Ryan Mathews 2.50 6.00
RR Ray Rice 2.00 5.00
SB Sam Bradford 2.00 5.00
TT Tim Tebow 3.00 8.00

2011 Score Retail Factory Set Packers Super Bowl Bonus

ONE PER SPECIAL RETAIL FACT.SET
SBCM Clay Matthews Prime 4.00 10.00
SBJN Jordy Nelson Prime 4.00 10.00
SBAR1 Aaron Rodgers SB patch 5.00 12.00
SBAR2 Aaron Rodgers MVP patch 5.00 12.00

2011 Score Retail Factory Set Rookie Jerseys

TWO PER RETAIL FACTORY SET
AD Andy Dalton 1.50 4.00
AG A.J. Green 2.00 5.00
BG Blaine Gabbert 2.50 6.00
CN Cam Newton 4.00 10.00
CP Christian Ponder .75 2.00
DM DeMarco Murray 1.50 4.00
DT Daniel Thomas 2.00 5.00
JJ Julio Jones 2.50 6.00
JL Jake Locker .75 2.00
MI Mark Ingram 1.25 3.00
RM Ryan Mallett .75 2.00
VM Von Miller 2.00 5.00

2011 Score Hot Rookies

COMPLETE SET (30) 10.00 25.00
*ARTIST PROOF: 3X TO 8X BASIC INSERT
*GLOSSY: .6X TO 1.5X BASIC INSERT
*GOLD ZONE: 1.2X TO 3X BASIC INSERT
*RED ZONE: 1.5X TO 4X BASIC INSERT
*SCORECARD: 1X TO 2.5X BASIC INSERT
END ZONE TOO SCARCE TO PRICE
1 A.J. Green .60 1.50
2 Alex Green .25 .60
3 Andy Dalton .50 1.25
4 Austin Pettis .25 .60
5 Blaine Gabbert .25 .60
6 Cam Newton 1.25 3.00
7 Christian Ponder .25 .60
8 Colin Kaepernick .40 1.00
9 Daniel Thomas .25 .60
10 Delone Carter .25 .60
11 DeMarco Murray .50 1.25
12 Greg Little .30 .75
13 Jake Locker .25 .60
14 Jamie Harper .25 .60
15 Jerrel Jernigan .25 .60
16 Jonathan Baldwin .25 .60
17 Julio Jones .75 2.00
18 Kyle Rudolph .25 .60
19 Leonard Hankerson .25 .60
20 Mark Ingram .40 1.00
21 Mikel LeShoure .25 .60
22 Randall Cobb .40 1.00
23 Ryan Mallett .25 .60
24 Ryan Williams .25 .60
25 Shane Vereen .30 .75
26 Taiwan Jones .25 .60
27 Titus Young .25 .60
28 Torrey Smith .25 .60
29 Vincent Brown .25 .60
30 Von Miller .40 1.00

2011 Score Hot Rookies Signatures

RANDOM INSERTS IN PACKS
1 A.J. Green 20.00 50.00
2 Alex Green
3 Andy Dalton
4 Austin Pettis
5 Blaine Gabbert
6 Cam Newton 75.00 150.00
7 Christian Ponder
8 Colin Kaepernick
9 Daniel Thomas
10 Delone Carter
11 DeMarco Murray 40.00 80.00
12 Greg Little
13 Jake Locker 8.00 20.00
14 Jamie Harper
15 Jerrel Jernigan
16 Jonathan Baldwin
17 Julio Jones 20.00 50.00
18 Kyle Rudolph
19 Leonard Hankerson
20 Mark Ingram
21 Mikel Leshoure
22 Randall Cobb 12.00 30.00
23 Ryan Mallett
24 Ryan Williams
25 Shane Vereen
26 Taiwan Jones
27 Titus Young
28 Torrey Smith 8.00 20.00
30 Von Miller

2011 Score In the Zone

COMPLETE SET (30) 6.00 15.00
*ARTIST PROOF: 4X TO 10X BASIC INSERT
*GLOSSY: .6X TO 1.5X BASIC INSERT
*GOLD ZONE: 1.5X TO 4X BASIC INSERT
*RED ZONE: 2X TO 5X BASIC INSERT
*SCORECARD: 1X TO 2.5X BASIC INSERT
END ZONE TOO SCARCE TO PRICE
SIGNATURES TOO SCARCE TO PRICE
1 Andre Johnson .40 1.00
2 Arian Foster .30 .75
3 Braylon Edwards .30 .75
4 Calvin Johnson .50 1.25
5 Chad Johnson .30 .75
6 Darren McFadden .30 .75
7 DeMarcus Ware .40 1.00
8 Dwayne Bowe .40 1.00
9 Frank Gore .40 1.00
10 Greg Jennings .30 .75
11 Jamaal Charles .40 1.00
12 Jared Allen .30 .75
13 Jeremy Maclin .30 .75
14 Joe Flacco .40 1.00
15 Josh Freeman .40 1.00
16 Mark Sanchez .30 .75
17 Matt Cassel .30 .75
18 Matt Ryan .40 1.00
19 Matt Schaub .30 .75
20 Mike Wallace .30 .75
21 Miles Austin .30 .75
22 Ndamukong Suh .40 1.00
23 Percy Harvin .30 .75
24 Philip Rivers .50 1.25
25 Rashard Mendenhall .30 .75
26 Roddy White .30 .75
27 Sam Bradford .30 .75
28 Shonn Greene .30 .75
29 Steve Smith .40 1.00
30 Tony Romo .40 1.00

2011 Score Millennium Men

COMPLETE SET (20) 6.00 15.00
*ARTIST PROOF: 4X TO 10X BASIC INSERT
*GLOSSY: .6X TO 1.5X BASIC INSERT
*GOLD ZONE: 1.5X TO 4X BASIC INSERT
*RED ZONE: 2X TO 5X BASIC INSERT
*SCORECARD: 1X TO 2.5X BASIC INSERT
END ZONE TOO SCARCE TO PRICE
SIGNATURES TOO SCARCE TO PRICE
1 Aaron Rodgers .75 2.00
2 Adrian Peterson .50 1.25
3 Antonio Gates .30 .75
4 Ben Roethlisberger .50 1.25
5 Brian Urlacher .50 1.25
6 Chris Johnson .30 .75
7 Donovan McNabb .40 1.00
8 Drew Brees .50 1.25
9 Eli Manning .40 1.00
10 Hines Ward .40 1.00
11 LaDainian Tomlinson .50 1.25
12 Larry Fitzgerald .40 1.00
13 Maurice Jones-Drew .30 .75
14 Peyton Manning 1.00 2.50
15 Randy Moss .40 1.00
16 Ray Lewis .50 1.25
17 Steven Jackson .30 .75
18 Tom Brady 1.25 3.00
19 Tony Gonzalez .40 1.00
20 Troy Polamalu .50 1.25

2011 Score Millennium Men Signatures

RANDOM INSERTS IN PACKS
10 Hines Ward 40.00 80.00
14 Peyton Manning 60.00 120.00
17 Steven Jackson
19 Tony Gonzalez 20.00 40.00

2011 Score Panini Authentic Autograph

320A Colin Kaepernick field 20.00 50.00
320B Colin Kaepernick stands 20.00 50.00

2011 Score Signatures

RANDOM INSERTS IN PACKS
20 Anquan Boldin 5.00 12.00
30 C.J. Spiller 8.00 20.00
42 Brandon LaFell 5.00 12.00
43 Jimmy Clausen 8.00 20.00
45 Jonathan Stewart 5.00 12.00
68 Colt McCoy 8.00 20.00
71 Josh Cribbs 5.00 12.00
77 Dez Bryant 12.00 30.00
91 Kyle Orton 5.00 12.00
93 Brandon Pettigrew 5.00 12.00
102 A.J. Hawk 5.00 12.00
111 Ryan Grant 8.00 20.00
116 DeMeco Ryans 5.00 12.00
124 Donald Brown 5.00 12.00
126 Jacob Tamme 5.00 12.00
128 Peyton Manning
142 Dexter McCluster 5.00 12.00
144 Eric Berry 8.00 20.00
149 Tony Moeaki 5.00 12.00
155 Jake Long 5.00 12.00
163 Percy Harvin 8.00 20.00
164 Sidney Rice 8.00 20.00
166 Toby Gerhart 6.00 15.00
193 Kevin Boss 5.00 12.00
200 Darrelle Revis 8.00 20.00
201 David Harris 5.00 12.00
205 Mark Sanchez
206 Santonio Holmes 8.00 20.00
207 Shonn Greene 8.00 20.00
215 Rolando McClain 5.00 12.00
216 Tyvon Branch 5.00 12.00
221 Jeremy Maclin 5.00 12.00
222 Kevin Kolb 5.00 12.00
229 Heath Miller 5.00 12.00
230 Hines Ward
237 Antoine Cason 5.00 12.00
241 Mike Tolbert 8.00 20.00
243 Ryan Mathews 8.00 20.00
245 Vincent Jackson 5.00 12.00
253 Troy Smith 5.00 12.00
260 Leon Washington 5.00 12.00
272 Steven Jackson 5.00 12.00
285 Kenny Britt 5.00 12.00
287 Michael Griffin 5.00 12.00
293 Brian Orakpo 6.00 15.00
301 A.J. Green 25.00 50.00
302 Aaron Williams 3.00 8.00
303 Adrian Clayborn 8.00 20.00
304 Ahmad Black 4.00 10.00
305 Akeem Ayers 3.00 8.00
306 Aldon Smith 8.00 20.00
307 Alex Green 8.00 20.00
308 Andy Dalton 15.00 40.00
309 Austin Pettis 3.00 8.00
310 Bilal Powell 5.00 12.00
311 Blaine Gabbert 3.00 8.00
312 Brandon Harris 3.00 8.00
315 Cam Newton 60.00 120.00
316 Cameron Heyward 4.00 10.00
317 Cameron Jordan 4.00 10.00
318 Cecil Shorts 3.00 8.00
319 Christian Ponder 3.00 8.00
320 Colin Kaepernick 5.00 12.00
322 Corey Liuget 3.00 8.00
324 D.J. Williams 3.00 8.00
325 Daniel Thomas 3.00 8.00
326 Da'Quan Bowers 8.00 20.00
328 Delone Carter 3.00 8.00
329 DeMarco Murray 20.00 50.00
331 Dion Lewis 4.00 10.00
333 Dwayne Harris 3.00 8.00
334 Clyde Gates 6.00 15.00
335 Evan Royster 3.00 8.00
336 Greg Jones 4.00 10.00
337 Greg Little 4.00 10.00
339 Greg Salas 8.00 20.00
340 J.J. Watt 40.00 80.00
342 Jacquizz Rodgers 3.00 8.00
343 Jake Locker 3.00 8.00
344 Jamie Harper 3.00 8.00
345 Jeremy Kerley 5.00 12.00
346 Jerrel Jernigan 3.00 8.00
347 Jimmy Smith 3.00 8.00
348 Jonathan Baldwin 8.00 20.00
350 Jordan Todman 3.00 8.00
351 Julio Jones 25.00 60.00
354 Kendall Hunter 6.00 15.00
356 Kyle Rudolph 3.00 8.00
357 Lance Kendricks 3.00 8.00
358 Leonard Hankerson 3.00 8.00
359 Luke Stocker 3.00 8.00
360 Marcell Dareus 3.00 8.00
361 Mark Ingram 5.00 12.00
362 Martez Wilson 3.00 8.00
364 Mikel Leshoure 8.00 20.00
369 Niles Paul 3.00 8.00
373 Prince Amukamara 8.00 20.00
375 Quinton Carter 5.00 12.00
377 Randall Cobb 8.00 20.00
379 Ricky Stanzi 3.00 8.00
382 Ronald Johnson 3.00 8.00
384 Ryan Kerrigan 4.00 10.00
385 Ryan Mallett 10.00 25.00
387 Ryan Williams 20.00 50.00
388 Shane Vereen 4.00 10.00
389 Stanley Havili 3.00 8.00
390 Stephen Paea 3.00 8.00
391 Stevan Ridley 3.00 8.00
393 Taiwan Jones 6.00 15.00
394 Tandon Doss 6.00 15.00
395 Titus Young 3.00 8.00
396 Torrey Smith 3.00 8.00
397 Tyler Sash 3.00 8.00
400 Von Miller 8.00 20.00

2012 Score

COMP.SET w/o SPs (400) 20.00 50.00
*ROOKIE VARIATION SP: 1.5 TO 4X RC
1 Aaron Rodgers .30 .75
2 A.J. Hawk .12 .30
3 Charles Woodson .20 .50
4 Clay Matthews .20 .50
5 Desmond Bishop .12 .30
6 Greg Jennings .12 .30
7 James Starks .12 .30
8 Jermichael Finley .12 .30
9 Jordy Nelson .15 .40
10 Ryan Grant .12 .30
11 Aldon Smith .12 .30
12 Alex Smith QB .15 .40
13 Mario Williams .12 .30
14 Frank Gore .15 .40
15 Kendall Hunter .15 .40
16 Michael Crabtree .12 .30
17 NaVorro Bowman .15 .40
18 Patrick Willis .15 .40
19 Ted Ginn Jr. .12 .30
20 Vernon Davis .12 .30
21 Darren Sproles .15 .40
22 Drew Brees .20 .50
23 Jimmy Graham .20 .50
24 Jonathan Vilma .12 .30
25 Lance Moore .12 .30
26 Mark Ingram .15 .40
27 Marques Colston .12 .30
28 Pierre Thomas .12 .30
29 Robert Meachem .12 .30
30 Roman Harper .12 .30
31 Ahmad Bradshaw .12 .30
32 Antrel Rolle .12 .30
33 Brandon Jacobs .12 .30
34 Eli Manning .15 .40
35 Hakeem Nicks .12 .30
36 Jason Pierre-Paul .12 .30
37 Justin Tuck .12 .30
38 Mathias Kiwanuka .12 .30
39 Michael Boley .12 .30
40 Victor Cruz .15 .40
41 Curtis Lofton .12 .30
42 Harry Douglas .12 .30
43 Jacquizz Rodgers .15 .40
44 John Abraham .12 .30
45 Julio Jones .20 .50
46 Matt Ryan .15 .40
47 Michael Turner .12 .30
48 Roddy White .12 .30
49 Sean Weatherspoon .12 .30
50 Tony Gonzalez .15 .40
51 Brandon Pettigrew .12 .30
52 Calvin Johnson .20 .50
53 Sheldon Brown .12 .30
54 Jahvid Best .12 .30
55 Kevin Smith .12 .30
56 Matthew Stafford .15 .40
57 Nate Burleson .12 .30
58 Ndamukong Suh .15 .40
59 Stephen Tulloch .12 .30
60 Titus Young .12 .30
61 Brian Urlacher .20 .50
62 Devin Hester .15 .40
63 Jay Cutler .12 .30
64 Johnny Knox .12 .30
65 Julius Peppers .15 .40
66 Lance Briggs .15 .40
67 Kellen Davis .12 .30
68 Matt Forte .12 .30
69 Roy Williams .12 .30
70 Andre Roberts .15 .40
71 Beanie Wells .12 .30
72 Daryl Washington .12 .30
73 Early Doucet III .12 .30
74 Kevin Kolb .12 .30
75 LaRod Stephens-Howling .12 .30
76 Larry Fitzgerald .15 .40
77 Paris Lenon .12 .30
78 Patrick Peterson .12 .30
79 Asante Samuel .15 .40
80 Brent Celek .12 .30
81 DeSean Jackson .15 .40
82 Michael Huff .12 .30
83 Jason Babin .12 .30
84 Jeremy Maclin .12 .30
85 LeSean McCoy .20 .50
86 Michael Vick .15 .40
87 Nnamdi Asomugha .12 .30
88 DeMarco Murray .15 .40
89 DeMarcus Ware .20 .50
90 Dez Bryant .20 .50
91 Felix Jones .12 .30
92 Jason Witten .15 .40
93 Laurent Robinson .12 .30
94 Miles Austin .12 .30
95 Sean Lee .20 .50
96 Tony Romo .15 .40
97 Terrelle Pryor .15 .40
98 David Hawthorne .12 .30
99 Doug Baldwin .20 .50
100 Aaron Curry .12 .30
101 Golden Tate .12 .30
102 Leon Washington .12 .30
103 Marshawn Lynch .15 .40
104 Sidney Rice .12 .30
105 Tarvaris Jackson .12 .30
106 Brandon LaFell .12 .30
107 Cam Newton .20 .50
108 Charles Johnson .12 .30
109 DeAngelo Williams .12 .30
110 Greg Olsen .15 .40
111 James Anderson .12 .30
112 Jon Beason .12 .30
113 Jonathan Stewart .12 .30
114 Steve Smith WR .15 .40
115 DeAngelo Hall .12 .30
116 Fred Davis .12 .30
117 Jabar Gaffney .12 .30
118 London Fletcher .15 .40
119 Rex Grossman .12 .30
120 Roy Helu Jr. .12 .30
121 Ryan Kerrigan .12 .30
122 Santana Moss .15 .40
123 Tim Hightower .12 .30
124 Adrian Clayborn .12 .30
125 Dezmon Briscoe .12 .30
126 Josh Freeman .15 .40
127 Kellen Winslow Jr. .12 .30
128 LeGarrette Blount .15 .40
129 Mike Williams .15 .40
130 Preston Parker .12 .30
131 Ronde Barber .12 .30
132 Chris Canty .12 .30
133 Adrian Peterson .20 .50
134 Chad Greenway .15 .40
135 Christian Ponder .12 .30
136 E.J. Henderson .12 .30
137 Jared Allen .12 .30
138 Michael Jenkins .12 .30
139 Percy Harvin .12 .30
140 Toby Gerhart .12 .30
141 Visanthe Shiancoe .12 .30
142 Brandon Gibson .12 .30
143 Brandon Lloyd .12 .30
144 Chris Long .12 .30
145 Danario Alexander .12 .30
146 James Laurinaitis .12 .30
147 Lance Kendricks .12 .30
148 Eddie Royal .12 .30
149 Sam Bradford .12 .30
150 Steven Jackson .12 .30
151 Aaron Hernandez .15 .40
152 BenJarvus Green-Ellis .15 .40
153 Deion Branch .12 .30
154 Jerod Mayo .12 .30
155 Shaun Phillips .12 .30
156 Rob Gronkowski .20 .50
157 Stevan Ridley .12 .30
158 Tom Brady .50 1.25
159 Wes Welker .15 .40
160 Anquan Boldin .12 .30
161 Ed Reed .15 .40
162 Haloti Ngata .12 .30
163 Joe Flacco .15 .40
164 Ray Lewis .20 .50
165 Ray Rice .12 .30
166 Ricky Williams .15 .40
167 Terrell Suggs .12 .30
168 Torrey Smith .12 .30
169 Andre Johnson .15 .40
170 Arian Foster .15 .40
171 Ben Tate .12 .30
172 Brian Cushing .12 .30
173 Brandon Carr .12 .30
174 DeMeco Ryans .12 .30
175 Kevin Walter .12 .30
176 Matt Schaub .12 .30
177 Owen Daniels .12 .30
178 Elvis Dumervil .12 .30
179 Champ Bailey .15 .40
180 Jay Ratliff .15 .40
181 Demaryius Thomas .20 .50
182 Eric Decker .12 .30
183 Knowshon Moreno .12 .30
184 Tim Tebow .20 .50
185 Von Miller .15 .40
186 Wesley Woodyard .12 .30
187 Willis McGahee .12 .30
188 Antonio Brown .20 .50
189 Ben Roethlisberger .20 .50
190 Heath Miller .12 .30
191 LaMarr Woodley .12 .30
192 James Harrison .15 .40
193 Lawrence Timmons .12 .30
194 Mike Wallace .12 .30
195 Rashard Mendenhall .12 .30
196 Ryan Clark .12 .30
197 Troy Polamalu .20 .50
198 A.J. Green .20 .50
199 Andre Caldwell .12 .30
200 Andy Dalton .15 .40
201 Brent Grimes .12 .30
202 Jermaine Gresham .12 .30
203 Jerome Simpson .12 .30
204 Lofa Tatupu .12 .30
205 Rey Maualuga .12 .30
206 Devery Henderson .12 .30
207 Chris Johnson .12 .30
208 Damian Williams .12 .30
209 Jake Locker .20 .50
210 Jared Cook .12 .30
211 Jason McCourty RC .20 .50
212 Jordan Babineaux .12 .30
213 Kenny Britt .12 .30
214 Matt Hasselbeck .12 .30
215 Nate Washington .12 .30
216 Darrelle Revis .12 .30
217 David Harris .12 .30
218 Dustin Keller .12 .30
219 Darnell Dockett .12 .30
220 LaDainian Tomlinson .20 .50
221 Mark Sanchez .12 .30
222 Plaxico Burress .12 .30
223 Santonio Holmes .12 .30
224 Shonn Greene .12 .30
225 Antonio Gates .15 .40
226 Antwan Barnes .12 .30
227 Eric Weddle .12 .30
228 Malcom Floyd .12 .30
229 Mike Tolbert .12 .30
230 Philip Rivers .20 .50
231 Ryan Mathews .15 .40
232 Takeo Spikes .12 .30
233 Vincent Jackson .12 .30
234 Carson Palmer .15 .40
235 Darren McFadden .12 .30
236 Darrius Heyward-Bey .12 .30
237 Denarius Moore .12 .30
238 Jacoby Ford .12 .30
239 Kamerion Wimbley .12 .30
240 Louis Murphy .12 .30
241 Michael Bush .12 .30
242 Rolando McClain .12 .30
243 Tyvon Branch .12 .30
244 Derrick Johnson .12 .30
245 Dexter McCluster .12 .30
246 Dwayne Bowe .15 .40
247 Jackie Battle .12 .30
248 Jamaal Charles .15 .40
249 Matt Cassel .12 .30
250 Steve Breaston .12 .30
251 Tamba Hali .12 .30
252 Thomas Jones .12 .30
253 Tony Moeaki .12 .30
254 Anthony Fasano .12 .30
255 Brandon Marshall .15 .40
256 Brian Hartline .15 .40
257 Cameron Wake .15 .40
258 Daniel Thomas .12 .30
259 Davone Bess .12 .30
260 Karlos Dansby .12 .30
261 Matt Moore .12 .30
262 Reggie Bush .12 .30
263 Yeremiah Bell .12 .30
264 C.J. Spiller .12 .30
265 David Nelson .12 .30
266 Fred Jackson .15 .40
267 George Wilson .12 .30
268 Marcell Dareus .12 .30
269 Nick Barnett .12 .30
270 Ryan Fitzpatrick .12 .30
271 Scott Chandler .12 .30
272 Steve Johnson .15 .40
273 Blaine Gabbert .12 .30
274 Daryl Smith .12 .30
275 Dawan Landry .12 .30
276 Jason Hill .12 .30
277 Jeremy Mincey .12 .30
278 Marcedes Lewis .12 .30
279 Maurice Jones-Drew .12 .30
280 Mike Thomas .15 .40
281 Paul Posluszny .12 .30
282 Ben Watson .12 .30
283 Colt McCoy .15 .40
284 D'Qwell Jackson .12 .30
285 Greg Little .12 .30
286 Jabaal Sheard .12 .30
287 Josh Cribbs .12 .30
288 Mohamed Massaquoi .12 .30
289 Montario Hardesty .12 .30
290 Peyton Hillis .12 .30
291 Antoine Bethea .12 .30
292 Austin Collie .12 .30
293 Dallas Clark .12 .30
294 Donald Brown .12 .30
295 Joseph Addai .12 .30
296 Pat Angerer .12 .30
297 Peyton Manning .40 1.00
298 Pierre Garcon .15 .40
299 Reggie Wayne .15 .40
300 Robert Mathis .12 .30
301A A.J. Jenkins RC .25 .60
301B A.J. Jenkins SP catch helmut 1.00 2.50
302A Alshon Jeffery RC .50 1.25
302B Alshon Jeffery SP run left 2.00 5.00
303 Andre Branch RC .25 .60
304A Andrew Luck RC 2.50 6.00
304B A.Luck SP pass 12.00 30.00
305 B.J. Coleman RC .25 .60
306A Bernard Pierce RC .25 .60
306B Bernard Pierce SP heisman 1.00 2.50
307 Bobby Wagner RC .40 1.00
308A Brandon Weeden RC .25 .60
308B B.Weeden SP pass 1.00 2.50
309A Brian Quick RC .25 .60
309B Brian Quick SP leap 1.00 2.50
310A Brock Osweiler RC .25 .60
310B Brock Osweiler SP pointing 1.00 2.50
311 Case Keenum RC .50 1.25
312 Chandler Harnish RC .25 .60
313A Chandler Jones RC .25 .60
313B Chandler Jones SP rt leg up 1.00 2.50
314A Chris Givens RC .25 .60
314B Chris Givens SP catch 1.00 2.50
315 Chris Rainey RC .25 .60
316A Coby Fleener RC .25 .60
316B Coby Fleener SP stretch ball 1.00 2.50
317 Courtney Upshaw RC .30 .75
318 Cyrus Gray RC .25 .60
319 Dan Herron RC .25 .60
320 Danny Coale RC .25 .60
321 David DeCastro RC .25 .60
322A David Wilson RC .25 .60
322B D.Wilson SP leap 1.00 2.50
323A DeVier Posey RC .25 .60
323B DeVier Posey SP catch 1.00 2.50
324 Devon Still RC .30 .75
325 Devon Wylie RC .25 .60
326A Dont'a Hightower RC .40 1.00
326B D.Hightower SP hands at waist 1.50 4.00
327 Dontari Poe RC .25 .60
328A Doug Martin RC .40 1.00
328B Doug Martin SP leap 1.50 4.00
329A Dre Kirkpatrick RC .25 .60
329B D.Kirkpatrick SP rt hand up 1.00 2.50
330A Dwayne Allen RC .25 .60
330B D.Allen SP heel on grnd 1.00 2.50
331A Fletcher Cox RC .40 1.00
331B Fletcher Cox SP run 1.50 4.00
332 George Iloka RC .25 .60
333A Isaiah Pead RC .25 .60
333B Isaiah Pead SP leap 1.00 2.50
334 Janoris Jenkins RC .30 .75
335 Jared Crick RC .25 .60
336 Jarius Wright RC .25 .60
337A Joe Adams RC .25 .60
337B Joe Adams SP stretch 1.00 2.50
338 Jonathan Martin RC .25 .60
339 Juron Criner RC .25 .60
340A Justin Blackmon RC .25 .60
340B J.Blackmon SP leap 1.00 2.50
341 Kellen Moore RC .30 .75
342A Kendall Wright RC .25 .60
342B Kendall Wright SP 1.00 2.50
343 Kirk Cousins RC 1.00 2.50
344 Ladarius Green RC .25 .60
345A Lamar Miller RC .40 1.00
345B L.Miller SP leap 1.50 4.00
346A LaMichael James RC .25 .60
346B L.James SP leap 1.00 2.50
347 Lavonte David RC .40 1.00
348A Luke Kuechly RC .60 1.50
348B Luke Kuechly SP no ball 2.50 6.00
349A Mark Barron RC .25 .60
349B Mark Barron SP lft hand up 1.00 2.50
350 Marvin Jones RC .25 .60
351 Marvin McNutt RC .25 .60
352A Matt Kalil RC .25 .60
352B Matt Kalil SP hands in front 1.00 2.50
353A Melvin Ingram RC .25 .60
353B Melvin Ingram SP looking left 1.00 2.50
354A Michael Brockers RC .25 .60
354B Michael Brockers SP helm 1.00 2.50
355A Michael Egnew RC .25 .60
355B Michael Egnew SP catch 1.00 2.50
356A Michael Floyd RC .25 .60
356B M.Floyd SP catch 1.00 2.50
357A Mohamed Sanu RC .40 1.00
357B M.Sanu SP ball in right hand 1.50 4.00
358A Morris Claiborne RC .25 .60
358B M.Claiborne SP hand on left side 1.00 2.50
359 Mychal Kendricks RC .40 1.00
360A Nick Foles RC .60 1.50
360B N.Foles SP feet together 2.50 6.00
361 Nick Perry RC .30 .75
362A Nick Toon RC .25 .60
362B Nick Toon SP leap 1.00 2.50
363 Orson Charles RC .25 .60
364A Quinton Coples RC .25 .60
364B Q.Coples SP run straight 1.00 2.50
365A Rueben Randle RC .25 .60
365B R.Randle SP ball by side 1.00 2.50
366 Riley Reiff RC .25 .60
367 Rishard Matthews RC .25 .60
368A Robert Griffin III RC .30 .75
368B R.Griffin III SP pass 8.00 20.00
369A Robert Turbin RC .25 .60
369B Robert Turbin SP catch 1.00 2.50
370 Ronnell Lewis RC .25 .60
371A Ronnie Hillman RC .25 .60
371B Ronnie Hillman SP leap 1.00 2.50
372A Russell Wilson RC 2.00 5.00
372B Russell Wilson SP running 10.00 25.00
373A Ryan Broyles RC .25 .60
373B Ryan Broyles SP 1.00 2.50
374 Ryan Lindley RC .25 .60
375A Ryan Tannehill RC .40 1.00
375B R.Tannehill SP pass 1.50 4.00
376A Shea McClellin RC .30 .75
376B S.McClellin SP right hand visible 1.25 3.00
377A Stephen Hill RC .25 .60
377B S.Hill SP feet together 1.00 2.50
378A T.Y. Hilton RC .50 1.25
378B T.Hilton SP helm 2.00 5.00
379 Terrance Ganaway RC .30 .75
380 Tommy Streeter RC .25 .60
381A Trent Richardson RC .25 .60

381B T.Richardson SP side 1.00 2.50
382 Vick Ballard RC .30 .75
383 Vinny Curry RC .30 .75
384A Whitney Mercilus RC .25 .60
384B W.Mercilus SP no ball 1.00 2.50
385 Zach Brown RC .25 .60
386 Alfred Morris RC .25 .60
387 B.J. Cunningham RC .25 .60
388 Bruce Irvin RC .30 .75
389 Bryce Brown RC .25 .60
390 Greg Childs RC .25 .60
391A Harrison Smith RC .25 .60
391B H.Smith SP no ball 1.00 2.50
392 Jeff Fuller RC .25 .60
393 Keshawn Martin RC .30 .75
394 Kevin Zeitler RC .25 .60
395 LaVon Brazill RC .40 1.00
396 Marc Tyler RC .25 .60
397 Michael Smith RC .30 .75
398A Stephon Gilmore RC .30 .75
398B S.Gilmore SP hands by head 1.25 3.00
399A T.J. Graham RC .25 .60
399B T.Graham SP left foot raised 1.00 2.50
400 Travis Benjamin RC .25 .60

2012 Score Artist's Proof

*1-300 VETS/32: 10X TO 25X BASIC CARDS
*301-400 ROOKIES/32: 5X TO 12X BASIC RC

2012 Score Glossy

*1-300 VETS: 1X TO 2.5X BASIC CARDS
*301-400 ROOKIES: .6X TO 1.5X BASIC CARDS
ONE GLOSSY PER PACK

2012 Score Gold Zone

*1-300 VETS: 3X TO 8X BASIC INSERTS
*301-400 ROOKIES: 1.5X TO 4X BASIC RC
RANDOM INSERTS IN PACKS

2012 Score Red Zone

*1-300 VETS/20: 12X TO 30X BASIC CARDS
*301-400 ROOKIES/20: 6X TO 15X BASIC RC
STATED PRINT RUN 20 SER.#'d SETS

2012 Score Scorecard

*1-300 VETS: 2.5X TO 6X BASIC CARDS
*301-400 ROOKIES: 1.2X TO 3X BASIC CARDS
RANDOM INSERTS IN PACKS
307 Bobby Wagner 1.25 3.00

2012 Score Complete Players

COMPLETE SET (20) 4.00 10.00
*GLOSSY: .6X TO 1.5X BASIC INSERTS
1 Cam Newton .50 1.25
2 LeSean McCoy .50 1.25
3 Darren Sproles .40 1.00
4 Percy Harvin .30 .75
5 Jason Pierre-Paul .30 .75
6 Terrell Suggs .30 .75
7 Ray Rice .30 .75
8 Chris Johnson .30 .75
9 Von Miller .40 1.00
10 Fred Jackson .40 1.00
11 Michael Vick .40 1.00
12 Maurice Jones-Drew .30 .75
13 Matt Forte .30 .75
14 Calvin Johnson .50 1.25
15 Jared Allen .30 .75
16 Tamba Hali .30 .75
17 Darren McFadden .30 .75
18 Jahvid Best .30 .75
19 Wes Welker .40 1.00
20 Ryan Mathews .40 1.00

2012 Score Hot Rookies

COMPLETE SET (30) 10.00 25.00
*GLOSSY: .6X TO 1.5X BASIC INSERTS
1 Andrew Luck 3.00 8.00
2 Robert Griffin III .40 1.00
3 Trent Richardson .30 .75
4 Justin Blackmon .30 .75
5 Ryan Tannehill .50 1.25
6 Michael Floyd .30 .75
7 Kendall Wright .30 .75
8 Brandon Weeden .30 .75
9 A.J. Jenkins .30 .75
10 Doug Martin .50 1.25
11 David Wilson .30 .75
12 Brian Quick .30 .75
13 Coby Fleener .30 .75
14 Stephen Hill .30 .75
15 Bernard Pierce .30 .75
16 Isaiah Pead .30 .75
17 Ryan Broyles .30 .75
18 Brock Osweiler .30 .75
19 LaMichael James .30 .75
20 Rueben Randle .30 .75
21 Nick Toon .30 .75
22 Russell Wilson 2.50 6.00
23 Mohamed Sanu .50 1.25
24 Lamar Miller .50 1.25
25 Chris Givens .30 .75
26 Alshon Jeffery .60 1.50
27 DeVier Posey .30 .75
28 T.J. Graham .30 .75
29 Ronnie Hillman .30 .75
30 Robert Turbin .30 .75

2012 Score Hot Rookies Toronto Fall Expo

CRACKED ICE/25: 1.5X TO 4X BASE HI
7 Andrew Luck 8.00 20.00
8 Robert Griffin III 8.00 20.00
9 Trent Richardson 2.50 6.00
10 Justin Blackmon 2.00 5.00
11 Russell Wilson 3.00 8.00
12 Doug Martin 2.00 5.00

2012 Score Hot Rookies Signatures

RANDOM INSERTS IN PACKS
1 Andrew Luck 100.00 200.00
2 Robert Griffin III 15.00 40.00
3 Trent Richardson
4 Justin Blackmon 6.00 15.00
5 Ryan Tannehill 10.00 25.00
6 Michael Floyd 6.00 15.00
7 Kendall Wright 6.00 15.00
8 Brandon Weeden 6.00 15.00
9 A.J. Jenkins 6.00 15.00
10 Doug Martin 10.00 25.00
13 Coby Fleener 6.00 15.00
16 Isaiah Pead 6.00 15.00
18 Brock Osweiler 6.00 15.00
21 Nick Toon 6.00 15.00
22 Russell Wilson 100.00 200.00
25 Chris Givens 6.00 15.00

2012 Score In the Zone

COMPLETE SET (30) 5.00 12.00
*GLOSSY: .6X TO 1.5X BASIC INSERTS
1 LeSean McCoy .50 1.25
2 Rob Gronkowski .50 1.25
3 Calvin Johnson .50 1.25
4 Jordy Nelson .40 1.00
5 Ray Rice .30 .75
6 Cam Newton .50 1.25
7 Adrian Peterson .50 1.25
8 Marshawn Lynch .40 1.00
9 Arian Foster .40 1.00
10 Ahmad Bradshaw .30 .75
11 BenJarvus Green-Ellis .40 1.00
12 Jimmy Graham .50 1.25
13 Laurent Robinson .30 .75
14 Maurice Jones-Drew .30 .75
15 Michael Turner .30 .75
16 Beanie Wells .30 .75
17 Darren Sproles .40 1.00
18 Mike Tolbert .30 .75
19 Dez Bryant .50 1.25
20 Eric Decker .30 .75
21 Greg Jennings .30 .75
22 Percy Harvin .30 .75
23 Rashard Mendenhall .30 .75
24 Victor Cruz .40 1.00
25 Vincent Jackson .30 .75
26 Wes Welker .40 1.00
27 Frank Gore .40 1.00
28 Jermichael Finley .30 .75
29 Larry Fitzgerald .40 1.00
30 Roddy White .30 .75

2012 Score In the Zone Signatures

3 Calvin Johnson
5 Ray Rice 15.00 40.00
6 Cam Newton
10 Ahmad Bradshaw
12 Jimmy Graham
15 Michael Turner 8.00 20.00
16 Beanie Wells 8.00 20.00
17 Darren Sproles 8.00 20.00
18 Mike Tolbert
22 Percy Harvin
25 Vincent Jackson
27 Frank Gore

2012 Score Numbers Game

COMPLETE SET (20) 4.00 10.00
*GLOSSY: .6X TO 1.5X BASIC INSERTS
1 Calvin Johnson .50 1.25
2 Wes Welker .40 1.00
3 Roddy White .30 .75
4 Rob Gronkowski .50 1.25
5 Maurice Jones-Drew .30 .75
6 Michael Turner .30 .75
7 LeSean McCoy .50 1.25
8 Ray Rice .30 .75
9 Drew Brees .50 1.25
10 Tom Brady 1.25 3.00
11 Aaron Rodgers .75 2.00
12 David Akers .30 .75
13 Brandon Banks .30 .75
14 Joe McKnight .30 .75
15 Patrick Peterson .30 .75
16 Brandon Tate .30 .75
17 D'Qwell Jackson .30 .75
18 NaVorro Bowman .40 1.00
19 Jared Allen .30 .75
20 Terrell Suggs .30 .75

2012 Score RC Flashbacks

18 Michael Irvin 1.25 3.00
57 Kurt Warner 1.00 2.50
72 Cris Carter 1.25 3.00
78 Rod Woodson 1.00 2.50
86 Tim Brown 1.25 3.00
101 Emmitt Smith 4.00 10.00
211 Thurman Thomas 1.00 2.50
214 Keyshawn Johnson 1.00 2.50
217 Mike Alstott .75 2.00
222 Ricky Williams 1.00 2.50
223 Donovan McNabb 1.00 2.50
228 Champ Bailey 1.00 2.50
230 Marvin Harrison 1.00 2.50
231 Eddie George 1.00 2.50
233 Peyton Manning 2.50 6.00
235 Randy Moss 1.00 2.50
236 Charles Woodson 1.50 4.00
246 Deion Sanders 1.50 4.00
252 Hines Ward 1.25 3.00
256 Kerry Collins .75 2.00
257 Barry Sanders 4.00 10.00
270 Troy Aikman 2.00 5.00
271 Michael Vick 1.00 2.50
272A Drew Brees 1.50 4.00
272B Andre Rison 1.00 2.50
274 Tiki Barber 1.00 2.50
276 Warrick Dunn .75 2.00
277 Marshall Faulk 1.00 2.50
283 LaDainian Tomlinson 1.25 3.00
288 Brian Urlacher 1.25 3.00
289 Tony Gonzalez 1.00 2.50
302 Junior Seau 1.00 2.50
306A Jason Witten 1.00 2.50
306B Jerome Bettis 1.25 3.00
310 Dallas Clark .75 2.00
316 Tom Brady 3.00 8.00
324 Ed Reed 1.00 2.50
331 Alex Smith QB 1.00 2.50
333 Sterling Sharpe 1.00 2.50
352 Aaron Rodgers 2.50 6.00
354 Roddy White .75 2.00
367 Frank Gore 1.00 2.50
371 Eli Manning 1.00 2.50
373 Larry Fitzgerald 1.00 2.50
374 Philip Rivers 1.25 3.00
381 Ben Roethlisberger 2.00 5.00
488 Jimmy Smith .75 2.00
506 Haywood Jeffires .75 2.00
611 Brett Favre 2.50 6.00
627 Mark Carrier .75 2.00

2012 Score Signatures

17 NaVorro Bowman 6.00 15.00
23 Jimmy Graham 8.00 20.00
26 Mark Ingram 8.00 20.00
43 Jacquizz Rodgers 6.00 15.00
79 Asante Samuel 8.00 20.00
107 Cam Newton 40.00 80.00
120 Roy Helu Jr. 5.00 12.00
145 Danario Alexander 5.00 12.00
147 Lance Kendricks 5.00 12.00
172 Brian Cushing 5.00 12.00
198 A.J. Green 8.00 20.00
208 Damian Williams 5.00 12.00
209 Jake Locker 15.00 30.00
256 Brian Hartline 6.00 15.00
301 A.J. Jenkins 3.00 8.00
304 Andrew Luck 125.00 200.00
307 Bobby Wagner 5.00 12.00
308 Brandon Weeden 10.00 25.00
310 Brock Osweiler 3.00 8.00
314 Chris Givens 3.00 8.00
316 Coby Fleener 3.00 8.00
318 Cyrus Gray 3.00 8.00
320 Danny Coale 3.00 8.00
321 David DeCastro 3.00 8.00
327 Dontari Poe 3.00 8.00
328 Doug Martin 5.00 12.00
330 Dwayne Allen 3.00 8.00
332 George Iloka 3.00 8.00
333 Isaiah Pead 6.00 15.00
335 Jared Crick 3.00 8.00
337 Joe Adams 3.00 8.00
338 Jonathan Martin 3.00 8.00
340 Justin Blackmon 3.00 8.00
341 Kellen Moore 4.00 10.00
342 Kendall Wright 3.00 8.00
343 Kirk Cousins 12.00 30.00
344 Ladarius Green 3.00 8.00
348 Luke Kuechly 8.00 20.00
350 Marvin Jones 3.00 8.00
351 Marvin McNutt 3.00 8.00
352 Matt Kalil 3.00 8.00
354 Michael Brockers 3.00 8.00
355 Michael Egnew 3.00 8.00
356 Michael Floyd 12.00 30.00
359 Mychal Kendricks 5.00 12.00
360 Nick Foles 8.00 20.00
362 Nick Toon 3.00 8.00
363 Orson Charles 3.00 8.00
366 Riley Reiff 6.00 15.00
368 Robert Griffin III 4.00 10.00
372 Russell Wilson 50.00 100.00
375 Ryan Tannehill 5.00 12.00
378 T.Y. Hilton 6.00 15.00
379 Terrance Ganaway 4.00 10.00
381 Trent Richardson 3.00 8.00
384 Whitney Mercilus 3.00 8.00
392 Jeff Fuller 3.00 8.00
396 Marc Tyler 3.00 8.00

2013 Score

COMPLETE SET (440) 50.00 100.00
COMP.SET w/o RC's (330) 15.00 40.00
ONE RC PER RETAIL; FIVE PER JUMBO
1 John Skelton .12 .30
2 Larry Fitzgerald .15 .40
3 Andre Roberts .12 .30
4 Michael Floyd .12 .30
5 Rashard Mendenhall .12 .30
6 Patrick Peterson .12 .30
7 Matt Ryan .15 .40
8 Julio Jones .20 .50
9 Roddy White .12 .30
10 Steven Jackson .12 .30
11 Jacquizz Rodgers .15 .40
12 Tony Gonzalez .15 .40
13 Sean Weatherspoon .12 .30
14 Joe Flacco .15 .40
15 Torrey Smith .12 .30
16 Jacoby Jones .12 .30
17 Ray Rice .12 .30
18 Bernard Pierce .12 .30
19 Dennis Pitta .12 .30
20 Ed Reed .15 .40
21 C.J. Spiller .12 .30
22 Fred Jackson .15 .40
23 Steve Johnson .15 .40
24 T.J. Graham .12 .30
25 Scott Chandler .12 .30
26 Tarvaris Jackson .12 .30
27 Cam Newton .20 .50
28 Steve Smith .15 .40
29 Brandon LaFell .12 .30
30 DeAngelo Williams .12 .30
31 Jonathan Stewart .12 .30
32 Greg Olsen .15 .40
33 Luke Kuechly .15 .40
34 Jay Cutler .12 .30
35 Brandon Marshall .15 .40
36 Alshon Jeffery .15 .40
37 Matt Forte .12 .30
38 Martellus Bennett .12 .30
39 Lance Briggs .15 .40
40 Andy Dalton .15 .40
41 A.J. Green .20 .50
42 Marvin Jones .15 .40
43 Mohamed Sanu .12 .30
44 BenJarvus Green-Ellis .15 .40
45 Jermaine Gresham .15 .40
46 Geno Atkins .12 .30
47 Brandon Weeden .12 .30
48 Josh Gordon .12 .30
49 Greg Little .12 .30
50 Trent Richardson .12 .30
51 Joe Haden .12 .30
52 Travis Benjamin .12 .30
53 D'Qwell Jackson .12 .30
54 Tony Romo .15 .40
55 Dez Bryant .20 .50
56 Miles Austin .12 .30
57 DeMarco Murray .15 .40
58 Jason Witten .15 .40
59 Morris Claiborne .12 .30
60 DeMarcus Ware .20 .50
61 Peyton Manning .40 1.00
62 Demaryius Thomas .15 .40
63 Eric Decker .12 .30
64 Willis McGahee .12 .30
65 Wes Welker .15 .40
66 Ronnie Hillman .12 .30
67 Von Miller .15 .40
68 Matthew Stafford .15 .40
69 Calvin Johnson .20 .50
70 Ryan Broyles .15 .40
71 Mikel Leshoure .12 .30
72 Brandon Pettigrew .12 .30
73 Ndamukong Suh .15 .40
74 Reggie Bush .12 .30
75 Aaron Rodgers .30 .75
76 James Jones .12 .30
77 Jordy Nelson .15 .40
78 Randall Cobb .15 .40
79 DuJuan Harris RC .20 .50
80 Clay Matthews .20 .50
81 Jermichael Finley .12 .30
82 Matt Schaub .12 .30
83 Andre Johnson .12 .30
84 Arian Foster .15 .40
85 Owen Daniels .12 .30
86 J.J. Watt .15 .40
87 Ben Tate .12 .30
88 Andrew Luck .30 .75
89 Reggie Wayne .15 .40
90 T.Y. Hilton .15 .40
91 Vick Ballard .12 .30
92 Dwayne Allen .12 .30
93 Coby Fleener .12 .30
94 Antoine Bethea .12 .30
95 Blaine Gabbert .12 .30
96 Cecil Shorts .12 .30
97 Justin Blackmon .12 .30
98 Maurice Jones-Drew .12 .30
99 Marcedes Lewis .12 .30
100 Paul Posluszny .12 .30
101 Chad Henne .12 .30
102 Jonathan Baldwin .12 .30
103 Jamaal Charles .15 .40
104 Anthony Fasano .12 .30
105 Tony Moeaki .12 .30
106 Alex Smith .15 .40
107 Derrick Johnson .12 .30
108 Dwayne Bowe .15 .40
109 Brian Hartline .12 .30
110 Mike Wallace .12 .30
111 Lamar Miller .12 .30
112 Dannell Ellerbe .12 .30
113 Cameron Wake .12 .30
114 Davone Bess .12 .30
115 Ryan Tannehill .15 .40
116 Matt Cassel .12 .30
117 Christian Ponder .12 .30
118 Jarius Wright .12 .30
119 Adrian Peterson .20 .50
120 Greg Jennings .12 .30
121 Kyle Rudolph .12 .30
122 Jared Allen .12 .30
123 Tom Brady .50 1.25
124 Danny Amendola .15 .40
125 Chandler Jones .12 .30
126 Stevan Ridley .12 .30
127 Shane Vereen .15 .40
128 Aaron Hernandez .15 .40
129 Rob Gronkowski .20 .50
130 Drew Brees .20 .50
131 Marques Colston .12 .30
132 Lance Moore .12 .30
133 Darren Sproles .15 .40
134 Mark Ingram .15 .40
135 Jimmy Graham .20 .50
136 Devery Henderson .12 .30
137 Eli Manning .15 .40
138 Hakeem Nicks .12 .30
139 Victor Cruz .15 .40
140 Brandon Myers .15 .40
141 David Wilson .12 .30
142 Andre Brown .15 .40
143 Jason Pierre-Paul .12 .30
144 Mark Sanchez .12 .30
145 Santonio Holmes .12 .30
146 Stephen Hill .12 .30
147 Joe McKnight .12 .30
148 Bilal Powell .12 .30
149 Jeremy Kerley .12 .30
150 Antonio Cromartie .12 .30
151 Matt Flynn .12 .30
152 Terrelle Pryor .15 .40
153 Denarius Moore .12 .30
154 Darren McFadden .15 .40
155 Jacoby Ford .12 .30
156 Richard Seymour .12 .30
157 Miles Burris .12 .30
158 Michael Vick .15 .40
159 DeSean Jackson .15 .40
160 Jeremy Maclin .12 .30
161 LeSean McCoy .20 .50
162 Bryce Brown .15 .40
163 Brent Celek .12 .30
164 Nick Foles .15 .40
165 Ben Roethlisberger .20 .50
166 Plaxico Burress .12 .30
167 Antonio Brown .20 .50
168 Lawrence Timmons .12 .30
169 Jonathan Dwyer .12 .30
170 Heath Miller .12 .30
171 Troy Polamalu .20 .50
172 Sam Bradford .12 .30
173 Jared Cook .12 .30
174 Lance Kendricks .12 .30
175 Chris Givens .12 .30
176 Isaiah Pead .12 .30
177 Daryl Richardson .12 .30
178 James Laurinaitis .15 .40
179 Philip Rivers .20 .50
180 Malcom Floyd .12 .30
181 Robert Meachem .12 .30
182 Vincent Brown .12 .30
183 Ryan Mathews .15 .40
184 Antonio Gates .15 .40
185 Eric Weddle .12 .30
186 Colin Kaepernick .15 .40
187 Michael Crabtree .12 .30
188 Frank Gore .15 .40
189 LaMichael James .12 .30
190 Vernon Davis .12 .30
191 Anquan Boldin .12 .30
192 Aldon Smith .12 .30
193 Russell Wilson .40 1.00
194 Sidney Rice .12 .30
195 Golden Tate .12 .30
196 Marshawn Lynch .15 .40
197 Robert Turbin .12 .30
198 Percy Harvin .12 .30
199 Richard Sherman .20 .50
200 Josh Freeman .15 .40
201 Vincent Jackson .12 .30
202 Mike Williams .15 .40
203 Doug Martin .15 .40
204 Kevin Ogletree .12 .30
205 Ronde Barber .12 .30
206 Lavonte David .12 .30
207 Jake Locker .15 .40
208 Kenny Britt .12 .30
209 Kendall Wright .12 .30
210 Nate Washington .12 .30
211 Chris Johnson .12 .30
212 Shonn Greene .12 .30
213 Zach Brown .12 .30
214 Robert Griffin III .12 .30
215 Pierre Garcon .15 .40
216 Santana Moss .15 .40
217 Alfred Morris .12 .30
218 Fred Davis .12 .30
219 Ryan Kerrigan .12 .30
220 London Fletcher .15 .40
221 John Skelton AM .12 .30
222 Matt Ryan AM .12 .30
223 Joe Flacco AM .12 .30
224 Tarvaris Jackson AM .10 .25
225 Cam Newton AM .15 .40
226 Jay Cutler AM .10 .25
227 Andy Dalton AM .12 .30
228 Brandon Weeden AM .10 .25
229 Tony Romo AM .12 .30
230 Peyton Manning AM .30 .75
231 Matthew Stafford AM .12 .30
232 Aaron Rodgers AM .25 .60
233 Matt Schaub AM .10 .25
234 Andrew Luck AM .25 .60
235 Blaine Gabbert AM .10 .25
236 Alex Smith AM .12 .30
237 Ryan Tannehill AM .12 .30
238 Christian Ponder AM .10 .25
239 Tom Brady AM .40 1.00
240 Drew Brees AM .15 .40
241 Eli Manning AM .12 .30
242 Mark Sanchez AM .10 .25
243 Carson Palmer AM .12 .30
244 Michael Vick AM .12 .30
245 Ben Roethlisberger AM .15 .40
246 Sam Bradford AM .10 .25
247 Philip Rivers AM .15 .40
248 Colin Kaepernick AM .12 .30
249 Russell Wilson AM .30 .75
250 Josh Freeman AM .12 .30
251 Jake Locker AM .12 .30
252 Robert Griffin III AM .10 .25
253 Joe Flacco RSB .12 .30
254 Anquan Boldin RSB .10 .25
255 Torrey Smith RSB .10 .25
256 Jacoby Jones RSB .10 .25
257 Ray Rice RSB .10 .25
258 Bernard Pierce RSB .10 .25
259 Dennis Pitta RSB .10 .25
260 Ed Dickson RSB .10 .25
261 Ray Lewis RSB .15 .40
262 Ed Reed RSB .12 .30
263 Haloti Ngata RSB .10 .25
264 Terrell Suggs RSB .10 .25
265 Bernard Pollard RSB .10 .25
266 Justin Tucker RSB .15 .40
267 Larry Fitzgerald F .12 .30
268 Matt Ryan F .12 .30
269 Ray Rice F .10 .25
270 Steve Johnson F .12 .30
271 Steve Smith F .12 .30
272 Jay Cutler F .10 .25
273 A.J. Green F .15 .40
274 Trent Richardson F .10 .25
275 Tony Romo F .12 .30
276 Peyton Manning F .30 .75
277 Calvin Johnson F .15 .40
278 Aaron Rodgers F .25 .60
279 Arian Foster F .12 .30
280 Reggie Wayne F .12 .30
281 Maurice Jones-Drew F .10 .25
282 Jamaal Charles F .12 .30
283 Cameron Wake F .10 .25
284 Adrian Peterson F .15 .40
285 Tom Brady F .40 1.00
286 Drew Brees F .15 .40
287 Eli Manning F .12 .30
288 Santonio Holmes F .10 .25
289 Darren McFadden F .12 .30
290 LeSean McCoy F .15 .40
291 Ben Roethlisberger F .15 .40
292 Sam Bradford F .10 .25
293 Philip Rivers F .15 .40
294 Frank Gore F .12 .30
295 Marshawn Lynch F .12 .30
296 Josh Freeman F .12 .30
297 Chris Johnson F .10 .25
298 Robert Griffin III F .10 .25
299 Patrick Peterson FF .10 .25
300 Julio Jones FF .15 .40
301 Torrey Smith FF .10 .25
302 C.J. Spiller FF .10 .25
303 Cam Newton FF .15 .40
304 Brandon Marshall FF .12 .30
305 Andy Dalton FF .12 .30
306 Josh Gordon FF .10 .25
307 DeMarco Murray FF .12 .30
308 Demaryius Thomas FF .12 .30
309 Ryan Broyles FF .12 .30
310 Randall Cobb FF .12 .30
311 J.J. Watt FF .12 .30
312 Andrew Luck FF .25 .60
313 Justin Blackmon FF .10 .25
314 Eric Berry FF .12 .30
315 Ryan Tannehill FF .12 .30
316 Christian Ponder FF .10 .25
317 Rob Gronkowski FF .15 .40
318 Jimmy Graham FF .15 .40
319 Hakeem Nicks FF .10 .25
320 Stephen Hill FF .10 .25
321 Denarius Moore FF .10 .25
322 Jeremy Maclin FF .10 .25
323 Jonathan Dwyer FF .10 .25
324 Chris Givens FF .10 .25
325 Ryan Mathews FF .12 .30
326 Colin Kaepernick FF .12 .30
327 Russell Wilson FF .30 .75
328 Doug Martin FF .12 .30
329 Kendall Wright FF .10 .25
330 Alfred Morris FF .10 .25
331 Aaron Dobson RC .30 .75
332 Aaron Mellette RC .30 .75
333 Ace Sanders RC .30 .75
334 Alec Lemon RC .40 1.00
335 Alec Ogletree RC .30 .75
336 Alex Okafor RC .30 .75
337 Andre Ellington RC .30 .75
338 Arthur Brown RC .30 .75
339 Barkevious Mingo RC .30 .75
340 Bjoern Werner RC .30 .75
341 Cornellius Carradine RC .30 .75
342 Darius Slay RC .30 .75
343 Chris Gragg RC .30 .75
344 Chris Harper RC .30 .75
345 Christine Michael RC .30 .75
346 Cierre Wood RC .30 .75
347 Cobi Hamilton RC .30 .75
348 David Amerson RC .30 .75
349 Eric Fisher RC .30 .75
350 Conner Vernon RC .30 .75
351 Cordarrelle Patterson RC .30 .75
352 Corey Fuller RC .30 .75
353 Damontre Moore RC .30 .75
354 Da'Rick Rogers RC .30 .75
355 Datone Jones RC .30 .75
356 DeAndre Hopkins RC .75 2.00
357 Dee Milliner RC .30 .75
358 Denard Robinson RC .30 .75
359 Dennis Johnson RC .30 .75
360 Johnathan Cyprien RC .30 .75
361 Dion Jordan RC .30 .75
362 Dion Sims RC .30 .75
363 Eddie Lacy RC .30 .75
364 EJ Manuel RC .30 .75
365 Eric Reid RC .40 1.00
366 Ezekiel Ansah RC .30 .75
367 Gavin Escobar RC .30 .75
368 Geno Smith RC .30 .75
369 Giovani Bernard RC .30 .75
370 Jamar Taylor RC .30 .75
371 Jarvis Jones RC .30 .75
372 Jasper Collins RC .30 .75
373 Jawan Jamison RC .30 .75
374 John Simon RC .50 1.25
375 Johnthan Banks RC .30 .75
376 Johnathan Hankins RC .30 .75
377 Johnathan Franklin RC .30 .75
378 Jordan Poyer RC .30 .75
379 Jordan Reed RC .50 1.25
380 Kawann Short RC .30 .75
381 Joseph Randle RC .30 .75
382 Josh Boyce RC .30 .75
383 Justin Hunter RC .30 .75
384 Keenan Allen RC .60 1.50
385 Kenjon Barner RC .30 .75
386 Kenny Stills RC .30 .75
387 Kenny Vaccaro RC .30 .75
388 Kerwynn Williams RC .30 .75
389 Kevin Minter RC .30 .75
390 Khaseem Greene RC .30 .75
391 Landry Jones RC .30 .75
392 Le'Veon Bell RC 1.00 2.50
393 Logan Ryan RC .40 1.00
394 Luke Joeckel RC .30 .75
395 Manti Te'o RC .40 1.00
396 Tyrann Mathieu RC .50 1.25
397 Marcus Lattimore RC .30 .75
398 Desmond Trufant RC .30 .75
399 Margus Hunt RC .30 .75
400 Knile Davis RC .30 .75
401 Markus Wheaton RC .30 .75
402 Marquess Wilson RC .50 1.25
403 Marquise Goodwin RC .30 .75
404 Matt Barkley RC .30 .75
405 Matt Elam RC .30 .75
406 Matt Scott RC .30 .75
407 Onterio McCalebb RC .40 1.00
408 Mike Gillislee RC .30 .75
409 Mike Glennon RC .30 .75
410 Montee Ball RC .30 .75
411 Nick Kasa RC .30 .75
412 Phillip Thomas RC .30 .75
413 Quinton Patton RC .30 .75
414 Ray Graham RC .30 .75
415 Ryan Otten RC .30 .75
416 Rex Burkhead RC .40 1.00
417 Sharrif Floyd RC .30 .75
418 Robert Woods RC .50 1.25
419 Rodney Smith RC .30 .75
420 Ryan Nassib RC .30 .75
421 Ryan Swope RC .30 .75
422 Sam Montgomery RC .30 .75
423 Sheldon Richardson RC .30 .75
424 Star Lotulelei RC .40 1.00
425 Stedman Bailey RC .30 .75
426 Stepfan Taylor RC .30 .75
427 Tavarres King RC .30 .75
428 Tavon Austin RC .40 1.00
429 Terrance Williams RC .30 .75
430 Theo Riddick RC .30 .75
431 Travis Kelce RC .75 2.00
432 Tyler Bray RC .30 .75
433 Tyler Eifert RC .30 .75
434 Tyler Wilson RC .30 .75
435 Sio Moore RC .30 .75
436 Chance Warmack RC .30 .75
437 Xavier Rhodes RC .30 .75
438 Zac Dysert RC .30 .75
439 Zach Ertz RC .60 1.50
440 Sean Renfree RC .40 1.00
441 Leon Sandcastle (Deion) SP 6.00 15.00

2013 Score Artist's Proof

*1-330 VETS/32: 10X TO 25X BASIC CARDS

2013 Score Black

*331-440 ROOKIES/25: 4X TO 10X BASIC RC
*441 SANDCASTLE: .8X TO 2X BASIC CARD

2013 Score Blue

*331-400 ROOKIES: 1X TO 2.5X BASIC RC
*441 SANDCASTLE: .4X TO 1X BASIC CARD
INSERTS IN WAL-MART RETAIL

2013 Score Gold Zone

*1-330 VETS/50: 8X TO 20X BASIC CARDS

2013 Score Purple

*331-400 ROOKIES/99: 1.5X TO 4X BASIC RC
*441 SANDCASTLE: .5X TO 1.2X BASIC CARD
STATED PRINT RUN 99 SER.#'d SETS

2013 Score Red

*331-400 ROOKIES: 1.2X TO 3X BASIC RC
*441 SANDCASTLE: .4X TO 1X BASIC CARD
INSERTS IN TARGET RETAIL

2013 Score Red Zone

*1-330 VETS/30: 10X TO 25X BASIC CARDS

2013 Score Scorecard

*1-330 VETS: 2.5X TO 6X BASIC CARDS
OVERALL ONE PARALLEL PER PACK

2013 Score Showcase

*1-330 VETS/99: 5X TO 12X BASIC CARDS

2013 Score Franchise Fabrics

*PRIME/25: .6X TO 1.5X BASIC JSY
FFAF Arian Foster 5.00 12.00
FFAG Antonio Gates 5.00 12.00
FFAP Adrian Peterson 6.00 15.00
FFCHJ Chris Johnson 4.00 10.00
FFCJ Calvin Johnson 6.00 15.00
FFCK Colin Kaepernick 5.00 12.00
FFCN Cam Newton 6.00 15.00
FFCS C.J. Spiller 4.00 10.00
FFDB Dwayne Bowe 5.00 12.00
FFDH Devin Hester 5.00 12.00
FFDJ DeSean Jackson 5.00 12.00
FFDM Darren McFadden 5.00 12.00
FFFG Frank Gore 5.00 12.00
FFHN Hakeem Nicks 4.00 10.00
FFJA Jared Allen 4.00 10.00
FFJF Joe Flacco 5.00 12.00
FFKB Kenny Britt 4.00 10.00
FFLF Larry Fitzgerald 5.00 12.00
FFLW Lardarius Webb 5.00 12.00
FFMA Miles Austin 4.00 10.00
FFMR Matt Ryan 5.00 12.00
FFRR Ray Rice 4.00 10.00
FFSJ Steve Johnson 5.00 12.00
FFTR Tony Romo 5.00 12.00
FFVD Vernon Davis 4.00 10.00

2013 Score Franchise Fabrics Signatures

*PRIME AU/25: .6X TO 1.5X BASIC AU/50
FFCS C.J. Spiller/25 8.00 20.00
FFJF Jacoby Ford/25 8.00 20.00
FFKB Kenny Britt/50 6.00 15.00
FFLF London Fletcher/25 10.00 25.00

2013 Score Future Franchise Fabrics

*PRIME/99: .5X TO 1.2X BASIC JSY
*PRIME/25: .6X TO 1.5X BASIC JSY
FRAJ A.J. Jenkins 3.00 8.00
FRAJE Alshon Jeffery 4.00 10.00
FRBP Bernard Pierce 3.00 8.00
FRCF Coby Fleener 3.00 8.00
FRCG Chris Givens 3.00 8.00
FRCU Courtney Upshaw 3.00 8.00
FRDB Dez Bryant 5.00 12.00
FRDH Dont'a Hightower 3.00 8.00
FRDM Doug Martin 4.00 10.00
FRDMO Denarius Moore 3.00 8.00
FRDW David Wilson 3.00 8.00
FRJB Justin Blackmon 3.00 8.00
FRJB Jonathan Baldwin 3.00 8.00
FRJJ Julio Jones 5.00 12.00
FRJW Jarius Wright 3.00 8.00
FRMC Morris Claiborne 3.00 8.00
FRMF Michael Floyd 3.00 8.00
FRMS Mohamed Sanu 3.00 8.00
FRRG Robert Griffin III 3.00 8.00
FRRM Ryan Mathews 4.00 10.00
FRRT Ryan Tannehill 4.00 10.00
FRRW Russell Wilson 10.00 25.00
FRSH Stephen Hill 3.00 8.00
FRTG T.J. Graham 3.00 8.00
FRVM Von Miller 4.00 10.00

2013 Score Future Franchise Fabrics Signatures

*PRIME/25: .6X TO 1.5X BASIC JSY AU/50
FRAM Alfred Morris/50* 6.00 15.00
FRBW Brandon Weeden/25* 8.00 20.00
FRCF Coby Fleener/50* 6.00 15.00
FRCG Chris Givens/50* 6.00 15.00
FRDT Daniel Thomas/50* 6.00 15.00
FRDW David Wilson/50* 10.00 25.00
FRJB Jonathan Baldwin/25* 8.00 20.00
FRJK Jeremy Kerley/50* 6.00 15.00
FRJW Jarius Wright/50* 8.00 20.00
FRKR Kyle Rudolph/50* 6.00 15.00
FRLJ LaMichael James/50* 6.00 15.00
FRMS Mohamed Sanu/50* 6.00 15.00
FRRH Ronnie Hillman/50* 6.00 15.00
FRTG T.J. Graham/50* 6.00 15.00

2013 Score Hot Rookies

COMPLETE SET (50) 20.00 50.00
ONE PER HOBBY PACK
*ART.PROOF/32: 2X TO 5X BASIC INSERTS
*RETAIL: .4X TO 1X BASIC INSERTS
*SHOWCASE/99: 1.2X TO 3X BASIC INSERTS
1 Geno Smith .30 .75
2 Matt Barkley .30 .75
3 Cordarrelle Patterson .30 .75
4 Eddie Lacy .30 .75
5 Keenan Allen .60 1.50
6 Mike Glennon .30 .75
7 DeAndre Hopkins .75 2.00
8 Tavon Austin .40 1.00
9 Tyler Wilson .30 .75
10 Robert Woods .50 1.25
11 Quinton Patton .30 .75
12 Ryan Nassib .30 .75
13 Giovani Bernard .30 .75
14 Justin Hunter .30 .75
15 Terrance Williams .30 .75
16 Markus Wheaton .30 .75
17 EJ Manuel .30 .75
18 Denard Robinson .30 .75
19 Johnathan Franklin .30 .75
20 Joseph Randle .30 .75
21 Tyler Eifert .30 .75
22 Zach Ertz .60 1.50
23 Aaron Dobson .30 .75
24 Knile Davis .30 .75
25 Landry Jones .30 .75
26 Montee Ball .30 .75
27 Andre Ellington .30 .75
28 Le'Veon Bell 1.00 2.50
29 Christine Michael .30 .75
30 Stedman Bailey .30 .75
31 Jawan Jamison .30 .75
32 Mike Gillislee .30 .75
33 Tavarres King .30 .75
34 Stepfan Taylor .30 .75
35 Ryan Swope .30 .75
36 Marquise Goodwin .30 .75
37 Marcus Lattimore .30 .75
38 Kenjon Barner .30 .75
39 Kenny Stills .30 .75
40 Cobi Hamilton .30 .75
41 Gavin Escobar .30 .75
42 Jordan Reed .50 1.25
43 Travis Kelce .75 2.00
44 Tyrann Mathieu .50 1.25
45 Dee Milliner .30 .75
46 Ezekiel Ansah .30 .75
47 Dion Jordan .30 .75
48 Manti Te'o .40 1.00
49 Sharrif Floyd .30 .75
50 Jarvis Jones .30 .75

2013 Score Hot Rookies Signatures

*SHOWCASE/25: .6X TO 1.5X BASIC AU/99
1 Geno Smith/99 5.00 12.00
2 Matt Barkley/99 5.00 12.00
3 Cordarrelle Patterson/99 5.00 12.00
4 Eddie Lacy/99 5.00 12.00
5 Keenan Allen/99 10.00 25.00
6 Mike Glennon/99 5.00 12.00
7 DeAndre Hopkins/99 12.00 30.00
8 Tavon Austin/99 6.00 15.00
9 Tyler Wilson/99 15.00 40.00
10 Robert Woods/99 8.00 20.00
11 Quinton Patton/99 12.00 30.00
12 Ryan Nassib/25 8.00 20.00
13 Giovani Bernard/99 5.00 12.00
14 Justin Hunter/25 8.00 20.00
15 Terrance Williams/25 8.00 20.00
16 Markus Wheaton/99 5.00 12.00
17 EJ Manuel/99 5.00 12.00
18 Denard Robinson/25
19 Johnathan Franklin/99 5.00 12.00
20 Joseph Randle/25 8.00 20.00
21 Tyler Eifert/25
22 Zach Ertz/99 10.00 25.00
23 Aaron Dobson/99 5.00 12.00
24 Knile Davis/99 5.00 12.00
25 Landry Jones/99 20.00 40.00
26 Montee Ball/99 5.00 12.00
27 Andre Ellington/99 5.00 12.00
28 Le'Veon Bell/99 15.00 40.00
29 Christine Michael/25
30 Stedman Bailey/25 25.00 50.00
32 Mike Gillislee/25
33 Tavarres King/99 5.00 12.00
34 Stepfan Taylor/99 5.00 12.00
35 Ryan Swope/99 5.00 12.00
36 Marquise Goodwin/99 5.00 12.00
37 Marcus Lattimore/99 5.00 12.00
38 Kenjon Barner/99 5.00 12.00
39 Kenny Stills/99 5.00 12.00
41 Gavin Escobar/99 10.00 25.00
42 Jordan Reed/25
43 Travis Kelce/99 12.00 30.00
44 Tyrann Mathieu/25
45 Dee Milliner/25 8.00 20.00
47 Dion Jordan/25 20.00 40.00
48 Manti Te'o/99 25.00 50.00
50 Jarvis Jones/99 5.00 12.00

2013 Score Inscriptions

1 A.J. Green SP
2 Aaron Hernandez SP
3 Adrian Peterson SP
4 Ronde Barber 8.00 20.00
5 Akeem Ayers 2.50 6.00
6 Alfred Morris 2.50 6.00
7 Andre Roberts 3.00 8.00
8 Andrew Luck SP
9 Andy Dalton 10.00 25.00
10 Anquan Boldin SP
11 Antonio Brown 8.00 20.00
12 Ben Roethlisberger SP 30.00 60.00
13 BenJarvus Green-Ellis SP
14 Brandon Pettigrew SP
15 Brent Celek SP
16 Bryce Brown 4.00 10.00
17 C.J. Spiller SP
18 Cam Newton SP 40.00 80.00
19 Cecil Shorts 2.50 6.00
20 Robert Mathis SP 5.00 12.00
21 Christian Ponder SP
22 Clay Matthews SP
23 Colin Kaepernick SP 15.00 40.00
24 Danario Alexander 2.50 6.00
25 DeMarcus Ware SP 10.00 25.00
26 Demaryius Thomas SP 8.00 20.00
27 Denarius Moore 3.00 8.00
28 DeSean Jackson 5.00 12.00
29 Dexter McCluster SP 5.00 12.00
30 Doug Martin SP 15.00 30.00
31 Drew Brees SP 30.00 80.00
32 Pierre Thomas SP 6.00 15.00
33 Dustin Keller SP
35 Frank Gore SP 8.00 20.00
36 Greg McElroy 4.00 10.00
37 J.J. Watt SP 30.00 60.00
38 Jamaal Charles SP 15.00 30.00
39 Jared Allen SP 15.00 30.00
40 Jared Cook SP
41 Jason Pierre-Paul SP 5.00 12.00
42 Jason Witten SP
43 Jeremy Maclin SP 6.00 15.00
44 Jermaine Gresham 3.00 8.00
45 Jermichael Finley SP 5.00 12.00
46 Jerod Mayo SP 5.00 12.00
47 Jimmy Graham SP
48 Joe Flacco SP 15.00 30.00
49 Jonathan Dwyer 2.50 6.00
50 Josh Freeman SP 5.00 12.00
51 Josh Gordon SP
52 Justin Blackmon SP
53 Kellen Davis SP 5.00 12.00
54 Kenny Britt 2.50 6.00
55 Knowshon Moreno SP 6.00 15.00
56 Kyle Rudolph 4.00 10.00
57 Lance Kendricks 2.50 6.00
58 LeSean McCoy 8.00 20.00
59 London Fletcher SP
60 Mark Ingram 6.00 15.00
61 Marshawn Lynch SP
62 Matt Forte SP
63 Matt Ryan SP 30.00 60.00
64 Matt Schaub SP 5.00 12.00
65 Matthew Stafford SP 25.00 50.00
66 Maurice Jones-Drew SP 6.00 15.00
67 Michael Floyd SP 5.00 12.00
68 Mike Wallace SP
69 Navorro Bowman SP 6.00 15.00
70 Niles Paul 2.50 6.00
71 Owen Daniels SP 5.00 12.00
72 Patrick Willis SP
73 Paul Posluszny SP 5.00 12.00
74 Peyton Manning SP
75 Randall Cobb SP 8.00 20.00
76 Rashard Mendenhall SP 5.00 12.00
77 Robert Griffin III SP 12.00 30.00
78 Roy Helu 2.50 6.00
79 Russell Wilson SP 50.00 100.00
80 Ryan Tannehill SP 20.00 50.00
81 Sam Bradford SP 12.00 30.00
82 Santana Moss SP
83 Mario Williams SP 6.00 15.00
84 Kevin Walter SP 6.00 15.00
85 Sean Lee 6.00 15.00
87 T.Y. Hilton 4.00 10.00
88 Jonathan Stewart SP
90 Torrey Smith SP
91 Trent Richardson SP
92 Vick Ballard SP 5.00 12.00
93 Von Miller SP 6.00 15.00
94 Antoine Bethea 3.00 8.00
95 Blaine Gabbert SP 5.00 12.00
96 James Starks 2.50 6.00
97 Jonathan Baldwin SP
98 Brian Cushing 5.00 12.00
99 Champ Bailey SP 15.00 30.00
100 Derrick Johnson SP 12.00 30.00

2013 Score Rookie Signatures

*BLUE: .5X TO 1.2X BASIC AU
*BLUE: .4X TO 1X BASIC SP AU
*PURPLE: .6X TO 1.5X BASIC AU
*PURPLE: .5X TO 1.2X BASIC SP AU

*RED/49: .8X TO 2X BASIC AU
*RED/49: .5X TO 1.2X BASIC SP AU
331 Aaron Dobson 3.00 8.00
332 Aaron Mellette 3.00 8.00
335 Alec Ogletree 3.00 8.00
336 Alex Okafor 3.00 8.00
337 Andre Ellington 3.00 8.00
338 Arthur Brown 3.00 8.00
340 Bjoern Werner 3.00 8.00
342 Darius Slay SP 8.00 20.00
343 Chris Gragg 3.00 8.00
344 Chris Harper 6.00 15.00
345 Christine Michael SP
349 Eric Fisher 8.00 20.00
350 Conner Vernon 3.00 8.00
351 Cordarrelle Patterson SP 3.00 8.00
352 Corey Fuller 3.00 8.00
353 Damontre Moore 3.00 8.00
354 Da'Rick Rogers 3.00 8.00
355 Datone Jones 8.00 20.00
356 DeAndre Hopkins 6.00 15.00
357 Dee Milliner SP 3.00 8.00
358 Denard Robinson SP
359 Dennis Johnson SP 3.00 8.00
360 Johnathan Cyprien 3.00 8.00
361 Dion Jordan SP 20.00 40.00
362 Dion Sims 3.00 8.00
363 Eddie Lacy 3.00 8.00
364 EJ Manuel SP 20.00 50.00
365 Eric Reid 4.00 10.00
367 Gavin Escobar 8.00 20.00
368 Geno Smith SP 3.00 8.00
369 Giovani Bernard 3.00 8.00
371 Jarvis Jones 3.00 8.00
372 Jasper Collins 3.00 8.00
377 Johnathan Franklin 3.00 8.00
378 Jordan Poyer SP 3.00 8.00
379 Jordan Reed SP
381 Joseph Randle SP 3.00 8.00
382 Josh Boyce 3.00 8.00
383 Justin Hunter SP 15.00 30.00
384 Keenan Allen 6.00 15.00
385 Kenjon Barner 3.00 8.00
386 Kenny Stills 3.00 8.00
387 Kenny Vaccaro 3.00 8.00
389 Kevin Minter 3.00 8.00
391 Landry Jones 15.00 30.00
392 Le'Veon Bell 15.00 30.00
395 Manti Te'o 4.00 10.00
396 Tyrann Mathieu SP
397 Marcus Lattimore 3.00 8.00
398 Desmond Trufant 3.00 8.00
399 Margus Hunt 5.00 12.00
400 Knile Davis 3.00 8.00
401 Markus Wheaton 3.00 8.00
403 Marquise Goodwin 8.00 20.00
404 Matt Barkley 10.00 25.00
405 Matt Elam 3.00 8.00
406 Matt Scott SP 5.00 12.00
407 Onterio McCalebb 4.00 10.00
408 Mike Gillislee SP
409 Mike Glennon 3.00 8.00
410 Montee Ball 3.00 8.00
411 Nick Kasa 3.00 8.00
412 Phillip Thomas SP 3.00 8.00
413 Quinton Patton 6.00 15.00
415 Ryan Otten 3.00 8.00
416 Rex Burkhead SP 15.00 30.00
418 Robert Woods 5.00 12.00
419 Rodney Smith 5.00 12.00
420 Ryan Nassib SP 10.00 25.00
421 Ryan Swope 3.00 8.00
422 Sam Montgomery SP 3.00 8.00
425 Stedman Bailey SP 12.50 25.00
426 Stepfan Taylor 3.00 8.00
427 Tavarres King 3.00 8.00
428 Tavon Austin 4.00 10.00
429 Terrance Williams SP 3.00 8.00
431 Travis Kelce 8.00 20.00
432 Tyler Bray 3.00 8.00
433 Tyler Eifert SP 3.00 8.00
434 Tyler Wilson 10.00 25.00
436 Chance Warmack 6.00 15.00
437 Xavier Rhodes 3.00 8.00
438 Zac Dysert
439 Zach Ertz 6.00 15.00

2013 Score Rookie Signatures Black

*BLACK/25: 1X TO 2.5X BASIC AU
351 Cordarrelle Patterson/25 8.00 20.00
363 Eddie Lacy/25 8.00 20.00
404 Matt Barkley/25 25.00 60.00
410 Montee Ball/25 8.00 20.00

2014 Score Previews

1 Johnny Manziel 3.00 8.00
2 Jadeveon Clowney 2.50 6.00
3 Blake Bortles 2.50 6.00
4 Teddy Bridgewater 3.00 8.00
5 Sammy Watkins 3.00 8.00
6 Greg Robinson 5.00 12.00

2014 Score

COMPLETE SET (440) 25.00 50.00
1 Carson Palmer .15 .40
2 Larry Fitzgerald .15 .40
3 Michael Floyd .12 .30
4 Andre Ellington .12 .30
5 Tyrann Mathieu .15 .40
6 Robert Housler .12 .30
7 Patrick Peterson .12 .30
8 Matt Ryan .15 .40
9 Julio Jones .20 .50
10 Roddy White .12 .30
11 Harry Douglas .12 .30
12 Steven Jackson .12 .30
13 Jacquizz Rodgers .12 .30
14 Levine Toilolo .12 .30
15 Joe Flacco .15 .40
16 Torrey Smith .12 .30
17 Marlon Brown .12 .30
18 Ray Rice .12 .30
19 Bernard Pierce .12 .30
20 Dennis Pitta .12 .30
21 Steve Smith .15 .40
22 Terrell Suggs .12 .30
23 EJ Manuel .12 .30
24 Steve Johnson .15 .40
25 Robert Woods .15 .40
26 C.J. Spiller .12 .30
27 Fred Jackson .15 .40
28 Mario Williams .12 .30
29 Kiko Alonso .12 .30
30A Cam Newton w/FB .20 .50
30B Cam Newton SP w/o FB 8.00 20.00
31 Greg Hardy .12 .30
32 Jerricho Cotchery .12 .30
33 DeAngelo Williams .12 .30
34 Jonathan Stewart .12 .30
35 Greg Olsen .15 .40
36 Luke Kuechly .15 .40
37 Jay Cutler .12 .30
38 Tim Jennings .12 .30
39 Brandon Marshall .12 .30
40 Alshon Jeffery .15 .40
41 Matt Forte .12 .30
42 Lance Briggs .15 .40
43 Martellus Bennett .12 .30
44 Andy Dalton .15 .40
45 A.J. Green .20 .50
46 Marvin Jones .12 .30
47 Giovani Bernard .12 .30
48 BenJarvus Green-Ellis .15 .40
49 Jermaine Gresham .12 .30
50 Tyler Eifert .15 .40
51 Geno Atkins .12 .30
52 Brian Hoyer .12 .30
53 Josh Gordon .12 .30
54 Ben Tate .12 .30
55 Jordan Cameron .12 .30
56 Joe Haden .12 .30
57 Barkevious Mingo .12 .30
58 Tony Romo .15 .40
59 Dez Bryant .20 .50
60 Terrance Williams .12 .30
61 DeMarco Murray .15 .40
62 Lance Dunbar .12 .30
63 Jason Witten .15 .40
64 Sean Lee .15 .40
65 Morris Claiborne .12 .30
66 Peyton Manning .40 1.00
67 Demaryius Thomas .15 .40
68 Wes Welker .15 .40
69 Montee Ball .12 .30
70 DeMarcus Ware .15 .40
71 Julius Thomas .12 .30
72 Von Miller .15 .40
73 Matthew Stafford .15 .40
74 Calvin Johnson .20 .50
75 Kris Durham .12 .30
76 Reggie Bush .12 .30
77 Golden Tate .15 .40
78 Brandon Pettigrew .12 .30
79 Nick Fairley .12 .30
80 Aaron Rodgers .40 1.00
81 Jordy Nelson .15 .40
82 Randall Cobb .15 .40
83 Andrew Quarless .12 .30
84 Julius Peppers .15 .40
85 Eddie Lacy .12 .30
86 Clay Matthews .20 .50
87 Case Keenum .15 .40
88 Andre Johnson .15 .40
89 DeAndre Hopkins .15 .40
90A Arian Foster w/FB .15 .40
90B Arian Foster SP w/o FB 4.00 10.00
91 Dennis Johnson .12 .30
92 Garrett Graham .12 .30
93 J.J. Watt .20 .50
94 Andrew Luck .25 .60
95 Reggie Wayne .15 .40
96 T.Y. Hilton .15 .40
97 Hakeem Nicks .12 .30
98 Trent Richardson .12 .30
99 Vick Ballard .12 .30
100 Vontae Davis .12 .30
101 Chad Henne .12 .30
102 Justin Blackmon .12 .30
103 Cecil Shorts .12 .30
104 Ace Sanders .12 .30
105 Toby Gerhart .12 .30
106 Marcedes Lewis .12 .30
107 Alex Smith .15 .40
108 Dwayne Bowe .15 .40
109 Derrick Johnson .12 .30
110 Jamaal Charles .15 .40
111 Knile Davis .12 .30
112 Eric Berry .15 .40
113 Justin Houston .12 .30
114 Ryan Tannehill .15 .40
115 Mike Wallace .12 .30
116 Brian Hartline .12 .30
117 Lamar Miller .12 .30
118 Daniel Thomas .12 .30
119 Charles Clay .12 .30
120 Cameron Wake .12 .30
121 Matt Cassel .12 .30
122 Cordarrelle Patterson .12 .30
123 Greg Jennings .12 .30
124 Adrian Peterson .20 .50
125 Xavier Rhodes .12 .30
126 Kyle Rudolph .12 .30
127 Captain Munnerlyn .12 .30
128 Tom Brady .50 1.25
129 Danny Amendola .15 .40
130 Kenbrell Thompkins .12 .30
131 Julian Edelman .20 .50
132 Stevan Ridley .12 .30
133 Darrelle Revis .12 .30
134A R.Gronkowski white .20 .50
134B R.Gronkowski SP red 5.00 12.00
135 Drew Brees .20 .50
136 Marques Colston .12 .30
137 Kenny Stills .12 .30
138 Khiry Robinson .15 .40
139 Jairus Byrd .12 .30
140 Pierre Thomas .12 .30
141 Mark Ingram .15 .40
142A J.Graham waist .20 .50
142B J.Graham SP shldr 5.00 12.00
143 Eli Manning .15 .40
144 Victor Cruz .15 .40
145 Rueben Randle .12 .30
146 Rashad Jennings .12 .30
147 David Wilson .12 .30
148 Prince Amukamara .12 .30
149 Jason Pierre-Paul .12 .30
150 Geno Smith .12 .30
151 Jeremy Kerley .12 .30
152 Eric Decker .12 .30
153 Chris Ivory .15 .40
154 Michael Vick .15 .40
155 Sheldon Richardson .12 .30
156 Justin Tuck .12 .30
157 Matt McGloin .15 .40
158 Andre Holmes RC .20 .50
159 Denarius Moore .12 .30
160 Darren McFadden .12 .30
161 James Jones .12 .30
162 Matt Schaub .12 .30
163 Nick Foles .15 .40
164 Arrelious Benn .12 .30
165 Jeremy Maclin .12 .30
166 Riley Cooper .15 .40
167 LeSean McCoy .20 .50
168 Bryce Brown .12 .30
169 Brent Celek .12 .30
170 Darren Sproles .15 .40
171 Ben Roethlisberger .20 .50
172 Antonio Brown .20 .50
173 Maurkice Pouncey .12 .30
174 Le'Veon Bell .15 .40
175 Heath Miller .12 .30
176 Troy Polamalu .20 .50
177 Philip Rivers .20 .50
178 Keenan Allen .15 .40
179 Eddie Royal .12 .30
180 Ryan Mathews .15 .40
181 Danny Woodhead .15 .40
182 Antonio Gates .12 .30
183 Manti Te'o .15 .40
184 Eric Weddle .12 .30
185A C.Kaepernick hand off .15 .40
185B Kaepernick SP celebrate 8.00 20.00
186 Anquan Boldin .12 .30
187 Michael Crabtree .12 .30
188 Frank Gore .15 .40
189 Kendall Hunter .12 .30
190 Vernon Davis .12 .30
191 Aldon Smith .12 .30
192 Patrick Willis .15 .40
193 Russell Wilson .30 .75
194 Doug Baldwin .15 .40
195 Percy Harvin .12 .30
196 Bruce Irvin .12 .30
197 Marshawn Lynch .15 .40
198 Zach Miller .12 .30
199 Richard Sherman .20 .50
200 Kam Chancellor .20 .50
201 Malcolm Smith RC .20 .50
202 Sam Bradford .12 .30
203 Tavon Austin .12 .30
204 Chris Givens .12 .30
205 Zac Stacy .12 .30
206 Daryl Richardson .12 .30
207 Jared Cook .12 .30
208 James Laurinaitis .15 .40
209 Mike Glennon .15 .40
210 Josh McCown .12 .30
211 Vincent Jackson .12 .30
212 Doug Martin .15 .40
213 Mike James .12 .30
214 Timothy Wright .12 .30
215 Lavonte David .12 .30
216 Jake Locker .15 .40
217 Dexter McCluster .15 .40
218 Kendall Wright .12 .30
219 Justin Hunter .12 .30
220 Nate Washington .12 .30
221 Chris Johnson .12 .30
222 Shonn Greene .12 .30
223 Delanie Walker .12 .30
224 Robert Griffin III .12 .30
225 Pierre Garcon .15 .40
226 Santana Moss .15 .40
227 Alfred Morris .12 .30
228 Andre Roberts .12 .30
229 Jordan Reed .12 .30
230 Brian Orakpo .12 .30
231 Peyton Manning H100 .40 1.00
232 Adrian Peterson H100 .20 .50
233 Drew Brees H100 .20 .50
234 Calvin Johnson H100 .20 .50
235 Tom Brady H100 .50 1.25
236 Aaron Rodgers H100 .40 1.00
237 LeSean McCoy H100 .20 .50
238 Jamaal Charles H100 .15 .40
239 A.J. Green H100 .20 .50
240 Brandon Marshall H100 .12 .30
241 Arian Foster H100 .15 .40
242 Dez Bryant H100 .20 .50
243 Jimmy Graham H100 .20 .50
244 Larry Fitzgerald H100 .15 .40
245 Tony Romo H100 .15 .40
246 Marshawn Lynch H100 .15 .40
247 Andrew Luck H100 .25 .60
248 Andre Johnson H100 .15 .40
249 Russell Wilson H100 .30 .75
250 Demaryius Thomas H100 .15 .40
251 Matthew Stafford H100 .15 .40
252 Julio Jones H100 .20 .50
253 Wes Welker H100 .15 .40
254 Cam Newton H100 .20 .50
255 J.J. Watt H100 .20 .50
256 Josh Gordon H100 .12 .30
257 Geno Atkins H100 .12 .30
258 Philip Rivers H100 .20 .50
259 Jordy Nelson H100 .15 .40
260 Alshon Jeffery H100 .15 .40
261 Matt Forte H100 .12 .30
262 Richard Sherman H100 .20 .50
263 Luke Kuechly H100 .15 .40
264 Von Miller H100 .15 .40
265 Rob Gronkowski H100 .20 .50
266 Colin Kaepernick H100 .15 .40
267 Patrick Peterson H100 .12 .30
268 Antonio Brown H100 .20 .50
269 Joe Haden H100 .12 .30
270 Percy Harvin H100 .12 .30
271 Earl Thomas H100 .15 .40
272 Vontaze Burfict H100 .12 .30
273 Reggie Wayne H100 .15 .40
274 Robert Mathis H100 .12 .30
275 Julius Thomas H100 .12 .30
276 Clay Matthews H100 .20 .50
277 Frank Gore H100 .15 .40
278 Robert Quinn H100 .15 .40
279 Vernon Davis H100 .12 .30
280 Vincent Jackson H100 .12 .30
281 Alfred Morris H100 .12 .30
282 DeSean Jackson H100 .15 .40
283 Mario Williams H100 .12 .30
284 NaVorro Bowman H100 .15 .40
285 Cameron Jordan H100 .12 .30
286 Reggie Bush H100 .12 .30
287 Victor Cruz H100 .15 .40
288 Eric Berry H100 .15 .40
289 Charles Tillman H100 .15 .40
290 Paul Posluszny H100 .12 .30
291 Anquan Boldin H100 .12 .30
292 Jordan Cameron H100 .12 .30
293 Ndamukong Suh H100 .15 .40
294 Joe Flacco H100 .15 .40
295 Lavonte David H100 .12 .30
296 Greg Hardy H100 .12 .30
297 Ben Roethlisberger H100 .20 .50
298 Derrick Johnson H100 .12 .30
299 Chris Johnson H100 .12 .30
300 Tamba Hali H100 .12 .30
301 Eric Decker H100 .12 .30
302 Nate Solder H100 .20 .50
303 Tyron Smith H100 .12 .30
304 Torrey Smith H100 .12 .30
305 Matt Ryan H100 .15 .40
306 Aldon Smith H100 .12 .30
307 Eli Manning H100 .15 .40
308 Doug Martin H100 .15 .40
309 Jay Cutler H100 .12 .30
310 Ray Rice H100 .12 .30
311 Justin Houston H100 .12 .30
312 Jason Witten H100 .15 .40
313 Jared Allen H100 .12 .30
314 Darrelle Revis H100 .12 .30
315 Dwayne Bowe H100 .15 .40
316 Tim Jennings H100 .12 .30
317 Matt Prater H100 .20 .50
318 Roddy White H100 .12 .30
319 Brian Orakpo H100 .12 .30
320 Cameron Wake H100 .12 .30
321 Pierre Garcon H100 .15 .40
322 Jason Pierre-Paul H100 .12 .30
323 Terrell Suggs H100 .12 .30
324 Keenan Allen H100 .15 .40
325 Robert Griffin III H100 .12 .30
326 Kiko Alonso H100 .12 .30
327 Demarco Murray H100 .15 .40
328 Devin McCourty H100 .12 .30
329 DeMarcus Ware H100 .15 .40
330 T.J. Ward H100 .12 .30
331 A.J. McCarron RC .25 .60
332 Aaron Donald RC .60 1.50
333 Aaron Murray RC .25 .60
334 Ahmad Dixon RC .25 .60
335 Allen Robinson RC .40 1.00
336 Andre Williams RC .25 .60
337 Anthony Barr RC .25 .60
338 Austin Seferian-Jenkins RC .25 .60
339 Bishop Sankey RC .25 .60
340 Blake Bortles RC .30 .75
341 Bradley Roby RC .25 .60
342 Brandin Cooks RC .40 1.00
343 Brandon Coleman RC .25 .60
344 Brett Smith RC .25 .60
345 Bruce Ellington RC .25 .60
346 C.J. Fiedorowicz RC .25 .60
347 C.J. Mosley RC .30 .75
348 Calvin Pryor RC .25 .60
349 Carlos Hyde RC .30 .75
350 Charles Sims RC .25 .60
351 Chris Borland RC .25 .60
352 Chris Smith RC .25 .60
353 Cody Latimer RC .30 .75
354 Connor Shaw RC .25 .60
355 Cyril Richardson RC .25 .60
356 Cyrus Kouandjio RC .30 .75
357 Darqueze Dennard RC .30 .75
358 Davante Adams RC .40 1.00
359 David Fales RC .25 .60
360 David Yankey RC .25 .60
361 De'Anthony Thomas RC .25 .60
362 Dee Ford RC .25 .60
363 Deone Bucannon RC .25 .60
364 Derek Carr RC 1.50 4.00
365 Devonta Freeman RC .40 1.00
366 Donte Moncrief RC .25 .60
367 Dri Archer RC .25 .60
368 Ed Reynolds RC .25 .60
369 Eric Ebron RC .30 .75
370 Greg Robinson RC .25 .60
371 Ha Ha Clinton-Dix RC .30 .75
372 Jace Amaro RC .25 .60
373 Jackson Jeffcoat RC .30 .75
374 Jadeveon Clowney RC .30 .75
375 Jake Matthews RC .25 .60
376 Jalen Saunders RC .25 .60
377 James White RC .50 1.25
378 James Wilder Jr. RC .30 .75
379 Jared Abbrederis RC .25 .60
380 Jarvis Landry RC .50 1.25
381 Jason Verrett RC .25 .60
382 Jeff Janis RC .25 .60
383 Jeremy Hill RC .30 .75
384 Jerick McKinnon RC .30 .75
385 Tom Savage RC .25 .60
386 Jimmy Garoppolo RC 2.00 5.00
387 Johnny Manziel RC .40 1.00
388 Jordan Matthews RC .40 1.00
389 Josh Huff RC .30 .75
390 Ka'Deem Carey RC .25 .60
391 Kelvin Benjamin RC .40 1.00
392 Kevin Norwood RC .25 .60
393 Khalil Mack RC 1.00 2.50
394 Kony Ealy RC .30 .75
395 Kyle Fuller RC .25 .60
396 Kyle Van Noy RC .30 .75
397 L'Damian Washington RC .30 .75
398 Lache Seastrunk RC .25 .60
399 Lamarcus Joyner RC .30 .75
400 Logan Thomas RC .25 .60
401 Louis Nix III RC .25 .60
402 Marcus Roberson RC .30 .75
403 Marcus Smith RC .25 .60
404 Marion Grice RC .25 .60
405 Marqise Lee RC .30 .75
406 Martavis Bryant RC .30 .75
407 Michael Campanaro RC .25 .60
408 Michael Sam RC .25 .60
409 Mike Davis RC .25 .60
410 Mike Evans RC .60 1.50
411 Odell Beckham Jr. RC .60 1.50
412 Paul Richardson RC .30 .75
413 Isaiah Crowell RC .30 .75
414 Ra'Shede Hageman RC .25 .60
415 Robert Herron RC .25 .60
416 Ryan Grant RC .25 .60
417 Ryan Shazier RC .40 1.00
418 Sammy Watkins RC .40 1.00
419 Scott Crichton RC .25 .60
420 Shaq Evans RC .25 .60
421 Shayne Skov RC .25 .60
422 Stephon Tuitt RC .40 1.00
423 Storm Johnson RC .25 .60
424 Tajh Boyd RC .25 .60
425 Taylor Lewan RC .25 .60
426 Teddy Bridgewater RC .40 1.00
427 Telvin Smith RC .25 .60
428 Terrance West RC .25 .60
429 Tevin Reese RC .25 .60
430 Timmy Jernigan RC .25 .60
431 TJ Jones RC .40 1.00
432 Travis Swanson RC .25 .60
433 Tre Mason RC .25 .60
434 Trent Murphy RC .25 .60
435 Trevor Reilly RC .25 .60
436 Troy Niklas RC .25 .60
437 Xavier Su'A-Filo RC .30 .75
438 Yawin Smallwood RC .25 .60
439 Zach Mettenberger RC .25 .60
440 Zack Martin RC .30 .75

2014 Score Artist's Proof

*1-330 VETS/35: 8X TO 20X BASIC CARDS
*331-440 ROOKIES/35: 5X TO 12X BASIC RC

2014 Score Gold Zone

*1-330 VETS/50: 4X TO 10X BASIC CARDS
*331-440 ROOKIES/50: 2.5X TO 6X BASIC RC

2014 Score Red Zone

*1-330 VETS/20: 10X TO 25X BASIC CARDS
*331-440 ROOKIES/20: 6X TO 15X BASIC RC

2014 Score Scorecard

*1-330 VETS: 2X TO 5X BASIC CARDS
*331-440 ROOKIES: 1X TO 2.5X BASIC RC
STATED ODDS 1:6

2014 Score Showcase

*1-330 VETS/99: 3X TO 8X BASIC CARDS
*331-440 ROOKIES/99: 2X TO 5X BASIC RC

2014 Score '89 Score Quarterbacks

1 Peyton Manning 2.50 6.00
2 Tom Brady 3.00 8.00
3 Drew Brees 1.25 3.00
4 Colin Kaepernick 1.00 2.50
5 Aaron Rodgers 3.00 8.00
6 Andrew Luck 3.00 8.00
7 Robert Griffin III .75 2.00
8 Russell Wilson 2.00 5.00

2014 Score Air Commanders Dual Jerseys

*PRIME/25: 1X TO 2.5X BASIC DUAL
ACCJ Jay Cutler 3.00 8.00
Alshon Jeffery
ACDG Andy Dalton 4.00 10.00
A.J. Green
ACFJ Joe Flacco 3.00 8.00
Jacoby Jones
ACMJ EJ Manuel 3.00 8.00
Steve Johnson
ACSB Alex Smith 3.00 8.00
Dwayne Bowe
ACTW Ryan Tannehill 3.00 8.00
Mike Wallace

2014 Score Air Mail Blue

*GOLD: .5X TO 1.2X BASIC INSERTS
*GREEN: .8X TO 2X BASIC INSERTS
*RED: .8X TO 2X BASIC INSERTS
STATED ODDS 1:24 OVERALL
AM1 Peyton Manning 2.00 5.00
AM2 Tom Brady 2.50 6.00
AM3 Josh Gordon .60 1.50
AM4 Pierre Garcon .75 2.00
AM5 Andrew Luck 1.25 3.00
AM6 Brandon Marshall .60 1.50
AM7 Jordy Nelson .75 2.00
AM8 Colin Kaepernick .75 2.00
AM9 Russell Wilson 1.50 4.00
AM10 DeSean Jackson .75 2.00

2014 Score Backfield Tandems Dual Jerseys

*PRIME/25: 1X TO 2.5X BASIC DUAL
BTBG Giovani Bernard 3.00 8.00
BenJarvus Green-Ellis
BTDC Knile Davis 4.00 10.00
Jamaal Charles
BTMD Daniel Thomas 2.50 6.00
Lamar Miller
BTMW Ryan Mathews 3.00 8.00
Danny Woodhead
BTSJ C.J. Spiller 3.00 8.00
Fred Jackson
BTWS DeAngelo Williams 2.50 6.00
Jonathan Stewart

2014 Score Behind The Numbers Blue

*GOLD: .5X TO 1.2X BASIC INSERTS
*GREEN: .6X TO 1.5X BASIC INSERTS
*RED: .5X TO 1.2X BASIC INSERTS
STATED ODDS 1:24 OVERALL
BN1 Jordy Nelson 1.00 2.50
BN2 Andre Johnson 1.00 2.50
BN3 Alshon Jeffery 1.00 2.50
BN4 Matthew Stafford 1.00 2.50
BN5 Vernon Davis .75 2.00
BN6 Matt Ryan 1.00 2.50
BN7 Nick Foles 1.00 2.50
BN8 Reggie Wayne 1.00 2.50
BN9 Wes Welker 1.00 2.50
BN10 Ryan Mathews 1.00 2.50
BN11 Alfred Morris .75 2.00
BN12 Marshawn Lynch 1.00 2.50
BN13 Julian Edelman 1.25 3.00
BN14 Dez Bryant 1.25 3.00
BN15 Josh Gordon .75 2.00
BN16 Ryan Tannehill 1.00 2.50
BN17 Victor Cruz 1.00 2.50
BN18 Mike Glennon 1.00 2.50

2014 Score Brothers In Arms Blue

*GOLD: .4X TO 1X BASIC INSERTS
*GREEN: .6X TO 1.5X BASIC INSERTS
*RED: .5X TO 1.2X BASIC INSERTS
STATED ODDS 1:6 OVERALL
BA1 L.Fitzgerald/P.Fanaika .60 1.50
BA2 J.Jones/R.White .75 2.00
BA3 Ray Rice .50 1.25
BA4 Fred Jackson .60 1.50
BA5 Newton/Tolbert/Chandler .75 2.00
BA6 Marshall/Jeffery/Mills .60 1.50
BA7 Sanu/G.Bernard/Eifert .60 1.50
BA8 G.Barnidge/B.Winn .50 1.25
BA9 J.Witten/M.Austin .60 1.50
BA10 D.Thomas/O.Franklin .60 1.50
BA11 C.Johnson/B.Pettigrew .75 2.00
BA12 N.Perry/C.Matthews .75 2.00
BA13 Garrett Graham .50 1.25
BA14 T.Hilton/G.Cherilus .60 1.50
BA15 Mike Brown .50 1.25
BA16 Dwayne Bowe .60 1.50
BA17 C.Clay/B.Hartline .50 1.25
BA18 Cassel/Kalil/Patterson .50 1.25
BA19 Thompkins/Hoomanawanui .50 1.25
BA20 Graham/Watson/Sproles .75 2.00
BA21 R.Barden/C.Snee .50 1.25
BA22 G.Smith/Hill/Colon .50 1.25
BA23 Brice Butler .50 1.25
BA24 LeSean McCoy .75 2.00
BA25 B.Roethlisberger/C.Hubbard .75 2.00
BA26 Royal/K.Allen/Brown .60 1.50
BA27 Colin Kaepernick .60 1.50
BA28 Doug Baldwin .60 1.50
BA29 Cory Harkey .50 1.25
BA30 M.Williams/D.Martin .60 1.50
BA31 Kendall Wright .50 1.25
BA32 P.Garcon/L.Hankerson .60 1.50

2014 Score Complete Players

STATED ODDS 1:12
CP1 Adrian Peterson .75 2.00
CP2 A.J. Green .75 2.00
CP3 Andre Johnson .60 1.50
CP4 Steve Smith .60 1.50
CP5 Vernon Davis .50 1.25
CP6 Jimmy Graham .75 2.00
CP7 Ray Rice .50 1.25
CP8 Roddy White .50 1.25
CP9 Patrick Peterson .50 1.25
CP10 Randall Cobb .60 1.50
CP11 Calvin Johnson .75 2.00
CP12 DeSean Jackson .60 1.50
CP13 Knowshon Moreno .50 1.25
CP14 Antonio Gates .50 1.25
CP15 Pierre Garcon .60 1.50
CP16 Richard Sherman .75 2.00
CP17 Rob Gronkowski .75 2.00
CP18 Jason Witten .60 1.50
CP19 Joe Haden .50 1.25
CP20 Maurice Jones-Drew .50 1.25
CP21 Victor Cruz .60 1.50
CP22 Ben Roethlisberger .75 2.00
CP23 Zac Stacy .50 1.25
CP24 Earl Thomas .60 1.50

2014 Score Destination End Zone Blue

*GOLD: .4X TO 1X BASIC INSERTS
*GREEN: .5X TO 1.2X BASIC INSERTS
*RED: .5X TO 1.2X BASIC INSERTS
STATED ODDS 1:24 OVERALL
DE1 Jamaal Charles 1.00 2.50
DE2 Marshawn Lynch 1.00 2.50
DE3 Eddie Lacy .75 2.00
DE4 Knowshon Moreno .75 2.00
DE5 Adrian Peterson 1.25 3.00
DE6 Frank Gore 1.00 2.50
DE7 Jimmy Graham 1.25 3.00
DE8 Demaryius Thomas 1.00 2.50
DE9 Dez Bryant 1.25 3.00
DE10 Vernon Davis .75 2.00
DE11 Calvin Johnson 1.25 3.00
DE12 Julius Thomas .75 2.00

2014 Score Field Commanders

COMPLETE SET (10) 8.00 20.00
STATED ODDS 1:24
FC1 Aaron Rodgers 1.50 4.00
FC2 Ben Roethlisberger .75 2.00
FC3 Colin Kaepernick .60 1.50
FC4 Drew Brees .75 2.00
FC5 Andrew Luck 1.00 2.50
FC6 Peyton Manning 1.50 4.00
FC7 Philip Rivers .75 2.00
FC8 Russell Wilson 1.25 3.00
FC9 Robert Griffin III .50 1.25
FC10 Tom Brady 2.00 5.00

2014 Score Franchise Blue

*GOLD: .4X TO 1X BASIC INSERTS
*GREEN: .5X TO 1.2X BASIC INSERTS
*RED: .5X TO 1.2X BASIC INSERTS
STATED ODDS 1:12 OVERALL
F1 Aaron Rodgers 2.50 6.00
F2 Adrian Peterson 1.25 3.00
F3 A.J. Green 1.25 3.00
F4 Arian Foster 1.00 2.50
F5 Matt Forte .75 2.00
F6 Calvin Johnson 1.25 3.00
F7 Cam Newton 1.25 3.00
F8 C.J. Spiller .75 2.00
F9 Colin Kaepernick 1.00 2.50
F10 Drew Brees 1.25 3.00
F11 Jamaal Charles 1.00 2.50
F12 Joe Flacco 1.00 2.50
F13 Julio Jones 1.25 3.00
F14 Larry Fitzgerald 1.00 2.50
F15 LeSean McCoy 1.25 3.00
F16 Andrew Luck 1.50 4.00
F17 Peyton Manning 2.50 6.00
F18 Philip Rivers 1.25 3.00
F19 Robert Griffin III .75 2.00
F20 Russell Wilson 2.00 5.00
F21 Tom Brady 3.00 8.00
F22 Tony Romo 1.00 2.50

2014 Score Franchise Fabrics

FFDT Demaryius Thomas 3.00 8.00
FFEM Eli Manning 3.00 8.00
FFJC Jamaal Charles 3.00 8.00
FFJF Joe Flacco 3.00 8.00
FFLF Larry Fitzgerald 3.00 8.00
FFMR Matt Ryan 3.00 8.00
FFTB Tom Brady 10.00 25.00
FFTR Tony Romo 3.00 8.00

2014 Score Future Franchise Fabrics

FFFAE Andre Ellington 2.50 6.00
FFFBM Barkevious Mingo 2.50 6.00
FFFBP Bernard Pierce 2.50 6.00
FFFJB Justin Blackmon 2.50 6.00
FFFJH Justin Houston 2.50 6.00
FFFKA Kiko Alonso 2.50 6.00
FFFMC Morris Claiborne 2.50 6.00
FFFMG Mike Gillislee 2.50 6.00

2014 Score Hot Rookies

COMPLETE SET (50) 25.00 60.00
HR1 Johnny Manziel .60 1.50
HR2 Teddy Bridgewater .60 1.50
HR3 Blake Bortles .50 1.25
HR4 Sammy Watkins .60 1.50
HR5 Mike Evans 1.00 2.50
HR6 Marqise Lee .50 1.25
HR7 Odell Beckham Jr. 1.00 2.50
HR8 Brandin Cooks .60 1.50
HR9 Kelvin Benjamin .60 1.50
HR10 Derek Carr 2.50 6.00
HR11 Jimmy Garoppolo 3.00 8.00
HR12 A.J. McCarron .40 1.00
HR13 Carlos Hyde .50 1.25
HR14 Ka'Deem Carey .40 1.00
HR15 Bishop Sankey .40 1.00
HR16 Allen Robinson .60 1.50
HR17 Davante Adams .60 1.50
HR18 Jordan Matthews .60 1.50
HR19 Paul Richardson .50 1.25
HR20 Eric Ebron .50 1.25
HR21 Charles Sims .40 1.00
HR22 Darqueze Dennard .50 1.25
HR23 Andre Williams .40 1.00
HR24 Terrance West .40 1.00
HR25 Devonta Freeman .60 1.50
HR26 Zach Mettenberger .40 1.00
HR27 Aaron Murray .40 1.00
HR28 Tom Savage .40 1.00
HR29 Jadeveon Clowney .50 1.25
HR30 Jace Amaro .40 1.00
HR31 Austin Seferian-Jenkins .40 1.00
HR32 Jarvis Landry .75 2.00
HR33 Donte Moncrief .40 1.00
HR34 Martavis Bryant .50 1.25
HR35 Bruce Ellington .40 1.00
HR36 Cody Latimer .50 1.25
HR37 Dri Archer .40 1.00
HR38 Jerick McKinnon .50 1.25
HR39 Jeremy Hill .50 1.25
HR40 Tre Mason .40 1.00
HR41 Troy Niklas .40 1.00
HR42 De'Anthony Thomas .40 1.00
HR43 Josh Huff .50 1.25
HR44 Logan Thomas .40 1.00
HR45 Anthony Barr .40 1.00
HR46 Ha Ha Clinton-Dix .50 1.25
HR47 John Brown .60 1.50
HR48 Kony Ealy .50 1.25
HR49 C.J. Mosley .50 1.25
HR50 Khalil Mack 1.50 4.00

2014 Score Hot Rookies Autographs

STATED PRINT RUN 25 SER.#'d SETS
HR1 Johnny Manziel 12.00 30.00
HR2 Teddy Bridgewater 40.00 80.00
HR3 Blake Bortles 10.00 25.00
HR4 Sammy Watkins 12.00 30.00
HR5 Mike Evans 25.00 60.00
HR6 Marqise Lee 10.00 25.00
HR7 Odell Beckham Jr. 40.00 80.00
HR8 Brandin Cooks
HR9 Kelvin Benjamin 12.00 30.00
HR10 Derek Carr 40.00 80.00
HR11 Jimmy Garoppolo 30.00 60.00
HR12 A.J. McCarron 40.00 80.00
HR13 Carlos Hyde 10.00 25.00
HR14 Ka'Deem Carey
HR15 Bishop Sankey 25.00 50.00
HR16 Allen Robinson
HR17 Davante Adams
HR18 Jordan Matthews 12.00 30.00
HR19 Paul Richardson
HR20 Eric Ebron 10.00 25.00
HR21 Charles Sims 8.00 20.00
HR22 Darqueze Dennard 10.00 25.00
HR23 Andre Williams 8.00 20.00
HR24 Terrance West
HR25 Devonta Freeman 12.00 30.00
HR26 Zach Mettenberger
HR27 Aaron Murray
HR28 Tom Savage
HR29 Jadeveon Clowney 10.00 25.00
HR30 Jace Amaro
HR31 Austin Seferian-Jenkins 10.00 25.00
HR32 Jarvis Landry
HR33 Donte Moncrief
HR34 Martavis Bryant
HR35 Bruce Ellington 8.00 20.00
HR36 Cody Latimer 10.00 25.00
HR37 Dri Archer
HR38 Jerick McKinnon
HR39 Jeremy Hill
HR40 Tre Mason
HR41 Troy Niklas 8.00 20.00
HR42 De'Anthony Thomas 8.00 20.00
HR43 Josh Huff 10.00 25.00
HR44 Logan Thomas
HR45 Anthony Barr 8.00 20.00
HR46 Ha Ha Clinton-Dix
HR47 John Brown
HR48 Kony Ealy 10.00 25.00
HR49 C.J. Mosley
HR50 Khalil Mack 15.00 40.00

2014 Score Hot Rookies Player of the Day Autographs

HRAW Asa Watson 3.00 8.00
HRCS Connor Shaw 5.00 12.00

2014 Score Inscriptions

IAA Akeem Ayers 3.00 8.00
IAB Andre Brown 3.00 8.00
IAB Arrelious Benn
IAD Aaron Dobson 3.00 8.00
IAE Andre Ellington
IAG Alex Green 3.00 8.00
IAH Andrew Hawkins 3.00 8.00
IAR Adrien Robinson 3.00 8.00
IBB Brice Butler 3.00 8.00
IBC Benny Cunningham
IBQ Brian Quick
IBR Bobby Rainey
ICB Cobi Hamilton 3.00 8.00
ICC Charles Clay 3.00 8.00
ICG Chris Gragg 3.00 8.00
ICG Chris Givens
ICH Chris Harper
ICH Chris Hogan
ICI Chris Ivory 4.00 10.00
ICK Case Keenum
ICP Chris Polk
ICR Chris Rainey
ICS Caleb Sturgis 3.00 8.00
ICU Courtney Upshaw 3.00 8.00
ICV Conner Vernon 3.00 8.00
ICW Chance Warmack 3.00 8.00
IDA Dwayne Allen
IDC David DeCastro 3.00 8.00
IDH Dwayne Harris 3.00 8.00
IDJ Dennis Johnson 3.00 8.00
IDJ Dion Jordan 3.00 8.00
IDJW D.J. Williams 3.00 8.00
IDL Dion Lewis 3.00 8.00
IDP Dennis Pitta 4.00 10.00
IDR Da'Rick Rogers
IDW Damian Williams
IEP Eric Page 3.00 8.00
IER Eric Reid 5.00 12.00
IEW Earl Wolff
IFG Frank Gore
IFJ Felix Jones 4.00 10.00
IGB Giovani Bernard
IGC Greg Childs 3.00 8.00
IGM Greg McElroy 6.00 15.00
IIP Isaiah Pead
IJB Jake Ballard 3.00 8.00
IJBOS Jon Bostic 3.00 8.00
IJBOY Jarrett Boykin
IJBR Justin Brown 3.00 8.00
IJC Jordan Cameron
IJH James Hanna 3.00 8.00
IJJ Janoris Jenkins 3.00 8.00
IJK Jeremy Kerley 4.00 10.00
IJR Joseph Randle
IJS Jimmy Smith 3.00 8.00
IJT Justin Tucker 6.00 15.00
IJT Jordan Todman 3.00 8.00
IKB Kenjon Barner
IKC Kirk Cousins 5.00 12.00
IKD Knile Davis
IKMA Keshawn Martin 3.00 8.00
IKMI Kevin Minter 3.00 8.00
IKS Kawann Short 3.00 8.00
IKW Kendall Wright
IKW Kerwynn Williams
ILW Luke Willson 4.00 10.00
IMB Marlon Brown
IMC Michael Cox 3.00 8.00
IME Michael Egnew
IMF Michael Floyd
IMS Malcolm Smith 40.00 80.00
IMS Matt Simms 3.00 8.00
IMW Markus Wheaton
INW Nate Washington
IPA Prince Amukamara 3.00 8.00
IPT Phillip Thomas 3.00 8.00
IRB Ronnie Brown
IRB Rex Burkhead 4.00 10.00
IRH Robert Housler 3.00 8.00
IRM Rahim Moore 3.00 8.00
IRN Ryan Nassib
IRR Rueben Randle
IRT Ryan Tannehill
IRT Robert Turbin 4.00 10.00
ITG Ted Ginn Jr. 3.00 8.00
ITH Trindon Holliday 3.00 8.00
ITM Tyrann Mathieu 4.00 10.00
ITW Terrance Williams
ITW Timothy Wright

2014 Score Numbers Game

COMPLETE SET (50) 12.00 30.00
STATED ODDS 1:6
NG1 R.Wilson/E.Manuel 1.25 3.00
NG2 M.Prater/D.bailey .75 2.00
NG3 J.Cutler/B.Hoyer .50 1.25
NG4 C.Kaepernick/G.Smith .60 1.50
NG5 M.Glennon/S.Bradford .60 1.50
NG6 T.Romo/N.Foles .60 1.50
NG7 D.Brees/M.Stafford .75 2.00
NG8 E.Manning/R.Griffin .60 1.50
NG9 R.Woods/D.Hopkins .60 1.50
NG10 P.Harvin/T.Austin .50 1.25
NG11 M.Colston/J.Gordon .50 1.25
NG12 A.Luck/T.Drady 2.00 5.00
NG13 K.Allen/T.Hilton .60 1.50
NG14 M.Brown/J.Blackmon .50 1.25
NG15 B.Marshall/M.Crabtree .50 1.25
NG16 A.Hawkins/D.Rogers .50 1.25
NG17 A.Jeffery/J.Wright .60 1.50
NG18 R.Tannehill/P.Rivers .75 2.00
NG19 P.Manning/A.Green 1.50 4.00
NG20 R.Cobb/J.Maclin .50 1.25
NG21 P.Peterson/L.Webb .50 1.25
NG22 F.Gore/R.Bush .60 1.50
NG23 M.Ingram/D.Martin .60 1.50
NG24 A.Foster/P.Thomas .50 1.25
NG25 J.Haden/V.Davis .50 1.25
NG26 B.Flowers/D.Revis .50 1.25
NG27 M.Lynch/R.Mathews .60 1.50
NG28 J.Charles/L.McCoy .75 2.00
NG29 R.Sherman/C.Bernard .75 2.00
NG30 E.Lacy/K.Moreno .50 1.25
NG31 A.Peterson/C.Spiller .75 2.00
NG32 E.Berry/E.Thomas .60 1.50
NG33 J.Kuhn/Z.Stacy .50 1.25
NG34 T.Mathieu/E.Weddle .60 1.50
NG35 S.Jackson/D.Woodhead .60 1.50
NG36 S.Lee/K.Alonso .60 1.50
NG37 D.Bryant/D.Thomas .75 2.00
NG38 E.Decker/J.Nelson .60 1.50
NG39 B.Pettigrew/R.Gronkowski .75 2.00
NG40 J.Reed/Z.Ertz .60 1.50
NG41 C.Patterson/A.Brown .75 2.00
NG42 W.Welker/T.Williams .60 1.50
NG43 V.Cruz/J.Graham .75 2.00
NG44 D.Ryans/L.Kuechly .60 1.50
NG45 V.Miller/R.Maualuga .60 1.50
NG46 C.Matthews/P.Wills .75 2.00
NG47 A.Smith/J.Watt .75 2.00
NG48 R.Quinn/M.Williams .60 1.50
NG49 L.Fitzgerald/J.Jones .75 2.00
NG50 M.Forte/S.Ridley .50 1.25

2014 Score Rookie Team Helmets

*GOLD/99: .6X TO 1.5X BASIC INSERTS
1 Johnny Manziel 2.50 6.00
2 Teddy Bridgewater 2.50 6.00
3 Blake Bortles 2.00 5.00
4 Sammy Watkins 2.50 6.00
5 Mike Evans 6.00 15.00
6 Marqise Lee 2.00 5.00
7 Odell Beckham Jr. 5.00 12.00
8 Brandin Cooks 2.50 6.00
9 Kelvin Benjamin 2.50 6.00
10 Derek Carr 10.00 25.00
11 Jimmy Garoppolo 12.00 30.00
12 A.J. McCarron 1.50 4.00
13 Carlos Hyde 2.00 5.00
14 Ka'Deem Carey 1.50 4.00
15 Bishop Sankey 1.50 4.00
16 Allen Robinson 2.50 6.00
17 Davante Adams 2.50 6.00
18 Jordan Matthews 2.50 6.00
19 Paul Richardson 2.00 5.00
20 Eric Ebron 2.00 5.00
21 Charles Sims 1.50 4.00
22 Lache Seastrunk 1.50 4.00
23 Andre Williams 1.50 4.00
24 Devonta Freeman 2.50 6.00
25 Zach Mettenberger 1.50 4.00
26 Aaron Murray 1.50 4.00
27 David Fales 1.50 4.00
28 Jadeveon Clowney 2.00 5.00
29 Jace Amaro 4.00 10.00
30 Jarvis Landry 3.00 8.00
31 Jeremy Hill 2.00 5.00
32 Tre Mason 1.50 4.00

2014 Score Shotgun Swatches

SSAS Alex Smith 3.00 8.00
SSEM EJ Manuel 2.50 6.00
SSJF Joe Flacco 3.00 8.00
SSNF Nick Foles 3.00 8.00
SSPM Peyton Manning 8.00 20.00
SSPR Philip Rivers 4.00 10.00

SSRG3 Robert Griffin III 2.50 6.00
SSRT Ryan Tannehill 3.00 8.00

2015 Score

1 Danny Lansanah RC .12 .30
2 Terrell Suggs .12 .30
3 Donald Brown .12 .30
4 James Starks .12 .30
5 Earl Thomas .15 .40
6 Tom Brady .50 1.25
7 Coby Fleener .12 .30
8 Nick Mangold .12 .30
9 Dexter McCluster .15 .40
10 Preston Parker .12 .30
11 Mike Glennon .15 .40
12 Ben Roethlisberger .20 .50
13 Keenan Allen .15 .40
14 Jordy Nelson .15 .40
15 Kam Chancellor .20 .50
16 Malcolm Butler .20 .50
17 Dwayne Allen .12 .30
18 Eric Decker .12 .30
19 Michael Griffin .12 .30
20 Victor Cruz .15 .40
21 Doug Martin .15 .40
22 Le'Veon Bell .15 .40
23 Malcom Floyd .12 .30
24 Randall Cobb .15 .40
25 Richard Sherman .20 .50
26 Rob Ninkovich .12 .30
27 Andre Johnson .15 .40
28 Jeremy Kerley .12 .30
29 Drew Brees .20 .50
30 Shane Vereen .15 .40
31 Bobby Rainey .12 .30
32 Antonio Brown .20 .50
33 Antonio Gates .12 .30
34 Davante Adams .15 .40
35 Bobby Wagner .12 .30
36 Jonas Gray RC .40 1.00
37 Donte Moncrief .15 .40
38 Jace Amaro .12 .30
39 Mark Ingram .15 .40
40 Jason Pierre-Paul .12 .30
41 Mike Evans .15 .40
42 Martavis Bryant .12 .30
43 Manti Te'o .15 .40
44 Andrew Quarless .12 .30
45 Colin Kaepernick .15 .40
46 LeGarrette Blount .15 .40
47 Robert Mathis .12 .30
48 Brandon Marshall .12 .30
49 Kenny Vaccaro .12 .30
50 Kirk Cousins .20 .50
51 Vincent Jackson .12 .30
52 Heath Miller .12 .30
53 Danny Woodhead .15 .40
54 Richard Rodgers .15 .40
55 Jerome Simpson .12 .30
56 Rob Gronkowski .20 .50
57 Brian Hoyer .12 .30
58 Sheldon Richardson .12 .30
59 Khiry Robinson .15 .40
60 Robert Griffin III .12 .30
61 Louis Murphy .15 .40
62 Markus Wheaton .12 .30
63 Eric Weddle .12 .30
64 Clay Matthews .20 .50
65 Carlos Hyde .12 .30
66 Julian Edelman .20 .50
67 Ryan Mallett .15 .40
68 Muhammad Wilkerson .12 .30
69 Nick Toon .12 .30
70 Alfred Morris .12 .30
71 Austin Seferian-Jenkins .12 .30
72 Cameron Heyward .12 .30
73 Derek Carr .20 .50
74 Julius Peppers .15 .40
75 Anquan Boldin .12 .30
76 Danny Amendola .15 .40
77 Arian Foster .15 .40
78 Tony Romo .15 .40
79 C.J. Spiller .12 .30
80 Trent Williams .12 .30
81 Gerald McCoy .12 .30
82 William Gay .12 .30
83 Albert Wilson .12 .30
84 Teddy Bridgewater .15 .40
85 Torrey Smith .12 .30
86 Brandon LaFell .12 .30
87 Alfred Blue .12 .30
88 Darren McFadden .12 .30
89 Marques Colston .12 .30
90 DeSean Jackson .15 .40
91 Lavonte David .12 .30
92 Lawrence Timmons .12 .30
93 Latavius Murray .12 .30
94 Matt Asiata .12 .30
95 Antoine Bethea .12 .30
96 Devin McCourty .12 .30
97 DeAndre Hopkins .15 .40
98 Joseph Randle .12 .30
99 Brandin Cooks .15 .40
100 Pierre Garcon .15 .40
101 Peyton Manning .40 1.00
102 James Harrison .15 .40
103 Roy Helu Jr. .12 .30
104 Jerick McKinnon .12 .30
105 Aldon Smith .12 .30
106 Preston Brown .12 .30
107 Brian Cushing .12 .30
108 Dez Bryant .20 .50
109 Brandon Browner .12 .30
110 Niles Paul .12 .30
111 C.J. Anderson .15 .40
112 Johnny Manziel .15 .40
113 James Jones .12 .30
114 Harrison Smith .12 .30
115 Vernon Davis .12 .30
116 EJ Manuel .12 .30
117 Damaris Johnson .12 .30
118 Terrance Williams .12 .30
119 Josh Hill RC .15 .40
120 Jordan Reed .12 .30
121 Ronnie Hillman .12 .30
122 Tashaun Gipson RC .15 .40
123 Andre Holmes .15 .40
124 Jarius Wright .12 .30
125 Aaron Lynch .12 .30
126 Fred Jackson .15 .40
127 Garrett Graham .12 .30
128 Jason Witten .15 .40
129 Cam Newton .20 .50
130 Andre Roberts .12 .30
131 Montee Ball .12 .30
132 Terrance West .12 .30
133 Mychal Rivera .12 .30
134 Charles Johnson .12 .30
135 Darnell Dockett .12 .30
136 Marcell Dareus .12 .30
137 J.J. Watt .20 .50
138 Gavin Escobar .12 .30
139 Jonathan Stewart .12 .30
140 Ryan Kerrigan .12 .30
141 Emmanuel Sanders .15 .40
142 Isaiah Crowell .12 .30
143 Khalil Mack .20 .50
144 Adrian Peterson .20 .50
145 Robert Quinn .15 .40
146 Anthony Dixon .12 .30
147 Jadeveon Clowney .12 .30
148 Cole Beasley .20 .50
149 Ted Ginn Jr. .12 .30
150 Andy Dalton .15 .40
151 Demaryius Thomas .15 .40
152 Andrew Hawkins .12 .30
153 Justin Tuck .12 .30
154 Kyle Rudolph .12 .30
155 Nick Foles .15 .40
156 Sammy Watkins .15 .40
157 Blake Bortles .12 .30
158 Dan Bailey .12 .30
159 Greg Olsen .15 .40
160 Jeremy Hill .12 .30
161 Owen Daniels .12 .30
162 Dwayne Bowe .15 .40
163 Charles Woodson .20 .50
164 Cordarrelle Patterson .12 .30
165 Austin Davis .15 .40
166 Robert Woods .15 .40
167 Denard Robinson .12 .30
168 Sean Lee .15 .40
169 Kelvin Benjamin .15 .40
170 Giovani Bernard .12 .30
171 T.J. Ward .12 .30
172 Travis Benjamin .12 .30
173 Drew Stanton .20 .50
174 Everson Griffen .12 .30
175 Tre Mason .15 .40
176 Percy Harvin .12 .30
177 Toby Gerhart .12 .30
178 Sam Bradford .12 .30
179 Jerricho Cotchery .12 .30
180 A.J. Green .20 .50
181 Von Miller .15 .40
182 Paul Kruger .12 .30
183 Carson Palmer .15 .40
184 Jay Cutler .12 .30
185 Zac Stacy .12 .30
186 LeSean McCoy .20 .50
187 Allen Hurns .12 .30
188 Mark Sanchez .12 .30
189 Philly Brown .12 .30
190 Mohamed Sanu .12 .30
191 DeMarcus Ware .15 .40
192 Donte Whitner .12 .30
193 Andre Ellington .12 .30
194 Matt Forte .12 .30
195 Benny Cunningham .15 .40
196 Mario Williams .12 .30
197 Allen Robinson .15 .40
198 Kiko Alonso .12 .30
199 Luke Kuechly .15 .40
200 A.J. Hawk .12 .30
201 Alex Smith .15 .40
202 Taylor Gabriel .12 .30
203 Larry Fitzgerald .15 .40
204 Alshon Jeffery .15 .40
205 Kenny Britt .12 .30
206 Ryan Tannehill .15 .40
207 Julius Thomas .12 .30
208 Darren Sproles .15 .40
209 Charles Johnson .12 .30
210 Brandon Tate .12 .30
211 Jamaal Charles .15 .40
212 Matthew Stafford .15 .40
213 Michael Floyd .12 .30
214 Martellus Bennett .12 .30
215 Jared Cook .12 .30
216 Lamar Miller .12 .30
217 Marqise Lee .12 .30
218 DeMarco Murray .15 .40
219 Mike Tolbert .12 .30
220 Carlos Dunlap .12 .30
221 Knile Davis .12 .30
222 Haloti Ngata .12 .30
223 John Brown .15 .40
224 Pernell McPhee .12 .30
225 Tavon Austin .12 .30
226 Ndamukong Suh .15 .40
227 Sen'Derrick Marks .12 .30
228 Jordan Matthews .15 .40
229 Matt Ryan .15 .40
230 Adam Jones .12 .30
231 De'Anthony Thomas .12 .30
232 Joique Bell .12 .30
233 John Carlson .12 .30
234 Ka'Deem Carey .12 .30
235 Stedman Bailey .12 .30
236 Knowshon Moreno .12 .30
237 Marcedes Lewis .12 .30
238 Zach Ertz .15 .40
239 Paul Worrilow .12 .30
240 Denarius Moore .12 .30
241 Travis Kelce .20 .50
242 Golden Tate .12 .30
243 Jaron Brown .12 .30
244 Jacquizz Rodgers .12 .30
245 Morgan Burnett .12 .30
246 Jordan Cameron .12 .30
247 Paul Posluszny .12 .30
248 Riley Cooper .15 .40
249 Devonta Freeman .15 .40
250 Joe Flacco .15 .40
251 Tamba Hali .12 .30
252 Calvin Johnson .20 .50
253 Patrick Peterson .12 .30
254 Kyle Fuller .12 .30
255 Aqib Talib .12 .30
256 Jarvis Landry .15 .40
257 Zach Mettenberger .12 .30
258 Brent Celek .12 .30
259 Kroy Biermann .12 .30
260 Justin Forsett .15 .40
261 Jeremy Maclin .12 .30
262 Theo Riddick .12 .30
263 Calais Campbell .12 .30
264 Eddie Royal .12 .30
265 Barry Church RC .15 .40
266 Kenny Stills .12 .30
267 Harry Douglas .12 .30
268 Ryan Mathews .15 .40
269 Julio Jones .20 .50
270 Justin Tucker .12 .30
271 Justin Houston .12 .30
272 Jeremy Ross RC .15 .40
273 Russell Wilson .25 .60
274 Jared Allen .12 .30
275 Lance Dunbar .12 .30
276 Brent Grimes .12 .30
277 Bishop Sankey .12 .30
278 Eli Manning .15 .40
279 Roddy White .12 .30
280 Lorenzo Taliaferro .12 .30
281 Derrick Johnson .12 .30
282 Eric Ebron .12 .30
283 Marshawn Lynch .15 .40
284 Andrew Luck .25 .60
285 Juwan Thompson .15 .40
286 Dion Sims .12 .30
287 Shonn Greene .12 .30
288 Andre Williams .12 .30
289 Kemal Ishmael RC .15 .40
290 Steve Smith .15 .40
291 Trent Richardson .12 .30
292 Ezekiel Ansah .12 .30
293 Robert Turbin .12 .30
294 Vontae Davis .12 .30
295 Bruce Ellington .12 .30
296 Cameron Wake .12 .30
297 Delanie Walker .12 .30
298 Rashad Jennings .12 .30
299 Devin Hester .15 .40
300 Kamar Aiken RC .15 .40
301 Philip Rivers .20 .50
302 Glover Quin .12 .30
303 Doug Baldwin .15 .40
304 Frank Gore .15 .40
305 Reggie Bush .12 .30
306 Geno Smith .12 .30
307 Kendall Wright .12 .30
308 Odell Beckham Jr. .20 .50
309 Antone Smith RC .15 .40
310 C.J. Mosley .20 .50
311 Jacoby Jones .12 .30
312 Aaron Rodgers .40 1.00
313 Jermaine Kearse .12 .30
314 Dan Herron .12 .30
315 Leodis McKelvin .12 .30
316 Darrelle Revis .12 .30
317 Justin Hunter .12 .30
318 Rueben Randle .12 .30
319 Matt Bryant .12 .30
320 Dennis Pitta .12 .30
321 Branden Oliver .15 .40
322 Eddie Lacy .12 .30
323 Jimmy Graham .20 .50
324 T.Y. Hilton .15 .40
325 Rod Streater .12 .30
326 Chris Ivory .15 .40
327 Brian Orakpo .12 .30
328 Larry Donnell RC .12 .30
329 Mason Crosby .12 .30
330 Elvis Dumervil .12 .30
331 Trae Waynes RC .25 .60
332 Kevin Johnson RC .25 .60
333 P.J. Williams RC .30 .75
334 Senquez Golson RC .25 .60
335 Davis Tull RC .25 .60
336 Ifo Ekpre-Olomu RC .25 .60
337 Eric Rowe RC .25 .60
338 Landon Collins RC .30 .75
339 Mario Alford RC .25 .60
340 Shane Ray RC .25 .60
341 Randy Gregory RC .25 .60
342 Arik Armstead RC .25 .60
343 Eli Harold RC .25 .60
344 Vic Beasley RC .30 .75
345 Bud Dupree RC .30 .75
346 Owamagbe Odighizuwa RC .30 .75
347 Danielle Hunter RC .30 .75
348 Austin Hill RC .25 .60
349 Leonard Williams RC .25 .60
350 Malcom Brown RC .25 .60
351 Eddie Goldman RC .25 .60
352 Derron Smith RC .25 .60
353 Carl Davis RC .30 .75
354 Danny Shelton RC .25 .60
355 Denzel Perryman RC .25 .60
356 Eric Kendricks RC .25 .60
357 Benardrick McKinney RC .25 .60
358 Shaq Thompson RC .30 .75
359 Dante Fowler Jr. RC .40 1.00
360 Kwon Alexander RC .30 .75
361 Byron Jones RC .40 1.00
362 Andrus Peat RC .25 .60
363 T.J. Clemmings RC .25 .60
364 Brandon Scherff RC .40 1.00
365 Ereck Flowers RC .30 .75
366 Jameis Winston RC .60 1.50
367 Garrett Grayson RC .25 .60
368 Marcus Mariota RC 1.00 2.50
369 Brett Hundley RC .25 .60
370 Sean Mannion RC .25 .60
371 Taylor Heinicke RC .40 1.00
372 Blake Sims RC .25 .60
373 Shane Carden RC .25 .60
374 Cody Fajardo RC .30 .75
375 Bryan Bennett RC .25 .60
376 Bryce Petty RC .25 .60
377 Michael Dyer RC .40 1.00
378 Malcolm Brown RC .30 .75
379 Jeremy Langford RC .25 .60
380 Melvin Gordon III RC .60 1.50
381 David Cobb RC .25 .60
382 Tevin Coleman RC .30 .75
383 Jay Ajayi RC .40 1.00
384 Cameron Artis-Payne RC .25 .60
385 Ameer Abdullah RC .40 1.00
386 Todd Gurley RC 1.00 2.50
387 Duke Johnson RC .40 1.00
388 Matt Jones RC .25 .60
389 Karlos Williams RC .25 .60
390 T.J. Yeldon RC .25 .60
391 David Johnson RC .60 1.50
392 Buck Allen RC .30 .75
393 Terrence Magee RC .40 1.00
394 Mike Davis RC .25 .60
395 Antwan Goodley RC .25 .60
396 Jesse James RC .30 .75
397 Nick O'Leary RC .25 .60
398 Maxx Williams RC .25 .60
399 Ben Koyack RC .40 1.00
400 Devin Funchess RC .40 1.00
401 E.J. Bibbs RC .30 .75
402 Dezmin Lewis RC .25 .60
403 Kevin White RC .30 .75
404 Jamison Crowder RC .30 .75
405 Justin Hardy RC .25 .60
406 Nelson Agholor RC .30 .75
407 Breshad Perriman RC .25 .60
408 Amari Cooper RC .75 2.00
409 Devin Smith RC .25 .60
410 Rashad Greene RC .25 .60
411 Vince Mayle RC .30 .75
412 Tony Lippett RC .25 .60
413 Sammie Coates RC .30 .75
414 Phillip Dorsett RC .25 .60
415 Stefon Diggs RC .60 1.50
416 Jaelen Strong RC .30 .75
417 Dorial Green-Beckham RC .25 .60
418 Kenny Bell RC .40 1.00
419 Ty Montgomery RC .25 .60
420 DeVante Parker RC .40 1.00
421 Tyler Lockett RC .40 1.00
422 Dres Anderson RC .25 .60
423 Trey Flowers RC .40 1.00
424 Josh Harper RC .25 .60
425 Chris Conley RC .25 .60
426 Deontay Greenberry RC .25 .60
427 MyCole Pruitt RC .25 .60
428 Bo Wallace RC .25 .60
429 DeAndrew White RC .40 1.00
430 J.J. Nelson RC .25 .60
431 DaVaris Daniels RC .25 .60
432 Ronald Darby RC .25 .60
433 Titus Davis RC .30 .75
434 Josh Robinson RC .25 .60
435 Tre McBride RC .25 .60
436 Jalen Collins RC .25 .60
437 Trey Williams RC .30 .75
438 Darren Waller RC .30 .75
439 Clive Walford RC .25 .60
440 Marcus Peters RC .40 1.00

2015 Score All Pro All-American Glossy

1 Le'Veon Bell .60 1.50
2 Demaryius Thomas .60 1.50
3 Aaron Rodgers 1.50 4.00
4 Justin Houston .50 1.25
5 Jordy Nelson .60 1.50
6 Darrelle Revis .50 1.25
7 Tony Romo .60 1.50
8 Ndamukong Suh .60 1.50
9 Rob Gronkowski .75 2.00
10 J.J. Watt .75 2.00
11 DeMarco Murray .60 1.50
12 Antonio Brown .75 2.00
13 Richard Sherman .75 2.00
14 Dez Bryant .75 2.00
15 Marshawn Lynch .60 1.50
16 Marcus Mariota 1.25 3.00
17 Todd Gurley 1.25 3.00
18 Melvin Gordon III .75 2.00
19 Jameis Winston .75 2.00
20 Amari Cooper 1.00 2.50

2015 Score All-Time Franchise

*GOLD: .5X TO 1.2X BASIC INSERTS
*RED: .6X TO 1.5X BASIC INSERTS
*GREEN: .6X TO 1.5X BASIC INSERTS
*BLACK: .75X TO 2X BASIC INSERTS
1 Walter Payton 1.00 2.50
2 Barry Sanders .75 2.00
3 Joe Montana 1.25 3.00
4 Jerry Rice .75 2.00
5 John Elway .75 2.00
6 Brett Favre 1.00 2.50
7 Dan Marino 1.00 2.50
8 Roger Staubach .60 1.50

2015 Score Dual Jerseys

DJBH G.Bernard/J.Hill 1.50 4.00
DJBH B.Bortles/C.Henne 1.50 4.00
DJBR D.Bryant/T.Romo 2.50 6.00
DJDB E.Dumervil/V.Burfict 1.50 4.00
DJDC O.Daniels/S.Chandler 1.50 4.00
DJDW M.Dareus/M.Williams 1.50 4.00
DJFP M.Floyd/P.Rivers 2.50 6.00
DJFS J.Flacco/S.Smith 2.00 5.00
DJLW J.Landry/S.Watkins 2.00 5.00
DJMI D.Thomas/L.Miller 2.00 5.00
DJOL E.Fisher/T.Williams 1.50 4.00
DJPN D.Poe/H.Ngata 1.50 4.00
DJRL A.Robinson/M.Lee 2.00 5.00
DJSK A.Smith/T.Kelce 2.50 6.00
DJTM D.Thomas/P.Manning 5.00 12.00

2015 Score Franchise

*GOLD: .5X TO 1.2X BASIC INSERTS
*RED: .6X TO 1.5X BASIC INSERTS
*GREEN: .6X TO 1.5X BASIC INSERTS
*BLACK: .78X TO 2X BASIC INSERTS
1 Tom Brady 2.50 6.00
2 Matt Ryan .75 2.00
3 Joe Flacco .75 2.00
4 A.J. Green 1.00 2.50
5 Tony Romo .75 2.00
6 Peyton Manning 2.00 5.00
7 Calvin Johnson 1.00 2.50
8 Drew Brees 1.00 2.50
9 Cam Newton 1.00 2.50
10 Ben Roethlisberger 1.00 2.50
11 Philip Rivers 1.00 2.50
12 Russell Wilson 1.25 3.00
13 Derek Carr 1.00 2.50
14 Aaron Rodgers 2.00 5.00
15 Andrew Luck 1.25 3.00
16 Jamaal Charles .75 2.00
17 Eli Manning .75 2.00
18 Colin Kaepernick .75 2.00
19 J.J. Watt 1.00 2.50
20 Teddy Bridgewater .75 2.00

2015 Score Gridiron Heritage

*GOLD: .5X TO 1.2X BASIC INSERTS
*RED: .6X TO 1.5X BASIC INSERTS
*GREEN: .6X TO 1.5X BASIC INSERTS
*BLACK: .75X TO 2X BASIC INSERTS
1 Earl Campbell 1.00 2.50
2 Roger Staubach 1.25 3.00
3 John Elway 1.50 4.00
4 John Riggins .75 2.00
5 Steve Largent 1.00 2.50
6 Paul Warfield .75 2.00
7 Brett Favre 2.00 5.00
8 Doug Flutie .75 2.00
9 Dan Hampton .60 1.50
10 Dan Marino 2.00 5.00
11 Ahman Green .75 2.00
12 Barry Sanders 1.50 4.00
13 Len Dawson 1.00 2.50
14 Fred Biletnikoff 1.00 2.50
15 Kurt Warner .75 2.00
16 Ozzie Newsome .75 2.00
17 Fran Tarkenton 1.00 2.50
18 Jim Kelly 1.00 2.50
19 Derrick Brooks .60 1.50
20 Joe Namath 1.25 3.00
21 Jerome Bettis 1.00 2.50
22 Michael Strahan .75 2.00
23 Tim Brown
24 Terry Bradshaw 1.25 3.00
25 Jerry Rice 1.50 4.00

2015 Score Ground Gainers

*DESERT: .5X TO 1.2X BASIC INSERTS
*GREEN: .5X TO 1.2X BASIC INSERTS
*BLACK: .6X TO 1.5X BASIC INSERTS
*BLUE: .6X TO 1.5X BASIC INSERTS
1 LeGarrette Blount 1.50 4.00
2 Eddie Lacy 1.25 3.00
3 Marshawn Lynch 1.50 4.00
4 DeMarco Murray 1.50 4.00
5 Jonathan Stewart 1.25 3.00
6 C.J. Anderson 1.50 4.00
7 Emmitt Smith 3.00 8.00
8 Frank Gore 1.50 4.00
9 Le'Veon Bell 1.50 4.00
10 Joique Bell 1.25 3.00
11 Mark Ingram 1.50 4.00
12 Dan Herron 1.25 3.00
13 Jeremy Hill 1.25 3.00
14 Franco Harris 2.00 5.00
15 Andre Williams 1.25 3.00
16 Ahman Green 1.50 4.00
17 Justin Forsett 1.50 4.00
18 Devonta Freeman 1.50 4.00

2015 Score Inscriptions

ONE AUTO OR MEM CARD PER BOX OVERALL
2 A.J. McCarron
3 Aaron Murray 5.00 12.00
4 Andre Ellington
5 Andre Williams 5.00 12.00
6 Allen Hurns 5.00 12.00
7 Anthony Hitchens 5.00 12.00
8 Arian Foster
9 Brandon LaFell 5.00 12.00
10 C.J. Spiller
11 Cameron Wake 5.00 12.00
12 Carson Palmer
13 Connor Shaw 5.00 12.00
14 Cory Harkey 5.00 12.00
15 Danny Lansanah 5.00 12.00
16 Demaryius Thomas
17 Denard Robinson
18 Derek Carr 10.00 25.00
19 Doug Martin
20 Drew Brees
21 Frank Gore
22 Fred Jackson 6.00 15.00
23 Latavius Murray 5.00 12.00
24 James Develin 8.00 20.00
25 James Wright 6.00 15.00
26 Jerrell Freeman 5.00 12.00
27 Jordy Nelson
28 Joseph Fauria
29 Justin Forsett
30 Justin Houston
31 Kerwynn Williams
32 Malcolm Smith 5.00 12.00
33 Marqise Lee
34 Marshawn Lynch
35 Matt Ryan
36 Mike Evans
37 Percy Harvin 5.00 12.00
38 Peyton Manning
39 Rob Gronkowski
40 Robert Herron
41 Ronnie Hillman
42 Ryan Mallett
43 Sam Barrington
44 Silas Redd 5.00 12.00
45 Steve Smith
46 Teddy Bridgewater
47 Tom Brady
48 Tom Savage 5.00 12.00
49 Tony Romo
50 Victor Cruz

2015 Score Jerseys

JAS Alex Smith 3.00 8.00
JBB Blake Bortles 2.50 6.00
JCC Charles Clay 2.50 6.00
JCM C.J. Mosley 4.00 10.00
JCW Cameron Wake 2.50 6.00
JDJ DeSean Jackson 3.00 8.00
JDM DeMarco Murray 3.00 8.00
JDP Dontari Poe 2.50 6.00
JDS Dion Sims 2.50 6.00
JDT Daniel Thomas 3.00 8.00
JEB Eric Berry 3.00 8.00
JED Elvis Dumervil 2.50 6.00
JEF Eric Fisher 2.50 6.00
JFJ Fred Jackson 3.00 8.00
JGB Giovani Bernard 2.50 6.00
JHN Haloti Ngata 2.50 6.00
JJF Joe Flacco 3.00 8.00
JJG Jermaine Gresham 3.00 8.00
JJH Jeremy Hill 2.50 6.00
JJJ Jacoby Jones 2.50 6.00
JJL Jarvis Landry 3.00 8.00
JLF Larry Fitzgerald 3.00 8.00
JLM Lamar Miller 2.50 6.00
JMD Marcell Dareus 2.50 6.00
JMF Malcom Floyd 2.50 6.00
JMW Mario Williams 2.50 6.00
JNF Nick Foles 3.00 8.00
JOD Owen Daniels 2.50 6.00
JPM Peyton Manning 12.00 30.00
JPR Philip Rivers 4.00 10.00
JRM Rey Maualuga 2.50 6.00
JRT Ryan Tannehill 3.00 8.00
JRW Robert Woods 3.00 8.00
JSB Sam Bradford 2.50 6.00
JSC Scott Chandler 2.50 6.00
JSW Sammy Watkins 3.00 8.00
JTH Tamba Hali 4.00 10.00
JTR Tony Romo 3.00 8.00
JTW Trent Williams 2.50 6.00
JVB Vontaze Burfict 2.50 6.00

2015 Score Photo Variations

*DESERT: .5X TO 1.2X BASIC INSERTS
*GREEN: .5X TO 1.2X BASIC INSERTS
*BLACK: .6X TO 1.5X BASIC INSERTS
*BLUE: .6X TO 1.5X BASIC INSERTS
6 Tom Brady 6.00 15.00
12 Ben Roethlisberger 2.50 6.00
25 Richard Sherman 2.50 6.00
32 Antonio Brown 2.50 6.00
33 Antonio Gates 1.50 4.00
45 Colin Kaepernick 2.00 5.00
56 Rob Gronkowski 2.50 6.00
64 Clay Matthews 2.50 6.00
69 Jimmy Graham 2.50 6.00
90 DeSean Jackson 2.00 5.00
96 Darrelle Revis 1.50 4.00
101 Peyton Manning 5.00 12.00
108 Dez Bryant 2.50 6.00
112 Johnny Manziel 2.00 5.00
129 Cam Newton 2.50 6.00
137 J.J. Watt 2.50 6.00
180 A.J. Green 2.50 6.00
198 LeSean McCoy 2.50 6.00
250 Joe Flacco 2.00 5.00
252 Calvin Johnson 2.50 6.00
269 Julio Jones 2.50 6.00
273 Russell Wilson 3.00 8.00
283 Marshawn Lynch 2.00 5.00
284 Andrew Luck 3.00 8.00
299 Devin Hester 2.00 5.00
302 Ndamukong Suh 2.00 5.00
308 Odell Beckham Jr. 2.50 6.00
312 Aaron Rodgers 5.00 12.00

2015 Score Playmakers

*DESERT: .5X TO 1.2X BASIC INSERTS
*GREEN: .5X TO 1.2X BASIC INSERTS
*BLACK: .6X TO 1.5X BASIC INSERTS
*BLUE: .6X TO 1.5X BASIC INSERTS
1 Rob Gronkowski 2.00 5.00
2 Jordy Nelson 1.50 4.00
3 Doug Baldwin 1.50 4.00
4 Dez Bryant 2.00 5.00
5 Kelvin Benjamin 1.50 4.00
6 Demaryius Thomas 1.50 4.00
7 Michael Irvin 2.00 5.00
8 Anquan Boldin 1.25 3.00
9 Antonio Brown 2.00 5.00
10 Calvin Johnson 2.00 5.00
11 Marques Colston 1.25 3.00
12 T.Y. Hilton 1.50 4.00
13 A.J. Green 2.00 5.00
14 John Stallworth 1.50 4.00
15 Odell Beckham Jr. 2.00 5.00
16 Donald Driver 2.00 5.00
17 Steve Smith 1.50 4.00
18 Julio Jones 2.00 5.00

2015 Score Precision Passers

*DESERT: .5X TO 1.2X BASIC INSERTS
*GREEN: .5X TO 1.2X BASIC INSERTS
*BLACK: .6X TO 1.5X BASIC INSERTS
*BLUE: .6X TO 1.5X BASIC INSERTS
1 Tom Brady 5.00 12.00
2 Aaron Rodgers 4.00 10.00
3 Russell Wilson 2.50 6.00
4 Tony Romo 1.50 4.00
5 Cam Newton 2.00 5.00
6 Peyton Manning 4.00 10.00
7 Troy Aikman 2.50 6.00
8 Colin Kaepernick 1.50 4.00
9 Ben Roethlisberger 2.00 5.00
10 Matthew Stafford 1.50 4.00
11 Drew Brees 2.00 5.00
12 Andrew Luck 2.50 6.00
13 Andy Dalton 1.50 4.00
14 Terry Bradshaw 2.50 6.00
15 Eli Manning 1.50 4.00
16 Brett Favre 4.00 10.00
17 Joe Flacco 1.50 4.00
18 Matt Ryan 1.50 4.00

2015 Score Quad Jerseys

QJDWWC Dareus/Williams/Woods/Chandler 2.50 6.00
QJFTJB Fasano/Thomas/Johnson/Berry 2.50 6.00
QJGBHS Green/Bernard/Hill/Sanu 3.00 8.00
QJLSTW Latimer/Sanders/Thomas/Welker 2.50 6.00
QJRBRL Robinson/Bortles/Robinson/Lee 2.50 6.00

2015 Score Rookie Helmets

1 Landon Collins 1.00 2.50
2 Devin Smith .75 2.00
3 Amari Cooper 2.50 6.00
4 Maxx Williams .75 2.00
5 Jameis Winston 2.00 5.00
6 Jaelen Strong 1.00 2.50
7 Dorial Green-Beckham .75 2.00
8 Dante Fowler Jr. 1.25 3.00
9 Leonard Williams .75 2.00
10 Ameer Abdullah 1.25 3.00
11 Todd Gurley 3.00 8.00
12 DeVante Parker 1.25 3.00
13 Randy Gregory .75 2.00
14 Marcus Mariota 3.00 8.00
15 Shane Ray .75 2.00
16 Kevin White 1.00 2.50
17 Melvin Gordon III 2.00 5.00
18 Devin Funchess 1.25 3.00
19 Sammie Coates 1.00 2.50
20 Brett Hundley .75 2.00

2015 Score Team Leaders

*GOLD: .5X TO 1.2X BASIC INSERTS
*RED: .6X TO 1.5X BASIC INSERTS
*GREEN: .6X TO 1.5X BASIC INSERTS
*BLACK: .75X TO 2X BASIC INSERTS
1 Gray/Gronkowski/Ninkovich/Brady 2.50 6.00
2 Jackson/Orton/Williams/Watkins .75 2.00
3 Wake/Miller/Wallace/Tannehill .75 2.00
4 Ivory/Decker/Smith/Richardson .75 2.00
5 Murray/Bryant/Mincey/Romo 1.00 2.50
6 Barwin/Maclin/McCoy/Sanchez 1.00 2.50
7 Williams/Manning/Pierre-Paul/Beckham Jr. 1.00 2.50
8 Morris/Jackson/Cousins/Kerrigan 1.00 2.50
9 Brown/Roethlisberger/Worilds/Bell 1.00 2.50
10 Green/Dalton/Dunlap/Hill 1.00 2.50
11 Dumervil/Flacco/Forsett/Smith .75 2.00
12 Hawkins/Hoyer/Kruger/West .60 1.50
13 Rodgers/Matthews/Lacy/Nelson 2.00 5.00
14 Tate/Bell/Stafford/Suh .75 2.00
15 Griffen/Jennings/Asiata/Bridgewater .75 2.00
16 Jeffery/Cutler/Forte/Young .75 2.00
17 Luck/Newsome/Hilton/Richardson 1.25 3.00
18 Foster/Hopkins/Watt/Fitzpatrick 1.00 2.50
19 Hurns/Bortles/Robinson/Marks .60 1.50
20 Sankey/Walker/Morgan/Mettenberger .75 2.00
21 Newton/Johnson/Stewart/Benjamin 1.00 2.50
22 Brees/Galette/Stills/Ingram 1.00 2.50
23 Jones/Biermann/Ryan/Jackson 1.00 2.50
24 Martin/McCoy/David/Evans .75 2.00
25 Anderson/Thomas/Manning/Miller 2.00 5.00
26 Smith/Charles/Houston/Kelce 1.00 2.50
27 Oliver/Liuget/Floyd/Rivers 1.00 2.50
28 Holmes/McFadden/Carr/Tuck 1.00 2.50
29 Baldwin/Lynch/Bennett/Wilson 1.25 3.00
30 Okafor/Ellington/Stanton/Floyd 1.00 2.50
31 Brooks/Boldin/Kaepernick/Gore .75 2.00
32 Davis/Britt/Quinn/Mason .75 2.00

2015 Score The Great Outdoors

*DESERT: .5X TO 1.2X BASIC INSERTS
*GREEN: .5X TO 1.2X BASIC INSERTS
*BLACK: .6X TO 1.5X BASIC INSERTS
*BLUE: .6X TO 1.5X BASIC INSERTS
1 LeSean McCoy 2.00 5.00
2 Ryan Tannehill 1.50 4.00
3 Tom Brady 5.00 12.00
4 Adam Vinatieri 1.25 3.00
5 Joe Namath 2.50 6.00
6 Ben Roethlisberger 2.00 5.00
7 Wes Welker 1.50 4.00
8 Curtis Martin 1.50 4.00
9 Jerome Bettis 2.00 5.00
10 Jay Cutler 1.25 3.00
11 Brett Favre 4.00 10.00
12 Peyton Manning 4.00 10.00
13 Calvin Johnson 2.00 5.00
14 Cordarrelle Patterson 1.25 3.00
15 Nick Foles 1.50 4.00
16 Joe Flacco 1.50 4.00
17 Brandon Marshall 1.25 3.00
18 Matt Forte 1.25 3.00

2015 Score Triple Jerseys

TJDHS Dalton/Hill/Sanu 3.00 8.00
TJDMB Dumervil/Miller/Burfict 3.00 8.00
TJFTS Flacco/Taliaferro/Suggs 3.00 8.00
TJHBL Hurns/Bortles/Lee 2.50 6.00
TJHLT Hartline/Landry/Tannehill 3.00 8.00
TJJBH Johnson/Berry/Houston 3.00 8.00
TJMWR Murray/Witten/Romo 3.00 8.00
TJSJW Spiller/Jackson/Watkins 3.00 8.00
TJSTK Smith/Thomas/Kelce 4.00 10.00
TJTMW Thomas/Manning/Welker 12.00 30.00

2015 Score Veteran Helmets

1 Peyton Manning 8.00 20.00
2 Tony Romo 3.00 8.00
3 Dez Bryant 4.00 10.00
4 Andrew Luck 5.00 12.00
5 Larry Fitzgerald 3.00 8.00
6 Joe Flacco 3.00 8.00
7 Antonio Brown 4.00 10.00
8 Philip Rivers 4.00 10.00
9 Keenan Allen 3.00 8.00

2016 Score

1 Carson Palmer .15 .40
2 Chris Johnson .12 .30
3 David Johnson .20 .50
4 Andre Ellington .12 .30
5 John Brown .15 .40
6 Larry Fitzgerald .15 .40
7 Michael Floyd .12 .30
8 Darren Fells RC .12 .30
9 Patrick Peterson .12 .30
10 Tyrann Mathieu .15 .40
11 Rashad Johnson .15 .40
12 Matt Ryan .15 .40
13 Devonta Freeman .15 .40
14 Terron Ward .12 .30
15 Tevin Coleman .15 .40
16 Julio Jones .20 .50
17 Justin Hardy .12 .30
18 Roddy White .12 .30
19 Jacob Tamme .12 .30
20 Devin Hester .15 .40
21 Vic Beasley Jr. .12 .30
22 Joe Flacco .15 .40
23 Justin Forsett .15 .40
24 Buck Allen .12 .30
25 Steve Smith .15 .40
26 Kamar Aiken .12 .30
27 Breshad Perriman .12 .30
28 Crockett Gillmore .12 .30
29 Jimmy Smith .12 .30
30 Terrell Suggs .12 .30
31 C.J. Mosley .15 .40
32 Tyrod Taylor .15 .40
33 EJ Manuel .12 .30
34 LeSean McCoy .20 .50
35 Karlos Williams .12 .30
36 Sammy Watkins .20 .50
37 Charles Clay .12 .30
38 Robert Woods .15 .40
39 Percy Harvin .12 .30
40 Mario Williams .12 .30
41 Jerry Hughes .12 .30
42 Corey Graham .12 .30
43 Cam Newton .20 .50
44 Jonathan Stewart .12 .30
45 Greg Olsen .15 .40
46 Ted Ginn Jr. .12 .30
47 Philly Brown .12 .30
48 Devin Funchess .12 .30
49 Kelvin Benjamin .15 .40
50 Luke Kuechly .15 .40
51 Josh Norman .12 .30
52 Jared Allen .12 .30
53 Kawann Short .12 .30
54 Jay Cutler .12 .30
55 Matt Forte .12 .30
56 Jeremy Langford .15 .40
57 Alshon Jeffery .15 .40
58 Martellus Bennett .12 .30
59 Kevin White .12 .30
60 Marquess Wilson .12 .30
61 Eddie Royal .12 .30
62 Lamarr Houston .12 .30
63 Pernell McPhee .12 .30
64 Andy Dalton .15 .40
65 Jeremy Hill .12 .30
66 Giovani Bernard .12 .30
67 A.J. Green .20 .50
68 Tyler Eifert .15 .40
69 Marvin Jones .12 .30
70 Mohamed Sanu .12 .30
71 Carlos Dunlap .12 .30
72 Geno Atkins .12 .30
73 Reggie Nelson .12 .30
74 Adam Jones .12 .30
75 Johnny Manziel .15 .40
76 Josh McCown .12 .30
77 Duke Johnson .12 .30
78 Isaiah Crowell .12 .30
79 Travis Benjamin .12 .30
80 Brian Hartline .12 .30
81 Gary Barnidge .12 .30
82 Karlos Dansby .12 .30
83 Danny Shelton .12 .30
84 Andrew Hawkins .12 .30
85 Tony Romo .15 .40
86 Darren McFadden .12 .30
87 DeMarcus Lawrence .20 .50
88 Lance Dunbar .12 .30
89 Jason Witten .15 .40
90 Dez Bryant .20 .50
91 Terrance Williams .12 .30
92 Cole Beasley .20 .50
93 Sean Lee .15 .40
94 Randy Gregory .15 .40
95 Peyton Manning .40 1.00
96 Brock Osweiler .12 .30
97 C.J. Anderson .15 .40
98 Ronnie Hillman .12 .30
99 Demaryius Thomas .15 .40
100 Emmanuel Sanders .20 .50
101 Owen Daniels .12 .30
102 Vernon Davis .12 .30
103 DeMarcus Ware .15 .40
104 Von Miller .15 .40
105 Brandon Marshall .12 .30
106 Evan Mathis .12 .30
107 Matthew Stafford .15 .40
108 Ameer Abdullah .12 .30
109 Joique Bell .12 .30
110 Calvin Johnson .20 .50
111 Golden Tate .12 .30
112 Theo Riddick .12 .30
113 Lance Moore .12 .30
114 Eric Ebron .12 .30
115 Ezekiel Ansah .12 .30
116 Haloti Ngata .12 .30
117 Aaron Rodgers .40 1.00
118 Eddie Lacy .12 .30
119 James Starks .12 .30
120 Randall Cobb .15 .40
121 James Jones .12 .30
122 Richard Rodgers .15 .40
123 Davante Adams .12 .30
124 Ty Montgomery .15 .40
125 Clay Matthews .20 .50
126 Julius Peppers .15 .40
127 Ha Ha Clinton-Dix .12 .30
128 Brian Hoyer .12 .30
129 Alfred Blue .12 .30
130 Arian Foster .15 .40
131 DeAndre Hopkins .15 .40
132 Nate Washington .12 .30
133 Jaelen Strong .12 .30
134 J.J. Watt .20 .50
135 Brian Cushing .12 .30
136 Jadeveon Clowney .12 .30
137 Andrew Luck .25 .60
138 Matt Hasselbeck .12 .30
139 Frank Gore .15 .40
140 T.Y. Hilton .15 .40
141 Donte Moncrief .15 .40
142 Andre Johnson .15 .40
143 Coby Fleener .12 .30
144 Phillip Dorsett .12 .30
145 Robert Mathis .12 .30
146 Mike Adams .12 .30
147 Adam Vinatieri .15 .40
148 Blake Bortles .12 .30
149 T.J. Yeldon .12 .30
150 Denard Robinson .12 .30
151 Allen Robinson .15 .40
152 Allen Hurns .12 .30
153 Julius Thomas .12 .30
154 Bryan Walters RC .15 .40
155 Aaron Colvin .12 .30
156 Dante Fowler Jr. .12 .30
157 Paul Posluszny .12 .30
158 Alex Smith .15 .40
159 Jamaal Charles .15 .40
160 Charcandrick West .12 .30
161 Knile Davis .12 .30
162 Jeremy Maclin .12 .30
163 Travis Kelce .20 .50
164 De'Anthony Thomas .12 .30
165 Chris Conley .12 .30
166 Derrick Johnson .12 .30
167 Justin Houston .12 .30
168 Marcus Peters .12 .30
169 Ryan Tannehill .15 .40
170 Lamar Miller .12 .30
171 Jay Ajayi .15 .40
172 Jarvis Landry .15 .40
173 Rishard Matthews .12 .30
174 Kenny Stills .12 .30
175 DeVante Parker .15 .40
176 Jordan Cameron .12 .30
177 Cameron Wake .12 .30
178 Ndamukong Suh .15 .40
179 Teddy Bridgewater .15 .40
180 Adrian Peterson .20 .50
181 Jerick McKinnon .12 .30
182 Stefon Diggs .15 .40
183 Mike Wallace .12 .30
184 Charles Johnson .12 .30
185 Kyle Rudolph .12 .30
186 Harrison Smith .12 .30
187 Everson Griffen .12 .30
188 Eric Kendricks .12 .30
189 Tom Brady .50 1.25
190 Dion Lewis .12 .30
191 LeGarrette Blount .15 .40
192 Rob Gronkowski .20 .50
193 Julian Edelman .20 .50
194 Danny Amendola .15 .40
195 Brandon LaFell .12 .30
196 Dont'a Hightower .12 .30
197 Chandler Jones .12 .30
198 Logan Ryan .12 .30
199 Drew Brees .20 .50
200 Mark Ingram .15 .40
201 Khiry Robinson .15 .40
202 Brandin Cooks .15 .40
203 Willie Snead .15 .40
204 Ben Watson .12 .30
205 Marques Colston .12 .30
206 Brandon Coleman .12 .30
207 Cameron Jordan .12 .30
208 Hau'oli Kikaha .12 .30
209 Eli Manning .15 .40
210 Rashad Jennings .12 .30
211 Andre Williams .12 .30
212 Shane Vereen .15 .40
213 Odell Beckham Jr. .20 .50
214 Rueben Randle .12 .30
215 Dwayne Harris .12 .30
216 Dominique Rodgers-Cromartie .12 .30
217 Jason Pierre-Paul .12 .30
218 Landon Collins .12 .30
219 Ryan Fitzpatrick .12 .30
220 Geno Smith .12 .30
221 Chris Ivory .15 .40
222 Stevan Ridley .12 .30

223 Brandon Marshall .12 .30
224 Eric Decker .12 .30
225 Jeremy Kerley .12 .30
226 Muhammad Wilkerson .12 .30
227 Devin Smith .12 .30
228 David Harris .12 .30
229 Derek Carr .20 .50
230 Latavius Murray .12 .30
231 Amari Cooper .20 .50
232 Michael Crabtree .12 .30
233 Marcel Reece .12 .30
234 Seth Roberts RC .15 .40
235 Khalil Mack .20 .50
236 Charles Woodson .20 .50
237 Malcolm Smith .20 .50
238 Sebastian Janikowski .12 .30
239 Sam Bradford .12 .30
240 Ryan Mathews .15 .40
241 DeMarco Murray .15 .40
242 Darren Sproles .15 .40
243 Jordan Matthews .15 .40
244 Zach Ertz .15 .40
245 Nelson Agholor .12 .30
246 Brandon Graham .12 .30
247 Brent Celek .12 .30
248 Fletcher Cox .12 .30
249 Ben Roethlisberger .20 .50
250 Landry Jones .12 .30
251 Le'Veon Bell .15 .40
252 DeAngelo Williams .12 .30
253 Antonio Brown .20 .50
254 Heath Miller .12 .30
255 Martavis Bryant .12 .30
256 Markus Wheaton .12 .30
257 Bud Dupree .12 .30
258 James Harrison .15 .40
259 Lawrence Timmons .15 .40
260 Philip Rivers .20 .50
261 Melvin Gordon .15 .40
262 Danny Woodhead .15 .40
263 Keenan Allen .15 .40
264 Malcom Floyd .12 .30
265 Steve Johnson .15 .40
266 Antonio Gates .12 .30
267 Ladarius Green .12 .30
268 Melvin Ingram .12 .30
269 Jeremiah Attaochu .12 .30
270 Eric Weddle .12 .30
271 Colin Kaepernick .15 .40
272 Blaine Gabbert .12 .30
273 Carlos Hyde .12 .30
274 Torrey Smith .12 .30
275 Anquan Boldin .12 .30
276 Garrett Celek RC .15 .40
277 Quinton Patton .12 .30
278 Aaron Lynch .12 .30
279 NaVorro Bowman .15 .40
280 Ahmad Brooks .12 .30
281 Russell Wilson .25 .60
282 Marshawn Lynch .15 .40
283 Thomas Rawls .12 .30
284 Jimmy Graham .20 .50
285 Doug Baldwin .15 .40
286 Jermaine Kearse .12 .30
287 Tyler Lockett .15 .40
288 Michael Bennett RC .12 .30
289 Richard Sherman .20 .50
290 Earl Thomas .15 .40
291 Bruce Irvin .12 .30
292 Nick Fules .15 .40
293 Todd Gurley .20 .50
294 Wes Welker .15 .40
295 Tavon Austin .12 .30
296 Kenny Britt .12 .30
297 Jared Cook .12 .30
298 James Laurinaitis .15 .40
299 Mark Barron .12 .30
300 Robert Quinn .15 .40
301 Trumaine Johnson .12 .30
302 Jameis Winston .20 .50
303 Doug Martin .15 .40
304 Charles Sims .12 .30
305 Mike Evans .15 .40
306 Vincent Jackson .12 .30
307 Austin Seferian-Jenkins .12 .30
308 Gerald McCoy .12 .30
309 Kwon Alexander .12 .30
310 Jacquies Smith RC .15 .40
311 Marcus Mariota .20 .50
312 Antonio Andrews .12 .30
313 Dexter McCluster .15 .40
314 Delanie Walker .12 .30
315 Kendall Wright .12 .30
316 Dorial Green-Beckham .12 .30
317 Harry Douglas .12 .30
318 Jurrell Casey .12 .30
319 Derrick Morgan .12 .30
320 Brian Orakpo .12 .30
321 Kirk Cousins .20 .50
322 Robert Griffin III .12 .30
323 Matt Jones .15 .40
324 Alfred Morris .12 .30
325 Pierre Garcon .15 .40
326 Jordan Reed .12 .30
327 Jamison Crowder .12 .30
328 DeSean Jackson .15 .40
329 Ryan Kerrigan .12 .30
330 Rashad Ross .12 .30
331 Paxton Lynch RC .25 .60
332 Jared Goff RC 1.50 4.00
333 Connor Cook RC .30 .75
334 Christian Hackenberg RC .25 .60
335 Carson Wentz RC 2.50 6.00
336 Cardale Jones RC .25 .60
337 Dak Prescott RC 1.25 3.00
338 Brandon Doughty RC .25 .60
339 Jacoby Brissett RC .30 .75
340 Nate Sudfeld RC .25 .60
341 Cody Kessler RC .25 .60
342 Kevin Hogan RC .30 .75
343 Trevone Boykin RC .25 .60
344 Ezekiel Elliott RC 1.25 3.00
345 Derrick Henry RC .60 1.50
346 Devontae Booker RC .30 .75
347 C.J. Prosise RC .25 .60
348 Paul Perkins RC .25 .60
349 Alex Collins RC .30 .75
350 Kenyan Drake RC .40 1.00
351 Kenneth Dixon RC .25 .60
352 Tra Carson RC .25 .60
353 Jonathan Williams RC .30 .75
354 Aaron Green RC .25 .60
355 Tre Madden RC .25 .60
356 Jordan Howard RC .60 1.50
357 Kelvin Taylor RC .25 .60
358 Jay Lee RC .25 .60
359 D.J. Foster RC .30 .75
360 Glenn Gronkowski RC .25 .60
361 Laquon Treadwell RC .30 .75
362 Michael Thomas RC .50 1.25
363 Corey Coleman RC .40 1.00
364 Josh Doctson RC .30 .75
365 Tyler Boyd RC .30 .75
366 Will Fuller RC .40 1.00
367 Pharoh Cooper RC .25 .60
368 Sterling Shepard RC .30 .75
369 Leonte Carroo RC .25 .60
370 De'Runnya Wilson RC .25 .60
371 Braxton Miller RC .25 .60
372 Demarcus Robinson RC .25 .60
373 Rashard Higgins RC .25 .60
374 Jordan Williams RC .25 .60
375 Tajae Sharpe RC .30 .75
376 Braion Addison RC .25 .60
377 Aaron Burbridge RC .25 .60
378 Nelson Spruce RC .25 .60
379 Daniel Braverman RC .25 .60
380 Byron Marshall RC .25 .60
381 Kenny Lawler RC .40 1.00
382 Hunter Henry RC .30 .75
383 Nick Vannett RC .25 .60
384 Jerell Adams RC .25 .60
385 Austin Hooper RC .25 .60
386 Laremy Tunsil RC .25 .60
387 Ronnie Stanley RC .30 .75
388 Taylor Decker RC .30 .75
389 Jack Conklin RC .40 1.00
390 Robert Nkemdiche RC .30 .75
391 A'Shawn Robinson RC .25 .60
392 Kenny Clark RC .25 .60
393 Adolphus Washington RC .25 .60
394 Jarran Reed RC .25 .60
395 Austin Johnson RC .25 .60
396 Maliek Collins RC .25 .60
397 Joey Bosa RC .50 1.25
398 DeForest Buckner RC .25 .60
399 Shaq Lawson RC .25 .60
400 Emmanuel Ogbah RC .30 .75
401 Shilique Calhoun RC .25 .60
402 Devon Cajuste RC .25 .60
403 Kevin Dodd RC .25 .60
404 Sheldon Rankins RC .30 .75
405 Reggie Ragland RC .25 .60
406 Darron Lee RC .25 .60
407 Jaylon Smith RC .25 .60
408 Leonard Floyd RC .30 .75
409 Myles Jack RC .30 .75
410 Su'a Cravens RC .25 .60
411 Scooby Wright RC .25 .60
412 Vernon Hargreaves III RC .40 1.00
413 Mackensie Alexander RC .25 .60
414 Eli Apple RC .30 .75
415 Kendall Fuller RC .30 .75
416 Keyarris Garrett RC .25 .60
417 Karl Joseph RC .25 .60
418 Jalen Ramsey RC .40 1.00
419 Jayron Kearse RC .25 .60
420 Vonn Bell RC .30 .75
421 Jeremy Cash RC .30 .75
422 Keith Marshall RC .25 .60
423 Will Redmond RC .40 1.00
424 Zack Sanchez RC .40 1.00
425 Andrew Billings RC .30 .75
426 Jonathan Bullard RC .25 .60
427 Noah Spence RC .25 .60
428 Brandon Allen RC .25 .60
429 Malcolm Mitchell RC .25 .60
430 Jeff Driskel RC .25 .60
431 Tyler Ervin RC .25 .60
432 Josh Ferguson RC .25 .60
433 Wendell Smallwood RC .25 .60
434 Cayleb Jones RC .25 .60
435 Jordan Payton RC .25 .60
436 Kolby Listenbee RC .25 .60
437 Kamalei Correa RC .25 .60
438 Thomas Duarte RC .25 .60
439 Jalin Marshall RC .40 1.00
440 Demarcus Ayers RC .25 .60

2016 Score Artist's Proof

*1-330 VETS/35: 5X TO 12X BASIC CARDS
*331-440 ROOKIES/35: 3X TO 8X BASIC RC

2016 Score Gold Zone

*1-330 VETS/50: 4X TO 10X BASIC CARDS
*331-440 ROOKIES/50. 2X TO 5X BASIC RC

2016 Score Jumbo Artist's Proof

*1-330 VETS/50: 4X TO 10X BASIC CARDS
*331-440 ROOKIES/50. 2X TO 5X BASIC RC

2016 Score Jumbo Gold Zone

*1-330 VETS/99: 3X TO 8X BASIC CARDS
*331-440 ROOKIES/99: 2X TO 5X BASIC RC

2016 Score Jumbo Jerseys

1 Todd Gurley 3.00 8.00
2 Amari Cooper 3.00 8.00
3 Jameis Winston 3.00 8.00
4 Marcus Mariota 3.00 8.00
5 Stefon Diggs 2.50 6.00
6 Devin Funchess 2.00 5.00
7 Melvin Gordon 2.50 6.00
8 Dorial Green-Beckham 2.00 5.00
9 Duke Johnson 2.00 5.00
10 Matt Jones 2.50 6.00
11 Karlos Williams 2.00 5.00
12 T.J. Yeldon 2.00 5.00
13 Odell Beckham Jr. 3.00 8.00
14 Blake Bortles 2.00 5.00
15 Teddy Bridgewater 2.50 6.00
16 Brandin Cooks 2.50 6.00
17 Devonta Freeman 2.50 6.00
18 Johnny Manziel 2.50 6.00
19 Allen Robinson 2.50 6.00
20 Davante Adams 2.00 5.00
21 Kelvin Benjamin 2.50 6.00
22 Jadeveon Clowney 2.00 5.00
23 Mike Evans 2.50 6.00
24 Jeremy Hill 2.00 5.00
25 Carlos Hyde 2.00 5.00
26 Jarvis Landry 2.50 6.00
27 Jordan Matthews 2.50 6.00
28 Donte Moncrief 2.50 6.00
29 Austin Seferian-Jenkins 2.00 5.00
30 Ameer Abdullah 2.00 5.00
31 Nelson Agholor 2.00 5.00
32 David Cobb 2.00 5.00
33 Jay Ajayi 2.50 6.00
34 Phillip Dorsett 2.00 5.00
35 David Johnson 3.00 8.00
36 Jeremy Langford 2.50 6.00
37 Breshad Perriman 2.00 5.00
38 Kevin White 2.00 5.00
39 Devin Smith 2.00 5.00
40 Bryce Petty 2.00 5.00

2016 Score Jumbo Red Zone

*1-330 VETS/35: 5X TO 12X BASIC CARDS
*331-440 ROOKIES/35: 3X TO 8X BASIC RC

2016 Score Scorecard

*1-330 VETS: 2X TO 5X BASIC CARDS
*331-440 ROOKIES: 1X TO 2.5X BASIC RC

2016 Score Showcase

*1-330 VETS/99: 3X TO 8X BASIC CARDS
*331-440 ROOKIES/99: 2X TO 5X BASIC RC
35 Karlos Williams 1.00 2.50

2016 Score All Americans

*GOLD: .5X TO 1.2X BASIC INSERTS
*RED: .6X TO 1.5X BASIC INSERTS
*GREEN: .8X TO 2X BASIC INSERTS
*BLACK: 1X TO 2.5X BASIC INSERTS
*GOLD/99: 1.2X TO 3X BASIC INSERTS
*RED/50: 1.5X TO 4X BASIC INSERTS
*GREEN/20: 2X TO 5X BASIC INSERTS
1 Marcus Mariota .75 2.00
2 Melvin Gordon .60 1.50
3 Amari Cooper .75 2.00
4 Danny Shelton .50 1.25
5 Kevin White .50 1.25
6 Jameis Winston .75 2.00
7 Mike Evans .60 1.50
8 Brandin Cooks .60 1.50
9 C.J. Mosley .60 1.50
10 Odell Beckham Jr. .75 2.00
11 Johnny Manziel .60 1.50
12 Tavon Austin .50 1.25
13 Jadeveon Clowney .50 1.25
14 Tyler Eifert .60 1.50
15 DeAndre Hopkins .60 1.50
16 Andrew Luck 1.00 2.50
17 Robert Griffin III .50 1.25
18 Sammy Watkins .75 2.00
19 Luke Kuechly .60 1.50
20 Mark Barron .50 1.25
21 Cam Newton .75 2.00
22 A.J. Green .75 2.00
23 J.J. Watt .75 2.00
24 Von Miller .60 1.50
25 Patrick Peterson .50 1.25

2016 Score Chain Reaction

*GOLD: .5X TO 1.2X BASIC INSERTS
*RED: .6X TO 1.5X BASIC INSERTS
*GREEN: .8X TO 2X BASIC INSERTS
*BLACK: 1X TO 2.5X BASIC INSERTS
*GOLD/99: 1.2X TO 3X BASIC INSERTS
*RED/50: 1.5X TO 4X BASIC INSERTS
*GREEN/20: 2X TO 5X BASIC INSERTS
1 Cam Newton 1.00 2.50
2 Aaron Rodgers 2.00 5.00
3 Tom Brady 2.50 6.00
4 Odell Beckham Jr. 1.00 2.50
5 John Brown .75 2.00
6 Jarvis Landry .75 2.00
7 Rob Gronkowski 1.00 2.50
8 Randall Cobb .75 2.00
9 Doug Martin .75 2.00
10 Donte Moncrief .75 2.00
11 Tavon Austin .60 1.50
12 Eric Decker .60 1.50
13 Danny Woodhead .75 2.00
14 Demaryius Thomas .75 2.00
15 Dez Bryant 1.00 2.50

2016 Score Dual Draft Autographs

1 J.Charles/M.Forte
2 M.Stafford/C.Matthews 25.00 60.00
3 D.Bryant/D.Thomas 25.00 60.00
4 A.Green/A.Dalton
5 A.Luck/B.Osweiler 30.00 80.00
6 D.Hopkins/T.Eifert
7 B.Bortles/T.Bridgewater 20.00 50.00
8 D.Carr/J.Garoppolo 30.00 80.00
9 J.Winston/M.Mariota 30.00 80.00
10 T.Gurley/T.Rawls 25.00 60.00

2016 Score Dual Jerseys

1 R.Tannehill/L.Miller 3.00 8.00
2 D.Carr/A.Cooper 4.00 10.00
3 A.Dalton/A.Green 4.00 10.00
4 J.Jones/M.Ryan 4.00 10.00
5 A.Brown/L.Bell 4.00 10.00
6 T.Benjamin/J.Manziel 3.00 8.00
7 A.Robinson/B.Bortles 3.00 8.00
8 M.Mariota/K.Wright 4.00 10.00
9 C.Newton/J.Stewart 4.00 10.00
10 J.Laurinaitis/T.Gurley 4.00 10.00

2016 Score Franchise

*GOLD: .5X TO 1.2X BASIC INSERTS
*RED: .6X TO 1.5X BASIC INSERTS
*GREEN: .8X TO 2X BASIC INSERTS
*BLACK: 1X TO 2.5X BASIC INSERTS
*GOLD/99: 1.2X TO 3X BASIC INSERTS
*RED/50: 1.5X TO 4X BASIC INSERTS
*GREEN/20: 2X TO 5X BASIC INSERTS
1 LeSean McCoy .75 2.00
2 Ryan Tannehill .60 1.50
3 Tom Brady 2.00 5.00
4 Chris Ivory .60 1.50
5 Joe Flacco .60 1.50
6 A.J. Green .75 2.00
7 Travis Benjamin .50 1.25
8 Antonio Brown .75 2.00
9 J.J. Watt .75 2.00
10 Andrew Luck 1.00 2.50
11 Blake Bortles .50 1.25
12 Marcus Mariota .75 2.00
13 Demaryius Thomas .60 1.50
14 Jamaal Charles .60 1.50
15 Amari Cooper .75 2.00
16 Melvin Gordon .60 1.50
17 Jason Witten .60 1.50
18 Odell Beckham Jr. .75 2.00
19 DeMarco Murray .60 1.50
20 Ryan Kerrigan .50 1.25
21 Matt Forte .50 1.25
22 Calvin Johnson .75 2.00
23 Aaron Rodgers 1.50 4.00
24 Adrian Peterson .75 2.00
25 Julio Jones .75 2.00
26 Cam Newton .75 2.00
27 Drew Brees .75 2.00
28 Jameis Winston .75 2.00
29 Larry Fitzgerald .60 1.50
30 Todd Gurley .75 2.00
31 NaVorro Bowman .60 1.50
32 Richard Sherman .75 2.00

2016 Score NFL Draft

*GOLD: .5X TO 1.2X BASIC INSERTS
*RED: .6X TO 1.5X BASIC INSERTS
*GREEN: .8X TO 2X BASIC INSERTS
*BLACK: 1X TO 2.5X BASIC INSERTS
*GOLD/99: 1.2X TO 3X BASIC INSERTS
*RED/50: 1.5X TO 4X BASIC INSERTS
*GREEN/20: 2X TO 5X BASIC INSERTS
1 Paxton Lynch .30 .75
2 Jared Goff 2.00 5.00
3 Connor Cook .40 1.00
4 Ezekiel Elliott 1.50 4.00
5 Derrick Henry .75 2.00
6 Laquon Treadwell .40 1.00
7 Michael Thomas .60 1.50
8 Corey Coleman .50 1.25
9 Joey Bosa .60 1.50
10 Jalen Ramsey .50 1.25

2016 Score No Fly Zone

*GOLD: .5X TO 1.2X BASIC INSERTS
*RED: .6X TO 1.5X BASIC INSERTS
*GREEN: .8X TO 2X BASIC INSERTS
*BLACK: 1X TO 2.5X BASIC INSERTS
*GOLD/99: 1.2X TO 3X BASIC INSERTS
*RED/50: 1.5X TO 4X BASIC INSERTS
*GREEN/20: 2X TO 5X BASIC INSERTS
1 Richard Sherman 1.00 2.50
2 Darrelle Revis .60 1.50
3 Charles Woodson 1.00 2.50
4 Josh Norman .60 1.50
5 Ronald Darby .60 1.50
6 Marcus Peters .60 1.50
7 Tyrann Mathieu .75 2.00
8 Davon House .60 1.50
9 Stephon Gilmore .60 1.50
10 Mike Adams .60 1.50

2016 Score Pepsi Rookie of the Week

1 Marcus Mariota 2.00 5.00
2 Jameis Winston 2.00 5.00
3 Kwon Alexander 1.25 3.00
4 Todd Gurley 2.00 5.00
5 Jameis Winston 2.00 5.00
6 Stefon Diggs 1.50 4.00
7 Amari Cooper 2.00 5.00
8 Kwon Alexander 1.25 3.00
9 Amari Cooper 2.00 5.00
10 Mario Edwards Jr. 1.50 4.00
11 Jameis Winston 2.00 5.00
12 Amari Cooper 2.00 5.00
13 Thomas Rawls 1.25 3.00
14 Tyler Lockett 1.50 4.00
15 Amari Cooper 2.00 5.00
16 Preston Smith 1.50 4.00
17 Tyler Lockett 1.50 4.00
18 Jameis Winston 2.00 5.00

2016 Score Quad Jerseys

1 Cbb/Bckhm/Snky/Mrta 6.00 15.00
2 Ctlr/White/Lngfrd/Jffry 5.00 12.00
3 Dnbr/Bsly/Wllms/Smth 6.00 15.00
4 Wnstn/Jnkns/Mrtn/Evns 6.00 15.00
5 Mrshll/Wre/Mllr/Tlb 5.00 12.00

2016 Score Reflections

*GOLD: .5X TO 1.2X BASIC INSERTS
*RED: .6X TO 1.5X BASIC INSERTS
*GREEN: .8X TO 2X BASIC INSERTS
*BLACK: 1X TO 2.5X BASIC INSERTS
*GOLD/99: 1.2X TO 3X BASIC INSERTS
*RED/50: 1.5X TO 4X BASIC INSERTS
*GREEN/20: 2X TO 5X BASIC INSERTS
1 M.Mariota/R.Wilson 1.00 2.50
2 R.Gronkowski/J.Witten .75 2.00
3 B.Bortles/B.Roethlisberger .75 2.00
4 A.Luck/P.Manning 1.50 4.00
5 C.Ivory/M.Lynch .60 1.50
6 C.Newton/M.Vick .75 2.00
7 L.McCoy/L.Bell .75 2.00
8 A.Cooper/J.Jones .75 2.00
9 M.Gordon/J.Charles .60 1.50
10 D.Carr/A.Rodgers 1.50 4.00
11 O.Beckham Jr./C.Johnson .75 2.00
12 C.Jones/J.Pierre-Paul .50 1.25
13 J.Landry/A.Boldin .60 1.50
14 T.Yeldon/A.Foster .60 1.50
15 J.Watt/D.Ware .75 2.00
16 A.Johnson/D.Bryant .75 2.00
17 J.Graham/A.Gates .75 2.00
18 J.Winston/E.Manning .75 2.00
19 S.Diggs/A.Brown .75 2.00
20 M.Evans/V.Jackson .60 1.50
21 A.Dalton/C.Palmer .60 1.50
22 J.Edelman/W.Welker .75 2.00
23 D.Grn-Bckhm/A.Green .75 2.00
24 D.Freeman/F.Gore .60 1.50

2016 Score Rookie Autographs

331 Paxton Lynch SP 12.00 30.00
332 Jared Goff SP 12.00 30.00
333 Connor Cook SP 5.00 12.00
334 Christian Hackenberg 3.00 8.00
335 Carson Wentz SP 50.00 100.00
336 Cardale JonesSP
337 Dak Prescott 30.00 80.00
338 Brandon Doughty 3.00 8.00
340 Nate Sudfeld 3.00 8.00
341 Cody Kessler 3.00 8.00
342 Kevin Hogan 4.00 10.00
343 Trevone Boykin SP 4.00 10.00
344 Ezekiel Elliott SP 60.00 120.00
345 Derrick Henry SP 10.00 25.00
346 Devontae Booker SP 5.00 12.00
347 C.J. Prosise 3.00 8.00
348 Paul Perkins 3.00 8.00
349 Alex Collins 4.00 10.00
350 Kenyan Drake 5.00 12.00
352 Tra Carson 3.00 8.00
353 Jonathan Williams 4.00 10.00
354 Aaron Green 3.00 8.00
355 Tre Madden 3.00 8.00
356 Jordan Howard 8.00 20.00
357 Kelvin Taylor 3.00 8.00
358 Jay Lee 3.00 8.00
360 Glenn Gronkowski 3.00 8.00
361 Laquon Treadwell SP 20.00 40.00
362 Michael Thomas 6.00 15.00
363 Corey Coleman 5.00 12.00
364 Josh Doctson 4.00 10.00
366 Will Fuller 5.00 12.00
367 Pharoh Cooper 3.00 8.00
368 Sterling Shepard 4.00 10.00
369 Leonte Carroo 3.00 8.00
370 De'Runnya Wilson 3.00 8.00
371 Braxton Miller 3.00 8.00
372 Demarcus Robinson 3.00 8.00
374 Jordan Williams 3.00 8.00
375 Tajae Sharpe 4.00 10.00
377 Aaron Burbridge 3.00 8.00
378 Nelson Spruce 3.00 8.00
379 Daniel Braverman 3.00 8.00
380 Byron Marshall 3.00 8.00
381 Kenny Lawler 5.00 12.00
382 Hunter Henry 4.00 10.00
383 Nick Vannett 3.00 8.00
384 Jerell Adams SP 4.00 10.00
385 Austin Hooper 3.00 8.00
386 Laremy Tunsil SP 4.00 10.00
388 Taylor Decker SP 5.00 12.00
389 Jack Conklin SP
391 A'Shawn Robinson 3.00 8.00
392 Kenny Clark
393 Adolphus Washington 3.00 8.00
394 Jarran Reed 3.00 8.00
395 Austin Johnson 3.00 8.00
396 Maliek Collins 3.00 8.00
397 Joey Bosa SP 8.00 20.00
398 DeForest Buckner 3.00 8.00
400 Emmanuel Ogbah 4.00 10.00
401 Shilique Calhoun 3.00 8.00
402 Devon Cajuste 3.00 8.00
403 Kevin Dodd 3.00 8.00
404 Sheldon Rankins
405 Reggie Ragland 3.00 8.00
406 Darron Lee 3.00 8.00
407 Jaylon Smith 3.00 8.00
409 Myles Jack 4.00 10.00
410 Su'a Cravens 3.00 8.00
411 Scooby Wright 3.00 8.00
412 Vernon Hargreaves III 5.00 12.00
413 Mackensie Alexander 3.00 8.00
414 Eli Apple 4.00 10.00
415 Kendall Fuller 4.00 10.00
417 Karl Joseph 3.00 8.00
420 Vonn Bell 4.00 10.00
421 Jeremy Cash 4.00 10.00
422 Keith Marshall 3.00 8.00
425 Andrew Billings 4.00 10.00
426 Jonathan Bullard 3.00 8.00
427 Noah Spence 3.00 8.00
428 Brandon Allen 3.00 8.00
429 Malcolm Mitchell 3.00 8.00
430 Jeff Driskel 3.00 8.00
432 Josh Ferguson 3.00 8.00
433 Wendell Smallwood
434 Cayleb Jones 3.00 8.00
435 Jordan Payton 3.00 8.00
436 Kolby Listenbee
437 Kamalei Correa 3.00 8.00
438 Thomas Duarte 3.00 8.00
440 Demarcus Ayers 3.00 8.00

2016 Score Rookie Autographs Artist's Proof

*ARTIST PROOF/35: .8X TO 2X BASIC AU
*ARTIST PROOF/35: .6X TO 1.5X BASIC SP AU
*ARTIST PROOF/25: 1X TO 2.5X BASIC AU
*ARTIST PROOF/25: .8X TO 2X BASIC SP AU
335 Carson Wentz/25 75.00 150.00
344 Ezekiel Elliott/25 100.00 200.00

2016 Score Rookie Autographs Gold Zone

*GOLD/30-50: .8X TO 2X BASIC AU
*GOLD/30-50: .6X TO 1.5X BASIC SP AU
*GOLD/25: 1X TO 2.5X BASIC AU
*GOLD/25: .8X TO 2X BASIC SP AU
335 Carson Wentz/25 75.00 150.00
344 Ezekiel Elliott/25 100.00 200.00

2016 Score Rookie Autographs Jumbo Artist's Proof

*ARTIST PROOF/35-50: .8X TO 2X BASIC AU
*ARTIST PROOF/35-50: .6X TO 1.5X BASIC SP AU
*ARTIST PROOF/15-25: 1X TO 2.5X BASIC AU
*ARTIST PROOF/15-25: .8X TO 2X BASIC SP AU
335 Carson Wentz/15 75.00 150.00
344 Ezekiel Elliott/15 100.00 200.00

2016 Score Rookie Autographs Jumbo Gold Zone

*GOLD/99: .6X TO 1.5X BASIC AU
*GOLD/99: .5X TO 1.2X BASIC SP AU
*GOLD/35-50: .8X TO 2X BASIC AU
*GOLD/35-50: .6X TO 1.5X BASIC SP AU
*GOLD/25: 1X TO 2.5X BASIC AU
*GOLD/25: .8X TO 2X BASIC SP AU
335 Carson Wentz/25 75.00 150.00
344 Ezekiel Elliott/25 100.00 200.00

2016 Score Rookie Autographs Red Zone

*RED/20: 1X TO 2.5X BASIC AU
*RED/20: .8X TO 2X BASIC AU
335 Carson Wentz 75.00 150.00
344 Ezekiel Elliott 100.00 200.00

2016 Score Rookie Autographs Scorecard

*SCORECARD: .5X TO 1.2X BASIC AU
*SCORECARD SP: .5X TO 1.2X BASIC SP AU
*SCORECARD: .4X TO 1X BASIC SP AU
*SCORECARD SP: .6X TO 1.5X BASIC AU

2016 Score Rookie Autographs Showcase

*SHOWCASE/75-99: .6X TO 1.5X BASIC AU
*SHOWCASE/75-99: .5X TO 1.2X BASIC SP AU
*SHOWCASE/35-50: .8X TO 2X BASIC AU
*SHOWCASE/35-50: .6X TO 1.5X BASIC SPAU
337 Dak Prescott/75 50.00 125.00
344 Ezekiel Elliott/35 100.00 200.00

2016 Score Rookie Helmets

1 Connor Cook 1.00 2.50
2 Jared Goff 5.00 12.00
3 Christian Hackenberg .75 2.00
4 Paxton Lynch .75 2.00
5 Carson Wentz 8.00 20.00
6 Devontae Booker 1.00 2.50
7 Ezekiel Elliott 4.00 10.00
8 Derrick Henry 2.00 5.00
9 Tyler Boyd 1.00 2.50
10 Corey Coleman 1.25 3.00
11 Josh Doctson 1.00 2.50
12 Michael Thomas 1.50 4.00
13 Laquon Treadwell 1.00 2.50
14 Joey Bosa 1.50 4.00
15 Vernon Hargreaves III 1.25 3.00
16 Jayron Kearse .75 2.00
17 Robert Nkemdiche 1.00 2.50
18 Jalen Ramsey 1.25 3.00

2016 Score Sack Attack

*GOLD: .5X TO 1.2X BASIC INSERTS
*RED: .6X TO 1.5X BASIC INSERTS
*GREEN: .8X TO 2X BASIC INSERTS
*BLACK: 1X TO 2.5X BASIC INSERTS
*GOLD/99: 1.2X TO 3X BASIC INSERTS
*RED/50: 1.5X TO 4X BASIC INSERTS
*GREEN/20: 2X TO 5X BASIC INSERTS
1 Chandler Jones .60 1.50
2 Carlos Dunlap .60 1.50
3 J.J. Watt 1.00 2.50
4 Justin Houston .60 1.50
5 Cameron Wake .60 1.50
6 Muhammad Wilkerson .60 1.50
7 Ezekiel Ansah .60 1.50
8 DeMarcus Ware .75 2.00
9 Michael Bennett .60 1.50
10 Brian Orakpo .60 1.50

2016 Score Sidelines

*GOLD: .5X TO 1.2X BASIC INSERTS
*RED: .6X TO 1.5X BASIC INSERTS
*GREEN: .8X TO 2X BASIC INSERTS
*BLACK: 1X TO 2.5X BASIC INSERTS
*GOLD/99: 1.2X TO 3X BASIC INSERTS
*RED/50: 1.5X TO 4X BASIC INSERTS
*GREEN/20: 2X TO 5X BASIC INSERTS
1 Peyton Manning 1.50 4.00
2 Tom Brady 2.00 5.00
3 Adrian Peterson .75 2.00
4 Ndamukong Suh .60 1.50
5 Aaron Rodgers 1.50 4.00
6 Dez Bryant .75 2.00
7 Andrew Luck 1.00 2.50
8 Larry Fitzgerald .60 1.50
9 Drew Brees .75 2.00
10 Marcus Mariota .75 2.00
11 Eli Manning .60 1.50
12 Rob Gronkowski .75 2.00
13 Russell Wilson 1.00 2.50
14 DeMarco Murray .60 1.50
15 Teddy Bridgewater .60 1.50
16 Tony Romo .60 1.50
17 Antonio Gates .50 1.25
18 Ben Roethlisberger .75 2.00
19 Jameis Winston .75 2.00
20 Carson Palmer .60 1.50
21 Odell Beckham Jr. .75 2.00
22 Cam Newton .75 2.00
23 Derek Carr .75 2.00
24 Steve Smith .60 1.50
25 Richard Sherman .75 2.00

2016 Score Signal Callers

*GOLD: .5X TO 1.2X BASIC INSERTS
*RED: .6X TO 1.5X BASIC INSERTS
*GREEN: .8X TO 2X BASIC INSERTS
*BLACK: 1X TO 2.5X BASIC INSERTS
*GOLD/99: 1.2X TO 3X BASIC INSERTS
*RED/50: 1.5X TO 4X BASIC INSERTS
*GREEN/20: 2X TO 5X BASIC INSERTS
1 Carson Palmer .60 1.50
2 Matt Ryan .60 1.50
3 Joe Flacco .60 1.50
4 Cam Newton .75 2.00
5 Andy Dalton .60 1.50
6 Tony Romo .60 1.50
7 Peyton Manning 1.50 4.00
8 Matthew Stafford .60 1.50
9 Aaron Rodgers 1.50 4.00
10 Andrew Luck 1.00 2.50
11 Blake Bortles .50 1.25
12 Alex Smith .60 1.50
13 Ryan Tannehill .60 1.50
14 Teddy Bridgewater .60 1.50
15 Tom Brady 2.00 5.00
16 Drew Brees .75 2.00
17 Eli Manning .60 1.50
18 Derek Carr .75 2.00
19 Sam Bradford .50 1.25
20 Ben Roethlisberger .75 2.00
21 Philip Rivers .75 2.00
22 Russell Wilson 1.00 2.50
23 Jameis Winston .75 2.00
24 Marcus Mariota .75 2.00

2016 Score Stoppers

*GOLD: .5X TO 1.2X BASIC INSERTS
*RED: .6X TO 1.5X BASIC INSERTS
*GREEN: .8X TO 2X BASIC INSERTS
*BLACK: 1X TO 2.5X BASIC INSERTS
*GOLD/99: 1.2X TO 3X BASIC INSERTS
*RED/50: 1.5X TO 4X BASIC INSERTS
*GREEN/20: 2X TO 5X BASIC INSERTS
1 Kam Chancellor 1.00 2.50
2 J.J. Watt 1.00 2.50
3 Von Miller .75 2.00
4 Paul Posluszny .60 1.50
5 Clay Matthews 1.00 2.50
6 Luke Kuechly .75 2.00
7 Harrison Smith .60 1.50
8 Mark Barron .60 1.50
9 James Harrison .75 2.00
10 T.J. McDonald .60 1.50

2016 Score Toe the Line

*GOLD: .5X TO 1.2X BASIC INSERTS
*RED: .6X TO 1.5X BASIC INSERTS
*GREEN: .8X TO 2X BASIC INSERTS
*BLACK: 1X TO 2.5X BASIC INSERTS
*GOLD/99: 1.2X TO 3X BASIC INSERTS
*RED/50: 1.5X TO 4X BASIC INSERTS
*GREEN/20: 2X TO 5X BASIC INSERTS
1 Antonio Brown 1.00 2.50
2 Julio Jones 1.00 2.50
3 DeAndre Hopkins .75 2.00
4 Odell Beckham Jr. 1.00 2.50
5 Mike Evans .75 2.00
6 Demaryius Thomas .75 2.00
7 Calvin Johnson 1.00 2.50
8 Amari Cooper 1.00 2.50
9 T.Y. Hilton .75 2.00
10 A.J. Green 1.00 2.50
11 Allen Robinson .75 2.00
12 Steve Smith .75 2.00
13 Travis Benjamin .60 1.50
14 Terrance Williams .60 1.50
15 Randall Cobb .75 2.00

2016 Score Triple Jerseys

1 Reed/Grcn/Jcksn SP 4.00 10.00
2 Ftzgrld/Flyd/Jhnsn SP 5.00 12.00
3 Jffry/Ctlr/White 4.00 10.00
4 Abdllh/Ebrn/Sttfrd 4.00 10.00
5 Ptty/Smth/Wllms 3.00 8.00
6 Prrmn/Alln/Wllms 4.00 10.00
7 Oswlr/Mnng/Mllr SP 10.00 25.00
8 GrnBckhm/Wrght/Wlkr SP 3.00 8.00
9 Mntgmry/Hndly/Adms 4.00 10.00
10 Brdgwtr/Dggs/Ptrsn 5.00 12.00

2016 Score Veteran Helmets

1 Chris Johnson 2.50 6.00
2 Julio Jones 4.00 10.00
3 Tyrod Taylor 3.00 8.00
4 Tyler Eifert 3.00 8.00
5 Andrew Luck 5.00 12.00
6 Travis Kelce 4.00 10.00
7 Adrian Peterson 4.00 10.00
8 Tom Brady 10.00 25.00
9 Drew Brees 4.00 10.00
10 DeMarco Murray 3.00 8.00
11 Anquan Boldin 2.50 6.00
12 Jimmy Graham 4.00 10.00

2017 Score

1 Jamie Collins .12 .30
2 Emmanuel Sanders .20 .50
3 Eric Kendricks .12 .30
4 Tyrell Williams .12 .30
5 Cliff Avril .12 .30
6 Kiko Alonso .12 .30
7 Zach Miller .12 .30
8 Brandin Cooks .15 .40
9 Ryan Tannehill .15 .40
10 Andrew Whitworth .12 .30
11 Paul Perkins .12 .30
12 Jalin Marshall .12 .30
13 Giovani Bernard .12 .30
14 Jason Witten .15 .40
15 Bryce Petty .12 .30
16 Carson Palmer .15 .40
17 Case Keenum .15 .40
18 Jeremy Langford .15 .40
19 Cameron Wake .12 .30
20 Matthew Stafford .15 .40
21 Sammy Watkins .20 .50
22 Antoine Bethea .12 .30
23 Mike Gillislee .12 .30
24 Trent Murphy .12 .30
25 David Amerson .12 .30
26 LeGarrette Blount .15 .40
27 Eli Rogers .12 .30
28 Terrance West .12 .30
29 Thomas Rawls .12 .30
30 Jack Doyle .12 .30
31 Darren Sproles .15 .40
32 Jordy Nelson .15 .40
33 Jacob Tamme .12 .30
34 Jimmy Graham .20 .50
35 Kendall Wright .12 .30
36 Blaine Gabbert .12 .30
37 Ezekiel Ansah .12 .30
38 Kirk Cousins .20 .50
39 Alfred Morris .12 .30
40 Devin Funchess .12 .30
41 Demaryius Thomas .15 .40
42 Carlos Dunlap .12 .30
43 Brian Quick .12 .30
44 Cameron Brate .12 .30
45 Dak Prescott .20 .50
46 Golden Tate III .12 .30
47 Marqise Lee .12 .30
48 Eddie Royal .12 .30
49 Dominique Rodgers-Cromartie .12 .30
50 Vic Beasley Jr. .12 .30
51 Theo Riddick .12 .30
52 Malcolm Jenkins .15 .40
53 Deion Jones .12 .30
54 David Johnson .20 .50
55 Allen Hurns .12 .30
56 Joe Flacco .15 .40
57 Blake Bortles .12 .30
58 Mike Wallace .12 .30
59 Cody Kessler .12 .30
60 Luke Kuechly .15 .40
61 Lawrence Timmons .15 .40
62 Tyrann Mathieu .15 .40
63 Paul Posluszny .12 .30
64 Robert Quinn .15 .40
65 Jalen Richard .12 .30
66 Adam Thielen .20 .50
67 Chris Ivory .15 .40
68 Rashad Jennings .12 .30
69 Eli Manning .15 .40
70 Ryan Mathews .15 .40
71 Jordan Reed .12 .30
72 Joe Thomas .12 .30
73 Tevin Coleman .15 .40
74 Tim Hightower .12 .30
75 C.J. Fiedorowicz .12 .30
76 Jaron Brown .12 .30
77 T.Y. Hilton .15 .40
78 David Harris .12 .30
79 Breshad Perriman .12 .30
80 Tyler Lockett .15 .40
81 Jordan Matthews .12 .30
82 Julius Peppers .15 .40
83 Fozzy Whittaker .12 .30
84 Ty Montgomery .12 .30
85 Markus Golden .12 .30
86 Damien Williams .12 .30
87 Carson Wentz .25 .60
88 Chris Thompson .12 .30
89 Kenny Stills .12 .30
90 Mohamed Sanu .12 .30
91 Travis Benjamin .12 .30
92 Derrick Morgan .12 .30
93 DeAngelo Williams .12 .30
94 Bruce Irvin .12 .30
95 Quincy Enunwa .12 .30
96 Brian Orakpo .12 .30
97 Marcus Mariota .20 .50
98 Russell Wilson .25 .60
99 Jarvis Landry .15 .40
100 Greg Olsen .15 .40
101 Cordarrelle Patterson .12 .30
102 Harrison Smith .12 .30
103 Jeremy Hill .12 .30
104 Vance McDonald .12 .30
105 LeSean McCoy .20 .50
106 Sammie Coates .12 .30
107 Telvin Smith .12 .30
108 Jamison Crowder .12 .30
109 Dont'a Hightower .12 .30
110 Davante Adams .15 .40
111 Nick Fairley .12 .30
112 Kerry Hyder RC .12 .30
113 Tavon Austin .12 .30
114 Terrell Suggs .12 .30
115 Donte Moncrief .15 .40
116 Le'Veon Bell .15 .40
117 Kyle Rudolph .12 .30
118 Brice Butler .12 .30
119 Julio Jones .20 .50
120 Alex Smith .15 .40
121 Danny Amendola .15 .40
122 Spencer Ware .12 .30
123 Taylor Gabriel .12 .30
124 Cole Beasley .20 .50
125 Tyrod Taylor .15 .40
126 Michael Crabtree .12 .30
127 C.J. Mosley .15 .40
128 Brock Osweiler .12 .30
129 Derek Carr .20 .50
130 Alfred Blue .12 .30
131 Melvin Gordon .15 .40
132 Ameer Abdullah .12 .30
133 Vontae Davis .12 .30
134 Jadeveon Clowney .12 .30
135 Michael Thomas .20 .50
136 Seth Roberts .12 .30
137 Mike Evans .15 .40
138 Quinton Patton .12 .30
139 DeAndre Hopkins .15 .40
140 Sterling Shepard .15 .40
141 Odell Beckham Jr. .20 .50
142 Matt Forte .12 .30
143 Navorro Bowman .15 .40
144 Lamar Miller .12 .30
145 Marcus Peters .12 .30
146 James Harrison .15 .40
147 Cameron Meredith .12 .30
148 Vontaze Burfict .12 .30
149 Anquan Boldin .12 .30
150 Doug Martin .15 .40
151 Trevor Siemian .12 .30
152 Byron Jones .12 .30
153 Todd Gurley II .20 .50
154 Leonard Williams .12 .30
155 Matt Jones .15 .40
156 Chandler Jones .12 .30
157 Robert Mathis .12 .30
158 Steve Smith Sr. .15 .40
159 Melvin Ingram .12 .30
160 John Brown .15 .40
161 Julian Edelman .20 .50
162 Chris Conley .12 .30
163 Derrick Henry .15 .40
164 Ted Ginn Jr. .12 .30
165 DeAndre Washington .12 .30
166 Will Fuller V .12 .30
167 Jared Goff .20 .50
168 Everson Griffen .12 .30
169 Doug Baldwin .15 .40
170 Mark Barron .12 .30
171 Willie Snead .15 .40
172 Kenny Vaccaro .12 .30
173 Jay Ajayi .15 .40
174 Frank Gore .15 .40
175 Kelvin Benjamin .15 .40
176 Eric Ebron .12 .30
177 Tyler Eifert .15 .40
178 Victor Cruz .15 .40
179 Terrance Williams .12 .30
180 Charles Clay .12 .30
181 Jay Cutler .12 .30
182 Phillip Dorsett .12 .30
183 Khalil Mack .20 .50
184 Amari Cooper .20 .50
185 DeForest Buckner .12 .30
186 Pierre Garcon .15 .40
187 Rishard Matthews .12 .30
188 Thomas Davis .12 .30
189 Lorenzo Alexander .12 .30
190 Casey Hayward .12 .30
191 Larry Fitzgerald .15 .40
192 Martellus Bennett .12 .30
193 Jamaal Charles .15 .40
194 DeVante Parker .15 .40
195 Antonio Gates .12 .30
196 Zach Brown .12 .30
197 Ben Roethlisberger .20 .50
198 Jurrell Casey .12 .30
199 James Bradberry .12 .30
200 Tom Brady .50 1.25
201 Corey Coleman .12 .30
202 Brandon Marshall .12 .30
203 Jeremy Maclin .12 .30
204 Richard Sherman .20 .50
205 Malcolm Butler .20 .50
206 C.J. Anderson .15 .40
207 Allen Robinson .15 .40
208 Robert Woods .15 .40
209 Reshad Jones .12 .30
210 Kenny Britt .12 .30
211 Chris Hogan .12 .30
212 Colin Kaepernick .15 .40
213 Patrick Peterson .12 .30
214 Jalen Ramsey .12 .30
215 DeMarcus Ware .15 .40
216 Coby Fleener .12 .30
217 Jesse James .12 .30
218 Joey Bosa .20 .50
219 Tyler Boyd .12 .30
220 Nelson Agholor .12 .30
221 Marcell Dareus .12 .30
222 Fletcher Cox .12 .30
223 Cameron Jordan .12 .30
224 Lance Kendricks .12 .30
225 Andrew Luck .25 .60
226 J.J. Watt .20 .50
227 Eric Decker .12 .30
228 Gary Barnidge .12 .30
229 Devonta Freeman .15 .40
230 Jonathan Stewart .12 .30
231 Alshon Jeffery .15 .40
232 Sam Bradford .12 .30
233 Kelechi Osemele .12 .30
234 Ndamukong Suh .15 .40
235 Brent Grimes .12 .30
236 Cam Newton .20 .50
237 Devontae Booker .12 .30
238 Geno Atkins .12 .30
239 Torrey Smith .12 .30
240 Rob Ninkovich .12 .30
241 Adam Humphries .12 .30
242 Drew Brees .20 .50
243 Matt Asiata .12 .30
244 Ryan Shazier .12 .30
245 Josh Sitton .12 .30
246 Jermaine Kearse .12 .30
247 J.J. Nelson .12 .30
248 Trent Williams .12 .30
249 Erik Walden .12 .30
250 Dwayne Allen .12 .30
251 Brandon Graham .12 .30
252 Tyreek Hill .20 .50
253 Eric Weddle .12 .30
254 Joe Haden .12 .30

255 Latavius Murray .12 .30
256 Eric Berry .15 .40
257 DeMarco Murray .15 .40
258 Clay Matthews .15 .40
259 Tajae Sharpe .12 .30
260 Keenan Allen .15 .40
261 Lane Johnson .12 .30
262 Randall Cobb .15 .40
263 Stefon Diggs .15 .40
264 Jaelen Strong .12 .30
265 Whitney Mercilus .12 .30
266 Darrelle Revis .12 .30
267 Ryan Kerrigan .12 .30
268 Janoris Jenkins .12 .30
269 Chris Harris .12 .30
270 Marvin Jones Jr. .12 .30
271 Pernell McPhee .12 .30
272 Tony Romo .15 .40
273 Marquise Goodwin .12 .30
274 Carlos Hyde .12 .30
275 Kamar Aiken .12 .30
276 Jameis Winston .15 .40
277 Adrian Peterson .20 .50
278 Larry Donnell .12 .30
279 Jordan Howard .20 .50
280 C.J. Prosise .12 .30
281 Rob Gronkowski .20 .50
282 Brandon LaFell .12 .30
283 Ha Ha Clinton-Dix .12 .30
284 Danny Trevathan .12 .30
285 Zach Ertz .15 .40
286 Von Miller .15 .40
287 Philip Rivers .20 .50
288 Justin Houston .12 .30
289 Desmond Trufant .12 .30
290 A.J. Green .20 .50
291 Ezekiel Elliott .25 .60
292 Bilal Powell .12 .30
293 Wendell Smallwood .12 .30
294 Richard Rodgers .15 .40
295 Virgil Green .12 .30
296 Eddie Lacy .12 .30
297 Darius Slay .12 .30
298 Aaron Rodgers .40 1.00
299 Jacquizz Rodgers .12 .30
300 Kwon Alexander .12 .30
301 Mark Ingram .15 .40
302 Vincent Jackson .12 .30
303 Dennis Pitta .12 .30
304 Andy Dalton .15 .40
305 Matt Ryan .15 .40
306 Terrelle Pryor Sr. .12 .30
307 Andrew Hawkins .12 .30
308 Sean Lee .15 .40
309 Jeremy Kerley .12 .30
310 Emmanuel Ogbah .12 .30
311 Aaron Donald .20 .50
312 Josh Norman .12 .30
313 Duke Johnson .12 .30
314 Dez Bryant .20 .50
315 Taylor Lewan .12 .30
316 Antonio Brown .20 .50
317 Julius Thomas .12 .30
318 Hunter Henry .12 .30
319 Tracy Porter .12 .30
320 T.J. Yeldon .12 .30
321 Marshal Yanda .12 .30
322 Aqib Talib .12 .30
323 Gerald McCoy .12 .30
324 Earl Thomas III .15 .40
325 Travis Kelce .20 .50
326 Delanie Walker .12 .30
327 Justin Pugh .12 .30
328 Landon Collins .12 .30
329 Isaiah Crowell .12 .30
330 DeSean Jackson .15 .40
331 J.SmthSchstr RC .60 1.50
332 Dawuane Smoot RC .25 .60
333 Noah Brown RC .30 .75
334 Malik Hooker RC .25 .60
335 Donnel Pumphrey RC .30 .75
336 T.J. Watt RC .75 2.00
337 Myles Garrett RC .75 2.00
338 Travis Rudolph RC .25 .60
339 Solomon Thomas RC .25 .60
340 Zay Jones RC .30 .75
341 O.J. Howard RC .30 .75
342 Shelton Gibson RC .25 .60
343 David Njoku RC .30 .75
344 Zach Cunningham RC .30 .75
345 Marquez White RC .25 .60
346 Dede Westbrook RC .25 .60
347 Leonard Fournette RC .75 2.00
348 KD Cannon RC .25 .60
349 Mitchell Trubisky RC 1.25 3.00
350 Corey Smith RC .40 1.00
351 Nathan Peterman RC .30 .75
352 Chris Wormley RC .25 .60
353 Seth Russell RC .30 .75
354 Desmond King RC .30 .75
355 Corey Clement RC .30 .75
356 Gerald Everett RC .25 .60
357 Jabrill Peppers RC .40 1.00
358 Amara Darboh RC .25 .60
359 Marshon Lattimore RC .30 .75
360 Caleb Brantley RC .25 .60
361 Deshaun Watson RC 1.50 4.00
362 Ricky Seals-Jones RC .25 .60
363 D'Onta Foreman RC .30 .75
364 Jordan Willis RC .25 .60
365 De'Veon Smith RC .60 1.50
366 Josh Malone RC .25 .60
367 Jonathan Allen RC .30 .75
368 Travin Dural RC .30 .75
369 Mike Williams RC .40 1.00
370 Gareon Conley RC .25 .60
371 Brad Kaaya RC .25 .60
372 Cameron Sutton RC .25 .60
373 Christian McCaffrey RC .60 1.50
374 Joe Mixon RC .50 1.25
375 Alvin Kamara RC 1.00 2.50
376 Malachi Dupre RC .25 .60
377 Reuben Foster RC .25 .60
378 Jehu Chesson RC .30 .75
379 Carl Lawson RC .25 .60
380 Jarrad Davis RC .30 .75
381 DeShone Kizer RC .25 .60
382 Sidney Jones RC .25 .60
383 Wayne Gallman RC .30 .75
384 Curtis Samuel RC .30 .75
385 Jake Butt RC .30 .75
386 Isaiah Ford RC .25 .60
387 Jamal Adams RC .25 .60
388 Josh Reynolds RC .25 .60
389 Cam Robinson RC .25 .60
390 Haason Reddick RC .25 .60
391 Jeremy McNichols RC .25 .60
392 Adoree' Jackson RC .30 .75
393 Samaje Perine RC .25 .60
394 Jamaal Williams RC .25 .60
395 John Ross RC .30 .75
396 Corey Davis RC .40 1.00
397 Malik McDowell RC .25 .60
398 James Quick RC .30 .75
399 Charles Harris RC .25 .60
400 Cordrea Tankersley RC .30 .75
401 C.J. Beathard RC .25 .60
402 DeMarcus Walker RC .25 .60
403 Patrick Mahomes II RC 3.00 8.00
404 Chad Hansen RC .25 .60
405 Jordan Leggett RC .25 .60
406 Taywan Taylor RC .25 .60
407 Tim Williams RC .30 .75
408 Stacy Coley RC .25 .60
409 Marlon Humphrey RC .25 .60
410 Quincy Wilson RC .25 .60
411 Chad Kelly RC .25 .60
412 Jerod Evans RC .30 .75
413 James Conner RC .50 1.25
414 Carlos Henderson RC .25 .60
415 Jeremy Sprinkle RC .25 .60
416 Cooper Kupp RC .40 1.00
417 Takkarist McKinley RC .25 .60
418 Ryan Switzer RC .30 .75
419 Elijah Qualls RC .25 .60
420 ArDarius Stewart RC .25 .60
421 Ryan Ramczyk RC .25 .60
422 Marlon Mack RC .40 1.00
423 Kareem Hunt RC .50 1.25
424 Brian Hill RC .25 .60
425 Evan Engram RC .30 .75
426 Elijah Hood RC .25 .60
427 Dalvin Cook RC .60 1.50
428 Chris Godwin RC .30 .75
429 Teez Tabor RC .30 .75
430 Tre'Davious White RC .25 .60
431 Davis Webb RC .25 .60
432 Taco Charlton RC .25 .60
433 Matthew Dayes RC .25 .60
434 Artavis Scott RC .25 .60
435 Cole Hikutini RC .25 .60
436 R. Joshua Dobbs RC .30 .75
437 Derek Barnett RC .30 .75
438 Fred Ross RC .25 .60
439 Bucky Hodges RC .25 .60
440 Raekwon McMillan RC .25 .60

2017 Score Artist's Proof

*1-330 VETS/35: 5X TO 12X BASIC CARDS
*331-440 ROOKIES/35: 3X TO 8X BASIC RC

2017 Score Black

*1-330 VETS: 2X TO 5X BASIC CARDS
*331-440 ROOKIES: 1X TO 2.5X BASIC RC

2017 Score Gold

*1-330 VETS: 2X TO 5X BASIC CARDS
*331-440 ROOKIES: 1X TO 2.5X BASIC RC

2017 Score Gold Zone

*1-330 VETS/50: 4X TO 10X BASIC CARDS
*331-440 ROOKIES/50: 2X TO 5X BASIC RC

2017 Score Red

*1-330 VETS: 2X TO 5X BASIC CARDS
*331-440 ROOKIES: 1X TO 2.5X BASIC RC

2017 Score Red Zone

*1-330 VETS/20: 10X TO 25X BASIC CARDS
*331-440 ROOKIES/20: 6X TO 15X BASIC RC

2017 Score Scorecard

*1-330 VETS: 2X TO 5X BASIC CARDS
*331-440 ROOKIES: 1X TO 2.5X BASIC RC

2017 Score Showcase

*1-330 VETS/99: 3X TO 8X BASIC CARDS
*331-440 ROOKIES/99: 2X TO 5X BASIC RC

2017 Score Big Man on Campus

*GOLD: .6X TO 1.5X BASIC INSERTS
*GREEN: .6X TO 1.5X BASIC INSERTS
*RED: .6X TO 1.5X BASIC INSERTS
1 John Ross .40 1.00
2 Mitchell Trubisky 1.50 4.00
3 Dede Westbrook .30 .75
4 JuJu Smith-Schuster .75 2.00
5 Jonathan Allen .40 1.00
6 Patrick Mahomes II 4.00 10.00
7 Dalvin Cook .75 2.00
8 David Njoku .40 1.00
9 Christian McCaffrey .75 2.00
10 Deshaun Watson 2.00 5.00
11 D'Onta Foreman .40 1.00
12 Mike Williams .50 1.25
13 Brad Kaaya .30 .75
14 Corey Davis .50 1.25
15 Leonard Fournette 1.00 2.50

2017 Score Color Rush

*GOLD: .6X TO 1.5X BASIC INSERTS
*GREEN: .6X TO 1.5X BASIC INSERTS
*RED: .6X TO 1.5X BASIC INSERTS
1 Matt Forte .60 1.50
2 LeGarrette Blount .75 2.00
3 A.J. Green 1.00 2.50
4 David Johnson 1.00 2.50
5 Melvin Gordon .75 2.00
6 Aaron Rodgers 2.00 5.00
7 Marcus Mariota 1.00 2.50
8 Matt Ryan .75 2.00
9 Julio Jones 1.00 2.50
10 Joe Flacco .75 2.00
11 Drew Brees 1.00 2.50
12 Ted Ginn Jr. .60 1.50
13 Ezekiel Elliott 1.25 3.00
14 Dez Bryant 1.00 2.50
15 Tyreek Hill 1.00 2.50
16 Russell Wilson 1.25 3.00
17 Tyler Lockett .75 2.00
18 Malcolm Jenkins .75 2.00
19 Odell Beckham Jr. 1.00 2.50
20 Antonio Brown 1.00 2.50

2017 Score Drive Team

*GOLD: .6X TO 1.5X BASIC INSERTS
*GREEN: .6X TO 1.5X BASIC INSERTS
*RED: .6X TO 1.5X BASIC INSERTS
1 Hll/Grn/Dltn 1.00 2.50
2 Frmn/Jns/Ryn 1.00 2.50
3 Jms/Wrnr/Ftzgrld .75 2.00
4 Nwtn/Stwrt/Bnjmn 1.00 2.50
5 Ftzgrld/Plmr/Jhnsn 1.00 2.50
6 Edlmn/Brdy/Blnt 2.50 6.00
7 Grse/Wrfld/Csnka 1.00 2.50
8 Brwn/Rthlsbrgr/Bll 1.00 2.50
9 Rd/Klly/Thms 1.00 2.50
10 Prsctt/Brynt/Elltt 1.25 3.00
11 Shrpe/Dvs/Elwy 1.50 4.00
12 Brs/Cks/Ingrm 1.00 2.50
13 Mnng/Bckhm/Jnngs 1.00 2.50
14 Rdgrs/Lcy/Nlsn 2.00 5.00
15 Irvn/Smth/Akmn 1.50 4.00
16 Gre/Hltn/Lck 1.25 3.00
17 Rce/Crg/Mntna 2.50 6.00
18 Crr/Cpr/Mrry 1.00 2.50
19 Hrrsn/Mnng/Jms 2.00 5.00
20 Wntz/Mtthws/Mthws 1.25 3.00

2017 Score Fantasy Stars

*GOLD: .6X TO 1.5X BASIC INSERTS
*GREEN: .6X TO 1.5X BASIC INSERTS
*RED: .6X TO 1.5X BASIC INSERTS
*BLACK: .6X TO 1.5X BASIC INSERTS
1 Andrew Luck 1.25 3.00
2 Cam Newton 1.00 2.50
3 Marvin Jones Jr. .60 1.50
4 Julio Jones 1.00 2.50
5 Marcus Mariota 1.00 2.50
6 Odell Beckham Jr. 1.00 2.50
7 Melvin Gordon .75 2.00
8 Derek Carr 1.00 2.50
9 Latavius Murray .60 1.50
10 Ezekiel Elliott 1.25 3.00
11 Aaron Rodgers 2.00 5.00
12 Drew Brees 1.00 2.50
13 David Johnson 1.00 2.50
14 Le'Veon Bell .75 2.00
15 Brandin Cooks .75 2.00
16 Adam Thielen 1.00 2.50
17 Matt Ryan .75 2.00

2017 Score Franchise Fabric

1 Will Fuller V 2.50 6.00
2 Connor Cook 2.50 6.00
3 Tyler Ervin 2.50 6.00
4 Michael Thomas 4.00 10.00
5 Leonte Carroo 2.50 6.00
6 Kenyan Drake 2.50 6.00
7 Derrick Henry 3.00 8.00
8 Wendell Smallwood 2.50 6.00
9 Josh Doctson 2.50 6.00
10 Tyler Boyd 2.50 6.00
11 Paul Perkins 2.50 6.00
12 DeAndre Washington 2.50 6.00
13 Trevor Davis 2.50 6.00
14 C.J. Prosise 2.50 6.00
15 Hunter Henry 2.50 6.00
16 Colin Kaepernick 3.00 8.00
17 Christian Hackenberg 2.50 6.00
18 Kenneth Dixon 2.50 6.00
19 Justin Hardy 2.50 6.00
20 Devontae Booker 2.50 6.00
21 Alex Collins 2.50 6.00
22 Keenan Reynolds 2.50 6.00
23 Devin Smith 2.50 6.00
24 Moritz Bohringer 2.50 6.00
25 Chris Conley 2.50 6.00
26 Jaelen Strong 2.50 6.00
27 Rashad Greene 2.50 6.00
28 Bryce Petty 2.50 6.00
29 Brett Hundley 2.50 6.00
30 Leonard Williams 2.50 6.00

2017 Score Huddle Up

*GOLD: .6X TO 1.5X BASIC INSERTS
*GREEN: .6X TO 1.5X BASIC INSERTS
*RED: .6X TO 1.5X BASIC INSERTS
1 Dak Prescott 1.25 3.00
2 Andrew Luck 1.50 4.00
3 Carson Wentz 1.50 4.00
4 Drew Brees 1.25 3.00
5 Matt Ryan 1.00 2.50
6 Cam Newton 1.25 3.00
7 Eli Manning 1.00 2.50
8 Tom Brady 3.00 8.00
9 Ben Roethlisberger 1.25 3.00
10 Aaron Rodgers 2.50 6.00

2017 Score Hype

*GOLD: .6X TO 1.5X BASIC INSERTS
*GREEN: .6X TO 1.5X BASIC INSERTS
*RED: .6X TO 1.5X BASIC INSERTS
1 Dalvin Cook 1.00 2.50
2 D'Onta Foreman .50 1.25
3 Mitchell Trubisky 2.00 5.00
4 Mike Williams .60 1.50
5 DeShone Kizer .40 1.00
6 Corey Davis .60 1.50
7 Jonathan Allen .50 1.25
8 John Ross .50 1.25
9 David Njoku .50 1.25
10 Leonard Fournette 1.25 3.00
11 Christian McCaffrey 1.00 2.50
12 Curtis Samuel .50 1.25
13 Deshaun Watson 2.50 6.00
14 JuJu Smith-Schuster 1.00 2.50
15 Brad Kaaya .40 1.00

2017 Score Inscriptions

3 La'el Collins/25
4 Kony Ealy/25 6.00 15.00
5 Rishard Matthews/25 6.00 15.00
6 Phil McConkey/25 8.00 20.00
7 Geno Smith/20 6.00 15.00
8 Tajae Sharpe/25 6.00 15.00
10 Trevor Siemian/25 6.00 15.00
11 Jermaine Kearse/25 6.00 15.00
13 Travis Benjamin/25 6.00 15.00
14 Charles Sims/25 6.00 15.00
16 Kyle Van Noy/25 6.00 15.00
17 Eric Weddle/25 6.00 15.00
20 Ottis Anderson/25 6.00 15.00
34 Rayfield Wright/25 8.00 20.00
44 Dexter Manley/25 8.00 20.00

2017 Score NFL Draft

1 Mitchell Trubisky 2.00 5.00
2 Patrick Mahomes II 5.00 12.00
3 Deshaun Watson 2.50 6.00
4 DeShone Kizer .40 1.00
5 JuJu Smith-Schuster 1.00 2.50
6 Jonathan Allen .50 1.25
7 Dede Westbrook .40 1.00
8 Dalvin Cook 1.00 2.50
9 Christian McCaffrey 1.00 2.50
10 O.J. Howard .50 1.25
11 John Ross .50 1.25
12 Curtis Samuel .50 1.25
13 Mike Williams .60 1.50
14 Corey Davis .60 1.50
15 Brad Kaaya .40 1.00
16 David Njoku .50 1.25
17 Leonard Fournette 1.25 3.00
18 D'Onta Foreman .50 1.25

2017 Score No Fly Zone

*GOLD: .6X TO 1.5X BASIC INSERTS
*GREEN: .6X TO 1.5X BASIC INSERTS
*RED: .6X TO 1.5X BASIC INSERTS
1 Josh Norman .60 1.50
2 Malcolm Butler 1.00 2.50
3 Harrison Smith .60 1.50
4 Marcus Peters .60 1.50
5 Casey Hayward .60 1.50
6 Richard Sherman 1.00 2.50
7 Chris Harris .60 1.50
8 Xavier Rhodes .60 1.50
9 Aqib Talib .60 1.50
10 Kam Chancellor 1.00 2.50
11 Patrick Peterson .60 1.50
12 Eric Berry .75 2.00
13 Tyrann Mathieu .75 2.00
14 Landon Collins .60 1.50
15 Reshad Jones .60 1.50

2017 Score Pro Bowl Jerseys

1 Joe Staley 2.00 5.00
2 Sebastian Janikowski 2.00 5.00
3 L.P. Ladouceur 2.00 5.00
4 Joe Thomas 2.00 5.00
5 Evan Mathis 2.00 5.00
6 Marshal Yanda 2.00 5.00
7 Mike Pouncey 2.00 5.00
8 Elvis Dumervil 2.00 5.00
9 Duane Brown 2.00 5.00
10 Joe Thomas 2.00 5.00
11 Trent Williams 2.00 5.00
12 Pat McAfee 2.50 6.00
13 Jahri Evans 2.00 5.00
14 Ryan Clady 2.00 5.00
15 Geno Atkins 2.00 5.00
16 Marshal Yanda 2.00 5.00
17 Travis Frederick 2.00 5.00
18 Andy Lee 2.00 5.00
19 Josh Sitton 2.00 5.00
20 Paul Soliai 2.00 5.00

2017 Score Reflections

*GOLD: .6X TO 1.5X BASIC INSERTS
*GREEN: .6X TO 1.5X BASIC INSERTS
*RED: .6X TO 1.5X BASIC INSERTS
1 J.Goff/K.Warner 1.25 3.00
2 B.Favre/C.Wentz 2.50 6.00
3 E.Smith/E.Elliott 2.00 5.00
4 A.Brown/J.Rice 2.00 5.00
5 K.Mack/V.Miller 1.25 3.00
6 A.Peterson/J.Brown 1.50 4.00
7 T.Bradshaw/B.Rthlsbrgr 2.00 5.00
8 D.Prescott/R.Staubach 1.50 4.00
9 M.Lynch/T.Gurley 1.25 3.00
10 L.Ftzgrld/O.Bckhm 1.25 3.00

2017 Score Rookie Autographs

331 JuJu Smith-Schuster 8.00 20.00
332 Dawuane Smoot 3.00 8.00
333 Noah Brown 4.00 10.00
334 Malik Hooker 3.00 8.00
335 Donnel Pumphrey 4.00 10.00
336 T.J. Watt 10.00 25.00
338 Travis Rudolph 3.00 8.00
339 Solomon Thomas 3.00 8.00
340 Zay Jones 4.00 10.00
341 O.J. Howard 4.00 10.00
342 Shelton Gibson 3.00 8.00
345 Marquez White 3.00 8.00
346 Dede Westbrook 3.00 8.00
347 Leonard Fournette 30.00 60.00
348 KD Cannon 3.00 8.00
349 Mitchell Trubisky 40.00 80.00
350 Corey Smith 5.00 12.00
352 Chris Wormley 3.00 8.00
353 Seth Russell 4.00 10.00
354 Desmond King 4.00 10.00
355 Corey Clement 4.00 10.00
356 Gerald Everett 3.00 8.00
357 Jabrill Peppers 5.00 12.00
358 Amara Darboh 3.00 8.00
359 Marshon Lattimore 4.00 10.00
361 Deshaun Watson 30.00 60.00
362 Ricky Seals-Jones 3.00 8.00
363 D'Onta Foreman 4.00 10.00
364 Jordan Willis 3.00 8.00
366 Josh Malone 3.00 8.00
367 Jonathan Allen 4.00 10.00
368 Travin Dural 4.00 10.00
369 Mike Williams 5.00 12.00
370 Gareon Conley 3.00 8.00
371 Brad Kaaya 3.00 8.00
372 Cameron Sutton 3.00 8.00
373 Christian McCaffrey 25.00 50.00
374 Joe Mixon 6.00 15.00
375 Alvin Kamara 12.00 30.00
376 Malachi Dupre 3.00 8.00
378 Jehu Chesson 4.00 10.00
379 Carl Lawson 3.00 8.00
381 DeShone Kizer 3.00 8.00
382 Sidney Jones 3.00 8.00
383 Wayne Gallman 4.00 10.00
384 Curtis Samuel 4.00 10.00
385 Jake Butt 4.00 10.00
386 Isaiah Ford 3.00 8.00
387 Jamal Adams 3.00 8.00
388 Josh Reynolds 3.00 8.00
390 Haason Reddick 3.00 8.00
391 Jeremy McNichols 3.00 8.00
393 Samaje Perine 3.00 8.00
394 Jamaal Williams 3.00 8.00
395 John Ross 4.00 10.00
396 Corey Davis 5.00 12.00
398 James Quick 4.00 10.00
399 Charles Harris 3.00 8.00
401 C.J. Beathard 3.00 8.00
402 DeMarcus Walker 3.00 8.00
403 Patrick Mahomes II 90.00 150.00
404 Chad Hansen 3.00 8.00
405 Jordan Leggett 3.00 8.00
406 Taywan Taylor 3.00 8.00
407 Tim Williams 4.00 10.00
408 Stacy Coley 3.00 8.00
410 Quincy Wilson 3.00 8.00
411 Chad Kelly 3.00 8.00
412 Jerod Evans 4.00 10.00
413 James Conner 6.00 15.00
414 Carlos Henderson 3.00 8.00
415 Jeremy Sprinkle 3.00 8.00
416 Cooper Kupp 5.00 12.00
418 Ryan Switzer 4.00 10.00
419 Elijah Qualls 3.00 8.00
420 ArDarius Stewart 3.00 8.00
421 Ryan Ramczyk 3.00 8.00
422 Marlon Mack 5.00 12.00
423 Kareem Hunt 15.00 40.00
424 Brian Hill 3.00 8.00
425 Evan Engram 4.00 10.00
426 Elijah Hood 3.00 8.00
427 Dalvin Cook 8.00 20.00
428 Chris Godwin 4.00 10.00
430 Tre'Davious White 3.00 8.00
431 Davis Webb 3.00 8.00
432 Taco Charlton 3.00 8.00
433 Matthew Dayes 3.00 8.00
434 Artavis Scott 3.00 8.00
436 R. Joshua Dobbs 4.00 10.00
437 Derek Barnett 4.00 10.00
440 Raekwon McMillan 3.00 8.00

2017 Score Rookie Autographs Artist's Proof

*ARTIST PROOF/35: .8X TO 2X BASIC AU
349 Mitchell Trubisky 75.00 150.00
373 Christian McCaffrey 50.00 100.00
403 Patrick Mahomes II 150.00 250.00

2017 Score Rookie Autographs Gold Zone

*GOLD/50: .8X TO 2X BASIC AU
349 Mitchell Trubisky 75.00 150.00
373 Christian McCaffrey 50.00 100.00
403 Patrick Mahomes II 150.00 250.00

2017 Score Rookie Autographs Red Zone

*RED/20: 1X TO 2.5X BASIC AU
373 Christian McCaffrey 50.00 125.00
403 Patrick Mahomes II 200.00 400.00

2017 Score Rookie Jerseys

1 Curtis Samuel 1.50 4.00
2 Dalvin Cook 3.00 8.00
3 Davis Webb 1.25 3.00
5 O.J. Howard 1.50 4.00
6 Dede Westbrook 1.25 3.00
7 Patrick Mahomes II 15.00 40.00
8 Leonard Fournette 4.00 10.00
9 Alvin Kamara 5.00 12.00
10 Mitchell Trubisky 6.00 15.00
11 Chad Kelly 1.25 3.00
12 Mike Williams 2.00 5.00
13 R. Joshua Dobbs 1.50 4.00
14 Christian McCaffrey 3.00 8.00
16 John Ross 1.50 4.00
17 D'Onta Foreman 1.50 4.00
18 Deshaun Watson 8.00 20.00
20 DeShone Kizer 1.25 3.00
21 James Conner 2.50 6.00
22 JuJu Smith-Schuster 3.00 8.00
23 Jeremy McNichols 1.25 3.00
25 Samaje Perine 1.25 3.00

2017 Score Sack Attack

*GOLD: .6X TO 1.5X BASIC INSERTS
*GREEN: .6X TO 1.5X BASIC INSERTS
*RED: .6X TO 1.5X BASIC INSERTS
1 Julius Peppers .75 2.00
2 Terrell Suggs .60 1.50
3 Joey Bosa 1.00 2.50
4 Lorenzo Alexander .60 1.50
5 Clay Matthews .75 2.00
6 Brian Orakpo .60 1.50
7 Cameron Wake .60 1.50
8 Cliff Avril .60 1.50
9 Dwight Freeney .60 1.50
10 Vic Beasley Jr. .60 1.50
11 DeMarcus Ware .75 2.00
12 Chandler Jones .60 1.50
13 Ryan Kerrigan .60 1.50
14 Von Miller .75 2.00
15 Michael Bennett .60 1.50

2017 Score Signal Callers

*GOLD: .6X TO 1.5X BASIC INSERTS
*GREEN: .6X TO 1.5X BASIC INSERTS
*RED: .6X TO 1.5X BASIC INSERTS
1 Ben Roethlisberger 1.00 2.50
2 Tony Romo .75 2.00
3 Derek Carr 1.00 2.50
4 Eli Manning .75 2.00
5 Tom Brady 2.50 6.00
6 Andy Dalton .75 2.00
7 Dak Prescott 1.00 2.50
8 Matt Ryan .75 2.00
9 Blake Bortles .60 1.50
10 Dan Marino 2.00 5.00
11 Carson Palmer .75 2.00
12 Joe Namath 1.25 3.00
13 Joe Flacco .75 2.00
14 Kirk Cousins 1.00 2.50
15 Cam Newton 1.00 2.50
16 Andrew Luck 1.25 3.00
17 Aaron Rodgers 2.00 5.00
18 Peyton Manning 2.00 5.00
19 Jameis Winston .75 2.00
20 John Elway 1.50 4.00
21 Ryan Tannehill .75 2.00
22 Roger Staubach 1.25 3.00
23 Matthew Stafford .75 2.00
24 Philip Rivers 1.00 2.50
25 Carson Wentz 1.25 3.00
26 Drew Brees 1.00 2.50
27 Russell Wilson 1.25 3.00
28 Brett Favre 2.00 5.00
29 Marcus Mariota 1.00 2.50
30 Terry Bradshaw 1.50 4.00

2017 Score Signatures

5 Phil McConkey/25
7 Jermaine Kearse/25
15 Geno Smith/20
19 Tom Matte/25
23 La'el Collins/25
25 Tajae Sharpe/25
27 Travis Benjamin/25
29 Kordell Stewart/25
33 Kony Ealy/25
37 Charles Sims/25
39 Latavius Murray/25
40 Joey Bosa/25
43 Rishard Matthews/25
44 Kyle Van Noy/25
45 Trevor Siemian/25

2017 Score Standout Numbers

*GOLD: .6X TO 1.5X BASIC INSERTS
*GREEN: .6X TO 1.5X BASIC INSERTS
*RED: .6X TO 1.5X BASIC INSERTS
1 Jamaal Charles .75 2.00
2 Jerry Rice 1.50 4.00
3 Warren Moon 1.00 2.50
4 Drew Brees 1.00 2.50
5 Tom Brady 2.50 6.00
6 Barry Sanders 1.50 4.00
7 Y.A. Tittle 1.00 2.50
8 Jim Brown 1.25 3.00
9 Emmitt Smith 1.50 4.00
10 Antonio Brown 1.00 2.50
11 Julio Jones 1.00 2.50
12 Gale Sayers 1.00 2.50
13 Ben Roethlisberger 1.00 2.50
14 Peyton Manning 2.00 5.00
15 Adrian Peterson 1.00 2.50

2018 Score

1 Carson Palmer .15 .40
2 David Johnson .20 .50
3 Larry Fitzgerald .15 .40
4 Adrian Peterson .20 .50
5 John Brown .15 .40
6 Tyrann Mathieu .15 .40
7 Patrick Peterson .12 .30
8 Jaron Brown .12 .30
9 D.J. Humphries .12 .30
10 J.J. Nelson .12 .30
11 Kerwynn Williams .12 .30
12 Matt Ryan .15 .40
13 Devonta Freeman .15 .40
14 Tevin Coleman .12 .30
15 Julio Jones .20 .50
16 Mohamed Sanu .12 .30
17 Vic Beasley Jr. .12 .30
18 Austin Hooper .12 .30
19 Taylor Gabriel .12 .30
20 Dontari Poe .12 .30
21 Adrian Clayborn .12 .30
22 Justin Hardy .12 .30
23 Joe Flacco .15 .40
24 Danny Woodhead .15 .40
25 Terrell Suggs .12 .30
26 Mike Wallace .12 .30
27 Justin Tucker .12 .30
28 Jeremy Maclin .12 .30
29 Alex Collins .12 .30
30 Breshad Perriman .12 .30
31 Brandon Williams .12 .30
32 Marlon Humphrey .12 .30
33 Tyrod Taylor .15 .40
34 LeSean McCoy .20 .50
35 Jordan Matthews .12 .30
36 Zay Jones .12 .30
37 Charles Clay .12 .30
38 E.J. Gaines .12 .30
39 Shaq Lawson .12 .30
40 Nathan Peterman .12 .30
41 Jordan Poyer .12 .30
42 Kelvin Benjamin .15 .40
43 Cam Newton .20 .50
44 Christian McCaffrey .20 .50
45 Luke Kuechly .15 .40
46 Jonathan Stewart .12 .30
47 Julius Peppers .15 .40
48 Greg Olsen .15 .40
49 Devin Funchess .12 .30
50 Curtis Samuel .12 .30
51 Ed Dickson .12 .30
52 Graham Gano .12 .30
53 Mitchell Trubisky .20 .50
54 Kevin White .12 .30
55 Jordan Howard .20 .50
56 Tarik Cohen .15 .40
57 Cameron Meredith .12 .30
58 Kendall Wright .12 .30
59 Danny Trevathan .12 .30
60 Josh Bellamy .12 .30
61 Kyle Long .12 .30
62 Eddie Jackson .12 .30
63 Andy Dalton .15 .40
64 A.J. Green .20 .50
65 Vontaze Burfict .12 .30
66 Joe Mixon .15 .40
67 Giovani Bernard .12 .30
68 Tyler Eifert .15 .40
69 Geno Atkins .12 .30
70 Dre Kirkpatrick .12 .30
71 Brandon LaFell .12 .30
72 Tyler Boyd .12 .30
73 DeShone Kizer .15 .40
74 Jabrill Peppers .12 .30
75 Myles Garrett .20 .50
76 Isaiah Crowell .12 .30
77 Corey Coleman .12 .30
78 Duke Johnson .12 .30
79 David Njoku .12 .30
80 Joe Thomas .12 .30
81 Jamie Collins .12 .30
82 Josh Gordon .12 .30
83 Dak Prescott .20 .50
84 Ezekiel Elliott .25 .60
85 Alfred Morris .12 .30
86 Dez Bryant .20 .50
87 Terrance Williams .12 .30
88 Sean Lee .15 .40
89 Jason Witten .15 .40
90 Dan Bailey .12 .30
91 Orlando Scandrick .12 .30
92 Jourdan Lewis .12 .30
93 DeMarcus Lawrence .12 .30
94 Trevor Siemian .12 .30
95 Paxton Lynch .12 .30
96 Von Miller .15 .40
97 C.J. Anderson .15 .40
98 Demaryius Thomas .15 .40
99 Emmanuel Sanders .20 .50
100 Aqib Talib .12 .30
101 Virgil Green .12 .30
102 Bennie Fowler .12 .30
103 Derek Wolfe .12 .30
104 Matthew Stafford .15 .40
105 Kenny Golladay .12 .30
106 Ameer Abdullah .12 .30
107 Golden Tate III .12 .30
108 Eric Ebron .12 .30
109 Marvin Jones Jr. .12 .30
110 Darius Slay .12 .30
111 Theo Riddick .12 .30
112 Haloti Ngata .12 .30
113 Ezekiel Ansah .12 .30
114 Aaron Rodgers .40 1.00
115 Jordy Nelson .15 .40
116 Aaron Jones .15 .40
117 Clay Matthews .15 .40
118 Davante Adams .15 .40
119 Randall Cobb .15 .40
120 Jamaal Williams .12 .30
121 Nick Perry .12 .30
122 Ha Ha Clinton-Dix .12 .30
123 Ty Montgomery .12 .30
124 Mason Crosby .12 .30
125 Deshaun Watson .25 .60
126 Lamar Miller .12 .30
127 J.J. Watt .20 .50
128 DeAndre Hopkins .15 .40
129 Will Fuller V .12 .30
130 Jadeveon Clowney .12 .30
131 D'Onta Foreman .12 .30
132 Zach Cunningham .12 .30
133 Whitney Mercilus .12 .30
134 Braxton Miller .12 .30
135 Andrew Luck .25 .60
136 Marlon Mack .12 .30
137 T.Y. Hilton .15 .40
138 Frank Gore .15 .40
139 Malik Hooker .12 .30
140 Adam Vinatieri .12 .30
141 Donte Moncrief .15 .40
142 Jack Doyle .12 .30
143 Ryan Kelly .12 .30
144 Jacoby Brissett .12 .30
145 Blake Bortles .12 .30
146 Leonard Fournette .20 .50
147 Allen Robinson .15 .40
148 Allen Hurns .12 .30
149 Jalen Ramsey .15 .40
150 Dede Westbrook .12 .30
151 Myles Jack .12 .30
152 Calais Campbell .12 .30
153 T.J. Yeldon .12 .30
154 Telvin Smith .12 .30
155 Alex Smith .15 .40
156 Kareem Hunt .15 .40
157 Eric Berry .15 .40
158 Travis Kelce .20 .50
159 Patrick Mahomes II .50 1.25
160 Tyreek Hill .20 .50
161 Marcus Peters .12 .30
162 Justin Houston .12 .30
163 Derrick Johnson .12 .30
164 De'Anthony Thomas .12 .30
165 Reggie Ragland .12 .30
166 Jared Goff .20 .50
167 Todd Gurley II .20 .50
168 Aaron Donald .20 .50
169 Sammy Watkins .20 .50
170 Cooper Kupp .15 .40
171 Robert Woods .15 .40
172 Alec Ogletree .12 .30
173 Tavon Austin .12 .30
174 Tyler Higbee .12 .30
175 Greg Zuerlein .12 .30
176 Philip Rivers .20 .50
177 Mike Williams .12 .30
178 Melvin Gordon .15 .40
179 Joey Bosa .20 .50
180 Keenan Allen .15 .40
181 Antonio Gates .12 .30
182 Melvin Ingram .12 .30
183 Hunter Henry .12 .30
184 Travis Benjamin .12 .30
185 Desmond King .12 .30
186 Ryan Tannehill .15 .40
187 Jarvis Landry .15 .40
188 Kenyan Drake .12 .30
189 Ndamukong Suh .15 .40
190 DeVante Parker .15 .40
191 Cameron Wake .12 .30
192 Kenny Stills .12 .30
193 Laremy Tunsil .12 .30
194 Kiko Alonso .12 .30
195 Julius Thomas .12 .30
196 Case Keenum .15 .40
197 Dalvin Cook .15 .40
198 Adam Thielen .20 .50
199 Stefon Diggs .15 .40
200 Jerick McKinnon .12 .30
201 Laquon Treadwell .12 .30
202 Danielle Hunter .12 .30
203 Kyle Rudolph .12 .30
204 Xavier Rhodes .12 .30
205 Anthony Barr .12 .30
206 Tom Brady .50 1.25
207 Julian Edelman .20 .50
208 Rob Gronkowski .20 .50
209 Chris Hogan .12 .30
210 Dont'a Hightower .12 .30
211 Brandin Cooks .15 .40
212 Dion Lewis .12 .30
213 Malcolm Butler .20 .50
214 Martellus Bennett .12 .30
215 Stephen Gostkowski .12 .30
216 Trey Flowers .12 .30
217 Drew Brees .20 .50
218 Michael Thomas .20 .50
219 Willie Snead .15 .40
220 Mark Ingram .15 .40
221 Alvin Kamara .15 .40
222 Marshon Lattimore .12 .30
223 Ted Ginn Jr. .12 .30
224 Kenny Vaccaro .12 .30
225 Coby Fleener .12 .30
226 Brandon Coleman .12 .30
227 Eli Manning .15 .40
228 Eli Apple .12 .30
229 Odell Beckham Jr. .20 .50
230 Sterling Shepard .15 .40
231 Evan Engram .12 .30
232 Jason Pierre-Paul .12 .30
233 Janoris Jenkins .12 .30
234 Wayne Gallman .12 .30
235 Paul Perkins .12 .30
236 Landon Collins .12 .30
237 Dominique Rodgers-Cromartie .12 .30
238 Josh McCown .12 .30
239 Matt Forte .12 .30
240 Jermaine Kearse .12 .30
241 Bilal Powell .12 .30
242 Robby Anderson .12 .30
243 Jamal Adams .15 .40
244 Elijah McGuire .12 .30
245 Quincy Enunwa .12 .30
246 Leonard Williams .12 .30
247 Austin Seferian-Jenkins .12 .30
248 Derek Carr .20 .50
249 Marshawn Lynch .15 .40
250 Khalil Mack .20 .50
251 Amari Cooper .20 .50
252 Navorro Bowman .15 .40
253 Marquette King .12 .30
254 Jared Cook .12 .30
255 Jalen Richard .12 .30
256 Mario Edwards Jr. .12 .30
257 Bruce Irvin .12 .30
258 Carson Wentz .25 .60
259 Ronald Darby .12 .30
260 Jay Ajayi .15 .40
261 LeGarrette Blount .15 .40
262 Alshon Jeffery .15 .40
263 Nelson Agholor .12 .30
264 Fletcher Cox .12 .30
265 Zach Ertz .15 .40
266 Jason Peters .12 .30
267 Torrey Smith .12 .30
268 Jake Elliott .15 .40
269 Ben Roethlisberger .20 .50
270 Le'Veon Bell .15 .40
271 Antonio Brown .20 .50
272 Joe Haden .12 .30
273 T.J. Watt .15 .40
274 Alejandro Villanueva .15 .40
275 Jesse James .12 .30
276 Ryan Shazier .12 .30
277 JuJu Smith-Schuster .20 .50
278 Eli Rogers .12 .30
279 James Conner .20 .50
280 C.J. Beathard .12 .30
281 Reuben Foster .12 .30
282 Carlos Hyde .12 .30
283 Eric Reid .15 .40
284 George Kittle .12 .30
285 Marquise Goodwin .12 .30
286 DeForest Buckner .12 .30
287 Jimmy Garoppolo .25 .60
288 Solomon Thomas .12 .30
289 Pierre Garcon .15 .40
290 Russell Wilson .25 .60
291 Richard Sherman .20 .50
292 Michael Bennett .12 .30
293 Tyler Lockett .15 .40
294 Jimmy Graham .20 .50
295 Doug Baldwin .15 .40
296 Earl Thomas III .15 .40
297 Chris Carson .15 .40
298 Kam Chancellor .20 .50
299 Paul Richardson .12 .30
300 Cliff Avril .12 .30
301 Jameis Winston .15 .40
302 Doug Martin .15 .40
303 Mike Evans .15 .40
304 Gerald McCoy .12 .30
305 DeSean Jackson .15 .40
306 Kwon Alexander .12 .30
307 Chris Godwin .12 .30
308 Vernon Hargreaves III .12 .30
309 O.J. Howard .12 .30
310 Cameron Brate .12 .30
311 Marcus Mariota .20 .50
312 Corey Davis .15 .40
313 DeMarco Murray .15 .40
314 Derrick Henry .20 .50
315 Logan Ryan .12 .30
316 Adoree' Jackson .12 .30
317 Rishard Matthews .12 .30
318 Delanie Walker .12 .30
319 Jurrell Casey .12 .30
320 Brian Orakpo .12 .30
321 Kirk Cousins .20 .50
322 Robert Kelley .12 .30
323 Josh Norman .12 .30
324 Terrelle Pryor .12 .30
325 Preston Smith .12 .30
326 Josh Doctson .12 .30
327 Chris Thompson .12 .30
328 Samaje Perine .12 .30
329 Jordan Reed .12 .30
330 Jamison Crowder .12 .30
331 Minkah Fitzpatrick RC .50 1.25
332 Denzel Ward RC .60 1.50
333 Joshua Jackson RC .50 1.25
334 Isaiah Oliver RC .25 .60
335 Arden Key RC .25 .60
336 Bradley Chubb RC .40 1.00
337 Austin Proehl RC .25 .60
338 Ian Thomas RC .25 .60
339 Carlton Davis RC .30 .75
340 Maurice Hurst RC .30 .75
341 Vita Vea RC .40 1.00
342 Roquan Smith RC .75 2.00
343 Malik Jefferson RC .30 .75
344 Harold Landry RC .25 .60
345 Rashaan Evans RC .40 1.00
346 Tremaine Edmunds RC .50 1.25
347 Ogbonnia Okoronkwo RC .40 1.00
348 Josh Rosen RC .75 2.00
349 Sam Darnold RC 1.50 4.00
350 Josh Allen RC 1.00 2.50
351 Baker Mayfield RC 2.50 6.00
352 Lamar Jackson RC 1.50 4.00
353 Mason Rudolph RC .60 1.50
354 Logan Woodside RC .40 1.00
355 Luke Falk RC .30 .75
356 Kurt Benkert RC .30 .75
357 Mike White RC .30 .75
358 Riley Ferguson RC .40 1.00
359 Saquon Barkley RC 2.00 5.00
360 Derrius Guice RC .50 1.25
361 Chase Edmonds RC .25 .60
362 Rasheem Green RC .25 .60
363 Ronald Jones II RC .25 .60
364 Josh Adams RC .50 1.25
365 Nick Chubb RC .75 2.00
366 Bo Scarbrough RC .30 .75
367 Kerryon Johnson RC .40 1.00
368 Royce Freeman RC .30 .75
369 Sony Michel RC .75 2.00
370 John Kelly RC .30 .75
371 Akrum Wadley RC .25 .60
372 Kalen Ballage RC .30 .75
373 Mark Walton RC .30 .75
374 Rashaad Penny RC .40 1.00
375 Derwin James RC .50 1.25
376 Ronnie Harrison RC .30 .75
377 Dallas Goedert RC .30 .75
378 Mark Andrews RC .40 1.00
379 Mike Gesicki RC .30 .75
380 Calvin Ridley RC .60 1.50
381 Christian Kirk RC .40 1.00
382 Courtland Sutton RC .40 1.00
383 James Washington RC .50 1.25
384 D.J. Moore RC .50 1.25
385 Anthony Miller RC .40 1.00
386 Deontay Burnett RC .30 .75
387 Marcell Ateman RC .30 .75
388 Michael Gallup RC .50 1.25
389 D.J. Chark RC .30 .75
390 Simmie Cobbs Jr. RC .40 1.00
391 Allen Lazard RC .25 .60
392 Dante Pettis RC .40 1.00
393 Deon Cain RC .30 .75

394 Jaleel Scott RC .25 .60
395 Jordan Lasley RC .25 .60
396 Auden Tate RC .25 .60
397 Dalton Schultz RC .30 .75
398 Equanimeous St. Brown RC .40 1.00
399 Hayden Hurst RC .30 .75
400 Anthony Averett RC .30 .75
401 Kamryn Pettway RC .40 1.00
402 Da'Shawn Hand RC .25 .60
403 Chase Litton RC .30 .75
404 Nyheim Hines RC .30 .75
405 Quadree Henderson RC .30 .75
406 Ray-Ray McCloud RC .25 .60
407 Richie James RC .25 .60
408 Ryan Izzo RC .25 .60
409 Donte Jackson RC .40 1.00
410 Trey Quinn RC .25 .60
411 DeAndre Goolsby RC .25 .60
412 Adam Breneman RC .30 .75
413 Jake Wieneke RC .30 .75
414 Daron Payne RC .40 1.00
415 Sam Hubbard RC .30 .75
416 Orlando Brown RC .40 1.00
417 Robert Foster RC .25 .60
418 Cedrick Wilson Jr. RC .25 .60
419 Duke Dawson RC .25 .60
420 Dorance Armstrong Jr. RC .25 .60
421 Javon Wims RC .25 .60
422 Billy Price RC .30 .75
423 J.T. Barrett RC .40 1.00
424 Shaquem Griffin RC .40 1.00
425 Marcus Allen RC .40 1.00
426 DaeSean Hamilton RC .30 .75
427 Troy Fumagalli RC .30 .75
428 Darren Carrington II RC .30 .75
429 Leighton Vander Esch RC .75 2.00
430 Jester Weah RC .25 .60
431 Justin Jackson RC .30 .75
432 Taven Bryan RC .25 .60
433 J'Mon Moore RC .25 .60
434 Lavon Coleman RC .30 .75
435 Steve Ishmael RC .25 .60
436 Austin Allen RC .30 .75
437 Jaylen Samuels RC .30 .75
438 Trey Marshall RC .30 .75
439 Kyle Lauletta RC .40 1.00
440 Harrison Phillips RC .25 .60
441 Nick Mullens
442 Saquon Barkley
443 Josh Allen
444 Josh Rosen
445 Baker Mayfield
446 Sam Darnold
447 Calvin Ridley
448 Lamar Jackson
449 Tre'Quan Smith
450 Leighton Vander Esch
451 Marquez Valdes-Scantling
452 Keke Coutee
453 Minkah Fitzpatrick
454 D.J. Chark Jr.
455 Nick Chubb
456 Rashaad Penny
457 Mason Rudolph
458 Mike White
459 Ito Smith
460 Michael Gallup
461 Phillip Lindsay
462 Derrius Guice
463 Darius Leonard
464 Christian Kirk
465 Anthony Miller
466 D.J. Moore
467 James Washington
468 Dante Pettis
469 Sony Michel
470 Jaylen Samuels

2018 Score Artist's Proof
*1-330 VETS/35: 5X TO 12X BASIC CARDS
*331-440 ROOKIES/35: 3X TO 8X BASIC RC

2018 Score Black
*1-330 VETS: 2X TO 5X BASIC CARDS
*331-440 ROOKIES: 1X TO 2.5X BASIC RC

2018 Score Gold
*1-330 VETS: 2X TO 5X BASIC CARDS
*331-440 ROOKIES: 1X TO 2.5X BASIC RC

2018 Score Gold Zone
*1-330 VETS/50: 4X TO 10X BASIC CARDS
*331-440 ROOKIES/50: 2X TO 5X BASIC RC

2018 Score Green
*1-330 VETS: 2X TO 5X BASIC CARDS
*331-440 ROOKIES: 1X TO 2.5X BASIC RC

2018 Score Red Zone
*1-330 VETS/20: 10X TO 25X BASIC CARDS
*331-440 ROOKIES/20: 6X TO 15X BASIC RC

2018 Score Scorecard
*1-330 VETS: 2X TO 5X BASIC CARDS
*331-440 ROOKIES: 1X TO 2.5X BASIC RC

2018 Score Showcase
*1-330 VETS/99: 3X TO 8X BASIC CARDS
*331-440 ROOKIES/99: 2X TO 5X BASIC RC
366 Bo Scarbrough 1.25 3.00

2018 Score All Hands Team
*BLACK: .6X TO 1.5X BASIC INSERTS
*GOLD: .6X TO 1.5X BASIC INSERTS
*GREEN: .6X TO 1.5X BASIC INSERTS
*PURPLE: .6X TO 1.5X BASIC INSERTS
*RED: .6X TO 1.5X BASIC INSERTS
1 Cole Beasley .75 2.00
2 Antonio Brown 1.00 2.50
3 Jason Witten .75 2.00
4 Marvin Jones Jr. .60 1.50
5 Julio Jones 1.00 2.50
6 Maurice Harris .60 1.50
7 DeAndre Hopkins .75 2.00
8 Paul Richardson .60 1.50
9 Mike Evans .75 2.00
10 Julian Edelman 1.00 2.50
11 Michael Thomas 1.00 2.50
12 Greg Olsen .75 2.00
13 Rob Gronkowski 1.00 2.50
14 Josh Gordon .60 1.50
15 A.J. Green 1.00 2.50

2018 Score Captains
*BLACK: .5X TO 1.2X BASIC INSERTS
*GOLD: .6X TO 1.5X BASIC INSERTS
*GREEN: .6X TO 1.5X BASIC INSERTS
*PURPLE: .6X TO 1.5X BASIC INSERTS
*RED: .6X TO 1.5X BASIC INSERTS
1 Larry Fitzgerald .75 2.00
2 Cam Newton 1.00 2.50
3 Julius Peppers .75 2.00
4 Joe Thomas .60 1.50
5 Dak Prescott 1.00 2.50
6 Jason Witten .75 2.00
7 Von Miller .75 2.00
8 Aqib Talib .60 1.50
9 Adam Vinatieri .60 1.50
10 Travis Kelce 1.00 2.50
11 Eric Berry .75 2.00
12 Tyreek Hill 1.00 2.50
13 Philip Rivers 1.00 2.50
14 Antonio Gates .60 1.50
15 Todd Gurley II 1.00 2.50
16 Ndamukong Suh .75 2.00
17 Kyle Rudolph .60 1.50
18 Tom Brady 2.50 6.00
19 Rob Gronkowski 1.00 2.50
20 Drew Brees 1.00 2.50
21 Eli Manning .75 2.00
22 Derek Carr 1.00 2.50
23 Khalil Mack 1.00 2.50
24 Ben Roethlisberger 1.00 2.50
25 Russell Wilson 1.25 3.00
26 Kam Chancellor 1.00 2.50
27 Gerald McCoy .60 1.50
28 Marcus Mariota 1.00 2.50
29 Kirk Cousins 1.00 2.50
30 J.J. Watt 1.00 2.50

2018 Score Collegiate Jerseys
*PRIME/25: 1X TO 2.5X BASIC JSY
1 Akrum Wadley 1.50 4.00
2 Anthony Miller 2.50 6.00
3 Baker Mayfield 15.00 40.00
4 Dalvin Cook 2.00 5.00
5 John Kelly 2.00 5.00
7 Christian Kirk 2.50 6.00
8 Courtland Sutton 2.50 6.00
9 JuJu Smith-Schuster 2.50 6.00
11 Patrick Mahomes II 6.00 15.00
12 Alvin Kamara 2.00 5.00
13 James Washington 3.00 8.00
14 J'Mon Moore 1.50 4.00
18 Mason Rudolph 4.00 10.00
19 Deshaun Watson 3.00 8.00
25 Sony Michel 5.00 12.00

2018 Score Defenders Jerseys
*PRIME/25: 1X TO 2.5X BASIC JSY
1 Deion Sanders 2.00 5.00
2 Tre'Davious White 1.50 4.00
3 Luke Kuechly 2.00 5.00
4 Geno Atkins 1.50 4.00
5 Vontaze Burfict 1.50 4.00
6 Jabrill Peppers 1.50 4.00
7 DeMarcus Lawrence 1.50 4.00
8 Aqib Talib 1.50 4.00
9 Von Miller 2.00 5.00
10 Chris Harris Jr. 1.50 4.00
11 Clay Matthews 2.00 5.00
12 Jadeveon Clowney 1.50 4.00
13 Jalen Ramsey 2.00 5.00
14 Myles Jack 1.50 4.00
15 Justin Houston 1.50 4.00
16 T.J. Watt 2.00 5.00
17 Ndamukong Suh 2.00 5.00
18 Reshad Jones 1.50 4.00
19 Harrison Smith 2.50 6.00
20 Dont'a Hightower 1.50 4.00
21 Leonard Williams 1.50 4.00
22 Khalil Mack 2.50 6.00
23 James Harrison 2.00 5.00
24 Melvin Ingram 1.50 4.00
25 Joey Bosa 2.50 6.00
26 Ronnie Lott 2.00 5.00
27 Earl Thomas III 2.00 5.00
28 Richard Sherman 2.50 6.00
29 Jaylon Smith 1.50 4.00
30 Darian Stewart 1.50 4.00

2018 Score Home and Away Jerseys
*PRIME/25: 1X TO 2.5X BASIC JSY
1 Amari Cooper 2.50 6.00
2 Amari Cooper 2.50 6.00
3 Nelson Agholor 1.50 4.00
4 Nelson Agholor 1.50 4.00
5 Teddy Bridgewater 2.00 5.00
6 Teddy Bridgewater 2.00 5.00
7 Jameis Winston 2.00 5.00
8 Jameis Winston 2.00 5.00
9 Marcus Mariota 2.50 6.00
10 Marcus Mariota 2.50 6.00
11 Patrick Mahomes II 6.00 15.00
12 Patrick Mahomes II 6.00 15.00
13 Andy Dalton 2.00 5.00
14 Andy Dalton 2.00 5.00
15 Russell Wilson 3.00 8.00
16 Russell Wilson 3.00 8.00
17 Blake Bortles 1.50 4.00
18 Blake Bortles 1.50 4.00
19 Eli Manning 2.00 5.00
20 Eli Manning 2.00 5.00

2018 Score Huddle Up
*BLACK: .6X TO 1.5X BASIC INSERTS
*GOLD: .6X TO 1.5X BASIC INSERTS
*GREEN: .6X TO 1.5X BASIC INSERTS
*PURPLE: .6X TO 1.5X BASIC INSERTS
*RED: .6X TO 1.5X BASIC INSERTS
1 New England Patriots .75 2.00
2 Pittsburgh Steelers .75 2.00
3 Houston Texans .75 2.00
4 Philadelphia Eagles .75 2.00
5 Dallas Cowboys .75 2.00
6 Los Angeles Rams .75 2.00
7 Seattle Seahawks .75 2.00
8 Minnesota Vikings .75 2.00
9 Green Bay Packers .75 2.00
10 Detroit Lions .75 2.00

2018 Score Inscriptions
1 D'Onta Foreman 6.00 15.00
2 Stephon Gilmore 6.00 15.00
3 Kyle Juszczyk 6.00 15.00
4 Karl Joseph 6.00 15.00
5 Sterling Shepard 8.00 20.00
6 Jack Doyle 6.00 15.00
7 Kyle Van Noy 6.00 15.00
8 Eric Kendricks 6.00 15.00
9 Jacoby Brissett 6.00 15.00
10 Pepper Johnson 6.00 15.00
11 Isaiah Crowell 6.00 15.00
12 Ray Guy 6.00 15.00
13 Christian Okoye 6.00 15.00
14 Vic Beasley Jr. 6.00 15.00
15 Fletcher Cox 6.00 15.00
16 Jeff Garcia 6.00 15.00
17 Mike Vrabel 8.00 20.00
18 Cooper Kupp 8.00 20.00
19 Chris Hogan 6.00 15.00
20 Adam Thielen 30.00 60.00
21 Alex Collins 6.00 15.00
22 Brett Keisel 6.00 15.00
23 Delanie Walker 6.00 15.00
24 Bill Bates 6.00 15.00
25 Zay Jones 6.00 15.00
26 Jamal Adams 8.00 20.00
27 Haloti Ngata 6.00 15.00
28 Andrew Luck
29 Steve Atwater 8.00 20.00
30 Jimmy Garoppolo 100.00 200.00
31 Ezekiel Elliott 30.00 60.00
32 Kareem Hunt
33 Christian McCaffrey 10.00 25.00
34 Deshaun Watson 30.00 60.00
35 Patrick Mahomes II 25.00 50.00
36 Leonard Fournette
37 Carson Wentz 40.00 80.00
38 LaVar Arrington 6.00 15.00
39 Michael Strahan 8.00 20.00
40 Drew Bledsoe
41 Tony Gonzalez 8.00 20.00
42 Dalvin Cook
43 Tedy Bruschi
44 Sterling Sharpe
45 Randy Moss 50.00 100.00
46 Ricky Watters 12.00 30.00
47 Rob Gronkowski 25.00 50.00
48 Stefon Diggs 8.00 20.00
49 Aaron Rodgers 150.00 250.00
50 Antonio Brown 25.00 50.00

2018 Score NFL Draft
*BLACK: .6X TO 1.5X BASIC INSERTS
*GOLD: .6X TO 1.5X BASIC INSERTS
*GREEN: .6X TO 1.5X BASIC INSERTS
*PURPLE: .6X TO 1.5X BASIC INSERTS
*RED: .6X TO 1.5X BASIC INSERTS
1 Sam Darnold 2.50 6.00
2 Josh Rosen 1.25 3.00
3 Bradley Chubb .60 1.50
4 Minkah Fitzpatrick .75 2.00
5 Josh Allen 1.50 4.00
6 Saquon Barkley 3.00 8.00
7 Joshua Jackson .75 2.00
8 Calvin Ridley 1.00 2.50
9 Arden Key .40 1.00
10 Connor Williams .75 2.00
11 Denzel Ward 1.00 2.50
12 Derwin James .75 2.00
13 Roquan Smith 1.25 3.00
14 Daron Payne .60 1.50
15 Harold Landry .40 1.00
16 Tremaine Edmunds .75 2.00
17 Baker Mayfield 4.00 10.00
18 Vita Vea .60 1.50
19 Christian Kirk .60 1.50
20 Ronnie Harrison .50 1.25
21 Derrius Guice .75 2.00
22 Courtland Sutton .60 1.50
23 Dallas Goedert .50 1.25
24 Rashaan Evans .60 1.50
25 Kerryon Johnson .60 1.50
26 Ronald Jones II .40 1.00
27 Mark Andrews .60 1.50
28 Luke Falk .50 1.25
29 D.J. Chark .50 1.25
30 Rashaad Penny .60 1.50

2018 Score Rookie Autographs
331 Minkah Fitzpatrick 6.00 15.00
332 Denzel Ward 8.00 20.00
333 Joshua Jackson 6.00 15.00
334 Isaiah Oliver
335 Arden Key 3.00 8.00
336 Bradley Chubb 5.00 12.00
337 Austin Proehl 3.00 8.00
338 Ian Thomas 3.00 8.00
339 Carlton Davis 4.00 10.00
340 Maurice Hurst 4.00 10.00
341 Vita Vea 5.00 12.00
342 Roquan Smith 10.00 25.00
343 Malik Jefferson 4.00 10.00
344 Harold Landry 3.00 8.00
345 Rashaan Evans 5.00 12.00
346 Tremaine Edmunds 6.00 15.00
347 Ogbonnia Okoronkwo 5.00 12.00
348 Josh Rosen 30.00 60.00
349 Sam Darnold 50.00 100.00
350 Josh Allen 30.00 60.00
351 Baker Mayfield EXCH 60.00 125.00
353 Mason Rudolph 8.00 20.00
354 Logan Woodside 5.00 12.00
355 Luke Falk 4.00 10.00
356 Kurt Benkert 4.00 10.00
357 Mike White 4.00 10.00
358 Riley Ferguson 5.00 12.00
359 Saquon Barkley 90.00 150.00
360 Derrius Guice EXCH 20.00 40.00
361 Chase Edmonds 3.00 8.00
362 Rasheem Green 3.00 8.00
363 Ronald Jones II 3.00 8.00
364 Josh Adams 6.00 15.00
365 Nick Chubb 10.00 25.00
366 Bo Scarbrough 4.00 10.00
367 Kerryon Johnson 5.00 12.00
368 Royce Freeman 4.00 10.00
369 Sony Michel 10.00 25.00
370 John Kelly 4.00 10.00
371 Akrum Wadley 3.00 8.00
372 Kalen Ballage 4.00 10.00
373 Mark Walton 4.00 10.00
374 Rashaad Penny
375 Derwin James 6.00 15.00
376 Ronnie Harrison 4.00 10.00
377 Dallas Goedert 4.00 10.00
378 Mark Andrews 5.00 12.00
379 Mike Gesicki 4.00 10.00
380 Calvin Ridley EXCH 8.00 20.00
381 Christian Kirk 5.00 12.00
382 Courtland Sutton 5.00 12.00
383 James Washington 6.00 15.00
384 D.J. Moore 6.00 15.00
385 Anthony Miller 5.00 12.00
386 Deontay Burnett 4.00 10.00
387 Marcell Ateman 4.00 10.00
388 Michael Gallup 6.00 15.00
389 D.J. Chark 4.00 10.00
390 Simmie Cobbs Jr. 5.00 12.00
391 Allen Lazard 3.00 8.00
392 Dante Pettis 5.00 12.00
393 Deon Cain 4.00 10.00
394 Jaleel Scott 3.00 8.00
395 Jordan Lasley 3.00 8.00
396 Auden Tate 3.00 8.00
397 Dalton Schultz 4.00 10.00
399 Hayden Hurst 4.00 10.00
400 Anthony Averett 4.00 10.00
401 Kamryn Pettway 5.00 12.00
402 Da'Shawn Hand 3.00 8.00
403 Chase Litton 4.00 10.00
404 Nyheim Hines 4.00 10.00
405 Quadree Henderson 4.00 10.00
406 Ray-Ray McCloud 3.00 8.00
407 Richie James 3.00 8.00
408 Ryan Izzo 3.00 8.00
409 Donte Jackson 5.00 12.00
411 DeAndre Goolsby 3.00 8.00
413 Jake Wieneke 4.00 10.00
414 Daron Payne 5.00 12.00
415 Sam Hubbard 4.00 10.00
416 Orlando Brown 5.00 12.00
417 Robert Foster 3.00 8.00
418 Cedrick Wilson Jr. 3.00 8.00
419 Duke Dawson 3.00 8.00
420 Dorance Armstrong Jr. 3.00 8.00
421 Javon Wims 3.00 8.00
422 Billy Price 4.00 10.00
423 J.T. Barrett 5.00 12.00
424 Shaquem Griffin 5.00 12.00
425 Marcus Allen 5.00 12.00
426 DaeSean Hamilton 4.00 10.00
427 Troy Fumagalli 4.00 10.00
428 Darren Carrington II 4.00 10.00
429 Leighton Vander Esch 10.00 25.00
430 Jester Weah 3.00 8.00
431 Justin Jackson 4.00 10.00
433 J'Mon Moore 3.00 8.00
434 Lavon Coleman 4.00 10.00
435 Steve Ishmael 3.00 8.00
436 Austin Allen 4.00 10.00
438 Trey Marshall 4.00 10.00
439 Kyle Lauletta 5.00 12.00
440 Harrison Phillips 3.00 8.00
441 Nick Mullens/75
442 Saquon Barkley/35
443 Josh Allen/35
444 Josh Rosen/35
445 Baker Mayfield/35
447 Calvin Ridley/49
448 Lamar Jackson/35
450 Leighton Vander Esch/75
451 Marquez Valdes-Scantling/75
453 Minkah Fitzpatrick/75
455 Nick Chubb/49
460 Michael Gallup/75
461 Phillip Lindsay/75
462 Derrius Guice/49
463 Darius Leonard/75
464 Christian Kirk/49
465 Anthony Miller/75
466 D.J. Moore/75
467 James Washington/75
468 Dante Pettis/75
470 Jaylen Samuels/75

2018 Score Rookie Autographs Artist's Proof
*AP/35: .6X TO 1.5X BASIC AU
349 Sam Darnold 75.00 150.00
350 Josh Allen 50.00 100.00
351 Baker Mayfield EXCH 75.00 150.00
359 Saquon Barkley 100.00 200.00

2018 Score Rookie Autographs Gold Zone
*GOLD/50: .6X TO 1.5X BASIC AU
349 Sam Darnold 75.00 150.00
350 Josh Allen 50.00 100.00
351 Baker Mayfield EXCH 75.00 150.00
359 Saquon Barkley 100.00 200.00

2018 Score Rookie Autographs Red Zone
*RED/20: 1X TO 2.5X BASIC AU
349 Sam Darnold 150.00 300.00
350 Josh Allen 75.00 150.00
351 Baker Mayfield EXCH 100.00 200.00
359 Saquon Barkley 200.00 300.00
374 Rashaad Penny 12.00 30.00

2018 Score Scoreboard
*BLACK: .6X TO 1.5X BASIC INSERTS
*GOLD: .6X TO 1.5X BASIC INSERTS
*GREEN: .6X TO 1.5X BASIC INSERTS
*PURPLE: .6X TO 1.5X BASIC INSERTS
*RED: .6X TO 1.5X BASIC INSERTS
1 Dalvin Cook .75 2.00
2 Kareem Hunt .75 2.00
3 Jared Goff 1.00 2.50
4 Tom Brady 2.50 6.00
5 Cam Newton 1.00 2.50
6 Aaron Rodgers 2.00 5.00
7 Mark Ingram .75 2.00
8 Russell Wilson 1.25 3.00
9 Dak Prescott 1.00 2.50
10 Matt Ryan .75 2.00
11 Antonio Brown 1.00 2.50
12 Andy Dalton .75 2.00
13 Jimmy Garoppolo 1.25 3.00
14 Leonard Fournette 1.00 2.50
15 Ben Roethlisberger 1.00 2.50

2018 Score Signatures
1 Jon Dorenbos 2.50 6.00
2 Jordan Poyer 2.50 6.00
3 Jerrell Freeman 2.50 6.00
4 Marcus Smith 2.50 6.00
5 Charles Tapper 2.50 6.00
6 Robert Nkemdiche 2.50 6.00
7 La'el Collins 2.50 6.00
8 Tajae Sharpe 2.50 6.00
9 Arthur Moats 2.50 6.00
10 Ottis Anderson 2.50 6.00
11 Spencer Ware 2.50 6.00
12 ArDarius Stewart 2.50 6.00
13 Aaron Ripkowski 2.50 6.00
14 Geronimo Allison 2.50 6.00
15 Jeff Driskel 2.50 6.00
16 Julius Thomas 2.50 6.00
17 Bashaud Breeland 2.50 6.00
18 Shaq Thompson 2.50 6.00
19 Kendall Fuller 2.50 6.00
20 Alex Mack 2.50 6.00
21 Nathan Peterman 2.50 6.00
22 Chad Williams 2.50 6.00
23 Blake Martinez 2.50 6.00
24 Solomon Thomas 2.50 6.00
25 Artie Burns 4.00 10.00
26 Vonn Bell 2.50 6.00
27 Rico Gathers 2.50 6.00
28 Dwayne Harris 2.50 6.00
29 Jalen Richard 2.50 6.00
30 Matt Breida 3.00 8.00
31 Cameron Brate 2.50 6.00
32 Byron Jones 2.50 6.00
33 Charles Sims 2.50 6.00
34 Sidney Jones 2.50 6.00
35 Desmond King 2.50 6.00
36 Travis Rudolph 2.50 6.00
37 Demarcus Robinson 2.50 6.00
38 Sean Davis 2.50 6.00
39 Kony Ealy 2.50 6.00
40 Aaron Burbridge 2.50 6.00

2019 Score
1 Patrick Mahomes II .50 1.25
2 Travis Kelce .20 .50
3 Steven Nelson .12 .30
4 Tyreek Hill .20 .50
5 Sammy Watkins .20 .50
6 Spencer Ware .12 .30
7 Dee Ford .12 .30
8 Anthony Hitchens .12 .30
9 Eric Berry .15 .40
10 Chris Conley .12 .30
11 Justin Houston .12 .30
12 Case Keenum .15 .40
13 Phillip Lindsay .20 .50
14 Emmanuel Sanders .20 .50
15 Todd Davis .12 .30
16 Royce Freeman .12 .30
17 Courtland Sutton .15 .40
18 Jeff Heuerman .12 .30
19 Bradley Chubb .15 .40
20 Von Miller .15 .40
21 Chris Harris Jr. .12 .30
22 Philip Rivers .20 .50
23 Melvin Gordon III .15 .40
24 Keenan Allen .15 .40
25 Derwin James .15 .40
26 Desmond King .12 .30
27 Austin Ekeler .12 .30
28 Mike Williams .12 .30
29 Tyrell Williams .12 .30
30 Melvin Ingram .12 .30
31 Antonio Gates .12 .30
32 Derek Carr .20 .50
33 Doug Martin .15 .40
34 Jared Cook .12 .30
35 Tahir Whitehead .12 .30
36 Maurice Hurst .12 .30
37 Jordy Nelson .15 .40
38 Marshawn Lynch .15 .40
39 Jalen Richard .12 .30
40 Seth Roberts .12 .30
41 Marquel Lee .12 .30
42 Deshaun Watson .25 .60
43 DeAndre Hopkins .15 .40
44 Alfred Blue .12 .30
45 Keke Coutee .12 .30
46 Demaryius Thomas .15 .40
47 Will Fuller V .12 .30
48 J.J. Watt .20 .50
49 Jadeveon Clowney .12 .30
50 Tyrann Mathieu .15 .40
51 Zach Cunningham .12 .30
52 Andrew Luck .25 .60
53 Marlon Mack .12 .30
54 T.Y. Hilton .15 .40
55 Darius Leonard .15 .40
56 Jordan Wilkins .15 .40
57 Nyheim Hines .15 .40
58 Eric Ebron .12 .30
59 Chester Rogers .12 .30
60 Adam Vinatieri .12 .30
61 Jabaal Sheard .12 .30
62 Blake Bortles .12 .30
63 Leonard Fournette .20 .50
64 Dede Westbrook .12 .30
65 D.J. Chark Jr. .12 .30
66 Telvin Smith .12 .30
67 Jalen Ramsey .15 .40
68 Myles Jack .12 .30
69 Calais Campbell .12 .30
70 Yannick Ngakoue .12 .30
71 A.J. Bouye .12 .30
72 Marcus Mariota .20 .50
73 Dion Lewis .12 .30
74 Corey Davis .15 .40
75 Kevin Byard .12 .30
76 Wesley Woodyard .12 .30
77 Derrick Henry .20 .50
78 Tajae Sharpe .12 .30
79 Jonnu Smith .12 .30
80 Jayon Brown .12 .30
81 Brian Orakpo .12 .30
82 Joe Flacco .15 .40
83 Lamar Jackson .20 .50
84 Terrell Suggs .12 .30
85 Michael Crabtree .12 .30
86 Alex Collins .12 .30
87 C.J. Mosley .15 .40
88 Gus Edwards .12 .30
89 Justin Tucker .12 .30
90 John Brown .15 .40
91 Mark Andrews .12 .30
92 Andy Dalton .15 .40
93 Joe Mixon .15 .40
94 Tyler Boyd .12 .30
95 A.J. Green .20 .50
96 C.J. Uzomah .12 .30
97 Jessie Bates .12 .30
98 Carlos Dunlap .12 .30
99 Geno Atkins .12 .30
100 Shawn Williams .12 .30
101 Tyler Eifert .15 .40
102 Baker Mayfield .30 .75
103 Nick Chubb .20 .50
104 Jarvis Landry .15 .40
105 Duke Johnson Jr. .12 .30
106 David Njoku .12 .30
107 Antonio Callaway .12 .30
108 Denzel Ward .15 .40
109 Myles Garrett .12 .30
110 Jabrill Peppers .12 .30
111 Jamie Collins .12 .30
112 Ben Roethlisberger .15 .40
113 James Conner .20 .50
114 Le'Veon Bell .15 .40
115 JuJu Smith-Schuster .20 .50
116 Antonio Brown .20 .50
117 T.J. Watt .15 .40
118 Alejandro Villanueva .15 .40
119 Terrell Edmunds .20 .50
120 Jon Bostic .12 .30
121 Joe Haden .12 .30
122 Josh Allen .20 .50
123 LeSean McCoy .20 .50
124 Chris Ivory .15 .40
125 Zay Jones .12 .30
126 Robert Foster .12 .30
127 Tremaine Edmunds .15 .40
128 Lorenzo Alexander .12 .30
129 Matt Milano .12 .30
130 Tre'Davious White .12 .30
131 Micah Hyde .12 .30
132 Ryan Tannehill .15 .40
133 Brock Osweiler .12 .30
134 Frank Gore .15 .40
135 Danny Amendola .15 .40
136 Kenyan Drake .12 .30
137 Kiko Alonso .12 .30
138 Xavien Howard .12 .30
139 Albert Wilson .12 .30
140 Kenny Stills .12 .30
141 T.J. McDonald .12 .30
142 Tom Brady .50 1.25
143 Sony Michel .20 .50
144 James White .15 .40
145 Kyle Van Noy .12 .30
146 Julian Edelman .20 .50
147 Cordarrelle Patterson .12 .30
148 Rob Gronkowski .20 .50
149 Stephen Gostkowski .12 .30
150 Josh Gordon .12 .30
151 Chris Hogan .12 .30
152 Sam Darnold .20 .50
153 Isaiah Crowell .12 .30
154 Quincy Enunwa .12 .30
155 Bilal Powell .12 .30
156 Robby Anderson .12 .30
157 Chris Herndon IV .12 .30
158 Jamal Adams .15 .40
159 Avery Williamson .12 .30
160 Leonard Williams .12 .30
161 Darron Lee .12 .30
162 Dak Prescott .20 .50
163 Cole Beasley .20 .50
164 Ezekiel Elliott .25 .60
165 DeMarcus Lawrence .12 .30
166 Sean Lee .15 .40
167 Leighton Vander Esch .15 .40
168 Amari Cooper .20 .50
169 Michael Gallup .20 .50
170 Jaylon Smith .12 .30
171 Zack Martin .12 .30
172 Tyron Smith .12 .30
173 Eli Manning .15 .40
174 Saquon Barkley .25 .60
175 Odell Beckham Jr. .20 .50
176 Sterling Shepard .15 .40
177 Landon Collins .12 .30
178 Evan Engram .12 .30
179 Alec Ogletree .12 .30
180 Wayne Gallman .12 .30
181 Olivier Vernon .12 .30
182 Lorenzo Carter .12 .30
183 Carson Wentz .25 .60
184 Jordan Hicks .12 .30
185 Josh Adams .15 .40
186 Zach Ertz .15 .40
187 Alshon Jeffery .15 .40
188 Nelson Agholor .12 .30
189 Michael Bennett .12 .30
190 Fletcher Cox .12 .30
191 Jay Ajayi .15 .40
192 Golden Tate III .15 .40
193 Alex Smith .15 .40
194 Derrius Guice .15 .40
195 Adrian Peterson .20 .50
196 Jordan Reed .12 .30
197 Mason Foster .12 .30
198 Chris Thompson .12 .30
199 Josh Doctson .12 .30
200 Trent Williams .12 .30
201 Vernon Davis .15 .40
202 Ryan Kerrigan .12 .30
203 Mitchell Trubisky .20 .50
204 Tarik Cohen .15 .40
205 Jordan Howard .20 .50
206 Allen Robinson II .15 .40
207 Khalil Mack .20 .50
208 Roquan Smith .20 .50
209 Kyle Fuller .12 .30
210 Danny Trevathan .12 .30
211 Eddie Jackson .12 .30
212 Trey Burton .12 .30
213 Matthew Stafford .15 .40
214 Kerryon Johnson .15 .40
215 Kenny Golladay .12 .30
216 LeGarrette Blount .15 .40
217 Jarrad Davis .12 .30
218 Marvin Jones Jr. .12 .30
219 Theo Riddick .12 .30
220 Ezekiel Ansah .12 .30
221 Darius Slay .12 .30
222 Luke Willson .12 .30
223 Aaron Rodgers .40 1.00
224 Aaron Jones .15 .40
225 Davante Adams .15 .40
226 Jimmy Graham .20 .50
227 Marquez Valdes-Scantling .15 .40
228 Randall Cobb .15 .40
229 Blake Martinez .12 .30
230 Clay Matthews .15 .40
231 Jaire Alexander .12 .30
232 Kyler Fackrell .12 .30
233 Kirk Cousins .20 .50
234 Latavius Murray .12 .30
235 Dalvin Cook .15 .40
236 Adam Thielen .20 .50
237 Harrison Smith .12 .30
238 Kyle Rudolph .12 .30
239 Stefon Diggs .15 .40
240 Danielle Hunter .12 .30
241 Laquon Treadwell .12 .30
242 Eric Kendricks .12 .30
243 Matt Ryan .20 .50
244 Julio Jones .20 .50
245 Tevin Coleman .12 .30
246 Devonta Freeman .15 .40
247 Ito Smith .12 .30
248 Calvin Ridley .15 .40
249 Mohamed Sanu .12 .30
250 Vic Beasley Jr. .12 .30
251 Damontae Kazee .12 .30
252 Takkarist McKinley .12 .30
253 Cam Newton .20 .50
254 Christian McCaffrey .20 .50
255 Luke Kuechly .15 .40
256 Julius Peppers .15 .40
257 D.J. Moore .15 .40
258 Greg Olsen .15 .40
259 Devin Funchess .12 .30
260 Mike Adams .12 .30
261 Shaq Thompson .12 .30
262 Mario Addison .12 .30
263 Drew Brees .20 .50
264 Alvin Kamara .15 .40
265 Michael Thomas .20 .50
266 Mark Ingram II .15 .40
267 Taysom Hill .12 .30
268 Tre'Quan Smith .12 .30
269 Cameron Jordan .12 .30
270 Marcus Davenport .12 .30
271 Sheldon Rankins .12 .30
272 Marshon Lattimore .12 .30
273 Jameis Winston .15 .40
274 Peyton Barber .12 .30
275 Mike Evans .15 .40
276 O.J. Howard .12 .30
277 Ronald Jones II .12 .30
278 DeSean Jackson .15 .40
279 Jason Pierre-Paul .12 .30
280 Lavonte David .12 .30
281 Gerald McCoy .12 .30
282 Adam Humphries .12 .30
283 Josh Rosen .20 .50
284 David Johnson .20 .50
285 Larry Fitzgerald .15 .40
286 Christian Kirk .12 .30
287 Chandler Jones .12 .30
288 Patrick Peterson .12 .30
289 Chad Williams .12 .30
290 Josh Bynes .12 .30
291 Budda Baker .12 .30
292 Chase Edmonds .12 .30
293 Jared Goff .20 .50
294 Marcus Peters .12 .30
295 Aaron Donald .20 .50
296 Todd Gurley II .20 .50
297 Cooper Kupp .15 .40
298 Robert Woods .15 .40
299 Brandin Cooks .15 .40
300 Cory Littleton .15 .40
301 Johnny Hekker .12 .30
302 John Johnson .12 .30
303 Ndamukong Suh .15 .40
304 Jimmy Garoppolo .20 .50
305 Nick Mullens .15 .40
306 Matt Breida .12 .30
307 George Kittle .12 .30
308 Fred Warner .12 .30
309 Marquise Goodwin .12 .30
310 Pierre Garcon .15 .40
311 Kyle Juszczyk .12 .30
312 DeForest Buckner .12 .30
313 Arik Armstead .12 .30
314 Russell Wilson .25 .60
315 Rashaad Penny .12 .30
316 Chris Carson .15 .40
317 Tyler Lockett .15 .40
318 Will Dissly .15 .40
319 Bobby Wagner .12 .30
320 Frank Clark .15 .40
321 Shaquill Griffin .12 .30
322 David Moore .12 .30
323 Nick Vannett .12 .30
324 C.J. Anderson .15 .40
325 Taylor Lewan .12 .30
326 Jack Doyle .12 .30
327 Andrew Whitworth .12 .30
328 Leonard Floyd .12 .30
329 Quenton Nelson .15 .40
330 Mike McGlinchey .12 .30
331 Daniel Jones RC 1.25 3.00
332 Dwayne Haskins RC 1.25 3.00
333 Will Grier RC .75 2.00
334 Drew Lock RC 1.25 3.00
335 Ryan Finley RC .50 1.25
336 Jarrett Stidham RC .75 2.00
337 Damien Harris RC .60 1.50
338 Bryce Love RC .40 1.00
339 David Montgomery RC 1.00 2.50
340 Rodney Anderson RC .30 .75
341 Karan Higdon RC .30 .75
342 Dexter Williams RC .30 .75
343 Jalin Moore Jr. RC .25 .60
344 David Blough RC .30 .75
345 Myles Gaskin RC .50 1.25
346 Miles Sanders RC .60 1.50
347 Marquise Brown RC .75 2.00
348 A.J. Brown RC .60 1.50
349 N'Keal Harry RC .75 2.00
350 Hakeem Butler RC .50 1.25
351 Parris Campbell RC .60 1.50
352 D.K. Metcalf RC .75 2.00
353 Anthony Johnson RC .30 .75
354 Deebo Samuel RC .60 1.50
355 JJ Arcega-Whiteside RC .40 1.00
356 Andy Isabella RC .40 1.00
357 Elijah Holyfield RC .40 1.00
358 Noah Fant RC .50 1.25
359 Irv Smith Jr. RC .50 1.25
360 Nick Bosa RC .75 2.00
361 Ed Oliver RC .40 1.00
362 Rashan Gary RC .50 1.25
363 Clelin Ferrell RC .40 1.00
364 Josh Allen RC 1.00 2.50
365 Quinnen Williams RC .25 .60
366 Gardner Minshew II RC .40 1.00
367 Dexter Lawrence RC .40 1.00
368 Montez Sweat RC .75 2.00
369 Devin White RC .75 2.00
370 Devin Bush II RC 1.00 2.50
371 Mack Wilson RC .30 .75
372 Jachai Polite RC .30 .75
373 D'Andre Walker RC .25 .60
374 Greedy Williams RC .75 2.00
375 Deandre Baker RC .60 1.50
376 Julian Love RC .30 .75
377 Deionte Thompson RC .30 .75
378 Johnathan Abram RC .25 .60
379 Brian Burns RC .30 .75
380 Kelvin Harmon RC .40 1.00
381 Byron Murphy RC .25 .60
382 Riley Ridley RC .40 1.00
383 Josh Jacobs RC 1.25 3.00
384 Kyler Murray RC 2.50 6.00
385 Hunter Renfrow RC .50 1.25
386 Alex Barnes RC .30 .75
387 Kyle Shurmur RC .50 1.25
388 Dillon Mitchell RC .30 .75
389 Anthony Ratliff-Williams RC .50 1.25
390 Benny Snell Jr. RC .75 2.00
391 Devin Singletary RC .30 .75
392 Darwin Thompson RC .40 1.00
393 Trayveon Williams RC .30 .75
394 Jaylon Ferguson RC .25 .60
395 Zach Allen RC .40 1.00
396 Christian Wilkins RC 1.00 2.50
397 Jeffery Simmons RC .25 .60
398 Darrell Henderson RC .60 1.50
399 Justice Hill RC .40 1.00
400 Caleb Wilson RC .25 .60
401 Antoine Wesley RC .25 .60
402 Lil'Jordan Humphrey RC .30 .75
403 Preston Williams RC .25 .60
404 Gary Jennings Jr. RC .40 1.00
405 David Sills V RC .75 2.00
406 Stanley Morgan Jr. RC .40 1.00
407 Mike Weber RC .40 1.00
408 L.J. Scott RC .40 1.00
409 Tyree Jackson RC .60 1.50
410 James Williams RC .25 .60
411 Clayton Thorson RC .40 1.00
412 Brett Rypien RC .30 .75
413 Trace McSorley RC .60 1.50
414 Emanuel Hall RC .25 .60
415 Eric Dungey RC 1.00 2.50
416 Jake Browning RC .60 1.50
417 Jacques Patrick RC .25 .60
418 Travis Homer RC .25 .60
419 Nick Brossette RC .30 .75
420 Jordan Scarlett RC .25 .60
421 Trayvon Mullen Jr. RC .40 1.00
422 T.J. Hockenson RC .60 1.50
423 Alexander Mattison RC .50 1.25
424 Terry McLaurin RC .30 .75
425 Chauncey Gardner-Johnson RC .25 .60
426 Germaine Pratt RC .30 .75
427 C.J. Conrad RC .25 .60
428 Terry Godwin II RC .30 .75
429 Jaylen Smith RC .25 .60
430 Miles Boykin RC .30 .75
431 Jakobi Meyers RC .25 .60
432 Amani Oruwariye RC .30 .75
433 Oshane Ximines RC .25 .60
434 Nasir Adderley RC .30 .75
435 Greg Dortch RC .30 .75
436 Rock Ya-Sin RC .30 .75
437 Darius Slayton RC .40 1.00
438 Johnnie Dixon RC .30 .75
439 Patrick Laird RC .50 1.25
440 Jalen Hurd RC .30 .75

2019 Score 30th Anniversary
*1-330 VETS/30: 6X TO 15X BASIC CARDS
*331-440 ROOKIES/30: 4X TO 10X BASIC RC

2019 Score Artist's Proof
*1-330 VETS/35: 5X TO 12X BASIC CARDS
*331-440 ROOKIES/35: 3X TO 8X BASIC RC

2019 Score Black
*1-330 VETS: 2X TO 5X BASIC CARDS
*331-440 ROOKIES: 1X TO 2.5X BASIC RC

2019 Score Gold
*1-330 VETS: 2X TO 5X BASIC CARDS
*331-440 ROOKIES: 1X TO 2.5X BASIC RC

2019 Score Gold Zone
*1-330 VETS/50: 4X TO 10X BASIC CARDS
*331-440 ROOKIES/50: 2X TO 5X BASIC RC

2019 Score Green
*1-330 VETS: 2X TO 5X BASIC CARDS
*331-440 ROOKIES: 1X TO 2.5X BASIC RC

2019 Score Purple
*1-330 VETS: 2X TO 5X BASIC CARDS
*331-440 ROOKIES: 1X TO 2.5X BASIC RC

2019 Score Red
*1-330 VETS: 2X TO 5X BASIC CARDS
*331-440 ROOKIES: 1X TO 2.5X BASIC RC

2019 Score Red Zone
*1-330 VETS/20: 10X TO 25X BASIC CARDS
*331-440 ROOKIES/20: 6X TO 15X BASIC RC

2019 Score Scorecard
*1-330 VETS: 2X TO 5X BASIC CARDS
*331-440 ROOKIES: 1X TO 2.5X BASIC RC

2019 Score Showcase
*1-330 VETS/100: 3X TO 8X BASIC CARDS
*331-440 ROOKIES/100: 2X TO 5X BASIC RC

2019 Score All Hands Team
*BLACK: .6X TO 1.5X BASIC INSERTS
*GOLD: .6X TO 1.5X BASIC INSERTS
*GREEN: .6X TO 1.5X BASIC INSERTS
*PURPLE: .6X TO 1.5X BASIC INSERTS
*RED: .5X TO 1.2X BASIC INSERTS
1 Keelan Cole .60 1.50
2 Nick Chubb 1.00 2.50
3 Alejandro Villanueva .75 2.00
4 Adam Thielen 1.00 2.50
5 Michael Thomas 1.00 2.50
6 T.J. Yeldon .75 2.00
7 Mike Williams .60 1.50
8 DeAndre Hopkins .75 2.00
9 Julio Jones 1.00 2.50
10 Antonio Brown 1.00 2.50

2019 Score Captains
*BLACK: .5X TO 1.2X BASIC INSERTS
*GOLD: .6X TO 1.5X BASIC INSERTS
*GREEN: .6X TO 1.5X BASIC INSERTS
*PURPLE: .6X TO 1.5X BASIC INSERTS
*RED: .6X TO 1.5X BASIC INSERTS
1 Larry Fitzgerald .75 2.00
2 Drew Brees 1.00 2.50
3 Russell Wilson 1.25 3.00
4 Dak Prescott 1.00 2.50
5 Cam Newton 1.00 2.50
6 Greg Olsen .75 2.00
7 Von Miller .75 2.00
8 J.J. Watt 1.00 2.50
9 Deshaun Watson 1.25 3.00
10 Andrew Luck 1.25 3.00
11 Adam Vinatieri .60 1.50
12 Jared Goff 1.00 2.50
13 Todd Gurley II 1.00 2.50
14 Tom Brady 2.50 6.00
15 Jamal Adams .75 2.00
16 Landon Collins .60 1.50
17 Myles Garrett .60 1.50
18 Sean Lee .75 2.00
19 Kirk Cousins 1.00 2.50
20 Everson Griffen .60 1.50
21 Kyle Rudolph .60 1.50
22 Mike Evans .75 2.00
23 Eli Manning .75 2.00
24 Matthew Stafford .75 2.00
25 Travis Kelce 1.00 2.50

26 DeAndre Hopkins .75 2.00
27 Eric Berry .75 2.00
28 Tyrann Mathieu .75 2.00
29 Marcus Mariota 1.00 2.50
30 Wesley Woodyard .60 1.50

2019 Score Celebration

*BLACK: .5X TO 1.2X BASIC INSERTS
*GOLD: .6X TO 1.5X BASIC INSERTS
*GREEN: .6X TO 1.5X BASIC INSERTS
*PURPLE: .6X TO 1.5X BASIC INSERTS
*RED: .6X TO 1.5X BASIC INSERTS
1 Phillip Lindsay 1.00 2.50
2 Ezekiel Elliott 1.25 3.00
3 Tyler Lockett .75 2.00
4 Dalvin Cook .75 2.00
5 David Njoku .60 1.50
6 Rob Gronkowski 1.00 2.50
7 Joe Mixon .75 2.00
8 Anthony Miller .75 2.00
9 DeAndre Hopkins .75 2.00
10 JuJu Smith-Schuster 1.00 2.50

2019 Score Collegiate Jerseys

*PRIME/25: 1X TO 2.5X BASIC JSY
1 Mitchell Trubisky 2.50 6.00
2 Saquon Barkley 3.00 8.00
3 Baker Mayfield 4.00 10.00
4 Patrick Mahomes II 6.00 15.00
5 JuJu Smith-Schuster 2.50 6.00
6 Marcus Mariota 2.50 6.00
7 Ezekiel Elliott 3.00 8.00
8 Sony Michel 2.50 6.00
9 Todd Gurley II 2.50 6.00
10 Deshaun Watson 3.00 8.00
11 Joey Bosa 2.00 5.00
12 Amari Cooper 2.50 6.00
13 Melvin Gordon III 2.00 5.00
14 Jared Goff 2.50 6.00
15 Stefon Diggs 2.00 5.00
16 Lamar Jackson 2.50 6.00
17 Mike Evans 2.00 5.00
18 Will Fuller V 1.50 4.00
19 Corey Davis 2.00 5.00
20 Alvin Kamara 2.00 5.00
21 Derrick Henry 2.50 6.00
22 Jordan Howard 2.50 6.00
23 Sam Darnold 2.50 6.00
24 Calvin Ridley 2.00 5.00
25 Josh Allen 6.00 15.00

2019 Score Defenders Jerseys

*PRIME/25: 1X TO 2.5X BASIC JSY
*PRIME/15: 1.2X TO 3X BASIC JSY
1 Khalil Mack 2.50 6.00
2 Jadeveon Clowney 1.50 4.00
3 T.J. Watt 2.00 5.00
4 Cameron Wake 1.50 4.00
5 Robert Quinn 2.00 5.00
6 Bradley Chubb 2.00 5.00
7 Tedy Bruschi 2.00 5.00
8 Shane Ray 1.50 4.00
9 Jabrill Peppers 1.50 4.00
10 Todd Davis 1.50 4.00
11 Howie Long 2.00 5.00
12 Aaron Donald 2.50 6.00
13 Ndamukong Suh 2.00 5.00
14 Lawrence Taylor 2.50 6.00
15 Ray Lewis 2.50 6.00
16 Bruce Smith 2.00 5.00
17 Terrell Suggs 1.50 4.00
18 Michael Bennett 1.50 4.00
19 Richard Sherman 2.00 5.00
20 Geno Atkins 1.50 4.00
21 Vincent Rey 1.50 4.00
22 Jason Taylor 2.00 5.00
23 Shaquem Griffin 2.00 5.00
24 Patrick Chung 2.00 5.00
25 Dan Hampton 1.50 4.00
26 John Randle 1.50 4.00
27 Michael Strahan 2.50 6.00
28 Leonard Williams 1.50 4.00
29 Joey Bosa 2.00 5.00
30 Harrison Smith 1.50 4.00

2019 Score Epix Game

*BLACK: .5X TO 1.2X BASIC INSERTS
*GOLD: .6X TO 1.5X BASIC INSERTS
*GREEN: .6X TO 1.5X BASIC INSERTS
*PURPLE: .6X TO 1.5X BASIC INSERTS
*RED: .6X TO 1.5X BASIC INSERTS
1 Jared Goff 1.00 2.50
2 Khalil Mack 1.00 2.50
3 Patrick Mahomes II 2.50 6.00
4 Drew Brees 1.00 2.50
5 Michael Thomas 1.00 2.50
6 Aaron Donald 1.00 2.50
7 James Conner 1.00 2.50
8 Saquon Barkley 1.25 3.00
9 Ezekiel Elliott 1.25 3.00
10 Baker Mayfield 1.50 4.00

2019 Score Fantasy Stars

*BLACK: .5X TO 1.2X BASIC INSERTS
*GOLD: .6X TO 1.5X BASIC INSERTS
*GREEN: .6X TO 1.5X BASIC INSERTS
*PURPLE: .6X TO 1.5X BASIC INSERTS
*RED: .6X TO 1.5X BASIC INSERTS
1 Patrick Mahomes II 2.50 6.00
2 Todd Gurley II 1.00 2.50
3 Ben Roethlisberger .75 2.00
4 Matt Ryan 1.00 2.50
5 Jared Goff 1.00 2.50
6 Drew Brees 1.00 2.50
7 Saquon Barkley 1.25 3.00
8 Cam Newton 1.00 2.50
9 Andrew Luck 1.25 3.00
10 Alvin Kamara .75 2.00
11 Christian McCaffrey 1.00 2.50
12 Adam Thielen 1.00 2.50
13 Tyreek Hill 1.00 2.50
14 Melvin Gordon III .75 2.00
15 Aaron Rodgers 2.00 5.00
16 Michael Thomas 1.00 2.50
17 Ezekiel Elliott 1.25 3.00
18 James Conner 1.00 2.50
19 Russell Wilson 1.25 3.00
20 Tom Brady 2.50 6.00

2019 Score Home and Away Jerseys Away

*PRIME/25: 1X TO 2.5X BASIC JSY
1 Andrew Luck 3.00 8.00
2 Russell Wilson 3.00 8.00
3 Allen Robinson II 2.00 5.00
4 Alshon Jeffery 2.00 5.00
5 Stefon Diggs 2.00 5.00
6 Chris Godwin 1.50 4.00
7 Patrick Mahomes II 6.00 15.00
8 Derek Carr 2.50 6.00
9 Jarvis Landry 2.00 5.00
10 Tyler Lockett 2.00 5.00

2019 Score Home and Away Jerseys Home

*PRIME/25: 1X TO 2.5X BASIC JSY
1 Ezekiel Elliott 3.00 8.00
2 Tarik Cohen 2.00 5.00
3 Michael Thomas 2.50 6.00
4 Jay Ajayi 2.00 5.00
5 Kyle Rudolph 1.50 4.00
6 Sammy Watkins 2.50 6.00
7 Marquise Goodwin 1.50 4.00
8 Baker Mayfield 4.00 10.00
9 Deshaun Watson 3.00 8.00
10 Lamar Jackson 2.50 6.00

2019 Score Huddle Up

*BLACK: .6X TO 1.5X BASIC INSERTS
*GOLD: .6X TO 1.5X BASIC INSERTS
*GREEN: .6X TO 1.5X BASIC INSERTS
*PURPLE: .6X TO 1.5X BASIC INSERTS
*RED: .6X TO 1.5X BASIC INSERTS
1 Baltimore Ravens .75 2.00
2 New York Giants FB .75 2.00
3 New England Patriots .75 2.00
4 Green Bay Packers .75 2.00
5 Pittsburgh Steelers .75 2.00
6 Los Angeles Rams .75 2.00
7 Kansas City Chiefs .75 2.00
8 Chicago Bears .75 2.00
9 New Orleans Saints .75 2.00
10 Detroit Lions .75 2.00

2019 Score Inscriptions

1 Patrick Mahomes II/25 100.00 200.00
3 Keyshawn Johnson/25 6.00 15.00
4 Andre Rison/25 8.00 20.00
5 Sterling Shepard/25 8.00 20.00
6 Brandon Graham/25 6.00 15.00
7 Everson Griffen/25 6.00 15.00
8 Jimmy Garoppolo/25 40.00 80.00
9 Mitchell Trubisky/25 25.00 50.00
10 Case Keenum/25 8.00 20.00
11 Vinny Testaverde/25 6.00 15.00
12 Joey Bosa/25 8.00 20.00
13 DeSean Jackson/25 8.00 20.00
14 Josh Gordon/25 6.00 15.00
15 Richard Sherman/25 10.00 25.00
16 Steven Jackson/25 6.00 15.00
17 Dante Hall/25 6.00 15.00
18 Mark Clayton/25 6.00 15.00
19 Josh Allen/25
20 Christian McCaffrey/25
21 Eric Weddle/25 6.00 15.00
22 Harrison Smith/25 6.00 15.00
23 Justin Tucker/25 10.00 25.00
24 Leonard Fournette/25 10.00 25.00
25 Randall Cunningham/25 8.00 20.00
26 Isaac Bruce/25 10.00 25.00
27 O.J. Howard/25 6.00 15.00
28 Mike Ditka/25
30 Chris Carson/25 8.00 20.00
31 DeAndre Hopkins/25 8.00 20.00
33 Trent Dilfer/25 6.00 15.00
34 Sam Darnold/25 30.00 60.00
36 Nick Chubb/25 10.00 25.00
37 Mark Ingram II/25 8.00 20.00
39 Andy Dalton/25 8.00 20.00
41 Tyreek Hill/25 EXCH 10.00 25.00
42 JuJu Smith-Schuster/25 EXCH 25.00 50.00
43 Alshon Jeffery/25 8.00 20.00
44 Amari Cooper/25 15.00 40.00
45 Josh Rosen/25 10.00 25.00
46 T.Y. Hilton/25 8.00 20.00
48 Clay Matthews/25 8.00 20.00
49 Saquon Barkley/25 60.00 125.00
50 A.J. Green/25 10.00 25.00

2019 Score NFL Draft

*BLACK: .6X TO 1.5X BASIC INSERTS
*GOLD: .6X TO 1.5X BASIC INSERTS
*GREEN: .6X TO 1.5X BASIC INSERTS
*PURPLE: .6X TO 1.5X BASIC INSERTS
*RED: .6X TO 1.5X BASIC INSERTS
1 Greedy Williams 1.25 3.00
2 Marquise Brown 1.25 3.00
3 Damien Harris 1.00 2.50
4 Nick Bosa 1.25 3.00
5 Dwayne Haskins 2.00 5.00
6 N'Keal Harry 1.25 3.00
7 Josh Jacobs 2.00 5.00
8 Quinnen Williams .40 1.00
9 Kyler Murray 4.00 10.00
10 A.J. Brown 1.00 2.50
11 Bryce Love .60 1.50
12 Josh Allen 1.50 4.00
13 Irv Smith Jr. .75 2.00
14 Daniel Jones 2.00 5.00
15 D.K. Metcalf 1.25 3.00
16 Darrell Henderson 1.00 2.50
17 Ed Oliver .60 1.50
18 JJ Arcega-Whiteside .60 1.50
19 Drew Lock 2.00 5.00
20 Devin White 1.25 3.00
21 David Montgomery 1.50 4.00
22 Anthony Johnson .50 1.25
23 Clelin Ferrell .60 1.50
24 Will Grier 1.25 3.00
25 Rashan Gary .75 2.00
26 Rodney Anderson .50 1.25
27 Kelvin Harmon .60 1.50
28 Noah Fant .75 2.00
29 Ryan Finley .75 2.00
30 Hakeem Butler .75 2.00

2019 Score Pro Bowl Jerseys

*PRIME/25: 1X TO 2.5X BASIC JSY
1 Budda Baker 1.50 4.00
2 Graham Gano 1.50 4.00
3 Michael Bennett 1.50 4.00
4 Earl Thomas III 2.00 5.00
5 Keanu Neal 1.50 4.00
6 Ryan Kerrigan 1.50 4.00
7 Pharoh Cooper 1.50 4.00
8 Chandler Jones 1.50 4.00
9 Deion Jones 1.50 4.00
10 Kyle Rudolph 1.50 4.00
11 Darius Slay 1.50 4.00
12 Travis Frederick 1.50 4.00
13 Mike Daniels 1.50 4.00
14 Kyle Juszczyk 1.50 4.00
15 Xavier Rhodes 1.50 4.00
16 Chris Boswell 1.50 4.00
17 Keenan Allen 2.00 5.00
18 Melvin Ingram 1.50 4.00
19 Yannick Ngakoue 1.50 4.00
20 Roosevelt Nix 1.50 4.00
21 Malik Jackson 1.50 4.00
22 Kevin Byard 1.50 4.00
23 Maurkice Pouncey 1.50 4.00
24 Jurrell Casey 1.50 4.00
25 Taylor Lewan 1.50 4.00

2019 Score Rookie Autographs

331 Daniel Jones 30.00 60.00
332 Dwayne Haskins 40.00 80.00
333 Will Grier 10.00 25.00
334 Drew Lock 15.00 40.00
335 Ryan Finley 6.00 15.00
336 Jarrett Stidham 15.00 40.00
337 Damien Harris 8.00 20.00
338 Bryce Love 5.00 12.00
339 David Montgomery 12.00 30.00
340 Rodney Anderson 4.00 10.00
341 Karan Higdon 4.00 10.00
342 Dexter Williams 4.00 10.00
343 Jalin Moore Jr. 3.00 8.00
344 David Blough 4.00 10.00
345 Myles Gaskin 6.00 15.00
346 Miles Sanders 8.00 20.00
348 A.J. Brown 8.00 20.00
349 N'Keal Harry 15.00 40.00
350 Hakeem Butler 6.00 15.00
351 Parris Campbell 8.00 20.00
352 D.K. Metcalf 12.00 30.00
353 Anthony Johnson 4.00 10.00
354 Deebo Samuel 8.00 20.00
355 JJ Arcega-Whiteside 5.00 12.00
356 Andy Isabella 5.00 12.00
357 Elijah Holyfield 5.00 12.00
358 Noah Fant 6.00 15.00
359 Irv Smith Jr. 6.00 15.00
360 Nick Bosa 10.00 25.00
361 Ed Oliver 5.00 12.00
362 Rashan Gary 6.00 15.00
363 Clelin Ferrell 5.00 12.00
366 Gardner Minshew II 5.00 12.00
367 Dexter Lawrence 5.00 12.00
369 Devin White 10.00 25.00
371 Mack Wilson 4.00 10.00
373 D'Andre Walker 3.00 8.00
374 Greedy Williams 10.00 25.00
375 Deandre Baker 8.00 20.00
376 Julian Love 4.00 10.00
377 Deionte Thompson 4.00 10.00
378 Johnathan Abram 3.00 8.00
379 Brian Burns 4.00 10.00
380 Kelvin Harmon 5.00 12.00
381 Byron Murphy 3.00 8.00
382 Riley Ridley 5.00 12.00
383 Josh Jacobs 15.00 40.00
384 Kyler Murray 90.00 150.00
385 Hunter Renfrow 6.00 15.00
386 Alex Barnes 4.00 10.00
387 Kyle Shurmur 6.00 15.00
388 Dillon Mitchell 4.00 10.00
389 Anthony Ratliff-Williams 6.00 15.00
390 Benny Snell Jr. 10.00 25.00
391 Devin Singletary 4.00 10.00
392 Darwin Thompson 5.00 12.00
393 Trayveon Williams 4.00 10.00
394 Jaylon Ferguson 3.00 8.00
395 Zach Allen 5.00 12.00
396 Christian Wilkins 12.00 30.00
397 Jeffery Simmons 3.00 8.00
398 Darrell Henderson 8.00 20.00
399 Justice Hill 5.00 12.00
400 Caleb Wilson 3.00 8.00
401 Antoine Wesley 3.00 8.00
402 Lil'Jordan Humphrey 4.00 10.00
403 Preston Williams 3.00 8.00
404 Gary Jennings Jr. 5.00 12.00
405 David Sills V 10.00 25.00
406 Stanley Morgan Jr. 5.00 12.00
407 Mike Weber 5.00 12.00
408 L.J. Scott 5.00 12.00
409 Tyree Jackson 8.00 20.00
410 James Williams 3.00 8.00
411 Clayton Thorson 5.00 12.00
412 Brett Rypien 4.00 10.00
413 Trace McSorley 8.00 20.00
414 Emanuel Hall 3.00 8.00
416 Jake Browning 8.00 20.00
417 Jacques Patrick 3.00 8.00
418 Travis Homer 3.00 8.00
419 Nick Brossette 4.00 10.00
420 Jordan Scarlett 3.00 8.00
421 Trayvon Mullen Jr. 5.00 12.00
422 T.J. Hockenson 8.00 20.00
423 Alexander Mattison
424 Terry McLaurin 4.00 10.00
425 Chauncey Gardner-Johnson 3.00 8.00
426 Germaine Pratt 4.00 10.00
427 C.J. Conrad 3.00 8.00
428 Terry Godwin II 4.00 10.00
429 Jaylen Smith 3.00 8.00
430 Miles Boykin 4.00 10.00
431 Jakobi Meyers 3.00 8.00
432 Amani Oruwariye 4.00 10.00
433 Oshane Ximines 3.00 8.00
434 Nasir Adderley 4.00 10.00
435 Greg Dortch 4.00 10.00
436 Rock Ya-Sin 4.00 10.00
437 Darius Slayton 5.00 12.00
438 Johnnie Dixon 4.00 10.00
439 Patrick Laird 6.00 15.00
440 Jalen Hurd 4.00 10.00

2019 Score Rookie Autographs Artist's Proof

*AP/35: .6X TO 1.5X BASIC AU
384 Kyler Murray 150.00 250.00

2019 Score Rookie Autographs Gold Zone

384 Kyler Murray 150.00 250.00

2019 Score Rookie Autographs Red Zone

*RED/20: 1X TO 2.5X BASIC AU
384 Kyler Murray 200.00 400.00

2019 Score Signal Callers

*BLACK: .5X TO 1.2X BASIC INSERTS
*GOLD: .6X TO 1.5X BASIC INSERTS
*GREEN: .6X TO 1.5X BASIC INSERTS
*PURPLE: .6X TO 1.5X BASIC INSERTS
*RED: .6X TO 1.5X BASIC INSERTS
1 Baker Mayfield 1.50 4.00
2 Tom Brady 2.50 6.00
3 Nick Mullens .75 2.00
4 Jimmy Garoppolo 1.00 2.50
5 Mitchell Trubisky 1.00 2.50
6 Josh Allen 1.00 2.50
7 Josh Rosen 1.00 2.50
8 Lamar Jackson 1.00 2.50
9 Matt Ryan 1.00 2.50
10 Cam Newton 1.00 2.50
11 Andy Dalton .75 2.00
12 Dak Prescott 1.00 2.50
13 Case Keenum .75 2.00
14 Matthew Stafford .75 2.00
15 Aaron Rodgers 2.00 5.00
16 Deshaun Watson 1.25 3.00
17 Andrew Luck 1.25 3.00
18 Patrick Mahomes II 2.50 6.00
19 Philip Rivers 1.00 2.50
20 Jared Goff 1.00 2.50
21 Carson Wentz 1.25 3.00
22 Kirk Cousins 1.00 2.50
23 Drew Brees 1.00 2.50
24 Sam Darnold 1.00 2.50
25 Ben Roethlisberger .75 2.00
26 Derek Carr 1.00 2.50
27 Russell Wilson 1.25 3.00
28 Marcus Mariota 1.00 2.50
29 Jameis Winston .75 2.00
30 Eli Manning .75 2.00

2019 Score Signatures

1 Josh Reynolds 2.50 6.00
2 Jake Elliott 2.50 6.00
3 Kyle Long 2.50 6.00
4 Kendall Fuller 2.50 6.00
5 Anthony Harris 2.50 6.00
6 Pat McAfee 30.00 60.00
7 Hunter Henry 2.50 6.00
8 Latavius Murray 2.50 6.00
9 Eric Kendricks 2.50 6.00
10 Greg Zuerlein 2.50 6.00
11 Bo Scarbrough 2.50 6.00
12 Yannick Ngakoue 2.50 6.00
13 Gilbert Brown 2.50 6.00
14 Linval Joseph 2.50 6.00
15 Adam Humphries 2.50 6.00
16 Cameron Jordan 2.50 6.00
17 Alex Mack 2.50 6.00
18 Kevin Byard 2.50 6.00
19 Larry Johnson 2.50 6.00
20 Dede Westbrook 2.50 6.00
21 Peyton Barber 2.50 6.00
22 Carl Nassib 2.50 6.00
23 Marquise Goodwin 2.50 6.00
24 Geno Atkins 2.50 6.00
25 Mohamed Sanu 2.50 6.00
26 Chris Godwin 2.50 6.00
27 Tyler Boyd 2.50 6.00
28 Marshon Lattimore 2.50 6.00
29 Brian Orakpo 2.50 6.00
30 Jurrell Casey 2.50 6.00
31 Luke Falk 2.50 6.00
32 Danny Amendola 3.00 8.00
33 Taylor Gabriel 2.50 6.00
34 Landon Collins 2.50 6.00
35 Allen Hurns 2.50 6.00
36 Lamar Miller 3.00 8.00
37 Robby Anderson 2.50 6.00
38 Christian Kirksey 2.50 6.00
39 Laquon Treadwell 2.50 6.00
40 Frank Clark 3.00 8.00

2019 Score Throwbacks

*BLACK: .5X TO 1.2X BASIC INSERTS
*GOLD: .6X TO 1.5X BASIC INSERTS
*GREEN: .6X TO 1.5X BASIC INSERTS
*PURPLE: .6X TO 1.5X BASIC INSERTS
*RED: .6X TO 1.5X BASIC INSERTS
1 Julio Jones 1.00 2.50
2 Matt Ryan 1.00 2.50
3 Aaron Rodgers 2.00 5.00
4 Clay Matthews .75 2.00
5 Mitchell Trubisky 1.00 2.50
6 Roquan Smith 1.00 2.50
7 Tarik Cohen .75 2.00
8 Jared Goff 1.00 2.50
9 Todd Gurley II 1.00 2.50
10 Aaron Donald 1.00 2.50
11 Brandin Cooks .75 2.00
12 Adrian Peterson 1.00 2.50
13 Ryan Kerrigan .60 1.50
14 Philip Rivers 1.00 2.50
15 Melvin Gordon III .75 2.00
16 Von Miller .75 2.00
17 Bradley Chubb .75 2.00
18 Phillip Lindsay 1.00 2.50
19 JuJu Smith-Schuster 1.00 2.50
20 Antonio Brown 1.00 2.50

2015 Score NFL Draft

COMPLETE SET (9) 60.00 100.00
COMP. SET w/o SPs (6) 30.00 60.00
DP1 Jameis Winston White 4.00 10.00
DP2 Kevin White 1.00 2.50
(issued at Draft Town event)
DP3 Marcus Mariota 3.00 8.00
(issued at Draft Town event)
DP4 Amari Cooper 2.50 6.00
(issued at Draft Town event)
DP5 Melvin Gordon 2.00 5.00
(issued at Draft Town event)
DP6 Todd Gurley 3.00 8.00
(issued at Draft Town event)
DPDF Dante Fowler 2.50 6.00
(issued at Draft Day event)
DPJW Jameis Winston Red 2.00 5.00
DPLW Leonard Williams 1.50 4.00
(issued at Draft Day event)

2009 Score Inscriptions

COMP.SET w/o RC's (300) 20.00 40.00
ROOKIE PRINT RUN 999 SER.#'d SETS
1 Adrian Wilson .20 .50
2 Anquan Boldin .20 .50
3 Dominique Rodgers-Cromartie .20 .50
4 Edgerrin James .25 .60
5 Kurt Warner .25 .60
6 Larry Fitzgerald .25 .60
7 Matt Leinart .20 .50
8 Steve Breaston .25 .60
9 Tim Hightower .20 .50
10 Chris Houston .20 .50
11 Curtis Lofton .20 .50
12 Harry Douglas .20 .50
13 Jerious Norwood .20 .50
14 John Abraham .20 .50
15 Matt Ryan .25 .60
16 Michael Jenkins .20 .50
17 Michael Turner .20 .50
18 Roddy White .20 .50
19 Demetrius Williams .20 .50
20 Derrick Mason .20 .50
21 Joe Flacco .25 .60
22 Le'Ron McClain .25 .60
23 Mark Clayton .20 .50
24 Ray Lewis .30 .75
25 Ray Rice .20 .50
26 Terrell Suggs .20 .50
27 Todd Heap .20 .50
28 Willis McGahee .20 .50
29 Derek Fine .20 .50
30 Fred Jackson .25 .60
31 James Hardy .25 .60
32 Lee Evans .25 .60
33 Leodis McKelvin .20 .50
34 Marshawn Lynch .25 .60
35 Paul Posluszny .20 .50
36 Steve Johnson .25 .60
37 Trent Edwards .20 .50
38 Charles Godfrey .20 .50
39 Chris Gamble .20 .50
40 Dante Rosario .20 .50
41 DeAngelo Williams .20 .50
42 Jake Delhomme .20 .50
43 Jon Beason .20 .50
44 Jonathan Stewart .20 .50
45 Muhsin Muhammad .20 .50
46 Steve Smith .25 .60
47 Alex Brown .20 .50
48 Brian Urlacher .30 .75
49 Desmond Clark .20 .50
50 Devin Hester .25 .60
51 Earl Bennett .25 .60
52 Greg Olsen .25 .60
53 Kyle Orton .20 .50
54 Lance Briggs .25 .60
55 Matt Forte .20 .50
56 Andre Caldwell .20 .50
57 Carson Palmer .25 .60
58 Cedric Benson .20 .50
59 Chad Ochocinco .20 .50
60 Dhani Jones .20 .50
61 Jerome Simpson .20 .50
62 Keith Rivers .20 .50
63 Reggie Kelly .20 .50
64 T.J. Houshmandzadeh .20 .50
65 Brady Quinn .20 .50
66 Braylon Edwards .20 .50
67 D'Qwell Jackson .20 .50
68 Jamal Lewis .25 .60
69 Jerome Harrison .20 .50
70 Josh Cribbs .20 .50
71 Kellen Winslow .20 .50
72 Shaun Rogers .20 .50
73 Steve Heiden .20 .50
74 DeMarcus Ware .25 .60
75 Felix Jones .20 .50
76 Jason Witten .25 .60
77 Marion Barber .25 .60
78 Patrick Crayton .20 .50
79 Roy Williams WR .20 .50
80 Tashard Choice .20 .50
81 Terrell Owens .25 .60
82 Terence Newman .20 .50
83 Tony Romo .25 .60
84 Brandon Marshall .25 .60
85 Brandon Stokley .20 .50
86 Champ Bailey .25 .60
87 Daniel Graham .20 .50
88 Eddie Royal .20 .50
89 Jay Cutler .20 .50
90 Peyton Hillis .25 .60
91 D.J. Williams .20 .50
92 Tony Scheffler .20 .50
93 Calvin Johnson .30 .75
94 Daunte Culpepper .25 .60
95 Ernie Sims .20 .50
96 Jerome Felton .20 .50
97 Jordon Dizon .20 .50
98 Kevin Smith .20 .50
99 Paris Lenon .20 .50
100 Rudi Johnson .20 .50
101 Shaun McDonald .20 .50
102 Aaron Rodgers .60 1.50
103 A.J. Hawk .20 .50
104 Brandon Jackson .25 .60
105 Donald Driver .25 .60
106 Donald Lee .20 .50
107 Greg Jennings .20 .50
108 James Jones .20 .50
109 Jermichael Finley .20 .50
110 Jordy Nelson .25 .60
111 Ryan Grant .25 .60
112 Amobi Okoye .20 .50
113 Andre Johnson .25 .60
114 Chester Pitts .20 .50
115 DeMeco Ryans .25 .60
116 Kevin Walter .25 .60
117 Kris Brown .20 .50
118 Mario Williams .25 .60
119 Matt Schaub .20 .50
120 Owen Daniels .20 .50
121 Steve Slaton .20 .50
122 Adam Vinatieri .20 .50
123 Anthony Gonzalez .20 .50
124 Dallas Clark .20 .50
125 Dominic Rhodes .20 .50
126 Dwight Freeney .20 .50
127 Joseph Addai .20 .50
128 Freddie Keiaho .20 .50
129 Mike Hart .25 .60
130 Peyton Manning .75 2.00
131 Reggie Wayne .25 .60
132 David Garrard .20 .50
133 Dennis Northcutt .20 .50
134 Derrick Harvey .20 .50
135 Josh Scobee .20 .50
136 Marcedes Lewis .20 .50
137 Mike Peterson .20 .50
138 Maurice Jones-Drew .20 .50
139 Quentin Groves .20 .50
140 Reggie Nelson .20 .50
141 Brian Williams .20 .50
142 Derrick Johnson .20 .50
143 Matt Cassel .20 .50
144 Dwayne Bowe .25 .60
145 Jamaal Charles .25 .60
146 Kolby Smith .20 .50
147 Larry Johnson .20 .50
148 Mark Bradley .20 .50
149 Tony Gonzalez .25 .60
150 Tyler Thigpen .20 .50
151 Anthony Fasano .20 .50
152 Chad Henne .25 .60
153 Chad Pennington .20 .50
154 Davone Bess .20 .50
155 Joey Porter .25 .60
156 Greg Camarillo .25 .60
157 Jake Long .20 .50
158 Ricky Williams .25 .60
159 Ronnie Brown .20 .50
160 Ted Ginn .20 .50
161 Adrian Peterson .30 .75
162 Bernard Berrian .20 .50
163 Chad Greenway .20 .50
164 Chester Taylor .20 .50
165 Erin Henderson .20 .50
166 Jared Allen .20 .50
167 John David Booty .25 .60
168 Sidney Rice .20 .50
169 Tarvaris Jackson .25 .60
170 Visanthe Shiancoe .25 .60
171 Brandon Meriweather .20 .50
172 Jerod Mayo .25 .60
173 Kevin Faulk .20 .50
174 LaMont Jordan .20 .50
175 Laurence Maroney .25 .60
176 Randy Moss .25 .60
177 Tedy Bruschi .25 .60
178 Terrence Wheatley .20 .50
179 Tom Brady 1.00 2.50
180 Wes Welker .25 .60
181 Adrian Arrington .20 .50
182 Devery Henderson .20 .50
183 Drew Brees .30 .75
184 Jeremy Shockey .20 .50
185 Jonathan Vilma .20 .50
186 Lance Moore .20 .50
187 Marques Colston .20 .50
188 Pierre Thomas .20 .50
189 Reggie Bush .20 .50
190 Scott Shanle .20 .50
191 Ahmad Bradshaw .20 .50
192 Antonio Pierce .20 .50
193 Brandon Jacobs .20 .50
194 Derrick Ward .20 .50
195 Domenik Hixon .20 .50
196 Eli Manning .25 .60
197 Justin Tuck .20 .50
198 Kenny Phillips .20 .50
199 Kevin Boss .20 .50
200 Steve Smith USC .25 .60
201 Calvin Pace .20 .50
202 Chansi Stuckey .20 .50
203 Dustin Keller .20 .50
204 Jerricho Cotchery .20 .50
205 Kellen Clemens .20 .50
206 Laveranues Coles .20 .50
207 Leon Washington .20 .50
208 Thomas Jones .20 .50
209 Vernon Gholston .20 .50
210 Chaz Schilens .20 .50
211 Darren McFadden .30 .75
212 JaMarcus Russell .20 .50
213 Johnnie Lee Higgins .20 .50
214 Justin Fargas .20 .50
215 Michael Bush .20 .50
216 Nnamdi Asomugha .20 .50
217 Sebastian Janikowski .20 .50
218 Zach Miller .20 .50
219 Brian Westbrook .20 .50
220 Correll Buckhalter .20 .50
221 DeSean Jackson .25 .60
222 Donovan McNabb .25 .60
223 Greg Lewis .20 .50
224 Hank Baskett .20 .50
225 Kevin Curtis .20 .50
226 Reggie Brown .20 .50
227 Stewart Bradley .20 .50
228 Ben Roethlisberger .30 .75
229 Heath Miller .20 .50
230 Hines Ward .25 .60
231 James Harrison .30 .75
232 Troy Polamalu .30 .75
233 Nate Washington .20 .50
234 Rashard Mendenhall .20 .50
235 Santonio Holmes .20 .50
236 Willie Parker .20 .50
237 Antonio Gates .25 .60
238 Chris Chambers .20 .50
239 Darren Sproles .25 .60
240 Eric Weddle .20 .50
241 Jacob Hester .20 .50
242 LaDainian Tomlinson .30 .75
243 Philip Rivers .30 .75
244 Shawne Merriman .20 .50
245 Vincent Jackson .20 .50
246 Brandon Jones .20 .50
247 Frank Gore .25 .60
248 Isaac Bruce .30 .75
249 Josh Morgan .20 .50
250 Michael Robinson .20 .50
251 Patrick Willis .25 .60
252 Reggie Smith .20 .50
253 Shaun Hill .20 .50
254 Vernon Davis .20 .50
255 Deion Branch .20 .50
256 John Carlson .25 .60
257 Julian Peterson .20 .50
258 Julius Jones .20 .50
259 Lofa Tatupu .20 .50
260 Matt Hasselbeck .20 .50
261 Nate Burleson .20 .50
262 Owen Schmitt .20 .50
263 T.J. Duckett .20 .50
264 Antonio Pittman .20 .50
265 Chris Long .25 .60
266 Donnie Avery .20 .50
267 Keenan Burton .20 .50
268 Marc Bulger .20 .50
269 Pisa Tinoisamoa .20 .50
270 Steven Jackson .20 .50
271 Torry Holt .25 .60
272 Antonio Bryant .20 .50
273 Aqib Talib .20 .50
274 Cadillac Williams .25 .60
275 Dexter Jackson .20 .50
276 Earnest Graham .20 .50
277 Gaines Adams .20 .50
278 Michael Clayton .20 .50
279 Ronde Barber .20 .50
280 Barrett Ruud .20 .50
281 Albert Haynesworth .20 .50
282 Bo Scaife .20 .50
283 Chris Johnson .20 .50
284 Justin Gage .20 .50
285 Keith Bulluck .20 .50
286 Kerry Collins .20 .50
287 LenDale White .20 .50
288 Rob Bironas .20 .50
289 Roydell Williams .20 .50
290 Vince Young .20 .50
291 Chris Cooley .20 .50
292 Chris Horton .25 .60
293 Clinton Portis .20 .50
294 Colt Brennan .25 .60
295 Devin Thomas .20 .50
296 Jason Campbell .20 .50
297 Kedric Golston .30 .75
298 Ladell Betts .20 .50
299 Malcolm Kelly .20 .50
300 Santana Moss .25 .60
301 Aaron Brown RC 1.00 2.50
302 Aaron Curry RC 1.25 3.00
303 Aaron Kelly RC .75 2.00
304 Aaron Maybin RC 1.00 2.50
305 Alphonso Smith RC .75 2.00
306 Andre Brown RC 1.00 2.50
307 Andre Smith RC .75 2.00
308 Anthony Hill RC .75 2.00
309 Arian Foster RC 2.00 5.00
310 Austin Collie RC .75 2.00
311 B.J. Raji RC 1.00 2.50
312 Brandon Gibson RC 1.00 2.50
313 Brandon Pettigrew RC .75 2.00
314 Brandon Tate RC 1.00 2.50
315 Brian Cushing RC .75 2.00
316 Brian Hartline RC 1.25 3.00
317 Brian Orakpo RC 1.00 2.50
318 Brian Robiskie RC .75 2.00
319 Brooks Foster RC .75 2.00
320 Cameron Morrah RC .75 2.00
321 Cedric Peerman RC .75 2.00
322 Chase Coffman RC .75 2.00
323 Chris Wells RC .75 2.00
324 Clay Matthews RC 3.00 8.00
325 Clint Sintim RC .75 2.00
326 Cornelius Ingram RC .75 2.00
327 Curtis Painter RC .75 2.00
328 Darius Butler RC 1.00 2.50
329 Darius Passmore RC .75 2.00
330 Darrius Heyward-Bey RC 1.25 3.00
331 Davon Drew RC .75 2.00
332 Demetrius Byrd RC 1.00 2.50
333 Deon Butler RC .75 2.00
334 Derrick Williams RC .75 2.00
335 Devin Moore RC .75 2.00
336 Dominique Edison RC .75 2.00
338 Eugene Monroe RC .75 2.00
339 Everette Brown RC .75 2.00
340 Gartrell Johnson RC .75 2.00
341 Glen Coffee RC .75 2.00
342 Graham Harrell RC .75 2.00
343 Hakeem Nicks RC 1.00 2.50
344 Hunter Cantwell RC .75 2.00
345 Jairus Byrd RC 1.25 3.00
346 James Casey RC 1.00 2.50
347 James Davis RC .75 2.00
348 James Laurinaitis RC .75 2.00
349 Jared Cook RC 1.00 2.50
350 Jarett Dillard RC .75 2.00
351 Jason Smith RC .75 2.00
352 Javon Ringer RC .75 2.00
353 Jeremiah Johnson RC .75 2.00
354 Jeremy Childs RC .75 2.00
355 Jeremy Maclin RC 1.00 2.50
356 John Parker Wilson RC .75 2.00
357 Johnny Knox RC 1.00 2.50
358 Josh Freeman RC .75 2.00
359 Juaquin Iglesias RC .75 2.00
360 Keith Null RC 1.00 2.50
361 Kenny Britt RC 1.25 3.00
362 Kenny McKinley RC .75 2.00
363 Kevin Ogletree RC 1.00 2.50
364 Knowshon Moreno RC .75 2.00
365 Kory Sheets RC 1.00 2.50
366 Larry English RC 1.00 2.50
367 LeSean McCoy RC 2.00 5.00
368 Louis Murphy RC .75 2.00
369 Malcolm Jenkins RC .75 2.00
370 Mark Sanchez RC .75 2.00
371 Matthew Stafford RC 5.00 12.00
372 Michael Crabtree RC 1.25 3.00
373 Mike Goodson RC 1.00 2.50
374 Mike Thomas RC .75 2.00
375 Mike Wallace RC 1.25 3.00
376 Mohamed Massaquoi RC .75 2.00
377 Nate Davis RC .75 2.00
378 Nathan Brown RC 1.00 2.50
379 P.J. Hill RC .75 2.00
380 Pat White RC 1.00 2.50
381 Patrick Chung RC .75 2.00
382 Patrick Turner RC .75 2.00
383 Percy Harvin RC .75 2.00
384 Quan Cosby RC .75 2.00
385 Quinn Johnson RC .75 2.00
386 Quinten Lawrence RC .75 2.00
387 Ramses Barden RC .75 2.00
388 Rashad Jennings RC 1.00 2.50
389 Rey Maualuga RC 1.25 3.00
390 Rhett Bomar RC .75 2.00
391 Richard Quinn RC 1.00 2.50
392 Shawn Nelson RC .75 2.00
393 Shonn Greene RC .75 2.00
394 Stephen McGee RC .75 2.00
395 Tom Brandstater RC 1.00 2.50
396 Tony Fiammetta RC .75 2.00
397 Travis Beckum RC .75 2.00
398 Tyrell Sutton RC .75 2.00
399 Tyson Jackson RC .75 2.00
400 Vontae Davis RC .75 2.00

2009 Score Inscriptions Artist's Proof

*VETS 1-300: 6X TO 15X BASIC CARDS
*ROOKIES 301-400: 1X TO 2.5X BASIC CARDS
ARTIST'S PROOF PRINT RUN 32

2009 Score Inscriptions Gold Zone

*VETS 1-300: 5X TO 12X BASIC CARDS
*ROOKIES 301-400: .8X TO 2X BASIC CARDS
GOLD ZONE PRINT RUN 50 SER.#'d SETS

2009 Score Inscriptions Red Zone

*VETS 1-300: 6X TO 15X BASIC CARDS
*ROOKIES 301-400: 1X TO 2.5X BASIC CARDS
RED ZONE PRINT RUN 30 SER.#'d SETS

2009 Score Inscriptions Scorecard

*VETS 1-300: 5X TO 12X BASIC CARDS
*ROOKIES 301-400: .8X TO 2X BASIC CARDS
STATED PRINT RUN 50 SER.#'d SETS

2009 Score Inscriptions 1989 Score

1 Matthew Stafford 4.00 10.00
2 Mark Sanchez .75 2.00
3 Darrius Heyward-Bey 1.25 3.00
4 Michael Crabtree 1.25 3.00
5 Knowshon Moreno .75 2.00
6 Josh Freeman .75 2.00
7 Jeremy Maclin 1.00 2.50
8 Percy Harvin .75 2.00
9 Hakeem Nicks 1.00 2.50
10 Chris Wells .75 2.00

2009 Score Inscriptions 1989 Score Autographs

STATED PRINT RUN 20 SER.#'d SETS
1 Matthew Stafford 125.00 250.00
2 Mark Sanchez 75.00 150.00
3 Darrius Heyward-Bey 40.00 80.00
4 Michael Crabtree 60.00 120.00
5 Knowshon Moreno 40.00 100.00
6 Josh Freeman 60.00 150.00
7 Jeremy Maclin 40.00 100.00
8 Percy Harvin 30.00 80.00
9 Hakeem Nicks 40.00 80.00
10 Chris Wells 50.00 120.00

2009 Score Inscriptions Autographs

VET PRINT RUN 10-499
*ROOK.AU/299-999: .25X TO .6X GOLD ZONE AU
*ROOK.AU/199: .3X TO .8X GOLD ZONE AU
*ROOK.AU/99: .4X TO 1X GOLD ZONE AU
ROOKIE PRINT RUN 45-999
SERIAL #'d UNDER 20 NOT PRICED
3 Dominique Rodgers-Cromartie/199 4.00 10.00
10 Chris Houston/182 4.00 10.00
12 Harry Douglas/50 5.00 12.00
19 Demetrius Williams/100 5.00 12.00
25 Ray Rice/299 3.00 8.00
29 Derek Fine/499 3.00 8.00
33 Leodis McKelvin/85 5.00 12.00
36 Steve Johnson/499 6.00 15.00
38 Charles Godfrey/399 3.00 8.00
40 Dante Rosario/499 3.00 8.00
51 Earl Bennett/399 4.00 10.00
56 Andre Caldwell/25 6.00 15.00
61 Jerome Simpson/299 3.00 8.00
70 Josh Cribbs/100 12.50 25.00
78 Patrick Crayton/100 5.00 12.00
90 Peyton Hillis/203 12.00 30.00
96 Jerome Felton/499 3.00 8.00
97 Jordon Dizon/22 6.00 15.00
100 Rudi Johnson/188 4.00 10.00
108 James Jones/100 5.00 12.00
109 Jermichael Finley/499 3.00 8.00
112 Amobi Okoye/499 3.00 8.00
115 DeMeco Ryans/249 5.00 12.00
129 Mike Hart/100 6.00 15.00
134 Derrick Harvey/499 3.00 8.00
139 Quentin Groves/449 3.00 8.00
140 Reggie Nelson/246 4.00 10.00
146 Kolby Smith/299 3.00 8.00
154 Davone Bess/100 5.00 12.00
157 Jake Long/499 3.00 8.00
167 John David Booty/199 5.00 12.00
168 Sidney Rice/75 5.00 12.00
171 Brandon Meriweather/499 3.00 8.00
174 LaMont Jordan/190 4.00 10.00
178 Terrence Wheatley/499 3.00 8.00
181 Adrian Arrington/214 4.00 10.00
182 Devery Henderson/499 3.00 8.00
187 Marques Colston/50 5.00 12.00
198 Kenny Phillips/499 3.00 8.00
209 Vernon Gholston /199 4.00 10.00
210 Chaz Schilens/499 3.00 8.00
215 Michael Bush/100 5.00 12.00
223 Greg Lewis/150 4.00 10.00
227 Stewart Bradley/126 4.00 10.00
241 Jacob Hester/499 3.00 8.00
249 Josh Morgan/263 3.00 8.00
264 Antonio Pittman/47 5.00 12.00
265 Chris Long/368 4.00 10.00
267 Keenan Burton/493 3.00 8.00
275 Dexter Jackson/499 3.00 8.00
277 Gaines Adams/499 3.00 8.00
292 Chris Horton/499 4.00 10.00
295 Devin Thomas/236 4.00 10.00
298 Ladell Betts/150 4.00 10.00
302 Aaron Curry/99 6.00 15.00
303 Aaron Kelly/799 2.50 6.00
306 Andre Brown/99 5.00 12.00
310 Austin Collie/599 2.50 6.00
311 B.J. Raji/299 6.00 15.00
312 Brandon Gibson/399 3.00 8.00
313 Brandon Pettigrew/99 4.00 10.00
314 Brandon Tate/99 5.00 12.00
315 Brian Cushing/99 4.00 10.00
317 Brian Orakpo/99 5.00 12.00
318 Brian Robiskie/99 4.00 10.00
319 Brooks Foster/499 2.50 6.00
320 Cameron Morrah/499 2.50 6.00
321 Cedric Peerman/99 4.00 10.00
322 Chase Coffman/99 4.00 10.00
324 Clay Matthews/99 20.00 50.00
325 Clint Sintim/99 4.00 10.00
326 Cornelius Ingram/499 2.50 6.00
329 Darius Passmore/999 2.50 6.00
332 Demetrius Byrd/499 3.00 8.00
333 Deon Butler/599 2.50 6.00
334 Derrick Williams/99 4.00 10.00
335 Devin Moore/799 2.50 6.00
336 Dominique Edison/599 2.50 6.00
339 Everette Brown/99 4.00 10.00
341 Glen Coffee/99 4.00 10.00
342 Graham Harrell/199 10.00 25.00
344 Hunter Cantwell/799 2.50 6.00
346 James Casey/399 3.00 8.00
348 James Laurinaitis/99 4.00 10.00
349 Jared Cook/299 3.00 8.00
350 Jarett Dillard/399 2.50 6.00
351 Jason Smith/99 4.00 10.00
352 Javon Ringer/99 4.00 10.00
353 Jeremiah Johnson/511 2.50 6.00
356 John Parker Wilson/99 4.00 10.00
357 Johnny Knox/299 3.00 8.00
358 Josh Freeman/99 4.00 10.00
362 Kenny McKinley/499 2.50 6.00

363 Kevin Ogletree/799 3.00 8.00
365 Kory Sheets/799 3.00 8.00
366 Larry English/99 5.00 12.00
367 LeSean McCoy/99 10.00 25.00
369 Malcolm Jenkins/99 4.00 10.00
370 Mark Sanchez/45 20.00 50.00
372 Michael Crabtree/199 5.00 12.00
373 Mike Goodson/599 3.00 8.00
374 Mike Thomas/99 4.00 10.00
375 Mike Wallace/599 4.00 10.00
376 Mohamed Massaquoi/99 4.00 10.00
377 Nate Davis/99 4.00 10.00
378 Nathan Brown/299 3.00 8.00
379 P.J. Hill/799 2.50 6.00
380 Pat White/99 5.00 12.00
382 Patrick Turner/599 2.50 6.00
383 Percy Harvin/99 4.00 10.00
384 Quan Cosby/799 2.50 6.00
385 Quinn Johnson/599 2.50 6.00
387 Ramses Barden/99 4.00 10.00
388 Rashad Jennings/99 5.00 12.00
389 Rey Maualuga/99 6.00 15.00
390 Rhett Bomar/99 4.00 10.00
392 Shawn Nelson/399 2.50 6.00
394 Stephen McGee/99 4.00 10.00
395 Tom Brandstater/99 5.00 12.00
396 Tony Fiammetta/599 2.50 6.00
397 Travis Beckum/499 2.50 6.00
398 Tyrell Sutton/590 2.50 6.00
399 Tyson Jackson/99 4.00 10.00
400 Vontae Davis/199 3.00 8.00

2009 Score Inscriptions Autographs Gold Zone

1-300 VET PRINT RUN 18-50
301-400 ROOKIE PRINT RUN 50
3 Dominique Rodgers-Cromartie/50 5.00 12.00
10 Chris Houston/50 5.00 12.00
12 Harry Douglas/50 5.00 12.00
19 Demetrius Williams/50 5.00 12.00
25 Ray Rice/50 5.00 12.00
29 Derek Fine/50 5.00 12.00
30 Fred Jackson/50 6.00 15.00
31 James Hardy/50 6.00 15.00
33 Leodis McKelvin/50 5.00 12.00
35 Paul Posluszny/50 5.00 12.00
36 Steve Johnson/50 10.00 25.00
38 Charles Godfrey/50 5.00 12.00
40 Dante Rosario/50 5.00 12.00
43 Jon Beason/44 5.00 12.00
51 Earl Bennett/50 6.00 15.00
56 Andre Caldwell/50 5.00 12.00
61 Jerome Simpson/50 5.00 12.00
70 Josh Cribbs/50 12.00 30.00
78 Patrick Crayton/50 5.00 12.00
90 Peyton Hillis/50 12.00 30.00
96 Jerome Felton/50 5.00 12.00
97 Jordon Dizon/50 5.00 12.00
100 Rudi Johnson/50 5.00 12.00
108 James Jones/50 5.00 12.00
109 Jermichael Finley/50 5.00 12.00
112 Amobi Okoye/50 5.00 12.00
115 DeMeco Ryans/50 6.00 15.00
121 Steve Slaton/50 5.00 12.00
129 Mike Hart/50 6.00 15.00
134 Derrick Harvey/50 5.00 12.00
139 Quentin Groves/50 5.00 12.00
140 Reggie Nelson/50 5.00 12.00
145 Jamaal Charles/50 6.00 15.00
146 Kolby Smith/50 5.00 12.00
150 Tyler Thigpen/50 5.00 12.00
152 Chad Henne/50 6.00 15.00
154 Davone Bess/50 5.00 12.00
157 Jake Long/50 5.00 12.00
165 Erin Henderson/50 5.00 12.00
167 John David Booty/50 6.00 15.00
168 Sidney Rice/50 5.00 12.00
169 Tarvaris Jackson/50 6.00 15.00
171 Brandon Meriweather/50 5.00 12.00
174 LaMont Jordan/50 5.00 12.00
178 Terrence Wheatley/50 5.00 12.00
181 Adrian Arrington/50 5.00 12.00
182 Devery Henderson/50 5.00 12.00
187 Marques Colston/50 5.00 12.00
188 Pierre Thomas/50 5.00 12.00
198 Kenny Phillips/50 5.00 12.00
203 Dustin Keller/50 5.00 12.00
209 Vernon Gholston/50 5.00 12.00
210 Chaz Schilens/50 5.00 12.00
215 Michael Bush/50 5.00 12.00
227 Stewart Bradley/50 5.00 12.00
234 Rashard Mendenhall/50 5.00 12.00
240 Eric Weddle/50 5.00 12.00
241 Jacob Hester/50 5.00 12.00
249 Josh Morgan/50 5.00 12.00
252 Reggie Smith/28 6.00 15.00
256 John Carlson/50 6.00 15.00
262 Owen Schmitt/50 5.00 12.00
264 Antonio Pittman/50 5.00 12.00
265 Chris Long/50 6.00 15.00
267 Keenan Burton/50 5.00 12.00
273 Aqib Talib/50 5.00 12.00
275 Dexter Jackson/50 5.00 12.00
277 Gaines Adams/50 5.00 12.00
292 Chris Horton/50 6.00 15.00
295 Devin Thomas/50 5.00 12.00
298 Ladell Betts/50 5.00 12.00
302 Aaron Curry/50 6.00 15.00
303 Aaron Kelly/50 4.00 10.00
306 Andre Brown/50 5.00 12.00
310 Austin Collie/50 4.00 10.00
311 B.J. Raji/50 8.00 20.00
312 Brandon Gibson/50 5.00 12.00
313 Brandon Pettigrew/50 4.00 10.00
314 Brandon Tate/50 5.00 12.00
315 Brian Cushing/50 4.00 10.00
317 Brian Orakpo/50 5.00 12.00
318 Brian Robiskie/50 4.00 10.00
319 Brooks Foster/50 4.00 10.00
320 Cameron Morrah/50 4.00 10.00
321 Cedric Peerman/50 4.00 10.00
322 Chase Coffman/50 4.00 10.00
323 Chris Wells/50 4.00 10.00
324 Clay Matthews/50 40.00 80.00
325 Clint Sintim/50 4.00 10.00
326 Cornelius Ingram/50 4.00 10.00
329 Darius Passmore/50 4.00 10.00
330 Darrius Heyward-Bey/50 6.00 15.00
332 Demetrius Byrd/50 5.00 12.00
333 Deon Butler/50 4.00 10.00
334 Derrick Williams/50 4.00 10.00
335 Devin Moore/50 4.00 10.00
336 Dominique Edison/50 4.00 10.00
337 Donald Brown/50 4.00 10.00
339 Everette Brown/50 4.00 10.00
341 Glen Coffee/50 4.00 10.00
342 Graham Harrell/50 10.00 25.00
343 Hakeem Nicks/50 5.00 12.00
344 Hunter Cantwell/50 4.00 10.00
346 James Casey/50 5.00 12.00
348 James Laurinaitis/50 4.00 10.00
349 Jared Cook/50 5.00 12.00
350 Jarett Dillard/50 4.00 10.00
351 Jason Smith/50 4.00 10.00
352 Javon Ringer/50 4.00 10.00
353 Jeremiah Johnson/50 4.00 10.00
355 Jeremy Maclin/50 5.00 12.00
356 John Parker Wilson/50 4.00 10.00
357 Johnny Knox/50 5.00 12.00
358 Josh Freeman/50 4.00 10.00
359 Juaquin Iglesias/50 4.00 10.00
361 Kenny Britt/50 6.00 15.00
362 Kenny McKinley/50 4.00 10.00
363 Kevin Ogletree/50 5.00 12.00
364 Knowshon Moreno/50 4.00 10.00
365 Kory Sheets/50 5.00 12.00
366 Larry English/50 5.00 12.00
367 LeSean McCoy/50 10.00 25.00
369 Malcolm Jenkins/50 4.00 10.00
370 Mark Sanchez/50 20.00 50.00
371 Matthew Stafford/50 50.00 120.00
372 Michael Crabtree/50 6.00 15.00
373 Mike Goodson/50 5.00 12.00
374 Mike Thomas/50 4.00 10.00
375 Mike Wallace/50 6.00 15.00
376 Mohamed Massaquoi/50 4.00 10.00
377 Nate Davis/50 4.00 10.00
378 Nathan Brown/50 5.00 12.00
379 P.J. Hill/50 4.00 10.00
380 Pat White/50 5.00 12.00
382 Patrick Turner/50 4.00 10.00
383 Percy Harvin/50 4.00 10.00
384 Quan Cosby/50 4.00 10.00
385 Quinn Johnson/50 4.00 10.00
387 Ramses Barden/50 4.00 10.00
388 Rashad Jennings/50 5.00 12.00
389 Rey Maualuga/50 6.00 15.00
390 Rhett Bomar/50 4.00 10.00
392 Shawn Nelson/50 4.00 10.00
393 Shonn Greene/50 4.00 10.00
394 Stephen McGee/50 4.00 10.00
395 Tom Brandstater/50 5.00 12.00
396 Tony Fiammetta/50 4.00 10.00
397 Travis Beckum/50 4.00 10.00
398 Tyrell Sutton/50 4.00 10.00
399 Tyson Jackson/50 4.00 10.00
400 Vontae Davis/50 4.00 10.00

2009 Score Inscriptions Autographs Red Zone

1-300 VET PRINT RUN 5-30
*ROOKIE/30: .5X TO 1.2X GOLD ZONE AU
301-400 ROOKIE PRINT RUN 30
SERIAL #'d UNDER 15 NOT PRICED
3 Dominique Rodgers-Cromartie/30 6.00 15.00
9 Tim Hightower/30 6.00 15.00
10 Chris Houston/30 6.00 15.00
11 Curtis Lofton/30 6.00 15.00
12 Harry Douglas/30 6.00 15.00
13 Jerious Norwood/30 6.00 15.00
19 Demetrius Williams/30 6.00 15.00
25 Ray Rice/30 6.00 15.00
29 Derek Fine/30 6.00 15.00
30 Fred Jackson/30 8.00 20.00
33 Leodis McKelvin/30 5.00 12.00
35 Paul Posluszny/30 6.00 15.00
36 Steve Johnson/30 12.00 30.00
37 Trent Edwards/30 6.00 15.00
38 Charles Godfrey/30 6.00 15.00
40 Dante Rosario/30 6.00 15.00
43 Jon Beason/30 6.00 15.00
51 Earl Bennett/30 8.00 20.00
56 Andre Caldwell/30 6.00 15.00
61 Jerome Simpson/30 6.00 15.00
62 Keith Rivers/30 6.00 15.00
64 T.J. Houshmandzadeh/30 6.00 15.00
70 Josh Cribbs/30 15.00 40.00
78 Patrick Crayton/30 6.00 15.00
88 Eddie Royal/30 6.00 15.00
90 Peyton Hillis/30 25.00 50.00
96 Jerome Felton/30 6.00 15.00
97 Jordon Dizon/30 6.00 15.00
98 Kevin Smith/30 6.00 15.00
100 Rudi Johnson/30 6.00 15.00
103 A.J. Hawk/30 6.00 15.00
107 Greg Jennings/30 6.00 15.00
109 Jermichael Finley/30 6.00 15.00
112 Amobi Okoye/30 6.00 15.00
115 DeMeco Ryans/30 8.00 20.00
121 Steve Slaton/20 6.00 15.00
129 Mike Hart/30 8.00 20.00
134 Derrick Harvey/30 6.00 15.00
139 Quentin Groves/30 6.00 15.00
140 Reggie Nelson/30 6.00 15.00
145 Jamaal Charles/30 8.00 20.00
146 Kolby Smith/30 6.00 15.00
147 Larry Johnson/30 6.00 15.00
150 Tyler Thigpen/30 6.00 15.00
154 Davone Bess/30 6.00 15.00
157 Jake Long/30 6.00 15.00
165 Erin Henderson/30 6.00 15.00
167 John David Booty/30 8.00 20.00
168 Sidney Rice/30 6.00 15.00
169 Tarvaris Jackson/30 8.00 20.00
171 Brandon Meriweather/30 6.00 15.00
172 Jerod Mayo/30 8.00 20.00
174 LaMont Jordan/20 6.00 15.00
178 Terrence Wheatley/30 6.00 15.00
181 Adrian Arrington/30 6.00 15.00
182 Devery Henderson/30 6.00 15.00
187 Marques Colston/30 6.00 15.00
188 Pierre Thomas/30 6.00 15.00
198 Kenny Phillips/30 6.00 15.00
203 Dustin Keller/30 6.00 15.00
209 Vernon Gholston /30 6.00 15.00
210 Chaz Schilens/30 6.00 15.00
214 Justin Fargas/30 6.00 15.00
215 Michael Bush/30 6.00 15.00
218 Zach Miller/30 6.00 15.00
224 Hank Baskett/30 6.00 15.00
227 Stewart Bradley/30 6.00 15.00
234 Rashard Mendenhall/15 12.00 30.00
241 Jacob Hester/30 6.00 15.00
249 Josh Morgan/30 6.00 15.00
251 Patrick Willis/30 8.00 20.00
252 Reggie Smith/30 6.00 15.00
254 Vernon Davis/15 12.00 30.00
256 John Carlson/30 8.00 20.00
262 Owen Schmitt/30 6.00 15.00
264 Antonio Pittman/30 6.00 15.00
265 Chris Long/30 8.00 20.00
266 Donnie Avery/30 6.00 15.00
267 Keenan Burton/30 6.00 15.00
273 Aqib Talib/30 6.00 15.00
275 Dexter Jackson/30 6.00 15.00
277 Gaines Adams/30 6.00 15.00
292 Chris Horton/30 8.00 20.00
294 Colt Brennan/30 8.00 20.00
295 Devin Thomas/30 6.00 15.00
370 Mark Sanchez/30 15.00 40.00
371 Matthew Stafford/30 50.00 120.00
372 Michael Crabtree/30 8.00 20.00

2009 Score Inscriptions Franchise

STATED PRINT RUN 499 SER.#'d SETS
*ART.PROOF/32: 1.5X TO 4X BASIC INSERTS
*GOLD ZONE/50: 1.2X TO 3X BASIC INSERTS
*RED ZONE/30: 1.5X TO 4X BASIC INSERTS
*SCORECARD/100: .8X TO 2X BASIC INSERTS
1 Adrian Peterson 1.00 2.50
2 Andre Johnson .75 2.00
3 Brady Quinn .60 1.50
4 Brandon Jacobs .60 1.50
5 Brandon Marshall .75 2.00
6 Braylon Edwards .60 1.50
7 Brian Westbrook .60 1.50
8 Calvin Johnson 1.00 2.50
9 Clinton Portis .60 1.50
10 DeAngelo Williams .60 1.50
11 Frank Gore .75 2.00
12 Greg Jennings .60 1.50
13 Larry Fitzgerald .75 2.00
14 Lee Evans .75 2.00
15 Marion Barber .75 2.00
16 Maurice Jones-Drew .60 1.50
17 Philip Rivers 1.00 2.50
18 Roddy White .60 1.50
19 Santonio Holmes .60 1.50
20 Dwayne Bowe .75 2.00

2009 Score Inscriptions Future Franchise

STATED PRINT RUN 499 SER.#'d SETS
*ART.PROOF/32: 1.5X TO 4X BASIC INSERTS
*GOLD ZONE/50: 1.2X TO 3X BASIC INSERTS
*RED ZONE/30: 1.5X TO 4X BASIC INSERTS
*SCORECARD/100: .8X TO 2X BASIC INSERTS
1 Brian Brohm .60 1.50
2 Chad Henne .75 2.00
3 Chris Johnson .60 1.50
4 Colt Brennan .75 2.00
5 Darren McFadden 1.00 2.50
6 Derrick Ward .60 1.50
7 DeSean Jackson .75 2.00
8 Eddie Royal .60 1.50
9 Erik Ainge .75 2.00
10 Joe Flacco .75 2.00
11 John David Booty .75 2.00
12 Jonathan Stewart .60 1.50
13 Kevin Smith .60 1.50
14 Matt Cassel .60 1.50
15 Matt Forte .60 1.50
16 Matt Ryan .75 2.00
17 Rashard Mendenhall .60 1.50
18 Ray Rice .60 1.50
19 Steve Slaton .60 1.50
20 Tashard Choice .60 1.50

2009 Score Inscriptions Hot Rookies

STATED PRINT RUN 499 SER.#'d SETS
*ART.PROOF/32: 1X TO 2.5X BASIC INSERTS
*GOLD ZONE/50: .8X TO 2X BASIC INSERTS
*RED ZONE/30: 1X TO 2.5X BASIC INSERTS
*SCORECARD/100: .6X TO 1.5X BASIC INSERTS
1 Aaron Curry 1.00 2.50
2 Brandon Pettigrew .60 1.50
3 Brandon Tate .75 2.00
4 Brian Robiskie .60 1.50
5 Chris Wells .60 1.50
6 Darrius Heyward-Bey 1.00 2.50
7 Deon Butler .60 1.50
8 Derrick Williams .60 1.50
10 Glen Coffee .60 1.50
11 Hakeem Nicks .75 2.00
12 Jeremy Maclin .75 2.00
13 Josh Freeman .60 1.50
14 Juaquin Iglesias .60 1.50
15 Kenny Britt 1.00 2.50
16 Knowshon Moreno .60 1.50
17 LeSean McCoy 1.50 4.00
18 Mark Sanchez .60 1.50
19 Matthew Stafford 3.00 8.00
20 Michael Crabtree 1.00 2.50
21 Mike Thomas .60 1.50
22 Mike Wallace 1.00 2.50
23 Mohamed Massaquoi .60 1.50
24 Pat White .75 2.00
25 Patrick Turner .60 1.50
26 Percy Harvin .60 1.50
27 Ramses Barden .60 1.50
28 Shonn Greene .60 1.50
29 Stephen McGee .60 1.50
30 Tyson Jackson .60 1.50

2009 Score Inscriptions Hot Rookies Autographs Gold Zone

GOLD ZONE PRINT RUN 50
*RED ZONE/23-30: .5X TO 1.2X GOLD ZONE/50
1 Aaron Curry 6.00 15.00
2 Brandon Pettigrew 4.00 10.00
3 Brandon Tate 5.00 12.00
4 Brian Robiskie 4.00 10.00
5 Chris Wells 12.00 30.00
6 Darrius Heyward-Bey 6.00 15.00
7 Deon Butler 4.00 10.00
8 Derrick Williams 4.00 10.00
10 Glen Coffee 4.00 10.00
11 Hakeem Nicks 5.00 12.00
12 Jeremy Maclin 5.00 12.00
13 Josh Freeman 4.00 10.00
14 Juaquin Iglesias 4.00 10.00
15 Kenny Britt 6.00 15.00
16 Knowshon Moreno 4.00 10.00
17 LeSean McCoy 10.00 25.00
18 Mark Sanchez 40.00 80.00
19 Matthew Stafford 25.00 60.00
20 Michael Crabtree 6.00 15.00
21 Mike Thomas 4.00 10.00
22 Mike Wallace 6.00 15.00
23 Mohamed Massaquoi 4.00 10.00
24 Pat White 5.00 12.00
25 Patrick Turner 4.00 10.00
26 Percy Harvin 4.00 10.00
27 Ramses Barden 4.00 10.00
28 Shonn Greene 4.00 10.00
29 Stephen McGee 4.00 10.00
30 Tyson Jackson 4.00 10.00

2009 Score Inscriptions Young Stars

STATED PRINT RUN 499 SER.#'d SETS
*ART.PROOF/32: 1.5X TO 4X BASIC INSERTS
*GOLD ZONE/50: 1.2X TO 3X BASIC INSERTS
*RED ZONE/30: 1.5X TO 4X BASIC INSERTS
*SCORECARD/100: .8X TO 2X BASIC INSERTS
1 Antoine Cason .60 1.50
2 Aqib Talib .60 1.50
3 Brandon Flowers .60 1.50
4 Chris Horton .75 2.00
5 Dan Connor .60 1.50
6 Davone Bess .60 1.50
7 Donnie Avery .60 1.50
8 Dustin Keller .60 1.50
9 Dwight Lowery .60 1.50
10 Felix Jones .60 1.50
11 Jerod Mayo .75 2.00
12 John Carlson .75 2.00
13 Josh Morgan .60 1.50
14 Leodis McKelvin .60 1.50
15 Le'Ron McClain .75 2.00
16 Malcolm Kelly .60 1.50
17 Martellus Bennett .60 1.50
18 Ryan Torain .60 1.50
19 Steve Johnson .75 2.00
20 Tim Hightower .60 1.50

2009 Score National Convention VIP Promos

Cards from this set were available to VIP guests at the 2009 National Sports Collectors Convention in Cleveland, Ohio. Each card was produced in the style of the 1989 Score product.

COMPLETE SET (6) 10.00 20.00
1 Mark Sanchez .50 1.25
2 Matthew Stafford 2.50 6.00
3 Matt Ryan 1.00 2.50
4 Larry Fitzgerald 1.00 2.50
5 Ben Roethlisberger 1.25 3.00
6 Brady Quinn .75 2.00

2002 Score QBC Materials

Issued in retail only blister packs, each card was slabbed by SCD Authentic and labeled as "Untouched." Packs contained one game-used jersey card or signed card and carried an initial SRP of $19.99. Signed cards were issued for the following players: Steve Young, Warren Moon, Jake Plummer, Aaron Brooks, and John Elway.

AUTOS TOO SCARCE TO PRICE
1 Donovan McNabb JSY 2.50 6.00
2 Jake Plummer JSY 2.00 5.00
3 Jeff Garcia JSY 2.00 5.00
4 Peyton Manning JSY 8.00 20.00
5 Rob Johnson JSY 2.50 6.00
6 Trent Dilfer JSY 2.00 5.00
7 Bernie Kosar JSY 2.50 6.00
8 Boomer Esiason JSY 2.50 6.00
9 Jim Everett JSY 2.50 6.00
10 Jim Kelly JSY 3.00 8.00
11 Steve Young JSY 4.00 10.00
12 Warren Moon JSY 3.00 8.00
13 Donovan McNabb FB 2.50 6.00
14 Jeff Garcia FB 2.00 5.00
15 Peyton Manning FB 8.00 20.00
16 Boomer Esiason FB 2.50 6.00
17 Jim Kelly FB 3.00 8.00
18 Steve Young FB 4.00 10.00
19 Warren Moon FB 3.00 8.00
20 Peyton Manning JSY 8.00 20.00
21 Doug Flutie JSY 2.50 6.00
22 Jeff Garcia JSY 2.00 5.00
23 Jake Plummer JSY 2.00 5.00
24 Aaron Brooks JSY 2.00 5.00
25 John Elway JSY 5.00 12.00
26 Boomer Esiason JSY 2.50 6.00
27 Warren Moon JSY 3.00 8.00
28 Jim Everett JSY 2.50 6.00
29 John Elway FB 5.00 12.00
30 Warren Moon FB 3.00 8.00
31 Jake Plummer FB 2.00 5.00
32 Peyton Manning FB 8.00 20.00
33 Jeff Garcia FB 2.00 5.00
34 Aaron Brooks FB 2.00 5.00
35 Doug Flutie FB 2.50 6.00
36 Boomer Esiason FB 2.50 6.00
37 Ken O'Brien JSY 2.00 5.00

1994 Score Board National Promos

Distributed during the 1994 National Sports Collectors Convention, this 20-card standard-size multi-sport set features four subsets: Salute to 1994 Draft Stars (1-5), Centers of Attention (6-9), Texas Heroes (10-13, 20), and Salute to Racing's Greatest (14-18). The borderless fronts feature color action cutouts on multi-colored metallic backgrounds. The players name, position, and team name appear randomly placed on arcs. The borderless backs feature a color head shot on a ghosted backgound. The players name and biography appear at the top with the player's stats and profile at the bottom. The cards are numbered on the back with an "NC" prefix. The sets were given away to attendees at Classic's National Convention Party. Each set included a certificate of authenticity, giving the set serial number out of a total of 9,900 sets produced. There were five different checklist cards created using the fronts of other cards in the set. The complete set price includes only one of the checklist cards.

COMPLETE SET (20) 20.00 40.00
10 Troy Aikman 1.00 2.50
12 Emmitt Smith 1.25 3.00
20A Troy Aikman CL 1.25 2.50
20E Emmitt Smith CL 1.25 3.00

1996-97 Score Board All Sport PPF

The 1996-97 All Sport Past Present and Future set was issued in two series in six-card packs. The product contains original vintage and rookie cards of the top athletes from baseball, basketball, football and hockey as well as new cards of tomorrow's stars from each sport. Release date for series one was October 1996; series two was February 1997. There was also a gold parallel produced for this set. Series one gold cards were inserted 1:10 packs while series two had gold cards inserted at a 1:5 ratio.

COMPLETE SET (200) 6.00 15.00
30 Troy Aikman .30 .75
31 Kerry Collins .15 .40
32 Steve Young .25 .60
33 Kordell Stewart .15 .40
34 Kevin Hardy .05 .15
35 Joey Galloway .15 .40
36 Simeon Rice .07 .20
37 Marcus Coleman .05 .15
38 Eric Moulds .20 .50
39 Ray Farmer .05 .15
40 Chris Darkins .05 .15
41 Amani Toomer .15 .40
42 Daryl Gardener .05 .15
43 Bobby Engram .08 .25
44 Stepfret Williams .07 .20
45 Eddie George .40 1.00
46 Tony Brackens .05 .15
47 Cedric Jones .05 .15
48 Jason Dunn .07 .20
49 Mike Alstott .20 .50
51 Danny Kanell .07 .20
52 Andre Johnson .07 .20
53 Rickey Dudley .07 .20
54 Jeff Hartings .07 .20
55 Regan Upshaw .05 .15
56 Alex Molden .07 .20
57 Terry Glenn .15 .40
58 Alex Van Dyke .07 .20
59 Karim Abdul-Jabbar .08 .25
87 Emmitt Smith .50 1.25
88 Drew Bledsoe .20 .50
89 Keyshawn Johnson .20 .50
90 Marshall Faulk .20 .50
91 Steve Young .25 .60
92 Lawrence Phillips .08 .25
93 Terry Glenn .15 .40
100 Troy Aikman CL (51-100) .15 .40
126 Emmitt Smith .50 1.25
127 Drew Bledsoe .20 .50
128 Steve McNair .15 .40
129 Marshall Faulk .20 .50
130 Keyshawn Johnson .20 .50
131 Lawrence Phillips .08 .25
132 Leeland McElroy .05 .15
133 Tony Banks .08 .25
134 Derrick Mayes .07 .20
135 Jonathan Ogden .30 .75
136 Zach Thomas .30 .75
137 Tim Biakabutuka .08 .25
138 Ray Mickens .05 .15
139 Ray Lewis .50 1.25
140 Marco Battaglia .05 .15
141 John Mobley .05 .15
142 Marvin Harrison .30 .75
143 Duane Clemons .07 .20
144 Lance Johnstone .07 .20
145 Eddie Kennison .10 .30
146 Bobby Hoying .10 .30
147 Brett Favre .40 1.00
148 Reggie Brown .05 .15
149 Walt Harris .05 .15
151 Marcus Jones .05 .15
152 Je'Rod Cherry .05 .15
153 Brian Dawkins .15 .40
154 Johnny McWilliams .07 .20
155 Brian Roche .05 .15
156 Muhsin Muhammad .15 .40
157 Lawyer Milloy .08 .25
158 Jermane Mayberry .05 .15
159 DeRon Jenkins .07 .20
187 Steve Young .25 .60
188 Kerry Collins .15 .40
189 Kevin Hardy .05 .15
190 Kordell Stewart .15 .40
191 Joey Galloway .15 .40
192 Simeon Rice .08 .25
193 Eddie George .40 1.00
194 Brett Favre .40 1.00
195 Emmitt Smith .50 1.25
200 Eddie George CL .15 .40

1996-97 Score Board All Sport PPF Gold

*GOLDS: 1.2X TO 3X BASIC CARDS
GOLD STATED ODDS SER.1 1:10/SER.2 1:5

1996-97 Score Board All Sport PPF Retro

Randomly inserted in series one packs at a rate of one in 35, this 10-card set was printed on old-style card stock.

COMPLETE SET (10) 12.00 30.00
R2 Keyshawn Johnson 1.00 2.50
R4 Emmitt Smith 3.00 8.00
R7 Troy Aikman 2.00 5.00
R9 Lawrence Phillips .40 2.00

1996-97 Score Board All Sport PPF Revivals

Randomly inserted in series two packs at a rate of one in 35, this 10-card set was printed on old-style card stock.

COMPLETE SET (10) 12.00 30.00
REV6 Emmitt Smith 2.50 6.00
REV7 Keyshawn Johnson 1.00 2.50
REV8 Eddie George 1.25 3.00
REV9 Brett Favre 3.00 8.00

1996-97 Score Board Autographed Collection

Each box of Score Board Autographed Collection contains 16 packs containing six cards. The 50-card regular set includes top athletes from all four major team sports. According to Score Board, a total of 1,500 sequentially numbered cases were produced.

COMPLETE SET (50) 5.00 12.00
18 Emmitt Smith .50 1.25
19 Kordell Stewart .15 .40
20 Lawrence Phillips .07 .20
21 Kerry Collins .15 .40
22 Drew Bledsoe .20 .50
23 Marshall Faulk .25 .60
24 Steve Young .25 .60
25 Joey Galloway .20 .50
26 Keyshawn Johnson .20 .50
27 Eddie George .75 2.00
28 Karim Abdul-Jabbar .07 .20
29 Terry Glenn .20 .50
30 Marvin Harrison .30 .75
31 Tim Biakabutuka .10 .30
32 Leeland McElroy .07 .20
33 Simeon Rice .07 .20
34 Kevin Hardy .07 .20
35 Rickey Dudley .07 .20
36 Zach Thomas .30 .75
37 Bobby Engram .07 .20

1996-97 Score Board Autographed Collection Autographs

Each box of Autographed Collection contains an average of four autographed cards. There are two different varieties: silver foil stamped cards with no individual serial numbering inserted at a rate of 1:7 packs, and Gold foil serial numbered autographs inserted at a rate of 1:16 packs.

1 Karim Abdul-Jabbar 2.00 5.00
5 Marco Battaglia 1.50 4.00
8 Michael Cheever 1.50 4.00
11 Chris Darkins 1.50 4.00
14 Donnie Edwards 1.50 4.00
15 Ray Farmer 1.50 4.00
17 Eddie George 15.00 40.00
19 Kevin Hardy 1.50 4.00
21 Jimmy Herndon 1.50 4.00
22 Bobby Hoying 2.00 5.00
24 Dietrich Jells 2.00 5.00
25 DeRon Jenkins 1.50 4.00
26 Andre Johnson 1.50 4.00
27 Danny Kanell 2.00 5.00
31 Derrick Mayes 2.00 5.00
33 Leeland McElroy 1.50 4.00
34 Ray Mickens 1.50 4.00
35 Roman Oben 1.50 4.00
36 Jason Odom 1.50 4.00
41 Jamain Stephens 1.50 4.00
42 Matt Stevens 1.50 4.00
43 Kordell Stewart 8.00 20.00
44 Zach Thomas 12.00 25.00

1996-97 Score Board Autographed Collection Autographs Gold

*UNLISTED GOLD: .6X TO 1.5X BASIC AU

1996-97 Score Board Autographed Collection Game Breakers

This 30-card insert set was printed on metallic stock and has two versions-- regular and gold. The insertion ratio is 1:10 packs for regular inserts and 1:50 for the gold foil version.

COMPLETE SET (30) 25.00 60.00
*GOLD: .8X TO 2X BASIC INSERTS
GB14 Emmitt Smith 3.00 8.00
GB15 Kordell Stewart 1.00 2.50
GB16 Kevin Hardy .60 1.50
GB17 Kerry Collins .75 2.00
GB18 Drew Bledsoe 1.25 3.00
GB19 Marshall Faulk 1.25 3.00
GB20 Steve Young 1.50 4.00
GB21 Lawrence Phillips .60 1.50
GB22 Keyshawn Johnson 1.50 4.00
GB23 Eddie George 1.50 4.00
GB24 Karim Abdul-Jabbar .60 1.50
GB25 Terry Glenn 1.00 2.50
GB26 Marvin Harrison 2.00 5.00
GB27 Tim Biakabutuka .60 1.50

1997-98 Score Board Autographed Collection

The 1998 Autographed Collection set was issued in one series totaling 50 cards with players from baseball, basketball, football and hockey. The product's major draw was an average of five autographed cards and one memorabilia redemption card per 18-pack box. The regular autographs were inserted 1:4.5 packs, the Blue Ribbon autographs were inserted 1:18 packs. The one-per box memorabilia redemption cards were not all redeemed due to the fact that Score Board, Inc. filed for bankruptcy a few months after the product's release. Score Board also released a "Strongbox Collection" that original retailed for around $125. Each Strongbox included a parallel of this 50-card set, one star player autographed baseball with holder, one star player autographed 8" x 10", one Athletic Excellence card and One Sports City USA card.

COMPLETE SET (50) 5.00 12.00
2 Brett Favre .60 1.50
6 Emmitt Smith .50 1.25
8 Steve Young .20 .50
10 Ike Hilliard .15 .40
13 Darrell Russell .07 .20
17 Jake Plummer .20 .50
19 Danny Wuerffel .10 .30
21 Kordell Stewart .15 .40
26 Warrick Dunn .30 .75
29 Rae Carruth .07 .20
31 Troy Aikman .25 .60
33 Peter Boulware .08 .25
34 David LaFleur .07 .20
35 Jim Druckenmiller .07 .20
38 Yatil Green .07 .20
40 Orlando Pace .08 .25
42 Byron Hanspard .08 .25
43 Troy Davis .07 .20
44 Reidel Anthony .07 .20
46 Tony Banks .10 .30
48 Tony Gonzalez .20 .50

1997-98 Score Board Autographed Collection Strongbox

*STRONGBOX: .8X TO 2X BASIC CARDS

1997-98 Score Board Autographed Collection Athletic Excellence

These 3 1/2" x 5" cards, were inserted one per Score Board "Strongbox Collection" box that originally retailed for around $125. Each Strongbox also included a parallel of the 1998 Autograph Collection 50 card set, one star player autographed baseball with holder, one star player autographed 8" x 10" and one Sports City USA card. Each card is sequentially numbered out of 750.

COMPLETE SET (12) 10.00 25.00
AE3 Warrick Dunn 1.50 4.00
AE7 Darrell Russell .75 2.00

1997-98 Score Board Autographed Collection Autographs

One autographed card was available in one in every 4.5 Score Board Autograph Collection packs. The cards have a circular player photograph in the middle with a white oval below that includes a player's autograph. The card backs read, "Congratulations! You have received an authentic Score Board autographed card." There were also Kerry Wood and Greg Jones cards produced that appear on the marketplace later, although not inserted into packs. The cards are unnumbered and listed below in alphabetical order.

1 John Allred FB 1.50 4.00
2 Darnell Autry FB 1.50 4.00
3 Pat Barnes FB 1.50 4.00
8 Jim Druckenmiller FB 1.50 4.00
12 Greg Jones FB 1.50 4.00
14 Dexter McCleon FB 1.50 4.00
15 Brad Otton FB 1.50 4.00
18 Jake Plummer FB 8.00 20.00
19 Scot Pollard FB 2.50 6.00
20 Antowain Smith FB 4.00 10.00
23 Reinard Wilson FB 1.50 4.00

1997-98 Score Board Autographed Collection Blue Ribbon Autographs

One Blue Ribbon autographed card was available in one in every 18 Score Board Autograph Collection packs. The cards have a circular player photograph with a blue ribbon border in the middle with a white oval below that includes a player's autograph. The cards are hand numbered out of the amounts listed below in the upper right hand corner. The card backs read, "Congratulations! You have received an authentic Score Board autographed card." The cards are unnumbered and listed below in alphabetical order. A Warrick Dunn card was later released through a home shopping network show. Some Kobe Bryant cards have surfaced in un-signed form and can often be found with forged autographs on the front. No authentic Kobe signed and numbered cards are known although the Congratulations Score Board message is included on the cardbacks.

8 Eddie George/240 30.00 60.00
13 Emmitt Smith/120 75.00 150.00
15 Steve Young/139 50.00 100.00
P1 Warrick Dunn/200 5.00 12.00

1997-98 Score Board Autographed Collection Sports City USA

These multi-player, city-themed cards were inserted one in nine Autographed Collection packs. There is also a Strongbox parallel found one per Score Board "Strongbox Collection" box that originally retailed for around $125. Each Strongbox also included a parallel of the 1998 Autograph Collection 50 card set, one star player autographed baseball with holder, one star player autographed 8" x 10"and one Athletic Excellence jumbo card..

COMPLETE SET (15) 10.00 25.00
SC1 A.Foyle/J.Smith/S.Young .75 2.00
SC2 M.White/Dunn/R.Anthony .75 2.00
SC4 K.Wood/Pippen/D.Autry .60 1.50
SC5 R.Allen/B.Favre 2.00 5.00
SC7 T.Thomas/D.Staley/J.D.Drew 1.00 2.50
SC8 A.Mourning/Y.Green .50 1.25
SC9 J.Thornton/C.Billups .40 1.00
SC10 E.Smith/Aikm/Jackman 1.50 4.00
SC11 K.Stewart/R.Dome .50 1.25
SC12 W.Helms/Hanspard/E.Gray .40 1.00
SC13 S.Marbury/D.Rudd .40 1.00
SC14 J.Payton/Barber/V.Horn .75 2.00
SC15 M.Drews/B.Westbrook/Pollard .75 2.00

1997-98 Score Board Autographed Collection Sports City USA Strongbox

*STRONGBOX/600: .8X TO 2X BASIC INSERTS

1996 Score Board Lasers

The 1996 Score Board Lasers set consists of 100-cards distributed in six-card packs. Each card features a color action player photo of a top NFL player printed on 24-point foil board with special effects stamping.

COMPLETE SET (100) 8.00 20.00
1 Brett Favre .75 2.00
2 Chris Warren .07 .20
3 J.J. Stokes .15 .40
4 Barry Sanders .60 1.50
5 Ben Coates .07 .20
6 Bryan Cox .02 .10
7 Carl Pickens .07 .20
8 Cris Carter .15 .40
9 Curtis Martin .30 .75
10 Dan Marino .75 2.00
11 Dave Brown .07 .20
12 Drew Bledsoe .25 .60
13 Edgar Bennett .07 .20
14 Herman Moore .07 .20
15 Jeff Blake .15 .40
16 Jerry Rice .40 1.00
17 Jim Kelly .15 .40
18 John Elway .75 2.00
19 Junior Seau .15 .40
20 Kerry Collins .15 .40
21 Kordell Stewart .15 .40
22 Leonard Russell .02 .10
23 Mark Brunell .25 .60
24 Marshall Faulk .20 .50
25 Mike Tomczak .02 .10
26 Reggie White .15 .40
27 Ricky Watters .07 .20
28 Rod Woodson .07 .20
29 Rodney Peete .02 .10
30 Stan Humphries .07 .20
31 Steve McNair .30 .75
32 Terry Allen .07 .20
33 Thurman Thomas .15 .40
34 Troy Aikman .40 1.00
35 Vinny Testaverde .07 .20
36 Chris T. Jones .15 .40
37 Deion Sanders .20 .50
38 Eric Metcalf .07 .20
39 Erik Kramer .02 .10
40 Emmitt Smith .60 1.50
41 Gus Frerotte .07 .20
42 Shannon Sharpe .07 .20
43 Jerome Bettis .15 .40
44 Jim Harbaugh .07 .20
45 Isaac Bruce .15 .40
46 Jeff Hostetler .07 .20
47 Ki-Jana Carter .07 .20
48 Marcus Allen .15 .40
49 Neil O'Donnell .07 .20
50 Rashaan Salaam .07 .20
51 Robert Brooks .15 .40
52 Steve Bono .07 .20
53 Scott Mitchell .07 .20
54 Terrell Davis .30 .75
55 Tim Brown .15 .40
56 Troy Vincent .02 .10
57 Warren Moon .07 .20
58 Tony Martin .07 .20
59 Rodney Hampton .07 .20
60 Steve Young .30 .75
61 Rick Mirer .07 .20
62 Mark Chmura .07 .20
63 Larry Centers .07 .20
64 Ken Dilger .07 .20
65 Joey Galloway .15 .40
66 Jim Everett .02 .10
67 Chris Chandler .07 .20
68 James O. Stewart .07 .20
69 Robert Smith .07 .20
70 Tamarick Vanover .15 .40
71 Wayne Chrebet .25 .60
72 Keyshawn Johnson RC .40 1.00
73 Kevin Hardy RC .15 .40
74 Lawrence Phillips RC .15 .40
75 Jonathan Ogden RC .40 1.00
76 Terry Glenn RC .40 1.00
77 Tim Biakabutuka RC .15 .40
78 Eddie George RC .50 1.25
79 Eric Moulds RC .50 1.25
80 John Mobley RC .02 .10
81 Amani Toomer RC .40 1.00
82 Marvin Harrison RC 1.00 2.50
83 Leeland McElroy RC .07 .20
84 Rickey Dudley RC .15 .40
85 Tony Banks RC .15 .40
86 Zach Thomas RC .30 .75
87 Alex Molden RC .02 .10
88 Daryl Gardener RC .07 .20
89 Jamal Anderson RC .20 .50
90 Karim Abdul-Jabbar RC .15 .40
91 Simeon Rice RC .40 1.00
92 Walt Harris RC .02 .10
93 Bobby Engram RC .15 .40
94 Kevin Williams .02 .10
95 Sean Gilbert .02 .10
96 Kevin Greene .07 .20
97 Regan Upshaw RC .02 .10
98 Marcus Jones RC .02 .10
99 Ray Lewis RC 3.00 8.00
100 Keyshawn Johnson CL .07 .20
P1 Emmitt Smith Promo .30 .75
NNO Emmitt Smith

1996 Score Board Lasers Autographs

Randomly inserted in packs at a rate of one in 150, this seven-card set features color player images over a black shadow player image and the player's autograph in the yellow bar near the bottom. Only 400 of each card was hand-signed. A Die Cut version was also produced and numbered of 100-sets made.

STATED ODDS 1:150
*DIE CUT/100: .6X TO 1.5X BASIC AU
DIE CUT/100 ODDS 1:930
1 Troy Aikman 30.00 80.00
2 Drew Bledsoe 12.00 30.00
3 Marshall Faulk 15.00 40.00
4 Keyshawn Johnson 10.00 25.00
5 Emmitt Smith 60.00 150.00
6 Kordell Stewart 10.00 25.00
7 Steve Young 20.00 50.00

1996 Score Board Lasers Images

Randomly inserted in packs at a rate of one in seven, this 30-card set features color player photos printed over a black shadow player image with gold foil highlights on a gray ray background. The backs carry another player photo and a paragraph about the player.

COMPLETE SET (30) 20.00 50.00
STATED ODDS 1:7
I1 Steve Bono .30 .75
I2 Kerry Collins .60 1.50
I3 Tim Biakabutuka .30 .75
I4 Rashaan Salaam .30 .75
I5 Jeff Blake .40 1.00
I6 Emmitt Smith 2.50 6.00
I7 Troy Aikman 1.50 4.00
I8 Deion Sanders .75 2.00
I9 John Elway 3.00 8.00
I10 Herman Moore .30 .75
I11 Brett Favre 3.00 8.00
I12 Eddie George .60 1.50
I13 Marvin Harrison 2.00 5.00
I14 Mark Brunell .60 1.50
I15 Dan Marino 3.00 8.00
I16 Karim Abdul-Jabbar .30 .75
I17 Cris Carter .60 1.50
I18 Drew Bledsoe 1.00 2.50
I19 Curtis Martin 1.25 3.00
I20 Keyshawn Johnson .60 1.50
I21 Chris T. Jones .30 .75
I22 Kordell Stewart .60 1.50
I23 Junior Seau .60 1.50
I24 Steve Young 1.25 3.00
I25 Jerry Rice 1.50 4.00
I26 Joey Galloway .40 1.00
I27 Lawrence Phillips .40 1.00
I28 Jonathan Ogden 1.00 2.50
I29 Jim Harbaugh .30 .75
I30 Neil O'Donnell .30 .75

1996 Score Board Lasers Sunday's Heroes

Randomly inserted in packs at a rate of one in 22, this 25-card set features color play images on a football textured suface background with rounded corners. The backs carry another color player photo and a paragraph about the player.

COMPLETE SET (25) 40.00 100.00
STATED ODDS 1:22
SH1 Tim Brown 1.25 3.00
SH2 Kerry Collins 1.25 3.00
SH3 Tim Biakabutuka .60 1.50
SH4 Rashaan Salaam .60 1.50
SH5 Jeff Blake 1.25 3.00
SH6 Ki-Jana Carter .60 1.50
SH7 Emmitt Smith 5.00 12.00
SH8 Troy Aikman 3.00 8.00
SH9 Deion Sanders 1.50 4.00
SH10 Terrell Davis 2.50 6.00
SH11 Barry Sanders 5.00 12.00
SH12 Brett Favre 6.00 15.00
SH13 Reggie White 1.25 3.00
SH14 Marshall Faulk 1.50 4.00
SH15 Mark Brunell 1.25 3.00
SH16 Kevin Hardy 1.25 3.00
SH17 Dan Marino 6.00 15.00
SH18 Drew Bledsoe 2.00 5.00
SH19 Curtis Martin 2.50 6.00
SH20 Keyshawn Johnson 1.25 3.00
SH21 Kordell Stewart 1.25 3.00
SH22 Steve Young 2.50 6.00
SH23 Jerry Rice 3.00 8.00
SH24 Chris Warren .60 1.50
SH25 Karim Abdul-Jabbar .60 1.50

1997 Score Board NFL Experience

The 1997 Score Board NFL Experience set was issued in 6-card packs with one series totaling 100-cards. A retail version and special Super Bowl Card Show version were produced with each box carrying a different assortment of insert cards. Score Board included a wide variety of "vintage" cards inserted in packs at the rate of 1:36. These included cards from the 1935 National Chicle set up to the near present. A blank-backed promo sheet was distributed at the 1997 NFL Experience Super Bowl Card Show in New Orleans. Each sheet features three members of the participating Super Bowl teams and is numbered of 5000 sheets produced.

COMPLETE SET (100) 5.00 12.00
1 Emmitt Smith .50 1.25
2 Kordell Stewart .15 .40
3 Antonio Freeman .15 .40
4 William Thomas .05 .15
5 Simeon Rice .08 .25
6 Drew Bledsoe .20 .50

7 Elvis Grbac .08 .25
8 Ken Dilger .05 .15
9 John Elway .60 1.50
10 Curtis Conway .08 .25
11 Adrian Murrell .08 .25
12 Karim Abdul-Jabbar .15 .40
13 Terry Allen .15 .40
14 Lawrence Phillips .05 .15
15 Barry Sanders .50 1.25
16 Shannon Sharpe .08 .25
17 Troy Aikman .30 .75
18 Kevin Greene .08 .25
19 Cris Carter .15 .40
20 Jim Kelly .15 .40
21 Eric Metcalf .08 .25
22 Joey Galloway .08 .25
23 Eddie George .15 .40
24 Scott Mitchell .08 .25
25 Neil O'Donnell .08 .25
26 Ben Coates .08 .25
27 Andre Reed .08 .25
28 Michael Jackson .08 .25
29 Keith Jackson .05 .15
30 J.J. Stokes .08 .25
31 Rickey Dudley .08 .25
32 Ricky Watters .08 .25
33 Marcus Allen .15 .40
34 Brett Favre .60 1.50
35 Kevin Hardy .05 .15
36 Jim Everett .05 .15
37 Zach Thomas .15 .40
38 Lamar Lathon .05 .15
39 LeShon Johnson .05 .15
40 Bruce Smith .08 .25
41 Junior Seau .15 .40
42 Tony Banks .08 .25
43 Brian Mitchell .05 .15
44 Chris T. Jones .05 .15
45 Ty Detmer .08 .25
46 Robert Brooks .08 .25
47 Derrick Thomas .15 .40
48 Dan Wilkinson .05 .15
49 Michael Sinclair .05 .15
50 Dave Brown .05 .15
51 Carl Pickens .08 .25
52 Jim Harbaugh .08 .25
53 Wayne Chrebet .15 .40
54 Warren Moon .15 .40
55 Steve Young .20 .50
56 Sean Gilbert .05 .15
57 Jerome Bettis .15 .40
58 Dan Marino .60 1.50
59 Terrell Davis .25 .60
60 Mark Brunell .20 .50
61 Kent Graham .05 .15
62 Rashaan Salaam .08 .25
63 Tony Martin .08 .25
64 Robert Smith .08 .25
65 Thurman Thomas .15 .40
66 Marshall Faulk .20 .50
67 Dale Carter .05 .15
68 Stan Humphries .08 .25
69 Isaac Bruce .15 .40
70 Warren Sapp .08 .25
71 Kerry Collins .15 .40
72 Jamal Anderson .15 .40
73 Chris Chandler .08 .25
74 Herman Moore .08 .25
75 Rodney Hampton .08 .25
76 Tim Brown .15 .40
77 Keenan McCardell .08 .25
78 Anthony Miller .05 .15
79 Jake Reed .08 .25
80 Earnest Byner .05 .15
81 Chris Warren .08 .25
82 Deion Sanders .15 .40
83 Mike Tomczak .05 .15
84 Curtis Martin .20 .50
85 John Friesz .05 .15
86 Gus Frerotte .05 .15
87 Vinny Testaverde .08 .25
88 Jason Dunn .05 .15
89 James O.Stewart .08 .25
90 Steve Bono .08 .25
91 Levon Kirkland .05 .15
92 Merton Hanks .05 .15
93 Marvin Harrison .15 .40
94 Reggie Brooks .05 .15
95 Reggie White .15 .40
96 Jeff Blake .08 .25
97 Terry Glenn .15 .40
98 Jerry Rice .30 .75
99 Keyshawn Johnson .15 .40
100 Edgar Bennett CL .05 .15
P1 Promo Sheet 1.20 3.00
NNO Barry Sanders JUMBO/2053 7.50 15.00

1997 Score Board NFL Experience Bayou Country

Randomly inserted at a rate of one in 35 Super Bowl packs, this 10-card set highlights 10 "championship caliber players" set on the backdrop of the Superdome in New Orleans, LA.

COMPLETE SET (10) 25.00 60.00
STATED ODDS 1:35 SUPER BOWL PACKS
BC1 Terry Allen 1.50 4.00
BC2 Emmitt Smith 5.00 12.00
BC3 Troy Aikman 3.00 8.00
BC4 Brett Favre 6.00 15.00
BC5 Jerry Rice 3.00 8.00
BC6 Curtis Martin 2.00 5.00
BC7 John Elway 6.00 15.00
BC8 Jerome Bettis 1.50 4.00
BC9 Kevin Greene 1.00 2.50
BC10 Karim Abdul-Jabbar 1.50 4.00

1997 Score Board NFL Experience Foundations

The franchise player from each of the 30-NFL teams is featured in this set. The cards were randomly inserted in the standard version of 1997 Score Board NFL Experience at the rate of 1:12 packs.

COMPLETE SET (30) 40.00 100.00
STATED ODDS 1:12
F1 Ray Lewis 1.50 4.00
F2 Bruce Smith .75 2.00
F3 Jeff Blake .75 2.00
F4 Terrell Davis 2.00 5.00
F5 Steve McNair 1.50 4.00
F6 Marshall Faulk 1.50 4.00
F7 Mark Brunell 1.50 4.00
F8 Derrick Thomas 1.25 3.00
F9 Karim Abdul-Jabbar 1.25 3.00
F10 Curtis Martin 1.50 4.00
F11 Keyshawn Johnson 1.25 3.00
F12 Tim Brown 1.25 3.00
F13 Kordell Stewart 1.25 3.00
F14 Junior Seau 1.25 3.00
F15 Joey Galloway .75 2.00
F16 Simeon Rice .75 2.00
F17 Jessie Tuggle .50 1.25
F18 Kerry Collins 1.25 3.00
F19 Rashaan Salaam .75 2.00
F20 Emmitt Smith 4.00 10.00
F21 Barry Sanders 4.00 10.00
F22 Brett Favre 5.00 12.00
F23 Cris Carter 1.25 3.00
F24 Jim Everett .50 1.25
F25 Amani Toomer 1.25 3.00
F26 Ricky Watters .75 2.00
F27 Tony Banks .75 2.00
F28 Jerry Rice 2.50 6.00
F29 Warren Sapp .75 2.00
F30 Terry Allen 1.25 3.00

1997 Score Board NFL Experience Season's Heroes

Randomly inserted at a rate of one in 18 Super Bowl packs, this 20-card set highlights the league's top stars. Each card features the Super Bowl XXXI logo and a football textured bottom portion on the front.

COMPLETE SET (20) 30.00 80.00
STATED ODDS 1:18 SUPER BOWL PACKS
SH1 Gus Frerotte .60 1.50
SH2 Terry Allen 1.50 4.00
SH3 Troy Aikman 3.00 8.00
SH4 Emmitt Smith 5.00 12.00
SH5 Ricky Watters 1.00 2.50
SH6 Brett Favre 6.00 15.00
SH7 Reggie White 1.50 4.00
SH8 Steve Young 2.00 5.00
SH9 Jerry Rice 3.00 8.00
SH10 Kevin Greene 1.00 2.50
SH11 Anthony Johnson .60 1.50
SH12 Thurman Thomas 1.50 4.00
SH13 Bruce Smith 1.00 2.50
SH14 Jerome Bettis 1.50 4.00
SH15 Rod Woodson 1.00 2.50
SH16 Eddie George 1.50 4.00
SH17 Terrell Davis 2.50 6.00
SH18 John Elway 6.00 15.00
SH19 Drew Bledsoe 2.00 5.00
SH20 Junior Seau 1.50 4.00

1997 Score Board NFL Experience Teams of the '90s

Randomly inserted in packs at a rate of one in 100, this 15-card set highlights players who have starred in Super Bowls during the 1990's. The cards are die-cut in an oval shape and use photography from the year's championship game.

COMPLETE SET (15) 40.00 100.00
STATED ODDS 1:100
WC1 Emmitt Smith 10.00 25.00
WC2 Bruce Smith 2.00 5.00
WC3 Steve Young 4.00 10.00
WC4 Thurman Thomas 3.00 8.00
WC5 Kordell Stewart 3.00 8.00
WC6 Ricky Watters 2.00 5.00
WC7 Ken Norton 1.25 3.00
WC8 Jeff Hostetler 2.00 5.00
WC9 Jim Kelly 3.00 8.00
WC10 Troy Aikman 6.00 15.00
WC11 Jerry Rice 6.00 15.00
WC12 Mark Rypien 2.00 5.00
WC13 Stan Humphries 2.00 5.00
WC14 Deion Sanders 3.00 8.00
WC15 Andre Reed 2.00 5.00

1997 Score Board NFL Experience Hard Target

These oversized (approximately 5" by 7") cards were distributed by Score Board at the 1997 NFL Experience Super Bowl Card Show in New Orleans. Each card is unnumbered and features a top NFL player on the cardfront with an explanation of Score Board's Wrapper Redemption program on the cardbacks. A different player was distributed each day of the card show.

COMPLETE SET (5) 6.00 15.00
1 Terrell Davis 2.00 5.00
2 Brett Favre 2.00 5.00
3 Eddie George 1.20 3.00
4 Keyshawn Johnson 1.00 2.50
5 Emmitt Smith 1.60 4.00

1997 Score Board Playbook

The 1997 Score Board Playbook set was issued in one series totaling 100-cards and was distributed in five-card packs with a suggested retail price of $3.99. The fronts feature color action player photos in four unique designs based on the player's playing position. The backs carry player information and statistical graphs and charts. Only 1,500 sequentially numbered cases were produced. A By the Numbers partial (50-cards) parallel set was later released in its own separate packaging.

COMPLETE SET (100) 6.00 15.00
1 Warren Moon .15 .40
2 Troy Aikman .30 .75
3 Jeff George .08 .25
4 Brett Favre .60 1.50
5 Jim Harbaugh .08 .25
6 Jeff Blake .08 .25
7 John Elway .60 1.50
8 Mark Brunell .20 .50
9 Steve McNair .20 .50
10 Kordell Stewart .15 .40
11 Drew Bledsoe .20 .50
12 Kerry Collins .15 .40
13 Dan Marino .60 1.50
14 Jim Druckenmiller RC .08 .25
15 Todd Collins .05 .15
16 Jake Plummer RC .60 1.50
17 Pat Barnes RC .05 .15
18 Vinny Testaverde .08 .25
19 Scott Mitchell .08 .25
20 Rob Johnson .15 .40
21 Elvis Grbac .08 .25
22 Danny Wuerffel RC .15 .40
23 Neil O'Donnell .08 .25
24 Tony Banks .08 .25
25 Stan Humphries .08 .25
26 Brad Johnson .15 .40
27 Trent Dilfer .15 .40
28 Ty Detmer .08 .25
29 Steve Young .20 .50
30 Gus Frerotte .05 .15
31 Leeland McElroy .05 .15
32 Byron Hanspard RC .08 .25
33 Jamal Anderson .15 .40
34 Thurman Thomas .15 .40
35 Antowain Smith RC .40 1.00
36 Tim Biakabutuka .08 .25
37 Raymont Harris .05 .15
38 Corey Dillon RC .60 1.50
39 Emmitt Smith .50 1.25
40 Terrell Davis .20 .50
41 Barry Sanders .50 1.25
42 Dorsey Levens .15 .40
43 Marshall Faulk .20 .50
44 Natrone Means .08 .25
45 Marcus Allen .15 .40
46 Karim Abdul-Jabbar .15 .40
47 Robert Smith .08 .25
48 Curtis Martin .20 .50
49 Troy Davis RC .08 .25
50 Tiki Barber RC 1.00 2.50
51 Adrian Murrell .08 .25
52 Napoleon Kaufman .15 .40
53 Ricky Watters .08 .25
54 Jerome Bettis .15 .40
55 Lawrence Phillips .05 .15
56 Garrison Hearst .08 .25
57 Warrick Dunn RC .50 1.25
58 Eddie George .15 .40
59 Terry Allen .15 .40
60 Michael Jackson .08 .25
61 Rae Carruth RC .05 .15
62 Carl Pickens .08 .25
63 Michael Irvin .15 .40
64 Shannon Sharpe .08 .25
65 Herman Moore .08 .25
66 Robert Brooks .08 .25
67 Antonio Freeman .15 .40
68 Marvin Harrison .15 .40
69 Keenan McCardell .08 .25
70 Jimmy Smith .08 .25
71 Cris Carter .15 .40
72 Ben Coates .08 .25
73 Terry Glenn .15 .40
74 Ike Hilliard RC .25 .60
75 Keyshawn Johnson .15 .40
76 Eddie Kennison .08 .25
77 Tim Brown .15 .40
78 Irving Fryar .08 .25
79 Jake Reed .08 .25
80 Isaac Bruce .15 .40
81 Tony Martin .08 .25
82 Jerry Rice .30 .75
83 Joey Galloway .08 .25
84 Reidel Anthony RC .15 .40
85 Yatil Green RC .08 .25
86 Tony Gonzalez RC .60 1.50
87 Simeon Rice .08 .25
88 Peter Boulware RC .15 .40
89 Bruce Smith .08 .25
90 Reinard Wilson RC .08 .25
91 Deion Sanders .15 .40
92 Bryant Westbrook RC .05 .15
93 Reggie White .15 .40
94 Dwayne Rudd RC .05 .15
95 Darrell Russell RC .05 .15
96 Greg Lloyd .05 .15
97 Junior Seau .15 .40
98 Shawn Springs RC .08 .25
99 Cortez Kennedy .05 .15
100 Kordell Stewart CL .08 .25

1997 Score Board Playbook Franchise Player

Randomly inserted in packs at the rate of one in six, this 30-card set features action color photos of the top player from each of the 30 NFL teams. The backs carry historical team information and a descriptive copy about the featured player.

COMPLETE SET (30) 20.00 50.00
STATED ODDS 1:6 PLAYBOOK
FP1 Simeon Rice .50 1.25
FP2 Jamal Anderson .75 2.00
FP3 Peter Boulware .75 2.00
FP4 Bruce Smith .50 1.25
FP5 Kerry Collins .75 2.00
FP6 Rashaan Salaam .50 1.25
FP7 Jeff Blake .50 1.25
FP8 Emmitt Smith 2.50 6.00
FP9 Terrell Davis 1.00 2.50
FP10 Barry Sanders 2.50 6.00
FP11 Brett Favre 3.00 8.00
FP12 Marshall Faulk 1.00 2.50
FP13 Mark Brunell 1.00 2.50
FP14 Derrick Thomas .75 2.00
FP15 Dan Marino 3.00 8.00
FP16 Brad Johnson .75 2.00
FP17 Drew Bledsoe 1.00 2.50
FP18 Troy Davis .50 1.25
FP19 Ike Hilliard .60 1.50
FP20 Keyshawn Johnson .75 2.00
FP21 Tim Brown .75 2.00
FP22 Ricky Watters .50 1.25
FP23 Jerome Bettis .75 2.00
FP24 Isaac Bruce .75 2.00
FP25 Junior Seau .75 2.00
FP26 Jerry Rice 1.50 4.00
FP27 Joey Galloway .50 1.25
FP28 Warrick Dunn 1.25 3.00
FP29 Eddie George .75 2.00
FP30 Gus Frerotte .30 .75

1997 Score Board Playbook Mirror Image

Randomly inserted in packs at the rate of one in 24, this 20-card set features color action dual photos (front and back) of the top veteran and rookie players printed on reflective mirror foil-board.

COMPLETE SET (20) 40.00 100.00
STATED ODDS 1:24 PLAYBOOK
1 Brett Favre 6.00 15.00
2 Warrick Dunn 2.50 6.00
3 Emmitt Smith 5.00 12.00
4 Steve Young 2.00 5.00
5 Terrell Davis 2.00 5.00
6 Kordell Stewart 1.50 4.00
7 Kerry Collins 1.50 4.00
8 John Elway 6.00 15.00
9 Barry Sanders 5.00 12.00
10 Drew Bledsoe 2.00 5.00
11 Troy Aikman 3.00 8.00
12 Curtis Martin 2.00 5.00
13 Mark Brunell 2.00 5.00
14 Terry Glenn 1.50 4.00
15 Antowain Smith 2.00 5.00
16 Reggie White 1.50 4.00
17 Jeff Blake 1.00 2.50
18 Darrell Russell .60 1.50
19 Terry Allen 1.50 4.00
20 Keyshawn Johnson 1.50 4.00

1997 Score Board Playbook Mirror Image Autographs

Randomly inserted in packs at the rate of one in 192, this seven-card set features color action photos of top players with the players autograph at the bottom. The cards were printed on mirror board with the backs certifying the authenticity of the autograph.

AUTO/110-915 ODDS 1:192 PLAYBOOK
MI1 Brett Favre/110 75.00 150.00
MI2 Warrick Dunn/915 12.00 30.00
MI3 Emmitt Smith/410 50.00 120.00
MI4 Steve Young/360 20.00 50.00
MI5 Terrell Davis/590 12.00 30.00
MI6 Kordell Stewart/550 10.00 25.00
MI7 Kerry Collins/200 12.00 30.00

1997 Score Board Playbook Title Quest

Randomly inserted in packs at the rate of 1:32 for cards TQ3-TQ12 and 1:192 for cards TQ1-TQ2, this 12-card set features color action photos of top players with foil stamping to signify the limited edition of the print run.

COMPLETE SET (12) 20.00 50.00
TQ1-TQ2: ODDS 1:192 PLAYBOOK
TQ3-TQ12: ODDS 1:32 PLAYBOOK
TQ1 Brett Favre 5.00 12.00
TQ2 Terrell Davis 1.50 4.00
TQ3 Emmitt Smith 4.00 10.00
TQ4 Drew Bledsoe 1.50 4.00
TQ5 Mark Brunell 1.50 4.00
TQ6 Warrick Dunn 2.00 5.00
TQ7 Jim Druckenmiller .75 2.00
TQ8 Derrick Thomas 1.25 3.00
TQ9 Rae Carruth .50 1.25
TQ10 Jerome Bettis 1.25 3.00
TQ11 Dan Marino 5.00 12.00
TQ12 Barry Sanders 4.00 10.00

1997 Score Board Playbook By The Numbers

COMPLETE SET (50) 5.00 12.00
*BY THE NUMB: SAME PRICE AS PLAYBOOK
GOLD MAG.ODDS 1:21 BY THE NUMBERS
SILVER MAG.ODDS 1:2 BY THE NUMBERS

1997 Score Board Playbook By The Numbers Magnified Gold

COMPLETE SET (50) 30.00 80.00
*MAG.GOLD STARS: 3X TO 8X BASIC CARDS
*MAG.GOLD RCs: 1.5X TO 4X BASIC CARDS
STATED PRINT RUN 200 SERIAL #'d SETS
STATED ODDS 1:21 BY THE NUMBERS

1997 Score Board Playbook By The Numbers Magnified Silver

COMPLETE SET (50) 10.00 25.00
*MAG SILV.STARS: .8X TO 2X BASIC CARDS
*MAG SILV.RCs: .8X TO 2X BASIC CARDS
STATED PRINT RUN 2000 SERIAL #'d SETS
STATED ODDS 1:2 BY THE NUMBERS

1997 Score Board Playbook By The Numbers Master Signings

Randomly inserted in packs at the rate of one in 1,268, this 120-card set features color photos of top players each pictured in four different one-of-a-kind versions: Home Uniform-Portrait Photo (A), Home Uniform-Action Photo (B), Away Uniform-Portrait Photo (C), and Away Uniform-Action Photo (D). The cards measure approximately 3" by 4.5" and display the pictured player's autograph.

1997 Score Board Playbook By The Numbers Red Zone Stats

Randomly inserted in packs at the rate of one in 20, this 10-card set features color action player photos on a red background with a portrait image of the same player in the foreground. Two oversized (3" by 4 1/2") parallel sets were randomly inserted as well: Gold Foil with only 100 sequentially numbered sets made (1:210 packs) and Silver Foil with 1000-sets produced (1:21 packs).

COMPLETE SET (10) 10.00 25.00
STATED ODDS 1:20 BY THE NUMBERS
*MAGNIFIED GOLD/100: 2.5X TO 6X
*MAGNIFIED SILVER/1000: .4X TO 1X
RZ1 Emmitt Smith 2.50 6.00
RZ2 Terry Allen .50 1.25
RZ3 Troy Aikman 1.50 4.00
RZ4 Brett Favre 3.00 8.00
RZ5 John Elway 3.00 8.00
RZ6 Drew Bledsoe 1.00 2.50
RZ7 Terrell Davis 1.00 2.50
RZ8 Karim Abdul-Jabbar .50 1.25
RZ9 Curtis Martin 1.00 2.50
RZ10 Warrick Dunn 1.25 3.00

1997 Score Board Playbook By The Numbers Standout Numbers

Randomly inserted in packs at the rate of one in four. This 30-card set features color action player photos with their outstanding statistical numbers in the background. Two oversized (3" by 4 1/2") parallel sets were randomly inserted as well: Gold Foil with only 270 sequentially numbered sets made (1:26 packs) and Silver Foil with 2700-sets produced (1:3 packs).

COMPLETE SET (30) 15.00 40.00
STATED ODDS 1:4 BY THE NUMBERS
*MAG.GOLDS: 1.2X TO 3X BASIC INSERTS
MAG.GOLD ODDS 1:26 BY THE NUMBERS
MAG.GOLD PRINT RUN 270 SER.#'d SETS
*MAG.SILVERS: .4X TO 1X BASIC INSERTS
MAG.SILVER ODDS 1:3 BY THE NUMBERS
MAG.SILVER PRINT RUN 2700 SER.#'d SETS
SN1 Drew Bledsoe .75 2.00
SN2 Emmitt Smith 2.00 5.00
SN3 Cris Carter .60 1.50
SN4 Brett Favre 2.50 6.00
SN5 Jerome Bettis .60 1.50
SN6 Mark Brunell .60 1.50
SN7 John Elway 2.50 6.00
SN8 Troy Aikman 1.25 3.00
SN9 Steve Young .75 2.00
SN10 Kordell Stewart .60 1.50
SN11 Reggie White .60 1.50
SN12 Isaac Bruce .60 1.50
SN13 Dan Marino 2.50 6.00
SN14 Kevin Greene .60 1.50
SN15 Tim Brown .60 1.50
SN16 Terry Glenn .60 1.50
SN17 Ricky Watters .40 1.00
SN18 Carl Pickens .40 1.00
SN19 Keyshawn Johnson .60 1.50
SN20 Barry Sanders 2.00 5.00
SN21 Marshall Faulk .75 2.00
SN22 James O.Stewart .60 1.50
SN23 Jerry Rice 1.25 3.00
SN24 Curtis Martin .75 2.00
SN25 Herman Moore .40 1.00
SN26 Terry Allen .60 1.50
SN27 Eddie George .60 1.50
SN28 Warrick Dunn 1.00 2.50
SN29 Marcus Allen .60 1.50
SN30 Terrell Davis .75 2.00

1997 Score Board Players Club

The 70 cards that make-up this set are a grouping from baseball, basketball, football and hockey players. Card fronts are full colored action shots, with professional team names air-brushed out. The card backs contain 1997 projected statistics and biographical information. Along with the number 1 Die-Cuts and Play Back inserts, vintage cards were the major draw to this product. One in 32 packs contained a vintage card from 1909-1979 from any of the four sports. An original Honus Wagner T206 card was offered as a redemption in 1:153,600 packs. Also, one vintage wax pack was available via redemption card in one in every 32 packs.

COMPLETE SET (70) 5.00 12.00
1 Brett Favre .60 1.50
2 Duce Staley .20 .50
5 Adonal Foyle .08 .25
10 Kordell Stewart .08 .25
11 Antowain Smith .07 .20
13 P.Boulware .08 .25
R.Wilson
14 Troy Davis .07 .20
20 Emmitt Smith .50 1.25
21 Troy Aikman .25 .60
25 Warrick Dunn .30 .75
26 Eddie George .20 .50
28 Joey Galloway .08 .25
33 Darnell Autry .07 .20
34 Steve Young .20 .50
38 Tony Gonzalez .30 .75
39 Jim Druckenmiller .07 .20
44 Corey Dillon .30 .75
46 Kerry Collins .08 .25
47 Byron Hanspard .08 .25
50 Rae Carruth .07 .20
51 Jake Plummer .20 .50
53 Darrell Russell .07 .20
54 Shawn Springs .07 .20
56 Bryant Westbrook .07 .20
59 Orlando Pace .08 .25
61 Ike Hilliard .08 .25
63 Reidel Anthony .07 .20
67 Zach Thomas .20 .50
70 Brett Favre CL .25 .60

1997 Score Board Players Club #1 Die-Cuts

Each player in this 20 card set, inserted one in 32 packs, was at one time selected as a first round selection in the professional draft. The cards are die-cut in the shape of a "1" and have gold foil on the left border. The backs contain pre-professional biographical information and (if applicable) statistics from their last college or minor league season. The card numbers have a "D" prefix.

COMPLETE SET (20) 25.00 60.00
D2 Troy Aikman 2.50 6.00
D3 Darrell Russell 1.25 3.00
D7 Orlando Pace 1.25 3.00
D15 Jim Druckenmiller 1.25 3.00
D18 Warrick Dunn 1.50 4.00
D19 Emmitt Smith 4.00 10.00

1997 Score Board Players Club Play Backs

This 15-card set highlights stars form all four major U.S. sports. The card fronts have a player photo superimposed on a photo of the player's jersey. To the left is a movie reel design with individual action shots. The backs have another player photograph and biographical information. The cards are numbered with a "PB" prefix.

COMPLETE SET (15) 30.00 80.00
STATED ODDS 1:32
PB1 Brett Favre 5.00 12.00
PB2 Kordell Stewart 1.25 3.00
PB3 Emmitt Smith 4.00 10.00
PB4 Troy Aikman 2.50 6.00
PB6 Steve Young 2.00 5.00
PB13 Kerry Collins 1.50 4.00

1997 Score Board Brett Favre Super Bowl XXXI

Special retail boxes of 1997 Pro Line contained one of these five Brett Favre Super Bowl XXXI cards. Each box included packs with 112-Pro Line cards along with one autographed card and one of these Favre cards. Each card features Favre along with "Super Bowl XXXI Champion" printed below the player image. Score Board logos are included on the cards instead of Pro Line.

COMPLETE SET (5) 3.00 8.00
COMMON CARD (BF1-BF5) .75 2.00

1997 Score Board Talk N' Sports

This product features phone cards with a couple twists, including trivia contests to win memorabilia and to check current sports scores. The 50-card regular set includes stars and prospects from all four major team sports. According to Score Board, a total of 1,500 sequentially numbered cases were produced.

COMPLETE SET (50) 4.00 10.00
1 Brett Favre .50 1.25
2 Marshall Faulk .15 .40
3 Steve Young .20 .50
4 Troy Aikman .25 .60
5 Kordell Stewart .08 .25
6 Kerry Collins .10 .30
7 Keyshawn Johnson .08 .25
8 Eddie George .10 .30
9 Terry Glenn .10 .30
10 Kevin Hardy .07 .20
11 Emmitt Smith .40 1.00
12 Karim Abdul-Jabbar .08 .25
13 Tony Banks .08 .25
14 Zach Thomas .20 .50
15 Mike Alstott .10 .30
16 Matt Stevens .07 .20
17 Troy Davis .07 .20
18 Warrick Dunn .25 .60
19 Yatil Green .07 .20
20 Rae Carruth .07 .20
21 Darrell Russell .07 .20
22 Peter Boulware .07 .20
23 Shawn Springs .07 .20

1997 Score Board Talk N' Sports Essentials

These 10 plastic acetate cards were randomly inserted at a rate of 1:24 Talk N' Sports packs.

COMPLETE SET (10) 25.00 60.00
E1 Brett Favre 5.00 12.00
E4 Emmitt Smith 4.00 10.00
E7 Eddie George 3.00 8.00
E8 Troy Davis 1.50 4.00
E9 Darrell Russell 1.50 4.00

1997 Score Board Talk N' Sports Phone Cards $1

COMPLETE SET (50) 8.00 20.00
*PIN NUMBER REVEALED: HALF VALUE

1997 Score Board Talk N' Sports Phone Cards $10

These $10 phone cards allow users to choose trivia contests to win memorabilia in lieu of the phone time. Entrants who choose the trivia contest forfeit their phone time, but if they answer 9 of 10 questions, they win a baseball bat autographed by one of these six players: Willie Mays, Hank Aaron, Barry Bonds, Ken Griffey Jr., Pete Rose or Chipper Jones. The $10 cards were inserted at a rate of 1:12 packs and expired on 5/20/1998. Each card is sequentially numbered out of 3,960.

COMPLETE SET (10) 12.00 30.00
*PIN NUMBER REVEALED: HALF VALUE
1 Brett Favre 3.00 8.00
3 Keyshawn Johnson 1.25 3.00
4 Steve Young 1.50 4.00
5 Kordell Stewart 1.00 2.50
7 Eddie George 1.25 3.00
8 Troy Aikman 2.00 5.00

1997 Score Board Talk N' Sports Phone Cards $20

These $20 phone cards allow users to choose sports updates in lieu of the phone time. The time on the card can be used interchangably for either phone calls or sports updates. The $20 cards were inserted at a rate of 1:36 packs and expired on 7/31/1998. Each card is sequentially numbered out of 1,440.

COMPLETE SET (10) 25.00 60.00
*PIN NUMBER REVEALED: HALF VALUE
1 Brett Favre 5.00 12.00
7 Eddie George 2.50 6.00
8 Troy Davis 2.00 5.00
9 Darrell Russell 2.00 5.00

1998 Score Board Jumbos

Score Board released these cards as singles direct to the public for $19.75 each. Each measures roughly 3 1/2" by 5," is die cut, and carries and announced print run.

COMPLETE SET (2) 12.00 30.00
JE7 John Elway 6.00 15.00
MVP3 Brett Favre 6.00 15.00
SB Super Bowl XXXII/5000 8.00 20.00

1976 Seahawks Post-Intelligencer

This 57-card set was issued at the start of training camp for the Seattle Seahawks first season. The cards measure approximately 6 1/2" by 3" and were printed in the sports section of the local newspaper. The fronts feature headshot drawings of the player and his background and have a black dotted line to help cut them out of the newspaper.

COMPLETE SET (57) 125.00 250.00
1 Jack Patera 3.00 6.00
2 Dave Williams WR 3.00 6.00
3 Bill Olds 3.00 6.00
4 Mike Curtis 4.00 8.00
5 Norm Evans 3.00 6.00
6 Ron Howard 3.00 6.00
7 John Demarie 3.00 6.00
8 Ken Geddes 3.00 6.00
9 Don Hansen 3.00 6.00
10 Rollie Woolsey 3.00 6.00
11 Sam McCullum 3.00 6.00
12 Eddie McMillan 3.00 6.00
13 Gordon Jolley 3.00 6.00
14 John McMakin 3.00 6.00
15 Nick Bebout 3.00 6.00
16 Carl Barisich 3.00 6.00
17 Gary Hayman 3.00 6.00
18 Al Matthews 3.00 6.00
19 Fred Hoaglin 3.00 6.00
20 Ahmad Rashad 6.00 12.00
21 Wayne Baker 3.00 6.00
22 Dave Brown 3.00 6.00
23 Larry Woods 3.00 6.00
24 Dave Tipton DE 3.00 6.00
25 Ed Bradley 3.00 6.00
26 Bob Penchion 3.00 6.00
27 Steve Niehaus 3.00 6.00
28 Gary Keithley 3.00 6.00
29 Bob Picard 3.00 6.00
30 Joe Owens 3.00 6.00
31 Steve Myer 3.00 6.00
32 Lyle Blackwood 3.00 6.00
33 Sherman Smith 3.00 6.00
34 Don Bitterlich 3.00 6.00
35 Neil Graff 3.00 6.00
36 Steve Taylor DB 3.00 6.00
37 Kerry Marbury 3.00 6.00
38 Charles Waddell 3.00 6.00
39 Art Kuehn 3.00 6.00
40 Jerry Davis 3.00 6.00
41 Sammy Green 3.00 6.00
42 Rocky Rasley 3.00 6.00
43 Ken Hutcherson 3.00 6.00
44 Dwayne Crump 3.00 6.00
45 Steve Raible 3.00 6.00
45 Larry Bates 3.00 6.00
46 Rondy Colbert 3.00 6.00
47 Randy Johnson 3.00 6.00
48 Andy Bolton 3.00 6.00
49 Jeff Lloyd 3.00 6.00
50 Don Dufek Jr. 3.00 6.00
51 Rick Engles 3.00 6.00
52 Alvis Darby 3.00 6.00
53 Ernie Jones DB 3.00 6.00
55 Jim Zorn 5.00 10.00
56 Don Clune 3.00 6.00
57 Bill Munson 4.00 8.00

1976 Seahawks Team Issue 8.5x11

These blank-backed photos measure approximately 8 1/2" by 11" and feature black-and-white full-bleed head shots of Seattle Seahawks players. The player's name, team name, facsimile autograph, and Seahawks logo appear near the bottom. The photos are unnumbered and checklisted below in alphabetical order. We've included all known photos. Any addtions to this list are appreciated.

COMPLETE SET (12) 60.00 120.00
1 Ed Bradley 5.00 10.00
2 Mike Curtis 6.00 12.00
3 Norm Evans 5.00 10.00
4 Ken Geddes 5.00 10.00
5 Sammy Green 5.00 10.00
6 Fred Hoaglin 5.00 10.00
7 Ron Howard 5.00 10.00
8 Eddie McMillan 5.00 10.00
9 Steve Niehaus 5.00 10.00
10 Jack Patera 5.00 10.00
11 Bob Penchion 5.00 10.00
12 Jim Zorn 7.50 15.00

1976-77 Seahawks Team Issue 5x7

These blank-backed photos measure approximately 5" by 7" and feature black-and-white full-bleed head shots of Seattle Seahawks players. The player's name, team, facsimile autograph, and Seahawks logo appear near the bottom. Some of the photos have the text and helmet printed in black ink while others use white ink. The photos are unnumbered and checklisted below in alphabetical order. We've included all known photos. Any addtions to this list are appreciated.

COMPLETE SET (37) 150.00 300.00
1 Sam Adkins 4.00 8.00
2 Steve August 4.00 8.00
3 Carl Barisich 4.00 8.00
4 Nick Bebout 4.00 8.00
5 Dennis Boyd 4.00 8.00
6 Dave Brown 4.00 8.00
7 Ron Coder 4.00 8.00
8 Mike Curtis 5.00 10.00
9 John DeMarie 4.00 8.00
10 Dan Doornink 4.00 8.00
11 Norm Evans 4.00 8.00
12 Efren Herrera 4.00 8.00
13 Fred Hoaglin 4.00 8.00
14 Ron Howard 4.00 8.00
15 Steve Largent 15.00 25.00
16 Steve Largent 15.00 25.00
17 John Leypoldt 4.00 8.00
18 Bob Lurtsema 4.00 8.00
19 Al Matthews 4.00 8.00
20 Sam McCullum 4.00 8.00
21 John McMakin 4.00 8.00
22 Bill Munson 5.00 10.00
23 Steve Myer 4.00 8.00
24 Steve Niehaus 4.00 8.00
25 Jack Patera CO 4.00 8.00
26 Steve Raible 4.00 8.00
27 John Sawyer 4.00 8.00
28 Sherman Smith 4.00 8.00
29 Don Testerman 4.00 8.00
30 Dave Tipton 4.00 8.00
31 Manu Tuiasosopo 4.00 8.00
32 Herman Weaver 4.00 8.00
33 Cornell Webster 4.00 8.00
34 Rollie Woolsey 4.00 8.00
35 Jim Zorn 7.50 15.00
36 Jim Zorn 7.50 15.00
37 Seahawk Mascot 4.00 8.00

1977 Seahawks Fred Meyer

Sponsored by Fred Meyer Department Stores and subtitled "Savings Selections Quality Service," this set consists of 14 photos (approximately 6" by 7 1/4") printed on thin glossy paper stock. The cards were reportedly given out one per week. The fronts feature either posed or action color player photos with black borders. The player's name, uniform number, and brief player information appear in one of the bottom corners. Most photos have a small color closeup in one of the lower corners; several others do not (photo numbers 3, 5, 12, 13A). Only Jim Zorn is represented twice in the set, by an action photo with a small color closeup and a portrait without an inset closeup. The backs are blank. The cards are unnumbered and checklisted below in alphabetical order. The set features a card of Steve Largent in his Rookie Card year.

COMPLETE SET (14) 75.00 150.00
1 Steve August 5.00 10.00
2 Autry Beamon 5.00 10.00
3 Terry Beeson 5.00 10.00
4 Dennis Boyd 5.00 10.00
5 Norm Evans 5.00 10.00
6 Sammy Green 5.00 10.00
7 Ron Howard 5.00 10.00
8 Steve Largent 20.00 40.00
9 Steve Myer 5.00 10.00
10 Steve Niehaus 5.00 10.00
11 Sherman Smith 5.00 10.00
12 Don Testerman 5.00 10.00
13A Jim Zorn 7.50 15.00
13B Jim Zorn 7.50 15.00

1978 Seahawks Nalley's

The 1978 Nalley's Chips Seattle Seahawks cards are actually the back panels of large (nine ounce) Nalley's boxes of Dippers, Barbecue Chips, and Potato Chips. The cards themselves measure approximately 9" by 10 3/4" and include a facsimile autograph. The back of the potato chip box features a color posed photo of the player with his facsimile autograph. One side of the box has the Seahawks game schedule, while the other side provides biographical and statistical information on the player. The front of the box includes the player's name and card number. The prices listed below refer to complete boxes.

COMPLETE SET (8) 350.00 500.00
1 Steve Largent 200.00 350.00
2 Autry Beamon 15.00 25.00
3 Jim Zorn 35.00 60.00
4 Sherman Smith 10.00 30.00
5 Ron Coder 15.00 25.00
6 Terry Beeson 15.00 25.00
7 Steve Niehaus 15.00 25.00
8 Ron Howard 15.00 25.00

1979 Seahawks Nalley's

The 1979 Nalley's Chips Seattle Seahawks cards are actually the back panels of large (nine ounce) Nalley's boxes of Dippers, Barbecue Chips, and Potato Chips. The cards themselves measure approximately 9" by 10 3/4" and include a facsimile autograph. The back of the potato chip box features a color photo of the player with his facsimile autograph. One side of the box has the Seahawks game schedule, while the other side provides biographical and statistical information on the player. The front of the box features the player's name and a card number that is a continuation of previous year's cards. The prices listed below refer to complete boxes.

COMPLETE SET (8) 75.00 135.00
9 Steve Myer 12.00 20.00
10 Tom Lynch 12.00 20.00
11 David Sims 12.00 20.00
12 John Yarno 12.00 20.00
13 Bill Gregory 12.00 20.00
14 Steve Raible 12.00 20.00
15 Dennis Boyd 12.00 20.00
16 Steve August 12.00 20.00

1979 Seahawks Police

The 1979 Seattle Seahawks Police set consists of 16 cards each measuring approximately 2 5/8" by 4 1/8". In addition to the local law enforcement agency, the set was sponsored by the Washington State Crime Prevention Association, the Kiwanis Club, and Coca-Cola, the logos of which all appear on the back of the cards. In addition to the 13 player cards, cards for the mascot, coach, and Sea Gal were issued. The set is unnumbered but has been listed below in alphabetical order by subject. The backs contain "Tips from the Seahawks". A 1979 copyright date can be found on the back of the cards.

COMPLETE SET (16) 12.50 25.00
1 Steve August .50 1.00
2 Autry Beamon .50 1.00
3 Terry Beeson .50 1.00
4 Dennis Boyd .50 1.00
5 Dave Brown .63 1.25
6 Efren Herrera .50 1.00
7 Steve Largent 6.00 12.00
8 Tom Lynch .50 1.00
9 Bob Newton .50 1.00
10 Jack Patera CO .63 1.25
11 Sea Gal (Keri Truscan) .50 1.00
12 Seahawk (Mascot) .50 1.00
13 David Sims .50 1.00
14 Sherman Smith .63 1.25
15 John Yarno .50 1.00
16 Jim Zorn 1.50 3.00

1980 Seahawks Nalley's

The 1980 Nalley's Chips Seattle Seahawks cards are actually the back panels of large (nine ounce) Nalley's boxes of Dippers, Barbecue Chips, and Potato Chips. The cards themselves measure approximately 9" by 10 3/4" and include a facsimile autograph. The back of the potato chip box features a color photo of the player with his facsimile autograph. One side of the box has the Seahawks game schedule, while the other side provides biographical and statistical information on the player. The front of the box features the player's name and a card number that is a continuation of previous year's cards. The prices listed below refer to complete boxes.

COMPLETE SET (8) 75.00 135.00
17 Keith Simpson 8.00 20.00
18 Michael Jackson 8.00 20.00
19 Manu Tuiasosopo 8.00 20.00
20 Sam McCullum 8.00 20.00
21 Keith Butler 8.00 20.00
22 Sam Adkins 8.00 20.00
23 Dan Doornink 8.00 20.00
24 Dave Brown 8.00 20.00

1980 Seahawks Police

The 1980 Seattle Seahawks set of 16 cards is numbered and contains the 1980 date on the back. The cards measure approximately 2 5/8" by 4 1/8". In addition to the local law enforcement agency, the set is sponsored by the Washington State Crime Prevention Association, the Kiwanis Club, Coca-Cola, and the Ernst Home Centers, each of which has their logo appearing on the back. Also appearing on the backs of the cards are "Tips from the Seahawks". The card backs have blue printing with red accent on white card stock. A stylized Seahawks helmet logo appears on the front.

COMPLETE SET (16) 7.50 15.00
1 Sam McCullum .30 .75
2 Dan Doornink .25 .60
3 Sherman Smith .40 1.00
4 Efren Herrera .25 .60
5 Bill Gregory .25 .60
6 Keith Simpson .25 .60
7 Manu Tuiasosopo .30 .75
8 Michael Jackson .25 .60
9 Steve Raible .25 .60
10 Steve Largent 2.50 6.00
11 Jim Zorn .75 2.00
12 Nick Bebout .25 .60
13 The Seahawk (mascot) .25 .60
14 Jack Patera CO .30 .75
15 Robert Hardy .25 .60
16 Keith Butler .25 .60

1980 Seahawks 7-Up

This "7-Up/Seahawks Collectors Series" (as noted on the cardbacks) measures approximately 2 3/8" by 3 1/4" and is printed on thin card stock. Each card was issued on a slightly larger panel (roughly 3 7/8" by 3 1/4") with both the left and right side of the panel being intended to be removed leaving a perforation on both sides of the final separated card. The cardfronts carry a color player photo enclosed in a white border with the Seahawks' helmet, player's name, and 7-Up logo in the bottom border. The card backs feature brief player vital statistics and sponsor logos. The cards are unnumbered and checklisted below alphabetically. Steve Largent and Jim Zorn were not included in the set due to their sponsorship of Darigold Dairy Products.

COMPLETE SET (10) 75.00 150.00
1 Steve August 6.00 15.00
2 Terry Beeson 6.00 15.00
3 Dan Doornink 6.00 15.00
4 Michael Jackson 6.00 15.00
5 Tom Lynch 6.00 15.00
6 Steve Myer 6.00 15.00
7 Steve Raible 6.00 15.00
8 Sherman Smith 8.00 20.00
9 Manu Tuiasosopo 6.00 15.00
10 John Yarno 6.00 15.00

1981 Seahawks 7-Up

Sponsored by 7-Up and issued by the Seahawks, usually through mail requests, these cards measure approximately 3 1/2" by 5 1/2" and are made of thin stock. The borderless cardfronts feature color player photos with the words "Seahawks Fan Mail Courtesy..." and the 7-Up logo. A facsimile autograph can also be found on the photo. However, the Steve Largent and Jim Zorn photos do not have the 7-Up logo due to their association with Darigold Milk products at the time. The backs carry a brief player biography. The cards are unnumbered and checklisted below in alphabetical order.

COMPLETE SET (31) 48.00 120.00
1 Sam Adkins 1.50 4.00
2 Steve August 1.50 4.00
3 Terry Beeson 1.50 4.00
4 Dennis Boyd 1.50 4.00
5 Dave Brown 2.50 6.00
6 Louis Bullard 1.50 4.00
7 Keith Butler 1.50 4.00
8 Ron Coder
9 Peter Cronan 1.50 4.00
10 Dan Doornink 1.50 4.00
11 Jacob Green 2.50 6.00
12 Bill Gregory 1.50 4.00
13 Robert Hardy 1.50 4.00

14 Efren Herrera 1.50 4.00
15 Michael Jackson 2.50 6.00
16 Art Kuehn 1.50 4.00
17 Steve Largent 10.00 25.00
18 Tom Lynch 1.50 4.00
19 Sam McCullum 2.50 6.00
20 Steve Myer 1.50 4.00
21 Jack Patera CO 1.50 4.00
22 Steve Raible 1.50 4.00
23 The Sea Gals 1.50 4.00
24 The Seahawk Mascot 1.50 4.00
25 Keith Simpson 1.50 4.00
26 Sherman Smith 2.50 6.00
27 Manu Tuiasosopo 2.50 6.00
28 Herman Weaver 1.50 4.00
29 Cornell Webster 1.50 4.00
30 John Yarno 1.50 4.00
31 Jim Zorn 4.00 10.00

1982 Seahawks Police

Similar to the 1980 set in design, this 16-card, numbered set is sponsored by the Washington State Crime Prevention Association, the Kiwanis Club, Coca-Cola, and Ernst Home Centers in addition to the local law enforcement agency. The cards measure approximately 2 5/8" by 4 1/8". A 1982 date and short "Tips from the Seahawks" appear on the backs. Card backs have blue print with red trim on white card stock. Cards of Jack Patera and Sam McCullum are reported to be more difficult to obtain than other cards in this set.

COMPLETE SET (16) 4.00 10.00
1 Sam McCullum SP .60 1.50
2 Manu Tuiasosopo .20 .50
3 Sherman Smith .30 .75
4 Karen Godwin (Sea Gal) .15 .40
5 Dave Brown .30 .75
6 Keith Simpson .15 .40
7 Steve Largent 1.50 4.00
8 Michael Jackson .15 .40
9 Kenny Easley .30 .75
10 Dan Doornink .15 .40
11 Jim Zorn .50 1.25
12 Jack Patera CO SP .60 1.50
13 Jacob Green .30 .75
14 Dave Krieg .60 1.50
15 Steve August .15 .40
16 Keith Butler .15 .40

1982 Seahawks 7-Up

Sponsored by 7-Up and issued by the Seahawks, usually through mail requests, these 15 cards measure approximately 3 1/2" by 5 1/2" and are printed on thin stock. The fronts feature color player action shots with "Seahawks Fan Mail Courtesy," the 7-Up logo, and a facsimile autograph (which sometimes appears on the card back). The Steve Largent and Jim Zorn cards carry the Darigold logo, "Gold-n-Soft Margarine," due to their association with Darigold Milk products at the time. The back carries a brief player biography, career highlights, or personal message. Some of the cards are horizontally oriented and some are vertically oriented. The cards are unnumbered and checklisted below in alphabetical order.

COMPLETE SET (15) 50.00 100.00
1 Edwin Bailey 2.50 6.00
2 Dave Brown 2.50 6.00
3 Kenny Easley 3.00 8.00
4 Ron Essink 2.50 6.00
5 Jacob Green 3.00 8.00
6 Robert Hardy 2.50 6.00
7 John Harris 2.50 6.00
8 David Hughes 2.50 6.00
9 Paul Johns HOR 2.50 6.00
10 Kerry Justin 2.50 6.00
11 Dave Krieg 4.00 10.00
12 Steve Largent 8.00 20.00
13 Keith Simpson 2.50 6.00
14 Manu Tuiasosopo 2.50 6.00
15 Jim Zorn HOR 3.00 8.00

1984 Seahawks GTE

Sponsored by GTE Communications and issued by the Seahawks, usually through mail requests or player appearances, these cards measure approximately 3 1/2" by 5 1/2" and are printed on thin stock. The fronts feature color player action shots with the GTE logo and facsimile autograph. The back carries a brief player biography. They are very similar to the 1988 set and may have been released over a period of years. The card's year can be determined by the varying information in the player bios on the backs or in very slight differences in the cropping of the player photos. The cards are unnumbered and checklisted below in alphabetical order. Any additions to the list below are appreciated.

COMPLETE SET (13) 40.00 80.00
1 Dan Doornink 2.00 5.00
2 Kenny Easley 2.00 5.00
3 Jacob Green 2.50 6.00
4 John Harris 2.00 5.00
5 Norm Johnson 2.00 5.00
6 Chuck Knox CO 2.50 6.00
7 Dave Krieg 3.00 8.00
8 Steve Largent 8.00 20.00
9 Joe Nash 2.00 5.00
10 Keith Simpson 2.00 5.00
11 Mike Tice 2.00 5.00
12 Curt Warner 3.00 8.00
13 Charle Young 2.00 5.00

1984 Seahawks Nalley's

The 1984 Nalley's Seahawks set was issued on large Nalley's Potato Chip boxes. The back of the box features a color photo of the player, with his facsimile autograph. One side of the box has the Seahawks 1984 schedule, while the other side provides biographical and statistical information on the player. The prices listed below refer to complete boxes. These cards are unnumbered and are listed below alphabetically.

COMPLETE SET (4) 30.00 80.00
1 Kenny Easley 5.00 12.00
2 Dave Krieg 6.00 15.00
3 Steve Largent 15.00 40.00
4 Curt Warner 8.00 20.00

1984 Seahawks Team Issue

These photos were issued by the Seahawks around 1984. Each measures roughly 8" by 10" and includes a black and white player photo and a blank cardback. The player's name, position and Seahawks helmet logo appear below the photo.

COMPLETE SET (23) 35.00 60.00
1 Edwin Bailey 1.25 3.00
2 Cullen Bryant 1.25 3.00
3 Keith Butler 1.25 3.00
4 Chris Castor 1.25 3.00
5 Bob Cryder 1.25 3.00
6 Zachary Dixon 1.25 3.00
7 Randy Edwards 1.25 3.00
8 John Harris S 1.25 3.00
9 David Hughes 1.25 3.00
10 Terry Jackson CB 1.25 3.00
11 Paul Johns 1.25 3.00
12 John Kaiser 1.25 3.00
13 Reggie McKenzie 1.50 4.00
14 Sam Merriman 1.25 3.00
15 Bryan Millard 1.50 4.00
16 Joe Nash 1.25 3.00
17 Shelton Robinson 1.25 3.00
18 Bruce Scholtz 1.25 3.00
19 Keith Simpson 1.25 3.00
20 Terry Taylor 1.25 3.00
21 Mike Tice 1.25 3.00
22 Daryl Turner 1.25 3.00
23 Jeff West 1.25 3.00

1985 Seahawks Police

This 16-card set of Seattle Seahawks is unnumbered; not even the uniform number is given. Cards measure approximately 2 5/8" by 4 1/8" and the backs contain "Tips from the Seahawks". The set was sponsored by Coca-Cola, McDonald's, KOMO-TV4, Kiwanis, the Washington State Crime Prevention Association, and local law enforcement agencies. Card backs are written in red and blue on white card stock. The year of issue is printed in the bottom right corner of the reverse.

COMPLETE SET (16) 3.00 8.00
1 Dave Brown .25 .60
2 Jeff Bryant .20 .50
3 Blair Bush .20 .50
4 Keith Butler .15 .40
5 Dan Doornink .15 .40
6 Kenny Easley .25 .60
7 Jacob Green .25 .60
8 John Harris .15 .40
9 Norm Johnson .25 .60
10 Chuck Knox CO .25 .60
11 Dave Krieg .60 1.50
12 Steve Largent 1.25 3.00
13 Joe Nash .20 .50
14 Bruce Scholtz .15 .40
15 Curt Warner .40 1.00
16 Fredd Young .25 .60

1986 Seahawks Police

This 16-card set of Seattle Seahawks is unnumbered; not even the uniform number is given explicitly on the front of the card. Cards measure approximately 2 5/8" by 4 1/8" and the backs contain "Tips from the Seahawks". The year of issue is not printed anywhere on the cards. The cards are unnumbered so they are ordered below alphabetically.

COMPLETE SET (16) 3.00 8.00
1 Edwin Bailey .15 .40
2 Dave Brown .25 .60
3 Jeff Bryant .20 .50
4 Blair Bush .20 .50
5 Keith Butler .15 .40
6 Kenny Easley .25 .60
7 Jacob Green .25 .60
8 Michael Jackson .15 .40
9 Chuck Knox CO .25 .60
10 Dave Krieg .40 1.00
11 Steve Largent 1.40 3.50
12 Joe Nash .20 .50
13 Bruce Scholtz .15 .40
14 Terry Taylor .15 .40
15 Curt Warner .30 .75
16 Fredd Young .25 .60

1987 Seahawks Ace Fact Pack

This 33-card set measures approximately 2 1/4" by 3 5/8". This set consists of 33 cards of which 22 are player cards and we have checklisted those cards alphabetically. The cards have rounded corners and a playing card type of design on the back. These cards were manufactured in West Germany (by Ace Fact Pack) and released in Great Britain. The set contains members of the Seattle Seahawks.

COMPLETE SET (33) 50.00 120.00
1 Edwin Bailey 1.25 3.00
2 Dave Brown 1.25 3.00
3 Jeff Bryant 1.25 3.00
4 Blair Bush 1.25 3.00
5 Keith Butler 1.25 3.00
6 Kenny Easley 2.00 5.00
7 Greg Gaines 1.25 3.00
8 Jacob Green 2.00 5.00
9 Norm Johnson 2.00 5.00
10 Dave Krieg 3.00 8.00
11 Steve Largent 12.00 30.00
12 Reggie Kinlaw 1.25 3.00
13 Ron Mattes 1.25 3.00
14 Bryan Millard 1.25 3.00
15 Eugene Robinson 2.00 5.00
16 Bruce Scholtz 1.25 3.00
17 Terry Taylor 1.25 3.00
18 Mike Tice 2.00 5.00
19 Daryl Turner 1.25 3.00
20 Curt Warner 2.50 6.00
21 John L. Williams 2.00 5.00
22 Fredd Young 2.00 5.00
23 Seahawks Helmet 1.25 3.00
24 Seahawks Information 1.25 3.00
25 Seahawks Uniform 1.25 3.00
26 Game Record Holders 1.25 3.00
27 Season Record Holders 1.25 3.00
28 Career Record Holders 1.25 3.00
29 Record 1977-86 1.25 3.00
30 1986 Team Statistics 1.25 3.00
31 All-Time Greats 1.25 3.00
32 Roll of Honour 1.25 3.00
33 Kingdome 1.25 3.00

1987 Seahawks Police

This 16-card set of Seattle Seahawks is unnumbered; not even the uniform number is given explicitly on the front of the card. Cards measure approximately 2 5/8" by 4 1/8". The backs contain a safety tip. The year of issue is not printed anywhere on the cards. The card fronts have a silver border and feature a blue and green Seahawks logo. The cards are listed below alphabetically for convenience.

COMPLETE SET (16) 3.00 8.00
1 Jeff Bryant .20 .50
2 Kenny Easley .25 .60
3 Bobby Joe Edmonds .15 .40
4 Jacob Green .25 .60
5 Chuck Knox CO .25 .60
6 Dave Krieg .50 1.25
7 Steve Largent 1.25 3.00
8 Ron Mattes .15 .40
9 Bryan Millard .15 .40
10 Eugene Robinson .25 .60
11 Bruce Scholtz .15 .40
12 Paul Skansi .15 .40
13 Curt Warner .25 .60
14 John L. Williams .25 .60
15 Mike Wilson T .15 .40
16 Fredd Young .20 .50

1987 Seahawks Snyder's/Franz

This 12-card set features players of the Seattle Seahawks. Cards were available only in Snyder's (distributed in the Spokane area) or Franz Bread (distributed in the Portland area) loaves. The set was co-produced by Mike Schechter Associates on behalf of the NFL Players Association. Cards are standard size, 2 1/2" by 3 1/2", in full color, and are numbered on the back. The card fronts have a color photo within a blue border and the backs are printed in black ink on white card stock.

COMPLETE SET (12) 30.00 75.00
1 Jeff Bryant 2.50 6.00
2 Keith Butler 2.50 6.00
3 Randy Edwards 2.50 6.00
4 Byron Franklin 2.50 6.00
5 Jacob Green 2.50 6.00
6 Dave Krieg 3.00 8.00
7 Bryan Millard 2.50 6.00
8 Paul Moyer 2.50 6.00
9 Eugene Robinson 3.00 8.00
10 Mike Tice 2.50 6.00
11 Daryl Turner 2.50 6.00
12 Curt Warner 3.00 8.00

1988 Seahawks Ace Fact Pack

Cards from this 33-card set measure approximately 2 1/4" by 3 5/8". This set consists of 22-player cards and 11-additional informational cards about the Seahawks team. We've checklisted the cards alphabetically beginning with the 22-players. The cards have square corners (as opposed to rounded like the 1987 sets) and a playing card design on the back printed in red. These cards were manufactured in West Germany (by Ace Fact Pack) and released primarily in Great Britain.

COMPLETE SET (33) 75.00 150.00
1 Edwin Bailey 1.50 4.00
2 Brian Bosworth 6.00 15.00
3 Jeff Bryant 1.50 4.00
4 Blair Bush 1.50 4.00
5 Raymond Butler 2.00 5.00
6 Bobby Joe Edmonds 1.50 4.00
7 Greg Gaines 1.50 4.00
8 Jacob Green 2.00 5.00
9 Norm Johnson 1.50 4.00
10 Dave Krieg 3.00 8.00
11 Steve Largent 20.00 50.00
12 Ron Mattes 1.50 4.00
13 Bryan Millard 1.50 4.00
14 Paul Moyer 1.50 4.00
15 Eugene Robinson 2.00 5.00
16 Bruce Scholtz 1.50 4.00
17 Terry Taylor 1.50 4.00
18 Mike Tice 1.50 4.00
19 Daryl Turner 1.50 4.00
20 Curt Warner 3.00 8.00
21 John L. Williams 2.00 5.00
22 Fredd Young 1.50 4.00
23 1987 Team Statistics 1.50 4.00
24 All-Time Greats 1.50 4.00
25 Career Record Holders 1.50 4.00
26 Game Record Holders 1.50 4.00
27 Kingdome 1.50 4.00
28 Record 1976-87 1.50 4.00
29 Roll Of Honour 1.50 4.00
30 Seahawks Helmet 1.50 4.00
31 Seahawks Helmet 1.50 4.00
32 Seahawks Uniform 1.50 4.00
33 Season Record Holders 1.50 4.00

1988 Seahawks Domino's

This 50-card set was sponsored by Domino's Pizza and features Seattle Seahawks players and personnel. The cards were first distributed as a starter set of nine cards (1-9) perforated along with a team photo. Later cards were issued in strips of four or five players (10-13, 14-17, 18-21, 22-25, 26-29, 30-33, 34-38, 39-42, 43-46, and 47-50) along with a promotional coupon for a discount on pizza at Domino's. One strip was available each week with every Domino's pizza ordered. The discount coupons on strips 5, 6, and 8 were supposedly removed prior to distribution to the general public. The cards measure approximately 2 1/2" by 3" whereas the team photo is approximately 12 1/2" by 8 1/2". The set was also partially sponsored by Coca-Cola Classic and KING-5 TV.

COMPLETE SET (51) 16.00 40.00
1 Steve Largent 4.00 10.00
2 Kelly Stouffer .30 .75
3 Bobby Joe Edmonds .30 .75
4 Patrick Hunter .20 .50
5 Ventrella .20 .50
Valle
Gellos
6 Edwin Bailey .20 .50
7 Alonzo Mitz .20 .50
8 Tommy Kane .30 .75
9 Chuck Knox CO .30 .75
10 Curt Warner .40 1.00
11 Alvin Powell .20 .50
12 Joe Nash .20 .50
13 Brian Blades 1.25 3.00
14 Blair Bush .30 .75
15 Melvin Jenkins .20 .50
16 Ruben Rodriguez .20 .50
17 Tommie Agee .20 .50
18 Eugene Robinson .40 1.00
19 Dwayne Harper .20 .50
20 Raymond Butler .20 .50
21 Jeff Kemp .40 1.00
22 Norm Johnson .30 .75
23 Bryan Millard .20 .50
24 Tony Woods .20 .50
25 Paul Skansi .20 .50
26 Jacob Green .30 .75
27 Randall Morris .20 .50
28 Mike Tice .30 .75
29 Kevin Harmon .20 .50
30 Dave Krieg .75 2.00
31 Nesby Glasgow .20 .50
32 Bruce Scholtz .20 .50
33 John Spagnola .20 .50
34 Jeff Bryant .30 .75
35 Stan Eisenhooth .20 .50
36 David Wyman .20 .50
37 Greg Gaines .20 .50
38 Charlie Jones NBC ANN .20 .50
39 Terry Taylor .20 .50
40 Vernon Dean .20 .50
41 Mike Wilson T .20 .50
42 Darrin Miller .20 .50
43 John L. Williams .40 1.00
44 Grant Feasel .20 .50
45 M.L. Johnson .20 .50
46 Ken Clarke .20 .50
47 Brian Bosworth 1.25 3.00
48 Ron Mattes .20 .50
49 Paul Moyer .20 .50
50 Rufus Porter .30 .75
NNO Team Photo 2.50 6.00

1988 Seahawks GTE

This 24-card set was sponsored by GTE and features members of the Seattle Seahawks. The cards measure approximately 3 5/8" by 5 1/2" and were used primarily for player appearances and for fan mailings. The fronts show full-bleed color player photos with the player's signature and uniform number inscribed across the picture. The horizontal backs have a brief career summary on the left portion; the right portion is blank but often has a greeting and/or the player's signature if the player or team signed and mailed out the card. They are very similar to the 1984 set and may have been released over a period of years. The card's year can be determined by the varying information in the player bios on the backs.

COMPLETE SET (24) 40.00 80.00
1 Edwin Bailey 1.25 3.00
2 Brian Bosworth 3.00 8.00
3 Dave Brown 1.25 3.00
4 Jeff Bryant 1.25 3.00
5 Bobby Joe Edmonds 1.25 3.00
6 Jacob Green 1.50 4.00
7 Michael Jackson 1.50 4.00
8 Norm Johnson 1.25 3.00
9 Jeff Kemp 1.50 4.00
10 Chuck Knox CO 1.50 4.00
11 Dave Krieg 3.00 8.00
12 Steve Largent 8.00 20.00
13 Ron Mattes 1.25 3.00
14 Bryan Millard 1.25 3.00
15 Paul Moyer 1.25 3.00
16 Eugene Robinson 1.50 4.00
17 Paul Skansi 1.25 3.00
18 Kelly Stouffer 1.25 3.00
19 Terry Taylor 1.25 3.00
20 Mike Tice 1.25 3.00
21 Daryl Turner 1.25 3.00
22 Curt Warner 2.00 5.00
23 John L. Williams 2.00 5.00
24 Fredd Young 1.25 3.00

1988 Seahawks Police

The 1988 Police Seattle Seahawks set contains 16 cards measuring approximately 2 5/8" by 4 1/8". There are 15 player cards and one coach card. The fronts have gray borders and color photos. The backs have safety tips. Terry Taylor's card was pulled from distribution after his suspension from the team. This unnumbered set is listed alphabetically below for convenience.

COMPLETE SET (15) 4.00 10.00
1 Brian Bosworth .25 .60
2 Jeff Bryant .15 .40
3 Raymond Butler .12 .30
4 Jacob Green .15 .40
5 Patrick Hunter .12 .30
6 Norm Johnson .15 .40
7 Chuck Knox CO .15 .40
8 Dave Krieg .25 .60
9 Steve Largent .75 2.00
10 Ron Mattes .12 .30
11 Bryan Millard .12 .30
12 Paul Moyer .12 .30
13 Terry Taylor SP 1.25 3.00
14 Curt Warner .25 .60
15 John L. Williams .25 .60
16 Fredd Young SP 1.25 3.00

1988 Seahawks Snyder's/Franz

This 12-card standard-size full-color set features players of the Seattle Seahawks. Cards were available only in Snyder's (distributed in the Spokane area) or Franz Bread (distributed in the Portland area) loaves. The set was co-produced by Mike Schechter Associates on behalf of the NFL Players Association. The card fronts have a color photo within a blue border and the backs are printed in black ink on white card stock.

COMPLETE SET (12) 30.00 60.00
1 Dave Krieg 4.00 10.00
2 Curt Warner 3.00 8.00
3 Byron Franklin 2.00 5.00
4 Eugene Robinson 2.50 6.00
5 Mike Tice 2.50 6.00
6 Daryl Turner 2.00 5.00
7 Paul Moyer 2.00 5.00
8 Bryan Millard 2.00 5.00
9 Jeff Bryant 2.00 5.00
10 Keith Butler 2.00 5.00
11 Randy Edwards 2.00 5.00
12 Jacob Green 2.50 6.00

1988 Seahawks Team Issue

This set of photos was issued by the Seahawks. Each measures roughly 8" by 10" and includes a black and white player photo on the front with his name, position, and team name below the photo. These were likely released over a period of years since many vary slightly in regards to type style and size. The backs are blank and unnumbered.

COMPLETE SET (15) 20.00 50.00
1 Brian Bosworth 4.00 10.00
2 Jacob Green 1.50 4.00
3 David Hollis 1.25 3.00
4 Melvin Jenkins 1.25 3.00
5 Norm Johnson 1.25 3.00
6 Jeff Kemp 1.50 4.00
7 Chuck Knox CO 1.50 4.00
8 David Krieg 1.50 4.00
9 Ron Mattes 1.25 3.00
10 Paul Moyer 1.25 3.00
11 Eugene Robinson 2.50 6.00
12 Paul Skansi 1.25 3.00
13 John L. Williams 1.50 4.00
14 Curt Warner 2.50 6.00
15 Tony Woods LB 1.25 3.00

1989 Seahawks Oroweat

The 1989 Oroweat Seahawks set contains 20 standard-size cards. The cards have attractive silver borders and color action shots and were produced by Pacific Trading Cards for Oroweat. The horizontally-oriented backs have light blue borders with bios, stats, and career highlights. One card was distributed in each specially marked loaf of Oroweat's Oatnut Bread, sold only in the Pacific Northwest. It has been reported that 1.5 million cards were distributed.

COMPLETE SET (20) 25.00 60.00
1 Paul Moyer .40 1.00
2 David Wyman .40 1.00
3 Tony Woods .60 1.50
4 Kelly Stouffer .40 1.00
5 Brian Blades 4.00 10.00
6 Norm Johnson .60 1.50
7 Curt Warner 1.00 2.50
8 John L. Williams 1.00 2.50
9 Edwin Bailey .40 1.00
10 Jacob Green .60 1.50
11 Paul Skansi .40 1.00
12 Jeff Bryant .40 1.00
13 Bruce Scholtz .40 1.00
14 Dave Krieg 2.00 5.00
15 Steve Largent 6.00 15.00
16 Joe Nash .40 1.00
17 Mike Wilson T .40 1.00
18 Ron Mattes .40 1.00
19 Grant Feasel .40 1.00
20 Bryan Millard .40 1.00

1989 Seahawks Police

The 1989 Police Seattle Seahawks set contains 16 cards measuring approximately 2 5/8" by 4 1/8". The fronts have light blue borders and color action photos; the vertically-oriented backs have safety tips. These cards were printed on very thin stock. The cards are unnumbered, so therefore are listed alphabetically by subject's name. The Largent card contains a list of Steve's records on the back instead of the typical safety tip found on all the other cards in the set.

COMPLETE SET (16) 2.50 6.00
1 Brian Blades .25 .60
2 Brian Bosworth .40 1.00
3 Jeff Bryant .12 .30
4 Jacob Green .15 .40
5 Chuck Knox CO .15 .40
6 Dave Krieg .30 .75
7 Steve Largent .75 2.00
8 Bryan Millard .12 .30
9 Rufus Porter .12 .30
10 Paul Moyer .12 .30
11 Eugene Robinson .25 .60
12 Ruben Rodriguez .12 .30
13 Kelly Stouffer .15 .40
14 Curt Warner .25 .60
15 John L. Williams .25 .60
16 Tony Woods .15 .40

1990 Seahawks Oroweat

This 50-card set of Seattle Seahawks was released in the Seattle area in various loaves of Oroweat products, Oat Nut, Health Nut, and Twelve Grain bread. The set was released in two series, 20 cards issued before the 1990 NFL season began and 30 cards released during the season. The fronts of the set feature full-color action shots within a silver border while the back of the card features a mix of statistical and biographical information. The cards each measure approximately 2 1/2" by 3 1/2" and were produced by Pacific Trading Cards for Oroweat. There are two #24 cards and no card #25.

COMPLETE SET (50) 20.00 50.00
1 Dave Krieg 1.00 2.50
2 Rick Donnelly .30 .75
3 Brian Blades 1.25 3.00
4 Cortez Kennedy 1.50 4.00
5 John L. Williams .80 2.00
6 Jeff Chadwick .60 1.50
7 Thom Kaumeyer .30 .75
8 Bryan Millard .30 .75
9 Eugene Robinson .60 1.50
10 Jacob Green .60 1.50
11 Willie Bouyer .30 .75
12 Jeff Bryant .30 .75
13 Chris Warren 3.20 8.00
14 Derrick Fenner .60 1.50
15 Paul Skansi .30 .75
16 Joe Cain .30 .75
17 Tommy Kane .30 .75
18 Tom Flores GM .60 1.50
19 Terry Wooden .30 .75
20 Tony Woods .80 2.00
21 Ricky Andrews .40 1.00
22 Joe Tofflemire .40 1.00
23 Ned Bolcar .40 1.00
24A Kelly Stouffer .80 2.00
24B Melvin Jenkins .40 1.00
26 Norm Johnson .80 2.00
27 Eric Hayes .40 1.00
28 Mike Morris .40 1.00
29 Edwin Bailey .40 1.00
30 Ron Heller TE .40 1.00
31 Darren Comeaux .40 1.00
32 Andy Heck .40 1.00
33 Ronnie Lee .40 1.00
34 Robert Blackmon .40 1.00
35 Joe Nash .40 1.00
36 Patrick Hunter .40 1.00
37 Darrick Brilz .40 1.00
38 Ron Mattes .40 1.00
39 Nesby Glasgow .40 1.00
40 Dwayne Harper .40 1.00
41 Chuck Knox CO .80 2.00
42 Travis McNeal .80 2.00
43 Derek Loville .80 2.00
44 David Wyman .80 2.00
45 Louis Clark .40 1.00
46 Grant Feasel .40 1.00
47 James Jones FB .40 1.00
48 Rufus Porter .80 2.00
49 Jeff Kemp .80 2.00
50 James Jefferson .80 2.00
NNO Title Card 1.60 4.00

1990 Seahawks Police

This 16-card set was issued in the Seattle area to promote the various saftey tips using members of the 1990 Seattle Seahawks. The cards measure approximately 2 5/8" by 4 1/8" and have solid green borders which frame a full-color photo of the player pictured. On the back is a safety tip. Since the cards are unnumbered, we have checklisted this set in alphabetical order.

COMPLETE SET (16) 2.40 6.00
1 Brian Blades .40 1.00
2 Grant Feasel .10 .30
3 Jacob Green .15 .40
4 Andy Heck .10 .30
5 James Jefferson .10 .30
6 Norm Johnson .15 .40
7 Cortez Kennedy .50 1.25
8 Chuck Knox CO .15 .40
9 Dave Krieg .25 .60
10 Travis McNeal .10 .30
11 Bryan Millard .10 .30
12 Rufus Porter .10 .30
13 Paul Skansi .10 .30
14 John L. Williams .25 .60
15 Tony Woods .15 .40
16 David Wyman .10 .30

1991 Seahawks Oroweat

This 50-card standard-size set was sponsored by Oroweat and produced by Pacific. One card was included in every Oroweat loaf of bread throughout Washington, Oregon, and western portions of Idaho. Although cards were not sold in complete sets, five-card packs were given out at one of the Seahawks' games. The title cards were only available in the five-card packs. The fronts of these cards feature glossy color action player photos, with the player's name written vertically in a purple stripe at the left side of the picture. The team name and position appear in a silver stripe below the picture. In a diagonal design, the horizontally oriented backs have biography, a color headshot of the player, statistics, and career summary.

COMPLETE SET (51) 16.00 40.00
1 Tommy Kane .40 1.00
2 Norm Johnson .40 1.00
3 Robert Blackmon .40 1.00
4 Mike Tice .40 1.00
5 Cortez Kennedy .80 2.00
6 Bryan Millard .40 1.00
7 Tony Woods .50 1.25
8 Paul Skansi .40 1.00
9 John L. Williams .80 2.00
10 Terry Wooden .40 1.00
11 Brian Blades .80 2.00
12 Jacob Green .40 1.00
13 Joe Nash .40 1.00
14 Eugene Robinson .80 2.00
15 Rufus Porter .40 1.00
16 Andy Heck .40 1.00
17 Derrick Fenner .80 2.00
18 Nesby Glasgow .40 1.00
19 Chris Warren 3.20 8.00
20 Dave Krieg 1.00 2.50
21 Vann McElroy .40 1.00
22 Jeff Bryant .40 1.00
23 Warren Wheat .40 1.00
24 Marcus Cotton .40 1.00
25 David Wyman .40 1.00
26 Joe Cain .40 1.00
27 Darrick Brilz .40 1.00
28 Eric Hayes .40 1.00
29 Ronnie Lee .40 1.00
30 Louis Clark .40 1.00
31 James Jones FB .40 1.00
32 Dwayne Harper .40 1.00
33 Grant Feasel .40 1.00
34 Trey Junkin .40 1.00
35 James Jefferson .40 1.00
36 Edwin Bailey .40 1.00
37 Derek Loville .80 2.00
38 Travis McNeal .40 1.00
39 Rick Donnelly .40 1.00
40 Rod Stephens .40 1.00
41 Darren Comeaux .40 1.00
42 Brian Davis .40 1.00
43 Bill Hitchcock .40 1.00
44 Jeff Chadwick .50 1.25
45 Patrick Hunter .50 1.25
46 David Daniels .40 1.00
47 Doug Thomas .40 1.00
48 Dan McGwire .50 1.25
49 John Kasay .80 2.00
50 Jeff Kemp .50 1.25
NNO Title Card 1.60 4.00

1992 Seahawks Oroweat

Inserted one card per Oroweat bread loaf, these 50 standard-size cards feature on their fronts white-bordered color player action shots. The player's name and position appear vertically in green lettering within a gray stripe on the left. The white-bordered horizontal back carries a color player close-up on the left and, alongside on the right, the player's name and position within a white strip near the top, followed below by biography, statistics, and career highlights within a green panel. The Oroweat and KIRO Newsradio logos on the back round out the card.

COMPLETE SET (51) 60.00 100.00
1 Brian Blades 2.00 4.00
2 Patrick Hunter .75 2.00
3 Jeff Bryant .75 2.00
4 Robert Blackmon .75 2.00
5 Joe Cain .75 2.00
6 Grant Feasel .75 2.00
7 Dan McGwire 1.25 2.50
8 David Wyman .75 2.00
9 Jacob Green 1.25 2.50
10 Theo Adams .75 2.00
11 Brian Davis .75 2.00
12 Andy Heck .75 2.00
13 Bill Hitchcock .75 2.00
14 Joe Nash .75 2.00
15 Rod Stephens .75 2.00
16 John Hunter .75 2.00
17 Paul Green .75 2.00
18 James Jones FB .75 2.00
19 Robb Thomas .75 2.00
20 Tony Woods .75 2.00
21 Dedrick Dodge .75 2.00
22 Tracy Johnson .75 2.00
23 Darrick Brilz .75 2.00
24 Joe Tofflemire .75 2.00
25 Louis Clark .75 2.00
26 Rueben Mayes 1.25 2.50
27 Natu Tuatagaloa .75 2.00
28 Terry Wooden .75 2.00
29 Tommy Kane .75 2.00
30 Stan Gelbaugh .75 2.00
31 Nesby Glasgow .75 2.00
32 Kelly Stouffer .75 2.00
33 Ray Roberts .75 2.00
34 Doug Thomas .75 2.00
35 David Daniels .75 2.00
36 John Kasay 2.00 4.00
37 Cortez Kennedy 1.25 2.50
38 Tyrone Rodgers .75 2.00
39 Bryan Millard .75 2.00
40 Eugene Robinson 2.00 4.00
41 Malcolm Frank .75 2.00
42 Dwayne Harper .75 2.00
43 Ron Heller TE .75 2.00
44 Rick Tuten .75 2.00
45 Trey Junkin .75 2.00
46 Bob Spitulski .75 2.00
47 Chris Warren 2.00 4.00
48 John L. Williams 1.25 2.50
49 Ronnie Lee .75 2.00
50 Rufus Porter .75 2.00
NNO Title 2.00 4.00
ad card

1993 Seahawks Oroweat

Produced by Pacific, this 50-card standard-size set was co-sponsored by Oroweat and KIRO News 710 AM. One card was included in each Oroweat loaf of bread throughout Washington, Oregon, and western portions of Idaho. Moreover, cello packs containing three player cards and one ad card were given away at home games. The fronts feature color action player photos that are tilted slightly to the left and set on a team color-coded gray and blue marbleized card face. The team helmet appears at the lower left corner, and the player's name and position are printed across the bottom of the picture. On a marbleized gray and blue background, the backs carry a second color player photo, biography, statistics, and player profile.

COMPLETE SET (50) 50.00 100.00
1 Cortez Kennedy 1.25 2.50
2 Robb Thomas 1.00 2.00
3 Rueben Mayes 1.00 2.00
4 Rick Tuten 1.00 2.00
5 Tracy Johnson 1.00 2.00
6 Michael Bates 1.00 2.00
7 Andy Heck 1.00 2.00
8 Stan Gelbaugh 1.00 2.00
9 Dan McGwire 1.25 2.50
10 Mike Keim 1.00 2.00
11 Grant Feasel 1.00 2.00
12 Brian Blades 2.00 4.00
13 Tyrone Rodgers 1.00 2.00
14 Paul Green 1.00 2.00
15 Rafael Robinson 1.00 2.00
16 John Kasay 2.00 4.00
17 Chris Warren 2.00 4.00
18 Michael Sinclair 1.25 2.50
19 John L. Williams 1.25 2.50
20 Bob Spitulski 1.00 2.00
21 Eugene Robinson 2.00 4.00
22 Patrick Hunter 1.00 2.00
23 Kevin Murphy 1.00 2.00
24 Dave McCloughan 1.00 2.00
25 Rick Mirer 4.00 8.00
26 Ray Donaldson 1.00 2.00
27 E.J. Junior 1.00 2.00
28 Jeff Bryant 1.00 2.00
29 Ferrell Edmunds 1.00 2.00
30 Tommy Kane 1.00 2.00
31 Terry Wooden 1.00 2.00
32 Doug Thomas 1.00 2.00
33 Carlton Gray 1.00 2.00
34 Kelvin Martin 1.00 2.00
35 Rod Stephens 1.00 2.00
36 Darrick Brilz 1.00 2.00
37 Joe Tofflemire 1.00 2.00
38 James Jefferson 1.00 2.00
39 Rufus Porter 1.00 2.00
40 Jeff Blackshear 1.00 2.00
41 Dwayne Harper 1.00 2.00
42 Ray Roberts 1.00 2.00
43 Robert Blackmon 1.00 2.00
44 Joe Nash 1.00 2.00
45 Michael McCrary 2.00 4.00
46 Trey Junkin 1.00 2.00
47 Natu Tuatagaloa 1.00 2.00
48 Bill Hitchcock 1.00 2.00
49 Jon Vaughn 1.00 2.00
50 Dean Wells 1.00 2.00

1994 Seahawks Oroweat

These 50 standard-size cards were produced by Pacific Trading Cards, Inc. for Oroweat. This occasion marks the sixth straight year that these two companies have worked together in a promotion. Seven different players were issued every two weeks throughout the regular season. The cards were found in loaves of Oatnut, Health Nut, and other variety breads sold throughout Washington, Oregon, Idaho, and Alaska. The fronts feature color player action shots on their blue-bordered fronts. The player's name and position appear at the lower right. The horizontal white-bordered back carries a color player close-up on the left, with the player's name, position, biography, and career highlights displayed alongside on the right within a gray panel highlighted by a ghosted Seahawks helmet. The cards are numbered on the back as "X of 50."

COMPLETE SET (50) 50.00 100.00
1 Brian Blades 1.25 2.50
2 Terrence Warren 1.00 2.00
3 Carlton Gray 1.00 2.00
4 Bob Spitulski 1.00 2.00
5 Dean Wells 1.00 2.00
6 Lamar Smith 7.50 15.00
7 Michael Bates 1.00 2.00
8 Duane Bickett 1.00 2.00
9 Cortez Kennedy 1.25 2.50
10 Dave McCloughan 1.00 2.00
11 Tracy Johnson 1.00 2.00
12 Eugene Robinson 2.00 4.00
13 Jeff Blackshear 1.00 2.00
14 Tyrone Rodgers 1.00 2.00
15 Trey Junkin 1.00 2.00
16 Ferrell Edmunds 1.00 2.00
17 Tony Brown 1.00 2.00
18 Orlando Watters 1.00 2.00
19 John Kasay 2.00 4.00
20 Rafael Robinson 1.00 2.00
21 Kelvin Martin 1.00 2.00
22 Stan Gelbaugh 1.00 2.00
23 Steve Smith 1.00 2.00
24 Ray Donaldson 1.00 2.00
25 Rufus Porter 1.00 2.00
26 Patrick Hunter 1.00 2.00
27 Terry Wooden 1.00 2.00
28 Sam Adams 2.00 4.00
29 Mack Strong 2.50 6.00
30 Chris Warren 1.25 2.50
31 Bill Hitchcock 1.00 2.00
32 David Brandon 1.00 2.00
33 Michael McCrary 2.00 4.00
34 Jon Vaughn 1.00 2.00
35 Paul Green 1.00 2.00
36 Mike Keim 1.00 2.00
37 Joe Tofflemire 1.00 2.00
38 Rick Tuten 1.00 2.00
39 Rick Mirer 2.00 4.00
40 Rod Stephens 1.00 2.00
41 Robert Blackmon 1.00 2.00
42 Howard Ballard 1.00 2.00
43 Michael Sinclair 1.00 2.00
44 Kevin Mawae 2.00 4.00
45 Brent Williams 1.00 2.00
46 Ray Roberts 1.00 2.00
47 Robb Thomas 1.00 2.00
48 Antonio Edwards 1.00 2.00
49 Dan McGwire 1.00 2.00
50 Joe Nash 1.00 2.00

1997 Seahawks Pacific Franz

This set was produced by Pacific Trading Cards and released in Franz Bread packages one card at a time. The card fronts feature both the Pacific Crown and Seattle Seahawks logos.

COMPLETE SET (16) 60.00 100.00
1 Howard Ballard 2.00 5.00
2 Bennie Blades 2.00 5.00
3 Brian Blades 2.50 6.00
4 Chad Brown 2.50 6.00
5 John Friesz 2.50 6.00
6 Joey Galloway 4.00 10.00
7 Walter Jones 2.00 5.00
8 Pete Kendall 2.00 5.00
9 Cortez Kennedy 2.50 6.00
10 Warren Moon 5.00 12.00
11 Winston Moss 2.00 5.00
12 Michael Sinclair 2.00 5.00
13 Shawn Springs 2.50 6.00
14 Chris Warren 3.00 8.00
15 Darryl Williams 2.00 5.00
16 Willie Williams 2.00 5.00

2006 Seahawks DAV

COMPLETE SET (10) 4.00 10.00
1 Shaun Alexander .50 1.50
2 Michael Boulware .40 1.00
3 Josh Brown .40 1.00
4 Bobby Engram .40 1.00
5 Bryce Fisher .30 .75
6 Matt Hasselbeck .60 1.50
7 Mack Strong .40 1.00
8 Lofa Tatupu .60 1.50
9 Marcus Trufant .40 1.00
10 Grant Wistrom .40 1.00

2006 Seahawks Topps

COMPLETE SET (12) 3.00 6.00
SEA1 Lofa Tatupu .25 .60
SEA2 Bobby Engram .25 .60
SEA3 Leroy Hill .25 .60
SEA4 Jerramy Stevens .30 .75
SEA5 Michael Boulware .25 .60
SEA6 Matt Hasselbeck .25 .60
SEA7 Shaun Alexander .25 .60
SEA8 Darrell Jackson .30 .75
SEA9 Marcus Trufant .25 .60
SEA10 Walter Jones .25 .60
SEA11 Nate Burleson .25 .60
SEA12 Kelly Jennings .30 .75

2007 Seahawks Topps

COMPLETE SET (12) 2.50 5.00
1 Shaun Alexander .40 1.00
2 Matt Hasselbeck .40 1.00
3 Deion Branch .40 1.00
4 Lofa Tatupu .40 1.00
5 Seneca Wallace .40 1.00
6 Maurice Morris .40 1.00
7 Marcus Pollard .40 1.00
8 D.J. Hackett .40 1.00
9 Walter Jones .40 1.00
10 Julian Peterson .40 1.00
11 Josh Brown .40 1.00
12 Patrick Kerney .40 1.00

2008 Seahawks Topps

COMPLETE SET (12) 2.00 4.00
1 Lawrence Jackson .40 1.00
2 Bobby Engram .40 1.00
3 Patrick Kerney .40 1.00
4 Lofa Tatupu .40 1.00
5 Matt Hasselbeck .40 1.00
6 Julius Jones .40 1.00
7 Maurice Morris .40 1.00
8 Deion Branch .40 1.00
9 Julian Peterson .40 1.00
10 Nate Burleson .40 1.00
11 Marcus Trufant .40 1.00
12 Walter Jones .40 1.00

2014 Seahawks Panini Super Bowl XLVIII

COMPLETE SET (10) 4.00 10.00
ISSUED AS PART OF 40-CARD FACT.SET
1 Russell Wilson 1.00 2.50
2 Marshawn Lynch .50 1.25
3 Golden Tate .50 1.25
4 Doug Baldwin .50 1.25
5 Max Unger .40 1.00
6 Richard Sherman .60 1.50
7 Earl Thomas .50 1.25
8 Kam Chancellor .60 1.50
9 Bobby Wagner .40 1.00
10 Steven Hauschka 1.25 3.00

2014 Seahawks Topps 5x7 Super Bowl XLIX

COMPLETE SET (8) 12.00 20.00
32 Russell Wilson 2.50 6.00
157 Derrick Coleman 1.00 2.50
230 Bobby Wagner 1.00 2.50
250 Terrelle Pryor 1.00 2.50
255 Marshawn Lynch 1.25 3.00
256 Bruce Irvin 1.00 2.50
296 Steven Hauschka 3.00 8.00
304 Malcolm Smith 1.50 4.00

2015 Seahawks Panini Super Bowl XLIX

COMPLETE SET (10) 12.50 25.00
1 Russell Wilson 1.50 4.00
2 Marshawn Lynch 1.00 2.50
3 Doug Baldwin 1.00 2.50
4 Luke Willson 1.00 2.50
5 Max Unger .75 2.00
6 Kam Chancellor 1.25 3.00
7 Richard Sherman 1.25 3.00
8 Earl Thomas 1.00 2.50
9 Bobby Wagner .75 2.00
10 Steven Hauschka 1.25 3.00

1982 Sears-Roebuck

These oversized 5" by 7" cards feature player photos on fronts. Reportedly these cards were issued in Sears 37 District Stores from January to December 1982. Reportedly because of the football players' strike, the promotion flopped, and consequently many cards were destroyed or thrown out. These cards look almost exactly like the Marketcom cards but say Sears Roebuck at the bottom of the reverse. These unnumbered cards are checklisted below in alphabetical order.

COMPLETE SET (14) 150.00 300.00
1 Ken Anderson 5.00 12.00
2 Terry Bradshaw 12.00 30.00
3 Earl Campbell 8.00 20.00
4 Rob Carpenter 4.00 10.00
5 Dwight Clark 4.00 10.00
6 Cris Collinsworth 4.00 10.00
7 Tony Dorsett 8.00 20.00
8 Dan Fouts 6.00 15.00

9 Mark Gastineau 5.00 12.00
10 Franco Harris 8.00 20.00
11 Joe Montana 40.00 100.00
12 Walter Payton 20.00 50.00
13 Randy White 6.00 15.00
14 Kellen Winslow 5.00 12.00

1993 Select

The 1993 Select set consists of 200 standard-size cards. Production was reportedly limited to 2,950 cases and cards were issued in 12-card packs. Rookie Cards include Jerome Bettis, Drew Bledsoe, Curtis Conway, Garrison Hearst, O.J. McDuffie, Natrone Means, Glyn Milburn and Rick Mirer.

COMPLETE SET (200) 7.50 20.00
1 Steve Young .75 2.00
2 Andre Reed .15 .40
3 Deion Sanders .50 1.25
4 Harold Green .07 .20
5 Wendell Davis .07 .20
6 Mike Johnson .07 .20
7 Troy Aikman .75 2.00
8 Johnny Mitchell .07 .20
9 Dale Carter .07 .20
10 Bruce Matthews .07 .20
11 Terrell Buckley .07 .20
12 Steve Emtman .07 .20
13 Neil Smith .30 .75
14 Tim Brown .30 .75
15 Chris Doleman .07 .20
16 Dan Marino 1.50 4.00
17 Terry McDaniel .07 .20
18 Neal Anderson .07 .20
19 Phil Simms .15 .40
20 Jeff Lageman .07 .20
21 Jerry Rice 1.00 2.50
22 Dermontti Dawson .15 .40
23 Reggie Cobb .07 .20
24 Junior Seau .30 .75
25 Darrell Green .07 .20
26 Chris Warren .15 .40
27 Randall Cunningham .30 .75
28 Bruce Smith .30 .75
29 Bryan Cox .07 .20
30 David Klingler .07 .20
31 Chip Lohmiller .07 .20
32 Eric Metcalf .15 .40
33 Ken Norton Jr. .15 .40
34 John Elway 1.50 4.00
35 Harris Barton .07 .20
36 Tim Barnett .07 .20
37 Rodney Hampton .15 .40
38 Desmond Howard .15 .40
39 Tom Rathman .07 .20
40 Derrick Thomas .30 .75
41 Randal Hill .07 .20
42 Steve Wisniewski .07 .20
43 Brett Favre 2.00 5.00
44 Darryl Talley .07 .20
45 Shane Conlan .07 .20
46 Anthony Miller .15 .40
47 Randall McDaniel .07 .20
48 Rod Woodson .30 .75
49 Eric Martin .07 .20
50 Ronnie Lott .15 .40
51 Chris Spielman .15 .40
52 Vincent Brown .07 .20
53 Donnell Woolford .07 .20
54 Richmond Webb .07 .20
55 Emmitt Smith 1.25 3.00
56 Haywood Jeffires .15 .40
57 Jim Kelly .30 .75
58 James Francis .07 .20
59 Steve Wallace .07 .20
60 Jarrod Bunch .07 .20
61 Lawrence Dawsey .07 .20
62 Steve Atwater .07 .20
63 Art Monk .15 .40
64 Eric Green .07 .20
65 Lawrence Taylor .30 .75
66 Ronnie Harmon .07 .20
67 Fred Barnett .15 .40
68 Cortez Kennedy .15 .40
69 Mark Collins .07 .20
70 Howie Long .30 .75
71 Jackie Harris .07 .20
72 Irving Fryar .15 .40
73 Jim Everett .15 .40
74 Troy Vincent .07 .20
75 Cris Carter .30 .75
76 Boomer Esiason .15 .40
77 Sam Mills .07 .20
78 Lorenzo White .07 .20
79 Andre Rison .15 .40
80 Quentin Coryatt .15 .40
81 Steve McMichael .15 .40
82 Nick Lowery .07 .20
83 Michael Irvin .30 .75
84 Thurman Thomas .30 .75
85 Bill Romanowski .07 .20
86 Carl Pickens .15 .40
87 Tim McDonald .07 .20
88 Bernie Kosar .15 .40
89 Greg Lloyd .15 .40
90 Barry Sanders 1.25 3.00
91 Shannon Sharpe .30 .75
92 Henry Thomas .07 .20
93 Barry Foster .15 .40
94 Antone Davis .07 .20
95 Stan Humphries .15 .40
96 Eric Swann .15 .40
97 Mike Pritchard .15 .40
98 Reggie White .30 .75
99 Jeff Hostetler .15 .40
100 Flipper Anderson .07 .20
101 Gary Clark .15 .40
102 Morten Andersen .07 .20
103 Leonard Russell .15 .40
104 Chris Hinton .07 .20
105 John Stephens .07 .20
106 Byron Evans .07 .20
107 Warren Moon .30 .75
108 Marv Cook .07 .20
109 Carlton Gray RC .07 .20
110 Jay Novacek .15 .40
111 Gary Anderson K .07 .20
112 Andre Tippett .07 .20
113 Cornelius Bennett .15 .40
114 Clyde Simmons .07 .20
115 Jeff George .30 .75
116 Audray McMillian .07 .20
117 Mark Carrier WR .15 .40
118 Vaughan Johnson .07 .20
119 Kevin Greene .15 .40
120 John Taylor .15 .40
121 Jerry Ball .07 .20
122 Pat Swilling .07 .20
123 George Teague RC .15 .40
124 Ricky Reynolds .07 .20
125 Marcus Allen .30 .75
126 Henry Jones .07 .20
127 Ricky Watters .30 .75
128 Leon Searcy .07 .20
129 Chris Miller .15 .40
130 Jim Harbaugh .30 .75
131 Luis Sharpe .07 .20
132 Simon Fletcher .07 .20
133 Eric Allen .07 .20
134 Carlton Haselrig .07 .20
135 Harvey Williams .15 .40
136 Leslie O'Neal .15 .40
137 Sterling Sharpe .30 .75
138 Tim Harris .07 .20
139 Mark Rypien .07 .20
140 Harry Galbreath .07 .20
141 Sean Gilbert .15 .40
142 Keith Jackson .15 .40
143 Mark Clayton .07 .20
144 Guy McIntyre .07 .20
145 Jessie Tuggle .07 .20
146 Leonard Marshall .07 .20
147 Willie Davis .30 .75
148 Herman Moore .30 .75
149 Charles Haley .15 .40
150 Amp Lee .07 .20
151 Gary Zimmerman .07 .20
152 Bennie Blades .07 .20
153 Pierce Holt .07 .20
154 Edgar Bennett .30 .75
155 Joe Montana 1.50 4.00
156 Ted Washington .07 .20
157 Hardy Nickerson .15 .40
158 Rohn Stark .07 .20
159 Brent Jones .15 .40
160 Eugene Robinson .07 .20
161 Pepper Johnson .07 .20
162 Dan Saleaumua .07 .20
163 Seth Joyner .07 .20
164 Bruce Armstrong .07 .20
165 Mike Munchak .15 .40
166 Drew Bledsoe RC 2.00 5.00
167 Curtis Conway RC .50 1.25
168 Lincoln Kennedy RC .07 .20
169 Dana Stubblefield RC .30 .75
170 Wayne Simmons RC .07 .20
171 Garrison Hearst RC .75 2.00
172 Jerome Bettis RC 3.00 8.00
173 Eric Curry RC .07 .20
174 Natrone Means RC .30 .75
175 Glyn Milburn RC .30 .75
176 Marvin Jones RC .07 .20
177 O.J.McDuffie RC .30 .75
178 Dan Williams RC .07 .20
179 Rick Mirer RC .30 .75
180 John Copeland RC .15 .40
181 Willie Roaf RC .50 1.25
182 Patrick Bates RC .07 .20
183 Troy Drayton RC .15 .40
184 Vincent Brisby RC .30 .75
185 Irv Smith RC .07 .20
186 Marion Butts .07 .20
187 Wayne Martin .07 .20
188 Brian Blades .15 .40
189 Mel Gray .15 .40
190 Mark Stepnoski .07 .20
191 Ernest Givins .15 .40
192 Steve Tasker .15 .40
193 Tim Grunhard .07 .20
194 Stanley Richard .07 .20
195 Jeff Wright .07 .20
196 Rodney Peete .07 .20
197 Tunch Ilkin .07 .20
198 Rich Camarillo .07 .20
199 Erik Williams .07 .20
200 Pete Stoyanovich .07 .20
S21 Jerry Rice SAMPLE 1.00 2.50

1993 Select Gridiron Skills

Featuring five quarterbacks and five wide receivers, this ten-card "Gridiron Skills" subset was randomly inserted throughout the foil packs. The insert rate of these chase cards was reportedly one in every two boxes or not less than one in 72 packs. The cards are numbered on the back as "X of 10."

COMPLETE SET (10) 30.00 80.00
1 Warren Moon 2.00 5.00
2 Steve Young 5.00 12.00
3 Dan Marino 10.00 25.00
4 John Elway 10.00 25.00
5 Troy Aikman 5.00 12.00
6 Sterling Sharpe 2.00 5.00
7 Jerry Rice 6.00 15.00
8 Andre Rison 1.00 2.50
9 Haywood Jeffires 1.00 2.50
10 Michael Irvin 2.00 5.00

1993 Select Young Stars

This 38-card standard-size set was sold in a hinged black leatherette box. Each set included a certificate of authenticity, providing the set serial number out of a total of 5,900 sets produced. Using Score's FX printing technology, the fronts display color action cutouts that extend beyond the arched-shape background. The cards are numbered on the back "X of 38."

COMP.FACT SET (38) 15.00 40.00
1 Brett Favre 4.00 10.00
2 Anthony Miller .30 .75
3 Rodney Hampton .30 .75
4 Cortez Kennedy .30 .75
5 Junior Seau .40 1.00
6 Ricky Watters .30 .75
7 Terry Allen .30 .75
8 Drew Bledsoe 6.00 15.00
9 Rick Mirer .40 1.00
10 Jeff Graham .30 .75
11 Barry Foster .30 .75
12 Eric Green .20 .50
13 Troy Aikman 2.50 6.00
14 Michael Haynes .30 .75
15 Johnny Mitchell .20 .50
16 Lawrence Dawsey .20 .50
17 Mo Lewis .20 .50
18 Andre Ware .30 .75
19 Neil O'Donnell .30 .75
20 Broderick Thomas .20 .50
21 Tim Barnett .20 .50
22 Fred Barnett .30 .75
23 Carl Pickens .30 .75
24 Santana Dotson .30 .75
25 Sean Gilbert .20 .50
26 Quentin Coryatt .20 .50
27 Arthur Marshall .20 .50
28 Dale Carter .20 .50
29 Henry Jones .20 .50
30 Terrell Buckley .20 .50
31 Tommy Vardell .20 .50
32 Russell Maryland .20 .50
33 Steve Emtman .20 .50
34 Jarrod Bunch .20 .50
35 Alfred Williams .20 .50
36 Brian Mitchell .20 .50
37 Chris Warren .30 .75
38 Deion Sanders 1.25 3.00

1994 Select Samples

These sample cards measure the standard size and preview the style of the 1994 Select football set and include four regular issue cards, one "Canton Bound" and one "Future Force" card. The fronts feature full-bleed color action player photos. A small, oval-shaped black-and-white action player photo with a gold-foil border carrying the team name appears in the lower left corner. Select's logo is superimposed in the lower right corner, with the player's last name printed in gold-foil letters over it. The horizontal backs carry a second color action photo on the left, with 1993 highlights, statistics and career totals on the right. The upper right corner of each card is cut off.

COMPLETE SET (7) 4.80 12.00
5 Rod Woodson .40 1.00
19 Junior Seau .50 1.25
33 Mark Carrier DB .40 1.00
218 Charlie Garner .60 1.50
CB4 Barry Sanders 2.00 5.00
FF2 Drew Bledsoe 1.20 3.00
NNO Title Card .40 1.00

1994 Select

The 1994 Select football set consists of 226 standard size cards. Production was reportedly limited to 3,950 individually numbered boxes and cases. Top rookie prospects are showcased in a Rookie (199-223) subset. Rookie cards include Derrick Alexander, Mario Bates, Trent Dilfer, Marshall Faulk, William Floyd, Greg Hill, Charles Johnson, Errict Rhett, Darnay Scott and Heath Shuler.

COMPLETE SET (225) 6.00 15.00
1 Emmitt Smith 1.00 2.50
2 Bruce Smith .15 .40
3 Randall McDaniel .05 .15
4 Drew Bledsoe .50 1.25
5 Rod Woodson .07 .20
6 Richard Dent .07 .20
7 Norm Johnson .02 .10
8 Jim Everett .07 .20
9 Harold Green .02 .10
10 John Elway 1.25 3.00
11 Barry Sanders 1.00 2.50
12 Sterling Sharpe .07 .20
13 Marcus Robertson .02 .10
14 Steve Wisniewski .02 .10
15 Irving Fryar .07 .20
16 Tyrone Hughes .07 .20
17 Garrison Hearst .15 .40
18 Randall Cunningham .15 .40
19 Junior Seau .15 .40
20 Rick Mirer .15 .40
21 Jerry Rice .60 1.50
22 Eric Metcalf .07 .20
23 Roosevelt Potts .02 .10
24 Neil Smith .07 .20
25 Jerome Bettis .30 .75
26 Keith Hamilton .02 .10
27 Hardy Nickerson .07 .20
28 Steve Tasker .07 .20
29 Johnny Johnson .02 .10
30 Tom Carter .02 .10
31 Andre Rison .07 .20
32 Cortez Kennedy .07 .20
33 Mark Carrier DB .02 .10
34 Shannon Sharpe .07 .20
35 Eric Swann .07 .20
36 Steve Young .50 1.25
37 Johnny Mitchell .02 .10
38 Dermontti Dawson .08 .20
39 Mike Johnson .02 .10
40 Troy Aikman .60 1.50
41 Pierce Holt .02 .10
42 Derrick Thomas .15 .40
43 Reggie Cobb .02 .10
44 Michael Jackson .07 .20
45 Lomas Brown .02 .10
46 Jeff Hostetler .07 .20
47 Pete Stoyanovich .02 .10
48 Reggie White .15 .40
49 Quentin Coryatt .02 .10
50 Cris Carter .30 .75
51 Sean Gilbert .02 .10
52 Chris Slade .02 .10
53 Ronnie Harmon .02 .10
54 Renaldo Turnbull .02 .10
55 Fred Barnett .07 .20
56 John Elliott .02 .10
57 Deion Sanders .30 .75
58 John Carney .02 .10
59 Louis Oliver .02 .10
60 Greg Lloyd .07 .20
61 Chris Hinton .02 .10
62 Ronald Moore .02 .10
63 Vincent Brown .02 .10
64 Tony McGee .02 .10
65 Erik Williams .02 .10
66 Thurman Thomas .15 .40
67 Neil O'Donnell .15 .40
68 Scott Mitchell .07 .20
69 Keith Byars .02 .10
70 Henry Ellard .07 .20
71 Chris Spielman .07 .20
72 LeRoy Butler .02 .10
73 Tim Brown .15 .40
74 Darrell Green .02 .10
75 Bruce Matthews .02 .10
76 Stan Humphries .07 .20
77 Will Wolford .02 .10
78 John Taylor .07 .20
79 Joe Montana 1.25 3.00
80 Chris Warren .07 .20
81 Michael Brooks .02 .10
82 Vance Johnson .02 .10
83 Rob Moore .07 .20
84 Herschel Walker .07 .20
85 Alvin Harper .07 .20
86 Wayne Martin .02 .10
87 Leslie O'Neal .02 .10
88 Flipper Anderson .02 .10
89 Tommy Vardell .02 .10
90 Mike Sherrard .02 .10
91 Chris Jacke .02 .10
92 Jim Kelly .15 .40
93 Jeff Graham .02 .10
94 Bryan Cox .02 .10
95 Michael Irvin .15 .40
96 Jeff Lageman .02 .10
97 Webster Slaughter .02 .10
98 Eugene Robinson .02 .10
99 Vencie Glenn .02 .10
100 Sean Jones .02 .10
101 Calvin Williams .07 .20
102 Jim Harbaugh .15 .40
103 Eric Curry .02 .10
104 Terry Allen .07 .20
105 Darryl Williams .02 .10
106 Gary Clark .07 .20
107 Marcus Allen .15 .40
108 Chip Lohmiller .02 .10
109 Vaughan Johnson .02 .10
110 Herman Moore .15 .40
111 Barry Foster .02 .10
112 Rocket Ismail .07 .20
113 Erric Pegram .02 .10
114 Anthony Miller .07 .20
115 Shane Conlan .02 .10
116 David Klingler .02 .10
117 Mark Collins .02 .10
118 Tony Bennett .02 .10
119 Donnell Woolford .02 .10
120 Reggie Brooks .07 .20
121 Sam Mills .02 .10
122 Greg Montgomery .02 .10
123 Kevin Greene .07 .20
124 Terry McDaniel .02 .10
125 Henry Jones .02 .10
126 Ricky Watters .07 .20
127 Dan Marino 1.25 3.00
128 Steve Atwater .02 .10
129 Ricky Proehl .02 .10
130 Ernest Givins .07 .20
131 John L. Williams .02 .10
132 John Randle .07 .20
133 Jay Novacek .07 .20
134 Boomer Esiason .07 .20
135 Jessie Hester .02 .10
136 Courtney Hawkins .02 .10
137 Ben Coates .07 .20
138 Stevon Moore .02 .10
139 Eric Allen .02 .10
140 Jessie Tuggle .02 .10
141 Marion Butts .02 .10
142 Brett Favre 1.25 3.00
143 Andre Reed .07 .20
144 Rodney Hampton .07 .20
145 Keith Sims .02 .10
146 Derek Brown RBK .02 .10
147 Eric Green .02 .10
148 Greg Robinson .02 .10
149 Nate Newton .02 .10
150 Mark Higgs .02 .10
151 Nick Lowery .02 .10
152 Craig Erickson .02 .10
153 Anthony Carter .07 .20
154 Simon Fletcher .02 .10
155 Ronnie Lott .07 .20
156 Gary Brown .02 .10
157 Brent Jones .07 .20
158 Jim Sweeney .02 .10
159 Robert Brooks .15 .40
160 Keith Jackson .02 .10
161 Daryl Johnston .07 .20
162 Tom Waddle .02 .10
163 Eric Martin .02 .10
164 Cornelius Bennett .07 .20
165 Tim McDonald .02 .10
166 Chris Doleman .02 .10
167 Gary Zimmerman .02 .10
168 Al Smith .02 .10
169 Mark Carrier WR .07 .20
170 Harris Barton .02 .10
171 Ray Childress .02 .10
172 Darryl Talley .02 .10
173 James Jett .02 .10
174 Mark Stepnoski .02 .10
175 Jeff Query .02 .10
176 Charles Haley .07 .20
177 Rod Bernstine .02 .10
178 Richmond Webb .02 .10
179 Rich Camarillo .02 .10
180 Pat Swilling .02 .10
181 Chris Miller .02 .10
182 Mike Pritchard .02 .10
183 Checklist NFC .02 .10
184 Natrone Means .15 .40
185 Erik Kramer .07 .20
186 Clyde Simmons .02 .10
187 Checklist AFC .02 .10
NFC
188 Warren Moon .15 .40
189 Michael Haynes .07 .20
190 Terry Kirby .15 .40
191 Brian Blades .07 .20
192 Haywood Jeffires .07 .20
193 Thomas Everett .02 .10
194 Morten Andersen .02 .10
195 Dana Stubblefield .07 .20
196 Ken Norton .07 .20
197 Art Monk .07 .20
198 Seth Joyner .02 .10
199 Heath Shuler RC .15 .40
200 Marshall Faulk RC 2.50 6.00
201 Charles Johnson RC .15 .40
202 Derrick Alexander WR RC .15 .40
203 Greg Hill RC .15 .40
204 Darnay Scott RC .40 1.00
205 Willie McGinest RC .15 .40
206 Thomas Randolph RC .02 .10
207 Errict Rhett RC .15 .40
208 William Floyd RC .15 .40
209 Johnnie Morton RC .75 2.00
210 David Palmer RC .15 .40
211 Dan Wilkinson RC .07 .20
212 Trent Dilfer RC .50 1.25
213 Antonio Langham RC .07 .20
214 Chuck Levy RC .02 .10
215 John Thierry RC .02 .10
216 Kevin Lee RC .02 .10
217 Aaron Glenn RC .15 .40
218 Charlie Garner RC .60 1.50
219 Jeff Burris RC .07 .20
220 LeShon Johnson RC .07 .20
221 Thomas Lewis RC .07 .20
222 Ryan Yarborough RC .02 .10
223 Mario Bates RC .15 .40
224 Checklist NFC .02 .10
AFC
225 Checklist AFC .02 .10
SR1 Marshall Faulk SR 12.00 30.00
SR2 Dan Wilkinson SR 3.00 8.00

1994 Select Canton Bound

This 12-card standard-size set feature veteran superstars bound for the Football Hall of Fame. Odds of finding a Canton Bound card are approximately one in 48 packs. Using Pinnacle's all-foil "Dufex" refractive printing technology, the fronts feature color action player photos. The player's name is printed in the top portion of the card. The horizontal backs carry another color player headshot on the left, with player information printed over a ghosted action shot on the right.

COMPLETE SET (12) 40.00 100.00
STATED ODDS 1:48
CB1 Emmitt Smith 8.00 20.00
CB2 Sterling Sharpe .60 1.50
CB3 Joe Montana 10.00 25.00
CB4 Barry Sanders 8.00 20.00
CB5 Jerry Rice 5.00 12.00
CB6 Ronnie Lott .60 1.50
CB7 Reggie White 1.25 3.00
CB8 Steve Young 4.00 10.00
CB9 Jerome Bettis 2.50 6.00
CB10 Bruce Smith 1.25 3.00
CB11 Troy Aikman 5.00 12.00
CB12 Thurman Thomas 1.25 3.00

1994 Select Future Force

This 12-card set measures the standard size. Odds of finding a Future Force card are approximately one in 48 packs. Using Pinnacle's all-foil refractive printing technology known as Dufex, the fronts feature color action player photos. The player's name in gold-foil is printed under the Future Force logo in a lower corner. The backs carry another color player headshot, with player information next to it. The cards are numbered on the back with an "FF" prefix.

COMPLETE SET (12) 7.50 20.00
STATED ODDS 1:48
FF1 Rick Mirer 1.25 3.00
FF2 Drew Bledsoe 4.00 10.00
FF3 Jerome Bettis 2.50 6.00
FF4 Reggie Brooks .60 1.50
FF5 Natrone Means 1.25 3.00
FF6 James Jett .30 .75
FF7 Terry Kirby 1.25 3.00
FF8 Vincent Brisby .30 .75
FF9 Gary Brown .30 .75
FF10 Tyrone Hughes .60 1.50
FF11 Dana Stubblefield .60 1.50
FF12 Garrison Hearst 1.25 3.00

1994 Select Franco Harris Autograph

This standard-size card features a borderless front with the back carrying a color close-up shot of Franco on the right and bio information on the left. This card was given away at the Pinnacle Party at the 15th National Sports Card Convention. Harris' autograph appears in black felt-tip pen in the brown bottom margin, along with hand serial numbering of a total of 5,000 produced.

1 Franco Harris 10.00 25.00

1996 Select Promos

These three promos were sent out to promote the 1996 Select release. Two base brand promo cards were produced and one Prime Cut insert promo (Dan Marino).

COMPLETE SET (3) 4.00 10.00
1 Troy Aikman .75 2.00
10 Dan Marino 1.50 4.00
19 Brett Favre 1.50 4.00

1996 Select

The 1996 Select set was issued in one hobby series totalling 200 standard-size cards. The set was issued in 10-card packs which had a suggested retail price of $1.99 each. Among the topical subsets are 1996 Rookies (151-180), Fluid and Fleet (181-195) and Checklists (196-200). Rookie Cards in this set include Tim Biakabutuka, Terry Glenn, Eddie George, Keyshawn Johnson, Leeland McElroy and Lawrence Phillips.

COMPLETE SET (200) 8.00 20.00
1 Troy Aikman .40 1.00
2 Marshall Faulk .20 .50
3 Kordell Stewart .15 .40
4 Larry Centers .07 .20
5 Tamarick Vanover .07 .20
6 Ken Norton Jr. .02 .10
7 Steve Tasker .02 .10
8 Dan Marino .75 2.00
9 Heath Shuler .07 .20
10 Anthony Miller .07 .20
11 Mario Bates .07 .20
12 Natrone Means .07 .20
13 Darren Woodson .07 .20
14 Chris Sanders .07 .20
15 Chris Warren .07 .20
16 Eric Metcalf .02 .10
17 Quentin Coryatt .02 .10
18 Jeff Hostetler .02 .10
19 Brett Favre .75 2.00
20 Curtis Martin .30 .75
21 Floyd Turner .02 .10
22 Curtis Conway .15 .40
23 Orlando Thomas .02 .10
24 Lee Woodall .02 .10
25 Darick Holmes .02 .10
26 Marcus Allen .15 .40
27 Ricky Watters .07 .20
28 Herman Moore .07 .20
29 Rodney Hampton .07 .20
30 Alvin Harper .02 .10
31 Jeff Blake .15 .40
32 Wayne Chrebet .25 .60
33 Jerry Rice .40 1.00
34 Dave Krieg .02 .10
35 Mark Brunell .25 .60
36 Terry Allen .07 .20
37 Emmitt Smith .60 1.50
38 Bryan Cox .02 .10
39 Tony Martin .07 .20
40 John Elway .75 2.00
41 Warren Moon .07 .20
42 Yancey Thigpen .07 .20
43 Jeff George .07 .20
44 Rodney Thomas .02 .10
45 Joey Galloway .15 .40
46 Jim Kelly .15 .40
47 Drew Bledsoe .25 .60
48 Greg Lloyd .07 .20
49 Michael Irvin .15 .40
50 Quinn Early .02 .10
51 Brent Jones .02 .10
52 Rashaan Salaam .07 .20
53 James O.Stewart .07 .20
54 Gus Frerotte .07 .20
55 Edgar Bennett .07 .20
56 Lamont Warren .02 .10
57 Napoleon Kaufman .15 .40
58 Kevin Williams .02 .10
59 Irving Fryar .07 .20
60 Trent Dilfer .15 .40
61 Eric Zeier .02 .10
62 Tyrone Wheatley .07 .20
63 Isaac Bruce .15 .40
64 Terrell Davis .30 .75
65 Lake Dawson .02 .10
66 Carnell Lake .02 .10
67 Kerry Collins .15 .40
68 Kyle Brady .02 .10
69 Rodney Peete .02 .10
70 Carl Pickens .07 .20
71 Robert Smith .07 .20
72 Rod Woodson .07 .20
73 Deion Sanders .25 .60
74 Sean Dawkins .02 .10
75 William Floyd .07 .20
76 Barry Sanders .60 1.50
77 Ben Coates .07 .20
78 Neil O'Donnell .07 .20
79 Bill Brooks .02 .10
80 Steve Bono .02 .10
81 Jay Novacek .02 .10
82 Bernie Parmalee .02 .10
83 Derek Loville .02 .10
84 Frank Sanders .07 .20
85 Robert Brooks .15 .40
86 Jim Harbaugh .07 .20
87 Rick Mirer .07 .20
88 Craig Heyward .02 .10
89 Greg Hill .07 .20
90 Andre Coleman .02 .10
91 Shannon Sharpe .07 .20
92 Hugh Douglas .07 .20
93 Andre Hastings .02 .10
94 Bryce Paup .02 .10
95 Jim Everett .02 .10
96 Brian Mitchell .02 .10
97 Jeff Graham .02 .10
98 Steve McNair .30 .75
99 Charlie Garner .07 .20
100 Willie McGinest .02 .10
101 Harvey Williams .02 .10
102 Daryl Johnston .07 .20
103 Cris Carter .15 .40
104 J.J. Stokes .15 .40
105 Garrison Hearst .07 .20
106 Mark Chmura .07 .20
107 Derrick Thomas .15 .40
108 Errict Rhett .07 .20
109 Terance Mathis .02 .10
110 Dave Brown .02 .10
111 Erric Pegram .02 .10
112 Scott Mitchell .07 .20
113 Aaron Bailey .02 .10
114 Stan Humphries .07 .20
115 Bruce Smith .07 .20
116 Rob Johnson .15 .40
117 O.J. McDuffie .07 .20
118 Brian Blades .02 .10
119 Steve Atwater .02 .10
120 Tyrone Hughes .02 .10
121 Michael Westbrook .15 .40
122 Ki-Jana Carter .07 .20
123 Adrian Murrell .07 .20
124 Steve Young .30 .75
125 Charles Haley .07 .20
126 Vincent Brisby .02 .10
127 Jerome Bettis .15 .40
128 Erik Kramer .02 .10
129 Roosevelt Potts .02 .10
130 Tim Brown .15 .40
131 Reggie White .15 .40
132 Jake Reed .07 .20
133 Junior Seau .15 .40
134 Stoney Case .02 .10
135 Kimble Anders .07 .20
136 Brett Perriman .02 .10
137 Todd Collins .07 .20
138 Sherman Williams .02 .10
139 Hardy Nickerson .02 .10
140 Ernie Mills .02 .10
141 Glyn Milburn .02 .10
142 Terry Kirby .07 .20
143 Bert Emanuel .07 .20
144 Aeneas Williams .02 .10
145 Aaron Craver .02 .10
146 Jackie Harris .02 .10
147 Thurman Thomas .15 .40
148 Aaron Hayden RC .02 .10
149 Antonio Freeman .15 .40
150 Kevin Greene .07 .20
151 Kevin Hardy RC .15 .40
152 Eric Moulds RC .60 1.50
153 Tim Biakabutuka RC .15 .40
154 Keyshawn Johnson RC .50 1.25
155 Jeff Lewis RC .07 .20
156 Stepfret Williams RC .07 .20
157 Tony Brackens RC .15 .40
158 Mike Alstott RC .50 1.25
159 Willie Anderson RC .02 .10
160 Marvin Harrison RC 1.25 3.00
161 Regan Upshaw RC .02 .10
162 Bobby Engram RC .15 .40
163 Leeland McElroy RC .07 .20
164 Alex Van Dyke RC .07 .20
165 Stanley Pritchett RC .07 .20
166 Cedric Jones RC .02 .10
167 Terry Glenn RC .50 1.25
168 Eddie George RC .60 1.50
169 Lawrence Phillips RC .15 .40
170 Jonathan Ogden RC .40 1.00
171 Danny Kanell RC .15 .40
172 Alex Molden RC .02 .10
173 Daryl Gardener RC .02 .10
174 Derrick Mayes RC .15 .40
175 Marco Battaglia RC .02 .10
176 Jon Stark RC .02 .10
177 Karim Abdul-Jabbar RC .15 .40
178 Stephen Davis RC .75 2.00
179 Rickey Dudley RC .15 .40
180 Eddie Kennison RC .15 .40
181 Barry Sanders FF .30 .75
182 Brett Favre FF .40 1.00
183 John Elway FF .40 1.00
184 Steve Young FF .15 .40
185 Michael Irvin FF .07 .20
186 Jerry Rice FF .20 .50
187 Emmitt Smith FF .30 .75
188 Isaac Bruce FF .15 .40
189 Chris Warren FF .07 .20
190 Errict Rhett FF .07 .20
191 Herman Moore FF .07 .20
192 Carl Pickens FF .07 .20
193 Cris Carter FF .15 .40
194 Terrell Davis FF .15 .40
195 Rodney Thomas FF .02 .10
196 Dan Marino CL .15 .40
197 Drew Bledsoe CL .07 .20
198 Emmitt Smith CL .15 .40
199 Jerry Rice CL .15 .40
200 Barry Sanders .15 .40
Elway CL

1996 Select Artist's Proofs

*AP STARS: 6X TO 15X BASIC CARDS
*AP RCs: 3X TO 8X BASIC CARDS
STATED ODDS 1:23

1996 Select Building Blocks

Randomly inserted in packs at a rate of one in 48, this 20-card standard-size horizontal set features first or second year players who are looked upon as important parts of their team's future. The cards are numbered as "X" of 20.

COMPLETE SET (20) 50.00 100.00
STATED ODDS 1:48
1 Curtis Martin 5.00 12.00
2 Terrell Davis 5.00 12.00
3 Darick Holmes .60 1.50
4 Rashaan Salaam 1.25 3.00
5 Ki-Jana Carter 1.25 3.00
6 Rodney Thomas .60 1.50
7 Kerry Collins 2.50 6.00
8 Eric Zeier .60 1.50
9 Steve McNair 5.00 12.00
10 Kordell Stewart 2.50 6.00
11 J.J. Stokes 2.50 6.00
12 Joey Galloway 2.50 6.00
13 Michael Westbrook 2.50 6.00
14 Mike Alstott 2.50 6.00
15 Tony Brackens .75 2.00
16 Terry Glenn 2.50 6.00
17 Kevin Hardy .75 2.00
18 Leeland McElroy .40 1.00
19 Tim Biakabutuka .75 2.00
20 Keyshawn Johnson 2.50 6.00

1996 Select Four-midable

Randomly inserted in packs at a rate of one in 18, this 16-card holographic set features players who participated in the 1995 NFL Conference Championship games. The set is broken down by team: Dallas Cowboys (1-4), Green Bay Packers (5-8), Pittsburgh Steelers (9-12) and the Indianapolis Colts (13-16). The cards are numbered as "X" of 16.

COMPLETE SET (16) 20.00 40.00
STATED ODDS 1:18
1 Troy Aikman 2.50 5.00
2 Michael Irvin 1.00 2.00
3 Emmitt Smith 4.00 8.00
4 Deion Sanders 1.50 3.00
5 Brett Favre 5.00 10.00
6 Robert Brooks 1.00 2.00
7 Edgar Bennett .40 1.00
8 Reggie White 1.00 2.00
9 Kordell Stewart 1.00 2.00
10 Yancey Thigpen .40 1.00
11 Neil O'Donnell .40 1.00
12 Greg Lloyd .40 1.00
13 Jim Harbaugh .40 1.00
14 Sean Dawkins .20 .50
15 Marshall Faulk 1.25 2.50
16 Quentin Coryatt .20 .50

1996 Select Prime Cuts

Randomly inserted in packs at a rate of one in 80, this 18-card die-cut set has three player's photos against a background which includes a football. The backs state that these cards are "1 of 1996 sets produced" and are numbered "X" of 18.

COMPLETE SET (18) 100.00 200.00
STATED ODDS 1:80
1 Emmitt Smith 8.00 20.00
2 Troy Aikman 5.00 12.00
3 Michael Irvin 2.00 5.00
4 Steve Young 4.00 10.00
5 Jerry Rice 5.00 12.00
6 Drew Bledsoe 3.00 8.00
7 Brett Favre 10.00 25.00
8 John Elway 10.00 25.00
9 Barry Sanders 8.00 20.00
10 Dan Marino 10.00 25.00
11 Isaac Bruce 2.00 5.00
12 Marshall Faulk 2.50 6.00
13 Errict Rhett 1.00 2.50
14 Chris Warren 1.00 2.50
15 Herman Moore 1.00 2.50
16 Deion Sanders 3.00 8.00
17 Joey Galloway 2.00 5.00
18 Curtis Martin 4.00 10.00

2001 Select

Playoff released Score Select as the hobby version of the basic Score product. This 330-card set was highlighted by the serial numbered rookies (numbered of 275-326) which were randomly inserted. The base card design follows that of the Score set along with a glossy coating on the cardfront. The cards were also printed on much thicker paper stock. An exchange card was inserted in packs that was good for an option to purchase a 2001 Score Supplemental factory set. It carried an expiration date of 12/01/2001.

COMP.SET w/o SPs (220) 12.50 30.00
271-330 ROOKIE PRINT RUN 275
1 David Boston .20 .50
2 Frank Sanders .20 .50
3 Jake Plummer .20 .50
4 Michael Pittman .25 .60
5 Rob Moore .20 .50
6 Thomas Jones .20 .50
7 Chris Chandler .25 .60
8 Doug Johnson .20 .50
9 Jamal Anderson .25 .60
10 Tim Dwight .25 .60
11 Brandon Stokley .20 .50
12 Chris Redman .30 .75
13 Jamal Lewis .30 .75
14 Qadry Ismail .20 .50
15 Ray Lewis .30 .75
16 Rod Woodson .30 .75
17 Shannon Sharpe .25 .60
18 Travis Taylor .20 .50
19 Trent Dilfer .20 .50
20 Elvis Grbac .25 .60
21 Eric Moulds .20 .50
22 Jay Riemersma .20 .50
23 Peerless Price .20 .50
24 Rob Johnson .25 .60
25 Sam Cowart .20 .50
26 Sammy Morris .20 .50
27 Shawn Bryson .20 .50
28 Donald Hayes .20 .50
29 Muhsin Muhammad .20 .50
30 Patrick Jeffers .20 .50
31 Reggie White DE .30 .75
32 Steve Beuerlein .25 .60
33 Tim Biakabutuka .20 .50
34 Wesley Walls .20 .50
35 Brian Urlacher .40 1.00
36 Cade McNown .25 .60
37 Dez White .25 .60
38 James Allen .20 .50
39 Marcus Robinson .25 .60
40 Marty Booker .20 .50
41 Akili Smith .20 .50
42 Corey Dillon .20 .50
43 Danny Farmer .20 .50
44 Peter Warrick .20 .50
45 Ron Dugans .20 .50
46 Takeo Spikes .20 .50
47 Courtney Brown .20 .50
48 Dennis Northcutt .20 .50
49 JaJuan Dawson .20 .50
50 Kevin Johnson .20 .50
51 Tim Couch .20 .50
52 Travis Prentice .20 .50
53 Anthony Wright .20 .50
54 Emmitt Smith .50 1.25
55 James McKnight .20 .50
56 Joey Galloway .25 .60
57 Rocket Ismail .25 .60
58 Randall Cunningham .25 .60
59 Troy Aikman .40 1.00
60 Brian Griese .20 .50
61 Ed McCaffrey .25 .60
62 Gus Frerotte .20 .50
63 John Elway .50 1.25
64 Mike Anderson .20 .50
65 Olandis Gary .20 .50
66 Rod Smith .25 .60
67 Terrell Davis .25 .60
68 Barry Sanders .50 1.25
69 Charlie Batch .20 .50
70 Germane Crowell .20 .50
71 Herman Moore .20 .50
72 James Stewart .20 .50
73 Johnnie Morton .25 .60
74 Robert Porcher .20 .50
75 Jim Harbaugh .25 .60
76 Ahman Green .25 .60
77 Antonio Freeman .30 .75
78 Bill Schroeder .25 .60
79 Brett Favre .60 1.50
80 Bubba Franks .20 .50
81 Dorsey Levens .25 .60
82 E.G. Green .20 .50
83 Edgerrin James .25 .60
84 Jerome Pathon .20 .50
85 Ken Dilger .20 .50
86 Marcus Pollard .20 .50
87 Marvin Harrison .25 .60
88 Peyton Manning .75 2.00
89 Terrence Wilkins .20 .50
90 Fred Taylor .20 .50
91 Hardy Nickerson .20 .50
92 Jimmy Smith .25 .60
93 Keenan McCardell .25 .60
94 Kyle Brady .20 .50
95 Mark Brunell .25 .60
96 Tony Brackens .20 .50
97 Derrick Alexander WR .20 .50
98 Sylvester Morris .20 .50
99 Tony Gonzalez .25 .60
100 Tony Richardson .20 .50
101 Kimble Anders .20 .50
102 Warren Moon .30 .75
103 Dan Marino .60 1.50
104 Jay Fiedler .25 .60
105 Lamar Smith .25 .60
106 O.J. McDuffie .20 .50
107 Oronde Gadsden .20 .50
108 Sam Madison .20 .50
109 Thurman Thomas .25 .60
110 Tony Martin .25 .60
111 Zach Thomas .25 .60
112 Cris Carter .30 .75
113 Daunte Culpepper .25 .60
114 Matthew Hatchette .20 .50
115 Randy Moss .25 .60
116 Robert Smith .20 .50
117 Drew Bledsoe .25 .60
118 J.R. Redmond .20 .50
119 Kevin Faulk .20 .50
120 Michael Bishop .25 .60
121 Terry Glenn .25 .60
122 Troy Brown .20 .50
123 Ty Law .30 .75
124 Aaron Brooks .20 .50
125 Darren Howard .20 .50
126 Jake Reed .25 .60
127 Jeff Blake .25 .60
128 Joe Horn .20 .50
129 La'Roi Glover .20 .50
130 Ricky Williams .25 .60
131 Willie Jackson .20 .50
132 Albert Connell .20 .50
133 Amani Toomer .20 .50
134 Ike Hilliard .20 .50
135 Jason Sehorn .25 .60
136 Jessie Armstead .20 .50
137 Kerry Collins .20 .50
138 Michael Strahan .25 .60
139 Ron Dayne .25 .60
140 Ron Dixon .20 .50
141 Tiki Barber .25 .60
142 Anthony Becht .20 .50
143 Chad Pennington .20 .50
144 Curtis Martin .25 .60
145 Dedric Ward .20 .50
146 Laveranues Coles .25 .60
147 Vinny Testaverde .20 .50
148 Wayne Chrebet .20 .50
149 Andre Rison .25 .60
150 Charles Woodson .30 .75
151 Darrell Russell .20 .50
152 Napoleon Kaufman .20 .50
153 Rich Gannon .25 .60

154 Tim Brown .30 .75
155 Tyrone Wheatley .25 .60
156 Chad Lewis .20 .50
157 Charles Johnson .20 .50
158 Donovan McNabb .25 .60
159 Duce Staley .20 .50
160 Hugh Douglas .20 .50
161 Na Brown .20 .50
162 Todd Pinkston .20 .50
163 James Thrash .25 .60
164 Bobby Shaw .20 .50
165 Hines Ward .25 .60
166 Jerome Bettis .30 .75
167 Kordell Stewart .20 .50
168 Levon Kirkland .20 .50
169 Plaxico Burress .20 .50
170 Richard Huntley .20 .50
171 Troy Edwards .20 .50
172 Jeff Graham .20 .50
173 Junior Seau .25 .60
174 Doug Flutie .25 .60
175 Charlie Garner .25 .60
176 Jeff Garcia .20 .50
177 Jerry Rice .60 1.50
178 Steve Young .40 1.00
179 Terrell Owens .25 .60
180 Brock Huard .20 .50
181 Darrell Jackson .25 .60
182 Derrick Mayes .20 .50
183 Ricky Watters .25 .60
184 Shaun Alexander .20 .50
185 Matt Hasselbeck .20 .50
186 John Randle .25 .60
187 Az-Zahir Hakim .20 .50
188 Isaac Bruce .30 .75
189 Kurt Warner .50 1.25
190 Marshall Faulk .25 .60
191 Torry Holt .25 .60
192 Trent Green .20 .50
193 Derrick Brooks .20 .50
194 Jacquez Green .20 .50
195 John Lynch .25 .60
196 Keyshawn Johnson .25 .60
197 Mike Alstott .20 .50
198 Reidel Anthony .20 .50
199 Shaun King .20 .50
200 Warren Sapp .25 .60
201 Warrick Dunn .20 .50
202 Ryan Leaf .20 .50
203 Carl Pickens .25 .60
204 Derrick Mason .20 .50
205 Eddie George .30 .75
206 Frank Wycheck .20 .50
207 Jevon Kearse .20 .50
208 Neil O'Donnell .25 .60
209 Steve McNair .25 .60
210 Yancey Thigpen .20 .50
211 Andre Reed .30 .75
212 Brad Johnson .25 .60
213 Bruce Smith .25 .60
214 Champ Bailey .25 .60
215 Darrell Green .30 .75
216 Deion Sanders .25 .60
217 Irving Fryar .25 .60
218 Jeff George .25 .60
219 Michael Westbrook .20 .50
220 Stephen Davis .20 .50
221 Terrell Owens AP .60 1.50
222 Peyton Manning AP 2.00 5.00
223 Stephen Davis AP .50 1.25
224 Marvin Harrison AP .60 1.50
225 Donovan McNabb AP .60 1.50
226 Edgerrin James AP .60 1.50
227 Eric Moulds AP .50 1.25
228 Daunte Culpepper AP .60 1.50
229 Eddie George AP .75 2.00
230 Cris Carter AP .75 2.00
231 Rich Gannon AP .60 1.50
232 Jeff Garcia AP .50 1.25
233 Jimmy Smith AP .60 1.50
234 Tony Gonzalez AP .60 1.50
235 Torry Holt AP .60 1.50
236 Jevon Kearse AP .50 1.25
237 Ray Lewis AP .75 2.00
238 Warren Sapp AP .60 1.50
239 Brian Urlacher AP 1.00 2.50
240 Champ Bailey AP .60 1.50
241 Peyton Manning LL 2.00 5.00
242 Jeff Garcia LL .50 1.25
243 Elvis Grbac LL .60 1.50
244 Daunte Culpepper LL .60 1.50
245 Brett Favre LL 1.50 4.00
246 Edgerrin James LL .60 1.50
247 Robert Smith LL .50 1.25
248 Eddie George LL .75 2.00
249 Mike Anderson LL .50 1.25
250 Corey Dillon LL .50 1.25
251 Torry Holt LL .60 1.50
252 Rod Smith LL .60 1.50
253 Isaac Bruce LL .75 2.00
254 Terrell Owens LL .60 1.50
255 Randy Moss LL .60 1.50
256 La'Roi Glover LL .50 1.25
257 Trace Armstrong LL .50 1.25
258 Warren Sapp LL .60 1.50
259 Hugh Douglas LL .50 1.25
260 Jason Taylor LL .75 2.00
261 Mike Anderson SS .50 1.25
262 Jamal Lewis SS .75 2.00
263 Sylvester Morris SS .50 1.25
264 Darrell Jackson SS .60 1.50
265 Peter Warrick SS .50 1.25
266 Ron Dayne SS .60 1.50
267 Shaun Alexander SS .50 1.25
268 Plaxico Burress SS .50 1.25
269 Brian Urlacher SS 1.00 2.50
270 Courtney Brown SS .50 1.25
271 Michael Vick RC 5.00 12.00
272 Drew Brees RC 60.00 125.00
273 Chris Weinke RC 2.50 6.00
274 Quincy Carter RC 2.50 6.00
275 Sage Rosenfels RC 2.50 6.00
276 Josh Heupel RC 3.00 8.00
277 David Rivers RC 2.00 5.00
278 Ben Leard RC 2.00 5.00
279 Marques Tuiasosopo RC 2.50 6.00
280 Mike McMahon RC 2.50 6.00
281 Deuce McAllister RC 3.00 8.00
282 LaMont Jordan RC 3.00 8.00
283 LaDainian Tomlinson RC 10.00 25.00
284 James Jackson RC 2.00 5.00
285 Anthony Thomas RC 3.00 8.00
286 Travis Henry RC 2.50 6.00
287 Travis Minor RC 2.50 6.00
288 Rudi Johnson RC 3.00 8.00
289 Michael Bennett RC 2.50 6.00
290 Kevan Barlow RC 2.50 6.00
291 Reggie White RC 2.00 5.00
292 Moran Norris RC 2.00 5.00
293 Ja'Mar Toombs RC 2.00 5.00
294 Heath Evans RC 2.50 6.00
295 David Terrell RC 2.50 6.00
296 Santana Moss RC 3.00 8.00
297 Rod Gardner RC 2.50 6.00
298 Quincy Morgan RC 2.50 6.00
299 Freddie Mitchell RC 2.00 5.00
300 Boo Williams RC 2.00 5.00
301 Reggie Wayne RC 4.00 10.00
302 Ronney Daniels RC 2.00 5.00
303 Bobby Newcombe RC 2.50 6.00
304 Vinny Sutherland RC 2.00 5.00
305 Cedrick Wilson RC 2.50 6.00
306 Robert Ferguson RC 3.00 8.00
307 Ken-Yon Rambo RC 2.00 5.00
308 Alex Bannister RC 2.00 5.00
309 Koren Robinson RC 2.50 6.00
310 Chad Johnson RC 4.00 10.00
311 Chris Chambers RC 2.00 5.00
312 Javon Green RC 2.00 5.00
313 Snoop Minnis RC 2.00 5.00
314 Scotty Anderson RC 2.00 5.00
315 Todd Heap RC 2.50 6.00
316 Alge Crumpler RC 3.00 8.00
317 Marcellus Rivers RC 2.00 5.00
318 Rashon Burns RC 2.00 5.00
319 Jamal Reynolds RC 2.00 5.00
320 Andre Carter RC 2.50 6.00
321 Justin Smith RC 4.00 10.00
322 Gerard Warren RC 2.50 6.00
323 Tommy Polley RC 2.00 5.00
324 Dan Morgan RC 2.50 6.00
325 Torrance Marshall RC 2.00 5.00
326 Correll Buckhalter RC 2.00 5.00
327 Derrick Gibson RC 2.00 5.00
328 Adam Archuleta RC 2.50 6.00
329 Jamar Fletcher RC 2.00 5.00
330 Nate Clements RC 2.50 6.00

2001 Select Chicago Collection

NOT PRICED DUE TO SCARCITY

2001 Select Final Score

STATED PRINT RUNS VARY ACCORDING
UNPRICED FINAL SCORE PRINT RUN 1-13

2001 Select Behind the Numbers

Randomly inserted in the hobby-only Score Select product, this 40-card set featured almost the same card design as the Behind the Numbers in the retail version with a few exceptions. This set was produced with a foilboard cardfront and highlighted with holofoil lettering, and they were produced on a much thicker card stock. The cards were serial numbered to the number of the featured player's pass attempts, rushes or receptions from the 2000 NFL/NCAA season.
STATED PRINT RUN 45-403
BN1 Brett Favre/338 3.00 8.00
BN2 Marshall Faulk/253 1.25 3.00
BN3 Michael Vick/87 2.00 5.00
BN4 Peyton Manning/357 4.00 10.00
BN5 David Terrell/63 1.50 4.00
BN6 Randy Moss/77 1.50 4.00
BN7 Kurt Warner/235 2.50 6.00
BN8 Edgerrin James/387 1.25 3.00
BN9 Drew Brees/309 30.00 60.00
BN10 Daunte Culpepper/297 1.25 3.00
BN11 Jeff Garcia/355 1.00 2.50
BN12 Mike Anderson/297 1.00 2.50
BN13 Jamal Lewis/309 1.50 4.00
BN14 Eddie George/403 1.50 4.00
BN15 Michael Bennett/310 1.25 3.00
BN16 Emmitt Smith/294 2.50 6.00
BN17 Chris Weinke/266 1.25 3.00
BN18 Tim Brown/76 2.00 5.00
BN19 Eric Moulds/94 1.25 3.00
BN20 Marvin Harrison/102 1.50 4.00
BN21 Deuce McAllister/105 2.00 5.00
BN22 Donovan McNabb/330 1.25 3.00
BN23 Fred Taylor/292 1.00 2.50
BN24 Santana Moss/45 2.00 5.00
BN25 Cris Carter/96 2.00 5.00
BN26 Robert Smith/295 1.00 2.50
BN27 LaDainian Tomlinson/369 3.00 8.00
BN28 Isaac Bruce/87 2.00 5.00
BN29 Terrell Owens/97 1.50 4.00
BN30 Torry Holt/82 1.50 4.00
BN31 Ricky Williams/248 1.25 3.00
BN32 Curtis Martin/316 1.25 3.00
BN33 Stephen Davis/332 1.00 2.50
BN34 Corey Dillon/315 1.00 2.50
BN35 Ed McCaffrey/101 1.50 4.00
BN36 Steve McNair/248 1.25 3.00
BN37 Rudi Johnson/324 1.50 4.00
BN38 Antonio Freeman/62 2.00 5.00
BN39 Jerry Rice/75 4.00 10.00
BN40 Aaron Brooks/113 1.25 3.00

2001 Select Complete Players

This 30-card set was randomly inserted in hobby-only packs of Score Select and was serial numbered to 550. The cardfronts are similar to that of the Complete Players from the retail version of Score with the differences being the thicker card stock on the Select version and the cardfronts using foilboard and holofoil lettering.
COMPLETE SET (30) 40.00 100.00
STATED PRINT RUN 550 SER.#'d SETS
CP1 Edgerrin James 1.00 2.50
CP2 Marshall Faulk 1.00 2.50
CP3 Kurt Warner 2.00 5.00
CP4 Daunte Culpepper 1.00 2.50
CP5 Donovan McNabb 1.00 2.50
CP6 Koren Robinson 1.00 2.50
CP7 Peyton Manning 3.00 8.00
CP8 Eddie George 1.25 3.00
CP9 Fred Taylor .75 2.00
CP10 Drew Brees 25.00 50.00
CP11 Randy Moss 1.00 2.50
CP12 Cris Carter 1.25 3.00
CP13 Steve Young 1.50 4.00
CP14 Marvin Harrison 1.00 2.50
CP15 Isaac Bruce 1.25 3.00
CP16 Terrell Owens 1.00 2.50
CP17 Mike Anderson .75 2.00
CP18 Jamal Lewis 1.25 3.00
CP19 Curtis Martin 1.00 2.50
CP20 Ricky Williams 1.00 2.50
CP21 Jerry Rice 2.50 6.00
CP22 Steve McNair 1.00 2.50
CP23 Michael Vick 1.25 3.00
CP24 Brett Favre 2.50 6.00
CP25 John Elway 2.00 5.00
CP26 Dan Marino 2.50 6.00
CP27 Barry Sanders 2.00 5.00
CP28 Michael Bennett 1.00 2.50
CP29 David Terrell 1.00 2.50
CP30 Emmitt Smith 2.00 5.00

2001 Select Franchise Tags Autographs

Randomly inserted in hobby-only Score Select packs, this 31-card set features a premium jersey swatch and an autograph on each of the 50 serial numbered cards for each player. The cardfronts have the jersey swatch displayed in a star shaped cut-out.
STATED PRINT RUN 50 SER.#'d SETS
FT1 Daunte Culpepper 20.00 50.00
FT2 Stephen Davis 15.00 40.00
FT3 Kurt Warner 40.00 100.00
FT4 Ricky Williams 20.00 50.00
FT5 Terrell Owens 20.00 50.00
FT6 Ricky Watters 20.00 50.00
FT7 Rich Gannon 20.00 50.00
FT8 Mike Anderson 15.00 40.00
FT9 Tony Gonzalez 25.00 60.00
FT10 Jerome Bettis 100.00 175.00
FT11 Peter Warrick
FT12 Tim Couch No Auto 10.00 25.00
FT13 Mark Brunell 20.00 50.00
FT14 Edgerrin James 20.00 50.00
FT15 Curtis Martin No Auto 12.00 30.00
FT16 Brett Favre 100.00 200.00
FT17 Donovan McNabb 20.00 50.00
FT18 Drew Bledsoe 20.00 50.00
FT19 Jake Plummer 15.00 40.00
FT20 Eric Moulds 15.00 40.00
FT21 Lamar Smith No Auto 12.00 30.00
FT22 Junior Seau 40.00 80.00
FT23 Wesley Walls 15.00 40.00
FT24 Jamal Anderson 20.00 50.00
FT25 Warren Sapp No Auto 12.00 30.00
FT26 Ron Dayne 20.00 50.00
FT27 Jamal Lewis 15.00 40.00
FT28 Cade McNown 20.00 50.00
FT29 Charlie Batch 15.00 40.00
FT30 Eddie George 25.00 60.00
FT31 Troy Aikman 90.00 150.00

2001 Select Future Franchise

Randomly inserted in packs of the hobby-only Score Select, this 31 card set was serial numbered to 550. The cardfronts contained a rainbow holofoil design with the 2001 draft pick, and a basic glossy back with the new teammate and the serial number on the back. The cardbacks also contained 'FF' as the card number's prefix.
COMPLETE SET (31) 50.00 120.00
STATED PRINT RUN 550 SER.#'d SETS
FF1 T.Couch/J.Jackson .75 2.00
FF2 P.Warrick/J.Smith .75 2.00
FF3 J.Bettis/C.Hampton 1.25 3.00
FF4 F.Taylor/M.Stroud 1.00 2.50
FF5 E.George/D.Alexander 1.25 3.00
FF6 J.Lewis/T.Heap 1.25 3.00
FF7 P.Manning/R.Wayne 3.00 8.00
FF8 D.Bledsoe/J.Holloway 1.00 2.50
FF9 C.Martin/S.Moss .75 2.00
FF10 E.Moulds/T.Henry .75 2.00
FF11 L.Smith/C.Chambers 1.00 2.50
FF12 T.Gonzalez/S.Minnis 1.00 2.50
FF13 R.Gannon/M.Tuiasosopo 1.00 2.50
FF14 R.Watters/K.Robinson 1.00 2.50
FF15 J.Seau/L.Tomlinson 2.50 6.00
FF16 B.Griese/K.Kasper .75 2.00
FF17 T.Owens/K.Barlow 1.00 2.50
FF18 R.Williams/D.McAllister 1.25 3.00
FF19 K.Warner/D.Lewis 2.00 5.00
FF20 M.Muhammad/C.Weinke 1.00 2.50
FF21 J.Anderson/M.Vick 1.25 3.00
FF22 B.Favre/R.Ferguson 2.50 6.00
FF23 R.Moss/M.Bennett 1.00 2.50
FF24 M.Robinson/D.Terrell 1.00 2.50
FF25 W.Dunn/K.Walker .75 2.00
FF26 J.Stewart/M.McMahon 1.00 2.50
FF27 J.Plummer/B.Newcombe .75 2.00
FF28 K.Collins/J.Palmer 1.00 2.50
FF29 E.Smith/Q.Carter 2.00 5.00
FF30 S.Davis/R.Gardner 1.00 2.50
FF31 D.McNabb/F.Mitchell 1.00 2.50

2001 Select Rookie Preview Autographs

Randomly inserted in hobby-only Score Select packs at a rate of 1:19, this 40-card autograph set was issued with print runs that varried by player. At the time of release there were 18 different players that were issued as exchange cards with an expiration date of 5-31-2003. The cardfronts were on a high gloss card stock with the autographs signed on holographic stickers along with the "Authentic Score Autograph" embossed logo.
RP1 Michael Vick/150 25.00 60.00
RP2 Drew Brees/150 75.00 150.00
RP3 Chris Weinke/250 5.00 12.00
RP5 Josh Heupel/450 5.00 12.00
RP6 David Terrell/150 5.00 12.00
RP7 Santana Moss/250 6.00 15.00
RP8 Freddie Mitchell/350 3.00 8.00
RP9 Reggie Wayne/250 12.00 30.00
RP10 Rod Gardner/50 6.00 15.00
RP11 Chris Chambers/450 3.00 8.00
RP12 Chad Johnson/450 5.00 12.00
RP13 Ken-Yon Rambo/550 3.00 8.00
RP14 Deuce McAllister/150 6.00 15.00
RP15 LaDainian Tomlinson/250 40.00 100.00
RP16 Travis Henry/450 4.00 10.00
RP17 Anthony Thomas/250 6.00 15.00
RP18 Michael Bennett/250 5.00 12.00
RP19 LaMont Jordan/350 5.00 12.00
RP20 Kevan Barlow/450 4.00 10.00
RP21 Reggie White/550 3.00 8.00
RP22 Sage Rosenfels/50 6.00 15.00
RP24 Mike McMahon/450 4.00 10.00
RP25 Quincy Morgan/450 4.00 10.00
RP28 Alex Bannister/450 3.00 8.00
RP29 Snoop Minnis/450 3.00 8.00
RP30 Cedrick Wilson/450 4.00 10.00
RP34 Correll Buckhalter/550 3.00 8.00
RP36 Jamal Reynolds/350 3.00 8.00
RP37 Richard Seymour/350 No Auto 2.50 6.00
RP42 James Jackson/350 3.00 8.00
RP43 Rudi Johnson/350 5.00 12.00
RP45 Travis Minor/750 4.00 10.00
RP46 Robert Ferguson/350 5.00 12.00
RP49 Justin Smith/350 6.00 15.00
RP50 Gerard Warren/350 4.00 10.00
RP51 Koren Robinson/50 6.00 15.00
RP52 T.J. Houshmandzadeh/450 4.00 10.00
RP53 Todd Heap/750 4.00 10.00
RP55 Alge Crumpler/750 5.00 12.00
RP60 Will Allen/750 5.00 12.00

2001 Select Rookie Roll Call Autographs

Randomly inserted in hobby-only Score Select packs, this 40-card autograph set was issued with a print run of 50 serial numbered sets. At the time of release there were 18 different players that were issued as exchange cards with an expiration date of 5-31-03. The cardfronts were on a high gloss card stock with the autographs done on hohographic stickers and an authentic Score autograph crimpted on the card.
STATED PRINT RUN 50 SER.#'d SETS
RP1 Michael Vick 50.00 120.00
RP2 Drew Brees 125.00 200.00
RP3 Chris Weinke 6.00 15.00
RP5 Josh Heupel 8.00 20.00
RP6 David Terrell 6.00 15.00
RP7 Santana Moss 8.00 20.00
RP8 Freddie Mitchell 5.00 12.00
RP9 Reggie Wayne 25.00 60.00
RP10 Rod Gardner 6.00 15.00
RP11 Chris Chambers 5.00 12.00
RP12 Chad Johnson 8.00 20.00
RP13 Ken-Yon Rambo 5.00 12.00
RP14 Deuce McAllister 8.00 20.00
RP15 LaDainian Tomlinson 75.00 150.00
RP16 Travis Henry 6.00 15.00
RP17 Anthony Thomas 8.00 20.00
RP18 Michael Bennett 6.00 15.00
RP19 LaMont Jordan 8.00 20.00
RP20 Kevan Barlow 6.00 15.00
RP21 Reggie White 5.00 12.00
RP22 Sage Rosenfels 6.00 15.00
RP24 Mike McMahon 6.00 15.00
RP25 Quincy Morgan 6.00 15.00
RP28 Alex Bannister 5.00 12.00
RP29 Snoop Minnis 5.00 12.00
RP30 Cedrick Wilson 6.00 15.00
RP34 Correll Buckhalter 5.00 12.00
RP36 Jamal Reynolds 5.00 12.00
RP37 Richard Seymour No Auto 4.00 10.00
RP42 James Jackson 5.00 12.00
RP43 Rudi Johnson 8.00 20.00
RP45 Travis Minor 6.00 15.00
RP46 Robert Ferguson 8.00 20.00
RP49 Justin Smith 10.00 25.00
RP50 Gerard Warren 6.00 15.00
RP51 Koren Robinson 6.00 15.00
RP52 T.J. Houshmandzadeh 6.00 15.00
RP53 Todd Heap 6.00 15.00
RP55 Alge Crumpler 8.00 20.00
RP60 Will Allen 8.00 20.00

2001 Select Settle the Score

Randomly inserted in the hobby-only Score Select packs, this 30-card set was comprised of two players per card, one on the foilboard front with gold holofoil highlights, and the other player on the back with a basic glossy coating along with being serial numbered to 550.
COMPLETE SET (30) 40.00 100.00
STATED PRINT RUN 550 SER.#'d SETS
SS1 K.Warner/S.McNair 2.00 5.00
SS2 R.Moss/I.Bruce 1.25 3.00
SS3 E.Smith/S.Davis 2.00 5.00
SS4 M.Faulk/R.Smith 1.00 2.50
SS5 E.George/R.Lewis 1.25 3.00
SS6 F.Taylor/J.Bettis 1.25 3.00
SS7 P.Manning/D.Bledsoe 3.00 8.00
SS8 D.Culpepper/A.Brooks 1.00 2.50
SS9 M.Harrison/E.Moulds 1.00 2.50
SS10 J.Rice/C.Carter 2.50 6.00
SS11 C.Martin/E.James 1.00 2.50
SS12 D.McNabb/R.Dayne 1.00 2.50
SS13 B.Favre/W.Sapp 2.50 6.00
SS14 T.Gonzalez/S.Sharpe 1.00 2.50
SS15 W.Chrebet/K.Johnson 1.00 2.50
SS16 T.Couch/C.McNown 1.00 2.50
SS17 T.Davis/J.Anderson 1.00 2.50
SS18 M.Anderson/J.Lewis 1.25 3.00
SS19 T.Owens/A.Freeman 1.25 3.00
SS20 B.Griese/R.Gannon .75 2.00
SS21 R.Watters/C.Garner 1.00 2.50
SS22 M.Muhammad/R.Williams 1.00 2.50
SS23 J.Garcia/E.Grbac 1.00 2.50
SS24 R.Smith/J.Smith 1.00 2.50
SS25 B.Urlacher/A.Green 1.50 4.00
SS26 D.Jackson/S.Morris 1.00 2.50
SS27 P.Warrick/T.Taylor .75 2.00
SS28 D.Marino/J.Elway 2.50 6.00
SS29 S.Young/M.Brunell 1.50 4.00
SS30 T.Aikman/J.Plummer .75 2.00

2001 Select Zenith Z-Team

Randomly inserted in the hobby-only Score Select packs, this 38-card set was die-cut and featured rainbow holofoil technology on the cardfront. The cards were serial numbered to 100.
STATED PRINT RUN 100 SER.#'d SETS
ZT1 Michael Vick 3.00 8.00
ZT2 Donovan McNabb 3.00 8.00
ZT3 Daunte Culpepper 3.00 8.00
ZT4 Kurt Warner 6.00 15.00
ZT5 Peyton Manning 10.00 25.00
ZT6 Brett Favre 8.00 20.00
ZT7 Dan Marino 8.00 20.00
ZT8 John Elway 6.00 15.00
ZT9 Steve Young 5.00 12.00
ZT10 Troy Aikman 5.00 12.00
ZT11 Chad Pennington 2.50 6.00
ZT12 Brian Griese 2.50 6.00
ZT13 Drew Brees 15.00 40.00
ZT14 David Terrell 3.00 8.00
ZT15 Eric Moulds 2.50 6.00
ZT16 Marvin Harrison 3.00 8.00
ZT17 Randy Moss 3.00 8.00
ZT18 Reggie Wayne 2.50 6.00
ZT19 Terrell Owens 3.00 8.00
ZT20 Jerry Rice 8.00 20.00
ZT21 Cris Carter 4.00 10.00
ZT22 Isaac Bruce 4.00 10.00
ZT23 Peter Warrick 2.50 6.00
ZT24 Deuce McAllister 4.00 10.00
ZT25 Edgerrin James 3.00 8.00
ZT26 Robert Smith 2.50 6.00
ZT27 Marshall Faulk 3.00 8.00
ZT28 Ricky Williams 3.00 8.00
ZT29 Michael Bennett 3.00 8.00
ZT30 Emmitt Smith 6.00 15.00
ZT31 Eddie George 4.00 10.00
ZT32 Jamal Lewis 4.00 10.00
ZT33 Ron Dayne 3.00 8.00
ZT34 Mike Anderson 2.50 6.00
ZT35 Barry Sanders 6.00 15.00
ZT36 Stephen Davis 2.50 6.00
ZT37 Koren Robinson 3.00 8.00
ZT38 LaDainian Tomlinson 6.00 15.00

2006 Select

This 430-card set was released in July, 2006. The set was issued into hobby outlets in five-card packs which came 20 packs to a box. Cards numbered 1-290 feature players sequenced in team alphabetical order by where they played in 2005. Cards numbered 291-330 featured rookies also in team alphabetical order while cards numbered 331-430 also featured 2006 NFL rookies. Cards numbered 331-430 were issued to a stated print run of 599 serial numbered copies.
COMP.SET w/o RC's (330) 25.00 50.00
331-430 RC PRINT RUN 599 SETS
UNPRICED BLACK PRINT RUN 6 SETS
1 Kurt Warner .25 .60
2 J.J. Arrington .20 .50
3 Anquan Boldin .20 .50
4 Larry Fitzgerald .25 .60
5 Marcel Shipp .20 .50
6 Bryant Johnson .20 .50
7 Bertrand Berry .20 .50
8 John Navarre .20 .50
9 Michael Vick .25 .60
10 Warrick Dunn .20 .50
11 Roddy White .20 .50
12 Alge Crumpler .25 .60
13 T.J. Duckett .20 .50
14 Michael Jenkins .20 .50
15 DeAngelo Hall .20 .50
16 Brian Finneran .20 .50
17 Kyle Boller .20 .50
18 Jamal Lewis .25 .60
19 Chester Taylor .25 .60
20 Derrick Mason .20 .50
21 Mark Clayton .20 .50
22 Todd Heap .20 .50
23 Ray Lewis .30 .75
24 Devard Darling .20 .50
25 J.P. Losman .25 .60
26 Willis McGahee .20 .50
27 Lee Evans .25 .60
28 Eric Moulds .20 .50
29 Lawyer Milloy .20 .50
30 Josh Reed .20 .50
31 Kelly Holcomb .20 .50
32 Jake Delhomme .20 .50
33 DeShaun Foster .25 .60
34 Steve Smith .30 .75
35 Julius Peppers .25 .60
36 Drew Carter .20 .50
37 Chris Gamble .20 .50
38 Stephen Davis .20 .50
39 Keary Colbert .20 .50
40 Nick Goings .20 .50
41 Eric Shelton .20 .50
42 Rex Grossman .20 .50
43 Thomas Jones .20 .50
44 Cedric Benson .20 .50
45 Muhsin Muhammad .20 .50
46 Brian Urlacher .30 .75
47 Mark Bradley .20 .50
48 Kyle Orton .20 .50
49 Tommie Harris .20 .50
50 Adrian Peterson .25 .60
51 Bernard Berrian .20 .50
52 Justin Gage .20 .50
53 Carson Palmer .25 .60
54 Rudi Johnson .20 .50
55 Chad Johnson .20 .50
56 T.J. Houshmandzadeh .20 .50
57 Chris Henry .20 .50
58 Chris Perry .25 .60
59 Jon Kitna .20 .50
60 Deltha O'Neal .20 .50
61 Charlie Frye .25 .60
62 Reuben Droughns .25 .60
63 Braylon Edwards .20 .50
64 Kellen Winslow .20 .50
65 Antonio Bryant .20 .50
66 Trent Dilfer .20 .50
67 Dennis Northcutt .20 .50
68 Drew Bledsoe .25 .60
69 Julius Jones .20 .50
70 Marion Barber .25 .60
71 Terry Glenn .25 .60
72 Keyshawn Johnson .25 .60
73 Roy Williams S .20 .50
74 Jason Witten .25 .60
75 Terence Newman .20 .50
76 Drew Henson .20 .50
77 Patrick Crayton .20 .50
78 Jake Plummer .20 .50
79 Mike Anderson .20 .50
80 Tatum Bell .20 .50
81 Ashley Lelie .20 .50
82 Rod Smith .25 .60
83 D.J. Williams .20 .50
84 Darius Watts .20 .50
85 Ron Dayne .25 .60
86 Jeb Putzier .20 .50
87 Joey Harrington .20 .50
88 Kevin Jones .20 .50
89 Roy Williams WR .20 .50
90 Mike Williams .20 .50
91 Charles Rogers .25 .60
92 Teddy Lehman .20 .50
93 Marcus Pollard .20 .50
94 Artose Pinner .20 .50
95 Brett Favre .60 1.50
96 Ahman Green .25 .60
97 Najeh Davenport .20 .50
98 Samkon Gado .20 .50
99 Javon Walker .25 .60
100 Donald Driver .25 .60
101 Aaron Rodgers .75 2.00
102 Robert Ferguson .20 .50
103 David Carr .20 .50
104 Domanick Davis .20 .50
105 Andre Johnson .25 .60
106 Jabar Gaffney .20 .50
107 Jonathan Wells .20 .50
108 Vernand Morency .20 .50
109 Corey Bradford .20 .50
110 Jerome Mathis .20 .50
111 Peyton Manning .75 2.00
112 Edgerrin James .25 .60
113 Marvin Harrison .25 .60
114 Reggie Wayne .25 .60
115 Dwight Freeney .20 .50
116 Dallas Clark .20 .50
117 Dominic Rhodes .20 .50
118 Jim Sorgi .20 .50
119 Brandon Stokley .20 .50
120 Bob Sanders .25 .60
121 Mike Doss .20 .50
122 Marlin Jackson .20 .50
123 Byron Leftwich .20 .50
124 Fred Taylor .20 .50
125 Jimmy Smith .25 .60
126 Matt Jones .20 .50
127 Ernest Wilford .20 .50
128 Greg Jones .20 .50
129 Mike Peterson .20 .50
130 Reggie Williams .25 .60
131 Rashean Mathis .20 .50
132 Trent Green .20 .50
133 Larry Johnson .20 .50
134 Priest Holmes .20 .50
135 Eddie Kennison .20 .50
136 Tony Gonzalez .25 .60
137 Kendrell Bell .20 .50
138 Samie Parker .20 .50
139 Dante Hall .20 .50
140 Tony Richardson .20 .50
141 Gus Frerotte .20 .50
142 Ronnie Brown .25 .60
143 Neil Rackers .20 .50
144 Chris Chambers .20 .50
145 Zach Thomas .25 .60
146 Cliff Russell .20 .50
147 David Boston .20 .50
148 Wes Welker .25 .60
149 Marty Booker .20 .50
150 Randy McMichael .20 .50
151 Daunte Culpepper .25 .60
152 Mewelde Moore .20 .50
153 Nate Burleson .20 .50
154 Troy Williamson .20 .50
155 Koren Robinson .20 .50
156 Erasmus James .20 .50
157 Marcus Robinson .20 .50
158 E.J. Henderson .20 .50
159 Brad Johnson .25 .60
160 Michael Bennett .20 .50
161 Travis Taylor .20 .50
162 Tom Brady 1.00 2.50
163 Corey Dillon .20 .50
164 Deion Branch .20 .50
165 Tedy Bruschi .25 .60
166 Ben Watson .20 .50
167 Daniel Graham .20 .50
168 Bethel Johnson .20 .50
169 Kevin Faulk .20 .50
170 David Givens .25 .60
171 Troy Brown .20 .50
172 Aaron Brooks .20 .50
173 Deuce McAllister .25 .60
174 Joe Horn .20 .50
175 Donte Stallworth .20 .50
176 Antowain Smith .20 .50
177 Devery Henderson .20 .50
178 Eli Manning .25 .60
179 Tiki Barber .25 .60
180 Plaxico Burress .20 .50
181 Jeremy Shockey .20 .50
182 Osi Umenyiora .20 .50
183 Gibril Wilson .20 .50
184 Brandon Jacobs .20 .50
185 Michael Strahan .25 .60
186 Will Allen .20 .50
187 Amani Toomer .20 .50
188 Chad Pennington .20 .50
189 Curtis Martin .25 .60
190 Laveranues Coles .20 .50
191 Jonathan Vilma .20 .50
192 Ty Law .30 .75
193 Cedric Houston .20 .50
194 Justin McCareins .20 .50
195 Jerald Sowell .20 .50
196 Josh Brown .20 .50
197 LaMont Jordan .25 .60
198 Randy Moss .25 .60
199 Jerry Porter .20 .50
200 Doug Gabriel .20 .50
201 Johnnie Morant .20 .50
202 Zack Crockett .20 .50
203 Derrick Burgess .20 .50
204 Donovan McNabb .25 .60
205 Brian Westbrook .20 .50
206 Reggie Brown .20 .50
207 Terrell Owens .25 .60
208 Ryan Moats .20 .50
209 Correll Buckhalter .20 .50
210 Jevon Kearse .20 .50
211 L.J. Smith .20 .50
212 Lamar Gordon .20 .50
213 Greg Lewis .20 .50
214 Ben Roethlisberger .40 1.00
215 Willie Parker .25 .60
216 Jerome Bettis .30 .75
217 Hines Ward .25 .60
218 Troy Polamalu .30 .75
219 Heath Miller .20 .50
220 Antwaan Randle El .20 .50
221 Duce Staley .20 .50
222 Cedrick Wilson .20 .50
223 James Farrior .20 .50
224 Drew Brees .30 .75
225 LaDainian Tomlinson .30 .75
226 Keenan McCardell .25 .60
227 Antonio Gates .30 .75
228 Shawne Merriman .25 .60
229 Philip Rivers .30 .75
230 Vincent Jackson .20 .50
231 Donnie Edwards .20 .50
232 Eric Parker .20 .50
233 Reche Caldwell .20 .50
234 Alex Smith QB .25 .60
235 Frank Gore .25 .60
236 Brandon Lloyd .20 .50
237 Kevan Barlow .20 .50
238 Rashaun Woods .20 .50
239 Arnaz Battle .20 .50
240 Matt Hasselbeck .20 .50
241 Shaun Alexander .20 .50
242 Darrell Jackson .25 .60
243 Jerramy Stevens .25 .60
244 Lofa Tatupu .20 .50
245 D.J. Hackett .20 .50
246 Bobby Engram .20 .50
247 Joe Jurevicius .20 .50
248 Maurice Morris .20 .50
249 Marc Bulger .20 .50
250 Steven Jackson .20 .50
251 Torry Holt .25 .60
252 Isaac Bruce .30 .75
253 Kevin Curtis .25 .60
254 Marshall Faulk .25 .60
255 Shaun McDonald .20 .50
256 Chris Simms .20 .50
257 Cadillac Williams .25 .60
258 Joey Galloway .25 .60
259 Michael Clayton .20 .50
260 Derrick Brooks .20 .50
261 Ronde Barber .20 .50
262 Michael Pittman .20 .50
263 Alex Smith TE .20 .50
264 Simeon Rice .20 .50
265 Steve McNair .25 .60
266 Chris Brown .20 .50
267 Drew Bennett .25 .60
268 Brandon Jones .20 .50
269 Adam Jones .20 .50
270 Keith Bulluck .20 .50
271 Ben Troupe .20 .50
272 Jarrett Payton .20 .50
273 Tyrone Calico .20 .50
274 Bobby Wade .20 .50
275 Troy Fleming .20 .50
276 Mark Brunell .25 .60
277 Clinton Portis .20 .50
278 Santana Moss .25 .60
279 Jason Campbell .20 .50
280 Chris Cooley .20 .50
281 Carlos Rogers .20 .50
282 Ladell Betts .20 .50
283 Patrick Ramsey .25 .60
284 Taylor Jacobs .20 .50
285 James Thrash .20 .50
286 Adrian Wilson .20 .50
287 London Fletcher .25 .60
288 Lance Briggs .25 .60
289 Robert Mathis .20 .50
290 Rod Coleman .20 .50
291 Bart Scott RC 1.00 2.50
292 Brian Moorman RC .30 .75
293 Shayne Graham RC .30 .75
294 Kevin Kaesviharn RC .30 .75
295 Leigh Bodden RC .40 1.00
296 Lousaka Polite RC .30 .75
297 Todd Devoe RC .30 .75
298 Scottie Vines .30 .75
299 Cullen Jenkins RC .40 1.00
300 Donovan Morgan RC .30 .75
301 C.C. Brown .30 .75
302 Demarcus Faggins RC .30 .75
303 Shantee Orr RC .30 .75
304 Vashon Pearson RC .30 .75
305 Reggie Hayward RC .30 .75
306 Paul Spicer RC .30 .75
307 Kenny Wright RC .30 .75
308 Rich Alexis RC .30 .75
309 Terrence Melton RC .30 .75
310 Willie Whitehead RC .30 .75
311 Kendrick Clancy RC .30 .75
312 Mark Brown RC .30 .75
313 Tommy Kelly .30 .75
314 Josh Parry RC .30 .75
315 Malcom Floyd RC .40 1.00
316 Mike Adams RC .50 1.25
317 Ben Emanuel RC .30 .75
318 Brandon Moore RC .30 .75
319 Chartric Darby RC .30 .75
320 Bryce Fisher RC .30 .75
321 D.D. Lewis RC .30 .75
322 Jimmy Williams DB RC .30 .75
323 Robert Pollard RC .30 .75
324 Chris Johnson RC .50 1.25
325 Edell Shepherd RC .30 .75
326 O.J. Small RC .30 .75
327 Brad Kassell RC .30 .75
328 M.Leinart/R.Bush .50 1.25
329 M.Leinart/V.Young .30 .75
330 White/Leinart/Bush .50 1.25
331 Matt Leinart RC 1.50 4.00
332 Chad Greenway RC 2.50 6.00
333 Devin Aromashodu RC 1.50 4.00
334 DeAngelo Williams RC 2.00 5.00
335 Travis Wilson RC 1.50 4.00
336 Leon Washington RC 1.50 4.00
337 Maurice Stovall RC 1.50 4.00
338 Michael Huff RC 2.00 5.00
339 Charlie Whitehurst RC 1.50 4.00
340 Vince Young RC 1.50 4.00
341 Jerious Norwood RC 1.50 4.00
342 D'Brickashaw Ferguson RC 1.50 4.00
343 Taurean Henderson RC 1.50 4.00
344 Dominique Byrd RC 1.50 4.00
345 Sinorice Moss RC 1.50 4.00
346 Martin Nance RC 1.50 4.00
347 Vernon Davis RC 2.00 5.00
348 Ko Simpson RC 2.00 5.00
349 Jerome Harrison RC 1.50 4.00
350 Jay Cutler RC 2.00 5.00
351 Alan Zemaitis RC 1.50 4.00
352 Haloti Ngata RC 2.00 5.00
353 Greg Lee RC 1.50 4.00
354 Laurence Maroney RC 1.50 4.00
355 Bobby Carpenter RC 1.50 4.00
356 Jonathan Orr RC 2.00 5.00
357 Marcedes Lewis RC 1.50 4.00
358 Brodrick Bunkley RC 2.00 5.00
359 Todd Watkins RC 1.50 4.00
360 Reggie Bush RC 2.50 6.00
361 Jimmy Williams RC 1.50 4.00
362 Maurice Drew RC 2.50 0.00
363 Mario Williams RC 2.50 6.00
364 Derek Hagan RC 2.00 5.00
365 Santonio Holmes RC 2.00 5.00
366 Tye Hill RC 1.50 4.00
367 Jason Avant RC 1.50 4.00
368 Tamba Hali RC 2.50 6.00
369 Joe Klopfenstein RC 1.50 4.00
370 LenDale White RC 1.50 4.00
371 DeMeco Ryans RC 2.00 5.00
372 Bruce Gradkowski RC 2.00 5.00
373 A.J. Hawk RC 2.00 5.00
374 Gabe Watson RC 1.50 4.00
375 Devin Hester RC 3.00 8.00
376 Demetrius Williams RC 1.50 4.00
377 Joseph Addai RC 1.50 4.00
378 Leonard Pope RC 2.50 6.00
379 Omar Jacobs RC 1.50 4.00
380 Brad Smith RC 2.00 5.00
381 Michael Robinson RC 1.50 4.00
382 Brodie Croyle RC 1.50 4.00
383 Anthony Fasano RC 1.50 4.00
384 Brian Calhoun RC 1.50 4.00
385 Chad Jackson RC 1.50 4.00
386 Drew Olson RC 1.50 4.00
387 Greg Jennings RC 2.50 6.00
388 Andre Hall RC 2.00 5.00
389 Ryan Gilbert RC 2.00 5.00
390 Tim Day RC 2.00 5.00
391 Brandon Williams RC 1.50 4.00
392 Mark Anderson RC 6.00 15.00
393 DonTrell Moore RC 2.00 5.00
394 Kellen Clemens RC 1.50 4.00
395 Ernie Sims RC 1.50 4.00
396 Cedric Humes RC 1.50 4.00
397 Brandon Kirsch RC 2.00 5.00
398 Tony Scheffler RC 2.50 6.00
399 Kelly Jennings RC 2.00 5.00
400 Manny Lawson RC 2.00 5.00
401 Terrence Whitehead RC 2.00 5.00
402 Marcus Vick RC 1.50 4.00
403 De'Arrius Howard RC 2.50 6.00
404 Wendell Mathis RC 2.00 5.00
405 Abdul Hodge RC 1.50 4.00
406 Owen Daniels RC 2.50 6.00
407 Mike Hass RC 1.50 4.00
408 Brett Elliott RC 2.50 6.00
409 Kamerion Wimbley RC 2.00 5.00
410 Jeremy Bloom RC 1.50 4.00
411 D.J. Shockley RC 2.00 5.00
412 Darnell Bing RC 2.00 5.00
413 Miles Austin RC 2.00 5.00
414 D'Qwell Jackson RC 1.50 4.00
415 Tarvaris Jackson RC 1.50 4.00
416 Mathias Kiwanuka RC 2.50 6.00
417 Mike Bell RC 1.50 4.00
418 Paul Pinegar RC 1.50 4.00
419 David Thomas RC 1.50 4.00
420 Hank Baskett RC 1.50 4.00
421 P.J. Daniels RC 1.50 4.00
422 Jon Alston RC 1.50 4.00
423 Reggie McNeal RC 1.50 4.00
424 Brandon Marshall RC 3.00 8.00
425 Gerald Riggs RC 2.00 5.00
426 Delanie Walker RC 3.00 8.00
427 Erik Meyer RC 1.50 4.00
428 Jeff Webb RC 2.00 5.00
429 Skyler Green RC 1.50 4.00
430 Thomas Howard RC 1.50 4.00

2006 Select Artist's Proof

*VETS 1-290: 10X TO 25X BASIC CARDS
*VETS 291-327: 6X TO 15X BASIC CARDS
*ROOKIES 328-330: 2X TO 5X BASIC CARDS
*ROOKIES 331-385: .8X TO 2X BASIC CARDS
STATED PRINT RUN 32 SER.#'d SETS

2006 Select Gold

*VETS 1-290: 6X TO 15X BASIC CARDS
*VETS 291-327: 4X TO 10X BASIC CARDS
*ROOKIES 328-330: 1.2X TO 3X BASIC CARDS
*ROOKIES 331-385: .6X TO 1.5X
GOLD PRINT RUN 50 SER.#'d SETS

2006 Select Red

*VETS 1-290: 10X TO 25X BASIC CARDS
*VETS 291-327: 6X TO 15X BASIC CARDS
*ROOKIES 328-330: 2X TO 5X BASIC CARDS
*ROOKIES 331-385: 1X TO 2.5X BASIC CARDS
RED PRINT RUN 25 SER.#'d SETS
360 Reggie Bush 6.00 15.00

2006 Select Scorecard

*VETS 1-290: 4X TO 10X BASIC CARDS
*VETS 291-327: 2.5X TO 6X BASIC CARDS
*ROOKIES 328-330: 1X TO 2.5X BASIC CARDS
*ROOKIES 331-385: .5X TO 1.2X
SCORECARD PRINT RUN 100 SER.#'d SETS

2006 Select Autographs Red

SERIAL #'d UNDER 25 NOT PRICED
UNPRICED BLACK SER.#'d TO 6
332 Chad Greenway/25 12.00 30.00
335 Travis Wilson/25 12.00 30.00
336 Leon Washington/25 25.00 60.00
341 Jerious Norwood/25 25.00 60.00
352 Haloti Ngata/25 12.00 30.00
355 Bobby Carpenter/25 12.00 30.00
367 Jason Avant/25 12.00 30.00
368 Tamba Hali/25 15.00 40.00
381 Michael Robinson/25 12.00 30.00
387 Greg Jennings/25 12.00 30.00
394 Kellen Clemens/25 15.00 40.00
399 Kelly Jennings/25 12.00 30.00
400 Manny Lawson/25 12.00 30.00
415 Tarvaris Jackson/25 12.00 30.00
416 Mathias Kiwanuka/25 20.00 50.00
424 Brandon Marshall/25 15.00 40.00

2006 Select Hot Rookies

STATED PRINT RUN 749 SER.#'d SETS
*ART.PROOF: 1X TO 2.5X BASIC INSERTS
ART.PROOF PRINT RUN 32 SER.#'d SETS
UNPRICED BLACK PRINT RUN 6 SETS
*GOLD: .8X TO 2X BASIC INSERTS
GOLD PRINT RUN 75 SER.#'d SETS
*RED: 1.2X TO 3X BASIC INSERTS
RED PRINT RUN 25 SER.#'d SETS
*SCORECARD: .6X TO 1.5X BASIC INSERTS
SCORECARD PRINT RUN 125 SER.#'d SETS
1 Matt Leinart .75 2.00
2 Vince Young .75 2.00
3 Jay Cutler 1.00 2.50
4 Reggie Bush 1.25 3.00
5 LenDale White .75 2.00
6 DeAngelo Williams 1.00 2.50
7 Laurence Maroney .75 2.00
8 Santonio Holmes 1.00 2.50
9 Sinorice Moss .75 2.00
10 Maurice Stovall .75 2.00
11 Brodie Croyle .75 2.00
12 Charlie Whitehurst .75 2.00
13 Reggie McNeal .75 2.00
14 Joseph Addai .75 2.00
15 Brian Calhoun .75 2.00
16 Maurice Drew 1.25 3.00
17 Vernon Davis 1.00 2.50
18 Chad Jackson .75 2.00
19 Demetrius Williams .75 2.00
20 Brandon Marshall 1.50 4.00

2006 Select Hot Rookies Inscriptions

STATED PRINT RUN 25 SER.#'d SETS
1 Matt Leinart 12.00 30.00
2 Vince Young 12.00 30.00
3 Jay Cutler 15.00 40.00
4 Reggie Bush 20.00 50.00
5 LenDale White 12.00 30.00
0 DeAngelo Williams 15.00 40.00

7 Laurence Maroney 12.00 30.00
8 Santonio Holmes 15.00 40.00
9 Sinorice Moss
10 Maurice Stovall 12.00 30.00
11 Brodie Croyle 12.00 30.00
12 Charlie Whitehurst 12.00 30.00
13 Reggie McNeal 12.00 30.00
14 Joseph Addai 12.00 30.00
15 Brian Calhoun 12.00 30.00
16 Maurice Drew 20.00 50.00
17 Vernon Davis 15.00 40.00
18 Chad Jackson 12.00 30.00
19 Demetrius Williams 12.00 30.00
20 Brandon Marshall 25.00 60.00

2006 Select Inscriptions

VETERAN STATED PRINT RUN 5-50
SERIAL #'d UNDER 25 NOT PRICED
32 Jake Delhomme/50 6.00 15.00
56 T.J. Houshmandzadeh/25 6.00 15.00
80 Tatum Bell/25 6.00 15.00
88 Kevin Jones/25 6.00 15.00
98 Samkon Gado/100 10.00 25.00
104 Domanick Davis/50 8.00 20.00
114 Reggie Wayne/50 8.00 20.00
116 Dallas Clark/25 10.00 25.00
123 Byron Leftwich/50 8.00 20.00
125 Jimmy Smith/25 10.00 25.00
188 Chad Pennington/30 6.00 15.00
190 Laveranues Coles/35 8.00 20.00
218 Troy Polamalu/37 50.00 100.00
227 Antonio Gates/34 12.00 30.00
253 Kevin Curtis/59 8.00 20.00
266 Chris Brown/50 6.00 15.00
331 Matt Leinart/100 6.00 15.00
332 Chad Greenway/250 8.00 20.00
333 Devin Aromashodu/250 5.00 12.00
334 DeAngelo Williams/100 8.00 20.00
335 Travis Wilson/100 6.00 15.00
336 Leon Washington/50 6.00 15.00
337 Maurice Stovall/100 6.00 15.00
338 Michael Huff/50 8.00 20.00
339 Charlie Whitehurst/50 6.00 15.00
340 Vince Young/100 6.00 15.00
341 Jerious Norwood/100 6.00 15.00
342 D'Brickashaw Ferguson/250 5.00 12.00
343 Taurean Henderson/250 5.00 12.00
344 Dominique Byrd/100 6.00 15.00
345 Sinorice Moss/100 6.00 15.00
346 Martin Nance/250 5.00 12.00
347 Vernon Davis/100 8.00 20.00
348 Ko Simpson/250 6.00 15.00
349 Jerome Harrison/200 5.00 12.00
350 Jay Cutler/100 25.00 60.00
351 Alan Zemaitis/100 6.00 15.00
352 Haloti Ngata/150 6.00 15.00
353 Greg Lee/250 5.00 12.00
354 Laurence Maroney/100 6.00 15.00
355 Bobby Carpenter/100 6.00 15.00
356 Jonathan Orr/250 6.00 15.00
357 Marcedes Lewis/250 5.00 12.00
358 Brodrick Bunkley/50 8.00 20.00
359 Todd Watkins/250 5.00 12.00
360 Reggie Bush/100 12.00 30.00
361 Jimmy Williams/250 5.00 12.00
362 Maurice Drew/100 15.00 40.00
363 Mario Williams/50 10.00 25.00
364 Derek Hagan/100 8.00 20.00
365 Santonio Holmes/100 8.00 20.00
366 Tye Hill/50 6.00 15.00
367 Jason Avant/125 6.00 15.00
368 Tamba Hali/250 8.00 20.00
369 Joe Klopfenstein/50 6.00 15.00
370 LenDale White/100 6.00 15.00
371 DeMeco Ryans/250 6.00 15.00
372 Bruce Gradkowski/100 8.00 20.00
373 A.J. Hawk/50 8.00 20.00
374 Gabe Watson/200 5.00 12.00
375 Devin Hester/50 12.00 30.00
376 Demetrius Williams/50 6.00 15.00
377 Joseph Addai/100 6.00 15.00
378 Leonard Pope/100 10.00 25.00
379 Omar Jacobs/125 6.00 15.00
380 Brad Smith/250 6.00 15.00
381 Michael Robinson/50 6.00 15.00
382 Brodie Croyle/100 6.00 15.00
383 Anthony Fasano/50 6.00 15.00
384 Brian Calhoun/100 6.00 15.00
385 Chad Jackson/100 6.00 15.00
386 Drew Olson/250 5.00 12.00
387 Greg Jennings/100 10.00 25.00
388 Andre Hall/250 6.00 15.00
391 Brandon Williams/50 6.00 15.00
394 Kellen Clemens/50 6.00 15.00
396 Cedric Humes/250 5.00 12.00
397 Brandon Kirsch/250 6.00 15.00
398 Tony Scheffler/250 8.00 20.00
399 Kelly Jennings/100 8.00 20.00
400 Manny Lawson/50 8.00 20.00
403 De'Arrius Howard/250 8.00 20.00
404 Wendell Mathis/250 6.00 15.00
405 Abdul Hodge/250 5.00 12.00
407 Mike Hass/250 5.00 12.00
409 Kamerion Wimbley/100 8.00 20.00
410 Jeremy Bloom/25 6.00 15.00
411 D.J. Shockley/100 8.00 20.00
412 Darnell Bing/100 8.00 20.00
413 Miles Austin/250 6.00 15.00
414 D'Qwell Jackson/100 6.00 15.00
415 Tarvaris Jackson/100 6.00 15.00
416 Mathias Kiwanuka/100 10.00 25.00
417 Mike Bell/250 5.00 12.00
418 Paul Pinegar/250 5.00 12.00
419 David Thomas/100 6.00 15.00
420 Hank Baskett/250 5.00 12.00
421 P.J. Daniels/250 5.00 12.00
422 Jon Alston/250 5.00 12.00
423 Reggie McNeal/250 5.00 12.00
424 Brandon Marshall/100 12.00 30.00
425 Gerald Riggs/250 6.00 15.00
426 Delanie Walker/250 10.00 25.00
427 Erik Meyer/250 5.00 12.00
428 Jeff Webb/250 6.00 15.00
429 Skyler Green/250 5.00 12.00
430 Thomas Howard/25 6.00 15.00

2006 Select Hot Rookies National Anaheim Embossed Promos

COMPLETE SET (10) 30.00 60.00
11 Brodie Croyle 1.00 2.50
12 Charlie Whitehurst 1.00 2.50
13 Reggie McNeal 1.00 2.50
14 Joseph Addai 1.00 2.50
15 Brian Calhoun 1.00 2.50
16 Maurice Drew 1.50 4.00
17 Vernon Davis 1.25 3.00
18 Chad Jackson 1.00 2.50
19 DeMetrius Williams 1.00 2.50
20 Brandon Marshall 2.00 5.00

2006 Select National Anaheim Blue Promos

COMPLETE SET (12) 30.00 60.00
*GOLD/100: .8X TO 2X BLUE
1 Mario Williams 1.00 2.50
2 Reggie Bush 1.00 2.50
3 Vince Young .60 1.50
4 A.J. Hawk .75 2.00
5 Vernon Davis .75 2.00
6 Matt Leinart .60 1.50
7 Jay Cutler .75 2.00
8 Laurence Maroney .60 1.50
9 Santonio Holmes .75 2.00
10 Chad Jackson .60 1.50
11 LenDale White .60 1.50
12 DeAngelo Williams .75 2.00

2007 Select

This 430-card set was released in July, 2007. The set was issued into the hobby in five-card packs, with a $4 SRP, which came 20 packs to a box. Cards numbered 1-288 feature veterans in team alphabetical order by division while cards numbered 289-430 feature 2007 NFL rookies. The rookie cards are broken up into two groups: Cards numbered 289-330 and cards numbered 331-430 which were issued to a stated print run of 599 serial numbered sets.

COMP.SET w/o RC's (288) 25.00 50.00
331-430 RC PRINT RUN 599 SER.#'d SETS
1 Tony Romo .40 1.00
2 Julius Jones .20 .50
3 Terry Glenn .25 .60
4 Terrell Owens .25 .60
5 Jason Witten .25 .60
6 Marion Barber .25 .60
7 Patrick Crayton .20 .50
8 Bradie James .20 .50
9 DeMarcus Ware .25 .60
10 Roy Williams S .20 .50
11 Eli Manning .25 .60
12 Plaxico Burress .20 .50
13 Jeremy Shockey .20 .50
14 Brandon Jacobs .20 .50
15 Sinorice Moss .25 .60
16 Antonio Pierce .20 .50
17 David Tyree .20 .50
18 Donovan McNabb .25 .60
19 Brian Westbrook .20 .50
20 Reggie Brown .20 .50
21 L.J. Smith .20 .50
22 Hank Baskett .25 .60
23 Jeremiah Trotter .20 .50
24 Trent Cole .20 .50
25 Lito Sheppard .20 .50
26 Jason Campbell .20 .50
27 Clinton Portis .20 .50
28 Santana Moss .25 .60
29 Brandon Lloyd .20 .50
30 Chris Cooley .20 .50
31 Sean Taylor .30 .75
32 Lemar Marshall .20 .50
33 Ladell Betts .20 .50
34 London Fletcher .25 .60
35 Rex Grossman .20 .50
36 Cedric Benson .20 .50
37 Muhsin Muhammad .20 .50
38 Bernard Berrian .20 .50
39 Desmond Clark .20 .50
40 Lance Briggs .25 .60
41 Robbie Gould .20 .50
42 Devin Hester .25 .60
43 Mark Anderson .25 .60
44 Brian Urlacher .30 .75
45 Jon Kitna .20 .50
46 Kevin Jones .20 .50
47 Roy Williams WR .20 .50
48 Mike Furrey .25 .60
49 Cory Redding .20 .50
50 Ernie Sims .20 .50
51 Tatum Bell .20 .50
52 Brian Calhoun .20 .50
53 Brett Favre .60 1.50
54 Vernand Morency .25 .60
55 Donald Driver .25 .60
56 Greg Jennings .20 .50
57 Aaron Kampman .25 .60
58 Charles Woodson .30 .75
59 A.J. Hawk .20 .50
60 Nick Barnett .20 .50
61 Aaron Rodgers .75 2.00
62 Tarvaris Jackson .20 .50
63 Chester Taylor .20 .50
64 Troy Williamson .20 .50
65 Jim Kleinsasser .20 .50
66 Dwight Smith .20 .50
67 Antoine Winfield .20 .50
68 E.J. Henderson .20 .50
69 Mewelde Moore .20 .50
70 Michael Vick .25 .60
71 Warrick Dunn .20 .50
72 Joe Horn .20 .50
73 Michael Jenkins .20 .50
74 Alge Crumpler .25 .60
75 DeAngelo Hall .20 .50
76 Keith Brooking .20 .50
77 Lawyer Milloy .20 .50
78 Jerious Norwood .20 .50
79 Matt Schaub .20 .50
80 Jake Delhomme .20 .50
81 DeShaun Foster .25 .60
82 Steve Smith .25 .60
83 Keyshawn Johnson .25 .60
84 Julius Peppers .25 .60
85 DeAngelo Williams .20 .50
86 Chris Draft .20 .50
87 Drew Brees .30 .75
88 Deuce McAllister .25 .60
89 Scott Fujita .20 .50
90 Marques Colston .20 .50
91 Terrance Copper .25 .60
92 Will Smith .20 .50
93 Charles Grant .20 .50
94 Devery Henderson .20 .50
95 Reggie Bush .20 .50
96 Jeff Garcia .20 .50
97 Cadillac Williams .25 .60
98 Joey Galloway .25 .60
99 Michael Clayton .20 .50
100 Alex Smith TE .20 .50
101 Ronde Barber .20 .50
102 Jermaine Phillips .20 .50
103 Derrick Brooks .20 .50
104 Matt Leinart .20 .50
105 Edgerrin James .25 .60
106 Anquan Boldin .20 .50
107 Larry Fitzgerald .25 .60
108 Neil Rackers .20 .50
109 Adrian Wilson .20 .50
110 Karlos Dansby .20 .50
111 Chike Okeafor .20 .50
112 Marc Bulger .20 .50
113 Steven Jackson .20 .50
114 Torry Holt .25 .60
115 Isaac Bruce .30 .75
116 Joe Klopfenstein .20 .50
117 Randy McMichael .20 .50
118 Will Witherspoon .20 .50
119 Drew Bennett .20 .50
120 Alex Smith QB .25 .60
121 Frank Gore .25 .60
122 Arnaz Battle .20 .50
123 Ashley Lelie .25 .60
124 Vernon Davis .20 .50
125 Walt Harris .20 .50
126 Brandon Moore .20 .50
127 Nate Clements .20 .50
128 Matt Hasselbeck .20 .50
129 Shaun Alexander .20 .50
130 Deion Branch .20 .50
131 Darrell Jackson .20 .50
132 Nate Burleson .20 .50
133 Julian Peterson .20 .50
134 Lofa Tatupu .20 .50
135 Mack Strong .20 .50
136 Josh Brown .20 .50
137 J.P. Losman .20 .50
138 Anthony Thomas .20 .50
139 Lee Evans .25 .60
140 Josh Reed .20 .50
141 Roscoe Parrish .20 .50
142 Aaron Schobel .20 .50
143 Donte Whitner .20 .50
144 Shaud Williams .20 .50
145 Daunte Culpepper .25 .60
146 Ronnie Brown .20 .50
147 Chris Chambers .20 .50
148 Marty Booker .20 .50
149 Derek Hagan .20 .50
150 Jason Taylor .25 .60
151 Vonnie Holliday .20 .50
152 Zach Thomas .25 .60
153 Channing Crowder .20 .50
154 Joey Porter .20 .50
155 Tom Brady 1.00 2.50
156 Laurence Maroney .25 .60
157 Chad Jackson .20 .50
158 Wes Welker .25 .60
159 Ben Watson .20 .50
160 Donte Stallworth .25 .60
161 Rosevelt Colvin .20 .50
162 Ty Warren .20 .50
163 Asante Samuel .20 .50
164 Adalius Thomas .20 .50
165 Tedy Bruschi .25 .60
166 Chad Pennington .20 .50
167 Thomas Jones .20 .50
168 Laveranues Coles .20 .50
169 Jerricho Cotchery .20 .50
170 Chris Baker .20 .50
171 Bryan Thomas .20 .50
172 Leon Washington .20 .50
173 Jonathan Vilma .20 .50
174 Eric Barton .20 .50
175 Erik Coleman .20 .50
176 Steve McNair .25 .60
177 Willis McGahee .20 .50
178 Derrick Mason .20 .50
179 Demetrius Williams .20 .50
180 Todd Heap .20 .50
181 Ray Lewis .30 .75
182 Trevor Pryce .20 .50
183 Bart Scott .25 .60
184 Terrell Suggs .20 .50
185 Mark Clayton .20 .50
186 Carson Palmer .25 .60
187 Rudi Johnson .20 .50
188 Chad Johnson .20 .50
189 T.J. Houshmandzadeh .20 .50
190 Robert Geathers .20 .50
191 Justin Smith .25 .60
192 Tory James .20 .50
193 Landon Johnson .20 .50
194 Shayne Graham .20 .50
195 Charlie Frye .25 .60
196 Reuben Droughns .25 .60
197 Braylon Edwards .20 .50
198 Travis Wilson .20 .50
199 Kellen Winslow .20 .50
200 Kamerion Wimbley .20 .50
201 Sean Jones .20 .50
202 Andra Davis .20 .50
203 Jamal Lewis .25 .60
204 Ben Roethlisberger .30 .75
205 Willie Parker .25 .60
206 Hines Ward .25 .60
207 Santonio Holmes .20 .50
208 Heath Miller .20 .50
209 Troy Polamalu .30 .75
210 James Farrior .20 .50
211 Cedrick Wilson .20 .50
212 Dunta Robinson .20 .50
213 Ahman Green .25 .60
214 Andre Johnson .25 .60
215 Jerome Mathis .20 .50
216 Owen Daniels .20 .50
217 DeMeco Ryans .25 .60
218 Wali Lundy .20 .50
219 Mario Williams .25 .60
220 Peyton Manning .75 2.00
221 Joseph Addai .20 .50
222 Marvin Harrison .25 .60
223 Reggie Wayne .25 .60
224 Dallas Clark .25 .60
225 Robert Mathis .20 .50
226 Cato June .20 .50
227 Adam Vinatieri .20 .50
228 Bob Sanders .25 .60
229 Dwight Freeney .20 .50
230 Byron Leftwich .20 .50
231 Fred Taylor .20 .50
232 Matt Jones .25 .60
233 Reggie Williams .25 .60
234 Marcedes Lewis .25 .50
235 Bobby McCray .20 .50
236 Rashean Mathis .20 .50
237 Maurice Jones-Drew .20 .50
238 Ernest Wilford .20 .50
239 Daryl Smith .20 .50
240 Vince Young .20 .50
241 LenDale White .25 .60
242 Brandon Jones .20 .50
243 Bo Scaife .20 .50
244 Keith Bulluck .20 .50
245 Chris Hope .20 .50
246 Kyle Vanden Bosch .20 .50
247 Roydell Williams .20 .50
248 Jay Cutler .20 .50
249 Travis Henry .25 .60
250 Javon Walker .25 .60
251 Rod Smith .25 .60
252 Tony Scheffler .25 .60
253 Elvis Dumervil .20 .50
254 Champ Bailey .25 .60
255 Mike Bell .25 .60
256 Brandon Marshall .25 .60
257 Al Wilson .20 .50
258 Trent Green .20 .50
259 Larry Johnson .20 .50
260 Eddie Kennison .20 .50
261 Samie Parker .20 .50
262 Tony Gonzalez .25 .60
263 Jared Allen .20 .50
264 Kawika Mitchell .20 .50
265 Tamba Hali .20 .50
266 Dante Hall .20 .50
267 Brodie Croyle .25 .60
268 Andrew Walter .20 .50
269 LaMont Jordan .25 .60
270 Dominic Rhodes .20 .50
271 Randy Moss .25 .60
272 Ronald Curry .20 .50
273 Courtney Anderson .20 .50
274 Derrick Burgess .20 .50
275 Warren Sapp .25 .60
276 Michael Huff .25 .60
277 Thomas Howard .20 .50
278 Kirk Morrison .20 .50
279 Philip Rivers .30 .75
280 LaDainian Tomlinson .30 .75
281 Vincent Jackson .20 .50
282 Lorenzo Neal .20 .50
283 Antonio Gates .30 .75
284 Shawne Merriman .20 .50
285 Shaun Phillips .20 .50
286 Michael Turner .20 .50
287 Jamal Williams .20 .50
288 Nate Kaeding .20 .50
289 Michael Okwo RC .60 1.50
290 Gary Russell RC .60 1.50
291 Josh Wilson RC .60 1.50
292 Thomas Clayton RC .60 1.50
293 Jerard Rabb RC .60 1.50
294 Roy Hall RC .75 2.00
295 LaMarr Woodley RC 1.00 2.50
296 Eric Wright RC .50 1.25
297 Dan Bazuin RC .60 1.50
298 A.J. Davis RC .50 1.25
299 Buster Davis RC .60 1.50
300 Stewart Bradley RC .50 1.25
301 Toby Korrodi RC .60 1.50
302 Marcus McCauley RC .50 1.25
303 DeMarcus Tank Tyler RC .50 1.25
304 Jon Abbate RC .50 1.25
305 Ikaika Alama-Francis RC .75 2.00
306 Tim Crowder RC .60 1.50
307 D'Juan Woods RC .50 1.25
308 Tim Shaw RC .60 1.50
309 Fred Bennett RC .50 1.25
310 Victor Abiamiri RC .50 1.25
311 Eric Weddle RC .60 1.50
312 Danny Ware RC .75 2.00
313 Quentin Moses RC .50 1.25
314 Ryan McBean RC .75 2.00
315 David Harris RC .50 1.25
316 David Irons RC .50 1.25
317 Syndric Steptoe RC .60 1.50
318 Eric Frampton RC .60 1.50
319 Jemalle Cornelius RC .60 1.50
320 Earl Everett RC .50 1.25
321 Alonzo Coleman RC .60 1.50
322 Josh Gattis RC .50 1.25
323 Zak DeOssie RC .60 1.50
324 Jon Beason RC .50 1.25
325 Joe Staley RC .60 1.50
326 Aaron Rouse RC .50 1.25
327 Reggie Ball RC .60 1.50
328 Rufus Alexander RC .50 1.25
329 Daymeion Hughes RC .50 1.25
330 Justin Durant RC .75 2.00
331 JaMarcus Russell RC 1.50 4.00
332 Paul Williams RC 1.50 4.00
333 Kenny Irons RC 1.50 4.00
334 Chris Davis RC 1.50 4.00
335 Darius Walker RC 1.50 4.00
336 Dwayne Bowe RC 1.50 4.00
337 Isaiah Stanback RC 1.50 4.00
338 Leon Hall RC 1.50 4.00
339 Sidney Rice RC 2.00 5.00
340 Amobi Okoye RC 2.00 5.00
341 Adrian Peterson RC 5.00 12.00
342 LaRon Landry RC 2.50 6.00
343 Lorenzo Booker RC 2.00 5.00
344 Craig Buster Davis RC 1.50 4.00
345 Mike Walker RC 2.50 6.00
346 Zach Miller RC 1.50 4.00
347 Levi Brown RC 1.50 4.00
348 Brian Leonard RC 1.50 4.00
349 Aundrae Allison RC 1.50 4.00
350 Brandon Siler RC 1.50 4.00
351 Calvin Johnson RC 5.00 12.00
352 Gaines Adams RC 2.00 5.00
353 Anthony Gonzalez RC 1.50 4.00
354 John Beck RC 1.50 4.00
355 Joe Thomas RC 2.50 6.00
356 Michael Bush RC 1.50 4.00
357 Courtney Taylor RC 1.50 4.00
358 Lawrence Timmons RC 2.50 6.00
359 Drew Stanton RC 1.50 4.00
360 Chansi Stuckey RC 2.00 5.00
361 Greg Olsen RC 2.50 6.00
362 Rhema McKnight RC 1.50 4.00
363 Antonio Pittman RC 1.50 4.00
364 Kevin Kolb RC 2.00 5.00
365 Alan Branch RC 1.50 4.00
366 Robert Meachem RC 2.00 5.00
367 Troy Smith RC 1.50 4.00
368 Jamaal Anderson RC 2.00 5.00
369 Tony Hunt RC 1.50 4.00
370 David Clowney RC 1.50 4.00
371 Brady Quinn RC 1.50 4.00
372 Michael Griffin RC 1.50 4.00
373 Jared Zabransky RC 1.50 4.00
374 Jason Hill RC 1.50 4.00
375 Trent Edwards RC 1.50 4.00
376 Dwayne Jarrett RC 2.00 5.00
377 DeShawn Wynn RC 1.50 4.00
378 Patrick Willis RC 2.50 6.00
379 Steve Smith USC RC 1.50 4.00
380 David Ball RC 1.50 4.00
381 Marshawn Lynch RC 3.00 8.00
382 Paul Posluszny RC 1.50 4.00
383 Johnnie Lee Higgins RC 1.50 4.00
384 Kolby Smith RC 1.50 4.00
385 Ted Ginn Jr. RC 2.00 5.00
386 Adam Carriker RC 1.50 4.00
387 Tyler Palko RC 2.50 6.00
388 Joel Filani RC 1.50 4.00
389 Garrett Wolfe RC 1.50 4.00
390 Ryne Robinson RC 2.00 5.00
391 Reggie Nelson RC 1.50 4.00
392 Dallas Baker RC 1.50 4.00
393 Dwayne Wright RC 1.50 4.00
394 Scott Chandler RC 2.50 6.00
395 Jordan Kent RC 2.00 5.00
396 Jarvis Moss RC 1.50 4.00
397 Jonathan Wade RC 1.50 4.00
398 Ben Grubbs RC 2.00 5.00
399 Jason Snelling RC 1.50 4.00
400 Jeff Rowe RC 1.50 4.00
401 Aaron Ross RC 1.50 4.00
402 Jarrett Hicks RC 2.00 5.00
403 Chris Henry RC 1.50 4.00
404 James Jones RC 1.50 4.00
405 Matt Spaeth RC 2.50 6.00
406 Brandon Meriweather RC 2.00 5.00
407 Nate Ilaoa RC 2.00 5.00
408 Brandon Myles RC 2.00 5.00
409 Ray McDonald RC 2.00 5.00
410 Chris Leak RC 1.50 4.00
411 Darrelle Revis RC 2.00 5.00
412 Ahmad Bradshaw RC 2.50 6.00
413 Tyler Thigpen RC 2.50 6.00
414 Justise Hairston RC 2.00 5.00
415 Charles Johnson RC 1.50 4.00
416 Anthony Spencer RC 2.00 5.00
417 Legedu Naanee RC 2.00 5.00
418 Kenneth Darby RC 1.50 4.00
419 Steve Breaston RC 1.50 4.00
420 Ben Patrick RC 2.00 5.00
421 Chris Houston RC 1.50 4.00
422 Jordan Palmer RC 2.00 5.00
423 Laurent Robinson RC 2.50 6.00
424 Selvin Young RC 1.50 4.00
425 Justin Harrell RC 1.50 4.00
426 Sabby Piscitelli RC 1.50 4.00
427 Yamon Figurs RC 1.50 4.00
428 Brandon Jackson RC 1.50 4.00
429 Jacoby Jones RC 1.50 4.00
430 H.B. Blades RC 1.50 4.00

2007 Select Artist's Proof

*VETS 1-288: 8X TO 20X BASIC CARDS
*ROOKIES 289-330: 2.5X TO 6X BASIC CARDS
*ROOKIES 331-430: .8X TO 2X BASIC CARDS
STATED PRINT RUN 32 SER.#'d SETS

2007 Select End Zone

UNPRICED END ZONE PRINT RUN 6

2007 Select Gold Zone

*VETS 1-288: 5X TO 12X BASIC CARDS
*ROOKIES 289-330: 2X TO 5X BASIC CARDS
*ROOKIES 331-430: .6X TO 1.5X BASIC CARDS
STATED PRINT RUN 50 SER.#'d SETS

2007 Select Red Zone

*VETS 1-288: 8X TO 20X BASIC CARDS
*ROOKIES 289-330: 2.5X TO 6X BASIC CARDS
*ROOKIES 331-430: .8X TO 2X BASIC CARDS
STATED PRINT RUN 30 SER.#'d SETS

2007 Select Scorecard

*VETS 1-288: 4X TO 10X BASIC CARDS
*ROOKIES 289-330: 1.5X TO 4X BASIC CARDS
*ROOKIES 331-430: .5X TO 1.2X BASIC CARDS
STATED PRINT RUN 100 SER.#'d SETS

2007 Select Autographs Gold Zone

GOLD ZONE PRINT RUN 10-40
*RED ZONE/25: .5X TO 1.2X GOLD AU/40
RED ZONE PRINT RUN 5-25
UNPRICED END ZONE PRINT RUN 1-5
SERIAL #'d UNDER 25 NOT PRICED
289 Michael Okwo/40 8.00 20.00
290 Gary Russell/40 8.00 20.00
291 Josh Wilson/40 8.00 20.00
292 Thomas Clayton/40 8.00 20.00
293 Jerard Rabb/40 8.00 20.00
295 LaMarr Woodley/40 12.00 30.00
297 Dan Bazuin/40 8.00 20.00
298 A.J. Davis/40 6.00 15.00
299 Buster Davis/40 8.00 20.00
300 Stewart Bradley/40 6.00 15.00
301 Toby Korrodi/40 8.00 20.00
302 Marcus McCauley/40 6.00 15.00
306 Tim Crowder/40 8.00 20.00
307 D'Juan Woods/40 6.00 15.00
308 Tim Shaw/40 8.00 20.00
309 Fred Bennett/40 6.00 15.00
310 Victor Abiamiri/40 6.00 15.00
312 Danny Ware/40 10.00 25.00
313 Quentin Moses/40 6.00 15.00
314 Ryan McBean/40 10.00 25.00
315 David Harris/40 6.00 15.00
316 David Irons/40 6.00 15.00
317 Syndric Steptoe/40 8.00 20.00
318 Eric Frampton/40 8.00 20.00
319 Jemalle Cornelius/40 8.00 20.00
320 Earl Everett/40 6.00 15.00
321 Alonzo Coleman/40 8.00 20.00
322 Josh Gattis/40 6.00 15.00
323 Zak DeOssie/40 8.00 20.00
324 Jon Beason/25 8.00 20.00
326 Aaron Rouse/40 6.00 15.00
327 Reggie Ball/40 8.00 20.00
328 Rufus Alexander/40 6.00 15.00
329 Daymeion Hughes/40 6.00 15.00
331 JaMarcus Russell/25 8.00 20.00
332 Paul Williams/25 8.00 20.00
333 Kenny Irons/25 8.00 20.00
334 Chris Davis/40 6.00 15.00
335 Darius Walker/40 6.00 15.00
336 Dwayne Bowe/25 8.00 20.00
337 Isaiah Stanback/40 6.00 15.00
338 Leon Hall/25 8.00 20.00
339 Sidney Rice/25 10.00 25.00
340 Amobi Okoye/25 10.00 25.00
341 Adrian Peterson/25 125.00 250.00
342 LaRon Landry/40 10.00 25.00
343 Lorenzo Booker/25 10.00 25.00
345 Mike Walker/40 10.00 25.00
346 Zach Miller/25 8.00 20.00
347 Levi Brown/40 6.00 15.00
348 Brian Leonard/25 10.00 25.00
349 Aundrae Allison/40 6.00 15.00
350 Brandon Siler/40 6.00 15.00
351 Calvin Johnson/25 25.00 60.00
352 Gaines Adams/25 10.00 25.00
353 Anthony Gonzalez/25 8.00 20.00
354 John Beck/25 8.00 20.00
355 Joe Thomas/40 10.00 25.00
356 Michael Bush/25 8.00 20.00
357 Courtney Taylor/40 6.00 15.00
358 Lawrence Timmons/25 12.00 30.00
359 Drew Stanton/25 8.00 20.00
360 Chansi Stuckey/40 8.00 20.00
361 Greg Olsen/25 12.00 30.00
362 Rhema McKnight/40 6.00 15.00
363 Antonio Pittman/25 8.00 20.00
364 Kevin Kolb/25 10.00 25.00
366 Robert Meachem/25 10.00 25.00
367 Troy Smith/25 8.00 20.00
368 Jamaal Anderson/40 8.00 20.00
369 Tony Hunt/25 8.00 20.00
370 David Clowney/40 6.00 15.00
371 Brady Quinn/25 8.00 20.00
372 Michael Griffin/40 6.00 15.00
373 Jared Zabransky/40 6.00 15.00
374 Jason Hill/25 8.00 20.00
375 Trent Edwards/25 8.00 20.00
376 Dwayne Jarrett/25 10.00 25.00
377 DeShawn Wynn/25 8.00 20.00
378 Patrick Willis/25 12.00 30.00
379 Steve Smith USC/25 8.00 20.00
380 David Ball/40 6.00 15.00
381 Marshawn Lynch/25 25.00 60.00
382 Paul Posluszny/25 8.00 20.00
383 Johnnie Lee Higgins/25 8.00 20.00
384 Kolby Smith/40 6.00 15.00
385 Ted Ginn Jr./25 10.00 25.00
386 Adam Carriker/40 6.00 15.00
387 Tyler Palko/40 10.00 25.00
388 Joel Filani/40 6.00 15.00
389 Garrett Wolfe/25 8.00 20.00
390 Ryne Robinson/40 8.00 20.00
391 Reggie Nelson/40 6.00 15.00
392 Dallas Baker/40 6.00 15.00
393 Dwayne Wright/40 6.00 15.00
394 Scott Chandler/40 10.00 25.00
395 Jordan Kent/40 8.00 20.00
397 Jonathan Wade/40 6.00 15.00
399 Jason Snelling/40 6.00 15.00
400 Jeff Rowe/40 6.00 15.00
401 Aaron Ross/40 6.00 15.00
402 Jarrett Hicks/40 8.00 20.00
403 Chris Henry/25 8.00 20.00
404 James Jones/40 6.00 15.00
405 Matt Spaeth/40 10.00 25.00
406 Brandon Meriweather/40 8.00 20.00
407 Nate Ilaoa/40 8.00 20.00
408 Brandon Myles/40 8.00 20.00
409 Ray McDonald/40 8.00 20.00
410 Chris Leak/25 8.00 20.00
411 Darrelle Revis/40 8.00 20.00
412 Ahmad Bradshaw/40 10.00 25.00
416 Anthony Spencer/40 8.00 20.00
418 Kenneth Darby/40 6.00 15.00
419 Steve Breaston/40 6.00 15.00
420 Ben Patrick/40 8.00 20.00
421 Chris Houston/40 6.00 15.00
422 Jordan Palmer/25 10.00 25.00
423 Laurent Robinson/40 10.00 25.00
424 Selvin Young/40 6.00 15.00
426 Sabby Piscitelli/40 6.00 15.00
427 Yamon Figurs/25 8.00 20.00
428 Brandon Jackson/25 8.00 20.00
429 Jacoby Jones/40 6.00 15.00
430 H.B. Blades/40 6.00 15.00

2007 Select Franchise

STATED PRINT RUN 749 SER.#'d SETS
*SCORECARD/100: .6X TO 1.5X BASIC INSERTS
SCORECARD PRINT RUN 100 SER.#'d SETS
*GOLD ZONE/50: 1X TO 2.5X BASIC INSERTS
GOLD ZONE PRINT RUN 50 SER.#'d SETS
*ART.PROOF/32: 1.5X TO 4X BASIC INSERTS
ARTIST'S PROOF PRINT RUN 32 SER.#'d SETS
*RED ZONE/30: 1.5X TO 4X BASIC INSERTS
RED ZONE PRINT RUN 30 SER.#'d SETS
UNPRICED END ZONE PRINT RUN 6
UNPRICED AUTO END ZONE PRINT RUN 1
UNPRICED AUTO RED ZONE PRINT RUN 5
1 LaDainian Tomlinson 1.00 2.50
2 Frank Gore .75 2.00
3 Shaun Alexander .60 1.50
4 Brett Favre 2.00 5.00
5 Reggie Bush .60 1.50
6 Jay Cutler .60 1.50
7 Larry Johnson .60 1.50
8 Maurice Jones-Drew .60 1.50
9 Carson Palmer .75 2.00
10 Vince Young .60 1.50
11 Matt Leinart .60 1.50
12 Tom Brady 3.00 8.00
13 Tony Romo 1.25 3.00
14 Willie Parker .75 2.00
15 Brian Urlacher 1.00 2.50
16 Roy Williams WR .60 1.50
17 Steven Jackson .60 1.50
18 Peyton Manning 2.50 6.00
19 Brian Westbrook .60 1.50
20 Steve Smith .75 2.00

2007 Select Hot Rookies

STATED PRINT RUN 749 SER.#'d SETS
*SCORECARD/100: .6X TO 1.5X BASIC INSERTS
SCORECARD PRINT RUN 100 SER.#'d SETS
*GOLD ZONE/50: 1X TO 2.5X BASIC INSERTS
GOLD ZONE PRINT RUN 50 SER.#'d SETS
*ART.PROOF/32: 1.2X TO 3X BASIC INSERTS
ARTIST'S PROOF PRINT RUN 32 SER.#'d SETS
*RED ZONE/25: 1.2X TO 3X BASIC INSERTS
RED ZONE PRINT RUN 25 SER.#'d SETS
UNPRICED END ZONE PRINT RUN 6
1 JaMarcus Russell .75 2.00
2 Brady Quinn .75 2.00
3 Adrian Peterson 2.50 6.00
4 Marshawn Lynch 1.50 4.00
5 Calvin Johnson 2.50 6.00
6 Ted Ginn Jr. 1.00 2.50
7 Dwayne Bowe .75 2.00
8 Robert Meachem 1.00 2.50
9 Dwayne Jarrett 1.00 2.50
10 Greg Olsen 1.25 3.00
11 Kevin Kolb 1.00 2.50
12 John Beck .75 2.00
13 Drew Stanton .75 2.00
14 Kenny Irons .75 2.00
15 Chris Henry .75 2.00
16 Brandon Jackson .75 2.00
17 Craig Buster Davis .75 2.00
18 Anthony Gonzalez .75 2.00
19 Sidney Rice 1.00 2.50
20 Steve Smith USC .75 2.00

2007 Select Hot Rookies Autographs Gold Zone

GOLD ZONE PRINT RUN 20 SER.#'d SETS
UNPRICED RED ZONE PRINT RUN 10
UNPRICED END ZONE PRINT RUN 5
1 JaMarcus Russell 10.00 25.00
2 Brady Quinn 10.00 25.00
3 Adrian Peterson 150.00 300.00
4 Marshawn Lynch 20.00 50.00
5 Calvin Johnson 60.00 120.00
6 Ted Ginn Jr. 12.00 30.00
7 Dwayne Bowe 10.00 25.00
8 Robert Meachem 12.00 30.00
9 Dwayne Jarrett 12.00 30.00
10 Greg Olsen 15.00 40.00
11 Kevin Kolb 12.00 30.00
12 John Beck 10.00 25.00
13 Drew Stanton 10.00 25.00
14 Kenny Irons 10.00 25.00
15 Chris Henry 10.00 25.00
16 Brandon Jackson 10.00 25.00
18 Anthony Gonzalez 10.00 25.00
19 Sidney Rice 12.00 30.00
20 Steve Smith USC 10.00 25.00

2007 Select Hot Rookies Inscriptions

STATED PRINT RUN 40 SER.#'d SETS
1 JaMarcus Russell 8.00 20.00
2 Brady Quinn 8.00 20.00
3 Adrian Peterson 125.00 250.00
4 Marshawn Lynch 15.00 40.00
5 Calvin Johnson 60.00 120.00
6 Ted Ginn Jr. 10.00 25.00
7 Dwayne Bowe 8.00 20.00
8 Robert Meachem 10.00 25.00
9 Dwayne Jarrett 10.00 25.00
10 Greg Olsen 12.00 30.00
11 Kevin Kolb 10.00 25.00
12 John Beck 8.00 20.00
13 Drew Stanton 8.00 20.00
14 Kenny Irons 8.00 20.00
15 Chris Henry 8.00 20.00
16 Brandon Jackson 8.00 20.00
18 Anthony Gonzalez 8.00 20.00
19 Sidney Rice 10.00 25.00
20 Steve Smith USC 8.00 20.00

2007 Select Inscriptions

STATED PRINT RUN 20-100
7 Patrick Crayton/20 8.00 20.00
38 Bernard Berrian/20 8.00 20.00
48 Mike Furrey/20 10.00 25.00
78 Jerious Norwood/20 8.00 20.00
90 Marques Colston/20 8.00 20.00
94 Devery Henderson/20 8.00 20.00
179 Demetrius Williams/20 8.00 20.00
217 DeMeco Ryans/20 10.00 25.00
255 Mike Bell/20 10.00 25.00
256 Brandon Marshall/20 10.00 25.00
281 Vincent Jackson/20 8.00 20.00
286 Michael Turner/20 8.00 20.00
289 Michael Okwo/100 6.00 15.00
290 Gary Russell/100 6.00 15.00
291 Josh Wilson/50 10.00 25.00
292 Thomas Clayton/50 10.00 25.00
293 Jerard Rabb/100 6.00 15.00
295 LaMarr Woodley/50 15.00 40.00
297 Dan Bazuin/100 6.00 15.00
298 A.J. Davis/50 8.00 20.00
299 Buster Davis/100 6.00 15.00
300 Stewart Bradley/100 5.00 12.00
301 Toby Korrodi/50 10.00 25.00
302 Marcus McCauley/50 8.00 20.00
306 Tim Crowder/50 10.00 25.00
307 D'Juan Woods/100 5.00 12.00
308 Tim Shaw/50 10.00 25.00
309 Fred Bennett/100 5.00 12.00
310 Victor Abiamiri/50 8.00 20.00
312 Danny Ware/100 8.00 20.00
313 Quentin Moses/50 8.00 20.00
314 Ryan McBean/100 8.00 20.00
315 David Harris/50 8.00 20.00
316 David Irons/100 5.00 12.00
317 Syndric Steptoe/100 6.00 15.00
318 Eric Frampton/100 6.00 15.00
319 Jemalle Cornelius/100 6.00 15.00
320 Earl Everett/50 8.00 20.00
321 Alonzo Coleman/50 10.00 25.00
322 Josh Gattis/50 8.00 20.00
323 Zak DeOssie/100 6.00 15.00
324 Jon Beason/40 8.00 20.00
326 Aaron Rouse/50 8.00 20.00
327 Reggie Ball/100 6.00 15.00
328 Rufus Alexander/100 5.00 12.00
329 Daymeion Hughes/100 5.00 12.00
331 JaMarcus Russell/40 8.00 20.00
332 Paul Williams/40 8.00 20.00
333 Kenny Irons/40 8.00 20.00
334 Chris Davis/50 8.00 20.00
335 Darius Walker/50 8.00 20.00
336 Dwayne Bowe/40 8.00 20.00
337 Isaiah Stanback/50 8.00 20.00
338 Leon Hall/40 8.00 20.00
339 Sidney Rice/40 10.00 25.00
340 Amobi Okoye/40 10.00 25.00
341 Adrian Peterson/40 125.00 250.00
342 LaRon Landry/50 12.00 30.00
343 Lorenzo Booker/40 10.00 25.00
345 Mike Walker/50 12.00 30.00
346 Zach Miller/40 8.00 20.00
347 Levi Brown/100 5.00 12.00
348 Brian Leonard/40 8.00 20.00
349 Aundrae Allison/50 8.00 20.00
350 Brandon Siler/100 5.00 12.00
351 Calvin Johnson/40 40.00 100.00
352 Gaines Adams/40 10.00 25.00
353 Anthony Gonzalez/40 8.00 20.00
354 John Beck/40 8.00 20.00
355 Joe Thomas/50 12.00 30.00
356 Michael Bush/40 8.00 20.00
357 Courtney Taylor/50 8.00 20.00
358 Lawrence Timmons/40 12.00 30.00
359 Drew Stanton/40 8.00 20.00
360 Chansi Stuckey/50 10.00 25.00
361 Greg Olsen/40 12.00 30.00
362 Rhema McKnight/100 5.00 12.00
363 Antonio Pittman/40 8.00 20.00
364 Kevin Kolb/40 10.00 25.00
366 Robert Meachem/40 10.00 25.00
367 Troy Smith/40 8.00 20.00
368 Jamaal Anderson/50 10.00 25.00
369 Tony Hunt/40 8.00 20.00
370 David Clowney/50 8.00 20.00
371 Brady Quinn/40 8.00 20.00
372 Michael Griffin/50 8.00 20.00
373 Jared Zabransky/50 8.00 20.00
374 Jason Hill/40 8.00 20.00
375 Trent Edwards/40 8.00 20.00
376 Dwayne Jarrett/40 10.00 25.00
377 DeShawn Wynn/40 8.00 20.00
378 Patrick Willis/40 12.00 30.00
379 Steve Smith USC/40 8.00 20.00
380 David Ball/50 8.00 20.00
381 Marshawn Lynch/40 15.00 40.00
382 Paul Posluszny/40 8.00 20.00
383 Johnnie Lee Higgins/40 8.00 20.00
384 Kolby Smith/50 8.00 20.00
385 Ted Ginn Jr./40 10.00 25.00
386 Adam Carriker/50 8.00 20.00
387 Tyler Palko/50 12.00 30.00
388 Joel Filani/50 8.00 20.00
389 Garrett Wolfe/40 8.00 20.00
390 Ryne Robinson/50 10.00 25.00
391 Reggie Nelson/50 8.00 20.00
392 Dallas Baker/50 8.00 20.00
393 Dwayne Wright/100 5.00 12.00
394 Scott Chandler/50 12.00 30.00
395 Jordan Kent/50 10.00 25.00
397 Jonathan Wade/100 5.00 12.00
399 Jason Snelling/50 8.00 20.00
400 Jeff Rowe/50 8.00 20.00
401 Aaron Ross/50 8.00 20.00
402 Jarrett Hicks/100 6.00 15.00
403 Chris Henry/40 8.00 20.00
404 James Jones/50 8.00 20.00
405 Matt Spaeth/50 12.00 30.00
406 Brandon Meriweather/50 10.00 25.00
407 Nate Ilaoa/100 6.00 15.00
408 Brandon Myles/100 6.00 15.00
409 Ray McDonald/50 10.00 25.00
410 Chris Leak/40 8.00 20.00
411 Darrelle Revis/50 10.00 25.00
412 Ahmad Bradshaw/100 8.00 20.00
416 Anthony Spencer/50 10.00 25.00
418 Kenneth Darby/100 5.00 12.00
419 Steve Breaston/50 8.00 20.00
420 Ben Patrick/50 10.00 25.00
421 Chris Houston/50 8.00 20.00
422 Jordan Palmer/40 10.00 25.00
423 Laurent Robinson/50 12.00 30.00
424 Selvin Young/50 8.00 20.00
426 Sabby Piscitelli/100 5.00 12.00
427 Yamon Figurs/40 8.00 20.00
428 Brandon Jackson/40 8.00 20.00
429 Jacoby Jones/50 8.00 20.00
430 H.B. Blades/100 5.00 12.00

2007 Select National Convention

COMPLETE SET (12) 10.00 25.00
1 Brett Favre 1.25 3.00
2 Reggie Bush .40 1.00
3 Peyton Manning 1.50 4.00
4 Vince Young .40 1.00
5 LaDainian Tomlinson .60 1.50
6 JaMarcus Russell .50 1.25
7 Adrian Peterson 1.50 4.00
8 Calvin Johnson 1.50 4.00
9 Brady Quinn .50 1.25
10 Ted Ginn Jr. .60 1.50
11 Marshawn Lynch 1.00 2.50
12 Troy Smith .50 1.25

2008 Select

This set was released on August 27, 2008. The base set consists of 440 cards. Cards 1-330 feature veterans, and cards 331-440 are rookies serial numbered of 999.

COMP.SET w/o RC's (330) 25.00 50.00
ROOKIE PRINT RUN 999 SER.#'d SETS
UNPRICED END ZONE PRINT RUN 6
1 Matt Leinart .20 .50
2 Kurt Warner .25 .60
3 Larry Fitzgerald .25 .60
4 Anquan Boldin .20 .50
5 Edgerrin James .25 .60
6 Neil Rackers .20 .50
7 Steve Breaston .20 .50
8 Antrel Rolle .20 .50
9 Karlos Dansby .20 .50
10 Joey Harrington .20 .50
11 Jerious Norwood .20 .50
12 Roddy White .20 .50
13 Michael Jenkins .20 .50
14 Joe Horn .20 .50
15 Keith Brooking .20 .50
16 Lawyer Milloy .20 .50
17 John Abraham .20 .50
18 Michael Turner .20 .50
19 Troy Smith .25 .60
20 Willis McGahee .20 .50
21 Musa Smith .20 .50
22 Derrick Mason .20 .50
23 Mark Clayton .20 .50
24 Bart Scott .20 .50
25 Demetrius Williams .20 .50
26 Yamon Figurs .20 .50
27 Ray Lewis .30 .75
28 Terrell Suggs .20 .50
29 Ed Reed .25 .60
30 Trent Edwards .20 .50
31 Marshawn Lynch .25 .60
32 Lee Evans .25 .60
33 Roscoe Parrish .20 .50
34 Paul Posluszny .20 .50
35 John DiGiorgio RC .25 .60
36 Angelo Crowell .20 .50
37 Jabari Greer RC .20 .50
38 Chris Kelsay .20 .50
39 Fred Jackson RC .60 1.50
40 Matt Moore .20 .50
41 Steve Smith .25 .60
42 DeAngelo Williams .20 .50
43 Brad Hoover .20 .50

44 Dante Rosario .20 .50
45 Julius Peppers .25 .60
46 Jon Beason .20 .50
47 Chris Harris .20 .50
48 D.J. Hackett .20 .50
49 Jake Delhomme .20 .50
50 Adrian Peterson .20 .50
51 Mark Anderson .20 .50
52 Desmond Clark .20 .50
53 Greg Olsen .25 .60
54 Devin Hester .25 .60
55 Brian Urlacher .30 .75
56 Jason McKie RC .25 .60
57 Lance Briggs .25 .60
58 Rex Grossman .20 .50
59 Carson Palmer .25 .60
60 Chad Johnson .20 .50
61 T.J. Houshmandzadeh .20 .50
62 Rudi Johnson .20 .50
63 Kenny Watson .20 .50
64 Dhani Jones .20 .50
65 Leon Hall .20 .50
66 Johnathan Joseph .20 .50
67 Derek Anderson .20 .50
68 Brady Quinn .20 .50
69 Jamal Lewis .25 .60
70 Josh Cribbs .20 .50
71 Kellen Winslow .20 .50
72 Braylon Edwards .20 .50
73 Joe Jurevicius .20 .50
74 D'Qwell Jackson .20 .50
75 Leigh Bodden .20 .50
76 Sean Jones .20 .50
77 Tony Romo .25 .60
78 Terrell Owens .25 .60
79 Marion Barber .20 .50
80 Jason Witten .25 .60
81 Patrick Crayton .25 .60
82 Anthony Henry .20 .50
83 DeMarcus Ware .25 .60
84 Terence Newman .20 .50
85 Greg Ellis .20 .50
86 Zach Thomas .25 .60
87 Keary Colbert .20 .50
88 Jay Cutler .20 .50
89 Tony Scheffler .20 .50
90 Selvin Young .20 .50
91 Brandon Marshall .25 .60
92 Brandon Stokley .20 .50
93 Champ Bailey .25 .60
94 John Lynch .25 .60
95 Dre Bly .20 .50
96 Elvis Dumervil .20 .50
97 Jon Kitna .20 .50
98 Tatum Bell .20 .50
99 Shaun McDonald .20 .50
100 Roy Williams WR .20 .50
101 Calvin Johnson .30 .75
102 Mike Furrey .25 .60
103 Ernie Sims .20 .50
104 Aveion Cason .20 .50
105 Aaron Rodgers .60 1.50
106 Brett Favre .60 1.50
107 Ryan Grant .25 .60
108 Greg Jennings .20 .50
109 Donald Driver .25 .60
110 Donald Lee .25 .60
111 James Jones .20 .50
112 Al Harris .20 .50
113 Nick Barnett .20 .50
114 Charles Woodson .30 .75
115 Aaron Kampman .25 .60
116 Mason Crosby .20 .50
117 Matt Schaub .20 .50
118 Ahman Green .25 .60
119 Andre Johnson .25 .60
120 Kevin Walter .25 .60
121 Owen Daniels .20 .50
122 Andre Davis .20 .50
123 DeMeco Ryans .25 .60
124 Mario Williams .25 .60
125 Dunta Robinson .20 .50
126 Chris Brown .20 .50
127 Peyton Manning .75 2.00
128 Joseph Addai .20 .50
129 Marvin Harrison .25 .60
130 Reggie Wayne .25 .60
131 Dallas Clark .20 .50
132 Anthony Gonzalez .20 .50
133 Kenton Keith .20 .50
134 Adam Vinatieri .20 .50
135 Bob Sanders .25 .60
136 Kolvin Haydon .20 .50
137 Freddie Keiaho .20 .50
138 David Garrard .20 .50
139 Fred Taylor .20 .50
140 Maurice Jones-Drew .20 .50
141 Greg Jones .20 .50
142 Dennis Northcutt .20 .50
143 Reggie Williams .25 .60
144 Marcedes Lewis .20 .50
145 Matt Jones .25 .60
146 Reggie Nelson .20 .50
147 Cleo Lemon .20 .50
148 Jerry Porter .20 .50
149 Damon Huard .20 .50
150 Brodie Croyle .25 .60
151 Larry Johnson .20 .50
152 Kolby Smith .20 .50
153 Tony Gonzalez .25 .60
154 Dwayne Bowe .25 .60
155 Donnie Edwards .20 .50
156 Jared Allen .20 .50
157 Patrick Surtain .20 .50
158 Derrick Johnson .20 .50
159 Ernest Wilford .20 .50
160 John Beck .20 .50
161 Ronnie Brown .20 .50
162 Greg Camarillo RC .60 1.50
163 Ted Ginn Jr. .20 .50
164 Derek Hagan .20 .50
165 Channing Crowder .20 .50
166 Joey Porter .20 .50
167 Jason Taylor .25 .60
168 Josh McCown .20 .50
169 Bernard Berrian .20 .50
170 Maurice Hicks .20 .50
171 Tarvaris Jackson .20 .50
172 Adrian Peterson .30 .75
173 Chester Taylor .20 .50
174 Bobby Wade .20 .50
175 Sidney Rice .20 .50
176 Robert Ferguson .20 .50
177 Darren Sharper .20 .50
178 Visanthe Shiancoe .30 .75
179 E.J. Henderson .20 .50
180 Cedric Griffin .20 .50
181 Chad Greenway .20 .50
182 Tom Brady 1.00 2.50
183 Randy Moss .25 .60
184 Laurence Maroney .25 .60
185 Wes Welker .25 .60
186 Sammy Morris .20 .50
187 Kevin Faulk .20 .50
188 Ben Watson .20 .50
189 Tedy Bruschi .25 .60
190 Rodney Harrison .20 .50
191 Mike Vrabel .20 .50
192 Drew Brees .30 .75
193 Reggie Bush .20 .50
194 Deuce McAllister .25 .60
195 Marques Colston .20 .50
196 David Patten .20 .50
197 Devery Henderson .20 .50
198 Scott Fujita .20 .50
199 Roman Harper .20 .50
200 Mike McKenzie .20 .50
201 Will Smith .20 .50
202 Billy Miller .20 .50
203 Sammy Knight .20 .50
204 Eli Manning .25 .60
205 Plaxico Burress .20 .50
206 Brandon Jacobs .20 .50
207 Ahmad Bradshaw .20 .50
208 David Tyree .20 .50
209 Amani Toomer .20 .50
210 Jeremy Shockey .20 .50
211 Steve Smith USC .25 .60
212 Aaron Ross .20 .50
213 Antonio Pierce .20 .50
214 Michael Strahan .25 .60
215 Jesse Chatman .20 .50
216 Calvin Pace .20 .50
217 Kellen Clemens .20 .50
218 Leon Washington .20 .50
219 Jerricho Cotchery .20 .50
220 Laveranues Coles .20 .50
221 Chris Baker .20 .50
222 Brad Smith .20 .50
223 Thomas Jones .20 .50
224 Darrelle Revis .20 .50
225 David Harris .20 .50
226 DeAngelo Hall .20 .50
227 Drew Carter .20 .50
228 Javon Walker .25 .60
229 JaMarcus Russell .20 .50
230 Justin Fargas .20 .50
231 Michael Bush .20 .50
232 Ronald Curry .20 .50
233 Zach Miller .20 .50
234 Thomas Howard .20 .50
235 Johnnie Lee Higgins .20 .50
236 Kirk Morrison .20 .50
237 Michael Huff .20 .50
238 Asante Samuel .20 .50
239 Donovan McNabb .25 .60
240 Brian Westbrook .20 .50
241 Correll Buckhalter .20 .50
242 Kevin Curtis .20 .50
243 Reggie Brown .20 .50
244 L.J. Smith .20 .50
245 Greg Lewis .20 .50
246 Lito Sheppard .20 .50
247 Omar Gaither .20 .50
248 Ben Roethlisberger .30 .75
249 Willie Parker .25 .60
250 Najeh Davenport .20 .50
251 Hines Ward .25 .60
252 Santonio Holmes .20 .50
253 Heath Miller .20 .50
254 Cedrick Wilson .20 .50
255 James Harrison RC 1.25 3.00
256 Ike Taylor .20 .50
257 James Farrior .20 .50
258 Troy Polamalu .30 .75
259 Philip Rivers .30 .75
260 LaDainian Tomlinson .30 .75
261 Darren Sproles .20 .50
262 Vincent Jackson .20 .50
263 Chris Chambers .20 .50
264 Antonio Gates .25 .60
265 Craig Buster Davis .20 .50
266 Malcom Floyd .20 .50
267 Antonio Cromartie .20 .50
268 Shawne Merriman .20 .50
269 DeShaun Foster .20 .50
270 Alex Smith QB .25 .60
271 Frank Gore .25 .60
272 Michael Robinson .20 .50
273 Vernon Davis .20 .50
274 Arnaz Battle .20 .50
275 Isaac Bruce .30 .75
276 Patrick Willis .25 .60
277 Nate Clements .20 .50
278 Jason Hill .20 .50
279 T.J. Duckett .20 .50
280 Matt Hasselbeck .20 .50
281 Julian Peterson .20 .50
282 Maurice Morris .20 .50
283 Bobby Engram .20 .50
284 Nate Burleson .20 .50
285 Deion Branch .20 .50
286 Lofa Tatupu .20 .50
287 Marcus Trufant .20 .50
288 Darryl Tapp .20 .50
289 Julius Jones .20 .50
290 Marc Bulger .20 .50
291 Stovon Jackson .20 .50
292 Brian Leonard .20 .50
293 Torry Holt .25 .60
294 Dante Hall .20 .50
295 Randy McMichael .20 .50
296 Drew Bennett .20 .50
297 Will Witherspoon .20 .50
298 Tye Hill .20 .50
299 Corey Chavous .20 .50
300 Warrick Dunn .20 .50
301 Brian Griese .20 .50
302 Jeff Garcia .20 .50
303 Cadillac Williams .25 .60
304 Earnest Graham .20 .50
305 Joey Galloway .25 .60
306 Ike Hilliard .20 .50
307 Michael Clayton .20 .50
308 Derrick Brooks .20 .50
309 Phillip Buchanon .20 .50
310 Alex Smith TE .30 .75
311 Ronde Barber .20 .50
312 Justin McCareins .20 .50
313 Jevon Kearse .20 .50
314 Vince Young .20 .50
315 LenDale White .20 .50
316 Justin Gage .20 .50
317 Roydell Williams .20 .50
318 Alge Crumpler .20 .50
319 Brandon Jones .20 .50
320 Michael Griffin .20 .50
321 Keith Bulluck .20 .50
322 Jason Campbell .20 .50
323 Clinton Portis .20 .50
324 Ladell Betts .20 .50
325 Santana Moss .20 .50
326 Chris Cooley .20 .50
327 Antwaan Randle El .20 .50
328 London Fletcher .25 .60
329 Shawn Springs .20 .50
330 LaRon Landry .25 .60
331 Jake Long RC 1.50 4.00
332 Chris Long RC 1.25 3.00
333 Matt Ryan RC 3.00 8.00
334 Darren McFadden RC 1.00 2.50
335 Glenn Dorsey RC 1.00 2.50
336 Vernon Gholston RC 1.00 2.50
337 Sedrick Ellis RC 1.00 2.50
338 Derrick Harvey RC 1.00 2.50
339 Keith Rivers RC 1.00 2.50
340 Jerod Mayo RC 1.50 4.00
341 Leodis McKelvin RC 1.25 3.00
342 Jonathan Stewart RC 1.50 4.00
343 D.Rodgers-Cromartie RC 1.25 3.00
344 Joe Flacco RC 2.00 5.00
345 Aqib Talib RC 1.50 4.00
346 Felix Jones RC 1.00 2.50
347 Rashard Mendenhall RC 1.00 2.50
348 Chris Johnson RC 1.25 3.00
349 Mike Jenkins RC 1.00 2.50
350 Antoine Cason RC 1.25 3.00
351 Lawrence Jackson RC 1.00 2.50
352 Kontwan Balmor RC 1.00 2.50
353 Dustin Keller RC 1.25 3.00
354 Kenny Phillips RC 1.00 2.50
355 Phillip Merling RC 1.00 2.50
356 Donnie Avery RC 1.25 3.00
357 Devin Thomas RC 1.00 2.50
358 Brandon Flowers RC 1.25 3.00
359 Jordy Nelson RC 3.00 8.00
360 Curtis Lofton RC 1.25 3.00
361 John Carlson RC 1.00 2.50
362 Tracy Porter RC 1.25 3.00
363 James Hardy RC 1.00 2.50
364 Eddie Royal RC 1.00 2.50
365 Matt Forte RC 1.50 4.00
366 Jordon Dizon RC 1.00 2.50
367 Jerome Simpson RC 1.25 3.00
368 Fred Davis RC 1.00 2.50
369 DeSean Jackson RC 2.00 5.00
370 Calais Campbell RC 1.25 3.00
371 Malcolm Kelly RC 1.00 2.50
372 Quentin Groves RC 1.25 3.00
373 Limas Sweed RC 1.00 2.50
374 Ray Rice RC 1.00 2.50
375 Brian Brohm RC 1.00 2.50
376 Chad Henne RC 1.25 3.00
377 Dexter Jackson RC 1.50 4.00
378 Martellus Bennett RC 1.25 3.00
379 Terrell Thomas RC 1.00 2.50
380 Kevin Smith RC 1.00 2.50
381 Anthony Alridge RC 1.00 2.50
382 Jacob Hester RC 1.00 2.50
383 Earl Bennett RC 1.50 4.00
384 Jamaal Charles RC 1.50 4.00
385 Dan Connor RC 1.00 2.50
386 Reggie Smith RC 1.00 2.50
387 Brad Cottam RC 1.00 2.50
388 Pat Sims RC 1.25 3.00
389 Dantrell Savage RC 1.25 3.00
390 Early Doucet RC 1.00 2.50
391 Harry Douglas RC 1.25 3.00
392 Steve Slaton RC 1.00 2.50
393 Jermichael Finley RC 1.00 2.50
394 Kevin O'Connell RC 1.00 2.50
395 Mario Manningham RC 1.00 2.50
396 Andre Caldwell RC 1.00 2.50
397 Will Franklin RC 1.25 3.00
398 Marcus Smith RC 1.25 3.00
399 Martin Rucker RC 1.00 2.50
400 Xavier Adibi RC 1.00 2.50
401 Craig Steltz RC 1.00 2.50
402 Tashard Choice RC 1.00 2.50
403 Lavelle Hawkins RC 1.25 3.00
404 Jacob Tamme RC 1.25 3.00
405 Keenan Burton RC 1.00 2.50
406 John David Booty RC 1.00 2.50
407 Ryan Torain RC 1.25 3.00
408 Tim Hightower RC 1.25 3.00
409 Dennis Dixon RC 1.00 2.50
410 Kellen Davis RC 1.00 2.50
411 Josh Johnson RC 1.00 2.50
412 Erik Ainge RC 1.00 2.50
413 Owen Schmitt RC 1.00 2.50
414 Marcus Thomas RC 1.25 3.00
415 Thomas Brown RC 1.00 2.50
416 Josh Morgan RC 1.00 2.50
417 Kevin Robinson RC 1.00 2.50
418 Colt Brennan RC 1.25 3.00
419 Paul Hubbard RC 1.00 2.50
420 Andre Woodson RC 1.00 2.50
421 Mike Hart RC 1.00 2.50
422 Matt Flynn RC 1.00 2.50
423 Chauncey Washington RC 1.25 3.00
424 Caleb Campbell RC 1.50 4.00
425 Peyton Hillis RC 1.50 4.00
426 Justin Forsett RC 1.25 3.00
427 Adrian Arrington RC 1.00 2.50
428 Cory Boyd RC 1.00 2.50
429 Allen Patrick RC 1.00 2.50
430 Marcus Monk RC 1.25 3.00
431 DJ Hall RC 1.00 2.50
432 Darrell Strong RC 1.25 3.00
433 Jason Rivers RC 1.00 2.50
434 Jed Collins RC 1.25 3.00
435 Paul Smith RC 1.00 2.50
436 Darius Reynaud RC 1.00 2.50
437 Ali Highsmith RC 1.00 2.50
438 Davone Bess RC 1.25 3.00
439 Erin Henderson RC 1.25 3.00
440 Kalvin McRae RC 1.00 2.50

2008 Select Artist's Proof

*VETS 1-330: 6X TO 15X BASIC CARDS
*ROOKIES 331-440: .8X TO 2X BASIC CARDS
STATED PRINT RUN 32 SER.#'d SETS

2008 Select Gold Zone

*VETS 1-330: 5X TO 12X BASIC CARDS
*ROOKIES 331-440: .6X TO 1.5X BASIC CARDS
STATED PRINT RUN 50 SER.#'d SETS

2008 Select Red Zone

*VETS 1-330: 6X TO 15X BASIC CARDS
*ROOKIES 331-440: .8X TO 2X BASIC CARDS
STATED PRINT RUN 30 SER.#'d SETS

2008 Select Scorecard

*VETS 1-330: 4X TO 10X BASIC CARDS
*ROOKIES 331-440: .5X TO 1.2X BASIC CARDS
STATED PRINT RUN 100 SER.#'d SETS

2008 Select Autographs Gold Zone

GOLD ZONE PRINT RUN 40-50
*RED ZONE/25-30: .5X TO 1.2X GOLD/40-50
RED ZONE PRINT RUN 25-30
UNPRICED END ZONE PRINT RUN 6
331 Jake Long/40 8.00 20.00
332 Chris Long/40 6.00 15.00
333 Matt Ryan/50 40.00 80.00
334 Darren McFadden/50 5.00 12.00
335 Glenn Dorsey/50 EXCH 5.00 12.00
336 Vernon Gholston/40 5.00 12.00
337 Sedrick Ellis/40 5.00 12.00
338 Derrick Harvey/40 5.00 12.00
339 Keith Rivers/40 5.00 12.00
340 Jerod Mayo/40 8.00 20.00
341 Leodis McKelvin/50 6.00 15.00
342 Jonathan Stewart/50 8.00 20.00
343 Dominique Rodgers-Cromartie/40 6.00 15.00
344 Joe Flacco/50 10.00 25.00
345 Aqib Talib/50 8.00 20.00
346 Felix Jones/50 5.00 12.00
347 Rashard Mendenhall/50 5.00 12.00
348 Chris Johnson/40 6.00 15.00
349 Mike Jenkins/50 5.00 12.00
350 Antoine Cason/50 6.00 15.00
351 Lawrence Jackson/50 5.00 12.00
352 Kentwan Balmer/50 5.00 12.00
353 Dustin Keller/40 6.00 15.00
354 Kenny Phillips/40 5.00 12.00
355 Phillip Merling/50 5.00 12.00
356 Donnie Avery/40 6.00 15.00
357 Devin Thomas/40 5.00 12.00
358 Brandon Flowers/50 6.00 15.00
359 Jordy Nelson/40 20.00 40.00
360 Curtis Lofton/50 6.00 15.00
361 John Carlson/50 5.00 12.00
362 Tracy Porter/50 6.00 15.00
363 James Hardy/40 5.00 12.00
364 Eddie Royal/40 5.00 12.00
365 Matt Forte/50 20.00 50.00
366 Jordon Dizon/50 5.00 12.00
367 Jerome Simpson/40 6.00 15.00
368 Fred Davis/50 5.00 12.00
369 DeSean Jackson/40 20.00 40.00
370 Calais Campbell/50 6.00 15.00
371 Malcolm Kelly/40 5.00 12.00
372 Quentin Groves/50 6.00 15.00
373 Limas Sweed/40 5.00 12.00
374 Ray Rice/40 5.00 12.00
375 Brian Brohm/50 5.00 12.00
376 Chad Henne/50 6.00 15.00
377 Dexter Jackson/50 8.00 20.00
378 Martellus Bennett/50 6.00 15.00
379 Terrell Thomas/50 5.00 12.00
380 Kevin Smith/40 EXCH 5.00 12.00
381 Anthony Alridge/50 5.00 12.00
382 Jacob Hester/50 5.00 12.00
383 Earl Bennett/40 8.00 20.00
384 Jamaal Charles/40 8.00 20.00
385 Dan Connor/50 5.00 12.00
386 Reggie Smith/50 5.00 12.00
387 Brad Cottam/50 5.00 12.00
388 Pat Sims/50 6.00 15.00
389 Dantrell Savage/50 6.00 15.00
390 Early Doucet/40 EXCH 5.00 12.00
391 Harry Douglas/40 EXCH 6.00 15.00
392 Steve Slaton/40 5.00 12.00
393 Jermichael Finley/50 5.00 12.00
394 Kevin O'Connell/40 5.00 12.00
395 Mario Manningham/40 5.00 12.00
396 Andre Caldwell/40 5.00 12.00
397 Will Franklin/50 6.00 15.00
398 Marcus Smith/50 6.00 15.00
399 Martin Rucker/50 5.00 12.00
400 Xavier Adibi/50 5.00 12.00
401 Craig Steltz/50 5.00 12.00
402 Tashard Choice/50 5.00 12.00
403 Lavelle Hawkins/50 6.00 15.00
404 Jacob Tamme/50 6.00 15.00
405 Keenan Burton/50 5.00 12.00
406 John David Booty/40 5.00 12.00
407 Ryan Torain/50 6.00 15.00
408 Tim Hightower/50 6.00 15.00
409 Dennis Dixon/40 5.00 12.00
410 Kellen Davis/50 5.00 12.00
411 Josh Johnson/40 5.00 12.00
412 Erik Ainge/40 5.00 12.00
413 Owen Schmitt/50 5.00 12.00
414 Marcus Thomas/50 6.00 15.00
415 Thomas Brown/50 5.00 12.00
416 Josh Morgan/50 5.00 12.00
417 Kevin Robinson/50 5.00 12.00
418 Colt Brennan/40 6.00 15.00
419 Paul Hubbard/50 5.00 12.00
420 Andre Woodson/40 5.00 12.00
421 Mike Hart/40 5.00 12.00
422 Matt Flynn/40 5.00 12.00
423 Chauncey Washington/50 6.00 15.00
424 Caleb Campbell/50 8.00 20.00
425 Peyton Hillis/50 8.00 20.00
426 Justin Forsett/50 6.00 15.00
427 Adrian Arrington/50 5.00 12.00
428 Cory Boyd/50 5.00 12.00
429 Allen Patrick/50 5.00 12.00
430 Marcus Monk/50 6.00 15.00
431 DJ Hall/50 5.00 12.00
432 Darrell Strong/50 6.00 15.00
433 Jason Rivers/50 5.00 12.00
434 Jed Collins/50 6.00 15.00
435 Paul Smith/50 5.00 12.00
436 Darius Reynaud/50 5.00 12.00
437 Ali Highsmith/50 5.00 12.00
438 Davone Bess/50 6.00 15.00
439 Erin Henderson/50 6.00 15.00
440 Kalvin McRae/50 5.00 12.00

2008 Select Franchise

STATED PRINT RUN 999 SER.#'d SETS
*SCORECARD/100: .8X TO 2X BASIC INSERTS
SCORECARD PRINT RUN 100 SER.#'d SETS
*GOLD ZONE/50: 1.2X TO 3X BASIC INSERTS
GOLD ZONE PRINT RUN 50 SER.#'d SETS
*ARTIST PROOF/32: 1.5X TO 4X BASIC INSERTS
ARTIST'S PROOF PRINT RUN 32 SER.#'d SETS
*RED ZONE/30: 1.5X TO 4X BASIC INSERTS
RED ZONE PRINT RUN 30 SER.#'d SETS
UNPRICED END ZONE PRINT RUN 6
1 Tony Romo .50 1.25
2 Tom Brady 2.00 5.00
3 Joseph Addai .40 1.00
4 Randy Moss .50 1.25
5 Terrell Owens .50 1.25
6 Aaron Rodgers 1.25 3.00
7 T.J. Houshmandzadeh .40 1.00
8 Ben Roethlisberger .60 1.50
9 Larry Johnson .40 1.00
10 Drew Brees .60 1.50
11 Jay Cutler .40 1.00
12 Eli Manning .50 1.25
13 Clinton Portis .40 1.00
14 Brian Westbrook .40 1.00
15 Torry Holt .50 1.25
16 Reggie Wayne .50 1.25
17 David Garrard .40 1.00
18 Steve Smith .50 1.25
19 Willie Parker .50 1.25
20 Edgerrin James .50 1.25
21 Andre Johnson .50 1.25
22 LaDainian Tomlinson .60 1.50
23 Donald Driver .50 1.25
24 Fred Taylor .40 1.00
25 Peyton Manning 1.50 4.00

2008 Select Future Franchise

STATED PRINT RUN 999 SER.#'d SETS
*SCORECARD/100: .8X TO 2X BASIC INSERTS
SCORECARD PRINT RUN 100 SER.#'d SETS
*GOLD ZONE/50: 1.2X TO 3X BASIC INSERTS
GOLD ZONE PRINT RUN 50 SER.#'d SETS
*ARTIST PROOF/32: 1.5X TO 4X BASIC INSERTS
ARTIST'S PROOF PRINT RUN 32 SER.#'d SETS
*RED ZONE/30: 1.5X TO 4X BASIC INSERTS
RED ZONE PRINT RUN 30 SER.#'d SETS
UNPRICED END ZONE PRINT RUN 6
1 JaMarcus Russell .40 1.00
2 Brady Quinn .40 1.00
3 Brandon Jacobs .40 1.00
4 Adrian Peterson .60 1.50
5 Dallas Clark .40 1.00
6 Brandon Marshall .50 1.25
7 Santonio Holmes .40 1.00
8 Dwayne Bowe .50 1.25
9 Laurence Maroney .50 1.25
10 Marion Barber .40 1.00
11 Greg Jennings .40 1.00
12 Trent Edwards .40 1.00
13 Wes Welker .50 1.25
14 Michael Turner .40 1.00
15 Derek Anderson .40 1.00
16 Kevin Curtis .40 1.00
17 Reggie Bush .40 1.00
18 Chris Cooley .40 1.00
19 Maurice Jones-Drew .40 1.00
20 Braylon Edwards .40 1.00
21 Willis McGahee .40 1.00
22 Vince Young .40 1.00
23 Frank Gore .50 1.25
24 Roddy White .40 1.00
25 Marques Colston .40 1.00

2008 Select Hot Rookies

STATED PRINT RUN 999 SER.#'d SETS
*SCORECARD/100: .6X TO 1.5X BASIC INSERTS
SCORECARD PRINT RUN 100 SER.#'d SETS
*GOLD ZONE/50: .8X TO 2X BASIC INSERTS
GOLD ZONE PRINT RUN 50 SER.#'d SETS
*ARTIST PROOF/32: 1X TO 2.5X BASIC INSERTS
ARTIST'S PROOF PRINT RUN 32 SER.#'d SETS
*RED ZONE/30: 1X TO 2.5X BASIC INSERTS
RED ZONE PRINT RUN 30 SER.#'d SETS
UNPRICED END ZONE PRINT RUN 6
1 Brian Brohm .40 1.00
2 Chad Henne .50 1.25
3 Chris Johnson .50 1.25
4 Darren McFadden .40 1.00
5 DeSean Jackson .75 2.00
6 Devin Thomas .40 1.00
7 Dexter Jackson .60 1.50
8 Donnie Avery .50 1.25
9 Eddie Royal .40 1.00
10 Felix Jones .40 1.00
11 Jamaal Charles .60 1.50
12 James Hardy .40 1.00
13 Jerome Simpson .50 1.25
14 Joe Flacco .75 2.00
15 Jonathan Stewart .60 1.50
16 Jordy Nelson 1.25 3.00
17 Kevin Smith .40 1.00
18 Limas Sweed .40 1.00
19 Malcolm Kelly .40 1.00
20 Mario Manningham .40 1.00
21 Matt Forte .60 1.50
22 Matt Ryan 1.25 3.00
23 Rashard Mendenhall .40 1.00
24 Ray Rice .40 1.00
25 Steve Slaton .40 1.00

2008 Select Hot Rookies Autographs Gold Zone

GOLD ZONE PRINT RUN 40 SER.#'d SETS
*RED ZONE/25: .5X TO 1.2X GOLD/40
RED ZONE PRINT RUN 25 SER.#'d SETS
UNPRICED END ZONE PRINT RUN 6
1 Brian Brohm 5.00 12.00
2 Chad Henne 6.00 15.00
3 Chris Johnson 6.00 15.00
4 Darren McFadden 5.00 12.00
5 DeSean Jackson 20.00 50.00
6 Devin Thomas 5.00 12.00
7 Dexter Jackson 8.00 20.00
8 Donnie Avery 6.00 15.00
9 Eddie Royal 5.00 12.00
10 Felix Jones 5.00 12.00
11 Jamaal Charles 8.00 20.00
12 James Hardy 5.00 12.00
13 Jerome Simpson 6.00 15.00
14 Joe Flacco 10.00 25.00
15 Jonathan Stewart 8.00 20.00
16 Jordy Nelson 20.00 40.00
17 Kevin Smith 5.00 12.00
18 Limas Sweed 5.00 12.00
19 Malcolm Kelly 5.00 12.00
20 Mario Manningham 5.00 12.00
21 Matt Forte 15.00 40.00
22 Matt Ryan 40.00 100.00
23 Rashard Mendenhall 5.00 12.00
24 Ray Rice 5.00 12.00
25 Steve Slaton 5.00 12.00

2008 Select Inscriptions

STATED PRINT RUN 25-750
331 Jake Long/375 4.00 10.00
332 Chris Long/50 5.00 12.00
333 Matt Ryan/25 60.00 120.00
334 Darren McFadden/25 6.00 15.00
335 Glenn Dorsey/500 No AU 1.25 3.00
336 Vernon Gholston/50 4.00 10.00
337 Sedrick Ellis/375 2.50 6.00
338 Derrick Harvey/450 2.50 6.00
339 Keith Rivers/50 4.00 10.00
340 Jerod Mayo/375 4.00 10.00
341 Leodis McKelvin/500 3.00 8.00
342 Jonathan Stewart/25 10.00 25.00
343 Dominique Rodgers-Cromartie/375 3.00 8.00
344 Joe Flacco/25 12.00 30.00
345 Aqib Talib/500 4.00 10.00
346 Felix Jones/25 6.00 15.00
347 Rashard Mendenhall/25 6.00 15.00
348 Chris Johnson/50 5.00 12.00
349 Mike Jenkins/375 2.50 6.00
350 Antoine Cason/500 3.00 8.00
351 Lawrence Jackson/500 2.50 6.00
352 Kentwan Balmer/500 2.50 6.00
353 Dustin Keller/50 5.00 12.00
354 Kenny Phillips/375 2.50 6.00
355 Phillip Merling/500 2.50 6.00
356 Donnie Avery/25 8.00 20.00
357 Devin Thomas/50 4.00 10.00
358 Brandon Flowers/500 3.00 8.00
359 Jordy Nelson/25 30.00 60.00
360 Curtis Lofton/750 3.00 8.00
361 John Carlson/375 2.50 6.00
362 Tracy Porter/750 5.00 12.00
363 James Hardy/25 6.00 15.00
364 Eddie Royal/25 6.00 15.00
365 Matt Forte/100 20.00 50.00
366 Jordon Dizon/750 2.50 6.00
367 Jerome Simpson/50 5.00 12.00
368 Frod Davis/375 2.50 6.00
369 DeSean Jackson/25 30.00 60.00
370 Calais Campbell/750 3.00 8.00
371 Malcolm Kelly/25 6.00 15.00
372 Quentin Groves/750 3.00 8.00
373 Limas Sweed/25 6.00 15.00
374 Ray Rice/50 4.00 10.00
375 Brian Brohm/25 6.00 15.00
376 Chad Henne/25 8.00 20.00
377 Dexter Jackson/50 6.00 15.00
378 Martellus Bennett/375 3.00 8.00
379 Terrell Thomas/500 2.50 6.00
380 Kevin Smith/50 4.00 10.00
381 Anthony Alridge/750 2.50 6.00
382 Jacob Hester/500 2.50 6.00
383 Earl Bennett/50 6.00 15.00
384 Jamaal Charles/50 6.00 15.00
385 Dan Connor/50 4.00 10.00
386 Reggie Smith/500 2.50 6.00
387 Brad Cottam/750 2.50 6.00
388 Pat Sims/500 3.00 8.00
389 Dantrell Savage/750 3.00 8.00
390 Early Doucet/50 EXCH 4.00 10.00
391 Harry Douglas/50 EXCH 5.00 12.00
392 Steve Slaton/50 4.00 10.00
393 Jermichael Finley/375 2.50 6.00
394 Kevin O'Connell/50 4.00 10.00
395 Mario Manningham/50 4.00 10.00
396 Andre Caldwell/50 4.00 10.00
397 Will Franklin/750 3.00 8.00
398 Marcus Smith/750 3.00 8.00
399 Martin Rucker/750 2.50 6.00
400 Xavier Adibi/375 2.50 6.00
401 Craig Steltz/76 4.00 10.00
402 Tashard Choice/100 4.00 10.00
403 Lavelle Hawkins/500 3.00 8.00
404 Jacob Tamme/500 3.00 8.00
405 Keenan Burton/500 2.50 6.00
406 John David Booty/50 4.00 10.00
407 Ryan Torain/500 3.00 8.00
408 Tim Hightower/750 6.00 15.00
409 Dennis Dixon/25 30.00 60.00
410 Kellen Davis/750 2.50 6.00
411 Josh Johnson/50 4.00 10.00
412 Erik Ainge/50 4.00 10.00
413 Owen Schmitt/750 2.50 6.00
414 Marcus Thomas/500 3.00 8.00
415 Thomas Brown/375 2.50 6.00
416 Josh Morgan/750 2.50 6.00
417 Kevin Robinson/750 2.50 6.00
418 Colt Brennan/25 8.00 20.00
419 Paul Hubbard/750 2.50 6.00
420 Andre Woodson/25 6.00 15.00
421 Mike Hart/50 4.00 10.00
422 Matt Flynn/50 4.00 10.00
423 Chauncey Washington/750 3.00 8.00
424 Caleb Campbell/750 4.00 10.00
425 Peyton Hillis/750 4.00 10.00
426 Justin Forsett/750 3.00 8.00
427 Adrian Arrington/750 2.50 6.00
428 Cory Boyd/750 2.50 6.00
429 Allen Patrick/500 2.50 6.00
430 Marcus Monk/656 3.00 8.00
431 DJ Hall/520 2.50 6.00
432 Darrell Strong/750 3.00 8.00
433 Jason Rivers/750 2.50 6.00
434 Jed Collins/604 3.00 8.00
435 Paul Smith/750 2.50 6.00
436 Darius Reynaud/375 2.50 6.00
437 Ali Highsmith/750 2.50 6.00
438 Davone Bess/750 3.00 8.00
439 Erin Henderson/750 3.00 8.00
440 Kalvin McRae/535 2.50 6.00

2008 Select Young Stars

STATED PRINT RUN 999 SER.#'d SETS
*SCORECARD/100: .8X TO 2X BASIC INSERTS
SCORECARD PRINT RUN 100 SER.#'d SETS
*GOLD ZONE/50: 1.2X TO 3X BASIC INSERTS
GOLD ZONE PRINT RUN 50 SER.#'d SETS
*ARTIST PROOF/32: 1.5X TO 4X BASIC INSERTS
ARTIST'S PROOF PRINT RUN 32 SER.#'d SETS
*RED ZONE/30: 1.5X TO 4X BASIC INSERTS
RED ZONE PRINT RUN 30 SER.#'d SETS
END ZONE PRINT RUN 6 SER.#'d SETS
1 Earnest Graham .40 1.00
2 Anthony Gonzalez .40 1.00
3 Ted Ginn Jr. .40 1.00
4 Marshawn Lynch .50 1.25
5 Calvin Johnson .60 1.50
6 Steve Smith USC .50 1.25
7 Kenny Watson .40 1.00
8 Vernon Davis .40 1.00
9 LenDale White .40 1.00
10 Vincent Jackson .40 1.00
11 Kolby Smith .40 1.00
12 Selvin Young .40 1.00
13 Patrick Willis .50 1.25
14 Lee Evans .50 1.25
15 Ahmad Bradshaw .40 1.00
16 Justin Fargas .40 1.00
17 Tarvaris Jackson .40 1.00
18 DeMeco Ryans .50 1.25
19 Fred Jackson 1.25 3.00
20 Patrick Crayton .50 1.25
21 James Jones .40 1.00
22 Michael Bush .40 1.00
23 Sidney Rice .40 1.00
24 LaRon Landry .50 1.25
25 Zach Miller .40 1.00

2013 Select

COMP.SET w/o SP's (100) 12.00 30.00
101-150 RETIRED: TWO PER BOX
151-250 ROOKIES: FOUR PER BOX
1 Tom Brady 1.00 2.50
2 Danny Amendola .30 .75
3 Rob Gronkowski .40 1.00
4 Ryan Tannehill .30 .75
5 Mike Wallace .25 .60
6 Lamar Miller .25 .60
7 Mark Sanchez .25 .60
8 Santonio Holmes .25 .60
9 Chris Ivory .30 .75
10 Fred Jackson .30 .75
11 Steve Johnson .30 .75
12 C.J. Spiller .25 .60
13 Joe Flacco .30 .75
14 Torrey Smith .25 .60
15 Jacoby Jones .25 .60
16 Ray Rice .25 .60
17 Andy Dalton .30 .75
18 A.J. Green .40 1.00
19 BenJarvus Green-Ellis .30 .75
20 Ben Roethlisberger .40 1.00
21 Antonio Brown .40 1.00
22 Troy Polamalu .40 1.00
23 Brandon Weeden .25 .60
24 Josh Gordon .25 .60
25 Trent Richardson .25 .60
26 Matt Schaub .25 .60
27 Andre Johnson .25 .60
28 Arian Foster .30 .75
29 Andrew Luck .60 1.50
30 Reggie Wayne .30 .75
31 Ahmad Bradshaw .25 .60
32 Jake Locker .30 .75
33 Kendall Wright .25 .60
34 Chris Johnson .25 .60
35 Blaine Gabbert .25 .60
36 Justin Blackmon .25 .60
37 Maurice Jones-Drew .25 .60
38 Peyton Manning .75 2.00
39 Wes Welker .30 .75
40 Demaryius Thomas .30 .75
41 Von Miller .30 .75
42 Philip Rivers .40 1.00
43 Danny Woodhead .30 .75
44 Antonio Gates .30 .75
45 Terrelle Pryor .30 .75
46 Denarius Moore .25 .60
47 Darren McFadden .30 .75
48 Alex Smith .30 .75
49 Dwayne Bowe .30 .75
50 Jamaal Charles .30 .75
51 Robert Griffin III .25 .60
52 Pierre Garcon .30 .75
53 Alfred Morris .25 .60
54 Eli Manning .30 .75
55 Victor Cruz .30 .75
56 Jason Pierre-Paul .25 .60
57 Tony Romo .30 .75
58 Dez Bryant .40 1.00
59 DeMarco Murray .30 .75
60 Jason Witten .30 .75
61 Michael Vick .30 .75
62 DeSean Jackson .30 .75
63 LeSean McCoy .40 1.00
64 Aaron Rodgers .60 1.50
65 Jordy Nelson .30 .75
66 Clay Matthews .40 1.00
67 Christian Ponder .25 .60
68 Greg Jennings .25 .60
69 Adrian Peterson .40 1.00
70 Jay Cutler .25 .60
71 Brandon Marshall .30 .75
72 Matt Forte .25 .60
73 Matthew Stafford .30 .75
74 Calvin Johnson .40 1.00
75 Reggie Bush .25 .60
76 Matt Ryan .30 .75
77 Julio Jones .40 1.00
78 Steven Jackson .25 .60
79 Cam Newton .40 1.00
80 Steve Smith .30 .75
81 Jonathan Stewart .25 .60
82 Drew Brees .40 1.00
83 Jimmy Graham .40 1.00
84 Mark Ingram .30 .75
85 Darrelle Revis .25 .60
86 Vincent Jackson .25 .60
87 Doug Martin .30 .75
88 Colin Kaepernick .30 .75
89 Anquan Boldin .25 .60
90 Frank Gore .30 .75
91 Patrick Willis .30 .75
92 Russell Wilson .75 2.00
93 Richard Sherman .40 1.00
94 Marshawn Lynch .30 .75
95 Sam Bradford .25 .60
96 Daryl Richardson .25 .60
97 Chris Givens .25 .60
98 Carson Palmer .30 .75
99 Larry Fitzgerald .30 .75
100 Rashard Mendenhall .25 .60
101 Andre Rison 1.00 2.50
102 Art Monk 1.25 3.00
103 Barry Sanders 2.00 5.00
104 Bart Starr 2.00 5.00
105 Bernie Kosar 1.00 2.50
106 Bill Romanowski .75 2.00
107 Bo Jackson 1.50 4.00
108 Bob Griese 1.25 3.00
109 Brett Favre 2.50 6.00
110 Charlie Joiner 1.00 2.50
111 Chuck Foreman .75 2.00
112 Cris Carter 1.25 3.00
113 D.D. Lewis .75 2.00
114 Dan Marino 2.50 6.00
115 Darrell Green 1.25 3.00
116 Daryle Lamonica .75 2.00
117 Deion Sanders 1.00 2.50
118 Don Maynard 1.00 2.50
119 Doug Flutie 1.00 2.50
120 Drew Bledsoe 1.00 2.50
121 Earl Campbell 1.25 3.00
122 Ed McCaffrey .75 2.00
123 Edgerrin James 1.00 2.50
124 Emmitt Smith 2.00 5.00
125 Franco Harris 1.25 3.00
126 Fred Taylor .75 2.00
127 Herman Moore .75 2.00
128 Jay Novacek 1.00 2.50
129 Jerome Bettis 1.25 3.00
130 Jerry Rice 2.00 5.00
131 Jim Kiick .75 2.00
132 Jim McMahon 1.00 2.50
133 Joe Montana 3.00 8.00
134 John Elway 2.00 5.00
135 John Taylor 1.00 2.50
136 Keith Jackson .75 2.00
137 Kurt Warner 1.00 2.50
138 LaDainian Tomlinson 1.00 2.50
139 Lenny Moore .75 2.00
140 Michael Irvin 1.25 3.00
141 Ozzie Newsome 1.00 2.50
142 Rod Woodson 1.00 2.50
143 Ron Jaworski 1.00 2.50
144 Shannon Sharpe 1.00 2.50
145 Steve Bartkowski 1.00 2.50
146 Steve Young 1.50 4.00
147 Terry Bradshaw 1.50 4.00
148 Tony Dorsett 1.25 3.00
149 Walter Payton 2.50 6.00
150 Warren Sapp 1.00 2.50
151 Aaron Dobson RC .50 1.25
152 Aaron Mellette RC .50 1.25
153 Ace Sanders RC .50 1.25
154 Alec Ogletree RC .50 1.25
155 Alex Okafor RC .50 1.25
156 Andre Ellington RC .50 1.25
157 Arthur Brown RC .50 1.25
158 Barkevious Mingo RC .50 1.25
159 Bjoern Werner RC .50 1.25
160 Blidi Wreh-Wilson RC .60 1.50
161 Brad Sorensen RC .50 1.25
162 Chance Warmack RC .50 1.25
163 Chris Gragg RC .50 1.25
164 Chris Harper RC .50 1.25
165 Chris Thompson RC .50 1.25
166 Christine Michael RC .50 1.25
167 Conner Vernon RC .50 1.25
168 Cordarrelle Patterson RC .50 1.25
169 Corey Fuller RC .50 1.25
170 Cornellius Carradine RC .50 1.25
171 D.J. Fluker RC .50 1.25
172 D.J. Hayden RC .50 1.25
173 Damontre Moore RC .50 1.25
174 Da'Rick Rogers RC .50 1.25
175 Datone Jones RC .50 1.25
176 DeAndre Hopkins RC 1.25 3.00
177 Dee Milliner RC .50 1.25
178 Denard Robinson RC .50 1.25
179 Dennis Johnson RC .50 1.25
180 Desmond Trufant RC .50 1.25
181 Dion Jordan RC .50 1.25
182 Dion Sims RC .50 1.25
183 Dustin Hopkins RC .50 1.25
184 Eddie Lacy RC .50 1.25
185 EJ Manuel RC .50 1.25
186 Eric Fisher RC .50 1.25
187 Eric Reid RC .60 1.50
188 Ezekiel Ansah RC .50 1.25
189 Gavin Escobar RC .50 1.25
190 Geno Smith RC .50 1.25
191 Giovani Bernard RC .50 1.25
192 Jamar Taylor RC .50 1.25
193 Jarvis Jones RC .50 1.25
194 Jasper Collins RC .50 1.25
195 Johnathan Cyprien RC .50 1.25
196 Johnathan Franklin RC .50 1.25
197 Johnthan Banks RC .50 1.25
198 Jordan Poyer RC .50 1.25
199 Jordan Reed RC .75 2.00
200 Joseph Randle RC .50 1.25
201 Josh Boyce RC .50 1.25
202 Justin Hunter RC .50 1.25
203 Keenan Allen RC 1.00 2.50
204 Kenjon Barner RC .50 1.25
205 Kenny Stills RC .50 1.25
206 Kenny Vaccaro RC .50 1.25
207 Kerwynn Williams RC .50 1.25
208 Kevin Minter RC .50 1.25
209 Knile Davis RC .50 1.25
210 Landry Jones RC .50 1.25
211 Le'Veon Bell RC 1.50 4.00
212 Manti Te'o RC .60 1.50
213 Marcus Davis RC .50 1.25
214 Marcus Lattimore RC .50 1.25
215 Margus Hunt RC .50 1.25
216 Markus Wheaton RC .50 1.25
217 Marquess Wilson RC .75 2.00
218 Marquise Goodwin RC .50 1.25
219 Matt Barkley RC .50 1.25
220 Matt Elam RC .50 1.25
221 Mike Gillislee RC .50 1.25
222 Mike Glennon RC .50 1.25
223 Montee Ball RC .50 1.25
224 Mychal Rivera RC .50 1.25
225 Nick Kasa RC .50 1.25
226 Phillip Thomas RC .50 1.25
227 Quinton Patton RC .50 1.25
228 Rex Burkhead RC .60 1.50
229 Robert Alford RC .50 1.25
230 Robert Woods RC .75 2.00
231 Rodney Smith RC .50 1.25
232 Ryan Nassib RC .50 1.25
233 Ryan Otten RC .50 1.25
234 Brice Butler RC .50 1.25
235 Sam Montgomery RC .50 1.25
236 Stedman Bailey RC .50 1.25
237 Steptan Taylor RC .50 1.25
238 Tavarres King RC .50 1.25
239 Tavon Austin RC .60 1.50
240 Terrance Williams RC .50 1.25
241 Theo Riddick RC .50 1.25
242 Travis Kelce RC 1.25 3.00
243 Tyler Bray RC .50 1.25
244 Tyler Eifert RC .50 1.25

245 Tyler Wilson RC .50 1.25
246 Tyrann Mathieu RC .75 2.00
247 Vance McDonald RC .60 1.50
248 Xavier Rhodes RC .50 1.25
249 Zac Dysert RC .50 1.25
250 Zach Ertz RC 1.00 2.50

2013 Select Prizm

*1-100 VETS: 1.5X TO 4X BASIC CARDS
*101-150 RETIRED: 1X TO 2.5X BASIC RET
*151-250 ROOKIES: .8X TO 2X BASIC RC
FOUR PRIZMS PER BOX OVERALL

2013 Select Greatest

*PRIZM/25: 2X TO 5X BASIC INSERTS
1 C.Newton/W.Moon 1.25 3.00
2 F.Tarkenton/R.Griffin 1.25 3.00
3 T.Bradshaw/T.Brady 3.00 8.00
4 J.Watt/W.Sapp 1.00 2.50
5 B.Rothlisbrgr/J.Elway 2.50 6.00
6 D.Brees/S.Jurgensen 1.25 3.00
7 E.George/R.Rice 1.00 2.50
8 A.Peterson/M.Faulk 1.25 3.00
9 A.Johnson/J.Rice 2.00 5.00
10 J.Witten/O.Newsome 1.00 2.50

2013 Select Hot Rookies Red

SIX INSERTS PER BOX OVERALL
*BLUE: .5X TO 1.2X BASIC RED
*BLUE PRIZM/25: 1X TO 2.5X BASIC RED
*RED PRIZM/25: 1X TO 2.5X BASIC RED
1 Cordarrelle Patterson .75 2.00
2 DeAndre Hopkins 2.00 5.00
3 Eddie Lacy .75 2.00
4 EJ Manuel .75 2.00
5 Geno Smith .75 2.00
6 Giovani Bernard .75 2.00
7 Johnathan Franklin .75 2.00
8 Keenan Allen 1.50 4.00
9 Knile Davis .75 2.00
10 Le'Veon Bell 2.50 6.00
11 Mike Gillislee .75 2.00
12 Montee Ball .75 2.00
13 Robert Woods 1.25 3.00
14 Stepfan Taylor .75 2.00
15 Quinton Patton .75 2.00
16 Terrance Williams .75 2.00
17 Tyler Eifert .75 2.00
18 Kenbrell Thompkins 1.25 3.00
19 Ace Sanders .75 2.00
20 Denard Robinson .75 2.00
21 Tyrann Mathieu 1.25 3.00
22 Aaron Dobson .75 2.00
23 Gavin Escobar .75 2.00
24 Tavon Austin 1.00 2.50
25 Vance McDonald 1.00 2.50
26 Justin Hunter .75 2.00
27 Manti Te'o 1.00 2.50
28 Stedman Bailey .75 2.00
29 Kiko Alonso 1.00 2.50
30 Zach Ertz 1.50 4.00

2013 Select Hot Stars Red

SIX INSERTS PER BOX OVERALL
*BLUE: .5X TO 1.2X BASIC INSERTS
*BLUE PRIZM/25: 2X TO 5X BASIC INSERTS
*RED PRIZM/25: 2X TO 5X BASIC INSERTS
1 C.J. Spiller .75 2.00
2 Mike Wallace .75 2.00
3 Tom Brady 3.00 8.00
4 Joe Flacco 1.00 2.50
5 A.J. Green 1.25 3.00
6 Trent Richardson .75 2.00
7 Ben Roethlisberger 1.25 3.00
8 Arian Foster 1.00 2.50
9 Andrew Luck 2.00 5.00
10 Maurice Jones-Drew .75 2.00
11 Chris Johnson .75 2.00
12 Peyton Manning 2.50 6.00
13 Jamaal Charles 1.00 2.50
14 Darren McFadden 1.00 2.50
15 Antonio Gates 1.00 2.50
16 Tony Romo 1.00 2.50
17 Victor Cruz 1.00 2.50
18 LeSean McCoy 1.25 3.00
19 Robert Griffin III .75 2.00
20 Matt Forte .75 2.00
21 Matthew Stafford 1.00 2.50
22 Aaron Rodgers 2.00 5.00
23 Adrian Peterson 1.25 3.00
24 Matt Ryan 1.00 2.50
25 Cam Newton 1.25 3.00
26 Drew Brees 1.25 3.00
27 Doug Martin 1.00 2.50
28 Larry Fitzgerald 1.00 2.50
29 Colin Kaepernick 1.00 2.50
30 Russell Wilson 2.50 6.00

2013 Select In Motion

SIX INSERTS PER BOX OVERALL
*PRIZM/25: 2X TO 5X BASIC INSERTS
1 Steve Johnson 1.00 2.50
2 Mike Wallace .75 2.00
3 Danny Amendola 1.00 2.50
4 Torrey Smith .75 2.00
5 A.J. Green 1.25 3.00
6 Antonio Brown 1.25 3.00
7 Andre Johnson .75 2.00
8 Reggie Wayne 1.00 2.50
9 Justin Blackmon .75 2.00
10 Kenny Britt .75 2.00
11 Wes Welker 1.00 2.50
12 Dwayne Bowe 1.00 2.50
13 Santonio Holmes .75 2.00
14 Vincent Brown .75 2.00
15 Dez Bryant 1.25 3.00
16 Hakeem Nicks .75 2.00
17 Jeremy Maclin .75 2.00
18 Pierre Garcon 1.00 2.50
19 Brandon Marshall 1.00 2.50
20 Calvin Johnson 1.25 3.00
21 Jordy Nelson 1.00 2.50
22 Greg Jennings .75 2.00
23 Julio Jones 1.25 3.00
24 Steve Smith 1.00 2.50
25 Marques Colston .75 2.00
26 Vincent Jackson .75 2.00
27 Larry Fitzgerald 1.00 2.50
28 Chris Givens .75 2.00
29 Anquan Boldin .75 2.00
30 Golden Tate .75 2.00

2013 Select Rookie Autographs

STATED PRINT RUN 199-499
EXCH EXPIRATION: 6/18/2015
*PRIZM/99-199: .5X TO 1.2X AU/299-499
*PRIZM/99: .4X TO 1X AU/199
152 Aaron Mellette/499 2.00 5.00
153 Ace Sanders/499 2.00 5.00
154 Alec Ogletree/499 2.00 5.00
155 Alex Okafor/299 2.00 5.00
157 Arthur Brown/299 2.00 5.00
158 Barkevious Mingo/499 2.00 5.00
159 Bjoern Werner/499 2.00 5.00
160 Blidi Wreh-Wilson/499 2.50 6.00
161 Brad Sorensen/499 2.00 5.00
162 Chance Warmack/299 2.00 5.00
163 Chris Gragg/299 2.00 5.00
164 Chris Harper/499 2.00 5.00
165 Chris Thompson/499 2.00 5.00
169 Corey Fuller/499 2.00 5.00
170 Cornellius Carradine/499 2.00 5.00
171 D.J. Fluker/499 2.00 5.00
172 D.J. Hayden/499 2.00 5.00
173 Damontre Moore/499 2.00 5.00
174 Da'Rick Rogers/499 2.00 5.00
175 Datone Jones/499 2.00 5.00
177 Dee Milliner/499 2.00 5.00
179 Dennis Johnson/499 2.00 5.00
180 Desmond Trufant/499 2.00 5.00
182 Dion Sims/499 2.00 5.00
183 Dustin Hopkins/499 2.00 5.00
186 Eric Fisher/499 2.00 5.00
187 Eric Reid/499 6.00 15.00
188 Ezekiel Ansah/499 2.00 5.00
192 Jamar Taylor/499 2.00 5.00
193 Jarvis Jones/499 4.00 10.00
195 Johnathan Cyprien/499 2.00 5.00
197 Johnthan Banks/499 2.00 5.00
198 Jordan Poyer/199 2.50 6.00
201 Josh Boyce/499 2.00 5.00
204 Kenjon Barner/499 2.00 5.00
206 Kenny Vaccaro/499 2.00 5.00
208 Kevin Minter/499 2.00 5.00
215 Margus Hunt/499 2.00 5.00
217 Marquess Wilson/499 3.00 8.00
220 Matt Elam/499 2.00 5.00
224 Mychal Rivera/499 2.00 5.00
225 Nick Kasa/499 2.00 5.00
226 Phillip Thomas/499 2.00 5.00
228 Rex Burkhead/499 6.00 15.00
229 Robert Alford/499 2.00 5.00
231 Rodney Smith/499 2.00 5.00
234 Brice Butler/499 2.00 5.00
235 Sam Montgomery/499 2.00 5.00
238 Tavarres King/499 2.00 5.00
241 Theo Riddick/499 2.00 5.00
242 Travis Kelce/499 15.00 40.00
243 Tyler Bray/499 2.00 5.00
246 Tyrann Mathieu/299 6.00 15.00
248 Xavier Rhodes/499 2.00 5.00
249 Zac Dysert/499 2.00 5.00
251 Alan Bonner/499 2.00 5.00
252 B.J. Daniels/499 3.00 8.00
253 Benny Cunningham/499 6.00 15.00
254 C.J. Anderson/499 8.00 20.00
255 Caleb Sturgis/199 6.00 15.00
256 Cierre Wood/199 2.50 6.00
257 Cobi Hamilton/499 2.00 5.00
258 D.J. Swearinger/499 2.00 5.00
259 Darius Slay/299 2.00 5.00
260 David Amerson/499 2.00 5.00
261 Earl Wolff/499 3.00 8.00
262 Jack Doyle/499 3.00 8.00
263 Jamie Collins/499 2.00 5.00
264 Jaron Brown/499 2.00 5.00
265 Jawan Jamison/499 2.00 5.00
266 Jeff Tuel/499 2.00 5.00
267 Jon Bostic/499 2.00 5.00
268 Justin Brown/499 3.00 8.00
269 Kawann Short/499 2.00 5.00
270 Kenbrell Thompkins/499 3.00 8.00
271 Khiry Robinson/499 3.00 8.00
272 Kiko Alonso/499 2.50 6.00
273 Latavius Murray/499 2.50 6.00
274 Luke Joeckel/199
275 Luke Willson/499 6.00 15.00
276 Marlon Brown/499 3.00 8.00
277 Matt McGloin/499 15.00 40.00
278 Matt Scott/199
279 Matt Simms/499 2.50 6.00
280 Michael Cox/499 8.00 20.00
281 Michael Ford/499 6.00 15.00
282 Mike James/499 3.00 8.00
283 Nick Moody/499 3.00 8.00
284 Onterio McCalebb/199
285 Russell Shepard/499 2.00 5.00
286 Ryan Griffin/499 2.00 5.00
287 Ryan Spadola/499 2.50 6.00
288 Levine Toilolo/499 3.00 8.00
289 Sio Moore/499 5.00 12.00
290 Zach Sudfeld/499 2.00 5.00
291 Ray Graham/499 2.00 5.00
292 Ryan Griffin/499 2.00 5.00
293 Sheldon Richardson/199
294 Spencer Ware/499 2.00 5.00
295 Zac Stacy/499 2.00 5.00

2013 Select Rookie Jersey Autographs

*PRIZM/99: .5X TO 1.2X JSY AU/399-499
151 Aaron Dobson/499 3.00 8.00
156 Andre Ellington/499 3.00 8.00
166 Christine Michael/499 3.00 8.00
168 Cordarrelle Patterson/399 3.00 8.00
176 DeAndre Hopkins/399 8.00 20.00
178 Denard Robinson/499 3.00 8.00
181 Dion Jordan/499 3.00 8.00
184 Eddie Lacy/399 3.00 8.00
185 EJ Manuel/399 3.00 8.00
189 Gavin Escobar/499 3.00 8.00
190 Geno Smith/399 3.00 8.00
191 Giovani Bernard/399 3.00 8.00
196 Johnathan Franklin/499 3.00 8.00
199 Jordan Reed/499 5.00 12.00
200 Joseph Randle/499 3.00 8.00
202 Justin Hunter/399 3.00 8.00
203 Keenan Allen/399 6.00 15.00
205 Kenny Stills/499 3.00 8.00
209 Knile Davis/499 3.00 8.00
210 Landry Jones/399 3.00 8.00
211 Le'Veon Bell/499 20.00 50.00
212 Manti Te'o/399 4.00 10.00
214 Marcus Lattimore/499 3.00 8.00
216 Markus Wheaton/399 3.00 8.00
218 Marquise Goodwin/499 3.00 8.00
219 Matt Barkley/399 3.00 8.00
221 Mike Gillislee/499 3.00 8.00
222 Mike Glennon/399 3.00 8.00
223 Montee Ball/499 3.00 8.00
227 Quinton Patton/499 3.00 8.00
230 Robert Woods/399 5.00 12.00
232 Ryan Nassib/399 3.00 8.00
236 Stedman Bailey/499 3.00 8.00
237 Stepfan Taylor/499 3.00 8.00
239 Tavon Austin/499 4.00 10.00
240 Terrance Williams/399 3.00 8.00
244 Tyler Eifert/499 3.00 8.00
245 Tyler Wilson/399 3.00 8.00
247 Vance McDonald/499 4.00 10.00
250 Zach Ertz/499 EXCH 6.00 15.00

2013 Select Signatures

*PRIZM/49: .5X TO 1.2X BASIC AU/99
*PRIZM/25: .5X TO 1.2X BASIC AU/49
1 Russell Wilson/25
3 Cecil Shorts/49 4.00 10.00
4 Clay Matthews/25
5 Danny Amendola/25
6 Doug Martin/25
7 Frank Gore/25
8 Nate Washington/99 4.00 10.00
9 Greg Olsen/25
10 Victor Cruz/49 5.00 12.00
11 Jay Cutler/25
12 Jeremy Maclin/49 4.00 10.00
13 Kyle Rudolph/25
15 Matthew Stafford/25
18 T.Y. Hilton/25
19 Peyton Manning/25
20 Andrew Luck/25 90.00 150.00
21 Rashard Mendenhall/25
22 Reggie Wayne/25
23 Danario Alexander/99 4.00 10.00
24 Cam Newton/25
25 Andy Dalton/25
26 Richard Sherman/99 90.00 150.00
27 Sam Bradford/25
29 David Wilson/40 4.00 10.00
30 Greg Jennings/25
31 C.J. Spiller/25 12.00 30.00
32 Jimmy Graham/25
33 London Fletcher/25 10.00 25.00
35 Jordy Nelson/25

2013 Select Stripes Jersey Autographs

*PRIZM/25: .5X TO 1.2X JSY AU/49
1 Matt Ryan/25
2 Darren McFadden/25
3 Demaryius Thomas/25
4 Kenny Britt/49 6.00 15.00
5 LeSean McCoy/25
6 Maurice Jones-Drew/25
7 Ryan Mathews/25
8 Ryan Tannehill/49 12.00 30.00
9 Jamaal Charles/25
12 Torrey Smith/25
14 Larry Fitzgerald/25
19 Josh Gordon/49
20 Jason Witten/25
21 A.J. Green/25
22 Steve Johnson/49
23 Champ Bailey/49
24 Alfred Morris/25

2014 Select

201-240 ROOKIE JSY AU PRINT RUN 99-149
EXCH EXPIRATION: 6/17/2016
1 Victor Cruz .40 1.00
2 Jimmy Graham .50 1.25
3 Golden Tate .40 1.00
4 Zac Stacy .30 .75
5 Julian Edelman .50 1.25
6 Larry Fitzgerald .40 1.00
7 Steve Smith .40 1.00
8 Rob Gronkowski .40 1.00
9 Josh McCown .30 .75
10 Andre Johnson .40 1.00
11 Julio Jones .50 1.25
12 Calvin Johnson .50 1.25
13 Jamaal Charles .40 1.00
14 Tony Romo .40 1.00
15 C.J. Spiller .30 .75
16 Matthew Stafford .40 1.00
17 Steve Johnson .40 1.00
18 Aaron Rodgers 1.00 2.50
19 Knowshon Moreno .30 .75
20 Julius Thomas .30 .75
21 Fred Jackson .40 1.00
22 Ben Tate .30 .75
23 Adrian Peterson .50 1.25
24 Andrew Luck .60 1.50
25 Marshawn Lynch .40 1.00
26 Cordarrelle Patterson .30 .75
27 Marques Colston .30 .75
28 Peyton Manning 1.00 2.50
29 Colin Kaepernick .40 1.00
30 Kendall Wright .30 .75
31 Nick Foles .40 1.00
32 J.J. Watt .50 1.25
33 Andre Ellington .30 .75
34 Hakeem Nicks .30 .75
35 Joe Flacco .40 1.00
36 Keenan Allen .40 1.00
37 Doug Martin .40 1.00
38 Michael Crabtree .30 .75
39 Alex Smith .40 1.00
40 T.Y. Hilton .40 1.00
41 Eddie Lacy .30 .75
42 Cam Newton .50 1.25
43 Shonn Greene .30 .75
44 Mike Wallace .30 .75
45 LeSean McCoy .50 1.25
46 Tom Brady 1.25 3.00
47 James Jones .30 .75
48 Andre Roberts .30 .75
49 Robert Griffin III .30 .75
50 Toby Gerhart .30 .75
51 Carson Palmer .40 1.00
52 DeAngelo Williams .30 .75
53 Ben Roethlisberger .50 1.25
54 DeMarco Murray .40 1.00
55 Tavon Austin .30 .75
56 Greg Olsen .40 1.00
57 Steven Jackson .30 .75
58 Jeremy Maclin .30 .75
59 Giovani Bernard .30 .75
60 Matt Forte .30 .75
61 Darren McFadden .30 .75
62 Eric Decker .30 .75
63 Demaryius Thomas .40 1.00
64 Brian Hoyer .30 .75
65 Drew Brees .50 1.25
66 Nate Washington .30 .75
67 Brandon Marshall .30 .75
68 Greg Jennings .30 .75
69 Vincent Jackson .30 .75
70 Maurice Jones-Drew .30 .75
71 Philip Rivers .50 1.25
72 Troy Polamalu .50 1.25
73 Clay Matthews .50 1.25
74 Matt Ryan .40 1.00
75 Rashad Jennings .30 .75
76 Cecil Shorts .30 .75
77 Arian Foster .40 1.00
78 Russell Wilson .75 2.00
79 Alfred Morris .30 .75
80 Ryan Mathews .40 1.00
81 Antonio Brown .50 1.25
82 Percy Harvin .30 .75
83 Dez Bryant .50 1.25
84 Geno Smith .30 .75
85 Derrick Johnson .30 .75
86 Andy Dalton .40 1.00
87 Alshon Jeffery .40 1.00
88 Torrey Smith .30 .75
89 Eli Manning .40 1.00
90 Brian Hartline .30 .75
91 Chris Long .30 .75
92 Jordan Cameron .30 .75
93 A.J. Green .50 1.25
94 Chris Johnson .30 .75
95 Brett Favre 1.50 4.00
96 Dan Marino 1.50 4.00
97 John Elway 1.25 3.00
98 Bo Jackson 1.00 2.50
99 Jerry Rice 1.25 3.00
100 Emmitt Smith 1.25 3.00
101 Greg Robinson RC .75 2.00
102 Jake Matthews RC .75 2.00
103 Justin Gilbert RC .75 2.00
104 Anthony Barr RC .75 2.00
105 Taylor Lewan RC .75 2.00
106 Aaron Donald RC 2.00 5.00
107 Kyle Fuller RC .75 2.00
108 Ryan Shazier RC 1.25 3.00
109 Zack Martin RC 1.00 2.50
110 C.J. Mosley RC 1.00 2.50
111 Calvin Pryor RC .75 2.00
112 Ja'Wuan James RC .75 2.00
113 Ha Ha Clinton-Dix RC 1.00 2.50
114 Dee Ford RC .75 2.00
115 Darqueze Dennard RC 1.00 2.50
116 Jason Verrett RC .75 2.00
117 Marcus Smith RC .75 2.00
118 Deone Bucannon RC .75 2.00
119 Dominique Easley RC .75 2.00
120 Jimmie Ward RC 1.00 2.50
121 Bradley Roby RC .75 2.00
122 Garrett Gilbert RC .75 2.00
123 Allen Hurns RC 1.00 2.50
124 David Fales RC .75 2.00
125 Keith Wenning RC 1.00 2.50
126 Zach Mettenberger RC .75 2.00
127 Stephen Morris RC .75 2.00
128 Christian Kirksey RC .75 2.00
129 Dustin Vaughan RC .75 2.00
130 Antonio Andrews RC .75 2.00
131 Isaiah Crowell RC 1.00 2.50
132 James White RC 1.50 4.00
133 Bashaud Breeland RC .75 2.00
134 Jordan Lynch RC 1.00 2.50
135 Jerick McKinnon RC 1.00 2.50
136 Orleans Darkwa RC 1.25 3.00
137 Lorenzo Taliaferro RC .75 2.00
138 Marion Grice RC .75 2.00
139 Rajion Neal RC .75 2.00
140 Branden Oliver RC 1.25 3.00
141 Storm Johnson RC .75 2.00
142 Alfred Blue RC .75 2.00
143 T.J. Carrie RC 1.00 2.50
144 Jay Prosch RC 1.25 3.00
145 E.J. Gaines RC .75 2.00
146 LaDarius Perkins RC .75 2.00
147 David Fluellen RC .75 2.00
148 Damien Williams RC .75 2.00
149 Telvin Smith RC .75 2.00
150 Silas Redd RC 1.00 2.50
151 Shayne Skov RC .75 2.00
152 Henry Josey RC .75 2.00
153 Zach Bauman RC 1.00 2.50
154 Preston Brown RC .75 2.00
155 Kyle Van Noy RC 1.00 2.50
156 Kapri Bibbs RC 1.00 2.50
157 Chris Borland RC .75 2.00
158 Brandon Coleman RC .75 2.00
159 Bruce Ellington RC .75 2.00
160 Taylor Gabriel RC 1.00 2.50
161 Devin Street RC .75 2.00
162 Glenn Winston RC 1.00 2.50
163 Jeff Janis RC .75 2.00
164 John Brown RC 1.25 3.00
165 Josh Huff RC 1.00 2.50
166 Kevin Norwood RC .75 2.00
167 L'Damian Washington RC 1.00 2.50
168 Martavis Bryant RC 1.00 2.50
169 Matt Hazel RC .75 2.00
170 Isaiah Burse RC .75 2.00
171 Jeremiah Attaochu RC .75 2.00
172 Robert Herron RC .75 2.00
173 Juwan Thompson RC 1.25 3.00
174 Stephon Tuitt RC 1.25 3.00
175 Tevin Reese RC .75 2.00
176 Jalen Saunders RC .75 2.00
177 Kony Ealy RC 1.00 2.50
178 Ryan Grant RC .75 2.00
179 Michael Sam RC .75 2.00
180 James Wright RC 1.00 2.50
181 Rashad Ross RC .75 2.00
182 Solomon Patton RC 1.00 2.50
183 Ted Bolser RC 1.00 2.50
184 Kain Colter RC 1.00 2.50
185 Trey Watts RC .75 2.00
186 C.J. Fiedorowicz RC .75 2.00
187 Crockett Gillmore RC 1.00 2.50
188 Jace Amaro RC .75 2.00
189 Richard Rodgers RC 1.25 3.00
190 Troy Niklas RC .75 2.00
191 Ego Ferguson RC .75 2.00
192 Timmy Jernigan RC .75 2.00
193 Walt Aikens RC 1.00 2.50
194 Bennie Fowler RC 1.00 2.50
195 Senorise Perry RC 1.00 2.50
196 Zurlon Tipton RC 1.00 2.50
197 Ryan Hewitt RC .75 2.00
198 Philly Brown RC 1.00 2.50
199 George Atkinson III RC .75 2.00
200 Jeff Mathews RC 1.00 2.50
201 Mike Evans JSY AU/149 RC 6.00 15.00
203 Donte Moncrief JSY AU/149 RC 2.50 6.00
206 A.J. McCarron JSY AU/149 RC 2.50 6.00
207 Bishop Sankey JSY AU/149 RC 2.50 6.00
208 Tom Savage JSY AU/149 RC 2.50 6.00
209 J.Matthews JSY AU/149 RC 4.00 10.00
210 Tajh Boyd JSY AU/149 RC 2.50 6.00
212 Marqise Lee JSY AU/149 RC 3.00 8.00
213 Brandin Cooks JSY AU/149 RC 4.00 10.00
214 Allen Robinson JSY AU/149 RC 4.00 10.00
216 Kelvin Benjamin JSY AU/149 RC 4.00 10.00
218 Seferian-Jenkins JSY AU/149 RC 2.50 6.00
219 Andre Williams JSY AU/149 RC 2.50 6.00
221 Derek Carr JSY AU/149 RC 25.00 50.00
222 Charles Sims JSY AU/149 RC 2.50 6.00
223 Aaron Murray JSY AU/149 RC 2.50 6.00
224 Tre Mason JSY AU/149 RC 2.50 6.00
225 T.Bridgewater JSY AU/99 RC 5.00 12.00
226 Jimmy Garoppolo JSY AU/149 RC 40.00 80.00
227 Terrance West JSY AU/149 RC 2.50 6.00
228 Blake Bortles JSY AU/99 RC 4.00 10.00
229 Dri Archer JSY AU/149 RC 2.50 6.00
230 Sammy Watkins JSY AU/99 RC 5.00 12.00
231 O.Beckham JSY AU/149 RC 40.00 80.00
232 Logan Thomas JSY AU/49 RC 3.00 8.00
233 Ka'Deem Carey JSY AU/149 RC 2.50 6.00
234 Johnny Manziel JSY AU/99 RC 10.00 25.00
235 Connor Shaw JSY AU/49 RC 3.00 8.00
236 Eric Ebron JSY AU/149 RC 3.00 8.00
237 Jeremy Hill JSY AU/149 RC 3.00 8.00
238 D.Freeman JSY AU/149 RC 10.00 25.00
240 Asa Watson JSY AU/149 RC 2.50 6.00

2014 Select Prizm

*1-100 VETS: 1.2X TO 3X BASIC CARDS
*101-200 ROOKIES: .8X TO 2X BASIC RC
*ROOK.JSY AU/49-99: .5X TO 1.2X JSY AU/149
*ROOK.JSY AU/49: .4X TO 1X JSY AU/99
*ROOK.JSY AU/35: .5X TO 1.2X JSY AU 49-99

2014 Select Prizm Blue

*1-100 VETS/50: 2.5X TO 6X BASIC CARDS
*101-200 ROOKIES/50: 1.2X TO 3X BASIC RC
*ROOK.JSY AU/20-25: .6X TO 1.5X JSY AU/149
*ROOK.JSY AU/20: .5X TO 1.2X JSY AU/99
*ROOK.JSY AU/15: .6X TO 1.5X JSY AU/49-99

2014 Select Prizm Fuchsia

*1-100 VETS/199: 1.5X TO 4X BASIC CARDS
*101-200 ROOKIES/199: .8X TO 2X BASIC RC
*ROOK.JSY AU/75: .5X TO 1.2X JSY AU/149
*ROOK.JSY AU/35: .6X TO 1.5X JSY AU/149
*ROOK.JSY AU/30-35: .5X TO 1.2X JSY AU/49-99

2014 Select Prizm Gold

*1-100 VETS/10: 6X TO 15X BASIC CARDS
*101-200 ROOKIES/10: 2.5X TO 6X BASIC RC

2014 Select Prizm Orange

*1-100 VETS/75: 2X TO 5X BASIC CARDS
*101-200 ROOKIES/75: 1X TO 2.5X BASIC RC
*ROOK.JSY AU/25-35: .6X TO 1.5X JSY AU/149
*ROOK.JSY AU/20-25: .5X TO 1.2X JSY AU/49-99

2014 Select Prizm Purple

*1-100 VETS/25: 4X TO 10X BASIC CARDS
*101-200 ROOKIES/25: 2X TO 5X BASIC RC
*ROOK.JSY AU/15: .8X TO 2X JSY AU/149
*ROOK.JSY AU/15: .6X TO 1.5X JSY AU/99

2014 Select Prizm Red

*1-100 VETS/99: 2X TO 5X BASIC CARDS
*101-200 ROOKIES/99: 1X TO 2.5X BASIC RC
*ROOK.JSY AU/50: .5X TO 1.2X JSY AU/149
*ROOK.JSY AU/30: .6X TO 1.5X JSY AU/149
*ROOK.JSY AU/25-30: .5X TO 1.2X JSY AU/49-99

2014 Select Rookies Mojo

*101-200 ROOKIES: .6X TO 1.5X BASIC RC
*ROOK.JSY AU/20-25: .6X TO 1.5X JSY AU/149
*ROOK.JSY AU/20: .5X TO 1.2X JSY AU/49
*ROOK.JSY AU/15: .6X TO 1.5X JSY AU/99-149
211 Khalil Mack JSY AU/20 15.00 40.00
217 De'Anthony Thomas JSY AU/25 4.00 10.00
239 Davante Adams JSY AU/15 8.00 20.00

2014 Select Rookies Mojo Blue

*101-200 ROOKIES/25: 2X TO 5X BASIC RC

2014 Select Rookies Mojo Red

*101-200 ROOKIES/75: 1X TO 2.5X BASIC RC
*ROOK.JSY AU/15: 1X TO 2.5X JSY AU/149
*ROOK.JSY AU/15: .8X TO 2X JSY AU/49
211 Khalil Mack JSY AU/15 25.00 50.00
215 Carlos Hyde JSY AU/15 8.00 20.00
217 De'Anthony Thomas JSY AU/15 6.00 15.00
239 Davante Adams JSY AU/10

2014 Select Defensive ROY Selections

DEF1 Jadeveon Clowney 1.50 4.00
DEF2 Khalil Mack 5.00 12.00
DEF3 Ryan Shazier 2.00 5.00
DEF4 Justin Gilbert 1.25 3.00
DEF5 C.J. Mosley 1.50 4.00
DEF6 Jason Verrett 1.25 3.00
DEF7 Kyle Fuller 1.25 3.00
DEF8 Aaron Donald WIN 8.00 20.00
DEF9 Calvin Pryor 1.25 3.00
DEF10 Ha Ha Clinton-Dix 1.50 4.00
DEF11 Jimmie Ward 1.50 4.00
DEF12 Ego Ferguson 1.25 3.00
DEF13 T.J. Carrie 1.50 4.00
DEF14 Preston Brown 1.25 3.00
DEF15 Anthony Hitchens 1.25 3.00
DEF16 Walt Aikens 1.50 4.00
DEF17 Christian Kirksey 1.25 3.00
DEF18 Telvin Smith 1.25 3.00
DEF19 Deone Bucannon 1.25 3.00
DEF20 Bradley Roby 1.25 3.00
DEF21 Dominique Easley 1.25 3.00
DEF22 Anthony Barr 1.25 3.00
DEF23 Darqueze Dennard 1.50 4.00
DEF24 Wild Card 1.25 3.00

2014 Select MVP Selections

1 Aaron Rodgers WIN 25.00 50.00
2 Peyton Manning 4.00 10.00
3 Andrew Luck 2.50 6.00
4 Tony Romo 1.50 4.00
5 Tom Brady 5.00 12.00
6 Ben Roethlisberger 2.00 5.00
7 Philip Rivers 2.00 5.00
8 Eli Manning 1.50 4.00
9 Matthew Stafford 1.50 4.00
10 Matt Ryan 1.50 4.00
11 Cam Newton 2.00 5.00
12 Drew Brees 2.00 5.00
13 Colin Kaepernick 1.50 4.00
14 Russell Wilson 3.00 8.00
15 Marshawn Lynch 1.50 4.00
16 Julio Jones 2.00 5.00
17 Calvin Johnson 2.00 5.00
18 Nick Foles 1.50 4.00
19 DeMarco Murray 1.50 4.00
20 Wild Card 1.25 3.00

2014 Select Offensive ROY Selections

OFF1 Blake Bortles 1.50 4.00
OFF2 Johnny Manziel 2.00 5.00
OFF3 Teddy Bridgewater 2.00 5.00
OFF4 Derek Carr 8.00 20.00
OFF5 Sammy Watkins 2.00 5.00
OFF6 Mike Evans 3.00 8.00
OFF7 Eric Ebron 1.50 4.00
OFF8 Odell Beckham Jr. WIN 20.00 50.00
OFF9 Brandin Cooks 2.00 5.00
OFF10 Alfred Blue 1.25 3.00
OFF11 Andre Williams 1.25 3.00
OFF12 Bishop Sankey 1.25 3.00
OFF13 Devonta Freeman 2.00 5.00
OFF14 Lorenzo Taliaferro 1.25 3.00
OFF15 Jeremy Hill 1.50 4.00
OFF16 Terrance West 1.25 3.00
OFF17 Allen Hurns 1.50 4.00
OFF18 Allen Robinson 2.00 5.00
OFF19 John Brown 2.00 5.00
OFF20 Jace Amaro 1.25 3.00
OFF21 Jarvis Landry 2.50 6.00
OFF22 Jordan Matthews 2.00 5.00
OFF23 Kelvin Benjamin 2.00 5.00
OFF24 Wild Card 1.25 3.00

2014 Select Rookie Autographs Mojo Red

*MOJO RED/15: .5X TO 1.2X FUCHSIA/75-199

2014 Select Rookie Autographs Prizm

*PRIZM AU/75-99: .4X TO 1X FUCHSIA/75-199
*PRIZM AU/25-35: .5X TO 1.2X FUCHSIA/75-199
RAJG Jimmy Garoppolo/75 50.00 100.00
RASW Sammy Watkins/25 6.00 15.00

2014 Select Rookie Autographs Prizm Blue

*BLUE/15-25: .5X TO 1.2X FUCHSIA/75-199
RAJG Jimmy Garoppolo/25 100.00 200.00

2014 Select Rookie Autographs Prizm Fuchsia

*BASE AU/149: .4X TO 1X FUCHSIA/175-199
*BASE AU/99: .3X TO .8X FUCHSIA/75
*BASE AU/49: .5X TO 1.2X FUCHSIA/199
RAAA Antonio Andrews/199 2.50 6.00
RAAB Anthony Barr/199 2.50 6.00
RAABL Alfred Blue/199 2.50 6.00
RAAD Ahmad Dixon/199 2.50 6.00
RAAH Allen Hurns/199 3.00 8.00
RAAW Asa Watson/199 2.50 6.00
RAAWI Andre Williams/75 3.00 8.00
RABC Brandon Coleman/199 2.50 6.00
RABCO Brandin Cooks/75 5.00 12.00
RABE Bruce Ellington/199 2.50 6.00
RABO Branden Oliver/199 4.00 10.00
RABS Bishop Sankey/75 3.00 8.00
RACB Chris Borland/199 2.50 6.00
RADB Deone Bucannon/199 2.50 6.00
RADC Derek Carr/75 30.00 80.00
RADD Darqueze Dennard/199 3.00 8.00
RADFR Devonta Freeman/75 8.00 20.00
RADM Donte Moncrief/199 2.50 6.00
RADS Devin Street/199 2.50 6.00
RAEE Eric Ebron/75 4.00 10.00
RAER Ed Reynolds/199 2.50 6.00
RAGG Garrett Gilbert/199 2.50 6.00
RAGR Greg Robinson/199 2.50 6.00
RAHC Ha Ha Clinton-Dix/199 3.00 8.00
RAHJ Henry Josey/199 2.50 6.00
RAIB Isaiah Burse/199 2.50 6.00
RAIC Isaiah Crowell/199 3.00 8.00
RAJA Jace Amaro/99 3.00 8.00
RAJAM Jake Matthews/199 2.50 6.00
RAJB John Brown/199 4.00 10.00
RAJG Jimmy Garoppolo/75 50.00 100.00
RAJH Jeremy Hill/75 4.00 10.00
RAJJ Jeff Janis/199 2.50 6.00
RAJL Jordan Lynch/199 3.00 8.00
RAJMC Jerick McKinnon/199 3.00 8.00
RAJOM Jordan Matthews/175 4.00 10.00
RAJV Jason Verrett/199 2.50 6.00
RAJW Jimmie Ward/199 3.00 8.00
RAJWR James Wright/199 3.00 8.00
RAKB Kelvin Benjamin/75 5.00 12.00
RAKE Kony Ealy/199 3.00 8.00
RAKF Kyle Fuller/199 2.50 6.00
RAKN Kevin Norwood/199 2.50 6.00
RAKV Kyle Van Noy/199 3.00 8.00
RAKW Keith Wenning/199 3.00 8.00
RALJ Lamarcus Joyner/199 3.00 8.00
RALT Lorenzo Taliaferro/199 2.50 6.00
RAMC Michael Campanaro/199 2.50 6.00
RAMG Marion Grice/199 2.50 6.00
RAMH Matt Hazel/199 2.50 6.00
RAML Marqise Lee/75 4.00 10.00
RAMR Marcus Roberson/199 3.00 8.00
RAMS Michael Sam/199 2.50 6.00
RAMSM Marcus Smith/199 2.50 6.00
RAOB Odell Beckham Jr./75 EXCH 30.00 80.00
RAPB Preston Brown/199 2.50 6.00
RAPBR Philly Brown/199
RAPD Pierre Desir/199 2.50 6.00
RARH Ra'Shede Hageman/199 2.50 6.00
RARHE Robert Herron/199 2.50 6.00
RARN Rajion Neal/199 2.50 6.00
RARR Richard Rodgers/199 4.00 10.00
RARRO Rashad Ross/199 2.50 6.00
RARS Ryan Shazier/199 4.00 10.00
RASC Scott Crichton/199 2.50 6.00
RASR Silas Redd/199 3.00 8.00
RASS Shayne Skov/199 2.50 6.00
RATJ Timmy Jernigan/199 2.50 6.00
RATL Taylor Lewan/199 2.50 6.00
RATM Tre Mason/75 3.00 8.00
RATMU Trent Murphy/199 2.50 6.00
RATN Troy Niklas/175 2.50 6.00
RATR Tevin Reese/199 2.50 6.00
RATRE Trevor Reilly/199 2.50 6.00
RATW Terrance West/199 2.50 6.00
RAYS Yawin Smallwood/199 2.50 6.00

2014 Select Rookie Autographs Prizm Orange

*ORANGE/20-35: .5X TO 1.2X FUCHSIA/75-199
RAJG Jimmy Garoppolo/35 60.00 125.00

2014 Select Rookie Autographs Prizm Purple

*PURPLE/15: .5X TO 1.2X FUCHSIA/75-199

2014 Select Rookie Autographs Prizm Red

*RED/50: .4X TO 1X FUCHSIA/75-199
*RED/25: .5X TO 1.2X FUCHSIA/75-199
RAJG Jimmy Garoppolo/50 75.00 150.00

2014 Select Rookie Jerseys

*BLUE/50: .6X TO 1.5X BASIC JSY/399
*FUCHSIA/199: .4X TO 1X BASIC JSY/399
*GOLD/10: 1.2X TO 3X BASIC JSY/399
*ORANGE/99: .5X TO 1.2X BASIC JSY/399
*PRIZM/299: .4X TO 1X BASIC JSY/399
*PURPLE/35: .8X TO 2X BASIC JSY/399
*RED/149: .4X TO 1X BASIC JSY/399
RJAJ A.J. McCarron 1.50 4.00
RJAM Aaron Murray 1.50 4.00
RJBB Blake Bortles 2.00 5.00
RJBS Bishop Sankey 1.50 4.00
RJDA Dri Archer 1.50 4.00
RJDC Derek Carr 5.00 12.00
RJJF Johnny Manziel 2.50 6.00
RJJH Jeremy Hill 2.00 5.00
RJJO Jordan Matthews 2.50 6.00
RJKB Kelvin Benjamin 2.50 6.00
RJME Mike Evans 4.00 10.00
RJOB Odell Beckham Jr. 4.00 10.00
RJSW Sammy Watkins 2.50 6.00
RJTB Teddy Bridgewater 2.50 6.00
RJTM Tre Mason 1.50 4.00

2014 Select Rookies Jersey Autographs Prizm

*BASE AU/40-99: .4X TO 1X PRISM AU/40-99
*BLUE/25: .6X TO 1.5X PRIZM AU/99
*BLUE/20-25: .5X TO 1.2X PRIZM AU/35-40
*BLUE/15: .4X TO 1X PRIZM AU/20-25
*FUCHSIA/30-75: .4X TO 1X PRISM AU/40-99
*ORANGE AU/15-35: .5X TO 1.2X PRIZM AU/25-99
*PURPLE/15: .8X TO 2X PRIZM AU/99
*PURPLE/15: .6X TO 1.5X PRIZM AU/40
*PURLE/15: .5X TO 1.2X PRIZM AU/20
*RED AU/50: .5X TO 1.2X PRIZM AU/99
*RED AU/30: .4X TO 1X PRIZM AU/40
*RED AU/25: .5X TO 1.2X PRIZM AU/35
*RED AU/15: .4X TO 1X PRIZM AU/20
RJAJ A.J. McCarron/25 5.00 12.00
RJBS Bishop Sankey/40
RJDA Dri Archer/99 3.00 8.00
RJDC Derek Carr/35 30.00 60.00
RJJH Jeremy Hill/40 5.00 12.00
RJJO Jordan Matthews/99 5.00 12.00
RJKB Kelvin Benjamin/35 6.00 15.00
RJME Mike Evans/25 12.00 30.00
RJOB Odell Beckham Jr./40 EXCH 30.00 80.00
RJSW Sammy Watkins/20 8.00 20.00
RJTB Teddy Bridgewater/20
RJTM Tre Mason/40 4.00 10.00

2014 Select Super Bowl Selections

1 Buffalo Bills 1.25 3.00
2 Miami Dolphins 1.25 3.00
3 New England Patriots WIN/T.Brady 15.00 30.00
4 New York Jets 1.00 2.50
Chris Johnson
Willie Colon
5 Baltimore Ravens 1.00 2.50
Torrey Smith
6 Cincinnati Bengals 1.00 2.50
Giovani Bernard
7 Cleveland Browns 1.00 2.50
Joe Haden
Barkevious Mingo
8 Pittsburgh Steelers 1.25 3.00
Le'Veon Bell
9 Houston Texans 1.25 3.00
10 Indianapolis Colts/A.Luck 2.00 5.00
11 Jacksonville Jaguars 1.25 3.00
12 Tennessee Titans 1.00 2.50
Nate Washington
13 Denver Broncos/P.Manning 3.00 8.00
14 Kansas City Chiefs 1.25 3.00
15 Oakland Raiders 1.00 2.50
Darren McFadden
16 San Diego Chargers 1.50 4.00
Philip Rivers
17 Dallas Cowboys 1.50 4.00
Dez Bryant
18 New York Giants 1.00 2.50
Peyton Hillis
19 Philadelphia Eagles 1.25 3.00
20 Washington Redskins 1.00 2.50
Robert Griffin III
Alfred Morris
21 Chicago Bears 1.00 2.50
Matt Forte
22 Detroit Lions 1.25 3.00
Matt Stafford
23 Green Bay Packers 1.00 2.50
Eddie Lacy
24 Minnesota Vikings 1.00 2.50
Cordarrelle Patterson
25 Atlanta Falcons 1.00 2.50
Steven Jackson
26 Carolina Panthers 1.50 4.00
Cam Newton
27 New Orleans Saints 1.25 3.00
28 Tampa Bay Buccaneers 1.25 3.00
Mike Evans
Vincent Jackson
29 Arizona Cardinals 1.25 3.00
Carson Palmer
30 St. Louis Rams 1.25 3.00
31 San Francisco 49ers 1.25 3.00
Colin Kaepernick
Frank Gore
32 Seattle Seahawks 1.25 3.00
Marshawn Lynch

2014 Select Signatures

6 Alshon Jeffery
7 Andre Ellington 3.00 8.00
13 Bryce Brown 3.00 8.00
17 Charles Clay 3.00 8.00
18 Chris Jones 3.00 8.00
29 Earl Thomas
34 Gavin Escobar 3.00 8.00
38 Greg Jennings
39 Hakeem Nicks
42 Joseph Randle
44 Kenbrell Thompkins 3.00 8.00
46 Knile Davis 3.00 8.00
55 Mike James 3.00 8.00
68 Rod Streater 3.00 8.00
72 Scott Chandler 3.00 8.00
75 T.Y. Hilton
78 Torrey Smith
79 Trindon Holliday
84 Barkevious Mingo 3.00 8.00
85 Jeremy Kerley 3.00 8.00
87 Ben Tate 3.00 8.00
88 Nick Toon 3.00 8.00
89 Dwayne Harris
91 Bill Romanowski 12.50 25.00
96 John Taylor
100 Vai Sikahema

2014 Select Signatures Prizm Blue

1 A.J. Green/15
6 Alshon Jeffery/15 6.00 15.00
7 Andre Ellington/15 5.00 12.00
10 Antonio Gates/15
13 Bryce Brown/25 5.00 12.00
14 C.J. Spiller/15 5.00 12.00
17 Charles Clay/25 5.00 12.00
18 Chris Jones/25 5.00 12.00
21 Danny Amendola/15
23 DeAndre Hopkins/15
25 DeMarcus Ware/15
29 Earl Thomas/15
34 Gavin Escobar/25 5.00 12.00
42 Joseph Randle/25 5.00 12.00
44 Kenbrell Thompkins/25 5.00 12.00
46 Knile Davis/25 5.00 12.00
49 Luke Kuechly/15
50 Manti Te'o/15
53 Michael Floyd/15 5.00 12.00
55 Mike James/25 5.00 12.00
63 Reggie Wayne/15
68 Rod Streater/25 5.00 12.00
69 Ryan Mathews/15 6.00 15.00
70 Ryan Tannehill/15
72 Scott Chandler/25 5.00 12.00
75 T.Y. Hilton/15
76 Terrance Williams/15 5.00 12.00
78 Torrey Smith/15 5.00 12.00
79 Trindon Holliday/25 5.00 12.00
81 Vincent Jackson/15 5.00 12.00
84 Barkevious Mingo/25 5.00 12.00
85 Jeremy Kerley/25 5.00 12.00
87 Ben Tate/25 5.00 12.00
88 Nick Toon/25 5.00 12.00
89 Dwayne Harris/25 5.00 12.00
91 Bill Romanowski/15
96 John Taylor/25 15.00 40.00
99 Trent Dilfer/15
100 Vai Sikahema/25 8.00 20.00

2014 Select Stars Jersey Autographs Prizm Orange

ASAD Andy Dalton 12.00 30.00

2014 Select Stars Jerseys

*BLUE/35: .8X TO 2X BASIC JSY/199
*FUCHSIA/99: .6X TO 1.5X BASIC JSY/199
*FUCHSIA/28: 1X TO 2.5X BASIC JSY/199
*ORANGE/50: .8X TO 2X BASIC JSY/199
*PRIZM/150: .5X TO 1.2X BASIC JSY/199
*PURPLE/20-25: 1X TO 2.5X BASIC JSY/199
*RED/75: .6X TO 1.5X BASIC JSY/199
SSAD Andy Dalton 2.50 6.00
SSAP Adrian Peterson 3.00 8.00
SSCK Colin Kaepernick 2.50 6.00
SSCN Cam Newton 3.00 8.00
SSDB Drew Brees 3.00 8.00
SSDM Dan Marino 8.00 20.00
SSDT Demaryius Thomas 2.50 6.00
SSEM Eli Manning 2.50 6.00
SSJB Jerome Bettis 5.00 12.00
SSJC Jay Cutler 2.00 5.00
SSJE John Elway 5.00 12.00
SSJM Joe Montana 10.00 25.00
SSML Marshawn Lynch 2.50 6.00
SSPM Peyton Manning 5.00 12.00
SSSY Steve Young 5.00 12.00

2016 Select

1 Rob Gronkowski .30 .75
2 Brice Butler .20 .50
3 Todd Gurley II .30 .75
4 Hunter Henry RC .40 1.00
5 Joe Haden .20 .50
6 Aaron Burbridge RC .30 .75
7 Kevin Greene .30 .75
8 Barry Sanders .50 1.25
9 Michael Irvin .30 .75
10 Cardale Jones .20 .50
11 Roger Lewis RC .30 .75
12 Demaryius Thomas .25 .60
13 Tom Brady .75 2.00
14 J.J. Watt .30 .75
15 Joe Namath .40 1.00
16 Aaron Donald .30 .75
17 Kirk Cousins .30 .75
18 Ben Roethlisberger .30 .75
19 Michael Thomas RC .60 1.50
20 Carson Wentz RC 3.00 8.00
21 Roger Staubach .40 1.00
22 Derrick Henry RC .75 2.00
23 Tony Romo .25 .60
24 Franco Harris .30 .75
25 Joey Bosa RC .60 1.50
26 Aaron Rodgers .60 1.50
27 Kurt Warner .25 .60
28 Blake Martinez RC .40 1.00
29 Mike Evans .25 .60
30 Christian Hackenberg RC .30 .75
31 Russell Wilson .40 1.00
32 Vic Beasley Jr. .20 .50
33 Trevor Siemian .20 .50
34 Jacoby Brissett RC .40 1.00
35 John Elway .50 1.25
36 Adrian Peterson .30 .75
37 Laquon Treadwell RC .40 1.00
38 Bo Jackson .40 1.00
39 Odell Beckham Jr. .30 .75
40 Cole Wick RC .40 1.00
41 Ryan Tannehill .25 .60
42 Cameron Meredith .20 .50
43 Tyler Boyd RC .40 1.00
44 Jalen Ramsey RC .50 1.25
45 Jonathan Williams RC .40 1.00
46 Alex Collins .25 .60
47 Larry Donnell .20 .50
48 Brandin Cooks .25 .60
49 Paul Perkins .20 .50
50 Connor Cook RC .40 1.00
51 Sterling Shepard RC .40 1.00
52 DeAndre Hopkins .25 .60
53 Jalin Marshall RC .50 1.25
54 Jordy Nelson .25 .60
55 Allen Robinson .25 .60
56 Tyler Higbee RC .30 .75
57 LeSean McCoy .30 .75
58 Braxton Miller RC .30 .75
59 Paxton Lynch RC .30 .75
60 LeGarrette Blount .25 .60
61 Steve Smith .25 .60
62 Doug Baldwin .25 .60
63 Jared Goff RC 2.00 5.00
64 Josh Doctson RC .40 1.00
65 Tyreek Hill RC 1.25 3.00
66 Alshon Jeffery .25 .60

67 Le'Veon Bell .25 .60
68 Brett Favre .60 1.50
69 Pharoh Cooper RC .30 .75
70 Dak Prescott RC 1.50 4.00
71 T.Y. Hilton .25 .60
72 Eddie Lacy .20 .50
73 Jarvis Landry .25 .60
74 Julio Jones .30 .75
75 Vincent Jackson .20 .50
76 Andrew Luck .40 1.00
77 Malcolm Mitchell RC .30 .75
78 Brock Osweiler .20 .50
79 Ray Lewis .30 .75
80 Dan Marino .60 1.50
81 Tajae Sharpe RC .40 1.00
82 Ezekiel Elliott RC 1.50 4.00
83 Jeremy Hill .20 .50
84 Julius Peppers .25 .60
85 Antonio Brown .30 .75
86 Will Fuller V RC .50 1.25
87 Marcus Mariota .30 .75
88 C.J. Prosise RC .30 .75
89 Terrelle Pryor .20 .50
90 Danny Amendola .25 .60
91 Terry Bradshaw .40 1.00
92 Frank Gore .25 .60
93 Jerry Rice .50 1.25
94 Kelvin Benjamin .25 .60
95 Austin Hooper .20 .50
96 Xavien Howard RC .40 1.00
97 Matt Ryan .25 .60
98 Cam Newton .30 .75
99 Richard Sherman .30 .75
100 DeForest Buckner RC .75 2.00
101 Jared Goff 3.00 8.00
102 Jordan Howard RC 2.00 5.00
103 Aaron Burbridge .50 1.25
104 Adam Thielen 3.00 8.00
105 C.J. Prosise .50 1.25
106 Matthew Stafford .60 1.50
107 David Johnson .75 2.00
108 Rob Gronkowski .75 2.00
109 Dwayne Allen .50 1.25
110 Tom Brady 2.00 5.00
111 Jarran Reed RC .75 2.00
112 Jordan Reed .50 1.25
113 Aaron Rodgers 1.50 4.00
114 Laquon Treadwell .60 1.50
115 Cam Newton .75 2.00
116 Michael Thomas 1.00 2.50
117 DeAndre Hopkins .60 1.50
118 Robert Kelley RC 1.25 3.00
119 Eli Manning .60 1.50
120 Tommylee Lewis RC 1.00 2.50
121 Jason Pierre-Paul .50 1.25
122 Josh Doctson .60 1.50
123 Adrian Peterson .75 2.00
124 Larry Fitzgerald .60 1.50
125 Carlos Hyde .50 1.25
126 Odell Beckham Jr. .75 2.00
127 DeForest Buckner .50 1.25
128 Russell Wilson 1.00 2.50
129 Eric Ebron .50 1.25
130 Travis Kelce .75 2.00
131 Jeremy Langford .60 1.50
132 Julian Edelman .75 2.00
133 Alex Smith .60 1.50
134 Leonte Carroo RC .75 2.00
135 Carson Wentz 5.00 12.00
136 Patrick Peterson .50 1.25
137 Delanie Walker .50 1.25
138 Ryan Mathews .60 1.50
139 Ezekiel Elliott 2.50 6.00
140 Trevor Davis RC .75 2.00
141 Jerome Bettis .75 2.00
142 Julio Jones .75 2.00
143 Amari Cooper .75 2.00
144 Le'Veon Bell .60 1.50
145 Chris Moore RC 1.00 2.50
146 Paxton Lynch .50 1.25
147 Demarcus Robinson RC .75 2.00
148 Sam Bradford .50 1.25
149 Gary Barnidge .50 1.25
150 Tyler Boyd .60 1.50
151 Michael Crabtree .50 1.25
152 Julius Thomas .50 1.25
153 Antonio Gates .50 1.25
154 Malcolm Mitchell .50 1.25
155 Clay Matthews .75 2.00
156 Peyton Manning 1.50 4.00
157 Derek Carr .75 2.00
158 Shannon Sharpe .75 2.00
159 Greg Olsen .60 1.50
160 Tyler Ervin RC .75 2.00
161 Joe Flacco .60 1.50
162 Keenan Allen .60 1.50
163 Blake Martinez .60 1.50
164 Mark Ingram .60 1.50
165 Connor Cook .60 1.50
166 Rashad Jennings .50 1.25
167 Derrick Henry 1.25 3.00
168 Sterling Shepard .60 1.50
169 J.J. Watt .75 2.00
170 Tyreek Hill 2.00 5.00
171 Curtis Martin .60 1.50
172 Kevin Greene .75 2.00
173 Braxton Miller .50 1.25
174 Marshall Faulk .60 1.50
175 D.J. Foster RC 1.00 2.50
176 Philip Rivers .75 2.00
177 DeSean Jackson .60 1.50
178 Steve Young 1.00 2.50
179 Jacoby Brissett .60 1.50
180 Jeremy Kerley .50 1.25
181 Joey Bosa 1.00 2.50
182 Khalil Mack .75 2.00
183 Brett Favre 1.50 4.00
184 Marshawn Lynch .60 1.50
185 Dak Prescott 1.50 4.00
186 Ricardo Louis .50 1.25
187 Devonta Freeman .60 1.50
188 Tajae Sharpe .60 1.50
189 Jalen Ramsey .75 2.00
190 Von Miller .60 1.50
191 John Riggins .60 1.50
192 Kurt Warner .60 1.50
193 Darren Sproles .60 1.50
194 Matt Jones .60 1.50
195 Darrelle Revis .50 1.25
196 Richard Sherman .75 2.00
197 Dez Bryant .75 2.00
198 Todd Gurley II .75 2.00
199 Jameis Winston .75 2.00
200 Will Fuller V .75 2.00
201 A.J. Green .30 .75
202 Karl Joseph RC .75 2.00
203 Brandon Marshall .50 1.25
204 Luke Kuechly .60 1.50
205 Curtis Martin .60 1.50
206 Paxton Lynch .50 1.25
207 Devonta Freeman .60 1.50
208 Stefon Diggs .60 1.50
209 Jakeem Grant RC .75 2.00
210 Jimmy Graham .75 2.00
211 Alex Smith .60 1.50
212 Keenan Allen .60 1.50
213 Brett Favre 1.50 4.00
214 Mark Ingram .60 1.50
215 Dak Prescott 2.50 6.00
216 Peyton Manning 1.50 4.00
217 Devontae Booker RC 1.00 2.50
218 Steve Young 1.00 2.50
219 James Bradberry RC 1.00 2.50
220 Joe Flacco .60 1.50
221 Allen Hurns .50 1.25
222 Kenneth Dixon RC .75 2.00
223 C.J. Anderson .60 1.50
224 Marshall Faulk .60 1.50
225 Daryl Worley RC .75 2.00
226 Philip Rivers .75 2.00
227 Doug Martin .60 1.50
228 Kenny Britt .50 1.25
229 Jared Goff 3.00 8.00
230 John Riggins .60 1.50
231 Ameer Abdullah .50 1.25
232 Kenyan Drake RC 1.25 3.00
233 Carson Palmer .60 1.50
234 Marshawn Lynch .60 1.50
235 David Johnson .75 2.00
236 Randall Cobb .60 1.50
237 Drew Brees .75 2.00
238 Travis Kelce .75 2.00
239 Jason Pierre-Paul .50 1.25
240 Greg Olsen .60 1.50
241 Andy Dalton .60 1.50
242 Kevin Greene .75 2.00
243 Carson Wentz 5.00 12.00
244 Matt Forte .20 .50
245 DeAndre Washington RC .75 2.00
246 Richard Rodgers .60 1.50
247 Jack Doyle .50 1.25
248 Trevone Boykin RC .75 2.00
249 Jason Witten .60 1.50
250 Jonathan Stewart .50 1.25
251 Antonio Gates .50 1.25
252 Kurt Warner .60 1.50
253 Clay Matthews .75 2.00
254 Matthew Stafford .60 1.50
255 DeMarco Murray .60 1.50
256 Ryan Fitzpatrick .50 1.25
257 Emmanuel Sanders .75 2.00
258 Tyler Eifert .60 1.50
259 Jay Cutler .50 1.25
260 Jordan Matthews .60 1.50
261 Jay Ajayi .60 1.50
262 Lamar Miller .50 1.25
263 Coby Fleener .50 1.25
264 Melvin Gordon .60 1.50
265 Derek Carr .75 2.00
266 Ryan Mathews .60 1.50
267 Marvin Jones Jr. .50 1.25
268 Tyrod Taylor .60 1.50
269 Jeremy Maclin .50 1.25
270 Josh Norman .50 1.25
271 Blake Bortles .50 1.25
272 Latavius Murray .50 1.25
273 Cody Kessler RC .75 2.00
274 Navorro Bowman .60 1.50
275 Derrick Henry 1.25 3.00
276 Sammy Watkins .75 2.00
277 Ezekiel Elliott 8.00 20.00
278 Von Miller .60 1.50
279 Jerome Bettis .75 2.00
280 Julian Edelman .75 2.00
281 Tyrann Mathieu .60 1.50
282 Kyle Rudolph .50 1.25
283 Corey Coleman RC 1.25 3.00
284 Nick Vannett RC .75 2.00
285 Derrick Johnson .50 1.25
286 Shannon Sharpe .75 2.00
287 Geno Atkins .50 1.25
288 Wendell Smallwood RC .75 2.00
289 J.J. Watt .75 2.00
290 Cam Newton .75 2.00
291 Richard Sherman .75 2.00
292 Russell Wilson 1.00 2.50
293 Julio Jones .75 2.00
294 Le'Veon Bell .60 1.50
295 Odell Beckham Jr. .75 2.00
296 Tom Brady 2.00 5.00
297 Aaron Rodgers 1.50 4.00
298 Rob Gronkowski .75 2.00
299 Adrian Peterson .75 2.00
300 Todd Gurley II .75 2.00

2016 Select Prizm
RANDOM INSERTS IN PACKS

2016 Select Prizm Copper
*COPPERVETS (201-300): .75X TO 2X BASIC CARDS
*COOPERROOK (201-300): .6X TO 1.5X BASIC CARDS
STATED PRINT RUN 49 SER.#'d SETS

2016 Select Prizm Light Blue
STATED PRINT RUN 125 SER.#'d SETS

2016 Select Prizm Orange
STATED PRINT RUN 49 SER.#'d SETS

2016 Select Prizm Purple
STATED PRINT RUN 75 SER.#'d SETS

2016 Select Prizm Red
STATED PRINT RUN 99 SER.#'d SETS

2016 Select Prizm Tie Dye
STATED PRINT RUN 25 SER.#'d SETS

2016 Select Prizm Tri Color
RANDOM INSERTS IN PACKS

2016 Select Autograph Materials Prizm
*COPPER/25: .5X TO 1.2X BASIC JSY AU/49
1 Allen Robinson/25 6.00 15.00
3 Ameer Abdullah/49 4.00 10.00
4 Marcus Allen/15 25.00 50.00
5 DeAngelo Williams/15 6.00 15.00
7 Lance Briggs/25
9 Marqise Lee/25 5.00 12.00
11 Jay Ajayi/49 8.00 20.00
13 Devin Funchess/49 4.00 10.00
14 EJ Manuel/15 6.00 15.00
15 Ronnie Brown/15 6.00 15.00
17 Doug Baldwin/25 10.00 25.00
19 Zach Ertz/49 5.00 12.00
21 Matt Jones/49 5.00 12.00
22 Blake Bortles/15 6.00 15.00
23 Charles Sims/49 4.00 10.00
24 Clay Matthews/15 25.00 50.00
25 Earl Campbell/15
27 Jordan Matthews/25 6.00 15.00
29 Allen Hurns/49 4.00 10.00
30 Larry Csonka/15 40.00 80.00
31 Jeremy Langford/49 5.00 12.00
32 Jay Cutler/15 6.00 15.00
33 T.J. Yeldon/49 4.00 10.00
34 Antonio Brown/15 50.00 100.00
35 Don Maynard/25 10.00 25.00
37 Roger Craig/25 15.00 40.00
39 Josh Gordon/49 8.00 20.00
41 Robert Woods/49 5.00 12.00
44 Jim McMahon/15 30.00 60.00
45 Jimmy Garoppolo/25 30.00 60.00
47 Edgerrin James/25
49 Malcolm Smith/49 6.00 15.00
51 Jan Stenerud/49 4.00 10.00
52 Richard Sherman/15 30.00 60.00
53 Carl Eller/49 8.00 20.00
54 Warren Moon/15
55 Dallas Clark/25 12.00 30.00
58 James White/49 5.00 12.00

2016 Select Die Cut Autographs Prizm
DCAA Ameer Abdullah/99 3.00 8.00
DCAD Aaron Donald/49 6.00 15.00
DCBP Bill Parcells/25 15.00 40.00
DCCH Cameron Heyward/99 3.00 8.00
DCCS Charles Sims/99 3.00 8.00
DCDM Dexter Manley/99 4.00 10.00
DCDT Desmond Trufant/99 3.00 8.00
DCEC Earl Campbell/25 15.00 40.00
DCGA Geno Atkins/99 3.00 8.00
DCJG Jimmy Garoppolo/49 50.00 100.00
DCJM Jim McMahon/25 12.00 30.00
DCKE Kony Ealy/99 3.00 8.00
DCLC La'el Collins/99 3.00 8.00
DCMJ Marvin Jones Jr./49 4.00 10.00
DCML Marqise Lee/49 4.00 10.00
DCOA Ottis Anderson/99 3.00 8.00
DCPM Phil McConkey/99 4.00 10.00
DCRB Rocky Bleier/49 12.00 30.00
DCRS Ryan Shazier/99 10.00 25.00
DCTB Travis Benjamin/99 3.00 8.00
DCTH Ted Hendricks/20 6.00 15.00
DCTM Tom Matte/99 3.00 8.00
DCTS Trevor Siemian/99 3.00 8.00

2016 Select Jumbo Rookie Signature Swatches Prizm
1 C.J. Prosise/75 4.00 10.00
2 Laquon Treadwell/75 5.00 12.00
3 Christian Hackenberg/75 4.00 10.00
4 Paul Perkins/75 4.00 10.00
5 Dak Prescott/99 EXCH 60.00 125.00
6 Sterling Shepard/99 5.00 12.00
7 Devontae Booker/99 5.00 12.00
8 Joey Bosa/99 8.00 20.00
9 Malcolm Mitchell/99 4.00 10.00
10 Keenan Reynolds/99 5.00 12.00
11 Cardale Jones/75 4.00 10.00
12 Leonte Carroo/99 4.00 10.00
13 Cody Kessler/99 4.00 10.00
14 Paxton Lynch/49 5.00 12.00
15 DeAndre Washington/99 4.00 10.00
16 Trevor Davis/99 4.00 10.00
17 Ezekiel Elliott/49 150.00 250.00
18 Jonathan Williams/99 5.00 12.00
19 Jacoby Brissett/99 5.00 12.00
20 Kenneth Dixon/99 4.00 10.00
21 Carson Wentz/49 60.00 125.00
22 Michael Thomas/75 8.00 20.00
23 Connor Cook/49 6.00 15.00
24 Pharoh Cooper/99 4.00 10.00
25 Demarcus Robinson/99 4.00 10.00
26 Tyler Boyd/75 5.00 12.00
27 Hunter Henry/99 5.00 12.00
28 Jordan Howard/99 10.00 25.00
29 Alex Collins/99 5.00 12.00
30 Kenyan Drake/99 6.00 15.00
31 Chris Moore/99 5.00 12.00
32 Moritz Bohringer/99 4.00 10.00
33 Corey Coleman/75 6.00 15.00
34 Ricardo Louis/99 4.00 10.00
35 Derrick Henry/49 30.00 80.00
36 Tyler Ervin/99 4.00 10.00
37 Jared Goff/49 30.00 80.00
38 Josh Doctson/75 5.00 12.00
39 Braxton Miller/99 4.00 10.00
40 Tajae Sharpe/99 5.00 12.00
41 Wendell Smallwood/99 4.00 10.00
42 Will Fuller V/75 6.00 15.00
43 Tyreek Hill/99 30.00 60.00

2016 Select Jumbo Rookie Signature Swatches Prizm Orange
*ORANGE/35-49: .5X TO 1.2X BASIC JSY AU/75-99
*ORANGE/30: .5X TO 1.2X BASIC JSY AU/49
JSCW Carson Wentz/30 100.00 200.00
JSDP Dak Prescott/49 EXCH 60.00 150.00
JSEE Ezekiel Elliott/30 200.00 300.00

2016 Select Jumbo Rookie Signature Swatches Prizm Purple
*PURPLE/49-60: .5X TO 1.2X BASIC JSY AU/75-99
*PURPLE/35: .4X TO 1X BASIC JSY AU/49
JSCW Carson Wentz/35 60.00 125.00
JSDP Dak Prescott/60 EXCH 60.00 150.00
JSEE Ezekiel Elliott/35 150.00 250.00

2016 Select Jumbo Rookie Signature Swatches Prizm Tie Dye
*TIE DYE/25: .6X TO 1.5X BASIC JSY AU/75-99
*TIE DYE/25: .5X TO 1.2X BASIC JSY AU/49
JSCW Carson Wentz 150.00 300.00
JSDP Dak Prescott EXCH 100.00 200.00
JSEE Ezekiel Elliott 300.00 500.00

2016 Select Jumbo Rookie Swatches Prizm
1 Devontae Booker 2.50 6.00
2 Braxton Miller 2.00 5.00
3 Jared Goff 10.00 25.00
4 Cardale Jones 2.00 5.00
5 Laquon Treadwell 2.50 6.00
6 Christian Hackenberg 2.00 5.00
7 Paxton Lynch 2.00 5.00
8 Connor Cook 2.50 6.00
9 Tyler Boyd 2.50 6.00
10 Dak Prescott 10.00 25.00
11 Ezekiel Elliott 10.00 25.00
12 C.J. Prosise 2.00 5.00
13 Josh Doctson 2.50 6.00
14 Carson Wentz 12.00 30.00
15 Michael Thomas 4.00 10.00
16 Cody Kessler 2.00 5.00
17 Sterling Shepard 2.50 6.00
18 Corey Coleman 3.00 8.00
19 Will Fuller V 3.00 8.00
20 Derrick Henry 5.00 12.00

2016 Select Prime Selections Prizm Nameplate
1 Jared Goff 30.00 80.00
2 Malcolm Mitchell 15.00 40.00
3 Demarcus Robinson 5.00 12.00
4 Carson Wentz 125.00 250.00
5 Kenyan Drake 8.00 20.00
6 Cody Kessler 5.00 12.00
7 Michael Thomas 25.00 50.00
8 Dak Prescott 100.00 200.00
9 Ricardo Louis 5.00 12.00
10 Ezekiel Elliott 250.00 400.00
11 Joey Bosa 25.00 50.00
12 Jacoby Brissett 6.00 15.00
13 Kenneth Dixon 5.00 12.00
14 Chris Moore 6.00 15.00
15 Leonte Carroo 5.00 12.00
16 Corey Coleman 8.00 20.00
17 Pharoh Cooper 5.00 12.00
18 Derrick Henry 12.00 30.00
19 Wendell Smallwood 5.00 12.00
20 Hunter Henry 12.00 30.00

2016 Select Rookie Autograph Materials Prizm
1 Paxton Lynch/49 5.00 12.00
2 Dak Prescott/99 EXCH 90.00 150.00
3 Tyler Boyd/75 5.00 12.00
4 Ezekiel Elliott/49 60.00 125.00
5 Jonathan Williams/99 5.00 12.00
6 Malcolm Mitchell/99 4.00 10.00
7 Kenneth Dixon/99 4.00 10.00
8 C.J. Prosise/75 4.00 10.00
9 Leonte Carroo/99 4.00 10.00
10 Christian Hackenberg/75 4.00 10.00
11 Pharoh Cooper/99 4.00 10.00
12 DeAndre Washington/99 4.00 10.00
13 Tyler Ervin/99 4.00 10.00
14 Hunter Henry/99 5.00 12.00
15 Jordan Howard/99 10.00 25.00
16 Jacoby Brissett/99 5.00 12.00
17 Kenyan Drake/99 6.00 15.00
18 Cardale Jones/75 4.00 10.00
19 Michael Thomas/75 8.00 20.00
20 Cody Kessler/99 4.00 10.00
21 Ricardo Louis/99 4.00 10.00
22 Demarcus Robinson/99 4.00 10.00
23 Wendell Smallwood/99 4.00 10.00
24 Jared Goff/49 50.00 100.00
25 Josh Doctson/75 5.00 12.00
26 Alex Collins/99 5.00 12.00
27 Tajae Sharpe/99 5.00 12.00
28 Carson Wentz/49 50.00 100.00
29 Moritz Bohringer/99 4.00 10.00
30 Connor Cook/49 6.00 15.00
31 Sterling Shepard/99 5.00 12.00
32 Derrick Henry/49 12.00 30.00
33 Will Fuller V/75 6.00 15.00
34 Joey Bosa/99 8.00 20.00
35 Keenan Reynolds/99 5.00 12.00
36 Braxton Miller/99 4.00 10.00
37 Laquon Treadwell/75 5.00 12.00
38 Chris Moore/99 5.00 12.00
39 Paul Perkins/75 4.00 10.00
40 Corey Coleman/75 6.00 15.00
41 Trevor Davis/99 4.00 10.00
42 Devontae Booker/99 5.00 12.00
43 Tyreek Hill/99 30.00 60.00

2016 Select Rookie Autograph Materials Prizm Copper
*COPPER/35-49: .4X TO 1X BASIC JSY AU/49
*COPPER/35-49: .5X TO 1.2X BASIC JSY AU/75-99
2 Dak Prescott/49 EXCH 125.00 200.00
4 Ezekiel Elliott/35 50.00 125.00

2016 Select Rookie Autograph Materials Prizm Tie Dye
*TIE DYE/25: .5X TO 1.2X BASIC JSY AU/49
*TIE DYE/25: .6X TO 1.5X BASIC JSY AU/75-99
2 Dak Prescott EXCH 125.00 250.00
4 Ezekiel Elliott 60.00 150.00

2016 Select Rookie Die Cut Autographs Prizm
1 Derrick Henry/25 12.00 30.00
2 Paxton Lynch/25 5.00 12.00
3 Braxton Miller/99 3.00 8.00
4 Jonathan Williams/99 4.00 10.00
5 Michael Thomas/49 40.00 80.00
6 C.J. Prosise/99 3.00 8.00
7 Tyler Boyd/99 4.00 10.00
8 Dak Prescott/99 60.00 125.00
9 Kenyan Drake/99 5.00 12.00
10 Malcolm Mitchell/99 3.00 8.00
11 Tyler Ervin/99 3.00 8.00
12 DeAndre Washington/99 3.00 8.00
13 Kevin Hogan/99 4.00 10.00
14 Jacoby Brissett/99 4.00 10.00
15 Connor Cook/25 6.00 15.00
16 Laquon Treadwell/49 5.00 12.00
17 Hunter Henry/99 4.00 10.00
18 Sterling Shepard/99 4.00 10.00
19 Chris Moore/99 4.00 10.00
20 Cardale Jones/49 4.00 10.00
21 Jared Goff/25 50.00 100.00
22 Trevor Davis/99 3.00 8.00
23 Wendell Smallwood/99 3.00 8.00
24 Kenneth Dixon/99 3.00 8.00
25 Pharoh Cooper/99 3.00 8.00
26 Christian Hackenberg/49 4.00 10.00
27 Jordan Howard/99 8.00 20.00
28 Devontae Booker/99 4.00 10.00
29 Corey Coleman/49 6.00 15.00
30 Leonte Carroo/99 3.00 8.00
31 Josh Doctson/49 5.00 12.00
32 Ezekiel Elliott/25 75.00 150.00
33 Will Fuller V/49 6.00 15.00
34 Carson Wentz/25 100.00 200.00
35 Demarcus Robinson/99 3.00 8.00
36 Paul Perkins/99 3.00 8.00
37 Alex Collins/99 4.00 10.00
38 Joey Bosa/99 6.00 15.00
39 Ricardo Louis/99 3.00 8.00
40 Cody Kessler/99 3.00 8.00

2016 Select Rookie Signatures Prizm
RSAB Aaron Burbridge/199 2.50 6.00
RSAB Andrew Billings/199 3.00 8.00
RSCC Connor Cook/49 5.00 12.00
RSCC Corey Coleman/49 6.00 15.00
RSCW Carson Wentz/49 60.00 125.00
RSDB Daniel Braverman/199 2.50 6.00
RSDH Derrick Henry/49 30.00 60.00
RSDP Dak Prescott/199 40.00 80.00
RSDW Daryl Worley/199 2.50 6.00
RSEE Ezekiel Elliott/49 150.00 250.00
RSJD Joey Bosa/49 8.00 20.00
RSJC Jeremy Cash/199 3.00 8.00
RSJG Jared Goff/49 75.00 150.00
RSJM Jalen Mills/199 3.00 8.00
RSJP Jordan Payton/199 2.50 6.00
RSJR Jalen Richard/199 3.00 8.00
RSJR Jalen Ramsey/199 4.00 10.00
RSJR Jarran Reed/199 2.50 6.00
RSJS Jaylon Smith/199 2.50 6.00
RSKG Keyarris Garrett/199 2.50 6.00
RSKL Kenny Lawler/199 4.00 10.00
RSKM Keith Marshall/199 2.50 6.00
RSKT Kelvin Taylor/199 2.50 6.00
RSKV Nick Vannett/199 2.50 6.00
RSLF Leonard Floyd/35 12.00 30.00
RSLT Laquon Treadwell/49 5.00 12.00
RSMT Michael Thomas/49 8.00 20.00
RSNS Noah Spence/199 2.50 6.00
RSPL Paxton Lynch/49 4.00 10.00
RSRH Rashard Higgins/199 2.50 6.00
RSRN Robert Nkemdiche/199 3.00 8.00
RSSL Shaq Lawson/199 2.50 6.00
RSTD Thomas Duarte/199 2.50 6.00
RSWJ William Jackson III/199 3.00 8.00

2016 Select Rookie Signatures Prizm Copper
*COPPER/49: .6X TO 1.5X BASIC AU/199

2016 Select Rookie Signatures Prizm Tie Dye
*TIE DYE/25: .8X TO 2X BASIC AU/199
*TIE DYE/25: .5X TO 1.2X BASIC AU/35-49
RSCW Carson Wentz 150.00 250.00
RSDH Derrick Henry 90.00 150.00
RSEE Ezekiel Elliott 300.00 450.00

2016 Select Signatures Prizm
*COPPER/35: .4X TO 1X BASIC AU/49
*COPPER/25: .5X TO 1.2X BASIC AU/35-43
SAA Ameer Abdullah/35 4.00 10.00
SAD Aaron Donald/35 6.00 15.00
SAH Allen Hurns/35 4.00 10.00
SAR Andre Reed/25 6.00 15.00
SBJ Byron Jones/49 4.00 10.00
SBM Bruce Matthews/43 4.00 10.00
SCH Charles Haley/35 12.00 30.00
SCJ Charlie Joiner/35 4.00 10.00
SDB Derrick Brooks/35 8.00 20.00
SDC Dwight Clark/25
SDF Devin Funchess/35 4.00 10.00
SDH Dan Hampton/35 4.00 10.00
SDM Don Majkowski/35 5.00 12.00
SDW Danny Woodhead/25 6.00 15.00
SEJ Ed Too Tall Jones/35 15.00 40.00
SGB Gary Barnidge/49 4.00 10.00
SGB Giovani Bernard/25 5.00 12.00
SIW Ickey Woods/49 4.00 10.00
SJA Jay Ajayi/35 5.00 12.00
SJF Justin Forsett/49 5.00 12.00
SJG Josh Gordon/35 4.00 10.00
SJK Jim Kiick/49 6.00 15.00
SJL Jeremy Langford/35 5.00 12.00
SJM Jordan Matthews/25 6.00 15.00
SJT Julius Thomas/35 4.00 10.00
SJW James White/49 5.00 12.00
SKA Keenan Allen/25 6.00 15.00
SKE Kony Ealy/49 4.00 10.00
SKS Kordell Stewart/35 15.00 40.00
SLM Lamar Miller/25 5.00 12.00
SME Mike Evans/25 6.00 15.00
SMJ Matt Jones/35 5.00 12.00
SMJ Marvin Jones/49 4.00 10.00
SSD Stefon Diggs/49 5.00 12.00
SSG Steve Grogan/49 6.00 15.00
STK Travis Kelce/35 6.00 15.00
SWG Walt Garrison/49 12.00 30.00
SWM Willie McGinest/35 10.00 25.00
SZE Zach Ertz/35 5.00 12.00

2016 Select Signatures Prizm Tie Dye
*TIE DYE/25: .5X TO 1.2X BASIC AU/49
*TIE DYE/15: .6X TO 1.5X BASIC AU/35-49
SKS Kordell Stewart/15 60.00 120.00

2016 Select Sparks Materials Prizm
1 Paxton Lynch 2.00 5.00
2 Will Fuller V 3.00 8.00
3 Tyler Boyd 2.50 6.00
4 Ezekiel Elliott 10.00 25.00
5 Josh Doctson 2.50 6.00
6 Devontae Booker 2.50 6.00
7 Jared Goff 12.00 30.00
8 Michael Thomas 4.00 10.00
9 Sterling Shepard 2.50 6.00
10 Laquon Treadwell 2.50 6.00
11 Connor Cook 2.50 6.00
12 Derrick Henry 5.00 12.00
13 Dak Prescott 10.00 25.00
14 C.J. Prosise 2.00 5.00
15 Braxton Miller 2.00 5.00
16 Carson Wentz 20.00 50.00
17 Cardale Jones 2.00 5.00
18 Cody Kessler 2.00 5.00
19 Christian Hackenberg 2.00 5.00
20 Corey Coleman 3.00 8.00

2016 Select Swatches Prizm
1 Jordan Matthews/199 2.50 6.00
2 Jarvis Landry/199 2.50 6.00
3 Ezekiel Elliott/199 10.00 25.00
4 Geno Atkins/199 2.00 5.00
5 Larry Fitzgerald/49 4.00 10.00
6 Tyrod Taylor/99 3.00 8.00
7 Doug Martin/199 2.50 6.00
8 C.J. Anderson/99 3.00 8.00
9 Davante Adams/199 2.00 5.00
10 Alfred Morris/99 2.50 6.00
11 Kelvin Benjamin/199 2.50 6.00
12 Kurt Warner/99 3.00 8.00
13 Le'Veon Bell/49 4.00 10.00
14 Tyler Eifert/199 2.50 6.00
15 Philip Rivers/199 3.00 8.00
16 Reggie Bush/199 2.00 5.00
17 Allen Robinson/199 2.50 6.00
18 Demaryius Thomas/99 3.00 8.00
19 Devonta Freeman/199 2.50 6.00
20 Arian Foster/199 2.50 6.00
21 Kevin White/199 2.00 5.00
22 Dak Prescott/199 10.00 25.00
23 Carson Wentz/199 20.00 50.00
24 Andy Dalton/199 2.50 6.00
25 Jared Goff/199 12.00 30.00
26 LeSean McCoy/99 4.00 10.00
27 Amari Cooper/199 3.00 8.00
28 Corey Coleman/199 3.00 8.00
29 Duke Johnson/199 2.00 5.00
30 Ryan Tannehill/99 3.00 8.00
31 Matt Jones/199 2.50 6.00
32 Antonio Gates/99 2.50 6.00
33 Adrian Peterson/49 5.00 12.00
34 Giovani Bernard/199 2.00 5.00
35 Alshon Jeffery/199 2.50 6.00
36 Sammy Watkins/199 3.00 8.00
37 Ameer Abdullah/199 2.00 5.00
38 Jordan Howard/199 5.00 12.00
39 Jeremy Langford/199 2.50 6.00
40 Jay Ajayi/199 2.50 6.00
41 Todd Gurley II/199 3.00 8.00
42 Will Fuller V/199 3.00 8.00
43 Paxton Lynch/199 2.00 5.00
44 Jeremy Hill/199 2.00 5.00
45 Michael Floyd/99 2.50 6.00
46 Von Miller/99 3.00 8.00
47 Brandin Cooks/199 2.50 6.00
48 Dez Bryant/99 4.00 10.00
49 Jimmy Garoppolo/199 4.00 10.00
50 DeVante Parker/199 2.50 6.00
51 Tyler Lockett/199 2.50 6.00
52 Derrick Henry/199 5.00 12.00
53 DeSean Jackson/99 3.00 8.00
54 A.J. Green/99 4.00 10.00
55 Sterling Shepard/199 2.50 6.00
56 Laquon Treadwell/199 2.50 6.00
57 Josh Doctson/199 2.50 6.00

2016 Select Swatches Prizm Orange
STATED PRINT RUN 49 SER.#'d SETS

2017 Select
1 Joe Williams RC .30 .75
2 Andy Dalton .25 .60
3 Jared Goff .30 .75
4 Eddie Jackson .25 .60
5 Aaron Jones RC .75 2.00
6 Carson Wentz .40 1.00
7 T.J. Logan RC .50 1.25
8 Zach Ertz .25 .60
9 Matt Breida RC .50 1.25
10 Jeremy Maclin .20 .50
11 Chad Williams RC .30 .75
12 Kelvin Benjamin .25 .60
13 Keenan Allen .25 .60
14 Golden Tate III .20 .50
15 Jaylon Smith .20 .50
16 Deshaun Watson RC 2.00 5.00
17 Amara Darboh .20 .50
18 Eli Manning .25 .60
19 Marcus Maye RC .30 .75
20 Antonio Gates .20 .50
21 Tyrod Taylor .25 .60
22 Blake Bortles .20 .50
23 Joe Flacco .25 .60
24 Danny Amendola .25 .60
25 T.Y. Hilton .25 .60
26 Martavis Bryant .20 .50
27 Curtis Samuel RC .40 1.00
28 Gerald Everett RC .30 .75
29 Dede Westbrook RC .30 .75
30 Tyler Eifert .25 .60
31 Marcus Mariota .30 .75
32 Joe Mixon RC .60 1.50
33 ArDarius Stewart RC .30 .75
34 Brian Hill RC .30 .75
35 David Johnson .30 .75
36 Jermaine Kearse .20 .50
37 Kendell Beckwith RC .30 .75
38 Davis Webb RC .30 .75
39 C.J. Beathard RC .30 .75
40 Jamaal Williams RC .30 .75
41 Carlos Henderson RC .30 .75
42 DeVante Parker .25 .60
43 Nathan Peterman RC .40 1.00
44 Alex Smith .25 .60
45 Emmanuel Sanders .30 .75
46 DeSean Jackson .25 .60
47 Buck Allen .20 .50
48 Doug Martin .25 .60
49 Michael Thomas .30 .75
50 Ty Montgomery .20 .50
51 Dalvin Cook RC .75 2.00
52 Stefon Diggs .25 .60
53 Sidney Jones RC .30 .75
54 Ryan Switzer RC .40 1.00
55 Philip Rivers .30 .75
56 C.J. Anderson .25 .60
57 Adoree' Jackson RC .40 1.00
58 Allen Hurns .20 .50
59 Cole Beasley .30 .75
60 Marlon Mack RC .50 1.25
61 Amari Cooper .30 .75
62 Vic Beasley Jr. .20 .50
63 Samaje Perine RC .30 .75
64 Alshon Jeffery .25 .60
65 Delanie Walker .20 .50
66 Ameer Abdullah .20 .50
67 Jalen Ramsey .20 .50
68 Kareem Hunt RC .60 1.50
69 JuJu Smith-Schuster RC .75 2.00
70 Lamar Miller .20 .50
71 Jarrad Davis RC .40 1.00
72 Mitchell Trubisky RC 1.50 4.00
73 Mike Evans .25 .60
74 Christian McCaffrey RC .75 2.00
75 Isaiah Crowell .20 .50
76 Bilal Powell .20 .50
77 Carl Lawson RC .30 .75
78 Michael Crabtree .20 .50
79 Greg Olsen .25 .60
80 Tre'Davious White RC .30 .75
81 Brandin Cooks .25 .60
82 Doug Baldwin .25 .60
83 Jay Cutler .20 .50
84 Austin Ekeler RC .30 .75
85 Jay Ajayi .25 .60
86 Dez Bryant .30 .75
87 Kirk Cousins .30 .75
88 Marvin Jones Jr. .20 .50
89 Cooper Kupp RC .50 1.25
90 Jake Butt RC .40 1.00
91 Carlos Hyde .20 .50
92 Kendall Wright .20 .50
93 Derek Barnett RC .40 1.00
94 Davante Adams .25 .60
95 Adrian Peterson .30 .75
96 Chris Godwin RC .40 1.00
97 Demaryius Thomas .25 .60
98 Wayne Gallman RC .40 1.00
99 Sammy Watkins .30 .75
100 Luke Kuechly .25 .60
101 Jordan Howard .50 1.25
102 Antonio Brown .50 1.25
103 Patrick Mahomes II RC 6.00 15.00
104 Russell Wilson .60 1.50
105 Myles Garrett RC 1.50 4.00
106 Ed Reed .40 1.00
107 LeSean McCoy .50 1.25
108 Ronnie Lott .40 1.00
109 Solomon Thomas RC .50 1.25
110 O.J. Howard RC .60 1.50
111 Devonta Freeman .40 1.00
112 A.J. Green .50 1.25
113 Rob Gronkowski .50 1.25
114 John Elway .75 2.00
115 Takkarist McKinley RC .50 1.25
116 Travis Kelce .50 1.25
117 Leonard Fournette RC 1.50 4.00
118 Dan Marino 1.00 2.50
119 Corey Davis RC .75 2.00
120 David Njoku RC .60 1.50
121 Kenny Golladay RC .75 2.00
122 LaDainian Tomlinson .40 1.00
123 James Harrison .40 1.00
124 T.J. Watt RC 1.50 4.00
125 Drew Bledsoe .40 1.00
126 Khalil Mack .50 1.25
127 Kurt Warner .40 1.00
128 Jason Witten .40 1.00
129 Kareem Hunt 1.00 2.50
130 Marshall Faulk .40 1.00
131 Matt Ryan .40 1.00
132 Ray Lewis .50 1.25
133 Hines Ward .40 1.00
134 Mark Brunell .40 1.00
135 Tarik Cohen RC 1.00 2.50
136 Joe Mixon 1.00 2.50
137 Michael Vick .40 1.00
138 Mike Williams RC .75 2.00
139 Odell Beckham Jr. .50 1.25
140 Malik Hooker RC .50 1.25
141 Kam Chancellor .50 1.25
142 Andrew Luck .60 1.50
143 Jeff Garcia .30 .75
144 Joey Bosa .50 1.25
145 Matthew Stafford .40 1.00
146 Peyton Manning 1.00 2.50
147 Zay Jones RC .60 1.50
148 Brett Favre 1.00 2.50
149 Derek Carr .50 1.25
150 John Ross III RC .60 1.50
151 Jerry Rice .75 2.00
152 Cooper Rush RC .60 1.50
153 Josh Norman .30 .75
154 Randy Moss .40 1.00
155 Christian McCaffrey 1.25 3.00
156 Warrick Dunn .30 .75
157 Haason Reddick RC .50 1.25
158 Jamal Adams RC .50 1.25
159 J.J. Watt .50 1.25
160 Earl Campbell .50 1.25
161 R. Joshua Dobbs RC .60 1.50
162 Von Miller .40 1.00
163 Jameis Winston .40 1.00
164 Deshaun Watson 3.00 8.00
165 Jabrill Peppers RC .75 2.00
166 John Riggins .40 1.00
167 Alvin Kamara RC 2.00 5.00
168 Mike Singletary .50 1.25
169 Brian Urlacher .50 1.25
170 Cooper Kupp .75 2.00
171 Taco Charlton RC .50 1.25
172 Ezekiel Elliott .60 1.50
173 Dalvin Cook 1.25 3.00
174 Emmitt Smith .75 2.00
175 Drew Brees .50 1.25
176 Jordy Nelson .40 1.00
177 Tyreek Hill .50 1.25
178 Steve Smith .40 1.00
179 Aaron Rodgers 1.00 2.50
180 Lawrence Taylor .50 1.25
181 Todd Gurley II .50 1.25
182 Marshawn Lynch .40 1.00
183 DeShone Kizer RC .50 1.25
184 Julio Jones .50 1.25
185 Tom Brady 1.25 3.00
186 DeAndre Hopkins .40 1.00
187 Ben Roethlisberger .50 1.25
188 Priest Holmes .30 .75
189 Howie Long .50 1.25
190 Cam Newton .50 1.25
191 Thurman Thomas .40 1.00
192 Chris Carson RC .75 2.00
193 Larry Fitzgerald .40 1.00
194 Curtis Martin .40 1.00
195 Dak Prescott .50 1.25
196 James Conner RC 1.00 2.50
197 Mitchell Trubisky 2.50 6.00
198 Brian Dawkins .30 .75
199 Joe Namath .60 1.50
200 Barry Sanders .75 2.00
201 Patrick Peterson .50 1.25
202 Von Miller .60 1.50
203 Cam Newton .75 2.00
204 J.J. Watt .75 2.00
205 Todd Gurley II .75 2.00
206 Myles Garrett 2.50 6.00
207 A.J. Green .75 2.00
208 James Harrison .60 1.50
209 John Ross III 1.00 2.50
210 Ben Roethlisberger .75 2.00
211 Russell Wilson 1.00 2.50
212 Gareon Conley RC .75 2.00
213 Antonio Brown .75 2.00
214 Jabrill Peppers 1.25 3.00
215 D'Onta Foreman RC 1.00 2.50
216 Julio Jones .75 2.00
217 Carson Wentz 1.00 2.50
218 Andrew Luck 1.00 2.50
219 Jimmy Garoppolo 6.00 15.00
220 Peyton Manning 1.50 4.00
221 Jordy Nelson .60 1.50
222 R. Joshua Dobbs 1.00 2.50
223 Jordan Howard .75 2.00
224 LeSean McCoy .75 2.00
225 Alvin Kamara 3.00 8.00
226 Dan Marino 1.50 4.00
227 James Conner 1.50 4.00
228 Joe Mixon 1.50 4.00
229 Chris Carson .75 2.00
230 DeShone Kizer .75 2.00
231 Matthew Stafford .60 1.50
232 Adam Thielen .75 2.00
233 Jamal Adams .75 2.00
234 Larry Fitzgerald .60 1.50
235 Joey Bosa .75 2.00
236 Landon Collins .50 1.25
237 Clay Matthews .60 1.50
238 Kareem Hunt 1.50 4.00
239 Travis Kelce .75 2.00
240 John Elway 1.25 3.00
241 Kam Chancellor .75 2.00
242 Marshawn Lynch .60 1.50
243 Eric Berry .60 1.50
244 Rob Gronkowski .75 2.00
245 Leonard Fournette 2.50 6.00
246 Cooper Kupp 1.25 3.00
247 Patrick Mahomes II 10.00 25.00
248 Aaron Rodgers 1.50 4.00
249 Le'Veon Bell .60 1.50
250 Dak Prescott .75 2.00
251 Marlon Humphrey RC .75 2.00
252 Kenny Golladay 1.25 3.00
253 Mitchell Trubisky 4.00 10.00
254 Josh Norman .50 1.25
255 Evan Engram RC 1.00 2.50
256 Aqib Talib .50 1.25
257 Kevin King RC 1.00 2.50
258 Matt Ryan .60 1.50
259 T.J. Watt 2.50 6.00
260 Tarik Cohen 1.50 4.00
261 Jourdan Lewis RC .75 2.00
262 Ezekiel Elliott 1.00 2.50
263 Jason Witten .60 1.50
264 Odell Beckham Jr. .75 2.00
265 Corey Davis 1.25 3.00
266 Khalil Mack .75 2.00
267 Cooper Rush 1.00 2.50
268 DeAndre Hopkins .60 1.50
269 Tom Brady 2.00 5.00
270 Drew Brees .75 2.00
271 Derek Carr .75 2.00
272 Marshon Lattimore RC 1.00 2.50
273 Ndamukong Suh .60 1.50
274 Tyrann Mathieu .60 1.50
275 Devonta Freeman .60 1.50
276 Taywan Taylor .50 1.25
277 Deshaun Watson 5.00 12.00
278 Jonathan Allen RC 1.00 2.50
279 Dalvin Cook 2.00 5.00
280 Tyreek Hill .75 2.00
281 Christian McCaffrey 2.00 5.00
282 Chris Thompson .50 1.25
283 Mike Williams 1.25 3.00
284 Charles Harris RC .75 2.00
285 Jameis Winston .60 1.50
286 Tom Brady 2.00 5.00
287 Dak Prescott .75 2.00
288 Ezekiel Elliott 1.00 2.50
289 Derek Carr .75 2.00
290 Aaron Rodgers 1.50 4.00
291 Antonio Brown .75 2.00
292 Rob Gronkowski .75 2.00
293 Von Miller .60 1.50
294 Russell Wilson 1.00 2.50
295 Matt Ryan .60 1.50
296 Ben Roethlisberger .75 2.00
297 Peyton Manning 1.50 4.00
298 Cam Newton .75 2.00
299 Dan Marino 1.50 4.00
300 John Elway 1.25 3.00
301A QB1
301B Baker Mayfield XRC
302A QB2
302B Sam Darnold XRC
303A QB3
303B Josh Allen XRC
304A QB4
304B Josh Rosen XRC
305A QB5
305B Lamar Jackson XRC
306A RB1
306B Saquon Barkley XRC
307A RB2
307B Rashaad Penny XRC
308A RB3
308B Sony Michel XRC
309A RB4
309B Nick Chubb XRC
310A RB5
310B Ronald Jones XRC
311A WR1
311B D.J. Moore XRC
312A WR2
312B Calvin Ridley XRC
313A WR3
313B Courtland Sutton XRC
314A WR4
314B Dante Pettis XRC
315A WR5
315B Christian Kirk XRC
316A TE1
316B Hayden Hurst XRC
317A TE2
317B Mike Gesicki XRC
318A TE3
318B Dallas Goedert XRC
319A TE4
319B Mark Andrews XRC
320A TE5
320B Jordan Akins XRC
321A XRC AU 1
321B Baker Mayfield AU
322A XRC AU 2
322B Saquon Barkley AU
323A XRC AU 3
323B Sam Darnold AU
324A XRC AU 4
324B Denzel Ward AU
325A XRC AU 5
325B Bradley Chubb AU

2017 Select Prizm Copper
*VETS/75: 1.5X TO 4X BASIC CARDS
*ROOK/75: 1X TO 2.5X BASIC CARDS

2017 Select Prizm Light Blue
*VETS/99: 1.5X TO 4X BASIC CARDS
*ROOK/99: 1X TO 2.5X BASIC CARDS

2017 Select Prizm Maroon
*VETS/99: 2.5X TO 6X BASIC CARDS
*ROOK/99: 1.5X TO 4X BASIC CARDS

2017 Select Prizm Neon Green
*VETS/49: 2X TO 5X BASIC CARDS
*ROOK/49: 1.2X TO 3X BASIC CARDS

2017 Select Prizm Orange
*VETS/49: 3X TO 8X BASIC CARDS
*ROOK/49: 2X TO 5X BASIC CARDS

2017 Select Prizm Purple
*VETS/75: 1.5X TO 4X BASIC CARDS
*ROOK/75: 1X TO 2.5X BASIC CARDS

2017 Select Prizm Silver
*VETS (1-100): 1.5X TO 4X BASIC CARDS
*ROOKIES: 1X TO 2.5X BASIC CARDS
*VETS (101-200): 1X TO 2.5X BASIC CARDS
*ROOKIES: .6X TO 1.5X BASIC CARDS
*VETS (201-300): .6X TO 1.5X BASIC CARDS
*ROOKIES: .4X TO 1X BASIC CARDS

2017 Select Prizm Tie Dye
*VETS (1-100): 4X TO 6X BASIC CARDS
*ROOKIES: 2.5X TO 6X BASIC CARDS
*VETS (101-200): 2.5X TO 6X BASIC CARDS
*ROOKIES: 1.5X TO 4X BASIC CARDS
*VETS (201-300): 1.5 TO 4X BASIC CARDS
*ROOKIES: 1X TO 2.5X BASIC CARDS
219 Jimmy Garoppolo 60.00 125.00

2017 Select Prizm Tri Color
*VETS (1-100): 2X TO 5X BASIC CARDS
*ROOKIES: 1.2X TO 3X BASIC CARDS
*VETS (101-200): 1.2X TO 3X BASIC CARDS
*ROOKIES: .8X TO 2X BASIC CARDS
*VETS (201-300): .8X TO 2X BASIC CARDS
*ROOKIES: .5X TO 1.2X BASIC CARDS

2017 Select Jumbo Rookie Signature Swatches Prizm
1 Mitchell Trubisky/25 30.00 80.00
2 Patrick Mahomes II/25 150.00 300.00
3 Deshaun Watson/25 125.00 250.00
4 DeShone Kizer/25 EXCH 6.00 15.00
5 Nathan Peterman/49 6.00 15.00
6 Davis Webb/49 5.00 12.00
7 R. Joshua Dobbs/25 8.00 20.00
8 C.J. Beathard/99 4.00 10.00
9 Leonard Fournette/25 20.00 50.00
10 Christian McCaffrey/49 25.00 60.00
11 Dalvin Cook/49 15.00 40.00
12 Joe Mixon/25 12.00 30.00
13 Alvin Kamara/99 30.00 80.00
14 Marlon Mack/25 10.00 25.00
15 Samaje Perine/99 4.00 10.00
16 Wayne Gallman/49 6.00 15.00
17 Kareem Hunt/99 8.00 20.00
18 D'Onta Foreman/49 6.00 15.00
19 James Conner/49 10.00 25.00
20 Jamaal Williams/49 5.00 12.00
21 David Njoku/99
22 O.J. Howard/49 6.00 15.00
23 Evan Engram/99 EXCH 5.00 12.00
24 Mike Williams/49 8.00 20.00
25 John Ross III/49 6.00 15.00
26 JuJu Smith-Schuster/49 12.00 30.00
27 Corey Davis/49 8.00 20.00
28 Dede Westbrook/99 4.00 10.00
29 Curtis Samuel/49 6.00 15.00
30 Amara Darboh/49 5.00 12.00
31 Carlos Henderson/49 5.00 12.00
32 Zay Jones/99 5.00 12.00
33 Cooper Kupp/49 8.00 20.00
34 Josh Reynolds/49 5.00 12.00
35 ArDarius Stewart/49 5.00 12.00
36 Chris Godwin/61 6.00 15.00
37 Taywan Taylor/99 4.00 10.00
38 Kenny Golladay/99 6.00 15.00
39 Mack Hollins/99 4.00 10.00
40 Jabrill Peppers/99 6.00 15.00
41 T.J. Watt/99 12.00 30.00
42 Aaron Jones/99 10.00 25.00

2017 Select Prime Selections Signatures Prizm Prime
1 Mitchell Trubisky 75.00 150.00
2 Deshaun Watson 150.00 250.00
4 Patrick Mahomes II 250.00 500.00
5 Nathan Peterman 8.00 20.00
6 R. Joshua Dobbs 8.00 20.00
7 C.J. Beathard 6.00 15.00
8 Dalvin Cook 30.00 60.00
9 Kareem Hunt 12.00 30.00
10 Leonard Fournette 50.00 100.00
11 Christian McCaffrey 40.00 80.00
12 Alvin Kamara 50.00 100.00
13 Samaje Perine 6.00 15.00
14 Jamaal Williams 12.00 30.00
15 D'Onta Foreman 8.00 20.00
16 O.J. Howard 8.00 20.00
17 Evan Engram 8.00 20.00
18 Corey Davis 10.00 25.00
19 Kenny Golladay 10.00 25.00
20 Mike Williams 10.00 25.00
21 John Ross III 8.00 20.00
22 Zay Jones 8.00 20.00
23 Cooper Kupp 10.00 25.00
24 Jabrill Peppers 10.00 25.00
25 Ryan Switzer 8.00 20.00

2017 Select Rookie Signature Memorabilia Prizm
1 Mitchell Trubisky/49 50.00 100.00
2 Patrick Mahomes II/99 150.00 300.00
3 Deshaun Watson/49 100.00 200.00
4 DeShone Kizer/99 EXCH 4.00 10.00
5 Nathan Peterman/199 4.00 10.00
6 Davis Webb/199 3.00 8.00
7 R. Joshua Dobbs/99 5.00 12.00
8 C.J. Beathard/199 3.00 8.00
9 Leonard Fournette/49 15.00 40.00
10 Christian McCaffrey/199 12.00 30.00
11 Dalvin Cook/199 10.00 25.00
12 Joe Mixon/99 8.00 20.00
13 Alvin Kamara/199 15.00 40.00
14 Marlon Mack/199 5.00 12.00
15 Samaje Perine/199 3.00 8.00
16 Wayne Gallman/199 4.00 10.00
17 Kareem Hunt/199 6.00 15.00
18 D'Onta Foreman/199 4.00 10.00
19 James Conner/199 6.00 15.00
20 Jamaal Williams/199 3.00 8.00
21 David Njoku/99
22 O.J. Howard/199 4.00 10.00
23 Evan Engram/199 EXCH 4.00 10.00
24 Mike Williams/99 6.00 15.00
25 John Ross III/199 4.00 10.00
26 JuJu Smith-Schuster/199 8.00 20.00
27 Corey Davis/199 5.00 12.00
28 Dede Westbrook/199 3.00 8.00
29 Curtis Samuel/199 4.00 10.00
30 Amara Darboh/199 3.00 8.00
31 Carlos Henderson/199 3.00 8.00
32 Zay Jones/199 4.00 10.00
33 Cooper Kupp/99 6.00 15.00
34 Josh Reynolds/99 4.00 10.00
35 ArDarius Stewart/199 3.00 8.00
36 Chris Godwin/49 6.00 15.00
37 Taywan Taylor/199 3.00 8.00
38 Kenny Golladay/199 5.00 12.00
39 Mack Hollins/199 3.00 8.00
40 Jabrill Peppers/199 5.00 12.00
41 T.J. Watt/199 10.00 25.00
42 Aaron Jones/199 8.00 20.00

2017 Select Rookie Signatures Prizm
1 Adam Shaheen/199 2.50 6.00
2 Adoree' Jackson/199
3 Brad Kaaya/199 2.50 6.00
4 Brian Hill/199 2.50 6.00
5 Chris Carson/199 4.00 10.00
6 Cordrea Tankersley/199
8 Donnel Pumphrey/199 3.00 8.00
9 Haason Reddick/199 2.50 6.00
10 Jabrill Peppers/199 5.00 12.00
11 Jake Butt/199 3.00 8.00
12 Jamal Adams/199 2.50 6.00
13 Jonathan Allen/199 3.00 8.00
14 Malik Hooker/199
15 Marlon Humphrey/199 2.50 6.00
16 Matt Breida/199 4.00 10.00
17 Ryan Switzer/199 3.00 8.00
18 Sidney Jones/199 2.50 6.00
19 Solomon Thomas/199 2.50 6.00
20 Stacy Coley/199 2.50 6.00
21 T.J. Watt/199 10.00 25.00
22 Taco Charlton/199 2.50 6.00
23 Derek Barnett/199
24 Malik McDowell/199 2.50 6.00
25 Matthew Dayes/199 2.50 6.00
26 Alvin Kamara/199 10.00 25.00
27 C.J. Beathard/199 2.50 6.00
28 Christian McCaffrey/49 10.00 25.00
29 Corey Davis/199 4.00 10.00
30 Dalvin Cook/99 10.00 25.00
31 Dede Westbrook/149 2.50 6.00
32 Deshaun Watson/25 100.00 200.00
33 Evan Engram/99 EXCH 4.00 10.00
34 John Ross III/99 4.00 10.00
35 Kareem Hunt/149 12.00 30.00
36 Leonard Fournette/25 15.00 40.00
37 Mike Williams/25 8.00 20.00
38 Mitchell Trubisky/25 60.00 125.00
39 Nathan Peterman/199 3.00 8.00
40 Patrick Mahomes II/25 150.00 300.00

2017 Select Rookie Signatures Prizm Light Blue
*L. BLUE/49: .6X TO 1.5X BASIC AU/149-199
*L. BLUE/25: .8X TO 2X BASIC AU/149-199
*L. BLUE/25: .6X TO 1.5X BASIC AU/99
*L. BLUE/15: 1X TO 2.5X BASIC AU/149-199
*L. BLUE/15: .8X TO 8X BASIC AU/99
*L. BLUE/15: .6X TO 1.5X BASIC AU/49
*L. BLUE/15: .5X TO 1.2X BASIC AU/25
37 Mike Williams/15 10.00 25.00
40 Patrick Mahomes II/15 200.00 400.00

2017 Select Rookie Signatures Prizm Tie Dye
*TIE DYE/25: .8X TO 2X BASIC AU/149-199
*TIE DYE/15: 1X TO 2.5X BASIC AU/149-199
*DIE CUT HAS SAME PRINT RUN AS REG. TIE DYE

2017 Select Signature Memorabilia Prizm
*PURPLE/49: .5X TO 1.2X BASIC JSY AU/99
*PURPLE/25: .5X TO 1.2X BASIC JSY AU/49
*PURPLE/15-20: .5X TO 1.2X BASIC JSY AU/25
*PURPLE/15-20: .4X TO 1X BASIC JSY AU/15
*TIE DYE/25: .6X TO 1.5X BASIC JSY AU/99
*TIE DYE/15-20: .8X TO 2X BASIC JSY AU/99
*TIE DYE/15-20: .6X TO 1.5X BASIC JSY AU/49
*TIE DYE/15-20: .5X TO 1.2X BASIC JSY AU/25
1 Geno Atkins/99 5.00 12.00
2 A.J. Green/15 15.00 40.00
3 Tyler Boyd/99 5.00 12.00
5 Priest Holmes/15 10.00 25.00
6 Aqib Talib/15 10.00 25.00
7 Trevor Siemian/15 10.00 25.00
8 Emmanuel Sanders/15 15.00 40.00
9 Andy Janovich/99 5.00 12.00
11 Ezekiel Elliott/15 40.00 80.00
12 Cole Beasley/25 12.00 30.00
13 Dan Bailey/99 10.00 25.00
14 Jaylon Smith/99 5.00 12.00
15 Zack Martin/99 5.00 12.00
16 Kiko Alonso/99 5.00 12.00
17 Jay Cutler/15 10.00 25.00
18 Julius Thomas/99 5.00 12.00
19 Darren Woodson/15 12.00 30.00
20 Joe Theismann/15 15.00 40.00
22 Mike Singletary/25 12.00 30.00
23 Mike Evans/15 12.00 30.00
24 Morten Andersen/99 5.00 12.00
25 Brett Keisel/99 5.00 12.00
26 Edgerrin James/20 12.00 30.00
27 Steve Largent/15 15.00 40.00
28 Len Dawson/15 15.00 40.00
29 Terrell Suggs/15 25.00 50.00
30 Jordy Nelson/15 12.00 30.00
31 Greg Olsen/25 10.00 25.00
32 Howie Long/15 15.00 40.00
33 Jack Doyle/99 5.00 12.00
34 Tevin Coleman/99 6.00 15.00
36 Michael Bennett/99 5.00 12.00
37 Thomas Rawls/25 8.00 20.00
38 Carlos Hyde/99 5.00 12.00
41 Clay Matthews/15 12.00 30.00
42 Aaron Ripkowski/15 15.00 40.00
43 Drew Bledsoe/15 50.00 100.00
45 Earl Thomas III/25 10.00 25.00
46 Jordan Howard/99 8.00 20.00
47 Sterling Shepard/99 6.00 15.00
48 Tyreek Hill/49 10.00 25.00
49 Heath Miller/25 8.00 20.00
51 Hines Ward/15 15.00 40.00
52 Tyler Lockett/99 6.00 15.00
53 Derek Carr/15 15.00 40.00
55 Jim Plunkett/25 10.00 25.00
56 Hunter Henry/99 5.00 12.00
57 Roger Craig/99 6.00 15.00
58 David Johnson/15 15.00 40.00

2017 Select Signatures Prizm
*L. BLUE/49: .6X TO 1.5X BASIC AU/149-199
*L. BLUE/25: .8X TO 2X BASIC AU/149-199
*L. BLUE/15: 1X TO 2.5X BASIC AU/149-199
*L. BLUE/15: .8X TO 2X BASIC AU/93-129
*L. BLUE/15: .6X TO 1.5X BASIC AU/45-49
*L. BLUE/15: .5X TO 1.2X BASIC AU/25
*L. BLUE/15: .4X TO 1X BASIC AU/15
*TIE DYE/25: .8X TO 2X BASIC AU/149-199
*TIE DYE/15: 1X TO 2.5X BASIC AU/149-199
1 Sterling Shepard/199 3.00 8.00
2 Jacoby Brissett/199 2.50 6.00
3 Sean Davis/199 2.50 6.00
4 Zach Ertz/25 6.00 15.00
5 Delanie Walker/199 2.50 6.00
6 Isaiah Crowell/199 2.50 6.00
7 Vernon Hargreaves III/199 2.50 6.00
8 Maurkice Pouncey/199 6.00 15.00
9 Fletcher Cox/99 6.00 15.00
10 Gilbert Brown/199 2.50 6.00
11 John Kuhn/199 2.50 6.00
12 Tyler Matakevich/199 2.50 6.00
13 Thomas Rawls/99 3.00 8.00
14 Adam Thielen/199 20.00 40.00
15 Mike Glennon/25 6.00 15.00
16 Jalen Richard/199 2.50 6.00
17 Dick Anderson/149 2.50 6.00
18 Melvin Ingram/199 2.50 6.00
19 Rishard Matthews/199 2.50 6.00
20 Geno Atkins/199 2.50 6.00
21 LeGarrette Blount/99 10.00 25.00
22 Jaylon Smith/199 5.00 12.00
23 Jonathan Stewart/99 3.00 8.00
24 Mike Shanahan/25 6.00 15.00
25 Jack Youngblood/99 8.00 20.00
26 Robby Anderson/199 2.50 6.00
27 Eric Weddle/49 8.00 20.00
28 Chris Spielman/49 12.00 30.00
29 Andre Reed/25 6.00 15.00
30 Duke Johnson/199 2.50 6.00
31 LaVar Arrington/99 6.00 15.00
32 Louis Lipps/194 2.50 6.00
33 Kabeer Gbaja-Biamila/149 2.50 6.00
34 Ozzie Newsome/25 6.00 15.00
35 Jordan Matthews/15 6.00 15.00
36 Mel Renfro/199 2.50 6.00
37 Chad Pennington/199 2.50 6.00
38 Bert Jones/199 2.50 6.00
39 Kellen Winslow/198 3.00 8.00
40 Jason Witten/15 EXCH 30.00 60.00
41 Billy Cannon/182 5.00 12.00
42 Paul Hornung/25 8.00 20.00
43 Rickey Jackson/155 2.50 6.00
44 Jeremy Shockey/49 4.00 10.00
45 Steve Tasker/155 2.50 6.00
46 Jack Conklin/113 4.00 10.00
47 Mike Holmgren/25 15.00 40.00
48 Ray Guy/129 2.50 6.00
49 Pepper Johnson/49 4.00 10.00
50 Mark Gastineau/45 4.00 10.00
51 Vince Ferragamo/93 8.00 20.00
52 Thurman Thomas/25 6.00 15.00
55 Taylor Gabriel/149 2.50 6.00
56 Clay Matthews Jr./99 3.00 8.00
57 Jerome Bettis/15 30.00 60.00
58 Jay Novacek/99 6.00 15.00
60 Antonio Brown/15 40.00 80.00

2017 Select Sparks Materials Prizm
1 David Njoku 3.00 8.00
2 Mitchell Trubisky 8.00 20.00
3 O.J. Howard 3.00 8.00
4 Deshaun Watson 10.00 25.00
5 DeShone Kizer 2.50 6.00
6 Leonard Fournette 8.00 20.00
7 Christian McCaffrey 6.00 15.00
8 Dalvin Cook 5.00 12.00
9 Joe Mixon 5.00 12.00
10 Alvin Kamara 10.00 25.00
11 Kareem Hunt 6.00 15.00
12 D'Onta Foreman 3.00 8.00
13 Evan Engram 3.00 8.00
14 Mike Williams 4.00 10.00
15 Corey Davis 5.00 12.00
16 Zay Jones 3.00 8.00
17 Cooper Kupp 4.00 10.00
18 Chris Godwin 3.00 8.00
19 Taywan Taylor 2.50 6.00
20 Kenny Golladay 4.00 10.00
21 Matthew Stafford 3.00 8.00
22 Kirk Cousins 4.00 10.00
23 Jordy Nelson 3.00 8.00
24 Marcus Mariota 4.00 10.00
25 Russell Wilson 5.00 12.00
26 Carlos Hyde 2.50 6.00
27 Blake Bortles 2.50 6.00
28 Frank Gore 3.00 8.00
29 Jamaal Charles 3.00 8.00
30 Thomas Rawls 2.50 6.00
31 Jameis Winston 3.00 8.00
32 Richard Sherman 4.00 10.00
33 Golden Tate III 2.50 6.00
34 C.J. Anderson 3.00 8.00
35 Carson Wentz 5.00 12.00
36 Kenyan Drake 2.50 6.00
37 Todd Gurley II 4.00 10.00
38 David Johnson 4.00 10.00
39 DeVante Parker 3.00 8.00
40 Devonta Freeman 3.00 8.00

2017 Select Swatches Prizm
*COPPER/75-99: .5X TO 1.2X BASIC JSY/199
*COPPER/75-99: .4X TO 1X BASIC JSY/99
*COPPER/49: .6X TO 1.5X BASIC JSY/199
*COPPER/49: .5X TO 1.2X BASIC JSY/99
*TIE DYE/25: .8X TO 2X BASIC JSY/199
*TIE DYE/25: .6X TO 1.5X BASIC JSY/99
1 ArDarius Stewart/99 2.50 6.00
2 C.J. Beathard/199 2.00 5.00
3 David Njoku/199 2.50 6.00
4 Davis Webb/99 2.50 6.00
5 Joe Williams/99 2.50 6.00
6 Josh Reynolds/99 2.50 6.00
7 Marlon Mack/99 4.00 10.00
8 Nathan Peterman/99 3.00 8.00
9 Samaje Perine/199 2.00 5.00
10 Jadeveon Clowney/199 2.00 5.00
11 Devin Funchess/199 2.00 5.00
12 Davante Adams/199 2.50 6.00
13 Mike Evans/199 2.50 6.00
14 Marshawn Lynch/199 2.50 6.00
15 Jarvis Landry/199 2.50 6.00
16 Marqise Lee/199 2.00 5.00
17 Khalil Mack/199 3.00 8.00
18 Paul Richardson/99 2.50 6.00
19 Keenan Allen/199 2.50 6.00
20 Tavon Austin/99 2.50 6.00
21 DeAndre Hopkins/199 2.50 6.00
22 Ameer Abdullah/99 2.50 6.00
23 Nelson Agholor/199 2.00 5.00
24 Buck Allen/99 2.50 6.00
25 Tevin Coleman/99 3.00 8.00
26 Jamison Crowder/199 2.00 5.00
27 Stefon Diggs/199 2.50 6.00
28 Melvin Gordon/199 2.50 6.00
29 Ty Montgomery/199 2.00 5.00
30 Joey Bosa/199 3.00 8.00
31 Josh Doctson/199 2.00 5.00
32 Ezekiel Elliott/199 4.00 10.00
33 Dak Prescott/99 4.00 10.00
34 Will Fuller V/199 2.00 5.00
35 Jared Goff/199 3.00 8.00
36 Derrick Henry/199 2.50 6.00
37 Hunter Henry/99 2.50 6.00
38 Jordan Howard/199 3.00 8.00
39 Malcolm Mitchell/99 3.00 8.00
40 Paul Perkins/99 2.50 6.00
41 Sterling Shepard/199 2.50 6.00
42 Wendell Smallwood/99 2.50 6.00
43 Michael Thomas/199 3.00 8.00
44 Doug Baldwin/99 3.00 8.00
45 Matt Ryan/199 2.50 6.00
46 DeMarco Murray/99 3.00 8.00
47 Robert Kelley/99 2.50 6.00
48 Danny Woodhead/99 3.00 8.00
49 Tyler Lockett/99 3.00 8.00
50 Earl Thomas III/199 2.50 6.00
51 Thomas Rawls/99 2.50 6.00
52 Latavius Murray/199 2.00 5.00
53 Luke Kuechly/199 2.50 6.00
54 Jamaal Charles/199 2.50 6.00
55 Isaiah Crowell/199 2.00 5.00
56 Tom Brady/99 10.00 25.00
57 Aaron Rodgers/99 8.00 20.00
58 Julio Jones/99 4.00 10.00

2018 Select
1 Ronald Jones II RC .60 1.50
2 Quenton Nelson RC .50 1.25
3 Nyheim Hines RC .40 1.00
4 Andrew Luck .40 1.00
5 Darius Leonard RC .75 2.00
6 Deon Cain RC .40 1.00
7 Jordan Wilkins RC .40 1.00
8 James Washington RC .60 1.50
9 Jaylen Samuels RC .40 1.00
10 Antonio Brown .30 .75
11 Ben Roethlisberger .30 .75
12 Mason Rudolph RC .75 2.00
13 Kerryon Johnson RC .50 1.25
14 Kyle Lauletta RC .50 1.25
15 Lorenzo Carter RC .30 .75
16 Odell Beckham Jr. .30 .75
17 Saquon Barkley RC 4.00 10.00
18 Sam Darnold RC 2.00 5.00
19 Adrian Peterson .30 .75
20 Derrius Guice RC .60 1.50
21 Dallas Goedert RC .40 1.00
22 Carson Wentz .40 1.00
23 Josh Adams RC .60 1.50
24 Josh Allen RC 1.25 3.00
25 LeSean McCoy .30 .75
26 Tremaine Edmunds RC .60 1.50
27 Todd Gurley II .30 .75
28 Jared Goff .30 .75
29 Antonio Callaway RC .40 1.00
30 Baker Mayfield RC 4.00 10.00
31 Denzel Ward RC .75 2.00
32 Myles Garrett .30 .75
33 Nick Chubb RC 1.00 2.50
34 Dante Pettis RC .50 1.25
35 Fred Warner .20 .50
36 Jimmy Garoppolo .40 1.00
37 Khalil Mack .30 .75
38 Anthony Miller RC .50 1.25
39 Roquan Smith RC 1.00 2.50
40 Tre'Quan Smith RC .50 1.25
41 Michael Thomas .30 .75
42 Alvin Kamara .25 .60
43 Drew Brees .30 .75
44 Rashaad Penny RC .50 1.25
45 Will Dissly RC .40 1.00
46 Russell Wilson .40 1.00
47 Derek Carr .30 .75
48 Jason Sanders RC .30 .75
49 Kalen Ballage RC .40 1.00
50 Ryan Tannehill .25 .60
51 Minkah Fitzpatrick RC .60 1.50
52 Mike Gesicki RC .40 1.00
53 Kirk Cousins .30 .75
54 Julio Jones .30 .75
55 Ito Smith RC .40 1.00
56 Devonta Freeman .25 .60
57 Calvin Ridley RC .75 2.00
58 Matt Ryan .25 .60
59 Ronnie Harrison RC .40 1.00
60 D.J. Chark Jr. RC .40 1.00
61 Jalen Ramsey .25 .60
62 Josh Rosen RC 1.00 2.50
63 David Johnson .30 .75
64 Chase Edmonds RC .30 .75
65 Christian Kirk RC .50 1.25
66 Patrick Mahomes II 1.50 4.00
67 Jaleel Scott RC .30 .75
68 Hayden Hurst RC .40 1.00
69 Kenny Young RC .30 .75
70 Lamar Jackson RC 2.00 5.00
71 Mark Andrews RC .50 1.25
72 Jordan Thomas RC .40 1.00
73 Keke Coutee RC .40 1.00
74 Deshaun Watson .40 1.00
75 Brennan Scarlett RC .30 .75
76 Courtland Sutton RC .50 1.25
77 DaeSean Hamilton RC .40 1.00
78 Bradley Chubb RC .50 1.25
79 Phillip Lindsay RC 1.25 3.00
80 Royce Freeman RC .40 1.00
81 Von Miller .25 .60
82 Cam Newton .30 .75
83 Christian McCaffrey .30 .75
84 D.J. Moore RC .60 1.50
85 Donte Jackson RC .50 1.25
86 Tom Brady .75 2.00
87 Sony Michel RC 1.00 2.50
88 Andy Dalton .25 .60
89 Jessie Bates RC .50 1.25
90 Mark Walton RC .40 1.00
91 Marcus Mariota .30 .75
92 Leighton Vander Esch RC 1.00 2.50
93 Ezekiel Elliott .40 1.00
94 Michael Gallup RC .60 1.50
95 Mike White RC .40 1.00
96 J'Mon Moore RC .30 .75
97 Marquez Valdes-Scantling RC .40 1.00
98 Aaron Rodgers .60 1.50
99 Derwin James RC .60 1.50
100 Philip Rivers .30 .75
101 Shaquem Griffin RC .75 2.00
102 Terrell Edmunds RC 1.50 4.00
103 Von Miller .40 1.00
104 Patrick Mahomes II 2.50 6.00
105 Saquon Barkley 6.00 15.00
106 Drew Brees .50 1.25
107 Sam Darnold 3.00 8.00
108 Tyreek Hill .50 1.25
109 Carson Wentz .60 1.50
110 James Conner .50 1.25
111 Aaron Donald .50 1.25
112 Matt Ryan .40 1.00
113 Khalil Mack .50 1.25
114 Derek Carr .50 1.25
115 Melvin Gordon III .40 1.00
116 Julio Jones .50 1.25
117 Adam Thielen .50 1.25
118 Harrison Smith .50 1.25
119 J.J. Watt .50 1.25
120 Christian McCaffrey .50 1.25
121 Ito Smith .60 1.50
122 Jerry Rice .75 2.00
123 Alvin Kamara .40 1.00
124 Brett Favre 1.00 2.50
125 Cam Newton .50 1.25
126 Steven Jackson .40 1.00
127 Keyshawn Johnson .40 1.00
128 Todd Gurley II .50 1.25
129 Deshaun Watson .60 1.50
130 Russell Wilson .60 1.50
131 Ryan Fitzpatrick .30 .75
132 Jared Goff .50 1.25
133 DeAndre Hopkins .40 1.00
134 Jarvis Landry .40 1.00
135 Michael Thomas .50 1.25
136 Calvin Ridley 1.25 3.00
137 D.J. Moore 1.00 2.50
138 Josh Rosen 1.50 4.00
139 Josh Allen 2.00 5.00
140 Kerryon Johnson .75 2.00
141 Phillip Lindsay 2.00 5.00
142 Courtland Sutton .75 2.00
143 Baker Mayfield 8.00 20.00
144 Royce Freeman .60 1.50
145 Derrius Guice 1.00 2.50
146 Stefon Diggs .40 1.00
147 Tre'Quan Smith .75 2.00
148 Marquez Valdes-Scantling .60 1.50
149 Lamar Jackson 3.00 8.00
150 Sony Michel 1.50 4.00
151 Christian Kirk .75 2.00
152 Nick Chubb 1.50 4.00
153 Mason Rudolph 1.25 3.00
154 Rashaad Penny .75 2.00
155 Dante Pettis .75 2.00
156 Aaron Rodgers 1.00 2.50
157 Justin Jackson RC .60 1.50
158 Adrian Peterson .50 1.25
159 Joe Mixon .60 1.50
160 Keke Coutee .60 1.50
161 Antonio Brown .50 1.25
162 Odell Beckham Jr. .50 1.25
163 Myles Garrett .50 1.25
164 Matthew Stafford .40 1.00
165 Travis Kelce .50 1.25
166 Tom Brady 1.25 3.00
167 Kalen Ballage .60 1.50
168 Marcus Mariota .50 1.25
169 Corey Davis .60 1.50
170 Jalen Ramsey .40 1.00
171 Leonard Fournette .50 1.25
172 Andrew Luck .60 1.50
173 Mark Walton .40 1.00
174 Kirk Cousins .50 1.25
175 Alex Smith .40 1.00
176 James Washington 1.00 2.50
177 Anthony Miller .75 2.00
178 Bradley Chubb .75 2.00
179 Kyle Lauletta .75 2.00
180 Michael Gallup 1.00 2.50
181 D.J. Chark Jr. .60 1.50
182 Ronald Jones II 1.00 2.50
183 Calais Campbell .30 .75
184 Clay Matthews .40 1.00
185 Troy Aikman .60 1.50
186 Eli Manning .40 1.00
187 Peyton Manning 1.00 2.50
188 Jimmy Garoppolo .60 1.50
189 Barry Sanders .75 2.00
190 Ben Roethlisberger .50 1.25
191 Mike White .40 1.00
192 Mitchell Trubisky .50 1.25
193 Alex Collins .30 .75
194 David Johnson .50 1.25
195 Roquan Smith 1.50 4.00
196 JuJu Smith-Schuster .50 1.25
197 Donte Jackson .50 1.25
198 Bo Jackson .60 1.50
199 Nyheim Hines .60 1.50
200 Jaylen Samuels 1.00 2.50
201 Tom Brady 2.00 5.00
202 Saquon Barkley 10.00 25.00
203 Sam Darnold 5.00 12.00
204 Baker Mayfield 20.00 50.00
205 Lamar Jackson 5.00 12.00
206 Josh Rosen 2.50 6.00
207 Josh Allen 3.00 8.00
208 D.J. Moore 1.50 4.00
209 Calvin Ridley 2.00 5.00
210 Aaron Rodgers 1.50 4.00
211 T.J. Watt .60 1.50
212 Tyreek Hill .75 2.00
213 Xavier Rhodes .50 1.25
214 Brandin Cooks .60 1.50
215 Matt Breida RC 1.00 2.50
216 Nick Mullens RC 2.50 6.00
217 Cameron Jordan .50 1.25
218 Ezekiel Elliott 1.00 2.50
219 Dak Prescott .75 2.00
220 Gus Edwards RC 2.00 5.00
221 Jameis Winston .60 1.50
222 Derrick Henry .75 2.00
223 Jordy Nelson .60 1.50
224 Phillip Lindsay 3.00 8.00
225 Kerryon Johnson 1.25 3.00
226 Sony Michel 2.50 6.00
227 Bradley Chubb 1.25 3.00
228 Le'Veon Bell .60 1.50
229 Sammy Watkins .75 2.00
230 Marshon Lattimore .50 1.25
231 Deshaun Watson 1.00 2.50
232 Patrick Mahomes II 4.00 10.00
233 Dalvin Cook .60 1.50
234 Leonard Fournette .75 2.00
235 Larry Fitzgerald .60 1.50
236 Xavien Howard .50 1.25
237 Brian Dawkins .75 2.00
238 Barry Sanders 1.25 3.00
239 Emmitt Smith 1.25 3.00
240 Terrell Davis .60 1.50
241 Justin Tucker .50 1.25
242 Pat McAfee .60 1.50
243 Evan Engram .50 1.25
244 Tony Gonzalez .60 1.50
245 Marshawn Lynch .60 1.50
246 Chris Hogan .50 1.25
247 JuJu Smith-Schuster .75 2.00
248 Josh Gordon .50 1.25
249 Chris Godwin .75 2.00
250 Kenny Golladay .75 2.00
251 Davante Adams .60 1.50
252 Tyler Lockett .60 1.50
253 Roquan Smith 2.50 6.00
254 Shaquem Griffin 1.25 3.00
255 Joey Bosa .75 2.00
256 Jordan Howard .75 2.00
257 Austin Ekeler .50 1.25
258 Aaron Jones .60 1.50
259 Keenan Allen .60 1.50
260 Derwin James 1.50 4.00
261 Terrell Edmunds 2.50 6.00
262 Zach Ertz .60 1.50
263 Jarvis Landry .60 1.50
264 DeAndre Hopkins .60 1.50
265 Sterling Shepard .60 1.50
266 Mason Rudolph 2.00 5.00
267 James Washington 1.50 4.00
268 Michael Gallup 1.50 4.00
269 Derrius Guice 1.50 4.00
270 Christian Kirk 1.25 3.00
271 Anthony Miller 1.25 3.00
272 Kyle Lauletta 1.25 3.00
273 Brett Favre 1.50 4.00
274 Randy Moss .60 1.50
275 John Riggins .60 1.50
276 Steve Largent .75 2.00
277 A.J. Green .75 2.00
278 Andy Dalton .60 1.50
279 T.Y. Hilton .60 1.50
280 Philip Rivers .75 2.00
281 Golden Tate III .50 1.25
282 Jerome Bettis .75 2.00
283 Len Dawson .75 2.00
284 Stefon Diggs .60 1.50
285 Rob Gronkowski .75 2.00
286 Robert Foster RC .75 2.00
287 Jamal Adams .60 1.50
288 Luke Kuechly .60 1.50
289 Demaryius Thomas .60 1.50
290 Darius Leonard 1.25 3.00
291 Case Keenum .60 1.50
292 Ray Lewis .75 2.00
293 Eddie George .60 1.50
294 Lawrence Taylor .75 2.00
295 Steve Young 1.00 2.50
296 Dante Hall .50 1.25
297 Nick Chubb 1.50 4.00
298 Odell Beckham Jr. .75 2.00
299 Harrison Butker .50 1.25
300 Brett Maher .50 1.25
301A QB1 50.00 100.00
302A QB2 40.00 80.00
303A QB3 12.00 30.00
304A QB4 12.00 30.00
305A QB5 12.00 30.00
306A RB1 15.00 40.00
307A RB2 10.00 25.00
308A RB3 10.00 25.00
309A RB4 10.00 25.00
310A RB5 10.00 25.00
311A WR1 25.00 50.00
312A WR2 8.00 20.00
313A WR3 8.00 20.00
314A WR4 8.00 20.00
315A WR5 8.00 20.00
316A TE1 8.00 20.00
317A TE2 8.00 20.00
318A DEF1 12.00 30.00
319A DEF2 12.00 30.00
320A DEF3 10.00 25.00
321A XRC AU1 125.00 250.00
322A XRC AU2 100.00 200.00
323A XRC AU3 60.00 125.00
324A XRC AU4 60.00 125.00
325A XRC AU5 60.00 15.00

2018 Select Prizm Blue
*VETS/175: 2X TO 5X BASIC CARDS
*ROOK/175: 1.2X TO 3X BASIC CARDS
30 Baker Mayfield 25.00 60.00

2018 Select Prizm Copper
*VETS/75: 1.5X TO 4X BASIC CARDS
*ROOK/75: 1X TO 2.5X BASIC CARDS
30 Baker Mayfield [illegible]

2018 Select Prizm Light Blue
*VETS/99: 1.5X TO 4X BASIC CARDS
*ROOK/99: 1X TO 2.5X BASIC CARDS
143 Baker Mayfield 30.00 80.00

2018 Select Prizm Maroon
*VETS/99: 2.5X TO 6X BASIC CARDS
*ROOK/99: 1.5X TO 4X BASIC CARDS
30 Baker Mayfield 30.00 80.00

2018 Select Prizm Neon Green
*VETS/49: 2X TO 5X BASIC CARDS
*ROOK/49: 1.2X TO 3X BASIC CARDS
104 Patrick Mahomes II 20.00 50.00
107 Sam Darnold 15.00 40.00
139 Josh Allen 12.00 30.00
141 Phillip Lindsay 12.00 30.00
143 Baker Mayfield 40.00 100.00

2018 Select Prizm Orange
*VETS/49: 3X TO 8X BASIC CARDS
*ROOK/49: 2X TO 5X BASIC CARDS
18 Sam Darnold 15.00 40.00
30 Baker Mayfield 40.00 100.00
66 Patrick Mahomes II 20.00 50.00
79 Phillip Lindsay 12.00 30.00
92 Leighton Vander Esch 12.00 30.00

2018 Select Prizm Purple
*VETS/75: 1.5X TO 4X BASIC CARDS
*ROOK/75: 1X TO 2.5X BASIC CARDS
143 Baker Mayfield 30.00 80.00

2018 Select Prizm Red
*VETS/49: 1.2 TO 3X BASIC CARDS
*ROOK/49: .8X TO 2X BASIC CARDS
203 Sam Darnold 15.00 40.00
204 Baker Mayfield 25.00 60.00
207 Josh Allen 12.00 30.00
224 Phillip Lindsay 12.00 30.00
232 Patrick Mahomes II 20.00 50.00

2018 Select Prizm Silver
*VETS (1-100): 1.5X TO 4X BASIC CARDS
*ROOKIES: 1X TO 2.5X BASIC CARDS
*VETS (101-200): 1X TO 2.5X BASIC CARDS
*ROOKIES: .6X TO 1.5X BASIC CARDS
*VETS (201-300): .6X TO 1.5X BASIC CARDS
*ROOKIES: .4X TO 1X BASIC CARDS
30 Baker Mayfield 12.00 30.00
143 Baker Mayfield 20.00 50.00
204 Baker Mayfield 20.00 50.00

2018 Select Prizm Tie Dye
*VETS (1-100): 4X TO 6X BASIC CARDS
*ROOKIES: 2.5X TO 6X BASIC CARDS
*VETS (101-200): 2.5X TO 6X BASIC CARDS
*ROOKIES: 1.5X TO 4X BASIC CARDS
*VETS (201-300): 1.5 TO 4X BASIC CARDS
*ROOKIES: 1X TO 2.5X BASIC CARDS
12 Mason Rudolph 12.00 30.00
18 Sam Darnold 25.00 60.00
30 Baker Mayfield 125.00 250.00
66 Patrick Mahomes II 75.00 150.00
70 Lamar Jackson 25.00 50.00
79 Phillip Lindsay 15.00 40.00
86 Tom Brady 60.00 125.00
92 Leighton Vander Esch 25.00 60.00
104 Patrick Mahomes II 75.00 150.00
107 Sam Darnold 25.00 60.00
139 Josh Allen 15.00 40.00
141 Phillip Lindsay 15.00 40.00
143 Baker Mayfield 125.00 250.00
149 Lamar Jackson 25.00 50.00
153 Mason Rudolph 12.00 30.00
166 Tom Brady 60.00 125.00
201 Tom Brady 60.00 125.00
203 Sam Darnold 25.00 60.00
204 Baker Mayfield 125.00 250.00
205 Lamar Jackson 25.00 50.00
207 Josh Allen 15.00 40.00
224 Phillip Lindsay 15.00 40.00
232 Patrick Mahomes II 75.00 150.00
266 Mason Rudolph 12.00 30.00

2018 Select Prizm Tri Color
*VETS (1-100): 2X TO 5X BASIC CARDS
*ROOKIES: 1.2X TO 3X BASIC CARDS
*VETS (101-200): 1.2X TO 3X BASIC CARDS
*ROOKIES: .8X TO 2X BASIC CARDS
*VETS (201-300): .8X TO 2X BASIC CARDS
*ROOKIES: .5X TO 1.2X BASIC CARDS
30 Baker Mayfield 25.00 60.00
143 Baker Mayfield 25.00 60.00
204 Baker Mayfield 30.00 80.00

2018 Select Prizm White
*VETS/75: 2.5X TO 6X BASIC CARDS
*ROOK/75: 1.5X TO 4X BASIC CARDS
30 Baker Mayfield 30.00 80.00

2018 Select Jumbo Rookie Signature Swatches Prizm
1 Baker Mayfield/35 125.00 250.00
2 Sam Darnold/35 60.00 125.00
3 Saquon Barkley/35 EXCH 60.00 125.00
4 Josh Allen/35 50.00 100.00
5 Josh Rosen/35 15.00 40.00
6 Lamar Jackson/35 30.00 80.00
7 Calvin Ridley/49 12.00 30.00
8 Derrius Guice/49 25.00 50.00
9 Sony Michel/49 20.00 50.00
10 Christian Kirk/49 8.00 20.00
11 Nick Chubb/49 15.00 40.00
12 Mason Rudolph/49 12.00 30.00
13 Rashaad Penny/49 8.00 20.00
14 D.J. Moore/49 10.00 25.00
15 Courtland Sutton/49 8.00 20.00
16 Dante Pettis/49 8.00 20.00
17 James Washington/99 8.00 20.00
18 Ronald Jones II/49 10.00 25.00
19 Kerryon Johnson/75 20.00 50.00
20 Anthony Miller/75 6.00 15.00
21 Bradley Chubb/49 8.00 20.00
22 Royce Freeman/99 5.00 12.00
23 Kyle Lauletta/49 8.00 20.00
24 Hayden Hurst/35 6.00 15.00
25 Mike Gesicki/49 6.00 15.00
26 Michael Gallup/75 8.00 20.00
27 Nyheim Hines/99 5.00 12.00
28 Jaleel Scott/49 5.00 12.00
29 DaeSean Hamilton/49 6.00 15.00
30 Keke Coutee/99 5.00 12.00
31 Ito Smith/75 5.00 12.00
32 Kalen Ballage/49 6.00 15.00
33 Mark Walton/99 5.00 12.00
34 Mike White/35 6.00 15.00
35 D.J. Chark Jr./99 5.00 12.00
36 Jaylen Samuels/99 5.00 12.00
37 J'Mon Moore/49 5.00 12.00
38 Daurice Fountain/99 5.00 12.00
39 Marquez Valdes-Scantling/99 5.00 12.00
41 Shaquem Griffin/75 6.00 15.00
42 Derwin James/99 8.00 20.00

2018 Select Jumbo Rookie Signature Swatches Prizm Copper
*COPPER35-49: .6X TO 1.5X BASIC JSY AU/75-99
*COPPER/25: .5X TO 1.2X BASIC JSY AU/35-49
*COPPER/15: .6X TO 1.5X BASIC JSY AU/35-49
1 Baker Mayfield/15 200.00 400.00
2 Sam Darnold/15 100.00 200.00
3 Saquon Barkley/15 EXCH 100.00 200.00

2018 Select Jumbo Rookie Signature Swatches Prizm Neon Orange Pulsar
*ORANGE/23: .8X TO 2X BASIC JSY AU/75-99
*ORANGE/23: .6X TO 1.5X BASIC JSY AU/35-49
[illegible]
2 Sam Darnold 100.00 200.00
3 Saquon Barkley EXCH 100.00 200.00

2018 Select Jumbo Rookie Signature Swatches Prizm Tie Dye
*TIE DYE/25: .6X TO 1.5X BASIC JSY AU/75-99
*TIE DYE/15: .6X TO 1.5X BASIC JSY AU/35-49
1 Baker Mayfield/15 200.00 400.00
2 Sam Darnold/15 100.00 200.00
3 Saquon Barkley/15 EXCH 100.00 200.00

2018 Select Jumbo Rookie Signature Swatches Prizm White
*WHITE/75: .4X TO 1X BASIC JSY AU/75-99
*WHITE/35-49: .5X TO 1.2X BASIC JSY AU/75-99
*WHITE/35-49: .4X TO 1X BASIC JSY AU/35-49
*WHITE/25: .5X TO 1.2X BASIC JSY AU/35-49
1 Baker Mayfield/25 150.00 300.00
2 Sam Darnold/25 75.00 150.00
3 Saquon Barkley/25 EXCH 75.00 150.00

2018 Select Jumbo Rookie Swatches Prizm
1 Mike Gesicki 3.00 8.00
2 Bradley Chubb 4.00 10.00
3 Mark Walton 3.00 8.00
4 Kalen Ballage 3.00 8.00
5 Ito Smith 3.00 8.00
6 Anthony Miller 4.00 10.00
7 DaeSean Hamilton 3.00 8.00
8 Jaleel Scott 2.50 6.00
9 Nyheim Hines 3.00 8.00
10 Michael Gallup 5.00 12.00
11 D.J. Chark Jr. 3.00 8.00
12 Hayden Hurst 3.00 8.00
13 Kyle Lauletta 4.00 10.00
14 Royce Freeman 3.00 8.00
15 Mike White 3.00 8.00
16 Keke Coutee 3.00 8.00
17 Kerryon Johnson 4.00 10.00
18 Ronald Jones II 5.00 12.00
19 James Washington 5.00 12.00
20 Dante Pettis 4.00 10.00
21 Courtland Sutton 4.00 10.00
22 Josh Allen 6.00 15.00
23 Rashaad Penny 4.00 10.00
24 Mason Rudolph 5.00 12.00
25 Saquon Barkley 12.00 30.00
26 Sam Darnold 10.00 25.00
27 Baker Mayfield 15.00 40.00
28 Derrius Guice 5.00 12.00
29 Calvin Ridley 5.00 12.00
30 Lamar Jackson 10.00 25.00
31 Josh Rosen 6.00 15.00
32 D.J. Moore 5.00 12.00
33 Nick Chubb 5.00 12.00
34 Christian Kirk 4.00 10.00
35 Sony Michel 5.00 12.00

2018 Select Phenomenon
*PRIZM: .6X TO 1.5X BASIC INSERTS
*TIE DYE/25: 1.2X TO 3X BASIC INSERTS
1 Patrick Mahomes II 2.50 6.00
2 Tom Brady 2.00 5.00
3 Russell Wilson 1.00 2.50
4 Saquon Barkley 4.00 10.00
5 Odell Beckham Jr. .75 2.00
6 Antonio Brown .75 2.00
7 Tyreek Hill .75 2.00
8 Shaquem Griffin .75 2.00
9 Baker Mayfield 5.00 12.00
10 Jalen Ramsey .60 1.50
11 J.J. Watt .75 2.00
12 Jared Goff .75 2.00
13 Aaron Rodgers 1.50 4.00
14 Ezekiel Elliott 1.00 2.50
15 Adrian Peterson .75 2.00
16 Todd Gurley II .75 2.00
17 Cam Newton .75 2.00
18 Sony Michel 1.50 4.00
19 Drew Brees .75 2.00
20 Calvin Ridley 1.25 3.00
21 Deshaun Watson 1.00 2.50
22 Rob Gronkowski .75 2.00
23 Julio Jones .75 2.00
24 Alvin Kamara .60 1.50
25 Josh Gordon .50 1.25

2018 Select Rookie Signatures Prizm
1 Saquon Barkley/25 EXCH 100.00 200.00
2 Leighton Vander Esch/199 12.00 30.00
3 D.J. Moore/99 6.00 15.00
4 Sony Michel/49 12.00 30.00
5 Nick Chubb/75 10.00 25.00
6 Quenton Nelson/199 4.00 10.00
7 Shaquem Griffin/199 4.00 10.00
8 Josh Allen/35 40.00 80.00
9 Josh Rosen/35 20.00 50.00
10 Chad Thomas/199 2.50 6.00
11 Carlton Davis/199 3.00 8.00
12 Baker Mayfield/25 125.00 250.00
13 Jaire Alexander/199 4.00 10.00
14 Isaiah Oliver/199 2.50 6.00
15 Jordan Akins/199 2.50 6.00
16 Roquan Smith/149 8.00 20.00
17 Dallas Goedert/199 3.00 8.00
18 Joshua Jackson/149 5.00 12.00
19 John Kelly/199 3.00 8.00
20 Tremaine Edmunds/199 5.00 12.00
21 Maurice Hurst/199 3.00 8.00
22 Mark Andrews/199 4.00 10.00
23 Fred Warner/199 2.50 6.00
24 Minkah Fitzpatrick/199 5.00 12.00
25 Denzel Ward/199
26 Lorenzo Carter/199 2.50 6.00
27 Jordan Wilkins/199 3.00 8.00
28 Nick Mullens/199 8.00 20.00
29 Braxton Berrios/199 2.50 6.00
30 Gus Edwards/199
31 Justin Jackson/199 3.00 8.00
33 Derwin James/199 5.00 12.00
34 Harold Landry/199 2.50 6.00
35 Will Dissly/199 3.00 8.00
36 Luke Falk/199 3.00 8.00
37 Trey Quinn/199 2.50 6.00
38 Phillip Lindsay/199 25.00 50.00
39 Darius Leonard/199 6.00 15.00
40 Christian Kirk/75 5.00 12.00

2018 Select Rookie Signatures Prizm Light Blue
*L.BLUE/35-49: .6X TO 1.5X BASIC AU/149-199
*L.BLUE/35-49: .5X TO 1.2X BASIC AU/75-99
*L.BLUE/25: .5X TO 1.2X BASIC AU/35-49
*L.BLUE/15-20: .6X TO 1.5X BASIC AU/35-49
*L.BLUE/15-20: .5X TO 1.2X BASIC AU/25
1 Saquon Barkley/15 EXCH 150.00 300.00

2018 Select Rookie Signatures Prizm Maroon
*MAROON/75: .5X TO 1.2X BASIC AU/149-199
*MAROON/75: .4X TO 1X BASIC AU/75-99
*MAROON/35-64: .5X TO 1.2X BASIC AU/75-99
*MAROON/35-64: .4X TO 1X BASIC AU/35-49
*MAROON/25: .5X TO 1.2X BASIC AU/35-49
*MAROON/20: .5X TO 1.2X BASIC AU/25
1 Saquon Barkley/20 EXCH 150.00 300.00

2018 Select Rookie Signatures Prizm Tie Dye
*TIE DYE/25: .8X TO 2X BASIC AU/149-199
*TIE DYE/25: .6X TO 1.5X BASIC AU/75-99
*TIE DYE/15: .6X TO 1.5X BASIC AU/35-49

2018 Select Rookie Signatures Prizm Tie Dye Die Cut
[illegible]

*TIE DYE/25: .6X TO 1.5X BASIC AU/75-99
*TIE DYE/15: .6X TO 1.5X BASIC AU/35-49

2018 Select Select Swatches Prizm

*COPPER/99: .5X TO 1.2X BASIC JSY/125-199
*COPPER/50: .6X TO 1.5X BASIC JSY/125-199
*TIE DYE/25: .8X TO 2X BASIC JSY/125-199
*WHITE/149: .4X TO 1X BASIC JSY/125-199
*WHITE/99: .5X TO 1.2X BASIC JSY/125-199
1 David Johnson/199 3.00 8.00
2 Warrick Dunn/125 2.00 5.00
3 Joe Flacco/199 2.50 6.00
4 Terrell Suggs/125 2.00 5.00
5 Saquon Barkley/199 10.00 25.00
6 Sam Darnold/199 8.00 20.00
7 Baker Mayfield/199 12.00 30.00
8 Lamar Jackson/199 8.00 20.00
9 Josh Allen/199 5.00 12.00
10 Josh Rosen/199 5.00 12.00
11 Calvin Ridley/199 4.00 10.00
12 D.J. Moore/199 4.00 10.00
13 Mason Rudolph/199 4.00 10.00
14 Sony Michel/199 4.00 10.00
15 Christian Kirk/199 3.00 8.00
16 Shaquem Griffin/199 3.00 8.00
17 Dak Prescott/199 3.00 8.00
18 Terrell Davis/125 2.50 6.00
19 Matthew Stafford/125 2.50 6.00
20 Edgerrin James/125 2.50 6.00
21 Blake Bortles/199 2.00 5.00
22 Travis Kelce/125 3.00 8.00
23 Antonio Gates/199 2.00 5.00
24 Dan Marino/199 6.00 15.00
25 Adam Thielen/125 3.00 8.00
26 Harry Carson/125 2.00 5.00
27 Quincy Enunwa/125 2.00 5.00
28 Robby Anderson/125 2.00 5.00
29 Marshawn Lynch/125 2.50 6.00
30 Alejandro Villanueva/125 2.50 6.00
31 Heath Miller/199 2.00 5.00
32 Matt Breida/125 2.50 6.00
33 Doug Baldwin/199 2.50 6.00
34 Tyler Lockett/125 2.50 6.00
35 Kurt Warner/199 2.50 6.00
36 DeSean Jackson/199 2.50 6.00
37 Jameis Winston/199 2.50 6.00
38 Derrick Henry/199 3.00 8.00
39 Chris Thompson/199 2.00 5.00
40 Carson Wentz/199 4.00 10.00
41 Marcus Mariota/125 3.00 8.00
42 Andrew Luck/125 4.00 10.00
43 Jared Goff/199 3.00 8.00
44 Deshaun Watson/199 4.00 10.00
45 James Conner/199 3.00 8.00
46 Davante Adams/199 2.50 6.00
47 Julio Jones/125 3.00 8.00
48 Patrick Chung/125 2.00 5.00
49 Michael Thomas/125 3.00 8.00
50 Alvin Kamara/125 2.50 6.00
51 DeMarcus Lawrence/194 2.00 5.00
52 Kiko Alonso/199 2.00 5.00
53 Earl Thomas III/199 2.50 6.00
54 Melvin Gordon III/125 2.50 6.00
55 Christian McCaffrey/199 3.00 8.00
56 Zach Ertz/125 2.50 6.00
57 JuJu Smith-Schuster/199 3.00 8.00
58 Mike Evans/125 2.50 6.00

2018 Select Sensations

*PRIZM: .6X TO 1.5X BASIC INSERTS
*TIE DYE/25: 1.2X TO 3X BASIC INSERTS
1 Deshaun Watson 1.00 2.50
2 Jared Goff .75 2.00
3 Patrick Mahomes II 2.00 5.00
4 Todd Gurley II .75 2.00
5 Ezekiel Elliott 1.00 2.50
6 Stefon Diggs .60 1.50
7 Tyreek Hill .75 2.00
8 JuJu Smith-Schuster .75 2.00
9 Evan Engram .50 1.25
10 Joey Bosa .75 2.00
11 Myles Garrett .75 2.00
12 T.J. Watt .60 1.50
13 Jalen Ramsey .60 1.50
14 Jamal Adams .60 1.50
15 Carson Wentz 1.00 2.50
16 Leonard Fournette .75 2.00
17 Corey Davis .60 1.50
18 Kenny Golladay .50 1.25
19 James Conner .75 2.00
20 Alvin Kamara .60 1.50
21 Michael Thomas .75 2.00
22 Cooper Kupp .60 1.50
23 Joe Mixon .60 1.50
24 Adam Thielen .75 2.00
25 Mitchell Trubisky .75 2.00

2018 Select Snapshots

*PRIZM: .6X TO 1.5X BASIC INSERTS
*TIE DYE/25: 1.2X TO 3X BASIC INSERTS
1 Patrick Mahomes II 2.00 5.00
2 Emmanuel Sanders .75 2.00
3 Keelan Cole .50 1.25
4 Baker Mayfield 5.00 12.00
5 Tom Brady 2.00 5.00
6 James Conner .75 2.00
7 Khalil Mack .75 2.00
8 Amari Cooper .75 2.00
9 Tyreek Hill .75 2.00
10 Calvin Ridley 1.25 3.00
11 Derwin James 1.00 2.50
12 Denzel Ward 1.25 3.00
13 Aaron Rodgers 1.50 4.00
14 Alvin Kamara .60 1.50
15 T.J. Watt .60 1.50
16 Saquon Barkley 4.00 10.00
17 J.J. Watt .75 2.00
18 Terrell Suggs .50 1.25
19 Ezekiel Elliott 1.00 2.50
20 David Johnson .75 2.00
21 Cam Newton .75 2.00
22 Christian McCaffrey .75 2.00
23 Kirk Cousins .75 2.00
24 Jared Goff .75 2.00
25 Michael Thomas .75 2.00

1995 Select Certified

The first year product from Pinnacle was offered in six card packs with a suggested retail price of $4.99/pack. The set contains 135 cards with seven checklist cards inserted at one per pack. Card fronts feature an all-foil silver black and white background with the player shot in color. The player's name is located at the bottom right. Card backs are horizontal with statistical and biographical information. Also, a NFL Super Bowl Instant Win Card was randomly inserted at a rate of one in 1,264,000 packs. Card #78 (Deion Sanders) was not issued in pack form, rather he was issued later in December '95 through a mail offering to Pinnacle direct dealers. Rookie cards include Jeff Blake, Ki-Jana Carter, Kerry Collins, Terrell Davis, Joey Galloway, Curtis Martin, Napoleon Kaufman, Rashaan Salaam, Kordell Stewert, J.J. Stokes, Rodney Thomas and Michael Westbrook. Three promo card were produced and priced below.

COMPLETE SET (135) 15.00 40.00
1 Marshall Faulk 1.50 4.00
2 Heath Shuler .20 .50
3 Garrison Hearst .40 1.00
4 Errict Rhett .20 .50
5 Jeff George .20 .50
6 Jerome Bettis .40 1.00
7 Jim Kelly .40 1.00
8 Rick Mirer .20 .50
9 Willie Davis .20 .50
10 Steve Young 1.00 2.50
11 Frik Kramer .08 .25
12 Natrone Means .20 .50
13 Jeff Blake RC 1.25 3.00
14 Neil O'Donnell .20 .50
15 Andre Rison .20 .50
16 Randall Cunningham .40 1.00
17 Emmitt Smith 2.00 5.00
18 Tim Brown .40 1.00
19 Shannon Sharpe .20 .50
20 Boomer Esiason .20 .50
21 Barry Sanders 2.00 5.00
22 Rodney Hampton .20 .50
23 Robert Brooks .40 1.00
24 Jim Everett .08 .25
25 Gary Brown .08 .25
26 Drew Bledsoe .50 1.25
27 Desmond Howard .20 .50
28 Cris Carter .40 1.00
29 Marcus Allen .40 1.00
30 Dan Marino 2.50 6.00
31 Warren Moon .20 .50
32 Dave Krieg .08 .25
33 Ben Coates .20 .50
34 Terance Mathis .20 .50
35 Mario Bates .20 .50
36 Andre Reed .20 .50
37 Dave Brown .20 .50
38 Jeff Graham .08 .25
39 Johnny Mitchell .08 .25
40 Carl Pickens .20 .50
41 Jeff Hostetler .20 .50
42 Vinny Testaverde .20 .50
43 Ricky Watters .20 .50
44 Troy Aikman 1.25 3.00
45 Byron Bam Morris .08 .25
46 John Elway 2.50 6.00
47 Junior Seau .40 1.00
48 Scott Mitchell .20 .50
49 Jerry Rice 1.25 3.00
50 Brett Favre 2.50 6.00
51 Chris Warren .20 .50
52 Chris Chandler .20 .50
53 Lorenzo White .08 .25
54 Craig Erickson .08 .25
55 Alvin Harper .08 .25
56 Steve Beuerlein .20 .50
57 Edgar Bennett .20 .50
58 Steve Bono .20 .50
59 Eric Green .08 .25
60 Jake Reed .20 .50
61 Terry Kirby .20 .50
62 Vincent Brisby .08 .25
63 Lake Dawson .20 .50
64 Torrance Small .08 .25
65 Mark Brunell .50 1.25
66 Haywood Jeffires .08 .25
67 Flipper Anderson .08 .25
68 Ronald Moore .08 .25
69 LeShon Johnson .20 .50
70 Rocket Ismail .20 .50
71 Herman Moore .40 1.00
72 Charlie Garner .40 1.00
73 Anthony Miller .20 .50
74 Greg Lloyd .20 .50
75 Michael Irvin .40 1.00
76 Stan Humphries .20 .50
77 Leroy Hoard .08 .25
78 Deion Sanders Mail Out 1.25 3.00
79 Darnay Scott .20 .50
80 Chris Miller .08 .25
81 Curtis Conway .40 1.00
82 Trent Dilfer .40 1.00
83 Bruce Smith .40 1.00
84 Reggie Brooks .20 .50
85 Frank Reich .08 .25
86 Henry Ellard .20 .50
87 Eric Metcalf .20 .50
88 Sean Gilbert .20 .50
89 Larry Centers .20 .50
90 Ricky Ervins .08 .25
91 Craig Heyward .20 .50
92 Rod Woodson .20 .50
93 Steve Walsh .08 .25
94 Fred Barnett .20 .50
95 William Floyd .20 .50
96 Harvey Williams .08 .25
97 Greg Hill .20 .50
98 Irving Fryar .20 .50
99 Kevin Williams WR .20 .50
100 Herschel Walker .20 .50
101 Sean Dawkins .20 .50
102 Michael Haynes .20 .50
103 Reggie White .40 1.00
104 Robert Smith .40 1.00
105 Todd Collins RC 2.50 6.00
106 Michael Westbrook RC .75 2.00
107 Frank Sanders RC .75 2.00
108 Christian Fauria RC .40 1.00
109 Stoney Case RC .20 .50
110 Jimmy Oliver RC .20 .50
111 Mark Bruener RC .40 1.00
112 Rodney Thomas RC .40 1.00
113 Chris T.Jones RC .20 .50
114 James A.Stewart RC .20 .50
115 Kevin Carter RC .75 2.00
116 Eric Zeier RC .75 2.00
117 Curtis Martin RC 6.00 15.00
118 James O. Stewart RC 2.00 5.00
119 Joe Aska RC .20 .50
120 Ken Dilger RC .75 2.00
121 Tyrone Wheatley RC 2.00 5.00
122 Ray Zellars RC .40 1.00
123 Kyle Brady RC .75 2.00
124 Chad May RC .20 .50
125 Napoleon Kaufman RC 2.00 5.00
126 Terrell Davis RC 5.00 12.00
127 Warren Sapp RC 2.50 6.00
128 Sherman Williams RC .20 .50
129 Kordell Stewart RC 3.00 8.00
130 Ki-Jana Carter RC .75 2.00
131 Terrell Fletcher RC .20 .50
132 Rashaan Salaam RC .40 1.00
133 J.J. Stokes RC .75 2.00
134 Kerry Collins RC 4.00 8.00
135 Joey Galloway RC 3.00 8.00
P7 Dan Marino Promo 2.00 5.00
P10 Steve Young Promo .75 2.00
P44 Troy Aikman Promo 1.00 2.50

1995 Select Certified Mirror Gold

COMPLETE SET (135) 125.00 300.00
*MIRROR GOLD STARS: 2X TO 5X HI COL.
*MIRROR GOLD RCs: 1X TO 2.5X
MIRROR GOLDS: STATED ODDS 1:5

1995 Select Certified Checklists

These cards were inserted one per pack in Select Certified and feature different members of the Quarterback Club on the card fronts with numerical checklists on the back.

COMPLETE SET (7) .60 1.50
1 Drew Bledsoe .15 .40
2 John Elway .25 .60
3 Dan Marino .25 .60
4 Brett Favre .25 .60
5 Troy Aikman .15 .40
6 Steve Young .10 .30
7 Rick Mirer .07 .20
R.Cunningham UER

1995 Select Certified Future

Randomly inserted at a rate of one in 19 packs, this 10 card set commemorates the introduction of 10 rookie players with unlimited future potential. Card fronts contain a shot of the player with his name directly underneath and the title "Certified Future" running along the right side. The background of the fronts are half blank and white and half gold. Card backs are horizontal with a brief summary on the player.

COMPLETE SET (10) 20.00 50.00
STATED ODDS 1:19
1 Ki-Jana Carter .75 2.00
2 Steve McNair 6.00 15.00
3 Kerry Collins 3.00 8.00
4 Michael Westbrook 1.25 3.00
5 Joey Galloway 3.00 8.00
6 J.J. Stokes 1.25 3.00
7 Rashaan Salaam .75 2.00
8 Tyrone Wheatley 2.00 5.00
9 Todd Collins 3.00 8.00
10 Curtis Martin 6.00 15.00

1995 Select Certified Gold Team

Randomly inserted at a rate of one in 41 packs, this 10 card set features 10 top position players using gold double-sided all-foil dufex technology. Card fronts contain a gold/black background with the player's name in black at the top and the "Gold Team" logo at the lower right. Card backs contain a headshot of the player against the same type background.

COMPLETE SET (10) 50.00 120.00
STATED ODDS 1:41
1 Jerry Rice 5.00 12.00
2 Emmitt Smith 8.00 20.00
3 Drew Bledsoe 2.00 5.00
4 Marshall Faulk 6.00 15.00
5 Troy Aikman 5.00 12.00
6 Barry Sanders 8.00 20.00
7 Dan Marino 10.00 25.00
8 Errict Rhett .75 2.00
9 Brett Favre 10.00 25.00
10 Steve McNair 7.50 20.00

1995 Select Certified Select Few

Randomly inserted at a rate of one in 32 packs, this 20 card set contains top veteran stars utilizing an all-foil dufex background. Card fronts have a headshot of the player against a football field background. Card backs have a shot of the player on the left against a stadium background and player commentary against a black background to the right. Cards are numbered out of 2,250. A parallel of this set exists that is numbered out of 1,028 and looks the same except the fronts are not dufexed. These cards were inserted at a rate of one card in a plastic holder inside sealed boxes.

COMPLETE SET (20) 50.00 120.00
STATED ODDS 1:32
PRICED CARDS ARE NUMBERED OF 2250
*1028 CARDS: .8X TO 2X BASIC INSERTS
1 Dan Marino 10.00 25.00
2 Emmitt Smith 8.00 20.00
3 Marshall Faulk 6.00 15.00
4 Barry Sanders 8.00 20.00
5 Drew Bledsoe 2.00 5.00
6 Brett Favre 10.00 25.00
7 Troy Aikman 5.00 12.00
8 Jerry Rice 5.00 12.00
9 Steve Young 4.00 10.00
10 Natrone Means .75 2.00
11 Byron Bam Morris .40 1.00
12 Frrict Rhett .75 2.00
13 John Elway 10.00 25.00
14 Heath Shuler .75 2.00
15 Ki-Jana Carter 1.25 3.00
16 Kerry Collins 5.00 12.00
17 Steve McNair 7.50 20.00
18 Rashaan Salaam .60 1.50
19 Tyrone Wheatley 3.00 8.00
20 J.J. Stokes 1.25 3.00

1996 Select Certified

The 1996 Select Certified set was issued in one series totalling 125 cards. The six-card packs retail for $4.99 each. The cards feature color player photos on 24-point silver mirror card stock. The set includes 30 rookie cards and a special Silver Spiral subset (116-125) which honors ten of the Quarterback Club's superstar elite. Too many promos were produced to properly catalog for this book. Many of the promos apparently were made for the various Mirror parallels and usually sell at a heavy discount over the base cards.

COMPLETE SET (125) 20.00 50.00
1 Isaac Bruce .30 .75
2 Rick Mirer .20 .50
3 Jake Reed .20 .50
4 Reggie White .30 .75
5 Harvey Williams .10 .30
6 Jim Everett .10 .30
7 Tony Martin .20 .50
8 Craig Heyward .10 .30
9 Tamarick Vanover .20 .50
10 Hugh Douglas .20 .50
11 Erik Kramer .10 .30
12 Charlie Garner .20 .50
13 Erric Pegram .10 .30
14 Scott Mitchell .20 .50
15 Michael Westbrook .30 .75
16 Robert Smith .20 .50
17 Kerry Collins .30 .75
18 Derek Loville .10 .30
19 Jeff Blake .30 .75
20 Terry Kirby .20 .50
21 Bruce Smith .20 .50
22 Stan Humphries .20 .50
23 Rodney Thomas .10 .30
24 Wayne Chrebet .30 .75
25 Napoleon Kaufman .30 .75
26 Marshall Faulk .40 1.00
27 Emmitt Smith 1.25 3.00
28 Natrone Means .20 .50
29 Neil O'Donnell .20 .50
30 Warren Moon .20 .50
31 Junior Seau .30 .75
32 Chris Sanders .20 .50
33 Barry Sanders 1.25 3.00
34 Jeff Graham .10 .30
35 Kordell Stewart .30 .75
36 Jim Harbaugh .20 .50
37 Chris Warren .20 .50
38 Cris Carter .30 .75
39 J.J. Stokes .30 .75
40 Tyrone Wheatley .20 .50
41 Terrell Davis .60 1.50
42 Mark Brunell .30 .75
43 Steve Young .60 1.50
44 Rodney Hampton .20 .50
45 Drew Bledsoe .50 1.25
46 Larry Centers .20 .50
47 Ken Norton Jr. .10 .30
48 Deion Sanders .50 1.25
49 Alvin Harper .10 .30
50 Trent Dilfer .30 .75
51 Steve McNair .60 1.50
52 Robert Brooks .30 .75
53 Edgar Bennett .20 .50
54 Troy Aikman .75 2.00
55 Dan Marino 1.50 4.00
56 Steve Bono .10 .30
57 Marcus Allen .30 .75
58 Rodney Peete .10 .30
59 Ben Coates .20 .50
60 Yancey Thigpen .20 .50
61 Tim Brown .30 .75
62 Jerry Rice 1.00 2.50
63 Quinn Early .10 .30
64 Ricky Watters .20 .50
65 Thurman Thomas .30 .75
66 Greg Lloyd .20 .50
67 Eric Metcalf .10 .30
68 Jeff George .20 .50
69 John Elway 1.50 4.00
70 Frank Sanders .20 .50
71 Curtis Conway .30 .75
72 Greg Hill .20 .50
73 Darick Holmes .10 .30
74 Herman Moore .20 .50
75 Carl Pickens .20 .50
76 Eric Zeier .10 .30
77 Curtis Martin .60 1.50
78 Rashaan Salaam .20 .50
79 Joey Galloway .30 .75
80 Jeff Hostetler .10 .30
81 Jim Kelly .30 .75
82 Dave Brown .10 .30
83 Sean Dawkins .10 .30
84 Michael Irvin .30 .75
85 Brett Favre 1.50 4.00
86 Cedric Jones RC .10 .30
87 Jeff Lewis RC .20 .50
88 Alex Van Dyke RC .20 .50
89 Regan Upshaw RC .10 .30
90 Karim Abdul-Jabbar RC .30 .75
91 Marvin Harrison RC 1.50 4.00
92 Stephen Davis RC .75 2.00
93 Terry Glenn RC .40 1.00
94 Kevin Hardy RC .30 .75
95 Stanley Pritchett RC .10 .30
96 Willie Anderson RC .10 .30
97 Lawrence Phillips RC .20 .50
98 Bobby Hoying RC .30 .75
99 Amani Toomer RC .75 2.00
100 Eddie George RC 2.00 5.00
101 Stepfret Williams RC .10 .30
102 Eric Moulds RC .30 .75
103 Simeon Rice RC .75 2.00
104 John Mobley RC .10 .30
105 Keyshawn Johnson RC 1.00 2.50
106 Daryl Gardener RC .10 .30
107 Tony Banks RC .30 .75
108 Bobby Engram RC .30 .75
109 Jonathan Ogden RC 1.00 2.50
110 Eddie Kennison RC .30 .75
111 Danny Kanell RC .20 .50
112 Tony Brackens RC .20 .50
113 Tim Biakabutuka RC .30 .75
114 Leeland McElroy RC .20 .50
115 Rickey Dudley RC .30 .75
116 Troy Aikman SS .40 1.00
117 Brett Favre SS .75 2.00
118 Drew Bledsoe SS .30 .75
119 Steve Young SS .30 .75
120 Kerry Collins SS .30 .75
121 John Elway SS .75 2.00
122 Dan Marino SS .75 2.00
123 Kordell Stewart SS .30 .75
124 Jeff Blake SS .20 .50
125 Jim Harbaugh SS .20 .50

1996 Select Certified Artist's Proofs

COMPLETE SET (125) 200.00 400.00
VETS/500: 2.5X TO 6X BASIC CARDS
ROOKIE STARS/500: 1.2X TO 3X BASIC RC
STATED ODDS 1:18
STATED PRINT RUN 500 SETS

1996 Select Certified Blue

COMPLETE SET (125) 500.00 1000.00
VETS/200: 5X TO 12X BASIC CARDS
STAR ROOKIES/200: 2.5X TO 6X BASIC RC
STATED ODDS 1:50
ANNOUNCED PRINT RUN 200

1996 Select Certified Mirror Blue

VETS/50: 12X TO 30X BASIC CARDS
ROOKIE STARS/50: 5X TO 12X BASIC RC
STATED ODDS 1:200
ANNOUNCED PRINT RUN 50

1996 Select Certified Mirror Gold

VETS/35: 15X TO 40X BASIC CARDS
ROOKIE STARS/35: 8X TO 20X BASIC RC
STATED ODDS 1:300
ANNOUNCED PRINT RUN 35 SETS

1996 Select Certified Mirror Red

VETS/90: 8X TO 20X BASIC CARDS
STAR ROOKIES/90: 4X TO 10X BASIC RC
MIRROR RED STATED ODDS 1:100
ANNOUNCED PRINT RUN 90

1996 Select Certified Mirror Red Premium Stock

VETS/20: 40X TO 100X BASIC CARDS
SS VETS/20: 30X TO 80X BASIC CARDS
STAR ROOKIES/20: 20X TO 50X BASIC RC
ANNOUNCED PRINT RUN 20

1996 Select Certified Premium Stock

COMPLETE SET (125) 30.00 80.00
*VETERANS: 1X TO 2.5X BASIC CARDS
*ROOKIES: .6X TO 1.5X BASIC CARDS
ANNOUNCED PRINT RUN LESS THAN 7000

1996 Select Certified Red

COMPLETE SET (125) 150.00 300.00
VETS/2000: 2X TO 5X BASIC CARDS
ROOKIES/2000: 1X TO 2.5X BASIC RC
STATED ODDS 1:5
ANNOUNCED PRINT RUN 2000

1996 Select Certified Gold Team

Randomly inserted in packs at a rate of one in 38, this 18-card set features color player photos of future Hall of Fame hopefuls printed with a special all-foil Dufex technology.

COMPLETE SET (18) 75.00 150.00
STATED ODDS 1:38
1 Emmitt Smith 6.00 15.00
2 Barry Sanders 6.00 15.00
3 Dan Marino 8.00 20.00
4 Steve Young 3.00 8.00
5 Troy Aikman 4.00 10.00
6 Jerry Rice 4.00 10.00
7 Rashaan Salaam .75 2.00
8 Marshall Faulk 2.00 5.00
9 Drew Bledsoe 2.50 6.00
10 Steve McNair 3.00 8.00
11 Brett Favre 8.00 20.00
12 Terrell Davis 3.00 8.00
13 Kordell Stewart 1.50 4.00
14 Keyshawn Johnson 3.00 8.00
15 Kerry Collins 1.50 4.00
16 Curtis Martin 3.00 8.00
17 Isaac Bruce 1.50 4.00
18 Terry Glenn 3.00 8.00

1996 Select Certified Thumbs Up

Randomly inserted in packs at a rate of one in 41, this 24-card set features color player photos of top rookie standouts and veteran superstars utilizing silver Prime frost to highlight each player's defining moments.

COMPLETE SET (24) 125.00 250.00
STATED ODDS 1:41
1 Steve Young 4.00 10.00
2 Jeff Blake 2.00 5.00
3 Dan Marino 10.00 25.00
4 Kerry Collins 2.00 5.00
5 John Elway 10.00 25.00
6 Neil O'Donnell 1.00 2.50
7 Brett Favre 8.00 20.00
8 Scott Mitchell 1.00 2.50
9 Troy Aikman 5.00 12.00
10 Jim Harbaugh 1.00 2.50
11 Drew Bledsoe 3.00 8.00
12 Jeff Hostetler .50 1.25
13 Marvin Harrison 10.00 25.00
14 Tim Biakabutuka .75 2.00
15 Eddie George 5.00 12.00
16 Tony Brackens .75 2.00
17 Karim Abdul-Jabbar .75 2.00
18 Daryl Gardener .20 .50
19 Alex Van Dyke .40 1.00
20 Terry Glenn 3.00 8.00
21 Eric Moulds 4.00 10.00
22 Eddie Kennison .75 2.00
23 Regan Upshaw .20 .50
24 Mike Alstott 3.00 8.00

1972 7-Eleven Slurpee Cups

Seven-Eleven stores released two series of football player cups in the early 1970s. Each white plastic cup measures roughly 5-1/4" tall, 3-1/4" in diameter at the mouth and 2" at the base. The fronts feature a color portrait of a player along with his name and team name. In many cases, a facsimile autograph appears between the bottom of the portrait and the player's name. All of the players pictured are helmetless. The backs include basic biographical information along with the 7-Eleven logo at the top and the player's team helmet at the bottom. The unnumbered cups are arranged below alphabetically. Both years are very similar in design. The 1972 release is distinguished by the smaller type face used on the player's name (1/16" tall) and the lack of the "Made in USA" tag that runs down the sides of the 1973 cups.

COMPLETE SET (60) 75.00 150.00
1 Donny Anderson 1.00 2.50
2 Elvin Bethea 1.00 2.50
3 Fred Biletnikoff 2.00 5.00
4 Bill Bradley .75 2.00
5 Terry Bradshaw 5.00 12.00
6 Larry Brown 1.00 2.50
7 Willie Brown 1.25 3.00
8 Norm Bulaich .75 2.00
9 Dick Butkus 3.00 8.00
10 Ray Chester .75 2.00
11 Bill Curry .75 2.00
12 Len Dawson 1.50 4.00
13 Willie Ellison .75 2.00
14 Ed Flanagan .75 2.00
15 Gary Garrison .75 2.00
16 Gale Gillingham .75 2.00
17 Joe Greene 1.50 4.00
18 Cedrick Hardman .75 2.00
19 Jim Hart 1.25 3.00
20 Ted Hendricks 1.25 3.00
21 Winston Hill .75 2.00
22 Ken Houston 1.25 3.00
23 Chuck Howley 1.00 2.50
24 Claude Humphrey .75 2.00
25 Roy Jefferson .75 2.00
26 Sonny Jurgensen 1.50 4.00
27 Leroy Kelly 1.25 3.00
28 Paul Krause 1.00 2.50
29 George Kunz .75 2.00
30 Jake Kupp .75 2.00
31 Ted Kwalick .75 2.00
32 Willie Lanier 1.25 3.00
33 Bob Lilly 1.50 4.00
34 Floyd Little 1.00 2.50
35 Larry Little 1.25 3.00
36 Tom Mack 1.00 2.50
37 Milt Morin .75 2.00
38 Mercury Morris 1.25 3.00
39 John Niland .75 2.00
40 Jim Otto 1.25 3.00
41 Steve Owens 1.00 2.50
42 Alan Page 1.25 3.00
43 Jim Plunkett 1.25 3.00
44 Mike Reid 1.25 3.00
45 Mel Renfro 1.25 3.00
46 Isiah Robertson .75 2.00
47 Andy Russell 1.00 2.50
48 Charlie Sanders 1.00 2.50
49 O.J. Simpson 2.50 6.00
50 Bubba Smith 1.25 3.00
51 Bill Stanfill 1.00 2.50
52 Jan Stenerud 1.25 3.00
53 Walt Sweeney .75 2.00
54 Bob Tucker .75 2.00
55 Jim Tyrer .75 2.00
56 Rick Volk .75 2.00
57 Gene Washington 49er 1.00 2.50
58 Dave Wilcox 1.00 2.50
59 Del Williams .75 2.00
60 Ron Yary 1.25 3.00
NNO Picture Checklist 6.00 15.00

1973 7-Eleven Slurpee Cups

Seven-Eleven stores released two series of football player cups in the early 1970s. Each white plastic cup measures roughly 5-1/4" tall, 3-1/4" in diameter at the mouth and 2" at the base. The fronts feature a color portrait of a player along with his name and team name. In many cases, a facsimile autograph appears between the bottom of the portrait and the player's name. All of the players pictured are helmetless. The backs include basic biographical information along with the 7-Eleven logo at the top and the player's team helmet at the bottom. The unnumbered cups are arranged below alphabetically. Both years are very similar in design. The 1973 issue is distinguished by the larger type face used on the player's name (1/8" tall) and the words "Made in USA" that run down the sides of the cups.

COMPLETE SET (1-80) 125.00 250.00
1 Dan Abramowicz 1.25 3.00
2 Ken Anderson 2.00 5.00
3 Jim Beirne 1.00 2.50
4 Ed Bell 1.00 2.50
5 Bob Berry 1.00 2.50
6 Jim Bertelsen 1.00 2.50
7 Marlin Briscoe 1.00 2.50
8 John Brockington 1.00 2.50
9 Larry Brown 1.25 3.00
10 Buck Buchanan 1.50 4.00
11 Dick Butkus 5.00 12.00
12 Larry Carwell 1.00 2.50
13 Rich Caster 1.00 2.50
14 Bobby Douglass 1.00 2.50
15 Pete Duranko 1.00 2.50
16 Cid Edwards 1.00 2.50
17 Mel Farr 1.00 2.50
18 Pat Fischer 1.00 2.50
19 Mike Garrett 1.25 3.00
20 Walt Garrison 1.25 3.00
21 George Goeddeke 1.00 2.50
22 Bob Gresham 1.00 2.50
23 Jack Ham 2.50 6.00
24 Chris Hanburger 1.25 3.00
25 Franco Harris 5.00 12.00
26 Calvin Hill 1.25 3.00
27 J.D. Hill 1.00 2.50
28 Marv Hubbard 1.00 2.50
29 Scott Hunter 1.00 2.50
30 Harold Jackson 1.25 3.00
31 Randy Jackson 1.00 2.50
32 Bob Johnson 1.00 2.50
33 Jim Johnson 1.50 4.00
34 Ron Johnson 1.00 2.50
35 Leroy Keyes 1.00 2.50
36 Greg Landry 1.25 3.00
37 Gary Larsen 1.00 2.50
38 Frank Lewis 1.00 2.50
39 Bob Lilly 2.00 5.00
40 Dale Lindsey 1.00 2.50
41 Larry Little 1.50 4.00
42 Spider Lockhart 1.00 2.50
43 Mike Lucci 1.00 2.50
44 Jim Lynch 1.00 2.50
45 Art Malone 1.00 2.50
46 Ed Marinaro 1.25 3.00
47 Jim Marshall 1.50 4.00
48 Ray May 1.00 2.50
49 Don Maynard 2.00 5.00
50 Don McCauley 1.00 2.50
51 Mike McCoy 1.00 2.50
52 Tom Mitchell 1.00 2.50
53 Tommy Nobis 1.25 3.00
54 Dan Pastorini 1.25 3.00
55 Mac Percival 1.00 2.50
56 Mike Phipps 1.25 3.00
57 Ed Podolak 1.00 2.50
58 John Reaves 1.00 2.50
59 Tim Rossovich 1.00 2.50
60 Bo Scott 1.00 2.50
61 Ron Sellers 1.00 2.50
62 Dennis Shaw 1.00 2.50
63 Mike Siani 1.00 2.50
64 O.J. Simpson 3.00 8.00
65 Bubba Smith 1.50 4.00
66 Larry Smith 1.00 2.50
67 Jackie Smith 1.50 4.00
68 Norm Snead 1.25 3.00
69 Jack Snow 1.25 3.00
70 Steve Spurrier 2.50 6.00
71 Doug Swift 1.00 2.50
72 Jack Tatum 1.50 4.00
73 Bruce Taylor 1.00 2.50
74 Otis Taylor 1.25 3.00
75 Bob Trumpy 1.25 3.00
76 Jim Turner 1.00 2.50
77 Phil Villapiano 1.25 3.00
78 Roger Wehrli 1.25 3.00
79 Ken Willard 1.00 2.50
80 Jack Youngblood 1.50 4.00
NNO Picture Checklist 10.00 25.00

1983 7-Eleven Discs

This set of 15 discs, each measuring approximately 1 3/4" in diameter, features an alternating portrait and action picture of each of the players listed below. The set was sponsored by 7-Eleven Stores (Southland Corporation) and distributed through an in-store promotion.

COMPLETE SET (15) 12.50 25.00
1 Franco Harris .75 2.00
2 Dan Fouts .75 2.00
3 Lee Roy Selmon .50 1.25
4 Nolan Cromwell .30 .75
5 Marcus Allen 2.50 6.00
6 Joe Montana 4.00 10.00
7 Kellen Winslow .50 1.25
8 Hugh Green .30 .75
9 Ted Hendricks .50 1.25
10 Danny White .50 1.25
11 Wes Chandler .30 .75
12 Jimmie Giles .30 .75
13 Jack Youngblood .40 1.00
14 Lester Hayes .40 1.00
15 Vince Ferragamo .40 1.00

1984 7-Eleven Discs

This set of 40 discs, each measuring approximately 1 3/4" in diameter, features an alternating portrait and action picture of each of the players listed below. The set was sponsored by 7-Eleven Stores (Southland Corporation) and distributed through an in-store promotion. The discs in the set are grouped into two subsets, East (E prefix) and West (W prefix). Some players were included in both subsets.

COMPLETE SET (40) 25.00 50.00
E1 Franco Harris .50 1.25
E2 Lawrence Taylor .50 1.25
E3 Mark Gastineau .20 .50
E4 Lee Roy Selmon .30 .75
E5 Ken Anderson .30 .75
E6 Walter Payton 2.00 5.00
E7 Ken Stabler .50 1.25
E8 Marcus Allen .60 1.50
E9 Fred Smerlas .20 .50
E10 Ozzie Newsome .30 .75
E11 Steve Bartkowski .30 .75
E12 Tony Dorsett .50 1.25
E13 John Riggins .40 1.00
E14 Billy Sims .30 .75
E15 Dan Marino 5.00 12.00
E16 Tony Collins .20 .50
E17 Curtis Dickey .20 .50
E18 Ron Jaworski .20 .50
E19 William Andrews .20 .50
E20 Joe Theismann .40 1.00
W1 Franco Harris .50 1.25
W2 Joe Montana 4.00 10.00
W3 Matt Blair .20 .50
W4 Warren Moon .40 1.00
W5 Marcus Allen .60 1.50
W6 John Riggins .40 1.00
W7 Walter Payton 2.00 5.00
W8 Vince Ferragamo .20 .50
W9 Billy Sims .30 .75
W10 Ken Anderson .30 .75
W11 Lynn Dickey .20 .50
W12 Tony Dorsett .50 1.25
W13 Bill Kenney .20 .50
W14 Ottis Anderson .30 .75
W15 Dan Fouts .40 1.00
W16 Eric Dickerson .40 1.00
W17 John Elway 5.00 12.00
W18 Ozzie Newsome .30 .75
W19 Curt Warner .20 .50
W20 Joe Theismann .40 1.00
NNO East Display Board 6.00 15.00
NNO West Display Board 6.00 15.00

1995 7-Eleven AT&T Phone Cards

1 Steve Young 2.50 6.00
2 Dan Marino 4.00 10.00
3 John Elway 4.00 10.00
4 Michael Irvin 2.00 5.00
5 Boomer Esiason 1.50 4.00

1996 7-Eleven Sprint Phone Cards

7-Eleven stores distributed these Sprint 15-minute phone cards. Each includes a photo of the player on front with the phone card use instructions on back. The cards are priced below in unused condition and originally carried an SRP of $5.99 each.

COMPLETE SET (12) 32.00 80.00
1 Troy Aikman 3.20 8.00
2 Drew Bledsoe 3.20 8.00
3 John Elway 4.80 12.00
4 Brett Favre 4.80 12.00
5 Jim Kelly 2.00 5.00
6 Erik Kramer 2.00 5.00
7 Dan Marino 4.80 12.00
8 Barry Sanders 4.80 12.00
9 Jerry Rice 3.20 8.00
10 Junior Seau 2.00 5.00
11 Emmitt Smith 4.80 12.00
12 Steve Young 2.40 6.00

1997 7-Eleven Promotion

This set was released 3-cards at a time via a 7-Eleven Stores wrapper redemption program from November 1997 to January 1998. For $1 and two wrappers from football card packs purchased at 7-Eleven stores, the collector would receive the 3-cards. Each was produced by a major card manufacturer and features a unique card design. Some include card numbers while others do not. We've cataloged the set below in the order of card release and/or card number.

COMPLETE SET (9) 4.80 12.00
1 John Elway CL .50 1.25
2 Barry Sanders 1.20 3.00
3 Steve Young .40 1.00
4 Troy Aikman .60 1.50
5 Terrell Davis .80 2.00
6 Junior Seau .30 .75
7 Drew Bledsoe .60 1.50
8 Rae Carruth .30 .75
9 Dan Marino 1.20 3.00

1981 Shell Posters

This set of 96 posters was distributed by Shell Oil Co. across the country, with each major city distributing players from the local team. Those cities without a close NFL issuing team distributed the National set of six popular players (indicated as "National" in the checklist below: numbers 18, 21, 28, 35, 45, and 79). The pictures used are actually black and white drawings by artists, suitable for framing. These posters measure approximately 10 7/8" by 13 7/8"; most were (facsimile) signed by the artist. They are frequently available and offered by the team set of six. Several different artists are responsible for the artwork; they are K. Akins (KA), Nick Galloway (NG) and Tanenbawm (T). Those drawings which are not signed are asterisked in the checklist below. New Orleans and Houston are supposedly tougher to find than the other teams. The posters are numbered below alphabetically by team and then player.

COMPLETE SET (96) 100.00 200.00
1 William Andrews NG 1.25 3.00
2 Steve Bartkowski NG 1.25 3.00
3 Buddy Curry NG 1.00 2.50
4 Wallace Francis NG 1.25 3.00
5 Mike Kenn NG 1.00 2.50
6 Jeff Van Note NG 1.00 2.50
7 Mike Barnes * 1.00 2.50
8 Roger Carr KA 1.00 2.50
9 Curtis Dickey KA 1.25 3.00
10 Bert Jones KA 1.25 3.00
11 Bruce Laird * 1.00 2.50
12 Randy McMillan * 1.00 2.50
13 Brian Baschnagel T 1.00 2.50
14 Vince Evans T 1.00 2.50
15 Gary Fencik T 1.00 2.50
16 Roland Harper T 1.00 2.50
17 Alan Page T 1.25 3.00
18 Walter Payton T 4.00 10.00
19 Ken Anderson T 1.50 4.00
20 Ross Browner T 1.00 2.50
21 Archie Griffin T 1.00 2.50
22 Pat McInally T 1.00 2.50
23 Anthony Munoz T 1.50 4.00
24 Reggie Williams T 1.25 3.00
25 Lyle Alzado KA 1.25 3.00
26 Joe DeLamielleure KA 1.25 3.00
27 Doug Dieken KA 1.00 2.50
28 Dave Logan KA 1.00 2.50
29 Reggie Rucker KA 1.25 3.00
30 Brian Sipe KA 1.25 3.00
31 Benny Barnes T 1.00 2.50
32 Bob Breunig T 1.00 2.50
33 D.D. Lewis T 1.00 2.50
34 Harvey Martin T 1.25 3.00
35 Drew Pearson T 1.25 3.00
36 Rafael Septien T 1.00 2.50
37 Al(Bubba) Baker KA 1.25 3.00
38 Dexter Bussey KA 1.00 2.50
39 Gary Danielson KA 1.00 2.50
40 Freddie Scott KA 1.00 2.50
41 Billy Sims KA 1.50 4.00
42 Tom Skladany KA 1.00 2.50
43 Robert Brazile T 1.25 3.00
44 Ken Burrough T 1.25 3.00
45 Earl Campbell T 2.50 6.00
46 Leon Gray T 1.00 2.50
47 Carl Mauck T 1.00 2.50
48 Ken Stabler T 1.50 4.00
49 Bob Baumhower NG 1.25 3.00
50 Jimmy Cefalo NG 1.25 3.00
51 A.J. Duhe NG 1.00 2.50
52 Nat Moore NG 1.25 3.00
53 Ed Newman NG 1.00 2.50
54 Uwe Von Schamann NG 1.00 2.50
55 Steve Grogan NG 1.25 3.00
56 John Hannah NG 1.25 3.00
57 Don Hasselbeck NG 1.00 2.50
58 Mike Haynes NG 1.25 3.00
59 Harold Jackson NG 1.25 3.00
60 Steve Nelson NG 1.00 2.50
61 Elois Grooms 1.25 3.00
62 Rickey Jackson NG 1.50 4.00
63 Archie Manning T 1.50 4.00
64 Tom Myers 1.25 3.00
65 Benny Ricardo T 1.25 3.00
66 George Rogers NG 1.25 3.00
67 Harry Carson NG 1.50 4.00
68 Dave Jennings NG 1.00 2.50
69 Gary Jeter NG 1.00 2.50
70 Phil Simms NG 1.50 4.00
71 Lawrence Taylor NG 2.00 5.00
72 Brad Van Pelt NG 1.25 3.00
73 Greg Buttle NG 1.00 2.50
74 Bruce Harper NG 1.00 2.50
75 Joe Klecko NG 1.25 3.00
76 Randy Rasmussen NG 1.00 2.50
77 Richard Todd NG 1.25 3.00
78 Wesley Walker NG 1.25 3.00
79 Ottis Anderson NG 1.00 2.50
80 Dan Dierdorf NG 1.25 3.00
81 Mel Gray NG 1.25 3.00
82 Jim Hart NG 1.25 3.00
83 E.J. Junior NG 1.25 3.00
84 Pat Tilley NG 1.25 3.00
85 Jimmie Giles NG 1.25 3.00
86 Charley Hannah NG 1.00 2.50
87 Bill Kollar NG 1.00 2.50
88 David Lewis NG 1.00 2.50
89 Lee Roy Selmon NG 1.50 4.00
90 Doug Williams NG 1.25 3.00
91 Joe Lavender T 1.00 2.50
92 Mark Moseley T 1.00 2.50
93 Mark Murphy * 1.00 2.50
94 Lemar Parrish T 1.00 2.50
95 John Riggins T 2.00 5.00
96 Joe Washington T 1.25 3.00

1926 Shotwell Red Grange Ad Back

Shotwell Candy issued two different sets featuring Red Grange. Each card in the "ad back" version measures roughly 2" by 3 1/8" (slightly larger than the blankbacks) and was printed on very thin newspaper type paper stock. Each features Red Grange in a black and white photo from the motion picture "One Minute to Play." The cards were issued as inserts into Shotwell Candies so many are found with creases and other damage from the original packaging. Many of the same photos were used in this version as the first 12-cards of the blankbacked set. However, the captions are worded differently. Each also includes an advertisement on the cardback for Shotwell Candies, a Grange album, and Grange photos. A second, presumably much more scarce, version of card #9 was confirmed in 2011 featuring a photo of Grange wearing his famous jersey #77. It has been speculated that this card may have been pulled early in production or issued very late in the promotion or even issued as a seperate sample card.

COMPLETE SET (12) 2500.00 4000.00
1 Red Grange (Getting Under Way) 250.00 400.00
2 Red Grange (A Forward Pass) 200.00 350.00
3 Red Grange (The start of one of those famous 50-yard runs) 200.00 350.00
4 Red Grange (Passing it Along) 250.00 400.00
5 Red Grange (Picking a High One) 200.00 350.00
6 Red Grange (Raccoon coat photo) 250.00 400.00
7 Red Grange (America's Most Famous Ice Man) 200.00 350.00
8 Red Grange (The Famous Smile) 200.00 350.00
9A Red Grange (Illinois Famous Half Back) 250.00 400.00
9B Red Grange SP

(Red calls this his lucky number)
10 Red Grange 250.00 400.00
(The Kick That Put it Over)
11 Red Grange 250.00 400.00
(On the Run)
12 Red Grange 250.00 400.00
(Himself)

1926 Shotwell Red Grange Blankbacked

Shotwell Candy issued two different sets featuring Red Grange. Each card in the blankbacked version measures roughly 1-15/16" by 3" and features a black and white photo from the motion picture "One Minute to Play." The cards were issued as inserts into Shotwell Candies. Photos that feature Grange in football attire generally fetch a slight premium over the movie photo cards.

COMPLETE SET (24) 5000.00 8000.00
WRAPPER 1000.00 1500.00
1 Red Grange 250.00 400.00
2 Red Grange 200.00 350.00
3 Red Grange 200.00 350.00
4 Red Grange 200.00 350.00
5 Red Grange 200.00 350.00
6 Red Grange 200.00 350.00
7 Red Grange 250.00 400.00
8 Red Grange 200.00 350.00
9 Red Grange 200.00 350.00
10 Red Grange 200.00 350.00
11 Red Grange 200.00 350.00
12 Red Grange 200.00 350.00
13 Red Grange 250.00 400.00
14 Red Grange 250.00 400.00
15 Red Grange 250.00 400.00
16 Red Grange 200.00 350.00
17 Red Grange 200.00 350.00
18 Red Grange 200.00 350.00
19 Red Grange 200.00 350.00
20 Red Grange 250.00 400.00
21 Red Grange 200.00 350.00
22 Red Grange 200.00 350.00
23 Red Grange 200.00 350.00
24 Red Grange 250.00 400.00

2005 Sioux City Bandits UIF

COMPLETE SET (30) 7.50 15.00
1 Nick Allison .30 .75
2 Jamal Argrow .30 .75
3 John Bowman .30 .75
4 Cody Butler .30 .75
5 Keith Chapman .30 .75
6 Jarrod DeGeorgia .30 .75
7 Clint Harrison .30 .75
8 Kenneth Horton .30 .75
9 Fred Jackson .30 .75
10 Patrick Jackson .30 .75
11 Jose Jefferson CO .30 .75
12 Jose Jefferson CO .30 .75
13 Cori Johnson .30 .75
14 Tristan Johnson .30 .75
15 Donavan Laviness .30 .75
16 Adam Lloyd .30 .75
17 Art Maulupe .30 .75
18 Corey Mayes .30 .75
19 Johnnie Ostermeyer .30 .75
20 Jon Paulsen .30 .75
21 David Perrigo .30 .75
22 Deron Rush .30 .75
23 Steve Schmidt .30 .75
24 Willie Simmons .30 .75
25 Derrick Smith Jr. .30 .75
26 Erv Strohbeen .30 .75
27 Anthony Thomas .30 .75
28 Spetlar Tonga .30 .75
29 Ken Ware .30 .75
30 Jesse Wavrunek .30 .75

2005 Sioux Falls Storm UIF

COMPLETE SET (6) 4.00 8.00
1 Shannon Poppinga .60 1.50
2 Adam Hicks .60 1.50
3 Mark Blackburn .60 1.50
4 Nate Fluit .60 1.50
5 James Jones .60 1.50
6 John Semchenko .60 1.50

2007 Sioux Falls Storm UIF

COMPLETE SET (6) 4.00 8.00
1 Trice Crump .60 1.50
2 Leo Hall Jr. .60 1.50
3 Paul Keizer .60 1.50
4 Justin Landis .60 1.50
5 Leif Murphy .60 1.50
6 James Terry .60 1.50

2008 Sioux Falls Storm UIF

COMPLETE SET (6) 2.50 6.00
1 Bryan Alberty .40 1.00
2 Mark Blackburn .40 1.00
3 Ya'Tarrie Brown .40 1.00
4 Cory Johnsen .40 1.00
5 Anthony Thomas .40 1.00
6 Sean Treasure .40 1.00

1993 SkyBox Celebrity Cycle Prototypes

Measuring the standard size, these two prototype cards feature celebrities and their bikes. On the fronts, the featured celebrity is pictured on his bike, and the varying backgrounds have a metallic sheen to them. The celebrity is identified by his name, position, and his team. (The mystery card pictures a Harley Davidson motocycle against an American flag background.) The backs are blank except for a red-inked stamp that reads "Unfinished SkyBox Prototype." The cards are unnumbered and checklisted below in alphabetical order.

1 Mitch Frerotte .80 2.00
2 Jerry Glanville CO .75 2.00

2000 SkyBox

Released as a 300-card base set, Skybox features 200-veteran cards, 50-base rookie cards and the same 50-rookies again in a short printed version. The Short Printed rookies (noted below with an "H" suffix on the card number) feature a horizontal photo on the cardfront instead of vertical and are sequentially numbered to 2000. SkyBox was packaged in 24-pack boxes with packs containing 10 cards and carried a suggested retail price of $2.99.

COMPLETE SET (300) 250.00 400.00
COMP.SET w/o SPs (250) 12.50 30.00
201-250 ROOKIE SP PRINT RUN 2000
1 Tim Couch .20 .50
2 Edgerrin James .20 .50
3 Wesley Walls .15 .40
4 Brian Griese .15 .40
5 Herman Moore .15 .40
6 Mark Brunell .20 .50
7 John Randle .25 .60
8 Victor Green .15 .40
9 Michael Sinclair .15 .40
10 Jevon Kearse .15 .40
11 Peter Boulware .15 .40
12 Kevin Johnson .15 .40
13 Vonnie Holliday .15 .40
14 Jason Taylor .20 .50
15 Cam Cleeland .15 .40
16 Jeff Graham .15 .40
17 Jacquez Green .15 .40
18 Chris McAlister .15 .40
19 Takeo Spikes .15 .40
20 Marvin Harrison .20 .50
21 Jay Fiedler .20 .50
22 Jake Reed .20 .50
23 Jerry Rice .60 1.50
24 Shaun King .15 .40
25 Donovan McNabb .20 .50
26 David Boston .15 .40
27 Curtis Enis .15 .40
28 Olandis Gary .20 .50
29 James Stewart .15 .40
30 Jimmy Smith .20 .50
31 Randy Moss .20 .50
32 Keyshawn Johnson .20 .50
33 Kevin Carter .15 .40
34 Stephen Davis .15 .40
35 Jay Riemersma .15 .40
36 Emmitt Smith .40 1.00
37 E.G. Green .15 .40
38 Dwayne Rudd .15 .40
39 Michael Strahan .20 .50
40 Troy Edwards .15 .40
41 Derrick Mayes .15 .40
42 Eddie George .20 .50
43 Bruce Smith .20 .50
44 Andre Wadsworth .15 .40
45 Bobby Engram .15 .40
46 Byron Chamberlain .15 .40
47 Antonio Freeman .20 .50
48 Hardy Nickerson .15 .40
49 Terry Glenn .20 .50
50 Wayne Chrebet .15 .40
51 London Fletcher RC .40 1.00
52 Michael Westbrook .15 .40
53 Rob Moore .15 .40
54 Eddie Kennison .15 .40
55 Ed McCaffrey .20 .50
56 Dorsey Levens .20 .50
57 Andre Rison .20 .50
58 Willie McGinest .20 .50
59 Tyrone Wheatley .15 .40
60 Kurt Warner .40 1.00
61 Stephen Alexander .15 .40
62 Jessie Tuggle .15 .40
63 Jim Miller .15 .40
64 Luther Elliss .15 .40
65 Bill Schroeder .20 .50
66 Elvis Grbac .15 .40
67 Ty Law .25 .60
68 Tim Brown .25 .60
69 Marshall Faulk .20 .50
70 Champ Bailey .20 .50
71 Charlie Batch .15 .40
72 Steve Beuerlein .20 .50
73 Rocket Ismail .20 .50
74 Kevin Hardy .15 .40
75 Zach Thomas .20 .50
76 Aaron Glenn .15 .40
77 Jerome Bettis .25 .60
78 Chris Chandler .20 .50
79 Marcus Robinson .20 .50
80 Derrick Alexander .15 .40
81 Drew Bledsoe .20 .50
82 Charles Woodson .25 .60
83 Isaac Bruce .25 .60
84 Darrell Green .20 .50
85 Tim Dwight .20 .50
86 Darnay Scott .20 .50
87 Chris Claiborne .15 .40
88 Tony Gonzalez .20 .50
89 Tony Simmons .15 .40
90 Rich Gannon .20 .50
91 Torry Holt .20 .50
92 Jamal Anderson .20 .50
93 Akili Smith .15 .40
94 Germane Crowell .15 .40
95 Lawyer Milloy .15 .40
96 Napoleon Kaufman .20 .50
97 Grant Wistrom .15 .40
98 Terance Mathis .15 .40
99 Karim Abdul-Jabbar .15 .40
100 Kerry Collins .15 .40
101 Troy Vincent .15 .40
102 Jermaine Fazande .15 .40
103 Warren Sapp .20 .50
104 Tony Banks .15 .40
105 Darrin Chiaverini .15 .40
106 Corey Bradford .15 .40
107 Tony Martin .20 .50
108 Jeff Blake .20 .50
109 Torrance Small .15 .40
110 Freddie Jones .15 .40
111 Warrick Dunn .15 .40
112 Tim Biakabutuka .20 .50
113 Rod Smith .20 .50
114 Kyle Brady .15 .40
115 Oronde Gadsden .20 .50
116 Dedric Ward .15 .40
117 Mikhael Ricks .15 .40
118 Bryant Young .15 .40
119 Michael Bates .15 .40
120 Junior Seau .20 .50
121 Bill Romanowski .15 .40
122 Reggie Barlow .15 .40
123 Jeff Garcia .15 .40
124 Peerless Price .20 .50
125 Jeff George .20 .50
126 Cornelius Bennett .15 .40
127 Amani Toomer .15 .40
128 Charles Johnson .15 .40
129 Cortez Kennedy .20 .50
130 Samari Rolle .15 .40
131 Eric Moulds .15 .40
132 Joey Galloway .20 .50
133 Peyton Manning .60 1.50
134 Robert Smith .15 .40
135 Jessie Armstead .15 .40
136 Will Blackwell .15 .40
137 Jon Kitna .15 .40
138 Kevin Dyson .20 .50
139 Jake Plummer .15 .40
140 Cade McNown .15 .40
141 Terrell Davis .20 .50
142 Johnnie Morton .20 .50
143 Fred Taylor .15 .40
144 Ed McDaniel .15 .40
145 Vinny Testaverde .15 .40
146 Az-Zahir Hakim .15 .40
147 Brad Johnson .20 .50
148 Antowain Smith .20 .50
149 Rob Konrad .15 .40
150 Sam Cowart .15 .40
151 Cris Carter .25 .60
152 Jason Sehorn .15 .40
153 Levon Kirkland .15 .40
154 Shawn Springs .15 .40
155 Frank Wycheck .20 .50
156 Troy Aikman .30 .75
157 Keenan McCardell .20 .50
158 Sam Madison .15 .40
159 Curtis Martin .20 .50
160 Hines Ward .20 .50
161 Steve Young .30 .75
162 Blaine Bishop .15 .40
163 Shannon Sharpe .20 .50
164 Michael Pittman .15 .40
165 Brett Favre .50 1.25
166 Damon Huard .15 .40
167 Keith Poole .15 .40
168 Curtis Conway .20 .50
169 Derrick Brooks .15 .40
170 Duce Staley .15 .40
171 Rob Johnson .20 .50
172 Pete Gonzalez .15 .40
173 Ken Dilger .15 .40
174 Ike Hilliard .15 .40
175 Bobby Taylor .15 .40
176 Ricky Watters .20 .50
177 Steve McNair .20 .50
178 Pat Johnson .15 .40
179 Carl Pickens .20 .50
180 Terrence Wilkins .15 .40
181 Rashaan Shehee .15 .40
182 Ricky Williams .20 .50
183 James Jett .20 .50
184 Terrell Owens .20 .50
185 John Lynch .20 .50
186 Muhsin Muhammad .15 .40
187 Ryan McNeil .15 .40
188 Jerome Pathon .15 .40
189 Daunte Culpepper .20 .50
190 Joe Jurevicius .15 .40
191 Kordell Stewart .15 .40
192 Christian Fauria .15 .40
193 Yancey Thigpen .15 .40
194 Patrick Jeffers .15 .40
195 Corey Dillon .15 .40
196 Tamarick Vanover .15 .40
197 Doug Flutie .20 .50
198 Rickey Dudley .15 .40
199 Charlie Garner .20 .50
200 Mike Alstott .15 .40
201 Courtney Brown RC .25 .60
201H Courtney Brown SP 2.00 5.00
202 Peter Warrick RC .20 .50
202H Peter Warrick SP 1.50 4.00
203 Thomas Jones RC .25 .60
203H Thomas Jones SP 2.00 5.00
204 Sylvester Morris RC .20 .50
204H Sylvester Morris SP 1.50 4.00
205 Chad Pennington RC .25 .60
205H Chad Pennington SP 2.00 5.00
206 Ron Dayne RC .30 .75
206H Ron Dayne SP 2.50 6.00
207 Todd Pinkston RC .20 .50
207H Todd Pinkston SP 1.50 4.00
208 Todd Husak RC .20 .50
208H Todd Husak SP 1.50 4.00
209 Chris Redman RC .20 .50
209H Chris Redman SP 1.50 4.00
210 Jerry Porter RC .30 .75
210H Jerry Porter SP 2.50 6.00
211 Michael Wiley RC .20 .50
211H Michael Wiley SP 1.50 4.00
212 J.R. Redmond RC .20 .50
212H J.R. Redmond SP 1.50 4.00
213 Dennis Northcutt RC .20 .50
213H Dennis Northcutt SP 1.50 4.00
214 Gari Scott RC .20 .50
214H Gari Scott SP 1.50 4.00
215 Bashir Yamini RC .20 .50
215H Bashir Yamini SP 1.50 4.00
216 Danny Farmer RC .20 .50
216H Danny Farmer SP 1.50 4.00
217 Corey Simon RC .25 .60
217H Corey Simon SP 2.00 5.00
218 Plaxico Burress RC .25 .60
218H Plaxico Burress SP 2.00 5.00
219 Chad Morton RC .25 .60
219H Chad Morton SP 2.00 5.00
220 Bubba Franks RC .20 .50
220H Bubba Franks SP 1.50 4.00
221 Shaun Alexander RC .30 .75
221H Shaun Alexander SP 2.50 6.00
222 Dez White RC .20 .50
222H Dez White SP 1.50 4.00
223 Mareno Philyaw RC .20 .50
223H Mareno Philyaw SP 1.50 4.00
224 Travis Taylor RC .20 .50
224H Travis Taylor SP 1.50 4.00
225 Brian Urlacher RC 1.00 2.50
225H Brian Urlacher SP 8.00 20.00
226 Jamal Lewis RC .30 .75
226H Jamal Lewis SP 2.50 6.00
227 Sherrod Gideon RC .20 .50
227H Sherrod Gideon SP 1.50 4.00
228 Shyrone Stith RC .20 .50
228H Shyrone Stith SP 1.50 4.00
229 Chris Cole RC .25 .60
229H Chris Cole SP 2.00 5.00
230 Darrell Jackson RC .20 .50
230H Darrell Jackson SP 1.50 4.00
231 Quinton Spotwood RC .20 .50
231H Quinton Spotwood SP 1.50 4.00
232 Tee Martin RC .20 .50
232H Tee Martin SP 1.50 4.00
233 Tim Rattay RC .25 .60
233H Tim Rattay SP 2.00 5.00
234 Marc Bulger RC .25 .60
234H Marc Bulger SP 2.00 5.00
235 Doug Johnson RC .20 .50
235H Doug Johnson SP 1.50 4.00
236 Joe Hamilton RC .20 .50
236H Joe Hamilton SP 1.50 4.00
237 Trevor Gaylor RC .20 .50
237H Trevor Gaylor SP 1.50 4.00
238 Travis Prentice RC .20 .50
238H Travis Prentice SP 1.50 4.00
239 R.Jay Soward RC .20 .50
239H R.Jay Soward SP 1.50 4.00
240 Trung Canidate RC .20 .50
240H Trung Canidate SP 1.50 4.00
241 Giovanni Carmazzi RC .20 .50
241H Giovanni Carmazzi SP 1.50 4.00
242 Reuben Droughns RC .20 .50
242H Reuben Droughns SP 1.50 4.00
243 Curtis Keaton RC .20 .50
243H Curtis Keaton SP 1.50 4.00
244 Laveranues Coles RC .25 .60
244H Laveranues Coles SP 2.00 5.00
245 Ron Dugans RC .20 .50
245H Ron Dugans SP 1.50 4.00
246 Mike Anderson RC .20 .50
246H Mike Anderson SP 1.50 4.00
247 Anthony Becht RC .20 .50
247H Anthony Becht SP 1.50 4.00
248 Raynoch Thompson RC .20 .50
248H Raynoch Thompson SP 1.50 4.00
249 Rob Morris RC .25 .60
249H Rob Morris SP 2.00 5.00
250 Chafie Fields RC .20 .50
250H Chafie Fields SP 1.50 4.00
P1 Tim Couch Promo .40 1.00

2000 SkyBox Star Rubies

COMPLETE SET (250) 60.00 120.00
*VETS 1-200: 2.5X TO 6X BASIC CARDS
*ROOKIES 201-250: 2X TO 5X
STAR RUBY STATED ODDS 1:12

2000 SkyBox Star Rubies Extreme

*VETS 1-200: 12X TO 30X BASIC CARDS
*ROOKIES 201-250: 10X TO 25X
EXTREME PRINT RUN 50 SER.#'d SETS

2000 SkyBox Preemptive Strike

Randomly inserted in packs at the rate of one in four, this 15-card set features full color player action photos set against a yellow background with a black box in the middle of the card with the Preemptive Strike logo.

COMPLETE SET (15) 5.00 12.00
STATED ODDS 1:4
*STAR RUBIES/100: 5X TO 12X BASIC INSERTS
STAR RUBIES PRINT RUN 100 SER.#'d SETS
1 Tim Couch .30 .75
2 Edgerrin James .30 .75
3 Jake Plummer .25 .60
4 Akili Smith .25 .60
5 Cade McNown .25 .60
6 Isaac Bruce .40 1.00
7 Marvin Harrison .30 .75
8 Troy Aikman .50 1.25
9 Germane Crowell .25 .60
10 Cris Carter .40 1.00
11 Keyshawn Johnson .30 .75
12 Donovan McNabb .30 .75
13 Charlie Batch .25 .60
14 Muhsin Muhammad .25 .60
15 Marcus Robinson .30 .75

2000 SkyBox Skylines

Randomly inserted in packs at the rate of one in 11, this 10-card set features black borders along the top and bottom the card with an overlayed color player action photo on the right side. Across the background is a panoramic photo of the city skyline that the featured player's team stadium is in.

COMPLETE SET (10) 7.50 20.00
STATED ODDS 1:11
*STAR RUBIES/50: 5X TO 12X BASIC INSERTS
STAR RUBIES PRINT RUN 50 SER.#'d SETS
1 Tim Couch .50 1.25
2 Edgerrin James .50 1.25
3 Terrell Davis .50 1.25
4 Jamal Anderson .50 1.25
5 Kurt Warner 1.00 2.50
6 Charlie Batch .40 1.00
7 Emmitt Smith 1.00 2.50
8 Peyton Manning 1.50 4.00
9 Cade McNown .40 1.00
10 Mark Brunell .50 1.25

2000 SkyBox Sole Train

Randomly inserted in packs at the rate of one in eight, this 10-card set features color player action photograpy on the left side of the card with a colored banner on the right with the words Sole Train and the player's name in silver foil.

COMPLETE SET (10) 5.00 12.00
STATED ODDS 1:8
*STAR RUBIES/100: 4X TO 10X BASIC INSERTS
STAR RUBIES PRINT RUN 100 SER.#'d SETS
1 Edgerrin James .40 1.00
2 Eddie George .40 1.00
3 Marshall Faulk .40 1.00
4 Emmitt Smith .75 2.00
5 Fred Taylor .30 .75
6 Stephen Davis .30 .75
7 Ricky Williams .40 1.00
8 Jamal Anderson .40 1.00
9 Warrick Dunn .30 .75
10 Jerome Bettis .50 1.25

2000 SkyBox Sunday's Best

Randomly inserted in packs at the rate of one in 24, this 10-card set features a die cut top in the shape of a semi-circle. Player action photos are set agains a stained glass background. The card stock is plastic and features gold foil highlights along the right side of the card.

COMPLETE SET (10) 12.50 30.00
STATED ODDS 1:24
*STAR RUBIES/50: 4X TO 10X BASIC INSERTS
STAR RUBIES PRINT RUN 50 SER.#'d SETS
1 Tim Couch .60 1.50
2 Edgerrin James .60 1.50
3 Terrell Davis .60 1.50
4 Peyton Manning 2.00 5.00
5 Marshall Faulk .60 1.50
6 Brett Favre 1.50 4.00
7 Emmitt Smith 1.25 3.00
8 Randy Moss .60 1.50
9 Fred Taylor .50 1.25
10 Ricky Williams .60 1.50

2000 SkyBox Superlatives

Randomly inserted in packs at the rate of one in 11, this 15-card set features a brushed foil background with centered player action photograpy. The word superlatives appears on the top of the card in gold foil, and towards the bottom of the card, the player's name and a brief comment appear also in gold foil.

COMPLETE SET (15) 10.00 25.00
STATED ODDS 1:11
*STAR RUBIES/50: 5X TO 12X BASIC INSERTS
STAR RUBIES PRINT RUN 50 SER.#'d SETS
1 Tim Couch .50 1.25
2 Edgerrin James .50 1.25
3 Randy Moss .50 1.25
4 Marshall Faulk .50 1.25
5 Fred Taylor .40 1.00
6 Jake Plummer .40 1.00
7 Vinny Testaverde .40 1.00
8 Troy Aikman .75 2.00
9 Drew Bledsoe .50 1.25
10 Stephen Davis .40 1.00
11 Marvin Harrison .50 1.25
12 Steve Young .75 2.00
13 Jimmy Smith .50 1.25
14 Ricky Williams .50 1.25
15 Kurt Warner 1.00 2.50

2000 SkyBox The Bomb

Randomly inserted in packs at the rate of one in 24, this 10-card set features a yellow and orange background. Next to player action photos, the words The Bomb appear in silver foil.

COMPLETE SET (10) 12.00 30.00
STATED ODDS 1:24
*STAR RUBIES/50: 3X TO 8X BASIC INSERTS
STAR RUBIES PRINT RUN 50
1 Tim Couch .60 1.50
2 Kurt Warner 1.25 3.00
3 Edgerrin James .60 1.50
4 Randy Moss .60 1.50
5 Keyshawn Johnson .60 1.50
6 Brett Favre 1.50 4.00
7 Peyton Manning 2.00 5.00
8 Eddie George .60 1.50
9 Isaac Bruce .75 2.00
10 Marvin Harrison .60 1.50

1999 SkyBox Dominion

Released as a 250-card set, the 1999 Skybox Dominion is comprised of 200 veteran player cards an 50 rookie cards. Base cards are accented with gray tone backgrounds and silver foil highlights. Skybox Dominion was packaged in 36-pack boxes with 10 cards per pack. Also inserted were the cross brand autographics cards which features hand signed cards of various players.

COMPLETE SET (250) 15.00 40.00
1 Randy Moss .15 .40
2 James Jett .12 .30
3 Lawyer Milloy .12 .30
4 Mike Alstott .12 .30
5 Courtney Hawkins .12 .30
6 Carl Pickens .15 .40
7 Marvin Harrison .15 .40
8 Robert Smith .12 .30
9 Fred Taylor .12 .30
10 Barry Sanders .30 .75
11 Tony Gonzalez .15 .40
12 Leroy Hoard .12 .30
13 Drew Bledsoe .15 .40
14 Cam Cleeland .12 .30
15 Steve Atwater .15 .40
16 Eric Moulds .12 .30
17 Herman Moore .15 .40
18 Rickey Dudley .12 .30
19 Jeff Blake .15 .40
20 Eddie George .15 .40
21 Antonio Freeman .15 .40
22 Stephen Alexander .12 .30
23 Larry Centers .12 .30
24 Chris Chandler .15 .40
25 James Stewart .12 .30
26 Randall Cunningham .15 .40
27 Mark Brunell .15 .40
28 David Palmer .12 .30
29 Eric Green .12 .30
30 Terry Glenn .15 .40
31 Jerry Rice .50 1.25
32 Ricky Proehl .12 .30
33 Tony Banks .15 .40
34 John Elway .30 .75
35 Johnnie Morton .15 .40
36 Tony Simmons .12 .30
37 Jon Kitna .12 .30
38 Trent Green .12 .30
39 Peyton Manning .60 1.50
40 Emmitt Smith .30 .75
41 Warrick Dunn .12 .30
42 Jerome Bettis .20 .50
43 Ricky Watters .15 .40
44 Rocket Ismail .15 .40
45 Ryan Leaf .15 .40
46 Jackie Harris .15 .40
47 Robert Holcombe .12 .30
48 Dorsey Levens .15 .40
49 Duce Staley .12 .30
50 Brett Favre .40 1.00
51 Andre Rison .15 .40
52 Curtis Conway .15 .40
53 Mark Chmura .12 .30
54 Doug Flutie .20 .50
55 Ernie Mills .12 .30
56 Jeff George .12 .30
57 Chris Warren .15 .40
58 Alonzo Mayes .12 .30
59 Freddie Jones .12 .30
60 Shannon Sharpe .15 .40
61 O.J. Santiago .12 .30
62 Shawn Springs .12 .30
63 Kent Graham .12 .30
64 Muhsin Muhammad .12 .30
65 Keith Poole .12 .30
66 Chris Spielman .15 .40
67 Curtis Enis .12 .30
68 Lamar Smith .12 .30
69 Charles Johnson .12 .30
70 Kerry Collins .12 .30
71 Charlie Batch .12 .30
72 Keenan McCardell .15 .40
73 Ty Detmer .12 .30
74 Mark Bruener .12 .30
75 Lamar Thomas .12 .30
76 Kwamie Lassiter RC .12 .30
77 Byron Bam Morris .12 .30
78 Michael Sinclair .12 .30
79 Darnay Scott .12 .30
80 Napoleon Kaufman .12 .30
81 Ed McCaffrey .15 .40
82 Reidel Anthony .12 .30
83 Kevin Greene .20 .50
84 Michael Irvin .20 .50
85 Charles Way .12 .30
86 Tim Brown .20 .50
87 Johnny McWilliams .12 .30
88 Brad Johnson .15 .40
89 Antonio Langham .12 .30
90 Bruce Smith .15 .40
91 Reggie Barlow .12 .30
92 Ty Law .20 .50
93 Bobby Engram .12 .30
94 Kimble Anders .12 .30
95 Dale Carter .12 .30
96 Jimmy Smith .15 .40
97 Marc Edwards .15 .40
98 Ken Dilger .12 .30
99 Adrian Murrell .12 .30
100 Terance Mathis .12 .30
101 Gary Anderson .12 .30
102 Garrison Hearst .12 .30
103 Ahman Green .15 .40
104 Daryl Johnston .15 .40
105 O.J. McDuffie .15 .40
106 Matthew Hatchette .15 .40
107 Chris Doleman .12 .30
108 Steve McNair .15 .40
109 Leon Johnson .12 .30
110 Terrell Davis .15 .40
111 Rob Moore .12 .30
112 Troy Aikman .25 .60
113 John Avery .12 .30
114 Frank Wycheck .15 .40
115 Curtis Martin .15 .40
116 Jim Harbaugh .15 .40
117 Sean Dawkins .12 .30
118 Glenn Foley .12 .30
119 Warren Sapp .15 .40
120 R.W. McQuarters .12 .30
121 Yancey Thigpen .12 .30
122 Frank Sanders .12 .30
123 Tim Dwight .15 .40
124 Pete Mitchell .12 .30
125 Steve Beuerlein .15 .40
126 Tyrone Davis .12 .30
127 Jamie Asher .12 .30
128 Corey Dillon .12 .30
129 Doug Pederson .12 .30
130 Deion Sanders .15 .40
131 J.J. Stokes .12 .30
132 Jermaine Lewis .12 .30
133 Gary Brown .12 .30
134 Derrick Alexander .12 .30
135 Tony McGee .12 .30
136 Kyle Brady .12 .30
137 Mikhael Ricks .12 .30
138 Germane Crowell .12 .30
139 Skip Hicks .12 .30
140 Ben Coates .15 .40
141 Will Blackwell .12 .30
142 Al Del Greco .12 .30
143 Jake Plummer .12 .30
144 Marshall Faulk .15 .40
145 Antowain Smith .12 .30
146 Corey Fuller .12 .30
147 Keyshawn Johnson .15 .40
148 John Randle .20 .50
149 Terrell Buckley .15 .40
150 Terry Kirby .12 .30
151 Robert Brooks .15 .40
152 Karim Abdul-Jabbar .12 .30
153 Jason Sehorn .15 .40
154 Elvis Grbac .12 .30
155 Andre Reed .20 .50
156 Ike Hilliard .12 .30
157 Jamal Anderson .15 .40
158 Jake Reed .15 .40
159 Rich Gannon .15 .40
160 Michael Jackson .12 .30
161 Bert Emanuel .15 .40
162 Charles Woodson .20 .50
163 Ray Lewis .20 .50
164 Trent Dilfer .12 .30
165 Oronde Gadsden .12 .30
166 Wesley Walls .15 .40
167 Joey Galloway .15 .40
168 Mo Lewis .12 .30
169 Darren Woodson .15 .40
170 Cris Carter .20 .50
171 Brian Mitchell .15 .40
172 Tim Biakabutuka .15 .40
173 Michael Westbrook .12 .30
174 Dan Marino .40 1.00
175 Greg Hill .12 .30
176 Priest Holmes .12 .30
177 Fred Lane .12 .30
178 Isaac Bruce .20 .50
179 Erik Kramer .15 .40
180 Steve Young .25 .60
181 Terry Fair .12 .30
182 Brian Griese .12 .30
183 Leslie Shepherd .12 .30
184 Kordell Stewart .12 .30
185 Charlie Jones .12 .30
186 Chris Calloway .12 .30
187 Wayne Chrebet .12 .30
188 Natrone Means .15 .40
189 David LaFleur .12 .30
190 Rod Smith WR .15 .40
191 Kevin Dyson .12 .30
192 Scott Mitchell .12 .30
193 Andre Wadsworth .12 .30
194 Vinny Testaverde .12 .30
195 Az-Zahir Hakim .12 .30
196 Joe Jurevicius .12 .30
197 Junior Seau .15 .40
198 Jason Elam .12 .30
199 Terrell Owens .15 .40
200 Jacquez Green .12 .30
201 Tim Couch RC .25 .60
202 Donovan McNabb RC 2.00 5.00
203 Cade McNown RC .20 .50
204 Akili Smith RC .20 .50
205 Kevin Faulk RC .20 .50
206 Sedrick Irvin RC .20 .50
207 Edgerrin James RC .30 .75
208 Ricky Williams RC .30 .75
209 D'Wayne Bates RC .20 .50
210 David Boston RC .20 .50
211 Torry Holt RC .40 1.00
212 Peerless Price RC .20 .50
213 Daunte Culpepper RC .30 .75
214 Troy Edwards RC .20 .50
215 Rob Konrad RC .20 .50
216 Joe Germaine RC .25 .60
217 James Johnson RC .20 .50
218 Brock Huard RC .20 .50
219 Cecil Collins RC .20 .50
220 J.Paulk/E.Baker RC .20 .50
221 Mar.Booker RC/J.Finn RC .20 .50
222 S.Covington/N.Williams RC .20 .50
223 K.Johnson/Chiaverini RC .25 .60
224 E.Ekuban/D.Nguyen RC .30 .75
225 A.Wilson/C.Plummer RC .30 .75
226 C.Claiborne/A.Gibson RC .20 .50
227 A.Brooks/D.Parker RC .25 .60
228 J.Tait/M.Cloud RC .20 .50
229 A.Katzenmoyer/Bishop RC .25 .60
230 Montgomery/Campbell RC .30 .75
231 N.Brown RC/C.Martin RC .20 .50
232 A.Zereoue/J.Tuman RC .20 .50
233 J.Fazande .20 .50
S.Heiden RC
234 K.Bailey/C.Rogers RC .20 .50
235 S.King/M.Gramatica RC .20 .50
236 J.Kearse/K.Daft RC .25 .60
237 C.Bailey/T.Alexander RC .40 1.00
238 K.Bailey/D.McDonald RC .20 .50
239 L.Glenn/T.Jackson RC .20 .50
240 T.Smith .25 .60
M.Johnson RC
241 R.Menendez/C.Yeast RC .20 .50
242 J.Weaver/J.Dearth RC .20 .50
243 J.Makovicka/S.Bryson RC .20 .50
244 D.Clark/J.Kleinsasser RC .30 .75
245 S.Bennett/A.Denson RC .20 .50
246 B.Miller .20 .50
W.McGarity RC
247 M.Lucky/J.Swift RC .20 .50
248 T.McGriff/M.Jenkins RC .25 .60
249 D.Driver RC/L.Parker RC 4.00 10.00
250 A.Winfield/D.Bly RC .30 .75
P54 Doug Flutie Promo .40 1.00

1999 SkyBox Dominion Atlantattitude

Randomly inserted in packs at the rate of one in 24, this 15-card set features top players battling to lead their team to Super Bowl XXXIV in Atlanta. Two parallel versions of this set were released also with the Plus version being printed on a refractive card stock and the Warp Tek individually serial numbered.

COMPLETE SET (15) 40.00 80.00
STATED ODDS 1:24
*PLUS REFRACT: 1.2X TO 3X BASIC INSERTS
PLUS STATED ODDS 1:240
1 Charlie Batch 1.50 4.00
2 Mark Brunell 1.50 4.00
3 Tim Couch .75 2.00
4 Terrell Davis 1.50 4.00
5 Warrick Dunn 1.50 4.00
6 Brett Favre 5.00 12.00
7 Peyton Manning 5.00 12.00
8 Dan Marino 5.00 12.00
9 Randy Moss 4.00 10.00
10 Jake Plummer 1.00 2.50
11 Barry Sanders 5.00 12.00
12 Akili Smith .60 1.50
13 Emmitt Smith 3.00 8.00
14 Fred Taylor 1.50 4.00
15 Ricky Williams 2.00 5.00

1999 SkyBox Dominion Atlantattitude Warp Tek

CARDS SERIAL #'d UNDER 20 NOT PRICED
4 Terrell Davis/30 30.00 80.00
5 Warrick Dunn/28 30.00 60.00
9 Randy Moss/84 40.00 80.00
11 Barry Sanders/20 125.00 250.00
13 Emmitt Smith/22 75.00 150.00
14 Fred Taylor/28 40.00 100.00
15 Ricky Williams/34 30.00 80.00

1999 SkyBox Dominion Gen Next

Randomly inserted in packs at the rate of one in 3, this 20-card set features 20 top rookies on a silver foil board background. Two parallels of this set were released also.

COMPLETE SET (20) 10.00 25.00
STATED ODDS 1:3
*PLUS GOLD: 1X TO 2.5X BASIC INSERTS
PLUS GOLD STATED ODDS 1:30
*WARP TEK GREEN: 3X TO 8X BASIC INSERTS
WARP TEK GREEN ODDS 1:300
1 D'Wayne Bates .20 .50
2 David Boston .25 .60
3 Cecil Collins .10 .30
4 Tim Couch .25 .60
5 Daunte Culpepper 1.25 3.00
6 Troy Edwards .20 .50
7 Kevin Faulk .25 .60
8 Joe Germaine .20 .50
9 Torry Holt .60 1.50
10 Brock Huard .25 .60
11 Sedrick Irvin .10 .30
12 Edgerrin James 1.25 3.00
13 James Johnson .20 .50
14 Kevin Johnson .25 .60
15 Shaun King .20 .50
16 Donovan McNabb 1.50 4.00
17 Cade McNown .20 .50
18 Akili Smith .20 .50
19 Ricky Williams .60 1.50
20 Amos Zereoue .25 .60

1999 SkyBox Dominion Goal 2 Go

Randomly inserted in packs at a rate of one in nine, This dual player 10 card insert set features one star player on the card front and card back.

COMPLETE SET (10) 10.00 25.00
STATED ODDS 1:9
*PLUS REFRACT: 1.2X TO 3X BASIC CARDS
PLUS STATED ODDS 1:90
*WARP TEK PRISM: 3X TO 8X BASIC CARDS
WARP TEK STATED ODDS 1:900
1 T.Davis .60 1.50
J.Anderson
2 B.Favre 2.00 5.00
J.Plummer
3 R.Moss 1.50 4.00
J.Rice
4 W.Dunn 2.00 5.00
B.Sanders
5 E.George .60 1.50
F.Taylor
6 E.Smith 1.25 3.00
M.Faulk
7 Key.Johnson .60 1.50
T.Owens
8 P.Manning 2.00 5.00
R.Leaf
9 D.Marino 2.00 5.00
J.Elway
10 C.McNown .60 1.50
C.Batch

1999 SkyBox Dominion Hats Off

Randomly inserted in packs, This six card insert set features and actual piece of the hat each respective player wore during the 1999 NFL draft. Each is hand numbered to diferent quantities for each player on the card front. Aslo on the card front is a head shot of the player wearing the hat used for the set. A signed version of each (except Couch) was also produced and serial numbered of 20.

1 Tim Couch/135 15.00 40.00
2 Donovan McNabb/130 30.00 80.00
3 Akili Smith/85 15.00 40.00
4 Ricky Williams/130 25.00 60.00
5 Daunte Culpepper/100 20.00 50.00
6 Cade McNown/120 20.00 50.00

1999 SkyBox Dominion Hats Off Autographs

Randomly inserted in packs, this five card insert set features an actual piece of the hat each respective player wore during the 1999 NFL draft along with an actual hand signed autograph. The cardfront is hand serial numbered to 20 of each issued. Please note that Tim Couch did not sign the Autographed version of Hats Off.

STATED PRINT RUN 20 SER.#'d SETS
2 Donovan McNabb 200.00 350.00
3 Akili Smith 20.00 50.00
4 Ricky Williams 100.00 200.00
5 Daunte Culpepper 30.00 80.00
6 Cade McNown 25.00 60.00

2000 SkyBox Dominion

Released as a 243-card set, 2000 Dominion is composed of 195 Veteran cards, 33 Rookies, and 15 Rookie Pairs cards. Base cards contain full color action photograpy that fades away into an all white border, and are accented with silver foil stamping. Dominion was packaged in 20-pack boxes with packs containing 10 cards and carried a suggested retail price of $1.49. Card numbers 214 and 226 were not released.

COMPLETE SET (243) 12.50 30.00
1 Tim Couch .15 .40
2 Byron Hanspard .12 .30
3 Jay Riemersma .12 .30
4 Cade McNown .12 .30
5 Darnay Scott .15 .40
6 Emmitt Smith .30 .75
7 Rod Smith .15 .40
8 James Stewart .12 .30
9 Marvin Harrison .15 .40
10 Keenan McCardell .15 .40
11 Andre Rison .15 .40
12 Jeff George .15 .40
13 Terry Glenn .15 .40
14 Cam Cleeland .12 .30
15 Curtis Martin .15 .40
16 Troy Edwards .12 .30
17 Mikhael Ricks .12 .30
18 Joey Galloway .15 .40
19 Az-Zahir Hakim .12 .30
20 Mike Alstott .12 .30
21 Samari Rolle .12 .30
22 Michael Pittman .12 .30
23 Tony Banks .12 .30
24 Bruce Smith .15 .40
25 Curtis Enis .12 .30
26 Jake Plummer .12 .30
27 Darren Woodson .15 .40
28 Bill Romanowski .12 .30
29 Antonio Freeman .15 .40
30 Terrence Wilkins .12 .30
31 Kevin Hardy .12 .30
32 Peerless Price .15 .40
33 Cris Carter .20 .50
34 Willie McGinest .15 .40
35 Kerry Collins .12 .30
36 Bryan Cox .12 .30
37 Tyrone Wheatley .12 .30
38 Jason Sehorn .12 .30
39 Jerry Rice .50 1.25
40 Christian Fauria .12 .30
41 Kevin Carter .12 .30
42 John Lynch .15 .40
43 Brad Johnson .15 .40
44 David Boston .12 .30
45 Peter Boulware .12 .30
46 Muhsin Muhammad .12 .30
47 Bobby Engram .12 .30
48 Kevin Johnson .12 .30
49 Charlie Batch .12 .30
50 Dorsey Levens .15 .40
51 Cornelius Bennett .12 .30
52 Kyle Brady .12 .30
53 Damon Huard .12 .30
54 Robert Smith .12 .30
55 Ty Law .20 .50
56 Amani Toomer .12 .30
57 Aaron Glenn .12 .30
58 Donovan McNabb .15 .40
59 Levon Kirkland .12 .30
60 Terrell Owens .15 .40
61 Sam Adams .12 .30
62 London Fletcher RC .30 .75
63 Steve McNair .15 .40
64 Stephen Davis .12 .30
65 Daunte Culpepper .15 .40
66 Andre Wadsworth .12 .30
67 Priest Holmes .12 .30
68 Patrick Jeffers .12 .30
69 Walt Harris .12 .30
70 Darrin Chiaverini .12 .30
71 Dat Nguyen .12 .30
72 Robert Porcher .12 .30
73 Bill Schroeder .15 .40
74 Tyrone Poole .12 .30
75 Bryce Paup .12 .30
76 O.J. McDuffie .15 .40
77 Jake Reed .15 .40
78 Ike Hilliard .12 .30
79 Victor Green .12 .30
80 Duce Staley .12 .30
81 Amos Zereoue .12 .30
82 Charlie Garner .15 .40
83 Shawn Springs .12 .30
84 Shaun King .12 .30
85 Eddie George .15 .40
86 Michael Westbrook .12 .30
87 Ricky Williams .15 .40
88 Chris Chandler .15 .40
89 Chris McAlister .12 .30
90 Steve Beuerlein .15 .40
91 Marty Booker .12 .30
92 Karim Abdul-Jabbar .12 .30
93 Brian Griese .12 .30
94 Germane Crowell .12 .30
95 Mark Chmura .12 .30
96 E.G. Green .12 .30
97 Elvis Grbac .12 .30

98 Tony Martin .15 .40
99 John Randle .20 .50
100 Michael Strahan .15 .40
101 Tim Brown .20 .50
102 Torrance Small .12 .30
103 Junior Seau .15 .40
104 Bryant Young .12 .30
105 Kurt Warner .30 .75
106 Trent Dilfer .12 .30
107 Kevin Dyson .15 .40
108 Stephen Alexander .12 .30
109 Tim Dwight .15 .40
110 Rob Johnson .15 .40
111 Tim Biakabutuka .15 .40
112 Akili Smith .12 .30
113 Terry Kirby .12 .30
114 Terrell Davis .15 .40
115 Herman Moore .12 .30
116 Vonnie Holliday .12 .30
117 Mark Brunell .15 .40
118 Derrick Alexander .12 .30
119 Oronde Gadsden .15 .40
120 Ed McDaniel .12 .30
121 Eddie Kennison .12 .30
122 Jessie Armstead .12 .30
123 Charles Woodson .20 .50
124 Troy Vincent .12 .30
125 Jeff Garcia .12 .30
126 Marshall Faulk .15 .40
127 Jacquez Green .12 .30
128 Frank Wycheck .15 .40
129 Champ Bailey .15 .40
130 Natrone Means .15 .40
131 Jamal Anderson .15 .40
132 Doug Flutie .15 .40
133 Michael Bates .12 .30
134 Corey Dillon .12 .30
135 Corey Fuller .12 .30
136 Olandis Gary .15 .40
137 Johnnie Morton .15 .40
138 Peyton Manning .50 1.25
139 Fred Taylor .12 .30
140 Tony Gonzalez .15 .40
141 Zach Thomas .15 .40
142 Drew Bledsoe .15 .40
143 Keith Poole .12 .30
144 Vinny Testaverde .12 .30
145 Rich Gannon .15 .40
146 Jeremiah Trotter RC .40 1.00
147 Freddie Jones .12 .30
148 Jon Kitna .12 .30
149 Isaac Bruce .20 .50
150 Warrick Dunn .12 .30
151 Yancey Thigpen .12 .30
152 Darrell Green .15 .40
153 Terance Mathis .12 .30
154 Eric Moulds .12 .30
155 Wesley Walls .12 .30
156 Carl Pickens .15 .40
157 Troy Aikman .25 .60
158 Dwayne Carswell .12 .30
159 David Sloan .12 .30
160 Edgerrin James .15 .40
161 Jimmy Smith .15 .40
162 Tamarick Vanover .12 .30
163 Sam Madison .12 .30
164 Tony Simmons .12 .30
165 Andre Hastings .12 .30
166 Keyshawn Johnson .15 .40
167 Napoleon Kaufman .15 .40
168 Hines Ward .15 .40
169 Jeff Graham .12 .30
170 Derrick Mayes .12 .30
171 Torry Holt .15 .40
172 Blaine Bishop .12 .30
173 Rob Moore .12 .30
174 Pat Johnson .12 .30
175 Antowain Smith .15 .40
176 Marcus Robinson .15 .40
177 Takeo Spikes .12 .30
178 Rocket Ismail .15 .40
179 Ed McCaffrey .15 .40
180 Brett Favre .40 1.00
181 Ken Dilger .12 .30
182 Carnell Lake .12 .30
183 Cris Dishman .12 .30
184 Randy Moss .15 .40
185 Lawyer Milloy .12 .30
186 Jake Delhomme RC .15 .40
187 Wayne Chrebet .12 .30
188 Darrell Russell .12 .30
189 Jerome Bettis .20 .50
190 Steve Young .25 .60
191 Ricky Watters .15 .40
192 Grant Wistrom .12 .30
193 Warren Sapp .15 .40
194 Jevon Kearse .12 .30
195 James Jett .15 .40
196 Courtney Brown RC .20 .50
197 Peter Warrick RC .15 .40
198 Thomas Jones RC .20 .50
199 Sylvester Morris RC .15 .40
200 Chad Pennington RC .20 .50
201 Ron Dayne RC .25 .60
202 Todd Pinkston RC .15 .40
203 Deon Dyer RC .15 .40
204 Chris Redman RC .15 .40
205 Jerry Porter RC .25 .60
206 Michael Wiley RC .15 .40
207 J.R. Redmond RC .15 .40
208 Dennis Northcutt RC .15 .40
209 Gari Scott RC .15 .40
210 Anthony Lucas RC .15 .40
211 Danny Farmer RC .15 .40
212 Marcus Knight RC .15 .40
213 Plaxico Burress RC .20 .50
215 Bubba Franks RC .15 .40
216 Shaun Alexander RC .25 .60
217 Dez White RC .15 .40
218 Mareno Philyaw RC .15 .40
219 Travis Taylor RC .15 .40
220 Kwame Cavil RC .15 .40
221 Jamal Lewis RC .25 .60
222 Sebastian Janikowski RC .25 .60
223 Shyrone Stith RC .15 .40
224 Ron Dugans RC .15 .40
225 Darrell Jackson RC .15 .40
227 Tee Martin RC .15 .40
228 Tim Rattay RC .20 .50
229 Marc Bulger RC .20 .50
230 Doug Johnson RC .15 .40
231 J.Hamilton RC .15 .40
T.Husak RC
232 T.Prentice RC .15 .40
R.Soward RC
233 T.Canidate RC .15 .40
R.Drghns RC
234 T.Brady RC 25.00 50.00
G.Carmazzi RC
235 L.Coles RC .20 .50
C.Fields RC
236 J.Jackson RC .20 .50
S.Gideon RC
237 T.Walters RC .15 .40
E.Kinney RC
238 R.Mealey RC .15 .40
J.Gdspeed RC
239 A.Becht RC .15 .40
Q.Spotwood RC
240 D.O'Neal RC .15 .40
N.Diggs RC
241 C.Simon RC .20 .50
C.Hovan RC
242 B.Urlacher RC .75 2.00
C.Moore RC
243 K.Bulluck RC .20 .50
R.Morris RC
244 R.Thompson RC .15 .40
D.Grant RC
245 J.Abraham RC .25 .60
S.Ellis RC
P1 Tim Couch Promo .40 1.00

2000 SkyBox Dominion Extra

COMPLETE SET (243) 40.00 100.00
*VETS 1-195: 1X TO 2.5X BASIC CARDS
*ROOKIES 196-245: .8X TO 25X
STATED ODDS 1:2

2000 SkyBox Dominion Characteristics

Randomly inserted in packs at the rate of one in 35, this 10-card set features all foil die cut cards with a Japanese Kanji character that best describes the featured player.

COMPLETE SET (10) 10.00 25.00
STATED ODDS 1:35
1 Brett Favre 1.50 4.00
2 Troy Aikman 1.00 2.50
3 Terrell Davis .60 1.50
4 Emmitt Smith 1.25 3.00
5 Peyton Manning 2.00 5.00
6 Randy Moss .60 1.50
7 Tim Couch .60 1.50
8 Eddie George .60 1.50
9 Kurt Warner 1.25 3.00
10 Edgerrin James .60 1.50

2000 SkyBox Dominion Go-To Guys

Randomly inserted in packs at the rate of one in 12, this 20-card set features an all-foil holographic background with two full color action shots of the showcased player.

COMPLETE SET (20) 7.50 20.00
STATED ODDS 1:12
1 Peyton Manning 1.50 4.00
2 Brett Favre 1.25 3.00
3 Troy Aikman .75 2.00
4 Kurt Warner 1.00 2.50
5 Randy Moss .50 1.25
6 Germane Crowell .40 1.00
7 Marvin Harrison .50 1.25
8 Jerry Rice 1.50 4.00
9 Muhsin Muhammad .40 1.00
10 Marcus Robinson .50 1.25
11 Isaac Bruce .60 1.50
12 Tim Brown .60 1.50
13 Stephen Davis .40 1.00
14 Cris Carter .60 1.50
15 Tim Couch .50 1.25
16 Ricky Williams .50 1.25
17 Dorsey Levens .50 1.25
18 Keyshawn Johnson .50 1.25
19 Mark Brunell .50 1.25
20 Jimmy Smith .50 1.25

2000 SkyBox Dominion Hard Corps

Randomly inserted in packs at the rate of one in six, this 10-card set features an all-white card stock with color player photos. The words Hard Corps appear across the front of the card in embossed silver printing.

COMPLETE SET (10) 2.50 6.00
STATED ODDS 1:6
1 Brett Favre .50 1.25
2 Eddie George .20 .50
3 Terrell Davis .20 .50
4 Randy Moss .20 .50
5 Marshall Faulk .20 .50
6 Ricky Williams .20 .50
7 Keyshawn Johnson .20 .50
8 Fred Taylor .15 .40
9 Steve Young .30 .75
10 Edgerrin James .20 .50

2000 SkyBox Dominion Turfs Up

Randomly inserted in packs at the rate of one in 18, this 10-card set features a rainbow colored background, color action player photos, and rainbow holofoil highlights.

COMPLETE SET (10) 6.00 15.00
STATED ODDS 1:18
1 Terrell Davis .50 1.25
2 Ricky Williams .50 1.25
3 Jamal Anderson .50 1.25
4 Marshall Faulk .50 1.25
5 Emmitt Smith 1.00 2.50
6 Eddie George .50 1.25
7 Fred Taylor .40 1.00
8 Edgerrin James .50 1.25
9 Warrick Dunn .40 1.00
10 Stephen Davis .40 1.00

1998 SkyBox Double Vision

This 32-card set was distributed in one-card packs with a suggested retail price of $5.99. The cards feature player color action photos and portraits printed on a large interactive slide that makes images appear and disappear. The slide mechanism combined with an acetate window background magically disappears. The borders are illustrated with team logos and colors. Every slide is sequentially numbered to 5000. The set includes the subset, "Strange but True" (Cards #22-32).

COMPLETE SET (32) 40.00 80.00
1 Dan Marino 3.00 8.00
2 John Elway 3.00 8.00
3 Troy Aikman 2.00 5.00
4 Steve Young 1.25 3.00
5 Terrell Davis 2.00 5.00
6 Barry Sanders 3.00 8.00
7 Jerry Rice 2.00 5.00
8 Kordell Stewart .60 1.50
9 Jake Plummer .60 1.50
10 Brett Favre 3.00 8.00
11 Drew Bledsoe 1.25 3.00
12 Tony Banks .40 1.00
13 Kerry Collins .40 1.00
14 Steve McNair .60 1.50
15 Warren Moon .40 1.00
16 Ryan Leaf .60 1.50
17 Peyton Manning 4.00 10.00
18 Elvis Grbac .40 1.00
19 Jeff Blake .40 1.00
20 Brad Johnson .60 1.50
21 Trent Dilfer .40 1.00
22 Scott Mitchell .30 .75
23 Dan Marino 3.00 8.00
24 John Elway 3.00 8.00
25 Troy Aikman 2.00 5.00
26 Steve Young 1.25 3.00
27 Terrell Davis 2.00 5.00
28 Barry Sanders 3.00 8.00
29 Jerry Rice 2.00 5.00
30 Kordell Stewart .60 1.50
31 Jake Plummer .60 1.50
32 Brett Favre 3.00 8.00

1992 SkyBox/Impel Impact/Primetime Promos

This two-card promotional standard-size set was distributed at the Super Bowl XXVI Show in Minneapolis in January, 1992. These cards were issued before Impel changed their corporate name to SkyBox and hence made some subtle changes in the promo cards to reflect their new identity. The Byner card displays a full-bleed photo of him running with the ball, superimposed on a gray background. His name and jersey number are printed in maroon, with the team name in white on a maroon bar. Against the background of a crowd, the Kelly card shows him with the ball cocked, ready to pass. The backs of both cards have an advertisement for Impel's new Impact and Primetime series. The Byner card is trimmed in red, while the Kelly card is trimmed in blue. The cards are unnumbered.

NNO Jim Kelly 1.20 3.00
NNO Earnest Byner .50 1.25

1992 SkyBox Impact Promos

These three standard-size cards were issued as a promo pack to show what the then-upcoming SkyBox Impact cards would be like. The fronts feature full-bleed color action photos, with the player's name in block lettering across the top of the picture. The team logo is superimposed at the lower left corner, and the SkyBox logo appears in the lower right corner. The backs show another color photo, career highlights, statistics, and the player's position by a diagram of "X's" and "O's." The photo displayed on the front of the Kelly card is almost identical to that used on the Impel promo given away at the Super Bowl XXVI card show.

COMPLETE SET (3) 1.60 4.00
1 Jim Kelly 1.00 2.50
2 Michael Dean Perry .40 1.00
3 Reggie Roby .40 1.00

1992 SkyBox Impact

The 1992 SkyBox Impact set consists of 350 standard-size cards that were issued in 12 and 24-card packs. The set includes the following subsets: Team Checklists (277-304), High Impact League Leaders (305-314), Sudden Impact Hardest Hitters (315-320), and Instant Impact Rookies (321-350). The key Rookie Cards in this set are Edgar Bennett, Steve Bono, Robert Brooks, Terrell Buckley, Marco Coleman, Steve Emtman and Carl Pickens. Five hundred Impact Playmakers cards featuring Magic Johnson and Jim Kelly bear autographs by both stars. These cards were randomly inserted in foil packs. Also, 2,500 gold foil-stamped Total Impact cards were autographed by Jim Kelly and randomly inserted in the foil packs.

COMPLETE SET (350) 5.00 12.00
1 Jim Kelly .08 .25
2 Andre Rison .02 .10
3 Michael Dean Perry .02 .10
4 Herman Moore .08 .25
5 Fred McAfee RC .01 .05
6 Ricky Proehl .01 .05
7 Jim Everett .02 .10
8 Mark Carrier DB .01 .05
9 Eric Martin .01 .05
10 John Elway .50 1.25
11 Michael Irvin .08 .25
12 Keith McCants .01 .05
13 Greg Lloyd .02 .10
14 Lawrence Taylor .08 .25
15 Mike Tomczak .01 .05
16 Cortez Kennedy .02 .10
17 William Fuller .01 .05
18 James Lofton .02 .10
19 Kevin Fagan .01 .05
20 Bill Brooks .01 .05
21 Roger Craig UER .02 .10
22 Jay Novacek .02 .10
23 Steve Sewell .01 .05
24 William Perry UER .02 .10
25 Jerry Rice .30 .75
26 James Joseph .01 .05
27 Timm Rosenbach .01 .05
28 Pat Terrell .01 .05
29 Jon Vaughn .01 .05
30 Steve Walsh .01 .05
31 James Hasty .01 .05
32 Dwight Stone .01 .05
33 Derrick Fenner UER .01 .05
34 Mark Bortz .01 .05
35 Dan Saleaumua .01 .05
36 Sammie Smith UER .01 .05
37 Antone Davis .01 .05
38 Steve Young .25 .60
39 Mike Baab .01 .05
40 Rick Fenney .01 .05
41 Chris Hinton .01 .05
42 Bart Oates .01 .05
43 Bryan Hinkle .01 .05
44 James Francis .01 .05
45 Ray Crockett .01 .05
46 Eric Dickerson .02 .10
47 Hart Lee Dykes .01 .05
48 Percy Snow .01 .05
49 Ron Hall .01 .05
50 Warren Moon .08 .25
51 Ed West .01 .05
52 Clarence Verdin .01 .05
53 Eugene Lockhart .01 .05
54 Andre Reed .02 .10
55 Kevin Ross .01 .05
56 Al Noga .01 .05
57 Wes Hopkins .01 .05
58 Rufus Porter .01 .05
59 Brian Mitchell .02 .10
60 Reggie Roby .01 .05
61 Rodney Peete .02 .10
62 Jeff Herrod .01 .05
63 Anthony Smith .01 .05
64 Brad Muster .01 .05
65 Jessie Tuggle .01 .05
66 Al Smith .01 .05
67 Jeff Hostetler .02 .10
68 John L. Williams .01 .05
69 Paul Gruber .01 .05
70 Cornelius Bennett .02 .10
71 William White .01 .05
72 Tom Rathman .01 .05
73 Boomer Esiason .02 .10
74 Neil Smith .08 .25
75 Sterling Sharpe .08 .25
76 James Jones DT .01 .05
77 David Treadwell .01 .05
78 Flipper Anderson .01 .05
79 Eric Allen .01 .05
80 Joe Jacoby .01 .05
81 Keith Sims .01 .05
82 Bubba McDowell .01 .05
83 Ronnie Lippett .01 .05
84 Cris Carter .20 .50
85 Chris Burkett .01 .05
86 Issiac Holt .01 .05
87 Duane Bickett .01 .05
88 Leslie O'Neal .02 .10
89 Gill Fenerty .01 .05
90 Pierce Holt .01 .05
91 Willie Drewrey .01 .05
92 Brian Blades .02 .10
93 Tony Martin .02 .10
94 Jessie Hester .01 .05
95 John Stephens .01 .05
96 Keith Willis UER .01 .05
97 Vai Sikahema UER .01 .05
98 Mark Higgs .01 .05
99 Steve McMichael .02 .10
100 Deion Sanders .20 .50
101 Marvin Washington .01 .05
102 Ken Norton .02 .10
103 Barry Word .01 .05
104 Sean Jones .01 .05
105 Ronnie Harmon .01 .05
106 Donnell Woolford .01 .05
107 Ray Agnew .01 .05
108 Lemuel Stinson .01 .05
109 Dennis Smith .01 .05
110 Lorenzo White .01 .05
111 Craig Heyward .02 .10
112 Jeff Query UER .01 .05
113 Gary Plummer .01 .05
114 John Taylor .02 .10
115 Rohn Stark .01 .05
116 Tom Waddle .01 .05
117 Jeff Cross .01 .05
118 Tim Green .01 .05
119 Anthony Munoz .02 .10
120 Mel Gray .02 .10
121 Ray Donaldson .01 .05
122 Dennis Byrd .01 .05
123 Carnell Lake .01 .05
124 Broderick Thomas .01 .05
125 Charles Mann .01 .05
126 Darion Conner .01 .05
127 John Roper .01 .05
128 Jack Del Rio UER .01 .05
129 Rickey Dixon .01 .05
130 Eddie Anderson .01 .05
131 Steve Broussard .01 .05
132 Michael Young .01 .05
133 Lamar Lathon .01 .05
134 Rickey Jackson .01 .05
135 Billy Ray Smith .01 .05
136 Tony Casillas .01 .05
137 Ickey Woods .01 .05
138 Ray Childress .01 .05
139 Vance Johnson .01 .05
140 Brett Perriman .08 .25
141 Calvin Williams .02 .10
142 Dino Hackett .01 .05
143 Jacob Green .01 .05
144 Robert Delpino .01 .05
145 Marv Cook .01 .05
146 Dwayne Harper .01 .05
147 Ricky Ervins .01 .05
148 Kelvin Martin .01 .05
149 Leroy Hoard .02 .10
150 Dan Marino .50 1.25
151 Richard Johnson CB UER .01 .05
152 Henry Ellard .02 .10
153 Al Toon .02 .10
154 Dermontti Dawson .02 .10
155 Robert Blackmon .01 .05
156 Howie Long .08 .25
157 David Fulcher .01 .05
158 Mike Merriweather .01 .05
159 Gary Anderson K .01 .05
160 John Friesz .02 .10
161 Eugene Robinson .01 .05
162 Brad Baxter .01 .05
163 Bennie Blades .01 .05
164 Harold Green .01 .05
165 Ernest Givins .02 .10
166 Deron Cherry .01 .05
167 Carl Banks .01 .05
168 Keith Jackson .02 .10
169 Pat Leahy .01 .05
170 Alvin Harper .02 .10
171 David Little .01 .05
172 Anthony Carter .02 .10
173 Willie Gault .02 .10
174 Bruce Armstrong .01 .05
175 Junior Seau .08 .25
176 Eric Metcalf .02 .10
177 Tony Mandarich .01 .05
178 Ernie Jones .01 .05
179 Albert Bentley .01 .05
180 Mike Pritchard .02 .10
181 Bubby Brister .01 .05
182 Vaughan Johnson .01 .05
183 Robert Clark UER .01 .05
184 Lawrence Dawsey .02 .10
185 Eric Green .01 .05
186 Jay Schroeder .01 .05
187 Andre Tippett .01 .05
188 Vinny Testaverde .02 .10
189 Wendell Davis .01 .05
190 Russell Maryland .01 .05
191 Chris Singleton .01 .05
192 Ken O'Brien .01 .05
193 Merril Hoge .01 .05
194 Steve Bono RC .08 .25
195 Earnest Byner .01 .05
196 Mike Singletary .02 .10
197 Gaston Green .01 .05
198 Mark Carrier WR .02 .10
199 Harvey Williams .08 .25
200 Randall Cunningham .08 .25
201 Cris Dishman .01 .05
202 Greg Townsend .01 .05
203 Christian Okoye .01 .05
204 Sam Mills .01 .05
205 Kyle Clifton .01 .05
206 Jim Harbaugh .08 .25
207 Anthony Thompson .01 .05
208 Rob Moore .02 .10
209 Irving Fryar .02 .10
210 Derrick Thomas .08 .25
211 Chris Miller .02 .10
212 Doug Smith .01 .05
213 Michael Haynes .02 .10
214 Phil Simms .02 .10
215 Charles Haley .02 .10
216 Burt Grossman .01 .05
217 Rod Bernstine .01 .05
218 Louis Lipps .01 .05
219 Dan McGwire .01 .05
220 Ethan Horton .01 .05
221 Michael Carter .01 .05
222 Neil O'Donnell .02 .10
223 Anthony Miller .02 .10
224 Eric Swann .02 .10
225 Thurman Thomas .08 .25
226 Jeff George .08 .25
227 Joe Montana .50 1.25
228 Leonard Marshall .01 .05
229 Haywood Jeffires .02 .10
230 Mark Clayton .02 .10
231 Chris Doleman .01 .05
232 Troy Aikman .30 .75
233 Gary Anderson RB .01 .05
234 Pat Swilling .01 .05
235 Ronnie Lott .02 .10
236 Brian Jordan .02 .10
237 Bruce Smith .08 .25
238 Tony Jones WR UER .01 .05
239 Tim McKyer .01 .05
240 Gary Clark .08 .25
241 Mitchell Price .01 .05
242 John Kasay .01 .05
243 Stephone Paige .01 .05
244 Jeff Wright .01 .05
245 Shannon Sharpe .08 .25
246 Keith Byars .01 .05
247 Charles Dimry .01 .05
248 Steve Smith .01 .05
249 Erric Pegram .02 .10
250 Bernie Kosar .02 .10
251 Peter Tom Willis .01 .05
252 Mark Ingram .01 .05
253 Keith McKeller .01 .05
254 Lewis Billups UER .01 .05
255 Alton Montgomery .01 .05
256 Jimmie Jones .01 .05
257 Brent Williams .01 .05
258 Gene Atkins .01 .05
259 Reggie Rutland .01 .05
260 Sam Seale UER .01 .05
261 Andre Ware .01 .05
262 Fred Barnett .08 .25
263 Randal Hill .01 .05
264 Patrick Hunter .01 .05
265 Johnny Rembert UER .01 .05
266 Monte Coleman .01 .05
267 Aaron Wallace .01 .05
268 Ferrell Edmunds .01 .05
269 Stan Thomas .01 .05
270 Robb Thomas .01 .05
271 Martin Bayless UER .01 .05
272 Dean Biasucci .01 .05
273 Keith Henderson .01 .05
274 Vinnie Clark .01 .05
275 Emmitt Smith .60 1.50
276 Mark Rypien .01 .05
277 Michael Haynes TC .01 .05
278 Jim Kelly TC .02 .10
279 Tom Waddle TC .01 .05
280 Mitchell Price TC .01 .05
281 Bernie Koasr TC .01 .05
282 Michael Irvin TC .02 .10
283 John Elway TC .20 .50
284 Mel Gray TC .01 .05
285 Sterling Sharpe TC .02 .10
286 Warren Moon TC .02 .10
287 Jeff George TC .02 .10
288 Derrick Thomas TC .02 .10
289 Ronnie Lott TC .01 .05
290 Robert Delpino TC .01 .05
291 Dan Marino TC .20 .50
292 Cris Carter CL .08 .25
293 Irving Fryar TC .01 .05
294 Gene Atkins TC .01 .05
295 Phil Simms TC .01 .05
296 Ken O'Brien TC .01 .05
297 Keith Jackson TC .01 .05
298 Ricky Proehl TC .01 .05
299 Bryan Hinkle TC .01 .05
300 John Friesz TC .01 .05
301 Jerry Rice TC .20 .50
302 Eugene Robinson TC .01 .05
303 Broderick Thomas TC .01 .05
304 Mark Rypien TC .01 .05
305 Jim Kelly LL .02 .10
306 Steve Young LL .10 .30
307 Thurman Thomas LL .02 .10
308 Emmitt Smith LL .30 .75
309 Haywood Jeffires LL .01 .05
310 Michael Irvin LL .02 .10
311 William Fuller LL .01 .05
312 Pat Swilling LL .01 .05
313 Ronnie Lott LL .01 .05
314 Deion Sanders LL .08 .25
315 Cornelius Bennett HH .01 .05
316 David Fulcher HH .01 .05
317 Ronnie Lott HH .01 .05
318 Pat Swilling HH .01 .05
319 Lawrence Taylor HH .02 .10
320 Derrick Thomas HH .02 .10
321 Steve Emtman RC .01 .05
322 Carl Pickens RC .08 .25
323 David Klingler RC .01 .05
324 Dale Carter RC .02 .10
325 Mike Gaddis RC .01 .05
326 Quentin Coryatt RC .01 .05
327 Darryl Williams RC .01 .05
328 Jeremy Lincoln RC .01 .05
329 Robert Jones RC .01 .05
330 Bucky Richardson RC .01 .05
331 Tony Brooks RC .01 .05
332 Alonzo Spellman RC .02 .10
333 Robert Brooks RC .25 .60
334 Marco Coleman RC .01 .05
335 Siran Stacy RC .01 .05
336 Tommy Maddox RC .60 1.50
337 Steve Israel RC .01 .05
338 Vaughn Dunbar RC .01 .05
339 Shane Collins RC .01 .05
340 Kevin Smith RC .01 .05
341 Chris Mims RC .01 .05
342 Chester McGlockton UER RC .02 .10
343 Tracy Scroggins RC .01 .05
344 Howard Dinkins RC .01 .05
345 Levon Kirkland RC .01 .05
346 Terrell Buckley RC .01 .05
347 Marquez Pope RC .01 .05
348 Phillippi Sparks RC .01 .05
349 Joe Bowden RC .01 .05
350 Edgar Bennett RC .08 .25
SP1 Jim Kelly 3.00 8.00
SP1AU Jim Kelly AU/2500* 15.00 40.00
SP2AU Kelly/Magic AU/500* 75.00 150.00

1992 SkyBox Impact Holograms

The 1992 SkyBox Impact Hologram set consists of six standard-size cards. The first two hologram cards (featuring Jim Kelly and Lawrence Taylor) were randomly inserted in 12-card foil packs. Four additional hologram cards were available as part of a mail-away promotion (H3-H6). The fronts feature full-bleed holograms with the player's last name in block lettering toward the bottom of the card. The cards are numbered with an "H" prefix.

COMPLETE SET (6) 8.00 20.00
H1-H2 RANDOM INSERTS IN PACKS
H3-H6 AVAILABLE VIA MAIL REDEMPT.
H1 Jim Kelly 1.00 2.50
H2 Lawrence Taylor 1.00 2.50
H3 Christian Okoye 2.00 4.00
H4 Mark Rypien 2.00 4.00
H5 Pat Swilling 2.00 4.00
H6 Ricky Ervins 2.00 4.00

1992 SkyBox Impact Major Impact

This 20-card standard-size set was randomly inserted into 1992 SkyBox Impact jumbo packs. The photos are separated from the text by a red stripe on AFC player cards (1-10) and by a blue stripe on NFC player cards (11-20).

COMPLETE SET (20) 6.00 15.00
RANDOM INSERTS IN JUMBO PACKS
M1 Cornelius Bennett .08 .25
M2 David Fulcher .05 .15
M3 Haywood Jeffires .08 .25
M4 Ronnie Lott .08 .25
M5 Dan Marino 1.25 3.00
M6 Warren Moon .25 .60
M7 Christian Okoye .05 .15
M8 Andre Reed .08 .25
M9 Derrick Thomas .25 .60
M10 Thurman Thomas .25 .60
M11 Troy Aikman .75 2.00
M12 Randall Cunningham .25 .60
M13 Michael Irvin .25 .60
M14 Jerry Rice .75 2.00
M15 Joe Montana 1.25 3.00
M16 Mark Rypien .05 .15
M17 Deion Sanders .50 1.25
M18 Emmitt Smith 1.50 4.00
M19 Pat Swilling .05 .15
M20 Lawrence Taylor .25 .60

1993 SkyBox Impact Promos

These standard-size cards were issued to preview the design of the 1993 SkyBox Impact football set. The fronts feature full-bleed color action player photos with an unfocused background to make the featured player stand out. The player's name is printed vertically with the team logo beneath it. The top of the back has a second color photo, with biography, expanded four-year statistics, and career totals filling out the rest of the back. The cards are numbered on the back.

COMPLETE SET (3) 2.00 4.00
IP1 Jim Kelly .75 2.00
IP2 Lawrence Taylor .40 1.00
IP4 Jim Kelly National .75 2.00
IP2A Lawrence Taylor AU/1993 10.00 25.00

1993 SkyBox Impact

The 1993 SkyBox Impact football set consists of 400 standard-size cards. Cards were issued in 12-card packs that included one Impact Colors card. The cards are checklisted below alphabetically according to teams. Subsets include Class of '83 (341-352), and Impact Rookies (361-400) which represents first and second round draft picks. Rookie Cards include Jerome Bettis, Drew Bledsoe, Curtis Conway, Garrison Hearst, O.J. McDuffie, Natrone Means, Glyn Milburn, Rick Mirer and Robert Smith. Randomly inserted in foil packs were 500 individually numbered redemption certificates that entitled the collector to an Impact Jim Kelly/Magic Johnson Header card signed by Kelly. As a bonus, certificates number 12 and number 32, which correspond to Kelly and Johnson's uniform numbers, respectively, received the autographed cards personally presented by the superstar.

COMPLETE SET (400) 6.00 15.00
1 Steve Broussard .01 .05
2 Michael Haynes .02 .10
3 Tony Smith RB .01 .05
4 Tory Epps .01 .05
5 Chris Hinton .01 .05
6 Bobby Hebert .01 .05
7 Tim McKyer .01 .05
8 Chris Miller .02 .10
9 Bruce Pickens .01 .05
10 Mike Pritchard .02 .10
11 Andre Rison .02 .10
12 Deion Sanders .20 .50
13 Pierce Holt .01 .05
14 Jessie Tuggle .01 .05
15 Don Beebe .01 .05
16 Cornelius Bennett .02 .10
17 Kenneth Davis .01 .05
18 Kent Hull .01 .05
19 Jim Kelly .08 .25
20 Mark Kelso .01 .05
21 Keith McKeller UER .01 .05
22 Andre Reed .02 .10
23 Jim Ritcher .01 .05
24 Bruce Smith .08 .25
25 Thurman Thomas .08 .25
26 Steve Christie .01 .05
27 Darryl Talley UER .01 .05
28 Pete Metzelaars .01 .05
29 Steve Tasker .02 .10
30 Henry Jones .01 .05
31 Neal Anderson .01 .05
32 Trace Armstrong .01 .05
33 Mark Bortz .01 .05
34 Mark Carrier DB .01 .05
35 Wendell Davis .01 .05
36 Richard Dent .02 .10
37 Jim Harbaugh .08 .25
38 Steve McMichael .02 .10
39 Craig Heyward .02 .10
40 William Perry .02 .10
41 Donnell Woolford .01 .05
42 Tom Waddle .01 .05
43 Anthony Morgan .01 .05
44 Jim Breech .01 .05
45 David Klingler .01 .05
46 Derrick Fenner .01 .05
47 David Fulcher .01 .05
48 James Francis .01 .05
49 Harold Green .01 .05
50 Carl Pickens .02 .10
51 Jay Schroeder .01 .05
52 Alex Gordon .01 .05
53 Eric Ball .01 .05
54 Eddie Brown .01 .05
55 Jay Hilgenberg UER .01 .05
56 Michael Jackson .02 .10
57 Bernie Kosar .02 .10
58 Kevin Mack .01 .05
59 Eric Metcalf .02 .10
60 Michael Dean Perry .02 .10
61 Tommy Vardell .01 .05
62 Leroy Hoard .02 .10
63 Clay Matthews .02 .10
64 Vinny Testaverde .02 .10
65 Mark Carrier WR .02 .10
66 Troy Aikman .30 .75
67 Lin Elliott RC .01 .05
68 Thomas Everett .01 .05
69 Alvin Harper .02 .10
70 Ray Horton .01 .05
71 Michael Irvin .08 .25
72 Russell Maryland .01 .05
73 Jay Novacek .02 .10
74 Emmitt Smith .60 1.50
75 Tony Casillas .01 .05
76 Robert Jones .01 .05
77 Ken Norton Jr. .02 .10
78 Daryl Johnston .08 .25
79 Charles Haley .02 .10
80 Leon Lett RC .02 .10
81 Steve Atwater .01 .05
82 Mike Croel .01 .05
83 John Elway .60 1.50
84 Simon Fletcher .01 .05
85 Vance Johnson .01 .05
86 Shannon Sharpe .08 .25
87 Rod Bernstine .01 .05
88 Robert Delpino .01 .05
89 Karl Mecklenburg .01 .05
90 Steve Sewell .01 .05
91 Tommy Maddox UER .08 .25
92 Arthur Marshall RC .01 .05
93 Dennis Smith .01 .05
94 Derek Russell .01 .05
95 Bennie Blades .01 .05
96 Michael Cofer .01 .05
97 Willie Green .01 .05
98 Herman Moore .08 .25
99 Rodney Peete .01 .05
100 Andre Ware .01 .05
101 Barry Sanders UER .50 1.25
102 Chris Spielman .02 .10
103 Jason Hanson .01 .05
104 Mel Gray .02 .10
105 Pat Swilling .01 .05
106 Bill Fralic .01 .05
107 Rodney Holman .01 .05
108 Brett Favre .75 2.00
109 Sterling Sharpe .08 .25
110 Reggie White .08 .25
111 Terrell Buckley .01 .05
112 Sanjay Beach .01 .05
113 Tony Bennett .01 .05
114 Jackie Harris .01 .05
115 Bryce Paup .02 .10
116 Shawn Patterson .01 .05
117 John Stephens .01 .05
118 Cris Dishman .01 .05
119 Ernest Givins .02 .10
120 Haywood Jeffires .02 .10
121 Lamar Lathon .01 .05
122 Warren Moon .08 .25
123 Lorenzo White .01 .05
124 Curtis Duncan .01 .05
125 Webster Slaughter .01 .05
126 Cody Carlson .01 .05
127 Leonard Harris .01 .05
128 Bruce Matthews .01 .05
129 Ray Childress .01 .05
130 Al Smith .01 .05
131 Jeff George .08 .25
132 Anthony Johnson .02 .10
133 Steve Emtman .01 .05
134 Quentin Coryatt .02 .10
135 Rodney Culver .01 .05
136 Jessie Hester .01 .05
137 Aaron Cox .01 .05
138 Clarence Verdin .01 .05
139 Joe Montana .60 1.50
140 Dave Krieg .02 .10
141 Harvey Williams .02 .10
142 Derrick Thomas .08 .25
143 Barry Word .01 .05
144 Christian Okoye .01 .05
145 Nick Lowery .01 .05
146 Dale Carter .01 .05
147 Willie Davis .08 .25
148 Tim Barnett .01 .05
149 Neil Smith UER .08 .25
150 Marcus Allen .08 .25
151 Nick Bell .01 .05
152 Tim Brown .08 .25
153 Eric Dickerson .02 .10
154 Willie Gault .01 .05
155 Howie Long .08 .25
156 Gaston Green .01 .05
157 Chester McGlockton .02 .10
158 Eddie Anderson .01 .05
159 Ethan Horton .01 .05
160 James Lofton .02 .10
161 Jeff Hostetler .02 .10
162 Terry McDaniel .01 .05
163 Flipper Anderson .01 .05
164 Shane Conlan .01 .05
165 Jim Everett .02 .10
166 Henry Ellard .02 .10
167 Cleveland Gary .01 .05
168 Todd Lyght .01 .05
169 Sean Gilbert .02 .10
170 Jim Price .01 .05
171 Bill Hawkins .01 .05
172 Mark Clayton .01 .05
173 Mark Higgs .01 .05
174 Dan Marino .60 1.50
175 Louis Oliver .01 .05
176 Reggie Roby .01 .05
177 Bobby Humphrey .01 .05
178 Troy Vincent .01 .05
179 Marco Coleman .01 .05
180 Aaron Craver .01 .05
181 Keith Jackson .02 .10
182 Mark Duper .01 .05
183 Pete Stoyanovich .01 .05
184 Irving Fryar .02 .10
185 Bryan Cox .01 .05
186 Terry Allen .08 .25
187 Anthony Carter .02 .10
188 Cris Carter .08 .25
189 Chris Doleman .01 .05
190 Rich Gannon .08 .25
191 Sean Salisbury .01 .05
192 Hassan Jones .01 .05
193 Steve Jordan .01 .05
194 Roger Craig .02 .10
195 Todd Scott .01 .05
196 Esera Tuaolo .01 .05
197 Ray Agnew .01 .05
198 Marv Cook .01 .05
199 Tommy Hodson .01 .05
200 Chris Singleton .01 .05
201 Michael Timpson .01 .05
202 Jon Vaughn UER .01 .05
203 Leonard Russell .02 .10
204 Scott Zolak .01 .05
205 Reyna Thompson .01 .05
206 Andre Tippett .01 .05
207 Morten Andersen UER .01 .05
208 Wesley Carroll .01 .05
209 Vince Buck .01 .05
210 Rickey Jackson .01 .05
211 Vaughan Johnson UER .01 .05
212 Eric Martin .01 .05
213 Sam Mills .01 .05
214 Steve Walsh .01 .05
215 Wade Wilson .01 .05
216 Vaughn Dunbar .01 .05
217 Brad Muster .01 .05
218 Dalton Hilliard .01 .05
219 Floyd Turner .01 .05
220 Stephen Baker .01 .05
221 Mark Jackson .01 .05
222 Jarrod Bunch .01 .05
223 Mark Collins .01 .05
224 Rodney Hampton .02 .10
225 Phil Simms .02 .10
226 Pepper Johnson .01 .05
227 Dave Meggett .01 .05
228 Derek Brown TE .01 .05
229 Mike Sherrard .01 .05
230 Lawrence Taylor .08 .25
231 Leonard Marshall .01 .05
232 Brad Baxter .01 .05
233 Dennis Byrd .01 .05
234 Ronnie Lott .02 .10
235 Boomer Esiason .02 .10
236 Browning Nagle .01 .05
237 Rob Moore .02 .10
238 Jeff Lageman .01 .05
239 Johnny Mitchell .01 .05
240 Chris Burkett .01 .05
241 Eric Thomas .01 .05
242 Johnny Johnson .01 .05
243 Eric Allen .01 .05
244 Fred Barnett .02 .10
245 Keith Byars .01 .05
246 Randall Cunningham .08 .25
247 Heath Sherman .01 .05
248 Calvin Williams .02 .10
249 Erik McMillan .01 .05
250 Byron Evans .01 .05
251 Seth Joyner .01 .05
252 Vai Sikahema .01 .05
253 Andre Waters .01 .05
254 Tim Harris .01 .05
255 Mark Bavaro .01 .05
256 Clyde Simmons .01 .05
257 Steve Beuerlein .02 .10
258 Randal Hill UER .01 .05
259 Ernie Jones .01 .05
260 Robert Massey .01 .05
261 Ricky Proehl UER .01 .05
262 Aeneas Williams .01 .05
263 Johnny Bailey .01 .05
264 Chris Chandler UER .02 .10
265 Anthony Thompson .01 .05
266 Gary Clark .02 .10
267 Chuck Cecil .01 .05
268 Rich Camarillo .01 .05
269 Neil O'Donnell .08 .25
270 Gerald Williams .01 .05
271 Greg Lloyd .02 .10
272 Eric Green .01 .05
273 Merril Hoge .01 .05
274 Ernie Mills .01 .05
275 Rod Woodson .08 .25
276 Gary Anderson K .01 .05
277 Barry Foster .02 .10
278 Jeff Graham .02 .10
279 Dwight Stone .01 .05
280 Kevin Greene .02 .10
281 Eric Bieniemy .01 .05
282 Marion Butts .01 .05
283 Gill Byrd .01 .05
284 Stan Humphries .02 .10
285 Anthony Miller .02 .10
286 Leslie O'Neal .02 .10
287 Junior Seau .08 .25
288 Ronnie Harmon .01 .05
289 Nate Lewis .01 .05
290 John Kidd .01 .05
291 Steve Young .30 .75
292 John Taylor .02 .10
293 Jerry Rice .40 1.00
294 Tim McDonald .01 .05
295 Brent Jones .02 .10
296 Tom Rathman .01 .05

297 Dexter Carter .01 .05
298 Mike Cofer .01 .05
299 Ricky Watters .08 .25
300 Mervyn Fernandez .01 .05
301 Amp Lee .01 .05
302 Kevin Fagan .01 .05
303 Roy Foster .01 .05
304 Bill Romanowski .01 .05
305 Brian Blades .02 .10
306 John L. Williams .01 .05
307 Tommy Kane .01 .05
308 John Kasay .01 .05
309 Chris Warren .02 .10
310 Rufus Porter .01 .05
311 Cortez Kennedy .02 .10
312 Dan McGwire .01 .05
313 Stan Gelbaugh .01 .05
314 Kelvin Martin .01 .05
315 Ferrell Edmunds .01 .05
316 Eugene Robinson .01 .05
317 Gary Anderson RB .01 .05
318 Reggie Cobb .01 .05
319 Lawrence Dawsey .01 .05
320 Courtney Hawkins .01 .05
321 Santana Dotson .02 .10
322 Ron Hall .01 .05
323 Keith McCants .01 .05
324 Martin Mayhew .01 .05
325 Anthony Munoz .02 .10
326 Steve DeBerg .01 .05
327 Vince Workman .01 .05
328 Earnest Byner .01 .05
329 Ricky Ervins .01 .05
330 Jim Lachey .01 .05
331 Chip Lohmiller .01 .05
332 Ricky Sanders UER .01 .05
333 Brad Edwards .01 .05
334 Tim McGee .01 .05
335 Darrell Green .01 .05
336 Charles Mann .01 .05
337 Wilber Marshall .01 .05
338 Brian Mitchell .02 .10
339 Art Monk .02 .10
340 Mark Rypien .01 .05
341 John Elway C83 .30 .75
342 Jim Kelly C83 .02 .10
343 Dan Marino C83 .30 .75
344 Eric Dickerson C83 .02 .10
345 Willie Gault C83 .01 .05
346 Ken O'Brien C83 .01 .05
347 Darrell Green C83 .01 .05
348 Richard Dent C83 .01 .05
349 Karl Mecklenburg C83 .01 .05
350 Henry Ellard C83 .01 .05
351 Roger Craig C83 .01 .05
352 Charles Mann C83 .01 .05
353 Checklist A UER .01 .05
354 Checklist B UER .01 .05
355 Checklist C UER .01 .05
356 Checklist D UER .01 .05
357 Checklist E UER .01 .05
358 Checklist F UER .01 .05
359 Checklist G UER .01 .05
360 Rookies Checklist UER .01 .05
361 Drew Bledsoe RC 1.00 2.50
362 Rick Mirer RC .08 .25
363 Garrison Hearst RC .30 .75
364 Marvin Jones RC .01 .05
365 John Copeland RC .02 .10
366 Eric Curry RC .01 .05
367 Curtis Conway RC .15 .40
368 Willie Roaf RC .10 .30
369 Lincoln Kennedy RC .01 .05
370 Jerome Bettis RC 1.50 4.00
371 Dan Williams RC .01 .05
372 Patrick Bates RC .01 .05
373 Brad Hopkins RC .01 .05
374 Steve Everitt RC .01 .05
375 Wayne Simmons RC .01 .05
376 Tom Carter RC .02 .10
377 Ernest Dye RC .01 .05
378 Lester Holmes RC .01 .05
379 Irv Smith RC .01 .05
380 Robert Smith RC .50 1.25
381 Darrien Gordon RC .01 .05
382 Deon Figures RC .01 .05
383 O.J.McDuffie RC .08 .25
384 Dana Stubblefield RC .08 .25
385 Todd Kelly RC .01 .05
386 Thomas Smith RC .02 .10
387 George Teague RC .02 .10
388 Carlton Gray RC .01 .05
389 Chris Slade RC .02 .10
390 Ben Coleman RC .01 .05
391 Ryan McNeil RC .08 .25
392 Demetrius DuBose RC .01 .05
393 Carl Simpson RC .01 .05
394 Coleman Rudolph RC .01 .05
395 Tony McGee RC .02 .10
396 Roger Harper RC .01 .05
397 Troy Drayton RC .02 .10
398 Michael Strahan RC .60 1.50
399 Natrone Means RC .08 .25
400 Glyn Milburn RC .08 .25

1993 SkyBox Impact Colors

COMPLETE SET (392) 30.00 60.00
*COLOR STARS: 1.5X TO 4X BASIC CARDS
*COLOR RCs: 1X TO 2.5X BASIC CARDS
ONE PER PACK

1993 SkyBox Impact Kelly/Magic

Jim Kelly and Magic Johnson, spokesmen for SkyBox International, selected a fantasy team of their favorite NFL players, Kelly's Heroes and Magic's Kingdom. Measuring the standard size, these 12 cards were foil stamped and randomly inserted into foil packs at a rate of one in 12. Kelly's pick at the position is on one side, while Magic's pick is found on the other side. The cards are numbered on the back with a "T" prefix.

COMPLETE SET (12) 8.00 20.00
STATED ODDS 1:12
AUTO.STATED ODDS 1:2071
1 Mag.Johnson .75 2.00
Kelly Hdr
2 D.Marino 2.00 5.00
Jim Kelly
3 J.Novacek .40 1.00
K.Jackson
4 B.Sanders 2.00 5.00
T.Thomas
5 E.Smith 3.00 6.00
B.Sanders
6 J.Rice 1.50 3.00
St.Sharpe
7 J.Rice 1.50 3.00
A.Reed
8 D.Thomas .75 2.00
P.Swilling
9 L.Taylor .75 2.00
D.Talley
10 R.Woodson .75 2.00
D.Green
11 S.Tasker .40 1.00
E.Patterson
12 C.Lohmiller .40 1.00
M.Andersen
AU1 Kelly Header AU/2500 12.50 30.00

1993 SkyBox Impact Update

Focusing on NFL players who switched teams through free agency, SkyBox issued this 20-card standard-size set to depict these players in their new uniforms. The set could be obtained by sending in five Impact foil pack wrappers plus 3.99 for postage and handling. Each borderless front features a color player action shot showing him in his new team's uniform. The cards are numbered on the back with a "U" prefix.

COMPLETE SET (20) 5.00 10.00
SET AVAILABLE VIA MAIL OFFER
U1 Pierce Holt .08 .25
U2 Vinny Testaverde .20 .50
U3 Rod Bernstine .08 .25
U4 Reggie White .60 1.25
U5 Mark Clayton .08 .25
U6 Joe Montana 4.00 8.00
U7 Marcus Allen .60 1.25
U8 Jeff Hostetler .20 .50
U9 Shane Conlan .08 .25
U10 Brad Muster .08 .25
U11 Mike Sherrard .08 .25
U12 Ronnie Lott .20 .50
U13 Steve Beuerlein .20 .50
U14 Gary Clark .20 .50
U15 Kevin Greene .20 .50
U16 Tim McDonald .08 .25
U17 Wilber Marshall .08 .25
U18 Keith Byars .08 .25
U19 Pat Swilling .08 .25
U20 Boomer Esiason .20 .50

1993 SkyBox Impact Rookie Redemption

One NFL Rookie Exchange card was randomly inserted in approximately every 180 foil packs and could be redeemed by mail for this special set of 28 NFL Draft First Round selections in their pro uniforms. Collectors could also receive the insert set by sending in a postcard for an entry in the second chance drawing. After the checklist card (No. 1) the cards are arranged consecutively in order of the draft, from the first pick to the 29th pick. (The 16th 1993 NFL first-round draft pick, Sean Dawkins, is not represented in this set because of his exclusive contract with another card company.) The cards are numbered on the back with an "R" prefix.

COMPLETE SET (29) 5.00 12.00
ONE SET PER REDEMPTION CARD BY MAIL
R1 Drew Bledsoe CL 1.00 2.50
R2 Drew Bledsoe 1.50 4.00
R3 Rick Mirer .15 .40
R4 Garrison Hearst .50 1.25
R5 Marvin Jones .02 .10
R6 John Copeland .05 .15
R7 Eric Curry .02 .10
R8 Curtis Conway .25 .60
R9 Willie Roaf .20 .50
R10 Lincoln Kennedy .02 .10
R11 Jerome Bettis 2.50 6.00
R12 Dan Williams .02 .10
R13 Patrick Bates .02 .10
R14 Brad Hopkins .02 .10
R15 Steve Everitt .02 .10
R16 Wayne Simmons .02 .10
R17 Tom Carter .05 .15
R18 Ernest Dye .02 .10
R19 Lester Holmes .02 .10
R20 Irv Smith .02 .10
R21 Robert Smith .75 2.00
R22 Darrien Gordon .02 .10
R23 Deon Figures .02 .10
R24 Leonard Renfro .02 .10
R25 O.J.McDuffie .15 .40
R26 Dana Stubblefield .15 .40
R27 Todd Kelly .02 .10
R28 Thomas Smith .05 .15
R29 George Teague .05 .15
NNO Rookie Redempt.Expired .02 .10

1994 SkyBox Impact Promos

These six standard-size promo cards feature on their fronts borderless color player action shots. The featured players stand out against faded backgrounds. The player's name appears within team-colored boxes in an upper corner. The horizontal back carries a color player action shot on the right, and upon which the player's NFL stats appear. His biography and career highlights appear to the left of the photo. The cards are numbered on the back with an "S" prefix. These six promo cards were also issued as a 7 1/2" by 8 1/2" unperforated sheet. Reportedly 55,000 sheets were produced to be given away at the National Sports Collectors Convention (August 2, 4-7, 1994).

COMPLETE SET (6) 3.20 8.00
S1 Marcus Allen 1.20 3.00
S2 Chris Doleman .30 .75
S3 Craig Erickson .30 .75
S4 Jim Kelly 1.20 3.00
S5 Reggie Roby .30 .75
S6 Rod Woodson .50 1.25
NNO National Promo Sheet 2.00 5.00

1994 SkyBox Impact

These 300 standard-size cards were issued in 12-card foil and 20-card jumbo packs. The checklist is alphabetical by team. Randomly inserted in packs and listed at the end of the checklist below is a Carolina Panthers Hologram card. Rookie Cards include Derrick Alexander, Marshall Faulk, William Floyd, Greg Hill, Charles Johnson and Heath Shuler. A Jim Kelly promo card was produced and given away at the 1994 Super Bowl Card Show in Atlanta.

COMPLETE SET (300) 6.00 15.00
1 Johnny Bailey .01 .05
2 Steve Beuerlein .02 .10
3 Gary Clark .02 .10
4 Garrison Hearst .08 .25
5 Ronald Moore .01 .05
6 Ricky Proehl .01 .05
7 Eric Swann .02 .10
8 Aeneas Williams .01 .05
9 Robert Massey .01 .05
10 Chuck Cecil .01 .05
11 Ken Harvey .01 .05
12 Michael Haynes .02 .10
13 Tony Smith RB .01 .05
14 Bobby Hebert .01 .05
15 Mike Pritchard .01 .05
16 Andre Rison .02 .10
17 Deion Sanders .15 .40
18 Pierce Holt .01 .05
19 Erric Pegram .01 .05
20 Jessie Tuggle .01 .05
21 Steve Broussard .01 .05
22 Don Beebe .01 .05
23 Cornelius Bennett .02 .10
24 Kenneth Davis .01 .05
25 Bill Brooks .01 .05
26 Jim Kelly .08 .25
27 Andre Reed .02 .10
28 Bruce Smith .08 .25
29 Darryl Talley .01 .05
30 Thurman Thomas .08 .25
31 Steve Tasker .02 .10
32 Neal Anderson .01 .05
33 Mark Carrier DB .01 .05
34 Richard Dent .02 .10
35 Jim Harbaugh .08 .25
36 Chris Gedney .01 .05
37 Tom Waddle .01 .05
38 Curtis Conway .08 .25
39 Dante Jones .01 .05
40 Donnell Woolford .01 .05
41 Tim Worley .01 .05
42 John Copeland .01 .05
43 David Klingler .01 .05
44 Derrick Fenner .01 .05
45 Harold Green .01 .05
46 Carl Pickens .02 .10
47 Tony McGee .01 .05
48 Darryl Williams .01 .05
49 Steve Everitt .01 .05
50 Michael Jackson .02 .10
51 Eric Metcalf .02 .10
52 Tommy Vardell .01 .05
53 Vinny Testaverde .02 .10
54 Mark Carrier WR .02 .10
55 Michael Dean Perry .02 .10
56 Eric Turner .01 .05
57 Troy Aikman .30 .75
58 Alvin Harper .02 .10
59 Michael Irvin .08 .25
60 Leon Lett .01 .05
61 Russell Maryland .01 .05
62 Jay Novacek .02 .10
63 Emmitt Smith .50 1.25
64 Ken Norton .02 .10
65 Charles Haley .02 .10
66 Daryl Johnston .02 .10
67 Kevin Smith .01 .05
68 James Washington .01 .05
69 Kevin Williams WR .02 .10
70 Bernie Kosar .02 .10
71 Mike Croel .01 .05
72 John Elway .60 1.50
73 Shannon Sharpe .02 .10
74 Rod Bernstine .01 .05
75 Simon Fletcher .01 .05
76 Arthur Marshall .01 .05
77 Glyn Milburn .02 .10
78 Dennis Smith .01 .05
79 Herman Moore .08 .25
80 Rodney Peete .01 .05
81 Barry Sanders .50 1.25
82 Mel Gray .01 .05
83 Erik Kramer .02 .10
84 Pat Swilling .01 .05
85 Willie Green .01 .05
86 Chris Spielman .02 .10
87 Robert Porcher .01 .05
88 Derrick Moore .01 .05
89 Edgar Bennett .08 .25
90 Tony Bennett .01 .05
91 LeRoy Butler .01 .05
92 Brett Favre .60 1.50
93 Jackie Harris .01 .05
94 Sterling Sharpe .02 .10
95 Darrell Thompson .01 .05
96 Reggie White .08 .25
97 Terrell Buckley .01 .05
98 Cris Dishman .01 .05
99 Ernest Givins .02 .10
100 Haywood Jeffires .02 .10
101 Warren Moon .08 .25
102 Lorenzo White .01 .05
103 Webster Slaughter .01 .05
104 Ray Childress .01 .05
105 Wilber Marshall .01 .05
106 Gary Brown .01 .05
107 Marcus Robertson .01 .05
108 Sean Jones .01 .05
109 Jeff George .08 .25
110 Steve Emtman .01 .05
111 Quentin Coryatt .01 .05
112 Sean Dawkins RC .08 .25
113 Jeff Herrod .01 .05
114 Roosevelt Potts .01 .05
115 Marcus Allen .08 .25
116 Kimble Anders .02 .10
117 Tim Barnett .01 .05
118 J.J. Birden .01 .05
119 Dale Carter .01 .05
120 Willie Davis .02 .10
121 Nick Lowery .01 .05
122 Joe Montana .60 1.50
123 Kevin Ross .01 .05
124 Neil Smith .02 .10
125 Derrick Thomas .08 .25
126 Keith Cash .01 .05
127 Tim Brown .08 .25
128 Rocket Ismail .02 .10
129 Ethan Horton .01 .05
130 Jeff Hostetler .02 .10
131 Patrick Bates .01 .05
132 Terry McDaniel .01 .05
133 Anthony Smith .01 .05
134 Greg Robinson .01 .05
135 James Jett .01 .05
136 Alexander Wright .01 .05
137 Flipper Anderson .01 .05
138 Shane Conlan .01 .05
139 Jim Everett .02 .10
140 Henry Ellard .02 .10
141 Jerome Bettis .20 .50
142 Troy Drayton .01 .05
143 Sean Gilbert .01 .05
144 Chris Miller .01 .05
145 Keith Byars .01 .05
146 Marco Coleman .01 .05
147 Bryan Cox .01 .05
148 Irving Fryar .02 .10
149 Mark Ingram .01 .05
150 Keith Jackson .01 .05
151 Terry Kirby .08 .25
152 Dan Marino .60 1.50
153 O.J.McDuffie .08 .25
154 Scott Mitchell .02 .10
155 Anthony Carter .02 .10
156 Cris Carter .15 .40
157 Chris Doleman .01 .05
158 Steve Jordan .01 .05
159 Qadry Ismail .08 .25
160 Randall McDaniel .02 .10
161 John Randle .02 .10
162 Robert Smith .08 .25
163 Henry Thomas .01 .05
164 Terry Allen .02 .10
165 Scottie Graham RC .02 .10
166 Drew Bledsoe .30 .75
167 Vincent Brown .01 .05
168 Ben Coates .02 .10
169 Leonard Russell .01 .05
170 Andre Tippett .01 .05
171 Vincent Brisby .02 .10
172 Michael Timpson .01 .05
173 Bruce Armstrong .01 .05
174 Morten Andersen UER .01 .05
175 Derek Brown RBK .01 .05
176 Quinn Early .02 .10
177 Rickey Jackson .01 .05
178 Vaughan Johnson .01 .05
179 Lorenzo Neal .01 .05
180 Sam Mills .01 .05
181 Irv Smith .01 .05
182 Renaldo Turnbull .01 .05
183 Wade Wilson .01 .05
184 Willie Roaf .01 .05
185 Michael Brooks .01 .05
186 Mark Jackson .01 .05
187 Rodney Hampton .02 .10
188 Phil Simms .02 .10
189 Dave Meggett .01 .05
190 Mike Sherrard .01 .05
191 Chris Calloway .01 .05
192 Brad Baxter .01 .05
193 Ronnie Lott .02 .10
194 Boomer Esiason .02 .10
195 Rob Moore .02 .10
196 Johnny Johnson .01 .05
197 Marvin Jones .01 .05
198 Mo Lewis .01 .05
199 Johnny Mitchell .01 .05
200 Brian Washington .01 .05
201 Eric Allen .01 .05
202 Fred Barnett .02 .10
203 Mark Bavaro .01 .05
204 Randall Cunningham .08 .25
205 Vaughn Hebron .01 .05
206 Seth Joyner .01 .05
207 Clyde Simmons .01 .05
208 Herschel Walker .02 .10
209 Calvin Williams .02 .10
210 Neil O'Donnell .08 .25
211 Eric Green .01 .05
212 Leroy Thompson .01 .05
213 Rod Woodson .02 .10
214 Barry Foster .01 .05
215 Jeff Graham .01 .05
216 Kevin Greene .02 .10
217 Deon Figures .01 .05
218 Greg Lloyd .02 .10
219 Marion Butts .01 .05
220 Chris Mims .01 .05
221 Eric Curry .01 .05
222 Ronnie Harmon .01 .05
223 Stan Humphries .02 .10
224 Nate Lewis .01 .05
225 Natrone Means .08 .25
226 Anthony Miller .02 .10
227 Leslie O'Neal .01 .05
228 Junior Seau .08 .25
229 Brent Jones .02 .10
230 Tim McDonald .01 .05
231 Tom Rathman .01 .05
232 Jerry Rice .30 .75
233 Dana Stubblefield .02 .10
234 John Taylor .02 .10
235 Ricky Watters .02 .10
236 Steve Young .25 .60
237 Amp Lee .01 .05
238 Robert Blackmon .01 .05
239 Brian Blades .02 .10
240 Cortez Kennedy .02 .10
241 Kelvin Martin .01 .05
242 Rick Mirer .08 .25
243 Eugene Robinson .01 .05
244 Chris Warren .02 .10
245 John L. Williams .01 .05
246 Jon Vaughn .01 .05
247 Reggie Cobb .01 .05
248 Horace Copeland .01 .05
249 Derrick Alexander WR RC .08 .25
250 Santana Dotson .02 .10
251 Craig Erickson .01 .05
252 Courtney Hawkins .01 .05
253 Hardy Nickerson .02 .10
254 Vince Workman .01 .05
255 Paul Gruber .01 .05
256 Reggie Brooks .02 .10
257 Tom Carter .01 .05
258 Andre Collins .01 .05
259 Darrell Green .01 .05
260 Desmond Howard .02 .10
261 Tim McGee .01 .05
262 Brian Mitchell .01 .05
263 Art Monk .02 .10
264 John Friesz .02 .10
265 Ricky Sanders .01 .05
266 Checklist .01 .05
267 Checklist .01 .05
268 Checklist .01 .05
269 Checklist .01 .05
270 Checklist .01 .05
271 Carolina Panthers .05 .15
272 Jacksonville Jaguars .05 .15
273 Dan Wilkinson RC .02 .10
274 Marshall Faulk RC 2.00 5.00
275 Heath Shuler RC .08 .25
276 Willie McGinest RC .08 .25
277 Trev Alberts RC .02 .10
278 Trent Dilfer RC .50 1.25
279 Bryant Young RC .15 .40
280 Sam Adams RC .02 .10
281 Antonio Langham RC .02 .10
282 Jamir Miller RC .02 .10
283 John Thierry RC .01 .05
284 Aaron Glenn RC .08 .25
285 Joe Johnson RC .01 .05
286 Bernard Williams RC .01 .05
287 Wayne Gandy RC .01 .05
288 Aaron Taylor RC .01 .05
289 Charles Johnson RC .08 .25
290 Dewayne Washington RC .02 .10
291 Todd Steussie RC .02 .10
292 Tim Bowens RC .02 .10
293 Johnnie Morton RC .20 .50
294 Rob Fredrickson RC .02 .10
295 Shante Carver RC .01 .05
296 Thomas Lewis RC .02 .10
297 Greg Hill RC .08 .25
298 Henry Ford RC .01 .05
299 Jeff Burris RC .02 .10
300 William Floyd RC .08 .25
NNO Carolina Panthers HOLO 7.50 20.00
P1 Jim Kelly Promo .30 .75

1994 SkyBox Impact Instant Impact

This 12-card standard-size set featured leading 1993 rookies. These were inserted one in every 30 packs. The cards are similar in design to the regular SkyBox Impact issue, except the SkyBox "Instant Impact" words are all in gold foil. Key players in this set include Drew Bledsoe and Natrone Means.

COMPLETE SET (12) 7.50 20.00
STATED ODDS 1:30
R1 Rick Mirer 1.25 2.50
R2 Jerome Bettis 2.50 5.00
R3 Reggie Brooks .40 1.00
R4 Terry Kirby 1.25 2.50
R5 Vincent Brisby .40 1.00
R6 James Jett .20 .50
R7 Drew Bledsoe 4.00 8.00
R8 Dana Stubblefield .40 1.00
R9 Natrone Means 1.25 2.50
R10 Curtis Conway 1.25 2.50
R11 O.J.McDuffie 1.25 2.50
R12 Garrison Hearst 1.25 2.50

1994 SkyBox Impact Quarterback Update

This 10-card standard-size set was issued one per special SkyBox retail box and could also be obtained through a redemption offer. The set depicts traded quarterbacks in their new uniforms and rookies. The cards are identical in design to the basic SkyBox Impact cards with a full-bleed photo and the player's name at the top. The horizontal backs offer a second photo of the player with a brief write-up.

COMPLETE SET (11) 1.50 4.00
SET AVAILABLE VIA MAIL REDEMPTION
ONE SET PER SPECIAL SKYBOX RETAIL BOX
1 Warren Moon .30 .75
2 Trent Dilfer .60 1.50
3 Jeff George .20 .50
4 Heath Shuler .30 .75
5 Jim Harbaugh .20 .50
6 Rodney Peete .08 .25
7 Chris Miller .08 .25
8 Jim Everett .08 .25
9 Scott Mitchell .20 .50
10 Erik Kramer .08 .25
NNO Checklist .08 .25

1994 SkyBox Impact Rookie Redemption

A redemption card randomly inserted in foil packs entitled the collector to receive this set. The set is arranged in draft order and presents the first twenty-nine players chosen in the 1994 NFL Draft. The card design used is very similar to the base SkyBox Impact issue along with an updated photo showing the player in his respective team's uniform. The exchange offer expired January 31, 1995.

COMPLETE SET (30) 7.50 15.00
SET AVAILABLE VIA MAIL REDEMPTION
1 Dan Wilkinson .07 .20
2 Marshall Faulk 5.00 10.00
3 Heath Shuler .20 .50
4 Willie McGinest .20 .50
5 Trev Alberts .07 .20
6 Trent Dilfer 1.25 2.50
7 Bryant Young .30 .75
8 Sam Adams .07 .20
9 Antonio Langham .07 .20
10 Jamir Miller .07 .20
11 John Thierry .02 .10
12 Aaron Glenn .20 .50
13 Joe Johnson .02 .10
14 Bernard Williams .02 .10
15 Wayne Gandy .02 .10
16 Aaron Taylor .02 .10
17 Charles Johnson .20 .50
18 Dewayne Washington .07 .20
19 Todd Steussie .07 .20
20 Tim Bowens .07 .20
21 Johnnie Morton .40 1.00
22 Rob Fredrickson .07 .20
23 Shante Carver .02 .10
24 Thomas Lewis .07 .20
25 Greg Hill .20 .50
26 Henry Ford .02 .10
27 Jeff Burris .07 .20
28 William Floyd .20 .50
29 Derrick Alexander WR .20 .50
30 Title .02 .10
Checklist Card
NNO Rookie Redempt.Expired .02 .10

1994 SkyBox Impact Ultimate Impact

This 15-card standard-size set was randomly inserted into packs and features leading NFL players. The cards were inserted one in every 15 packs. Similar in design to the Instant Impact cards, the major difference are the words "SkyBox Ultimate Impact" printed in silver foil.

COMPLETE SET (15) 25.00 60.00
STATED ODDS 1:15
U1 Troy Aikman 2.50 6.00
U2 Emmitt Smith UER 4.00 10.00
U3 Michael Irvin .75 2.00
U4 Joe Montana 5.00 12.00
U5 Jerry Rice 2.50 6.00
U6 Sterling Sharpe .30 .75
U7 Steve Young 2.00 5.00
U8 Ricky Watters .30 .75
U9 Barry Sanders 4.00 10.00
U10 John Elway 5.00 12.00
U11 Reggie White .75 2.00
U12 Jim Kelly .75 2.00
U13 Thurman Thomas .75 2.00
U14 Dan Marino 5.00 12.00
U15 Brett Favre 5.00 12.00

1995 SkyBox Impact Samples

This 6-card promotion or sample panel was issued to promote the 1995 SkyBox Impact product. Each card includes a card number on the back and could be detached individually using the perforations applied in the printing process. A seventh card was issued separately to round out the set.

COMPLETE SET (7) 2.00 5.00
S1 Chris Spielman .30 .75
S2 Ronald Moore .20 .50
S3 Bernie Parmalee .20 .50
S4 Tyrone Hughes .20 .50
S5 Brett Favre Countdown 1.25 3.00
S6 Bryan Cox Impact Power .20 .50
S7 William Floyd More Attitude .40 1.00
NNO Uncut Panel S1-S6 1.50 4.00

1995 SkyBox Impact

This 200-card standard-size set is considered the base issue released by SkyBox.. The cards were issued in 12-card foil packs with a suggested retail price of $1.29 or 20-card jumbo packs with a suggested retail price of $1.99. . Featured in the set are 148 player cards. The set is broken down by teams and includes these subsets: Something Special (149-158), Sophomores (159-168), Impact Rookies (169-198) and Checklists (199-200). Rookie Cards in this set include Jeff Blake, Ki-Jana Carter, Kerry Collins, Joey Galloway, Steve McNair, and Rashaan Salaam. There was also a rookie running back set randomly inserted at a rate of one set per special retail box. A promo sheet was produced and is priced below in complete sheet form.

COMPLETE SET (200) 6.00 15.00
1 Garrison Hearst .08 .25
2 Ronald Moore .01 .05
3 Eric Swann .02 .10
4 Aeneas Williams .01 .05
5 Jeff George .02 .10
6 Craig Heyward .02 .10
7 Terance Mathis .02 .10
8 Andre Rison .02 .10
9 Cornelius Bennett .02 .10
10 Jim Kelly .08 .25
11 Andre Reed .02 .10
12 Bruce Smith .08 .25
13 Thurman Thomas .08 .25
14 Frank Reich .01 .05
15 Lamar Lathon .01 .05
16 Darion Conner .01 .05
17 Randy Baldwin .01 .05
18 Don Beebe .01 .05
19 Mark Carrier DB .01 .05
20 Jeff Graham .01 .05
21 Raymont Harris .01 .05
22 Alonzo Spellman .01 .05
23 Lewis Tillman .01 .05
24 Steve Walsh .01 .05
25 Jeff Blake RC .25 .60
26 Carl Pickens .02 .10
27 Darnay Scott .02 .10
28 Dan Wilkinson .02 .10
29 Derrick Alexander WR .08 .25
30 Leroy Hoard .01 .05
31 Antonio Langham .01 .05
32 Vinny Testaverde .02 .10
33 Eric Turner .01 .05
34 Troy Aikman .30 .75
35 Charles Haley .02 .10
36 Alvin Harper .01 .05
37 Michael Irvin .08 .25
38 Daryl Johnston .02 .10
39 Jay Novacek .02 .10
40 Leon Lett .01 .05
41 Emmitt Smith .50 1.25
42 John Elway .60 1.50
43 Glyn Milburn .01 .05
44 Anthony Miller .02 .10
45 Leonard Russell .01 .05
46 Shannon Sharpe .02 .10
47 Scott Mitchell .02 .10
48 Herman Moore .08 .25
49 Barry Sanders .50 1.25
50 Chris Spielman .02 .10
51 Edgar Bennett .02 .10
52 Robert Brooks .08 .25
53 Brett Favre .60 1.60
54 Bryce Paup .02 .10
55 Sterling Sharpe .02 .10
56 Reggie White .08 .25
57 Ray Childress .01 .05
58 Haywood Jeffires .01 .05
59 Webster Slaughter .01 .05
60 Lorenzo White .01 .05
61 Trev Alberts .01 .05
62 Quentin Coryatt .02 .10
63 Sean Dawkins .02 .10
64 Marshall Faulk .40 1.00
65 Jeff Lageman .01 .05
66 Steve Beuerlein .02 .10
67 Desmond Howard .02 .10
68 Kelvin Martin .01 .05
69 Reggie Cobb .01 .05
70 Marcus Allen .08 .25
71 Greg Hill .02 .10
72 Joe Montana .60 1.50
73 Neil Smith .02 .10
74 Derrick Thomas .08 .25
75 Tim Brown .08 .25
76 Rocket Ismail .02 .10
77 Jeff Hostetler .02 .10
78 Chester McGlockton .02 .10
79 Harvey Williams .01 .05
80 Tim Bowens .01 .05
81 Irving Fryar .02 .10
82 Keith Jackson .01 .05
83 Terry Kirby .02 .10
84 Dan Marino .60 1.50
85 O.J. McDuffie .08 .25
86 Bernie Parmalee .02 .10
87 Terry Allen .02 .10
88 Cris Carter .08 .25
89 Qadry Ismail .02 .10
90 Warren Moon .02 .10
91 Jake Reed .02 .10
92 Drew Bledsoe .20 .50
93 Vincent Brisby .01 .05
94 Ben Coates .02 .10
95 Michael Timpson .01 .05
96 Jim Everett .01 .05
97 Michael Haynes .02 .10
98 Willie Roaf .01 .05
99 Michael Brooks .01 .05
100 Dave Brown .02 .10
101 Rodney Hampton .02 .10
102 Thomas Lewis .02 .10
103 Dave Meggett .01 .05
104 Boomer Esiason .02 .10
105 Johnny Johnson .01 .05
106 Johnny Mitchell .01 .05
107 Rob Moore .02 .10
108 Fred Barnett .02 .10
109 Randall Cunningham .08 .25
110 Charlie Garner .08 .25
111 Herschel Walker .02 .10
112 Barry Foster .02 .10
113 Eric Green .01 .05
114 Charles Johnson .02 .10
115 Greg Lloyd .02 .10
116 Byron Bam Morris .01 .05
117 Neil O'Donnell .02 .10
118 Rod Woodson .02 .10
119 Flipper Anderson .01 .05
120 Jerome Bettis .08 .25
121 Troy Drayton .01 .05
122 Sean Gilbert .02 .10
123 Ronnie Harmon .01 .05
124 Stan Humphries .02 .10
125 Shawn Jefferson .01 .05
126 Natrone Means .02 .10
127 Leslie O'Neal .02 .10
128 Junior Seau .08 .25
129 William Floyd .02 .10
130 Brent Jones .01 .05
131 Jerry Rice .30 .75
132 Deion Sanders .20 .50
133 Dana Stubblefield .02 .10
134 Ricky Watters .02 .10
135 Bryant Young .02 .10
136 Steve Young .25 .60
137 Brian Blades .02 .10
138 Cortez Kennedy .02 .10
139 Rick Mirer .02 .10
140 Chris Warren .02 .10
141 Horace Copeland .01 .05
142 Trent Dilfer .08 .25
143 Hardy Nickerson .01 .05
144 Errict Rhett .02 .10
145 Henry Ellard .02 .10
146 Brian Mitchell .01 .05
147 Heath Shuler .02 .10
148 Tydus Winans .01 .05
149 Steve Tasker .02 .10
150 Jeff Burris .01 .05
151 Tyrone Hughes .02 .10
152 Mel Gray .01 .05
153 Kevin Williams WR .02 .10
154 Andre Coleman .01 .05
155 Corey Sawyer .01 .05
156 Darrien Gordon .01 .05
157 Aaron Glenn .01 .05
158 Eric Metcalf .02 .10
159 Errict Rhett SS .02 .10
160 Marshall Faulk SS .15 .40
161 Darnay Scott SS .02 .10
162 William Floyd SS .01 .05
163 Charlie Garner SS .02 .10
164 Heath Shuler SS .02 .10
165 Trent Dilfer SS .08 .25
166 Willie McGinest SS .02 .10
167 Byron Bam Morris SS .01 .05
168 Mario Bates SS .02 .10
169 Ki-Jana Carter RC .08 .25
170 Tony Boselli RC .08 .25
171 Steve McNair RC 1.00 2.50
172 Michael Westbrook RC .08 .25
173 Kerry Collins RC .75 2.00
174 Kevin Carter RC .08 .25
175 Mike Mamula RC .01 .05
176 Joey Galloway RC .50 1.25
177 Kyle Brady RC .08 .25
178 J.J. Stokes RC .08 .25
179 Warren Sapp RC .50 1.25
180 Rob Johnson RC .30 .75
181 Tyrone Wheatley RC .40 1.00
182 Napoleon Kaufman RC .40 1.00
183 James O. Stewart RC .40 1.00
184 Dino Philyaw RC .01 .05
185 Rashaan Salaam RC .02 .10
186 Tyrone Poole RC .08 .25
187 Ty Law RC .50 1.25
188 Joe Aska RC .01 .05
189 Mark Bruener RC .02 .10
190 Derrick Brooks RC .50 1.25
191 Jack Jackson RC .01 .05
192 Ray Zellars RC .02 .10
193 Eddie Goines RC .01 .05
194 Chris Sanders RC .02 .10
195 Charlie Simmons RC .01 .05
196 Lee DeRamus RC .01 .05
197 Frank Sanders RC .08 .25
198 Rodney Thomas RC .02 .10
199 Checklist A 1-128 .01 .05
200 Checklist B 129-200 .01 .05
M1 Brett Favre SkyMotion 15.00 30.00
M2 Brett Favre SkyMotion 15.00 30.00

1995 SkyBox Impact Countdown

This 10 card horizontally designed standard-size set was randomly inserted into packs at a rate of one in 30. The cards feature the player's photo against a solid green UV coated background with a digital clock reading across the middle. The player is identified in the upper right corner and the words "Countdown to Impact" are located in the right bottom. The horizontal back has another action photo as well as player information. The digital time on the front is repeated on the back.

COMPLETE SET (10) 20.00 50.00
STATED ODDS 1:20 H/R, 1:60 SPEC.RET
C1 Barry Sanders 5.00 10.00
C2 Jerry Rice 3.00 6.00
C3 Steve Young 2.50 5.00
C4 Troy Aikman 3.00 6.00
C5 Dan Marino 6.00 12.00
C6 Emmitt Smith 5.00 10.00
C7 Junior Seau .75 2.00
C8 Drew Bledsoe 2.00 4.00
C9 Brett Favre 6.00 12.00
C10 Deion Sanders 2.00 4.00

1995 SkyBox Impact Future Hall of Famers

These cards are inserted in hobby packs at a rate of one in 60. This standard-size set features players who appear headed for the Pro Football Hall of Fame. All cards have an "HF" prefix. Card #HF2 featuring Joe Montana was pulled from packaging very early in the process due to licensing concerns. However, some cards have surfaced in the hobby.

COMP.SHORT SET (7) 30.00 80.00
STATED ODDS 1:60 HOBBY
HF1 Jerry Rice 5.00 12.00
HF2 Joe Montana SP 200.00 400.00
HF3 Steve Young 4.00 10.00
HF4 John Elway 10.00 25.00
HF5 Dan Marino 10.00 25.00
HF6 Emmitt Smith 8.00 20.00
HF7 Barry Sanders 8.00 20.00
HF8 Troy Aikman 5.00 12.00

1995 SkyBox Impact More Attitude

This 15 card standard-size set was randomly inserted into packs at a rate of one in nine. Players featured in this set are leading rookies and other young stars. The fronts feature the player's photo superimposed over a football field with the words "Same Game, More Attitude" along the sidelines. The "NFL on Fox" logo is located in the lower right corner. The backs have biographical information, a player photo and a brief player write-up. The cards are numbered with an "F" prefix.

COMPLETE SET (15) 10.00 25.00
STATED ODDS 1:9 H/R, 1:27 SPEC.RET
F1 Ki-Jana Carter .25 .60
F2 Steve McNair 3.00 6.00
F3 Michael Westbrook .25 .60
F4 Kerry Collins 1.50 4.00
F5 Joey Galloway 1.50 3.00
F6 J.J.Stokes .25 .60
F7 James O. Stewart 1.25 2.50
F8 Rashaan Salaam .08 .25
F9 Trent Dilfer 1.00 2.00
F10 William Floyd .30 .75
F11 Marshall Faulk 4.00 8.00
F12 Errict Rhett .30 .75
F13 Heath Shuler .30 .75
F14 Drew Bledsoe 2.00 4.00
F15 Ben Coates .30 .75

1995 SkyBox Impact Power

This standard-size set was randomly inserted into packs. This set is subdivided into De-Terminators (IP1-IP10) and Stars of the Ozone (IP11-IP30). The approximate ratio for finding these cards are one in three packs. The player's name is printed on the left in gold foil, while the words "Impact Power" are on the bottom of the card. The upper right corner either has either set name. The backs feature an action photo as well as some player performance information. All cards are numbered with an "IP" prefix. Card #IP25 featuring Joe Montana was pulled from packaging very early in the process due to licensing concerns. However, some cards have surfaced in the hobby.

COMP.SHORT SET (29) 10.00 25.00
STATED ODDS 1:3 H/R, 1:9 SPEC.RET
IP1 Junior Seau .40 1.00
IP2 Reggie White .40 1.00
IP3 Eric Swann .15 .40
IP4 Bruce Smith .40 1.00
IP5 Rod Woodson .15 .40
IP6 Derrick Thomas .40 1.00
IP7 Chester McGlockton .15 .40
IP8 Cortez Kennedy .15 .40
IP9 Deion Sanders 1.00 2.00
IP10 Bryan Cox .07 .20
IP11 Jerry Rice 1.50 3.00
IP12 Sterling Sharpe .15 .40
IP13 Tim Brown .40 1.00
IP14 Marshall Faulk 2.00 4.00
IP15 Brett Favre 3.00 6.00
IP16 Chris Warren .15 .40
IP17 Herman Moore .40 1.00
IP18 Steve Young 1.25 2.50
IP19 Andre Rison .15 .40
IP20 Thurman Thomas .40 1.00
IP21 Marcus Allen .40 1.00
IP22 Michael Irvin .40 1.00
IP23 Emmitt Smith 2.50 5.00
IP24 John Elway 3.00 6.00
IP25 Joe Montana SP 300.00 600.00
IP26 Barry Sanders 2.50 5.00
IP27 Troy Aikman 1.50 3.00
IP28 Natrone Means .15 .40
IP29 Ben Coates .15 .40
IP30 Errict Rhett .15 .40

1995 SkyBox Impact Rookie Running Backs

This nine card set was inserted at a rate of one set per special retail box. Cardfronts look identical to the rookie design of the player's regular card. The cardbacks have a different card number.

COMPLETE SET (9) 4.00 8.00
ONE SET PER SPECIAL RETAIL BOX
1 Ki-Jana Carter .30 .75
2 Tyrone Wheatley .60 1.50
3 Napoleon Kaufman .60 1.50
4 James O. Stewart .60 1.50
5 Rashaan Salaam .30 .75
6 Ray Zellars .20 .50
7 Rodney Thomas .20 .50
8 Curtis Martin 1.50 4.00
NNO Cover .10 .30
Checklist Card

1995 SkyBox Impact Fox Announcers

SkyBox issued this promo set to announce its affiliation with Fox. The seven-card set features the Fox Network NFL Sunday announcers. The fronts display photos of the announcers while the backs carry information about them.

COMPLETE SET (8) 8.00 20.00
1 P.Summerall 2.00 5.00
J.Madden
2 James Brown 2.00 5.00
Jimmy Johnson
T.Bradshaw
H.Long
3 Dick Stockton .80 2.00
Matt Millen
4 Kevin Harlan .80 2.00
Jerry Glanville
5 Joe Buck .80 2.00
Tim Green DE
6 Kenny Albert 1.20 3.00
Anthony Munoz
7 Thom Brennaman .80 2.00
Ron Pitts
NNO Cover Card .40 1.00

1996 SkyBox Impact Samples

This 3 card promotion or sample panel was issued to promote the 1996 SkyBox Impact product. Each card includes a card number on the back and could be detached individually using the perforations applied in the printing process.

COMPLETE SET (3) 1.50 4.00
S1 Brett Favre 1.25 3.00
S2 William Floyd Excelerators .20 .50
S3 Daryl Johnston Inspiration .30 .75
NNO Uncut Panel 1.50 4.00

1996 SkyBox Impact

The 1996 Skybox Impact set was issued in one series totalling 200 cards. The 10-card packs retail for $1.49 each. Dealers had the option of ordering either a 30 box case or a 12 box case. Each box contains 24 packs. The set contains the topical subsets: Rookies (149-188), Inspirations (189-193) and Brett Favre Highlights (194-198). The regular cards are grouped alphabetically within teams and checklisted below alphabetically according to teams. A Brett Favre instant win card is included in every pack. Among the prizes available were 1,995 Favre SkyMotion cards, 1,995 Favre Lenticular Cards and 1995 Favre Season Highlight All-In-One Cards. These winning cards were exchanged one every 480 packs. Exchange cards for the SkyMotion card as well as a SkyMint Coin were inserted one every 360 packs. These two cards expired on 1/24/97. Rookie Cards in this set include Karim Abdul-Jabbar, Tim Biakabutuka, Tommie Frazier, Eddie George, Terry Glenn, Keyshawn Johnson, Danny Kanell, and Leeland McElroy. A 3-card (cards numbered S1-S3) promo sheet was produced as well and priced below in complete sheet form.

COMPLETE SET (200) 6.00 15.00
1 Garrison Hearst .07 .20
2 Rob Moore .07 .20
3 Frank Sanders .07 .20
4 Eric Swann .02 .10
5 Aeneas Williams .02 .10
6 Bert Emanuel .07 .20
7 Jeff George .07 .20
8 Craig Heyward .02 .10
9 Terance Mathis .02 .10
10 Eric Metcalf .02 .10
11 Leroy Hoard .02 .10
12 Michael Jackson .07 .20
13 Andre Rison .07 .20
14 Vinny Testaverde .07 .20
15 Eric Turner .02 .10
16 Darick Holmes .02 .10
17 Jim Kelly .10 .30
18 Bryce Paup .02 .10
19 Bruce Smith .07 .20
20 Thurman Thomas .10 .30
21 Mark Carrier WR .02 .10
22 Kerry Collins .10 .30
23 Derrick Moore .02 .10
24 Tyrone Poole .02 .10
25 Curtis Conway .10 .30
26 Jeff Graham .02 .10
27 Erik Kramer .02 .10
28 Rashaan Salaam .07 .20
29 Jeff Blake .10 .30
30 Ki-Jana Carter .07 .20
31 Carl Pickens .07 .20
32 Darnay Scott .07 .20
33 Troy Aikman .30 .75
34 Charles Haley .07 .20
35 Michael Irvin .10 .30
36 Daryl Johnston .07 .20
37 Jay Novacek .02 .10
38 Deion Sanders .15 .40
39 Emmitt Smith .50 1.25
40 Steve Atwater .02 .10
41 Terrell Davis .25 .60
42 John Elway .60 1.50
43 Anthony Miller .07 .20
44 Shannon Sharpe .07 .20
45 Scott Mitchell .07 .20
46 Herman Moore .07 .20
47 Brett Perriman .02 .10
40 Darry Sanders .50 1.25
49 Edgar Bennett .07 .20
50 Robert Brooks .10 .30
51 Mark Chmura .07 .20
52 Brett Favre .60 1.50
53 Reggie White .10 .30
54 Mel Gray .02 .10
55 Steve McNair .25 .60
56 Chris Sanders .07 .20
57 Rodney Thomas .02 .10
58 Quentin Coryatt .02 .10
59 Sean Dawkins .02 .10
60 Ken Dilger .07 .20
61 Marshall Faulk .15 .40
62 Jim Harbaugh .07 .20
63 Tony Boselli .02 .10
64 Mark Brunell .20 .50
65 Keenan McCardell .10 .30
66 James O.Stewart .07 .20
67 Marcus Allen .10 .30
68 Steve Bono .02 .10
69 Neil Smith .07 .20
70 Derrick Thomas .10 .30
71 Tamarick Vanover .07 .20
72 Bryan Cox .02 .10
73 Irving Fryar .07 .20
74 Eric Green .02 .10
75 Dan Marino .60 1.50
76 O.J. McDuffie .07 .20
77 Bernie Parmalee .02 .10
78 Cris Carter .10 .30
79 Qadry Ismail .07 .20
80 Warren Moon .07 .20
81 Jake Reed .07 .20
82 Robert Smith .07 .20
83 Drew Bledsoe .20 .50
84 Ben Coates .07 .20
85 Curtis Martin .25 .60
86 Willie McGinest .02 .10
87 Dave Meggett .02 .10
88 Mario Bates .07 .20
89 Quinn Early .02 .10
90 Jim Everett .02 .10
91 Michael Haynes .02 .10
92 Renaldo Turnbull .02 .10
93 Dave Brown .02 .10
94 Rodney Hampton .07 .20
95 Thomas Lewis .02 .10
96 Phillippi Sparks .02 .10
97 Tyrone Wheatley .07 .20
98 Kyle Brady .02 .10
99 Hugh Douglas .07 .20
100 Mo Lewis .02 .10
101 Adrian Murrell .07 .20
102 Tim Brown .10 .30
103 Jeff Hostetler .02 .10
104 Rocket Ismail .02 .10
105 Chester McGlockton .02 .10
106 Harvey Williams .02 .10
107 Fred Barnett .02 .10
108 William Fuller .02 .10
109 Charlie Garner .07 .20
110 Rodney Peete .02 .10
111 Ricky Watters .07 .20
112 Calvin Williams .02 .10
113 Byron Bam Morris .02 .10
114 Neil O'Donnell .07 .20
115 Erric Pegram .02 .10
116 Kordell Stewart .10 .30
117 Yancey Thigpen .07 .20
118 Rod Woodson .07 .20
119 Jerome Bettis .10 .30
120 Isaac Bruce .10 .30
121 Troy Drayton .02 .10
122 Leslie O'Neal .02 .10
123 Aaron Hayden RC .02 .10
124 Stan Humphries .07 .20
125 Natrone Means .07 .20
126 Junior Seau .10 .30
127 William Floyd .07 .20
128 Brent Jones .02 .10
129 Derek Loville .02 .10
130 Ken Norton .02 .10
131 Jerry Rice .30 .75
132 J.J. Stokes .10 .30
133 Steve Young .25 .60
134 Brian Blades .02 .10
135 Joey Galloway .10 .30
136 Cortez Kennedy .02 .10
137 Rick Mirer .07 .20
138 Chris Warren .07 .20
139 Trent Dilfer .10 .30
140 Alvin Harper .02 .10
141 Jackie Harris .02 .10
142 Hardy Nickerson .02 .10
143 Errict Rhett .07 .20
144 Terry Allen .07 .20
145 Henry Ellard .02 .10
146 Brian Mitchell .02 .10
147 Heath Shuler .07 .20
148 Michael Westbrook .10 .30
149 Karim Abdul-Jabbar RC .10 .30
150 Mike Alstott RC .40 1.00
151 Marco Battaglia RC .02 .10
152 Tim Biakabutuka RC .10 .30
153 Sean Boyd RC .07 .20
154 Tony Brackens RC .10 .30
155 Duane Clemons RC .02 .10
156 Marcus Coleman RC .02 .10
157 Chris Darkins RC .02 .10
158 Rickey Dudley RC .10 .30
159 Jason Dunn RC .07 .20
160 Bobby Engram RC .10 .30
161 Daryl Gardener RC .02 .10
162 Eddie George RC .50 1.25
163 Terry Glenn RC .40 1.00
164 Kevin Hardy RC .10 .30
165 Marvin Harrison RC 1.00 2.50
166 Dietrich Jells RC .02 .10
167 DeRon Jenkins RC .07 .20
168 Darrius Johnson RC .02 .10
169 Keyshawn Johnson RC .40 1.00
170 Lance Johnstone RC .07 .20
171 Cedric Jones RC .02 .10
172 Marcus Jones RC .02 .10
173 Danny Kanell RC .10 .30
174 Eddie Kennison RC .10 .30
175 Jevon Langford RC .02 .10
176 Markco Maddox RC .07 .20
177 Derrick Mayes RC .10 .30
178 Leeland McElroy RC .07 .20
179 Dell McGee RC .02 .10
180 Johnny McWilliams RC .07 .20
181 Alex Molden RC .02 .10
182 Eric Moulds RC .50 1.25
183 Jonathan Ogden RC .40 1.00
184 Lawrence Phillips RC .10 .30
185 Simeon Rice RC .30 .75
186 Amani Toomer RC .40 1.00
187 Regan Upshaw RC .02 .10
188 Jerome Woods RC .02 .10
189 Darrell Green I .02 .10
190 Daryl Johnston I .07 .20
191 Sam Mills I .02 .10
192 Earnest Byner I .02 .10
193 Herschel Walker I .07 .20
194 Brett Favre Highlights .20 .50
195 Brett Favre Highlights .20 .50
196 Brett Favre Highlights .20 .50
197 Brett Favre Highlights .20 .50
198 Brett Favre Highlights .20 .50
199 Checklist .02 .10
200 Checklist .02 .10
BF1 Brett Favre SkyMotion 5.00 12.00
BF1X Favre SkyMotion EXCH .40 1.00
BF2 Brett Favre SkyMint 10.00 25.00
BF2X Favre SkyMint EXCH .40 1.00

1996 SkyBox Impact Excelerators

Randomly inserted in packs at a rate of one in 12, this 15-card standard-size set highlights some of the NFL's fastest players. The set is sequenced in alphabetical order.

COMPLETE SET (15) 12.50 30.00
STATED ODDS 1:12
1 Robert Brooks 1.00 2.00
2 Isaac Bruce 1.00 2.00
3 William Floyd .60 1.25
4 Joey Galloway 1.00 2.00
5 Michael Irvin 1.00 2.00
6 Napoleon Kaufman 1.00 2.00
7 Anthony Miller .60 1.25
8 Herman Moore .60 1.25
9 Barry Sanders 4.00 8.00
10 Chris Sanders .60 1.25
11 Kordell Stewart 1.00 2.00
12 Rodney Thomas .25 .60
13 Tamarick Vanover .60 1.25
14 Ricky Watters .60 1.25
15 Michael Westbrook 1.00 2.00

1996 SkyBox Impact Intimidators

Randomly inserted in packs at a rate of one in 20, this 10-card standard-size set focuses on some of the most respected NFL players. The cards are sequenced in alphabetical order.

COMPLETE SET (10) 20.00 50.00
STATED ODDS 1:20
1 Terrell Davis 3.00 6.00
2 Hugh Douglas 1.00 2.00
3 Dan Marino 8.00 15.00
4 Curtis Martin 3.00 6.00
5 Carl Pickens 1.00 2.00
6 Errict Rhett 1.00 2.00
7 Jerry Rice 4.00 8.00
8 Emmitt Smith 6.00 12.00
9 Eric Swann .40 1.00
10 Chris Warren 1.00 2.00

1996 SkyBox Impact More Attitude

Randomly inserted in packs at a rate of one in 3, this 20-card standard-size set features leading 1996 NFL Rookies. The cards are sequenced roughly in alphabetical order.

COMPLETE SET (20) 12.50 25.00
STATED ODDS 1:3
1 Karim Abdul-Jabbar .25 .60
2 Tim Biakabutuka .25 .60
3 Bobby Engram .25 .60
4 Daryl Gardener .07 .20
5 Eddie George 1.25 2.50
6 Terry Glenn 1.00 2.00
7 Kevin Hardy .25 .60
8 Marvin Harrison 2.50 5.00
9 DeRon Jenkins .15 .40
10 Keyshawn Johnson 1.00 2.00
11 Cedric Jones .07 .20
12 Eddie Kennison .25 .60
13 Jevon Langford .07 .20
14 Leeland McElroy .15 .40
15 Johnny McWilliams .15 .40
16 Eric Moulds 1.25 2.50
17 Lawrence Phillips .25 .60
18 Jonathan Ogden .75 2.00
19 Simeon Rice .75 1.50
20 Amani Toomer 1.00 2.00

1996 SkyBox Impact No Surrender

Randomly inserted in hobby packs only at a rate of one in 40, this 20-card standard-size set featrues players who always give their best on the field. The set is sequenced in alphabetical order.

COMPLETE SET (20) 30.00 80.00
STATED ODDS 1:40 HOBBY
1 Marcus Allen 2.00 5.00
2 Jeff Blake 2.00 5.00
3 Drew Bledsoe 3.00 8.00
4 Ben Coates 1.25 3.00
5 Brett Favre 10.00 25.00
6 Terry Glenn 5.00 10.00
7 Jim Harbaugh 1.25 3.00
8 Kevin Hardy 1.50 3.00
9 Keyshawn Johnson 5.00 10.00
10 Dan Marino 10.00 25.00
11 Leeland McElroy 1.00 2.00
12 Steve McNair 4.00 10.00
13 Herman Moore 1.25 3.00
14 Lawrence Phillips 1.50 3.00
15 Errict Rhett 1.25 3.00
16 Jerry Rice 5.00 12.00
17 Simeon Rice 4.00 8.00
18 Barry Sanders 8.00 20.00
19 Rodney Thomas .60 1.50
20 Tyrone Wheatley 1.25 3.00

1996 SkyBox Impact VersaTeam

Randomly inserted in packs at a rate of one in 120, this 10-card standard-size set features players who are multi-skilled. The set is sequenced in alphabetical order.

COMPLETE SET (10) 30.00 80.00
STATED ODDS 1:120
1 Tim Brown 2.50 6.00
2 Terrell Davis 5.00 12.00
3 John Elway 12.50 30.00
4 Marshall Faulk 3.00 8.00
5 Joey Galloway 2.50 6.00
6 Curtis Martin 5.00 12.00
7 Deion Sanders 3.00 8.00
8 Kordell Stewart 2.50 6.00
9 Chris Warren 1.50 4.00
10 Steve Young 5.00 12.00

1996 SkyBox Impact Rookies

The SkyBox Impact Rookies set was issued in one series totalling 150 cards. The set contains the topical subsets: All-Time Impact Rookies (71-120), Rookie Sleepers (121-140) and Rookie Record Holders (141-148). The cards were packaged 10-cards per pack with 36-packs per box and carried a suggested retail price of $1.49 per pack. The Draft Exchange card (expired 7/22/97) mentions several prize levels on the cardback instructions in error. In fact, there was only one Draft Exchange card which was good for all five prize cards.

COMPLETE SET (150) 5.00 12.00
1 Leeland McElroy RC .02 .10
2 Johnny McWilliams .01 .05
3 Simeon Rice RC .20 .50
4 DeRon Jenkins .01 .05
5 Jermaine Lewis RC .07 .20
6 Ray Lewis RC 2.00 5.00
7 Jonathan Ogden .30 .75
8 Eric Moulds UER RC .40 1.00
9 Tim Biakabutuka RC .07 .20
10 Muhsin Muhammad RC .40 1.00
11 Winslow Oliver .01 .05
12 Bobby Engram RC .07 .20
13 Walt Harris .01 .05
14 Willie Anderson .01 .05
15 Marco Battaglia .01 .05
16 Jevon Langford .01 .05
17 Kavika Pittman RC .01 .05
18 Stepfret Williams .01 .05
19 Tory James RC .02 .10
20 Jeff Lewis RC .02 .10
21 John Mobley .01 .05
22 Detron Smith .01 .05
23 Derrick Mayes RC .07 .20
24 Eddie George RC .40 1.00
25 Marvin Harrison RC .75 2.00
26 Dedric Mathis .01 .05
27 Tony Brackens RC .07 .20
28 Kevin Hardy RC .07 .20
29 Jerome Woods .01 .05
30 Karim Abdul-Jabbar RC .07 .20
31 Daryl Gardener .01 .05
32 Jerris McPhail .01 .05
33 Stanley Pritchett .01 .05
34 Zach Thomas RC .20 .50
35 Duane Clemons .01 .05
36 Moe Williams RB RC .20 .50
37 Tedy Bruschi RC 1.50 4.00
38 Terry Glenn RC .30 .75
39 Alex Molden .01 .05
40 Ricky Whittle .01 .05
41 Cedric Jones .01 .05
42 Danny Kanell RC .07 .20
43 Amani Toomer RC .30 .75
44 Marcus Coleman .01 .05
45 Keyshawn Johnson RC .30 .75
46 Ray Mickens .01 .05
47 Alex Van Dyke RC .02 .10
48 Rickey Dudley RC .07 .20
49 Lance Johnstone .02 .10
50 Brian Dawkins RC .40 1.00
51 Jason Dunn .01 .05
52 Ray Farmer .01 .05
53 Bobby Hoying RC .07 .20
54 Jermane Mayberry .01 .05
55 Bryan Still RC .02 .10
56 Tony Banks RC .07 .20
57 Ernie Conwell .01 .05
58 Eddie Kennison RC .07 .20
59 Jerald Moore RC .02 .10
60 Lawrence Phillips RC .07 .20
61 Israel Ifeanyi .01 .05
62 Terrell Owens RC .75 2.00
63 Iheanyi Uwaezuoke RC .07 .20
64 Mike Alstott RC .30 .75
65 Marcus Jones .01 .05
66 Nilo Silvan .01 .05
67 Regan Upshaw .01 .05
68 Stephen Davis RC .50 1.25
69 Troy Aikman AIR .20 .50
70 Terry Allen AIR .02 .10
71 Edgar Bennett AIR .02 .10
72 Jerome Bettis AIR .02 .10
73 Drew Bledsoe AIR .15 .40
74 Tim Brown AIR .07 .20
75 Mark Brunell AIR .15 .40
76 Cris Carter AIR .07 .20
77 Kerry Collins AIR .07 .20
78 Terrell Davis AIR .15 .40
79 John Elway AIR .40 1.00
80 Marshall Faulk AIR .07 .20
81 Brett Favre AIR .40 1.00
82 Joey Galloway AIR .07 .20
83 Rodney Hampton AIR .01 .05
84 Jim Harbaugh AIR .02 .10
85 Michael Irvin AIR .02 .10
86 Chris T. Jones AIR .07 .20
87 Napoleon Kaufman AIR .07 .20
88 Jim Kelly AIR .07 .20
89 Dan Marino AIR .40 1.00
90 Curtis Martin AIR .15 .40
91 Terance Mathis AIR .01 .05
92 Steve McNair AIR .20 .50
93 Anthony Miller AIR .02 .10
94 Scott Mitchell AIR .01 .05
95 Herman Moore AIR .02 .10
96 Brett Perriman AIR .01 .05
97 Carl Pickens AIR .02 .10
98 Jerry Rice AIR .20 .50
99 Andre Rison AIR .02 .10
100 Rashaan Salaam AIR .02 .10
101 Barry Sanders AIR .30 .75
102 Chris Sanders AIR .02 .10
103 Deion Sanders AIR .07 .20
104 Frank Sanders AIR .02 .10
105 Bruce Smith AIR .02 .10
106 Emmitt Smith AIR .30 .75
107 Robert Smith AIR .02 .10
108 Kordell Stewart AIR .07 .20
109 J.J. Stokes AIR .07 .20
110 Yancey Thigpen AIR .02 .10
111 Thurman Thomas AIR .02 .10
112 Eric Turner AIR .01 .05
113 Tamarick Vanover AIR .02 .10
114 Chris Warren AIR .02 .10
115 Ricky Watters AIR .02 .10
116 Michael Westbrook AIR .07 .20
117 Reggie White AIR .07 .20
118 Steve Young AIR .15 .40
119 Jeff Blake AIR .02 .10
120 Robert Brooks AIR .02 .10
121 Isaac Bruce RS .07 .20
122 Mark Chmura RS .02 .10
123 Wayne Chrebet RS .10 .30
124 Ben Coates RS .02 .10
125 Ken Dilger RS .02 .10
126 Bert Emanuel RS .02 .10
127 Gus Frerotte RS .02 .10
128 Kevin Greene RS .02 .10
129 Erik Kramer RS .01 .05
130 Greg Lloyd RS .02 .10
131 Tony Martin RS .01 .05
132 Brian Mitchell RS .01 .05
133 Bryce Paup RS .01 .05
134 Jake Reed RS .02 .10
135 Errict Rhett RS .02 .10
136 Yancey Thigpen RS .02 .10
137 Tamarick Vanover RS .02 .10
138 Chris Warren RS .02 .10
139 Marcus Allen RS .07 .20
140 Jerome Bettis RS .07 .20
141 Tim Brown RRH .07 .20
142 Mark Carrier RRH .01 .05
143 Marshall Faulk RRH .07 .20
144 Tyrone Hughes RRH .01 .05
145 Dan Marino RRH .40 1.00
146 Curtis Martin RRH .15 .40
147 Barry Sanders RRH .30 .75
148 Orlando Thomas RRH .01 .05
149 Checklist (1-107) UER .01 .05
150 Checklist (108-150 inserts) .01 .05
NNO Draft Exchange Card .40 1.00

1996 SkyBox Impact Rookies All-Rookie Team

Randomly inserted in packs at a rate of one in six, this 10-card set features color action player photos of five rookies from the AFC and five from the NFC who are the top at their position. The backs carry a paragraph stating why the pictured player was selected for this set.

COMPLETE SET (10) 5.00 12.00
STATED ODDS 1:6
1 Karim Abdul-Jabbar .25 .60
2 Tim Biakabutuka .25 .60
3 Eddie George 1.50 3.00
4 Marvin Harrison 3.00 6.00
5 Keyshawn Johnson 1.25 2.50
6 Eddie Kennison .25 .60
7 Lawrence Phillips .25 .60
8 Zach Thomas .75 1.50
9 Amani Toomer 1.25 2.50
10 Simeon Rice .75 1.50

1996 SkyBox Impact Rookies Draft Board

Randomly inserted in packs at a rate of one in 48, this 20-card set features nulti-player cards which depict two or three players with something in common from the draft.

COMPLETE SET (20) 50.00 100.00
STATED ODDS 1:48
1 Glenn / Dudley / Hoying 2.50 6.00
2 S.Rice / K.Hardy 4.00 10.00
3 E.Smith / E.Rhett 7.50 15.00
4 D.Sanders / Swyr / D.Brks 3.00 6.00
5 T.Allen / M.Allen 2.00 5.00
6 J.Mobley / A.Reed 1.25 3.00
7 D.Bledsoe / Mirer / M.Brunell 3.00 8.00
8 J.Elway / J.Kelly / D.Marino 6.00 15.00
9 C.Pickens / A.Miller 1.25 3.00
10 Freeman / R.Brks / C.Jnes 2.00 5.00
11 Bettis / Watters / T.Brown 2.00 5.00
12 J.Rice / H.Moore / M.Irvin 5.00 10.00
13 T.Davis / Hampton / Hearst 3.00 8.00
14 K.Collins / K.Carter / K.Brady 2.00 5.00
15 B.Sanders / T.Thomas 6.00 15.00
16 R.Lewis/Jr.Lewis/Jf.Lewis 4.00 10.00
17 S.Young / T.Aikman 5.00 10.00
18 C.Martin / Warren / J.Ander. 3.00 8.00
19 K.Stew / Sala / Westbrook 2.00 5.00
20 T.Banks / M.Muhammad 2.50 6.00

1996 SkyBox Impact Rookies 1996 Rookies

Randomly inserted in packs at a rate of one in 144, this 10-card set features color player photos of top Rookie stars of 1996. Only 1,996 of each card was produced and are individually numbered.

COMPLETE SET (10) 40.00 100.00
STATED ODDS 1:144
STATED PRINT RUN 1996 SER.#d SETS
1 Karim Abdul-Jabbar 1.50 4.00
2 Tim Biakabutuka 1.50 4.00
3 Rickey Dudley 1.50 4.00
4 Eddie George 8.00 20.00
5 Terry Glenn 6.00 15.00
6 Marvin Harrison 15.00 40.00
7 Keyshawn Johnson 6.00 15.00
8 Eddie Kennison 1.50 4.00
9 Lawrence Phillips 1.50 4.00
10 Amani Toomer 6.00 15.00

1996 SkyBox Impact Rookies 1996 Rookies Autographs

This six-card set was inserted as a chip-topper within cases of 1996 SkyBox Impact Rookies. There was one inserted for every six-box case, two inserted in every twelve-box case, and three inserted in every twenty-box case. The cards are autographed on the front and have a SkyBox seal of authenticity.

A1 Karim Abdul-Jabbar 7.50 20.00
A2 Rickey Dudley 7.50 20.00
A3 Marvin Harrison 25.00 60.00
A4 Eddie Kennison 10.00 25.00
A5 Lawrence Phillips 7.50 20.00
A6 Amani Toomer 10.00 25.00

1996 SkyBox Impact Rookies Rookie Rewind

Randomly inserted in hobby packs only at a rate of one in 36, this 10-card set features color player images of some of today's up-and-coming stars on a spiral background. The backs carry a paragraph about the players ability in his Rookie season.

COMPLETE SET (10) 15.00 30.00
STATED ODDS 1:36 HOBBY
1 Jamal Anderson .60 1.50
2 Jeff Blake 1.00 2.50
3 Robert Brooks 1.00 2.50
4 Mark Brunell 1.50 4.00
5 Brett Favre 5.00 12.00
6 Aaron Hayden .30 .75
7 Derek Loville .30 .75
8 Emmitt Smith 4.00 10.00
9 Robert Smith .60 1.50
10 Tamarick Vanover .60 1.50

1997 SkyBox Impact

The 1997 SkyBox Impact set was issued in one series totalling 250 cards and was distributed in eight-card packs with a suggested retail of $1.59. The fronts features a color player image with 3-D illustrated graphics. The backs carry another player image, player information and key statistics. In addition to the popular Autographics inserts, a separate Karim Abdul-Jabbar Sample signed card was randomly insderted into packs. SkyBox Impact included 250 of the 500 signed cards, with the balance being distributed as a chiptopper through the Fleer/SkyBox Surprise insert program across various card brands..

COMPLETE SET (250) 6.00 15.00
1 Carl Pickens .10 .30
2 Ray Lewis .30 .75
3 Darrell Green .10 .30
4 Brett Favre .75 2.00
5 Todd Collins .07 .20
6 Errict Rhett .07 .20
7 John Elway .75 2.00
8 Troy Aikman .40 1.00
9 Steve McNair .25 .60
10 Kordell Stewart .20 .50
11 Drew Bledsoe .25 .60
12 Kerry Collins .20 .50
13 Dan Marino .75 2.00
14 Ricky Watters .10 .30
15 Marvin Harrison .20 .50
16 Simeon Rice .10 .30
17 Qadry Ismail .10 .30
18 Andre Coleman .07 .20
19 Keyshawn Johnson .20 .50
20 Barry Sanders .60 1.50
21 Rickey Dudley .10 .30
22 Emmitt Smith .60 1.50
23 Erik Kramer .07 .20
24 Tony Boselli .07 .20
25 Steve Young .25 .60
26 Rod Woodson .10 .30
27 Eddie George .20 .50
28 Curtis Martin .25 .60
29 Amani Toomer .10 .30
30 Terrell Davis .25 .60
31 Jim Everett .07 .20
32 Marcus Allen .20 .50
33 Karim Abdul-Jabbar .20 .50
34 Thurman Thomas .20 .50
35 Cortez Kennedy .07 .20
36 Jerome Bettis .20 .50
37 Kevin Carter .07 .20
38 Gilbert Brown .10 .30
39 Bert Emanuel .10 .30
40 Kyle Brady .07 .20
41 Trent Dilfer .20 .50
42 Garrison Hearst .10 .30
43 Kevin Greene .10 .30
44 Bryan Cox .07 .20
45 Desmond Howard .10 .30
46 Larry Centers .10 .30
47 Quentin Coryatt .07 .20
48 Michael Jackson .10 .30
49 John Randle .10 .30
50 Mark Brunell .25 .60
51 William Thomas .07 .20
52 Glyn Milburn .07 .20
53 Mike Alstott .20 .50
54 Chris Spielman .07 .20
55 Junior Seau .20 .50
56 Brian Blades .07 .20
57 Lamar Lathon .07 .20
58 Derrick Thomas .20 .50
59 Dave Brown .07 .20
60 Frank Wycheck .07 .20
61 Chris Slade .07 .20
62 Neil Smith .10 .30
63 Ashley Ambrose .07 .20
64 Alex Molden .07 .20
65 Edgar Bennett .10 .30
66 Alvin Harper .07 .20
67 Jamal Anderson .20 .50
68 Eddie Kennison .10 .30
69 Ken Norton .07 .20
70 Zach Thomas .20 .50
71 Leeland McElroy .07 .20
72 Terry Allen .20 .50
73 Raymont Harris .07 .20
74 Ken Dilger .07 .20
75 Jason Dunn .07 .20
76 Robert Smith .10 .30
77 William Roaf .07 .20
78 Bruce Smith .10 .30
79 Vinny Testaverde .10 .30
80 Jerry Rice .40 1.00
81 Tim Brown .20 .50
82 James O.Stewart .10 .30
83 Andre Reed .10 .30
84 Herman Moore .10 .30
85 Stan Humphries .10 .30
86 Chris Warren .10 .30
87 Tyrone Wheatley .10 .30
88 Michael Irvin .20 .50
89 Dan Wilkinson .07 .20
90 Tony Banks .10 .30
91 Chester McGlockton .07 .20
92 Reggie White .20 .50
93 Elvis Grbac .10 .30
94 Willie Davis .07 .20
95 Greg Lloyd .07 .20
96 Ben Coates .10 .30
97 Rashaan Salaam .07 .20
98 Eric Swann .07 .20
99 Hugh Douglas .07 .20
100 Henry Ellard .07 .20
101 Rod Smith WR .20 .50
102 Tim Biakabutuka .10 .30
103 Chad Brown .07 .20
104 Kevin Hardy .07 .20
105 Chris T. Jones .07 .20
106 Antonio Freeman .20 .50
107 Lamont Warren .07 .20
108 Derrick Alexander DE .07 .20
109 Brett Perriman .07 .20
110 Antonio Langham .07 .20
111 Eric Moulds .20 .50
112 O.J. McDuffie .10 .30
113 Eric Metcalf .10 .30
114 Ray Zellars .07 .20
115 Marco Coleman .07 .20
116 Terry Kirby .10 .30
117 Darren Woodson .07 .20
118 Charles Johnson .10 .30
119 Sam Mills .07 .20
120 Rodney Hampton .10 .30
121 Rick Mirer .07 .20
122 Derrick Brooks .20 .50
123 Greg Hill .07 .20
124 John Mobley .07 .20
125 Chris Sanders .07 .20
126 Kent Graham .07 .20
127 Michael Westbrook .10 .30
128 Harvey Williams .07 .20
129 Keenan McCardell .10 .30
130 Neil O'Donnell .10 .30
131 LeRoy Butler .07 .20
132 Willie McGinest .07 .20
133 Ki-Jana Carter .07 .20
134 Robert Jones .07 .20
135 Jim Harbaugh .10 .30
136 Wesley Walls .10 .30
137 Jackie Harris .07 .20
138 Jermaine Lewis .20 .50
139 Jake Reed .10 .30
140 John Friesz .07 .20
141 Jerris McPhail .07 .20
142 Charlie Garner .10 .30
143 Bryce Paup .07 .20
144 Tony Martin .10 .30
145 Shannon Sharpe .10 .30
146 Terrell Owens .25 .60
147 Curtis Conway .10 .30
148 Jamie Asher .07 .20
149 Lawrence Phillips .07 .20
150 Deion Sanders .20 .50
151 Frank Sanders .10 .30
152 Joey Galloway .10 .30
153 Mel Gray .07 .20
154 Robert Brooks .10 .30
155 Jeff George .10 .30
156 Michael Haynes .07 .20
157 Chris Chandler .10 .30
158 Adrian Murrell .10 .30
159 Tamarick Vanover .10 .30
160 Marshall Faulk .25 .60
161 Thomas Lewis .07 .20
162 Ty Detmer .10 .30
163 Darnay Scott .10 .30
164 Byron Bam Morris .07 .20
165 Scott Mitchell .10 .30
166 Brad Johnson .20 .50
167 Dave Meggett .07 .20
168 Bobby Engram .10 .30
169 Natrone Means .10 .30
170 Eric Pegram .07 .20
171 Leonard Russell .07 .20
172 Muhsin Muhammad .10 .30
173 Aeneas Williams .07 .20
174 Fred Barnett .07 .20
175 William Floyd .10 .30
176 Kimble Anders .07 .20
177 Darick Holmes .07 .20
178 Willie Green .07 .20
179 Rodney Thomas .07 .20
180 Derrick Alexander WR .10 .30
181 Sean Dawkins .07 .20
182 Dorsey Levens .20 .50
183 Napoleon Kaufman .20 .50
184 Mario Bates .07 .20
185 Yancey Thigpen .10 .30
186 Johnnie Morton .10 .30
187 Gus Frerotte .07 .20
188 Terance Mathis .10 .30
189 Tyrone Hughes .07 .20
190 Wayne Chrebet .20 .50
191 Tony Brackens .07 .20
192 Hardy Nickerson .07 .20
193 Daryl Johnston .10 .30
194 Irving Fryar .10 .30
195 Jeff Blake .10 .30
196 Charles Way .10 .30
197 Brian Mitchell .07 .20
198 Brent Jones .10 .30
199 Mark Chmura .10 .30
200 Terry Glenn .20 .50
201 Cris Carter .20 .50
202 Steve Atwater .07 .20
203 Rob Moore .10 .30
204 Anthony Johnson .07 .20
205 Warren Moon .20 .50
206 Darrien Gordon .07 .20
207 Isaac Bruce .20 .50
208 Reidel Anthony RC .20 .50
209 Darnell Autry RC .10 .30
210 Tiki Barber RC 1.25 3.00
211 Pat Barnes RC .20 .50
212 Terry Battle RC .07 .20
213 Michael Booker RC .07 .20
214 Peter Boulware RC .20 .50
215 Chris Canty RC .07 .20
216 Rae Carruth RC .07 .20
217 Troy Davis RC .10 .30
218 Corey Dillon RC .75 2.00
219 Jim Druckenmiller RC .10 .30
220 Warrick Dunn RC .60 1.50
221 James Farrior RC .20 .50
222 Tarik Glenn RC .20 .50
223 Tony Gonzalez RC .75 2.00
224 Yatil Green RC .10 .30
225 Byron Hanspard RC .10 .30
226 Ike Hilliard RC .30 .75
227 Kenny Holmes RC .20 .50
228 Walter Jones RC .30 .75
229 Tom Knight RC .07 .20
230 David LaFleur RC .07 .20
231 Kenard Lang RC .10 .30
232 Kevin Lockett RC .10 .30
233 Tremain Mack RC .07 .20
234 Sam Madison RC .20 .50
235 Chris Naeole RC .07 .20
236 Orlando Pace RC .20 .50
237 Jake Plummer RC .75 2.00
238 Dwayne Rudd RC .20 .50
239 Darrell Russell RC .07 .20
240 Jamie Sharper RC .10 .30
241 Sedrick Shaw RC .10 .30
242 Antowain Smith RC .50 1.25
243 Shawn Springs RC .10 .30
244 Bryant Westbrook RC .07 .20
245 Reinard Wilson RC .10 .30
246 Danny Wuerffel RC .20 .50
247 Renaldo Wynn RC .07 .20
248 Checklist .07 .20
249 Checklist .07 .20
250 Checklist .07 .20
S1 Karim Abdul-Jabbar Sample .10 .30
S1AU Abdul-Jabb. AUTO/500 25.00 50.00

1997 SkyBox Impact Rave

*STARS: 10X TO 25X HI COLUMN
*RCs: 8X TO 20X HI
STATED ODDS 1:36 HOBBY
STATED PRINT RUN 150 SERIAL #'d SETS

1997 SkyBox Impact Boss

Randomly inserted in packs at a rate of one in six, this 20-card set features color player photos printed on embossed and spot UV-coated cards. The backs carry player information. A "Super Boss" parallel version was also inserted at the rate of 1:36 and printed on colorful foil card stock.

COMPLETE SET (20) 15.00 40.00
STATED ODDS 1:6
*SUPER BOSS: 1.5X TO 3X BASIC INSERTS
1 Karim Abdul-Jabbar .60 1.50
2 Troy Aikman 1.25 3.00
3 Tim Biakabutuka .40 1.00
4 Mark Brunell .75 2.00
5 Rae Carruth .15 .40
6 Kerry Collins .60 1.50
7 Corey Dillon 2.50 6.00
8 Jim Druckenmiller .25 .60
9 Warrick Dunn 1.25 3.00
10 Brett Favre 2.50 6.00
11 Eddie George .60 1.50
12 Marvin Harrison .60 1.50
13 Keyshawn Johnson .60 1.50
14 Eddie Kennison .40 1.00
15 Dan Marino 2.50 6.00
16 Curtis Martin .75 2.00
17 Steve McNair .75 2.00
18 Orlando Pace .40 1.00
19 Barry Sanders 2.00 5.00
20 Steve Young .75 2.00

1997 SkyBox Impact Excelerators

Randomly inserted in packs at a rate of one in 48, this 12-card set displays color images of players with great speed. The raised and textured thermographics feature metallic ink on a die-cut design.

COMPLETE SET (12) 30.00 60.00
STATED ODDS 1:48
1 Mark Brunell 3.00 8.00
2 Rae Carruth 1.00 2.50
3 Terrell Davis 3.00 8.00
4 Joey Galloway 1.50 4.00
5 Marvin Harrison 2.50 6.00
6 Keyshawn Johnson 2.50 6.00
7 Eddie Kennison 1.50 4.00
8 Steve McNair 3.00 8.00
9 Jerry Rice 5.00 12.00
10 Emmitt Smith 8.00 20.00
11 Shawn Springs 1.50 4.00
12 Kordell Stewart 2.50 6.00

1997 SkyBox Impact Instant Impact

Randomly inserted in packs at the rate of one in 24, this 15-card set features color photos of top selections from the 1997 NFL Draft. The cards were printed with silver foil.

COMPLETE SET (15) 15.00 40.00
STATED ODDS 1:24
1 Reidel Anthony 1.50 4.00
2 Darnell Autry 1.00 2.50
3 Tiki Barber 10.00 25.00
4 Peter Boulware 1.50 4.00
5 Troy Davis 1.00 2.50
6 Jim Druckenmiller 1.00 2.50
7 Warrick Dunn 5.00 12.00
8 Yatil Green 1.00 2.50
9 Ike Hilliard 2.50 6.00
10 Orlando Pace 1.50 4.00
11 Darrell Russell .60 1.50
12 Sedrick Shaw 1.00 2.50
13 Shawn Springs 1.00 2.50
14 Bryant Westbrook .60 1.50
15 Danny Wuerffel 1.50 4.00

1997 SkyBox Impact Rave Reviews

Randomly inserted in packs at a rate of one in 288, this 12-card set features color player images printed over a rainbow holofoil. The backs carry a commentary about the player by former All-Pro Ronnie Lott.

COMPLETE SET (12) 125.00 250.00
STATED ODDS 1:288
1 Terrell Davis 5.00 12.00
2 John Elway 15.00 40.00
3 Brett Favre 15.00 40.00
4 Joey Galloway 2.50 6.00
5 Eddie George 4.00 10.00
6 Terry Glenn 4.00 10.00
7 Dan Marino 15.00 40.00
8 Curtis Martin 5.00 12.00
9 Jerry Rice 8.00 20.00
10 Barry Sanders 12.50 30.00
11 Deion Sanders 4.00 10.00
12 Emmitt Smith 12.50 30.00

1997 SkyBox Impact Total Impact

Randomly inserted in retail packs only at a rate of one in 36, this 10-card set features color player images of top NFL stars printed on plastic over a white background.

COMPLETE SET (10) 25.00 60.00
STATED ODDS 1:36 RETAIL
1 Karim Abdul-Jabbar 2.50 6.00
2 Troy Aikman 5.00 12.00
3 Drew Bledsoe 3.00 8.00
4 Isaac Bruce 2.50 6.00
5 Kerry Collins 2.50 6.00
6 John Elway 10.00 25.00
7 Terry Glenn 2.50 6.00
8 Lawrence Phillips 1.00 2.50
9 Deion Sanders 2.50 6.00
10 Kordell Stewart 2.50 6.00

2003 SkyBox LE

Released in January of 2004, this set contains 160 cards including 60 veterans and 100 rookies. Rookies are serial numbered to 99. Boxes contained 18 packs of 3 cards. SRP was $3.99.

COMP.SET w/o RC's (60) 8.00 20.00
61-160 ROOKIE PRINT RUN 99
1 Emmitt Smith .50 1.25
2 Eric Moulds .20 .50
3 William Green .20 .50
4 Clinton Portis .20 .50
5 Tony Gonzalez .25 .60
6 Aaron Brooks .20 .50
7 Chad Pennington .20 .50
8 Jerry Rice .60 1.50
9 LaDainian Tomlinson .30 .75
10 Torry Holt .25 .60
11 Warren Sapp .25 .60
12 Steve McNair .25 .60
13 Marc Bulger .20 .50
14 Patrick Ramsey .25 .60
15 Peerless Price .20 .50
16 Jamal Lewis .25 .60
17 Rich Gannon .25 .60
18 Plaxico Burress .20 .50
19 Drew Brees .30 .75
20 Eddie George .25 .60
21 Ray Lewis .30 .75
22 Drew Bledsoe .25 .60
23 Antonio Bryant .20 .50
24 David Carr .20 .50
25 Priest Holmes .20 .50
26 Ricky Williams .25 .60
27 Peyton Manning .75 2.00
28 Daunte Culpepper .25 .60
29 Jeremy Shockey .20 .50
30 Tiki Barber .25 .60
31 Koren Robinson .25 .60
32 Keyshawn Johnson .30 .75
33 Laveranues Coles .20 .50
34 Brian Urlacher .30 .75
35 Jake Plummer .20 .50
36 Edgerrin James .25 .60
37 Marvin Harrison .25 .60
38 Tom Brady 1.25 3.00
39 Curtis Martin .25 .60
40 Donovan McNabb .25 .60

41 Hines Ward .25 .60
42 Charlie Garner .25 .60
43 Tommy Maddox .20 .50
44 Terrell Owens .25 .60
45 Shaun Alexander .20 .50
46 Ahman Green .25 .60
47 Fred Taylor .20 .50
48 Randy Moss .25 .60
49 Deuce McAllister .25 .60
50 Quincy Carter .20 .50
51 Jeff Garcia .20 .50
52 Marshall Faulk .25 .60
53 Dante Hall .20 .50
54 Michael Vick .25 .60
55 Stephen Davis .20 .50
56 Corey Dillon .20 .50
57 Travis Henry .20 .50
58 Chad Johnson .20 .50
59 Joey Harrington .20 .50
60 Brett Favre .60 1.50
61 Bryant Johnson RC 8.00 20.00
62 Terence Newman RC 8.00 20.00
63 Labrandon Toefield RC 5.00 12.00
64 Visanthe Shiancoe RC 8.00 20.00
65 Josh Brown RC 10.00 25.00
66 Andre Woolfolk RC 5.00 12.00
67 Jeremi Johnson RC 5.00 12.00
68 Michael Doss RC 8.00 20.00
69 Talman Gardner RC 5.00 12.00
70 Arnaz Battle RC 8.00 20.00
71 Troy Polamalu RC 75.00 135.00
72 Brock Forsey RC 6.00 15.00
73 Domanick Davis RC 6.00 15.00
74 Onterrio Smith RC 5.00 12.00
75 Kassim Osgood RC 8.00 20.00
76 Asante Samuel RC 12.00 30.00
77 Terrell Suggs RC 6.00 15.00
78 Boss Bailey RC 6.00 15.00
79 Larry Johnson RC 6.00 15.00
80 Teyo Johnson RC 6.00 15.00
81 Chris Simms RC 5.00 12.00
82 Walter Young RC 5.00 12.00
83 Dave Ragone RC 5.00 12.00
84 E.J. Henderson RC 6.00 15.00
85 Billy McMullen RC 5.00 12.00
86 Taylor Jacobs RC 5.00 12.00
87 Sam Aiken RC 6.00 15.00
88 Avon Cobourne RC 5.00 12.00
89 J.R. Tolver RC 6.00 15.00
90 Doug Gabriel RC 6.00 15.00
91 Chris Brown RC 5.00 12.00
92 Musa Smith RC 5.00 12.00
93 Charles Rogers RC 6.00 15.00
94 Seth Marler RC 5.00 12.00
95 DeWayne Robertson RC 6.00 15.00
96 Shaun McDonald RC 6.00 15.00
97 Reno Mahe RC 6.00 15.00
98 Carson Palmer RC 10.00 25.00
99 Dallas Clark RC 8.00 20.00
100 Johnathan Sullivan RC 5.00 12.00
101 Brandon Lloyd RC 8.00 20.00
102 Ken Dorsey RC 6.00 15.00
103 Kelley Washington RC 5.00 12.00
104 Tony Hollings RC 6.00 15.00
105 Bethel Johnson RC 5.00 12.00
106 Antonio Gates RC 75.00 135.00
107 Tyler Brayton RC 6.00 15.00
108 Michael Haynes RC 5.00 12.00
109 Andre Johnson RC 12.00 30.00
110 Nate Burleson RC 6.00 15.00
111 Sammy Davis RC 6.00 15.00
112 Nick Barnett RC 8.00 20.00
113 Willis McGahee RC 6.00 15.00
114 Casey Fitzsimmons RC 6.00 15.00
115 Donald Lee RC 6.00 15.00
116 L.J. Smith RC 8.00 20.00
117 Tyrone Calico RC 5.00 12.00
118 Anquan Boldin RC 8.00 20.00
119 Jason Witten RC 20.00 50.00
120 George Wrighster RC 5.00 12.00
121 William Joseph RC 5.00 12.00
122 Kevin Curtis RC 5.00 12.00
123 Anthony Adams RC 6.00 15.00
124 Kyle Boller RC 5.00 12.00
125 Artose Pinner RC 5.00 12.00
126 Rashean Mathis RC 5.00 12.00
127 Justin Fargas RC 8.00 20.00
128 Pisa Tinoisamoa RC 8.00 20.00
129 Justin Griffith RC 6.00 15.00
130 Quentin Griffin RC 6.00 15.00
131 Cortez Hankton RC 6.00 15.00
132 B.J. Askew RC 6.00 15.00
133 Arlen Harris RC 5.00 12.00
134 Dan Klecko RC 6.00 15.00
135 Lee Suggs RC 5.00 12.00
136 Byron Leftwich RC 6.00 15.00
137 David Tyree RC 6.00 15.00
138 Aaron Walker RC 6.00 15.00
139 Marcus Trufant RC 6.00 15.00
140 Rex Grossman RC 6.00 15.00
141 Bennie Joppru RC 5.00 12.00
142 Kevin Williams RC 8.00 20.00
143 Jerome McDougle RC 5.00 12.00
144 Ken Hamlin RC 8.00 20.00
145 Zuriel Smith RC 5.00 12.00
146 Brooks Bollinger RC 6.00 15.00
147 Ike Taylor RC 8.00 20.00
148 Brad Pyatt RC 5.00 12.00
149 DeJuan Groce RC 8.00 20.00
150 Keenan Howry RC 5.00 12.00
151 Seneca Wallace RC 6.00 15.00
152 Richard Angulo RC 5.00 12.00
153 Jimmy Kennedy RC 6.00 15.00
154 Ty Warren RC 6.00 15.00
155 Nnamdi Asomugha RC 8.00 20.00
156 Chris Kelsay RC 6.00 15.00
157 Terry Pierce RC 5.00 12.00
158 Victor Hobson RC 5.00 12.00
159 Brian St.Pierre RC 5.00 12.00
160 Dewayne White RC 5.00 12.00

2003 SkyBox LE Artist Proofs

*VETS 1-60: 8X TO 20X BASIC CARDS
STATED PRINT RUN 50 SER.#'d SETS

2003 SkyBox LE Executive Proofs

UNPRICED EXEC.PROOF PRINT RUN 1

2003 SkyBox LE Gold Proofs

*VETS 1-60: 4X TO 10X BASIC CARDS
STATED PRINT RUN 150 SER.#'d SETS

2003 SkyBox LE Jersey Proofs

STATED PRINT RUN 175 SER.#'d SETS
UNPRICED GOLD PRINT RUN 10
1 Emmitt Smith 10.00 25.00
2 Eric Moulds 4.00 10.00
4 Clinton Portis 4.00 10.00
5 Tony Gonzalez 5.00 12.00
7 Chad Pennington 4.00 10.00
8 Jerry Rice 12.00 30.00
9 LaDainian Tomlinson 6.00 15.00
10 Torry Holt 5.00 12.00
11 Warren Sapp 5.00 12.00
12 Steve McNair 5.00 12.00
21 Ray Lewis 6.00 15.00
22 Drew Bledsoe 5.00 12.00
24 David Carr 4.00 10.00
25 Priest Holmes 4.00 10.00
26 Ricky Williams 5.00 12.00
27 Peyton Manning 15.00 40.00
28 Daunte Culpepper 5.00 12.00
29 Jeremy Shockey 4.00 10.00
30 Tiki Barber 5.00 12.00
32 Keyshawn Johnson 6.00 15.00
34 Brian Urlacher 6.00 15.00
35 Jake Plummer 4.00 10.00
36 Edgerrin James 5.00 12.00
37 Marvin Harrison 5.00 12.00
39 Curtis Martin 5.00 12.00
40 Donovan McNabb 5.00 12.00
41 Hines Ward 5.00 12.00
42 Charlie Garner 5.00 12.00
44 Terrell Owens 5.00 12.00
45 Shaun Alexander 4.00 10.00
46 Ahman Green 5.00 12.00
47 Fred Taylor 4.00 10.00
48 Randy Moss 5.00 12.00
49 Deuce McAllister 5.00 12.00
52 Marshall Faulk 5.00 12.00
54 Michael Vick 5.00 12.00
55 Stephen Davis 4.00 10.00
56 Corey Dillon 4.00 10.00
59 Joey Harrington 4.00 10.00
60 Brett Favre 12.00 30.00

2003 SkyBox LE Photographer's Proofs

*VETS 1-60: 15X TO 40X BASIC CARDS
STATED PRINT RUN 25 SER.#'d SETS

2003 SkyBox LE Retail

COMPLETE SET (60) 8.00 20.00
*VETS 1-60: .3X TO .8X BASIC CARDS

2003 SkyBox LE History of the Draft Jerseys

Randomly inserted in packs, this set features game worn jersey swatches. Each card is serial numbered to the last two digits of the year in which the player was drafted. A Silver and Gold parallel of this set exist. Silver cards feature silver highlights and are serial numbered to 50. Gold cards feature gold highlights and are serial numbered to 10. Gold cards are not priced due to scarcity.

STATED PRINT RUN 90-99
*SILVER/50: .5X TO 1.2X JSY/90-99
SILVER PRINT RUN 50 SER.#'d SETS
UNPRICED GOLD PRINT RUN 10
HDAG Ahman Green/98 4.00 10.00
HDAT Amani Toomer/96 3.00 8.00
HDBF Brett Favre/91 10.00 25.00
HDCD Corey Dillon/97 3.00 8.00
HDCG Charlie Garner/94 4.00 10.00
HDCM Curtis Martin/95 4.00 10.00
HDCW Charles Woodson/98 5.00 12.00
HDDB Derrick Brooks/95 3.00 8.00
HDDB Drew Bledsoe/93 4.00 10.00
HDDC Daunte Culpepper/99 4.00 10.00
HDDM Donovan McNabb/99 4.00 10.00
HDEG Eddie George/96 4.00 10.00
HDEJ Edgerrin James/99 4.00 10.00
HDEM Eric Moulds/96 3.00 8.00
HDES Emmitt Smith/90 8.00 20.00
HDFT Fred Taylor/98 3.00 8.00
HDHW Hines Ward/98 4.00 10.00
HDIB Isaac Bruce/94 5.00 12.00
HDJG Joey Galloway/95 4.00 10.00
HDJK Jevon Kearse/99 3.00 8.00
HDJP Jake Plummer/97 3.00 8.00
HDKC Kerry Collins/95 3.00 8.00
HDKJ Keyshawn Johnson/96 5.00 12.00
HDMA Mike Alstott/96 3.00 8.00
HDMF Marshall Faulk/94 4.00 10.00
HDMH Marvin Harrison/96 4.00 10.00
HDPM Peyton Manning/98 12.00 30.00
HDRL Ray Lewis/96 5.00 12.00
HDRM Randy Moss/98 4.00 10.00
HDRW Ricky Williams/99 4.00 10.00
HDSD Stephen Davis/96 3.00 8.00
HDSM Steve McNair/95 4.00 10.00
HDSR Simeon Rice/96 3.00 8.00
HDTB Tiki Barber/97 4.00 10.00
HDTC Tim Couch/99 3.00 8.00
HDTG Tony Gonzalez/97 4.00 10.00
HDTH Torry Holt/99 4.00 10.00
HDTO Terrell Owens/96 4.00 10.00
HDWS Warren Sapp/95 4.00 10.00
HDZT Zach Thomas/96 4.00 10.00

2003 SkyBox LE League Leaders

Inserted at a rate of 1:18, this set highlights some of the NFL's statistical league leaders. An Executive Proof parallel of this set exists. Executive Proof cards features an authentic signature of Fleer's Executive Vice President, Lloyd J. Pawlak, on the back of the card. Each card is serial numbered to 1 and is not priced due to scarcity.

COMPLETE SET (10) 12.00 30.00
STATED ODDS 1:18
UNPRICED EXEC.PROOF PRINT RUN 1
1 Ricky Williams 1.00 2.50
2 Marvin Harrison 1.00 2.50
3 Chad Pennington .75 2.00
4 Terrell Owens 1.00 2.50
5 Brian Urlacher 1.25 3.00
6 Shaun Alexander .75 2.00
7 Marshall Faulk 1.00 2.50
8 Ray Lewis 1.25 3.00
9 Randy Moss 1.00 2.50
10 Peyton Manning 3.00 8.00

2003 SkyBox LE League Leaders Jerseys

Randomly inserted in packs, this set features game worn jersey swatches. Each card is serial numbered to 75. A Silver and Gold parallel of this set exist. Silver cards feature silver highlights and are serial numbered to 50. Gold cards feature gold highlights and are serial numbered to 10. Gold cards are not priced due to scarcity.

STATED PRINT RUN 75 SER.#'d SETS
*SILVER/50: .5X TO 1.2X BASE JSY/75
SILVER PRINT RUN 50 SER.#'d SETS
UNPRICED GOLD PRINT RUN 10
LLBU Brian Urlacher 8.00 20.00
LLCP Chad Pennington 5.00 12.00
LLMF Marshall Faulk 6.00 15.00
LLMH Marvin Harrison 6.00 15.00
LLPM Peyton Manning 20.00 50.00
LLRL Ray Lewis 8.00 20.00
LLRM Randy Moss 6.00 15.00
LLRW Ricky Williams 6.00 15.00
LLSA Shaun Alexander 5.00 12.00
LLTO Terrell Owens 6.00 15.00

2003 SkyBox LE Rare Form

Inserted at a rate of 1:288, this set features die cut designed cards and highlights 10 NFL superstars. An Executive Proof parallel of this set exists. Executive Proof cards features an authentic signature of Fleer's Executive Vice President, Lloyd J. Pawlak, on the back of the card. Each card is serial numbered to 1 and is not priced due to scarcity.

STATED ODDS 1:288
UNPRICED EXEC.PROOF PRINT RUN 1
1 Brett Favre 8.00 20.00
2 Emmitt Smith 6.00 15.00
3 Michael Vick 3.00 8.00
4 Clinton Portis 2.50 6.00
5 Jeremy Shockey 2.50 6.00
6 Jerry Rice 8.00 20.00
7 David Carr 2.50 6.00
8 Peyton Manning 10.00 25.00
9 Randy Moss 3.00 8.00
10 Brian Urlacher 4.00 10.00

2003 SkyBox LE Rare Form Jerseys Silver Proofs

SILVER PRINT RUN 50 SER.#'d SETS
*BASE JSY/54-84: .4X TO 1X JSY/50
*BASE JSY/22-26: .6X TO 1.5X JSY/50
BASE JSY PRINT RUN 4-84
UNPRICED GOLD PRINT RUN 10
RFBF Brett Favre 20.00 50.00
RFBU Brian Urlacher 10.00 25.00
RFCP Clinton Portis 6.00 15.00
RFDC David Carr 6.00 15.00
RFES Emmitt Smith 15.00 40.00
RFJR Jerry Rice 20.00 50.00
RFJS Jeremy Shockey 6.00 15.00
RFMV Michael Vick 8.00 20.00
RFPM Peyton Manning 25.00 60.00
RFRM Randy Moss 8.00 20.00

2003 SkyBox LE Sky's the Limit

Inserted at a rate of 1:6, this set highlights some of the biggest stars in the NFL. An Executive Proof parallel of this set exists. Executive Proof cards features an authentic signature of Fleer's Executive Vice President, Lloyd J. Pawlak, on the back of the card. Each card is serial numbered to 1 and is not priced due to scarcity.

COMPLETE SET (20) 25.00 60.00
STATED ODDS 1:6
UNPRICED EXEC.PROOF PRINT RUN 1
1 Donovan McNabb 1.00 2.50
2 Jeremy Shockey .75 2.00
3 Michael Vick 1.00 2.50
4 Peyton Manning 3.00 8.00
5 Randy Moss 1.00 2.50
6 Clinton Portis .75 2.00
7 Joey Harrington .75 2.00
8 Ricky Williams 1.00 2.50
9 Deuce McAllister 1.00 2.50
10 LaDainian Tomlinson 1.25 3.00
11 Priest Holmes .75 2.00
12 Carson Palmer 1.00 2.50
13 Byron Leftwich .60 1.50
14 Andre Johnson 1.25 3.00
15 Larry Johnson .60 1.50
16 Rex Grossman .60 1.50
17 Terence Newman .75 2.00
18 David Carr .75 2.00
19 Daunte Culpepper 1.00 2.50
20 Brian Urlacher 1.25 3.00

2003 SkyBox LE Sky's the Limit Jerseys

Randomly inserted in packs, this set features game worn jersey swatches. Each card is serial numbered to 99. A Silver and Gold parallel of this set exist. Silver cards feature silver highlights and are serial numbered to 50. Gold cards feature gold highlights and are serial numbered to 10.

PRINT RUN 99 SERIAL #'d SETS
*SILVER/50: .5X TO 1.2X JSY/99
SILVER PRINT RUN 50 SER.#'d SETS
UNPRICED GOLD PRINT RUN 10
SLAJ Andre Johnson 8.00 20.00
SLBL Byron Leftwich 4.00 10.00
SLBU Brian Urlacher 8.00 20.00
SLCP Clinton Portis 5.00 12.00
SLCP Carson Palmer 6.00 15.00
SLDC David Carr 5.00 12.00
SLDC Daunte Culpepper 6.00 15.00
SLDM Donovan McNabb 6.00 15.00
SLDM Deuce McAllister 6.00 15.00
SLJH Joey Harrington 5.00 12.00
SLJS Jeremy Shockey 5.00 12.00
SLLJ Larry Johnson 4.00 10.00
SLLT LaDainian Tomlinson 8.00 20.00
SLMV Michael Vick 6.00 15.00
SLPH Priest Holmes 5.00 12.00
SLPM Peyton Manning 20.00 50.00
SLRG Rex Grossman 4.00 10.00
SLRM Randy Moss 6.00 15.00
SLRW Ricky Williams 6.00 15.00
SLTN Terence Newman 5.00 12.00

2004 SkyBox LE

SkyBox LE was produced by Fleer and initially released in late September 2004. The base set consists of 160-cards including 100-rookies serial numbered of 99. Hobby boxes contained 16-packs of 3-cards and retail boxes contained 24-packs of 5-cards each. Four parallel sets and a variety of inserts can be found seeded in hobby and retail packs highlighted by the Future Legends Autographed Patches and a variety of other game used jersey inserts. Some signed cards were issued via mail-in exchange or redemption cards with a number of those EXCH cards not yet appearing live on the secondary market as of the printing of this book.

COMP.SET w/o SP's (60) 7.50 20.00
ROOKIE/99 ODDS 1:29 HOB
ROOKIE PRINT RUN 99 SER.#'d SETS
UNPRICED PURPLE PRINT RUN 1
1 Anquan Boldin .20 .50
2 Quincy Carter .20 .50
3 Chad Pennington .20 .50
4 Brett Favre .60 1.50
5 Marc Bulger .20 .50
6 David Carr .20 .50
7 Byron Leftwich .20 .50
8 Hines Ward .25 .60
9 Drew Bledsoe .25 .60
10 Domanick Davis .20 .50
11 Plaxico Burress .20 .50
12 Mark Brunell .25 .60
13 Terrell Owens .25 .60
14 Peyton Manning .75 2.00
15 Matt Hasselbeck .20 .50
16 Willis McGahee .20 .50
17 Fred Taylor .20 .50
18 Torry Holt .25 .60
19 Priest Holmes .20 .50
20 Charlie Garner .25 .60
21 Brian Urlacher .30 .75
22 Corey Dillon .20 .50
23 Daunte Culpepper .25 .60
24 Clinton Portis .20 .50
25 Chad Johnson .20 .50
26 Tom Brady 1.25 3.00
27 Deuce McAllister .25 .60
28 Randy Moss .25 .60
29 A.J. Feeley .20 .50
30 Steve McNair .25 .60
31 Aaron Brooks .20 .50
32 Carson Palmer .25 .60
33 Jeremy Shockey .20 .50
34 Emmitt Smith .50 1.25
35 Jeff Garcia .20 .50
36 Kurt Warner .25 .60
37 Andre Johnson .25 .60
38 LaDainian Tomlinson .30 .75
39 Ray Lewis .30 .75
40 Charles Rogers .20 .50
41 Rich Gannon .25 .60
42 Jake Delhomme .20 .50
43 Marvin Harrison .25 .60
44 Shaun Alexander .20 .50
45 Ricky Williams .25 .60
46 Eddie George .25 .60
47 Edgerrin James .25 .60
48 Chris Chambers .20 .50
49 Jamal Lewis .25 .60
50 Joey Harrington .20 .50
51 Jerry Rice .60 1.50
52 Kyle Boller .20 .50
53 Ahman Green .25 .60
54 Donovan McNabb .25 .60
55 Stephen Davis .20 .50
56 Tony Gonzalez .25 .60
57 Marshall Faulk .25 .60
58 Michael Vick .25 .60
59 Jake Plummer .20 .50
60 Curtis Martin .25 .60
61 Eli Manning RC 20.00 50.00
62 Robert Gallery RC 3.00 8.00
63 Larry Fitzgerald RC 10.00 25.00
64 Philip Rivers RC 8.00 20.00
65 Sean Taylor RC 15.00 40.00
66 Kellen Winslow RC 2.50 6.00
67 Roy Williams RC 2.50 6.00
68 DeAngelo Hall RC 4.00 10.00
69 Reggie Williams RC 2.50 6.00
70 Dunta Robinson RC 2.50 6.00
71 Ben Roethlisberger RC 20.00 50.00
72 Jonathan Vilma RC 3.00 8.00
73 Lee Evans RC 4.00 10.00
74 Tommie Harris RC 3.00 8.00
75 Michael Clayton RC 3.00 8.00
76 D.J. Williams RC 4.00 10.00
77 Tim Euhus RC 2.50 6.00
78 Kenechi Udeze RC 3.00 8.00
79 Vince Wilfork RC 4.00 10.00
80 J.P. Losman RC 2.50 6.00
81 Jared Lorenzen RC 3.00 8.00
82 Steven Jackson RC 4.00 10.00
83 Ricky Ray RC 4.00 10.00
84 Chris Perry RC 2.50 6.00
85 Jason Babin RC 4.00 10.00
86 Chris Gamble RC 2.50 6.00
87 Michael Jenkins RC 2.50 6.00
88 Kevin Jones RC 3.00 8.00
89 Rashaun Woods RC 2.50 6.00
90 Ben Watson RC 3.00 8.00
91 Karlos Dansby RC 3.00 8.00
92 Teddy Lehman RC 2.50 6.00
93 Ben Troupe RC 2.50 6.00
94 Tatum Bell RC 2.50 6.00
95 Julius Jones RC 2.50 6.00
96 Devery Henderson RC 2.50 6.00
97 Drew Henson RC 2.50 6.00
98 Darius Watts RC 2.50 6.00
99 Greg Jones RC 2.50 6.00
100 Luke McCown RC 2.50 6.00
101 Keary Colbert RC 2.50 6.00
102 Mewelde Moore RC 3.00 8.00
103 Ben Hartsock RC 2.50 6.00
104 Derrick Hamilton RC 2.50 6.00
105 Bernard Berrian RC 2.50 6.00
106 Chris Cooley RC 3.00 8.00
107 Devard Darling RC 2.50 6.00
108 Matt Schaub RC 2.50 6.00
109 Carlos Francis RC 2.50 6.00
110 Will Poole RC 4.00 10.00
111 Samie Parker RC 2.50 6.00
112 Derrick Knight RC 2.50 6.00
113 Jerricho Cotchery RC 3.00 8.00
114 Rod Rutherford RC 2.50 6.00
115 Ernest Wilford RC 3.00 8.00
116 Cedric Cobbs RC 2.50 6.00
117 Johnnie Morant RC 2.50 6.00
118 Craig Krenzel RC 2.50 6.00
119 Maurice Mann RC 2.50 6.00
120 Michael Turner RC 2.50 6.00
121 Ryan Dinwiddie RC 2.50 6.00
122 Drew Carter RC 3.00 8.00
123 P.K. Sam RC 2.50 6.00
124 Jamaar Taylor RC 2.50 6.00
125 Ryan Krause RC 2.50 6.00
126 Triandos Luke RC 2.50 6.00
127 Andy Hall RC 2.50 6.00
128 Josh Harris RC 2.50 6.00
129 Jim Sorgi RC 3.00 8.00
130 Jason Fife RC 2.50 6.00
131 Clarence Moore RC 2.50 6.00
132 Jeff Smoker RC 3.00 8.00
133 John Navarre RC 2.50 6.00
134 Justin Jenkins RC 2.50 6.00
135 Adimchinobe Echemandu RC 3.00 8.00
136 Jammal Lord RC 2.50 6.00
137 Erik Jensen RC 2.50 6.00
138 Cody Pickett RC 2.50 6.00
139 Casey Bramlet RC 2.50 6.00
140 Quincy Wilson RC 2.50 6.00
141 Thomas Tapeh RC 3.00 8.00
142 Matt Brandt RC 2.50 6.00
143 Bruce Perry RC 2.50 6.00
144 Mark Jones RC 2.50 6.00
145 Keith Smith RC 2.50 6.00
146 B.J. Symons RC 2.50 6.00
147 Patrick Crayton RC 4.00 10.00
148 Daryl Smith RC 2.50 6.00
149 Demorrio Williams RC 4.00 10.00
150 Casey Clausen RC 3.00 8.00
151 Jarrett Payton RC 3.00 8.00
152 Kris Wilson RC 3.00 8.00
153 Renaldo Works RC 2.50 6.00
154 Shawn Andrews RC 3.00 8.00
155 Ricardo Colclough RC 2.50 6.00
156 Travis LaBoy RC 3.00 8.00
157 Bob Sanders RC 5.00 12.00
158 Chad Lavalais RC 2.50 6.00
159 Derrick Strait RC 2.50 6.00
160 Darnell Dockett RC 4.00 10.00

2004 SkyBox LE Black Border Red

*VETS: 6X TO 15X BASIC CARDS
*ROOKIES: .4X TO 1X BASIC CARDS
STATED PRINT RUN 50 SER.#'d SETS

2004 SkyBox LE Gold

*VETS: 3X TO 8X BASIC CARDS
*ROOKIES: .25X TO .6X BASIC CARDS
STATED PRINT RUN 150 SER.#'d SETS

2004 SkyBox LE Black Border Platinum

*VETS: 8X TO 20X BASIC CARDS
*ROOKIES: .5X TO 1.2X BASIC CARDS
STATED PRINT RUN 35 SER.#'d SETS

2004 SkyBox LE Future Legends

STATED ODDS 1:16
UNPRICED EXEC.PROOF #'d OF 1
1FL Tatum Bell .60 1.50
2FL Bernard Berrian .60 1.50
3FL Michael Clayton .75 2.00
4FL Lee Evans 1.00 2.50
5FL Devery Henderson .60 1.50
6FL Michael Jenkins .60 1.50
7FL Greg Jones .60 1.50
8FL Julius Jones .60 1.50
9FL Kevin Jones .75 2.00
10FL J.P. Losman .60 1.50
11FL Eli Manning 5.00 12.00
12FL Chris Perry .60 1.50
13FL Ben Troupe .60 1.50
14FL Philip Rivers 2.00 5.00
15FL Ben Roethlisberger 5.00 12.00
16FL Matt Schaub .60 1.50
17FL Sean Taylor 4.00 10.00
18FL Roy Williams WR .60 1.50
19FL Kellen Winslow Jr. .60 1.50
20FL Rashaun Woods .60 1.50
21FL Reggie Williams .60 1.50
22FL Steven Jackson 1.00 2.50
23FL Larry Fitzgerald 2.50 6.00
24FL Drew Henson .60 1.50
25FL Luke McCown .60 1.50

2004 SkyBox LE Future Legends Autographed Patches

STATED PRINT RUN 25 SER.#'d SETS
UNPRICED DUAL AU PRINT RUN 1
BR Ben Roethlisberger 150.00 300.00
CP Chris Perry 12.00 30.00
DH Devery Henderson 12.00 30.00
EM Eli Manning 175.00 300.00
JL J.P. Losman 12.00 30.00
KW Kellen Winslow Jr. 12.00 30.00
MC Michael Clayton 15.00 40.00
PR Philip Rivers 60.00 125.00
RW Roy Williams WR 12.00 30.00
RW2 Rashaun Woods 12.00 30.00
RW3 Reggie Williams 12.00 30.00
WP Will Poole 20.00 50.00

2004 SkyBox LE Future Legends Jerseys Silver

SILVER PRINT RUN 75
*COPPER/50: .5X TO 1.2X SLVR/75
COPPER PRINT RUN 50
*GOLD PATCH/25: .8X TO 2X SLVR/75
GOLD PROOF PATCH PRINT RUN 25
FLBB Bernard Berrian 2.50 6.00
FLBR Ben Roethlisberger 12.00 30.00
FLBT Ben Troupe 2.50 6.00
FLCP Chris Perry 2.50 6.00
FLDH Devery Henderson 2.50 6.00
FLDH Drew Henson 2.50 6.00
FLEM Eli Manning 10.00 25.00
FLGJ Greg Jones 2.50 6.00
FLJJ Julius Jones 2.50 6.00
FLJL J.P. Losman 2.50 6.00
FLKJ Kevin Jones 3.00 8.00
FLKW Kellen Winslow Jr. 2.50 6.00
FLLE Lee Evans 4.00 10.00
FLLF Larry Fitzgerald 5.00 12.00
FLLM Luke McCown 2.50 6.00
FLMC Michael Clayton 3.00 8.00
FLMJ Michael Jenkins 2.50 6.00
FLMS Matt Schaub 2.50 6.00
FLPR Philip Rivers 4.00 10.00
FLRW Rashaun Woods 2.50 6.00
FLRW2 Reggie Williams 2.50 6.00
FLRW3 Roy Williams WR 2.50 6.00
FLSJ Steven Jackson 4.00 10.00
FLST Sean Taylor 6.00 15.00
FLTB Tatum Bell 2.50 6.00

2004 SkyBox LE Jersey Silver

SILVER PRINT RUN 250 SER.#'d SETS
*COPPER/99: .5X TO 1.2X SILVER/250
COPPER PRINT RUN 99 SER.#'d SETS
UNPRICED EXEC.PRPL PRINT RUN 1
*GOLD PATCH/50: 1X TO 2.5X SILVER/250
GOLD PATCH SER.#'d OF 50 SETS
*PLATINUM/15: 1.5X TO 4X SLVR/250
PLATINUM PATCH PRINT RUN 15
1 Anquan Boldin 2.00 5.00
2 Quincy Carter 2.00 5.00
3 Chad Pennington 2.00 5.00
4 Brett Favre 6.00 15.00
5 Marc Bulger 2.00 5.00
6 David Carr 2.00 5.00
7 Byron Leftwich 2.00 5.00
8 Hines Ward 2.50 6.00
9 Drew Bledsoe 2.50 6.00
10 Domanick Davis 2.00 5.00
11 Plaxico Burress 2.00 5.00
12 Mark Brunell 2.50 6.00
13 Terrell Owens 2.50 6.00
14 Peyton Manning 8.00 20.00
15 Matt Hasselbeck 2.00 5.00
16 Willis McGahee 2.00 5.00
17 Fred Taylor 2.00 5.00
18 Torry Holt 2.50 6.00
19 Priest Holmes 2.00 5.00
20 Charlie Garner 2.50 6.00
21 Brian Urlacher 3.00 8.00
22 Corey Dillon 2.00 5.00
23 Daunte Culpepper 2.50 6.00
24 Clinton Portis 2.00 5.00
25 Chad Johnson 2.00 5.00
26 Tom Brady 12.00 30.00
27 Deuce McAllister 2.50 6.00
28 Randy Moss 2.50 6.00
29 A.J. Feeley 2.00 5.00
30 Steve McNair 2.50 6.00
31 Aaron Brooks 2.00 5.00
32 Carson Palmer 2.50 6.00
33 Jeremy Shockey 2.00 5.00
34 Emmitt Smith 5.00 12.00
35 Jeff Garcia 2.00 5.00
36 Kurt Warner 2.50 6.00
37 Andre Johnson 2.50 6.00
38 LaDainian Tomlinson 3.00 8.00
39 Ray Lewis 3.00 8.00
40 Charles Rogers 2.00 5.00
41 Rich Gannon 2.50 6.00
42 Jake Delhomme 2.00 5.00
43 Marvin Harrison 2.50 6.00
44 Shaun Alexander 2.00 5.00
45 Ricky Williams 2.50 6.00
46 Eddie George 2.50 6.00
47 Edgerrin James 2.50 6.00
48 Chris Chambers 2.00 5.00
49 Jamal Lewis 2.50 6.00
50 Joey Harrington 2.00 5.00
51 Jerry Rice 6.00 15.00
52 Kyle Boller 2.00 5.00
53 Ahman Green 2.50 6.00
54 Donovan McNabb 2.50 6.00
55 Stephen Davis 2.00 5.00
56 Tony Gonzalez 2.50 6.00
57 Marshall Faulk 2.50 6.00
58 Michael Vick 2.50 6.00
59 Jake Plummer 2.00 5.00
60 Curtis Martin 2.50 6.00

2004 SkyBox LE LEgends of the Draft Autographed Patches

STATED PRINT RUN 25 SER.#'d SETS
UNPRICED DUAL AU PRINT RUN 1
AJ Andre Johnson 15.00 40.00
BL Byron Leftwich 12.00 30.00
JL Jamal Lewis 15.00 40.00
KB Kyle Boller 12.00 30.00
PM Peyton Manning 75.00 150.00

2004 SkyBox LE LEgends of the Draft Jerseys Silver

SILVER PRINT RUN 81-103
*COPPER/50: .5X TO 1.2X SILVER
COPPER PRINT RUN 50
*GOLD PATCH/25: 1X TO 2.5X SILVER
GOLD PROOF PATCH PRINT RUN 25
LDAB Anquan Boldin/103 3.00 8.00
LDAF A.J. Feeley/101 3.00 8.00
LDAJ Andre Johnson/103 4.00 10.00
LDBF Brett Favre/91 10.00 25.00
LDBL Byron Leftwich/103 3.00 8.00
LDBS Barry Sanders/89 12.00 30.00
LDBU Brian Urlacher/100 5.00 12.00
LDBW Brian Westbrook/102 3.00 8.00
LDCC Chris Chambers/101 3.00 8.00
LDCJ Chad Johnson/101 3.00 8.00
LDCP Bo Jackson/87 10.00 25.00
LDCP Clinton Portis/102 3.00 8.00
LDDC David Carr/102 3.00 8.00
LDDD Domanick Davis/103 3.00 8.00
LDDF DeShaun Foster/102 4.00 10.00
LDDM Dan Marino/83 12.00 30.00
LDDM Donovan McNabb/99 4.00 10.00
LDDM2 Deuce McAllister/100 4.00 10.00
LDDS Deion Sanders/89 6.00 15.00
LDES Emmitt Smith/90 8.00 20.00
LDJE John Elway/83 12.00 30.00
LDJH Joey Harrington/100 3.00 8.00
LDJL Jamal Lewis/100 4.00 10.00
LDJM Joe Montana/86 15.00 40.00
LDJR Jerry Rice/85 10.00 25.00
LDJS Jeremy Shockey/102 3.00 8.00
LDKB Kyle Boller/103 3.00 8.00
LDLA LaVar Arrington/100 3.00 8.00
LDLT Lawrence Taylor/81 8.00 20.00
LDLT2 LaDainian Tomlinson/101 5.00 12.00
LDMV Michael Vick/101 4.00 10.00
LDPM Peyton Manning/98 12.00 30.00
LDRJ Rudi Johnson/101 3.00 8.00
LDRM Randy Moss/98 4.00 10.00
LDSM Santana Moss/101 4.00 10.00
LDSY Steve Young/84 10.00 25.00
LDTA Troy Aikman/89 10.00 25.00
LDTB Tom Brady/100 20.00 50.00
LDTC Tyrone Calico/103 4.00 10.00
LDWM Willis McGahee/100 3.00 8.00

2004 SkyBox LE Rare Form

STATED ODDS 1:256
UNPRICED EXECUTIVE PROOF #'d TO 1
1RF Randy Moss 1.25 3.00
2RF Donovan McNabb 1.25 3.00
3RF Chad Pennington 1.00 2.50
4RF Tom Brady 6.00 15.00
5RF Brett Favre 3.00 8.00
6RF Priest Holmes 1.00 2.50
7RF Ricky Williams 1.25 3.00
8RF Byron Leftwich 1.00 2.50
9RF Carson Palmer 1.25 3.00
10RF Michael Vick 1.25 3.00

2004 SkyBox LE Rare Form Jerseys Copper

COPPER PRINT RUN 50 SER.#'d SETS
*GOLD PATCH/25: .8X TO 2X COP/50
GOLD PATCH PRINT RUN 25
*SILVER/84: .4X TO 1X COP/50
*SILVER/31-34: .5X TO 1.2X COP/50
SILVER STATED PRINT RUN 4-84
RFBF Brett Favre 12.00 30.00
RFBL Byron Leftwich 4.00 10.00
RFCP Chad Pennington 4.00 10.00
RFCP2 Carson Palmer 5.00 12.00
RFDM Donovan McNabb 5.00 12.00
RFMV Michael Vick 5.00 12.00
RFPH Priest Holmes 4.00 10.00
RFRM Randy Moss 5.00 12.00
RFRW Ricky Williams 5.00 12.00
RFTB Tom Brady 25.00 60.00

2004 SkyBox LE Sky's the Limit

COMPLETE SET (20) 15.00 40.00
STATED ODDS 1:4
UNPRICED EXEC.PROOF #'d TO 1
1SL Eli Manning 3.00 8.00
2SL Peyton Manning 2.00 5.00
3SL Philip Rivers 1.25 3.00
4SL LaDainian Tomlinson .75 2.00
5SL Steven Jackson .60 1.50
6SL Marshall Faulk .60 1.50
7SL Ben Roethlisberger 3.00 8.00
8SL Hines Ward .60 1.50
9SL Reggie Williams .40 1.00
10SL Byron Leftwich .50 1.25
11SL Kevin Jones .50 1.25
12SL Joey Harrington .50 1.25
13SL Larry Fitzgerald 1.50 4.00
14SL Anquan Boldin .50 1.25
15SL Roy Williams WR .40 1.00
16SL Charles Rogers .50 1.25
17SL Julius Jones .40 1.00
18SL Emmitt Smith 1.25 3.00
19SL Tatum Bell .40 1.00
20SL Clinton Portis .50 1.25

2004 SkyBox LE Sky's the Limit Jerseys Silver

STATED PRINT RUN 99 SER.#'d SETS
*COPPER/50: .5X TO 1.2X SLVR/99
COPPER PRINT RUN 50 SER.#'d SETS
*GOLD PATCH/25: .8X TO 2X SLVR/99
GOLD PATCH SER.#'d OF 25 SETS
UNPRICED DUAL PLATINUM #'d TO 10
UNPRICED DUAL PURPLE #'d TO 1
SLAB Anquan Boldin 3.00 8.00
SLBL Byron Leftwich 3.00 8.00
SLBR Ben Roethlisberger 15.00 40.00
SLCP Clinton Portis 3.00 8.00
SLCR Charles Rogers 3.00 8.00
SLEM Eli Manning 20.00 40.00
SLES Emmitt Smith 8.00 20.00
SLHW Hines Ward 4.00 10.00
SLJH Joey Harrington 3.00 8.00
SLJJ Julius Jones 2.00 5.00
SLKJ Kevin Jones 3.00 8.00
SLLF Larry Fitzgerald 8.00 20.00
SLLT LaDainian Tomlinson 5.00 12.00
SLMF Marshall Faulk 4.00 10.00
SLPM Peyton Manning 12.00 30.00
SLPR Philip Rivers 10.00 25.00
SLRW Reggie Williams 3.00 8.00
SLRW2 Roy Williams WR 2.00 5.00
SLSJ Steven Jackson 3.00 8.00
SLTB Tatum Bell 3.00 8.00

1999 SkyBox Molten Metal

Released as a 151-card set, 1999 Skybox Molten Metal is comprised of 125 veteran cards and 26 short-printed rookies found one in every five packs. Rookie cards are printed on actual metal cards. Packaged in five card packs, Molten Metal carried a suggested retail of $5.99.

COMPLETE SET (151) 40.00 100.00
COMP.SET w/o SP's (125) 12.50 30.00
1 Terrell Davis .30 .75
2 Chris Chandler .30 .75
3 Terry Glenn .30 .75
4 Jon Kitna .25 .60
5 Bubby Brister .25 .60
6 Jermaine Lewis .25 .60
7 Doug Flutie .40 1.00
8 Napoleon Kaufman .25 .60
9 Yancey Thigpen .25 .60
10 Bobby Engram .25 .60
11 Barry Sanders .60 1.50
12 Ben Coates .30 .75
13 Joey Galloway .30 .75
14 Charlie Batch .25 .60
15 Jerome Bettis .40 1.00
16 Brad Johnson .30 .75
17 Brian Griese .25 .60
18 Jeff Lewis .25 .60
19 Jake Plummer .25 .60
20 Mark Brunell .30 .75
21 Robert Smith .25 .60
22 Steve Young .50 1.25
23 Derrick Mayes .25 .60
24 Wayne Chrebet .25 .60
25 Rich Gannon .30 .75
26 Steve McNair .30 .75
27 Charles Johnson .25 .60
28 Stephen Alexander .25 .60
29 Jeff Blake .30 .75
30 Tony Gonzalez .30 .75
31 Eddie Kennison .30 .75
32 Hines Ward .30 .75
33 Isaac Bruce .40 1.00
34 Peyton Manning 1.25 3.00
35 Doug Pederson .25 .60
36 Stephen Davis .25 .60
37 Terance Mathis .25 .60
38 Herman Moore .30 .75
39 Fred Taylor .25 .60
40 Courtney Hawkins .25 .60
41 Michael Westbrook .25 .60
42 Vinny Testaverde .25 .60
43 Jacquez Green .25 .60
44 Rocket Ismail .30 .75
45 Curtis Martin .30 .75
46 Tim Brown .40 1.00
47 Kevin Dyson .25 .60
48 Steve Beuerlein .30 .75
49 Adrian Murrell .25 .60
50 Randall Cunningham .30 .75
51 Jerry Rice 1.00 2.50
52 Tim Biakabutuka .30 .75
53 Muhsin Muhammad .25 .60
54 Antonio Freeman .30 .75
55 Cris Carter .40 1.00
56 Lawrence Phillips .30 .75
57 Michael Irvin .40 1.00
58 Terrell Owens .30 .75
59 Warrick Dunn .25 .60
60 Leslie Shepherd .25 .60
61 O.J. McDuffie .30 .75
62 Byron Hanspard .25 .60
63 Trent Dilfer .25 .60
64 Eric Moulds .25 .60
65 Scott Mitchell .25 .60
66 Marc Edwards .30 .75
67 Dorsey Levens .30 .75
68 Dan Marino .75 2.00
69 Jason Sehorn .30 .75
70 Junior Seau .30 .75
71 Reidel Anthony .25 .60
72 Rob Moore .25 .60
73 Deion Sanders .30 .75
74 Rickey Dudley .25 .60
75 Keyshawn Johnson .30 .75
76 Eddie George .30 .75
77 E.G. Green .25 .60
78 Terry Kirby .25 .60
79 John Avery .25 .60
80 Pete Mitchell .25 .60
81 Natrone Means .30 .75
82 Mike Alstott .25 .60
83 Carl Pickens .30 .75
84 Karim Abdul-Jabbar .25 .60
85 Kerry Collins .25 .60
86 Erik Kramer .30 .75
87 Robert Holcombe .25 .60
88 Willie Jackson .25 .60
89 Marcus Pollard .25 .60
90 Bam Morris .25 .60
91 Gary Brown .25 .60
92 Freddie Jones .25 .60
93 Kurt Warner RC 4.00 10.00
94 Priest Holmes .25 .60
95 Duce Staley .25 .60
96 Skip Hicks .25 .60
97 Frank Sanders .25 .60
98 Corey Dillon .25 .60
99 Shannon Sharpe .30 .75
100 Randy Moss .30 .75
101 Sean Dawkins .25 .60
102 Marshall Faulk .30 .75
103 Mark Chmura .25 .60
104 Keenan McCardell .30 .75
105 Jimmy Smith .30 .75
106 Jim Harbaugh .30 .75
107 Jamal Anderson .30 .75
108 Elvis Grbac .25 .60
109 Ed McCaffrey .30 .75
110 Drew Bledsoe .30 .75
111 Curtis Conway .30 .75
112 Billy Joe Tolliver .25 .60
113 J.J. Stokes .25 .60
114 Curtis Enis .25 .60
115 Antowain Smith .25 .60
116 Troy Aikman .50 1.25
117 Ricky Watters .30 .75
118 Kordell Stewart .25 .60
119 Derrick Alexander .25 .60
120 Emmitt Smith .60 1.50
121 Billy Joe Hobert .25 .60
122 Johnnie Morton .30 .75
123 Rod Smith .30 .75
124 Marvin Harrison .30 .75
125 Brett Favre .75 2.00
126 Craig Yeast RC .60 1.50
127 Ricky Williams RC 1.00 2.50
128 Brandon Stokley RC .75 2.00
129 Akili Smith RC .60 1.50
130 Peerless Price RC .60 1.50
131 Joe Montgomery RC .60 1.50
132 Cade McNown RC .60 1.50
133 Donovan McNabb RC 2.00 5.00
134 Shaun King RC .60 1.50
135 James Johnson RC .60 1.50
136 Kevin Johnson RC .75 2.00
137 Edgerrin James RC 1.00 2.50
138 Terry Jackson RC .60 1.50
139 Sedrick Irvin RC .60 1.50
140 Brock Huard RC .60 1.50
141 Torry Holt RC 1.25 3.00
142 Amos Zereoue RC .60 1.50
143 Kevin Faulk RC .60 1.50
144 Troy Edwards RC .60 1.50
145 Donald Driver RC 12.00 30.00
146 Daunte Culpepper RC 1.00 2.50
147 Tim Couch RC .75 2.00
148 Cecil Collins RC .60 1.50
149 David Boston RC .60 1.50
150 Champ Bailey RC 1.25 3.00
151 Olandis Gary RC 1.00 2.50
P133 Donovan McNabb Promo 1.25 3.00

1999 SkyBox Molten Metal Gridiron Gods

Randomly inserted in packs at the rate of one in six, this 20-card set features the NFL's finest an all-foil card. Three parallel versions of this set were released. The parallels are printed on metal.

COMPLETE SET (20) 25.00 50.00
STATED ODDS 1:6
*BLUE CARDS: 2.5X TO 6X BRONZE
BLUE STATED PRINT RUN 99 SER.#'d SETS
*GOLD CARDS: 1.5X TO 4X BRONZE
GOLD STATED ODDS 1:72
*SILVER CARDS: .8X TO 2X BRONZE
SILVER STATED ODDS 1:24
GG1 Randy Moss 2.50 6.00
GG2 Keyshawn Johnson 1.00 2.50
GG3 Mike Alstott 1.00 2.50
GG4 Brian Griese 1.00 2.50
GG5 Tim Couch .75 2.00
GG6 Troy Aikman 2.00 5.00
GG7 Warrick Dunn 1.00 2.50
GG8 Mark Brunell 1.00 2.50
GG9 Jerry Rice 2.00 5.00
GG10 Dorsey Levens 1.00 2.50
GG11 Fred Taylor 1.00 2.50
GG12 Emmitt Smith 2.00 5.00
GG13 Edgerrin James 2.50 6.00
GG14 Eddie George 1.00 2.50
GG15 Drew Bledsoe 1.25 3.00
GG16 Deion Sanders 1.00 2.50
GG17 Charlie Batch 1.00 2.50
GG18 Kordell Stewart .60 1.50
GG19 Brad Johnson 1.00 2.50
GG20 Akili Smith .60 1.50

1999 SkyBox Molten Metal Patchworks

Randomly inserted in packs at the rate of one in 360, this set features players paired with a swatch of a game-worn jersey. Some cards were available from the Millenium factory sets only and are listed with an "FS" notation. A few extra cards appeared on the market sometime after Fleer closed out old inventory.

STATED ODDS 1:360 HOBBY
1 Drew Bledsoe 10.00 25.00
2 Mark Brunell 8.00 20.00
3 Randall Cunningham FS 10.00 25.00
4 Terrell Davis 10.00 25.00
5 Marshall Faulk FS 10.00 25.00
6 Brett Favre 30.00 80.00
7 Antonio Freeman FS 10.00 25.00
8 Dorsey Levens FS 8.00 20.00
9 Peyton Manning 30.00 80.00
10 Dan Marino 30.00 80.00
11 Curtis Martin 10.00 25.00
12 Keenan McCardell FS 6.00 15.00
13 Herman Moore 6.00 15.00
14 Johnnie Morton 6.00 15.00
15 Randy Moss 10.00 25.00
16 Jake Plummer FS 8.00 20.00
17 Jerry Rice 25.00 60.00
18 Fred Taylor FS 8.00 20.00
19 Steve Young 15.00 40.00

1999 SkyBox Molten Metal Perfect Fit

Randomly inserted in packs at the rate of one in 24, this 10-card set features top players on a foil semi-circular die-cut card. Three parallel versions, printed on metal, were released for this set also.

COMPLETE SET (10) 30.00 60.00
STATED ODDS 1:24
*GOLD CARDS: 1.2X TO 3X BRONZE
GOLD STATED ODDS 1:216
*RED CARDS: 6X TO 12X BRONZE
RED STATED PRINT RUN 25 SER.#'d SETS
*SILVER CARDS: .6X TO 1.5X BRONZE
SILVER STATED ODDS 1:72
PF1 Barry Sanders 5.00 12.00
PF2 Brett Favre 5.00 12.00
PF3 Dan Marino 5.00 12.00
PF4 Edgerrin James 3.00 8.00
PF5 Emmitt Smith 3.00 8.00
PF6 Fred Taylor 1.50 4.00
PF7 Randy Moss 4.00 10.00
PF8 Terrell Davis 1.50 4.00
PF9 Tim Couch 1.50 4.00
PF10 Peyton Manning 5.00 12.00

1999 SkyBox Molten Metal Top Notch

Randomly inserted in packs at the rate of one one in 12, this 15-card set feature top notch players printed on an all-foil card. Three parallel versions, printed on metal, were released for this set also.

COMPLETE SET (15) 25.00 50.00
STATED ODDS 1:12
*GOLD CARDS: 1.2X TO 3X BRONZE
GOLD STATED ODDS 1:108
*GREEN CARDS: 3X TO 8X BRONZE
GREEN STATED PRINT RUN 75 SER.#'d SETS
*SILVER CARDS: .6X TO 1.5X BRONZE
SILVER STATED ODDS 1:36
TN1 Jake Plummer .75 2.00
TN2 Cade McNown 1.00 2.50
TN3 Tim Couch 1.25 3.00
TN4 Emmitt Smith 2.50 6.00
TN5 Charlie Batch 1.25 3.00
TN6 Donovan McNabb 5.00 12.00
TN7 Steve Young 1.50 4.00
TN8 Brian Griese 1.25 3.00
TN9 Doug Flutie 1.25 3.00
TN10 Edgerrin James 4.00 10.00
TN11 Fred Taylor 1.25 3.00
TN12 Keyshawn Johnson 1.25 3.00
TN13 Mark Brunell 1.25 3.00
TN14 Randy Moss 3.00 8.00
TN15 Ricky Williams 2.00 5.00

1999 SkyBox Molten Metal Millennium Gold

COMP.FACT.SET (127) 25.00 60.00
*GOLD STARS: .6X TO 1.5X BASIC CARDS
STATED PRINT RUN 2000 SETS

1999 SkyBox Molten Metal Millennium Silver

COMPLETE SET (125) 12.50 30.00
*MILL.SILVERS: .4X TO 1X BASIC CARDS
STATED PRINT RUN 3400 SETS

1999 SkyBox Molten Metal Player's Party

COMPLETE SET (125) 30.00 50.00
*SINGLES: .5X TO 1.2X BASIC CARDS

1993 SkyBox Premium

Having dropped "Primetime" from the set name, the 1993 Skybox Premium set consists of 270 standard-size cards. Cards were issued in 10-card packs. The fronts display borderless color action player photos with backgrounds that are split horizontally or vertically into team colors. The player's name and team logo appear near the top. The backs carry a second color action photo, career synopsis, biography, four-year stats and career totals. Rookie Cards include Jerome Bettis, Drew Bledsoe, Curtis Conway, Garrison Hearst, O.J. McDuffie, Natrone Means, Rick Mirer and Robert Smith. Two 6-card promo panel sheets were produced and are listed below. The sheets were given away at the 1993 National Sports Collectors Convention in Chicago.

COMPLETE SET (270) 10.00 25.00
1 Eric Martin .02 .10
2 Earnest Byner .02 .10
3 Ricky Proehl .02 .10
4 Mark Carrier WR .07 .20
5 Shannon Sharpe .15 .40
6 Anthony Thompson .02 .10
7 Drew Bledsoe RC 2.00 5.00
8 Tom Carter RC .07 .20
9 Ryan McNeil RC .15 .40
10 Troy Aikman .60 1.50
11 Robert Jones .02 .10
12 Rodney Peete .02 .10
13 Wendell Davis .02 .10
14 Thurman Thomas .15 .40
15 John Stephens .02 .10
16 Rodney Hampton .07 .20
17 Eric Bieniemy .02 .10
18 Santana Dotson .07 .20
19 Jeff George .15 .40
20 John L. Williams .02 .10
21 Barry Word .02 .10
22 Chris Miller .07 .20
23 Jeff Hostetler .07 .20
24 Dwight Stone .02 .10
25 Brad Baxter .02 .10
26 Randall Cunningham .15 .40
27 Mark Higgs .02 .10
28 Vaughn Dunbar .02 .10
29 Ricky Ervins .02 .10
30 Johnny Bailey .02 .10
31 Michael Jackson .07 .20
32 Mike Croel .02 .10
33 Steve Young .60 1.50
34 Deon Figures RC .02 .10
35 Robert Smith RC 1.00 2.50
36 Irv Smith RC .02 .10
37 Charles Haley .07 .20
38 Cris Dishman .02 .10
39 Barry Sanders 1.00 2.50
40 Jim Harbaugh .15 .40
41 Darryl Talley .02 .10
42 Jackie Harris .02 .10
43 Phil Simms .07 .20
44 Marion Butts .02 .10
45 Anthony Munoz .07 .20
46 Steve Emtman .02 .10
47 Kelvin Martin .02 .10
48 Joe Montana 1.25 3.00
49 Andre Rison .07 .20
50 Ethan Horton .02 .10
51 Kevin Greene .07 .20
52 Browning Nagle .02 .10
53 Tim Harris .02 .10
54 Keith Byars .02 .10
55 Terry Allen .15 .40
56 Chip Lohmiller .02 .10
57 Robert Massey .02 .10
58 Michael Dean Perry .07 .20
59 Tommy Maddox .15 .40
60 Jerry Rice .75 2.00
61 Lincoln Kennedy RC .02 .10
62 Jerome Bettis RC 3.00 8.00
63 Coleman Rudolph RC .02 .10
64 Emmitt Smith 1.50 3.00
65 Curtis Duncan .02 .10
66 Andre Ware .02 .10
67 Neal Anderson .02 .10
68 Jim Kelly .15 .40
69 Reggie White .15 .40
70 Dave Meggett .02 .10
71 Junior Seau .15 .40
72 Courtney Hawkins .02 .10
73 Clarence Verdin .02 .10
74 Tommy Kane .02 .10
75 Dale Carter .02 .10
76 Michael Haynes .07 .20
77 Willie Gault .02 .10
78 Eric Green .02 .10
79 Ronnie Lott .07 .20
80 Vai Sikahema .02 .10
81 Mark Ingram .02 .10
82 Anthony Carter .07 .20
83 Mark Rypien .02 .10
84 Gary Clark .07 .20
85 Bernie Kosar .07 .20
86 Cleveland Gary .02 .10
87 Tom Rathman .02 .10
88 Tony McGee RC .07 .20
89 Rick Mirer RC .15 .40
90 John Copeland RC .07 .20
91 Michael Irvin .15 .40
92 Wilber Marshall .02 .10
93 Mel Gray .07 .20
94 Craig Heyward .07 .20
95 Don Beebe .02 .10
96 Andre Tippett .02 .10
97 Derek Brown TE .02 .10
98 Ronnie Harmon .02 .10
99 Derrick Fenner .02 .10
100 Rodney Culver .02 .10
101 Cortez Kennedy .07 .20
102 Marcus Allen .15 .40
103 Steve Broussard .02 .10
104 Tim Brown .15 .40
105 Merril Hoge .02 .10
106 Chris Burkett .02 .10
107 Fred Barnett .07 .20
108 Dan Marino 1.25 3.00
109 Chris Doleman .02 .10
110 Art Monk .07 .20
111 Ernie Jones .02 .10
112 Jay Hilgenberg .02 .10
113 Jim Everett .07 .20
114 John Taylor .07 .20
115 Steve Everitt RC .02 .10
116 Carlton Gray RC .02 .10
117 Eric Curry RC .02 .10
118 Ken Norton Jr. .07 .20
119 Lorenzo White .02 .10
120 Pat Swilling .02 .10
121 William Perry .07 .20
122 Brett Favre 2.00 4.00
123 Jon Vaughn .02 .10
124 Mark Jackson .02 .10
125 Stan Humphries .07 .20
126 Harold Green .02 .10
127 Anthony Johnson .07 .20
128 Brian Blades .07 .20
129 Willie Davis .15 .40
130 Bobby Hebert .02 .10
131 Terry McDaniel .02 .10
132 Jeff Graham .07 .20
133 Jeff Lageman .02 .10
134 Andre Waters .02 .10
135 Steve Walsh .02 .10
136 Cris Carter .15 .40
137 Tim McGee .02 .10
138 Chuck Cecil .02 .10
139 John Elway 1.25 3.00
140 Todd Lyght .02 .10
141 Brent Jones .07 .20
142 Patrick Bates RC .02 .10
143 Darrien Gordon RC .02 .10
144 Michael Strahan RC 1.25 3.00
145 Jay Novacek .07 .20
146 Warren Moon .15 .40
147 Rodney Holman .02 .10
148 Anthony Morgan .02 .10
149 Sterling Sharpe .15 .40
150 Leonard Russell .07 .20
151 Lawrence Taylor .15 .40
152 Leslie O'Neal .07 .20
153 Carl Pickens .07 .20
154 Aaron Cox .02 .10
155 Ferrell Edmunds .02 .10
156 Neil O'Donnell .15 .40
157 Tony Smith RB .02 .10
158 James Lofton .07 .20
159 George Teague RC .07 .20
160 Boomer Esiason .07 .20
161 Eric Allen .02 .10
162 Floyd Turner .02 .10
163 Esera Tuaolo .02 .10
164 Darrell Green .02 .10
165 Steve Beuerlein .07 .20
166 Vance Johnson .02 .10
167 Flipper Anderson .02 .10
168 Ricky Watters .15 .40
169 Marvin Jones RC .02 .10
170 Dana Stubblefield RC .15 .40
171 Willie Roaf RC .25 .60
172 Russell Maryland .02 .10
173 Ernest Givins .07 .20
174 Willie Green .02 .10
175 Bruce Smith .15 .40
176 Terrell Buckley .02 .10
177 Scott Zolak .02 .10
178 Mike Sherrard .02 .10
179 Lawrence Dawsey .02 .10
180 Jay Schroeder .02 .10
181 Quentin Coryatt .07 .20
182 Harvey Williams .07 .20
183 Natrone Means RC .15 .40
184 Eric Dickerson .07 .20
185 Gaston Green .02 .10
186 Thomas Smith RC .07 .20
187 Johnny Johnson .02 .10
188 Marco Coleman .02 .10
189 Wade Wilson .02 .10
190 Rich Gannon .15 .40
191 Brian Mitchell .07 .20
192 Eric Metcalf .07 .20
193 Robert Delpino .02 .10
194 Shane Conlan .02 .10
195 Dexter Carter .02 .10
196 Garrison Hearst RC .60 1.50
197 Chris Slade RC .07 .20
198 Troy Drayton RC .07 .20
199 Lin Elliott .02 .10
200 Haywood Jeffires .07 .20
201 Herman Moore .15 .40
202 Cornelius Bennett .07 .20
203 Mark Clayton .02 .10
204 Marv Cook .02 .10
205 Stephen Baker .02 .10
206 Gary Anderson RB .02 .10
207 Eddie Brown .02 .10
208 Will Wolford .02 .10
209 Derrick Thomas .15 .40
210 Seth Joyner .02 .10
211 Mike Pritchard .07 .20
212 Rod Woodson .15 .40
213 Todd Kelly RC .02 .10
214 Rob Moore .07 .20
215 Keith Jackson .07 .20
216 Wesley Carroll .02 .10
217 Steve Jordan .02 .10
218 Ricky Sanders .02 .10
219 Tommy Vardell .02 .10
220 Rod Bernstine .02 .10
221 Henry Ellard .07 .20
222 Amp Lee .02 .10
223 O.J.McDuffie RC .15 .40
224 Carl Simpson RC .02 .10
225 Dan Williams RC .02 .10
226 Thomas Everett .02 .10
227 Webster Slaughter .02 .10
228 Trace Armstrong .02 .10
229 Kenneth Davis .02 .10
230 Tony Bennett .02 .10
231 Reyna Thompson .02 .10
232 Anthony Miller .07 .20
233 Reggie Cobb .02 .10
234 Mark Duper .02 .10
235 Chris Warren .07 .20
236 Christian Okoye .02 .10
237 Irving Fryar .07 .20
238 Deion Sanders .30 .75
239 Barry Foster .07 .20
240 Ernest Dye RC .02 .10
241 Calvin Williams .07 .20
242 Louis Oliver .02 .10
243 Dalton Hilliard .02 .10
244 Roger Craig .07 .20
245 Randal Hill .02 .10
246 Vinny Testaverde .07 .20
247 Steve Atwater .02 .10
248 Jim Price .02 .10
249 Martin Harrison RC .02 .10
250 Curtis Conway RC .30 .75
251 Demetrius DuBose RC .02 .10
252 Leonard Renfro RC .02 .10
253 Alvin Harper .07 .20
254 Leonard Harris .02 .10
255 Tom Waddle .02 .10
256 Andre Reed .07 .20
257 Sanjay Beach .02 .10
258 Michael Timpson .02 .10
259 Nate Lewis .02 .10
260 Steve DeBerg .02 .10
261 David Klingler .02 .10
262 Dan McGwire .02 .10
263 Dave Krieg .07 .20
264 Brad Muster .02 .10
265 Nick Bell .02 .10
266 Checklist 1 .02 .10
267 Checklist 2 .02 .10
268 Checklist 3 .02 .10
269 Checklist 4 .02 .10
270 Checklist 5 .02 .10
P1 Promo Panel .75 2.00
P2 Promo Panel .75 2.00

1993 SkyBox Premium Poster Cards

This ten-card standard-size set was randomly inserted in SkyBox packs. The fronts feature black-bordered reproductions of the Costacos Brothers Sports Posters. The back carries a color player action shot in its upper half, with the player's name appearing within a gold-colored stripe under the photo. The player's career highlights and team logo appear in the white bottom half. The cards are numbered on the back with a "CB" prefix.

COMPLETE SET (10) 2.00 5.00
CB1 Dallas Cowboys Defense .15 .40
CB2 Aikman .50 1.25
Irvin
Smith
Mary
CB3 Barry Foster .08 .25
CB4 Art Monk .08 .25
CB5 Jerry Rice .40 1.00
CB6 Barry Sanders .75 2.00
CB7 Deion Sanders .20 .50
CB8 Junior Seau .20 .50
CB9 Derrick Thomas .20 .50
CB10 Steve Young .25 .60

1993 SkyBox Premium Prime Time Rookies

The chances of finding one of these ten standard-size inserts in 1993 SkyBox Premium 12-card foil packs was one-in-18. Chris Mortensen of The Sporting News and ESPN selected these ten rookies who, in his estimation, would be "prime time" players during 1993 and beyond. Each front features a color action shot of the rookie in his college uniform against a two-tone (black and gold) metallic background. The player's name appears at the top of the broad black stripe at the left edge, and Mortensen's facsimile signature and set title appear at the bottom of that stripe. The back carries a color player photo in its upper half, with the player's name appearing within a gold-colored stripe beneath. The player's position and Mortensen's scouting report, along with a head shot of Mortensen, appear in the white bottom half. The cards are numbered on the back with a "PR" prefix.

COMPLETE SET (10) 15.00 30.00
1 Patrick Bates .75 2.00
2 Drew Bledsoe 6.00 15.00
3 Darrien Gordon .75 2.00
4 Garrison Hearst 2.50 6.00
5 Marvin Jones .75 2.00
6 Terry Kirby .75 2.00
7 Natrone Means 1.50 4.00
8 Rick Mirer 1.25 3.00
9 Willie Roaf 3.00 8.00
10 Dan Williams .75 2.00

1993 SkyBox Premium Thunder and Lightning

The chances of finding one of these nine standard-size inserts in 1993 SkyBox Premium 12-card foil packs were one-in-nine. Each borderless and horizontal card features two players from the same team with a color action shot of each player appearing on either side. The player photo on the "Thunder" side has multiple ghosted images and appears upon a black- and gold-metallic background. The player photo on the "Lightning" side appears upon a black- and silver-metallic background, which is highlighted by filaments of lightning. Each side carries its player's name in white lettering near the bottom. The cards are numbered on the "Lightning" side with a "TL" prefix.

COMPLETE SET (9) 7.50 20.00
1 J.Kelly 1.50 4.00
T.Thomas
2 Cunningham 1.50 4.00
Barnett
3 D.Marino 3.00 8.00
K.Jackson
4 S.Mills .60 1.50
V.Johnson
5 W.Moon 1.00 2.50
H.Jeffires
6 T.Aikman 2.00 5.00
M.Irvin
7 B.Favre 3.00 8.00
St.Sharpe
8 J.Rice 2.50 6.00
S.Young
9 D.Smith .60 1.50
S.Atwater

1994 SkyBox Premium Promos

Issued to preview the design of SkyBox's '94 Premium set, these seven standard-size promo cards feature on their borderless fronts color player action shots set on ghosted and colorized backgrounds. The player's name, position, and ghosted team logo appear in a white rectangle in an upper corner. The back carries a color player close-up on the right, with the player's team logo, name, position, career highlights, and statistics displayed alongside on the left.The S4 Jim Kelly card was also given away in Tuff Stuff.

COMPLETE SET (7) 3.20 8.00
S1 Tom Carter .40 1.00
S2 Gary Clark .40 1.00
S3 James Jett .50 1.25
S4 Jim Kelly 1.00 2.50
S5 Ronnie Lott .50 1.25
S6 John Taylor .40 1.00
NNO Sample Commemorative .20 .50

1994 SkyBox Premium

These 200 standard-size cards feature borderless color player action photos. The featured players stand out against a faded background. The player's name appears in either upper corner with the SkyBox logo in either lower corner. The cards were issued in 10-card foil packs with a suggested retail price of $1.99. The cards are grouped alphabetically within teams, and checklisted below alphabetically according to teams. The set closes with Rookies (157-200). Rookie Cards include Mario Bates, Trent Dilfer, Marshall Faulk, William Floyd, Byron Bam Morris, Errict Rhett, Darnay Scott and Heath Shuler.

COMPLETE SET (200) 7.50 20.00
1 Steve Beuerlein .05 .15
2 Gary Clark .05 .15
3 Garrison Hearst .10 .30
4 Ronald Moore .01 .05
5 Eric Swann .05 .15
6 Chuck Cecil .01 .05
7 Seth Joyner .01 .05
8 Clyde Simmons .01 .05
9 Andre Rison .05 .15
10 Deion Sanders .15 .40
11 Erric Pegram .01 .05
12 Steve Broussard .01 .05
13 Chris Doleman .01 .05
14 Jeff George .10 .30
15 Cornelius Bennett .05 .15
16 Jim Kelly .10 .30
17 Andre Reed .05 .15
18 Bruce Smith .10 .30
19 Darryl Talley .01 .05
20 Thurman Thomas .10 .30
21 Mark Carrier DB .01 .05
22 Dante Jones .01 .05
23 Curtis Conway .10 .30
24 Tim Worley .01 .05
25 Erik Kramer .05 .15
26 John Copeland .01 .05
27 David Klingler .01 .05
28 Derrick Fenner .01 .05
29 Harold Green .01 .05
30 Carl Pickens .05 .15
31 Tony McGee .01 .05
32 Steve Everitt .01 .05
33 Michael Jackson .05 .15
34 Eric Metcalf .05 .15
35 Vinny Testaverde .05 .15
36 Michael Dean Perry .05 .15
37 Troy Aikman .50 1.25
38 Alvin Harper .05 .15
39 Michael Irvin .10 .30
40 Jay Novacek .05 .15
41 Emmitt Smith .75 2.00
42 Charles Haley .05 .15
43 Daryl Johnston .05 .15
44 Kevin Williams WR .05 .15
45 Rodney Peete .01 .05
46 John Elway 1.00 2.50
47 Shannon Sharpe .05 .15
48 Rod Bernstine .01 .05
49 Glyn Milburn .05 .15
50 Mike Pritchard .01 .05
51 Anthony Miller .05 .15
52 Herman Moore .10 .30
53 Barry Sanders .75 2.00
54 Scott Mitchell .05 .15
55 Pat Swilling .01 .05
56 Willie Green .01 .05
57 Edgar Bennett .10 .30
58 Brett Favre 1.00 2.50
59 Sterling Sharpe .05 .15
60 Reggie White .10 .30
61 Sean Jones .01 .05
62 Reggie Cobb .01 .05
63 Haywood Jeffires .05 .15
64 Lorenzo White .01 .05
65 Webster Slaughter .01 .05
66 Gary Brown .01 .05
67 Steve Emtman .01 .05
68 Quentin Coryatt .01 .05
69 Sean Dawkins RC .10 .30
70 Jim Harbaugh .10 .30
71 Tony Bennett .01 .05
72 Marcus Allen .10 .30
73 Steve Bono .05 .15
74 Dale Carter .01 .05
75 Joe Montana 1.00 2.50
76 Neil Smith .05 .15
77 Derrick Thomas .10 .30
78 Keith Cash .01 .05
79 Tim Brown .10 .30
80 Rocket Ismail .05 .15
81 Jeff Hostetler .05 .15
82 Patrick Bates .01 .05
83 James Jett .01 .05
84 Jerome Bettis .25 .60
85 Chris Miller .01 .05
86 Marc Boutte .01 .05
87 Sean Gilbert .01 .05
88 Keith Jackson .01 .05
89 Terry Kirby .10 .30
90 Dan Marino 1.00 2.50
91 Bryan Cox .01 .05
92 Bernie Kosar .05 .15
93 Qadry Ismail .10 .30
94 Robert Smith .10 .30
95 Terry Allen .05 .15
96 Scottie Graham RC .05 .15
97 Warren Moon .10 .30
98 Drew Bledsoe .40 1.00
99 Ben Coates .05 .15
100 Leonard Russell .01 .05
101 Vincent Brisby .05 .15
102 Marion Butts .01 .05
103 Morten Andersen .01 .05
104 Derek Brown RBK .01 .05
105 Michael Haynes .05 .15
106 Sam Mills .01 .05
107 Lorenzo Neal .01 .05
108 Willie Roaf .01 .05
109 Jim Everett .05 .15
110 Michael Brooks .01 .05
111 Rodney Hampton .05 .15
112 Dave Brown .05 .15
113 Dave Meggett .01 .05
114 Ronnie Lott .05 .15
115 Boomer Esiason .05 .15
116 Rob Moore .05 .15
117 Johnny Johnson .01 .05
118 Marvin Jones .01 .05
119 Johnny Mitchell .01 .05
120 Fred Barnett .05 .15
121 Randall Cunningham .10 .30
122 Herschel Walker .05 .15
123 Calvin Williams .05 .15
124 Neil O'Donnell .10 .30
125 Eric Green .01 .05
126 Leroy Thompson .01 .05
127 Rod Woodson .05 .15
128 Barry Foster .01 .05
129 Deon Figures .01 .05
130 John L. Williams .01 .05
131 Chris Mims .01 .05
132 Darrien Gordon .01 .05
133 Stan Humphries .05 .15
134 Natrone Means .10 .30
135 Junior Seau .10 .30
136 Brent Jones .05 .15
137 Jerry Rice .50 1.25
138 Dana Stubblefield .05 .15
139 John Taylor .05 .15
140 Ricky Watters .05 .15
141 Steve Young .40 1.00
142 Ken Norton Jr. .05 .15
143 Brian Blades .05 .15
144 Cortez Kennedy .05 .15
145 Kelvin Martin .01 .05
146 Rick Mirer .10 .30
147 Chris Warren .05 .15
148 Eric Curry .01 .05
149 Santana Dotson .05 .15
150 Craig Erickson .01 .05
151 Hardy Nickerson .05 .15
152 Paul Gruber .01 .05
153 Reggie Brooks .05 .15
154 Tom Carter .01 .05
155 Desmond Howard .05 .15
156 Ken Harvey .01 .05
157 Dan Wilkinson RC .05 .15
158 Marshall Faulk RC 2.00 5.00
159 Heath Shuler RC .10 .30
160 Willie McGinest RC .10 .30
161 Trev Alberts RC .05 .15
162 Trent Dilfer RC .50 1.25
163 Bryant Young RC .20 .50
164 Sam Adams RC .05 .15
165 Antonio Langham RC .05 .15
166 Jamir Miller RC .05 .15
167 John Thierry RC .01 .05
168 Aaron Glenn RC .10 .30
169 Joe Johnson RC .01 .05
170 Bernard Williams RC .01 .05
171 Wayne Gandy RC .01 .05
172 Aaron Taylor RC .01 .05
173 Charles Johnson RC .10 .30
174 Dewayne Washington RC .05 .15
175 Todd Steussie RC .05 .15
176 Tim Bowens RC .05 .15
177 Johnnie Morton RC .50 1.25
178 Rob Fredrickson .05 .15
179 Shante Carver RC .01 .05
180 Thomas Lewis RC .05 .15
181 Greg Hill RC .10 .30
182 Henry Ford RC .01 .05
183 Jeff Burris RC .05 .15
184 William Floyd RC .10 .30
185 Derrick Alexander WR RC .10 .30
186 Glenn Foley RC .10 .30
187 Charlie Garner RC .50 1.25
188 Errict Rhett RC .10 .30
189 Chuck Levy RC .01 .05
190 Byron Bam Morris RC .05 .15
191 Donnell Bennett RC .10 .30
192 LeShon Johnson RC .05 .15
193 Mario Bates RC .10 .30
194 David Palmer RC .10 .30
195 Darnay Scott RC .25 .60
196 Lake Dawson RC .05 .15
197 Checklist .01 .05
198 Checklist .01 .05
199 Checklist .01 .05
200 Checklist for Inserts .01 .05
NNO NFL Anniv.Commemor. .10 .30

1994 SkyBox Premium Inside the Numbers

This 20-card standard-size set was issued one per special retail pack. The borderless fronts feature the player's name and team logo in the upper left corner. The SkyBox logo in the lower right corner is done in gold foil. A player photo and a brief write-up are on the back.

COMPLETE SET (20) 4.00 10.00
ONE PER SPECIAL RETAIL PACK
1 Jim Kelly .25 .60
2 Ronnie Lott .10 .30
3 Morten Andersen .02 .10
4 Reggie White .25 .60
5 Terry Kirby .25 .60
6 Marcus Allen .25 .60
7 Thurman Thomas .25 .60
8 Joe Montana 2.00 5.00
9 Tom Carter .02 .10
10 Jerome Bettis .50 1.25
11 Sterling Sharpe .10 .30
12 Andre Rison .10 .30
13 Reggie Brooks .10 .30
14 Hardy Nickerson .10 .30
15 Ricky Watters .10 .30
16 Gary Brown .02 .10
17 Natrone Means .25 .60
18 LeShon Johnson .07 .20
19 Errict Rhett .15 .40
20 Trent Dilfer .60 1.50

1994 SkyBox Premium Quarterback Autographs

This three card set was released via a mail redemption offer inserted into 1994 SkyBox packs. The set came mounted in a stand-up plastic card display and is usually found in this form.

1 Trent Dilfer 25.00 50.00
2 Jim Kelly 40.00 80.00
3 Ken Stabler 20.00 50.00

1994 SkyBox Premium Revolution

This 15-card standard-size set was randomly inserted at a rate of one in 20. An up-close color photo on front is surrounded by a silver border. The back is a solid color (depending on team) with career highlights. The cards are numbered with an "R" prefix.

COMPLETE SET (15) 12.50 30.00
STATED ODDS 1:20
R1 Jim Kelly .40 1.00
R2 Thurman Thomas .40 1.00
R3 Troy Aikman 1.50 4.00
R4 Michael Irvin .40 1.00
R5 Emmitt Smith 2.50 6.00
R6 John Elway 3.00 8.00
R7 Barry Sanders 2.50 6.00
R8 Sterling Sharpe .30 .75
R9 Joe Montana 3.00 8.00
R10 Jerome Bettis .75 2.00
R11 Dan Marino 3.00 8.00
R12 Drew Bledsoe 1.25 3.00
R13 Jerry Rice 1.50 4.00
R14 Steve Young 1.25 3.00
R15 Rick Mirer .30 .75

1994 SkyBox Premium Prime Time Rookies

Randomly inserted at a rate of one in 96, this 10-card standard-size set reflects ESPN's Chris Mortensen's rookie picks. Metallic, full-bleed fronts have the player superimposed over a background of team logos. The photos are from either college or training camp. Horizontal backs have a photo and comments from Mortensen. The cards are numbered with a "PT" suffix.

COMPLETE SET (10) 20.00 40.00
STATED ODDS 1:96
PT1 Trent Dilfer 2.50 6.00
PT2 Heath Shuler .60 1.50
PT3 Marshall Faulk 8.00 20.00
PT4 Charlie Garner 1.50 4.00
PT5 Errict Rhett .60 1.50
PT6 Greg Hill .60 1.50
PT7 William Floyd .60 1.50
PT8 Charles Johnson .60 1.50
PT9 Derrick Alexander WR .60 1.50
PT10 David Palmer .60 1.50

1994 SkyBox Premium SkyTech Stars

Randomly inserted in packs at a rate of one in six, these full-bleed, metallic cards feature 30 top players. The fronts have a player photo over a blurred background. The backs have a player photo to the right with highlights and statistics to the left. The cards are numbered with an "ST" prefix.

COMPLETE SET (30) 12.50 30.00
STATED ODDS 1:6
ST1 Troy Aikman 1.25 3.00
ST2 Emmitt Smith 2.00 5.00
ST3 Michael Irvin .30 .75
ST4 John Elway 2.50 6.00
ST5 Sterling Sharpe .15 .40
ST6 Joe Montana 2.50 6.00
ST7 Drew Bledsoe 1.00 2.50
ST8 Rick Mirer .30 .75
ST9 Junior Seau .30 .75
ST10 Jerome Bettis .60 1.50
ST11 Rod Woodson .15 .40
ST12 Tim Brown .30 .75
ST13 Jeff George .30 .75
ST14 Brett Favre 2.50 6.00
ST15 Reggie White .30 .75
ST16 Cortez Kennedy .15 .40
ST17 Ricky Watters .15 .40
ST18 Shannon Sharpe .15 .40
ST19 Reggie Brooks .15 .40
ST20 Heath Shuler .15 .40
ST21 Marshall Faulk 2.50 6.00
ST22 Thurman Thomas .30 .75
ST23 Barry Foster .05 .15
ST24 Sean Gilbert .05 .15
ST25 Jerry Rice 1.25 3.00
ST26 Andre Rison .15 .40
ST27 Barry Sanders 2.00 5.00
ST28 Jim Kelly .30 .75
ST29 Steve Young 1.00 2.50
ST30 Dan Marino 2.50 6.00

1995 SkyBox Premium Samples

This 6-card promotion or sample panel was issued to promote the 1995 SkyBox Premium product. Each card includes a card number on the back and could be detached individually using the perforations applied in the printing process.

COMPLETE SET (6) 2.00 5.00
S1 Trent Dilfer Promise .40 1.00
S2 Eric Turner Quickstrike .30 .75
S3 William Floyd .30 .75
S4 Dave Meggett .30 .75
S5 Daryl Johnston Mirror Image .30 .75
William Floyd
S6 Brett Favre Style Points 1.25 3.00
Trent Dilfer
NNO Uncut Panel 2.00 5.00

1995 SkyBox Premium

Issued as a 200 card set in 10 card packs with a suggested retail price of $2.19/pack. Card fronts have a borderless design featuring the player on a half-action half metallic background with a "ripped" effect dividing the two sections, along with a gold foil logo and player name. Card backs show a headshot with biographical and career statistics. Subsets include: Stylepoints (139-148), Mirror Image (149-158) and Rookies (159-198). Rookie Cards include Jeff Blake, Ki-Jana Carter, Kerry Collins, Joey Galloway, Napoleon Kaufman, Steve McNair, Rashaan Salaam, Chris Sanders, Kordell Stewart, J.J Stokes, Rodney Thomas and Michael Westbrook. A complete rookie receiver set was also available at one set per special retail box. A 6-card SkyBox promo sheet was produced and priced below as an uncut sheet. A number of John Elway cards (#36) were signed and released through SkyBox's instant win contest. Each autographed card was embossed with a SkyBox stamp.

COMPLETE SET (200) 7.50 20.00
1 Garrison Hearst .15 .40
2 Dave Krieg .02 .10
3 Rob Moore .07 .20
4 Eric Swann .07 .20
5 Larry Centers .07 .20
6 Jeff George .07 .20
7 Craig Heyward .07 .20
8 Terance Mathis .07 .20
9 Eric Metcalf .07 .20
10 Jim Kelly .15 .40
11 Andre Reed .07 .20
12 Bruce Smith .15 .40
13 Cornelius Bennett .07 .20
14 Randy Baldwin .02 .10
15 Don Beebe .02 .10
16 Barry Foster .07 .20
17 Lamar Lathon .02 .10
18 Frank Reich .02 .10
19 Jeff Graham .02 .10
20 Raymont Harris .02 .10
21 Lewis Tillman .02 .10
22 Michael Timpson .02 .10
23 Jeff Blake RC .40 1.00
24 Carl Pickens .07 .20
25 Darnay Scott .07 .20
26 Dan Wilkinson .07 .20
27 Derrick Alexander WR .15 .40
28 Leroy Hoard .02 .10
29 Antonio Langham .02 .10
30 Andre Rison .07 .20
31 Eric Turner .02 .10
32 Troy Aikman .50 1.25
33 Michael Irvin .15 .40
34 Daryl Johnston .07 .20
35 Emmitt Smith .75 2.00
36 John Elway 1.00 2.50
37 Glyn Milburn .02 .10
38 Anthony Miller .07 .20
39 Shannon Sharpe .07 .20
40 Scott Mitchell .07 .20
41 Herman Moore .15 .40
42 Barry Sanders .75 2.00
43 Chris Spielman .07 .20
44 Edgar Bennett .07 .20
45 Robert Brooks .15 .40
46 Brett Favre 1.00 2.50
47 Reggie White .15 .40
48 Mel Gray .02 .10
49 Haywood Jeffires .02 .10
50 Gary Brown .02 .10
51 Craig Erickson .02 .10
52 Quentin Coryatt .07 .20
53 Sean Dawkins .07 .20
54 Marshall Faulk .60 1.50
55 Steve Beuerlein .07 .20
56 Reggie Cobb .02 .10
57 Desmond Howard .07 .20
58 Ernest Givins .02 .10
59 Jeff Lageman .02 .10
60 Marcus Allen .15 .40
61 Steve Bono .07 .20
62 Greg Hill .07 .20
63 Willie Davis .07 .20
64 Tim Brown .15 .40
65 Rocket Ismail .07 .20
66 Jeff Hostetler .07 .20
67 Chester McGlockton .07 .20
68 Tim Bowens .02 .10
69 Irving Fryar .07 .20
70 Eric Green .02 .10
71 Terry Kirby .07 .20
72 Dan Marino 1.00 2.50
73 O.J. McDuffie .15 .40
74 Bernie Parmalee .07 .20
75 Dewayne Washington .07 .20
76 Cris Carter .15 .40
77 Qadry Ismail .07 .20
78 Warren Moon .07 .20
79 Jake Reed .07 .20
80 Drew Bledsoe .30 .75
81 Vincent Brisby .02 .10
82 Ben Coates .07 .20
83 Dave Meggett .02 .10
84 Mario Bates .07 .20
85 Jim Everett .02 .10
86 Michael Haynes .07 .20
87 Tyrone Hughes .07 .20
88 Dave Brown .07 .20
89 Rodney Hampton .07 .20
90 Thomas Lewis .07 .20
91 Herschel Walker .07 .20
92 Mike Sherrard .02 .10
93 Boomer Esiason .07 .20
94 Aaron Glenn .02 .10
95 Johnny Johnson .02 .10
96 Johnny Mitchell .02 .10
97 Ronald Moore .02 .10
98 Fred Barnett .07 .20
99 Randall Cunningham .15 .40
100 Charlie Garner .15 .40
101 Ricky Watters .07 .20
102 Calvin Williams .15 .40
103 Charles Johnson .07 .20
104 Byron Bam Morris .02 .10
105 Neil O'Donnell .07 .20
106 Rod Woodson .07 .20
107 Jerome Bettis .15 .40
108 Troy Drayton .02 .10
109 Sean Gilbert .07 .20
110 Chris Miller .02 .10
111 Leonard Russell .02 .10
112 Ronnie Harmon .02 .10
113 Stan Humphries .07 .20
114 Shawn Jefferson .02 .10
115 Natrone Means .07 .20
116 Junior Seau .15 .40
117 William Floyd .07 .20
118 Brent Jones .02 .10
119 Jerry Rice .50 1.25
120 Deion Sanders .30 .75
121 Dana Stubblefield .07 .20
122 Bryant Young .07 .20
123 Steve Young .40 1.00
124 Brian Blades .07 .20
125 Cortez Kennedy .07 .20
126 Rick Mirer .07 .20
127 Ricky Proehl .02 .10
128 Chris Warren .07 .20
129 Horace Copeland .02 .10
130 Trent Dilfer .15 .40
131 Alvin Harper .02 .10
132 Jackie Harris .02 .10
133 Hardy Nickerson .02 .10
134 Errict Rhett .07 .20
135 Henry Ellard .07 .20
136 Brian Mitchell .02 .10
137 Heath Shuler .07 .20
138 Tydus Winans .02 .10
139 Brett Favre .40 1.00
Bledsoe
140 Marshall Faulk .25 .60
Floyd
141 Brett Favre .30 .75
Dilfer
142 Dan Marino .40 1.00
Favre
143 Errict Rhett .15 .40
Dilfer
144 Jerry Rice .20 .50
Turner
145 Andre Rison .07 .20
E.Turner
146 Barry Sanders .25 .60
Meggett
147 Emmitt Smith .25 .60
Johnston
148 Steve Young .40 1.00
Favre
149 Emmitt Smith .25 .60
Rhett
150 Marshall Faulk .30 .75
B.Sanders
151 Jerry Rice .20 .50
D.Scott
152 William Floyd .07 .20
Johnston
153 Dan Marino .30 .75
Dilfer
154 John Elway .30 .75
Shuler
155 Byron Bam Morris .02 .10
Means
156 Dan Wilkinson .07 .20
R.White
157 Mario Bates .07 .20
Hampton
158 Junior Seau .15 .40
M.Jones
159 Ki-Jana Carter RC .15 .40
160 Tony Boselli RC .15 .40
161 Steve McNair RC 1.50 4.00
162 Michael Westbrook RC .15 .40
163 Kerry Collins RC .75 2.00
164 Kevin Carter RC .15 .40
165 Mike Mamula RC .02 .10
166 Joey Galloway RC .75 2.00
167 Kyle Brady RC .15 .40
168 J.J. Stokes RC .15 .40
169 Warren Sapp RC .75 2.00
170 Rob Johnson RC .50 1.25
171 Tyrone Wheatley RC .60 1.50
172 Napoleon Kaufman RC .60 1.50
173 James O. Stewart RC .60 1.50
174 Joe Aska RC .02 .10
175 Rashaan Salaam RC .07 .20
176 Tyrone Poole RC .15 .40
177 Ty Law RC .75 2.00
178 Dino Philyaw RC .02 .10
179 Mark Bruener RC .07 .20
180 Derrick Brooks RC .75 2.00
181 Jack Jackson RC .02 .10
182 Ray Zellars RC .07 .20
183 Eddie Goines RC .02 .10
184 Chris Sanders RC .07 .20
185 Charlie Simmons RC .02 .10
186 Lee DeRamus RC .02 .10
187 Frank Sanders RC .15 .40

188 Rodney Thomas RC .07 .20
189 Steve Stenstrom RC .02 .10
190 Stoney Case RC .02 .10
191 Tyrone Davis RC .02 .10
192 Kordell Stewart RC .75 2.00
193 Christian Fauria RC .07 .20
194 Todd Collins RC .50 1.25
195 Sherman Williams RC .02 .10
196 Lovell Pinkney RC .02 .10
197 Eric Zeier RC .15 .40
198 Zack Crockett RC .07 .20
199 Checklist A .02 .10
200 Checklist B .02 .10
AU36 John Elway AUTO 75.00 150.00
AU46 Brett Favre AUTO/250 125.00 250.00

1995 SkyBox Premium Inside the Numbers

This 20 card set was issued one per special retail pack. The card design is very similar to the base issue card except for the player write-ups.

COMPLETE SET (20) 10.00 20.00
ONE PER SPECIAL RETAIL PACK
1 William Floyd .10 .30
2 Marshall Faulk 1.00 2.50
3 Warren Moon .10 .30
4 Cris Carter .25 .60
5 Deion Sanders .50 1.25
6 Drew Bledsoe .50 1.25
7 Natrone Means .10 .30
8 Herschel Walker .10 .30
9 Ben Coates .10 .30
10 Mel Gray .05 .15
11 Barry Sanders 1.25 3.00
12 Steve Young .60 1.50
13 Rashaan Salaam .10 .30
14 Andre Reed .10 .30
15 Tyrone Hughes .10 .30
16 Eric Turner .05 .15
17 Ki-Jana Carter .25 .60
18 Dan Marino 1.50 4.00
19 Errict Rhett .10 .30
20 Jerry Rice .75 2.00

1995 SkyBox Premium Paydirt Gold

Randomly inserted at a rate of one in four packs, this 30 card set focuses on players who "just get it done". Card fronts have a silver-foil background with an alternating image of "SkyBox" and "Paydirt" logos. The player's name runs along the bottom of the card in gold foil with line of scrimmage numbers along the left of the card. Card backs include a team color background with a action shot of the player on the right and a brief commentary directly underneath. A parallel of this set was produced called "Paydirt Colors". The players name and the line of scrimmage numbers are done in one of four colors: green, blue, purple or a reddish-pink. These were reportedly produced at less than five percent of the production run. Card backs are numbered with a "PD" prefix.

COMPLETE GOLD SET (30) 20.00 50.00
STATED ODDS 1:4
*COLORS: 2.5X TO 6X BASIC INSERTS
*COLOR ROOKIES: 2.5X TO 6X BASE CARD HI
COLORS STATED PRINT RUN 5% OF TOTAL
PD1 Troy Aikman 1.25 3.00
PD2 J.J. Stokes .08 .25
PD3 Ki-Jana Carter .08 .25
PD4 Steve McNair 2.00 4.00
PD5 Jerome Bettis .40 1.00
PD6 Tim Brown .40 1.00
PD7 Cris Carter .40 1.00
PD8 John Elway 2.50 6.00
PD9 Marshall Faulk 1.50 4.00
PD10 Brett Favre 2.50 6.00
PD11 Michael Westbrook .08 .25
PD12 Rodney Hampton .20 .50
PD13 Michael Irvin .40 1.00
PD14 Dan Marino 2.50 6.00
PD15 Natrone Means .20 .50
PD16 Dave Meggett .08 .25
PD17 Joey Galloway 1.00 2.00
PD18 Herman Moore .40 1.00
PD19 Byron Bam Morris .08 .25
PD20 Carl Pickens .20 .50
PD21 Errict Rhett .20 .50
PD22 Kerry Collins 1.00 2.00
PD23 Barry Sanders 2.00 5.00
PD24 Deion Sanders .75 2.00
PD25 Emmitt Smith 2.00 5.00
PD26 Drew Bledsoe .75 2.00
PD27 Ricky Watters .20 .50
PD28 Rod Woodson .20 .50
PD29 Chris Warren .20 .50
PD30 Steve Young 1.00 2.50

1995 SkyBox Premium Promise

This 14-card set was randomly inserted at a rate of one in 24 packs and featues young stars. Card fronts have a team color background with the title "The Promise" in gold foil running across the player shot. Card backs are horizontal with an action shot at the left and a brief commentary to the right. Cards are numbered with a "P" prefix.

COMPLETE SET (14) 12.50 25.00
STATED ODDS 1:24
P1 Derrick Alexander WR 1.25 3.00
P2 Mario Bates .75 2.00
P3 Trent Dilfer 1.50 4.00
P4 Marshall Faulk 5.00 12.00
P5 William Floyd .75 2.00
P6 Aaron Glenn .75 2.00
P7 Raymont Harris .75 2.00
P8 Greg Hill .75 2.00
P9 Charles Johnson 1.25 3.00
P10 Byron Bam Morris .75 2.00
P11 Errict Rhett 1.25 3.00
P12 Darnay Scott 1.25 3.00
P13 Heath Shuler 1.25 3.00
P14 Dan Wilkinson .75 2.00

1995 SkyBox Premium Quickstrike

This 10 card set was randomly inserted at a rate of one in 15 packs and features players who can turn a game around in the blink of an eye. Card fronts feature a color-foil background with numbers. The title "Quickstrike" is in gold foil and the player's name is in black in the middle of the card. Card backs are horizontal with a team color background and a brief commentary. Cards are numbered with a "Q" prefix.

COMPLETE SET (10) 8.00 20.00
STATED ODDS 1:15
Q1 Chris Warren .25 .60
Q2 Marshall Faulk 2.00 5.00
Q3 William Floyd .25 .60
Q4 Jerry Rice 1.50 4.00
Q5 Eric Turner .10 .30
Q6 Tim Brown .50 1.25
Q7 Deion Sanders 1.00 2.50
Q8 Emmitt Smith 2.50 6.00
Q9 Rod Woodson .25 .60
Q10 Steve Young 1.25 3.00

1995 SkyBox Premium Rookie Receivers

This eight card set was inserted as a set at a rate of one per special retail box. Cardfronts look identical to the rookie design in the regular set. Cardbacks are numbered differently as "X" of 7.

COMPLETE SET (8) 2.50 6.00
ONE SET PER SPECIAL RETAIL BOX
1 Michael Westbrook .60 1.25
2 Joey Galloway .75 2.00
3 J.J.Stokes .30 .75
4 Frank Sanders .30 .75
5 Chris Sanders .20 .50
6 Tyrone Davis .20 .50
7 Jimmy Oliver .20 .50
NNO Cover .10 .30
Checklist Card

1995 SkyBox Premium Prime Time Rookies

Officially titled "Prime Time Rookies", this 10 card set was randomly inserted into packs at a rate of one in 96 and features rookies tabbed for stardom. Card fronts have a clock in the background with a shot of the player in his college uniform and the player's name in gold foil surrounding the "SkyBox" logo. Card backs are horizontal with biographical information and a brief commentary. Cards are numbered with a "PT" prefix.

COMPLETE SET (10) 25.00 60.00
STATED ODDS 1:96
PT1 Ki-Jana Carter 1.00 2.50
PT2 Kerry Collins 5.00 12.00
PT3 Joey Galloway 5.00 12.00
PT4 Steve McNair 10.00 25.00
PT5 Rashaan Salaam .50 1.25
PT6 James O. Stewart 4.00 10.00
PT7 J.J. Stokes 1.00 2.50
PT8 Rodney Thomas .50 1.25
PT9 Michael Westbrook 1.00 2.50
PT10 Tyrone Wheatley 4.00 10.00

1996 SkyBox Premium Samples

This 3-card promotion or sample panel was issued to promote the 1996 SkyBox Premium product. Each card includes a card number on the back and could be detached individually using the perforations applied in the printing process.

COMPLETE SET (3) 1.50 4.00
S1 Brett Favre 1.25 3.00
S2 Leeland McElroy .20 .50
S3 Kordell Stewart/Quentin Coryatt Panorama.30 .75
NNO Uncut Panel 1.50 4.00

1996 SkyBox Premium

The 1996 Skybox set was issued in one series totalling 250 cards. The fronts feature borderless color player photos with foil stamping and UV coating. The set contains the topical subsets: Rookies (179-228), PrimeTime Rookie Retrospective (229-238) and Panorama (239-248). A 3-card (cards numbered S1-S3) promo sheet was produced and is priced below in complete sheet form.

COMPLETE SET (250) 7.50 20.00
1 Larry Centers .08 .25
2 Boomer Esiason .08 .25
3 Garrison Hearst .08 .25
4 Rob Moore .08 .25
5 Frank Sanders .08 .25
6 Eric Swann .02 .10
7 Bert Emanuel .08 .25
8 Jeff George .08 .25
9 Craig Heyward .02 .10
10 Terance Mathis .02 .10
11 Eric Metcalf .02 .10
12 Derrick Alexander WR .08 .25
13 Leroy Hoard .02 .10
14 Michael Jackson .08 .25
15 Vinny Testaverde .08 .25
16 Eric Turner .02 .10
17 Darick Holmes .02 .10
18 Jim Kelly .20 .50
19 Bryce Paup .02 .10
20 Andre Reed .08 .25
21 Bruce Smith .08 .25
22 Thurman Thomas .20 .50
23 Tim Tindale RC .02 .10
24 Mark Carrier WR .02 .10
25 Kerry Collins .20 .50
26 Willie Green .02 .10
27 Kevin Greene .08 .25
28 Tyrone Poole .02 .10
29 Curtis Conway .20 .50
30 Bryan Cox .02 .10
31 Erik Kramer .02 .10
32 Nate Lewis .02 .10
33 Rashaan Salaam .08 .25
34 Alonzo Spellman .02 .10
35 Michael Timpson .02 .10
36 Jeff Blake .20 .50
37 Ki-Jana Carter .08 .25
38 David Dunn .02 .10
39 Carl Pickens .08 .25
40 Darnay Scott .08 .25
41 Troy Aikman .50 1.25
42 Charles Haley .08 .25
43 Michael Irvin .20 .50
44 Daryl Johnston .08 .25
45 Jay Novacek .02 .10
46 Deion Sanders .30 .75
47 Emmitt Smith .75 2.00
48 Kevin Williams .02 .10
49 Steve Atwater .02 .10
50 Terrell Davis .40 1.00
51 John Elway 1.00 2.50
52 Anthony Miller .08 .25
53 Shannon Sharpe .08 .25
54 Mike Sherrard .02 .10
55 Scott Mitchell .08 .25
56 Herman Moore .08 .25
57 Johnnie Morton .08 .25
58 Brett Perriman .02 .10
59 Barry Sanders .75 2.00
60 Edgar Bennett .08 .25
61 Robert Brooks .20 .50
62 Mark Chmura .08 .25
63 Brett Favre 1.00 2.50
64 Antonio Freeman .20 .50
65 Keith Jackson .02 .10
66 Reggie White .20 .50
67 Chris Chandler .08 .25
68 Mel Gray .02 .10
69 Steve McNair .40 1.00
70 Chris Sanders .08 .25
71 Rodney Thomas .02 .10
72 Quentin Coryatt .02 .10
73 Sean Dawkins .02 .10
74 Ken Dilger .08 .25
75 Marshall Faulk .25 .60
76 Jim Harbaugh .08 .25
77 Lamont Warren .02 .10
78 Tony Boselli .02 .10
79 Mark Brunell .30 .75
80 Willie Jackson .08 .25
81 Natrone Means .08 .25
82 James O.Stewart .08 .25
83 Marcus Allen .20 .50
84 Kimble Anders .08 .25
85 Steve Bono .02 .10
86 Lake Dawson .02 .10
87 Neil Smith .08 .25
88 Derrick Thomas .20 .50
89 Tamarick Vanover .08 .25
90 Fred Barnett .02 .10
91 Terry Kirby .08 .25
92 Dan Marino 1.00 2.50
93 O.J. McDuffie .08 .25
94 Bernie Parmalee .02 .10
95 Richmond Webb .02 .10
96 Cris Carter .20 .50
97 Scottie Graham .02 .10
98 Qadry Ismail .08 .25
99 Warren Moon .08 .25
100 Jake Reed .08 .25
101 Robert Smith .08 .25
102 Drew Bledsoe .30 .75
103 Vincent Brisby .02 .10
104 Ben Coates .08 .25
105 Curtis Martin .40 1.00
106 Dave Meggett .02 .10
107 Chris Slade .02 .10
108 Mario Bates .08 .25
109 Jim Everett .02 .10
110 Michael Haynes .02 .10
111 Tyrone Hughes .02 .10
112 Renaldo Turnbull .02 .10
113 Dave Brown .02 .10
114 Chris Calloway .02 .10
115 Rodney Hampton .08 .25
116 Thomas Lewis .02 .10
117 Tyrone Wheatley .08 .25
118 Kyle Brady .02 .10
119 Hugh Douglas .08 .25
120 Aaron Glenn .02 .10
121 Jeff Graham .02 .10
122 Adrian Murrell .08 .25
123 Neil O'Donnell .08 .25
124 Tim Brown .20 .50
125 Nolan Harrison .02 .10
126 Billy Joe Hobert .08 .25
127 Jeff Hostetler .02 .10
128 Napoleon Kaufman .20 .50
129 Chester McGlockton .02 .10
130 Harvey Williams .02 .10
131 Charlie Garner .08 .25
132 Andy Harmon .02 .10
133 Chris T. Jones .08 .25
134 Mike Mamula .02 .10
135 Rodney Peete .02 .10
136 Bobby Taylor .02 .10
137 Ricky Watters .08 .25
138 Jerome Bettis .20 .50
139 Greg Lloyd .08 .25
140 Jim Miller .20 .50
141 Ernie Mills .02 .10
142 Kordell Stewart .20 .50
143 Yancey Thigpen .08 .25
144 Rod Woodson .08 .25
145 Andre Coleman .02 .10
146 Terrell Fletcher .02 .10
147 Aaron Hayden RC .02 .10
148 Stan Humphries .08 .25
149 Junior Seau .20 .50
150 Isaac Bruce .20 .50
151 Kevin Carter .02 .10
152 Todd Kinchen .02 .10
153 Leslie O'Neal .02 .10
154 Steve Walsh .02 .10
155 William Floyd .08 .25
156 Merton Hanks .02 .10
157 Brent Jones .02 .10
158 Derek Loville .02 .10
159 Ken Norton .02 .10
160 Jerry Rice .50 1.25
161 J.J. Stokes .20 .50
162 Steve Young .40 1.00
163 Brian Blades .02 .10
164 Christian Fauria .02 .10
165 Joey Galloway .20 .50
166 Rick Mirer .08 .25
167 Chris Warren .08 .25
168 Trent Dilfer .20 .50
169 Alvin Harper .02 .10
170 Jackie Harris .02 .10
171 Hardy Nickerson .02 .10
172 Errict Rhett .08 .25
173 Terry Allen .08 .25
174 Henry Ellard .02 .10
175 Gus Frerotte .08 .25
176 Brian Mitchell .02 .10
177 Heath Shuler .08 .25
178 Michael Westbrook .20 .50
179 Karim Abdul-Jabbar RC .20 .50
180 Mike Alstott RC .50 1.25
181 Willie Anderson RC .02 .10
182 Marco Battaglia RC .02 .10
183 Tim Biakabutuka RC .20 .50
184 Tony Brackens RC .20 .50
185 Duane Clemons RC .02 .10
186 Marcus Coleman RC .02 .10
187 Ernie Conwell RC .02 .10
188 Chris Darkins RC .02 .10
189 Stephen Davis RC .75 2.00
190 Brian Dawkins RC .60 1.50
191 Rickey Dudley RC .20 .50
192 Jason Dunn RC .08 .25
193 Bobby Engram RC .20 .50
194 Daryl Gardener RC .02 .10
195 Eddie George RC .60 1.50
196 Terry Glenn RC .50 1.25
197 Kevin Hardy RC .20 .50
198 Walt Harris RC .02 .10
199 Marvin Harrison RC 1.25 3.00
200 Bobby Hoying RC .20 .50
201 Israel Ifeanyi RC .02 .10
202 DeRon Jenkins RC .02 .10
203 Keyshawn Johnson RC .50 1.25
204 Lance Johnstone RC .08 .25
205 Cedric Jones RC .02 .10
206 Marcus Jones RC .02 .10
207 Eddie Kennison RC .20 .50
208 Jevon Langford RC .02 .10
209 Dedric Mathis RC .02 .10
210 Jermane Mayberry RC .02 .10
211 Leeland McElroy RC .08 .25
212 Johnny McWilliams RC .08 .25
213 Ray Mickens RC .02 .10
214 John Mobley RC .02 .10
215 Jerald Moore RC .08 .25
216 Eric Moulds RC .60 1.50
217 Muhsin Muhammad RC .50 1.25
218 Jonathan Ogden RC .50 1.25
219 Lawrence Phillips RC .20 .50
220 Kavika Pittman RC .02 .10
221 Stanley Pritchett RC .08 .25
222 Simeon Rice RC .50 1.25
223 Detron Smith RC .02 .10
224 Bryan Still RC .08 .25
225 Amani Toomer RC .50 1.25
226 Regan Upshaw RC .02 .10
227 Alex Van Dyke RC .08 .25
228 Stepfret Williams RC .08 .25
229 Coryatt/McGlck/Pckns/Brks .08 .25
230 D.Crtr/E.Bnn/Blds/Hrst .20 .50
231 Means/Mirer/Bettis/R.Smith .08 .25
232 McDffie/Cnwy/Faulk/G.Hill .20 .50
233 Shuler/Dilfr/Flyd/C.Johnsn .08 .25
234 Rhett/Dawkns/Bates/K.Cartr .08 .25
235 K.Cllns/McNair/Gallo/Salm .20 .50
236 Stokes/Westb/Brdy/K.Stew. .20 .50
237 Johnson/George/McElroy/Phillips .08 .25
238 Engram/Dudley/Moulds/Biak .08 .25
239 K.Stewart/Q.Coryatt P .20 .50
240 Robert Brooks P .08 .25
241 H.Jones/T.Mathis P .02 .10
242 M.Seay/A.Pupunu P .02 .10
243 R.Brooks/W.Beamon P .08 .25
244 49ers Halloween P .02 .10
245 Garrison Hearst P .02 .10
246 Z.Crockett/J.Seau P .20 .50
247 K.Williams/D.Evans P .02 .10
248 T.Jacobs/A.Freeman P .08 .25
249 Checklist Card 1 .02 .10
250 Checklist Card 2 .02 .10

1996 SkyBox Premium Rubies

COMP.RUBY SET (248) 250.00 500.00
*RUBY STARS: 10X TO 25X BASIC CARDS
*RUBY RCs: 5X TO 12X BASIC CARDS
ONE PER HOBBY BOX

1996 SkyBox Premium Close-ups

Randomly inserted in retail packs only at the rate of one in 30, this 10-card set features tight photography profiles of some of the top NFL players.

COMPLETE SET (10) 20.00 50.00
RANDOM INS.IN RETAIL PACKS
1 Troy Aikman 4.00 10.00
2 Drew Bledsoe 2.50 6.00
3 Isaac Bruce 1.50 4.00
4 Terrell Davis 3.00 8.00
5 John Elway 8.00 20.00
6 Barry Sanders 6.00 15.00
7 Emmitt Smith 6.00 15.00
8 Kordell Stewart 1.50 4.00
9 Tamarick Vanover .75 2.00
10 Ricky Watters .75 2.00

1996 SkyBox Premium Brett Favre MVP

Randomly inserted in packs of Skybox Impact cards (1-3A) and SkyBox packs (3B-5), this six-card set honors the different facets of Brett Favre's game. The set is tied together by a two-part Exchange Card for the Lenticular #3 card. Collectors had to get both Exchange Cards to claim the lenticular card.

COMPLETE SET (7) 30.00 80.00
1-3A: RANDOM INSERTS IN IMPACT PACKS
3B-5: RANDOM INSERTS IN SKYBOX PACKS
1 Brett Favre Foil 5.00 12.00
2 Brett Favre Acrylic 5.00 12.00
3A Brett Favre Lent.Exch.A .10 .30
3B Brett Favre Lent.Exch.B .10 .30
3C Brett Favre Lent.Prize 15.00 40.00
4 Brett Favre Die Cut 6.00 15.00
5 Brett Favre Leather 6.00 15.00

1996 SkyBox Premium Inside the Numbers

COMPLETE SET (20) 10.00 25.00
ONE PER SPECIAL RETAIL PACK
1 Troy Aikman 1.25 3.00
2 Robert Brooks .50 1.25
3 Mark Brunell .50 1.25
4 Larry Centers .25 .60
5 Andre Coleman .08 .25
6 Brett Favre 2.50 6.00
7 Charlie Garner .25 .60
8 Mel Gray .08 .25
9 Greg Lloyd .25 .60
10 Dan Marino 2.50 6.00
11 Warren Moon .25 .60
12 Bryce Paup .08 .25
13 Carl Pickens .25 .60
14 Barry Sanders 2.00 5.00
15 Deion Sanders .75 2.00
16 Eric Swann .08 .25
17 Thurman Thomas .50 1.25
18 Tamarick Vanover .25 .60
19 Reggie White .50 1.25
20 Steve Young 1.00 2.50

1996 SkyBox Premium Next Big Thing

Randomly inserted in packs at a rate of one in 40, this 15-card set features player photos of top NFL prospects.

COMPLETE SET (15) 25.00 60.00
STATED ODDS 1:40
1 Mark Brunell 3.00 8.00
2 Rickey Dudley 1.25 3.00
3 Bobby Engram 1.25 3.00
4 Antonio Freeman 2.00 5.00
5 Eddie George 4.00 10.00
6 Terry Glenn 3.00 8.00
7 Marvin Harrison 8.00 20.00
8 Keyshawn Johnson 3.00 8.00
9 Napoleon Kaufman 2.00 5.00
10 Steve McNair 4.00 10.00
11 Alex Molden .40 1.00
12 Frank Sanders 1.00 2.50
13 Kordell Stewart 2.00 5.00
14 Amani Toomer 3.00 8.00
15 Alex Van Dyke .60 1.50

1996 SkyBox Premium Prime Time Rookies

Randomly inserted in hobby packs only at a rate of one in 96, this 10-card set features color photos of 1996's first year superstars.

COMPLETE SET (10) 30.00 80.00
STATED ODDS 1:96 HOBBY
1 Tim Biakabutuka 2.00 5.00
2 Rickey Dudley 2.00 5.00
3 Bobby Engram 2.00 5.00
4 Eddie George 6.00 15.00
5 Terry Glenn 5.00 12.00
6 Marvin Harrison 12.50 30.00
7 Keyshawn Johnson 5.00 12.00
8 Leeland McElroy 1.00 2.50
9 Eric Moulds 6.00 15.00
10 Lawrence Phillips 2.00 5.00

1996 SkyBox Premium Autographs

Randomly inserted in packs at a rate of one in 900, this six-card set features color photos of players who served as SkyBox spokesmen in 1996. Each card was hand-signed by the featured player.

COMPLETE SET (6) 100.00 200.00
STATED ODDS 1:900
A1 Trent Dilfer 20.00 40.00
A2 Brett Favre 75.00 150.00
A3 William Floyd 7.50 20.00
A4 Daryl Johnston 20.00 40.00
A5 Dave Meggett 7.50 20.00
A6 Eric Turner 20.00 40.00

1996 SkyBox Premium Thunder and Lightning

Randomly inserted in packs at a rate of one in 72, this 10-card set features two cards in one. The color photo of the player designated as the "Lightning" is encased in a sleeve with a color photos of the player designated as the "Thunder."

COMPLETE SET (10) 75.00 150.00
STATED ODDS 1:72
1 E.Smith 7.50 20.00
T.Aikman
2 B.Sanders 7.50 20.00
S.Mitchell
3 M.Faulk 7.50 20.00
J.Harbaugh
4 D.Marino 10.00 25.00
O.J.McDuffie
5 J.Rice 10.00 25.00
S.Young
6 J.Blake 5.00 12.00
C.Pickens
7 B.Favre 10.00 25.00
R.Brooks
8 C.Martin 7.50 20.00
D.Bledsoe
9 E.Rhett 4.00 10.00
T.Dilfer
10 R.Mirer 4.00 10.00
C.Warren

1996 SkyBox Premium V

Randomly inserted in packs at a rate of one in 18, this 10-card set showcases top players produced with a die cut "V" card design.

COMPLETE SET (10) 15.00 30.00
STATED ODDS 1:18
1 Ki-Jana Carter 1.00 2.50
2 Kerry Collins 2.00 5.00
3 Trent Dilfer 2.00 5.00
4 Joey Galloway 2.00 5.00
5 Herman Moore 1.00 2.50
6 Errict Rhett 1.00 2.50
7 Rashaan Salaam 1.00 2.50
8 Deion Sanders 3.00 8.00
9 Thurman Thomas 2.00 5.00
10 Reggie White 2.00 5.00

1997 SkyBox Premium

The 1997 SkyBox set was issued in one series totalling 250 cards. The set features color action player images printed on 20 pt. card stock with colorful holographic foil enhancements. The backs carry player information and career statistics with a faint player photo in the background. The set features 40-rookies (208-247) and 3-checklists (248-250)

COMPLETE SET (250) 12.50 30.00
1 Brett Favre 1.25 2.50
2 Michael Bates .08 .25
3 Jeff Graham .08 .25
4 Terry Glenn .25 .60
5 Stephen Davis .25 .60
6 Wesley Walls .15 .40
7 Barry Sanders .75 2.00
8 Chris Sanders .08 .25
9 O.J. McDuffie .15 .40
10 Ken Dilger .08 .25
11 Kimble Anders .15 .40
12 Keenan McCardell .15 .40
13 Ki-Jana Carter .08 .25
14 Gary Brown .08 .25
15 Andre Rison .15 .40
16 Edgar Bennett .15 .40
17 Jerome Bettis .25 .60
18 Ted Johnson .08 .25
19 John Friesz .08 .25
20 Tony Brackens .08 .25
21 Bryan Cox .08 .25
22 Eric Moulds .25 .60
23 Johnnie Morton .15 .40
24 Brad Johnson .25 .60
25 Byron Bam Morris .08 .25
26 Anthony Johnson .08 .25
27 Jim Harbaugh .15 .40
28 Keyshawn Johnson .25 .60
29 Cary Blanchard .08 .25
30 Curtis Conway .15 .40
31 Herschel Walker .15 .40
32 Thurman Thomas .25 .60
33 Frank Sanders .15 .40
34 Lawrence Phillips .08 .25
35 Scottie Graham .08 .25
36 Jim Everett .08 .25
37 Dale Carter .08 .25
38 Ashley Ambrose .08 .25
39 Mark Chmura .15 .40
40 James O.Stewart .15 .40
41 John Mobley .08 .25
42 Terrell Davis .30 .75
43 Ben Coates .15 .40
44 Jeff George .15 .40
45 Ty Detmer .15 .40
46 Isaac Bruce .25 .60
47 Chris Warren .15 .40
48 Steve Walsh .08 .25
49 Bruce Smith .15 .40
50 Cris Carter .25 .60
51 Jamal Anderson .25 .60
52 Tim Biakabutuka .15 .40
53 Steve Young .30 .75
54 Eric Turner .08 .25
55 Jessie Tuggle .08 .25
56 Chris T. Jones .08 .25
57 Daryl Johnston .15 .40
58 Randall Cunningham .25 .60
59 Trent Dilfer .25 .60
60 Mark Brunell .30 .75
61 Warren Moon .25 .60
62 Terry Kirby .15 .40
63 Eddie George .25 .60
64 Neil Smith .15 .40
65 Gilbert Brown .15 .40
66 Emmitt Smith .75 2.00
67 Chad Brown .08 .25
68 Jamie Asher .08 .25
69 Willie McGinest .08 .25
70 Tim Brown .25 .60
71 Quentin Coryatt .08 .25
72 Mario Bates .08 .25
73 Fred Barnett .08 .25
74 Hugh Douglas .08 .25
75 Eric Swann .08 .25
76 Chris Chandler .15 .40
77 Larry Centers .15 .40
78 Vinny Testaverde .15 .40
79 Jermaine Lewis .25 .60
80 Junior Seau .25 .60
81 Kevin Greene .15 .40
82 Ricky Watters .15 .40
83 Billy Davis RC .08 .25
84 Michael Westbrook .15 .40
85 Charles Way .15 .40
86 Andre Reed .15 .40
87 Darrell Green .15 .40
88 Troy Aikman .50 1.25
89 Jim Pyne .08 .25
90 Dan Marino 1.00 2.50
91 Elvis Grbac .15 .40
92 Mel Gray .08 .25
93 Marcus Allen .25 .60
94 Terry Allen .25 .60
95 Karim Abdul-Jabbar .25 .60
96 Rick Mirer .08 .25
97 Bert Emanuel .15 .40
98 John Elway 1.00 2.50
99 Tony Martin .15 .40
100 Zach Thomas .25 .60
101 Harvey Williams .08 .25
102 Jason Sehorn .15 .40
103 Lawyer Milloy .15 .40
104 Thomas Lewis .08 .25
105 Michael Irvin .25 .60
106 James Hundon RC .25 .60
107 Willie Green .08 .25
108 Bobby Engram .15 .40
109 Mike Alstott .25 .60
110 Greg Lloyd .08 .25
111 Shannon Sharpe .15 .40
112 Desmond Howard .15 .40
113 Jason Elam .15 .40
114 Qadry Ismail .15 .40
115 William Thomas .08 .25
116 Marshall Faulk .30 .75
117 Tyrone Wheatley .15 .40
118 Tommy Vardell .08 .25
119 Rashaan Salaam .08 .25
120 Brian Mitchell .08 .25
121 Terance Mathis .15 .40
122 Dorsey Levens .25 .60
123 Todd Collins .08 .25
124 Derrick Alexander WR .15 .40
125 Stan Humphries .15 .40
126 Kordell Stewart .25 .60
127 Kent Graham .08 .25
128 Yancey Thigpen .15 .40
129 Bryan Still .08 .25
130 Carl Pickens .15 .40
131 Ray Lewis .40 1.00
132 Curtis Martin .30 .75
133 Kerry Collins .25 .60
134 Ed McCaffrey .15 .40
135 Darick Holmes .08 .25
136 Glyn Milburn .08 .25
137 Rickey Dudley .15 .40
138 Terrell Owens .30 .75
139 Kevin Williams .08 .25
140 Reggie White .25 .60
141 Darnay Scott .15 .40
142 Brett Perriman .08 .25
143 Neil O'Donnell .15 .40
144 Natrone Means .08 .25
145 Jerris McPhail .08 .25
146 Lamar Lathon .08 .25
147 Michael Jackson .15 .40
148 Simeon Rice .15 .40
149 Greg Hill .08 .25
150 Erik Kramer .08 .25
151 Quinn Early .08 .25
152 Tamarick Vanover .15 .40
153 Derrick Thomas .25 .60
154 Nilo Silvan .08 .25
155 Deion Sanders .25 .60
156 Lorenzo Neal .08 .25
157 Steve McNair .30 .75
158 Levon Kirkland .08 .25
159 Bobby Hebert .08 .25
160 William Floyd .15 .40
161 Leeland McElroy .08 .25
162 Chester McGlockton .08 .25
163 Michael Haynes .08 .25
164 Aeneas Williams .08 .25
165 Hardy Nickerson .08 .25
166 Ray Zellars .08 .25
167 Ifeanyi Uwaezuoke .15 .40
168 Chris Slade .08 .25
169 Herman Moore .15 .40
170 Rob Moore .15 .40
171 Andre Hastings .08 .25
172 Antonio Freeman .25 .60
173 Tony Boselli .08 .25
174 Drew Bledsoe .30 .75
175 Sam Mills .08 .25
176 Robert Smith .15 .40
177 Jimmy Smith .15 .40
178 Alex Molden .08 .25
179 Joey Galloway .15 .40
180 Irving Fryar .15 .40
181 Wayne Chrebet .25 .60
182 Dave Brown .08 .25
183 Robert Brooks .15 .40
184 Tony Banks .15 .40
185 Eric Metcalf .15 .40
186 Napoleon Kaufman .25 .60
187 Frank Wycheck .08 .25
188 Donnell Woolford .08 .25
189 Kevin Turner .08 .25
190 Eddie Kennison .15 .40
191 Cortez Kennedy .08 .25
192 Raymont Harris .08 .25
193 Ronnie Harmon .08 .25
194 Kevin Hardy .08 .25
195 Gus Frerotte .08 .25
196 Marvin Harrison .25 .60
197 Jeff Blake .15 .40
198 Mike Tomczak .08 .25
199 William Roaf .08 .25
200 Jerry Rice .50 1.25
201 Jake Reed .15 .40
202 Ken Norton .08 .25
203 Errict Rhett .08 .25
204 Adrian Murrell .15 .40
205 Rodney Hampton .15 .40
206 Scott Mitchell .15 .40
207 Jason Dunn .08 .25
208 Mike Adams RC .08 .25
209 John Allred RC .08 .25
210 Reidel Anthony RC .25 .60
211 Darnell Autry RC .15 .40
212 Tiki Barber RC 1.50 4.00
213 Will Blackwell RC .15 .40
214 Peter Boulware RC .25 .60
215 Macey Brooks RC .25 .60
216 Rae Carruth RC .08 .25
217 Troy Davis RC .15 .40
218 Corey Dillon RC 1.00 2.50
219 Jim Druckenmiller RC .15 .40
220 Warrick Dunn RC .75 2.00
221 Marc Edwards RC .08 .25
222 James Farrior RC .25 .60
223 Tony Gonzalez RC 1.00 2.50
224 Jay Graham RC .15 .40
225 Yatil Green RC .15 .40
226 Byron Hanspard RC .15 .40
227 Ike Hilliard RC .30 .75
228 Leon Johnson RC .15 .40
229 Damon Jones RC .08 .25
230 Freddie Jones RC .15 .40
231 Joey Kent RC .25 .60
232 David LaFleur RC .08 .25
233 Kevin Lockett RC .15 .40
234 Sam Madison RC .25 .60
235 Brian Manning RC .08 .25
236 Ronnie McAda RC .08 .25
237 Orlando Pace RC .25 .60
238 Jake Plummer RC 1.00 2.50
239 Keith Poole RC .25 .60
240 Darrell Russell RC .08 .25
241 Sedrick Shaw RC .15 .40
242 Antowain Smith RC .60 1.50
243 Shawn Springs RC .15 .40
244 Duce Staley RC 2.00 5.00
245 Dedric Ward RC .15 .40
246 Bryant Westbrook RC .08 .25
247 Danny Wuerffel RC .25 .60
248 Checklist .08 .25
249 Checklist .08 .25
250 Checklist .08 .25
S1 Terrell Davis Sample .75 2.00

1997 SkyBox Premium Rubies

*RUBY STARS: 40X TO 100X HI COL.
*RUBY RCs: 15X TO 40X HI COL.
STATED PRINT RUN 50 SERIAL #'d SETS

1997 SkyBox Premium Autographics

The Autographics inserts set was distributed across the line of 1997 SkyBox football products and includes 68-different cards. SkyBox Impact packs contained 48-different cards inserted at the rate of 1:120 packs. Each card features an authentic player signature along with an embossed SkyBox seal. SkyBox Premium packs included 65-cards inserted at the rate of 1:72 packs. SkyBox E-X2000 included 51-cards random inserted at the rate of 1:60 packs. We've combined the listings below since many cards were inserted in more than one product type (S= SkyBox Premium, IM= SkyBox Impact, EX= SkyBox E-X2000, MU= Metal Universe). The first 100-signed of each card was printed with holographic foil layering and individually numbered; called Century Marks. Brett Favre and Reggie White were only produced as Century Marks. All other cards were printed in both versions. The unnumbered cards are listed below alphabetically.

ODDS: 1:120 IMPACT/1:500 METAL UNIV
1:72 SKYBOX/1:60 E-X2000
5-CARDS/SKYBOX HOT PACK 1:288 ODDS
1 K.Jabbar EX/IM/MU/S 10.00 25.00
2 Larry Allen IM/S 12.00 30.00
3 Terry Allen IM/S 10.00 25.00
4 Mike Alstott IM/MU/S 10.00 25.00
5 Darnell Autry EX/IM/MU/S 4.00 10.00
6 Tony Banks IM 6.00 15.00
7 Pat Barnes EX/S 4.00 10.00
8 Jeff Blake S 10.00 25.00
9 Michael Booker IM/S 4.00 10.00
10 Rueben Brown EX/S 4.00 10.00
11 Rae Carruth EX/IM/MU/S 4.00 10.00
12 Cris Carter EX/IM/S 20.00 40.00
13 Ben Coates EX/IM/S 6.00 15.00
14 Ernie Conwell EX/IM/S 4.00 10.00
15 Terrell Davis EX/IM/S 15.00 30.00
16 Ty Detmer EX/IM/MU/S 6.00 15.00
17 Ken Dilger EX/IM/S 4.00 10.00
18 Corey Dillon IM/S 10.00 25.00
19 Jim Druckenmiller EX/S 6.00 15.00
20 Rickey Dudley EX/IM/S 6.00 15.00
22 Antonio Freeman EX/IM/S 10.00 25.00
23 Daryl Gardener EX/IM/S 4.00 10.00
24 Chris Gedney IM/S 4.00 10.00
25 Eddie George S 10.00 25.00
26 Hunter Goodwin EX/IM/S 4.00 10.00
27 Marvin Harrison EX/S 12.00 30.00
28 Garrison Hearst EX/S 6.00 15.00
29 William Henderson EX/IM/S 10.00 25.00
30 Michael Jackson EX/IM/S 6.00 15.00
31 Tory James EX/IM/S 4.00 10.00
32 Rob Johnson EX/IM/S 10.00 25.00
33 Chris T. Jones IM/S 4.00 10.00
34 Pete Kendall EX/S 4.00 10.00
35 Eddie Kennison EX/MU/S 6.00 15.00
36 David LaFleur EX/IM/S 4.00 10.00
37 Jeff Lewis EX/IM/S 4.00 10.00
38 Thomas Lewis IM/S 4.00 10.00
39 Kevin Lockett EX/IM/S 4.00 10.00
40 Brian Manning IM/MU/S 4.00 10.00
41 Dan Marino S 200.00 400.00
42 Ed McCaffrey 8.00 20.00
EX/IM/MU/S
43 Keenan McCardell EX/S 10.00 25.00
44 Glyn Milburn EX/IM/S 4.00 10.00
45 Alex Molden EX/IM/S 4.00 10.00
46 Johnnie Morton IM/S 6.00 15.00
47 Winslow Oliver EX/S 4.00 10.00
48 Jerry Rice MU 125.00 200.00
49 Rashaan Salaam EX/S 4.00 10.00
50 Frank Sanders EX/IM/S 6.00 15.00
51 Shannon Sharpe EX/IM/MU/S 15.00 40.00
52 Sedrick Shaw EX/IM/S 6.00 15.00
53 Alex Smith EX/IM/S 4.00 10.00
54 Antowain Smith EX/S 10.00 25.00
55 Emmitt Smith EX 100.00 200.00
56 Jimmy Smith IM/S 5.00 12.00
57 Shawn Springs S 6.00 15.00
58 James O.Stewart EX/IM/S 6.00 15.00
59 Kordell Stewart IM 10.00 25.00
60 Rodney Thomas EX/S 4.00 10.00
61 Amani Toomer EX/IM/S 10.00 25.00
62 Floyd Turner EX/IM/S 4.00 10.00
63 Alex Van Dyke EX/IM/S 4.00 10.00
64 Mike Vrabel IM/MU/S 25.00 50.00
65 Charles Way EX/S 4.00 10.00
66 Chris Warren EX/MU/S 4.00 10.00
68 Ricky Whittle EX/IM/S 4.00 10.00
69 Sherman Williams/EX/IM/S 4.00 10.00
70 Jon Witman EX/IM/S 6.00 15.00

1997 SkyBox Premium Autographics Century Mark

*CENT.MARKS: .5X TO 1.2X BASIC AUTOS
21 Brett Favre EX 250.00 400.00
41 Dan Marino S 200.00 400.00
48 Jerry Rice MU 125.00 250.00
55 Emmitt Smith EX 150.00 250.00
67 Reggie White EX/S 75.00 135.00

1997 SkyBox Premium Close-ups

Randomly inserted in packs at the rate of one in 18, this 10-card set features NFL stars with unusual personal commentary on the cardback. The cardfronts include three small action photos and one larger "close-up" photo.

COMPLETE SET (10) 25.00 60.00
STATED ODDS 1:18
1 Terrell Davis 3.00 8.00
2 Troy Aikman 5.00 12.00
3 Drew Bledsoe 3.00 8.00
4 Steve McNair 3.00 8.00
5 Jerry Rice 5.00 12.00
6 Kordell Stewart 2.50 6.00
7 Kerry Collins 2.50 6.00
8 John Elway 10.00 25.00
9 Deion Sanders 2.50 6.00
10 Joey Galloway 1.50 4.00

1997 SkyBox Premium Inside the Numbers

This set is essentially a parallel version of the base 1997 SkyBox Premium cards with a slightly re-designed cardback that includes the words "Inside the Numbers." They were released one per special retail pack.

COMPLETE SET (8) 6.00 15.00
ONE PER SPECIAL RETAIL PACK
1 Brett Favre 2.00 5.00
32 Thurman Thomas .50 1.25
46 Isaac Bruce .50 1.25
47 Chris Warren .30 .75
49 Bruce Smith .30 .75
66 Emmitt Smith 1.50 4.00
98 John Elway 2.00 5.00
140 Reggie White .50 1.25

1997 SkyBox Premium Larger Than Life

Randomly inserted in packs at the rate of one in 360, this 10-card set features color action photos of the players considered to become legends of the NFL.

COMPLETE SET (10) 125.00 250.00
STATED ODDS 1:360
1 Emmitt Smith 15.00 40.00
2 Barry Sanders 15.00 40.00
3 Curtis Martin 6.00 15.00
4 Dan Marino 20.00 50.00
5 Keyshawn Johnson 5.00 12.00
6 Marvin Harrison 5.00 12.00
7 Terry Glenn 5.00 12.00
8 Eddie George 5.00 12.00
9 Brett Favre 20.00 50.00
10 Karim Abdul-Jabbar 5.00 12.00

1997 SkyBox Premium Players

Randomly inserted in packs at the rate of one in 192, this 15-card set features color action photos of the NFL's best showing how they get the job done.

COMPLETE SET (15) 100.00 250.00
STATED ODDS 1:192
1 Eddie George 4.00 10.00
2 Terry Glenn 4.00 10.00
3 Karim Abdul-Jabbar 4.00 10.00
4 Emmitt Smith 12.50 30.00
5 Dan Marino 15.00 40.00
6 Brett Favre 15.00 40.00
7 Keyshawn Johnson 4.00 10.00
8 Curtis Martin 5.00 12.00
9 Marvin Harrison 4.00 10.00
10 Barry Sanders 12.50 30.00
11 Jerry Rice 8.00 20.00
12 Terrell Davis 5.00 12.00
13 Troy Aikman 8.00 20.00
14 Drew Bledsoe 5.00 12.00
15 John Elway 15.00 40.00

1997 SkyBox Premium Prime Time Rookies

Randomly inserted in packs at the rate of one in 96, this 10-card set features color action photos of the rookies that SkyBox predicts will become top players.

COMPLETE SET (10) 30.00 80.00
STATED ODDS 1:96
1 Jim Druckenmiller 2.50 6.00
2 Antowain Smith 10.00 25.00
3 Rae Carruth 1.50 4.00
4 Yatil Green 2.50 6.00
5 Ike Hilliard 5.00 12.00
6 Reidel Anthony 4.00 10.00
7 Orlando Pace 4.00 10.00
8 Peter Boulware 4.00 10.00
9 Warrick Dunn 12.50 30.00
10 Troy Davis 2.50 6.00

1997 SkyBox Premium Reebok

Issued one per pack, these cards are essentially a parallel to 15-different 1997 SkyBox cards featuring the company's spokesmen. The differentiating factor is the Reebok logo on the cardback along with the Reebok website address at the bottom of the cardback. The address was printed in five different colors each with different unannounced insertion ratios: Bronze (easiest to pull), Silver (next easiest), Gold (third easiest), and Red and Green (the toughest two). Therefore, each of the 15-cards has 5-different color variations.

COMP.BRONZE SET (15) 1.25 3.00
*REEBOK GREENS: 25X TO 50X BRONZES
*REEBOK GOLDS: 2X TO 5X BRONZES
*REEBOK REDS: 12.5X TO 25X BRONZES
*REEBOK SILVERS: .8X TO 2X BRONZES
OVERALL REEBOK ODDS ONE PER PACK
12 Keenan McCardell .10 .30
37 Dale Carter .07 .20
38 Ashley Ambrose .07 .20
43 Ben Coates .10 .30
66 Emmitt Smith .40 1.00
95 Karim Abdul-Jabbar .15 .40
98 John Elway .50 1.25
110 Greg Lloyd .07 .20
123 Todd Collins .07 .20
161 Leeland McElroy .07 .20
169 Herman Moore .10 .30
175 Sam Mills .07 .20
180 Irving Fryar .10 .30
202 Ken Norton .07 .20
205 Rodney Hampton .10 .30

1997 SkyBox Premium Rookie Preview

Randomly inserted in packs at the rate of one in six, this 15-card set features color action photos of top 1997 rookies and encapsulates their college highlights.

COMPLETE SET (15) 6.00 15.00
STATED ODDS 1:6
1 Reidel Anthony .60 1.50
2 Tiki Barber 4.00 10.00
3 Peter Boulware .60 1.50
4 Rae Carruth .25 .60
5 Jim Druckenmiller .40 1.00
6 Warrick Dunn 2.00 5.00
7 James Farrior .60 1.50
8 Yatil Green .40 1.00
9 Byron Hanspard .40 1.00
10 Ike Hilliard .75 2.00
11 Orlando Pace .60 1.50
12 Darrell Russell .25 .60
13 Antowain Smith 1.50 4.00
14 Shawn Springs .40 1.00
15 Bryant Westbrook .25 .60

1998 SkyBox Premium

The 1998 SkyBox set was issued in one series totalling 250 cards and was distributed in eight-card packs with a suggested retail price of $2.69. The set features color action player photos highlighted by gold holo-foil stamping on thick 20 pt. card stock. The set contains the topical subsets: One for the Ages (196-210), and Rookies (211-250) seeded 1:4 packs.

COMPLETE SET (250) 30.00 80.00
1 John Elway 1.00 2.50
2 Drew Bledsoe .40 1.00
3 Antonio Freeman .25 .60
4 Merton Hanks .08 .25
5 James Jett .15 .40
6 Ricky Proehl .08 .25
7 Deion Sanders .25 .60
8 Frank Sanders .15 .40
9 Bruce Smith .15 .40
10 Tiki Barber .25 .60
11 Isaac Bruce .25 .60
12 Mark Brunell .25 .60
13 Quinn Early .08 .25
14 Terry Glenn .25 .60
15 Darrien Gordon .08 .25
16 Keith Byars .08 .25
17 Terrell Davis .25 .60
18 Charlie Garner .15 .40
19 Eddie Kennison .15 .40
20 Keenan McCardell .15 .40
21 Eric Moulds .25 .60
22 Jimmy Smith .15 .40
23 Reidel Anthony .15 .40
24 Rae Carruth .08 .25
25 Michael Irvin .25 .60
26 Dorsey Levens .25 .60
27 Derrick Mayes .15 .40
28 Adrian Murrell .15 .40
29 Dwayne Rudd .08 .25
30 Leslie Shepherd .08 .25
31 Jamal Anderson .15 .40
32 Robert Brooks .15 .40
33 Sean Dawkins .08 .25
34 Cris Dishman .08 .25
35 Rickey Dudley .08 .25
36 Bobby Engram .15 .40
37 Chester McGlockton .08 .25
38 Terrell Owens .25 .60
39 Wayne Chrebet .25 .60
40 Dexter Coakley .08 .25
41 Kerry Collins .15 .40
42 Trent Dilfer .25 .60
43 Bobby Hoying .15 .40
44 Glyn Milburn .08 .25
45 Rob Moore .15 .40
46 Jake Reed .15 .40
47 Dana Stubblefield .08 .25
48 Reggie White .25 .60
49 Natrone Means .15 .40
50 Troy Aikman .50 1.25
51 Aaron Bailey .08 .25
52 William Floyd .08 .25
53 Eric Metcalf .08 .25
54 Warrick Dunn .25 .60
55 Chad Lewis .15 .40
56 Curtis Martin .25 .60
57 Tony Martin .15 .40
58 John Randle .15 .40
59 Jeff Burris .08 .25
60 Larry Centers .08 .25
61 Bert Emanuel .15 .40
62 Sean Gilbert .08 .25
63 David Palmer .08 .25
64 Eric Bieniemy .08 .25
65 Peter Boulware .08 .25
66 Charles Johnson .08 .25
67 Jerris McPhail .08 .25
68 Scott Mitchell .15 .40
69 Chris Sanders .08 .25
70 Ken Dilger .08 .25
71 Brad Johnson .25 .60
72 Danny Kanell .15 .40
73 Fred Lane .08 .25
74 Warren Sapp .15 .40
75 Carl Pickens .15 .40
76 Cris Carter .25 .60
77 Marshall Faulk .30 .75
78 Keyshawn Johnson .25 .60
79 Tony McGee .08 .25
80 Muhsin Muhammad .15 .40
81 Kordell Stewart .25 .60
82 Karl Williams .08 .25
83 Willie Davis .08 .25
84 David Dunn .08 .25
85 Marvin Harrison .25 .60
86 Michael Jackson .08 .25
87 John Mobley .08 .25
88 Shawn Springs .08 .25
89 Wesley Walls .15 .40
90 Jermaine Lewis .15 .40
91 Ed McCaffrey .15 .40
92 Chris Calloway .08 .25
93 Lamont Warren .08 .25
94 Ricky Watters .15 .40
95 Tony Banks .15 .40
96 Tony Brackens .08 .25
97 Gary Brown .08 .25
98 Howard Griffith .08 .25
99 Ray Lewis .25 .60
100 Jeff Blake .15 .40
101 Charlie Jones .08 .25
102 Glenn Foley .15 .40
103 Jay Graham .08 .25
104 James McKnight .25 .60
105 Steve McNair .25 .60
106 Chad Scott .08 .25
107 Rod Smith WR .15 .40
108 Jason Taylor .15 .40
109 Corey Dillon .25 .60
110 Eddie George .25 .60
111 Jim Harbaugh .15 .40
112 Warren Moon .25 .60
113 Shannon Sharpe .15 .40
114 Darnell Autry .08 .25
115 Brett Favre 1.25 2.50
116 Jeff George .15 .40
117 Tony Gonzalez .25 .60
118 Garrison Hearst .25 .60
119 Randal Hill .08 .25
120 Eric Swann .08 .25
121 Jamie Asher .08 .25
122 Tim Brown .25 .60
123 Stephen Davis .08 .25
124 Chris Chandler .15 .40
125 Jerry Rice .50 1.25
126 Troy Davis .08 .25
127 Ronnie Harmon .08 .25
128 Andre Rison .15 .40
129 Duce Staley .30 .75
130 Charles Way .08 .25
131 Bryant Westbrook .08 .25
132 Mike Alstott .25 .60
133 Gus Frerotte .08 .25
134 Travis Jervey .15 .40
135 Daryl Johnston .15 .40
136 Jake Plummer .25 .60
137 Junior Seau .25 .60
138 Robert Smith .25 .60
139 Thurman Thomas .25 .60
140 Karim Abdul-Jabbar .25 .60
141 Jerome Bettis .25 .60
142 Byron Hanspard .08 .25
143 Raymont Harris .08 .25
144 Willie McGinest .08 .25
145 Barry Sanders .75 2.00
146 Irv Smith .08 .25
147 Michael Strahan .15 .40
148 Frank Wycheck .08 .25
149 Steve Broussard .08 .25
150 Joey Galloway .15 .40
151 Courtney Hawkins .08 .25
152 O.J. McDuffie .15 .40
153 Herman Moore .15 .40
154 Chris Penn .08 .25
155 O.J. Santiago .08 .25
156 Yancey Thigpen .08 .25
157 Jason Sehorn .15 .40
158 Ben Coates .15 .40
159 Ernie Conwell .08 .25
160 Dale Carter .08 .25
161 Jeff Graham .08 .25
162 Rob Johnson .15 .40
163 Damon Jones .08 .25
164 Mark Chmura .15 .40
165 Curtis Conway .15 .40
166 Elvis Grbac .15 .40
167 Andre Hastings .08 .25
168 Terry Kirby .08 .25
169 Aeneas Williams .08 .25
170 Derrick Alexander WR .15 .40
171 Troy Brown .15 .40
172 Irving Fryar .15 .40
173 Jerald Moore .08 .25
174 Andre Reed .15 .40
175 James Stewart .15 .40
176 Chris Warren .15 .40
177 Will Blackwell .08 .25
178 Erik Kramer .08 .25
179 Dan Marino 1.00 2.50
180 Terance Mathis .15 .40
181 Johnnie Morton .15 .40
182 J.J. Stokes .15 .40
183 Rodney Thomas .08 .25
184 Steve Young .30 .75
185 Kimble Anders .15 .40
186 Napoleon Kaufman .25 .60
187 Orlando Pace .08 .25
188 Antowain Smith .25 .60
189 Emmitt Smith .75 2.00
190 Terry Allen .25 .60
191 Mark Bruener .08 .25
192 Rodney Harrison .15 .40
193 Billy Joe Hobert .08 .25
194 Leon Johnson .08 .25
195 Freddie Jones .08 .25
196 John Elway OFA .40 1.00
197 Brett Favre .30 .75
Atwater OFA
198 Brett Favre .30 .75
Atwater OFA
199 D.Levens .15 .40
Traylor OFA
200 Packers .25 .60
Broncos OFA
201 M.Chmura .08 .25
Braxton OFA
202 Atwater .15 .40
Levens
Roman. OFA
203 R.Brooks .15 .40
R.Crockett OFA
204 Tim McKyer OFA .08 .25
205 Allen Aldridge OFA .08 .25
206 T.Davis .25 .60
R.Smith OFA
207 Bill Romanowski OFA .08 .25
208 Elway .40 1.00
R.Smith
McCaff.OFA
209 Ray Crockett OFA .08 .25
210 John Elway OFA .40 1.00
211 Robert Edwards RC 1.00 2.50
212 Roland Williams RC .75 2.00
213 Joe Jurevicius RC 1.50 4.00
214 Wilmont Perry RC .75 2.00
215 Robert Holcombe RC 1.00 2.50
216 Larry Shannon RC .75 2.00
217 Skip Hicks RC 1.00 2.50
218 Pat Johnson RC 1.00 2.50
219 Pat Palmer RC .75 2.00
220 John Dutton RC .75 2.00
221 Az-Zahir Hakim RC 1.50 4.00
222 Mikhael Ricks RC 1.00 2.50
223 Rashaan Shehee RC 1.00 2.50
224 Ryan Leaf RC 1.50 4.00
225 Alvis Whitted RC 1.00 2.50
226 Marcus Nash RC .75 2.00
227 Fred Taylor RC 2.50 6.00
228 Hines Ward RC 5.00 12.00
229 Chris Fuamatu-Ma'afala RC 1.00 2.50
230 Jerome Pathon RC 1.50 4.00
231 Peyton Manning RC 15.00 40.00
232 Charles Woodson RC 3.00 8.00
233 Jon Ritchie RC 1.00 2.50
234 Scott Frost RC .75 2.00
235 John Avery RC 1.00 2.50
236 Jonathan Linton RC 1.00 2.50
237 Jacquez Green RC 1.00 2.50
238 Andre Wadsworth RC 1.00 2.50
239 Cam Quayle RC .75 2.00
240 Randy Moss RC 6.00 15.00
241 Raymond Priester RC .75 2.00
242 Donald Hayes RC 1.00 2.50
243 Brian Griese RC 3.00 8.00
244 Brian Alford RC .75 2.00
245 Kevin Dyson RC 1.50 4.00
246 Jammi German RC .75 2.00
247 Cameron Cleeland RC .75 2.00
248 Curtis Enis RC .75 2.00
249 Terry Hardy RC .75 2.00
250 Tony Simmons RC 1.00 2.50
NNO Checklist Card .08 .25
P136 Jake Plummer Promo .60 1.50

1998 SkyBox Premium Fleet Farms

COMPLETE SET (250) 90.00 150.00
*STARS: 1.5X TO 4X BASIC CARDS
*ROOKIES: .15X TO .4X BASIC CARDS
ONE PER FLEET FARMS PACK

1998 SkyBox Premium Star Rubies

*RUBY STARS: 25X TO 60X HI COL.
1-210 PRINT RUN 50 SERIAL #'d SETS
*RUBY RCs: 4X TO 10X
211-250 PRINT RUN 35 SERIAL #'d SETS
115 Brett Favre 100.00 200.00
231 Peyton Manning 250.00 400.00

1998 SkyBox Premium Autographics

The Autographics inserts were distributed across the line of 1998 SkyBox football products and included 73 different cards. The cards were inserted in E-X2001 packs at the rate of 1:48, Metal Universe at 1:68, SkyBox Premium at 1:68, and SkyBox thunder at 1:112. This set features borderless color player portraits with the player's signature in black across the bottom. A blue ink parallel version was also produced with a print run of 50 sets. 23 of the players also had special retail redemption cards with an expiration date of April 30, 1999. A Peyton Manning card appeared on the secondary market much later and could have been released sometime after Fleer closed and sold off inventroy remainders. The Manning card was never inserted into packs and it is not yet certain whether the card was released signed or unsigned. However, a very small number of legitimate signed copies of the card can be found on the secondary market.

ODDS: 1:48 E-X2001/1:68 METAL UNIVERSE
1:68 SKYBOX PREMIUM/1:112 SKY.THUNDER
*BLUE SIGS/50: .8X TO 2X BASIC AU
BLUE SIGNATURES PRINT RUN 50 SETS
1 Kevin Abrams S/ST 4.00 10.00
2 Mike Alstott MU/S 15.00 40.00
3 Jamie Asher MU/S/ST* 4.00 10.00
4 John Avery S 6.00 15.00
5 Tavian Banks MU/S/ST* 6.00 15.00
6 Pat Barnes MU/ST 4.00 10.00
7 Jerome Bettis MU/S* 50.00 100.00
8 Eric Bjornson MU/S* 4.00 10.00
9 Peter Boulware MU/ST* 4.00 10.00
10 Troy Brown MU/S/ST 10.00 25.00
11 Mark Bruener MU/S* 4.00 10.00
12 Mark Brunell MU/ST* 12.50 30.00
13 Rae Carruth MU/S/ST 4.00 10.00
14 Ray Crockett S/ST* 4.00 10.00
15 Germane Crowell S/ST 6.00 15.00
16 Stephen Davis MU/S* 10.00 25.00
17 Troy Davis MU/ST 4.00 10.00
18 Sean Dawkins MU/ST 4.00 10.00
19 Trent Dilfer S/ST 10.00 25.00
20 Corey Dillon MU/S 8.00 20.00
21 Jim Druckenmiller S/ST 4.00 10.00
22 Kevin Dyson MU/S/ST 6.00 15.00
23 Marc Edwards S/ST 4.00 10.00
24 Robert Edwards S/ST 6.00 15.00
25 Bobby Engram MU/S/ST 6.00 15.00
26 Curtis Enis S/ST 4.00 10.00
27 William Floyd MU/ST 6.00 15.00
28 Glenn Foley MU/ST 6.00 15.00
29 Chris Fuamatu-Ma'afala MU/S/ST* 6.00 15.00
30 Joey Galloway MU/S/ST* 6.00 15.00
31 Jeff George MU/ST 10.00 25.00
32 Ahman Green S/ST 20.00 50.00
33 Jacquez Green S/ST 6.00 15.00
34 Yatil Green MU/S/ST 4.00 10.00
35 Byron Hanspard MU/S* 4.00 10.00
36 Marvin Harrison MU/S* 15.00 30.00
37 Skip Hicks S/ST 6.00 15.00
38 Robert Holcombe MU/S 6.00 15.00
39 Bobby Hoying MU/S 6.00 15.00
40 Travis Jervey MU/S/ST 4.00 10.00
41 Rob Johnson MU/S 6.00 15.00
42 Freddie Jones MU/S/ST 4.00 10.00
43 Eddie Kennison S/ST 6.00 15.00
44 Fred Lane MU/S 10.00 25.00
45 Ryan Leaf EX 6.00 15.00
46 Dorsey Levens MU/ST 6.00 15.00
47 Jeff Lewis S 4.00 10.00
48 Jermaine Lewis MU/ST 6.00 15.00
49 Dan Marino S 75.00 150.00
50 Curtis Martin MU/S/ST* 20.00 50.00
51 Steve Matthews MU/ST 4.00 10.00
52 Alonzo Mayes S/ST 4.00 10.00
53 Keenan McCardell MU/ST* 6.00 15.00
54 Willie McGinest S/ST* 10.00 25.00
55 James McKnight S 6.00 15.00
56 Glyn Milburn MU/ST* 4.00 10.00
57 Randy Moss MU/ST 125.00 200.00
58 Marcus Nash MU/S/ST 4.00 10.00
59 Terrell Owens S/ST* 20.00 40.00
60 Jason Peter S/ST 4.00 10.00
61 Jake Plummer MU 10.00 25.00
62 John Randle MU/ST 10.00 25.00
63 Shannon Sharpe MU/S* 15.00 40.00
64 Jimmy Smith MU/ST 6.00 15.00
65 Robert Smith MU/ST 6.00 15.00
66 Duce Staley MU/S 10.00 25.00
67 Kordell Stewart S* 10.00 25.00
68 Fred Taylor MU/S/ST 10.00 25.00
69 Rodney Thomas MU/S/ST* 4.00 10.00
70 Kevin Turner MU/S/ST 4.00 10.00
71 Hines Ward MU/S/ST* 15.00 40.00
72 Charles Way MU/S* 4.00 10.00
73 Frank Wycheck MU/ST 4.00 10.00
74 Peyton Manning SP
(unsigned release after Fleer closed)
NNO E-X2001 Checklist Card .02 .10
NNO Premium Checklist Card .02 .10
NNO Premium Retail Checklist .02 .10

1998 SkyBox Premium D'stroyers

Randomly inserted into packs at the rate of one in six, this 15-card set features color action photos of top young stars printed on prismatic foil cards.

COMPLETE SET (15) 12.50 30.00
STATED ODDS 1:6
1D Antowain Smith .60 1.50
2D Corey Dillon 1.00 2.50
3D Charles Woodson 1.00 2.50
4D Randy Moss 3.00 8.00
5D Deion Sanders 1.00 2.50
6D Robert Edwards .30 .75
7D Herman Moore .30 .75
8D Mark Brunell 1.00 2.50
9D Dorsey Levens .30 .75
10D Curtis Enis .30 .75
11D Drew Bledsoe 1.50 4.00
12D Steve McNair 1.00 2.50
13D Keyshawn Johnson .60 1.50
14D Bobby Hoying .30 .75
15D Trent Dilfer .60 1.50

1998 SkyBox Premium Intimidation Nation

Randomly inserted into packs at the rate of one in 360, this 15-card set features color player head photots printed on gold holo-foiled background and silver foil-stamped cards.

COMPLETE SET (15) 125.00 250.00
STATED ODDS 1:360
1IN Terrell Davis 4.00 10.00
2IN Emmitt Smith 8.00 20.00
3IN Barry Sanders 10.00 25.00
4IN Brett Favre 10.00 25.00
5IN Eddie George 4.00 10.00
6IN Jerry Rice 8.00 20.00
7IN John Elway 15.00 40.00
8IN Mark Brunell 4.00 10.00
9IN Troy Aikman 8.00 20.00
10IN Peyton Manning 40.00 100.00
11IN Ryan Leaf 4.00 10.00
12IN Curtis Martin 4.00 10.00
13IN Dan Marino 15.00 40.00
14IN Warrick Dunn 4.00 10.00
15IN Jake Plummer 4.00 10.00

1998 SkyBox Premium Prime Time Rookies

Randomly inserted into packs at the rate of one in 96, this 10-card set features color photos of top rookies printed on horizontal cards with "TV color Bars" and the Prime Time Rookies logo with matte silver-foil stamping.

COMPLETE SET (10) 60.00 120.00
STATED ODDS 1:96
1PT Curtis Enis 2.00 5.00
2PT Robert Edwards 3.00 8.00
3PT Fred Taylor 4.00 10.00
4PT Robert Holcombe 3.00 8.00
5PT Ryan Leaf 4.00 10.00
6PT Peyton Manning 15.00 40.00
7PT Randy Moss 10.00 25.00
8PT Charles Woodson 6.00 15.00
9PT Andre Wadsworth 3.00 8.00
10PT Kevin Dyson 4.00 10.00

1998 SkyBox Premium Rap Show

Randomly inserted in packs at the rate of one in 36, this 15-card set features color photos of the star players everyone is talking about printed on silver foil cards with a silver foil-stamped quote from one of his peers.

COMPLETE SET (15) 30.00 60.00
STATED ODDS 1:36
1 John Elway 5.00 12.00
2 Drew Bledsoe 2.00 5.00
3 Corey Dillon 1.25 3.00
4 Brett Favre 5.00 12.00
5 Barry Sanders 4.00 10.00
6 Eddie George 1.25 3.00
7 Emmitt Smith 4.00 10.00
8 Jake Plummer 1.25 3.00
9 Joey Galloway .75 2.00
10 Ricky Watters .75 2.00
11 Mike Alstott 1.25 3.00
12 Kordell Stewart 1.25 3.00
13 Antonio Freeman 1.25 3.00
14 Terrell Davis 1.25 3.00
15 Warrick Dunn 1.25 3.00

1998 SkyBox Premium Soul of the Game

Randomly inserted in packs at the rate of one in 18, this 15-card set features black-and-white photos of some of the NFL's best veterans presented in a unique die-cut around the shape of a record album emerging from the album sleeve.

COMPLETE SET (15) 15.00 30.00
STATED ODDS 1:18
1 Troy Aikman 2.00 5.00
2 Dorsey Levens 1.00 2.50
3 Deion Sanders 1.00 2.50
4 Antonio Freeman 1.00 2.50
5 Dan Marino 4.00 10.00
6 Keyshawn Johnson 1.00 2.50
7 Terry Glenn 1.00 2.50
8 Tim Brown 1.00 2.50
9 Curtis Martin 1.00 2.50
10 Bobby Hoying .60 1.50
11 Kordell Stewart 1.00 2.50
12 Jerry Rice 2.00 5.00
13 Steve McNair 1.00 2.50
14 Joey Galloway .60 1.50
15 Steve Young 1.25 3.00

1999 SkyBox Premium

Issued in late October of 1999, This set contained 210 veteran player cards with 40 rookie cards also availble. The rookie cards were available in two forms a regular issue which featured a head shot non action photo and a short printed version with a full player action shot which was inserted 1 in 8 packs. Also randomly inserted were the Autographics cross brand insert of hand signed autographs at a rate of 1 in 68 packs. Boxes contained 24 packs with 8 cards per pack.

COMPLETE SET (290) 150.00 300.00
COMP.SET w/o SPs (250) 25.00 50.00
1 Randy Moss .20 .50
2 Jamie Asher .15 .40
3 Joey Galloway .20 .50
4 Kent Graham .15 .40
5 Leslie Shepherd .15 .40
6 Levon Kirkland .15 .40
7 Marcus Pollard .15 .40
8 O.J. McDuffie .20 .50
9 Bill Romanowski .20 .50
10 Priest Holmes .15 .40
11 Tim Biakabutuka .20 .50
12 Duce Staley .15 .40
13 Isaac Bruce .25 .60
14 Jay Riemersma .15 .40
15 Karim Abdul-Jabbar .15 .40
16 Kevin Dyson .15 .40
17 Rickey Dudley .15 .40
18 Rocket Ismail .20 .50
19 Billy Davis .15 .40
20 James Jett .15 .40
21 Jerome Bettis .25 .60
22 Michael McCrary .15 .40
23 Michael Westbrook .15 .40
24 Oronde Gadsden .15 .40
25 Brad Johnson .20 .50
26 Shawn Springs .15 .40
27 Cris Carter .25 .60
28 Ed McCaffrey .20 .50
29 Gary Brown .15 .40
30 Hines Ward .20 .50
31 Hugh Douglas .20 .50
32 Jamir Miller .15 .40
33 Michael Bates .15 .40
34 Peyton Manning .75 2.00
35 Tony Banks .20 .50
36 Charles Way .15 .40
37 Charlie Batch .15 .40
38 Jake Reed .20 .50
39 Mark Brunell .20 .50
40 Skip Hicks .15 .40
41 Steve Young .30 .75
42 Wesley Walls .20 .50
43 Antonio Langham .15 .40
44 Antowain Smith .15 .40
45 Brian Griese .15 .40
46 Jessie Armstead .20 .50
47 Thurman Thomas .20 .50
48 Jeff George .15 .40
49 Jessie Tuggle .15 .40
50 Jim Harbaugh .20 .50
51 Marvin Harrison .20 .50
52 Randall Cunningham .20 .50
53 Stephen Alexander .15 .40
54 Tiki Barber .20 .50
55 Billy Joe Tolliver .15 .40
56 Bruce Smith .20 .50
57 Eddie George .20 .50
58 Eugene Robinson .20 .50
59 John Elway .40 1.00
60 Kent Dilger .15 .40
61 Rodney Harrison .15 .40
62 Ty Detmer .15 .40
63 Andre Reed .25 .60
64 Dorsey Levens .20 .50
65 Eddie Kennison .20 .50
66 Freddie Jones .15 .40
67 Jacquez Green .15 .40
68 Jason Elam .15 .40
69 Marc Edwards .20 .50
70 Terance Mathis .15 .40
71 Alonzo Mayes .15 .40
72 Andre Wadsworth .15 .40
73 Barry Sanders .40 1.00
74 Derrick Alexander .15 .40
75 Garrison Hearst .15 .40
76 Leon Johnson .15 .40
77 Mike Alstott .15 .40
78 Shawn Jefferson .15 .40
79 Andre Hastings .15 .40
80 Eric Moulds .15 .40
81 Ryan Leaf .20 .50
82 Takeo Spikes .15 .40
83 Terrell Davis .20 .50
84 Tim Dwight .20 .50
85 Trent Dilfer .15 .40
86 Vonnie Holliday .15 .40
87 Antonio Freeman .20 .50
88 Carl Pickens .20 .50
89 Chris Chandler .20 .50
90 Dale Carter .15 .40
91 La'Roi Glover RC .40 1.00
92 Natrone Means .20 .50
93 Reidel Anthony .15 .40
94 Brett Favre .50 1.25
95 Bubby Brister .15 .40
96 Cameron Cleeland .15 .40
97 Chris Calloway .15 .40
98 Corey Dillon .15 .40
99 Greg Hill .15 .40
100 Vinny Testaverde .15 .40
101 Trent Green .15 .40
102 Sam Gash .15 .40
103 Mikhael Ricks .15 .40
104 Emmitt Smith .40 1.00
105 Doug Flutie .25 .60
106 Deion Sanders .20 .50
107 Charles Johnson .15 .40
108 Byron Bam Morris .15 .40
109 Andre Rison .20 .50
110 Doug Pederson .15 .40
111 Marshall Faulk .20 .50
112 Tim Brown .25 .60
113 Warren Sapp .20 .50
114 Bryan Still .15 .40
115 Chris Penn .15 .40
116 Jamal Anderson .20 .50
117 Keyshawn Johnson .20 .50
118 Ricky Proehl .15 .40
119 Robert Brooks .20 .50
120 Tony Gonzalez .20 .50
121 Ty Law .25 .60
122 Elvis Grbac .15 .40
123 Jeff Blake .20 .50
124 Mark Chmura .15 .40
125 Junior Seau .20 .50
126 Mo Lewis .15 .40
127 Ray Buchanan .15 .40
128 Robert Holcombe .15 .40
129 Tony Simmons .15 .40
130 David Palmer .15 .40
131 Ike Hilliard .15 .40
132 Mike Vanderjagt .15 .40
133 Rae Carruth .15 .40
134 Sean Dawkins .15 .40
135 Shannon Sharpe .20 .50
136 Curtis Conway .20 .50
137 Darrell Green .25 .60
138 Germane Crowell .15 .40
139 J.J. Stokes .15 .40
140 Kevin Hardy .15 .40
141 Rob Moore .15 .40
142 Robert Smith .15 .40
143 Wayne Chrebet .15 .40
144 Yancey Thigpen .15 .40
145 Jerome Pathon .15 .40
146 John Mobley .15 .40
147 Kerry Collins .15 .40
148 Peter Boulware .15 .40
149 Matthew Hatchette .20 .50
150 Kordell Stewart .15 .40
151 Koy Detmer .15 .40
152 Sedrick Shaw .15 .40
153 Steve Beuerlein .20 .50
154 Zach Thomas .20 .50
155 Adrian Murrell .15 .40
156 Bobby Engram .15 .40
157 Bryan Cox .20 .50
158 Drew Bledsoe .20 .50
159 Jerry Rice .60 1.50
160 Keenan McCardell .20 .50
161 Steve McNair .20 .50
162 Terry Fair .15 .40
163 Derrick Brooks .25 .60
164 Eric Green .15 .40
165 Erik Kramer .20 .50
166 Frank Sanders .15 .40
167 Fred Taylor .15 .40
168 Johnnie Morton .20 .50
169 R.W. McQuarters .15 .40
170 Terry Glenn .20 .50
171 Frank Wycheck .20 .50
172 John Avery .15 .40
173 Kevin Turner .15 .40
174 Larry Centers .15 .40
175 Michael Irvin .25 .60
176 Rich Gannon .20 .50
177 Ricky Watters .20 .50
178 Rodney Thomas .15 .40
179 Scott Mitchell .15 .40
180 Chad Brown .15 .40
181 John Randle .25 .60
182 Michael Strahan .20 .50
183 Muhsin Muhammad .15 .40
184 Reggie Barlow .15 .40
185 Rod Smith .20 .50
186 Dan Marino .50 1.25
187 Dexter Coakley .15 .40
188 Jermaine Lewis .15 .40
189 Jon Kitna .15 .40
190 Napoleon Kaufman .15 .40
191 Will Blackwell .15 .40
192 Aaron Glenn .15 .40
193 Ben Coates .20 .50
194 Curtis Enis .15 .40
195 Herman Moore .20 .50
196 Jake Plummer .15 .40
197 Jimmy Smith .20 .50
198 Terrell Owens .20 .50
199 Warrick Dunn .15 .40
200 Charles Woodson .25 .60
201 Ahman Green .20 .50
202 Mark Bruener .15 .40
203 Ray Lewis .25 .60
204 Tony Martin .20 .50
205 Troy Aikman .30 .75
206 Curtis Martin .20 .50
207 Darnay Scott .15 .40
208 Derrick Mayes .15 .40
209 Keith Poole .15 .40
210 Warren Moon .25 .60
211 Chris Claiborne RC .25 .60
211S Chris Claiborne SP .60 1.50
212 Ricky Williams RC .40 1.00
212S Ricky Williams SP 1.00 2.50
213 Tim Couch RC .30 .75
213S Tim Couch SP .75 2.00
214 Champ Dailey RC .50 1.25
214S Champ Bailey SP 1.25 3.00
215 Torry Holt RC .50 1.25
215S Torry Holt SP 1.25 3.00
216 Donovan McNabb RC 1.50 4.00
216S Donovan McNabb SP 4.00 10.00
217 David Boston RC .25 .60
217S David Boston SP .60 1.50
218 Chris McAlister RC .25 .60
218S Chris McAlister SP .60 1.50
219 Michael Bishop RC .30 .75
219S Michael Bishop SP .75 2.00
220 Daunte Culpepper RC .40 1.00
220S Daunte Culpepper SP 1.00 2.50
221 Joe Germaine RC .30 .75
221S Joe Germaine SP .75 2.00
222 Edgerrin James RC .40 1.00
222S Edgerrin James SP 1.00 2.50
223 Jevon Kearse RC .30 .75
223S Jevon Kearse SP .75 2.00
224 Ebenezer Ekuban RC .25 .60
224S Ebenezer Ekuban SP .60 1.50
225 Scott Covington RC .25 .60
225S Scott Covington SP .60 1.50
226 Aaron Brooks RC .30 .75
226S Aaron Brooks SP .75 2.00
227 Cecil Collins RC .25 .60
227S Cecil Collins SP .60 1.50
228 Akili Smith RC .25 .60
228S Akili Smith SP .60 1.50
229 Shaun King RC .25 .60
229S Shaun King SP .60 1.50
230 Chad Plummer RC .25 .60
230S Chad Plummer SP .60 1.50
231 Peerless Price RC .25 .60
231S Peerless Price SP .60 1.50
232 Antoine Winfield RC .25 .60
232S Antoine Winfield SP .60 1.50
233 Antuan Edwards RC .25 .60
233S Antuan Edwards SP .60 1.50
234 Rob Konrad RC .25 .60
234S Rob Konrad SP .60 1.50
235 Troy Edwards RC .25 .60
235S Troy Edwards SP .60 1.50
236 Terry Jackson RC .25 .60
236S Terry Jackson SP .60 1.50
237 Jim Kleinsasser RC .40 1.00
237S Jim Kleinsasser SP 1.00 2.50
238 Joe Montgomery RC .25 .60
238S Joe Montgomery SP .60 1.50
239 Desmond Clark RC .30 .75
239S Desmond Clark SP .75 2.00
240 Lamar King RC .25 .60
240S Lamar King SP .60 1.50
241 Dameane Douglas RC .25 .60
241S Dameane Douglas SP .60 1.50
242 Martin Gramatica RC .25 .60
242S Martin Gramatica SP .60 1.50
243 Jim Finn RC .25 .60
243S Jim Finn SP .60 1.50
244 Andy Katzenmoyer RC .30 .75
244S Andy Katzenmoyer SP .75 2.00
245 Dee Miller RC .25 .60
245S Dee Miller SP .60 1.50
246 D'Wayne Bates RC .25 .60
246S D'Wayne Bates SP .60 1.50
247 Amos Zereoue RC .25 .60
247S Amos Zereoue SP .60 1.50
248 Karsten Bailey RC .25 .60
248S Karsten Bailey SP .60 1.50
249 Kevin Johnson RC .30 .75
249S Kevin Johnson SP .75 2.00
250 Cade McNown RC .25 .60
250S Cade McNown SP .60 1.50

1999 SkyBox Premium Shining Star Rubies

*RUBY VETS/30: 30X TO 80X BASIC CARDS
*RUBY ROOKIES/30: 10X TO 25X
*RUBY SINGLES/15: 4X TO 10X BASE CI's

1999 SkyBox Premium 2000 Men

Randomly inserted in packs, This 15 card insert set features Stars who will make an impact well into the new millenium. Star include such players as Randy Moss, Peyton Manning, and Warrick Dunn. Cards are individually serial numbered to 100 of each card made.

COMPLETE SET (15) 150.00 400.00
STATED PRINT RUN 100 SER.#'d SETS
1TM Warrick Dunn 8.00 20.00
2TM Tim Couch 3.00 8.00
3TM Fred Taylor 8.00 20.00
4TM Jake Plummer 5.00 12.00
5TM Jerry Rice 15.00 40.00
6TM Edgerrin James 12.50 30.00
7TM Mark Brunell 8.00 20.00
8TM Peyton Manning 25.00 60.00
9TM Randy Moss 20.00 50.00
10TM Terrell Davis 12.00 30.00
11TM Charlie Batch 8.00 20.00
12TM Dan Marino 25.00 60.00
13TM Emmitt Smith 15.00 40.00
14TM Brett Favre 25.00 60.00
15TM Barry Sanders 25.00 60.00

1999 SkyBox Premium Autographics

Randomly inserted in Hobby packs at a rate of 1 in 68 and 1 in 90 for the retail version packs, These Cards are hand signed on the front of each. The Autographics are a cross brand autographed insert set. Key players found within Skybox Premium Packs include Randy Moss, Ricky Williams and Akili Smith.

STATED ODDS 1:68H, 1:90R
*RED FOIL STARS: 1X TO 2.5X BASIC AUTOS
*RED FOIL ROOKIES: .8X TO 2X BASIC AUTOS
RED FOIL STATED PRINT RUN 50 SER.#'d SETS
1 St.Alexander EX/MM/MU/S 5.00 12.00
2 Mike Alstott D/EX/S 12.50 30.00
3 C.Bailey D/EX/MM/MU/S 20.00 40.00
4 Karsten Bailey EX/MM/MU/S 5.00 12.00
5 Charlie Batch EX/MM/MU/S 7.50 20.00
6 D.Bates D/EX/MM/MU/S 5.00 12.00
7 Michael Bishop D/EX/MM/S 7.50 20.00
8 Dre Bly D/EX/MM/MU/S 7.50 20.00
9 David Boston D/EX/MM/S 12.50 30.00
10 Gary Brown D/EX/MM/S 5.00 12.00
11 Na Brown D/EX/MM/S 5.00 12.00
12 Tim Brown D/EX/MM/S 12.50 30.00
13 Troy Brown EX/MM/MU/S 12.50 30.00
14 M.Bruener D/EX/MM/MU/S 5.00 12.00
15 Mark Brunell D/EX/MM/S 7.50 20.00
16 Shawn Bryson EX 5.00 12.00
17 W.Chrebet EX/MM/MU/S 12.50 30.00
18 Chris Claiborne D/EX/MM/S 5.00 12.00
19 C.Cleeland D/EX/MM/MU/S 5.00 12.00
20 Cecil Collins D/EX/MM/S 5.00 12.00
21 D.Culpepper D/EX/MM 15.00 40.00
22 Cunningham D/EX/MM 12.50 30.00
23 Terrell Davis EX/MU/S 15.00 40.00
24 Ty Detmer D/EX/MM/S 5.00 12.00
25 J.DeVries D/EX/MM/MU/S 5.00 12.00
26 Troy Edwards D/EX/MM/S 5.00 12.00
27 Kevin Faulk D/EX/MM/S 7.50 20.00
28 Marshall Faulk D/EX/MM/S 15.00 40.00
29 Doug Flutie EX/MM/MU/S 12.50 30.00
30 Oronde Gadsden MU/S 7.50 20.00
31 Joey Galloway D/EX/MM/S 7.50 20.00
32 Eddie George D/MM/S 12.50 30.00
33 M.Gramatica EX/MM/MU/S 5.00 12.00
34 Anthony Gray MM/MU/S 5.00 12.00
35 Ahman Green D/EX/MM/S 12.50 30.00
36 Brian Griese D/EX/MM/S 12.50 30.00
37 H.Griffith EX/MM/MU/S 5.00 12.00
38 M.Harrison MM/MU/S 12.00 30.00
39 C.Hawkins D/MM/MU/S 5.00 12.00
40 V.Holliday D/EX/MM/MU/S 5.00 12.00
41 Priest Holmes MM 12.50 30.00
42 Torry Holt D/EX/MM 12.50 30.00
43 Sedrick Irvin D/S 5.00 12.00
44 Edg.James D/EX/MM/MU 25.00 50.00
45 Patrick Jeffers D/MU/S 5.00 12.00
46 James Johnson D/MM/S 5.00 12.00
47 Kevin Johnson D/EX/MM/S 7.50 20.00
48 Freddie Jones D/EX/MM/S 5.00 12.00
49 Jevon Kearse D/EX/MM/S 12.50 30.00
50 Shaun King D/EX/MM/S 5.00 12.00
51 Jon Kitna EX/MM/MU/S 7.50 20.00
52 Rob Konrad D/EX/MM/S 5.00 12.00
53 Dorsey Levens MU/S 7.50 20.00
54 Peyton Manning D/EX/MM 75.00 150.00
55 D.McDonald D/EX/MM/MU/S 5.00 12.00
56 Don.McNabb D/EX/MM/S 20.00 50.00
57 Cade McNown D/EX/MM/S 5.00 12.00
58 Eric Moss D/MM/S 5.00 12.00
59 Randy Moss EX/MM/S 40.00 80.00
60 Eric Moulds EX/MM/S 7.50 20.00
61 Marcus Nash EX/MM/MU/S 5.00 12.00
62 Terrell Owens D/EX/MM 15.00 40.00
63 J.Pathon EX/MM/MU/S 5.00 12.00
64 Jake Plummer D/EX/MM 12.50 30.00
65 Peerless Price EX/MM 12.50 30.00
66 M.Ricks D/EX/MM/MU/S 5.00 12.00
67 F.Sanders EX/MM/MU/S 5.00 12.00
68 T.Simmons D/EX/MM/MU/S 5.00 12.00
69 Akili Smith D/S 5.00 12.00
70 Ant.Smith EX/MM/MU/S 7.50 20.00
71 L.C. Stevens D/EX/MM/S 5.00 12.00
72 M.Strahan EX/MM/MU/S 25.00 50.00
73 T.Streets D/EX/MM/MU/S 7.50 20.00
74 Fred Taylor MM 12.50 30.00
75 Lamar Thomas EX/MM 5.00 12.00
76 Jerame Tuman D/EX/MM/S 12.50 30.00
77 K.Turner D/EX/MM/MU/S 5.00 12.00
78 Kurt Warner MM 50.00 100.00
79 T.Wheatley D/EX/MM/MU/S 7.50 20.00
80 Ricky Williams D/EX/MM/S 12.50 30.00
81 F.Wycheck D/EX/MM/MU/S 5.00 12.00
82 A.Zereoue EX/MM/MU/S 7.50 20.00
CL1 Dominion CL .02 .10
CL2 E-X Century CL .02 .10
CL3 Metal Universe CL .02 .10
CL4 Premium CL .02 .10

1999 SkyBox Premium Box Tops

Randomly inserted in packs at a rate of 1 in 12, This insert set features players done with a color action shot fetauring the team logo set in the Background. Key players found within the set include Randy Moss, Emmitt Smith, and Brett Favre.

COMPLETE SET (15) 20.00 40.00
STATED ODDS 1:12
1BT Terrell Davis .75 2.00
2BT Troy Aikman 1.50 4.00
3BT Peyton Manning 2.50 6.00
4BT Mark Brunell .75 2.00
5BT Eddie George .75 2.00
6BT Corey Dillon .75 2.00
7BT Dan Marino 2.50 6.00
8BT Brett Favre 2.50 6.00
9BT Barry Sanders 2.50 6.00
10BT Emmitt Smith 1.50 4.00
11BT Fred Taylor .75 2.00
12BT Jerry Rice 1.50 4.00
13BT Jamal Anderson .75 2.00
14BT Joey Galloway .50 1.25
15BT Randy Moss 2.00 5.00

1999 SkyBox Premium DejaVu

Randomly inserted in packs at a rate of 1 in 36 packs, This 15 card insert set features a dual player format showing a current rookie with a veteran player whom were both selected the same pick in the NFL draft.

COMPLETE SET (15) 25.00 50.00
STATED ODDS 1:36
*DIE CUT/99: 2X TO 5X HI COL.
DIE CUTS PRINT RUN 99 SER.#'d SETS

1DV A.Smith 3.00 8.00
B.Sanders
2DV C.McNown .75 2.00
W.Dunn
3DV C.Collins .60 1.50
J.McPhail
4DV C.Bailey .75 2.00
C.Conway
5DV D.Culpepper 2.00 5.00
M.Irvin
6DV D.Boston .75 2.00
T.Biakabutuka
7DV D.McNabb 2.50 6.00
M.Faulk
8DV E.James 2.00 5.00
M.Westbrook
9DV K.Faulk .75 2.00
J.Kent
10DV K.Johnson .75 2.00
J.Pathon
11DV R.Williams 1.00 2.50
D.Sanders
12DV S.King .60 1.50
G.Crowell
13DV T.Couch 3.00 8.00
T.Aikman
14DV T.Holt 1.50 4.00
T.Brown
15DV T.Edwards .60 1.50
E.Metcalf

1999 SkyBox Premium Genuine Coverage

Randomly inserted in packs, These cards have an actual piece of NFL game worn jersey swatch on the card front. Cards are individually hand numbered on card front to a specific amount of swatches made for each individual player. Key stars found within the set include Randy Moss, Brett Favre, and Drew Bledsoe.

COMPLETE SET (6) 75.00 150.00
*MULTI-COLORED SWATCHES: .6X TO 1.5X
1GC Mark Brunell/420 10.00 25.00
2GC Randy Moss/265 15.00 40.00
3GC Herman Moore/400 7.50 20.00
4GC Brett Favre/410 20.00 50.00
5GC Randall Cunningham/425 7.50 20.00
6GC Drew Bledsoe/440 12.50 30.00

1999 SkyBox Premium Prime Time Rookies

Randomly inserted in packs at a rate of 1 in 96, This 15 card insert set whch features key rookie players such as Tim Couch and Ricky Williams done on a clear platic card stock with a silver holo foil stamping.

COMPLETE SET (15) 75.00 150.00
STATED ODDS 1:96
1PR Ricky Williams 4.00 10.00
2PR Tim Couch 2.00 5.00
3PR Edgerrin James 8.00 20.00
4PR Daunte Culpepper 8.00 20.00
5PR David Boston 2.00 5.00
6PR Akili Smith .75 2.00
7PR Cecil Collins .75 2.00
8PR Cade McNown 1.25 3.00
9PR Torry Holt 5.00 12.00
10PR Donovan McNabb 10.00 25.00
11PR Kevin Johnson .75 2.00
12PR Shaun King .75 2.00
13PR Champ Bailey 2.50 6.00
14PR Troy Edwards 1.25 3.00
15PR Kevin Faulk 1.25 3.00

1999 SkyBox Premium Prime Time Rookies Autographs

These cards are a parallel of the regular Prime Time Rookies insert set. They were limited to a print run of 25 cards each. Tim Couch was the only player not to sign for the set. Cards were signed and hand numbered to 25 on card front for each respective player.

STATED PRINT RUN 25 SERIAL #'d SETS
1PR Ricky Williams 50.00 120.00
3PR Edgerrin James 50.00 120.00
5PR David Boston 30.00 80.00
6PR Akili Smith 25.00 60.00
7PR Cecil Collins 20.00 50.00
8PR Cade McNown 25.00 60.00
9PR Torry Holt 75.00 150.00
10PR Donovan McNabb 125.00 250.00
11PR Kevin Johnson 25.00 60.00
12PR Shaun King 25.00 60.00
14PR Troy Edwards 20.00 50.00
15PR Kevin Faulk 30.00 80.00

1999 SkyBox Premium Year 2

Randomly inserted in packs at the rate of one in six, this 15-card set features 1998 rookies on a card that evaluates their rookie performances.

COMPLETE SET (15) 6.00 15.00
STATED ODDS 1:6
1Y2 Ahman Green .60 1.50
2Y2 Terry Fair .25 .60
3Y2 Charlie Batch .60 1.50
4Y2 Ryan Leaf .60 1.50
5Y2 Skip Hicks .25 .60
6Y2 John Avery .25 .60
7Y2 Charles Woodson .60 1.50
8Y2 Jacquez Green .25 .60
9Y2 Kevin Dyson .40 1.00
10Y2 Marcus Nash .40 1.00
11Y2 Robert Holcombe .25 .60
12Y2 Germane Crowell .25 .60
13Y2 Curtis Enis .25 .60
14Y2 Tim Dwight .60 1.50
15Y2 Brian Griese .60 1.50

1992 SkyBox Prime Time Previews

This five-card standard-size set was issued in cello packs to provide collectors with samples of SkyBox's Prime Time series. The fronts feature cut-out action color player photos superimposed on a computer generated gray background accented with a row of thin black lines. The player's name is printed across the top. The player's jersey number is team color-coded while his team name is printed vertically in a team color-coded bar along the edge of the card. For example, the Elway card has a Broncos "purple" background featuring the picture of a horse. The backs display action color player photos on the upper half of the card. Biographical information, statistics, and career highlights appear below a team color-coded stripe on a white background. Except for the title card, the cards are numbered on the back at the upper right corner.

COMPLETE SET (5) 4.00 10.00
A Jerry Rice 1.20 3.00
B Deion Sanders .60 1.50
C John Elway 2.40 6.00
D Vaughn Dunbar .20 .50
NNO Title Card .20 .50

1992 SkyBox Prime Time

The 1992 SkyBox Prime Time football set consists of 360 standard-size cards. The cards were issued in 12-card packs. . The player's jersey number is team color-coded while his team name is printed vertically in a team color-coded bar along the edge of the card. The cards of rookies, including many in their NFL uniforms, have the round and the draft pick number on their fronts. The backs display action color player photos on the upper half of the card. Team MVP's (four of them without player photos) and Costacos Poster Art cards (PC) are scattered throughout the set. There are five uncorrected errors involving misnumbered cards: see card numbers 38, 61, 138, 216, and 267. Rookie Cards include Edgar Bennett, Robert Brooks, Terrell Buckley, Robert Brooks, Dale Carter, Marco Coleman, Quentin Coryatt, Steve Emtman and Carl Pickens. Randomly inserted in packs and listed at the end of the checklist below are a Jim Kelly hologram card (H1) and a Steve Emtman Horse-Power card (S1).

COMPLETE SET (360) 10.00 25.00
1 Deion Sanders .40 1.00
2A Shane Collins UER RC .02 .10
2B Sean Lumpkin UER RC .02 .10
3 James Patton RC .02 .10
4 Reggie Roby .02 .10
5 Merril Hoge .02 .10
6 Vinny Testaverde .07 .20
7 Boomer Esiason .07 .20
8 Troy Aikman .75 2.00
9 Tommy Jeter RC .02 .10
10 Brent Williams .02 .10
11 Mark Rypien .02 .10
12 Jim Kelly .15 .40
13 Dan Marino 1.25 3.00
14 Bill Cowher CO RC .30 .75
15 Leslie O'Neal .07 .20
16 Joe Montana 1.25 3.00
17 William Fuller .02 .10
18 Paul Gruber .02 .10
19 Bernie Kosar .07 .20
20 Rickey Jackson .02 .10
21 Earnest Byner .02 .10
22 Emmitt Smith 1.50 4.00
23 Neal Anderson PC .02 .10
24 Greg Lloyd .07 .20
25 Ronnie Harmon .02 .10
26 Ray Donaldson .02 .10
27 Kevin Ross .02 .10
28 Irving Fryar .07 .20
29 John L. Williams .02 .10
30 Chris Hinton .02 .10
31 Tracy Scroggins RC .02 .10
32 Rohn Stark .02 .10
33 David Fulcher .02 .10
34 Thurman Thomas .15 .40
35 Christian Okoye .02 .10
36 Vaughn Dunbar RC .02 .10
37 Joel Steed RC .02 .10
39 Dermontti Dawson .08 .20
40 Mark Higgs .02 .10
41 Flipper Anderson UER .02 .10
42 Ronnie Lott .07 .20
43 Jim Everett .07 .20
44 Burt Grossman .02 .10
45 Charles Haley .07 .20
46 Ricky Proehl .02 .10
47 Marquez Pope RC .02 .10
48 David Treadwell .02 .10
49 William White .02 .10
50 John Elway 1.25 3.00
51 Mark Carrier WR .07 .20
52 Brian Blades .07 .20
53 Keith McKeller .02 .10
54 Art Monk .07 .20
55 Lamar Lathon .02 .10
56 Pat Swilling .02 .10
57 Steve Broussard .02 .10
58 Derrick Thomas .15 .40
59 Keith Jackson .07 .20
60 Leonard Marshall .02 .10
62 Andy Heck .02 .10
63 Mark Carrier DB .02 .10
64 Neil O'Donnell .07 .20
65 Broderick Thomas MVP .02 .10
66 Erik Kramer .07 .20
67 Joe Montana PC .60 1.50
68 Robert Delpino MVP .02 .10
69 Steve Israel RC .02 .10
70 Herman Moore .15 .40
71 Jacob Green .02 .10
72 Lorenzo White .02 .10
73 Nick Lowery .02 .10
74 Eugene Robinson .02 .10
75 Carl Banks .02 .10
76 Bruce Smith .15 .40
77 Mark Rypien MVP .02 .10
78 Anthony Munoz .07 .20
79 Clayton Holmes RC .02 .10
80 Jerry Rice .75 2.00
81 Henry Ellard .07 .20
82 Tim McGee .02 .10
83 Al Toon .07 .20
84 Haywood Jeffires .07 .20
85 Mike Singletary .07 .20
86 Thurman Thomas PC .07 .20
87 Jessie Hester .02 .10
88 Michael Irvin .15 .40
89 Jack Del Rio .02 .10
90 Eagles MVP .02 .10
91 Jeff Herrod .02 .10
92 Michael Dean Perry .07 .20
93 Louis Oliver .02 .10
94 Dan McGwire .02 .10
95 Cris Carter MVP .07 .20
96 Dale Carter RC .07 .20
97 Cornelius Bennett .07 .20
98 Edgar Bennett RC .15 .40
99 Steve Young .60 1.50
100 Warren Moon .15 .40
101 Deion Sanders MVP .25 .60
102 Mel Gray .07 .20
103 Mark Murphy .02 .10
104 Jeff George .15 .40
105 Anthony Miller .07 .20
106 Tom Rathman .02 .10
107 Fred McAfee RC .02 .10
108 Paul Siever RC .02 .10
109 Lemuel Stinson .02 .10
110 Vance Johnson .02 .10
111 Jay Schroeder .02 .10
112 Calvin Williams .07 .20
113 Cortez Kennedy .07 .20
114 Quentin Coryatt RC .02 .10
115 Ronnie Lippett .02 .10
116 Brad Baxter .02 .10
117 Bubba McDowell .02 .10
118 Cris Carter .40 1.00
119 John Stephens .02 .10
120 James Hasty .02 .10
121 Bubby Brister .02 .10
122 Robert Jones RC .02 .10
123 Sterling Sharpe .15 .40
124 Jason Hanson RC .07 .20
125 Sam Mills .02 .10
126 Ernie Jones .02 .10
127 Chester McGlockton RC .07 .20
128 Troy Vincent RC .02 .10
129 Chuck Smith RC .02 .10
130 Tim McKyer .02 .10
131 Tom Newberry .02 .10
132 Leonard Wheeler RC .02 .10
133 Patrick Rowe RC .02 .10
134 Eric Swann .07 .20
135 Jeremy Lincoln RC .02 .10
136 Brian Noble .02 .10
137 Allen Pinkett .02 .10
139 Eric Green .02 .10
140 Louis Lipps .02 .10
141 Chris Singleton .02 .10
142 Gary Clark .15 .40
143 Tim Green .02 .10
144 Dennis Green CO RC .07 .20
145 Gary Anderson K .02 .10
146 Mark Clayton .07 .20
147 Kelvin Martin .02 .10
148 Mike Holmgren CO RC .15 .40
149 Gaston Green .02 .10
150 Terrell Buckley RC .02 .10
151 Robert Brooks RC .50 1.25
152 Anthony Smith .02 .10
153 Jay Novacek .07 .20
154 Webster Slaughter .02 .10
155 John Roper .02 .10
156 Steve Emtman RC .02 .10
157 Tony Sacca RC .02 .10
158 Ray Crockett .02 .10
159 Jerry Rice MVP .40 1.00
160 Alonzo Spellman RC .07 .20
161 Deion Sanders PC .25 .60
162 Robert Clark .02 .10
163 Mark Ingram .02 .10
164 Ricardo McDonald RC .02 .10
165 Emmitt Smith PC .75 2.00
166 Tommy Maddox RC 1.25 3.00
167 Tom Myslinski RC .02 .10
168 Packers MVP .02 .10
169 Ernest Givins .07 .20
170 Eugene Robinson MVP .02 .10
171 Roger Craig .07 .20
172 Irving Fryar MVP .02 .10
173 Jeff Herrod MVP .02 .10
174 Chris Mims RC .02 .10
175 Bart Oates .02 .10
176 Michael Irvin MVP .15 .40
177 Lawrence Dawsey .07 .20
178 Warren Moon MVP .07 .20
179 Timm Rosenbach .02 .10
180 Bobby Ross CO RC .02 .10
181 Chris Burkett MVP .02 .10
182 Tony Brooks RC .02 .10
183 Clarence Verdin .02 .10
184 Bernie Kosar PC .02 .10
185 Eric Martin .02 .10
186 Jeff Bryant .02 .10
187 Carnell Lake .02 .10
188 Darren Woodson RC .15 .40
189 Dwayne Harper .02 .10
190 Bernie Kosar MVP .02 .10
191 Keith Sims .02 .10
192 Rich Gannon .15 .40
193 Broderick Thomas .02 .10
194 Michael Young .02 .10
195 Cris Dishman .02 .10
196 Wes Hopkins .02 .10
197 Christian Okoye PC .02 .10
198 David Little .02 .10
199 Chris Crooms RC .02 .10
200 Lawrence Taylor .15 .40
201 Marc Boutte RC .02 .10
202 Mark Carrier DB PC .02 .10
203 Keith McCants .02 .10
204 Dwayne Sabb RC .02 .10
205 Brian Mitchell .07 .20
206 Keith Byars .02 .10
207 Jeff Hostetler .07 .20
208 Percy Snow .02 .10
209 Lawrence Taylor MVP .07 .20
210 Troy Auzenne RC .02 .10
211 Warren Moon PC .07 .20
212 Mike Pritchard .07 .20
213 Eric Dickerson .07 .20
214 Harvey Williams .15 .40
215 Phil Simms .07 .20
217 Marco Coleman RC .02 .10
218 Phillippi Sparks RC .02 .10
219 Gerald Dixon RC .02 .10
220 Steve Walsh .02 .10
221 Russell Maryland .02 .10
222 Eddie Anderson .02 .10
223 Shane Dronett RC .02 .10
224 Todd Collins RC .02 .10
225 Leon Searcy RC .02 .10
226 Andre Rison .07 .20
227 James Lofton .07 .20
228 Ken O'Brien .02 .10
229 Mike Tomczak .02 .10
230 Nick Bell .02 .10
231 Ben Smith .02 .10
232 Wendell Davis MVP .02 .10
233 Craig Thompson RC .02 .10
234 Dana Hall RC .02 .10
235 Larry Webster RC .02 .10
236 Jerry Rice PC .40 1.00
237 Rod Bernstine .02 .10
238 David Klingler RC .02 .10
239 Greg Skrepenak RC .02 .10
240 Mark Wheeler RC .02 .10
241 Kevin Smith RC .02 .10
242 Charles Mann .02 .10
243 Lions MVP .02 .10
244 Curtis Whitley RC .02 .10
245 Ronnie Harmon MVP .02 .10
246 Brent Jones .07 .20
247 Robert Harris RC .02 .10
248 Ted Marchibroda CO .02 .10
249 Willie Gault .07 .20
250 Siran Stacy RC .02 .10
251 Dennis Byrd .02 .10
252 Corey Harris RC .02 .10
253 Al Noga .02 .10
254 David Shula CO RC .02 .10
255 Rob Moore .07 .20
256 Marv Cook .02 .10
257 John Elway MVP .60 1.50
258 Harold Green .02 .10
259 Tom Flores CO .02 .10
260 Andre Reed .07 .20
261 Anthony Thompson .02 .10
262 Issiac Holt .02 .10
263 Mike Evans RC .02 .10
264 Jimmy Smith RC 2.00 5.00
265 Anthony Carter .07 .20
266 Ashley Ambrose RC .15 .40
268 Sean Gilbert RC .07 .20
269 Ken Norton Jr. .07 .20
270 Barry Word .02 .10
271 Pat Swilling MVP .02 .10
272 Dan Marino PC .60 1.50
273 David Fulcher MVP .02 .10
274 William Perry .07 .20
275 Ed West .02 .10
276 Gene Atkins .02 .10
277 Neal Anderson .02 .10
278 Dino Hackett .02 .10
279 Greg Townsend .02 .10
280 Andre Tippett .02 .10
281 Darryl Williams RC .02 .10
282 Kurt Barber RC .02 .10
283 Pat Terrell .02 .10
284 Derrick Thomas PC .07 .20
285 Eddie Robinson RC .02 .10
286 Howie Long .15 .40
287 Cardinals MVP .02 .10
288 Thurman Thomas MVP .07 .20
289 Wendell Davis .02 .10
290 Jeff Cross .02 .10
291 Duane Bickett .02 .10
292 Tony Smith RC .02 .10
293 Jerry Ball .02 .10
294 Jessie Tuggle .02 .10
295 Chris Burkett .02 .10
296 Eugene Chung RC .02 .10
297 Chris Miller .07 .20
298 Albert Bentley .02 .10
299 Richard Johnson CB .02 .10
300 Randall Cunningham .15 .40
301 Courtney Hawkins RC .07 .20
302 Ray Childress .02 .10
303 Rodney Peete .07 .20
304 Kevin Fagan .02 .10
305 Ronnie Lott MVP .02 .10
306 Michael Carter .02 .10
307 Derrick Thomas MVP .07 .20
308 Jarvis Williams .02 .10
309 Greg Lloyd MVP .07 .20
310 Ethan Horton .02 .10
311 Ricky Ervins .02 .10
312 Bennie Blades .02 .10
313 Troy Aikman PC .40 1.00
314 Bruce Armstrong .02 .10
315 Leroy Hoard .07 .20
316 Gary Anderson RB .02 .10
317 Steve McMichael .07 .20
318 Junior Seau .15 .40
319 Mark Thomas RC .02 .10
320 Fred Barnett .15 .40
321 Mike Merriweather .02 .10
322 Keith Willis .02 .10
323 Brett Perriman .15 .40
324 Michael Haynes .07 .20
325 Jim Harbaugh .15 .40
326 Sammie Smith .02 .10
327 Robert Delpino .02 .10
328 Tony Mandarich .02 .10
329 Mark Bortz .02 .10
330 Ray Ethridge RC .02 .10
331 J.Williams/L.Oliver PC .02 .10
332 Dan Marino MVP .60 1.50
333 Dwight Stone .02 .10
334 Billy Ray Smith .02 .10
335 Darion Conner .02 .10
336 Howard Dinkins RC .02 .10
337 Robert Porcher RC .15 .40
338 Chris Doleman .02 .10
339 Alvin Harper .07 .20
340 John Taylor .07 .20
341 Ray Agnew .02 .10
342 Jon Vaughn .02 .10
343 James Brown RC .02 .10
344 Michael Irvin PC .15 .40
345 Neil Smith .15 .40
346 Vaughan Johnson .02 .10
347 Atlanta Falcons/Buffalo Bills CL .02 .10
348 Chicago Bears/Cincinnati Bengals CL .02 .10
349 Cleveland Browns/Dallas Cowboys CL .02 .10
350A Detroit Lions/Denver Broncos CL .02 .10
350B Eric Metcalf UER .15 .40
351 Green Bay Packers/Houston Oilers CL .02 .10
352 Indianapolis Colts/Kansas City Chiefs CL.02 .10
353 Los Angeles Raiders .02 .10
Los Angeles Rams CL
354A Miami Dolphins/Minnesota Vikings CL.02 .10
354B James Francis UER .02 .10
355 New England Patriots .02 .10
New Orleans Saints CL
356 New York Giants/New York Jets CL .02 .10
357A Philadelphia Eagles .02 .10
Phoenix Cardinals CL
357B John Fina UER RC .02 .10
358A Pittsburgh Steelers .02 .10
San Diego Chargers CL
358B Carl Pickens UER RC .15 .40
359 San Francisco 49ers/Seattle Seahawks CL.02 .10
360 Tampa Bay Buccaneers .02 .10
Washington Redskins CL
H1 Jim Kelly HOLO 1.00 2.50
S1 Steve Emtman PC .30 .75

1992 SkyBox Prime Time Poster Cards

Randomly inserted throughout 1992 SkyBox Prime Time foil packs, these cards present the same poster image as the regularly issued "Costacos" cards except that the borders of the cards are silver foil-stamped. A 16th Costacos Poster Art checklist card rounds out the insert set. The cards measure the standard size and are numbered on the back with an "M" prefix. These metallic insert cards were available in 10,000 numbered cases distributed only to the hobby. SkyBox estimated that two Costacos metallic poster cards would be found in each 36-pack box. The poster cards take the featured player out of the football arena and into an imaginary setting highlighting his nickname, image, or reputation.

COMPLETE SET (16) 12.00 30.00
RANDOM INSERTS IN FOIL PACKS
M1 Bernie Kosar .15 .40
M2 Mark Carrier DB .07 .20
M3 Neal Anderson .07 .20
M4 Thurman Thomas .30 .75
M5 Deion Sanders .75 2.00
M6 Joe Montana 2.50 6.00
M7 Jerry Rice 1.50 4.00
M8 Jarvis Williams .07 .20
Louis Oliver
M9 Dan Marino 2.50 6.00
M10 Derrick Thomas .30 .75
M11 Christian Okoye .07 .20
M12 Warren Moon .30 .75
M13 Michael Irvin .30 .75
M14 Troy Aikman 1.50 4.00
M15 Emmitt Smith 3.00 8.00
M16 Checklist .07 .20

1996 SkyBox SkyMotion

The 1996 Skybox SkyMotion is a hobby only set issued in one series totalling 60 cards. The two-card packs retail for $4.99 each. The fronts feature color player motion-photos on paper stock with 3.5 seconds of game action. The four-color backs carry action photos plus career statistics and player biographical information.

COMPLETE SET (60) 15.00 40.00
1 Troy Aikman .75 2.00
2 Marcus Allen .30 .75
3 Jeff Blake .30 .75
4 Drew Bledsoe .50 1.25
5 Tim Brown .30 .75
6 Isaac Bruce .30 .75
7 Mark Brunell .50 1.25
8 Cris Carter .30 .75
9 Ben Coates .15 .40
10 Kerry Collins .30 .75
11 Curtis Conway .30 .75
12 Terrell Davis .60 1.50
13 Trent Dilfer .30 .75
14 Hugh Douglas .15 .40
15 John Elway 1.50 4.00
16 Marshall Faulk .40 1.00
17 Brett Favre 1.50 4.00
18 William Floyd .07 .20
19 Joey Galloway .30 .75
20 Jeff George .15 .40
21 Rodney Hampton .15 .40
22 Jim Harbaugh .15 .40
23 Aaron Hayden RC .07 .20
24 Jeff Hostetler .07 .20
25 Tyrone Hughes .07 .20
26 Michael Irvin .30 .75
27 Daryl Johnston .15 .40
28 Jim Kelly .30 .75
29 Greg Lloyd .15 .40
30 Dan Marino 1.50 4.00
31 Curtis Martin .60 1.50
32 Chester McGlockton .07 .20
33 Steve McNair .60 1.50
34 Eric Metcalf .07 .20
35 Scott Mitchell .15 .40
36 Herman Moore .15 .40
37 Bryce Paup .07 .20
38 Carl Pickens .15 .40
39 Errict Rhett .15 .40
40 Jerry Rice .75 2.00
41 Rashaan Salaam .15 .40
42 Barry Sanders 1.25 3.00
43 Chris Sanders .15 .40
44 Deion Sanders .50 1.25
45 Junior Seau .30 .75
46 Heath Shuler .15 .40
47 Bruce Smith .15 .40
48 Emmitt Smith 1.25 3.00
49 Kordell Stewart .30 .75
50 Eric Swann .07 .20
51 Derrick Thomas .30 .75
52 Thurman Thomas .30 .75
53 Eric Turner .07 .20
54 Tamarick Vanover .15 .40
55 Chris Warren .15 .40
56 Ricky Watters .15 .40
57 Michael Westbrook .30 .75
58 Reggie White .30 .75
59 Rod Woodson .15 .40
60 Steve Young .60 1.50
P1 Trent Dilfer Promo .40 1.00
SM1 Trent Dilfer Promo .40 1.00

1996 SkyBox SkyMotion Gold

COMPLETE SET (60) 200.00 400.00
*GOLDS: 2.5X TO 6X BASIC CARDS
STATED ODDS 1:2 BOXES

1996 SkyBox SkyMotion Big Bang

Randomly inserted in packs at a rate of one in nine, this 10-card set features photos of top rated 1996 NFL rookies on sharp lenticular 3D cards.

COMPLETE SET (10) 12.50 30.00
STATED ODDS 1:9
1 Tim Biakabutuka 1.00 2.50
2 Rickey Dudley 1.00 2.50
3 Eddie George 4.00 10.00
4 Terry Glenn 2.50 6.00
5 Kevin Hardy .60 1.50
6 Marvin Harrison 6.00 15.00
7 Keyshawn Johnson 2.00 5.00
8 Leeland McElroy .60 1.50
9 Lawrence Phillips .60 1.50
10 Simeon Rice 1.25 3.00

1996 SkyBox SkyMotion Team Galaxy

Randomly inserted in packs at a rate of one in 35, this five-card set features color player photos of five of the NFL's top players on lenticular 3D cards.

COMPLETE SET (5) 12.50 30.00
STATED ODDS 1:35
1 Karim Abdul-Jabbar 1.50 4.00
2 Brett Favre 8.00 20.00
3 Curtis Martin 2.50 6.00
4 Jerry Rice 4.00 10.00
5 Emmitt Smith 5.00 12.00

1998 SkyBox Thunder

The 1998 SkyBox Thunder set was issued in one series totalling 250 cards. The fronts feature color player photos. The backs carry player information. The base set was broken down into three tiers: 1-100 (3-4 perpack), 101-200 (3 per pack), and 201-250 (1 per pack).

COMPLETE SET (250) 25.00 50.00
1 Reggie White .20 .50
2 Elvis Grbac .10 .30
3 Ed McCaffrey .10 .30
4 O.J. McDuffie .10 .30
5 Scott Mitchell .10 .30
6 Byron Hanspard .07 .20
7 John Randle .10 .30
8 Shawn Jefferson .07 .20
9 Peter Boulware .07 .20
10 Karl Williams .07 .20
11 Napoleon Kaufman .20 .50
12 Barry Minter .07 .20
13 Cris Dishman .07 .20
14 James Stewart .10 .30
15 Marcus Robertson .07 .20
16 Rodney Harrison .10 .30
17 Michael Barrow .07 .20
18 Michael Sinclair .07 .20
19 Dewayne Washington .07 .20
20 Phillippi Sparks .07 .20
21 Ernie Conwell .07 .20
22 Ken Dilger .07 .20
23 Johnnie Morton .10 .30
24 Eric Swann .07 .20
25 Curtis Conway .10 .30
26 Duce Staley .30 .75
27 Darrell Green .10 .30
28 Quinn Early .07 .20
29 LeRoy Butler .07 .20
30 Winfred Tubbs .07 .20
31 Darren Woodson .07 .20
32 Marcus Allen .20 .50
33 Glenn Foley .10 .30
34 Tom Knight .07 .20
35 Sam Shade .07 .20
36 James McKnight .20 .50
37 Leeland McElroy .07 .20
38 Earl Holmes RC .25 .60
39 Ryan McNeil .07 .20
40 Cris Carter .20 .50
41 Jessie Armstead .07 .20
42 Bryce Paup .07 .20
43 Chris Slade .07 .20
44 Eric Metcalf .07 .20
45 Jim Harbaugh .10 .30
46 Terry Kirby .07 .20
47 Donnie Edwards .07 .20
48 Darryl Williams .07 .20
49 Neil Smith .10 .30
50 Warren Sapp .10 .30
51 Jason Taylor .10 .30
52 Irving Fryar .10 .30
53 Jeff George .10 .30
54 Yancey Thigpen .07 .20
55 Ricky Proehl .07 .20
56 Kevin Greene .10 .30
57 Joel Steed .07 .20
58 Larry Allen .07 .20
59 Thurman Thomas .20 .50
60 Aaron Glenn .07 .20
61 Natrone Means .10 .30
62 Chris Calloway .07 .20
63 Chuck Smith .07 .20
64 Chidi Ahanotu .07 .20
65 [illegible]
66 Jonathan Ogden .07 .20
67 Drew Bledsoe CL .20 .50
68 John Mobley CL .07 .20
69 Antowain Smith CL .10 .30
70 Aeneas Williams .07 .20
71 Brian Williams .07 .20
72 Derrick Thomas .20 .50
73 Ted Johnson .07 .20
74 Troy Drayton .07 .20
75 Mike Pritchard .07 .20
76 Darnay Scott .10 .30
77 James Jett .10 .30
78 Dwayne Rudd .07 .20
79 Marvin Harrison .20 .50
80 Dermontti Dawson .15 .40
81 Keith Lyle .07 .20
82 Steve Atwater .07 .20
83 Tyrone Wheatley .10 .30
84 Tony Brackens .07 .20
85 Dale Carter .07 .20
86 Robert Porcher .07 .20
87 Merton Hanks .07 .20
88 Leon Johnson .07 .20
89 Simeon Rice .10 .30
90 Robert Brooks .10 .30
91 William Thomas .07 .20
92 Wesley Walls .10 .30
93 Chester McGlockton .07 .20
94 Chris Chandler .10 .30
95 Michael Strahan .10 .30
96 Ray Zellars .07 .20
97 Dexter Coakley .07 .20
98 Rob Johnson .10 .30
99 Eric Green .07 .20
100 Darrien Gordon .07 .20
101 Gary Brown .07 .20
102 Reidel Anthony .10 .30
103 Keenan McCardell .10 .30
104 Leslie O'Neal .07 .20
105 Bryant Westbrook .07 .20
106 Derrick Alexander .10 .30
107 Jeff Blake .10 .30
108 Ben Coates .10 .30
109 Shawn Springs .07 .20
110 Robert Smith .20 .50
111 Karim Abdul-Jabbar .20 .50
112 Willie Davis .07 .20
113 Mark Chmura .10 .30
114 Terry Allen .20 .50
115 Will Blackwell .07 .20
116 Jamal Anderson .20 .50
117 Dana Stubblefield .07 .20
118 Trent Dilfer .20 .50
119 Jermaine Lewis .10 .30
120 Chad Brown .07 .20
121 Tamarick Vanover .07 .20
122 Tony Martin .10 .30
123 Larry Centers .07 .20
124 J.J. Stokes .10 .30
125 Danny Kanell .10 .30
126 Wayne Chrebet .20 .50
127 Kerry Collins .10 .30
128 Tony Banks .10 .30
129 Randal Hill .07 .20
130 Jimmy Smith .10 .30
131 Tim Brown .20 .50
132 Zach Thomas .20 .50
133 Rod Smith .10 .30
134 Frank Wycheck .07 .20
135 Garrison Hearst .20 .50
136 Bruce Smith .10 .30
137 Hardy Nickerson .07 .20
138 Sean Dawkins .07 .20
139 Willie McGinest .07 .20
140 Kimble Anders .10 .30
141 Michael Westbrook .10 .30
142 Chris Doleman .07 .20
143 Ricky Watters .10 .30
144 Levon Kirkland .07 .20
145 Rob Moore .10 .30
146 Eddie Kennison .10 .30
147 Rickey Dudley .07 .20
148 Jay Graham .07 .20
149 Brad Johnson .20 .50
150 Bobby Hoying .10 .30
151 Sherman Williams .07 .20
152 Charles Way .07 .20
153 Adrian Murrell .10 .30
154 Chris Sanders .07 .20
155 Greg Hill .07 .20
156 Rae Carruth .07 .20
157 Mike Alstott .20 .50
158 Terance Mathis .10 .30
159 Antonio Freeman .20 .50
160 Junior Seau .20 .50
161 Chris Warren .10 .30
162 Shannon Sharpe .10 .30
163 Derrick Rodgers .07 .20
164 Charles Johnson .07 .20
165 Marshall Faulk .25 .60
166 Jamie Asher .07 .20
167 Michael Jackson .07 .20
168 Terrell Owens .20 .50
169 Jason Sehorn .10 .30
170 Raymont Harris .07 .20
171 Jake Reed .10 .30
172 Kevin Hardy .07 .20
173 Jerald Moore .07 .20
174 Michael Irvin .20 .50
175 Freddie Jones .07 .20
176 Steve McNair .20 .50
177 Carnell Lake .07 .20
178 Troy Brown .10 .30
179 Hugh Douglas .07 .20
180 Andre Rison .10 .30
181 Leslie Shepherd .07 .20
182 Andre Hastings .07 .20
183 Fred Lane .07 .20
184 Andre Reed .10 .30
185 Darrell Russell .07 .20
186 Frank Sanders .10 .30
187 Derrick Brooks .20 .50
188 Charlie Garner .10 .30
189 Bert Emanuel .10 .30
190 Terrell Buckley .07 .20
191 Carl Pickens .10 .30
192 Tiki Barber .20 .50
193 Pete Mitchell .07 .20
194 Gilbert Brown .07 .20
195 Isaac Bruce .20 .50
196 Ray Lewis .20 .50
197 Warren Moon .20 .50
198 Tony Gonzalez .20 .50
199 John Mobley .07 .20
200 Gus Frerotte .07 .20
201 Brett Favre 1.50 3.00
202 Terrell Davis .20 .50
203 Dan Marino 1.50 3.00
204 Barry Sanders 1.00 2.50
205 Steve Young .30 .75
206 Deion Sanders .25 .60
207 Kordell Stewart .25 .60
208 Eddie George .20 .50
209 Jake Plummer .20 .50
210 Warrick Dunn .25 .60
211 John Elway 1.50 3.00
212 Terry Glenn .25 .60
213 Mark Brunell .20 .50
214 Corey Dillon .20 .50
215 Joey Galloway .25 .60
216 Dorsey Levens .25 .60
217 Troy Aikman .60 1.50
218 Keyshawn Johnson .25 .60
219 Jerome Bettis .20 .50
220 [illegible]
221 Herman Moore .25 .60
222 Emmitt Smith 1.00 2.50
223 Jerry Rice .60 1.50
224 Drew Bledsoe .50 1.25
225 Antowain Smith .25 .60
226 Stephen Alexander RC .50 1.25
227 John Avery RC .25 .60
228 Kevin Dyson RC .75 2.00
229 Robert Edwards RC .25 .60
230 Greg Ellis RC .40 1.00
231 Curtis Enis RC .25 .60
232 Chris Fuamatu-Ma'afala RC .50 1.25
233 Ahman Green RC 2.00 5.00
234 Jacquez Green RC .50 1.25
235 Az-Zahir Hakim RC .75 2.00
236 Skip Hicks RC .50 1.25
237 Joe Jurevicius RC .25 .60
238 Ryan Leaf RC .75 2.00
239 Peyton Manning RC 8.00 20.00
240 Alonzo Mayes RC .40 1.00
241 R.W. McQuarters RC .50 1.25
242 Randy Moss RC 5.00 12.00
243 Marcus Nash RC .40 1.00
244 Jerome Pathon RC .75 2.00
245 Jason Peter RC .40 1.00
246 Brian Simmons RC .50 1.25
247 Takeo Spikes RC .75 2.00
248 Fred Taylor RC 1.25 3.00
249 Andre Wadsworth RC .50 1.25
250 Charles Woodson RC 2.00 5.00
P162 Shannon Sharpe Promo .30 .75
P231 C.Enis Chicago Promo/5000* .50 1.25

1998 SkyBox Thunder Rave

*1-200 VETS: 30X TO 60X BASE CARDS
*201-225 VETS: 20X TO 40X BASIC CARDS
*226-250 ROOKIES: 3X TO 8X
STATED PRINT RUN 150 SER.#'d SETS

1998 SkyBox Thunder Super Rave

*1-200 STARS: 40X TO100X BASIC CARDS
*201-225 STARS: 30X TO 80X BASIC CARDS
*226-250 ROOKIES: 10X TO 25X
STATED PRINT RUN 25 SER.#'d SETS

1998 SkyBox Thunder Boss

Randomly inserted in packs at a rate of one in 8, this 20-card set is an insert to the SkyBox Thunder base set. The sculpted embossed card fronts feature color action photos with an illusional three-dimensional background.

COMPLETE SET (20) 15.00 30.00
STATED ODDS 1:8
1B Troy Aikman 2.50 6.00
2B Drew Bledsoe 2.00 5.00
3B Tim Brown .75 2.00
4B Antonio Freeman .75 2.00
5B Joey Galloway 1.00 2.50
6B Terry Glenn 1.00 2.50
7B Bobby Hoying .50 1.25
8B Michael Irvin .75 2.00
9B Keyshawn Johnson 1.00 2.50
10B Dorsey Levens 1.00 2.50
11B Curtis Martin 1.00 2.50
12B John Mobley .30 .75
13B Jake Plummer .75 2.00
14B John Randle .50 1.25
15B Deion Sanders 1.00 2.50
16B Junior Seau .75 2.00
17B Shannon Sharpe .50 1.25
18B Bruce Smith .50 1.25
19B Robert Smith .75 2.00
20B Dana Stubblefield .30 .75

1998 SkyBox Thunder Destination Endzone

Randomly inserted in packs at a rate of one in 96, this 15-card set is an insert to the SkyBox Thunder base set. The tri-fold cards are printed and stamped with silver holofoil.

COMPLETE SET (15) 125.00 250.00
STATED ODDS 1:96
1DE Jerome Bettis 3.00 8.00
2DE Mark Brunell 3.00 8.00
3DE Terrell Davis 3.00 8.00
4DE Corey Dillon 3.00 8.00
5DE Warrick Dunn 3.00 8.00
6DE John Elway 15.00 40.00
7DE Brett Favre 15.00 40.00
8DE Eddie George 2.00 5.00
9DE Dorsey Levens 1.25 3.00
10DE Curtis Martin 3.00 8.00
11DE Herman Moore 1.25 3.00
12DE Barry Sanders 12.50 30.00
13DE Emmitt Smith 12.50 30.00
14DE Kordell Stewart 2.00 5.00
15DE Steve Young 4.00 10.00

1998 SkyBox Thunder Number Crushers

Randomly inserted in packs at a rate of one in 16, this 10-card set is an insert to the SkyBox Thunder base set. The fronts feature a color action photo on a square-cut grade background. The backs offer a pull-down strip that shows the numbers for some of the NFL's best through a die-cut window.

COMPLETE SET (10) 15.00 35.00
STATED ODDS 1:16
1NC Troy Aikman 2.50 6.00
2NC Jerome Bettis 1.25 3.00
3NC Tim Brown 1.25 3.00
4NC Mark Brunell 1.25 3.00
5NC Dan Marino 5.00 12.00
6NC Herman Moore .50 1.25
7NC Rob Moore .50 1.25
8NC Jerry Rice 2.50 6.00
9NC Shannon Sharpe .75 2.00
10NC Emmitt Smith 4.00 10.00

1998 SkyBox Thunder Quick Strike

Randomly inserted in packs at a rate of one in 300, this 12-card set is an insert to the SkyBox Thunder base set. The cards feature color action photos and resemble a match book. It is complete with a staple and simulated strike area at the bottom.

COMPLETE SET (12) 125.00 250.00
STATED ODDS 1:300
1QS Terrell Davis 5.00 12.00
2QS John Elway 20.00 50.00
3QS Brett Favre 20.00 50.00
4QS Joey Galloway 3.00 8.00
5QS Eddie George 3.00 8.00
6QS Keyshawn Johnson 3.00 8.00
7QS Dan Marino 20.00 50.00
8QS Jerry Rice 10.00 25.00
9QS Barry Sanders 15.00 40.00
10QS Deion Sanders 5.00 12.00
11QS Kordell Stewart 3.00 8.00
12QS Steve Young 6.00 15.00

1998 SkyBox Thunder StarBurst

Randomly inserted in packs at a rate of one in 32, this 10-card set is an insert to the SkyBox Thunder base set. The fronts feature color action photos of some of the 1st and 2nd year players on a background of gold holo foil-stamped starburst design.

COMPLETE SET (10) 30.00 60.00
STATED ODDS 1:32
1SB Tiki Barber 1.25 3.00
2SB Corey Dillon 1.25 3.00
3SB Warrick Dunn 1.25 3.00
4SB Curtis Enis .60 1.50
5SB Ryan Leaf .60 1.50
6SB Peyton Manning 8.00 20.00
7SB Randy Moss 5.00 12.00
8SB Jake Plummer 1.25 3.00
9SB Antowain Smith 1.25 3.00
10SB [illegible]

1992 Slam Thurman Thomas

This ten-card set showcases Thurman Thomas, the All-Pro Buffalo Bills' running back. The backs combine to present a biography of Thomas' life. The production run was reportedly 25,000 sets, and for every 25 sets ordered, the dealer received a limited edition (only 1,000 were reportedly produced) autograph card. Also a free promo card, numbered "Promo 1" in the upper right corner, was issued with every ten-card set. The fronts feature mostly color action or posed player photos inside a white frame. The card face shades from purple to white and back to purple. The player's name and the card subtitle are gold foil stamped in the bottom border. On a blue background inside a white frame, the backs carry career highlights, statistics, and a special "Slam-O-Meter" feature that summarizes his performance at that level.

COMPLETE SET (11) 4.00 10.00
COMMON THOMAS (1-10) .40 1.00
AU Thurman Thomas AUTO 20.00 50.00

1993 Slam Jerome Bettis

This six-card set is comprised of five numbered cards and one unnumbered promo, and spotlights Jerome Bettis. One card in each sealed factory set was hand autographed by Bettis. A promo card and the four other numbered cards were included with each factory set. Each factory set also came with a certificate of authenticity, which carried the production number out of 5,000 numbered sets produced. The cards measure 2 1/2" by 3 5/8" and feature on their fronts blue-bordered color action shots of Bettis in his Notre Dame uniform. His name and the card's title appear in gold foil within the bottom margin. The words "1st Round Pick" appear in gold foil within the top margin. The blue back is framed by a white line and carries a quote about Bettis from his coach at Notre Dame, Lou Holtz. Below this, each card carries stats and a graph representing Jerome's on-field yearly performance. Aside from the promo card, the cards are numbered on the back.

COMPLETE SET (6) 4.00 10.00
COMPLETE FACT.SET (6) 10.00 25.00
COMMON BETTIS (1-5) .75 2.00
P1 Jerome Bettis Promo .75 2.00
1AU Jerome Bettis AU 8.00 20.00
2AU Jerome Bettis AU 8.00 20.00
3AU Jerome Bettis AU 8.00 20.00
4AU Jerome Bettis AU 8.00 20.00
5AU Jerome Bettis AU 8.00 20.00

1978 Slim Jim

The 1978 Slim Jim football discs were issued on the backs of Slim Jim packages with each package back containing two discs. There were six package colors (flavors): blue (mild), green (pizza), dark green (pepperoni), maroon (salami), orange (bacon), and red (spicy). The large display boxes originally contained 12 small packages and each large box featured one Slim Jim player disc. It is thought that all 70 discs appeared on at least one large box. The complete set consists of 35 connected pairs or 70 individual discs. The individual discs measure approximately 2 3/8" in diameter whereas the complete panel is 3" by 5 3/4". The discs themselves are either yellow, red or brown with black lettering. The same two players are always paired on a particular package. The discs are numbered for convenience in alphabetical order below and prices are for single punched or neatly cut out discs.

COMPLETE SET (70) 200.00 400.00
*UNCUT BOXES: .6X TO 1.5X PAIRS
*LARGE OUTER BOXES: 2X TO 4X
1 Lyle Alzado 3.00 8.00
2 Otis Armstrong 2.50 6.00
3 Jerome Barkum 1.50 4.00
4 Bill Bergey 2.00 5.00
5 Elvin Bethea 3.00 8.00
6 Fred Biletnikoff 6.00 15.00
7 Rocky Bleier 5.00 12.00
8 Willie Buchanon 1.50 4.00
9 Doug Buffone 1.50 4.00
10 Dexter Bussey 1.50 4.00
11 John Cappelletti 3.00 8.00
12 Fred Carr 1.50 4.00
13 Tommy Casanova 1.50 4.00
14 Richard Caster 1.50 4.00
15 Bob Chandler 1.50 4.00
16 Larry Csonka 10.00 20.00
17 Isaac Curtis 2.00 5.00
18 Joe DeLamielleure 3.00 8.00
19 Dan Dierdorf 3.00 8.00
20 Glenn Doughty 1.50 4.00
21 Billy Joe DuPree 2.00 5.00
22 John Dutton 1.50 4.00
23 Glen Edwards 1.50 4.00
24 Leon Gray 1.50 4.00
25 Mel Gray 2.00 5.00
26 Joe Greene 6.00 15.00
27 Jack Gregory 1.50 4.00
28 Steve Grogan 3.00 8.00
29 John Hannah 4.00 10.00
30 Jim Hart 2.50 6.00
31 Tommy Hart 1.50 4.00
32 Ron Howard 1.50 4.00
33 Claude Humphrey 2.00 5.00
34 Wilbur Jackson 1.50 4.00
35 Ron Jaworski 3.00 8.00
36 Ron Jessie 1.50 4.00
37 Billy Johnson 2.00 5.00
38 Charlie Joiner 3.00 8.00
39 Paul Krause 3.00 8.00
40 Larry Little 4.00 10.00
41 Archie Manning 5.00 12.00
42 Ron McDole 1.50 4.00
43 Lydell Mitchell 2.00 5.00
44 Nat Moore 2.00 5.00
45 Robert Newhouse 2.50 6.00
46 Riley Odoms 1.50 4.00
47 Alan Page 4.00 10.00
48 Lemar Parrish 2.00 5.00
49 Walter Payton 30.00 60.00
50 Greg Pruitt 2.00 5.00
51 Ahmad Rashad 4.00 10.00
52 Golden Richards 2.00 5.00
53 John Riggins 6.00 15.00
54 Isiah Robertson 1.50 4.00
55 Charlie Sanders 2.50 6.00
56 Clarence Scott 1.50 4.00
57 Lee Roy Selmon 6.00 15.00
58 Otis Sistrunk 2.50 6.00
59 Darryl Stingley 2.50 6.00
60 Bruce Taylor 1.50 4.00
61 Emmitt Thomas 2.00 5.00
62 Mike Thomas 1.50 4.00
63 Gene Upshaw 3.00 8.00
64 Jeff Van Note 1.50 4.00
65 Brad Van Pelt 1.50 4.00
66 Gene Washington 49ers 2.00 5.00
67 Ted Washington 1.50 4.00
68 Roger Wehrli 2.00 5.00
69 Clarence Williams 1.50 4.00
70 Don Woods 1.50 4.00

1974 Southern California Sun WFL Team Issue 8X10

These photos measure roughly 8" x 10" and include black and white images with the player's name in the lower right below the photo and the team name in the upper left corner above the photo. The backs are blank.

1 Anthony Davis 10.00 20.00
2 Dave Roller 7.50 15.00

1974 Southern California Sun WFL Team Sheets

These team issued sheets feature player photos, measuring roughly 8" x 10" overall, with black and white images of either three or four players. The format varies from eight small photos of four players to a sheet to three larger photos on one sheet. The team name and year are included near the bottom and each player's name is printed below his image.

COMPLETE SET (11) 75.00 125.00
1 Booker Brown/Joe Carollo 7.50 15.00
Jack Conners/Dennis Crane
2 Alonzo Emery/Wayne Estabrook 7.50 15.00
Kevin Fletcher/Kevin Grady
3 Steve Gunther/Tim Guy/Ike Harris 7.50 15.00
John Hoffman DE
4 Gene Howard/Clay Jefferies 7.50 15.00
Eric Johnson DB/Kermit Johnson
5 Jimmie Jones RB/Durwood Keeton 7.50 15.00
Younger Klippert/Ed Kezirian
6 Ken Lee/Terry Lindsey 7.50 15.00
Jacque MacKinnon/Greg Mason
7 Ralph Nelson/Jim Bowman 7.50 15.00
Charles DeJurnett
8 Eric Patton/Ed Philpott/Dan Pride/Bill Reid 7.50 15.00
9 Dave Roller/Mike Ryan 7.50 15.00
Steve Schroder/Ted Seifert
10 Neal Skarin/Dave Szymakowski 7.50 15.00
Ron Thomas WR/ Gary Valbuena
11 Cleveland Vann/Jim Williams DB 7.50 15.00
Dave Williams WR

1975 Southern California Sun WFL Team Issue 5X7

These photos were released by the team to fulfill fan requests. Each measures roughly 5" x 7" and includes a black and white image with no player names or writing on the fronts. The backs are blank.

1975 Southern California Sun WFL Team Issue 5X7

1 Kevin Fletcher 6.00 12.00
2 Jim Jones 6.00 12.00
3 Jim Norton 6.00 12.00
4 Scott Palmer 6.00 12.00
5 Don Parish 6.00 12.00
6 Ron Thomas 6.00 12.00

1975 Southern California Sun WFL Team Issue 8X10

These team issued photos measure roughly 8" x 10" and feature black and white player images with no names or identification on the fronts. The photo backs sometimes contain hand written player identification.

1 Kermit Johnson 7.50 15.00
2 Jimmie Lee Jones 7.50 15.00
3 Younger Klippert 7.50 15.00
4 Daryle Lamonica 10.00 20.00
5 James McAlister 7.50 15.00
6 Bill Reid 7.50 15.00
7 Paul Seiler 7.50 15.00
8 Dave Williams 7.50 15.00

1993 SP

The 270 standard-size cards comprising Upper Deck's SP set were issued in 12-card packs. After a Premier Prospects (1-18) subset, the cards are arranged alphabetically according to and within teams. Rookie Cards include Jerome Bettis, Drew Bledsoe, Reggie Brooks, Mark Brunell, Curtis Conway, Garrison Hearst, Qadry Ismail, O.J. McDuffie, Rick Mirer, Dana Stubblefield and Kevin Williams. A Joe Montana promo card was issued to promote the debut of the set and closely resembles his regular 1993 SP card. The promo card is not marked as such, but its card number (19) contrasts with Montana's card number (122) in the regular series.

COMPLETE SET (270) 25.00 60.00
1 Curtis Conway RC 1.25 3.00
2 John Copeland RC .30 .75
3 Kevin Williams RC .60 1.50
4 Dan Williams RC .30 .75
5 Patrick Bates RC .30 .75
6 Jerome Bettis RC 8.00 20.00
7 O.J.McDuffie RC 1.25 3.00
8 Robert Smith RC 2.00 5.00
9 Drew Bledsoe RC 6.00 15.00
10 Irv Smith RC .30 .75
11 Marvin Jones RC .30 .75
12 Victor Bailey RC .30 .75
13 Garrison Hearst RC 2.00 5.00
14 Natrone Means RC 1.25 3.00
15 Todd Kelly RC .30 .75
16 Rick Mirer RC 1.25 3.00
17 Eric Curry RC .30 .75
18 Reggie Brooks RC .60 1.50
19 Eric Dickerson .20 .50
20 Roger Harper RC .10 .30
21 Michael Haynes .20 .50
22 Bobby Hebert .10 .30
23 Lincoln Kennedy RC .10 .30
24 Chris Miller .20 .50
25 Mike Pritchard .20 .50
26 Andre Rison .20 .50
27 Deion Sanders .60 1.50
28 Cornelius Bennett .20 .50
29 Kenneth Davis .10 .30
30 Henry Jones .10 .30
31 Jim Kelly .40 1.00
32 John Parrella RC .10 .30
33 Andre Reed .20 .50
34 Bruce Smith .40 1.00
35 Thomas Smith RC .20 .50
36 Thurman Thomas .40 1.00
37 Neal Anderson .10 .30
38 Myron Baker RC .10 .30
39 Mark Carrier DB .10 .30
40 Richard Dent .20 .50
41 Chris Gedney RC .10 .30
42 Jim Harbaugh .40 1.00
43 Craig Heyward .20 .50
44 Carl Simpson RC .10 .30
45 Alonzo Spellman .10 .30
46 Derrick Fenner .10 .30
47 Harold Green .10 .30
48 David Klingler .10 .30
49 Ricardo McDonald .10 .30
50 Tony McGee RC .20 .50
51 Carl Pickens .20 .50
52 Steve Tovar RC .10 .30
53 Alfred Williams .10 .30
54 Darryl Williams .10 .30
55 Jerry Ball .10 .30
56 Mike Caldwell RC .10 .30
57 Mark Carrier WR .20 .50
58 Steve Everitt RC .10 .30
59 Dan Footman RC .10 .30
60 Pepper Johnson .10 .30
61 Bernie Kosar .20 .50
62 Eric Metcalf .20 .50
63 Michael Dean Perry .20 .50
64 Troy Aikman 1.25 2.50
65 Charles Haley .20 .50
66 Michael Irvin .40 1.00
67 Robert Jones .10 .30
68 Derrick Lassic RC .10 .30
69 Russell Maryland .10 .30
70 Ken Norton Jr. .20 .50
71 Darrin Smith RC .20 .50
72 Emmitt Smith 2.50 5.00
73 Steve Atwater .10 .30
74 Rod Bernstine .10 .30
75 Jason Elam RC .40 1.00
76 John Elway 2.00 5.00
77 Simon Fletcher .10 .30
78 Tommy Maddox .40 1.00
79 Glyn Milburn RC .40 1.00
80 Derek Russell .10 .30
81 Shannon Sharpe .40 1.00
82 Bennie Blades .10 .30
83 Willie Green .10 .30
84 Antonio London RC .10 .30
85 Ryan McNeil RC .40 1.00
86 Herman Moore .40 1.00
87 Rodney Peete .10 .30
88 Barry Sanders 1.50 4.00
89 Chris Spielman .20 .50
90 Pat Swilling .10 .30
91 Mark Brunell RC 5.00 12.00
92 Terrell Buckley .10 .30
93 Brett Favre 3.00 6.00
94 Jackie Harris .10 .30
95 Sterling Sharpe .40 1.00
96 John Stephens .10 .30
97 Wayne Simmons RC .10 .30
98 George Teague RC .20 .50
99 Reggie White .40 1.00
100 Micheal Barrow RC .40 1.00
101 Cody Carlson .10 .30
102 Ray Childress .10 .30
103 Brad Hopkins RC .10 .30
104 Haywood Jeffires .20 .50
105 Wilber Marshall .10 .30
106 Warren Moon .40 1.00
107 Webster Slaughter .10 .30
108 Lorenzo White .10 .30
109 John Baylor .10 .30
110 Duane Bickett .10 .30
111 Quentin Coryatt .20 .50
112 Steve Emtman .10 .30
113 Jeff George .40 1.00
114 Jessie Hester .10 .30
115 Anthony Johnson .20 .50
116 Reggie Langhorne .10 .30
117 Roosevelt Potts RC .10 .30
118 Marcus Allen .40 1.00
119 J.J. Birden .10 .30
120 Willie Davis .40 1.00
121 Jaime Fields RC .10 .30
122 Joe Montana 2.00 5.00
123 Will Shields RC .40 1.00
124 Neil Smith .40 1.00
125 Derrick Thomas .40 1.00
126 Harvey Williams .20 .50
127 Tim Brown .40 1.00
128 Billy Joe Hobert RC .40 1.00
129 Jeff Hostetler .20 .50
130 Ethan Horton .10 .30
131 Rocket Ismail .20 .50
132 Howie Long .40 1.00
133 Terry McDaniel .10 .30
134 Greg Robinson RC .10 .30
135 Anthony Smith .10 .30
136 Flipper Anderson .10 .30
137 Marc Boutte .10 .30
138 Shane Conlan .10 .30
139 Troy Drayton RC .20 .50
140 Henry Ellard .20 .50
141 Jim Everett .20 .50
142 Cleveland Gary .10 .30
143 Sean Gilbert .20 .50
144 Robert Young .10 .30
145 Marco Coleman .10 .30
146 Bryan Cox .10 .30
147 Irving Fryar .20 .50
148 Keith Jackson .10 .30
149 Terry Kirby RC .40 1.00
150 Dan Marino 2.00 5.00
151 Scott Mitchell .40 1.00
152 Louis Oliver .10 .30
153 Troy Vincent .10 .30
154 Anthony Carter .20 .50
155 Cris Carter .40 1.00
156 Roger Craig .20 .50
157 Chris Doleman .10 .30
158 Qadry Ismail RC .75 2.00
159 Steve Jordan .10 .30
160 Randall McDaniel .10 .30
161 Audray McMillian .10 .30
162 Barry Word .10 .30
163 Vincent Brown .10 .30
164 Marv Cook .10 .30
165 Sam Gash RC .40 1.00
166 Pat Harlow .10 .30
167 Greg McMurtry .10 .30
168 Todd Rucci RC .10 .30
169 Leonard Russell .20 .50
170 Scott Sisson RC .10 .30
171 Chris Slade RC .20 .50
172 Morten Andersen .10 .30
173 Derek Brown RBK RC .20 .50
174 Reggie Freeman RC .10 .30
175 Rickey Jackson .10 .30
176 Eric Martin .10 .30
177 Wayne Martin .10 .30
178 Brad Muster .10 .30
179 Willie Roaf RC .75 2.00
180 Renaldo Turnbull .10 .30
181 Derek Brown TE .10 .30
182 Marcus Buckley RC .10 .30
183 Jarrod Bunch .10 .30
184 Rodney Hampton .20 .50
185 Ed McCaffrey .40 1.00
186 Kanavis McGhee .10 .30
187 Mike Sherrard .10 .30
188 Phil Simms .20 .50
189 Lawrence Taylor .40 1.00
190 Kurt Barber .10 .30
191 Boomer Esiason .20 .50
192 Johnny Johnson .10 .30
193 Ronnie Lott .20 .50
194 Johnny Mitchell .10 .30
195 Rob Moore .20 .50
196 Adrian Murrell RC .40 1.00
197 Browning Nagle .10 .30
198 Marvin Washington .10 .30
199 Eric Allen .10 .30
200 Fred Barnett .20 .50
201 Randall Cunningham .40 1.00
202 Byron Evans .10 .30
203 Tim Harris .10 .30
204 Seth Joyner .10 .30
205 Leonard Renfro RC .10 .30
206 Heath Sherman .10 .30
207 Clyde Simmons .10 .30
208 Johnny Bailey .10 .30
209 Steve Beuerlein .20 .50
210 Chuck Cecil .10 .30
211 Larry Centers RC .40 1.00
212 Gary Clark .20 .50
213 Ernest Dye RC .10 .30
214 Ken Harvey .10 .30
215 Randal Hill .10 .30
216 Ricky Proehl .10 .30
217 Deon Figures RC .10 .30
218 Barry Foster .20 .50
219 Eric Green .10 .30
220 Kevin Greene .20 .50
221 Carlton Haselrig .10 .30
222 Andre Hastings RC .20 .50
223 Greg Lloyd .20 .50
224 Neil O'Donnell .40 1.00
225 Rod Woodson .40 1.00
226 Marion Butts .10 .30
227 Darren Carrington RC .10 .30
228 Darrien Gordon RC .10 .30
229 Ronnie Harmon .10 .30
230 Stan Humphries .20 .50
231 Anthony Miller .20 .50
232 Chris Mims .10 .30
233 Leslie O'Neal .10 .30
234 Junior Seau .40 1.00
235 Dana Hall .10 .30
236 Adrian Hardy .10 .30
237 Brent Jones .20 .50
238 Tim McDonald .10 .30
239 Tom Rathman .10 .30
240 Jerry Rice 1.50 3.00
241 Dana Stubblefield RC .40 1.00
242 Ricky Watters .40 1.00
243 Steve Young 1.25 2.50
244 Brian Blades .20 .50
245 Ferrell Edmunds .10 .30
246 Carlton Gray RC .10 .30
247 Cortez Kennedy .20 .50
248 Kelvin Martin .10 .30
249 Dan McGwire .10 .30
250 Jon Vaughn .10 .30
251 Chris Warren .20 .50
252 John L. Williams .10 .30
253 Reggie Cobb .10 .30
254 Horace Copeland RC .20 .50
255 Lawrence Dawsey .10 .30
256 Demetrius DuBose RC .10 .30
257 Craig Erickson .20 .50
258 Courtney Hawkins .10 .30
259 John Lynch RC 3.00 8.00
260 Hardy Nickerson .20 .50
261 Lamar Thomas RC .10 .30
262 Carl Banks .10 .30
263 Tom Carter RC .20 .50
264 Brad Edwards .10 .30
265 Kurt Gouveia .10 .30
266 Desmond Howard .20 .50
267 Charles Mann .10 .30
268 Art Monk .20 .50
269 Mark Rypien .10 .30
270 Ricky Sanders .10 .30
P1 Joe Montana Promo 2.00 5.00

1993 SP All-Pros

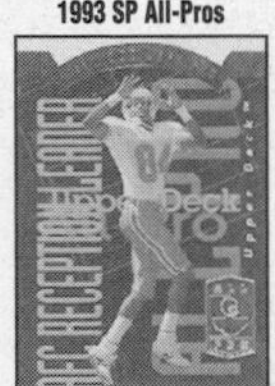

Randomly inserted in 1993 SP football packs at a rate of approximately one in 15, these 15 standard-size cards are distinguished by the gold-foil-accented arcs cut into their top edges, and feature on their fronts color player action cut-outs superposed upon black backgrounds that carry multicolored lettering.

COMPLETE SET (15) 50.00 120.00
STATED ODDS 1:15
AP1 Steve Young 5.00 12.00
AP2 Warren Moon 2.50 6.00
AP3 Troy Aikman 6.00 15.00
AP4 Dan Marino 10.00 25.00
AP5 Barry Sanders 8.00 20.00
AP6 Barry Foster 2.00 5.00
AP7 Emmitt Smith 10.00 25.00
AP8 Thurman Thomas 3.00 8.00
AP9 Jerry Rice 8.00 20.00
AP10 Sterling Sharpe 3.00 8.00
AP11 Anthony Miller 2.00 5.00
AP12 Haywood Jeffires 2.00 5.00
AP13 Junior Seau 3.00 8.00
AP14 Reggie White 3.00 8.00
AP15 Derrick Thomas 3.00 8.00

1994 SP

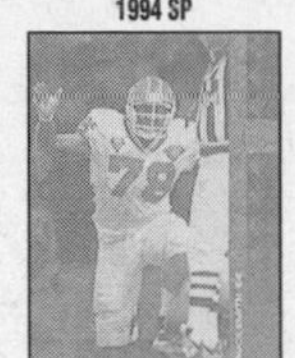

These 200 standard-size cards feature all-foil player photos that are full-bleed except on the right where a black-and-gold variegated strip carrying the "Upper Deck SP" logo edges the picture. The small hologram on the cardbacks were printed primarily in gold foil (with two variations on the gold Upper Deck name -- either horizontal or vertical) but silver foil holograms are known to exist. The silver hologram was used on the Die Cut parallels. After beginning with Premier Prospects (1-20), the cards are checklisted according to teams. Inserted approximately one in every other case, are special Dan Marino (300th touchdown pass) and Jerry Rice (127th touchdown) cards. Numbered RB1 and RB2, respectively, the cards are horizontal with a gold die cut design. A Joe Montana Promo card was produced and priced below.

COMPLETE SET (200) 12.00 30.00
1 Dan Wilkinson RC .50 1.25
2 Heath Shuler RC .30 .75
3 Marshall Faulk RC 6.00 15.00
4 Willie McGinest RC .75 2.00
5 Trent Dilfer RC 2.00 5.00
6 Bryant Young RC .75 2.00
7 Antonio Langham RC .15 .40
8 John Thierry RC .15 .40
9 Aaron Glenn RC .50 1.25
10 Charles Johnson RC .50 1.25
11 Dewayne Washington RC .15 .40
12 Johnnie Morton RC 1.25 3.00
13 Greg Hill RC .30 .75
14 William Floyd RC .30 .75
15 Derrick Alexander WR RC .50 1.25
16 Darnay Scott RC .50 1.25
17 Errict Rhett RC .50 1.25
18 Charlie Garner RC 1.25 3.00
19 Thomas Lewis RC .15 .40
20 David Palmer FOIL RC .50 1.25
21 Andre Reed .10 .30
22 Thurman Thomas .20 .50
23 Bruce Smith .10 .30
24 Jim Kelly .20 .50
25 Cornelius Bennett .10 .30
26 Bucky Brooks RC .05 .15
27 Jeff Burris RC .10 .30
28 Jim Harbaugh .20 .50
29 Tony Bennett .05 .15
30 Quentin Coryatt .05 .15
31 Floyd Turner .05 .15
32 Roosevelt Potts .05 .15
33 Jeff Herrod .05 .15
34 Irving Fryar .10 .30
35 Bryan Cox .05 .15
36 Dan Marino 1.50 4.00
37 Terry Kirby .20 .50
38 Michael Stewart .05 .15
39 Bernie Kosar .10 .30
40 Aubrey Beavers RC .05 .15
41 Vincent Brisby .05 .15
42 Ben Coates .10 .30
43 Drew Bledsoe .75 2.00
44 Marion Butts .05 .15
45 Chris Slade .05 .15
46 Michael Timpson .05 .15
47 Ray Crittenden RC .05 .15
48 Rob Moore .10 .30
49 Johnny Mitchell .05 .15
50 Art Monk .10 .30
51 Boomer Esiason .10 .30
52 Ronnie Lott .10 .30
53 Ryan Yarborough RC .05 .15
54 Carl Pickens .10 .30
55 David Klingler .05 .15
56 Harold Green .05 .15
57 John Copeland .05 .15
58 Louis Oliver .05 .15
59 Corey Sawyer .10 .30
60 Michael Jackson .10 .30
61 Mark Rypien .05 .15
62 Vinny Testaverde .10 .30
63 Eric Metcalf .10 .30
64 Eric Turner .05 .15
65 Haywood Jeffires .05 .15
66 Micheal Barrow .05 .15
67 Cody Carlson .05 .15
68 Gary Brown .05 .15
69 Bucky Richardson .05 .15
70 Al Smith .05 .15
71 Eric Green .05 .15
72 Neil O'Donnell .20 .50
73 Barry Foster .05 .15
74 Greg Lloyd .10 .30
75 Rod Woodson .10 .30
76 Byron Bam Morris RC .10 .30
77 John L. Williams .05 .15
78 Anthony Miller .10 .30
79 Mike Pritchard .05 .15
80 John Elway 1.50 4.00
81 Shannon Sharpe .10 .30
82 Steve Atwater .05 .15
83 Simon Fletcher .05 .15
84 Glyn Milburn .10 .30
85 Mark Collins .05 .15
86 Keith Cash .05 .15
87 Willie Davis .10 .30
88 Joe Montana 1.50 4.00
89 Marcus Allen .20 .50
90 Neil Smith .10 .30
91 Derrick Thomas .20 .50
92 Tim Brown .20 .50
93 Jeff Hostetler .10 .30
94 Terry McDaniel .05 .15
95 Rocket Ismail .10 .30
96 Rob Fredrickson RC .10 .30
97 Harvey Williams .05 .15
98 Steve Wisniewski .05 .15
99 Stan Humphries .10 .30
100 Natrone Means .20 .50
101 Leslie O'Neal .10 .30
102 Junior Seau .20 .50
103 Ronnie Harmon .05 .15
104 Shawn Jefferson .05 .15
105 Howard Ballard .05 .15
106 Rick Mirer .20 .50
107 Cortez Kennedy .10 .30
108 Chris Warren .10 .30
109 Brian Blades .10 .30
110 Sam Adams RC .10 .30
111 Gary Clark .10 .30
112 Steve Beuerlein .10 .30
113 Ronald Moore .05 .15
114 Eric Swann .10 .30
115 Clyde Simmons .05 .15
116 Seth Joyner .05 .15
117 Troy Aikman .75 2.00
118 Charles Haley .10 .30
119 Alvin Harper .10 .30
120 Michael Irvin .20 .50
121 Daryl Johnston .10 .30
122 Emmitt Smith 1.25 3.00
123 Shante Carver RC .05 .15
124 Dave Brown .10 .30
125 Rodney Hampton .10 .30
126 Dave Meggett .05 .15
127 Chris Calloway .05 .15
128 Mike Sherrard .05 .15
129 Carlton Bailey .05 .15
130 Randall Cunningham .20 .50
131 William Fuller .05 .15
132 Eric Allen .05 .15
133 Calvin Williams .10 .30
134 Herschel Walker .10 .30
135 Bernard Williams RC .05 .15
136 Henry Ellard .10 .30
137 Ethan Horton .05 .15
138 Desmond Howard .10 .30
139 Reggie Brooks .10 .30
140 John Friesz .10 .30
141 Tom Carter .05 .15
142 Terry Allen .10 .30
143 Adrian Cooper .05 .15
144 Qadry Ismail .20 .50
145 Warren Moon .20 .50
146 Henry Thomas .05 .15
147 Todd Steussie RC .10 .30
148 Cris Carter .30 .75
149 Andy Heck .05 .15
150 Curtis Conway .20 .50
151 Erik Kramer .10 .30
152 Lewis Tillman .05 .15
153 Dante Jones .05 .15
154 Alonzo Spellman .05 .15
155 Herman Moore .20 .50
156 Broderick Thomas .05 .15
157 Scott Mitchell .10 .30
158 Barry Sanders 1.25 3.00
159 Chris Spielman .10 .30
160 Pat Swilling .05 .15
161 Bennie Blades .05 .15
162 Sterling Sharpe .10 .30
163 Brett Favre 1.50 4.00
164 Reggie Cobb .05 .15
165 Reggie White .20 .50
166 Sean Jones .05 .15
167 George Teague .05 .15
168 LeShon Johnson RC .10 .30
169 Courtney Hawkins .05 .15
170 Jackie Harris .05 .15
171 Craig Erickson .05 .15
172 Santana Dotson .10 .30
173 Eric Curry .05 .15
174 Hardy Nickerson .10 .30
175 Derek Brown RBK .05 .15
176 Jim Everett .10 .30
177 Michael Haynes .10 .30
178 Tyrone Hughes .10 .30
179 Wayne Martin .05 .15
180 Willie Roaf .05 .15
181 Irv Smith .05 .15
182 Jeff George .20 .50
183 Andre Rison .10 .30
184 Eric Pegram .05 .15
185 Bert Emanuel RC .40 1.00
186 Chris Doleman .05 .15
187 Ron George .05 .15
188 Chris Miller .05 .15
189 Troy Drayton .05 .15
190 Chris Chandler .10 .30
191 Jerome Bettis .40 1.00
192 Jimmie Jones .05 .15
193 Sean Gilbert .10 .30
194 Jerry Rice .75 2.00
195 Brent Jones .10 .30
196 Deion Sanders .40 1.00
197 Steve Young .60 1.50
198 Ricky Watters .10 .30
199 Dana Stubblefield .10 .30
200 Ken Norton Jr. .10 .30
RB1 Dan Marino RB 10.00 25.00
RB2 Jerry Rice RB 12.50 25.00
P16 Joe Montana Promo 1.50 4.00

1994 SP Die Cuts

COMPLETE SET (200) 40.00 80.00
*STARS: .8X TO 2X BASIC CARDS
*RCs: .5X TO 1.2X BASIC CARDS
ONE PER PACK

1994 SP Holoviews

Randomly inserted in SP packs at a rate of one in five, this set showcases 40 top veteran players and rookies. Card fronts feature a player photo with a black and blue right border. A hologram featuring a close-up of the player and game action from the Pro Bowl is toward the bottom. The back contains a player photo and a write-up.

COMPLETE SET (40) 20.00 40.00
STATED ODDS 1:5
*DIE CUTS: 4X TO 10X BASIC INSERTS
DIE CUT STATED ODDS 1:75
PB1 Jamir Miller .60 1.50
PB2 Andre Rison 1.00 2.50
PB3 Bucky Brooks .60 1.50
PB4 Thurman Thomas 1.00 2.50
PB5 John Thierry .60 1.50
PB6 Dan Wilkinson .60 1.50
PB7 Darnay Scott .75 2.00
PB8 Antonio Langham .60 1.50
PB9 Troy Aikman 2.00 5.00
PB10 Emmitt Smith 3.00 8.00
PB11 John Elway 4.00 10.00
PB12 Barry Sanders 3.00 8.00
PB13 Johnnie Morton .75 2.00
PB14 Reggie White 1.25 3.00
PB15 Brett Favre 4.00 10.00
PB16 LeShon Johnson .60 1.50
PB17 Joe Montana 4.00 10.00
PB18 Greg Hill .60 1.50
PB19 Calvin Jones .60 1.50
PB20 Tim Brown 1.00 2.50
PB21 Isaac Bruce 1.00 2.50
PB22 Jerome Bettis 1.25 3.00
PB23 Dan Marino 4.00 10.00
PB24 O.J.McDuffie .60 1.50
PB25 Willie McGinest .60 1.50
PB26 Mario Bates .60 1.50
PB27 Rodney Hampton .60 1.50
PB28 Thomas Lewis .60 1.50
PB29 Aaron Glenn .60 1.50
PB30 Barry Foster .60 1.50
PB31 Charles Johnson .60 1.50
PB32 Steve Young 1.50 4.00
PB33 Jerry Rice 2.50 6.00
PB34 Bryant Young .75 2.00
PB35 William Floyd .75 2.00
PB36 Sam Adams .60 1.50
PB37 Rick Mirer .75 2.00
PB38 Errict Rhett .75 2.00
PB39 Reggie Brooks .60 1.50
PB40 Heath Shuler .75 2.00

1995 SP

Issued as a 200 card set, these cards were available in eight card packs at a suggested retail price of $4.19/pack. The set is broken down into 180 player cards and 20 Premier Prospect cards, which features top rookies. Rookie Cards include Jeff Blake, Ki-Jana Carter, Kerry Collins, Terrell Davis, Joey Galloway, Curtis Martin, Steve McNair, Rashaan Salaam, J.J. Stokes, Tamarick Vanover and Michael Westbrook. A couple of "one-shot" inserts were also available: a Dan Marino Record Breaker and a Joe Montana Tribute. The Marino Record Breaker card is a horizontal etched-foil card saluting his record breaking 343 career touchdown passes. This card was randomly inserted at a rate of one in 383 packs. The Montana Tribute card is also a horizontal etched-foil card showcasing his extraordinary career. It was also randomly inserted at a rate of one in 383 packs. A Joe Montana All-Pro Promo card was produced and priced below.

COMPLETE SET (200) 20.00 50.00
1 Ki-Jana Carter RC .75 2.00
2 Eric Zeier RC .75 2.00
3 Steve McNair RC 4.00 10.00
4 Michael Westbrook RC .75 2.00
5 Kerry Collins RC 2.50 6.00
6 Joey Galloway RC 2.00 5.00
7 Kevin Carter RC .75 2.00
8 Mike Mamula RC .20 .50
9 Kyle Brady RC .75 2.00
10 J.J. Stokes RC .75 2.00
11 Tyrone Poole RC .75 2.00
12 Rashaan Salaam RC .40 1.00
13 Sherman Williams RC .20 .50
14 Luther Elliss RC .20 .50
15 James O. Stewart RC 1.25 3.00
16 Tamarick Vanover RC .75 2.00
17 Napoleon Kaufman RC 1.25 3.00
18 Curtis Martin RC 6.00 12.00
19 Tyrone Wheatley RC 1.25 3.00
20 Frank Sanders RC .75 2.00
21 Devin Bush .07 .20
22 Terance Mathis .15 .40
23 Bert Emanuel .30 .75
24 Eric Metcalf .15 .40
25 Craig Heyward .15 .40
26 Jeff George .15 .40
27 Mark Carrier WR .15 .40
28 Pete Metzelaars .07 .20
29 Frank Reich .07 .20
30 Sam Mills .15 .40
31 John Kasay .07 .20
32 Willie Green .15 .40
33 Jeff Graham .07 .20
34 Curtis Conway .30 .75
35 Steve Walsh .07 .20
36 Erik Kramer .07 .20
37 Michael Timpson .07 .20
38 Mark Carrier DB .07 .20
39 Troy Aikman .75 2.00
40 Michael Irvin .30 .75
41 Charles Haley .15 .40
42 Deion Sanders .50 1.25
43 Jay Novacek .15 .40
44 Emmitt Smith 1.25 3.00
45 Herman Moore .30 .75
46 Scott Mitchell UER .15 .40
47 Bennie Blades .07 .20
48 Johnnie Morton .15 .40
49 Chris Spielman .15 .40
50 Barry Sanders 1.25 3.00
51 Edgar Bennett .15 .40
52 Reggie White .30 .75
53 Sean Jones .07 .20
54 Mark Ingram .07 .20
55 Robert Brooks .30 .75
56 Brett Favre 1.50 4.00
57 Lovell Pinkney RC .20 .50
58 Chris Miller .07 .20
59 Isaac Bruce .50 1.25
60 Roman Phifer .07 .20
61 Sean Gilbert .15 .40
62 Jerome Bettis .30 .75
63 Derrick Alexander DE RC .30 .75
64 Cris Carter .30 .75
65 Jake Reed .15 .40
66 Robert Smith .30 .75
67 David Palmer .15 .40
68 Warren Moon .15 .40
69 Ray Zellars RC .40 1.00
70 Jim Everett .07 .20
71 Michael Haynes .15 .40
72 Quinn Early .15 .40
73 Willie Roaf .07 .20
74 Mario Bates .15 .40
75 Mike Sherrard .07 .20
76 Chris Calloway .07 .20
77 Dave Brown .15 .40
78 Thomas Lewis .15 .40
79 Herschel Walker .15 .40
80 Rodney Hampton .15 .40
81 Fred Barnott .15 .40
82 Calvin Williams .15 .40
83 Randall Cunningham .30 .75
84 Charlie Garner .30 .75
85 Bobby Taylor RC 1.25 3.00
86 Ricky Watters .15 .40
87 Dave Krieg .07 .20
88 Rob Moore .15 .40
89 Eric Swann .15 .40
90 Clyde Simmons .07 .20
91 Seth Joyner .07 .20
92 Garrison Hearst .30 .75
93 Jerry Rice .75 2.00
94 Bryant Young .15 .40
95 Brent Jones .07 .20
96 Ken Norton .15 .40
97 William Floyd .15 .40
98 Steve Young .60 1.50
99 Warren Sapp RC 2.00 5.00
100 Trent Dilfer .30 .75
101 Alvin Harper .07 .20
102 Hardy Nickerson .07 .20
103 Derrick Brooks RC 2.00 5.00
104 Errict Rhett .15 .40
105 Henry Ellard .15 .40
106 Ken Harvey .07 .20
107 Gus Frerotte .15 .40
108 Brian Mitchell .07 .20
109 Terry Allen .15 .40
110 Heath Shuler .15 .40
111 Jim Kelly .30 .75
112 Andre Reed .15 .40
113 Bruce Smith .30 .75
114 Darick Holmes RC .40 1.00
115 Bryce Paup .15 .40
116 Cornelius Bennett .15 .40
117 Carl Pickens .15 .40
118 Darnay Scott .15 .40
119 Jeff Blake RC .75 2.00
120 Steve Tovar .07 .20
121 Tony McGee .07 .20
122 Dan Wilkinson .15 .40
123 Craig Powell RC .07 .20
124 Vinny Testaverde .15 .40
125 Eric Turner .07 .20
126 Leroy Hoard .07 .20
127 Lorenzo White .07 .20
128 Andre Rison .15 .40
129 Shannon Sharpe .15 .40
130 Terrell Davis RC 3.00 8.00
131 Anthony Miller .15 .40
132 Mike Pritchard .07 .20
133 Steve Atwater .07 .20
134 John Elway 1.50 4.00
135 Haywood Jeffires .07 .20
136 Gary Brown .07 .20
137 Al Smith .07 .20
138 Rodney Thomas RC .40 1.00
139 Chris Chandler .15 .40
140 Mel Gray .07 .20
141 Craig Erickson .07 .20
142 Sean Dawkins .15 .40
143 Ken Dilger RC .75 2.00
144 Ellis Johnson RC .20 .50
145 Quentin Coryatt .15 .40
146 Marshall Faulk 1.00 2.50
147 Tony Boselli RC .75 2.00
148 Rob Johnson RC 1.25 3.00
149 Desmond Howard .15 .40
150 Steve Beuerlein .15 .40
151 Reggie Cobb .07 .20
152 Jeff Lageman .07 .20
153 Willie Davis .15 .40
154 Marcus Allen .30 .75
155 Neil Smith .15 .40
156 Greg Hill .15 .40
157 Steve Bono .15 .40
158 Derrick Thomas .30 .75
159 Jeff Hostetler .15 .40
160 Harvey Williams .07 .20
161 Rocket Ismail .15 .40
162 Chester McGlockton .15 .40
163 Terry McDaniel .07 .20
164 Tim Brown .30 .75
165 Terry Kirby .15 .40
166 Irving Fryar .15 .40
167 O.J. McDuffie .30 .75
168 Bryan Cox .07 .20
169 Eric Green .07 .20
170 Dan Marino 1.50 4.00
171 Ben Coates .15 .40
172 Vincent Brisby .07 .20
173 Chris Slade .07 .20
174 Ty Law RC 1.50 4.00
175 Vincent Brown .07 .20
176 Drew Bledsoe .50 1.25
177 Johnny Mitchell .07 .20
178 Boomer Esiason .15 .40
179 Wayne Chrebet RC 2.00 5.00
180 Mo Lewis .07 .20
181 Ronald Moore .07 .20
182 Aaron Glenn .07 .20
183 Mark Bruener RC .40 1.00
184 Neil O'Donnell .15 .40
185 Charles Johnson .15 .40
186 Greg Lloyd .15 .40
187 Rod Woodson .15 .40
188 Byron Bam Morris .07 .20
189 Terrell Fletcher RC .20 .50
190 Terrance Shaw UER RC .20 .50
191 Stan Humphries .15 .40
192 Junior Seau .30 .75
193 Leslie O'Neal .15 .40
194 Natrone Means .15 .40
195 Christian Fauria RC .40 1.00
196 Rick Mirer .15 .40
197 Sam Adams .07 .20
198 Cortez Kennedy .15 .40
199 Eugene Robinson .07 .20
200 Chris Warren .15 .40
DM1 Dan Marino Tribute 7.50 20.00
JM1 Joe Montana Salute 7.50 20.00
JMAP Joe Montana Promo 1.50 4.00
NNO Dan Marino TRI Jumbo 10.00 25.00
NNO Joe Montana SAL Jumbo 10.00 25.00
P113 Dan Marino Promo 1.25 3.00

1995 SP All-Pros

Randomly inserted at a rate of one in five packs, this 20 card set features a double die cut design of the top NFL players. The parallel All-Pro Gold set was randomly inserted into packs at a rate of one in 62 packs. It is identical to the silver, except with gold foil. Cards are numbered with an "AP" prefix.

COMPLETE SET (20) 15.00 40.00
SILVER STATED ODDS 1:5
*GOLD: 1.2X TO 3X SILVER
GOLD STATED ODDS 1:62
1 Marshall Faulk 1.50 4.00
2 Natrone Means .75 2.00
3 Emmitt Smith 3.00 8.00
4 Brett Favre 4.00 10.00
5 Michael Westbrook .75 2.00
6 Jerry Rice 2.50 6.00
7 John Elway 4.00 10.00
8 Troy Aikman 2.00 5.00
9 Rashaan Salaam .60 1.50
10 Jerome Bettis 1.00 2.50
11 Drew Bledsoe 1.00 2.50
12 Kerry Collins 1.00 2.50
13 Dan Marino 4.00 10.00
14 Tyrone Wheatley .75 2.00
15 Steve McNair 2.50 6.00
16 Steve Young 1.50 4.00
17 Eric Zeier .60 1.50
18 Errict Rhett .75 2.00
19 Michael Irvin 1.25 3.00
20 Barry Sanders 3.00 8.00

1995 SP Holoviews

Randomly inserted at a rate of one in five packs, this 40 card set features the NFL's top stars and rookies utilizing the Upper Deck "Holoview" technology. Card fronts contain the holoview at the left with the player's name, team name and position underneath. An action photo of the player makes up the rest of the front. Card backs contain a player shot on the left with commentary on the right.

COMPLETE SET (40) 25.00 60.00
STATED ODDS 1:5
*DIE CUTS: .8X TO 2X BASIC INSERTS
DIE CUT STATED ODDS 1:75
1 Joe Montana 3.00 8.00
2 Dan Marino 4.00 10.00
3 Drew Bledsoe 1.25 3.00
4 Ben Coates .40 1.00
5 Curtis Martin 4.00 10.00
6 Kyle Brady .60 1.50
7 Marshall Faulk 2.50 6.00
8 Ki-Jana Carter .60 1.50
9 Leroy Hoard .20 .50
10 James O. Stewart 1.25 3.00
11 Mark Bruener .30 .75
12 Charles Johnson .40 1.00
13 Rod Woodson .40 1.00
14 John Elway 4.00 10.00
15 Tim Brown .75 2.00
16 Napoleon Kaufman 1.25 3.00
17 Natrone Means .40 1.00
18 Jimmy Oliver .05 .15
19 Christian Fauria .30 .75
20 Joey Galloway 1.50 4.00
21 Chris Warren .40 1.00
22 Kerry Collins 2.00 5.00
23 Mario Bates .40 1.00
24 Jerome Bettis .75 2.00
25 William Floyd .40 1.00
26 Jerry Rice 2.00 5.00
27 J.J. Stokes .60 1.50
28 Steve Young 1.50 4.00
29 Troy Aikman 2.00 5.00
30 Michael Irvin .75 2.00
31 Emmitt Smith 3.00 8.00
32 Rodney Hampton .40 1.00
33 Heath Shuler .40 1.00
34 Michael Westbrook .60 1.50
35 Barry Sanders 3.00 8.00
36 Brett Favre 3.00 8.00
37 Cris Carter .75 2.00
38 Warren Moon .40 1.00
39 James A.Stewart .05 .15
40 Errict Rhett .40 1.00

1996 SP

The 1996 SP set was issued in one series totalling 188 cards. The 8-card packs retail for $4.39 each. The set contains the topical subset Premier Prospects (1-20). The fronts feature color action player photos with a small player head portrait insert and a silver foil border around two-thirds of the card. The backs display another player photo with biographical information and statistics.

COMPLETE SET (188) 40.00 100.00
1 Keyshawn Johnson RC 3.00 8.00
2 Kevin Hardy RC .30 .75
3 Simeon Rice RC 1.25 3.00
4 Jonathan Ogden RC 6.00 12.00
5 Eddie George RC 4.00 10.00
6 Terry Glenn RC 2.50 6.00
7 Terrell Owens RC 8.00 20.00
8 Tim Biakabutuka RC .75 2.00
9 Lawrence Phillips RC .30 .75
10 Alex Molden RC .15 .40
11 Regan Upshaw RC .15 .40
12 Rickey Dudley RC .50 1.25
13 Duane Clemons RC .15 .40
14 John Mobley RC .30 .75
15 Eddie Kennison RC .75 2.00
16 Karim Abdul-Jabbar RC .50 1.25
17 Eric Moulds RC 1.50 4.00
18 Marvin Harrison RC 6.00 15.00
19 Stepfret Williams RC .15 .40
20 Stephen Davis RC 3.00 8.00
21 Deion Sanders .50 1.25
22 Emmitt Smith 1.25 3.00
23 Troy Aikman .75 2.00
24 Michael Irvin .30 .75
25 Herschel Walker .15 .40
26 Kavika Pittman RC .07 .20
27 Andre Hastings .07 .20
28 Jerome Bettis .30 .75
29 Mike Tomczak .07 .20
30 Kordell Stewart .30 .75
31 Charles Johnson .07 .20
32 Greg Lloyd .15 .40
33 Brett Favre 1.50 4.00
34 Mark Chmura .15 .40
35 Edgar Bennett .15 .40
36 Robert Brooks .15 .40
37 Craig Newsome .07 .20
38 Reggie White .30 .75
39 Jim Harbaugh .15 .40
40 Marshall Faulk .40 1.00
41 Sean Dawkins .07 .20
42 Quentin Coryatt .07 .20
43 Ray Buchanan .07 .20
44 Ken Dilger .15 .40
45 Jerry Rice .75 2.00
46 J.J. Stokes .30 .75
47 Steve Young .60 1.50
48 Derek Loville .07 .20
49 Terry Kirby .15 .40
50 Ken Norton .07 .20
51 Tamarick Vanover .15 .40
52 Marcus Allen .30 .75
53 Steve Bono .07 .20
54 Neil Smith .15 .40
55 Derrick Thomas .30 .75
56 Dale Carter .07 .20
57 Terance Mathis .07 .20
58 Eric Metcalf .07 .20
59 Jamal Anderson RC .60 1.50
60 Bert Emanuel .15 .40
61 Craig Heyward .07 .20
62 Cornelius Bennett .07 .20
63 Tony Martin .15 .40
64 Stan Humphries .15 .40
65 Andre Coleman .07 .20
66 Junior Seau .30 .75
67 Terrell Fletcher .07 .20
68 John Carney .07 .20
69 Charlie Jones RC .15 .40
70 Ricky Watters .15 .40
71 Charlie Garner .15 .40
72 Bobby Hoying RC .30 .75
73 Jason Dunn RC .15 .40
74 Bobby Taylor .07 .20
75 Irving Fryar .15 .40
76 Jim Kelly .30 .75
77 Thurman Thomas .30 .75
78 Bruce Smith .15 .40
79 Bryce Paup .07 .20
80 Darick Holmes .07 .20
81 Andre Reed .15 .40
82 Glyn Milburn .07 .20
83 Brett Perriman .07 .20
84 Herman Moore .15 .40
85 Scott Mitchell .15 .40
86 Barry Sanders 1.25 3.00
87 Johnnie Morton .15 .40
88 Dan Marino 1.50 4.00
89 O.J. McDuffie .15 .40
90 Stanley Pritchett RC .07 .20
91 Zach Thomas RC 2.00 5.00
92 Daryl Gardener RC .07 .20
93 Rashaan Salaam .15 .40
94 Erik Kramer .07 .20
95 Curtis Conway .30 .75
96 Bobby Engram RC .30 .75
97 Walt Harris RC .07 .20
98 Bryan Cox .07 .20
99 John Elway 1.50 4.00
100 Terrell Davis .60 1.50
101 Anthony Miller .15 .40
102 Shannon Sharpe .15 .40
103 Tory James RC .30 .75
104 Jeff Lewis RC .15 .40
105 Joey Galloway .30 .75
106 Chris Warren .15 .40
107 Rick Mirer .15 .40
108 Cortez Kennedy .07 .20
109 Michael Sinclair .07 .20
110 John Friesz .07 .20
111 Warren Moon .15 .40
112 Cris Carter .30 .75
113 Jake Reed .15 .40
114 Robert Smith .15 .40
115 John Randle .15 .40
116 Orlando Thomas .07 .20
117 Jeff Hostetler .07 .20
118 Tim Brown .30 .75
119 Joe Aska .07 .20
120 Napoleon Kaufman .30 .75
121 Terry McDaniel .07 .20
122 Harvey Williams .07 .20
123 Trent Dilfer .30 .75
124 Reggie Brooks .07 .20
125 Alvin Harper .07 .20
126 Mike Alstott RC 2.00 5.00
127 Hardy Nickerson .07 .20
128 Mario Bates .15 .40
129 Jim Everett .07 .20
130 Tyrone Hughes .07 .20
131 Michael Haynes .07 .20
132 Eric Allen .07 .20
133 Isaac Bruce .30 .75
134 Kevin Carter .07 .20
135 Leslie O'Neal .07 .20
136 Tony Banks RC .30 .75
137 Chris Chandler .15 .40
138 Steve McNair .60 1.50
139 Chris Sanders .15 .40
140 Ronnie Harmon .07 .20
141 Willie Davis .07 .20
142 Michael Westbrook .30 .75
143 Terry Allen .15 .40
144 Brian Mitchell .07 .20
145 Henry Ellard .07 .20
146 Gus Frerotte .15 .40
147 Kerry Collins .30 .75
148 Sam Mills .07 .20
149 Wesley Walls .15 .40
150 Kevin Greene .15 .40
151 Muhsin Muhammad RC 1.50 4.00
152 Winslow Oliver .07 .20
153 Jeff Blake .30 .75
154 Carl Pickens .15 .40
155 Darnay Scott .15 .40
156 Garrison Hearst .15 .40
157 Marco Battaglia RC .07 .20
158 Drew Bledsoe .50 1.25
159 Curtis Martin .60 1.50
160 Shawn Jefferson .07 .20
161 Ben Coates .15 .40
162 Lawyer Milloy RC .75 2.00
163 Tyrone Wheatley .15 .40
164 Rodney Hampton .15 .40
165 Chris Calloway .07 .20
166 Dave Brown .07 .20
167 Amani Toomer RC 1.50 4.00
168 Vinny Testaverde .15 .40
169 Michael Jackson .15 .40
170 Eric Turner .07 .20
171 DeRon Jenkins .07 .20
172 Jermaine Lewis RC .30 .75
173 Frank Sanders .15 .40
174 Rob Moore .15 .40
175 Kent Graham .07 .20
176 Leeland McElroy RC .15 .40
177 Larry Centers .15 .40
178 Eric Swann .07 .20
179 Mark Brunell .50 1.25
180 Willie Jackson .15 .40
181 James O. Stewart .15 .40
182 Natrone Means .15 .40
183 Tony Brackens RC .30 .75
184 Adrian Murrell .15 .40
185 Neil O'Donnell .15 .40
186 Hugh Douglas .15 .40
187 Wayne Chrebet .40 1.00
188 Alex Van Dyke RC .15 .40
SP13 Dan Marino Promo 1.25 3.00

1996 SP Explosive

Randomly inserted in packs at a rate of one in 360, this 20-card set features 20 of the most explosive players in the NFL. The cards carry a circular player portrait over a larger player image in the background and are die-cut in an "x" shape.

STATED ODDS 1:360
X1 Emmitt Smith 50.00 120.00
X2 Jerry Rice 30.00 80.00
X3 Rashaan Salaam 10.00 25.00
X4 Brett Favre 50.00 120.00
X5 Napoleon Kaufman 10.00 25.00
X6 Tim Biakabutuka 10.00 25.00
X7 John Elway 40.00 100.00
X8 Steve Young 25.00 60.00
X9 Isaac Bruce 12.00 30.00
X10 Troy Aikman 30.00 80.00
X11 Drew Bledsoe 15.00 40.00
X12 Carl Pickens 10.00 25.00
X13 Dan Marino 50.00 120.00
X14 Eddie George 12.00 30.00
X15 Joey Galloway 12.00 30.00
X16 Deion Sanders 25.00 60.00
X17 Curtis Martin 25.00 60.00
X18 Marshall Faulk 12.00 30.00
X19 Keyshawn Johnson 15.00 40.00
X20 Barry Sanders 40.00 100.00

1996 SP Focus on the Future

Randomly inserted in packs at a rate of one in 30, this 30-card set features some of the future young stars of the NFL. The cards display a color action player photo with a slide film image of the player beside it. The player's name and the photographer are printed on the slide border. The backs carry player information.

COMPLETE SET (30) 75.00 200.00
STATED ODDS 1:30
F1 Leeland McElroy .60 1.50
F2 Frank Sanders .60 1.50
F3 Darick Holmes .60 1.50
F4 Eric Moulds 4.00 10.00
F5 Kerry Collins 4.00 10.00
F6 Tim Biakabutuka .60 1.50
F7 Ki-Jana Carter .60 1.50
F8 Jeff Blake 2.50 6.00
F9 John Mobley .60 1.50
F10 Johnnie Morton .60 1.50
F11 Eddie George 5.00 12.00
F12 Steve McNair 5.00 12.00
F13 Marshall Faulk 4.00 10.00
F14 Kevin Hardy .60 1.50
F15 Greg Hill .60 1.50
F16 Mario Bates .60 1.50
F17 Karim Abdul-Jabbar 1.25 3.00
F18 Drew Bledsoe 4.00 10.00
F19 Curtis Martin 5.00 12.00
F20 Danny Kanell .60 1.50
F21 Keyshawn Johnson 4.00 10.00
F22 Napoleon Kaufman 1.25 3.00
F23 Rickey Dudley .60 1.50
F24 Kordell Stewart 2.50 6.00
F25 Lawrence Phillips .60 1.50
F26 Isaac Bruce 2.50 6.00
F27 J.J. Stokes 1.25 3.00
F28 Joey Galloway 2.50 6.00
F29 Errict Rhett .60 1.50
F30 Mike Alstott 2.50 6.00

1996 SP Holoviews

Randomly inserted in packs at a rate of one in seven, this 48-card set features the top 1996 rookies along with veteran players. Utilizing "holoview" technology, the fronts carry a color action player image and a head portrait on a background with the team logo running throughout. The backs contain player information.

COMPLETE SET (48) 75.00 150.00
STATED ODDS 1:7
*DIE CUTS: .8X TO 2X BASIC INSERTS
DIE CUT STATED ODDS 1:74
1 Jerry Rice 2.50 6.00
2 Herman Moore .50 1.25
3 Kerry Collins 1.00 2.50
4 Brett Favre 5.00 12.00
5 Junior Seau 1.00 2.50
6 Troy Aikman 2.50 6.00
7 John Elway 5.00 12.00
8 Steve Young 2.00 5.00
9 Reggie White 1.00 2.50
10 Kordell Stewart 1.00 2.50
11 Drew Bledsoe 1.50 4.00
12 Jeff Blake 1.00 2.50
13 Dan Marino 5.00 12.00
14 Curtis Martin 2.00 5.00
15 Marshall Faulk 1.25 3.00
16 Greg Lloyd .50 1.25
17 Cris Carter 1.00 2.50
18 Isaac Bruce 1.00 2.50
19 Joey Galloway 1.00 2.50
20 Barry Sanders 4.00 10.00
21 Emmitt Smith 4.00 10.00
22 Edgar Bennett .50 1.25
23 Rashaan Salaam .50 1.25
24 Steve McNair 2.00 5.00
25 Tamarick Vanover .50 1.25
26 Deion Sanders 1.50 4.00
27 Keyshawn Johnson 2.50 6.00
28 Kevin Hardy .25 .60
29 Simeon Rice .50 1.25
30 Lawrence Phillips .25 .60
31 Tim Biakabutuka .50 1.25
32 Terry Glenn 2.00 5.00
33 Rickey Dudley .25 .60
34 Regan Upshaw .25 .60
35 Eddie George 3.00 8.00
36 John Mobley .25 .60
37 Eddie Kennison .50 1.25
38 Marvin Harrison 6.00 15.00
39 Leeland McElroy .25 .60
40 Eric Moulds 2.50 6.00
41 Alex Van Dyke .25 .60
42 Mike Alstott 1.50 4.00
43 Jeff Lewis .25 .60
44 Bobby Engram .25 .60
45 Derrick Mayes .25 .60
46 Karim Abdul-Jabbar .50 1.25
47 Stepfret Williams .25 .60
48 Stephen Davis 4.00 10.00

1996 SP SPx Force

Randomly inserted in packs at a rate of one in 950, this multi-holoview die-cut set features the game's best players at quarterback, running back, wide receiver, and rookies. Printed on 32-point stock, each card displays color player portraits of four different players with the players' and teams' names printed either above or below each player's picture. The fifth card of this set features the top player from each category with each card signed by one of the four players pictured on the card. The Barry Sanders #5 card was actually a redemption for a signed card. The expiration date was 12/19/97. The insertion rate for the signed cards was one in every 8820 packs.

COMPLETE SET (4) 40.00 100.00
STATED ODDS 1:950
AUTO STATED ODDS 1:8820
FR1 K.John/Phill/Glenn/Biak 7.50 20.00
FR2 BSan/ESmi/Faulk/CMart 15.00 40.00
FR3 Marino/Favre/Bled/Aikmn 15.00 40.00
FR4 Rice/Moore/Pick/Bruce 10.00 25.00
SPX5A Key.Johnson AUTO 50.00 120.00
SPX5B Dan Marino AUTO 100.00 250.00
SPX5C Jerry Rice AUTO 60.00 150.00
SPX5D Barry Sanders AUTO 125.00 250.00

1997 SP Authentic

The 1997 SP Authentic set was issued in one series totalling 198 cards and distributed in five-card packs with a suggested retail price of $4.99. The fronts features color player photos, while the backs carry player information. The set contains the topical subset: Future Watch (1-30).

COMPLETE SET (198) 50.00 100.00
1 Orlando Pace RC .75 2.00
2 Darrell Russell RC .20 .50
3 Shawn Springs RC .40 1.00
4 Peter Boulware RC 1.50 4.00
5 Bryant Westbrook RC .40 1.00
6 Walter Jones RC 1.25 3.00
7 Ike Hilliard RC 1.50 4.00
8 James Farrior RC 1.25 3.00
9 Tom Knight RC .20 .50
10 Warrick Dunn RC 4.00 10.00
11 Tony Gonzalez RC 10.00 25.00
12 Reinard Wilson RC .40 1.00
13 Yatil Green RC .40 1.00
14 Reidel Anthony RC .75 2.00
15 Kenny Holmes RC .20 .50
16 Dwayne Rudd RC .20 .50
17 Renaldo Wynn RC .20 .50
18 David LaFleur RC .20 .50
19 Antowain Smith RC 2.50 6.00
20 Jim Druckenmiller RC .40 1.00
21 Rae Carruth RC .20 .50
22 Byron Hanspard RC .40 1.00
23 Jake Plummer RC 4.00 10.00
24 Joey Kent RC .40 1.00
25 Corey Dillon RC 4.00 10.00
26 Danny Wuerffel RC 2.00 5.00
27 Will Blackwell RC .20 .50
28 Troy Davis RC .40 1.00
29 Darnell Autry RC .40 1.00
30 Pat Barnes RC .40 1.00
31 Kent Graham .20 .50
32 Simeon Rice .30 .75
33 Frank Sanders .30 .75
34 Rob Moore .30 .75
35 Eric Swann .20 .50
36 Chris Chandler .30 .75
37 Jamal Anderson .50 1.25
38 Terance Mathis .30 .75
39 Bert Emanuel .30 .75
40 Michael Booker .20 .50
41 Vinny Testaverde .30 .75
42 Byron Bam Morris .20 .50
43 Michael Jackson .30 .75
44 Derrick Alexander WR .30 .75
45 Jamie Sharper RC .75 2.00
46 Kim Herring RC .20 .50
47 Todd Collins .20 .50
48 Thurman Thomas .50 1.25
49 Andre Reed .30 .75
50 Quinn Early .20 .50
51 Bryce Paup .20 .50
52 Lonnie Johnson .20 .50
53 Kerry Collins .50 1.25
54 Anthony Johnson .20 .50
55 Tim Biakabutuka .30 .75
56 Muhsin Muhammad .30 .75
57 Sam Mills .20 .50
58 Wesley Walls .30 .75
59 Rick Mirer .20 .50
60 Raymont Harris .20 .50
61 Curtis Conway .30 .75
62 Bobby Engram .30 .75
63 Bryan Cox .20 .50
64 John Allred RC .20 .50
65 Jeff Blake .30 .75
66 Ki-Jana Carter .20 .50
67 Darnay Scott .30 .75
68 Carl Pickens .30 .75
69 Dan Wilkinson .20 .50
70 Troy Aikman 1.25 2.50
71 Emmitt Smith 2.00 4.00
72 Michael Irvin .50 1.25
73 Deion Sanders .50 1.25
74 Anthony Miller .20 .50
75 Antonio Anderson RC .20 .50
76 John Elway 2.00 5.00
77 Terrell Davis .60 1.50
78 Rod Smith WR .50 1.25
79 Shannon Sharpe .30 .75
80 Neil Smith .30 .75
81 Trevor Pryce RC .75 2.00
82 Scott Mitchell .30 .75
83 Barry Sanders 1.50 4.00
84 Herman Moore .30 .75
85 Johnnie Morton .30 .75
86 Matt Russell RC .20 .50
87 Brett Favre 2.50 5.00
88 Edgar Bennett .30 .75
89 Robert Brooks .30 .75
90 Antonio Freeman .50 1.25
91 Reggie White .50 1.25
92 Craig Newsome .20 .50
93 Jim Harbaugh .30 .75
94 Marshall Faulk .60 1.50
95 Sean Dawkins .20 .50
96 Marvin Harrison .50 1.25
97 Quentin Coryatt .20 .50
98 Tarik Glenn RC .40 1.00
99 Mark Brunell .60 1.50
100 Natrone Means .30 .75
101 Keenan McCardell .30 .75
102 Jimmy Smith .30 .75
103 Tony Brackens .20 .50
104 Kevin Hardy .20 .50
105 Elvis Grbac .30 .75
106 Marcus Allen .50 1.25
107 Greg Hill .20 .50
108 Derrick Thomas .50 1.25
109 Dale Carter .20 .50
110 Dan Marino 2.00 5.00
111 Karim Abdul-Jabbar .30 .75
112 Brian Manning RC .20 .50
113 Daryl Gardener .20 .50
114 Troy Drayton .20 .50
115 Zach Thomas .50 1.25
116 Jason Taylor RC 8.00 20.00
117 Brad Johnson .50 1.25
118 Robert Smith .30 .75
119 John Randle .30 .75
120 Cris Carter .50 1.25
121 Jake Reed .30 .75
122 Randall Cunningham .50 1.25
123 Drew Bledsoe .60 1.50
124 Curtis Martin .60 1.50
125 Terry Glenn .50 1.25
126 Willie McGinest .20 .50
127 Chris Canty RC .20 .50
128 Sedrick Shaw RC .40 1.00
129 Heath Shuler .20 .50
130 Mario Bates .20 .50
131 Ray Zellars .20 .50
132 Andre Hastings .20 .50
133 Dave Brown .20 .50
134 Tyrone Wheatley .30 .75
135 Rodney Hampton .30 .75
136 Chris Calloway .20 .50
137 Tiki Barber RC 8.00 20.00
138 Neil O'Donnell .30 .75
139 Adrian Murrell .30 .75
140 Wayne Chrebet .50 1.25
141 Keyshawn Johnson .50 1.25
142 Hugh Douglas .20 .50
143 Jeff George .30 .75
144 Napoleon Kaufman .50 1.25
145 Tim Brown .50 1.25
146 Desmond Howard .30 .75
147 Rickey Dudley .30 .75
148 Terry McDaniel .20 .50
149 Ty Detmer .30 .75
150 Ricky Watters .30 .75
151 Chris T. Jones .20 .50
152 Irving Fryar .30 .75
153 Mike Mamula .20 .50
154 Jon Harris RC .20 .50
155 Kordell Stewart .50 1.25
156 Jerome Bettis .50 1.25
157 Charles Johnson .30 .75
158 Greg Lloyd .20 .50
159 George Jones RC .20 .50
160 Terrell Fletcher .20 .50
161 Stan Humphries .30 .75
162 Tony Martin .30 .75
163 Eric Metcalf .30 .75
164 Junior Seau .50 1.25
165 Rod Woodson .30 .75
166 Steve Young .60 1.50
167 Terry Kirby .30 .75
168 Garrison Hearst .30 .75
169 Jerry Rice 1.25 2.50
170 Ken Norton .20 .50
171 Kevin Greene .30 .75
172 Lamar Smith .50 1.25
173 Warren Moon .50 1.25
174 Chris Warren .30 .75
175 Cortez Kennedy .20 .50
176 Joey Galloway .30 .75
177 Tony Banks .30 .75
178 Isaac Bruce .50 1.25
179 Eddie Kennison .30 .75
180 Kevin Carter .20 .50
181 Craig Heyward .20 .50
182 Trent Dilfer .50 1.25
183 Errict Rhett .20 .50
184 Mike Alstott .50 1.25
185 Hardy Nickerson .20 .50
186 Ronde Barber RC 10.00 25.00
187 Steve McNair .60 1.50
188 Eddie George .50 1.25
189 Chris Sanders .20 .50
190 Blaine Bishop .20 .50
191 Derrick Mason RC 4.00 10.00
192 Gus Frerotte .20 .50
193 Terry Allen .50 1.25
194 Brian Mitchell .20 .50
195 Alvin Harper .20 .50
196 Jeff Hostetler .20 .50
197 Leslie Shepherd .20 .50
198 Stephen Davis .50 1.25
A1 Aikman Audio Blue 1.50 4.00
A2 Aikman Audio Pro Bowl 4.00 10.00
A3 Aikman Audio White/500 15.00 30.00

1997 SP Authentic Mark of a Legend

Randomly inserted in packs at the rate of one in 168, these exchange cards included a white instructional sticker mounted to the cardfront with redemption rules. Collectors could mail the redemptions to Upper Deck before 10/30/1998 in exchange for a hand-signed unnumbered player card. Each unnumbered prize card was personally signed by the featured player and some were issued in either a silver foiled or non-foiled white paper stock version, or both. Apparently a very small number of Joe Namath signed cards were released but little else is known as to the exact quantity.

COMPLETE SET (7) 250.00 400.00
STATED ODDS 1:168
1 Tony Dorsett 30.00 60.00
1X Tony Dorsett EXCH 2.50 6.00
2 Bob Griese 25.00 50.00
2X Bob Griese EXCH 2.50 6.00
3 Franco Harris wht 30.00 60.00
3X Franco Harris EXCH 2.50 6.00
4 Steve Largent 25.00 50.00
4X Steve Largent EXCH 2.50 6.00
5 Joe Montana 60.00 120.00
5X Joe Montana EXCH 5.00 12.00
6 Joe Namath SP
7A Gale Sayers Wht 30.00 60.00
7B Gale Sayers Silv 30.00 60.00
7X Gale Sayers EXCH 2.50 6.00
8 Roger Staubach 50.00 80.00
8X Roger Staubach EXCH 3.00 8.00

1997 SP Authentic ProFiles

Randomly inserted in packs at the rate of one in five, this 40-card set features color photos of the league's most dominant players. The backs carry player information.

COMPLETE SET (40) 30.00 80.00
STATED ODDS 1:5
*DIE CUTS: .6X TO 1.5X BASIC INSERTS
DIE CUT STATED ODDS 1:12
*DIE CUT 100: 2.5X TO 6X BASIC INSERTS
STATED PRINT RUN 100 SERIAL #'d SETS
P1 Dan Marino 5.00 12.00
P2 Kordell Stewart 1.25 3.00
P3 Emmitt Smith 4.00 10.00
P4 Brett Favre 5.00 12.00
P5 Marcus Allen 1.25 3.00
P6 Jerry Rice 2.50 6.00
P7 Jeff George .75 2.00
P8 Mark Brunell 1.50 4.00
P9 Eddie George 1.25 3.00
P10 Cris Carter 1.25 3.00
P11 Tim Biakabutuka .75 2.00
P12 Ike Hilliard .75 2.00
P13 Darrell Russell .08 .25
P14 Jim Druckenmiller .20 .50
P15 Rae Carruth .08 .25
P16 Warrick Dunn 5.00 12.00
P17 Herman Moore .75 2.00
P18 Deion Sanders 1.25 3.00
P19 Drew Bledsoe 1.50 4.00
P20 Jeff Blake .75 2.00
P21 Keyshawn Johnson 1.25 3.00
P22 Curtis Martin 1.50 4.00
P23 Michael Irvin 1.25 3.00
P24 Barry Sanders 4.00 10.00
P25 Carl Pickens .75 2.00
P26 Steve McNair 1.50 4.00
P27 Terry Allen 1.25 3.00
P28 Terrell Davis 1.50 4.00
P29 Lawrence Phillips .50 1.25
P30 Marshall Faulk 1.50 4.00
P31 Karim Abdul-Jabbar .75 2.00
P32 Steve Young 1.50 4.00
P33 Tim Brown 1.25 3.00
P34 Antowain Smith 2.50 6.00
P35 Kerry Collins 1.25 3.00
P36 Reggie White 1.25 3.00
P37 John Elway 5.00 12.00
P38 Jerome Bettis 1.25 3.00
P39 Troy Aikman 2.50 6.00
P40 Junior Seau 1.25 3.00

1997 SP Authentic Sign of the Times

Randomly inserted in packs at the rate of one in 24, this set featured redemption cards for favorite current NFL stars with a white instructional sticker mounted to the cardfront. Collectors could redeem the cards for signed prize cards which are listed below. The cards are unnumbered and checklisted below in alphabetical order. Foiled and non-foiled versions of some cards were mailed as redemptions. While some player's cards have been found in both versions, others have only been reported as non-foiled.

STATED ODDS 1:24
1 Karim Abdul-Jabbar 8.00 20.00
2 Troy Aikman 40.00 80.00
3 Terry Allen 8.00 20.00
4 Reidel Anthony 6.00 15.00
5 Jerome Bettis 50.00 100.00
6 Will Blackwell 6.00 15.00
7 Jeff Blake 8.00 20.00
8 Robert Brooks 8.00 20.00
9 Tim Brown 12.00 30.00
10 Isaac Bruce 10.00 25.00
11 Rae Carruth 8.00 20.00
12 Kerry Collins 10.00 25.00
13 Terrell Davis 12.00 30.00
14 Jim Druckenmiller 6.00 15.00
15 Warrick Dunn 8.00 20.00
16 Marshall Faulk 10.00 25.00
17 Joey Galloway 8.00 20.00
18 Eddie George 10.00 25.00
19 Tony Gonzalez 25.00 50.00
20 George Jones 6.00 15.00
21 Napoleon Kaufman 8.00 20.00
22A Dan Marino silver 50.00 100.00
22B Dan Marino white 50.00 100.00
23 Curtis Martin SP 25.00 50.00
24 Herman Moore 8.00 20.00
25A Jerry Rice silver 75.00 150.00
25B Jerry Rice white SP 75.00 150.00
26 Rashaan Salaam 6.00 15.00
27 Antowain Smith 10.00 25.00
28 Emmitt Smith SP 100.00 200.00

1997 SP Authentic Traditions

Randomly inserted in packs at the rate of one in 1440, this six-card insert set includes silver foil cards with photos of a top NFL star along with the retired counterpart from the same team and position. The cards originally included a white instructional sticker on the cardfront that advised the collector to exchange it for a card signed by both players. The redemption offer expired on 9/30/98. We price only the autographed prize cards.

STATED ODDS 1:1440
TD1 D.Marino/B.Griese 150.00 300.00
TD2 T.Aikman/R.Staubach 125.00 250.00
TD3 J.Rice/J.Montana 300.00 500.00
TD4 J.Bettis/F.Harris 125.00 250.00
TD5 E.Smith/T.Dorsett 200.00 350.00
TD6 J.Galloway/S.Largent 75.00 135.00

1998 SP Authentic

This set was released in one series with a total of 126-cards. The first 42-cards (1998 draft picks and Time Warp subsets) were short-printed and serial numbered to 2000-sets produced. A Die Cut parallel of all cards was produced and numbered of 500-sets.

COMP.SET w/o SP's (84) 20.00 40.00
*HAND NUMBERED RC: .3X TO .8X
1 Andre Wadsworth RC 8.00 20.00
2 Corey Chavous RC 8.00 20.00
3 Keith Brooking RC 12.00 30.00
4 Duane Starks RC 5.00 12.00
5 Pat Johnson RC 5.00 12.00
6 Jason Peter RC 5.00 12.00
7 Curtis Enis RC 6.00 15.00
8 Takeo Spikes RC 8.00 20.00
9 Greg Ellis RC 6.00 15.00
10 Marcus Nash RC 5.00 12.00
11 Brian Griese RC 12.00 30.00
12 Germane Crowell RC 6.00 15.00
13 Vonnie Holliday RC 8.00 20.00
14 Peyton Manning RC 400.00 600.00
15 Jerome Pathon RC 5.00 12.00
16 Fred Taylor RC 20.00 40.00
17 John Avery RC 5.00 12.00
18 Randy Moss RC 80.00 200.00
19 Robert Edwards RC 5.00 12.00
20 Tony Simmons RC 5.00 12.00
21 Shaun Williams RC 5.00 12.00
22 Joe Jurevicius RC 8.00 20.00
23 Charles Woodson RC 40.00 80.00
24 Tra Thomas RC 5.00 12.00
25 Grant Wistrom RC 6.00 15.00
26 Ryan Leaf RC 8.00 20.00
27 Ahman Green RC 15.00 40.00
28 Jacquez Green RC 5.00 12.00
29 Kevin Dyson RC 8.00 20.00
30 Stephen Alexander RC 6.00 15.00
31 John Elway TW 6.00 15.00
32 Jerry Rice TW 5.00 12.00
33 Emmitt Smith TW 6.00 15.00
34 Steve Young TW 3.00 8.00
35 Jerome Bettis TW 2.50 6.00
36 Deion Sanders TW 2.50 6.00
37 Andre Rison TW 1.50 4.00
38 Warren Moon TW 2.50 6.00
39 Mark Brunell TW 2.00 5.00
40 Ricky Watters TW 1.50 4.00
41 Dan Marino TW 8.00 20.00
42 Brett Favre TW 10.00 25.00
43 Jake Plummer .40 1.00
44 Adrian Murrell .25 .60
45 Eric Swann .15 .40
46 Jamal Anderson .40 1.00
47 Chris Chandler .25 .60
48 Jim Harbaugh .25 .60
49 Michael Jackson .15 .40
50 Jermaine Lewis .25 .60
51 Rob Johnson .25 .60
52 Antowain Smith .40 1.00
53 Thurman Thomas .40 1.00
54 Kerry Collins .25 .60
55 Fred Lane .15 .40
56 Rae Carruth .15 .40
57 Erik Kramer .15 .40
58 Curtis Conway .25 .60
59 Corey Dillon .40 1.00
60 Neil O'Donnell .25 .60
61 Carl Pickens .25 .60
62 Troy Aikman .75 2.00
63 Emmitt Smith 1.25 3.00
64 Deion Sanders .40 1.00
65 Terrell Davis .40 1.00
66 John Elway 1.50 4.00
67 Rod Smith .25 .60
68 Scott Mitchell .25 .60
69 Barry Sanders 1.25 3.00
70 Herman Moore .25 .60
71 Brett Favre 1.50 4.00
72 Dorsey Levens .40 1.00
73 Antonio Freeman .40 1.00
74 Marshall Faulk .50 1.25
75 Marvin Harrison .40 1.00
76 Mark Brunell .40 1.00
77 Keenan McCardell .25 .60
78 Jimmy Smith .25 .60
79 Andre Rison .25 .60
80 Elvis Grbac .25 .60
81 Derrick Alexander .25 .60
82 Dan Marino 1.50 4.00
83 Karim Abdul-Jabbar .40 1.00
84 O.J. McDuffie .25 .60
85 Brad Johnson .40 1.00
86 Cris Carter .40 1.00
87 Robert Smith .40 1.00
88 Drew Bledsoe .60 1.50
89 Terry Glenn .40 1.00
90 Ben Coates .25 .60
91 Lamar Smith .25 .60
92 Danny Wuerffel .25 .60
93 Tiki Barber .40 1.00
94 Danny Kanell .25 .60
95 Ike Hilliard .25 .60
96 Curtis Martin .40 1.00
97 Keyshawn Johnson .40 1.00
98 Glenn Foley .25 .60
99 Jeff George .25 .60
100 Tim Brown .40 1.00
101 Napoleon Kaufman .40 1.00
102 Bobby Hoying .25 .60
103 Charlie Garner .25 .60
104 Irving Fryar .25 .60
105 Kordell Stewart .40 1.00
106 Jerome Bettis .40 1.00
107 Charles Johnson .15 .40
108 Tony Banks .25 .60
109 Isaac Bruce .40 1.00
110 Natrone Means .25 .60
111 Junior Seau .40 1.00
112 Steve Young .50 1.25
113 Jerry Rice .75 2.00
114 Garrison Hearst .40 1.00
115 Ricky Watters .25 .60
116 Warren Moon .40 1.00
117 Joey Galloway .25 .60
118 Trent Dilfer .40 1.00
119 Warrick Dunn .50 1.25
120 Mike Alstott .40 1.00
121 Steve McNair .40 1.00
122 Eddie George .40 1.00
123 Yancey Thigpen .15 .40
124 Gus Frerotte .15 .40
125 Terry Allen .40 1.00
126 Michael Westbrook .25 .60
AE13 Dan Marino SAMPLE 1.25 3.00

1998 SP Authentic Die Cuts

*DIE CUT VETS 43-126: 3X TO 8X
*DIE CUT TIME WARP 31-42: .6X TO 1.5X
*DIE CUT ROOKIE 1-30: .3X TO .8X
DIE CUT PRINT RUN 500 SER.#'d SETS
14 Peyton Manning 450.00 800.00
18 Randy Moss 50.00 120.00

1998 SP Authentic Maximum Impact

The Maximum Impact insert set featured cards of top veteran and young NFL stars. Each card was randomly seeded in packs at a rate of 1:4. An SE Die Cut version of each card was also produced with each numbered as a 1-of-1 insert.

COMPLETE SET (30) 20.00 50.00
STATED ODDS 1:4
SE1 Brett Favre 2.00 5.00
SE2 Warrick Dunn .60 1.50
SE3 Junior Seau .50 1.25
SE4 Steve Young .60 1.50
SE5 Herman Moore .30 .75
SE6 Antowain Smith .50 1.25
SE7 John Elway 2.00 5.00
SE8 Troy Aikman 1.00 2.50
SE9 Dorsey Levens .50 1.25
SE10 Kordell Stewart .50 1.25
SE11 Peyton Manning 8.00 20.00
SE12 Eddie George .50 1.25
SE13 Dan Marino 2.00 5.00
SE14 Joey Galloway .30 .75
SE15 Mark Brunell .50 1.25
SE16 Jake Plummer .50 1.25
SE17 Curtis Enis .30 .75
SE18 Corey Dillon .50 1.25
SE19 Rob Johnson .30 .75
SE20 Barry Sanders 1.50 4.00
SE21 Deion Sanders .50 1.25
SE22 Napoleon Kaufman .50 1.25
SE23 Ryan Leaf .50 1.25
SE24 Jerry Rice 1.00 2.50
SE25 Drew Bledsoe .50 1.25
SE26 Jerome Bettis .50 1.25
SE27 Emmitt Smith 1.50 4.00
SE28 Tim Brown .50 1.25
SE29 Curtis Martin .50 1.25
SE30 Terrell Davis .50 1.25

1998 SP Authentic Player's Ink Green

These signed cards were randomly inserted in 1998 SP Authentic packs. There are three background color versions for each player with varying insertion ratios: overall odds 1:23, silver cards numbered of 100, and golds numbered to the player's jersey number. Some cards were issued in packs as mail order redemptions while others were standard inserts. The redemption cards were a standard Player's Ink card featuring the player's photo along with an attached sticker that included the rules for the redemption program. The expiration date for the trade cards was 7/15/1999. Note that some players also signed in two different colored inks.

STATED ODDS 1:23 OVERALL
AW Andre Wadsworth 8.00 20.00
BG Brian Griese 10.00 25.00
BH Bobby Hoying 8.00 20.00
CD Corey Dillon 8.00 20.00
CE Curtis Enis 8.00 20.00
DL Dorsey Levens 8.00 20.00
DM Dan Marino 75.00 150.00
EG Eddie George 10.00 25.00
FL Fred Lane 10.00 25.00
FT Fred Taylor 12.00 30.00
GC Germane Crowell 5.00 12.00
JA Jamal Anderson 8.00 20.00
JM Johnnie Morton 8.00 20.00
JP Jake Plummer 10.00 25.00
JR Jerry Rice 100.00 200.00
KJ Keyshawn Johnson 10.00 25.00
KM Keenan McCardell 8.00 20.00
KS Kordell Stewart 8.00 20.00
MA Mike Alstott 10.00 25.00
MJ Michael Jackson 5.00 12.00
MN Marcus Nash 5.00 12.00
PA Jerome Pathon 5.00 12.00
RE Robert Edwards 8.00 20.00
RL Ryan Leaf 8.00 20.00
RM Randy Moss 50.00 100.00
SH Skip Hicks 8.00 20.00
SS Shannon Sharpe 8.00 20.00
TA Troy Aikman 30.00 60.00
TS Takeo Spikes 8.00 20.00
TV Tamarick Vanover 5.00 12.00

1998 SP Authentic Player's Ink Gold

These signed cards are the Gold parallel to the base Player's Ink inserts. Each card is numbered to the player's jersey number. Some cards were issued in packs as mail order redemptions while others were standard inserts. The expiration date for the trade cards was 7/15/99.

GOLDS SERIAL #'d TO PLAYER'S JERSEY NO.
CARDS SERIAL #'d UNDER 25 NOT PRICED
AW Andre Wadsworth/90 20.00 50.00
CD Corey Dillon/28 25.00 60.00
CE Curtis Enis/39 25.00 60.00
DL Dorsey Levens/25 25.00 60.00
EG Eddie George/27 50.00 100.00
FL Fred Lane/32 20.00 50.00
FT Fred Taylor/28 60.00 120.00
JA Jamal Anderson/32 25.00 60.00
JM Johnnie Morton/87 20.00 50.00
JR Jerry Rice/80 125.00 250.00
KM Keenan McCardell/87 20.00 50.00
MA Mike Alstott/40 30.00 80.00
MJ Michael Jackson/81 20.00 50.00
RE Robert Edwards/47 20.00 50.00
SS Shannon Sharpe/84 20.00 50.00
TS Takeo Spikes/51 15.00 40.00
TV Tamarick Vanover/87 20.00 50.00

1998 SP Authentic Player's Ink Silver

*SILVERS: .8X TO 2X GREENS
JR Jerry Rice 75.00 150.00
RM Randy Moss 50.00 120.00

1998 SP Authentic Special Forces

Specila Forces features top players at key offensive positions. Each card was randomly inserted in packs and serial numbered of 1000.

COMPLETE SET (30) 100.00 200.00
STATED PRINT RUN 1000 SERIAL #'d SETS
S1 Kordell Stewart 2.00 5.00
S2 Charles Woodson 3.00 8.00
S3 Terrell Davis 2.00 5.00
S4 Brett Favre 8.00 20.00
S5 Joey Galloway 1.25 3.00
S6 Warrick Dunn 2.50 6.00
S7 Ryan Leaf 2.00 5.00
S8 Drew Bledsoe 3.00 8.00
S9 Takeo Spikes 1.25 3.00
S10 Barry Sanders 6.00 15.00
S11 Troy Aikman 4.00 10.00
S12 John Elway 8.00 20.00
S13 Jerome Bettis 2.00 5.00
S14 Karim Abdul-Jabbar 2.00 5.00
S15 Tony Gonzalez 2.00 5.00
S16 Steve Young 2.50 6.00
S17 Napoleon Kaufman 2.00 5.00
S18 Andre Wadsworth 1.25 3.00
S19 Herman Moore 1.25 3.00
S20 Fred Taylor 4.00 10.00
S21 Deion Sanders 2.00 5.00
S22 Peyton Manning 15.00 40.00
S23 Jerry Rice 4.00 10.00
S24 Dan Marino 8.00 20.00
S25 Antonio Freeman 2.00 5.00
S26 Curtis Enis 1.25 3.00
S27 Jake Plummer 2.00 5.00
S28 Steve McNair 2.00 5.00
S29 Mark Brunell 2.00 5.00
S30 Robert Edwards 1.25 3.00

1999 SP Authentic

Released as a 145-card base set, the 1999 SP Authentic set features 90 veteran cards and 55 rookie cards. Base cards are printed on white card stock with gold foil highlights. Rookie cards are sequentially numbered out of 1999. The set was released in boxes containing 24 packs of 5 cards each, and carried a suggested retail price of $4.99.

COMP.SET w/o SPs (90) 12.00 30.00
*HAND NUMBERED RCs: .3X TO .8X
1 Jake Plummer .25 .60
2 Adrian Murrell .25 .60
3 Frank Sanders .25 .60
4 Jamal Anderson .30 .75
5 Chris Chandler .30 .75
6 Terance Mathis .25 .60
7 Priest Holmes .25 .60
8 Jermaine Lewis .25 .60
9 Antowain Smith .25 .60
10 Doug Flutie .40 1.00
11 Eric Moulds .25 .60
12 Muhsin Muhammad .25 .60
13 Tim Biakabutuka .30 .75
14 Wesley Walls .30 .75
15 Curtis Enis .25 .60
16 Bobby Engram .25 .60
17 Corey Dillon .25 .60
18 Darnay Scott .25 .60
19 Terry Kirby .25 .60
20 Ty Detmer .25 .60
21 Troy Aikman .50 1.25
22 Michael Irvin .40 1.00
23 Emmitt Smith .60 1.50
24 Terrell Davis .30 .75

25 Brian Griese .25 .60
26 Rod Smith .30 .75
27 Shannon Sharpe .30 .75
28 Barry Sanders .60 1.50
29 Charlie Batch .25 .60
30 Herman Moore .30 .75
31 Johnnie Morton .30 .75
32 Brett Favre .75 2.00
33 Antonio Freeman .30 .75
34 Dorsey Levens .30 .75
35 Mark Chmura .25 .60
36 Peyton Manning 1.25 3.00
37 Marvin Harrison .30 .75
38 Mark Brunell .30 .75
39 Fred Taylor .25 .60
40 Jimmy Smith .30 .75
41 Elvis Grbac .25 .60
42 Andre Rison .30 .75
43 Dan Marino .75 2.00
44 O.J. McDuffie .30 .75
45 Yatil Green .25 .60
46 Randall Cunningham .30 .75
47 Randy Moss .30 .75
48 Robert Smith .25 .60
49 Cris Carter .40 1.00
50 Drew Bledsoe .30 .75
51 Ben Coates .30 .75
52 Terry Glenn .30 .75
53 Eddie Kennison .30 .75
54 Cam Cleeland .25 .60
55 Ike Hilliard .25 .60
56 Gary Brown .25 .60
57 Kerry Collins .25 .60
58 Vinny Testaverde .25 .60
59 Keyshawn Johnson .30 .75
60 Wayne Chrebet .25 .60
61 Curtis Martin .30 .75
62 Tim Brown .40 1.00
63 Napoleon Kaufman .25 .60
64 Charles Woodson .40 1.00
65 Duce Staley .25 .60
66 Charles Johnson .25 .60
67 Kordell Stewart .25 .60
68 Jerome Bettis .40 1.00
69 Marshall Faulk .30 .75
70 Isaac Bruce .40 1.00
71 Trent Green .25 .60
72 Jim Harbaugh .30 .75
73 Junior Seau .30 .75
74 Natrone Means .30 .75
75 Steve Young .50 1.25
76 Jerry Rice 1.00 2.50
77 Terrell Owens .30 .75
78 Lawrence Phillips .30 .75
79 Joey Galloway .30 .75
80 Ricky Watters .30 .75
81 Jon Kitna .25 .60
82 Warrick Dunn .25 .60
83 Trent Dilfer .25 .60
84 Mike Alstott .25 .60
85 Eddie George .30 .75
86 Steve McNair .30 .75
87 Yancey Thigpen .25 .60
88 Brad Johnson .30 .75
89 Skip Hicks .25 .60
90 Michael Westbrook .25 .60
91 Ricky Williams RC 6.00 15.00
92 Tim Couch RC 4.00 10.00
93 Akili Smith RC 3.00 8.00
94 Edgerrin James RC 5.00 12.00
95 Donovan McNabb RC 15.00 40.00
96 Torry Holt RC 6.00 15.00
97 Cade McNown RC 3.00 8.00
98 Shaun King RC 3.00 8.00
99 Daunte Culpepper RC 5.00 12.00
100 Brock Huard RC 3.00 8.00
101 Chris Claiborne RC 3.00 8.00
102 James Johnson RC 3.00 8.00
103 Rob Konrad RC 3.00 8.00
104 Peerless Price RC 3.00 8.00
105 Kevin Faulk RC 3.00 8.00
106 Andy Katzenmoyer RC 4.00 10.00
107 Troy Edwards RC 3.00 8.00
108 Kevin Johnson RC 4.00 10.00
109 Mike Cloud RC 3.00 8.00
110 David Boston RC 3.00 8.00
111 Champ Bailey RC 6.00 15.00
112 D'Wayne Bates RC 3.00 8.00
113 Joe Germaine RC 4.00 10.00
114 Antoine Winfield RC 3.00 8.00
115 Fernando Bryant RC 3.00 8.00
116 Jevon Kearse RC 4.00 10.00
117 Chris McAlister RC 3.00 8.00
118 Brandon Stokley RC 6.00 15.00
119 Karsten Bailey RC 3.00 8.00
120 Daylon McCutcheon RC 3.00 8.00
121 Jermaine Fazande RC 3.00 8.00
122 Joel Makovicka RC 3.00 8.00
123 Ebenezer Ekuban RC 3.00 8.00
124 Joe Montgomery RC 3.00 8.00
125 Sean Bennett RC 3.00 8.00
126 Na Brown RC 3.00 8.00
127 De'Mond Parker RC 3.00 8.00
128 Sedrick Irvin RC 3.00 8.00
129 Terry Jackson RC 3.00 8.00
130 Jeff Paulk RC 3.00 8.00
131 Cecil Collins RC 3.00 8.00
132 Bobby Collins RC 3.00 8.00
133 Amos Zereoue RC 3.00 8.00
134 Travis McGriff RC 3.00 8.00
135 Larry Parker RC 4.00 10.00
136 Wane McGarity RC 3.00 8.00
137 Cecil Martin RC 3.00 8.00
138 Al Wilson RC 5.00 12.00
139 Jim Kleinsasser RC 5.00 12.00
140 Dat Nguyen RC 5.00 12.00
141 Marty Booker RC 3.00 8.00
142 Reginald Kelly RC 3.00 8.00
143 Scott Covington RC 3.00 8.00
144 Antuan Edwards RC 3.00 8.00
145 Craig Yeast RC 3.00 8.00
WPA W.Payton AU/100 400.00 600.00
WPSP W.Payton Jsy AU/34 1000.00 1500.00

1999 SP Authentic Excitement

*VETS/250: 6X TO 15X BASIC CARDS
*ROOKIES/250: .5X TO 1.2X BASE RC
STATED PRINT RUN 250 SER.#'d SETS
95 Donovan McNabb 40.00 100.00

1999 SP Authentic Excitement Gold

STATED PRINT RUN 25 SER.#'d SETS
*VETS/25: 15X TO 40X BASIC CARDS
*ROOKIES/25: 1.2X TO 3X BASIC RC
95 Donovan McNabb 100.00 200.00

1999 SP Authentic Athletic

Randomly inserted in packs at the rate of one in 10, this 10-card set features NFL players who have proven their athletic prowess in the league. Card backs carry an "A" prefix.
COMPLETE SET (10) 15.00 30.00
STATED ODDS 1:10
A1 Randy Moss 4.00 10.00
A2 Steve McNair 1.25 3.00
A3 Jamal Anderson 1.25 3.00
A4 Curtis Martin 1.25 3.00
A5 Kordell Stewart .75 2.00
A6 Barry Sanders 4.00 10.00
A7 Fred Taylor 1.25 3.00
A8 Doug Flutie 1.25 3.00
A9 Emmitt Smith 2.50 6.00
A10 Steve Young 1.50 4.00

1999 SP Authentic Buy Back Autographs

Randomly inserted in packs at the rate of one in 576, this set features authentic player autographs on previously issued Upper Deck cards. Each card was hand serial numbered and contained a silver holographic tracking sticker on the cardbacks. Some cards were released in redemption form with an expiration date of 7/3/2000.
BUY BACK AU/1-117 ODDS 1:576
SERIAL #'d UNDER 12 NOT PRICED
1 T.Aikman 93SP/12 60.00 150.00
2 T.Aikman 94SP/42 40.00 80.00
3 T.Aikman 95SP/94 25.00 60.00
4 T.Aikman 95SPC/24 50.00 100.00
6 T.Aikman 96SP/28 50.00 100.00
8 T.Aikman 98SPA/24 50.00 100.00
10 J.Anderson 96SP/15 20.00 50.00
12 J.Anderson 98SPA/20 20.00 50.00
13 J.Bettis 93SP/25 90.00 150.00
14 J.Bettis 94SP/42 50.00 80.00
15 J.Bettis 95SP/93 50.00 80.00
16 J.Bettis 95SPC/25 60.00 100.00
19 J.Bettis 98SPA/63 50.00 80.00
20 D.Bledsoe 93SP/14 60.00 120.00
21 D.Bledsoe 94SP/28 20.00 50.00
22 D.Bledsoe 95SP/98 15.00 40.00
23 D.Bledsoe 95SPC/25 20.00 50.00
28 D.Bledsoe 98SPA/117 20.00 50.00
30 T.Brown 93SP/19 20.00 50.00
31 T.Brown 94SP/36 15.00 40.00
32 T.Brown 95SPC/25 15.00 40.00
34 T.Brown 98SP/25 15.00 40.00
38 M.Brunell 98SPA/21 25.00 60.00
39 W.Chrebet 95SP/43 15.00 40.00
40 W.Chrebet 96SP/14 20.00 50.00
41 T.Davis 96SP/14 125.00 250.00
43 T.Davis 98SPA/62 20.00 50.00
45 W.Dunn 98SPAMI/50 15.00 40.00
46 M.Faulk 94SP/28 125.00 250.00
47 M.Faulk 95SP/17 30.00 80.00
48 M.Faulk 95SPC/23 30.00 80.00
50 M.Faulk 96SP/40 20.00 50.00
51 M.Faulk 98SPA/28 30.00 80.00
52 J.Galloway 95SP/30 15.00 40.00
53 J.Galloway 95SPC/48 15.00 40.00
55 J.Galloway 98SPA/68 15.00 40.00
56 E.George 96SP/17 100.00 200.00
58 E.George 98SPA/65 20.00 50.00
59 E.George 98SPAMI/48 20.00 50.00
60 B.Johnson 98SPA/70 15.00 40.00
61 P.Manning 98UDEnc/60 175.00 300.00
62 P.Manning 98UDECT/16 300.00 500.00
63 D.Marino 95SP/100 50.00 100.00
64 D.Marino 95SPC/25 75.00 150.00
65 D.Marino 96SP/37 60.00 120.00
67 D.Marino 98SPA/44 50.00 100.00
68 D.Marino 99SP/28 50.00 100.00
69 N.Means 95SP/64 12.00 30.00
70 H.Moore 93SP/18 15.00 40.00
71 H.Moore 94SP/45 12.00 30.00
72 H.Moore 95SP/84 12.00 30.00
73 H.Moore 95SPC/25 12.00 30.00
74 H.Moore 96SP/40 12.00 30.00
75 H.Moore 98SPA/30 12.00 30.00
76 J.Plummer 98SPA/112 20.00 50.00
78 J.Plummer 98SPAMI/98 15.00 40.00
80 J.Rice 95SP/80 50.00 100.00
81 J.Rice 95SPC/28 100.00 200.00
85 J.Rice 98SPA/61 75.00 150.00

1999 SP Authentic Maximum Impact

Randomly inserted in packs at the rate of one in four, this 10-card set showcases game-breaking stars on colored card stock with gold foil highlights. Card backs carry an "MI" prefix.
COMPLETE SET (10) 6.00 15.00
STATED ODDS 1:4
MI1 Jerry Rice 1.25 3.00
MI2 Eddie George .60 1.50
MI3 Marshall Faulk .75 2.00
MI4 Keyshawn Johnson .60 1.50
MI5 Terrell Davis .60 1.50
MI6 Warrick Dunn .60 1.50
MI7 Jerome Bettis .60 1.50
MI8 Drew Bledsoe .75 2.00
MI9 Curtis Martin .60 1.50
MI10 Brett Favre 2.00 5.00

1999 SP Authentic New Classics

Randomly seeded in packs at the rate of one in 23, this 10-card set focuses on young players and future top NFL performers. Card backs carry an "NC" prefix.
COMPLETE SET (10) 15.00 40.00
STATED ODDS 1:23
NC1 Steve McNair 1.50 4.00
NC2 Jon Kitna 1.50 4.00
NC3 Curtis Enis .60 1.50
NC4 Peyton Manning 5.00 12.00
NC5 Fred Taylor 1.50 4.00
NC6 Randy Moss 5.00 12.00
NC7 Donovan McNabb 6.00 15.00
NC8 Terrell Owens 1.50 4.00
NC9 Keyshawn Johnson 1.50 4.00
NC10 Ricky Williams 2.50 6.00

1999 SP Authentic NFL Headquarters

Randomly inserted in packs at the rate of one in 10, this 10-card set pays tribute to the top ten quarterbacks in the NFL. Card backs carry an "HQ" prefix.
COMPLETE SET (10) 15.00 40.00
STATED ODDS 1:10
HQ1 Brett Favre 4.00 10.00
HQ2 Jake Plummer .75 2.00
HQ3 Charlie Batch 1.25 3.00
HQ4 Akili Smith 1.00 2.50
HQ5 Troy Aikman 2.50 6.00
HQ6 Drew Bledsoe 1.50 4.00
HQ7 Dan Marino 4.00 10.00
HQ8 Jon Kitna 1.25 3.00
HQ9 Mark Brunell 1.25 3.00
HQ10 Tim Couch 1.25 3.00

1999 SP Authentic Player's Ink Green

Randomly inserted in packs at the rate of one in 23, this 40-card set features authentic player autographs. Two versions of this set were released and some cards were issued via mail redemption cards that carried an expiration date of 7/10/2000. The redemption cards were a standard Player's Ink card featuring the player's photo, a punched hole in the card, and an attached sticker that included the rules for the redemption program. Base inserts feature a green background, while the Level 2 Purple version features a purple background. Note: Ricky Williams only signed the Level 2 Purple version.
STATED ODDS 1:23
AFA Antonio Freeman 6.00 15.00
ASA Akili Smith 6.00 15.00
BHA Brock Huard 6.00 15.00
BJA Brad Johnson 8.00 20.00
BRA Mark Brunell 8.00 20.00
CBA Champ Bailey 12.00 30.00
CDA Corey Dillon 8.00 20.00
CHA Charlie Batch 8.00 20.00
CLA Mike Cloud 6.00 15.00
CMA Cade McNown 6.00 15.00
DBA David Boston 8.00 20.00
DCA Daunte Culpepper 10.00 25.00
DFA Doug Flutie 10.00 25.00
DMA Dan Marino 75.00 150.00
DRA Drew Bledsoe 10.00 25.00
DRAX Drew Bledsoe EXCH 2.00 5.00
EDA Ed McCaffrey 8.00 20.00
EGA Eddie George 8.00 20.00
EJA Edgerrin James 8.00 20.00
EMA Eric Moulds 8.00 20.00
HMA Herman Moore 6.00 15.00
JAA Jamal Anderson 8.00 20.00
JBA Jerome Bettis 25.00 60.00
JGA Joey Galloway 6.00 15.00
JPA Jake Plummer 10.00 25.00
JRA Jerry Rice 50.00 100.00
KFA Kevin Faulk 8.00 20.00
MBA Michael Bishop 6.00 15.00
MFA Marshall Faulk 12.00 30.00
NMA Natrone Means 6.00 15.00
PMA Peyton Manning 60.00 120.00
PMAX Peyton Manning EXCH 4.00 10.00
RMA Randy Moss 20.00 50.00
SKA Shaun King 6.00 15.00
SSA Shannon Sharpe 12.00 30.00
TAA Troy Aikman 40.00 80.00
TCA Tim Couch 8.00 20.00
TDA Terrell Davis 15.00 40.00
TEA Troy Edwards 8.00 20.00
THA Torry Holt 10.00 25.00
TOA Terrell Owens 10.00 25.00
WCA Wayne Chrebet 8.00 20.00

1999 SP Authentic Player's Ink Purple

*LEVEL 2 PURPLE/100: .8X TO 2X GREEN AU
RWA Ricky Williams 40.00 100.00

1999 SP Authentic Rookie Blitz

Randomly inserted in packs at the rate of one in 11, this 19-card set showases this year's rookie crop on a card stock with a white border and gold background. Card fronts also contain gold foil highlights. Card backs carry an "RB" prefix.
COMPLETE SET (19) 20.00 50.00
STATED ODDS 1:11
RB1 Edgerrin James 4.00 10.00
RB2 Tim Couch 1.00 2.50
RB3 Daunte Culpepper 4.00 10.00
RB4 Champ Bailey 1.25 3.00
RB5 Donovan McNabb 5.00 12.00
RB6 Kevin Johnson 1.00 2.50
RB7 Shaun King 1.00 2.50
RB8 Peerless Price 1.00 2.50
RB9 David Boston 1.00 2.50
RB10 Ricky Williams 2.00 5.00
RB11 Akili Smith 1.00 2.50
RB12 Kevin Faulk 1.00 2.50
RB13 D'Wayne Bates .75 2.00
RB14 Brock Huard 1.00 2.50
RB15 Rob Konrad .75 2.00
RB16 Torry Holt 2.50 6.00
RB17 Troy Edwards 1.00 2.50
RB18 Cade McNown 1.00 2.50
RB19 Cecil Collins .75 2.00

1999 SP Authentic Supremacy

Randomly inserted in packs at the rate of one in 23, this 12-card set focuses on the NFL's most impressive athletes and showcases their top talents. Card backs carry an "S" prefix.
COMPLETE SET (12) 30.00 60.00
STATED ODDS 1:23
S1 Terrell Davis 1.50 4.00
S2 Joey Galloway 1.00 2.50
S3 Dan Marino 5.00 12.00
S4 Brett Favre 5.00 12.00
S5 Emmitt Smith 3.00 8.00
S6 Barry Sanders 5.00 12.00
S7 Curtis Martin 1.50 4.00
S8 Jamal Anderson 1.50 4.00
S9 Jake Plummer 1.00 2.50
S10 Randy Moss 5.00 12.00
S11 Tim Couch 1.50 4.00
S12 Peyton Manning 5.00 12.00

2000 SP Authentic

Released as a 150-card set, SP Authentic is comprised of 90 veteran base cards and 60 shortprinted rookie cards sequentially numbered to 1250. Card stock is white bordered and embossed along the edges of the cards with full color player action photography and silver foil highlights. SP Authentic was packaged in 24-pack boxes with packs containing five cards each and carried a suggested retail price of $4.99. An Update set of 21-cards was issued in April 2001 as part of 3-card packs distributed directly to Upper Deck hobby accounts.
COMP.SET w/o RC's (90) 6.00 15.00
91-171 ROOKIE PRINT RUN 1250
1 Jake Plummer .20 .50
2 David Boston .20 .50
3 Frank Sanders .20 .50
4 Chris Chandler .25 .60
5 Jamal Anderson .25 .60
6 Shawn Jefferson .20 .50
7 Tony Banks .20 .50
8 Shannon Sharpe .25 .60
9 Rob Johnson .25 .60
10 Antowain Smith .25 .60
11 Muhsin Muhammad .20 .50
12 Steve Beuerlein .25 .60
13 Cade McNown .20 .50
14 Curtis Enis .20 .50
15 Marcus Robinson .25 .60
16 Akili Smith .20 .50
17 Corey Dillon .20 .50
18 Tim Couch .25 .60
19 Kevin Johnson .20 .50
20 Errict Rhett .25 .60
21 Troy Aikman .40 1.00
22 Emmitt Smith .50 1.25
23 Rocket Ismail .25 .60
24 Joey Galloway .25 .60
25 Terrell Davis .25 .60
26 Olandis Gary .25 .60
27 Ed McCaffrey .25 .60
28 Brian Griese .20 .50
29 Charlie Batch .20 .50
30 Germane Crowell .20 .50
31 James O. Stewart .20 .50
32 Brett Favre .60 1.50
33 Antonio Freeman .25 .60
34 Dorsey Levens .25 .60
35 Peyton Manning .75 2.00
36 Edgerrin James .25 .60
37 Marvin Harrison .25 .60
38 Mark Brunell .25 .60
39 Fred Taylor .20 .50
40 Jimmy Smith .25 .60
41 Elvis Grbac .20 .50
42 Tony Gonzalez .25 .60
43 James Johnson .20 .50
44 Oronde Gadsden .25 .60
45 Damon Huard .20 .50
46 Randy Moss .25 .60
47 Cris Carter .30 .75
48 Daunte Culpepper .25 .60
49 Drew Bledsoe .25 .60
50 Terry Glenn .25 .60
51 Ricky Williams .25 .60
52 Jeff Blake .25 .60
53 Keith Poole .20 .50
54 Kerry Collins .20 .50
55 Amani Toomer .20 .50
56 Ike Hilliard .20 .50
57 Wayne Chrebet .20 .50
58 Curtis Martin .25 .60
59 Vinny Testaverde .20 .50
60 Tim Brown .30 .75
61 Rich Gannon .25 .60
62 Tyrone Wheatley .20 .50
63 Duce Staley .20 .50
64 Donovan McNabb .25 .60
65 Troy Edwards .20 .50
66 Jerome Bettis .30 .75
67 Kordell Stewart .20 .50
68 Marshall Faulk .25 .60
69 Kurt Warner .50 1.25
70 Isaac Bruce .30 .75
71 Torry Holt .25 .60
72 Ryan Leaf .25 .60
73 Jim Harbaugh .25 .60
74 Jermaine Fazande .20 .50
75 Jerry Rice .75 2.00
76 Terrell Owens .25 .60
77 Jeff Garcia .20 .50
78 Ricky Watters .25 .60
79 Jon Kitna .20 .50
80 Derrick Mayes .20 .50
81 Shaun King .20 .50
82 Mike Alstott .20 .50
83 Keyshawn Johnson .25 .60
84 Warrick Dunn .20 .50
85 Eddie George .25 .60
86 Steve McNair .25 .60
87 Jevon Kearse .20 .50
88 Brad Johnson .25 .60
89 Stephen Davis .20 .50
90 Michael Westbrook .20 .50
91 Anthony Lucas RC 2.50 6.00
92 Avion Black RC 2.50 6.00
93 Dante Hall RC 2.50 6.00
94 Darrell Jackson RC 2.50 6.00
95 Deltha O'Neal RC 2.50 6.00
96 Erron Kinney RC 2.50 6.00
97 Doug Chapman RC 2.50 6.00
98 Frank Murphy RC 2.50 6.00
99 Gari Scott RC 2.50 6.00
100 Giovanni Carmazzi RC 2.50 6.00
101 JaJuan Dawson RC 2.50 6.00
102 Jarious Jackson RC 3.00 8.00
103 Rashard Anderson RC 2.50 6.00
104 Michael Wiley RC 2.50 6.00
105 Spergon Wynn RC 2.50 6.00
106 Muneer Moore RC 2.50 6.00
107 Ahmed Plummer RC 2.50 6.00
108 Chad Morton RC 3.00 8.00
109 Rob Morris RC 3.00 8.00
110 Ron Dixon RC 2.50 6.00
111 Rondell Mealey RC 2.50 6.00
112 Sebastian Janikowski RC 4.00 10.00
113 Shaun Ellis RC 3.00 8.00
114 Rogers Beckett RC 2.50 6.00
115 Shyrone Stith RC 2.50 6.00
116 Tim Rattay RC 3.00 8.00
117 Todd Husak RC 2.50 6.00
118 Tom Brady RC 3000.00 6000.00
119 Trevor Gaylor RC 2.50 6.00
120 Windrell Hayes RC 2.50 6.00
121 Anthony Becht RC 2.50 6.00
122 Brian Urlacher RC 20.00 50.00
123 Bubba Franks RC 2.50 6.00
124 Chad Pennington RC 3.00 8.00
125 Chris Redman RC 2.50 6.00
126 Corey Simon RC 3.00 8.00
127 Curtis Keaton RC 2.50 6.00
128 Danny Farmer RC 2.50 6.00
129 Dennis Northcutt RC 2.50 6.00
130 Dez White RC 2.50 6.00
131 J.R. Redmond RC 2.50 6.00
132 Jamal Lewis RC 4.00 10.00
133 Jerry Porter RC 4.00 10.00
134 Joe Hamilton RC 2.50 6.00
135 Laveranues Coles RC 3.00 8.00
136 R.Jay Soward RC 2.50 6.00
137 Reuben Droughns RC 2.50 6.00
138 Ron Dayne RC 4.00 10.00
139 Ron Dugans RC 2.50 6.00
140 Shaun Alexander RC 4.00 10.00
141 Sylvester Morris RC 2.50 6.00
142 Tee Martin RC 2.50 6.00
143 Thomas Jones RC 3.00 8.00
144 Todd Pinkston RC 2.50 6.00
145 Travis Prentice RC 2.50 6.00
146 Travis Taylor RC 2.50 6.00
147 Trung Canidate RC 2.50 6.00
148 Courtney Brown RC 3.00 8.00
149 Plaxico Burress RC 3.00 8.00
150 Peter Warrick RC 2.50 6.00
151 Billy Volek RC 4.00 10.00
152 Bobby Shaw RC 2.50 6.00
153 Brad Hoover RC 3.00 8.00
154 Brian Finneran RC 4.00 10.00
155 Charles Lee RC 2.50 6.00
156 Chris Cole RC 3.00 8.00
157 Clint Stoerner RC 5.00 12.00
158 Doug Johnson RC 2.50 6.00
159 Frank Moreau RC 2.50 6.00
160 Jake Delhomme RC 3.00 8.00
161 KaRon Coleman RC 2.50 6.00
162 Kevin McDougal RC 2.50 6.00
163 Larry Foster RC 2.50 6.00
164 Mike Anderson RC 2.50 6.00
165 Patrick Pass RC 2.50 6.00
166 Reggie Jones RC 2.50 6.00
167 Sammy Morris RC 2.50 6.00
168 Shockmain Davis RC 2.50 6.00
169 Terrelle Smith RC 2.50 6.00
170 Ronney Jenkins RC 2.50 6.00
171 Troy Walters RC 2.50 6.00
PM Peyton Manning Sample 1.00 2.50

2000 SP Authentic Buy Back Autographs

Randomly inserted in packs at the rate of one in 71, this set features original Upper Deck cards from previous year's releases. Each card is signed and numbered and comes with a UDA certificate of authenticity. UDA holograms on this certificate carry a "BAH" prefix and then a number. Several cards were issued via redemption cards which carried an expiration date of 8/03/2001. Curtis Martin and Fred Taylor mail redemption cards were produced but they never signed for the set.
STATED ODDS 1:71
1 T.Aikman 94SP/55 30.00 60.00
2 T.Aikman 96SP/27 30.00 80.00
3 T.Aikman 98SPA/65 30.00 60.00
4 T.Aikman 99SPA/385 25.00 50.00
4 T.Couch 99SPANFL/251 7.50 20.00
4A T.Aikman 93SP/8
5 M.Alstott 98SPA/204 15.00 40.00
6 M.Alstott 99SPA/400 15.00 40.00
7 J.Anderson 97SPA
8 J.Anderson 98SPA/133 10.00 25.00
9 J.Anderson 99SPA/584 6.00 15.00
10 C.Bailey 99SPARB/426 10.00 25.00
11 C.Batch 99SPA/285 7.50 20.00
12 C.Batch 99SPANFL/354 7.50 20.00
13 D.Bledsoe 94SP/50 40.00 80.00
14 D.Bledsoe 96SP/21 50.00 120.00
15 D.Bledsoe 95SP/74 25.00 50.00
16 D.Bledsoe 99SPA/156 20.00 50.00
17 T.Brown 93SP/26 30.00 60.00
18 T.Brown 94SP/302 7.50 20.00
19 T.Brown 95SP/123 10.00 25.00
20 T.Brown 96SP/24 30.00 60.00
22 T.Brown 98SPA/121 10.00 25.00
23 T.Brown 99SPA/464 7.50 20.00
24 I.Bruce 95SP/217 10.00 25.00
25 I.Bruce 96SP/33 30.00 60.00
26 I.Bruce 97SPA/16 40.00 80.00
27 I.Bruce 98SPA/147 10.00 25.00
28 I.Bruce 99SPA/555 7.50 20.00
29 M.Brunell 96SP/46 20.00 50.00
30 M.Brunell 97SPA/11 100.00 200.00
31 M.Brunell 99SPA/620 8.00 20.00
32 C.Carter 93SP/21 25.00 60.00
33 C.Carter 94SP/20 25.00 60.00
34 C.Carter 98SPA/68 15.00 30.00
35 C.Carter 99SPA/300 15.00 30.00
36 C.Carter 00SPA/180 15.00 30.00
37 C.Chandler 94SP/35 10.00 25.00
38 C.Chandler 95SP/361 6.00 15.00
39 C.Chandler 96SP/18 15.00 40.00
41 C.Chandler 98SPA/153 6.00 15.00
42 C.Chandler 99SPA/595 6.00 15.00
43 W.Chrebet 99SPA/267 7.50 20.00
44 K.Collins 95SP/114 30.00 80.00
45 K.Collins 96SP/32 15.00 40.00
46 K.Collins 98SPA/202 7.50 20.00
47 K.Collins 99SPA/605 7.50 20.00
48 T.Couch 99SPARB/400 7.50 20.00
50 T.Davis 99SPA/237 20.00 40.00
52 T.Davis 98SPA/43 40.00 80.00
53 T.Dilfer 96SP/12 30.00 60.00
54 T.Dilfer 98SPA/65 10.00 25.00
55 T.Dilfer 99SPA/288 6.00 15.00
56 K.Faulk 99SPARB/394 7.50 20.00
57 M.Faulk 95SP/38 30.00 80.00
58 M.Faulk 96SP/25 50.00 100.00
59 M.Faulk 98SPA/65 25.00 50.00
60 M.Faulk 99SPA/74 25.00 50.00
61 D.Flutie 99SPA/293 10.00 25.00
62 D.Flutie 99SPAA/395 10.00 25.00
64 A.Freeman 98SPA/137 10.00 25.00
65 A.Freeman 99SPA/507 7.50 20.00
67 J.Galloway 96SP/123 10.00 25.00
68 J.Galloway 98SPA/200 10.00 25.00
69 J.Galloway 99SPA/273 10.00 25.00
70 J.Galloway 99SPAS/415 7.50 20.00
72 E.George 98SPA/121 10.00 25.00
73 E.George 99SPA/155 10.00 25.00
74 T.Holt 99SPARB/400 10.00 25.00
75 B.Johnson 99SPA/381 10.00 25.00
77 Ky.Johnson 98SPA/102 10.00 25.00
78 Ky.Johnson 99SPA/310 7.50 20.00
79 J.Kitna 99SPA/240 6.00 15.00
80 J.Kitna 99SPANC/396 6.00 15.00
82 D.Levens 98SPA/196 10.00 25.00
82 D.Levens 99SPA/620 6.00 15.00
83 P.Manning 99SPA/131 30.00 80.00
84 H.Moore 94SP/333 7.50 20.00
85 H.Moore 96SP/221 7.50 20.00
86 H.Moore 99SPA/270 7.50 20.00
87 E.Moulds 99SPA/291 7.50 20.00
88 R.Moss 99SPA/50 60.00 120.00
89 T.Owens 99SPA/450 15.00 40.00
90 T.Owens 99SPANC/282 15.00 40.00
91 J.Plummer 99SPA/280 10.00 25.00
92 J.Plummer 99SPASUP/165 10.00 25.00
93 S.Sharpe 94SP/77 12.00 30.00
94 S.Sharpe 95SP/281 10.00 25.00
95 S.Sharpe 96SP/62 12.00 30.00
97 S.Sharpe 99SPA/554 10.00 25.00
98 Ak.Smith 99SPARB/417 10.00 25.00
99 K.Stewart 96SP/67 30.00 60.00
100 K.Stewart 98SPA/169 10.00 25.00
101 K.Stewart 99SPA/600 10.00 25.00
102 V.Testeverde 99SPA/290 7.50 20.00
104 R.Watters 94SP/45 12.00 30.00
105 R.Watters 96SP/39 12.00 30.00
106 R.Watters 98SPA/148 7.50 20.00
107 R.Watters 99SPA/430 7.50 20.00

2000 SP Authentic New Classics

Randomly inserted in packs at the rate of one in 11, this 10-card set features a white border with a fade to a square colored player portrait style shot. Gold foil highlights outline the picture and display the player's name and number below the photo.
COMPLETE SET (10) 5.00 12.00
STATED ODDS 1:11
NC1 Peter Warrick .40 1.00
NC2 Courtney Brown .50 1.25
NC3 Trung Canidate .40 1.00
NC4 Dennis Northcutt .40 1.00
NC5 J.R. Redmond .40 1.00
NC6 Daunte Culpepper .50 1.25
NC7 Edgerrin James .50 1.25
NC8 Marcus Robinson .50 1.25
NC9 Shaun King .40 1.00
NC10 Ricky Williams .50 1.25

2000 SP Authentic Rookie Fusion

Randomly inserted in packs at the rate of one in 18, this seven card set features white borders and player action photography set against a green background. The cards are highlighted with silver foil.
COMPLETE SET (7) 6.00 15.00
STATED ODDS 1:18
RF1 Plaxico Burress .60 1.50
RF2 Chad Pennington .60 1.50
RF3 Travis Taylor .50 1.25
RF4 Ron Dayne .75 2.00
RF5 Thomas Jones .60 1.50
RF6 Jamal Lewis .75 2.00
RF7 Sylvester Morris .50 1.25

2000 SP Authentic Sign of the Times

Randomly inserted in packs at the rate of one in 23, this 81-card set features a player acton shot on the left side of the card set against a gray tone background where another player action shot appears. The right side of the card has a "Sign of the Times" logo running from bottom to top. Most of the players signed in this area of the card. Some were issued via mail redemption cards that carried an expiration date of 8/17/2001 with five of those players never signing for the product. We've cataloged those five players as EXCH below since that is the only form in which they can be collected. Those cards feature no autograph but are otherwise like any other card in the set with the additional feature of a hole punched through to indicate that they were for redemption.
STATED ODDS 1:23
AF Antonio Freeman 6.00 15.00
AL Anthony Lucas 5.00 12.00
AS Akili Smith 5.00 12.00
BF Bubba Franks 5.00 12.00
BG Brian Griese 5.00 12.00
BJ Brad Johnson 6.00 15.00
BU Brian Urlacher 20.00 50.00
CA Trung Canidate 5.00 12.00
CB Charlie Batch 5.00 12.00
CH Champ Bailey 6.00 15.00
CK Curtis Keaton 5.00 12.00
CL Chris Coleman UER 5.00 12.00
CM Cade McNown 5.00 12.00
CO Courtney Brown 6.00 15.00
CP Chad Pennington 6.00 15.00
CR Chris Chandler/7*
CS Corey Simon 6.00 15.00
DB David Boston 5.00 12.00
DC Daunte Culpepper 6.00 15.00
DF Danny Farmer 5.00 12.00
DJ Darrell Jackson 5.00 12.00
DL Chris Claiborne 5.00 12.00
DM Dan Marino/23*
DN Dennis Northcutt 5.00 12.00
DR Reuben Droughns 5.00 12.00
DU Ron Dugans 5.00 12.00
DW Dez White 5.00 12.00
EG Eddie George 6.00 15.00
EJ Edgerrin James 6.00 15.00
EM Eric Moulds 5.00 12.00
FB Mike Alstott 5.00 12.00
FL Doug Flutie 6.00 15.00
GC Giovanni Carmazzi 5.00 12.00
GF Gus Frerotte 5.00 12.00
GO Tony Gonzalez 10.00 25.00
HM Herman Moore 5.00 12.00
JD JaJuan Dawson 5.00 12.00
JH Joe Hamilton 5.00 12.00
JJ J.J. Stokes 6.00 15.00
JK Jon Kitna 5.00 12.00
JL Jamal Lewis 8.00 20.00
JN Joe Namath 40.00 80.00
JO Kevin Johnson 5.00 12.00
JR J.R. Redmond 5.00 12.00
KC Kwame Cavil 5.00 12.00
KE Kerry Collins 5.00 12.00
KF Kevin Faulk 5.00 12.00
KJ Keyshawn Johnson 6.00 15.00
KS Kordell Stewart 5.00 12.00
KW Kurt Warner 20.00 50.00
LC Laveranues Coles 6.00 15.00
MB Mark Brunell 6.00 15.00
MH Marvin Harrison 6.00 15.00
MO Corey Moore 5.00 12.00
MW Michael Wiley 5.00 12.00
OG Olandis Gary 6.00 15.00
PB Plaxico Burress 6.00 15.00
PM Peyton Manning 50.00 100.00
PW Peter Warrick SP
QI Qadry Ismail 5.00 12.00
RB Rob Johnson 6.00 15.00
RD Ron Dayne 8.00 20.00
RE Chris Redman 5.00 12.00
RL Ray Lucas 5.00 12.00
RM Randy Moss 40.00 80.00
SA Shaun Alexander 25.00 50.00
SD Stephen Davis 5.00 12.00
SG Sherrod Gideon 5.00 12.00
SM Sylvester Morris 5.00 12.00
SY Steve Young 40.00 80.00
TC Tim Couch 6.00 15.00
TD Trent Dilfer 5.00 12.00
TE Troy Edwards 5.00 12.00
TG Trevor Gaylor 5.00 12.00
TH Torry Holt 6.00 15.00
TJX Thomas Jones EXCH 6.00 15.00
TM1 Tee Martin 5.00 12.00
TP Travis Prentice 5.00 12.00
TR Tim Rattay 6.00 15.00
TT Travis Taylor 5.00 12.00
TW Troy Walters 5.00 12.00
WC Wayne Chrebet 5.00 12.00
WH Windrell Hayes 5.00 12.00

2000 SP Authentic Sign of the Times Gold

Randomly seeded in packs, this 82-card set parallels the base Sign of the Times set enhanced with a gold background, Each card was sequentially numbered to the featured player's jersey number. Some were issued via mail redemption cards that carried an expiration date of 8/17/2001.
STATED PRINT RUN 5-92
SERIAL #'d UNDER 20 NOT PRICED
AF Antonio Freeman/86 10.00 25.00
AL Anthony Lucas/87 8.00 20.00
BF Bubba Franks/88 8.00 20.00
BU Brian Urlacher/54 50.00 100.00
CH Champ Bailey/24 25.00 60.00
CK Curtis Keaton/29 15.00 40.00
CO Courtney Brown/92 10.00 25.00
CS Corey Simon/90 10.00 25.00
DB David Boston/89 8.00 20.00
DJ Darrell Jackson/82 8.00 20.00
DL Chris Claiborne/50 10.00 25.00
DN Dennis Northcutt/86 8.00 20.00
DR Reuben Droughns/21 15.00 40.00
EG Eddie George/27 20.00 50.00
EJ Edgerrin James/32 15.00 40.00
EM Eric Moulds/80 8.00 20.00
FB Mike Alstott/40 10.00 25.00
GO Tony Gonzalez/88 15.00 40.00
JD JaJuan Dawson/88 8.00 20.00
JJ J.J. Stokes/83 10.00 25.00
JL Jamal Lewis/31 15.00 40.00
JO Kevin Johnson/85 8.00 20.00
JR J.R. Redmond/21 15.00 40.00
KC Kwame Cavil/82 8.00 20.00
LC Laveranues Coles/87 10.00 25.00
MH Marvin Harrison/88 15.00 40.00
MW Michael Wiley/33 12.00 30.00
OG Olandis Gary/22 20.00 50.00
PB Plaxico Burress/88 10.00 25.00
QI Qadry Ismail/87 8.00 20.00
RD Ron Dayne/27 25.00 60.00
SA Shaun Alexander/37 15.00 40.00
SD Stephen Davis/46 10.00 25.00
SM Sylvester Morris/82 8.00 20.00
TE Troy Edwards/81 8.00 20.00
TH Torry Holt/88 15.00 40.00
TW Troy Walters/82 8.00 20.00
WC Wayne Chrebet/80 8.00 20.00
WH Windrell Hayes/86 8.00 20.00

2000 SP Authentic SP Athletic

Randomly inserted in packs at the rate of one in 11, this 10-card set features a rectangular color box with a player action photograph and the words SP Athletic along the left border of the card from bottom to top. Cards are accented with gold foil.
COMPLETE SET (10) 3.00 8.00
STATED ODDS 1:11
A1 Marshall Faulk .50 1.25
A2 Kevin Johnson .40 1.00
A3 Olandis Gary .50 1.25
A4 Jeff Garcia .40 1.00
A5 Akili Smith .40 1.00
A6 Donovan McNabb .50 1.25
A7 Rob Johnson .50 1.25
A8 Marcus Robinson .50 1.25
A9 Shaun King .40 1.00
A10 Troy Edwards .40 1.00

2000 SP Authentic Supremacy

Randomly inserted in packs at the rate of one in eight, this 15-card set is white bordered and features players in action. The background is colored in tracing the pose that the featured player is in and is accented with gold foil.
COMPLETE SET (15) 10.00 25.00
STATED ODDS 1:8
S1 Mark Brunell .60 1.50
S2 Terrell Davis .60 1.50
S3 Jamal Anderson .60 1.50
S4 Jerry Rice 2.00 5.00
S5 Emmitt Smith 1.25 3.00
S6 Troy Aikman 1.00 2.50
S7 Randy Moss .60 1.50
S8 Brad Johnson .60 1.50
S9 Brett Favre 1.50 4.00
S10 Keyshawn Johnson .60 1.50
S11 Fred Taylor .50 1.25
S12 Kurt Warner 1.25 3.00
S13 Tim Couch .60 1.50
S14 Eddie George .60 1.50
S15 Drew Bledsoe .60 1.50

2001 SP Authentic

This set was issued in December, 2001. The set was issued in five card packs which were packed 24 to a box. Cards numbered 91-190 featured rookies and were printed to different amounts. Cards numbered 91-93, which had a jersey swatch and an autograph, had a print run of 250 sets. Cards numbered 94-120 had a jersey swatch and were printed to 800 (except for a few cards which we have notated specific print runs in our checklist). Cards number 121-150 had a stated print run of 550 sets and were autographed. Cards numbered 151-190 also had a print run of 800 sets. Some cards were issued in packs via mail redemptions. Of those, cards #121 Adam Archuleta and #122 Alex Bannister were never fulfilled.
COMP.SET w/o SP's (90) 7.50 20.00
91-93 JSY AU RC PRINT RUN 250
94-120 JSY RC PRINT RUN 106-800
151-190 ROOKIE PRINT RUN 800
1 Jake Plummer .20 .50
2 Thomas Jones .20 .50
3 Frank Sanders .20 .50
4 Jamal Anderson .25 .60
5 Chris Chandler .25 .60
6 Tony Martin .25 .60
7 Jamal Lewis .30 .75
8 Elvis Grbac .25 .60
9 Travis Taylor .20 .50
10 Peerless Price .20 .50
11 Rob Johnson .25 .60
12 Eric Moulds .20 .50
13 Muhsin Muhammad .20 .50
14 Isaac Byrd .20 .50
15 Wesley Walls .20 .50
16 James Allen .20 .50
17 Marcus Robinson .25 .60
18 Brian Urlacher .40 1.00
19 Jon Kitna .20 .50
20 Peter Warrick .20 .50
21 Corey Dillon .20 .50
22 Kevin Johnson .20 .50
23 JaJuan Dawson .20 .50
24 Tim Couch .20 .50
25 Rocket Ismail .25 .60
26 Emmitt Smith .50 1.25
27 Joey Galloway .25 .60
28 Terrell Davis .25 .60
29 Mike Anderson .20 .50
30 Brian Griese .20 .50
31 Ed McCaffrey .25 .60
32 Charlie Batch .20 .50
33 James O. Stewart .20 .50
34 Johnnie Morton .25 .60
35 Brett Favre .60 1.50
36 Antonio Freeman .30 .75
37 Bill Schroeder .25 .60
38 Ahman Green .25 .60
39 Peyton Manning .75 2.00
40 Edgerrin James .25 .60
41 Marvin Harrison .25 .60
42 Mark Brunell .25 .60
43 Fred Taylor .20 .50
44 Jimmy Smith .25 .60
45 Tony Gonzalez .25 .60
46 Trent Green .20 .50
47 Oronde Gadsden .20 .50
48 Jay Fiedler .25 .60
49 Lamar Smith .25 .60
50 Randy Moss .25 .60
51 Cris Carter .30 .75
52 Daunte Culpepper .25 .60
53 Drew Bledsoe .25 .60
54 Terry Glenn .25 .60
55 Antowain Smith .25 .60
56 Ricky Williams .25 .60
57 Joe Horn .20 .50
58 Aaron Brooks .20 .50
59 Kerry Collins .20 .50
60 Tiki Barber .25 .60
61 Ron Dayne .25 .60
62 Vinny Testaverde .20 .50
63 Wayne Chrebet .20 .50
64 Curtis Martin .25 .60
65 Tim Brown .30 .75
66 Rich Gannon .25 .60
67 Jerry Rice .60 1.50
68 Duce Staley .20 .50
69 Donovan McNabb .25 .60
70 Kordell Stewart .20 .50
71 Jerome Bettis .30 .75
72 Marshall Faulk .25 .60
73 Kurt Warner .50 1.25
74 Isaac Bruce .30 .75
75 Doug Flutie .25 .60
76 Junior Seau .25 .60
77 Jeff Garcia .20 .50
78 Garrison Hearst .25 .60
79 Terrell Owens .25 .60
80 Ricky Watters .25 .60
81 Matt Hasselbeck .20 .50
82 Brad Johnson .25 .60
83 Warrick Dunn .20 .50
84 Mike Alstott .20 .50
85 Kevin Dyson .20 .50
86 Eddie George .30 .75
87 Steve McNair .25 .60
88 Champ Bailey .25 .60
89 Michael Westbrook .20 .50
90 Stephen Davis .20 .50
91 Michael Vick JSY AU RC 250.00 500.00
92 Rod Gardner JSY AU RC 10.00 25.00
93 Freddie Mitchell JSY AU RC 8.00 20.00
94 Koren Robinson JSY/500 RC 6.00 15.00
95 David Terrell JSY/500 RC 6.00 15.00
96 Michael Bennett JSY RC 8.00 20.00
97 Robert Ferguson JSY RC 10.00 25.00
98 Deuce McAllister JSY RC 10.00 25.00
99 Travis Henry JSY RC 8.00 20.00
100 Andre Carter JSY RC 8.00 20.00
101 Drew Brees JSY RC 400.00 800.00
102 Santana Moss JSY/500 RC 8.00 20.00
103 Chris Weinke JSY/390 RC 8.00 20.00
104 Chad Johnson JSY/160 RC 30.00 80.00
105 Reggie Wayne JSY RC 30.00 60.00
106 Kevan Barlow JSY/500 RC 6.00 15.00
107 C.Chambers JSY/500 RC 12.00 30.00
108 Todd Heap JSY/500 RC 12.00 30.00
109 A.Thomas JSY/500 RC 8.00 20.00
110 James Jackson JSY/500 RC 5.00 12.00
111 Rudi Johnson JSY/500 RC 8.00 20.00
112 Mike McMahon JSY RC 8.00 20.00
113 Josh Heupel JSY RC 10.00 25.00
114 Travis Minor JSY/500 RC 6.00 15.00
115 Quincy Morgan JSY/500 RC 6.00 15.00
116 Dan Morgan JSY/500 RC 6.00 15.00
117 Jesse Palmer JSY/500 RC 6.00 15.00
118 Sage Rosenfels JSY/300 RC 15.00 40.00
119 M.Tuiasosopo JSY RC 6.00 15.00
120 L.Tomlinson JSY/500 RC 75.00 150.00
123 Alge Crumpler AU RC 8.00 20.00
124 Arnold Jackson AU RC 5.00 12.00
125 Bobby Newcombe AU RC 6.00 15.00
126 Brand Manumaleuna AU RC 6.00 15.00
127 Cedrick Wilson AU RC 6.00 15.00
128 Brian Allen AU RC 5.00 12.00
129 Dee Brown AU RC 5.00 12.00
130 Damerien McCants AU RC 6.00 15.00
131 Dave Dickenson AU RC 6.00 15.00
132 Derrick Blaylock AU RC 6.00 15.00
133 Eddie Berlin AU RC 5.00 12.00
134 Francis St.Paul AU RC 5.00 12.00
135 Jamar Fletcher AU RC 5.00 12.00
136 Josh Booty AU RC 6.00 15.00
137 Scotty Anderson AU RC 5.00 12.00
138 Ken-Yon Rambo AU RC 5.00 12.00
139 Kenyatta Walker AU RC 5.00 12.00
140 Kevin Kasper AU RC 5.00 12.00
141 Snoop Minnis AU RC 5.00 12.00
142 Houshmandzadeh AU RC 10.00 25.00
143 Quincy Carter AU RC 6.00 15.00
144 Ronney Daniels AU RC 5.00 12.00
145 Sedrick Hodge AU RC 5.00 12.00
146 Steve Smith AU RC 40.00 80.00
147 Tim Hasselbeck AU RC 6.00 15.00
148 Vinny Sutherland AU RC 5.00 12.00
149 Richard Seymour AU RC 8.00 20.00
150 Jamie Winborn AU 6.00 15.00
151 Gerard Warren RC 2.50 6.00
152 Justin Smith RC 4.00 10.00
153 David Martin RC 2.00 5.00
154 Jamal Reynolds RC 2.00 5.00
155 Dominic Rhodes RC 2.50 6.00
156 Nate Clements RC 2.50 6.00
157 Michael Lewis RC 3.00 8.00
158 Andre King RC 2.00 5.00
159 Benjamin Gay RC 2.50 6.00
160 Correll Buckhalter RC 2.00 5.00
161 Roderick Robinson RC 2.00 5.00
162 Moran Norris RC 2.00 5.00
163 Onome Ojo RC 2.00 5.00
164 Will Allen RC 3.00 8.00
165 Jonathan Carter RC 2.00 5.00
166 LaMont Jordan RC 3.00 8.00
167 DeLawrence Grant RC 2.00 5.00
168 Derrick Gibson RC 2.00 5.00
169 A.J. Feeley RC 2.50 6.00
170 Tim Baker RC 2.00 5.00
171 Kendrell Bell RC 3.00 8.00
172 Zeke Moreno RC 2.50 6.00
173 Carlos Polk RC 2.00 5.00
174 Ken Lucas RC 2.50 6.00
175 Heath Evans RC 2.50 6.00
176 Elvis Joseph RC 2.00 5.00

177 Damione Lewis RC	2.50	6.00
178 Tommy Polley RC	2.00	5.00
179 Fred Smoot RC	2.50	6.00
180 Jason Brookins RC	3.00	8.00
181 Nick Goings RC	3.00	8.00
182 Drew Bennett RC	3.00	8.00
183 Justin McCareins RC	2.50	6.00
184 Kabeer Gbaja-Biamila RC	3.00	8.00
185 Edgerton Hartwell RC	2.00	5.00
186 Robert Carswell RC	2.00	5.00
187 Aaron Schobel RC	3.00	8.00
188 Dan Alexander RC	2.50	6.00
189 Jamie Winborn RC	2.50	6.00
190 Karon Riley RC	2.00	5.00
EG Eddie George SAMPLE	1.50	3.00

2001 SP Authentic Rookie Gold 100

STATED PRINT RUN 100 SER.#'d SETS

91 Michael Vick	30.00	80.00
92 Rod Gardner	15.00	40.00
93 Freddie Mitchell	12.00	30.00
94 Koren Robinson	15.00	40.00
95 David Terrell	15.00	40.00
96 Michael Bennett	15.00	40.00
97 Robert Ferguson	20.00	50.00
98 Deuce McAllister	20.00	50.00
99 Travis Henry	15.00	40.00
100 Andre Carter	15.00	40.00
101 Drew Brees	500.00	100.00
102 Santana Moss	20.00	50.00
103 Chris Weinke	15.00	40.00
104 Chad Johnson	20.00	50.00
105 Reggie Wayne	20.00	50.00
106 Kevan Barlow	15.00	40.00
107 Chris Chambers	12.00	30.00
108 Todd Heap	15.00	40.00
109 Anthony Thomas	20.00	50.00
110 James Jackson	12.00	30.00
111 Rudi Johnson	20.00	50.00
112 Mike McMahon	15.00	40.00
113 Josh Heupel	20.00	50.00
114 Travis Minor	15.00	40.00
115 Quincy Morgan	15.00	40.00
116 Dan Morgan	15.00	40.00
117 Jesse Palmer	15.00	40.00
118 Sage Rosenfels	25.00	60.00
119 Marques Tuiasosopo	15.00	40.00
120 LaDainian Tomlinson	100.00	200.00
121 Adam Archuleta	15.00	40.00
122 Alex Bannister	12.00	30.00
123 Alge Crumpler	20.00	50.00
124 Arnold Jackson	12.00	30.00
125 Bobby Newcombe	15.00	40.00
126 Brandon Manumaleuna	15.00	40.00
127 Cedrick Wilson	15.00	40.00
128 Brian Allen	12.00	30.00
129 Dee Brown	12.00	30.00
130 Darnerien McCants	15.00	40.00
131 Dave Dickenson	15.00	40.00
132 Derrick Blaylock	15.00	40.00
133 Eddie Berlin	12.00	30.00
134 Francis St.Paul	12.00	30.00
135 Jamar Fletcher	12.00	30.00
136 Josh Booty	15.00	40.00
137 Scotty Anderson	12.00	30.00
138 Ken-Yon Rambo	12.00	30.00
139 Kenyatta Walker	12.00	30.00
140 Kevin Kasper	12.00	30.00
141 Snoop Minnis	12.00	30.00
142 T.J. Houshmandzadeh	15.00	40.00
143 Quincy Carter	15.00	40.00
144 Ronney Daniels	12.00	30.00
145 Sedrick Hodge	12.00	30.00
146 Steve Smith	40.00	100.00
147 Tim Hasselbeck	15.00	40.00
148 Vinny Sutherland	12.00	30.00
149 Richard Seymour	20.00	50.00
150 Jamie Winborn	15.00	40.00
151 Gerard Warren	15.00	40.00
152 Justin Smith	25.00	60.00
153 David Martin	12.00	30.00
154 Jamal Reynolds	12.00	30.00
155 Dominic Rhodes	15.00	40.00
156 Nate Clements	15.00	40.00
157 Michael Lewis	20.00	50.00
158 Andre King	12.00	30.00
159 Benjamin Gay	15.00	40.00
160 Correll Buckhalter	12.00	30.00
161 Roderick Robinson	12.00	30.00
162 Moran Norris	12.00	30.00
163 Onome Ojo	12.00	30.00
164 Will Allen	20.00	50.00
165 Jonathan Carter	12.00	30.00
166 LaMont Jordan	20.00	50.00
167 DeLawrence Grant	12.00	30.00
168 Derrick Gibson	12.00	30.00
169 A.J. Feeley	15.00	40.00
170 Tim Baker	12.00	30.00
171 Kendrell Bell	20.00	50.00
172 Zeke Moreno	15.00	40.00
173 Carlos Polk	12.00	30.00
174 Ken Lucas	15.00	40.00
175 Heath Evans	15.00	40.00
176 Elvis Joseph	12.00	30.00
177 Damione Lewis	15.00	40.00
178 Tommy Polley	12.00	30.00
179 Fred Smoot	15.00	40.00
180 Jason Brookins	20.00	50.00
181 Nick Goings	20.00	50.00
182 Drew Bennett	20.00	50.00
183 Justin McCareins	15.00	40.00
184 Kabeer Gbaja-Biamila	20.00	50.00
185 Edgerton Hartwell	12.00	30.00
186 Robert Carswell	12.00	30.00
187 Aaron Schobel	20.00	50.00
188 Dan Alexander	15.00	40.00
189 Jamie Winborn	15.00	40.00
190 Karon Riley	12.00	30.00

2001 SP Authentic Sign of the Times

Inserted in packs at stated odds of one in 27, these 39 cards feature signature of a mix of great players past and present.
STATED ODDS 1:47
*GOLD/25: .8X TO 2X BASIC AUTO
GOLD PRINT RUN 25 SER.#'d SETS

BJ Brad Johnson	8.00	20.00
CB Charlie Batch	6.00	15.00
CT Charley Taylor	6.00	15.00
DB Drew Bledsoe	12.00	30.00
DBR Drew Brees	300.00	600.00
DC Daunte Culpepper	8.00	20.00
DF Doug Flutie	12.00	30.00
DM Dan Marino	60.00	125.00
EJ Ed Too Tall Jones SP	8.00	20.00
HL Howie Long	20.00	50.00
JDL Jeff Blake	8.00	20.00
JBR Jim Brown	50.00	100.00
JGA Jeff Garcia	6.00	15.00
JK Jim Kelly	20.00	50.00
JM Joe Montana	60.00	125.00
JN Joe Namath	40.00	100.00
JP Jim Plunkett	12.00	30.00
JPL Jake Plummer	6.00	15.00
JR John Riggins	20.00	50.00
JS Junior Seau	25.00	50.00
JU Johnny Unitas	250.00	400.00
JY Jack Youngblood	6.00	15.00
KW Kurt Warner	25.00	50.00
MA Marcus Allen	20.00	35.00
PH Paul Hornung	20.00	50.00
PM Peyton Manning DP	60.00	125.00
PW Peter Warrick	6.00	15.00
RM Randy Moss SP	50.00	100.00
RS Roger Staubach	50.00	100.00
RW Ricky Williams	8.00	20.00
SD Stephen Davis	6.00	15.00
SY Steve Young	25.00	60.00
TB Terry Bradshaw	50.00	100.00
TDA Terrell Davis	15.00	40.00
TDI Trent Dilfer	6.00	15.00
TH Torry Holt	8.00	20.00
TO Terrell Owens	15.00	40.00
VT Vinny Testaverde SP	6.00	15.00

2001 SP Authentic Stat Jerseys

Inserted at packs at stated odds of one in 23, these 61 cards have game-worn swatches of the featured player. Each card is serial numbered to a significant stat involved in that player's career.
STAT JERSEY/13-1681 ODDS 1:23
#'d/23 or LESS NOT PRICED DUE TO SCARCITY

SPAF Antonio Freeman/1424	3.00	8.00
SPAT Amani Toomer/1094	2.00	5.00
SPBF1 Brett Favre/255	10.00	25.00
SPBF2 Brett Favre/260	10.00	25.00
SPBG1 Brian Griese/102	4.00	10.00
SPBG2 Brian Griese/327	2.50	6.00
SPBS1 Barry Sanders/99	12.00	30.00
SPBS2 Barry Sanders/1000	5.00	12.00
SPCM Curtis Martin/1204	2.50	6.00
SPCW2 Chris Weinke/223	4.00	10.00
SPDB1 Drew Brees/194	50.00	100.00
SPDB2 Drew Brees/349	40.00	80.00
SPDC1 Daunte Culpepper/40	6.00	15.00
SPDC2 Daunte Culpepper/470	3.00	8.00
SPDF Doug Flutie/129	5.00	12.00
SPDM2 Dan Marino/48	15.00	40.00
SPDM3 Dan Marino/420	8.00	20.00
SPES1 Emmitt Smith/156	10.00	25.00
SPFT Fred Taylor/1399	2.00	5.00
SPIB Isaac Bruce/1471	3.00	8.00
SPIH Ike Hilliard/787	2.00	5.00
SPJA Jesse Armstead/529	2.50	6.00
SPJE John Elway/300	6.00	15.00
SPJF1 Jay Fiedler/225	4.00	10.00
SPJF2 Jay Fiedler/1173	2.50	6.00
SPJK1 Jim Kelly/237	5.00	12.00
SPJK2 Jim Kelly/403	4.00	10.00
SPJR Jerry Rice/1281	6.00	15.00
SPJS Junior Seau/1058	2.50	6.00
SPJSM Jimmy Smith/1213	2.50	6.00
SPLT1 LaDainian Tomlinson/113	10.00	25.00
SPLT2 LaDainian Tomlinson/196	6.00	15.00
SPMA Mike Alstott/1219	2.00	5.00
SPMBR Mark Brunell/236	4.00	10.00
SPMB1 Michael Bennett/55	6.00	15.00
SPMB2 Michael Bennett/1681	2.50	6.00
SPMF1 Marshall Faulk/26	10.00	25.00
SPMF2 Marshall Faulk/1359	2.50	6.00
SPMV1 Michael Vick/32	15.00	40.00
SPMV2 Michael Vick/1234	10.00	25.00
SPPM1 Peyton Manning/33	25.00	60.00
SPPM2 Peyton Manning/87	15.00	40.00
SPPM3 Peyton Manning/94	15.00	40.00
SPPM4 Peyton Manning/231	12.00	30.00
SPPM5 Peyton Manning/440	10.00	25.00
SPRD Ron Dayne/770	2.50	6.00
SPRL Ray Lewis/137	6.00	15.00
SPRM1 Randy Moss/43	6.00	15.00
SPRM2 Randy Moss/226	4.00	10.00
SPSD Stephen Davis/1318	2.00	5.00
SPSE1 Jason Sehorn/260	4.00	10.00
SPSE2 Jason Sehorn/995	2.50	6.00
SPTA1 Troy Aikman/23	15.00	40.00
SPTA2 Troy Aikman/165	8.00	20.00
SPTC Tim Couch/1483	2.00	5.00
SPWD1 Warrick Dunn/422	2.50	6.00
SPWD2 Warrick Dunn/1133	2.00	5.00
SPWS1 Warren Sapp/58	6.00	15.00
SPWS2 Warren Sapp/1066	2.50	6.00

2002 SP Authentic

Released in late-December 2002, this set contains 94 veterans and 150 rookies. In addition, four base cards, 91-94, were only available autographed. Stated odds for these cards is 1:300. Subset cards 95-124 were #'d to 2000 and cards 125-154 were #'d to 1150. Rookie cards 155-184 were also #'d to 1150. Rookie cards 185-214 were all signed and #'d to 1150. Cards 215-234 all featured jersey swatches and were #'d to either 850 or 350. Cards 235-244 features autographs and jersey swatches and were #'d to 250. Some cards were issued as redemption cards with an expiration date of 12/13/2005. Note that #236 was intended to be Ashley Lelie but he never signed cards for the set.

COMP.SET w/o SP's (90)	10.00	25.00
155-184 ROOKIE PRINT RUN 1150		
185-214 ROOKIE AU PRINT RUN 1150		
ROOKIE JSY PRINT RUN 850		
235-244 RC JSY AU PRINT RUN 250		
1 Tom Brady	25.00	60.00
2 Antowain Smith	.30	.75
3 Troy Brown	.25	.60
4 Kurt Warner	.30	.75
5 Marshall Faulk	.30	.75
6 Isaac Bruce	.40	1.00
7 Kordell Stewart	.25	.60
8 Jerome Bettis	.40	1.00
9 Plaxico Burress	.25	.60
10 Hines Ward	.30	.75
11 Donovan McNabb	.30	.75
12 Duce Staley	.25	.60
13 Dorsey Levens	.30	.75
14 Antonio Freeman	.40	1.00
15 Jerry Rice	.75	2.00
16 Rich Gannon	.30	.75
17 Tim Brown	.40	1.00
18 Jim Miller	.25	.60
19 Marty Booker	.25	.60
20 Brian Urlacher	.40	1.00
21 Jamal Lewis	.30	.75
22 Chris Redman	.25	.60
23 Ray Lewis	.40	1.00
24 Brett Favre	.75	2.00
25 Ahman Green	.30	.75
26 Terry Glenn	.30	.75
27 Keyshawn Johnson	.30	.75
28 Keenan McCardell	.30	.75
29 Michael Pittman	.30	.75
30 Curtis Martin	.30	.75
31 Vinny Testaverde	.25	.60
32 Chad Pennington	.25	.60
33 Wayne Chrebet	.25	.60
34 Terrell Owens	.30	.75
35 Garrison Hearst	.25	.60
36 Jay Fiedler	.30	.75
37 Ricky Williams	.30	.75
38 Chris Chambers	.25	.60
39 Shaun Alexander	.25	.60
40 Darrell Jackson	.30	.75
41 Drew Bledsoe	.30	.75
42 Travis Henry	.25	.60
43 Eric Moulds	.25	.60
44 Stephen Davis	.25	.60
45 Rod Gardner	.25	.60
46 Brian Griese	.25	.60
47 Olandis Gary	.30	.75
48 Shannon Sharpe	.30	.75
49 Tim Couch	.25	.60
50 Kevin Johnson	.25	.60
51 Steve McNair	.30	.75
52 Eddie George	.30	.75
53 Aaron Brooks	.25	.60
54 Deuce McAllister	.30	.75
55 Joe Horn	.25	.60
56 Michael Vick	.30	.75
57 Warrick Dunn	.25	.60
58 Kerry Collins	.25	.60
59 Tiki Barber	.30	.75
60 Amani Toomer	.25	.60
61 Jake Plummer	.25	.60
62 David Boston	.25	.60
63 Thomas Jones	.25	.60
64 Edgerrin James	.30	.75
65 Marvin Harrison	.30	.75
66 Mark Brunell	.30	.75
67 Jimmy Smith	.30	.75
68 Fred Taylor	.25	.60
69 Corey Dillon	.25	.60
70 Jon Kitna	.25	.60
71 Michael Westbrook	.25	.60
72 Trent Green	.25	.60
73 Priest Holmes	.25	.60
74 Tony Gonzalez	.30	.75
75 Daunte Culpepper	.30	.75
76 Michael Bennett	.25	.60
77 Randy Moss	.30	.75
78 Drew Brees	.75	2.00
79 Curtis Conway	.30	.75
80 Junior Seau	.30	.75
81 Quincy Carter	.25	.60
82 Emmitt Smith	.60	1.50
83 Joey Galloway	.30	.75
84 Cory Schlesinger	.25	.60
85 James Stewart	.25	.60
86 Az-Zahir Hakim	.25	.60
87 Rodney Peete	.30	.75
88 Lamar Smith	.25	.60
89 Corey Bradford	.25	.60
90 Jermaine Lewis	.25	.60
91 Peyton Manning AU	50.00	100.00
92 Anthony Thomas AU	10.00	25.00
93 LaDainian Tomlinson AU	15.00	40.00
94 Jeff Garcia AU	8.00	20.00
95 Kurt Warner SC	1.00	2.50
96 Brett Favre SC	2.50	6.00
97 Michael Vick SC	1.00	2.50
98 Donovan McNabb SC	1.00	2.50
99 Daunte Culpepper SC	1.00	2.50
100 Tom Brady SC	6.00	15.00
101 Drew Brees SC	2.50	6.00
102 Kordell Stewart SC	.75	2.00
103 Steve McNair SC	1.00	2.50
104 Peyton Manning SC	3.00	8.00
105 Mark Brunell SC	1.00	2.50
106 Jeff Garcia SC	.75	2.00
107 Aaron Brooks SC	.75	2.00
108 Rich Gannon SC	1.00	2.50
109 Tim Couch SC	.75	2.00
110 Jake Plummer SC	.75	2.00
111 Drew Bledsoe SC	1.00	2.50
112 Brian Griese SC	.75	2.00
113 Quincy Carter SC	.75	2.00
114 Vinny Testaverde SC	.75	2.00
115 Chad Pennington SC	.75	2.00
116 Brad Johnson SC	1.00	2.50
117 Trent Dilfer SC	.75	2.00
118 Jim Miller SC	.75	2.00
119 Tommy Maddox SC	.75	2.00
120 Trent Green SC	.75	2.00
121 Rodney Peete SC	1.00	2.50
122 Jay Fiedler SC	1.00	2.50
123 Kerry Collins SC	.75	2.00
124 Chris Redman SC	.75	2.00
125 Marshall Faulk SS	1.25	3.00
126 Donovan McNabb SS	1.25	3.00
127 Michael Vick SS	1.25	3.00
128 Brett Favre SS	3.00	8.00
129 Peyton Manning SS	4.00	10.00
130 Kurt Warner SS	1.25	3.00
131 Curtis Martin SS	1.25	3.00
132 Randy Moss SS	1.25	3.00
133 Edgerrin James SS	1.25	3.00
134 Jerome Bettis SS	1.50	4.00
135 Emmitt Smith SS	2.50	6.00
136 LaDainian Tomlinson SS	1.50	4.00
137 Jeff Garcia SS	1.00	2.50
138 Kordell Stewart SS	1.00	2.50
139 Anthony Thomas SS	1.25	3.00
140 Tom Brady SS	8.00	20.00
141 Daunte Culpepper SS	1.25	3.00
142 Drew Bledsoe SS	1.25	3.00
143 Ricky Williams SS	1.25	3.00
144 Warrick Dunn SS	1.00	2.50
145 Steve McNair SS	1.25	3.00
146 Rich Gannon SS	1.25	3.00
147 Jake Plummer SS	1.00	2.50
148 Jerry Rice SS	3.00	8.00
149 Mark Brunell SS	1.25	3.00
150 Brian Griese SS	1.00	2.50
151 Eddie George SS	1.25	3.00
152 Tim Couch SS	1.00	2.50
153 Keyshawn Johnson SS	1.25	3.00
154 Shannon Sharpe SS	1.25	3.00
155 Phillip Buchanon RC	2.50	6.00
156 Brian Allen RC	2.00	5.00
157 Brian Westbrook RC	15.00	30.00
158 Lito Sheppard RC	2.50	6.00
159 Daryl Jones RC	1.50	4.00
160 Javin Hunter RC	1.50	4.00
161 Derrick Lewis RC	1.50	4.00
162 Javon Walker RC	2.50	6.00
163 Tank Williams RC	2.00	5.00
164 Shaun Hill RC	5.00	12.00
165 Napoleon Harris RC	2.00	5.00
166 Herb Haygood RC	1.50	4.00
167 Jake Schifino RC	1.50	4.00
168 Quentin Jammer RC	2.50	6.00
169 Jason McAddley RC	2.00	5.00
170 Jerramy Stevens RC	2.50	6.00
171 Jesse Chatman RC	1.50	4.00
172 Larry Ned RC	1.50	4.00
173 Najeh Davenport RC	1.50	4.00
174 Lamont Thompson RC	2.00	5.00
175 Darrell Hill RC	1.50	4.00
176 Ryan Sims RC	2.50	6.00
177 Ryan Denney RC	1.50	4.00
178 Jamin Elliott RC	1.50	4.00
179 Sam Simmons RC	1.50	4.00
180 Seth Burford RC	1.50	4.00
181 Tellis Redmon RC	1.50	4.00
182 Ben Leber RC	1.50	4.00
183 Kendall Newson RC	1.50	4.00
184 Marques Anderson RC	2.00	5.00
185 Adrian Peterson AU RC	6.00	15.00
187 Antwoine Womack AU RC	5.00	12.00
188 Brandon Doman AU RC	5.00	12.00
189 Craig Nall AU RC	6.00	15.00
190 Chad Hutchinson AU RC	5.00	12.00
191 Chester Taylor AU RC	8.00	20.00
192 Damien Anderson AU RC	5.00	12.00
193 Deion Branch AU RC	12.50	25.00
194 Dusty Bonner AU RC	5.00	12.00
195 Ed Reed AU RC	20.00	50.00
196 Eric McCoo AU RC	5.00	12.00
197 J.T. O'Sullivan AU RC	6.00	15.00
198 Kalimba Edwards AU RC	6.00	15.00
100 Jonathan Wells AU RC	6.00	15.00
200 Josh Scobey AU RC	6.00	15.00
201 Kelly Campbell AU RC	6.00	15.00
202 Kurt Kittner AU RC	5.00	12.00
203 Lamar Gordon AU RC	6.00	15.00
204 Lee Mays AU RC	5.00	12.00
205 Leonard Henry AU RC	5.00	12.00
206 Luke Staley AU RC	5.00	12.00
207 Justin Peelle AU RC	5.00	12.00
208 Randy Fasani AU RC	5.00	12.00
209 Ricky Williams AU RC	6.00	15.00
210 Ronald Curry AU RC	5.00	12.00
211 Travis Stephens AU RC	5.00	12.00
212 Wendell Bryant AU RC	5.00	12.00
213 Woody Dantzler AU RC	6.00	15.00
214 Kahlil Hill AU RC	5.00	12.00
215 Donte Stallworth JSY RC	6.00	15.00
216 Joey Harrington AU/280 RC	6.00	15.00
217 Cliff Russell JSY RC	4.00	10.00
218 Clinton Portis JSY RC	6.00	15.00
219 Daniel Graham JSY RC	5.00	12.00
220 David Garrard JSY RC	5.00	12.00
221 DeShaun Foster JSY RC	6.00	15.00
222 Julius Peppers JSY RC	8.00	20.00
223 Jeremy Shockey JSY RC	6.00	15.00
224 Patrick Ramsey JSY RC	5.00	12.00
225 Josh Reed JSY RC	5.00	12.00
226 LaDell Betts JSY RC	6.00	15.00
227 Mike Williams JSY/350 RC	4.00	10.00
228 Reche Caldwell JSY RC	5.00	12.00
229 Rohan Davey JSY RC	6.00	15.00
230 Ron Johnson JSY RC	5.00	12.00
231 Roy Williams JSY/350 RC	5.00	12.00
232 T.J. Duckett JSY RC	4.00	10.00
233 Tim Carter JSY RC	5.00	12.00
234 William Green JSY RC	5.00	12.00
235 Randle El JSY AU RC	10.00	25.00
237 David Carr JSY AU RC	10.00	25.00
238 Andre Davis JSY AU RC	10.00	25.00
239 Eric Crouch JSY AU RC	15.00	40.00
240 Antonio Bryant JSY AU RC	15.00	40.00
241 Jabar Gaffney JSY AU RC	10.00	25.00
242 Marquise Walker JSY AU RC	10.00	25.00
243 Maurice Morris JSY AU RC	8.00	20.00
244 Josh McCown JSY AU RC	15.00	40.00
AP1 Walter Payton AU/34	500.00	750.00
SW1 Walter Payton JSY/150	40.00	100.00
SW1 W.Payton Gold JSY/34	60.00	150.00
SCPS Payt/Smith JSY/250	30.00	80.00
SCPSG Payt/Smith Gld JSY/34	125.00	250.00

2002 SP Authentic Gold

*VETS 1-90: 10X TO 25X BASIC CARDS
1-90 VETERAN PRINT RUN 50
91-94 VET AUTO PRINT RUN 25
*ROOKIE JSY 215-234: 1X TO 2.5X
215-234 ROOKIE JSY PRINT RUN 25
235-244 JSY AU PRINT RUN 25

91 Peyton Manning AU	75.00	150.00
92 Anthony Thomas AU	15.00	40.00
93 LaDainian Tomlinson AU	25.00	60.00
94 Jeff Garcia AU	15.00	40.00

2002 SP Authentic Sign of the Times

Inserted at a rate of 1:96, this set features authentic autographs from many of the NFL's top stars. There is also a gold parallel version #'d to 25. Some cards were issued via redemption with an exchange expiration of 12/13/2005. Finally Upper Deck announced print runs on some cards as noted below.
STATED ODDS 1:96
*GOLD/25: .8X TO 2X BASIC AU
GOLD/25: .5X TO 1.2X BASIC AU/63-150
*GOLD/25: .4X TO 1X BASIC AU/25

STAB Aaron Brooks SP	5.00	12.00
STAG Ahman Green SP/76 *	12.00	30.00
STAS Antowain Smith	6.00	15.00
STBJ Brad Johnson SP	6.00	15.00
STBR Drew Brees SP	40.00	80.00
STBT Antonio Bryant SP/75 *	8.00	20.00
STCA David Carr SP/25 *	20.00	50.00
STCH Chad Hutchinson	5.00	12.00
STDB Drew Bledsoe SP/75 *	20.00	50.00
STDC Daunte Culpepper SP	15.00	30.00
STDG David Garrard	6.00	15.00
STER Antwaan Randle El/235 *	6.00	15.00
STES Emmitt Smith SP/77 *	150.00	250.00
STFM Freddie Mitchell SP	5.00	12.00
STJG Jabar Gaffney SP	5.00	12.00
STJP Jake Plummer	5.00	12.00
STJR John Riggins	25.00	50.00
STLT LaDainian Tomlinson	25.00	60.00
STMB Marty Booker	5.00	12.00
STMM Maurice Morris SP	6.00	15.00
STMV Michael Vick	12.00	30.00
STPE Julius Peppers/150 *	60.00	100.00
STPM Peyton Manning	60.00	120.00
STRC Rosevelt Colvin	10.00	25.00
STRG Rich Gannon SP/63 *	10.00	25.00
STTC Tim Couch SP	5.00	12.00
STTG Tony Gonzalez SP	6.00	15.00

2002 SP Authentic Threads

Inserted at a rate of 1:52, this set features jersey swatches from top NFL rookies. There is also a gold parallel #'d to 25.

STATED ODDS 1:52
*GOLD/25: .8X TO 2X BASIC JSY
GOLD PRINT RUN 25 SER.#'d SETS

AT1AB Antonio Bryant	4.00	10.00
AT1AL Ashley Lelie	2.50	6.00
AT1DC David Carr	2.50	6.00
AT1DF DeShaun Foster	4.00	10.00
AT1DS Donte Stallworth	4.00	10.00
AT1EC Eric Crouch	4.00	10.00
AT1JH Joey Harrington	2.50	6.00
AT1JP Julius Peppers	6.00	15.00
AT1JW Javon Walker	4.00	10.00
AT1MM Maurice Morris	3.00	8.00
AT1MW Marquise Walker	2.50	6.00
AT1PR Patrick Ramsey	3.00	8.00

2002 SP Authentic Threads Doubles

Inserted at a rate of 1:70, this set features jersey swatches from top NFL rookies, along with top veterans. There is also a gold parallel #'d to 25.
STATED ODDS 1:70
*GOLD/25: .8X TO 2X BASIC DUAL
GOLD PRINT RUN 25 SER.#'d SETS

AT2CB R.Caldwell/D.Brees	8.00	20.00
AT2CC D.Carr/T.Couch	2.50	6.00
AT2CW D.Carr/K.Warner	3.00	8.00
AT2HC J.Harrington/D.Culpepper	3.00	8.00
AT2HM J.Harrington/D.McNabb	3.00	8.00
AT2MF M.Morris/M.Faulk	3.00	8.00
AT2RB P.Ramsey/T.Brady	20.00	50.00
AT2SM D.Stallworth/P.Manning	10.00	25.00

2002 SP Authentic Threads Triples

Randomly inserted into packs, and serial #'d to 250, this set features three jersey swatches from top NFL stars. There is also a gold parallel #'d to 10.
STATED PRINT RUN 250 SER.#'d SETS
UNPRICED TRIPLE GOLD PRINT RUN 10

AT3BP Bledsoe/Price/Reed	6.00	15.00
AT3CC Carr/Crouch/Manning	20.00	50.00
AT3CD Crouch/Dayne/Williams	8.00	20.00
AT3CH Carr/Harrington/Ramsey	6.00	15.00
AT3CM Culpepper/McNabb/Vick	6.00	15.00
AT3CW Crouch/Warner/Faulk	8.00	20.00
AT3FM Foster/Mitchell/Stokes	8.00	20.00
AT3FW Favre/Warner/Manning	20.00	50.00
AT3PB Plummer/Boston/McCown	8.00	20.00
AT3PL Portis/Lewis/S.Moss	8.00	20.00
AT3SS Stllwrth/Stphns/Mnnng	20.00	50.00
AT3WG Walker/Griese/Howard	6.00	15.00

2002 SP Authentic Threads Quads

Randomly inserted into packs, and serial #'d to 100, this set features four jersey swatches from top NFL stars. There is also a gold parallel #'d to 25.
STATED PRINT RUN 100 SER.#'d SETS
*GOLD/25: .8X TO 2X BASIC QUAD
GOLD PRINT RUN 25 SER.#'d SETS

CB Eric Crouch	10.00	25.00
Tim Brown		
Eddie George		
Charles Woodson		
CH David Carr	10.00	25.00
Joey Harrington		
Patrick Ramsey		
Rohan Davey		
CW Eric Crouch	10.00	25.00
Kurt Warner		
Marshall Faulk		
Isaac Bruce		
SL Shock/Lewis/Moss/Sapp	10.00	25.00
SS Stall/Steph/Mann/Lewis	25.00	60.00
WG Kurt Warner	8.00	20.00
Brian Griese		
Rich Gannon		
Quincy Carter		

2002 SP Authentic Sign of the Times Hawaii Trade Conference

This card, featuring HOFer John Riggins, was distributed by Upper Deck to attendees of the Hawaii Trade Conference in 2001. Each card was serial numbered to 500.

JR John Riggins/500	15.00	40.00

2003 SP Authentic

Released in January of 2004, this set consists of 269 cards, including 90 veterans and 179 rookies. Rookies 91-120 are serial numbered to 2200. Cards 121-150 make up the Star Status (SS) subset and are serial numbered to 1200. Rookies 151-211 are serial numbered to 1200. Rookies 212-240 are serial numbered to 1200 and feature authentic player autographs on the card. Please note that Chris Simms (#212) is serial numbered to 250. Rookies 241-270 feature event worn patch swatches. The patch cards of Bryant Johnson, Kyle Boller, Seneca Wallace, Byron Leftwich, and Carson Palmer also feature an authentic player autograph on the card. Non-autographed patch cards are serial numbered to 850, while autographed patches are serial numbered to 250. Several players were issued as exchange cards in packs with an expiration date of 12/29/2006. Please note that card number 267 was not released due to a production error. Boxes contained 24 packs of 5 cards. SRP was $4.99.

COMP.SET w/o SP's (90)	7.50	20.00
91-120 ROOKIE PRINT RUN 2200		
151-211 ROOKIE PRINT RUN 1200		
213-240 AU RC PRINT RUN 1200		
1 Donovan McNabb	.30	.75
2 Tim Couch	.25	.60
3 Joey Harrington	.25	.60
4 Brett Favre	.75	2.00
5 Jeff Garcia	.25	.60
6 Kerry Collins	.25	.60
7 Michael Vick	.30	.75
8 David Carr	.25	.60
9 Steve McNair	.30	.75
10 Chad Pennington	.25	.60
11 Patrick Ramsey	.30	.75
12 Rich Gannon	.30	.75
13 Kurt Warner	.30	.75
14 Brad Johnson	.30	.75
15 Jay Fiedler	.25	.60
16 Jake Plummer	.25	.60
17 Mark Brunell	.30	.75
18 Peyton Manning	1.00	2.50
19 Brian Griese	.25	.60
20 Kordell Stewart	.25	.60
21 Kelly Holcomb	.25	.60
22 Josh McCown	.30	.75
23 Matt Hasselbeck	.25	.60
24 Marc Bulger	.25	.60
25 Chris Redman	.25	.60
26 Rodney Peete	.25	.60
27 Jake Delhomme	.25	.60
28 Jon Kitna	.25	.60
29 Trent Green	.25	.60
30 Quincy Carter	.25	.60
31 Chad Hutchinson	.25	.60
32 Edgerrin James	.30	.75
33 Deuce McAllister	.30	.75
34 Ricky Williams	.30	.75
35 Priest Holmes	.25	.60
36 Curtis Martin	.30	.75
37 Shaun Alexander	.25	.60
38 Eddie George	.30	.75
39 Marshall Faulk	.30	.75
40 Garrison Hearst	.25	.60
41 Ahman Green	.30	.75
42 Corey Dillon	.25	.60
43 Jamal Lewis	.30	.75
44 William Green	.25	.60
45 Travis Henry	.25	.60
46 Mike Alstott	.25	.60
47 Amos Zereoue	.25	.60
48 Stephen Davis	.25	.60
49 Duce Staley	.25	.60
50 Fred Taylor	.25	.60
51 Anthony Thomas	.30	.75
52 Charlie Garner	.30	.75
53 Kevan Barlow	.25	.60
54 Brian Urlacher	.40	1.00
55 Junior Seau	.30	.75
56 Zach Thomas	.30	.75
57 Ray Lewis	.40	1.00
58 Jerry Porter	.25	.60
59 Marty Booker	.25	.60
60 Javon Walker	.30	.75
61 Donald Driver	.30	.75
62 Amani Toomer	.25	.60
63 Peerless Price	.25	.60
64 Santana Moss	.30	.75
65 Laveranues Coles	.25	.60
66 Troy Brown	.25	.60
67 Chris Chambers	.25	.60
68 Rod Smith	.30	.75
69 Ashley Lelie	.25	.60
70 Plaxico Burress	.25	.60
71 Keyshawn Johnson	.40	1.00
72 Isaac Bruce	.40	1.00
73 Torry Holt	.30	.75
74 Koren Robinson	.30	.75
75 Derrick Mason	.25	.60
76 Kevin Johnson	.25	.60
77 Andre' Davis	.25	.60
78 Antonio Bryant	.25	.60
79 Eric Moulds	.25	.60
80 Jerry Rice	.75	2.00
81 Tim Brown	.40	1.00
82 Antwaan Randle El	.25	.60
83 Donte Stallworth	.25	.60
84 Randy Moss	.30	.75
85 Chad Johnson	.25	.60
86 Hines Ward	.30	.75
87 Rod Gardner	.25	.60
88 Marvin Harrison	.30	.75
89 David Boston	.25	.60
90 Julius Peppers	.40	1.00
91 Dewayne White RC	1.00	2.50
92 Casey Fitzsimmons RC	1.25	3.00
93 Aaron Moorehead RC	1.25	3.00
94 Jimmy Farris RC	1.00	2.50
95 Eric Parker RC	1.50	4.00
96 Michael Haynes RC	1.00	2.50
97 J.J. Moses RC	1.00	2.50
98 Ken Hamlin RC	1.50	4.00
99 William Joseph RC	1.00	2.50
100 Alonzo Jackson RC	1.00	2.50
101 Tyler Brayton RC	1.25	3.00
102 Eddie Moore RC	1.00	2.50
103 Cleo Lemon RC	1.50	4.00
104 Arlen Harris RC	1.00	2.50
105 Cortez Hankton RC	1.25	3.00
106 Angelo Crowell RC	1.25	3.00
107 Johnathan Sullivan RC	1.00	2.50
108 Pisa Tinoisamoa RC	1.50	4.00
109 Boss Bailey RC	1.25	3.00
110 Tommy Jones RC	1.00	2.50
111 E.J. Henderson RC	1.25	3.00
112 Jimmy Kennedy RC	1.25	3.00
113 Nnamdi Asomugha RC	1.50	4.00
114 Hanik Milligan RC	1.00	2.50
115 Sammy Davis RC	1.25	3.00
116 Drayton Florence RC	1.50	4.00
117 Andre Woolfolk RC	1.00	2.50
118 Dennis Weathersby RC	1.00	2.50
119 Mike Doss RC	1.50	4.00
120 Troy Polamalu RC	20.00	50.00
121 Clinton Portis SS	1.00	2.50
122 Daunte Culpepper SS	1.25	3.00
123 Jeremy Shockey SS	1.00	2.50
124 Drew Brees SS	1.50	4.00
125 Marshall Faulk SS	1.25	3.00
126 Emmitt Smith SS	2.50	6.00
127 Terrell Owens SS	1.25	3.00
128 Ricky Williams SS	1.25	3.00
129 Deuce McAllister SS	1.25	3.00
130 Ahman Green SS	1.25	3.00
131 Chad Pennington SS	1.00	2.50
132 Plaxico Burress SS	1.00	2.50
133 Steve McNair SS	1.25	3.00
134 Keyshawn Johnson SS	1.50	4.00
135 Jeff Garcia SS	1.00	2.50
136 Drew Bledsoe SS	1.25	3.00
137 Jerry Rice SS	3.00	8.00
138 Randy Moss SS	1.25	3.00
139 David Carr SS	1.00	2.50
140 Joey Harrington SS	1.00	2.50
141 Michael Vick SS	1.25	3.00
142 Tom Brady SS	6.00	15.00
143 Brian Urlacher SS	1.50	4.00
144 Brett Favre SS	3.00	8.00
145 Kurt Warner SS	1.25	3.00
146 LaDainian Tomlinson SS	1.50	4.00
147 Aaron Brooks SS	1.00	2.50
148 Edgerrin James SS	1.25	3.00
149 Peyton Manning SS	2.50	6.00
150 Donovan McNabb SS	1.25	3.00
151 Jason Gesser RC	1.50	4.00
152 Ken Dorsey RC	1.50	4.00
153 Jason Johnson RC	1.25	3.00
154 Avon Cobourne RC	1.25	3.00
155 Andrew Pinnock RC	1.50	4.00
156 Kirk Farmer RC	1.50	4.00
157 Reno Mahe RC	1.50	4.00
158 Lon Sheriff RC	1.25	3.00
159 Marquel Blackwell RC	1.25	3.00
160 Quentin Griffin RC	1.50	4.00
161 Rashean Mathis RC	1.25	3.00
162 Lee Suggs RC	1.25	3.00
163 Jeremi Johnson RC	1.25	3.00
164 Ovie Mughelli RC	1.50	4.00
165 Nick Barnett RC	2.00	5.00
166 Brock Forsey RC	1.50	4.00
167 Malaefou MacKenzie RC	1.25	3.00
168 Ahmaad Galloway RC	1.50	4.00
169 Cecil Sapp RC	1.25	3.00
170 Kerry Carter RC	1.25	3.00
171A Terrence Edwards RC	1.25	3.00
171B Dahrran Diedrick RC	1.25	3.00
172 Joffrey Reynolds RC	1.25	3.00
173 Sultan McCullough RC	1.25	3.00
174 Brandon Drumm RC	1.25	3.00
175 Casey Moore RC	1.25	3.00
176 Gerald Hayes RC	1.50	4.00
178 Jamal Burke RC	1.25	3.00
179 Antonio Chatman RC	2.00	5.00
180 Reggie Newhouse RC	1.25	3.00
181 Chris Horn RC	1.50	4.00
182 Denero Marriott RC	1.25	3.00
183 DeAndrew Rubin RC	1.25	3.00
184 Taco Wallace RC	1.25	3.00
185 Doug Gabriel RC	1.50	4.00
186 Willie Ponder RC	1.25	3.00
187 David Tyree RC	1.50	4.00
188 Kevin Walter RC	3.00	8.00
189 Zuriel Smith RC	1.25	3.00
190 Keenan Howry RC	1.25	3.00
191 C.J. Jones RC	1.25	3.00
192 Arnaz Battle RC	2.00	5.00
193 Walter Young RC	1.25	3.00
194 Anthony Adams RC	1.50	4.00
195 Jerome McDougle RC	1.25	3.00
196 Will Heller RC	1.50	4.00
197 Cecil Moore RC	1.25	3.00
198 Mike Seidman RC	1.25	3.00
199 Jason Witten RC	25.00	60.00
200 L.J. Smith RC	2.00	5.00
201 Bennie Joppru RC	1.25	3.00
202 Donald Lee RC	1.50	4.00
203 Aaron Walker RC	1.50	4.00
204 Antonio Brown RC	1.25	3.00
205 George Wrighster RC	1.25	3.00
206 Danny Curley RC	1.25	3.00
207 Mike Banks RC	1.25	3.00
208 Mike Pinkard RC	1.25	3.00
209 Ryan Hoag RC	1.25	3.00
210 Brad Pyatt RC	1.25	3.00
211 Charles Rogers RC	1.50	4.00
212 Chris Simms AU/250 RC	8.00	20.00
213 Nate Hybl AU RC	4.00	10.00
214 Brandon Lloyd AU RC	5.00	12.00
215 ReShard Lee AU RC	5.00	12.00
216 Dwone Hicks AU RC	3.00	8.00
217 Tony Romo AU RC	125.00	250.00
218 Brett Engemann AU RC	3.00	8.00
219 Nick Maddox AU RC	3.00	8.00
220 James MacPherson AU RC	4.00	10.00
221 Juston Wood AU RC	3.00	8.00
222 Adrian Madise AU RC	3.00	8.00
223 Shaun McDonald AU RC	4.00	10.00
224 Carl Ford AU RC	3.00	8.00
225 Vishante Shiancoe AU RC	8.00	20.00
226 Gibran Hamdan AU RC	3.00	8.00
227 Brooks Bollinger AU RC	4.00	10.00
228 B.J. Askew AU RC	4.00	10.00
229 Domanick Davis AU RC	4.00	10.00
230 LaBrandon Toefield AU RC	3.00	8.00
231 Bobby Wade AU RC	4.00	10.00
232 Justin Gage AU RC	4.00	10.00
233 Billy McMullen AU RC	3.00	8.00
234 David Kircus AU RC	4.00	10.00
235 J.R. Tolver AU RC	4.00	10.00
236 Sam Aiken AU RC	4.00	10.00
237 LaTarence Dunbar AU RC	3.00	8.00
238 Kassim Osgood AU RC	5.00	12.00
239 Tony Hollings AU RC	4.00	10.00
240 Justin Griffith AU RC	4.00	10.00
241 Brian St.Pierre JSY RC	4.00	10.00
242 Kevin Curtis JSY RC	4.00	10.00
243 Dallas Clark JSY RC	6.00	15.00
244 Willis McGahee JSY RC	5.00	12.00
245 Terence Newman JSY RC	6.00	15.00
246 Justin Fargas JSY AU RC	12.00	30.00
247 Artose Pinner JSY RC	4.00	10.00
248 Kelley Washington JSY RC	4.00	10.00
249 DeWayne Robertson JSY RC	5.00	12.00
250 Nate Burleson JSY RC	5.00	12.00
251 Kliff Kingsbury JSY RC	6.00	15.00
252 Bethel Johnson JSY RC	4.00	10.00
253 Anquan Boldin JSY RC	6.00	15.00
254 Bryant Johnson JSY AU RC	12.00	30.00
255 Terrell Suggs JSY AU RC	30.00	80.00
256 Musa Smith JSY RC	4.00	10.00
257 Chris Brown JSY RC	4.00	10.00
258 Marcus Trufant JSY RC	5.00	12.00
259 Teyo Johnson JSY RC	5.00	12.00
260 Tyrone Calico JSY RC	4.00	10.00
261 Dave Ragone JSY AU RC	8.00	20.00
262 Kyle Boller JSY AU RC	8.00	20.00
263 Onterrio Smith JSY AU RC	8.00	20.00
264 Rex Grossman JSY RC	5.00	12.00
265 Larry Johnson JSY RC	5.00	12.00
266 Seneca Wallace JSY AU RC	10.00	25.00
268 Taylor Jacobs JSY AU RC	8.00	20.00
269 Byron Leftwich JSY AU RC	10.00	25.00
270 Carson Palmer JSY AU RC	40.00	100.00

2003 SP Authentic Gold

*VETS 1-90: 12X TO 30X BASIC CARDS
*ROOKIES 91-120: 2.5X TO 6X
*SS 121-150: 3X TO 8X BASIC CARDS
*ROOKIES 151-211: 2X TO 5X
*ROOKIE AU: .6X TO 1.5X BASE AU/250
*ROOKIE AU: 1.5X TO 4X BASE AU/1200
*ROOKIE JSY: 1X TO 2.5X BASIC JSY
*ROOK.JSY AUs: 1.2X TO 3X BASE CARD HI
STATED PRINT RUN 25 SERIAL #'d SETS

120 Troy Polamalu	150.00	300.00
217 Tony Romo AU	900.00	1500.00
270 Carson Palmer JSY AU	125.00	250.00

2003 SP Authentic Buy Back Autographs

Randomly inserted in packs, this set features nine authentic player autographs on original 1993 SP cards. Each card is signed and numbered and comes with a certificate of authenticity.
NOT PRICED DUE TO SCARCITY

2003 SP Authentic Sign of the Times

Randomly inserted in packs, this set features authentic player autographs on the cards. Each card is machine numbered to varying quantities. Some cards were also issued without any serial numbering. Please note that Justin Fargas, Joe Montana, Matt Hasselbeck, Ray Lewis, Lee Suggs, Terrell Owens, Terrell Suggs, and Zach Thomas were issued as exchange cards in packs with an expiration date of 12/29/2006. A Gold parallel of this set was also issued with each card serial numbered to 25.
STATED PRINT RUN 12-900
SERIAL #'d UNDER 20 NOT PRICED

AB Aaron Brooks/250	8.00	20.00
AL Mike Alstott/275	8.00	20.00
BA Barry Sanders/43	100.00	200.00
BJ Bryant Johnson/475	10.00	25.00
BL Byron Leftwich/75	12.00	30.00
BR Troy Brown/600	6.00	15.00
BS Bart Starr/120	90.00	150.00
BU Brian Urlacher/250	15.00	40.00
CP Chad Pennington/141	12.00	30.00
DA David Boston/250	8.00	20.00
DB Drew Brees/250	40.00	80.00
DC David Carr/250	8.00	20.00
DM Deuce McAllister/250	10.00	25.00
DO Donovan McNabb/75	25.00	60.00
DR Drew Bledsoe/250	10.00	25.00
JB Jim Brown/75	50.00	100.00
JE Jerry Porter/600	6.00	15.00
JF Justin Fargas/475	10.00	25.00
JG Jeff Garcia/50	12.00	30.00
JL Jamal Lewis/400	8.00	20.00
JM Joe Montana/21	125.00	250.00
JN Joe Namath/35	75.00	150.00
JW Javon Walker/600	8.00	20.00
KH Kelly Holcomb/475	6.00	15.00
KR Koren Robinson/530	8.00	20.00
LS Lynn Swann/125	200.00	400.00
MA Marcus Allen/21	40.00	80.00
MH Matt Hasselbeck/275	12.00	30.00
PH Priest Holmes/75	12.00	30.00
PM Peyton Manning/900	60.00	100.00
PO Clinton Portis/520	6.00	15.00
PP Peerless Price/350	6.00	15.00
RG Rod Gardner/215	8.00	20.00
RI John Riggins/105	30.00	80.00
RW Ricky Williams/50	15.00	40.00
SA Shaun Alexander/250	8.00	20.00
SU Lee Suggs/375	6.00	15.00
TA Troy Aikman/97	50.00	120.00
TB Tim Brown/246	20.00	50.00
TC Tyrone Calico/200	8.00	20.00
TE Teyo Johnson/250	10.00	25.00
TG Trent Green/200	8.00	20.00
TM Tommy Maddox/592	6.00	15.00
TO Terrell Owens/286	15.00	40.00
TS Terrell Suggs/475	12.00	30.00
ZT Zach Thomas/350	8.00	20.00

2003 SP Authentic Sign of the Times Gold

PRINT RUN 25 SERIAL #'d SETS

AB Aaron Brooks	15.00	40.00
AL Mike Alstott	15.00	40.00
BA Barry Sanders	75.00	150.00
BJ Bryant Johnson	20.00	50.00
BL Byron Leftwich	15.00	40.00
BR Troy Brown	15.00	40.00
BS Bart Starr	125.00	200.00
BU Brian Urlacher	25.00	60.00
CP Chad Pennington	15.00	40.00
DA David Boston	15.00	40.00
DB Drew Brees	60.00	120.00
DC David Carr	15.00	40.00
DM Deuce McAllister	20.00	50.00
DO Donovan McNabb	20.00	50.00
DR Drew Bledsoe	20.00	50.00
JB Jim Brown	60.00	120.00
JE Jerry Porter	15.00	40.00
JF Justin Fargas	20.00	50.00
JG Jeff Garcia	15.00	40.00
JL Jamal Lewis	20.00	50.00
JM Joe Montana	100.00	200.00
JN Joe Namath	60.00	120.00
JW Javon Walker	20.00	50.00
KH Kelly Holcomb	15.00	40.00
KR Koren Robinson	20.00	50.00
LS Lynn Swann	300.00	600.00
MA Marcus Allen	40.00	80.00
MH Matt Hasselbeck	15.00	40.00
PH Priest Holmes	15.00	40.00
PM Peyton Manning	75.00	150.00
PO Clinton Portis	15.00	40.00
PP Peerless Price	15.00	40.00
RG Rod Gardner	15.00	40.00
RI John Riggins	30.00	80.00
RW Ricky Williams	20.00	50.00
SA Shaun Alexander	15.00	40.00
SU Lee Suggs	12.00	30.00
TA Troy Aikman	50.00	100.00
TB Tim Brown	25.00	60.00
TC Tyrone Calico	12.00	30.00
TE Teyo Johnson	15.00	40.00
TG Trent Green	15.00	40.00
TM Tommy Maddox	15.00	40.00
TO Terrell Owens	20.00	50.00
TS Terrell Suggs	25.00	60.00
ZT Zach Thomas	20.00	50.00

2003 SP Authentic Threads

Inserted at a rate of 1:24, this set features jersey swatches of NFL superstars and promising rookies. A Gold parallel of this set exists featuring cards with gold highlights with each being serial numbered to 25.
OVERALL THREADS STATED ODDS 1:24
ANNOUNCED PRINT RUN 450
*GOLD/25: 1X TO 2.5X BASIC JSY/450
GOLD STATED PRINT RUN 25 SER.#'d SETS

JCAB Anquan Boldin	4.00	10.00
JCAG Ahman Green	4.00	10.00
JCAJ Andre Johnson	6.00	15.00
JCBF Brett Favre	10.00	25.00
JCBJ Bethel Johnson	3.00	8.00
JCBR Bryant Johnson	4.00	10.00
JCCL Dallas Clark	4.00	10.00
JCCP Chad Pennington	3.00	8.00
JCCU Daunte Culpepper	4.00	10.00
JCDC David Carr	3.00	8.00
JCDR Dave Ragone	3.00	8.00
JCEJ Edgerrin James	4.00	10.00
JCES Emmitt Smith	8.00	20.00

JCHO Torry Holt 4.00 10.00
JCJP Jake Plummer 3.00 8.00
JCJR Jerry Rice 10.00 25.00
JCKB Kyle Boller 2.50 6.00
JCKC Kevin Curtis 2.50 6.00
JCKE Kelley Washington 2.50 6.00
JCKK Kliff Kingsbury 4.00 10.00
JCKW Kurt Warner 4.00 10.00
JCLJ Larry Johnson 3.00 8.00
JCMC Donovan McNabb 4.00 10.00
JCMH Marvin Harrison 4.00 10.00
JCMS Musa Smith 2.50 6.00
JCMV Michael Vick 4.00 10.00
JCNB Nate Burleson 3.00 8.00
JCOS Onterrio Smith 2.50 6.00
JCPA Carson Palmer 12.00 30.00
JCPH Priest Holmes 3.00 8.00
JCPM Peyton Manning 12.00 30.00
JCPO Clinton Portis 3.00 8.00
JCPP Peerless Price 3.00 8.00
JCRG Rich Gannon 4.00 10.00
JCRS Rod Smith 4.00 10.00
JCSM Santana Moss 4.00 10.00
JCST Steve McNair 4.00 10.00
JCTB Tom Brady 20.00 50.00
JCTC Tyrone Calico 2.50 6.00
JCTH Travis Henry 3.00 8.00
JCTJ Teyo Johnson 3.00 8.00
JCWM Willis McGahee 3.00 8.00

2003 SP Authentic Threads Doubles

Randomly inserted in packs, each card in this set pairs two players along with a jersey swatch of each player. The cards are serial numbered to 345. A Gold parallel of this set exists featuring cards with gold highlights. The gold cards are serial numbered to 25.

DOUBLE STATED PRINT RUN 345
*GOLD/25: 1X TO 2.5X DUAL/345
GOLD PRINT RUN 25 SER.#'d SETS
ABBJ Boldin/Br.Johnson 4.00 10.00
BFAG Favre/Green 10.00 25.00
CPKW Palmer/Washington 12.00 30.00
CPSM Pennington/Moss 4.00 10.00
DCAJ Carr/Johnson 6.00 15.00
DCDR Carr/Ragone 3.00 8.00
DCNB Culpepper/Burleson 4.00 10.00
DCOS Culpepper/O.Smith 4.00 10.00
DMMV McNabb/Vick 4.00 10.00
EJCP James/Portis 4.00 10.00
ESCP E.Smith/Portis 8.00 20.00
JFTJ Fargas/Johnson 5.00 12.00
JPCP Plummer/Portis 3.00 8.00
JPRS Plummer/R.Smith 4.00 10.00
JRRG Rice/Gannon 10.00 25.00
KBMS Boller/M.Smith 3.00 8.00
KKBJ Kingsbury/Be.Johnson 5.00 12.00
KWKC Warner/Curtis 3.00 8.00
KWTH Warner/Holt 4.00 10.00
LJPH Johnson/Holmes 3.00 8.00
MVPP Vick/Price 4.00 10.00
OSNB O.Smith/Burleson 4.00 10.00
PMCP Manning/Palmer 12.00 30.00
PMDC Manning/Clark 12.00 30.00
PMMH Manning/Harrison 12.00 30.00
RGTJ Gannon/T.Johnson 4.00 10.00
SMTC McNair/Calico 4.00 10.00
TBBJ Brady/Be.Johnson 20.00 50.00
TBKK Brady/Kingsbury 20.00 50.00
THWM Henry/McGahee 3.00 8.00

2003 SP Authentic Threads Triples

Randomly inserted in packs, each card in this set features three players along with a jersey swatch of each player. The cards are serial numbered to 175. A Gold parallel of this set exists featuring cards with gold highlights. The gold cards are serial numbered to 25.

TRIPLE PRINT RUN 175 SER.#'d SETS
*GOLD/25: .8X TO 2X TRIPLE/175
GOLD STATED PRINT RUN 25 SER.#'d SETS
HMJ Harrison/Manning/James 15.00 40.00
HWC Holt/Warner/James 5.00 12.00
JBK Johnson/Brady/Kingsbury 25.00 60.00
JCR Johnson/Carr/Ragone 6.00 15.00
MCB Moss/Culpepper/Burleson 5.00 12.00
MPJ McGahee/Portis/James 3.00 8.00
MPM Moss/Penn/Martin 5.00 12.00
PPS Portis/Plummer/Smith 5.00 12.00
RGJ Rice/Gannon/Johnson 12.00 30.00
VCP Vick/Carr/Palmer 5.00 12.00

2003 SP Authentic Promo Strips

These three-card strips were issued by Upper Deck to promote the 2003 SP Authentic card release. Each was serial numbered on the front to 1000 and released primarily at the 2004 Super Bowl XXXVIII Card Show in Houston. We've numbered them below according to alphabetical order starting with the player to the far left on the strip.

1 Plaxico Burress .75 2.00
Travis Henry
Kelly Holcomb
2 Trent Green 1.50 4.00
Ray Lewis
Donte Stallworth
3 Edgerrin James 1.50 4.00
Zach Thomas
Tim Brown
4 Santana Moss 1.25 3.00
Donovan McNabb
Rodney Peete
5 Amos Zereoue 1.25 3.00
Marvin Harrison
Chad Hutchinson

2004 SP Authentic

SP Authentic initially released in late-December 2004 and was one of the most popular releases of the year. The base set consists of 216-cards including 60-rookies serial numbered to 1199, 35-rookie autographs serial numbered to 990 and 31-rookie jersey autographs numbered between 299 and 799. Hobby boxes contained 24-packs of 5-cards and carried an S.R.P. of $4.99 per pack. Two parallel sets and a variety of inserts can be found seeded in packs highlighted by the Scripts for Success and Sign of the Times autograph inserts.

COMP.SET w/o SP's (90) 10.00 25.00
91-150 ROOKIE PRINT RUN 1199
151-185 ROOKIE AU PRINT RUN 990
186-200 JSY AU RC PRINT RUN 799
201-206 JSY AU RC PRINT RUN 499
207-216 JSY AU RC PRINT RUN 299
1 Josh McCown .30 .75
2 Anquan Boldin .25 .60
3 Michael Vick .30 .75
4 Peerless Price .25 .60
5 Todd Heap .25 .60
6 Kyle Boller .25 .60
7 Jamal Lewis .30 .75
8 Drew Bledsoe .30 .75
9 Travis Henry .25 .60
10 Eric Moulds .25 .60
11 Steve Smith .40 1.00
12 Stephen Davis .25 .60
13 Jake Delhomme .25 .60
14 Rex Grossman .25 .60
15 Brian Urlacher .40 1.00
16 Thomas Jones .25 .60
17 Chad Johnson .25 .60
18 Rudi Johnson .25 .60
19 Carson Palmer .30 .75
20 William Green .25 .60
21 Andre Davis .25 .60
22 Jeff Garcia .25 .60
23 Roy Williams S .25 .60
24 Eddie George .30 .75
25 Keyshawn Johnson .30 .75
26 Ashley Lelie .25 .60
27 Jake Plummer .25 .60
28 Champ Bailey .30 .75
29 Charles Rogers .25 .60
30 Joey Harrington .25 .60
31 Ahman Green .30 .75
32 Brett Favre .75 2.00
33 Javon Walker .25 .60
34 David Carr .25 .60
35 Domanick Davis .25 .60
36 Andre Johnson .30 .75
37 Marvin Harrison .30 .75
38 Edgerrin James .30 .75
39 Peyton Manning 1.00 2.50
40 Byron Leftwich .25 .60
41 Fred Taylor .25 .60
42 Trent Green .25 .60
43 Tony Gonzalez .30 .75
44 Priest Holmes .25 .60
45 Ricky Williams .30 .75
46 Chris Chambers .25 .60
47 Jay Fiedler .25 .60
48 Daunte Culpepper .30 .75
49 Randy Moss .30 .75
50 Onterrio Smith .25 .60
51 Tom Brady 1.50 4.00
52 Troy Brown .25 .60
53 Corey Dillon .25 .60
54 Deuce McAllister .30 .75
55 Aaron Brooks .25 .60
56 Joe Horn .25 .60
57 Amani Toomer .25 .60
58 Kurt Warner .30 .75
59 Jeremy Shockey .25 .60
60 Chad Pennington .25 .60
61 Santana Moss .30 .75
62 Curtis Martin .30 .75
63 Rich Gannon .30 .75
64 Jerry Rice .75 2.00
65 Jerry Porter .25 .60
66 Terrell Owens .30 .75
67 Jevon Kearse .25 .60
68 Donovan McNabb .30 .75
69 Hines Ward .30 .75
70 Plaxico Burress .25 .60
71 Tommy Maddox .25 .60
72 Drew Brees .40 1.00
73 LaDainian Tomlinson .40 1.00
74 Tim Rattay .25 .60
75 Brandon Lloyd .30 .75
76 Kevan Barlow .25 .60
77 Shaun Alexander .25 .60
78 Koren Robinson .25 .60
79 Matt Hasselbeck .25 .60
80 Marshall Faulk .30 .75
81 Torry Holt .30 .75
82 Marc Bulger .25 .60
83 Brad Johnson .30 .75
84 Joey Galloway .30 .75
85 Steve McNair .30 .75
86 Derrick Mason .25 .60
87 Chris Brown .25 .60
88 Mark Brunell .30 .75
89 Laveranues Coles .25 .60
90 Clinton Portis .25 .60
91 Triandos Luke RC 1.50 4.00
92 Keith Smith RC 1.50 4.00
93 Shaun Phillips RC 2.00 5.00
94 D.J. Williams RC 2.50 6.00
95 Keiwan Ratliff RC 1.50 4.00
96 Madieu Williams RC 1.50 4.00
97 Chris Cooley RC 2.00 5.00
98 Stuart Schweigert RC 2.00 5.00
99 Sloan Thomas RC 2.00 5.00
100 Chad Lavalais RC 1.50 4.00
101 Jared Allen RC 25.00 50.00
102 Brian Jones RC 1.50 4.00
103 Matt Ware RC 2.50 6.00
104 Daryl Smith RC 1.50 4.00
105 J.R. Reed RC 1.50 4.00
106 D.J. Hackett RC 1.50 4.00
107 Jeris McIntyre RC 1.50 4.00
108 Dexter Reid RC 1.50 4.00
109 Courtney Anderson RC 1.50 4.00
110 Courtney Watson RC 1.50 4.00
111 Larry Croom RC 1.50 4.00
112 Jonathan Smith RC 1.50 4.00
113 Vernon Carey RC 1.50 4.00
114 Michael Gaines RC 1.50 4.00
115 Chris Snee RC 3.00 8.00
116 Nathan Vasher RC 2.50 6.00
117 Teddy Lehman RC 1.50 4.00
118 Marcus Tubbs RC 1.50 4.00
119 Ben Utecht RC 2.00 5.00
120 Maurice Mann RC 1.50 4.00
121 Thomas Tapeh RC 2.00 5.00
122 Will Allen RC 2.00 5.00
123 Demorrio Williams RC 2.50 6.00
124 Ran Carthon RC 1.50 4.00
125 Tim Euhus RC 1.50 4.00
126 Bradlee Van Pelt RC 2.00 5.00
127 Patrick Crayton RC 2.50 6.00
128 Ryan Krause RC 1.50 4.00
129 Joey Thomas RC 1.50 4.00
130 Antwan Odom RC 1.50 4.00
131 Karlos Dansby RC 2.00 5.00
132 Junior Siavii RC 1.50 4.00
133 Jamaar Taylor RC 1.50 4.00
134 Kendrick Starling RC 1.50 4.00
135 Wes Welker RC 8.00 20.00
136 Igor Olshansky RC 2.00 5.00
137 Mark Jones RC 1.50 4.00
138 Bruce Thornton RC 1.50 4.00
139 Michael Boulware RC 2.50 6.00
140 Matt Mauck RC 1.50 4.00
141 Clarence Moore RC 1.50 4.00
142 Derrick Strait RC 1.50 4.00
143 Jarrett Payton RC 2.00 5.00
144 Dontarrious Thomas RC 2.00 5.00
145 Shawntae Spencer RC 1.50 4.00
146 Bob Sanders RC 8.00 20.00
147 Darnell Dockett RC 2.50 6.00
148 Sean Taylor RC 10.00 25.00
149 Jason Babin RC 2.50 6.00
150 Ricardo Colclough RC 1.50 4.00
151 Brandon Chillar AU RC 4.00 10.00
152 Clarence Farmer AU RC 3.00 8.00
153 B.J. Symons AU RC 3.00 8.00
154 John Navarre AU RC 3.00 8.00
155 P.K. Sam AU RC 3.00 8.00
156 Casey Clausen AU RC 4.00 10.00
157 Drew Henson AU RC 3.00 8.00
157B Drew Henson AU/50 ERR 3.00 8.00
158 Kris Wilson AU RC 4.00 10.00
159 Vince Wilfork AU RC 8.00 20.00
160 Michael Turner AU RC 10.00 25.00
161 Jonathan Vilma AU RC 4.00 10.00
162 Samie Parker AU RC 3.00 8.00
163 B.J. Sams AU RC 3.00 8.00
164 A.Echemandu AU RC 4.00 10.00
165 Ernest Wilford AU RC 4.00 10.00
166 Troy Fleming AU RC 3.00 8.00
167 Tommie Harris AU RC 4.00 10.00
168 Jammal Lord AU RC 3.00 8.00
169 Kenechi Udeze AU RC 4.00 10.00
170 Chris Gamble AU RC 3.00 8.00
171 Carlos Francis AU RC 3.00 8.00
172 Mewelde Moore AU RC 4.00 10.00
173 Jared Lorenzen AU RC 4.00 10.00
174 Jeff Smoker AU RC 4.00 10.00
175 Ben Hartsock AU RC 3.00 8.00
176 Jerricho Cotchery AU RC 4.00 10.00
177 Josh Harris AU RC 3.00 8.00
178 Cody Pickett AU RC 3.00 8.00
179 Quincy Wilson AU RC 3.00 8.00
180 Will Smith AU RC 4.00 10.00
181 Ahmad Carroll AU RC 3.00 8.00
182 B.J. Johnson AU RC 3.00 8.00
183 Dunta Robinson AU RC 3.00 8.00
184 Craig Krenzel AU RC 3.00 8.00
185 Johnnie Morant AU RC 3.00 8.00
186 Cedric Cobbs JSY AU RC 6.00 15.00
187 Matt Schaub JSY AU RC 6.00 15.00
188 Bernard Berrian JSY AU RC 6.00 15.00
189 Devard Darling JSY AU RC 6.00 15.00
190 Ben Watson JSY AU RC 8.00 20.00
191 Darius Watts JSY AU RC 6.00 15.00
192 DeAngelo Hall JSY AU RC 10.00 25.00
193 Ben Troupe JSY AU RC 6.00 15.00
194 Mich Jenkins JSY AU RC 6.00 15.00
195 Keary Colbert JSY AU RC 6.00 15.00
196 Robert Gallery JSY AU RC 8.00 20.00
197 Greg Jones JSY AU RC 6.00 15.00
198 Mich.Clayton JSY AU RC 8.00 20.00
199 Luke McCown JSY AU RC 6.00 15.00
200 Derrick Hamilton JSY AU RC 6.00 15.00
201 Ras.Woods JSY AU RC 8.00 20.00
202 Chris Perry JSY AU RC 8.00 20.00
203 D.Henderson JSY AU RC 8.00 20.00
204 Tatum Bell JSY AU RC 8.00 20.00
205 Lee Evans JSY AU RC 12.00 30.00
206 J.P. Losman JSY AU RC 8.00 20.00
207 Kel.Winslow JSY AU RC 10.00 25.00
208 Reg.Williams JSY AU RC 10.00 25.00
209 Julius Jones JSY AU RC 10.00 25.00
210 S.Jackson JSY AU RC 15.00 40.00
211 Kevin Jones JSY AU RC 12.00 30.00
212 Roy Williams JSY AU RC 10.00 25.00
213 Roethlisberger JSY AU RC 350.00 700.00
214 Philip Rivers JSY AU RC 250.00 500.00
215 L.Fitzgerald JSY AU RC 150.00 300.00
216 Eli Manning JSY AU RC 250.00 500.00

2004 SP Authentic Black

UNPRICED BLACK PRINT RUN 10

2004 SP Authentic Gold

*VETS: 6X TO 15X BASIC CARDS
*ROOKIES 91-150: 1.5X TO 4X
1-150 STATED PRINT RUN 50
*ROOKIE JSY AU 186-200: 1.2X TO 3X
*ROOK.JSY AU 201-206: 1X TO 2.5X
*ROOK.JSY AU 207-216: .8X TO 2X
186-216 JSY AU PRINT RUN 25
101 Jared Allen 100.00 200.00
135 Wes Welker 60.00 120.00
187 Matt Schaub JSY AU 25.00 60.00
210 Steven Jackson JSY AU 40.00 100.00
213 Roethlisberger JSY AU 1000.00 1500.00
214 Philip Rivers JSY AU 350.00 700.00
215 Larry Fitzgerald JSY AU 350.00 700.00
216 Eli Manning JSY AU 750.00 1500.00

2004 SP Authentic Artifacts Jerseys

STATED PRINT RUN 75 SER.#'d SETS
AABF Brett Favre 8.00 20.00
AABL Byron Leftwich 2.50 6.00
AABR Ben Roethlisberger 20.00 50.00
AACH Chad Pennington 2.50 6.00
AACL Clinton Portis 2.50 6.00
AACP Chris Perry 2.50 6.00
AADB Drew Bledsoe 3.00 8.00
AADC David Carr 2.50 6.00
AADE Deuce McAllister 3.00 8.00
AADH Devery Henderson 2.50 6.00
AADM Donovan McNabb 3.00 8.00
AAEJ Edgerrin James 3.00 8.00
AAEM Eli Manning 20.00 50.00
AAGJ Greg Jones 2.50 6.00
AAJJ Julius Jones 2.50 6.00
AAJP J.P. Losman 2.50 6.00
AAJR Jerry Rice 8.00 20.00
AAJS Jeremy Shockey 2.50 6.00
AAKC Keary Colbert 2.50 6.00
AAKJ Kevin Jones 3.00 8.00
AAKU Kurt Warner 3.00 8.00
AAKW Kellen Winslow Jr. 2.50 6.00
AALE Lee Evans 4.00 10.00
AALF Larry Fitzgerald 10.00 25.00
AALT LaDainian Tomlinson 4.00 10.00
AAMC Michael Clayton 3.00 8.00
AAMF Marshall Faulk 3.00 8.00
AAMJ Michael Jenkins 2.50 6.00
AAPH Priest Holmes 2.50 6.00
AAPM Peyton Manning 10.00 25.00
AAPR Philip Rivers 8.00 20.00
AARE Reggie Williams 2.50 6.00
AARG Robert Gallery 3.00 8.00
AARI Ricky Williams 3.00 8.00
AARM Randy Moss 3.00 8.00
AARO Roy Williams WR 2.50 6.00
AARW Rashaun Woods 2.50 6.00
AASJ Steven Jackson 4.00 10.00
AASM Steve McNair 3.00 8.00
AATB Tatum Bell 2.50 6.00
AATO Tom Brady 15.00 40.00

2004 SP Authentic Scripts for Success Autographs

STATED ODDS 1:24
SSAG Ahman Green/100* 10.00 25.00
SSAR Antwaan Randle El 6.00 15.00
SSBF Brett Favre SP 100.00 200.00
SSBH Ben Hartsock 4.00 10.00
SSBJ B.J. Sams 4.00 10.00
SSBS B.J. Symons 4.00 10.00
SSBT Ben Troupe 4.00 10.00
SSBW Ben Watson 5.00 12.00
SSCA Carlos Francis 4.00 10.00
SSCG Chris Gamble 4.00 10.00
SSCJ Chad Johnson 6.00 15.00
SSCP Cody Pickett 4.00 10.00
SSDA Dante Hall 6.00 15.00
SSDB Drew Bledsoe SP 15.00 40.00
SSDH Derrick Hamilton 4.00 10.00
SSDM Derrick Mason 6.00 15.00
SSDR Dunta Robinson 4.00 10.00
SSDV Devery Henderson 4.00 10.00
SSDW Darius Watts 4.00 10.00
SSEW Ernest Wilford 5.00 12.00
SSHE Todd Heap 6.00 15.00
SSHO Joe Horn 6.00 15.00
SSJC Jerricho Cotchery 5.00 12.00
SSJM Johnnie Morant 4.00 10.00
SSJN John Navarre 4.00 10.00
SSJO Josh McCown 8.00 20.00
SSJP Jesse Palmer 6.00 15.00
SSJS Jeff Smoker 5.00 12.00
SSJV Jonathan Vilma 5.00 12.00
SSKC Keary Colbert 4.00 10.00
SSKU Kenechi Udeze 5.00 12.00
SSLE Lee Evans 6.00 15.00
SSLM Luke McCown 4.00 10.00
SSMJ Michael Jenkins 4.00 10.00
SSMM Mewelde Moore 5.00 12.00
SSMS Matt Schaub 4.00 10.00
SSMT Michael Turner 6.00 15.00
SSMV Michael Vick SP 30.00 80.00
SSPK P.K. Sam 4.00 10.00
SSRA Rashaun Woods 4.00 10.00
SSRJ Rudi Johnson 6.00 15.00
SSRW Roy Williams S 6.00 15.00
SSSP Samie Parker 4.00 10.00
SSTG Tony Gonzalez 8.00 20.00
SSTH Tommie Harris 5.00 12.00
SSTR Travis Henry 6.00 15.00
SSVW Vince Wilfork 8.00 20.00
SSWS Will Smith 5.00 12.00
SSZT Zach Thomas 8.00 20.00

2004 SP Authentic Sign of the Times

STATED ODDS 1:72
SOTAM Archie Manning 12.00 30.00
SOTAR Andy Reid 8.00 20.00
SOTBE Tatum Bell 5.00 12.00
SOTBF Brett Favre SP 125.00 200.00
SOTBL Byron Leftwich 6.00 15.00
SOTBP Bill Parcells 25.00 50.00
SOTBR Ben Roethlisberger 75.00 150.00
SOTBS Barry Sanders SP 60.00 120.00
SOTCH Chris Perry 5.00 12.00
SOTCJ Chad Johnson 6.00 15.00
SOTCP Chad Pennington 6.00 15.00
SOTDA David Carr 6.00 15.00
SOTDC Daunte Culpepper 8.00 20.00
SOTDE Deuce McAllister 8.00 20.00
SOTDH Dante Hall 6.00 15.00
SOTDM Donovan McNabb/50* 20.00 50.00
SOTDR Drew Henson 6.00 15.00
SOTEM Eli Manning 40.00 100.00
SOTGJ Greg Jones 5.00 12.00
SOTHL Howie Long 20.00 50.00
SOTJE John Elway SP 50.00 120.00
SOTJF John Fox 6.00 15.00
SOTJG Jon Gruden 8.00 20.00
SOTJJ Julius Jones 5.00 12.00
SOTJM Josh McCown 8.00 20.00
SOTJO Joe Montana SP 60.00 120.00
SOTJP J.P. Losman 5.00 12.00
SOTKB Kyle Boller 6.00 15.00
SOTKE Kellen Winslow Jr. 5.00 12.00
SOTKJ Kevin Jones 6.00 15.00
SOTKW Kellen Winslow Sr. 10.00 25.00
SOTLT LaDainian Tomlinson/50* 60.00 120.00
SOTMA Derrick Mason 6.00 15.00
SOTMB Mark Brunell 8.00 20.00
SOTMV Michael Vick/50 * 20.00 50.00
SOTPM Peyton Manning 60.00 120.00
SOTPR Philip Rivers 150.00 300.00
SOTRE Reggie Williams 5.00 12.00
SOTRG Rex Grossman 6.00 15.00
SOTRO Robert Gallery 6.00 15.00
SOTRS Roger Staubach SP 35.00 60.00
SOTRW Roy Williams S 6.00 15.00
SOTSJ Steven Jackson 8.00 20.00
SOTSM Steve McNair SP 20.00 40.00
SOTTA Troy Aikman 40.00 80.00
SOTTG Tony Gonzalez 8.00 20.00
SOTTH Travis Henry 6.00 15.00
SOTWI Roy Williams WR 5.00 12.00

2004 SP Authentic Sign of the Times Dual

STATED PRINT RUN 50 SER.#'d SETS
AE A.Manning/E.Manning 125.00 250.00
JG J.Johnson/J.Gruden 20.00 50.00
LE J.Losman/L.Evans 20.00 50.00
LG H.Long/R.Gallery 40.00 80.00
MM E.Manning/P.Manning 250.00 500.00
PJ C.Perry/S.Jackson 25.00 60.00
PR B.Parcells/A.Reid 25.00 60.00
RR P.Rivers/Roethlisberger 250.00 500.00
SJ B.Sanders/K.Jones 60.00 120.00
WW Winslow Sr./Winslow Jr. 25.00 60.00

2004 SP Authentic Sign of the Times Gold

*GOLD/25: .8X TO 2X BASIC AUTO
GOLD PRINT RUN 25 SER.#'d SETS
SOTBF Brett Favre 125.00 250.00
SOTBR Ben Roethlisberger 175.00 350.00
SOTBS Barry Sanders 100.00 200.00
SOTEM Eli Manning 150.00 300.00
SOTJE John Elway 100.00 200.00
SOTJO Joe Montana 125.00 250.00
SOTLT LaDainian Tomlinson 100.00 200.00
SOTPM Peyton Manning 100.00 200.00
SOTPR Philip Rivers 200.00 400.00
SOTSJ Steven Jackson 15.00 40.00

2004 SP Authentic Sign of the Times Triple

UNPRICED TRIPLE PRINT RUN 10 SETS

2005 SP Authentic

This 257-card set was released in December, 2005. The set was issued through the hobby in five-card packs with a $4.99 SRP which came 24 packs to a box. The first 90 cards of the set feature veterans in alphabetical order by team while the rest of the set features rookies. Cards numbered 91-180 were issued to a stated print run of 750 serial nuimbered sets while cards numbered 181-220 and 254-257 were issued to a stated print run of 850 serial numbered sets. The set also had a subset of rookies which were both signed and have a player-worn swatch and those cards were issued to stated print runs between 99 and 899 serial numbered copies. A few players did not return their signatures in time for pack out and those cards could be redeemed until December 20, 2008.

COMP.SET w/o RC's (90) 10.00 25.00
91-180 ROOKIE PRINT RUN 750
181-220/254-257 ROOKIE AU PRINT RUN 850
221-253 ROOKIE JSY AUPRINT RUN 99-899
UNPRICED NFL LOGO PATCHES #'d TO 1
1 Kurt Warner .30 .75
2 Larry Fitzgerald .40 1.00
3 Anquan Boldin .25 .60
4 Michael Vick .30 .75
5 Alge Crumpler .30 .75
6 Warrick Dunn .25 .60
7 Kyle Boller .25 .60
8 Jamal Lewis .30 .75
9 J.P. Losman .25 .60
10 Willis McGahee .25 .60
11 Lee Evans .30 .75
12 Jake Delhomme .25 .60
13 DeShaun Foster .30 .75
14 Muhsin Muhammad .25 .60
15 Walter Payton 1.00 2.50
16 Brian Urlacher .40 1.00
17 Carson Palmer .30 .75
18 Rudi Johnson .25 .60
19 Chad Johnson .25 .60
20 Lee Suggs .25 .60
21 Antonio Bryant .25 .60
22 Julius Jones .25 .60
23 Drew Bledsoe .30 .75
24 Keyshawn Johnson .30 .75
25 Tatum Bell .25 .60
26 Jake Plummer .25 .60
27 Roy Williams WR .25 .60
28 Kevin Jones .25 .60
29 Jeff Garcia .25 .60
30 Brett Favre .75 2.00
31 Ahman Green .30 .75
32 Javon Walker .25 .60
33 David Carr .25 .60
34 Andre Johnson .30 .75
35 Domanick Davis .25 .60
36 Peyton Manning 1.00 2.50
37 Edgerrin James .30 .75
38 Reggie Wayne .30 .75
39 Byron Leftwich .25 .60
40 Fred Taylor .25 .60
41 Jimmy Smith .30 .75
42 Priest Holmes .25 .60
43 Larry Johnson .25 .60
44 Trent Green .25 .60
45 Randy McMichael .25 .60
46 Chris Chambers .25 .60
47 Ricky Williams .30 .75
48 Daunte Culpepper .30 .75
49 Nate Burleson .25 .60
50 Tom Brady 1.50 4.00
51 Corey Dillon .25 .60
52 David Givens .25 .60
53 Aaron Brooks .25 .60
54 Deuce McAllister .30 .75
55 Joe Horn .25 .60
56 Eli Manning .60 1.50
57 Jeremy Shockey .25 .60
58 Tiki Barber .30 .75
59 Chad Pennington .25 .60
60 Santana Moss .30 .75
61 Curtis Martin .30 .75
62 Randy Moss .30 .75
63 LaMont Jordan .30 .75
64 Kerry Collins .25 .60
65 Donovan McNabb .30 .75
66 Brian Westbrook .25 .60
67 Terrell Owens .30 .75
68 Ben Roethlisberger .60 1.50
69 Hines Ward .30 .75
70 Jerome Bettis .40 1.00
71 Drew Brees .40 1.00
72 Antonio Gates .40 1.00
73 LaDainian Tomlinson .40 1.00
74 Kevan Barlow .25 .60
75 Brandon Lloyd .25 .60
76 Matt Hasselbeck .25 .60
77 Shaun Alexander .25 .60
78 Darrell Jackson .25 .60
79 Marc Bulger .25 .60
80 Steven Jackson .25 .60
81 Torry Holt .30 .75
82 Brian Griese .25 .60
83 Michael Clayton .25 .60
84 Michael Pittman .25 .60
85 Steve McNair .30 .75
86 Drew Bennett .30 .75
87 Chris Brown .25 .60
88 Clinton Portis .25 .60
89 Patrick Ramsey .30 .75
90 Laveranues Coles .25 .60
91 Nehemiah Broughton RC 2.00 5.00
92 Madison Hedgecock RC 2.50 6.00
93 Damien Nash RC 2.00 5.00
94 Michael Boley RC 2.50 6.00
95 Lionel Gates RC 1.50 4.00
96 Noah Herron RC 1.50 4.00
97 Bo Scaife RC 2.00 5.00
98 Joel Dreessen RC 2.00 5.00
99 Rasheed Marshall RC 2.00 5.00
100 Andre Maddox RC 1.50 4.00
101 Tab Perry RC 1.50 4.00
102 Dante Ridgeway RC 1.50 4.00
103 Patrick Estes RC 1.50 4.00
104 Billy Bajema RC 1.50 4.00
105 Paris Warren RC 2.00 5.00
106 LeRon McCoy RC 1.50 4.00
107 Adam Bergen RC 1.50 4.00
108 Manuel White RC 2.00 5.00
109 Stephen Spach RC 1.50 4.00
110 Donte Nicholson RC 1.50 4.00
111 Brodney Pool RC 2.00 5.00
112 Stanford Routt RC 2.00 5.00
113 Josh Bullocks RC 2.00 5.00
114 Ronald Bartell RC 2.00 5.00
115 Nick Collins RC 3.00 8.00
116 Darrent Williams RC 2.50 6.00
117 Justin Miller RC 1.50 4.00
118 Kelvin Hayden RC 2.00 5.00
119 Bryant McFadden RC 2.00 5.00
120 Oshiomogho Atogwe RC 2.00 5.00
121 Stanley Wilson RC 2.00 5.00
122 Eric Green RC 1.50 4.00
123 Michael Hawkins RC 1.50 4.00
124 Marcus Spears RC 1.50 4.00
125 Ellis Hobbs RC 2.50 6.00
126 Scott Starks RC 2.00 5.00
127 Domonique Foxworth RC 2.00 5.00
128 Sean Considine RC 1.50 4.00
129 James Sanders RC 1.50 4.00
130 Travis Daniels RC 2.00 5.00
131 Vincent Fuller RC 2.00 5.00
132 Marviel Underwood RC 2.00 5.00
133 Jerome Carter RC 1.50 4.00
134 Kerry Rhodes RC 2.00 5.00
135 Fred Amey RC 1.50 4.00
136 Eric King RC 1.50 4.00
137 Derrick Johnson CB RC 1.50 4.00
138 Luis Castillo RC 2.00 5.00
139 Shaun Cody RC 2.00 5.00
140 Matt Roth RC 1.50 4.00
141 Jonathan Babineaux RC 1.50 4.00
142 Justin Tuck RC 6.00 15.00
143 Sione Pouha RC 1.50 4.00
144 Daven Holly RC 1.50 4.00
145 Vincent Burns RC 1.50 4.00
146 Derrick Johnson RC 2.00 5.00
147 Lofa Tatupu RC 2.00 5.00
148 Odell Thurman RC 2.50 6.00
149 Rick Razzano RC 1.50 4.00
150 Channing Crowder RC 2.00 5.00
151 Kirk Morrison RC 2.50 6.00
152 Alfred Fincher RC 2.00 5.00
153 Jordan Beck RC 2.00 5.00
154 Darryl Blackstock RC 1.50 4.00
155 Leroy Hill RC 2.50 6.00
156 Jammal Brown RC 2.50 6.00
157 Alex Barron RC 1.50 4.00
158 Chris Spencer RC 2.50 6.00
159 Logan Mankins RC 2.50 6.00
160 David Baas RC 1.50 4.00
161 Michael Roos RC 1.50 4.00
162 Kurt Campbell RC 1.50 4.00
163 Khalif Barnes RC 1.50 4.00
164 Antonio Perkins RC 2.00 5.00
165 Vonta Leach RC 2.00 5.00
166 Brady Poppinga RC 2.50 6.00
167 Trent Cole RC 2.50 6.00
168 Dave Rayner RC 1.50 4.00
169 Bill Swancutt RC 1.50 4.00
170 Eric Moore RC 1.50 4.00
171 Justin Green RC 2.50 6.00
172 Shaun Suisham RC 1.50 4.00
173 C.J. Mosley RC 1.50 4.00
174 Ryan Riddle RC 1.50 4.00
175 Darrell Shropshire RC 1.50 4.00
176 Boomer Grigsby RC 2.50 6.00
177 Rian Wallace RC 2.00 5.00
178 Lance Mitchell RC 2.00 5.00
179 Nick Speegle RC 1.50 4.00
180 Tyson Thompson RC 1.50 4.00
181 Dan Orlovsky AU RC 4.00 10.00
182 Anthony Davis AU RC 4.00 10.00
183 Kay-Jay Harris AU RC 4.00 10.00
184 Walter Reyes AU RC 4.00 10.00
185 Darren Sproles AU RC 10.00 25.00
186 Marlin Jackson AU RC 4.00 10.00
187 Corey Webster AU RC 5.00 12.00
188 Marion Barber AU RC 4.00 10.00
189 Chris Henry AU RC 5.00 12.00
190 Derek Anderson AU RC 5.00 12.00
191 David Pollack AU RC 4.00 10.00
192 Anttaj Hawthorne AU RC 4.00 10.00
193 David Greene AU RC 4.00 10.00
194 Erasmus James AU RC 4.00 10.00
195 Ryan Fitzpatrick AU RC 6.00 15.00
196 Derrick Johnson AU 5.00 12.00
197 Barrett Ruud AU RC 5.00 12.00
198 Kevin Burnett AU RC 5.00 12.00
200 J.R. Russell AU RC 4.00 10.00
201 Larry Brackins AU RC 4.00 10.00
202 Thomas Davis AU RC 4.00 10.00
203 Fred Gibson AU RC 4.00 10.00
204 Craphonso Thorpe AU RC 4.00 10.00
205 Brandon Jacobs AU RC 10.00 208.00
206 Taylor Stubblefield AU RC 4.00 10.00
207 Shawne Merriman AU RC 8.00 20.00
208 Travis Johnson AU RC 4.00 10.00
209 Adrian McPherson AU RC 4.00 10.00
210 Brandon Jones AU RC 5.00 12.00
211 Jerome Mathis AU RC 6.00 15.00
212 Alex Smith TE AU RC 4.00 10.00
213 Fabian Washington AU RC 4.00 10.00
214 Mike Nugent AU RC 5.00 12.00
215 Chase Lyman AU RC 4.00 10.00
216 Roydell Williams AU RC 5.00 12.00
217 Matt Cassel AU RC 10.00 25.00
218 Alvin Pearman AU RC 4.00 10.00
219 DeMarcus Ware AU RC 20.00 40.00
220 Mike Patterson AU RC 4.00 10.00
221 C.Roby JSY/899 AU RC 6.00 15.00
222 E.Shelton JSY/899 AU RC 6.00 15.00
223 S.LeFors JSY/899 AU RC 6.00 15.00
224 Frank Gore JSY/899 AU RC 25.00 60.00
225 Ryan Moats JSY/899 AU RC 6.00 15.00
226 A.Walter JSY/899 AU RC 6.00 15.00
227 A.Jones JSY/899 AU RC 6.00 15.00
228 C.Rogers JSY/699 AU RC 10.00 25.00
229 T.Murphy JSY/899 AU RC 6.00 15.00
230 Kyle Orton JSY/699 AU RC 8.00 20.00
231 C.Fason JSY/699 AU RC 6.00 15.00
232 V.Morency JSY/699 AU RC 6.00 15.00
233 R.Parrish JSY/699 AU RC 6.00 15.00
234 V.Jackson JSY/699 AU RC 10.00 25.00
235 M.Bradley JSY/699 AU RC 6.00 15.00
236 Re.Brown JSY/599 AU RC 6.00 15.00
237 Ro.White JSY/499 AU RC 10.00 25.00
238 M.Clayton JSY/499 AU RC 6.00 15.00
239 Antrel Rolle JSY/499 AU RC 10.00 25.00
240 Maurice Clarett JSY/499 AU 6.00 15.00
241 J.Arrington JSY/699 AU RC 8.00 20.00
242 Matt Jones JSY/399 AU RC 6.00 15.00
243 Ro.Brown JSY/299 AU RC 12.00 30.00
244 C.Frye JSY/499 AU RC 6.00 15.00
245 J.Campbell JSY/299 AU RC 6.00 15.00
246 T.Willmsn JSY/299 AU RC 8.00 20.00
247 B.Edwrd JSY/299 AU RC 8.00 20.00
248 A.Smith JSY/299 AU RC 60.00 120.00
249 C.Willms JSY/299 AU RC 8.00 20.00
250 H.Miller JSY/299 AU RC 15.00 40.00
251 C.Benson JSY/99 AU RC 25.00 30.00
252 A.Rodgers JSY/99 AU RC 1500.00 2500.00
253 M.Williams JSY/99 AU 15.00 40.00
254 Chris Carr AU RC 4.00 10.00
255 Deandra Cobb AU RC 4.00 10.00
256 James Kilian AU RC 4.00 10.00
257 Airese Currie AU RC 4.00 10.00

2005 SP Authentic Gold

*VETS 1-90: 8X TO 20X BASIC CARDS
*ROOK.91-180: 1.5X TO 4X BASIC CARDS
*RK.JSY AU/25 : 1.2X TO 3X JSY AU/399-899
*ROOK.JSY AU/25 : 1X TO 2.5X JSY AU/299
*ROOK.JSY AU/25 : .8X TO 2X JSY AU/99
STATED PRINT RUN 25 SER.#'d SETS
224 Frank Gore JSY AU 150.00 250.00
237 Roddy White JSY AU 30.00 80.00
248 Alex Smith QB JSY AU 250.00 500.00
250 Heath Miller JSY AU 100.00 200.00
252 Aaron Rodgers JSY AU 4500.00 5500.00

2005 SP Authentic Rookie Gold 100

*GOLD 100: .6X TO 1.5X BASIC CARDS

2005 SP Authentic Rookie Fabrics Bronze

STATED PRINT RUN 100 SER.#'d SETS
*GOLD TRIPLES: .6X TO 1.5X BASIC INSERTS
GOLD TRIPLE PRINT RUN 50 SER.#'d SETS
*SILVER DOUBLE: .5X TO 1.2X BASE INSERT
SILVER DOUBLE PRINT RUN 75 SER.#'d SETS
RFAN Antrel Rolle 4.00 10.00
RFAR Aaron Rodgers 50.00 100.00
RFAS Alex Smith QB 10.00 25.00
RFBE Braylon Edwards 2.50 6.00
RFCA Carlos Rogers 4.00 10.00
RFCB Cedric Benson 2.50 6.00
RFCF Charlie Frye 2.50 6.00
RFCI Ciatrick Fason 2.50 6.00
RFCR Courtney Roby 2.50 6.00
RFCW Cadillac Williams 2.50 6.00
RFES Eric Shelton 2.50 6.00
RFFG Frank Gore 5.00 12.00
RFJA J.J. Arrington 3.00 8.00
RFJC Jason Campbell 2.50 6.00
RFKO Kyle Orton 2.50 6.00
RFMB Mark Bradley 2.50 6.00
RFMC Mark Clayton 2.50 6.00
RFMJ Matt Jones 2.50 6.00
RFMO Maurice Clarett 2.50 6.00
RFMW Mike Williams 3.00 8.00
RFRB Ronnie Brown 3.00 8.00
RFRE Reggie Brown 2.50 6.00
RFRM Ryan Moats 2.50 6.00
RFRP Roscoe Parrish 2.50 6.00
RFRW Roddy White 4.00 10.00
RFSL Stefan LeFors 2.50 6.00
RFTM Terrence Murphy 2.50 6.00
RFTW Troy Williamson 2.50 6.00
RFVJ Vincent Jackson 4.00 10.00
RFVM Vernand Morency 3.00 8.00

2005 SP Authentic Rookie Fabrics Autographs

STATED PRINT RUN 15 SER.#'d SETS
RFAN Antrel Rolle 30.00 80.00
RFAR Aaron Rodgers 500.00 800.00
RFAS Alex Smith QB 75.00 150.00
RFBE Braylon Edwards 20.00 50.00
RFCB Cedric Benson 20.00 50.00
RFCF Charlie Frye 20.00 50.00
RFCI Ciatrick Fason 20.00 50.00
RFCR Courtney Roby 20.00 50.00
RFCW Cadillac Williams 20.00 50.00
RFES Eric Shelton 20.00 50.00
RFFG Frank Gore 40.00 100.00
RFJA J.J. Arrington 25.00 60.00
RFJC Jason Campbell 75.00 150.00
RFKO Kyle Orton 100.00 200.00
RFMB Mark Bradley 20.00 50.00
RFMC Mark Clayton 20.00 50.00
RFMJ Matt Jones 20.00 50.00
RFMO Maurice Clarett 20.00 50.00
RFMW Mike Williams 50.00 125.00
RFRB Ronnie Brown 100.00 200.00
RFRE Reggie Brown 20.00 50.00
RFRM Ryan Moats 20.00 50.00
RFRP Roscoe Parrish 20.00 50.00
RFRW Roddy White 30.00 80.00
RFSL Stefan LeFors 20.00 50.00
RFTM Terrence Murphy 20.00 50.00
RFTW Troy Williamson 20.00 50.00
RFVJ Vincent Jackson 30.00 80.00
RFVM Vernand Morency 20.00 50.00

2005 SP Authentic Scripts for Success Autographs

STATED ODDS 1:24
SSAB Anquan Boldin 6.00 15.00
SSAC Airese Currie 4.00 10.00
SSAG Alge Crumpler 6.00 15.00
SSAH Ahman Green SP 10.00 25.00
SSAJ Adam Jones 6.00 15.00
SSAM Adrian McPherson 6.00 15.00
SSAR Antrel Rolle 6.00 15.00
SSAW Andrew Walter 8.00 15.00
SSCH Chad Owens 6.00 15.00
SSCJ Chad Johnson 10.00 25.00
SSCO Courtney Roby 4.00 10.00
SSDB Drew Bennett 4.00 10.00
SSDD Domanick Davis 4.00 10.00
SSDG David Greene 6.00 15.00
SSDM Donovan McNabb SP 20.00 50.00
SSDO Dan Orlovsky 6.00 15.00
SSEJ Edgerrin James SP 12.00 30.00
SSES Eric Shelton 4.00 10.00
SSFG Frank Gore 10.00 25.00
SSJH Joe Horn 4.00 10.00
SSJK James Kilian 4.00 10.00
SSJL J.P. Losman 6.00 15.00
SSKC Keary Colbert 6.00 15.00
SSKO Kyle Orton 10.00 25.00
SSLE Lee Evans 4.00 10.00
SSLJ Larry Johnson 10.00 25.00
SSLT LaDainian Tomlinson 15.00 40.00
SSMA Marion Barber 8.00 20.00
SSMB Marc Bulger 6.00 15.00
SSMB Mark Bradley 6.00 15.00
SSMC Michael Clayton 4.00 10.00
SSMM Muhsin Muhammad 6.00 15.00
SSMN Mike Nugent 4.00 10.00
SSMO Maurice Clarett 4.00 10.00
SSNB Nate Burleson 6.00 15.00
SSPM Peyton Manning SP 60.00 100.00
SSRB Reggie Brown 6.00 15.00
SSRJ Rudi Johnson 6.00 15.00
SSRM Ryan Moats 6.00 15.00
SSRP Roscoe Parrish 6.00 15.00
SSRW Roddy White 8.00 20.00
SSSL Stefan LeFors 4.00 10.00
SSTD Thomas Davis 4.00 10.00
SSTG Trent Green 6.00 15.00
SSTM Terrence Murphy 4.00 10.00
SSVJ Vincent Jackson 10.00 25.00
SSVM Vernand Morency 6.00 15.00

2005 SP Authentic Sign of the Times

SOTAD Andre Reed 10.00 25.00
SOTAG Antonio Gates 10.00 25.00
SOTAH Ahman Green SP 10.00 25.00
SOTAR Aaron Rodgers SP 200.00 350.00
SOTAS Alex Smith QB SP 30.00 60.00
SOTBD Brian Dawkins 10.00 25.00
SOTBE Braylon Edwards 10.00 25.00
SOTBF Brett Favre SP 125.00 200.00
SOTBK Bernie Kosar 10.00 25.00
SOTBL Byron Leftwich 6.00 15.00
SOTBO Bo Jackson 40.00 80.00
SOTBR Ben Roethlisberger SP 60.00 120.00
SOTBS Barry Sanders SP 100.00 175.00
SOTBT Drew Bennett 8.00 20.00
SOTCB Cedric Benson 6.00 15.00
SOTCF Charlie Frye 6.00 15.00
SOTCP Carson Palmer SP 10.00 25.00
SOTCW Cadillac Williams SP 8.00 20.00
SOTDA Dan Marino SP 100.00 200.00
SOTDE Deuce McAllister SP 10.00 25.00
SOTDM Donovan McNabb SP 25.00 50.00
SOTEJ Edgerrin James SP 10.00 25.00
SOTEM Eli Manning SP 60.00 100.00
SOTJA J.J. Arrington 8.00 20.00
SOTJC Jason Campbell 6.00 15.00
SOTJE John Elway SP 75.00 150.00
SOTJK Jim Kelly SP 20.00 40.00
SOTLJ LaMont Jordan 8.00 20.00
SOTMA Marcus Allen 20.00 40.00
SOTMJ Matt Jones SP 8.00 20.00
SOTMM Muhsin Muhammad 6.00 15.00
SOTMV Michael Vick SP 30.00 60.00
SOTMW Mike Williams SP 10.00 25.00
SOTPM Peyton Manning SP 60.00 120.00
SOTRB Ronnie Brown SP 10.00 25.00
SOTRE Reggie Brown 6.00 15.00
SOTRG Reggie Wayne 15.00 30.00
SOTRW Roddy White 10.00 25.00
SOTRY Roy Williams WR SP 8.00 20.00
SOTSJ Steven Jackson 6.00 15.00
SOTTA Troy Aikman SP 30.00 60.00
SOTTB Tiki Barber 15.00 30.00
SOTTG Trent Green 6.00 15.00
SOTTW Troy Williamson 6.00 15.00

2005 SP Authentic Sign of the Times Gold

*GOLD/25: .8X TO 2X BASIC AUTO
*GOLD/25: .6X TO 1.5X BASIC AU SP
GOLD PRINT RUN 25 SER.#'d SETS
SOTAR Aaron Rodgers 500.00 650.00
SOTAS Alex Smith QB 50.00 120.00
SOTBF Brett Favre 150.00 300.00
SOTBO Bo Jackson 75.00 150.00
SOTBR Ben Roethlisberger 60.00 150.00
SOTBS Barry Sanders 125.00 250.00
SOTDA Dan Marino 125.00 250.00
SOTEM Eli Manning 75.00 150.00
SOTJE John Elway 75.00 150.00
SOTMV Michael Vick 40.00 80.00
SOTPM Peyton Manning 125.00 200.00

2005 SP Authentic Sign of the Times Dual

DUAL PRINT RUN 50 SER.#'d SETS
UNPRICED TRIPLE PRINT RUN 15 SETS
UNPRICED QUAD PRINT RUN 5 SETS
BJ M.Bulger/S.Jackson 15.00 40.00
BO C.Benson/K.Orton 20.00 50.00
BR D.Bennett/C.Roby 12.00 30.00
BW Ro.Brown/C.Will 30.00 80.00
CG J.Campbell/D.Greene 20.00 50.00
DM D.Davis/V.Morency 10.00 25.00
EF B.Edwards/C.Fyre 20.00 50.00
EP L.Evans/R.Parrish 12.00 30.00
GJ A.Gates/V.Jackson 30.00 60.00
JB J.Jones/M.Barber 15.00 40.00
LJ Leftwich/M.Jones 15.00 40.00
LS S.LeFors/E.Shelton 10.00 25.00
NT N.Burleson/T.Williamson 12.00 30.00
RF Roethlisberger/Frye 40.00 100.00
RM Re.Brown/R.Moats 15.00 40.00
SG A.Smith QB/F.Gore 60.00 120.00
SR A.Smith QB/A.Rodgers 250.00 400.00
VW M.Vick/R.White 25.00 50.00
WW Ro.Will.WR/M.Williams 20.00 50.00

2005 SP Authentic Sign of the Times Triple

EWW Edwards/Wllmson/Williams 15.00 40.00
JAD Jones/Aikman/Dorsett 75.00 15.00
MMF P.Mann/Marino/Fouts 200.00 350.00
MRD McNabb/Brown/Dawkins 25.00 60.00
RFH Rodgers/Favre/Hornung 200.00 400.00
RMK Roeth/Montana/Kelly 100.00 200.00
SJH B.Sanders/Bo/F.Harris 125.00 250.00
SMP Smith QB/Montana/Plnktt 125.00 250.00
VMP Vick/Manning/Palmer 60.00 120.00
WBB Williams/Brown/Benson 15.00 40.00

2005 SP Authentic UD Promo

Cards in this set were inserted in select copies of Tuff Stuff magazine in early 2006. Each card is a parallel to the basic issue #1-90 veterans group in 2005 SP Authentic with the addition of "UD Promo" printed in foil on the cardfronts.

*UD PROMOS: .8X TO 2X BASIC CARDS

2006 SP Authentic

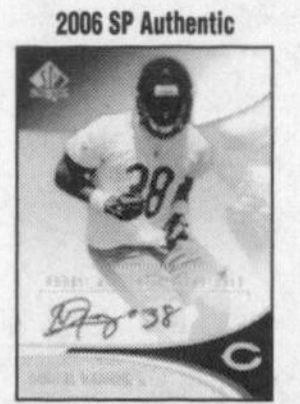

This 260-card set was released in January, 2007. The set was issued into the hobby in five-card packs, with a $5 SRP, which came 24 packs to a box. Cards numbered 1-90 feature players in alphabetical team order and cards numbered 91-260 feature 2006 rookies. The rookies are broken down into the following groupings: Cards numbered 91-120 and 251 were issued to a stated print run of 750 serial numbered sets, Cards numbered 121-180 were issued to a stated print run of 1399 serial numbered sets, cards numbered 181-226 were issued to a stated print run of 1175 serial numbered copies unless noted in our checklist. The set concludes with cards containing both player-worn jersey swatches and signatures from cards numbered 227-260. Those cards, with the exception of card numbered 251, have stated print runs of between 99 and 999 serial numbered copies.

COMP.SET w/o RC's (90) 8.00 20.00
91-120/251 PRINT RUN 750 SER.#'d SETS
121-180 PRINT RUN 1399 SER.#'d SETS
181-226 AU PRINT RUN 1175 UNLESS NOTED
227-260 JSY AU PRINT RUN 99-999
1 Edgerrin James .30 .75
2 Larry Fitzgerald .30 .75
3 Anquan Boldin .25 .60
4 Michael Vick .30 .75
5 Warrick Dunn .25 .60
6 Alge Crumpler .30 .75
7 Steve McNair .30 .75
8 Jamal Lewis .30 .75
9 Derrick Mason .25 .60
10 Willis McGahee .25 .60
11 Lee Evans .30 .75
12 Jake Delhomme .25 .60
13 Steve Smith .40 1.00
14 DeShaun Foster .30 .75
15 Rex Grossman .25 .60
16 Thomas Jones .25 .60
17 Brian Urlacher .40 1.00
18 Carson Palmer .30 .75
19 Chad Johnson .25 .60
20 Rudi Johnson .25 .60
21 Charlie Frye .30 .75
22 Braylon Edwards .25 .60
23 Reuben Droughns .30 .75
24 Drew Bledsoe .30 .75
25 Terrell Owens .30 .75
26 Julius Jones .25 .60
27 Jake Plummer .25 .60
28 Tatum Bell .25 .60
29 Javon Walker .30 .75
30 Kevin Jones .25 .60
31 Roy Williams WR .25 .60
32 Brett Favre .75 2.00
33 Donald Driver .30 .75
34 David Carr .25 .60
35 Ron Dayne .30 .75
36 Andre Johnson .30 .75
37 Peyton Manning 1.00 2.50
38 Marvin Harrison .30 .75
39 Reggie Wayne .30 .75
40 Byron Leftwich .25 .60
41 Fred Taylor .25 .60
42 Matt Jones .25 .60
43 Trent Green .25 .60
44 Larry Johnson .25 .60
45 Tony Gonzalez .30 .75
46 Daunte Culpepper .30 .75
47 Ronnie Brown .30 .75
48 Chris Chambers .25 .60
49 Chester Taylor .30 .75
50 Troy Williamson .25 .60
51 Tom Brady 1.25 3.00
52 Corey Dillon .25 .60
53 Troy Brown .25 .60
54 Drew Brees .40 1.00
55 Deuce McAllister .30 .75
56 Joe Horn .25 .60
57 Eli Manning .30 .75
58 Tiki Barber .30 .75
59 Plaxico Burress .25 .60
60 Laveranues Coles .25 .60
61 Chad Pennington .25 .60
62 Aaron Brooks .25 .60
63 Randy Moss .30 .75
64 LaMont Jordan .30 .75
65 Donovan McNabb .30 .75
66 Brian Westbrook .25 .60
67 Ben Roethlisberger .50 1.25
68 Willie Parker .30 .75
69 Hines Ward .30 .75
70 Philip Rivers .40 1.00
71 LaDainian Tomlinson .40 1.00
72 Antonio Gates .40 1.00
73 Alex Smith QB .30 .75
74 Frank Gore .30 .75
75 Antonio Bryant .25 .60
76 Matt Hasselbeck .25 .60
77 Shaun Alexander .25 .60
78 Darrell Jackson .30 .75
79 Marc Bulger .25 .60
80 Steven Jackson .25 .60
81 Torry Holt .30 .75
82 Chris Simms .25 .60
83 Cadillac Williams .30 .75
84 Joey Galloway .30 .75
85 Travis Henry .25 .60
86 Drew Bennett .30 .75
87 David Givens .30 .75
88 Mark Brunell .30 .75
89 Clinton Portis .25 .60
90 Santana Moss .30 .75
91 Bernard Pollard RC 4.00 10.00
92 Brodie Croyle RC 3.00 8.00
93 Cedric Griffin RC 4.00 10.00
94 Marques Colston RC 5.00 12.00
95 Daniel Bullocks RC 3.00 8.00
96 Darryl Tapp RC 4.00 10.00
97 David Thomas RC 3.00 8.00
98 Montell Owens RC 4.00 10.00
99 DeMeco Ryans RC 4.00 10.00
100 Devin Hester RC 6.00 15.00
101 Donte Whitner RC 4.00 10.00
102 D'Qwell Jackson RC 3.00 8.00
103 Patrick Cobbs RC 4.00 10.00
104 Haloti Ngata RC 4.00 10.00
105 Lawrence Vickers RC 4.00 10.00
106 Jeff King RC 4.00 10.00
107 Jeremy Bloom RC 3.00 8.00
108 Johnathan Joseph RC 4.00 10.00
109 DeDe Dorsey RC 4.00 10.00
110 Marcus Vick RC 3.00 8.00
111 Bobby Carpenter RC 3.00 8.00
112 Manny Lawson RC 4.00 10.00
113 Nick Mangold RC 4.00 10.00
114 Quinn Sypniewski RC 4.00 10.00
115 Richard Marshall RC 3.00 8.00
116 Rocky McIntosh RC 3.00 8.00
117 Roman Harper RC 4.00 10.00
118 Tamba Hali RC 5.00 12.00
119 Tony Scheffler RC 5.00 12.00
120 Wali Lundy RC 3.00 8.00
121 A.J. Nicholson RC 2.50 6.00
122 Abdul Hodge RC 2.50 6.00
123 Adam Jennings RC 3.00 8.00
124 Alan Zemaitis RC 2.50 6.00
125 Andrew Whitworth RC 2.50 6.00
126 Anthony Schlegel RC 3.00 8.00
127 Anthony Smith RC 4.00 10.00
128 Antoine Bethea RC 4.00 10.00
129 Barry Cofield RC 4.00 10.00
130 Brandon Johnson RC 3.00 8.00
131 Calvin Lowry RC 4.00 10.00
132 Shaun Bodiford RC 3.00 8.00
133 Charlie Peprah RC 3.00 8.00
134 Claude Wroten RC 2.50 6.00
135 Clint Ingram RC 4.00 10.00
136 Cortland Finnegan RC 4.00 10.00
137 Daryn Colledge RC 4.00 10.00
138 David Anderson RC 3.00 8.00
139 David Kirtman RC 3.00 8.00
140 Boone Stutz RC 3.00 8.00
141 Delanie Walker RC 5.00 12.00
142 Sam Hurd RC 2.50 6.00
143 Derrick Martin RC 3.00 8.00
144 Willie Andrews RC 3.00 8.00
145 Dusty Dvoracek RC 4.00 10.00
146 Elvis Dumervil RC 4.00 10.00
147 Eric Smith RC 3.00 8.00
148 Freddie Keiaho RC 3.00 8.00
149 Gabe Watson RC 2.50 6.00
150 Gerris Wilkinson RC 2.50 6.00
151 Greg Blue RC 3.00 8.00
152 Guy Whimper RC 2.50 6.00
153 Jamar Williams RC 3.00 8.00
154 James Anderson RC 2.50 6.00
155 Jason Spitz RC 4.00 10.00
156 Jeff Webb RC 3.00 8.00
157 Jeremy Mincey RC 4.00 10.00
158 Jeremy Trueblood RC 3.00 8.00
159 Omar Gaither RC 3.00 8.00
160 Jon Alston RC 2.50 6.00
161 Julian Jenkins RC 3.00 8.00
162 Keith Ellison RC 3.00 8.00
163 Kevin McMahan RC 3.00 8.00
164 Kyle Williams RC 4.00 10.00
165 Leon Williams RC 3.00 8.00
166 Mark Anderson RC 5.00 12.00
167 LaJuan Ramsey RC 4.00 10.00
168 Nate Salley RC 3.00 8.00
169 Rob Ninkovich RC 15.00 30.00
170 Parys Haralson RC 3.00 8.00
171 Pat Watkins RC 3.00 8.00
172 Paul McQuistan RC 2.50 6.00
173 Rashad Butler RC 2.50 6.00
174 Ray Edwards RC 4.00 10.00
175 Reed Doughty RC 3.00 8.00
176 Ronnie Prude RC 3.00 8.00
177 Stephen Tulloch RC 3.00 8.00
178 Tim Jennings RC 4.00 10.00
179 Jarrad Page RC 4.00 10.00
180 Victor Adeyanju RC 3.00 8.00
181 Andre Hall AU RC 5.00 12.00
182 Anthony Fasano AU RC 4.00 10.00
183 Antonio Cromartie AU RC 10.00 20.00
184 Ashton Youboty AU RC 4.00 10.00
185 Kamerion Wimbley AU RC 5.00 12.00
186 Brad Smith AU RC 5.00 12.00
187 Brodrick Bunkley AU RC 5.00 12.00
188 Bruce Gradkowski AU RC 8.00 20.00
189 Chad Greenway AU RC 8.00 20.00
190 Cory Rodgers AU RC 4.00 10.00
191 D.J. Shockley AU RC 5.00 12.00
192 Danieal Manning AU RC 6.00 15.00
193 Darnell Bing AU RC 5.00 12.00
194 Darrell Hackney AU RC 5.00 12.00
195 D.Ferguson AU RC 4.00 10.00
196 Dominique Byrd AU RC 4.00 10.00
197 Drew Olson AU RC 4.00 10.00
198 Ernie Sims AU RC 4.00 10.00
199 Garrett Mills AU/99 RC 20.00 50.00
200 Gerald Riggs AU RC 5.00 12.00
201 Greg Jennings AU RC 6.00 15.00
202 Greg Lee AU RC 4.00 10.00
203 Hank Baskett AU RC 4.00 10.00
204 Ingle Martin AU RC 5.00 12.00
205 Jason Allen AU RC 5.00 12.00
206 Jerome Harrison AU RC 8.00 20.00
207 Jimmy Williams AU RC 4.00 10.00
208 John McCargo AU RC 4.00 10.00
209 Josh Betts AU RC 5.00 12.00
210 Leonard Pope AU RC 6.00 15.00
211 Marques Hagans AU RC 4.00 10.00
212 Martin Nance AU RC 4.00 10.00
213 Mathias Kiwanuka AU RC 6.00 15.00
214 Mike Bell AU RC 4.00 10.00
215 Mike Hass AU RC 4.00 10.00
216 Owen Daniels AU RC 6.00 15.00
217 P.J. Daniels AU RC 4.00 10.00
218 Reggie McNeal AU RC 4.00 10.00
219 Skyler Green AU RC 4.00 10.00
220 Terrence Whitehead AU RC 5.00 12.00
221 Thomas Howard AU RC 4.00 10.00
222 Tye Hill AU RC 4.00 10.00
223 Will Blackmon AU RC 4.00 10.00
224 Willie Reid AU RC 5.00 12.00
225 Winston Justice AU RC 5.00 12.00
226 Jay Cutler AU/99 RC 150.00 300.00
227 Joseph Addai AU/99 RC 20.00 50.00
228 Br.Williams JSY/999 AU RC 6.00 15.00
229 B.Calhoun JSY/999 AU RC 6.00 15.00
230 Ch.Jackson JSY/699 AU RC 6.00 15.00
231 C.Whitehurst JSY/999 AU RC 6.00 15.00
232 DeA.Willms JSY/175 AU RC 12.00 30.00
233 Dem.Williams JSY/999 AU RC 6.00 15.00
234 Derek Hagan JSY/999 AU RC 8.00 20.00
235 Jason Avant JSY/999 AU RC 6.00 15.00
236 J.Norwood JSY/999 AU RC 6.00 15.00
237 J.Klopfenstein JSY/999 AU RC 6.00 15.00
238 K.Clemens JSY/999 AU RC 6.00 15.00
239 K.Jennings JSY/199 AU RC 10.00 25.00
240 L.Maroney JSY/999 AU RC 6.00 15.00
241 L.White JSY/999 AU RC 5.00 12.00
242 L.Washington JSY/999 AU RC 6.00 15.00
243 M.Lewis JSY/999 AU RC 6.00 15.00
244 M.McNeill JSY/260 AU RC 8.00 20.00
245 Ma.Williams JSY/699 AU RC 12.00 30.00
246 M.Leinart JSY/299 AU RC 12.00 30.00
247 M.Drew JSY/999 AU RC 15.00 40.00
248 M.Stovall JSY/999 AU RC 6.00 15.00
249 M.Huff JSY/999 AU RC 8.00 20.00
250 M.Robinson JSY/999 AU RC 6.00 15.00
251 Omar Jacobs/750 RC 3.00 8.00
252 R.Bush JSY/299 AU RC 15.00 40.00
253 S.Holmes JSY/399 AU RC 10.00 25.00
254 Si.Moss JSY/99 AU RC 15.00 40.00
255 T.Jackson JSY/999 AU RC 6.00 15.00
256 T.Wilson JSY/999 AU RC 6.00 15.00
257 V.Davis JSY/699 AU RC 8.00 20.00
258 V.Young JSY/270 AU RC 8.00 20.00
259 A.J. Hawk JSY/399 AU RC 10.00 25.00
260 B.Marshall JSY/999 AU RC 15.00 40.00

2006 SP Authentic Gold

*VETS 1-90: 8X TO 20X BASIC CARDS
*ROOKIE 91-120/251: 1X TO 2.5X
*ROOKIE 121-180: 1.2X TO 3X BASIC CARDS
*ROOK.181-225: 1.2X TO 3X BASE AU/1175
*ROOK.228-260: 1.5X TO 3X JSY AU/699-999
STATED PRINT RUN 25 SER.#'d SETS
MULTI-COLORED PATCHES: .6X TO 1.2X
199 Garrett Mills AU 15.00 40.00
201 Greg Jennings AU 20.00 50.00
232 DeAngelo Williams JSY AU 40.00 100.00
247 Maurice Drew JSY AU 125.00 250.00

2006 SP Authentic Rookie Autographed NFL Logo Patches

UNPRICED NFL LOGO PRINT RUN 1

2006 SP Authentic Rookie Autographed Patches

UNPRICED PATCH EXCH PRINT RUN 5
ISSUED VIA MIAL EXCHANGE CARDS

2006 SP Authentic Autographs

SPAC Alge Crumpler 5.00 12.00
SPAF Anthony Fasano 4.00 10.00
SPAG Antonio Gates 6.00 15.00
SPAV Jason Avant 4.00 10.00
SPBF Brett Favre SP 75.00 150.00
SPBG Bruce Gradkowski 5.00 12.00
SPBR Ben Roethlisberger SP 60.00 120.00
SPBU Marc Bulger SP 4.00 10.00
SPBW Brandon Williams 4.00 10.00
SPCG Chad Greenway 6.00 15.00
SPCR Cory Rodgers 4.00 10.00
SPCW Charlie Whitehurst 4.00 10.00
SPDB Darnell Bing 5.00 12.00
SPDG David Givens 5.00 12.00
SPDH Derek Hagan 5.00 12.00
SPDM Danieal Manning 6.00 15.00
SPDO Drew Olson 4.00 10.00
SPDS D.J. Shockley 5.00 12.00
SPDW Demetrius Williams 4.00 10.00
SPEM Eli Manning SP 40.00 80.00
SPFT Fran Tarkenton 20.00 40.00
SPGJ Greg Jennings 6.00 15.00
SPHA Mike Hass 4.00 10.00
SPHI Tye Hill 4.00 10.00
SPIM Ingle Martin 5.00 12.00
SPJA Jason Allen 5.00 12.00
SPJK Joe Klopfenstein 4.00 10.00
SPJM John McCargo 4.00 10.00
SPJN Jerious Norwood 4.00 10.00
SPJW Jimmy Williams 4.00 10.00
SPKC Kevin Curtis 5.00 12.00
SPKJ Keyshawn Johnson 5.00 12.00
SPLJ Larry Johnson SP 4.00 10.00
SPLP Leonard Pope 6.00 15.00
SPLW Leon Washington 4.00 10.00
SPMB Mike Bell 4.00 10.00
SPMH Marques Hagans 4.00 10.00
SPMO Joe Montana SP 100.00 200.00
SPMR Michael Robinson 4.00 10.00
SPMS Maurice Stovall 4.00 10.00
SPPD P.J. Daniels 4.00 10.00
SPPR Philip Rivers 12.00 30.00
SPRB Ronde Barber 8.00 20.00
SPRJ Rudi Johnson 4.00 10.00
SPRW Reggie Wayne 10.00 25.00
SPSG Skyler Green 4.00 10.00
SPTA Lofa Tatupu 6.00 15.00
SPTD Tony Dorsett SP 25.00 50.00
SPTH T.J. Houshmandzadeh 4.00 10.00
SPTJ Tarvaris Jackson 4.00 10.00
SPTW Travis Wilson 4.00 10.00
SPWR Willie Reid 5.00 12.00

2006 SP Authentic Chirography

CHAH A.J. Hawk 20.00 40.00
CHAY Ashton Youboty 3.00 8.00
CHBB Brodrick Bunkley 4.00 10.00
CHBC Brian Calhoun 3.00 8.00
CHBE Drew Bennett 4.00 10.00
CHBG Bob Griese SP
CHBL Brandon Lloyd 3.00 8.00
CHBM Brandon Marshall 8.00 20.00
CHBS Brad Smith 4.00 10.00
CHBU Reggie Bush SP 10.00 25.00
CHBW Brandon Williams 3.00 8.00
CHCB Cedric Benson 8.00 20.00
CHCJ Chad Jackson 3.00 8.00
CHCL Mark Clayton 3.00 8.00
CHDB Dominique Byrd 3.00 8.00
CHDC Dwight Clark 8.00 20.00
CHDF D'Brickashaw Ferguson 3.00 8.00
CHDM Dan Marino SP 100.00 200.00
CHDS D.J. Shockley 4.00 10.00
CHDW DeAngelo Williams SP 25.00 50.00
CHES Ernie Sims 3.00 8.00
CHFO DeShaun Foster 4.00 10.00
CHGM Garrett Mills 4.00 10.00
CHGR Gerald Riggs 4.00 10.00
CHJA Joseph Addai SP 12.00 30.00
CHJB Josh Betts 4.00 10.00
CHJC Jay Cutler 4.00 10.00
CHJE John Elway SP 75.00 150.00
CHJH Jerome Harrison 3.00 8.00
CHJJ Julius Jones 6.00 15.00
CHJT Joe Theismann 15.00 30.00
CHJW Jason Witten 20.00 40.00
CHKC Kellen Clemens 6.00 15.00
CHKO Kyle Orton 3.00 8.00
CHKS Ken Stabler SP 25.00 60.00
CHLE Byron Leftwich 3.00 8.00
CHLG L.C. Greenwood SP 40.00 80.00
CHLM Laurence Maroney 3.00 8.00
CHLT Lofa Tatupu 8.00 20.00
CHMA Matt Leinart SP
CHMB Marc Bulger 3.00 8.00
CHMC Deuce McAllister 4.00 10.00
CHMH Michael Huff 4.00 10.00
CHMI Michael Clayton 3.00 8.00
CHML Marcedes Lewis 3.00 8.00
CHMM Muhsin Muhammad 3.00 8.00
CHMW Mario Williams 5.00 12.00
CHNB Nate Burleson 3.00 8.00
CHOD Owen Daniels 5.00 12.00
CHPM Peyton Manning 60.00 100.00
CHRB Reggie Brown 3.00 8.00
CHTA Troy Aikman 40.00 100.00
CHTG Trent Green 3.00 8.00
CHTJ Thomas Jones 3.00 8.00
CHVY Vince Young SP 8.00 20.00
CHWB Will Blackmon 3.00 8.00
CHWP Willie Parker 6.00 15.00

2006 SP Authentic Chirography Gold

*GOLD/25: .6X TO 1.5X BASIC AUTO
GOLD STATED PRINT RUN 10-25
CHBU Reggie Bush 15.00 40.00
CHDM Dan Marino 125.00 250.00
CHJE John Elway 100.00 200.00
CHKS Ken Stabler 25.00 60.00
CHLM Laurence Maroney 5.00 12.00
CHMA Matt Leinart 25.00 60.00
CHPM Peyton Manning 75.00 150.00
CHTA Troy Aikman 50.00 120.00
CHVY Vince Young 12.00 30.00

2006 SP Authentic Chirography Duals

STATED PRINT RUN 10-50
SERIAL #'d UNDER 25 NOT PRICED
BB Burleson/R.Brown/50 10.00 25.00
BL R.Bush/M.Leinart/50 12.00 30.00
CJ Clemens/T.Jackson/50 12.00 30.00
DC M.Drew/B.Calhoun/50 20.00 50.00
DL V.Davis/M.Lewis/50 15.00 40.00
DM Dorsett/L.Maroney/25 30.00 80.00
GC Gates/Crumpler/50 15.00 40.00
HB M.Huff/D.Bing/50 12.00 30.00
HH S.Holmes/A.Hawk/50 30.00 60.00
JG L.Johnson/T.Green/50 12.00 30.00
JM C.Jackson/S.Moss/50 12.00 30.00
JS Jacobs/Shockley/50 10.00 25.00
JW J.Jones/J.Witten/25 25.00 50.00
MA P.Mann/Addai/50 75.00 150.00
MD G.Mills/O.Daniels/50 10.00 25.00
MJ T.Jones/Muhammad/50 12.00 30.00
MR E.Mann/Rivers/50 40.00 80.00
MW Maroney/DeA.Will/50 20.00 50.00
PH Palmer/Housh/50
RP Roeth/Parker/50 40.00 80.00
TS L.Tatupu/E.Sims/50 12.00 30.00
WF Ma.Will/Ferg/50 12.00 30.00
WR B.Williams/Robinson/50 10.00 25.00
YW V.Young/L.White/50 10.00 25.00

2006 SP Authentic Chirography Triples

TRIPLE STATED PRINT RUN 20
BJG Bledsoe/Jones/Green 30.00 60.00
CCJ Cutler/Clemens/Jackson 50.00 100.00
HMS Hagan/Marshall/Stovall 20.00 50.00
MMM Marino/Mann/Montna 300.00 500.00
MWA Maroney/Williams/Addai 25.00 60.00
TJW Tmlinsn/Jhnsn/Williams 60.00 120.00
WDC White/Drew/Calhoun 25.00 60.00
WHH Williams/Hawk/Huff 40.00 80.00
WJM Whitehrst/Jacobs/Mrtin 20.00 50.00
WWA Wilson/Williams/Avant

2006 SP Authentic Chirography Quads

UNPRICED QUAD PRINT RUN 5 SER.#'d SETS

2006 SP Authentic Rookie Exclusives Autographs

STATED PRINT RUN 100 UNLESS NOTED
REAAC Antonio Cromartie/75 12.50 30.00
REAAD Joseph Addai 5.00 12.00
REAAH A.J. Hawk 6.00 15.00
REAAV Jason Avant 5.00 12.00
REABM Brandon Marshall 10.00 25.00
REABS Brad Smith 6.00 15.00
REABW Brandon Williams 5.00 12.00
REACA Brian Calhoun 5.00 12.00
REACJ Chad Jackson 5.00 12.00
REACW Charlie Whitehurst 5.00 12.00
READB Dominique Byrd 5.00 12.00
READF D'Brickashaw Ferguson 5.00 12.00
READH Derek Hagan 6.00 15.00
READS D.J. Shockley 6.00 15.00
READW DeAngelo Williams 15.00 40.00
REAES Ernie Sims 5.00 12.00
REAGJ Greg Jennings 8.00 20.00
REAHA Mike Hass 5.00 12.00
REAIM Ingle Martin 6.00 15.00
REAJA Jason Allen 6.00 15.00
REAJC Jay Cutler 6.00 15.00
REAJK Joe Klopfenstein 5.00 12.00
REAJN Jerious Norwood 5.00 12.00
REAJW Jimmy Williams 5.00 12.00
REAKC Kellen Clemens 5.00 12.00
REALM Laurence Maroney 5.00 12.00
REALP Leonard Pope 8.00 20.00
REALW LenDale White 5.00 12.00
REAMD Maurice Drew/85 25.00 60.00
REAMH Michael Huff 6.00 15.00
REAML Marcedes Lewis 5.00 12.00
REAMR Michael Robinson 5.00 12.00
REAMS Maurice Stovall 5.00 12.00
REAMW Mario Williams 8.00 20.00
REAPD P.J. Daniels 5.00 12.00
REARB Reggie Bush 8.00 20.00
REASG Skyler Green 5.00 12.00
REASH Santonio Holmes 6.00 15.00
REASM Sinorice Moss/25 10.00 25.00
REATJ Tarvaris Jackson 5.00 12.00
REATW Travis Wilson 5.00 12.00
REAVD Vernon Davis 6.00 15.00
REAVY Vince Young 8.00 20.00
REAWA Leon Washington 5.00 12.00
REAWI Demetrius Williams 5.00 12.00

2006 SP Authentic Rookie Exclusives Jerseys

STATED PRINT RUN 150 SER.#'d SETS
REJAH A.J. Hawk 5.00 12.00
REJBC Brian Calhoun 4.00 10.00
REJBM Brandon Marshall 8.00 20.00
REJBW Brandon Williams 4.00 10.00
REJCJ Chad Jackson 4.00 10.00
REJCW Charlie Whitehurst 4.00 10.00
REJDH Derek Hagan 5.00 12.00
REJDW DeAngelo Williams 5.00 12.00
REJJA Jason Avant 4.00 10.00
REJJC Jay Cutler 5.00 12.00
REJJK Joe Klopfenstein 4.00 10.00
REJJN Jerious Norwood 4.00 10.00
REJKC Kellen Clemens 4.00 10.00
REJLE Matt Leinart 4.00 10.00
REJLM Laurence Maroney 4.00 10.00
REJLW LenDale White 4.00 10.00
REJMD Maurice Drew 6.00 15.00
REJMH Michael Huff 5.00 12.00
REJML Marcedes Lewis 4.00 10.00
REJMR Michael Robinson 4.00 10.00
REJMS Maurice Stovall 4.00 10.00
REJMW Mario Williams 6.00 15.00
REJOJ Omar Jacobs 4.00 10.00
REJRB Reggie Bush 6.00 15.00
REJSH Santonio Holmes 5.00 12.00
REJSM Sinorice Moss 4.00 10.00
REJTJ Tarvaris Jackson 4.00 10.00
REJTW Travis Wilson 4.00 10.00
REJVD Vernon Davis 5.00 12.00
REJVY Vince Young 4.00 10.00
REJWA Leon Washington 4.00 10.00
REJWI Demetrius Williams 4.00 10.00

2007 SP Authentic

This 298-card set was released in February, 2008. The set was issued into the hobby in five-card packs with an $4.99 SRP which came 24 packs to a box. Cards numbered 1-100 feature veterans in first name alphabetical order (with a couple of exceptions) while cards numbered 101-298 feature 2007 NFL rookies. Within the rookies, cards numbered 201-265 are signed by the player and cards numbered 266-298 have both signatures and a game-worn player swatch.

COMP.SET w/o RC's (100) 8.00 20.00
101-160 ROOKIE PRINT RUN 1399
161-200 ROOKIE PRINT RUN 999
201-230 AU RC PRINT RUN 1199
231-250 AU RC PRINT RUN 999
251-265 AU RC PRINT RUN 399
266-288 JSY AU RC PRINT RUN 725
289-298 JSY AU RC PRINT RUN 399
1 Ahman Green .25 .60
2 A.J. Hawk .20 .50
3 Alex Smith QB .25 .60
4 Andre Johnson .25 .60
5 Antonio Gates .30 .75
6 Ben Roethlisberger .30 .75
7 Bernard Berrian .20 .50
8 Brandon Jacobs .20 .50
9 Braylon Edwards .20 .50
10 Brett Favre .60 1.50
11 Brian Urlacher .30 .75
12 Brian Westbrook .20 .50
13 Brodie Croyle .25 .60
14 Byron Leftwich .20 .50
15 Cadillac Williams .25 .60
16 Carson Palmer .25 .60
17 Cedric Benson .20 .50
18 Chad Johnson .20 .50
19 Chad Pennington .20 .50
20 Champ Bailey .25 .60
21 Derek Anderson .20 .50
22 Chester Taylor .20 .50
23 Chris Brown .20 .50
24 Chris Chambers .20 .50
25 Clinton Portis .20 .50
26 Darrell Jackson .20 .50
27 Deuce McAllister .25 .60
28 Dominic Rhodes .20 .50
29 Donald Driver .25 .60
30 Donovan McNabb .25 .60
31 Donte Stallworth .25 .60
32 Drew Brees .30 .75
33 Edgerrin James .25 .60
34 Eli Manning .25 .60
35 Frank Gore .25 .60
36 Fred Taylor .20 .50
37 Greg Jennings .20 .50
38 Hines Ward .25 .60
39 Jake Delhomme .20 .50
40 Jamal Lewis .25 .60
41 Jason Campbell .20 .50
42 Jason Taylor .25 .60
43 Jason Witten .25 .60
44 Javon Walker .25 .60
45 Jay Cutler .20 .50
46 Jerious Norwood .20 .50
47 Jerry Porter .25 .60
48 Jon Kitna .20 .50
49 Joseph Addai .20 .50
50 Julius Jones .20 .50
51 LaDainian Tomlinson .30 .75
52 Larry Johnson .20 .50
53 Larry Fitzgerald .25 .60
54 Laurence Maroney .25 .60
55 Marc Bulger .20 .50
56 Marion Barber .25 .60
57 Mark Clayton .20 .50
58 Marques Colston .20 .50
59 Marvin Harrison .25 .60
60 Matt Hasselbeck .20 .50
61 Matt Jones .25 .60
62 Matt Leinart .20 .50
63 Matt Schaub .20 .50
64 Maurice Jones-Drew .20 .50
65 Jeff Garcia .20 .50
66 Mike Alstott .20 .50
67 David Garrard .20 .50
68 Peyton Manning .75 2.00
69 Philip Rivers .30 .75
70 Plaxico Burress .20 .50
71 Randy Moss .25 .60
72 Reggie Brown .20 .50
73 Reggie Bush .20 .50
74 Reggie Wayne .25 .60
75 Rex Grossman .20 .50
76 Ronnie Brown .20 .50
77 Roy Williams S .20 .50
78 Roy Williams WR .20 .50
79 Rudi Johnson .20 .50
80 Shaun Alexander .20 .50
81 Shawne Merriman .20 .50
82 Steven Jackson .20 .50
83 Steve McNair .25 .60
84 Steve Smith .25 .60
85 T.J. Houshmandzadeh .20 .50
86 Tarvaris Jackson .20 .50
87 Tedy Bruschi .25 .60
88 Terrell Owens .25 .60
89 Thomas Jones .20 .50
90 Tom Brady 1.00 2.50
91 Torry Holt .25 .60
92 Travis Henry .25 .60
93 Trent Green .20 .50
94 Vince Young .20 .50
95 Vincent Jackson .20 .50
96 Walter Jones .20 .50
97 Warrick Dunn .20 .50
98 Willie Parker .25 .60
99 Willis McGahee .20 .50
100 Tony Romo .40 1.00
101 Deon Anderson RC 3.00 8.00
102 Ben Patrick RC 3.00 8.00
103 Reagan Mauia RC 2.50 6.00
104 Derek Schouman RC 3.00 8.00
105 Keyunta Dawson RC 3.00 8.00
106 Usama Young RC 3.00 8.00
107 Syndric Steptoe RC 3.00 8.00
108 Martrez Milner RC 2.50 6.00
109 Brandon McDonald RC 2.50 6.00
110 Jason Snelling RC 4.00 10.00
111 Derek Stanley RC 3.00 8.00
112 Ed Johnson RC 3.00 8.00
113 Jacob Bender RC 2.50 6.00
114 Charles Ali RC 3.00 8.00
115 Tanard Jackson RC 2.50 6.00
116 Paul Soliai RC 2.50 6.00
117 Marvin White RC 2.50 6.00
118 Jared Gaither RC 2.50 6.00
119 Baraka Atkins RC 2.50 6.00
120 Marcus Thomas RC 3.00 8.00
121 Fred Bennett RC 2.50 6.00
122 Dashon Goldson RC 4.00 10.00
123 Kareem Brown RC 3.00 8.00
124 Courtney Bryan RC 2.50 6.00
125 Joe Cohen RC 2.50 6.00
126 Jay Richardson RC 3.00 8.00
127 Greg Peterson RC 3.00 8.00
120 Dallas Sartz RC 3.00 8.00
129 Brandon Harrison RC 2.50 6.00
130 Tarell Brown RC 4.00 10.00
131 Matt Gutierrez RC 4.00 10.00
132 Edmond Miles RC 3.00 8.00
133 Clifton Ryan RC 3.00 8.00
134 Antwan Barnes RC 4.00 10.00
135 Tim Shaw RC 3.00 8.00
136 Eric Frampton RC 3.00 8.00
137 William Gay RC
138 Nick Graham RC 3.00 8.00
139 Matt Toeaina RC 3.00 8.00
140 John Wendling RC 3.00 8.00
141 Mason Crosby RC 3.00 8.00
142 C.J. Wallace RC 3.00 8.00
143 Prescott Burgess RC 2.50 6.00
144 Oscar Lua RC 3.00 8.00
145 Chase Pittman RC 3.00 8.00
146 Zachary Diles RC 3.00 8.00
147 Kelvin Smith RC 3.00 8.00
148 Marvin Mitchell RC 3.00 8.00
149 Trumaine McBride RC 3.00 8.00
150 Edgar Jones RC 3.00 8.00
151 Abraham Wright RC 2.50 6.00
152 Nick Folk RC 4.00 10.00
153 Brandon Siler RC 2.50 6.00
154 Clint Session RC 3.00 8.00
155 Nedu Ndukwe RC 4.00 10.00
156 C.J. Wilson RC 3.00 8.00
157 Desmond Bishop RC 4.00 10.00
158 Melvin Bullitt RC 3.00 8.00
159 Courtney Brown RC 3.00 8.00
160 Troy Smith RC 2.50 6.00
161 Levi Brown RC 2.50 6.00
162 Justin Harrell RC 2.50 6.00
163 Jarvis Moss RC 2.50 6.00
164 Aaron Ross RC 2.50 6.00
165 Jon Beason RC 2.50 6.00
166 Anthony Spencer RC 3.00 8.00
167 Joe Staley RC 3.00 8.00
168 Ben Grubbs RC 3.00 8.00
169 Arron Sears RC 3.00 8.00
170 Eric Weddle RC 3.00 8.00
171 Justin Blalock RC 2.50 6.00
172 Chris Houston RC 2.50 6.00
173 David Harris RC 2.50 6.00
174 Justin Durant RC 4.00 10.00
175 Turk McBride RC 3.00 8.00
176 Josh Wilson RC 3.00 8.00
177 Tim Crowder RC 3.00 8.00
178 Victor Abiamiri RC 2.50 6.00
179 Ikaika Alama-Francis RC 4.00 10.00
180 Ryan Kalil RC 2.50 6.00
181 Samson Satele RC 3.00 8.00
182 Gerald Alexander RC 2.50 6.00
183 Corey Graham RC 2.50 6.00
184 Sabby Piscitelli RC 2.50 6.00
185 Quincy Black RC 4.00 10.00
186 Daniel Coats RC 3.00 8.00
187 Tony Ugoh RC 2.50 6.00
188 David Jones RC 2.50 6.00
189 DeMarcus Tank Tyler RC 2.50 6.00
190 Chad Nkang RC 2.50 6.00
191 Jonathan Wade RC 2.50 6.00
192 Brandon Mebane RC 3.00 8.00
193 Stewart Bradley RC 2.50 6.00
194 Aaron Rouse RC 2.50 6.00
195 Michael Okwo RC 3.00 8.00
196 Anthony Waters RC 3.00 8.00
197 Ray McDonald RC 3.00 8.00
198 Clifton Dawson RC 4.00 10.00
199 Brian Robison RC 4.00 10.00
200 Jay Moore RC 3.00 8.00
201 Dante Rosario AU RC 6.00 15.00
202 Ahmad Bradshaw AU RC 6.00 15.00
203 Roy Hall AU RC UER 6.00 15.00
204 Aundrae Allison AU RC 4.00 10.00
205 Brent Celek AU RC 4.00 10.00
206 Chansi Stuckey AU RC 5.00 12.00
207 Courtney Taylor AU RC 4.00 10.00
208 Dallas Baker AU RC 4.00 10.00
209 Darius Walker AU RC 4.00 10.00
210 David Ball AU RC 4.00 10.00
211 David Clowney AU RC 4.00 10.00
212 David Irons AU RC 4.00 10.00
213 Daymeion Hughes AU RC 4.00 10.00
214 DeShawn Wynn AU RC 4.00 10.00
215 Jordan Kent AU RC 5.00 12.00
216 Dwayne Wright AU RC 4.00 10.00
217 Eric Wright AU RC 4.00 10.00
218 Gary Russell AU RC 5.00 12.00
219 Mike Walker AU RC 8.00 20.00
220 Isaiah Stanback AU RC 4.00 10.00
221 Jamaal Anderson AU RC 5.00 12.00
222 Jared Zabransky AU RC 4.00 10.00
223 Jeff Rowe AU RC 4.00 10.00
224 Joel Filani AU RC 4.00 10.00
225 Jordan Palmer AU RC 5.00 12.00
226 Kenneth Darby AU RC 4.00 10.00
227 Kolby Smith AU RC 4.00 10.00
228 Thomas Clayton AU RC 5.00 12.00
229 Steve Breaston AU RC 10.00 25.00
230 James Jones AU RC 8.00 20.00
231 Marcus McCauley AU RC 4.00 10.00
232 Alan Branch AU RC 4.00 10.00
233 Michael Griffin AU RC 4.00 10.00
234 Paul Posluszny AU RC 4.00 10.00
235 Quentin Moses AU RC 4.00 10.00
236 Lawrence Timmons AU RC 6.00 15.00
237 Scott Chandler AU RC 6.00 15.00
238 Jacoby Jones AU RC 4.00 10.00
239 Tyler Thigpen AU RC 6.00 15.00
240 Laurent Robinson AU RC 6.00 15.00
241 John Broussard AU RC 5.00 12.00
242 Zach Miller AU RC 4.00 10.00
243 Matt Spaeth AU RC 6.00 15.00
244 Ryne Robinson AU RC 5.00 12.00
245 Danny Ware AU RC 6.00 15.00
246 Legedu Naanee AU RC 5.00 12.00
247 Le'Ron McClain AU RC 6.00 15.00
248 Kevin Boss AU RC 6.00 15.00
249 Orenthal O'Neal AU RC 4.00 10.00
250 Amobi Okoye AU RC 5.00 12.00
251 Darrelle Revis AU RC 12.00 30.00
252 LaRon Landry AU RC 10.00 25.00
253 Chris Leak AU RC 6.00 15.00
254 Craig Davis AU RC 6.00 15.00
255 Leon Hall AU RC 6.00 15.00
256 Reggie Nelson AU RC 6.00 15.00
257 Adam Carriker AU RC 6.00 15.00
258 H.B. Blades AU RC 6.00 15.00
259 LaMarr Woodley AU RC 12.00 30.00
260 Korey Hall AU RC 8.00 20.00
261 Rhema McKnight AU RC 6.00 15.00
262 B.Meriweather AU RC 8.00 20.00
263 Matt Moore AU RC 10.00 25.00
264 Selvin Young AU RC 6.00 15.00
265 Tyler Palko AU RC 10.00 25.00
266 A.Gonzalez JSY AU RC 6.00 15.00
267 A.Pittman JSY AU RC 6.00 15.00
268 Br.Jackson JSY AU RC 6.00 15.00
269 Brian Leonard JSY AU RC 6.00 15.00
270 Chris Henry JSY AU RC 6.00 15.00
271 Drew Stanton JSY AU RC 6.00 15.00
273 Garrett Wolfe JSY AU RC 6.00 15.00
274 Greg Olsen JSY AU RC 10.00 25.00
275 Jason Hill JSY AU RC 6.00 15.00
276 Joe Thomas JSY AU RC 10.00 25.00
277 John Beck JSY AU RC 6.00 15.00
278 J.Lee Higgins JSY AU RC 6.00 15.00
279 Kenny Irons JSY AU RC 6.00 15.00
280 Kevin Kolb JSY AU RC 8.00 20.00
281 Lorenzo Booker JSY AU RC 8.00 20.00
282 Michael Bush JSY AU RC 6.00 15.00
283 Patrick Willis JSY AU RC 10.00 25.00
284 Paul Williams JSY AU RC 6.00 15.00
285 Steve Smith JSY AU RC 6.00 15.00
286 Tony Hunt JSY AU RC 6.00 15.00
287 Trent Edwards JSY AU RC 6.00 15.00
288 Yamon Figurs JSY AU RC 6.00 15.00
289 A.Peterson JSY AU RC 150.00 300.00
290 Brady Quinn JSY AU RC 10.00 25.00
291 C.Johnson JSY AU RC 75.00 150.00
292 J.Russell JSY AU RC 10.00 25.00
293 M.Lynch JSY AU RC 30.00 60.00
294 Dwayne Bowe JSY AU RC 10.00 25.00
295 Sidney Rice JSY AU RC 12.00 30.00
296 R.Meachem JSY AU RC 12.00 30.00
297 Dwayne Jarrett JSY AU RC 12.00 30.00
298 Ted Ginn JSY AU RC 12.00 30.00

2007 SP Authentic Gold

*VETS 1-100: 8X TO 20X BASIC CARDS
*ROOK 101-160: 1.2X TO 3X BASE RC/1399
*ROOKIE 161-200: 1.2X TO 3X BASE RC/999
*RK 201-230: 1.2X TO 3X BASE AU RC/1199
*RK 231-250: 1.2X TO 3X BASE AU RC/999
*ROOK 251-265: .8X TO 2X BASE AU RC/399
*RK.JSY AU 266-288: 1.2X TO 3X JSY AU/725
*RK.JSY AU 289-298: .6X TO 1.5X JSY AU/399
GOLD PRINT RUN 25 SER.#'d SETS
289 Adrian Peterson JSY AU 900.00 1500.00
291 Calvin Johnson JSY AU 400.00 800.00
293 Marshawn Lynch JSY AU 125.00 250.00

2007 SP Authentic Autographs

SPAAAP Adrian Peterson 150.00 250.00
SPAABF Brett Favre SP 125.00 200.00
SPAABJ Brandon Jackson 4.00 10.00
SPAACD Craig Buster Davis 4.00 10.00
SPAACH Chris Henry RB 4.00 10.00
SPAACJ Chad Johnson SP 8.00 20.00
SPAADB Drew Brees 30.00 60.00
SPAADJ Dwayne Jarrett 5.00 12.00
SPAAGO Greg Olsen 6.00 15.00
SPAAJC Jerricho Cotchery 8.00 20.00
SPAAJN Jerious Norwood 8.00 20.00
SPAAJP Jordan Palmer 5.00 12.00
SPAAJT Joe Thomas 6.00 15.00
SPAALB Lorenzo Booker 5.00 12.00
SPAALJ Larry Johnson SP 8.00 20.00
SPAALL LaRon Landry 6.00 15.00
SPAAMB Marc Bulger SP 8.00 20.00
SPAAMG Michael Griffin 4.00 10.00
SPAAML Matt Leinart 8.00 20.00
SPAAPW Paul Williams 4.00 10.00
SPAASC Scott Chandler 6.00 15.00
SPAATG Ted Ginn SP 5.00 12.00
SPAATH T.J. Houshmandzadeh SP 8.00 20.00
SPAAZM Zach Miller 4.00 10.00

2007 SP Authentic Autographs Gold

*GOLD/25: .8X TO 2X BASIC INSERTS
GOLD PRINT RUN 25 SER.#'d SETS
SPAAAP Adrian Peterson 200.00 400.00
SPAABF Brett Favre 100.00 200.00

2007 SP Authentic By The Letter Autographs

SERIAL NUMBERING BETWEEN 10-99
OVERALL PRINT RUNS ARE HIGHER
BTLAB Anquan Boldin/10 20.00 50.00
BTLAS1 Aaron Schobel/25 12.00 30.00
BTLAS2 Aaron Schobel/75 12.00 30.00
BTLBF Brett Favre/25 150.00 300.00
BTLBJ Bo Jackson/15 50.00 120.00
BTLBR Reggie Brown/75 12.00 30.00
BTLBS Barry Sanders/15 100.00 200.00
BTLCB Champ Bailey/75 25.00 50.00
BTLCC1 Chris Cooley/25 12.00 30.00
BTLCC2 Chris Cooley/75 10.00 25.00
BTLCR Roger Craig/99 15.00 40.00
BTLCW Cadillac Williams/25 15.00 40.00
BTLDB Drew Brees/15 60.00 120.00
BTLDM Dan Marino/15 125.00 250.00
BTLDP Drew Pearson/99 12.00 30.00
BTLDW1 DeMarcus Ware/60 20.00 50.00
BTLDW2 DeMarcus Ware/75 15.00 40.00
BTLES Emmitt Smith/15 100.00 200.00
BTLFG Frank Gore/25 15.00 40.00
BTLHE1 Heath Evans/50 10.00 25.00
BTLHE2 Heath Evans/70 10.00 25.00
BTLHN Haloti Ngata/70 10.00 25.00
BTLJA Joseph Addai/25 12.00 30.00
BTLJC Jason Campbell/35 12.00 30.00
BTLJM Joe Montana/15 125.00 250.00
BTLJN Joe Namath/15 75.00 150.00
BTLJT1 Jeremiah Trotter/40 10.00 25.00
BTLJT2 Jeremiah Trotter/45 10.00 25.00
BTLJT3 Jeremiah Trotter/70 10.00 25.00
BTLKB Keith Brooking/50 10.00 25.00
BTLLE Lee Evans/25 12.00 30.00
BTLLJ Larry Johnson/20 10.00 25.00
BTLLT LaDainian Tomlinson/10 40.00 100.00
BTLMA Matt Leinart/15 12.00 30.00
BTLMB Marc Bulger/25 12.00 30.00
BTLMC Marques Colston/50 15.00 40.00
BTLML1 Matt Light/25 12.00 30.00
BTLML2 Matt Light/50 10.00 25.00
BTLML3 Matt Light/70 10.00 25.00
BTLML4 Matt Light/75 10.00 25.00
BTLMS Mike Singletary/15 25.00 60.00
BTLNB1 Nick Barnett/35 10.00 25.00
BTLNB2 Nick Barnett/50 10.00 25.00
BTLNB3 Nick Barnett/70 10.00 25.00
BTLNM1 Nick Mangold/65 8.00 20.00
BTLNM2 Nick Mangold/70 8.00 20.00
BTLPC1 Patrick Crayton/50 12.00 30.00
BTLPC2 Patrick Crayton/55 12.00 30.00
BTLPC3 Patrick Crayton/60 12.00 30.00
BTLPH Paul Hornung/50 20.00 50.00
BTLQJ1 Quentin Jammer/50 8.00 20.00
BTLQJ2 Quentin Jammer/55 8.00 20.00
BTLRB Reggie Bush/15 40.00 100.00
BTLRC1 Ronald Curry/45 10.00 25.00
BTLRC2 Ronald Curry/65 10.00 25.00
BTLRC3 Ronald Curry/75 8.00 20.00
BTLRG Roberto Garza/75 12.00 30.00
BTLRO Ronnie Brown/25 15.00 40.00
BTLSA1 Bob Sanders/40 12.00 30.00
BTLSA2 Bob Sanders/70 10.00 25.00
BTLSH1 Steve Hutchinson/90 10.00 25.00
BTLSH2 Steve Hutchinson/25 10.00 25.00
BTLST1 Mack Strong/25 12.00 30.00
BTLST2 Mack Strong/65 12.00 30.00
BTLST3 Mack Strong/75 12.00 30.00
BTLTR Tony Romo/25 40.00 100.00
BTLTW1 Ty Warren/35 10.00 25.00
BTLTW2 Ty Warren/70 10.00 25.00
BTLTW3 Ty Warren/75 10.00 25.00
BTLWP Willie Parker/25 15.00 40.00

2007 SP Authentic Chirography

*GOLD/25: .8X TO 2X BASIC INSERTS
GOLD PRINT RUN 25 SER.#'d SETS
CAAC Adam Carriker 4.00 10.00
CAAG Anthony Gonzalez SP 4.00 10.00
CAAS Alex Smith QB SP 15.00 40.00
CABM Brandon Meriweather 5.00 12.00
CABQ Brady Quinn SP 8.00 20.00
CABR Ronnie Brown SP 15.00 30.00
CACB Champ Bailey SP 20.00 40.00
CACH Korey Hall 5.00 12.00
CACL Chris Leak 4.00 10.00
CACW Cadillac Williams SP 10.00 25.00
CADD Donald Driver
CADR Darrelle Revis 5.00 12.00
CADS Drew Stanton SP 4.00 10.00
CAEM Eli Manning SP 40.00 80.00
CAIS Isaiah Stanback 4.00 10.00
CAJA Joseph Addai 8.00 20.00
CAJB John Beck 4.00 10.00
CAJC Jason Campbell 8.00 20.00
CAJH Jason Hill 4.00 10.00
CAKI Kenny Irons 4.00 10.00
CALE Lee Evans 10.00 25.00
CALT Lawrence Timmons 8.00 20.00
CAMB Marion Barber 10.00 25.00
CAMC Marques Colston 8.00 20.00
CAML Marshawn Lynch 8.00 20.00
CAMM Matt Moore 6.00 15.00
CAPR Philip Rivers 15.00 30.00
CAPW Patrick Willis 6.00 15.00
CARB Reggie Bush 25.00 60.00
CARN Reggie Nelson 4.00 10.00
CASR Sidney Rice 5.00 12.00
CATH Tony Hunt 4.00 10.00
CATO LaDainian Tomlinson SP 30.00 60.00
CATP Tyler Palko 6.00 15.00
CAVY Vince Young 20.00 50.00

2007 SP Authentic Chirography Duals

STATED PRINT RUN 50 SER.#'d SETS
AH J.Higgins/A.Allison 8.00 20.00
CW Carriker/L.Woodley 15.00 30.00
FN L.Naanee/J.Filani 8.00 20.00
GA M.Griffin/Anderson 10.00 25.00
HW J.Hill/P.Williams 15.00 30.00
JB B.Jcksn/Booker 8.00 20.00
KE K.Kolb/T.Edwards 8.00 20.00
LB C.Leak/J.Beck 6.00 15.00
LC Chandler/Leonard 10.00 25.00
MB D.Bowe/R.Meachem 8.00 20.00
NL L.Landry/R.Nelson 10.00 25.00
OM G.Olsen/Z.Miller 10.00 25.00
PB M.Bush/A.Pittman 12.00 30.00
PS Stanback/J.Palmer 8.00 20.00
SF S.Smith/Figurs 6.00 15.00
WB P.Willis/H.Blades 15.00 40.00
WH T.Hunt/G.Wolfe 6.00 15.00
WS D.Wright/K.Smith 6.00 15.00

2007 SP Authentic Chirography Triples

STATED PRINT RUN 25 SER.#'d SETS
BKE Kolb/Beck/Edw 15.00 40.00
JGB Johnson/Ginn Jr./Bowe 100.00 200.00
LMP Leak/Moore/Palko 15.00 40.00
OMC Olsen/Miller/Chandler 15.00 40.00
PLI Peterson/Lynch/Irons 125.00 250.00
QRS Russell/Quinn/Stant 30.00 80.00
WBH Hunt/Wolfe/Bush 20.00 50.00

2007 SP Authentic Sign of the Times

SOTTAB Anquan Boldin 8.00 20.00
SOTTAO Amobi Okoye 5.00 12.00
SOTTAP Antonio Pittman 4.00 10.00
SOTTBA Dallas Baker 4.00 10.00
SOTTBE Drew Bennett SP 8.00 20.00
SOTTBL Brian Leonard 4.00 10.00
SOTTBR Alan Branch 4.00 10.00
SOTTCJ Calvin Johnson SP 40.00 80.00
SOTTCT Chester Taylor SP 8.00 20.00
SOTTDB Dwayne Bowe SP 5.00 12.00
SOTTDC David Clowney 4.00 10.00
SOTTFG Frank Gore 10.00 25.00
SOTTGW Garrett Wolfe 4.00 10.00
SOTTJA Jamaal Anderson 5.00 12.00

SOTTJH Johnnie Lee Higgins 4.00 10.00
SOTTJL John Lynch 10.00 25.00
SOTTJR Jeff Rowe 4.00 10.00
SOTTJT Jason Taylor
SOTTKK Kevin Kolb 5.00 12.00
SOTTLF Larry Fitzgerald 15.00 40.00
SOTTLH Leon Hall 4.00 10.00
SOTTMB Michael Bush 4.00 10.00
SOTTMJ Maurice Jones-Drew
SOTTPM Peyton Manning SP 60.00 120.00
SOTTPP Paul Posluszny 4.00 10.00
SOTTRB Reggie Brown 8.00 20.00
SOTTRM Robert Meachem 5.00 12.00
SOTTRW Roy Williams S
SOTTSJ Steven Jackson
SOTTSS Steve Smith USC 4.00 10.00
SOTTTE Trent Edwards 4.00 10.00
SOTTTR Tony Romo SP 75.00 150.00
SOTTWP Willie Parker SP 10.00 25.00
SOTTYF Yamon Figurs 4.00 10.00

2007 SP Authentic Sign of the Times Gold

*GOLD/25: .8X TO 2X BASIC AUTOS
GOLD PRINT RUN 25 SER.#'d SETS
SOTTTR Tony Romo 100.00 200.00

2007 SP Authentic Sign of the Times Duals

STATED PRINT RUN 75 SER.#'d SETS
BT Timmons/Booker 15.00 30.00
DB C.Davis/D.Bowe 6.00 15.00
GG T.Ginn Jr./A.Gonzalez 15.00 40.00
GP A.Gonzalez/A.Pittman 20.00 50.00
HB L.Hall/A.Branch 8.00 20.00
HM C.Henry RB/Z.Miller 10.00 25.00
HP P.Posluszny/T.Hunt 6.00 15.00
HS K.Hall/C.Stuckey 8.00 20.00
II K.Irons/D.Irons 10.00 25.00
JC Jackson/Carriker 12.00 30.00
JS D.Jarrett/S.Smith USC 8.00 20.00
LD C.Davis/L.Landry 10.00 25.00
NW D.Wynn/R.Nelson 10.00 25.00
OM Meriwthr/Olsen 12.00 30.00
PH Palmer/Higgins 10.00 25.00
RB Revis/Blades 15.00 30.00
WW P.Williams/D.Wright 10.00 25.00
ZN J.Zabransky/L.Naanee 10.00 25.00

2007 SP Authentic Sign of the Times Triples

STATED PRINT RUN 25
BJS Bush/Jrrtt/Smith 40.00 100.00
LDB Bowe/Davis/Landry 30.00 80.00
LWB Leak/Baker/Wynn 25.00 60.00
MOM Meri/Olsn/Moss 20.00 50.00
QWM Quinn/Walker/McKni 50.00 120.00
SBO Bush/Okoye/Smith
WMW McCau/Williams/Wright 20.00 50.00

2007 SP Authentic Sign of the Times Quads

UNPRICED QUAD PRINT RUN 15

2008 SP Authentic

This set was released on January 30, 2009. The base set consists of 303 cards. Cards 1-100 feature veterans, and cards 101-200 are rookies serial numbered of 999-1399. Cards 201-270 are autographed rookies serial numbered of 399-999, and cards 271-305 are autographed jersey rookies serial numbered of 499-999. This product was released with 5 cards per pack and 24 packs per hobby box. A retail version was also produced with a simple "SP" logo on the cardfronts for the first 100 veteran players instead of "SP Authentic." The Retail base rookies (101-140) were created with a new design and include no brand logos on the fronts while the Retail rookie autographs (141-175) have the simple "SP" logo on the fronts along with a unique design.

COMP.SET w/o RC's (100) 8.00 20.00
101-160 ROOKIE PRINT RUN 1399
161-200 ROOKIE PRINT RUN 999
201-230 AU RC PRINT RUN 1199
231-250 AU RC PRINT RUN 999
251-270 AU RC PRINT RUN 399-499
271-298 JSY AU RC PRINT RUN 999
299-305 JSY AU RC PRINT RUN 499
UNPRICED NFL LOGO AU PRINT RUN 1
1 Marshawn Lynch .25 .60
2 Trent Edwards .20 .50
3 Roscoe Parrish .20 .50
4 Jason Taylor .25 .60
5 Ronnie Brown .20 .50
6 Chad Pennington .20 .50
7 Tom Brady 1.00 2.50
8 Laurence Maroney .25 .60
9 Randy Moss .25 .60
10 Darrelle Revis .20 .50
11 Jerricho Cotchery .20 .50
12 Thomas Jones .20 .50
13 Ray Lewis .30 .75
14 Ed Reed .25 .60
15 Willis McGahee .20 .50
16 Carson Palmer .25 .60
17 T.J. Houshmandzadeh .20 .50
18 Chad Johnson .20 .50
19 Kellen Winslow .20 .50
20 Derek Anderson .20 .50
21 Braylon Edwards .20 .50
22 Ben Roethlisberger .30 .75
23 Willie Parker .25 .60
24 Matt Schaub .20 .50
25 DeMeco Ryans .25 .60
26 Andre Johnson .25 .60
27 Darius Walker .20 .50
28 Peyton Manning .75 2.00
29 Reggie Wayne .25 .60
30 Joseph Addai .20 .50
31 David Garrard .20 .50
32 Maurice Jones-Drew .20 .50
33 Fred Taylor .20 .50
34 Vince Young .20 .50
35 LenDale White .20 .50
36 Alge Crumpler .20 .50
37 Jay Cutler .20 .50
38 Brandon Marshall .25 .60
39 Jason Witten .25 .60
40 Brodie Croyle .25 .60
41 Larry Johnson .20 .50
42 Derrick Johnson .20 .50
43 JaMarcus Russell .20 .50
44 Ronald Curry .20 .50
45 Jeremy Shockey .20 .50
46 Antonio Gates .25 .60
47 LaDainian Tomlinson .30 .75
48 Antonio Cromartie .20 .50
49 Philip Rivers .30 .75
50 Tony Romo .25 .60
51 Terrell Owens .25 .60
52 DeMarcus Ware .25 .60
53 Marion Barber .20 .50
54 Eli Manning .25 .60
55 Brandon Jacobs .20 .50
56 Plaxico Burress .20 .50
57 Antonio Pierce .20 .50
58 Donovan McNabb .25 .60
59 Brian Dawkins .30 .75
60 Brian Westbrook .20 .50
61 Chris Cooley .20 .50
62 Jason Campbell .20 .50
63 Clinton Portis .20 .50
64 Brian Urlacher .30 .75
65 Lance Briggs .25 .60
66 Devin Hester .25 .60
67 Roy Williams WR .20 .50
68 Calvin Johnson .30 .75
69 Brett Favre .60 1.50
70 Aaron Rodgers .60 1.50
71 Ryan Grant .25 .60
72 Greg Jennings .20 .50
73 Tarvaris Jackson .20 .50
74 Adrian Peterson .30 .75
75 Sidney Rice .20 .50
76 Michael Turner .20 .50
77 Jerious Norwood .20 .50
78 Jake Delhomme .20 .50
79 DeAngelo Williams .20 .50
80 Steve Smith .25 .60
81 Julius Peppers .25 .60
82 Drew Brees .30 .75
83 Reggie Bush .20 .50
84 Marques Colston .20 .50
85 Jonathan Vilma .20 .50
86 Joey Galloway .25 .60
87 Jeff Garcia .20 .50
88 Earnest Graham .20 .50
89 Kurt Warner .25 .60
90 Edgerrin James .25 .60
91 Larry Fitzgerald .25 .60
92 Anquan Boldin .20 .50
93 Marc Bulger .20 .50
94 Steven Jackson .20 .50
95 Torry Holt .25 .60
96 J.T. O'Sullivan .20 .50
97 Frank Gore .25 .60
98 Nate Clements .20 .50
99 Matt Hasselbeck .20 .50
100 Deion Branch .20 .50
101 Kregg Lumpkin RC 3.00 8.00
102 Donovan Woods RC 2.50 6.00
103 Joe Mays RC 2.00 5.00
104 Anthony Alridge RC 2.00 5.00
105 Beau Bell RC 2.50 6.00
106 Brad Cottam RC 2.00 5.00
107 Brandon Flowers RC 2.50 6.00
108 Darrell Strong RC 2.50 6.00
109 Mike Tolbert RC 3.00 8.00
110 Bryan Kehl RC 2.00 5.00
111 Andy Studebaker RC 2.50 6.00
112 Duane Brown RC 2.00 5.00
113 Mike Humpal RC 3.00 8.00
114 Corey Clark RC 2.00 5.00
115 Josh Sitton RC 3.00 8.00
116 Curtis Lofton RC 2.50 6.00
117 Lance Leggett RC 3.00 8.00
118 Gary Barnidge RC 3.00 8.00
119 Marcus Dixon RC 2.00 5.00
120 Dominique Barber RC 2.00 5.00
121 Reggie Smith RC 2.00 5.00
122 John Sullivan RC 2.50 6.00
123 Jabari Arthur RC 2.50 6.00
124 Maurice Leggett RC 2.50 6.00
125 Jehuu Caulcrick RC 2.50 6.00
126 Philip Wheeler RC 2.50 6.00
127 Jo-Lonn Dunbar RC 2.50 6.00
128 Josh Barrett RC 2.00 5.00
129 Danny Amendola RC 6.00 15.00
130 Kenny Iwebema RC 2.00 5.00
131 Lance Ball RC 2.00 5.00
132 Caleb Hanie RC 3.00 8.00
133 Chris Chamberlain RC 2.00 5.00
134 Marcus Howard RC 3.00 8.00
135 Shaheer McBride RC 2.00 5.00
136 Orlando Scandrick RC 2.00 5.00
137 Quentin Groves RC 2.50 6.00
138 Quintin Demps RC 2.50 6.00
139 John Greco RC 2.50 6.00
140 Jamey Richard RC 2.00 5.00
141 Corey Lynch RC 2.00 5.00
142 Orlando Scandrick RC 2.00 5.00
143 Lex Hilliard RC 2.50 6.00
144 Tyrell Johnson RC 2.00 5.00
145 Martellus Bennett RC 2.50 6.00
146 Simeon Castille RC 2.00 5.00
147 Steve Johnson RC 6.00 15.00
148 Steven Justice RC 2.00 5.00
149 Terrell Thomas RC 2.00 5.00
150 Thomas Brown RC 2.00 5.00
151 Thomas DeCoud RC 2.00 5.00
152 Matt Slater RC 3.00 8.00
153 Tom Zbikowski RC 2.50 6.00
154 Jaymar Johnson RC 2.00 5.00
155 Brian Johnston RC 2.00 5.00
156 Trevor Laws RC 2.00 5.00
157 Will Franklin RC 2.50 6.00
158 Xavier Adibi RC 2.00 5.00
159 Chaz Schilens RC 2.50 6.00
160 Zack Bowman RC 2.50 6.00
161 Tim Hightower RC 2.50 6.00
162 Barry Richardson RC 2.00 5.00
163 Pierre Garcon RC 10.00 25.00
164 Tyvon Branch RC 2.50 6.00
165 Marcus Henry RC 2.00 5.00
166 Carl Nicks RC 2.50 6.00
167 Chauncey Washington RC 2.50 6.00
168 Chilo Rachal RC 2.00 5.00
169 Chris Williams RC 2.00 5.00
170 Craig Stevens RC 2.00 5.00
171 Jordan Dizon RC 2.00 5.00
172 Dantrell Savage RC 2.50 6.00
173 Clifton Smith RC 3.00 8.00
174 Drew Radovich RC 2.50 6.00
175 Jerome Felton RC 2.00 5.00
176 Haruki Nakamura RC 2.00 5.00
177 Olaniyi Sobomehin RC 2.00 5.00
178 Jamie Silva RC 2.50 6.00
179 Brandon Carr RC 2.50 6.00
180 Jeff Otah RC 2.00 5.00
181 William Hayes RC 2.00 5.00
182 Jerome Simpson RC 2.50 6.00
183 Anthony Collins RC 2.00 5.00
184 Alex Hall RC 2.50 6.00
185 Branden Albert RC 2.50 6.00
186 Jalen Parmele RC 2.50 6.00
187 Stanford Keglar RC 2.00 5.00
188 Louis Rankin RC 2.50 6.00
189 Maurice Purify RC 3.00 8.00
190 Darnell Jenkins RC 2.50 6.00
191 Pat Sims RC 2.50 6.00
192 Patrick Lee RC 2.00 5.00
193 Roy Schuening RC 2.00 5.00
194 Lynell Hamilton RC 3.00 8.00
195 Joey LaRocque RC 2.00 5.00
196 Terrence Wheatley RC 2.00 5.00
197 Tracy Porter RC 2.50 6.00
198 Brett Swain RC 2.00 5.00
199 Wesley Woodyard RC 3.00 8.00
200 Xavier Omon RC 2.00 5.00
201 Allen Patrick AU RC 3.00 8.00
202 Marcus Monk AU RC 4.00 10.00
203 Anthony Morelli AU RC 3.00 8.00
204 Antoine Cason AU RC 4.00 10.00
205 Aqib Talib AU RC 5.00 12.00
206 Ben Moffitt AU RC 3.00 8.00
207 Chris Long AU RC 20.00 40.00
208 Bruce Davis AU RC 4.00 10.00
209 Calais Campbell AU RC 4.00 10.00
210 Mario Urrutia AU RC 3.00 8.00
211 Chevis Jackson AU RC 3.00 8.00
212 Chris Ellis AU RC 3.00 8.00
213 Josh Morgan AU RC 3.00 8.00
214 Craig Steltz AU RC 3.00 8.00
215 DJ Hall AU RC 3.00 8.00
216 Dan Connor AU RC 3.00 8.00
217 Darius Reynaud AU RC 3.00 8.00
218 DeJuan Tribble AU RC 3.00 8.00
219 DeMario Pressley AU RC 4.00 10.00
220 Dennis Keyes AU RC 3.00 8.00
221 Derrick Harvey AU RC 3.00 8.00
222 Owen Schmitt AU RC 3.00 8.00
223 Dwight Lowery AU RC 12.50 25.00
224 Erik Ainge AU RC 3.00 8.00
225 Erin Henderson AU RC 4.00 10.00
226 DaJuan Morgan AU RC 4.00 10.00
227 Frank Okam AU RC 3.00 8.00
228 Matt Flynn AU RC 12.00 30.00
229 Phillip Merling AU RC SP 15.00 30.00
230 Ryan Clady AU RC 4.00 10.00
231 Davone Bess AU RC 4.00 10.00
232 Fred Davis AU RC 3.00 8.00
234 Gosder Cherilus AU RC 4.00 10.00
235 Tashard Choice AU RC 6.00 15.00
236 J Leman AU RC 3.00 8.00
237 Jack Ikegwuonu AU RC 3.00 8.00
238 Jacob Hester AU RC 3.00 8.00
239 Jacob Tamme AU RC 6.00 15.00
240 Sedrick Ellis AU RC 3.00 8.00
241 Jermichael Finley AU RC 3.00 8.00
242 John Carlson AU RC 3.00 8.00
243 Jonathan Goff AU RC 3.00 8.00
245 Shawn Crable AU RC 3.00 8.00
246 Josh Johnson AU RC 3.00 8.00
247 Justin Forsett AU RC 5.00 12.00
248 Justin King AU RC 4.00 10.00
249 Keenan Burton AU RC 3.00 8.00
250 Sam Baker AU RC 3.00 8.00
251 Colt Brennan AU/399 RC 6.00 15.00
252 Adrian Arrington AU/399 RC 5.00 12.00
253 Alex Brink AU/399 RC 6.00 15.00
254 Ali Highsmith AU/399 RC 5.00 12.00
255 Keith Rivers AU/499 RC 5.00 12.00
256 Kellen Davis AU/399 RC 5.00 12.00
257 Kenny Phillips AU/399 RC 5.00 12.00
258 Geno Hayes AU/399 RC 5.00 12.00
259 Paul Smith AU/399 RC 5.00 12.00
260 Lavelle Hawkins AU/499 RC 6.00 15.00
261 L.Jackson AU/399 RC 5.00 12.00
262 Leodis McKelvin AU/399 RC 6.00 15.00
263 Andre Woodson AU/399 RC 5.00 12.00
264 Mike Hart AU/499 RC 5.00 12.00
265 Martin Rucker AU/399 RC 5.00 12.00
266 Dennis Dixon AU/399 RC 5.00 12.00
267 Paul Hubbard AU/399 RC 5.00 12.00
268 Peyton Hillis AU/399 RC 10.00 25.00
269 R.Grice-Mullins AU/399 RC 5.00 12.00
270 V.Gholston AU/399 RC 5.00 12.00
271 Jerome Simpson JSY AU RC 8.00 20.00
272 Dexter Jackson JSY AU RC 10.00 25.00
273 Donnie Avery JSY AU RC 8.00 20.00
275 Jake Long JSY AU RC 12.00 30.00
276 Dustin Keller JSY AU RC 8.00 20.00
277 James Hardy JSY AU RC 6.00 15.00
278 Andre Caldwell JSY AU RC 6.00 15.00
279 Jordy Nelson JSY AU RC 25.00 50.00
280 Kevin Smith JSY AU RC 6.00 15.00
281 Eddie Royal JSY AU RC 6.00 15.00
282 M.Manningham JSY AU RC 6.00 15.00
283 Earl Bennett JSY AU RC 10.00 25.00
284 Harry Douglas JSY AU RC 8.00 20.00
285 Ray Rice JSY AU RC 10.00 25.00
286 Steve Slaton JSY AU RC 6.00 15.00
288 Chris Johnson JSY AU RC 10.00 25.00
289 Kevin O'Connell JSY AU RC 6.00 15.00
290 DeSean Jackson JSY AU RC 12.00 30.00
291 Early Doucet JSY AU RC 6.00 15.00
292 Felix Jones JSY AU RC 6.00 15.00
293 Jamaal Charles JSY AU RC 12.00 30.00
294 J.David Booty JSY AU RC 6.00 15.00
295 Joe Flacco JSY AU RC 30.00 80.00
297 Malcolm Kelly JSY AU RC 6.00 15.00
298 Matt Forte JSY AU RC 15.00 40.00
299 McFadden JSY AU/499 RC 10.00 25.00
300 Matt Ryan JSY AU/499 RC 75.00 150.00
301 Brian Brohm JSY AU/499 RC 10.00 25.00
302 C.Henne JSY AU/499 RC 12.00 30.00
303 D.Thomas JSY AU/499 RC 10.00 25.00
304 Mendenhall JSY AU/499 RC 10.00 25.00
305 J.Stewart JSY AU/499 RC 12.00 30.00

2008 SP Authentic Gold

*JSY AU 271-298: 1.2X TO 3X BASE JSY AU/999
*JSY AU 299-305: 1X TO 2.5X BASE JSY AU/499
STATED PRINT RUN 25 SER.#'d SETS
279 Jordy Nelson JSY AU 60.00 125.00
295 Joe Flacco JSY AU 200.00 400.00
298 Matt Forte JSY AU 175.00 300.00
299 Darren McFadden JSY AU 30.00 80.00
300 Matt Ryan JSY AU 250.00 500.00

2008 SP Authentic Retail

COMP.SET w/o RC's (100) 8.00 20.00
*1-100 RETAIL VETS: .4X TO 1X HOBBY
1-100 VETS HAVE SP BRAND LOGO ON FRONT
101-140 RCs HAVE NO BRAND LOGO
141-175 AU RC's HAVE SP BRAND LOGO ON FRONT
101 Adrian Arrington RC 1.00 2.50
102 Anthony Morelli RC 1.00 2.50
103 Calais Campbell RC 1.25 3.00
104 Colt Brennan RC 1.25 3.00
105 Chevis Jackson RC 1.00 2.50
106 Chris Williams RC 1.00 2.50
107 Craig Stevens RC 1.00 2.50
108 Curtis Lofton RC 1.25 3.00
109 Dan Connor RC 1.00 2.50
110 Davone Bess RC 1.25 3.00
111 Dennis Dixon RC 1.00 2.50
112 Derrick Harvey RC 1.00 2.50
113 D.Rodgers-Cromartie RC 1.25 3.00
114 Dre Moore RC 1.00 2.50
115 Erik Ainge RC 1.00 2.50
116 Erin Henderson RC 1.25 3.00
117 Frank Okam RC 1.00 2.50
118 Haruki Nakamura RC 1.00 2.50
119 Jack Ikegwuonu RC 1.00 2.50
120 Jeff Otah RC 1.00 2.50
121 Jerod Mayo RC 1.50 4.00
122 Jonathan Goff RC 1.00 2.50
123 Jordon Dizon RC 1.00 2.50
124 Justin King RC 1.25 3.00
125 Kenny Phillips RC 1.00 2.50
126 Kentwan Balmer RC 1.00 2.50
127 King Dunlap RC 1.00 2.50
128 Leodis McKelvin RC 1.25 3.00
129 Mike Jenkins RC 1.00 2.50
130 Owen Schmitt RC 1.00 2.50
131 Patrick Lee RC 1.00 2.50
132 Peyton Hillis RC 1.50 4.00
133 Quentin Groves RC 1.25 3.00
134 Ryan Clady RC 1.25 3.00
135 Sam Baker RC 1.00 2.50
136 Josh Morgan RC 1.00 2.50
137 Tracy Porter RC 1.25 3.00
138 Vernon Gholston RC 1.00 2.50
139 Will Franklin RC 1.25 3.00
140 Xavier Omon RC 1.00 2.50
141 Andre Caldwell AU RC 5.00 12.00
142 Chad Henne AU RC 6.00 15.00
143 DeSean Jackson AU RC 25.00 50.00
144 Chris Johnson AU RC 10.00 25.00
145 Felix Jones AU RC 5.00 12.00
146 Chris Long AU RC 6.00 15.00
147 Darren McFadden AU RC
148 Joe Flacco AU RC 40.00 80.00
149 Ray Rice AU RC 5.00 12.00
150 Matt Ryan AU RC 40.00 100.00
152 Alex Brink AU RC 6.00 15.00
153 Thomas Brown AU RC 5.00 12.00
154 Mike Jenkins AU 5.00 12.00
155 Kellen Davis AU RC 5.00 12.00
156 Andre Woodson AU RC 5.00 12.00
157 Quintin Demps AU RC 6.00 15.00
158 Aqib Talib AU RC 8.00 20.00
159 Matt Flynn AU RC 5.00 12.00
160 Xavier Adibi AU RC 5.00 12.00
161 Shawn Crable AU RC 5.00 12.00
162 Trevor Laws AU RC 5.00 12.00
163 Tom Zbikowski AU RC 6.00 15.00
164 Erik Ainge AU 5.00 12.00
165 Josh Johnson AU RC 5.00 12.00
166 Terrell Thomas AU RC 5.00 12.00
167 Malcolm Kelly AU RC 5.00 12.00
168 Davone Bess AU 6.00 15.00
169 John David Booty AU RC 5.00 12.00
170 Lawrence Jackson AU RC 5.00 12.00
171 DeMario Pressley AU RC 6.00 15.00
172 Brian Brohm AU RC 5.00 12.00
173 Calais Campbell AU 6.00 15.00
174 Ryan Torain AU RC 6.00 15.00
175 Mario Urrutia AU RC 5.00 12.00

2008 SP Authentic Autographs

*GOLD VETS/25: .5X TO 1.2X BASIC AU
*GOLD ROOKIES/25: .8X TO 2X BASIC AU
GOLD PRINT RUN 25 SER.#'d SETS
SPAM Anthony Morelli 3.00 8.00
SPAP Adrian Peterson SP 60.00 120.00
SPBD Bruce Davis 4.00 10.00
SPBF Brett Favre SP 100.00 200.00
SPCE Chris Ellis 3.00 8.00
SPCJ Chris Johnson 5.00 12.00
SPCL Chris Long 4.00 10.00
SPCP Clinton Portis 8.00 20.00
SPCS Craig Steltz 3.00 8.00
SPDD Dennis Dixon 8.00 20.00
SPDM Darren McFadden SP 3.00 8.00
SPDR Dominique Rodgers-Cromartie 4.00 10.00
SPDT Devin Thomas 3.00 8.00
SPER Erin Henderson 4.00 10.00
SPFJ Felix Jones 3.00 8.00
SPGC Gosder Cherilus 4.00 10.00
SPGR Bob Griese 12.00 30.00
SPHD Harry Douglas 4.00 10.00
SPJL Jamal Lewis 10.00 25.00
SPJS Jonathan Stewart 12.00 30.00
SPMK Malcolm Kelly 3.00 8.00
SPMR Matt Ryan SP 125.00 250.00
SPOS Owen Schmitt 3.00 .8.00
SPPM Peyton Manning 60.00 120.00
SPPW Patrick Willis 10.00 25.00
SPRT Rashard Mendenhall 3.00 8.00
SPSY Steve Young SP 30.00 60.00
SPVG Vernon Gholston 3.00 8.00
SPYT Y.A. Tittle 12.00 30.00

2008 SP Authentic By the Letter Autographs

SER.#'d 4-56, TOTAL PRINT RUNS 30-224
BLAH A.J. Hawk G/100* 15.00 40.00
BLAM Archie Manning/98* 20.00 50.00
BLAS Aaron Schobel/175* 10.00 25.00
BLBA Marion Barber/96* 20.00 50.00
BLBB Brian Bosworth/96* 15.00 40.00
BLBC Brodie Croyle/84* 12.00 30.00
BLBJ Bert Jones/100* 12.00 30.00
BLBR Ben Roethlisberger/56* 100.00 200.00
BLBW Ben Watson/96* 10.00 25.00
BLCB Chuck Bednarik/96* 12.00 30.00
BLCP Clinton Portis/102* 12.00 30.00
BLDA Dorek Anderson/96* 12.00 30.00
BLDB Dwayne Bowe/96* 15.00 40.00
BLDG David Garrard/98* 15.00 40.00
BLDJ Daryl Johnston/168* 30.00 60.00
BLDM Don Maynard/98* 12.00 30.00
BLEM Eli Manning/98* 50.00 120.00
BLFT Fran Tarkenton/99* 25.00 50.00
BLHA A.J. Hawk W/105* 15.00 40.00
BLJK Jerry Kramer/96* 20.00 50.00
BLJT Joe Theismann/72* 40.00 80.00
BLKW Kellen Winslow Sr./98* 15.00 40.00
BLLJ Larry Johnson/70* 12.00 30.00
BLMF Marshall Faulk/50* 30.00 60.00
BLML Marshawn Lynch/80* 15.00 40.00
BLOA Ottis Anderson/112* 12.00 30.00
BLPH Paul Hornung/119* 15.00 40.00
BLPW Patrick Willis/138* 15.00 40.00
BLRA Tom Rathman/105* 15.00 40.00
BLRC Roger Craig/100* 12.00 30.00
BLRO Tony Romo/100* 50.00 100.00
BLRW Rod Woodson/98* 25.00 60.00
BLSI Billy Sims/224* 12.00 30.00
BLSY Steve Young/50* 60.00 120.00
BLTA Troy Aikman/30* 75.00 150.00
BLTR Tom Rathman/105* 15.00 40.00
BLWI Roy Williams WR/64* 12.00 30.00
BLYT Y.A. Tittle/102* 25.00 50.00

2008 SP Authentic Chirography

*GOLD VETS/25: .5X TO 1.2X BASIC AU
*GOLD ROOKIES/25: .8X TO 2X BASIC AU
GOLD PRINT RUN 25 SER.#'d SETS
UNPRICED QUAD AUTO PRIINT RUN 10
CHAT Aqib Talib 5.00 12.00
CHBB Brian Brohm 3.00 8.00
CHBD Bruce Davis 4.00 10.00
CHBR Ben Roethlisberger SP 60.00 120.00
CHCE Chris Ellis 3.00 8.00
CHCH Chad Henne 4.00 10.00
CHCJ Chris Johnson 4.00 10.00
CHCN Chad Johnson SP 6.00 15.00
CHCS Craig Steltz 3.00 8.00
CHDJ DeSean Jackson 6.00 15.00
CHDM Don Maynard 10.00 25.00
CHDT Devin Thomas 3.00 8.00
CHEH Erin Henderson 4.00 10.00
CHFJ Felix Jones 3.00 8.00
CHFT Fran Tarkenton 20.00 40.00
CHGC Gosder Cherilus 4.00 10.00
CHJA Joseph Addai SP 8.00 20.00
CHJF Joe Flacco 30.00 60.00
CHJK Jim Kelly SP
CHJL Jamal Lewis 10.00 25.00
CHKA Anthony Morelli 3.00 8.00
CHKS Kevin Smith 3.00 8.00
CHKW Kellen Winslow Sr. SP 15.00 40.00
CHLH Lester Hayes 10.00 25.00
CHLJ Larry Johnson SP EXCH
CHLO Jake Long 5.00 12.00
CHMB Marc Bulger 8.00 20.00
CHMF Matt Forte 10.00 25.00
CHMK Malcolm Kelly 3.00 8.00
CHOS Owen Schmitt 3.00 8.00
CHPM Peyton Manning SP 60.00 120.00
CHRM Rashard Mendenhall 3.00 8.00
CHSY Steve Young SP 40.00 80.00
CHTR Tony Romo 40.00 80.00
CHWP Emmitt Smith SP 100.00 175.00

2008 SP Authentic Chirography Duals

STATED PRINT RUN 10-100
DK F.Davis/D.Keller/100 8.00 20.00
JM L.Jackson/P.Merling/90 10.00 25.00
WD K.Warner/E.Doucet/100 15.00 40.00
BG R.Gabriel/M.Bulger/50 12.00 30.00
GF Sayers/McFad/15 10.00 25.00
GH Griese/Henne/20 30.00 60.00
HC Hester/Cason/80 8.00 20.00
HF Henne/Flacco/50 25.00 60.00
JC Charles/LJ/20 EXCH 25.00 50.00
KE Kelly/Edwrds/20 50.00 80.00
LC J.Long/Cherilus/80 10.00 25.00
MA Mann/Addai/20 75.00 150.00
MT Y.Tittle/E.Manning/30 50.00 100.00
MW P.Willis/Eli/30 50.00 100.00
PW Phillips/R.Wdson/80 25.00 60.00
RH Hart/Rice/85 20.00 40.00
SS B.Sims/K.Smith/80 15.00 40.00
ST Sayers/Tomlin/20 60.00 120.00
TK D.Thms/Klly/100 8.00 20.00
WW Ware/Willis/50 30.00 60.00

2008 SP Authentic Chirography Triples

STATED PRINT RUN 25 SER.#'d SETS
BFS Btks/Frte/Syrs/25 125.00 200.00
FRB Favre/Rodgers/Brohm
PGP Port/Gore/Phillps/25 EXCH 25.00 60.00
PTC Theis/Prtis/Cmpbl/25 30.00 60.00
TPM Tittle/Phillips/Eli/25 40.00 80.00
WCB Bswrth/Cnnr/Wllis/25 30.00 60.00

2008 SP Authentic Immortals Autographs

STATED PRINT RUN 15-55
UNPRICED QUAD AUTO PRINT RUN 5
UNPRICED TRIPLE AUTO PRINT RUN 5-10
SPIBG Bob Griese/35 15.00 40.00
SPIBJ Bo Jackson/35 50.00 100.00
SPIBS Barry Sanders/15 125.00 200.00
SPIFH Franco Harris/35 25.00 50.00
SPIFT Fran Tarkenton/35 25.00 50.00
SPIJK Jerry Kramer/50 15.00 40.00
SPIJR Jerry Rice/15 125.00 200.00
SPIJT Joe Theismann/55 15.00 40.00
SPIKA Ken Anderson/55 15.00 40.00
SPIPH Paul Hornung/35 15.00 40.00
SPIRG Roman Gabriel/55 15.00 40.00
SPISI Billy Sims/35 15.00 40.00
SPISY Steve Young/35 40.00 80.00
SPIYT Y.A. Tittle/35 15.00 40.00

2008 SP Authentic Immortals Autographs Dual

STATED PRINT RUN 5-20
AT O.Anderson/Y.Tittle/40 20.00 40.00
JB Bosworth/Bo/20 60.00 120.00

2008 SP Authentic Retail Pro Bowl Performers

ONE PER RETAIL PACK
PBP1 Aaron Kampman .40 1.00
PBP2 Adrian Peterson .50 1.25
PBP3 Andre Johnson .40 1.00
PBP4 Antonio Cromartie .30 .75
PBP5 Ben Roethlisberger .50 1.25
PBP6 Bob Sanders .40 1.00
PBP7 Braylon Edwards .30 .75
PBP8 Carson Palmer .40 1.00
PBP9 Steve Smith .40 1.00
PBP10 Chad Johnson .30 .75
PBP11 Champ Bailey .40 1.00
PBP12 Chris Chambers .30 .75
PBP13 Deuce McAllister .40 1.00
PBP14 DeMarcus Ware .40 1.00
PBP15 Derrick Burgess .30 .75
PBP16 Devin Hester .40 1.00
PBP17 Drew Brees .50 1.25
PBP18 Dwight Freeney .30 .75
PBP19 Ed Reed .40 1.00
PBP20 Edgerrin James .40 1.00
PBP21 Steven Jackson .30 .75
PBP22 Fred Taylor .30 .75
PBP23 Hines Ward .40 1.00
PBP24 Roy Williams WR .30 .75
PBP25 Jason Taylor .40 1.00
PBP26 Jason Witten .40 1.00
PBP27 John Lynch .40 1.00
PBP28 LaDainian Tomlinson .50 1.25
PBP29 Larry Fitzgerald .40 1.00
PBP30 Larry Johnson .30 .75
PBP31 Lofa Tatupu .30 .75
PBP32 Marvin Harrison .40 1.00
PBP33 Peyton Manning 1.25 3.00
PBP34 Randy Moss .40 1.00
PBP35 Ray Lewis .50 1.25
PBP36 Reggie Wayne .40 1.00
PBP37 Shawne Merriman .30 .75
PBP38 Terrell Owens .40 1.00
PBP39 T.J. Houshmandzadeh .30 .75
PBP40 Tom Brady 1.50 4.00
PBP41 Tony Gonzalez .40 1.00
PBP42 Troy Polamalu .50 1.25
PBP43 Tony Romo .40 1.00
PBP44 Torry Holt .40 1.00
PBP45 Matt Hasselbeck .30 .75

2008 SP Authentic Retail Rookie Authentics Jerseys

RA1 John David Booty 2.00 5.00
RA2 Brian Brohm 2.00 5.00
RA3 Andre Caldwell 2.00 5.00
RA4 Jamaal Charles 3.00 8.00
RA5 Glenn Dorsey 2.00 5.00
RA6 Early Doucet 2.00 5.00
RA7 Harry Douglas 2.50 6.00
RA8 Joe Flacco 4.00 10.00
RA9 Matt Forte 3.00 8.00
RA10 James Hardy 2.00 5.00
RA11 Chad Henne 2.50 6.00
RA12 DeSean Jackson 4.00 10.00
RA13 Chris Johnson 2.50 6.00
RA14 Felix Jones 2.00 5.00
RA15 Dustin Keller 2.50 6.00
RA16 Malcolm Kelly 2.00 5.00
RA17 Jake Long 3.00 8.00
RA18 Mario Manningham 2.00 5.00
RA19 Darren McFadden 2.00 5.00
RA20 Rashard Mendenhall 2.00 5.00
RA21 Jordy Nelson 6.00 15.00
RA22 Kevin O'Connell 2.00 5.00
RA23 Ray Rice 2.00 5.00
RA24 Matt Ryan 6.00 15.00
RA25 Jerome Simpson 2.50 6.00
RA26 Steve Slaton 2.00 5.00
RA27 Kevin Smith 2.00 5.00
RA28 Jonathan Stewart 3.00 8.00
RA29 Limas Sweed 2.00 5.00
RA30 Devin Thomas 2.00 5.00

2008 SP Authentic Retro Rookie Jerseys Autographs

STATED PRINT RUN 75 SER.#'d SETS
RRAS Aaron Schobel 10.00 25.00
RRBA Marion Barber 15.00 40.00
RRBB Brian Bosworth 20.00 50.00
RRBC Brodie Croyle 12.00 30.00
RRBF Brett Favre 125.00 250.00
RRBS Barry Sanders 75.00 150.00
RRDA Derek Anderson 10.00 25.00
RRDB Dick Butkus 40.00 80.00
RRDC Dallas Clark 15.00 40.00
RRDW DeMarcus Ware 12.00 30.00
RRFH Franco Harris 20.00 50.00
RRFT Fran Tarkenton 20.00 50.00
RRGS Gale Sayers 20.00 50.00
RRHW Herschel Walker
RRJA Joseph Addai 10.00 25.00
RRJE John Elway 75.00 150.00
RRJG Jeff Garcia 10.00 25.00
RRJN Joe Namath 60.00 120.00
RRJT Joe Theismann 20.00 50.00
RRKA Ken Anderson 15.00 40.00
RRKU Kurt Warner 40.00 80.00
RRKW Kellen Winslow Sr. 15.00 40.00
RRMB Marc Bulger 10.00 25.00
RRPH Paul Hornung 20.00 50.00
RRPM Peyton Manning 75.00 150.00
RRRC Roger Craig 15.00 40.00
RRRM Rod Woodson
RRSI Billy Sims 20.00 50.00
RRTM Tom Rathman
RRTR Tony Romo 50.00 100.00
RRWW Wes Welker 25.00 50.00

2008 SP Authentic Rookie Leatherheads Autographs

STATED PRINT RUN 50-150
LHAC Andre Caldwell/99 6.00 15.00
LHBB Brian Brohm/75 6.00 15.00
LHCH Chad Henne/150 8.00 20.00
LHCJ Chris Johnson/150 8.00 20.00
LHDA Donnie Avery/99 8.00 20.00
LHDJ DeSean Jackson/150 12.00 30.00
LHDK Dustin Keller/150 8.00 20.00
LHDM Darren McFadden/125 6.00 15.00
LHDT Devin Thomas/150 6.00 15.00
LHEB Earl Bennett/150 10.00 25.00
LHED Early Doucet/150 6.00 15.00
LHER Eddie Royal/150 6.00 15.00
LHFJ Felix Jones/150 6.00 15.00
LHHD Harry Douglas/150 8.00 20.00
LHJA Dexter Jackson/150 10.00 25.00
LHJB John David Booty/99 6.00 15.00
LHJC Jamaal Charles/150 10.00 25.00
LHJF Joe Flacco/150 12.00 30.00
LHJH James Hardy/150 6.00 15.00
LHJL Jake Long/150 10.00 25.00
LHJN Jordy Nelson/150 15.00 40.00
LHJS Jerome Simpson/150 8.00 20.00
LHKO Kevin O'Connell/99 6.00 15.00
LHKS Kevin Smith/150 6.00 15.00
LHMF Matt Forte/150 10.00 25.00
LHMK Malcolm Kelly/99 6.00 15.00
LHMM Mario Manningham/99 6.00 15.00
LHMR Matt Ryan/50 75.00 150.00
LHRM Rashard Mendenhall/99 8.00 20.00
LHRR Ray Rice/150 6.00 15.00
LHSS Steve Slaton/150 6.00 15.00
LHST Jonathan Stewart/99 10.00 25.00

2008 SP Authentic Sign of the Times

*GOLD VETS/25: .5X TO 1.2X BASIC AUTO
*GOLD ROOKIES/25: .8X TO 2X BASIC AUTO
GOLD PRINT RUN 25 SER.#'d SETS
UNPRICED QUAD PRINT RUN 10
SOTAB Alex Brink 4.00 10.00
SOTAC Andre Caldwell 3.00 8.00
SOTAM Anthony Morelli 3.00 8.00
SOTAP Adrian Peterson SP 50.00 100.00
SOTBB Brian Bosworth 20.00 40.00
SOTBD Bruce Davis 4.00 10.00
SOTBJ Bert Jones 5.00 12.00
SOTBS Barry Sanders 60.00 120.00
SOTCA Antoine Cason 4.00 10.00
SOTCC Calais Campbell 4.00 10.00
SOTCJ Chad Johnson SP 8.00 20.00
SOTDA Donnie Avery 4.00 10.00
SOTDT DeJuan Tribble 4.00 10.00
SOTEA Erik Ainge 3.00 8.00
SOTEM Eli Manning 30.00 60.00
SOTFD Fred Davis 3.00 8.00
SOTFH Franco Harris SP 20.00 40.00
SOTFO Frank Okam 3.00 8.00
SOTJH James Hardy 3.00 8.00
SOTJL Jack Lambert
SOTJT Joe Theismann 12.00 30.00
SOTLM Leodis McKelvin 4.00 10.00
SOTLT LaDainian Tomlinson 30.00 80.00
SOTMC Darren McFadden 3.00 8.00
SOTMF Marshall Faulk 20.00 40.00
SOTPH Paul Hornung 15.00 30.00
SOTPM Peyton Manning 60.00 120.00
SOTRW Roy Williams WR 8.00 20.00
SOTSA Bob Sanders
SOTSI Billy Sims 10.00 25.00
SOTST Bart Starr SP 75.00 150.00
SOTSY Steve Young SP 40.00 80.00
SOTTA Troy Aikman SP 50.00 100.00
SOTWO Rod Woodson 40.00 80.00
SOTWW Wes Welker

2008 SP Authentic Sign of the Times Duals

STATED PRINT RUN 20-100
AL D.Anderson/J.Lewis/50 8.00 20.00
AM O.Andrsn/Eli/20 50.00 100.00
BG D.Bess/Grice-Mullen
BP Booty/Peterson/20 60.00 120.00
CD Rodgers-Cromartie/Doucet/99 20.00 40.00
CH D.Connor/A.Hawk/80 12.00 30.00
CK A.Caldwell/M.Kelly/99 10.00 25.00
DC F.Dvs/Carlson/90 10.00 25.00
GH Griese/Henne/50 15.00 40.00
GW F.Gore/P.Willis/50 30.00 60.00
HH Henne/Hart/50 20.00 40.00
JC F.Jns/Charles/75 30.00 60.00
JR Jhnstn/Rthmn/100 30.00 60.00
MD K.Davis/M.Monk/80 10.00 25.00
MJ McFad/Jones/20 20.00 50.00
MM P.Manning/Eli/20 125.00 200.00
MP D.Mrgn/Philips/50 8.00 20.00
MS Mendn/Stwrt/50 15.00 40.00
RD J.Russell/E.Doucet
RM Roeth/Mendenhl/20 60.00 120.00
SB B.Snders/K.Smth/20 75.00 150.00
SF Sayers/Forte/50 30.00 80.00
TC Theis/Cmpbll/50 EXCH 20.00 50.00
TF Tomlinson/M.Faulk/50 40.00 80.00
TM Tmlin/McFad/20 40.00 100.00
WC C.Campbell/D.Ware/80 12.00 30.00

2008 SP Authentic Sign of the Times Triples

STATED PRINT RUN 25-50
RJM McKlvn/Rdgrs-Crmrt/Jnkns 8.00 20.00
LJH Jcksn/Lynch/Hwkn EXCH 30.00 60.00
MTP Tittle/Eli/Phillips 50.00 100.00
SSS K.Smth/Sndrs/Sms 75.00 150.00

2008 SP Authentic SP Numbers Signatures

STATED PRINT RUN 15-150
NPAP Adrian Peterson/15 125.00 200.00
NPBB Brian Brohm/35 12.00 30.00
NPBG Bob Griese/35 15.00 40.00
NPBJ Bo Jackson/15 60.00 120.00
NPBO Brian Bosworth/150 15.00 40.00
NPCB Chuck Bednarik/150 12.00 30.00
NPCH Chad Henne/150 8.00 20.00
NPCL Chris Long/150 8.00 20.00
NPDB Dick Butkus/45 40.00 80.00
NPDM Don Maynard/150 12.00 30.00
NPDT Devin Thomas/150 6.00 15.00
NPEM Eli Manning/99 50.00 100.00
NPFA Marshall Faulk/35 25.00 50.00
NPFJ Felix Jones/150 3.00 8.00
NPFT Fran Tarkenton/35 30.00 60.00
NPJF Joe Flacco/150 6.00 15.00
NPJK Jim Kelly/15 40.00 80.00
NPJS Jeremy Shockey/35 12.00 30.00
NPJT Joe Theismann/150 15.00 40.00
NPKA Ken Anderson/150 12.00 30.00
NPKR Jerry Kramer/135 12.00 30.00
NPKS Kevin Smith/150 6.00 15.00
NPLH Lester Hayes/150 12.00 30.00
NPLT LaDainian Tomlinson/15 40.00 80.00
NPMB Marion Barber/35 12.00 30.00
NPMC Darren McFadden
NPMF Matt Forte/150 15.00 40.00
NPMR Matt Ryan/75 50.00 100.00
NPOA Ottis Anderson/150 10.00 25.00
NPPH Paul Hornung/135 15.00 40.00
NPPM Peyton Manning/99 75.00 150.00
NPPW Patrick Willis/150 10.00 25.00
NPRG Roman Gabriel/150 15.00 40.00
NPRM Rashard Mendenhall/150 6.00 15.00
NPRW Rod Woodson/135 20.00 50.00
NPSY Steve Young
NPTR Tony Romo/99 50.00 100.00
NPWI Roy Williams WR/15 20.00 40.00
NPYT Y.A. Tittle/135 15.00 40.00

2008 SP Authentic SP Star Signatures

SPSS1 Patrick Willis 10.00 25.00
SPSS2 Kenny Irons 8.00 20.00
SPSS3 Aaron Ross 8.00 20.00
SPSS4 Craig Davis 8.00 20.00
SPSS5 Chris Henry RB 10.00 25.00
SPSS6 Jerious Norwood 8.00 20.00
SPSS7 Kevin Boss 8.00 20.00
SPSS8 Yamon Figurs 8.00 20.00
SPSS9 Garrett Wolfe 10.00 25.00
SPSS10 Ahmad Bradshaw 8.00 20.00
SPSS11 Bernard Berrian 8.00 20.00
SPSS12 John Lynch 10.00 25.00
SPSS13 Greg Jennings 8.00 20.00
SPSS14 Anquan Boldin 8.00 20.00
SPSS15 Marques Colston 8.00 20.00
SPSS16 Willie Parker 10.00 25.00
SPSS17 Ted Ginn Jr. 8.00 20.00
SPSS18 Brandon Jacobs 12.00 30.00
SPSS19 Mark Clayton 8.00 20.00
SPSS20 Jerricho Cotchery 8.00 20.00
SPSS21 Champ Bailey 10.00 25.00
SPSS22 Darrell Jackson 8.00 20.00
SPSS23 Brady Quinn 8.00 20.00
SPSS24 John Beck 8.00 20.00
SPSS25 Derek Anderson 8.00 20.00

2009 SP Authentic

COMP.SET w/o RC's (100) 8.00 20.00
101-200 SP STATED ODDS 1:6
201-300 ROOKIE PRINT RUN 999
301-370 ROOKIE AU PRINT RUN 299-999
371-400 JSY AU RC PRINT RUN 475-999
EXCH EXPIRATION: 1/26/2012
1 Tony Romo .25 .60
2 Marion Barber .25 .60
3 Roy Williams WR .20 .50
4 Jason Witten .25 .60
5 Eli Manning .25 .60
6 Brandon Jacobs .20 .50
7 Ahmad Bradshaw .20 .50
8 Steve Smith USC .25 .60
9 Donovan McNabb .25 .60
10 Brian Westbrook .20 .50
11 DeSean Jackson .25 .60
12 Jason Campbell .20 .50
13 Clinton Portis .20 .50
14 Santana Moss .25 .60
15 Trent Edwards .20 .50
16 Marshawn Lynch .25 .60
17 Terrell Owens .25 .60
18 Chad Pennington .20 .50
19 Ronnie Brown .20 .50
20 Ted Ginn .20 .50
21 Tom Brady 1.00 2.50
22 Randy Moss .25 .60
23 Wes Welker .25 .60
24 Jerod Mayo .25 .60
25 Kellen Clemens .20 .50
26 Thomas Jones .20 .50
27 Jerricho Cotchery .20 .50
28 Bart Scott .20 .50
29 Kurt Warner .25 .60
30 Anquan Boldin .20 .50
31 Larry Fitzgerald .25 .60
32 Shaun Hill .20 .50
33 Frank Gore .25 .60
34 Patrick Willis .25 .60
35 Matt Hasselbeck .20 .50
36 T.J. Houshmandzadeh .20 .50
37 Lofa Tatupu .20 .50
38 Marc Bulger .20 .50
39 Steven Jackson .20 .50
40 Donnie Avery .20 .50
41 Kyle Orton .20 .50
42 Eddie Royal .20 .50
43 Brian Dawkins .20 .50
44 Matt Cassel .20 .50
45 Larry Johnson .20 .50
46 Dwayne Bowe .25 .60
47 JaMarcus Russell .20 .50
48 Darren McFadden .30 .75
49 Nnamdi Asomugha .20 .50
50 Philip Rivers .30 .75
51 LaDainian Tomlinson .30 .75
52 Shawne Merriman .20 .50
53 Jay Cutler .20 .50
54 Matt Forte .20 .50
55 Brian Urlacher .30 .75
56 Daunte Culpepper .25 .60
57 Kevin Smith .20 .50
58 Calvin Johnson .30 .75
59 Aaron Rodgers .60 1.50
60 Ryan Grant .25 .60
61 Greg Jennings .20 .50
62 Brett Favre 2.50 6.00
63 Adrian Peterson .30 .75
64 Bernard Berrian .20 .50
65 Joe Flacco .25 .60
66 Ray Lewis .30 .75
67 Ed Reed .25 .60
68 Carson Palmer .25 .60
69 Chad Ochocinco .20 .50
70 Laveranues Coles .20 .50
71 Brady Quinn .20 .50
72 Jamal Lewis .25 .60
73 Braylon Edwards .20 .50
74 Ben Roethlisberger .30 .75
75 James Harrison .30 .75
76 Troy Polamalu .30 .75
77 Matt Ryan .25 .60
78 Michael Turner .20 .50
79 Roddy White .20 .50
80 Jake Delhomme .20 .50
81 DeAngelo Williams .20 .50
82 Jonathan Stewart .20 .50
83 Drew Brees .30 .75
84 Reggie Bush .20 .50
85 Marques Colston .20 .50
86 Luke McCown .20 .50
87 Derrick Ward .20 .50
88 Antonio Bryant .20 .50
89 Matt Schaub .20 .50
90 Steve Slaton .20 .50
91 Andre Johnson .25 .60
92 Peyton Manning .75 2.00
93 Joseph Addai .20 .50
94 Reggie Wayne .25 .60
95 David Garrard .20 .50
96 Maurice Jones-Drew .20 .50
97 John Henderson .20 .50
98 Kerry Collins .20 .50
99 Chris Johnson .20 .50
100 LenDale White .20 .50
101 Archie Manning 1.50 4.00
102 Lem Barney 1.25 3.00
103 Steve Young 2.50 6.00

104 Dan Marino 4.00 10.00
105 Drew Bledsoe 1.50 4.00
106 Jim Kelly 2.00 5.00
107 Joe Theismann 2.00 5.00
108 Ken Anderson 1.50 4.00
109 Randall Cunningham 1.50 4.00
110 Mike Singletary 2.00 5.00
111 Terry Bradshaw 2.50 6.00
112 Warren Moon 2.00 5.00
113 Y.A. Tittle 2.00 5.00
114 Barry Sanders 3.00 8.00
115 Billy Sims 1.50 4.00
116 Christian Okoye 1.25 3.00
117 Earl Campbell 2.00 5.00
118 Franco Harris 2.00 5.00
119 Alan Page 1.25 3.00
120 Paul Hornung 2.00 5.00
121 Bob Griese 2.00 5.00
122 Doug Flutie 1.50 4.00
123 Thurman Thomas 1.50 4.00
124 Andre Reed 1.50 4.00
125 Phil Simms 1.50 4.00
126 Don Maynard 1.50 4.00
127 Herman Moore 1.25 3.00
128 Jerry Rice 4.00 10.00
129 Tim Brown 2.00 5.00
130 Steve Largent 2.00 5.00
131 T.Romo/J.Witten 1.50 4.00
132 M.Barber/F.Jones 1.50 4.00
133 E.Manning/B.Jacobs 1.50 4.00
134 D.McNabb/B.Westbrook 1.50 4.00
135 J.Campbell/C.Portis 1.25 3.00
136 M.Lynch/T.Edwards 1.50 4.00
137 R.Williams/R.Brown 1.50 4.00
138 R.Moss/T.Brady 1.50 4.00
139 T.Jones/L.Washington 1.25 3.00
140 A.Boldin/L.Fitzgerald 1.50 4.00
141 T.Spikes/P.Willis 1.50 4.00
142 Hasselbeck/Houshmandzadeh 1.25 3.00
143 D.Avery/S.Jackson 1.25 3.00
144 E.Royal/B.Marshall 1.50 4.00
145 D.Bowe/M.Cassel 1.50 4.00
146 J.Russell/D.McFadden 2.00 5.00
147 V.Jackson/P.Rivers 2.00 5.00
148 D.Sproles/L.Tomlinson 2.00 5.00
149 J.Cutler/M.Forte 1.25 3.00
150 L.Briggs/B.Urlacher 2.00 5.00
151 C.Johnson/K.Smith 2.00 5.00
152 A.Rodgers/G.Jennings 4.00 10.00
153 J.Allen/A.Peterson 2.00 5.00
154 E.Reed/R.Lewis 2.00 5.00
155 C.Ochocinco/C.Palmer 1.50 4.00
156 B.Quinn/B.Edwards 1.25 3.00
157 Holmes/Roethlisberger 2.00 5.00
158 M.Turner/M.Ryan 1.50 4.00
159 J.Stewart/D.Williams 1.25 3.00
160 D.Brees/R.Bush 2.50 6.00
161 R.Barber/B.Ruud 1.25 3.00
162 A.Johnson/S.Slaton 1.50 4.00
163 P.Manning/R.Wayne 5.00 12.00
164 D.Garrard/M.Jones-Drew 1.25 3.00
165 C.Johnson/L.White 1.25 3.00
166 Barber/Witten/Romo 1.50 4.00
167 Jacobs/Manning/Smith 1.50 4.00
168 Westbrook/McNabb/Jackson 1.50 4.00
169 Portis/Moss/Campbell 1.50 4.00
170 Owens/Evans/Lynch 1.50 4.00
171 Pennington/Porter/Brown 1.50 4.00
172 Brady/Moss/Welker 6.00 15.00
173 Keller/Jones/Cotchery 1.25 3.00
174 Boldin/Fitzgerald/Warner 1.50 4.00
175 Bruce/Gore/Morgan 2.00 5.00
176 Hasselbeck/Housh/Jones 1.25 3.00
177 Avery/Jackson/Bulger 1.25 3.00
178 Royal/Marshall/Orton 1.50 4.00
179 Johnson/Cassel/Bowe 1.50 4.00
180 Russell/Bush/McFadden 2.00 5.00
181 Tomlinson/Gates/Rivers 2.00 5.00
182 Merriman/Cromartie/Jammer 1.25 3.00
183 Cutler/Olsen/Forte 1.50 4.00
184 Urlacher/Brown/Briggs 2.00 5.00
185 Smith/Johnson/Peterson 2.00 5.00
186 Grant/Rodgers/Jennings 4.00 10.00
187 Berrian/Peterson/Tylr 2.00 5.00
188 Reed/Lewis/Landry 2.00 5.00
189 Ochocinco/Coles/Palmer 1.50 4.00
190 Lewis/Edwards/Quinn 1.50 4.00
191 Ward/Parker/Roeth 2.00 5.00
192 Polamalu/Harrison/Woodley 2.00 5.00
193 Turner/White/Ryan 1.50 4.00
194 Smith/Williams/Stewart 1.50 4.00
195 Brees/Bush/Colston 2.00 5.00
196 Ward/Bryant/Winslow 1.25 3.00
197 Slaton/Johnson/Schaub 1.50 4.00
198 Manning/Wayne/Clark 5.00 12.00
199 Jones-Drew/Garrard/Lewis 1.25 3.00
200 Vanden Bosch/Finnegan/Bulluck 1.25 3.00
201 Greg Toler RC 2.00 5.00
202 Herman Johnson RC 2.50 6.00
203 LaRod Stephens-Howling RC 4.00 10.00
204 Christopher Owens RC 2.00 5.00
205 Lawrence Sidbury RC 2.00 5.00
206 William Middleton RC 2.00 5.00
207 Paul Kruger RC 3.00 8.00
208 Lardarius Webb RC 3.00 8.00
209 Jason Phillips RC 2.50 6.00
210 Aaron Maybin RC 2.50 6.00
211 Andy Levitre RC 2.50 6.00
212 Nic Harris RC 2.50 6.00
213 Sherrod Martin RC 2.00 5.00
214 Corvey Irvin RC 2.00 5.00
215 Duke Robinson RC 2.00 5.00
216 Captain Munnerlyn RC 2.50 6.00
217 Henry Melton RC 2.00 5.00
218 Derek Kinder RC 2.00 5.00
219 D.J. Moore RC 2.50 6.00
220 Marcus Freeman RC 2.00 5.00
221 Jonathan Luigs RC 2.00 5.00
222 Morgan Trent RC 2.50 6.00
223 Kevin Huber RC 2.00 5.00
224 Fui Vakapuna RC 2.50 6.00
225 Freddie Brown RC 2.00 5.00
226 Ricky Jean-Francois RC 2.50 6.00
227 David Veikune RC 2.50 6.00
228 Coye Francies RC 2.00 5.00
229 Victor Butler RC 2.50 6.00
230 Jason Williams RC 2.50 6.00
231 Curtis Taylor RC 2.50 6.00
232 Clinton McDonald RC 2.50 6.00
233 Manuel Johnson RC 2.00 5.00
234 Ellis Lankster RC 2.00 5.00
235 Darcel McBath RC 2.00 5.00
236 David Bruton RC 2.00 5.00
237 Kareem Huggins RC 3.00 8.00
238 DeAndre Levy RC 2.50 6.00
239 Will Davis RC 2.00 5.00
240 Aaron Brown RC 2.50 6.00
241 T.J. Lang RC 2.50 6.00
242 Jamon Meredith RC 2.00 5.00
243 Jarius Wynn RC 2.50 6.00
244 Antoine Caldwell RC 2.00 5.00
245 Glover Quin RC 2.50 6.00
246 James Casey RC 2.50 6.00
247 Brice McCain RC 2.00 5.00
248 Jerraud Powers RC 2.00 5.00
249 Louis Murphy RC 2.00 5.00
250 Jaimie Thomas RC 2.00 5.00
251 Tiquan Underwood RC 2.00 5.00
252 Eben Britton RC 2.50 6.00
253 Terrance Knighton RC 3.00 8.00
254 Derek Cox RC 3.00 8.00
255 Zach Miller RC 2.50 6.00
256 Alex Magee RC 2.50 6.00
257 Donald Washington RC 2.50 6.00
258 Colin Brown RC 2.50 6.00
259 Javarris Williams RC 2.50 6.00
260 Jake O'Connell RC 2.00 5.00
261 John Matthews RC 2.50 6.00
262 John Parker Wilson RC 2.00 5.00
263 Spencer Adkins RC 2.00 5.00
264 Phil Loadholt RC 2.50 6.00
265 Jasper Brinkley RC 2.50 6.00
266 Jamarca Sanford RC 2.50 6.00
267 Ron Brace RC 2.50 6.00
268 Sebastian Vollmer RC 2.50 6.00
269 Brian Hoyer RC 3.00 8.00
270 Connor Barwin RC 2.50 6.00
271 Chip Vaughn RC 2.00 5.00
272 DeAndre Wright RC 2.00 5.00
273 Clint Sintim RC 2.00 5.00
274 William Beatty RC 2.00 5.00
275 Matt Slauson RC 3.00 8.00
276 Mike Mitchell RC 2.00 5.00
277 Matt Shaughnessy RC 2.50 6.00
278 Slade Norris RC 2.00 5.00
279 Fenuki Tupou RC 2.00 5.00
280 Brandon Gibson RC 2.50 6.00
281 Kraig Urbik RC 2.50 6.00
282 Joe Burnett RC 3.00 8.00
283 Evander Hood RC 3.00 8.00
284 Brandon Underwood RC 2.00 5.00
285 Louis Vasquez RC 2.50 6.00
286 Vaughn Martin RC 2.00 5.00
287 Kevin Ellison RC 2.00 5.00
288 Brandon Hughes RC 2.00 5.00
289 Ronald Talley RC 2.50 6.00
290 Scott McKillop RC 2.00 5.00
291 Bear Pascoe RC 2.50 6.00
292 Courtney Greene RC 2.00 5.00
293 Bradley Fletcher RC 2.00 5.00
294 Darell Scott RC 2.00 5.00
295 Shawn Nelson RC 2.00 5.00
296 Sammie Stroughter RC 2.00 5.00
297 Kyle Moore RC 2.50 6.00
298 Dominique Edison RC 2.00 5.00
299 David Johnson RC 2.50 6.00
300 Marko Mitchell RC 2.00 5.00
301 Asher Allen AU RC 3.00 8.00
302 Anthony Hill AU RC 3.00 8.00
303 Alex Mack AU RC 3.00 8.00
304 Bernard Scott AU RC 5.00 12.00
305 Julian Edelman AU RC 150.00 300.00
306 Cornelius Ingram AU RC 3.00 8.00
307 Cody Brown AU RC 3.00 8.00
308 DeAngelo Smith AU RC 5.00 12.00
309 Eric Wood AU RC 3.00 8.00
310 Gerald McRath AU RC 4.00 10.00
311 Jairus Byrd AU RC 8.00 20.00
312 Jarett Dillard AU RC 3.00 8.00
313 Malcolm Jenkins AU RC 3.00 8.00
314 Jarron Gilbert AU RC 4.00 10.00
315 Johnny Knox AU RC 4.00 10.00
316 Rashad Johnson AU RC 3.00 8.00
317 Kevin Barnes AU RC 3.00 8.00
318 Keenan Lewis AU RC 5.00 12.00
319 Kenny McKinley AU RC 3.00 8.00
320 Keith Null AU RC 4.00 10.00
321 Roy Miller AU RC 3.00 8.00
322 Mike Teel AU RC 6.00 15.00
323 Max Unger AU RC 5.00 12.00
324 Quinn Johnson AU RC 3.00 8.00
325 Quinten Lawrence AU RC 3.00 8.00
326 Mike Mickens AU RC 3.00 8.00
327 Richard Quinn AU RC 4.00 10.00
328 Ryan Mouton AU RC 3.00 8.00
329 Sean Smith AU RC 3.00 8.00
330 Tony Fiammetta AU RC 3.00 8.00
331 Austin Collie AU/799 RC 3.00 8.00
332 Andre Smith AU/799 RC 3.00 8.00
333 Travis Beckum AU/799 RC 3.00 8.00
334 Brooks Foster AU/799 RC 3.00 8.00
335 Cedric Peerman AU/799 RC 3.00 8.00
336 Darius Butler AU/799 RC 4.00 10.00
337 Eugene Monroe AU/799 RC 3.00 8.00
338 Fili Moala AU/799 RC 3.00 8.00
339 Frank Summers AU/799 RC 5.00 12.00
340 Gartrell Johnson AU/799 RC 3.00 8.00
341 Louis Delmas AU/799 RC 8.00 20.00
342 Mike Goodson AU/799 RC 4.00 10.00
343 M.Johnson AU/799 RC 3.00 8.00
344 Curtis Painter AU/799 RC 3.00 8.00
345 Patrick Chung AU/799 RC 5.00 12.00
346 C.Ogbonnaya AU/999 RC 4.00 10.00
347 R.Jennings AU/799 RC 6.00 15.00
348 Alphonso Smith AU/799 RC 3.00 8.00
349 Victor Harris AU/799 RC 4.00 10.00
350 William Moore AU/799 RC 3.00 8.00
351 Brian Cushing AU/299 RC 8.00 20.00
352 Brian Hartline AU/299 RC 12.50 25.00
354 B.J. Raji AU/299 RC 12.50 25.00
355 Brandon Tate AU/299 RC 10.00 25.00
356 Chase Coffman AU/299 RC 5.00 12.00
357 Clay Matthews AU/299 RC 40.00 80.00
359 Everette Brown AU/299 RC 5.00 12.00
360 Graham Harrell AU/299 RC 20.00 40.00
362 J.Laurinaitis AU/299 RC 10.00 25.00
363 Larry English AU/299 RC 6.00 15.00
364 Terrance Taylor AU/999 RC 4.00 10.00
365 Michael Oher AU/299 RC 25.00 60.00
366 Rudy Carpenter AU/299 RC 6.00 15.00
367 Rey Maualuga AU/299 RC 8.00 20.00
368 Kaluka Maiava AU/999 RC 3.00 8.00
370 Vontae Davis AU/299 RC 5.00 12.00
371 A.Brown JSY AU/999 RC 10.00 25.00
372 A.Curry JSY AU/999 RC 12.00 30.00
373 Rhett Bomar JSY AU/999 RC 8.00 20.00
374 B.Pettigrew JSY AU/999 RC 10.00 25.00
375 B.Robiskie JSY AU/999 RC 8.00 20.00
376 Deon Butler JSY AU/999 RC 8.00 20.00
377 Chris Wells JSY AU/499 RC 8.00 20.00
378 D.Brown JSY AU/499 RC 10.00 25.00
379 D.Heyward-Bey JSY AU/499 RC 12.00 30.00
380 D.Williams JSY AU/999 RC 8.00 20.00
381 Glen Coffee JSY AU/999 RC 8.00 20.00
382 H.Nicks JSY AU/999 RC 10.00 25.00
383 J.Freeman JSY AU/999 RC 8.00 20.00
384 J.Iglesias JSY AU/999 RC 8.00 20.00
385 J.Maclin JSY AU/999 RC 10.00 25.00
386 J.Ringer JSY AU/999 RC 8.00 20.00
387 Jason Smith JSY AU/999 RC 8.00 20.00
388 Kenny Britt JSY AU/999 RC 12.00 30.00
389 K.Moreno JSY AU/499 RC 8.00 20.00
390 L.McCoy JSY AU/999 RC 15.00 40.00
391 M.Crabtree JSY AU/499 RC 12.00 30.00
392 M.Massaquoi JSY AU/999 RC 8.00 20.00
393 M.Sanchez JSY AU/499 RC 12.00 30.00
394 M.Thomas JSY AU/999 RC 8.00 20.00
395 M.Wallace JSY AU/999 RC 12.00 30.00
396 Nate Davis JSY AU/999 RC 8.00 20.00
397 P.Harvin JSY AU/999 RC 8.00 20.00
398 P.Turner JSY AU/999 RC 8.00 20.00
399 Pat White JSY AU/999 RC 10.00 25.00
400 R.Barden JSY AU/999 RC 8.00 20.00
401 S.Greene JSY AU/999 RC 8.00 20.00
402 S.McGee JSY AU/999 RC 8.00 20.00
403 M.Stafford JSY AU/499 RC 75.00 150.00
404 T.Jackson JSY AU/999 RC 8.00 20.00

2009 SP Authentic Bronze

*ROOKIES: .5X TO 1.2X BASIC CARDS
STATED PRINT RUN 150 SER.#'d SETS

2009 SP Authentic Gold

*201-300 ROOK/50: .8X TO 2X BASIC RC/999
201-300 ROOKIE PRINT RUN 50
*ROOKIE JSY AU/25: 1.2X TO 3X BASIC RC
371-404 ROOKIE JSY AU PRINT RUN 25
383 Josh Freeman JSY AU 25.00 60.00
390 LeSean McCoy JSY AU 175.00 350.00
393 Mark Sanchez JSY AU 175.00 300.00
397 Percy Harvin JSY AU 25.00 60.00
403 Matthew Stafford JSY AU 350.00 600.00

2009 SP Authentic Autographs

OVERALL AUTO ODDS 1:8 HOB
*GOLD/25: .6X TO 1.5X BASIC INSERTS
GOLD PRINT RUN 25 SER.#'d SETS
SPAB Andre Brown 4.00 10.00
SPAN Shawn Andrews 4.00 10.00
SPBC Brian Cushing 3.00 8.00
SPBO Brian Orakpo 8.00 20.00
SPBP Brandon Pettigrew 3.00 8.00
SPBU Deon Butler 3.00 8.00
SPCM Clay Matthews 25.00 60.00
SPCO Christian Okoye 6.00 15.00
SPDB Donald Brown 8.00 20.00
SPDW Derrick Williams 3.00 8.00
SPEC Earl Campbell 20.00 50.00
SPGC Greg Camarillo 5.00 12.00
SPHC Harry Carson 10.00 25.00
SPJF Josh Freeman 3.00 8.00
SPJP Joey Porter 6.00 15.00
SPJS Jason Smith 3.00 8.00
SPJY Jack Youngblood 10.00 25.00
SPLB Lem Barney 8.00 20.00
SPMW Mike Wallace 5.00 12.00
SPPT Patrick Turner 3.00 8.00
SPPW Pat White
SPQJ Quentin Jammer 6.00 15.00
SPRB Ramses Barden 3.00 8.00
SPSA Stacy Andrews 4.00 10.00
SPSG Shonn Greene 10.00 25.00
SPTJ Tyson Jackson 3.00 8.00
SPWA DeMarcus Ware 10.00 25.00
SPWM Warren Moon 15.00 40.00

2009 SP Authentic By the Letter Autographs

SER.#'d 3-90, TOTAL PRINT RUNS 21-98
EXCH EXPIRATION: 1/26/2012
LETTERS SPELL THE PLAYER'S TEAM NAME
BLSAH Albert Haynesworth/40* 15.00 40.00
BLSAK Alex Karras/72* 12.00 30.00
BLSAP Alan Page/42* 25.00 60.00
BLSBR Derrick Brooks/90* 25.00 50.00
BLSBW Brian Westbrook/24* 15.00 40.00
BLSCM Craig Morton/98* 10.00 25.00
BLSCO Christian Okoye/96* 12.00 30.00
BLSCP Clinton Portis/24* 15.00 40.00
BLSDB Drew Bledsoe/24* 30.00 60.00
BLSDE DeSean Jackson/45* 15.00 40.00
BLSDJ Deacon Jones/68* 12.00 30.00
BLSDR Drew Brees/24* 75.00 135.00
BLSDS Donnie Shell/64* 15.00 40.00
BLSDW DeMarcus Ware/35* 15.00 40.00
BLSGA Roman Gabriel/68* 10.00 25.00
BLSGC Greg Camarillo/96* 10.00 25.00
BLSHC Harry Carson/96* 12.00 30.00
BLSJA Jared Allen/98* 40.00 80.00
BLSJP Joey Porter/56* 15.00 40.00
BLSLB Lance Briggs/50* 25.00 50.00
BLSLE Lem Barney/95* 10.00 25.00
BLSLM Lance Moore/72* 40.00 80.00
BLSMC Matt Cassel/36* 15.00 40.00
BLSMD Maurice Jones-Drew/35* 15.00 40.00
BLSMF Matt Forte/30* 25.00 60.00
BLSMT Michael Turner/21* 25.00 50.00
BLSMW Mario Williams/50* 12.00 30.00
BLSPH Paul Hornung/63* 15.00 40.00
BLSPM Peyton Manning/60* 100.00 200.00
BLSPS Phil Simms/20* 15.00 40.00
BLSPW Patrick Willis/40* 30.00 60.00
BLSRB Rocky Bleier/64* 30.00 80.00
BLSRC Randall Cunningham/24* 40.00 80.00
BLSRL Ray Lewis/24* 125.00 200.00
BLSRW Reggie Wayne/35* 15.00 40.00
BLSSI Billy Sims/95* 12.00 30.00
BLSWO Rod Woodson/20* EXCH 40.00 80.00
BLSWP William Perry/70* 15.00 40.00

2009 SP Authentic Chirography

OVERALL AUTO ODDS 1:8 HOB
EXCH EXPIRATION: 1/26/2012
*GOLD/25: .6X TO 1.5X BASIC AUTO
CHAM Anthony Munoz 10.00 25.00
CHBC Brian Cushing 5.00 12.00
CHBP Brandon Pettigrew 3.00 8.00
CHBR Brian Robiskie 3.00 8.00
CHCF Glen Coffee 3.00 8.00
CHCM Clay Matthews 25.00 60.00
CHCP Clinton Portis 10.00 25.00
CHDB Drew Bledsoe 15.00 30.00
CHDQ D'Qwell Jackson 4.00 10.00
CHEM Eli Manning 30.00 60.00
CHFG Frank Gore 6.00 15.00
CHGC Greg Camarillo 5.00 12.00
CHJC Jason Campbell 6.00 15.00
CHJM Jerod Mayo 5.00 12.00
CHJP Joey Porter 6.00 15.00
CHJR Javon Ringer 3.00 8.00
CHJS Jason Smith 3.00 8.00
CHJY Jack Youngblood 10.00 25.00
CHKW Kurt Warner 40.00 80.00
CHMC Matt Cassel 6.00 15.00
CHML Marshawn Lynch 6.00 15.00
CHNA Nnamdi Asomugha 6.00 15.00
CHND Nate Davis 5.00 12.00
CHPH Percy Harvin 3.00 8.00
CHPM Peyton Manning 60.00 120.00
CHPW Pat White 4.00 10.00
CHRB Ronnie Brown 6.00 15.00
CHRM Rey Maualuga 6.00 15.00
CHSG Shonn Greene 12.00 30.00
CHSM Stephen McGee 6.00 15.00
CHST Matthew Stafford 25.00 60.00
CHSZ Mark Sanchez 12.00 30.00
CHTR Tony Romo 30.00 60.00

2009 SP Authentic Chirography Duals

STATED PRINT RUN 25-75
AJ J.Allen/T.Jackson/50 25.00 50.00
AP A.Curry/P.Willis/50 12.00 30.00
BC A.Curry/D.Butler/75 12.00 30.00
BJ J.Porter/R.Brown/75 12.00 30.00
BK K.Warner/A.Boldin/50 25.00 50.00
BN H.Nicks/A.Brown/75 12.00 30.00
CH G.Harrell/M.Crabtree/50 20.00 50.00
CS M.Sanchez/M.Cassel/50 20.00 50.00
FD N.Davis/J.Freeman/50 12.00 30.00
GC F.Gore/G.Coffee/50 15.00 40.00
GS G.Coffee/S.Greene/75 25.00 60.00
JC C.Wells/J.Ringer/50 15.00 40.00
JL Jones-Drew/M.Lynch/50 12.00 30.00
JS J.Smith/J.Laurinaitis/75 10.00 25.00
MY A.Munoz/R.Yary/50 15.00 40.00
PC C.Portis/J.Campbell/25 15.00 40.00
RR R.Barden/R.Bomar/75 10.00 25.00
RW C.Wells/B.Robiskie/50 15.00 40.00
SC M.Schaub/S.Slaton/25 20.00 50.00
SP M.Stafford/B.Pettigrew/50 40.00 100.00
SW S.Slaton/P.White/50 15.00 40.00
TC Tarkenton/Cunningham/25 40.00 80.00
WC A.Curry/D.Ware/50 12.00 30.00
WP B.Pettigrew/D.Williams/75 10.00 25.00
WS M.Sanchez/P.White/25 40.00 80.00
YO M.Olsen/J.Youngblood/35 30.00 60.00
XLIII Roethlisberger/Warner/50 125.00 200.00

2009 SP Authentic Chirography Triples

STATED PRINT RUN 10-35
BMD Bomar/Davis/McGee/35 12.00 30.00
CLE English/Laurin/Curry/35 15.00 40.00
CNB Crabtree/Nicks/Britt/25 20.00 50.00
OSU Laurin/Robiskie/Wells/25 30.00 60.00
PIT Hood/Smmrs/Wllace/25 40.00 100.00
SDC Byrd/English/Johnson/35 12.00 30.00
SSF Frman/Sanchz/Stffrd/25 100.00 200.00
USC Maual/Mtthws/Cshing/25 40.00 80.00

2009 SP Authentic Dynasties Autographs

STATED PRINT RUN 20 SER.#'d SETS
SADES Emmitt Smith 100.00 200.00
SADFH Franco Harris 40.00 80.00
SADJH Jack Ham 40.00 80.00
SADJK Jerry Kramer 25.00 50.00
SADJR Jerry Rice 100.00 200.00
SADLG L.C. Greenwood 30.00 60.00
SADPH Paul Hornung 30.00 60.00
SADRB Rocky Bleier 40.00 80.00
SADRC Roger Craig 30.00 60.00
SADRL Ronnie Lott 50.00 100.00
SADSH Donnie Shell 30.00 60.00
SADSY Steve Young 60.00 120.00
SADTA Troy Aikman 60.00 120.00
SADTB Terry Bradshaw
SADTR Tom Rathman 30.00 60.00

2009 SP Authentic Immortals Autographs

STATED PRINT RUN 25 SER.#'d SETS
EXCH EXPIRATION: 1/26/2012
ISBS Barry Sanders 75.00 150.00
ISFH Franco Harris
ISJH Jack Ham 25.00 50.00
ISJT Joe Theismann 25.00 50.00
ISJY Jack Youngblood 15.00 40.00
ISKW Kellen Winslow Sr. 15.00 30.00
ISLB Lem Barney 15.00 30.00
ISLG L.C. Greenwood 30.00 60.00
ISLT Lawrence Taylor 30.00 60.00
ISMO Merlin Olsen 20.00 40.00
ISPS Phil Simms 25.00 50.00
ISRB Rocky Bleier 25.00 50.00
ISRC Randall Cunningham 25.00 50.00
ISRL Ronnie Lott 25.00 60.00
ISRY Ron Yary 15.00 30.00
ISSL Steve Largent 20.00 40.00
ISSY Steve Young 40.00 80.00
ISTA Troy Aikman 50.00 100.00
ISTT Thurman Thomas 25.00 50.00

2009 SP Authentic Immortals Autographs Duals

STATED PRINT RUN 15 SER.#'d SETS
EXCH EXPIRATION: 1/26/2012
SBS L.Barney/D.Shell 25.00 50.00
SHC F.Harris/E.Campbell 40.00 80.00
SJO M.Olsen/D.Jones 30.00 60.00
SMB D.Maynard/F.Biletnikoff 30.00 60.00
SSK A.Karras/B.Smith 25.00 50.00
SSS B.Sanders/G.Sayers 125.00 200.00
STC Taylor/Carson EXCH 40.00 80.00

2009 SP Authentic Rookie Super Patch Autographs

STATED PRINT RUN 99 SER.#'d SETS
RSPAC Aaron Curry 12.00 30.00
RSPBP Brandon Pettigrew 8.00 20.00
RSPBR Donald Brown 8.00 20.00
RSPCW Chris Wells 8.00 20.00
RSPDB Deon Butler 8.00 20.00
RSPDH Darrius Heyward-Bey 12.00 30.00
RSPDW Derrick Williams 8.00 20.00
RSPGC Glen Coffee 8.00 20.00
RSPHN Hakeem Nicks 10.00 25.00
RSPJF Josh Freeman 8.00 20.00
RSPJI Juaquin Iglesias 8.00 20.00
RSPJM Jeremy Maclin 12.00 30.00
RSPJR Javon Ringer 8.00 20.00
RSPJS Jason Smith 8.00 20.00
RSPKB Kenny Britt 12.00 30.00
RSPKM Knowshon Moreno 8.00 20.00
RSPLM LeSean McCoy 25.00 60.00
RSPMC Michael Crabtree 12.00 30.00
RSPMM Mohamed Massaquoi 8.00 20.00
RSPMS Matthew Stafford 50.00 100.00
RSPMW Mike Wallace 12.00 30.00
RSPND Nate Davis 8.00 20.00
RSPPH Percy Harvin 8.00 20.00
RSPPT Patrick Turner 8.00 20.00
RSPPW Pat White 10.00 25.00
RSPRB Ramses Barden 8.00 20.00
RSPSA Mark Sanchez 20.00 50.00
RSPSG Shonn Greene 8.00 20.00
RSPSM Stephen McGee 8.00 20.00
RSPTJ Tyson Jackson 8.00 20.00

2009 SP Authentic Sign of the Times

OVERALL AUTO ODDS 1:8 HOB
*GOLD/25: .6X TO 1.5X BASIC AUTO
EXCH EXPIRATION: 1/26/2012
STAB Anquan Boldin 8.00 20.00
STAC Aaron Curry 5.00 12.00
STAN Shawn Andrews 4.00 10.00
STBA Lem Barney 8.00 20.00
STBM Brandon Marshall 8.00 20.00
STDW DeMarcus Ware 10.00 25.00
STEV Lee Evans 5.00 12.00
STHN Hakeem Nicks 4.00 10.00
STJA Jared Allen 20.00 50.00
STJF Josh Freeman 3.00 8.00
STJR Javon Ringer 3.00 8.00
STKB Kenny Britt 5.00 12.00
STKM Knowshon Moreno 8.00 20.00
STKW Kurt Warner 40.00 80.00
STLB Lance Briggs 12.50 25.00
STLS LeSean McCoy 12.00 30.00
STMA Mark Sanchez 40.00 80.00
STMC Matt Cassel 10.00 25.00
STMF Matt Forte 8.00 20.00
STMJ Maurice Jones-Drew 8.00 20.00
STMS Matthew Stafford 40.00 100.00
STMW Mario Williams 5.00 12.00
STND Nate Davis 5.00 12.00
STPT Patrick Turner 3.00 8.00
STRB Ramses Barden 3.00 8.00
STRW Reggie Wayne 15.00 30.00
STRY Ron Yary 12.00 30.00
STSA Stacy Andrews 4.00 10.00
STSM Stephen McGee 6.00 15.00
STSS Steve Slaton 6.00 15.00
STTH Mike Thomas EXCH 3.00 8.00
STTJ Tyson Jackson 3.00 8.00
STTR Tony Romo 30.00 60.00

2009 SP Authentic Sign of the Times Duals

STATED PRINT RUN 10-100
EXCH EXPIRATION: 1/26/2012
AA St.Andrws/Sh.Andrws/100 8.00 20.00
AW J.Allen/M.Williams/50 20.00 50.00
BH B.Berrian/P.Harvin/50 8.00 20.00
BO D.Brees/K.Orton/50 50.00 100.00
CB Cassel/Bowe/50 8.00 20.00
CM Cunning/Moon/25 40.00 80.00
DD D.Williams/D.Butler/100 6.00 15.00
FI J.Iglesias/M.Forte/50 6.00 15.00
JC A.Curry/T.Jackson/100 6.00 15.00
JM Maclin/D.Jcksn/50 15.00 40.00
KK A.Karras/J.Kramer/50 30.00 60.00
LP J.Porter/R.Lewis/50 40.00 80.00
LW P.Willis/R.Lott/50 40.00 80.00
MB K.Moreno/D.Brown/50 10.00 25.00
NT H.Nicks/B.Tate/100 8.00 20.00
RS Schaub/Romo/50 30.00 60.00
SB Barney/B.Smth/75 15.00 40.00
SG Greene/Sanchez/50 10.00 25.00
SS Sanchz/Staffrd/25 40.00 80.00
SW S.Slaton/P.White/50 15.00 40.00
TT Turner/Tomlinson/25 30.00 60.00
WB D.Brown/C.Wells/50 8.00 20.00
WC D.Clark/R.Wayne/50 30.00 60.00
WF Forte/Westbrook/50 15.00 40.00
WR Robiskie/Hartline/100 10.00 25.00
NYG H.Carsn/L.Tylr/25 EXCH

2009 SP Authentic Sign of the Times Quads

STATED PRINT RUN 10-25
OLINE Yary/Andrews/Munoz/Andrews/25 20.00 40.00

2009 SP Authentic Sign of the Times Triples

STATED PRINT RUN 10-50
EXCH EXPIRATION: 1/26/2012
CMH Maclin/Harvin/Crabtree/25
HBN Britt/Heyward-Bey/Nicks/50 20.00 50.00
SSF Stafford/Frman/Sanchez/25 125.00 250.00
USC Csh/Malga/Mthw/50 40.00 80.00
WBM Brown/Wells/McCoy/25 20.00 50.00
49ER Crabtree/Davis/Coffee/25 30.00 80.00
SBQB Eli/Roeth/Manning/25 150.00 250.00

2009 SP Authentic Retail

COMP.SET w/o RC's (100) 8.00 20.00
1 Jason Campbell .15 .40
2 Clinton Portis .15 .40
3 Santana Moss .20 .50
4 Kerry Collins .15 .40
5 Chris Johnson .15 .40
6 LenDale White .15 .40
7 Luke McCown .15 .40
8 Derrick Ward .15 .40
9 Antonio Bryant .15 .40
10 Marc Bulger .15 .40
11 Steven Jackson .15 .40
12 Donnie Avery .15 .40
13 Matt Hasselbeck .15 .40
14 T.J. Houshmandzadeh .15 .40
15 Kyle Williams RC .15 .40
16 Alex Smith QB .25 .60
17 Frank Gore .20 .50
18 Patrick Willis .20 .50
19 Philip Rivers .25 .60
20 LaDainian Tomlinson .25 .60
21 Shawne Merriman .15 .40
22 Ben Roethlisberger .25 .60
23 James Harrison .25 .60
24 Troy Polamalu .25 .60
25 DeSean Jackson .20 .50
26 Donovan McNabb .20 .50
27 Brian Westbrook .15 .40
28 JaMarcus Russell .15 .40
29 Darren McFadden .25 .60
30 Nnamdi Asomugha .15 .40
31 Kellen Clemens .15 .40
32 Thomas Jones .15 .40
33 Jerricho Cotchery .15 .40
34 Bart Scott .15 .40
35 Eli Manning .20 .50
36 Brandon Jacobs .15 .40
37 Ahmad Bradshaw .15 .40
38 Steve Smith USC .20 .50
39 Drew Brees .25 .60
40 Reggie Bush .15 .40
41 Marques Colston .15 .40
42 Tom Brady .75 2.00
43 Randy Moss .20 .50
44 Wes Welker .20 .50
45 Jerod Mayo .20 .50
46 Tarvaris Jackson .20 .50
47 Adrian Peterson .25 .60
48 Bernard Berrian .15 .40
49 Chad Pennington .15 .40
50 Ronnie Brown .15 .40
51 Ted Ginn Jr. .15 .40
52 Matt Cassel .15 .40
53 Larry Johnson .15 .40
54 Dwayne Bowe .20 .50
55 David Garrard .15 .40
56 Maurice Jones-Drew .15 .40
57 John Henderson .15 .40
58 Peyton Manning .60 1.50
59 Joseph Addai .15 .40
60 Reggie Wayne .20 .50
61 Matt Schaub .15 .40
62 Steve Slaton .15 .40
63 Andre Johnson .20 .50
64 Aaron Rodgers .50 1.25
65 Ryan Grant .20 .50
66 Greg Jennings .15 .40
67 Daunte Culpepper .20 .50
68 Kevin Smith .15 .40
69 Calvin Johnson .25 .60
70 Kyle Orton .15 .40
71 Eddie Royal .15 .40
72 Brian Dawkins .15 .40
73 Tony Romo .20 .50
74 Marion Barber .20 .50
75 Roy Williams WR .15 .40
76 Jason Witten .20 .50
77 Brady Quinn .15 .40
78 Jamal Lewis .20 .50
79 Braylon Edwards .15 .40
80 Carson Palmer .20 .50
81 Chad Johnson .15 .40
82 Laveranues Coles .15 .40
83 Jay Cutler .15 .40
84 Matt Forte .15 .40
85 Brian Urlacher .25 .60
86 Jake Delhomme .15 .40
87 DeAngelo Williams .15 .40
88 Jonathan Stewart .15 .40
89 Trent Edwards .15 .40
90 Marshawn Lynch .20 .50
91 Terrell Owens .20 .50
92 Joe Flacco .20 .50
93 Ray Lewis .25 .60
94 Ed Reed .20 .50
95 Matt Ryan .20 .50
96 Michael Turner .15 .40
97 Roddy White .15 .40
98 Kurt Warner .20 .50
99 Anquan Boldin .15 .40
100 Larry Fitzgerald .20 .50
101 Aaron Maybin RC 1.00 2.50
102 Aaron Curry RC 1.25 3.00
103 Rhett Bomar RC .75 2.00
104 Brandon Pettigrew RC .75 2.00
105 Brian Robiskie RC .75 2.00
106 Deon Butler RC .75 2.00
107 Chris Wells RC .75 2.00
108 Donald Brown RC .75 2.00
109 Darrius Heyward-Bey RC 1.25 3.00
110 Derrick Williams RC .75 2.00
111 Kevin Ellison RC .75 2.00
112 Hakeem Nicks RC 1.00 2.50
113 Josh Freeman RC .75 2.00
114 Juaquin Iglesias RC .75 2.00
115 Jeremy Maclin RC 1.00 2.50
116 Javon Ringer RC .75 2.00
117 Jason Smith RC .75 2.00
118 Kenny Britt RC 1.25 3.00
119 Knowshon Moreno RC .75 2.00
120 LeSean McCoy RC 2.00 5.00
121 Michael Crabtree RC 1.25 3.00
122 Mohamed Massaquoi RC .75 2.00
123 Mark Sanchez RC .75 2.00
124 Mike Thomas RC .75 2.00
125 Sherrod Martin RC .75 2.00
126 Nate Davis RC .75 2.00
127 Percy Harvin RC .75 2.00
128 Patrick Turner RC .75 2.00
129 Pat White RC 1.00 2.50
130 Ramses Barden RC .75 2.00
131 Shonn Greene RC .75 2.00
132 Louis Murphy RC .75 2.00
133 Matthew Stafford RC 4.00 10.00
134 Tyson Jackson RC .75 2.00
135 Andre Brown RC 1.00 2.50
136 Antoine Caldwell RC .75 2.00
137 Asher Allen RC .75 2.00
138 Austin Collie RC .75 2.00
139 Bear Pascoe RC 1.00 2.50
140 Bernard Scott RC 1.25 3.00
141 Bradley Fletcher RC .75 2.00
142 Brandon Gibson RC 1.00 2.50
143 Brian Hartline RC 1.25 3.00
144 Brooks Foster RC .75 2.00
145 Cedric Peerman RC .75 2.00
146 Christopher Owens RC .75 2.00
147 Connor Barwin RC 1.00 2.50
148 Cornelius Ingram RC .75 2.00
149 Tony Fiammetta RC .75 2.00
150 Curtis Painter RC .75 2.00
151 Darius Butler RC 1.00 2.50
152 David Veikune RC 1.00 2.50
153 DeAngelo Smith RC 1.00 2.50
154 Johnny Knox RC 1.00 2.50
155 Donald Washington RC 1.00 2.50
156 Eben Britton RC 1.00 2.50
157 Eric Wood RC .75 2.00
158 Evander Hood RC 1.25 3.00
159 Fili Moala RC .75 2.00
160 Gartrell Johnson RC .75 2.00
161 Glen Coffee RC .75 2.00
162 Greg Toler RC .75 2.00
163 Jairus Byrd RC 1.25 3.00
164 James Casey RC 1.00 2.50
165 Brandon Hughes RC .75 2.00
166 Jamon Meredith RC .75 2.00
167 Jared Cook RC 1.00 2.50
168 Jarron Gilbert RC 1.00 2.50
169 Jason Phillips RC 1.00 2.50
170 Jason Williams RC 1.00 2.50
171 Jasper Brinkley RC 1.00 2.50
172 Jonathan Luigs RC .75 2.00
173 Kaluka Maiava RC .75 2.00
174 Keenan Lewis RC 1.25 3.00
175 Kevin Barnes RC .75 2.00
176 Kraig Urbik RC 1.00 2.50
177 Larry English RC 1.00 2.50
178 Lawrence Sidbury RC .75 2.00
179 Louis Delmas RC 1.00 2.50
180 Louis Vasquez RC 1.00 2.50
181 Marcus Freeman RC .75 2.00
182 Matt Shaughnessy RC 1.00 2.50
183 Max Unger RC 1.25 3.00
184 Mike Goodson RC 1.00 2.50
185 Mike Teel RC .75 2.00
186 Everette Brown RC .75 2.00
187 Mike Wallace RC 1.25 3.00
188 Nic Harris RC 1.00 2.50
189 Patrick Chung RC .75 2.00
190 Brian Orakpo RC 1.00 2.50
191 Paul Kruger RC 1.25 3.00
192 Phil Loadholt RC 1.00 2.50
193 Spencer Adkins RC .75 2.00
194 Rashad Johnson RC .75 2.00
195 Robert Ayers RC .75 2.00
196 Sen'Derrick Marks RC .75 2.00
197 Stephen McGee RC .75 2.00
198 Tom Brandstater RC 1.00 2.50
199 Travis Beckum RC .75 2.00
200 Victor Harris RC 1.00 2.50

2009 SP Authentic Retail Rookie Signatures

RANDOM INSERTS IN SP RETAIL PACKS
RSAB Alex Boone 5.00 12.00
RSAC Austin Collie 3.00 8.00
RSAM Alex Mack 3.00 8.00
RSBF Brooks Foster 3.00 8.00
RSBG Brandon Gibson 4.00 10.00
RSBH Brian Hartline 8.00 20.00
RSBR Brian Robiskie 3.00 8.00
RSBT Brandon Tate 4.00 10.00
RSCC Chase Coffman 3.00 8.00
RSCH Cullen Harper 3.00 8.00
RSDB Demetrius Byrd 4.00 10.00
RSEM Eugene Monroe 3.00 8.00
RSGH Graham Harrell 8.00 20.00
RSGJ Gartrell Johnson 3.00 8.00
RSHC Hunter Cantwell 3.00 8.00
RSJD Jarett Dillard 3.00 8.00
RSJE Malcolm Jenkins 3.00 8.00
RSJM Jeremy Maclin
RSJR Javon Ringer 3.00 8.00
RSJW Jaison Williams 4.00 10.00
RSKL Keenan Lewis 5.00 12.00
RSKM Knowshon Moreno 30.00 60.00
RSMC Michael Crabtree
RSMS Matthew Stafford
RSQC Quan Cosby 3.00 8.00
RSRB Rhett Bomar 3.00 8.00
RSRJ Rashad Jennings 4.00 10.00
RSSA Mark Sanchez
RSSG Shonn Greene 10.00 25.00
RSSM Stephen McGee 3.00 8.00
RSSS Sean Smith 3.00 8.00
RSTB Travis Beckum 3.00 8.00
RSTJ Tyson Jackson 3.00 8.00
RSVD Vontae Davis 3.00 8.00
RSVH Victor Harris 4.00 10.00
RSWM William Moore 3.00 8.00

2009 SP Authentic Retail Star Signatures

RANDOM INSERTS IN SP RETAIL PACKS
SRAB Alan Branch
SRAH Ali Highsmith
SRAT Aqib Talib
SRAW Andre Woodson
SRCB Cedric Benson
SRCJ Chad Jackson
SRCL Chris Long
SRCS Chansi Stuckey
SRDA Derek Anderson
SRDC David Clowney
SRDJ D'Qwell Jackson
SRDL Donald Lee
SRDM Darren McFadden
SRDR Darrelle Revis
SRDS DeSean Jackson
SRDV Kellen Davis 5.00 12.00
SRER Eddie Royal 5.00 12.00
SRES Ernie Sims
SRFT Fred Taylor
SRGC Gosder Cherilus
SRGO Greg Olsen
SRGW Garrett Wolfe 5.00 12.00
SRJF Joe Flacco
SRJH Justise Hairston
SRJK Jordan Kent
SRJM Jerod Mayo
SRJO Calvin Johnson
SRJS Jonathan Stewart
SRKP Kenny Phillips
SRLE Lee Evans
SRLO Jake Long
SRMB Marc Bulger
SRML Matt Leinart
SRMM Mario Manningham
SRMR Matt Ryan
SRMS Matt Schaub
SROS Owen Schmitt
SRPM Phillip Merling
SRRB Reggie Bush
SRRM Rashard Mendenhall 8.00 20.00
SRRU Martin Rucker
SRSC Scott Chandler
SRSH Jeremy Shockey
SRSI Jerome Simpson
SRSK Sam Keller
SRTC Ted Ginn Jr.

2010 SP Authentic

COMP.SET w/o RC's (100) 8.00 20.00
101-134 RC JSY AU PRINT RUN 199-499
135-184 ROOKIE AU PRINT RUN 599
185-233 ROOKIE PRINT RUN 999
EXCH EXPIRATION: 2/17/2013
1 A.J. Hawk .20 .50
2 Aaron Rodgers .60 1.50
3 Adrian Peterson .30 .75
4 Ahmad Bradshaw .20 .50
5 Alex Smith QB .25 .60
6 Andre Johnson .25 .60
7 Anquan Boldin .20 .50
8 Ben Roethlisberger .30 .75
9 Brady Quinn .25 .60
10 Brandon Jacobs .20 .50
11 Brandon Marshall .25 .60
12 Braylon Edwards .20 .50
13 Brent Celek .20 .50
14 Brett Favre .60 1.50
15 Calvin Johnson .30 .75
16 Cadillac Williams .20 .50
17 Carson Palmer .25 .60
18 Cedric Benson .20 .50
19 Chad Henne .25 .60
20 Chad Johnson .20 .50
21 Charles Woodson .30 .75
22 Chris Johnson .20 .50
23 Chris Wells .20 .50
24 Dallas Clark .20 .50
25 Darren McFadden .20 .50
26 David Garrard .20 .50
27 DeAngelo Williams .20 .50
28 DeSean Jackson .25 .60
29 Devery Henderson .20 .50
30 Devin Hester .25 .60
31 Donovan McNabb .25 .60
32 Drew Brees .30 .75
33 Eli Manning .25 .60
34 Felix Jones .20 .50
35 Frank Gore .25 .60
36 Greg Jennings .20 .50
37 Hines Ward .25 .60
38 Peyton Hillis .25 .60
39 Jamaal Charles .25 .60
40 Jason Campbell .20 .50
41 Jason Witten .25 .60
42 Jay Cutler .20 .50
43 Jerome Harrison .20 .50
44 Joe Flacco .25 .60
45 Jonathan Stewart .20 .50
46 Joseph Addai .20 .50
47 Josh Freeman .25 .60
48 Hakeem Nicks .20 .50
49 Kellen Winslow .25 .60
50 Kevin Kolb .20 .50
51 Knowshon Moreno .20 .50
52 Kyle Orton .20 .50
53 LaDainian Tomlinson .30 .75
54 Larry Fitzgerald .25 .60
55 Mario Manningham .20 .50
56 Marion Barber .25 .60
57 Mark Sanchez .20 .50
58 Marques Colston .20 .50
59 Matt Cassel .20 .50
60 Matt Forte .20 .50
61 Matt Hasselbeck .20 .50
62 LeSean McCoy .30 .75
63 Michael Vick .25 .60
64 Matt Ryan .25 .60
65 Matt Schaub .20 .50
66 Matthew Stafford .25 .60
67 Maurice Jones-Drew .20 .50
68 Michael Crabtree .20 .50
69 Michael Turner .20 .50
70 Miles Austin .20 .50
71 Patrick Willis .25 .60
72 Percy Harvin .20 .50
73 Peyton Manning .75 2.00
74 Philip Rivers .30 .75
75 Pierre Thomas .20 .50
76 Randy Moss .25 .60
77 Rashard Mendenhall .20 .50
78 Arian Foster .25 .60
79 Ray Rice .20 .50
80 Reggie Wayne .25 .60
81 Ricky Williams .25 .60
82 Roddy White .20 .50
83 Ronnie Brown .20 .50
84 Ryan Grant .25 .60
85 Santana Moss .25 .60
86 Santonio Holmes .20 .50
87 Shonn Greene .20 .50
88 Sidney Rice .20 .50
89 Steve Smith USC .20 .50
90 Austin Collie .20 .50
91 Steven Jackson .20 .50
92 Terrell Owens .25 .60
93 Thomas Jones .20 .50
94 Tom Brady .75 2.00
95 Tony Romo .25 .60
96 Troy Polamalu .30 .75
97 Vernon Davis .20 .50
98 Vince Young .20 .50
99 Vincent Jackson .20 .50
100 Wes Welker .25 .60
101 C.J. Spiller JSY AU/299 RC 8.00 20.00
102 Colt McCoy JSY AU/299 RC 10.00 25.00
103 Dez Bryant JSY AU/299 RC 75.00 135.00
104 Jahvid Best JSY AU/199 RC 10.00 25.00
105 J.Clausen JSY AU/299 RC 8.00 20.00
106 R.Mathews JSY AU/299 RC 8.00 20.00
107 S.Bradford JSY AU/299 RC 10.00 25.00
108 Tim Tebow JSY AU/299 RC 50.00 100.00
109 D.Thomas JSY AU/199 RC 60.00 100.00
110 N.Suh JSY AU/299 RC 15.00 40.00
111 G.McCoy JSY AU/299 RC 8.00 20.00
112 Eric Berry JSY AU/299 RC 15.00 40.00
113 D.Williams JSY AU/499 RC 8.00 20.00
114 Eric Decker JSY AU/199 RC 12.00 30.00
115 A.Edwards JSY AU/499 RC 8.00 20.00
116 Taylor Price JSY AU/499 RC 6.00 15.00
117 M.Williams JSY AU/499 RC 6.00 15.00
118 Mike Kafka JSY AU/199 RC 12.00 30.00
119 J.Dwyer JSY AU/499 RC 6.00 15.00
120 R.McClain JSY AU/499 RC 6.00 15.00
121 D.McCluster JSY AU/499 RC 8.00 20.00
122 E.Sanders JSY AU/199 RC 15.00 40.00
123 Jordan Shipley JSY AU/499 RC 6.00 15.00
124 M.Gilyard JSY AU/399 RC 6.00 15.00
125 J.McKnight JSY AU/499 RC 6.00 15.00
126 J.Gresham JSY AU/199 RC 10.00 25.00
127 Arrelious Benn JSY AU/399 RC 6.00 15.00
128 Grnkwski JSY AU/499 RC 30.00 80.00
129 Toby Gerhart JSY AU/399 RC 6.00 15.00
130 Ben Tate JSY AU/499 RC 12.00 30.00
131 M.Hardesty JSY AU/499 RC 6.00 15.00
132 Golden Tate JSY AU/499 RC 12.50 25.00
133 M.Easley JSY AU/499 RC 6.00 15.00
134 A.Roberts JSY AU/499 RC 10.00 25.00
135 Carlos Dunlap AU RC EXCH 6.00 15.00
136 Russell Okung AU RC EXCH 8.00 20.00
137 Tyson Alualu AU RC 3.00 8.00

138 Brandon Graham AU RC 4.00 10.00
139 Earl Thomas AU RC 10.00 25.00
140 Jason Pierre-Paul AU RC 5.00 12.00
141 Derrick Morgan AU RC 3.00 8.00
142 Bryan Bulaga AU RC 6.00 15.00
143 Sean Weatherspoon AU RC 3.00 8.00
144 Kareem Jackson AU RC 3.00 8.00
145 Dan Williams AU RC 3.00 8.00
146 Jermaine Cunningham AU RC 3.00 8.00
147 Jared Odrick AU RC 6.00 15.00
148 David Nelson AU RC 5.00 12.00
149 Jerry Hughes AU RC 3.00 8.00
150 Sergio Kindle AU RC 3.00 8.00
151 Taylor Mays AU RC 3.00 8.00
152 Rennie Curran AU RC 3.00 8.00
153 Brian Price AU RC 3.00 8.00
154 John Skelton AU RC 4.00 10.00
155 Jonathan Crompton AU RC 3.00 8.00
156 Dan LeFevour AU RC 3.00 8.00
157 Joe Webb AU RC 6.00 15.00
158 Tony Pike AU RC 3.00 8.00
159 Sean Canfield AU RC 3.00 8.00
160 Zac Robinson AU RC 4.00 10.00
161 NaVorro Bowman AU RC 8.00 20.00
162 Lamarr Houston AU RC 4.00 10.00
163 Trent Williams AU RC 8.00 20.00
164 Sean Lee AU RC 12.50 25.00
165 Jarrett Brown AU RC 3.00 8.00
166 James Starks AU RC 4.00 10.00
167 Charles Scott AU RC 3.00 8.00
168 LeGarrette Blount AU RC 6.00 15.00
169 Koa Misi AU RC 4.00 10.00
170 Stafon Johnson AU RC 3.00 8.00
171 Jimmy Graham AU RC 25.00 50.00
172 Jacoby Ford AU RC 3.00 8.00
173 David Reed AU RC 3.00 8.00
174 Riley Cooper AU RC 3.00 8.00
175 Kerry Meier AU RC 4.00 10.00
176 Carlton Mitchell AU RC 3.00 8.00
177 Dezmon Briscoe AU RC 3.00 8.00
178 Antonio Brown AU RC 75.00 150.00
179 Patrick Robinson AU RC 4.00 10.00
180 Rusty Smith AU RC 5.00 12.00
181 Levi Brown AU RC 3.00 8.00
182 Anthony Dixon AU RC 3.00 8.00
183 Aaron Hernandez AU RC 12.00 30.00
184 Joe Haden AU RC 5.00 12.00
185 Brandon Spikes RC 2.00 5.00
186 Donald Butler RC 2.00 5.00
187 Phillip Dillard RC 2.00 5.00
188 Terrence Austin RC 2.50 6.00
189 Ed Wang RC 3.00 8.00
190 Stevenson Sylvester RC 3.00 8.00
191 Charles Brown RC 2.00 5.00
192 Anthony Davis RC 2.50 6.00
193 Mike Iupati RC 3.00 8.00
194 Maurkice Pouncey RC 5.00 12.00
195 Rodger Saffold RC 2.00 5.00
196 Chris Cook RC 2.00 5.00
197 Terrence Cody RC 2.00 5.00
198 Nate Allen RC 3.00 8.00
199 T.J. Ward RC 3.00 8.00
200 Morgan Burnett RC 2.50 6.00
201 Torell Troup RC 2.00 5.00
202 Ed Dickson RC 2.00 5.00
203 Linval Joseph RC 2.00 5.00
204 Daryl Washington RC 2.00 5.00
205 Javier Arenas RC 2.00 5.00
206 Jason Worilds RC 2.00 5.00
207 Brody Eldridge RC 3.00 8.00
208 Tony Moeaki RC 2.50 6.00
209 Mike Neal RC 3.00 8.00
210 Devin McCourty RC 2.50 6.00
211 Pat Angerer RC 2.00 5.00
212 Roddrick Muckelroy RC 2.00 5.00
213 Perry Riley RC 2.50 6.00
214 Kyle Wilson RC 2.00 5.00
215 Everson Griffen RC 2.00 5.00
216 Darryl Sharpton RC 2.00 5.00
217 Dennis Pitta RC 2.00 5.00
218 Thaddeus Gibson RC 2.50 6.00
219 Garrett Graham RC 2.00 5.00
220 Michael Hoomanawanui RC 3.00 8.00
221 John Conner RC 2.00 5.00
222 Deji Karim RC 2.50 6.00
223 Anthony McCoy RC 2.00 5.00
224 Trindon Holliday RC 6.00 15.00
225 David Gettis RC 2.00 5.00
226 Kyle Williams RC 3.00 8.00
227 Jevan Snead RC 2.00 5.00
228 Dorin Dickerson RC 2.00 5.00
229 Brandon LaFell RC 3.00 8.00
230 Major Wright RC 2.00 5.00
231 Andrew Quarless RC 2.00 5.00
232 Daniel Te'o-Nesheim RC 2.50 6.00
233 Nate Byham RC 2.00 5.00

2010 SP Authentic Gold

*ROOK.JSY AU: 1X TO 2.5X RC JSY AU/399-499
*ROOK.JSY AU: .8X TO 2X RC JSY AU/299
*ROOK.JSY AU: .6X TO 1.5X RC JSY AU/199
*ROOKIE AU: 1.2X TO 3X BASE RC AU/599
*ROOKIE 185-233: 1X TO 2.5X BASE RC/999
GOLD PRINT RUN 25 SER.#'d SETS
EXCH EXPIRATION: 2/17/2013
103 Dez Bryant JSY AU 200.00 350.00
108 Tim Tebow JSY AU 150.00 300.00
109 Demaryius Thomas JSY AU 75.00 150.00
110 Ndamukong Suh JSY AU 30.00 80.00
128 Rob Gronkowski JSY AU 150.00 250.00

2010 SP Authentic Championship Patch Autographs

EXCH EXPIRATION: 2/17/2013
AH Aaron Hernandez 20.00 40.00
CM Colt McCoy 6.00 15.00
DM Derrick Morgan 5.00 12.00
DN David Nelson 12.00 30.00
DT Demaryius Thomas 12.00 30.00
ET Earl Thomas 20.00 40.00
HU Jerry Hughes 5.00 12.00
JC Jermaine Cunningham 5.00 12.00
JD Jonathan Dwyer 5.00 12.00
JH Joe Haden 15.00 40.00
JS Jordan Shipley 5.00 12.00
KJ Kareem Jackson 12.00 30.00
LB LeGarrette Blount 15.00 40.00
MC Mardy Gilyard EXCH 5.00 12.00
RC Riley Cooper 5.00 12.00
RM Rolando McClain 15.00 40.00
SK Sergio Kindle 5.00 12.00
TP Tony Pike 5.00 12.00
TT Tim Tebow 60.00 120.00
TW T.J. Ward 8.00 20.00

2010 SP Authentic Chirography

AB Anquan Boldin 10.00 25.00
AM Archie Manning 20.00 40.00
AP Adrian Peterson 60.00 120.00
BC Brent Celek 5.00 12.00
BM Brandon Marshall 8.00 20.00
BO Brian Orakpo 5.00 12.00
BR Ben Roethlisberger 50.00 100.00
BS Brandon Spikes 4.00 10.00
DB Drew Brees 40.00 80.00
DE Derrick Morgan 5.00 12.00
DF Doug Flutie 10.00 25.00
DM Dan Marino 75.00 150.00
DW Damian Williams 4.00 10.00
DX Dexter McCluster 5.00 12.00
ED Eric Decker 5.00 12.00
GJ Greg Jennings 5.00 12.00
GT Golden Tate 5.00 12.00
HE Herman Moore 5.00 12.00
HM Heath Miller 8.00 20.00
JA James Starks 5.00 12.00
JB Jahvid Best 4.00 10.00
JD Jonathan Dwyer 4.00 10.00
JF Joe Flacco 20.00 40.00
JG Jermaine Gresham 4.00 10.00
JM Joe McKnight 4.00 10.00
JO Josh Freeman 8.00 20.00
JS Jordan Shipley 4.00 10.00
KJ Kareem Jackson 4.00 10.00
KM Knowshon Moreno 5.00 12.00
MB Marion Barber 8.00 20.00
MF Matt Forte 5.00 12.00
MH Montario Hardesty 6.00 15.00
MJ Maurice Jones-Drew 8.00 20.00
MK Mike Kafka 5.00 12.00
MR Matt Ryan 25.00 50.00
MT Michael Turner 5.00 12.00
MW Mike Wallace 5.00 12.00
NA Nnamdi Asomugha 15.00 40.00
PW Patrick Willis 6.00 15.00
RC Rennie Curran 4.00 10.00
RM Ryan Mathews 4.00 10.00
RW Reggie Wayne 10.00 25.00
SG Shonn Greene 8.00 20.00
SK Sergio Kindle 5.00 12.00
TO Tony Pike 4.00 10.00
TP Taylor Price 4.00 10.00
TT Tim Tebow SP 60.00 120.00
WI DeAngelo Williams 8.00 20.00
YT Y.A. Tittle 12.00 30.00

2010 SP Authentic Chirography Duals

DUAL AUTO STATED PRINT RUN 5-15
BM J.Best/R.Mathews/15 15.00 40.00
BW L.Briggs/P.Willis/15 15.00 40.00
CR R.Craig/T.Rathman/15 15.00 40.00
GG Gresham/R.Gronkowski/15 30.00 60.00
HB P.Hornung/R.Bleier/15 40.00 80.00
HG A.Hawk/V.Gholston/15 20.00 50.00
HM C.Matthews/A.Hawk/15 50.00 100.00
HT J.Theismann/Hornung/15 40.00 80.00
JG CJohnson/D.Garrard/15 20.00 50.00
JH Houshmnd/C.Johnson/15 20.00 50.00
KT S.Kindle/E.Thomas/15 15.00 40.00
MB Breaston/Manningham/15 15.00 40.00
MH H.Miller/M.Schaub/15 15.00 40.00
MS G.McCoy/N.Suh/15 40.00 80.00
RC B.Cushing/D.Ryans/15 15.00 40.00
SR D.Rosario/J.Stewart/15 15.00 40.00
WB M.Williams/A.Benn/15 25.00 60.00
WS J.Shockey/R.Wayne/15 20.00 50.00

2010 SP Authentic College Pride Patch Autographs

EXCH EXPIRATION: 2/17/2013
AB Arrelious Benn 6.00 15.00
AM Archie Manning
AP Adrian Peterson 60.00 120.00
BS Barry Sanders 75.00 150.00
BT Ben Tate 6.00 15.00
CH Chad Henne 25.00 60.00
CM Colt McCoy 15.00 40.00
CS C.J. Spiller 6.00 15.00
DF Doug Flutie
DT Demaryius Thomas 15.00 40.00
DW Damian Williams
EC Earl Campbell
EM Eli Manning 40.00 80.00
GT Golden Tate 8.00 20.00
JB Jahvid Best 6.00 15.00
JD Jonathan Dwyer 6.00 15.00
JM Joe McKnight 6.00 15.00
JS Jordan Shipley 6.00 15.00
MH Montario Hardesty 6.00 15.00
MK Mike Kafka 8.00 20.00
MO Craig Morton 12.00 30.00
MR Matt Ryan 20.00 50.00
MS Matt Schaub
PM Peyton Manning 125.00 200.00
RM Ryan Mathews 6.00 15.00
SB Sam Bradford 40.00 100.00
SI Billy Sims 10.00 25.00
TG Toby Gerhart 6.00 15.00
TT Tim Tebow 60.00 120.00

2010 SP Authentic Retro Rookie Patch Autographs

STATED PRINT RUN 5-25
EXCH EXPIRATION: 2/18/2013
AP Adrian Peterson/5
BB Brian Bosworth/15 40.00 80.00
BJ Bo Jackson/5
BS Barry Sanders/5
DB Drew Bledsoe/15
DS DeSean Jackson/15 30.00 60.00
EM Eli Manning/5
FG Frank Gore/35 EXCH 25.00 50.00
GJ Greg Jennings/15 40.00 80.00
HM Heath Miller/35 25.00 50.00
JE John Elway/5
KW Kellen Winslow Sr/15 30.00 60.00
MR Matt Ryan/5
PM Peyton Manning/5
PW Patrick Willis/35 30.00 60.00
RB Ronnie Brown/35 20.00 50.00
SI Billy Sims/15 30.00 60.00
SY Steve Young/15

2010 SP Authentic Rookie Super Jersey Autographs

STATED PRINT RUN 25 SER.#'d SETS
EXCH EXPIRATION: 2/17/2013
AB Arrelious Benn 10.00 25.00
AR Andre Roberts 12.00 30.00
BT Ben Tate 10.00 25.00
CM Colt McCoy 12.00 30.00
CS C.J. Spiller 10.00 25.00
DM Dexter McCluster 12.00 30.00
DT Demaryius Thomas 25.00 60.00
DW Damian Williams 10.00 25.00
ED Eric Decker 12.00 30.00
ES Emmanuel Sanders 15.00 40.00
GT Golden Tate 12.00 30.00
JB Jahvid Best 10.00 25.00
JC Jimmy Clausen 10.00 25.00
JD Jonathan Dwyer 10.00 25.00
JG Jermaine Gresham 10.00 25.00
JM Joe McKnight 10.00 25.00
JS Jordan Shipley 10.00 25.00
MC Rolando McClain 10.00 25.00
ME Marcus Easley 10.00 25.00
MG Mardy Gilyard 10.00 25.00
MH Montario Hardesty 10.00 25.00
MK Mike Kafka 12.00 30.00
MW Mike Williams 40.00 80.00
NS Ndamukong Suh 75.00 150.00
RG Rob Gronkowski 40.00 80.00
RM Ryan Mathews 10.00 25.00
SB Sam Bradford 12.00 30.00
TG Toby Gerhart 10.00 25.00
TP Taylor Price 10.00 25.00
TT Tim Tebow 75.00 150.00

2010 SP Authentic Sign of the Times

AB Arrelious Benn 4.00 10.00
AH Aaron Hernandez 4.00 10.00
AP Adrian Peterson 60.00 120.00
AR Andre Roberts 5.00 12.00
BC Brian Cushing 5.00 12.00
BG Brandon Graham 5.00 12.00
BS Billy Sims 8.00 20.00
CJ Chris Johnson 10.00 25.00
CS C.J. Spiller 4.00 10.00
DM Donovan McNabb 15.00 30.00
DT Demaryius Thomas 10.00 25.00
EB Eric Berry 10.00 25.00
EC Earl Campbell 15.00 30.00
EM Eli Manning 40.00 80.00
ES Emmanuel Sanders 6.00 15.00
ET Earl Thomas 10.00 25.00
FG Frank Gore 6.00 15.00
GT Golden Tate 5.00 12.00
JC Jason Campbell 5.00 12.00
JF Jacoby Ford 4.00 10.00
JH Jerry Hughes 5.00 12.00
JI Jimmy Clausen 4.00 10.00
JL James Laurinaitis 6.00 15.00
JO Joe Haden 6.00 15.00
JP Jason Pierre-Paul 6.00 15.00
JS John Skelton 10.00 25.00
KB Kenny Britt 5.00 12.00
KK Kevin Kolb 8.00 20.00
LB Lance Briggs 8.00 20.00
LE Lee Evans 6.00 15.00
LT LaDainian Tomlinson 15.00 30.00
ME Marcus Easley 4.00 10.00
MG Mardy Gilyard 5.00 12.00
MI Mike Williams 4.00 10.00
MM Mario Manningham 5.00 12.00
MO Michael Oher 10.00 25.00
MS Mark Sanchez
MW Mike Sims-Walker 5.00 12.00
PM Peyton Manning 100.00 175.00
RC Riley Cooper 5.00 12.00
RG Rob Gronkowski 20.00 40.00
RO Rolando McClain 4.00 10.00
SB Sam Bradford 5.00 12.00
SL Steve Largent 15.00 30.00
SW Sean Weatherspoon 5.00 12.00
TG Toby Gerhart 4.00 10.00
TM Taylor Mays 4.00 10.00
TR Tony Romo 25.00 50.00
VJ Vincent Jackson 5.00 12.00
WM Warren Moon 30.00 60.00

2010 SP Authentic Sign of the Times Duals

DUAL AUTO PRINT RUN 5-15
BH P.Hornung/T.Brown/15 40.00 80.00
BL M.Lynch/Jahvid Best/15 20.00 50.00
BM J.Best/R.Mathews/15 20.00 50.00
CM C.Matthews/B.Cushing/15 50.00 100.00
CS M.Sanchez/M.Cassel/15 30.00 60.00
DJ D.Williams/J.McKnight/15 15.00 40.00
GH R.Gronkowski/Hernandez/15 50.00 100.00
GL Laurinaitis/V.Gholston/15 20.00 50.00
HG S.Holmes/T.Ginn/15 20.00 50.00
HL A.Hawk/J.Laurinaitis/15 30.00 60.00
JM D.Jackson/J.Maclin/15 20.00 50.00
KJ D.Jackson/K.Kolb/15 20.00 50.00
ME M.Wallace/E.Sanders/15 30.00 60.00
MS B.Marshall/Sims-Walker/15 15.00 40.00
RS Weatherspoon/R.McClain/15 15.00 40.00
SC E.Campbell/B.Sanders/15 125.00 200.00
SJ B.Jackson/B.Sims/15 60.00 120.00
SL S.Smith USC/M.Leinart/15 20.00 50.00
TB A.Benn/G.Tate/15 20.00 50.00
WC W.Welker/M.Crabtree/15 60.00 120.00
WG F.Gore/R.Wayne/15 20.00 50.00
WT D.Williams/G.Tate/15 15.00 40.00

2011 SP Authentic

COMP.SET w/o SP's (100) 8.00 20.00
101-200 FUTURE WATCH ODDS 1:4
201-234 JSY AU PRINT RUN 299-699
1 Tyrod Taylor .60 1.50
2 Anthony Castonzo .30 .75
3 Mark Herzlich .30 .75
4 Da'Quan Bowers .30 .75
5 Colin McCarthy .40 1.00
6 Dwayne Harris .30 .75
7 Jeremy Kerley .50 1.25
8 Nick Fairley .30 .75
9 Jamie Harper .30 .75
10 Greg Little .40 1.00
11 Lester Jean .30 .75
12 Bruce Carter .30 .75
13 Ras-I Dowling .30 .75
14 Aaron Williams .30 .75
15 Austin Pettis .30 .75
16 Anthony Allen .30 .75
17 Ryan Kerrigan .40 1.00
18 D.J. Williams .30 .75
19 Pat Devlin .50 1.25
20 Drake Nevis .30 .75
21 Andy Dalton .60 1.50
22 Nate Solder .30 .75
23 Brandon Saine .50 1.25
24 Ronald Johnson .30 .75
25 Allen Bailey .30 .75
26 Cameron Jordan .40 1.00
27 Prince Amukamara .30 .75
28 Ryan Whalen .30 .75
29 Dane Sanzenbacher .30 .75
30 Von Miller .50 1.25
31 Terrence Toliver .40 1.00
32 Kelvin Sheppard .30 .75
33 Armon Binns .40 1.00
34 DeMarco Murray .60 1.50
35 Damien Berry .40 1.00
36 Stevan Ridley .30 .75
37 Virgil Green .30 .75
38 Vai Taua .30 .75
39 Edmond Gates .30 .75
40 Aldon Smith .30 .75
41 Noel Devine .50 1.25
42 Akeem Ayers .30 .75
43 Leonard Hankerson .30 .75
44 Bilal Powell .40 1.00
45 Ricky Stanzi .30 .75
46 Jarvis Jenkins .30 .75
47 Greg Salas .30 .75
48 Jerrel Jernigan .30 .75
49 Mike Pouncey .50 1.25
50 Jeremy Beal .40 1.00
51 Cecil Shorts .30 .75
52 T.J. Yates .30 .75
53 Mason Foster .30 .75
54 Derrick Locke .40 1.00
55 Jimmy Smith .30 .75
56 Nathan Enderle .30 .75
57 J.J. Watt 1.50 4.00
58 Titus Young .30 .75
59 Vincent Brown .30 .75
60 Luke Stocker .30 .75
61 Quan Sturdivant .40 1.00
62 Evan Royster .30 .75
63 Jake Locker .30 .75
64 Christian Ponder .30 .75
65 Jock Sanders .40 1.00
66 Ross Homan .40 1.00
67 Cameron Heyward .40 1.00
68 Lance Kendricks .30 .75
69 Jeff Maehl .30 .75
70 Roy Helu .30 .75
71 Graig Cooper .40 1.00
72 Colin Kaepernick .50 1.25
73 Dion Lewis .40 1.00
74 Niles Paul .30 .75
75 Delone Carter .30 .75
76 Tyron Smith .40 1.00
77 Adrian Clayborn .30 .75
78 Marvin Austin .30 .75
79 Kendall Hunter .30 .75
80 Daniel Thomas .30 .75
81 Marcell Dareus .30 .75
82 Greg Jones .40 1.00
83 Stephen Paea .30 .75
84 Jordan Todman .30 .75
85 Mikel Leshoure .30 .75
86 Shane Vereen .40 1.00
87 Jacquizz Rodgers .30 .75
88 Tandon Doss .30 .75
89 A.J. Green .75 2.00
90 Kyle Rudolph .30 .75
91 Torrey Smith .30 .75
92 Ryan Mallett .30 .75
93 John Clay .50 1.25
94 Cam Newton 1.50 4.00
95 Mark Ingram .50 1.25
96 Jonathan Baldwin .30 .75
97 Ryan Williams .30 .75
98 Blaine Gabbert .30 .75
99 Randall Cobb .50 1.25
100 Julio Jones 1.00 2.50
101 Austin Pettis FW .50 1.25
102 Lance Kendricks FW .50 1.25
103 Andy Dalton FW 1.00 2.50
104 Mikel Leshoure FW .50 1.25
105 Daniel Thomas FW .50 1.25
106 Marcell Dareus FW .50 1.25
107 D.J. Williams FW .50 1.25
108 Colin Kaepernick FW .75 2.00
109 Stevan Ridley FW .50 1.25
110 Cameron Heyward FW .60 1.50
111 Noel Devine FW .75 2.00
112 Evan Royster FW .50 1.25
113 John Clay FW .75 2.00
114 Kelvin Sheppard FW .50 1.25
115 Jake Locker FW .50 1.25
116 Delone Carter FW .50 1.25
117 Tyrod Taylor FW 1.00 2.50
118 Von Miller FW .75 2.00
119 Christian Ponder FW .50 1.25
120 Anthony Castonzo FW .50 1.25
121 Dane Sanzenbacher FW .50 1.25
122 J.J. Watt FW 2.50 6.00
123 Dwayne Harris FW .50 1.25
124 Kendall Hunter FW .50 1.25
125 Virgil Green FW .50 1.25
126 Luke Stocker FW .50 1.25
127 Terrence Toliver FW .60 1.50
128 Greg Little FW .60 1.50
129 Greg Jones FW .60 1.50
130 Quan Sturdivant FW .60 1.50
131 Derrick Locke FW .60 1.50
132 Vincent Brown FW .50 1.25
133 Adrian Clayborn FW .50 1.25
134 Ras-I Dowling FW .50 1.25
135 Greg Salas FW .50 1.25
136 Jerrel Jernigan FW .50 1.25
137 Niles Paul FW .50 1.25
138 Prince Amukamara FW .50 1.25
139 Leonard Hankerson FW .50 1.25
140 Pat Devlin FW .75 2.00
141 Roy Helu FW .50 1.25
142 Jeremy Kerley FW .75 2.00
143 Ronald Johnson FW .50 1.25
144 Titus Young FW .50 1.25
145 Ricky Stanzi FW .50 1.25
146 DeMarco Murray FW 1.00 2.50
147 Tyron Smith FW .60 1.50
148 Cameron Jordan FW .60 1.50
149 A.J. Green FW 1.25 3.00
150 Julio Jones FW 1.50 4.00
151 Cam Newton FW 2.50 6.00
152 Ryan Mallett FW .50 1.25
153 Shane Vereen FW .60 1.50
154 Mark Ingram FW .75 2.00
155 Cecil Shorts FW .50 1.25
156 Jonathan Baldwin FW .50 1.25
157 Randall Cobb FW .75 2.00
158 Tandon Doss FW .50 1.25
159 Torrey Smith FW .50 1.25
160 Kyle Rudolph FW .50 1.25
161 Blaine Gabbert FW .50 1.25
162 Ryan Williams FW .50 1.25
163 Nick Fairley FW .50 1.25
164 Jordan Todman FW .50 1.25
165 Dion Lewis FW .60 1.50
166 Jacquizz Rodgers FW .50 1.25
167 Edmond Gates FW .50 1.25
168 Da'Quan Bowers FW .50 1.25
169 Drew Brees FW 1.25 3.00
170 Steven Jackson FW .75 2.00
171 Aaron Rodgers FW 2.00 5.00
172 Rocket Ismail FW 1.00 2.50
173 Troy Aikman FW 1.50 4.00
174 Bob Griese FW 1.25 3.00
175 Tony Dorsett FW 1.25 3.00
176 Roman Gabriel FW .75 2.00
177 Bo Jackson FW 1.50 4.00
178 John Elway FW 2.00 5.00
179 Paul Hornung FW 1.25 3.00
180 Warren Moon FW 1.25 3.00
181 Jerry Rice FW 2.00 5.00
182 Gale Sayers FW 1.25 3.00
183 George Rogers FW 1.00 2.50
184 Tim Brown FW 1.25 3.00
185 Thurman Thomas FW 1.00 2.50
186 Doug Flutie FW 1.00 2.50
187 John Cappelletti FW .75 2.00
188 Bernie Kosar FW 1.00 2.50
189 Kellen Winslow Sr. FW 1.00 2.50
190 Jim Kelly FW 1.25 3.00
191 Barry Sanders FW 2.00 5.00
192 Steve Young FW 1.50 4.00
193 Floyd Little FW .75 2.00
194 Dan Marino FW 2.50 6.00
195 Charles White FW .75 2.00
196 Brian Bosworth FW 1.00 2.50
197 Earl Campbell FW 1.25 3.00
198 Drew Bledsoe FW 1.00 2.50
199 Mike Singletary FW 1.25 3.00
200 Billy Sims FW 1.00 2.50
201 Jake Locker JSY AU/299 20.00 50.00
202 Mark Ingram JSY AU/299 15.00 40.00
203 A.J. Green JSY AU/299 30.00 80.00
204 Cam Newton JSY AU/299 75.00 150.00
205 Blaine Gabbert JSY AU/299 20.00 50.00
206 Ryan Williams JSY AU/299 20.00 50.00
207 Julio Jones JSY AU/299 40.00 100.00
208 Ryan Mallett JSY AU/299 20.00 50.00
209 Randall Cobb JSY AU/699 12.00 30.00
210 Greg Salas JSY AU/699 10.00 25.00
211 Jerrel Jernigan JSY AU/699 8.00 20.00
212 Leonard Hankerson JSY AU/699 10.00 25.00
213 Kendall Hunter JSY AU/699 12.00 30.00
214 Niles Paul JSY AU/699 8.00 20.00
215 Terrence Toliver JSY AU/699 8.00 20.00
216 DeMarco Murray JSY AU/699 15.00 40.00
217 Tandon Doss JSY AU/699 8.00 20.00
218 Ronald Johnson JSY AU/699 8.00 20.00
219 Greg Little JSY AU/699 10.00 25.00
220 Titus Young JSY AU/699 8.00 20.00
221 Vincent Brown JSY AU/699 8.00 20.00
222 Mikel Leshoure JSY AU/699 8.00 20.00
223 Jacquizz Rodgers JSY AU/699 8.00 20.00
224 Jonathan Baldwin JSY AU/699 8.00 20.00
225 Jordan Todman JSY AU/699 8.00 20.00
226 Shane Vereen JSY AU/699 10.00 25.00
227 Torrey Smith JSY AU/699 8.00 20.00
228 Austin Pettis JSY AU/699 8.00 20.00
229 Christian Ponder JSY AU/699 8.00 20.00
230 Kyle Rudolph JSY AU/699 8.00 20.00
231 Daniel Thomas JSY AU/699 8.00 20.00
232 Andy Dalton JSY AU/699 15.00 40.00
233 Colin Kaepernick JSY AU/699 12.00 30.00
234 Delone Carter JSY AU/699 8.00 20.00
MCPATCH Marques Colston Patch/4

2011 SP Authentic Autographs Gold

*1-100 ROOKIE/15: 1.2X TO 3X BASIC AU
1-100 ROOKIE PRINT RUN 15
101-200 FUTURE WATCH PRINT RUN 5-25
OVERALL AUTO STATED ODDS 1:12
21 Andy Dalton/15 30.00 60.00
34 DeMarco Murray/15 15.00 40.00
57 J.J. Watt/15 250.00 400.00
63 Jake Locker/15 8.00 20.00
64 Christian Ponder/15 75.00 150.00
72 Colin Kaepernick/15 12.00 30.00
89 A.J. Green/15 75.00 150.00
92 Ryan Mallett/15 25.00 60.00
94 Cam Newton/15 500.00 800.00
95 Mark Ingram/15 30.00 80.00
98 Blaine Gabbert/15 8.00 20.00
100 Julio Jones/15 125.00 200.00
101 Austin Pettis FW/35 12.00 30.00
102 Lance Kendricks FW/35 8.00 20.00
103 Andy Dalton FW/35 30.00 60.00
105 Daniel Thomas FW/35 8.00 20.00
106 Marcell Dareus FW/35 8.00 20.00
107 D.J. Williams FW/35 8.00 20.00
108 Colin Kaepernick FW/35 12.00 30.00
109 Stevan Ridley FW/35 20.00 50.00
110 Cameron Heyward FW/35 12.00 30.00
111 Noel Devine FW/35 12.00 30.00
112 Evan Royster FW/35 15.00 40.00
113 John Clay FW/35 12.00 30.00
114 Kelvin Sheppard FW/35 8.00 20.00
116 Delone Carter FW/35 8.00 20.00
117 Tyrod Taylor FW/35 15.00 40.00
118 Von Miller FW/35 20.00 50.00
120 Anthony Castonzo FW/35 8.00 20.00
121 Dane Sanzenbacher FW/35 30.00 60.00
122 J.J. Watt FW/35 175.00 300.00
123 Dwayne Harris FW/35 8.00 20.00
126 Luke Stocker FW/35 8.00 20.00
127 Terrence Toliver FW/35 10.00 25.00
128 Greg Little FW/35 10.00 25.00
129 Greg Jones FW/35 10.00 25.00
130 Quan Sturdivant FW/35 10.00 25.00
132 Vincent Brown FW/35 15.00 40.00
133 Adrian Clayborn FW/35 25.00 50.00
134 Ras-I Dowling FW/35 8.00 20.00
135 Greg Salas FW/35 15.00 40.00
136 Jerrel Jernigan FW/35 8.00 20.00
137 Niles Paul FW/35 12.00 30.00
138 Prince Amukamara FW/35 20.00 50.00
140 Pat Devlin FW/35 20.00 50.00
141 Roy Helu FW/35 8.00 20.00
142 Jeremy Kerley FW/35 12.00 30.00
143 Ronald Johnson FW/35 8.00 20.00
146 DeMarco Murray FW/35 15.00 40.00
147 Tyron Smith FW/35
148 Cameron Jordan FW/35 10.00 25.00
150 Julio Jones FW/35 75.00 200.00
165 Dion Lewis FW/35 10.00 25.00
167 Edmond Gates FW/35
168 Da'Quan Bowers FW/35 20.00 50.00
183 George Rogers FW/35 20.00 40.00
187 John Cappelletti FW/35 20.00 40.00
193 Floyd Little FW/35 12.00 30.00
195 Charles White FW/35 12.00 30.00
200 Billy Sims FW/35 25.00 50.00

2011 SP Authentic Autographs

OVERALL AUTO STATED ODDS 1:12
GROUP A ANNC'D ODDS 1:818
GROUP B ANNC'D ODDS 1:552
GROUP C ANNC'D ODDS 1:236
GROUP D ANNC'D ODDS 1:145
GROUP E ANNC'D ODDS 1:47
EXCH EXPIRATION: 1/12/2014
1 Tyrod Taylor E 5.00 12.00
2 Anthony Castonzo E 2.50 6.00
3 Mark Herzlich B 6.00 15.00
4 Da'Quan Bowers B 20.00 40.00
5 Colin McCarthy D 3.00 8.00
6 Dwayne Harris D 8.00 20.00
7 Jeremy Kerley C 4.00 10.00
8 Nick Fairley A EXCH 5.00 12.00
9 Jamie Harper A 5.00 12.00
10 Greg Little C 6.00 15.00
11 Lestar Jean A EXCH 20.00 40.00
12 Bruce Carter A 8.00 20.00
13 Ras-I Dowling E 2.50 6.00
14 Aaron Williams A 8.00 20.00
15 Austin Pettis D 4.00 10.00
16 Anthony Allen E 2.50 6.00
17 Ryan Kerrigan C 5.00 12.00
18 D.J. Williams E 2.50 6.00
19 Pat Devlin E 5.00 12.00
20 Drake Nevis D 2.50 6.00
21 Andy Dalton C 12.00 30.00
22 Nate Solder E 2.50 6.00
23 Brandon Saine E 8.00 20.00
24 Ronald Johnson C 2.50 6.00
25 Allen Bailey E 2.50 6.00
26 Cameron Jordan D 3.00 8.00
27 Prince Amukamara E 6.00 15.00
28 Ryan Whalen E 2.50 6.00
29 Dane Sanzenbacher D 6.00 15.00
30 Von Miller E 6.00 15.00
31 Terrence Toliver D 3.00 8.00
32 Kelvin Sheppard E 2.50 6.00
33 Armon Binns E 3.00 8.00
34 DeMarco Murray D 5.00 12.00
35 Damien Berry D 3.00 8.00
36 Stevan Ridley A 25.00 50.00
37 Virgil Green C 4.00 10.00
38 Vai Taua E EXCH 2.50 6.00
39 Edmond Gates D EXCH 2.50 6.00
40 Aldon Smith B 12.00 30.00
41 Noel Devine E 5.00 12.00
42 Akeem Ayers C 5.00 12.00
43 Leonard Hankerson A 12.00 30.00
44 Bilal Powell D 3.00 8.00
45 Ricky Stanzi A 8.00 20.00
46 Jarvis Jenkins C 6.00 15.00
47 Greg Salas B 6.00 15.00
48 Jerrel Jernigan E 2.50 6.00
49 Mike Pouncey E 5.00 12.00
50 Jeremy Beal B 3.00 8.00
51 Cecil Shorts E 2.50 6.00
52 T.J. Yates A 15.00 30.00
53 Mason Foster E 5.00 12.00
54 Derrick Locke E 3.00 8.00
55 Jimmy Smith D 6.00 15.00
56 Nathan Enderle C 5.00 12.00
57 J.J. Watt C 50.00 80.00
58 Titus Young A 20.00 40.00
59 Vincent Brown E 5.00 12.00
60 Luke Stocker E 5.00 12.00
61 Quan Sturdivant E 3.00 8.00
62 Evan Royster E 6.00 15.00
63 Jake Locker B 2.50 6.00
64 Christian Ponder B 10.00 25.00
65 Jock Sanders E 4.00 10.00
66 Ross Homan D 6.00 15.00
67 Cameron Heyward E 5.00 12.00
68 Lance Kendricks E 2.50 6.00
69 Jeff Maehl D EXCH 6.00 15.00
70 Roy Helu E 2.50 6.00
71 Graig Cooper E 3.00 8.00
73 Dion Lewis D 3.00 8.00
74 Niles Paul C 6.00 15.00
75 Delone Carter E 2.50 6.00
76 Tyron Smith B EXCH 12.00 30.00
77 Adrian Clayborn C 8.00 20.00
79 Kendall Hunter C 8.00 20.00
80 Daniel Thomas B 2.50 6.00
81 Marcell Dareus A 2.50 6.00
82 Greg Jones E 3.00 8.00
83 Stephen Paea D 2.50 6.00
84 Jordan Todman A 8.00 20.00
85 Mikel Leshoure B 25.00 50.00
86 Shane Vereen A 3.00 8.00
87 Jacquizz Rodgers B EXCH 8.00 20.00
88 Tandon Doss A 20.00 40.00
89 A.J. Green A 40.00 80.00
90 Kyle Rudolph A 8.00 20.00
91 Torrey Smith C 2.50 6.00
92 Ryan Mallett A 15.00 40.00
93 John Clay C 4.00 10.00
94 Cam Newton A 250.00 500.00
95 Mark Ingram B 10.00 25.00
96 Jonathan Baldwin A 12.00 30.00
97 Ryan Williams A 15.00 40.00
98 Blaine Gabbert B 2.50 6.00
99 Randall Cobb A 8.00 20.00
100 Julio Jones B 40.00 80.00

2011 SP Authentic Sign of the Times

OVERALL AUTO STATED ODDS 1:12
GROUP A ANNC'D ODDS 1:1021
GROUP B ANNC'D ODDS 1:677
GROUP C ANNC'D ODDS 1:252
GROUP D ANNC'D ODDS 1:45
STAB Allen Bailey D 2.50 6.00
STAC Adrian Clayborn D 6.00 15.00
STAD Andy Dalton C 12.00 30.00
STAG A.J. Green A 25.00 50.00
STAI Troy Aikman A 30.00 60.00
STAM Mike Alstott A 12.00 30.00
STAP Alan Page A 10.00 25.00
STAR Aaron Rodgers A 125.00 225.00
STAU Austin Pettis D 2.50 6.00
STBB Brian Bosworth A 20.00 40.00
STBC Bruce Carter D 2.50 6.00
STBG Blaine Gabbert A 2.50 6.00
STBI Armon Binns D 3.00 8.00
STBJ Bo Jackson A 60.00 120.00
STBK Bernie Kosar A 15.00 30.00
STBO Bob Griese A 20.00 40.00
STBR Tim Brown A 25.00 50.00
STBS Barry Sanders A 60.00 120.00
STCA John Cappelletti B 8.00 20.00
STCH Cameron Heyward D 3.00 8.00
STCJ Cameron Jordan D 3.00 8.00
STCK Colin Kaepernick D 4.00 10.00
STCL John Clay C 4.00 10.00
STCM Colin McCarthy D 3.00 8.00
STCN Cam Newton A 60.00 120.00
STCP Christian Ponder C 10.00 25.00
STCS Cecil Shorts A 6.00 15.00
STCW Charles White B 6.00 15.00
STDB Da'Quan Bowers B 8.00 20.00
STDC Delone Carter B 2.50 6.00
STDH Dwayne Harris D 2.50 6.00
STDL Derrick Locke D 3.00 8.00
STDM DeMarco Murray C 5.00 12.00
STDN Drake Nevis C 2.50 6.00
STDS Dane Sanzenbacher B 8.00 20.00
STDT Daniel Thomas C 2.50 6.00
STDW D.J. Williams D 2.50 6.00
STEC Earl Campbell A 20.00 40.00
STEG Edmond Gates B 2.50 6.00
STER Evan Royster D 2.50 6.00
STFL Floyd Little B 10.00 25.00
STGJ Greg Jones D 5.00 12.00
STGL Greg Little D 3.00 8.00
STGP Greg Pruitt C 8.00 20.00
STGR George Rogers B 8.00 20.00
STGS Greg Salas D 2.50 6.00
STHE Roy Helu D 5.00 12.00
STJB Jonathan Baldwin A 6.00 15.00
STJE John Elway A 75.00 150.00
STJJ Jerrel Jernigan D 2.50 6.00
STJK Jeremy Kerley D 4.00 10.00
STJL Jake Locker A 2.50 6.00
STJO Julio Jones A 25.00 50.00
STJR Jerry Rice A 100.00 200.00
STJS Jimmy Smith B 2.50 6.00
STKE Jim Kelly A 25.00 50.00
STKH Kendall Hunter D 5.00 12.00
STKJ Keith Jackson B 12.50 25.00
STKS Kelvin Sheppard D 2.50 6.00
STLE Dion Lewis B 3.00 8.00
STLH Leonard Hankerson B 6.00 15.00
STLK Lance Kendricks D 2.50 6.00
STLR Lee Roy Jordan B 8.00 20.00
STLS Lee Roy Selmon B 25.00 50.00
STMD Marcell Dareus B 2.50 6.00
STMH Mark Herzlich D 2.50 6.00
STMI Mark Ingram A 30.00 60.00
STML Mikel Leshoure A 6.00 15.00
STMO Craig Morton B 6.00 15.00
STND Noel Devine D 6.00 15.00
STNE Nathan Enderle C 2.50 6.00
STNF Nick Fairley A 2.50 6.00
STNP Niles Paul D 5.00 12.00
STPA Prince Amukamara D 6.00 15.00
STPD Pat Devlin C 6.00 15.00
STPH Paul Hornung A 20.00 40.00
STRC Roger Craig A 8.00 20.00
STRD Ras-I Dowling D 2.50 6.00
STRG Roman Gabriel A 8.00 20.00
STRH Ross Homan D 5.00 12.00
STRJ Ronald Johnson D 2.50 6.00
STRK Ryan Kerrigan D 5.00 12.00
STRM Ryan Mallett A 8.00 20.00
STRS Ricky Stanzi A 8.00 20.00
STRW Ryan Whalen D 2.50 6.00
STRY Ron Yary B 6.00 15.00
STSI Billy Sims B 8.00 20.00
STSM Tyron Smith C 6.00 15.00
STSP Stephen Paea D 2.50 6.00
STST Luke Stocker B 5.00 12.00
STSY Steve Young A 25.00 50.00
STTA Tyrod Taylor D 5.00 12.00
STTH Thurman Thomas A 15.00 40.00
STTS Torrey Smith B 2.50 6.00
STTT Terrence Toliver D 3.00 8.00
STTY Titus Young C 6.00 15.00
STVB Vincent Brown D 2.50 6.00
STVM Von Miller C 6.00 15.00
STWI Ryan Williams A 15.00 30.00

2011 SP Authentic Sign of the Times Duals

STATED PRINT RUN 15 SER.#'d SETS
ST2AY S.Young/T.Aikman 50.00 100.00
ST2BH T.Brown/P.Hornung 30.00 60.00
ST2CS B.Sims/E.Campbell 40.00 80.00
ST2DR E.Royster/N.Devine 12.00 30.00
ST2FD M.Dareus/N.Fairley
ST2GJ J.Jones/A.J. Green 60.00 120.00
ST2GL B.Gabbert/J.Locker
ST2GN B.Gabbert/C.Newton 40.00 80.00
ST2HP R.Helu/N.Paul 40.00 80.00
ST2IJ M.Ingram/J.Jones 50.00 100.00
ST2JH L.Hankerson/R.Johnson 15.00 40.00
ST2JL J.Jones/G.Little 50.00 100.00
ST2KK B.Kosar/J.Kelly 50.00 100.00
ST2MH D.Murray/K.Hunter 12.00 30.00
ST2ML J.Locker/R.Mallett
ST2MT D.Thomas/D.Murray 12.00 30.00
ST2RW G.Rogers/C.White 15.00 40.00
ST2SL G.Little/T.Smith 15.00 40.00
ST2SW C.White/B.Sims 15.00 40.00
ST2YP A.Pettis/T.Young 15.00 40.00

2011 SP Authentic Signature Threads

STATED PRINT RUN 25-99
THAD Andy Dalton/25 40.00 80.00
THAG A.J. Green/25 75.00 150.00
THAP Austin Pettis/99 10.00 25.00
THBG Blaine Gabbert/25 12.00 30.00
THCN Cam Newton/25 250.00 500.00
THCP Christian Ponder/25 12.00 30.00
THDC Delone Carter/99 10.00 25.00
THDM DeMarco Murray/25 25.00 60.00
THDT Daniel Thomas/25 12.00 30.00
THGL Greg Little/99 12.00 30.00
THGS Greg Salas/99 10.00 25.00
THJB Jonathan Baldwin/25 12.00 30.00
THJE Jerrel Jernigan/99 10.00 25.00
THJJ Julio Jones/25 50.00 120.00
THJL Jake Locker/25 12.00 30.00
THJR Jacquizz Rodgers/25 20.00 50.00
THJT Jordan Todman/25 12.00 30.00
THKH Kendall Hunter/99 10.00 25.00
THKR Kyle Rudolph/99 10.00 25.00
THLH Leonard Hankerson/25 12.00 30.00
THMI Mark Ingram/25 20.00 50.00
THML Mikel Leshoure/25 25.00 60.00
THNP Niles Paul/99 10.00 25.00
THRC Randall Cobb/99 15.00 40.00
THRJ Ronald Johnson/99 10.00 25.00
THRM Ryan Mallett/25 12.00 30.00
THRW Ryan Williams/25 30.00 80.00
THSV Shane Vereen/25 15.00 40.00
THTD Tandon Doss/25 12.00 30.00
THTS Torrey Smith/25 12.00 30.00
THTT Terrence Toliver/99 12.00 30.00
THTY Titus Young/99 10.00 25.00
THVB Vincent Brown/99 10.00 25.00

2012 SP Authentic

COMP.SET w/o RC's (100) 8.00 20.00
ROOKIE JSY AU/425-885 ODDS 1:24
EXCH EXPIRATION: 1/8/2015
1 A.J. Jenkins .25 .60
2 Aaron Corp .25 .60
3 Alameda Ta'amu .30 .75
4 Stephon Gilmore .30 .75
5 Alshon Jeffery .50 1.25
6 Andre Branch .25 .60
7 Dont'a Hightower .40 1.00
8 Darius Hanks .40 1.00
9 Jarrett Lee .40 1.00
10 Robert Griffin III .30 .75
11 Bobby Rainey .25 .60
12 Antwon Bailey .30 .75
13 Cordy Glenn .30 .75
14 Bobby Wagner .40 1.00
15 Brandon Thompson .30 .75
16 Brandon Weeden .25 .60
17 Lavonte David .40 1.00
18 Case Keenum .50 1.25
19 Chandler Harnish .25 .60
20 Tyler Hansen .25 .60
21 Jayron Hosley .40 1.00
22 David DeCastro .25 .60
23 Dontari Poe .25 .60
24 Cliff Harris .40 1.00
25 Courtney Upshaw .30 .75
26 Da'Jon McKnight .30 .75
27 Dan Herron .25 .60
28 Evan Rodriguez .30 .75
29 Derek Moye .40 1.00
30 Shea McClellin .30 .75
31 Devon Wylie .25 .60
32 Dominique Davis .30 .75
33 Doug Martin .40 1.00
34 Janoris Jenkins .30 .75
35 Dwayne Allen .25 .60
36 Amini Silatolu .25 .60
37 Foswhitt Whittaker .25 .60
38 Gerell Robinson .25 .60
39 Greg Childs .25 .60
40 Isaiah Pead .25 .60
41 Harrison Smith .25 .60
42 Jamell Fleming .25 .60
43 Jerry Franklin .30 .75
44 Jarrett Boykin .60 1.50
45 Jeff Fuller .25 .60
46 James-Michael Johnson .30 .75
47 Joe Adams .25 .60
48 Jeremy Ebert .25 .60
49 Kevin Koger .40 1.00
50 Jonathan Martin .25 .60
51 Jordan Jefferson .30 .75
52 Jordan White .30 .75
53 Junior Hemingway .40 1.00
54 Juron Criner .25 .60
55 Kendall Wright .25 .60
56 Keshawn Martin .30 .75
57 Jermaine Kearse .40 1.00
58 Kirk Cousins 1.00 2.50
59 Ladarius Green .25 .60
60 LaMichael James .25 .60
61 Kendall Reyes .25 .60
62 Lavasier Tuinei .40 1.00
63 Alfred Morris .25 .60
64 Lennon Creer .25 .60
65 Luke Kuechly .60 1.50
66 Marc Tyler .25 .60
67 Laron Byrd .30 .75
68 Marquis Maze .25 .60
69 Nigel Bradham .30 .75
70 Alfonzo Dennard .25 .60
71 Matt Kalil .25 .60
72 Rodney Stewart .30 .75
73 Michael Egnew .25 .60
74 Dan Persa .30 .75
75 Mike Willie .40 1.00
76 Micanor Regis .25 .60
77 Mike Martin .30 .75
78 Orson Charles .25 .60
79 Pat Edwards .30 .75
80 Quinton Coples .25 .60
81 Justin Blackmon .25 .60
82 Riley Reiff .25 .60
83 Rishard Matthews .25 .60
84 Ronnell Lewis .25 .60
85 Ronnie Hillman .25 .60
86 Nelson Rosario .25 .60
87 Russell Wilson 4.00 10.00
88 Stephfon Green .40 1.00
89 T.J. Graham .25 .60
90 Mychal Kendricks .40 1.00
91 Eric Page .30 .75
92 Thomas Mayo .25 .60
93 Jared Crick .25 .60
94 Travis Benjamin .25 .60
95 David Molk .40 1.00
96 Tyler Shoemaker .30 .75
97 Tim Benford .25 .60
98 Vontaze Burfict .30 .75
99 Whitney Mercilus .25 .60
100 Rhett Ellison .30 .75
101 Trent Richardson SP 1.00 2.50
102 Cyrus Gray SP 1.00 2.50
103 Nick Toon SP 1.00 2.50
104 Brock Osweiler SP 1.00 2.50
105 Jarius Wright SP 1.00 2.50
106 Ryan Broyles SP 1.00 2.50
107 Michael Brockers SP 1.00 2.50
108 Michael Floyd SP 1.00 2.50
109 Mohamed Sanu SP 1.50 4.00
110 Bernard Pierce SP 1.00 2.50
111 Rueben Randle SP 1.00 2.50
112 DeVier Posey SP 1.00 2.50
113 Ryan Lindley SP 1.00 2.50
114 Marvin McNutt SP 1.00 2.50
115 Tauren Poole SP 1.00 2.50
116 Kellen Moore SP 1.25 3.00
117 Dre Kirkpatrick SP 1.00 2.50
118 Nick Foles SP 2.50 6.00
119 Stephen Hill SP 1.00 2.50
120 Brian Quick SP 1.00 2.50
121 Dwight Jones SP 1.00 2.50
122 B.J. Cunningham SP 1.00 2.50
123 Ryan Tannehill SP 1.50 4.00
124 Edwin Baker SP 1.25 3.00
125 Coby Fleener SP 1.00 2.50
126 Brandon Bolden SP 1.00 2.50
127 Mark Barron SP 1.00 2.50
128 Davin Meggett SP 1.00 2.50
129 Marvin Jones SP 1.00 2.50
130 Melvin Ingram SP 1.00 2.50
131 Roger Staubach SP 2.00 5.00
132 Ty Detmer SP 1.00 2.50
133 Andre Ware SP 1.25 3.00
134 Troy Aikman SP 2.00 5.00
135 Jerry Rice SP 2.50 6.00
136 Herschel Walker SP 1.50 4.00
137 John Elway SP 2.50 6.00

138 Charles White SP	1.00	2.50
139 Tony Dorsett SP	1.50	4.00
140 Earl Campbell SP	1.50	4.00
141 Jim Kelly SP	1.50	4.00
142 Joe Theismann SP	1.25	3.00
143 Dan Marino SP	3.00	8.00
144 Steve Young SP	2.00	5.00
145 Bo Jackson SP	2.00	5.00
146 Barry Sanders SP	2.50	6.00
147 Billy Sims SP	1.25	3.00
148 Aaron Rodgers SP	2.50	6.00
149 Drew Brees SP	2.00	5.00
150 Tim Tebow SP	2.00	5.00
151 Andrew Luck	30.00	60.00
251 Nick Foles JSY AU/885	20.00	50.00
252 Doug Martin JSY AU/885	8.00	20.00
253 Kellen Moore JSY AU/885	6.00	15.00
254 Case Keenum JSY AU/885	50.00	100.00
255 D.Allen JSY AU/885	5.00	12.00
256 Coby Fleener JSY AU/885	5.00	12.00
257 Juron Criner JSY AU/885	5.00	12.00
258 Kirk Cousins JSY AU/885	25.00	50.00
259 Dwight Jones JSY AU/885	5.00	12.00
260 K. Wright JSY AU/885	5.00	12.00
261 Dan Herron JSY AU/885	5.00	12.00
262 DeVier Posey JSY AU/885	5.00	12.00
263 Ryan Broyles JSY AU/885	5.00	12.00
264 B.Weeden JSY AU/885	5.00	12.00
265 B.Cunningham JSY AU/885	5.00	12.00
266 Alshon Jeffery JSY AU/885	12.00	30.00
267 Jeff Fuller JSY AU/885	5.00	12.00
268 Mohamed Sanu JSY AU/885	8.00	20.00
269 L.James JSY AU/885	5.00	12.00
270 Rueben Randle JSY AU/885	5.00	12.00
271 Nick Toon JSY AU/885	5.00	12.00
272 Russell Wilson JSY AU/885	50.00	100.00
273 T.Richardson JSY AU/425	8.00	20.00
274 R.Griffin III JSY AU/425	10.00	25.00
275 Michael Floyd JSY AU/425	8.00	20.00
276 Isaiah Pead JSY AU/425	8.00	20.00
277 J.Blackmon JSY AU/425	8.00	20.00
278 B.Osweiler JSY AU/425	8.00	20.00
279 R.Tannehill JSY AU/425	12.00	30.00
280 Stephen Hill JSY AU/425	8.00	20.00
NNO QB Draft Trade AU	350.00	500.00

2012 SP Authentic Rookie Patch Autographs Gold

*GOLD/25: 1.2X TO 3X BASE JSY AU/885
*GOLD/25: .8X TO 2X BASE JSY AU/425

251 Nick Foles	100.00	200.00
252 Doug Martin	30.00	80.00
258 Kirk Cousins	60.00	120.00
272 Russell Wilson	300.00	500.00
273 Trent Richardson	75.00	150.00
274 Robert Griffin III	25.00	60.00
278 Brock Osweiler	20.00	50.00
279 Ryan Tannehill	30.00	80.00

2012 SP Authentic 1994 SP

*DIE CUT: .8X TO 2X BASIC INSERTS

94SP1 Troy Aikman	1.50	4.00
94SP2 Bernie Kosar	1.00	2.50
94SP3 John Elway	2.00	5.00
94SP4 Billy Sims	1.00	2.50
94SP5 Barry Sanders	2.00	5.00
94SP6 Bo Jackson	1.50	4.00
94SP7 Steve Young	1.50	4.00
94SP8 Tony Dorsett	1.25	3.00
94SP9 Thurman Thomas	1.00	2.50
94SP10 Drew Brees	1.25	3.00
94SP11 Earl Campbell	1.25	3.00
94SP12 Charles White	.75	2.00
94SP13 Aaron Rodgers	2.00	5.00
94SP14 Herschel Walker	1.25	3.00
94SP15 Tim Tebow	1.25	3.00
94SP16 Mike Alstott	.75	2.00
94SP17 Dan Marino	2.50	6.00
94SP18 Ty Detmer	.75	2.00
94SP19 Roger Staubach	1.50	4.00
94SP20 Andre Ware	.75	2.00
94SP21 Aaron Corp	.60	1.50
94SP22 Michael Egnew	.60	1.50
94SP23 Jeremy Ebert	.60	1.50
94SP24 Jordan White	.75	2.00
94SP25 Pat Edwards	.75	2.00
94SP26 Ladarius Green	.60	1.50
94SP27 Alshon Jeffery	1.25	3.00
94SP28 Devon Wylie	.60	1.50
94SP29 B.J. Cunningham	.60	1.50
94SP30 Mark Barron	.60	1.50
94SP31 Brandon Weeden	.60	1.50
94SP32 Brian Quick	.60	1.50
94SP33 Case Keenum	1.25	3.00
94SP34 Chandler Harnish	.60	1.50
94SP35 Matt Kalil	.60	1.50
94SP36 Harrison Smith	.60	1.50
94SP37 Shea McClellin	.75	2.00
94SP38 Davin Meggett	.60	1.50
94SP39 Coby Fleener	.60	1.50
94SP40 Cyrus Gray	.60	1.50
94SP41 Dan Herron	.60	1.50
94SP42 Alfred Morris	.60	1.50
94SP43 DeVier Posey	.60	1.50
94SP44 Rueben Randle	.60	1.50
94SP45 Doug Martin	1.00	2.50
94SP46 Dwight Jones	.60	1.50
94SP47 Edwin Baker	.75	2.00
94SP48 Jeff Fuller	.60	1.50
94SP49 Juron Criner	.60	1.50
94SP50 Joe Adams	.60	1.50
94SP51 Isaiah Pead	.60	1.50
94SP52 Jarius Wright	.60	1.50
94SP53 Ronnie Hillman	.60	1.50
94SP54 Michael Brockers	.60	1.50
94SP55 Brock Osweiler	.60	1.50
94SP56 Luke Kuechly	1.50	4.00
94SP57 Kellen Moore	.75	2.00
94SP58 Justin Blackmon	.60	1.50
94SP59 Kendall Wright	.60	1.50
94SP60 Rhett Ellison	.75	2.00
94SP61 Tauren Poole	.60	1.50
94SP62 Melvin Ingram	.60	1.50
94SP63 Kirk Cousins	2.50	6.00
94SP64 LaMichael James	.60	1.50
94SP65 Stephen Hill	.60	1.50
94SP66 Marvin Jones	.60	1.50
94SP67 Whitney Mercilus	.60	1.50
94SP68 Marquis Maze	.60	1.50
94SP69 Robert Griffin III	.75	2.00
94SP70 Rishard Matthews	.60	1.50
94SP71 Dwayne Allen	.60	1.50
94SP72 Michael Floyd	.60	1.50
94SP73 Mohamed Sanu	1.00	2.50
94SP74 Nick Foles	1.50	4.00
94SP75 Trent Richardson	.60	1.50
94SP76 T.J. Graham	.60	1.50
94SP77 Ryan Broyles	.60	1.50
94SP78 Nick Toon	.60	1.50
94SP79 Russell Wilson	5.00	12.00
94SP80 Quinton Coples	.60	1.50
94SP81 Ryan Lindley	.60	1.50
94SP82 Stephon Gilmore	.75	2.00
94SP83 Dre Kirkpatrick	.60	1.50
94SP84 Ryan Tannehill	1.00	2.50
94SP85 Dont'a Hightower	1.00	2.50
94SP86 Lavonte David	1.00	2.50
94SP87 Travis Benjamin	.60	1.50
94SP88 A.J. Jenkins	.60	1.50
94SP89 Marvin McNutt	.60	1.50
94SP90 Dontari Poe	.60	1.50
94SP91 Dominique Davis	.75	2.00
94SP92 Junior Hemingway	1.00	2.50
94SP93 Jarrett Boykin	1.50	4.00
94SP94 Orson Charles	.60	1.50
94SP95 Andre Branch	.60	1.50
94SP96 Bernard Pierce	.60	1.50
94SP97 Courtney Upshaw	.75	2.00
94SP98 Keshawn Martin	.75	2.00
94SP99 Greg Childs	.60	1.50
94SP100 Janoris Jenkins	.75	2.00

2012 SP Authentic 1994 SP Autographs

EXCH EXPIRATION: 1/8/2015

94SP1 Troy Aikman		
94SP2 Bernie Kosar		
94SP3 John Elway		
94SP4 Billy Sims	10.00	25.00
94SP5 Barry Sanders		
94SP6 Bo Jackson		
94SP7 Steve Young		
94SP8 Tony Dorsett		
94SP9 Thurman Thomas	12.00	30.00
94SP10 Drew Brees		
94SP11 Earl Campbell	12.00	30.00
94SP12 Charles White		
94SP13 Aaron Rodgers		
94SP14 Herschel Walker		
94SP15 Tim Tebow		
94SP16 Mike Alstott		
94SP17 Dan Marino		
94SP18 Ty Detmer	8.00	20.00
94SP19 Roger Staubach		
94SP20 Andre Ware		
94SP21 Aaron Corp	5.00	12.00
94SP22 Michael Egnew		
94SP23 Jeremy Ebert	5.00	12.00
94SP24 Jordan White		
94SP25 Pat Edwards	6.00	15.00
94SP26 Ladarius Green		
94SP27 Alshon Jeffery	10.00	25.00
94SP28 Devon Wylie	5.00	12.00
94SP29 B.J. Cunningham	5.00	12.00
94SP30 Mark Barron		
94SP31 Brandon Weeden		
94SP32 Brian Quick		
94SP33 Case Keenum	10.00	25.00
94SP34 Chandler Harnish	5.00	12.00
94SP35 Matt Kalil	10.00	25.00
94SP36 Harrison Smith	10.00	25.00
94SP37 Shea McClellin	6.00	15.00
94SP38 Davin Meggett	6.00	15.00
94SP39 Coby Fleener		
94SP40 Cyrus Gray		
94SP41 Dan Herron		
94SP42 Alfred Morris	5.00	12.00
94SP43 DeVier Posey		
94SP44 Rueben Randle		
94SP45 Doug Martin		
94SP46 Dwight Jones		
94SP47 Edwin Baker	6.00	15.00
94SP48 Jeff Fuller	5.00	12.00
94SP49 Juron Criner		
94SP50 Joe Adams	8.00	20.00
94SP51 Isaiah Pead		
94SP52 Jarius Wright	5.00	12.00
94SP53 Ronnie Hillman	5.00	12.00
94SP54 Michael Brockers	5.00	12.00
94SP55 Brock Osweiler	5.00	12.00
94SP56 Luke Kuechly	15.00	40.00
94SP57 Kellen Moore		
94SP58 Justin Blackmon		
94SP59 Kendall Wright		
94SP60 Rhett Ellison	6.00	15.00
94SP61 Tauren Poole		
94SP62 Melvin Ingram		
94SP63 Kirk Cousins	15.00	40.00
94SP64 LaMichael James	5.00	12.00
94SP65 Stephen Hill	12.00	30.00
94SP66 Marvin Jones		
94SP67 Whitney Mercilus	6.00	15.00
94SP68 Marquis Maze		
94SP69 Robert Griffin III EXCH		
94SP70 Rishard Matthews	5.00	12.00
94SP71 Dwayne Allen		
94SP72 Michael Floyd	5.00	12.00
94SP73 Mohamed Sanu		
94SP74 Nick Foles	25.00	60.00
94SP75 Trent Richardson		
94SP76 T.J. Graham	5.00	12.00
94SP77 Ryan Broyles	20.00	40.00
94SP78 Nick Toon		
94SP79 Russell Wilson	100.00	200.00
94SP80 Quinton Coples	5.00	12.00
94SP81 Ryan Lindley		
94SP82 Stephon Gilmore	6.00	15.00
94SP83 Dre Kirkpatrick EXCH	5.00	12.00
94SP84 Ryan Tannehill		
94SP85 Dont'a Hightower		
94SP86 Lavonte David		
94SP87 Travis Benjamin	5.00	12.00
94SP88 A.J. Jenkins		
94SP89 Marvin McNutt	10.00	25.00
94SP90 Dontari Poe	5.00	12.00
94SP91 Dominique Davis	6.00	15.00
94SP93 Jarrett Boykin	12.00	30.00
94SP94 Orson Charles		
94SP95 Andre Branch	8.00	20.00
94SP96 Bernard Pierce	20.00	40.00
94SP97 Courtney Upshaw	6.00	15.00
94SP98 Keshawn Martin		
94SP99 Greg Childs	5.00	12.00
94SP100 Janoris Jenkins	12.00	30.00

2012 SP Authentic Autographs

OVERALL AUTO ODDS 1:12
EXCH EXPIRATION: 1/8/2015

1 A.J. Jenkins	3.00	8.00
2 Aaron Corp	3.00	8.00
3 Alameda Ta'amu	4.00	10.00
4 Stephon Gilmore	4.00	10.00
5 Alshon Jeffery	10.00	25.00
6 Andre Branch	3.00	8.00
7 Dont'a Hightower	5.00	12.00
8 Darius Hanks	5.00	12.00
9 Jarrett Lee	5.00	12.00
10 Robert Griffin III EXCH	10.00	25.00
11 Bobby Rainey	3.00	8.00
12 Antwon Bailey	4.00	10.00
13 Cordy Glenn EXCH	5.00	12.00
14 Bobby Wagner	5.00	12.00
15 Brandon Thompson	4.00	10.00
16 Brandon Weeden	8.00	20.00
17 Lavonte David	5.00	12.00
18 Case Keenum	6.00	15.00
19 Chandler Harnish	3.00	8.00
20 Tyler Hansen	3.00	8.00
22 David DeCastro	3.00	8.00
23 Dontari Poe	3.00	8.00
24 Cliff Harris	5.00	12.00
25 Courtney Upshaw	4.00	10.00
26 Da'Jon McKnight	4.00	10.00
27 Dan Herron	5.00	12.00
28 Evan Rodriguez	4.00	10.00
29 Derek Moye	5.00	12.00
30 Shea McClellin	4.00	10.00
31 Devon Wylie	5.00	12.00
32 Dominique Davis	4.00	10.00
33 Doug Martin	5.00	12.00
34 Janoris Jenkins	4.00	10.00
35 Dwayne Allen	3.00	8.00
36 Amini Silatolu	3.00	8.00
37 Foswhitt Whittaker	3.00	8.00
38 Gerell Robinson	3.00	8.00
39 Greg Childs	3.00	8.00
40 Isaiah Pead	3.00	8.00
41 Harrison Smith	6.00	15.00
42 Jamell Fleming	3.00	8.00
43 Jerry Franklin	4.00	10.00
44 Jarrett Boykin	8.00	20.00
45 Jeff Fuller	3.00	8.00
46 James-Michael Johnson	4.00	10.00
47 Joe Adams	3.00	8.00
48 Jeremy Ebert	3.00	8.00
49 Kevin Koger	5.00	12.00
50 Jonathan Martin	4.00	10.00
51 Jordan Jefferson	4.00	10.00
52 Jordan White	4.00	10.00
54 Juron Criner	3.00	8.00
55 Kendall Wright	3.00	8.00
56 Keshawn Martin	4.00	10.00
57 Jermaine Kearse	6.00	15.00
58 Kirk Cousins	30.00	60.00
59 Ladarius Green	3.00	8.00
60 LaMichael James	3.00	8.00
61 Kendall Reyes	3.00	8.00
62 Lavasier Tuinei	5.00	12.00
63 Alfred Morris	3.00	8.00
65 Luke Kuechly	10.00	25.00
66 Marc Tyler	3.00	8.00
67 Laron Byrd	4.00	10.00
68 Marquis Maze	5.00	12.00
69 Nigel Bradham	4.00	10.00
70 Alfonzo Dennard	3.00	8.00
71 Matt Kalil	3.00	8.00
72 Rodney Stewart	4.00	10.00
73 Michael Egnew	3.00	8.00
74 Dan Persa	4.00	10.00
75 Mike Willie	5.00	12.00
76 Micanor Regis	3.00	8.00
77 Mike Martin	8.00	20.00
78 Orson Charles	3.00	8.00
79 Pat Edwards	4.00	10.00
80 Quinton Coples	3.00	8.00
81 Justin Blackmon	3.00	8.00
82 Riley Reiff	6.00	15.00
83 Rishard Matthews	3.00	8.00
84 Ronnell Lewis	3.00	8.00
85 Ronnie Hillman	3.00	8.00
86 Nelson Rosario	3.00	8.00
87 Russell Wilson	50.00	100.00
88 Stephfon Green	5.00	12.00
89 T.J. Graham	3.00	8.00
90 Mychal Kendricks	5.00	12.00
91 Eric Page	4.00	10.00
92 Thomas Mayo	3.00	8.00
93 Jared Crick	3.00	8.00
94 Travis Benjamin	3.00	8.00
95 David Molk	5.00	12.00
96 Tyler Shoemaker	5.00	12.00
97 Tim Benford	3.00	8.00
98 Vontaze Burfict EXCH	4.00	10.00
99 Whitney Mercilus	3.00	8.00
100 Rhett Ellison	4.00	10.00
101 Trent Richardson SP	25.00	50.00
102 Cyrus Gray SP	6.00	15.00
103 Nick Toon SP		
104 Brock Osweiler SP	10.00	25.00
105 Jarius Wright SP	5.00	12.00
106 Ryan Broyles SP		
107 Michael Brockers SP	5.00	12.00
108 Michael Floyd SP	20.00	40.00
109 Mohamed Sanu SP	8.00	20.00
110 Bernard Pierce SP	20.00	40.00
111 Rueben Randle SP	5.00	12.00
112 DeVier Posey SP	8.00	20.00
113 Ryan Lindley SP	5.00	12.00
114 Marvin McNutt SP	8.00	20.00
115 Tauren Poole SP	5.00	12.00
116 Kellen Moore SP	6.00	15.00
117 Dre Kirkpatrick SP	10.00	25.00
118 Nick Foles SP	25.00	60.00
119 Stephen Hill SP	10.00	25.00
120 Brian Quick SP		
121 Dwight Jones SP	5.00	12.00
122 B.J. Cunningham SP	5.00	12.00
123 Ryan Tannehill SP	8.00	20.00
124 Edwin Baker SP	6.00	15.00
125 Coby Fleener SP	5.00	12.00
126 Brandon Bolden SP	5.00	12.00
127 Mark Barron SP	12.00	30.00
128 Davin Meggett SP	5.00	12.00
129 Marvin Jones SP	5.00	12.00
130 Melvin Ingram SP	5.00	12.00
131 Roger Staubach SP	40.00	80.00
132 Ty Detmer SP	8.00	20.00
133 Andre Ware SP	10.00	25.00
134 Troy Aikman SP	40.00	80.00
135 Jerry Rice SP		
136 Herschel Walker SP	25.00	50.00
137 John Elway SP	75.00	150.00
138 Charles White SP	8.00	20.00
139 Tony Dorsett SP EXCH	30.00	60.00
140 Earl Campbell SP	15.00	40.00
141 Jim Kelly SP	40.00	80.00
142 Joe Theismann SP	20.00	40.00
143 Dan Marino SP		
144 Steve Young SP	40.00	80.00
145 Bo Jackson SP	30.00	60.00
146 Barry Sanders SP		
147 Billy Sims SP	10.00	25.00
148 Aaron Rodgers SP	125.00	200.00
149 Drew Brees SP	40.00	80.00
150 Tim Tebow SP		
151 Andrew Luck SP	350.00	550.00
NNO QB Trade Card	250.00	400.00

2012 SP Authentic Autographs Gold

*1-100 GOLD/15: 1.2X TO 3X BASIC AU
1-100 ROOKIE PRINT RUN 15

10 Robert Griffin III EXCH	30.00	80.00
16 Brandon Weeden	20.00	50.00
58 Kirk Cousins	50.00	100.00
60 LaMichael James		
63 Alfred Morris	10.00	25.00
81 Justin Blackmon	10.00	25.00
87 Russell Wilson		

2012 SP Authentic Canvas Collection

STATED ODDS 1:6

CC1 Bobby Wagner	1.25	3.00
CC2 Aaron Corp	.75	2.00
CC3 Jarrett Lee	1.25	3.00
CC4 Alfonzo Dennard	.75	2.00
CC5 Andre Branch	.75	2.00
CC6 Jared Crick	.75	2.00
CC7 Harrison Smith	.75	2.00
CC8 B.J. Cunningham	.75	2.00
CC9 Bernard Pierce	.75	2.00
CC10 Bobby Rainey	.75	2.00
CC11 Brandon Bolden	.75	2.00
CC12 Brandon Thompson	1.00	2.50
CC13 Brian Quick	.75	2.00
CC14 Jayron Hosley	1.25	3.00
CC15 Chandler Harnish	.75	2.00
CC16 Dontari Poe	.75	2.00
CC17 Alfred Morris	.75	2.00
CC18 Coby Fleener	.75	2.00
CC19 Dan Persa	1.00	2.50
CC20 Cyrus Gray	.75	2.00
CC21 Da'Jon McKnight	1.00	2.50
CC22 Mychal Kendricks	1.25	3.00
CC23 Davin Meggett	.75	2.00
CC24 Derek Moye	1.25	3.00
CC25 DeVier Posey	.75	2.00
CC26 Shea McClellin	1.00	2.50
CC27 Devon Wylie	.75	2.00
CC28 Dominique Davis	1.00	2.50
CC29 Dre Kirkpatrick	.75	2.00
CC30 Dwight Jones	.75	2.00
CC31 Amini Silatolu	.75	2.00
CC32 Foswhitt Whittaker	.75	2.00
CC33 Rueben Randle	.75	2.00
CC34 Greg Childs	.75	2.00
CC35 Kendall Reyes	.75	2.00
CC36 Janoris Jenkins	1.00	2.50
CC37 Jarius Wright	.75	2.00
CC38 Jarrett Boykin	2.00	5.00
CC39 Edwin Baker	1.00	2.50
CC40 Jermaine Kearse	1.25	3.00
CC41 Darius Hanks	1.25	3.00
CC42 Tim Benford	.75	2.00
CC43 Jonathan Martin	.75	2.00
CC44 Jordan Jefferson	1.00	2.50
CC45 Jordan White	1.00	2.50
CC46 Junior Hemingway	1.25	3.00
CC47 Ladarius Green	.75	2.00
CC48 Kellen Moore	1.00	2.50
CC49 Keshawn Martin	1.00	2.50
CC50 Cordy Glenn	1.00	2.50
CC51 Jamell Fleming	.75	2.00
CC52 Kevin Koger	1.25	3.00
CC53 Dont'a Hightower	1.25	3.00
CC54 Lennon Creer	.75	2.00
CC55 Laron Byrd	1.00	2.50
CC56 Marc Tyler	.75	2.00
CC58 Marvin Jones	.75	2.00
CC59 Marvin McNutt	.75	2.00
CC60 Michael Brockers	.75	2.00
CC61 Matt Kalil	.75	2.00
CC62 Melvin Ingram	.75	2.00
CC63 Michael Egnew	.75	2.00
CC64 Michael Floyd	.75	2.00
CC65 David DeCastro	.75	2.00
CC66 Mike Willie	1.25	3.00
CC67 Mohamed Sanu	1.25	3.00
CC68 Eric Page	1.00	2.50
CC69 Lavasier Tuinei	1.25	3.00
CC70 Nick Foles	2.00	5.00
CC71 Nick Toon	.75	2.00
CC72 Orson Charles	.75	2.00
CC73 Pat Edwards	1.00	2.50
CC74 Riley Reiff	.75	2.00
CC75 Rishard Matthews	.75	2.00
CC76 Stephen Hill	.75	2.00
CC77 Ronnell Lewis	.75	2.00
CC78 Ryan Broyles	.75	2.00
CC79 Ryan Lindley	.75	2.00
CC80 Ryan Tannehill	1.25	3.00
CC81 Stephfon Green	1.25	3.00
CC82 Tyler Hansen	.75	2.00
CC83 Tauren Poole	.75	2.00
CC84 Tyler Shoemaker	1.00	2.50
CC85 Travis Benjamin	.75	2.00
CC86 Trent Richardson	.75	2.00
CC87 Brock Osweiler	.75	2.00
CC88 Rhett Ellison	1.00	2.50
CC89 Whitney Mercilus	.75	2.00
CC90 Lavonte David	1.25	3.00

2012 SP Authentic Canvas Legends

CL1 Bo Jackson	4.00	10.00
CL2 Steve Young	4.00	10.00
CL3 Herschel Walker	3.00	8.00
CL4 Bernie Kosar	2.50	6.00
CL5 Jerry Rice	5.00	12.00
CL6 Roger Staubach	4.00	10.00
CL7 Tim Brown	3.00	8.00
CL8 Joe Theismann	2.50	6.00
CL9 Billy Sims	2.50	6.00
CL10 Barry Sanders	5.00	12.00
CL11 Tony Dorsett	3.00	8.00
CL12 Dan Marino	6.00	15.00
CL13 John Elway	5.00	12.00
CL14 Jim Plunkett	2.50	6.00
CL15 Earl Campbell	3.00	8.00
CL16 Troy Aikman	4.00	10.00
CL17 Charles White	2.00	5.00
CL18 Aaron Rodgers	5.00	12.00
CL19 Drew Brees	3.00	8.00
CL20 Tim Tebow	3.00	8.00

2012 SP Authentic Canvas Rookie SP

CR1 Robert Griffin III	1.50	4.00
CR2 Kendall Wright	1.25	3.00
CR3 Courtney Upshaw	1.50	4.00
CR4 Marquis Maze	1.25	3.00
CR5 Gerell Robinson	1.25	3.00
CR6 Juron Criner	1.25	3.00
CR7 Joe Adams	1.25	3.00
CR8 Doug Martin	2.00	5.00
CR9 Luke Kuechly	3.00	8.00
CR10 Isaiah Pead	1.25	3.00
CR11 Dwayne Allen	1.25	3.00
CR12 Case Keenum	2.50	6.00
CR13 A.J. Jenkins	1.25	3.00
CR14 Kirk Cousins	5.00	12.00
CR15 T.J. Graham	1.25	3.00
CR16 Quinton Coples	1.25	3.00
CR17 Dan Herron	1.25	3.00
CR18 Brandon Weeden	1.25	3.00
CR19 Justin Blackmon	1.25	3.00
CR20 LaMichael James	1.25	3.00
CR21 Ronnie Hillman	1.25	3.00
CR22 Alshon Jeffery	2.50	6.00
CR23 Stephon Gilmore	1.50	4.00
CR24 Jeff Fuller	1.25	3.00
CR25 Russell Wilson	10.00	25.00

2012 SP Authentic Rookie Threads Autographs

RTBO Brock Osweiler/335	5.00	12.00
RTBW Brandon Weeden/335	5.00	12.00
RTCG Cyrus Gray/335	5.00	12.00
RTCK Case Keenum/335	25.00	50.00
RTDJ Dwight Jones/335	5.00	12.00
RTDM Doug Martin/335	8.00	20.00
RTDP DeVier Posey/335	5.00	12.00
RTIP Isaiah Pead/335	5.00	12.00
RTJB Justin Blackmon/75	8.00	20.00
RTJC Juron Criner/335	5.00	12.00
RTJE Alshon Jeffery/335	10.00	25.00
RTJF Jeff Fuller/335	5.00	12.00
RTKC Kirk Cousins/335	20.00	50.00
RTKM Kellen Moore/335	6.00	15.00
RTKW Kendall Wright/335	5.00	12.00
RTLJ LaMichael James/335	5.00	12.00
RTMF Michael Floyd/165	8.00	20.00
RTMI Melvin Ingram/335	5.00	12.00
RTMS Mohamed Sanu/335	8.00	20.00
RTNF Nick Foles/335	20.00	40.00
RTNT Nick Toon/335	5.00	12.00
RTRB Ryan Broyles/335	5.00	12.00
RTRG Robert Griffin III/75	10.00	25.00
RTRR Rueben Randle/335	5.00	12.00
RTRT Ryan Tannehill/75	12.00	30.00
RTRW Russell Wilson/335	60.00	125.00
RTSH Stephen Hill/165	6.00	15.00
RTTR Trent Richardson/75	15.00	40.00

2012 SP Authentic Sign of the Times

STAB Andre Branch	3.00	8.00
STAD Alfonzo Dennard	3.00	8.00
STAJ A.J. Jenkins		
STAM Alfred Morris	3.00	8.00
STAR Aaron Rodgers		
STAW Andre Ware	6.00	15.00
STBA Mark Barron	3.00	8.00
STBC B.J. Cunningham	3.00	8.00
STBJ Bo Jackson	40.00	80.00
STBK Bernie Kosar	6.00	15.00
STBO Jarrett Boykin	8.00	20.00
STBP Bernard Pierce	6.00	15.00
STBQ Brian Quick	3.00	8.00
STBS Barry Sanders	50.00	120.00
STBW Brandon Weeden	3.00	8.00
STCF Coby Fleener	3.00	8.00
STCG Cyrus Gray	3.00	8.00
STCH Chandler Harnish	3.00	8.00
STCK Case Keenum	6.00	15.00
STCU Courtney Upshaw	4.00	10.00
STDA Dwayne Allen	3.00	8.00
STDB Drew Brees		
STDD Dominique Davis	4.00	10.00
STDH Dan Herron	3.00	8.00
STDJ Dwight Jones	3.00	8.00
STDK Dre Kirkpatrick	3.00	8.00
STDM Dan Marino		
STDO Doug Martin	5.00	12.00
STDP DeVier Posey	3.00	8.00
STDW Devon Wylie	3.00	8.00
STEB Jeremy Ebert	3.00	8.00
STEC Earl Campbell	20.00	50.00
STED Edwin Baker	6.00	15.00
STEL John Elway		
STGC Greg Childs	3.00	8.00
STHA Casey Hayward	3.00	8.00
STHI Dont'a Hightower EXCH	5.00	12.00
STHS Harrison Smith	6.00	15.00
STHW Herschel Walker	20.00	40.00
STIP Isaiah Pead	3.00	8.00
STJA Joe Adams	3.00	8.00
STJB Justin Blackmon	6.00	15.00
STJC Juron Criner	3.00	8.00
STJE Alshon Jeffery	6.00	15.00
STJF Jeff Fuller	3.00	8.00
STJJ Janoris Jenkins	4.00	10.00
STJP Jim Plunkett		
STJR Johnny Rodgers	6.00	15.00
STJW Jarius Wright	3.00	8.00
STKC Kirk Cousins	20.00	40.00
STKE Keshawn Martin	4.00	10.00
STKM Kellen Moore	4.00	10.00
STKW Kendall Wright		
STLD Lavonte David	5.00	12.00
STLG Ladarius Green	3.00	8.00
STLJ LaMichael James	3.00	8.00
STLK Luke Kuechly	8.00	20.00
STMB Michael Brockers	3.00	8.00
STMC Marvin McNutt	5.00	12.00
STMF Michael Floyd	8.00	20.00
STMI Melvin Ingram	3.00	8.00
STMJ Marvin Jones	3.00	8.00
STMK Matt Kalil	3.00	8.00
STMM Marquis Maze	4.00	10.00
STMS Mohamed Sanu	5.00	12.00
STMY Mychal Kendricks	5.00	12.00
STNF Nick Foles	15.00	40.00
STNT Nick Toon	3.00	8.00
STOC Orson Charles	3.00	8.00
STOS Brock Osweiler	3.00	8.00
STPE Pat Edwards	4.00	10.00
STPO Dontari Poe	3.00	8.00
STQC Quinton Coples	3.00	8.00
STRB Ryan Broyles	6.00	15.00
STRG Robert Griffin III EXCH	12.00	30.00
STRH Ronnie Hillman	3.00	8.00
STRL Ryan Lindley	3.00	8.00
STRM Rishard Matthews	3.00	8.00
STRR Rueben Randle	3.00	8.00
STRS Roger Staubach EXCH	40.00	80.00
STRT Ryan Tannehill	5.00	12.00
STRW Russell Wilson	60.00	100.00
STSG Stephon Gilmore	4.00	10.00
STSH Stephen Hill		
STSI Billy Sims	6.00	15.00
STSM Shea McClellin	4.00	10.00
STSS Steve Sewell	5.00	12.00
STSY Steve Young	30.00	60.00
STTA Troy Aikman		
STTB Travis Benjamin	3.00	8.00
STTD Tony Dorsett		
STTG T.J. Graham	3.00	8.00
STTH Thurman Thomas		
STTR Trent Richardson	25.00	60.00
STTT Tim Tebow		
STVB Vontaze Burfict EXCH	4.00	10.00
STWA Bobby Wagner	5.00	12.00
STWH Jordan White	4.00	10.00
STWM Whitney Mercilus	3.00	8.00

2012 SP Authentic Sign of the Times Duals

ST21 M.Barron/D.Kirkpatrick/35	10.00	25.00
ST22 B.Quick/A.Jenkins/35	10.00	25.00
ST23 A.Toon/N.Toon/35	25.00	50.00
ST25 K.Cousins/N.Foles/35	60.00	125.00
ST28 A.Ware/C.Keenum/35	25.00	50.00
ST214 D.Martin/K.Moore/35	15.00	40.00
ST215 K.Martin/D.Posey/35	12.00	30.00
ST219 L.James/R.Hillman/35	10.00	25.00

2012 SP Authentic Sign of the Times Triple

ST32 White/Sims/Broyles/20	40.00	80.00
ST39 Lindley/Keenum/Moore/20		
ST313 Allen/Fleener/Egnew/20		

2012 SP Authentic Stadium Authentics

STATED ODDS 1:110
*BOWL LOGO: .5X TO 1.2X BASIC INSERTS

SAAC Anthony Carter	8.00	20.00
SAAG Archie Griffin	8.00	20.00
SAAR Aaron Rodgers	15.00	40.00
SABB Brian Bosworth	8.00	20.00
SABO Brock Osweiler	4.00	10.00
SABS Barry Sanders	15.00	40.00
SACW Charles White	6.00	15.00
SADB Drew Brees	8.00	20.00
SADM Dan Marino	20.00	50.00
SAEC Earl Campbell	10.00	25.00
SAEL John Elway	12.00	30.00
SAHW Herschel Walker	10.00	25.00
SAJK Jim Kelly	10.00	25.00
SAJW Jarius Wright	4.00	10.00
SAKC Kirk Cousins	15.00	40.00
SAKM Kellen Moore	5.00	12.00
SALJ LaMichael James	4.00	10.00
SARC Roger Craig	8.00	20.00
SARG Robert Griffin III	5.00	12.00
SARR Rueben Randle	4.00	10.00
SARS Roger Staubach	12.00	30.00
SARW Russell Wilson	15.00	30.00
SASH Stephen Hill	4.00	10.00
SASY Steve Young	10.00	25.00
SATB Tim Brown	10.00	25.00
SATR Trent Richardson	4.00	10.00
SAWA Charlie Ward	8.00	20.00
SAWM Warren Moon	10.00	25.00

2012 SP Authentic Stadium Authentics Autographs

SAABJ Bo Jackson		
SAABW Brandon Weeden		
SAADM Doug Martin	15.00	40.00
SAAJR Johnny Rodgers	20.00	40.00
SAAMF Michael Floyd	30.00	80.00
SAANF Nick Foles	15.00	40.00
SAARB Ryan Broyles	40.00	80.00
SAART Ryan Tannehill		
SAATT Tim Tebow	75.00	150.00

2013 SP Authentic

COMP.SET w/o RC's (100) 8.00 20.00
101-150 SP STATED ODDS 1:12
ROOKIE JSY AU/325-650 ODDS 1:24

1 Brad Sorensen	.25	.60
2 B.J. Daniels	.40	1.00
3 Dayne Crist	.30	.75
4 Geno Smith	.25	.60
5 Jeff Tuel	.25	.60
6 Jordan Rodgers	.30	.75
7 Matt Barkley	.25	.60
8 Matt Scott	.25	.60
9 Bennie Logan	.30	.75
10 D.J. Swearinger	.25	.60
11 Ryan Nassib	.25	.60
12 Justin Pugh	.25	.60
13 Tyler Wilson	.25	.60
14 Zac Dysert	.25	.60
15 Zach Maynard	.30	.75
16 Cameron Marshall	.25	.60
17 Chris Thompson	.25	.60
18 Cierre Wood	.25	.60
19 Damontre Moore	.25	.60
20 David Amerson	.25	.60
21 Dennis Johnson	.25	.60
22 Jawan Jamison	.25	.60
23 Johnathan Franklin	.25	.60
24 Kenjon Barner	.25	.60
25 Knile Davis	.25	.60
26 Le'Veon Bell	.75	2.00
27 Mike Gillislee	.25	.60
28 Montee Ball	.25	.60
29 Ray Graham	.25	.60
30 Rex Burkhead	.30	.75
31 Robbie Rouse	.25	.60
32 Stefphon Jefferson	.30	.75
33 Stepfan Taylor	.25	.60
34 Zach Ertz	.50	1.25
35 Aaron Dobson	.25	.60
36 Aaron Mellette	.25	.60
37 Brandon Kaufman	.25	.60
38 Chris Harper	.25	.60
39 Dion Jordan	.25	.60
40 Cobi Hamilton	.25	.60
41 Conner Vernon	.25	.60
42 Corey Fuller	.25	.60
43 Kiko Alonso	.30	.75
44 DeAndre Hopkins	.60	1.50
45 Blidi Wreh-Wilson	.30	.75
46 Dee Milliner	.25	.60
47 Margus Hunt	.25	.60
48 Erik Highsmith	.30	.75
49 Desmond Trufant	.25	.60
50 Keenan Davis	.40	1.00
51 Keenan Allen	.50	1.25
52 Marcus Davis	.25	.60
53 Markus Wheaton	.25	.60
54 Marquess Wilson	.40	1.00
55 Marquise Goodwin	.25	.60
56 Eric Reid	.30	.75
57 Sam Montgomery	.25	.60
58 Russell Shepard	.25	.60
59 Ryan Swope	.25	.60
60 Bjoern Werner	.25	.60
61 Jordan Reed	.40	1.00
62 Joseph Fauria	.25	.60
63 Michael Williams	.30	.75
64 Nick Kasa	.25	.60
65 Philip Lutzenkirchen	.40	1.00
66 Jon Bostic	.25	.60
67 Jordan Hill	.40	1.00
68 Gavin Escobar	.25	.60
69 Matt Elam	.25	.60
70 Tyrone Goard	.25	.60
71 T.J. McDonald	.25	.60
72 Barkevious Mingo	.25	.60
73 Xavier Rhodes	.25	.60
74 Datone Jones	.25	.60
75 Kawann Short	.25	.60
76 Sharrif Floyd	.25	.60
77 Sheldon Richardson	.25	.60
78 Alec Ogletree	.25	.60
79 Spencer Ware	.25	.60
80 Dion Sims	.25	.60
81 Lane Johnson	.30	.75
82 Robert Alford	.25	.60
83 Kevin Minter	.25	.60
84 Vince Williams	.40	1.00
85 Brandon Jenkins	.30	.75
86 D.J. Fluker	.25	.60
87 Sylvester Williams	.25	.60
88 Khaseem Greene	.25	.60
89 Ezekiel Ansah	.25	.60
90 Eric Fisher	.25	.60
91 Manti Te'o	.30	.75
92 Tavon Austin	.30	.75
93 Theo Riddick	.25	.60
94 Josh Boyce	.25	.60
95 Travis Kelce	.60	1.50
96 Vance McDonald	.30	.75
97 Kenny Vaccaro	.25	.60
98 Arthur Brown	.25	.60
99 Onterio McCalebb	.30	.75
100 EJ Manuel	.25	.60
101 Andre Ellington SP	.75	2.00
102 Justin Hunter SP	.75	2.00
103 Robert Woods SP	1.25	3.00
104 Luke Joeckel SP	.75	2.00
105 Terrance Williams SP	.75	2.00
106 Collin Klein SP	1.00	2.50
107 Kenny Stills SP	.75	2.00
108 Marcus Lattimore SP	.75	2.00
109 Tavon Austin SP	1.00	2.50
110 Denard Robinson SP	.75	2.00
111 Eddie Lacy SP	.75	2.00
112 Mike Glennon SP	.75	2.00
113 Giovani Bernard SP	.75	2.00
114 Cordarrelle Patterson SP	.75	2.00
115 Joseph Randle SP	.75	2.00
116 Star Lotulelei SP	1.00	2.50
117 Da'Rick Rogers SP	.75	2.00
118 Jarvis Jones SP	.75	2.00
119 Landry Jones SP	.75	2.00
120 Tyler Bray SP	.75	2.00
121 Tavarres King SP	.75	2.00
122 Stedman Bailey SP	.75	2.00
123 Alex Okafor SP	.75	2.00
124 EJ Manuel SP	.75	2.00
125 Tyler Eifert SP	.75	2.00
126 Jerry Rice SP	2.50	6.00
127 John Elway SP	2.50	6.00
128 Dan Marino SP	3.00	8.00
129 Aaron Rodgers SP	2.50	6.00
130 Joe Namath SP	2.00	5.00
131 Barry Sanders SP	2.50	6.00
132 Alan Page SP	1.00	2.50
133 Herschel Walker SP	1.50	4.00
134 Brian Bosworth SP	1.25	3.00
135 Eddie George SP	1.25	3.00
136 Lawrence Taylor SP	1.50	4.00
137 Vinny Testaverde SP	1.00	2.50
138 Bruce Smith SP	1.25	3.00
139 Ronnie Lott SP	1.25	3.00
140 Ty Detmer SP	1.00	2.50
141 Andrew Luck SP	4.00	10.00
142 Joe Theismann SP	1.50	4.00
143 Jason White SP	1.00	2.50
144 Warren Sapp SP	1.25	3.00
145 Ron Dayne SP	1.25	3.00
146 Doug Flutie SP	1.25	3.00
147 Earl Campbell SP	1.50	4.00
148 Archie Griffin SP	1.00	2.50
149 Warren Moon SP	1.50	4.00
150 Steve Young SP	2.00	5.00
151 Le'Veon Bell JSY AU/650	50.00	100.00
152 Robert Woods JSY AU/650	8.00	20.00
153 Ryan Nassib JSY AU/650	10.00	25.00
154 M.Wheaton JSY AU/650	5.00	12.00
155 T.Williams JSY AU/650	5.00	12.00
156 Aaron Dobson JSY AU/650	5.00	12.00
157 Cobi Hamilton JSY AU/650	5.00	12.00
158 M.Glennon JSY AU/650	5.00	12.00
159 G.Bernard JSY AU/650	5.00	12.00
160 Tyler Eifert JSY AU/650	5.00	12.00
161 Tavarres King JSY AU/650	5.00	12.00
163 Justin Hunter JSY AU/650	12.00	30.00
164 Montee Ball JSY AU/650	5.00	12.00
166 Zach Ertz JSY AU/650	10.00	25.00
167 Mike Gillislee JSY AU/650	5.00	12.00
168 Kenny Stills JSY AU/650	5.00	12.00
169 J.Franklin JSY AU/650	5.00	12.00
170 M.Lattimore JSY AU/650	5.00	12.00
171 Joseph Randle JSY AU/650	5.00	12.00
172 Tyler Wilson JSY AU/325	6.00	15.00
173 Zac Dysert JSY AU/650	5.00	12.00
174 Kenjon Barner JSY AU/650	5.00	12.00
175 D.Robinson JSY AU/650	5.00	12.00
176 Keenan Allen JSY AU/325	12.00	30.00
177 Eddie Lacy JSY AU/650	5.00	12.00
178 Tavon Austin JSY AU/325	8.00	20.00
179 Landry Jones JSY AU/325	6.00	15.00
180 C.Patterson JSY AU/325	6.00	15.00
181 D.Hopkins JSY AU/650	30.00	60.00
182 EJ Manuel JSY AU/650	5.00	12.00
183 Geno Smith JSY AU/325	6.00	15.00
184 Manti Te'o JSY AU/325	8.00	20.00
185 Matt Barkley JSY AU/325	6.00	15.00

2013 SP Authentic Canvas

C1-C90 STATED ODDS 1:6
C91-C113 STATED ODDS 1:72
C114-C135 STATED ODDS 1:144

CC1 Brad Sorensen	.75	2.00
CC2 Dayne Crist	1.00	2.50
CC3 Geno Smith	.75	2.00
CC4 D.J. Swearinger	.75	2.00
CC5 Jordan Rodgers	1.00	2.50
CC6 Matt Barkley	.75	2.00
CC7 Matt Scott	.75	2.00
CC8 Matt McGloin	2.50	6.00
CC9 Matt Elam	.75	2.00
CC10 Ryan Nassib	.75	2.00
CC11 Travis Kelce	2.00	5.00
CC12 Tyler Wilson	.75	2.00
CC13 Zac Dysert	.75	2.00
CC14 Chris Harper	.75	2.00
CC15 Chris Thompson	.75	2.00
CC16 Cierre Wood	.75	2.00
CC17 Damontre Moore	.75	2.00
CC18 D.J. Harper	1.00	2.50
CC19 Dennis Johnson	.75	2.00
CC20 Jawan Jamison	.75	2.00
CC21 Johnathan Franklin	.75	2.00
CC22 Kenjon Barner	.75	2.00
CC23 Knile Davis	.75	2.00
CC24 Le'Veon Bell	2.50	6.00
CC25 Mike Gillislee	.75	2.00
CC26 Montee Ball	.75	2.00
CC27 Ray Graham	.75	2.00
CC28 Rex Burkhead	1.00	2.50
CC29 Vance McDonald	1.00	2.50
CC30 Stefphon Jefferson	1.00	2.50
CC31 Stepfan Taylor	.75	2.00
CC32 Zach Ertz	1.50	4.00
CC33 Aaron Dobson	.75	2.00
CC34 Aaron Mellette	.75	2.00
CC35 Brandon Kaufman	.75	2.00
CC36 Dion Jordan	.75	2.00
CC37 Cobi Hamilton	.75	2.00
CC38 Sylvester Williams	.75	2.00
CC39 Corey Fuller	.75	2.00
CC40 DeAndre Hopkins	2.00	5.00
CC41 Blidi Wreh-Wilson	1.00	2.50
CC42 Dee Milliner	.75	2.00
CC43 Erik Highsmith	1.00	2.50
CC44 Desmond Trufant	.75	2.00
CC45 Keenan Davis	1.25	3.00
CC46 Keenan Allen	1.50	4.00
CC47 Marcus Davis	.75	2.00
CC48 Markus Wheaton	.75	2.00
CC49 Marquess Wilson	1.25	3.00
CC50 Marquise Goodwin	1.00	2.50
CC51 Eric Reid	1.00	2.50
CC52 B.J. Daniels	1.25	3.00
CC53 Russell Shepard	.75	2.00
CC54 Ryan Swope	.75	2.00
CC55 Bjoern Werner	.75	2.00
CC56 Jordan Reed	1.25	3.00
CC57 Justin Pugh	.75	2.00
CC58 Michael Williams	1.00	2.50
CC59 Nick Kasa	.75	2.00
CC60 T.J. McDonald	.75	2.00
CC61 Jon Bostic	.75	2.00
CC62 Kiko Alonso	1.00	2.50
CC63 Gavin Escobar	.75	2.00
CC64 Tommy Bohanon	1.00	2.50
CC66 Xavier Rhodes	.75	2.00
CC67 Datone Jones	.75	2.00
CC68 Kawann Short	.75	2.00
CC69 Sharrif Floyd	.75	2.00
CC70 Sheldon Richardson	.75	2.00
CC71 Alec Ogletree	.75	2.00
CC72 Spencer Ware	.75	2.00
CC73 Dion Sims	.75	2.00
CC74 Lane Johnson	1.00	2.50
CC75 Dan Buckner	.75	2.00
CC76 Kevin Minter	.75	2.00
CC77 Vince Williams	1.25	3.00
CC78 Brandon Jenkins	1.00	2.50
CC79 D.J. Fluker	.75	2.00
CC80 Khaseem Greene	.75	2.00
CC81 Ezekiel Ansah	.75	2.00
CC82 Eric Fisher	.75	2.00
CC83 Manti Te'o	1.00	2.50
CC84 Tavon Austin	1.00	2.50
CC85 Theo Riddick	.75	2.00
CC86 Josh Boyce	.75	2.00
CC87 Kenny Vaccaro	.75	2.00
CC88 Arthur Brown	.75	2.00
CC89 Onterio McCalebb	1.00	2.50
CC90 EJ Manuel	.75	2.00
CC91 Andre Ellington	1.25	3.00
CC92 Justin Hunter	1.25	3.00
CC93 Robert Woods	2.00	5.00
CC94 Luke Joeckel	1.25	3.00
CC95 Terrance Williams	1.25	3.00
CC96 Collin Klein	1.50	4.00
CC97 Kenny Stills	1.25	3.00
CC98 Marcus Lattimore	1.25	3.00
CC99 Denard Robinson	1.25	3.00
CC100 Eddie Lacy	1.25	3.00
CC101 Mike Glennon	1.25	3.00
CC102 Giovani Bernard	1.25	3.00
CC103 Cordarrelle Patterson	1.25	3.00
CC104 Joseph Randle	1.25	3.00
CC105 Star Lotulelei	3.00	8.00
CC106 Da'Rick Rogers	1.25	3.00
CC107 Jarvis Jones	1.25	3.00
CC108 Landry Jones	1.25	3.00
CC109 Tyler Bray	1.25	3.00
CC110 Tavarres King	1.25	3.00
CC111 Stedman Bailey	1.25	3.00
CC112 Alex Okafor	1.25	3.00
CC113 Tyler Eifert	1.25	3.00
CC114 Jerry Rice	5.00	12.00
CC115 John Elway	5.00	12.00
CC116 Dan Marino	6.00	15.00
CC117 Aaron Rodgers	5.00	12.00
CC118 Joe Namath	4.00	10.00
CC119 Barry Sanders	5.00	12.00
CC120 Herschel Walker	3.00	8.00
CC121 Tedy Bruschi	2.50	6.00
CC122 Eddie George	2.50	6.00
CC123 Lawrence Taylor	3.00	8.00
CC124 Jason White	2.00	5.00
CC125 Bruce Smith	2.50	6.00
CC126 Alan Page	2.00	5.00
CC127 Ron Dayne	2.00	5.00
CC128 Roman Gabriel	2.00	5.00
CC129 Ozzie Newsome	2.00	5.00
CC130 Warren Sapp	2.50	6.00
CC131 Doug Flutie	2.50	6.00
CC132 Earl Campbell	3.00	8.00
CC133 Archie Griffin	2.00	5.00
CC134 Warren Moon	3.00	8.00
CC136 Steve Young	4.00	10.00

2013 SP Authentic 1996 SP

STATED ODDS 1:6

96SP1 Andre Ellington	.60	1.50
96SP2 B.J. Daniels	1.00	2.50
96SP3 D.J. Swearinger	.60	1.50

96SP4 Geno Smith .60 1.50
96SP5 Jarvis Jones .60 1.50
96SP6 Jordan Rodgers .75 2.00
96SP7 Matt Barkley .60 1.50
96SP8 Matt Scott .60 1.50
96SP9 David Amerson .60 1.50
96SP10 Dion Jordan .60 1.50
96SP11 Ryan Nassib .60 1.50
96SP12 Sam Montgomery .60 1.50
96SP13 Tyler Wilson .60 1.50
96SP14 Zac Dysert .60 1.50
96SP15 Justin Pugh .60 1.50
96SP16 Bennie Logan .75 2.00
96SP17 D.J. Fluker .60 1.50
96SP18 Brad Sorensen .60 1.50
96SP19 Kenny Vaccaro .60 1.50
96SP20 Kiko Alonso 1.00 2.50
96SP21 Jordan Hill 1.00 2.50
96SP22 Jawan Jamison .60 1.50
96SP23 Johnathan Franklin .60 1.50
96SP24 Kenjon Barner .60 1.50
96SP25 Knile Davis .60 1.50
96SP26 Le'Veon Bell 2.00 5.00
96SP27 Mike Gillislee .60 1.50
96SP28 Montee Ball .60 1.50
96SP29 Ray Graham .60 1.50
96SP30 Rex Burkhead .75 2.00
96SP31 Robert Woods 1.00 2.50
96SP32 Chris Thompson .60 1.50
96SP33 Stepfan Taylor .60 1.50
96SP34 Zach Ertz 1.25 3.00
96SP35 Aaron Dobson .60 1.50
96SP36 Aaron Mellette .60 1.50
96SP37 Vance McDonald .75 2.00
96SP38 Chris Harper .60 1.50
96SP39 Sylvester Williams .60 1.50
96SP40 Cordarrelle Patterson .60 1.50
96SP41 Conner Vernon .60 1.50
96SP42 Corey Fuller .60 1.50
96SP43 Da'Rick Rogers .60 1.50
96SP44 DeAndre Hopkins 1.50 4.00
96SP45 Denard Robinson .60 1.50
96SP46 Marquise Goodwin .60 1.50
96SP47 Eddie Lacy .60 1.50
96SP48 Erik Highsmith .75 2.00
96SP49 Justin Hunter .60 1.50
96SP50 T.J. McDonald .60 1.50
96SP51 Keenan Allen 1.25 3.00
96SP52 Marcus Davis .60 1.50
96SP53 Markus Wheaton .60 1.50
96SP54 Marquess Wilson 1.00 2.50
96SP55 Marcus Lattimore .60 1.50
96SP56 Robert Alford .60 1.50
96SP57 Star Lotulelei .75 2.00
96SP58 Russell Shepard .60 1.50
96SP59 Ryan Swope .60 1.50
96SP60 Bjoern Werner .60 1.50
96SP61 Jordan Reed 1.00 2.50
96SP62 Joseph Randle .60 1.50
96SP63 Mike Glennon .60 1.50
96SP64 Travis Kelce 1.50 4.00
96SP65 Eric Reid .75 2.00
96SP66 Matt Elam .60 1.50
96SP67 Desmond Trufant .60 1.50
96SP68 Gavin Escobar .60 1.50
96SP69 Stedman Bailey .60 1.50
96SP70 Tyler Bray .60 1.50
96SP71 Damontre Moore .60 1.50
96SP72 Barkevious Mingo .60 1.50
96SP73 Xavier Rhodes .60 1.50
96SP74 Datone Jones .60 1.50
96SP75 Kawann Short .60 1.50
96SP76 Sharrif Floyd .60 1.50
96SP77 Sheldon Richardson .60 1.50
96SP78 Alec Ogletree .60 1.50
96SP79 Landry Jones .60 1.50
96SP80 Luke Joeckel .60 1.50
96SP81 Ezekiel Ansah .60 1.50
96SP82 Spencer Ware .60 1.50
96SP83 Kevin Minter .60 1.50
96SP84 Margus Hunt .60 1.50
96SP85 Arthur Brown .60 1.50
96SP86 Dee Milliner .60 1.50
96SP87 Giovani Bernard .60 1.50
96SP88 Jon Bostic .60 1.50
96SP89 Cobi Hamilton .60 1.50
96SP90 Eric Fisher .60 1.50
96SP91 Manti Te'o .75 2.00
96SP92 Tavon Austin .75 2.00
96SP93 Theo Riddick .60 1.50
96SP94 Josh Boyce .60 1.50
96SP95 Terrance Williams .60 1.50
96SP96 Tyler Eifert .60 1.50
96SP97 Kenny Stills .60 1.50
96SP98 Tavarres King .60 1.50
96SP99 Lane Johnson .75 2.00
96SP100 EJ Manuel .60 1.50
96SP101 Warren Sapp .75 2.00
96SP102 Steve Young 1.25 3.00
96SP103 Bo Jackson 1.25 3.00
96SP104 Clinton Portis .60 1.50
96SP105 Archie Griffin .60 1.50
96SP106 Jerry Rice 1.50 4.00
96SP107 Billy Sims .75 2.00
96SP108 Ron Dayne .75 2.00
96SP109 Joe Montana 2.50 6.00
96SP110 Rick Mirer .60 1.50
96SP111 Ronnie Lott .75 2.00
96SP112 Paul Hornung 1.00 2.50
96SP113 Drew Brees 1.00 2.50
96SP114 Lawrence Taylor 1.00 2.50
96SP115 Thurman Thomas .75 2.00
96SP116 Anthony Carter .75 2.00
96SP117 Charlie Ward .60 1.50
96SP118 John Hannah .60 1.50
96SP119 Doug Flutie .75 2.00
96SP120 Barry Sanders 1.50 4.00
96SP121 Aaron Rodgers 2.00 5.00
96SP122 Andrew Luck 2.50 6.00
96SP123 Joe Namath 1.25 3.00
96SP124 LaDainian Tomlinson .75 2.00
96SP125 Jason White .60 1.50
96SP126 Roman Gabriel .60 1.50
96SP127 Keith Jackson .60 1.50
96SP128 Natrone Means .60 1.50
96SP129 Daryle Lamonica .60 1.50
96SP130 Jerome Bettis 1.00 2.50
96SP131 Herschel Walker 1.00 2.50
96SP132 Ozzie Newsome .75 2.00
96SP133 Alan Page .60 1.50
96SP134 Dan Marino 2.00 5.00
96SP135 Tedy Bruschi .75 2.00
96SP136 Ray Guy .60 1.50
96SP137 John Elway 1.50 4.00
96SP138 Warren Moon 1.00 2.50
96SP139 Ickey Woods .60 1.50
96SP140 Eddie George .75 2.00
96SP141 Kordell Stewart .60 1.50
96SP142 Joe Theismann 1.00 2.50
96SP143 Earl Campbell 1.00 2.50
96SP144 Brian Bosworth .75 2.00
96SP145 Robert Smith .60 1.50
96SP146 Drew Bledsoe .75 2.00
96SP147 Eric Dickerson .75 2.00
96SP148 Roger Craig .75 2.00
96SP149 Jake Plummer .60 1.50
96SP150 Ty Detmer .60 1.50

2013 SP Authentic 1996 SP Autographs

UNPRICED GROUP A ODDS 1:16,320
UNPRICED GROUP B ODDS 1:1335
UNPRICED GROUP C ODDS 1:875
GROUP D STATED ODDS 1:750
GROUP E STATED ODDS 1:280
OVERALL STATED ODDS 1:25
UNPRICED 2014 INSERT ODDS 1:2336
96SP2 B.J. Daniels E 6.00 15.00
96SP9 David Amerson E 4.00 10.00
96SP16 Bennie Logan E 5.00 12.00
96SP17 D.J. Fluker E 4.00 10.00
96SP18 Brad Sorensen E 4.00 10.00
96SP20 Kiko Alonso E 5.00 12.00
96SP21 Jordan Hill E 6.00 15.00
96SP25 Knile Davis C 25.00 50.00
96SP37 Vance McDonald E 5.00 12.00
96SP39 Sylvester Williams E 4.00 10.00
96SP48 Erik Highsmith E 5.00 12.00
96SP50 T.J. McDonald E 4.00 10.00
96SP58 Russell Shepard E 4.00 10.00
96SP64 Travis Kelce E 12.00 30.00
96SP68 Gavin Escobar E 4.00 10.00
96SP73 Xavier Rhodes E 4.00 10.00
96SP75 Kawann Short E 4.00 10.00
96SP82 Spencer Ware E 4.00 10.00
96SP84 Margus Hunt E 4.00 10.00
96SP93 Theo Riddick E 4.00 10.00
96SP94 Josh Boyce E 4.00 10.00
96SP99 Lane Johnson E 5.00 12.00
96SP107 Billy Sims D 6.00 15.00
96SP108 Ron Dayne D 6.00 15.00
96SP116 Anthony Carter D 6.00 15.00
96SP118 John Hannah D 8.00 20.00
96SP125 Jason White D 5.00 12.00
96SP127 Keith Jackson D 5.00 12.00
96SP128 Natrone Means D 5.00 12.00
96SP136 Ray Guy D 5.00 12.00
96SP139 Ickey Woods D 5.00 12.00
96SP145 Robert Smith D 6.00 15.00
96SP148 Roger Craig D 6.00 15.00
96SP149 Jake Plummer D 5.00 12.00
96SP150 Ty Detmer D 5.00 12.00

2013 SP Authentic Autographs

UNPRICED GROUP A ODDS 1:3766
GROUP B STATED ODDS 1:706
GROUP C STATED ODDS 1:165
GROUP D STATED ODDS 1:30
OVERALL STATED ODDS 1:25
1 Brad Sorensen D 2.50 6.00
2 B.J. Daniels D 4.00 10.00
3 Dayne Crist D 3.00 8.00
5 Jeff Tuel D 2.50 6.00
6 Jordan Rodgers D 3.00 8.00
7 Matt Barkley B
8 Matt Scott D 2.50 6.00
9 Bennie Logan D 3.00 8.00
11 Ryan Nassib B 5.00 12.00
12 Justin Pugh D 2.50 6.00
14 Zac Dysert B 6.00 15.00
15 Zach Maynard D 3.00 8.00
16 Cameron Marshall D 2.50 6.00
17 Chris Thompson D 2.50 6.00
20 David Amerson D 2.50 6.00
22 Jawan Jamison D 2.50 6.00
23 Johnathan Franklin B 5.00 12.00
24 Kenjon Barner B 6.00 15.00
25 Knile Davis D 2.50 6.00
27 Mike Gillislee D 2.50 6.00
28 Montee Ball B 5.00 12.00
29 Ray Graham D 2.50 6.00
30 Rex Burkhead D 8.00 20.00
31 Robbie Rouse D 2.50 6.00
32 Stefphon Jefferson D 3.00 8.00
33 Stepfan Taylor B 12.00 30.00
34 Zach Ertz B
35 Aaron Dobson B 5.00 12.00
36 Aaron Mellette D 2.50 6.00
37 Brandon Kaufman D 2.50 6.00
38 Chris Harper D 2.50 6.00
39 Dion Jordan B 5.00 12.00
40 Cobi Hamilton B
41 Conner Vernon D 2.50 6.00
42 Corey Fuller D 2.50 6.00
43 Kiko Alonso D 3.00 8.00
44 DeAndre Hopkins B 12.00 30.00
45 Blidi Wreh-Wilson D 3.00 8.00
47 Margus Hunt D 2.50 6.00
48 Erik Highsmith D 3.00 8.00
49 Desmond Trufant D 2.50 6.00
50 Keenan Davis D 4.00 10.00
51 Keenan Allen B
52 Marcus Davis D 2.50 6.00
53 Markus Wheaton B 5.00 12.00
55 Marquise Goodwin B
58 Russell Shepard D 2.50 6.00
59 Ryan Swope D 2.50 6.00
60 Bjoern Werner B 8.00 20.00
61 Jordan Reed D 4.00 10.00
62 Joseph Fauria D 2.50 6.00
63 Michael Williams D 3.00 8.00
64 Nick Kasa D 2.50 6.00
65 Philip Lutzenkirchen D 4.00 10.00
67 Jordan Hill D 5.00 12.00
68 Gavin Escobar D 6.00 15.00
71 T.J. McDonald D 2.50 6.00
72 Barkevious Mingo B
73 Xavier Rhodes D 5.00 12.00
74 Datone Jones D 2.50 6.00
75 Kawann Short D 2.50 6.00
76 Sharrif Floyd D 2.50 6.00
79 Spencer Ware D 2.50 6.00
80 Dion Sims D 2.50 6.00
81 Lane Johnson D 3.00 8.00
82 Robert Alford D 2.50 6.00
83 Kevin Minter D 2.50 6.00
86 D.J. Fluker D 2.50 6.00
87 Sylvester Williams D 2.50 6.00
88 Khaseem Greene D 2.50 6.00
90 Eric Fisher D 2.50 6.00
91 Manti Te'o B 6.00 15.00
92 Tavon Austin B
93 Theo Riddick D 2.50 6.00
94 Josh Boyce D 2.50 6.00
95 Travis Kelce D 8.00 20.00
96 Vance McDonald D 3.00 8.00
97 Kenny Vaccaro B 5.00 12.00
98 Arthur Brown D 2.50 6.00
100 EJ Manuel B
101 Andre Ellington C 10.00 25.00
102 Justin Hunter C 10.00 25.00
103 Robert Woods C 5.00 12.00
104 Luke Joeckel C 4.00 10.00
105 Terrance Williams C 4.00 10.00
107 Kenny Stills C 8.00 20.00
108 Marcus Lattimore C 4.00 10.00
109 Tavon Austin C 5.00 12.00
110 Denard Robinson C 6.00 15.00
111 Eddie Lacy C 4.00 10.00
114 Cordarrelle Patterson C 4.00 10.00
115 Joseph Randle C 4.00 10.00
117 Da'Rick Rogers C 4.00 10.00
118 Jarvis Jones C 4.00 10.00
119 Landry Jones C 4.00 10.00
120 Tyler Bray C 4.00 10.00
121 Tavarres King C 4.00 10.00
123 Alex Okafor C 4.00 10.00
124 EJ Manuel C 4.00 10.00
125 Tyler Eifert C 4.00 10.00
137 Vinny Testaverde C 6.00 15.00
139 Ronnie Lott A 12.00 30.00
140 Ty Detmer C 5.00 12.00
143 Jason White C 6.00 15.00
145 Ron Dayne C 6.00 15.00

2013 SP Authentic Rookie Patch Autographs Silver

*PATCH/25: 1.2X TO 3X BASIC JSY AU/650
*PATCH/15: 1X TO 2.5X BASIC JSY AU/325
176 Keenan Allen/15 60.00 120.00
177 Eddie Lacy/25 15.00 40.00
180 Cordarrelle Patterson/15 15.00 40.00
182 EJ Manuel/25 15.00 40.00

2013 SP Authentic Rookie Threads Autographs

RTAD Aaron Dobson/275 4.00 10.00
RTBA Montee Ball/275 4.00 10.00
RTCP Cordarrelle Patterson/50 6.00 15.00
RTDH DeAndre Hopkins/275 10.00 25.00
RTEL Eddie Lacy/50 6.00 15.00
RTEM EJ Manuel/275 4.00 10.00
RTJF Johnathan Franklin/275 4.00 10.00
RTJH Justin Hunter/275 10.00 25.00
RTJR Joseph Randle/275 4.00 10.00
RTKA Keenan Allen/275 8.00 20.00
RTKS Kenny Stills/275 4.00 10.00
RTLJ Landry Jones/275 4.00 10.00
RTMB Matt Barkley/50 12.00 30.00
RTML Marcus Lattimore/275 4.00 10.00
RTMT Manti Te'o/50 8.00 20.00
RTRN Ryan Nassib/275 8.00 20.00
RTRW Robert Woods/275 6.00 15.00
RTTA Tavon Austin/50 8.00 20.00
RTTW Tyler Wilson/50 6.00 15.00
RTWH Markus Wheaton/275 4.00 10.00
RTWI Terrance Williams/275 4.00 10.00
RTZD Zac Dysert/275 4.00 10.00
RTZE Zach Ertz/275 8.00 20.00

2013 SP Authentic Sign of the Times

UNPRICED GROUP A ODDS 1:1985
UNPRICED GROUP B ODDS 1:760
GROUP C STATED ODDS 1:350
GROUP D STATED ODDS 1:32
OVERALL STATED ODDS 1:28
UNPRICED 2014 INSERT ODDS 1:2336
STAD Aaron Dobson C 3.00 8.00
STAE Andre Ellington C 8.00 20.00
STAM Aaron Mellette D 2.50 6.00
STBA Montee Ball C 3.00 8.00
STBD B.J. Daniels D 4.00 10.00
STBJ Barrett Jones D 2.50 6.00
STBK Brandon Kaufman D 2.50 6.00
STBR Tyler Bray B 5.00 12.00
STBS Barry Sanders A 75.00 150.00
STCF Corey Fuller D 2.50 6.00
STCH Cobi Hamilton D 2.50 6.00
STCP Cordarrelle Patterson B 5.00 12.00
STCV Conner Vernon D 2.50 6.00
STDB Dan Buckner D 2.50 6.00
STDC Dayne Crist D 3.00 8.00
STDH D.J. Harper D 3.00 8.00
STDI Dion Jordan C 3.00 8.00
STDR Da'Rick Rogers C 3.00 8.00
STDT Desmond Trufant D 2.50 6.00
STEM EJ Manuel B 12.00 30.00
STER Denard Robinson D 4.00 10.00
STFR Johnathan Franklin D 2.50 6.00
STGA Mitchell Gale D 2.50 6.00
STGI Mike Gillislee D 2.50 6.00
STGO Marquise Goodwin C 3.00 8.00
STGU Ray Guy D 6.00 15.00
STHA Chris Harper D 2.50 6.00
STHO DeAndre Hopkins B 15.00 40.00
STJE John Elway A 120.00 200.00
STJH Justin Hunter B 20.00 50.00
STJJ Jawan Jamison D 2.50 6.00
STJN Joe Namath A 75.00 150.00
STJO Luke Joeckel C 3.00 8.00
STJP Jake Plummer C 6.00 15.00
STJR Jerry Rice A 200.00 300.00
STJT Jeff Tuel D 4.00 10.00
STJW Jesse Williams D 4.00 10.00
STKB Kenjon Barner D 2.50 6.00
STKD Knile Davis D 2.50 6.00
STKE Travis Kelce D 8.00 20.00
STML Marcus Lattimore C 3.00 8.00
STMS Matt Scott D 2.50 6.00
STMW Markus Wheaton C 3.00 8.00
STPJ Justin Pugh D 2.50 6.00
STRA Joseph Randle C 3.00 8.00
STRB Rex Burkhead D 8.00 20.00
STRD Ron Dayne C 5.00 12.00
STRE Jordan Reed D 4.00 10.00
STRN Ryan Nassib C 6.00 15.00
STRO Jordan Rodgers D 3.00 8.00
STRR Robbie Rouse D 2.50 6.00
STRS Ryan Swope D 2.50 6.00
STSD Seth Doege D 4.00 10.00
STSI Dion Sims D 2.50 6.00
STSO Brad Sorensen D 2.50 6.00
STSR Rodney Smith D 2.50 6.00
STTA Stepfan Taylor D 2.50 6.00
STTE Tyler Eifert C 3.00 8.00
STTK Tavarres King D 2.50 6.00
STVM Vance McDonald D 3.00 8.00
STWG William Gholston D 4.00 10.00
STWI Terrance Williams C 3.00 8.00
STXR Xavier Rhodes D 6.00 15.00
STZD Zac Dysert C 3.00 8.00
STZE Zach Ertz C 6.00 15.00
STZM Zach Maynard D 3.00 8.00

2013 SP Authentic Sign of the Times Dual

ST2AT K.Allen/M.Te'o/25 30.00 60.00
ST2BB G.Bernard/L.Bell/25
ST2DH K.Davis/C.Hamilton/25 25.00 50.00
ST2HA D.Hopkins/T.Austin/25 25.00 60.00
ST2JS L.Jones/K.Stills/25 25.00 50.00

2014 SP Authentic

COMP.SET w/o SP's (100) 10.00 25.00
101-130 SP STATED ODDS 1:7
101-150 SP STATED ODDS 1:10
151-200 AM STATED ODDS 1:4
ROOKIE JSY AU/325-650 ODDS 1:24
EXCH EXPIRATION 11/22/2016
1 Sammy Watkins .40 1.00
2 Johnny Manziel .40 1.00
3 Bishop Sankey .25 .60
4 Eric Ebron .30 .75
5 Teddy Bridgewater .40 1.00
6 Robert Herron .25 .60
7 James Wilder Jr. .30 .75
8 C.J. Mosley .30 .75
9 Marqise Lee .30 .75
10 Derek Carr 1.50 4.00
11 Ka'Deem Carey .25 .60
12 Darqueze Dennard .30 .75
13 Michael Sam .25 .60
14 Ha Ha Clinton-Dix .30 .75
15 Zach Mettenberger .25 .60
16 Jared Abbrederis .25 .60
17 Marion Grice .25 .60
18 Zack Martin .30 .75
19 Kelvin Benjamin .40 1.00
20 Aaron Murray .25 .60
21 Carlos Hyde .30 .75
22 Jace Amaro .25 .60
23 Kenny Shaw .40 1.00
24 Kyle Fuller .25 .60
25 David Fales .25 .60
26 Donte Moncrief .25 .60
27 Antonio Andrews .25 .60
28 Shayne Skov .25 .60
29 Odell Beckham Jr. .60 1.50
30 Brett Smith .25 .60
31 Dri Archer .25 .60
32 Jeremy Gallon .50 1.25
33 Scott Crichton .25 .60
34 Calvin Pryor .25 .60
35 Tommy Rees .30 .75
36 Josh Huff .30 .75
37 Tyler Gaffney .25 .60
38 Dee Ford .25 .60
39 Allen Robinson .40 1.00
40 Keith Wenning .30 .75
41 Jeremy Hill .30 .75
42 Jerick Mckinnon .30 .75
43 Austin Seferian-Jenkins .25 .60
44 Rajion Neal .25 .60
45 Jeff Mathews .30 .75
46 Bruce Ellington .25 .60
47 Chris Borland .25 .60
48 Alfred Blue .25 .60
49 Mike Evans .60 1.50
50 Blake Bortles .30 .75
51 De'Anthony Thomas .25 .60
52 Kevin Norwood .25 .60
53 Devonta Freeman .40 1.00
54 Ra'Shede Hageman .25 .60
55 Tom Savage .25 .60
56 Mike Davis .25 .60
57 Jerome Smith .25 .60
58 Yawin Smallwood .25 .60
59 Brandin Cooks .40 1.00
60 Tajh Boyd .25 .60
61 Lache Seastrunk .25 .60
62 Troy Niklas .25 .60
63 Cody Latimer .30 .75
64 LaDarius Perkins .25 .60
65 Logan Thomas .25 .60
66 Ryan Grant .25 .60
67 Silas Redd .30 .75
68 Kony Ealy .30 .75
69 Jarvis Landry .50 1.25
70 Stephen Morris .25 .60
71 Terrance West .25 .60
72 Jason Verrett .25 .60
73 Taylor Lewan .25 .60
74 Kapri Bibbs .30 .75
75 Jordan Lynch .30 .75
76 TJ Jones .40 1.00
77 Chris Davis .25 .60
78 Damien Williams .25 .60
79 Davante Adams .40 1.00
80 Keith Price .40 1.00
81 Charles Sims .25 .60
82 Tevin Reese .25 .60
83 Stephon Tuitt .40 1.00
84 Jake Matthews .25 .60
85 Casey Pachall .40 1.00
86 Devin Street .25 .60
87 Lorenzo Taliaferro .25 .60
88 Khalil Mack 1.00 2.50
89 Paul Richardson .30 .75
90 Bryn Renner .25 .60
91 Andre Williams .25 .60
92 Quincy Enunwa .40 1.00
93 Anthony Barr .25 .60
94 George Atkinson III .25 .60
95 Jimmy Garoppolo 2.00 5.00
96 Brandon Coleman .25 .60
97 Joe Don Duncan .25 .60
98 Shaquelle Evans .25 .60
99 James White .50 1.25
100 Martavis Bryant .30 .75
101 Teddy Bridgewater SP 1.00 2.50
102 Marqise Lee SP .75 2.00
103 Carlos Hyde SP .75 2.00
104 Eric Ebron SP .75 2.00
105 Derek Carr SP 4.00 10.00
106 Brandin Cooks SP 1.00 2.50
107 Josh Huff SP .75 2.00
108 Davante Adams SP 1.00 2.50
109 De'Anthony Thomas SP .60 1.50
110 Jimmy Garoppolo SP 10.00 25.00
111 Mike Evans SP 1.50 4.00
112 Bishop Sankey SP .60 1.50
113 Cody Latimer SP .75 2.00
114 Dri Archer SP .60 1.50
115 Johnny Manziel SP 1.00 2.50
116 Sammy Watkins SP 1.00 2.50
117 Terrance West SP .60 1.50
118 Jarvis Landry SP 1.25 3.00
119 Paul Richardson SP .75 2.00
120 Aaron Murray SP .60 1.50
121 Odell Beckham Jr. SP 1.50 4.00
122 Charles Sims SP .60 1.50
123 Tajh Boyd SP .60 1.50
124 Allen Robinson SP 1.00 2.50
125 Logan Thomas SP .60 1.50
126 Jeremy Hill SP .75 2.00
127 Blake Bortles SP .75 2.00
128 Kelvin Benjamin SP 1.00 2.50
129 Austin Seferian-Jenkins SP .60 1.50
130 Tom Savage SP .60 1.50
131 Drew Brees SP 1.50 4.00
132 LaDainian Tomlinson SP 1.25 3.00
133 Jerry Rice SP 2.50 6.00
134 Peyton Manning SP 3.00 8.00
135 Warren Moon SP 1.50 4.00
136 Tim Brown SP 1.50 4.00
137 Matthew Stafford SP 1.25 3.00
138 Bo Jackson SP 2.00 5.00
139 John Elway SP 2.50 6.00
140 Earl Campbell SP 1.50 4.00
141 Hines Ward SP 1.25 3.00
142 Thurman Thomas SP 1.25 3.00
143 Ben Roethlisberger SP 1.50 4.00
144 Terrell Davis SP .60 1.50
145 Dan Marino SP 3.00 8.00
146 Eric Dickerson SP 1.25 3.00
147 Joe Namath SP 2.00 5.00
148 Jerome Bettis SP 1.50 4.00
149 Steve Young SP 2.00 5.00
150 Bernie Kosar SP 1.25 3.00
151 Peyton Manning AM 1.50 4.00
152 Jerry Rice AM 1.25 3.00
153 Bo Jackson AM 1.00 2.50
154 Matthew Stafford AM .60 1.50
155 Dan Marino AM 1.50 4.00
156 Jim Plunkett AM .60 1.50
157 Drew Brees AM .75 2.00
158 LaDainian Tomlinson AM .60 1.50
159 Irving Fryar AM .50 1.25
160 Steve Young AM 1.00 2.50
161 Doug Flutie AM .60 1.50
162 Jerome Bettis AM .75 2.00
163 John Elway AM 1.25 3.00
164 Warren Moon AM .75 2.00
165 Joe Namath AM 1.00 2.50
166 Earl Campbell AM .75 2.00
167 Ben Roethlisberger AM .75 2.00
168 Terrell Davis AM .30 .75
169 Charlie Ward AM .50 1.25
170 Rick Mirer AM .50 1.25
171 Ka'Deem Carey AM .50 1.25
172 Chris Davis AM .50 1.25
173 Andre Williams AM .50 1.25
174 Blake Bortles AM .60 1.50
175 Allen Robinson AM .75 2.00
176 Jordan Lynch AM .60 1.50
177 Jimmy Garoppolo AM 4.00 10.00
178 Jalen Saunders AM .50 1.25
179 Sammy Watkins AM .75 2.00
180 Johnny Manziel AM .75 2.00
181 Derek Carr AM 3.00 8.00
182 Aaron Murray AM .50 1.25
183 Kelvin Benjamin AM .75 2.00
184 Tajh Boyd AM .50 1.25
185 Teddy Bridgewater AM .75 2.00
186 Mike Evans AM 1.25 3.00
187 Bishop Sankey AM .50 1.25
188 Carlos Hyde AM .60 1.50
189 Marqise Lee AM .60 1.50
190 Michael Sam AM .50 1.25
191 Johnny Manziel AM .75 2.00
192 Teddy Bridgewater AM .75 2.00
193 Blake Bortles AM .60 1.50
194 Sammy Watkins AM .75 2.00
195 Zach Mettenberger AM .60 1.50
196 Tommy Rees AM .60 1.50
197 Jimmy Garoppolo AM 4.00 10.00
198 Derek Carr AM 3.00 8.00
199 Brett Smith AM .50 1.25
200 Eric Ebron AM .60 1.50
201 Tajh Boyd JSY AU/550 5.00 12.00
202 Kelvin Benjamin JSY AU/550 8.00 20.00
203 Ka'Deem Carey JSY AU/550 5.00 12.00
204 Davante Adams JSY AU/550 15.00 40.00
205 L.Seastrunk JSY AU/550 5.00 12.00
206 Aaron Murray JSY AU/550 5.00 12.00
207 Martavis Bryant JSY AU/550 6.00 15.00
208 Terrance West JSY AU/550 5.00 12.00
209 P.Richardson JSY AU/550 EX 20.00 40.00
210 Charles Sims JSY AU/550 5.00 12.00
211 Tom Savage JSY AU/550 5.00 12.00
212 Allen Robinson JSY AU/550 8.00 20.00
213 Donte Moncrief JSY AU/550 5.00 12.00
214 Marqise Lee JSY AU/550 6.00 15.00
215 Carlos Hyde JSY AU/550 6.00 15.00
216 Z.Mettenberger JSY AU/550 5.00 12.00
217 Brandin Cooks JSY AU/550 8.00 20.00
218 Jeremy Hill JSY AU/550 6.00 15.00
219 Josh Huff JSY AU/550 6.00 15.00
220 Devonta Freeman JSY AU/550 20.00 40.00
221 Logan Thomas JSY AU/550 5.00 12.00
222 Jarvis Landry JSY AU/550 15.00 40.00
223 D.Thomas JSY AU/550 EXCH 5.00 12.00
224 Bruce Ellington JSY AU/550 5.00 12.00
225 A.Williams JSY AU/550 EXCH 12.00 30.00
226 Derek Carr JSY AU/350 50.00 100.00
227 Beckham JSY AU/350 EXCH 50.00 100.00
228 Eric Ebron JSY AU/350 12.00 30.00
229 Bishop Sankey JSY AU/350 8.00 20.00
230 Mike Evans JSY AU/350 20.00 50.00
231 J.Garoppolo JSY AU/350 100.00 200.00
232 J.Manziel JSY AU/150 EXCH 12.00 30.00
233 T.Bridgewater JSY AU/150 25.00 60.00
234 Blake Bortles JSY AU/150 10.00 25.00
235 Sammy Watkins JSY AU/150 12.00 30.00

2014 SP Authentic Autographs

1 Sammy Watkins B 8.00 20.00
2 Johnny Manziel A EXCH 15.00 40.00
3 Bishop Sankey C 3.00 8.00
4 Eric Ebron B 6.00 15.00
5 Teddy Bridgewater B 6.00 15.00
6 Robert Herron D 2.50 6.00
7 James Wilder Jr. D 3.00 8.00
8 C.J. Mosley D 3.00 8.00
9 Marqise Lee C 4.00 10.00
10 Derek Carr B
11 Ka'Deem Carey E 2.50 6.00
12 Darqueze Dennard E 3.00 8.00
13 Michael Sam C 3.00 8.00
14 Ha Ha Clinton-Dix E 3.00 8.00
15 Zach Mettenberger E 2.50 6.00
16 Jared Abbrederis E 2.50 6.00
17 Marion Grice E 2.50 6.00
19 Kelvin Benjamin B 8.00 20.00
20 Aaron Murray D 2.50 6.00
21 Carlos Hyde C 4.00 10.00
23 Kenny Shaw E 4.00 10.00
24 Kyle Fuller D 2.50 6.00
25 David Fales C 3.00 8.00
26 Donte Moncrief A
27 Antonio Andrews A
28 Shayne Skov E 2.50 6.00
29 Odell Beckham Jr. A
30 Brett Smith D 2.50 6.00
31 Dri Archer D 2.50 6.00
32 Jeremy Gallon E 8.00 20.00
33 Scott Crichton E 2.50 6.00
34 Calvin Pryor B 5.00 12.00
35 Tommy Rees D 3.00 8.00
36 Josh Huff E 3.00 8.00
37 Tyler Gaffney E 2.50 6.00
38 Dee Ford E 2.50 6.00
39 Allen Robinson C 5.00 12.00
40 Keith Wenning E 3.00 8.00
41 Jeremy Hill C 4.00 10.00
42 Jerick Mckinnon C 4.00 10.00
44 Rajion Neal E 2.50 6.00
45 Jeff Mathews D 3.00 8.00
46 Bruce Ellington E 2.50 6.00
47 Chris Borland E 2.50 6.00
48 Alfred Blue E 2.50 6.00
49 Mike Evans B 12.00 30.00
50 Blake Bortles B 5.00 12.00
52 Kevin Norwood E 2.50 6.00
53 Devonta Freeman D 10.00 25.00
54 Ra'Shede Hageman E 2.50 6.00
55 Tom Savage E 2.50 6.00
56 Mike Davis E 2.50 6.00
57 Jerome Smith E 2.50 6.00
58 Yawin Smallwood A
59 Brandin Cooks B 8.00 20.00
60 Tajh Boyd B 5.00 12.00
62 Troy Niklas E 2.50 6.00
63 Cody Latimer C 4.00 10.00
64 LaDarius Perkins E 2.50 6.00
65 Logan Thomas E 2.50 6.00
66 Ryan Grant D 2.50 6.00
67 Silas Redd E 3.00 8.00
68 Kony Ealy C 4.00 10.00
69 Jarvis Landry E 5.00 12.00
70 Stephen Morris E 2.50 6.00
71 Terrance West E 5.00 12.00
72 Jason Verrett D 2.50 6.00
73 Taylor Lewan D 2.50 6.00
74 Kapri Bibbs D 3.00 8.00
75 Jordan Lynch E 3.00 8.00
76 TJ Jones E 4.00 10.00
77 Chris Davis E 6.00 15.00
78 Damien Williams D 4.00 10.00
79 Davante Adams C 5.00 12.00
80 Keith Price E 4.00 10.00
81 Charles Sims A 6.00 15.00
82 Tevin Reese B 5.00 12.00
83 Stephon Tuitt A EXCH 10.00 25.00
84 Jake Matthews D 2.50 6.00
85 Casey Pachall E 4.00 10.00
86 Devin Street E 2.50 6.00
87 Lorenzo Taliaferro E 2.50 6.00
89 Paul Richardson A
90 Bryn Renner E 2.50 6.00
91 Andre Williams A
92 Quincy Enunwa B 12.00 30.00
93 Anthony Barr E 2.50 6.00
94 George Atkinson III E 2.50 6.00
95 Jimmy Garoppolo C 75.00 150.00
96 Brandon Coleman D 2.50 6.00
97 Joe Don Duncan E 2.50 6.00
98 Shaquelle Evans B 5.00 12.00
99 James White E 5.00 12.00
100 Martavis Bryant A EXCH 8.00 20.00
101 Teddy Bridgewater B 10.00 25.00
102 Marqise Lee B 8.00 20.00
103 Carlos Hyde C 6.00 15.00
104 Eric Ebron C 8.00 20.00
105 Derek Carr B
106 Brandin Cooks A 15.00 40.00
107 Josh Huff C
108 Davante Adams C 8.00 20.00
110 Jimmy Garoppolo B 75.00 150.00
111 Mike Evans B 12.00 30.00
112 Bishop Sankey C 5.00 12.00
113 Cody Latimer C
114 Dri Archer C 6.00 15.00
115 Johnny Manziel A EXCH
116 Sammy Watkins B 12.00 30.00
117 Terrance West C 6.00 15.00
118 Jarvis Landry B
120 Aaron Murray C 5.00 12.00
121 Odell Beckham Jr. A
123 Tajh Boyd C 6.00 15.00
124 Allen Robinson C 8.00 20.00
125 Logan Thomas C 6.00 15.00
126 Jeremy Hill C 8.00 20.00
127 Blake Bortles B 8.00 20.00
128 Kelvin Benjamin B 10.00 25.00
130 Tom Savage C 5.00 12.00
131 Drew Brees C EXCH
132 LaDainian Tomlinson C 20.00 50.00
133 Jerry Rice A
134 Peyton Manning A
135 Warren Moon D
136 Tim Brown D 10.00 25.00
137 Matthew Stafford C
138 Bo Jackson B EXCH 90.00 150.00
139 John Elway B 200.00 300.00
140 Earl Campbell D 15.00 40.00
141 Hines Ward D 30.00 30.00
142 Thurman Thomas B EXCH 10.00 25.00
143 Ben Roethlisberger C 20.00 50.00
144 Terrell Davis D 6.00 15.00
145 Dan Marino B 25.00 60.00
146 Eric Dickerson D 15.00 40.00
147 Joe Namath B
148 Jerome Bettis D
149 Steve Young C 25.00 50.00
151 Peyton Manning AM B 100.00 200.00
152 Jerry Rice AM C
153 Bo Jackson AM B EXCH
154 Matthew Stafford AM C
155 Dan Marino AM C 75.00 150.00
156 Jim Plunkett AM D 8.00 20.00
157 Drew Brees AM B EXCH
158 LaDainian Tomlinson AM C 10.00 25.00
159 Irving Fryar AM E 8.00 20.00
160 Steve Young AM C 15.00 40.00
161 Doug Flutie AM D 8.00 20.00
162 Jerome Bettis AM C
163 John Elway AM C 100.00 200.00
164 Warren Moon AM C
165 Joe Namath AM C 90.00 150.00
166 Earl Campbell AM C 20.00 50.00
167 Ben Roethlisberger AM C
168 Terrell Davis AM E 4.00 10.00
169 Charlie Ward AM E 6.00 15.00
170 Rick Mirer AM A
171 Ka'Deem Carey AM E 6.00 15.00
172 Chris Davis AM E 10.00 25.00
174 Blake Bortles AM C 8.00 20.00
176 Jordan Lynch AM D 6.00 15.00
177 Jimmy Garoppolo AM D 75.00 150.00
178 Jalen Saunders AM A
179 Sammy Watkins AM D 8.00 20.00
180 Johnny Manziel AM B EXCH 15.00 40.00
181 Derek Carr AM D 20.00 40.00
182 Aaron Murray AM E 5.00 12.00
183 Kelvin Benjamin AM C 10.00 25.00
184 Tajh Boyd AM C 6.00 15.00
185 Teddy Bridgewater AM C 10.00 25.00
186 Mike Evans AM D 12.00 30.00
187 Bishop Sankey AM D
189 Marqise Lee AM E 5.00 12.00
190 Michael Sam AM E 6.00 15.00
191 Johnny Manziel AM B EXCH 15.00 40.00
192 Teddy Bridgewater AM C 10.00 25.00
193 Blake Bortles AM C 8.00 20.00
194 Sammy Watkins AM D 10.00 25.00
195 Zach Mettenberger AM E 4.00 10.00
196 Tommy Rees AM E 5.00 12.00
197 Jimmy Garoppolo AM E 75.00 150.00
198 Derek Carr AM C
199 Brett Smith AM D 5.00 12.00
200 Eric Ebron AM C 8.00 20.00

2014 SP Authentic Autographs Inscriptions

6 Robert Herron/25 6.00 15.00
7 James Wilder Jr./25 8.00 20.00
8 C.J. Mosley/25 8.00 20.00
11 Ka'Deem Carey/25 6.00 15.00
12 Darqueze Dennard/25 8.00 20.00
13 Michael Sam/25 6.00 15.00
14 Ha Ha Clinton-Dix/25 8.00 20.00
15 Zach Mettenberger/25
16 Jared Abbrederis/25 20.00 40.00
17 Marion Grice/25 6.00 15.00
19 Kelvin Benjamin/25 10.00 25.00
20 Aaron Murray/25 6.00 15.00
21 Carlos Hyde/25 8.00 20.00
23 Kenny Shaw/25 10.00 25.00
24 Kyle Fuller/25 6.00 15.00
25 David Fales/25 6.00 15.00
26 Donte Moncrief/25
28 Shayne Skov/25 6.00 15.00
30 Brett Smith/25 6.00 15.00
31 Dri Archer/25 6.00 15.00
32 Jeremy Gallon/25 40.00 80.00
33 Scott Crichton/25 6.00 15.00
34 Calvin Pryor/25 6.00 15.00
35 Tommy Rees/25 8.00 20.00
36 Josh Huff/25 8.00 20.00
37 Tyler Gaffney/25 6.00 15.00
38 Dee Ford/25 6.00 15.00
39 Allen Robinson/25 10.00 25.00
40 Keith Wenning/25 8.00 20.00
41 Jeremy Hill/25 30.00 60.00
42 Jerick Mckinnon/25
44 Rajion Neal/25 6.00 15.00
45 Jeff Mathews/25 8.00 20.00
46 Bruce Ellington/25 6.00 15.00
47 Chris Borland/25 6.00 15.00
48 Alfred Blue/25 6.00 15.00
52 Kevin Norwood/25 6.00 15.00
53 Devonta Freeman/25 15.00 40.00
54 Ra'Shede Hageman/25 6.00 15.00
55 Tom Savage/25 6.00 15.00
56 Mike Davis/25 6.00 15.00
57 Jerome Smith/25 6.00 15.00
59 Brandin Cooks/25 10.00 25.00
60 Tajh Boyd/25 6.00 15.00
62 Troy Niklas/25 6.00 15.00
63 Cody Latimer/25 8.00 20.00
64 LaDarius Perkins/25 6.00 15.00
65 Logan Thomas/25 6.00 15.00
66 Ryan Grant/25 6.00 15.00
67 Silas Redd/25 8.00 20.00
68 Kony Ealy/25 8.00 20.00
69 Jarvis Landry/25 12.00 30.00
70 Stephen Morris/25 6.00 15.00
71 Terrance West/25 6.00 15.00
72 Jason Verrett/25 6.00 15.00
73 Taylor Lewan/25 6.00 15.00
74 Kapri Bibbs/25 8.00 20.00
75 Jordan Lynch/25 25.00 50.00
76 TJ Jones/25 10.00 25.00
77 Chris Davis/25 6.00 15.00
78 Damien Williams/25 6.00 15.00
79 Davante Adams/25 25.00 50.00
80 Keith Price/25 10.00 25.00
81 Charles Sims/25 50.00 100.00
82 Tevin Reese/25 6.00 15.00
83 Stephon Tuitt/25 10.00 25.00
84 Jake Matthews/25
85 Casey Pachall/25
86 Devin Street/25 6.00 15.00
87 Lorenzo Taliaferro/25 6.00 15.00
89 Paul Richardson/25
90 Bryn Renner/25 6.00 15.00
91 Andre Williams/25 30.00 60.00
92 Quincy Enunwa/25 25.00 50.00
93 Anthony Barr/25 6.00 15.00
94 George Atkinson III/25 6.00 15.00
96 Brandon Coleman/25 6.00 15.00
97 Joe Don Duncan/25 6.00 15.00
98 Shaquelle Evans/25 6.00 15.00
99 James White/25 12.00 30.00
100 Martavis Bryant/25

2014 SP Authentic Canvas

C1-C90 STATED ODDS 1:6
C91-C113 STATED ODDS 1:45
C1 Johnny Manziel 1.00 2.50
C2 Sammy Watkins 1.00 2.50
C3 Bishop Sankey .60 1.50
C4 Eric Ebron .75 2.00
C5 Jimmy Garoppolo 5.00 12.00
C6 Anthony Barr .60 1.50
C7 Davante Adams 1.00 2.50
C8 Zack Martin .75 2.00
C9 Lache Seastrunk .60 1.50
C10 Tom Savage .60 1.50
C11 Bruce Ellington .60 1.50
C12 Mike Evans 1.50 4.00
C13 Jarvis Landry 1.25 3.00
C14 Jeremy Hill .75 2.00
C15 Tajh Boyd .60 1.50
C16 Khalil Mack 2.50 6.00
C17 Cody Latimer .75 2.00
C18 Ka'Deem Carey .60 1.50
C19 Dri Archer .60 1.50
C20 Teddy Bridgewater 1.00 2.50
C21 Ha Ha Clinton-Dix .75 2.00
C22 Odell Beckham Jr. 1.50 4.00
C23 Austin Seferian-Jenkins .60 1.50
C24 Kelvin Benjamin 1.00 2.50
C25 Zach Mettenberger .60 1.50
C26 C.J. Mosley .75 2.00
C27 Allen Robinson 1.00 2.50
C28 De'Anthony Thomas .60 1.50
C29 Paul Richardson .75 2.00
C30 David Fales .60 1.50
C31 Taylor Lewan .60 1.50
C32 Jace Amaro .60 1.50
C33 Keith Wenning .75 2.00
C34 Andre Williams .60 1.50
C35 Logan Thomas .60 1.50
C36 Donte Moncrief .60 1.50
C37 Troy Niklas .60 1.50
C38 Drew Brees 1.00 2.50
C39 Ben Roethlisberger 1.00 2.50
C40 LaDainian Tomlinson .75 2.00
C41 Peyton Manning SP 3.00 8.00
C42 John Elway SP 2.50 6.00
C43 Marqise Lee SP 1.25 3.00
C44 Blake Bortles SP 1.25 3.00
C45 Derek Carr SP 6.00 15.00
C46 Carlos Hyde SP 1.25 3.00
C47 Brandin Cooks SP 1.50 4.00
C48 Darqueze Dennard SP 1.25 3.00
C49 Josh Huff SP 1.25 3.00
C50 Aaron Murray SP 1.00 2.50

2014 SP Authentic Canvas Autographs

C1 Johnny Manziel B 8.00 20.00
C2 Sammy Watkins B 8.00 20.00
C3 Bishop Sankey C 3.00 8.00
C4 Eric Ebron B 6.00 15.00
C5 Jimmy Garoppolo C
C6 Anthony Barr C 3.00 8.00
C7 Davante Adams C 5.00 12.00
C8 Zack Martin A
C9 Lache Seastrunk A
C10 Tom Savage C 3.00 8.00
C11 Bruce Ellington C 3.00 8.00
C12 Mike Evans B 12.00 30.00
C13 Jarvis Landry A
C14 Jeremy Hill C 4.00 10.00
C15 Tajh Boyd B 5.00 12.00
C16 Khalil Mack A
C17 Cody Latimer C 4.00 10.00
C18 Ka'Deem Carey B 5.00 12.00
C19 Dri Archer C 3.00 8.00
C20 Teddy Bridgewater B 8.00 20.00
C21 Ha Ha Clinton-Dix C 4.00 10.00
C22 Odell Beckham Jr. B 30.00 60.00
C23 Austin Seferian-Jenkins A
C24 Kelvin Benjamin B 8.00 20.00
C25 Zach Mettenberger C 3.00 8.00
C26 C.J. Mosley C 4.00 10.00
C27 Allen Robinson C 5.00 12.00
C28 De'Anthony Thomas A
C29 Paul Richardson A
C30 David Fales C 3.00 8.00
C31 Taylor Lewan C 3.00 8.00
C32 Jace Amaro A
C33 Keith Wenning C 4.00 10.00
C34 Andre Williams A
C35 Logan Thomas C 3.00 8.00
C36 Donte Moncrief A
C37 Troy Niklas C 3.00 8.00
C38 Drew Brees B 50.00 100.00
C39 Ben Roethlisberger B
C40 LaDainian Tomlinson B 15.00 40.00
C41 Peyton Manning SP A
C42 John Elway SP A
C43 Marqise Lee SP B 6.00 15.00
C44 Blake Bortles SP A
C45 Derek Carr SP A
C46 Carlos Hyde SP B 6.00 15.00
C47 Brandin Cooks SP B
C48 Darqueze Dennard SP B 6.00 15.00
C49 Josh Huff SP B 6.00 15.00
C50 Aaron Murray SP B 5.00 12.00

2014 SP Authentic Future Watch Autographs

FW1 Matthew Stafford
FW2 Peyton Manning
FW3 Jerry Rice
FW4 Hines Ward
FW5 Drew Brees
FW6 Ben Roethlisberger
FW7 Sammy Watkins 10.00 25.00
FW8 Teddy Bridgewater
FW9 Carlos Hyde 8.00 20.00
FW10 Mike Evans 20.00 50.00
FW11 Blake Bortles 8.00 20.00
FW12 Ka'Deem Carey 6.00 15.00
FW13 Marqise Lee 8.00 20.00
FW14 Johnny Manziel 10.00 25.00
FW15 Donte Moncrief
FW16 Kelvin Benjamin
FW17 Derek Carr 100.00 200.00
FW18 Bishop Sankey 6.00 15.00
FW19 Odell Beckham Jr.
FW20 Jimmy Garoppolo
FW22 Allen Robinson 10.00 25.00
FW23 Zach Mettenberger 6.00 15.00
FW24 Dri Archer 6.00 15.00
FW25 Brandin Cooks 40.00 80.00
FW26 Aaron Murray 6.00 15.00
FW27 Devonta Freeman 15.00 40.00
FW28 Jarvis Landry
FW29 David Fales 6.00 15.00
FW30 Eric Ebron 8.00 20.00
FW31 Davante Adams 10.00 25.00
FW32 Logan Thomas 6.00 15.00
FW34 Paul Richardson 8.00 20.00
FW35 Tom Savage 6.00 15.00
FW36 Martavis Bryant 8.00 20.00
FW39 Cody Latimer 8.00 20.00
FW40 Tajh Boyd 6.00 15.00
FW41 Jeremy Hill 8.00 20.00
FW42 Jared Abbrederis 6.00 15.00

2014 SP Authentic Sign of the Times

UNPRICED GROUP A ODDS 1:8,033
UNPRICED GROUP B ODDS 1:2,142
GROUP C STATED ODDS 1:515
GROUP D STATED ODDS 1:164
OVERALL STATED ODDS 1:116
SOTTAM Aaron Murray D 2.50 6.00
SOTTBB Blake Bortles B 30.00 60.00
SOTTBC Brandin Cooks C
SOTTBJ Bo Jackson A EXCH 90.00 150.00

SOTTBR Ben Roethlisberger B 30.00 60.00
SOTTCH Carlos Hyde D 3.00 8.00
SOTTCW Charlie Ward D 2.50 6.00
SOTTDB Drew Brees A
SOTTDC Derek Carr B 30.00 80.00
SOTTDF Dan Fouts B 30.00 60.00
SOTTEE Eric Ebron C 4.00 10.00
SOTTJE John Elway B 200.00 300.00
SOTTJG Jimmy Garoppolo D 75.00 150.00
SOTTJM Johnny Manziel A
SOTTJN Joe Namath B 75.00 125.00
SOTTJR Jerry Rice B 50.00 100.00
SOTTJW Jason White D 2.50 6.00
SOTTKB Kelvin Benjamin C 5.00 12.00
SOTTLT LaDainian Tomlinson B
SOTTME Mike Evans C 8.00 20.00
SOTTML Marqise Lee D 3.00 8.00
SOTTMS Matthew Stafford B
SOTTOB Odell Beckham Jr. C EXCH 40.00 80.00
SOTTPM Peyton Manning A 150.00 250.00
SOTTSA Bishop Sankey D 2.50 6.00
SOTTSW Sammy Watkins B 50.00 100.00
SOTTSY Steve Young B
SOTTTB Teddy Bridgewater B
SOTTTD Terrell Davis C 8.00 20.00
SOTTTL Logan Thomas D 2.50 6.00

2014 SP Authentic Super F/X

*SILVER/80-88: .5X TO 1.2X BASIC INSERTS
*SILVER/22-34: .6X TO 1.5X BASIC INSERTS
1 Peyton Manning 10.00 25.00
2 Joe Namath 10.00 25.00
3 John Elway 5.00 12.00
4 Dan Marino 6.00 15.00
5 Drew Brees 4.00 10.00
6 Ben Roethlisberger 6.00 15.00
7 Johnny Manziel 1.50 4.00
8 Blake Bortles 1.25 3.00
9 Teddy Bridgewater 1.50 4.00
10 Derek Carr 6.00 15.00
11 Jimmy Garoppolo 8.00 20.00
12 Zach Mettenberger 1.00 2.50
13 Aaron Murray 1.00 2.50
14 Tajh Boyd 1.00 2.50
15 Tom Savage 1.00 2.50
16 David Fales 1.00 2.50
17 Stephen Morris 1.00 2.50
18 Logan Thomas 1.00 2.50
19 Brett Smith 1.00 2.50
20 Sammy Watkins 6.00 15.00
21 Marqise Lee 1.25 3.00
22 Mike Evans 2.50 6.00
23 Kelvin Benjamin 1.50 4.00
24 Brandin Cooks 1.50 4.00
25 Allen Robinson 1.50 4.00
26 Odell Beckham Jr. 8.00 20.00
27 Davante Adams 1.50 4.00
28 Paul Richardson 1.25 3.00
29 Jarvis Landry 2.00 5.00
30 Robert Herron 1.00 2.50
31 Jared Abbrederis 1.00 2.50
32 Charles Sims 1.00 2.50
33 Ka'Deem Carey 1.00 2.50
34 Carlos Hyde 1.25 3.00
35 Bishop Sankey 1.00 2.50
36 Jeremy Hill 1.25 3.00
37 Devonta Freeman 1.50 4.00
38 Lache Seastrunk 1.00 2.50
39 De'Anthony Thomas 1.00 2.50
40 Eric Ebron 1.25 3.00
41 Jace Amaro 1.00 2.50
42 Austin Seferian-Jenkins 1.00 2.50

1995 SP Championship

This is the first effort for the retail version of SP and comes as a 225 card set in six card packs with a suggested retail price of $2.99. The set breaks down into 180 regular player cards and 45 Future Champions cards which highlight the top 1995 rookies in game-action photographs. Rookies include Jeff Blake, Ki-Jana Carter, Kerry Collins, Terrell Davis, Joey Galloway, Steve McNair, Kordell Stewert, J.J. Stokes, Tamarick Vanover and Michael Westbrook.

COMPLETE SET (225) 20.00 50.00
1 Frank Sanders RC .30 .75
2 Stoney Case RC .07 .20
3 Lorenzo Styles RC .07 .20
4 Todd Collins RC 1.00 2.50
5 Darick Holmes RC .15 .40
6 Brian DeMarco RC .07 .20
7 Tyrone Poole RC .30 .75
8 Kerry Collins RC 1.50 4.00
9 Rashaan Salaam RC .15 .40
10 Steve Stenstrom RC .07 .20
11 Ki-Jana Carter RC .30 .75
12 Eric Zeier RC .30 .75
13 Sherman Williams RC .07 .20
14 Terrell Davis RC 2.00 5.00
15 David Dunn RC .07 .20
16 Luther Elliss RC .07 .20
17 Craig Newsome RC .07 .20
18 Antonio Freeman RC .75 2.00
19 Steve McNair RC 2.50 6.00
20 Anthony Cook RC .07 .20
21 Rodney Thomas RC .15 .40
22 Ellis Johnson RC .07 .20
23 Ken Dilger RC .30 .75
24 James O. Stewart RC .75 2.00
25 Pete Mitchell RC .15 .40
26 Tamarick Vanover RC .30 .75
27 Orlando Thomas RC .07 .20
28 Corey Fuller RC .07 .20
29 Curtis Martin RC 2.50 6.00
30 Ty Law RC 1.00 2.50
31 Roell Preston RC .10 .30
32 Mark Fields RC .30 .75
33 Tyrone Wheatley RC .75 2.00
34 Kyle Brady RC .30 .75
35 Napoleon Kaufman RC 1.00 2.50
36 Kordell Stewart RC 1.25 3.00
37 Mark Bruener RC .15 .40
38 Terrance Shaw RC .07 .20
39 Terrell Fletcher RC .07 .20
40 J.J. Stokes RC .30 .75
41 Christian Fauria RC .15 .40
42 Joey Galloway RC 1.25 3.00
43 Kevin Carter RC .30 .75
44 Warren Sapp RC 1.25 3.00
45 Michael Westbrook RC .30 .75
46 Clyde Simmons .05 .15
47 Rob Moore .10 .30
48 Seth Joyner .05 .15
49 Dave Krieg .05 .15
50 Garrison Hearst .20 .50
51 Aeneas Williams .05 .15
52 Terance Mathis .10 .30
53 Bert Emanuel .20 .50
54 Chris Doleman .05 .15
55 Craig Heyward .10 .30
56 Jeff George .10 .30
57 Eric Metcalf .10 .30
58 Jim Kelly .20 .50
59 Andre Reed .10 .30
60 Russell Copeland .05 .15
61 Bruce Smith .20 .50
62 Cornelius Bennett .10 .30
63 Jeff Burris .05 .15
64 Mark Carrier WR .10 .30
65 Pete Metzelaars .05 .15
66 Frank Reich .05 .15
67 Sam Mills .10 .30
68 John Kasay .05 .15
69 Willie Green .10 .30
70 Curtis Conway .20 .50
71 Erik Kramer .05 .15
72 Donnell Woolford .05 .15
73 Mark Carrier DB .05 .15
74 Jeff Graham .05 .15
75 Raymont Harris .05 .15
76 Carl Pickens .10 .30
77 Darnay Scott .10 .30
78 Jeff Blake RC .50 1.25
79 Dan Wilkinson .10 .30
80 Tony McGee .05 .15
81 Eric Bieniemy .05 .15
82 Vinny Testaverde .10 .30
83 Eric Turner .05 .15
84 Leroy Hoard .05 .15
85 Lorenzo White .05 .15
86 Antonio Langham .05 .15
87 Andre Rison .10 .30
88 Troy Aikman .60 1.50
89 Michael Irvin .20 .50
90 Charles Haley .10 .30
91 Daryl Johnston .10 .30
92 Jay Novacek .10 .30
93 Emmitt Smith 1.00 2.50
94 Shannon Sharpe .10 .30
95 Anthony Miller .10 .30
96 Mike Pritchard .05 .15
97 Glyn Milburn .05 .15
98 Simon Fletcher .05 .15
99 John Elway 1.25 3.00
100 Henry Thomas .05 .15
101 Herman Moore .20 .50
102 Scott Mitchell .10 .30
103 Bennie Blades .05 .15
104 Chris Spielman .10 .30
105 Barry Sanders 1.00 2.50
106 Mark Ingram .05 .15
107 Edgar Bennett .10 .30
108 Reggie White .20 .50
109 Sean Jones .05 .15
110 Robert Brooks .20 .50
111 Brett Favre 1.25 3.00
112 Chris Chandler .10 .30
113 Haywood Jeffires .05 .15
114 Gary Brown .05 .15
115 Al Smith .05 .15
116 Ray Childress .05 .15
117 Mel Gray .05 .15
118 Jim Harbaugh .10 .30
119 Sean Dawkins .10 .30
120 Roosevelt Potts .05 .15
121 Marshall Faulk .75 2.00
122 Tony Bennett .05 .15
123 Quentin Coryatt .10 .30
124 Desmond Howard .10 .30
125 Tony Boselli .20 .50
126 Steve Beuerlein .10 .30
127 Jeff Lageman .05 .15
128 Rob Johnson RC .75 2.00
129 Ernest Givins .05 .15
130 Willie Davis .10 .30
131 Marcus Allen .20 .50
132 Neil Smith .10 .30
133 Greg Hill .10 .30
134 Steve Bono .10 .30
135 Lake Dawson .10 .30
136 Dan Marino 1.25 3.00
137 Terry Kirby .10 .30
138 Irving Fryar .10 .30
139 O.J. McDuffie .20 .50
140 Bryan Cox .05 .15
141 Eric Green .05 .15
142 Cris Carter .20 .50
143 Robert Smith .20 .50
144 John Randle .10 .30
145 Jake Reed .10 .30
146 Dewayne Washington .10 .30
147 Warren Moon .10 .30
148 Dave Meggett .05 .15
149 Ben Coates .10 .30
150 Vincent Brisby .05 .15
151 Willie McGinest .10 .30
152 Chris Slade .05 .15
153 Drew Bledsoe .40 1.00
154 Eric Allen .05 .15
155 Mario Bates .10 .30
156 Jim Everett .05 .15
157 Renaldo Turnbull .05 .15
158 Tyrone Hughes .10 .30
159 Michael Haynes .10 .30
160 Mike Sherrard .05 .15
161 Dave Brown .10 .30
162 Chris Calloway .05 .15
163 Keith Hamilton .05 .15
164 Rodney Hampton .10 .30
165 Herschel Walker .10 .30
166 Adrian Murrell .10 .30
167 Johnny Mitchell .05 .15
168 Boomer Esiason .10 .30
169 Mo Lewis .05 .15
170 Brad Baxter .05 .15
171 Aaron Glenn .05 .15
172 Jeff Hostetler .10 .30
173 Harvey Williams .05 .15
174 Tim Brown .20 .50
175 Terry McDaniel .05 .15
176 Pat Swilling .05 .15
177 Rocket Ismail .10 .30
178 Randall Cunningham .20 .50
179 Calvin Williams .10 .30
180 Ricky Watters .10 .30
181 Charlie Garner .20 .50
182 Fred Barnett .10 .30
183 Rodney Peete .05 .15
184 Neil O'Donnell .10 .30
185 Charles Johnson .10 .30
186 Rod Woodson .10 .30
187 Byron Bam Morris .05 .15
188 Kevin Greene .10 .30
189 Greg Lloyd .10 .30
190 Chris Miller .05 .15
191 Isaac Bruce .30 .75
192 Roman Phifer .05 .15
193 Jerome Bettis .20 .50
194 Carlos Jenkins .05 .15
195 Troy Drayton .05 .15
196 Andre Coleman .05 .15
197 Natrone Means .10 .30
198 Leslie O'Neal .10 .30
199 Junior Seau .20 .50
200 Tony Martin .10 .30
201 Stan Humphries .10 .30
202 Steve Young .50 1.25
203 Jerry Rice .60 1.50
204 Brent Jones .05 .15
205 Dana Stubblefield .10 .30
206 Lee Woodall .05 .15
207 Merton Hanks .05 .15
208 Rick Mirer .10 .30
209 Brian Blades .10 .30
210 Chris Warren .10 .30
211 Sam Adams .05 .15
212 Cortez Kennedy .10 .30
213 Eugene Robinson .05 .15
214 Alvin Harper .05 .15
215 Trent Dilfer .20 .50
216 Hardy Nickerson .05 .15
217 Errict Rhett .10 .30
218 Eric Curry .05 .15
219 Jackie Harris .05 .15
220 Henry Ellard .10 .30
221 Terry Allen .10 .30
222 Brian Mitchell .05 .15
223 Ken Harvey .05 .15
224 Gus Frerotte .10 .30
225 Heath Shuler .10 .30
P116 Joe Montana Promo 1.25 3.00

1995 SP Championship Die Cuts

COMPLETE SET (225) 75.00 150.00
*STARS: 1.5X TO 3X BASIC CARDS
*RCs: .6X TO 1.5X BASIC CARDS
ONE PER PACK

1995 SP Championship Playoff Showcase

This 20 card set was randomly inserted into packs at a rate of one in 15 and features top NFL stars who have made a great impact for their team in the playoffs. Cards are numbered with a "PS" prefix and have a gold hologram in the lower right corner. The parallel "Playoff Showcase Die Cut" cards are similar to the regular cards. The exceptions include a die cut design at the top, the silver foil replaced with gold foil and the hologram on the back of the card being in silver.

COMPLETE SET (20) 50.00 100.00
STATED ODDS 1:15
*DIE CUTS: .6X TO 1.5X BASIC INSERTS
DIE CUTS: STATED ODDS 1:20
PS1 Troy Aikman 5.00 10.00
PS2 Jerry Rice 5.00 10.00
PS3 Isaac Bruce 2.50 5.00
PS4 Rodney Peete .40 1.00
PS5 Rashaan Salaam .60 1.25
PS6 Brett Favre 8.00 20.00
PS7 Alvin Harper .40 1.00
PS8 Cris Carter 1.50 3.00
PS9 Michael Westbrook 1.25 2.50
PS10 Jeff George 1.00 2.00
PS11 Natrone Means 1.00 2.00
PS12 Dan Marino 10.00 20.00
PS13 Steve Bono 1.00 2.00
PS14 Greg Lloyd 1.00 2.00
PS15 Jim Kelly 1.50 3.00
PS16 Jeff Hostetler 1.00 2.00
PS17 Marshall Faulk 6.00 12.00
PS18 John Elway 10.00 20.00
PS19 Jeff Blake 2.00 4.00
PS20 Andre Rison 1.00 2.00

2007 SP Chirography

This 147-card set was released in December, 2007. The set was issued in three-card packs with an $50 SRP which came eight packs to a box. The first 100 cards in this set feature veterans in team alphabetical order while the final 47 cards in this set feature signed Rookie Cards. Those cards were signed in quantities between 75 and 699 cards and we have notated that information in our checklist. In addition, a few players did not return their signatures in time for pack out and those cards could be exchanged until December 10, 2009. Cards numbered 119, 140 and 141 were never issued.

AU ROOKIE PRINT RUN 5-699 SER.#'d SETS
1 Edgerrin James .60 1.50
2 Anquan Boldin .50 1.25
3 Matt Leinart .50 1.25
4 DeAngelo Hall .50 1.25
5 Warrick Dunn .50 1.25
6 Jeff Garcia .50 1.25
7 Ray Lewis .75 2.00
8 Willis McGahee .50 1.25
9 Steve McNair .60 1.50
10 Lee Evans .60 1.50
11 J.P. Losman .50 1.25
12 Anthony Thomas .50 1.25
13 Jake Delhomme .50 1.25
14 Steve Smith .60 1.50
15 DeAngelo Williams .50 1.25
16 Brian Urlacher .75 2.00
17 Rex Grossman .50 1.25
18 Cedric Benson .50 1.25
19 Chad Johnson .50 1.25
20 Carson Palmer .60 1.50
21 Rudi Johnson .50 1.25
22 Jamal Lewis .60 1.50
23 Derek Anderson .50 1.25
24 Braylon Edwards .50 1.25
25 Julius Jones .50 1.25
26 Tony Romo 1.00 2.50
27 Terrell Owens .60 1.50
28 Marion Barber .60 1.50
29 Jay Cutler .50 1.25
30 Travis Henry .60 1.50
31 Javon Walker .60 1.50
32 Tatum Bell .50 1.25
33 Jon Kitna .50 1.25
34 Roy Williams WR .50 1.25
35 Brett Favre 1.50 4.00
36 A.J. Hawk .50 1.25
37 Greg Jennings .50 1.25
38 Ahman Green .60 1.50
39 Andre Johnson .60 1.50
40 Matt Schaub .50 1.25
41 Peyton Manning 2.00 5.00
42 Reggie Wayne .60 1.50
43 Joseph Addai .50 1.25
44 Marvin Harrison .60 1.50
45 David Garrard .50 1.25
46 Fred Taylor .50 1.25
47 Maurice Jones-Drew .50 1.25
48 Larry Johnson .50 1.25
49 Tony Gonzalez .60 1.50
50 Damon Huard .60 1.50
51 Ronnie Brown .50 1.25
52 Zach Thomas .60 1.50
53 Chris Chambers .50 1.25
54 Troy Williamson .50 1.25
55 Tarvaris Jackson .50 1.25
56 Chester Taylor .50 1.25
57 Tom Brady 2.50 6.00
58 Randy Moss .60 1.50
59 Laurence Maroney .60 1.50
60 Reggie Bush .50 1.25
61 Drew Brees .75 2.00
62 Deuce McAllister .60 1.50
63 Marques Colston .50 1.25
64 Eli Manning .60 1.50
65 Brandon Jacobs .50 1.25
66 Plaxico Burress .50 1.25
67 Chad Pennington .50 1.25
68 Thomas Jones .50 1.25
69 Laveranues Coles .50 1.25
70 LaMont Jordan .60 1.50
71 Josh McCown .50 1.25
72 Ronald Curry .50 1.25
73 Donovan McNabb .60 1.50
74 Reggie Brown .50 1.25
75 Brian Westbrook .50 1.25
76 Ben Roethlisberger .75 2.00
77 Willie Parker .60 1.50
78 Hines Ward .60 1.50
79 LaDainian Tomlinson .75 2.00
80 Philip Rivers .75 2.00
81 Antonio Gates .75 2.00
82 Shawne Merriman .50 1.25
83 Alex Smith QB .60 1.50
84 Frank Gore .60 1.50
85 Ashley Lelie .60 1.50
86 Matt Hasselbeck .50 1.25
87 Shaun Alexander .50 1.25
88 Deion Branch .50 1.25
89 Torry Holt .60 1.50
90 Marc Bulger .50 1.25
91 Steven Jackson .50 1.25
92 Cadillac Williams .60 1.50
93 Chris Brown .50 1.25
94 Joey Galloway .60 1.50
95 Vince Young .50 1.25
96 David Givens .50 1.25
97 LenDale White .80 1.50
98 Clinton Portis .60 1.25
99 Santana Moss .60 1.50
100 Jason Campbell .50 1.25
101 Adrian Peterson AU/199 RC 100.00 200.00
102 Brady Quinn AU/199 RC 6.00 15.00
103 Calvin Johnson AU/149 RC 40.00 80.00
104 Dwayne Bowe AU/199 RC 6.00 15.00
105 JaMarcus Russell AU/199 RC 6.00 15.00
106 Marshawn Lynch AU/199 RC 15.00 40.00
107 Ted Ginn Jr. AU/199 RC 8.00 20.00
108 Anthony Gonzalez AU/399 RC 4.00 10.00
109 Brian Leonard AU/399 RC 4.00 10.00
110 Darrelle Revis AU/399 RC 15.00 40.00
111 Drew Stanton AU/399 RC 4.00 10.00
112 Dwayne Jarrett AU/399 RC 5.00 12.00
113 Kevin Kolb AU/399 RC 5.00 12.00
114 LaRon Landry AU/399 RC 6.00 15.00
115 Leon Hall AU/399 RC 4.00 10.00
116 Robert Meachem AU/349 RC 10.00 20.00
117 Sidney Rice AU/99 RC 20.00 40.00
118 Antonio Pittman AU/699 RC 3.00 8.00
120 Chris Henry RB AU/699 RC 3.00 8.00
121 Garrett Wolfe AU/699 RC 3.00 8.00
122 Isaiah Stanback AU/699 RC 3.00 8.00
123 Jamaal Anderson AU/79 RC 7.50 20.00
124 Jason Hill AU/699 RC 3.00 8.00
125 Jeff Rowe AU/699 RC 3.00 8.00
126 John Beck AU/699 RC 3.00 8.00
127 Jordan Palmer AU/699 RC 4.00 10.00
128 Lawrence Timmons AU/699 RC 5.00 12.00
129 Lorenzo Booker AU/699 RC 4.00 10.00
130 Michael Bush AU/699 RC 3.00 8.00
131 Michael Griffin AU/699 RC 3.00 8.00
132 Patrick Willis AU/15 RC 50.00 100.00
133 Paul Posluszny AU/699 RC 3.00 8.00
134 Steve Smith AU/699 RC 8.00 20.00
135 Tony Hunt AU/109 RC 3.00 8.00
136 Trent Edwards AU/299 RC 3.00 8.00
137 Yamon Figurs AU/699 RC 3.00 8.00
138 Zach Miller AU/699 RC 3.00 8.00
139 Chris Leak AU/699 RC 3.00 8.00
142 Greg Olsen AU/699 RC 5.00 12.00
143 Kenny Irons AU/75 RC 7.50 20.00
144 Reggie Nelson AU/699 RC 3.00 8.00
145 David Clowney AU/699 RC 3.00 8.00
146 DeShawn Wynn AU/699 RC 3.00 8.00
147 Joe Thomas AU/699 RC 5.00 12.00
148 Johnnie Lee Higgins AU/699 RC 3.00 8.00
149 Paul Williams AU/699 RC 3.00 8.00

2007 SP Chirography Biography of a Rookie Autographs Gold

GOLD AU PRINT RUN 1-99
*SILVER/75: .4X TO 1X GOLD AU/99
*SILVER/50: .5X TO 1.2X GOLD AU/99
SILVER PRINT RUN 50-75
*EMERALD/50: .5X TO 1.2X GOLD AU/99
*EMERALD/25: .6X TO 1.5X GOLD AU/99
EMERALD PRINT RUN 25-50
UNPRICED SAPPHIRE PRINT RUN 1
UNPRICED BRONZE PRINT RUN 1
BORAP Antonio Pittman 3.00 8.00
BORBR John Broussard 4.00 10.00
BORCD Chris Davis 3.00 8.00
BORCH Chris Henry RB 3.00 8.00
BORDW DeShawn Wynn 3.00 8.00
BORGW Garrett Wolfe 3.00 8.00
BORHI Johnnie Lee Higgins 3.00 8.00
BORIS Isaiah Stanback 3.00 8.00
BORJB John Beck 3.00 8.00
BORJH Jason Hill 3.00 8.00
BORJP Jordan Palmer 4.00 10.00
BORMB Michael Bush 3.00 8.00
BORPP Paul Posluszny 3.00 8.00
BORSC Scott Chandler 5.00 12.00
BORTH Tony Hunt 3.00 8.00
BORWI Paul Williams 3.00 8.00
BORYF Yamon Figurs 3.00 8.00
BORZM Zach Miller 3.00 8.00

2007 SP Chirography Dual Autographs Gold

GOLD PRINT RUN 1-25
UNPRICED SILVER PRINT RUN 1
UNPRICED EMERALD PRINT RUN 1
CDHB L.Hall/A.Branch/25
CDOM B.Meriweather/G.Olsen/25 12.00 30.00

2007 SP Chirography First Signs Gold

GOLD PRINT RUN 99 SER.#'d SETS
*SILVER/75: .4X TO 1X GOLD AU/99
*SILVER/50: .5X TO 1.2X GOLD AU/99
SILVER PRINT RUN 50-75
*EMERALD/50: .5X TO 1.2X GOLD AU/99
*EMERALD/25: .6X TO 1.5X GOLD AU/99
EMERALD PRINT RUN 10-50
UNPRICED SAPPHIRE PRINT RUN 1
UNPRICED BRONZE PRINT RUN 1
FSAP Antonio Pittman 3.00 8.00
FSBR John Broussard 4.00 10.00
FSCH Chris Henry RB 3.00 8.00
FSCL Chris Leak 3.00 8.00
FSDW DeShawn Wynn 3.00 8.00
FSGO Greg Olsen 5.00 12.00
FSGW Garrett Wolfe 3.00 8.00
FSIS Isaiah Stanback 3.00 8.00
FSJA Jamaal Anderson 4.00 10.00
FSJB John Beck 3.00 8.00
FSJH Jason Hill 3.00 8.00
FSJP Jordan Palmer 4.00 10.00
FSJR Jeff Rowe 3.00 8.00
FSMB Michael Bush 3.00 8.00
FSMG Michael Griffin 3.00 8.00
FSPP Paul Posluszny 3.00 8.00
FSRN Reggie Nelson 3.00 8.00
FSSS Steve Smith USC 3.00 8.00
FSTH Tony Hunt 3.00 8.00
FSTT Tyler Thigpen 5.00 12.00
FSYF Yamon Figurs 3.00 8.00
FSZM Zach Miller 3.00 8.00

2007 SP Chirography Football Heroes Autographs Gold

GOLD PRINT RUN 4-99
*EMERALD/50: .5X TO 1.2X GOLD AU/99
*EMERALD/25: .6X TO 1.5X GOLD AU/99
*EMERALD/25: .6X TO 1.5X GOLD AU/75
EMERALD PRINT RUN 5-50
UNPRICED SAPPHIRE PRINT RUN 1
UNPRICED BRONZE PRINT RUN 1
SERIAL #'d UNDER 25 NOT PRICED
FHAD Joseph Addai/50 8.00 20.00
FHAG Anthony Gonzalez/50 4.00 10.00
FHAP Adrian Peterson/15 125.00 250.00
FHBF Brett Favre/15 100.00 200.00
FHBQ Brady Quinn/15
FHBU Reggie Bush/15
FHCL Chris Leak/99 3.00 8.00
FHCW Cadillac Williams/50 10.00 25.00
FHDB Dwayne Bowe/50 15.00 40.00
FHDM Dan Marino/15 75.00 150.00
FHDS Drew Stanton/99 3.00 8.00
FHES Emmitt Smith/15 75.00 150.00
FHGO Greg Olsen/99 5.00 12.00
FHGW Garrett Wolfe/99 3.00 8.00
FHJA Brandon Jacobs/99 6.00 15.00
FHJB John Beck/99 3.00 8.00
FHJJ Julius Jones/75 6.00 15.00
FHJM Joe Montana/15
FHJN Joe Namath/15 40.00 80.00
FHJR JaMarcus Russell/15 6.00 15.00
FHJT Joe Theismann/99 10.00 25.00
FHKK Kevin Kolb/75 4.00 10.00
FHLL LaRon Landry/99 5.00 12.00
FHLT LaDainian Tomlinson/15 20.00 50.00
FHMB Michael Bush/99 3.00 8.00
FHML Marshawn Lynch/25 10.00 25.00
FHPH Paul Hornung/75 10.00 25.00
FHPI Antonio Pittman/99 3.00 8.00
FHPM Peyton Manning/15 75.00 150.00
FHRC Roger Craig/50 10.00 25.00
FHSH Santonio Holmes/15
FHSS Steve Smith USC/99 3.00 8.00
FHSY Steve Young/15 75.00 150.00
FHTH Tony Hunt/99 3.00 8.00
FHWP Willie Parker/15 15.00 40.00

2007 SP Chirography Football Heroes Autographs Silver

*SILVER/75: .4X TO 1X GOLD AU/99
*SILVER/50: .5X TO 1.2X GOLD AU/99
*SILVER/50: .5X TO 1.2X GOLD AU/75
*SILVER/25: .5X TO 1.2X GOLD AU/50
SILVER PRINT RUN 10-75
FHMA Marcus Allen/50 15.00 40.00

2007 SP Chirography NFL Imagery Autographs Gold

GOLD PRINT RUN 1-99
*SILVER/75: .4X TO 1X GOLD AU/99
*SILVER/50: .5X TO 1.2X GOLD AU/99
*SILVER/25: .5X TO 1.2X GOLD AU/50
SILVER PRINT RUN 10-75
*EMERALD/50: .5X TO 1.2X GOLD AU/99
EMERALD PRINT RUN 5-50
UNPRICED SAPPHIRE PRINT RUN 1
UNPRICED BRONZE PRINT RUN 1
NFLIAG Anthony Gonzalez/50 4.00 10.00
NFLIAP Adrian Peterson/15 100.00 200.00
NFLIBL Brian Leonard/99 3.00 8.00
NFLIBQ Brady Quinn/15 6.00 15.00
NFLICH Chris Henry RB/99 3.00 8.00
NFLICL Chris Leak/99 3.00 8.00
NFLIDJ Dwayne Jarrett/99 4.00 10.00
NFLIDS Drew Stanton/99 3.00 8.00
NFLIDW DeShawn Wynn/99 3.00 8.00
NFLIGO Greg Olsen/99 5.00 12.00
NFLIGW Garrett Wolfe/99 3.00 8.00
NFLIHI Johnnie Lee Higgins/99 3.00 8.00
NFLIIS Isaiah Stanback/99 3.00 8.00
NFLIJA Joseph Addai/50 8.00 20.00
NFLIJB John Broussard/99 4.00 10.00
NFLIJB John Beck/99 3.00 8.00
NFLIJH Jason Hill/99 3.00 8.00
NFLIJT Joe Thomas/99 5.00 12.00
NFLILL LaRon Landry/99 5.00 12.00
NFLIPP Paul Posluszny/99 3.00 8.00
NFLIRB Reggie Bush/15 12.00 30.00
NFLIRM Robert Meachem/50 8.00 20.00
NFLISS Steve Smith USC/99 3.00 8.00
NFLIYF Yamon Figurs/99 3.00 8.00

2007 SP Chirography Notable Notations Autographs Gold

GOLD PRINT RUN 5-50
UNPRICED SILVER PRINT RUN 1
NNJB John Beck/50 4.00 10.00
NNJT Joe Thomas/50 6.00 15.00
NNRC Roger Craig/25 12.00 30.00

2007 SP Chirography Rookie Signatures Gold

GOLD PRINT RUN 1-25
UNPRICED SAPPHIRE AU PRINT RUN 1
101 Adrian Peterson 150.00 300.00
103 Calvin Johnson 75.00 150.00
104 Dwayne Bowe 12.00 30.00
106 Marshawn Lynch 12.00 30.00
110 Darrelle Revis 20.00 50.00
113 Kevin Kolb 6.00 15.00
117 Sidney Rice 40.00 100.00
134 Steve Smith USC 12.00 30.00

2007 SP Chirography Signature Running Backs Gold

STATED PRINT RUN 15-99 SER.#'d SETS
*SILVER/75: .4X TO 1X GOLD AU/99
*SILVER/50: .5X TO 1.2X GOLD AU/99
*SILVER/50: .5X TO 1.2X GOLD AU/75
SILVER PRINT RUN 10-75
*EMERALD/50: .5X TO 1.2X GOLD AU/99
*EMERALD/25: .6X TO 1.5X GOLD AU/99
EMERALD PRINT RUN 5-50
UNPRICED SAPPHIRE PRINT RUN 1
UNPRICED BRONZE PRINT RUN 1
SBDW DeShawn Wynn/99 3.00 8.00
SBFG Frank Gore/75 8.00 20.00
SBML Marshawn Lynch/25 10.00 25.00
SBRC Roger Craig/99 8.00 20.00
SBTH Tony Hunt/99 3.00 8.00

2007 SP Chirography Signature Numbers Gold

GOLD PRINT RUN 4-99
*SILVER/75: .4X TO 1X GOLD AU/99
*SILVER/50: .5X TO 1.2X GOLD AU/99
*SILVER/25: .5X TO 1.2X GOLD AU/50
SILVER PRINT RUN 10-75
*EMERALD/50: .5X TO 1.2X GOLD AU/99
*EMERALD/25: .6X TO 1.5X GOLD AU/99
EMERALD PRINT RUN 5-50
UNPRICED SAPPHIRE PRINT RUN 1
UNPRICED BRONZE PRINT RUN 1
SERIAL #'d UNDER 25 NOT PRICED
SNAG Anthony Gonzalez/99 3.00 8.00
SNCL Chris Leak/99 3.00 8.00
SNCW Cadillac Williams/50 10.00 25.00
SNDJ Dwayne Jarrett/99 4.00 10.00
SNGO Greg Olsen/99 5.00 12.00
SNJB John Beck/99 3.00 8.00
SNLD Len Dawson/35 15.00 40.00
SNML Marshawn Lynch/25 10.00 25.00
SNRC Roger Craig/50 10.00 25.00
SNRN Reggie Nelson/99 3.00 8.00
SNTH Tony Hunt/99 3.00 8.00

2007 SP Chirography Signature Quarterbacks Gold

GOLD PRINT RUN 15-99
*SILVER/75: .4X TO 1X GOLD AU/99
SILVER PRINT RUN 10-75
*EMERALD/50: .5X TO 1.2X GOLD AU/99
EMERALD PRINT RUN 5-50
UNPRICED SAPPHIRE PRINT RUN 1
UNPRICED BRONZE PRINT RUN 1
SQCL Chris Leak/99 3.00 8.00
SQDS Drew Stanton/99 3.00 8.00
SQJB John Beck/99 3.00 8.00
SQJP Jordan Palmer/99 4.00 10.00
SQTR Tony Romo/25 90.00 150.00

2007 SP Chirography Signature Receivers Gold

GOLD PRINT RUN 50-99
*SILVER/75: .4X TO 1X GOLD AU/99
*SILVER/50: .5X TO 1.2X GOLD AU/75
*SILVER/50: .4X TO 1X GOLD AU/50
SILVER PRINT RUN 50-75
*EMERALD/50: .5X TO 1.2X GOLD AU/99
*EMERALD/25: .6X TO 1.5X GOLD AU/75
*EMERALD/25: .5X TO 1.2X GOLD AU/50
EMERALD PRINT RUN 25-50
UNPRICED SAPPHIRE PRINT RUN 1
UNPRICED BRONZE PRINT RUN 1
SRAG Anthony Gonzalez/99 3.00 8.00
SRBB Bernard Berrian/75 6.00 15.00
SRCJ Chad Johnson/75 6.00 15.00
SRDB Dwayne Bowe/75 3.00 8.00
SRDP Drew Pearson/99 8.00 20.00
SRJB John Broussard/99 4.00 10.00
SRRB Reggie Brown/75 6.00 15.00
SRRM Robert Meachem/50 8.00 20.00

2007 SP Chirography Signatures Gold

GOLD PRINT RUN 15-99
*SILVER/75: .4X TO 1X GOLD AU/99
*SILVER/50: .5X TO 1.2X GOLD AU/99
*SILVER/50: .5X TO 1.2X GOLD AU/75
SILVER PRINT RUN 10-75
*EMERALD/50: .5X TO 1.2X GOLD AU/99
*EMERALD/50: .4X TO 1X GOLD AU/50
*EMERALD/25: .6X TO 1.5X GOLD AU/99
*EMERALD/25: .6X TO 1.5X GOLD AU/75
EMERALD PRINT RUN 5-50
UNPRICED SAPPHIRE PRINT RUN 1
UNPRICED BRONZE PRINT RUN 1
SERIAL #'d UNDER 25 NOT PRICED
CSCD Chris Davis/99 3.00 8.00
CSCH Chris Henry RB/99 3.00 8.00
CSDJ Dwayne Jarrett/50 5.00 12.00
CSDP Drew Pearson/99 8.00 20.00
CSDS Drew Stanton/99 3.00 8.00
CSGJ Greg Jennings/99 6.00 15.00
CSGO Greg Olsen/99 5.00 12.00
CSGW Garrett Wolfe/99 3.00 8.00
CSJB John Beck/99 3.00 8.00
CSJJ Julius Jones/75 6.00 15.00
CSJM Jim McMahon/30 20.00 50.00
CSKK Kevin Kolb/75 4.00 10.00
CSLL LaRon Landry/99 5.00 12.00
CSML Marshawn Lynch/25 10.00 25.00
CSRC Roger Craig/50 10.00 25.00
CSSS Steve Smith USC/99 3.00 8.00
CSTH Tony Hunt/99 3.00 8.00

2007 SP Chirography Signs of Defense Gold

GOLD PRINT RUN 99 SER.#'d SETS
*SILVER/75: .4X TO 1X GOLD AU/99
*SILVER/50: .5X TO 1.2X GOLD AU/99
SILVER PRINT RUN 50-75
*EMERALD/50: .5X TO 1.2X GOLD AU/99
*EMERALD/25: .6X TO 1.5X GOLD AU/99
EMERALD PRINT RUN 25-50
UNPRICED SAPPHIRE PRINT RUN 1
UNPRICED BRONZE PRINT RUN 1
SODAC Adam Carriker 3.00 8.00
SODBM Brandon Meriweather 4.00 10.00
SODJA Jamaal Anderson 4.00 10.00
SODJL John Lynch 12.00 30.00
SODLW LaMarr Woodley 8.00 20.00
SODMG Michael Griffin 3.00 8.00
SODPP Paul Posluszny 3.00 8.00
SODRN Reggie Nelson 3.00 8.00

2007 SP Chirography Signs of September Dual Autographs Gold

GOLD PRINT RUN 2-50
UNPRICED SILVER PRINT RUN 1
UNPRICED EMERALD PRINT RUN 1
SERIAL #'d UNDER 50 NOT PRICED
AC A.Carriker/J.Anderson 6.00 15.00
AM J.Anderson/B.Meriweather 6.00 15.00
BK K.Kolb/J.Beck 6.00 15.00
BW A.Branch/L.Woodley 12.00 30.00
DN C.Davis/L.Naanee 6.00 15.00
DR D.Walker/R.McKnight 5.00 12.00
GD G.Wolfe/D.Ball 5.00 12.00
GM B.Meriweather/M.Griffin 6.00 15.00
HP P.Posluszny/T.Hunt 5.00 12.00
II K.Irons/D.Irons 5.00 12.00
LS C.Leak/D.Stanton 5.00 12.00
MP T.Palko/M.Moore 8.00 20.00
NL R.Nelson/L.Landry 8.00 20.00
OM G.Olsen/Z.Miller 8.00 20.00
PB P.Posluszny/H.Blades 5.00 12.00
PI K.Irons/A.Pittman 5.00 12.00
PP T.Palko/A.Pittman 8.00 20.00
RB G.Russell/D.Baker 6.00 15.00
SB M.Bush/K.Smith 5.00 12.00
WB L.Booker/D.Wynn 6.00 15.00
WM D.Wright/M.McCauley 5.00 12.00

2007 SP Chirography Triple Signatures Gold

GOLD PRINT RUN 1-25
UNPRICED SILVER PRINT RUN 1
UNPRICED EMERALD PRINT RUN 1
HWH Henry RB/Hunt/Wolfe 6.00 15.00
LWB Leak/Baker/Wynn 6.00 15.00
OMC Olsen/Miller/Chandler 10.00 25.00

2001 SP Game Used Edition

Upper Deck released SP Game Used Edition in mid July of 2001. The packs contained 3 cards per pack and 1 of which was a jersey card. The base set design had a black and white photo in the background with a color photo on top of that. The cardbacks contained the featured players statistics and a quick summary about the player, along with the Upper Deck hologram.

COMP.SET w/o SP's (90) 50.00 100.00
ROOKIE PRINT RUN 500 SER.#'d SETS
1 Jake Plummer .60 1.50
2 David Boston .60 1.50
3 Frank Sanders .60 1.50
4 Jamal Anderson .75 2.00
5 Doug Johnson .60 1.50
6 Shawn Jefferson .60 1.50
7 Jamal Lewis 1.00 2.50
8 Shannon Sharpe .75 2.00
9 Qadry Ismail .60 1.50
10 Shawn Bryson .60 1.50
11 Rob Johnson .75 2.00
12 Eric Moulds .60 1.50
13 Muhsin Muhammad .60 1.50
14 Brad Hoover .75 2.00
15 Tim Biakabutuka .60 1.50
16 Cade McNown .75 2.00
17 Marcus Robinson .75 2.00
18 Brian Urlacher 1.25 3.00
19 Akili Smith .60 1.50
20 Peter Warrick .60 1.50
21 Corey Dillon .60 1.50
22 Kevin Johnson .60 1.50
23 Rickey Dudley .60 1.50
24 Tim Couch .60 1.50
25 Tony Banks .60 1.50
26 Emmitt Smith 1.50 4.00
27 Carl Pickens .75 2.00
28 Terrell Davis .75 2.00
29 Mike Anderson .60 1.50
30 Brian Griese .60 1.50
31 Ed McCaffrey .75 2.00
32 Charlie Batch .60 1.50
33 Germane Crowell .60 1.50
34 James O. Stewart .60 1.50
35 Brett Favre 2.00 5.00
36 Antonio Freeman 1.00 2.50
37 Ahman Green .75 2.00
38 Peyton Manning 2.50 6.00
39 Edgerrin James .75 2.00
40 Marvin Harrison .75 2.00
41 Mark Brunell .75 2.00
42 Fred Taylor .60 1.50
43 Jimmy Smith .75 2.00
44 Tony Gonzalez .75 2.00
45 Derrick Alexander .60 1.50
46 Oronde Gadsden .60 1.50
47 Ray Lucas .00 1.50
48 Lamar Smith .75 2.00
49 Randy Moss .75 2.00
50 Cris Carter 1.00 2.50
51 Daunte Culpepper .75 2.00
52 Drew Bledsoe .75 2.00
53 Terry Glenn .75 2.00
54 Ricky Williams .75 2.00
55 Jeff Blake .75 2.00
56 Joe Horn .60 1.50
57 Aaron Brooks .60 1.50
58 Kerry Collins .60 1.50
59 Tiki Barber .75 2.00
60 Ron Dayne .75 2.00
61 Vinny Testaverde .60 1.50
62 Wayne Chrebet .60 1.50
63 Curtis Martin .75 2.00
64 Tim Brown 1.00 2.50
65 Rich Gannon .75 2.00
66 Tyrone Wheatley .75 2.00
67 Duce Staley .60 1.50
68 Donovan McNabb .75 2.00
69 Kordell Stewart .60 1.50
70 Jerome Bettis 1.00 2.50
71 Marshall Faulk .75 2.00
72 Kurt Warner 1.50 4.00
73 Isaac Bruce 1.00 2.50
74 Doug Flutie .75 2.00
75 Curtis Conway .75 2.00
76 Jeff Garcia .60 1.50
77 Jerry Rice 2.00 5.00
78 Charlie Garner .75 2.00
79 Terrell Owens .75 2.00
80 Ricky Watters .75 2.00
81 Matt Hasselbeck .60 1.50
82 Levon Kirkland .60 1.50
83 Keyshawn Johnson .75 2.00
84 Brad Johnson .75 2.00
85 Mike Alstott .60 1.50
86 Eddie George 1.00 2.50
87 Steve McNair .75 2.00
88 Jeff George .75 2.00
89 Michael Westbrook .60 1.50
90 Stephen Davis .60 1.50
91 Michael Vick JSY RC 6.00 15.00
92 Chris Weinke JSY RC 3.00 8.00
93 Drew Brees JSY RC 50.00 100.00
94 Deuce McAllister JSY RC 4.00 10.00
95 Michael Bennett JSY RC 3.00 8.00
96 LaDain Tomlinson JSY RC 15.00 40.00
97 Kevan Barlow JSY RC 3.00 8.00
98 Travis Minor JSY RC 3.00 8.00
99 Rudi Johnson JSY RC 4.00 10.00
100 Todd Heap JSY RC 3.00 8.00
101 Freddie Mitchell JSY RC 2.50 6.00
102 Santana Moss JSY RC 4.00 10.00
103 Reggie Wayne JSY RC 5.00 12.00
104 Koren Robinson JSY RC 3.00 8.00
105 Josh Heupel JSY RC 4.00 10.00
106 Rod Gardner JSY RC 3.00 8.00
107 Quincy Morgan JSY RC 3.00 8.00
108 Chad Johnson JSY RC 4.00 10.00
109 Dan Morgan JSY RC 3.00 8.00
110 Gerard Warren JSY RC 3.00 8.00
111 Chris Chambers JSY RC 2.50 6.00
112 James Jackson JSY RC 2.50 6.00
113 Jesse Palmer JSY RC 3.00 8.00
114 Sage Rosenfels JSY RC 3.00 8.00
115 Mike McMahon JSY RC 3.00 8.00
116 M.Tuiasosopo JSY RC 3.00 8.00
117 Robert Ferguson JSY RC 4.00 10.00
118 Travis Henry JSY RC 3.00 8.00
119 Richard Seymour JSY RC 4.00 10.00
120 Andre Carter JSY RC 3.00 8.00
121 LaMont Jordan RC 2.50 6.00
122 Vinny Sutherland RC 1.50 4.00
123 Nate Clements RC 2.00 5.00
124 David Terrell RC 2.00 5.00
125 A.J. Feeley RC 2.00 5.00
126 David Rivers RC 1.50 4.00
127 Snoop Minnis RC 1.50 4.00
128 Josh Booty RC 2.00 5.00
129 Correll Buckhalter RC 1.50 4.00
130 Will Allen RC 2.50 6.00
131 Dan Alexander RC 2.00 5.00
132 Leonard Davis RC 2.50 6.00
133 Anthony Thomas RC 2.50 6.00
134 Alge Crumpler RC 2.50 6.00
135 Jamal Reynolds RC 1.50 4.00
136 Ken-Yon Rambo RC 1.50 4.00
137 Bobby Newcombe RC 2.00 5.00
138 Alex Bannister RC 1.50 4.00
139 Jabari Holloway RC 1.50 4.00
140 Jamar Fletcher RC 1.50 4.00
141 Adam Archuleta RC 2.00 5.00
142 Heath Evans RC 2.00 5.00
143 Scotty Anderson RC 1.50 4.00
144 Moran Norris RC 1.50 4.00
145 Justin Smith RC 3.00 8.00
146 Quincy Carter RC 2.00 5.00
147 Ronney Daniels RC 1.50 4.00
148 Ben Leard RC 1.50 4.00
149 Fred Smoot RC 2.00 5.00
150 Milton Wynn RC 1.50 4.00

2001 SP Game Used Edition Authentic Fabric

Randomly inserted in packs of 2001 SP Game-Used Edition at a rate of 1:1, this 78-card set featured jersey swatches from the top players from the NFL. Each swatch is about 1 square inch. The card numbers were the players initials. A gold parallel set was also produced with each card serial numbered to 25. Finally, some cards were produced in an autographed version serial numbered of 25 as well.

STATED ODDS ONE PER PACK
*GOLD/25: 1.5X TO 4X BASIC JSY
*GOLD/25: 1X TO 2.5X BASIC JSY SP
GOLD STATED PRINT RUN 25 SER.#'d SETS
AF Antonio Freeman 5.00 12.00
AG Ahman Green 4.00 10.00
AL Mike Alstott 3.00 8.00
AS Akili Smith 3.00 8.00
AT Amani Toomer 3.00 8.00
AZ Az Zahir Hakim 3.00 8.00
BA Tiki Barber 4.00 10.00
BF Brett Favre 10.00 25.00
BG Brian Griese 3.00 8.00
BJ Brad Johnson 4.00 10.00
BO David Boston 3.00 8.00
BR Drew Brees 20.00 50.00
BS Bart Starr SP 20.00 50.00
CB Champ Bailey 4.00 10.00
CC Chris Chambers 3.00 8.00
CD Corey Dillon 3.00 8.00
CH Chris Chandler 4.00 10.00
CO Curtis Conway 4.00 10.00
CW Charles Woodson 5.00 12.00
DB Drew Bledsoe 4.00 10.00
DC Daunte Culpepper SP 6.00 15.00
DF Bubba Franks 3.00 8.00
DL Dorsey Levens SP 12.00 30.00
DM Deuce McAllister 5.00 12.00
EJ Edgerrin James SP 6.00 15.00
EM Eric Moulds 3.00 8.00
FM Freddie Mitchell 3.00 8.00
FS Frank Sanders 3.00 8.00
FT Fran Tarkenton SP 15.00 40.00
IB Isaac Bruce 5.00 12.00
IH Ike Hilliard 3.00 8.00
JA Jamal Anderson 4.00 10.00
JB Jerome Bettis 6.00 15.00
JE John Elway SP 15.00 40.00
JG Jeff Garcia 3.00 8.00
JJ J.J. Stokes 3.00 8.00
JL Jamal Lewis SP 12.00 30.00
JM Joe Montana 15.00 40.00
JP Jake Plummer 3.00 0.00
JR Jerry Rice 10.00 25.00
JS Junior Seau 4.00 10.00
JU Johnny Unitas SP 20.00 50.00
KC Kerry Collins 3.00 8.00
KS Kordell Stewart 3.00 8.00
KW Kurt Warner 8.00 20.00

LT LaDainian Tomlinson SP 10.00 25.00
MA Marcus Allen SP 10.00 25.00
MB Mark Brunell 4.00 10.00
MC Ed McCaffrey 4.00 10.00
MF Marshall Faulk 4.00 10.00
MP Michael Pittman 4.00 10.00
MT Marques Tuiasosopo 4.00 10.00
MV Michael Vick 5.00 12.00
MW Michael Westbrook 3.00 8.00
PB Plaxico Burress 3.00 8.00
PM Peyton Manning 12.00 30.00
PW Peter Warrick 3.00 8.00
RD Ron Dayne 4.00 10.00
RL Ray Lewis 5.00 12.00
RM Randy Moss SP 6.00 15.00
RS Rod Smith 4.00 10.00
SD Stephen Davis 3.00 8.00
SE Jason Sehorn 4.00 10.00
SK Shaun King 3.00 8.00
SM Justin Smith 6.00 15.00
TA Troy Aikman SP 12.00 30.00
TB Terry Bradshaw SP 20.00 50.00
TC Tim Couch 3.00 8.00
TD Terrell Davis 4.00 10.00
TG Terry Glenn 4.00 10.00
TH Torry Holt 4.00 10.00
TJ Thomas Jones 3.00 8.00
TO Terrell Owens 4.00 10.00
WD Warrick Dunn 3.00 8.00
WE Chris Weinke 4.00 10.00
WP Walter Payton SP 15.00 40.00
WS Warren Sapp 4.00 10.00
FTA Fred Taylor 3.00 8.00

2001 SP Game Used Edition Authentic Fabric Autographs

Randomly inserted in packs of 2001 SP Game-Used Edition , this set featured jersey swatches from the top players from the NFL. Each swatch is about 1 square inch. The card numbers were the players initials, and carried an 'A' suffix. The cards were also autographed,and were serial numbered to 25.

STATED PRINT RUN 25 SER.#'d SETS
AZA Az Zahir Hakim 20.00 50.00
BJA Brad Johnson 25.00 60.00
BRA Drew Brees 150.00 300.00
BSA Bart Starr 125.00 250.00
CDA Corey Dillon 20.00 50.00
DCA Daunte Culpepper 25.00 60.00
DMA Deuce McAllister 30.00 80.00
EJA Edgerrin James 75.00 150.00
FTA Fran Tarkenton 30.00 80.00
JEA John Elway 150.00 250.00
JGA Jeff Garcia 20.00 50.00
JMA Joe Montana 100.00 175.00
JPA Jake Plummer 20.00 50.00
JRA Jerry Rice 150.00 250.00
JUA Johnny Unitas 250.00 400.00
KWA Kurt Warner 50.00 125.00
MBA Mark Brunell 25.00 60.00
MFA Marshall Faulk 25.00 60.00
PMA Peyton Manning 150.00 250.00
RDA Ron Dayne 25.00 60.00
RMA Randy Moss 75.00 150.00
TAA Troy Aikman 75.00 150.00
TBA Terry Bradshaw 100.00 200.00
TCA Tim Couch 20.00 50.00

2001 SP Game Used Edition Authentic Fabric Duals

Randomly inserted in packs of 2001 SP Game Used Edition, this 15-card set featured jersey swatches from the top players from the NFL. Each swatch is about 1 square inch. The card numbers had a "2C" prefix and the players initials. These cards had 2 players' jersey swatches on them, and were serial numbered to 50.

STATED PRINT RUN 50 SER.#'d SETS
2CAD M.Alstott/W.Dunn 12.00 30.00
2CAS T.Aikman/E.Smith 75.00 150.00
2CBM M.Brunell/K.McCardell 15.00 40.00
2CBS F.Sanders/D.Boston 12.00 30.00
2CCM C.Carter/R.Moss 20.00 50.00
2CCS D.Chapman/R.Smith 12.00 30.00
2CDC R.Dayne/K.Collins 15.00 40.00
2CFF B.Favre/A.Freeman 50.00 120.00
2CJS K.Johnson/W.Sapp 15.00 40.00
2CMJ P.Manning/E.James 60.00 150.00
2COG T.Owens/J.Garcia 15.00 40.00
2CSB K.Stewart/J.Bettis 20.00 50.00
2CWB C.Woodson/T.Brown 20.00 50.00
2CWD P.Warrick/C.Dillon 12.00 30.00
2CWH K.Warner/T.Holt 50.00 120.00

2001 SP Game Used Edition Authentic Fabric Triples

Randomly inserted in packs of 2001 SP Game Used Edition, this 6-card set featured jersey swatches from the top players from the NFL. Each swatch is about 1 square inch. These cards had 3 players' jersey swatches on them, and were serial numbered to 25.

STATED PRINT RUN 25 SER.#'d SETS
3CCMC Carter/Moss/Culpepper 30.00 80.00
3CDCB Dayne/Collins/Barber 25.00 60.00
3CDGJ Davis/George/James 30.00 80.00
3CFWM Favre/Warner/Manning 100.00 200.00
3CHHB Holt/Hakim/Bruce 30.00 80.00
3CLLD J.Lewis/R.Lewis/Dilfer 30.00 80.00

2003 SP Game Used Edition

Released in July of 2003, this set consists of 181 cards, including 90 veterans, 50 rookies, and 41 memorabilia cards featuring game worn jersey swatches. The rookies are serial numbered to 600. Boxes contained 6 packs of 3 cards, with a jersey or autograph card in each pack. SRP was $29.99.

COMP.SET w/o SP's (90) 30.00 60.00
1 Chad Hutchinson .60 1.50
2 Quincy Carter .60 1.50
3 Joey Galloway .75 2.00
4 Kerry Collins .60 1.50
5 Jeremy Shockey .60 1.50
6 Amani Toomer .60 1.50
7 A.J. Feeley .60 1.50
8 Duce Staley .60 1.50
9 Dorsey Levens .75 2.00
10 Ladell Betts .60 1.50
11 Patrick Ramsey .75 2.00
12 Anthony Thomas .75 2.00
13 Marty Booker .60 1.50
14 Brian Urlacher 1.00 2.50
15 Joey Harrington .60 1.50
16 James Stewart .60 1.50
17 Az-Zahir Hakim .60 1.50
18 Donald Driver .75 2.00
19 Javon Walker .75 2.00
20 Kordell Stewart .60 1.50
21 Randy Moss .75 2.00
22 Shaun Hill 1.00 2.50
23 Brian Finneran .60 1.50
24 T.J. Duckett .60 1.50
25 Warrick Dunn .60 1.50
26 Rodney Peete .60 1.50
27 Stephen Davis .60 1.50
28 Muhsin Muhammad .60 1.50
29 Aaron Brooks .60 1.50
30 Deuce McAllister .75 2.00
31 Joe Horn .60 1.50
32 Keyshawn Johnson 1.00 2.50
33 Brad Johnson .75 2.00
34 Keenan McCardell .75 2.00
35 Jake Plummer .60 1.50
36 Josh McCown .75 2.00
37 Thomas Jones .60 1.50
38 Tai Streets .60 1.50
39 Kevan Barlow .60 1.50
40 Garrison Hearst .60 1.50
41 Maurice Morris .60 1.50
42 Matt Hasselbeck .60 1.50
43 Koren Robinson .75 2.00
44 Marc Bulger .60 1.50
45 Trung Canidate .60 1.50
46 Emmitt Smith 1.50 4.00
47 Alex Van Pelt .60 1.50
48 Travis Henry .60 1.50
49 Eric Moulds .60 1.50
50 Jason Taylor .75 2.00
51 Jay Fiedler .60 1.50
52 Randy McMichael .60 1.50
53 Tom Brady 4.00 10.00
54 Antowain Smith .75 2.00
55 Troy Brown .60 1.50
56 Curtis Martin .75 2.00
57 Vinny Testaverde .60 1.50
58 Santana Moss .75 2.00
59 Jamal Lewis .75 2.00
60 Chris Redman .60 1.50
61 Ray Lewis 1.00 2.50
62 Jon Kitna .60 1.50
63 Peter Warrick .60 1.50
64 Kelly Holcomb .60 1.50
65 William Green .60 1.50
66 Kevin Johnson .60 1.50
67 Amos Zereoue .60 1.50
68 Tommy Maddox .60 1.50
69 Hines Ward .75 2.00
70 Corey Bradford .60 1.50
71 Jonathan Wells .60 1.50
72 Jabar Gaffney .60 1.50
73 Edgerrin James .75 2.00
74 David Garrard .60 1.50
75 Mark Brunell .75 2.00
76 Jimmy Smith .75 2.00
77 Steve McNair .75 2.00
78 Kevin Dyson .60 1.50
79 Terrell Davis .75 2.00
80 Shannon Sharpe .75 2.00
81 Rod Smith .75 2.00
82 Trent Green .60 1.50
83 Priest Holmes .60 1.50
84 Tony Gonzalez .75 2.00
85 Jerry Rice 2.00 5.00
86 Charlie Garner .75 2.00
87 Jerry Porter .60 1.50
88 Reche Caldwell .60 1.50
89 Tim Dwight .60 1.50
90 Junior Seau .75 2.00
91 Carson Palmer RC 5.00 12.00
92 Byron Leftwich RC 3.00 8.00
93 Dave Ragone RC 2.50 6.00
94 Kyle Boller RC 2.50 6.00
95 Rex Grossman RC 3.00 8.00
96 Chris Simms RC 2.50 6.00
97 Kliff Kingsbury RC 4.00 10.00
98 Jason Gesser RC 3.00 8.00
99 Brad Banks RC 3.00 8.00
100 Ken Dorsey RC 3.00 8.00
101 Juston Wood RC 2.50 6.00
102 Brian St.Pierre RC 2.50 6.00
103 Domanick Davis RC 3.00 8.00
104 Quentin Griffin RC 3.00 8.00
105 B.J. Askew RC 3.00 8.00
106 Onterrio Smith RC 2.50 6.00
107 Seneca Wallace RC 3.00 8.00
108 Artose Pinner RC 2.50 6.00
109 Justin Fargas RC 4.00 10.00
110 Chris Brown RC 2.50 6.00
111 Willis McGahee RC 3.00 8.00
112 Larry Johnson RC 3.00 8.00
113 Lee Suggs RC 2.50 6.00
114 Billy McMullen RC 2.50 6.00
115 Sultan McCullough RC 2.50 6.00
116 Musa Smith RC 2.50 6.00
117 Earnest Graham RC 4.00 10.00
118 Antwone Savage RC 2.50 6.00
119 Kirk Farmer RC 3.00 8.00
120 Kareem Kelly RC 2.50 6.00
121 J.R. Tolver RC 3.00 8.00
122 Tyrone Calico RC 2.50 6.00
123 Kevin Curtis RC 2.50 6.00
124 Bobby Wade RC 3.00 8.00
125 Justin Gage RC 3.00 8.00
126 Bryant Johnson RC 4.00 10.00
127 Doug Gabriel RC 3.00 8.00
128 Teyo Johnson RC 3.00 8.00
129 Brandon Lloyd RC 4.00 10.00
130 Kelley Washington RC 2.50 6.00
131 Talman Gardner RC 2.50 6.00
132 Anquan Boldin RC 4.00 10.00
133 Taylor Jacobs RC 2.50 6.00
134 Andre Johnson RC 6.00 15.00
135 Charles Rogers RC 3.00 8.00
136 Antonio Bryant JSY 3.00 8.00
137 Donovan McNabb JSY/99 6.00 15.00
138 Rod Gardner JSY 3.00 8.00
139 Ahman Green JSY 4.00 10.00
140 Brett Favre JSY/99 15.00 40.00
141 Daunte Culpepper JSY 4.00 10.00
142 Michael Bennett JSY 3.00 8.00
143 Michael Vick JSY/99 6.00 15.00
144 Jeff Garcia JSY 3.00 8.00
145 Terrell Owens JSY 4.00 10.00
146 Shaun Alexander JSY 3.00 8.00
147 Torry Holt JSY 4.00 10.00
148 Isaac Bruce JSY 5.00 12.00
149 Marshall Faulk JSY/99 6.00 15.00
150 Kurt Warner JSY/99 6.00 15.00
151 Drew Bledsoe JSY 4.00 10.00
152 Josh Reed JSY 3.00 8.00
153 Peerless Price JSY 3.00 8.00
154 David Boston JSY 3.00 8.00
155 Ricky Williams JSY/99 6.00 15.00
156 Chris Chambers JSY 3.00 8.00
157 Wayne Chrebet JSY 3.00 8.00
158 Chad Pennington JSY/99 5.00 12.00
159 Laveranues Coles JSY 3.00 8.00
160 Corey Dillon JSY 3.00 8.00
161 Tim Couch JSY 3.00 8.00
162 Jerome Bettis JSY 5.00 12.00
163 Plaxico Burress JSY 3.00 8.00
164 Antwaan Randle El JSY 3.00 8.00
165 David Carr JSY/99 5.00 12.00
166 Marvin Harrison JSY 4.00 10.00
167 Peyton Manning JSY 12.00 30.00
168 Fred Taylor JSY 3.00 8.00
169 Eddie George JSY 4.00 10.00
170 Clinton Portis JSY/99 5.00 12.00
171 Ashley Lelie JSY 3.00 8.00
172 Rich Gannon JSY 4.00 10.00
173 Phillip Buchanon JSY 3.00 8.00
174 Tim Brown JSY 5.00 12.00
175 LaDainian Tomlinson JSY 5.00 12.00
176 Drew Brees JSY/99 8.00 20.00
177 Jason Johnson RC 2.50 6.00
178 Sam Aiken RC 3.00 8.00
179 Nate Burleson RC 3.00 8.00
180 Tony Romo RC 20.00 50.00
181 Arnaz Battle RC 4.00 10.00

2003 SP Game Used Edition Gold Rookies

*GOLD/50: .8X TO 2X BASIC CARDS
GOLD PRINT RUN 50 SER.#'d SETS
180 Tony Romo 60.00 150.00

2003 SP Game Used Edition Field Fabrics

Randomly inserted into packs, this set features game worn jersey swatches. According to Upper Deck, the average print run per card is approximately 800. A gold parallel version also exists, with each card serial numbered to 75.

ANNOUNCED AVERAGE PRINT RUN 800
*GOLD/75: .8X TO 2X JSY/800
GOLD PRINT RUN 75 SER.#'d SETS
BF Brett Favre 8.00 20.00
BJ Brad Johnson 3.00 8.00
BU Brian Urlacher 4.00 10.00
DM Deuce McAllister 3.00 8.00
EM Eric Moulds 2.50 6.00
ES Emmitt Smith 6.00 15.00
JL Jamal Lewis 3.00 8.00
JR Jerry Rice 8.00 20.00
KJ Keyshawn Johnson 4.00 10.00
PM Peyton Manning 10.00 25.00
PP Peerless Price 2.50 6.00
RM Randy Moss 3.00 8.00
RW Ricky Williams 3.00 8.00
TG Tony Gonzalez 3.00 8.00
TO Terrell Owens 3.00 8.00

2003 SP Game Used Edition Field Fabrics Autographs

Randomly inserted into packs, this set features game worn jersey swatches, and authentic player autographs. Each card is serial numbered to 100. Please note that Rod Gardner was issued in packs as an exchange card, with an expiration date of 6/24/2006, but he never signed for the set.

STATED PRINT RUN 100 SER.#'d SETS
SDM Deuce McAllister 15.00 40.00
SPM Peyton Manning 60.00 120.00
STG Tony Gonzalez 15.00 40.00
STH Travis Henry 12.00 30.00

2003 SP Game Used Edition Formations Four Wide

Randomly inserted into packs, this set features four game worn jersey swatches. Each card is serial numbered to 25. A gold version serial numbered to 10 was also issued.

STATED PRINT RUN 25 SER.#'d SETS
UNPRICED GOLD PRINT RUN 10
FBBH Favre/Brunell/Brooks/Hassel.
FPSM Faulk/Port/E.Smith/McAll. 50.00 120.00
GRBG Gannon/Rice/Brown/Garner
JETS Penn/Martin/Moss/Chrebet
MCCV Mann/Couch/Carr/Vick 60.00 150.00
MFCH McNbb/Favre/Culp/Harrin. 60.00 150.00
RHOJ Rice/Harrison/Owens/Key.Johnson
WFBH Warner/Faulk/Bruce/Holt
WGAB R.Will/Green/Alex/Bettis 25.00 60.00

2003 SP Game Used Edition Formations Trips

Randomly inserted into packs, this set features three game worn jersey swatches. Each card is serial numbered to 35. A gold version, serial numbered to 15 also exists.

STATED PRINT RUN 35 SER.#'d SETS
*GOLD/15: 5X TO 1.2X BASIC TRIO/35
BHM Bledsoe/Henry/Moulds 15.00 40.00
CVM Culpepper/Vick/McNabb 15.00 40.00
FBV Favre/Bledsoe/Vick 40.00 100.00
FSG Faulk/E.Smith/Green 40.00 100.00
GRB Gannon/Rice/Brown 40.00 100.00
MJH Manning/E.James/Harrison 50.00 120.00
OHG Owens/Hearst/Garcia 15.00 40.00
PCH Pennington/Carr/Harrington 12.00 30.00
RHO Rice/Harrison/Owens 40.00 100.00
WCG Warner/Couch/Gannon 15.00 40.00

2003 SP Game Used Edition Formations Twins

Randomly inserted into packs, this set features two game worn jersey swatches. Each card is serial numbered to 50. A gold version, serial numbered to 25 also exists.

PRINT RUN 50 SER. #'d SETS
*GOLD: .6X TO 1.5X TWIN JSY/50
GOLD STATED PRINT RUN 25
BM D.Bledsoe/E.Moulds 10.00 25.00
BT D.Brees/L.Tomlinson 12.00 30.00
CM D.Culpepper/R.Moss 10.00 25.00
FG B.Favre/A.Green 25.00 60.00
FS M.Faulk/E.Smith 20.00 50.00
GO J.Garcia/T.Owens 10.00 25.00
MH P.Manning/M.Harrison 30.00 80.00
PM C.Pennington/S.Moss 10.00 25.00
VM M.Vick/D.McNabb 10.00 25.00
WH K.Warner/T.Holt 10.00 25.00

2003 SP Game Used Edition Formations Wing

Randomly inserted into packs, this set features game worn jersey swatches. The average print run for these cards (according to Upper Deck) is 750, unless noted below. A gold version, serial numbered to 50 or 25 also exists.

ANNOUNCED PRINT RUN 99-750
*GOLD/50: .8X TO 2X JSY/750
*GOLD/25: .8X TO 2X JSY/99
GOLD STATED PRINT RUN 25-50
AT Anthony Thomas/750* 2.50 6.00
BU Brian Urlacher/750* 3.00 8.00
CM Curtis Martin/750* 2.50 6.00
CP1 Clinton Portis/750* 2.00 5.00
CP2 Chad Pennington/99 4.00 10.00
DB1 Drew Brees/750* 3.00 8.00
DB2 Drew Bledsoe/99 5.00 12.00
DC David Carr/750* 2.00 5.00
DM Donovan McNabb/99 5.00 12.00
ES Emmitt Smith/99 10.00 25.00
GH Garrison Hearst/750* 2.00 5.00
JG Jeff Garcia/99 4.00 10.00
JH Joey Harrington/750* 2.00 5.00
JL Jamal Lewis/750* 2.50 6.00
JR Jerry Rice/99 12.00 30.00
KJ Keyshawn Johnson/750* 3.00 8.00
KW Kurt Warner/750* 2.50 6.00
LT LaDainian Tomlinson/99 6.00 15.00
MF Marshall Faulk/99 5.00 12.00
MV Michael Vick/750* 2.50 6.00
PH Priest Holmes/99 4.00 10.00
PM Peyton Manning/99 15.00 40.00
RM Randy Moss/99 5.00 12.00
SM Santana Moss/750* 2.50 6.00
TG Trent Green/750* 2.00 5.00
TH Travis Henry/750* 2.00 5.00
TO Terrell Owens/99 5.00 12.00

2003 SP Game Used Edition Patch Singles

Randomly inserted into packs, this set features game worn patch swatches. Each card is serial numbered to 99.

STATED PRINT RUN 99 SER. #'d SETS
AG Ahman Green 8.00 20.00
AR Antwaan Randle El 6.00 15.00
AT Anthony Thomas 8.00 20.00
BF Brett Favre 20.00 50.00
BO David Boston 6.00 15.00
BR Drew Brees 10.00 25.00
BU Brian Urlacher 10.00 25.00
CD Corey Dillon 6.00 15.00
CP Chad Pennington 6.00 15.00
DB Drew Bledsoe 8.00 20.00
DC David Carr 6.00 15.00
DC Daunte Culpepper 8.00 20.00
DM Deuce McAllister 8.00 20.00
DN Donovan McNabb 8.00 20.00
EG Eddie George 8.00 20.00
EJ Edgerrin James 8.00 20.00
ES Emmitt Smith 15.00 40.00
FT Fred Taylor 6.00 15.00
GH Garrison Hearst 6.00 15.00
JB Jerome Bettis 10.00 25.00
JG Jeff Garcia 6.00 15.00
JR Jerry Rice 20.00 50.00
KJ Keyshawn Johnson 10.00 25.00
KW Kurt Warner 8.00 20.00
LT LaDainian Tomlinson 10.00 25.00
MF Marshall Faulk 8.00 20.00
MV Michael Vick 8.00 20.00
PB Plaxico Burress 6.00 15.00
PH Priest Holmes 6.00 15.00
PM Peyton Manning 25.00 60.00
RM Randy Moss 8.00 20.00
RW Ricky Williams 8.00 20.00
SA Shaun Alexander 6.00 15.00
SM Steve McNair 8.00 20.00
TB Tom Brady 40.00 100.00
TC Tim Couch 6.00 15.00
TG Trent Green 6.00 15.00
TH Torry Holt 8.00 20.00
TO Terrell Owens 8.00 20.00
CPO Clinton Portis 6.00 15.00

2003 SP Game Used Edition Patch Doubles

Randomly inserted into packs, this set features two game worn patch swatches. Each card is serial numbered to 50.

STATED PRINT RUN 50 SER.#'d SETS
BE D.Bledsoe/E.Moulds 10.00 25.00
BF D.Brees/L.Tomlinson 12.00 30.00
BP T.Brady/C.Pennington 50.00 125.00
BR P.Burress/A.Randle E. 8.00 20.00
BT M.Brunell/F.Taylor 10.00 25.00
CM T.Couch/P.Manning 30.00 80.00
DM D.Culpepper/R.Moss 10.00 25.00
DT C.Dillon/A.Thomas 10.00 25.00
FG B.Favre/A.Green 25.00 60.00
GD C.Portis/A.Lelie 8.00 20.00
GH T.Green/P.Holmes 8.00 20.00
GO J.Garcia/T.Owens 10.00 25.00
JM Key.Johnson/R.Moss 12.00 30.00
JP E.James/C.Portis 10.00 25.00
JW E.James/R.Williams 10.00 25.00
MC S.McNair/D.Culpepper 10.00 25.00
MG S.McNair/E.George 10.00 25.00
MH P.Manning/M.Harrison 30.00 80.00
MP C.Martin/C.Pennington 10.00 25.00
RB J.Rice/T.Brown 25.00 60.00
RG J.Rice/R.Gannon 15.00 40.00
VM M.Vick/D.McNabb 10.00 25.00
WF K.Warner/M.Faulk 10.00 25.00
WM R.Williams/D.McAllister 10.00 25.00

2003 SP Game Used Edition Patch Triples

Randomly inserted into packs, this set features three game worn patch swatches. Each card is serial numbered to 25.

STATED PRINT RUN 25 SER.#'d SETS
AMC Brooks/McNabb/Culp 15.00 40.00
BFB Brooks/Favre/Brunell 40.00 100.00
BPM Bledsoe/Penn/Manning 50.00 120.00
CCV Carr/Couch/Vick 15.00 40.00
CCW Warner/Carr/Favre 40.00 100.00
CVM Culpepper/Vick/McNabb 15.00 40.00
FTB Flutie/Toml/Bledsoe 20.00 50.00
GBC Garvia/Brees/Carr 20.00 50.00
GMC Garcia/Manning/Couch 50.00 120.00
MJR R.Moss/Johnson/Rice 40.00 100.00
MMP S.Moss/Martin/Pennington 15.00 40.00
MVD McNair/Vick/Brooks 15.00 40.00
OHG Owens/Hearst/Garcia 15.00 40.00
WFB Warner/Favre/Brady 80.00 200.00

2003 SP Game Used Edition Patch Autographs

Randomly inserted into packs, this set features patch swatches and authentic player autographs. Each card is serial numbered to various quantities. The autograph is on the card, and is not a sticker or a cut autograph. Some cards were issued in packs as exchange cards with an expiration date of 6/24/2003.

STATED PRINT RUN 25-75
AB Aaron Brooks/50 12.00 30.00
BR Mark Brunell/40 15.00 40.00
CP Chad Pennington/25 20.00 50.00
DB Drew Brees/50 40.00 80.00
JF Jay Fiedler/50 12.00 30.00
JG Jeff Garcia/25 20.00 50.00
LT LaDainian Tomlinson/25 40.00 100.00
MB Michael Bennett/75 12.00 30.00
PM Peyton Manning/75 75.00 150.00
SA Shaun Alexander/50 12.00 30.00
SC Carson Palmer/25 150.00 300.00
TC Tim Couch/40 12.00 30.00
TG Trent Green/50 12.00 30.00
TR Travis Henry/50 12.00 30.00

2003 SP Game Used Edition Significant Signatures

Randomly inserted into packs, this set features authentic player autographs on card fronts. Each card is serial numbered to various quantities, with the majority of them being numbered to 99. Please note that Tony Gonzalez and Willis McGahee were issued in packs as exchange cards with an expiration date of 6/24/2003.

STATED PRINT RUN 25-99
UNPRICED DUAL AUTOs #'d TO 10
AB Aaron Brooks/99 8.00 20.00
AT Anthony Thomas/99 10.00 25.00
BB Brad Banks/99 10.00 25.00
BE Michael Bennett/99 8.00 20.00
BF Brett Favre/25 150.00 250.00
BL Byron Leftwich/25 15.00 40.00
CB Chris Brown/99 8.00 20.00
CP Chad Pennington/50 10.00 25.00
CS Chris Simms/99 8.00 20.00
DB Drew Brees/50 40.00 80.00
DC David Carr/25 15.00 40.00
DE Deuce McAllister/25 20.00 50.00
EG Earnest Graham/99 12.00 30.00
GR Trent Green/99 8.00 20.00
JF1 Justin Fargas/99 12.00 30.00
JF2 Jay Fiedler/99 8.00 20.00
JG Jeff Garcia/25 15.00 40.00
JR Jerry Rice/25 100.00 200.00
KD Ken Dorsey/99 10.00 25.00
KK1 Kareem Kelly/99 8.00 20.00
KK2 Kliff Kingsbury/99 12.00 30.00
KW Kelley Washington/99 8.00 20.00
LJ Larry Johnson/99 10.00 25.00
LT LaDainian Tomlinson/25 50.00 120.00
MB Mark Brunell/99 10.00 25.00
PM1 Peyton Manning/50 60.00 120.00
PM2 Peyton Manning/99 50.00 100.00
QG Quentin Griffin/99 10.00 25.00
RG Rod Gardner/99 8.00 20.00
SA Shaun Alexander/40 10.00 25.00
SC Carson Palmer/25 100.00 200.00
SW Seneca Wallace/99 10.00 25.00
TC Tim Couch/40 10.00 25.00
TG Tony Gonzalez/50 12.00 30.00
TJ Taylor Jacobs/99 8.00 20.00
TS Terrell Suggs/99 15.00 40.00
WM Willis McGahee/50 10.00 25.00

2004 SP Game Used Edition

SP Game Used Edition initially released in mid-July 2004. The base set consists of 200-cards including 100-rookies serial numbered to 425. Hobby boxes contained 6-packs of 3-cards and carried an S.R.P. of $29.99 per pack. One parallel set and a variety of game jersey and autographed inserts can be found seeded in packs highlighted by the Rookie Exclusives Autographs, the Authentic Fabric Autograph Duals and the Legendary Fabric Autograph inserts.

1 Anquan Boldin .60 1.50
2 Marcel Shipp .60 1.50
3 Josh McCown .75 2.00
4 Michael Vick .75 2.00
5 T.J. Duckett .60 1.50
6 Peerless Price .60 1.50
7 Jamal Lewis .75 2.00
8 Todd Heap .60 1.50
9 Kyle Boller .60 1.50
10 Drew Bledsoe .75 2.00
11 Travis Henry .60 1.50
12 Eric Moulds .60 1.50
13 Jake Delhomme .60 1.50
14 Stephen Davis .60 1.50
15 Julius Peppers .75 2.00
16 Anthony Thomas .75 2.00
17 Rex Grossman .60 1.50
18 Brian Urlacher 1.00 2.50
19 Carson Palmer .75 2.00
20 Chad Johnson .60 1.50
21 Rudi Johnson .60 1.50
22 Jeff Garcia .60 1.50
23 Dennis Northcutt .60 1.50
24 Andre Davis .60 1.50
25 Quincy Carter .60 1.50
26 Roy Williams S .60 1.50
27 Keyshawn Johnson .75 2.00
28 Quentin Griffin .60 1.50
29 Jake Plummer .60 1.50
30 Ashley Lelie .60 1.50
31 Shannon Sharpe .75 2.00
32 Joey Harrington .60 1.50
33 Charles Rogers .60 1.50
34 Az-Zahir Hakim .60 1.50
35 Brett Favre 2.00 5.00
36 Javon Walker .60 1.50
37 Ahman Green .75 2.00
38 Andre Johnson .75 2.00
39 David Carr .60 1.50
40 Domanick Davis .60 1.50
41 Peyton Manning 2.50 6.00
42 Edgerrin James .75 2.00
43 Marvin Harrison .75 2.00
44 Byron Leftwich .60 1.50
45 Fred Taylor .60 1.50
46 Jimmy Smith .75 2.00
47 Priest Holmes .60 1.50
48 Trent Green .60 1.50
49 Dante Hall .60 1.50
50 Tony Gonzalez .75 2.00
51 Ricky Williams .75 2.00
52 Jay Fiedler .60 1.50
53 Chris Chambers .60 1.50
54 Randy Moss .75 2.00
55 Daunte Culpepper .75 2.00
56 Moe Williams .60 1.50
57 Tom Brady 4.00 10.00
58 Deion Branch .60 1.50
59 Corey Dillon .60 1.50
60 Deuce McAllister .75 2.00
61 Aaron Brooks .60 1.50
62 Joe Horn .60 1.50
63 Jeremy Shockey .60 1.50
64 Amani Toomer .60 1.50
65 Michael Strahan .75 2.00
66 Curtis Martin .75 2.00
67 Chad Pennington .60 1.50
68 Santana Moss .75 2.00
69 Jerry Rice 2.00 5.00
70 Tim Brown 1.00 2.50
71 Jerry Porter .60 1.50
72 Donovan McNabb .75 2.00
73 Brian Westbrook .60 1.50
74 Terrell Owens .75 2.00
75 Hines Ward .75 2.00
76 Plaxico Burress .60 1.50
77 Duce Staley .60 1.50
78 LaDainian Tomlinson 1.00 2.50
79 Quentin Jammer .60 1.50
80 Drew Brees 1.00 2.50
81 Brandon Lloyd .75 2.00
82 Kevan Barlow .60 1.50
83 Tim Rattay .60 1.50
84 Matt Hasselbeck .60 1.50
85 Shaun Alexander .60 1.50
86 Darrell Jackson .75 2.00
87 Marc Bulger .60 1.50
88 Torry Holt .75 2.00
89 Marshall Faulk .75 2.00
90 Isaac Bruce 1.00 2.50
91 Brad Johnson .75 2.00
92 Derrick Brooks .60 1.50
93 Warren Sapp .75 2.00
94 Steve McNair .75 2.00
95 Derrick Mason .60 1.50
96 Eddie George .75 2.00
97 Clinton Portis .60 1.50
98 Mark Brunell .75 2.00
99 Laveranues Coles .60 1.50
100 LaVar Arrington .60 1.50
101 Ben Troupe RC 3.00 8.00
102 Chris Gamble RC 3.00 8.00
103 DeAngelo Hall RC 5.00 12.00
104 Dunta Robinson RC 3.00 8.00
105 Jason Shivers RC 3.00 8.00
106 Keary Colbert RC 3.00 8.00
107 Craig Krenzel RC 3.00 8.00
108 Philip Rivers RC 10.00 25.00
109 Roy Williams RC 3.00 8.00
110 Will Allen RC 4.00 10.00
111 Bob Sanders RC 6.00 15.00
112 Kris Wilson RC 4.00 10.00
113 D.J. Williams RC 5.00 12.00
114 Devery Henderson RC 3.00 8.00
115 Carlos Francis RC 3.00 8.00
116 Jonathan Vilma RC 4.00 10.00
117 Luke McCown RC 3.00 8.00
118 Michael Turner RC 3.00 8.00
119 Richard Seigler RC 3.00 8.00
120 Jared Lorenzen RC 4.00 10.00
121 P.K. Sam RC 3.00 8.00
122 Justin Smiley RC 4.00 10.00
123 Marquise Hill RC 3.00 8.00
124 Ernest Wilford RC 4.00 10.00
125 Jerricho Cotchery RC 4.00 10.00
126 Kevin Jones RC 4.00 10.00
127 Michael Boulware RC 5.00 12.00
128 Jarrett Payton RC 4.00 10.00
129 Sean Taylor RC 20.00 40.00
130 Will Smith RC 4.00 10.00
131 Bernard Berrian RC 3.00 8.00
132 Ahmad Carroll RC 3.00 8.00
133 Derrick Hamilton RC 3.00 8.00
134 Dwan Edwards RC 3.00 8.00
135 Jeff Smoker RC 4.00 10.00
136 Kenechi Udeze RC 4.00 10.00
137 Mewelde Moore RC 4.00 10.00
138 Joey Thomas RC 3.00 8.00
139 Sean Jones RC 3.00 8.00
140 Will Poole RC 5.00 12.00
141 Casey Clausen RC 4.00 10.00
142 Stuart Schweigert RC 4.00 10.00
143 Cody Pickett RC 3.00 8.00
144 Derrick Strait RC 3.00 8.00
145 Greg Jones RC 3.00 8.00
146 John Navarre RC 3.00 8.00
147 Larry Fitzgerald RC 12.00 30.00
148 Michael Clayton RC 4.00 10.00
149 Rashaun Woods RC 3.00 8.00
150 Shawn Andrews RC 4.00 10.00
151 B.J. Symons RC 3.00 8.00
152 Cedric Cobbs RC 3.00 8.00
153 Darius Watts RC 3.00 8.00
154 B.J. Johnson RC 3.00 8.00
155 Max Starks RC 4.00 10.00
156 Josh Harris RC 3.00 8.00
157 Kendrick Starling RC 3.00 8.00
158 Brandon Miree RC 3.00 8.00
159 Robert Gallery RC 4.00 10.00
160 Tatum Bell RC 3.00 8.00
161 Ben Hartsock RC 3.00 8.00
162 Derek Abney RC 3.00 8.00
163 Ricardo Colclough RC 3.00 8.00
164 Justin Jenkins RC 3.00 8.00
165 Chris Cooley RC 4.00 10.00
166 Julius Jones RC 3.00 8.00
167 Matt Mauck RC 3.00 8.00
168 Vernon Carey RC 3.00 8.00
169 John Standeford RC 3.00 8.00
170 Teddy Lehman RC 3.00 8.00
171 Ben Roethlisberger RC 25.00 60.00
172 Ben Utecht RC 4.00 10.00
173 D.J. Hackett RC 3.00 8.00
174 Drew Henson RC 3.00 8.00
175 Rich Gardner RC 4.00 10.00
176 Karlos Dansby RC 4.00 10.00
177 Matt Schaub RC 3.00 8.00
178 Darrion Scott RC 4.00 10.00
179 Keyaron Fox RC 4.00 10.00
180 Tommie Harris RC 4.00 10.00
181 Ben Watson RC 4.00 10.00
182 Chris Perry RC 3.00 8.00
183 Travelle Wharton RC 3.00 8.00
184 Eli Manning RC 15.00 40.00
185 Demorrio Williams RC 5.00 12.00
186 Kellen Winslow RC 3.00 8.00
187 Jason Babin RC 5.00 12.00
188 Quincy Wilson RC 3.00 8.00
189 Samie Parker RC 3.00 8.00
190 Vince Wilfork RC 5.00 12.00
191 Antwan Odom RC 3.00 8.00
192 Josh Davis RC 4.00 10.00
193 Courtney Watson RC 3.00 8.00
194 Devard Darling RC 3.00 8.00
195 J.P. Losman RC 3.00 8.00
196 Johnnie Morant RC 3.00 8.00
197 Lee Evans RC 5.00 12.00
198 Michael Jenkins RC 3.00 8.00
199 Reggie Williams RC 3.00 8.00
200 Steven Jackson RC 5.00 12.00

2004 SP Game Used Edition Gold

*1-100 VETS: 1.2X TO 3X BASIC CARDS
1-100 VETERAN/100 ODDS 1:7
VETERAN PRINT RUN 100 SER.#'d SETS
*101-200 ROOKIES: .8X TO 2X
101-200 ROOKIES PRINT RUN 50

2004 SP Game Used Edition Authentic All-Pro Fabric

RANDOM INSERTS IN PACKS
AG Ahman Green 3.00 8.00
BF Brett Favre 8.00 20.00
CJ Chad Johnson 2.50 6.00
CP Clinton Portis 2.50 6.00
DC Daunte Culpepper 3.00 8.00
DM Donovan McNabb 3.00 8.00
JL Jamal Lewis 3.00 8.00
PH Priest Holmes 2.50 6.00
PM Peyton Manning 10.00 25.00
RM Randy Moss 3.00 8.00
SD Stephen Davis 2.50 6.00
SM Steve McNair 3.00 8.00

2004 SP Game Used Edition Authentic Fabric

ONE GAME USED OR AUTO CARD PER PACK
*GOLD/100: .8X TO 2X BASIC JSY
GOLD PRINT RUN 100 SER.#'d SETS
AFAB Anquan Boldin 2.00 5.00
AFAG Ahman Green 2.50 6.00
AFAJ Andre Johnson 2.50 6.00
AFBF Brett Favre 6.00 15.00
AFBL Byron Leftwich 2.00 5.00
AFBR Aaron Brooks 2.00 5.00
AFBU Brian Urlacher 3.00 8.00
AFCA Carson Palmer 2.50 6.00
AFCD Corey Dillon 2.00 5.00
AFCJ Chad Johnson 2.00 5.00
AFCL Clinton Portis 2.00 5.00
AFCP Chad Pennington 2.00 5.00
AFCR Charles Rogers 2.00 5.00
AFDA David Carr 2.00 5.00
AFDB Derrick Brooks 2.00 5.00
AFDC Daunte Culpepper 2.50 6.00
AFDD Domanick Davis 2.00 5.00
AFDE Deuce McAllister 2.50 6.00
AFDH Dante Hall 2.00 5.00
AFDK Derrick Mason 2.00 5.00
AFDM Donovan McNabb 2.50 6.00
AFDR Drew Bledsoe 2.50 6.00
AFDS Duce Staley 2.00 5.00
AFEJ Edgerrin James 2.50 6.00
AFEM Eric Moulds 2.00 5.00
AFES Emmitt Smith 5.00 12.00
AFFT Fred Taylor 2.00 5.00
AFHA Matt Hasselbeck 2.00 5.00
AFHW Hines Ward 2.50 6.00
AFIB Isaac Bruce 3.00 8.00
AFJB Jerome Bettis 3.00 8.00
AFJK Jevon Kearse 2.00 5.00
AFJL Jamal Lewis 2.50 6.00
AFJP Jake Plummer SP 2.00 5.00
AFJR Jerry Rice 6.00 15.00
AFJS Jeremy Shockey 2.00 5.00
AFJU Junior Seau 3.00 8.00
AFKB Kyle Boller 2.00 5.00
AFKM Keenan McCardell 2.00 5.00
AFKW Kurt Warner 2.50 6.00
AFLA LaVar Arrington 2.00 5.00
AFLC Laveranues Coles 2.00 5.00
AFLT LaDainian Tomlinson 3.00 8.00
AFLY John Lynch 2.50 6.00
AFMA Mark Brunell 2.50 6.00
AFMB Marc Bulger 2.00 5.00
AFMF Marshall Faulk 2.50 6.00
AFMH Marvin Harrison 2.50 6.00
AFMS Michael Strahan 2.50 6.00
AFMV Michael Vick 2.50 6.00
AFPH Priest Holmes 2.00 5.00
AFPM Peyton Manning 8.00 20.00
AFPP Peerless Price 2.00 5.00
AFRG Rex Grossman 2.00 5.00
AFRL Ray Lewis 3.00 8.00
AFRM Randy Moss 2.50 6.00
AFRO Roy Williams S 2.00 5.00
AFRW Ricky Williams 2.50 6.00
AFSA Shaun Alexander 2.00 5.00
AFSD Stephen Davis 2.00 5.00
AFSM Steve McNair 2.50 6.00
AFSS Shannon Sharpe SP 2.50 6.00
AFTB Tom Brady 12.00 30.00
AFTG Tony Gonzalez 2.50 6.00
AFTH Torry Holt 2.50 6.00
AFTJ Thomas Jones 2.00 5.00
AFTL Ty Law 3.00 8.00
AFTO Terrell Owens 2.50 6.00
AFTR Trent Green 2.00 5.00
AFTS Terrell Suggs 2.00 5.00
AFTY Troy Brown 2.00 5.00
AFWM Willis McGahee 2.00 5.00
AFWS Warren Sapp 2.50 6.00

2004 SP Game Used Edition Authentic Fabric Autographs

ONE GAME USED OR AUTO CARD PER PACK
STATED PRINT RUN 100 SER.#'d SETS
AG Ahman Green 10.00 25.00
BF Brett Favre 100.00 200.00
BL Byron Leftwich 8.00 20.00
CJ Chad Johnson 8.00 20.00
CP Chad Pennington 8.00 20.00
DA David Carr 8.00 20.00
DB Drew Bledsoe 10.00 25.00
DC Daunte Culpepper 10.00 25.00
DD Domanick Davis 8.00 20.00
DE Deuce McAllister 10.00 25.00
DH Dante Hall 8.00 20.00
DM Donovan McNabb 35.00 60.00
JH Joe Horn 8.00 20.00
JP Jesse Palmer 8.00 20.00
KB Kyle Boller 8.00 20.00
KS Ken Stabler 25.00 60.00
LT LaDainian Tomlinson 25.00 60.00
MA Mark Brunell 10.00 25.00
PM Peyton Manning 60.00 120.00
RW Ricky Williams 10.00 25.00
SM Steve McNair 10.00 25.00
TA Troy Aikman 60.00 100.00
TB Tom Brady 200.00 300.00
TG Tony Gonzalez 10.00 25.00
WM Willis McGahee 8.00 20.00
ZT Zach Thomas 10.00 25.00

2004 SP Game Used Edition Authentic Fabric Autographs Dual

STATED PRINT RUN 15-50
BB M.Brunell/D.Bledsoe/50 15.00 40.00
BP T.Brady/C.Penn/15
CD D.Carr/D.Davis/50 12.00 30.00
CM D.Culpepper/D.McNabb/15 30.00 80.00
DK D.Bledsoe/K.Boller/50 15.00 40.00
DS D.Culpepper/S.McNair/50 15.00 40.00
DT D.Bledsoe/T.Brady/50 100.00 200.00
EF J.Elway/B.Favre/15 150.00 350.00
FG B.Favre/A.Green/15 150.00 250.00
GH T.Gonzalez/D.Hall/50 15.00 40.00
HM T.Henry/W.McGahee/50 12.00 30.00
JJ Ch.Johnson/R.Johnson/50 12.00 30.00
LC B.Leftwich/Culpepper/50 20.00 50.00
LP Leftwich/Penning/50 12.00 30.00
MB W.McGahee/D.Bledsoe/50 15.00 40.00
MH D.McAllister/J.Horn/50 15.00 40.00
ML S.McNair/B.Leftwich/50 30.00 80.00
MM S.McNair/P.Manning/15 125.00 200.00
MW McNabb/Westbrk/50 15.00 40.00
PD P.Manning/D.Bledsoe/50 60.00 120.00
PK P.Manning/K.Boller/50 50.00 100.00
PT P.Manning/T.Brady/15 250.00 400.00
RZ Ri.Will./Z.Thomas/50 15.00 40.00
ST K.Stabler/F.Tarkenton/50 40.00 100.00
TB J.Theismann/M.Brunell/50 20.00 50.00
TK T.Brady/K.Boller/50 100.00 200.00
WT Ri.Will./Tomlinson/50 30.00 80.00

2004 SP Game Used Edition Authentic Fabric Duals

STATED PRINT RUN 100 SER.#'d SETS
BA D.Brooks/L.Arrington 8.00 20.00
BF M.Bulger/M.Faulk 6.00 15.00
BH I.Bruce/T.Holt 8.00 20.00
BL T.Brady/T.Law 30.00 80.00
BM A.Brooks/D.McAllister 6.00 15.00
BP M.Brunell/C.Portis 6.00 15.00
BW J.Bettis/H.Ward 8.00 20.00
CB L.Coles/M.Brunell 6.00 15.00
CD D.Carr/D.Davis 5.00 12.00
CM D.Culpepper/R.Moss 6.00 15.00
DD J.Delhomee/S.Davis 5.00 12.00
DF D.McNabb/F.Mitchell 6.00 15.00
FG B.Favre/A.Green 15.00 40.00
FM B.Favre/P.Manning 20.00 50.00
GG T.Green/T.Gonzalez 6.00 15.00
GU R.Grossman/B.Urlacher 8.00 20.00
HA M.Hasselbeck/S.Alexander 5.00 12.00
HH P.Holmes/D.Hall 5.00 12.00
HP P.Holmes/C.Portis 5.00 12.00
JJ C.Johnson/R.Johnson 5.00 12.00
LL J.Lewis/R.Lewis 8.00 20.00
LP B.Leftwich/C.Pennington 5.00 12.00
LS B.Leftwich/J.Smith 6.00 15.00
MB W.McGahee/D.Bledsoe 6.00 15.00
MG S.McNair/E.George 6.00 15.00
MH P.Manning/M.Harrison 20.00 50.00
MM S.McNair/P.Manning 20.00 50.00
MW D.McNabb/B.Westbrook 6.00 15.00
PM C.Pennington/S.Moss 6.00 15.00
RJ J.Rice/K.Johnson 15.00 40.00
SB E.Smith/A.Boldin 12.00 30.00
VP M.Vick/P.Price 12.00 30.00
WC R.Williams/C.Chambers 6.00 15.00
WN Ro.Williams/T.Newman 6.00 15.00

2004 SP Game Used Edition Authentic Fabric Quads

UNPRICED QUAD PRINT RUN 10 SETS

2004 SP Game Used Edition Authentio Fabric Triples

STATED PRINT RUN 25 SER.#'d SETS
BHF Bulger/Holt/M.Faulk 15.00 40.00
CDJ Carr/Davis/Johnson 15.00 40.00
CMS Culpepper/Moss/O.Smith 15.00 40.00
FGW Favre/Green/Walker 40.00 100.00
GHH Green/Holmes/Hall 12.00 30.00
MHJ Manning/Harrison/James 30.00 80.00
MWM McNabb/Westbrook/Mitchell 15.00 40.00
PBL Plummer/Bailey/Lelie 15.00 40.00
PMM Pennington/Martin/S.Moss 15.00 40.00
VPD Vick/Price/Dunn 25.00 60.00

2004 SP Game Used Edition Authentic Patches

STATED PRINT RUN 100 SER.#'d SETS
UNPRICED TRIPLE PRINT RUN 10
APAB Anquan Boldin 4.00 10.00
APCJ Chad Johnson 4.00 10.00
APCP Chad Pennington 4.00 10.00
APDD Domanick Davis 4.00 10.00
APDH Dante Hall 4.00 10.00
APDN Donovan McNabb 5.00 12.00
APEJ Edgerrin James 5.00 12.00
APGO Tony Gonzalez 5.00 12.00
APJH Joey Harrington 4.00 10.00
APJN Joe Namath 10.00 25.00
APJO Joe Horn 4.00 10.00
APJP Jake Plummer 4.00 10.00
APJS Jeremy Shockey 4.00 10.00
APLC Laveranues Coles 4.00 10.00
APLT LaDainian Tomlinson 6.00 15.00
APMA Mark Brunell 5.00 12.00
APMV Michael Vick 5.00 12.00
APPH Priest Holmes 4.00 10.00
APPM Peyton Manning 10.00 25.00
APRG Rex Grossman 4.00 10.00
APRW Roy Williams S 4.00 10.00
APTB Tom Brady 25.00 60.00
APTG Trent Green 4.00 10.00
APTH Torry Holt 5.00 12.00

2004 SP Game Used Edition Authentic Patches Autographs

STATED PRINT RUN 25 SER.#'d SETS
UNPRICED DUAL AU PRINT RUN 5
AG Ahman Green 15.00 40.00
BL Byron Leftwich 12.00 30.00
CJ Chad Johnson 12.00 30.00
CPO Chad Pennington 12.00 30.00
DB Drew Bledsoe 15.00 40.00
DD Domanick Davis 12.00 30.00
DH Dante Hall 12.00 30.00
DN Donovan McNabb 40.00 80.00
IB Isaac Bruce 20.00 50.00
JN Joe Namath 100.00 200.00
JO Joe Horn 12.00 30.00
KB Kyle Boller 12.00 30.00
LT LaDainian Tomlinson 30.00 80.00
MA Mark Brunell 15.00 40.00
PM Peyton Manning 100.00 200.00
RW Roy Williams S 12.00 30.00
SM Steve McNair 40.00 80.00
TB Tom Brady 175.00 300.00
TG Tony Gonzalez 30.00 60.00

TH Todd Heap 12.00 30.00
WM Willis McGahee 12.00 30.00
ZT Zach Thomas 15.00 40.00

2004 SP Game Used Edition Authentic Patches Dual

STATED PRINT RUN 25 SER.#'d SETS
BD B.Favre/D.Culpepper 40.00 100.00
BP T.Brady/C.Pennington 80.00 200.00
FC B.Favre/D.Carr 40.00 100.00
MH R.Moss/M.Harrison 15.00 40.00
MM P.Manning/S.McNair 50.00 125.00
MV D.McNabb/M.Vick 30.00 80.00
PJ C.Portis/E.James 15.00 40.00

2004 SP Game Used Edition Awesome Authentics

STATED PRINT RUN 100 SER.#'d SETS
AAAB Anquan Boldin 4.00 10.00
AAAG Ahman Green 5.00 12.00
AABF Brett Favre 12.00 30.00
AABL Byron Leftwich 4.00 10.00
AACH Chad Pennington 4.00 10.00
AACJ Chad Johnson 4.00 10.00
AACP Clinton Portis 4.00 10.00
AADA David Carr 4.00 10.00
AADC Daunte Culpepper 5.00 12.00
AADE Deuce McAllister 5.00 12.00
AADH Dante Hall 4.00 10.00
AADM Donovan McNabb 5.00 12.00
AAEJ Edgerrin James 5.00 12.00
AAHE Todd Heap 4.00 10.00
AAJH Joey Harrington 4.00 10.00
AAJL Jamal Lewis 5.00 12.00
AAJP Jake Plummer 4.00 10.00
AAJS Jeremy Shockey 4.00 10.00
AALC Laveranues Coles 4.00 10.00
AALT LaDainian Tomlinson 6.00 15.00
AAMA Mark Brunell 5.00 12.00
AAMB Marc Bulger 4.00 10.00
AAMF Marshall Faulk 5.00 12.00
AAMH Marvin Harrison 5.00 12.00
AAMV Michael Vick 10.00 25.00
AAPH Priest Holmes 4.00 10.00
AAPM Peyton Manning 15.00 40.00
AARM Randy Moss 5.00 12.00
AARO Roy Williams S 4.00 10.00
AARW Ricky Williams 5.00 12.00
AASM Steve McNair 5.00 12.00
AATB Tom Brady 25.00 60.00
AATH Torry Holt 5.00 12.00

2004 SP Game Used Edition Legendary Fabric Autographs

STATED PRINT RUN 50 SER.#'d SETS
AM Archie Manning 15.00 40.00
BS Barry Sanders 100.00 200.00
FT Fran Tarkenton 20.00 50.00
HL Howie Long 50.00 100.00
JE John Elway 100.00 200.00
JM Joe Montana 100.00 200.00
JN Joe Namath 75.00 150.00
JT Joe Theismann 20.00 50.00
KS Ken Stabler 25.00 60.00
KW Kellen Winslow 20.00 50.00
RS Roger Staubach 60.00 120.00
TA Troy Aikman 50.00 100.00

2004 SP Game Used Edition Rookie Exclusives Autographs

STATED PRINT RUN 100 SER.#'d SETS
REBB Bernard Berrian 12.00 30.00
REBC Brandon Chillar 15.00 40.00
REBJ B.J. Symons 12.00 30.00
REBR Ben Roethlisberger 100.00 200.00
REBT Ben Troupe 12.00 30.00
REBW Ben Watson 15.00 40.00
RECC Cedric Cobbs 12.00 30.00
RECH Chris Perry 12.00 30.00
RECP Cody Pickett 12.00 30.00
REDD Devard Darling 12.00 30.00
REDH DeAngelo Hall 20.00 50.00
REDR Drew Henson 12.00 30.00
REEM Eli Manning 175.00 300.00
REEW Ernest Wilford 15.00 40.00
REGJ Greg Jones 12.00 30.00
REJC Jerricho Cotchery 15.00 40.00
REJM Johnnie Morant 12.00 30.00
REJN John Navarre 12.00 30.00
REJP J.P. Losman 12.00 30.00
REJV Jonathan Vilma 15.00 40.00
REKC Keary Colbert 12.00 30.00
REKJ Kevin Jones 15.00 40.00
REKU Kenechi Udeze 15.00 40.00
REKW Kellen Winslow Jr. 12.00 30.00
RELE Lee Evans 20.00 50.00
RELF Larry Fitzgerald 75.00 150.00
RELM Luke McCown 12.00 30.00
REMC Michael Clayton 15.00 40.00
REMJ Michael Jenkins 12.00 30.00
REMS Matt Schaub 15.00 40.00
REPR Philip Rivers 50.00 120.00
RERA Rashaun Woods 12.00 30.00
RERE Reggie Williams 12.00 30.00
RERG Robert Gallery 15.00 40.00
RERW Roy Williams WR 12.00 30.00
RESJ Steven Jackson 20.00 50.00
RESP Samie Parker 12.00 30.00
RETH Tommie Harris 15.00 40.00
REVW Vince Wilfork 20.00 50.00
REWS Will Smith 15.00 40.00

2004 SP Game Used Edition SIGnificance

STATED PRINT RUN 100 SER.#'d SETS
*GOLD/10: .8X TO 2X BASIC AU
GOLD STATED PRINT RUN 10
UNPRICED NUMBERS PRINT RUN 4-12
AG Ahman Green 10.00 25.00
AM Archie Manning 12.00 30.00
BL Brandon Lloyd 10.00 25.00
BP Bill Parcells 30.00 60.00
BY Byron Leftwich 8.00 20.00
CJ Chad Johnson 8.00 20.00
DC Daunte Culpepper 10.00 25.00
DD Domanick Davis 8.00 20.00
DE Deuce McAllister 10.00 25.00
DH Dante Hall 8.00 20.00
DM Derrick Mason 8.00 20.00
GO Tony Gonzalez 10.00 25.00
GR Jon Gruden 10.00 25.00
HE Todd Heap 8.00 20.00
HL Howie Long 30.00 60.00
JF John Fox 8.00 20.00
JH Joe Horn 8.00 20.00
JJ Jimmy Johnson 12.00 30.00
JO Joey Galloway 10.00 25.00
JP Jesse Palmer 8.00 20.00
JT Joe Theismann 12.00 30.00
KB Kyle Boller 8.00 20.00
KS Ken Stabler 20.00 50.00
MA Mark Brunell 10.00 25.00
RE Andy Reid 10.00 25.00
TH Travis Henry 8.00 20.00
TS Tony Siragusa 10.00 25.00
WM Willis McGahee 8.00 20.00

2004 SP Game Used Edition SIGnificance Extra

EXTRA PRINT RUN 25 SETS
UNPRICED GOLD PRINT RUN 5
BT M.Brunell/J.Theismann 30.00 80.00
JA J.Johnson CO/Aikman 60.00 120.00
LS H.Long/K.Stabler 60.00 120.00
MB J.Montana/T.Brady 500.00 750.00
ME J.Montana/J.Elway 125.00 250.00
MM A.Manning/P.Manning 90.00 150.00
PF Pennington/Favre 125.00 250.00
SA R.Staubach/T.Aikman 100.00 200.00
ST B.Sanders/Tomlinson 125.00 250.00
TS F.Tarkenton/K.Stabler 40.00 100.00

2002 SP Legendary Cuts

Released in late-December, this set contains 210 cards including 90 veterans, 30 veterans short-prints, and 90 rookies. Cards 91-100 were #'d to 2500, cards 101-110 were #'d to 1500, and cards 111-120 were #'d to 800. Rookies 121-150 were #'d to 500 and rookies 151-210 were #'d to 1100. Boxes contained 12 packs of 4 cards, and carried an SRP of $9.99

COMP.SET w/o SP's (90) 15.00 40.00
151-210 ROOKIE PRINT RUN 1100
1 Tom Brady 2.50 6.00
2 Antowain Smith .40 1.00
3 Troy Brown .30 .75
4 Drew Bledsoe .40 1.00
5 Travis Henry .30 .75
6 Eric Moulds .30 .75
7 Ricky Williams .40 1.00
8 Jay Fiedler .40 1.00
9 Chris Chambers .30 .75
10 Curtis Martin .40 1.00
11 Chad Pennington .30 .75
12 Wayne Chrebet .30 .75
13 Jerome Bettis .50 1.25
14 Tommy Maddox .30 .75
15 Hines Ward .40 1.00
16 Tim Couch .30 .75
17 Kevin Johnson .30 .75
18 Jamal Lewis .40 1.00
19 Chris Redman .30 .75
20 Corey Dillon .30 .75
21 Michael Westbrook .30 .75
22 Peyton Manning 1.25 3.00
23 Edgerrin James .40 1.00
24 Marvin Harrison .40 1.00
25 Qadry Ismail .30 .75
26 Mark Brunell .40 1.00
27 Jimmy Smith .40 1.00
28 Stacey Mack .30 .75
29 Fred Taylor .30 .75
30 Steve McNair .40 1.00
31 Eddie George .40 1.00
32 Kevin Dyson .40 1.00
33 James Allen .30 .75
34 Corey Bradford .30 .75
35 Shannon Sharpe .40 1.00
36 Brian Griese .30 .75
37 Ed McCaffrey .40 1.00
38 Jerry Rice 1.00 2.50
39 Rich Gannon .40 1.00
40 Tim Brown .50 1.25
41 Trent Green .30 .75
42 Priest Holmes .30 .75
43 Tony Gonzalez .40 1.00
44 LaDainian Tomlinson .50 1.25
45 Drew Brees 1.00 2.50
46 Curtis Conway .40 1.00
47 Donovan McNabb .40 1.00
48 Duce Staley .30 .75
49 Antonio Freeman .50 1.25
50 James Thrash .40 1.00
51 Kerry Collins .30 .75
52 Tiki Barber .40 1.00
53 Amani Toomer .30 .75
54 Emmitt Smith .75 2.00
55 Quincy Carter .30 .75
56 Joey Galloway .40 1.00
57 Stephen Davis .30 .75
58 Champ Bailey .40 1.00
59 Anthony Thomas .40 1.00
60 Jim Miller .30 .75
61 Brian Urlacher .50 1.25
62 Brett Favre 1.00 2.50
63 Ahman Green .40 1.00
64 Robert Ferguson .40 1.00
65 Randy Moss .40 1.00
66 Daunte Culpepper .40 1.00
67 Moe Williams .30 .75
68 James Stewart .30 .75
69 Az-Zahir Hakim .30 .75
70 Keyshawn Johnson .40 1.00
71 Brad Johnson .40 1.00
72 Mike Alstott .30 .75
73 Michael Vick .40 1.00
74 Warrick Dunn .30 .75
75 Shawn Jefferson .30 .75
76 Aaron Brooks .30 .75
77 Deuce McAllister .40 1.00
78 Joe Horn .30 .75
79 Rodney Peete .40 1.00
80 Steve Smith .50 1.25
81 Terrell Owens .40 1.00
82 Jeff Garcia .30 .75
83 Garrison Hearst .30 .75
84 Kurt Warner .40 1.00
85 Marshall Faulk .40 1.00
86 Torry Holt .40 1.00
87 Jake Plummer .30 .75
88 David Boston .30 .75
89 Shaun Alexander .30 .75
90 Trent Dilfer .30 .75
91 Tom Brady VM 4.00 10.00
92 Michael Vick VM .60 1.50
93 LaDainian Tomlinson VM .75 2.00
94 Rich Gannon VM .60 1.50
95 Randy Moss VM .60 1.50
96 Aaron Brooks VM .50 1.25
97 Mark Brunell VM .60 1.50
98 Jeff Garcia VM .50 1.25
99 Ahman Green VM .60 1.50
100 Shaun Alexander VM .50 1.25
101 Ricky Williams TG .75 2.00
102 Bruce Smith TG .75 2.00
103 Curtis Martin TG .75 2.00
104 Brian Urlacher TG 1.00 2.50
105 Jerome Bettis TG 1.00 2.50
106 Ray Lewis TG 1.00 2.50
107 Edgerrin James TG .75 2.00
108 Junior Seau TG .75 2.00
109 Priest Holmes TG .60 1.50
110 Warren Sapp TG .75 2.00
111 Emmitt Smith RI 2.00 5.00
112 Jerry Rice RI 2.50 6.00
113 Brett Favre RI 2.50 6.00
114 Marshall Faulk RI 1.00 2.50
115 Drew Bledsoe RI 1.00 2.50
116 Tim Brown RI 1.25 3.00
117 Donovan McNabb RI 1.00 2.50
118 Peyton Manning RI 3.00 8.00
119 Kurt Warner RI 1.00 2.50
120 Shannon Sharpe RI 1.00 2.50
121 Andre Davis RC 1.50 4.00
122 Antonio Bryant RC 2.50 6.00
123 Antwaan Randle El RC 2.00 5.00
124 Ashley Lelie RC 1.50 4.00
125 Ben Leber RC 1.50 4.00
126 Chad Hutchinson RC 1.50 4.00
127 Clinton Portis RC 2.50 6.00
128 David Carr RC 1.50 4.00
129 Deion Branch RC 2.50 6.00
130 DeShaun Foster RC 2.50 6.00
131 Donte Stallworth RC 2.50 6.00
132 Jabar Gaffney RC 1.50 4.00
133 Javon Walker RC 2.50 6.00
134 Jeremy Shockey RC 2.50 6.00
135 Joey Harrington RC 1.50 4.00
136 Josh McCown RC 2.50 6.00
137 Josh Reed RC 2.00 5.00
138 Julius Peppers RC 4.00 10.00
139 Marquise Walker RC 1.50 4.00
140 Maurice Morris RC 2.00 5.00
141 Patrick Ramsey RC 2.00 5.00
142 Quentin Jammer RC 2.50 6.00
143 Randy Fasani RC 1.50 4.00
144 Reche Caldwell RC 2.00 5.00
145 Rohan Davey RC 2.50 6.00
146 Ron Johnson RC 2.00 5.00
147 Roy Williams RC 1.50 4.00
148 T.J. Duckett RC 1.50 4.00
149 Travis Stephens RC 1.50 4.00
150 William Green RC 2.00 5.00
151 Albert Haynesworth RC 2.00 5.00
152 Alex Brown RC 2.00 5.00
153 Andra Davis RC 1.25 3.00
154 Andre Gurode RC 3.00 8.00
155 Anthony Weaver RC 1.25 3.00
156 Brandon Doman RC 1.25 3.00
157 Brian Westbrook RC 2.50 6.00
158 Brian Williams RC 1.25 3.00
159 Lamont Brightful RC 1.25 3.00
160 Charles Grant RC 2.00 5.00
161 Chester Taylor RC 2.00 5.00
162 Cliff Russell RC 1.25 3.00
163 Daniel Graham RC 1.50 4.00
164 David Garrard RC 1.50 4.00
165 James Mungro RC 2.00 5.00
166 Dennis Johnson RC 1.25 3.00
167 Derek Ross RC 1.50 4.00
168 Dwight Freeney RC 2.50 6.00
169 Ed Reed RC 8.00 20.00
170 Carlos Hall RC 1.25 3.00
171 Jarrod Baxter RC 1.25 3.00
172 Jason McAddley RC 1.50 4.00
173 Jerramy Stevens RC 2.00 5.00
174 Jesse Chatman RC 1.25 3.00
175 John Henderson RC 1.50 4.00
176 Jon McGraw RC 1.25 3.00
177 Jonathan Wells RC 1.50 4.00
178 Justin Peelle RC 1.25 3.00
179 Kalimba Edwards RC 1.50 4.00
180 Keyou Craver RC 1.25 3.00
181 Kurt Kittner RC 1.25 3.00
182 LaDell Betts RC 2.00 5.00
183 Lamar Gordon RC 1.50 4.00
184 Lamont Thompson RC 1.50 4.00
185 Larry Tripplett RC 1.25 3.00
186 Randy McMichael RC 2.00 5.00
187 Lito Sheppard RC 2.00 5.00
188 Marques Anderson RC 1.50 4.00
189 Michael Lewis RC 1.50 4.00
190 Mike Pearson RC 1.25 3.00
191 Mike Rumph RC 1.25 3.00
192 Najeh Davenport RC 1.25 3.00
193 Napoleon Harris RC 1.50 4.00
194 Phillip Buchanon RC 2.00 5.00
195 Quinn Gray RC 1.50 4.00
196 Raonall Smith RC 1.25 3.00
197 Ricky Williams RC 1.50 4.00
198 Robert Thomas RC 1.25 3.00
199 Rocky Calmus RC 1.50 4.00
200 Ryan Denney RC 1.25 3.00
201 Ryan Sims RC 2.00 5.00
202 Jamal Robertson RC 1.25 3.00
203 Shaun Hill RC 2.00 5.00
204 Tank Williams RC 1.50 4.00
205 Tellis Redmon RC 1.25 3.00
206 Tim Carter RC 1.50 4.00
207 Tony Fisher RC 1.25 3.00
208 Travis Fisher RC 1.50 4.00
209 Verron Haynes RC 1.25 3.00
210 Wendell Bryant RC 1.25 3.00

2002 SP Legendary Cuts Autographs

Inserted at a rate of 1:192, this set features authentic cut autographs from many of the NFL's elite retired players. Please note that all print runs were provided by Upper Deck.

STATED ODDS 1:192
PRINT RUN UNDER 20 NOT PRICED
LCAH Arnie Herber/25* 500.00 800.00
LCAW Alex Wojciechowicz/28* 125.00 250.00
LCBN Bronko Nagurski/75* 250.00 500.00
LCDF Dan Fortmann/30* 60.00 150.00
LCJU Johnny Unitas/29* 350.00 600.00
LCKS Ken Strong/120* 60.00 150.00
LCLG Lou Groza/20* 60.00 150.00
LCRB Red Badgro/57* 50.00 120.00
LCRF Ray Flaherty/25* 100.00 200.00
LCRN Ray Nitschke/115* 175.00 300.00
LCSL Sid Luckman/22* 175.00 300.00
LCTL Tom Landry/20* 350.00 600.00
LCVL Vince Lombardi/240* 450.00 700.00
LCWP Walter Payton/65* 350.00 600.00

2002 SP Legendary Cuts Rookie Recruits Jerseys

Randomly inserted into packs, this set features event-worn swatches from many of the NFL's top 2002 rookies. There was also a gold parallel version #'d to 75.

STATED ODDS 1:17
*GOLD/75: .6X TO 1.5X BASIC JSY
GOLD PRINT RUN 75 SER.#'d SETS
RRAB Antonio Bryant 4.00 10.00
RRAD Andre Davis 2.50 6.00
RRAL Ashley Lelie 2.50 6.00
RRCP Clinton Portis 3.00 8.00
RRCR Cliff Russell 2.50 6.00
RRDC David Carr 2.50 6.00
RRDG Daniel Graham 3.00 8.00
RRDS Donte Stallworth 4.00 10.00
RREC Eric Crouch 3.00 8.00
RREL Antwaan Randle El 3.00 8.00
RRFO DeShaun Foster 4.00 10.00
RRJG Jabar Gaffney 2.50 6.00
RRJH Joey Harrington 2.50 6.00
RRJM Josh McCown 4.00 10.00
RRJP Julius Peppers 6.00 15.00
RRJR Josh Reed 3.00 8.00
RRJS Jeremy Shockey 4.00 10.00
RRJW Javon Walker 4.00 10.00
RRLB LaDell Betts 4.00 10.00
RRMM Maurice Morris 3.00 8.00
RRPR Patrick Ramsey 3.00 8.00
RRRC Reche Caldwell 3.00 8.00
RRRD Rohan Davey 4.00 10.00
RRRJ Ron Johnson 3.00 8.00
RRRO Roy Williams 2.50 6.00
RRTC Tim Carter 3.00 8.00
RRTJ T.J. Duckett 2.50 6.00
RRTS Travis Stephens 2.50 6.00
RRWA Marquise Walker 2.50 6.00
RRWG William Green 3.00 8.00

2002 SP Legendary Cuts SP Classic Threads

Randomly inserted into packs, this set features game-worn swatches from many of the NFL's top players. Each card was #'d to 350. There was also a gold parallel version #'d to 75.

STATED PRINT RUN 350 SER.#'d SETS
*GOLD/75: .6X TO 1.5X BASIC JSY
GOLD PRINT RUN 75 SER.#'d SETS
CCAB Aaron Brooks 2.50 6.00
CCAG Ahman Green 3.00 8.00
CCAT Anthony Thomas 3.00 8.00
CCBF Brett Favre 8.00 20.00
CCBG Brian Griese 2.50 6.00
CCBO David Boston 2.50 6.00
CCBR Drew Brees 8.00 20.00
CCBY Tom Brady 10.00 25.00
CCCD Corey Dillon 2.50 6.00
CCCM Curtis Martin 3.00 8.00
CCCW Chris Weinke 2.50 6.00
CCDB Drew Bledsoe 3.00 8.00
CCDC Daunte Culpepper 3.00 8.00
CCDM Dan Marino 10.00 25.00
CCEG Eddie George 3.00 8.00
CCEJ Edgerrin James 3.00 8.00
CCES Emmitt Smith 8.00 20.00
CCGH Garrison Hearst 2.50 6.00
CCJB Jerome Bettis 6.00 15.00
CCJE John Elway 8.00 20.00
CCJG Jeff Garcia 2.50 6.00
CCJK Jim Kelly 5.00 12.00
CCJL Jamal Lewis 3.00 8.00
CCJR Jerry Rice 8.00 20.00
CCKC Kerry Collins 2.50 6.00
CCKJ Keyshawn Johnson 3.00 8.00
CCKW Kurt Warner 3.00 8.00
CCLT LaDainian Tomlinson 4.00 10.00
CCMA Marcus Allen 4.00 10.00
CCMC Donovan McNabb 3.00 8.00
CCMF Marshall Faulk 3.00 8.00
CCMH Marvin Harrison 3.00 8.00
CCMV Michael Vick 3.00 8.00
CCPH Priest Holmes 2.50 6.00
CCPM Peyton Manning 10.00 25.00
CCRG Rich Gannon 3.00 8.00
CCRM Randy Moss 3.00 8.00
CCRW Ricky Williams 3.00 8.00
CCSM Steve McNair 3.00 8.00
CCTB Tim Brown 4.00 10.00
CCTC Tim Couch 2.50 6.00
CCWP Walter Payton 20.00 50.00

2008 SP Legendary Cuts Mystery Cut Signatures

EXCHANGE DEADLINE 12/31/2010

2008 SP Rookie Edition

This set was released on November 26, 2008. The base set consists of 413 cards. Cards 1-100 are veterans, while cards 101-150 are rookies. Cards 151-200 are short printed rookies produced to look like cards from 1993 SP, cards 201-250 are rookies printed to look like cards from 1994 SP, cards 251-300 are rookies printed to look like cards from 1995 SP, and cards 301-350 are rookies printed to look like cards from 1996 SP. Cards 352-392 are legends printed to look like cards from 1996 SP, and cards 394-434 are legends printed to look like cards from 1993 SP.

COMP.SET w/o SP's (150) 25.00 50.00
ROOKIE STATED ODDS 4:1
LEGENDS STATED ODDS 1:3.5
1 Marshawn Lynch .25 .60
2 Trent Edwards .20 .50
3 Roscoe Parrish .20 .50
4 Jason Taylor .25 .60
5 Ronnie Brown .20 .50
6 Hines Ward .25 .60
7 Tom Brady 1.00 2.50
8 Laurence Maroney .25 .60
9 Randy Moss .25 .60
10 Thomas Jones .20 .50
11 Jerricho Cotchery .20 .50
12 Brett Favre 1.50 4.00
13 Ray Lewis .30 .75
14 Ed Reed .25 .60
15 Willis McGahee .20 .50
16 Carson Palmer .25 .60
17 T.J. Houshmandzadeh .20 .50
18 Dwayne Bowe .25 .60
19 Kellen Winslow .20 .50
20 Derek Anderson .20 .50
21 Braylon Edwards .20 .50
22 Ben Roethlisberger .30 .75
23 Willie Parker .25 .60
24 Wes Welker .25 .60
25 DeMeco Ryans .25 .60
26 Andre Johnson .25 .60
27 Darius Walker .20 .50
28 Peyton Manning .75 2.00
29 Reggie Wayne .25 .60
30 Joseph Addai .20 .50
31 David Garrard .20 .50
32 Maurice Jones-Drew .20 .50
33 Fred Taylor .20 .50
34 Vince Young .20 .50
35 LenDale White .20 .50
36 Alge Crumpler .20 .50
37 Jay Cutler .20 .50
38 Brandon Marshall .25 .60
39 John Lynch .25 .60
40 Brodie Croyle .25 .60
41 Larry Johnson .20 .50
42 Derrick Johnson .20 .50
43 JaMarcus Russell .20 .50
44 Ronald Curry .20 .50
45 Jake Delhomme .20 .50
46 Antonio Gates .25 .60
47 LaDainian Tomlinson .30 .75
48 Antonio Cromartie .20 .50
49 Philip Rivers .30 .75
50 Tony Romo .25 .60
51 Terrell Owens .25 .60
52 DeMarcus Ware .25 .60
53 Marion Barber .20 .50
54 Eli Manning .25 .60
55 Brandon Jacobs .20 .50
56 Plaxico Burress .20 .50
57 Antonio Pierce .20 .50
58 Donovan McNabb .25 .60
59 Brian Dawkins .30 .75
60 Brian Westbrook .20 .50
61 Chris Cooley .20 .50
62 Jason Campbell .20 .50
63 Clinton Portis .20 .50
64 Brian Urlacher .30 .75
65 Lance Briggs .25 .60
66 Devin Hester .25 .60
67 Roy Williams WR .20 .50
68 Calvin Johnson .30 .75
69 Ernie Sims .20 .50
70 Aaron Rodgers .60 1.50
71 Ryan Grant .25 .60
72 Greg Jennings .20 .50
73 Tarvaris Jackson .20 .50
74 Adrian Peterson .30 .75
75 Sidney Rice .20 .50
76 Michael Turner .20 .50
77 Roddy White .20 .50
78 Jason Witten .25 .60
79 DeAngelo Williams .20 .50
80 Steve Smith .25 .60
81 Julius Peppers .25 .60
82 Drew Brees .30 .75
83 Reggie Bush .20 .50
84 Marques Colston .20 .50
85 Jonathan Vilma .20 .50
86 Joey Galloway .25 .60
87 Jeff Garcia .20 .50
88 Cadillac Williams .25 .60
89 Kurt Warner .25 .60
90 Edgerrin James .25 .60
91 Larry Fitzgerald .25 .60
92 Anquan Boldin .20 .50
93 Marc Bulger .20 .50
94 Steven Jackson .20 .50
95 Torry Holt .25 .60
96 J.T. O'Sullivan .20 .50
97 Frank Gore .25 .60
98 Nate Clements .20 .50
99 Matt Hasselbeck .20 .50
100 Deion Branch .20 .50
101 Alex Brink RC .50 1.25
102 Andre Woodson RC .40 1.00
103 Brian Brohm RC .40 1.00
104 Dorien Bryant RC .50 1.25
105 Colt Brennan RC .50 1.25
106 Calais Campbell RC .50 1.25
107 Chad Henne RC .50 1.25
108 Chris Johnson RC .50 1.25
109 Chris Long RC .50 1.25
110 Jacob Tamme RC .50 1.25
111 Dan Connor RC .40 1.00
112 Dennis Dixon RC .40 1.00
113 DeSean Jackson RC .75 2.00
114 Dennis Keyes RC .40 1.00
115 Darren McFadden RC .40 1.00
116 D.Rodgers-Cromartie RC .50 1.25
117 Devin Thomas RC .40 1.00
118 Erik Ainge RC .40 1.00
119 Early Doucet RC .40 1.00
120 Erin Henderson RC .50 1.25
121 Fred Davis RC .40 1.00
122 Felix Jones RC .40 1.00
123 Matt Forte RC .60 1.50
124 Glenn Dorsey RC .40 1.00
125 John David Booty RC .40 1.00
126 Jamaal Charles RC .60 1.50
127 Joe Flacco RC .75 2.00
128 Jonathan Goff RC .40 1.00
129 Jake Long RC .60 1.50
130 Jordy Nelson RC 1.25 3.00
131 Jonathan Stewart RC .60 1.50
132 Davone Bess RC .50 1.25
133 Kalvin McRae RC .40 1.00
134 Kenny Phillips RC .40 1.00
135 Kevin Smith RC .40 1.00
136 Leodis McKelvin RC .50 1.25
137 Limas Sweed RC .40 1.00
138 Matt Flynn RC .40 1.00
139 Mike Hart RC .40 1.00
140 Aqib Talib RC .60 1.50
141 Malcolm Kelly RC .40 1.00
142 Mario Manningham RC .40 1.00
143 Matt Ryan RC 1.25 3.00
144 Paul Smith RC .40 1.00
145 Rashard Mendenhall RC .40 1.00
146 Ray Rice RC .40 1.00
147 Sedrick Ellis RC .40 1.00
148 Donnie Avery RC .50 1.25
149 Tashard Choice RC .40 1.00
150 Vernon Gholston RC .40 1.00
151 Alex Brink 93 .75 2.00
152 Andre Caldwell 93 .60 1.50
153 Allen Patrick 93 .60 1.50
154 Andre Woodson 93 .60 1.50
155 Brian Brohm 93 .60 1.50
156 Dorien Bryant 93 .75 2.00
157 Colt Brennan 93 .75 2.00
158 Chris Ellis 93 .60 1.50
159 Chad Henne 93 .75 2.00
160 Chris Johnson 93 .75 2.00
161 Chris Long 93 .75 2.00
162 Donnie Avery 93 .75 2.00
163 Davone Bess 93 .75 2.00
164 Dan Connor 93 .60 1.50
165 Dennis Dixon 93 .60 1.50
166 DeSean Jackson 93 1.25 3.00
167 Darren McFadden 93 .60 1.50
168 Erik Ainge 93 .60 1.50
169 Early Doucet 93 .60 1.50
170 Fred Davis 93 .60 1.50
171 Felix Jones 93 .60 1.50
172 Matt Forte 93 1.00 2.50
173 Geno Hayes 93 .60 1.50
174 Chevis Jackson 93 .60 1.50
175 John David Booty 93 .60 1.50
176 Jamaal Charles 93 1.00 2.50
177 Joe Flacco 93 1.25 3.00
178 Peyton Hillis 93 1.00 2.50
179 Jake Long 93 1.00 2.50
180 Jordy Nelson 93 2.00 5.00
181 Jonathan Stewart 93 1.00 2.50
182 Justin Forsett 93 .75 2.00
183 Kevin O'Connell 93 .60 1.50
184 Kenny Phillips 93 .60 1.50
185 Kevin Smith 93 .60 1.50
186 Lance Ball 93 .60 1.50
187 Leodis McKelvin 93 .75 2.00
188 Limas Sweed 93 .60 1.50
189 Marcus Monk 93 .75 2.00
190 Matt Flynn 93 .60 1.50
191 Mike Hart 93 .60 1.50
192 Mike Jenkins 93 .60 1.50
193 Malcolm Kelly 93 .60 1.50
194 Mario Manningham 93 .60 1.50
195 Dre Moore 93 .60 1.50
196 Matt Ryan 93 2.00 5.00
197 Ryan Clady 93 .75 2.00
198 Rashard Mendenhall 93 .60 1.50
199 Ray Rice 93 .60 1.50
200 Tashard Choice 93 .60 1.50
201 Alex Brink 94 1.00 2.50
202 Aqib Talib 94 1.25 3.00
203 Andre Woodson 94 .75 2.00
204 Brian Brohm 94 .75 2.00
205 Dorien Bryant 94 1.00 2.50
206 Colt Brennan 94 1.00 2.50
207 Calais Campbell 94 1.00 2.50
208 Chad Henne 94 1.00 2.50
209 Chris Johnson 94 1.00 2.50
210 Chris Long 94 1.00 2.50
211 Donnie Avery 94 1.00 2.50
212 Davone Bess 94 1.00 2.50
213 Dennis Dixon 94 .75 2.00
214 DeSean Jackson 94 1.50 4.00
215 Darren McFadden 94 .75 2.00
216 Dominique Rodgers-Cromartie 94 1.00 2.50
217 Erik Ainge 94 .75 2.00
218 Early Doucet 94 .75 2.00
219 Fred Davis 94 .75 2.00
220 Felix Jones 94 .75 2.00
221 Matt Forte 94 1.25 3.00
222 Harry Douglas 94 1.00 2.50
223 John David Booty 94 .75 2.00
224 Jamaal Charles 94 1.25 3.00
225 Joe Flacco 94 1.50 4.00
226 James Hardy 94 .75 2.00
227 Josh Johnson 94 .75 2.00
228 Jordy Nelson 94 2.50 6.00
229 Jonathan Stewart 94 1.25 3.00
230 Keenan Burton 94 .75 2.00
231 Kenny Phillips 94 .75 2.00
232 Keith Rivers 94 .75 2.00
233 Kevin Smith 94 .75 2.00
234 Lavelle Hawkins 94 1.00 2.50
235 Leodis McKelvin 94 1.00 2.50
236 Limas Sweed 94 .75 2.00
237 Matt Flynn 94 .75 2.00
238 Mike Hart 94 .75 2.00
239 Adrian Arrington 94 .75 2.00
240 Malcolm Kelly 94 .75 2.00
241 Mario Manningham 94 .75 2.00
242 Matt Ryan 94 2.50 6.00
243 Phillip Merling 94 .75 2.00
244 Darius Reynaud 94 .75 2.00
245 Rashard Mendenhall 94 .75 2.00
246 Ray Rice 94 .75 2.00
247 Ryan Torain 94 1.00 2.50
248 Thomas Brown 94 .75 2.00
249 Tashard Choice 94 .75 2.00
250 Vernon Gholston 94 .75 2.00
251 Alex Brink 95 1.25 3.00
252 Allen Patrick 95 1.00 2.50
253 Aqib Talib 95 1.50 4.00
254 Andre Woodson 95 1.00 2.50
255 Brian Brohm 95 1.00 2.50
256 Dorien Bryant 95 1.25 3.00
257 Colt Brennan 95 1.25 3.00
258 Chad Henne 95 1.25 3.00
259 Chris Johnson 95 1.25 3.00
260 Chris Long 95 1.25 3.00
261 Davone Bess 95 1.25 3.00
262 Dennis Dixon 95 1.00 2.50
263 DeSean Jackson 95 2.00 5.00
264 Darren McFadden 95 1.00 2.50
265 Erik Ainge 95 1.00 2.50
266 Early Doucet 95 1.00 2.50
267 Fred Davis 95 1.00 2.50
268 Felix Jones 95 1.00 2.50
269 Matt Forte 95 1.50 4.00
270 Geno Hayes 95 1.00 2.50
271 Harry Douglas 95 1.25 3.00
272 John David Booty 95 1.00 2.50
273 Jamaal Charles 95 1.50 4.00
274 Joe Flacco 95 2.00 5.00
275 Peyton Hillis 95 1.50 4.00
276 Jacob Hester 95 1.00 2.50
277 Josh Johnson 95 1.00 2.50
278 Jordy Nelson 95 3.00 8.00
279 Jonathan Stewart 95 1.50 4.00
280 Keenan Burton 95 1.00 2.50
281 Kenny Phillips 95 1.00 2.50
282 Kevin Smith 95 1.00 2.50
283 Lance Ball 95 1.00 2.50
284 Lavelle Hawkins 95 1.25 3.00
285 Limas Sweed 95 1.00 2.50
286 Matt Flynn 95 1.00 2.50
287 Mike Hart 95 1.00 2.50
288 Adrian Arrington 95 1.00 2.50
289 Malcolm Kelly 95 1.00 2.50
290 Mario Manningham 95 1.00 2.50
291 Marcus Monk 95 1.25 3.00
292 Matt Ryan 95 3.00 8.00
293 Mario Urrutia 95 1.00 2.50
294 Paul Hubbard 95 1.00 2.50
295 Rashard Mendenhall 95 1.00 2.50
296 Ray Rice 95 1.00 2.50
297 Ryan Torain 95 1.25 3.00
298 Thomas Brown 95 1.00 2.50
299 Tashard Choice 95 1.00 2.50
300 Yvenson Bernard 95 1.50 4.00
301 Alex Brink 96 1.25 3.00
302 Chevis Jackson 96 1.00 2.50
303 Andre Caldwell 96 1.00 2.50
304 Allen Patrick 96 1.00 2.50
305 Kevin O'Connell 96 1.00 2.50
306 Andre Woodson 96 1.00 2.50
307 Brian Brohm 96 1.00 2.50
308 Mike Jenkins 96 1.00 2.50
309 Tom Zbikowski 96 1.25 3.00
310 Dorien Bryant 96 1.25 3.00
311 Colt Brennan 96 1.25 3.00
312 Chad Henne 96 1.25 3.00
313 Chris Johnson 96 1.25 3.00
314 Chris Long 96 1.25 3.00
315 Donnie Avery 96 1.25 3.00
316 Davone Bess 96 1.25 3.00
317 Dennis Dixon 96 1.00 2.50
318 DeSean Jackson 96 2.00 5.00
319 Darren McFadden 96 1.00 2.50
320 DeMario Pressley 96 1.25 3.00
321 Dre Moore 96 1.00 2.50
322 Erik Ainge 96 1.00 2.50
323 Early Doucet 96 1.00 2.50
324 Fred Davis 96 1.00 2.50
325 Felix Jones 96 1.00 2.50
326 Matt Forte 96 1.50 4.00
327 Harry Douglas 96 1.25 3.00
328 John David Booty 96 1.00 2.50
329 Jamaal Charles 96 1.50 4.00
330 Joe Flacco 96 2.00 5.00
331 Jordy Nelson 96 3.00 8.00
332 Jonathan Stewart 96 1.50 4.00
333 Kalvin McRae 96 1.00 2.50
334 Kenny Phillips 96 1.00 2.50
335 Kevin Smith 96 1.00 2.50
336 Lavelle Hawkins 96 1.25 3.00
337 Limas Sweed 96 1.00 2.50
338 Marcus Monk 96 1.25 3.00
339 Matt Flynn 96 1.00 2.50
340 Mike Hart 96 1.00 2.50
341 Adrian Arrington 96 1.00 2.50
342 Malcolm Kelly 96 1.00 2.50
343 Mario Manningham 96 1.00 2.50
344 Ben Moffitt 96 1.00 2.50
345 Matt Ryan 96 3.00 8.00
346 Mario Urrutia 96 1.00 2.50
347 Rashard Mendenhall 96 1.00 2.50
348 Ray Rice 96 1.00 2.50
349 Ryan Torain 96 1.25 3.00
350 Tashard Choice 96 1.00 2.50
352 Bob Griese 96 1.25 3.00
353 Bert Jones 96 .75 2.00
354 Bruce Smith 96 1.00 2.50
355 Barry Sanders 96 2.00 5.00
356 Dick Butkus 96 1.50 4.00
357 Daryl Johnston 96 1.00 2.50
359 Franco Harris 96 1.25 3.00
360 Fran Tarkenton 96 1.25 3.00
363 Bo Jackson 96 1.50 4.00
365 John Elway 96 2.00 5.00
366 Joe Greene 96 1.25 3.00
367 Jack Ham 96 1.00 2.50
368 Jerry Kramer 96 1.00 2.50
369 Jim Kelly 96 1.25 3.00
372 Joe Theismann 96 1.25 3.00
373 Ken Anderson 96 1.00 2.50
376 Jerry Rice 96 2.50 6.00
377 Emmitt Smith 96 2.00 5.00
379 Ottis Anderson 96 .75 2.00
380 Paul Hornung 96 1.25 3.00
381 Roger Craig 96 1.00 2.50
382 Roman Gabriel 96 .75 2.00
383 Chuck Bednarik 96 1.00 2.50
384 Rod Woodson 96 1.00 2.50
385 Billy Sims 96 1.00 2.50
386 Archie Manning 96 1.00 2.50
387 Bart Starr 96 2.00 5.00
388 Steve Young 96 1.50 4.00
389 Troy Aikman 96 1.50 4.00
391 Tom Rathman 96 1.00 2.50
392 Y.A. Tittle 96 1.25 3.00
394 Bob Griese 93 1.25 3.00
395 Bert Jones 93 .75 2.00
396 Bruce Smith 93 1.00 2.50
397 Barry Sanders 93 2.00 5.00
398 Dick Butkus 93 1.50 4.00
399 Daryl Johnston 93 1.00 2.50
401 Franco Harris 93 1.25 3.00
402 Fran Tarkenton 93 1.25 3.00
405 Bo Jackson 93 1.50 4.00
407 John Elway 93 2.00 5.00
408 Joe Greene 93 1.25 3.00
409 Jack Ham 93 1.00 2.50
410 Jim Kelly 93 1.25 3.00
411 Jerry Kramer 93 1.00 2.50
414 Joe Theismann 93 1.25 3.00
415 Ken Anderson 93 1.00 2.50
418 Roger Staubach 93 1.50 4.00
419 Chuck Bednarik 93 1.00 2.50
421 Ottis Anderson 93 .75 2.00
422 Paul Hornung 93 1.25 3.00
423 Roger Craig 93 1.00 2.50
424 Roman Gabriel 93 .75 2.00
426 Rod Woodson 93 1.00 2.50
427 Billy Sims 93 1.00 2.50
428 Archie Manning 93 1.00 2.50
429 Bart Starr 93 2.00 5.00
430 Steve Young 93 1.50 4.00
431 Troy Aikman 93 1.50 4.00
433 Tom Rathman 93 1.00 2.50
434 Y.A. Tittle 93 1.25 3.00

2008 SP Rookie Edition Autographs

STATED ODDS 1:7
152 Andre Caldwell 93 3.00 8.00
153 Allen Patrick 93 3.00 8.00
154 Andre Woodson 93 3.00 8.00
155 Brian Brohm 93 3.00 8.00
156 Dorien Bryant 93 4.00 10.00
157 Colt Brennan 93 4.00 10.00
158 Chris Ellis 93 3.00 8.00
159 Chad Henne 93 4.00 10.00
160 Chris Johnson 93 4.00 10.00
161 Chris Long 93 4.00 10.00
162 Donnie Avery 93 4.00 10.00
163 Davone Bess 93 4.00 10.00
164 Dan Connor 93 3.00 8.00
165 Dennis Dixon 93 10.00 20.00
166 DeSean Jackson 93 8.00 20.00
167 Darren McFadden 93 3.00 8.00
168 Erik Ainge 93 3.00 8.00
169 Early Doucet 93 3.00 8.00
170 Fred Davis 93 3.00 8.00
171 Felix Jones 93 3.00 8.00
172 Matt Forte 93 12.00 30.00
173 Geno Hayes 93 3.00 8.00
174 Chevis Jackson 93 3.00 8.00
175 John David Booty 93 3.00 8.00
176 Jamaal Charles 93 5.00 12.00
177 Joe Flacco 93 12.00 30.00
178 Peyton Hillis 93 6.00 15.00
179 Jake Long 93 5.00 12.00
180 Jordy Nelson 93 10.00 25.00
181 Jonathan Stewart 93 5.00 12.00
182 Justin Forsett 93 4.00 10.00
183 Kevin O'Connell 93 3.00 8.00
184 Kenny Phillips 93 3.00 8.00
185 Kevin Smith 93 3.00 8.00
186 Lance Ball 93 3.00 8.00
187 Leodis McKelvin 93 4.00 10.00
188 Limas Sweed 93 3.00 8.00
189 Marcus Monk 93 4.00 10.00
190 Matt Flynn 93 3.00 8.00
191 Mike Hart 93 3.00 8.00
192 Mike Jenkins 93 3.00 8.00
193 Malcolm Kelly 93 3.00 8.00
194 Mario Manningham 93 6.00 15.00
195 Dre Moore 93 3.00 8.00
196 Matt Ryan 93 40.00 80.00
197 Ryan Clady 93 4.00 10.00
198 Rashard Mendenhall 93 3.00 8.00
199 Ray Rice 93 3.00 8.00
200 Tashard Choice 93 3.00 8.00
201 Alex Brink 94 4.00 10.00
202 Aqib Talib 94 5.00 12.00
203 Andre Woodson 94 3.00 8.00
204 Brian Brohm 94 3.00 8.00
205 Dorien Bryant 94 4.00 10.00
206 Colt Brennan 94 4.00 10.00
207 Calais Campbell 94
208 Chad Henne 94 4.00 10.00
209 Chris Johnson 94 4.00 10.00
210 Chris Long 94 4.00 10.00
211 Donnie Avery 94 4.00 10.00
212 Davone Bess 94 4.00 10.00
213 Dennis Dixon 94 10.00 20.00
214 DeSean Jackson 94 8.00 20.00
215 Darren McFadden 94 3.00 8.00
216 Dominique Rodgers-Cromartie 94 4.00 10.00
217 Erik Ainge 94 3.00 8.00
218 Early Doucet 94 3.00 8.00
220 Felix Jones 94 3.00 8.00
221 Matt Forte 94 12.00 30.00
222 Harry Douglas 94 4.00 10.00
223 John David Booty 94 3.00 8.00
224 Jamaal Charles 94 5.00 12.00
225 Joe Flacco 94 12.00 30.00
226 James Hardy 94 3.00 8.00
227 Josh Johnson 94 3.00 8.00
228 Jordy Nelson 94 10.00 25.00
229 Jonathan Stewart 94 5.00 12.00
230 Keenan Burton 94 3.00 8.00
231 Kenny Phillips 94 3.00 8.00
232 Keith Rivers 94 3.00 8.00
233 Kevin Smith 94 3.00 8.00
234 Lavelle Hawkins 94 4.00 10.00
235 Leodis McKelvin 94 4.00 10.00
236 Limas Sweed 94 3.00 8.00
237 Matt Flynn 94 3.00 8.00
238 Mike Hart 94 3.00 8.00
239 Adrian Arrington 94 3.00 8.00
240 Malcolm Kelly 94 3.00 8.00
241 Mario Manningham 94 6.00 15.00
242 Matt Ryan 94 40.00 80.00
243 Phillip Merling 94 3.00 8.00
244 Darius Reynaud 94 3.00 8.00
246 Ray Rice 94 3.00 8.00
247 Ryan Torain 94 4.00 10.00
248 Thomas Brown 94 3.00 8.00
249 Tashard Choice 94 3.00 8.00
250 Vernon Gholston 94 4.00 10.00
252 Allen Patrick 95 4.00 10.00
253 Aqib Talib 95 6.00 15.00
254 Andre Woodson 95 4.00 10.00
255 Brian Brohm 95 3.00 8.00
256 Dorien Bryant 95 5.00 12.00
257 Colt Brennan 95 4.00 10.00
258 Chad Henne 95 5.00 12.00
259 Chris Johnson 95 4.00 10.00
260 Chris Long 95 4.00 10.00
261 Davone Bess 95 4.00 10.00
263 DeSean Jackson 95 8.00 20.00
264 Darren McFadden 95 3.00 8.00
265 Erik Ainge 95 4.00 10.00
268 Felix Jones 95 3.00 8.00
269 Matt Forte 95 15.00 40.00
271 Harry Douglas 95 5.00 12.00
272 John David Booty 95 3.00 8.00
273 Jamaal Charles 95 6.00 15.00
274 Joe Flacco 95 12.00 30.00
275 Peyton Hillis 95 6.00 15.00
277 Josh Johnson 95 4.00 10.00
278 Jordy Nelson 95 12.00 30.00
279 Jonathan Stewart 95 6.00 15.00
280 Keenan Burton 95 4.00 10.00
281 Kenny Phillips 95 4.00 10.00
282 Kevin Smith 95 4.00 10.00
283 Lance Ball 95 4.00 10.00
284 Lavelle Hawkins 95 5.00 12.00
285 Limas Sweed 95 4.00 10.00
286 Matt Flynn 95 4.00 10.00
287 Mike Hart 95 4.00 10.00
288 Adrian Arrington 95 4.00 10.00
289 Malcolm Kelly 95 4.00 10.00
291 Marcus Monk 95 5.00 12.00
292 Matt Ryan 95 50.00 100.00
293 Mario Urrutia 95
294 Paul Hubbard 95
297 Ryan Torain 95 5.00 12.00
298 Thomas Brown 95 4.00 10.00
299 Tashard Choice 95 3.00 8.00
302 Chevis Jackson 96
303 Andre Caldwell 96 4.00 10.00
304 Allen Patrick 96
306 Andre Woodson 96
307 Brian Brohm 96
308 Mike Jenkins 96 4.00 10.00
309 Tom Zbikowski 96 5.00 12.00
310 Dorien Bryant 96
311 Colt Brennan 96
312 Chad Henne 96
313 Chris Johnson 96 4.00 10.00
314 Chris Long 96 8.00 20.00
315 Donnie Avery 96 5.00 12.00
316 Davone Bess 96 5.00 12.00

318 DeSean Jackson 96 10.00 25.00
319 Darren McFadden 96
320 DeMario Pressley 96 5.00 12.00
321 Dre Moore 96
322 Erik Ainge 96
325 Felix Jones 96 3.00 8.00
326 Matt Forte 96 15.00 40.00
327 Harry Douglas 96
328 John David Booty 96 4.00 10.00
329 Jamaal Charles 96 6.00 15.00
330 Joe Flacco 96 12.00 30.00
331 Jordy Nelson 96 12.00 30.00
332 Jonathan Stewart 96 30.00 80.00
334 Kenny Phillips 96 4.00 10.00
335 Kevin Smith 96 4.00 10.00
337 Limas Sweed 96 4.00 10.00
338 Marcus Monk 96 5.00 12.00
339 Matt Flynn 96 4.00 10.00
340 Mike Hart 96 4.00 10.00
341 Adrian Arrington 96 4.00 10.00
342 Malcolm Kelly 96
344 Ben Moffitt 96 4.00 10.00
345 Matt Ryan 96 40.00 100.00
346 Mario Urrutia 96
349 Ryan Torain 96 6.00 15.00
350 Tashard Choice 96
353 Bert Jones 96 15.00 30.00
354 Bruce Smith 96 30.00 60.00
355 Barry Sanders 96
356 Dick Butkus 96 50.00 100.00
357 Daryl Johnston 96 25.00 50.00
359 Franco Harris 96 40.00 80.00
363 Bo Jackson 96 40.00 80.00
365 John Elway 96 50.00 100.00
367 Jack Ham 96
368 Jerry Kramer 96
372 Joe Theismann 96 20.00 40.00
376 Jerry Rice 96 100.00 175.00
377 Emmitt Smith 96
379 Ottis Anderson 96 10.00 25.00
380 Paul Hornung 96 20.00 40.00
381 Roger Craig 96 15.00 30.00
382 Roman Gabriel 96 20.00 40.00
385 Billy Sims 96
388 Steve Young 96 40.00 80.00
391 Tom Rathman 96 15.00 40.00
392 Y.A. Tittle 96 25.00 50.00
395 Bert Jones 93 15.00 30.00
396 Bruce Smith 93 30.00 60.00
397 Barry Sanders 93
398 Dick Butkus 93 50.00 100.00
399 Daryl Johnston 93 20.00 40.00
401 Franco Harris 93
405 Bo Jackson 93
407 John Elway 93
409 Jack Ham 93 30.00 60.00
411 Jerry Kramer 93 15.00 30.00
414 Joe Theismann 93
418 Roger Staubach 93 75.00 125.00
421 Ottis Anderson 93
422 Paul Hornung 93 20.00 40.00
423 Roger Craig 93 15.00 30.00
424 Roman Gabriel 93 20.00 40.00
427 Billy Sims 93 15.00 30.00
428 Archie Manning 93
430 Steve Young 93 50.00 80.00
433 Tom Rathman 93
434 Y.A. Tittle 93

2007 SP Rookie Threads

This 160-card set was released in September, 2007. The set was issued into the hobby in five-card packs, with a $50 SRP, which came six packs to a box. Cards numbered 1-100 feature veterans while cards 101-160 feature 2007 NFL rookies, all of whom signed the cards. Those cards were issued to stated print runs of between 150 and 250 serial numbered sets. For those players who signed 150 cards we have notated that information in our checklist.

COMP.SET w/o RC's (100) 25.00 50.00
AU ROOKIE PRINT RUN 150-250
1 Matt Leinart .50 1.25
2 Anquan Boldin .50 1.25
3 Larry Fitzgerald .60 1.50
4 Edgerrin James .60 1.50
5 Michael Vick .60 1.50
6 Warrick Dunn .50 1.25
7 Alge Crumpler .60 1.50
8 Steve McNair .60 1.50
9 Mark Clayton .50 1.25
10 Ray Lewis .75 2.00
11 J.P. Losman .50 1.25
12 Lee Evans .60 1.50
13 Anthony Thomas .50 1.25
14 Jake Delhomme .50 1.25
15 Steve Smith .60 1.50
16 DeShaun Foster .60 1.50
17 Brian Urlacher .75 2.00
18 Cedric Benson .50 1.25
19 Rex Grossman .50 1.25
20 Bernard Berrian .50 1.25
21 Chad Johnson .50 1.25
22 Rudi Johnson .50 1.25
23 Carson Palmer .60 1.50
24 T.J. Houshmandzadeh .50 1.25
25 Jamal Lewis .60 1.50
26 Braylon Edwards .50 1.25
27 Kellen Winslow .50 1.25
28 Julius Jones .50 1.25
29 Tony Romo 1.00 2.50
30 Terrell Owens .60 1.50
31 Javon Walker .60 1.50
32 Travis Henry .60 1.50
33 Jay Cutler .50 1.25
34 Champ Bailey .60 1.50
35 Tatum Bell .50 1.25
36 Roy Williams WR .50 1.25
37 Jon Kitna .50 1.25
38 Donald Driver .60 1.50
39 Brett Favre 1.50 4.00
40 A.J. Hawk .50 1.25
41 Ahman Green .60 1.50
42 Matt Schaub .50 1.25
43 Andre Johnson .60 1.50
44 Reggie Wayne .60 1.50
45 Joseph Addai .50 1.25
46 Marvin Harrison .60 1.50
47 Peyton Manning 2.00 5.00
48 Byron Leftwich .50 1.25
49 Fred Taylor .50 1.25
50 Maurice Jones-Drew .50 1.25
51 Tony Gonzalez .60 1.50
52 Larry Johnson .50 1.25
53 Damon Huard .60 1.50
54 Chris Chambers .50 1.25
55 Ronnie Brown .50 1.25
56 Chester Taylor .50 1.25
57 Troy Williamson .50 1.25
58 Tarvaris Jackson .50 1.25
59 Tedy Bruschi .60 1.50
60 Laurence Maroney .60 1.50
61 Tom Brady 2.50 6.00
62 Reggie Bush .50 1.25
63 Drew Brees .75 2.00
64 Deuce McAllister .60 1.50
65 Eli Manning .60 1.50
66 Plaxico Burress .50 1.25
67 Brandon Jacobs .50 1.25
68 Chad Pennington .50 1.25
69 Leon Washington .50 1.25
70 Laveranues Coles .50 1.25
71 Jerricho Cotchery .50 1.25
72 Ronald Curry .50 1.25
73 Dominic Rhodes .50 1.25
74 Donovan McNabb .60 1.50
75 Brian Westbrook .50 1.25
76 Reggie Brown .50 1.25
77 Ben Roethlisberger .75 2.00
78 Hines Ward .60 1.50
79 Willie Parker .60 1.50
80 Santonio Holmes .50 1.25
81 Philip Rivers .75 2.00
82 Antonio Gates .75 2.00
83 Shawne Merriman .50 1.25
84 LaDainian Tomlinson .75 2.00
85 Alex Smith QB .60 1.50
86 Frank Gore .60 1.50
87 Shaun Alexander .50 1.25
88 Matt Hasselbeck .50 1.25
89 Deion Branch .50 1.25
90 Torry Holt .60 1.50
91 Steven Jackson .50 1.25
92 Marc Bulger .50 1.25
93 Chris Simms .50 1.25
94 Cadillac Williams .60 1.50
95 Joey Galloway .60 1.50
96 Keith Bulluck .50 1.25
97 Vince Young .50 1.25
98 Jason Campbell .50 1.25
99 Santana Moss .60 1.50
100 Clinton Portis .50 1.25
101 Daymeion Hughes AU RC 8.00 20.00
102 Eric Wright AU RC 8.00 20.00
103 Leon Hall AU RC 8.00 20.00
104 Gaines Adams AU RC 10.00 25.00
105 LaMarr Woodley AU RC 20.00 40.00
106 Quentin Moses AU RC 8.00 20.00
107 Amobi Okoye AU RC 10.00 25.00
108 Lawrence Timmons AU RC 12.00 30.00
109 Joe Thomas AU RC 12.00 30.00
110 Brady Quinn AU/150 RC 10.00 25.00
111 Chris Leak AU RC 8.00 20.00
112 Drew Stanton AU RC 8.00 20.00
113 JaMarcus Russell AU/150 RC 10.00 25.00
114 Jeff Rowe AU RC 8.00 20.00
115 John Beck AU RC 8.00 20.00
116 Jordan Palmer AU RC 10.00 25.00
117 Kevin Kolb AU RC 10.00 25.00
118 Matt Moore AU RC 12.00 30.00
119 Trent Edwards AU RC 8.00 20.00
120 Jamaal Anderson AU RC 10.00 25.00
121 Tyler Palko AU RC 12.00 30.00
122 Adrian Peterson AU/150 RC 100.00 200.00
123 Antonio Pittman AU RC 8.00 20.00
124 Brandon Jackson AU RC 8.00 20.00
125 Brian Leonard AU RC 8.00 20.00
126 Chris Henry RB AU RC 8.00 20.00
127 Darius Walker AU RC 8.00 20.00
128 Dwayne Wright AU RC 8.00 20.00
129 Garrett Wolfe AU RC 8.00 20.00
130 Kenneth Darby AU RC 8.00 20.00
131 Kenny Irons AU RC 8.00 20.00
132 Kolby Smith AU RC 8.00 20.00
133 Lorenzo Booker AU RC 10.00 25.00
134 Marshawn Lynch AU RC 15.00 40.00
135 Michael Bush AU RC 8.00 20.00
136 Selvin Young AU RC 8.00 20.00
137 Tony Hunt AU RC 8.00 20.00
138 LaRon Landry AU RC 12.00 30.00
139 Scott Chandler AU RC 12.00 30.00
140 Greg Olsen AU RC 12.00 30.00
141 Zach Miller AU RC 8.00 20.00
142 Anthony Gonzalez AU RC 8.00 20.00
143 Aundrae Allison AU RC 8.00 20.00
144 Calvin Johnson AU/150 RC 50.00 100.00
145 Chansi Stuckey AU RC 10.00 25.00
146 Craig Buster Davis AU RC 8.00 20.00
147 Dallas Baker AU RC 8.00 20.00
148 David Ball AU RC 8.00 20.00
149 David Clowney AU RC 8.00 20.00
150 Dwayne Rowe AU RC 8.00 20.00
151 Dwayne Jarrett AU RC 10.00 25.00
152 Jason Hill AU RC 8.00 20.00
153 Johnnie Lee Higgins AU RC 8.00 20.00
154 Rhema McKnight AU RC 8.00 20.00
155 Robert Meachem AU RC 10.00 25.00
156 Sidney Rice AU RC 8.00 20.00
157 Steve Smith USC AU RC 8.00 20.00
158 Syvelle Newton AU RC 10.00 25.00
159 Ted Ginn Jr. AU RC 10.00 25.00
160 Legedu Naanee AU RC 10.00 25.00

2007 SP Rookie Threads Rookie Lettermen Black

*BLACK/25: .6X TO 1.5X BASIC AU/250
STATED PRINT RUN 5-25
SERIAL #'d UNDER 25 NOT PRICED

2007 SP Rookie Threads Rookie Lettermen Gold

*GOLD/75-99: .5X TO 1.2X BASIC AU/250
STATED PRINT RUN 25-99
122 Adrian Peterson AU/25 150.00 300.00

2007 SP Rookie Threads Rookie Lettermen Silver

*SILVER/150-199: .4X TO 1X BASIC AU/250
STATED PRINT RUN 75-199
122 Adrian Peterson AU/75 100.00 200.00

2007 SP Rookie Threads Double Coverage

COMMON CARD 4.00 10.00
SEMISTARS 5.00 12.00
UNLISTED STARS 6.00 15.00
DCAC Alge Crumpler 5.00 12.00
DCAG Antonio Gates 6.00 15.00
DCAP Adrian Peterson 8.00 20.00
DCAR Aaron Rodgers 20.00 50.00
DCBE Tatum Bell 4.00 10.00
DCBF Brett Favre 12.00 30.00
DCBL Byron Leftwich 4.00 10.00
DCBQ Brady Quinn 2.50 6.00
DCBR Ben Roethlisberger 6.00 15.00
DCBU Brian Urlacher 6.00 15.00
DCBW Brian Westbrook 4.00 10.00
DCCB Cedric Benson 4.00 10.00
DCCJ Calvin Johnson 8.00 20.00
DCCM Curtis Martin 5.00 12.00
DCCP Chad Pennington 4.00 10.00
DCCS Chris Simms 4.00 10.00
DCCW Cadillac Williams 5.00 12.00
DCDB Drew Brees 6.00 15.00
DCDC Daunte Culpepper 5.00 12.00
DCDM Donovan McNabb 5.00 12.00
DCEM Eli Manning 5.00 12.00
DCGI Ted Ginn Jr. 3.00 8.00
DCGO Tony Gonzalez 5.00 12.00
DCJA Joseph Addai 4.00 10.00
DCJH Joe Horn 4.00 10.00
DCJN Jerious Norwood 4.00 10.00
DCJO Chad Johnson 8.00 20.00
DCJP Julius Peppers 5.00 12.00
DCJR JaMarcus Russell 2.50 6.00
DCJS Jeremy Shockey 4.00 10.00
DCLJ Larry Johnson 4.00 10.00
DCLM Laurence Maroney 5.00 12.00
DCLT LaDainian Tomlinson 6.00 15.00
DCMB Marc Bulger 4.00 10.00
DCMC Deuce McAllister 5.00 12.00
DCMF Marshall Faulk 10.00 25.00
DCMH Marvin Harrison 5.00 12.00
DCML Matt Leinart 4.00 10.00
DCMM Muhsin Muhammad 4.00 10.00
DCMS Michael Strahan 5.00 12.00
DCMV Michael Vick 5.00 12.00
DCPA Carson Palmer 5.00 12.00
DCPB Plaxico Burress 4.00 10.00
DCPH Priest Holmes 5.00 12.00
DCPM Peyton Manning 15.00 30.00
DCRB Ronnie Brown 4.00 10.00
DCRL Ray Lewis 6.00 15.00
DCRS Rod Smith 5.00 12.00
DCRW Reggie Wayne 5.00 12.00
DCSJ Steven Jackson 4.00 10.00
DCSM Steve McNair 5.00 12.00
DCTB Tom Brady 15.00 30.00
DCTE Tedy Bruschi 10.00 25.00
DCTG Trent Green 4.00 10.00
DCTH T.J. Houshmandzadeh 4.00 10.00
DCTR Tony Romo 8.00 20.00
DCTW Troy Williamson 4.00 10.00
DCWI Roy Williams WR 4.00 10.00
DCWM Willis McGahee 4.00 10.00
DCWP Willie Parker 5.00 12.00

2007 SP Rookie Threads Draft Day Ink

DDIAA Aundrae Allison 3.00 8.00
DDIAB Alan Branch 3.00 8.00
DDIAG Anthony Gonzalez 3.00 8.00
DDIAP Adrian Peterson
DDIBM Brandon Meriweather 4.00 10.00
DDIBQ Brady Quinn
DDICD Craig Buster Davis 3.00 8.00
DDICH Chris Henry RB 3.00 8.00
DDICJ Calvin Johnson
DDIDI David Irons 3.00 8.00
DDIDJ Dwayne Jarrett 4.00 10.00
DDIDS Drew Stanton 3.00 8.00
DDIDW Dwayne Wright 3.00 8.00
DDIGO Greg Olsen 5.00 12.00
DDIGW Garrett Wolfe 3.00 8.00
DDIHI Johnnie Lee Higgins 3.00 8.00
DDIIS Isaiah Stanback 3.00 8.00
DDIJA Jamaal Anderson 4.00 10.00
DDIJH Jason Hill 3.00 8.00
DDIJR JaMarcus Russell
DDIJT Joe Thomas 5.00 12.00
DDIKI Kenny Irons 3.00 8.00
DDILL LaRon Landry
DDIMG Michael Griffin 3.00 8.00
DDIML Marshawn Lynch 25.00 50.00
DDIMM Marcus McCauley 3.00 8.00
DDIPI Antonio Pittman 3.00 8.00
DDIPW Paul Williams 3.00 8.00
DDIRM Robert Meachem 4.00 10.00
DDISN Syvelle Newton 4.00 10.00
DDISS Steve Smith USC 3.00 8.00
DDITE Trent Edwards 12.00 30.00
DDITG Ted Ginn Jr. 4.00 10.00
DDIWI Patrick Willis 5.00 12.00
DDIYF Yamon Figurs 3.00 8.00

2007 SP Rookie Threads Maximum Threads

STATED PRINT RUN 50 SER.#'d SETS
MTAG Ahman Green 6.00 15.00
MTAJ Andre Johnson 6.00 15.00
MTAN Anthony Gonzalez 3.00 8.00
MTAP Adrian Peterson 10.00 25.00
MTAS Alex Smith QB 6.00 15.00
MTBF Brett Favre 15.00 40.00
MTBL Byron Leftwich 5.00 12.00
MTBQ Brady Quinn 3.00 8.00
MTBR Ben Roethlisberger 8.00 20.00
MTBW Brian Westbrook 5.00 12.00
MTCB Champ Bailey 6.00 15.00
MTCJ Calvin Johnson 10.00 25.00
MTCP Clinton Portis 5.00 12.00
MTCS Chris Simms 5.00 12.00
MTCT Chester Taylor 5.00 12.00
MTCU Jay Cutler 5.00 12.00
MTDB Dwayne Bowe 3.00 8.00
MTDD Donald Driver 6.00 15.00
MTDM Donovan McNabb 6.00 15.00
MTDR Drew Brees 8.00 20.00
MTEJ Edgerrin James 6.00 15.00
MTFM Eli Manning 6.00 15.00
MTEV Lee Evans 6.00 15.00
MTFG Frank Gore 6.00 15.00
MTFT Fred Taylor 5.00 12.00
MTGA Gaines Adams 4.00 10.00
MTGO Greg Olsen 5.00 12.00
MTHO T.J. Houshmandzadeh 5.00 12.00
MTHW Hines Ward 6.00 15.00
MTIB Isaac Bruce 8.00 20.00
MTJJ Julius Jones 5.00 12.00
MTJL J.P. Losman 5.00 12.00
MTJR JaMarcus Russell 3.00 8.00
MTJS Jeremy Shockey 5.00 12.00
MTJS2 Jeremy Shockey 5.00 12.00
MTJT Joe Thomas 5.00 12.00
MTLE Matt Leinart 5.00 12.00
MTLF Larry Fitzgerald 6.00 15.00
MTLJ Larry Johnson 5.00 12.00
MTLM Laurence Maroney 6.00 15.00
MTLT LaDainian Tomlinson 8.00 20.00
MTMB Marc Bulger 5.00 12.00
MTMC Marques Colston 5.00 12.00
MTMH Matt Hasselbeck 5.00 12.00
MTML Marshawn Lynch 6.00 15.00
MTPE Chad Pennington 5.00 12.00
MTPM Peyton Manning 15.00 40.00
MTPR Philip Rivers 8.00 20.00
MTRB Ronnie Brown 5.00 12.00
MTRJ Rudi Johnson 5.00 12.00
MTRM Robert Meachem 4.00 10.00
MTRW Roy Williams WR 5.00 12.00
MTSA Shaun Alexander 5.00 12.00
MTSM Shawne Merriman 5.00 12.00
MTST Steve McNair 6.00 15.00
MTTA Jason Taylor 6.00 15.00
MTTB Tom Brady 15.00 40.00
MTTG Ted Ginn Jr. 4.00 10.00
MTTH Todd Heap 5.00 12.00
MTTO Terrell Owens 6.00 15.00
MTTR Tony Romo 10.00 25.00
MTVY Vince Young 5.00 12.00
MTWD Warrick Dunn 5.00 12.00
MTWM Willis McGahee 5.00 12.00
MTWP Willie Parker 6.00 15.00

2007 SP Rookie Threads Phenom Flashbacks Jerseys

PHFAH A.J. Hawk 2.00 5.00
PHFDW DeAngelo Williams 2.00 5.00
PHFLM Laurence Maroney 2.50 6.00
PHFLW Leon Washington 2.00 5.00
PHFMJ Maurice Jones-Drew 2.00 5.00
PHFML Matt Leinart 2.00 5.00
PHFRB Reggie Bush 2.00 5.00
PHFSH Santonio Holmes 2.00 5.00
PHFVY Vince Young 2.00 5.00
PHFWH LenDale White 2.50 6.00

2007 SP Rookie Threads Rookie Exclusive Autographs

STATED PRINT RUN 89-100
REAG Anthony Gonzalez 5.00 12.00
REAP Adrian Peterson 125.00 250.00
REBA Dallas Baker 5.00 12.00
REBM Brandon Meriweather 6.00 15.00
REBQ Brady Quinn 5.00 12.00
RECD Craig Buster Davis 5.00 12.00
RECH Chris Henry RB 5.00 12.00
RECJ Calvin Johnson 60.00 120.00
RECS Chansi Stuckey 6.00 15.00
REDA David Ball 5.00 12.00
REDB Dwayne Bowe 5.00 12.00
REDH Daymeion Hughes 5.00 12.00
REDI David Irons 5.00 12.00
REDJ Dwayne Jarrett 6.00 15.00
REDR Darrelle Revis 6.00 15.00
REDW Darius Walker 5.00 12.00
REEW Eric Wright 5.00 12.00
REGA Gaines Adams 6.00 15.00
REGR Gary Russell 6.00 15.00
REHB H.B. Blades/89 5.00 12.00
REIS Isaiah Stanback 5.00 12.00
REJB John Beck 5.00 12.00
REJF Joel Filani 5.00 12.00
REJH Jason Hill 5.00 12.00
REJR JaMarcus Russell 5.00 12.00
REJT Joe Thomas 8.00 20.00
REKI Kenny Irons 5.00 12.00
REKK Kevin Kolb 6.00 15.00
RELH Leon Hall 5.00 12.00
RELL LaRon Landry 8.00 20.00
RELT Lawrence Timmons 8.00 20.00
REMG Michael Griffin 5.00 12.00
REML Marshawn Lynch 15.00 30.00
REMM Marcus McCauley 5.00 12.00
REPI Antonio Pittman 5.00 12.00
REPW Patrick Willis 8.00 20.00
RERM Robert Meachem 6.00 15.00
RERO Jeff Rowe 5.00 12.00
RESB Steve Breaston 5.00 12.00
RESC Scott Chandler 8.00 20.00
RESR Sidney Rice 6.00 15.00
RESS Steve Smith USC 5.00 12.00
RESY Selvin Young 5.00 12.00
RETG Ted Ginn Jr. 6.00 15.00
RETH Tony Hunt 5.00 12.00
RETM Tyrone Moss 5.00 12.00
RETP Tyler Palko 8.00 20.00
REWI Paul Williams 5.00 12.00
REYF Yamon Figurs 5.00 12.00
REZM Zach Miller 5.00 12.00

2007 SP Rookie Threads Rookie STATure

STATED PRINT RUN 9-45
SERIAL #'d UNDER 15 NOT PRICED
RSTAG Anthony Gonzalez/13
RSTBJ Brandon Jackson/10
RSTBL Brian Leonard/45 6.00 15.00
RSTBQ Brady Quinn/37 4.00 10.00
RSTCJ Calvin Johnson/15 30.00 80.00
RSTDB Dwayne Bowe/12
RSTDJ Dwayne Jarrett/12
RSTDS Drew Stanton/12
RSTGW Garrett Wolfe/19 8.00 20.00
RSTHI Jason Hill/13
RSTJB John Beck/32 8.00 20.00
RSTJH Johnnie Lee Higgins/13
RSTJR JaMarcus Russell/28 10.00 25.00
RSTJT Joe Thomas/39 6.00 15.00
RSTKK Kevin Kolb/30 5.00 12.00
RSTPW Patrick Willis/11
RSTSS Steve Smith USC/9
RSTTE Trent Edwards/17 10.00 25.00
RSTTH Tony Hunt/14
RSTTS Troy Smith/30 8.00 20.00
RSTWI Paul Williams/17 8.00 20.00

2007 SP Rookie Threads Rookie Threads Silver

*BRONZE/225: .5X TO 1.2X BASIC INSERTS
BRONZE PRINT RUN 225 SER.#'d SETS
*GOLD/150: .5X TO 1.2X BASIC INSERTS
GOLD PRINT RUN 150 SER.#'d SETS
*GOLD HOLO/99: .6X TO 1.5X BASIC INSERTS
GOLD HOLO.PRINT RUN 99 SER.#'d SETS
*GOLD PATCH: .6X TO 1.5X BASIC INSERTS
GOLD PATCH CARDS NOT SERIAL #'d
RTAG Anthony Gonzalez 1.50 4.00
RTAP Adrian Peterson 5.00 12.00
RTAP2 Adrian Peterson 5.00 12.00
RTBJ Brandon Jackson 1.50 4.00
RTBL Brian Leonard 1.50 4.00
RTBQ Brady Quinn 1.50 4.00
RTBQ2 Brady Quinn 1.50 4.00
RTCH Chris Henry RB 1.50 4.00
RTCJ Calvin Johnson 5.00 12.00
RTCJ2 Calvin Johnson 5.00 12.00
RTDB Dwayne Bowe 1.50 4.00
RTDB2 Dwayne Bowe 1.50 4.00
RTDJ Dwayne Jarrett 2.00 5.00
RTDS Drew Stanton 1.50 4.00
RTGA Gaines Adams 2.00 5.00
RTGO Greg Olsen 2.50 6.00
RTGW Garrett Wolfe 1.50 4.00
RTHI Johnnie Lee Higgins 1.50 4.00
RTJB John Beck 1.50 4.00
RTJH Jason Hill 1.50 4.00
RTJR JaMarcus Russell 1.50 4.00
RTJR2 JaMarcus Russell 1.50 4.00
RTJT Joe Thomas 2.50 6.00
RTKI Kenny Irons 1.50 4.00
RTKK Kevin Kolb 2.00 5.00
RTLB Lorenzo Booker 2.00 5.00
RTMB Michael Bush 1.50 4.00
RTML Marshawn Lynch 3.00 8.00
RTML2 Marshawn Lynch 3.00 8.00
RTPI Antonio Pittman 1.50 4.00
RTPW Patrick Willis 2.50 6.00
RTRM Robert Meachem 2.00 5.00
RTRM2 Robert Meachem 2.00 5.00
RTSR Sidney Rice 2.00 5.00
RTSS Steve Smith USC 1.50 4.00
RTTE Trent Edwards 1.50 4.00
RTTG Ted Ginn Jr. 2.00 5.00
RTTG2 Ted Ginn Jr. 2.00 5.00
RTTH Tony Hunt 1.50 4.00
RTTS Troy Smith 1.50 4.00
RTWI Paul Williams 1.50 4.00
RTYF Yamon Figurs 1.50 4.00

2007 SP Rookie Threads Rookie Threads Autographs

STATED PRINT RUN 25 SER.#'d SETS
UNPRICED HOLOFOIL PRINT RUN 10
RTAG Anthony Gonzalez 8.00 20.00
RTAP Adrian Peterson 100.00 200.00
RTAP2 Adrian Peterson 100.00 200.00
RTBJ Brandon Jackson 8.00 20.00
RTBL Brian Leonard 8.00 20.00
RTBQ Brady Quinn 8.00 20.00
RTBQ2 Brady Quinn 8.00 20.00
RTCJ Calvin Johnson 60.00 120.00
RTCJ2 Calvin Johnson 60.00 120.00
RTDB Dwayne Bowe 8.00 20.00
RTDB2 Dwayne Bowe 8.00 20.00
RTDJ Dwayne Jarrett 10.00 25.00
RTGO Greg Olsen 12.00 30.00
RTGW Garrett Wolfe 8.00 20.00
RTHI Johnnie Lee Higgins 8.00 20.00
RTJH Jason Hill 8.00 20.00
RTJR JaMarcus Russell 8.00 20.00
RTJR2 JaMarcus Russell 8.00 20.00
RTJT Joe Thomas 12.00 30.00
RTKI Kenny Irons 8.00 20.00
RTKK Kevin Kolb 10.00 25.00
RTMB Michael Bush 8.00 20.00
RTML Marshawn Lynch 25.00 50.00
RTML2 Marshawn Lynch 15.00 40.00
RTPI Antonio Pittman 8.00 20.00
RTPW Patrick Willis 12.00 30.00
RTRM Robert Meachem 10.00 25.00
RTRM2 Robert Meachem 10.00 25.00
RTSR Sidney Rice 10.00 25.00
RTSS Steve Smith USC 8.00 20.00
RTTE Trent Edwards 8.00 20.00
RTTG Ted Ginn Jr. 10.00 25.00
RTTG2 Ted Ginn Jr. 10.00 25.00
RTTH Tony Hunt 8.00 20.00
RTWI Paul Williams 8.00 20.00
RTYF Yamon Figurs 8.00 20.00

2007 SP Rookie Threads Rookie Threads Dual

UNPRICED BRONZE PATCH SER.#'d TO 10
UNPRICED GOLD PATCH SER.#'d TO 1
AW G.Adams/P.Willis 2.50 6.00
BE J.Beck/T.Edwards 1.50 4.00
BR J.Russell/D.Bowe 1.50 4.00
EL T.Edwards/M.Lynch 3.00 8.00
GB T.Ginn Jr./J.Beck 3.00 8.00
GG T.Ginn Jr./A.Gonzalez 4.00 10.00
HB C.Henry RB/L.Booker 3.00 8.00
HF J.Higgins/Y.Figurs 3.00 8.00
HL C.Henry RB/M.Lynch 3.00 8.00
HW J.Hill/P.Williams 3.00 8.00
IH K.Irons/T.Hunt 3.00 8.00
JR C.Johnson/J.Russell 8.00 20.00
JS C.Johnson/D.Stanton 8.00 20.00
LB B.Leonard/M.Bush 3.00 8.00
MB R.Meachem/D.Bowe 2.00 5.00
PJ A.Peterson/B.Jackson 10.00 25.00
PL A.Peterson/M.Lynch 10.00 25.00
PR A.Peterson/S.Rice 10.00 25.00
QR B.Quinn/J.Russell 1.50 4.00
QT B.Quinn/J.Thomas 2.50 6.00
RB J.Russell/M.Bush 5.00 12.00
SD D.Jarrett/S.Smith USC 3.00 8.00
SK D.Stanton/K.Kolb 2.00 5.00
SP T.Smith/A.Pittman 3.00 8.00
WO G.Wolfe/G.Olsen 5.00 12.00

2007 SP Rookie Threads Rookie Threads Triple

UNPRICED BRONZE PATCH SER.#'d TO 5
UNPRICED GOLD PATCH SER.#'d TO 1
ATW Adams/Thomas/Willis 6.00 15.00
GBB Ginn Jr./Beck/Booker 3.00 8.00
GGR Ginn Jr./Gonzalez/Rice 8.00 20.00
GSG Ginn Jr./Smith/Gonzalez 8.00 20.00
JHS Jarrett/Hill/Smith USC 3.00 8.00
JIH Jackson/Irons/Hunt 8.00 20.00
JJS Johnson/Jarrett/Smith USC 10.00 25.00
JMB Johnson/Meachem/Bowe 10.00 25.00
JRP Johnson/Russell/Peterson 15.00 40.00
JTR Johnson/Thomas/Russell 10.00 25.00
PHL Peterson/Henry RB/Lynch 12.00 30.00
PLB Pittman/Leonard/Booker 5.00 12.00
QRS Quinn/Russell/Smith 2.50 6.00
QSE Quinn/Stanton/Edwards 2.50 6.00
RBH Russell/Bush/Higgins 6.00 15.00
RWF Rice/Williams/Figurs 6.00 15.00
SBK Stanton/Beck/Kolb 3.00 8.00

2007 SP Rookie Threads Scripted in Time Autographs

STATED PRINT RUN 99-100
SITAB Anquan Boldin 6.00 15.00
SITAS Alex Smith QB 8.00 20.00
SITBA Marion Barber 8.00 20.00
SITBB Bernard Berrian 6.00 15.00
SITBF Brett Favre 100.00 200.00
SITBJ Bo Jackson 30.00 60.00
SITBM Brandon Marshall 8.00 20.00
SITBR Ronnie Brown 6.00 15.00
SITCA Jason Campbell 6.00 15.00
SITCB Champ Bailey 8.00 20.00
SITCJ Chad Johnson 6.00 15.00
SITCL Mark Clayton 6.00 15.00
SITCT Chester Taylor 6.00 15.00
SITCW Cadillac Williams 8.00 20.00
SITDB Drew Bennett 6.00 15.00
SITDD Donald Driver 15.00 30.00
SITDJ Darrell Jackson GRN 6.00 15.00
SITDJ2 Darrell Jackson WHT 6.00 15.00
SITDP Drew Pearson 8.00 20.00
SITDR Drew Brees 40.00 80.00
SITEM Eli Manning 40.00 80.00
SITFG Frank Gore 8.00 20.00
SITGJ Greg Jennings 6.00 15.00
SITJA Joseph Addai 6.00 15.00
SITJB Brandon Jacobs 6.00 15.00
SITJC Jerricho Cotchery 6.00 15.00
SITJL John Lynch
SITJL2 John Lynch
SITJT Joe Theismann 10.00 25.00
SITLE Lee Evans 8.00 20.00
SITLF Larry Fitzgerald 8.00 20.00
SITMA Marcus Allen 15.00 30.00
SITMB Marc Bulger/99 6.00 15.00
SITMC Marques Colston 6.00 15.00
SITML Matt Leinart 6.00 15.00
SITMS Matt Schaub 6.00 15.00
SITPH Paul Hornung 15.00 40.00
SITPM Peyton Manning 75.00 150.00
SITPM2 Peyton Manning 75.00 150.00
SITPR Philip Rivers 10.00 25.00
SITRB Reggie Brown 6.00 15.00
SITRC Roger Craig 8.00 20.00
SITTH T.J. Houshmandzadeh 6.00 15.00
SITVJ Vincent Jackson 6.00 15.00
SITWP Willie Parker 8.00 20.00

2007 SP Rookie Threads Signing Day Autographs

SDAAA Aundrae Allison 3.00 8.00
SDAAB Alan Branch 3.00 8.00
SDAAC Adam Carriker 3.00 8.00
SDAAO Amobi Okoye 4.00 10.00
SDAAP Antonio Pittman 3.00 8.00
SDABA David Ball 3.00 8.00
SDABJ Brandon Jackson 3.00 8.00
SDABL Brian Leonard 3.00 8.00
SDABM Brandon Meriweather 4.00 10.00
SDABO Dwayne Bowe 3.00 8.00
SDACD Craig Buster Davis 3.00 8.00
SDACH Chris Houston 3.00 8.00
SDACL Chris Leak 3.00 8.00
SDACS Chansi Stuckey 4.00 10.00
SDACT Courtney Taylor 3.00 8.00
SDADB Dallas Baker 3.00 8.00
SDADC David Clowney 3.00 8.00
SDADH Daymeion Hughes 3.00 8.00
SDADI David Irons 3.00 8.00
SDADR Darrelle Revis 4.00 10.00
SDADS Drew Stanton 3.00 8.00
SDADT Drew Tate 4.00 10.00
SDADW Darius Walker 3.00 8.00
SDAEW Eric Wright 3.00 8.00
SDAGA Gaines Adams 4.00 10.00
SDAGO Greg Olsen 5.00 12.00
SDAGR Gary Russell 4.00 10.00
SDAGW Garrett Wolfe 3.00 8.00
SDAHB H.B. Blades 3.00 8.00
SDAIS Isaiah Stanback 3.00 8.00
SDAJA Jamaal Anderson 4.00 10.00
SDAJF Joel Filani 3.00 8.00
SDAJH Jason Hill 3.00 8.00
SDAJP Jordan Palmer 4.00 10.00
SDAJR Jeff Rowe 3.00 8.00
SDAJT Joe Thomas 5.00 12.00
SDAJZ Jared Zabransky 3.00 8.00
SDAKD Kenneth Darby 3.00 8.00
SDAKS Kolby Smith 3.00 8.00
SDALB Lorenzo Booker 4.00 10.00
SDALH Leon Hall 3.00 8.00
SDALL LaRon Landry 5.00 12.00
SDALN Legedu Naanee 4.00 10.00
SDALT Lawrence Timmons 5.00 12.00
SDALW LaMarr Woodley 8.00 20.00
SDAMA Marcus McCauley 3.00 8.00
SDAMB Michael Bush 3.00 8.00
SDAMG Michael Griffin 3.00 8.00
SDAMM Matt Moore 5.00 12.00
SDAPP Paul Posluszny 3.00 8.00
SDAPW Patrick Willis 5.00 12.00
SDAQM Quentin Moses 3.00 8.00
SDARM Rhema McKnight 3.00 8.00
SDARN Reggie Nelson 3.00 8.00
SDASC Scott Chandler 5.00 12.00
SDASN Syvelle Newton 4.00 10.00
SDASY Selvin Young 8.00 20.00
SDATE Trent Edwards 15.00 40.00
SDATH Tony Hunt 3.00 8.00
SDATM Tyrone Moss 3.00 8.00
SDATP Tyler Palko 5.00 12.00
SDAWR Dwayne Wright 3.00 8.00
SDAWY DeShawn Wynn 3.00 8.00
SDAYF Yamon Figurs 3.00 8.00
SDAZM Zach Miller 3.00 8.00

2007 SP Rookie Threads SP Multi Marks Autographs Dual

STATED PRINT RUN 75 SER.#'d SETS
AR J.Addai/J.Russell 10.00 25.00
AS S.Rice/A.Allison 8.00 20.00
BB C.Bailey/R.Brown 8.00 20.00
BE M.Bulger/T.Edwards 6.00 15.00
BH D.Bennett/J.Hill 6.00 15.00
BL Leinart/R.Bush 30.00 80.00
BM B.Jacobs/M.Barber 15.00 40.00
BR D.Revis/H.Blades 8.00 20.00
BS A.Smith QB/J.Beck 8.00 20.00
BW B.Berrian/P.Williams 6.00 15.00
CO G.Olsen/S.Chandler 10.00 25.00
DB C.Davis/D.Bowe 6.00 15.00
DD D.Brees/D.Stanton 30.00 60.00
DJ D.Driver/G.Jennings 10.00 25.00
DM R.Meachem/C.Davis 8.00 20.00
EL M.Leinart/T.Edwards 6.00 15.00
FH T.Houshmandzadeh/Y.Figurs 6.00 15.00
FJ V.Jackson/Y.Figurs 6.00 15.00
FM F.Gore/M.Bush 8.00 20.00
GE L.Evans/A.Gonzalez 8.00 20.00
GP T.Ginn Jr./A.Pittman 8.00 20.00
GY S.Young/M.Griffin 6.00 15.00
HH L.Hall/D.Hughes 6.00 15.00
HJ V.Jackson/J.Higgins 6.00 15.00
HL M.Lynch/D.Hughes 12.00 30.00
HP J.Palmer/J.Higgins 8.00 20.00
HW L.Hall/L.Woodley 12.00 30.00
JB D.Jackson/D.Baker 6.00 15.00
JC B.Jackson/A.Carriker 6.00 15.00
JJ Chad John/Cal.Jhn 40.00 100.00
JM C.Johnson/Meachem 40.00 100.00
JT C.Taylor/B.Jackson 6.00 15.00
LB L.Landry/D.Bowe 10.00 25.00
LC J.Campbell/C.Leak 6.00 15.00
LH L.Hall/L.Landry 10.00 25.00
QS Quinn/Stanton 12.00 30.00
RB J.Russell/D.Bowe 6.00 15.00
RC Cotchery/Rivers 15.00 40.00
RP A.Pittman/G.Russell 8.00 20.00
SK M.Schaub/K.Kolb 15.00 40.00
WJ De.Williams/Jarrett 8.00 20.00
WW D.Walker/G.Wolfe 6.00 15.00

2007 SP Rookie Threads SP Multi Marks Autographs Triple

STATED PRINT RUN 25 SER.#'d SETS
AAC Anderson/Adams/Carriker
ARD Addai/Russell/Davis 25.00 60.00
BHL Henry RB/Leonard/Booker 20.00 50.00
CBW Brown/Will/Camp 25.00 60.00
ESQ Quinn/Stanton/Edwrd 20.00 50.00
FSQ Fvre/A.Smt/Qnn 150.00 250.00
GGP Ginn Jr./Pittman/Gonzalez 40.00 80.00
HWB Hall/Branch/Woodley 20.00 50.00
JBC Boldin/Cotchery/Johnson
JSC Johnson/Clowney/Stuckey
JTA Johnson/Adams/Thomas
LNB Leak/Nelson/Baker 15.00 40.00
MOC Olsen/Miller/Chandler 20.00 50.00
NML Nelson/Landry/Meriweather 15.00 40.00
PBR Beck/Palmer/Rowe 20.00 50.00
RHW Hall/Revis/Wright 25.00 60.00
RLB Russell/Landry/Bowe 30.00 80.00
SHB Bennett/Hill/Smith USC 20.00 50.00
TAO Adams/Thomas/Olsen
WBL Lynch/Wolfe/Bush 30.00 80.00
WTB Willis/Timmons/Blades 20.00 50.00
WWM Wright/McCauley/Williams 20.00 50.00
YRC Cmpbll/Yng/Russ 20.00 50.00

2008 SP Rookie Threads

This set was released on October 2, 2008. The base set consists of 160 cards. Cards 1-100 feature veterans, and cards 101-160 are rookies serial numbered of various quantities ranging from 152-402 that feature autographs and jersey swatches.

COMP.SET w/o RC's (100) 25.00 50.00
ROOKIE AU ANNOUNCED PRINT RUN 152-402
ACTUAL ROOKIE AU SERIAL #'s 18-87
1 Matt Leinart .40 1.00
2 Anquan Boldin .40 1.00
3 Larry Fitzgerald .50 1.25
4 Edgerrin James .50 1.25
5 Warrick Dunn .40 1.00
6 DeAngelo Hall .40 1.00
7 Todd Heap .40 1.00
8 Ray Lewis .60 1.50
9 Ed Reed .50 1.25
10 Trent Edwards .40 1.00
11 Marshawn Lynch .50 1.25
12 Lee Evans .50 1.25
13 Steve Smith .50 1.25
14 DeAngelo Williams .40 1.00
15 Julius Peppers .50 1.25
16 Brian Urlacher .60 1.50
17 Devin Hester .50 1.25
18 Rex Grossman .40 1.00
19 Carson Palmer .50 1.25
20 T.J. Houshmandzadeh .40 1.00
21 Rudi Johnson .40 1.00
22 Braylon Edwards .40 1.00
23 Kellen Winslow Jr. .40 1.00
24 Jamal Lewis .50 1.25
25 Terrell Owens .50 1.25
26 Tony Romo .50 1.25
27 Marion Barber .40 1.00
28 Jay Cutler .40 1.00
29 Brandon Marshall .50 1.25
30 Champ Bailey .50 1.25
31 Willis McGahee .40 1.00
32 Jon Kitna .40 1.00
33 Calvin Johnson .60 1.50
34 Brett Favre 1.25 3.00
35 Greg Jennings .40 1.00
36 Ryan Grant .50 1.25
37 A.J. Hawk .40 1.00
38 DeMeco Ryans .50 1.25
39 Andre Johnson .50 1.25
40 Matt Schaub .40 1.00
41 Peyton Manning 1.50 4.00
42 Reggie Wayne .50 1.25
43 Bob Sanders .50 1.25
44 David Garrard .40 1.00
45 Maurice Jones-Drew .40 1.00
46 Fred Taylor .40 1.00
47 Brodie Croyle .50 1.25
48 Larry Johnson .40 1.00
49 Derrick Johnson .40 1.00
50 Chad Johnson .40 1.00
51 Jason Taylor .50 1.25
52 John Beck .40 1.00
53 Tarvaris Jackson .40 1.00
54 Adrian Peterson .60 1.50
55 Darren Sharper .40 1.00
56 Tom Brady 2.00 5.00
57 Laurence Maroney .50 1.25
58 Randy Moss .50 1.25
59 Wes Welker .50 1.25
60 Drew Brees .60 1.50
61 Marques Colston .40 1.00
62 Reggie Bush .40 1.00
63 Eli Manning .50 1.25
64 Antonio Pierce .40 1.00
65 Aaron Ross .40 1.00
66 Brandon Jacobs .40 1.00
67 Thomas Jones .40 1.00
68 Kellen Clemens .40 1.00
69 Jerricho Cotchery .40 1.00
70 JaMarcus Russell .40 1.00
71 Kirk Morrison .40 1.00
72 Ronald Curry .40 1.00
73 Donovan McNabb .50 1.25
74 Brian Dawkins .60 1.50
75 Brian Westbrook .40 1.00
76 Ben Roethlisberger .60 1.50
77 Willie Parker .50 1.25
78 Santonio Holmes .40 1.00
79 LaDainian Tomlinson .60 1.50
80 Antonio Cromartie .40 1.00
81 Shawne Merriman .40 1.00
82 Antonio Gates .50 1.25
83 Frank Gore .50 1.25
84 Alex Smith QB .50 1.25
85 Patrick Willis .50 1.25
86 Matt Hasselbeck .40 1.00
87 Clinton Portis .40 1.00
88 Deion Branch .40 1.00
89 Marc Bulger .40 1.00
90 Torry Holt .50 1.25
91 Steven Jackson .40 1.00
92 Jeff Garcia .40 1.00
93 Cadillac Williams .50 1.25
94 Joey Galloway .50 1.25
95 Vince Young .40 1.00
96 LenDale White .40 1.00
97 Alge Crumpler .40 1.00
98 Jason Campbell .40 1.00
99 Chris Cooley .40 1.00
100 LaRon Landry .50 1.25
AA59 A.Arrington AU/252* RC 5.00 12.00
AH12 Ali Highsmith AU/252* RC 5.00 12.00
AT14 Aqib Talib AU/250* RC 8.00 20.00
AW43 A.Woodson AU/252* RC 5.00 12.00
BB39 Brian Brohm AU/250* RC 5.00 12.00
BD13 Bruce Davis AU/250* RC 6.00 15.00
BE46 Davone Bess AU/352* RC 6.00 15.00
CB41 Colt Brennan AU/252* RC 6.00 15.00
CC15 Calais Campbell AU/248* RC 6.00 15.00
CH38 Chad Henne AU/250* RC 12.00 30.00
CJ44 Chris Johnson AU/252* RC 6.00 15.00
CL45 Chris Long AU/252* RC 10.00 25.00
DA17 Donnie Avery AU/250* RC 6.00 15.00
DB10 D.Bryant AU/348* RC UER 6.00 15.00
DC16 Dan Connor AU/252* RC 5.00 12.00
DD47 Dennis Dixon AU/250* RC 12.50 25.00
DJ37 D.Jackson AU/154* RC 8.00 20.00
DM1 D.McFadden AU/152* RC 5.00 12.00
EA49 Erik Ainge AU/250* RC 5.00 12.00
ED48 Early Doucet AU/252* RC 5.00 12.00
FD51 Fred Davis AU/250* RC 5.00 12.00
FJ50 Felix Jones AU/250* RC 5.00 12.00
FO5 Matt Forte AU/250* RC 20.00 50.00
JB54 J.David Booty AU/250* RC 5.00 12.00
JC52 J.Charles AU/245* RC 12.00 30.00
JF53 Joe Flacco AU/252* RC 20.00 50.00
JH19 Jacob Hester AU/252* RC 5.00 12.00
JJ22 Josh Johnson AU/245* RC 5.00 12.00
JK23 Justin King AU/252* RC 6.00 15.00
JL20 Jake Long AU/248* RC 8.00 20.00
JL21 J Leman AU/250* RC 5.00 12.00
JN55 Jordy Nelson AU/252* RC 25.00 60.00
JS2 J.Stewart AU/245* RC 8.00 20.00
KO26 K.O'Connell AU/248* RC 5.00 12.00
KP25 Kenny Phillips AU/256* RC 5.00 12.00
KR24 Keith Rivers AU/252* RC 5.00 12.00
KS57 Kevin Smith AU/250* RC 5.00 12.00
LH27 Lavelle Hawkins AU/252* RC 6.00 15.00
LJ28 L.Jackson AU/259* RC 5.00 12.00
LM30 Leodis McKelvin AU/248* RC 6.00 15.00
LS58 Limas Sweed AU/250* RC 5.00 12.00
MF4 Matt Flynn AU/250* RC 5.00 12.00
MH6 Mike Hart AU/248* RC 5.00 12.00
MJ7 Mike Jenkins AU/252* RC 5.00 12.00
MK60 Malcolm Kelly AU/250* RC 5.00 12.00
MR40 Matt Ryan AU/152* RC 50.00 100.00
PH56 Philip Wheeler AU/252* RC 6.00 15.00
PS29 Paul Smith AU/250* RC 5.00 12.00
QG31 Quentin Groves AU/252* RC 6.00 15.00
RM42 R.Mendenhall AU/250* RC 5.00 12.00
RR8 Ray Rice AU/252* RC 5.00 12.00
SB32 Sam Baker AU/250* RC 5.00 12.00
SC33 Shawn Crable AU/402* RC 5.00 12.00
SS9 Steve Slaton AU/252* RC 5.00 12.00
TC11 Tashard Choice AU/252* RC 5.00 12.00
TZ35 Tom Zbikowski AU/252* RC 6.00 15.00
VG34 Vernon Gholston AU/248* RC 5.00 12.00
XA36 Xavier Adibi AU/250* RC 5.00 12.00

2008 SP Rookie Threads Flashback Fabrics 175-200

FF DIE CUT PRINT RUN 175-200
*SQUARE/99-115: .4X TO 1X JSY/175-200
SQUARE DIE CUT PRINT RUN 99-115
*DIAMOND/85: .4X TO 1X JSY/175-200
DIAMOND DIE CUT PRINT RUN 85
*TRAPEZOID/50-60: .4X TO 1X JSY/175-200
TRAPEZOID DIE CUT PRINT RUN 50-60
*UD LOGO/25-30: .5X TO 1.2X JSY/175-200
UD LOGO DIE CUT PRINT RUN 25-30
*SHIELD/15-20: .5X TO 1.2X JSY/175-200
SHIELD DIE CUT PRINT RUN 15-20
SERIAL #'d 1/1 TOO SCARCE TO PRCE
FFAG Anthony Gonzalez 2.00 5.00
FFAH A.J. Hawk 2.00 5.00
FFAP Adrian Peterson 3.00 8.00
FFAS Alex Smith QB 2.50 6.00
FFAV Jason Avant 2.00 5.00
FFBE Braylon Edwards 2.00 5.00
FFBM Brandon Marshall 2.50 6.00
FFBQ Brady Quinn 2.00 5.00
FFBR Ben Roethlisberger 3.00 8.00
FFCF Charlie Frye 2.00 5.00
FFCH Chris Henry RB 2.50 6.00
FFCJ Calvin Johnson 3.00 8.00
FFCP Carson Palmer/175 2.50 6.00
FFCW Cadillac Williams 2.50 6.00
FFDB Dwayne Bowe 2.50 6.00
FFDS Drew Stanton 3.00 8.00
FFEM Eli Manning 2.50 6.00
FFFG Frank Gore 2.50 6.00
FFGA Gaines Adams 2.00 5.00
FFGO Greg Olsen 2.50 6.00
FFGW Garrett Wolfe 2.50 6.00
FFJA Chad Jackson 2.50 6.00
FFJB John Beck 2.00 5.00
FFJC Jason Campbell 2.00 5.00
FFJK Joe Klopfenstein 2.00 5.00
FFJR JaMarcus Russell 2.00 5.00
FFJT Joe Thomas 2.50 6.00
FFKI Kenny Irons 2.00 5.00
FFKK Kevin Kolb 2.00 5.00
FFLE Matt Leinart 2.00 5.00
FFLF Larry Fitzgerald 2.50 6.00
FFLM Laurence Maroney 2.50 6.00
FFLW LenDale White/175 2.00 5.00
FFLY Marshawn Lynch 2.50 6.00
FFMC Mark Clayton 2.00 5.00
FFMH Michael Huff 2.00 5.00
FFMJ Maurice Jones-Drew 2.00 5.00
FFML Marcedes Lewis 2.00 5.00
FFPW Patrick Willis 2.50 6.00
FFRB Reggie Bush 2.00 5.00

FFRM Robert Meachem 2.00 5.00
FFRO Ronnie Brown 2.00 5.00
FFSH Santonio Holmes 2.00 5.00
FFSJ Steven Jackson 2.00 5.00
FFSM Sinorice Moss 2.50 6.00
FFSR Sidney Rice 2.00 5.00
FFSS Steve Smith USC 2.50 6.00
FFTE Trent Edwards 2.00 5.00
FFTJ Tarvaris Jackson 2.00 5.00
FFTS Troy Smith 2.50 6.00
FFTW Travis Wilson 2.00 5.00
FFVY Vince Young/175 2.00 5.00
FFWI Troy Williamson/175 2.00 5.00

2008 SP Rookie Threads Legendary Numbers 99

STARS PRINT RUN 99 SER.#'d SETS
*INITIALS/50: .5X TO 1.2X STARS/99
PLAYER INITIALS PRINT RUN 50
*BADGE/15: .6X TO 1.5X BASIC JSY/99
BADGE DIE CUT PRINT RUN 15
JERSEY 1/1 TOO SCARCE TO PRICE
*JSY NUM/80: .4X TO 1X BASIC JSY/99
*JSY NUM/20-40: .5X TO 1.2X BASIC JSY/99
JERSEY NUMBER PRINT RUN 7-40
LNBJ Bo Jackson 8.00 20.00
LNBS Barry Sanders 8.00 20.00
LNDM Dan Marino 10.00 25.00
LNGS Gale Sayers 8.00 20.00
LNHW Herschel Walker 5.00 12.00
LNJE John Elway 8.00 20.00
LNJM Jim McMahon 5.00 12.00
LNJR Jerry Rice 10.00 25.00
LNJT Joe Theismann 5.00 12.00
LNKA Ken Anderson 4.00 10.00
LNKS Ken Stabler 5.00 12.00
LNMO Joe Montana 15.00 40.00
LNRC Roger Craig 4.00 10.00
LNTB Terry Bradshaw 6.00 15.00

2008 SP Rookie Threads Multi Marks Dual

DUAL PRINT RUN 15-399
UNPRICED SIX PRINT RUN 6
UNPRICED EIGHT PRINT RUN 8
MMD1 Stewart/Mendenhall/75 12.00 30.00
MMD2 L.Sweed/J.Hardy/299 8.00 20.00
MMD3 Sweed/Mendenhall/25 10.00 25.00
MMD4 B.Brohm/C.Henne/99 12.00 30.00
MMD5 J.Long/C.Long/299 8.00 20.00
MMD6 B.Brohm/M.Ryan/99 25.00 60.00
MMD7 J.Booty/C.Henne/99 12.00 30.00
MMD8 J.Charles/M.Forte/299 15.00 40.00
MMD10 Avery/De.Jackson/299 10.00 25.00
MMD11 K.Smith/S.Slaton/199 6.00 15.00
MMD12 G.Sayers/Peterson/99 75.00 150.00
MMD13 Woodson/E.Ainge/299 6.00 15.00
MMD14 D.Dixon/J.Booty/99 10.00 25.00
MMD15 McFadden/F.Jones/55 8.00 20.00
MMD16 J.Charles/J.Hester/206 6.00 15.00
MMD17 C.Jhnsn/Menden/75 10.00 25.00
MMD18 J.Stewart/D.Dixon/25 15.00 40.00
MMD19 T.Choice/J.Charles/299 10.00 25.00
MMD20 G.Sayers/M.Forte/99 40.00 80.00
MMD21 D.Avery/E.Doucet/299 6.00 15.00
MMD22 M.Ryan/H.Douglas/299 25.00 60.00
MMD23 Woodson/O'Connell/299 6.00 15.00
MMD24 Hawkins/D.Jcksn/299 10.00 25.00
MMD25 B.Brohm/J.Nelson/44 15.00 40.00
MMD26 Woodson/B.Brohm/199 8.00 20.00
MMD27 K.Rivers/S.Ellis/299 6.00 15.00
MMD28 Ca.Jhnsn/Colston/150 30.00 80.00
MMD30 Rathman/Johnston/25 25.00 50.00
MMD31 Rathman/R.Craig/25 35.00 60.00
MMD32 C.Steltz/C.Jackson/299 5.00 12.00
MMD33 M.Barber/F.Jones/25 10.00 25.00
MMD34 R.Rice/M.Hart/299 5.00 12.00
MMD35 T.Choice/F.Jones/299 5.00 12.00
MMD36 V.Gholston/C.Long/99 8.00 20.00
MMD38 B.Croyle/D.Bowe/25 8.00 20.00
MMD39 Garrard/J.Campbell/50 12.00 30.00
MMD40 Y.Tittle/P.Hornung/99 20.00 40.00
MMD41 P.Hornung/J.Kramer/99 20.00 40.00
MMD43 B.Jones/K.Anderson/35 15.00 30.00
MMD45 Zbikowski/Jenkins/399 6.00 15.00
MMD46 M.Bulger/R.Gabriel/15 30.00 60.00
MMD47 Campbell/Theismann/50 20.00 40.00
MMD48 D.Keller/J.Carlson/288 6.00 15.00
MMD49 Ross/A.Bradshaw/250 8.00 20.00
MMD50 Woodson/J.Booty/199 8.00 20.00

2008 SP Rookie Threads Multi Marks Triple

STATED PRINT RUN 15-75
MMT1 Rice/Forte/Johnson/35 25.00 60.00
MMT2 Rodgers/Brohm/Flynn
MMT3 Ryan/Brohm/Flacco/15 60.00 125.00
MMT4 Kelly/Sweed/Jackson
MMT5 Keller/Carlson/Davis/55 8.00 20.00
MMT6 Sweed/Royal/Hardy
MMT7 Smith/Forte/Hart/35 30.00 60.00
MMT8 Henn/O'Cnn/Wdson/55 20.00 40.00
MMT9 Slaton/Rice/Johnson/35 15.00 40.00
MMT10 Bennett/Jackson/Avery
MMT11 Royal/Bennett/Doucet
MMT12 McFad/Jones/Stewart/15 20.00 50.00
MMT13 Flynn/Doucet/Hester
MMT14 McKlvn/Rdgr-Crm/Jnkns/55 10.00 25.00
MMT15 Long/Gholston/Hrvy/55 10.00 25.00
MMT16 Nelson/Douglas/Cldwll/75 15.00 40.00
MMT17 Booty/Dixon/Ainge/35 20.00 40.00
MMT18 Hester/Hillis/Schmitt/55 6.00 15.00
MMT19 Mann/Clark/Add/15 EXCH
MMT20 Andrsn/Edwrds/Brohm
MMT21 Peterson/Lynch/Portis/15 100.00 200.00
MMT22 Ware/Brbr/Jnes/15 25.00 60.00
MMT23 Lambert/Ham/Blount
MMT24 Thomas/Davis/Kelly
MMT25 Flacco/Rice/Zbikow/55 25.00 50.00

2008 SP Rookie Threads Multi Marks Quad

STATED PRINT RUN 5-45
SERIAL #'d UNDER 15 NOT PRICED
MMQ3 Swd/Bnn/Jcksn/Avry/25 15.00 40.00
MMQ4 Forte/Rice/Hstr/Smth/40 15.00 40.00
MMQ5 O'Cnn/Bty/Wdsn/Brnn/25 12.00 30.00
MMQ6 Lng/Ghol/Hrvy/Jcksn/40 10.00 25.00
MMQ7 McKlv/R-Cr/Jnk/Csn/45 12.00 30.00
MMQ9 Doucet/Royal/Douglas/Caldwell
MMQ10 Kllr/Dvis/Crlsn/Bnntt/45 12.00 30.00
MMQ11 Cnnr/Rvrs/Adibi/Dvs/45 10.00 25.00
MMQ12 Tittle/Tarkenton/Gabriel/Griese
MMQ13 Garcia/Garrard/Campbell/Bulger
MMQ14 Theismann/Anderson/Jones/Stabler

2008 SP Rookie Threads Rookie Lettermen College Autographs

*SINGLES: .4X TO 1X BASE AU RC
ANNOUNCED PRINT RUN 72-126
ACTUAL CARD SERIAL NUMBERING
DM1 Darren McFadden JSY AU/72* 15.00 40.00
FO5 Matt Forte JSY AU/120* 15.00 40.00
JS2 Jonathan Stewart JSY AU/120* 20.00 50.00
MF4 Matt Flynn JSY AU/120* 5.00 12.00
MH6 Mike Hart JSY AU/120* 5.00 12.00
MJ7 Mike Jenkins JSY AU/120* 5.00 12.00
RR8 Ray Rice JSY AU/126* 5.00 12.00
SS9 Steve Slaton JSY AU/120* 5.00 12.00
AA59 Adrian Arrington JSY AU/120* 5.00 12.00
AH12 Ali Highsmith JSY AU/120* 5.00 12.00
AT14 Aqib Talib JSY AU/120* 8.00 20.00
AW43 Andre Woodson JSY AU/120* 5.00 12.00
BB39 Brian Brohm JSY AU/120* 5.00 12.00
BD13 Bruce Davis JSY AU/124* 6.00 15.00
BE46 Davone Bess JSY AU/126* 6.00 15.00
CB41 Colt Brennan JSY AU/120* 6.00 15.00
CC15 Calais Campbell JSY AU/120* 6.00 15.00
CH38 Chad Henne JSY AU/120* 12.00 30.00
CJ44 Chris Johnson JSY AU/120* 25.00 60.00
CL45 Chris Long JSY AU/120* 6.00 15.00
DA17 Donnie Avery JSY AU/126* 6.00 15.00
DB10 Dorien Bryant JSY AU/126* 6.00 15.00
DC16 Dan Connor JSY AU/117* 5.00 12.00
DD47 Dennis Dixon JSY AU/126* 12.50 25.00
DJ37 DeSean Jackson JSY AU/120* 12.00 30.00
EA49 Erik Ainge JSY AU/126* 5.00 12.00
ED48 Early Doucet JSY AU/120* 5.00 12.00
FD51 Fred Davis JSY AU/120* 5.00 12.00
FJ50 Felix Jones JSY AU/120* 5.00 12.00
JB54 John David Booty JSY AU/120* 5.00 12.00
JC52 Jamaal Charles JSY AU/120* 20.00 50.00
JF53 Joe Flacco JSY AU/120* 15.00 40.00
JH19 Jacob Hester JSY AU/120* 5.00 12.00
JJ22 Josh Johnson JSY AU/120* 5.00 12.00
JK23 Justin King JSY AU/126* 6.00 15.00
JL20 Jake Long JSY AU/120* 8.00 20.00
JL21 J Leman JSY AU/120* 5.00 12.00
JN55 Jordy Nelson JSY AU/121* 20.00 40.00
KO26 Kevin O'Connell JSY AU/117* 5.00 12.00
KP25 Kenny Phillips JSY AU/120* 5.00 12.00
KR24 Keith Rivers JSY AU/120* 5.00 12.00
KS57 Kevin Smith JSY AU/120* 5.00 12.00
LH27 Lavelle Hawkins JSY AU/120* 6.00 15.00
LJ28 Lawrence Jackson JSY AU/120* 5.00 12.00
LM30 Leodis McKelvin JSY AU/116* 6.00 15.00
LS58 Limas Sweed JSY AU/120* 5.00 12.00
MK60 Malcolm Kelly JSY AU/120* 5.00 12.00
MR40 Matt Ryan JSY AU/78* 60.00 120.00
PH56 Philip Wheeler JSY AU/121* 6.00 15.00
PS29 Paul Smith JSY AU/120* 5.00 12.00
QG31 Quentin Groves JSY AU/120* 6.00 15.00
RM42 Rashard Mendenhall JSY AU/120* 5.00 12.00
SB32 Sam Baker JSY AU/120* 5.00 12.00
SC33 Shawn Crable JSY AU/120* 5.00 12.00
TC11 Tashard Choice JSY AU/121* 5.00 12.00
TZ35 Tom Zbikowski JSY AU/126* 6.00 15.00
VG34 Vernon Gholston JSY AU/126* 5.00 12.00
XA36 Xavier Adibi JSY AU/120* 5.00 12.00

2008 SP Rookie Threads Rookie Lettermen College Nickname Autographs

*SINGLES: .5X TO 1.2X BASE AU RC
ANNOUNCED PRINT RUN 45-60
ACTUAL CARD SERIAL NUMBERING
DM1 Darren McFadden JSY AU/48* 20.00 50.00
FO5 Matt Forte JSY AU/54* 20.00 50.00
JS2 Jonathan Stewart JSY AU/50* 20.00 50.00
MF4 Matt Flynn JSY AU/48* 6.00 15.00
MH6 Mike Hart JSY AU/50* 6.00 15.00
MJ7 Mike Jenkins JSY AU/50* 12.00 30.00
RR8 Ray Rice JSY AU/56* 6.00 15.00
SS9 Steve Slaton JSY AU/48* 25.00 50.00
AA59 Adrian Arrington JSY AU/50* 6.00 15.00
AH12 Ali Highsmith JSY AU/48* 6.00 15.00
AT14 Aqib Talib JSY AU/56* 10.00 25.00
AW43 Andre Woodson JSY AU/48* 6.00 15.00
BB39 Brian Brohm JSY AU/54* 6.00 15.00
BD13 Bruce Davis JSY AU/54* 8.00 20.00
BE46 Davone Bess JSY AU/48* 8.00 20.00
CB41 Colt Brennan JSY AU/48* 8.00 20.00
CC15 Calais Campbell JSY AU/50* 8.00 20.00
CH38 Chad Henne JSY AU/50* 40.00 80.00
CJ44 Chris Johnson JSY AU/49* 25.00 60.00
CL45 Chris Long JSY AU/54* 12.00 30.00
DA17 Donnie Avery JSY AU/49* 8.00 20.00
DB10 Dorien Bryant JSY AU/60* 8.00 20.00
DC16 Dan Connor JSY AU/48* 6.00 15.00
DD47 Dennis Dixon JSY AU/50* 15.00 30.00
DJ37 DeSean Jackson JSY AU/50* 12.00 30.00
EA49 Erik Ainge JSY AU/52* 6.00 15.00
ED48 Early Doucet JSY AU/48* 6.00 15.00
FD51 Fred Davis JSY AU/49* 6.00 15.00
FJ50 Felix Jones JSY AU/48* 6.00 15.00
JB54 John David Booty JSY AU/49* 6.00 15.00
JC52 Jamaal Charles JSY AU/54* 25.00 60.00
JF53 Joe Flacco JSY AU/56* 20.00 50.00
JH19 Jacob Hester JSY AU/48* 6.00 15.00
JJ22 Josh Johnson JSY AU/49* 6.00 15.00
JK23 Justin King JSY AU/48* 8.00 20.00
JL20 Jake Long JSY AU/50* 10.00 25.00
JL21 J Leman JSY AU/56* 6.00 15.00
JN55 Jordy Nelson JSY AU/56* 25.00 50.00
KO26 Kevin O'Connell JSY AU/48* 6.00 15.00
KP25 Kenny Phillips JSY AU/50* 6.00 15.00
KR24 Keith Rivers JSY AU/49* 6.00 15.00
KS57 Kevin Smith JSY AU/49* 6.00 15.00
LH27 Lavelle Hawkins JSY AU/50* 8.00 20.00
LJ28 Lawrence Jackson JSY AU/49* 6.00 15.00
LM30 Leodis McKelvin JSY AU/49* 8.00 20.00
LS58 Limas Sweed JSY AU/54* 6.00 15.00
MK60 Malcolm Kelly JSY AU/49* 6.00 15.00
MR40 Matt Ryan JSY AU/48* 60.00 120.00
PH56 Philip Wheeler JSY AU/52* 8.00 20.00
PS29 Paul Smith JSY AU/45* 6.00 15.00
QG31 Quentin Groves JSY AU/48* 8.00 20.00
RM42 Rashard Mendenhall JSY AU/56* 6.00 15.00
SB32 Sam Baker JSY AU/49* 6.00 15.00
SC33 Shawn Crable JSY AU/50* 6.00 15.00
TC11 Tashard Choice JSY AU/52* 6.00 15.00
TZ35 Tom Zbikowski JSY AU/52* 8.00 20.00
VG34 Vernon Gholston JSY AU/48* 6.00 15.00
XA36 Xavier Adibi JSY AU/48* 6.00 15.00

2008 SP Rookie Threads Rookie Numbers Silver 135

SILVER PRINT RUN 135
*HOLOFOIL/30: .5X TO 1.2X SILVER/135
HOLOFOIL PRINT RUN 30
*GOLD/72-87: .4X TO 1X SILVER JSY
*GOLD/17-39: .5X TO 1.2X SILVER JSY
GOLD PRINT RUN 1-87
*HOLO.PATCH/75: .6X TO 1.5X SLVR/135
HOLOFOIL PATCH PRINT RUN 75
RNAC Andre Caldwell 1.50 4.00
RNBB Brian Brohm 1.50 4.00
RNCH Chad Henne 2.00 5.00
RNCJ Chris Johnson 2.00 5.00
RNDA Donnie Avery 2.00 5.00
RNDJ DeSean Jackson 3.00 8.00
RNDK Dustin Keller 2.00 5.00
RNDM Darren McFadden 1.50 4.00
RNDT Devin Thomas 1.50 4.00
RNDX Dexter Jackson 2.50 6.00
RNEB Earl Bennett 2.50 6.00
RNED Early Doucet 1.50 4.00
RNER Eddie Royal 1.50 4.00
RNFJ Felix Jones 1.50 4.00
RNFO Matt Forte 2.50 6.00
RNGD Glenn Dorsey 1.50 4.00
RNHD Harry Douglas 2.00 5.00
RNJB John David Booty 1.50 4.00
RNJC Jamaal Charles 2.50 6.00
RNJF Joe Flacco 3.00 8.00
RNJH James Hardy 1.50 4.00
RNJL Jake Long 2.50 6.00
RNJN Jordy Nelson 5.00 12.00
RNJS Jonathan Stewart 2.50 6.00
RNKO Kevin O'Connell 1.50 4.00
RNKS Kevin Smith 1.50 4.00
RNLS Limas Sweed 1.50 4.00
RNMK Malcolm Kelly 1.50 4.00
RNMM Mario Manningham 1.50 4.00
RNMR Matt Ryan 5.00 12.00
RNRM Rashard Mendenhall 1.50 4.00
RNRR Ray Rice 1.50 4.00
RNSI Jerome Simpson 2.00 5.00
RNSS Steve Slaton 1.50 4.00

2008 SP Rookie Threads Rookie Super Swatch Blue 175

BLUE PRINT RUN 175 SER.#'d SETS
*GREEN/99: .4X TO 1X BLUE/175
GREEN PRINT RUN 99 SER.#'d SETS
*SILVER HOLO/55: .4X TO 1X BLUE/175
SILVER HOLOFOIL PRINT RUN 55
*GOLD HOLO/25: .5X TO 1.2X BLUE/175
GOLD HOLOFOIL PRINT RUN 25
*GOLD PATCH/25: .6X TO 1.5X BLUE/175
GOLD PATCH PRINT RUN 25
UNPRICED AUTO PRINT RUN 5-15
RSSAC Andre Caldwell 1.50 4.00
RSSBB Brian Brohm 1.50 4.00
RSSBE Earl Bennett 2.50 6.00
RSSCH Chad Henne 2.00 5.00
RSSCJ Chris Johnson 2.00 5.00
RSSDA Donnie Avery 2.00 5.00
RSSDJ DeSean Jackson 3.00 8.00
RSSDK Dustin Keller 2.00 5.00
RSSDM Darren McFadden 1.50 4.00
RSSDT Devin Thomas 1.50 4.00
RSSDX Dexter Jackson 2.50 6.00
RSSED Early Doucet 1.50 4.00
RSSER Eddie Royal 1.50 4.00
RSSFJ Felix Jones 1.50 4.00
RSSGD Glenn Dorsey 1.50 4.00
RSSHD Harry Douglas 2.00 5.00
RSSJB John David Booty 1.50 4.00
RSSJC Jamaal Charles 2.50 6.00
RSSJF Joe Flacco 3.00 8.00
RSSJH James Hardy 1.50 4.00
RSSJL Jake Long 2.50 6.00
RSSJN Jordy Nelson 5.00 12.00
RSSJS Jonathan Stewart 2.50 6.00
RSSKO Kevin O'Connell 1.50 4.00
RSSKS Kevin Smith 1.50 4.00
RSSLS Limas Sweed 1.50 4.00
RSSMF Matt Forte 2.50 6.00
RSSMK Malcolm Kelly 1.50 4.00
RSSMM Mario Manningham 1.50 4.00
RSSMR Matt Ryan 5.00 12.00
RSSRM Rashard Mendenhall 1.50 4.00
RSSRR Ray Rice 1.50 4.00
RSSSI Jerome Simpson 2.00 5.00
RSSSS Steve Slaton 1.50 4.00

2008 SP Rookie Threads Rookie Super Swatch Autographs

UNPRICED AUTO PRINT RUN 5-15

2008 SP Rookie Threads Rookie Threads 250

STATED PRINT RUN 250 SER.#'d SETS
*199: .4X TO 1X BASIC JSY/250
*125: .5X TO 1.2X BASIC JSY/250
*99: .5X TO 1.2X BASIC JSY/250
*75: .5X TO 1.2X BASIC JSY/250
*50: .5X TO 1.2X BASIC JSY/250
*25: .6X TO 1.5X BASIC JSY/250
*JSY NUM/72-87: .5X TO 1.2X JSY/250
*JSY NUM/17-39: .6X TO 1.5X JSY/250
*PATCH/99: .6X TO 1.5X JSY/250
*PATCH/75: .6X TO 1.5X JSY/250
*PATCH/25: .8X TO 2X JSY/250
*PATCH/15: .8X TO 2X JSY/250
*PATCH JSY #/72-87: .6X TO 1.5X JSY/250
*PATCH JSY #/17-39: .8X TO 2X JSY/250
RTAC Andre Caldwell 1.25 3.00
RTBB Brian Brohm 1.25 3.00
RTCH Chad Henne 1.50 4.00
RTCJ Chris Johnson 1.50 4.00
RTDA Donnie Avery 1.50 4.00
RTDJ DeSean Jackson 2.50 6.00
RTDK Dustin Keller 1.50 4.00
RTDM Darren McFadden 1.25 3.00
RTDT Devin Thomas 1.25 3.00
RTDX Dexter Jackson 2.00 5.00
RTEB Earl Bennett 2.00 5.00
RTED Early Doucet 1.25 3.00
RTER Eddie Royal 1.25 3.00
RTFJ Felix Jones 1.25 3.00
RTFO Matt Forte 2.00 5.00
RTGD Glenn Dorsey 1.25 3.00
RTHD Harry Douglas 1.50 4.00
RTJB John David Booty 1.25 3.00
RTJC Jamaal Charles 2.00 5.00
RTJF Joe Flacco 2.50 6.00
RTJH James Hardy 1.25 3.00
RTJL Jake Long 2.00 5.00
RTJN Jordy Nelson 4.00 10.00
RTJS Jonathan Stewart 2.00 5.00
RTKO Kevin O'Connell 1.25 3.00
RTKS Kevin Smith 1.25 3.00
RTLS Limas Sweed 1.25 3.00
RTMK Malcolm Kelly 1.25 3.00
RTMM Mario Manningham 1.25 3.00
RTMR Matt Ryan 4.00 10.00
RTRM Rashard Mendenhall 1.25 3.00
RTRR Ray Rice 1.25 3.00
RTSI Jerome Simpson 1.50 4.00
RTSS Steve Slaton 1.25 3.00

2008 SP Rookie Threads Rookie Threads Autographs 50

AUTO PRINT RUN 50 SER.#'d SETS
*AUTO POSIT/24-25: .5X TO 1.2X AU/50
AUTO POSITION PRINT RUN 24-25
AUTO/1 TOO SCARCE TO PRICE
*PATCH AU/24-25: .6X TO 1.5X AU/50
PATCH AUTO/1 TOO SCARCE TO PRICE
RTAC Andre Caldwell 5.00 12.00
RTBB Brian Brohm 5.00 12.00
RTCH Chad Henne 6.00 15.00
RTCJ Chris Johnson 6.00 15.00
RTDA Donnie Avery 6.00 15.00
RTDJ DeSean Jackson 20.00 50.00
RTDK Dustin Keller 6.00 15.00
RTDM Darren McFadden 12.00 30.00
RTDT Devin Thomas 5.00 12.00
RTDX Dexter Jackson 8.00 20.00
RTEB Earl Bennett 8.00 20.00
RTED Early Doucet 5.00 12.00
RTER Eddie Royal 5.00 12.00
RTFJ Felix Jones 5.00 12.00
RTFO Matt Forte 20.00 50.00
RTHD Harry Douglas 6.00 15.00
RTJB John David Booty 5.00 12.00
RTJC Jamaal Charles 20.00 50.00
RTJF Joe Flacco 15.00 40.00
RTJH James Hardy 5.00 12.00
RTJL Jake Long 8.00 20.00
RTJN Jordy Nelson 15.00 40.00
RTJS Jonathan Stewart 8.00 20.00
RTKO Kevin O'Connell 5.00 12.00
RTKS Kevin Smith 5.00 12.00
RTLS Limas Sweed 5.00 12.00
RTMK Malcolm Kelly 5.00 12.00
RTMM Mario Manningham 10.00 25.00
RTMR Matt Ryan 50.00 100.00
RTRM Rashard Mendenhall 5.00 12.00
RTRR Ray Rice 5.00 12.00
RTSI Jerome Simpson 6.00 15.00
RTSS Steve Slaton 5.00 12.00

2008 SP Rookie Threads Dual Threads 160

DUAL PRINT RUN 160 SER.#'d SETS
*DUAL/99: .5X TO 1.2X DUAL JSY/160
*DUAL/75: .5X TO 1.2X DUAL JSY/160
*DUAL/50: .5X TO 1.2X DUAL JSY/160
*DUAL PATCH/35: .8X TO 2X DUAL JSY/160
*DUAL/25: .6X TO 1.5X DUAL JSY/160
*DUAL/15: .6X TO 1.5X DUAL JSY/160
DUAL/2 TOO SCARCE TO PRICE
DTBR B.Brohm/M.Ryan 6.00 15.00
DTBS S.Slaton/B.Brohm 1.25 3.00
DTCM J.Long/C.Henne 2.00 5.00
DTDD G.Dorsey/E.Doucet 1.25 3.00
DTDF D.McFadden/F.Jones 1.50 4.00
DTDR E.Doucet/M.Ryan 6.00 15.00
DTFC J.Charles/M.Forte 2.00 5.00
DTFO J.Flacco/K.O'Connell 2.50 6.00
DTHF C.Henne/J.Flacco 2.50 6.00
DTHK J.Hardy/M.Kelly 1.25 3.00
DTJJ J.Stewart/J.Booty 2.00 5.00
DTJS C.Johnson/K.Smith 1.50 4.00
DTKT M.Kelly/D.Thomas 1.25 3.00
DTMJ D.McFadden/D.Jackson 3.00 8.00
DTMM Mendenhall/McFadden 1.50 4.00
DTMR E.Royal/M.Manningham 1.25 3.00
DTNB J.Nelson/E.Bennett 4.00 10.00
DTOB K.O'Connell/J.Booty 1.25 3.00
DTRJ C.Johnson/R.Rice 1.50 4.00
DTSJ D.Jackson/J.Simpson 2.00 5.00

2008 SP Rookie Threads Trio Threads 100

TRIPLE PRINT RUN 100 SER.#'d SETS
*TRIPLE/60: .4X TO 1X TRIPLE/100
*TRIPLE/45: .4X TO 1X TRIPLE/100
*TRIPLE/25: .5X TO 1.2X TRIPLE/100
*TRIPLE/15: .5X TO 1.2X TRIPLE/100
*TRIPLE PATCH/20: .6X TO 1.5X TRIPLE/100
TRIPLE/5 TOO SCARCE TO PRICE
TRIPLE 1/1 TOO SCARCE TO PRICE
ABR Avery/Bennett/Royal 1.50 4.00
BHB Brohm/Henne/Booty 2.00 5.00
BRO Brohm/Ryan/O'Connell 5.00 12.00
DMC Dorsey/McFad/Charles 8.00 20.00
DTS Dglas/Thmas/Simpsn 2.00 5.00
FBO Flacco/Booty/O'Conn 3.00 8.00
JJS Jcksn/Simpson/Jcksn 3.00 8.00
JKS Kelly/Simpson/Jackson 2.50 6.00
JNT Nelson/Thoms/Jcksn 5.00 12.00
KDK Keller/Doucet/Kelly 2.00 5.00
LMR McFadden/Long/Ryan 5.00 12.00
MFC McFad/Forte/Charles 8.00 20.00
MJM McFad/Jones/Mend 1.50 4.00
RJS Rice/Johnson/Smith 2.00 5.00
RRM McFadd/Royal/Ryan 5.00 12.00

2008 SP Rookie Threads Rookie Threads Foursome 75

QUAD PRINT RUN 75 SER.#'d SETS
*QUAD/50: .4X TO 1X QUAD JSY/75
*QUAD PATCH/15: .8X TO 2X QUAD JSY/75
QUAD 1/1 TOO SCARCE TO PRICE
AKFR Avery/Kell/Flacco/Rice 4.00 10.00
BHBO Brhm/Hen/Bty/O'Con 2.50 6.00
FBRO Flaco/Booty/Ryan/O'Con 6.00 15.00
JCRK Cald/Royal/Kelly/Jcksn 2.00 5.00
JSTS Jhnsn/Smith/Thm/Simp 2.50 6.00
MJRM McFad/Jnes/Rice/Mend 2.00 5.00
MLRT McFad/Long/Ryan/Thm 6.00 15.00

2008 SP Rookie Threads Scripted in Time

STATED PRINT RUN 5-304
SERIAL #'d UNDER 20 NOT PRICED
STAO Amobi Okoye/304 5.00 12.00
STBJ Bo Jackson/34 30.00 60.00
STBR Brian Brohm/120 3.00 8.00
STBS Barry Sanders/20 75.00 150.00
STBS Bob Sanders/21
STCA Calvin Johnson/304 30.00 60.00
STCH Chad Henne/304 4.00 10.00
STCJ Chad Johnson/60 6.00 15.00
STCP Clinton Portis/80 6.00 15.00
STDB Dwayne Bowe/82 6.00 15.00
STDM Darren McFadden/41
STEM Eli Manning/90 30.00 60.00
STFJ Felix Jones/255 3.00 8.00
STJS Jonathan Stewart/41 5.00 12.00
STKS Kevin Smith/304 3.00 8.00
STLH Lavelle Hawkins/230 4.00 10.00
STLJ Larry Johnson/41 8.00 20.00
STMB Marion Barber/41 8.00 20.00
STMH Mike Hart/204 3.00 8.00
STML Marshawn Lynch/46 10.00 25.00
STMR Matt Ryan/50 50.00 100.00
STPH Paul Hornung/101 15.00 40.00
STPM Peyton Manning/50 50.00 100.00
STRM Rashard Mendenhall/230 3.00 8.00
STRR Ray Rice/230 3.00 8.00
STSS Steve Slaton/154 3.00 8.00
STTC Tashard Choice/255 3.00 8.00
STTM Tom Brady/25 125.00 250.00
STYT Y. A. Tittle/80 12.00 30.00

2008 SP Rookie Threads Signature Draft Choice

STATED PRINT RUN 50-280
SDCAW Andre Woodson/241 3.00 8.00
SDCBB Brian Brohm/71 3.00 8.00
SDCCC Calais Campbell/224 4.00 10.00
SDCCH Chad Henne/210 4.00 10.00
SDCCL Chris Long/114 4.00 10.00
SDCDA Donnie Avery/280 4.00 10.00
SDCDC Dan Connor/136 3.00 8.00
SDCDD Dennis Dixon/116 6.00 15.00
SDCDJ DeSean Jackson/141 6.00 15.00
SDCDM Darren McFadden/55 10.00 25.00
SDCED Early Doucet/280 3.00 8.00
SDCFD Fred Davis/229 3.00 8.00
SDCFJ Felix Jones/280 3.00 8.00
SDCHD Harry Douglas/280 4.00 10.00
SDCJL Jake Long/229 5.00 12.00
SDCJN Jordy Nelson/180 12.50 25.00
SDCJS Jonathan Stewart/61 5.00 12.00
SDCKP Kenny Phillips/254 3.00 8.00
SDCKS Kevin Smith/121 3.00 8.00
SDCLS Limas Sweed/199 3.00 8.00
SDCMJ Mike Jenkins/99 3.00 8.00
SDCMK Malcolm Kelly/149 3.00 8.00
SDCMR Matt Ryan/50 50.00 100.00
SDCRC Ryan Clady/99 4.00 10.00
SDCRM Rashard Mendenhall/50 3.00 8.00

2008 SP Rookie Threads Signing Day

STATED PRINT RUN 20-329
SDAA Adrian Arrington/280 3.00 8.00
SDAM Anthony Morelli/254 3.00 8.00
SDAT Aqib Talib/231 5.00 12.00
SDAW Andre Woodson/120 3.00 8.00
SDBB Brian Brohm/71 3.00 8.00
SDCB Colt Brennan/96 4.00 10.00
SDCC Calais Campbell/329 4.00 10.00
SDCH Chad Henne/180 4.00 10.00
SDCL Chris Long/116 4.00 10.00
SDDA Donnie Avery/111 4.00 10.00
SDDB Davone Bess/116 4.00 10.00
SDDD Dennis Dixon/128 6.00 15.00
SDDJ DeSean Jackson/181 12.00 30.00
SDDK Dustin Keller/280 4.00 10.00
SDDM Darren McFadden/51 10.00 25.00
SDEA Erik Ainge/131 3.00 8.00
SDED Early Doucet/201 3.00 8.00
SDFD Fred Davis/249 3.00 8.00
SDFJ Felix Jones/280 3.00 8.00
SDFO Matt Forte/280 15.00 40.00
SDJB John David Booty/116 3.00 8.00
SDJC Jamaal Charles/131 10.00 25.00
SDJF Joe Flacco/20 6.00 15.00
SDJL Jake Long/180 5.00 12.00
SDJN Jordy Nelson/180 12.50 25.00
SDJS Jonathan Stewart/71 5.00 12.00
SDKP Kenny Phillips/180 3.00 8.00
SDKS Kevin Smith/131 3.00 8.00
SDLS Limas Sweed/280 3.00 8.00
SDMH Mike Hart/116 3.00 8.00
SDMJ Mike Jenkins/231 3.00 8.00
SDMR Matt Ryan/51 50.00 100.00
SDRM Rashard Mendenhall/65 3.00 8.00
SDRR Ray Rice/254 3.00 8.00
SDSS Steve Slaton/136 3.00 8.00
SDTC Tashard Choice/181 3.00 8.00

2008 SP Rookie Threads SP Authentics

STATED PRINT RUN 10-284
SERIAL #'d UNDER 20 NOT PRICED
SPAA Adrian Arrington/244 3.00 8.00
SPAB Ahmad Bradshaw/244 5.00 12.00
SPAC Antoine Cason/244 4.00 10.00
SPAH A.J. Hawk/60 6.00 15.00
SPAO Amobi Okoye/240 5.00 12.00
SPAP Adrian Peterson/25 75.00 150.00
SPAT Aqib Talib/234 5.00 12.00
SPAW Andre Woodson/100 3.00 8.00
SPBB Brian Brohm/45 10.00 25.00
SPBC Brodie Croyle/20 8.00 20.00
SPBK Bo Jackson/35 30.00 60.00
SPBO Dwayne Bowe/60 6.00 15.00
SPBR Bert Jones/80 8.00 20.00
SPBS Bob Sanders/40 12.00 30.00
SPBU Dick Butkus/35 30.00 60.00
SPBW Ben Watson/80 5.00 12.00
SPCA Jason Campbell/60 6.00 15.00
SPCB Colt Brennan/60 8.00 20.00
SPCC Calais Campbell/184 4.00 10.00
SPCH Chad Henne/184 4.00 10.00
SPCJ Chris Johnson/244 4.00 10.00
SPCL Chris Long/60 4.00 10.00
SPCP Clinton Portis/120 6.00 15.00
SPCR Roger Craig/60 10.00 25.00
SPDB Davone Bess/80 4.00 10.00
SPDC Dan Connor/195 3.00 8.00
SPDD Dennis Dixon/80 3.00 8.00
SPDM Don Maynard/30 12.00 30.00
SPDT DeJuan Tribble/217 3.00 8.00
SPEA Erik Ainge/80 3.00 8.00
SPED Early Doucet/244 3.00 8.00
SPFD Fred Davis/249 3.00 8.00
SPFG Frank Gore/60 8.00 20.00
SPFJ Felix Jones/244 3.00 8.00
SPFO Matt Forte/159 12.00 30.00
SPHD Harry Douglas/284 4.00 10.00
SPJA Joseph Addai/25
SPJB John David Booty/80 3.00 8.00
SPJC Jamaal Charles/80 5.00 12.00
SPJD Daryl Johnston/60 20.00 40.00
SPJM Jim Kelly/20 50.00 80.00
SPJN Jordy Nelson/244 12.00 30.00
SPJS Jonathan Stewart/50 5.00 12.00
SPJT Joe Theismann/60 12.00 30.00
SPJW Jerious Norwood/244 5.00 12.00
SPJX DeSean Jackson/80 12.00 30.00
SPKB Kevin Boss/155 6.00 15.00
SPKO Kevin O'Connell/80 3.00 8.00
SPKP Kenny Phillips/244 3.00 8.00
SPKR Keith Rivers/224 3.00 8.00
SPKS Kevin Smith/80 3.00 8.00
SPLG L.C. Greenwood/99 15.00 40.00
SPLO Jake Long/244 5.00 12.00
SPLS Limas Sweed/182 3.00 8.00
SPMB Marc Bulger/60 6.00 15.00
SPMC Darren McFadden/35 10.00 25.00
SPMH Mike Hart/80 3.00 8.00
SPMJ Mike Jenkins/144 3.00 8.00
SPML Marshawn Lynch/35 8.00 20.00
SPMO DaJuan Morgan/209 4.00 10.00
SPMR Matt Ryan/35 50.00 100.00
SPPH Paul Hornung/60 12.00 30.00
SPPL Phillip Merling/259 3.00 8.00
SPPM Peyton Manning/75 50.00 100.00
SPPS Paul Smith/259 3.00 8.00
SPPW Patrick Willis/284 6.00 15.00
SPRC Ryan Clady/244 4.00 10.00
SPRM Rashard Mendenhall/60 5.00 12.00
SPRR Ray Rice/259 3.00 8.00
SPSB Sam Baker/244 3.00 8.00
SPSC Shawn Crable/244 3.00 8.00
SPSM Billy Sims/80 10.00 25.00
SPSS Steve Slaton/80 3.00 8.00
SPTC Tashard Choice/120 3.00 8.00
SPTR Tony Romo/175 30.00 80.00

2008 SP Rookie Threads Stitch in Time 99

STATED PRINT RUN 99 SER.#'d SETS
*JSY/50: .5X TO 1.2X JSY/99
*JSY/15: .6X TO 1.5X JSY/99
JERSEY 1/1 TOO SCARCE TO PRICE
*JSY NUMBER/72-82: .4X TO 1X JSY/99
*JSY NUMBER/20-50: .5X TO 1.2X JSY/99
JERSEY NUMBER PRINT RUN 1-82
STAH A.J. Hawk 1.50 4.00
STBS Barry Sanders 8.00 20.00
STDA Derek Anderson 1.50 4.00
STDJ DeSean Jackson 2.50 6.00
STDK Dustin Keller 1.50 4.00
STDM Darren McFadden 5.00 12.00
STED Early Doucet 1.25 3.00
STER Ed Reed 2.00 5.00
STGD Glenn Dorsey 1.25 3.00
STJS Jonathan Stewart 2.00 5.00
STLT LaDainian Tomlinson 2.50 6.00
STMA Dan Marino 10.00 25.00
STMJ Maurice Jones-Drew 1.50 4.00
STMR Matt Ryan 6.00 15.00
STRC Roger Craig 4.00 10.00
STRM Rashard Mendenhall 1.25 3.00

2008 SP Rookie Threads Super Swatch 25

STATED PRINT RUN 25 SER.#'d SETS
*SUPER SWATCH/15: .5X TO 1.2X JSY/25
SUPER SWATCH/5 TOO SCARCE TO PRICE
SS PATCH/10 TOO SCARCE TO PRICE
UNPRICED AUTO PRINT RUN 5
SUPER SWATCH 1/1 TOO SCARCE TO PRICE
SSAP Adrian Peterson 6.00 15.00
SSBF Brett Favre 12.00 30.00
SSBR Ben Roethlisberger 6.00 15.00
SSBW Ben Watson 4.00 10.00
SSCU Jay Cutler 4.00 10.00
SSDA Derek Anderson 4.00 10.00
SSDH Devin Hester 5.00 12.00
SSER Ed Reed 5.00 12.00
SSFG Frank Gore 5.00 12.00
SSLJ Larry Johnson 4.00 10.00
SSML Marshawn Lynch 5.00 12.00
SSPW Patrick Willis 5.00 12.00
SSRY Roy Williams WR 4.00 10.00
SSTB Tom Brady 20.00 50.00
SSTG Tony Gonzalez 5.00 12.00
SSTR Tony Romo 5.00 12.00
SSVY Vince Young 4.00 10.00

1999 SP Signature

This set was released in one series initially with a total of 170-cards. The cards feature current NFL stars as well as a group (#131-170) of past football greats and were released 3-cards per pack. Ten rookies stated to be included in the initial print run missed the product pack out. These cards were distributed roughly 4-months later directly through the Upper Deck dealer/distributor network in 2-card generic packs. The ten rookie cards can often be found missing the gold foil on the cardfronts.

COMPLETE SET (180) 200.00 400.00
COMP.SET w/o SP's (170) 50.00 100.00
1 Jake Plummer .25 .60
2 Mario Bates .25 .60
3 Adrian Murrell .25 .60
4 Jamal Anderson .30 .75
5 Chris Chandler .30 .75
6 Bob Christian .25 .60
7 O.J. Santiago .25 .60
8 Jim Harbaugh .30 .75
9 Priest Holmes .25 .60
10 Ray Lewis .40 1.00
11 Michael Jackson .25 .60
12 Tony Siragusa .40 1.00
13 Doug Flutie .40 1.00
14 Antowain Smith .25 .60
15 Eric Moulds .25 .60
16 William Floyd .30 .75
17 Fred Lane .25 .60
18 Muhsin Muhammad .25 .60
19 Bobby Engram .25 .60
20 Curtis Enis .25 .60
21 Curtis Conway .30 .75
22 Corey Dillon .25 .60
23 Carl Pickens .30 .75
24 Ashley Ambrose .25 .60
25 Darnay Scott .25 .60
26 Troy Aikman .50 1.25
27 Jason Garrett .40 1.00
28 Emmitt Smith .60 1.50
29 Deion Sanders .30 .75
30 John Elway .60 1.50
31 Terrell Davis .30 .75
32 Ed McCaffrey .30 .75
33 John Mobley .25 .60
34 Maa Tanuvasa .25 .60
35 Ray Crockett .25 .60
36 Barry Sanders .60 1.50
37 Herman Moore .30 .75
38 Charlie Batch .25 .60
39 Robert Porcher .25 .60
40 Tommy Vardell .30 .75
41 Brett Favre .75 2.00
42 Antonio Freeman .30 .75
43 Darick Holmes .25 .60
44 Robert Brooks .30 .75
45 Peyton Manning 1.25 3.00
46 Marshall Faulk .30 .75
47 Torrance Small .25 .60
48 Lamont Warren .30 .75
49 Zack Crockett .25 .60
50 Mark Brunell .30 .75
51 Pete Mitchell .25 .60
52 Fred Taylor .25 .60
53 Jimmy Smith .30 .75
54 Andre Rison .30 .75
55 Rich Gannon .30 .75
56 Donnell Bennett .25 .60
57 Dan Marino .75 2.00
58 Karim Abdul-Jabbar .25 .60
59 Troy Drayton .25 .60
60 Jason Taylor .30 .75
61 Cris Carter .40 1.00
62 Randy Moss .30 .75
63 Robert Smith .25 .60
64 Leroy Hoard .25 .60
65 Randall Cunningham .30 .75
66 Derrick Alexander DE .25 .60
67 Drew Bledsoe .30 .75
68 Robert Edwards .25 .60
69 Willie McGinest .30 .75
70 Chris Slade .25 .60
71 Terry Glenn .30 .75
72 Ty Law .40 1.00
73 Kerry Collins .25 .60
74 Sean Dawkins .25 .60
75 Cam Cleeland .25 .60
76 Sammy Knight .25 .60
77 Danny Kanell .25 .60
78 Gary Brown .25 .60
79 Chris Calloway .25 .60
80 Curtis Martin .30 .75
81 Keyshawn Johnson .30 .75
82 Vinny Testaverde .25 .60
83 Leon Johnson .25 .60
84 Kyle Brady .25 .60
85 Tim Brown .40 1.00
86 Jeff George .25 .60
87 Rickey Dudley .25 .60
88 Napoleon Kaufman .25 .60
89 James Jett .25 .60
90 Harvey Williams .25 .60
91 Koy Detmer .25 .60
92 Duce Staley .25 .60
93 Charlie Garner .30 .75
94 Jerome Bettis .40 1.00
95 Kordell Stewart .25 .60
96 Courtney Hawkins .25 .60
97 Hines Ward .30 .75
98 Isaac Bruce .40 1.00
99 Tony Banks .30 .75
100 Greg Hill .25 .60
101 Keith Lyle .25 .60
102 Ryan Leaf .30 .75
103 Craig Whelihan .25 .60
104 Charlie Jones .25 .60
105 Junior Seau .30 .75
106 Natrone Means .30 .75
107 Rodney Harrison .25 .60
108 Steve Young .50 1.25
109 Garrison Hearst .25 .60
110 Jerry Rice 1.00 2.50
111 Chris Doleman .25 .60
112 Roy Barker .25 .60
113 Ricky Watters .30 .75
114 Jon Kitna .25 .60
115 Joey Galloway .30 .75
116 Chad Brown .25 .60
117 Michael Sinclair .25 .60
118 Warrick Dunn .25 .60
119 Mike Alstott .25 .60
120 Bert Emanuel .30 .75
121 Hardy Nickerson .25 .60
122 Eddie George .30 .75
123 Steve McNair .30 .75
124 Yancey Thigpen .25 .60
125 Frank Wycheck .30 .75
126 Jackie Harris .30 .75
127 Terry Allen .30 .75
128 Trent Green .25 .60
129 Jamie Asher .25 .60
130 Brian Mitchell .30 .75
131 Lance Alworth .50 1.25
132 Fred Biletnikoff .50 1.25
133 Mel Blount .40 1.00
134 Cliff Branch .40 1.00
135 Harold Carmichael .30 .75
136 Larry Csonka .50 1.25
137 Eric Dickerson .40 1.00
138 Randy Gradishar .30 .75
139 Joe Greene .50 1.25
140 Jack Ham .50 1.25
141 Ted Hendricks .30 .75
142 Charlie Joiner .30 .75
143 Ed Jones .30 .75
144 Billy Kilmer .40 1.00
145 Paul Krause .30 .75
146 James Lofton .30 .75
147 Archie Manning .40 1.00
148 Don Maynard .40 1.00
149 Ozzie Newsome .40 1.00
150 Jim Otto .30 .75
151 Lee Roy Selmon .30 .75
152 Billy Sims .40 1.00
153 Mike Singletary .50 1.25
154 Ken Stabler .60 1.50
155 John Stallworth .40 1.00
156 Roger Staubach .60 1.50
157 Charley Taylor .30 .75
158 Paul Warfield .50 1.25
159 Kellen Winslow .40 1.00
160 Jack Youngblood .30 .75
161 Bill Bergey .30 .75
162 Raymond Berry .40 1.00
163 Chuck Howley .30 .75
164 Rocky Bleier .40 1.00
165 Russ Francis .30 .75
166 Drew Pearson .40 1.00
167 Mercury Morris .30 .75
168 Dick Anderson .30 .75
169 Earl Morrall .30 .75
170 Jim Hart .30 .75
171 Ricky Williams RC 2.00 5.00
172 Cade McNown RC 1.25 3.00
173 Tim Couch RC 1.50 4.00
174 Daunte Culpepper RC 2.00 5.00
175 Akili Smith RC 1.25 3.00
176 Brock Huard RC 1.25 3.00
177 Donovan McNabb RC 4.00 10.00
178 Michael Bishop RC 1.50 4.00
179 Shaun King RC 1.25 3.00
180 Torry Holt RC 2.50 6.00

1999 SP Signature Autographs

Inserted one per pack, these cards include an authentic autograph of the featured player. Each card appears to be a parallel of the base card along with a different card number and congratulations message on the cardback. A parallel Gold version was also produced and randomly seeded at the rate of 1:59.

ONE AUTOGRAPH PER PACK
AA Ashley Ambrose 4.00 10.00
AF Antonio Freeman 15.00 40.00
AK Akili Smith 8.00 20.00
AM Adrian Murrell 4.00 10.00
AN Dick Anderson 6.00 15.00
AS Antowain Smith 6.00 15.00
BB Bill Bergey 6.00 15.00
BC Bob Christian 4.00 10.00
BE Bobby Engram 6.00 15.00
BH Brock Huard 15.00 40.00
BT Bert Emanuel 4.00 10.00
CB Charlie Batch 6.00 15.00
CC Chris Chandler 6.00 15.00
CD Corey Dillon 8.00 20.00
CE Curtis Enis 6.00 15.00
CG Charlie Garner 6.00 15.00
CJ Charlie Joiner 6.00 15.00
CK Ray Crockett 4.00 10.00
CL Cameron Cleeland 4.00 10.00
CP Mike Singletary 12.00 30.00
CS Chris Slade 4.00 10.00
CT Charley Taylor 6.00 15.00
CW Curtis Conway 6.00 15.00
CY Chris Calloway 4.00 10.00
DA Derrick Alexander DE 4.00 10.00
DB Donnell Bennett 4.00 10.00
DC Daunte Culpepper 30.00 80.00
DE Roy Barker 4.00 10.00
DH Darick Holmes 4.00 10.00
DM Dan Marino 40.00 80.00
DP Drew Pearson 8.00 20.00
EG Eddie George 25.00 50.00
EJ Ed Too Tall Jones 12.50 30.00
EM Eric Moulds 6.00 15.00
ES Emmitt Smith 100.00 200.00
FL Fred Lane 8.00 20.00
FW Frank Wycheck 6.00 15.00
GA Joey Galloway 10.00 25.00
GB Gary Brown 4.00 10.00
GE Jeff George 15.00 40.00
GH Garrison Hearst 6.00 15.00
GN Trent Green 8.00 20.00
GR Randy Gradishar 6.00 15.00
HC Harold Carmichael 6.00 15.00
HL Greg Hill 4.00 10.00
HM Herman Moore 6.00 15.00
HN Hardy Nickerson 6.00 15.00
HT Jim Hart 6.00 15.00
HV Harvey Williams 4.00 10.00
HW Hines Ward 25.00 60.00
HY Chuck Howley 8.00 20.00
IB Isaac Bruce 8.00 20.00
JG Jason Garrett 12.00 30.00
JH Jack Ham 15.00 40.00
JJ James Jett 4.00 10.00
JK Jackie Harris 4.00 10.00
JL James Lofton 8.00 20.00
JM John Mobley 4.00 10.00
JP Jake Plummer 30.00 60.00
JR Junior Seau 75.00 150.00
JS Jimmy Smith 6.00 15.00
JT Jason Taylor 15.00 40.00
JY Jack Youngblood 6.00 15.00
KA Karim Abdul-Jabbar 4.00 10.00
KB Kyle Brady 4.00 10.00
KD Koy Detmer 6.00 15.00
KI Jon Kitna 5.00 15.00
KJ Keyshawn Johnson 10.00 25.00
KL Keith Lyle 4.00 10.00
KR Brian Mitchell 6.00 15.00
KS Ken Stabler 15.00 40.00
KW Kellen Winslow 6.00 15.00
LB Chad Brown 4.00 10.00
LH Leroy Hoard 4.00 10.00
LJ Leon Johnson 4.00 10.00
LS Lee Roy Selmon 10.00 25.00
LW Lamont Warren 4.00 10.00
MA Mike Alstott 30.00 60.00
MB Mario Bates 4.00 10.00
MF Marshall Faulk 25.00 60.00
MG Archie Manning 12.50 30.00
MI Michael Bishop 15.00 40.00
MJ Michael Jackson 4.00 10.00
MK Mark Brunell 15.00 40.00
ML Mel Blount 15.00 30.00
MM Muhsin Muhammad 6.00 15.00
MN Donovan McNabb 60.00 120.00
MO Earl Morrall 8.00 20.00
MS Michael Sinclair 4.00 10.00
MT Maa Tanuvasa 4.00 10.00
MY Mercury Morris 6.00 15.00
ND Ricky Watters 6.00 15.00
NM Natrone Means 6.00 15.00
NO Sean Dawkins 4.00 10.00
NY Don Maynard 6.00 15.00
OJ O.J. Santiago 4.00 10.00
OZ Ozzie Newsome 8.00 20.00
PH Priest Holmes 8.00 20.00
PK Paul Krause 6.00 15.00
PT Pete Mitchell 4.00 10.00
PW Paul Warfield 8.00 20.00
QB Cade McNown 8.00 20.00
RB Robert Brooks 12.00 30.00
RD Rickey Dudley 4.00 10.00
RE Robert Edwards 6.00 15.00
RF Russ Francis 8.00 20.00
RH Rodney Harrison 8.00 20.00
RL Ray Lewis 40.00 80.00
RM Randy Moss 75.00 150.00
RP Robert Porcher 4.00 10.00
RW Ricky Williams 40.00 100.00
RY Raymond Berry 8.00 20.00
SD Charlie Jones 4.00 10.00
SH Shaun King 8.00 20.00
SK Sammy Knight 4.00 10.00
ST Duce Staley 8.00 20.00
SW John Stallworth 15.00 30.00
TA Troy Aikman 60.00 120.00
TB Tim Brown 40.00 100.00
TC Tim Couch 20.00 50.00

TE Jamie Asher 4.00 10.00
TH Ted Hendricks 8.00 20.00
TL Ty Law 8.00 20.00
TO Torrance Small 4.00 10.00
TR Troy Drayton 4.00 10.00
TS Tony Siragusa 8.00 20.00
TV Tommy Vardell 4.00 10.00
WF William Floyd 4.00 10.00
WH Craig Whelihan 4.00 10.00
WM Willie McGinest 6.00 15.00
WP Torry Holt 20.00 50.00
ZC Zack Crockett 4.00 10.00

1999 SP Signature Autographs Gold

*GOLDS: .8X TO 2X BASIC AU
*GOLDS: .6X TO 1.5X BASIC AU SP
AK Akili Smith 60.00 150.00
BH Brock Huard 60.00 150.00
DC Daunte Culpepper 125.00 250.00
JR Junior Seau 200.00 400.00
MN Donovan McNabb 150.00 300.00
QB Cade McNown 60.00 150.00
SH Shaun King 60.00 150.00

1999 SP Signature Montana Great Performances

Joe Montana is the subject of this 10-card insert set. Each features a moment in time of Montana's Hall of Fame career. A signed parallel version entitled Signature Performances was also produced and seeded at the rate of 1:47 packs. A Gold Version of each Signature card was seeded an average of 1:880 packs.
COMPLETE SET (10) 30.00 60.00
COMMON CARD (J1-J10) 3.00 8.00

1999 SP Signature Montana Signature Performances

COMMON CARD (J1A-J10A) 40.00 100.00
AUTO STATED ODDS 1:47
COMMON GOLD AUTO 125.00 250.00
GOLD STATED ODDS 1:880

1999 SP Signature UD Authentics

Not much is known about the official release of this card, but it is thought that it was issued as a replacement for other redemption cards that could not be fufilled. There is a large SP Signature logo printed in foil on the cardfront.
TD Terrell Davis 15.00 30.00

2003 SP Signature

Released in November of 2003, this set contains 200 cards, including 100 veterans and 100 rookies. Rookies 101-170 are serial numbered to 750. Rookies 171-200 are serial numbered to 250. Each 3-card pack contained an authentic player autograph card, and had an SRP of $49.99. Boxes contained 5 packs.
101-170 ROOKIE PRINT RUN 750
171-200 ROOKIE PRINT RUN 250
1 Michael Vick 1.25 3.00
2 Aaron Brooks 1.00 2.50
3 Jim Brown 2.50 6.00
4 Steve Young 2.50 6.00
5 Jeff Garcia 1.00 2.50
6 Warren Moon 2.00 5.00
7 John Elway 3.00 8.00
8 Troy Aikman 2.50 6.00
9 Drew Brees 1.50 4.00
10 Chad Pennington 1.00 2.50
11 Fran Tarkenton 2.00 5.00
12 Joe Namath 3.00 8.00
13 Dan Marino 4.00 10.00
14 Terry Bradshaw 2.50 6.00
15 Edgerrin James 1.25 3.00
16 Joe Montana 6.00 15.00
17 Ken Stabler 2.50 6.00
18 Peyton Manning 4.00 10.00
19 Johnny Unitas 4.00 10.00
20 Barry Sanders 3.00 8.00
21 Jim Kelly 2.00 5.00
22 Michael Bennett 1.00 2.50
23 Phil Simms 2.00 5.00
24 David Carr 1.00 2.50
25 Deuce McAllister 1.25 3.00
26 Clinton Portis 1.00 2.50
27 Brad Johnson 1.25 3.00
28 Tim Couch 1.00 2.50
29 Archie Manning 1.50 4.00
30 Ahman Green 1.25 3.00
31 Priest Holmes 1.00 2.50
32 Marcus Allen 2.00 5.00
33 Ricky Williams 1.25 3.00
34 Walter Payton 6.00 15.00
35 Anthony Thomas 1.25 3.00
36 Eddie George 1.25 3.00
37 Shaun Alexander 1.00 2.50
38 Rich Gannon 1.25 3.00
39 Jay Fiedler 1.00 2.50
40 Travis Henry 1.00 2.50
41 Chad Johnson 1.00 2.50
42 Eric Moulds 1.00 2.50
43 Julius Peppers 1.50 4.00
44 John Riggins 1.50 4.00
45 Antonio Bryant 1.00 2.50
46 Laveranues Coles 1.00 2.50
47 Josh McCown 1.25 3.00
48 Matt Hasselbeck 1.00 2.50
49 William Green 1.00 2.50
50 Peerless Price 1.00 2.50
51 Kerry Collins 1.00 2.50
52 Zach Thomas 1.25 3.00
53 Bruiser Kinard 1.50 4.00
54 Brian Urlacher 1.50 4.00
55 Junior Seau 1.25 3.00
56 Jamal Lewis 1.25 3.00
57 Duce Staley 1.00 2.50
58 Chris Redman 1.00 2.50
59 Kordell Stewart 1.00 2.50
60 Chad Hutchinson 1.00 2.50
61 Kevan Barlow 1.00 2.50
62 Charlie Garner 1.25 3.00
63 Fred Taylor 1.00 2.50
64 Jerome Bettis 1.50 4.00
65 Donte Stallworth 1.00 2.50
66 Rod Smith 1.25 3.00
67 Antwaan Randle El 1.00 2.50
68 Brian Griese 1.00 2.50
69 Corey Dillon 1.00 2.50
70 Chris Chambers 1.00 2.50
71 Steve McNair 1.25 3.00
72 Jake Plummer 1.00 2.50
73 Keyshawn Johnson 1.50 4.00
74 Marvin Harrison 1.25 3.00
75 Plaxico Burress 1.00 2.50
76 Tim Brown 1.50 4.00
77 Mark Brunell 1.25 3.00
78 Curtis Martin 1.25 3.00
79 Cal Hubbard 1.50 4.00
80 Isaac Bruce 1.50 4.00
81 Terrell Owens 1.25 3.00
82 Santana Moss 1.25 3.00
83 Tommy Maddox 1.00 2.50
84 Randy Moss 1.25 3.00
85 Drew Bledsoe 1.25 3.00
86 Az-Zahir Hakim 1.00 2.50
87 Rod Gardner 1.00 2.50
88 Tom Brady 6.00 15.00
89 David Boston 1.00 2.50
90 Trent Green 1.00 2.50
91 Jeremy Shockey 1.00 2.50
92 Daunte Culpepper 1.25 3.00
93 Emmitt Smith 2.50 6.00
94 Jerry Rice 3.00 8.00
95 LaDainian Tomlinson 1.50 4.00
96 Marshall Faulk 1.25 3.00
97 Kurt Warner 1.25 3.00
98 Brett Favre 3.00 8.00
99 Doak Walker 2.00 5.00
100 Donovan McNabb 1.25 3.00
101 Ken Dorsey RC 2.00 5.00
102 Kirk Farmer RC 2.00 5.00
103 Nate Hybl RC 2.00 5.00
104 Marquel Blackwell RC 1.50 4.00
105 Brett Engemann RC 1.50 4.00
106 Tony Romo RC 15.00 40.00
107 Derick Armstrong RC 2.00 5.00
108 Lon Sheriff RC 1.50 4.00
109 Casey Moore RC 1.50 4.00
110 Jason Gesser RC 2.00 5.00
111 Brock Forsey RC 2.00 5.00
112 Willis McGahee RC 2.00 5.00
113 Nick Maddox RC 1.50 4.00
114 LaBrandon Toefield RC 1.50 4.00
115 Kareem Kelly RC 1.50 4.00
116 Malaefou MacKenzie RC 1.50 4.00
117 Troy Polamalu RC 12.00 30.00
118 Terence Newman RC 2.50 6.00
119 Marcus Trufant RC 2.00 5.00
120 Terrell Suggs RC 2.00 5.00
121 DeWayne Robertson RC 2.00 5.00
122 Justin Griffith RC 2.00 5.00
123 Lee Suggs RC 1.50 4.00
124 Bryant Johnson RC 2.50 6.00
125 Andre Woolfolk RC 1.50 4.00
126 Cedric Henry RC 1.50 4.00
127 Billy McMullen RC 1.50 4.00
128 Charles Rogers RC 2.00 5.00
129 David Kircus RC 2.00 5.00
130 Jerome McDougle RC 1.50 4.00
131 Ryan Hoag RC 1.50 4.00
132 Mike Pinkard RC 1.50 4.00
133 Shaun McDonald RC 2.00 5.00
134 Bobby Wade RC 2.00 5.00
135 Kassim Osgood RC 2.50 6.00
136 Ovie Mughelli RC 2.00 5.00
137 Doug Gabriel RC 2.00 5.00
138 Aaron Walker RC 2.00 5.00
139 Brandon Lloyd RC 2.50 6.00
140 Donald Lee RC 2.00 5.00
141 George Wrighster RC 1.50 4.00
142 Antwone Savage RC 1.50 4.00
143 Keenan Howry RC 1.50 4.00
144 Kevin Walter RC 4.00 10.00
145 Gerald Hayes RC 2.00 5.00
146 Walter Young RC 1.50 4.00
147 Casey Fitzsimmons RC 2.00 5.00
148 Vishante Shiancoe RC 2.50 6.00
149 Lance Briggs RC 12.00 30.00
150 Zuriel Smith RC 1.50 4.00
151 Terrence Edwards RC 1.50 4.00
152 Arnaz Battle RC 2.50 6.00
153 DeAndrew Rubin RC 1.50 4.00
154 Pisa Tinoisamoa RC 2.50 6.00
155 David Tyree RC 2.00 5.00
156 Bradie James RC 2.50 6.00
157 Anquan Boldin RC 2.50 6.00
158 Kevin Curtis RC 1.50 4.00
159 Taylor Jacobs RC 1.50 4.00
160 Cato June RC 3.00 8.00
161 Jason Witten RC 6.00 15.00
162 Mike Seidman RC 1.50 4.00
163 Dallas Clark RC 2.50 6.00
164 Gibran Hamdan RC 1.50 4.00
165 Kliff Kingsbury RC 2.50 6.00
166 Brooks Bollinger RC 2.00 5.00
167 Nick Barnett RC 2.50 6.00
168 Rex Grossman RC 2.00 5.00
169 Byron Leftwich RC 2.00 5.00
170 Kyle Boller RC 1.50 4.00
171 Chris Brown RC 2.50 6.00
172 Carl Ford RC 2.50 6.00
173 Kelley Washington RC 2.50 6.00
174 Charles Tillman RC 12.00 30.00
175 Ken Hamlin RC 4.00 10.00
176 Bennie Joppru RC 2.50 6.00
177 Nate Burleson RC 3.00 8.00
178 Boss Bailey RC 3.00 8.00
179 LaTarence Dunbar RC 2.50 6.00
180 Adrian Madise RC 2.50 6.00
181 J.R. Tolver RC 3.00 8.00
182 Tyrone Calico RC 2.50 6.00
183 Justin Gage RC 3.00 8.00
184 Teyo Johnson RC 3.00 8.00
185 B.J. Askew RC 3.00 8.00
186 Sam Aiken RC 3.00 8.00
187 Andre Johnson RC 6.00 15.00
188 Bethel Johnson RC 2.50 6.00
189 Artose Pinner RC 2.50 6.00
190 Quentin Griffin RC 3.00 8.00
191 Musa Smith RC 2.50 6.00
192 Larry Johnson RC 3.00 8.00
193 Onterrio Smith RC 2.50 6.00
194 Justin Fargas RC 4.00 10.00
195 Dwone Hicks RC 2.50 6.00
196 Brian St.Pierre RC 2.50 6.00
197 Dave Ragone RC 2.50 6.00
198 Seneca Wallace RC 3.00 8.00
199 Chris Simms RC 2.50 6.00
200 Carson Palmer RC 5.00 12.00

2003 SP Signature Autographs Black Ink

Randomly inserted in packs, this set features authentic player autographs on foil stickers in black ink. Please note that Taylor Jacobs and Terence Newman were issued as exchange cards in packs, with the exchange expiration date being 10/30/2006. The below print runs were provided by Upper Deck.
COMMON CARD 6.00 15.00
SEMISTARS 8.00 20.00
UNLISTED STARS 10.00 25.00
AB Anquan Boldin 15.00 40.00
AJ Andre Johnson 20.00 50.00
AM Archie Manning 15.00 40.00
BY Byron Leftwich 12.00 30.00
CP Chad Pennington 12.00 30.00
DA David Boston SP/25* 15.00 40.00
DB Drew Brees SP/20* 40.00 80.00
DM Dan Marino SP 75.00 150.00
FT Fran Tarkenton SP 20.00 50.00
JM Joe Montana 60.00 120.00
JN Joe Namath SP 60.00 120.00
KS Ken Stabler SP 25.00 50.00
LJ Larry Johnson 10.00 25.00
PH Priest Holmes SP/25* 30.00 80.00
PM Peyton Manning 60.00 120.00
SC Carson Palmer 20.00 50.00
TM Tommy Maddox SP/25* 15.00 40.00

2003 SP Signature Autographs Blue Ink

Randomly inserted in packs, this set features authentic player autographs on foil stickers in blue ink. Please note that Taylor Jacobs and Terence Newman were issued as exchange cards in packs, with the exchange expiration date being 10/30/2006. The below print runs were provided by Upper Deck.
OVERALL AUTOGRAPH ODDS ONE PER PACK
SERIAL #'d UNDER 25 NOT PRICED
AA Aaron Brooks 6.00 15.00
AB Anquan Boldin 12.00 30.00
AH Az-Zahir Hakim 4.00 10.00
AJ Andre Johnson 20.00 50.00
AM Archie Manning SP/25* 30.00 60.00
AP Artose Pinner 6.00 15.00
AR Arnaz Battle 6.00 15.00
AT Anthony Thomas 6.00 15.00
BB Brad Banks 5.00 12.00
BJ Brad Johnson SP/25* 15.00 40.00
BL Brandon Lloyd 6.00 15.00
BO Brooks Bollinger 6.00 15.00
BR Bryant Johnson 6.00 15.00
BY Byron Leftwich 10.00 25.00
CA Tyrone Calico 6.00 15.00
CB Chris Brown 6.00 15.00
CP Chad Pennington SP 12.00 30.00
CS Chris Simms SP 15.00 40.00
DB Drew Brees SP 30.00 60.00
DC David Carr 6.00 15.00
DO Donovan McNabb SP/19*
DR DeWayne Robertson 5.00 12.00
EG Earnest Graham 6.00 15.00
FA Justin Fargas 6.00 15.00
IB Isaac Bruce 6.00 15.00
JB Jim Brown SP 50.00 100.00
JF Jay Fiedler 6.00 15.00
JG Jeff Garcia SP/24*
JO Teyo Johnson 6.00 15.00
KA Kareem Kelly 4.00 10.00
KB Kyle Boller 6.00 15.00
KC Kevin Curtis 6.00 15.00
KD Ken Dorsey 6.00 15.00
KK Kliff Kingsbury 5.00 12.00
KW Kelley Washington 6.00 15.00
LJ Larry Johnson 6.00 15.00
LS Lee Suggs 6.00 15.00
MB Michael Bennett 6.00 15.00
MM Malaefou MacKenzie 4.00 10.00
MO Warren Moon 20.00 40.00
MS Musa Smith 6.00 15.00
MT Marcus Trufant 6.00 15.00
NB Nate Burleson 6.00 15.00
OS Onterrio Smith 6.00 15.00
PM Peyton Manning 50.00 100.00
PO Clinton Portis SP/25* 25.00 60.00
QG Quentin Griffin 6.00 15.00
RA Dave Ragone 6.00 15.00
RE Rex Grossman 8.00 20.00
RG Rod Gardner 5.00 12.00
RM Randy Moss SP/10*
RW Ricky Williams SP/25* 25.00 60.00
SA Shaun Alexander 6.00 15.00
SC Carson Palmer 15.00 40.00
SM Santana Moss 8.00 20.00
SP Brian St.Pierre 6.00 15.00
SW Seneca Wallace 6.00 15.00
TC Tim Couch 4.00 10.00
TJ Taylor Jacobs 6.00 15.00
TN Terence Newman 6.00 15.00
TS Terrell Suggs 8.00 20.00
WM Willis McGahee SP 12.00 30.00

2003 SP Signature Autographs Blue Ink Numbered

Randomly inserted in packs, this set features authentic player autographs on foil stickers in blue ink. With the exception of Brett Favre, whose card is serial numbered to 7, each card in this set is serial numberd to 100. Please note that Taylor Jacobs and Terence Newman were issued as exchange cards in packs, with the exchange expiration date being 10/30/2006. The Brett Favre card is not priced due to scarcity.
STATED PRINT RUN 100 SER.#'d SETS
AA Aaron Brooks 10.00 25.00
AB Anquan Boldin 20.00 50.00
AH Az-Zahir Hakim 8.00 20.00
AJ Andre Johnson 25.00 60.00
AM Archie Manning 20.00 50.00
AP Artose Pinner 10.00 25.00
AR Arnaz Battle 10.00 25.00
AT Anthony Thomas 12.00 30.00
BB Brad Banks 8.00 20.00
BL Brandon Lloyd 10.00 25.00
BO Brooks Bollinger 10.00 25.00
BR Bryant Johnson 10.00 25.00
BY Byron Leftwich 12.00 30.00
CA Tyrone Calico 12.00 30.00
CB Chris Brown 10.00 25.00
CP Chad Pennington 12.00 30.00
CS Chris Simms 12.00 30.00
DR DeWayne Robertson 8.00 20.00
EG Earnest Graham 12.00 30.00
FA Justin Fargas 10.00 25.00
IB Isaac Bruce 10.00 25.00
JB Jim Brown 30.00 80.00
JF Jay Fiedler 10.00 25.00
JO Teyo Johnson 10.00 25.00
KA Kareem Kelly 8.00 20.00
KB Kyle Boller 10.00 25.00
KC Kevin Curtis 10.00 25.00
KD Ken Dorsey 10.00 25.00
KK Kliff Kingsbury 8.00 20.00
KW Kelley Washington 12.00 30.00
LJ Larry Johnson 12.00 30.00
LS Lee Suggs 10.00 25.00
MB Michael Bennett 10.00 25.00
MM Malaefou MacKenzie 8.00 20.00
MS Musa Smith 10.00 25.00
MT Marcus Trufant 10.00 25.00
NB Nate Burleson 10.00 25.00
OS Onterrio Smith 10.00 25.00
PM Peyton Manning 60.00 120.00
QG Quentin Griffin 10.00 25.00
RA Dave Ragone 10.00 25.00
RE Rex Grossman 15.00 40.00
RG Rod Gardner 8.00 20.00
SA Shaun Alexander 12.00 30.00
SC Carson Palmer 20.00 50.00
SM Santana Moss 12.00 30.00
SP Brian St.Pierre 10.00 25.00
SW Seneca Wallace 10.00 25.00
TC Tim Couch 8.00 20.00
TG Trent Green 10.00 25.00
TJ Taylor Jacobs 12.00 30.00
TN Terence Newman 12.00 30.00
TS Terrell Suggs 12.00 30.00

2003 SP Signature Autographs Green Ink

Randomly inserted in packs, this set features authentic player autographs on foil stickers in green ink. Each card is serial numbered to 50. The Seneca Wallace card exists with or without the serial numbering on the front. Please note that Taylor Jacobs, Terence Newman, and Terrell Owens were issued as exchange cards in packs, with the exchange expiration date being 10/30/2006.
COMMON CARD 10.00 25.00
SEMISTARS 12.50 30.00
UNLISTED STARS 15.00 40.00
STATED PRINT RUN 50 SER.#'d SETS
AB Anquan Boldin 25.00 60.00
AJ Andre Johnson 40.00 100.00
AM Archie Manning 30.00 80.00
BA Barry Sanders 60.00 120.00
BY Byron Leftwich 20.00 50.00
CP Chad Pennington 12.50 30.00
DB Drew Brees 30.00 60.00
DC David Carr 15.00 40.00
DM Dan Marino 60.00 120.00
EG Earnest Graham 15.00 40.00
FT Fran Tarkenton 20.00 50.00
JB Jim Brown 50.00 100.00
JE John Elway 75.00 150.00
JK Jim Kelly 40.00 80.00
JM Joe Montana 75.00 150.00
JN Joe Namath 60.00 120.00
JR John Riggins 25.00 60.00
KS Ken Stabler 30.00 60.00
LJ Larry Johnson 15.00 40.00
MA Marcus Allen 25.00 50.00
MO Warren Moon 20.00 50.00
PH Priest Holmes 20.00 50.00
PM Peyton Manning 75.00 150.00
SC Carson Palmer 20.00 50.00
SM Santana Moss 20.00 50.00
SY Steve Young 40.00 80.00
TB Terry Bradshaw 40.00 100.00
TS Terrell Suggs 20.00 50.00
WM Willis McGahee 25.00 60.00

2003 SP Signature Autographs Red Ink

Randomly inserted in packs, this set features authentic player autographs on foil stickers in red ink. Warren Moon signed his cards in purple ink. Each card is serial numbered to 100. Please note that Taylor Jacobs, Terence Newman, and Terrell Owens were issued as exchange cards in packs, with the exchange expiration date being 10/30/2006.
COMMON CARD 6.00 15.00
SEMISTARS 8.00 20.00
UNLISTED STARS 10.00 25.00
STATED PRINT RUN 100 SER. #'d SETS
AB Anquan Boldin 20.00 50.00
AJ Andre Johnson 25.00 60.00
AM Archie Manning 20.00 50.00
BA Barry Sanders 60.00 100.00
BY Byron Leftwich 12.00 30.00
CP Chad Pennington 12.00 30.00
DB Drew Brees 30.00 60.00
FT Fran Tarkenton 15.00 40.00
JB Jim Brown 40.00 100.00
JE John Elway 75.00 125.00
JK Jim Kelly
JM Joe Montana 60.00 120.00
JN Joe Namath 50.00 100.00
JR John Riggins 20.00 40.00
KS Ken Stabler 25.00 50.00
LJ Larry Johnson 12.00 30.00
MA Marcus Allen 25.00 50.00
MO Warren Moon Purple 25.00 60.00
PH Priest Holmes 15.00 40.00
PM Peyton Manning 60.00 120.00
RE Rex Grossman 12.00 30.00
SA Shaun Alexander 10.00 25.00
SC Carson Palmer 20.00 50.00
SY Steve Young 35.00 60.00
TB Terry Bradshaw 40.00 80.00
TO Terrell Owens 30.00 60.00
WM Willis McGahee 15.00 40.00

2003 SP Signature Dual Autographs

Randomly inserted in packs, this set features two authentic player autographs on foil stickers. Please note that the Ken Dorsey/Terrell Owens card was issued as an exchange card in packs. The exchange deadline is 10/30/2006. Each card is serial numbered to 75.
STATED PRINT RUN 75 SER.#'d SETS
ABKK A.Brooks/K.Kelly 10.00 25.00
BJAB B.Johnson/A.Boldin 10.00 25.00
CPKW C.Palmer/K.Washington 12.00 30.00
CPSM C.Pennington/S.Moss 12.00 30.00
CPVT Pennington/Testaverde 10.00 25.00
DBDB D.Brees/D.Boston 30.00 60.00
DCAJ D.Carr/A.Johnson 30.00 60.00
JMKD J.Montana/K.Dorsey 60.00 150.00
JNCP J.Namath/C.Pennington 40.00 100.00
KDTO K.Dorsey/T.Owens 12.00 30.00
MBOS M.Bennett/O.Smith 10.00 25.00
PHLJ P.Holmes/L.Johnson 12.00 30.00
PMAM P.Manning/A.Manning 75.00 150.00
PSCS P.Simms/C.Simms 12.00 30.00
RGAT R.Grossman/A.Thomas 8.00 20.00
TMBS T.Maddox/B.St.Pierre 10.00 25.00

2003 SP Signature SP Legendary Cuts

Randomly inserted in packs, this set features authentic player autograph cuts of NFL legends.
STATED PRINT RUN 11-45
SER.#'d UNDER 20 NOT PRICED
LCBK Bruiser Kinard/22 150.00 300.00
LCCH Cal Hubbard/22 150.00 300.00
LCDW Doak Walker/16 150.00 300.00
LCWP Walter Payton/45 400.00 750.00

2009 SP Signature

COMP.SET w/o RC's (200) 40.00 80.00
OVERALL AUTO STATED ODDS 1.5:1
EXCH EXPIRATION: 11/19/2011
1 John Abraham .25 .60
2 Joseph Addai .25 .60
3 Jared Allen .25 .60
4 Derek Anderson .25 .60
5 Oshiomogho Atogwe .25 .60
6 Donnie Avery .25 .60
7 Champ Bailey .30 .75
8 Ronde Barber .25 .60
9 Marion Barber .30 .75
10 Jon Beason .25 .60
11 Cedric Benson .25 .60
12 Bernard Berrian .25 .60
13 Anquan Boldin .25 .60
14 Dwayne Bowe .30 .75
15 Ahmad Bradshaw .25 .60
16 Tom Brady 1.25 3.00
17 Deion Branch .25 .60
18 Steve Breaston .30 .75
19 Drew Brees .40 1.00
20 Lance Briggs .30 .75
21 Keith Brooking .25 .60
22 Ronnie Brown .25 .60
23 Isaac Bruce .40 1.00
24 Antonio Bryant .25 .60
25 Marc Bulger .25 .60
26 Reggie Bush .25 .60
27 Greg Camarillo .30 .75
28 Jason Campbell .25 .60
29 John Carlson .30 .75
30 Matt Cassel .25 .60
31 Jamaal Charles .30 .75
32 Tashard Choice .25 .60
33 Dallas Clark .25 .60
34 Michael Clayton .25 .60
35 Kellen Clemens .25 .60
36 Laveranues Coles .25 .60
37 Kerry Collins .25 .60
38 Marques Colston .25 .60
39 Chris Cooley .25 .60
40 Jerricho Cotchery .25 .60
41 Daunte Culpepper .30 .75
42 Kevin Curtis .25 .60
43 Jay Cutler .25 .60
44 Owen Daniels .25 .60
45 Karlos Dansby .25 .60
46 Brian Dawkins .25 .60
47 Jake Delhomme .25 .60
48 Quintin Demps .25 .60
49 Donald Driver .30 .75
50 Braylon Edwards .25 .60
51 Trent Edwards .25 .60
52 Shaun Ellis .25 .60
53 Lee Evans .30 .75
54 Justin Fargas .25 .60
55 James Farrior .25 .60
56 Kevin Faulk .25 .60
57 Miles Austin .25 .60
58 Larry Fitzgerald .30 .75
59 Joe Flacco .30 .75
60 Matt Forte .25 .60
61 Dwight Freeney .25 .60
62 Justin Gage .25 .60
63 David Garrard .25 .60
64 Antonio Gates .30 .75
65 Ted Ginn .25 .60
66 Anthony Gonzalez .25 .60
67 Tony Gonzalez .30 .75
68 Frank Gore .30 .75
69 Earnest Graham .25 .60
70 Ryan Grant .30 .75
71 Chad Greenway .25 .60
72 Brian Griese .25 .60
73 Michael Griffin .25 .60
74 Jason Hanson .25 .60
75 James Harrison .40 1.00
76 Rodney Harrison .25 .60
77 Matt Hasselbeck .25 .60
78 A.J. Hawk .25 .60
79 Albert Haynesworth .25 .60
80 Chad Henne .30 .75
81 Devin Hester .30 .75
82 Johnnie Lee Higgins .25 .60
83 Tim Hightower .25 .60
84 Shaun Hill .25 .60
85 Peyton Hillis .30 .75
86 Domenik Hixon .25 .60
87 Torry Holt .30 .75
88 T.J. Houshmandzadeh .25 .60
89 DeSean Jackson .30 .75
90 D'Qwell Jackson .25 .60
91 Steven Jackson .25 .60
92 Tarvaris Jackson .30 .75
93 Vincent Jackson .25 .60
94 Brandon Jacobs .25 .60
95 Bradie James .25 .60
96 Greg Jennings .25 .60
97 Andre Johnson .30 .75
98 Calvin Johnson .40 1.00
99 Chad Ochocinco .25 .60
100 Chris Johnson .25 .60
101 Larry Johnson .25 .60
102 Dhani Jones .25 .60
103 Julius Jones .25 .60
104 Brett Favre Vikings 6.00 15.00
105 Thomas Jones .25 .60
106 Maurice Jones-Drew .25 .60
107 Dustin Keller .25 .60
108 Jamal Lewis .30 .75
109 Ray Lewis .40 1.00
110 Marshawn Lynch .30 .75
111 Eli Manning .30 .75
112 Peyton Manning 1.00 2.50
113 Brandon Marshall .30 .75
114 Derrick Mason .25 .60
115 Jerod Mayo .30 .75
116 Le'Ron McClain .30 .75
117 Darren McFadden .40 1.00
118 Willis McGahee .25 .60
119 Donovan McNabb .30 .75
120 Rashard Mendenhall .25 .60
121 Shawne Merriman .25 .60
122 Zach Miller .25 .60
123 Lance Moore .25 .60
124 Mewelde Moore .25 .60
125 Maurice Morris .25 .60
126 Kirk Morrison .25 .60
127 Randy Moss .30 .75
128 Santana Moss .30 .75
129 Muhsin Muhammad .25 .60
130 Jerious Norwood .25 .60
131 Kyle Orton .25 .60
132 Terrell Owens .30 .75
133 Carson Palmer .30 .75
134 Willie Parker .25 .60
135 Julius Peppers .30 .75
136 Julian Peterson .25 .60
137 Mike Peterson .25 .60
138 Adrian Peterson .40 1.00
139 Antonio Pierce .25 .60
140 Troy Polamalu .40 1.00
141 Joey Porter .30 .75
142 Clinton Portis .25 .60
143 Brady Quinn .25 .60
144 Ed Reed .30 .75
145 Darrelle Revis .25 .60
146 Dominic Rhodes .25 .60
147 Philip Rivers .40 1.00
148 Aaron Rodgers .75 2.00
149 Dominique Rodgers-Cromartie .25 .60
150 Ben Roethlisberger .40 1.00
151 Tony Romo .30 .75
152 Eddie Royal .25 .60
153 JaMarcus Russell .25 .60
154 Barrett Ruud .25 .60
155 Matt Ryan .30 .75
156 DeMeco Ryans .30 .75
157 Bob Sanders .30 .75
158 Matt Schaub .25 .60
159 Tony Scheffler .25 .60
160 Richard Seymour .25 .60
161 Ernie Sims .25 .60
162 Steve Slaton .25 .60
163 Alex Smith QB .40 1.00
164 Kevin Smith .25 .60
165 Kolby Smith .25 .60
166 Steve Smith USC .30 .75
167 Steve Smith .30 .75
168 Darren Sproles .30 .75
169 Jonathan Stewart .25 .60
170 Chester Taylor .25 .60
171 Fred Taylor .25 .60
172 Tyler Thigpen .25 .60
173 Pierre Thomas .25 .60
174 LaDainian Tomlinson .40 1.00
175 Justin Tuck .25 .60
176 Michael Turner .25 .60
177 Brian Urlacher .40 1.00
178 Jonathan Vilma .25 .60
179 Kevin Walter .30 .75
180 Derrick Ward .25 .60
181 Hines Ward .30 .75
182 DeMarcus Ware .30 .75
183 Kurt Warner .30 .75
184 Leon Washington .25 .60
185 Reggie Wayne .30 .75
186 Eric Weddle .25 .60
187 Wes Welker .30 .75
188 Brian Westbrook .25 .60
189 LenDale White .25 .60
190 Roddy White .25 .60
191 Cadillac Williams .30 .75
192 DeAngelo Williams .25 .60
193 Mario Williams .30 .75
194 Ricky Williams .30 .75
195 Roy Williams WR .25 .60
196 Patrick Willis .30 .75
197 Adrian Wilson .25 .60
198 Kellen Winslow .25 .60
199 Jason Witten .30 .75
200 Charles Woodson .40 1.00
201 Ramses Barden AU RC 6.00 15.00
202 Rhett Bomar AU RC 6.00 15.00
203 Tom Brandstater AU RC 8.00 20.00
204 Kenny Britt AU RC 10.00 25.00
205 Aaron Brown AU RC 8.00 20.00
206 Andre Brown AU RC 8.00 20.00
207 Donald Brown AU RC 6.00 15.00
208 Deon Butler AU RC 6.00 15.00
209 Patrick Chung AU RC 6.00 15.00
210 Glen Coffee AU RC 6.00 15.00
211 Austin Collie AU RC 6.00 15.00
212 Michael Crabtree AU RC 10.00 25.00
213 Aaron Curry AU RC EXCH 10.00 25.00
214 Brian Cushing AU RC 6.00 15.00
215 James Davis AU RC 6.00 15.00
216 Nate Davis AU RC 6.00 15.00
217 Vontae Davis AU RC 6.00 15.00
218 Louis Delmas AU RC 8.00 20.00
219 Josh Freeman AU RC 6.00 15.00
220 Mike Goodson AU RC 8.00 20.00
221 Shonn Greene AU RC 6.00 15.00
222 Brian Hartline AU RC 12.00 30.00
223 Percy Harvin AU RC 20.00 50.00
224 Darius Heyward-Bey AU RC 10.00 25.00
225 Juaquin Iglesias AU RC 6.00 15.00
226 Tyson Jackson AU RC 6.00 15.00
227 Malcolm Jenkins AU RC 6.00 15.00
228 Gartrell Johnson AU RC 6.00 15.00
229 Manuel Johnson AU RC 6.00 15.00
230 Johnny Knox AU RC 8.00 20.00
231 Jeremy Maclin AU RC 8.00 20.00
232 Mohamed Massaquoi AU RC 6.00 15.00
233 Clay Matthews AU RC 25.00 50.00
234 LeSean McCoy AU RC 40.00 80.00
235 Stephen McGee AU RC 6.00 15.00
236 Kenny McKinley AU RC EXCH 6.00 15.00
237 Knowshon Moreno AU RC 6.00 15.00
238 Louis Murphy AU RC
239 Hakeem Nicks AU RC 8.00 20.00
240 Keith Null AU RC EXCH 8.00 20.00
241 Brian Orakpo AU RC 8.00 20.00
242 Curtis Painter AU RC 6.00 15.00
243 Cedric Peerman AU RC 6.00 15.00
244 Brandon Pettigrew AU RC 6.00 15.00
245 Richard Quinn AU RC 8.00 20.00
246 B.J. Raji AU RC 8.00 20.00
247 Javon Ringer AU RC 6.00 15.00
248 Mark Sanchez AU SP RC 60.00 150.00
249 Bernard Scott AU RC EXCH 10.00 25.00
250 Jason Smith AU RC 6.00 15.00
251 Matthew Stafford AU RC 100.00 200.00
252 Frank Summers AU RC 10.00 25.00
253 Brandon Tate AU RC 8.00 20.00
254 Mike Teel AU RC 6.00 15.00
255 Mike Thomas AU RC 6.00 15.00
256 Patrick Turner AU RC 6.00 15.00
257 Mike Wallace AU RC 10.00 25.00
258 Chris Wells AU RC 30.00 80.00
259 Pat White AU RC 8.00 20.00
260 Derrick Williams AU RC 6.00 15.00

2009 SP Signature Draft Years Autographs

STATED PRINT RUN 20-199
AW P.Willis/J.Anderson/20 12.00 30.00
BR L.Robinson/Breaston/99 6.00 15.00
CJ V.Jackson/M.Clayton/99 5.00 12.00
DH K.Hall/B.Davis/199 5.00 12.00
FJ M.Flynn/J.Johnson/115 5.00 12.00
FR M.Ryan/J.Flacco/50 40.00 80.00
HH K.Hall/J.Hairston/199 5.00 12.00
HM S.Holmes/B.Marshall/35 10.00 25.00
JC D.Clark/L.Johnson/15 10.00 25.00
MO O.O'Neal/Q.Moses/199 5.00 12.00
NA J.Addai/M.Colston/50 8.00 20.00
PT A.Patrick/R.Torain/199 5.00 12.00
SF J.Stewart/M.Forte/50 12.00 30.00
SM Mendenhall/S.Slaton/50 12.00 30.00
ST J.Shockey/C.Taylor/35 8.00 20.00
TB T.Brown/R.Torain/199 5.00 12.00
WC M.Clayton/M.Williams/30 8.00 20.00

2009 SP Signature Party of Four Autographs

STATED PRINT RUN 10-99
AHIB Brown/Norwood/Houston/Anderson/35 8.00 20.00
ALBY Leinrt/Bsh/Add/Yng/15 60.00 100.00
ARIB Robinson/Burton/Anderson/Brown/45 8.00 20.00
BCME Branch/Carriker/McDonald/Ellis/60 6.00 15.00
CBDF Finley/Bennett/Chandler/Davis/50 8.00 20.00
CCSK Cotchery/Stuckey/Clowney/Keller/35 8.00 20.00
CHBH Clowney/Hubbard/Broussard/Hall/50 8.00 20.00
CLAK Carriker/Avery/Burton/Long/35 10.00 25.00
CMBM Balmer/McDonald/Smith/Morgan/15 15.00 40.00
CMFF Flc/Uhr/Frgs/McCl/35 50.00 80.00
CRKA Arrington/Robinson/Clowney/Kent/75 6.00 15.00
DBJK Breaston/Kelly/Davis/Jones/35 10.00 25.00
DHAH Adibi/Hayes/Davis/Hall/40 8.00 20.00
DRFR Rdgrs/Flco/Ryn/Dlh/20 125.00 200.00
FTMS Stwrt/Smth/Frt/Mndn/25 25.00 50.00
GNWG Nelson/Garrard 12.00 30.00
Groves/Sims-Walker/25
HIKD Keyes/Irons/Houston/Demps/15 10.00 25.00
ILPM Lowery/Phillips/Weddle/Morgan/50 8.00 20.00
JJFM Jhnsn/Mndn/Frte/Jns/20 25.00 50.00
JJSF Jones/Frte/Jhnsn/Stwrt/20 15.00 40.00
JYFT Young/Torain/Jones/Forsett/15 12.00 30.00
KHAJ Kelly/Jackson/Arrington/Hawkins/35 8.00 20.00
MFSR Stwrt/Flco/McF/Ryn/15 75.00 125.00
MGBS Smth USC/Brstn/Mrshl/Gnn/35 10.00 25.00
MHRM Mndn/Rssll/Rly/Mllr/35 20.00 40.00
MOPR Lattimore/O'Neal/Brown/Patrick/99 5.00 12.00
OPFB Patrick/Brown/Forsett/O'Neal/35 10.00 25.00
OPFS O'Neal/Forsett/Schmitt/Patrick/35 10.00 25.00
RHFJ Russell/Hester/Flynn/Jones/15 10.00 25.00
SBRM Beck/Moore/Reilly/Palmer/40 8.00 20.00
SJBJ Spncr/Ltmr/Jns/Will/15 25.00 50.00
SKAJ Jhnsn/Kolb/Ainge/Stanton/35 12.00 30.00
SRKF Shockey/Spaeth/Finley/Rosario/25 12.00 30.00
TRHB Robinson/Broussard/Hall/Taylor/75 6.00 15.00
WJK Revis/King/Weddle/Jenkins/35 8.00 20.00
WJM Jenkins/Weddle/Revis/Morgan/35 8.00 20.00
WWHH Hwkns/Sms-Wlkr/Will/Hbbrd/50 10.00 25.00
YRTC Young/Torain/Clady/Royal/15 10.00 25.00

2009 SP Signature Reflections Dual Autographs

STATED PRINT RUN 5-99
RAJ Brink/Jones/30 10.00 25.00
RBB Cantwell/Brohm/25 10.00 25.00
RBC Clayton/Brown/50 8.00 20.00
RBD Davis/Quinn/50 10.00 25.00
RBG Groves/Balmer/99 5.00 12.00
RBL Broussard/Lee/50 8.00 20.00
RBM Manningham/Brown/50 8.00 20.00
RBR Robinson/Burton/50 8.00 20.00
RCB Bennett/Celek/50 8.00 20.00
RCP Clayton/Patrick/50 8.00 20.00
RCR Rucker/Chandler/50 8.00 20.00
RCT Burton/Clowney/50 8.00 20.00
RCW Clowney/Sims-Walker/50 10.00 25.00
RDB Null/Davis/50 12.00 30.00
RDH Davis/Hawkins/50 8.00 20.00
RDK Hall/Lattimore/99 5.00 12.00
RDM Davis/Monk/99 5.00 12.00
RDW Davis/Wheeler/50 8.00 20.00
REN Johnson/Moore/50 8.00 20.00
RFB Lattimore/Hairston/99 5.00 12.00
RFM McFadden/Stewart/25 20.00 50.00
RHB Mack/Smith/50 8.00 15.00
RHC Hall/Crable/99 5.00 12.00
RHF Henne/Flynn/50 10.00 25.00
RHL Hall/Lee/50 8.00 20.00
RIJ Leonhard/Moore/50 8.00 20.00
RIM Moore/Morgan/50 8.00 20.00
RJB Brown/Jones/50 8.00 20.00
RJC Davis/Chandler/50 8.00 20.00
RKA Arrington/Kent/25 10.00 25.00
RKB Beckum/Bennett/50 10.00 25.00
RKC Burton/Kent/50 8.00 20.00
RKM King/Steltz/99 5.00 12.00
RLG Long/Groves/50 8.00 20.00
RLP Hawkins/Williams/50 8.00 20.00
RLW Walker/Lattimore/99 5.00 12.00
RMB Balmer/McDonald/99 5.00 12.00
RMD Demps/Morgan/99 5.00 12.00
RME Moses/Johnson/50 8.00 20.00
RMK Miller/Keller/25 10.00 25.00
RNE Moore/Robinson/50 8.00 20.00
RNK Nelson/Kelly/45 10.00 25.00
ROE Ellis/Okam/40 8.00 20.00
ROP O'Neal/Patrick/50 8.00 20.00
RPJ Jenkins/Phillips/50 8.00 20.00
RPT Lattimore/Torain/99 5.00 12.00
RRB Manningham/Broussard/50 8.00 20.00
RRC Pettigrew/Celek/50 8.00 20.00
RRJ Jenkins/Smith/20 10.00 25.00
RRM Moore/Rosario/50 8.00 20.00
RRW Burton/Robinson/50 8.00 20.00
RSC Spaeth/Celek/50 8.00 20.00
RTM Mendenhall/Torain/50 12.00 30.00
RTY Torain/Lattimore/25 10.00 25.00
RWH Collie/Wayne/20 12.00 30.00
RWR Robinson/Williams/50 8.00 20.00

2009 SP Signature Rivalries Autographs

STATED PRINT RUN 10-35
AS B.Smith/O.Anderson/25 25.00 50.00
BH A.Hawk/L.Briggs/20 15.00 40.00
BJ B.Jacobs/M.Barber/25 12.00 30.00
FB M.Forte/N.Barnett/25 10.00 25.00
HB A.Boldin/S.Holmes/35 8.00 20.00
LB T.Barber/R.Lewis/25 40.00 80.00
TG J.Theismann/B.Griese/25 25.00 50.00

2009 SP Signature Signature Duals

STATED PRINT RUN 10-99
AF Addai/Painter/25 20.00 50.00
AP Lattimore/Patrick/99 5.00 12.00
AR Avery/Royal/25 10.00 25.00
BD Bennett/Davis/99 6.00 15.00
BF Brink/Moffitt/90 5.00 12.00
BG Monroe/L.Jackson/50 8.00 20.00
BJ Burton/V.Jackson/25 10.00 25.00
BW Burton/Sims-Walker/99 6.00 15.00
CB Pettigrew/Nelson/25 6.00 15.00
CC Clowney/Greene/50 5.00 12.00
CK Clowney/Keller/99 5.00 12.00
CL Long/Carriker/25 10.00 25.00
CN Cosby/Coffman/50 8.00 20.00
CR Clowney/Burton/99 5.00 12.00
CS Chandler/Spaeth/99 5.00 12.00
CT Thigpen/Cassel/25 10.00 25.00
DB Brown/Douglas/70 6.00 15.00
DI Harris/Ikegwuonu/75 8.00 20.00
DW P.Williams/C.Davis/99 5.00 12.00
EG S.Nelson/Ellis/99 5.00 12.00
ET Kent/Rowe/99 5.00 12.00
EY Rowe/Reilly/99 5.00 12.00
FB Flynn/Brohm/25 25.00 50.00
FG Garcia/Flacco/25 25.00 60.00
FH Forsett/Hawkins/99 6.00 15.00
FR Ryan/Flacco/15 50.00 100.00
FS Forte/Slaton/25 15.00 40.00
HF Flynn/Cantwell/30 25.00 50.00
HG Ham/Greene/25 30.00 60.00
HH K.Hall/Hawk/25 10.00 25.00
HL D.Lee/K.Hall/25 10.00 25.00
JB Barber/Jacobs/25 15.00 50.00
JC Chandler/G.Johnson/50 8.00 20.00
JJ V.Jackson/Ochocinco/25 10.00 25.00
JM F.Jones/Mendenhall/25 20.00 50.00
JS K.Smith/C.Johnson/25 10.00 25.00
KD Monk/Broussard/99 5.00 12.00
KM Flynn/K.Hall/99 15.00 30.00
KP Kelly/Allison/25 10.00 25.00
KR Rodgers-Cromartie/Keyes/50 8.00 20.00
LB Breaston/Leinart/15 10.00 25.00
LK C.Long/J.King/25 10.00 25.00
MB Balmer/McDonald/99 5.00 12.00
MC McDonald/Butler-Beaton/99 5.00 12.00
MJ Moala/T.Jackson/50 10.00 25.00
MK Burton/Manningham/99 5.00 12.00
MM Bennett/Spaeth/99 6.00 15.00
MR Rosario/M.Moore/99 5.00 12.00
MS H.Miller/Pettigrew/25 6.00 15.00
MT Quinn/Marshall/25 12.00 30.00
NK Monk/Burton/99 5.00 12.00
OB O'Neal/T.Brown/99 5.00 12.00
OF Flacco/Oher/25 50.00 100.00
PB T.Brown/Patrick/99 5.00 12.00
PH Patrick/Hubbard/99 5.00 12.00
PK Patrick/Kelly/25 10.00 25.00
RF Ryan/Flacco/15 50.00 100.00
RJ M.Jenkins/V.Harris/25 10.00 25.00
RK V.Harris/L.Hall/25 10.00 25.00
RM Lattimore/Hairston/99 5.00 12.00
RR R.Robinson/Burton/99 5.00 12.00
RT T.Clayton/Torain/99 5.00 12.00
SA Slaton/Brink/25 10.00 25.00
SO Manningham/Monk/99 5.00 12.00
SS K.Smith/Stanton/25 10.00 25.00
TB T.Brown/Walker/99 5.00 12.00
TC Torain/Clady/99 5.00 12.00
TO O'Neal/Torain/99 5.00 12.00
WC D.Walker/T.Clayton/99 5.00 12.00
WH Hartline/Camarillo/25 15.00 40.00
WO Oher/Willis/25 40.00 80.00
WR Sims-Walker/Dillard/30 10.00 25.00
WS Willis/Curry/25 10.00 25.00
WT D.Walker/Torain/99 5.00 12.00
WW P.Willis/D.Ware/25 15.00 40.00
YH Manningham/Hawkins/99 5.00 12.00

2009 SP Signature Signature Eight

EIGHT AUTO PRINT RUN 5-50
EBCMLBG Linebackers/20 25.00 50.00
EBMBSAK Wide Receivers/20 25.00 50.00
EBWSJHG Retired Defense/20 150.00 250.00
ECOPFTB Young RBs/20 30.00 60.00
ECSBRDF First Tight Ends/50 25.00 50.00
ECWWRHH First Young Rec/20
EDBRCFR Quarterbacks/20 100.00 200.00
EHIKJDM First Young Def/20 30.00 60.00
EMPRBSM Steelers/20 50.00 100.00
ESMRBFJ Young QBs/50 30.00 60.00
ESRCKBF Second Tight Ends/30 25.00 50.00
ETRKBHA Second Young Rec/20
EWSHHHW Second Young Def/25 25.00 50.00

2009 SP Signature Signature Fours

STATED PRINT RUN 5-85
AKHA Hawkins/Kelly/Avery/Arrington/35 8.00 20.00
APRH Mack/Anderson/Patrick/Rucker/25 10.00 25.00
AWRH Reynaud/Allison/Hawkins/Williams/35 8.00 20.00
BBFD Frt/Dvs/Brsrd/Bntt/25 20.00 50.00
BCLK King/Carriker/Bulger/Long/15 12.00 30.00
BCSW Burton/Smith 12.00 30.00
Cotchery/Sims-Walker/25
BEMS Smith/Evns/Brtn/Mchm/25 12.00 30.00
BFFJ Jhn/Fln/Flco/Brnk/35 25.00 60.00
BFFR Flco/Flnn/Brhm/Ryn/15 60.00 100.00
BHHA Hardy/Bennett/Arrington/Hawkins/35 10.00 25.00
BJFM Mndn/Jns/Barbr/Frte/15 30.00 60.00
BMOE Okam/Ellis/McDonald/Branch/35 8.00 20.00
BWFJ Woodson/Johnson/Flynn/Brink/35 8.00 20.00
BWHA Sms/Hrtn/Arng/Brstn/35 12.00 30.00
CABH Caldwell/Bennett/Avery/Hawkins/35 10.00 25.00
CBDF Finley/Bennett/Chandler/Davis/60 8.00 20.00
CBHA Bennett/Clowney/Arrington/Hawkins/40 10.00 25.00
CDWH Hawkins/Davis/Williams/Crumpler/35 8.00 20.00
CPMJ Mrshl/Prsn/Bldn/Jhns/15 25.00 50.00
CSCF Celek/Chandler/Finley/Spaeth/35 8.00 20.00
CSCM Miller/Clark/Shockey/Crumpler/15 10.00 25.00
CSKA Clowney/Ainge/Stuckey/Keller/45 10.00 25.00
CWMK Shockey/Miller/Crumpler/Watson/15 10.00 25.00
CWWH Sims-Walker 10.00 25.00
Hawkins/Burton/Clowney/50
DBCF Cmpbl/Blgr/Flco/Dlh/15 25.00 60.00
DBFR Dlhm/Flco/Blgr/Ryn/15 60.00 100.00
DHHH Highsmith/Hall/Davis/Hayes/50 8.00 20.00
GFAJ Andrsn/Frgm/Grs/Jns/15 30.00 60.00
HIJD Houston/Demps/Jenkins/Weddle/85 8.00 20.00
HIJM Jenkins/Houston/Phillips/Morgan/35 8.00 20.00
HWIJ Rodgers-Cromartie 8.00 20.00
Houston/Jenkins/Weddle/35
JFTC Jons/Frte/Chrls/Stwrt/15 30.00 60.00
JJAL Jons/Lnch/Add/Jhnsn/15 25.00 50.00
JJFM Jhns/Mndn/Frte/Jnes/15 25.00 50.00
KCDI Kolb/Celek/Ikegwuonu/Demps/35 8.00 20.00
MLJG Jackson/Long/Groves/Moses/35 10.00 25.00
MRSM Mndn/Bryant/Davis/Rssll/15 15.00 40.00
MSFM McF/Frte/Mndn/Stwrt/15 40.00 80.00
NHIJ Nelson/Jenkins/Ikegwuonu/Houston/35 8.00 20.00
NWIJ Rodgers-Cromartie 10.00 25.00
Jenkins/Weddle/Nelson/35
OPFT Forsett/O'Neal/Lattimore/Torain/15 12.00 30.00
RBRD Rosario/Cook/Davis/Rucker/70 8.00 20.00

RBSM Mndn/Dvis/Baker/Rus/35 15.00 40.00
RCOB Clayton/Lattimore/Brown/O'Neal/55 6.00 15.00
RRHB Broussard/Robinson/Hall/Robinson/35 8.00 20.00
SBFJ Brnk/Jhnon/Flynn/Stn/35 15.00 40.00
SBRF Rucker/Finley/Bennett/Spaeth/35 8.00 20.00
SDHA Davis/Hall/Sims/Adibi/35 8.00 20.00
SEBG Groves/Ellis/Spencer/Balmer/75 8.00 20.00
SHSW Wills/Hwk/Sms/Sngl/20 30.00 60.00
SSMS Mndn/Smt/Stwrt/Slfn/15 25.00 60.00
TRKF Rowe/Taylor/Forsett/Kent/45 10.00 25.00
WSSJ Sm No AU/Sng/Wd/Jn/15 30.00 80.00
WWMC Wtn/My/Mny/Wlkr/25 30.00 60.00
YCFT Torain/Yng/Clytn/Forsett/15 12.00 30.00
YCTB Brown/Clayton/Young/Torain/15 10.00 25.00

2009 SP Signature Signature Six

STATED PRINT RUN 10-50
DB1 Ikegwuonu/Demps/Houston
Landry/Weddle/Jenkins/30 15.00 40.00
DB2 Jenkins/Jenkins/Rolle/Rodgers-
Cromartie/Houston/Nelson/30 15.00 40.00
LB1 Rs/Sg/Ss/Ws/Wr/Hk/15 50.00 80.00
LB2 Hall/Spencer/Wheeler/Davis
Highsmith/Adibi/30 15.00 40.00
LB3 Adibi/Sims/Davis/Wheeler/Hayes/Hall/30 15.00 40.00
QB1 Rg/Bg/Fc/An/Cp/Dh/30 125.00 200.00
QB2 Bn/Ag/Fc/Bh/Fn/Jn/30 40.00 80.00
QB3 Jn/Bm/Fc/Fn/Bn/Hn/30 40.00 80.00
QB4 Beck/Moore/Thigpen/Rowe
Kolb/Stanton/20 20.00 50.00
QB5 Palmer/Rowe/Ainge/Johnson
Moore/Brink/30 20.00 50.00
RB1 O'Neal/Brown/Patrick/Forsett
Hester/Clayton/30 15.00 40.00
RB2 Ge/Ad/Jn/Ps/Sr/Jn/15 100.00 200.00
RB3 Jn/Ps/Ft/Ad/Pk/Bh/15 100.00 200.00
RB6 Wynn/Mendenhall/Williams
Forsett/Patrick/Brown/30 20.00 50.00
TE1 Shockey/Clark/Miller
Finley/Rosario/Crumpler/15 25.00 60.00
TE2 Finley/Bennett/Spaeth
Celek/Rucker/Davis/30 15.00 40.00
WR1 Bt/Ky/Cd/Ar/Ay/Ry/30 15.00 40.00
WR2 Robinson/Hawkins/Williams/Broussard
Kent/Reynaud/30 15.00 40.00
WR4 Sims-Walker/Arrington/Hubbard
Taylor/Clowney/Bennett/30 15.00 40.00
WR5 Clowney/Kent/Robinson/Hall
Hawkins/Williams/30 15.00 40.00
DEF1 Morgan/Houston/Demps
Henderson/Steltz/Bing/40 15.00 40.00
DEF2 Branch/Jackson/Balmer
Carriker/Long/Groves/30 15.00 40.00
DEF3 Moses/Long/McDonald
Taylor/Anderson/Branch/30 15.00 40.00
DEF4 Taylor/McDonald/Balmer
Moses/Groves/Jackson/30 15.00 40.00
DEF5 Morgan/King/Jenkins/Jenkins
Jammer/Gholston/30 15.00 40.00
RBX2 Ft/Ss/Sm/St/Ge/Cg/30 40.00 80.00
DSTR Tp/Sn/Bn/Wn/Hm/Ws/15 50.00 100.00
PITT Reilly/Baker/Miller/Davis
Mendenhall/Sweed/30 25.00 60.00
JET1 Cotchery/Keller/Clowney/Hawkins
Williams/Crumpler/30 15.00 40.00
JET2 Clowney/Revis/Stuckey
Ainge/Keller/Cotchery/30 15.00 40.00
PACK Fn/Fl/Le/Hk/Bm/Hl/50 30.00 60.00
QBLG Tl/An/Ts/Js/Gr/Gr/15 50.00 100.00
RBLG Jk/Ss/Hn/Sm/Hr/Cg/15 175.00 300.00

2009 SP Signature Signature Trios

STATED PRINT RUN 5-109
ABM Morgan/Burton/Avery/49 8.00 20.00
AFH Lattimore/Forsett/Hawkins/99 6.00 15.00
AHR Hawkins/Reynaud/Arrington/99 5.00 12.00
APH Hubbard/Patrick/Anderson/25 10.00 25.00
ARN Avery/Nelson/Royal/25 12.00 30.00
BBD Broussard/Bennett/Davis/99 6.00 15.00
BBF Brohm/Lee/Flynn/25 10.00 25.00
BDF Bennett/Finley/Davis/99 8.00 20.00
BFF Lee/Brohm/Hall/25 10.00 25.00
BFJ Flynn/Johnson/Cantwell/20 10.00 25.00
BFR Flacco/Brennan/Ryan/15 60.00 100.00
BGE Branch/Ellis/Groves/49 8.00 20.00
BJD Jones/Demps/Breaston/99 6.00 15.00
BKA Burton/Bennett/Kelly/49 10.00 25.00
BMB Brink/Moore/Beck/70 6.00 15.00
BOS Brink/Okam/Slaton/25 10.00 25.00
BSM Lewis/Mendenhall/Davis/20 10.00 25.00
BSS Butks/Syrs/Sngltry/15 60.00 120.00
BWW Willms/Sims-Wlkr/Rbnsn/99 6.00 15.00
CBA Bennett/Caldwell/Arrington/49 10.00 25.00
CBS Breaston/Smith USC/Cotchery/25 12.00 30.00
CKS Keller/Shockey/Clark/25 10.00 25.00
CLA Burton/Long/Carriker/49 10.00 25.00
COB Clayton/Brown/O'Neal/99 5.00 12.00
CSK Clowney/Keller/Stuckey/49 8.00 20.00
CSR Coffman/Chandler/Spaeth/20 10.00 25.00
CWH Hawkins/Williams/Crumpler/25 10.00 25.00
DBC Delhomme/Bulger/Campbell/25 10.00 25.00
DCH Rivers/Hayes/Crable/70 6.00 15.00
DHW Mayo/Rivers/Henderson/25 12.00 30.00
DRS Delhomme/Stewart/Rosario/25 10.00 25.00
FAJ Grse/Andrsn/A.Mnn/20 25.00 60.00
FSH Hart/Schmitt/Forsett/60 8.00 20.00
FSJ Forte/Johnsn/Slatn/25 30.00 60.00
FSM Slaton/Forte/Mndnhll/25 25.00 50.00
GJW Gore/Jacobs/Portis/20 15.00 40.00
HBK Highsmith/Keyes/Morelli/109 5.00 12.00
HFF Hall/Lee/Finley/49 8.00 20.00
HMT Manning/Tittle/Griese/25 25.00 60.00
HSW Maualuga/Hawk/Willis/20 15.00 40.00
JAK Simpson/Jackson/Avery/25 10.00 25.00
JBJ Johnson/Bennett/Lattimore/20 10.00 25.00
JDM Moore/Demps/Morgan/40 8.00 20.00
JEB English/Johnson/Byrd/20 12.00 30.00
JJA Jackson/Addai/Johnson/25 15.00 40.00
JJG Johnson/Gore/Jones/25 12.00 30.00
JRF Jones/Forsett/Rowe/25 12.00 30.00
LMS Lynch/Stewart/McClain/25 15.00 40.00
MCT Clady/Torain/Marshall/25 12.00 30.00
MFS Forte/Mndnhll/Slton/25 25.00 50.00
MJG Marshall/Ginn/Johnson/15 15.00 40.00
MRM Mndnhll/Miller/Rssll/49 15.00 40.00
MRR Rosario/Goodson/Robinson/20 10.00 25.00
MTC Marshall/McKinley/Clady/20 10.00 25.00
NRB Robinson/Norwood/Brown/25 10.00 25.00
OBD Olsen/Bennett/Davis/55 10.00 25.00
PCK Williams/Portis/Campbell/20 12.00 30.00
PRH Mack/Rucker/Patrick/99 5.00 12.00
RBF Beckum/Bennett/Finley/20 10.00 25.00
RBS Russell/Baker/Spaeth/65 8.00 20.00
RFR Romo/Ryan/Flacco/15 75.00 135.00
RHA Hubbard/Burton/Arrington/99 5.00 12.00
SBM Rowe/Stanton/Moore/99 5.00 12.00
SCK Shockey/Clark/Keller/25 15.00 40.00
SFM Forte/Mndnhll/Stwrt/25 25.00 50.00
SHW Sims/Hall/Wheeler/49 8.00 20.00
SJE Ellis/Spencer/Jackson/99 6.00 15.00
SMR Rowe/Stanton/Moore/99 5.00 12.00
TJJ Johnson/Taylor/Jones/25 10.00 25.00
TKB Kent/Taylor/Broussard/99 5.00 12.00
WJR Williams/Jones/Robinson/99 5.00 12.00
WMB Willis/Smith/McDonald/25 15.00 40.00
WRK Kent/Robinson/Williams/99 5.00 12.00
WSS Sngltry/Smith/Wdson/25 40.00 80.00
WWR Willis/Ware/Revis/25 30.00 80.00
YTB Hairston/Brown/Lattimore/99 5.00 12.00

2009 SP Signature Triple Scripts

STATED PRINT RUN 10-99
ABK Burton/Bennett/Kelly/50 10.00 25.00
AHA Burton/Arrington/Hawkins/99 5.00 12.00
AHB Anderson/Houston/Baker/50 8.00 20.00
BCM Branch/Carriker/Moses/75 6.00 15.00
BDF Finley/Bennett/Davis/75 6.00 15.00
BFF Flynn/Flacco/Brink/50 20.00 50.00
BFJ Brink/Flynn/Johnson/99 8.00 20.00
BHK Branch/Highsmith/Keyes/99 5.00 12.00
BMC Clayton/McDnld/Balmer/99 5.00 12.00
BNR Robinsn/Brown/Moore/25 10.00 25.00
BSH Smith USC/Burtn/Hwkins/99 6.00 15.00
BSS Butkus/Sayrs/Singltry/25 60.00 120.00
CAW Clark/Wheeler/Addai/25 10.00 25.00
CGR Craig/Gore/Rathman/25 20.00 40.00
CJB Broussard/Clowney/Jones/99 5.00 12.00
CLK King/Long/Carriker/50 10.00 25.00
CMB Carriker/Balmer/McDonald/99 5.00 12.00
COP Clayton/Lattimore/O'Neal/99 5.00 12.00
CRF Finley/Crumpler/Rosario/50 8.00 20.00
CSC Chandler/Spaeth/Celek/99 5.00 12.00
CSK Coffman/Spaeth/Chandler/50 8.00 20.00
CWR Clowney/Robinson/Sims-Walker/99 6.00 15.00
DBC Dlhmme/Cmpbll/Bulgr/25 10.00 25.00
DHH Hall/Davis/Hayes/50 8.00 20.00
DHM Davis/Hall/Maualuga/25 10.00 25.00
DKA Kent/Arrington/Davis/99 5.00 12.00
DMR Dlhmme/Mre/Rbisn/99 10.00 25.00
DMS Stewart/Delhomme/Goodson/25 12.00 30.00
FBJ Brink/Johnson/Flynn/99 12.00 30.00
HCH Crable/Hall/Hayes/50 8.00 20.00
HFF Flynn/Hall/Finley/50 25.00 50.00
HGG Greene/Grnwd/Ham/25 60.00 120.00
HJH Houston/Harris/Jenkins/50 8.00 20.00
HJM Jackson/Holmes/Marshall/25 12.00 30.00
HKM Morgan/Harris/Keyes/50 8.00 20.00
HLF Lee/Hall/Flynn/75 6.00 15.00
HWB Wheeler/Brown/Hart/25 6.00 15.00
JBF Bush/Forte/Jones/25 25.00 50.00
JBJ Bennett/Jenkins/Lattimore/99 8.00 20.00
JCW Jackson/Clowney/Sims-Walker/50 8.00 20.00
JDM Morgan/Demps/Jenkins/99 5.00 12.00
JFS Jones/Schmitt/Forsett/25 12.00 30.00
JMS Mndnhll/Jhnsn/Stwrt/25 20.00 50.00
JSM Mndnhll/Jones/Stwrt/25 25.00 50.00
KHA Kelly/Arrington/Hawkins/50 8.00 20.00
LBG Groves/Balmer/Long/50 10.00 25.00
LJE Jackson/Ellis/Long/50 10.00 25.00
MHA Mnninghm/Arringtn/Hwkns/75 6.00 15.00
MLB Burton/Lee/Manningham/99 5.00 12.00
MRA Ainge/Rowe/Moore/75 6.00 15.00
MRR Goodson/Robinson/Rosario/75 8.00 20.00
OPB O'Neal/Patrick/Brown/99 5.00 12.00
PRH Rucker/Patrick/Mack/99 5.00 12.00
RBF Bennett/Finley/Rosario/50 8.00 20.00
RBS Davis/Baker/Russell/25 10.00 25.00
RCJ Cotchery/Jackson/Royal/25 10.00 25.00
RCW Sims-Wlkr/Reynd/Clowny/99 6.00 15.00
RFS Forsett/Schmitt/Rowe/75 8.00 20.00
RHN Naanee/Robinson/Hawkins/99 5.00 12.00
RPJ Jnkns/Phillps/Rdgrs-Crom/50 8.00 20.00
RTC Royal/Clady/Torain/25 10.00 25.00
RWC Williams/Clowney/Robinson/99 5.00 12.00
SBJ Spencer/Jenkins/Lattimore/50 10.00 25.00
SBM Rowe/Palmer/Moore/50 8.00 20.00
SCM Miller/Clark/Shockey/25 15.00 40.00
SFF Flacco/Flynn/Stanton/25 25.00 60.00
SGW Sngltry/Wilis/Grne/25 40.00 80.00
SHH Hayes/Hall/Sims/50 8.00 20.00
SJE Smith/Jackson/Ellis/99 6.00 15.00
SJK Kent/Smith/Jones/99 6.00 15.00
SJM Slatn/Mndnhll/Jones/25 25.00 50.00
SMJ Jones/Mndnhll/Stwrt/25 25.00 50.00
SMR Moore/Stanton/Rowe/99 10.00 25.00
STS Smith/Stewart/Torain/25 15.00 40.00
TJL Lynch/Johnson/Taylor/25 12.00 30.00
TMA Andrsn/Tittle/A.Mnn/25 30.00 60.00
TWH Hubbard/Taylor/Sims-Walker/99 6.00 15.00
WHA Adibi/Willis/Hall/25 12.00 30.00
WRJ Jnkins/Weddle/Rdgrs-Crom/50 8.00 20.00
WST Smith/Walker/Torain/25 10.00 25.00
WTC Torain/Clady/Walker/99 5.00 12.00

1963-66 Spalding Advisory Staff Photos

Spalding released a number of player photos during the 1960s. Each measures roughly 8" by 10" and carries a black and white photo of the player surrounding by a white border. Included below the photo is a note that the player is a member of Spalding's advisory staff. Some include the Spalding logo while other do not. The photos are blankbacked and unnumbered and checklisted below in alphabetical order. Since many of the photos differ in type style and design, it is thought that they were released over a number of years. Any additions to the list below are appreciated.

1 Jon Arnett 7.50 15.00
2 Ronnie Bull 7.50 15.00
3 Gail Cogdill 7.50 15.00
4 John David Crow 7.50 15.00
5 Len Dawson 12.50 25.00
6 Sonny Gibbs 7.50 15.00
7 Pete Retzlaff 7.50 15.00
8 Fran Tarkenton 15.00 30.00
9 Norm Van Brocklin 15.00 30.00
10 Bill Wade 7.50 15.00

1966 Spalding Brown Frame Photos

These photos are similar to other Spalding photos of the era except for the brown wood grain frame border that surrounds the picture. Spalding released a number of player photos during the 1960s. Each measures roughly 8" by 10" and carries a black and white photo of the player. The photos are blankbacked and unnumbered and checklisted below in alphabetical order. Any additions to the list below are appreciated.

1 Roman Gabriel 10.00 20.00
2 Johnny Unitas 30.00 50.00

1967 Spalding Red Border Photos

This group of photos is similar to other Spalding photos of the era except for the red border that surrounds the picture. Spalding released a number of player photos during the 1960s. Each measures roughly 8" by 10" and carries a black and white photo of the player. The photos are blankbacked and unnumbered and checklisted below in alphabetical order. Any additions to the list below are appreciated.

1 Norm Snead 10.00 15.00
2 Johnny Unitas 30.00 50.00

1968 Spalding Green Frame Photos

This group of photos is similar to other Spalding photos of the era except for the green frame border that surrounds the picture. Spalding released a number of player photos during the 1960s. Each measures roughly 8" by 10" and carries a black and white photo of the player. The photos are blankbacked and unnumbered and checklisted below in alphabetical order. Any additions to the list below are appreciated.

COMPLETE SET (5) 60.00 120.00
1 Len Dawson 10.00 20.00
2 Bobby Mitchell 10.00 20.00
3 Fran Tarkenton 15.00 30.00
4 Charley Taylor 10.00 20.00
5 Johnny Unitas 20.00 40.00

1993 Spectrum QB Club Tribute Sheets

These 8 1/2" by 11" blank-backed sheets pay tribute to NFL quarterbacks and feature color player photos and 24-karat gold player signature reproductions, all on a black marbleized background. Each sheet (except numbers 11 and 12 below) has two color photos of the honored player. The photo on the left is an action shot; the one on the right is a closeup. The player's 24K gold facsimile autograph, and the sheet's production number, appear between the two photos. The gold foil stamped player's name is shown near the top, and the gold foil stamped set title rests at the bottom. The sheets are unnumbered and checklisted below in alphabetical order.

COMPLETE SET (12) 15.00 40.00
PROMO/5000: .3X TO .8X BASIC CARDS
*COLL.EDITION/1500: .5X TO 1.2X BASIC CARDS
1 Troy Aikman 1.25 3.00
2 Randall Cunningham .75 2.00
3 John Elway 2.50 6.00
4 Boomer Esiason .60 1.50
5 Brett Favre 2.50 6.00
6 Jim Kelly 1.00 2.50
7 Dan Marino 2.50 6.00
8 Warren Moon .60 1.50
9 Phil Simms .60 1.50
10 Steve Young 1.25 3.00
11 AFC Stars .60 1.50
12 NFC Stars .60 1.50
13 Bob Griese .75 2.00

1926 Sport Company of America

This 151-card set encompasses athletes from a multitude of different sports. There are 49-cards representing baseball and 14-cards for football. Each includes a black-and-white player photo within a fancy frame border. The player's name and sport are printed at the bottom. The backs carry a short player biography and statistics. The cards originally came in a small glassine envelope along with a coupon that could be redeemed for sporting equipment and are often still found in this form. The cards are unnumbered and have been checklisted below in alphabetical order within sport. We've assigned prefixes to the card numbers which serves to group the cards by sport (BB- baseball, FB- football).

FB1 Peggy Flournoy 100.00 200.00
FB1B Peggy Flournoy AD 125.00 250.00
FB2 Benny Friedman 175.00 300.00
FB3 Ed Garbisch 100.00 200.00
FB4 Red Grango Promo 1500.00 2500.00
FB5 Homer Hazel 100.00 200.00
FB6 Walter Koppisch 125.00 250.00
FB6B Walter Koppisch AD 150.00 300.00
FB7 Edward McGinley 100.00 200.00
FB8 Edward McMillan 125.00 250.00
FB8B Edward McMillan AD 150.00 300.00
FB9 Harry Stuhldreher 250.00 500.00
FB9B Harry Stuhldreher AD 300.00 600.00
FB10 Brick Muller 100.00 200.00
FB11 Ernie Nevers 1000.00 1500.00
FB12 Swede Oberlander 100.00 200.00
FB12B Swede Oberlander AD 125.00 250.00
FB13 Edward Tryon 125.00 250.00
FB14 Ed Weir 100.00 200.00
FB15 George Wilson 125.00 250.00
FB15B George Wilson AD 150.00 300.00

1992 Sport Decks Promo Aces

Produced by Junior Card and Toy Inc. and given away at the 1992 National Sports Collectors Convention in Atlanta, this four-card standard-size set was produced to promote the premier edition of Sport Decks NFL playing cards. One card was given away on each of the four days of the convention. The color action player cut-outs on the fronts stand out against a full-bleed background that has a metallic sheen to it. A metallic bar overlays the photo at the top and bottom; the top bar carries the card's number, suit, and the Team NFL logo, while the bottom bar has the team helmet, player's name and position, and the Sport Decks logo. All cards come in two varieties, with either gold or silver metallic bars on their fronts. The production figures for the silver were reportedly approximately 6,000, and for the gold, approximately 1,000. On a white background with hot pink and black lettering, the backs carry an advertisement, logos, and a list of players featured in the different card sets. All these cards are Aces, and this is indicated below by the number one followed by a letter indicating the suit. The silver versions are valued individually below.

COMPLETE SET (4) 12.00 30.00
*GOLD CARDS: 1.5X TO 3X SILVERS
1C Emmitt Smith 6.00 15.00
1D Thurman Thomas .80 2.00
1H Dan Marino 6.00 15.00
1S Mark Rypien .40 1.00

1992 Sport Decks

This 55-card standard-size set was issued in a box as if it were a playing card deck. According to Sport Decks, 294,632 decks were produced and 7,500 certified uncut sheets. The design of these cards differ from the promo deck in that a Team NFL logo appears in the ghosted top stripe (promo issue has a NFL logo) and TM (trademark) is printed by the helmet. The back differs from the promo issue in that the Team NFL logo appears again, which slightly alters the back design. Since the set is similar to a playing card set, the set is arranged just like a card deck and checklisted below accordingly. In the checklist below S means Spades, D means Diamonds, C means Clubs, H means Hearts, and JK means Joker. The cards are checklisted below in playing card order by suits and numbers are assigned to Aces (1), Jacks (11), Queens (12), and Kings (13). The jokers are unnumbered and listed at the end.

COMP.FACT SET (55) 3.20 8.00
1C Troy Aikman .40 1.00
1D Jim Kelly .07 .20
1H Dan Marino .80 2.00
1S Mark Rypien .01 .05
2C Rodney Peete .01 .05
2D John Friesz .01 .05
2H Anthony Munoz .02 .10
2S Phil Simms .02 .10
3C Cris Carter .07 .20
3D Gaston Green .01 .05
3H Nick Bell .01 .05
3S Pat Swilling .01 .05
4C Randal Hill .01 .05
4D Hugh Millen .01 .05
4H Michael Dean Perry .01 .05
4S Jim Harbaugh .02 .10
5C Jeff Hostetler .02 .10
5D Dan McGwire .01 .05
5H Haywood Jeffires .01 .05
5S Mike Singletary .02 .10
6C Flipper Anderson .01 .05
6D Eric Green .01 .05
6H Bubby Brister .01 .05
6S Lawrence Taylor .02 .10
7C Chris Miller .01 .05
7D Christian Okoye .01 .05
7H Andre Reed .02 .10
7S John Taylor .01 .05
8C Anthony Carter .02 .10
8D Ronnie Lott .02 .10
8H Anthony Miller .02 .10
8S Keith Jackson .02 .10
9C Timm Rosenbach .01 .05
9D Rob Moore .02 .10
9H Ken O'Brien .01 .05
9S Vinny Testaverde .02 .10
10C Sterling Sharpe .02 .10
10D Mark Clayton .01 .05
10H Bernie Kosar .02 .10
10S Andre Rison .02 .10
11C Ricky Ervins .01 .05
11D Thurman Thomas .07 .20
11H Derrick Thomas .02 .10
11S Michael Irvin .07 .20
12C Jerry Rice .40 1.00
12D John Elway .80 2.00
12H Jeff George .02 .10
12S Earnest Byner .01 .05
13C Emmitt Smith .80 2.00
13D Warren Moon .07 .20
13H Boomer Esiason .02 .10
13S Randall Cunningham .07 .20
JK1 Eric Dickerson .02 .10
JK2 Jim Everett .02 .10
NNO Title Card .01 .05

1994 Sportflics Samples

This seven-card standard-size set was issued to preview the 1994 Sportflics series. When tilted, the full-bleed fronts show two different action photos of the same player. The backs carry another player photo as well as statistics and/or player profile. The cards are very similar to the regular issue Sportflics cards with only slight differences as noted below, usually on the cardback. The upper right corner of each card is cut off to indicate that these are samples.

COMPLETE SET (7) 3.00 7.50
3 Flipper Anderson .25 .60
50 Reggie Brooks .25 .60
70 Herman Moore .40 1.00
145 Chuck Levy .25 .60
180 Jerome Bettis .80 2.00
HH1 Dante Jones 1.60 4.00
Barry Sanders
NNO Sportflics Ad Card .10 .30

1994 Sportflics

This set consists of 184 standard size motion cards which offer a different photo depending on how they are held. The set closes with Rookies (143-175) and Starflics (176-184) subsets. The fronts have the player's name in a yellow banner up the left side with three footballs at the bottom. At bottom right, the team helmet and logo can be viewed. Horizontal backs have two player photos, statistics and highlights. Rookie Cards include Marshall Faulk, William Floyd, Errict Rhett, Darnay Scott and Heath Shuler.

COMPLETE SET (184) 10.00 25.00
1 Deion Sanders .25 .60
2 Leslie O'Neal .02 .10
3 Flipper Anderson .02 .10
4 Anthony Carter .07 .20
5 Thurman Thomas .10 .30
6 Johnny Mitchell .02 .10
7 Jeff Hostetler .07 .20
8 Renaldo Turnbull .02 .10
9 Chris Warren .07 .20
10 Darrell Green .02 .10
11 Randall Cunningham .10 .30
12 Barry Sanders .75 2.00
13 Jeff Cross .02 .10
14 Glyn Milburn .07 .20
15 Willie Davis .07 .20
16 Tony McGee .02 .10
17 Gary Clark .07 .20
18 Michael Jackson .07 .20
19 Alvin Harper .07 .20
20 Tim Worley .02 .10
21 Quentin Coryatt .02 .10
22 Michael Brooks .02 .10
23 Boomer Esiason .07 .20
24 Ricky Watters .07 .20
25 Craig Erickson .02 .10
26 Willie Green .02 .10
27 Brett Favre 1.00 2.50
28 John Elway 1.00 2.50
29 Steve Beuerlein .07 .20
30 Emmitt Smith .75 2.00
31 Troy Aikman .50 1.25
32 Cody Carlson .02 .10
33 Brian Mitchell .02 .10
34 Herschel Walker .07 .20
35 Bruce Smith .07 .20
36 Harold Green .02 .10
37 Erric Pegram .02 .10
38 Ronnie Harmon .02 .10
39 Brian Blades .07 .20
40 Sterling Sharpe .07 .20
41 Leonard Russell .02 .10
42 Cleveland Gary .02 .10
43 Tom Waddle .02 .10
44 Lawrence Dawsey .02 .10
45 Jerry Rice .50 1.25
46 Terry Allen .07 .20
47 Reggie Langhorne .02 .10
48 Derek Brown RBK .02 .10
49 Terry Kirby .07 .20
50 Reggie Brooks .07 .20
51 Calvin Williams .07 .20
52 Cornelius Bennett .07 .20
53 Russell Maryland .02 .10
54 Rob Moore .07 .20
55 Dana Stubblefield .07 .20
56 Rod Woodson .07 .20
57 Rodney Hampton .07 .20
58 Neil Smith .07 .20
59 Anthony Smith .02 .10
60 Neal Anderson .02 .10
61 Drew Bledsoe .40 1.00
62 John Copeland .02 .10
63 David Klingler .02 .10
64 Phil Simms .07 .20
65 Vincent Brisby .07 .20
66 Richard Dent .07 .20
67 Eric Metcalf .07 .20
68 Eric Curry .02 .10
69 Victor Bailey .02 .10
70 Herman Moore .10 .30
71 Steve Jordan .02 .10
72 Jerome Bettis .25 .60
73 Natrone Means .10 .30
74 Webster Slaughter .02 .10
75 Jackie Harris .02 .10
76 Michael Irvin .10 .30
77 Steve Emtman .02 .10
78 Eugene Robinson .02 .10
79 Tim Brown .10 .30
80 Derrick Thomas .10 .30
81 Vinny Testaverde .07 .20
82 Mark Jackson .02 .10
83 Ricky Proehl .02 .10
84 Stan Humphries .07 .20
85 Garrison Hearst .10 .30
86 Jim Kelly .10 .30
87 Brent Jones .07 .20
88 Eric Martin .02 .10
89 Wilber Marshall .02 .10
90 Chris Spielman .07 .20
91 Eric Green .02 .10
92 Andre Rison .07 .20
93 Andre Reed .07 .20
94 Carl Pickens .07 .20
95 Junior Seau .10 .30
96 Dwight Stone .02 .10
97 Mike Sherrard .02 .10
98 Vincent Brown .02 .10
99 Cris Carter .25 .60
100 Mark Higgs .02 .10
101 Steve Young .30 .75
102 Mark Carrier WR .07 .20
103 Barry Foster .02 .10
104 Tommy Vardell .02 .10
105 Shannon Sharpe .07 .20
106 Reggie White .10 .30
107 Ernest Givins .07 .20
108 Marcus Allen .10 .30
109 James Jett .02 .10
110 Keith Jackson .02 .10
111 Irving Fryar .07 .20
112 Ronnie Lott .07 .20
113 Cortez Kennedy .07 .20
114 Ronald Moore .02 .10
115 Rick Mirer .07 .20
116 Neil O'Donnell .07 .20
117 Courtney Hawkins .02 .10
118 Johnny Johnson .02 .10
119 Ben Coates .07 .20
120 Dan Marino 1.00 2.50
121 Sean Gilbert .02 .10
122 Rocket Ismail .07 .20
123 Joe Montana 1.00 2.50
124 Roosevelt Potts .02 .10
125 Gary Brown .02 .10
126 Reggie Cobb .02 .10
127 Marion Butts .02 .10
128 Scott Mitchell .07 .20
129 John L. Williams .02 .10
130 Jeff George .07 .20
131 Bobby Hebert .02 .10
132 John Friesz .07 .20
133 Anthony Miller .07 .20
134 Jim Harbaugh .07 .20
135 Erik Kramer .07 .20
136 Jim Everett .07 .20
137 Michael Haynes .07 .20
138 Rod Bernstine .02 .10
139 Chris Miller .02 .10
140 Henry Ellard .07 .20
141 William Fuller .02 .10
142 Warren Moon .10 .30
143 Lamar Smith RC .50 1.25
144 Charlie Garner RC .40 1.00
145 Chuck Levy RC .02 .10
146 Dan Wilkinson RC .07 .20
147 Perry Klein RC .02 .10
148 William Floyd RC .07 .20
149 Lake Dawson RC .07 .20
150 David Palmer RC .10 .30
151 James Bostic RC .07 .20
152 Marshall Faulk RC 2.00 5.00
153 Greg Hill RC .10 .30
154 Heath Shuler RC .10 .30
155 Errict Rhett RC .10 .30
156 Sam Adams RC .07 .20
157 Charles Johnson RC .10 .30
158 Ryan Yarborough RC .02 .10
159 Thomas Lewis RC .07 .20
160 Willie McGinest RC .10 .30
161 Jamir Miller RC .07 .20
162 Calvin Jones RC .02 .10
163 Donnell Bennett RC .10 .30
164 Trev Alberts RC .07 .20
165 LeShon Johnson RC .07 .20
166 Johnnie Morton RC .25 .60
167 Derrick Alexander WR RC .10 .30
168 Jeff Cothran RC .02 .10
169 Bucky Brooks RC .02 .10
170 Bert Emanuel RC .10 .30
171 Darnay Scott RC .25 .60
172 Kevin Lee RC .02 .10
173 Mario Bates RC .07 .20
174 Bryant Young RC .20 .50
175 Trent Dilfer RC .40 1.00
176 Joe Montana SF .50 1.25
177 Emmitt Smith SF .40 1.00
178 Troy Aikman SF .25 .60
179 Steve Young SF .10 .30
180 Jerome Bettis SF .10 .30
181 John Elway SF .50 1.25
182 Dan Marino SF .50 1.25
183 Brett Favre SF .50 1.25
184 Barry Sanders SF .40 1.00
FTF1 T.Kirby 1.50 4.00
L.Russell

1994 Sportflics Artist's Proofs

COMPLETE SET (184) 125.00 300.00
*STARS: 5X TO 12X BASIC CARDS
*RCs: 3X TO 8X BASIC CARDS
STATED ODDS 1:24

1994 Sportflics Head-To-Head

Randomly inserted in packs at a rate of one in 72, this set pairs a top offensive player with a top defensive player. Horizontally designed cards feature the defensive player on the left and the offensive player on the right. The images are a close-up and a three-dimensional view. The backs have a photo of both players and a brief write-up. The cards are numbered with an "HH" prefix.

COMPLETE SET (10) 20.00 50.00
STATED ODDS 1:72
HH1 B.Sanders 5.00 12.00
D.Jones
HH2 E.Smith 5.00 12.00
C.Bailey
HH3 D.Marino 6.00 15.00
R.Woodson
HH4 J.Rice 3.00 8.00
D.Sanders
HH5 J.Bettis 1.50 4.00
V.Johnson
HH6 T.Aikman 3.00 8.00
Reg.White
HH7 S.Young 2.00 5.00
R.Turnbull
HH8 St.Sharpe .50 1.25
E.Allen
HH9 J.Montana 6.00 15.00
Anth.Smith
HH10 J.Elway 6.00 15.00
N.Smith

1994 Sportflics Rookie Rivalry

Randomly inserted at a rate of one in 24, this 10-card set features two rookies from the same position. Surrounding the photos are the player's name along the right border with the position at upper right. The backs are split to show both players with a brief write-up. The cards are numbered with an "RR" prefix.

COMPLETE SET (10) 10.00 25.00
STATED ODDS 1:18
RR1 M.Faulk 4.00 10.00
W.Floyd
RR2 D.Wilkinson .40 1.00
S.Adams
RR3 H.Shuler 1.00 2.50
T.Dilfer
RR4 J.Miller .40 1.00
T.Alberts
RR5 J.Morton .60 1.50
C.Johnson
RR6 C.Levy 1.00 2.50
C.Garner
RR7 T.Lewis .60 1.50
D.Alexander WR
RR8 I.Bruce 4.00 10.00
D.Scott
RR9 D.Palmer .40 1.00
R.Yarborough
RR10 Le.Johnson .60 1.50
D.Bennett

1994 Sportflics Pride of Texas

These four Sportflics cards were given away at the Pinnacle Booth during the National Convention in Houston. Thus they feature athletes from Texas professional sport franchises: Dallas Cowboys (1), Houston Oilers (2), and Dallas Stars (3-4). On the fronts, the standard-size cards display a color player cutout on a background consisting of the Houston skyline. A Special "The Pride of Texas" logo appears on each front. The backs carry biography and a brief player profile. The tagline on the bottom of each back indicates that just 2,500 of each card were produced.

COMPLETE SET (4) 6.00 15.00
N1 Alvin Harper 1.50 4.00
N2 Gary Brown 1.50 4.00

1995 Sportflix

This 175 card set was issued through both hobby and retail outlets for the first time and breaks down into 118 regular cards, 30 rookie cards, 20 Game Winners cards and seven checklists. Rookie Cards include Kerry Collins, Terrell Davis, Joey Galloway, Steve McNair, Rashaan Salaam, Kordell Stewart, J.J. Stokes and Michael Westbrook. . Three Promo cards were produced and priced at the end of our checklist.

COMPLETE SET (175) 10.00 25.00
1 Troy Aikman .40 1.00
2 Rodney Hampton .07 .20
3 Jerry Rice .40 1.00
4 Reggie White .10 .30
5 Mark Ingram .02 .10
6 Chris Spielman .07 .20
7 Curtis Conway .10 .30
8 Erik Kramer .02 .10
9 Emmitt Smith .60 1.50
10 Alvin Harper .02 .10
11 Junior Seau .10 .30
12 Mike Pritchard .02 .10
13 Ricky Ervins .02 .10
14 Jim Harbaugh .07 .20
15 Dan Marino .75 2.00
16 Marshall Faulk .50 1.25
17 Lorenzo White .02 .10
18 Cortez Kennedy .07 .20
19 Rocket Ismail .07 .20
20 Eric Metcalf .07 .20
21 Chris Chandler .07 .20
22 John Elway .75 2.00
23 Boomer Esiason .07 .20
24 Herman Moore .10 .30
25 Deion Sanders .25 .60
26 Charles Johnson .07 .20
27 Daryl Johnston .07 .20
28 Dave Krieg .02 .10
29 Jim Kelly .10 .30
30 Warren Moon .07 .20
31 Lewis Tillman .02 .10
32 Bruce Smith .10 .30
33 Jake Reed .07 .20
34 Craig Heyward .07 .20
35 Frank Reich .02 .10
36 Stan Humphries .07 .20
37 Charles Haley .07 .20
38 Andre Rison .07 .20
39 James Jett .07 .20
40 Jay Novacek .07 .20
41 Gary Brown .02 .10
42 Steve Bono .07 .20
43 Cris Carter .10 .30
44 Steve Atwater .02 .10
45 Andre Reed .07 .20
46 Greg Lloyd .07 .20
47 Mark Seay .07 .20
48 Dave Meggett .02 .10
49 Steve Beuerlein .07 .20
50 Jeff Graham .02 .10
51 Barry Sanders .60 1.50
52 Willie Davis .07 .20
53 Robert Smith .10 .30
54 Steve Walsh .02 .10
55 Michael Irvin .10 .30
56 Natrone Means .07 .20
57 Chris Warren .07 .20
58 Tim Brown .10 .30
59 Steve Young .30 .75
60 Jerome Bettis .10 .30
61 Shannon Sharpe .07 .20
62 Errict Rhett .07 .20
63 Scott Mitchell .07 .20
64 Leroy Hoard .02 .10
65 Garrison Hearst .10 .30
66 Terance Mathis .07 .20
67 Sean Gilbert .07 .20
68 Fred Barnett .07 .20
69 Hardy Nickerson .02 .10
70 Jim Everett .02 .10
71 Randall Cunningham .10 .30
72 Carl Pickens .07 .20
73 Jeff Hostetler .07 .20
74 Marcus Allen .10 .30
75 Jeff George .07 .20
76 Brett Favre .75 2.00
77 Chris Miller .02 .10
78 Craig Erickson .02 .10
79 Herschel Walker .07 .20
80 Bert Emanuel .10 .30
81 Leonard Russell .02 .10
82 Ricky Watters .07 .20
83 Robert Brooks .10 .30
84 Dave Brown .07 .20
85 Henry Ellard .07 .20
86 Barry Foster .07 .20
87 Johnny Mitchell .02 .10
88 Eric Allen .02 .10
89 Darnay Scott .07 .20
90 Harvey Williams .02 .10
91 Neil O'Donnell .07 .20
92 Drew Bledsoe .25 .60
93 Ken Harvey .02 .10
94 Irving Fryar .07 .20
95 Rod Woodson .07 .20
96 Anthony Miller .07 .20
97 Mario Bates .07 .20
98 Jeff Blake RC .30 .75
99 Rick Mirer .07 .20
100 William Floyd .07 .20
101 Michael Haynes .07 .20
102 Flipper Anderson .02 .10
103 Greg Hill .07 .20
104 Mark Brunell .25 .60
105 Vinny Testaverde .07 .20
106 Heath Shuler .07 .20
107 Ronald Moore .02 .10
108 Ernest Givins .02 .10
109 Mike Sherrard .02 .10
110 Charlie Garner .10 .30
111 Trent Dilfer .10 .30
112 Byron Bam Morris .02 .10
113 Lake Dawson .07 .20
114 Brian Blades .07 .20
115 Brent Jones .02 .10
116 Ronnie Harmon .02 .10
117 Eric Green .02 .10
118 Ben Coates .07 .20
119 Ki-Jana Carter RC .10 .30
120 Steve McNair RC 1.25 3.00
121 Michael Westbrook RC .10 .30
122 Kerry Collins RC .75 2.00
123 Joey Galloway RC .60 1.50
124 Kyle Brady RC .10 .30
125 J.J. Stokes RC .10 .30
126 Tyrone Wheatley RC .50 1.25
127 Rashaan Salaam RC .07 .20
128 Napoleon Kaufman RC .50 1.25
129 Frank Sanders RC .10 .30
130 Stoney Case RC .02 .10
131 Todd Collins RC .50 1.25
132 Lovell Pinkney RC .02 .10
133 Sherman Williams RC .02 .10
134 Rob Johnson RC .40 1.00
135 Mark Bruener RC .07 .20
136 Lee DeRamus RC .02 .10
137 Chad May RC .02 .10
138 James A.Stewart RC .02 .10
139 Ray Zellars RC .07 .20
140 Dave Barr RC .02 .10
141 Kordell Stewart RC .60 1.50
142 Jimmy Oliver RC .02 .10
143 Terrell Fletcher RC .02 .10
144 James O. Stewart RC .50 1.25
145 Terrell Davis RC 1.00 2.50
146 Joe Aska RC .02 .10
147 John Walsh RC .02 .10
148 Tyrone Davis RC .02 .10
149 Emmitt Smith GW .30 .75
150 Barry Sanders GW .30 .75
151 Jerry Rice GW .20 .50
152 Steve Young GW .15 .40
153 Dan Marino GW .40 1.00
154 Troy Aikman GW .20 .50
155 Drew Bledsoe GW .10 .30
156 John Elway GW .40 1.00
157 Brett Favre GW .40 1.00
158 Michael Irvin GW .07 .20
159 Heath Shuler GW .07 .20
160 Warren Moon GW .02 .10
161 Jim Kelly GW .10 .30
162 Randall Cunningham GW .07 .20
163 Jeff Hostetler GW .07 .20
164 Dave Brown GW .07 .20
165 Neil O'Donnell GW .07 .20
166 Rick Mirer GW .07 .20
167 Jim Everett GW .02 .10
168 Boomer Esiason GW .07 .20
169 Dan Marino CL .20 .50
170 Drew Bledsoe CL .10 .30
171 John Elway CL .10 .30
172 Emmitt Smith CL .15 .40
173 Steve Young CL .10 .30
174 Barry Sanders CL .10 .30
175 Jerry Rice/Seau CL .10 .30
P1 Troy Aikman Promo .50 1.25
P6 J.J. Stokes Lightning Promo .30 .75
P92 Drew Bledsoe Promo .40 1.00

1995 Sportflix Artist's Proofs

COMPLETE SET (175) 250.00 500.00
*STARS: 6X TO 15X BASIC CARDS
*RCs: 4X TO 10X BASIC CARDS
STATED ODDS 1:36

1995 Sportflix Man 2 Man

Randomly inserted at a rate of one in eight jumbo packs, this 12 card set features two players at the same position. Card fronts include a background of a football field with both player's names located between them in the middle. Card backs contain seperate commentary for each player.

COMPLETE SET (12) 20.00 50.00
RANDOM INSERTS IN JUMBO PACKS
1 D.Marino 5.00 12.00
T.Aikman
2 E.Smith 4.00 10.00
M.Faulk
3 D.Bledsoe 1.50 4.00
K.Collins
4 S.Young 3.00 8.00
S.McNair
5 B.Sanders 4.00 10.00
Ki.Carter
6 J.Elway 5.00 12.00
H.Shuler
7 B.Morris .20 .50
R.Salaam
8 N.Means .50 1.25
R.Watters
9 J.Rice 2.50 6.00
J.J.Stokes
10 K.Stewart 1.50 4.00
W.Moon
11 B.Favre 5.00 12.00
J.Blake
12 J.Galloway 1.50 4.00
M.Westbrook

1995 Sportflix ProMotion

Randomly inserted into packs at a rate of one in 48 packs, this 12 card set utilizes a color morph multi-phase animated shot that follows these players through 36 phases of movement. Card fronts feature a team color background with the team helmet and the word "Motion" at the bottom at the beginning of the phase. The fronts then phase into an action shot of the player. Card backs are horizontal with a headshot against a brown background and contain a brief summary on the player. Cards are numbered with a "PM" prefix.

COMPLETE SET (12) 30.00 80.00
PM1 Steve Young 3.00 8.00
PM2 Troy Aikman 4.00 10.00
PM3 Dan Marino 8.00 20.00
PM4 Drew Bledsoe 2.50 6.00
PM5 John Elway 8.00 20.00
PM6 Jim Kelly 1.25 3.00
PM7 Jerry Rice 4.00 10.00
PM8 Michael Irvin 1.25 3.00
PM9 Emmitt Smith 6.00 15.00
PM10 Marshall Faulk 5.00 12.00
PM11 Natrone Means .75 2.00
PM12 Ki-Jana Carter 1.25 3.00

1995 Sportflix Rolling Thunder

Randomly inserted into packs at a rate of one in 12, this 12 card set features some of the most elusive running backs in the NFL. Card fronts contain two moving circles against a brown background with the title "Rolling Thunder" to the left of the card and the player's name at the bottom. Card backs contain an action-shot with a brief summary.

COMPLETE SET (12) 12.50 30.00
1 Emmitt Smith 4.00 10.00
2 Barry Sanders 4.00 10.00
3 Marshall Faulk 3.00 8.00
4 Ki-Jana Carter .75 2.00
5 Rashaan Salaam .50 1.25
6 Tyrone Wheatley 3.00 8.00
7 Natrone Means .50 1.25
8 Jerome Bettis .75 2.00
9 Errict Rhett .50 1.25
10 Byron Bam Morris .25 .60
11 William Floyd .50 1.25
12 Mario Bates .50 1.25

1995 Sportflix Rookie Lightning

Randomly inserted into one in 36 packs, this 12 card set features some of the hottest young rookie stars. Card fronts have a clear background with the words "Rookie" and "Lightning" alternating along the right. Two shots of the player are alternated with the player's name at the bottom. Card backs are clear and have numbering out of 12.

COMPLETE SET (12) 15.00 40.00
1 Ki-Jana Carter .50 1.25
2 Steve McNair 5.00 12.00
3 Michael Westbrook .50 1.25
4 Kerry Collins 2.50 6.00
5 Joey Galloway 2.50 6.00
6 J.J. Stokes .50 1.25
7 Tyrone Wheatley 2.00 5.00
8 Rashaan Salaam .30 .75
9 Napoleon Kaufman 2.00 5.00
10 Kordell Stewart 2.50 6.00
11 James O. Stewart 2.00 5.00
12 Todd Collins 2.00 5.00

1933 Sport Kings

The cards in this 48-card set measure 2 3/8" by 2 7/8". The 1933 Sport Kings set, issued by the Goudey Gum Company, contains cards for the most famous athletic heroes of the times. No less than 18 different sports are represented in the set. The baseball cards of Cobb, Hubbell, and Ruth, and the football cards of Rockne, Grange and Thorpe command premium prices. The cards were issued in one-card penny packs which came 100 packs to a box along with a piece of gum. The catalog designation for this set is R338.

COMPLETE SET 10000.00 16000.00
4 Red Grange RC FB 500.00 800.00
6 Jim Thorpe RC FB 600.00 1000.00
35 Knute Rockne RC FB 350.00 600.00

1934 Sport Kings Varsity Game

Goudey Gum Co. produced this 24-card set in wax packs under the Sport Kings Gum label. The year of issue is thought to be 1934, one year after the first set of Sport Kings. Each 2 3/8" by 2 7/8" card features the same front, but a slightly different back. The backs contain a card number followed by play results under the headings of kick off, rush, forward pass, punt, place kick, and goal after touchdown. The play results were designed to be used in a football card game played with the set. The first few words, when available, of the top line of text are included below to help identify each card.

- 1 Game Card 12.50 25.00
- 2 Game Card 12.50 25.00
- 3 Game Card 12.50 25.00
- 4 Game Card 12.50 25.00
- 5 Game Card 12.50 25.00
- 6 Game Card 12.50 25.00
- 7 Game Card 12.50 25.00
- 8 Game Card 12.50 25.00
- 9 Game Card 12.50 25.00
- 10 Game Card 12.50 25.00
- 11 Game Card 12.50 25.00
- 12 Game Card 12.50 25.00
- 13 Game Card SP 125.00 200.00
- 14 Game Card 12.50 25.00
- 15 Game Card 12.50 25.00
- 16 Game Card 12.50 25.00
- 17 Game Card 12.50 25.00
- 18 Game Card 12.50 25.00
- 19 Game Card SP 75.00 150.00
- 20 Game Card 12.50 25.00
- 21 Game Card SP 75.00 150.00
- 22 Game Card 12.50 25.00
- 23 Game Card 12.50 25.00
- 24 Game Card SP 75.00 150.00

2007 Sportkings

- 1 Troy Aikman 5.00 12.00
- 8 Tony Dorsett 4.00 10.00
- 38 Bart Starr 8.00 20.00
- 41 Thurman Thomas 4.00 10.00
- 42 Sammy Baugh 6.00 15.00
- 43 Reggie White 5.00 12.00
- 48 Steve Young 4.00 10.00

2007 Sportkings Mini

*MINIS: 1X TO 2X BASIC
ONE PER PACK
ANNOUNCED PRINT RUN 93 SETS

2007 Sportkings Autograph Gold

*GOLD: 1.2X TO 2X BASIC
RANDOM INSERTS IN PACKS
ANNOUNCED PRINT RUN 10 SETS

- ABS Bart Starr 90.00 150.00

2007 Sportkings Autograph Silver

RANDOM INSERTS IN PACKS
ANNOUNCED PRINT RUN B/WN 95-99 PER

- ABS Bart Starr 60.00 100.00
- ASY Steve Young 20.00 40.00
- ATA Troy Aikman 35.00 60.00
- ATD Tony Dorsett 20.00 40.00
- ATT Thurman Thomas 15.00 30.00

2007 Sportkings Autograph Memorabilia Gold

*GOLD/10: 1.2X TO 2X SILVER/40
ANNOUNCED PRINT RUN 10 SETS

2007 Sportkings Autograph Memorabilia Silver

RANDOM INSERTS IN PACKS
ANNOUNCED PRINT RUN 40 SETS

- AMRB Reggie Bush Jsy 25.00 50.00
- AMSY Steve Young Jsy 25.00 50.00
- AMTA Troy Aikman Jsy 50.00 80.00
- AMTD Tony Dorsett Jsy 25.00 50.00
- AMTT Thurman Thomas Jsy 20.00 40.00

2007 Sportkings Cityscapes Silver

ANNOUNCED PRINT RUN 20 SETS
*GOLD: .5X TO 1.2X BASIC
GOLD ANNOUNCED PRINT RUN 10 SETS
RANDOM INSERTS IN PACKS

- CS01 T.Dorsett/T.Aikman 20.00 40.00

2007 Sportkings Decades Silver

ANNOUNCED PRINT RUN 20 SETS
*GOLD: .5X TO 1.2X BASIC
GOLD ANNOUNCED PRINT RUN 10 SETS
RANDOM INSERTS IN PACKS

- D06 Aikman/Roy/Clemens 40.00 80.00
- D07 Adu/Jackson/Bush 40.00 80.00

2007 Sportkings Double Memorabilia Silver

RANDOM INSERTS IN PACKS
ANNOUNCED PRINT RUN 4-40 SETS
DM15, DM16 ANNOUNCED PRINT RUN 4 PER
NO DM15, DM16 PRICING DUE TO SCARCITY

- DM9 Reggie Bush 10.00 25.00
- DM10 Reggie White 15.00 40.00
- DM14 Troy Aikman 15.00 40.00

2007 Sportkings Double Memorabilia Gold

*GOLD: .6X TO 1.5X BASIC
RANDOM INSERTS IN PACKS
ANNOUNCED PRINT RUN 10 SETS
DM15, DM16 ANNOUNCED PRINT RUN 1 PER
NO DM15, DM16 PRICING DUE TO SCARCITY

2007 Sportkings Future Sportkings Autograph

- COMMON CARD 10.00 25.00

ANNOUNCED PRINT RUN B/WN 95-99 PER
*GOLD: 1.2X TO 2X BASIC
GOLD ANNOUNCED PRINT RUN 10 SETS
RANDOM INSERTS IN PACKS

- FSARB Reggie Bush 20.00 40.00

2007 Sportkings Patch Silver

ANNOUNCED PRINT RUN 20 SETS
P28-P30 ANNOUNCED PRINT RUN 4 PER
NO P28-P30 PRICING DUE TO SCARCITY
*GOLD: .6X TO 1.2X BASIC
GOLD ANNOUNCED PRINT RUN 10 SETS
GOLD P28-P30 ANCD. PRINT RUN 1 PER
GOLD P28-P30 NO PRICING AVAILABLE
RANDOM INSERTS IN PACKS

- P13 Troy Aikman Jsy 15.00 40.00
- P20 Reggie Bush Jsy 10.00 30.00
- P21 Reggie White Jsy 15.00 40.00
- P24 Steve Young Jsy 15.00 40.00
- P25 Tony Dorsett Jsy 12.50 30.00
- P27 Thurman Thomas Jsy 10.00 30.00

2007 Sportkings Single Memorabilia Silver

RANDOM INSERTS IN PACKS
ANNOUNCED PRINT RUN 90 SETS
SM3, SM13 ANNOUNCED PRINT RUN 4 PER
NO SM3, SM13 PRICING DUE TO SCARCITY

- SM20 Reggie Bush Jsy 4.00 15.00
- SM21 Reggie White Jsy 8.00 20.00
- SM26 Steve Young Jsy 4.00 15.00
- SM28 Thurman Thomas Jsy 4.00 15.00
- SM29 Tony Dorsett Jsy 4.00 15.00
- SM30 Troy Aikman Pants 8.00 20.00
- SM31 Troy Aikman Jsy 8.00 20.00
- SM43 Reggie White Cleats 8.00 20.00

2007 Sportkings Triple Memorabilia Silver

ANNOUNCED PRINT RUN 10 SETS
TM7, TM8 ANNOUNCED PRINT RUN 4 PER
NO TM7, TM8 PRICING DUE TO SCARCITY
GOLD ANNOUNCED PRINT RUN 1 SET
NO GOLD PRICING DUE TO SCARCITY
RANDOM INSERTS IN PACKS

- TM06 Reggie Bush 15.00 40.00
- TM10 Aikman/Young/Dorsett 40.00 80.00
- TM13 Jackson/Adu/Bush 20.00 50.00

2007 Sportkings National Convention Preview

- 1 Troy Aikman 1.00 2.50

2008 Sportkings

FIVE CARDS PER BOX

- 50 Jim Brown 6.00 12.00
- 51 Barry Sanders 7.50 15.00
- 52 Michael Irvin 4.00 8.00
- 58 John Elway 7.50 15.00
- 66 Vince Lombardi 10.00 20.00
- 74 Deion Sanders 6.00 12.00
- 86 Drew Pearson 4.00 8.00
- 96 Dan Marino 6.00 12.00
- 101 Bo Jackson 6.00 12.00
- 106 Joe Montana 15.00 30.00

2008 Sportkings Mini

*MINI: 1X TO 2X BASIC
ONE PER BOX

- 106 Joe Montana 15.00 30.00

2008 Sportkings 1933 Redemption

UNPRICED ANNOUNCED PRINT RUN 1

2008 Sportkings Autograph Silver

ANNOUNCED PRINT RUN B/WN 20-90 PER
RANDOM INSERTS IN PACKS

- MI Michael Irvin/40 * 20.00 40.00
- BJ1 Bo Jackson/30 * 30.00 60.00
- BJ2 Bo Jackson/30 * 30.00 60.00
- BSA Barry Sanders/40 * 50.00 100.00
- DP1 Drew Pearson/40 * 10.00 25.00
- DP2 Drew Pearson/40 * 10.00 25.00
- JE1 John Elway/30 * 40.00 80.00
- JE2 John Elway/30 * 40.00 80.00
- JE3 John Elway/30 * 40.00 80.00
- MI2 Michael Irvin/40 * 20.00 40.00
- BSA2 Barry Sanders/40 * 50.00 100.00
- DMA1 Dan Marino/40 * 60.00 120.00
- DMA2 Dan Marino/40 * 60.00 120.00
- DSA1 Deion Sanders/20 * 40.00 80.00
- DSA2 Deion Sanders/20 * 40.00 80.00
- DSA3 Deion Sanders/20 * 40.00 80.00
- JBR1 Jim Brown/90 * 30.00 60.00
- JBR2 Jim Brown/90 * 30.00 60.00
- JMO1 Joe Montana/40 * 50.00 100.00
- JMO2 Joe Montana/40 * 50.00 100.00
- JMO3 Joe Montana/40 * 50.00 100.00

2008 Sportkings Autograph Memorabilia Silver

ANNOUNCED PRINT RUN B/WN 15-50 PER
NO GOLD PRICING DUE TO SCARCITY
RANDOM INSERTS IN PACKS

- BJ1 Bo Jackson/25 * 40.00 80.00
- BJ2 Bo Jackson/25 * 40.00 80.00
- BS Barry Sanders/40 * 50.00 100.00
- DMA1 Dan Marino/40 * 100.00 150.00
- DMA2 Dan Marino/40 * 100.00 150.00
- DP1 Drew Pearson/40 * 15.00 30.00
- DP2 Drew Pearson/40 * 15.00 30.00
- DSA1 Deion Sanders/15 * 50.00 100.00
- DSA2 Deion Sanders/15 * 50.00 100.00
- DSA3 Deion Sanders/15 * 50.00 100.00
- JE John Elway/20 * 50.00 100.00
- JMO1 Joe Montana/40 * 75.00 125.00
- JMO2 Joe Montana/40 * 75.00 125.00
- MI Michael Irvin/40 * 25.00 50.00

2008 Sportkings Cityscapes Double Silver

RANDOM INSERTS IN PACKS

- 1 P.Roy/J.Elway 30.00 60.00
- 2 D.Sanders/D.Wilkins 15.00 40.00
- 4 B.Hull/M.Irvin 15.00 40.00
- 9 J.Montana/J.Marichal 20.00 50.00
- 10 B.Sanders/B.Hull 20.00 50.00

2008 Sportkings Cityscapes Triple Silver

RANDOM INSERTS IN PACKS

- 2 Irvin/Aikman/Hull 20.00 50.00
- 4 Montana/Young/Marichal 40.00 80.00

2008 Sportkings Decades Silver

RANDOM INSERTS IN PACKS

- 2 Brown/Plante/Marichal 20.00 50.00
- 3 Turcotte/Montana/Pele 75.00 125.00
- 4 Marino/Messier/Parish 30.00 60.00
- 5 Hull/Irvin/Olajuwon 20.00 50.00

2008 Sportkings Double Memorabilia Silver

RANDOM INSERTS IN PACKS

- 1 M.Irvin/T.Dorsett 10.00 25.00
- 5 T.Aikman/M.Irvin 10.00 25.00
- 6 B.Sanders/D.Sanders 15.00 40.00
- 11 J.Montana/S.Young 30.00 60.00
- 13 Bo Jackson BB-FB 20.00 50.00
- 14 Deion Sanders BB-FB 15.00 40.00

2008 Sportkings Papercuts

RANDOM INSERTS IN PACKS
ANNOUNCED PRINT RUN B/WN 1-10 PER
NO PRICING DUE TO SCARCITY

2008 Sportkings Passing the Torch Silver

RANDOM INSERTS IN PACKS

- 3 J.Montana/S.Young 30.00 60.00
- 10 J.Brown/B.Sanders 30.00 60.00
- 13 B.Sanders/R.Bush 10.00 25.00
- 14 D.Pearson/M.Irvin 10.00 25.00

2008 Sportkings Patch Silver

RANDOM INSERTS IN PACKS

- 2 Barry Sanders 20.00 50.00
- 6 Dan Marino 40.00 80.00
- 7 Drew Pearson 12.50 30.00
- 13 Deion Sanders 15.00 40.00
- 14 John Elway 15.00 40.00
- 20 Michael Irvin 12.50 30.00
- 22 Joe Montana 40.00 80.00

2008 Sportkings Single Memorabilia Silver

RANDOM INSERTS IN PACKS

- 3 Barry Sanders 10.00 25.00
- 7 Bo Jackson 8.00 20.00
- 12 Drew Pearson 6.00 15.00
- 20 Jim Brown 10.00 25.00
- 22 Joe Montana 10.00 25.00
- 24 John Elway 10.00 25.00
- 30 Michael Irvin 6.00 15.00
- 43 Dan Marino 15.00 40.00
- 44 Deion Sanders 10.00 25.00

2008 Sportkings Triple Memorabilia Silver

RANDOM INSERTS IN PACKS

- 4 Elway/Montana/Marino 50.00 100.00
- 12 Aikman/Dorsett/Irvin 10.00 25.00
- 13 Jackson/Sanders/Brown 30.00 60.00

2008 Sportkings National Convention VIP Promo

- 5 Jim Brown / Red Grange 4.00 10.00
- 15 Vince Lombardi / Knute Rockne 5.00 12.00

2009 Sportkings

- COMPLETE SET (52) 250.00 450.00
- COMMON CARD (109-160) 5.00 12.00
- SEMISTARS 6.00 15.00
- UNLISTED STARS 8.00 20.00
- 114 Doug Flutie 6.00 15.00
- 125 Joe Namath 8.00 20.00
- 126 Jerry Rice 8.00 20.00
- 135 Bronko Nagurski 8.00 20.00
- 156 Kurt Warner 6.00 15.00
- 158 Lawrence Taylor 8.00 20.00

2009 Sportkings Mini

*MINI: .6X TO 1.5X BASIC CARDS
STATED ODDS ONE PER BOX
UNPRICED SILVER PRINT RUN 7 SETS
UNPRICED GOLD PRINT RUN 3 SETS

2009 Sportkings Autograph Silver

ANNOUNCED PRINT RUN B/WN 15-70 PER
UNPRICED GOLD PRINT RUN 10

- DF1 Doug Flutie/30* 30.00 60.00
- DF2 Doug Flutie/30* 30.00 60.00
- JN1 Joe Namath/25* 60.00 120.00
- JN2 Joe Namath/25* 60.00 120.00
- JR1 Jerry Rice/20* 75.00 150.00
- JR2 Jerry Rice/20* 75.00 150.00
- KW1 Kurt Warner/25* 25.00 50.00
- KW2 Kurt Warner/25* 25.00 50.00
- KW3 Kurt Warner/25* 25.00 50.00
- LT1 Lawrence Taylor/40* 30.00 60.00
- LT2 Lawrence Taylor/40* 30.00 60.00

2009 Sportkings Autograph Memorabilia Silver

ANNOUNCED PRINT RUN B/WN 15-40 PER
UNPRICED GOLD PRINT RUN 10
RANDOM INSERTS IN PACKS

- DF1 Doug Flutie Jsy/30* 20.00 40.00
- DF2 Doug Flutie Jsy/30* 20.00 40.00
- JN1 Joe Namath Jsy/25* 60.00 120.00
- JN2 Joe Namath Jsy/25* 60.00 120.00
- JR1 Jerry Rice Jsy/20* 75.00 150.00
- JR2 Jerry Rice Jsy/20* 75.00 150.00
- KW1 Kurt Warner Jsy/25* 30.00 60.00
- KW2 Kurt Warner Jsy/25* 30.00 60.00
- LT1 Lawrence Taylor Jsy/40* 30.00 60.00
- LT2 Lawrence Taylor Jsy/40* 30.00 60.00

2009 Sportkings Cityscapes Double Silver

ANNOUNCED PRINT RUN 19 SETS
UNPRICED GOLD PRINT RUN 1
RANDOM INSERTS IN PACKS

- 1 R.Jackson Jsy/J.Namath Jsy 25.00 50.00
- 2 J.Rice Jsy/J.Montana Jsy 40.00 80.00
- 3 D.Flutie Jsy/T.Thomas Jsy 15.00 30.00
- 6 L.Taylor Jsy/J.Namath Jsy 20.00 40.00
- 7 D.Flutie Jsy/B.Hull Jsy 20.00 40.00

2009 Sportkings Cityscapes Triple Silver

ANNOUNCED PRINT RUN 19 SETS
UNPRICED GOLD PRINT RUN 1
RANDOM INSERTS IN PACKS

- 1 Reggie/Namath/Pele 50.00 100.00
- 2 Rice/Montana/Cepeda 60.00 120.00
- 3 Taylor/Reggie/P.Esposito 25.00 50.00
- 4 Flutie/Bo.Hull/T.Esposito 20.00 40.00

2009 Sportkings Decades Silver

ANNOUNCED PRINT RUN 19 SETS
UNPRICED GOLD PRINT RUN 1
RANDOM INSERTS IN PACKS

- 1 Pele/Namath/Cepeda 50.00 100.00
- 3 Taylor/Wallace/Schmidt 40.00 80.00
- 4 Rice/Lennox/Kersee 40.00 80.00

2009 Sportkings Double Memorabilia Silver

ANNOUNCED PRINT RUN B/WN 1-19
UNPRICED GOLD PRINT RUN 1
RANDOM INSERTS IN PACKS

- 1 Warner/L.Tylr/19* 20.00 40.00
- 2 Rice/Montana/19* 40.00 80.00
- 5 Namath/Montana/19* 30.00 60.00
- 13 Doug Flutie/19* 15.00 30.00

2009 Sportkings Patch Silver

ANNOUNCED PRINT RUN B/WN 4-19
UNPRICED GOLD PRINT RUN 1 SET
RANDOM INSERTS IN PACKS

- 14 Lawrence Taylor/4* 15.00 30.00
- 15 Joe Namath/4*
- 16 Jerry Rice/4* 40.00 80.00
- 17 Doug Flutie/4* 20.00 40.00

2009 Sportkings Single Memorabilia Silver

ANNOUNCED PRINT RUN B/WN 4-29
UNPRICED GOLD PRINT RUN B/WN 1-4
RANDOM INSERTS IN PACKS

- 2 Doug Flutie Jsy/29* 12.00 30.00
- 5 Jerry Rice Jsy/29* 30.00 60.00
- 6 Lawrence Taylor Jsy/29* 10.00 25.00
- 7 Joe Namath Jsy/29* 20.00 50.00

2009 Sportkings Triple Memorabilia Silver

ANNOUNCED PRINT RUN B/WN 3-19
UNPRICED GOLD PRINT RUN 1 SET
RANDOM INSERTS IN PACKS

- 1 Flutie/Namath/Montana/19* 40.00 80.00
- 2 Rice/Young/Montana/19* 60.00 120.00
- 4 Taylor/Sanders/Rice/19* 40.00 80.00

2009 Sportkings Vintage Memorabilia

RANDOM INSERTS IN PACKS
ANNOUNCED PRINT RUN 1 SET
NO PRICING DUE TO SCARCITY

- 1 Knute Rockne Jkt

2009 Sportkings National Convention VIP Promo

- COMPLETE SET (7)
- 2 Leslie/Namath/Flutie/Tretiak/Oliva/Taro 5.00 12.00
- 4 West/Nelson/Perry/Martin/Fats/Rice 5.00 12.00
- 5 Lewis/Jackson/Thorpe/Warner/Seabiscuit/Joyner-Kersee 5.00 12.00
- 6 Taylor/Chinaglia/Gyarmati/Karolyi/Rudolph/C.Smith 4.00 10.00
- 7 Morenz/Pollard/Johnson/Nagurski/S.Smith/Pele 5.00 12.00

2010 Sportkings

- COMPLETE SET (48) 150.00 300.00
- COMP.SET w/o ALI SP (47) 100.00 200.00
- 175 Warren Sapp 4.00 10.00
- 189 Johnny Unitas 6.00 15.00
- 190 Joe Greene 5.00 12.00
- 201 Raymond Berry 5.00 12.00
- 203 Bob Lilly 5.00 12.00

2010 Sportkings Mini

- COMPLETE SET (48) 175.00 350.00

*MINI: .5X TO 1.2X BASIC CARDS
STATED ODDS 1:2

2010 Sportkings Autograph Silver

ANNOUNCED PRINT RUN 10-50
UNPRICED GOLD PRINT RUN 5-10

- ABL1 Bob Lilly/40* 12.00 25.00
- ABL2 Bob Lilly/40* 12.00 25.00
- AJG1 Joe Greene/40* 15.00 30.00
- AJG2 Joe Greene/40* 15.00 30.00
- AWS1 Warren Sapp/40* 12.00 25.00
- AWS2 Warren Sapp/40* 12.00 25.00
- ARBE1 Raymond Berry/25* 20.00 40.00
- ARBE2 Raymond Berry/25* 20.00 40.00
- ARBE3 Raymond Berry/25* 20.00 40.00

2010 Sportkings Autograph Memorabilia Silver

ANNOUNCED PRINT RUN 10-40
UNPRICED GOLD PRINT RUN 5-10

- AMBL1 Bob Lilly Jsy/40* 15.00 30.00
- AMBL2 Bob Lilly Jsy/40* 15.00 30.00
- AMJG1 Joe Greene Jsy/40* 25.00 50.00
- AMJG2 Joe Greene Jsy/40* 25.00 50.00
- AMWS1 Warren Sapp Jsy/40* 15.00 30.00
- AMWS2 Warren Sapp Jsy/40* 15.00 30.00
- AMRBE1 Raymond Berry Jsy/25* 20.00 40.00
- AMRBE2 Raymond Berry Jsy/25* 20.00 40.00
- AMRBE3 Raymond Berry Jsy/25* 20.00 40.00

2010 Sportkings Double Memorabilia Silver

STATED PRINT RUN 20 UNLESS NOTED

- DM8 W.Sapp/L.Taylor 15.00 40.00

2010 Sportkings Patch Silver

STATED PRINT RUN 20
UNPRICED GOLD PRINT RUN 10

- P6 Warren Sapp 10.00 25.00
- P8 Lawrence Taylor 10.00 25.00

2010 Sportkings Single Memorabilia Silver

STATED PRINT RUN 26 UNLESS NOTED

- SM17 Joe Greene 12.00 25.00
- SM20 Raymond Berry 6.00 12.00
- SM29 Warren Sapp 6.00 12.00

2010 Sportkings Triple Memorabilia Silver

SILVER PRINT RUN 4-20
UNPRICED GOLD PRINT RUN 1-10

- TM5 Sapp/Taylor/Greene 15.00 30.00

2010 Sportkings National Convention VIP Promo

- 9 Warren Sapp 1.25 3.00
- 18 Joe Greene 1.50 4.00
- 22 Bob Lilly 1.25 3.00

2012 Sportkings

- 229 Gale Sayers 4.00 10.00
- 230 Franco Harris 4.00 10.00
- 231 Bob Waterfield 4.00 10.00
- 232 Roosevelt Brown 4.00 10.00
- 233 Paul Hornung 5.00 12.00

2012 Sportkings Mini

*MINI: .5X TO 1.2X BASIC CARDS
RANDOM INSERT IN PACKS

2012 Sportkings Premium Back

*SINGLES: .5X TO 1.2X BASIC CARDS
STATED ODDS ONE PER PACK

2012 Sportkings Autograph Memorabilia Silver

ANNOUNCED PRINT RUN 15-50

- AMFH1 Franco Harris 25.00 50.00
- AMFH2 Franco Harris 25.00 50.00
- AMGS1 Gale Sayers 30.00 60.00
- AMGS2 Gale Sayers 30.00 60.00

2012 Sportkings Autographs Silver

ANNOUNCED PRINT RUN 15-130

- AFH1 Franco Harris 20.00 40.00
- AFH2 Franco Harris 20.00 40.00
- AGS1 Gale Sayers 25.00 50.00
- AGS2 Gale Sayers 25.00 50.00
- AGS3 Gale Sayers 25.00 50.00
- APHO1 Paul Hornung 20.00 40.00
- APHO2 Paul Hornung 20.00 40.00

2012 Sportkings Cityscapes Double Silver

ANNOUNCED PRINT RUN 30

- CS4 F.Harris/D.Parker 10.00 20.00
- CS12 G.Sayers/R.Sandberg 20.00 40.00

2012 Sportkings Single Memorabilia Silver

ANNOUNCED PRINT RUN 90

- SM14 Franco Harris 7.50 15.00

2012 Sportkings Triple Memorabilia Silver

ANNOUNCED PRINT RUN 30

- TM5 Robinson/Petty/Sayers 15.00 30.00

2013 Sportkings

- COMPLETE SET (48) 60.00 120.00
- 263 Cookie Gilchrist 3.00 8.00
- 274 Frank Gifford 3.00 8.00
- 277 Jack Ham 3.00 8.00
- 278 Bob Hayes 3.00 8.00
- 281 Don Hutson 3.00 8.00
- 286 Lenny Moore 3.00 8.00
- 290 Bill Parcells 4.00 10.00
- 295 Eddie Robinson 3.00 8.00

2013 Sportkings Mini

*MINI: .5X TO 1.2X BASIC CARDS
STATED ODDS 1:2

2013 Sportkings Premium Back

*PREM.BACK: .5X TO 1.2X BASIC CARDS
ONE PREMIUM BACK PER BOX

2013 Sportkings Anthology Autographs

ANNOUNCED PRINT RUN 72

- ANBG1 Bob Griese 20.00 50.00
- ANBG2 Bob Griese 20.00 50.00
- ANBK1 Bob Kuechenberg 15.00 40.00
- ANBK2 Bob Kuechenberg 15.00 40.00
- ANDA1 Dick Anderson 15.00 40.00
- ANDA2 Dick Anderson 15.00 40.00
- ANDS1 Don Shula 30.00 60.00
- ANDS2 Don Shula 30.00 60.00
- ANGY1 Yepremian, Garo 15.00 40.00
- ANGY2 Yepremian, Garo 15.00 40.00
- ANHT1 Howard Twilley 15.00 40.00
- ANHT2 Howard Twilley 15.00 40.00
- ANJK1 Jim Kiick 15.00 40.00
- ANJK2 Jim Kiick 15.00 40.00
- ANJL1 Jim Langer 15.00 40.00
- ANJL2 Jim Langer 15.00 40.00
- ANLL1 Larry Little 15.00 40.00
- ANLL2 Larry Little 15.00 40.00
- ANMF1 Manny Fernandez 15.00 40.00
- ANMF2 Manny Fernandez 15.00 40.00
- ANMM1 Mercury Morris 15.00 40.00
- ANMM2 Mercury Morris 15.00 40.00
- ANNB1 Nick Buoniconti
- ANNB2 Nick Buoniconti
- ANPW1 Paul Warfield 15.00 40.00
- ANPW2 Paul Warfield 15.00 40.00

2013 Sportkings Autographs Silver

PRINT RUN 15-60

- ABPA1 Bill Parcells/20* 30.00 60.00
- ABPA2 Bill Parcells/20* 30.00 60.00
- ABPA3 Bill Parcells/20* 30.00 60.00
- ABPA4 Bill Parcells/20* 30.00 60.00
- AFG1 Frank Gifford/50* 10.00 25.00
- AFG2 Frank Gifford/50* 10.00 25.00
- AFG3 Frank Gifford/50* 10.00 25.00
- AFG4 Frank Gifford/50* 10.00 25.00
- AJH1 Jack Ham/60* 8.00 20.00
- AJH2 Jack Ham/60* 8.00 20.00
- AJH3 Jack Ham/60* 8.00 20.00
- ALM1 Lenny Moore/50* 10.00 25.00
- ALM2 Lenny Moore/50* 10.00 25.00
- ALM3 Lenny Moore/50* 10.00 25.00
- ALM4 Lenny Moore/50* 10.00 25.00

2013 Sportkings Decades Silver

ANNOUNCED PRINT RUN 40

- D4 Howe/Hays/Robi/Jack 12.00 30.00

2013 Sportkings Four Sport Silver

ANNOUNCED PRINT RUN 19

- FSQM2 Vale/Pipp/Hays/Ortiz 10.00 25.00

2013 Sportkings Papercuts

STATED PRINT RUN 1 SER. #'d SET
UNPRICED DUE TO SCARCITY

- PCBH Bob Hayes
- PCDH Don Hutson

2013 Sportkings Single Memorabilia Silver

ANNOUNCED PRINT RUN 90

- SM2 Bob Hayes 6.00 15.00

1953 Sport Magazine Premiums

This 10-card set features 5 1/2" by 7" color portraits and was issued as a subscription premium by Sport Magazine. These photos were taken by noted sports photographer Ozzie Sweet. Each features a top player from a number of different sports. The photo backs are blank and unnumbered. We've checklisted the set below in alphabetical order.

- COMPLETE SET (10) 30.00 60.00
- 3 Elroy Hirsch FB 7.50 15.00
- 7 John Olszewski FB 4.00 8.00

1968-73 Sport Pix

These 8" by 10" blank backed photos feature black and white photos with the players name and the words "Sport Pix" on the bottom. The address for Sport Pix is also on the bottom. Since the cards are not numbered, we have sequenced them in alphabetical order.

- COMPLETE SET (22) 150.00 300.00
- 1 Sammy Baugh 7.50 15.00
- 2 Jim Brown 10.00 20.00
- 3 Billy Cannon 5.00 10.00
- 4 Red Grange 7.50 15.00
- 6 Paul Hornung 7.50 15.00
- 7 Sam Huff 6.00 12.00
- 13 Bobby Mitchell 5.00 10.00
- 15 Bronko Nagurski 6.00 12.00 — Not in football uniform
- 17 Jim Taylor 6.00 12.00
- 18 Jim Thorpe 7.50 15.00
- 19 Y.A. Tittle 6.00 12.00
- 20 Johnny Unitas 10.00 20.00

1996 Sportscall Phone Cards

This set of phone cards was released in 1996 in pack form with 36 packs to a box and 4-cards per pack. Each card includes a color player photo (with airbrushed helmet logos) surrounded by a black border on the cardfronts. The cardbacks contain instructions on the use of the card which expired in late 1996. The cards measure standard size and have square corners.

- COMPLETE SET (400) 30.00 80.00
- 1 Michael Irvin .40 1.00
- 2 Cory Fleming .08 .25
- 3 Daryl Johnston .20 .50
- 4 Larry Brown .08 .25
- 5 Emmitt Smith 1.60 4.00
- 6 Sherman Williams .08 .25
- 7 Chris Boniol .08 .25
- 8 Jason Garrett .30 .75
- 9 Wade Wilson .08 .25
- 10 Troy Aikman 1.00 2.50
- 11 Dana Stubblefield .20 .50
- 12 Rickey Jackson .08 .25
- 13 John Taylor .08 .25
- 14 J.J. Stokes .40 1.00
- 15 Brent Jones .08 .25
- 16 Jerry Rice 1.00 2.50
- 17 Ricky Ervins .08 .25
- 18 William Floyd .20 .50
- 19 Elvis Grbac .20 .50
- 20 Steve Young .80 2.00
- 21 Michael Zordich .08 .25
- 22 Ricky Watters .20 .50
- 23 Kelvin Martin .08 .25
- 24 Randall Cunningham .40 1.00
- 25 Rodney Peete .08 .25
- 26 Toi Cook .08 .25
- 27 Eric Davis .08 .25
- 28 Tim McDonald .08 .25
- 29 Merton Hanks .08 .25
- 30 Ken Norton .08 .25
- 31 Brett Favre 2.00 5.00
- 32 George Teague .08 .25
- 33 Charlie Garner .20 .50
- 34 Gary Anderson K .08 .25
- 35 William Fuller .08 .25
- 36 Calvin Williams .08 .25
- 37 Fred Barnett .08 .25
- 38 Antone Davis .08 .25
- 39 Mike Mamula .08 .25
- 40 Greg Jackson .08 .25
- 41 Kevin Butler .08 .25
- 42 Craig Newsome .08 .25
- 43 Chris Jacke .08 .25
- 44 John Jurkovic .08 .25
- 45 Sean Jones .08 .25
- 46 Reggie White .40 1.00
- 47 Robert Brooks .20 .50
- 48 Mark Ingram .08 .25
- 49 Edgar Bennett .20 .50
- 50 Ty Detmer .20 .50
- 51 Rob Moore .20 .50
- 52 Dave Krieg .08 .25
- 53 Robert Green .08 .25
- 54 Donnell Woolford .08 .25
- 55 Chris Zorich .08 .25
- 56 Michael Timpson .08 .25
- 57 Curtis Conway .20 .50
- 58 Rashaan Salaam .20 .50
- 59 Lewis Tillman .08 .25
- 60 Erik Kramer .08 .25
- 61 Ken Harvey .08 .25
- 62 Scott Galbraith .08 .25
- 63 Michael Westbrook .40 1.00
- 64 Henry Ellard .08 .25
- 65 Reggie Brooks .08 .25
- 66 Brian Mitchell .08 .25
- 67 Terry Allen .20 .50
- 68 Gus Frerotte .20 .50
- 69 Clyde Simmons .08 .25
- 70 Frank Sanders .40 1.00
- 71 Pete Metzelaars .08 .25
- 72 Eric Guliford .08 .25
- 73 Mark Carrier .08 .25
- 74 Derrick Moore .08 .25
- 75 Jack Trudeau .08 .25
- 76 Frank Reich .08 .25
- 77 Kerry Collins .40 1.00
- 78 James Washington .08 .25
- 79 Stanley Richard .20 .50
- 80 Darrell Green .08 .25
- 81 Rodney Holman .08 .25
- 82 Brett Perriman .08 .25
- 83 Herman Moore .20 .50
- 84 Scott Mitchell .20 .50
- 85 Tyrone Poole .08 .25
- 86 Carlton Bailey .08 .25
- 87 Sam Mills .08 .25
- 88 Lamar Lathon .08 .25
- 89 Lawyer Tillman .08 .25
- 90 Don Beebe .08 .25
- 91 Chris Spielman .08 .25
- 92 Tracy Scroggins .08 .25
- 93 Jason Hanson .08 .25
- 94 Aubrey Matthews .08 .25
- 95 Darryl Talley .08 .25
- 96 J.J. Birden .08 .25
- 97 Craig Heyward .08 .25
- 98 Eric Metcalf .08 .25
- 99 Bobby Hebert .08 .25
- P1 Troy Aikman Prototype .80 2.00
- 100 Jeff George .20 .50
- 101 Ed McCaffrey .20 .50
- 102 Anthony Miller .20 .50
- 103 Shannon Sharpe .20 .50
- 104 Glyn Milburn .08 .25
- 105 Aaron Craver .08 .25
- 106 Terrell Davis 2.00 5.00
- 107 Bill Musgrave .08 .25
- 108 Hugh Millen .08 .25
- 109 John Elway 2.00 5.00
- 110 Bennie Blades .08 .25
- 111 Keith Byars .08 .25
- 112 Terry Kirby .20 .50
- 113 Bernie Parmalee .08 .25
- 114 Bernie Kosar .08 .25
- 115 Dan Marino 2.00 5.00
- 116 Steve Atwater .08 .25
- 117 Simon Fletcher .08 .25
- 118 Michael Perry .08 .25
- 119 Jason Elam .20 .50
- 120 Mike Pritchard .08 .25
- 121 Troy Vincent .08 .25
- 122 Chris Singleton .08 .25
- 123 Steve Emtman .08 .25
- 124 Trace Armstrong .08 .25
- 125 Pete Stoyanovich .08 .25
- 126 Randal Hill .08 .25
- 127 Gary Clark .08 .25
- 128 Eric Green .08 .25
- 129 O.J. McDuffie .20 .50
- 130 Irving Fryar .08 .25
- 131 Ray Childress .08 .25
- 132 Haywood Jeffires .08 .25
- 133 Todd McNair .08 .25
- 134 Gary Brown .08 .25
- 135 Rodney Thomas .08 .25
- 136 Will Furrer .08 .25
- 137 Steve McNair .80 2.00
- 138 Chris Chandler .20 .50
- 139 Aubrey Beavers .08 .25
- 140 Gene Atkins .08 .25
- 141 Rocket Ismail .08 .25
- 142 Tim Brown .40 1.00
- 143 Derrick Fenner .08 .25
- 144 Napoleon Kaufman .40 1.00
- 145 Harvey Williams .08 .25
- 146 Billy Joe Hobert .08 .25
- 147 Vince Evans .08 .25
- 148 Jeff Hostetler .08 .25
- 149 Mel Gray .08 .25
- 150 Chris Dishman .08 .25
- 151 Quinn Early .08 .25
- 152 Derek Brown RB .08 .25
- 153 Jim Everett .08 .25
- 154 Albert Lewis .08 .25
- 155 Jeff Gossett .08 .25
- 156 Terry McDaniel .08 .25
- 157 Aundray Bruce .08 .25
- 158 Chester McGlockton .08 .25
- 159 Pat Swilling .08 .25
- 160 James Jett .08 .25
- 161 Kimble Anders .20 .50
- 162 Greg Hill .20 .50
- 163 Steve Bono .08 .25
- 164 J.J. McCleskey .08 .25
- 165 Eric Allen .08 .25
- 166 Renaldo Turnbull .08 .25
- 167 Wayne Martin .08 .25
- 168 Torrance Small .08 .25
- 169 Michael Haynes .08 .25
- 170 Irv Smith .08 .25
- 171 Dan Saleaumua .08 .25
- 172 Neil Smith .20 .50
- 173 Lin Elliott .08 .25
- 174 Tamarick Vanover .20 .50
- 175 Derrick Walker .08 .25
- 176 Willie Davis .08 .25
- 177 Webster Slaughter .08 .25
- 178 Lake Dawson .08 .25
- 179 Keith Cash .08 .25
- 180 Leroy Thompson .08 .25
- 181 Leslie O'Neal .08 .25
- 182 John Carney .08 .25
- 183 Alfred Pupunu .08 .25
- 184 Mark Seay .08 .25
- 185 Shawn Jefferson .08 .25
- 186 Tony Martin .20 .50
- 187 Louie Aguiar .08 .25
- 188 Marcus Allen .40 1.00
- 189 Mark Collins .08 .25
- 190 Dale Carter .08 .25
- 191 Kelvin Pritchett .08 .25
- 192 Joel Smeenge .08 .25
- 193 Mike Hollis .08 .25
- 194 Desmond Howard .20 .50
- 195 Ernest Givins .08 .25
- 196 Reggie Cobb .08 .25
- 197 James O.Stewart .50 1.25
- 198 Steve Beuerlein .20 .50
- 199 Mark Brunell .80 2.00
- 200 Junior Seau .20 .50
- 201 Mark Higgs .08 .25
- 202 Kevin Smith .08 .25
- 203 John Elliott .08 .25
- 204 Doug Riesenberg .08 [illegible]
- 205 Chad Hennings [illegible] .25
- 206 Charles Haley [illegible] .50
- 207 Tony Tolbert .08 .25
- 208 Scott Case .08 .25
- 209 Russell Maryland .08 .25
- 210 Robert Jones .08 .25
- 211 Mark Stepnoski .08 .25
- 212 Richmond Webb .08 .25
- 213 Broderick Thompson .08 .25
- 214 Bart Oates .08 .25
- 215 Jesse Sapolu .08 .25
- 216 Luther Elliss .08 .25
- 217 Kent Graham .08 .25
- 218 Lomas Brown .08 .25
- 219 Browning Nagle .08 .25
- 220 Blake Brockermeyer .08 .25
- 221 Kent Hull .08 .25
- 222 Todd Steussie .08 .25
- 223 Chad May .08 .25
- 224 Robert Young .08 .25
- 225 Brock Marion .08 .25
- 226 Darren Woodson .20 .50
- 227 Tony Boselli .08 .25
- 228 Derek Brown .08 .25
- 229 Jeff Novak .08 .25
- 230 Bruce Matthews .08 .25
- 231 Alvin Harper .08 .25
- 232 Jackie Harris .08 .25
- 233 Lawrence Dawsey .08 .25
- 234 Hardy Nickerson .08 .25
- 235 Errict Rhett .20 .50
- 236 Trent Dilfer .40 1.00
- 237 Reggie Roby .08 .25
- 238 Thomas Everett .08 .25
- 239 Kevin Greene .20 .50
- 240 Kordell Stewart .50 1.25
- 241 Corey Miller .08 .25
- 242 Mike Croel .08 .25
- 243 Herschel Walker .20 .50
- 244 Tyrone Wheatley .20 .50
- 245 Rodney Hampton .20 .50
- 246 Phillippi Sparks .08 .25
- 247 Dave Brown .08 .25
- 248 Derrick Brooks .40 1.00
- 249 Warren Sapp .08 .25
- 250 Horace Copeland .08 .25
- 251 Craig Erickson .08 .25
- 252 Dave Meggett .08 .25
- 253 Scott Zolak .08 .25
- 254 Chris Calloway .08 .25
- 255 Michael Brooks .08 .25
- 256 Mike Sherrard .08 .25
- 257 Howard Cross .08 .25
- 258 Thomas Lewis .08 .25
- 259 Bill Bates .08 .25
- 260 Deion Sanders .60 1.50
- 261 Kevin Williams .08 .25
- 262 Jay Novacek .08 .25
- 263 Derek Loville .08 .25
- 264 Randy Baldwin .08 .25
- 265 Ronnie Harmon .08 .25
- 266 Natrone Means .20 .50
- 267 Stan Humphries .20 .50
- 268 Ray Buchanan .08 .25
- 269 Trev Alberts .08 .25
- 270 Roosevelt Potts .08 .25
- 271 Dixon Edwards .08 .25
- 272 Lorenzo White .08 .25
- 273 Derek Kennard .08 .25
- 274 Morten Andersen .08 .25
- 275 Terance Mathis .20 .50
- 276 Barry Sanders 2.00 5.00
- 277 Seth Joyner .08 .25
- 278 Larry Centers .20 .50
- 279 Garrison Hearst .20 .50
- 280 Raymont Harris UER .08 .25
- 281 Mario Bates .20 .50
- 282 Darren Smith .08 .25
- 283 Godfrey Myles .08 .25
- 284 Clayton Holmes .08 .25
- 285 Erik Williams .08 .25
- 286 Leon Lett .08 .25
- 287 Larry Allen .08 .25
- 288 Mark Tuinei .08 .25
- 289 Ron Stone .08 .25
- 290 Nate Newton .08 .25
- 291 Sean Landeta .08 .25
- 292 Mark Carrier DB .08 .25
- 293 Jim Kelly .40 1.00
- 294 Todd Collins QB .20 .50
- 295 Steve Walsh .08 .25
- 296 Tony Casillas .08 .25
- 297 Nick Lowery .08 .25
- 298 Kyle Brady .08 .25
- 299 Ronald Moore .08 .25
- 300 Boomer Esiason .20 .50
- 301 Robert Smith .20 .50
- 302 Warren Moon .40 1.00
- 303 Shane Conlan UER .08 .25
- 304 Todd Lyght .08 .25
- 305 Sean Gilbert .08 .25
- 306 Alex Wright .08 .25
- 307 Isaac Bruce .40 1.00
- 308 Leonard Russell .08 .25
- 309 Jerome Bettis .40 1.00
- 310 Chris Miller .08 .25
- 311 James Harris DE .08 .25
- 312 Jack Del Rio .08 .25
- 313 Esera Tuaolo .08 .25
- 314 Jeff Brady .08 .25
- 315 Fuad Reveiz .08 .25
- 316 David Palmer .08 .25
- 317 Adrian Cooper .08 .25
- 318 Andrew Jordan .08 .25
- 319 Jake Reed .20 .50
- 320 Amp Lee .08 .25
- 321 Doug Pelfrey .08 .25
- 322 Derek Ware .08 .25
- 323 Darnay Scott .20 .50
- 324 Tony McGee .08 .25
- 325 Carl Pickens .20 .50
- 326 Eric Bieniemy .08 .25
- 327 Harold Green .08 .25
- 328 David Klingel .08 .25
- 329 Jeff Blake .40 1.00
- 330 Mike Saxon .08 .25
- 331 Cortez Kennedy .08 .25
- 332 Ricky Proehl .08 .25
- 333 Joey Galloway .40 1.00
- 334 Brian Blades .08 .25
- 335 Steve Broussard .08 .25
- 336 Chris Warren .20 .50
- 337 John Friesz .08 .25
- 338 Rick Mirer .20 .50
- 339 Keith Rucker .08 .25
- 340 Dan Wilkinson .08 .25
- 341 Yancy Thigpen .20 .50
- 342 Carnell Lake .08 .25
- 343 Byron Bam Morris .08 .25
- 344 Rod Woodson .08 .25
- 345 John L. Williams .08 .25
- 346 Deon Figures .08 .25
- 347 Erric Pegram .08 .25
- 348 Mike Tomczak .08 .25
- 349 Neil O'Donnell .20 .50
- 350 Sam Adams .08 .25
- 351 Todd Collins .08 .25
- 352 Jim Kelly .40 1.00
- 353 Carl Banks .08 .25
- 354 Derrick Alexander WR .08 .25
- 355 Michael Jackson .20 .50
- 356 Andre Rison .08 .25
- 357 Earnest Byner .08 .25
- 358 Eric Zeier .08 .25
- 359 Vinny Testaverde .20 .50
- 360 Greg Lloyd .20 .50
- 361 Mark Pike .08 .25
- 362 Cornelius Bennett .08 .25
- 363 Bruce Smith .20 .50
- 364 Steve Christie .08 .25
- 365 Steve Tasker .08 .25
- 366 Andre Reed .08 .25
- 367 Russell Copeland .08 .25
- 368 Bill Brooks .08 .25
- 369 Carwell Gardner .08 .25
- 370 Alex Van Pelt .40 1.00
- 371 Ben Coates .20 .50
- 372 Curtis Martin .60 1.50
- 373 Drew Bledsoe .80 2.00
- 374 Jeff Herrod .08 .25
- 375 Freddie Joe Nunn .08 .25
- 376 Sean Dawkins .08 .25
- 377 Tony Bennett .08 .25
- 378 Quentin Coryatt .08 .25
- 379 Marshall Faulk .40 1.00
- 380 Jim Harbaugh .20 .50
- 381 Myron Guyton UER .08 .25
- 382 Darren Carrington .08 .25
- 383 Irv Eatman .08 .25
- 384 Blaine Bishop .08 .25
- 385 Rickey Sanders .08 .25
- 386 Tim Bowens .08 .25
- 387 Vincent Brown .08 .25
- 388 Willie McGinest .08 .25
- 389 Matt Bahr .08 .25
- 390 Vincent Brisby .08 .25
- 391 Darren Smith .08 .25
- 392 John Copeland .08 .25
- 393 Bryce Paup .08 .25
- 394 Phil Hansen .08 .25
- 395 Romon Phifer .08 .25
- 396 J.T. Thomas .08 .25
- 397 Jeff Criswell .08 .25
- 398 Mo Lewis .08 .25
- 399 Anthony Smith .08 .25
- 400 Steve Wisniewski .08 .25

1977-79 Sportscaster Series 1

- COMPLETE SET (24) 17.50 35.00
- 115 Johnny Unitas 2.00 4.00
- 120 Jets vs. Colts .75 1.50

1977-79 Sportscaster Series 2

- COMPLETE SET (24) 30.00 60.00
- 204 George Blanda 1.00 2.00

1977-79 Sportscaster Series 3

- COMPLETE SET (24) 15.00 30.00
- 307 O.J. Simpson 1.50 4.00
- 320 Joe Namath 2.50 6.00

1977-79 Sportscaster Series 5

- COMPLETE SET (24) 12.50 25.00
- 523 Gale Sayers 2.00 4.00

1977-79 Sportscaster Series 6

- COMPLETE SET (24) 12.50 25.00
- 613 Red Grange 2.00 4.00
- 618 Jimmy Brown 2.50 5.00

1977-79 Sportscaster Series 7

- COMPLETE SET (24) 15.00 30.00

715 1967 Green Bay Packers .75 2.00

1977-79 Sportscaster Series 8
COMPLETE SET (24) 12.50 25.00
806 Fran Tarkenton 1.25 2.50

1977-79 Sportscaster Series 9
COMPLETE SET (24) 15.00 30.00
922 The Rose Bowl .75 1.50

1977-79 Sportscaster Series 10
COMPLETE SET (24) 17.50 35.00
1024 Tony Dorsett 2.00 4.00

1977-79 Sportscaster Series 11
COMPLETE SET (25) 20.00 40.00
1113 Larry Csonka and Jim Kiick 1.50 3.00

1977-79 Sportscaster Series 12
COMPLETE SET (24) 12.50 25.00
1206 A Very Warlike Game .75 1.50
1209 Joe Greene 2.00 4.00

1977-79 Sportscaster Series 13
COMPLETE SET (24) 12.50 25.00
1306 Archie Griffin 1.00 2.50
1321 Miami Dolphins vs. Kansas City 1.00 2.00

1977-79 Sportscaster Series 16
COMPLETE SET (24) 15.00 30.00
1612 Paul Hornung 1.50 3.00

1977-79 Sportscaster Series 17
COMPLETE SET (24) 10.00 20.00
1701 Jim Taylor 1.25 2.50
1715 Ken Stabler 2.00 4.00

1977-79 Sportscaster Series 20
COMPLETE SET (24) 7.50 15.00
2020 Ken Anderson 1.25 2.50

1977-79 Sportscaster Series 21
COMPLETE SET (24) 15.00 30.00
2118 College AS Game 1.00 2.00

1977-79 Sportscaster Series 22
COMPLETE SET (24) 15.00 30.00
2216 Lingo 1.50 4.00

1977-79 Sportscaster Series 23
COMPLETE SET (24) 20.00 40.00
2311 Super Bowl .75 1.50

1977-79 Sportscaster Series 24
COMPLETE SET (24) 10.00 20.00
2405 Bert Jones .75 1.50

1977-79 Sportscaster Series 25
COMPLETE SET (24) 10.00 20.00
2523 Charley Taylor .75 1.50

1977-79 Sportscaster Series 26
COMPLETE SET (24) 15.00 30.00
2611 Presidents in Sport 5.00 10.00
Gerald Ford
2614 Walter Payton 4.00 8.00

1977-79 Sportscaster Series 27
COMPLETE SET (24) 12.50 25.00
2706 Packers vs. Bears .50 1.00

1977-79 Sportscaster Series 29
COMPLETE SET (24) 17.50 35.00
2907 Defensive Formations 3.00 6.00
2916 NFL History .75 1.50

1977-79 Sportscaster Series 31
COMPLETE SET (24) 12.50 25.00
3102 Trick Plays .75 1.50

1977-79 Sportscaster Series 32
COMPLETE SET (24) 17.50 35.00
3203 Offensive Alignments .75 1.50

1977-79 Sportscaster Series 33
COMPLETE SET (24) 10.00 20.00
3301 Holding .75 1.50
3314 Chuck Foreman .75 1.50
3322 Gene Upshaw 1.00 2.00

1977-79 Sportscaster Series 34
COMPLETE SET (24) 15.00 30.00
3418 Preston Pearson .75 2.00

1977-79 Sportscaster Series 35
COMPLETE SET (24) 15.00 30.00
3518 Jim Bakken .50 1.00

1977-79 Sportscaster Series 36
COMPLETE SET (24) 15.00 30.00
3617 Goal Line Defense .75 1.50
3620 Two-Minute Offense 1.50 3.00

1977-79 Sportscaster Series 37
Please note that cards number 4 and 17 are not listed. Any information on the two missing cards is very appreciated.
COMPLETE SET (24) 12.50 25.00
3715 Legal and Illegal .25 .50
3717 Lynn Swann 2.00 5.00

1977-79 Sportscaster Series 38
COMPLETE SET (24) 20.00 40.00
3822 Jack Youngblood 1.00 2.00

1977-79 Sportscaster Series 39
COMPLETE SET (24) 7.50 15.00
3917 Ball Control .75 1.50
3921 Grabbing the Face Mask .75 1.50
3922 Harvey Martin 1.00 2.00

1977-79 Sportscaster Series 40
COMPLETE SET (24) 10.00 20.00
4004 Pass Interference .75 1.50
4010 Rick Upchurch .50 1.00

1977-79 Sportscaster Series 42
COMPLETE SET (24) 15.00 30.00
4213 Curley Culp .50 1.00
4224 Cheerleading .75 1.50

1977-79 Sportscaster Series 43
COMPLETE SET (24) 12.50 25.00
4312 Holding the Ball .75 1.50

1977-79 Sportscaster Series 44
COMPLETE SET (24) 12.50 25.00
4422 Punting 1.25 2.50
4424 Special Team Defense .50 1.00

1977-79 Sportscaster Series 45
Card number 11 is not in our checklist. Any information on this missing card is greatly appreciated.
COMPLETE SET (24) 20.00 40.00
4504 Throwing the Ball 1.50 3.00
4509 Punt Returns 1.00 2.00

1977-79 Sportscaster Series 46
COMPLETE SET (24) 12.50 25.00
4601 NFL Draft 1.25 2.50
4613 Kickoff Returns 2.00 4.00

1977-79 Sportscaster Series 47
COMPLETE SET (24) 17.50 35.00
4721 Tom Jackson 2.00 4.00

1977-79 Sportscaster Series 50
COMPLETE SET (24) 15.00 30.00
5001 Equipment .75 1.50
5020 Ernie Nevers 1.00 2.00

1977-79 Sportscaster Series 53
COMPLETE SET (24) 15.00 30.00
5310 The Sidelines .75 1.50
5317 Joe Namath GM 1.50 4.00

1977-79 Sportscaster Series 54
COMPLETE SET (24) 15.00 30.00
5414 Joe Kapp 1.00 2.00
5420 Jim Thorpe 4.00 8.00

1977-79 Sportscaster Series 55
COMPLETE SET (24) 12.50 25.00
5501 Dave Casper 1.00 2.00

1977-79 Sportscaster Series 56
COMPLETE SET (24) 37.50 75.00
5615 Ray Guy 2.50 5.00
5618 Great Moments 7.50 15.00

1977-79 Sportscaster Series 57
COMPLETE SET (24) 40.00 80.00
5701 Willie Lanier 2.50 5.00

1977-79 Sportscaster Series 59
COMPLETE SET (24) 50.00 100.00
5902 Roger Staubach 5.00 10.00

1977-79 Sportscaster Series 60
COMPLETE SET (24) 37.50 75.00
6004 Whizzer White 4.00 8.00

1977-79 Sportscaster Series 61
COMPLETE SET (24) 50.00 100.00
6120 Heisman Trophy 5.00 10.00

1977-79 Sportscaster Series 62
COMPLETE SET (24) 40.00 80.00
6214 Eddie Lee Ivery 2.00 4.00

1977-79 Sportscaster Series 63
COMPLETE SET (24) 30.00 60.00
6302 17-0 Dolphins 5.00 10.00
6316 Outland Award 1.00 2.00

1977-79 Sportscaster Series 64
COMPLETE SET (24) 25.00 50.00
6411 Harvard Stadium 2.00 4.00
6419 Floyd Little 2.50 5.00

1977-79 Sportscaster Series 65
COMPLETE SET (24) 40.00 80.00
6524 Franco Harris 3.00 8.00

1977-79 Sportscaster Series 66
COMPLETE SET (24) 37.50 75.00
6607 The Four Horsemen 7.50 15.00

1977-79 Sportscaster Series 67
COMPLETE SET (24) 40.00 80.00
6705 The Bahr Family 2.50 5.00

1977-79 Sportscaster Series 68
COMPLETE SET (24) 40.00 80.00
6806 Incredible Playoff 2.00 4.00
6820 John Cappelletti 2.50 5.00

1977-79 Sportscaster Series 69
COMPLETE SET (24) 40.00 80.00
6902 Terry Bradshaw 5.00 10.00
6912 First Televised 1.00 2.00
6915 Indian HOF 4.00 8.00

1977-79 Sportscaster Series 70
COMPLETE SET (24) 30.00 60.00
7010 Pro Bowl 2.50 5.00

1977-79 Sportscaster Series 71
COMPLETE SET (24) 40.00 80.00
7101 Dave Jennings 2.00 4.00
7123 Chuck Noll 6.00 12.00

1977-79 Sportscaster Series 72
COMPLETE SET (24) 50.00 100.00
7217 Joe Paterno 10.00 20.00
Jeff Hostetler
7221 Greg Pruitt 2.50 5.00

1977-79 Sportscaster Series 73
COMPLETE SET (24) 40.00 80.00
7306 Bear Bryant 10.00 20.00

1977-79 Sportscaster Series 75
COMPLETE SET (24) 30.00 60.00
7502 Nick Buoniconti 2.50 5.00

1977-79 Sportscaster Series 76
COMPLETE SET (24) 30.00 60.00
7605 NFL Hall of Fame 2.00 4.00
7624 Walter Camp All- 2.00 4.00

1977-79 Sportscaster Series 78
COMPLETE SET (24) 150.00 300.00
7809 Tom Landry 7.50 15.00
7820 Rating Passers 5.00 10.00

1977-79 Sportscaster Series 79
COMPLETE SET (24) 60.00 120.00
7922 College Football 10.00 20.00

1977-79 Sportscaster Series 80
COMPLETE SET (24) 62.50 125.00
8019 Jim Marshall 4.00 8.00

1977-79 Sportscaster Series 81
COMPLETE SET (24) 62.50 125.00
8118 Dan Pastorini 3.00 6.00
8122 Billy Sims 4.00 8.00

1977-79 Sportscaster Series 82
COMPLETE SET (24) 50.00 100.00
8203 Jerome Holland 2.00 4.00
8221 Tom Cousineau 2.50 5.00

1977-79 Sportscaster Series 83
COMPLETE SET (24) 62.50 125.00
8310 Ed Too Tall Jones 4.00 8.00

1977-79 Sportscaster Series 85
COMPLETE SET (24) 62.50 125.00
8502 Barefoot Athletes 3.00 6.00
8510 Protecting the 3.00 6.00
8520 Lou Holtz FB 10.00 20.00

1977-79 Sportscaster Series 86
COMPLETE SET (24) 50.00 100.00
8601 Grambling 3.00 6.00

1977-79 Sportscaster Series 88
COMPLETE SET (24) 50.00 100.00
8811 Ernie Davis 7.50 15.00

1977-79 Sportscaster Series 101
COMPLETE SET (24) 62.50 125.00
10117 Pat Haden 2.00 5.00

1977-79 Sportscaster Series 102
COMPLETE SET (24) 75.00 150.00
10220 NCAA Records 4.00 8.00
Steve Owens

1977-79 Sportscaster Series 103
COMPLETE SET (24) 87.50 175.00
10301 Jim Turner 4.00 8.00
10316 Longest Runs 4.00 8.00

1987 Sports Cube Game
3 1/2" by 5 3/8" cards with nine black and white portrait shots on front and questions on the back
COMPLETE SET (3) 8.00 20.00
1 James Naismith 6.00 15.00
Babe Ruth
America's Cup
Knute
3 Joe Louis 3.20 8.00
Bill Klem
Ken Anderson
Thurman Muns

1977 Sports Illustrated Ad Cards
This set is a multi-sport set and features cards with action player photos from various sports as they appeared on different covers of Sports Illustrated Magazine. The cards measure approximately 3 1/2" by 4 3/4" with the backs displaying the player's name and team name and information on how to subscribe to the magazine at a special rate. It was issued by Mrs. Carter Breads.
COMPLETE SET 12.50 25.00
4 Oakland Raiders 2.50 5.00
5 Michigan Wolverines FB 2.50 5.00

1999 Sports Illustrated
The 1999 Sports Illustrated set was issued in one series totalling 150 cards and was distributed in seven-card packs with a suggested retail price of $15. The fronts feature color action player photos printed on 20 pt. card stock. The backs carry another player photo with biographical information and career statistics. The set includes the following two subsets: Super Bowl MVPs (1-30) and Fresh Faces (126-150).
COMPLETE SET (150) 30.00 60.00
1 Bart Starr MVP .75 2.00
2 Bart Starr MVP .75 2.00
3 Joe Namath MVP .60 1.50
4 Len Dawson MVP .30 .75
5 Chuck Howley MVP .20 .50
6 Roger Staubach MVP .40 1.00
7 Jake Scott MVP .20 .50
8 Larry Csonka MVP .30 .75
9 Franco Harris MVP .30 .75
10 Fred Biletnikoff MVP .30 .75
11 H.Martin .25 .60
R.White MVP
12 Terry Bradshaw MVP .75 2.00
13 Terry Bradshaw MVP .75 2.00
14 Jim Plunkett MVP .25 .60
15 Joe Montana MVP 1.00 2.50
16 Marcus Allen MVP .30 .75
17 Joe Montana MVP 1.00 2.50
18 Richard Dent MVP .20 .50
19 Phil Simms MVP .30 .75
20 Doug Williams MVP .25 .60
21 Jerry Rice MVP .75 2.00
22 Joe Montana MVP 1.00 2.50
23 Ottis Anderson MVP .20 .50
24 Mark Rypien MVP .20 .50
25 Troy Aikman MVP .40 1.00
26 Emmitt Smith MVP .50 1.25
27 Steve Young MVP .40 1.00
28 Larry Brown MVP .20 .50
29 Desmond Howard MVP .25 .60
30 Terrell Davis MVP .25 .60
31 Y.A. Tittle .30 .75
32 Paul Hornung .30 .75
33 Gale Sayers .30 .75
34 Garo Yepremian .20 .50
35 Bert Jones .20 .50
36 Joe Washington .20 .50
37 Joe Theismann .30 .75
38 Roger Craig .25 .60
39 Mike Singletary .30 .75
40 Bobby Bell .20 .50
41 Ken Houston .20 .50
42 Lenny Moore .20 .50
43 Mark Moseley .20 .50
44 Chuck Bednarik .25 .60
45 Ted Hendricks .20 .50
46 Steve Largent .30 .75
47 Bob Lilly .25 .60
48 Don Maynard .25 .60
49 John Mackey .20 .50
50 Anthony Munoz .25 .60
51 Bobby Mitchell .25 .60
52 Jim Brown .50 1.25
53 Otto Graham .25 .60
54 Earl Morrall .20 .50
55 Danny White .25 .60
56 Karim Abdul-Jabbar .20 .50
57 Charlie Garner .25 .60
58 Jeff Blake .25 .60
59 Reggie White .30 .75
60 Derrick Thomas .30 .75
61 Duce Staley .20 .50
62 Tim Brown .30 .75
63 Elvis Grbac .20 .50
64 Tony Banks .25 .60
65 Rob Johnson .25 .60
66 Danny Kanell .20 .50
67 Marshall Faulk .25 .60
68 Warrick Dunn .20 .50
69 Dan Marino .60 1.50
70 Jimmy Smith .25 .60
71 John Elway .50 1.25
72 Charles Way .20 .50
73 Ricky Watters .25 .60
74 Terry Glenn .25 .60
75 Bobby Hoying .20 .50
76 Curtis Martin .25 .60
77 Trent Dilfer .20 .50
78 Emmitt Smith .50 1.25
79 Irving Fryar .25 .60
80 Troy Aikman .40 1.00
81 Barry Sanders .50 1.25
82 Brett Favre .60 1.50
83 Robert Smith .20 .50
84 Dorsey Levens .25 .60
85 Cris Carter .30 .75
86 Jeff George .20 .50
87 Jerome Bettis .30 .75
88 Warren Moon .30 .75
89 Steve Young .40 1.00
90 Fred Lane .20 .50
91 Jerry Rice .75 2.00
92 Natrone Means .25 .60
93 Mike Alstott .20 .50
94 Kordell Stewart .20 .50
95 Jake Plummer .20 .50
96 Jamal Anderson .25 .60
97 Corey Dillon .20 .50
98 Deion Sanders .25 .60
99 Mark Brunell .25 .60
100 Garrison Hearst .20 .50
101 Andre Rison .25 .60
102 Antowain Smith .20 .50
103 Drew Bledsoe .25 .60
104 Eddie George .25 .60
105 Keyshawn Johnson .25 .60
106 Isaac Bruce .30 .75
107 Rob Moore .20 .50
108 Steve McNair .25 .60
109 Terrell Davis .25 .60
110 Carl Pickens .25 .60
111 Wayne Chrebet .20 .50
112 Kerry Collins .20 .50
113 Eric Metcalf .20 .50
114 Joey Galloway .25 .60
115 Shannon Sharpe .25 .60
116 Robert Brooks .25 .60
117 Glenn Foley .20 .50
118 Yancey Thigpen .20 .50
119 Frank Sanders .20 .50
120 Herman Moore .25 .60
121 Antonio Freeman .25 .60
122 Michael Irvin .30 .75
123 Brad Johnson .25 .60
124 James Stewart .20 .50
125 Jim Harbaugh .25 .60
126 Peyton Manning FF 2.50 6.00
127 Ryan Leaf FF .30 .75
128 Curtis Enis FF .25 .60
129 Fred Taylor FF .25 .60
130 Randy Moss FF .75 2.00
131 John Avery FF .25 .60
132 Charles Woodson FF .40 1.00
133 Robert Edwards FF .25 .60
134 Charlie Batch FF .25 .60
135 Brian Griese FF .25 .60
136 Skip Hicks FF .25 .60
137 Jacquez Green FF .25 .60
138 Robert Holcombe FF .25 .60
139 Kevin Dyson FF .25 .60
140 Rodney Williams FF .25 .60
141 Ahman Green FF .30 .75
142 Tavian Banks FF .25 .60
143 Donald Hayes FF .25 .60
144 Tony Simmons FF .25 .60
145 Pat Johnson FF .25 .60
146 Marcus Nash FF .25 .60
147 Germane Crowell FF .25 .60
148 R.W. McQuarters FF .25 .60
149 Jonathan Quinn FF .25 .60
150 Andre Wadsworth FF .25 .60
P35 Gale Sayers Promo 1.25 3.00

1999 Sports Illustrated Autographs
Inserted one per pack, this 35-card set features color action images of retired NFL "Greats of the Game" on a Sports Illustrated cover background with gold foil stamping and a facsimile autograph printed in the wide bottom margin. The card back is the official Certificate of Authenticity. The cards are unnumbered and checklisted below in alphabetical order.
ONE PER PACK
1 Ottis Anderson 6.00 15.00
2 Chuck Bednarik 12.50 25.00
3 Bobby Bell 8.00 20.00
4 Terry Bradshaw 125.00 250.00
5 Jim Brown 50.00 100.00
6 Roger Craig 8.00 20.00
7 Len Dawson 60.00 120.00
8 Otto Graham 15.00 50.00
9 Franco Harris 40.00 100.00
10 Ted Hendricks 6.00 15.00
11 Paul Hornung SP 100.00 200.00
12 Ken Houston 6.00 15.00
13 Bert Jones 6.00 15.00
14 Steve Largent 8.00 20.00
15 Bob Lilly 6.00 15.00
16 John Mackey 6.00 15.00
17 Don Maynard 8.00 20.00
18 Bobby Mitchell 6.00 15.00
19 Joe Montana 150.00 300.00
20 Lenny Moore 6.00 15.00
21 Earl Morrall 6.00 15.00
22 Mark Moseley 6.00 15.00
23 Anthony Munoz 6.00 15.00
24 Joe Namath 125.00 250.00
25 Jim Plunkett 6.00 15.00
26 Gale Sayers 20.00 40.00
27 Mike Singletary 30.00 60.00
28 Bart Starr 125.00 250.00
29 Roger Staubach 150.00 250.00
30 Joe Theismann 20.00 50.00
31 Y.A. Tittle 50.00 100.00
32 Joe Washington 6.00 15.00
33 Danny White 8.00 20.00
34 Doug Williams 12.00 30.00
35 Garo Yepremian 6.00 15.00

1999 Sports Illustrated Canton Calling
Randomly inserted in hobby packs at the rate of one in 12, this eight-card set features color action photos of top current NFL stars who are headed for Canton. A gold parallel version of this set was also produced with an insertion rate of 1:120.

COMPLETE SET (8) 30.00 60.00
STATED ODDS 1:12 HOBBY
*GOLDS: 1.5X TO 4X BASIC INSERTS
GOLD STATED ODDS 1:120
1 Warren Moon 1.50 4.00
2 Emmitt Smith 5.00 12.00
3 Jerry Rice 3.00 8.00
4 Brett Favre 6.00 15.00
5 Barry Sanders 5.00 12.00
6 Dan Marino 6.00 15.00
7 John Elway 6.00 15.00
8 Troy Aikman 3.00 8.00

1999 Sports Illustrated Covers
Randomly inserted one per pack, this 60-card set features standard-size card reproductions of actual Sports Illustrated Covers with copy on feature story.
COMPLETE SET (60) 10.00 25.00
ONE PER PACK
1 Jim Brown .30 .75
2 Y.A. Tittle .20 .50
3 Dallas Cowboys .10 .30
4 Joe Namath .30 .75
5 Bart Starr .30 .75
6 Earl Morrall .10 .30
7 Minnesota Vikings .10 .30
8 Kansas City Chiefs .10 .30
9 Len Dawson .20 .50
10 Monday Night FB .10 .30
11 Jim Plunkett .20 .50
12 Garo Yepremian .10 .30
13 Larry Csonka .20 .50
14 Terry Bradshaw .30 .75
15 Franco Harris .20 .50
16 Bert Jones .10 .30
17 H.Martin .10 .30
R.White
18 Roger Staubach .30 .75
19 Marcus Allen .30 .75
20 Joe Washington .10 .30
21 Dan Marino 1.25 3.00
22 Joe Theismann .20 .50
23 Roger Craig .20 .50
24 Mike Singletary .20 .50
25 Chicago Bears .10 .30
26 Phil Simms .20 .50
27 Vinny Testaverde .20 .50
28 Doug Williams .10 .30
29 Jerry Rice .60 1.50
30 Herschel Walker .20 .50
31 Joe Montana .60 1.50
32 Ottis Anderson .10 .30
33 Rocket Ismail .20 .50
34 Bruce Smith .20 .50
35 Thurman Thomas .20 .50
36 Mark Rypien .10 .30
37 Jim Harbaugh .20 .50
38 Randall Cunningham .30 .75
39 Troy Aikman .60 1.50
40 Reggie White .30 .75
41 Junior Seau .30 .75
42 Emmitt Smith 1.00 2.50
43 Natrone Means .20 .50
44 Ricky Watters .20 .50
45 Pittsburgh Steelers .10 .30
46 S.Young .40 1.00
T.Aikman
47 Steve Young .40 1.00
48 Deion Sanders .30 .75
49 Elvis Grbac .20 .50
50 Packers vs. Chiefs .10 .30
51 Brett Favre 1.25 3.00
52 M.Brunell .30 .75
K.Collins
53 Antonio Freeman .30 .75
54 Desmond Howard .20 .50
55 AFC Central QB's .20 .50
56 Warrick Dunn .30 .75
57 Jerome Bettis .30 .75
58 John Elway 1.25 3.00
59 Brent Jones .10 .30
60 Terrell Davis .30 .75

1989 Sports Illustrated for Kids I
Since its debut issue in January 1989, SI for Kids has included a perforated sheet of nine standard-size cards bound into each magazine. The cards were consecutively numbered 1-324 through December 1991. The athletes featured represent an extremely wide spectrum of sports. Each card features color photos with variously colored borders. The borders are as follows: aqua (1-108), green (109-207), woodgrain (208-216), red (217-315), marble (316-324). The player's name is printed in a white bar at the top, while his or her sport appears at the bottom. The backs carry biographical information, career highlights, and a trivia question with answer. The cards' magazine issue date appears on the back in very small type. Although originally distributed in sheet form, the cards are frequently traded as singles. Thus, they are priced individually. The value of an intact sheet is equal to the sum of the nine cards plus a premium of up to 20%.
3 Howie Long FB .40 1.00
7 Doug Williams FB .40 1.00
17 Herschel Walker FB .40 1.00
59 Jerry Rice FB 2.50 6.00
65 Al Toon FB .40 1.00
76 Boomer Esiason FB .40 1.00
78 Mike Singletary FB .40 1.00
84 Dan Marino FB 4.00 10.00
86 Eric Dickerson FB .40 1.00
94 Reggie Roby FB .40 1.00
98 Bobby Hebert FB .40 1.00
103 John Elway FB 4.00 10.00
105 Mike Rozier FB .40 1.00

1990 Sports Illustrated for Kids I
110 Randall Cunningham FB .30 .75
168 Joe Montana FB 4.00 10.00
180 Bobby Humphrey FB .10 .30
185 Ronnie Lott FB .30 .75
194 Bernie Kosar FB .20 .50
198 Bo Jackson FB .30 .75
202 Barry Sanders FB 3.00 8.00
206 Flipper Anderson FB .10 .30

1991 Sports Illustrated for Kids I
218 Don Majkowski FB .10 .30
225 Lawrence Taylor FB .40 1.00
232 Warren Moon FB .30 .75
234 Karl Mecklenburg FB .10 .30
277 Ottis Anderson FB .15 .40
284 Thurman Thomas FB 1.00 2.50
291 Derrick Thomas FB .30 .75
295 Emmitt Smith FB 3.00 8.00
298 Art Monk FB .20 .50
306 Mark Carrier FB .10 .30
311 Keith Jackson FB .10 .30
315 Morten Andersen FB .10 .30
320 Jim Thorpe .60 1.50
Track and Field
Football

Baseball
322 Red Grange FB .60 1.50

1992 Sports Illustrated for Kids II
Since its debut issue in January 1989, SI for Kids has included a perforated sheet of nine standard-size cards bound into each magazine. In January 1992, the card numbers started over again at 1. This listing comprises the cards contained from that magazine through the last 2000 issue. The athletes featured represent an extremely wide spectrum of sports. Each card features color photos with borders of various designs and colors. The borders are as follows: navy (1-9, 19-99), clouds (10-18, 55-63, 226-234), marble (100-108, 208-216, 316-324), pink (109-207), purple (217-225), blue (235-315), gold/silver (325-486), clouds (487-495) and gold/silver (496-621). The athlete's name is printed at the top while his or her sport appears at the bottom. The backs carry biographical information, career highlights, and a trivia question with answer. The cards' magazine issue date appears on the back in very small type. Although originally distributed in sheet form, the cards are frequently traded as singles. Thus, they are priced individually. The value of an intact sheet is equal to the sum of the nine cards plus a premium of up to 20 percent. The cards labeled as "MC" were issued in SI for Kids as part of a milk promotion.
3 Jim Kelly FB .40 1.00
5 Christian Okoye FB .10 .30
23 Mark Rypien FB .10 .30
69 Deion Sanders FB 1.00 2.50
74 Troy Aikman FB 2.50 6.00
76 Marcus Allen FB .40 1.00
82 Leonard Russell FB .10 .30
89 Anthony Carter FB .10 .30
94 Haywood Jeffires FB .10 .30
99 Bruce Smith FB .20 .50
106 Jim Brown FB 1.00 2.50

1993 Sports Illustrated for Kids II
113 Dan Marino FB 4.00 10.00
115 Anthony Munoz FB .20 .50
119 Steve Young FB 2.00 5.00
123 Andre Rison FB .20 .50
133 Rod Woodson FB .20 .50
138 Junior Seau FB .30 .75
180 Sterling Sharpe FB .20 .50
183 Nick Lowery FB .10 .30
188 Randall Cunningham FB .30 .75
192 Cortez Kennedy FB .10 .30
194 Barry Foster FB .10 .30
203 Brett Favre FB 3.00 8.00
205 Clyde Simmons .10 .30
Football
210 Johnny Unitas FB 1.25 3.00

1994 Sports Illustrated for Kids II
240 Phil Simms FB .20 .50
248 Tim Brown FB .30 .75
256 Emmitt Smith FB 2.00 5.00
263 Ricky Watters FB .20 .50
272 Jerome Bettis FB .40 1.00
283 Reggie White FB .30 .75
291 Drew Bledsoe FB .75 2.00
296 John Taylor FB .20 .50
302 Joe Montana FB 4.00 10.00
304 Renaldo Turnbull FB .10 .30
310 Eric Metcalf FB .20 .50
315 Seth Joyner FB .10 .30
321 Walter Payton FB 1.00 2.50

1996 Sports Illustrated for Kids II
437 John Elway FB 2.00 5.00
441 Terance Mathis FB .20 .50
445 Deion Sanders FB .60 1.50
450 Brett Favre FB 2.00 5.00
454 Barry Sanders FB .75 2.00
kid photo
459 Troy Aikman FB .40 1.00
kid photo
467 Kordell Stewart FB .40 1.00
476 Jim Harbaugh FB .20 .50
483 Darrell Green FB .20 .50
501 Herman Moore FB .20 .50
502 Danny Wuerffel FB .20 .50
510 Bryce Paup FB .10 .30
511 Ricky Watters FB .20 .50
517 Willie Roaf FB .10 .30
521 Jeff George FB .20 .50
526 Neil O'Donnell FB .10 .30
531 Darren Bennett FB .10 .30
532 Curtis Martin FB .40 1.00
538 Doug Flutie FB .60 1.50

1997 Sports Illustrated for Kids II
548 Brian Mitchell FB .10 .30
554 Terrell Davis FB 1.50 4.00
558 Stan Humphries FB .10 .30
592 Jerome Bettis FB .40 1.00
604 Drew Bledsoe FB .50 1.25
610 Mark Chmura FB .20 .50
615 Simeon Rice FB .20 .50
620 Mark Brunell FB .40 1.00
625 Troy Aikman FB .60 1.50
cartoon
632 Jerry Rice FB .60 1.50
636 Vinny Testaverde FB .20 .50
640 Rod Woodson FB .20 .50
644 Dan Marino FB 1.25 3.00

1998 Sports Illustrated for Kids II
649 Tim Brown FB .30 .75
671 Barry Sanders FB 2.00 5.00
687 Rob Moore FB .10 .30
694 Brett Favre FB 1.25 3.00
704 Warrick Dunn FB .40 1.00
719 Jason Sehorn FB .10 .30
723 Eddie George FB .40 1.00
724 Bruce Smith FB .20 .50
733 Barry Sanders FB 1.25 3.00
740 Cris Carter FB .30 .75
747 Mike Alstott FB .20 .50
750 Dana Stubblefield FB .10 .30
752 Steve Young FB .50 1.25

1999 Sports Illustrated for Kids II
757 Ricky Watters FB .10 .30
761 Deion Sanders FB .40 1.00
766 Randall Cunningham FB .30 .75
774 Kevin Greene FB .10 .30
788 John Elway FB 1.25 3.00
791 Jerry Rice FB .60 1.50
797 Emmitt Smith FB .75 2.00
806 Jamal Anderson FB .20 .50
812 Randy Moss FB 2.00 5.00
822 O.J. McDuffie FB .10 .30
824 Terrell Davis FB .75 2.00
829 Vinny Testaverde FB .20 .50
834 Gary Anderson FB .10 .30
843 Brett Favre FB 1.25 3.00
844 Shannon Sharpe FB .20 .50
848 Antonio Freeman FB .30 .75
855 Ray Lewis FB .30 .75
858 Jake Plummer FB .40 1.00
862 Ty Law FB .10 .30

2000 Sports Illustrated for Kids II
867 Jim Thorpe .40 1.00
Football
874 Peyton Manning FB 2.00 5.00
887 Kurt Warner FB 1.00 2.50
902 Jimmy Smith FB .20 .50
915 Edgerrin James FB .75 2.00
917 Kevin Carter FB .10 .30
932 Steve Beuerlein FB .20 .50
938 Marvin Harrison FB .30 .75
943 Jevon Kearse FB .20 .50
947 Randy Moss FB 1.25 3.00
949 Tim Dwight FB .20 .50
959 Stephen Davis FB .20 .50
963 Warren Sapp FB .20 .50

2001 Sports Illustrated for Kids
Since its debut issue in January 1989, SI for Kids has included a perforated sheet of nine standard-size cards bound into each magazine. In December 2000, for the second time, the card numbers started over again at 1. The athletes featured represent an extremely wide spectrum of sports. The athlete's name is printed at the top while his or her sport appears at the bottom. The backs carry biographical information, career highlights, and a trivia question with answer. The cards' magazine issue date appears on the back in very small type. Although originally distributed in sheet form, the cards are frequently traded as singles. Thus, they are priced individually. The value of an intact sheet is equal to the sum of the nine cards plus a premium of up to 20 percent.
COMPLETE SET (108) 25.00 50.00
3 Junior Seau FB .10 .30
5 Mark Brunell FB .15 .40
14 Daunte Culpepper FB .20 .50
18 Keyshawn Johnson FB .15 .40
21 Isaac Bruce FB .15 .40
26 Wayne Chrebet FB .15 .40
32 Brian Mitchell FB .08 .25
44 Aaron Brooks FB .15 .40
48 Jamal Lewis FB .20 .50
56 Donovan McNabb FB .20 .50
64 La'Roi Glover FB .08 .25
81 Eddie George FB .15 .40
86 Marshall Faulk FB .40 1.00
95 Jeff Garcia FB .10 .30
100 Champ Bailey FB .10 .30
104 Randy Moss FB .40 1.00

2002 Sports Illustrated for Kids
112 Matt Stover FB .08 .25
114 Courtney Brown FB .08 .25
118 Corey Dillon FB .15 .40
123 Michael Strahan FB .10 .30
129 Brett Favre FB 1.00 2.50
133 Curtis Martin FB .15 .40
140 Jerome Bettis FB .15 .40
145 Eric Crouch FB .40 1.00
153 Anthony Thomas FB .20 .50
158 Kurt Warner FB .20 .50
165 LaDainian Tomlinson FB .60 1.50
170 Tom Brady FB .40 1.00
172 Emmitt Smith FB .40 1.00
177 Marvin Harrison FB .15 .40
181 Andre Johnson FB .30 .75
189 Tim Couch FB .10 .30
194 Ty Law FB .10 .30
201 Terrell Owens FB .15 .40
203 Kordell Stewart FB .10 .30
208 Steve McNair FB .15 .40
213 Ahman Green FB .15 .40
218 Ronde Barber FB .10 .30
222 Brian Urlacher FB .25 .60

2003 Sports Illustrated for Kids
Since its debut issue in January 1989, SI for Kids has included a perforated sheet of nine standard-size cards bound into each magazine. In January 2001, for the second time, the card numbers started over at 1. Listed below are the cards issued in magazines that carry 2003 cover dates. The athletes featured represent an extremely wide spectrum of sports. Although originally distributed in sheet form, the cards are frequently traded as singles. Thus, they are priced individually. The value of an intact sheet is equal to the sum of the nine cards plus a premium of up to 20 percent.
230 Rich Gannon FB .10 .30
234 LaVar Arrington FB .20 .50
235 Mike Brown S FB .08 .25
239 Drew Bledsoe FB .15 .40
245 Deuce McAllister FB .15 .40
252 Peerless Price FB .07 .20
253 Willis McGahee FB .50 1.25
258 Joe Horn FB .10 .30
263 Brad Johnson FB .10 .30
270 Clinton Portis FB .60 1.50
272 Plaxico Burress FB .25 .60
281 Donald Driver FB .20 .50
285 Jason Taylor FB .10 .30
290 Chad Pennington FB .25 .60
294 Priest Holmes FB .20 .50
302 Tommy Maddox FB .10 .30
304 Shaun Alexander FB .20 .50
308 Charlie Garner FB .10 .30
312 Eli Manning FB 2.00 5.00
314 Torry Holt FB .10 .30
318 Tony Gonzalez FB .10 .30
320 Tiki Barber FB .10 .30
327 Kellen Winslow Jr. FB .60 1.25
329 Trent Green FB .10 .30
333 Takeo Spikes FB .07 .20

2004 Sports Illustrated for Kids
ONE NINE-CARD SHEET PER MAGAZINE
341 Emmitt Smith FB .50 1.25
345 Stephen Davis FB .15 .40
351 Simeon Rice FB .10 .30
353 Jason White FB .40 1.00
357 Chad Johnson FB .10 .30
365 Marc Bulger FB .15 .40
369 Mike Vanderjagt FB .07 .20
375 Steve Smith FB .15 .40
379 Dwight Freeney FB .10 .30
394 Tony Parrish FB .07 .20
399 Steve McNair FB .15 .40
409 Santana Moss FB .10 .30
411 Daunte Culpepper FB .15 .40
420 David Greene FB .07 .20
421 Derrick Mason FB .10 .30
426 Michael Strahan FB .07 .20
431 Darren Sproles FB .20 .50
438 Darrell Jackson FB .10 .30
440 Patrick Kerney FB .07 .20

2005 Sports Illustrated for Kids
444 Andre Johnson FB .10 .30
446 Tiki Barber FB .10 .30
452 Ben Roethlisberger FB 1.50 4.00
454 Adrian Peterson FB 2.50 6.00
461 Javon Walker FB .10 .30
465 Curtis Martin FB .15 .40
474 Ed Reed FB .10 .30
480 Tedy Bruschi FB .15 .40
484 Jake Plummer FB .08 .25
492 Bert Berry FB .08 .25
494 Joe Horn FB .10 .30
498 Drew Brees FB .15 .40
503 Willis McGahee FB .15 .40
506 Keith Brooking FB .07 .20
513 Brian Westbrook FB .10 .30
516 Kabeer Gbaja-Biamila FB .07 .20
518 Matt Leinart FB 1.00 2.50
524 Keith Bulluck FB .07 .20
528 Antonio Gates FB .20 .50
532 Vince Young FB 2.00 5.00
537 Shaun Alexander FB .20 .50

2006 Sports Illustrated for Kids
3 Jimmy Smith FB .07 .20
4 Carson Palmer FB .20 .50
12 Warrick Dunn FB .10 .30
17 Torry Holt FB .10 .30
21 Santana Moss FB .08 .25
26 Edgerrin James FB .10 .30
32 Michael Vick FB .15 .40
36 Robert Mathis FB .07 .20
42 Larry Johnson FB .20 .50
44 Anquan Boldin FB .08 .25
50 Tom Brady FB .60 1.50
52 Osi Umenyiora FB .08 .25
57 LaDainian Tomlinson FB .30 .75
65 Eli Manning FB .30 .75
70 Nathan Vasher FB .08 .25
75 Jake Delhomme FB .08 .25
76 DeAngelo Hall FB .08 .25
86 Willie Parker FB .10 .30
88 Larry Fitzgerald FB .10 .30
92 Reggie Wayne FB .10 .30
98 Matt Hasselbeck FB .08 .25
102 Cadillac Williams FB .25 .60
108 Champ Bailey FB .08 .25

2007 Sports Illustrated for Kids
ONE NINE-CARD SHEET PER MAGAZINE
111 Tom Brady FB .60 1.50
120 Jimmy Clausen HS FB .75 2.00
124 Marvin Austin HS FB .60 1.50
127 Frank Gore FB .10 .30
131 Philip Rivers FB .15 .40
140 Reggie Bush FB .75 2.00
146 Devin Hester FB .40 1.00
158 Vince Young FB .60 1.50
168 Tony Romo FB 1.00 2.50
173 Maurice Jones-Drew FB .40 1.00
183 Brian Urlacher FB .10 .30
187 Darren McFadden FB 2.00 5.00
192 Steven Jackson FB .10 .30
198 Jonathan Vilma FB .08 .25
201 Jason Taylor FB .08 .25
203 Drew Brees FB .10 .30
210 Joseph Addai FB .40 1.00
211 Julius Peppers FB .10 .30

2008 Sports Illustrated for Kids
217 Reggie White FB .10 .30
218 Jerry Rice FB .40 1.00
219 Walter Payton FB .75 2.00
220 Jim Brown FB .30 .75
221 Johnny Unitas FB .50 1.25
222 Deion Sanders FB .20 .50
223 Anthony Munoz FB .10 .30
224 Joe Greene FB .10 .30
225 John Elway FB .50 1.25
227 Derek Anderson FB .20 .50
231 Terrell Owens FB .20 .50
239 Brett Favre FB .75 2.00
252 Ryan Grant FB .10 .30
258 T.J. Houshmandzadeh FB .08 .25
266 Randy Moss FB .10 .30
275 Adrian Peterson FB .20 .50
277 Chase Daniel FB .15 .40
280 Antonio Cromartie FB .08 .25
288 Fred Taylor FB .08 .25
291 Knowshon Moreno FB .08 .25
296 Marques Colston FB .10 .30
300 Clinton Portis FB .08 .25
301 Mario Williams FB .08 .25
307 Peyton Manning FB .25 .60
311 Brett Favre FB .40 1.00
318 Justin Tuck FB .08 .25
322 Sam Bradford FB .10 .30
325 Adrian Peterson ART FB .20 .50
326 Reggie Bush ART FB .10 .30
327 Devin Hester ART FB .10 .30
328 Marion Barber ART FB .10 .30
329 Aaron Rodgers ART FB .30 .75
330 LaDainian Tomlinson ART FB .10 .30
331 Chris Chambers ART FB .08 .25
332 Brian Westbrook ART FB .08 .25
333 Frank Gore ART FB .08 .25

2009 Sports Illustrated for Kids
334 Ronde Barber FB
338 Barry Sanders FB
344 Ed Reed ART FB
348 Larry Fitzgerald ART FB
356 James Harrison FB
366 Michael Turner FB
371 Tim Tebow FB
375 DeMarcus Ware FB
379 Kurt Warner FB
386 DeAngelo Williams FB
389 Andre Johnson FB
393 Patrick Willis FB
399 Chad Pennington FB
400 Chris Johnson FB
407 Colt McCoy FB
411 Jared Allen FB
415 Roddy White FB
420 Thomas Jones FB
426 Joe Flacco FB
427 Darren Sharper FB

2010 Sports Illustrated for Kids
437 Cedric Benson FB
439 Elvis Dumervil FB
446 Peyton Manning FB
450 Vernon Davis FB
459 Mark Sanchez FB
468 Chad Ochocinco FB
474 Ray Rice FB
475 Matt Schaub FB
480 Darrelle Revis FB
488 Miles Austin FB

500 Maurice Jones-Drew FB
504 Terrelle Pryor FB .60 1.50
509 Aaron Rodgers FB
514 Frank Gore FB
518 Randy Moss FB
525 Clay Matthews FB
526 Arian Foster FB

2011 Sports Illustrated for Kids

3 LaMichael James FB
7 Brandon Lloyd FB
14 Tom Brady FB
24 Rashard Mendenhall FB
33 Andrew Luck FB 1.00 2.50
42 Kellen Moore FB
47 BenJarvus Green-Ellis FB
52 Denard Robinson FB
57 Philip Rivers FB
64 Tamba Hali FB
68 Adrian Peterson FB
75 Michael Turner FB
77 Drew Brees FB
86 Ndamukong Suh FB
90 LeSean McCoy FB
91 Darren McFadden FB
95 Calvin Johnson FB

2012 Sports Illustrated for Kids

100 Case Keenum FB
104 Eli Manning FB
108 Jared Allen FB
109 Victor Cruz FB
113 Maurice Jones-Drew FB
120 Ron Gronkowski FB
132 Matthew Stafford FB
137 Tyrann Mathieu FB
141 Eli Manning FB
150 Ray Rice FB
156 Aaron Rodgers FB
157 Jason Babin FB
164 Matt Barkley FB
169 Wes Welker FB
176 Alex Smith FB
180 Montee Ball FB
181 Marshawn Lynch FB
185 Andrew Luck FB
192 Jamaal Charles FB
194 Geno Smith FB
196 A.J. Green FB

2013 Sports Illustrated for Kids

199 Clay Matthews FB .20 .50
203 Peyton Manning FB .50 1.25
207 Kenjon Barner FB .40 1.00
210 Johnny Manziel FB
215 Alfred Morris FB
221 Joe Flacco FB
225 J.J. Watt FB
227 Brandon Marshall FB
235 Russell Wilson FB
245 Jadeveon Clowney FB
251 C.J. Spiller FB
254 Dez Bryant FB
260 Aldon Smith FB
264 Jimmy Graham FB
265 Teddy Bridgewater FB
275 Colin Kaepernick FB
277 Marqise Lee FB
279 Luke Kuechly FB
280 Julio Jones FB
284 Adrian Peterson FB
286 Braxton Miller FB
294 Slobber Griffin III FB
Dog head caricature
297 Troy Poodle-malu FB
Dog head caricature

2015 Sports Illustrated for Kids

388 Antonio Brown FB
396 Melvin Gordon FB
398 Ezekiel Elliott FB .75 2.00
402 Le'Veon Bell FB
410 Aaron Rodgers FB
414 Kyle Emanuel FB
420 Odell Beckham Jr. FB
425 J.J. Watt FB

1976 Sportstix

These ten blank-backed irregularly shaped stickers measure approximately 3 1/2" in diameter and feature borderless color player action photos. Team markings were crudely obliterated from the players' helmets. The numbering is a continuation from other non-football Sportstix. The stickers came in packs of five, with stickers 31-35 in packs marked "Series 3B" and stickers 36-40 in packs marked "Series 4B." The player's name, along with the sticker's number& appears in black lettering (except the Drew Pearson and Gary Huff stickers have white lettering). The stickers are numbered on the front.

COMPLETE SET (11) 100.00 175.00
31 Carl Eller 6.00 15.00
Minnesota Vikings
32 Fred Biletnikoff UER 10.00 25.00
Oakland Raiders
(Misspelled
33 Terry Metcalf 5.00 12.00
St. Louis Cardinals
34 Gary Huff 4.00 10.00
Chicago Bears
35 Steve Bartkowski 6.00 15.00
Atlanta Falcons
36 Dan Pastorini 5.00 12.00
Houston Oilers
37 Drew Pearson UER 7.50 20.00
Dallas Cowboys
(Photo is of
GI
38 Bert Jones 5.00 12.00
Baltimore Colts
39 Otis Armstrong 5.00 12.00
Denver Broncos
40 Don Woods 4.00 10.00
San Diego Chargers
C Dick Butkus 15.00 40.00
Chicago Bears

1997 Sprint Phone Cards

This set of 4-phone cards was produced for Sprint. Each unnumbered card carries 15-minutes worth of phone time with an expiration date of 10/03/98. A color player portrait was included on the cardfronts with instructions on the use of the card on back. Each was also numbered of 27,800 sets made. Although the phone cards measure roughly 2 1/8" by 3 3/8" loose, we've included pricing below for cards still mounted on their paper backers which measure 3 1/2" by 7." The backers include more detailed cardlike player information on the backs and a description of the set on the fronts.

COMPLETE SET (4) 8.00 20.00
1 Marcus Allen .80 2.00
2 Brett Favre 3.20 8.00
3 Dan Marino 3.20 8.00
4 Steve Young 1.20 3.00

2009 SP Threads

COMP.SET w/o RC's (100) 15.00 40.00
ROOKIE AU ANNOUNCED PRINT RUNS 120-126
ACTUAL ROOKIE AUTO SERIAL #'s 11-30
EXCH EXPIRATION: 10/7/2011
1 Aaron Rodgers .75 2.00
2 Adrian Peterson .40 1.00
3 Andre Johnson .30 .75
4 Anquan Boldin .25 .60
5 Antonio Bryant .25 .60
6 Ben Roethlisberger .40 1.00
7 Bernard Berrian .25 .60
8 Bob Sanders .30 .75
9 Brady Quinn .25 .60
10 Brandon Jacobs .25 .60
11 Brandon Marshall .30 .75
12 Braylon Edwards .25 .60
13 Brian Urlacher .40 1.00
14 Brian Westbrook .25 .60
15 Calvin Johnson .40 1.00
16 Carson Palmer .30 .75
17 Chad Ochocinco .25 .60
18 Chad Pennington .25 .60
19 Champ Bailey .30 .75
20 Chris Johnson .25 .60
21 Chris Long .30 .75
22 Clinton Portis .25 .60
23 Darren McFadden .40 1.00
24 Darren Sproles .30 .75
25 David Garrard .25 .60
26 DeAngelo Williams .25 .60
27 DeMarcus Ware .30 .75
28 DeMeco Ryans .30 .75
29 Derrick Johnson .25 .60
30 Donnie Avery .25 .60
31 Donovan McNabb .30 .75
32 D'Qwell Jackson .25 .60
33 Drew Brees .40 1.00
34 Dwayne Bowe .30 .75
35 Ed Reed .30 .75
36 Eddie Royal .25 .60
37 Eli Manning .30 .75
38 Frank Gore .30 .75
39 Greg Jennings .25 .60
40 Hines Ward .30 .75
41 Jamal Lewis .30 .75
42 JaMarcus Russell .25 .60
43 James Harrison .40 1.00
44 Jared Allen .25 .60
45 Jason Campbell .25 .60
46 Jay Cutler .25 .60
47 Jeremy Shockey .25 .60
48 Jerod Mayo .30 .75
49 Jerricho Cotchery .25 .60
50 Joe Flacco .30 .75
51 Joey Porter .30 .75
52 John Abraham .25 .60
53 Julius Peppers .30 .75
54 Justin Tuck .25 .60
55 Kellen Winslow .25 .60
56 Kevin Smith .25 .60
57 Kurt Warner .30 .75
58 LaDainian Tomlinson .40 1.00
59 Lance Briggs .30 .75
60 Larry Fitzgerald .30 .75
61 Larry Johnson .25 .60
62 Laveranues Coles .25 .60
63 Lee Evans .30 .75
64 LenDale White .25 .60
65 Lofa Tatupu .25 .60
66 Marc Bulger .25 .60
67 Marion Barber .30 .75
68 Marques Colston .25 .60
69 Marshawn Lynch .30 .75
70 Matt Forte .25 .60
71 Matt Hasselbeck .25 .60
72 Matt Ryan .30 .75
73 Maurice Jones-Drew .25 .60
74 Michael Turner .25 .60
75 Patrick Willis .30 .75
76 Peyton Manning 1.00 2.50
77 Philip Rivers .40 1.00
78 Randy Moss .30 .75
79 Ray Lewis .40 1.00
80 Reggie Bush .25 .60
81 Reggie Wayne .30 .75
82 Roddy White .25 .60
83 Ryan Grant .30 .75
84 Santana Moss .30 .75
85 Stephen Cooper RC .30 .75
86 Steve Breaston .30 .75
87 Steve Slaton .25 .60
88 Steve Smith .30 .75
89 Steven Jackson .25 .60
90 T.J. Houshmandzadeh .25 .60
91 Terrell Owens .30 .75
92 Thomas Jones .25 .60
93 Tom Brady 1.25 3.00
94 Tony Gonzalez .30 .75
95 Tony Romo .30 .75
96 Vincent Jackson .25 .60
97 Warrick Dunn .25 .60
98 Wes Welker .30 .75
99 Willie Parker .25 .60
100 Willis McGahee .25 .60
101 Aaron Brown RC 1.50 4.00
102 Alex Magee RC 1.50 4.00
103 Andre Brown RC 1.50 4.00
104 Andy Levitre RC 1.50 4.00
105 Antoine Caldwell RC 1.25 3.00
106 Asher Allen RC 1.25 3.00
107 Austin Collie RC 1.25 3.00
108 Bear Pascoe RC 1.50 4.00
109 Bernard Scott RC 2.00 5.00
110 Bradley Fletcher RC 1.25 3.00
111 Brandon Gibson RC 1.50 4.00
112 Brian Hartline RC 2.00 5.00
113 Brooks Foster RC 1.25 3.00
114 Cedric Peerman RC 1.25 3.00
115 Chip Vaughn RC 1.25 3.00
116 Chris Owens RC 1.25 3.00
117 Cody Brown RC 1.25 3.00
118 Cody Glenn RC 1.50 4.00
119 Connor Barwin RC 1.50 4.00
120 Cornelius Ingram RC 1.25 3.00
121 Corvey Irvin RC 1.25 3.00
122 Curtis Painter RC 1.25 3.00
123 Darcel McBath RC 1.25 3.00
124 Darius Butler RC 1.50 4.00
125 David Veikune RC 1.50 4.00
126 DeAndre Levy RC 1.50 4.00
127 DeAngelo Smith RC 1.50 4.00
128 Deon Butler RC 1.25 3.00
129 Derek Cox RC 2.00 5.00
130 Donald Washington RC 1.50 4.00
131 Darell Scott RC 1.25 3.00
132 Eben Britton RC 1.50 4.00
133 Eric Wood RC 1.25 3.00
134 Evander Hood RC 2.00 5.00
135 Fenuki Tupou RC 1.25 3.00
136 Fili Moala RC 1.25 3.00
137 Gartrell Johnson RC 1.25 3.00
138 Gerald McRath RC 1.50 4.00
139 Glen Coffee RC 1.25 3.00
140 Greg Toler RC 1.25 3.00
141 Henry Melton RC 1.25 3.00
142 Jairus Byrd RC 2.00 5.00
143 James Casey RC 1.50 4.00
144 Brandon Hughes RC 1.25 3.00
145 Jamon Meredith RC 1.25 3.00
146 Jared Cook RC 1.50 4.00
147 Jarron Gilbert RC 1.50 4.00
148 Jason Phillips RC 1.50 4.00
149 Jason Williams RC 1.50 4.00
150 Jasper Brinkley RC 1.50 4.00
151 Jerraud Powers RC 1.25 3.00
152 Jonathan Luigs RC 1.25 3.00
153 Kaluka Maiava RC 1.25 3.00
154 Keenan Lewis RC 2.00 5.00
155 Kevin Barnes RC 1.25 3.00
156 Kraig Urbik RC 1.50 4.00
157 Kyle Moore RC 1.50 4.00
158 Lardarius Webb RC 2.00 5.00
159 Larry English RC 1.50 4.00
160 Lawrence Sidbury RC 1.25 3.00
161 Louis Delmas RC 1.50 4.00
162 Louis Vasquez RC 1.50 4.00
163 Marcus Freeman RC 1.25 3.00
164 Matt Shaughnessy RC 1.50 4.00
165 Max Unger RC 2.00 5.00
166 Michael Hamlin RC 1.25 3.00
167 Mike Goodson RC 1.50 4.00
168 Mike Mitchell RC 1.25 3.00
169 Mike Teel RC 1.25 3.00
170 Mike Thomas RC 1.25 3.00
171 Mike Wallace RC 2.00 5.00
172 Morgan Trent RC 1.50 4.00
173 Nic Harris RC 1.50 4.00
174 Patrick Chung RC 1.25 3.00
175 Patrick Turner RC 1.25 3.00
176 Paul Kruger RC 2.00 5.00
177 Phil Loadholt RC 1.50 4.00
178 Ramses Barden RC 1.25 3.00
179 Rashad Johnson RC 1.25 3.00
180 Richard Quinn RC 1.50 4.00
181 Robert Ayers RC 1.25 3.00
182 Robert Brewster RC 1.25 3.00
183 Ron Brace RC 1.50 4.00
184 Roy Miller RC 1.25 3.00
185 Ryan Mouton RC 1.25 3.00
186 Scott McKillop RC 1.25 3.00
187 Sebastian Vollmer RC 1.50 4.00
188 Sen'Derrick Marks RC 1.25 3.00
189 Sherrod Martin RC 1.25 3.00
190 Stanley Arnoux RC 1.50 4.00
191 Stephen McGee RC 1.25 3.00
192 T.J. Lang RC 1.50 4.00
193 Terrance Knighton RC 2.00 5.00
194 Terrance Taylor RC 1.50 4.00
195 Tom Brandstater RC 1.50 4.00
196 Travis Beckum RC 1.25 3.00
197 Tyrone Mckenzie RC 1.50 4.00
198 Victor Harris RC 1.50 4.00
199 William Beatty RC 1.25 3.00
200 William Middleton RC 1.25 3.00
201 M.Massaquoi AU/126* RC 5.00 12.00
203 Alex Mack/120* AU RC 5.00 12.00
204 Andre Smith AU/120* RC 5.00 12.00
205 B.J. Raji AU/120* RC 6.00 15.00
207 B.Pettigrew AU/126* RC 5.00 12.00
208 Brian Cushing AU/126* RC 5.00 12.00
209 Brian Robiskie AU/120* RC 5.00 12.00
210 Rhett Bomar AU/120* RC 5.00 12.00
211 Chase Coffman AU/126* RC 5.00 12.00
213 Chris Wells AU/120* RC 5.00 12.00
214 Hunter Cantwell AU/120* RC 5.00 12.00
215 D.J. Moore AU/120* RC 6.00 15.00
216 D.Heyward-Bey AU RC 8.00 20.00
217 S.Smith AU/120* RC 5.00 12.00
218 Demetrius Byrd AU/120* RC 6.00 15.00
219 D.Williams AU/120* RC 5.00 12.00
220 D.Robinson AU/120* RC 5.00 12.00
221 Eugene Monroe AU/120* RC 5.00 12.00
223 Clint Sintim AU/120* RC 5.00 12.00
224 R.Jennings AU/120* RC 6.00 15.00
225 Aaron Curry AU/120* RC 8.00 20.00
226 Hakeem Nicks AU/120* RC 15.00 40.00
227 J.Iglesias AU/120* RC 5.00 12.00
228 Brian Orakpo AU/120* RC 10.00 25.00
229 J.Laurinaitis AU/121* RC 12.00 30.00
230 Jason Smith AU/120* RC 5.00 12.00
231 Javon Ringer AU/120* RC 5.00 12.00
232 Jeremy Maclin AU/120* RC 6.00 15.00
233 Nate Davis AU/120* RC 5.00 12.00
234 Josh Freeman AU/126* RC 5.00 12.00
235 Kenny Britt AU/120* RC 12.00 30.00
236 K.Moreno AU/120* RC 5.00 12.00
237 Louis Murphy AU/120* RC 5.00 12.00
238 Malcolm Jenkins AU/126* RC 5.00 12.00
239 James Davis AU/120* RC 5.00 12.00
240 M.Sanchez AU/126* RC 15.00 40.00
241 M.Stafford AU/120* RC 40.00 100.00
242 M.Crabtree AU/120* RC 8.00 20.00
243 Michael Johnson AU/126* RC 5.00 12.00
244 Michael Oher AU/120* RC 25.00 60.00
245 Donald Brown AU/120* RC 5.00 12.00
246 Pat White AU/120* RC 12.00 30.00
247 Jarett Dillard AU/126* RC 5.00 12.00
248 Percy Harvin AU/120* RC 5.00 12.00
249 Peria Jerry AU/120* RC 5.00 12.00
250 Rey Maualuga AU/120* RC 8.00 20.00
251 Brandon Tate AU/120* RC 6.00 15.00
252 Alphonso Smith AU/120* RC 5.00 12.00
253 Shonn Greene AU/120* RC 5.00 12.00
254 C.Matthews AU/120* RC 40.00 80.00
255 Devin Moore AU/120* RC 5.00 12.00
256 LeSean McCoy AU/120* RC 12.00 30.00
257 Travis Beckum AU/120* RC 5.00 12.00
258 T.Jackson AU/126* RC 5.00 12.00
259 V.Davis AU/120* RC 5.00 12.00
260 W.Moore AU/120* RC 5.00 12.00

2009 SP Threads Rookie Lettermen Autographs Gold

*GOLD: .5X TO 1.2X BASE AUTO
GOLD AU ANNCD PRINT RUNS 33-42
LETTERS SPELL PLAYERS LAST NAME
EXCH EXPIRATION: 10/7/2011

2009 SP Threads Rookie Lettermen College Autographs

*COLLEGE: .4X TO 1X BASE AUTO
COLLEGE AU ANNCD PRINT RUNS 72-126
ACTUAL COLLEGE AUTO SER.#'s 7-28
EXCH EXPIRATION: 10/7/2011

2009 SP Threads Rookie Lettermen College Nickname Autographs

*COLL.NICKNAME: .4X TO 1X BASE AUTO
COLL.NICKNAME ANNCD PRINT RUNS 63-72
ACTUAL NICKNAME AUTO SER.#'s 5-17
EXCH EXPIRATION: 10/7/2011

2009 SP Threads Die Cut

AP1 Michael Crabtree 1.25 3.00
AP2 Matt Ryan 1.25 3.00
AP3 JaMarcus Russell 1.00 2.50
AP4 Brett Favre 3.00 8.00
AP5 Paul Hornung 2.00 5.00
AP6 Terry Bradshaw 2.50 6.00
AP7 David Garrard 1.00 2.50
AP8 Steve Young 2.50 6.00
AP9 Tony Romo 1.25 3.00
AP10 Eli Manning 1.25 3.00
AP11 Roy Williams WR 1.00 2.50
AP12 Don Maynard 1.50 4.00
AP13 Brady Quinn 1.00 2.50
AP14 Bernard Berrian 1.00 2.50
AP15 Brandon Marshall 1.25 3.00
AP16 Marques Colston 1.00 2.50
AP17 Braylon Edwards 1.00 2.50
AP18 Peyton Manning 4.00 10.00
AP19 Felix Jones 1.00 2.50
AP20 Barry Sanders 3.00 8.00
AP21 Bob Sanders 1.25 3.00
AP22 Emmitt Smith 3.00 8.00
AP23 Quentin Jammer 1.00 2.50
AP24 Champ Bailey 1.25 3.00
AP25 Reggie Bush 1.00 2.50
AP26 Rod Woodson 1.50 4.00
AP27 Brandon Jacobs 1.00 2.50
AP28 Adrian Peterson 1.50 4.00
AP29 Donald Brown .75 2.00
AP30 Wes Welker 1.25 3.00
AP31 Chris Johnson 1.00 2.50
AP32 Franco Harris 2.00 5.00
AP33 Roger Craig 1.50 4.00
AP34 Bo Jackson 2.50 6.00
AP35 Brian Orakpo 1.00 2.50
AP36 Chris Wells .75 2.00
AP37 Ernie Sims 1.00 2.50
AP38 Greg Jennings 1.00 2.50
AP39 Willie Parker 1.00 2.50
AP40 Gale Sayers 2.00 5.00
AP41 James Laurinaitis .75 2.00
AP42 Jake Delhomme 1.00 2.50
AP43 Joe Flacco 1.25 3.00
AP44 Tom Rathman 1.25 3.00
AP45 Jeremy Maclin 1.00 2.50
AP46 Jonathan Stewart 1.00 2.50
AP47 Chris Cooley 1.00 2.50
AP48 Knowshon Moreno .75 2.00
AP49 Le'Ron McClain 1.25 3.00
AP50 Calvin Johnson 1.50 4.00
AP51 Marc Bulger 1.00 2.50
AP52 Patrick Willis 1.25 3.00
AP53 LeSean McCoy 2.00 5.00
AP54 Marion Barber 1.25 3.00
AP55 Mark Sanchez .75 2.00
AP56 Rashard Mendenhall 1.00 2.50
AP57 Jack Youngblood 2.50 6.00
AP58 Reggie Brown 1.00 2.50
AP59 Jack Ham 1.50 4.00
AP60 Steve Breaston 1.25 3.00
AP61 Santonio Holmes 1.00 2.50
AP62 Steve Slaton 1.00 2.50
AP63 Matthew Stafford 4.00 10.00
AP64 Vince Young 1.00 2.50
AP65 Darren McFadden 1.50 4.00
AP66 Joseph Addai 1.00 2.50
AP67 Chad Pennington 1.00 2.50
AP68 Eddie Royal 1.00 2.50
AP69 Josh Freeman .75 2.00
AP70 Kevin Smith 1.00 2.50
AP71 Frank Gore 1.25 3.00
AP72 Ed Jones 1.25 3.00
AP73 Ronde Barber 1.00 2.50
AP74 Jim Kelly 2.00 5.00
AP75 Deacon Jones 1.50 4.00
AP76 DeSean Jackson 1.25 3.00
AP77 Malcolm Jenkins .75 2.00
AP78 Marshawn Lynch 1.25 3.00
AP79 Jeff Garcia 1.00 2.50
AP80 Jerry Rice 4.00 10.00
AP81 Dustin Keller 1.00 2.50
AP82 Dwayne Bowe 1.25 3.00
AP83 Vincent Jackson 1.00 2.50
AP84 T.J. Houshmandzadeh 1.00 2.50
AP85 Chad Ochocinco 1.00 2.50
AP86 Roger Staubach 2.50 6.00
AP87 Reggie Wayne 1.25 3.00
AP88 Larry Johnson 1.00 2.50
AP89 Jerricho Cotchery 1.00 2.50
AP90 Matt Forte 1.00 2.50
AP91 A.J. Hawk 1.00 2.50
AP92 Aaron Curry 1.25 3.00
AP93 Donald Driver 1.25 3.00
AP94 Laurence Maroney 1.25 3.00
AP95 Nate Davis .75 2.00
AP96 Hakeem Nicks 1.00 2.50
AP97 Donnie Avery 1.00 2.50
AP98 Rey Maualuga 1.25 3.00
AP99 Kellen Winslow Sr. 1.50 4.00
AP100 Percy Harvin .75 2.00

2009 SP Threads Die Cut Autographs

STATED PRINT RUN 5-25
AP1 Michael Crabtree/15
AP5 Paul Hornung/15 15.00 40.00
AP7 David Garrard/15 6.00 15.00
AP11 Roy Williams WR/15 6.00 15.00
AP14 Bernard Berrian/15
AP15 Brandon Marshall/15
AP16 Marques Colston/15 6.00 15.00
AP17 Braylon Edwards/15 6.00 15.00
AP19 Felix Jones/25 20.00 40.00
AP21 Bob Sanders/15
AP23 Quentin Jammer/15 6.00 15.00
AP24 Champ Bailey/15 20.00 40.00
AP25 Reggie Bush/25 15.00 40.00
AP26 Rod Woodson/15 40.00 80.00
AP27 Brandon Jacobs/15 6.00 15.00
AP29 Donald Brown/15
AP30 Wes Welker/15 40.00 80.00
AP31 Chris Johnson/15 6.00 15.00
AP33 Roger Craig/15 8.00 20.00
AP35 Brian Orakpo/15 8.00 20.00
AP36 Chris Wells/15 6.00 15.00
AP37 Ernie Sims/25 6.00 15.00
AP38 Greg Jennings/15 6.00 15.00
AP39 Willie Parker/15 6.00 15.00
AP40 Gale Sayers/15 30.00 60.00
AP41 James Laurinaitis/25 6.00 15.00
AP42 Jake Delhomme/15 6.00 15.00
AP43 Joe Flacco/15
AP44 Tom Rathman/25 15.00 30.00
AP45 Jeremy Maclin/15 8.00 20.00
AP46 Jonathan Stewart/15 6.00 15.00
AP47 Chris Cooley/15 12.00 30.00
AP48 Knowshon Moreno/15 6.00 15.00
AP49 Le'Ron McClain/25 8.00 20.00
AP51 Marc Bulger/15
AP52 Patrick Willis/15
AP53 LeSean McCoy/15
AP54 Marion Barber/15
AP56 Rashard Mendenhall/15
AP58 Reggie Brown/15
AP59 Jack Ham/15
AP60 Steve Breaston/25 8.00 20.00
AP61 Santonio Holmes/15
AP62 Steve Slaton/15
AP69 Josh Freeman/15 6.00 15.00
AP75 Deacon Jones/25 15.00 40.00
AP79 Jeff Garcia/25 6.00 15.00
AP81 Dustin Keller/25 6.00 15.00
AP88 Larry Johnson/15 6.00 15.00
AP89 Jerricho Cotchery/25 6.00 15.00
AP90 Matt Forte/25 20.00 40.00
AP96 Hakeem Nicks/15 8.00 20.00
AP98 Rey Maualuga/15 10.00 25.00

2009 SP Threads Dual Threads

STATED PRINT RUN 199 SER.#'d SETS
AR Avery/Royal 2.50 6.00
BB Brees/R.Bush 4.00 10.00
BR Bowe/Royal 3.00 8.00
CK Cotchery/Keller 2.50 6.00
CM Colston/Meachem 2.50 6.00
EB E.Manning/B.Jacobs 3.00 8.00
EC Bailey/Royal 3.00 8.00
EE T.Edwards/L.Evans 3.00 8.00
EL T.Edwards/Lynch 3.00 8.00
EP E.Manning/Burress 3.00 8.00
FR Flacco/R.Rice 3.00 8.00
GJ Garrard/Jones-Drew 2.50 6.00
GM F.Gore/McFadden 4.00 10.00
HF A.Hawk/Forte 2.50 6.00
HH Hasselbeck/Houshmandzadeh 2.50 6.00
JA D.Jackson/Avery 3.00 8.00
JB T.Jackson/Booty 3.00 8.00
JF E.James/L.Fitzgerald 3.00 8.00
JP A.Peterson/T.Jackson 4.00 10.00
KC K.Smith/C.Johnson 4.00 10.00
KJ Kolb/D.Jackson 3.00 8.00
KR Keller/Gates 3.00 8.00
LB Leinart/R.Bush 2.50 6.00
LE Lynch/L.Evans 3.00 8.00
LF L.Fitzgerald/Leinart 3.00 8.00
LG Lynch/F.Gore 3.00 8.00
LR R.Lewis/E.Reed 10.00 25.00
MA P.Manning/Addai 2.50 6.00
MC McNabb/J.Campbell 3.00 8.00
MF Mendenhall/Forte 2.50 6.00
MH K.Morrison/Huff 2.50 6.00
MJ McNabb/D.Jackson 3.00 8.00
ML Merriman/R.Lewis 4.00 10.00
MM R.Moss/Maroney 3.00 8.00
MP Mendenhall/W.Parker 4.00 10.00
MS Slaton/McFadden 4.00 10.00
MY V.Young/McNabb 3.00 8.00
OE T.Edwards/T.Owens 3.00 8.00
PB Pennington/R.Brown 2.50 6.00
PC Campbell/Portis 2.50 6.00
PR P.Manning/Wayne 10.00 25.00
QE Quinn/B.Edwards 2.50 6.00
QP Quinn/C.Palmer 3.00 8.00
RF Ryan/Forte 3.00 8.00
RM J.Russell/McFadden 4.00 10.00
RR R.Lewis/R.Rice 6.00 15.00
RS Ryan/J.Stewart 3.00 8.00
RY J.Russell/V.Young 2.50 6.00
SE Sweed/B.Edwards 3.00 8.00
SJ J.Stewart/Jarrett 2.50 6.00
SM Sweed/Mendenhall 4.00 10.00
SP Peppers/J.Stewart 3.00 8.00
SS Schaub/Slaton 2.50 6.00
TJ Jones-Drew/F.Taylor 2.50 6.00
WH A.Hawk/Woodson 5.00 12.00
WQ Quinn/K.Winslow 2.50 6.00
WW Welker/B.Watson 3.00 8.00
YJ C.Johnson/V.Young 2.50 6.00

2009 SP Threads Foursome Fabrics

STATED PRINT RUN 25 SER.#'d SETS
2008 Ryan/Flcco/McFd/Frte 10.00 25.00
AUB1 Cmpbll/Brwn/Will/Jhnsn 6.00 15.00
BOLT Merr/Tmlin/Gats/Jcksn 10.00 25.00
CANE Lwis/Jhnsn/Gore/Jmes 10.00 25.00
DENV Cutler/Mrshll/Royal/Baily 8.00 20.00
LSU1 Rssell/Add/Bowe/Clayton 6.00 15.00
MICH Brady/Wdsn/Mnnhm/Long 30.00 80.00
NYG1 Eli/Jcbs/Mnnhm/Burress 8.00 20.00
OSU1 Hlmes/Hawk/Gnzalz/Vrabl 6.00 15.00
PATS Brady/Moss/Mrny/Vrabel 30.00 80.00
PHIL McNb/Wstbrk/Jcksn/Kolb 8.00 20.00
PITT Roeth/Holms/Prkr/Sweed 10.00 25.00
SBQB P.Mann/Brady/Roeth/Eli 20.00 50.00
TEX1 V.Yng/Sweed/Ross/Chrles 6.00 15.00
USC1 Palmr/Bush/Leinart/Booty 8.00 20.00
VOLS P.Mann/Lwis/Wittn/Mchm 8.00 20.00

2009 SP Threads Multi Marks Dual

STATED PRINT RUN 5-75
SERIAL #'d UNDER 25 NOT PRICED
BG D.Brown/Greene/50 25.00 50.00
BJ Barber/F.Jones/25 30.00 60.00
BT Byrd/Tate/50 12.00 30.00
DS Delhomme/J.Stewart/25 15.00 40.00
FB Forte/Briggs/25 20.00 50.00
JM M.Johnson/Mack/40 6.00 15.00
JR D.Jackson/Royal/50 12.00 30.00
ML Maualuga/Laurinaitis/75 10.00 25.00
MW Moreno/C.Wells/25 40.00 100.00
NH Nicks/Heyward-Bey/25 20.00 40.00
SW Schaub/M.Williams/50 12.00 30.00
WS D.Williams/J.Stewart/25 15.00 40.00
WW P.Willis/M.Williams/50 8.00 20.00

2009 SP Threads Multi Marks Quad

HOGS McFadden/F.Jones/Hillis/Monk/20

2009 SP Threads Multi Marks Triple

STATED PRINT RUN 5-50
BGR D.Brown/Greene/Ringer/50 25.00 60.00
CMH Crabtree/Maclin/Harvin/25 20.00 50.00
JMM M.Johnson/Mack/Monroe/50
WBB Warner/Boldin/Breaston/15 25.00 60.00
MJS Eli/Jacobs/S.Smith/25 60.00 120.00
MWM Moreno/Wells/McCoy/50 20.00 50.00
PHI D.Jackson/Kolb/Maclin/25

2009 SP Threads Rookie Threads Dual Swatch

STATED PRINT RUN 299 SER.#'d SETS
*PATCH/50: .6X TO 1.5X DUAL JSY/299
*TRIPLE/199: .5X TO 1.2X DUAL JSY/299
RTAB Andre Brown 2.00 5.00
RTAC Aaron Curry 2.50 6.00
RTBO Rhett Bomar 1.50 4.00
RTBP Brandon Pettigrew 1.50 4.00
RTBR Brian Robiskie 1.50 4.00
RTBU Deon Butler 1.50 4.00
RTCW Chris Wells 5.00 12.00
RTDB Donald Brown 1.50 4.00
RTDH Darrius Heyward-Bey 2.50 6.00
RTDW Derrick Williams 1.50 4.00
RTGC Glen Coffee 1.50 4.00
RTHN Hakeem Nicks 2.00 5.00
RTJF Josh Freeman 1.50 4.00
RTJI Juaquin Iglesias 1.50 4.00
RTJM Jeremy Maclin 2.00 5.00
RTJR Javon Ringer 1.50 4.00
RTJS Jason Smith 1.50 4.00
RTKB Kenny Britt 2.50 6.00
RTKM Knowshon Moreno 1.50 4.00
RTLM LeSean McCoy 4.00 10.00
RTMC Michael Crabtree 2.50 6.00
RTMM Mohamed Massaquoi 1.50 4.00
RTMS Mark Sanchez 1.50 4.00
RTMT Mike Thomas 1.50 4.00
RTMW Mike Wallace 2.50 6.00
RTND Nate Davis 1.50 4.00
RTPH Percy Harvin 1.50 4.00
RTPT Patrick Turner 1.50 4.00
RTPW Pat White 2.00 5.00
RTRB Ramses Barden 1.50 4.00
RTSG Shonn Greene 1.50 4.00
RTSM Stephen McGee 1.50 4.00
RTST Matthew Stafford 6.00 15.00
RTTJ Tyson Jackson 1.50 4.00

2009 SP Threads Rookie Threads Dual Swatch Autographs

STATED PRINT RUN 10-30
RTAB Andre Brown 6.00 15.00
RTBO Rhett Bomar 5.00 12.00
RTBP Brandon Pettigrew 5.00 12.00
RTBU Deon Butler 5.00 12.00
RTDW Derrick Williams 5.00 12.00
RTGC Glen Coffee 5.00 12.00
RTHN Hakeem Nicks 6.00 15.00
RTJF Josh Freeman
RTJI Juaquin Iglesias 5.00 12.00
RTJM Jeremy Maclin/10 6.00 15.00
RTJR Javon Ringer 5.00 12.00
RTKB Kenny Britt 8.00 20.00
RTKM Knowshon Moreno/10 5.00 12.00
RTLM LeSean McCoy 12.00 30.00
RTMC Michael Crabtree/10 8.00 20.00
RTMM Mohamed Massaquoi 5.00 12.00
RTMS Mark Sanchez/10 50.00 120.00
RTMT Mike Thomas 5.00 12.00
RTMW Mike Wallace 15.00 40.00
RTND Nate Davis 5.00 12.00
RTPH Percy Harvin 5.00 12.00
RTPT Patrick Turner 5.00 12.00
RTPW Pat White 6.00 15.00
RTSM Stephen McGee 5.00 12.00
RTST Matthew Stafford 50.00 120.00
RTTJ Tyson Jackson 5.00 12.00

2009 SP Threads SP Threads Patch

PATCH PRINT RUN 25 SER.#'d SETS
TAB Anquan Boldin 5.00 12.00
TAC Alge Crumpler 5.00 12.00
TAG Anthony Gonzalez 5.00 12.00
TAH A.J. Hawk 5.00 12.00
TAJ Andre Johnson 6.00 15.00
TAP Adrian Peterson 8.00 20.00
TAS Alex Smith QB 8.00 20.00
TBD Brian Dawkins 5.00 12.00
TBE Braylon Edwards 5.00 12.00
TBF Brett Favre 15.00 40.00
TBJ Bo Jackson 15.00 40.00
TBO Dwayne Bowe 6.00 15.00
TBQ Brady Quinn 5.00 12.00
TBS Barry Sanders 20.00 50.00
TBU Brian Urlacher 8.00 20.00
TCH Jamaal Charles 6.00 15.00
TCJ Calvin Johnson 8.00 20.00
TCP Carson Palmer 6.00 15.00
TCW Charles Woodson 8.00 20.00
TDA Donnie Avery 5.00 12.00
TDB Drew Brees
TDG David Garrard 5.00 12.00
TDJ DeSean Jackson 6.00 15.00
TDK Derrick Brooks 5.00 12.00
TDM Darren McFadden 8.00 20.00
TDO Donovan McNabb 6.00 15.00
TDW DeAngelo Williams 5.00 12.00
TEJ Edgerrin James 6.00 15.00
TEM Eli Manning 6.00 15.00
TER Ed Reed 6.00 15.00
TES Emmitt Smith 15.00 40.00
TFG Frank Gore 6.00 15.00
TFJ Felix Jones 5.00 12.00
TFR Fred Taylor 5.00 12.00
TGJ Greg Jennings 5.00 12.00
THA Marvin Harrison 6.00 15.00
THC Chad Henne 6.00 15.00
THD Harry Douglas 5.00 12.00
THJ James Hardy 6.00 15.00
THU Michael Huff 5.00 12.00
THW Hines Ward 6.00 15.00
TJA Jamal Lewis 6.00 15.00
TJB John David Booty 6.00 15.00
TJC Jason Campbell 5.00 12.00
TJF Joe Flacco 6.00 15.00
TJH Jack Ham
TJL Jake Long 5.00 12.00
TJO Chad Ochocinco 5.00 12.00
TJP Julius Peppers 6.00 15.00
TJR JaMarcus Russell 5.00 12.00
TJS Jonathan Stewart 5.00 12.00
TJT Joe Theismann 12.00 30.00
TKS Kevin Smith 5.00 12.00
TKW Kellen Winslow 8.00 20.00
TLE Lee Evans 6.00 15.00
TLF Larry Fitzgerald 6.00 15.00
TLM Laurence Maroney 6.00 15.00
TLS Limas Sweed 6.00 15.00
TLT LaDainian Tomlinson 8.00 20.00
TLW LenDale White 5.00 12.00
TLY Marshawn Lynch 6.00 15.00
TMA Marc Bulger 5.00 12.00
TMC Marques Colston 5.00 12.00
TMF Matt Forte 5.00 12.00
TMH Matt Hasselbeck 5.00 12.00
TMJ Maurice Jones-Drew 5.00 12.00
TML Matt Leinart 5.00 12.00
TMM Mario Manningham 5.00 12.00
TMO Randy Moss 6.00 15.00
TMR Matt Ryan 6.00 15.00
TMV Mike Vrabel 5.00 12.00
TNE Jordy Nelson 6.00 15.00
TPI Antonio Pierce 5.00 12.00
TPM Peyton Manning 20.00 50.00
TPO Clinton Portis 5.00 12.00
TPW Patrick Willis 6.00 15.00
TRB Reggie Bush 5.00 12.00
TRE Eddie Royal 5.00 12.00
TRL Ray Lewis 8.00 20.00
TRM Rashard Mendenhall 8.00 20.00
TRO Ronnie Brown 8.00 20.00
TRR Ray Rice 10.00 25.00
TSH Santonio Holmes 5.00 12.00
TSI Ernie Sims 5.00 12.00
TSL Steve Largent 12.00 30.00
TSS Steve Smith 6.00 15.00
TST Steve Slaton 5.00 12.00
TTA Troy Aikman 15.00 40.00
TTB Tom Brady 25.00 60.00
TTE Trent Edwards 5.00 12.00
TTJ Tarvaris Jackson 6.00 15.00
TTO Terrell Owens 6.00 15.00
TTR Tony Romo 6.00 15.00
TVJ Vincent Jackson 5.00 12.00
TVY Vince Young 5.00 12.00
TWP Willie Parker 5.00 12.00
TWW Wes Welker 6.00 15.00

2009 SP Threads Stitch in Time Autographs

SITAB Anquan Boldin 6.00 15.00
SITAS Anthony Spencer 5.00 12.00
SITBA Dallas Baker 4.00 10.00
SITBB Brian Brohm 4.00 10.00
SITBC Brent Celek 4.00 10.00
SITBE Martellus Bennett 4.00 10.00
SITBU Marc Bulgor 4.00 10.00
SITCJ Chris Johnson 8.00 20.00
SITCL Chris Long 5.00 12.00
SITCS Chansi Stuckey 4.00 10.00
SITCW Chris Wells
SITDA Donnie Avery 4.00 10.00
SITDB Dwayne Bowe 5.00 12.00
SITDC Dan Connor 4.00 10.00
SITDJ D'Qwell Jackson 4.00 10.00
SITDM Devin Moore 4.00 10.00
SITDR Darrelle Revis 8.00 20.00
SITDW Darius Walker 4.00 10.00
SITEM Eli Manning 40.00 80.00
SITER Eddie Royal 6.00 15.00
SITES Ernie Sims 4.00 10.00
SITEW Eric Weddle 4.00 10.00
SITGJ Greg Jennings 6.00 15.00
SITHM Heath Miller 6.00 15.00
SITJD Jake Delhomme 4.00 10.00
SITJF Joe Flacco 10.00 25.00
SITJJ James Jones 4.00 10.00
SITJM Jeremy Maclin 5.00 12.00
SITJN Jordy Nelson 5.00 12.00
SITJS Jonathan Stewart 6.00 15.00
SITKM Knowshon Moreno
SITLE Le'Ron McClain 5.00 12.00
SITLL LaRon Landry 4.00 10.00
SITLM LeSean McCoy 10.00 25.00
SITLN Legedu Naanee 4.00 10.00
SITLS Limas Sweed 5.00 12.00
SITMB Marion Barber
SITMC Michael Crabtree 6.00 15.00
SITMJ Mike Jenkins 4.00 10.00
SITML Matt Leinart
SITMM Marcus Monk 4.00 10.00
SITMR Matt Ryan 25.00 50.00
SITMS Mark Sanchez 50.00 120.00
SITMY Jerod Mayo 5.00 12.00
SITPH Percy Harvin 4.00 10.00
SITQM Quentin Moses 4.00 10.00
SITRE Mike Reilly 4.00 10.00
SITRM Rashard Mendenhall 6.00 15.00
SITRO Dominique Rodgers-Cromartie 4.00 10.00
SITRR Ray Rice 4.00 10.00
SITRT Ryan Torain 6.00 15.00
SITSB Steve Breaston 5.00 12.00
SITSH Santonio Holmes
SITSS Steve Slaton
SITSY Selvin Young 4.00 10.00
SITTA Terrance Taylor 5.00 12.00
SITTT Tyler Thigpen 4.00 10.00
SITVG Vernon Gholston 4.00 10.00
SITVJ Vincent Jackson 4.00 10.00

2009 SP Threads Tri Threads

STATED PRINT RUN 99 SER.#'d SETS
AFR Favre/Ryan/Aikman 12.00 30.00
BFR Ryan/Flacco/Brohm 5.00 12.00
BHH Brdshw/F.Hrris/Ham 12.00 30.00
BLG R.Brown/F.Gore/Lynch 5.00 12.00
DPS Dorsett/Ptrsn/B.Sndrs 15.00 40.00
FSM Slaton/Forte/DMcFadden 6.00 15.00
GWR Gonzalez/Welker/Royal 5.00 12.00
JFR Fitz/D.Jackson/Royal 5.00 12.00
JJM D.Jcksn/F.Jns/Mnnnghm 5.00 12.00
JRS Royal/D.Jackson/Sweed 5.00 12.00
LBM Leinart/Brees/E.Manning 6.00 15.00
MOB TO/R.Moss/Burress 5.00 12.00
MRM Roeth/Eli/McNabb 6.00 15.00
PML Ptrsn/McFad/Lynch 6.00 15.00
RYC J.Rice/Craig/S.Young 20.00 50.00
SAT Staub/Theis/Aikman 12.00 30.00

1996 SPx

The Upper Deck SPx was issued in one series totalling 50 cards. The 1-card packs originally retailed for $2.99. The 50-card set features limited, state-of-the art holoview printed on 32 point card stock. The cards all feature a die-cut design and have two photos on the front. The backs have a color player photo, vital statistics, recent season as well as career totals as well as some text. There are no Rookie Cards in this set. Two promo cards were produced and distributed by Upper Deck in various ways, including card show give-aways. Special cards inserted into these packs included Joe Montana tribute and Dan Marino record breaker cards as well as autographed cards of these players. The Montana tribute was inserted one every 95 packs, the Marino record breaker was one every 81 packs while the autographed cards were each inserted one every 433 packs.

COMPLETE SET (50) 10.00 25.00
1 Frank Sanders .40 1.00
2 Terance Mathis .20 .50
3 Todd Collins .40 1.00
4 Kerry Collins .75 2.00
5 Carl Pickens .40 1.00
6 Darnay Scott .40 1.00
7 Ki-Jana Carter .40 1.00
8 Eric Zeier .20 .50
9 Andre Rison .40 1.00
10 Sherman Williams .20 .50
11 Troy Aikman 1.50 4.00
12 Michael Irvin .75 2.00
13 Emmitt Smith 2.50 6.00
14 Shannon Sharpe .40 1.00
15 John Elway 3.00 8.00
16 Barry Sanders 2.50 6.00
17 Brett Favre 3.00 8.00
18 Rodney Thomas .20 .50
19 Marshall Faulk 1.00 2.50
20 James O.Stewart .40 1.00
21 Greg Hill .40 1.00
22 Tamarick Vanover .40 1.00
23 Dan Marino 3.00 8.00
24 Cris Carter .75 2.00
25 Warren Moon .40 1.00
26 Drew Bledsoe 1.00 2.50
27 Ben Coates .40 1.00
28 Curtis Martin 1.25 3.00
29 Mario Bates .40 1.00
30 Tyrone Wheatley .40 1.00
31 Rodney Hampton .40 1.00
32 Kyle Brady .20 .50
33 Jeff Hostetler .20 .50
34 Napoleon Kaufman .75 2.00
35 Tim Brown .75 2.00
36 Charles Johnson .20 .50
37 Rod Woodson .40 1.00
38 Natrone Means .40 1.00
39 J.J. Stokes .75 2.00
40 Steve Young 1.50 4.00
41 Brent Jones .20 .50
42 Jerry Rice 1.50 4.00
43 Joe Montana 3.00 8.00
44 Rick Mirer .40 1.00
45 Chris Warren .40 1.00
46 Joey Galloway .75 2.00
47 Isaac Bruce .75 2.00
48 Jerome Bettis .75 2.00
49 Errict Rhett .40 1.00
50 Michael Westbrook .75 2.00
UDT13 Dan Marino RB 5.00 12.00
UDT13A Dan Marino RB AU 40.00 100.00
UDT19 Joe Montana Tribute 5.00 12.00
UDT19A Joe Montana TRI AU 40.00 100.00
P1 Dan Marino Promo 2.00 5.00
P2 Joe Montana Promo 2.00 5.00

1996 SPx Gold

COMPLETE SET (50) 25.00 60.00
*GOLDS: 1X TO 2.5X BASIC CARDS
STATED ODDS 1:7

1996 SPx HoloFame

Randomly inserted in retail packs at a rate of one in 24, this 10-card set includes Upper Deck's top 10 predictions to make it to the NFL Hall of Fame. The words "Holofame Collection" are printed on both sides of the card with all cards having an "HM" prefix.

COMPLETE SET (10) 25.00 60.00
STATED ODDS 1:24
HM1 Troy Aikman 2.50 6.00
HM2 Emmitt Smith 4.00 10.00
HM3 Barry Sanders 4.00 10.00
HM4 Steve Young 2.50 6.00
HM5 Jerry Rice 2.50 6.00
HM6 John Elway 5.00 12.00
HM7 Marshall Faulk 1.50 4.00
HM8 Dan Marino 5.00 12.00
HM9 Drew Bledsoe 1.50 4.00
HM10 Natrone Means .60 1.50

1997 SPx

The 1997 SPx set was issued in one series totaling 50 cards and was distributed in one card packs with a suggested retail of $3.49. The 50-card set features color player photos of the best players and rookies of the NFL in an all new Holoview, Hologram and Light F/X design. A lenticular player portrait appears on the right side of the card front. The backs carry player information and statistics.

COMPLETE SET (50) 12.50 30.00
1 Jerry Rice 1.50 4.00
2 Steve Young 1.00 2.50
3 Karim Abdul-Jabbar .75 2.00
4 Dan Marino 3.00 8.00
5 Bobby Engram .50 1.25
6 Rashaan Salaam .30 .75
7 Marvin Harrison .75 2.00
8 Jim Harbaugh .50 1.25
9 Marshall Faulk 1.00 2.50
10 Eric Moulds .75 2.00
11 Thurman Thomas .75 2.00
12 Tamarick Vanover .50 1.25
13 Steve Bono .50 1.25
14 Warren Moon .75 2.00
15 Cris Carter .75 2.00
16 Carl Pickens .50 1.25
17 Ki Jana Carter .30 .75
18 Jeff Blake .50 1.25
19 Tim Biakabutuka .50 1.25
20 Kerry Collins .75 2.00
21 Leeland McElroy .30 .75
22 Simeon Rice .50 1.25
23 John Elway 3.00 8.00
24 Terrell Davis 1.00 2.50
25 Jeff Lewis .30 .75
26 Terry Glenn .75 2.00
27 Curtis Martin 1.00 2.50
28 Drew Bledsoe 1.00 2.50
29 Lawrence Phillips .30 .75
30 Isaac Bruce .75 2.00
31 Eddie Kennison .50 1.25
32 Keyshawn Johnson .75 2.00
33 Stepfret Williams .30 .75
34 Emmitt Smith 2.50 6.00
35 Troy Aikman 1.50 4.00
36 Deion Sanders .75 2.00
37 Joey Galloway .50 1.25
38 Rick Mirer .30 .75
39 Rickey Dudley .50 1.25
40 Jeff Hostetler .30 .75
41 Junior Seau .75 2.00
42 Derrick Mayes .50 1.25
43 Brett Favre 3.00 8.00
44 Edgar Bennett .50 1.25
45 Barry Sanders 2.50 6.00
46 Herman Moore .50 1.25

47 Kordell Stewart .75 2.00
48 Jerome Bettis .75 2.00
49 Eddie George .75 2.00
50 Steve McNair 1.00 2.50
P80 Jerry Rice Promo 1.25 3.00

1997 SPx Gold

COMPLETE SET (50) 60.00 120.00
*GOLD STARS: 1.5X TO 3X HI COL.

1997 SPx HoloFame

Randomly inserted in packs at a rate of one in 75, this 20-card set features 20 of the NFL's most collectible players. A small circular framed player portrait is centered on the die-cut "X" end of the card front. The word "Holofame" is printed in the top of the portrait frame with the player's name below.

COMPLETE SET (20) 100.00 200.00
STATED ODDS 1:75
HX1 Jerry Rice 6.00 15.00
HX2 Emmitt Smith 10.00 25.00
HX3 Karim Abdul-Jabbar 3.00 8.00
HX4 Brett Favre 10.00 25.00
HX5 Curtis Martin 4.00 10.00
HX6 Eddie Kennison 2.00 5.00
HX7 Troy Aikman 6.00 15.00
HX8 Steve Young 4.00 10.00
HX9 Tim Biakabutuka 2.00 5.00
HX10 Reggie White 3.00 8.00
HX11 Terry Glenn 3.00 8.00
HX12 Lawrence Phillips 1.25 3.00
HX13 Dan Marino 12.50 30.00
HX14 Deion Sanders 3.00 8.00
HX15 Terrell Davis 4.00 10.00
HX16 Marvin Harrison 3.00 8.00
HX17 Eddie George 3.00 8.00
HX18 Marshall Faulk 4.00 10.00
HX19 Keyshawn Johnson 3.00 8.00
HX20 Barry Sanders 10.00 25.00

1997 SPx ProMotion

Randomly inserted in packs at a rate of one in 433, this six-card set features color action player photos and two images highlighting different angles of the player on a Holoview die-cut card.

COMPLETE SET (6) 60.00 150.00
STATED ODDS 1:433
1 Dan Marino 20.00 50.00
2 Joe Montana 20.00 50.00
3 Troy Aikman 10.00 25.00
4 Barry Sanders 15.00 40.00
5 Karim Abdul-Jabbar 5.00 12.00
6 Eddie George 5.00 12.00

1997 SPx ProMotion Autographs

Randomly inserted in packs at a rate of one in 4331, this six-card set is an autographed version of the regular Pro Motion set. Each autograph is limited to 100 cards, and each card is individually numbered.

AUTO/100 STATED ODDS 1:4331
STATED PRINT RUN 100 SETS
1 Dan Marino 125.00 250.00
2 Joe Montana 125.00 250.00
3 Troy Aikman 75.00 150.00
4 Barry Sanders 100.00 200.00
5 Karim Abdul-Jabbar 25.00 60.00
6 Eddie George 30.00 80.00

1998 SPx

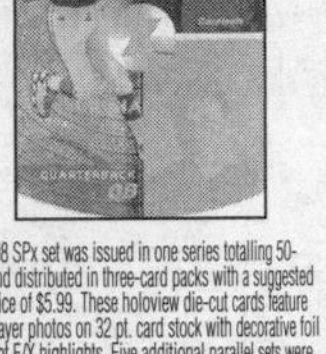

The 1998 SPx set was issued in one series totalling 50-cards and distributed in three-card packs with a suggested retail price of $5.99. These holoview die-cut cards feature color player photos on 32 pt. card stock with decorative foil and Light F/X highlights. Five additional parallel sets were inserted with the overall ratio of one per pack. The Piece of History trade program included trade insert cards that could be reedemed for game used NFL equipment (1:892 packs). The redemption program expired on 12/1/1998.

COMPLETE SET (50) 30.00 80.00
1 Jake Plummer .75 2.00
2 Byron Hanspard .30 .75
3 Vinny Testaverde .50 1.25
4 Antowain Smith .75 2.00
5 Kerry Collins .50 1.25
6 Rae Carruth .30 .75
7 Darnell Autry .30 .75
8 Rick Mirer .30 .75
9 Jeff Blake .50 1.25
10 Carl Pickens .50 1.25
11 Troy Aikman 1.50 4.00
12 Emmitt Smith 3.00 6.00
13 Deion Sanders .75 2.00
14 John Elway 3.00 8.00
15 Terrell Davis .75 2.00
16 Herman Moore .50 1.25
17 Barry Sanders 2.50 6.00
18 Brett Favre 3.00 8.00
19 Reggie White .75 2.00
20 Marshall Faulk 1.00 2.50
21 Mark Brunell .75 2.00
22 Elvis Grbac .50 1.25
23 Marcus Allen .75 2.00
24 Karim Abdul-Jabbar .75 2.00
25 Dan Marino 3.00 8.00
26 Cris Carter .75 2.00
27 Drew Bledsoe 1.25 3.00
28 Curtis Martin .75 2.00
29 Heath Shuler .30 .75
30 Ike Hilliard .50 1.25
31 Keyshawn Johnson .75 2.00
32 Jeff George .50 1.25
33 Napoleon Kaufman .75 2.00
34 Darrell Russell .30 .75
35 Ricky Watters .50 1.25
36 Kordell Stewart .75 2.00
37 Jerome Bettis .75 2.00
38 Junior Seau .75 2.00
39 Steve Young 1.00 2.50
40 Jerry Rice 2.00 4.00
41 Joey Galloway .50 1.25
42 Chris Warren .50 1.25
43 Orlando Pace .30 .75
44 Isaac Bruce .75 2.00
45 Tony Banks .50 1.25
46 Trent Dilfer .75 2.00
47 Warrick Dunn .75 2.00
48 Steve McNair .75 2.00
49 Eddie George .75 2.00
50 Terry Allen .75 2.00

1998 SPx Bronze

COMP.BRONZE SET (50) 75.00 150.00
*BRONZE STARS: .8X TO 2X BASIC CARDS
STATED ODDS 1:3 HOBBY

1998 SPx Gold

COMP.GOLD SET (50) 250.00 500.00
*GOLD STARS: 2X TO 5X BASIC CARDS
STATED ODDS 1:17

1998 SPx Grand Finale

GRAND FINALE/50: 12X TO 30X
ANNOUNCED PRINT RUN 50

1998 SPx Silver

COMP.SILVER SET (50) 125.00 250.00
*SILVER STARS: 1.2X TO 3X BASIC CARDS
STATED ODDS 1:6 HOBBY

1998 SPx Steel

COMP.STEEL SET (50) 50.00 100.00
*STEEL STARS: .6X TO 1.2X BASIC CARDS
STATED ODDS 1:1 HOBBY

1998 SPx HoloFame

Randomly inserted in hobby packs at the rate of one in 54, this 20-card set features images of impact players embossed on Holoview cards with silver decorative foil.

COMPLETE SET (20) 75.00 200.00
STATED ODDS 1:54
HF1 Troy Aikman 8.00 20.00
HF2 Emmitt Smith 12.50 30.00
HF3 John Elway 15.00 40.00
HF4 Terrell Davis 4.00 10.00
HF5 Herman Moore 2.50 6.00
HF6 Reggie White 4.00 10.00
HF7 Brett Favre 15.00 40.00
HF8 Napoleon Kaufman 4.00 10.00
HF9 Dan Marino 15.00 40.00
HF10 Karim Abdul-Jabbar 4.00 10.00
HF11 Cris Carter 4.00 10.00
HF12 Drew Bledsoe 6.00 15.00
HF13 Curtis Martin 4.00 10.00
HF14 Kordell Stewart 4.00 10.00
HF15 Junior Seau 4.00 10.00
HF16 Steve Young 5.00 12.00
HF17 Jerry Rice 8.00 20.00
HF18 Marshall Faulk 5.00 12.00
HF19 Eddie George 4.00 10.00
HF20 Terry Allen 4.00 10.00

1998 SPx ProMotion

Randomly inserted in hobby packs at the rate of one in 252, this 10-card set features color photos of some of the NFL's elite athletes on silver and copper Holoview cards.

COMPLETE SET (10) 150.00 400.00
STATED ODDS 1:252
P1 Troy Aikman 20.00 50.00
P2 Emmitt Smith 30.00 80.00
P3 Terrell Davis 10.00 25.00
P4 Brett Favre 40.00 100.00
P5 Marcus Allen 10.00 25.00
P6 Dan Marino 40.00 100.00
P7 Drew Bledsoe 15.00 40.00
P8 Ike Hilliard 6.00 15.00
P9 Warrick Dunn 10.00 25.00
P10 Eddie George 10.00 25.00

1998 SPx Finite

The SPx Finite set was issued in two series for a totoal of 370-cards. Series one was issued with a total of 190-cards and Series two with a total of 180-cards. Each card was individually serial numbered. Series One contains: base cards (#1-90; 7600-sets), Playmakers (#91-120; 5500-sets), Youth Movement (#121-150; 3000-sets), Pure Energy (#151-170; 2500-sets), and Heroes of the Game (#171-180; 1250-sets). Series Two contains: base cards (#191-280; 10,100-sets, #218/221/239; 1998-sets), Extreme Talent (#281-310; 7200-sets), the New School (311-340; 4000-sets, #321/338/339; 1700-sets), Sixth Sense (#341-360; 2700-sets), and Uncommon Valor (#361-370; 1620-sets). Each card was printed with two parallel color variations.

COMP.SERIES 1 (190) 400.00 750.00
COMP.SERIES 2 (180) 400.00 750.00
1 Jake Plummer .50 1.25
2 Eric Swann .50 1.25
3 Rob Moore .50 1.25
4 Jamal Anderson .60 1.50
5 Byron Hanspard .50 1.25
6 Cornelius Bennett .60 1.50
7 Michael Jackson .50 1.25
8 Peter Boulware .50 1.25
9 Jermaine Lewis .50 1.25
10 Antowain Smith .60 1.50
11 Bruce Smith .60 1.50
12 Bryce Paup .50 1.25
13 Rae Carruth .50 1.25
14 Michael Bates .50 1.25
15 Fred Lane .50 1.25
16 Darnell Autry .50 1.25
17 Curtis Conway .60 1.50
18 Erik Kramer .50 1.25
19 Corey Dillon .50 1.25
20 Darnay Scott .60 1.50
21 Reinard Wilson .50 1.25
22 Troy Aikman 1.00 2.50
23 David LaFleur .50 1.25
24 Emmitt Smith 1.50 4.00
25 John Elway 1.25 3.00
26 John Mobley .50 1.25
27 Terrell Davis .60 1.50
28 Rod Smith .60 1.50
29 Bryant Westbrook .50 1.25
30 Scott Mitchell .60 1.50
31 Barry Sanders 1.25 3.00
32 Dorsey Levens .60 1.50
33 Antonio Freeman .75 2.00
34 Reggie White .75 2.00
35 Marshall Faulk .60 1.50
36 Marvin Harrison .60 1.50
37 Ken Dilger .50 1.25
38 Mark Brunell .60 1.50
39 Keenan McCardell .60 1.50
40 Renaldo Wynn .50 1.25
41 Marcus Allen .75 2.00
42 Elvis Grbac .60 1.50
43 Andre Rison .60 1.50
44 Yatil Green .50 1.25
45 Zach Thomas .60 1.50
46 Karim Abdul-Jabbar .50 1.25
47 John Randle .75 2.00
48 Brad Johnson .60 1.50
49 Jake Reed .60 1.50
50 Danny Wuerffel .60 1.50
51 Andre Hastings .50 1.25
52 Drew Bledsoe .60 1.50
53 Terry Glenn .60 1.50
54 Ty Law .75 2.00
55 Danny Kanell .50 1.25
56 Tiki Barber .60 1.50
57 Jessie Armstead .50 1.25
58 Glenn Foley .50 1.25
59 James Farrior .50 1.25
60 Wayne Chrebet .50 1.25
61 Tim Brown .75 2.00
62 Napoleon Kaufman .50 1.25
63 Darrell Russell .50 1.25
64 Bobby Hoying .60 1.50
65 Irving Fryar .60 1.50
66 Charlie Garner .60 1.50
67 Will Blackwell .50 1.25
68 Kordell Stewart .50 1.25
69 Levon Kirkland .50 1.25
70 Tony Banks .60 1.50
71 Ryan McNeil .50 1.25
72 Isaac Bruce .75 2.00
73 Tony Martin .60 1.50
74 Junior Seau .60 1.50
75 Natrone Means .60 1.50
76 Jerry Rice 2.00 5.00
77 Garrison Hearst .50 1.25
78 Terrell Owens .60 1.50
79 Warren Moon .75 2.00
80 Joey Galloway .60 1.50
81 Chad Brown .50 1.25
82 Warrick Dunn .50 1.25
83 Mike Alstott .50 1.25
84 Hardy Nickerson .50 1.25
85 Steve McNair .60 1.50
86 Chris Sanders .50 1.25
87 Darryll Lewis .50 1.25
88 Gus Frerotte .50 1.25
89 Terry Allen .60 1.50
90 Chris Dishman .50 1.25
91 Kordell Stewart PM .60 1.50
92 Jerry Rice PM 2.50 6.00
93 Michael Irvin PM 1.00 2.50
94 Brett Favre PM 2.00 5.00
95 Jeff George PM .75 2.00
96 Joey Galloway PM .75 2.00
97 John Elway PM 1.50 4.00
98 Troy Aikman PM 1.25 3.00
99 Steve Young PM 1.25 3.00
100 Andre Rison PM .75 2.00
101 Ben Coates PM .75 2.00
102 Robert Brooks PM .75 2.00
103 Dan Marino PM 2.00 5.00
104 Isaac Bruce PM 1.00 2.50
105 Junior Seau PM .75 2.00
106 Jake Plummer PM .60 1.50
107 Curtis Conway PM .75 2.00
108 Jeff Blake PM .75 2.00
109 Rod Smith PM .75 2.00
110 Barry Sanders PM 1.50 4.00
111 Deion Sanders PM .75 2.00
112 Drew Bledsoe PM .75 2.00
113 Emmitt Smith PM 1.50 4.00
114 Herman Moore PM .75 2.00
115 Dorsey Levens PM .75 2.00
116 Jimmy Smith PM .75 2.00
117 Tony Martin PM .75 2.00
118 Carl Pickens PM .75 2.00
119 Keyshawn Johnson PM .75 2.00
120 Cris Carter PM 1.00 2.50
121 Warrick Dunn YM .75 2.00
122 Marshall Faulk YM 1.00 2.50
123 Trent Dilfer YM 1.00 2.50
124 Napoleon Kaufman YM .75 2.00
125 Corey Dillon YM .75 2.00
126 Darrell Russell YM .75 2.00
127 Danny Kanell YM .75 2.00
128 Reidel Anthony YM .75 2.00
129 Steve McNair YM 1.00 2.50
130 Ike Hilliard YM .75 2.00
131 Tony Banks YM 1.00 2.50
132 Yatil Green YM .75 2.00
133 J.J. Stokes YM 1.00 2.50
134 Fred Lane YM .75 2.00
135 Bryant Westbrook YM .75 2.00
136 Jake Plummer YM .75 2.00
137 Byron Hanspard YM .75 2.00
138 Rae Carruth YM .75 2.00
139 Keyshawn Johnson YM 1.00 2.50
140 Jim Druckenmiller YM .75 2.00
141 Amani Toomer YM .75 2.00
142 Troy Davis YM .75 2.00
143 Antowain Smith YM 1.00 2.50
144 Shawn Springs YM .75 2.00
145 Rickey Dudley YM .75 2.00
146 Terry Glenn YM 1.00 2.50
147 Johnnie Morton YM 1.00 2.50
148 David LaFleur YM .75 2.00
149 Eddie Kennison YM .75 2.00
150 Bobby Hoying YM 1.00 2.50
151 Junior Seau PE 1.50 4.00
152 Shannon Sharpe PE 1.50 4.00
153 Bruce Smith PE 1.50 4.00
154 Brett Favre PE 4.00 10.00
155 Emmitt Smith PE 3.00 8.00
156 Keenan McCardell PE 1.50 4.00
157 Kordell Stewart PE 1.25 3.00
158 Troy Aikman PE 2.50 6.00
159 Steve Young PE 2.50 6.00
160 Tim Brown PE 2.00 5.00
161 Eddie George PE 1.50 4.00
162 Herman Moore PE 1.50 4.00
163 Dan Marino PE 4.00 10.00
164 Dorsey Levens PE 1.50 4.00
165 Jerry Rice PE 5.00 12.00
166 Warren Sapp PE 1.50 4.00
167 Robert Smith PE 1.25 3.00
168 Mark Brunell PE 1.50 4.00
169 Terrell Davis PE 1.50 4.00
170 Jerome Bettis PE 2.00 5.00
171 Dan Marino HG 6.00 15.00
172 Barry Sanders HG 5.00 12.00
173 Marcus Allen HG 3.00 8.00
174 Brett Favre HG 6.00 15.00
175 Warrick Dunn HG 2.00 5.00
176 Eddie George HG 2.50 6.00
177 John Elway HG 5.00 12.00
178 Troy Aikman HG 4.00 10.00
179 Cris Carter HG 3.00 8.00
180 Terrell Davis HG 2.50 6.00
181 Peyton Manning/1998 RC 60.00 120.00
182 Ryan Leaf/1998 RC 5.00 12.00
183 Andre Wadsworth/1998 RC 6.00 15.00
184 Charles Woodson/1998 RC 15.00 40.00
185 Curtis Enis/1998 RC 5.00 12.00
186 Grant Wistrom/1998 RC 4.00 10.00
187 Fred Taylor/1998 RC 8.00 20.00
188 Takeo Spikes/1998 RC 5.00 12.00
189 Kevin Dyson/1998 RC 5.00 12.00
190 Robert Edwards/1998 RC 5.00 12.00
191 Adrian Murrell .30 .75
192 Simeon Rice .40 1.00
193 Frank Sanders .30 .75
194 Chris Chandler .40 1.00
195 Terance Mathis .30 .75
196 Keith Brooking RC .50 1.25
197 Jim Harbaugh .50 1.25
198 Errict Rhett .40 1.00
199 Pat Johnson RC .40 1.00
200 Rob Johnson .40 1.00
201 Andre Reed .50 1.25
202 Thurman Thomas .40 1.00
203 Kerry Collins .30 .75
204 William Floyd .30 .75
205 Sean Gilbert .30 .75
206 Bobby Engram .30 .75
207 Edgar Bennett .40 1.00
208 Walt Harris .30 .75
209 Carl Pickens .40 1.00
210 Neil O'Donnell .40 1.00
211 Tony McGee .30 .75
212 Deion Sanders .40 1.00
213 Michael Irvin .50 1.25
214 Greg Ellis RC .40 1.00
215 Shannon Sharpe .40 1.00
216 Neil Smith .40 1.00
217 Marcus Nash RC .30 .75
218 Brian Griese/1998 RC 8.00 20.00
219 Johnnie Morton .40 1.00
220 Herman Moore .40 1.00
221 Charlie Batch/1998 RC 6.00 15.00
222 Robert Brooks .40 1.00
223 Mark Chmura .30 .75
224 Brett Favre 1.00 2.50
225 Jerome Pathon RC .40 1.00
226 Zack Crockett .30 .75
227 Dan Footman .30 .75
228 Jimmy Smith .40 1.00
229 Bryce Paup .30 .75
230 James Stewart .30 .75
231 Derrick Thomas .50 1.25
232 Derrick Alexander .40 1.00
233 Tony Gonzalez .40 1.00
234 Dan Marino 1.00 2.50
235 O.J. McDuffie .40 1.00
236 Troy Drayton .30 .75
237 Cris Carter .50 1.25
238 Robert Smith .30 .75
239 Randy Moss/1998 RC 20.00 50.00
240 Lamar Smith .30 .75
241 Sean Dawkins .30 .75
242 Alex Molden .30 .75
243 Ben Coates .40 1.00
244 Ted Johnson .30 .75
245 Sedrick Shaw .30 .75
246 Ike Hilliard .30 .75
247 Jason Sehorn .40 1.00
248 Michael Strahan .40 1.00
249 Keyshawn Johnson .40 1.00
250 Curtis Martin .40 1.00
251 Jeff George .40 1.00
252 Rickey Dudley .30 .75
253 James Jett .30 .75
254 Bobby Taylor UER .40 1.00
255 Rodney Peete .40 1.00
256 William Thomas .40 1.00
257 Jerome Bettis .50 1.25
258 Charles Johnson .30 .75
259 Chris Fuamatu-Ma'afala RC .40 1.00
260 Eddie Kennison .30 .75
261 Az-Zahir Hakim RC .40 1.00
262 Robert Holcombe RC .30 .75
263 Bryan Still .30 .75
264 Mikhael Ricks RC .40 1.00
265 Charlie Jones .30 .75
266 J.J. Stokes .40 1.00
267 Marc Edwards .30 .75
268 Steve Young .60 1.50
269 Ricky Watters .40 1.00
270 Cortez Kennedy .40 1.00
271 Shawn Springs .30 .75
272 Trent Dilfer .40 1.00
273 Warren Sapp .40 1.00
274 Reidel Anthony .30 .75
275 Yancey Thigpen .30 .75
276 Chris Sanders .30 .75
277 Eddie George .40 1.00
278 Leslie Shepherd .30 .75
279 Skip Hicks RC .40 1.00
280 Dana Stubblefield .30 .75
281 John Elway ET 1.25 3.00
282 Brett Favre ET 1.50 4.00
283 Junior Seau ET .60 1.50
284 Barry Sanders ET 1.25 3.00
285 Jerry Rice ET 2.00 5.00
286 Antonio Freeman ET .75 2.00
287 Peyton Manning ET 10.00 25.00
288 Warrick Dunn ET .50 1.25
289 Steve Young ET 1.00 2.50
290 Dan Marino ET 1.50 4.00
291 Jerome Bettis ET .75 2.00
292 Ryan Leaf ET .60 1.50
293 Deion Sanders ET .60 1.50
294 Eddie George ET .60 1.50
295 Joey Galloway ET .60 1.50
296 Troy Aikman ET 1.00 2.50
297 Andre Wadsworth ET .75 2.00
298 Terrell Davis ET .60 1.50
299 Steve McNair ET .60 1.50
300 Jake Plummer ET .50 1.25
301 Emmitt Smith ET 1.25 3.00
302 Isaac Bruce ET .75 2.00
303 Kordell Stewart ET .50 1.25
304 Dorsey Levens ET .60 1.50
305 Antowain Smith ET .60 1.50
306 Drew Bledsoe ET .60 1.50
307 Marshall Faulk ET .60 1.50
308 Herman Moore ET .60 1.50
309 Mark Brunell ET .60 1.50
310 Charles Woodson ET 2.00 5.00
311 Peyton Manning NS 12.00 30.00
312 Curtis Enis NS 1.00 2.50
313 Terry Fair NS RC 1.00 2.50
314 Andre Wadsworth NS 1.25 3.00
315 Anthony Simmons NS RC .75 2.00
316 Jacquez Green NS RC 1.00 2.50
317 Takeo Spikes NS 1.00 2.50
318 Vonnie Holliday NS RC 1.00 2.50
319 Kyle Turley NS RC 1.00 2.50
320 Keith Brooking NS 1.25 3.00
321 Randy Moss NS/1700 10.00 25.00
322 Shaun Williams NS RC 1.00 2.50
323 Greg Ellis NS 1.00 2.50
324 Mikhael Ricks NS 1.00 2.50
325 Charles Woodson NS 3.00 8.00
326 Corey Chavous NS RC 1.00 2.50
327 Stephen Alexander NS RC 1.00 2.50
328 Marcus Nash NS .75 2.00
329 Tra Thomas NS RC .75 2.00
330 Duane Starks NS RC .75 2.00
331 John Avery NS RC 1.00 2.50
332 Kevin Dyson NS 1.00 2.50
333 Fred Taylor NS 1.50 4.00
334 Grant Wistrom NS .75 2.00
335 Ryan Leaf NS 1.00 2.50
336 Robert Edwards NS 1.00 2.50
337 Jason Peter NS RC .75 2.00
338 Brian Griese NS 2.50 6.00
339 Charlie Batch NS 2.00 5.00
340 Pat Johnson NS/4000 1.00 2.50
341 John Elway SS 3.00 8.00
342 Curtis Enis SS 1.50 4.00
343 Antonio Freeman SS 2.00 5.00
344 Mark Brunell SS 1.50 4.00
345 Robert Edwards SS 1.50 4.00
346 Ryan Leaf SS 1.50 4.00
347 Steve Young SS 2.50 6.00
348 Jerome Bettis SS 2.00 5.00
349 Antowain Smith SS 1.50 4.00
350 Tim Brown SS 2.00 5.00
351 Peyton Manning SS 12.00 30.00
352 Troy Aikman SS 2.50 6.00
353 Natrone Means SS 1.50 4.00
354 Dan Marino SS 4.00 10.00
355 Junior Seau SS 1.50 4.00
356 Brad Johnson SS 1.50 4.00
357 Jerry Rice SS 5.00 12.00
358 Drew Bledsoe SS 1.50 4.00
359 Fred Taylor SS 2.50 6.00
360 Emmitt Smith SS 3.00 8.00
361 Terrell Davis UV 2.00 5.00
362 Kordell Stewart UV 1.50 4.00
363 Barry Sanders UV 4.00 10.00
364 Jake Plummer UV 1.50 4.00
365 Brett Favre UV 5.00 12.00
366 Curtis Enis UV 2.00 5.00
367 Eddie George UV 2.00 5.00
368 Napoleon Kaufman UV 1.50 4.00
369 Randy Moss UV 8.00 20.00
370 Warrick Dunn UV 1.50 4.00
S8 Troy Aikman Sample .40 1.00
S234 Dan Marino Sample .75 2.00

1998 SPx Finite Radiance

*1-90 VETS/3800: .6X TO 1.5X BASIC CARDS
1-90 STATED PRINT RUN 3800
*91-120 VETS/2750: .6X TO 1.5X BASIC CARDS
91-120 PM STATED PRINT RUN 2750
*121-150 VETS/1500: .6X TO 1.5X BASIC CARDS
121-150 YM STATED PRINT RUN 1500
*151-170 VETS/1000: .8X TO 2X BASIC CARDS
151-170 PE STATED PRINT RUN 1000
*171-180 VETS/100: 2X TO 5X BASIC CARDS
171-180 HG STATED PRINT RUN 100
*181-190 ROOKIES/50: 1X TO 2.5X BASIC RC
181-190 PRINT RUN 50 SERIAL #'d SETS
*191-280 VETS/5050: .6X TO 1.5X BASIC CARDS
*191-280 ROOKIES/1700: .4X TO 1X
191-280 STATED PRINT RUN 1700-5050
*281-310 VETS/3600: .6X TO 1.5X BASIC CARDS
281-310 ET STATED PRINT RUN 3600
*311-340 VETS/2000: .6X TO 1.5X BASIC CARDS
*311-340 ROOKIES/850: .6X TO 1.5X
311-340 NS PRINT RUN 850-2000
*341-360 RADIANCE STARS: .8X TO 2X
341-360 SS PRINT RUN 900 SER.#'d SETS
*361-370 RADIANCE STARS: .8X TO 2X
*361-370 RAD.ROOKIES: .6X TO 1.5X
361-370 UV PRINT RUN 540 SER.#'d SETS
181 Peyton Manning 500.00 750.00
239 Randy Moss/1700 30.00 80.00

1998 SPx Finite Spectrum

*1-90 SPECTRUM STARS: 1.2X TO 3X HI
1-90 PRINT RUN 1900 SERIAL #'d SETS
*91-120 SPECTRUM PM STARS: 1.2X TO 3X
91-120 PM PRINT RUN 1375 SERIAL #'d SETS
*121-150 SPECTRUM YM STARS: 1.2X TO 3X
121 150 YM PRINT RUN 750 SERIAL #'d SETS
*151-170 SPECTRUM PE STARS: 6X TO 15X
151-170 PE PRINT RUN 50 SERIAL #'d SETS
171-180 HG PRINT RUN 1 SERIAL #'d SET
181-190 PRINT RUN 1 SERIAL #'d SET
*191-280 SPECTRUM STARS: 3X TO 8X
*191-280 SPECTRUM RCs: 1.2X TO 3X
*218/221/239 SPECTRUM RCs: .5X TO 1.2X
191-280 PRINT RUN 325 SERIAL #'d SETS
*281-310 SPECTRUM ET STARS: 4X TO 10X
*281-310 SPECTRUM ROOKIES: 1.2X TO 3X
281-310 ET PRINT RUN 150 SERIAL #'d SETS
*311-340 SPECTRUM NS: 3X TO 8X
*321/338/339 SPECTRUM NS: 1.5X TO 4X
311-340 NS PRINT RUN 50 SERIAL #'d SETS
*341-360 SPECTRUM SS STARS: 8X TO 20X
*341-360 SPECTRUM SS ROOKIES: 3X TO 8X
341-360 SS PRINT RUN 25 SERIAL #'d SETS

1998 SPx Finite UD Authentics

Randomly inserted into packs, this four-card set features color player photos signed by the player. The numbers after the players' names indicate how many cards each player signed (according to Upper Deck) although none are serial numbered. A parallel version of the set was also produced with signatures in red ink.The red ink versions are believed to be limited to the jersey number of each of the 4 players respectively. The Marino and Montana cards carry a 1999 copyright date.

DM1 Dan Marino/400* '99 50.00 120.00
JM Joe Montana/1984* '99 40.00 100.00
RS1 Roger Staubach/463* 30.00 80.00
TA1 Troy Aikman/1992* 40.00 80.00
MB Mark Brunell white 10.00 25.00

1999 SPx

Released as a 135-card set, 1999 SPx football features 90 veteran player cards and 45 rookies sequentially numbered to 1999 where 26 of the rookie cards are acutally autographed. Card numbers 130-135 are signed and numbered out of 500. Packaged in 18 pack boxes with three cards per pack, SPx carried a suggested retail price of $5.99.

COMPLETE SET (135) 1000.00 2000.00
COMP.SET w/o RCs (90) 12.50 25.00
*HAND NUMBERED RCs: .5X TO .8X
1 Jake Plummer .25 .60
2 Adrian Murrell .25 .60
3 Frank Sanders .25 .60
4 Jamal Anderson .30 .75
5 Chris Chandler .30 .75
6 Terance Mathis .25 .60
7 Tony Banks .30 .75
8 Priest Holmes .25 .60
9 Jermaine Lewis .25 .60
10 Antowain Smith .25 .60
11 Doug Flutie .40 1.00
12 Eric Moulds .25 .60
13 Tim Biakabutuka .30 .75
14 Steve Beuerlein .30 .75
15 Muhsin Muhammad .25 .60
16 Bobby Engram .25 .60
17 Curtis Conway .30 .75
18 Curtis Enis .25 .60
19 Corey Dillon .25 .60
20 Jeff Blake .30 .75
21 Carl Pickens .30 .75
22 Ty Detmer .25 .60
23 Terry Kirby .25 .60
24 Leslie Shepherd .25 .60
25 Troy Aikman .50 1.25
26 Emmitt Smith .60 1.50
27 Deion Sanders .30 .75
28 Terrell Davis .30 .75
29 Rod Smith .30 .75
30 Bubby Brister .25 .60
31 Barry Sanders .60 1.50
32 Herman Moore .30 .75
33 Charlie Batch .25 .60
34 Brett Favre .75 2.00
35 Antonio Freeman .30 .75
36 Dorsey Levens .30 .75
37 Peyton Manning 1.25 3.00
38 Marvin Harrison .30 .75
39 Jerome Pathon .25 .60
40 Mark Brunell .30 .75
41 Jimmy Smith .30 .75
42 Fred Taylor .25 .60
43 Elvis Grbac .25 .60
44 Andre Rison .30 .75
45 Warren Moon .40 1.00
46 Dan Marino .75 2.00
47 Karim Abdul-Jabbar .25 .60
48 O.J. McDuffie .30 .75
49 Randall Cunningham .30 .75
50 Robert Smith .25 .60
51 Randy Moss .30 .75
52 Drew Bledsoe .30 .75
53 Terry Glenn .30 .75
54 Tony Simmons .25 .60
55 Danny Wuerffel .30 .75
56 Cam Cleeland .25 .60
57 Kerry Collins .25 .60
58 Gary Brown .25 .60
59 Ike Hilliard .25 .60
60 Vinny Testaverde .25 .60
61 Curtis Martin .30 .75
62 Keyshawn Johnson .30 .75
63 Rich Gannon .30 .75
64 Napoleon Kaufman .25 .60
65 Tim Brown .40 1.00
66 Duce Staley .25 .60
67 Doug Pederson .25 .60
68 Charles Johnson .25 .60
69 Kordell Stewart .25 .60
70 Jerome Bettis .40 1.00
71 Trent Green .25 .60
72 Marshall Faulk .30 .75
73 Ryan Leaf .30 .75
74 Natrone Means .30 .75
75 Jim Harbaugh .30 .75
76 Steve Young .50 1.25
77 Garrison Hearst .25 .60
78 Jerry Rice 1.00 2.50
79 Terrell Owens .30 .75
80 Ricky Watters .30 .75
81 Joey Galloway .30 .75
82 Jon Kitna .25 .60
83 Warrick Dunn .25 .60
84 Trent Dilfer .25 .60
85 Mike Alstott .25 .60
86 Steve McNair .30 .75
87 Eddie George .30 .75
88 Yancey Thigpen .25 .60
89 Skip Hicks .25 .60
90 Michael Westbrook .25 .60
91 Amos Zereoue RC 3.00 8.00
92 Chris Claiborne AU RC 5.00 12.00
93 Scott Covington RC 3.00 8.00
94 Jeff Paulk RC 3.00 8.00
95 Brandon Stokley AU RC 10.00 25.00
96 Antoine Winfield RC 3.00 8.00
97 Reginald Kelly RC 3.00 8.00
98 Jermaine Fazande AU RC 5.00 12.00
99 Andy Katzenmoyer RC 4.00 10.00
100 Craig Yeast RC 3.00 8.00
101 Joe Montgomery RC 3.00 8.00
102 Darrin Chiaverini RC 3.00 8.00
103 Travis McGriff RC 3.00 8.00
104 Jevon Kearse RC 4.00 10.00
104X Jevon Kearse EXCH 1.50 4.00
(never issued as an AUTO)
105 Joel Makovicka AU RC 5.00 12.00
106 Aaron Brooks RC 3.00 8.00
107 Chris McAlister RC 3.00 8.00
108 Jim Kleinsasser RC 5.00 12.00
109 Ebenezer Ekuban RC 3.00 8.00
110 Karsten Bailey RC 3.00 8.00
111 Sedrick Irvin AU RC 5.00 12.00
112 D'Wayne Bates AU RC 5.00 12.00
113 Joe Germaine AU RC 6.00 15.00
114 Cecil Collins AU RC 5.00 12.00
115 Mike Cloud RC 3.00 8.00
116 James Johnson RC 3.00 8.00
117 Champ Bailey AU RC 12.00 30.00
118 Rob Konrad RC 3.00 8.00
119 Peerless Price AU RC 5.00 12.00
120 Kevin Faulk AU RC 5.00 12.00
121 Dameane Douglas RC 3.00 8.00
122 Kevin Johnson AU RC 6.00 15.00
123 Troy Edwards AU RC 5.00 12.00
124 Edgerrin James AU RC 8.00 20.00
125 David Boston AU RC 5.00 12.00
126 Michael Bishop AU RC 6.00 15.00
127 Shaun King AU SP RC 20.00 40.00
127X Shaun King EXCH 3.00 8.00
128 Brock Huard AU RC 5.00 12.00
129 Torry Holt AU RC 12.00 30.00
130 Cade McNown AU/500 RC 8.00 20.00
131 Tim Couch AU/500 RC 10.00 25.00
132 Donovan McNabb AU RC 12.00 30.00
132X Donovan McNabb EXCH 2.00 5.00
133 Akili Smith AU/500 RC 8.00 20.00
134 D.Culpepper AU/500 RC 10.00 25.00
134X Daunte Culpepper EXCH 2.00 5.00
135 Ricky Williams AU/500 RC 20.00 50.00
S8 Troy Aikman Sample .75 2.00

1999 SPx Radiance

*RADIANCE VETS: 6X TO 15X BASIC CARD
RADIANCE PRINT RUN 100 SER.#'d SETS
8 Priest Holmes 15.00 40.00
91 Amos Zereoue 8.00 20.00
92 Chris Claiborne 8.00 20.00
93 Scott Covington 8.00 20.00
94 Jeff Paulk 8.00 20.00
95 Brandon Stokley 10.00 25.00
96 Antoine Winfield 8.00 20.00
97 Reginald Kelly 8.00 20.00
98 Jermaine Fazande 8.00 20.00
99 Andy Katzenmoyer 10.00 25.00
100 Craig Yeast 8.00 20.00
101 Joe Montgomery 8.00 20.00
102 Darrin Chiaverini 8.00 20.00
103 Travis McGriff 8.00 20.00
104 Jevon Kearse 10.00 25.00
105 Joel Makovicka 8.00 20.00
106 Aaron Brooks 8.00 20.00
107 Chris McAlister 8.00 20.00
108 Jim Kleinsasser 12.00 30.00
109 Ebenezer Ekuban 8.00 20.00
110 Karsten Bailey 8.00 20.00
111 Sedrick Irvin 8.00 20.00
112 D'Wayne Bates 8.00 20.00
113 Joe Germaine 10.00 25.00
114 Cecil Collins 8.00 20.00
115 Mike Cloud 8.00 20.00
116 James Johnson 8.00 20.00
117 Champ Bailey 15.00 40.00
118 Rob Konrad 8.00 20.00
119 Peerless Price 8.00 20.00
120 Kevin Faulk 8.00 20.00
121 Dameane Douglas 8.00 20.00
122 Kevin Johnson 10.00 25.00
123 Troy Edwards 8.00 20.00
124 Edgerrin James 12.00 30.00
125 David Boston 8.00 20.00
126 Michael Bishop 10.00 25.00
127 Shaun King 8.00 20.00
128 Brock Huard 8.00 20.00
129 Torry Holt 15.00 40.00
130 Cade McNown 8.00 20.00
131 Tim Couch 10.00 25.00
132 Donovan McNabb 25.00 60.00
133 Akili Smith 8.00 20.00
134 Daunte Culpepper 8.00 20.00
135 Ricky Williams 12.00 30.00

1999 SPx Highlight Heroes

Randomly inserted in packs at the rate of one in nine, this 10-card set showcases NFL superstars like Jake Plummer and Fred Taylor. Card backs carry an "H" prefix.

COMPLETE SET (10) 10.00 25.00
STATED ODDS 1:9
H1 Jake Plummer .75 2.00
H2 Doug Flutie 1.25 3.00
H3 Garrison Hearst .75 2.00
H4 Fred Taylor 1.25 3.00
H5 Dorsey Levens 1.25 3.00
H6 Kordell Stewart .75 2.00
H7 Marshall Faulk 1.50 4.00
H8 Steve Young 1.50 4.00
H9 Troy Aikman 2.50 6.00
H10 Jerome Bettis 1.25 3.00

1999 SPx Masters

Randomly seeded in packs at the rate of one in 17, this 15-card set features the best players at their respective positions. Card backs carry an "M" prefix.

COMPLETE SET (15) 35.00 80.00
STATED ODDS 1:17
M1 Dan Marino 5.00 12.00
M2 Barry Sanders 5.00 12.00
M3 Peyton Manning 5.00 12.00
M4 Joey Galloway 1.00 2.50
M5 Steve Young 2.00 5.00
M6 Warrick Dunn 1.50 4.00
M7 Deion Sanders 1.50 4.00
M8 Fred Taylor 1.50 4.00
M9 Charlie Batch 1.50 4.00
M10 Jamal Anderson 1.50 4.00
M11 Jake Plummer 1.00 2.50
M12 Terrell Davis 1.50 4.00
M13 Eddie George 1.50 4.00
M14 Mark Brunell 1.50 4.00
M15 Randy Moss 4.00 10.00

1999 SPx Prolifics

Randomly inserted in packs at the rate of one in 17, this 15-card set focuses on top NFL Touchdown producers. Card backs carry a "P" prefix.

COMPLETE SET (15) 25.00 60.00
STATED ODDS 1:17
P1 John Elway 5.00 12.00
P2 Barry Sanders 5.00 12.00
P3 Jamal Anderson 1.50 4.00
P4 Terrell Owens 1.50 4.00
P5 Marshall Faulk 2.00 5.00
P6 Napoleon Kaufman 1.50 4.00
P7 Antonio Freeman 1.50 4.00
P8 Doug Flutie 1.50 4.00
P9 Vinny Testaverde 1.00 2.50
P10 Jerry Rice 3.00 8.00
P11 Eric Moulds 1.50 4.00
P12 Emmitt Smith 3.00 8.00
P13 Brett Favre 5.00 12.00
P14 Randall Cunningham 1.50 4.00
P15 Keyshawn Johnson 1.50 4.00

1999 SPx Spxcitement

Randomly inserted in packs at the rate of one in three, this 20-card set features some of the NFL's most exciting players. Card backs carry an "S" prefix.

COMPLETE SET (20) 12.50 30.00
STATED ODDS 1:3
S1 Troy Aikman 1.25 3.00
S2 Edgerrin James 2.50 6.00
S3 Jerry Rice 1.25 3.00
S4 Daunte Culpepper 2.50 6.00
S5 Antowain Smith .60 1.50
S6 Kevin Faulk .60 1.50
S7 Steve McNair .60 1.50
S8 Antonio Freeman .60 1.50
S9 Torry Holt 1.25 3.00
S10 Napoleon Kaufman .60 1.50
S11 Curtis Martin .60 1.50
S12 Randall Cunningham .60 1.50
S13 Eric Moulds .60 1.50
S14 Priest Holmes 1.00 2.50
S15 David Boston .60 1.50
S16 Herman Moore .40 1.00
S17 Champ Bailey .60 1.50
S18 Vinny Testaverde .40 1.00
S19 Garrison Hearst .40 1.00
S20 Jon Kitna .60 1.50

1999 SPx Spxtreme

Randomly seeded in packs at the rate of one in six, this 20-card set salutes extreme talents of the NFL. Card backs carry an "X" prefix.

COMPLETE SET (20) 15.00 40.00
STATED ODDS 1:6
X1 Emmitt Smith 2.00 5.00
X2 Brock Huard .60 1.50
X3 David Boston 1.00 2.50
X4 Edgerrin James 3.00 8.00
X5 Kevin Faulk 1.00 2.50
X6 Daunte Culpepper 3.00 8.00
X7 Charlie Batch 1.00 2.50
X8 Torry Holt 1.50 4.00
X9 Andre Rison .60 1.50
X10 Karim Abdul-Jabbar .60 1.50
X11 Kordell Stewart .60 1.50
X12 Curtis Enis .40 1.00
X13 Terrell Owens 1.00 2.50
X14 Curtis Martin 1.00 2.50
X15 Ricky Watters .60 1.50
X16 Corey Dillon 1.00 2.50
X17 Tim Brown 1.00 2.50
X18 Warrick Dunn 1.00 2.50
X19 Drew Bledsoe 1.25 3.00
X20 Eddie George 1.00 2.50

1999 SPx Starscape

Randomly inserted in packs at the rate of one in nine, this 10-card set contains veterans and young stars and dates a specific career achievement on each card. Card backs carry an "ST" prefix.

COMPLETE SET (10) 7.50 20.00
STATED ODDS 1:9
ST1 Randy Moss 2.50 6.00
ST2 Keyshawn Johnson 1.00 2.50
ST3 Curtis Enis .40 1.00
ST4 Jerome Bettis 1.00 2.50
ST5 Mark Brunell 1.00 2.50
ST6 Antowain Smith 1.00 2.50
ST7 Joey Galloway .60 1.50
ST8 Drew Bledsoe 1.25 3.00
ST9 Corey Dillon 1.00 2.50
ST10 Steve McNair 1.00 2.50

1999 SPx Winning Materials

Randomly inserted inpacks at the rate of one in 252, this 10-card set features swatches of game-used jerseys and game-used footballs. Tim Couch and Jerry Rice cards are autographed and numbered.

STATED ODDS 1:252
BFS Brett Favre 15.00 40.00
CMS Cade McNown 5.00 12.00
DBS David Boston 5.00 12.00
DCS Daunte Culpepper 8.00 20.00
DMS Dan Marino 15.00 40.00
JRA Jerry Rice AUTO/80 150.00 300.00
JRS Jerry Rice 20.00 50.00
MCS Donovan McNabb 15.00 40.00
RWS Ricky Williams 8.00 20.00
TCS Tim Couch 6.00 15.00
THS Torry Holt 10.00 25.00

2000 SPx

Released in early November 2000, SPx features a 162-card base set comprised of 90 veteran player cards, 42 Rookie Stars sequentially numbered to 1350, 27 Signed Rookie Jersey cards sequentially numbered to 2000, and three Signed Rookie Jersey Stars sequentially numbered to 500. Several rookies were issued via redemption cards which carried an expiration date of 7/20/2001. Thomas Jones was one of these players and ultimately signed a small number of cards to be mailed out. Although they are serial numbered to 2000, it is commonly believed that far fewer actually exist as live cards. Base cards feature action photography and foil highlights. SPx was packaged in 18-pack boxes with packs containing four cards and carried a suggested retail price of $6.99.

COMP.SET w/o SP's (90) 7.50 20.00
91-132 ROOKIE PRINT RUN 1350
160-162 JSY AU ROOKIE PRINT RUN 500
1 Jake Plummer .25 .60
2 David Boston .25 .60
3 Frank Sanders .25 .60
4 Chris Chandler .30 .75
5 Jamal Anderson .30 .75
6 Shawn Jefferson .25 .60
7 Qadry Ismail .25 .60
8 Tony Banks .25 .60
9 Shannon Sharpe .30 .75
10 Rob Johnson .30 .75
11 Eric Moulds .25 .60
12 Muhsin Muhammad .25 .60
13 Steve Beuerlein .30 .75
14 Cade McNown .25 .60
15 Marcus Robinson .30 .75
16 Akili Smith .25 .60
17 Corey Dillon .30 .75
18 Darnay Scott .30 .75
19 Tim Couch .30 .75
20 Kevin Johnson .25 .60
21 Errict Rhett .25 .60
22 Troy Aikman .50 1.25
23 Emmitt Smith .60 1.50
24 Joey Galloway .30 .75
25 Terrell Davis .30 .75
26 Olandis Gary .30 .75
27 Brian Griese .25 .60
28 Charlie Batch .25 .60
29 Germane Crowell .25 .60
30 James Stewart .25 .60
31 Brett Favre .75 2.00
32 Antonio Freeman .30 .75
33 Dorsey Levens .30 .75
34 Peyton Manning 1.00 2.50
35 Edgerrin James .30 .75
36 Marvin Harrison .30 .75
37 Mark Brunell .30 .75
38 Fred Taylor .25 .60
39 Jimmy Smith .30 .75
40 Keenan McCardell .30 .75
41 Elvis Grbac .25 .60

42 Tony Gonzalez .30 .75
43 Tony Martin .30 .75
44 Jay Fiedler .30 .75
45 Damon Huard .25 .60
46 Randy Moss .30 .75
47 Robert Smith .25 .60
48 Cris Carter .40 1.00
49 Daunte Culpepper .30 .75
50 Drew Bledsoe .30 .75
51 Terry Glenn .30 .75
52 Ricky Williams .30 .75
53 Jeff Blake .30 .75
54 Keith Poole .25 .60
55 Kerry Collins .25 .60
56 Amani Toomer .25 .60
57 Ike Hilliard .25 .60
58 Ray Lucas .25 .60
59 Curtis Martin .30 .75
60 Vinny Testaverde .25 .60
61 Tim Brown .40 1.00
62 Rich Gannon .30 .75
63 Tyrone Wheatley .25 .60
64 Napoleon Kaufman .30 .75
65 Duce Staley .25 .60
66 Donovan McNabb .30 .75
67 Troy Edwards .25 .60
68 Jerome Bettis .40 1.00
69 Kordell Stewart .25 .60
70 Marshall Faulk .30 .75
71 Kurt Warner .60 1.50
72 Isaac Bruce .40 1.00
73 Torry Holt .30 .75
74 Ryan Leaf .30 .75
75 Jim Harbaugh .30 .75
76 Jerry Rice 1.00 2.50
77 Terrell Owens .30 .75
78 Jeff Garcia .25 .60
79 Ricky Watters .30 .75
80 Jon Kitna .25 .60
81 Derrick Mayes .25 .60
82 Shaun King .25 .60
83 Mike Alstott .25 .60
84 Keyshawn Johnson .30 .75
85 Eddie George .30 .75
86 Steve McNair .30 .75
87 Jevon Kearse .25 .60
88 Brad Johnson .30 .75
89 Stephen Davis .25 .60
90 Michael Westbrook .25 .60
91 Anthony Lucas RC 2.50 6.00
92 Avion Black RC 2.50 6.00
93 Corey Moore RC 2.50 6.00
94 Chris Cole RC 3.00 8.00
95 Chris Hovan RC 3.00 8.00
96 Dante Hall RC 2.50 6.00
97 Darrell Jackson RC 2.50 6.00
98 Deltha O'Neal RC 2.50 6.00
99 Doug Chapman RC 2.50 6.00
S1 Peyton Manning Sample 1.50 4.00
100 Doug Johnson RC 2.50 6.00
101 Erron Kinney RC 2.50 6.00
102 Frank Moreau RC 2.50 6.00
103 Patrick Pass RC 2.50 6.00
104 Gari Scott RC 2.50 6.00
105 Giovanni Carmazzi RC 2.50 6.00
106 JaJuan Dawson RC 2.50 6.00
107 James Williams RC 2.50 6.00
108 Jarious Jackson RC 3.00 8.00
109 John Abraham RC 4.00 10.00
110 Keith Bulluck RC 3.00 8.00
111 Jonas Lewis RC 2.50 6.00
112 Mike Green RC 3.00 8.00
113 Ronney Jenkins RC 2.50 6.00
114 Michael Wiley RC 2.50 6.00
115 Mike Anderson RC 2.50 6.00
116 Mareno Philyaw RC 2.50 6.00
117 Muneer Moore RC 2.50 6.00
118 Paul Smith RC 2.50 6.00
119 Raynoch Thompson RC 2.50 6.00
120 Rob Morris RC 3.00 8.00
121 Ron Dixon RC 2.50 6.00
122 Rondell Mealey RC 2.50 6.00
123 Sebastian Janikowski RC 4.00 10.00
124 Shaun Ellis RC 3.00 8.00
125 Charles Lee RC 2.50 6.00
126 Shyrone Stith RC 2.50 6.00
127 Thomas Hamner RC 2.50 6.00
128 Tim Rattay RC 3.00 8.00
129 Todd Husak RC 2.50 8.00
130 Tom Brady RC 1000.00 2000.00
131 Trevor Gaylor RC 2.50 6.00
132 Windrell Hayes RC 2.50 6.00
133 Anthony Becht JSY AU RC 6.00 15.00
134 Brian Urlacher JSY AU RC 30.00 80.00
135 Bubba Franks JSY AU RC 6.00 15.00
136 C Pennington JSY AU RC 8.00 20.00
137 C.Redman JSY AU RC 6.00 15.00
138 Corey Simon JSY AU RC 8.00 20.00
139 Curtis Keaton JSY AU RC 6.00 15.00
139X Curtis Keaton EXCH .50 1.25
140 Danny Farmer JSY AU RC 6.00 15.00
141 D.Northcutt JSY AU RC 6.00 15.00
142 Dez White JSY AU RC 6.00 15.00
143 J.Redmond JSY AU RC 6.00 15.00
144 Jamal Lewis JSY AU RC 10.00 25.00
145 Jerry Porter JSY AU RC 10.00 25.00
146 Joe Hamilton EXCH 1.25 3.00
147 L.Coles JSY AU RC 8.00 20.00
148 R.Jay Soward JSY AU RC 6.00 15.00
149 R.Droughns JSY AU RC 6.00 15.00
150 Ron Dayne JSY AU RC 10.00 25.00
151 Ron Dugans JSY AU RC 6.00 15.00
152 S.Alexander JSY AU RC 10.00 25.00
153 Sylvester Morris JSY AU RC 6.00 15.00
154 Tee Martin JSY AU RC 6.00 15.00
155 Th.Jones JSY AU RC SP 8.00 20.00
156 Todd Pinkston JSY AU RC 6.00 15.00
157 Travis Prentice JSY AU RC 6.00 15.00
158 Travis Taylor JSY AU RC 6.00 15.00
159 Trung Canidate JSY AU RC 6.00 15.00
160 Courtney Brown JSY AU RC 12.00 30.00
161 Peter Warrick JSY AU RC 10.00 25.00
162 Plaxico Burress JSY AU RC 12.00 30.00

2000 SPx Spectrum

*VETS 1-90: 12X TO 30X BASIC CARDS
*ROOKIES 91-132: 1.2X TO 3X
*ROOKIE JSY AU 133-159: 1.2X TO 3X
*ROOKIE JSY AU 160-162: .8X TO 2X
SPECTRUM PRINT RUN 25 SER.#'d SETS
130 Tom Brady 4000.00 6000.00
134 Brian Urlacher JSY AU 125.00 350.00
146 Joe Hamilton JSY AU EXCH .75 2.00
155 Thomas Jones JSY AU 25.00 60.00

2000 SPx Highlight Heroes

Randomly inserted in packs at the rate of one in eight, this 12-card set features top NFL stars on a foil insert with foil stamping highlights.

COMPLETE SET (12) 6.00 15.00
STATED ODDS 1:8
HH1 Fred Taylor .40 1.00
HH2 Eddie George .50 1.25
HH3 Marshall Faulk .50 1.25
HH4 Shaun King .40 1.00
HH5 Cris Carter .60 1.50
HH6 Emmitt Smith 1.00 2.50
HH7 Jerry Rice 1.50 4.00
HH8 Tim Couch .50 1.25
HH9 Keyshawn Johnson .50 1.25
HH10 Troy Aikman .75 2.00
HH11 Terrell Davis .50 1.25
HH12 Ricky Williams .50 1.25

2000 SPx Powerhouse

Randomly inserted in packs at the rate of one in nine, this 10-card set features top 2000 draft picks expected to excel in the years to come.

STATED ODDS 1:9
PH1 Akili Smith .30 .75
PH2 Kevin Johnson .30 .75
PH3 Olandis Gary .40 1.00
PH4 Jeff Garcia .30 .75
PH5 Germane Crowell .30 .75
PH6 Donovan McNabb .40 1.00
PH7 Rob Johnson .40 1.00
PH8 Marcus Robinson .40 1.00
PH9 Shaun King .30 .75
PH10 Troy Edwards .30 .75

2000 SPx Prolifics

Randomly seeded in packs at the rate of one in 18, this 12-card set features full color player action shots with gold foil highlights.

COMPLETE SET (12) 10.00 25.00
STATED ODDS 1:18
P1 Stephen Davis .60 1.50
P2 Terrell Davis .75 2.00
P3 Jamal Anderson .75 2.00
P4 Jerry Rice 2.50 6.00
P5 Emmitt Smith 1.50 4.00
P6 Troy Aikman 1.25 3.00
P7 Cris Carter 1.00 2.50
P8 Brett Favre 2.00 5.00
P9 Mark Brunell .75 2.00
P10 Tim Couch .75 2.00
P11 Eddie George .75 2.00
P12 Marshall Faulk .75 2.00

2000 SPx Rookie Starscape

Randomly inserted in packs at the rate of one in 18, this 12-card set features top rookies in action on a card with a white background and foil stamping highlights.

COMPLETE SET (12) 12.50 30.00
STATED ODDS 1:18
RS1 Thomas Jones .60 1.50
RS2 Courtney Brown .60 1.50
RS3 Peter Warrick .50 1.25
RS4 Jamal Lewis .75 2.00
RS5 Sylvester Morris .50 1.25
RS6 Plaxico Burress .60 1.50
RS7 Travis Taylor .50 1.25
RS8 Chad Pennington .60 1.50
RS9 Ron Dayne .75 2.00
RS10 Shaun Alexander .75 2.00
RS11 Giovanni Carmazzi .50 1.25
RS12 Ron Dugans .50 1.25

2000 SPx Spxcitement

Randomly inserted in packs at the rate one in five, this 10-card set features top 2000 draft picks on a card with a border along the left side where the player's name is displayed and one on the right side where the team name is displayed.

COMPLETE SET (10) 3.00 8.00
STATED ODDS 1:5
XC1 Plaxico Burress .25 .60
XC2 Peter Warrick .20 .50
XC3 Travis Taylor .20 .50
XC4 Ron Dayne .30 .75
XC5 Thomas Jones .25 .60
XC6 Danny Farmer .20 .50
XC7 Bubba Franks .20 .50
XC8 Laveranues Coles .25 .60
XC9 Chad Pennington .25 .60
XC10 J.R. Redmond .20 .50

2000 SPx Spxtreme

Randomly inserted in packs at the rate of one in 12, this 18-card set focuses on each of these player's most signifigant individual career achievements.

COMPLETE SET (18) 15.00 40.00
STATED ODDS 1:12
X1 Isaac Bruce 1.00 2.50
X2 Cade McNown .60 1.50
X3 Daunte Culpepper .75 2.00
X4 Donovan McNabb .75 2.00
X5 Brett Favre 2.00 5.00
X6 Peyton Manning 2.50 6.00
X7 Edgerrin James .75 2.00
X8 Jon Kitna .60 1.50
X9 Mark Brunell .75 2.00
X10 Brad Johnson .75 2.00
X11 Jevon Kearse .60 1.50
X12 Curtis Martin .75 2.00
X13 Steve McNair .75 2.00
X14 Ricky Williams .75 2.00
X15 Stephen Davis .60 1.50
X16 Kurt Warner 1.50 4.00
X17 Marvin Harrison .75 2.00
X18 Randy Moss .75 2.00

2000 SPx Winning Materials

Randomly inserted in packs at the rate of one in 83, this 36-card set features a swatch of both a game jersey and ball.

STATED ODDS 1:83
WMBF Brett Favre 15.00 40.00
WMBG Brian Griese 5.00 12.00
WMCB Courtney Brown 6.00 15.00
WMCM Cade McNown 5.00 12.00
WMCP Chad Pennington 5.00 12.00
WMCR Chris Redman 4.00 10.00
WMDF Bubba Franks 4.00 10.00
WMDW Dez White 4.00 10.00
WMEG Eddie George 6.00 15.00
WMEJ Edgerrin James 6.00 15.00
WMJJ J.J. Stokes 6.00 15.00
WMJL Jamal Lewis 6.00 15.00
WMJP Jerry Porter 6.00 15.00
WMJR Jerry Rice 12.00 30.00
WMKJ Keyshawn Johnson 6.00 15.00
WMKW Kurt Warner 12.00 30.00
WMMC Steve McNair 6.00 15.00
WMMF Marshall Faulk 6.00 15.00
WMNE J.R. Redmond 5.00 12.00
WMPB Plaxico Burress 5.00 12.00
WMPM Peyton Manning 12.00 30.00
WMPW Peter Warrick 4.00 10.00
WMRD Ron Dayne 6.00 15.00
WMRD Reuben Droughns 4.00 10.00
WMRJ R.Jay Soward 5.00 12.00
WMRM Randy Moss 6.00 15.00
WMSA Shaun Alexander 6.00 15.00
WMSK Shaun King 5.00 12.00
WMSM Sylvester Morris 5.00 12.00
WMTC Trung Canidate 4.00 10.00
WMTD Terrell Davis 6.00 15.00
WMTH Torry Holt 6.00 15.00
WMTJ Thomas Jones 5.00 12.00
WMTM Tee Martin 4.00 10.00
WMTO Terrell Owens 6.00 15.00
WMWD Warrick Dunn 5.00 12.00

2000 SPx Winning Materials Autographs

Randomly inserted in packs, this 15-card set features a swatch of a game jersey and a game ball as well as an authentic player autograph. Each card is individually serial numbered to 225 of each. Some cards were issued via mail redemption cards that carried an expiration date of 7/20/2001.

STATED PRINT RUN 225 SER.#'d SETS
AWMCP Chad Pennington 12.00 30.00
AWMEG Eddie George 12.00 30.00
AWMEJ Edgerrin James 12.00 30.00
AWMJL Jamal Lewis 15.00 40.00
AWMKJ Keyshawn Johnson 12.00 30.00
AWMKW Kurt Warner 25.00 60.00
AWMPM Peyton Manning 60.00 150.00
AWMPW Peter Warrick 10.00 25.00
AWMRD Ron Dayne 15.00 40.00
AWMRM Randy Moss 30.00 80.00
AWMSA Shaun Alexander 15.00 40.00
AWMTC Tim Couch 12.00 30.00
AWMTD Terrell Davis 20.00 50.00
AWMTM Tee Martin 10.00 25.00
AWMTT Travis Taylor 10.00 25.00

2001 SPx

Released in late December, SPx features 90 veterans along with 66 rookies. Each rookie player has two versions of their card, one featuring platinum blue foil and the other featuring gold foil on the front. Rookie redemption cards for Bronze and Silver versions were also inserted in packs but both of those foil color versions were never actually released. Josh Heupel originally was only available in packs as an exchange card and is considered a short-print.

COMP.SET w/o SP's (90) 7.50 20.00
1 Jake Plummer .20 .50
2 David Boston .20 .50
3 Jamal Anderson .25 .60
4 Chris Chandler .25 .60
5 Tony Martin .25 .60
6 Elvis Grbac .25 .60
7 Qadry Ismail .20 .50
8 Ray Lewis .30 .75
9 Rob Johnson .25 .60
10 Shawn Bryson .20 .50
11 Eric Moulds .20 .50
12 Tim Biakabutuka .20 .50
13 Jeff Lewis .20 .50
14 Muhsin Muhammad .20 .50
15 Shane Matthews .20 .50
16 Marcus Robinson .25 .60
17 Brian Urlacher .40 1.00
18 Jon Kitna .20 .50
19 Peter Warrick .20 .50
20 Corey Dillon .20 .50
21 Tim Couch .20 .50
22 Travis Prentice .20 .50
23 Kevin Johnson .20 .50
24 Rocket Ismail .25 .60
25 Emmitt Smith .50 1.25
26 Joey Galloway .25 .60
27 Terrell Davis .25 .60
28 Brian Griese .20 .50
29 Rod Smith .25 .60
30 Ed McCaffrey .25 .60
31 Charlie Batch .20 .50
32 Germane Crowell .20 .50
33 James O. Stewart .20 .50
34 Brett Favre .60 1.50
35 Antonio Freeman .30 .75
36 Ahman Green .25 .60
37 Peyton Manning .75 2.00
38 Edgerrin James .25 .60
39 Marvin Harrison .25 .60
40 Mark Brunell .25 .60
41 Fred Taylor .20 .50
42 Jimmy Smith .25 .60
43 Tony Gonzalez .25 .60
44 Trent Green .20 .50
45 Priest Holmes .20 .50
46 Lamar Smith .25 .60
47 Jay Fiedler .25 .60
48 Oronde Gadsden .20 .50
49 Daunte Culpepper .25 .60
50 Randy Moss .25 .60
51 Cris Carter .30 .75
52 Drew Bledsoe .25 .60
53 Troy Brown .20 .50
54 Ricky Williams .25 .60
55 Joe Horn .20 .50
56 Aaron Brooks .20 .50
57 Albert Connell .20 .50
58 Kerry Collins .20 .50
59 Tiki Barber .25 .60
60 Ron Dayne .25 .60
61 Vinny Testaverde .20 .50
62 Wayne Chrebet .20 .50
63 Curtis Martin .25 .60
64 Tim Brown .30 .75
65 Jerry Rice .60 1.50
66 Rich Gannon .25 .60
67 Duce Staley .20 .50
68 Donovan McNabb .25 .60
69 Kordell Stewart .20 .50
70 Jerome Bettis .30 .75
71 Marshall Faulk .25 .60
72 Kurt Warner .50 1.25
73 Isaac Bruce .30 .75
74 Torry Holt .25 .60
75 Doug Flutie .25 .60
76 Junior Seau .25 .60
77 Jeff Garcia .20 .50
78 Garrison Hearst .25 .60
79 Terrell Owens .25 .60
80 Ricky Watters .25 .60
81 Matt Hasselbeck .20 .50
82 Brad Johnson .25 .60
83 Keyshawn Johnson .25 .60
84 Warrick Dunn .20 .50
85 Mike Alstott .20 .50
86 Kevin Dyson .20 .50
87 Eddie George .30 .75
88 Steve McNair .25 .60
89 Michael Westbrook .20 .50
90 Stephen Davis .20 .50
91B D.McAllister JSY AU/250 RC 15.00 40.00
91G D.McAllister JSY AU/250 RC 15.00 40.00
92B F.Mitchell JSY AU/250 RC 10.00 25.00
92G F.Mitchell JSY AU/250 RC 10.00 25.00
93B Koren Robinson/999 RC 2.00 5.00
93G Koren Robinson/999 RC 2.00 5.00
94B David Terrell/999 RC 2.00 5.00
94G David Terrell/999 RC 2.00 5.00
95B M.Vick JSY AU/250 RC 25.00 60.00
95G M.Vick JSY AU/250 RC 25.00 60.00
96B M.Bennett JSY AU/550 RC 8.00 20.00
96G M.Bennett JSY AU/550 RC 8.00 20.00
97B Robert Ferguson/999 RC 2.50 6.00
97G Robert Ferguson/999 RC 2.50 6.00
98B Rod Gardner/999 RC 2.00 5.00
98G Rod Gardner/999 RC 2.00 5.00
99B Travis Henry JSY AU/550 RC 8.00 20.00
99G Travis Henry JSY AU/550 RC 8.00 20.00
100B C.Johnson JSY AU/550 RC 10.00 25.00
100G C.Johnson JSY AU/550 RC 10.00 25.00
101B D.Brees JSY AU/250 RC 800.00 1200.00
101G D.Brees JSY AU/250 RC 800.00 1200.00
102B S Moss JSY AU/550 RC 10.00 25.00
102G S Moss JSY AU/550 RC 10.00 25.00
103B C Weinke JSY AU/550 RC 8.00 20.00
103G C Weinke JSY AU/550 RC 8.00 20.00
104B R Seymour JSY AU/900 RC 10.00 25.00
104G R Seymour JSY AU/900 RC 10.00 25.00
105B Reggie Wayne/999 RC 3.00 8.00
105G Reggie Wayne/999 RC 3.00 8.00
106B K.Barlow JSY AU/550 RC 8.00 20.00
106G K.Barlow JSY AU/550 RC 8.00 20.00
107B Chambers JSY AU/900 RC 6.00 15.00
107G Chambers JSY AU/900 RC 6.00 15.00
108B Todd Heap JSY AU/900 RC 12.00 30.00
108G Todd Heap JSY AU/900 RC 12.00 30.00
109B A.Thomas JSY AU/550 RC 10.00 25.00
109G A.Thomas JSY AU/550 RC 10.00 25.00
110B J.Jackson JSY AU/550 RC 6.00 15.00
110G J.Jackson JSY AU/550 RC 6.00 15.00
111B R.Johnson JSY AU/900 RC 10.00 25.00
111G R.Johnson JSY AU/900 RC 10.00 25.00
112B M.McMahon JSY AU/900 RC 8.00 20.00
112G M.McMahon JSY AU/900 RC 8.00 20.00
113B J.Heupel JSY AU/900 RC 10.00 25.00
113G J.Heupel JSY AU/900 RC 10.00 25.00
114B T.Minor JSY AU/900 RC 8.00 20.00
114G T.Minor JSY AU/900 RC 8.00 20.00
115B Quincy Morgan/999 RC 2.00 5.00
115G Quincy Morgan/999 RC 2.00 5.00
116B D.Morgan JSY AU/900 RC 8.00 20.00
116G D.Morgan JSY AU/900 RC 8.00 20.00
117B J.Palmer JSY AU/900 RC 8.00 20.00
117G J.Palmer JSY AU/900 RC 8.00 20.00
118B S.Rosenfels JSY AU/900 RC 8.00 20.00
118G S.Rosenfels JSY AU/900 RC 8.00 20.00
119B Tuiasosopo JSY AU/900 RC 8.00 20.00
119G Tuiasosopo JSY AU/900 RC 8.00 20.00
120B Damerien McCants/999 RC 2.00 5.00
120G Damerien McCants/999 RC 2.00 5.00
121B Snoop Minnis/999 RC 1.50 4.00
121G Snoop Minnis/999 RC 1.50 4.00
122B L.Tomlinson JSY/250 RC 15.00 40.00
122G L.Tomlinson JSY/250 RC 15.00 40.00
123B Quincy Carter/999 RC 2.00 5.00
123G Quincy Carter/999 RC 2.00 5.00
124B Arnold Jackson/999 RC 1.50 4.00
124G Arnold Jackson/999 RC 1.50 4.00
125B Justin McCareins/999 RC 2.00 5.00
125G Justin McCareins/999 RC 2.00 5.00
126B Eddie Berlin/999 RC 1.50 4.00
126G Eddie Berlin/999 RC 1.50 4.00
127B Quentin McCord/999 RC 2.00 5.00
127G Quentin McCord/999 RC 2.00 5.00
128B Vinny Sutherland/999 RC 1.50 4.00
128G Vinny Sutherland/999 RC 1.50 4.00
129B Willie Middlebrooks/999 RC 2.00 5.00
129G Willie Middlebrooks/999 RC 2.00 5.00
130B Dan Alexander/999 RC 2.00 5.00
130G Dan Alexander/999 RC 2.00 5.00
131B Dee Brown/999 RC 1.50 4.00
131G Dee Brown/999 RC 1.50 4.00
132B Andre Carter/999 RC 2.00 5.00
132G Andre Carter/999 RC 2.00 5.00
133B Justin Smith/999 RC 3.00 8.00
133G Justin Smith/999 RC 3.00 8.00
134B Houshmandzadeh/999 RC 2.00 5.00
134G Houshmandzadeh/999 RC 2.00 5.00
135B Andre King/999 RC 1.50 4.00
135G Andre King/999 RC 1.50 4.00
136B Nick Goings/999 RC 2.50 6.00
136G Nick Goings/999 RC 2.50 6.00
137B Scotty Anderson/999 RC 1.50 4.00
137G Scotty Anderson/999 RC 1.50 4.00
138B David Martin/999 RC 1.50 4.00
138G David Martin/999 RC 1.50 4.00
139B Derrick Blaylock/999 RC 2.00 5.00
139G Derrick Blaylock/999 RC 2.00 5.00
140B Onome Ojo/999 RC 1.50 4.00
140G Onome Ojo/999 RC 1.50 4.00
141B Jonathan Carter/999 RC 1.50 4.00
141G Jonathan Carter/999 RC 1.50 4.00
142B LaMont Jordan/999 RC 2.50 6.00
142G LaMont Jordan/999 RC 2.50 6.00
143B Dominic Rhodes/999 RC 2.00 5.00
143G Dominic Rhodes/999 RC 2.00 5.00
145B A.J. Feeley/999 RC 2.00 5.00
145G A.J. Feeley/999 RC 2.00 5.00
146B Correll Buckhalter/999 RC 1.50 4.00
146G Correll Buckhalter/999 RC 1.50 4.00
147B Steve Smith/999 RC 5.00 12.00
147G Steve Smith/999 RC 5.00 12.00
148B Dave Dickenson/999 RC 2.00 5.00
148G Dave Dickenson/999 RC 2.00 5.00
149B Cedrick Wilson/999 RC 2.00 5.00
149G Cedrick Wilson/999 RC 2.00 5.00
150B Jamie Winborn/999 RC 2.00 5.00
150G Jamie Winborn/999 RC 2.00 5.00
151B Alex Bannister/999 RC 1.50 4.00
151G Alex Bannister/999 RC 1.50 4.00
152B Heath Evans/999 RC 2.00 5.00
152G Heath Evans/999 RC 2.00 5.00
153B Josh Booty/999 RC 2.00 5.00
153G Josh Booty/999 RC 2.00 5.00
154B Adam Archuleta/999 RC 2.00 5.00
154G Adam Archuleta/999 RC 2.00 5.00
155B Francis St.Paul/999 RC 1.50 4.00
155G Francis St.Paul/999 RC 1.50 4.00
156B Andre Dyson/999 RC 1.50 4.00
156G Andre Dyson/999 RC 1.50 4.00
RM Randy Moss SAMPLE .75 2.00

2001 SPx Winning Materials

This set features some of the NFL's best on memorabilia cards featuring swatches of jerseys, pants, or footballs. Inserted at a rate of 1:18, making it a one per box insert.

WIN MATERIAL/20-750 ODDS 1:18
WMAC1 Andre Carter/750 3.00 8.00
WMAC2 Andre Carter/250 4.00 10.00
WMAS1 Akili Smith/300 3.00 8.00
WMAS2 Akili Smith/20 8.00 20.00
WMAT1 Anthony Thomas/500 4.00 10.00
WMAT2 Anthony Thomas/100 6.00 15.00
WMBE1 Michael Bennett/500 3.00 8.00
WMBE2 Michael Bennett/100 5.00 12.00
WMBF1 Brett Favre/300 10.00 25.00
WMBF2 Brett Favre/20 25.00 60.00
WMBO1 David Boston/300 3.00 8.00
WMBO2 David Boston/20 8.00 20.00
WMCG1 Charlie Garner/500 3.00 8.00
WMCG2 Charlie Garner/100 5.00 12.00
WMCH1 Chris Chambers/500 2.50 6.00
WMCH2 Chris Chambers/100 4.00 10.00
WMCW1 Chris Weinke/750 3.00 8.00
WMCW2 Chris Weinke/250 4.00 10.00
WMDB1 Drew Brees/500 30.00 80.00
WMDB2 Drew Brees/100 50.00 125.00
WMDB3 Drew Brees/250 40.00 100.00
WMDB4 Drew Brees/750 40.00 80.00
WMDF1 Doug Flutie/750 3.00 8.00
WMDF2 Doug Flutie/250 4.00 10.00
WMDT1 David Terrell/750 3.00 8.00
WMDT2 David Terrell/250 4.00 10.00
WMDU1 Deuce McAllister/750 4.00 10.00
WMDU2 Deuce McAllister/250 5.00 12.00
WMEG1 Elvis Grbac/500 3.00 8.00
WMEG2 Elvis Grbac/100 5.00 12.00
WMEJ1 Edgerrin James/300 4.00 10.00
WMEJ2 Edgerrin James/20 10.00 25.00
WMFM1 Freddie Mitchell/500 2.50 6.00
WMFM2 Freddie Mitchell/100 4.00 10.00
WMGA1 Rod Gardner/750 3.00 8.00
WMGA2 Rod Gardner/250 4.00 10.00
WMHE1 Travis Henry/300 4.00 10.00
WMHE2 Travis Henry/20 10.00 25.00
WMJF1 Jay Fiedler/750 3.00 8.00
WMJF2 Jay Fiedler/250 4.00 10.00
WMJJ1 James Jackson/300 3.00 8.00
WMJJ2 James Jackson/20 8.00 20.00
WMJP1 Jake Plummer/300 3.00 8.00
WMJP2 Jake Plummer/20 8.00 20.00
WMJR1 Jerry Rice/750 8.00 20.00
WMJR2 Jerry Rice/250 10.00 25.00
WMJS1 Junior Seau/750 3.00 8.00
WMJS2 Junior Seau/250 4.00 10.00
WMKB1 Kevan Barlow/500 3.00 8.00
WMKB2 Kevan Barlow/100 5.00 12.00
WMKR1 Koren Robinson/750 3.00 8.00
WMKR2 Koren Robinson/250 4.00 10.00
WMKW1 Kurt Warner/300 8.00 20.00
WMKW2 Kurt Warner/20 20.00 50.00
WMLT1 LaDainian Tomlinson/300 10.00 25.00
WMLT2 LaDainian Tomlinson/20 25.00 60.00
WMMA1 Mike Alstott/750 2.50 6.00
WMMA2 Mike Alstott/250 3.00 8.00
WMMB1 Mark Brunell/300 4.00 10.00
WMMB2 Mark Brunell/20 10.00 25.00
WMMF1 Marshall Faulk/300 4.00 10.00
WMMF2 Marshall Faulk/20 10.00 25.00
WMMO1 Dan Morgan/500 3.00 8.00
WMMO2 Dan Morgan/100 5.00 12.00
WMMT1 Marques Tuiasosopo/750 3.00 8.00
WMMT2 Marques Tuiasosopo/250 4.00 10.00
WMMV1 Michael Vick/750 6.00 15.00
WMMV2 Michael Vick/250 8.00 20.00
WMPA1 Jesse Palmer/500 3.00 8.00
WMPA2 Jesse Palmer/100 5.00 12.00
WMPM1 Peyton Manning/750 10.00 25.00
WMPM2 Peyton Manning/250 12.00 30.00
WMPW1 Peter Warrick/300 3.00 8.00
WMPW2 Peter Warrick/20 8.00 20.00
WMQM1 Quincy Morgan/750 3.00 8.00
WMQM2 Quincy Morgan/250 4.00 10.00
WMRD1 Ron Dayne/500 3.00 8.00
WMRD2 Ron Dayne/100 5.00 12.00
WMRF1 Robert Ferguson/750 4.00 10.00
WMRF2 Robert Ferguson/250 5.00 12.00
WMRG1 Rich Gannon/300 4.00 10.00
WMRG2 Rich Gannon/20 10.00 25.00
WMSE1 Jason Sehorn/500 3.00 8.00
WMSE2 Jason Sehorn/100 5.00 12.00
WMSM1 Santana Moss/750 4.00 10.00
WMSM2 Santana Moss/250 5.00 12.00
WMTA1 Troy Aikman/300 6.00 15.00
WMTA2 Troy Aikman/20 15.00 40.00
WMTB1 Tiki Barber/750 3.00 8.00
WMTB2 Tiki Barber/250 4.00 10.00
WMTC1 Tim Couch/750 2.50 6.00
WMTC2 Tim Couch/250 3.00 8.00
WMTJ1 Thomas Jones/500 2.50 6.00
WMTJ2 Thomas Jones/100 4.00 10.00
WMTO1 Terrell Owens/300 4.00 10.00
WMTO2 Terrell Owens/20 10.00 25.00
WMWA1 Reggie Wayne/750 5.00 12.00
WMWA2 Reggie Wayne/250 6.00 15.00

2002 SPx

Released in December 2002, this product features 90 veterans and 88 rookies. Cards 91-150 were serial #'d to 1500, cards 151-175 featured jersey swatches and autographs (if noted below) and were #'d to either 999, 650, or 250. Some cards were issued only as exchange cards with an expiration date of 11/26/2005. Boxes contained 18 packs of 4 cards.

COMP.SET w/o SP's (90) 7.50 20.00
91-150 ROOKIE PRINT RUN 1500
151-175 ROOKIE JSY PRINT RUN 250-999
1 Drew Bledsoe .25 .60
2 Peerless Price .20 .50
3 Travis Henry .20 .50
4 Ricky Williams .25 .60
5 Jay Fiedler .25 .60
6 Tom Brady 1.50 40.00
7 Troy Brown .20 .50
8 Antowain Smith .25 .60
9 Santana Moss .25 .60
10 Curtis Martin .25 .60
11 Vinny Testaverde .20 .50
12 Jamal Lewis .25 .60
13 Chris Redman .20 .50
14 Travis Taylor .20 .50
15 Corey Dillon .20 .50
16 T.J. Houshmandzadeh .20 .50
17 Peter Warrick .20 .50
18 Courtney Brown .20 .50
19 Kevin Johnson .20 .50
20 Tim Couch .20 .50
21 Hines Ward .25 .60
22 Jerome Bettis .30 .75
23 Kordell Stewart .20 .50
24 Corey Bradford .20 .50
25 Jermaine Lewis .20 .50
26 Edgerrin James .25 .60
27 Marvin Harrison .25 .60
28 Peyton Manning .75 2.00
29 Jimmy Smith .25 .60
30 Mark Brunell .25 .60
31 Fred Taylor .20 .50
32 Eddie George .25 .60
33 Steve McNair .25 .60
34 Brian Griese .20 .50
35 Shannon Sharpe .25 .60
36 Rod Smith .25 .60
37 Trent Green .20 .50
38 Johnnie Morton .25 .60
39 Priest Holmes .20 .50
40 Jerry Rice .60 1.50
41 Rich Gannon .25 .60
42 Tim Brown .30 .75
43 Drew Brees .60 1.50
44 Junior Seau .25 .60
45 LaDainian Tomlinson .30 .75
46 Emmitt Smith .50 1.25
47 Quincy Carter .20 .50
48 Rocket Ismail .25 .60
49 Amani Toomer .20 .50
50 Kerry Collins .20 .50
51 Ron Dayne .25 .60
52 Donovan McNabb .25 .60
53 Duce Staley .20 .50
54 Antonio Freeman .30 .75
55 Rod Gardner .20 .50
56 Stephen Davis .20 .50
57 Brian Urlacher .30 .75
58 Anthony Thomas .25 .60
59 Jim Miller .20 .50
60 Marty Booker .20 .50
61 Az-Zahir Hakim .20 .50
62 James Stewart .20 .50
63 Ahman Green .25 .60
64 Brett Favre .60 1.50
65 Robert Ferguson .25 .60
66 Terry Glenn .25 .60
67 Randy Moss .25 .60
68 Daunte Culpepper .25 .60
69 Michael Bennett .20 .50
70 Michael Vick .25 .60
71 Warrick Dunn .20 .50
72 Rodney Peete .25 .60
73 Muhsin Muhammad .20 .50
74 Aaron Brooks .20 .50
75 Deuce McAllister .25 .60
76 Keyshawn Johnson .25 .60
77 Michael Pittman .25 .60
78 Brad Johnson .25 .60
79 Thomas Jones .20 .50
80 David Boston .20 .50
81 Jake Plummer .20 .50
82 Terrell Owens .25 .60
83 Garrison Hearst .20 .50
84 Jeff Garcia .20 .50
85 Darrell Jackson .25 .60
86 Shaun Alexander .20 .50
87 Trent Dilfer .20 .50
88 Isaac Bruce .30 .75
89 Kurt Warner .25 .60
90 Marshall Faulk .25 .60
91 Saleem Rasheed RC 1.50 4.00
92 Jason McAddley RC 2.00 5.00
93 Brandon Doman RC 1.50 4.00
94 Mike Rumph RC 1.50 4.00
95 Wendell Bryant RC 1.50 4.00
96 Bryan Thomas RC 1.50 4.00
97 Anthony Weaver RC 1.50 4.00
98 Chester Taylor RC 2.50 6.00
99 Ed Reed RC 6.00 15.00
100 Lamar Gordon RC 2.00 5.00
101 Tellis Redmon RC 1.50 4.00
102 Ben Leber RC 1.50 4.00
103 Javin Hunter RC 1.50 4.00
104 Javon Walker RC 2.50 6.00
105 Shaun Hill RC 2.50 6.00
106 Raonall Smith RC 1.50 4.00
107 Darrell Hill RC 1.50 4.00
108 Kalimba Edwards RC 2.00 5.00
109 Robert Thomas RC 1.50 4.00
110 Craig Nall RC 2.00 5.00
111 Marques Anderson RC 2.00 5.00
112 Najeh Davenport RC 1.50 4.00
113 Jonathan Wells RC 2.00 5.00
114 Dwight Freeney RC 3.00 8.00
115 Larry Tripplett RC 1.50 4.00
116 T.J. Duckett RC 1.50 4.00
117 John Henderson RC 2.00 5.00
118 Albert Haynesworth RC 2.50 6.00
119 Tank Williams RC 2.00 5.00
120 Ryan Sims RC 2.50 6.00
121 Leonard Henry RC 1.50 4.00
122 Clinton Portis RC 2.50 6.00
123 Josh Reed RC 2.00 5.00
124 Chad Hutchinson RC 1.50 4.00
125 Deion Branch RC 2.50 6.00
126 Rocky Calmus RC 2.00 5.00
127 Donte Stallworth RC 2.50 6.00
128 Daryl Jones RC 1.50 4.00
129 Joey Harrington RC 1.50 4.00
130 Napoleon Harris RC 2.00 5.00
131 Phillip Buchanon RC 2.50 6.00
132 Patrick Ramsey RC 2.00 5.00
133 Brian Westbrook RC 3.00 8.00
134 Freddie Milons RC 1.50 4.00
135 Lito Sheppard RC 2.50 6.00
136 Michael Lewis RC 2.00 5.00
137 Jamin Elliott RC 1.50 4.00
138 Lee Mays RC 1.50 4.00
139 Verron Haynes RC 1.50 4.00
140 Jesse Chatman RC 1.50 4.00
141 Quentin Jammer RC 2.50 6.00
142 Seth Burford RC 1.50 4.00
143 Julius Peppers RC 4.00 10.00
144 William Green RC 2.00 5.00
145 DeShaun Foster RC 2.50 6.00
146 Daniel Graham RC 2.00 5.00
147 David Garrard RC 2.00 5.00
148 Reche Caldwell RC 2.00 5.00
149 Randy Fasani RC 1.50 4.00
150 J.T. O'Sullivan RC 2.00 5.00
151 Josh McCown JSY AU RC 8.00 20.00
152 Kurt Kittner JSY AU RC 5.00 12.00
153 Kahlil Hill JSY AU RC 5.00 12.00
154 Ladell Betts JSY AU RC 8.00 20.00
155 Ron Johnson JSY AU RC 6.00 15.00
156 Maurice Morris JSY AU RC 6.00 15.00
157 Andre Davis JSY AU RC 5.00 12.00
158 Antonio Bryant JSY AU RC 8.00 20.00
159 Roy Williams JSY AU RC 5.00 12.00
160 Lam Thompson JSY AU RC 6.00 15.00
161 Cliff Russell JSY AU RC 5.00 12.00
162 Woody Dantzler JSY AU RC 6.00 15.00
163 Travis Stephens JSY AU RC 5.00 12.00
164 Tony Fisher JSY AU RC 5.00 12.00
165 Eric McCoo JSY AU RC 5.00 12.00
166 Eric Crouch JSY AU RC 8.00 20.00
167 Rohan Davey JSY AU RC 8.00 20.00
168 Marquise Walker JSY AU RC 5.00 12.00
169 Jeremy Shockey JSY RC 5.00 12.00
170 Tim Carter JSY AU RC 6.00 15.00
171 Atrews Bell JSY AU RC 5.00 12.00
172 Ant Randle El JSY AU RC 6.00 15.00
173 Ricky Williams JSY AU RC 6.00 15.00
174 Mike Williams JSY AU 5.00 12.00
175 Adrian Peterson JSY AU RC 6.00 15.00
176 Jab Gaffney JSY AU/650 RC 5.00 12.00
177 Ashley Lelie JSY AU/250 RC 6.00 15.00
178 David Carr JSY AU/250 RC 6.00 15.00

2002 SPx Supreme Signatures

Inserted at a rate of 1:36, this set features authentic player signatures on a horizontal card design. Print runs on the two short-printed cards were announced by Upper Deck and listed below.

STATED ODDS 1:36
SSAG Ahman Green 8.00 20.00
SSAM Archie Manning 20.00 50.00
SSAT Anthony Thomas 6.00 15.00
SSBE Michael Bennett 5.00 12.00
SSBJ Brad Johnson 6.00 15.00
SSBO David Boston 5.00 12.00
SSCC Chris Chambers 5.00 12.00
SSCW Chris Weinke 5.00 12.00
SSDB Drew Brees 30.00 80.00
SSFM Freddie Mitchell 5.00 12.00
SSJB Jim Brown 40.00 80.00
SSJE John Elway/52* 60.00 120.00
SSJG Jeff Garcia/62* 15.00 40.00
SSJL Jamal Lewis 6.00 15.00
SSJR John Riggins 20.00 50.00
SSKJ Kevin Johnson 5.00 12.00
SSKS Kordell Stewart 5.00 12.00
SSMM Mike McMahon 5.00 12.00
SSMO Dan Morgan 5.00 12.00
SSMT Marques Tuiasosopo 5.00 12.00
SSMV Michael Vick 12.00 30.00
SSPH Priest Holmes 10.00 25.00
SSPM Peyton Manning 50.00 100.00
SSQM Quincy Morgan 5.00 12.00
SSSM Santana Moss 6.00 15.00
SSSR Sage Rosenfels 6.00 15.00
SSTC Tim Couch 5.00 12.00

2002 SPx Winning Materials

Inserted at a rate of 1:28 for veterans and 1:85 for rookies, this set features swatches of game used material. In addition, there is a gold parallel with veterans #'d/250, and rookies #'d/50. Finally, most card were also produced in an "NFL Logo" version with each card serial numbered from 1-5 copies.

VETERAN STATED ODDS 1:28
ROOKIE STATED ODDS 1:85
*GOLD VETS/250: .5X TO 1.2X BASE JSY
*GOLD VETS/250: .4X TO 1X BASE SP
*GOLD ROOKIES/50: .8X TO 2X BASE JSY
*GOLD ROOKIES/50: .6X TO 1.5X BASE SP
UNPRICED NFL LOGO PRINT RUN 1-5
WMAT Anthony Thomas 4.00 10.00
WMBF Brett Favre 10.00 25.00
WMBL Mark Brunell 4.00 10.00
WMBO David Boston 3.00 8.00
WMBR Tom Brady SP 25.00 60.00
WMCW Chris Weinke 3.00 8.00
WMDB Drew Bledsoe 4.00 10.00
WMDM Donovan McNabb 4.00 10.00
WMDT David Terrell 3.00 8.00
WMDW Drew Brees 10.00 25.00
WMEJ Edgerrin James 4.00 10.00
WMES Emmitt Smith 8.00 20.00
WMJB Jerome Bettis 5.00 12.00
WMJG Jeff Garcia 3.00 8.00
WMJR Jerry Rice 10.00 25.00
WMKC Kerry Collins 3.00 8.00
WMKW Kurt Warner SP 5.00 12.00
WMLT LaDainian Tomlinson 5.00 12.00
WMMA Mike Anderson 3.00 8.00
WMMF Marshall Faulk SP 5.00 12.00
WMMV Michael Vick 4.00 10.00
WMPM Peyton Manning 12.00 30.00
WMRAB Antonio Bryant SP 4.00 10.00
WMRAL Ashley Lelie 3.00 8.00
WMRCP Clinton Portis 4.00 10.00
WMRDC David Carr 3.00 8.00
WMRDF DeShaun Foster 5.00 12.00
WMRDS Donte Stallworth SP 4.00 10.00
WMRJG Jabar Gaffney 3.00 8.00
WMRJH Joey Harrington 3.00 8.00
WMRJM Josh McCown SP 4.00 10.00
WMRJP Julius Peppers 6.00 15.00
WMRJR Josh Reed 4.00 10.00
WMRM Randy Moss 4.00 10.00
WMRMW Marquise Walker 3.00 8.00
WMRPR Patrick Ramsey SP 3.00 8.00
WMRW Ricky Williams 4.00 10.00
WMRWG William Green 4.00 10.00
WMSM Steve McNair 4.00 10.00
WMTO Terrell Owens 4.00 10.00
WMVT Vinny Testaverde 3.00 8.00

2003 SPx

Released in October of 2003, this set consists of 218 cards, including 110 veterans and 108 rookies. Rookies 111-190 were serial numbered to 1500 and were inserted at a rate of 1:6. Rookies 191-220 feature jersey swatches and autographs and were inserted at a rate of 1:18. Each rookie jersey autograph was serial numbered to 1100 with the exceptions noted below. Please note that cards 209 and 214 were not released. Boxes contained 18 packs of 4 cards. Pack SRP was $6.99.

COMP.SET w/o SP's (110) 10.00 25.00
111-190 ROOKIE/1500 ODDS 1:6
1 Peyton Manning 1.00 2.50
2 Aaron Brooks .25 .60
3 Joey Harrington .25 .60
4 Tim Couch .25 .60
5 Jeff Garcia .25 .60
6 Jay Fiedler .25 .60
7 Chad Hutchinson .25 .60
8 Tommy Maddox .25 .60
9 Drew Brees .40 1.00
10 Trent Green .25 .60
11 Patrick Ramsey .30 .75
12 Daunte Culpepper .30 .75
13 Kurt Warner .30 .75
14 Brad Johnson .30 .75
15 Rich Gannon .30 .75
16 Jake Plummer .25 .60
17 Steve McNair .30 .75
18 Mark Brunell .30 .75
19 Drew Bledsoe .30 .75
20 Kordell Stewart .25 .60
21 Kelly Holcomb .25 .60
22 Josh McCown .30 .75
23 Matt Hasselbeck .25 .60
24 Marc Bulger .25 .60
25 Chris Redman .25 .60
26 Rodney Peete .25 .60
27 Jake Delhomme .25 .60
28 Jon Kitna .25 .60
29 Kerry Collins .25 .60
30 Quincy Carter .25 .60
31 Ricky Williams .30 .75
32 Clinton Portis .25 .60
33 Deuce McAllister .30 .75
34 Ahman Green .30 .75
35 Priest Holmes .25 .60
36 Curtis Martin .30 .75
37 Michael Bennett .25 .60
38 Eddie George .30 .75
39 Marshall Faulk .30 .75
40 Garrison Hearst .25 .60
41 Shaun Alexander .25 .60
42 Corey Dillon .25 .60
43 Jamal Lewis .30 .75
44 William Green .25 .60
45 Travis Henry .25 .60
46 Randy Moss .30 .75
47 Terrell Owens .30 .75
48 Peerless Price .25 .60
49 David Boston .25 .60
50 Eric Moulds .25 .60
51 Marvin Harrison .30 .75
52 Laveranues Coles .25 .60
53 Santana Moss .30 .75
54 Troy Brown .25 .60
55 Chris Chambers .25 .60
56 Tim Brown .40 1.00
57 Rod Smith .30 .75
58 Hines Ward .30 .75
59 Keyshawn Johnson .40 1.00
60 Isaac Bruce .40 1.00
61 Torry Holt .30 .75
62 Koren Robinson .30 .75
63 Chad Johnson .25 .60
64 Derrick Mason .25 .60
65 Antonio Bryant .25 .60
66 Kevin Johnson .25 .60
67 Todd Heap .25 .60
68 Tony Gonzalez .30 .75
69 Jeremy Shockey .25 .60
70 Brian Urlacher .40 1.00
71 Emmitt Smith/500 4.00 10.00
72 Edgerrin James/500 2.00 5.00
73 LaDainian Tomlinson/500 2.50 6.00
74 Brett Favre/500 5.00 12.00
75 Donovan McNabb/500 2.00 5.00
76 Tom Brady/500 10.00 25.00
77 Michael Vick/500 2.00 5.00
78 David Carr/500 1.50 4.00
79 Jerry Rice/500 5.00 12.00
80 Chad Pennington/500 1.50 4.00
81 Joey Harrington XCT .25 .60
82 Clinton Portis XCT .25 .60
83 Jeremy Shockey XCT .25 .60
84 David Boston XCT .25 .60
85 Marshall Faulk XCT .30 .75
86 Emmitt Smith XCT .60 1.50
87 Terrell Owens XCT .30 .75
88 Randy Moss XCT .30 .75
89 Deuce McAllister XCT .30 .75
90 Ahman Green XCT .30 .75
91 Peerless Price XCT .25 .60
92 Plaxico Burress XCT .25 .60
93 Marvin Harrison XCT .30 .75
94 Keyshawn Johnson XCT .40 1.00
95 Laveranues Coles XCT .25 .60
96 Drew Bledsoe XCT .30 .75
97 Eric Moulds XCT .25 .60
98 Chad Pennington XCT .25 .60
99 Jerry Rice XCT .75 2.00
100 David Carr XCT .25 .60
101 Michael Vick XCT .30 .75
102 Tom Brady XCT 1.50 4.00
103 Donovan McNabb XCT .30 .75
104 Brett Favre XCT .75 2.00
105 Kurt Warner XCT .30 .75
106 LaDainian Tomlinson XCT .40 1.00
107 Drew Brees XCT .40 1.00
108 Edgerrin James XCT .30 .75
109 Peyton Manning XCT 1.00 2.50
110 Ricky Williams XCT .30 .75
111 Brooks Bollinger RC 2.00 5.00
112 Gibran Hamden RC 1.50 4.00
113 Jason Johnson RC 1.50 4.00
114 Tony Romo RC 12.00 30.00
115 Juston Wood RC 1.50 4.00
116 Kirk Farmer RC 2.00 5.00
117 Kliff Kingsbury RC 2.50 6.00
118 Jason Gesser RC 2.00 5.00
119 Brad Banks RC 2.00 5.00
120 Rob Adamson RC 1.50 4.00
121 Ken Dorsey RC 2.00 5.00
122 Curt Anes RC 1.50 4.00
123 George Wrighster RC 1.50 4.00
124 Brett Engemann RC 1.50 4.00
125 Aaron Walker RC 2.00 5.00
126 Nate Hybl RC 2.00 5.00
127 Chris Simms RC 1.50 4.00
128 Marquel Blackwell RC 1.50 4.00
129 Domanick Davis RC 2.00 5.00
130 Quentin Griffin RC 2.00 5.00
131 B.J. Askew RC 2.00 5.00
132 Earnest Graham RC 2.50 6.00
133 Sultan McCullough RC 1.50 4.00
134 Dahrran Diedrick RC 1.50 4.00
135 Cecil Sapp RC 1.50 4.00
136 LaBrandon Toefield RC 1.50 4.00
137 ReShard Lee RC 2.50 6.00
138 Dwone Hicks RC 1.50 4.00
139 Brock Forsey RC 2.00 5.00
140 Bethel Johnson RC 1.50 4.00
141 Andrew Pinnock RC 2.00 5.00
142 Ahmaad Galloway RC 2.00 5.00
143 J.T. Wall RC 1.50 4.00
144 Tom Lopienski RC 1.50 4.00
145 Justin Griffith RC 2.00 5.00
146 Lee Suggs RC 1.50 4.00
147 Nick Maddox RC 1.50 4.00
148 Jeremi Johnson RC 1.50 4.00
149 Doug Gabriel RC 2.00 5.00
150 Bobby Wade RC 2.00 5.00
151 Justin Gage RC 2.00 5.00

152 Arnaz Battle RC 2.50 6.00
153 Brandon Lloyd RC 2.50 6.00
154 Talman Gardner RC 1.50 4.00
155 Kareem Kelly RC 1.50 4.00
156 Billy McMullen RC 1.50 4.00
157 Antwone Savage RC 1.50 4.00
158 J.R. Tolver RC 2.00 5.00
159 Kassim Osgood RC 2.50 6.00
160 Shaun McDonald RC 2.00 5.00
161 Sam Aiken RC 2.00 5.00
162 Adrian Madise RC 1.50 4.00
163 Charles Rogers RC 2.00 5.00
164 David Kircus RC 2.00 5.00
165 Zuriel Smith RC 1.50 4.00
166 LaTarence Dunbar RC 1.50 4.00
167 Willie Ponder RC 1.50 4.00
168 David Tyree RC 2.00 5.00
169 Kevin Walter RC 4.00 10.00
170 Keenan Howry RC 1.50 4.00
171 Walter Young RC 1.50 4.00
172 DeAndrew Rubin RC 1.50 4.00
173 Carl Ford RC 1.50 4.00
174 Taco Wallace RC 1.50 4.00
175 Travis Anglin RC 1.50 4.00
176 Ryan Hoag RC 1.50 4.00
177 Ronald Bellamy RC 2.00 5.00
178 Terrence Edwards RC 1.50 4.00
179 Jerel Myers RC 1.50 4.00
180 Mike Bush RC 1.50 4.00
181 Dan Curley RC 1.50 4.00
182 Carl Morris RC 1.50 4.00
183 Reggie Newhouse RC 1.50 4.00
184 Troy Polamalu RC 15.00 40.00
185 Cecil Moore RC 1.50 4.00
186 Bennie Joppru RC 1.50 4.00
187 Donald Lee RC 2.00 5.00
188 Jason Witten RC 8.00 20.00
189 Mike Seidman RC 1.50 4.00
190 Vishante Shiancoe RC 2.50 6.00
191 Anquan Boldin JSY AU RC 10.00 25.00
192 Kyle Boller JSY AU/450 RC 8.00 20.00
193 Chris Brown JSY AU RC 6.00 15.00
194 Nate Burleson JSY AU RC 8.00 20.00
195 Tyro Calico JSY AU/450 RC 8.00 20.00
196 Dallas Clark JSY AU RC 10.00 25.00
197 Kevin Curtis JSY AU RC 6.00 15.00
198 Kliff Kingsbury JSY AU RC 10.00 25.00
199 Justin Fargas JSY AU RC 10.00 25.00
200 Grossman JSY AU/450 RC 10.00 25.00
201 Taylor Jacobs JSY AU RC 6.00 15.00
202 An Johnson JSY AU/250 RC 90.00 150.00
203 Malae MacKenzie JSY AU RC 6.00 15.00
204 Bryant Johnson JSY AU RC 10.00 25.00
205 Larry Johnson JSY AU RC 8.00 20.00
206 T Johnson JSY AU/450 RC 10.00 25.00
207 Leftwich JSY AU/250 RC 10.00 25.00
208 McGahee JSY AU/450 RC 10.00 25.00
210 C.Palmer JSY AU/250 RC 20.00 50.00
211 Artose Pinner JSY AU RC 6.00 15.00
212 Dave Ragone JSY AU RC 6.00 15.00
213 Terrell Suggs JSY AU RC 15.00 40.00
215 Onterio Smith JSY AU RC 6.00 15.00
216 Musa Smith JSY AU RC 6.00 15.00
217 Brian St.Pierre JSY AU RC 6.00 15.00
218 Marcus Trufant JSY AU RC 8.00 20.00
219 Seneca Wallace JSY AU RC 8.00 20.00
220 Kell Washington JSY AU RC 6.00 15.00

2003 SPx Spectrum

*VETS 1-70/81-110: 8X TO 20X
*VETS 71-80: 1.2X TO 3X
*ROOKIES 111-190: 1.2X TO 3X
1-190 STATED PRINT RUN 50
*ROOK.JSY AU: 1.2X TO 3X JSY AU/1100
*ROOK.JSY AU: 1X TO 2.5X JSY AU/450
*ROOK.JSY AU: .8X TO 2X JSY AU/250
191-218 JSY AU PRINT RUN 25
114 Tony Romo 100.00 200.00
184 Troy Polamalu 50.00 120.00
200 Rex Grossman JSY AU 30.00 80.00
208 Willis McGahee JSY AU 50.00 120.00

2003 SPx Supreme Signatures

Randomly inserted into packs, this set features authentic on-card player autographs. In addition, a Spectrum parallel version exists, with each card serial numbered to 50. Please note that Michael Vick, Onterrio Smith, Clinton Portis and Quentin Griffin were issued in packs as exchange cards, with an expiration date of 10/8/2006.
SSAB Aaron Brooks 6.00 15.00
SSAH Az-Zahir Hakim 6.00 15.00
SSAM Archie Manning 8.00 20.00
SSBB Brad Banks 8.00 20.00
SSBJ Bryant Johnson 10.00 25.00
SSBL Byron Leftwich 8.00 20.00
SSBR Brad Johnson 8.00 20.00
SSBS Brian St.Pierre 6.00 15.00
SSCH Chad Pennington 6.00 15.00
SSCP Carson Palmer 15.00 40.00
SSCS Chris Simms 6.00 15.00
SSDC David Carr SP 10.00 25.00
SSDR Dave Ragone 6.00 15.00
SSEG Earnest Graham 10.00 25.00
SSIB Isaac Bruce 8.00 20.00
SSJG Jeff Garcia 6.00 15.00
SSJK Jim Kelly SP 30.00 60.00
SSKB Kyle Boller 6.00 15.00
SSKB Kevan Barlow 6.00 15.00
SSKK Kareem Kelly 6.00 15.00
SSKL Kliff Kingsbury 10.00 25.00
SSKW Kelley Washington 6.00 15.00
SSLS Lee Suggs 6.00 15.00
SSMB Mark Brunell 8.00 20.00
SSMH Matt Hasselbeck SP 25.00 60.00
SSMI Michael Bennett SP 6.00 15.00
SSMV Michael Vick 12.00 30.00
SSOS Onterrio Smith 6.00 15.00
SSPM Peyton Manning 60.00 100.00
SSPO Clinton Portis 12.00 30.00
SSQG Quentin Griffin 8.00 20.00
SSRG Rod Gardner 6.00 15.00
SSRS Rod Smith SP 8.00 20.00
SSTB Tom Brady SP 125.00 250.00
SSTC Tim Couch 6.00 15.00
SSTG Trent Green 6.00 15.00
SSTH Travis Henry 6.00 15.00
SSTJ Taylor Jacobs 6.00 15.00
SSTS Terrell Suggs 12.00 30.00

2003 SPx Supreme Signatures Spectrum

*SPECTRUM/50: .6X TO 1.5X BASIC AUTO
PRINT RUN 50 SERIAL #'d SETS
SSJK Jim Kelly 30.00 60.00
SSMH Matt Hasselbeck 20.00 50.00
SSTB Tom Brady 125.00 250.00

2003 SPx Winning Materials

Randomly inserted into packs, this set features game worn jersey swatches. Each card also features the NFL logo on a large rubber square. Each card was serial numbered to 350 unless noted below. A version featuring the US Flag on the rubber square also exists, with each card serial numbered to 25.
STATED PRINT RUN 220-350
*TEAM LOGO/147-250: .5X TO 1.2X BASE JSY
*TEAM LOGO/50-99: .6X TO 1.5X BASE JSY
TEAM LOGO PRINT RUN 50-250
*TL SPECTRUM/50: .6X TO 1.5X BASE JSY
TEAM LOGO SPECTRUM PRINT RUN 50
*USA FLAGS/25: 1X TO 2.5X BASE JSY
USA FLAG PRINT RUN 25
AB Aaron Brooks 2.00 5.00
AJ Andre Johnson 6.00 12.00
AN Anquan Boldin 3.00 8.00
AP Artose Pinner 2.00 5.00
BJ Bryant Johnson 3.00 8.00
BL Byron Leftwich 2.50 6.00
BR Tim Brown 3.00 8.00
CC Chris Chambers/300 2.00 5.00
CD Corey Dillon/266 2.00 5.00
CJ Chad Johnson/220 2.00 5.00
CM Curtis Martin 2.50 6.00
CP Chad Pennington 2.00 5.00
DC David Carr 2.00 5.00
DM Donovan McNabb 2.50 6.00
EJ Edgerrin James 2.50 6.00
EM Eric Moulds/264 2.00 5.00
ES Emmitt Smith 5.00 12.00
JH Joey Harrington 2.00 5.00
JP Julius Peppers 3.00 8.00
JR Jerry Rice/300 6.00 15.00
KC Kevin Curtis 2.00 5.00
KJ Keyshawn Johnson/268 3.00 8.00
KW Kurt Warner 2.50 6.00
LJ Larry Johnson 2.50 6.00
MB Mark Brunell 2.50 6.00
MF Marshall Faulk 2.50 6.00
MH Marvin Harrison/278 2.50 6.00
MT Marcus Trufant 2.50 6.00
PM Peyton Manning 8.00 20.00
PO Clinton Portis 2.00 5.00
PR Priest Holmes 2.00 5.00
RS Rod Smith/300 2.50 6.00
RW Ricky Williams 2.50 6.00
SC Carson Palmer 4.00 10.00
SH Jeremy Shockey 2.00 5.00
SW Seneca Wallace 2.50 6.00
TB Tom Brady 20.00 50.00
TJ Taylor Jacobs 2.00 5.00
TN Terence Newman 3.00 8.00
WG William Green 2.00 5.00
WM Willis McGahee 2.50 6.00

2003 SPx Winning Materials Patches

Randomly inserted into packs, this set features game worn jersey patches. Each card is serial numbered to 75 unless noted below.
STATED PRINT RUN 15-75
BF Brett Favre 50.00 120.00
BJ Bryant Johnson 15.00 40.00
CP Chad Pennington 25.00 60.00
DC David Carr 10.00 25.00
DM Donovan McNabb 25.00 60.00
JR Jerry Rice 40.00 100.00
LT LaDainian Tomlinson 20.00 50.00
MV Michael Vick 25.00 60.00
PM Peyton Manning 30.00 80.00
PO Clinton Portis 25.00 60.00
RM Randy Moss 25.00 60.00
RW Ricky Williams 12.00 30.00
SM Santana Moss/47 12.00 30.00
SW Seneca Wallace 12.00 30.00
TC Tim Couch 10.00 25.00

2003 SPx Winning Materials Patches Autographs

Randomly inserted into packs, this set features game worn patch swatches and authentic player autographs. Each card is serial numbered to various quantities. Please note that Michael Vick and Terrell Owens were issued in packs as exchange cards with an expiration date of 10/8/2006.
STATED PRINT RUN 25-50
BL Byron Leftwich/25 25.00 60.00
CP Chad Pennington/50 30.00 80.00
DB Drew Brees/50 50.00 100.00
JG Jeff Garcia/50 25.00 60.00
JR Jerry Rice/25 125.00 250.00
LT LaDainian Tomlinson/50 30.00 80.00
MV0 Michael Vick/25 60.00 100.00
PM Peyton Manning/50 100.00 175.00
RM Randy Moss/50 50.00 100.00
SA Shaun Alexander/50 30.00 80.00
SC Carson Palmer/25 100.00 200.00
TC Tim Couch/50 20.00 50.00
TO Terrell Owens/50 30.00 80.00

2004 SPx

SPx initially released in early-November 2004. The base set consists of 221-cards including 65-rookies serial numbered to 1650, 25-rookies serial numbered to 799, and 30-rookie jersey autographs numbered between 375 and 1499. Finally, the Larry Fitzgerald JSY AU card #219 was serial numbered to just 100-copies. Hobby boxes contained 18-packs of 5-cards and carried an S.R.P. of $6.99 per pack. One basic parallel set and four Player Printing Plate 1/1 parallels can be found seeded in packs. The balance of the inserts consists of jersey memorabilia cards and autographed cards.
COMP.SET w/o SP's (100) 15.00 30.00
101-165 RC PRINT RUN 1650 SER.#'d SETS
166-190 RC PRINT RUN 799 SER.#'d SETS
191-221 JSY AU RC #'d TO 1499 UNLESS NOTED
UNPRICED PRINT.PLATE #'d TO 1
1 Anquan Boldin .25 .60
2 Marcel Shipp .25 .60
3 Josh McCown .30 .75
4 Peerless Price .25 .60
5 Michael Vick .30 .75
6 T.J. Duckett .25 .60
7 Kyle Boller .25 .60
8 Todd Heap .25 .60
9 Jamal Lewis .30 .75
10 Travis Henry .25 .60
11 Drew Bledsoe .30 .75
12 Eric Moulds .25 .60
13 Jake Delhomme .25 .60
14 Steve Smith .40 1.00
15 Stephen Davis .25 .60
16 Brian Urlacher .40 1.00
17 Rex Grossman .25 .60
18 Thomas Jones .25 .60
19 Chad Johnson .25 .60
20 Carson Palmer .30 .75
21 Rudi Johnson .25 .60
22 William Green .25 .60
23 Jeff Garcia .25 .60
24 Andre Davis .25 .60
25 Roy Williams S .25 .60
26 Eddie George .30 .75
27 Keyshawn Johnson .30 .75
28 Jake Plummer .25 .60
29 Ashley Lelie .25 .60
30 Quentin Griffin .25 .60
31 Charles Rogers .25 .60
32 Olandis Gary .25 .60
33 Joey Harrington .25 .60
34 Brett Favre .75 2.00
35 Javon Walker .25 .60
36 Ahman Green .30 .75
37 Andre Johnson .30 .75
38 Domanick Davis .25 .60
39 David Carr .25 .60
40 Peyton Manning 1.00 2.50
41 Edgerrin James .30 .75
42 Marvin Harrison .30 .75
43 Byron Leftwich .25 .60
44 Jimmy Smith .30 .75
45 Fred Taylor .25 .60
46 Trent Green .25 .60
47 Priest Holmes .25 .60
48 Dante Hall .25 .60
49 Tony Gonzalez .30 .75
50 A.J. Feeley .25 .60
51 Marty Booker .25 .60
52 Chris Chambers .25 .60
53 Zach Thomas .40 1.00
54 Randy Moss .30 .75
55 Daunte Culpepper .30 .75
56 Onterrio Smith .25 .60
57 Troy Brown .25 .60
58 Corey Dillon .25 .60
59 Tom Brady 1.50 4.00
60 Deuce McAllister .30 .75
61 Joe Horn .25 .60
62 Aaron Brooks .25 .60
63 Jeremy Shockey .25 .60
64 Kurt Warner .30 .75
65 Tiki Barber .30 .75
66 Chad Pennington .25 .60
67 Curtis Martin .30 .75
68 Santana Moss .30 .75
69 Rich Gannon .30 .75
70 Jerry Rice .75 2.00
71 Warren Sapp .30 .75
72 Donovan McNabb .30 .75
73 Terrell Owens .30 .75
74 Jevon Kearse .25 .60
75 Brian Westbrook .25 .60
76 Hines Ward .30 .75
77 Duce Staley .25 .60
78 Tommy Maddox .25 .60
79 LaDainian Tomlinson .40 1.00
80 Drew Brees .40 1.00
81 Tim Rattay .25 .60
82 Kevan Barlow .25 .60
83 Brandon Lloyd .30 .75
84 Shaun Alexander .25 .60
85 Matt Hasselbeck .25 .60
86 Koren Robinson .25 .60
87 Marc Bulger .25 .60
88 Marshall Faulk .30 .75
89 Torry Holt .30 .75
90 Isaac Bruce .40 1.00
91 Brad Johnson .30 .75
92 Keenan McCardell .25 .60
93 Derrick Brooks .25 .60
94 Steve McNair .30 .75
95 Chris Brown .25 .60
96 Derrick Mason .25 .60
97 Clinton Portis .25 .60
98 Mark Brunell .30 .75
99 Laveranues Coles .25 .60
100 LaVar Arrington .25 .60
101 B.J. Johnson RC 1.25 3.00
102 Craig Krenzel RC 1.25 3.00
103 Will Smith RC 1.50 4.00
104 Jamaar Taylor RC 1.25 3.00
105 Tommie Harris RC 1.50 4.00
106 Shawn Andrews RC 1.50 4.00
107 Kendrick Starling RC 1.25 3.00
108 Jeris McIntyre RC 1.25 3.00
109 Jason Babin RC 2.00 5.00
110 Marcus Tubbs RC 1.25 3.00
111 Triandos Luke RC 1.25 3.00
112 Karlos Dansby RC 1.50 4.00
113 Vernon Carey RC 1.25 3.00
114 Ryan Krause RC 1.25 3.00
115 Daryl Smith RC 1.25 3.00
116 Ricardo Colclough RC 1.25 3.00
117 Michael Boulware RC 2.00 5.00
118 Chris Cooley RC 1.50 4.00
119 Tank Johnson RC 1.25 3.00
120 Marquise Hill RC 1.25 3.00
121 Teddy Lehman RC 1.25 3.00
122 Antwan Odom RC 1.25 3.00
123 Sean Jones RC 1.25 3.00
124 Junior Siavii RC 1.25 3.00
125 Joey Thomas RC 1.25 3.00
126 Shawntae Spencer RC 1.25 3.00
127 Dontarrious Thomas RC 1.50 4.00
128 Travis LaBoy RC 1.50 4.00
129 Justin Jenkins RC 1.25 3.00
130 Dwan Edwards RC 1.25 3.00
131 Derrick Strait RC 1.25 3.00
132 Matt Ware RC 2.00 5.00
133 Jared Lorenzen RC 1.50 4.00
134 Demorrio Williams RC 2.00 5.00
135 Bob Sanders RC 2.50 6.00
136 Justin Smiley RC 1.50 4.00
137 Casey Bramlet RC 1.25 3.00
138 Jake Grove RC 1.25 3.00
139 Thomas Tapeh RC 1.50 4.00
140 Igor Olshansky RC 1.50 4.00
141 Stuart Schweigert RC 1.50 4.00
142 Cody Pickett RC 1.25 3.00
143 Derrick Ward RC 2.00 5.00
144 Gilbert Gardner RC 1.25 3.00
145 D.J. Hackett RC 1.25 3.00
146 Marquis Cooper RC 1.25 3.00
147 Courtney Watson RC 1.25 3.00
148 Jim Sorgi RC 1.50 4.00
149 Caleb Miller RC 1.25 3.00
150 Casey Clausen RC 1.50 4.00
151 Jammal Lord RC 1.25 3.00
152 Sloan Thomas RC 1.50 4.00
153 Keyaron Fox RC 1.50 4.00
154 Adimchinobe Echemandu RC 1.50 4.00
155 Ryan Dinwiddie RC 1.25 3.00
156 Kris Wilson RC 1.50 4.00
157 D.J. Williams RC 2.00 5.00
158 Tim Euhus RC 1.25 3.00
159 Bradlee Van Pelt RC 1.50 4.00
160 Keiwan Ratliff RC 1.25 3.00
161 Darnell Dockett RC 2.00 5.00
162 Troy Fleming RC 1.25 3.00
163 Tramon Douglas RC 1.25 3.00
164 Jeremy LeSueur RC 1.25 3.00
165 Matt Mauck RC 1.25 3.00
166 Sean Taylor RC 15.00 40.00
167 B.J. Symons RC 2.50 6.00
168 Quincy Wilson RC 2.50 6.00
169 Ernest Wilford RC 3.00 8.00
170 Jerricho Cotchery RC 3.00 8.00
171 Michael Turner RC 2.50 6.00
172 Samie Parker RC 2.50 6.00
173 Andy Hall RC 2.50 6.00
174 Keith Smith RC 2.50 6.00
175 Josh Harris RC 2.50 6.00
176 Maurice Mann RC 2.50 6.00
177 Jonathan Vilma RC 3.00 8.00
178 Jeff Smoker RC 3.00 8.00
179 Ben Hartsock RC 2.50 6.00
180 Chris Gamble RC 2.50 6.00
181 Derrick Hamilton RC 2.50 6.00
182 John Navarre RC 2.50 6.00
183 P.K. Sam RC 2.50 6.00
184 Kenechi Udeze RC 3.00 8.00
185 Mewelde Moore RC 3.00 8.00
186 Carlos Francis RC 2.50 6.00
187 Dunta Robinson RC 2.50 6.00
188 Johnnie Morant RC 2.50 6.00
189 Ahmad Carroll RC 2.50 6.00
190 Vince Wilfork RC 4.00 10.00
191 Tatum Bell JSY AU RC 5.00 12.00
192 Cedric Cobbs JSY AU RC 5.00 12.00
193 Darius Watts JSY AU RC 5.00 12.00
194 Jul.Jones JSY AU/375 RC 8.00 20.00
195 Robert Gallery JSY AU RC 6.00 15.00
196 DeAngelo Hall JSY AU RC 8.00 20.00
197 Ben Watson JSY AU RC 6.00 15.00
198 Ben Troupe JSY AU RC 5.00 12.00
199 Matt Schaub JSY AU RC 5.00 12.00
200 Michael Jenkins JSY AU RC 5.00 12.00
201 Luke McCown JSY AU RC 5.00 12.00
202 Devery Henderson JSY AU RC 5.00 12.00
203 Bernard Berrian JSY AU RC 5.00 12.00
204 Keary Colbert JSY AU RC 5.00 12.00
205 Devard Darling JSY AU RC 5.00 12.00
206 Lee Evans JSY AU RC 8.00 20.00
207 Greg Jones JSY AU RC 5.00 12.00
208 Mich.Clayton JSY AU RC 6.00 15.00
209 Re.Williams JSY AU RC 5.00 12.00
210 C.Perry JSY AU/799 RC 5.00 12.00
211 Rash.Woods JSY AU RC 5.00 12.00
212 J.P. Losman JSY AU RC 5.00 12.00
213 Kevin Jones JSY AU RC 6.00 15.00
214 K.Winslow JSY AU/375 RC 8.00 20.00
215 S.Jackson JSY AU/375 RC 12.00 30.00
216 Hamilton JSY AU RC 5.00 12.00
217 Ro.Will.JSY AU/375 RC 8.00 20.00
218 P.Rivers JSY AU/375 RC 75.00 150.00
219 Fitzgerald JSY AU/100 RC 100.00 200.00
220 Roethlis.JSY AU/375 RC 100.00 200.00
221 Manning JSY AU/375 RC 75.00 150.00

2004 SPx Spectrum Gold

*VETS 1-100: 8X TO 20X BASIC CARDS
*ROOKIES 101-165: 1.2X TO 3X
*ROOKIES 166-190: 1X TO 2.5X
*ROOK.AU: 1.5X TO 4X AU/799-1499
*ROOKIE AU: 1X TO 2.5X AU/375
STATED PRINT RUN 25 SER.#'d SETS
199 Matt Schaub JSY AU 30.00 80.00
218 Philip Rivers JSY AU 150.00 300.00
219 Larry Fitzgerald JSY AU 125.00 250.00
220 Roethlisberger JSY AU 250.00 500.00
221 Eli Manning JSY AU 350.00 600.00

2004 SPx Rookie Swatch Supremacy

STATED ODDS 1:18
SWRBB Bernard Berrian 2.00 5.00
SWRBR Ben Roethlisberger 15.00 40.00
SWRBT Ben Troupe 2.00 5.00
SWRBW Ben Watson 2.50 6.00
SWRCC Cedric Cobbs 2.00 5.00
SWRCP Chris Perry 2.00 5.00
SWRDD Devard Darling 2.00 5.00
SWRDE Devery Henderson 2.00 5.00
SWRDH DeAngelo Hall 3.00 8.00
SWRDW Darius Watts 2.00 5.00
SWREM Eli Manning 15.00 40.00
SWRGJ Greg Jones 2.00 5.00
SWRHA Derrick Hamilton 2.00 5.00
SWRJJ Julius Jones 2.00 5.00
SWRJP J.P. Losman 2.00 5.00
SWRKC Keary Colbert 2.00 5.00
SWRKJ Kevin Jones 2.50 6.00
SWRKW Kellen Winslow Jr. 2.00 5.00
SWRLE Lee Evans 3.00 8.00
SWRLF Larry Fitzgerald 8.00 20.00
SWRLM Luke McCown 2.00 5.00
SWRMC Michael Clayton 2.50 6.00
SWRMJ Michael Jenkins 2.00 5.00
SWRPR Philip Rivers 10.00 25.00
SWRRA Rashaun Woods 2.00 5.00
SWRRG Robert Gallery 2.50 6.00
SWRRO Roy Williams WR 2.00 5.00
SWRRW Reggie Williams 2.00 5.00
SWRSJ Steven Jackson 3.00 8.00
SWRTB Tatum Bell 2.00 5.00

2004 SPx Rookie Winning Materials

STATED ODDS 1:126
WMRBB Bernard Berrian 2.50 6.00
WMRBR Ben Roethlisberger 15.00 40.00
WMRBT Ben Troupe 2.50 6.00
WMRBW Ben Watson 3.00 8.00
WMRCC Cedric Cobbs 2.50 6.00
WMRCP Chris Perry 2.50 6.00
WMRDD Devard Darling 2.50 6.00
WMRDE Devery Henderson 2.50 6.00
WMRDH DeAngelo Hall 4.00 10.00
WMRDW Darius Watts 2.50 6.00
WMREM Eli Manning 15.00 40.00
WMRGJ Greg Jones 2.50 6.00
WMRHA Derrick Hamilton 2.50 6.00
WMRJJ Julius Jones 2.50 6.00
WMRJP J.P. Losman 2.50 6.00
WMRKC Keary Colbert 2.50 6.00
WMRKJ Kevin Jones 3.00 8.00
WMRKW Kellen Winslow Jr. 2.50 6.00
WMRLE Lee Evans 4.00 10.00
WMRLF Larry Fitzgerald 10.00 25.00
WMRLM Luke McCown 2.50 6.00
WMRMC Michael Clayton 3.00 8.00
WMRMJ Michael Jenkins 2.50 6.00
WMRPR Philip Rivers 8.00 20.00
WMRRA Rashaun Woods 2.50 6.00
WMRRG Robert Gallery 3.00 8.00
WMRRO Roy Williams WR 2.50 6.00
WMRRW Reggie Williams 2.50 6.00
WMRSJ Steven Jackson 4.00 10.00
WMRTB Tatum Bell 2.50 6.00

2004 SPx Super Scripts Autographs

STATED ODDS 1:54
SSAG Ahman Green 6.00 15.00
SSAR Andy Reid CO 6.00 15.00
SSBC Brandon Chillar 6.00 15.00
SSBF Brett Favre SP 100.00 200.00
SSBH Ben Hartsock 5.00 12.00
SSBL Brandon Lloyd 6.00 15.00
SSBW Brian Westbrook 5.00 12.00
SSBY Byron Leftwich 5.00 12.00
SSCC Chris Chambers 5.00 12.00
SSCF Clarence Farmer 5.00 12.00
SSCJ Chad Johnson 5.00 12.00
SSCP Chad Pennington 5.00 12.00
SSDB Drew Bledsoe 6.00 15.00
SSDC David Carr 5.00 12.00
SSDD Domanick Davis 5.00 12.00
SSDE Deuce McAllister 6.00 15.00
SSDH Dante Hall 5.00 12.00
SSDM Derrick Mason 5.00 12.00
SSDO Donovan McNabb SP 20.00 50.00
SSEL Antwaan Randle El 5.00 12.00
SSHE Todd Heap 5.00 12.00
SSJF Justin Fargas 6.00 15.00
SSJG Jon Gruden CO 10.00 25.00
SSJH Joe Horn 5.00 12.00
SSJJ Jimmy Johnson CO 10.00 25.00
SSJO Joey Galloway 6.00 15.00
SSJP Jesse Palmer 5.00 12.00
SSKB Kyle Boller 5.00 12.00
SSKD Ken Dorsey 5.00 12.00
SSKW Kelley Washington 5.00 12.00
SSLT LaDainian Tomlinson 20.00 50.00
SSMB Mark Brunell 6.00 15.00
SSMV Michael Vick SP 20.00 50.00
SSPM Peyton Manning 40.00 80.00
SSRG Rex Grossman 5.00 12.00
SSRJ Rudi Johnson 5.00 12.00
SSRW Roy Williams S 5.00 12.00
SSSM Steve McNair 15.00 30.00
SSTB Tom Brady SP 125.00 200.00
SSTG Tony Gonzalez 12.00 30.00
SSTH Travis Henry 5.00 12.00
SSWM Willis McGahee 5.00 12.00
SSZT Zach Thomas 10.00 25.00

2004 SPx Super Scripts Triple Autographs

STATED PRINT RUN 10-25
SERIAL #'d TO 10 NOT PRICED
GBL Grssmn/Boll/Left/25 30.00 80.00
GSL Gallery/Stblr/Long/25 50.00 120.00
JCR J.Jhnsn/Crdn/Reid/25 40.00 100.00
JJJ Jcksn/J.Jnes/K.Jnes/25 30.00 80.00
MBM McNr/C.Brwn/Msn/25 75.00 150.00
RRM River/Roeth/E.Mann/25 350.00 600.00
SEA B.Snd/Elwy/Aik/25 200.00 400.00
TMG Tomlin/McAllis/A.Green/25 50.00 120.00
TST Theis/Stabler/Tarken/25 100.00 200.00
WWE Roy/Reg/Evns/25 ERR 50.00 120.00

2004 SPx Swatch Supremacy

STATED ODDS 1:18
SWAG Ahman Green 2.50 6.00
SWAR Antwaan Randle El 2.00 5.00
SWBL Byron Leftwich 2.00 5.00
SWBW Brian Westbrook 2.00 5.00
SWCB Chris Brown 2.00 5.00
SWCC Chris Chambers 2.00 5.00
SWCJ Chad Johnson 2.00 5.00
SWCP Chad Pennington 2.00 5.00
SWDC Daunte Culpepper 2.50 6.00
SWDD Domanick Davis 2.00 5.00
SWDE Derrick Mason 2.00 5.00
SWDH Dante Hall 2.00 5.00
SWDM Deuce McAllister 2.50 6.00
SWDO Donovan McNabb 2.50 6.00
SWHE Todd Heap 2.00 5.00
SWJG Joey Galloway 2.50 6.00
SWJH Joe Horn 2.00 5.00
SWJW Javon Walker 2.00 5.00
SWKB Kyle Boller 2.00 5.00
SWLT LaDainian Tomlinson 3.00 8.00
SWMB Mark Brunell 2.50 6.00
SWMV Michael Vick 2.50 6.00
SWPM Peyton Manning 8.00 20.00
SWRG Rex Grossman 2.00 5.00
SWRJ Rudi Johnson 2.00 5.00
SWRW Roy Williams S 2.00 5.00
SWTB Tom Brady 12.00 30.00
SWTG Tony Gonzalez 2.50 6.00
SWTH Travis Henry 2.00 5.00
SWZT Zach Thomas 2.50 6.00

2004 SPx Swatch Supremacy Autographs

STATED PRINT RUN 100 SER.#'d SETS
SWAAG Ahman Green 10.00 25.00
SWAAR Antwaan Randle El 8.00 20.00
SWABL Byron Leftwich 8.00 20.00
SWABW Brian Westbrook 8.00 20.00
SWACB Chris Brown 8.00 20.00
SWACC Chris Chambers 8.00 20.00
SWACJ Chad Johnson 8.00 20.00
SWACP Chad Pennington 8.00 20.00
SWADC Daunte Culpepper 10.00 25.00
SWADD Domanick Davis 8.00 20.00
SWADE Derrick Mason 8.00 20.00
SWADH Dante Hall 8.00 20.00
SWADM Deuce McAllister 10.00 25.00
SWADO Donovan McNabb 15.00 40.00
SWAHE Todd Heap 8.00 20.00
SWAJG Joey Galloway 10.00 25.00
SWAJH Joe Horn 8.00 20.00
SWAKB Kyle Boller 8.00 20.00
SWALT LaDainian Tomlinson 25.00 50.00
SWAMB Mark Brunell 10.00 25.00
SWAMV Michael Vick 25.00 50.00
SWAPM Peyton Manning 60.00 120.00
SWARG Rex Grossman 8.00 20.00
SWARJ Rudi Johnson 8.00 20.00
SWARW Roy Williams S 8.00 20.00
SWATB Tom Brady 125.00 250.00
SWATG Tony Gonzalez 10.00 25.00
SWATH Travis Henry 8.00 20.00
SWAZT Zach Thomas 10.00 25.00

2004 SPx Winning Materials

STATED ODDS 1:72
WMAC L.Arrington/L.Coles 3.00 8.00
WMBD T.Brady/C.Dillon 20.00 50.00
WMBM A.Brooks/D.McAllister 4.00 10.00
WMBP M.Brunell/C.Portis 4.00 10.00
WMCJ D.Carr/A.Johnson 4.00 10.00
WMCM D.Culpepper/R.Moss 4.00 10.00
WMDF S.Davis/D.Foster 4.00 10.00
WMDT D.Bledsoe/T.Henry 4.00 10.00
WMFG B.Favre/A.Green 10.00 25.00
WMFH M.Faulk/T.Holt 4.00 10.00
WMFM B.Favre/D.McNabb 10.00 25.00
WMGG T.Green/T.Gonzalez 4.00 10.00
WMHA M.Hasselbeck/S.Alexander 3.00 8.00
WMHR J.Harrington/C.Rogers 3.00 8.00
WMHW P.Holmes/Ri.Williams 4.00 10.00
WMMJ P.Manning/E.James 12.00 30.00
WMMM C.Martin/S.Moss 4.00 10.00
WMMO D.McNabb/T.Owens 4.00 10.00
WMMR R.Moss/J.Rice 10.00 25.00
WMMV S.McNair/M.Vick 4.00 10.00
WMPG J.Plummer/Q.Griffin 3.00 8.00
WMPJ C.Palmer/Ru.Johnson 4.00 10.00
WMPL C.Pennington/B.Leftwich 3.00 8.00
WMPS P.Manning/S.McNair 12.00 30.00
WMRG J.Rice/R.Gannon 10.00 25.00
WMSK M.Strahan/J.Kearse 4.00 10.00
WMSU J.Seau/B.Urlacher 5.00 12.00
WMSW J.Shockey/K.Warner 4.00 10.00
WMTH L.Tomlinson/P.Holmes 5.00 12.00
WMVB M.Vick/T.Brady 20.00 50.00

2004 SPx Winning Materials Autographs

STATED PRINT RUN 25 SER.#'d SETS
BF T.Brady/B.Favre 300.00 500.00
BH Fitzgerald/Re.Williams 75.00 150.00
JJ K.Jones/S.Jackson 25.00 60.00
MG D.McAllister/A.Green 30.00 60.00
MM P.Manning/S.McNair 100.00 200.00
PE P.Manning/E.Manning 150.00 300.00
PL Pennington/Leftwich 20.00 50.00
RR P.Rivers/Roethlisberger 200.00 350.00
SA R.Staubach/T.Aikman 100.00 200.00
TB J.Theismann/M.Brunell 30.00 80.00
TC Tarkenton/Culpepper 30.00 80.00
TM Tomlinson/D.McAllister 25.00 60.00
VM M.Vick/D.McNabb 60.00 120.00
WJ Ro.Williams WR/K.Jones 20.00 50.00
WW Winslow Jr./Winslow Sr. 30.00 80.00

2005 SPx

This 232-card set was released in September, 2005. The set was issued in four-card packs with an $6.99 SRP which came 18 packs to a box. Cards numbered 1-100 feature veteran players in team alphabetical order while cards numbered 101-223 are all 2005 rookies. Cards numbered 191-200 have two different players pictured (both regular rookie and rookies with both signatures and player-worn jersey swatches). Cards numbered 101-170 was issued to a stated print run of 1199 serial numbered sets. Cards numbered 171-190 and the non-signed no jersey swatch 191-200 cards were issued to a stated print run of 499 serial numbered sets. The signed jersey cards 191-200 and all the cards 201-223 were issued to a stated print run of 1275 serial numbered sets.
COMP.SET w/o SP's (100) 15.00 30.00
101-170 RC PRINT RUN 1199 SER.#'d SETS
171 200 RC PRINT RUN 400 SER.#'d SETS
JSY AU RC PRINT RUN 150-1275
1 Larry Fitzgerald .40 1.00
2 Anquan Boldin .25 .60
3 Josh McCown .30 .75
4 Michael Vick .30 .75
5 Alge Crumpler .30 .75
6 Peerless Price .25 .60
7 Ray Lewis .40 1.00
8 Jamal Lewis .30 .75
9 Kyle Boller .25 .60
10 J.P. Losman .25 .60
11 Willis McGahee .25 .60
12 Eric Moulds .25 .60
13 Jake Delhomme .25 .60
14 DeShaun Foster .30 .75
15 Steve Smith .40 1.00
16 Brian Urlacher .40 1.00
17 Rex Grossman .25 .60
18 Muhsin Muhammad .25 .60
19 Carson Palmer .30 .75
20 Rudi Johnson .25 .60
21 Chad Johnson .25 .60
22 Julius Jones .25 .60
23 Keyshawn Johnson .30 .75
24 Roy Williams S .25 .60
25 Tatum Bell .25 .60
26 Jake Plummer .25 .60
27 Ashley Lelie .25 .60
28 Roy Williams WR .25 .60
29 Kevin Jones .25 .60
30 Joey Harrington .25 .60
31 Brett Favre .75 2.00
32 Ahman Green .30 .75
33 Javon Walker .25 .60
34 David Carr .25 .60
35 Andre Johnson .30 .75
36 Domanick Davis .25 .60
37 Peyton Manning 1.00 2.50
38 Reggie Wayne .30 .75
39 Edgerrin James .30 .75
40 Marvin Harrison .30 .75
41 Byron Leftwich .25 .60
42 Fred Taylor .25 .60
43 Jimmy Smith .30 .75
44 Priest Holmes .25 .60
45 Larry Johnson .25 .60
46 Trent Green .25 .60
47 A.J. Feeley .25 .60
48 Chris Chambers .25 .60
49 Randy McMichael .25 .60
50 Daunte Culpepper .30 .75
51 Nate Burleson .25 .60
52 Michael Bennett .25 .60
53 Tom Brady 1.50 4.00
54 Corey Dillon .25 .60
55 Deion Branch .25 .60
56 David Givens .25 .60
57 Aaron Brooks .25 .60
58 Deuce McAllister .30 .75
59 Joe Horn .25 .60
60 Eli Manning .60 1.50
61 Jeremy Shockey .25 .60
62 Tiki Barber .30 .75
63 Chad Pennington .25 .60
64 Curtis Martin .30 .75
65 Laveranues Coles .25 .60
66 Kerry Collins .25 .60
67 Jerry Porter .25 .60
68 Randy Moss .30 .75
69 Donovan McNabb .30 .75
70 Terrell Owens .30 .75
71 Brian Dawkins .40 1.00
72 Brian Westbrook .25 .60
73 Ben Roethlisberger .60 1.50
74 Jerome Bettis .40 1.00
75 Hines Ward .30 .75
76 Duce Staley .25 .60
77 Drew Brees .40 1.00
78 LaDainian Tomlinson .40 1.00
79 Antonio Gates .40 1.00
80 Eric Parker .25 .60
81 Tim Rattay .25 .60
82 Kevan Barlow .25 .60
83 Eric Johnson .25 .60
84 Shaun Alexander .25 .60
85 Darrell Jackson .25 .60
86 Matt Hasselbeck .25 .60
87 Marc Bulger .25 .60
88 Steven Jackson .25 .60
89 Marshall Faulk .30 .75
90 Torry Holt .30 .75
91 Michael Pittman .25 .60
92 Brian Griese .25 .60
93 Michael Clayton .25 .60
94 Steve McNair .30 .75
95 Drew Bennett .30 .75
96 Billy Volek .25 .60
97 Chris Brown .25 .60
98 Clinton Portis .25 .60
99 Patrick Ramsey .30 .75
100 Santana Moss .30 .75
101 Matt Jones RC 1.25 3.00
102 Jonathan Babineaux RC 1.25 3.00
103 Darrent Williams RC 2.00 5.00
104 Timmy Chang RC 1.25 3.00
105 Kelvin Hayden RC 1.50 4.00
106 Paris Warren RC 1.50 4.00
107 Stanley Wilson RC 1.50 4.00
108 Walter Reyes RC 1.25 3.00
109 Roydell Williams RC 1.50 4.00
110 Chase Lyman RC 1.25 3.00
111 Anthony Davis RC 1.25 3.00
112 Rasheed Marshall RC 1.50 4.00
113 Jerome Carter RC 1.25 3.00
114 Mike Nugent RC 1.50 4.00
115 Brodney Pool RC 1.50 4.00
116 Sean Considine RC 1.25 3.00
117 Chris Rix RC 1.50 4.00
118 Donte Nicholson RC 1.25 3.00
119 Dustin Fox RC 1.50 4.00
120 Oshiomogho Atogwe RC 1.50 4.00
121 Vincent Fuller RC 1.50 4.00
122 Josh Bullocks RC 1.50 4.00
123 Ronald Bartell RC 1.50 4.00
124 Brock Berlin RC 1.25 3.00
125 Fabian Washington RC 1.25 3.00
126 Domonique Foxworth RC 1.50 4.00
127 Bryant McFadden RC 1.50 4.00
128 Marlin Jackson RC 1.25 3.00
129 Eric Green RC 1.25 3.00
130 Justin Miller RC 1.25 3.00
131 Lofa Tatupu RC 1.50 4.00
132 Justin Tuck RC 1.50 4.00
133 Kurt Campbell RC 1.25 3.00
134 Darryl Blackstock RC 1.25 3.00
135 Kevin Burnett RC 1.50 4.00
136 Marviel Underwood RC 1.50 4.00
137 Kirk Morrison RC 2.00 5.00
138 Alfred Fincher RC 1.50 4.00
139 Lance Mitchell RC 1.50 4.00
140 Barrett Ruud RC 1.50 4.00
141 David Pollack RC 1.25 3.00
142 Bill Swancutt RC 1.25 3.00
143 DeMarcus Ware RC 4.00 10.00
144 Steve Savoy RC 1.25 3.00
145 Matt Roth RC 1.25 3.00
146 Shaun Cody RC 1.50 4.00
147 Dan Cody RC 1.25 3.00
148 Jordan Beck RC 1.50 4.00
149 Kevin Everett RC 2.00 5.00
150 Anttaj Hawthorne RC 1.25 3.00
151 Mike Patterson RC 1.25 3.00
152 Jerome Collins RC 1.50 4.00
153 Dante Ridgeway RC 1.25 3.00
164 Bryan Randall RC 1.50 4.00
155 Marcus Maxwell RC 1.25 3.00
156 Airese Currie RC 1.25 3.00
157 Chad Owens RC 1.25 3.00
158 Brandon Jacobs RC 1.50 4.00
159 Manuel White RC 1.50 4.00
160 Ellis Hobbs RC 2.00 5.00
161 Lionel Gates RC 1.25 3.00
162 Ryan Fitzpatrick RC 2.00 5.00
163 Noah Herron RC 1.25 3.00
164 Kay-Jay Harris RC 1.25 3.00
165 T.A. McLendon RC 1.25 3.00
166 Kerry Rhodes RC 1.50 4.00
167 Nick Collins RC 2.00 5.00
168 Eric Moore RC 1.25 3.00
169 Harry Williams RC 1.50 4.00
170 Luis Castillo RC 1.50 4.00
171 James Kilian RC 2.00 5.00
172 Matt Cassel RC 2.00 5.00
173 Alvin Pearman RC 2.00 5.00
174 Dan Orlovsky RC 2.00 5.00
175 Damien Nash RC 2.50 6.00
176 Jason White RC 3.00 8.00
177 Craig Bragg RC 2.00 5.00
178 Craphonso Thorpe RC 2.00 5.00
179 Derrick Johnson RC 2.50 6.00
180 Derek Anderson RC 2.50 6.00
181 Darren Sproles RC 3.00 8.00
182 Cedric Houston RC 3.00 8.00
183 Jerome Mathis RC 3.00 8.00
184 Larry Brackins RC 2.00 5.00
185 Fred Gibson RC 2.00 5.00
186 J.R. Russell RC 2.00 5.00
187 Alex Smith TE RC 2.00 5.00
188 Deandra Cobb RC 2.00 5.00
189 Tab Perry RC 2.00 5.00
190 Travis Johnson RC 2.00 5.00
191A Marion Barber RC 2.00 5.00
191B Andrew Walter JSY AU RC 5.00 12.00
192A Erasmus James RC 2.00 5.00
192B V.Morency JSY AU RC 5.00 12.00
193A Marcus Spears RC 2.00 5.00
193B Antrel Rolle JSY AU RC 8.00 20.00
194A Channing Crowder RC 2.50 6.00
194B Adam Jones JSY AU RC 5.00 12.00
195A Odell Thurman RC 3.00 8.00
195B M.Clarett JSY AU/250 10.00 25.00
196A Shawne Merriman RC 3.00 8.00
196B Mark Bradley JSY AU RC 5.00 12.00
197A Adrian McPherson RC 2.00 5.00
197B Eric Shelton JSY AU RC 5.00 12.00
198A Chris Henry RC 2.50 6.00
198B Kyle Orton JSY AU RC 6.00 15.00
199A Thomas Davis RC 2.00 5.00
199B Ryan Moats JSY AU RC 5.00 12.00
200A Corey Webster RC 2.50 6.00
200B Frank Gore JSY AU RC 12.00 30.00
201 J.J. Arrington JSY AU RC 6.00 15.00
202 M.Williams JSY AU/250 12.00 30.00
203 V.Jackson JSY AU RC 8.00 20.00
204 Stefan LeFors JSY AU RC 5.00 12.00
206 T.Murphy JSY AU RC 5.00 12.00
207 Courtney Roby JSY AU RC 5.00 12.00
208 Carlos Rogers JSY AU RC 8.00 20.00
209 Charlie Frye JSY AU RC 4.00 10.00
210 Mark Clayton JSY AU RC 5.00 12.00
211 Roddy White JSY AU RC 8.00 20.00
212 Jason Campbell JSY AU RC 5.00 12.00
213 Roscoe Parrish JSY AU RC 5.00 12.00
214 Reggie Brown JSY AU RC 5.00 12.00
215 Heath Miller JSY AU RC 10.00 25.00
216 Williamson JSY AU/250 RC 10.00 25.00
217 Ciatrick Fason JSY AU RC 5.00 12.00
218 C.Benson JSY AU/150 RC 12.00 30.00
219 B.Edwards JSY AU/250 RC 8.00 20.00
220 Ro.Brown JSY AU/250 RC 10.00 25.00
221 C.Williams JSY AU/250 RC 8.00 20.00
222 A.Smith QB JSY AU/250 RC 40.00 100.00
223 A.Rodgers JSY AU/250 RC 400.00 700.00

2005 SPx Spectrum

*VETS/25: 6X TO 15X BASIC CARDS
*101-170 ROOK/25: 2X TO 5X BASE/1199
*171-200 ROOK/25: 1.2X TO 3X BASE/499
*ROOK.JSY AU/25: 1X TO 2.5X JSY AU/250
*ROOK.JSY AU/25: 1.2X TO 3X JSY AU/499
*ROOK.JSY AU/25: 1.5X TO 4X JSY AU/1275
222 Alex Smith QB JSY AU 200.00 400.00
223 Aaron Rodgers JSY AU 1500.00 2000.00

2005 SPx Holoview

COMPLETE SET (29) 40.00 100.00
STATED ODDS 1:126
UNPRICED DIE CUT PRINT RUN 10 SETS
1 Adam Jones 1.50 4.00
2 Antrel Rolle 2.50 6.00
3 Mark Bradley 1.50 4.00
4 Alex Smith QB 6.00 15.00
5 Andrew Walter 1.50 4.00
6 Braylon Edwards 1.50 4.00
7 J.J. Arrington 2.00 5.00
8 Charlie Frye 1.50 4.00
9 Carlos Rogers 2.50 6.00
10 Ciatrick Fason 1.50 4.00
11 Maurice Clarett 1.50 4.00
12 Cadillac Williams 1.50 4.00
13 Matt Jones 1.50 4.00
14 Courtney Roby 1.50 4.00
15 Frank Gore 3.00 8.00
16 Kyle Orton 1.50 4.00
17 Eric Shelton 1.50 4.00
18 Stefan LeFors 1.50 4.00
19 Ryan Moats 1.50 4.00
20 Jason Campbell 1.50 4.00
21 Mark Clayton 1.50 4.00
22 Ronnie Brown 2.00 5.00
23 Reggie Brown 1.50 4.00
24 Roscoe Parrish 1.50 4.00
25 Roddy White 2.50 6.00
26 Terrence Murphy 1.50 4.00
27 Vincent Jackson 2.50 6.00
28 Troy Williamson 1.50 4.00
29 Vernand Morency 1.50 4.00

2005 SPx Rookie Swatch Supremacy

STATED ODDS 1:18
RSAJ Adam Jones 2.00 5.00
RSAN Antrel Rolle 3.00 8.00
RSAR Aaron Rodgers 20.00 50.00
RSAS Alex Smith QB 8.00 20.00
RSAW Andrew Walter 2.00 5.00
RSBE Braylon Edwards 2.00 5.00
RSCA Carlos Rogers 3.00 8.00
RSCF Charlie Frye 2.00 5.00
RSCI Ciatrick Fason 2.00 5.00
RSCR Courtney Roby 2.00 5.00
RSCW Cadillac Williams 2.00 5.00
RSES Eric Shelton 2.00 5.00
RSFG Frank Gore 6.00 15.00
RSJA J.J. Arrington 2.50 6.00
RSJC Jason Campbell 2.00 5.00
RSKO Kyle Orton 2.00 5.00
RSMB Mark Bradley 2.00 5.00
RSMC Mark Clayton 2.00 5.00
RSMO Maurice Clarett 2.00 5.00
RSRB Ronnie Brown 2.50 6.00
RSRE Reggie Brown 2.00 5.00
RSRM Ryan Moats 2.00 5.00
RSRP Roscoe Parrish 2.00 5.00
RSRW Roddy White 3.00 8.00
RSTW Troy Williamson 2.00 5.00
RSVJ Vincent Jackson 3.00 8.00
RSVM Vernand Morency 2.00 5.00

2005 SPx Rookie Winning Materials

STATED ODDS 1:126
RWMAJ Adam Jones 2.50 6.00
RWMAN Antrel Rolle SP 4.00 10.00
RWMAR Aaron Rodgers SP 40.00 80.00
RWMAS Alex Smith QB 10.00 25.00
RWMAW Andrew Walter 2.50 6.00
RWMBE Braylon Edwards 2.50 6.00
RWMCA Carlos Rogers 4.00 10.00

RWMCF Charlie Frye 2.50 6.00
RWMCI Ciatrick Fason 2.50 6.00
RWMCR Courtney Roby 2.50 6.00
RWMCW Cadillac Williams 2.50 6.00
RWMES Eric Shelton 2.50 6.00
RWMFG Frank Gore 5.00 12.00
RWMJA J.J. Arrington 3.00 8.00
RWMJC Jason Campbell 2.50 6.00
RWMKO Kyle Orton 2.50 6.00
RWMMB Mark Bradley 2.50 6.00
RWMMC Mark Clayton 2.50 6.00
RWMMO Maurice Clarett 2.50 6.00
RWMRB Ronnie Brown 3.00 8.00
RWMRE Reggie Brown 2.50 6.00
RWMRM Ryan Moats 2.50 6.00
RWMRP Roscoe Parrish 2.50 6.00
RWMRW Roddy White 4.00 10.00
RWMTW Troy Williamson 2.50 6.00
RWMVJ Vincent Jackson 4.00 10.00
RWMVM Vernand Morency 2.50 6.00

2005 SPx Rookie Winning Materials Autographs

STATED PRINT RUN 25 SER.#'d SETS
AJ Adam Jones 15.00 40.00
AN Antrel Rolle 25.00 60.00
AR Aaron Rodgers 350.00 500.00
AS Alex Smith QB 60.00 150.00
AW Andrew Walter 15.00 40.00
BE Braylon Edwards 30.00 80.00
CA Carlos Rogers 25.00 60.00
CB Cedric Benson 15.00 40.00
CF Charlie Frye 15.00 40.00
CI Ciatrick Fason 15.00 40.00
CR Courtney Roby 15.00 40.00
CW Cadillac Williams 15.00 40.00
ES Eric Shelton 15.00 40.00
FG Frank Gore 75.00 150.00
HM Heath Miller 30.00 80.00
JA J.J. Arrington 20.00 50.00
JC Jason Campbell 15.00 40.00
KO Kyle Orton 15.00 40.00
MB Mark Bradley 15.00 40.00
MC Mark Clayton 15.00 40.00
MO Maurice Clarett 15.00 40.00
MW Mike Williams 20.00 50.00
RB Ronnie Brown 40.00 100.00
RE Reggie Brown 15.00 40.00
RM Ryan Moats 15.00 40.00
RP Roscoe Parrish 15.00 40.00
RW Roddy White 25.00 60.00
TW Troy Williamson 15.00 40.00
VJ Vincent Jackson 25.00 60.00
VM Vernand Morency 15.00 40.00

2005 SPx Super Scripts Autographs

STATED ODDS 1:126
SSAB Aaron Brooks 5.00 12.00
SSAG Antonio Gates 12.00 30.00
SSAN Anquan Boldin 5.00 12.00
SSBF Brett Favre SP 125.00 200.00
SSCB Chris Brown 5.00 12.00
SSCE Chris Berman SP 60.00 100.00
SSDD Domanick Davis 5.00 12.00
SSDP Dan Patrick SP
SSDT Drew Bennett 7.50 20.00
SSEJ Edgerrin James 12.00 30.00
SSEM Eli Manning 50.00 100.00
SSFT Fred Taylor 5.00 12.00
SSJJ Julius Jones SP 60.00 100.00
SSKC Keary Colbert 5.00 12.00
SSKM Kenny Mayne SP
SSLA LaMont Jordan 12.00 30.00
SSLC Linda Cohn SP 15.00 40.00
SSLE Lee Evans 5.00 12.00
SSLJ Larry Johnson 12.00 30.00
SSMB Marc Bulger 7.50 20.00
SSMC Michael Clayton 7.50 20.00
SSMV Michael Vick SP 40.00 80.00
SSNB Nate Burleson 7.50 20.00
SSPM Peyton Manning 50.00 100.00
SSSJ Steven Jackson
SSSS Stuart Scott SP 25.00 50.00
SSTG Trent Green 7.50 20.00
SSTI Tiki Barber 12.00 30.00

2005 SPx Super Scripts Quad Autographs

STATED PRINT RUN 25 SER.#'d SETS
BJD Bldin/L.Jhn/D.Dvs/C.Brwn 25.00 60.00
BWB Brsn/Cadil/Ro.Brw/J.Arr 40.00 100.00
EWW Edw/M.Wil/Wmsn/Whi 25.00 60.00
MMA Marin/Mntana/Aik/Stau 350.00 600.00
RFM Roeth/Favre/Eli/P.Mnn 450.00 700.00
RSF Rdgr/A.Smth/Fry/Camp 250.00 400.00
SSA B.Sndrs/Syrs/Allen/Dors 350.00 500.00
VJT Vick/C.Jhn/Tmlin/Jrdn 30.00 80.00
VMB Vick/McNab/Roeth/Left 75.00 150.00
WBW Wyn/Bldn/Ro.Wl/Clytn 40.00 100.00

2005 SPx Swatch Supremacy

STATED ODDS 1:18
SWAB Anquan Boldin 2.00 5.00
SWAG Antonio Gates 3.00 8.00
SWAH Ahman Green 2.50 6.00
SWAM Archie Manning SP 5.00 12.00
SWBD Brian Dawkins 3.00 8.00
SWBF Brett Favre 6.00 15.00
SWBL Byron Leftwich 2.00 5.00
SWBR Ben Roethlisberger SP 6.00 15.00
SWCB Chris Brown 2.00 5.00
SWCJ Chad Johnson 2.00 5.00
SWCP Carson Palmer 2.50 6.00
SWDB Drew Bledsoe 2.50 6.00
SWDD Domanick Davis 2.00 5.00
SWDE Deuce McAllister 2.50 6.00
SWDM Donovan McNabb 2.50 6.00
SWDW Drew Bennett 2.50 6.00
SWEM Eli Manning 5.00 12.00
SWFT Fred Taylor 2.00 5.00
SWJH Joe Horn 2.00 5.00
SWJJ Julius Jones 2.00 5.00
SWJL J.P. Losman 2.00 5.00
SWKC Keary Colbert 2.00 5.00
SWKS Ken Stabler 6.00 15.00
SWLA LaMont Jordan 2.50 6.00
SWLE Lee Evans 2.50 6.00
SWLJ Larry Johnson 2.00 5.00
SWLT LaDainian Tomlinson 3.00 8.00
SWMB Marc Bulger 2.00 5.00
SWMC Michael Clayton 2.00 5.00
SWMM Muhsin Muhammad 2.00 5.00
SWMO Merlin Olsen SP 5.00 12.00
SWMV Michael Vick SP 3.00 8.00
SWNB Nate Burleson 2.00 5.00
SWPM Peyton Manning 8.00 20.00
SWRE Reggie Wayne 2.50 6.00
SWRJ Rudi Johnson 2.00 5.00
SWRS Roger Staubach SP 10.00 25.00
SWRW Roy Williams WR 2.00 5.00
SWSJ Steven Jackson 2.00 5.00
SWTG Trent Green 2.00 5.00
SWTI Tiki Barber 2.50 6.00

2005 SPx Swatch Supremacy Autographs

STATED PRINT RUN 50 SER.#'d SETS
AB Anquan Boldin 12.50 30.00
AG Antonio Gates 20.00 50.00
AH Ahman Green 20.00 50.00
AM Archie Manning 12.00 30.00
BD Brian Dawkins 30.00 60.00
BF Brett Favre 125.00 250.00
BL Byron Leftwich 20.00 50.00
BR Ben Roethlisberger 60.00 120.00
CB Chris Brown 12.50 30.00
CJ Chad Johnson 20.00 50.00
CP Carson Palmer 40.00 80.00
DB Drew Bledsoe 30.00 60.00
DD Domanick Davis 12.50 30.00
DE Deuce McAllister 20.00 50.00
DW Drew Bennett 15.00 40.00
EM Eli Manning 75.00 135.00
FT Fred Taylor 12.50 30.00
JH Joe Horn 12.50 30.00
JJ Julius Jones 20.00 50.00
JL J.P. Losman 15.00 40.00
KC Keary Colbert 12.50 30.00
KS Ken Stabler 40.00 80.00
LA LaMont Jordan 20.00 50.00
LE Lee Evans 12.50 30.00
LJ Larry Johnson 20.00 50.00
LT LaDainian Tomlinson 50.00 100.00
MB Marc Bulger 15.00 40.00
MC Michael Clayton 15.00 40.00
MM Muhsin Muhammad 12.50 30.00
MO Merlin Olsen 20.00 50.00
MV Michael Vick 20.00 50.00
NB Nate Burleson 15.00 40.00
PM Peyton Manning 60.00 120.00
RE Reggie Wayne 20.00 50.00
RJ Rudi Johnson 12.50 30.00
RS Roger Staubach 60.00 120.00
RW Roy Williams WR 15.00 40.00
TG Trent Green 15.00 40.00
TI Tiki Barber 25.00 50.00

2005 SPx Winning Materials

*PATCHES: 1X TO 2.5X BASIC JERSEYS
AL A.Green/L.Tomlinson 4.00 10.00
BA D.Bennett/A.Boldin 3.00 8.00
BB C.Brown/D.Bennett 3.00 8.00
BJ C.Brown/L.Jordan 3.00 8.00
CC M.Clayton/K.Colbert 2.50 6.00
DH D.McAllister/J.Horn 3.00 8.00
DM B.Dawkins/D.McNabb 4.00 10.00
ET J.Elway/J.Theismann 6.00 15.00
EW L.Evans/Ro.Will.WR 3.00 8.00
FM B.Favre/P.Manning 10.00 25.00
FR B.Favre/B.Roethlisberger 8.00 20.00
GT A.Gates/L.Tomlinson 4.00 10.00
JB S.Jackson/M.Bulger 2.50 6.00
JD J.Jones/D.Bledsoe 3.00 8.00
JJ R.Johnson/C.Johnson 2.50 6.00
LE J.P.Losman/L.Evans 3.00 8.00
LT B.Leftwich/F.Taylor 2.50 6.00
MJ D.McAllister/L.Jordan 3.00 8.00
MM D.McNabb/P.Manning 10.00 25.00
MT E.Manning/T.Barber 6.00 15.00
PL C.Palmer/B.Leftwich 3.00 8.00
RM Roethlisberger/E.Manning 6.00 15.00
SS G.Sayers/M.Singletary 4.00 10.00
TS Theismann/Staubach SP 5.00 12.00
VG M.Vick/T.Green 3.00 8.00
VT M.Vick/L.Tomlinson 4.00 10.00
WB R.Wayne/A.Boldin 3.00 8.00
WM R.Wayne/P.Manning 10.00 25.00

2005 SPx Winning Materials Autographs

STATED PRINT RUN 25 SER.#'d SETS
AL A.Green/L.Tomlinson 25.00 60.00
BA D.Bennett/A.Boldin 25.00 60.00
BB C.Brown/D.Bennett 25.00 60.00
BJ C.Brown/L.Jordan 25.00 60.00
CC M.Clayton/K.Colbert 25.00 60.00
DH D.McAllister/J.Horn 25.00 60.00
ET J.Elway/J.Theismann 75.00 150.00
EW L.Evans/Ro.Will.WR 25.00 60.00
FM B.Favre/P.Manning 250.00 400.00
FR Favre/Roethlisberger 250.00 400.00
GB T.Green/M.Bulger 20.00 50.00
GT A.Gates/L.Tomlinson 60.00 120.00
JB S.Jackson/M.Bulger 20.00 50.00
JD J.Jones/D.Bledsoe 40.00 100.00
JG L.Johnson/T.Green 20.00 50.00
JJ R.Johnson/C.Johnson 20.00 50.00
LE J.P.Losman/L.Evans 25.00 60.00
LT B.Leftwich/F.Taylor 20.00 50.00
MJ D.McAllister/L.Jordan 25.00 60.00
MM D.McNabb/P.Manning 100.00 200.00
MT E.Manning/T.Barber 125.00 200.00
PL C.Palmer/B.Leftwich 25.00 60.00
RM Roethlisberger/E.Manning 150.00 300.00
SS G.Sayers/M.Singletary 90.00 150.00
TS J.Theismann/R.Staubach 60.00 120.00
VG M.Vick/T.Green 30.00 80.00
VT M.Vick/L.Tomlinson 50.00 120.00
WB R.Wayne/A.Boldin 25.00 60.00
WM R.Wayne/P.Manning 100.00 175.00

2006 SPx

This 213-card set was released in September, 2006. The set was issued in four-card packs with an $6.99 SRP which came 18 packs to a box. Cards numbered 1-90 feature veteran players in team alphabetical order while cards 91-213 feature 2006 rookies. Withiin the rookie subset, cards numbered 181-213 feature both player-worn swatches and signatures. Cards numbered 91-180 were issued to a stated print run of 1299 serial numbered cards, while cards 181-187 were issued to a stated print run of 399 serial numbered copies and cards numbered 188-213 were issued to a stated print run of 1650 serial numbered sets.

COMP.SET w/o RC's (90) 12.50 30.00
91-180 ROOKIE PRINT RUN 1299
181-187 RC JSY AU PRINT RUN 399
188-213 RC JSY AU PRINT RUN 1650
1 Edgerrin James .30 .75
2 Kurt Warner .30 .75
3 Larry Fitzgerald .30 .75
4 Michael Vick .30 .75
5 Warrick Dunn .25 .60
6 Michael Jenkins .25 .60
7 Jamal Lewis .30 .75
8 Kyle Boller .25 .60
9 Derrick Mason .25 .60
10 Willis McGahee .25 .60
11 Lee Evans .30 .75
12 Jake Delhomme .25 .60
13 Steve Smith .40 1.00
14 DeShaun Foster .30 .75
15 Rex Grossman .25 .60
16 Muhsin Muhammad .25 .60
17 Thomas Jones .25 .60
18 Carson Palmer .30 .75
19 Chad Johnson .25 .60
20 Rudi Johnson .25 .60
21 Charlie Frye .30 .75
22 Reuben Droughns .30 .75
23 Braylon Edwards .25 .60
24 Drew Bledsoe .30 .75
25 Terrell Owens .30 .75
26 Julius Jones .25 .60
27 Jake Plummer .25 .60
28 Tatum Bell .25 .60
29 Rod Smith .30 .75
30 Kevin Jones .25 .60
31 Roy Williams WR .25 .60
32 Brett Favre .75 2.00
33 Ahman Green .30 .75
34 Donald Driver .30 .75
35 David Carr .25 .60
36 Andre Johnson .30 .75
37 Peyton Manning 1.00 2.50
38 Marvin Harrison .30 .75
39 Reggie Wayne .30 .75
40 Byron Leftwich .25 .60
41 Fred Taylor .25 .60
42 Ernest Wilford .25 .60
43 Larry Johnson .25 .60
44 Trent Green .25 .60
45 Tony Gonzalez .30 .75
46 Daunte Culpepper .30 .75
47 Ronnie Brown .30 .75
48 Chris Chambers .25 .60
49 Troy Williamson .25 .60
50 Chester Taylor .30 .75
51 Brad Johnson .30 .75
52 Tom Brady 1.25 3.00
53 Deion Branch .25 .60
54 Corey Dillon .25 .60
55 Drew Brees .40 1.00
56 Deuce McAllister .30 .75
57 Donte Stallworth .25 .60
58 Eli Manning .30 .75
59 Tiki Barber .30 .75
60 Plaxico Burress .25 .60
61 Chad Pennington .25 .60
62 Curtis Martin .30 .75
63 Randy Moss .30 .75
64 LaMont Jordan .30 .75
65 Aaron Brooks .25 .60
66 Donovan McNabb .30 .75
67 Brian Westbrook .25 .60
68 Ben Roethlisberger .50 1.25
69 Hines Ward .30 .75
70 Willie Parker .30 .75
71 LaDainian Tomlinson .40 1.00
72 Philip Rivers .40 1.00
73 Antonio Gates .40 1.00
74 Alex Smith QB .30 .75
75 Antonio Bryant .25 .60
76 Frank Gore .30 .75
77 Shaun Alexander .25 .60
78 Matt Hasselbeck .25 .60
79 Nate Burleson .25 .60
80 Marc Bulger .25 .60
81 Steven Jackson .25 .60
82 Torry Holt .30 .75
83 Cadillac Williams .30 .75
84 Joey Galloway .30 .75
85 Chris Simms .25 .60
86 Billy Volek .25 .60
87 Drew Bennett .30 .75
88 Clinton Portis .25 .60
89 Santana Moss .30 .75
90 Mark Brunell .30 .75
91 Haloti Ngata RC 3.00 8.00
92 Willie Reid RC 3.00 8.00
93 Kamerion Wimbley RC 3.00 8.00
94 Donte Whitner RC 3.00 8.00
95 Ethan Kilmer RC 3.00 8.00
96 Johnathan Joseph RC 3.00 8.00
97 Brodie Croyle RC 2.50 6.00
98 Bobby Carpenter RC 2.50 6.00
99 Antonio Cromartie RC 3.00 8.00
100 Eric Winston RC 2.50 6.00
101 Nick Mangold RC 3.00 8.00
102 Manny Lawson RC 3.00 8.00
103 Claude Wroten RC 2.50 6.00
104 D'Qwell Jackson RC 2.50 6.00
105 Richard Marshall RC 2.50 6.00
106 Tamba Hali RC 4.00 10.00
107 Ko Simpson RC 3.00 8.00
108 Danieal Manning RC 4.00 10.00
109 Gabe Watson RC 2.50 6.00
110 Kevin McMahan RC 3.00 8.00
111 Jai Lewis RC 3.00 8.00
112 Darryl Tapp RC 3.00 8.00
113 John McCargo RC 2.50 6.00
114 Jeff King RC 3.00 8.00
115 Charles Davis RC 3.00 8.00
116 Calvin Lowry RC 4.00 10.00
117 Delanie Walker RC 5.00 12.00
118 Roman Harper RC 3.00 8.00
119 Nate Salley RC 3.00 8.00
120 Cooper Wallace RC 3.00 8.00
121 Bernard Pollard RC 3.00 8.00
122 Derrick Ross RC 3.00 8.00
123 Ingle Martin RC 3.00 8.00
124 Wali Lundy RC 2.50 6.00
125 Marcus Vick RC 2.50 6.00
126 Cedric Humes RC 2.50 6.00
127 Marques Hagans RC 2.50 6.00
128 Taurean Henderson RC 2.50 6.00
129 Marques Colston RC 4.00 10.00
130 Devin Aromashodu RC 2.50 6.00
131 Jonathan Orr RC 3.00 8.00
132 Skyler Green RC 2.50 6.00
133 Jeff Webb RC 3.00 8.00
134 Jon Alston RC 2.50 6.00
135 Daniel Bullocks RC 2.50 6.00
136 Anthony Schlegel RC 3.00 8.00
137 Adam Jennings RC 3.00 8.00
138 Gerris Wilkinson RC 2.50 6.00
139 James Anderson RC 2.50 6.00
140 Owen Daniels RC 4.00 10.00
141 Ray Edwards RC 4.00 10.00
142 Chris Gocong RC 3.00 8.00
143 Babatunde Oshinowo RC 3.00 8.00
144 Marvin Philip RC 4.00 10.00
145 Stanley McClover RC 3.00 8.00
146 DeMeco Ryans RC 3.00 8.00
147 Tony Scheffler RC 4.00 10.00
148 T.J. Williams RC 4.00 10.00
149 P.J. Daniels RC 2.50 6.00
150 Bennie Brazell RC 3.00 8.00
151 Will Blackmon RC 2.50 6.00
152 Bruce Gradkowski RC 3.00 8.00
153 Drew Olson RC 2.50 6.00
154 Darnell Bing RC 3.00 8.00
155 Darrell Hackney RC 3.00 8.00
156 Cory Rodgers RC 2.50 6.00
157 DonTrell Moore RC 3.00 8.00
158 Ernie Sims RC 2.50 6.00
159 Jay Cutler RC 3.00 8.00
160 D.J. Shockley RC 3.00 8.00
161 Martin Nance RC 2.50 6.00
162 Joseph Addai RC 2.50 6.00
163 Leonard Pope RC 4.00 10.00
164 Anthony Fasano RC 2.50 6.00
165 Mathias Kiwanuka RC 4.00 10.00
166 Greg Jennings RC 4.00 10.00
167 Greg Lee RC 2.50 6.00
168 Jerome Harrison RC 2.50 6.00
169 Jimmy Williams RC 2.50 6.00
170 Josh Betts RC 3.00 8.00
171 Ashton Youboty RC 2.50 6.00
172 Terrence Whitehead RC 3.00 8.00
173 Brad Smith RC 3.00 8.00
174 D'Brickashaw Ferguson RC 2.50 6.00
175 Mike Hass RC 2.50 6.00
176 Reggie McNeal RC 2.50 6.00
177 Dominique Byrd RC 2.50 6.00
178 Winston Justice RC 3.00 8.00
179 Chad Greenway RC 4.00 10.00
180 Tye Hill RC 2.50 6.00
181 Chad Jackson JSY AU RC 8.00 20.00
182 DeA.Williams JSY AU RC 10.00 25.00
183 Vince Young JSY AU RC 8.00 20.00
184 S.Holmes JSY AU RC 10.00 25.00
185 Sinorice Moss JSY AU RC 8.00 20.00
186 Matt Leinart JSY AU RC 8.00 20.00
187 Reggie Bush JSY AU RC 12.00 30.00
188 LenDale White JSY AU RC 5.00 12.00
189 Vernon Davis JSY AU RC 6.00 15.00
190 L.Maroney JSY AU RC 5.00 12.00
191 A.J. Hawk JSY AU RC 10.00 25.00
192 Marcus McNeill JSY AU RC 5.00 12.00
193 Kelly Jennings JSY AU RC 6.00 15.00
194 B.Williams JSY AU RC 5.00 12.00
195 Brian Calhoun JSY AU RC 5.00 12.00
196 Travis Wilson JSY AU RC 5.00 12.00
197 C.Whitehurst JSY AU RC 5.00 12.00
198 Omar Jacobs JSY AU RC 5.00 12.00
199 J.Klopfenstein JSY AU RC 5.00 12.00
200 Derek Hagan JSY AU RC 6.00 15.00
201 Michael Huff JSY AU RC 6.00 15.00
202 Maurice Stovall JSY AU RC 5.00 12.00
203 Maurice Drew JSY AU RC 12.00 30.00
204 Jason Avant JSY AU RC 5.00 12.00
205 K.Clemens JSY AU RC 5.00 12.00
206 J.Norwood JSY AU RC 5.00 12.00
207 T.Jackson JSY AU RC 5.00 12.00
208 B.Marshall JSY AU RC 12.50 25.00
209 Dem.Williams JSY AU RC 5.00 12.00
210 L.Washington JSY AU RC 5.00 12.00
211 M.Robinson JSY AU RC 5.00 12.00
212 Marcedes Lewis JSY AU RC 5.00 12.00
213 Mario Williams JSY AU RC 8.00 20.00

2006 SPx Spectrum

*VETS 1-90: 5X TO 12X BASIC CARDS
*ROOKIES 91-150: 1X TO 2.5X BASIC CARDS
COMMON ROOK.AU (151-180) 12.00 30.00
ROOKIE AU SEMISTARS 15.00 40.00
ROOKIE AU UNL.STARS 20.00 50.00
*ROOKIE JSY AU: 1X TO 2.5X JSY AU/399
*ROOKIE JSY AU: 1.5X TO 4X JSY AU/1650
STATED PRINT RUN 25 SER.#'d SETS
166 Greg Jennings AU 30.00 80.00
203 Maurice Drew JSY AU 100.00 250.00
208 Brandon Marshall JSY AU 75.00 150.00

2006 SPx Rookie Autographed Jerseys Gold

*GOLD/99: .5X TO 1.2X JSY AU/399
*GOLD/350: .5X TO 1.2X JSY AU/1650
GOLD STATED PRINT RUN 99-350
UNPRICED NFL LOGO SER.#'d TO 1

2006 SPx Rookie Autographs Gold

ANNOUNCED PRINT RUN 299 SETS
151 Will Blackmon 5.00 12.00
152 Bruce Gradkowski 6.00 15.00
153 Drew Olson 5.00 12.00
154 Darnell Bing 6.00 15.00
155 Darrell Hackney 6.00 15.00
156 Cory Rodgers 5.00 12.00
157 DonTrell Moore 6.00 15.00
158 Ernie Sims 5.00 12.00
159 Jay Cutler 6.00 15.00
160 D.J. Shockley 6.00 15.00
161 Martin Nance 5.00 12.00
162 Joseph Addai 5.00 12.00
163 Leonard Pope 8.00 20.00
164 Anthony Fasano 5.00 12.00
165 Mathias Kiwanuka 8.00 20.00
166 Greg Jennings 8.00 20.00
167 Greg Lee 5.00 12.00
168 Jerome Harrison 5.00 12.00
169 Jimmy Williams 5.00 12.00
170 Josh Betts 6.00 15.00
171 Ashton Youboty 5.00 12.00
172 Terrence Whitehead 6.00 15.00
173 Brad Smith 6.00 15.00
174 D'Brickashaw Ferguson 5.00 12.00
175 Mike Hass 5.00 12.00
176 Reggie McNeal 5.00 12.00
177 Dominique Byrd 5.00 12.00
178 Winston Justice 6.00 15.00
179 Chad Greenway 8.00 20.00
180 Tye Hill 5.00 12.00

2006 SPx Rookie Swatch Supremacy

STATED ODDS 1:50
SWAH A.J. Hawk 2.50 6.00
SWBC Brian Calhoun 2.00 5.00
SWBU Reggie Bush 3.00 8.00
SWCH Chad Jackson 2.00 5.00
SWDW DeAngelo Williams 2.50 6.00
SWKC Kellen Clemens 2.00 5.00
SWLE Matt Leinart 2.00 5.00
SWLM Laurence Maroney 2.00 5.00
SWLW LenDale White 2.00 5.00
SWMD Maurice Drew 3.00 8.00
SWMH Michael Huff 2.50 6.00
SWML Marcedes Lewis 2.00 5.00
SWMR Michael Robinson 2.00 5.00
SWMS Maurice Stovall 2.00 5.00
SWMW Mario Williams 3.00 8.00
SWOJ Omar Jacobs 2.00 5.00
SWSH Santonio Holmes 2.50 6.00
SWSM Sinorice Moss 2.00 5.00
SWVD Vernon Davis 2.50 6.00
SWVY Vince Young 2.00 5.00

2006 SPx Rookie Winning Materials

STATED ODDS 1:126
WMRAH A.J. Hawk 3.00 8.00
WMRBM Brandon Marshall 5.00 12.00
WMRBU Reggie Bush 4.00 10.00
WMRBW Brandon Williams 2.50 6.00
WMRCA Brian Calhoun 2.50 6.00
WMRCJ Chad Jackson 2.50 6.00
WMRDH Derek Hagan 3.00 8.00
WMRDW DeAngelo Williams 3.00 8.00
WMRJA Jason Avant 2.50 6.00
WMRJK Joe Klopfenstein 2.50 6.00
WMRJN Jerious Norwood 2.50 6.00
WMRKC Kellen Clemens 2.50 6.00
WMRLE Matt Leinart 2.50 6.00
WMRLM Laurence Maroney 2.50 6.00
WMRLW LenDale White 2.50 6.00
WMRMD Maurice Drew 4.00 10.00
WMRMH Michael Huff 3.00 8.00
WMRML Marcedes Lewis 2.50 6.00
WMRMR Michael Robinson 2.50 6.00
WMRMS Maurice Stovall 2.50 6.00
WMRMW Mario Williams 4.00 10.00
WMROJ Omar Jacobs 2.50 6.00
WMRSH Santonio Holmes 3.00 8.00
WMRSM Sinorice Moss 2.50 6.00
WMRTJ Tarvaris Jackson 2.50 6.00
WMRTR Travis Wilson 2.50 6.00
WMRVD Vernon Davis 3.00 8.00
WMRVY Vince Young 2.50 6.00
WMRWA Leon Washington 2.50 6.00
WMRWH Charlie Whitehurst 2.50 6.00
WMRWI Demetrius Williams 2.50 6.00

2006 SPx Rookie Winning Materials Autographs

STATED PRINT RUN 25 SER.#'d SETS
WMRAH A.J. Hawk 30.00 80.00
WMRBM Brandon Marshall 30.00 60.00
WMRBU Reggie Bush 20.00 50.00
WMRBW Brandon Williams 12.00 30.00
WMRCA Brian Calhoun 12.00 30.00
WMRCJ Chad Jackson 12.00 30.00
WMRDH Derek Hagan 15.00 40.00
WMRDW DeAngelo Williams 40.00 100.00
WMRJA Jason Avant 12.00 30.00
WMRJK Joe Klopfenstein 12.00 30.00
WMRJN Jerious Norwood 12.00 30.00
WMRKC Kellen Clemens 12.00 30.00
WMRLE Matt Leinart 12.00 30.00
WMRLM Laurence Maroney 12.00 30.00
WMRLW LenDale White 12.00 30.00
WMRMD Maurice Drew 30.00 80.00
WMRMH Michael Huff 15.00 40.00
WMRML Marcedes Lewis 12.00 30.00
WMRMR Michael Robinson 12.00 30.00
WMRMS Maurice Stovall 12.00 30.00
WMRMW Mario Williams 20.00 50.00
WMROJ Omar Jacobs 12.00 30.00
WMRSH Santonio Holmes 25.00 60.00
WMRSM Sinorice Moss 12.00 30.00
WMRTJ Tarvaris Jackson 12.00 30.00
WMRTR Travis Wilson 12.00 30.00
WMRVD Vernon Davis 15.00 40.00
WMRVY Vince Young 12.00 30.00
WMRWA Leon Washington 12.00 30.00
WMRWH Charlie Whitehurst 12.00 30.00
WMRWI Demetrius Williams 12.00 30.00

2006 SPx SPxcellence

STATED PRINT RUN 650 SER.#'d SETS
UNPRICED AUTO PRINT RUN 10
SPAC Alge Crumpler 2.50 6.00
SPAD Joseph Addai 1.25 3.00
SPAH A.J. Hawk 1.50 4.00
SPAV Jason Avant 1.25 3.00
SPBL Drew Bledsoe 2.50 6.00
SPBM Brandon Marshall 2.50 6.00
SPBR Ben Roethlisberger 4.00 10.00
SPCG Chad Greenway 2.00 5.00
SPCL Mark Clayton 2.00 5.00
SPCP Carson Palmer 2.50 6.00
SPCS Chris Simms 2.00 5.00
SPCW Charlie Whitehurst 1.25 3.00
SPDB Dominique Byrd 1.25 3.00
SPDG David Givens 2.50 6.00
SPDR DeMeco Ryans 1.50 4.00
SPDW Demetrius Williams 1.25 3.00
SPEM Eli Manning 2.50 6.00
SPHI Tye Hill 1.25 3.00
SPJA Tarvaris Jackson 1.25 3.00
SPJC Jay Cutler 1.50 4.00
SPJH Jerome Harrison 1.25 3.00
SPKC Kellen Clemens 1.25 3.00
SPKO Kyle Orton 2.00 5.00
SPLE Matt Leinart 1.25 3.00
SPLJ Larry Johnson 2.00 5.00
SPLM Laurence Maroney 1.25 3.00
SPLP Leonard Pope 2.00 5.00
SPLW LenDale White 1.25 3.00
SPMC Michael Clayton 2.00 5.00
SPMD Maurice Drew 2.00 5.00
SPMH Michael Huff 1.50 4.00
SPML Marcedes Lewis 1.25 3.00
SPMR Michael Robinson 1.25 3.00
SPMS Maurice Stovall 1.25 3.00
SPMW Mario Williams 2.00 5.00
SPOJ Omar Jacobs 1.25 3.00
SPPM Peyton Manning 8.00 20.00
SPRB Reggie Bush 2.50 6.00
SPRJ Rudi Johnson 2.00 5.00
SPRM Reggie McNeal 1.25 3.00
SPRO Ronnie Brown 2.50 6.00
SPSM Sinorice Moss 1.25 3.00
SPSS Steve Smith 3.00 8.00
SPTB Tedy Bruschi 2.50 6.00
SPTH T.J. Houshmandzadeh 2.00 5.00
SPTJ Thomas Jones 2.00 5.00
SPVD Vernon Davis 1.50 4.00
SPVY Vince Young 1.25 3.00
SPWA Leon Washington 1.25 3.00
SPWP Willie Parker 2.50 6.00

2006 SPx SPxclusives

STATED PRINT RUN 650 SER.#'d SETS
UNPRICED AUTO PRINT RUN 10
EXAG Antonio Gates 3.00 8.00
EXBC Brian Calhoun 2.50 6.00
EXBE Braylon Edwards 3.00 8.00
EXBF Brett Favre 6.00 15.00
EXBL Byron Leftwich 2.00 5.00
EXBU Reggie Bush 2.50 6.00
EXCB Cedric Benson 3.00 8.00
EXCJ Chad Jackson 2.50 6.00
EXCW Cadillac Williams 3.00 8.00
EXDB Drew Bledsoe 3.00 8.00
EXDF DeShaun Foster 2.00 5.00
EXDM Deuce McAllister 2.00 5.00
EXDR Drew Bennett 1.50 4.00
EXDW DeAngelo Williams 2.00 5.00
EXES Ernie Sims 2.50 6.00
EXFE D'Brickashaw Ferguson 2.50 6.00
EXGJ Greg Jones 1.50 4.00
EXJA Joseph Addai 1.50 4.00
EXJC Jay Cutler 2.00 5.00
EXJJ Julius Jones 3.00 8.00
EXJO LaMont Jordan 2.00 5.00
EXJW Jason Witten 2.00 5.00
EXKC Kevin Curtis 1.50 4.00
EXKJ Keyshawn Johnson 2.00 5.00
EXLJ Larry Johnson 3.00 8.00
EXLT LaDainian Tomlinson 3.00 8.00
EXML Matt Leinart 1.50 4.00
EXMW Mike Williams 3.00 8.00
EXPM Peyton Manning 5.00 12.00
EXPR Philip Rivers 3.00 8.00
EXRB Ronde Barber 1.50 4.00
EXRW Reggie Wayne 2.00 5.00
EXSH Santonio Holmes 4.00 10.00
EXSS Steve Smith 3.00 8.00
EXTA Lofa Tatupu 2.50 6.00
EXTB Tiki Barber 3.00 8.00
EXTG Trent Green 2.00 5.00
EXVD Vernon Davis 4.00 10.00
EXVY Vince Young 1.50 4.00
EXWI Jimmy Williams 2.50 6.00

2006 SPx SPxclusives Autographs

UNPRICED AUTO PRINT RUN 10

2006 SPx Super Scripts Autographs

STATED ODDS 1:252
SSAG Antonio Gates 10.00 25.00
SSAH A.J. Hawk SP 25.00 50.00
SSBE Braylon Edwards 6.00 15.00
SSBL Byron Leftwich 6.00 15.00
SSBR Ben Roethlisberger SP 50.00 100.00
SSBU Reggie Bush SP 10.00 25.00
SSCJ Chad Jackson SP 15.00 30.00
SSCS Chris Simms 6.00 15.00
SSDB Drew Bennett 8.00 20.00
SSDF DeShaun Foster 8.00 20.00
SSDG David Givens 8.00 20.00
SSDH Derek Hagan 5.00 12.00
SSDW DeAngelo Williams SP
SSFE D'Brickashaw Ferguson 4.00 10.00
SSGL Greg Lee 6.00 15.00
SSHA Andre Hall 5.00 12.00
SSJC Jay Cutler SP 8.00 20.00
SSJH Jerome Harrison 4.00 10.00
SSJW Jason Witten 20.00 40.00
SSKC Kevin Curtis 8.00 20.00
SSKO Kyle Orton 6.00 15.00
SSLJ LaMont Jordan 8.00 20.00
SSLL Brandon Lloyd 6.00 15.00
SSLM Laurence Maroney SP 12.00 30.00
SSLT LaDainian Tomlinson 40.00 80.00
SSLW LenDale White SP 15.00 30.00
SSMC Reggie McNeal 4.00 10.00
SSML Matt Leinart SP 25.00 60.00
SSMM Muhsin Muhammad 6.00 15.00
SSMW Mario Williams 12.50 30.00
SSPM Peyton Manning 50.00 100.00
SSPR Philip Rivers 12.00 30.00
SSRB Ronde Barber 6.00 15.00
SSRM Ryan Moats 4.00 10.00
SSRW Reggie Wayne 12.50 30.00
SSSH Santonio Holmes 15.00 40.00
SSSM Sinorice Moss SP 5.00 12.00
SSSS Steve Smith SP 10.00 25.00
SSTA Lofa Tatupu 6.00 15.00
SSVD Vernon Davis 5.00 12.00
SSVY Vince Young SP
SSWP Willie Parker SP

2006 SPx Swatch Supremacy

STATED ODDS 1:26
SWBE Braylon Edwards 4.00 10.00
SWBF Brett Favre 8.00 20.00
SWBL Byron Leftwich 3.00 8.00
SWBR Ben Roethlisberger 8.00 20.00
SWBT Tom Brady 6.00 15.00
SWCB Champ Bailey 3.00 8.00
SWCF Charlie Frye 4.00 10.00
SWCP Carson Palmer 4.00 10.00
SWCW Cadillac Williams 4.00 10.00
SWDB Drew Bledsoe 4.00 10.00
SWDC Daunte Culpepper 4.00 10.00
SWDM Deuce McAllister 3.00 8.00
SWDR Drew Brees SP 3.00 8.00
SWEJ Edgerrin James 4.00 10.00
SWGR Trent Green 3.00 8.00
SWHW Hines Ward 5.00 12.00
SWJJ Julius Jones 4.00 10.00
SWJO Larry Johnson 4.00 10.00
SWJT Jason Taylor 3.00 8.00
SWKO Kyle Orton 3.00 8.00
SWKW Kurt Warner 3.00 8.00
SWLJ LaMont Jordan 3.00 8.00
SWLT LaDainian Tomlinson 4.00 10.00
SWMC Donovan McNabb 4.00 10.00
SWMV Michael Vick 4.00 10.00
SWPH Priest Holmes 3.00 8.00
SWPM Peyton Manning 6.00 15.00
SWRB Ronnie Brown 4.00 10.00
SWRE Reggie Brown 3.00 8.00
SWRM Randy Moss 4.00 10.00
SWRW Roy Williams S 3.00 8.00
SWSA Shaun Alexander 4.00 10.00
SWSJ Steven Jackson 4.00 10.00
SWTB Tatum Bell 3.00 8.00
SWTG Tony Gonzalez 3.00 8.00
SWWA Reggie Wayne 3.00 8.00
SWWP Willie Parker 4.00 10.00

2006 SPx Winning Combo Autographs

STATED PRINT RUN 50 SER.#'d SETS
WCBA R.Brown/J.Avant 12.00 30.00
WCBB T.Barber/R.Barber 40.00 80.00
WCBC M.Bulger/K.Curtis 15.00 40.00
WCBH D.Bing/M.Huff 15.00 40.00
WCBJ B.Bunkley/W.Justice 15.00 40.00
WCBL D.Byrd/M.Lewis 12.00 30.00
WCBT L.Tomlinson/R.Bush 40.00 80.00
WCBW L.White/R.Bush 20.00 50.00
WCCW D.Williams/K.Clemens 12.00 30.00
WCEA B.Edwards/J.Avant 12.00 30.00
WCEW B.Edwards/T.Wilson 12.00 30.00
WCFD D.Foster/M.Drew 25.00 60.00
WCFJ D.Ferguson/W.Justice 15.00 40.00
WCFS A.Fasano/M.Stovall 12.00 30.00
WCGD A.Gates/V.Davis 20.00 50.00
WCGJ C.Greenway/T.Jackson 20.00 50.00
WCHH Housh/M.Hass 12.00 30.00
WCHJ O.Jacobs/S.Holmes 15.00 40.00
WCHW A.Hawk/M.Williams 25.00 60.00
WCIW T.Wilson/C.Ingram 20.00 50.00
WCJH K.Jennings/T.Hill 15.00 40.00
WCJM T.Jones/L.Maroney 12.00 30.00
WCJW L.Johnson/D.Williams 25.00 60.00
WCKB D.Byrd/J.Klopfenstein 12.00 30.00
WCKL Clemens/.Washington 12.00 30.00
WCLB M.Leinart/R.Bush 20.00 50.00
WCMJ C.Jackson/S.Moss 12.00 30.00
WCML P.Manning/M.Leinart 75.00 150.00
WCMW D.Mason/D.Williams 12.00 30.00
WCOD D.Olson/M.Drew 30.00 60.00
WCOJ K.Orton/T.Jackson 12.00 30.00
WCPJ W.Parker/O.Jacobs 15.00 40.00
WCRW P.Rivers/C.Whitehurst 30.00 60.00
WCSH S.Holmes/S.Smith 30.00 60.00
WCSP D.Shockley/L.Pope 20.00 50.00
WCSR D.Ryans/E.Sims 15.00 40.00
WCTB L.Tatupu/D.Bing 15.00 40.00
WCVY M.Vick/V.Young 15.00 40.00
WCWB Ro.Brown/C.Williams 15.00 40.00
WCWC B.Williams/B.Calhoun 12.00 30.00
WCWF J.Witten/A.Fasano 30.00 60.00
WCWH J.Williams/M.Huff 15.00 40.00
WCWS E.Sims/L.Washington 12.00 30.00
WCYC J.Cutler/V.Young 15.00 40.00

2006 SPx Winning Materials

STATED ODDS 1:18
WMVAC Alge Crumpler SP 3.00 8.00
WMVAG Antonio Gates 4.00 10.00
WMVAR Aaron Rodgers 12.00 30.00
WMVBA Ronde Barber 2.50 6.00
WMVBD Brian Dawkins 4.00 10.00
WMVBE Braylon Edwards 2.50 6.00
WMVBF Brett Favre 8.00 20.00
WMVBL Byron Leftwich 2.50 6.00
WMVBR Ben Roethlisberger 6.00 15.00
WMVBU Brian Urlacher SP 4.00 10.00
WMVCF Charlie Frye 3.00 8.00
WMVCL Michael Clayton 2.50 6.00
WMVCP Carson Palmer 3.00 8.00
WMVCS Chris Simms 2.50 6.00
WMVCW Cadillac Williams 3.00 8.00
WMVDB Drew Bledsoe 3.00 8.00
WMVDF DeShaun Foster 3.00 8.00
WMVDG David Givens 3.00 8.00
WMVDM Deuce McAllister 3.00 8.00
WMVEM Eli Manning 5.00 12.00
WMVGJ Greg Jones 2.50 6.00
WMVJJ Julius Jones 2.50 6.00
WMVJO LaMont Jordan 3.00 8.00
WMVJW Jason Witten 3.00 8.00
WMVKC Kevin Curtis 3.00 8.00
WMVKJ Keyshawn Johnson 3.00 8.00
WMVKO Kyle Orton 2.50 6.00
WMVLJ Larry Johnson 2.50 6.00
WMVLT LaDainian Tomlinson 4.00 10.00
WMVMC Mark Clayton 2.50 6.00
WMVMM Muhsin Muhammad 2.50 6.00
WMVMV Michael Vick 3.00 8.00
WMVNB Nate Burleson 2.50 6.00
WMVPM Peyton Manning 6.00 15.00
WMVPR Philip Rivers 4.00 10.00
WMVRB Reggie Brown 2.50 6.00
WMVRJ Rudi Johnson 2.50 6.00
WMVRM Ryan Moats 2.50 6.00
WMVRO Ronnie Brown 3.00 8.00
WMVRW Reggie Wayne 3.00 8.00
WMVSS Steve Smith 4.00 10.00
WMVTB Tiki Barber 3.00 8.00
WMVTE Tedy Bruschi 3.00 8.00
WMVTG Trent Green 2.50 6.00
WMVTH T.J. Houshmandzadeh SP 2.50 6.00
WMVTJ Thomas Jones 2.50 6.00
WMVTP Troy Polamalu 4.00 10.00
WMVTW Troy Williamson 2.50 6.00
WMVWP Willie Parker 3.00 8.00

2006 SPx Winning Materials Autographs

STATED PRINT RUN 25 SER.#'d SETS
WMVAC Alge Crumpler 12.00 30.00
WMVBA Ronde Barber 10.00 25.00
WMVBD Brian Dawkins 40.00 80.00
WMVBE Braylon Edwards 10.00 25.00
WMVBF Brett Favre 125.00 200.00
WMVBL Byron Leftwich 10.00 25.00
WMVBR Ben Roethlisberger 75.00 150.00
WMVCF Charlie Frye 12.00 30.00
WMVCL Michael Clayton 10.00 25.00
WMVCP Carson Palmer 12.00 30.00
WMVCS Chris Simms 10.00 25.00
WMVCW Cadillac Williams 12.00 30.00
WMVDB Drew Bledsoe
WMVDF DeShaun Foster 12.00 30.00
WMVDG David Givens 12.00 30.00
WMVDM Deuce McAllister 12.00 30.00
WMVEM Eli Manning 90.00 150.00
WMVGJ Greg Jones 10.00 25.00
WMVJJ Julius Jones 10.00 25.00
WMVJO LaMont Jordan 12.00 30.00
WMVJW Jason Witten 40.00 80.00
WMVKC Kevin Curtis 12.00 30.00
WMVKJ Keyshawn Johnson
WMVKO Kyle Orton 10.00 25.00
WMVLJ Larry Johnson 10.00 25.00
WMVLT LaDainian Tomlinson 40.00 80.00
WMVMC Mark Clayton 10.00 25.00
WMVMM Muhsin Muhammad 10.00 25.00
WMVMV Michael Vick 40.00 80.00
WMVNB Nate Burleson 10.00 25.00
WMVPM Peyton Manning 100.00 200.00
WMVPR Philip Rivers 15.00 40.00
WMVRB Reggie Brown 10.00 25.00
WMVRJ Rudi Johnson 10.00 25.00
WMVRM Ryan Moats 10.00 25.00
WMVRO Ronnie Brown 12.00 30.00
WMVRW Reggie Wayne 12.00 30.00
WMVSS Steve Smith 15.00 40.00
WMVTB Tiki Barber 30.00 60.00
WMVTG Trent Green 10.00 25.00
WMVTH T.J. Houshmandzadeh 10.00 25.00
WMVTJ Thomas Jones 10.00 25.00
WMVWP Willie Parker 12.00 30.00

2007 SPx

This 223-card set was released in August, 2007. The set was issued into the hobby in three-card packs, with an $19.99 SRP, which came 10 packs to a box. Cards numbered 1-100 feature veterans in team alphabetical order while cards 101-224 feature 2007 NFL rookies. The Rookie Cards are broken down like this: Cards numbered 101-160 were issued to a stated print run of 899 serial numbered cards; cards numbered 161-190 were signed by the player and those cards were issued to a stated print run of 499 serial numbered cards; and the set concludes with cards with both player-worn jersey swatches and autographs which were issued to stated print runs between 299 and 599 serial numbered copies.

COMP.SET w/o RC's (100) 20.00 40.00
101-160 ROOKIE PRINT RUN 899
161-190 AU ROOKIE PRINT RUN 499
191-224 JSY AU ROOKIE PRINT RUN 299-599
UNPRICED NFL LOGO AUs #'d TO 1
1 Matt Leinart .30 .75
2 Anquan Boldin .30 .75
3 Larry Fitzgerald .40 1.00
4 Edgerrin James .40 1.00
5 Michael Vick .40 1.00
6 Warrick Dunn .30 .75
7 DeAngelo Hall .30 .75
8 Steve McNair .40 1.00
9 Willis McGahee .30 .75
10 Ray Lewis .50 1.25
11 J.P. Losman .30 .75
12 Lee Evans .40 1.00
13 Anthony Thomas .30 .75
14 Jake Delhomme .30 .75
15 Steve Smith .40 1.00
16 DeAngelo Williams .30 .75
17 Brian Urlacher .50 1.25
18 Cedric Benson .30 .75
19 Rex Grossman .30 .75
20 Carson Palmer .40 1.00
21 Chad Johnson .30 .75
22 Rudi Johnson .30 .75
23 Charlie Frye .40 1.00
24 Braylon Edwards .30 .75
25 Jamal Lewis .40 1.00
26 Tony Romo .60 1.50
27 Terrell Owens .40 1.00
28 Julius Jones .30 .75
29 Marion Barber .40 1.00
30 Jay Cutler .30 .75
31 Javon Walker .40 1.00
32 Travis Henry .40 1.00
33 Roy Williams WR .30 .75
34 Mike Furrey .40 1.00
35 Tatum Bell .30 .75
36 Greg Jennings .30 .75
37 Brett Favre 1.00 2.50
38 A.J. Hawk .30 .75
39 Matt Schaub .30 .75
40 Andre Johnson .40 1.00
41 Ahman Green .40 1.00
42 Peyton Manning 1.25 3.00
43 Marvin Harrison .40 1.00
44 Reggie Wayne .40 1.00
45 Joseph Addai .40 1.00
46 Fred Taylor .30 .75
47 Maurice Jones-Drew .30 .75
48 Byron Leftwich .30 .75
49 Damon Huard .40 1.00
50 Larry Johnson .30 .75
51 Tony Gonzalez .40 1.00
52 Zach Thomas .40 1.00
53 Ronnie Brown .30 .75
54 Chris Chambers .30 .75
55 Tarvaris Jackson .30 .75
56 Chester Taylor .30 .75
57 Troy Williamson .30 .75
58 Tom Brady 1.50 4.00
59 Donte Stallworth .40 1.00
60 Laurence Maroney .40 1.00
61 Reggie Bush .30 .75
62 Deuce McAllister .40 1.00
63 Drew Brees .50 1.25
64 Marques Colston .30 .75
65 Eli Manning .40 1.00
66 Plaxico Burress .30 .75
67 Brandon Jacobs .30 .75
68 Chad Pennington .30 .75
69 Thomas Jones .30 .75
70 Laveranues Coles .30 .75
71 LaMont Jordan .40 1.00
72 Randy Moss .40 1.00
73 Nnamdi Asomugha .30 .75
74 Donovan McNabb .40 1.00
75 Brian Westbrook .30 .75
76 Reggie Brown .30 .75
77 Ben Roethlisberger .50 1.25
78 Hines Ward .40 1.00
79 Willie Parker .40 1.00
80 LaDainian Tomlinson .50 1.25
81 Philip Rivers .50 1.25
82 Antonio Gates .50 1.25
83 Frank Gore .40 1.00
84 Alex Smith QB .40 1.00
85 Ashley Lelie .40 1.00
86 Matt Hasselbeck .30 .75
87 Shaun Alexander .30 .75
88 Deion Branch .30 .75
89 Marc Bulger .30 .75
90 Torry Holt .40 1.00
91 Steven Jackson .30 .75
92 Cadillac Williams .40 1.00
93 Chris Simms .30 .75
94 Joey Galloway .40 1.00
95 Vince Young .30 .75
96 David Givens .30 .75
97 LenDale White .40 1.00
98 Jason Campbell .30 .75
99 Santana Moss .40 1.00
100 Clinton Portis .30 .75
101 Levi Brown RC 2.50 6.00
102 Adam Carriker RC 2.50 6.00
103 Jarvis Moss RC 2.50 6.00
104 Aaron Ross RC 2.50 6.00
105 Chris Houston RC 2.50 6.00
106 Michael Griffin RC 2.50 6.00
107 Justin Harrell RC 2.50 6.00
108 Joe Staley RC 3.00 8.00

109 Jon Beason RC 2.50 6.00
110 Anthony Spencer RC 3.00 8.00
111 Ben Grubbs RC 3.00 8.00
112 Charles Johnson RC 2.50 6.00
113 Marcus McCauley RC 2.50 6.00
114 Justin Blalock RC 2.50 6.00
115 Tim Crowder RC 3.00 8.00
116 Brandon Meriweather RC 3.00 8.00
117 Arron Sears RC 3.00 8.00
118 Zach Miller RC 2.50 6.00
119 Turk McBride RC 3.00 8.00
120 Ryan Kalil RC 2.50 6.00
121 Tony Ugoh RC 2.50 6.00
122 David Harris RC 2.50 6.00
123 Jonathan Wade RC 2.50 6.00
124 Josh Wilson RC 3.00 8.00
125 Demarcus Tank Tyler RC 2.50 6.00
126 Tanard Jackson RC 2.50 6.00
127 Jordan Kent RC 3.00 8.00
128 Ray McDonald RC 3.00 8.00
129 Quentin Moses RC 2.50 6.00
130 Eric Weddle RC 3.00 8.00
131 Victor Abiamiri RC 2.50 6.00
132 Josh Beekman RC 2.50 6.00
133 Brandon Siler RC 2.50 6.00
134 Aundrae Allison RC 2.50 6.00
135 Ben Patrick RC 3.00 8.00
136 Chris Davis RC 2.50 6.00
137 A.J. Davis RC 2.50 6.00
138 Scott Chandler RC 4.00 10.00
139 Mason Crosby RC 3.00 8.00
140 Zak DeOssie RC 3.00 8.00
141 Matt Spaeth RC 4.00 10.00
142 James Jones RC 2.50 6.00
143 Mike Walker RC 4.00 10.00
144 Martrez Milner RC 2.50 6.00
145 Michael Okwo RC 3.00 8.00
146 Steve Breaston RC 2.50 6.00
147 Isaiah Stanback RC 2.50 6.00
148 Laurent Robinson RC 4.00 10.00
149 Brandon Mebane RC 3.00 8.00
150 Quinn Pitcock RC 3.00 8.00
151 Roy Hall RC 4.00 10.00
152 Buster Davis RC 3.00 8.00
153 Alan Branch RC 2.50 6.00
154 Josh Gattis RC 2.50 6.00
155 Aaron Rouse RC 2.50 6.00
156 Tim Shaw RC 3.00 8.00
157 Sabby Piscitelli RC 2.50 6.00
158 Rufus Alexander RC 2.50 6.00
159 Marcus Thomas RC 3.00 8.00
160 Tarell Brown RC 4.00 10.00
161 Chris Leak AU RC 5.00 12.00
162 Amobi Okoye AU RC 6.00 15.00
163 Tyler Palko AU RC 8.00 20.00
164 Craig Buster Davis AU RC 5.00 12.00
165 Courtney Taylor AU RC 5.00 12.00
166 Tyrone Moss AU RC 5.00 12.00
167 Darrelle Revis AU RC 6.00 15.00
168 David Ball AU RC 5.00 12.00
169 David Clowney AU RC 5.00 12.00
170 Daymeion Hughes AU RC 5.00 12.00
171 DeShawn Wynn AU RC 5.00 12.00
172 Drew Tate AU RC 6.00 15.00
173 Dwayne Wright AU RC 5.00 12.00
174 Eric Wright AU RC 5.00 12.00
175 Kenneth Darby AU RC 5.00 12.00
176 H.B. Blades AU RC 5.00 12.00
177 Jamaal Anderson AU RC 6.00 15.00
178 Jared Zabransky AU RC 5.00 12.00
179 Rhema McKnight AU RC 5.00 12.00
180 Jeff Rowe AU RC 5.00 12.00
181 LaRon Landry AU RC 8.00 20.00
182 Jordan Palmer AU RC 6.00 15.00
183 Kolby Smith AU RC 5.00 12.00
184 LaMarr Woodley AU RC 10.00 25.00
185 Lawrence Timmons AU RC 8.00 20.00
186 Leon Hall AU RC 5.00 12.00
187 Matt Moore AU RC 8.00 20.00
188 Gary Russell AU RC 6.00 15.00
189 Paul Posluszny AU RC 5.00 12.00
190 Reggie Nelson AU RC 5.00 12.00
191 Antonio Pittman JSY AU RC 6.00 15.00
192 A.Gonzalez JSY AU/399 RC 8.00 20.00
193 Gaines Adams JSY AU RC 8.00 20.00
194 Brandon Jackson JSY AU RC 6.00 15.00
195 Brian Leonard JSY AU RC 6.00 15.00
196 J.Higgins JSY AU RC 6.00 15.00
197 Chris Henry RB JSY AU RC 6.00 15.00
198 Patrick Willis JSY AU RC 10.00 25.00
199 Drew Stanton JSY AU RC 6.00 15.00
200 D.Bowe JSY AU/399 RC 8.00 20.00
201 Greg Olsen JSY AU RC 10.00 25.00
202 John Beck JSY AU RC 6.00 15.00
203 Jason Hill JSY AU RC 6.00 15.00
204 Paul Williams JSY AU RC 6.00 15.00
205 Joe Thomas JSY AU RC 10.00 25.00
206 Lorenzo Booker JSY AU RC 8.00 20.00
207 Yamon Figurs JSY AU RC 6.00 15.00
208 Kenny Irons JSY AU RC 6.00 15.00
209 Kevin Kolb JSY AU/399 RC 10.00 25.00
210 Garrett Wolfe JSY AU RC 6.00 15.00
211 Michael Bush JSY AU RC 6.00 15.00
212 R.Meachem JSY AU/399 RC 10.00 25.00
213 Sidney Rice JSY AU/399 RC 8.00 20.00
214 Steve Smith JSY AU RC 12.00 30.00
215 Tony Hunt JSY AU RC 6.00 15.00
217 T.Edwards JSY AU/399 RC 8.00 20.00
218 A.Peterson JSY AU/299 RC 125.00 250.00
219 B.Quinn JSY AU/299 RC 10.00 25.00
220 Ca.Johnson JSY AU/299 RC 100.00 175.00
221 D.Jarrett JSY AU/299 RC 12.00 30.00
222 J.Russell JSY AU/299 RC 10.00 25.00
223 M.Lynch JSY AU/299 RC 20.00 50.00
224 Ted Ginn Jr. JSY AU/299 RC 12.00 30.00

2007 SPx Gold Rookies

*ROOKIES 101-160: .5X TO 1.2X BASIC RC/899
101-160 PRINT RUN 699 SER.#'d SETS
*ROOKIE AU: .5X TO 1.2X BASIC RC/499
*ROOKIE JSY AU: .6X TO 1.5X BASIC RC/599
*ROOKIE JSY AU: .6X TO 1.5X BASIC RC/399
161-217 PRINT RUN 199 SER.#'d SETS
218 Adrian Peterson JSY AU/99 125.00 250.00

2007 SPx Gold Holofoil Rookies

*ROOKIES 101-160: 1X TO 2.5X BASIC RC/899
*ROOK.AU 161-190: 1X TO 2.5X BASE RC/499
*ROOKIE JSY AU: 1.2X TO 3X BASIC RC/599
STATED PRINT RUN 25 SER.#'d SETS
218 Adrian Peterson JSY/FB AU 250.00 500.00

2007 SPx Silver Holofoil Rookies

*ROOKIES 101-160: .6X TO 1.5X BASIC RC/899
101-160 PRINT RUN 299 SER.#'d SETS
*ROOK.AU 161-190: .6X TO 1.5X BASE RC/499
161-190 PRINT RUN 99 SER.#'d SETS

2007 SPx Endorsements Autographs

ENAB Anquan Boldin 6.00 15.00
ENAO Amobi Okoye 5.00 12.00
ENAP Adrian Peterson SP 150.00 250.00
ENBE Drew Bennett 4.00 10.00
ENBL Brian Leonard SP 8.00 20.00
ENBO Dwayne Bowe SP 10.00 25.00
ENBQ Brady Quinn SP 8.00 20.00
ENBR Reggie Brown 4.00 10.00
ENCD Craig Buster Davis 6.00 15.00
ENCJ Calvin Johnson SP 75.00 150.00
ENCL Chris Leak 6.00 15.00
ENCO Jerricho Cotchery 5.00 12.00
ENCT Chester Taylor 4.00 10.00
ENDB Drew Brees SP 30.00 60.00
ENDJ Dwayne Jarrett 6.00 15.00
ENDP Drew Pearson 8.00 20.00
ENDS Drew Stanton SP 8.00 20.00
ENES Emmitt Smith SP 125.00 200.00
ENGO Greg Olsen 6.00 15.00
ENHB H.B. Blades 5.00 12.00
ENHO T.J. Houshmandzadeh 6.00 15.00
ENJC Jason Campbell 6.00 15.00
ENJR JaMarcus Russell SP 10.00 25.00
ENJT Joe Thomas 6.00 15.00
ENLE Lee Evans 5.00 12.00
ENLJ Larry Johnson SP 10.00 25.00
ENLL LaRon Landry 6.00 15.00
ENLN Legedu Naanee 5.00 12.00
ENLT Lawrence Timmons 6.00 15.00
ENLW LaMarr Woodley 8.00 20.00
ENMB Michael Bush 6.00 15.00
ENML Marshawn Lynch SP 15.00 40.00
ENNA Joe Namath SP 40.00 80.00
ENPM Peyton Manning 50.00 100.00
ENPP Paul Posluszny 8.00 20.00
ENRB Reggie Bush SP 50.00 100.00
ENRM Robert Meachem SP 10.00 25.00
ENRN Reggie Nelson 5.00 12.00
ENRW Reggie Wayne SP 10.00 25.00
ENSC Scott Chandler 6.00 15.00
ENSM Matt Schaub 6.00 15.00
ENSY Selvin Young 6.00 15.00
ENTG Ted Ginn Jr. SP 10.00 25.00
ENTH Joe Theismann SP 15.00 30.00
ENWP Willie Parker 8.00 20.00

2007 SPx Freshman Tandems Dual Jerseys

FT2AO G.Adams/G.Olsen 4.00 10.00
FT2AT G.Adams/J.Thomas 4.00 10.00
FT2AW G.Adams/P.Willis 4.00 10.00
FT2BH M.Bush/T.Hunt 2.50 6.00
FT2ES T.Edwards/T.Smith 2.50 6.00
FT2GG T.Ginn Jr./A.Gonzalez 3.00 8.00
FT2HL C.Henry RB/M.Lynch 5.00 12.00
FT2HW J.Higgins/P.Williams 2.50 6.00
FT2IW K.Irons/G.Wolfe 2.50 6.00
FT2JG C.Johnson/T.Ginn Jr. 10.00 25.00
FT2JJ C.Johnson/D.Stanton 10.00 25.00
FT2JS D.Jarrett/S.Smith USC 3.00 8.00
FT2KS K.Kolb/D.Stanton 3.00 8.00
FT2LB B.Leonard/L.Booker 3.00 8.00
FT2LH B.Leonard/T.Hunt 2.50 6.00
FT2MB R.Meachem/D.Bowe 3.00 8.00
FT2MR R.Meachem/S.Rice 3.00 8.00
FT2PG A.Pittman/A.Gonzalez 2.50 6.00
FT2PJ A.Peterson/B.Jackson 12.00 30.00
FT2PL A.Peterson/M.Lynch 12.00 30.00
FT2QB B.Quinn/J.Beck 2.50 6.00
FT2QR B.Quinn/J.Russell 2.50 6.00
FT2QT B.Quinn/J.Thomas 4.00 10.00
FT2QW J.Russell/C.Johnson 10.00 25.00
FT2RB J.Russell/D.Bowe 2.50 6.00
FT2SB D.Stanton/J.Beck 2.50 6.00
FT2SF T.Smith/Y.Figurs 2.50 6.00
FT2SH S.Smith USC/J.Hill 2.50 6.00
FT2SP T.Smith/A.Pittman 2.50 6.00
FT2WH P.Willis/J.Hill 4.00 10.00

2007 SPx Freshman Tandems Dual Jerseys Autographs

STATED PRINT RUN 25 SER.#'d SETS
FT2AO G.Adams/G.Olsen 20.00 50.00
FT2AT G.Adams/J.Thomas 20.00 50.00
FT2AW G.Adams/P.Willis 20.00 50.00
FT2BH M.Bush/T.Hunt 12.00 30.00
FT2GG T.Ginn Jr./A.Gonzalez 15.00 40.00
FT2HL C.Henry RB/M.Lynch 30.00 80.00
FT2HW J.Higgins/P.Williams 12.00 30.00
FT2IW G.Wolfe/K.Irons 12.00 30.00
FT2JG C.Johnson/T.Ginn Jr. 60.00 150.00
FT2JJ C.Johnson/D.Stanton 60.00 150.00
FT2JS D.Jarrett/S.Smith USC 15.00 40.00
FT2KS D.Stanton/K.Kolb 15.00 40.00
FT2LB B.Leonard/L.Booker 15.00 40.00
FT2LH B.Leonard/T.Hunt 12.00 30.00
FT2MB R.Meachem/D.Bowe 15.00 40.00
FT2MR R.Meachem/S.Rice 15.00 40.00
FT2PG A.Pittman/A.Gonzalez 12.00 30.00
FT2PJ A.Peterson/B.Jackson 200.00 400.00
FT2PL A.Peterson/M.Lynch 200.00 400.00
FT2QB B.Quinn/J.Beck 12.00 30.00
FT2QR B.Quinn/J.Russell 12.00 30.00
FT2QT B.Quinn/J.Thomas 20.00 50.00
FT2QW C.Johnson/J.Russell 40.00 100.00
FT2RB J.Russell/D.Bowe 12.00 30.00
FT2SB D.Stanton/J.Beck 12.00 30.00
FT2SH J.Hill/S.Smith USC 12.00 30.00
FT2WH J.Hill/P.Willis 20.00 50.00

2007 SPx Freshman Tandems Triple Jerseys

UNPRICED AUTO STATED PRINT RUN 10
ATW Adams/Thomas/Willis 5.00 12.00
BHL Booker/Hunt/Leonard 4.00 10.00
BHR Bush/Higgins/Russell 3.00 8.00
BKS Beck/Kolb/Stanton 4.00 10.00
GGS Ginn Jr./Gonzalez/Smith 4.00 10.00
GSJ Gonzalez/Smith USC/Jarrett 4.00 10.00
HJS Hill/Jarrett/Smith USC 4.00 10.00
HLJ Hunt/Leonard/Jackson 3.00 8.00
IWB Irons/Wolfe/Booker 4.00 10.00
JMG Johnson/Meachem/Ginn Jr. 12.00 30.00
LPD Lynch/Pittman/Jackson 6.00 15.00
PJB Peterson/Jackson/Bush 15.00 40.00
PLI Peterson/Lynch/Irons 15.00 40.00
QES Quinn/Edwards/Stanton 3.00 8.00
RJB Russell/Johnson/Bowe 12.00 30.00
RJP Russell/Johnson/Peterson 20.00 50.00
RJT Russell/Johnson/Thomas 12.00 30.00
RMB Rice/Meachem/Bowe 4.00 10.00
RQK Russell/Quinn/Kolb 4.00 10.00
SPG Smith/Pittman/Gonzalez 3.00 8.00

2007 SPx Freshman Tandems Quad Jerseys

GRJS Gonz/Rice/Jarr/Smith 8.00 20.00
HBLJ Hunt/Book/Leon/Jcksn 6.00 15.00
JGJR Jhnsn/Ginn/Meach/Hill 12.00 30.00
LLPH Lynch/Leon/Petersn/Hunt 15.00 40.00
MBSJ Meach/Bowe/Smith/Jarrett 10.00 25.00
PLIB Ptrson/Lynch/Irons/Bush 15.00 40.00
QKEB Quinn/Kolb/Edwrds/Beck 10.00 25.00
QRSK Quinn/Russell/Smith/Kolb 10.00 25.00
RQPL Russell/Quinn/Ptrson/Lynch 12.00 30.00
SGGP Smith/Ginn/Gonz/Pittman 10.00 25.00

2007 SPx Super Scripts Autographs

SSAP Adrian Peterson SP 125.00 250.00
SSAS Alex Smith QB SP 8.00 20.00
SSBF Brett Favre SP 125.00 200.00
SSBJ Bo Jackson SP 40.00 80.00
SSBM Brandon Meriweather 6.00 15.00
SSBQ Brady Quinn SP 5.00 12.00
SSBU Michael Bush 5.00 12.00
SSCB Champ Bailey 15.00 40.00
SSCD Craig Buster Davis 5.00 12.00
SSCJ Calvin Johnson SP 60.00 120.00
SSCW Cadillac Williams SP 8.00 20.00
SSDB Dwayne Bowe SP 5.00 12.00
SSDH Daymeion Hughes 5.00 12.00
SSDJ Dwayne Jarrett 6.00 15.00
SSDM Dan Marino SP 125.00 250.00
SSDR Darrelle Revis 10.00 25.00
SSDS Drew Stanton SP 6.00 15.00
SSDW Darius Walker 5.00 12.00
SSEW Eric Wright 5.00 12.00
SSFG Frank Gore SP 20.00 40.00
SSGA Gaines Adams SP
SSIS Isaiah Stanback 5.00 12.00
SSJA Joseph Addai SP 6.00 15.00
SSJP Joel Filani 3.00 12.00
SSJM Joe Montana SP 100.00 200.00
SSJR JaMarcus Russell SP 6.00 15.00
SSKI Kenny Irons 5.00 12.00
SSLB Lorenzo Booker 6.00 15.00
SSLF Larry Fitzgerald SP 15.00 40.00
SSLG L.C. Greenwood 15.00 30.00
SSLL LaRon Landry 8.00 20.00
SSLY Marshawn Lynch SP 12.00 30.00
SSMB Marc Bulger SP 6.00 15.00
SSMC Marques Colston 5.00 12.00
SSMG Michael Griffin 5.00 12.00
SSML Matt Leinart SP 6.00 15.00
SSPR Philip Rivers SP 25.00 50.00
SSRB Ronnie Brown SP 15.00 30.00
SSRC Roger Craig 10.00 25.00
SSRN Reggie Nelson 5.00 12.00
SSSS Steve Smith USC SP 12.00 30.00
SSTG Ted Ginn Jr. 6.00 15.00
SSTH T.J. Houshmandzadeh 5.00 12.00
SSVY Vince Young SP 20.00 50.00

2007 SPx Winning Materials Jersey Number

*DUAL: .5X TO 1.2X BASIC JSYs
*PATCH/10: 1.5X TO 4X BASIC JSYs
*DUAL PATCH/10: 2X TO 5X BASIC JSYs
PATCH PRINT RUN 10 SER.#'d SETS
WMAG Anthony Gonzalez 1.50 4.00
WMAP Adrian Peterson 10.00 25.00
WMAR Aaron Rodgers 10.00 25.00
WMBE Cedric Benson 4.00 10.00
WMBF1 Brett Favre 8.00 20.00
WMBF2 Brett Favre 8.00 20.00
WMBJ Brad Johnson 3.00 8.00
WMBL1 Byron Leftwich 3.00 8.00
WMBL2 Byron Leftwich 3.00 8.00
WMBO Anquan Boldin 3.00 8.00
WMBQ Brady Quinn 1.50 4.00
WMBR1 Ben Roethlisberger 6.00 15.00
WMBR2 Ben Roethlisberger 6.00 15.00
WMBU Michael Bush 4.00 10.00
WMCB1 Champ Bailey 3.00 8.00
WMCB2 Champ Bailey 3.00 8.00
WMCF Charlie Frye 3.00 8.00
WMCH Chris Brown 2.50 6.00
WMCJ Calvin Johnson 8.00 20.00
WMCP Carson Palmer 4.00 10.00
WMCS1 Chris Simms 2.50 6.00
WMCS2 Chris Simms 2.50 6.00
WMCU1 Daunte Culpepper 3.00 8.00
WMCU2 Daunte Culpepper 3.00 8.00
WMCW Cadillac Williams 3.00 8.00
WMDB Drew Brees 3.00 8.00
WMDC David Carr 3.00 8.00
WMDE Derrick Mason 2.50 6.00
WMDF DeShaun Foster 3.00 8.00
WMDJ Dwayne Jarrett 4.00 10.00
WMDM Dan Marino 10.00 25.00
WMDO1 Donovan McNabb 4.00 10.00
WMDO2 Donovan McNabb 4.00 10.00
WMDR1 Drew Bledsoe 4.00 10.00
WMDR2 Drew Bledsoe 4.00 10.00
WMDS Drew Stanton 4.00 10.00
WMDW Dwayne Bowe 3.00 8.00
WMEJ Edgerrin James 4.00 10.00
WMEM Eli Manning 4.00 10.00
WMGA Gaines Adams 3.00 8.00
WMGO Tony Gonzalez 3.00 8.00
WMGR Trent Green 3.00 8.00
WMHM Heath Miller 2.50 6.00
WMHW Hines Ward 4.00 10.00
WMIB Isaac Bruce 3.00 8.00
WMJA Brandon Jackson 1.50 4.00
WMJB John Beck 4.00 10.00
WMJD1 Jake Delhomme 3.00 8.00
WMJD2 Jake Delhomme 3.00 8.00
WMJH Joe Horn 3.00 8.00
WMJJ Julius Jones 3.00 8.00
WMJL Jamal Lewis 3.00 8.00
WMJO1 Chad Johnson 3.00 8.00
WMJO2 Chad Johnson 3.00 8.00
WMJP1 Jake Plummer 3.00 8.00
WMJP2 Jake Plummer 3.00 8.00
WMJR JaMarcus Russell 1.50 4.00
WMJS Jeremy Shockey 3.00 8.00
WMJT Joe Thomas 3.00 8.00
WMJU Julius Peppers 3.00 8.00
WMJV Jonathan Vilma 3.00 8.00
WMKI Kenny Irons 2.50 6.00
WMKJ Kevin Jones 2.50 6.00
WMKK Kevin Kolb 2.00 5.00
WMLT LaDainian Tomlinson 4.00 10.00
WMMA Mark Brunell 3.00 8.00
WMMB Marc Bulger 3.00 8.00
WMMC1 Deuce McAllister 3.00 8.00
WMMC2 Deuce McAllister 3.00 8.00
WMME Robert Meachem 4.00 10.00
WMMH Marvin Harrison 4.00 10.00
WMML Marshawn Lynch 3.00 8.00
WMMV Michael Vick 4.00 10.00
WMMW Mike Williams 2.50 6.00
WMOL Greg Olsen 2.50 6.00
WMOW Terrell Owens 4.00 10.00
WMPH Priest Holmes 3.00 8.00
WMPI Antonio Pittman 2.50 6.00
WMPM Peyton Manning 6.00 15.00
WMRE Antwaan Randle El 2.50 6.00
WMRM Randy Moss 4.00 10.00
WMRO Ronnie Brown 3.00 8.00
WMSA Shaun Alexander 4.00 10.00
WMSJ Steven Jackson 4.00 10.00
WMSR Sidney Rice 2.00 5.00
WMSS Steve Smith USC 1.50 4.00
WMST Donte Stallworth 3.00 8.00
WMTB Tatum Bell 3.00 8.00
WMTG Ted Ginn Jr. 4.00 10.00
WMTH Torry Holt 3.00 8.00
WMTO Tom Brady 5.00 12.00
WMTS Troy Smith 1.50 4.00
WMUR Brian Urlacher 4.00 10.00
WMWM Willis McGahee 3.00 8.00

2007 SPx Winning Materials Jersey Number Dual Autographs

STATED PRINT RUN 10-25
SERIAL #'d UNDER 25 NOT PRICED
WMBO Anquan Boldin/25 15.00 30.00
WMBR1 Ben Roethlisberger/25
WMBR2 Ben Roethlisberger/25
WMCB1 Champ Bailey/25 25.00 50.00
WMCB2 Champ Bailey/25 25.00 50.00
WMDB Drew Brees/25 40.00 80.00
WMEM Eli Manning/25 50.00 80.00
WMLT LaDainian Tomlinson/25 60.00 120.00
WMMB Marc Bulger/25 25.00 50.00
WMPM Peyton Manning/25 100.00 175.00
WMRO Ronnie Brown/25 25.00 50.00

2007 SPx Winning Materials Stat

*DUAL: .5X TO 1.2X BASIC JSYs
*PATCH/10: 1.5X TO 4X BASIC JSYs
*DUAL PATCH/10: 2X TO 5X BASIC JSYs
PATCH PRINT RUN 10 SER.#'d SETS
WMSAG Anthony Gonzalez 1.50 4.00
WMSAH Ahman Green 3.00 8.00
WMSAP1 Adrian Peterson 10.00 25.00
WMSAP2 Adrian Peterson 10.00 25.00
WMSAR Aaron Rodgers 12.00 30.00
WMSBA Ronde Barber 2.50 6.00
WMSBF1 Brett Favre 8.00 20.00
WMSBF2 Brett Favre 8.00 20.00
WMSBL1 Byron Leftwich 3.00 8.00
WMSBL2 Byron Leftwich 3.00 8.00
WMSBO Anquan Boldin 3.00 8.00
WMSBQ1 Brady Quinn 1.50 4.00
WMSBQ2 Brady Quinn 1.50 4.00
WMSBR Ben Roethlisberger 6.00 15.00
WMSBU Michael Bush 4.00 10.00
WMSCB Champ Bailey 3.00 8.00
WMSCJ1 Calvin Johnson 8.00 20.00
WMSCJ2 Calvin Johnson 8.00 20.00
WMSCP Carson Palmer 4.00 10.00
WMSCU Daunte Culpepper 3.00 8.00
WMSDO2 Donovan McNabb 4.00 10.00
WMSDB Drew Brees 3.00 8.00
WMSDC David Carr 3.00 8.00
WMSDJ Dwayne Jarrett 4.00 10.00
WMSDO1 Donovan McNabb 4.00 10.00
WMSDR Drew Bledsoe 4.00 10.00
WMSDW Dwayne Bowe 4.00 10.00
WMSEM Eli Manning 4.00 10.00
WMSGA Gaines Adams 3.00 8.00
WMSGO Tony Gonzalez 3.00 8.00
WMSGR Trent Green 3.00 8.00
WMSHA Matt Hasselbeck 3.00 8.00
WMSHO Torry Holt 3.00 8.00
WMSHU Tony Hunt 4.00 10.00
WMSHW Hines Ward 4.00 10.00
WMSJA Javon Walker 3.00 8.00
WMSJB John Beck 1.50 4.00
WMSJD Jake Delhomme 3.00 8.00
WMSJH Joe Horn 3.00 8.00
WMSJJ Julius Jones 3.00 8.00
WMSJL Jamal Lewis 3.00 8.00
WMSJM Joe Montana 10.00 25.00
WMSJO Joe Theismann 4.00 10.00
WMSJP1 Jake Plummer 3.00 8.00
WMSJP2 Jake Plummer 3.00 8.00
WMSJR1 JaMarcus Russell 2.50 6.00
WMSJR2 JaMarcus Russell 2.50 6.00
WMSJS1 Jeremy Shockey 3.00 8.00
WMSJS2 Jeremy Shockey 3.00 8.00
WMSJT Joe Thomas 3.00 8.00
WMSKB Kyle Boller 2.50 6.00
WMSKC Keary Colbert 2.50 6.00
WMSKI Kenny Irons 2.50 6.00
WMSKJ Keyshawn Johnson 3.00 8.00
WMSKK Kevin Kolb 2.00 5.00
WMSKO Kyle Orton 2.50 6.00
WMSLE Matt Leinart 5.00 12.00
WMSLT1 LaDainian Tomlinson 4.00 10.00
WMSLT2 LaDainian Tomlinson 4.00 10.00
WMSLT3 LaDainian Tomlinson 4.00 10.00
WMSMB Marc Bulger 3.00 8.00
WMSMC Deuce McAllister 3.00 8.00
WMSME Robert Meachem 4.00 10.00
WMSMH Marvin Harrison 4.00 10.00
WMSML Marshawn Lynch 3.00 8.00
WMSMM Muhsin Muhammad 3.00 8.00
WMSMV1 Michael Vick 4.00 10.00
WMSMV2 Michael Vick 4.00 10.00
WMSOW Terrell Owens 4.00 10.00
WMSPH Priest Holmes 3.00 8.00
WMSPI Antonio Pittman 1.50 4.00
WMSPM1 Peyton Manning 6.00 15.00
WMSPM2 Peyton Manning 6.00 15.00
WMSPO Clinton Portis 3.00 8.00
WMSPR Philip Rivers 4.00 10.00
WMSRB Reggie Bush 8.00 20.00
WMSRM Randy Moss 4.00 10.00
WMSRO Ronnie Brown 3.00 8.00
WMSRS Rod Smith 3.00 8.00
WMSRW1 Reggie Wayne 3.00 8.00
WMSRW2 Reggie Wayne 3.00 8.00
WMSRW3 Reggie Wayne 3.00 8.00
WMSSA Shaun Alexander 4.00 10.00
WMSSJ Steven Jackson 4.00 10.00
WMSSR Sidney Rice 2.00 5.00
WMSSS Steve Smith USC 1.50 4.00
WMSTB Tatum Bell 3.00 8.00
WMSTE Tedy Bruschi 4.00 10.00
WMSTG Ted Ginn Jr. 4.00 10.00
WMSTH T.J. Houshmandzadeh 3.00 8.00
WMSTJ Thomas Jones 3.00 8.00
WMSTO1 Tom Brady 5.00 12.00
WMSTO2 Tom Brady 5.00 12.00
WMSTS Troy Smith 2.50 6.00
WMSTW Troy Williamson 2.50 6.00
WMSUR Brian Urlacher 4.00 10.00
WMSWM1 Willis McGahee 3.00 8.00
WMSWM2 Willis McGahee 3.00 8.00
WMSWP Willie Parker 4.00 10.00

2007 SPx Winning Trios Jerseys

BHS Bulger/Holt/Jackson 6.00 15.00
BMB Brady/Maroney/Bruschi 10.00 25.00
BMC Bush/McAllister/Colston 12.00 30.00
BWS Bell/Walker/Smith 5.00 12.00
CBS Culpepper/Brown/Seau 5.00 12.00
CWM Curtis/Willmsn/Muham 5.00 12.00
FBL Favre/Brady/Leinart 12.00 30.00
FSM Frye/Smith/Manning 5.00 12.00
GHH Green/Holmes/Hall 5.00 12.00
JOB Jones/Owens/Bledsoe 6.00 15.00
JTJ Jones/Taylor/Jackson 5.00 12.00
LDR Maroney/Williams/Bush 10.00 25.00
LEB Leinart/James/Boldin 6.00 15.00
LTD Left/Taylor/Jones-Drew 5.00 12.00
MBB Manning/Brady/Brees 12.00 30.00
MHW Manning/Harrison/Wayne 10.00 25.00
MWB McNabb/Westbrk/Brown 6.00 15.00
MWF Manning/Wayne/Freeney 10.00 25.00
OBM Orton/Benson/Muham 6.00 15.00
PJH Palmer/Johnson/Housh 6.00 15.00
PRF Palmer/Roethr/Frye 8.00 20.00
PWB Polamalu/Will.S/Barber 6.00 15.00
RPW Roeth/Parker/Ward 8.00 20.00
RTG Rivers/Tomlinson/Gates 8.00 20.00
SBS Strahan/Burress/Shockey 5.00 12.00
TJA Tomlin/Johnson/Alexander 8.00 20.00
WMF Williams/McGahee/Foster 5.00 12.00
YLC Young/Leinart/Bush 15.00 40.00
YWG Young/Brown/Givens 8.00 20.00

2008 SPx

COMP.SET w/o RC's (90) 25.00 50.00
91-150 ROOKIE PRINT RUN 999
151-177 JSY AU RC PRINT RUN 599
179-185 JSY AU RC PRINT RUN 325
186-225 AU RC PRINT RUN 399
UNPRICED NFL LOGO AU PRINT RUN 1
1 A.J. Hawk .30 .75
2 Adrian Peterson .50 1.25
3 Alex Smith .40 1.00
4 Andre Johnson .40 1.00
5 Antonio Cromartie .30 .75
6 Antonio Gates .40 1.00
7 Fran Tarkenton .60 1.50
8 Ben Roethlisberger .50 1.25
9 Brandon Jacobs .30 .75
10 Donovan McNabb .40 1.00
11 Braylon Edwards .30 .75
12 Brett Favre 1.00 2.50
13 Brian Dawkins .50 1.25
14 Brian Urlacher .50 1.25
15 Brian Westbrook .30 .75
16 Brodie Croyle .40 1.00
17 Calvin Johnson .50 1.25
18 Cadillac Williams .40 1.00
19 Carson Palmer .40 1.00
20 Chad Johnson .30 .75
21 Champ Bailey .40 1.00
22 Charles Woodson .50 1.25
23 Marc Bulger .30 .75
24 Clinton Portis .30 .75
25 Dallas Clark .30 .75
26 David Garrard .30 .75
27 DeAngelo Williams .30 .75
28 Deion Branch .30 .75
29 DeMarcus Ware .40 1.00
30 Matt Leinart .30 .75
31 Derek Anderson .30 .75
32 Devin Hester .40 1.00
33 Donte Stallworth .30 .75
34 Drew Brees .50 1.25
35 Dwayne Bowe .40 1.00
36 Ed Reed .40 1.00
37 Edgerrin James .40 1.00
38 Eli Manning .40 1.00
39 Gale Sayers .60 1.50
40 Frank Gore .40 1.00
41 Fred Taylor .30 .75
42 Barry Sanders 1.00 2.50
43 Greg Jennings .30 .75
44 JaMarcus Russell .30 .75
45 Jason Campbell .30 .75
46 Jason Taylor .40 1.00
47 Jay Cutler .30 .75
48 Jeff Garcia .30 .75
49 Y.A. Tittle .60 1.50
50 Joseph Addai .30 .75
51 Kellen Winslow Jr. .30 .75
52 Joe Montana 2.00 5.00
53 LaDainian Tomlinson .50 1.25
54 Larry Fitzgerald .40 1.00
55 Larry Johnson .30 .75
56 Laurence Maroney .40 1.00
57 Jerry Rice 1.25 3.00
58 Paul Hornung .60 1.50
59 Lofa Tatupu .30 .75
60 Kurt Warner .40 1.00
61 Marshawn Lynch .40 1.00
62 Marvin Harrison .40 1.00
63 Matt Hasselbeck .30 .75
64 Maurice Jones-Drew .30 .75
65 Michael Strahan .40 1.00
66 Hines Ward .40 1.00
67 Reggie Wayne .40 1.00
68 Peyton Manning 1.25 3.00
69 Plaxico Burress .30 .75
70 Randy Moss .40 1.00
71 Reggie Bush .30 .75
72 Bob Griese .60 1.50
73 Ronnie Brown .30 .75
74 Jim Brown .75 2.00
75 Shawne Merriman .30 .75
76 Jamal Lewis .40 1.00
77 Steve Smith .40 1.00
78 Steven Jackson .30 .75
79 Terrell Owens .40 1.00
80 Joey Galloway .40 1.00
81 Tom Brady 1.50 4.00
82 Tony Gonzalez .40 1.00
83 Tony Romo .40 1.00
84 Torry Holt .40 1.00
85 Troy Polamalu .50 1.25
86 Vince Young .30 .75
87 Warrick Dunn .30 .75
88 Wes Welker .40 1.00
89 Willie Parker .40 1.00
90 Willis McGahee .30 .75
91 Marcus Thomas RC 2.00 5.00
92 Caleb Campbell RC 2.50 6.00
93 Xavier Omon RC 1.50 4.00
94 Spencer Larsen RC 1.50 4.00
95 Barry Richardson RC 1.50 4.00
96 Beau Bell RC 2.00 5.00
97 Brandon Flowers RC 2.00 5.00
98 Chauncey Washington RC 2.00 5.00
99 Cory Boyd RC 1.50 4.00
100 Chris Williams RC 1.50 4.00
101 Craig Stevens RC 1.50 4.00
102 Darius Reynaud RC 1.50 4.00
103 DeJuan Tribble RC 1.50 4.00
104 Dennis Keyes RC 1.50 4.00
105 Erin Henderson RC 2.00 5.00
106 Brad Cottam RC 1.50 4.00
107 Jamie Silva RC 2.00 5.00
108 Gosder Cherilus RC 2.00 5.00
109 Jacob Hester RC 1.50 4.00
110 Jehuu Caulcrick RC 2.00 5.00
111 Trae Williams RC 1.50 4.00
112 Jonathan Goff RC 1.50 4.00
113 Jonathan Hefney RC 1.50 4.00
114 Jordon Dizon RC 1.50 4.00
115 Josh Barrett RC 1.50 4.00
116 Josh Johnson RC 1.50 4.00
117 Justin Forsett RC 2.00 5.00
118 Justin King RC 2.00 5.00
119 Kalvin McRae RC 1.50 4.00
120 Keenan Burton RC 1.50 4.00
121 Kellen Davis RC 1.50 4.00
122 Keon Lattimore RC 2.00 5.00
123 Lance Leggett RC 2.50 6.00
124 Lavelle Hawkins RC 2.00 5.00
125 Marcus Monk RC 2.00 5.00
126 Mario Urrutia RC 1.50 4.00
127 Curtis Lofton RC 2.00 5.00
128 Martin Rucker RC 1.50 4.00
129 Will Franklin RC 2.00 5.00
130 Phillip Merling RC 1.50 4.00
131 Wesley Woodyard RC 2.50 6.00
132 Josh Morgan RC 1.50 4.00
133 Owen Schmitt RC 1.50 4.00
134 Paul Hubbard RC 1.50 4.00
135 Paul Smith RC 1.50 4.00
136 Philip Wheeler RC 2.00 5.00
137 Quentin Groves RC 2.00 5.00
138 Quintin Demps RC 2.00 5.00
139 Roy Schuening RC 1.50 4.00
140 Ryan Torain RC 2.00 5.00
141 Simeon Castille RC 1.50 4.00
142 T.C. Ostrander RC 2.00 5.00
143 Jerod Mayo RC 2.50 6.00
144 Tom Zbikowski RC 2.00 5.00
145 Thomas DeCoud RC 1.50 4.00
146 Tracy Porter RC 2.00 5.00
147 Trevor Laws RC 1.50 4.00
148 Trevor Scott RC 2.00 5.00
149 Vince Hall RC 1.50 4.00
150 Xavier Adibi RC 1.50 4.00
151 Donnie Avery JSY AU RC 6.00 15.00
152 Chad Henne JSY AU RC 6.00 15.00
153 Chris Johnson JSY AU RC 6.00 15.00
154 Earl Bennett JSY AU RC 8.00 20.00
155 Glenn Dorsey JSY AU RC 5.00 12.00
156 Harry Douglas JSY AU RC 6.00 15.00
157 Early Doucet JSY AU RC 5.00 12.00
158 Andre Caldwell JSY AU RC 5.00 12.00
159 Felix Jones JSY AU RC 5.00 12.00
160 Dustin Keller JSY AU RC 6.00 15.00
161 Jake Long JSY AU RC 8.00 20.00
162 Joe Flacco JSY AU RC 15.00 40.00
163 J.David Booty JSY AU RC 5.00 12.00
164 Jordy Nelson JSY AU RC 15.00 40.00
165 Jerome Simpson JSY AU RC 6.00 15.00
166 Kevin Smith JSY AU RC 5.00 12.00
167 Limas Sweed JSY AU RC 5.00 12.00
168 Malcolm Kelly JSY AU RC 5.00 12.00
169 M.Manningham JSY AU RC 10.00 25.00
170 James Hardy JSY AU RC 5.00 12.00
171 Matt Forte JSY AU RC 12.00 30.00
172 Dexter Jackson JSY AU RC 8.00 20.00
173 Eddie Royal JSY AU RC 5.00 12.00
174 R.Mendenhall JSY AU RC 5.00 12.00
175 Ray Rice JSY AU RC 5.00 12.00
176 Steve Slaton JSY AU RC 5.00 12.00
177 Kevin O'Connell JSY AU RC 5.00 12.00
179 Jamaal Charles JSY AU RC 10.00 25.00
180 Brian Brohm JSY AU RC 6.00 15.00
181 Devin Thomas JSY AU RC 6.00 15.00
182 D.McFadden JSY AU RC 6.00 15.00
183 DeS.Jackson JSY AU RC 8.00 20.00
184 J.Stewart JSY AU RC 8.00 20.00
185 Matt Ryan JSY AU RC 50.00 100.00
186 Yvenson Bernard AU RC 5.00 12.00
187 Alex Brink AU RC 4.00 10.00
188 Ali Highsmith AU RC 3.00 8.00
189 Allen Patrick AU RC 3.00 8.00
190 Antoine Cason AU RC 4.00 10.00
191 Aqib Talib AU RC 10.00 25.00
192 Ben Moffitt AU RC 3.00 8.00
193 Anthony Morelli AU RC 3.00 8.00
194 Bruce Davis AU RC 4.00 10.00
195 Calais Campbell AU RC 4.00 10.00
196 Chevis Jackson AU RC 3.00 8.00
197 Chris Ellis AU RC 3.00 8.00
198 Craig Steltz AU RC 3.00 8.00
199 DJ Hall AU RC 3.00 8.00
200 Dan Connor AU RC 3.00 8.00
201 DeMario Pressley AU RC 4.00 10.00
202 Derrick Harvey AU RC 3.00 8.00
203 D.Rodgers-Cromartie AU RC 4.00 10.00
204 Chris Long AU RC 4.00 10.00
205 Dre Moore AU RC 3.00 8.00
206 Fred Davis AU RC 3.00 8.00
207 Dwight Lowery AU RC 4.00 10.00
208 Davone Bess AU RC 4.00 10.00
209 Frank Okam AU RC 3.00 8.00
210 Dennis Dixon AU RC 8.00 20.00
211 Leodis McKelvin AU RC 4.00 10.00
212 Jack Ikegwuonu AU RC 3.00 8.00
213 Jacob Tamme AU RC 4.00 10.00
214 J Leman AU RC 3.00 8.00
215 John Carlson AU RC 3.00 8.00
216 Keith Rivers AU RC 3.00 8.00
217 Geno Hayes AU RC 3.00 8.00
218 Lawrence Jackson AU RC 3.00 8.00
219 Martellus Bennett AU RC 4.00 10.00
220 Ryan Clady AU RC 4.00 10.00
221 Sam Baker AU RC 3.00 8.00
222 Sedrick Ellis AU RC 3.00 8.00
223 Shawn Crable AU RC 3.00 8.00
224 Terrell Thomas AU RC 3.00 8.00
225 Vernon Gholston AU RC 3.00 8.00

2008 SPx Gold Holofoil Rookies

*ROOKIES 91-150: 1.2X TO 3X BASIC CARDS
*ROOKIE JSY AU 151-177: 1.2X TO 3X
*ROOKIE JSY AU 179-185: 1.2X TO 3X
*ROOKIE AU 186-225: 1X TO 2.5X
STATED PRINT RUN 25 SER.#'d SETS
162 Joe Flacco JSY AU 60.00 125.00
185 Matt Ryan JSY AU 200.00 350.00

2008 SPx Green Holofoil Rookies

*ROOKIES/499: .5X TO 1.2X BASIC CARDS
91-150 ROOKIE PRINT RUN 499
*ROOK.JSY AU/199: .6X TO 1.5X BASIC CARDS
151-177 JSY AU PRINT RUN 199
*ROOK.JSY AU/99: .6X TO 1.5X BASIC CARDS
179-185 JSY AU PRINT RUN 99
*ROOKIE AU/199: .6X TO 1.5X BASIC CARDS
186-225 ROOKIE AU PRINT RUN 199
162 Joe Flacco JSY AU 20.00 50.00
182 Darren McFadden JSY AU/99 10.00 25.00
185 Matt Ryan JSY AU/99 40.00 100.00

2008 SPx Platinum

UNPRICED PLATINUM PRINT RUN 1
EACH PLAYER HAS MULTIPLE 1/1 PLAT.
WITH DIFFERING STAT LINES ON FRONT

2008 SPx Silver Holofoil Rookies

*SILVER HOLO/299: .6X TO 1.5X BASIC RC
*SILVER HOLO AU/99: .6X TO 1.5X BASIC RC
STATED PRINT RUN 99-299

2008 SPx Rookie Materials Autographs SPX Triple

STATED PRINT RUN 25 SER.#'d SETS
RMAC Andre Caldwell 8.00 20.00
RMBB Brian Brohm 8.00 20.00
RMCH Chad Henne 10.00 25.00
RMCJ Chris Johnson 10.00 25.00
RMCL Chris Long 10.00 25.00
RMDA Donnie Avery 10.00 25.00
RMDJ DeSean Jackson 25.00 60.00
RMDK Dustin Keller 10.00 25.00
RMDM Darren McFadden 8.00 20.00
RMDT Devin Thomas 8.00 20.00
RMEB Earl Bennett 12.00 30.00
RMED Early Doucet 8.00 20.00
RMER Eddie Royal 8.00 20.00
RMFJ Felix Jones 8.00 20.00
RMFO Matt Forte 25.00 60.00
RMGD Glenn Dorsey 8.00 20.00
RMHD Harry Douglas 10.00 25.00
RMJA Dexter Jackson 12.00 30.00
RMJB John David Booty 8.00 20.00
RMJC Jamaal Charles 12.00 30.00
RMJF Joe Flacco 50.00 100.00
RMJH James Hardy 8.00 20.00
RMJL Jake Long 12.00 30.00
RMJN Jordy Nelson 30.00 60.00
RMJS Jonathan Stewart 12.00 30.00
RMKO Kevin O'Connell 8.00 20.00
RMKS Kevin Smith 8.00 20.00
RMLS Limas Sweed 8.00 20.00
RMMK Malcolm Kelly 8.00 20.00
RMMM Mario Manningham 15.00 40.00
RMMR Matt Ryan 40.00 100.00
RMRM Rashard Mendenhall 8.00 20.00
RMRR Ray Rice 8.00 20.00
RMSI Jerome Simpson 10.00 25.00
RMSS Steve Slaton 8.00 20.00

2008 SPx Rookie Materials SPX Dual 199

SPX DUAL PRINT RUN 199
*NFL DUAL/199: .4X TO 1X SPX DUAL/199
*JER.# DUAL/175: .4X TO 1X SPX DUAL/199
*POSIT.DUAL/149: .4X TO 1X SPX DUAL/199
*FOOTBALL/119: .4X TO 1X SPX DUAL/199
*AFC/NFC DUAL/99: .4X TO 1X SPX DUAL/199
*NFL SHIELD/99: .4X TO 1X SPX DUAL/199
*SPX PATCH/99: .5X TO 1.2X SPX DUAL/199
*SPX TRIPLE/99: .4X TO 1X SPX DUAL/199
*SPX NEW DUAL/75: .5X TO 1.2X SPX/199
*LOGO X LOGO/75: .5X TO 1.2X SPX DUAL/199
*AFC/NFC TRIPLE/50: .5X TO 1.2X
*NFL PATCH DUAL/50: .5X TO 1.2X
*UNIQUE SHAPE/50: .5X TO 1.2X SPX/199
*FOOTBALL/35: .6X TO 1.5X SPX DUAL/199
*LOGO X LOGO/35: .6X TO 1.5X SPX DUAL/199
*JER.# DUAL/25: .6X TO 1.5X SPX DUAL/199
*SPX TRIP PATCH/25: .8X TO 2X SPX DUAL/199
*POSIT.DUAL/25: .6X TO 1.5X SPX DUAL/199
*AFC/NFC PATCH/15: 1X TO 2.5X DUAL/199
*NFL PATCH TRIPLE/15: 1X TO 2.5X DUAL/199
*UNIQUE SHAPE/15: .8X TO 2X SPX DUAL/199
*NFL SHIELD/5: 1.2X TO 3X SPX DUAL/199
UNPRICED NFL LOGO PATCH #'d TO 1
UNPRICED SPX NEW LOGO TRIPLE #'d TO 1
RMAC Andre Caldwell 1.50 4.00
RMBB Brian Brohm 1.50 4.00
RMCH Chad Henne 2.00 5.00
RMCJ Chris Johnson 2.00 5.00
RMCL Chris Long 2.00 5.00
RMDA Donnie Avery 2.00 6.00
RMDJ DeSean Jackson 3.00 8.00
RMDK Dustin Keller 2.00 5.00
RMDM Darren McFadden 1.50 4.00
RMDT Devin Thomas 1.50 4.00
RMEB Earl Bennett 2.50 6.00
RMED Early Doucet 1.50 4.00
RMER Eddie Royal 1.50 4.00
RMFJ Felix Jones 1.50 4.00
RMFO Matt Forte 2.50 6.00
RMGD Glenn Dorsey 1.50 4.00
RMHD Harry Douglas 2.00 5.00
RMJA Dexter Jackson 2.50 6.00
RMJB John David Booty 1.50 4.00
RMJC Jamaal Charles 2.50 6.00
RMJF Joe Flacco 3.00 8.00
RMJH James Hardy 1.50 4.00
RMJL Jake Long 2.50 6.00
RMJN Jordy Nelson 5.00 12.00
RMJS Jonathan Stewart 5.00 12.00
RMKO Kevin O'Connell 1.50 4.00
RMKS Kevin Smith 1.50 4.00
RMLS Limas Sweed 1.50 4.00
RMMK Malcolm Kelly 1.50 4.00
RMMM Mario Manningham 1.50 4.00
RMMR Matt Ryan 8.00 20.00
RMRM Rashard Mendenhall 1.50 4.00
RMRR Ray Rice 1.50 4.00
RMSI Jerome Simpson 2.00 5.00
RMSS Steve Slaton 1.50 4.00

2008 SPx Signature Supremacy

SSAA Adrian Arrington 2.50 6.00
SSAC Andre Caldwell 2.50 6.00
SSAS Aaron Schobel 4.00 10.00
SSAV Donnie Avery 3.00 8.00
SSBD Bruce Davis 3.00 8.00
SSBM Ben Moffitt 3.00 8.00
SSBS Bob Sanders 15.00 40.00
SSBW Ben Watson 4.00 10.00
SSCC Calais Campbell 3.00 8.00
SSCJ Chris Johnson 3.00 8.00
SSCL Chris Long 3.00 8.00
SSCW Cadillac Williams 5.00 12.00
SSDA Derek Anderson 4.00 10.00
SSDB Dorien Bryant 3.00 8.00
SSDD Dennis Dixon 2.50 6.00
SSDJ Dexter Jackson 4.00 10.00
SSDK Dustin Keller 3.00 8.00
SSDL Donald Lee 5.00 12.00
SSDT Devin Thomas 2.50 6.00
SSES Emmitt Smith 75.00 150.00
SSFD Fred Davis 2.50 6.00
SSFO Matt Forte 12.00 30.00
SSGJ Frank Gore 8.00 20.00
SSHA Mike Hart 2.50 6.00
SSJB Jacob Hester 2.50 6.00
SSJC Jerricho Cotchery 4.00 10.00
SSJF Joe Flacco 12.00 30.00
SSJG Jeff Garcia EXCH
SSJH James Hardy 2.50 6.00
SSJL Jamal Lewis EXCH
SSLH Lavelle Hawkins 3.00 8.00
SSLT LaDainian Tomlinson 15.00 30.00
SSMB Marion Barber 4.00 10.00
SSME Rashard Mendenhall 2.50 6.00
SSMF Matt Flynn 6.00 15.00
SSMH Michael Huff 4.00 10.00
SSMK Malcolm Kelly 2.50 6.00
SSMS Matt Schaub 4.00 10.00
SSPW Patrick Willis 6.00 15.00
SSRR Ray Rice 2.50 6.00
SSSS Steve Slaton 2.50 6.00
SSTB Tom Brady 90.00 150.00
SSTR Tony Romo 25.00 60.00
SSTT Terrell Thomas 2.50 6.00
SSTZ Tom Zbikowski 3.00 8.00
SSWH Philip Wheeler 3.00 8.00
SSWW Wes Welker 15.00 30.00
SSXA Xavier Adibi 2.50 6.00
SSYT Y.A. Tittle 10.00 25.00

2008 SPx Super Scripts Autographs

UNPRICED TRIPLE AU PRINT RUN 20
UNPRICED QUAD AU PRINT RUN 15
UNPRICED SIX AU PRINT RUN 6
UNPRICED EIGHT AU PRINT RUN 8
SSS1 A.J. Hawk 10.00 25.00
SSS2 Aaron Schobel 4.00 10.00
SSS3 Adrian Arrington 2.50 6.00
SSS4 Andre Caldwell 2.50 6.00
SSS5 Patrick Willis 8.00 20.00
SSS6 Kevin O'Connell 2.50 6.00
SSS7 Devin Thomas 2.50 6.00
SSS8 Steve Young 20.00 40.00
SSS9 Dexter Jackson 4.00 10.00
SSS10 Ben Moffitt 2.50 6.00
SSS12 Bruce Davis 3.00 8.00
SSS13 Calais Campbell 3.00 8.00
SSS15 Chad Henne 3.00 8.00
SSS16 Cadillac Williams 5.00 12.00
SSS17 Chris Long 3.00 8.00
SSS18 Derek Anderson 4.00 10.00
SSS19 Derrick Harvey 2.50 6.00
SSS20 Daryl Johnston 12.50 25.00
SSS21 DeMarcus Ware 8.00 20.00
SSS22 Dennis Dixon 5.00 12.00
SSS23 Early Doucet 2.50 6.00
SSS24 Erin Henderson 3.00 8.00
SSS25 Eli Manning 30.00 80.00
SSS26 Fred Davis 2.50 6.00
SSS27 Frank Gore 8.00 20.00
SSS28 Jacob Hester 2.50 6.00
SSS29 James Hardy 2.50 6.00
SSS30 Jacob Tamme 3.00 8.00
SSS31 Joe Flacco 20.00 50.00
SSS32 Joe Namath
SSS33 Jonathan Stewart 4.00 10.00
SSS34 Jordy Nelson 15.00 30.00
SSS35 Keith Rivers 2.50 6.00
SSS36 Kenny Phillips 2.50 6.00
SSS37 Lawrence Jackson 2.50 6.00
SSS38 LaDainian Tomlinson 25.00 50.00
SSS39 Lavelle Hawkins 3.00 8.00
SSS40 Limas Sweed 2.50 6.00
SSS41 Jerome Simpson 3.00 8.00
SSS42 Malcolm Kelly 2.50 6.00
SSS43 Mario Urrutia 2.50 6.00
SSS44 Martin Rucker 2.50 6.00
SSS45 Matt Flynn 2.50 6.00
SSS46 Marc Bulger 4.00 10.00
SSS47 Michael Huff 4.00 10.00
SSS48 Rashard Mendenhall 2.50 6.00
SSS49 Y.A. Tittle 10.00 25.00
SSS50 Xavier Adibi 2.50 6.00
SSS53 Aaron Ross 4.00 10.00
SSS54 Buster Davis 4.00 10.00
SSS55 Quentin Groves 3.00 8.00
SSS57 Mike Hart 5.00 12.00
SSS58 Antoine Cason 3.00 8.00
SSS59 Peyton Hillis 8.00 20.00

2008 SPx Super Scripts Autographs Dual

STATED PRINT RUN 75-99
SSD1 A.J. Hawk/Ernie Sims
SSD2 Sam Baker/Jake Long 5.00 12.00
SSD3 M.Schaub/D.Anderson 6.00 15.00
SSD4 Chad Henne/Mike Hart 4.00 10.00
SSD5 Joe Flacco/Matt Schaub 25.00 50.00
SSD6 A.Bradshaw/Felix Jones 3.00 8.00
SSD7 Cal.Campbell/B.Davis/99 4.00 10.00
SSD8 C.Williams/Chris Johnson 4.00 10.00
SSD9 Aqib Talib/Mike Jenkins
SSD10 S.Ellis/L.Jackson 6.00 15.00
SSD11 D.Garrard/Joe Flacco 20.00 50.00
SSD12 D.Thomas/DeS.Jackson 12.00 30.00
SSD13 J.Hardy/J.Nelson 12.50 25.00
SSD14 Matt Forte/Earl Bennett 20.00 40.00
SSD15 Gore/Norwood 8.00 20.00
SSD16 G.Dorsey/Jacob Hester 8.00 20.00
SSD17 Brodie Croyle/DJ Hall 10.00 25.00
SSD18 J.D.Booty/Fred Davis 3.00 8.00
SSD19 J.Campbell/A.Woodson 12.50 25.00

SSD20 L.McKelvin/D.Lowery 4.00 10.00
SSD21 C.Brennan/D.Bess 8.00 20.00
SSD22 S.Slaton/Alex Brink 8.00 20.00
SSD23 J.D.Booty/S.Ellis/99 3.00 8.00
SSD24 J.Stewart/M.Barber 20.00 50.00
SSD25 J.Addai/S.Slaton 8.00 20.00
SSD26 A.Cason/M.Jenkins 4.00 10.00
SSD27 K.Phillips/M.Blount
SSD28 Mendenhall/Matt Forte 5.00 12.00
SSD29 L.Sweed/Dar.Jackson 3.00 8.00
SSD30 D.Ware/D.Connor 8.00 20.00
SSD31 M.Kelly/DeS.Jackson 10.00 25.00
SSD32 Marc Bulger/Erik Ainge 8.00 20.00
SSD33 A.Arrington/Chad Henne 4.00 10.00
SSD34 D.Thomas/J.Cotchery 8.00 20.00
SSD35 Dan Connor/Justin King 8.00 20.00
SSD36 Chris Johnson/F.Jones 4.00 10.00
SSD37 Cason/Jack Ikegwuonu 4.00 10.00
SSD38 W.Welker/T.Brady 125.00 250.00
SSD39 K.Boss/M.Rucker 8.00 20.00
SSD40 Jo.Johnson/D.Dixon 10.00 25.00

2008 SPx Super Scripts Autographs Triple

SUPER SCRIPTS TRIPLE AU PRINT RUN 20
SST2 C.Long/Dorsey/L.Jackson 20.00 40.00
SST3 D.Anderson/Bulger/Brennan 25.00 50.00
SST6 Gore/K.Smith/C.Johnson 20.00 50.00
SST8 Flacco/Roethlis/Garrard 60.00 120.00
SST10 Tomlin/Sayers/B.Sanders 125.00 200.00
SST11 Bulger/Schaub/Eli 40.00 80.00
SST12 Barber/Romo/Choice 50.00 100.00
SST14 R.Rice/McFadden/Menden 8.00 20.00
SST15 S.Ellis/T.Thomas/Booty 15.00 40.00
SST16 A.Wdson/Flacco/O'Connell 50.00 100.00
SST18 Ryan/Brohm/Henne 60.00 120.00
SST20 Ware/Connor/Butkus 40.00 80.00

2008 SPx Winning Combos 99

STATED PRINT RUN 99 SER.#'d SETS
*COMBOS/49: .5X TO 1.2X COMBO/99
*COMBOS/25: .6X TO 1.5X COMBO/99
*COMBOS/5: 1.2X TO 3X COMBO/99
*COMBOS PATCH/15: 1X TO 2.5X COMBO/99
WC1 D.Ware/A.Hawk 3.00 8.00
WC2 A.Peterson/C.Johnson 4.00 10.00
WC3 B.Croyle/G.Dorsey 5.00 12.00
WC4 A.Samuel/Bo.Sanders 3.00 8.00
WC5 O'Connell/D.Anderson 2.50 6.00
WC6 B.Watson/T.Gonzalez 3.00 8.00
WC7 B.Sanders/D.Sanders 6.00 15.00
WC8 B.Marshall/Jay Cutler 5.00 12.00
WC9 B.Edwards/Manningham 2.50 6.00
WC10 E.James/Anquan Boldin 4.00 10.00
WC11 B.Brohm/Dan Marino 10.00 25.00
WC12 B.Westbrook/D.McNabb 5.00 12.00
WC13 C.Johnson/L.Sweed 4.00 10.00
WC14 C.Henne/Roethlisberger 6.00 15.00
WC15 C.Bailey/Manningham 3.00 8.00
WC16 R.Wayne/M.Harrison 4.00 10.00
WC17 C.Portis/Devin Thomas 2.50 6.00
WC18 F.Harris/B.Jackson 10.00 25.00
WC19 D.Clark/P.Manning 6.00 15.00
WC20 Dar.Jackson/C.Taylor 2.50 6.00
WC21 McFadden/B.Sanders 12.00 30.00
WC22 M.Hasselbeck/D.Branch 3.00 8.00
WC23 D.Garrard/F.Taylor 3.00 8.00
WC24 E.Bennett/Mic.Clayton 4.00 10.00
WC25 De.Williams/D.Foster 3.00 8.00
WC26 R.Lewis/S.Merriman 4.00 10.00
WC27 De.Jackson/L.Fitzgerald 5.00 12.00
WC28 D.Hester/B.Urlacher 6.00 15.00
WC29 E.Royal/S.Smith 2.50 6.00
WC30 A.Gates/D.Sproles 4.00 10.00
WC31 D.Brees/R.Bush 5.00 12.00
WC32 E.James/W.McGahee 4.00 10.00
WC33 E.Smith/F.Taylor 10.00 25.00
WC34 D.Keller/J.Shockey 3.00 8.00
WC35 Dorsey/J.Russell 5.00 12.00
WC36 G.Jennings/E.Doucet 2.50 6.00
WC37 D.Bowe/M.Colston 3.00 8.00
WC38 G.Olsen/B.Berrian 3.00 8.00
WC39 H.Ward/S.Holmes 5.00 12.00
WC40 J.Campbell/C.Cooley 5.00 12.00
WC41 J.Witten/H.Miller 5.00 12.00
WC42 J.Garcia/J.Galloway 3.00 8.00
WC43 J.Shockey/M.Strahan 3.00 8.00
WC44 F.Gore/F.Taylor 3.00 8.00
WC45 J.Galloway/M.Kelly 3.00 8.00
WC46 Cal.Johnson/Rwilliams WR 4.00 10.00
WC47 J.Stewart/R.Mendenhall 4.00 10.00
WC48 J.Nelson/D.Bowe 8.00 20.00
WC49 J.Addai/Kevin Smith 2.50 6.00
WC50 J.Shockey/K.Winslow 4.00 10.00
WC51 J.Peppers/A.Schobel 3.00 8.00
WC52 C.Bailey/D.Bly 4.00 10.00
WC53 D.Jackson/J.Simpson 4.00 10.00
WC54 R.Williams/E.Sims 3.00 8.00
WC55 B.Favre/A.Rodgers 12.00 30.00
WC56 L.Tomlinson/G.Sayers 8.00 20.00
WC57 L.Tomlinson/K.Smith 4.00 10.00
WC58 L.Johnson/J.Stewart 5.00 12.00
WC59 L.White/F.Jones 2.50 6.00
WC60 L.Tatupu/A.Pierce 3.00 8.00
WC61 M.Kelly/V.Jackson 2.50 6.00
WC62 M.Bulger/C.Pennington 3.00 8.00
WC63 M.Lynch/T.Edwards 4.00 10.00
WC64 M.Forte/B.Jacobs 6.00 15.00
WC65 M.Leinart/A.Boldin 4.00 10.00
WC66 M.Ryan/C.Palmer 8.00 20.00
WC67 M.Strahan/D.Freeney 5.00 12.00
WC68 S.Slaton/M.Jones-Drew 2.50 6.00
WC69 G.Dorsey/J.Long 4.00 10.00
WC70 P.Rivers/E.Manning 5.00 12.00
WC71 P.Burress/Eli 5.00 12.00
WC72 P.Burress/Br.Jacobs 3.00 8.00
WC73 R.Mendenhall/Cad.Williams 3.00 8.00
WC74 R.Wayne/P.Manning 8.00 20.00
WC75 R.Curry/K.Morrison 3.00 8.00
WC76 R.Barber/T.Barber 2.50 6.00
WC77 R.Brown/Cad.Williams 3.00 8.00
WC78 R.Johnson/C.Johnson 3.00 8.00
WC79 R.Grant/G.Jones 5.00 12.00
WC80 S.Alexander/M.Hasselbeck 3.00 8.00
WC81 S.McNair/S.Young 5.00 12.00
WC82 S.Slaton/C.Benson 2.50 6.00
WC83 S.Jackson/B.Westbrook 4.00 10.00
WC84 T.Owens/Terry Glenn 5.00 12.00
WC85 D.Sproles/V.Jackson 4.00 10.00
WC86 T.Brady/J.Elway 10.00 25.00
WC87 T.Brady/R.Moss 10.00 25.00
WC88 T.Gonzalez/B.Croyle 4.00 10.00
WC89 T.Romo/M.Ryan 8.00 20.00
WC90 T.Holt/I.Bruce 4.00 10.00
WC91 T.Polamalu/J.Booty 6.00 15.00
WC92 F.Tarkenton/S.Rice 4.00 10.00
WC93 V.Davis/F.Gore 3.00 8.00
WC94 V.Young/G.Dorsey 5.00 12.00
WC95 W.Payton/C.Benson 12.00 30.00
WC96 W.Dunn/M.Jenkins 3.00 8.00
WC97 W.Welker/L.Maroney 4.00 10.00
WC98 W.Parker/Ray Rice 3.00 8.00
WC99 W.McGahee/R.Lewis 4.00 10.00
WC100 J.Taylor/R.Brown 3.00 8.00

2008 SPx Winning Materials SPX 149

SPX STATED PRINT RUN 149
*AFC/NFC/5: 1.2X TO 3X SPX/149
*AFC/NFC DUAL/75: .4X TO 1X SPX/149
*AFC/NFC DUAL PAT/25: .8X TO 2X SPX/149
*FOOTBALLS/39: .5X TO 1.2X SPX/149
*JERSEY #/75: .4X TO 1X SPX/149
*JSY # DUAL/25: .6X TO 1.5X SPX/149
*NFL/99: .4X TO 1X SPX/149
*NFL DUAL/50: .5X TO 1.2X SPX/149
*NFL PATCH/25: .8X TO 2X SPX/149
*SPX PATCH/50: .5X TO 1.2X SPX/149
*SPX DUAL/99: .4X TO 1X SPX/149
*SPX DUAL PAT/15-25: 1.2X TO 3X SPX/149
*TEAM LOGO/25: .6X TO 1.5X SPX/149
*UD LOGOS/99: .4X TO 1X SPX/149
*UNIQUE SHAPE/50: .5X TO 1.2X SPX/149
WMAB Anquan Boldin 2.00 5.00
WMAC Andre Caldwell 1.50 4.00
WMAH A.J. Hawk 2.00 5.00
WMAN Derek Anderson 2.00 5.00
WMAP Adrian Peterson 3.00 8.00
WMAS Aaron Schobel 2.00 5.00
WMBA Brandon Jacobs 2.00 5.00
WMBB Brian Brohm 1.50 4.00
WMBC Brodie Croyle 2.50 6.00
WMBE Braylon Edwards 2.00 5.00
WMBF Brett Favre 6.00 15.00
WMBJ Bo Jackson 5.00 12.00
WMBO Dwayne Bowe 2.50 6.00
WMBQ Brady Quinn 2.00 5.00
WMBR Ben Roethlisberger 3.00 8.00
WMBS Bob Sanders 2.50 6.00
WMBU Marc Bulger 2.00 5.00
WMBW Brian Westbrook 2.00 5.00
WMBZ Brian Bosworth 4.00 10.00
WMCA Jason Campbell 2.00 5.00
WMCB Champ Bailey 2.50 6.00
WMCH Chad Henne 2.00 5.00
WMCJ Calvin Johnson 3.00 8.00
WMCO Chris Johnson 2.00 5.00
WMCP Clinton Portis 2.00 5.00
WMCU Jay Cutler 2.00 5.00
WMCW Cadillac Williams 2.50 6.00
WMDA Donnie Avery 2.00 5.00
WMDE Dexter Jackson 2.50 6.00
WMDG David Garrard 2.00 5.00
WMDH Devin Hester 2.50 6.00
WMDJ DeSean Jackson 3.00 8.00
WMDK Dustin Keller 2.00 5.00
WMDL Donald Lee 2.50 6.00
WMDM Darren McFadden 1.50 4.00
WMDR Darrell Jackson 2.00 5.00
WMDT Devin Thomas 1.50 4.00
WMDW DeMarcus Ware 2.50 6.00
WMEB Earl Bennett 2.50 6.00
WMED Early Doucet 1.50 4.00
WMEM Eli Manning 2.50 6.00
WMER Ed Reed 2.50 6.00
WMES Ernie Sims 2.00 5.00
WMFG Frank Gore 2.50 6.00
WMFJ Felix Jones 1.50 4.00
WMFO Matt Forte 2.50 6.00
WMGD Glenn Dorsey 1.50 4.00
WMGJ Greg Jennings 2.00 5.00
WMGO Tony Gonzalez 2.50 6.00
WMGS Gale Sayers 4.00 10.00
WMHD Harry Douglas 2.00 5.00
WMJA Joseph Addai 2.00 5.00
WMJB John David Booty 1.50 4.00
WMJC Jamaal Charles 2.50 6.00
WMJE Jerricho Cotchery 2.00 5.00
WMJF Joe Flacco 3.00 8.00
WMJH James Hardy 1.50 4.00
WMJL Jake Long 2.50 6.00
WMJN Jordy Nelson 5.00 12.00
WMJO Chad Johnson 2.00 5.00
WMJR JaMarcus Russell 2.00 5.00
WMJS Jonathan Stewart 5.00 12.00
WMKO Kevin O'Connell 1.50 4.00
WMKS Kevin Smith 1.50 4.00
WMLE Matt Leinart 2.00 5.00
WMLJ Larry Johnson 2.00 5.00
WMLS Limas Sweed 1.50 4.00
WMLT LaDainian Tomlinson 3.00 8.00
WMMB Marion Barber 2.00 5.00
WMMC Mark Clayton 2.00 5.00
WMME Rashard Mendenhall 1.50 4.00
WMMK Malcolm Kelly 1.50 4.00
WMML Marshawn Lynch 2.50 6.00
WMMM Mario Manningham 1.50 4.00
WMMR Matt Ryan 5.00 12.00
WMMS Matt Schaub 2.00 5.00
WMMV Mike Vrabel 2.00 5.00
WMNO Jerious Norwood 2.00 5.00
WMPM Peyton Manning 8.00 20.00
WMPR Philip Rivers 3.00 8.00
WMPW Patrick Willis 2.50 6.00
WMRC Roger Craig 3.00 8.00
WMRM Randy Moss 2.50 6.00
WMRO Eddie Royal 1.50 4.00
WMRR Ray Rice 1.50 4.00
WMRW Roy Williams WR 2.00 5.00
WMSA Asante Samuel 2.00 5.00
WMSH Jeremy Shockey 2.00 5.00
WMSI Jerome Simpson 2.00 5.00
WMSS Steve Slaton 1.50 4.00
WMTO Tom Brady 10.00 25.00
WMTP Troy Polamalu 3.00 8.00
WMTR Tony Romo 2.50 6.00
WMVY Vince Young 2.00 5.00
WMWA Ben Watson 2.00 5.00
WMWH Michael Huff 2.00 5.00
WMWP Willie Parker 2.50 6.00
WMWW1 Wes Welker 2.50 6.00
WMWW2 Wes Welker 2.50 6.00

2008 SPx Winning Materials Autographs SPX Triple

UNPRICED AUTO PRINT RUN 10

2008 SPx Winning Trios Autographs

UNPRICED TRIO AU PRINT RUN 10

2008 SPx Winning Trios 99

UNPRICED TRIO AU PRINT RUN 10
*TRIOS/49: .5X TO 1.2X TRIOS/99
*TRIOS/25: .6X TO 1.5X TRIOS/99
*TRIOS/5: 1.2X TO 3X TRIOS/99
*TRIOS PATCH/5: 1.5X TO 4X TRIOS/99
WT1 Sayers/Peterson/Mndnhll 4.00 10.00
WT2 Bulger/Henne/O'Connell 3.00 8.00
WT3 D.Jcksn/Simpsn/Dx.Jcksn 6.00 15.00
WT4 Portis/Roeth/De.Jackson 6.00 15.00
WT5 Portis/J.Campbell/M.Kelly 6.00 15.00
WT6 Brohm/Henne/M.Ryan 8.00 20.00
WT7 Royl/Simpsn/Dex.Jcksn 2.50 6.00
WT8 Sweed/J.Nelson/D.Thomas 8.00 20.00
WT9 Ch.Jhnsn/Dr.Jcksn/D.Andersn 4.00 10.00
WT10 B.Sndrs/Tomlin/McFadd 15.00 40.00
WT11 D.Anderson/Quinn/Brohm 2.50 6.00
WT12 D.Jackson/Doucet/D.Jackson 6.00 15.00
WT13 Williams/Johnson/E.Smith 10.00 25.00
WT14 D.Andersn/Edwrds/Stewrt 8.00 20.00
WT15 H.Walker/Stewart/Forte 10.00 25.00
WT16 Tomlin/Petrsn/Charles 10.00 25.00
WT17 Russell/Flacco/Ryan 10.00 25.00
WT18 Shockey/Winslow Sr./Keller 3.00 8.00
WT19 Gore/Norwood/Slaton 6.00 15.00
WT20 Bulger/Flacco/O'Connell 8.00 20.00
WT21 F.Jones/Flacco/J.Nelson 5.00 12.00
WT22 Lynch/Stewart/Forte 6.00 15.00
WT23 Caldwell/J.Simpson/D.Jackson 4.00 10.00
WT24 McFadden/J.Long/Ryan 8.00 20.00
WT25 Sims/K.Smith/R.Will WR 2.50 6.00
WT26 F.Jons/C.Jhnsn/K.Smith 3.00 8.00
WT27 Romo/Barber/T.Owens 15.00 40.00
WT28 Clayton/Croyle/Forte 8.00 20.00
WT29 Norwood/Lynch/C.Johnson 6.00 15.00
WT30 Brohm/Booty/O'Connell 2.50 6.00
WT31 Schaub/Ryan/K.Anderson 15.00 40.00
WT32 Henne/J.Long/Manningham 4.00 10.00
WT33 P.Mann/Schaub/Flacco 10.00 25.00
WT34 Eli/Roethlis/Rivers 8.00 20.00
WT35 R.Rice/Slaton/K.Smith 2.50 6.00
WT36 Favre/P.Manning/Brady 20.00 50.00
WT37 O'Connell/Watson/Welker 6.00 15.00
WT38 L.Jhnsn/Croyle/Charles 5.00 12.00
WT39 Eli/Brohm/Romo 10.00 25.00
WT40 Roethlis/Sweed/Menden 2.50 6.00
WT41 R.Rice/Menden/K.Smith 2.50 6.00
WT42 Cotchery/Welker/E.Benn 6.00 15.00

2009 SPx

COMP.SET w/o RC's (90) 15.00 40.00
91-100 JSY AU RC PRINT RUN 275
101-123 JSY AU RC PRINT RUN 549
124-163 AU RC PRINT RUN 299
164-223 ROOKIE PRINT RUN 799
1 Aaron Rodgers 1.00 2.50
2 Adrian Peterson .50 1.25
3 Adrian Wilson .30 .75
4 Albert Haynesworth .30 .75
5 Andre Johnson .40 1.00
6 Anquan Boldin .30 .75
7 Antonio Bryant .30 .75
8 Antonio Gates .40 1.00
9 Ben Roethlisberger .50 1.25
10 Bob Sanders .40 1.00
11 Brady Quinn .30 .75
12 Brandon Jacobs .30 .75
13 Brandon Marshall .40 1.00
14 Braylon Edwards .30 .75
15 Brian Westbrook .30 .75
16 Calvin Johnson .50 1.25
17 Carson Palmer .40 1.00
18 Chad Pennington .30 .75
19 Charles Woodson .50 1.25
20 Chris Johnson .30 .75
21 Clinton Portis .30 .75
22 Darren McFadden .50 1.25
23 Darren Sproles .40 1.00
24 David Garrard .30 .75
25 DeAngelo Williams .30 .75
26 DeMarcus Ware .40 1.00
27 DeSean Jackson .40 1.00
28 Donnie Avery .30 .75
29 Donovan McNabb .40 1.00
30 Drew Brees .50 1.25
31 Dwayne Bowe .40 1.00
32 Ed Reed .40 1.00
33 Eddie Royal .30 .75
34 Eli Manning .40 1.00
35 Frank Gore .40 1.00
36 Greg Jennings .30 .75
37 Hines Ward .40 1.00
38 Jake Delhomme .30 .75
39 Jamal Lewis .40 1.00
40 James Farrior .30 .75
41 James Harrison .50 1.25
42 Jason Witten .40 1.00
43 Jay Cutler .30 .75
44 Joe Flacco .40 1.00
45 Joey Porter .40 1.00
46 Jonathan Stewart .30 .75
47 Julius Peppers .40 1.00
48 Justin Tuck .30 .75
49 Kevin Smith .30 .75
50 Kevin Williams .30 .75
51 Kurt Warner .40 1.00
52 LaDainian Tomlinson .50 1.25
53 Lance Briggs .40 1.00
54 Lance Moore .30 .75
55 Larry Fitzgerald .40 1.00
56 Lee Evans .40 1.00
57 Le'Ron McClain .40 1.00
58 Mario Williams .40 1.00
59 Marion Barber .40 1.00
60 Marshawn Lynch .40 1.00
61 Matt Cassel .30 .75
62 Matt Forte .30 .75
63 Matt Ryan .40 1.00
64 Matt Schaub .30 .75
65 Maurice Jones-Drew .30 .75
66 Michael Turner .30 .75
67 Nnamdi Asomugha .30 .75
68 Patrick Willis .40 1.00
69 Peyton Manning 1.25 3.00
70 Philip Rivers .50 1.25
71 Randy Moss .40 1.00
72 Ray Lewis .50 1.25
73 Reggie Wayne .40 1.00
74 Roddy White .30 .75
75 Ronde Barber .30 .75
76 Ronnie Brown .30 .75
77 Ryan Grant .40 1.00
78 Santana Moss .40 1.00
79 Steve Slaton .30 .75
80 Steve Smith .40 1.00
81 Steven Jackson .30 .75
82 T.J. Houshmandzadeh .30 .75
83 Terrell Owens .40 1.00
84 Thomas Jones .30 .75
85 Tom Brady 1.50 4.00
86 Tony Gonzalez .40 1.00
87 Tony Romo .40 1.00
88 Troy Polamalu .50 1.25
89 Walter Jones .30 .75
90 Wes Welker .40 1.00
91 M.Stafford JSY AU/275 RC 30.00 80.00
92 M.Crabtree JSY AU/275 RC 10.00 25.00
93 M.Sanchez JSY AU/275 RC 12.00 30.00
94 C.Wells JSY AU/275 RC 6.00 15.00
95 K.Moreno JSY AU/275 RC 6.00 15.00
96 D.Brown JSY AU/275 RC 6.00 15.00
97 J.Freeman JSY AU/275 RC 6.00 15.00
98 D.Hey-Bey JSY AU/275 RC 10.00 25.00
99 J.Maclin JSY AU/275 RC 8.00 20.00
100 Pat White JSY AU/275 RC 8.00 20.00
101 Brian Robiskie JSY AU RC 5.00 12.00
102 Aaron Curry JSY AU/546 RC 8.00 20.00
103 Derrick Williams JSY AU RC 5.00 12.00
104 LeSean McCoy JSY AU RC 12.00 30.00
105 Stephen McGee JSY AU RC 5.00 12.00
106 Rhett Bomar JSY AU RC 5.00 12.00
107 Ramses Barden JSY AU RC 5.00 12.00
108 Javon Ringer JSY AU RC 5.00 12.00
109 Andre Brown JSY AU RC 6.00 15.00
110 Juaquin Iglesias JSY AU RC 5.00 12.00
111 Patrick Turner JSY AU RC 5.00 12.00
112 Tyson Jackson JSY AU RC 5.00 12.00
113 Nate Davis JSY AU RC 5.00 12.00
114 Glen Coffee JSY AU RC 5.00 12.00
115 Percy Harvin JSY AU RC 5.00 12.00
116 M.Massaquoi JSY AU RC 5.00 12.00
117 Shonn Greene JSY AU RC 5.00 12.00
118 Mike Thomas JSY AU RC 5.00 12.00
119 Kenny Britt JSY AU RC 8.00 20.00
120 Mike Wallace JSY AU RC 8.00 20.00
121 B.Pettigrew JSY AU RC 5.00 12.00
122 Hakeem Nicks JSY AU RC 6.00 15.00
123 Jason Smith JSY AU RC 5.00 12.00
124 Brian Orakpo AU RC 5.00 12.00
125 Frank Summers AU RC 6.00 15.00
126 Tom Brandstater AU RC 5.00 12.00
127 Gartrell Johnson AU RC 4.00 10.00
128 Eugene Monroe AU RC 4.00 10.00
129 B.J. Raji AU RC 5.00 12.00
130 Vontae Davis AU RC 4.00 10.00
131 Mike Goodson AU RC 5.00 12.00
132 Clay Matthews AU RC 40.00 80.00
133 Michael Johnson AU RC 4.00 10.00
134 Peria Jerry AU RC 4.00 10.00
135 Brian Cushing AU RC 4.00 10.00
136 Brandon Tate AU RC 5.00 12.00
137 Louis Delmas AU RC 5.00 12.00
138 Malcolm Jenkins AU RC 4.00 10.00
139 Cedric Peerman AU RC 4.00 10.00
140 Bear Pascoe AU RC 5.00 12.00
141 Curtis Painter AU RC 4.00 10.00
142 James Laurinaitis AU RC 8.00 20.00
143 Travis Beckum AU RC 4.00 10.00
144 Clint Sintim AU RC 4.00 10.00
145 Patrick Chung AU RC 6.00 15.00
146 Marko Mitchell AU RC 4.00 10.00
147 Austin Collie AU RC 4.00 10.00
148 Chase Coffman AU RC 4.00 10.00
149 Andre Smith AU RC 4.00 10.00
150 Demetrius Byrd AU RC 5.00 12.00
151 Deon Butler AU RC 4.00 10.00
152 Alphonso Smith AU RC 4.00 10.00
153 Brandon Gibson AU RC 5.00 12.00
154 Brian Hartline AU RC 12.50 25.00
155 James Davis AU RC 4.00 10.00
156 Alex Mack AU RC 4.00 10.00
157 Rey Maualuga AU RC 6.00 15.00
158 Jarett Dillard AU RC 4.00 10.00
159 Robert Ayers AU RC 4.00 10.00
160 Jared Cook AU RC 5.00 12.00
161 Brooks Foster AU RC 4.00 10.00
162 Larry English AU RC 5.00 12.00
163 Rashad Jennings AU RC 5.00 12.00
164 Aaron Brown RC 2.00 5.00
165 Connor Barwin RC 2.00 5.00
166 Evander Hood RC 2.50 6.00
167 David Veikune RC 2.00 5.00
168 Bernard Scott RC 2.50 6.00
169 Darcel McBath RC 1.50 4.00
170 Keith Null RC 2.00 5.00
171 Andy Levitre RC 2.00 5.00
172 Louis Murphy RC 1.50 4.00
173 Eric Wood RC 1.50 4.00
174 Freddie Brown RC 1.50 4.00
175 Cody Brown RC 1.50 4.00
176 Kenny McKinley RC 1.50 4.00
177 Paul Kruger RC 2.50 6.00
178 Johnny Knox RC 2.00 5.00
179 Sebastian Vollmer RC 2.00 5.00
180 Shawn Nelson RC 1.50 4.00
181 Jairus Byrd RC 2.50 6.00
182 Anthony Hill RC 1.50 4.00
183 Eben Britton RC 2.00 5.00
184 Max Unger RC 2.50 6.00
185 Ron Brace RC 2.00 5.00
186 Mike Teel RC 1.50 4.00
187 Sherrod Martin RC 1.50 4.00
188 Fili Moala RC 1.50 4.00
189 Aaron Maybin RC 2.00 5.00
190 Chris Ogbonnaya RC 2.00 5.00
191 Louis Vasquez RC 2.00 5.00
192 Javarris Williams RC 2.00 5.00
193 D.J. Moore RC 2.00 5.00
194 Sean Smith RC 1.50 4.00
195 Brandon Williams RC 2.00 5.00
196 William Beatty RC 1.50 4.00
197 Fui Vakapuna RC 2.00 5.00
198 David Bruton RC 1.50 4.00
199 Quinn Johnson RC 1.50 4.00
200 Kraig Urbik RC 2.00 5.00
201 LaRod Stephens-Howling RC 6.00 12.00
202 Tony Fiammetta RC 1.50 4.00
203 William Moore RC 1.50 4.00
204 Eddie Williams RC 2.00 5.00
205 Manuel Johnson RC 1.50 4.00
206 Tiquan Underwood RC 1.50 4.00
207 Marlon Lucky RC 1.50 4.00
208 Julian Edelman RC 30.00 60.00
209 Dominique Edison RC 1.50 4.00
210 Michael Oher RC 2.50 6.00
211 Sen'Derrick Marks RC 1.50 4.00
212 Mike Mitchell RC 1.50 4.00
213 DeAndre Levy RC 2.00 5.00
214 Sammie Stroughter RC 1.50 4.00
215 Derek Kinder RC 1.50 4.00
216 Richard Quinn RC 2.00 5.00
217 Kaluka Maiava RC 1.50 4.00
218 Keenan Lewis RC 2.50 6.00
219 Kyle Moore RC 2.00 5.00
220 Victor Butler RC 2.00 5.00
221 Everette Brown RC 1.50 4.00
222 Phil Loadholt RC 2.00 5.00
223 Darius Butler RC 2.00 5.00

2009 SPx Rookies Silver

*RK.JSY AU 91-99: 1X TO 2.5X JSY AU/275
*RK.JSY AU 101-123: 1.2X TO 3X JSY AU/549
91-123 JSY AU PRINT RUN 25
*ROOK.AU 124-163: .5X TO 1.2X AU/299
124-163 ROOKIE AU PRINT RUN 99
*ROOKIE 164-223: .5X TO 1.2X RC/799
164-223 ROOKIE PRINT RUN 399
91 Matthew Stafford JSY AU 150.00 300.00
93 Mark Sanchez JSY AU 25.00 60.00

2009 SPx Rookies Gold Holofoil

*ROOK.AU 124-163: .6X TO 1.5X AU/299
*ROOKIE 164-223: 1X TO 2.5X RC/799
124-163 ROOKIE AU PRINT RUN 25

2009 SPx Rookie Materials

STATED PRINT RUN 249 SER.#'d SETS
*DUAL PATCH/99: .8X TO 2X BASIC JSY/299
*GOLD DUAL/99: .6X TO 1.5X BASIC JSY/299
*GREEN DUAL/149: .5X TO 1.2X BASIC JSY/299
RMAB Andre Brown 1.50 4.00
RMAC Aaron Curry 2.00 5.00
RMBO Rhett Bomar 1.25 3.00
RMBP Brandon Pettigrew 1.25 3.00
RMBR Brian Robiskie 1.25 3.00
RMCW Chris Wells 1.25 3.00
RMDB Donald Brown 1.25 3.00
RMDH Darrius Heyward-Bey 2.00 5.00
RMDW Derrick Williams 1.25 3.00
RMGC Glen Coffee 1.25 3.00
RMHN Hakeem Nicks 1.50 4.00
RMJF Josh Freeman 1.25 3.00
RMJI Juaquin Iglesias 1.25 3.00
RMJM Jeremy Maclin 1.50 4.00
RMJR Javon Ringer 1.25 3.00
RMJS Jason Smith 1.25 3.00
RMKB Kenny Britt 2.00 5.00
RMKM Knowshon Moreno 1.25 3.00
RMLM LeSean McCoy 3.00 8.00
RMMC Michael Crabtree 2.00 5.00
RMMM Mohamed Massaquoi 1.25 3.00
RMMS Mark Sanchez 1.25 3.00
RMMT Mike Thomas 1.25 3.00
RMMW Mike Wallace 2.00 5.00
RMND Nate Davis 1.25 3.00
RMPH Percy Harvin 1.25 3.00
RMPT Patrick Turner 1.25 3.00
RMPW Pat White 1.50 4.00
RMRB Ramses Barden 1.25 3.00
RMSG Shonn Greene 1.25 3.00
RMSM Stephen McGee 1.25 3.00
RMST Matthew Stafford 6.00 15.00
RMTJ Tyson Jackson 1.25 3.00

2009 SPx Rookie Materials Autographs

STATED PRINT RUN 25-50
RMAB Andre Brown 8.00 20.00
RMAC Aaron Curry 10.00 25.00
RMBO Rhett Bomar 6.00 15.00
RMBP Brandon Pettigrew 6.00 15.00
RMBR Brian Robiskie 6.00 15.00
RMCW Chris Wells 6.00 15.00
RMDB Donald Brown 6.00 15.00
RMDH Darrius Heyward-Bey 10.00 25.00
RMDW Derrick Williams 6.00 15.00
RMGC Glen Coffee 6.00 15.00
RMHN Hakeem Nicks 8.00 20.00
RMJF Josh Freeman 6.00 15.00
RMJI Juaquin Iglesias 6.00 15.00
RMJM Jeremy Maclin 8.00 20.00
RMJR Javon Ringer 6.00 15.00
RMJS Jason Smith 6.00 15.00
RMKB Kenny Britt 10.00 25.00
RMKM Knowshon Moreno 6.00 15.00
RMLM LeSean McCoy 25.00 60.00
RMMC Michael Crabtree 10.00 25.00
RMMM Mohamed Massaquoi 6.00 15.00
RMMS Mark Sanchez/25 40.00 80.00
RMMT Mike Thomas 6.00 15.00
RMMW Mike Wallace 10.00 25.00
RMND Nate Davis
RMPH Percy Harvin 6.00 15.00
RMPT Patrick Turner 6.00 15.00
RMPW Pat White 8.00 20.00
RMRB Ramses Barden 6.00 15.00
RMSG Shonn Greene 6.00 15.00
RMSM Stephen McGee 6.00 15.00
RMST Matthew Stafford/25 75.00 150.00
RMTJ Tyson Jackson 6.00 15.00

2009 SPx Shadow Box

ANNOUNCED PRINT RUN 10-100
ANNC'D PRINT RUN OF 10 NOT PRICED
SAJ Andre Johnson/50* 10.00 25.00
SAM Archie Manning/50* 15.00 40.00
SAP Adrian Peterson/10*
SBF Brett Favre/10*
SBR Ben Roethlisberger/10*
SBS Barry Sanders/10*
SBW Brian Westbrook/50* 10.00 25.00
SCJ Chris Johnson/100* 15.00 40.00
SCW Chris Wells/25* 15.00 40.00
SDB Donald Brown/25* 20.00 50.00
SDG Darrell Green/75* 10.00 25.00
SDH Devin Hester/75* 12.00 30.00
SDJ Daryl Johnston/75*
SDW DeAngelo Williams/75* 10.00 25.00
SEM Eli Manning/10*
SER Ed Reed/100* 15.00 40.00
SGJ Greg Jennings/100* 10.00 25.00
SGS Gale Sayers/25* 15.00 40.00
SJF Joe Flacco/25* 20.00 50.00
SJH James Harrison/100* 12.00 30.00
SJO Calvin Johnson/25* 15.00 40.00
SJR Jerry Rice/10*
SJS Jonathan Stewart/75* 10.00 25.00
SJV Javon Ringer/25*
SKM Knowshon Moreno/25* 30.00 60.00
SKS Kevin Smith/100* 8.00 20.00
SKW Kurt Warner/10*
SLF Larry Fitzgerald/25* 20.00 50.00
SMC Michael Crabtree/10*
SMR Matt Ryan/10*
SMS Mike Singletary/50* 15.00 40.00
SMT Michael Turner/75* 8.00 20.00
SPM Peyton Manning/10*
SRA Tom Rathman/100* 12.00 30.00
SRC Roger Craig/100* 10.00 25.00
SSI Billy Sims/100* 10.00 25.00
SSS Steve Slaton/100* 12.00 30.00
SST Matthew Stafford/10*
SSZ Mark Sanchez/10*
STB Tom Brady/10*
STP Troy Polamalu/100* 15.00 40.00
STR Tony Romo/10*
STT Thurman Thomas 15.00 40.00

2009 SPx Shadow Box Autographs

COMMON CARD 25.00 50.00
UNLISTED STARS 30.00 60.00
SBW Brian Westbrook 30.00 60.00
SCJ Chris Johnson 40.00 80.00
SDB Donald Brown 50.00 100.00
SDG Darrell Green 30.00 60.00
SGJ Greg Jennings 25.00 50.00
SJS Jonathan Stewart 30.00 60.00
SJV Javon Ringer 25.00 60.00
SKM Knowshon Moreno 50.00 120.00
SKS Kevin Smith 20.00 50.00
SMT Michael Turner 25.00 50.00
SRC Roger Craig 25.00 50.00
SSS Steve Slaton 25.00 50.00

2009 SPx Super Scripts Autographs

SAB Anquan Boldin 7.50 15.00
SAC Adam Carriker 3.00 8.00
SAS Alex Smith QB 8.00 20.00
SBC Brent Celek 7.50 15.00
SBE Braylon Edwards
SBM Brandon Marshall 7.50 15.00
SBR Thomas Brown 3.00 8.00
SCB Colt Brennan 5.00 12.00
SCH Chad Henne 7.50 15.00
SCJ Chris Johnson 10.00 20.00
SCL Chris Long 4.00 10.00
SCR Alge Crumpler 3.00 8.00
SCS Chansi Stuckey 3.00 8.00
SDB Dwayne Bowe 5.00 12.00
SDK Dustin Keller 3.00 8.00
SDL Donald Lee 3.00 8.00
SDO Dominique Rodgers-Cromartie 3.00 8.00
SDR Darrelle Revis 8.00 20.00
SDW Darius Walker 3.00 8.00
SEM Eli Manning 40.00 80.00
SEW Eric Weddle 3.00 8.00
SFG Frank Gore 7.50 15.00
SHM Heath Miller 7.50 15.00
SHO Chris Houston 3.00 8.00
SJA Joseph Addai 5.00 12.00
SJD Jake Delhomme 7.50 15.00
SJF Joe Flacco 15.00 30.00
SJJ James Jones 3.00 8.00
SJN Jordy Nelson 7.50 15.00
SJO Larry Johnson 7.50 15.00
SJS Jonathan Stewart
SJU Julius Jones 6.00 15.00
SKB Kevin Boss 5.00 12.00
SKP Kenny Phillips 3.00 8.00
SKS Kevin Smith 3.00 8.00
SLB Lance Ball 3.00 8.00
SLJ Lawrence Jackson 3.00 8.00
SLL LaRon Landry 7.50 15.00
SLM Leodis McKelvin 3.00 8.00
SMC Le'Ron McClain 5.00 12.00
SMM Mario Manningham 7.50 15.00
SPW Patrick Willis 5.00 12.00
SRB Reggie Brown 3.00 8.00
SRC Ryan Clady 3.00 8.00
SRW Reggie Wayne 7.50 15.00
STH Tyler Thigpen 3.00 8.00
STT Terrell Thomas 3.00 8.00
SVJ Vincent Jackson 3.00 8.00
SVY Vince Young
SWI DeAngelo Williams

2009 SPx Super Scripts Autographs Dual

DUAL STATED PRINT RUN 25-99
DAR Royal/Avery/50 8.00 20.00
DBF Flynn/Brohm/50 25.00 50.00
DBJ Breaston/J.Jones/50 6.00 15.00
DBW Butler/M.Wallace/50 15.00 30.00
DCF Flacco/Clayton/50 20.00 40.00
DCJ Clowney/J.Jones/50 5.00 12.00
DCS Clowney/Stuckey/50 5.00 12.00
DDB T.Brown/Douglas/50 6.00 15.00
DDH Hawkins/C.Davis/99 5.00 12.00
DDJ J.Jones/Driver/50 20.00 40.00
DFF Flynn/Finley/50 30.00 80.00
DFR Flacco/Ryan/25 50.00 100.00
DFS Forte/Slaton/25 20.00 40.00
DGB Goodson/A.Brown/99 8.00 20.00
DJB B.Jacobs/Barber/25 15.00 40.00
DJC Chandlr/V.Jcksn/50 6.00 15.00
DJD Jenkins/V.Davis/50 6.00 15.00
DJH Hall/B.Jackson/45 8.00 20.00
DJM F.Jones/Mndnhll/50 15.00 40.00
DJS C.Johnson/K.Smith/50 12.00 30.00
DJT Thigpen/L.Johnson/50 8.00 20.00
DKP Hall/Hillis/50 12.00 30.00
DLM McClain/Lynch/50 10.00 25.00
DMA Arringtn/Mnninghm/50 8.00 20.00
DMB McGee/Bomar/50 6.00 15.00
DMF Flacco/McClain/50 20.00 40.00
DMH Spaeth/Miller/50 15.00 30.00
DMS Monroe/J.Smith/50 6.00 15.00
DNB T.Brown/Norwood/50 6.00 15.00
DOC Chandler/Olsen/50 6.00 15.00
DPH Patrick/Hubbard/99 6.00 15.00
DRD Hall/Hughes/50 5.00 12.00
DRR Ryan/Russell/25 30.00 80.00
DRT Torain/Royal/50 8.00 20.00
DSM McFad/Stewart/25 10.00 25.00
DTB T.Brown/Torain/99 6.00 15.00
DTC Thigpen/Charles/50 10.00 25.00
DTH Torain/Hillis/50 12.00 30.00
DWT D.Williams/Tate/50 15.00 40.00
DYT Torain/S.Young/50 6.00 15.00

2009 SPx Super Scripts Autographs Triple

TRIPLE STATED PRINT RUN 10-25
TOL Monroe/J.Smith/A.Smith 15.00 40.00
TARI Boldin/Leinart/Breaston 15.00 40.00
TDEF Ware/Willis/Revis 30.00 60.00
TOSU Jenkins/Wells/Laurinaitis 20.00 50.00
TQB1 Ryan/Flacco/Brennan 40.00 100.00
TRB1 Slaton/Forte/C.Johnson 30.00 60.00
TRB2 J.Stewart/K.Smith/McFad 12.00 30.00
TRBT McClain/J.Stewart/Lynch 15.00 40.00
TRBY D.Williams/B.Jacobs/Gore 15.00 40.00
TREC Welker/Marshall/Housh 30.00 60.00
TRET Demps/Breaston/J.Jones 10.00 25.00
TRLB Cushing/Curry/Matthews 40.00 80.00
TRQB Stafford/Sanchez/Freemn 60.00 120.00
TRRB Wells/Moreno/McCoy 25.00 60.00
TRTD Bennett/Hardy/Keller 12.00 30.00
TRWR Crabtree/Maclin/Harvin 20.00 50.00
TWR1 Royal/Avery/Nelson 12.00 30.00
TWR2 Burton/Morgan/Avery 10.00 25.00

2009 SPx Winning Combos

STATED PRINT RUN 99 SER.#'d SETS
*GOLD/35: .5X TO 1.2X BASIC COMBOS
*GREEN/59: .5X TO 1.2X BASIC INSERTS
*PATCH/25: .8X TO 2X BASIC JSY
AR Avery/Royal 3.00 8.00
AW Quinn/D.Anderson 3.00 8.00
BR Brady/Roethlisberger 15.00 40.00
CH Crabtree/Heyward-Bey 2.50 6.00
CJ Curry/T.Jackson 2.50 6.00
EA Elway/Aikman 12.00 30.00
FJ C.Johnson/Fitzgerald 5.00 12.00
FR Ryan/Flacco 8.00 20.00
FW Freeman/P.White 2.00 5.00
JJ Jennings/D.Jackson 4.00 10.00
JL Maclin/McCoy 4.00 10.00
JS K.Smith/F.Jones 3.00 8.00
LK Lee/Keller 3.00 8.00
MM McFadden/Mendenhall 3.00 8.00
MP Palmer/McNabb 4.00 10.00
MR Rodgers/E.Manning 10.00 25.00
MW Moreno/Wells 1.50 4.00
NB Nicks/Barden 2.00 5.00
PP A.Peterson/Portis 5.00 12.00
RM Robiskie/Massaquoi 4.00 10.00
SG Sanchez/Greene 10.00 25.00
SJ C.Johnson/Slaton 3.00 8.00
SP Stafford/Pettigrew 8.00 20.00
SS Stafford/Sanchez 8.00 20.00
WF Forte/Westbrook 3.00 8.00
WH Woodson/Hawk 5.00 12.00
WO Owens/Ward 4.00 10.00
WS Stewart/D.Williams 3.00 8.00

2009 SPx Winning Combos Patch Autographs

PATCH AUTO STATED PRINT RUN 15
AR Avery/Royal
AW Quinn/D.Anderson 12.00 30.00
BR Brady/Roethlisberger 200.00 350.00
CH Crabtree/Heyward-Bey 12.00 30.00
CJ Curry/T.Jackson 20.00 50.00
EA Elway/Aikman 100.00 175.00
FR Ryan/Flacco 50.00 100.00
FW Freeman/P.White 10.00 25.00
JJ Jennings/D.Jackson 15.00 40.00
JL Maclin/McCoy 40.00 80.00
JS K.Smith/F.Jones 12.00 30.00
LK Lee/Keller
MM McFadden/Mendenhall 12.00 30.00
MR Rodgers/E.Manning 200.00 350.00
MW Moreno/Wells 8.00 20.00
NB Nicks/Barden 10.00 25.00
PP A.Peterson/Portis 100.00 200.00
SC Sanchez/Greene 8.00 20.00
SJ C.Johnson/Slaton 30.00 60.00
SP Stafford/Pettigrew 50.00 100.00
SS Stafford/Sanchez 40.00 100.00
WS Stewart/D.Williams 12.00 30.00

2009 SPx Fantastic Foursome

STATED PRINT RUN 20 SER.#'d SETS
QBS Cutler/Brees/Romo/Schaub 8.00 20.00
RBS Lynch/Gore/J.Lewis/Bush 6.00 15.00
RQB Staff/Snchz/Frman/McGee 15.00 40.00
RRB Mrno/D.Brwn/Wells/McCy 8.00 20.00
RWR Hywrd/Crbtr/Maclin/Harvin 5.00 12.00
WRS Housh/Clstn/L.Evans/Hstr 6.00 15.00
EAGL McNb/Wstbrk/Jcksn/Kolb 6.00 15.00
FISH R.Brwn/Hen/Whte/Penn 4.00 10.00
GNTS Pierce/Eli/LT/Simms 8.00 20.00
PATS Brady/Moss/Welkr/Watsn 25.00 60.00
PTHR D.Will/Stwrt/Pepprs/Smith 6.00 15.00
RAVN Flac/Rice/Claytn/McGhee 6.00 15.00
STLR Roeth/Ward/Pola/Holmes 8.00 20.00
TITN C.Jhnsn/White/V.Yng/Britt 8.00 20.00
VIKN Petrsn/S.Rce/Jcksn/Booty 8.00 20.00

2009 SPx Winning Materials

STATED PRINT RUN 65-349
*BLUE DUAL/50: .6X TO 1.5X BASIC JSY
*BRONZE DUAL/99: .5X TO 1.2X BASIC JSY
*BRONZE DUAL/24: .8X TO 2X BASIC JSY
*GREEN DUAL/149: .5X TO 1.2X BASIC JSY
*PATCH/99: .6X TO 1.5X BASIC JSY
*PATCH/35: .8X TO 2X BASIC JSY
*PATCH PLAT/15-25: 1X TO 2.5X BASIC JSY
WAC Aaron Curry/349 2.00 5.00
WAJ Andre Johnson/99 3.00 8.00
WAK Aaron Kampman/99 5.00 12.00
WAN Derek Anderson/159 2.50 6.00
WAP Antonio Pierce/249 3.00 8.00
WAV Donnie Avery/349 2.50 6.00
WBA Marion Barber/149 3.00 8.00
WBR Tom Brady/249 12.00 30.00
WBS Barry Sanders/249 8.00 20.00
WBU Deon Butler/349 1.25 3.00
WCC Chris Cooley/249 2.50 6.00
WCD Craig Davis/249 2.50 6.00
WCH Jamaal Charles/349 3.00 8.00
WCJ Calvin Johnson/349 4.00 10.00
WCO Jerricho Cotchery/249 2.50 6.00
WCP Carson Palmer/249 3.00 8.00
WCR Michael Crabtree/349 2.00 5.00
WCW Charles Woodson/249 4.00 10.00
WDA Daryl Johnston/249 6.00 15.00
WDB Drew Brees/249 4.00 10.00
WDE Derrick Brooks/249 2.50 6.00
WDG David Garrard/249 2.50 6.00
WDH Devin Hester/249 3.00 8.00
WDJ DeSean Jackson/349 3.00 8.00
WDK Dustin Keller/249 2.50 6.00
WDM Donovan McNabb/249 3.00 8.00
WDO Donald Brown/349 1.25 3.00
WDW DeAngelo Williams/249 2.50 6.00
WEC Earl Campbell/249 5.00 12.00
WEJ Edgerrin James/349 3.00 8.00
WEM Eli Manning/249 3.00 8.00
WER Eddie Royal/349 2.50 6.00
WES Ernie Sims/249 2.50 6.00
WFG Frank Gore/349 3.00 8.00
WFH Franco Harris/249 6.00 15.00
WFJ Felix Jones/349 2.50 6.00
WFT Fred Taylor/175 2.50 6.00
WGD Glenn Dorsey/249 2.50 6.00
WGJ Greg Jennings/249 2.50 6.00
WHE Chad Henne/349 3.00 8.00
WHW Hines Ward/125 5.00 12.00
WIB Isaac Bruce/249 4.00 10.00
WIE Brian Robiskie/349 1.25 3.00
WJC Jay Cutler/349 2.50 6.00
WJE John Elway/249 8.00 20.00
WJF Joe Flacco/349 3.00 8.00
WJK Jim Kelly/249 5.00 12.00
WJL Jamal Lewis/249 3.00 8.00
WJN Joe Namath/249 6.00 15.00
WJO Chris Johnson/349 2.50 6.00
WJP Julius Peppers/125 3.00 8.00
WJR Jerry Rice/249 10.00 25.00
WJS Jonathan Stewart/349 2.50 6.00
WJT Joe Theismann/249 5.00 12.00
WJW Jason Witten/225 3.00 8.00
WKM Knowshon Moreno/349 1.25 3.00
WKS Kevin Smith/349 2.50 6.00
WKW Kellen Winslow Jr./249 2.50 6.00
WLE Lee Evans/349 3.00 8.00
WLF Larry Fitzgerald/249 3.00 8.00
WLT Lawrence Taylor/249 6.00 15.00
WMB Marc Bulger/249 2.50 6.00
WMC Darren McFadden/349 4.00 10.00
WME Rashard Mendenhall/349 2.50 6.00
WMF Matt Forte/349 2.50 6.00
WMH Marvin Harrison/249 3.00 8.00
WML Marshawn Lynch/349 3.00 8.00
WMO Merlin Olsen/249 3.00 8.00
WMR Matt Ryan/349 3.00 8.00
WMS Mike Singletary/249 5.00 12.00
WMV Mike Vrabel/249 2.50 6.00
WNE Jordy Nelson/349 3.00 8.00
WOA Ottis Anderson/249 4.00 10.00
WPB Plaxico Burress/349 2.50 6.00
WPE Adrian Peterson/349 4.00 10.00
WPM Peyton Manning/249 10.00 25.00
WPS Phil Simms/249 4.00 10.00
WPW Patrick Willis/349 3.00 8.00
WRA Ray Lewis/249 4.00 10.00
WRB Ronnie Brown/349 2.50 6.00
WRC Roger Craig/249 4.00 10.00
WRL Ronnie Lott/249 4.00 10.00
WRM Randy Moss/249 3.00 8.00
WRO Ben Roethlisberger/249 4.00 10.00
WSA Mark Sanchez/349 1.25 3.00
WSC Matt Schaub/249 2.50 6.00
WSH Santonio Holmes/249 2.50 6.00
WSI Billy Sims/249 4.00 10.00
WSL Steve Largent/249 5.00 12.00
WSS Steve Slaton/349 2.50 6.00
WST Matthew Stafford/349 6.00 15.00
WTB Terry Bradshaw/249 6.00 15.00
WTH T.J. Houshmandzadeh/249 2.50 6.00
WLW LenDale White/65 3.00 8.00
WVJ Vincent Jackson/249 2.50 6.00
WWA Javon Walker/349 2.50 6.00
WWE Chris Wells/349 1.25 3.00
WWI Kellen Winslow Sr./249 4.00 10.00

2009 SPx Winning Trios

STATED PRINT RUN 50 SER.#'d SETS
*GREEN/15: .6X TO 1.5X BASIC TRIO/50
*PATCH/25: .6X TO 1.5X BASIC TRIO/50
ARI Fitz/Boldin/Warner 5.00 12.00
BAL Flacco/R.Lewis/Reed 6.00 15.00
DB1 Reed/Polamalu/Woodson 10.00 25.00
PHI McNabb/Wstbrk/D.Jcksn 5.00 12.00
PIT Roethlis/Parker/Holmes 6.00 15.00
QB1 P.Mann/Brees/Warner 15.00 40.00
RC1 Curry/T.Jackson/J.Smith 4.00 10.00
RCR Harvin/Pettigrew/Nicks 2.50 6.00
REC Mrshll/Bldin/Housh 5.00 12.00
RQB Stafford/Sanchez/Frmn 15.00 40.00
RRB Moreno/Wells/D.Brown 2.50 6.00
RWR Crabtr/Hywrd-Bey/Mclin 4.00 10.00
SQB Eli/P.Mann/Rodgers 20.00 50.00
WR1 A.Johnsn/Fitz/C.Johnsn 6.00 15.00
YRD C.Johnson/Jenn/Wayne 6.00 15.00

2009 SPx X-Factor Autographs

XAA Aundrae Allison 3.00 8.00
XAS Anthony Spencer 4.00 10.00
XAV Donnie Avery 3.00 8.00
XBA Sam Baker 3.00 8.00
XBB Brian Brohm 3.00 8.00
XBD Buster Davis 3.00 8.00
XBU Keenan Burton 3.00 8.00
XCD Craig Davis 3.00 8.00
XCH Chris Henry RB 3.00 8.00
XCJ Calvin Johnson 15.00 40.00
XCT Courtney Taylor 3.00 8.00
XDA Chris Davis 3.00 8.00
XDB Drew Bennett 3.00 8.00
XDC David Clowney 3.00 8.00
XDI David Irons 3.00 8.00
XDJ DeSean Jackson 4.00 10.00
XDM Darren McFadden 7.50 20.00
XDR Dante Rosario 3.00 8.00
XDS Drew Stanton 5.00 12.00
XJA Chevis Jackson 3.00 8.00
XJB John David Booty 4.00 10.00
XJF Justin Forsett 4.00 10.00
XJJ Josh Johnson 3.00 8.00
XJK Jordan Kent 3.00 8.00
XJO Jacoby Jones 3.00 8.00
XJS Jerome Simpson 3.00 8.00
XJT Jacob Tamme 3.00 8.00
XKB Kentwan Balmer 3.00 8.00
XKH Korey Hall 4.00 10.00
XKW Kelley Washington 3.00 8.00
XLH Lavelle Hawkins 3.00 8.00
XLR Laurent Robinson 3.00 8.00
XMF Matt Flynn 6.00 15.00
XMK Malcolm Kelly 3.00 8.00
XMM Matt Moore 4.00 10.00
XMR Matt Ryan 25.00 50.00
XMS Matt Spaeth 3.00 8.00
XPH Paul Hubbard 3.00 8.00
XQD Quintin Demps 3.00 8.00
XQG Quentin Groves 3.00 8.00
XQM Quentin Moses 3.00 8.00
XRB Reggie Bush 10.00 25.00
XRM Rashard Mendenhall 7.50 20.00
XRT Ryan Torain 3.00 8.00
XSB Steve Breaston 4.00 10.00
XSJ Steven Jackson 7.50 15.00
XSS Steve Smith USC 7.50 15.00
XSY Selvin Young 3.00 8.00

2010 SPx

COMP.SET w/o RC's (100) 8.00 20.00
101-112 ROOK.JSY AU PRINT RUN 99
113-135 ROOK.JSY AU PRINT RUN 375
136-184 ROOKIE AU PRINT RUN 140
186-234 ROOKIE PRINT RUN 599
UNPRICED ROOK.PATCH AU GOLD #'d TO 1
UNPRICED ROOK.PATCH AU SLVR #'d TO 10
1 Devin Hester .30 .75

2 Aaron Rodgers .75 2.00
3 Vincent Jackson .25 .60
4 Larry Fitzgerald .30 .75
5 Jeremy Maclin .25 .60
6 Adrian Peterson .40 1.00
7 Jamaal Charles .30 .75
8 Matt Forte .25 .60
9 Calvin Johnson .40 1.00
10 Philip Rivers .40 1.00
11 Matt Cassel .25 .60
12 Mario Manningham .25 .60
13 Kyle Orton .25 .60
14 Joseph Addai .25 .60
15 Jay Cutler .25 .60
16 Percy Harvin .25 .60
17 Jason Witten .30 .75
18 Thomas Jones .25 .60
19 Tony Romo .30 .75
20 Chad Henne .30 .75
21 Pierre Thomas .25 .60
22 Carson Palmer .30 .75
23 Cadillac Williams .25 .60
24 Andre Johnson .30 .75
25 Roddy White .25 .60
26 Rashard Mendenhall .25 .60
27 Brady Quinn .30 .75
28 Ryan Grant .30 .75
29 Drew Brees .40 1.00
30 Sidney Rice .25 .60
31 Matthew Stafford .30 .75
32 Ricky Williams .30 .75
33 DeSean Jackson .30 .75
34 Cedric Benson .25 .60
35 Lee Evans .30 .75
36 Santana Moss .30 .75
37 Steven Jackson .25 .60
38 Matt Hasselbeck .25 .60
39 Darren McFadden .25 .60
40 Ben Roethlisberger .40 1.00
41 Steve Smith USC .25 .60
42 Chad Johnson .25 .60
43 Brent Celek .25 .60
44 Vince Young .25 .60
45 Shonn Greene .25 .60
46 Ray Rice .25 .60
47 Wes Welker .30 .75
48 Dallas Clark .25 .60
49 Josh Freeman .30 .75
50 Miles Austin .25 .60
51 Michael Crabtree .25 .60
52 Marion Barber .30 .75
53 DeAngelo Williams .25 .60
54 Chris Wells .25 .60
55 Brett Favre .75 2.00
56 Mike Sims-Walker .25 .60
57 Frank Gore .30 .75
58 Jerricho Cotchery .25 .60
59 Felix Jones .25 .60
60 Michael Turner .25 .60
61 Peyton Manning 1.00 2.50
62 Patrick Willis .30 .75
63 Joe Flacco .30 .75
64 Anquan Boldin .25 .60
65 Santonio Holmes .25 .60
66 Knowshon Moreno .25 .60
67 Hines Ward .30 .75
68 Kevin Kolb .25 .60
69 Vernon Davis .25 .60
70 LaDainian Tomlinson .40 1.00
71 David Garrard .25 .60
72 Maurice Jones-Drew .25 .60
73 Randy Moss .30 .75
74 Matt Leinart .25 .60
75 Troy Polamalu .40 1.00
76 Matt Moore .25 .60
77 Jonathan Stewart .25 .60
78 Matt Ryan .30 .75
79 Donovan McNabb .30 .75
80 Eli Manning .30 .75
81 Greg Jennings .25 .60
82 Brandon Marshall .30 .75
83 Jerome Harrison .25 .60
84 Reggie Wayne .30 .75
85 Ronnie Brown .25 .60
86 Tom Brady 1.00 2.50
87 Jason Campbell .25 .60
88 Matt Schaub .25 .60
89 Braylon Edwards .25 .60
90 Brandon Jacobs .25 .60
91 Marques Colston .25 .60
92 Mark Sanchez .25 .60
93 Chris Johnson .25 .60
94 Alex Smith QB .30 .75
95 Steve Smith .30 .75
96 T.J. Houshmandzadeh .25 .60
97 Mike Wallace .25 .60
98 Kellen Winslow .25 .60
99 Clinton Portis .25 .60
100 Terrell Owens .30 .75
101 Sam Bradford JSY AU RC 10.00 25.00
102 Tim Tebow JSY AU RC 75.00 150.00
103 C.J. Spiller JSY AU RC 8.00 20.00
104 Ryan Mathews JSY AU RC 8.00 20.00
105 Jahvid Best JSY AU RC 12.00 30.00
106 Jimmy Clausen JSY AU RC 8.00 20.00
107 Colt McCoy JSY AU RC 10.00 25.00
108 D.Thomas JSY AU RC 30.00 40.00
109 Dez Bryant JSY AU RC 50.00 100.00
110 N.Suh JSY AU RC 40.00 100.00
111 Brandon LaFell JSY AU RC 12.00 30.00
112 Gerald McCoy JSY AU RC 8.00 20.00
113 Dexter McCluster JSY AU RC 6.00 15.00
114 Arrelious Benn JSY AU RC 5.00 12.00
115 Toby Gerhart JSY AU RC 5.00 12.00
116 Eric Berry JSY AU RC 12.00 30.00
117 R.McClain JSY AU RC 5.00 12.00
118 J.Gresham JSY AU RC 5.00 12.00
119 Ben Tate JSY AU RC 5.00 12.00
120 Montario Hardesty JSY AU RC 5.00 12.00
121 R.Gronkowski JSY AU RC 30.00 60.00
122 Golden Tate JSY AU RC 6.00 15.00
123 Mike Kafka JSY AU RC 6.00 15.00
124 Damian Williams JSY AU RC 5.00 12.00
125 E.Sanders JSY AU RC 8.00 20.00
126 Jordan Shipley JSY AU RC 5.00 12.00
127 Eric Decker JSY AU RC 6.00 15.00
128 Andre Roberts JSY AU RC 10.00 25.00
129 Armanti Edwards JSY AU RC 6.00 15.00
130 Taylor Price JSY AU RC 5.00 12.00
131 Mardy Gilyard JSY AU RC 5.00 12.00
132 Mike Williams JSY AU RC 12.00 30.00
133 Marcus Easley JSY AU RC 5.00 12.00
134 Joe McKnight JSY AU RC 5.00 12.00
135 Jonathan Dwyer JSY AU RC 5.00 12.00
136 Carlos Dunlap AU RC 5.00 12.00
137 Russell Okung AU RC 5.00 12.00
138 Tyson Alualu AU RC 5.00 12.00
139 Brandon Graham AU RC 10.00 25.00
140 Earl Thomas AU RC 15.00 40.00
141 Jason Pierre-Paul AU RC 8.00 20.00
142 Derrick Morgan AU RC 5.00 12.00
143 Bryan Bulaga AU RC 5.00 12.00
144 Sean Weatherspoon AU RC 5.00 12.00
145 Kareem Jackson AU RC 5.00 12.00
146 Dan Williams AU RC 10.00 25.00
147 J.Cunningham AU RC 15.00 30.00
148 Jared Odrick AU RC 12.50 25.00
149 Sean Lee AU RC 15.00 30.00
150 Jerry Hughes AU RC 5.00 12.00
151 Sergio Kindle AU RC 5.00 12.00
152 Taylor Mays AU RC 5.00 12.00
153 Rennie Curran AU RC 5.00 12.00
154 Brandon Spikes AU RC 5.00 12.00
155 John Skelton AU RC 10.00 25.00
156 Jonathan Crompton AU RC 5.00 12.00
157 Dan LeFevour AU RC 5.00 12.00
158 Joe Webb AU RC 5.00 12.00
159 Tony Pike AU RC 5.00 12.00
160 Sean Canfield AU RC 5.00 12.00
161 Zac Robinson AU RC 6.00 15.00
162 Trent Williams AU RC 6.00 15.00
163 Ed Dickson AU RC 5.00 12.00
164 NaVorro Bowman AU RC 12.00 30.00
165 Koa Misi AU RC 6.00 15.00
166 Jarrett Brown AU RC 6.00 15.00
167 James Starks AU RC 6.00 15.00
168 Charles Scott AU RC 5.00 12.00
169 LeGarrette Blount AU RC 10.00 25.00
170 Brian Price AU RC 5.00 12.00
171 Stafon Johnson AU RC 5.00 12.00
173 Jacoby Ford AU RC 5.00 12.00
174 David Reed AU RC 5.00 12.00
175 Riley Cooper AU RC 10.00 25.00
176 Kerry Meier AU RC 10.00 25.00
177 Carlton Mitchell AU RC 5.00 12.00
178 Dezmon Briscoe AU RC 8.00 20.00
179 Antonio Brown AU RC 30.00 60.00
180 Patrick Robinson AU RC 6.00 15.00
181 Rusty Smith AU RC 12.00 30.00
182 Levi Brown AU RC 5.00 12.00
183 Anthony Dixon AU RC 5.00 12.00
184 Aaron Hernandez AU RC 12.00 30.00
186 Andrew Quarless RC 1.50 4.00
187 Donald Butler RC 1.50 4.00
188 Anthony Davis RC 2.00 5.00
189 Mike Iupati RC 2.50 6.00
190 Maurkice Pouncey RC 2.00 5.00
191 Rodger Saffold RC 1.50 4.00
192 Chris Cook RC 1.50 4.00
193 Phillip Dillard RC 1.50 4.00
194 Nate Allen RC 2.50 6.00
195 T.J. Ward RC 2.50 6.00
196 Tony Moeaki RC 2.00 5.00
197 Victor Cruz RC 3.00 8.00
198 Lamarr Houston RC 2.00 5.00
199 Linval Joseph RC 1.50 4.00
200 Daryl Washington RC 1.50 4.00
201 Javier Arenas RC 1.50 4.00
202 Jason Worilds RC 1.50 4.00
203 Devin McCourty RC 2.00 5.00
204 Jevan Snead RC 1.50 4.00
205 Mike Neal RC 2.50 6.00
206 Clay Harbor RC 1.50 4.00
207 Pat Angerer RC 4.00 10.00
208 Charles Brown RC 1.50 4.00
209 Terrence Cody RC 1.50 4.00
210 Corey Wootton RC 1.50 4.00
211 Kyle Wilson RC 1.50 4.00
212 Everson Griffen RC 1.50 4.00
213 Darryl Sharpton RC 1.50 4.00
214 Perry Riley RC 2.00 5.00
215 Dennis Pitta RC 1.50 4.00
216 Thaddeus Gibson RC 2.00 5.00
217 Garrett Graham RC 1.50 4.00
218 Roddrick Muckelroy RC 1.50 4.00
219 Michael Hoomanawanui RC 2.50 6.00
220 John Conner RC 1.50 4.00
221 Deji Karim RC 2.00 5.00
222 Nate Byham RC 1.50 4.00
223 Anthony McCoy RC 1.50 4.00
224 Trindon Holliday RC 5.00 12.00
225 David Gettis RC 1.50 4.00
226 Kyle Williams RC 2.50 6.00
227 Myron Rolle RC 2.00 5.00
228 Terrence Austin RC 2.00 5.00
229 Marc Mariani RC 2.50 6.00
230 Dorin Dickerson RC 1.50 4.00
231 Jameson Konz RC 2.00 5.00
232 Tim Toone RC 2.00 5.00
233 Major Wright RC 1.50 4.00
234 Daniel Te'o-Nesheim RC 2.00 5.00

2010 SPx Fantastic Foursome Jerseys

STATED PRINT RUN 25 SER.#'d SETS
BBSM Brdfrd/Brynt/Spillr/Mthws 8.00 20.00
BTBT Bryant/Thoms/Benn/Tate
BTCM Brdfrd/Tebw/Clsen/McCy 8.00 20.00
MKTM Marin/Klly/Trkntn/Moon 20.00 50.00
MWCB Mann/Wyne/Clark/Brwn 25.00 50.00
PTJG Ptrsn/Tmlinsn/Jhnsn/Gre 15.00 40.00
RBSP Rmo/Brdy/Snchz/Palmr 15.00 40.00
RJBB Rmo/Jones/Brbr/Brynt 15.00 30.00
SMBT Spillr/Mathws/Best/Tate 8.00 20.00
SWPB Sandrs/Will/Palmr/Brwn

2010 SPx Rookie Materials

STATED PRINT RUN 375 SER.#'d SETS
RMAB Arrelious Benn 3.00 8.00
RMAE Armanti Edwards 2.00 5.00
RMAR Andre Roberts 2.00 5.00
RMBL Brandon LaFell 2.50 6.00
RMBT Ben Tate 1.50 4.00
RMCM Colt McCoy 2.00 5.00
RMCS C.J. Spiller 1.50 4.00
RMDB Dez Bryant 4.00 10.00
RMDM Dexter McCluster 2.00 5.00
RMDT Demaryius Thomas 4.00 10.00
RMDW Damian Williams 1.50 4.00
RMEB Eric Berry 6.00 15.00
RMED Eric Decker 2.00 5.00
RMES Emmanuel Sanders 2.50 6.00
RMGM Gerald McCoy 1.50 4.00
RMGT Golden Tate 2.00 5.00
RMJB Jahvid Best 3.00 8.00
RMJC Jimmy Clausen 1.50 4.00
RMJD Jonathan Dwyer 1.50 4.00
RMJG Jermaine Gresham 1.50 4.00
RMJM Joe McKnight 1.50 4.00
RMJS Jordan Shipley 1.50 4.00
RMMA Ryan Mathews 1.50 4.00
RMME Marcus Easley 1.50 4.00
RMMG Mardy Gilyard 1.50 4.00
RMMH Montario Hardesty 1.50 4.00
RMMK Mike Kafka 2.00 5.00
RMMW Mike Williams 1.50 4.00
RMNS Ndamukong Suh 10.00 25.00
RMRG Rob Gronkowski 5.00 12.00
RMRM Rolando McClain 4.00 10.00
RMSB Sam Bradford 2.00 5.00
RMTG Toby Gerhart 4.00 10.00
RMTP Taylor Price 1.50 4.00
RMTT Tim Tebow 5.00 12.00

2010 SPx Rookie Materials Autographs

STATED PRINT RUN 3-20
RMAB Arrelious Benn/20 10.00 25.00
RMAE Armanti Edwards/20 12.00 30.00
RMAR Andre Roberts/20 12.00 30.00
RMBL Brandon LaFell/20 15.00 40.00
RMBT Ben Tate/20 10.00 25.00
RMCM Colt McCoy/3
RMCS C.J. Spiller/3
RMDM Dexter McCluster/20 12.00 30.00
RMDT Demaryius Thomas/3
RMDW Damian Williams/20 10.00 25.00
RMEB Eric Berry/20 15.00 40.00
RMED Eric Decker/20 12.00 30.00
RMES Emmanuel Sanders/20 15.00 40.00
RMGM Gerald McCoy/20 10.00 25.00
RMGT Golden Tate/20 12.00 30.00
RMJB Jahvid Best/3
RMJC Jimmy Clausen/3
RMJD Jonathan Dwyer/20 10.00 25.00
RMJG Jermaine Gresham/20 10.00 25.00
RMJM Joe McKnight/20 10.00 25.00
RMJS Jordan Shipley/20 10.00 25.00
RMMA Ryan Mathews/3
RMME Marcus Easley/20 10.00 25.00
RMMG Mardy Gilyard/20 10.00 25.00
RMMH Montario Hardesty/20 10.00 25.00
RMMK Mike Kafka/3
RMMW Mike Williams/20
RMNS Ndamukong Suh/3
RMRG Rob Gronkowski/20 40.00 80.00
RMRM Rolando McClain/20 10.00 25.00
RMSB Sam Bradford/3
RMTG Toby Gerhart/20 10.00 25.00
RMTP Taylor Price/20 10.00 25.00
RMTT Tim Tebow/3

2010 SPx Shadow Box

AUTOS TOO SCARCE TO PRICE
SBAB Arrelious Benn 10.00 25.00
SBAM Archie Manning 12.00 30.00
SBAP Adrian Peterson 50.00 100.00
SBAR Aaron Rodgers 40.00 80.00
SBBF Brett Favre 90.00 150.00
SBBL Drew Bledsoe 15.00 40.00
SBBR Drew Brees 40.00 80.00
SBBS Barry Sanders 40.00 80.00
SBBT Ben Tate
SBCM Colt McCoy 15.00 40.00
SBCP Carson Palmer 12.00 30.00
SBCS C.J. Spiller 20.00 50.00
SBDB Dez Bryant 50.00 100.00
SBDM Dexter McCluster 12.00 30.00
SBDT Demaryius Thomas 25.00 50.00
SBDW Damian Williams 12.00 30.00
SBEC Earl Campbell
SBEM Eli Manning 30.00 60.00
SBFG Frank Gore 15.00 40.00
SBGT Golden Tate 10.00 25.00
SBJB Jahvid Best 15.00 40.00
SBJC Jimmy Clausen 12.00 30.00
SBJD Jonathan Dwyer
SBJM Joe McKnight 12.00 30.00
SBJO Chris Johnson 30.00 60.00
SBJS Jordan Shipley 15.00 40.00
SBLT LaDainian Tomlinson 15.00 40.00
SBMC Donovan McNabb 30.00 60.00
SBMR Matt Ryan 15.00 40.00
SBPM Peyton Manning 50.00 100.00
SBPR Philip Rivers 15.00 40.00
SBRC Randall Cunningham 15.00 40.00
SBRM Ryan Mathews 20.00 50.00
SBSB Sam Bradford 40.00 100.00
SBSI Billy Sims 15.00 40.00
SBTB Tom Brady 40.00 80.00
SBTG Toby Gerhart 12.00 30.00
SBTH Thurman Thomas 20.00 50.00
SBTI Tim Brown 15.00 40.00
SBTR Tony Romo 20.00 50.00
SBTT Tim Tebow 50.00 100.00
SBWM Warren Moon 10.00 25.00

2010 SPx Super Scripts Autographs

SSAC Austin Collie 8.00 20.00
SSAP Adrian Peterson
SSBC Brent Celek 4.00 10.00
SSBF Brett Favre 125.00 250.00
SSBH Brian Hartline 5.00 12.00
SSBM Brandon Marshall
SSBO Brian Orakpo 6.00 15.00
SSCA Matt Cassel 10.00 25.00
SSCH Chad Henne 5.00 12.00
SSCJ Chad Johnson
SSCM Clay Matthews 20.00 40.00
SSCO Marques Colston
SSDB Drew Brees 50.00 100.00
SSDJ DeSean Jackson
SSDK Dustin Keller 5.00 12.00
SSDR Dominique Rodgers-Cromartie 5.00 12.00
SSDW DeMarcus Ware 8.00 20.00
SSEM Eli Manning 40.00 80.00
SSFG Frank Gore
SSFJ Felix Jones
SSHM Heath Miller 8.00 20.00
SSJA Joseph Addai 4.00 10.00
SSJC Jason Campbell
SSJF Joe Flacco 20.00 40.00
SSJM Josh Morgan 5.00 12.00
SSKO Kyle Orton 6.00 15.00
SSLC LeSean McCoy 8.00 20.00
SSLE Larry English 5.00 12.00
SSLM Le'Ron McClain 8.00 20.00
SSMA Rey Maualuga 12.50 25.00
SSMC Donovan McNabb 15.00 30.00
SSMF Matt Forte
SSMJ Maurice Jones-Drew 8.00 20.00
SSMM Mario Manningham 8.00 20.00
SSMO Matt Moore 6.00 15.00
SSMR Matt Ryan
SSMS Mark Sanchez
SSMW Mike Wallace 8.00 20.00
SSNA Nnamdi Asomugha 12.00 30.00
SSOH Michael Oher 15.00 30.00
SSPH Percy Harvin 4.00 10.00
SSPM Peyton Manning 100.00 200.00
SSPW Patrick Willis
SSRM Rashard Mendenhall 8.00 20.00
SSRR Ray Rice 8.00 20.00
SSSB Steve Breaston 5.00 12.00
SSSG Shonn Greene 8.00 20.00
SSTR Tony Romo 20.00 40.00
SSVJ Vincent Jackson 10.00 25.00
SSWW Wes Welker 20.00 40.00

2010 SPx Winning Combos Dual Jerseys

STATED PRINT RUN 99 SER.#'d SETS
WCAL A.Hawk/L.Briggs 4.00 10.00
WCBB F.Biletnikoff/A.Boldin 6.00 15.00
WCBH T.Brady/C.Henne 10.00 25.00
WCBJ M.Barber/F.Jones 5.00 12.00
WCBT D.Bryant/D.Thomas 6.00 15.00
WCCM J.Clausen/C.McCoy 8.00 20.00
WCCS J.Charles/J.Shipley 4.00 10.00
WCCT J.Clausen/J.Theismann 5.00 12.00
WCFR M.Ryan/D.Flutie 6.00 15.00
WCGJ D.Garrard/C.Johnson 5.00 12.00
WCGS N.Suh/G.McCoy 10.00 25.00
WCHP P.Hornung/A.Page 6.00 15.00
WCHW A.Hawk/D.Ware 4.00 10.00
WCMM M.Ryan/M.Sanchez 6.00 15.00
WCMS M.Sanchez/E.Manning 5.00 12.00
WCPJ A.Peterson/C.Johnson 8.00 20.00
WCQB S.Bradford/T.Tebow 6.00 15.00
WCRJ R.Mathews/J.Best 2.00 5.00
WCRS T.Romo/M.Sanchez 6.00 15.00
WCSM C.Spiller/R.Mathews 2.00 5.00
WCTB A.Benn/G.Tate 2.50 6.00
WCTD D.Thomas/J.Dwyer 6.00 15.00
WCTS F.Tarkenton/M.Stafford 8.00 20.00
WCWG F.Gore/R.Wayne 5.00 12.00
WCWM D.Williams/J.McKnight 4.00 10.00
WCWO M.Williams/B.Orakpo 4.00 10.00

2010 SPx Winning Combos Dual Jerseys Patch

*PATCH/25: .6X TO 1.5X BASIC DUAL/99
PATCH PRINT RUN 25 SER.#'d SETS
WCJW B.Jackson/C.Williams 12.00 30.00
WCMB P.Manning/D.Brees 20.00 50.00

2010 SPx Winning Materials Patch

STATED PRINT RUN 25-125
WMPAB Anquan Boldin/125 4.00 10.00
WMPAH A.J. Hawk/25 5.00 12.00
WMPAL Mike Alstott/125 8.00 20.00
WMPAP Adrian Peterson/125 6.00 15.00
WMPAR Aaron Rodgers/125 10.00 25.00
WMPBJ Brandon Jacobs/125 4.00 10.00
WMPBM Brandon Marshall/125 5.00 12.00
WMPBN Donald Brown/125 4.00 10.00
WMPBO Brian Orakpo/125 4.00 10.00
WMPBP Brandon Pettigrew/125 4.00 10.00
WMPBR Ronnie Brown/125 4.00 10.00
WMPBS Barry Sanders/125 12.00 30.00
WMPBU Brian Urlacher/125 6.00 15.00
WMPCA Jason Campbell/125 4.00 10.00
WMPCB Champ Bailey/125 5.00 12.00
WMPCC Chris Cooley/125 8.00 20.00
WMPCH Chad Henne/125 8.00 20.00
WMPCJ Calvin Johnson/125 6.00 15.00
WMPCO Jerricho Cotchery/125 4.00 10.00
WMPCR Michael Crabtree/125 4.00 10.00
WMPCW Cadillac Williams/125 4.00 10.00
WMPDB Drew Brees/25 8.00 20.00
WMPDH Darrius Heyward-Bey/125 5.00 12.00
WMPDJ DeSean Jackson/125 5.00 12.00
WMPDM Dan Marino/125 15.00 40.00
WMPDO Donovan McNabb/125 5.00 12.00
WMPDW DeAngelo Williams/125 4.00 10.00
WMPEM Eli Manning/25 6.00 15.00
WMPFG Frank Gore/125 5.00 12.00
WMPFR Josh Freeman/125 5.00 12.00
WMPHA Albert Haynesworth/125 4.00 10.00
WMPHM Heath Miller/25 5.00 12.00
WMPHN Hakeem Nicks/125 4.00 10.00
WMPJA Jamaal Charles/125 5.00 12.00
WMPJF Joe Flacco/125 5.00 12.00
WMPJM Jeremy Maclin/125 4.00 10.00
WMPJN Chris Johnson/125 4.00 10.00
WMPJO Chad Johnson/125 4.00 10.00
WMPJP Julius Peppers/125 5.00 12.00
WMPJR Jerry Rice/125 10.00 25.00
WMPJS Jonathan Stewart/125 4.00 10.00
WMPJW Jason Witten/125 5.00 12.00
WMPKB Kenny Britt/125 4.00 10.00
WMPKM Knowshon Moreno/125 4.00 10.00
WMPLB Lance Briggs/125 5.00 12.00
WMPLE Lee Evans/125 5.00 12.00
WMPLF Larry Fitzgerald/25 6.00 15.00
WMPLM LeSean McCoy/125 6.00 15.00
WMPLT LaDainian Tomlinson/125 6.00 15.00
WMPMB Marc Bulger/125 4.00 10.00
WMPMC Darren McFadden/125 4.00 10.00
WMPMI Mike Wallace/125 4.00 10.00
WMPMM Mohamed Massaquoi/125 5.00 12.00
WMPMR Matt Ryan/125 5.00 12.00
WMPMS Mark Sanchez/125 4.00 10.00
WMPMT Michael Turner/125 4.00 10.00
WMPMW Mario Williams/125 5.00 12.00
WMPPA Alan Page/125 6.00 15.00
WMPPM Peyton Manning/25 15.00 40.00
WMPPO Clinton Portis/125 4.00 10.00
WMPPR Philip Rivers/25 8.00 20.00
WMPRC Roger Craig/125 6.00 15.00
WMPRL Ray Lewis/125 8.00 20.00
WMPRM Rashard Mendenhall/125 4.00 10.00
WMPRW Reggie Wayne/125 5.00 12.00
WMPSA Bob Sanders/125 5.00 12.00
WMPSI Mike Singletary/125 8.00 20.00
WMPSL Steve Largent/125 6.00 15.00
WMPSM Shawne Merriman/125 4.00 10.00
WMPSS Steve Smith/125 5.00 12.00
WMPST Matthew Stafford/125 5.00 12.00
WMPTB Tim Brown/125 8.00 20.00
WMPTH Todd Heap/125 4.00 10.00
WMPTO Tom Brady/125 15.00 40.00
WMPVY Vince Young/25 8.00 20.00
WMPWE Chris Wells/125 4.00 10.00
WMPWI Ricky Williams/25 6.00 15.00
WMPWO Charles Woodson/125 12.50 25.00

2010 SPx Winning Trios Jerseys

STATED PRINT RUN 50 SER.#'d SETS
*PATCH/15: .6X TO 1.5X BASIC TRIO/50
WTBTB Bryant/Thomas/Benn 12.00 30.00
WTBTC Brdfrd/Tbw/Clsn 10.00 25.00
WTGCS Gore/Crabtree/Smith 6.00 15.00
WTHWB Henne/Williams/Brown 8.00 20.00
WTMJM Maclin/Jackson/McCoy 6.00 15.00
WTMKM Marino/Kelly/Moon 25.00 50.00
WTPJS Ptrsn/Jhnsn/Stwrt 8.00 20.00
WTRFH Ryan/Flutie/Hasselbeck 8.00 20.00
WTRRP Ryan/Romo/Palmer 10.00 25.00
WTRSS Ryan/Sanchez/Stafford 10.00 25.00
WTSBF Sanders/Brown/Flutie 20.00 40.00
WTSBJ Sndrs/Ptrsn/Jhnsn 15.00 40.00
WTSMB Spiller/Mathews/Best 3.00 8.00
WTWHW Willis/Hawk/Ware 6.00 15.00

2011 SPx

1-42 STATED PRINT RUN 350
43-72 JSY AU PRINT RUN 150-225
ONE SPx PACK PER 1:6 SP AUTH. BOXES
1 Earl Campbell 1.50 4.00
2 Bernie Kosar 1.25 3.00
3 Jim Kelly 1.50 4.00
4 Barry Sanders 2.50 6.00
5 Tim Brown 1.50 4.00
6 Thurman Thomas 1.25 3.00
7 Doug Flutie 1.25 3.00
8 Dan Marino 3.00 8.00
9 Jerry Rice 2.50 6.00
10 Paul Hornung 1.50 4.00
11 John Elway 2.50 6.00
12 Bo Jackson 2.00 5.00
13 Troy Aikman 2.00 5.00
14 Steve Young 2.00 5.00
15 Tony Dorsett 1.50 4.00
16 Herschel Walker 1.50 4.00
17 Warren Moon 1.50 4.00
18 Archie Griffin 1.25 3.00
19 Eddie George 1.25 3.00
20 Cris Carter 1.50 4.00
21 Drew Brees 1.50 4.00
22 Aaron Rodgers 2.50 6.00
23 Dion Lewis 1.50 4.00
24 Dwayne Harris 1.25 3.00
25 Kris Durham 1.25 3.00
26 Edmond Gates 1.25 3.00
27 Aldon Smith 1.25 3.00
28 Evan Royster 1.25 3.00
29 Jamie Harper 1.25 3.00
30 Bilal Powell 1.50 4.00
31 Marcell Dareus 1.25 3.00
32 Roy Helu 1.25 3.00
33 Prince Amukamara 1.25 3.00
34 Ronald Johnson 1.25 3.00
35 Jeremy Kerley 2.00 5.00
36 Cecil Shorts 1.25 3.00
37 Tyrod Taylor 2.50 6.00
38 Ricky Stanzi 1.25 3.00
39 Jordan Todman 1.25 3.00
40 Kyle Rudolph 1.25 3.00
41 Von Miller 2.00 5.00
42 Stevan Ridley 1.25 3.00
43 Ryan Williams JSY AU/150 8.00 20.00
44 Austin Pettis JSY AU/225 6.00 15.00
45 Christian Ponder JSY AU/225 6.00 15.00
46 Colin Kaepernick JSY AU/150 12.00 30.00
47 Daniel Thomas JSY AU/225 6.00 15.00
48 DeMarco Murray JSY AU/225 12.00 30.00
49 Tandon Doss JSY AU/225 6.00 15.00
50 Greg Little JSY AU/225 12.00 30.00
51 Jonathan Baldwin JSY AU/150 8.00 20.00
52 Greg Salas JSY AU/225 6.00 15.00
53 Jerrel Jernigan JSY AU/225 6.00 15.00
54 Leonard Hankerson JSY AU/225 6.00 15.00
55 Kendall Hunter JSY AU/225 12.00 30.00
56 Niles Paul JSY AU/225 6.00 15.00
57 Mikel Leshoure JSY AU/225 6.00 15.00
58 Torrey Smith JSY AU/225 6.00 15.00
59 Shane Vereen JSY AU/225 8.00 20.00
60 Andy Dalton JSY AU/225 12.00 30.00
61 Randall Cobb JSY AU/225 10.00 25.00
62 Titus Young JSY AU/225 6.00 15.00
63 Vincent Brown JSY AU/225 6.00 15.00
64 Julio Jones JSY AU/150 40.00 80.00
65 Jake Locker JSY AU/150 8.00 20.00
66 Mark Ingram JSY AU/150 12.00 30.00
67 A.J. Green JSY AU/150 40.00 80.00
68 Cam Newton JSY AU/150 75.00 150.00
69 Blaine Gabbert JSY AU/150 8.00 20.00
70 Jacquizz Rodgers JSY AU/225 6.00 15.00
71 Delone Carter JSY AU/225 6.00 15.00
72 Ryan Mallett JSY AU/150 8.00 20.00

2011 SPx Jersey Autographs Gold

GOLD/30: .8X TO 2X BASIC JSY AU/225
GOLD/30: .6X TO 1.5X BASIC JSY AU/150
STATED PRINT RUN 30 SER.#'d SETS
48 DeMarco Murray 25.00 60.00
60 Andy Dalton 75.00 150.00
64 Julio Jones 75.00 150.00
65 Jake Locker 12.00 30.00
67 A.J. Green 75.00 150.00
68 Cam Newton 200.00 400.00

2012 SPx

COMP.SET w/o RC's (50) 6.00 15.00
51-77 JSY AUTO PRINT RUN 399
78-85 JSY AUTO PRINT RUN 199
86-145 AUTO PRINT RUN 225
146-205 ROOKIE PRINT RUN 750
AUTO EXCH EXPIRATION: 6/7/2014
QB DRAFT EXPIRATION: 6/1/2015
1 Aaron Rodgers .60 1.50
2 Bernie Kosar .30 .75
3 Billy Cannon .25 .60
4 Billy Sims .30 .75
5 Bo Jackson .50 1.25
6 Bob Lilly .30 .75
7 Charles White .25 .60
8 Chris Spielman .25 .60
9 Cornelius Bennett .25 .60
10 Danny Wuerffel .25 .60
11 Daryl Johnston .30 .75
12 Dave Casper .25 .60
13 Drew Brees .40 1.00
14 Dwight Stephenson .40 1.00
15 Earl Campbell .40 1.00
16 Eric Metcalf .25 .60
17 Floyd Little .25 .60
18 Gale Sayers .40 1.00
19 Gary Beban .25 .60
20 George Rogers .25 .60
21 Gino Torretta .25 .60
22 Harry Carson .25 .60
23 Herman Moore .25 .60
24 Herschel Walker .40 1.00
25 Jason White .30 .75
26 Jerry Rice .60 1.50
27 Jim Plunkett .30 .75
28 Joe Washington .25 .60
29 John Cappelletti .25 .60
30 Johnny Rodgers .30 .75
31 Keith Jackson .25 .60
32 Kellen Winslow Sr. .30 .75
33 Lawrence Taylor .30 .75
34 Lee Roy Jordan .25 .60
35 Marques Colston .25 .60
36 Mike Alstott .25 .60
37 Ozzie Newsome .30 .75
38 Rocket Ismail .30 .75
39 Randy White .30 .75
40 Roger Staubach .50 1.25
41 Roman Gabriel .25 .60
42 Ron Dayne .25 .60
43 Ron Yary .25 .60
44 Steve Young .50 1.25
45 Thurman Thomas .30 .75
46 Todd Marinovich .25 .60
47 Tony Dorsett .40 1.00
48 Troy Aikman .50 1.25
49 Ty Detmer .25 .60
50 Warren Moon .40 1.00
51 Nick Foles JSY AU 15.00 40.00
52 Juron Criner JSY AU 5.00 12.00
53 Kendall Wright JSY AU 5.00 12.00
54 Kellen Moore JSY AU 6.00 15.00
55 Doug Martin JSY AU 8.00 20.00
56 Case Keenum JSY AU 25.00 50.00
57 Coby Fleener JSY AU 5.00 12.00
58 Isaiah Pead JSY AU 5.00 12.00
59 Kirk Cousins JSY AU 20.00 50.00
60 Jarius Wright JSY AU 5.00 12.00
61 B.J. Cunningham JSY AU 8.00 20.00
62 Dwight Jones JSY AU 5.00 12.00
63 Marquis Maze JSY AU 5.00 12.00
64 Mohamed Sanu JSY AU 8.00 20.00
65 Dan Herron JSY AU 5.00 12.00
66 DeVier Posey JSY AU 5.00 12.00
67 Ryan Broyles JSY AU 5.00 12.00
68 Brandon Weeden JSY AU 10.00 25.00
69 Dwayne Allen JSY AU 5.00 12.00
70 Cyrus Gray JSY AU 5.00 12.00
71 Jeff Fuller JSY AU 5.00 12.00
72 Ryan Tannehill JSY AU 8.00 20.00
73 Bernard Pierce JSY AU 5.00 12.00
74 Melvin Ingram JSY AU 5.00 12.00
75 Russell Wilson JSY AU 75.00 125.00
76 Nick Toon JSY AU 5.00 12.00
77 Rueben Randle JSY AU 5.00 12.00
78 Richardson JSY AU/199 8.00 20.00
79 Robert Griffin III JSY AU/199 10.00 25.00
80 LaMichael James JSY AU/199 15.00 40.00
81 Justin Blackmon JSY AU/199 8.00 20.00
82 Brock Osweiler JSY AU/199 8.00 20.00
83 Alshon Jeffery JSY AU/199 15.00 40.00
84 Michael Floyd JSY AU/199 8.00 20.00
85 Stephen Hill JSY AU/199 8.00 20.00
86 Mark Barron AU EXCH 10.00 25.00
87 Dre Kirkpatrick AU 3.00 8.00
88 Stephen Garcia AU 5.00 12.00
89 Courtney Upshaw AU 4.00 10.00
90 Brian Quick AU 3.00 8.00
91 Gerell Robinson AU 3.00 8.00
92 Ladarius Green AU 3.00 8.00
93 Greg Childs AU 3.00 8.00
94 Joe Adams AU 6.00 15.00
95 Keshawn Martin AU 4.00 10.00
96 Luke Kuechly AU 20.00 40.00
97 Audie Cole AU 3.00 8.00
98 Alameda Ta'amu AU EXCH 4.00 10.00
99 Edwin Baker AU 6.00 15.00
100 Brandon Thompson AU 4.00 10.00
101 Stephon Gilmore AU 6.00 15.00
102 Dominique Davis AU 4.00 10.00
104 Eric Page AU 4.00 10.00
105 Shea McClellin AU 10.00 25.00
106 Quinton Coples AU 3.00 8.00
107 Orson Charles AU 3.00 8.00
108 Pat Edwards AU 4.00 10.00
109 A.J. Jenkins AU 3.00 8.00
110 Riley Reiff AU 3.00 8.00
111 Marvin McNutt AU 3.00 8.00
112 Bobby Wagner AU 5.00 12.00
113 Davin Meggett AU 3.00 8.00
114 Mike Willie AU 5.00 12.00
115 Travis Benjamin AU 6.00 15.00
116 Tyler Hansen AU 3.00 8.00
117 Dontari Poe AU EXCH 3.00 8.00
118 Brandon Bolden AU 3.00 8.00
119 Jason Ford AU 3.00 8.00
120 Marvin Jones AU 3.00 8.00
121 Alfred Morris AU 3.00 8.00
122 Andre Branch AU 5.00 12.00
123 Alfonzo Dennard AU 3.00 8.00
124 Janoris Jenkins AU 4.00 10.00
125 Rodney Stewart AU 4.00 10.00
126 Michael Brockers AU 3.00 8.00
127 Jermaine Kearse AU 5.00 12.00
128 Ronnell Lewis AU 3.00 8.00
129 T.J. Graham AU 3.00 8.00
130 Bobby Rainey AU 3.00 8.00
131 Derek Moye AU 5.00 12.00
132 Aaron Corp AU 3.00 8.00
133 Rishard Matthews AU 3.00 8.00
134 Ryan Lindley AU 3.00 8.00
135 Da'Jon McKnight AU 4.00 10.00
136 Jonathan Martin AU 3.00 8.00
137 David DeCastro AU 3.00 8.00
138 Dont'a Hightower AU 12.00 30.00
139 Tauren Poole AU 3.00 8.00
140 Marc Tyler AU 3.00 8.00
141 Matt Kalil AU EXCH 3.00 8.00
142 Jarrett Boykin AU 12.50 30.00
143 Ronnie Hillman AU 3.00 8.00
144 Whitney Mercilus AU 3.00 8.00
145 Jordan White AU 4.00 10.00
146 Josh Chapman 1.25 3.00
147 Darius Hanks 2.00 5.00
148 Vontaze Burfict 1.50 4.00
149 Tyler Shoemaker 1.50 4.00
150 Michael Egnew 1.25 3.00
151 Billy Winn 2.00 5.00
152 Mychal Kendricks 2.00 5.00
153 Tank Carder 2.00 5.00
154 Stephfon Green 2.00 5.00
155 Casey Hayward 1.25 3.00
156 Nigel Bradham 1.50 4.00
157 Kendall Reyes 1.25 3.00
158 Shaun Prater 2.00 5.00
159 Donnie Fletcher 1.25 3.00
160 Josh Norman 1.50 4.00
161 Leonard Johnson 1.50 4.00
162 Bryce Beall 1.25 3.00
163 Jordan Jefferson 1.50 4.00
164 Lennon Creer 1.25 3.00
165 Jarrett Lee 2.00 5.00
166 Evan Rodriguez 1.50 4.00
167 Jermaine Thomas 1.50 4.00
168 Kevin Koger 2.00 5.00
169 Laron Byrd 1.50 4.00
170 Brian Linthicum 1.50 4.00
171 Junior Hemingway 2.00 5.00
172 Duane Bennett 1.50 4.00
173 Cliff Harris 2.00 5.00
174 Lavonte David 2.00 5.00
175 James-Michael Johnson 1.50 4.00
176 Marshall Lobbestael 1.50 4.00
177 Jeremy Ebert 1.25 3.00
178 Bradie Ewing 1.50 4.00
179 Harrison Smith 1.25 3.00
180 Trenton Robinson 1.50 4.00
181 Levy Adcock 1.25 3.00
182 Markelle Martin 1.50 4.00
183 Lavasier Tuinei 2.00 5.00
184 Bobby Massie 1.25 3.00
185 Cody Johnson 1.50 4.00
186 Thomas Mayo 1.25 3.00
187 Jamell Fleming 1.25 3.00
188 Dan Persa 1.50 4.00
189 Trevor Guyton 1.50 4.00
190 Brian Reader 1.50 4.00
191 Antwon Bailey 1.50 4.00
192 David Paulson 2.00 5.00
193 Coryell Judie 1.25 3.00
194 Keenan Robinson 1.50 4.00
195 Jared Crick 1.25 3.00
196 Foswhitt Whittaker 1.25 3.00
197 Travis Lewis 1.50 4.00
198 Nelson Rosario 1.25 3.00
199 Rhett Ellison 1.50 4.00
200 Cam Johnson 2.00 5.00
201 Jayron Hosley 2.00 5.00
202 Devon Wylie 1.25 3.00
203 George Iloka 1.25 3.00
204 Tim Benford 1.25 3.00
205 Brandon Carswell 1.50 4.00
206 Andrew Luck AU/99 400.00 600.00
NNO QB Draft Trade AU 250.00 400.00

2012 SPx Rookie Patch Autographs Spectrum

*51-77 PATCH/25: 1.2X TO 3X
*78-85 PATCH/25: .8X TO 2X
STATED PRINT RUN 25 SER.#'d SETS
55 Doug Martin 25.00 60.00
68 Brandon Weeden 30.00 80.00
72 Ryan Tannehill 25.00 60.00
75 Russell Wilson 150.00 250.00
80 LaMichael James 30.00 80.00

2012 SPx Finite Rookies

STATED PRINT RUN 99-499
*RADIANCE/99: .8X TO 2X BASIC INSERT/499
*RADIANCE/50: .8X TO 2X BASIC INSERT/199
OVERALL STATED ODDS 1:9
FAB Andre Branch/499 1.00 2.50
FAJ A.J. Jenkins/499 1.00 2.50
FBA Mark Barron/299 1.25 3.00
FBB Brandon Bolden/499 1.00 2.50
FBC B.J. Cunningham/499 1.00 2.50
FBO Jarrett Boykin/499 2.50 6.00
FBP Bernard Pierce/499 1.00 2.50
FBQ Brian Quick/499 1.00 2.50
FBW Brandon Weeden/299 1.25 3.00
FCF Coby Fleener/499 1.00 2.50
FCG Cyrus Gray/499 1.00 2.50
FCH Chandler Harnish/499 1.00 2.50
FCK Case Keenum/299 2.50 6.00
FCU Courtney Upshaw/299 1.50 4.00
FDA Dwayne Allen/499 1.00 2.50
FDH Dan Herron/299 1.25 3.00
FDJ Dwight Jones/299 1.25 3.00
FDK Dre Kirkpatrick/499 1.00 2.50
FDM Doug Martin/299 2.00 5.00
FDP DeVier Posey/499 1.00 2.50
FGC Greg Childs/499 1.00 2.50
FGR Gerell Robinson/499 1.00 2.50
FIP Isaiah Pead/499 1.00 2.50
FJA Joe Adams/499 1.00 2.50
FJB Justin Blackmon/99 2.00 5.00
FJC Juron Criner/299 1.25 3.00
FJE Alshon Jeffery/99 4.00 10.00
FJF Jeff Fuller/299 1.25 3.00
FJK Jermaine Kearse/499 1.50 4.00
FJW Jarius Wright/499 1.00 2.50
FKC Kirk Cousins/499 4.00 10.00
FKM Keshawn Martin/499 1.25 3.00
FKW Kendall Wright/99 2.00 5.00
FLJ LaMichael James/99 2.00 5.00
FLK Luke Kuechly/299 3.00 8.00
FMA Marquis Maze/499 1.00 2.50
FMB Michael Brockers/299 1.25 3.00
FMF Michael Floyd/99 2.00 5.00
FMI Melvin Ingram/499 1.00 2.50
FMJ Marvin Jones/499 1.00 2.50
FMK Matt Kalil/299 1.25 3.00
FMM Marvin McNutt/499 1.00 2.50
FMO Kellen Moore/299 1.50 4.00
FMS Mohamed Sanu/299 2.00 5.00
FMT Marc Tyler/499 1.00 2.50
FNF Nick Foles/299 3.00 8.00
FNT Nick Toon/299 1.25 3.00
FOS Brock Osweiler/99 2.00 5.00
FQC Quinton Coples/299 1.25 3.00
FRB Ryan Broyles/299 1.25 3.00
FRG Robert Griffin III/99 2.50 6.00
FRH Ronnie Hillman/299 1.25 3.00
FRL Ryan Lindley/499 1.00 2.50
FRR Rueben Randle/499 1.00 2.50
FRT Ryan Tannehill/99 3.00 8.00
FRW Russell Wilson/499 10.00 25.00
FSH Stephen Hill/99 2.00 5.00
FTJ T.J. Graham/499 1.00 2.50
FTP Tauren Poole/299 1.25 3.00
FTR Trent Richardson/99 2.00 5.00

2012 SPx Shadow Box

AR Aaron Rodgers 40.00 80.00
BJ Bo Jackson 15.00 40.00
BK Bernie Kosar 12.00 30.00
BS Barry Sanders 30.00 60.00
CW Charles White 8.00 20.00
DB Drew Brees 25.00 60.00
DM Dan Marino 25.00 60.00
EC Earl Campbell 12.00 30.00
GR George Rogers 8.00 20.00
HW Herschel Walker 8.00 20.00
JB Justin Blackmon 8.00 20.00
JE John Elway 20.00 50.00
JK Jim Kelly 12.00 30.00
JP Jim Plunkett 10.00 25.00
JR Johnny Rodgers 10.00 25.00
LJ LaMichael James 8.00 20.00
MF Michael Floyd 8.00 20.00
RG Robert Griffin III 10.00 25.00
SY Steve Young 12.00 30.00
TA Troy Aikman 12.00 30.00
TR Trent Richardson 8.00 20.00

2012 SPx Shadow Slot Autographs

EXCH EXPIRATION: 6/6/2014
SHBJ Bo Jackson
SHBK Bernie Kosar 15.00 40.00
SHBS Barry Sanders
SHCW Charles White EXCH 10.00 25.00
SHDB Drew Brees 30.00 60.00
SHDM Dan Marino
SHEC Earl Campbell EXCH 15.00 40.00
SHGR George Rogers 10.00 25.00
SHHW Herschel Walker
SHJB Justin Blackmon
SHJE John Elway
SHJK Jim Kelly EXCH 75.00 125.00
SHJP Jim Plunkett 12.00 30.00
SHJR Johnny Rodgers 12.00 30.00
SHLJ LaMichael James EXCH 6.00 15.00
SHMF Michael Floyd EXCH 6.00 15.00
SHRG Robert Griffin III
SHSY Steve Young 30.00 60.00
SHTA Troy Aikman
SHTR Trent Richardson

2012 SPx Shadow Slots Pose 1

OVERALL STATED ODDS 1:6
*POSE TWO: .4X TO 1X POSE ONE
*POSE THREE: .5X TO 1.2X POSE ONE
*POSE FOUR: .5X TO 1.2X POSE ONE
AR1 Aaron Rodgers 3.00 8.00
BJ1 Bo Jackson 2.50 6.00
BK1 Bernie Kosar 1.50 4.00
BS1 Barry Sanders 3.00 8.00
CW1 Charles White 1.25 3.00
DB1 Drew Brees 2.00 5.00
DM1 Dan Marino 5.00 12.00
EC1 Earl Campbell 2.00 5.00
GR1 George Rogers 1.25 3.00
HW1 Herschel Walker 2.00 5.00
JB1 Justin Blackmon .75 2.00
JE1 John Elway 3.00 8.00
JK1 Jim Kelly 2.00 5.00
JP1 Jim Plunkett 1.50 4.00
JR1 Johnny Rodgers 1.50 4.00
LJ1 LaMichael James .75 2.00
MF1 Michael Floyd .75 2.00
RG1 Robert Griffin III 1.00 2.50
SY1 Steve Young 2.50 6.00
TA1 Troy Aikman 2.50 6.00
TR1 Trent Richardson .75 2.00

2012 SPx Signature Supremacy

OVERALL STATED ODDS 1:9
SUPAC Aaron Corp 2.50 6.00
SUPAD Alfonzo Dennard 2.50 6.00
SUPAF Antonio Freeman 8.00 20.00
SUPAR Aaron Rodgers
SUPBK Bernie Kosar
SUPBP Bernard Pierce 2.50 6.00
SUPBS Billy Sims 6.00 15.00
SUPBW Brandon Weeden 2.50 6.00
SUPCF Coby Fleener 2.50 6.00
SUPCG Cyrus Gray 2.50 6.00
SUPDH Dan Herron 6.00 15.00
SUPDJ Dwight Jones 4.00 10.00
SUPDP DeVier Posey 5.00 12.00
SUPDS Dwight Stephenson 8.00 20.00
SUPDW Devon Wylie 2.50 6.00
SUPEC Earl Campbell
SUPEL John Elway
SUPFW Foswhitt Whittaker 2.50 6.00
SUPGC Greg Childs 2.50 6.00
SUPGT Gino Torretta
SUPIP Isaiah Pead 5.00 12.00
SUPJB Justin Blackmon 6.00 15.00
SUPJC Juron Criner 4.00 10.00
SUPJJ Jordan Jefferson 3.00 8.00
SUPJK Jermaine Kearse 4.00 10.00
SUPJO Daryl Johnston
SUPKM Keshawn Martin 3.00 8.00
SUPKW Kendall Wright 6.00 15.00
SUPLJ LaMichael James 2.50 6.00
SUPLK Luke Kuechly 8.00 20.00
SUPMC Marvin McNutt 2.50 6.00
SUPME Michael Egnew 2.50 6.00
SUPMI Melvin Ingram 2.50 6.00
SUPMM Marquis Maze 6.00 15.00
SUPMO Kellen Moore 12.50 25.00
SUPNT Nick Toon 8.00 20.00
SUPON Ozzie Newsome 6.00 15.00
SUPQC Quinton Coples 6.00 15.00
SUPRG Robert Griffin III 20.00 50.00
SUPRI Rocket Ismail 8.00 20.00
SUPRL Ryan Lindley 2.50 6.00
SUPRO Johnny Rodgers 6.00 15.00
SUPRW Russell Wilson 75.00 125.00
SUPSA Shaun Alexander
SUPSH Stephen Hill 2.50 6.00
SUPTA Troy Aikman
SUPTD Tony Dorsett
SUPTG T.J. Graham 2.50 6.00
SUPWA Joe Washington 8.00 20.00
SUPWM Warren Moon 15.00 30.00

2012 SPx Super Scripts Autographs

OVERALL AUTO STATED ODDS 1:9
EXCH EXPIRATION: 6/6/2014
SSAB Andre Branch 3.00 8.00
SSAJ A.J. Jenkins 3.00 8.00
SSAL Mike Alstott 15.00 30.00
SSBB Brandon Bolden 3.00 8.00
SSBJ B.J. Cunningham 3.00 8.00
SSBO Jarrett Boykin 8.00 20.00
SSBQ Brian Quick 3.00 8.00
SSCH Chandler Harnish 3.00 8.00
SSCK Case Keenum 6.00 15.00
SSCS Chris Spielman
SSCU Courtney Upshaw 4.00 10.00
SSDA Dwayne Allen 3.00 8.00
SSDB Drew Brees 25.00 50.00
SSDC Dave Casper 8.00 20.00
SSDD David DeCastro 3.00 8.00
SSDK Dre Kirkpatrick 3.00 8.00
SSDM Doug Martin 5.00 12.00
SSDW Danny Wuerffel
SSFL Floyd Little
SSGA Roman Gabriel 8.00 20.00
SSGL Cordy Glenn 4.00 10.00
SSHW Herschel Walker 25.00 50.00
SSJA Joe Adams 3.00 8.00
SSJE Alshon Jeffery 15.00 30.00
SSJF Jeff Fuller 6.00 15.00
SSJP Jim Plunkett 10.00 25.00
SSJR Jerry Rice 75.00 150.00
SSJW Jarius Wright 6.00 15.00
SSKC Kirk Cousins 12.00 30.00
SSKE Jim Kelly
SSLT Lawrence Taylor 10.00 25.00
SSMA Dan Marino 100.00 200.00
SSMB Michael Brockers 3.00 8.00
SSMF Michael Floyd 15.00 30.00
SSMK Matt Kalil EXCH 8.00 20.00

Card	Low	High
SSMS Mohamed Sanu	6.00	15.00
SSNF Nick Foles	15.00	40.00
SSOS Brock Osweiler	3.00	8.00
SSRB Ryan Broyles	6.00	15.00
SSRH Ronnie Hillman	3.00	8.00
SSRR Rueben Randle	6.00	15.00
SSRS Roger Staubach	40.00	80.00
SSRT Ryan Tannehill	5.00	12.00
SSSY Steve Young	30.00	60.00
SSTM Todd Marinovich EXCH	15.00	30.00
SSTP Tauren Poole	3.00	8.00
SSTR Trent Richardson EXCH	20.00	50.00
SSTT Thurman Thomas		
SSVB Vontaze Burfict	4.00	10.00
SSWH Jason White EXCH	10.00	25.00

2012 SPx Winning Big Materials

STATED PRINT RUN 199 SER.#'d SETS
UNPRICED PATCH PRINT RUN 10

Card	Low	High
WM1 Alshon Jeffery	4.00	10.00
WM2 Brock Osweiler	2.00	5.00
WM3 Brandon Weeden	2.00	5.00
WM4 Case Keenum	4.00	10.00
WM5 Isaiah Pead	2.00	5.00
WM6 Dan Herron	2.00	5.00
WM7 Dwayne Allen	2.00	5.00
WM8 DeVier Posey	2.00	5.00
WM9 Doug Martin	3.00	8.00
WM10 Dwight Jones	2.00	5.00
WM11 Jeff Fuller	2.00	5.00
WM12 B.J. Cunningham	2.00	5.00
WM13 Justin Blackmon	2.00	5.00
WM14 Kellen Moore	2.50	6.00
WM15 Kirk Cousins	8.00	20.00
WM16 Coby Fleener	2.00	5.00
WM17 LaMichael James	2.00	5.00
WM18 Rueben Randle	2.00	5.00
WM19 Mohamed Sanu	4.00	10.00
WM20 Michael Floyd	2.00	5.00
WM21 Juron Criner	2.00	5.00
WM22 Kendall Wright	2.00	5.00
WM23 Nick Foles	5.00	12.00
WM24 Nick Toon	2.00	5.00
WM25 Jarius Wright	2.00	5.00
WM26 Robert Griffin III	2.50	6.00
WM27 Russell Wilson	15.00	40.00
WM28 Ryan Broyles	2.00	5.00
WM29 Ryan Tannehill	3.00	8.00
WM30 Trent Richardson	4.00	10.00

2012 SPx Winning Combos Dual Jerseys

STATED PRINT RUN 299 SER.#'d SETS
*PATCH/25: 1X TO 2.5X BASIC DUAL/299

Card	Low	High
WM21 C.Keenum/K.Moore	4.00	10.00
WM22 D.Herron/D.Posey	4.00	10.00
WM23 R.Randle/S.Hill	2.00	5.00
WM24 K.Cousins/B.Cunningham	8.00	20.00
WM25 N.Foles/B.Osweiler	5.00	12.00
WM26 M.Floyd/K.Wright	2.00	5.00
WM27 J.Blackmon/B.Weeden	2.00	5.00
WM28 L.James/D.Martin	3.00	8.00
WM29 R.Tannehill/J.Fuller	3.00	8.00
WM210 R.Griffin/T.Richardson	2.50	6.00
WM211 A.Jeffery/M.Sanu	4.00	10.00
WM212 C.Fleener/D.Allen	2.00	5.00
WM213 R.Wilson/N.Toon	15.00	40.00
WM214 R.Broyles/J.Criner	4.00	10.00
WM215 B.Pierce/I.Pead	2.00	5.00

2012 SPx Winning Quad Jerseys

STATED PRINT RUN 75 SER.#'d SETS

Card	Low	High
WM41 Griff/Tnhll/Osw/Fles	10.00	25.00
WM42 Wdn/Csins/Wlsn/Knm	20.00	50.00
WM43 Blkmn/Flyd/Wrght/Jfry	8.00	20.00
WM44 Sanu/Hill/Toon/Criner	6.00	15.00
WM45 Rrdsn/Jmes/Mrtin/Pead	6.00	15.00

2012 SPx Winning Trios Triple Jerseys

STATED PRINT RUN 99 SER.#'d SETS

Card	Low	High
WM31 Griffin/Richrdsn/Blackmn	4.00	10.00
WM32 Richrdsn/James/Martin	5.00	12.00
WM33 Sanu/Wright/Posey	5.00	12.00
WM34 Pead/Pierce/Herron	3.00	8.00
WM35 Wilson/Moore/Keenum	25.00	60.00
WM36 Floyd/Wright/Jeffery	6.00	15.00
WM37 Weeden/Foles/Cousins	12.00	30.00
WM38 Floyd/Randle/Hill	3.00	8.00
WM39 Toon/Broyles/Cunningham	3.00	8.00
WM310 Tannehill/Fuller/Gray	5.00	12.00

2013 SPx

Card	Low	High
COMP.SET w/o AU's (50)	6.00	15.00

51-74 ROOKIE JSY AU PRINT RUN 475
75-83 ROOKIE JSY AU PRINT RUN 175
84-133 ROOKIE AU PRINT RUN 299
EXCH EXPIRATION: 5/20/2015

Card	Low	High
1 Steve Owens	.25	.60
2 Anthony Carter	.25	.60
3 Bo Jackson	.50	1.25
4 Steve Young	.50	1.25
5 Bruce Smith	.30	.75
6 Joe Washington	.25	.60
7 Rodney Peete	.25	.60
8 Gary Beban	.25	.60
9 Andy Katzenmoyer	.25	.60
10 Ken MacAfee	.25	.60
11 Ty Detmer	.25	.60
12 Johnny Lattner	.25	.60
13 Dan Marino	.75	2.00
14 Archie Griffin	.25	.60
15 Tommie Frazier	.25	.60
16 Barry Sanders	.60	1.50
17 Warren Sapp	.30	.75
18 Rocky Bleier	.30	.75
19 Jerry Rice	.60	1.50
20 Johnny Rodgers	.25	.60
21 Alan Page	.25	.60
22 Tim Tebow	.30	.75
23 Vinny Testaverde	.25	.60
24 Roman Gabriel	.25	.60
25 Roger Craig	.30	.75
26 Andre Ware	.25	.60
27 Bart Starr	.60	1.50
28 George Rogers	.25	.60
29 Ronnie Lott	.30	.75
30 Earl Campbell	.40	1.00
31 Charlie Ward	.25	.60
32 Jake Plummer	.25	.60
33 Jason White	.25	.60
34 Robert Smith	.25	.60
35 Ken Stabler	.40	1.00
36 Archie Manning	.30	.75
37 Daryle Lamonica	.25	.60
38 Aaron Rodgers	.60	1.50
39 Billy Cannon	.25	.60
40 Tedy Bruschi	.30	.75
41 Joe Namath	.50	1.25
42 John Elway	.60	1.50
43 Paul Hornung	.40	1.00
44 Doug Flutie	.30	.75
45 Drew Bledsoe	.30	.75
46 Eddie George	.30	.75
47 Jim Kelly	.40	1.00
48 Jerome Bettis	.40	1.00
49 John Hannah	.25	.60
50 Warren Moon	.40	1.00
51 Robert Woods JSY AU	8.00	20.00
52 Cobi Hamilton JSY AU	5.00	12.00
53 Stedman Bailey JSY AU	5.00	12.00
54 T.Williams JSY AU	5.00	12.00
55 EJ Manuel JSY AU	5.00	12.00
56 Zach Ertz JSY AU	10.00	25.00
57 Montee Ball JSY AU	5.00	12.00
58 J.Franklin JSY AU	5.00	12.00
59 D.Robinson JSY AU	5.00	12.00
60 Le'Veon Bell JSY AU	15.00	30.00
61 Ryan Nassib JSY AU	5.00	12.00
62 Aaron Dobson JSY AU	5.00	12.00
63 Mike Gillislee JSY AU	5.00	12.00
64 Justin Hunter JSY AU	5.00	12.00
65 Keenan Allen JSY AU	12.00	30.00
66 M.Lattimore JSY AU	5.00	12.00
67 Joseph Randle JSY AU	5.00	12.00
68 Tyler Eifert JSY AU	5.00	12.00
69 Giovani Bernard JSY AU	5.00	12.00
70 Kenjon Barner JSY AU	5.00	12.00
71 Tyler Bray JSY AU	5.00	12.00
72 D.Hopkins JSY AU	8.00	20.00
73 Markus Wheaton JSY AU	5.00	12.00
74 Andre Ellington JSY AU	5.00	12.00
75 Eddie Lacy JSY AU/175	6.00	15.00
76 Geno Smith JSY AU/175	6.00	15.00
77 M.Barkley JSY AU/175	12.00	30.00
78 M.Glennon JSY AU/175	6.00	15.00
79 Tyler Wilson JSY AU/175	6.00	15.00
80 T.Austin JSY AU/175	8.00	20.00
81 Manti Te'o JSY AU/175	8.00	20.00
82 L.Jones JSY AU/175	6.00	15.00
83 C.Patterson JSY AU/175	6.00	15.00
84 Seth Doege AU	4.00	10.00
85 Zac Dysert AU	5.00	12.00
86 Dyrell Roberts AU	4.00	10.00
87 Stepfan Taylor AU	2.50	6.00
88 Erik Highsmith AU	3.00	8.00
89 Sharrif Floyd AU	2.50	6.00
90 Desmond Trufant AU	6.00	15.00
91 Rex Burkhead AU	15.00	30.00
92 Luke Joeckel AU	2.50	6.00
93 Nick Kasa AU	2.50	6.00
94 Kenny Stills AU	2.50	6.00
95 Dayne Crist AU	3.00	8.00
96 Theo Riddick AU	2.50	6.00
97 Chris Thompson AU	6.00	15.00
98 D.J. Fluker AU	2.50	6.00
99 Jordan Reed AU	4.00	10.00
100 Knile Davis AU	6.00	15.00
101 Matt Scott AU	5.00	12.00
102 Gavin Escobar AU	2.50	6.00
103 Collin Klein AU	3.00	8.00
104 Blidi Wreh-Wilson AU	3.00	8.00
105 Chris Harper AU	2.50	6.00
106 Tavarres King AU	5.00	12.00
107 Travis Kelce AU	12.00	30.00
108 Ryan Swope AU	2.50	6.00
109 Dee Milliner AU	2.50	6.00
110 Aaron Mellette AU	2.50	6.00
111 Keenan Davis AU	4.00	10.00
112 Dion Jordan AU	2.50	6.00
113 Brad Sorensen AU	2.50	6.00
114 Jawan Jamison AU	2.50	6.00
115 Da'Rick Rogers AU	2.50	6.00
116 Redney Smith AU	2.50	6.00
117 Alec Ogletree AU	2.50	6.00
118 Conner Vernon AU	2.50	6.00
119 Jarvis Jones AU	2.50	6.00
120 Spencer Ware AU	2.50	6.00
121 Philip Lutzenkirchen AU	4.00	10.00
122 Lane Johnson AU	3.00	8.00
123 Emory Blake AU	2.50	6.00
124 Roy Roundtree AU	6.00	15.00
125 Onterio McCalebb AU	3.00	8.00
126 Ray Graham AU	2.50	6.00
127 Dennis Johnson AU	2.50	6.00
128 Star Lotulelei AU	3.00	8.00
129 Jeff Tuel AU	2.50	6.00
130 Marquess Wilson AU	4.00	10.00
131 Alex Okafor AU	2.50	6.00
132 Marquise Goodwin AU	2.50	6.00
133 Josh Boyce AU	2.50	6.00
134 Corey Fuller AU	2.50	6.00
135 Robbie Rouse AU	2.50	6.00
136 Barkevious Mingo AU	2.50	6.00
137 Ezekiel Ansah AU	2.50	6.00
138 Cierre Wood AU	2.50	6.00
139 Sheldon Richardson AU EXCH	2.50	6.00
140 Jordan Rodgers AU	5.00	12.00
141 Kenny Vaccaro AU	2.50	6.00
142 Dan Buckner AU	2.50	6.00
143 Bjoern Werner AU	2.50	6.00

2013 SPx 1996 Inserts

Card	Low	High
961 Aaron Rodgers	2.50	6.00
962 Bart Starr	3.00	8.00
963 Vinny Testaverde	1.00	2.50
964 Archie Griffin	1.00	2.50
965 Bo Jackson	3.00	8.00
966 Brian Bosworth	2.50	6.00
967 Jim Kelly	1.50	4.00
968 Dan Fouts	1.25	3.00
969 Doug Flutie	1.25	3.00
9610 Drew Bledsoe	2.00	5.00
9611 Earl Campbell	1.50	4.00
9612 Jake Plummer	1.00	2.50
9613 Jerry Rice	2.50	6.00
9614 Joe Namath	5.00	12.00
9615 John Hannah	2.00	5.00
9616 Ken Stabler	3.00	8.00
9617 Lawrence Taylor	3.00	8.00
9618 John Elway	2.50	6.00
9619 Ricky Watters	1.00	2.50
9620 Rocky Bleier	1.50	4.00
9621 Roman Gabriel	1.00	2.50
9622 Steve Young	2.00	5.00
9623 Dan Marino	3.00	8.00
9624 Ty Detmer	1.00	2.50
9625 Warren Moon	1.50	4.00
9626 Manti Te'o	1.00	2.50
9627 Geno Smith	.75	2.00
9628 Matt Barkley	3.00	8.00
9629 Mike Glennon	.75	2.00
9630 Tyler Wilson	.75	2.00
9631 EJ Manuel	.75	2.00
9632 Landry Jones	.75	2.00
9633 Cobi Hamilton	.75	2.00
9634 Ryan Nassib	.75	2.00
9635 Collin Klein	1.00	2.50
9636 Giovani Bernard	.75	2.00
9637 Le'Veon Bell	3.00	8.00
9638 Montee Ball	.75	2.00
9639 Andre Ellington	.75	2.00
9640 Eddie Lacy	.75	2.00
9641 Dennis Johnson	.75	2.00
9642 Joseph Randle	.75	2.00
9643 Knile Davis	.75	2.00
9644 Justin Hunter	.75	2.00
9645 Keenan Allen	1.50	4.00
9646 Robert Woods	1.25	3.00
9647 Tavon Austin	1.00	2.50
9648 Terrance Williams	.75	2.00
9649 Aaron Dobson	.75	2.00
9650 Marquess Wilson	1.25	3.00

2013 SPx 1997 Inserts

Card	Low	High
971 Joe Namath	6.00	15.00
972 Steve Young	2.50	6.00
973 Archie Griffin	1.25	3.00
974 Archie Manning	3.00	8.00
975 Dan Fouts	1.50	4.00
976 Bo Jackson	2.50	6.00
977 Bruce Smith	1.50	4.00
978 Doug Flutie	1.50	4.00
979 Dan Marino	4.00	10.00
9710 Don Maynard	1.50	4.00
9711 Tim Brown	2.00	5.00
9712 Jerome Bettis	2.50	6.00
9713 Jim Kelly	2.00	5.00
9714 John Elway	3.00	8.00
9715 Ken MacAfee	1.25	3.00
9716 Nick Buoniconti	1.25	3.00
9717 Paul Hornung	2.00	5.00
9718 Ricky Watters	1.25	3.00
9719 Warren Moon	2.00	5.00
9720 Roger Craig	1.50	4.00
9721 Ronnie Lott	1.50	4.00
9722 Aaron Rodgers	3.00	8.00
9723 Tedy Bruschi		
9724 Vinny Testaverde	1.25	3.00
9725 Warren Sapp	1.50	4.00
9726 Manti Te'o	1.25	3.00
9727 Geno Smith	1.00	2.50
9728 Matt Barkley	1.00	2.50
9729 Mike Glennon	1.00	2.50
9730 Tyler Wilson	1.00	2.50
9731 EJ Manuel	1.00	2.50
9732 Landry Jones	1.00	2.50
9733 Cobi Hamilton	1.00	2.50
9734 Ryan Nassib	1.00	2.50
9735 Collin Klein	1.25	3.00
9736 Giovani Bernard	1.00	2.50
9737 Le'Veon Bell	3.00	8.00
9738 Montee Ball	1.00	2.50
9739 Andre Ellington	1.00	2.50
9740 Eddie Lacy	1.00	2.50
9741 Dennis Johnson	1.00	2.50
9742 Joseph Randle	1.00	2.50
9743 Knile Davis	1.00	2.50
9744 Justin Hunter	1.00	2.50
9745 Keenan Allen	2.00	5.00
9746 Robert Woods	1.50	4.00
9747 Tavon Austin	1.25	3.00
9748 Terrance Williams	1.00	2.50
9749 Aaron Dobson	1.00	2.50
9750 Marquess Wilson	1.50	4.00

2013 SPx Die Cut Autographs

1-50 UNPRICED VET PRINT RUN 5
*84-143 ROOK/25: 1X TO 2.5X BASIC AU/299
84-143 ROOKIE PRINT RUN 25

2013 SPx Finite

STATED ODDS 3:10
STATED PRINT RUN 899 SER.#'d SETS
*RADIANCE/99: .6X TO 1.5X BASIC INSERT/899

Card	Low	High
FIAD Aaron Dobson	.75	2.00
FIAE Andre Ellington	.75	2.00
FIAR Aaron Rodgers	2.00	5.00
FIBA Matt Barkley	.75	2.00
FIBJ Bo Jackson	2.00	5.00
FIBS Barry Sanders	2.50	6.00
FICP Cordarrelle Patterson	.75	2.00
FIDF Dan Fouts	1.25	3.00
FIDH DeAndre Hopkins	2.00	5.00
FIDM Dan Marino	3.00	8.00
FIEG Eddie George	1.50	4.00
FIEL Eddie Lacy	.75	2.00
FIEM EJ Manuel	.75	2.00
FIGB Giovani Bernard	.75	2.00
FIGL Mike Glennon	.75	2.00
FIGS Geno Smith	.75	2.00
FIJE John Elway	2.50	6.00
FIJH Justin Hunter	.75	2.00
FIJJ Jawan Jamison	.75	2.00
FIJK Jim Kelly	1.50	4.00
FIJR Jerry Rice	2.50	6.00
FIKA Keenan Allen	1.50	4.00
FILB Le'Veon Bell	3.00	8.00
FILJ Landry Jones	.75	2.00
FIMB Montee Ball	.75	2.00
FIMG Mike Gillislee	.75	2.00
FIML Marcus Lattimore	.75	2.00
FIMT Manti Te'o	1.00	2.50
FIRN Ryan Nassib	.75	2.00
FIRW Robert Woods	1.25	3.00
FISB Stedman Bailey	.75	2.00
FISM Bruce Smith	1.25	3.00
FIST Bart Starr	2.50	6.00
FISY Steve Young	2.00	5.00
FITA Tavon Austin	1.00	2.50
FITB Tyler Bray	.75	2.00
FITE Tyler Eifert	.75	2.00
FITK Tavarres King	.75	2.00
FITW Tyler Wilson	.75	2.00
FIWH Markus Wheaton	.75	2.00
FIWI Terrance Williams	.75	2.00
FIZE Zach Ertz	1.50	4.00

2013 SPx Rookie Jersey Autographs Variations 25

*PHOTO VAR/25: .5X TO 1.2X JSY AU/175

2013 SPx Rookie Patch Autographs

*51-74 PATCH AU/30: 1X TO 2.5X JSY AU/475
*75-83 PATCH AU/30: .6X TO 1.5X JSY AU/175

Card	Low	High
55 EJ Manuel	12.00	30.00
57 Montee Ball	12.00	30.00
59 Denard Robinson	12.00	30.00
76 Geno Smith	12.00	30.00
80 Tavon Austin	15.00	40.00

2013 SPx Shadow Box

STATED ODDS 1:100

Card	Low	High
SHAC Anthony Carter	6.00	15.00
SHAG Archie Griffin	6.00	15.00
SHAM Archie Manning	15.00	40.00
SHAR Aaron Rodgers	15.00	40.00
SHBB Brian Bosworth	8.00	20.00
SHBC Billy Cannon	10.00	25.00
SHBE Gary Beban	10.00	25.00
SHBJ Bo Jackson	15.00	40.00
SHBS Bruce Smith	6.00	15.00
SHCW Chris Weinke	6.00	15.00
SHDB Drew Bledsoe	12.00	30.00
SHDF Dan Fouts	8.00	20.00
SHDL Daryle Lamonica	6.00	15.00
SHDM Don Maynard	6.00	15.00
SHEC Earl Campbell	6.00	15.00
SHFL Doug Flutie	6.00	15.00
SHGB Giovani Bernard	3.00	8.00
SHGS Geno Smith	3.00	8.00
SHJB Jerome Bettis	15.00	40.00
SHJE John Elway	20.00	50.00
SHJH Justin Hunter	3.00	8.00
SHJK Jim Kelly	10.00	25.00
SHJN Joe Namath	40.00	80.00
SHJR Jerry Rice	15.00	40.00
SHKS Ken Stabler	6.00	15.00
SHMA Dan Marino	25.00	50.00
SHMB Matt Barkley	10.00	25.00
SHPH Paul Hornung	8.00	20.00
SHRC Roger Craig	8.00	20.00
SHST Bart Starr	12.00	30.00
SHSY Steve Young	10.00	25.00
SHTB Tedy Bruschi	8.00	20.00

2013 SPx Signatures

Card	Low	High
SPxAD Aaron Dobson	4.00	10.00
SPxAG Archie Griffin		
SPxAK Andy Katzenmoyer	6.00	15.00
SPxBA Bart Starr		
SPxBM Barkevious Mingo	4.00	10.00
SPxBS Bruce Smith		
SPxBW Bjoern Werner	4.00	10.00
SPxCH Cobi Hamilton	4.00	10.00
SPxCK Collin Klein	6.00	15.00
SPxDB Drew Bledsoe	30.00	60.00
SPxDH DeAndre Hopkins	10.00	25.00
SPxDJ Dennis Johnson	4.00	10.00
SPxDM Dan Marino		
SPxDR Da'Rick Rogers	4.00	10.00
SPxEH Erik Highsmith	5.00	12.00
SPxEL Eddie Lacy	4.00	10.00
SPxEM EJ Manuel	4.00	10.00
SPxGA Roman Gabriel		
SPxGB Giovani Bernard	4.00	10.00
SPxGL Mike Glennon		
SPxGS Geno Smith		
SPxJB Jerome Bettis		
SPxJE John Elway		
SPxJH Justin Hunter	4.00	10.00
SPxJO Josh Boyce	4.00	10.00
SPxJR Joseph Randle	4.00	10.00
SPxKA Keenan Allen	8.00	20.00
SPxKB Kenjon Barner	4.00	10.00
SPxKD Knile Davis	4.00	10.00
SPxKS Kenny Stills	4.00	10.00
SPxLJ Landry Jones	4.00	10.00
SPxMB Matt Barkley		
SPxME Aaron Mellette	4.00	10.00
SPxMG Mike Gillislee	6.00	15.00
SPxML Marcus Lattimore	4.00	10.00
SPxMO Montee Ball	4.00	10.00
SPxMW Markus Wheaton	4.00	10.00
SPxRB Rocky Bleier	8.00	20.00
SPxRN Ryan Nassib		
SPxRW Robert Woods	6.00	15.00
SPxSB Stedman Bailey	8.00	20.00
SPxST Stepfan Taylor		
SPxSY Steve Young		
SPxTA Tavon Austin	5.00	12.00
SPxTD Ty Detmer	6.00	15.00
SPxTW Tyler Wilson	4.00	10.00
SPxWM Warren Moon		
SPxZD Zac Dysert		

2013 SPx Super Scripts Autographs

Card	Low	High
SSAD Aaron Dobson	4.00	10.00
SSAE Andre Ellington	4.00	10.00
SSAR Aaron Rodgers		
SSBA Matt Barkley		
SSBB Brian Bosworth		
SSBS Barry Sanders	50.00	100.00
SSCH Cobi Hamilton	4.00	10.00
SSCK Collin Klein	5.00	12.00
SSCP Cordarrelle Patterson	4.00	10.00
SSDF Doug Flutie		
SSDH DeAndre Hopkins	10.00	25.00
SSDM Dee Milliner		
SSDR Denard Robinson	4.00	10.00
SSEL Eddie Lacy	4.00	10.00
SSEM EJ Manuel	4.00	10.00
SSGB Giovani Bernard	4.00	10.00
SSGS Geno Smith		
SSHU Justin Hunter	4.00	10.00
SSJF Johnathan Franklin	4.00	10.00
SSJH John Hannah	6.00	15.00
SSJR Joseph Randle	4.00	10.00
SSKA Keenan Allen		
SSKB Kenjon Barner	4.00	10.00
SSKS Kenny Stills	4.00	10.00
SSLB Le'Veon Bell		
SSLJ Landry Jones		
SSMB Montee Ball		
SSMG Mike Glennon		
SSML Marcus Lattimore	4.00	10.00
SSMS Matt Scott	4.00	10.00
SSMT Manti Te'o	12.00	30.00
SSMW Markus Wheaton	4.00	10.00
SSRC Roger Craig		
SSRI Jerry Rice		
SSRN Ryan Nassib	4.00	10.00
SSRO Da'Rick Rogers	8.00	20.00
SSRS Robert Smith	10.00	25.00
SSRW Robert Woods	6.00	15.00
SSTA Tavon Austin	5.00	12.00
SSTB Tedy Bruschi		
SSTK Tavarres King	4.00	10.00
SSTW Terrance Williams	4.00	10.00
SSTY Tyler Wilson		
SSVT Vinny Testaverde	8.00	20.00
SSWI Marquess Wilson	4.00	10.00
SSWS Warren Sapp		
SSZD Zac Dysert	4.00	10.00
SSZE Zach Ertz	8.00	20.00

2013 SPx UD Premier Jersey Autographs

*PATCH/15: .8X TO 2X JSY AU/120
*PATCH/15: .6X TO 1.5X JSY AU/70

Card	Low	High
1 Marcus Lattimore/125	10.00	25.00
2 Torrance Williams/125	6.00	15.00
3 Tyler Eifert/125	8.00	20.00
4 Le'Veon Bell/125	20.00	50.00
5 Robert Woods/125	10.00	25.00
6 Montee Ball/125	6.00	15.00
7 Cobi Hamilton/125	6.00	15.00
8 DeAndre Hopkins/125	15.00	40.00
9 Aaron Dobson/125	6.00	15.00
10 Johnathan Franklin/125	6.00	15.00
11 EJ Manuel/125	6.00	15.00
12 Joseph Randle/125	6.00	15.00
13 Tyler Bray/125	6.00	15.00
14 Kenjon Barner/125	6.00	15.00
15 Landry Jones/125	6.00	15.00
16 Justin Hunter/125	6.00	15.00
17 Giovani Bernard/125	6.00	15.00
18 Andre Ellington/125	6.00	15.00
19 Mike Gillislee/125	6.00	15.00
20 Markus Wheaton/125	6.00	15.00
21 Cordarrelle Patterson/70	8.00	20.00
22 Manti Te'o/70	10.00	25.00
23 Mike Glennon/70	8.00	20.00
24 Geno Smith/70	8.00	20.00
25 Keenan Allen/70	15.00	40.00
26 Tyler Wilson/70	8.00	20.00
27 Eddie Lacy/70	8.00	20.00
28 Tavon Austin/70	10.00	25.00
29 Matt Barkley/70	15.00	40.00
30 Ryan Nassib/70	8.00	20.00

2013 SPx Winning Big Materials

Card	Low	High
WBAD Aaron Dobson	2.00	5.00
WBAE Andre Ellington	2.00	5.00
WBBA Montee Ball	2.00	5.00
WBBJ Bo Jackson	8.00	20.00
WBBR Tyler Bray	2.00	5.00
WBBS Billy Sims	4.00	10.00
WBCP Cordarrelle Patterson	2.00	5.00
WBDH DeAndre Hopkins	5.00	12.00
WBDL Daryle Lamonica	3.00	8.00
WBDM Dan Marino	10.00	25.00
WBEC Earl Campbell	5.00	12.00
WBEL Eddie Lacy	2.00	5.00
WBEM EJ Manuel	2.00	5.00
WBGB Giovani Bernard	2.00	5.00
WBGS Geno Smith	2.00	5.00
WBHU Justin Hunter	2.00	5.00
WBHW Herschel Walker	5.00	12.00
WBJE John Elway	8.00	20.00
WBJK Jim Kelly	5.00	12.00
WBJR Jerry Rice	6.00	15.00
WBKA Keenan Allen	4.00	10.00
WBLB Le'Veon Bell	6.00	15.00
WBLJ Landry Jones	2.00	5.00
WBMB Matt Barkley	2.00	5.00
WBMG Mike Glennon	2.00	5.00
WBML Marcus Lattimore	2.00	5.00
WBMT Manti Te'o	2.50	6.00
WBON Ozzie Newsome	4.00	10.00
WBPH Paul Hornung	5.00	12.00
WBRC Roger Craig	4.00	10.00
WBRN Ryan Nassib	2.00	5.00
WBRW Robert Woods	3.00	8.00
WBSA Barry Sanders	8.00	20.00
WBTA Tavon Austin	2.50	6.00
WBTB Tedy Bruschi	4.00	10.00
WBTD Ty Detmer	3.00	8.00
WBTE Tyler Eifert	5.00	12.00
WBTW Terrance Williams	2.00	5.00
WBWH Markus Wheaton	2.00	5.00
WBWI Tyler Wilson	2.00	5.00

2013 SPx Winning Combos Dual Jerseys

STATED PRINT RUN 225 SER.#'d SETS
*PATCH/25: .8X TO 2X DUAL JSY/225

Card	Low	High
WCAH K.Allen/J.Hunter	5.00	12.00
WCBB L.Bell/G.Bernard	8.00	20.00
WCBL E.Lacy/M.Ball	2.50	6.00
WCBS M.Barkley/G.Smith	2.50	6.00
WCEM J.Elway/D.Marino	10.00	25.00
WCER J.Elway/J.Rice	8.00	20.00
WCHL D.Lamonica/P.Hornung	6.00	15.00
WCKT J.Kelly/V.Testaverde	5.00	12.00
WCPA C.Patterson/T.Austin	3.00	8.00
WCWG T.Wilson/M.Glennon	4.00	10.00

2013 SPx Winning Trios Triple Jerseys

STATED PRINT RUN 99 SER.#'d SETS

Card	Low	High
WTAAH Hunter/Allen/Austin	5.00	12.00
WTAPA Austin/Allen/Patterson	5.00	12.00
WTBLH Lamonica/Bettis/Hornung	15.00	40.00
WTBSG Glennon/Barkley/Smith	2.50	6.00
WTEMK Kelly/Elway/Marino	15.00	40.00
WTERM Marino/Elway/Rice	15.00	40.00
WTLBB Lacy/Ball/Bell	10.00	25.00
WTRSE Rice/Elway/Sanders	15.00	40.00
WTSJC Sndrs/Jcksn/Cmpbll	12.00	30.00
WTSWG Smith/Glennon/Wilson	3.00	8.00

2014 SPx

Card	Low	High
COMP.SET w/o AU's (50)	6.00	15.00

51-85 ROOK.JSY AU PRINT RUN 125-425
86-145 ROOKIE AU PRINT RUN 299

Card	Low	High
1 Peyton Manning	.75	2.00
2 Bo Jackson	.50	1.25
3 Tim Brown	.40	1.00
4 John Elway	.60	1.50
5 LaDainian Tomlinson	.30	.75
6 Jerry Rice	.60	1.50
7 Joe Namath	.50	1.25
8 Hines Ward	.30	.75
9 Anthony Carter	.25	.60
10 Steve Young	.50	1.25
11 Archie Griffin	.25	.60
12 Andrew Luck	.50	1.25
13 Eric Dickerson	.30	.75
14 Jim Kelly	.40	1.00
15 Barry Sanders	.60	1.50
16 Tedy Bruschi	.30	.75
17 Deuce McAllister	.30	.75
18 Jerome Bettis	.40	1.00
19 Ozzie Newsome	.30	.75
20 Joe Montana	1.00	2.50
21 Thurman Thomas	.30	.75
22 Charley Taylor	.25	.60
23 Dan Marino	.75	2.00
24 Mike Vrabel	.25	.60
25 George Rogers	.25	.60
26 Joe Theismann	.40	1.00
27 Ron Dayne	.30	.75
28 Drew Brees	.40	1.00
29 Terrell Davis	.15	.40
30 Bernie Kosar	.30	.75
31 Mike Alstott	.30	.75
32 Bart Starr	.60	1.50
33 Earl Campbell	.40	1.00
34 Dan Fouts	.30	.75
35 Roger Craig	.30	.75
36 Warren Moon	.40	1.00
37 Ben Roethlisberger	.40	1.00
38 Garrison Hearst	.25	.60
39 Jim Plunkett	.30	.75
40 Paul Hornung	.40	1.00
41 Drew Bledsoe	.30	.75
42 D.J. Shockley	.25	.60
43 Kordell Stewart	.25	.60
44 Brian Bosworth	.30	.75
45 Doug Flutie	.30	.75
46 Chris Weinke	.25	.60
47 Daryle Lamonica	.25	.60
48 Roman Gabriel	.25	.60
49 Ty Detmer	.25	.60
50 Randall Cunningham	.30	.75
51 Aaron Murray JSY AU/425	4.00	10.00
52 Mike Evans JSY AU/249	12.00	30.00
53 Eric Ebron JSY AU/425	6.00	15.00
54 Bishop Sankey JSY AU/425	4.00	10.00
55 Jarvis Landry JSY AU/425	8.00	20.00
56 Stephen Morris JSY AU/425	4.00	10.00
57 Kelvin Benjamin JSY AU/425	6.00	15.00
58 Jeremy Hill JSY AU/425	5.00	12.00
59 Lache Seastrunk JSY AU/425	4.00	10.00
60 Donte Moncrief JSY AU/425	4.00	10.00
61 Tajh Boyd JSY AU/425	4.00	10.00
62 Odell Beckham Jr. JSY AU/425	25.00	50.00
63 Charles Sims JSY AU/425	4.00	10.00
64 Paul Richardson JSY AU/425	8.00	20.00
65 Jared Abbrederis JSY AU/425	4.00	10.00
66 Logan Thomas JSY AU/425	4.00	10.00
67 Josh Huff JSY AU/425	5.00	12.00
68 Andre Williams JSY AU/425	4.00	10.00
69 Devonta Freeman JSY AU/425	6.00	15.00
70 Martavis Bryant JSY AU/425	5.00	12.00
71 Carlos Hyde JSY AU/425	5.00	12.00
72 Brandin Cooks JSY AU/425	6.00	15.00
73 Terrance West JSY AU/425	4.00	10.00
74 Allen Robinson JSY AU/425	6.00	15.00
75 Davante Adams JSY AU/425	8.00	20.00
76 Derek Carr JSY AU/249	30.00	60.00
77 Sammy Watkins JSY AU/249	8.00	20.00
78 Bruce Ellington JSY AU/425	4.00	10.00
79 Jimmy Garoppolo JSY AU/249	50.00	100.00
80 Marqise Lee JSY AU/249	6.00	15.00
81 Ka'Deem Carey JSY AU/249	5.00	12.00
82 Zach Mettenberger JSY AU/249	5.00	12.00
83 Johnny Manziel JSY AU/125	10.00	25.00
84 Teddy Bridgewater JSY AU/125	10.00	25.00
85 Blake Bortles JSY AU/125	8.00	20.00
86 David Fales AU	2.50	6.00
87 Dri Archer AU	2.50	6.00
89 Darqueze Dennard AU	3.00	8.00
90 Tevin Reese AU	2.50	6.00
91 Jordan Lynch AU	3.00	8.00
92 Marion Grice AU	2.50	6.00
93 Robert Herron AU	2.50	6.00
96 Brett Smith AU	2.50	6.00
97 James Wilder Jr. AU	3.00	8.00
98 Mike Davis AU	2.50	6.00
99 Jason Verrett AU	2.50	6.00
100 Quincy Enunwa AU	4.00	10.00
101 Keith Price AU	4.00	10.00
102 James White AU	5.00	12.00
103 De'Anthony Thomas AU	2.50	6.00
104 Lamarcus Joyner AU	3.00	8.00
105 Troy Niklas AU	5.00	12.00
106 Tom Savage AU	8.00	20.00
107 Antonio Andrews AU	2.50	6.00
108 Ryan Grant AU	2.50	6.00
110 Arthur Lynch AU	2.50	6.00
111 James Franklin AU	3.00	8.00
112 Tyler Gaffney AU	2.50	6.00
113 TJ Jones AU	4.00	10.00
114 Jace Amaro AU	2.50	6.00
115 Richard Rodgers AU	4.00	10.00
117 Rajion Neal AU	2.50	6.00
118 Devin Street AU	6.00	15.00
119 Kyle Fuller AU	2.50	6.00
120 Xavier Grimble AU	3.00	8.00
121 Chase Rettig AU	2.50	6.00
122 Jerick Mckinnon AU	3.00	8.00
123 Brandon Coleman AU	2.50	6.00
124 Louchiez Purifoy AU	2.50	6.00
125 Ha Ha Clinton-Dix AU	3.00	8.00
126 Tommy Rees AU	3.00	8.00
127 Storm Johnson AU	2.50	6.00
128 Jalen Saunders AU	2.50	6.00
129 Calvin Pryor AU	2.50	6.00
130 Anthony Barr AU	2.50	6.00
131 Brendon Kay AU	3.00	8.00
132 Kapri Bibbs AU	3.00	8.00
133 Jeff Janis AU	2.50	6.00
134 Jake Matthews AU	2.50	6.00
135 Ryan Shazier AU	4.00	10.00
136 Bryn Renner AU	2.50	6.00
137 Silas Redd AU	3.00	8.00
138 Cody Latimer AU	4.00	10.00
139 Khalil Mack AU	10.00	25.00
140 Timmy Jernigan AU	2.50	6.00
141 Casey Pachall AU	4.00	10.00
142 George Atkinson III AU	2.50	6.00
143 Jeremy Gallon AU	5.00	12.00
144 Taylor Lewan AU	2.50	6.00
145 Travis Swanson AU	2.50	6.00

2014 SPx 1996 Inserts

STATED ODDS 1:5

Card	Low	High
96AL Andrew Luck	1.50	4.00
96AM Aaron Murray	.60	1.50
96AR Allen Robinson	1.00	2.50
96BB Blake Bortles	.75	2.00
96BC Brandin Cooks	1.00	2.50
96BR Ben Roethlisberger	1.25	3.00
96BS Bishop Sankey	.60	1.50
96BT Tajh Boyd	.60	1.50
96CH Carlos Hyde	.75	2.00
96CS Charles Sims	.60	1.50
96DB Drew Brees	1.25	3.00
96DC Derek Carr	4.00	10.00
96DF David Fales	.60	1.50
96EE Eric Ebron	.75	2.00
96JA Jace Amaro	.60	1.50
96JG Jimmy Garoppolo	5.00	12.00
96JH Jeremy Hill	.75	2.00
96JL Jarvis Landry	1.25	3.00
96JM Johnny Manziel	1.00	2.50
96KB Kelvin Benjamin	1.00	2.50
96KC Ka'Deem Carey	.60	1.50
96LS Lache Seastrunk	.60	1.50
96LT LaDainian Tomlinson	1.00	2.50
96ME Mike Evans	1.50	4.00
96ML Marqise Lee	.75	2.00
96OB Odell Beckham Jr.	1.50	4.00
96PM Peyton Manning	2.50	6.00
96SW Sammy Watkins	1.00	2.50
96TB Teddy Bridgewater	1.00	2.50
96ZM Zach Mettenberger	.60	1.50

2014 SPx 1997 Inserts

STATED ODDS 1:10

Card	Low	High
97AL Andrew Luck	2.00	5.00
97AM Aaron Murray	.75	2.00
97AR Allen Robinson	1.25	3.00
97BB Blake Bortles	1.00	2.50
97BC Brandin Cooks	1.25	3.00
97BR Ben Roethlisberger	1.50	4.00
97BS Bishop Sankey	.75	2.00
97BT Tajh Boyd	.75	2.00
97CH Carlos Hyde	1.00	2.50
97CS Charles Sims	.75	2.00
97DB Drew Brees	1.50	4.00
97DC Derek Carr	5.00	12.00
97DF David Fales	.75	2.00
97EE Eric Ebron	1.00	2.50
97JA Jace Amaro	.75	2.00
97JG Jimmy Garoppolo	6.00	15.00
97JH Jeremy Hill	1.00	2.50
97JL Jarvis Landry	1.50	4.00
97JM Johnny Manziel	1.25	3.00
97KB Kelvin Benjamin	1.25	3.00
97KC Ka'Deem Carey	.75	2.00
97LS Lache Seastrunk	.75	2.00
97LT LaDainian Tomlinson	1.25	3.00
97ME Mike Evans	2.00	5.00
97ML Marqise Lee	1.00	2.50
97OB Odell Beckham Jr.	2.00	5.00
97PM Peyton Manning	5.00	12.00
97SW Sammy Watkins	1.25	3.00
97TB Teddy Bridgewater	1.25	3.00
97ZM Zach Mettenberger	.75	2.00

2014 SPx Die Cut Autographs

Card	Low	High
86 David Fales	6.00	15.00
87 Dri Archer	6.00	15.00
88 LaDarius Perkins	6.00	15.00
89 Darqueze Dennard	8.00	20.00
90 Tevin Reese	6.00	15.00
91 Jordan Lynch	8.00	20.00
92 Marion Grice	6.00	15.00
93 Robert Herron	6.00	15.00
94 Stephon Tuitt	10.00	25.00
95 Austin Seferian-Jenkins	6.00	15.00
96 Brett Smith	6.00	15.00
97 James Wilder Jr.	8.00	20.00
98 Mike Davis	6.00	15.00
99 Jason Verrett	6.00	15.00
100 Quincy Enunwa	10.00	25.00
101 Keith Price	10.00	25.00
102 James White	12.00	30.00
103 De'Anthony Thomas	6.00	15.00
104 Lamarcus Joyner	8.00	20.00
105 Troy Niklas	6.00	15.00
106 Tom Savage	6.00	15.00
107 Antonio Andrews	6.00	15.00
108 Ryan Grant	6.00	15.00
109 Marcus Roberson	8.00	20.00
110 Arthur Lynch	6.00	15.00
111 James Franklin	8.00	20.00
112 Tyler Gaffney	6.00	15.00
113 TJ Jones	10.00	25.00
114 Jace Amaro	6.00	15.00
115 Richard Rodgers	10.00	25.00
117 Rajion Neal	6.00	15.00
118 Devin Street	6.00	15.00
119 Kyle Fuller	6.00	15.00
120 Xavier Grimble	8.00	20.00
121 Chase Rettig	6.00	15.00
122 Jerick Mckinnon	8.00	20.00
123 Brandon Coleman	6.00	15.00
124 Louchiez Purifoy	6.00	15.00
125 Ha Ha Clinton-Dix	8.00	20.00
126 Tommy Rees	8.00	20.00
127 Storm Johnson	6.00	15.00
128 Jalen Saunders	6.00	15.00
129 Calvin Pryor	6.00	15.00
130 Anthony Barr	6.00	15.00
131 Brendon Kay	8.00	20.00
132 Kapri Bibbs	8.00	20.00
133 Jeff Janis	6.00	15.00
134 Jake Matthews	6.00	15.00
135 Ryan Shazier	10.00	25.00
136 Bryn Renner	6.00	15.00
137 Silas Redd	8.00	20.00
138 Cody Latimer	8.00	20.00
139 Khalil Mack	25.00	60.00
140 Timmy Jernigan	6.00	15.00
141 Casey Pachall	10.00	25.00
142 George Atkinson III	6.00	15.00
143 Jeremy Gallon	12.00	30.00
144 Taylor Lewan	6.00	15.00
145 Travis Swanson	6.00	15.00

2014 SPx Finite

FINITE/799-999 ODDS 3:10
*RADIANCE/99: 1X TO 2.5X BASIC VET/999
*RADIANCE/99: .8X TO 2X BASIC ROOK/799

Card	Low	High
FIAL Andrew Luck/999	1.25	3.00
FIAM Aaron Murray/799	.75	2.00
FIAR Allen Robinson/799	1.25	3.00
FIBB Blake Bortles/799	1.00	2.50
FIBC Brandin Cooks/799	1.25	3.00
FIBJ Bo Jackson/999	1.50	4.00
FIBS Barry Sanders/999	1.50	4.00
FIBT Tajh Boyd/799	.75	2.00
FICH Carlos Hyde/799	1.00	2.50
FICS Charles Sims/799	.75	2.00
FIDA Davante Adams/799	1.25	3.00
FIDC Derek Carr/799	5.00	12.00
FIDF Devonta Freeman/799	1.25	3.00
FIDM Dan Marino/999	2.00	5.00
FIDO Donte Moncrief/799	.75	2.00
FIDT De'Anthony Thomas/799	.75	2.00
FIED Eric Dickerson/999	.75	2.00
FIEE Eric Ebron/799	1.00	2.50
FIJA Jace Amaro/799	.75	2.00
FIJE John Elway/999	1.50	4.00
FIJG Jimmy Garoppolo/799	6.00	15.00
FIJH Jeremy Hill/799	1.00	2.50
FIJK Jim Kelly/999	1.00	2.50
FIJL Jarvis Landry/799	1.50	4.00
FIJM Johnny Manziel/799	1.25	3.00
FIJR Jerry Rice/999	1.50	4.00
FIKB Kelvin Benjamin/799	1.25	3.00
FIKC Ka'Deem Carey/799	.75	2.00
FILS Lache Seastrunk/799	.75	2.00
FIMB Martavis Bryant/799	1.00	2.50
FIME Mike Evans/799	2.00	5.00
FIML Marqise Lee/799	1.00	2.50
FIOB Odell Beckham Jr./799	2.00	5.00
FIPM Peyton Manning/999	5.00	12.00
FISB Bishop Sankey/799	.75	2.00
FISW Sammy Watkins/799	1.25	3.00
FISY Steve Young/999	1.25	3.00
FITB Teddy Bridgewater/799	1.25	3.00
FITI Tim Brown/999	1.00	2.50
FITS Tom Savage/799	.75	2.00
FITT Thurman Thomas/999	.75	2.00
FIZM Zach Mettenberger/799	.75	2.00

2014 SPx Rookie Patch Autographs

*PATCH/25-50: 1X TO 2.5X BASIC JSY RC

Card	Low	High
83 Johnny Manziel/25	25.00	60.00

2014 SPx Signatures

UNPRICED GROUP A ODDS 1:825
GROUP B ODDS 1:340
OVERALL STATED ODDS 1:240

Card	Low	High
SPxAL Andrew Luck A		
SPxBB Blake Bortles A	5.00	12.00
SPxBR Ben Roethlisberger A		
SPxBS Barry Sanders A		
SPxCH Carlos Hyde B	5.00	12.00
SPxCW Chris Weinke B	5.00	12.00
SPxEE Eric Ebron A		
SPxJE John Elway A		
SPxJM Johnny Manziel A		
SPxJN Joe Namath A		
SPxLS Lache Seastrunk A		
SPxMA Mike Alstott B	10.00	25.00
SPxML Marqise Lee A		
SPxMV Mike Vrabel B	8.00	20.00
SPxOB Odell Beckham Jr. A		
SPxPM Peyton Manning A		
SPxSB Bishop Sankey B	4.00	10.00
SPxSW Sammy Watkins A		
SPxTB Teddy Bridgewater A		

2014 SPx Super Scripts Autographs

UNPRICED GROUP A ODDS 1:3360
UNPRICED GROUP B ODDS 1:1120
GROUP C ODDS 1:336
OVERALL STATED ODDS 1:240

Card	Low	High
SSAL Andrew Luck A		
SSAM Aaron Murray C	3.00	8.00
SSBB Blake Bortles B	6.00	15.00
SSBR Ben Roethlisberger A		
SSDB Drew Brees A		
SSDC Derek Carr B		
SSJM Johnny Manziel B		
SSJR Jerry Rice A		
SSKB Kelvin Benjamin B		
SSKC Ka'Deem Carey C	3.00	8.00
SSLT LaDainian Tomlinson B		
SSMA Mike Alstott B		
SSME Mike Evans B		
SSMJ Joe Montana A		
SSML Marqise Lee C	4.00	10.00
SSPM Peyton Manning A		
SSSW Sammy Watkins B		
SSTB Teddy Bridgewater B		

2014 SPx UD Premier Jersey Autographs

*PATCH/20: .8X TO 2X BASIC JSY AU/125

Card	Low	High
1 Jimmy Garoppolo/125	50.00	100.00
2 Aaron Murray/125		
3 Zach Mettenberger/125	5.00	12.00
4 Tajh Boyd/125	5.00	12.00
5 Stephen Morris/125	5.00	12.00
6 Logan Thomas/125	5.00	12.00
7 Bruce Ellington/125	5.00	12.00
8 Kelvin Benjamin/125	8.00	20.00
9 Martavis Bryant/125	6.00	15.00
10 Allen Robinson/125	8.00	20.00
11 Brandin Cooks/125	8.00	20.00
12 Jarvis Landry/125	10.00	25.00
13 Donte Moncrief/125	5.00	12.00
14 Paul Richardson/125	10.00	25.00
15 Bishop Sankey/125	5.00	12.00
16 Jeremy Hill/125	6.00	15.00
17 Charles Sims/125	5.00	12.00
18 Lache Seastrunk/125	5.00	12.00
19 De'Anthony Thomas/125	5.00	12.00
20 Eric Ebron/125	6.00	15.00
21 Teddy Bridgewater/50	10.00	25.00
22 Johnny Manziel/50	10.00	25.00
23 Blake Bortles/50	8.00	20.00
24 Derek Carr/50	50.00	100.00
25 Sammy Watkins/50	10.00	25.00
26 Mike Evans/50	15.00	40.00
27 Marqise Lee/50	8.00	20.00
28 Odell Beckham Jr./50	50.00	100.00
29 Carlos Hyde/50	8.00	20.00
30 Ka'Deem Carey/50	6.00	15.00

2014 SPx Winning Big Materials

STATED ODDS 1:10

Card	Low	High
WBAM Aaron Murray	1.25	3.00
WBAR Allen Robinson	2.00	5.00
WBBB Blake Bortles	1.50	4.00
WBBC Brandin Cooks	2.00	5.00
WBBJ Bo Jackson	4.00	10.00
WBBS Barry Sanders	5.00	12.00
WBCH Carlos Hyde	1.50	4.00
WBDB Drew Brees	3.00	8.00
WBDC Derek Carr	8.00	20.00
WBDF Dan Fouts	2.50	6.00
WBEC Earl Campbell	3.00	8.00
WBJB Jerome Bettis	3.00	8.00
WBJE John Elway	5.00	12.00
WBJG Jimmy Garoppolo	10.00	25.00
WBJM Johnny Manziel	2.00	5.00
WBJN Joe Namath	8.00	20.00
WBJR Jerry Rice	5.00	12.00
WBKB Kelvin Benjamin	2.00	5.00
WBKC Ka'Deem Carey	1.25	3.00
WBLS Lache Seastrunk	1.25	3.00
WBME Mike Evans	3.00	8.00
WBML Marqise Lee	1.50	4.00
WBOB Odell Beckham Jr.	3.00	8.00
WBON Ozzie Newsome	2.50	6.00
WBPM Peyton Manning	12.00	30.00
WBSA Bishop Sankey	1.25	3.00
WBSW Sammy Watkins	2.00	5.00
WBSY Steve Young	4.00	10.00
WBTB Teddy Bridgewater	2.00	5.00
WBTD Terrell Davis	1.25	3.00

2014 SPx Winning Combos Dual Jerseys

STATED ODDS 1:40
*PATCH/25: .8X TO 2X BASIC INSERTS

Card	Low	High
WCBC B.Bortles/D.Carr	8.00	20.00
WCBM J.Manziel/B.Bortles	6.00	15.00
WCCM E.Campbell/W.Moon	5.00	12.00
WCCS K.Carey/B.Sankey	1.50	4.00
WCEB M.Evans/K.Benjamin	4.00	10.00
WCFK D.Flutie/B.Kosar	4.00	10.00
WCFP D.Fouts/J.Plunkett	6.00	15.00
WCGB T.Boyd/J.Garoppolo	12.00	30.00
WCGD E.George/T.Davis	4.00	10.00
WCHS B.Sankey/C.Hyde	2.00	5.00
WCJD B.Jackson/T.Davis	6.00	15.00
WCKY J.Kelly/S.Young	6.00	15.00
WCMB J.Manziel/Bridgewater	2.50	6.00
WCMM P.Manning/J.Montana	12.00	30.00
WCMR D.Marino/J.Rice	8.00	20.00

WCNE J.Namath/J.Elway 10.00 25.00
WCPD P.Manning/D.Brees 10.00 25.00
WCSH L.Seastrunk/J.Hill 2.00 5.00
WCWL S.Watkins/M.Lee 2.50 6.00
WCZA Mettenberger/A.Murray 1.50 4.00

2014 SPx Winning Trios Triple Jerseys

STATED ODDS 1:40
*PATCH/15: 1X TO 2.5X BASIC INSERTS
WTBBR Benjamin/Beckham Jr./Robinson 5.00 12.00
WTBMB Bridgewater/Manziel/Bortles 8.00 20.00
WTBMY Brees/Marino/Young 10.00 25.00
WTCGT Campbell/George/Thomas 6.00 15.00
WTCMM Carr/Murray/Mettenberger 6.00 15.00
WTMEN Manning/Elway/Namath 15.00 40.00
WTSHC Sankey/Hyde/Carey 4.00 10.00
WTSJB Sanders/Jackson/Bettis 10.00 25.00
WTWLE Watkins/Lee/Evans 6.00 15.00

1991 Stadium Club

The 1991 Stadium Club set contains 500 standard-size cards. Cards were issued in 12-card packs. . Rookie Cards include Mike Croel, Ricky Ervins, Brett Favre, Jeff Graham, Randal Hill, Russell Maryland, Leonard Russell, Ricky Watters and Harvey Williams. In conjunction with Super Bowl XXVI in Minneapolis, Topps issued cellophane packs containing Stadium Club cards. These cards differ from the basic issue in that an embossed Super Bowl XXVI logo appears at the top right or left corner of the card front.

COMPLETE SET (500) 25.00 60.00
1 Pepper Johnson .08 .25
2 Emmitt Smith 2.00 5.00
3 Deion Sanders .60 1.50
4 Andre Collins .08 .25
5 Eric Metcalf .15 .40
6 Richard Dent .15 .40
7 Eric Martin .08 .25
8 Marcus Allen .30 .75
9 Gary Anderson K .08 .25
10 Joey Browner .08 .25
11 Lorenzo White .08 .25
12 Bruce Smith .30 .75
13 Mark Boyer .08 .25
14 Mike Piel .08 .25
15 Albert Bentley .08 .25
16 Bennie Blades .08 .25
17 Jason Staurovsky .08 .25
18 Anthony Toney .08 .25
19 Dave Krieg .15 .40
20 Harvey Williams RC .30 .75
21 Bubba Paris .08 .25
22 Tim McGee .08 .25
23 Brian Noble .08 .25
24 Vinny Testaverde .15 .40
25 Doug Widell .08 .25
26 John Jackson WR RC .08 .25
27 Marion Butts .15 .40
28 Deron Cherry .08 .25
29 Don Warren .08 .25
30 Rod Woodson .30 .75
31 Mike Baab .08 .25
32 Greg Jackson RC .08 .25
33 Jerry Robinson .08 .25
34 Dalton Hilliard .08 .25
35 Brian Jordan .15 .40
36 James Thornton UER .08 .25
37 Michael Irvin .30 .75
38 Billy Joe Tolliver .08 .25
39 Jeff Herrod .08 .25
40 Scott Norwood .08 .25
41 Ferrell Edmunds .08 .25
42 Andre Waters .08 .25
43 Kevin Glover .08 .25
44 Ray Berry .08 .25
45 Timm Rosenbach .08 .25
46 Reuben Davis .08 .25
47 Charles Wilson .08 .25
48 Todd Marinovich RC .08 .25
49 Harris Barton .08 .25
50 Jim Breech .08 .25
51 Ron Holmes .08 .25
52 Chris Singleton .08 .25
53 Pat Leahy .08 .25
54 Tom Newberry .08 .25
55 Greg Montgomery .08 .25
56 Robert Blackmon .08 .25
57 Jay Hilgenberg .08 .25
58 Rodney Hampton .30 .75
59 Brett Perriman .30 .75
60 Ricky Watters RC 2.00 5.00
61 Howie Long .30 .75
62 Frank Cornish .08 .25
63 Chris Miller .15 .40
64 Keith Taylor .08 .25
65 Tony Paige .08 .25
66 Gary Zimmerman .08 .25
67 Mark Royals RC .08 .25
68 Ernie Jones .08 .25
69 David Grant .08 .25
70 Shane Conlan .08 .25
71 Jerry Rice 1.00 2.50
72 Christian Okoye .08 .25
73 Eddie Murray .08 .25
74 Reggie White .30 .75
75 Jeff Graham RC .30 .75
76 Mark Jackson .08 .25
77 David Grayson .08 .25
78 Dan Stryzinski .08 .25
79 Sterling Sharpe .30 .75
80 Cleveland Gary .08 .25
81 Johnny Meads .08 .25
82 Howard Cross .08 .25
83 Ken O'Brien .08 .25
84 Brian Blades .15 .40
85 Ethan Horton .08 .25
86 Bruce Armstrong .08 .25
87 James Washington RC .08 .25
88 Eugene Daniel .08 .25
89 James Lofton .15 .40
90 Louis Oliver .08 .25
91 Boomer Esiason .15 .40
92 Seth Joyner .15 .40
93 Mark Carrier WR .30 .75
94 Brett Favre UER RC 10.00 25.00
95 Lee Williams .08 .25
96 Neal Anderson .15 .40
97 Brent Jones .30 .75
98 John Alt .08 .25
99 Rodney Peete .15 .40
100 Steve Broussard .08 .25
101 Cedric Mack .08 .25
102 Pat Swilling .15 .40
103 Stan Humphries .30 .75
104 Darrell Thompson .08 .25
105 Reggie Langhorne .08 .25
106 Kenny Davidson .08 .25
107 Jim Everett .15 .40
108 Keith Millard .08 .25
109 Garry Lewis .08 .25
110 Jeff Hostetler .15 .40
111 Lamar Lathon .08 .25
112 Johnny Bailey .08 .25
113 Cornelius Bennett .15 .40
114 Travis McNeal .08 .25
115 Jeff Lageman .08 .25
116 Nick Bell RC .08 .25
117 Calvin Williams .15 .40
118 Shawn Lee RC .08 .25
119 Anthony Munoz .15 .40
120 Jay Novacek .30 .75
121 Kevin Fagan .08 .25
122 Leo Goeas .08 .25
123 Vance Johnson .08 .25
124 Brent Williams .08 .25
125 Clarence Verdin .08 .25
126 Luis Sharpe .08 .25
127 Darrell Green .08 .25
128 Barry Word .08 .25
129 Steve Walsh .08 .25
130 Bryan Hinkle .08 .25
131 Ed West .08 .25
132 Jeff Campbell .08 .25
133 Dennis Byrd .08 .25
134 Nate Odomes .08 .25
135 Trace Armstrong .08 .25
136 Jarvis Williams .08 .25
137 Warren Moon .30 .75
138 Eric Moten RC .08 .25
139 Tony Woods .08 .25
140 Phil Simms .15 .40
141 Ricky Reynolds .08 .25
142 Frank Stams .08 .25
143 Kevin Mack .08 .25
144 Wade Wilson .15 .40
145 Shawn Collins .08 .25
146 Roger Craig .15 .40
147 Jeff Feagles RC .08 .25
148 Norm Johnson .08 .25
149 Terance Mathis .15 .40
150 Reggie Cobb .08 .25
151 Chip Banks .08 .25
152 Darryl Pollard .08 .25
153 Karl Mecklenburg .08 .25
154 Ricky Proehl .08 .25
155 Pete Stoyanovich .08 .25
156 John Stephens .08 .25
157 Ron Morris .08 .25
158 Steve DeBerg .08 .25
159 Mike Munchak .15 .40
160 Brett Maxie .08 .25
161 Don Beebe .08 .25
162 Martin Mayhew .08 .25
163 Merril Hoge .08 .25
164 Kelvin Pritchett RC .15 .40
165 Jim Jeffcoat .08 .25
166 Myron Guyton .08 .25
167 Ickey Woods .08 .25
168 Andre Ware .15 .40
169 Gary Plummer .08 .25
170 Henry Ellard .15 .40
171 Scott Davis .08 .25
172 Randall McDaniel .08 .25
173 Randal Hill RC .15 .40
174 Anthony Bell .08 .25
175 Gary Anderson RB .08 .25
176 Byron Evans .08 .25
177 Tony Mandarich .08 .25
178 Jeff George .40 1.00
179 Art Monk .15 .40
180 Mike Kenn .08 .25
181 Sean Landeta .08 .25
182 Shaun Gayle .08 .25
183 Michael Carter .08 .25
184 Robb Thomas .08 .25
185 Richmond Webb .08 .25
186 Carnell Lake .08 .25
187 Rueben Mayes .08 .25
188 Issiac Holt .08 .25
189 Leon Seals .08 .25
190 Al Smith .08 .25
191 Steve Atwater .08 .25
192 Greg McMurtry .08 .25
193 Al Toon .15 .40
194 Cortez Kennedy .30 .75
195 Gill Byrd .08 .25
196 Carl Zander .08 .25
197 Robert Brown .08 .25
198 Buford McGee .08 .25
199 Mervyn Fernandez .08 .25
200 Mike Dumas RC .08 .25
201 Rob Burnett RC .15 .40
202 Brian Mitchell .15 .40
203 Randall Cunningham .30 .75
204 Sammie Smith .08 .25
205 Ken Clarke .08 .25
206 Floyd Dixon .08 .25
207 Ken Norton .15 .40
208 Tony Siragusa RC .60 1.50
209 Louis Lipps .08 .25
210 Chris Martin .08 .25
211 Jamie Mueller .08 .25
212 Dave Waymer .08 .25
213 Donnell Woolford .08 .25
214 Paul Gruber .08 .25
215 Ken Harvey .15 .40
216 Henry Jones RC .15 .40
217 Tommy Barnhardt RC .08 .25
218 Arthur Cox .08 .25
219 Pat Terrell .08 .25
220 Curtis Duncan .08 .25
221 Jeff Jaeger .08 .25
222 Scott Stephen RC .08 .25
223 Rob Moore .40 1.00
224 Chris Hinton .08 .25
225 Marv Cook .08 .25
226 Patrick Hunter RC .08 .25
227 Earnest Byner .08 .25
228 Troy Aikman 1.25 3.00
229 Kevin Walker RC .08 .25
230 Keith Jackson .15 .40
231 Russell Maryland RC .30 .75
232 Charles Haley .15 .40
233 Nick Lowery .08 .25
234 Erik Howard .08 .25
235 Leonard Smith .08 .25
236 Tim Irwin .08 .25
237 Simon Fletcher .08 .25
238 Thomas Everett .08 .25
239 Reggie Roby .08 .25
240 Leroy Hoard .15 .40
241 Wayne Haddix .08 .25
242 Gary Clark .30 .75
243 Eric Andolsek .08 .25
244 Jim Wahler RC .08 .25
245 Vaughan Johnson .08 .25
246 Kevin Butler .08 .25
247 Steve Tasker .15 .40
248 LeRoy Butler .15 .40
249 Darion Conner .08 .25
250 Eric Turner RC .15 .40
251 Kevin Ross .08 .25
252 Stephen Baker .08 .25
253 Harold Green .15 .40
254 Rohn Stark .08 .25
255 Joe Nash .08 .25
256 Jesse Sapolu .08 .25
257 Willie Gault .15 .40
258 Jerome Brown .08 .25
259 Ken Willis .08 .25
260 Courtney Hall .08 .25
261 Hart Lee Dykes .08 .25
262 William Fuller .15 .40
263 Stan Thomas .08 .25
264 Dan Marino 1.50 4.00
265 Ron Cox .08 .25
266 Eric Green .08 .25
267 Anthony Carter .15 .40
268 Jerry Ball .08 .25
269 Ron Hall .08 .25
270 Dennis Smith .08 .25
271 Eric Hill .08 .25
272 Dan McGwire RC .08 .25
273 Lewis Billups UER .08 .25
274 Rickey Jackson .08 .25
275 Jim Sweeney .08 .25
276 Pat Beach .08 .25
277 Kevin Porter .08 .25
278 Mike Sherrard .08 .25
279 Andy Heck .08 .25
280 Ron Brown .08 .25
281 Lawrence Taylor .30 .75
282 Anthony Pleasant .08 .25
283 Wes Hopkins .08 .25
284 Jim Lachey .08 .25
285 Tim Harris .08 .25
286 Tory Epps .08 .25
287 Wendell Davis .08 .25
288 Bubba McDowell .08 .25
289 Bubby Brister .08 .25
290 Chris Zorich RC .30 .75
291 Mike Merriweather .08 .25
292 Burt Grossman .08 .25
293 Erik McMillan .08 .25
294 John Elway 1.50 4.00
295 Toi Cook RC .08 .25
296 Tom Rathman .08 .25
297 Matt Bahr .08 .25
298 Chris Spielman .15 .40
299 F.J.Nunn w .15 .40
Aikman
Emmitt
300 Jim C. Jensen .08 .25
301 David Fulcher UER .08 .25
302 Tommy Hodson .08 .25
303 Stephone Paige .08 .25
304 Greg Townsend .08 .25
305 Dean Biasucci .08 .25
306 Jimmie Jones .08 .25
307 Eugene Marve .08 .25
308 Flipper Anderson .08 .25
309 Darryl Talley .08 .25
310 Mike Croel RC .08 .25
311 Thane Gash .08 .25
312 Perry Kemp .08 .25
313 Heath Sherman .08 .25
314 Mike Singletary .15 .40
315 Chip Lohmiller .08 .25
316 Tunch Ilkin .08 .25
317 Junior Seau .50 1.25
318 Mike Gann .08 .25
319 Tim McDonald .08 .25
320 Kyle Clifton .08 .25
321 Dan Owens .08 .25
322 Tim Grunhard .08 .25
323 Stan Brock .08 .25
324 Rodney Holman .08 .25
325 Mark Ingram .15 .40
326 Browning Nagle RC .08 .25
327 Joe Montana 2.00 5.00
328 Carl Lee .08 .25
329 John L. Williams .08 .25
330 David Griggs .08 .25
331 Clarence Kay .08 .25
332 Irving Fryar .15 .40
333 Doug Smith DT RC .15 .40
334 Kent Hull .08 .25
335 Mike Wilcher .08 .25
336 Ray Donaldson .08 .25
337 Mark Carrier DB UER .08 .25
338 Kelvin Martin .08 .25
339 Keith Byars .08 .25
340 Wilber Marshall .08 .25
341 Ronnie Lott .15 .40
342 Blair Thomas .08 .25
343 Ronnie Harmon .08 .25
344 Brian Brennan .08 .25
345 Charles McRae RC .08 .25
346 Michael Cofer .08 .25
347 Keith Willis .08 .25
348 Bruce Kozerski .08 .25
349 Dave Meggett .15 .40
350 John Taylor .15 .40
351 Johnny Holland .08 .25
352 Steve Christie .08 .25
353 Ricky Ervins RC .15 .40
354 Robert Massey .08 .25
355 Derrick Thomas .30 .75
356 Tommy Kane .08 .25
357 Melvin Bratton .08 .25
358 Bruce Matthews .15 .40
359 Mark Duper .15 .40
360 Jeff Wright RC .08 .25
361 Barry Sanders 1.50 4.00
362 Chuck Webb RC .08 .25
363 Darryl Grant .08 .25
364 William Roberts .08 .25
365 Reggie Rutland .08 .25
366 Clay Matthews .15 .40
367 Anthony Miller .15 .40
368 Mike Prior .08 .25
369 Jessie Tuggle .08 .25
370 Brad Muster .08 .25
371 Jay Schroeder .08 .25
372 Greg Lloyd .30 .75
373 Mike Cofer .08 .25
374 James Brooks .15 .40
375 Danny Noonan UER .08 .25
376 Latin Berry RC .08 .25
377 Brad Baxter .08 .25
378 Godfrey Myles RC .08 .25
379 Morten Andersen .08 .25
380 Keith Woodside .08 .25
381 Bobby Humphrey .08 .25
382 Mike Golic .08 .25
383 Keith McCants .08 .25
384 Anthony Thompson .08 .25
385 Mark Clayton .15 .40
386 Neil Smith .30 .75
387 Bryan Millard .08 .25
388 Mel Gray UER .15 .40
389 Ernest Givins .15 .40
390 Reyna Thompson .08 .25
391 Eric Bieniemy RC .08 .25
392 Jon Hand .08 .25
393 Mark Rypien .15 .40
394 Bill Romanowski .08 .25
395 Thurman Thomas .30 .75
396 Jim Harbaugh .30 .75
397 Don Mosebar .08 .25
398 Andre Rison .15 .40
399 Mike Johnson .08 .25
400 Dermontti Dawson .15 .40
401 Herschel Walker .15 .40
402 Joe Prokop .08 .25
403 Eddie Brown .08 .25
404 Nate Newton .15 .40
405 Damone Johnson RC .08 .25
406 Jessie Hester .08 .25
407 Jim Arnold .08 .25
408 Ray Agnew .08 .25
409 Michael Brooks .08 .25
410 Keith Sims .08 .25
411 Carl Banks .08 .25
412 Jonathan Hayes .08 .25
413 Richard Johnson CB RC .08 .25
414 Darryll Lewis RC .15 .40
415 Jeff Bryant .08 .25
416 Leslie O'Neal .15 .40
417 Andre Reed .15 .40
418 Charles Mann .08 .25
419 Keith DeLong .08 .25
420 Bruce Hill .08 .25
421 Matt Brock RC .08 .25
422 Johnny Johnson .08 .25
423 Mark Bortz .08 .25
424 Ben Smith .08 .25
425 Jeff Cross .08 .25
426 Irv Pankey .08 .25
427 Hassan Jones .08 .25
428 Andre Tippett .08 .25
429 Tim Worley .08 .25
430 Daniel Stubbs .08 .25
431 Max Montoya .08 .25
432 Jumbo Elliott .08 .25
433 Duane Bickett .08 .25
434 Nate Lewis RC .08 .25
435 Leonard Russell RC .30 .75
436 Hoby Brenner .08 .25
437 Ricky Sanders .08 .25
438 Pierce Holt .08 .25
439 Derrick Fenner .08 .25
440 Drew Hill .08 .25
441 Will Wolford .08 .25
442 Albert Lewis .08 .25
443 James Francis .08 .25
444 Chris Jacke .08 .25
445 Mike Farr .08 .25
446 Stephen Braggs .08 .25
447 Michael Haynes .30 .75
448 Freeman McNeil UER .08 .25
449 Kevin Donnalley RC .08 .25
450 John Offerdahl .08 .25
451 Eric Allen .08 .25
452 Keith McKeller .08 .25
453 Kevin Greene .15 .40
454 Ronnie Lippett .08 .25
455 Ray Childress .08 .25
456 Mike Saxon .08 .25
457 Mark Robinson .08 .25
458 Greg Kragen .08 .25
459 Steve Jordan .08 .25
460 John Johnson RC .08 .25
461 Sam Mills .08 .25
462 Bo Jackson .40 1.00
463 Mark Collins .08 .25
464 Percy Snow .08 .25
465 Jeff Bostic .08 .25
466 Jacob Green .08 .25
467 Dexter Carter .08 .25
468 Rich Camarillo .08 .25
469 Bill Brooks .08 .25
470 John Carney .08 .25
471 Don Majkowski .08 .25
472 Ralph Tamm RC .08 .25
473 Fred Barnett .30 .75
474 Jim Covert .08 .25
475 Kenneth Davis .08 .25
476 Jerry Gray .08 .25
477 Broderick Thomas .08 .25
478 Chris Doleman .08 .25
479 Haywood Jeffires .15 .40
480 Craig Heyward .15 .40
481 Markus Koch .08 .25
482 Tim Krumrie .08 .25
483 Robert Clark .08 .25
484 Mike Rozier .08 .25
485 Danny Villa .08 .25
486 Gerald Williams .08 .25
487 Steve Wisniewski .08 .25
488 J.B. Brown .08 .25
489 Eugene Robinson .08 .25
490 Ottis Anderson .15 .40
491 Tony Stargell .08 .25
492 Jack Del Rio .15 .40
493 Lamar Rogers RC .08 .25
494 Ricky Nattiel .08 .25
495 Dan Saleaumua .08 .25
496 Checklist 1-100 .08 .25
497 Checklist 101-200 .08 .25
498 Checklist 201-300 .08 .25
499 Checklist 301-400 .08 .25
500 Checklist 401-500 .08 .25

1991 Stadium Club Super Bowl XXVI

COMPLETE SET (300) 560.00 1400.00
*STARS: 6X TO 12X BASIC CARDS
*ROOKIES: 2.5X TO 6X BASIC CARDS
94 Brett Favre UER 150.00 300.00

1992 Stadium Club

The 1992 Stadium Club football set was issued in three series and totaled 700 standard-size cards. The first two series consisted of 300 cards followed by a less abundant 100-card high series. The set includes 30 Members Choice (291-310, 601-610) cards. Rookie Cards include Edgar Bennett, Steve Bono, Robert Brooks, Terrell Buckley, Quentin Coryatt, Amp Lee, Dale Carter, Steve Emtman, Johnny Mitchell and Darren Woodson. Members of both NFL Properties and the NFL Players Association were included in the third series. Two different 9-card promo sheets were distributed at the 1992 National Sports Collector's Convention. They are differentiated by the card show date printed on the sheet backs.

COMPLETE SET (700) 75.00 150.00
COMP.SERIES 1 (300) 6.00 15.00
COMP.SERIES 2 (300) 6.00 15.00
COMP.HIGH SER.(100) 60.00 120.00
1 Mark Rypien .05 .15
2 Carlton Bailey RC .05 .15
3 Kevin Glover .05 .15
4 Vance Johnson .05 .15
5 Jim Jeffcoat .05 .15
6 Dan Saleaumua .05 .15
7 Darion Conner .05 .15
8 Don Maggs .05 .15
9 Richard Dent .08 .25
10 Mark Murphy .05 .15
11 Wesley Carroll .05 .15
12 Chris Burkett .05 .15
13 Steve Wallace .05 .15
14 Jacob Green .05 .15
15 Roger Ruzek .05 .15
16 J.B. Brown .05 .15
17 Dave Meggett .08 .25
18 D.J. Johnson .05 .15
19 Rich Gannon .10 .30
20 Kevin Mack .05 .15
21A Reggie Cobb ERR .05 .15
21B Reggie Cobb COR .05 .15
22 Nate Lewis .05 .15
23 Doug Smith .05 .15
24 Irving Fryar .08 .25
25 Anthony Thompson .05 .15
26 Duane Bickett .05 .15
27 Don Majkowski .05 .15
28 Mark Schlereth RC .05 .15
29 Melvin Jenkins .05 .15
30 Michael Haynes .08 .25
31 Greg Lewis .05 .15
32 Kenneth Davis .05 .15
33 Derrick Thomas .10 .30
34 David Williams .05 .15
35 Neal Anderson .05 .15
36 Andre Collins .05 .15
37 Jesse Solomon .05 .15
38 Barry Sanders 1.00 2.50
39 Jeff Gossett .05 .15
40 Rickey Jackson .05 .15
41 Ray Berry .05 .15
42 Leroy Hoard .08 .25
43 Eric Thomas .05 .15
44 Brian Washington .05 .15
45 Pat Terrell .05 .15
46 Eugene Robinson .05 .15
47 Luis Sharpe .05 .15
48 Jerome Brown .05 .15
49 Mark Collins .05 .15
50 Johnny Holland .05 .15
51 Tony Paige .05 .15
52 Willie Green .05 .15
53 Steve Atwater .05 .15
54 Brad Muster .05 .15
55 Cris Dishman .05 .15
56 Eddie Anderson .05 .15
57 Sam Mills .05 .15
58 Donald Evans .05 .15
59 Jon Vaughn .05 .15
60 Marion Butts .05 .15
61 Rodney Holman .05 .15
62 Dwayne White RC .05 .15
63 Martin Mayhew .05 .15
64 Jonathan Hayes .05 .15
65 Andre Rison .08 .25
66 Calvin Williams .08 .25
67 James Washington .05 .15
68 Tim Harris .05 .15
69 Jim Ritcher .05 .15
70 Johnny Johnson .05 .15
71 John Offerdahl .05 .15
72 Herschel Walker .08 .25
73 Perry Kemp .05 .15
74 Erik Howard .05 .15
75 Lamar Lathon .05 .15
76 Greg Kragen .05 .15
77 Jay Schroeder .05 .15
78 Jim Arnold .05 .15
79 Chris Miller .08 .25
80 Deron Cherry .05 .15
81 Jim Harbaugh .10 .30
82 Gill Fenerty .05 .15
83 Fred Stokes .05 .15
84 Roman Phifer .05 .15
85 Clyde Simmons .05 .15
86 Vince Newsome .05 .15
87 Lawrence Dawsey .08 .25
88 Eddie Brown .05 .15
89 Greg Montgomery .05 .15
90 Jeff Lageman .05 .15
91 Terry Wooden .05 .15
92 Nate Newton .05 .15
93 David Richards .05 .15
94 Derek Russell .05 .15
95 Steve Jordan .05 .15
96 Hugh Millen .05 .15
97 Mark Duper .05 .15
98 Sean Landeta .05 .15
99 James Thornton .05 .15
100 Darrell Green .05 .15
101 Harris Barton .05 .15
102 John Alt .05 .15
103 Mike Farr .05 .15
104 Bob Golic .05 .15
105 Gene Atkins .05 .15
106 Gary Anderson K .05 .15
107 Norm Johnson .05 .15
108 Eugene Daniel .05 .15
109 Kent Hull .05 .15
110 John Elway 1.00 2.50
111 Rich Camarillo .05 .15
112 Charles Wilson .05 .15
113 Matt Bahr .05 .15
114 Mark Carrier WR .08 .25
115 Richmond Webb .05 .15
116 Charles Mann .05 .15
117 Tim McGee .05 .15
118 Wes Hopkins .05 .15
119 Mo Lewis .05 .15
120 Warren Moon .10 .30
121 Damone Johnson .05 .15
122 Kevin Gogan .05 .15
123 Joey Browner .05 .15
124 Tommy Kane .05 .15
125 Vincent Brown .05 .15
126 Barry Word .05 .15
127 Michael Brooks .05 .15
128 Jumbo Elliott .05 .15
129 Marcus Allen .10 .30
130 Tom Waddle .05 .15
131 Jim Dombrowski .05 .15
132 Aeneas Williams .08 .25
133 Clay Matthews .08 .25
134 Thurman Thomas .10 .30
135 Dean Biasucci .05 .15
136 Moe Gardner .05 .15
137 James Campen .05 .15
138 Tim Johnson .05 .15
139 Erik Kramer .08 .25
140 Keith McCants .05 .15
141 John Carney .05 .15
142 Tunch Ilkin .05 .15
143 Louis Oliver .05 .15
144 Bill Maas .05 .15
145 Wendell Davis .05 .15
146 Pepper Johnson .05 .15
147 Howie Long .10 .30
148 Brett Maxie .05 .15
149 Tony Casillas .05 .15
150 Michael Carter .05 .15
151 Byron Evans .05 .15
152 Lorenzo White .05 .15
153 Larry Kelm .05 .15
154 Andy Heck .05 .15
155 Harry Newsome .05 .15
156 Chris Singleton .05 .15
157 Mike Kenn .05 .15
158 Jeff Faulkner .05 .15
159 Ken Lanier .05 .15
160 Darryl Talley .05 .15
161 Louie Aguiar RC .05 .15
162 Danny Copeland .05 .15
163 Kevin Porter .05 .15
164 Trace Armstrong .05 .15
165 Dermontti Dawson .08 .25
166 Fred McAfee RC .05 .15
167 Ronnie Lott .08 .25
168 Tony Mandarich .05 .15
169 Howard Cross .05 .15
170 Vestee Jackson .05 .15
171 Jeff Herrod .05 .15
172 Randy Hilliard RC .05 .15
173 Robert Wilson .05 .15
174 Joe Walter RC .05 .15
175 Chris Spielman .08 .25
176 Darryl Henley .05 .15
177 Jay Hilgenberg .05 .15
178 John Kidd .05 .15
179 Doug Widell .05 .15
180 Seth Joyner .05 .15
181 Nick Bell .05 .15
182 Don Griffin .05 .15
183 Johnny Meads .05 .15
184 Jeff Bostic .05 .15
185 Johnny Hector .05 .15
186 Jessie Tuggle .05 .15
187 Robb Thomas .05 .15
188 Shane Conlan .05 .15
189 Michael Zordich RC .05 .15
190 Emmitt Smith 1.50 3.00
191 Robert Blackmon .05 .15
192 Carl Lee .05 .15
193 Harry Galbreath .05 .15
194 Ed King .05 .15
195 Stan Thomas .05 .15
196 Andre Waters .05 .15
197 Pat Harlow .05 .15
198 Zefross Moss .05 .15
199 Bobby Hebert .05 .15
200 Doug Riesenberg .05 .15
201 Mike Croel .05 .15
202 Jeff Jaeger .05 .15
203 Gary Plummer .05 .15
204 Chris Jacke .05 .15
205 Neil O'Donnell .08 .25
206 Mark Bortz .05 .15
207 Tim Barnett .05 .15
208 Jerry Ball .05 .15
209 Chip Lohmiller .05 .15
210 Jim Everett .08 .25
211 Tim McKyer .05 .15
212 Aaron Craver .05 .15
213 John L. Williams .05 .15
214 Simon Fletcher .05 .15
215 Walter Reeves .05 .15
216 Terance Mathis .08 .25
217 Mike Pitts .05 .15
218 Bruce Matthews .05 .15
219 Howard Ballard .05 .15
220 Leonard Russell .08 .25
221 Michael Stewart .05 .15
222 Mike Merriweather .05 .15
223 Ricky Sanders .05 .15
224 Ray Horton .05 .15
225 Michael Jackson .08 .25
226 Bill Romanowski .05 .15
227 Steve McMichael UER .08 .25
228 Chris Martin .05 .15
229 Tim Green .05 .15
230 Karl Mecklenburg .05 .15
231 Felix Wright .05 .15
232 Charles McRae .05 .15
233 Pete Stoyanovich .05 .15
234 Stephen Baker .05 .15
235 Herman Moore .10 .30
236 Terry McDaniel .05 .15
237 Dalton Hilliard .05 .15
238 Gill Byrd .05 .15
239 Leon Seals .05 .15
240 Rod Woodson .10 .30
241 Curtis Duncan .05 .15
242 Keith Jackson .08 .25
243 Mark Stepnoski .08 .25
244 Art Monk .08 .25
245 Matt Stover .05 .15
246 John Roper .05 .15
247 Rodney Hampton .08 .25
248 Steve Wisniewski .05 .15
249 Bryan Millard .05 .15
250 Todd Lyght .05 .15
251 Marvin Washington .05 .15
252 Eric Swann .08 .25
253 Bruce Kozerski .05 .15
254 Jon Hand .05 .15
255 Scott Fulhage .05 .15
256 Chuck Cecil .05 .15
257 Eric Martin .05 .15
258 Eric Metcalf .08 .25
259 T.J. Turner .05 .15
260 Kirk Lowdermilk .05 .15
261 Keith McKeller .05 .15
262 Wymon Henderson .05 .15
263 David Alexander .05 .15
264 George Jamison .05 .15
265 Ken Norton Jr. .08 .25
266 Jim Lachey .05 .15
267 Bo Orlando RC .05 .15
268 Nick Lowery .05 .15
269 Keith Van Horne .05 .15
270 Dwight Stone .05 .15
271 Keith DeLong .05 .15
272 James Francis .05 .15
273 Greg McMurtry .05 .15
274 Ethan Horton .05 .15
275 Stan Brock .05 .15
276 Ken Harvey .05 .15
277 Ronnie Harmon .05 .15
278 Mike Pritchard .08 .25
279 Kyle Clifton .05 .15
280 Anthony Johnson .08 .25
281 Esera Tuaolo .05 .15
282 Vernon Turner .05 .15
283 David Griggs .05 .15
284 Dino Hackett .05 .15
285 Carwell Gardner .05 .15
286 Ron Hall .05 .15
287 Reggie White .10 .30
288 Checklist 1-100 .05 .15
289 Checklist 101-200 .05 .15
290 Checklist 201-300 .05 .15
291 Mark Clayton MC .05 .15
292 Pat Swilling MC .05 .15
293 Ernest Givins MC .05 .15
294 Broderick Thomas MC .05 .15
295 John Friesz MC .05 .15
296 Cornelius Bennett MC .05 .15
297 Anthony Carter MC .08 .25
298 Earnest Byner MC .05 .15
299 Michael Irvin MC .10 .30
300 Cortez Kennedy MC .05 .15
301 Barry Sanders MC .60 1.50
302 Mike Croel MC .05 .15
303 Emmitt Smith MC .75 2.00
304 Leonard Russell MC .05 .15
305 Neal Anderson MC .05 .15
306 Derrick Thomas MC .08 .25
307 Mark Rypien MC .05 .15
308 Reggie White MC .08 .25
309 Rod Woodson MC .08 .25
310 Rodney Hampton MC .08 .25
311 Carnell Lake .05 .15
312 Robert Delpino .05 .15
313 Brian Blades .08 .25
314 Marc Spindler .05 .15
315 Scott Norwood .05 .15
316 Frank Warren .05 .15
317 David Treadwell .05 .15
318 Steve Broussard .05 .15
319 Lorenzo Lynch .05 .15
320 Ray Agnew .05 .15
321 Derrick Walker .05 .15
322 Vinson Smith RC .05 .15
323 Gary Clark .10 .30
324 Charles Haley .08 .25
325 Keith Byars .05 .15
326 Winston Moss .05 .15
327 Paul McJulien UER RC .05 .15
328 Tony Covington .05 .15
329 Mark Carrier DB .05 .15
330 Mark Tuinei .05 .15
331 Tracy Simien RC .05 .15
332 Jeff Wright .05 .15
333 Bryan Cox .08 .25
334 Lonnie Young .05 .15
335 Clarence Verdin .05 .15
336 Dan Fike .05 .15
337 Steve Sewell .05 .15
338 Gary Zimmerman .05 .15
339 Barney Bussey .05 .15
340 William Perry .08 .25
341 Jeff Hostetler .08 .25
342 Doug Smith .05 .15
343 Cleveland Gary .05 .15
344 Todd Marinovich .05 .15
345 Rich Moran .05 .15
346 Tony Woods .05 .15
347 Vaughan Johnson .05 .15
348 Marv Cook .05 .15
349 Pierce Holt .05 .15
350 Gerald Williams .05 .15
351 Kevin Butler .05 .15
352 William White .05 .15
353 Henry Rolling .05 .15
354 James Joseph .05 .15
355 Vinny Testaverde .08 .25
356 Scott Radecic .05 .15
357 Lee Johnson .05 .15
358 Steve Tasker .08 .25
359 David Lutz .05 .15
360 Audray McMillian UER .05 .15
361 Brad Baxter .05 .15
362 Mark Dennis .05 .15
363 Eric Pegram .08 .25
364 Sean Jones .05 .15
365 William Roberts .05 .15
366 Steve Young .40 1.00
367 Joe Jacoby .05 .15
368 Richard Brown RC .05 .15
369 Keith Kartz .05 .15
370 Freddie Joe Nunn .05 .15
371 Darren Comeaux .05 .15
372 Larry Brown DB .05 .15
373 Haywood Jeffires .08 .25
374 Tom Newberry .05 .15
375 Steve Bono RC .10 .30
376 Kevin Ross .05 .15
377 Kelvin Pritchett .05 .15
378 Jessie Hester .05 .15
379 Mitchell Price .05 .15
380 Barry Foster .08 .25
381 Reyna Thompson .05 .15
382 Cris Carter .30 .75
383 Lemuel Stinson .05 .15
384 Rod Bernstine .05 .15
385 James Lofton .08 .25
386 Kevin Murphy .05 .15
387 Greg Townsend .05 .15
388 Edgar Bennett RC .10 .30
389 Rob Moore .08 .25
390 Eugene Lockhart .05 .15
391 Bern Brostek .05 .15
392 Craig Heyward .08 .25
393 Ferrell Edmunds .05 .15
394 John Kasay .05 .15
395 Jesse Sapolu .05 .15
396 Jim Breech .05 .15
397 Neil Smith .10 .30
398 Bryce Paup .10 .30
399 Tony Tolbert .05 .15
400 Bubby Brister .05 .15
401 Dennis Smith .05 .15
402 Dan Owens .05 .15
403 Steve Beuerlein .08 .25
404 Rick Tuten .05 .15
405 Eric Allen .05 .15
406 Eric Hill .05 .15
407 Don Warren .05 .15
408 Greg Jackson .05 .15
409 Chris Doleman .05 .15
410 Anthony Munoz .08 .25
411 Michael Young .05 .15
412 Cornelius Bennett .08 .25
413 Ray Childress .05 .15
414 Kevin Call .05 .15
415 Burt Grossman .05 .15
416 Scott Miller .05 .15
417 Tim Newton .05 .15
418 Robert Young .05 .15
419 Tommy Vardell RC .05 .15
420 Michael Walter .05 .15
421 Chris Port RC .05 .15
422 Carlton Haselrig RC .05 .15
423 Rodney Peete .08 .25
424 Scott Stephen .05 .15
425 Chris Warren .10 .30
426 Scott Galbraith RC .05 .15
427 Fuad Reveiz UER .05 .15
428 Irv Eatman .05 .15
429 David Szott .05 .15
430 Brent Williams .05 .15
431 Mike Horan .05 .15
432 Brent Jones .08 .25
433 Paul Gruber .05 .15
434 Carlos Huerta .05 .15
435 Scott Case .05 .15
436 Greg Davis .05 .15
437 Ken Clarke .05 .15
438 Alfred Williams .05 .15
439 Jim C. Jensen .05 .15
440 Louis Lipps .05 .15
441 Larry Roberts .05 .15
442 James Jones DT .05 .15
443 Don Mosebar .05 .15
444 Quinn Early .08 .25
445 Robert Brown .05 .15
446 Tom Thayer .05 .15
447 Michael Irvin .10 .30
448 Jarrod Bunch .05 .15
449 Riki Ellison .05 .15
450 Joe Phillips .05 .15
451 Ernest Givins .08 .25
452 Glenn Parker .05 .15
453 Brett Perriman UER .10 .30
454 Jayice Pearson RC .05 .15
455 Mark Jackson .05 .15
456 Siran Stacy RC .05 .15
457 Rufus Porter .05 .15
458 Michael Ball .05 .15
459 Craig Taylor .05 .15
460 George Thomas RC .05 .15
461 Alvin Wright .05 .15
462 Ron Hallstrom .05 .15
463 Mike Mooney RC .05 .15
464 Dexter Carter .05 .15
465 Marty Carter RC .05 .15
466 Pat Swilling .05 .15
467 Mike Golic .05 .15
468 Reggie Roby .05 .15
469 Randall McDaniel .08 .25
470 John Stephens .05 .15
471 Ricardo McDonald RC .05 .15
472 Wilber Marshall .05 .15
473 Jim Sweeney .05 .15
474 Ernie Jones .05 .15
475 Bennie Blades .05 .15
476 Don Beebe .05 .15
477 Grant Feasel .05 .15
478 Ernie Mills .05 .15
479 Tony Jones T .05 .15
480 Jeff Uhlenhake .05 .15
481 Gaston Green .05 .15
482 John Taylor .08 .25
483 Anthony Smith .05 .15
484 Tony Bennett .05 .15
485 David Brandon RC .05 .15
486 Shawn Jefferson .05 .15
487 Christian Okoye .05 .15
488 Leonard Marshall .05 .15
489 Jay Novacek .08 .25
490 Harold Green .05 .15
491 Bubba McDowell .05 .15
492 Gary Anderson RB .05 .15
493 Terrell Buckley RC .05 .15
494 Jamie Dukes RC .05 .15
495 Morten Andersen .05 .15
496 Henry Thomas .05 .15
497 Bill Lewis .05 .15
498 Jeff Cross .05 .15
499 Hardy Nickerson .08 .25
500 Henry Ellard .08 .25
501 Joe Bowden RC .05 .15
502 Brian Noble .05 .15
503 Mike Cofer .05 .15
504 Jeff Bryant .05 .15
505 Lomas Brown .05 .15
506 Chip Banks .05 .15
507 Keith Traylor .05 .15
508 Mark Kelso .05 .15
509 Dexter McNabb RC .05 .15
510 Gene Chilton RC .05 .15
511 George Thornton .05 .15
512 Jeff Criswell .05 .15
513 Brad Edwards .05 .15
514 Ron Heller .05 .15

515 Tim Brown .10 .30
516 Keith Hamilton RC .08 .25
517 Mark Higgs .05 .15
518 Tommy Barnhardt .05 .15
519 Brian Jordan .08 .25
520 Ray Crockett .05 .15
521 Karl Wilson .05 .15
522 Ricky Reynolds .05 .15
523 Max Montoya .05 .15
524 David Little .05 .15
525 Alonzo Mitz RC .05 .15
526 Darryll Lewis .05 .15
527 Keith Henderson .05 .15
528 LeRoy Butler .05 .15
529 Rob Burnett .05 .15
530 Chris Chandler .10 .30
531 Maury Buford .05 .15
532 Mark Ingram .05 .15
533 Mike Saxon .05 .15
534 Bill Fralic .05 .15
535 Craig Patterson RC .05 .15
536 John Randle .08 .25
537 Dwayne Harper .05 .15
538 Chris Hakel RC .05 .15
539 Maurice Hurst .05 .15
540 Warren Powers UER .05 .15
541 Will Wolford .05 .15
542 Dennis Gibson .05 .15
543 Jackie Slater .05 .15
544 Floyd Turner .05 .15
545 Guy McIntyre .05 .15
546 Eric Green .05 .15
547 Rohn Stark .05 .15
548 William Fuller .05 .15
549 Alvin Harper .08 .25
550 Mark Clayton .08 .25
551 Natu Tuatagaloa RC .05 .15
552 Fred Barnett .10 .30
553 Bob Whitfield RC .05 .15
554 Courtney Hall .05 .15
555 Brian Mitchell .08 .25
556 Patrick Hunter .05 .15
557 Rick Bryan .05 .15
558 Anthony Carter .08 .25
559 Jim Wahler .05 .15
560 Joe Morris .05 .15
561 Tony Zendejas .05 .15
562 Mervyn Fernandez .05 .15
563 Jamie Williams .05 .15
564 Darrell Thompson .05 .15
565 Adrian Cooper .05 .15
566 Chris Goode .05 .15
567 Jeff Davidson RC .05 .15
568 James Hasty .05 .15
569 Chris Mims RC .05 .15
570 Ray Seals RC .05 .15
571 Myron Guyton .05 .15
572 Todd McNair .05 .15
573 Andre Tippett .05 .15
574 Kirby Jackson .05 .15
575 Mel Gray .08 .25
576 Stephone Paige .05 .15
577 Scott Davis .05 .15
578 John Gesek .05 .15
579 Earnest Byner .05 .15
580 John Friesz .08 .25
581 Al Smith .05 .15
582 Flipper Anderson .05 .15
583 Amp Lee RC .05 .15
584 Greg Lloyd .08 .25
585 Cortez Kennedy .08 .25
586 Keith Sims .05 .15
587 Terry Allen .10 .30
588 David Fulcher .05 .15
589 Chris Hinton .05 .15
590 Tim McDonald .05 .15
591 Bruce Armstrong .05 .15
592 Sterling Sharpe .10 .30
593 Tom Rathman .05 .15
594 Bill Brooks .05 .15
595 Broderick Thomas .05 .15
596 Jim Wilks .05 .15
597 Tyrone Braxton UER .05 .15
598 Checklist 301-400 UER .05 .15
599 Checklist 401-500 .05 .15
600 Checklist 501-600 .05 .15
601 Andre Reed MC .30 .75
602 Troy Aikman MC 2.00 4.00
603 Dan Marino MC 2.50 6.00
604 Randall Cunningham MC .30 .75
605 Jim Kelly MC .60 1.50
606 Deion Sanders MC .75 2.00
607 Junior Seau MC .60 1.50
608 Jerry Rice MC 2.00 4.00
609 Bruce Smith MC .30 .75
610 Lawrence Taylor MC .60 1.50
611 Todd Collins RC .20 .50
612 Ty Detmer .60 1.50
613 Browning Nagle .20 .50
614 Tony Sacca UER RC .20 .50
615 Boomer Esiason .30 .75
616 Billy Joe Tolliver .20 .50
617 Leslie O'Neal .30 .75
618 Mark Wheeler RC .20 .50
619 Eric Dickerson .30 .75
620 Phil Simms .30 .75
621 Troy Vincent RC .20 .50
622 Jason Hanson RC .30 .75
623 Andre Reed .30 .75
624 Russell Maryland .20 .50
625 Steve Emtman RC .20 .50
626 Sean Gilbert RC .30 .75
627 Dana Hall RC .20 .50
628 Dan McGwire .20 .50
629 Lewis Billups .20 .50
630 Darryl Williams RC .20 .50
631 Dwayne Sabb RC .20 .50
632 Mark Royals .20 .50
633 Cary Conklin .20 .50
634 Al Toon .30 .75
635 Junior Seau .60 1.50
686B Greg Skrepenak UER RC .20 .50
637 Deion Sanders 1.50 3.00
638 Steve DeOssie .20 .50
639 Randall Cunningham .60 1.50
640 Jim Kelly .60 1.50
641 Michael Brandon RC .20 .50
642 Clayton Holmes RC .20 .50
643 Webster Slaughter .20 .50
644 Ricky Proehl .20 .50
645 Jerry Rice 2.50 5.00
646 Carl Banks .20 .50
647 J.J.Birden .20 .50
648 Tracy Scroggins RC .20 .50
649 Alonzo Spellman RC .30 .75
650 Joe Montana 3.00 8.00
651 Courtney Hawkins RC .30 .75
652 Corey Widmer RC .20 .50
653 Robert Brooks RC 1.50 4.00
654 Darren Woodson RC .60 1.50
655 Derrick Fenner .20 .50
656 Steve Christie .20 .50
657 Chester McGlockton RC .30 .75
658 Steve Israel RC .20 .50
659 Robert Harris RC .20 .50
660 Dan Marino 3.00 8.00
661 Ed McCaffrey 2.00 5.00
662 Johnny Mitchell RC .20 .50
663 Timm Rosenbach .20 .50
664 Anthony Miller .30 .75
665 Merril Hoge .20 .50
666 Eugene Chung RC .20 .50
667 Rueben Mayes .20 .50
668 Martin Bayless .20 .50
669 Ashley Ambrose RC .60 1.50
670 Michael Cofer UER .20 .50
671 Shane Dronett RC .20 .50
672 Bernie Kosar .30 .75
673 Mike Singletary .30 .75
674 Mike Lodish RC .20 .50
675 Phillippi Sparks RC .20 .50
676 Joel Steed RC .20 .50
677 Kevin Fagan .20 .50
678 Randal Hill .20 .50
679 Ken O'Brien .20 .50
680 Lawrence Taylor .60 1.50
681 Harvey Williams .60 1.50
682 Quentin Coryatt RC .20 .50
683 Brett Favre 30.00 60.00
684 Robert Jones RC .20 .50
685 Michael Dean Perry .30 .75
686A Bruce Smith .60 1.50
687 Troy Auzenne RC .20 .50
688 Thomas McLemore RC .20 .50
689 Dale Carter RC .30 .75
690 Marc Boutte RC .20 .50
691 Jeff George .60 1.50
692 Dion Lambert RC UER .20 .50
693 Vaughn Dunbar RC .20 .50
694 Derek Brown TE RC .20 .50
695 Troy Aikman 2.50 5.00
696 John Fina RC .20 .50
697 Kevin Smith RC .20 .50
698 Corey Miller RC .20 .50
699 Lance Olberding RC .20 .50
700 Checklist 601-700 UER .20 .50
P1 Promo Sheet Natl. 4.00 10.00
P2 Promo Sheet Diam.Day 5.00 12.00

1992 Stadium Club No.1 Draft Picks

Featuring three of the past Number One draft picks plus Rocket Ismail (who was apparently considered to be equivalent due to his early CFL signing), this four-card standard-size set was randomly inserted into Stadium Club high series packs.

COMPLETE SET (4) 17.50 35.00
RANDOM INSERTS IN HIGH SERIES PACKS
1 Jeff George 6.00 12.00
2 Russell Maryland 4.00 8.00
3 Steve Emtman 4.00 8.00
4 Rocket Ismail 5.00 10.00

1992 Stadium Club QB Legends

Featuring some of the greatest quarterbacks in NFL history, this six-card standard-size set was randomly inserted into Stadium Club second series packs. Topps estimates that an average of one card would be found in every 72 packs.

COMPLETE SET (6) 8.00 20.00
RANDOM INSERTS IN SER.2 PACKS
1 Y.A. Tittle 1.25 2.50
2 Bart Starr 1.75 3.50
3 Johnny Unitas 1.75 3.50
4 George Blanda 1.25 2.50
5A Roger Staubach ERR 2.50 6.00
5B Roger Staubach COR 2.50 6.00
6 Terry Bradshaw 2.50 6.00

1993 Stadium Club

The 1993 Stadium Club football set was issued in two series of 250 cards each and a third 50-card series for a total of 550 standard-size cards. The cards were distributed in 14 and 23-card packs. The third, or high series, was also packaged as a 51-card factory set that included one First Day Issue. Cards from the Members Choice subsets are numbered 241-250 and 491-500. Rookie Cards include Reggie Brooks, Jerome Bettis, Drew Bledsoe, Garrison Hearst, Terry Kirby, O.J. McDuffie, Natrone Means, Glyn Milburn, Rick Mirer and Kevin Williams. The nine-card promo sheet was distributed at the 1993 National Sports Collector's Convention. It is not considered part of the complete set.

COMPLETE SET (550) 15.00 40.00
COMP.SERIES 1 (250) 10.00 25.00
COMP.SERIES 2 (250) 6.00 15.00
COMP.HIGH SERIES (50) 4.00 8.00
COMP.HIGH FACT.SET (51) 5.00 12.00
1 Sterling Sharpe .08 .25
2 Chris Burkett .05 .15
3 Santana Dotson .08 .25
4 Michael Jackson .08 .25
5 Neal Anderson .05 .15
6 Bryan Cox .05 .15
7 Dennis Gibson .05 .15
8 Jeff Graham .08 .25
9 Roger Ruzek .05 .15
10 Duane Bickett .05 .15
11 Charles Mann .05 .15
12 Tommy Maddox .15 .40
13 Vaughn Dunbar .05 .15
14 Gary Plummer .05 .15
15 Chris Miller .08 .25
16 Chris Warren .08 .25
17 Alvin Harper .08 .25
18 Eric Dickerson .08 .25
19 Mike Jones .05 .15
20 Ernest Givins .08 .25
21 Natrone Means RC .15 .40
22 Doug Riesenberg .05 .15
23 Barry Word .05 .15
24 Sean Salisbury .05 .15
25 Derrick Fenner .05 .15
26 David Howard .05 .15
27 Mark Kelso .05 .15
28 Todd Lyght .05 .15
29 Dana Hall .05 .15
30 Eric Metcalf .08 .25
31 Jason Hanson .05 .15
32 Dwight Stone .05 .15
33 Johnny Mitchell .05 .15
34 Reggie Roby .05 .15
35 Terrell Buckley .05 .15
36 Steve McMichael .08 .25
37 Marty Carter .05 .15
38 Seth Joyner .05 .15
39 Rohn Stark .05 .15
40 Eric Curry RC .05 .15
41 Tommy Barnhardt .05 .15
42 Karl Mecklenburg .05 .15
43 Darion Conner .05 .15
44 Ronnie Harmon .05 .15
45 Cortez Kennedy .08 .25
46 Tim Brown .15 .40
47 Bill Lewis .05 .15
48 Randall McDaniel .08 .25
49 Curtis Duncan .05 .15
50 Troy Aikman .60 1.50
51 David Klingler .05 .15
52 Brent Jones .08 .25
53 Dave Krieg .08 .25
54 Bruce Smith .15 .40
55 Vincent Brown .05 .15
56 O.J. McDuffie RC .15 .40
57 Cleveland Gary .05 .15
58 Larry Centers RC .15 .40
59 Pepper Johnson .05 .15
60 Dan Marino 1.25 3.00
61 Robert Porcher .05 .15
62 Jim Harbaugh .15 .40
63 Sam Mills .05 .15
64 Gary Anderson RB .05 .15
65 Neil O'Donnell .08 .25
66 Keith Byars .05 .15
67 Jeff Herrod .05 .15
68 Marion Butts .05 .15
69 Terry McDaniel .05 .15
70 John Elway 1.25 3.00
71 Steve Broussard .05 .15
72 Kelvin Martin .05 .15
73 Tom Carter RC .08 .25
74 Bryce Paup .08 .25
75 Jim Kelly UER .08 .25
76 Bill Romanowski .05 .15
77 Andre Collins .05 .15
78 Mike Farr .05 .15
79 Henry Ellard .08 .25
80 Dale Carter .05 .15
81 Johnny Bailey .05 .15
82 Garrison Hearst RC .60 1.50
83 Brent Williams .05 .15
84 Ricardo McDonald .05 .15
85 Emmitt Smith 1.00 2.00
86 Vai Sikahema .05 .15
87 Jackie Harris .05 .15
88 Alonzo Spellman .05 .15
89 Mark Wheeler .05 .15
90 Dalton Hilliard .05 .15
91 Mark Higgs .05 .15
92 Aaron Wallace .05 .15
93 Earnest Byner .05 .15
94 Stanley Richard .05 .15
95 Cris Carter .15 .40
96 Bobby Houston RC .05 .15
97 Craig Heyward .08 .25
98 Bernie Kosar .08 .25
99 Mike Croel .05 .15
100 Deion Sanders .40 1.00
101 Warren Moon .08 .25
102 Christian Okoye .05 .15
103 Ricky Watters .15 .40
104 Eric Swann .08 .25
105 Rodney Hampton .08 .25
106 Daryl Johnston .08 .25
107 Andre Reed .08 .25
108 Jerome Bettis RC 4.00 8.00
109 Eugene Daniel .05 .15
110 Leonard Russell .08 .25
111 Darryl Williams .05 .15
112 Rod Woodson .15 .40
113 Boomer Esiason .08 .25
114 James Hasty .05 .15
115 Marc Boutte .05 .15
116 Tom Waddle .05 .15
117 Lawrence Dawsey .05 .15
118 Mark Collins .05 .15
119 Willie Gault .05 .15
120 Barry Sanders 1.00 2.50
121 Leroy Hoard .08 .25
122 Anthony Munoz .08 .25
123 Jesse Sapolu .05 .15
124 Art Monk .08 .25
125 Randal Hill .05 .15
126 John Offerdahl .05 .15
127 Carlos Jenkins .05 .15
128 Al Smith .05 .15
129 Michael Irvin .15 .40
130 Kenneth Davis .05 .15
131 Curtis Conway RC .30 .75
132 Steve Atwater .05 .15
133 Neil Smith .15 .40
134 Steve Everitt RC .05 .15
135 Chris Mims .05 .15
136 Rickey Jackson .05 .15
137 Edgar Bennett .15 .40
138 Mike Pritchard .08 .25
139 Richard Dent .08 .25
140 Barry Foster .08 .25
141 Eugene Robinson .05 .15
142 Jackie Slater .05 .15
143 Paul Gruber .05 .15
144 Rob Moore .08 .25
145 Robert Smith RC 1.00 2.50
146 Lorenzo White .05 .15
147 Tommy Vardell .05 .15
148 Dave Meggett .05 .15
149 Vince Workman .05 .15
150 Terry Allen .15 .40
151 Howie Long .15 .40
152 Charles Haley .08 .25
153 Pete Metzelaars .05 .15
154 John Copeland RC .08 .25
155 Aeneas Williams .05 .15
156 Ricky Sanders .05 .15
157 Andre Ware .05 .15
158 Tony Paige .05 .15
159 Jerome Henderson .05 .15
160 Harold Green .05 .15
161 Wymon Henderson .05 .15
162 Andre Rison .08 .25
163 Donald Evans .05 .15
164 Todd Scott .05 .15
165 Steve Emtman .05 .15
166 William Fuller .05 .15
167 Michael Dean Perry .08 .25
168 Randall Cunningham .15 .40
169 Toi Cook .05 .15
170 Browning Nagle .05 .15
171 Darryl Henley .05 .15
172 George Teague RC .08 .25
173 Derrick Thomas .15 .40
174 Jay Novacek .08 .25
175 Mark Carrier DB .05 .15
176 Kevin Fagan .05 .15
177 Nate Lewis .05 .15
178 Courtney Hawkins .05 .15
179 Robert Blackmon .05 .15
180 Rick Mirer RC .15 .40
181 Mike Lodish .05 .15
182 Jarrod Bunch .05 .15
183 Anthony Smith .05 .15
184 Brian Noble .05 .15
185 Eric Bieniemy .05 .15
186 Keith Jackson .08 .25
187 Eric Martin .05 .15
188 Vance Johnson .05 .15
189 Kevin Mack .05 .15
190 Rich Camarillo .05 .15
191 Ashley Ambrose .05 .15
192 Ray Childress .05 .15
193 Jim Arnold .05 .15
194 Ricky Ervins .05 .15
195 Gary Anderson K .05 .15
196 Eric Allen .05 .15
197 Roger Craig .08 .25
198 Jon Vaughn .05 .15
199 Tim McDonald .05 .15
200 Broderick Thomas .05 .15
201 Jessie Tuggle .05 .15
202 Alonzo Mitz .05 .15
203 Harvey Williams .08 .25
204 Russell Maryland .05 .15
205 Marvin Washington .05 .15
206 Jim Everett .08 .25
207 Trace Armstrong .05 .15
208 Steve Young .60 1.50
209 Tony Woods .05 .15
210 Brett Favre 2.00 4.00
211 Nate Odomes .05 .15
212 Ricky Proehl .05 .15
213 Jim Dombrowski .05 .15
214 Anthony Carter .08 .25
215 Tracy Simien .05 .15
216 Clay Matthews .08 .25
217 Patrick Bates RC .05 .15
218 Jeff George .15 .40
219 David Fulcher .05 .15
220 Phil Simms .08 .25
221 Eugene Chung .05 .15
222 Reggie Cobb .05 .15
223 Jim Sweeney .05 .15
224 Greg Lloyd .08 .25
225 Sean Jones .05 .15
226 Marvin Jones RC .05 .15
227 Bill Brooks .05 .15
228 Moe Gardner .05 .15
229 Louis Oliver .05 .15
230 Flipper Anderson .05 .15
231 Marc Spindler .05 .15
232 Jerry Rice .75 2.00
233 Chip Lohmiller .05 .15
234 Nolan Harrison .05 .15
235 Heath Sherman .05 .15
236 Reyna Thompson .05 .15
237 Derrick Walker .05 .15
238 Rufus Porter .05 .15
239 Checklist 1-125 .05 .15
240 Checklist 126-250 .05 .15
241 John Elway MC .60 1.50
242 Troy Aikman MC .30 .75
243 Steve Emtman MC .05 .15
244 Ricky Watters MC .08 .25
245 Barry Foster MC .05 .15
246 Dan Marino MC .60 1.50
247 Reggie White MC .08 .25
248 Thurman Thomas MC .08 .25
249 Broderick Thomas MC .05 .15
250 Joe Montana MC .60 1.50
251 Tim Goad .05 .15
252 Joe Nash .05 .15
253 Anthony Johnson .08 .25
254 Carl Pickens .08 .25
255 Steve Beuerlein .08 .25
256 Anthony Newman .05 .15
257 Corey Miller .05 .15
258 Steve DeBerg .05 .15
259 Johnny Holland .05 .15
260 Jerry Ball .05 .15
261 Siupeli Malamala RC .05 .15
262 Steve Wisniewski .05 .15
263 Kelvin Pritchett .05 .15
264 Chris Gardocki .05 .15
265 Henry Thomas .05 .15
266 Arthur Marshall RC .05 .15
267 Quinn Early .08 .25
268 Jonathan Hayes .05 .15
269 Erric Pegram .08 .25
270 Clyde Simmons .05 .15
271 Eric Moten .05 .15
272 Brian Mitchell .08 .25
273 Adrian Cooper .05 .15
274 Gaston Green .05 .15
275 John Taylor .08 .25
276 Jeff Uhlenhake .05 .15
277 Phil Hansen .05 .15
278A Kevin Williams ERR RC .15 .40
278B Kevin Williams COR RC .15 .40
279 Robert Massey .05 .15
280A Drew Bledsoe ERR RC 3.00 8.00
280B Drew Bledsoe COR RC 2.00 5.00
281 Walter Reeves .05 .15
282A Carlton Gray ERR RC .08 .25
282B Carlton Gray COR RC .08 .25
283 Derek Brown TE .05 .15
284 Martin Mayhew .05 .15
285 Sean Gilbert .08 .25
286 Jessie Hester .05 .15
287 Mark Clayton .05 .15
288 Blair Thomas .05 .15
289 J.J. Birden .05 .15
290 Shannon Sharpe .15 .40
291 Richard Fain RC .05 .15
292 Gene Atkins .05 .15
293 Burt Grossman .05 .15
294 Chris Doleman .05 .15
295 Pat Swilling .05 .15
296 Mike Kenn .05 .15
297 Merril Hoge .05 .15
298 Don Mosebar .05 .15
299 Kevin Smith .08 .25
300 Darrell Green .05 .15
301A Dan Footman ERR RC .08 .25
301B Dan Footman COR RC .08 .25
302 Vestee Jackson .05 .15
303 Carwell Gardner .05 .15
304 Amp Lee .05 .15
305 Bruce Matthews .05 .15
306 Antone Davis .05 .15
307 Dean Biasucci .05 .15
308 Maurice Hurst .05 .15
309 John Kasay .05 .15
310 Lawrence Taylor .08 .25
311 Ken Harvey .05 .15
312 Willie Davis .08 .25
313 Tony Bennett .05 .15
314 Jay Schroeder .05 .15
315 Darren Perry .05 .15
316A Troy Drayton ERR RC .08 .25
316B Troy Drayton COR RC .08 .25
317A Dan Williams ERR RC .08 .25
317B Dan Williams COR RC .08 .25
318 Michael Haynes .08 .25
319 Renaldo Turnbull .05 .15
320 Junior Seau .15 .40
321 Ray Crockett .05 .15
322 Will Furrer .05 .15
323 Byron Evans .05 .15
324 Jim McMahon .08 .25
325 Robert Jones .05 .15
326 Eric Davis .05 .15
327 Jeff Cross .05 .15
328 Kyle Clifton .05 .15
329 Haywood Jeffires .08 .25
330 Jeff Hostetler .08 .25
331 Darryl Talley .05 .15
332 Keith McCants .05 .15
333 Mo Lewis .05 .15
334 Matt Stover .05 .15
335 Ferrell Edmunds .05 .15
336 Matt Brock .05 .15
337 Ernie Mills .05 .15
338 Shane Dronett .05 .15
339 Brad Muster .05 .15
340 Jesse Solomon .05 .15
341 John Randle .08 .25
342 Chris Spielman .08 .25
343 David Whitmore .05 .15
344 Glenn Parker .05 .15
345 Marco Coleman .05 .15
346 Kenneth Gant .05 .15
347 Cris Dishman .05 .15
348 Kenny Walker .05 .15
349A Roosevelt Potts ERR RC .08 .25
349B Roosevelt Potts COR RC .08 .25
350 Reggie White .15 .40
351 Gerald Robinson .05 .15
352 Mark Rypien .05 .15
353 Stan Humphries .08 .25
354 Chris Singleton .05 .15
355 Herschel Walker .08 .25
356 Ron Hall .05 .15
357 Ethan Horton .05 .15
358 Anthony Pleasant .05 .15
359A Thomas Smith ERR RC .08 .25
359B Thomas Smith COR RC .08 .25
360 Audray McMillian .05 .15
361 D.J. Johnson .05 .15
362 Ron Heller .05 .15
363 Bern Brostek .05 .15
364 Ronnie Lott .08 .25
365 Reggie Johnson .05 .15
366 Lin Elliott .05 .15
367 Lemuel Stinson .05 .15
368 William White .05 .15
369 Ernie Jones .05 .15
370 Tom Rathman .05 .15
371 Tommy Kane .05 .15
372 David Brandon .05 .15
373 Lee Johnson .05 .15
374 Wade Wilson .05 .15
375 Nick Lowery .05 .15
376 Bubba McDowell .05 .15
377A Wayne Simmons ERR RC .08 .25
377B Wayne Simmons COR RC .08 .25
378 Calvin Williams .08 .25
379 Courtney Hall .05 .15
380 Troy Vincent .05 .15
381 Tim McGee .05 .15
382 Russell Freeman RC .05 .15
383 Steve Tasker .08 .25
384A Michael Strahan ERR RC 1.25 3.00
384B Michael Strahan COR RC 1.00 2.50
385 Greg Skrepenak .05 .15
386 Jake Reed .08 .25
387 Pete Stoyanovich .05 .15
388 Levon Kirkland .05 .15
389 Mel Gray .08 .25
390 Brian Washington .05 .15
391 Don Griffin .05 .15
392 Desmond Howard .08 .25
393 Luis Sharpe .05 .15
394 Mike Johnson .05 .15
395 Andre Tippett .05 .15
396 Donnell Woolford .05 .15
397A Demetrius DuBose ERR RC .08 .25
397B Demetrius DuBose COR RC .08 .25
398 Pat Terrell .05 .15
399 Todd McNair .05 .15
400 Ken Norton .08 .25
401 Keith Hamilton .05 .15
402 Andy Heck .05 .15
403 Jeff Gossett .05 .15
404 Dexter McNabb .05 .15
405 Richmond Webb .05 .15
406 Irving Fryar .08 .25
407 Brian Hansen .05 .15
408 David Little .05 .15
409A Glyn Milburn ERR RC .15 .40
409B Glyn Milburn COR RC .08 .25
410 Doug Dawson .05 .15
411 Scott Mersereau .05 .15
412 Don Beebe .05 .15
413 Vaughan Johnson .05 .15
414 Jack Del Rio .05 .15
415A Darrien Gordon ERR RC .08 .25
415B Darrien Gordon COR RC .08 .25
416 Mark Schlereth .05 .15
417 Lomas Brown .05 .15
418 William Thomas .05 .15
419 James Francis .05 .15
420 Quentin Coryatt .08 .25
421 Tyji Armstrong .05 .15
422 Hugh Millen .05 .15
423 Adrian White RC .05 .15
424 Eddie Anderson .05 .15
425 Mark Ingram .05 .15
426 Ken O'Brien .05 .15
427 Simon Fletcher .05 .15
428 Tim McKyer .05 .15
429 Leonard Marshall .05 .15
430 Eric Green .05 .15
431 Leonard Harris .05 .15
432 Darin Jordan RC .05 .15
433 Erik Howard .05 .15
434 David Lang .05 .15
435 Eric Turner .05 .15
436 Michael Cofer .05 .15
437 Jeff Bryant .05 .15
438 Charles McRae .05 .15
439 Henry Jones .05 .15
440 Joe Montana 1.25 3.00
441 Morten Andersen .05 .15
442 Jeff Jaeger .05 .15
443 Leslie O'Neal .08 .25
444 LeRoy Butler .05 .15
445 Steve Jordan .05 .15
446 Brad Edwards .05 .15
447 J.B. Brown .05 .15
448 Kerry Cash .05 .15
449 Mark Tuinei .05 .15
450 Rodney Peete .05 .15
451 Sheldon White .05 .15
452 Wesley Carroll .05 .15
453 Brad Baxter .05 .15
454 Mike Pitts .05 .15
455 Greg Montgomery .05 .15
456 Kenny Davidson .05 .15
457 Scott Fulhage .05 .15
458 Greg Townsend .05 .15
459 Rod Bernstine .05 .15
460 Gary Clark .08 .25
461 Hardy Nickerson .08 .25
462 Sean Landeta .05 .15
463 Rob Burnett .05 .15
464 Fred Barnett .08 .25
465 John L. Williams .05 .15
466 Anthony Miller .08 .25
467 Roman Phifer .05 .15
468 Rich Moran .05 .15
469A Willie Roaf ERR RC .30 .75
469B Willie Roaf COR RC .20 .50
470 William Perry .08 .25
471 Marcus Allen .15 .40
472 Carl Lee .05 .15
473 Kurt Gouveia .05 .15
474 Jarvis Williams .05 .15
475 Alfred Williams .05 .15
476 Mark Stepnoski .05 .15
477 Steve Wallace .05 .15
478 Pat Harlow .05 .15
479 Chip Banks .05 .15
480 Cornelius Bennett .08 .25
481A Ryan McNeil RC ERR .08 .25
481B Ryan McNeil RC COR .15 .40
482 Norm Johnson .05 .15
483 Dermontti Dawson .08 .25
484 Dwayne White .05 .15
485 Derek Russell .05 .15
486 Lionel Washington .05 .15
487 Eric Hill .05 .15
488 Micheal Barrow RC .15 .40
489 Checklist 251-375 UER .05 .15
490 Checklist 376-500 UER .05 .15
491 Emmitt Smith MC .60 1.50
492 Derrick Thomas MC .08 .25
493 Deion Sanders MC .15 .40
494 Randall Cunningham MC .08 .25
495 Sterling Sharpe MC .08 .25
496 Barry Sanders MC .50 1.25
497 Thurman Thomas MC .08 .25
498 Brett Favre MC .75 2.00
499 Vaughan Johnson MC .05 .15
500 Steve Young MC .30 .75
501 Marvin Jones MC .05 .15
502 Reggie Brooks MC RC .08 .25
503 Eric Curry MC .05 .15
504 Drew Bledsoe MC .75 2.00
505 Glyn Milburn MC .08 .25
506 Jerome Bettis MC 1.50 4.00
507 Robert Smith MC .40 1.00
508 Dana Stubblefield MC RC .15 .40
509 Tom Carter MC .08 .25
510 Rick Mirer MC .15 .40
511 Russell Copeland RC .08 .25
512 Deon Figures RC .05 .15
513 Tony McGee RC .08 .25
514 Derrick Lassic RC .05 .15
515 Everett Lindsay RC .05 .15
516 Derek Brown RBK RC .05 .15
517 Harold Alexander RC .05 .15
518 Tom Scott RC .05 .15
519 Elvis Grbac RC 1.25 3.00
520 Terry Kirby RC .15 .40
521 Doug Pelfrey RC .05 .15
522 Horace Copeland RC .08 .25
523 Irv Smith RC .05 .15
524 Lincoln Kennedy RC .05 .15
525 Jason Elam RC .15 .40
526 Qadry Ismail RC .15 .40
527 Artie Smith RC .05 .15
528 Tyrone Hughes RC .08 .25
529 Lance Gunn RC .05 .15
530 Vincent Brisby RC .15 .40
531 Patrick Robinson RC .05 .15
532 Rocket Ismail .08 .25
533 Willie Beamon RC .05 .15
534 Vaughn Hebron RC .05 .15
535 Darren Drozdov RC .15 .40
536 James Jett RC .15 .40
537 Michael Bates RC .05 .15
538 Tom Rouen RC .05 .15
539 Michael Husted RC .05 .15
540 Greg Robinson RC .05 .15
541 Carl Banks .05 .15
542 Kevin Greene .08 .25
543 Scott Mitchell .15 .40
544 Michael Brooks .05 .15
545 Shane Conlan .05 .15
546 Vinny Testaverde .08 .25
547 Robert Delpino .05 .15
548 Bill Fralic .05 .15
549 Carlton Bailey .05 .15
550 Johnny Johnson .05 .15
NNO Jerry Rice RB 4.00 10.00
P1 Promo Sheet 2.00 5.00

1993 Stadium Club First Day

COMPLETE SET (550) 400.00 800.00
*VETS: 5X TO 12X BASIC CARDS
*ROOKIES: 2.5X TO 6X BASIS RC
STATED ODDS 1:24

1993 Stadium Club Master Photos I

Inserted one in every 24 packs, Master Photo redemption cards were redeemable for three Stadium Club Master Photos. The first series featured 12 different Master Photos. Carrying uncropped versions of regular Stadium Club cards, the front gives 17 percent more photo area than a regular card. The back has a narrative of the player along with a full-color graphic presentation of a key statistic.

COMPLETE SET (12) 6.00 15.00
ONE PER SERIES 1 HOBBY BOX
*TRADE CARD: .3X to .8X MASTER PHOTO
PRICES ARE PER SINGLE LARGE CARD
1 Barry Foster .30 .75
2 Barry Sanders 2.00 5.00
3 Reggie Cobb .30 .75
4 Cortez Kennedy .30 .75
5 Steve Young 1.25 3.00
6 Ricky Watters .40 1.00
7 Rob Moore .30 .75
8 Derrick Thomas .50 1.25
9 Jeff George .40 1.00
10 Sterling Sharpe .40 1.00
11 Bruce Smith .50 1.25
12 Deion Sanders .75 2.00

1993 Stadium Club Master Photos II

Inserted one in every 24 second series packs, Master Photo redemption cards were redeemable (until 6/1/94) for three Stadium Club Master Photos II. Redemption cards for complete sets were also produced. The second series featured 12 different 5" by 7" Master Photos. Carrying uncropped versions of regular Stadium Club cards, the front gives 17 percent more photo area than a regular card. The back has a narrative player profile with the player's name printed vertically down the center of the card.

COMPLETE SET (12) 4.00 8.00
ONE PER SERIES 2 HOBBY BOX
*TRADE CARD: .3X TO .8X MASTER PHOTOHI
PRICES ARE PER SINGLE LARGE CARD
1 Morten Andersen .40 1.00
2 Ken Norton Jr. .30 .75
3 Clyde Simmons .30 .75
4 Roman Phifer .30 .75
5 Greg Townsend .30 .75
6 Darryl Talley .30 .75
7 Herschel Walker .40 1.00
8 Reggie White .60 1.50
9 Jesse Solomon .30 .75
10 Joe Montana 2.50 6.00
11 John Taylor .40 1.00
12 Cornelius Bennett .50 1.25

1993 Stadium Club Super Teams

Measuring the standard-size, one of these Super Team cards was randomly inserted in approximately every 24 first and second series Stadium Club packs. Each of the 28 NFL teams is represented by a card. Team cards featuring a division winner (Cowboys, 49ers, Lions, Bills, Oilers, Chiefs), conference championship team (Cowboys, Bills) or Super Bowl XXVIII winner (Cowboys) were redeemable for the following prizes: (1) 12 Stadium Club cards of players from the winning team, embossed with gold foil division winning logo (Division Winner card); (2) 12 Master Photos of the winning team, with special embossed gold foil Conference logo (AFC or NFC Conference Championship card); and (3) complete set of all 500 Stadium Club cards with official gold foil embossed Super Bowl logo (Super Bowl XXVIII Winner card; winners were also entered into a random drawing to win an official Super Bowl game ball). If the team pictured on the Super Team card won more than one title, the collector could claim all of the corresponding prizes won by that card. The backs are white and filled with instructions and conditions of the promotion which expired 6/1/94. The cards are unnumbered and checklisted below alphabetically according to team name with the winning cards marked "WIN." Winning cards sent to Topps were also returned with a "redeemed " stamp on the card back. A Members Only edition of this set was issued as well, which had the team's 1992 won-loss record on its back. Prices for the redeemed versions and Member's Only versions are included with the respective listings.

COMPLETE SET (28) 40.00 75.00
STATED ODDS 1:24 H/R, 1:15 JUM
1 Bears/Harbaugh 1.00 2.50
2 Bengals/Klingler .60 1.50
3 Bills/Jim Kelly WIN 2.00 4.00
4 Broncos/Elway 5.00 12.00
5 Browns/Kosar .60 1.50
6 Buccaneers/Cobb .60 1.50
7 Cardinals/Swann .60 1.50
8 Chargers/Humphries .60 1.50
9 Chiefs/D.Thomas WIN 2.00 4.00
10 Colts/Emtman .60 1.50
11 Cowboys/E.Smith WIN 6.00 15.00
12 Dolphins/Marino 5.00 12.00
13 Eagles/R.Cunningham 1.25 3.00
14 Falcons/D.Sanders 2.00 4.00
15 49ers/S.Young WIN 4.00 8.00
16 Giants/L.Taylor 1.00 2.50
17 Jets/B.Baxter .60 1.50
18 Lions/B.Sanders WIN 5.00 12.00
19 Oilers/W.Moon WIN 2.00 4.00
20 Packers/B.Favre 8.00 20.00
21 Patriots/B.Williams .60 1.50
22 Raiders/H.Long 1.25 3.00
23 Rams/C.Gary .60 1.50
24 Redskins/M.Rypien .60 1.50
25 Saints/S.Mills .60 1.50
26 Seahawks/C.Kennedy .60 1.50
27 Steelers/B.Foster .60 1.50
28 Vikings/T.Allen 1.00 2.50

1993 Stadium Club Super Teams Division Winners

Collectors who redeemed a Super Team card of a division winner received a Super Team card redemption set. If the team also won the conference championship, collectors were entitled to receive a master photo set of the team. Finally, if the team was the Super Bowl XXVIII champion, they received additionally a factory set of 1993 Stadium Club cards with official gold foil embossed Super Bowl logo. The cards are similar in design to the basic Stadium Club issue except the words "Division Winner" are gold foil-stamped on the front.

COMPLETE BAG BILLS (13) 2.80 7.00
COMPLETE BAG CHIEFS (13) 4.00 10.00
COMPLETE BAG COWBOYS (13 6.00 15.00
COMPLETE BAG 49ERS (13) 4.80 12.00
COMPLETE BAG LIONS (13) 3.20 8.00
COMPLETE BAG OILERS (13) 2.80 7.00
B27 Mark Kelso .20 .50
B54 Bruce Smith .40 1.00
B75 Jim Kelly .40 1.00
B107 Andre Reed .40 1.00
B153 Pete Metzelaars .20 .50
B211 Nate Odomes .20 .50
B227 Bill Brooks .20 .50
B331 Darryl Talley .20 .50
B383 Steve Tasker .20 .50
B412 Don Beebe .20 .50
B439 Henry Jones .20 .50
B480 Cornelius Bennett .30 .75
F29 Dana Hall .20 .50
F52 Brent Jones .30 .75
F76 Bill Romanowski .20 .50
F103 Ricky Watters .40 1.00
F123 Jesse Sapolu .20 .50
F176 Kevin Fagan .20 .50
F199 Tim McDonald .20 .50
F208 Steve Young 1.00 2.50
F232 Jerry Rice 1.20 3.00
F275 John Taylor .30 .75
F326 Eric Davis .20 .50
F370 Tom Rathman .20 .50
L7 Dennis Gibson .20 .50
L31 Jason Hanson .20 .50
L61 Robert Porcher .20 .50
L120 Barry Sanders 2.00 5.00
L231 Marc Spindler .20 .50
L263 Kelvin Pritchett .20 .50
L295 Pat Swilling .30 .75
L321 Ray Crockett .20 .50
L342 Chris Spielman .20 .50
L368 William White .20 .50
L389 Mel Gray .30 .75
L450 Rodney Peete .20 .50
020 Ernest Givins .30 .75
0101 Warren Moon .40 1.00
0128 Al Smith .20 .50
0146 Lorenzo White .30 .75
0166 William Fuller .20 .50
0192 Ray Childress .30 .75
0225 Sean Jones .20 .50
0305 Bruce Matthews .20 .50
0329 Haywood Jeffires .30 .75
0347 Cris Dishman .20 .50
0376 Bubba McDowell .20 .50
0455 Greg Montgomery .20 .50
CH80 Dale Carter .30 .75
CH133 Neil Smith .30 .75
CH173 Derrick Thomas .40 1.00
CH203 Harvey Williams .30 .75
CH215 Tracy Simien .20 .50
CH268 Jonathan Hayes .20 .50
CH289 J.J. Birden .30 .75
CH312 Willie Davis .30 .75
CH375 Nick Lowery .20 .50
CH399 Todd McNair .20 .50
CH440 Joe Montana 1.20 3.00
CH471 Marcus Allen .40 1.00
CO17 Alvin Harper .30 .75
CO50 Troy Aikman 1.20 3.00
CO85 Emmitt Smith 2.00 5.00
CO106 Daryl Johnston .30 .75
CO129 Michael Irvin .40 1.00
CO152 Charles Haley .30 .75
CO174 Jay Novacek .30 .75
CO204 Russell Maryland .20 .50
CO278 Kevin Williams WR .30 .75
CO299 Kevin Smith .20 .50
CO325 Robert Jones .20 .50
CO400 Ken Norton Jr. .30 .75
DW3 Bills .40 1.00
J.Kelly Stamped
DW9 Chiefs .40 1.00
D.Thomas Stamped
DW11 Cowboys 1.20 3.00
E.Smith Stamped
DW15 49ers .60 1.50
S.Young Stamped
DW18 Lions .70 1.75
B.Sanders Stamped
DW19 Oilers .40 1.00
W.Moon Stamped

1993 Stadium Club Super Teams Conference Winners

Collectors who redeemed a Super Team card of a conference winner received a master photo team set stamped with the conference logo along with the Super Team card featuring the conference logo.

COMP.BAG BILLS (13) 2.80 7.00
COMP.BAG COWBOYS (13) 6.00 15.00
CW3 Cowboys 1.00 2.50
E.Smith
CW11 Bills .40 1.00
Jim Kelly

1993 Stadium Club Super Teams Master Photos

Featuring either the NFC Champion Dallas Cowboys or the AFC Champion Buffalo Bills, these 12 Master Photos measure approximately 5" by 7" each. Collectors who redeemed the conference winner's Super Team card received that teams' Master Photo as well as a Super Team card featuring the conference logo. Carrying uncropped versions of regular Stadium Club cards, the fronts give 17 percent more photo area than a regular card. A gold-foil "N" for NFC or "A" for AFC edged by stars appears beneath each picture. The backs are blank except for Team NFL, NFLPA, and Topps logos. The cards are unnumbered and checklisted below in alphabetical order by team.

COMP.BAG BILLS (12) 4.00 10.00
COMP.BAG COWBOYS (12) 8.00 20.00
B1 Don Beebe .30 .75
B2 Cornelius Bennett .40 1.00
B3 Bill Brooks .30 .75
B4 Henry Jones .30 .75
B5 Jim Kelly .60 1.50
B6 Mark Kelso .30 .75
B7 Pete Metzelaars .30 .75

B8 Nate Odomes .30 .75
B9 Andre Reed .40 1.00
B10 Bruce Smith .40 1.00
B11 Darryl Talley .30 .75
B12 Steve Tasker .30 .75
CO1 Troy Aikman 1.50 4.00
CO2 Charles Haley .40 1.00
CO3 Alvin Harper .40 1.00
CO4 Michael Irvin .60 1.50
CO5 Daryl Johnston .40 1.00
CO6 Robert Jones .30 .75
CO7 Russell Maryland .30 .75
CO8 Ken Norton Jr. .30 .75
CO9 Jay Novacek .40 1.00
CO10 Emmitt Smith 3.00 8.00
CO11 Kevin Smith .30 .75
CO12 Kevin Williams WR .40 1.00

1993 Stadium Club Super Teams Super Bowl

COMPLETE SET (500) 30.00 75.00
*STARS: 1X to 2.5X BASIC CARDS
*ROOKIES: .6X to 1.5X BASIC CARDS
SB3 Cowboys 1.50 4.00
Emmitt Smith

1993 Stadium Club Members Only Parallel

COMP.FACT.SET (603) 80.00 200.00
*1-550 VETS: 1.2X TO 3X BASIC CARDS
*1-550 ROOKIES: .8X TO 2X BASIC CARDS
*SUPER TEAMS: .2X TO.5X BASIC INSERTS
*MASTER PHOTOS: .4X TO 1X BASIC INSERT
NNO Jerry Rice RB AUTO 25.00 50.00

1993 Stadium Club Pre-Production Samples

COMPLETE SET (9) 6.00 15.00
1 Sterling Sharpe 1.00 2.50
41 Tommy Barnhardt .60 1.50
45 Cortez Kennedy .60 1.50
81 Johnny Bailey .60 1.50
86 Vai Sikahema .60 1.50
95 Cris Carter 1.25 3.00
102 Christian Okoye .75 2.00
139 Richard Dent .75 2.00
222 Reggie Cobb .60 1.50

1994 Stadium Club

This 630 standard size set was released in three series. Foil packs contained 12 player cards plus one info card or unnumbered checklist card. In the first two series, one in every eight packs contained a special insert card as opposed to an information card. Frequent Scorer Point cards were randomly packed one in every three packs. For 30 frequent scorer points of his favorite player, the collector received a Finest quality upgrade card of that player. Topical subsets included in this set are Chalk Talk (371-374), Best Defense (435-445), and Red Zone (511-525). Collectors who attended the Super Bowl show XXIX in Miami could trade five wrappers for a cellophane pack of '94 Stadium Club cards embossed with the Super Bowl XXIX logo. Rookie Cards in this set include Mario Bates, Bert Emanuel, Marshall Faulk, William Floyd, Bernie Parmalee, Errict Rhett, Darnay Scott and Heath Shuler.

COMPLETE SET (630) 25.00 60.00
COMP.SERIES 1 (270) 10.00 25.00
COMP.SERIES 2 (270) 10.00 25.00
COMP.HIGH SERIES (90) 5.00 10.00
1 Dan Wilkinson RC .08 .25
2 Chip Lohmiller .05 .15
3 Roosevelt Potts .05 .15
4 Martin Mayhew .05 .15
5 Shane Conlan .05 .15
6 Sam Adams RC .08 .25
7 Mike Kenn .05 .15
8 Tim Goad .05 .15
9 Tony Jones T .05 .15
10 Ronald Moore .05 .15
11 Mark Bortz .05 .15
12 Darren Carrington .05 .15
13 Eric Martin .05 .15
14 Eric Allen .05 .15
15 Aaron Glenn RC .15 .40
16 Bryan Cox .05 .15
17 Levon Kirkland .05 .15
18 Qadry Ismail .15 .40
19 Shane Dronett .05 .15
20 Chris Spielman .08 .25
21 Rob Fredrickson RC .08 .25
22 Wayne Simmons .05 .15
23 Glenn Montgomery .05 .15
24 Jason Sehorn RC .25 .60
25 Nick Lowery .05 .15
26 Dennis Brown .05 .15
27 Kenneth Davis .05 .15
28 Shante Carver RC .05 .15
29 Ryan Yarborough RC .05 .15
30 Cortez Kennedy .08 .25
31 Anthony Pleasant .05 .15
32 Jessie Tuggle .05 .15
33 Herschel Walker .08 .25
34 Andre Collins .05 .15
35 William Floyd RC .15 .40
36 Harold Green .05 .15
37 Courtney Hawkins .05 .15
38 Curtis Conway .15 .40
39 Ben Coates .08 .25
40 Natrone Means .15 .40
41 Eric Hill .05 .15
42 Keith Kartz .05 .15
43 Alexander Wright .05 .15
44 Willie Roaf .05 .15
45 Vencie Glenn .05 .15
46 Ronnie Lott .08 .25
47 George Koonce .05 .15
48 Rod Woodson .08 .25
49 Tim Grunhard .05 .15
50 Cody Carlson .05 .15
51 Bryant Young RC .25 .60
52 Jay Novacek .08 .25
53 Darryl Talley .05 .15
54 Harry Colon .05 .15
55 Dave Meggett .05 .15
56 Aubrey Beavers RC .05 .15
57 James Folston .05 .15
58 Willie Davis .08 .25
59 Jason Elam .08 .25
60 Eric Metcalf .08 .25
61 Bruce Armstrong .05 .15
62 Ron Heller .05 .15
63 LeRoy Butler .05 .15
64 Terry Obee .05 .15
65 Kurt Gouveia .05 .15
66 Pierce Holt .05 .15
67 David Alexander .05 .15
68 Deral Boykin .05 .15
69 Carl Pickens .08 .25
70 Broderick Thomas .05 .15
71 Barry Sanders CT .50 1.25
72 Qadry Ismail CT .15 .40
73 Thurman Thomas CT .15 .40
74 Junior Seau .15 .40
75 Vinny Testaverde .08 .25
76 Tyrone Hughes .08 .25
77 Nate Newton .05 .15
78 Eric Swann .08 .25
79 Brad Baxter .05 .15
80 Dana Stubblefield .08 .25
81 Jumbo Elliott .05 .15
82 Steve Wisniewski .05 .15
83 Eddie Robinson .05 .15
84 Isaac Davis .05 .15
85 Cris Carter .25 .60
86 Mel Gray .05 .15
87 Cornelius Bennett .08 .25
88 Neil O'Donnell .15 .40
89 Jon Hand .05 .15
90 John Elway 1.25 3.00
91 Bill Hitchcock .05 .15
92 Neil Smith .08 .25
93 Joe Johnson RC .05 .15
94 Edgar Bennett .15 .40
95 Vincent Brown .05 .15
96 Tommy Vardell .05 .15
97 Donnell Woolford .05 .15
98 Lincoln Kennedy .05 .15
99 O.J. McDuffie .15 .40
100 Heath Shuler RC .15 .40
101 Jerry Rice BO .30 .75
102 Erik Williams BO .05 .15
103 Randall McDaniel BO .05 .25
104 Dermontti Dawson BO .08 .25
105 Nate Newton BO .05 .15
106 Harris Barton BO .05 .15
107 Shannon Sharpe BO .08 .25
108 Sterling Sharpe BO .08 .25
109 Steve Young BO .25 .60
110 Emmitt Smith BO .50 1.25
111 Thurman Thomas BO .15 .40
112 Kyle Clifton .05 .15
113 Desmond Howard .08 .25
114 Quinn Early .08 .25
115 David Klingler .05 .15
116 Bern Brostek .05 .15
117 Gary Clark .08 .25
118 Courtney Hall .05 .15
119 Joe King .05 .15
120 Quentin Coryatt .05 .15
121 Johnnie Morton RC .75 2.00
122 Andre Reed .08 .25
123 Eric Davis .05 .15
124 Jack Del Rio .05 .15
125 Greg Lloyd .08 .25
126 Bubba McDowell .05 .15
127 Mark Jackson .05 .15
128 Jeff Jaeger .05 .15
129 Chris Warren .08 .25
130 Tom Waddle .05 .15
131 Tony Smith RB .05 .15
132 Todd Collins .05 .15
133 Mark Bavaro .05 .15
134 Joe Phillips .05 .15
135 Chris Jacke .05 .15
136 Glyn Milburn .08 .25
137 Keith Jackson .05 .15
138 Steve Tovar .05 .15
139 Tim Johnson .05 .15
140 Brian Washington .05 .15
141 Troy Drayton .05 .15
142 Dewayne Washington RC .08 .25
143 Erik Williams .05 .15
144 Eric Turner .05 .15
145 John Taylor .08 .25
146 Richard Cooper .05 .15
147 Van Malone .05 .15
148 Tim Ruddy RC .05 .15
149 Henry Jones .05 .15
150 Tim Brown .15 .40
151 Stan Humphries .08 .25
152 Harry Newsome .05 .15
153 Craig Erickson .05 .15
154 Gary Anderson K .05 .15
155 Ray Childress .05 .15
156 Howard Cross .05 .15
157 Heath Sherman .05 .15
158 Terrell Buckley .05 .15
159 J.B. Brown .05 .15
160 Joe Montana 1.25 3.00
161 David Wyman .05 .15
162 Norm Johnson .05 .15
163 Rod Stephens .05 .15
164 Willie McGinest RC .15 .40
165 Barry Sanders 1.00 2.50
166 Marc Logan .05 .15
167 Anthony Newman .05 .15
168 Russell Maryland .05 .15
169 Luis Sharpe .05 .15
170 Jim Kelly .15 .40
171 Tre Johnson RC .05 .15
172 Johnny Mitchell .05 .15
173 David Palmer RC .15 .40
174 Bob Dahl .05 .15
175 Aaron Wallace .05 .15
176 Chris Gardocki .05 .15
177 Hardy Nickerson .08 .25
178 Jeff Query .05 .15
179 Leslie O'Neal .05 .15
180 Kevin Greene .08 .25
181 Alonzo Spellman .05 .15
182 Reggie Brooks .08 .25
183 Dana Stubblefield .08 .25
184 Tyrone Hughes .08 .25
185 Drew Bledsoe GE .15 .40
186 Ronald Moore GE .05 .15
187 Jason Elam GE .05 .15
188 Rick Mirer GE .15 .40
189 Willie Roaf GE .05 .15
190 Jerome Bettis GE .15 .40
191 Brad Hopkins .05 .15
192 Derek Brown RBK .05 .15
193 Nolan Harrison .05 .15
194 John Randle .08 .25
195 Carlton Bailey .05 .15
196 Kevin Williams WR .08 .25
197 Greg Hill RC .15 .40
198 Mark McMillian .05 .15
199 Brad Edwards .05 .15
200 Dan Marino 1.25 3.00
201 Ricky Watters .08 .25
202 George Teague .05 .15
203 Steve Beuerlein .08 .25
204 Jeff Burris RC .08 .25
205 Steve Atwater .05 .15
206 John Thierry RC .05 .15
207 Patrick Hunter .05 .15
208 Wayne Gandy .05 .15
209 Derrick Moore .05 .15
210 Phil Simms .08 .25
211 Kirk Lowdermilk .05 .15
212 Patrick Robinson .05 .15
213 Kevin Mitchell .05 .15
214 Jonathan Hayes .05 .15
215 Michael Dean Perry .08 .25
216 John Fina .05 .15
217 Anthony Smith .05 .15
218 Paul Gruber .05 .15
219 Carnell Lake .05 .15
220 Carl Lee .05 .15
221 Steve Christie .05 .15
222 Greg Montgomery .05 .15
223 Reggie Brooks .08 .25
224 Derrick Thomas .15 .40
225 Eric Metcalf .08 .25
226 Michael Haynes .08 .25
227 Bobby Hebert .05 .15
228 Tyrone Hughes .08 .25
229 Donald Frank .05 .15
230 Vaughan Johnson .05 .15
231 Eric Thomas .05 .15
232 Ernest Givins .08 .25
233 Charles Haley .08 .25
234 Darrell Green .05 .15
235 Harold Alexander .05 .15
236 Dwayne Sabb .05 .15
237 Horrio Borton .05 .15
238 Randall Cunningham .15 .40
239 Ray Buchanan .05 .15
240 Sterling Sharpe .08 .25
241 Chris Mims .05 .15
242 Mark Carrier DB .05 .15
243 Ricky Proehl .05 .15
244 Michael Brooks .05 .15
245 Sean Gilbert .05 .15
246 David Lutz .05 .15
247 Kelvin Martin .05 .15
248 Scottie Graham RC .08 .25
249 Irving Fryar .08 .25
250 Ricardo McDonald .05 .15
251 Marvcus Patton .05 .15
252 Errict Rhett RC .15 .40
253 Winston Moss .05 .15
254 Rod Bernstine .05 .15
255 Terry Wooden .05 .15
256 Antonio Langham RC .08 .25
257 Tommy Barnhardt .05 .15
258 Marvin Washington .05 .15
259 Bo Orlando .05 .15
260 Marcus Allen .15 .40
261 Mario Bates RC .15 .40
262 Marco Coleman .05 .15
263 Doug Riesenberg .05 .15
264 Jesse Sapolu .05 .15
265 Dermontti Dawson .08 .25
266 Fernando Smith RC .05 .15
267 David Szott .05 .15
268 Steve Christie .05 .15
269 Bruce Matthews .05 .15
270 Michael Irvin .15 .40
271 Seth Joyner .05 .15
272 Santana Dotson .08 .25
273 Vincent Brisby .08 .25
274 Rohn Stark .05 .15
275 John Copeland .05 .15
276 Toby Wright .05 .15
277 David Griggs .05 .15
278 Aaron Taylor .05 .15
279 Chris Doleman .05 .15
280 Reggie Brooks .08 .25
281 Flipper Anderson .05 .15
282 Alvin Harper .08 .25
283 Chris Hinton .05 .15
284 Kelvin Pritchett .05 .15
285 Russell Copeland .05 .15
286 Dwight Stone .05 .15
287 Jeff Gossett .05 .15
288 Larry Allen RC .60 1.50
289 Kevin Mawae RC .15 .40
290 Mark Collins .05 .15
291 Chris Zorich .05 .15
292 Vince Buck .05 .15
293 Gene Atkins .05 .15
294 Webster Slaughter .05 .15
295 Steve Young .50 1.25
296 Dan Williams .05 .15
297 Jessie Armstead .05 .15
298 Victor Bailey .05 .15
299 John Carney .05 .15
300 Emmitt Smith 1.00 2.50
301 Bucky Brooks RC .05 .15
302 Mo Lewis .05 .15
303 Eugene Daniel .05 .15
304 Tyji Armstrong .05 .15
305 Eugene Chung .05 .15
306 Rocket Ismail .08 .25
307 Sean Jones .05 .15
308 Rick Cunningham .05 .15
309 Ken Harvey .05 .15
310 Jeff George .15 .40
311 Jon Vaughn .05 .15
312 Roy Barker RC .05 .15
313 Micheal Barrow .05 .15
314 Ryan McNeil .05 .15
315 Pete Stoyanovich .05 .15
316 Darryl Williams .05 .15
317 Renaldo Turnbull .05 .15
318 Eric Green .05 .15
319 Nate Lewis .05 .15
320 Mike Flores .05 .15
321 Derek Russell .05 .15
322 Marcus Spears RC .05 .15
323 Corey Miller .05 .15
324 Derrick Thomas .15 .40
325 Steve Everitt .05 .15
326 Brent Jones .08 .25
327 Marshall Faulk RC 2.50 6.00
328 Don Beebe .05 .15
329 Harry Swayne .05 .15
330 Boomer Esiason .08 .25
331 Don Mosebar .05 .15
332 Isaac Bruce RC 2.00 5.00
333 Rickey Jackson .05 .15
334 Daryl Johnston .08 .25
335 Lorenzo Lynch .05 .15
336 Brian Blades .08 .25
337 Michael Timpson .05 .15
338 Reggie Cobb .05 .15
339 Joe Walter .05 .15
340 Barry Foster .05 .15
341 Richmond Webb .05 .15
342 Pat Swilling .05 .15
343 Shaun Gayle .05 .15
344 Reggie Roby .05 .15
345 Chris Calloway .05 .15
346 Doug Dawson .05 .15
347 Rob Burnett .05 .15
348 Dana Hall .05 .15
349 Horace Copeland .05 .15
350 Shannon Sharpe .08 .25
351 Rich Miano .05 .15
352 Henry Thomas .05 .15
353 Dan Saleaumua .05 .15
354 Kevin Ross .05 .15
355 Morten Andersen .05 .15
356 Anthony Blaylock .05 .15
357 Stanley Richard .05 .15
358 Albert Lewis .05 .15
359 Darren Woodson .08 .25
360 Drew Bledsoe .40 1.00
361 Eric Mahlum .05 .15
362 Trent Dilfer RC .60 1.50
363 William Roberts .05 .15
364 Robert Brooks .15 .40
365 Jason Hanson .05 .15
366 Troy Vincent .05 .15
367 William Thomas .05 .15
368 Lonnie Johnson RC .05 .15
369 Jamir Miller RC .08 .25
370 Michael Jackson .08 .25
371 Charlie Ward CT RC .15 .40
372 Shannon Sharpe CT .08 .25
373 Jackie Slater CT .05 .15
374 Steve Young CT .25 .60
375 Bobby Wilson .05 .15
376 Paul Frase .05 .15
377 Dale Carter .05 .15
378 Robert Delpino .05 .15
379 Bert Emanuel RC .15 .40
380 Rick Mirer .15 .40
381 Carlos Jenkins .05 .15
382 Gary Brown .05 .15
383 Doug Pelfrey .05 .15
384 Dexter Carter .05 .15
385 Chris Miller .05 .15
386 Charles Johnson RC .15 .40
387 James Joseph .05 .15
388 Darrin Smith .05 .15
389 James Jett .05 .15
390 Junior Seau .15 .40
391 Chris Slade .05 .15
392 Jim Harbaugh .15 .40
393 Herman Moore .15 .40
394 Thomas Randolph RC .05 .15
395 Lamar Thomas .05 .15
396 Reggie Rivers .05 .15
397 Larry Centers .15 .40
398 Chad Brown .05 .15
399 Terry Kirby .15 .40
400 Bruce Smith .15 .40
401 Keenan McCardell RC .75 2.00
402 Tim McDonald .05 .15
403 Robert Smith .15 .40
404 Matt Brock .05 .15
405 Tony McGee .05 .15
406 Ethan Horton .05 .15
407 Michael Haynes .08 .25
408 Steve Jackson .05 .15
409 Erik Kramer .08 .25
410 Jerome Bettis .25 .60
411 D.J. Johnson .05 .15
412 John Alt .05 .15
413 Jeff Lageman .05 .15
414 Rick Tuten .05 .15
415 Jeff Robinson .05 .15
416 Kevin Lee RC .05 .15
417 Thomas Lewis RC .08 .25
418 Kerry Cash .05 .15
419 Chuck Levy RC .05 .15
420 Mark Ingram .05 .15
421 Dennis Gibson .05 .15
422 Tyronne Drakeford .05 .15
423 James Washington .05 .15
424 Dante Jones .05 .15
425 Eugene Robinson .05 .15
426 Johnny Johnson .05 .15
427 Brian Mitchell .05 .15
428 Charles Mincy .05 .15
429 Mark Carrier WR .08 .25
430 Vince Workman .05 .15
431 James Francis .05 .15
432 Clay Matthews .05 .15
433 Randall McDaniel .05 .25
434 Brad Ottis .05 .15
435 Bruce Smith .15 .40
436 Cortez Kennedy BD .05 .15
437 John Randle BD .08 .25
438 Neil Smith BD .08 .25
439 Cornelius Bennett BD .08 .25
440 Junior Seau BD .08 .25
441 Derrick Thomas BD .08 .25
442 Rod Woodson BD .08 .25
443 Terry McDaniel BD .05 .15
444 Tim McDonald BD .05 .15
445 Mark Carrier DB BD .05 .15
446 Irv Smith .05 .15
447 Steve Wallace .05 .15
448 Cris Dishman .05 .15
449 Bill Brooks .05 .15
450 Jeff Hostetler .08 .25
451 Brentson Buckner RC .05 .15
452 Ken Ruettgers .05 .15
453 Marc Boutte .05 .15
454 John Offerdahl .05 .15
455 Allen Aldridge .05 .15
456 Steve Emtman .05 .15
457 Andre Rison .08 .25
458 Shawn Jefferson .05 .15
459 Todd Steussie RC .08 .25
460 Scott Mitchell .08 .25
461 Tom Carter .05 .15
462 Donnell Bennett RC .15 .40
463 James Jones DT .05 .15
464 Antone Davis .05 .15
465 Jim Everett .08 .25
466 Tony Tolbert .05 .15
467 Merril Hoge .05 .15
468 Michael Bates .05 .15
469 Phil Hansen .05 .15
470 Rodney Hampton .08 .25
471 Aeneas Williams .05 .15
472 Al Del Greco .05 .15
473 Todd Lyght .05 .15
474 Joel Steed .05 .15
475 Merton Hanks .08 .25
476 Tony Stargell .05 .15
477 Greg Robinson .05 .15
478 Roger Duffy .05 .15
479 Simon Fletcher .05 .15
480 Reggie White .15 .40
481 Lee Johnson .05 .15
482 Wayne Martin .05 .15
483 Thurman Thomas .15 .40
484 Warren Moon .15 .40
485 Sam Rogers RC .05 .15
486 Erric Pegram .05 .15
487 Will Wolford .05 .15
488 Duane Young .05 .15
489 Keith Hamilton .05 .15
490 Haywood Jeffires .08 .25
491 Trace Armstrong .05 .15
492 J.J. Birden .05 .15
493 Ricky Ervins .05 .15
494 Robert Blackmon .05 .15
495 William Perry .08 .25
496 Robert Massey .05 .15
497 Jim Jeffcoat .05 .15
498 Pat Harlow .05 .15
499 Jeff Cross .05 .15
500 Jerry Rice .60 1.50
501 Darnay Scott RC .40 1.00
502 Clyde Simmons .05 .15
503 Henry Rolling .05 .15
504 James Hasty .05 .15
505 Leroy Thompson .05 .15
506 Darrell Thompson .05 .15
507 Tim Bowens RC .08 .25
508 Gerald Perry .05 .15
509 Mike Croel .05 .15
510 Sam Mills .05 .15
511 Steve Young RZ .25 .60
512 Hardy Nickerson RZ .08 .25
513 Cris Carter RZ .08 .25
514 Boomer Esiason RZ .05 .15
515 Bruce Smith RZ .08 .25
516 Emmitt Smith RZ .50 1.25
517 Eugene Robinson RZ .05 .15
518 Gary Brown RZ .05 .15
519 Jerry Rice RZ .30 .75
520 Troy Aikman RZ .30 .75
521 Marcus Allen RZ .08 .25
522 Junior Seau RZ .08 .25
523 Sterling Sharpe RZ .08 .25
524 Dana Stubblefield RZ .08 .25
525 Tom Carter RZ .05 .15
526 Pete Metzelaars .05 .15
527 Russell Freeman .05 .15
528 Keith Cash .05 .15
529 Willie Drewrey .05 .15
530 Randal Hill .05 .15
531 Pepper Johnson .05 .15
532 Rob Moore .08 .25
533 Todd Kelly .05 .15
534 Keith Byars .05 .15
535 Mike Fox .05 .15
536 Brett Favre 1.25 3.00
537 Terry McDaniel .05 .15
538 Darren Perry .05 .15
539 Maurice Hurst .05 .15
540 Troy Aikman .60 1.50
541 Junior Seau .15 .40
542 Steve Broussard .05 .15
543 Lorenzo White .05 .15
544 Terry McDaniel .05 .15
545 Henry Thomas .05 .15
546 Tyrone Hughes .08 .25
547 Mark Collins .05 .15
548 Gary Anderson K .05 .15
549 Darrell Green .05 .15
550 Jerry Rice .50 1.25
551 Cornelius Bennett .08 .25
552 Aeneas Williams .05 .15
553 Eric Metcalf .08 .25
554 Jumbo Elliott .05 .15
555 Mo Lewis .05 .15
556 Darren Carrington .05 .15
557 Kevin Greene .08 .25
558 John Elway 1.00 2.50
559 Eugene Robinson .05 .15
560 Drew Bledsoe .30 .75
561 Fred Barnett .08 .25
562 Bernie Parmalee RC .15 .40
563 Bryce Paup .08 .25
564 Donnell Woolford .05 .15
565 Terance Mathis .08 .25
566 Santana Dotson .08 .25
567 Randall McDaniel .05 .25
568 Stanley Richard .05 .15
569 Brian Blades .08 .25
570 Jerome Bettis .20 .50
571 Neil Smith .08 .25
572 Andre Reed .08 .25
573 Michael Bankston .05 .15
574 Dana Stubblefield .08 .25
575 Rod Woodson .08 .25
576 Ken Harvey .05 .15
577 Andre Rison .08 .25
578 Darion Conner .05 .15
579 Michael Strahan .15 .40
580 Barry Sanders .75 2.00
581 Pepper Johnson .05 .15
582 Lewis Tillman .05 .15
583 Jeff George .15 .40
584 Michael Haynes .08 .25
585 Herschel Walker .08 .25
586 Tim Brown .15 .40
587 Jim Kelly .15 .40
588 Ricky Watters .08 .25
589 Randall Cunningham .15 .40
590 Troy Aikman .50 1.25
591 Ken Norton Jr. .08 .25
592 Cortez Kennedy .08 .25
593 Ricky Ervins .05 .15
594 Cris Carter .20 .50
595 Sterling Sharpe .08 .25
596 John Randle .08 .25
597 Shannon Sharpe .08 .25
598 Ray Crittenden RC .05 .15
599 Barry Foster .05 .15
600 Deion Sanders .25 .60
601 Seth Joyner .05 .15
602 Chris Warren .08 .25
603 Tom Rathman .05 .15
604 Brett Favre 1.00 2.50
605 Marshall Faulk .75 2.00
606 Terry Allen .08 .25
607 Ben Coates .08 .25
608 Brian Washington .05 .15
609 Henry Ellard .08 .25
610 Dave Meggett .05 .15
611 Stan Humphries .08 .25
612 Warren Moon .15 .40
613 Marcus Allen .15 .40
614 Ed McDaniel .05 .15
615 Joe Montana 1.00 2.50
616 Jeff Hostetler .08 .25
617 Johnny Johnson .05 .15
618 Andre Coleman RC .05 .15
619 Willie Davis .08 .25
620 Rick Mirer .15 .40
621 Dan Marino 1.00 2.50
622 Rob Moore .08 .25
623 Byron Bam Morris RC .08 .25
624 Natrone Means .15 .40
625 Steve Young .30 .75
626 Jim Everett .08 .25
627 Michael Brooks .05 .15
628 Dermontti Dawson .08 .25
629 Reggie White .15 .40
630 Emmitt Smith .60 1.50
0 Micheal Barrow TSC 2.00 4.00
CC1 Best Offense/Defense Cover Card .02 .10
CC2 Chain Gang Cover Card .02 .10
CC3 Chalk Talk Cover Card .02 .10
CC4 Draft Picks Cover Card .02 .10
CC5 Dynasty Destiny Cover Card .02 .10
CC6 Extreme Cover Card .02 .10
CC7 Great Expectations Cover Card .02 .10
CC8 Super Team Cover Card .02 .10
CL1 Checklist Card 1 .02 .10
CL2 Checklist Card 3 .02 .10
CL3 Checklist Card 2 .02 .10

1994 Stadium Club First Day

COMPLETE SET (630) 300.00 600.00
COMP.SERIES 1 (270) 125.00 250.00
COMP.SERIES 2 (270) 125.00 250.00
COMP.HIGH SERIES (90) 50.00 100.00
*VETS: 3X TO 8X BASIC CARDS
*ROOKIES: 1.5X TO 4X BASIC RC
STATED ODDS 1:12

1994 Stadium Club Super Bowl XXIX

COMPLETE SET (540) 320.00 800.00
*STARS: 3X TO 8X BASIC CARDS
*RCs: 2X TO 5X BASIC CARDS

1994 Stadium Club Bowman's Best

Randomly inserted at a rate of one in every three packs, this 44-card insert set subdivides into Black (BK1-BK17), Blue (BU1-BU17), and Mirror Images (18-27). The Black subset features veteran favorites; the Blue subset spotlights rookie stars; and the Mirror Images subset matches veteran stars with up-and-coming rookies.

COMPLETE SET (45) 20.00 50.00
STATED ODDS 1:3 SER.3
*REFRACT: 1X TO 2.5X BASIC INSERTS
REFRACTOR STATED ODDS 1:12 SER.3
BK1 Jerry Rice 1.25 3.00
BK2 Deion Sanders .50 1.25
BK3 Reggie White .30 .75
BK4 Dan Marino 2.50 6.00
BK5 Natrone Means .30 .75
BK6 Rick Mirer .30 .75
BK7 Michael Irvin .30 .75
BK8 John Elway 2.50 6.00
BK9 Junior Seau .30 .75
BK10 Drew Bledsoe .75 2.00
BK11 Sterling Sharpe .15 .40
BK12 Brett Favre 2.50 6.00
BK13 Troy Aikman 1.25 3.00
BK14 Barry Sanders 2.00 5.00
BK15 Steve Young 1.00 2.50
BK16 Emmitt Smith 2.00 5.00
BK17 Joe Montana 2.50 6.00
BU1 Marshall Faulk 3.00 8.00
BU2 Derrick Alexander WR .15 .40
BU3 Darnay Scott .40 1.00
BU4 Gus Frerotte .50 1.25
BU5 Jeff Blake 1.00 2.50
BU6 Charles Johnson .15 .40
BU7 Thomas Lewis .07 .20
BU8 Charlie Garner .50 1.25
BU9 Aaron Glenn .15 .40
BU10 William Floyd .15 .40
BU11 Antonio Langham .07 .20
BU12 Errict Rhett .15 .40
BU13 Heath Shuler .15 .40
BU14 Jeff Burris .07 .20
BU15 Dan Wilkinson .07 .20
BU16 Rob Fredrickson .07 .20
BU17 Tim Bowens .07 .20
18 Deion Sanders .75 2.00
A.Glenn
19 Barry Sanders 2.50 6.00
M.Faulk
20 Will.Floyd .07 .20
D.Johnston UER
21 Reggie White .15 .40
T.Bowens
22 Troy Aikman 1.25 3.00
H.Shuler
23 Antonio Langham .15 .40
Woolford
24 Errict Rhett .15 .40
R.Hampton
25 Jeff Burris .15 .40
T.Hughes
26 Henry Thomas .15 .40
D.Wikinson
27 Jerry Rice 1.25 3.00
D.Alexander WR
28 Emmitt Smith 1.50 4.00
Bam Morris

1994 Stadium Club Dynasty and Destiny

Randomly inserted in packs at a rate of one in 24, this six-card standard-size set matches a current star (Destiny) with one from yesteryear (Dynasty). The card fronts are full-bleed with the Dynasty player at the top and the Destiny player at the bottom. The player's names are in gold foil. The backs have two up-close photos with statistical comparisons.

COMPLETE SET (6) 10.00 20.00
COMP.SERIES 1 (3) 6.00 12.00
COMP.SERIES 2 (3) 4.00 8.00
STATED ODDS 1:24 HOB/RET, 1:15JUM
1 E.Smith/W.Payton 3.00 8.00
2 S.Largent/T.Waddle .75 2.00
3 R.White/C.Kennedy .75 2.00
4 T.Aikman/D.Fouts 1.50 4.00
5 J.Seau/M.Singletary 1.25 3.00
6 Sh.Sharpe/O.Newsome .75 2.00

1994 Stadium Club Expansion Team Redemption

Randomly inserted in third series packs at a rate of one in 24, this six-card standard-size set is a redemption product. As a way of introducing two new NFL franchises to the hobby - the Charlotte Panthers and Jacksonville Jaguars - these special expansion team cards were redeemable for Finest cards of top players on each team in their new uniforms. Each of the three cards per franchise has the team logo and either "offense", "defense" or "special teams" on front. The "offense" card can be redeemed for a set of cards featuring offensive players from that team, etc. A complete set (44) redemption card was randomly inserted at a rate of one in 336. The expiration date was February 20, 1996.

JAGUARS PRIZE SET (22) 10.00 20.00
PANTHERS PRIZE SET (22) 10.00 20.00
J1 James O. Stewart 1.50 4.00
J2 Kelvin Pritchett .40 1.00
J3 Mike Dumas .40 1.00
J4 Brian DeMarco .40 1.00
J5 James Williams LB .40 1.00
J6 Ernest Givins .40 1.00
J7 Harry Colon .40 1.00
J8 Derek Brown TE .40 1.00
J9 Santo Stephens .40 1.00
J10 Jeff Lageman .40 1.00
J11 Bryan Barker .40 1.00
J12 Dave Widell .40 1.00
J13 Willie Jackson .60 1.50
J14 Vinnie Clark .40 1.00
J15 Mickey Washington .40 1.00
J16 Le'Shai Maston .40 1.00
J17 Darren Carrington .40 1.00
J18 Steve Beuerlein .50 1.25
J19 Mark Williams .40 1.00
J20 Keith Goganious .40 1.00
J21 Shawn Bouwens .40 1.00
J22 Chris Hudson .40 1.00
P1 Kerry Collins 4.00 10.00
P2 Rod Smith .40 1.00
P3 Willie Green .40 1.00
P4 Greg Kragen .40 1.00
P5 Blake Brockermeyer .40 1.00
P6 Bob Christian .40 1.00
P7 Carlton Bailey .40 1.00
P8 Bubba McDowell .40 1.00
P9 Matt Elliott .40 1.00
P10 Tyrone Poole .60 1.50
P11 John Kasay .50 1.25
P12 Gerald Williams .40 1.00
P13 Derrick Moore .40 1.00
P14 Don Beebe .40 1.00
P15 Sam Mills .50 1.25
P16 Darion Conner .40 1.00
P17 Eric Guliford .40 1.00
P18 Mike Fox .40 1.00
P19 Pete Metzelaars .40 1.00
P20 Frank Reich .50 1.25
P21 Mark Carrier WR .60 1.50
P22 Vince Workman .40 1.00
NNO Jaguars Defense .20 .50
NNO Jaguars Offense .20 .50
NNO Jaguars Spec.Teams .20 .50
NNO Panthers Defense .20 .50
NNO Panthers Offense .20 .50
NNO Panthers Spec.Teams .20 .50
NNO Panthers .20 .50
Jaguars

1994 Stadium Club Frequent Scorer Points Upgrades

Ten top offensive players were featured in this standard-size set. To obtain a Frequent Scorer Upgrade card, collectors had to accumulate 30 points of an individual player and redeem them by May 15, 1995. These upgrades are identical to the basic cards with the exception of a chromium like metallic gloss and Frequent Scorer logo on front.

COMPLETE SET (10) 15.00 40.00
ONE CARD VIA MAIL PER 30 FS POINTS
55 Dave Meggett .30 .75
75 Vinny Testaverde .75 1.50
129 Chris Warren .75 1.50
151 Stan Humphries .75 1.50
200 Dan Marino 10.00 20.00
310 Jeff George 1.50 3.00
327 Marshall Faulk 8.00 15.00
360 Drew Bledsoe 4.00 8.00
374 Steve Young 4.00 8.00
380 Rick Mirer 1.50 3.00

1994 Stadium Club Ring Leaders

Randomly inserted in packs at a rate of one in 24, this 12-card set showcases players that have won more than one championship ring including the Grey Cup (CFL Championship). The set features the premier of Stadium Club's "Power Matrix Technology," which makes the cards shine and glow. The player and two gold rings are on the front with a small photo and championship highlights on a horizontally designed back.

COMPLETE SET (12) 15.00 40.00
STATED ODDS 1:24 SERIES 2
1 Emmitt Smith 5.00 12.00
2 Steve Young 2.50 6.00
3 Deion Sanders 1.25 3.00
4 Warren Moon .75 2.00
5 Thurman Thomas .75 2.00
6 Jerry Rice 3.00 8.00
7 Sterling Sharpe .40 1.00
8 Barry Sanders 5.00 12.00
9 Reggie White .75 2.00
10 Michael Irvin .75 2.00
11 Ronnie Lott .40 1.00
12 Herschel Walker .40 1.00

1994 Stadium Club Super Teams

Measuring the standard size, this 28-card set of Super Team cards was randomly inserted in foil packs. Each of the 28 NFL teams is represented by a card. Team cards featuring a division winner, conference championship team, or Super Bowl XXX winner were redeemable for the following special prizes: (1) 10 Stadium Club cards of this team foil embossed with a "division winner" logo (Division winner card); (2) 10 Master Photos of this team foil-embossed with the conference logo (AFC or NFC Conference Championship card); and (3) 540-card set of Stadium Club Football cards foil-embossed with the Super Bowl logo (Super Bowl XXX Winner card; winners were also entered into a random drawing to win an official Super Bowl game ball). If a team wins more than one title, the collector could claim all the corresponding prizes won by that Team Card. Prizes could be redeemed only between 2/1/95 and 6/1/95. Winning cards sent to Topps were returned with a "redeemed" stamp on the back. Teams that would have stamps are the Chargers, Cowboys, Dolphins, 49ers, Steelers, and Vikings. The fronts display full-bleed color action photos that have a metallic sheen to them. The backs are white and are completely filled with instructions and conditions of the promotion.

COMPLETE SET (28) 30.00 80.00
STATED ODDS 1:24 HOB/RET, 1:15JUM
1 Cardinals/S.Beuerlein 1.25 3.00
2 Falcons/Drew Hill .75 2.00
3 Bills/Jim Kelly 1.25 3.00
4 Bears/Joe Cain .75 2.00
5 Bengals/D.Fenner .75 2.00
6 Browns/Tom.Vardell .75 2.00
7 Cowboys/E.Smith WIN 5.00 12.00
8 Broncos/John Elway 4.00 10.00
9 Lions/Barry Sanders 4.00 10.00
10 Packers/Brett Favre 8.00 20.00
11 Oilers/Gary Brown .75 2.00
12 Colts/Zefross Moss .75 2.00
13 Chiefs/Joe Montana 2.50 6.00
14 Raiders/Howie Long .75 2.00
15 Rams/Jerome Bettis 1.25 3.00
16 Dolphins/Fryar WIN 1.50 4.00
17 Vikings/Cris Carter WIN 1.50 4.00
18 Patriots/Drew Bledsoe 2.50 6.00
19 Saints/Rickey Jackson .75 2.00
20 Giants/Phil Simms .75 2.00
21 Jets/Boomer Esiason .75 2.00
22 Eagles/H.Walker .75 2.00
23 Steelers/O'Donnell WIN 1.50 4.00
24 Chargers/Means WIN 1.50 4.00
25 49ers/Rice/Young WIN 5.00 12.00
26 Seahawks/Rick Mirer .75 2.00
27 Buccaneers/C.Erickson .75 2.00
28 Redskins/R.Brooks .75 2.00

1994 Stadium Club Super Teams Division Winners

Each of these individual team bag sets was available via mail redemption as prizes for Divison Winner cards from the 1994 Stadium Club Super Teams set. Collectors could redeem the Winner card for a ten-player set and that team's Super Team card emblazened with a "Divison Winner" gold foil logo. Other than the special logo, the cards are essentially parallels to the base brand Stadium Club cards. The sets are most commonly sold individually as team sets.

COMPLETE BAG CHARGERS (11) 2.00 5.00
COMPLETE BAG COWBOYS (11) 4.00 10.00
COMPLETE BAG DOLPHINS (11) 3.20 8.00
COMPLETE BAG 49ERS (11) 4.00 10.00
COMPLETE BAG VIKINGS (11) 2.00 5.00
COMPLETE BAG STEELERS (11) 2.00 5.00
7DW Cowboys 1.00 2.50
Smith
Aikman
16DW Dolphins .25 .60
Fryar
17DW Vikings .25 .60
C.Carter
23DW Steelers .15 .40
O'Donnell
24DW Chargers .25 .60
N.Means
25DW 49ers .50 1.25
Rice
Young
D16 Bryan Cox .15 .40
D56 Aubrey Beavers .15 .40
D99 O.J. McDuffie .40 1.00
D200 Dan Marino 1.60 4.00
D249 Irving Fryar .25 .60
D262 Marco Coleman .15 .40
D341 Richmond Webb .15 .40
D399 Terry Kirby .40 1.00
D507 Tim Bowens .25 .60
D562 Bernie Parmalee .40 1.00
F35 William Floyd .40 1.00
F51 Bryant Young .60 1.50
F80 Dana Stubblefield .25 .60
F201 Ricky Watters .25 .60
F295 Steve Young .60 1.50
F326 Brent Jones .25 .60
F402 Tim McDonald .15 .40
F475 Merton Hanks .15 .40
F500 Jerry Rice .80 2.00
F600 Deion Sanders .50 1.25
V18 Qadry Ismail .40 1.00
V85 Cris Carter .40 1.00
V124 Jack Del Rio .15 .40
V142 Dewayne Washington .25 .60
V173 David Palmer .25 .60
V194 John Randle .25 .60
V352 Henry Thomas .15 .40
V433 Randall McDaniel .15 .40
V459 Todd Steussie .25 .60
V484 Warren Moon .25 .60
CH12 Darren Carrington .15 .40
CH40 Natrone Means .40 1.00
CH84 Isaac Davis .15 .40
CH151 Stan Humphries .25 .60
CH179 Leslie O'Neal .25 .60
CH299 John Carney .15 .40
CH357 Stanley Richard .15 .40
CH390 Junior Seau .40 1.00
CH421 Dennis Gibson .15 .40
CH458 Shawn Jefferson .15 .40
CO52 Jay Novacek .25 .60
CO168 Russell Maryland .15 .40
CO233 Charles Haley .25 .60
CO270 Michael Irvin .40 1.00
CO282 Alvin Harper .25 .60
CO300 Emmitt Smith 1.60 4.00
CO334 Daryl Johnston .25 .60
CO359 Darren Woodson .15 .40
CO423 James Washington .15 .40
CO540 Troy Aikman .80 2.00

1994 Stadium Club Super Teams Master Photos

Each of these individual team bag sets was available via mail redemption as prizes for AFC and NFC Conference Winner cards from the 1994 Stadium Club Super Teams set. Collectors could redeem the Conference Winner card for a ten-player Master Photos set and that team's Super Team card emblazened with a "Conference Winner" gold foil logo. The cards are essentially Master Photo versions of the regular Stadium Club cards and have been numbered according to the base brand card. The sets are most commonly sold individually as team sets.

COMPLETE BAG CHARGERS (11) 3.00 7.50
COMPLETE BAG 49ERS (11) 6.40 16.00
24CW Chargers .30 .75
N.Means

25CW 49ers Rice Young	.60	1.50
F35 William Floyd	.40	1.00
F51 Bryant Young	.50	1.25
F80 Dana Stubblefield	.30	.75
F201 Ricky Watters	.30	.75
F295 Steve Young	1.20	3.00
F326 Brent Jones	.30	.75
F402 Tim McDonald	.20	.50
F475 Merton Hanks	.20	.50
F500 Jerry Rice	1.60	4.00
F600 Deion Sanders	.60	1.50
CH12 Darren Carrington	.20	.50
CH40 Natrone Means	.40	1.00
CH84 Isaac Davis	.20	.50
CH151 Stan Humphries	.30	.75
CH179 Leslie O'Neal	.20	.50
CH299 John Carney	.20	.50
CH357 Stanley Richard	.20	.50
CH390 Junior Seau	.40	1.00
CH421 Dennis Gibson	.20	.50
CH458 Shawn Jefferson	.20	.50

1994 Stadium Club Super Teams Super Bowl

COMPLETE SET (541)	24.00	60.00
*STARS: 1X TO 2.5X BASIC CARDS		
*ROOKIES: .6X TO 1.5X BASIC CARDS		
SB25 Jerry Rice	1.50	4.00

1994 Stadium Club Members Only Parallel

COMP.FACT.SET (722)	100.00	200.00
*VETS 1-630: 1.5X TO 4X BASIC CARDS		
*ROOKIES 1-630: 1X TO 2.5X BASIC CARDS		
*BOW.BEST: .8X TO 2X BASIC INSERTS		
*DYN-DESTINY: .3X TO .8X BASIC INSERTS		
*RING LEADERS: .3X TO .8X BASIC INSERTS		
*SUPER TEAMS: .2X TO .5X BASIC INSERTS		

1994 Stadium Club Members Only 50

Issued to Stadium Club members, this 50-card standard-size set features 45 regular Stadium Club cards as well as five Stadium Club Finest cards. The fronts have full-bleed color action player photos. The player's name is printed in the bottom left corner, the words "Topps Stadium Club Members Only" in gold-foil appear in one of the top corners. On a black background, the horizontal backs carry a color player close-up shot, along with a player profile.

COMPLETE SET (50)	6.00	15.00
1 Jerry Rice	1.25	3.00
2 Erik Williams	.08	.25
3 Nate Newton	.08	.25
4 Jesse Sapolu	.08	.25
5 Randall McDaniel	.08	.25
6 Harris Barton	.08	.25
7 Jay Novacek	.15	.40
8 Michael Irvin	.30	.75
9 Steve Young	1.00	2.50
10 Jerome Bettis	.60	1.50
11 Daryl Johnston	.15	.40
12 Neil Smith	.15	.40
13 Cortez Kennedy	.15	.40
14 Ray Childress	.08	.25
15 Leslie O'Neal	.08	.25
16 Derrick Thomas	.15	.40
17 Junior Seau	.30	.75
18 Greg Lloyd	.15	.40
19 Rod Woodson	.15	.40
20 Nate Odomes	.08	.25
21 Dennis Smith	.08	.25
22 Steve Atwater	.08	.25
23 Reggie White	.30	.75
24 John Randle	.15	.40
25 Sean Gilbert	.08	.25
26 Richard Dent	.15	.40
27 Rickey Jackson	.08	.25
28 Hardy Nickerson	.08	.25
29 Renaldo Turnbull	.08	.25
30 Deion Sanders	.60	1.50
31 Eric Allen	.08	.25
32 Tim McDonald	.08	.25
33 Mark Carrier DB	.08	.25
34 Tim Brown	.30	.75
35 Richmond Webb	.08	.25
36 Keith Sims	.08	.25
37 Bruce Matthews	.08	.25
38 Steve Wisniewski	.08	.25
39 Howard Ballard	.08	.25
40 Shannon Sharpe	.15	.40
41 Anthony Miller	.15	.40
42 John Elway	2.40	6.00
43 Thurman Thomas	.30	.75
44 Marcus Allen	.30	.75
45 Andre Rison	.15	.40
46 Drew Bledsoe	1.25	3.00
47 Willie Roaf	.08	.25
48 Reggie Brooks	.08	.25
49 Dana Stubblefield	.15	.40
50 Rick Mirer	.30	.75

1995 Stadium Club

This 450-card standard-size set was issued in two series in both 12-card foil packs and 26-card jumbo packs. Subsets include Extreme Corps/Expansion Teams (181-210/406-435) and Draft Picks (211-225/436-450), which were seeded at a rate of one per pack, thus making them slightly tougher to find (per card) than the regular cards. Each of those subset cards was printed in a Diffraction parallel version with series one Diffraction featuring text in soild red foil against silver holofoil and series two with solid green foil against gold.

COMPLETE SET (450)	25.00	60.00
COMP.SERIES 1 (225)	12.50	30.00
COMP.SERIES 2 (225)	12.50	30.00
1 Steve Young	.50	1.25
2 Stan Humphries	.07	.20
3 Chris Boniol RC	.02	.10
4 Darren Perry	.02	.10
5 Vinny Testaverde	.07	.20
6 Aubrey Beavers	.02	.10
7 Dewayne Washington	.07	.20
8 Marion Butts	.02	.10
9 George Koonce	.02	.10
10 Joe Cain	.02	.10
11 Mike Johnson	.02	.10
12 Dale Carter	.07	.20
13 Greg Biekert	.02	.10
14 Aaron Pierce	.02	.10
15 Aeneas Williams	.02	.10
16 Stephen Grant RC	.02	.10
17 Henry Jones	.02	.10
18 James Williams LB	.02	.10
19 Andy Harmon	.02	.10
20 Anthony Miller	.07	.20
21 Kevin Ross	.02	.10
22 Erik Howard	.02	.10
23 Brian Blades	.07	.20
24 Trent Dilfer	.15	.40
25 Roman Phifer	.02	.10
26 Bruce Kozerski	.02	.10
27 Henry Ellard	.07	.20
28 Rich Camarillo	.02	.10
29 Richmond Webb	.02	.10
30 George Teague	.02	.10
31 Antonio Langham	.02	.10
32 Barry Foster	.07	.20
33 Bruce Armstrong	.02	.10
34 Tim McDonald	.02	.10
35 James Harris DE	.02	.10
36 Lomas Brown	.02	.10
37 Jay Novacek	.07	.20
38 John Thierry	.02	.10
39 John Elliott	.02	.10
40 Terry McDaniel	.02	.10
41 Shawn Lee	.02	.10
42 Shane Dronett	.02	.10
43 Cornelius Bennett	.07	.20
44 Steve Bono	.07	.20
45 Byron Evans	.02	.10
46 Eugene Robinson	.02	.10
47 Tony Bennett	.02	.10
48 Michael Bankston	.02	.10
49 Willie Roaf	.02	.10
50 Bobby Houston	.02	.10
51 Ken Harvey	.02	.10
52 Bruce Matthews	.02	.10
53 Lincoln Kennedy	.02	.10
54 Todd Lyght	.02	.10
55 Paul Gruber	.02	.10
56 Corey Sawyer	.02	.10
57 Myron Guyton	.02	.10
58 John Jackson T	.02	.10
59 Sean Jones	.02	.10
60 Pepper Johnson	.02	.10
61 Steve Walsh	.02	.10
62 Corey Miller	.02	.10
63 Fuad Reveiz	.02	.10
64 Rickey Jackson	.02	.10
65 Scott Mitchell	.07	.20
66 Michael Irvin	.15	.40
67 Andre Reed	.07	.20
68 Mark Seay	.07	.20
69 Keith Byars	.02	.10
70 Marcus Allen	.15	.40
71 Shannon Sharpe	.07	.20
72 Eric Hill	.02	.10
73 James Washington	.02	.10
74 Greg Jackson	.02	.10
75 Chris Warren	.07	.20
76 Will Wolford	.02	.10
77 Anthony Smith	.02	.10
78 Cris Dishman	.02	.10
79 Carl Pickens	.07	.20
80 Tyrone Hughes	.07	.20
81 Chris Miller	.02	.10
82 Clay Matthews	.07	.20
83 Lonnie Marts	.02	.10
84 Jerome Henderson	.02	.10
85 Ben Coates	.07	.20
86 Deon Figures	.02	.10
87 Anthony Pleasant	.02	.10
88 Guy McIntyre	.02	.10
89 Jake Reed	.07	.20
90 Rodney Hampton	.07	.20
91 Santana Dotson	.02	.10
92 Jeff Blackshear RC	.02	.10
93 Willie Clay	.02	.10
94 Nate Newton	.07	.20
95 Bucky Brooks	.02	.10
96 Lamar Lathon	.02	.10
97 Tim Grunhard	.02	.10
98 Harris Barton	.02	.10
99 Brian Mitchell	.02	.10
100 Natrone Means	.07	.20
101 Sean Dawkins	.07	.20
102 Chris Slade	.02	.10
103 Tom Rathman	.02	.10
104 Fred Barnett	.07	.20
105 Gary Brown	.02	.10
106 Leonard Russell	.02	.10
107 Alfred Williams	.02	.10
108 Kelvin Martin	.02	.10
109 Alexander Wright	.02	.10
110 O.J. McDuffie	.15	.40
111 Mario Bates	.07	.20
112 Tony Casillas	.02	.10
113 Michael Timpson	.02	.10
114 Robert Brooks	.15	.40
115 Rob Burnett	.02	.10
116 Mark Collins	.02	.10
117 Chris Calloway	.02	.10
118 Courtney Hawkins	.02	.10
119 Marvcus Patton	.02	.10
120 Greg Lloyd	.07	.20
121 Ryan McNeil	.02	.10
122 Gary Plummer	.02	.10
123 Dwayne Sabb	.02	.10
124 Jessie Hester	.02	.10
125 Terance Mathis	.07	.20
126 Steve Atwater	.02	.10
127 Lorenzo Lynch	.02	.10
128 James Francis	.02	.10
129 John Fina	.02	.10
130 Emmitt Smith	1.25	2.50
131 Bryan Cox	.02	.10
132 Robert Blackmon	.02	.10
133 Kenny Davidson	.02	.10
134 Eugene Daniel	.02	.10
135 Vince Buck	.02	.10
136 Leslie O'Neal	.07	.20
137 James Jett	.07	.20
138 Johnny Johnson	.02	.10
139 Michael Zordich	.02	.10
140 Warren Moon	.07	.20
141 William White	.02	.10
142 Carl Banks	.02	.10
143 Marty Carter	.02	.10
144 Keith Hamilton	.02	.10
145 Alvin Harper	.02	.10
146 Corey Harris	.02	.10
147 Elijah Alexander RC	.02	.10
148 Darrell Green	.02	.10
149 Yancey Thigpen RC	.07	.20
150 Deion Sanders	.40	1.00
151 Burt Grossman	.02	.10
152 J.B. Brown	.02	.10
153 Johnny Bailey	.02	.10
154 Harvey Williams	.02	.10
155 Jeff Blake RC	.40	1.00
156 Al Smith	.02	.10
157 Chris Doleman	.02	.10
158 Garrison Hearst	.15	.40
159 Bryce Paup	.07	.20
160 Herman Moore	.15	.40
161 Cortez Kennedy	.07	.20
162 Marquez Pope	.02	.10
163 Quinn Early	.07	.20
164 Broderick Thomas	.02	.10
165 Jeff Herrod	.02	.10
166 Robert Jones	.02	.10
167 Mo Lewis	.02	.10
168 Ray Crittenden	.02	.10
169 Raymont Harris	.02	.10
170 Bruce Smith	.15	.40
171 Dana Stubblefield	.07	.20
172 Charles Haley	.07	.20
173 Charles Johnson	.07	.20
174 Shawn Jefferson	.02	.10
175 Leroy Hoard	.02	.10
176 Bernie Parmalee	.07	.20
177 Scottie Graham	.07	.20
178 Edgar Bennett	.07	.20
179 Aubrey Matthews	.02	.10
180 Don Beebe	.02	.10
181 Eric Swann EC SP	.10	.30
182 Jeff George EC SP	.10	.30
183 Jim Kelly EC SP	.25	.60
184 Sam Mills EC SP	.10	.30
185 Mark Carrier DB EC SP	.07	.20
186 Dan Wilkinson EC SP	.10	.30
187 Eric Turner EC SP	.07	.20
188 Troy Aikman EC SP	.75	2.00
189 John Elway EC SP	1.50	4.00
190 Barry Sanders EC SP	1.25	3.00
191 Brett Favre EC SP	2.00	4.00
192 Micheal Barrow EC SP	.07	.20
193 Marshall Faulk EC SP	1.00	2.50
194 Steve Beuerlein EC SP	.10	.30
195 Neil Smith EC SP	.10	.30
196 Jeff Hostetler EC SP	.10	.30
197 Jerome Bettis EC SP	.25	.60
198 Dan Marino EC SP	1.50	4.00
199 Cris Carter EC SP	.25	.60
200 Drew Bledsoe EC SP	.40	1.00
201 Jim Everett EC SP	.07	.20
202 Dave Brown EC SP	.10	.30
203 Boomer Esiason EC SP	.10	.30
204 Randall Cunningham EC SP	.10	.30
205 Rod Woodson EC SP	.10	.30
206 Junior Seau EC SP	.25	.60
207 Jerry Rice EC SP	.75	2.00
208 Rick Mirer EC SP	.10	.30
209 Errict Rhett EC SP	.10	.30
210 Heath Shuler EC SP	.10	.30
211 Bobby Taylor SP RC	.25	.60
212 Jesse James SP RC	.07	.20
213 Devin Bush SP RC	.07	.20
214 Luther Elliss SP RC	.07	.20
215 Kerry Collins SP RC	1.00	2.50
216 Derrick Alexander SP RC	.07	.20
217 Rashaan Salaam SP RC	.10	.30
218 J.J. Stokes SP RC	.25	.60
219 Todd Collins SP RC	.75	2.00
220 Ki-Jana Carter SP RC	.25	.60
221 Kyle Brady SP RC	.25	.60
222 Kevin Carter SP RC	.25	.60
223 Tony Boselli SP RC	.25	.60
224 Scott Gragg SP RC	.07	.20
225 Warren Sapp SP RC	.75	2.00
226 Ricky Reynolds	.02	.10
227 Roosevelt Potts	.02	.10
228 Jessie Tuggle	.02	.10
229 Anthony Newman	.02	.10
230 Randall Cunningham	.15	.40
231 Jason Elam	.07	.20
232 Darnay Scott	.07	.20
233 Tom Carter	.02	.10
234 Micheal Barrow	.02	.10
235 Steve Tasker	.07	.20
236 Howard Cross	.02	.10
237 Charles Wilson	.02	.10
238 Rob Fredrickson	.02	.10
239 Russell Maryland	.02	.10
240 Dan Marino	1.25	3.00
241 Rafael Robinson	.02	.10
242 Ed McDaniel	.02	.10
243 Brett Perriman	.07	.20
244 Chuck Levy	.02	.10
245 Errict Rhett	.07	.20
246 Tracy Simien	.02	.10
247 Steve Everitt	.02	.10
248 John Jurkovic	.02	.10
249 Johnny Mitchell	.02	.10
250 Mark Carrier DB	.02	.10
251 Merton Hanks	.02	.10
252 Joe Johnson	.02	.10
253 Andre Coleman	.02	.10
254 Ray Buchanan	.02	.10
255 Jeff George	.07	.20
256 Shane Conlan	.02	.10
257 Gus Frerotte	.07	.20
258 Doug Pelfrey	.02	.10
259 Glenn Montgomery	.02	.10
260 John Elway	1.25	3.00
261 Larry Centers	.07	.20
262 Calvin Williams	.07	.20
263 Gene Atkins	.02	.10
264 Tim Brown	.15	.40
265 Leon Lett	.02	.10
266 Martin Mayhew	.02	.10
267 Arthur Marshall	.02	.10
268 Maurice Hurst	.02	.10
269 Greg Hill	.07	.20
270 Junior Seau	.15	.40
271 Rick Mirer	.07	.20
272 Jack Del Rio	.02	.10
273 Lewis Tillman	.02	.10
274 Renaldo Turnbull	.02	.10
275 Dan Footman	.02	.10
276 John Taylor	.02	.10
277 Russell Copeland	.02	.10
278 Tracy Scroggins	.02	.10
279 Lou Benfatti	.02	.10
280 Rod Woodson	.07	.20
281 Troy Drayton	.02	.10
282 Quentin Coryatt	.07	.20
283 Craig Heyward	.07	.20
284 Jeff Cross	.02	.10
285 Hardy Nickerson	.02	.10
286 Dorsey Levens	.30	.75
287 Derek Russell	.02	.10
288 Seth Joyner	.02	.10
289 Kimble Anders	.07	.20
290 Drew Bledsoe	.30	.75
291 Bryant Young	.07	.20
292 Chris Zorich	.02	.10
293 Michael Strahan	.15	.40
294 Kevin Greene	.07	.20
295 Aaron Glenn	.02	.10
296 Jimmy Spencer RC	.02	.10
297 Eric Turner	.02	.10
298 William Thomas	.02	.10
299 Dan Wilkinson	.07	.20
300 Troy Aikman	.60	1.50
301 Terry Wooden	.02	.10
302 Heath Shuler	.07	.20
303 Jeff Burris	.02	.10
304 Mark Stepnoski	.02	.10
305 Chris Mims	.02	.10
306 Todd Steussie	.02	.10
307 Johnnie Morton	.07	.20
308 Darryl Talley	.02	.10
309 Nolan Harrison	.02	.10
310 Dave Brown	.07	.20
311 Brent Jones	.02	.10
312 Curtis Conway	.15	.40
313 Ronald Humphrey	.02	.10
314 Richie Anderson RC	.20	.50
315 Jim Everett	.02	.10
316 Willie Davis	.07	.20
317 Ed Cunningham	.02	.10
318 Willie McGinest	.07	.20
319 Sean Gilbert	.07	.20
320 Brett Favre	1.50	3.00
321 Bennie Thompson	.02	.10
322 Neil O'Donnell	.07	.20
323 Vince Workman	.02	.10
324 Terry Kirby	.07	.20
325 Simon Fletcher	.02	.10
326 Ricardo McDonald	.02	.10
327 Duane Young	.02	.10
328 Jim Harbaugh	.07	.20
329 D.J. Johnson	.02	.10
330 Boomer Esiason	.07	.20
331 Donnell Woolford	.02	.10
332 Mike Sherrard	.02	.10
333 Tyrone Legette	.02	.10
334 Larry Brown DB	.02	.10
335 William Floyd	.07	.20
336 Reggie Brooks	.07	.20
337 Patrick Bates	.02	.10
338 Jim Jeffcoat	.02	.10
339 Ray Childress	.02	.10
340 Cris Carter	.15	.40
341 Charlie Garner	.15	.40
342 Bill Hitchcock	.02	.10
343 Levon Kirkland	.02	.10
344 Robert Porcher	.02	.10
345 Darryl Williams	.02	.10
346 Vincent Brisby	.02	.10
347 Kenyon Rasheed RC	.02	.10
348 Floyd Turner	.02	.10
349 Bob Whitfield	.02	.10
350 Jerome Bettis	.15	.40
351 Brad Baxter	.02	.10
352 Darrin Smith	.02	.10
353 Lamar Thomas	.02	.10
354 Lorenzo Neal	.02	.10
355 Erik Kramer	.02	.10
356 Dwayne Harper	.02	.10
357 Doug Evans RC	.15	.40
358 Jeff Feagles	.02	.10
359 Ray Crockett	.02	.10
360 Neil Smith	.07	.20
361 Troy Vincent	.02	.10
362 Don Griffin	.02	.10
363 Michael Brooks	.02	.10
364 Carlton Gray	.02	.10
365 Thomas Smith	.02	.10
366 Ken Norton	.07	.20
367 Tony McGee	.02	.10
368 Eric Metcalf	.07	.20
369 Mel Gray	.02	.10
370 Barry Sanders	1.00	2.50
371 Rocket Ismail	.07	.20
372 Chad Brown	.07	.20
373 Qadry Ismail	.07	.20
374 Anthony Prior	.02	.10
375 Kevin Lee	.02	.10
376 Robert Young	.02	.10
377 Kevin Williams WR	.07	.20
378 Tydus Winans	.02	.10
379 Ricky Watters	.07	.20
380 Jim Kelly	.15	.40
381 Eric Swann	.07	.20
382 Mike Pritchard	.02	.10
383 Derek Brown RBK	.02	.10
384 Dennis Gibson	.02	.10
385 Byron Bam Morris	.02	.10
386 Reggie White	.15	.40
387 Jeff Graham	.02	.10
388 Marshall Faulk	.75	2.00
389 Joe Phillips	.02	.10
390 Jeff Hostetler	.07	.20
391 Irving Fryar	.07	.20
392 Stevon Moore	.02	.10
393 Bert Emanuel	.15	.40
394 Leon Searcy	.02	.10
395 Robert Smith	.15	.40
396 Michael Bates	.02	.10
397 Thomas Lewis	.07	.20
398 Joe Bowden	.02	.10
399 Steve Tovar	.02	.10
400 Jerry Rice	.60	1.50
401 Toby Wright	.02	.10
402 Daryl Johnston	.07	.20
403 Vincent Brown	.02	.10
404 Marvin Washington	.02	.10
405 Chris Spielman	.07	.20
406 Willie Jackson ET SP	.10	.30
407 Harry Boatswain ET SP	.07	.20
408 Kelvin Pritchett ET SP	.07	.20
409 Dave Widell ET SP	.07	.20
410 Frank Reich ET SP	.07	.20
411 Corey Mayfield ET SP RC	.07	.20
412 Pete Metzelaars ET SP	.07	.20
413 Keith Goganious ET SP	.07	.20
414 John Kasay ET SP	.07	.20
415 Ernest Givins ET SP	.07	.20
416 Randy Baldwin ET SP	.07	.20
417 Shawn Bouwens ET SP	.07	.20
418 Mike Fox ET SP	.07	.20
419 Mark Carrier WR ET SP	.10	.30
420 Steve Beuerlein ET SP	.10	.30
421 Steve Lofton ET SP	.07	.20
422 Jeff Lageman ET SP	.07	.20
423 Paul Butcher ET SP	.07	.20
424 Mark Brunell ET SP	.40	1.00
425 Vernon Turner ET SP	.07	.20
426 Tim McKyer ET SP	.07	.20
427 James Williams ET SP	.07	.20
428 Tommy Barnhardt ET SP	.07	.20
429 Rogerick Green ET SP	.07	.20
430 Desmond Howard ET SP	.10	.30
431 Darion Conner ET SP	.07	.20
432 Reggie Clark ET SP	.07	.20
433 Eric Guliford ET SP	.07	.20
434 Rob Johnson SP RC	.50	1.25
435 Sam Mills ET SP	.10	.30
436 Kordell Stewart SP RC	.75	2.00
437 James O. Stewart SP RC	.60	1.50
438 Zach Wiegert SP	.07	.20
439 Ellis Johnson SP RC	.07	.20
440 Matt O'Dwyer SP RC	.07	.20
441 Anthony Cook SP RC	.07	.20
442 Ron Davis SP RC	.07	.20
443 Chris Hudson SP RC	.07	.20
444 Hugh Douglas SP RC	.25	.60
445 Tyrone Poole RC SP	.25	.60
446 Korey Stringer SP RC	.20	.50
447 Ruben Brown SP RC	.25	.60
448 Brian DeMarco SP RC	.07	.20
449 Michael Westbrook SP RC	.25	.60
450 Steve McNair SP RC	1.50	4.00

1995 Stadium Club Diffraction

*DIFFRACTION: .5X TO 1.2X BASIC CARDS
RANDOM INSERTS IN ALL PACKS
SERIES ONE PRINTED WITH RED FOIL
SERIES TWO PRINTED WITH GREEN FOIL
*MEMBERS ONLY: .4X TO 1X BASIC INSERTS

1995 Stadium Club Members Only Parallel

COMPLETE SET (550)	80.00	200.00
COMP.SERIES 1 (275)	40.00	100.00
COMP.SERIES 2 (275)	40.00	100.00
*VETS 1-450: 1.5X TO 4X BASIC CARDS		
*ROOKIES 1-450: .6X TO 1.5X BASIC CARDS		
*POWER SURGE: .2X TO .5X BASIC INSERTS		
*GRND ATTACK: .2X TO .5X BASIC INSERTS		
*METALISTS: .2X TO .5X BASIC INSERTS		
*MVPs: .3X TO .8X BASIC INSERTS		
*NEMESES: .2X TO .5X BASIC INSERTS		
*NIGHTMARES: .2X TO .5X BASIC INSERTS		

1995 Stadium Club Ground Attack

Randomly inserted into series two packs at a rate of one in 14 retail packs and one in 18 hobby packs, this 15 card set focuses on some of the best NFL backfield combinations. Card backs are also numbered with a "G" prefix.

COMPLETE SET (15)	15.00	40.00
STATED ODDS 1:18H,1:6J,1:12R SER.2		
STATED ODDS 1:16 SPEC.RET SER.2		
G1 Emmitt Smith Daryl Johnston	3.00	8.00
G2 Brett Favre Edgar Bennett	5.00	12.00
G3 Bernie Parmalee Irving Spikes	.60	1.50
G4 John Elway Glen Milburn	5.00	12.00
G5 Rick Mirer Chris Warren	.75	2.00
G6 Greg Hill Marcus Allen	.75	2.00
G7 Errict Rhett Vince Workman	.75	2.00
G8 Byron Bam Morris Erric Pegram	.60	1.50
G9 Derek Brown RBK Mario Bates	.60	1.50
G10 Steve Young William Floyd	2.00	5.00
G11 Charlie Garner Randall Cunningham	1.25	3.00
G12 Lewis Tillman Raymont Harris	.60	1.50
G13 Harvey Williams Jeff Hostetler	.60	1.50
G14 Garrison Hearst Larry Centers	.75	2.00
G15 Marshall Faulk Roosevelt Potts	2.50	6.00

1995 Stadium Club Metalists

This eight-card standard-size set was randomly inserted in series one retail packs at a rate of one in 18 and hobby packs at a rate of one in 24. This set boasts being the first-ever laser-cut card that makes for better precision in the making of the cards. Card backs are numbered with a "M" prefix.

COMPLETE SET (8)	12.50	30.00
STATED ODDS 1:24H, 1:9J, 1:28R SER.1		
STATED ODDS 1:21 SPEC.RET SER.1		
M1 Jerry Rice	2.50	6.00
M2 Barry Sanders	3.00	8.00
M3 John Elway	4.00	10.00
M4 Dana Stubblefield	.30	.75
M5 Emmitt Smith	3.00	8.00
M6 Deion Sanders	1.25	3.00
M7 Marshall Faulk	1.25	3.00
M8 Steve Young	1.50	4.00

1995 Stadium Club MVPs

This eight card set was randomly inserted in series two packs at a rate of one in 24 hobby packs and one in 18 retail packs. . Card backs are numbered with a "MVP" prefix.

COMPLETE SET (8)	10.00	25.00
STATED ODDS 1:24H, 1:9J, 1:24R SER.2		
STATED ODDS 1:28 SPEC.RET SER.2		
MVP1 Jerry Rice	2.00	4.00
MVP2 Boomer Esiason	.30	.75
MVP3 Randall Cunningham	.40	1.00
MVP4 Marcus Allen	.40	1.00
MVP5 John Elway	4.00	8.00
MVP6 Dan Marino	4.00	8.00
MVP7 Emmitt Smith	3.00	6.00
MVP8 Steve Young	1.50	3.00

1995 Stadium Club Nemeses

This 15-card standard-size set was randomly inserted in series one packs at a rate of one in 24. Card backs are numbered with a "N" prefix.

COMPLETE SET (15)	25.00	60.00
STATED ODDS 1:24H, 1:9J, 1:16SP.RET SER.1		
N1 Barry Sanders Jack Del Rio	5.00	12.00
N2 Reggie White Lomas Brown	1.50	4.00
N3 Terry McDaniel Anthony Miller	1.00	2.50
N4 Brett Favre Chris Spielman	5.00	12.00
N5 Junior Seau Chris Warren	2.00	5.00
N6 Cortez Kennedy Steve Wisniewski	1.00	2.50
N7 Rod Woodson Tim Brown	2.00	5.00
N8 Troy Aikman Michael Brooks	3.00	8.00
N9 Bruce Smith Bruce Armstrong	1.50	4.00
N10 Jerry Rice Donnell Woolford	3.00	8.00
N11 Emmitt Smith Seth Joyner	4.00	10.00
N12 Dan Marino Cornelius Bennett	5.00	12.00
N13 Marshall Faulk Bryan Cox	3.00	8.00
N14 Stan Humphries Greg Lloyd	1.50	4.00
N15 Michael Irvin Deion Sanders	2.00	5.00

1995 Stadium Club Nightmares

This 30 card standard-size set was randomly inserted in both series one and series two packs. Cards NM1-NM15 were inserted in series one at a rate of one in 24 hobby packs. Cards NM16-NM30 were inserted in series two at a rate of one in 18 hobby packs. The fronts have a color player photo with a dark, morbid background. The backs are horizontal with a head shot and player commentary done by Topps' comic character Vampirella. Card backs are also numbered with a "NM" prefix.

COMPLETE SET (30)	40.00	100.00
COMP.SERIES 1 (15)	30.00	70.00
COMP.SERIES 2 (15)	12.00	30.00
NM1-NM15 ODDS 1:24H, 1:9J SER.1		
NM16-NM30 ODDS 1:18H, 1:6J SER.2		
NM1 Drew Bledsoe	.75	2.00
NM2 Barry Sanders	4.00	10.00
NM3 Reggie White	.75	2.00
NM4 Michael Irvin	.75	2.00
NM5 Jerry Rice	3.00	8.00
NM6 Jerome Bettis	.75	2.00
NM7 Dan Marino	6.00	15.00
NM8 Bruce Smith	.75	2.00
NM9 Steve Young	2.00	5.00
NM10 Junior Seau	.75	2.00
NM11 Emmitt Smith	4.00	10.00
NM12 Deion Sanders	1.50	4.00
NM13 Rod Woodson	.50	1.25
NM14 Marshall Faulk	1.50	4.00
NM15 Troy Aikman	2.50	6.00
NM16 Stan Humphries	.50	1.25
NM17 Chris Warren	.50	1.25
NM18 Jack Del Rio	.30	.75
NM19 Randall Cunningham	.75	2.00
NM20 Natrone Means	.50	1.25
NM21 Dana Stubblefield	.50	1.25
NM22 Jim Kelly	.75	2.00
NM23 Cris Carter	.75	2.00
NM24 Cornelius Bennett	.50	1.25
NM25 Errict Rhett	.50	1.25
NM26 Terry McDaniel	.30	.75
NM27 Rodney Hampton	.50	1.25
NM28 Brett Favre	6.00	15.00
NM29 Bryan Cox	.30	.75
NM30 John Elway	6.00	15.00

1995 Stadium Club Power Surge

This 24 card standard-size set was randomly inserted in both series one and series two packs. Cards P1-P12 were inserted in series one at a rate of one in 18. Cards PS1-PS12 were inserted in series two at a rate of one in 36 hobby and one in 28 retail. The fronts have a full-color action photo with the player's name on the left side and the words "Power Surge" at the bottom. The fronts are done in a new foil technology called Power Matrix that gives it a holographic-silver look to the background. The backs are horizontal with a color head shot of the player and player information including statistics. Card backs are either numbered with a "P" or "PS" prefix.

COMPLETE SET (24)	30.00	80.00
COMP.SERIES 1 (12)	20.00	50.00
COMP.SERIES 2 (12)	12.50	30.00
P1-P12 ODDS 1:18H, 1:28R SER.1		
PS1-PS12 ODDS 1:36H, 1:28R SER.2		
P1 Steve Young	2.50	6.00
P2 Natrone Means	.40	1.00
P3 Cris Carter	.75	2.00
P4 Junior Seau	.75	2.00
P5 Barry Sanders	5.00	12.00
P6 Michael Irvin	.75	2.00
P7 John Elway	6.00	15.00
P8 Emmitt Smith	5.00	12.00
P9 Greg Lloyd	.40	1.00
P10 Jerry Rice	3.00	8.00
P11 Marshall Faulk	4.00	10.00
P12 Drew Bledsoe	1.50	4.00
PS1 Dan Marino	6.00	15.00
PS2 Ken Harvey	.20	.50
PS3 Chris Warren	.40	1.00
PS4 Henry Ellard	.40	1.00
PS5 Marshall Faulk	1.25	3.00
PS6 Irving Fryar	.40	1.00
PS7 Kevin Ross	.20	.50
PS8 Vince Workman	.20	.50
PS9 Ray Buchanan	.20	.50
PS10 Tony Martin	.40	1.00
PS11 D.J.Johnson	.20	.50
PS12 Steve Young	2.50	6.00

1995 Stadium Club Members Only 50

Topps produced a 50-card boxed set for each of the four major sports. With their club membership, members received one set of their choice and had the option of purchasing additional sets for $10.00 each. The set consists of 45 Stadium Club cards (reflecting the 44 starting players from the 1995 Pro Bowl and a special card of Jerry Rice and Emmitt Smith who were both elected to the starting team but did not play due to injuries) and five Finest cards (representing Topps' selection of the Top Rookies of 1994). The fronts carry the distinctive Topps Stadium Club Members Only gold foil seal.

COMP.FACT.SET (50)	6.00	15.00
1 Tim Brown Oakland Raiders	.30	.75
2 Richmond Webb Miami Dolphins	.07	.20
3 Keith Sims	.07	.20
4 Dermontti Dawson Pittsburgh Steelers	.15	.40
5 Duval Love Pittsburgh Steelers	.07	.20
6 Bruce Armstrong New England Patriots	.07	.20
7 Ben Coates New England Patriots	.15	.40
8 Andre Reed Buffalo Bills	.15	.40
9 John Elway Denver Broncos	1.60	4.00
10 Marshall Faulk	.80	2.00
11 Natrone Means San Diego Chargers	.15	.40
12 Charles Haley Dallas Cowboys	.07	.20
13 John Randle Minnesota Vikings	.15	.40
14 Leon Lett Dallas Cowboys	.07	.20
15 William Fuller Philadelphia Eagles	.07	.20
16 Ken Harvey Washington Redskins	.07	.20
17 Chris Spielman Detroit Lions	.07	.20
18 Bryce Paup Green Bay Packers	.07	.20
19 Deion Sanders	.60	1.50
20 Aeneas Williams	.07	.20
21 Darren Woodson Dallas Cowboys	.07	.20
22 Merton Hanks San Francisco 49ers	.07	.20
23 Michael Irvin Dallas Cowboys	.30	.75
24 William Roaf New Orleans Saints	.07	.20
25 Nate Newton Dallas Cowboys	.07	.20
26 Mark Stepnoski	.07	.20
27 Randall McDaniel Minnesota Vikings	.07	.20
28 Lomas Brown Detroit Lions	.07	.20
29 Brent Jones San Francisco 49ers	.07	.20
30 Cris Carter Minnesota Vikings	.30	.75
31 Steve Young San Francisco 49ers	.80	2.00
32 Barry Sanders Detroit Lions	1.60	4.00
33 Jerome Bettis Los Angeles Rams	.30	.75
34 Bruce Smith Buffalo Bills	.15	.40
35 Michael Dean Perry Cleveland Browns	.07	.20
36 Cortez Kennedy Seattle Seahawks	.07	.20
37 Leslie O'Neal San Diego Chargers	.07	.20
38 Derrick Thomas Kansas City Chiefs	.15	.40
39 Junior Seau San Diego Chargers	.15	.40
40 Greg Lloyd Pittsburgh Steelers	.07	.20
41 Rod Woodson Pittsburgh Steelers	.15	.40
42 Terry McDaniel Oakland Raiders	.07	.20
43 Eric Turner Cleveland Browns	.07	.20
44 Carnell Lake Pittsburgh Steelers	.07	.20
45 J.Rice E.Smith	1.60	4.00
46 William Floyd 9ers	.15	.40
47 Tim Bowens Miami Dolphins	.07	.20
48 Heath Shuler	.15	.40
49 Bryant Young	.15	.40
50 Marshall Faulk	.80	2.00

1996 Stadium Club

This 360-card set was issued in two series totalling 180 cards each. The set was distributed in 10-card packs with a suggested retail price of $2.50. Each pack of both Series I and Series II cards contained eight regular cards and two foil subset cards. Series I contains 135 regular cards with textured foil stamping and 45 double foil stamped subset cards from the following categories: Draft Picks (136-153), Shining Moments (154-171, highlights milestones or great plays from the '95 season), and Golden Moments (172-180, features record-breaking performances from the '95 season). Series 2 contained 135 regular cards stamped with etched gold foil and UV coated and 45-subset cards of rookies, free agents and traded veterans showcased in their new uniforms. Several Protoype cards were produced that look nearly exactly like base cards. The only difference is found is the base cards have a white ghosting on the team name printed on the cardbacks. There were likely more prototype cards printed than listed below.

COMPLETE SET (360)	30.00	60.00
COMP.SERIES 1 (180)	15.00	30.00
COMP.SERIES 2 (180)	15.00	30.00
1 Kyle Brady	.02	.10
2 Mickey Washington	.02	.10
3 Seth Joyner	.02	.10
4 Vinny Testaverde	.08	.25
5 Thomas Randolph	.02	.10
6 Heath Shuler	.08	.25
7 Ty Law	.20	.50
8 Blake Brockermeyer	.02	.10
9 Darryll Lewis	.02	.10
10 Jeff Blake	.20	.50
11 Tyrone Hughes	.02	.10
12 Horace Copeland	.02	.10
13 Roman Phifer	.02	.10
14 Eugene Robinson	.02	.10
15 Anthony Miller	.08	.25
16 Robert Smith	.08	.25
17 Chester McGlockton	.02	.10
18 Marty Carter	.02	.10
19 Scott Mitchell	.08	.25
20 O.J. McDuffie	.08	.25
21 Stan Humphries	.08	.25
22 Eugene Daniel	.02	.10
23 Devin Bush	.02	.10
24 Darick Holmes	.02	.10
25 Ricky Watters	.08	.25
26 J.J. Stokes	.20	.50
27 George Koonce	.02	.10
28 Tamarick Vanover	.08	.25
29 Yancey Thigpen	.08	.25
30 Troy Aikman	.50	1.25
31 Rashaan Salaam	.08	.25
32 Anthony Cook	.02	.10
33 Tim McKyer	.02	.10
34 Dale Carter	.02	.10
35 Marvin Washington	.02	.10
36 Terry Allen	.08	.25
37 Keith Goganious	.02	.10
38 Pepper Johnson	.02	.10
39 Dave Brown	.02	.10
40 Levon Kirkland	.02	.10
41 Ken Dilger	.08	.25
42 Harvey Williams	.02	.10
43 Robert Blackmon	.02	.10
44 Kevin Carter	.02	.10
45 Warren Moon	.08	.25
46 Allen Aldridge	.02	.10
47 Terance Mathis	.02	.10
48 Junior Seau	.20	.50
49 William Fuller	.02	.10
50 Lee Woodall	.02	.10
51 Aeneas Williams	.02	.10
52 Thomas Smith	.02	.10
53 Chris Slade	.02	.10
54 Eric Allen	.02	.10
55 David Sloan	.02	.10
56 Hardy Nickerson	.02	.10
57 Michael Irvin	.20	.50
58 Corey Sawyer	.02	.10
59 Eric Green	.02	.10
60 Reggie White	.20	.50
61 Isaac Bruce	.20	.50
62 Darrell Green	.02	.10
63 Aaron Glenn	.02	.10
64 Mark Brunell	.30	.75
65 Mark Carrier WR	.02	.10
66 Mel Gray	.02	.10
67 Phillippi Sparks	.02	.10
68 Ernie Mills	.02	.10
69 Rick Mirer	.08	.25
70 Neil Smith	.08	.25
71 Terry McDaniel	.02	.10
72 Terrell Davis	.40	1.00
73 Alonzo Spellman	.02	.10
74 Jessie Tuggle	.02	.10
75 Terry Kirby	.08	.25
76 David Palmer	.02	.10
77 Calvin Williams	.02	.10
78 Shaun Gayle	.02	.10
79 Bryant Young	.08	.25
80 Jim Harbaugh	.08	.25
81 Michael Jackson	.08	.25
82 Dave Meggett	.02	.10
83 Henry Thomas	.02	.10
84 Jim Kelly	.20	.50
85 Frank Sanders	.08	.25
86 Daryl Johnston	.08	.25
87 Alvin Harper	.02	.10
88 John Copeland	.02	.10
89 Mark Chmura	.08	.25
90 Jim Everett	.02	.10
91 Bobby Houston	.02	.10
92 Willie Jackson	.08	.25
93 Carlton Bailey	.02	.10
94 Todd Lyght	.02	.10
95 Ken Harvey	.02	.10
96 Erric Pegram	.02	.10
97 Anthony Smith	.02	.10
98 Kimble Anders	.08	.25
99 Steve McNair	.40	1.00
100 Jeff George	.08	.25
101 Michael Timpson	.02	.10
102 Brent Jones	.02	.10
103 Mike Mamula	.02	.10
104 Jeff Cross	.02	.10
105 Craig Newsome	.02	.10
106 Howard Cross	.02	.10
107 Terry Wooden	.02	.10
108 Randall McDaniel	.05	.15
109 Andre Reed	.08	.25
110 Steve Atwater	.02	.10
111 Larry Centers	.08	.25
112 Tony Bennett	.02	.10
113 Drew Bledsoe	.30	.75
114 Terrell Fletcher	.02	.10
115 Warren Sapp	.02	.10
116 Deion Sanders	.30	.75
117 Bryce Paup	.02	.10
118 Mario Bates	.08	.25
119 Steve Tovar	.02	.10
120 Barry Sanders	.75	2.00
121 Tony Boselli	.02	.10
122 Micheal Barrow	.02	.10
123 Sam Mills	.02	.10
124 Tim Brown	.20	.50
125 Darren Perry	.02	.10
126 Brian Blades	.02	.10
127 Tyrone Wheatley	.08	.25
128 Derrick Thomas	.20	.50
129 Edgar Bennett	.08	.25
130 Cris Carter	.20	.50
131 Stephen Grant	.02	.10
132 Kevin Williams	.02	.10
133 Darnay Scott	.08	.25
134 Rod Stephens	.02	.10
135 Ken Norton	.02	.10
136 Tim Biakabutuka SP RC	.20	.50
137 Willie Anderson SP RC	.02	.10
138 Lawrence Phillips SP RC	.20	.50
139 Jonathan Ogden SP RC	1.25	3.00
140 Simeon Rice SP RC	.50	1.25
141 Alex Van Dyke SP RC	.08	.25
142 Jerome Woods SP RC	.02	.10
143 Eric Moulds RC	.75	2.00
144 Mike Alstott SP RC	.60	1.50
145 Marvin Harrison SP RC	1.50	4.00
146 Duane Clemons SP RC	.02	.10
147 Regan Upshaw SP RC	.02	.10
148 Eddie Kennison SP RC	.20	.50
149 John Mobley SP RC	.02	.10
150 Keyshawn Johnson SP RC	.60	1.50
151 Marco Battaglia SP RC	.02	.10
152 Rickey Dudley SP RC	.20	.50
153 Kevin Hardy SP RC	.20	.50
154 Curtis Martin SM SP	.40	1.00
155 Dan Marino SM SP	1.00	2.50
156 Rashaan Salaam SM SP	.08	.25
157 Joey Galloway SM SP	.20	.50
158 John Elway SM SP	1.00	2.50
159 Marshall Faulk SM SP	.25	.60
160 Jerry Rice SM SP	.50	1.25
161 Darren Bennett SM SP	.02	.10
162 Tamarick Vanover SM SP	.08	.25
163 Orlando Thomas SM SP	.02	.10
164 Jim Kelly SM SP	.20	.50
165 Larry Brown SM SP	.02	.10
166 Errict Rhett SM SP	.08	.25
167 Warren Moon SM SP	.02	.10
168 Hugh Douglas SM SP	.02	.10
169 Jim Everett SM SP	.02	.10
170 AFC Championship Game SP	.02	.10
171 Larry Centers SM SP	.08	.25
172 Marcus Allen GM SP	.20	.50
173 Morten Andersen GM SP	.02	.10
174 Brett Favre GM SP	1.00	2.50
175 Jerry Rice GM SP	.50	1.25
176 Glyn Milburn GM SP	.02	.10
177 Thurman Thomas GM SP	.08	.25
178 Michael Irvin GM SP	.08	.25
179 Barry Sanders GM SP	.75	2.00

180 Dan Marino GM SP	1.00	2.50
181 Joey Galloway	.20	.50
182 Dwayne Harper	.02	.10
183 Antonio Langham	.02	.10
184 Chris Zorich	.02	.10
185 Willie McGinest	.02	.10
186 Wayne Chrebet	.30	.75
187 Dermontti Dawson	.08	.20
188 Charlie Garner	.08	.25
189 Quentin Coryatt	.02	.10
190 Rodney Hampton	.08	.25
191 Kelvin Pritchett	.02	.10
192 Willie Green	.02	.10
193 Garrison Hearst	.08	.25
194 Tracy Scroggins	.02	.10
195 Rocket Ismail	.02	.10
196 Michael Westbrook	.20	.50
197 Troy Drayton	.02	.10
198 Rob Fredrickson	.02	.10
199 Sean Lumpkin	.02	.10
200 John Elway	1.00	2.50
201 Bernie Parmalee	.02	.10
202 Chris Chandler	.08	.25
203 Lake Dawson	.02	.10
204 Orlando Thomas	.02	.10
205 Carl Pickens	.08	.25
206 Kurt Schulz	.02	.10
207 Clay Matthews	.02	.10
208 Winston Moss	.02	.10
209 Sean Dawkins	.02	.10
210 Emmitt Smith	.75	2.00
211 Mark Carrier DB	.02	.10
212 Clyde Simmons	.02	.10
213 Derrick Brooks	.20	.50
214 William Floyd	.08	.25
215 Aaron Hayden	.02	.10
216 Brian DeMarco	.02	.10
217 Ben Coates	.08	.25
218 Renaldo Turnbull	.02	.10
219 Adrian Murrell	.08	.25
220 Marcus Allen	.20	.50
221 Brett Maxie	.02	.10
222 Trev Alberts	.02	.10
223A Darren Woodson	.08	.25
223B Kordell Stewart UER	.20	.50
224 Brian Mitchell	.02	.10
225 Michael Haynes	.02	.10
226 Sean Jones	.02	.10
227 Eric Zeier	.02	.10
228 Herman Moore	.08	.25
229 Shane Conlan	.02	.10
230 Chris Warren	.08	.25
231 Dana Stubblefield	.08	.25
232 Andre Coleman	.02	.10
234 Ray Crockett	.02	.10
235 Craig Heyward	.02	.10
236 Mike Fox	.02	.10
237 Derek Brown RBK	.02	.10
238 Thomas Lewis	.02	.10
239 Hugh Douglas	.08	.25
240 Tom Carter	.02	.10
241 Toby Wright	.02	.10
242 Jason Belser	.02	.10
243 Rodney Peete	.02	.10
244 Napoleon Kaufman	.20	.50
245 Merton Hanks	.02	.10
246 Harry Colon	.02	.10
247 Greg Hill	.08	.25
248 Vincent Brisby	.02	.10
249 Eric Hill	.02	.10
250 Brett Favre	.75	2.00
251 Leroy Hoard	.02	.10
252 Eric Guliford	.02	.10
253 Stanley Richard	.08	.25
254 Carlos Jenkins	.02	.10
255 D'Marco Farr	.02	.10
256 Carlton Gray	.02	.10
257 Derek Loville	.02	.10
258 Ray Buchanan	.02	.10
259 Jake Reed	.08	.25
260 Dan Marino	1.00	2.50
261 Brad Baxter	.02	.10
262 Pat Swilling	.02	.10
263 Andy Harmon	.02	.10
264 Harold Green	.02	.10
265 Shannon Sharpe	.08	.25
266 Erik Kramer	.02	.10
267 Lamar Lathon	.02	.10
268 Stevon Moore	.02	.10
269 Tony Martin	.08	.25
270 Bruce Smith	.08	.25
271 James Washington	.02	.10
272 Tyrone Poole	.02	.10
273 Eric Swann	.02	.10
274 Dexter Carter	.02	.10
275 Greg Lloyd	.08	.25
276 Michael Zordich	.02	.10
277 Steve Wisniewski	.02	.10
278 Chris Calloway	.02	.10
279 Irv Smith	.02	.10
280 Steve Young	.40	1.00
281 James O.Stewart	.08	.25
282 Blaine Bishop	.02	.10
283 Rob Moore	.08	.25
284 Eric Metcalf	.02	.10
285 Kerry Collins	.20	.50
286 Dan Wilkinson	.02	.10
287 Curtis Conway	.20	.50
288 Jay Novacek	.02	.10
289 Henry Ellard	.02	.10
290 Curtis Martin	.40	1.00
291 Brett Perriman	.02	.10
292 Jeff Lageman	.02	.10
293 Trent Dilfer	.20	.50
294 Cortez Kennedy	.02	.10
295 Jeff Hostetler	.02	.10
296 Mark Fields	.02	.10
297 Qadry Ismail	.08	.25
298 Steve Bono	.02	.10
299 Tony Tolbert	.02	.10
300 Jerry Rice	.50	1.25
301 Marvcus Patton	.02	.10
302 Robert Brooks	.20	.50
303 Terry Ray RC	.02	.10
304 John Thierry	.02	.10
305 Errict Rhett	.08	.25
306 Ricardo McDonald	.02	.10
307 Antonio London	.02	.10
308 Lonnie Johnson	.02	.10
309 Mark Collins	.02	.10
310 Marshall Faulk	.25	.60
311 Anthony Pleasant	.02	.10
312 Howard Griffith	.02	.10
313 Roosevelt Potts	.02	.10
314 Jim Flanigan	.02	.10
315 Omar Ellison RC	.02	.10
316 Boomer Esiason SP	.08	.25
317 Leslie O'Neal SP	.02	.10
318 Jerome Bettis SP	.20	.50
319 Larry Brown SP	.02	.10
320 Neil O'Donnell SP	.08	.25
321 Andre Rison SP	.08	.25
322 Cornelius Bennett SP	.02	.10
323 Quinn Early SP	.02	.10
324 Bryan Cox SP	.02	.10
325 Irving Fryar SP	.08	.25
326 Eddie Robinson SP	.02	.10
327 Chris Doleman SP	.02	.10
328 Sean Gilbert SP	.02	.10
329 Steve Walsh SP	.02	.10
330 Kevin Greene SP	.08	.25
331 Chris Spielman SP	.02	.10
332 Jeff Graham SP	.02	.10
333 Anthony Dorsett SP RC	.02	.10
334 Amani Toomer SP RC	.60	1.50
335 Walt Harris SP RC	.02	.10
336 Ray Mickens SP RC	.02	.10
337 Danny Kanell SP RC	.20	.50
338 Daryl Gardener SP RC	.02	.10
339 Jonathan Ogden SP	1.00	2.50
340 Eddie George SP RC	.75	2.00
341 Jeff Lewis SP RC	.08	.25
342 Terrell Owens SP RC	1.50	4.00
343 Brian Dawkins SP RC	.75	2.00
344 Tim Biakabutuka SP	.20	.50
345 Marvin Harrison SP	.60	1.50
346 Lawyer Milloy SP RC	.25	.60
347 Eric Moulds SP	.30	.75
348 Alex Van Dyke SP	.08	.25
349 John Mobley SP	.02	.10
350 Kevin Hardy SP	.20	.50
351 Ray Lewis SP RC	6.00	15.00
352 Lawrence Phillips SP	.20	.50
353 Stepfret Williams SP RC	.08	.25
354 Bobby Engram SP RC	.20	.50
355 Leeland McElroy SP RC	.08	.25
356 Marco Battaglia SP	.02	.10
357 Rickey Dudley SP	.20	.50
358 Bobby Hoying SP RC	.20	.50
359 Cedric Jones SP RC	.02	.10
360 Keyshawn Johnson SP	.20	.50
P19 Scott Mitchell Prototype	.20	.50
P31 Rashaan Salaam Prototype	.30	.75
P56 Hardy Nickerson Prototype	.20	.50
NNO Checklist Card 1	.02	.10
NNO Checklist Card 2	.02	.10
NNO Checklist Card 3	.02	.10
NNO Checklist Card 4	.02	.10

1996 Stadium Club Dot Matrix

*DOT MATRIX: 4X TO 10X BASIC CARDS
STATED ODDS 1:12H/R, 1:4J SER.1
STATED ODDS 1:12H, 1:16R SER.2

1996 Stadium Club Match Proofs

*MATCH PROOFS: 15X TO 40X BASIC CARDS
STATED ODDS 1:240 SER.1
STATED ODDS 1:150H, 1:200R SER.2

1996 Stadium Club Brace Yourself

Randomly inserted in Series II hobby packs at the rate of 1:24, and retail packs at a rate of 1:32, this 10 card set features embossed, holographic foil cards of 10 gridiron giants.

COMPLETE SET (10)	25.00	60.00
STATED ODDS 1:24 HOB, 1:32 RET SER.2		
BY1 Dan Marino	8.00	20.00
BY2 Marshall Faulk	2.00	5.00
BY3 Greg Lloyd	1.00	2.50
BY4 Steve Young	2.50	6.00
BY5 Emmitt Smith	6.00	15.00
BY6 Junior Seau	1.50	4.00
BY7 Chris Warren	1.00	2.50
BY8 Jerry Rice	5.00	10.00
BY9 Troy Aikman	3.00	8.00
BY10 Barry Sanders	5.00	12.00

1996 Stadium Club Contact Prints

Randomly inserted in Series I packs at the rate of 1:12, with a ratio of 1:4 in the jumbo packs, this 10-card set features color action player photos printed on triple diffraction foil stamped cards with a full update of the player's history on the back.

COMPLETE SET (10)	6.00	15.00
SER.1 ODDS 1:12 HOB/RET, 1:4 JUM		
CP1 K.Norton/D.Bledsoe	1.00	2.50
CP2 B.Sanders/C.Zorich	1.50	4.00
CP3 C.Harris/H.Williams	.60	1.50
CP4 S.Mills/T.Thomas	1.00	2.50
CP5 B.Paup/D.Moore	.60	1.50
CP6 Fredrickson/C.Warren	.75	2.00
CP7 D.Walker/Parmalee	.60	1.50
CP8 D.Thomas/Frerotte	1.00	2.50
CP9 Nickerson/Rob.Smith	.75	2.00
CP10 R.White/D.Brown	1.00	2.50

1996 Stadium Club Cut Backs

This eight-card set was distributed in hobby only packs of Stadium Club Series I at the rate of 1:36, with a ratio of 1:12 in the hobby jumbo packs. The set features color action player photos of eight of the best running backs in the NFL and are printed on precisely-cut laser designed cards.

COMPLETE SET (8)	15.00	40.00
STATED ODDS 1:36 HOB, 1:12 JUM SER.1		
C1 Emmitt Smith	6.00	15.00
C2 Barry Sanders	6.00	15.00
C3 Curtis Martin	2.50	6.00
C4 Chris Warren	1.50	4.00
C5 Errict Rhett	1.50	4.00
C6 Rodney Hampton	1.50	4.00
C7 Ricky Watters	2.00	5.00
C8 Terry Allen	2.00	5.00

1996 Stadium Club Fusion

Randomly inserted in Stadium Club Series II hobby packs at a rate of one in 24, this 16-card set features color action player photos of havoc-wreaking teammates on laser-cut cards which when "fused" with the appropriate teammate card creates a larger image.

COMPLETE SET (16)	30.00	80.00
STATED ODDS 1:24 SER.2 HOBBY		
F1A Steve Young	2.50	6.00
F1B Jerry Rice	4.00	10.00
F2A Drew Bledsoe	1.50	4.00
F2B Curtis Martin	2.00	5.00
F3A Trent Dilfer	1.25	3.00
F3B Errict Rhett	1.25	3.00
F4A Jeff Hostetler	1.00	2.50
F4B Tim Brown	1.50	4.00
F5A Brett Favre	8.00	20.00
F5B Robert Brooks	1.25	3.00
F6A Jim Harbaugh	1.25	3.00
F6B Marshall Faulk	2.00	5.00
F7A Rashaan Salaam	1.25	3.00
F7B Erik Kramer	1.00	2.50
F8A Scott Mitchell	1.00	2.50
F8B Barry Sanders	5.00	12.00

1996 Stadium Club Laser Sites

Randomly inserted in Stadium Club Series one packs at the rate of one in 36, with an insertion rate of one in twelve hobby jumbo packs, this hobby-only set features color player photos of eight of the best quarterbacks printed on intricate laser cut designs with diffraction foil stamping.

COMPLETE SET (8)	15.00	40.00
STATED ODDS 1:36 HOB, 1:12 JUM SER.1		
LS1 Brett Favre	8.00	20.00
LS2 Dan Marino	6.00	15.00
LS3 Steve Young	2.50	6.00
LS4 Troy Aikman	3.00	8.00
LS5 Jim Harbaugh	1.25	3.00
LS6 Scott Mitchell	1.00	2.50
LS7 Erik Kramer	1.00	2.50
LS8 Warren Moon	1.50	4.00

1996 Stadium Club Namath Finest

Randomly inserted at the rate of 1:24 regular packs, and 1:8 jumbo packs in Stadium Club Series 1 cards, this 10-card set features reprints of Joe Namath Topps cards. The Finest Refractor version of this set was randomly inserted at the rate of one in 96 hobby, and 1:32 jumbo series 1 packs.

COMPLETE SET (10)	40.00	80.00
COMMON CARD (1-10)	4.00	10.00
STATED ODDS 1:24 HOB/RET, 1:8 JUM SER.1		
*REFRACTORS: .8X TO 2X BASIC INSERTS		
REF.STAT.ODDS 1:96 H/R, 1:32 JUM SER.1		
1 Joe Namath 1965	5.00	12.00

1996 Stadium Club New Age

Randomly inserted in series 2 hobby packs at a rate of 1:24, and retail series 2 packs at 1:32, this 20-card set features NFL draft picks and first-year rookies on an etched dot matrix card.

COMPLETE SET (20)	20.00	50.00
STATED ODDS 1:24 HOB, 1:32 RET SER.2		
NA1 Alex Van Dyke	.75	2.00
NA2 Lawrence Phillips	1.25	3.00
NA3 Tim Biakabutuka	1.00	2.50
NA4 Reggie Brown	.75	2.00
NA5 Duane Clemons	.75	2.00
NA6 Marco Battaglia	.75	2.00
NA7 Cedric Jones	.75	2.00
NA8 Jerome Woods	.75	2.00
NA9 Eric Moulds	1.25	3.00
NA10 Kevin Hardy	1.00	2.50
NA11 Rickey Dudley	.75	2.00
NA12 Regan Upshaw	.75	2.00
NA13 Eddie Kennison	1.00	2.50
NA14 Jonathan Ogden	3.00	8.00
NA15 John Mobley	.75	2.00
NA16 Mike Alstott	3.00	8.00
NA17 Alex Molden	.75	2.00
NA18 Marvin Harrison	4.00	10.00
NA19 Simeon Rice	1.50	4.00
NA20 Keyshawn Johnson	2.00	5.00

1996 Stadium Club Photo Gallery

Randomly inserted in series two hobby packs at a rate of 1:18, and at 1:24 in series two retail packs, this 21-card set features the league's top players. Printed on ultra-smooth cast-coated stock with an exclusive Topps high gloss laminate, each card displays a customized design that compliments the outstanding photography.

COMPLETE SET (21)	50.00	120.00
STATED ODDS 1:18 HOB, 1:24 RET SER.2		
PG1 Emmitt Smith	5.00	12.00
PG2 Jeff Blake	1.25	3.00
PG3 Junior Seau	1.25	3.00
PG4 Robert Brooks	1.25	3.00
PG5 Barry Sanders	5.00	12.00
PG6 Drew Bledsoe	1.50	4.00
PG7 Joey Galloway	1.25	3.00
PG8 Marshall Faulk	1.50	4.00
PG9 Mark Brunell	1.25	3.00
PG10 Jerry Rice	5.00	12.00
PG11 Rashaan Salaam	1.00	2.50
PG12 Troy Aikman	3.00	8.00
PG13 Steve Young	2.50	6.00
PG14 Tim Brown	1.25	3.00
PG15 Brett Favre	8.00	20.00
PG16 Kerry Collins	1.25	3.00
PG17 John Elway	5.00	12.00
PG18 Curtis Martin	2.50	6.00
PG19 Deion Sanders	2.00	5.00
PG20 Dan Marino	6.00	15.00
PG21 Chris Warren	1.00	2.50

1996 Stadium Club Pro Bowl

This 20 card standard-size set was inserted at a ratio of 1:24 series one retail packs. The front of the card has the players picture on a holographic enhanced silver foil background with the player's name on the bottom of the card.The back of the card has a color snapshot and biographical materials. The cards are numbered with a "PB" prefix.

COMPLETE SET (20)	40.00	100.00
STATED ODDS 1:24 RET. SER.1		
PB1 Brett Favre	8.00	20.00
PB2 Bruce Smith	1.50	4.00
PB3 Ricky Watters	1.25	3.00
PB4 Yancey Thigpen	1.00	2.50
PB5 Barry Sanders	5.00	12.00
PB6 Jim Harbaugh	1.25	3.00
PB7 Michael Irvin	2.00	5.00
PB8 Chris Warren	1.25	3.00
PB9 Dana Stubblefield	1.25	3.00
PB10 Jeff Blake	1.25	3.00
PB11 Emmitt Smith	6.00	15.00
PB12 Bryce Paup	1.00	2.50
PB13 Steve Young	2.50	6.00
PB14 Kevin Greene	1.00	2.50
PB15 Jerry Rice	5.00	12.00
PB16 Curtis Martin	2.50	6.00
PB17 Reggie White	1.50	4.00
PB18 Derrick Thomas	2.00	5.00
PB19 Cris Carter	1.50	4.00
PB20 Greg Lloyd	1.25	3.00

1996 Stadium Club Members Only Parallel

COMPLETE SET (476)	125.00	250.00
*1-360 VETS: 1.2X TO 3X BASIC CARDS		
*1-360 ROOKIES: .5X TO 1.2X BASIC RC		
*C1-C8 CUT BACKS: .1X TO .3X BASIC INSERT		
*F1-F8 FUSION: .1X TO .3X BASIC INSERT		
*N1-N10 NAMATH: .04X TO .1X BASIC INSERT		
*BY1-BY10 BRACE YS: .1X TO .3X BASIC INSERT		
*CP1-CP10 CONTACT: .3X TO .8X BASIC INSERT		
*NA1-NA20 NEW AGE: .1X TO .3X BASIC INSERT		
*PB1-PB20 PRO BOWL: .1X TO .3X BASIC INSERT		
*PG1-PG21 PHOTO: .15X TO .4X BASIC INSERT		
*LS1-LS8 LASER: .1X TO .3X BASIC INSERT		
351 Ray Lewis	10.00	25.00

1996 Stadium Club Members Only 50

Topps produced a 50-card boxed set for each of the four major sports again in 1996. With their club membership, members received one set of their choice and had the option of purchasing additional sets for $10.00 each. The set consists of 45 Stadium Club cards and five Finest styled cards. The fronts carry the distinctive Topps Stadium Club Members Only gold foil seal.

COMP.FACT SET (50)	6.00	15.00
1 Bruce Smith	.10	.30
2 Chester McGlockton	.07	.20
3 Dan Saleaumua	.07	.20
4 Neil Smith	.07	.20
5 Bryce Paup	.07	.20
6 Junior Seau	.20	.50
7 Greg Lloyd	.07	.20
8 Dale Carter	.07	.20
9 Terry McDaniel	.07	.20
10 Carnell Lake	.07	.20
11 Steve Atwater	.07	.20
12 Jerry Rice	.60	1.50
13 Lomas Brown	.07	.20
14 Nate Newton	.07	.20
15 Kevin Glover	.07	.20
16 Randall McDaniel	.07	.20
17 William Roaf	.07	.20
18 Mark Chmura	.07	.20
19 Herman Moore	.10	.30
20 Brett Favre	1.20	3.00
21 Emmitt Smith	1.00	2.50
22 Barry Sanders	1.20	3.00
23 Carl Pickens	.10	.30
24 Richmond Webb	.07	.20
25 Keith Sims	.07	.20
26 Dermontti Dawson	.15	.40
27 Steve Wisniewski	.07	.20
28 Bruce Armstrong	.07	.20
29 Ben Coates	.10	.30
30 Tim Brown	.20	.50
31 Jeff Blake	.20	.50
32 Marshall Faulk	.20	.50
33 Chris Warren	.10	.30
34 Reggie White	.20	.50
35 John Randle	.10	.30
36 Eric Swann	.07	.20
37 Charles Haley	.07	.20
38 Ken Harvey	.07	.20
39 Jessie Tuggle	.07	.20
40 Lee Woodall	.07	.20
41 Aeneas Williams	.07	.20
42 Eric Davis	.07	.20
43 Darren Woodson	.07	.20
44 Merton Hanks	.07	.20
45 Dan Marino	1.20	3.00
46 Kordell Stewart MC F	.80	2.00
47 Rashaan Salaam MC F	.10	.30
48 Joey Galloway MC F	.80	2.00
49 Kerry Collins MC F	.60	1.50
50 Curtis Martin MC F	1.00	2.50

1996 Stadium Club Sunday Night Redemption

Topps inserted Sunday Night Redemption cards randomly in 1996 Stadium Club series 1 packs (1:24 hobby and retail, 1:20 jumbo). Each card featured two numbers that were to be compared to the final scores of each week's NFL Sunday Night football game. Matching numbers (winning cards) were redeemable for two special jumbo (roughly 4" by 6") Finest cards featuring players that participated in that NFL game. The cards are arranged below in the order in which they were awarded each week. Note that there was no Sunday Night Football game in NFL Week 8. The contest expired 3/3/1997 and only the prize cards are listed below.

COMPLETE SET (32)	120.00	300.00
1A Rodney Hampton	1.60	4.00
1B Jim Kelly	3.20	8.00
2A Dan Marino	12.00	30.00
2B Frank Sanders	3.20	8.00
3A Trent Dilfer	2.40	6.00
3B John Elway	12.00	30.00
4A Eric Metcalf	1.60	4.00
4B Ricky Watters	2.40	6.00
5A Terry Allen	2.40	6.00
5B Keyshawn Johnson	8.00	20.00
6A Jeff Blake	3.20	8.00
6B Steve McNair	6.00	15.00
7A Marshall Faulk	4.00	10.00
7B Eric Zeier	1.60	4.00
9A Drew Bledsoe	6.00	15.00
9B Bruce Smith	2.40	6.00
10A Jim Everett	1.60	4.00
10B Steve Young	4.80	12.00
11A Dave Brown	1.60	4.00
11B Kerry Collins	4.00	10.00
12A Tim Brown	3.20	8.00
12B Cris Carter	3.20	8.00
13A Isaac Bruce	3.20	8.00
13B Brett Favre	12.00	30.00
14A Curtis Martin	6.00	15.00
14B Junior Seau	2.40	6.00
15A Warren Moon	3.20	8.00
15B Barry Sanders	12.00	30.00
16A Mark Brunell	6.00	15.00
16B Chris Warren	1.60	4.00
17A Terrell Davis	12.00	30.00
17B Stan Humphries	1.60	4.00

1997 Stadium Club Prototypes

P1 Junior Seau Prototype	.30	.75
P20 Curtis Martin Prototype	.40	1.00
P21 Deion Sanders Prototype	.50	1.25
P30 Kerry Collins Prototype	.20	.60
P47 Shannon Sharpe Prototype	.40	1.00
P84 Edgar Bennett Prototype	.20	.50

1997 Stadium Club

The 1997 Stadium Club was issued in two series of 170 cards each and was distributed in six-card retail packs with a suggested price of $2. Hobby packs contained nine cards with a price of $3.00. The Series 1 set consists of only the odd numbered cards while Series 2 consists of the even numbered ones. Six prototype cards were released for Series 1. These cards contain only very subtle differences versus the regular base cards. Most noteably they can be differentiated by the white line of text below the copyrights and licensing logos instead of above. Included in eight of every nine Series 2 packs was a Pro Bowl ballot which offered collectors a chance to win a grand prize of a trip to the Pro Bowl in Hawaii. One hundred runners up could win an uncut sheet of Stadium Club Football Series 2 with the official Pro Bowl logo stamped on it. A checklist for Stadium Club Series 2 was included in every ninth pack.

COMPLETE SET (340)	25.00	60.00
COMP.SERIES 1 (170)	15.00	30.00
COMP.SERIES 2 (170)	15.00	30.00
1 Junior Seau	.30	.75
2 Michael Irvin	.30	.75
3 Marcus Allen	.30	.75
4 Dale Carter	.10	.30
5 Darnell Autry RC	.20	.50
6 Isaac Bruce	.30	.75
7 Darrell Green	.20	.50
8 Joey Galloway	.20	.50
9 Steve Atwater	.10	.30
10 Kordell Stewart	.30	.75
11 Tony Brackens	.10	.30
12 Gus Frerotte	.10	.30
13 Henry Ellard	.10	.30
14 Charles Way	.20	.50
15 Jim Druckenmiller RC	.20	.50
16 Orlando Thomas	.10	.30
17 Terrell Davis	.40	1.00
18 Jim Schwantz	.10	.30
19 Derrick Thomas	.30	.75
20 Curtis Martin	.40	1.00
21 Deion Sanders	.30	.75
22 Bruce Smith	.20	.50
23 Jake Reed	.20	.50
24 Leeland McElroy	.10	.30
25 Jerome Bettis	.30	.75
26 Neil Smith	.20	.50
27 Terry Allen	.30	.75
28 Gilbert Brown	.20	.50
29 Steve McNair	.40	1.00
30 Kerry Collins	.30	.75
31 Thurman Thomas	.30	.75
32 Kenny Holmes RC	.30	.75
33 Karim Abdul-Jabbar	.30	.75
34 Steve Young	.40	1.00
35 Jerry Rice	.60	1.50
36 Jeff George	.20	.50
37 Errict Rhett	.10	.30
38 Mike Alstott	.30	.75
39 Tim Brown	.30	.75
40 Keyshawn Johnson	.30	.75
41 Jim Harbaugh	.20	.50
42 Kevin Hardy	.10	.30
43 Kevin Greene	.20	.50
44 Eric Metcalf	.20	.50
45 Troy Aikman	.60	1.50
46 Marshall Faulk	.40	1.00
47 Shannon Sharpe	.20	.50
48 Warren Moon	.30	.75
49 Mark Brunell	.40	1.00
50 Dan Marino	1.25	3.00
51 Byron Hanspard RC	.20	.50
52 Chris Chandler	.20	.50
53 Wayne Chrebet	.30	.75
54 Antonio Langham	.10	.30
55 Barry Sanders	1.00	2.50
56 Curtis Conway	.20	.50
57 Ricky Watters	.20	.50
58 William Thomas	.10	.30
59 Chris Warren	.20	.50
60 Terry Glenn	.30	.75
61 Peter Boulware RC	.30	.75
62 Chad Cota	.10	.30
63 Eddie Kennison	.20	.50
64 Lamar Smith	.30	.75
65 Brett Favre	1.50	3.00
66 Michael Westbrook	.20	.50
67 Larry Centers	.20	.50
68 Trent Dilfer	.30	.75
69 Stevon Moore	.10	.30
70 John Elway	1.25	3.00
71 Bryce Paup	.10	.30
72 Quentin Coryatt	.10	.30
73 Rashaan Salaam	.10	.30
74 Thomas Lewis	.10	.30
75 Drew Bledsoe	.40	1.00
76 Cris Carter	.30	.75
77 Joe Bowden	.10	.30
78 Allen Aldridge	.10	.30
79 Zach Thomas	.30	.75
80 Emmitt Smith	1.00	2.50
81 Daryl Johnston	.20	.50
82 Vinny Testaverde	.20	.50
83 James O.Stewart	.20	.50
84 Edgar Bennett	.20	.50
85 Shawn Springs RC	.20	.50
86 Elvis Grbac	.20	.50
87 Levon Kirkland	.10	.30
88 Jeff Graham	.10	.30
89 Terrell Fletcher	.10	.30
90 Eddie George	.30	.75
91 Jessie Tuggle	.10	.30
92 Terrell Owens	.40	1.00
93 Wayne Martin	.10	.30
94 Dwayne Harper	.10	.30
95 Mark Collins	.10	.30
96 Marvcus Patton	.10	.30
97 Napoleon Kaufman	.30	.75
98 Keenan McCardell	.20	.50
99 Ty Detmer	.20	.50
100 Reggie White	.30	.75
101 William Floyd	.20	.50
102 Scott Mitchell	.20	.50
103 Robert Blackmon	.10	.30
104 Dan Wilkinson	.10	.30
105 Warren Sapp	.20	.50
106 Dave Meggett	.10	.30
107 Brian Mitchell	.10	.30
108 Tyrone Poole	.10	.30
109 Derrick Alexander WR	.20	.50
110 David Palmer	.10	.30
111 James Farrior RC	.30	.75
112 Chad Brown	.10	.30
113 Marty Carter	.10	.30
114 Lawrence Phillips	.10	.30
115 Wesley Walls	.20	.50
116 John Friesz	.10	.30
117 Roman Phifer	.10	.30
118 Jason Sehorn	.20	.50
119 Henry Thomas	.10	.30
120 Natrone Means	.20	.50
121 Ty Law	.20	.50
122 Tony Gonzalez RC	1.50	4.00
123 Kevin Williams	.10	.30
124 Regan Upshaw	.10	.30
125 Antonio Freeman	.30	.75
126 Jessie Armstead	.10	.30
127 Pat Barnes RC	.30	.75
128 Charlie Garner	.20	.50
129 Irving Fryar	.20	.50
130 Rickey Dudley	.20	.50
131 Rodney Harrison RC	.60	1.50
132 Brent Jones	.20	.50
133 Neil O'Donnell	.20	.50
134 Darryll Lewis	.10	.30
135 Jason Belser	.10	.30
136 Mark Chmura	.20	.50
137 Seth Joyner	.10	.30
138 Herschel Walker	.20	.50
139 Santana Dotson	.10	.30
140 Carl Pickens	.20	.50
141 Terance Mathis	.20	.50
142 Walt Harris	.10	.30
143 John Mobley	.10	.30
144 Gabe Northern	.10	.30
145 Herman Moore	.20	.50
146 Michael Jackson	.20	.50
147 Chris Sanders	.10	.30
148 LeShon Johnson	.10	.30
149 Darrell Russell RC	.10	.30
150 Winslow Oliver	.10	.30
151 Tamarick Vanover	.20	.50
152 Tony Martin	.20	.50
153 Lamar Lathon	.10	.30
154 Ray Mickens	.10	.30
155 Derrick Brooks	.30	.75
156 Warrick Dunn RC	1.25	3.00
157 Tim McDonald	.10	.30
158 Keith Lyle	.10	.30
159 Terry McDaniel	.10	.30
160 Andre Hastings	.10	.30
161 Phillippi Sparks	.10	.30
162 Tedy Bruschi	.60	1.50
163 Bryant Westbrook RC	.10	.30
164 Victor Green	.10	.30
165 Jimmy Smith	.20	.50
166 Greg Biekert	.10	.30
167 Frank Sanders	.20	.50
168 Chris Doleman	.10	.30
169 Phil Hansen	.10	.30
170 Walter Jones RC	.50	1.25
171 Mark Carrier WR	.10	.30
172 Greg Hill	.10	.30
173 Erik Kramer	.10	.30
174 Chris Spielman	.10	.30
175 Tom Knight RC	.10	.30
176 Sam Mills	.10	.30
177 Robert Smith	.20	.50
178 Dorsey Levens	.30	.75
179 Chris Slade	.10	.30
180 Troy Vincent	.10	.30
181 Mario Bates	.10	.30
182 Ed McCaffrey	.20	.50
183 Mike Mamula	.10	.30
184 Chad Hennings	.10	.30
185 Stan Humphries	.20	.50
186 Reinard Wilson RC	.20	.50
187 Kevin Carter	.10	.30
188 Qadry Ismail	.20	.50
189 Cortez Kennedy	.10	.30
190 Eric Swann	.10	.30
191 Corey Dillon RC	1.50	4.00
192 Renaldo Wynn	.10	.30
193 Bobby Hebert	.10	.30
194 Fred Barnett	.10	.30
195 Ray Lewis	.50	1.25
196 Robert Jones	.10	.30
197 Brian Williams	.10	.30
198 Willie McGinest	.10	.30
199 Jake Plummer RC	1.50	4.00
200 Aeneas Williams	.10	.30
201 Ashley Ambrose	.10	.30
202 Cornelius Bennett	.10	.30
203 Mo Lewis	.10	.30
204 James Hasty	.10	.30
205 Carnell Lake	.10	.30
206 Heath Shuler	.10	.30
207 Dana Stubblefield	.10	.30
208 Corey Miller	.10	.30
209 Ike Hilliard RC	.50	1.25
210 Bryant Young	.10	.30
211 Hardy Nickerson	.10	.30
212 Blaine Bishop	.10	.30
213 Marcus Robertson	.10	.30
214 Tony Bennett	.10	.30
215 Kent Graham	.10	.30
216 Steve Bono	.20	.50
217 Will Blackwell RC	.20	.50
218 Tyrone Braxton	.10	.30
219 Eric Moulds	.30	.75
220 Rod Woodson	.20	.50
221 Anthony Johnson	.10	.30
222 Willie Davis	.10	.30
223 Darrin Smith	.10	.30
224 Rick Mirer	.10	.30
225 Marvin Harrison	.30	.75
226 Terrell Buckley	.10	.30
227 Joe Aska	.10	.30
228 Yatil Green RC	.20	.50
229 William Fuller	.10	.30
230 Eddie Robinson	.10	.30
231 Brian Blades	.10	.30
232 Michael Sinclair	.10	.30
233 Ken Harvey	.10	.30
234 Harvey Williams	.10	.30
235 Simeon Rice	.20	.50
236 Chris T. Jones	.10	.30
237 Bert Emanuel	.20	.50
238 Corey Sawyer	.10	.30
239 Chris Calloway	.10	.30
240 Jeff Blake	.20	.50
241 Alonzo Spellman	.10	.30
242 Bryan Cox	.10	.30
243 Antowain Smith RC	1.00	2.50
244 Tim Biakabutuka	.20	.50
245 Ray Crockett	.10	.30
246 Dwayne Rudd	.10	.30
247 Glyn Milburn	.10	.30
248 Gary Plummer	.10	.30
249 O.J. McDuffie	.20	.50
250 Willie Clay	.10	.30
251 Jim Everett	.10	.30
252 Eugene Daniel	.10	.30
253 Corey Widmer	.10	.30
254 Mel Gray	.10	.30
255 Ken Norton	.10	.30
256 Johnnie Morton	.20	.50
257 Courtney Hawkins	.10	.30
258 Ricardo McDonald	.10	.30
259 Todd Lyght	.10	.30
260 Micheal Barrow	.10	.30
261 Aaron Glenn	.10	.30
262 Jeff Herrod	.10	.30
263 Troy Davis RC	.20	.50
264 Eric Hill	.10	.30
265 Darrien Gordon	.10	.30
266 Lake Dawson	.10	.30
267 John Randle	.20	.50
268 Henry Jones	.10	.30
269 Mickey Washington	.10	.30
270 Amani Toomer	.20	.50
271 Steve Grant	.10	.30
272 Adrian Murrell	.20	.50
273 Derrick Witherspoon	.10	.30
274 Albert Lewis	.10	.30
275 Ben Coates	.20	.50
276 Reidel Anthony RC	.30	.75
277 Jim Schwantz	.10	.30
278 Aaron Hayden	.10	.30
279 Ryan McNeil	.10	.30
280 LeRoy Butler	.10	.30
281 Craig Newsome	.10	.30
282 Bill Romanowski	.10	.30
283 Michael Bankston	.10	.30
284 Kevin Smith	.10	.30
285 Byron Bam Morris	.10	.30
286 Darnay Scott	.20	.50
287 David LaFleur RC	.10	.30
288 Randall Cunningham	.30	.75
289 Eric Davis	.10	.30
290 Todd Collins	.10	.30
291 Steve Tovar	.10	.30
292 Jermaine Lewis	.30	.75
293 Alfred Williams	.10	.30
294 Brad Johnson	.30	.75
295 Charles Johnson	.20	.50
296 Ted Johnson	.10	.30
297 Merton Hanks	.10	.30
298 Andre Coleman	.10	.30
299 Keith Jackson	.10	.30
300 Terry Kirby	.20	.50
301 Tony Banks	.20	.50
302 Terrance Shaw	.10	.30
303 Bobby Engram	.20	.50
304 Hugh Douglas	.10	.30
305 Lawyer Milloy	.20	.50
306 James Jett	.20	.50
307 Joey Kent RC	.30	.75
308 Rodney Hampton	.20	.50
309 Dewayne Washington	.10	.30
310 Kevin Lockett RC	.20	.50
311 Ki-Jana Carter	.10	.30
312 Jeff Lageman	.10	.30
313 Don Beebe	.10	.30
314 Willie Williams	.10	.30
315 Tyrone Wheatley	.20	.50
316 Leslie O'Neal	.10	.30
317 Quinn Early	.10	.30
318 Sean Gilbert	.10	.30
319 Tim Bowens	.10	.30
320 Sean Dawkins	.10	.30
321 Ken Dilger	.10	.30
322 George Koonce	.10	.30
323 Jevon Langford	.10	.30
324 Mike Caldwell	.10	.30
325 Orlando Pace RC	.30	.75
326 Garrison Hearst	.20	.50
327 Mike Tomczak	.10	.30
328 Rob Moore	.20	.50
329 Andre Reed	.20	.50
330 Kimble Anders	.20	.50
331 Qadry Ismail	.20	.50
332 Eric Allen	.10	.30
333 Dave Brown	.10	.30
334 Bennie Blades	.10	.30
335 Jamal Anderson	.30	.75
336 John Lynch	.20	.50
337 Tyrone Hughes	.10	.30
338 Ronnie Harmon	.10	.30
339 Rae Carruth RC	.10	.30
340 Robert Brooks	.20	.50
CL1 Checklist Card 1	.05	.15
CL2 Checklist Card 2	.05	.15
CL3H Checklist Card co-signers	.05	.15
CL4H Checklist Card inserts	.05	.15

1997 Stadium Club First Day

*STARS: 6X TO 15X BASIC CARDS
*RCs: 3X TO 8X BASIC CARDS
STATED ODDS 1:24 RETAIL

1997 Stadium Club One of a Kind

*VETS: 12X TO 30X BASIC CARDS
*ROOKIE STARS: 8X TO 20X BASIC RC
STATED ODDS 1:48 HOB/RET, 1:30 JUM

1997 Stadium Club Aerial Assault

Randomly inserted in Series 1 hobby and retail packs at a rate of 1:12 (1:4 jumbo), this 10-card set features color images of star quarterbacks on a background of a map of the United States and printed on high quality card stock.

COMPLETE SET (10)	20.00	50.00
STATED ODDS 1:12 HOB/RET, 1:4 JUM		
AA1 Dan Marino	5.00	12.00
AA2 Mark Brunell	1.50	4.00
AA3 Troy Aikman	2.50	6.00
AA4 Ty Detmer	.75	2.00
AA5 John Elway	5.00	12.00
AA6 Drew Bledsoe	1.50	4.00
AA7 Steve Young	1.50	4.00
AA8 Vinny Testaverde	.75	2.00
AA9 Kerry Collins	1.25	3.00
AA10 Brett Favre	5.00	12.00

1997 Stadium Club Bowman's Best Previews

Randomly inserted in Series one hobby and retail packs at a rate of one in 24 (1:8 jumbo), this 15-card set features a preview look at the 1997 Bowman's Best set. Refractor (1:96 hobby and retail packs, 1:32 jumbo) and Atomic Refractor (1:192 packs, 1:64 jumbo) parallels were also produced.

COMPLETE SET (15)	40.00	80.00
STATED ODDS 1:24 HOB/RET, 1:8 JUM		
*REFRACTOR: 1X TO 2.5X BASIC INSERT		
REFRACTOR STATED ODDS 1:96		
*ATOMIC REF: 1.5X TO 4X BASIC INSERT		
ATOMIC REFRACTOR ODDS 1:192		
BBP1 Dan Marino	6.00	15.00
BBP2 Terry Allen	1.50	4.00
BBP3 Jerome Bettis	2.00	5.00
BBP4 Kevin Greene	1.50	4.00
BBP5 Junior Seau	2.00	5.00
BBP6 Brett Favre	6.00	15.00
BBP7 Isaac Bruce	2.00	5.00
BBP8 Michael Irvin	2.00	5.00
BBP9 Kerry Collins	2.00	5.00
BBP10 Karim Abdul-Jabbar	1.50	4.00
BBP11 Keenan McCardell	1.50	4.00
BBP12 Ricky Watters	1.50	4.00
BBP13 Mark Brunell	2.00	5.00
BBP14 Jerry Rice	4.00	10.00
BBP15 Drew Bledsoe	2.00	5.00

1997 Stadium Club Bowman's Best Rookie Previews

Randomly inserted in Series two packs at the rate of one in 24, this 15-card set features color photos of the top rookies printed on chromium card stock. Refractor (1:96 packs) and Atomic Refractor (1:192 packs) parallels were also produced.

COMPLETE SET (15)	20.00	40.00
STATED ODDS 1:24		
*REFRACTOR: 1X TO 2.5X BASIC INSERT		
REFRACTOR STATED ODDS 1:96		
*ATOMIC REF: 2X TO 5X BASIC INSERT		
ATOMIC REFRACTOR ODDS 1:192		
BBP1 Orlando Pace	1.50	4.00
BBP2 David LaFleur	.60	2.50
BBP3 James Farrior	1.50	4.00
BBP4 Tony Gonzalez	5.00	12.00
BBP5 Ike Hilliard	1.50	4.00
BBP6 Antowain Smith	2.50	6.00
BBP7 Tom Knight	.60	2.50
BBP8 Troy Davis	1.00	3.00
BBP9 Yatil Green	1.00	3.00
BBP10 Jim Druckenmiller	1.00	3.00
BBP11 Bryant Westbrook	.60	2.50
BBP12 Darrell Russell	.60	2.50
BBP13 Rae Carruth	.60	2.50
BBP14 Shawn Springs	1.00	3.00
BBP15 Peter Boulware	1.50	4.00

1997 Stadium Club Co-Signers

Randomly inserted in Series I hobby only packs at the rate of one in 63 and Series 2 hobby only packs at the rate of one in 68, this set features color player photos on double-sided cards printed on rainbow foilboard and featuring autographs of top players with the certified autograph stamp.

SERIES 1 OVERALL STATED ODDS 1:63		
SERIES 2 OVERALL STATED ODDS 1:68		
CO1 Abdul-Jab/E.George	100.00	200.00
CO2 T.Armstrong/A.Spellman	12.50	30.00
CO3 S.Atwater/K.Hardy	12.50	30.00
CO4 F.Barnett/L.Dawson	15.00	40.00
CO5 B.Bishop/D.Green	20.00	50.00
CO6 J.Blake/G.Frerotte	50.00	100.00
CO7 S.Bono/C.Carter	50.00	100.00
CO8 T.Brown/I.Bruce	50.00	100.00
CO9 W.Chrebet/M.Washington	12.50	30.00
CO10 C.Conway/E.Kennison	12.50	30.00
CO11 E.Davis/J.Sehorn	15.00	40.00
CO12 T.Davis/T.Thomas	50.00	100.00
CO13 K.Dilger/K.Graham	15.00	40.00
CO14 S.Grant/M.Patton	12.50	30.00
CO15 K.Hamilton/M.Tomczak	12.50	30.00
CO16 R.Hampton/D.Meggett	20.00	50.00
CO17 M.Hanks/A.Williams	12.50	30.00
CO19 B.Jones/W.Walls	12.50	30.00
CO20 C.Lake/T.McDonald	12.50	30.00
CO21 T.Lewis/K.Lyle	12.50	30.00
CO22 L.McElroy/J.Lageman	12.50	30.00
CO23 R.Mickens/W.Davis	12.50	30.00
CO24 H.Moore/D.Howard	12.50	30.00
CO25 S.Moore/W.Thomas	12.50	30.00
CO26 A.Murrell/L.Kirkland	12.50	30.00
CO27 S.Rice/W.Oliver	15.00	40.00
CO28 B.Romanowski/G.Plummer	12.50	30.00
CO29 J.Seau/C.Spielman	30.00	60.00
CO30 C.Slade/K.Greene	12.50	30.00
CO31 D.Thomas/C.Jones	60.00	100.00
CO32 O.Thomas/B.Engram	15.00	40.00
CO33 A.Toomer/T.Randolph	20.00	50.00
CO34 S.Tovar/E.Johnson	12.50	30.00
CO35 H.Walker/A.Johnson	20.00	50.00
CO36 D.Woodson/A.Glenn	20.00	50.00
CO37 Abdul-Jabbar/T.Thomas	40.00	80.00
CO38 B.Bishop/T.McDonald	12.50	30.00
CO39 J.Blake/D.Thomas	60.00	120.00
CO41 C.Carter/M.Harrison	60.00	120.00
CO42 C.Conway/W.Walls	12.50	30.00
CO43 W.Davis/A.Toomer	15.00	40.00
CO44 L.Dawson/R.Mickens	10.00	25.00
CO45 K.Dilger/E.Johnson	12.50	30.00
CO46 B.Engram/T.Lewis	12.50	30.00
CO47 G.Frerotte/C.T.Jones	20.00	50.00
CO48 E.George/T.Davis	50.00	100.00
CO49 A.Glenn/E.Davis	12.50	30.00
CO50 K.Graham/S.Tovar	10.00	25.00
CO51 D.Green/C.Lake	25.00	50.00
CO52 K.Greene/S.Atwater	12.50	30.00
CO53 R.Hampton/A.Johnson	15.00	40.00
CO54 K.Hardy/M.Hanks	12.50	30.00
CO55 D.Howard/T.Brown	40.00	80.00
CO56 E.Kennison/B.Jones	12.50	20.00
CO57 L.Kirkland/S.Rice	12.50	30.00
CO58 J.Lageman/A.Murrell	10.00	25.00
CO59 K.Lyle/W.Chrebet	15.00	40.00
CO60 D.Meggett/H.Walker	15.00	40.00
CO61 H.Moore/I.Bruce	40.00	80.00
CO62 W.Oliver/L.McElroy	10.00	25.00
CO63 M.Patton/K.Hamilton	10.00	25.00
CO64 G.Plummer/J.Seau	30.00	60.00
CO65 T.Randolph/F.Barnett	10.00	25.00
CO66 A.Spellman/S.Grant	10.00	25.00
CO67 C.Spielman/S.Moore	10.00	25.00
CO68 W.Thomas/B.Romanowski	12.50	30.00
CO69 M.Tomczak/T.Armstrong	10.00	25.00
CO70 M.Washington/O.Thomas	10.00	25.00
CO71 A.Williams/C.Slade	12.50	30.00
CO72 D.Woodson/J.Sehorn	15.00	40.00
CO73 T.Armstrong/K.Hamilton	6.00	15.00
CO74 S.Atwater/C.Slade	6.00	15.00
CO75 F.Barnett/A.Toomer	10.00	25.00
CO76 T.Brown/H.Moore	20.00	50.00
CO77 I.Bruce/D.Howard	25.00	60.00
CO78 W.Chrebet/T.Lewis	10.00	25.00
CO79 E.Davis/D.Woodson	8.00	20.00
CO80 T.Davis/Abdul-Jabbar	15.00	40.00
CO81 W.Davis/L.Dawson	8.00	20.00
CO82 B.Engram/M.Washington	6.00	15.00
CO83 S.Grant/M.Tomczak	6.00	15.00
CO84 M.Hanks/K.Greene	8.00	20.00
CO85 M.Harrison/S.Bono	15.00	40.00
CO86 A.Johnson/D.Meggett	6.00	15.00
CO87 E.Johnson LB/K.Graham	6.00	15.00
CO88 B.Jones/C.Conway	10.00	25.00
CO89 C.T.Jones/J.Blake	10.00	25.00
CO90 C.Lake/B.Bishop	6.00	15.00
CO91 T.McDonald/D.Green	25.00	50.00
CO92 R.Mickens/T.Randolph	6.00	15.00
CO93 S.Moore/G.Plummer	6.00	15.00
CO94 A.Murrell/L.McElroy	6.00	15.00
CO95 W.Oliver/L.Kirkland	6.00	15.00
CO96 M.Patton/A.Spellman	6.00	15.00
CO98 S.Rice/J.Lageman	10.00	25.00
CO99 J.Seau/B.Romanowski	30.00	60.00

CO100 J.Sehorn/A.Glenn 8.00 20.00
CO101 D.Thomas/G.Frerotte 60.00 120.00
CO102 O.Thomas/K.Lyle 6.00 15.00
CO103 T.Thomas/E.George 30.00 80.00
CO104 W.Thomas/C.Spielman 6.00 15.00
CO105 S.Tovar/K.Dilger 6.00 15.00
CO106 H.Walker/R.Hampton 12.00 30.00
CO107 W.Walls/E.Kennison 15.00 30.00
CO108 A.Williams/K.Hardy 8.00 20.00

1997 Stadium Club Grid Kids

Randomly inserted in Series 1 packs at a rate of one in 36 (1:12 jumbo), this 20-card set features color photos of 1997 top draft picks in their NFL game uniforms.

COMPLETE SET (20) 30.00 60.00
STATED ODDS 1:36 HOB/RET, 1:12 JUM
GK1 Orlando Pace 1.25 3.00
GK2 Darrell Russell .50 1.25
GK3 Shawn Springs .75 2.00
GK4 Peter Boulware 1.25 3.00
GK5 Bryant Westbrook .50 1.25
GK6 Darnell Autry .75 2.00
GK7 Ike Hilliard 2.00 5.00
GK8 James Farrior 1.25 3.00
GK9 Jake Plummer 6.00 15.00
GK10 Tony Gonzalez 6.00 15.00
GK11 Yatil Green .75 2.00
GK12 Corey Dillon 6.00 15.00
GK13 Dwayne Rudd .50 1.25
GK14 Renaldo Wynn .50 1.25
GK15 David LaFleur .50 1.25
GK16 Antowain Smith 4.00 10.00
GK17 Jim Druckenmiller .75 2.00
GK18 Rae Carruth .50 1.25
GK19 Tom Knight .50 1.25
GK20 Byron Hanspard .75 2.00

1997 Stadium Club Never Compromise

Randomly inserted in Series 2 packs at the rate of one in 12, this 40-card set features color action photos of 10 top veterans and 30 top rookies.

COMPLETE SET (40) 60.00 150.00
STATED ODDS 1:12 SERIES 2
NC1 Orlando Pace 1.50 4.00
NC2 Corey Dillon 2.50 6.00
NC3 Tony Gonzalez 3.00 8.00
NC4 Tom Knight .75 2.00
NC5 Deion Sanders 2.00 5.00
NC6 Dwayne Rudd 1.25 3.00
NC7 Warrick Dunn 2.50 6.00
NC8 Kenny Holmes 1.25 3.00
NC9 Will Blackwell 1.25 3.00
NC10 Shawn Springs 1.25 3.00
NC11 Rae Carruth .75 2.00
NC12 Edgar Bennett 1.50 4.00
NC13 Walter Jones 2.00 5.00
NC14 Reidel Anthony 1.25 3.00
NC15 Troy Davis 1.25 3.00
NC16 Mark Brunell 1.50 4.00
NC17 Pat Barnes 1.25 3.00
NC18 Reggie White 1.50 4.00
NC19 Darrell Russell .75 2.00
NC20 Ike Hilliard 1.50 4.00
NC21 Emmitt Smith 4.00 10.00
NC22 David LaFleur .75 2.00
NC23 Yatil Green .75 2.00
NC24 Barry Sanders 4.00 10.00
NC25 Bryant Westbrook .75 2.00
NC26 Lawrence Phillips 1.25 3.00
NC27 Peter Boulware 1.50 4.00
NC28 Joey Kent .75 2.00
NC29 Kevin Lockett .75 2.00
NC30 Derrick Thomas 1.50 4.00
NC31 Antowain Smith 2.00 5.00
NC32 James Farrior 1.50 4.00
NC33 Kordell Stewart 1.50 4.00
NC34 Byron Hanspard 1.25 3.00
NC35 Jim Druckenmiller 1.25 3.00
NC36 Reinard Wilson 1.25 3.00
NC37 Darnell Autry 1.25 3.00
NC38 Steve Young 2.50 6.00
NC39 Renaldo Wynn .75 2.00
NC40 Jake Plummer 2.50 6.00

1997 Stadium Club Offensive Strikes

Randomly inserted in Series 1 hobby and retail packs at a rate of one in 12 (1:4 jumbo), this 10-card set was divided into two subsets: Ground Control running backs (GC1-GC5) and five Air Force wide receivers (AF1-AF5). The cards were printed on borderless foilboard stock.

COMPLETE SET (10) 10.00 25.00
STATED ODDS 1:12 HOBY/RET, 1:4 JUM
AF1 Jerry Rice 2.00 5.00
AF2 Carl Pickens UER .60 1.50
AF3 Shannon Sharpe .60 1.50
AF4 Herman Moore .60 1.50
AF5 Terry Glenn 1.00 2.50
GC1 Barry Sanders 3.00 8.00
GC2 Curtis Martin 1.25 3.00
GC3 Emmitt Smith 3.00 8.00
GC4 Terrell Davis 1.25 3.00
GC5 Eddie George 1.00 2.50

1997 Stadium Club Triumvirate I

Randomly inserted in Series one retail packs at a rate of one in 36, this 36-card set features color player photos on the first-ever laser-cut chromium cards. Three players from selected NFL teams were chosen and the cards can be interlinked using the complex die cut pattern. Refractor (1:144 packs) and Atomic Refractor (1:288) parallels were also produced of each card.

COMP.SERIES 1 SET (18) 60.00 120.00
STATED ODDS 1:36 SER.1 RETAIL
*REFRACTORS: .8X TO 2X BASIC INSERTS
REFRACTOR STATED ODDS 1:144
*ATOMIC REF: 1.2X TO 3X BASIC INSERTS
ATOMIC REF.STATED ODDS 1:288
T1A Emmitt Smith 6.00 15.00
T1B Troy Aikman 4.00 10.00
T1C Michael Irvin 2.00 5.00
T2A Curtis Martin 2.50 6.00
T2B Drew Bledsoe 2.50 6.00
T2C Terry Glenn 2.00 5.00
T3A Barry Sanders 6.00 15.00
T3B Scott Mitchell 1.25 3.00
T3C Herman Moore 1.25 3.00
T4A William Floyd 1.25 3.00
T4B Steve Young 2.50 6.00
T4C Jerry Rice 4.00 10.00
T5A Terrell Davis 2.50 6.00
T5B John Elway 8.00 20.00
T5C Shannon Sharpe 1.25 3.00
T6A Edgar Bennett 1.25 3.00
T6B Brett Favre 8.00 20.00
T6C Antonio Freeman 2.00 5.00

1997 Stadium Club Triumvirate II

Randomly inserted in Series two retail only packs at a rate of one in 36, this 36-card set features color player photos on the first-ever laser-cut chromium cards. Three players from selected NFL teams were chosen and the cards can be interlinked using the complex die cut pattern. Refractor (1:144 packs) and Atomic Refractor (1:288) parallels were also produced of each card.

COMP.SERIES 2 SET (18) 75.00 150.00
STATED ODDS 1:36 SER.2 RETAIL
*REFRACTOR: .8X TO 2X BASIC INSERTS
REFRACTOR STATED ODDS 1:144
*ATOMIC REF: 1.2X TO 3X BASIC INSERTS
ATOMIC REF.STATED ODDS 1:288
T1A John Elway 8.00 20.00
T1B Drew Bledsoe 2.50 6.00
T1C Dan Marino 8.00 20.00
T2A Troy Aikman 4.00 10.00
T2B Brett Favre 8.00 20.00
T2C Steve Young 2.50 6.00
T3A Terrell Davis 2.50 6.00
T3B Eddie George 2.00 5.00
T3C Curtis Martin 2.50 6.00
T4A Emmitt Smith 6.00 15.00
T4B Ricky Watters 1.25 3.00
T4C Barry Sanders 6.00 15.00
T5A Peter Boulware .75 2.00
T5B Shawn Springs .75 2.00
T5C Tony Gonzalez 2.50 6.00
T6A Jake Plummer 2.50 6.00
T6B Orlando Pace .75 2.00
T6C Jim Druckenmiller .75 2.00

1997 Stadium Club Members Only Parallel

COMPLETE SET (486) 125.00 250.00
*1-340 VETS: 1.2X TO 3X BASIC CARDS
*1-340 ROOKIE STARS: .8X TO 2X
*TRIUMVIRATE 1: .2X TO .5X BASIC INSERTS
*TRIUMVIRATE 2: .2X TO .5X BASIC INSERTS
*AERIAL ASSAULT: .3X TO .8X BASIC INSERTS
*OFFEN.STRIKES: .4X TO 1X BASIC INSERTS
*GRID KIDS: .3X TO .8X BASIC INSERTS
*NEVER COMPROM: .3X TO .8X BASIC INSERTS
*BOW.BEST: .25X TO .6X BASIC INSERTS
*BOW.BEST ROOKIES: .25X TO .6X BASIC INSERTS

1997 Stadium Club Members Only 55

This 55-card 1997 Stadium Club Members Only set reflects Topps' selection of the 50 top NFL players. The five Finest-quality cards (51-55) represent Topps' selection of the top rookies from 1996. The fronts feature color action player photos with gold foil highlights including the "Members Only" seal. The backs carry player information.

COMP.FACT SET (55) 6.00 15.00
1 Brett Favre 1.20 3.00
2 Lamar Lathon .07 .20
3 Derrick Thomas .10 .30
4 Rod Woodson .10 .30
5 Dan Marino 1.20 3.00
6 Ashley Ambrose .07 .20
7 Herman Moore .10 .30
8 Larry Centers .10 .30
9 Cris Carter .20 .50
10 Jerry Rice .60 1.50
11 Hardy Nickerson .07 .20
12 Darrell Green .07 .20
13 Tim Brown .20 .50
14 Terrell Davis 1.00 2.50
15 Curtis Martin .40 1.00
16 Carl Pickens .10 .30
17 Darren Woodson .07 .20
18 Wesley Walls .10 .30
19 David Meggett .07 .20
20 Junior Seau .10 .30
21 Merton Hanks .07 .20
22 Terry Allen .10 .30
23 Keenan McCardell .10 .30
24 Shannon Sharpe .10 .30
25 Reggie White .20 .50
26 Chad Brown .07 .20
27 Aeneas Williams .07 .20
28 Vinny Testaverde .10 .30
29 Rickey Watters .07 .20
30 Drew Bledsoe .50 1.25
31 Kevin Greene .10 .30
32 Tony Martin .10 .30
33 Ben Coates .10 .30
34 Isaac Bruce .20 .50
35 Troy Aikman .60 1.50
36 LeRoy Butler .07 .20
37 Kimble Anders .10 .30
38 Levon Kirkland .07 .20
39 Willie McGinest .07 .20
40 Barry Sanders 1.20 3.00
41 Eric Davis .07 .20
42 Gus Frerotte .10 .30
43 Jerome Bettis .20 .50
44 Steve Young .50 1.25
45 Emmitt Smith 1.00 2.50
46 Sam Mills .07 .20
47 Mark Brunell .50 1.25
48 Kerry Collins .20 .50
49 Deion Sanders .40 1.00
50 John Elway 1.20 3.00
51 Keyshawn Johnson FIN .40 1.00
52 Terry Glenn FIN .20 .50
53 Eddie Kennison FIN .20 .50
54 Karim Abdul-Jabbar FIN .10 .30
55 Eddie George FIN .60 1.50

1998 Stadium Club Promos

COMPLETE SET (5) 3.00 8.00
PP2 Michael Jackson .40 1.00
PP3 John Elway 2.00 4.00
PP4 Warrick Dunn .50 1.25
PP5 Chris Slade .40 1.00
PP6 Darrell Green .60 1.50

1998 Stadium Club

The 1998 Stadium Club Set was issued with a total of 195-standard size cards and distributed in nine-card packs with a suggested retail price of $3. The fronts feature color action player photos printed on embossed, thick 20 pt. stock with a holographic foil logo. The set contains the subset: Draft Picks (181-210).

COMPLETE SET (195) 25.00 60.00
1 Barry Sanders 1.00 2.50
2 Tony Martin .20 .50
3 Fred Lane .10 .30
4 Darren Woodson .10 .30
5 Andre Reed .20 .50
6 Blaine Bishop .10 .30
7 Robert Brooks .20 .50
8 Tony Banks .20 .50
9 Charles Way .10 .30
10 Mark Brunell .30 .75
11 Darrell Green .20 .50
12 Aeneas Williams .10 .30
13 Rob Johnson .20 .50
14 Deion Sanders .30 .75
15 Marshall Faulk .40 1.00
16 Stephen Boyd .10 .30
17 Adrian Murrell .20 .50
18 Wayne Chrebet .30 .75
19 Michael Sinclair .10 .30
20 Dan Marino 1.25 3.00
21 Willie Davis .10 .30
22 Chris Warren .20 .50
23 John Mobley .10 .30
24 Shannon Sharpe .20 .50
25 Thurman Thomas .30 .75
26 Corey Dillon .30 .75
27 Zach Thomas .30 .75
28 James Jett .20 .50
29 Eric Metcalf .10 .30
30 Drew Bledsoe .50 1.25
31 Scott Greene .10 .30
32 Simeon Rice .20 .50
33 Robert Smith .30 .75
34 Keenan McCardell .20 .50
35 Jessie Armstead .10 .30
36 Jerry Rice .60 1.50
37 Eric Green .10 .30
38 Terrell Owens .30 .75
39 Tim Brown .30 .75
40 Vinny Testaverde .20 .50
41 Brian Stablein .10 .30
42 Bert Emanuel .20 .50
43 Terry Glenn .30 .75
44 Chad Cota .10 .30
45 Jermaine Lewis .20 .50
46 Derrick Thomas .30 .75
47 O.J. McDuffie .20 .50
48 Frank Wycheck .10 .30
49 Steve Broussard .10 .30
50 Terrell Davis .30 .75
51 Eric Allen .10 .30
52 Napoleon Kaufman .30 .75
53 Dan Wilkinson .10 .30
54 Kerry Collins .20 .50
55 Frank Sanders .20 .50
56 Jeff Burris .10 .30
57 Michael Westbrook .20 .50
58 Michael McCrary .10 .30
59 Bobby Hoying .20 .50
60 Jerome Bettis .30 .75
61 Amp Lee .10 .30
62 Levon Kirkland .10 .30
63 Dana Stubblefield .10 .30
64 Terance Mathis .20 .50
65 Mark Chmura .20 .50
66 Bryant Westbrook .10 .30
67 Rod Smith .20 .50
68 Derrick Alexander .20 .50
69 Jason Taylor .20 .50
70 Eddie George .30 .75
71 Elvis Grbac .20 .50
72 Junior Seau .30 .75
73 Marvin Harrison .30 .75
74 Neil O'Donnell .20 .50
75 Johnnie Morton .20 .50
76 John Randle .20 .50
77 Danny Kanell .20 .50
78 Charlie Garner .20 .50
79 J.J. Stokes .20 .50
80 Troy Aikman .60 1.50
81 Gus Frerotte .10 .30
82 Jake Plummer .30 .75
83 Andre Hastings .10 .30
84 Steve Atwater .10 .30
85 Larry Centers .10 .30
86 Kevin Hardy .10 .30
87 Willie McGinest .10 .30
88 Joey Galloway .20 .50
89 Charles Johnson .10 .30
90 Warrick Dunn .30 .75
91 Derrick Rodgers .10 .30
92 Aaron Glenn .10 .30
93 Shawn Jefferson .10 .30
94 Antonio Freeman .30 .75
95 Jake Reed .20 .50
96 Reidel Anthony .20 .50
97 Cris Dishman .10 .30
98 Jason Sehorn .20 .50
99 Herman Moore .20 .50
100 John Elway 1.25 3.00
101 Brad Johnson .30 .75
102 Jeff George .20 .50
103 Emmitt Smith 1.00 2.50
104 Steve McNair .30 .75
105 Ed McCaffrey .20 .50
106 Errict Rhett .20 .50
107 Dorsey Levens .30 .75
108 Michael Jackson .10 .30
109 Carl Pickens .20 .50
110 James Stewart .20 .50
111 Karim Abdul-Jabbar .30 .75
112 Jim Harbaugh .20 .50
113 Yancey Thigpen .10 .30
114 Chad Brown .10 .30
115 Chris Sanders .10 .30
116 Cris Carter .30 .75
117 Glenn Foley .20 .50
118 Ben Coates .20 .50
119 Jamal Anderson .30 .75
120 Steve Young .40 1.00
121 Scott Mitchell .20 .50
122 Rob Moore .20 .50
123 Bobby Engram .20 .50
124 Rod Woodson .20 .50
125 Terry Allen .30 .75
126 Warren Sapp .20 .50
127 Irving Fryar .20 .50
128 Isaac Bruce .30 .75
129 Rae Carruth .10 .30
130 Sean Dawkins .10 .30
131 Andre Rison .20 .50
132 Kevin Greene .20 .50
133 Warren Moon .30 .75
134 Keyshawn Johnson .30 .75
135 Jay Graham .10 .30
136 Mike Alstott .30 .75
137 Peter Boulware .10 .30
138 Doug Evans .10 .30
139 Jimmy Smith .20 .50
140 Kordell Stewart .30 .75
141 Tamarick Vanover .10 .30
142 Chris Slade .10 .30
143 Freddie Jones .10 .30
144 Erik Kramer .10 .30
145 Ricky Watters .20 .50
146 Chris Chandler .20 .50
147 Garrison Hearst .30 .75
148 Trent Dilfer .30 .75
149 Bruce Smith .20 .50
150 Brett Favre 1.25 3.00
151 Will Blackwell .10 .30
152 Rickey Dudley .10 .30
153 Natrone Means .20 .50
154 Curtis Conway .20 .50
155 Tony Gonzalez .30 .75
156 Jeff Blake .20 .50
157 Michael Irvin .30 .75
158 Curtis Martin .30 .75
159 Tim McDonald .10 .30
160 Wesley Walls .20 .50
161 Michael Strahan .20 .50
162 Reggie White .30 .75
163 Jeff Graham .10 .30
164 Ray Lewis .30 .75
165 Antowain Smith .30 .75
166 Ryan Leaf RC 1.00 2.50
167 Jerome Pathon RC 1.00 2.50
168 Duane Starks RC .50 1.25
169 Brian Simmons RC .75 2.00
170 Pat Johnson RC .75 2.00
171 Keith Brooking RC 1.00 2.50
172 Kevin Dyson RC 1.00 2.50
173 Robert Edwards RC .75 2.00
174 Grant Wistrom RC .75 2.00
175 Curtis Enis RC .50 1.25
176 John Avery RC .75 2.00
177 Jason Peter RC .50 1.25
178 Brian Griese RC 2.00 5.00
179 Tavian Banks RC .75 2.00
180 Andre Wadsworth RC .75 2.00
181 Skip Hicks RC .75 2.00
182 Hines Ward RC 5.00 10.00
183 Greg Ellis RC .50 1.25
184 Robert Holcombe RC .75 2.00
185 Joe Jurevicius RC 1.00 2.50
186 Takeo Spikes RC 1.00 2.50
187 Ahman Green RC 2.00 5.00
188 Jacquez Green RC .75 2.00
189 Randy Moss RC 5.00 12.00
190 Charles Woodson RC 2.50 6.00
191 Fred Taylor RC 1.50 4.00
192 Marcus Nash RC .50 1.25
193 Germane Crowell RC .75 2.00
194 Tim Dwight RC 1.00 2.50
195 Peyton Manning RC 8.00 20.00
H1 Checklist Card 1 .05 .15
H2 Checklist Card 2 .05 .15

1998 Stadium Club First Day

*FIRST DAY STARS: 3X TO 8X BASIC CARDS
*FIRST DAY RCs: 1.5X TO 4X BASIC CARDS
STATED ODDS 1:47 RETAIL
STATED PRINT RUN 200 SER.#'d SETS

1998 Stadium Club One of a Kind

*ONE OF KIND STARS: 5X TO 12X BASIC CARDS
*ONE OF KIND RC'S: 2X TO 5X BASIC CARDS
STATED ODDS 1:32 HOBBY
STATED PRINT RUN 150 SER.#'d SETS

1998 Stadium Club Chrome

Randomly inserted in packs at the rate of one in 12, this 20-card partial parallel set features 20 players picked from the base set and printed in Chrome. A Refractor version of this set was also produced with an insertion rate of 1:48 packs.

COMPLETE SET (20) 60.00 120.00
STATED ODDS 1:12 H/R, 1:6 JUM
*REFRACTORS: 1X TO 2X BASIC INSERTS
REFRACTOR ODDS 1:48 H/R, 1:24 JUM
*JUMBOS: .4X TO 1X BASIC INSERTS
JUMBO ODDS ONE PER BOX
*JUMBO REFRACT: 2X TO 5X BASIC INSERTS
JUMBO REFRACTOR ODDS 1:12 HTA BOXES
SCC1 John Elway 6.00 15.00
SCC2 Mark Brunell 1.50 4.00
SCC3 Jerome Bettis 1.50 4.00
SCC4 Steve Young 2.00 5.00
SCC5 Herman Moore 1.00 2.50
SCC6 Emmitt Smith 5.00 12.00
SCC7 Warrick Dunn 1.50 4.00
SCC8 Dan Marino 6.00 15.00
SCC9 Kordell Stewart 1.50 4.00
SCC10 Barry Sanders 5.00 12.00
SCC11 Tim Brown 1.50 4.00
SCC12 Dorsey Levens 1.50 4.00
SCC13 Eddie George 1.50 4.00
SCC14 Jerry Rice 3.00 8.00
SCC15 Terrell Davis 1.50 4.00
SCC16 Napoleon Kaufman 1.50 4.00
SCC17 Troy Aikman 3.00 8.00
SCC18 Drew Bledsoe 2.50 6.00
SCC19 Antonio Freeman 1.50 4.00
SCC20 Brett Favre 6.00 15.00

1998 Stadium Club Co-Signers

Randomly inserted in hobby packs only at the rate of one in 235, this 12-card set features color photos and autographs of eight different players printed two to a card. Both co-signers are featured on the same side and stamped with the gold foil Topps "Certified Autograph Issue" stamp.

CO1-CO4: STATED ODDS 1:9400H, 1:5640J
CO5-CO8: STATED ODDS 1:3133H, 1:1880J
CO9-CO12: STATED ODDS 1:261H, 1:157J
OVERALL STATED ODDS 1:235H, 1:141J
CO1 P.Manning/R.Leaf 250.00 400.00
CO2 D.Marino/K.Stewart 75.00 200.00
CO3 E.George/C.Dillon 20.00 50.00
CO4 D.Levens/M.Alstott 30.00 80.00
CO5 R.Leaf/D.Marino 75.00 200.00
CO6 P.Manning/K.Stewart 200.00 350.00
CO7 E.George/M.Alstott 25.00 60.00
CO8 D.Levens/C.Dillon 20.00 50.00
CO9 P.Manning/D.Marino 250.00 500.00
CO10 R.Leaf/K.Stewart 12.00 30.00
CO11 E.George/D.Levens 20.00 50.00
CO12 M.Alstott/C.Dillon 20.00 50.00

1998 Stadium Club Double Threat

Randomly inserted one per eight packs, this 10-card set features color action photos of rookie quarterbacks, running backs and wide receivers paired with a photo of a teammate at a different offensive position.

COMPLETE SET (10) 15.00 40.00
STATED ODDS 1:8 H/R, 1:4 JUM
DT1 M.Faulk / P.Manning 6.00 15.00
DT2 C.Conway / C.Enis 1.00 2.50
DT3 D.Bledsoe / R.Edwards 2.00 5.00
DT4 W.Dunn / J.Green 1.00 2.50
DT5 J.Elway / M.Nash 4.00 10.00
DT6 M.Brunell / F.Taylor 1.00 2.50
DT7 E.George / K.Dyson 1.00 2.50
DT8 M.Jackson / P.Johnson 1.00 2.50
DT9 T.Glenn / T.Simmons 1.00 2.50
DT10 N.Means / R.Leaf 1.00 2.50

1998 Stadium Club Leading Legends

Leading Legends insert cards were randomly seeded at the rate of 1:12 retail packs. Each card was printed on plastic card stock with gold foil layering on the cardfront.

COMPLETE SET (10) 20.00 40.00
STATED ODDS 1:12 RETAIL
1 John Elway 4.00 10.00
2 Brett Favre 4.00 10.00
3 Dan Marino 4.00 10.00
4 Warren Moon 1.00 2.50
5 Jerry Rice 2.00 5.00
6 Barry Sanders 3.00 8.00
7 Bruce Smith .60 1.50
8 Emmitt Smith 3.00 8.00
9 Reggie White 1.00 2.50
10 Steve Young 1.25 3.00

1998 Stadium Club Prime Rookies

Randomly inserted into packs at the rate of one in eight, this 10-card set features color action photos of the season's top draftees.

COMPLETE SET (10) 15.00 40.00
STATED ODDS 1:8 H/R, 1:4 JUM
PR1 Ryan Leaf .60 1.50
PR2 Andre Wadsworth .40 1.00
PR3 Fred Taylor 1.00 2.50
PR4 Kevin Dyson .60 1.50
PR5 Charles Woodson 1.50 4.00
PR6 Robert Edwards .30 .75
PR7 Grant Wistrom .40 1.00
PR8 Curtis Enis .30 .75
PR9 Randy Moss 4.00 10.00
PR10 Peyton Manning 6.00 15.00

1998 Stadium Club Triumvirate Luminous

Randomly inserted into hobby packs only at the rate of one in 24, this 15-card hobby-exclusive set features color photos of three outstanding teammates printed on die-cut cards that combine to form one Triumvirate. A parallel Luminescent set was also produced with an insertion rate of one in 96 packs. An Illuminator parallel version of the set was seeded at the rate of 1:192 packs.

COMPLETE SET (15) 35.00 80.00
STATED ODDS 1:24 H, 1:12 JUM HOB
*LUMINESCENTS: 1X TO 2X BASIC INSERTS
LUMINESCENT ODDS 1:96 H, 1:48 JUM HOB
*ILLUMINATORS: 1.5X TO 3X BASIC INSERTS
ILLUMINATOR ODDS 1:192 H, 1:96 JUM HOB
T1A Terrell Davis 2.00 5.00
T1B John Elway 8.00 20.00
T1C Shannon Sharpe 1.25 3.00
T2A Barry Sanders 5.00 12.00
T2B Scott Mitchell 1.25 3.00
T2C Herman Moore 1.25 3.00
T3A Dorsey Levens 2.00 5.00
T3B Brett Favre 8.00 20.00
T3C Antonio Freeman 2.00 5.00
T4A Emmitt Smith 6.00 15.00
T4B Troy Aikman 4.00 10.00
T4C Michael Irvin 2.00 5.00
T5A Napoleon Kaufman 2.00 5.00
T5B Jeff George 1.25 3.00
T5C Tim Brown 2.00 5.00

1999 Stadium Club Promos

COMPLETE SET (6) 2.50 6.00
PP1 Antowain Smith .40 1.00
PP2 Warren Sapp .50 1.25
PP3 Ty Law .40 1.00
PP4 Emmitt Smith 1.25 3.00
PP5 Randall Cunningham .50 1.25
PP6 Tim Dwight .30 .75

1999 Stadium Club

Released as a 200-card set, 1999 Stadium Club features 150 base veterans, 25 Transactions cards, and 25 Draft Picks seeded at one in three packs. Base cards are full-bleed color on a 20-point card stock. Stadium Club was packaged in 24-pack boxes with six cards per pack and carried a suggested retail price of $2.00 per pack.

COMPLETE SET (200) 25.00 60.00
COMP.SET w/o SP's (175) 7.50 20.00
UNPRICED PRINT.PLATES #'d TO 1
1 Dan Marino .60 1.50
2 Andre Reed .30 .75
3 Michael Westbrook .20 .50
4 Isaac Bruce .30 .75
5 Curtis Martin .25 .60
6 Courtney Hawkins .20 .50
7 Charles Way .20 .50
8 Terrell Owens .25 .60
9 Warrick Dunn .20 .50
10 Jake Plummer .20 .50
11 Chad Brown .20 .50
12 Yancey Thigpen .20 .50
13 Lamar Thomas .20 .50
14 Keenan McCardell .25 .60
15 Shannon Sharpe .25 .60
16 Robert Brooks .25 .60
17 Cameron Cleeland .20 .50
18 Derrick Thomas .30 .75
19 Mark Brunell .25 .60
20 Jamal Anderson .25 .60
21 Germane Crowell .20 .50
22 Rod Smith .25 .60
23 Ty Law .30 .75
24 Cris Carter .30 .75
25 Terrell Davis .25 .60
26 Takeo Spikes .20 .50
27 Tim Biakabutuka .25 .60
28 Jermaine Lewis .20 .50
29 Adrian Murrell .20 .50
30 Doug Flutie .30 .75
31 Curtis Enis .20 .50
32 Skip Hicks .20 .50
33 Steve McNair .25 .60
34 Charles Woodson .30 .75
35 Jessie Armstead .25 .60
36 Shawn Springs .20 .50
37 Levon Kirkland .20 .50
38 Freddie Jones .20 .50
39 Warren Sapp .25 .60
40 Emmitt Smith .50 1.25
41 Reidel Anthony .20 .50
42 Tony Simmons .20 .50
43 Andre Hastings .20 .50
44 Byron Bam Morris .20 .50
45 Jimmy Smith .25 .60
46 Antonio Freeman .25 .60
47 Herman Moore .25 .60
48 Muhsin Muhammad .20 .50
49 Chris Chandler .25 .60
50 John Elway .50 1.25
51 Aeneas Williams .20 .50
52 Bobby Engram .20 .50
53 Keith Poole .20 .50
54 Zach Thomas .25 .60
55 Mike Alstott .20 .50
56 Junior Seau .25 .60
57 Aaron Glenn .20 .50
58 Darrell Green .30 .75
59 Thurman Thomas .25 .60
60 Troy Aikman .40 1.00
61 Bill Romanowski .25 .60
62 Wesley Walls .25 .60
63 Andre Wadsworth .20 .50
64 Robert Smith .20 .50
65 Elvis Grbac .20 .50
66 Terry Fair .20 .50
67 Ben Coates .25 .60
68 Bert Emanuel .25 .60
69 Jacquez Green .20 .50
70 Barry Sanders .50 1.25
71 James Jett .20 .50
72 Gary Brown .20 .50
73 Stephen Alexander .20 .50
74 Wayne Chrebet .20 .50
75 Drew Bledsoe .25 .60
76 John Lynch .25 .60
77 Jake Reed .25 .60
78 Marvin Harrison .25 .60
79 Johnnie Morton .25 .60
80 Brett Favre .60 1.50
81 Charlie Batch .20 .50
82 Antowain Smith .20 .50
83 Mikhael Ricks .20 .50
84 Derrick Mayes .20 .50
85 John Mobley .20 .50
86 Ernie Mills .20 .50
87 Jeff Blake .25 .60
88 Curtis Conway .25 .60
89 Bruce Smith .25 .60
90 Peyton Manning 1.00 2.50
91 Tyrone Davis .20 .50
92 Ray Buchanan .20 .50
93 Tim Dwight .25 .60
94 O.J. McDuffie .25 .60
95 Vonnie Holliday .20 .50
96 Jon Kitna .20 .50
97 Trent Dilfer .20 .50
98 Jerome Bettis .30 .75
99 Dedric Ward .20 .50
100 Fred Taylor .20 .50
101 Ike Hilliard .20 .50
102 Frank Wycheck .25 .60
103 Eric Moulds .20 .50
104 Rob Moore .20 .50
105 Ed McCaffrey .25 .60
106 Carl Pickens .25 .60
107 Priest Holmes .25 .60
108 Kevin Hardy .20 .50
109 Terry Glenn .25 .60
110 Keyshawn Johnson .25 .60
111 Karim Abdul-Jabbar .20 .50
112 Stephen Boyd .20 .50
113 Ahman Green .25 .60
114 Duce Staley .20 .50
115 Vinny Testaverde .20 .50
116 Napoleon Kaufman .20 .50
117 Frank Sanders .20 .50
118 Peter Boulware .20 .50
119 Kevin Greene .30 .75
120 Steve Young .40 1.00
121 Darnay Scott .20 .50
122 Deion Sanders .25 .60
123 Corey Dillon .20 .50
124 Randall Cunningham .25 .60
125 Eddie George .25 .60
126 Derrick Alexander .20 .50
127 Mark Chmura .20 .50
128 Michael Sinclair .20 .50
129 Rickey Dudley .20 .50
130 Joey Galloway .25 .60
131 Michael Strahan .25 .60
132 Ricky Proehl .20 .50
133 Natrone Means .25 .60
134 Dorsey Levens .25 .60
135 Andre Rison .25 .60
136 Alonzo Mayes .20 .50
137 John Randle .30 .75
138 Terance Mathis .20 .50
139 Rae Carruth .20 .50
140 Jerry Rice .75 2.00
141 Michael Irvin .30 .75
142 Oronde Gadsden .20 .50
143 Jerome Pathon .20 .50
144 Ricky Watters .25 .60
145 J.J. Stokes .20 .50
146 Kordell Stewart .20 .50
147 Tim Brown .30 .75
148 Garrison Hearst .20 .50
149 Tony Gonzalez .25 .60
150 Randy Moss .25 .60
151 Daunte Culpepper RC .50 1.25
152 Amos Zereoue RC .30 .75
153 Champ Bailey RC .60 1.50
154 Peerless Price RC .30 .75
155 Edgerrin James RC .50 1.25
156 Joe Germaine RC .40 1.00
157 David Boston RC .30 .75
158 Kevin Faulk RC .30 .75
159 Troy Edwards RC .30 .75
160 Akili Smith RC .30 .75
161 Kevin Johnson RC .40 1.00
162 Rob Konrad RC .30 .75
163 Shaun King RC .30 .75
164 James Johnson RC .30 .75
165 Donovan McNabb RC 1.00 2.50
166 Torry Holt RC .60 1.50
167 Mike Cloud RC .30 .75
168 Sedrick Irvin RC .30 .75
169 Cade McNown RC .30 .75
170 Ricky Williams RC .50 1.25
171 Karsten Bailey RC .30 .75
172 Cecil Collins RC .30 .75
173 Brock Huard RC .30 .75
174 D'Wayne Bates RC .30 .75
175 Tim Couch RC .40 1.00
176 Torrance Small .20 .50
177 Warren Moon .30 .75
178 Rocket Ismail .25 .60
179 Marshall Faulk .25 .60
180 Trent Green .20 .50
181 Sean Dawkins .20 .50
182 Pete Mitchell .20 .50
183 Jeff Graham .20 .50
184 Eddie Kennison .25 .60
185 Kerry Collins .20 .50
186 Eric Green .20 .50
187 Kyle Brady .20 .50
188 Tony Martin .25 .60
189 Jim Harbaugh .25 .60
190 Erik Kramer .25 .60
191 Steve Atwater .25 .60
192 Chad Bratzke .20 .50
193 Charles Johnson .20 .50
194 Damon Gibson .20 .50
195 Jeff George .20 .50
196 Scott Mitchell .20 .50
197 Terry Kirby .20 .50
198 Rich Gannon .25 .60
199 Chris Spielman .25 .60
200 Brad Johnson .25 .60

1999 Stadium Club First Day

COMPLETE SET (200) 300.00 600.00
*STARS: 6X TO 15X HI COL.
*RCs: 1.5X TO 4X
STATED PRINT RUN 150 SER.#'d SETS
STATED ODDS 1:38 RETAIL

1999 Stadium Club One of a Kind

COMPLETE SET (200) 300.00 600.00
*STARS: 6X TO 15X HI COL.
*RCs: 1.5X TO 4X
STATED PRINT RUN 150 SER.#'d SETS
STATED ODDS 1:48 HOBBY

1999 Stadium Club 3X3 Luminous

Randomly inserted in hobby and retail packs at the rate of one in 36 and HTA packs at the rate of one in 18, this 15-card set features intricate laser cut cards that when combined with the other three cards that carry the same number in this set form a jumbo card called a Triumvirate. An example of a triumvirate is Brett Favre, number T1A, Troy Aikman, number T1B, and Jake Plummer, number T1C.

COMPLETE SET (15) 25.00 60.00
STATED ODDS 1:36 HOB/RET, 1:18 HTA
*LUMINESCENT: .8X TO 2X BASIC INSERTS
LUMINESCENT ODDS 1:144 H/R,1:72 HTA
*ILLUMINATOR: 1.2X TO 3X BASIC INSERTS
ILLUMINATOR ODDS 1:288 H/R,1:144 HTA
T1A Brett Favre 5.00 12.00
T1B Troy Aikman 3.00 8.00
T1C Jake Plummer 1.00 2.50
T2A Jamal Anderson 1.50 4.00
T2B Emmitt Smith 3.00 8.00
T2C Barry Sanders 5.00 12.00
T3A Antonio Freeman 1.50 4.00
T3B Randy Moss 4.00 10.00
T3C Jerry Rice 3.00 8.00
T4A Peyton Manning 5.00 12.00
T4B John Elway 5.00 12.00
T4C Dan Marino 5.00 12.00
T5A Fred Taylor 1.50 4.00
T5B Terrell Davis 1.50 4.00
T5C Curtis Martin 1.50 4.00

1999 Stadium Club Chrome Previews

Randomly inserted in packs at one in 24, and HTA packs at one in six, this 20-card set previews the base set for the 1999 Stadium Club Chrome to be released late in the 1999 season.

COMPLETE SET (20) 50.00 100.00
STATED ODDS 1:24 HOB/RET, 1:6 HTA
*REFRACTORS: .8X TO 2X HI COL.
REFRACTOR STATED ODDS 1:96H/R,1:24HTA
*JUMBOS: .3X TO .8X BASIC INSERTS
JUMBOS STATED ODDS 1:96H/R,1:24HTA
*JUMBO REF.: 1X TO 2.5X BASIC INSERTS
JUMBO REF.ODDS 1:12 HOBBY BOXES
C1 Randy Moss 3.00 8.00
C2 Terrell Davis 1.25 3.00
C3 Peyton Manning 4.00 10.00
C4 Fred Taylor 1.25 3.00
C5 John Elway 4.00 10.00
C6 Steve Young 1.50 4.00
C7 Brett Favre 4.00 10.00
C8 Jamal Anderson 1.25 3.00
C9 Barry Sanders 4.00 10.00
C10 Dan Marino 4.00 10.00
C11 Jerry Rice 2.50 6.00
C12 Emmitt Smith 2.50 6.00
C13 Randall Cunningham 1.25 3.00
C14 Troy Aikman 2.50 6.00
C15 Akili Smith .75 2.00
C16 Donovan McNabb 4.00 10.00
C17 Edgerrin James 3.00 8.00
C18 Torry Holt 2.00 5.00
C19 Ricky Williams 1.50 4.00
C20 Tim Couch 1.00 2.50

1999 Stadium Club Co-Signers

Randomly inserted in packs, cards CS1 and CS2 can be found one in every 2854 hobby packs and one in 1142 HTA packs, and cards CS3-CS6 can be found one in every 840 hobby packs and one in 476 HTA packs. This puts an overall pull at one in 840 packs. This 6-card set features two authentic autographs on each card. Some players were released as redemptions with an expiration date of 4/30/2000.

CS1/CS2 STATED ODDS 1:2854H,1:1142HTA
CS3-CS6 STATED ODDS 1:1189H,1:476HTA
OVERALL STATED ODDS 1:840 HOB
CS1 T.Davis/R.Williams 25.00 60.00
CS2 T.Davis/E.James 25.00 60.00
CS3 D.Marino/T.Couch 60.00 120.00
CS4 P.Manning/T.Couch 60.00 120.00
CS5 R.Moss/J.Rice 150.00 250.00
CS6 D.Marino/Testaverde 60.00 120.00

1999 Stadium Club Emperors of the Zone

Randomly inserted in hobby packs at the rate of one in 12 and HTA packs at the rate of one in four, this 10-card set showcases NFL touchdown producers on an all-black card front highlighted with silver foil. Card backs carry an "E" prefix.

COMPLETE SET (10) 12.50 30.00
STATED ODDS 1:12 HOB/RET, 1:4 HTA
E1 Ricky Williams .75 2.00
E2 Brett Favre 2.00 5.00
E3 Donovan McNabb 2.00 5.00
E4 Peyton Manning 2.00 5.00
E5 Terrell Davis .60 1.50
E6 Jamal Anderson .60 1.50
E7 Edgerrin James 1.50 4.00
E8 Fred Taylor .60 1.50
E9 Tim Couch .50 1.25
E10 Randy Moss 1.50 4.00

1999 Stadium Club Lone Star Signatures

Randomly inserted in packs with overall odds of one in 697, this 11-card set features authentic autographs from some of football's finest. The set includes players such as Randy Moss, Edgerrin James, and Tim Couch. Card backs carry an "LS" prefix.

OVERALL STATED ODDS 1:697
LS1 Randy Moss 40.00 80.00
LS2 Jerry Rice 60.00 120.00
LS3 Peyton Manning 60.00 120.00
LS4 Vinny Testaverde 10.00 25.00
LS5 Tim Couch 12.50 30.00
LS6 Dan Marino 75.00 150.00
LS7 Edgerrin James 15.00 40.00
LS8 Fred Taylor 12.50 30.00
LS9 Garrison Hearst 10.00 25.00
LS10 Antonio Freeman 15.00 40.00
LS11 Torry Holt 15.00 40.00

1999 Stadium Club Never Compromise

Randomly inserted in packs Hobby and Retail packs at the rate of one in 12, and HTA packs at the rate of one in four, this 30-card set sports three different subsets. The 10-card Rookies subset features photography from the 1999 rookie shoot, the 10-card Stars subset features current veterans, and the 10-card Legends set features players most likely to be inducted into the Football Hall of Fame. Card backs carry an "NC" prefix.

COMPLETE SET (30) 30.00 60.00
STATED ODDS 1:12 HOB/RET, 1:4 HTA
NC1 Tim Couch .60 1.50
NC2 David Boston .50 1.25
NC3 Daunte Culpepper .75 2.00
NC4 Donovan McNabb 1.50 4.00
NC5 Ricky Williams .75 2.00
NC6 Troy Edwards .50 1.25
NC7 Akili Smith .50 1.25
NC8 Torry Holt 1.00 2.50
NC9 Cade McNown .50 1.25
NC10 Edgerrin James .75 2.00
NC11 Randy Moss .60 1.50
NC12 Peyton Manning 2.50 6.00
NC13 Eddie George .60 1.50
NC14 Fred Taylor .50 1.25
NC15 Jamal Anderson .60 1.50
NC16 Joey Galloway .60 1.50
NC17 Terrell Davis .60 1.50
NC18 Keyshawn Johnson .60 1.50
NC19 Antonio Freeman .60 1.50
NC20 Jake Plummer .50 1.25
NC21 Steve Young 1.00 2.50
NC22 Barry Sanders 1.25 3.00
NC23 Dan Marino 1.50 4.00
NC24 Emmitt Smith 1.25 3.00
NC25 Brett Favre 1.50 4.00
NC26 Randall Cunningham .60 1.50
NC27 John Elway 1.25 3.00
NC28 Drew Bledsoe .60 1.50
NC29 Jerry Rice 2.00 5.00
NC30 Troy Aikman 1.00 2.50

2000 Stadium Club Promos

This 6-card set was released at various Topps sponsored events and through its dealer network to promote the 2000 football release. The cards look very similar to the base set except for the card numbering scheme.

COMPLETE SET (6) 2.00 5.00
PP1 Peyton Manning 1.00 2.50
PP2 Antonio Freeman .30 .75
PP3 O.J. McDuffie .30 .75
PP4 Junior Seau .30 .75
PP5 Mark Brunell .30 .75
PP6 Ed McCaffrey .30 .75

2000 Stadium Club

Released as a 175-card set, Stadium Club is composed of 150 base cards and 25 short printed Rookie cards inserted at one in four, and one in one HTA. Base cards feature full color crystal clear action photography and highlight some of the key moments and plays from the 1999 season. Stadium Club HTA was packaged in 12-pack boxes with each pack containing 18 cards including one rookie card and carried a suggested retail price of $6.00. Regular packing was 24-pack boxes with packs containing seven cards and carried a suggested retail price of $2.50.

COMPLETE SET (175) 20.00 50.00
COMP.SET w/o RC's (150) 7.50 20.00
151-175 ROOKIE STATED ODDS 1:4
1 Peyton Manning .60 1.50
2 Pete Mitchell .15 .40
3 Napoleon Kaufman .20 .50
4 Mikhael Ricks .15 .40
5 Mike Alstott .15 .40
6 Brad Johnson .20 .50
7 Tony Gonzalez .20 .50
8 Germane Crowell .15 .40
9 Marcus Robinson .20 .50
10 Stephen Davis .15 .40
11 Terance Mathis .15 .40
12 Jake Plummer .15 .40
13 Qadry Ismail .15 .40
14 Cade McNown .15 .40
15 Zach Thomas .20 .50
16 Curtis Martin .20 .50
17 Torrance Small .15 .40
18 Steve McNair .20 .50
19 Jim Harbaugh .20 .50
20 Keyshawn Johnson .20 .50
21 Antonio Freeman .20 .50
22 Ed McCaffrey .20 .50
23 Elvis Grbac .15 .40
24 Peerless Price .20 .50
25 Jerome Bettis .25 .60
26 Yancey Thigpen .15 .40
27 Jake Delhomme RC .20 .50
28 Keith Poole .15 .40
29 Carl Pickens .20 .50
30 Jerry Rice .60 1.50
31 Rob Moore .15 .40
32 Reidel Anthony .15 .40
33 Jimmy Smith .20 .50
34 Ray Lucas .15 .40
35 Troy Aikman .30 .75
36 Steve Beuerlein .20 .50
37 Charlie Batch .15 .40
38 Derrick Mayes .15 .40
39 Tim Brown .25 .60

40 Eddie George .20 .50
41 O.J. McDuffie .20 .50
42 Ike Hilliard .15 .40
43 Bill Schroeder .20 .50
44 Jim Miller .15 .40
45 Chris Chandler .20 .50
46 Fred Taylor .15 .40
47 Ricky Watters .20 .50
48 Tyrone Wheatley .15 .40
49 Bruce Smith .20 .50
50 Marshall Faulk .20 .50
51 Kevin Carter .15 .40
52 Champ Bailey .20 .50
53 Troy Edwards .15 .40
54 Doug Flutie .20 .50
55 Charles Johnson .15 .40
56 Michael Westbrook .15 .40
57 Frank Wycheck .20 .50
58 Drew Bledsoe .20 .50
59 Terrence Wilkins .15 .40
60 Ricky Williams .20 .50
61 Rod Smith .20 .50
62 Errict Rhett .20 .50
63 Vinny Testaverde .15 .40
64 Jacquez Green .15 .40
65 Curtis Conway .20 .50
66 Wayne Chrebet .15 .40
67 Albert Connell .15 .40
68 Kordell Stewart .15 .40
69 Bert Emanuel .15 .40
70 Randy Moss .20 .50
71 Akili Smith .15 .40
72 Brian Griese .15 .40
73 Frank Sanders .15 .40
74 Wesley Walls .15 .40
75 Michael Pittman .15 .40
76 Steve Young .30 .75
77 Jevon Kearse .15 .40
78 Az-Zahir Hakim .15 .40
79 James Stewart .15 .40
80 Brett Favre .50 1.25
81 Dan Marino .50 1.25
82 Joe Horn .20 .50
83 Mark Brunell .20 .50
84 Eddie Kennison .15 .40
85 Deion Sanders .20 .50
86 Priest Holmes .15 .40
87 Terry Glenn .20 .50
88 Olandis Gary .20 .50
89 Patrick Jeffers .15 .40
90 Emmitt Smith .40 1.00
91 J.J. Stokes .20 .50
92 Warrick Dunn .15 .40
93 Damon Huard .15 .40
94 Herman Moore .15 .40
95 Corey Dillon .15 .40
96 Joey Galloway .20 .50
97 Jamal Anderson .20 .50
98 Junior Seau .20 .50
99 Robert Smith .15 .40
100 Edgerrin James .20 .50
101 Derrick Alexander .15 .40
102 Johnnie Morton .20 .50
103 Sean Dawkins .15 .40
104 Derrick Brooks .15 .40
105 Rickey Dudley .15 .40
106 Keenan McCardell .20 .50
107 Kerry Collins .15 .40
108 Kevin Johnson .15 .40
109 Eric Moulds .15 .40
110 Terrell Davis .20 .50
111 Shawn Jefferson .15 .40
112 Donovan McNabb .20 .50
113 Torry Holt .20 .50
114 Marvin Harrison .20 .50
115 Amani Toomer .15 .40
116 Tony Martin .20 .50
117 Curtis Enis .15 .40
118 Tiki Barber .20 .50
119 Freddie Jones .15 .40
120 Muhsin Muhammad .15 .40
121 Shaun King .15 .40
122 Isaac Bruce .25 .60
123 Duce Staley .15 .40
124 Hardy Nickerson .15 .40
125 Corey Bradford .15 .40
126 Kevin Hardy .15 .40
127 Hines Ward .20 .50
128 Charlie Garner .20 .50
129 Warren Sapp .20 .50
130 Tim Couch .20 .50
131 Kevin Dyson .20 .50
132 Rocket Ismail .20 .50
133 Tim Dwight .20 .50
134 Darnay Scott .20 .50
135 Jeff George .20 .50
136 Dorsey Levens .20 .50
137 Jeff Blake .20 .50
138 Jon Kitna .15 .40
139 Rich Gannon .20 .50
140 Cris Carter .25 .60
141 Jeff Graham .15 .40
142 James Johnson .15 .40
143 Tim Biakabutuka .20 .50
144 Bobby Engram .15 .40
145 Tony Banks .15 .40
146 Shannon Sharpe .20 .50
147 Antowain Smith .20 .50
148 Terrell Owens .20 .50
149 Rob Johnson .20 .50
150 Kurt Warner .40 1.00
151 Thomas Jones RC .60 1.50
152 Chad Pennington RC .60 1.50
153 Ron Dayne RC .75 2.00
154 Tee Martin RC .50 1.25
155 Reuben Droughns RC .50 1.25
156 Jerry Porter RC .75 2.00
157 R.Jay Soward RC .50 1.25
158 Sylvester Morris RC .50 1.25
159 Todd Pinkston RC .50 1.25
160 Courtney Brown RC .60 1.50
161 Travis Taylor RC .50 1.25
162 Ron Dugans RC .50 1.25
163 Laveranues Coles RC .60 1.50
164 Joe Hamilton RC .50 1.25
165 Curtis Keaton RC .50 1.25
166 Bubba Franks RC .50 1.25
167 Dennis Northcutt RC .50 1.25
168 Chris Redman RC .50 1.25
169 Travis Prentice RC .50 1.25
170 Shaun Alexander RC .75 2.00
171 Jamal Lewis RC .75 2.00
172 Peter Warrick RC .50 1.25
173 J.R. Redmond RC .50 1.25
174 Trung Canidate RC .50 1.25
175 Plaxico Burress RC .60 1.50

2000 Stadium Club Beam Team

Randomly inserted in packs at the rate of one in 171 and one in 66 HTA, this 30-card set features all foil laser cut base cards with borders to match each specific player's team colors. Each card is sequentially numbered to 500.

COMPLETE SET (30) 50.00 100.00
BEAM TEAM/500 ODDS 1:171, 1:66 HTA
STATED PRINT RUN 500 SER.#'d SETS
BT1 Brett Favre 4.00 10.00
BT2 Stephen Davis 1.25 3.00
BT3 Germane Crowell 1.25 3.00
BT4 Jevon Kearse 1.25 3.00
BT5 Edgerrin James 1.50 4.00
BT6 Randy Moss 1.50 4.00
BT7 Isaac Bruce 2.00 5.00
BT8 Charlie Garner 1.50 4.00
BT9 Eddie George 1.50 4.00
BT10 Kurt Warner 3.00 8.00
BT11 Rocket Ismail 1.50 4.00
BT12 Doug Flutie 1.50 4.00
BT13 Jimmy Smith 1.50 4.00
BT14 Eric Moulds 1.25 3.00
BT15 Marvin Harrison 1.50 4.00
BT16 Ricky Watters 1.50 4.00
BT17 Marcus Robinson 1.50 4.00
BT18 Mark Brunell 1.50 4.00
BT19 Tim Dwight 1.50 4.00
BT20 Peyton Manning 5.00 12.00
BT21 Patrick Jeffers 1.25 3.00
BT22 Az-Zahir Hakim 1.25 3.00
BT23 Fred Taylor 1.25 3.00
BT24 Tim Biakabutuka 1.50 4.00
BT25 Marshall Faulk 1.50 4.00
BT26 Shannon Sharpe 1.50 4.00
BT27 Tony Gonzalez 1.50 4.00
BT28 Steve McNair 1.50 4.00
BT29 Antonio Freeman 1.50 4.00
BT30 Keyshawn Johnson 1.50 4.00

2000 Stadium Club Capture the Action

Randomly inserted in packs at the rate of one in eight and one in two HTA, this 30-card set features Quarterbacks, Receivers, Running Backs, and Defensive Players. Each card has full color action shots and is enhanced with silver foil stamping.

COMPLETE SET (30) 15.00 40.00
STATED ODDS 1:8, 1:2 HTA
*GAME VIEW/100: 3X TO 8X BASIC INSERTS
GAME VIEW/100 STATED ODDS 1:454
GAME VIEW PRINT RUN 100 SER.#'d SETS
CA1 Brett Favre 1.25 3.00
CA2 Drew Bledsoe .50 1.25
CA3 Dan Marino 1.25 3.00
CA4 Peyton Manning 1.50 4.00
CA5 Kurt Warner 1.00 2.50
CA6 Brad Johnson .50 1.25
CA7 Steve Beuerlein .50 1.25
CA8 Troy Aikman .75 2.00
CA9 Edgerrin James .50 1.25
CA10 Marshall Faulk .50 1.25
CA11 Stephen Davis .40 1.00
CA12 Eddie George .50 1.25
CA13 Emmitt Smith 1.00 2.50
CA14 Curtis Martin .50 1.25
CA15 Ricky Williams .50 1.25
CA16 Jimmy Smith .50 1.25
CA17 Marvin Harrison .50 1.25
CA18 Muhsin Muhammad .40 1.00
CA19 Keyshawn Johnson .50 1.25
CA20 Marcus Robinson .50 1.25
CA21 Antonio Freeman .50 1.25
CA22 Randy Moss .50 1.25
CA23 Tim Brown .60 1.50
CA24 Cris Carter .60 1.50
CA25 Isaac Bruce .60 1.50
CA26 Zach Thomas .50 1.25
CA27 Warren Sapp .50 1.25
CA28 Jevon Kearse .40 1.00
CA29 Junior Seau .50 1.25
CA30 Kevin Carter .40 1.00

2000 Stadium Club Co-Signers

Randomly inserted in Hobby Packs at the rate of one in 2270 and one in 880 HTA, this 6-card set pairs up players of the same position on a dual autographed card.

STATED ODDS 1:2270 HOB, 1:880 HTA
CS1 P.Manning/K.Warner 175.00 300.00
CS2 E.James/M.Faulk 50.00 100.00
CS3 S.Davis/E.George 20.00 50.00
CS4 J.Smith/C.Carter 20.00 50.00
CS5 M.Harrison/I.Bruce 50.00 100.00
CS6 J.Kitna/C.McNown 20.00 50.00

2000 Stadium Club Goal to Go

Randomly inserted in packs at the rate of one in eight and one in three HTA, this 15-card set features color action shots with black borders on the left side and bottom of the card. Each card is enhanced with red foil highlights.

COMPLETE SET (16) 5.00 12.00
STATED ODDS 1:8, 1:3 HTA
G1 Cris Carter .40 1.00
G2 Stephen Davis .25 .60
G3 Marvin Harrison .30 .75
G4 Edgerrin James .30 .75
G5 Zach Thomas .30 .75
G6 Terrell Davis .30 .75
G7 Leroy Hoard .25 .60
G8 Kurt Warner .60 1.50
G9 Tony Gonzalez .30 .75
G10 James Stewart .25 .60
G11 Isaac Bruce .40 1.00
G12 Emmitt Smith .60 1.50
G13 Dorsey Levens .30 .75
G14 Jevon Kearse .25 .60
G15 Eddie George .30 .75
G16 Warren Sapp .30 .75

2000 Stadium Club Lone Star Signatures

Randomly inserted in packs with overall odds of one in 202 and one in 79 HTA, this 30-card set features authentic player autographs and the gold foil "Topps Certified Autograph" stamp. Card number LS17 was not released.

OVERALL STATED ODDS 1:202, 1:79 HTA
ANNOUNCED PRINT RUNS 100-575
LS1 Edgerrin James 6.00 15.00
LS2 Stephen Davis 5.00 12.00
LS3 Marshall Faulk 12.00 30.00
LS4 Eddie George 8.00 20.00
LS5 Isaac Bruce 8.00 20.00
LS6 Jimmy Smith 6.00 15.00
LS7 Cris Carter 12.00 30.00
LS8 Kurt Warner 25.00 50.00
LS9 Marvin Harrison 6.00 15.00
LS10 Kevin Carter 5.00 12.00
LS11 Ron Dayne 8.00 20.00
LS12 Chad Pennington 6.00 15.00
LS13 Sylvester Morris 5.00 12.00
LS14 Thomas Jones 6.00 15.00
LS15 Shaun Alexander 8.00 20.00
LS16 Chris Redman 5.00 12.00
LS18 Peter Warrick 5.00 12.00
LS19 Jon Kitna 5.00 12.00
LS20 Cade McNown 5.00 12.00
LS21 Az-Zahir Hakim 5.00 12.00
LS22 Amani Toomer 5.00 12.00
LS23 Wesley Walls 5.00 12.00
LS24 Marcus Robinson 6.00 15.00
LS25 Zach Thomas 6.00 15.00
LS26 Tony Gonzalez 12.00 30.00
LS27 Muhsin Muhammad 5.00 12.00
LS28 Ed McCaffrey 8.00 20.00
LS29 Eric Moulds 5.00 12.00
LS30 Peyton Manning 50.00 100.00
LS31 Joe Montana 75.00 150.00

2000 Stadium Club Pro Bowl Jerseys

Randomly inserted in packs overall at the rate of one in 353 and one in 137 HTA, this 18-card set features swatches of authentic player worn Pro Bowl jerseys in the shape of the 2000 Pro Bowl Logo.

OVERALL STATED ODDS 1:353, 1:137 HTA
ANNOUNCED PRINT RUNS 300-900
CCWR Cris Carter 5.00 12.00
EGRB Eddie George 4.00 10.00
EJRB Edgerrin James 4.00 10.00
FWTE Frank Wycheck 4.00 10.00
HNLB Hardy Nickerson 3.00 8.00
IBWR Isaac Bruce 5.00 12.00
JKDE Jevon Kearse 3.00 8.00
KHILB Kevin Hardy 3.00 8.00
KJWR Keyshawn Johnson 4.00 10.00
MFRB Marshall Faulk 4.00 10.00
MMWR Muhsin Muhammad 3.00 8.00
PBOLB Peter Boulware 3.00 8.00
RMWR Randy Moss 4.00 10.00
SBQB Steve Beuerlein 4.00 10.00
SDRB Stephen Davis 3.00 8.00
TLCB Todd Lyght 3.00 8.00
WSLM Warren Sapp 4.00 10.00
WWTE Wesley Walls 3.00 8.00

2000 Stadium Club Pro Bowl Jerseys Autographs

Randomly inserted in Hobby packs at the rate of one in 5474 and one in 2116 HTA, this 5-card set features swatches of Pro Bowl worn jerseys coupled with authentic player autographs. Each card contains the gold foil "Topps Certified Stamp." A total of 50 sets were produced.

JSY AU/50 ODDS 1:5474 HOB, 1:2116 HTA
STATED PRINT RUN 50 SETS
APA1 Eddie George 50.00 100.00
APA2 Edgerrin James 60.00 120.00
APA3 Marshall Faulk 60.00 120.00
APA4 Stephen Davis 40.00 80.00
APA5 Isaac Bruce 50.00 100.00

2000 Stadium Club Pro Bowl Jerseys Combos

Randomly inserted in HTA packs at the rate of one in 523, this 6-card set features two players of the same position in opposing leagues coupled with a swatch of game worn jersey from each. Each card is hand numbered out of 50.

COMBO JSY/50 ODDS 1:523 HTA
STATED PRINT RUN 50 SER.#'d SETS
APC1 J.Kearse/W.Sapp 12.00 30.00
APC2 M.Faulk 12.00 30.00
E.James
APC3 K.Johnson/R.Moss 12.00 30.00
APC4 F.Wycheck/W.Walls 12.00 30.00
APC5 S.Davis/E.George 12.00 30.00
APC6 C.Carter/I.Bruce 15.00 40.00

2000 Stadium Club Tunnel Vision

Randomly inserted at one per box, this 8-card set features jumbo style cards with action photography and colored borders along the top and bottom of the card, and opens up to a close up action shot.

COMPLETE SET (8) 5.00 12.00
ONE PER BOX
TV1 Edgerrin James .40 1.00
TV2 Brett Favre 1.00 2.50
TV3 Marshall Faulk .40 1.00
TV4 Emmitt Smith .75 2.00
TV5 Peyton Manning 1.25 3.00
TV6 Eddie George .40 1.00
TV7 Kurt Warner .75 2.00
TV8 Fred Taylor .30 .75

2001 Stadium Club

Topps released Stadium Club in July of 2001. The set had 175 cards and 50 of those were short printed rookies. Cards 126-175 were all rookies that were available in packs at a rate of 1:4. The cardfronts featured a borderless action photo with a gold-foil bar for the player's name and position.

COMPLETE SET (175) 60.00 120.00
COMP.SET w/o SPs (125) 7.50 20.00
ROOKIE STATED ODDS 1:4
1 Peyton Manning .60 1.50
2 Akili Smith .15 .40
3 Brian Griese .15 .40
4 Wayne Chrebet .15 .40
5 Oronde Gadsden .15 .40
6 Marvin Harrison .20 .50
7 Charles Johnson .15 .40
8 Jay Fiedler .20 .50
9 Kerry Collins .15 .40
10 Troy Aikman .30 .75
11 Donovan McNabb .20 .50
12 Ike Hilliard .15 .40
13 Warrick Dunn .15 .40
14 Derrick Alexander .15 .40
15 Jake Plummer .15 .40
16 Corey Dillon .15 .40
17 Ahman Green .20 .50
18 Keenan McCardell .20 .50
19 Derrick Mason .15 .40
20 Jerry Rice .50 1.25
21 Emmitt Smith .40 1.00
22 Dedric Ward .15 .40
23 Jamal Anderson .20 .50
24 Charlie Garner .20 .50
25 Vinny Testaverde .15 .40
26 Shaun Alexander .15 .40
27 Terry Glenn .20 .50
28 Cade McNown .20 .50
29 Germane Crowell .15 .40
30 Jeff Graham .15 .40
31 Rich Gannon .20 .50
32 Jevon Kearse .15 .40
33 Shannon Sharpe .20 .50
34 Marcus Robinson .20 .50
35 Rod Smith .20 .50
36 Curtis Martin .20 .50
37 Robert Smith .15 .40
38 Marshall Faulk .20 .50
39 Tony Richardson .15 .40
40 Travis Prentice .15 .40
41 Edgerrin James .20 .50
42 Duce Staley .15 .40
43 Keyshawn Johnson .20 .50
44 Joe Horn .15 .40
45 Shawn Bryson .15 .40
46 Ray Lewis .25 .60
47 Fred Taylor .15 .40
48 Jeff George .20 .50
49 Sean Dawkins .15 .40
50 Daunte Culpepper .20 .50
51 Chris Chandler .20 .50
52 Tim Couch .15 .40
53 Trent Dilfer .15 .40
54 Steve McNair .20 .50
55 Kordell Stewart .15 .40
56 Aaron Brooks .15 .40
57 Michael Pittman .20 .50
58 Bill Schroeder .20 .50
59 Junior Seau .20 .50
60 Kurt Warner .40 1.00
61 Drew Bledsoe .20 .50
62 Steve Beuerlein .20 .50
63 Mike Anderson .15 .40
64 Brad Johnson .20 .50
65 Tim Brown .25 .60
66 Qadry Ismail .15 .40
67 Doug Flutie .20 .50
68 Terrell Owens .20 .50
69 Rocket Ismail .20 .50
70 Charlie Batch .15 .40
71 Jerome Pathon .15 .40
72 Peter Warrick .15 .40
73 Hines Ward .20 .50
74 Ron Dayne .20 .50
75 Lamar Smith .20 .50
76 Amani Toomer .16 .40
77 Joey Galloway .20 .50
78 James Allen .15 .40
79 Isaac Bruce .25 .60
80 David Boston .15 .40
81 James Thrash .20 .50
82 Tony Gonzalez .20 .50
83 Jason Taylor .25 .60
84 Ricky Watters .20 .50
85 Terance Mathis .15 .40
86 Troy Brown .15 .40
87 Mark Brunell .20 .50
88 Rob Johnson .20 .50
89 Freddie Jones .15 .40
90 Eddie George .25 .60
91 Tiki Barber .20 .50
92 Donald Hayes .15 .40
93 Muhsin Muhammad .15 .40
94 Johnnie Morton .20 .50
95 Warren Sapp .20 .50
96 Bobby Shaw .15 .40
97 Randy Moss .20 .50
98 Jerome Bettis .25 .60
99 Antonio Freeman .25 .60
100 Jamal Lewis .25 .60
101 Andre Rison .20 .50
102 Kevin Faulk .15 .40
103 Jon Kitna .15 .40
104 Shawn Jefferson .15 .40
105 Kevin Johnson .15 .40
106 Torry Holt .20 .50
107 Cris Carter .25 .60
108 Chad Lewis .15 .40
109 Stephen Davis .15 .40
110 Jeff Blake .20 .50
111 Elvis Grbac .20 .50
112 Ed McCaffrey .20 .50
113 Tim Biakabutuka .15 .40
114 Trent Green .15 .40
115 Jeff Garcia .15 .40
116 Jacquez Green .15 .40
117 Shaun King .15 .40
118 Jimmy Smith .20 .50
119 James Stewart .15 .40
120 Brian Urlacher .30 .75
121 Tyrone Wheatley .20 .50
122 J.R. Redmond .15 .40
123 Eric Moulds .15 .40
124 Ricky Williams .20 .50
125 Brett Favre .50 1.25
126 Koren Robinson RC .60 1.50
127 Richard Seymour RC .75 2.00
128 Jamal Reynolds RC .50 1.25
129 Kevin Kasper RC .50 1.25
130 LaMont Jordan RC .75 2.00
131 Reggie Wayne RC 1.00 2.50
132 Travis Henry RC .60 1.50
133 Alge Crumpler RC .75 2.00
134 Quincy Carter RC .60 1.50
135 Michael Bennett RC .60 1.50
136 Jamie Winborn RC .60 1.50
137 Josh Heupel RC .75 2.00
138 Will Allen RC .75 2.00
139 Scotty Anderson RC .50 1.25
140 LaDainian Tomlinson RC 2.50 6.00
141 Freddie Mitchell RC .50 1.25
142 Gerard Warren RC .60 1.50
143 Chad Johnson RC .75 2.00
144 Todd Heap RC .60 1.50
145 Leonard Davis RC .75 2.00
146 Kevan Barlow RC .60 1.50
147 Correll Buckhalter RC .50 1.25
148 Fred Smoot RC .60 1.50
149 Steve Smith RC 1.50 4.00
150 David Terrell RC .60 1.50
151 Chris Chambers RC .50 1.25
152 Mike McMahon RC .60 1.50
153 Rudi Johnson RC .75 2.00
154 Marques Tuiasosopo RC .60 1.50
155 Deuce McAllister RC .75 2.00
156 Marcus Stroud RC .60 1.50
157 Bobby Newcombe RC .60 1.50
158 Rod Gardner RC .60 1.50
159 Drew Brees RC 15.00 40.00
160 Jesse Palmer RC .60 1.50
161 Derrick Gibson RC .50 1.25
162 James Jackson RC .50 1.25
163 Dan Morgan RC .60 1.50
164 Michael Vick RC 1.25 3.00
165 Snoop Minnis RC .50 1.25
166 Anthony Thomas RC .75 2.00
167 Andre Carter RC .60 1.50
168 Travis Minor RC .60 1.50
169 Quincy Morgan RC .60 1.50
170 Justin Smith RC 1.00 2.50
171 Tay Cody RC .50 1.25
172 Santana Moss RC .75 2.00
173 Sage Rosenfels RC .60 1.50
174 Robert Ferguson RC .75 2.00
175 Chris Weinke RC .60 1.50

2001 Stadium Club Common Threads

Common Threads were inserted in 2001 Stadium Club HTA packs only. The 6-card set featured one player from the Pro Bowl and one player from the Senior Bowl. Each card had a jersey swatch from each of the featured players. The card numbers carried a 'CT' prefix.

RANDOM INSERTS IN HTA PACKS
CTCR D.Culpepper/D.Rivers 3.00 8.00
CTDM C.Dillon/T.Minor 2.50 6.00
CTGT E.George/L.Tomlinson 12.00 30.00
CTHW M.Harrison/R.Wayne 5.00 12.00
CTJB E.James/K.Barlow 3.00 8.00
CTMJ E.Moulds/C.Johnson 4.00 10.00

2001 Stadium Club Common Threads Autographs

Common Threads were inserted in 2001 Stadium Club HTA packs only. The set featured one player from the Pro Bowl and one player from the Senior Bowl. Each card had jersey swatches from each of the featured players and autographs. The card numbers carried a 'CTA' prefix.

RANDOM INSERTS IN HTA PACKS
CTACR D.Culpepper/D.Rivers 30.00 80.00
CTAHW M.Harrison/R.Wayne 40.00 100.00
CTAJB E.James/K.Barlow 30.00 80.00
CTMJ E.Moulds/C.Johnson 25.00 60.00

2001 Stadium Club Co-Signers

Randomly inserted in packs of 2001 Stadium Club, this 5-card set contained a dual autographed cards from some of the top players from the NFL. Please note that 4 of the 5 cards were issued in packs as exchange cards. The exchange deadline printed on the cards is 06/30/2003.

COAL M.Anderson/J.Lewis 20.00 40.00
COCG D.Culpepper/J.Garcia 25.00 50.00
COFB B.Favre/A.Brooks 150.00 300.00

2001 Stadium Club Highlight Reels

Highlight Reels were inserted in packs of 2001 Stadium Club at a rate of 1:6 retail and 1:4 in HTA packs. The 5-card set featured some of the greatest moments in pro football history, the cardfronts showed the an image and the cardbacks told the story. Each card carried an 'HR' prefix for the card numbers.

COMPLETE SET (5) 6.00 15.00
STATED ODDS 1:6 HOB/RET, 1:4 HTA
HRAA Alan Ameche .60 1.50
HRBG Bob Griese 1.00 2.50
HRBS Bart Starr 2.00 5.00
HRJE John Elway 1.50 4.00
HRJN Joe Namath 1.50 4.00

2001 Stadium Club In Focus

In Focus cards were inserted in packs of 2001 Stadium Club at a rate of 1:8 retail and 1:6 in HTA packs. The cardfronts have a horizontal view and they are highlighted with silver-foil lettering. The cards had an 'IF' prefix for the card numbering.

COMPLETE SET (15) 7.50 20.00
STATED ODDS 1:8 HOB/RET, 1:6 HTA
IF1 Peyton Manning 1.25 3.00
IF2 Marshall Faulk .40 1.00
IF3 Torry Holt .40 1.00
IF4 Daunte Culpepper .40 1.00
IF5 Edgerrin James .40 1.00
IF6 Marvin Harrison .40 1.00
IF7 Jeff Garcia .30 .75
IF8 Robert Smith .30 .75
IF9 Randy Moss .40 1.00
IF10 Mike Anderson .30 .75
IF11 Corey Dillon .30 .75
IF12 Rod Smith .40 1.00
IF13 Brett Favre 1.00 2.50
IF14 Eddie George .50 1.25
IF15 Terrell Owens .40 1.00

2001 Stadium Club Lone Star Signatures

Randomly inserted in packs of 2001 Stadium Club, this 23-card set featured a mixture of veterans and rookies. The stated odds for the players vary according to the group they are associated with. There were 10 stated groups in which the players were broken into. The overall stated odds were 1:84 packs. Each card carried a 'LS' prefix for the card number.

GROUP 1 ODDS 1:13,802H, 1:14,515R
GROUP 2 ODDS 1:8971H, 1:9117R
GROUP 3 ODDS 1:1701H, 1:1698R
GROUP 4 ODDS 1:2719H, 1:2707R
GROUP 5 ODDS 1:4542H, 1:4559R
GROUP 6 ODDS 1:3385H, 1:3456R
GROUP 7 ODDS 1:451 HOB/RET
GROUP 8 ODDS 1:451 HOB/RET
GROUP 9 ODDS 1:693 HOB/RET
GROUP 10 ODDS 1:225 HOB/RET
OVERALL ODDS: 1:84 HOB/RET
LSAT Anthony Thomas 8 8.00 20.00
LSDA Dan Alexander 7 6.00 15.00
LSDB Drew Brees 7 200.00 400.00
LSDC Daunte Culpepper 2 6.00 15.00
LSDM Deuce McAllister 1 10.00 25.00
LSDT David Terrell 3 6.00 15.00
LSEG Eddie George 3 8.00 20.00
LSEJ Edgerrin James 1 8.00 20.00
LSJB Josh Booty 10 6.00 15.00
LSJH Joe Horn 7 5.00 12.00
LSJP Jesse Palmer 10 6.00 15.00
LSKB Kevan Barlow 9 6.00 15.00
LSKW Kenyatta Walker 10 5.00 12.00
LSLT LaDainian Tomlinson 7 40.00 80.00
LSMA Mike Anderson 7 5.00 12.00
LSMF Marshall Faulk 3 15.00 30.00
LSMH Marvin Harrison 6 15.00 30.00
LSMV Michael Vick 4 30.00 80.00
LSQM Quincy Morgan 8 6.00 15.00
LSRW Reggie Wayne 3 25.00 50.00
LSSD Stephen Davis 4 5.00 12.00
LSTH Travis Henry 7 6.00 15.00
LSTO Terrell Owens 5 15.00 40.00

2001 Stadium Club Pro Bowl Jerseys

Pro Bowl Jerseys were inserted into packs of 2001 Stadium Club at a rate of 1:44. This 33-card set featured a jersey swatch from a player who played in the 2001 Pro Bowl. The cards carried an 'SP' prefix for the card number, and had a Topps Authentic sticker on the back to ensure authenticity.

OVERALL STATED ODDS 1:44 HOB/RET
SPBM Brock Marion 2.00 5.00
SPCB Champ Bailey 2.50 6.00
SPCC Cris Carter 3.00 8.00
SPDA Donnie Abraham 2.00 5.00
SPDC Daunte Culpepper 2.50 6.00
SPDH Desmond Howard 2.50 6.00
SPEGE Eddie George 3.00 8.00
SPEJ Edgerrin James 2.50 6.00
SPHD Hugh Douglas 2.00 5.00
SPJA Jessie Armstead 2.00 5.00
SPJC Jeff Christy 2.00 5.00
SPJK Jevon Kearse 2.00 5.00
SPJO Jonathan Ogden 2.50 6.00
SPJS Jimmy Smith 2.50 6.00
SPJT Jeremiah Trotter 2.00 5.00
SPKM Keith Mitchell 2.00 5.00
SPLA Larry Allen 3.00 8.00
SPLE Luther Elliss 2.00 5.00
SPLG La'Roi Glover 2.00 5.00
SPMC Marco Coleman 2.00 5.00
SPMG Martin Gramatica 2.00 5.00
SPMH Marvin Harrison 2.50 6.00
SPRA Richie Anderson 2.00 5.00
SPRB Ruben Brown 2.00 5.00
SPRG Robert Griffith 2.00 5.00
SPRS Rod Smith 2.50 6.00
SPRW Rod Woodson 3.00 8.00
SPSA Stephen Alexander 2.00 5.00
SPTA Trace Armstrong 2.00 5.00
SPTG Tony Gonzalez 2.50 6.00
SPTO Terrell Owens 2.50 6.00
SPTV Troy Vincent 2.50 6.00
SPWS Warren Sapp 2.50 6.00

2001 Stadium Club Pro Bowl Jerseys Autographs

Pro Bowl Jersey Autographs were random inserts in packs of 2001 Stadium Club. This 3-card set featured a jersey swatch from a player who played in the 2001 Pro Bowl along with his autograph. The cards carried an 'SPA' prefix for the card number, and had a Topps Authentic sticker on the back to ensure authenticity.

RANDOM INSERTS IN HTA PACKS
SPADC Daunte Culpepper 12.00 30.00
SPAEJ Edgerrin James 12.00 30.00
SPAMH Marvin Harrison 12.00 30.00

2001 Stadium Club Stepping Up

Stepping Up was a random insert in 2001 Stadium Club packs and was seeded at a rate of 1:8 and 1:6 HTA. The 15-card set featured some of the players that 'stepped up' to the challenge of the NFL. The cards carried an 'SU' prefix for the card numbering.

COMPLETE SET (15) 12.50 25.00
STATED ODDS 1:8 HOB/RET, 1:6 HTA
SU1 David Terrell .40 1.00
SU2 LaDainian Tomlinson 1.50 4.00
SU3 Michael Vick .75 2.00
SU4 Koren Robinson .40 1.00
SU5 Michael Bennett .40 1.00
SU6 Chad Johnson .50 1.25
SU7 Drew Brees 10.00 25.00
SU8 Reggie Wayne .60 1.50
SU9 Freddie Mitchell .30 .75
SU10 Chris Weinke .40 1.00
SU11 Rod Gardner .40 1.00
SU12 Chris Chambers .30 .75
SU13 Deuce McAllister .50 1.25
SU14 Santana Moss .50 1.25
SU15 Robert Ferguson .50 1.25

2002 Stadium Club

This 200-card base set includes 125 veterans and 75 rookies. The rookies were inserted at a rate of 1:4. Boxes contained 24 packs of six cards. HTA jumbo packs contained 15 cards. Hobby pack SRP was $2.99 and HTA jumbo pack SRP was $5.99.

COMPLETE SET (200) 40.00 80.00
COMP.SET w/o SP's (125) 10.00 25.00
126-200 ROOKIE STATED ODDS 1:4
1 Randy Moss .20 .50
2 Kordell Stewart .15 .40
3 Marvin Harrison .20 .50
4 Chris Weinke .15 .40
5 James Allen .15 .40
6 Michael Pittman .20 .50
7 Quincy Carter .15 .40
8 Mike Anderson .15 .40
9 Mike McMahon .15 .40
10 Chris Chambers .15 .40
11 Laveranues Coles .20 .50
12 Curtis Conway .20 .50
13 Brad Johnson .20 .50
14 Shaun Alexander .15 .40
15 Jerry Rice .50 1.25
16 Rod Gardner .15 .40
17 Derrick Mason .15 .40
18 Tom Brady 1.25 3.00
19 Jimmy Smith .20 .50
20 Tim Couch .15 .40
21 Jim Miller .15 .40
22 Eric Moulds .15 .40
23 Michael Vick .20 .50
24 Jon Kitna .15 .40
25 Johnnie Morton .20 .50
26 Priest Holmes .15 .40
27 Aaron Brooks .15 .40
28 Duce Staley .15 .40
29 LaDainian Tomlinson .25 .60
30 Lamar Smith .15 .40
31 Rod Smith .20 .50
32 Richard Huntley .15 .40
33 Antonio Freeman .25 .60
34 Amani Toomer .15 .40
35 Hines Ward .20 .50
36 Marshall Faulk .20 .50
37 Steve McNair .20 .50
38 Tim Brown .25 .60
39 Curtis Martin .20 .50
40 Kevin Johnson .15 .40
41 Rob Johnson .20 .50
42 Qadry Ismail .15 .40
43 Daunte Culpepper .20 .50
44 Willie Jackson .15 .40
45 Jeff Garcia .15 .40
46 Matt Hasselbeck .15 .40
47 Corey Bradford .15 .40
48 Snoop Minnis .15 .40
49 Ron Dayne .20 .50
50 Peyton Manning .60 1.50
51 Drew Bledsoe .20 .50
52 Terry Glenn .20 .50
53 Warrick Dunn .15 .40
54 Mark Brunell .20 .50
55 James Stewart .15 .40
56 Muhsin Muhammad .15 .40
57 Jake Plummer .15 .40
58 Terance Mathis .15 .40
59 Rocket Ismail .20 .50
60 Joe Horn .15 .40
61 Wayne Chrebet .15 .40
62 James Thrash .20 .50
63 Stephen Davis .15 .40
64 Isaac Bruce .25 .60
65 Peter Warrick .15 .40
66 Anthony Thomas .20 .50
67 Maurice Smith .15 .40
68 Tony Gonzalez .20 .50
69 Michael Bennett .15 .40
70 Ike Hilliard .15 .40
71 Plaxico Burress .15 .40
72 Darrell Jackson .20 .50
73 Kevan Barlow .15 .40
74 Ray Lewis .25 .60
75 Emmitt Smith .40 1.00
76 Bill Schroeder .15 .40
77 Az-Zahir Hakim .15 .40
78 Troy Brown .15 .40
79 Keyshawn Johnson .20 .50
80 Tim Dwight .15 .40
81 Peerless Price .15 .40
82 Marty Booker .15 .40
83 Terrell Davis .20 .50
84 Dominic Rhodes .15 .40
85 Jay Fiedler .20 .50
86 Rich Gannon .20 .50
87 Terrell Owens .20 .50
88 Donald Hayes .15 .40
89 Thomas Jones .15 .40
90 Ricky Williams .20 .50
91 Donovan McNabb .20 .50
92 Eddie George .20 .50
93 Germane Crowell .15 .40
94 David Terrell .15 .40
95 Alex Van Pelt .15 .40
96 Antowain Smith .20 .50
97 Jerome Bettis .25 .60
98 Mike Alstott .15 .40
99 Doug Flutie .20 .50
100 Kurt Warner .20 .50
101 Cris Carter .25 .60
102 Oronde Gadsden .15 .40
103 Ahman Green .20 .50
104 Corey Dillon .15 .40
105 Marcus Robinson .20 .50
106 Shannon Sharpe .20 .50
107 Kerry Collins .15 .40
108 Garrison Hearst .15 .40
109 David Boston .15 .40
110 Travis Henry .15 .40
111 James Jackson .15 .40
112 Fred Taylor .15 .40
113 Edgerrin James .20 .50
114 Vinny Testaverde .15 .40
115 Todd Pinkston .15 .40
116 Koren Robinson .15 .40
117 Torry Holt .20 .50
118 Brian Griese .15 .40
119 Trent Green .15 .40
120 James McKnight .15 .40
121 Charlie Garner .20 .50
122 Tiki Barber .20 .50
123 Joey Galloway .20 .50
124 Quincy Morgan .15 .40
125 Brett Favre .50 1.25
126 Joey Harrington RC .60 1.50
127 Ashley Lelie RC .60 1.50
128 Terry Charles RC .60 1.50
129 Charles Grant RC 1.00 2.50
130 Levar Fisher RC .60 1.50
131 Larry Tripplett RC .60 1.50
132 Quentin Jammer RC 1.00 2.50
133 Ron Johnson RC .75 2.00
134 Maurice Morris RC .75 2.00
135 Roy Williams RC .60 1.50
136 Kurt Kittner RC .60 1.50
137 Dennis Johnson RC .60 1.50
138 Seth Burford RC .60 1.50
139 Michael Lewis RC .75 2.00
140 William Green RC .75 2.00
141 Rohan Davey RC 1.00 2.50
142 Rocky Calmus RC .75 2.00
143 Robert Thomas RC .60 1.50
144 Travis Stephens RC .60 1.50
145 Ladell Betts RC 1.00 2.50
146 Daniel Graham RC .75 2.00
147 Chester Taylor RC 1.00 2.50
148 Tim Carter RC .75 2.00
149 Lito Sheppard RC 1.00 2.50
150 David Carr RC .60 1.50
151 Alex Brown RC 1.00 2.50
152 John Henderson RC .75 2.00
153 Jamar Martin RC .75 2.00
154 Raonall Smith RC .60 1.50
155 Leonard Henry RC .60 1.50
156 T.J. Duckett RC .60 1.50
157 Patrick Ramsey RC .75 2.00
158 Antwaan Randle El RC .75 2.00
159 Luke Staley RC .60 1.50
160 Jon McGraw RC .60 1.50
161 Phillip Buchanon RC 1.00 2.50
162 Dwight Freeney RC 1.25 3.00
163 Mike Rumph RC .60 1.50
164 Albert Haynesworth RC 1.00 2.50
165 Antonio Bryant RC 1.00 2.50
166 Josh Reed RC .75 2.00
167 Eric Crouch RC 1.00 2.50
168 Reche Caldwell RC .75 2.00
169 Adrian Peterson RC .75 2.00
170 Jonathan Wells RC .75 2.00
171 Wendell Bryant RC .60 1.50
172 Tellis Redmon RC .60 1.50
173 Josh McCown RC 1.00 2.50
174 DeShaun Foster RC 1.00 2.50
175 Cliff Russell RC .60 1.50
176 David Garrard RC .75 2.00
177 Brian Westbrook RC 1.25 3.00
178 Anthony Weaver RC .60 1.50
179 Bryan Thomas RC .60 1.50
180 Kalimba Edwards RC .75 2.00
181 Javon Walker RC 1.00 2.50
182 Marquise Walker RC .60 1.50
183 Deion Branch RC 1.00 2.50
184 Lamar Gordon RC .75 2.00
185 Jeremy Shockey RC 1.00 2.50
186 Clinton Portis RC 1.00 2.50
187 Napoleon Harris RC .75 2.00
188 Freddie Milons RC .60 1.50
189 Julius Peppers RC 1.50 4.00
190 Andre Davis RC .60 1.50
191 Travis Fisher RC .75 2.00
192 Chad Hutchinson RC .60 1.50
193 Najeh Davenport RC .60 1.50
194 Ed Reed RC 4.00 10.00
195 Donte Stallworth RC 1.00 2.50
196 Brandon Doman RC .60 1.50
197 Zak Kustok RC .60 1.50
198 Randy Fasani RC .60 1.50
199 J.T. O'Sullivan RC .75 2.00
200 Jabar Gaffney RC .60 1.50

2002 Stadium Club Photographer's Proofs

*1-125 VETS: 6X TO 15X BASIC CARDS
*126-200 ROOKIES: 1.5X TO 4X
STATED ODDS 1:21
STATED PRINT RUN 199 SER.#'d SETS

2002 Stadium Club Super Bowl Predictor Red

*1-125 RED VETS: 20X TO 50X BASIC CARDS
*126-200 RED ROOKIES: 5X TO 12X BASIC RC
ANNOUNCED PRINT RUN 29 SETS

2002 Stadium Club Co-Signers

Inserted in hobby packs only at a rate of 1:640, this set features cards that have authentic autographs from two NFL stars.

STATED ODDS 1:640
CSCH D.Carr/J.Harrington 25.00 60.00
CSFW B.Favre/K.Warner 125.00 250.00
CSGF W.Green/D.Foster 15.00 40.00
CSOB T.Owens/D.Boston 40.00 80.00
CSWB K.Warner/T.Brady 250.00 400.00

2002 Stadium Club Fabric of Champions

Inserted at a rate of 1:87, this 8-card insert set offers a piece of game-used relic honoring NFL players who have won a championship on the college or pro level. The cards are sequentially numbered to 1499. There is a gold parallel sequentially numbered to 25.

FABRIC/1499 STATED ODDS 1:87
STATED PRINT RUN 1499 SER.#'d SETS
*GOLD/25: 1X TO 2.5X BASIC JSY
GOLD/25 STATED ODDS 1:1581
GOLD PRINT RUN 25 SER.#'d SETS
FCAF Antonio Freeman 4.00 10.00
FCJK Jevon Kearse 2.50 6.00
FCPH Priest Holmes 2.50 6.00
FCRL Ray Lewis 4.00 10.00
FCRS Rod Smith 3.00 8.00
FCSY Steve Young 6.00 15.00
FCTD Terrell Davis 4.00 10.00
FCWD Warrick Dunn 2.50 6.00

2002 Stadium Club Highlight Material

Inserted at a rate of 1:31, this 18-card insert features top pro bowlers with a swatch of their game-used jersey from the 2002 NFC/AFC Pro Bowl. There is also a gold parallel available, which is serial #'d to 25. The gold version was inserted at a rate of 1:702.

STATED ODDS 1:31
*GOLD/25: 1X TO 2.5X BASIC JSY
GOLD/25 STATED ODDS 1:702
GOLD STATED PRINT RUN 25 SER.#'d SETS
HMAG Ahman Green 3.00 8.00
HMBU Brian Urlacher 4.00 10.00
HMDB David Boston 2.50 6.00
HMGH Garrison Hearst 2.50 6.00
HMHD Hugh Douglas 2.50 6.00
HMJA Jessie Armstead 2.50 6.00
HMJG Jeff Garcia 2.50 6.00
HMJR John Randle 3.00 8.00
HMJS Junior Seau 3.00 8.00
HMKS Kordell Stewart 2.50 6.00
HMKW Kurt Warner 3.00 8.00
HMMA Mike Alstott 2.50 6.00
HMMH Marvin Harrison 3.00 8.00
HMMS Michael Strahan 3.00 8.00
HMRG Rich Gannon 3.00 8.00
HMSS Steve Smith 4.00 10.00
HMTB Tim Brown 4.00 10.00
HMTO Terrell Owens 3.00 8.00

2002 Stadium Club Lone Star Signatures

Inserted in packs at a rate of 1:92, this 19-card insert set offers signatures from top NFL veterans and rookies. The cards feature the Topps Certified Autograph Issue stamp and the Topps Genuine Issue sticker.

OVERALL STATED ODDS 1:92
LSAP Adrian Peterson 6.00 15.00
LSAS Antowain Smith 6.00 15.00
LSBF Brett Favre 100.00 175.00
LSCC Chris Chambers 5.00 12.00
LSDB David Boston
LSDC David Carr 5.00 12.00
LSDF DeShaun Foster 8.00 20.00
LSJA John Abraham 6.00 15.00
LSJH Joey Harrington 5.00 12.00
LSJR Josh Reed 6.00 15.00
LSJT James Thrash 6.00 15.00
LSKK Kurt Kittner 5.00 12.00
LSKW Kurt Warner 25.00 60.00
LSMB Marty Booker 5.00 12.00
LSMP Mike Pearson 5.00 12.00
LSRW Roy Williams 5.00 12.00
LSTB Tom Brady 200.00 350.00
LSTO Terrell Owens 12.00 30.00
LSWG William Green 6.00 15.00

2002 Stadium Club Reel Time

Inserted in packs at a rate of 1:12, this 25-card insert set features players found on the highlight reels almost daily.

COMPLETE SET (25) 25.00 60.00
STATED ODDS 1:12
RT1 Marshall Faulk 1.00 2.50
RT2 Peyton Manning 3.00 8.00
RT3 Randy Moss 1.00 2.50
RT4 Stephen Davis .75 2.00
RT5 Jeff Garcia .75 2.00
RT6 Donovan McNabb 1.00 2.50
RT7 Edgerrin James 1.00 2.50
RT8 Trent Green .75 2.00
RT9 Eddie George 1.00 2.50
RT10 Ahman Green 1.00 2.50
RT11 Plaxico Burress .75 2.00
RT12 David Boston .75 2.00
RT13 Tom Brady 6.00 15.00
RT14 Marvin Harrison 1.00 2.50
RT15 Brett Favre 2.50 6.00
RT16 Ricky Williams 1.00 2.50
RT17 Kordell Stewart .75 2.00
RT18 Curtis Martin 1.00 2.50
RT19 Anthony Thomas 1.00 2.50
RT20 Shaun Alexander .75 2.00
RT21 LaDainian Tomlinson 1.25 3.00
RT22 Kurt Warner 1.00 2.50
RT23 Jerome Bettis 1.25 3.00
RT24 Priest Holmes .75 2.00
RT25 Terrell Owens 1.00 2.50

2002 Stadium Club Touchdown Treasures

Inserted at a rate of 1:516, this five-card insert set was issued exclusively in hobby packs. The cards contain game-used pylon pieces from the Super Bowl XXXVI end zones. There is also a gold parallel of this set with each card serial numbered to 25 (gold stated odds 1:2067 packs).

PYLON/75 STATED ODDS 1:516
STATED PRINT RUN 75 SER.#'d SETS
*GOLD/25: .6X TO 1.5X BASIC PYLON
GOLD/25 STATED ODDS 1:2067
GOLD PRINT RUN 25 SER.#'d SETS
TTDP David Patten 6.00 15.00
TTKW Kurt Warner 12.00 30.00
TTRP Ricky Proehl 8.00 20.00
TTTB Tom Brady 40.00 80.00
TTTL Ty Law 10.00 25.00

2008 Stadium Club

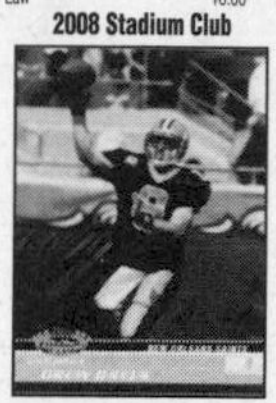

COMP.SET w/o RC's (100) 25.00 50.00
ROOKIE/1799 ODDS 1:2 HOB, 1:7 RET
1 Drew Brees .50 1.25
2 Tom Brady 1.50 4.00
3 Peyton Manning 1.25 3.00
4 Carson Palmer .40 1.00
5 Ben Roethlisberger .50 1.25
6 Eli Manning .40 1.00
7 Tony Romo .40 1.00
8 Tarvaris Jackson .30 .75
9 Vince Young .30 .75
10 Steven Jackson .30 .75
11 Willie Parker .40 1.00
12 Clinton Portis .30 .75
13 Adrian Peterson .50 1.25
14 LaDainian Tomlinson .50 1.25
15 Marion Barber .30 .75
16 Brian Westbrook .30 .75
17 Fred Taylor .30 .75
18 Marshawn Lynch .40 1.00
19 Joseph Addai .30 .75
20 Willis McGahee .30 .75
21 Frank Gore .40 1.00
22 Reggie Wayne .40 1.00
23 Anquan Boldin .30 .75
24 Randy Moss .40 1.00
25 Plaxico Burress .30 .75
26 Terrell Owens .40 1.00
27 Andre Johnson .40 1.00
28 Larry Fitzgerald .40 1.00
29 Braylon Edwards .30 .75
30 Steve Smith .40 1.00
31 Jon Kitna .30 .75
32 Matt Hasselbeck .30 .75
33 Derek Anderson .30 .75
34 Jay Cutler .30 .75
35 Kurt Warner .40 1.00
36 Donovan McNabb .40 1.00
37 Philip Rivers .50 1.25
38 Jason Campbell .30 .75
39 David Garrard .30 .75
40 Jeff Garcia .30 .75
41 Marc Bulger .30 .75
42 Jamal Lewis .40 1.00
43 Edgerrin James .40 1.00
44 Thomas Jones .30 .75
45 Lendale White .30 .75
46 Justin Fargas .30 .75
47 Brandon Jacobs .30 .75
48 Ryan Grant .40 1.00
49 Earnest Graham .30 .75
50 Chad Johnson .30 .75
51 Brandon Marshall .40 1.00
52 Roddy White .30 .75
53 Marques Colston .30 .75
54 Torry Holt .40 1.00
55 Wes Welker .40 1.00
56 Bobby Engram .30 .75
57 T.J. Houshmandzadeh .30 .75
58 Jerricho Cotchery .30 .75
59 Kevin Curtis .30 .75
60 Derrick Mason .30 .75
61 Donald Driver .40 1.00
62 Jason Witten .40 1.00
63 Tony Gonzalez .40 1.00
64 Kellen Winslow .30 .75
65 Antonio Gates .40 1.00
66 Chris Cooley .30 .75
67 Matt Schaub .30 .75
68 Laurence Maroney .40 1.00
69 Joey Galloway .40 1.00
70 Jeremy Shockey .30 .75
71 Dwayne Bowe .40 1.00
72 Dallas Clark .30 .75
73 Maurice Jones-Drew .30 .75
74 Ray Lewis .50 1.25
75 Michael Strahan .40 1.00
76 Derrick Brooks .30 .75
77 Ed Reed .40 1.00
78 Brian Urlacher .50 1.25
79 Jason Taylor .40 1.00
80 Bob Sanders .40 1.00
81 Patrick Kerney .30 .75
82 Albert Haynesworth .30 .75
83 Antonio Cromartie .30 .75
84 Mike Vrabel .30 .75
85 DeMarcus Ware .40 1.00
86 Ronde Barber .30 .75
87 James Harrison RC 3.00 8.00
88 Patrick Willis .40 1.00
89 Mario Williams .40 1.00
90 Osi Umenyiora .30 .75
91 Damon Huard .30 .75
92 Joey Harrington .30 .75
93 Roy Williams WR .30 .75
94 Champ Bailey .40 1.00
95 Shawne Merriman .30 .75
96 Chester Taylor .30 .75
97 Ron Dayne .30 .75
98 Santonio Holmes .30 .75
99 Lee Evans .40 1.00
100 Chris Chambers .30 .75
101 Matt Ryan RC 3.00 8.00
102 Brian Brohm RC 1.00 2.50
103 Chad Henne RC 1.25 3.00
104 Joe Flacco RC 2.00 5.00
105 Andre Woodson RC 1.00 2.50
106 John David Booty RC 1.00 2.50
107 Josh Johnson RC 1.00 2.50
108 Colt Brennan RC 1.25 3.00
109 Dennis Dixon RC 1.00 2.50
110 Erik Ainge RC 1.00 2.50
111 Darren McFadden RC 1.00 2.50
112 Rashard Mendenhall RC 1.00 2.50
113 Jonathan Stewart RC 1.50 4.00
114 Felix Jones RC 1.00 2.50
115 Jamaal Charles RC 1.50 4.00
116 Ray Rice RC 1.00 2.50
117 Chris Johnson RC 1.25 3.00
118 Mike Hart RC 1.00 2.50
119 Matt Forte RC 1.50 4.00
120 Kevin Smith RC 1.00 2.50
121 Steve Slaton RC 1.00 2.50
122 Malcolm Kelly RC 1.00 2.50
123 Limas Sweed RC 1.00 2.50
124 DeSean Jackson RC 2.00 5.00
125 James Hardy RC 1.00 2.50
126 Mario Manningham RC 1.00 2.50
127 Devin Thomas RC 1.00 2.50
128 Early Doucet RC 1.00 2.50
129 Andre Caldwell RC 1.00 2.50
130 Jordy Nelson RC 3.00 8.00
131 Eddie Royal RC 1.00 2.50
132 Earl Bennett RC 1.50 4.00
133 Fred Davis RC 1.00 2.50
134 Dustin Keller RC 1.25 3.00
135 John Carlson RC 1.00 2.50
136 Chris Long RC 1.25 3.00
137 Jake Long RC 1.50 4.00
138 Glenn Dorsey RC 1.00 2.50
139 Sedrick Ellis RC 1.00 2.50
140 Vernon Gholston RC 1.00 2.50
141 Kevin O'Connell RC 1.00 2.50
142 Leodis McKelvin RC 1.25 3.00
143 Keith Rivers RC 1.00 2.50
144 Mike Jenkins RC 1.00 2.50
145 Derrick Harvey RC 1.00 2.50
146 Phillip Merling RC 1.00 2.50
147 Kentwan Balmer RC 1.00 2.50
148 Dan Connor RC 1.00 2.50
149 D.Rodgers-Cromartie RC 1.25 3.00
150 Aqib Talib RC 1.50 4.00
151 Sam Baker RC 1.00 2.50
152 Adrian Arrington RC 1.00 2.50
153 Donnie Avery RC 1.25 3.00
154 Marcus Henry RC 1.00 2.50
155 Dexter Jackson RC 1.50 4.00
156 Jerome Simpson RC 1.25 3.00
157 Keenan Burton RC 1.00 2.50
158 Tashard Choice RC 1.00 2.50
159 Harry Douglas RC 1.25 3.00
160 Marcus Griffin RC 1.00 2.50
161 DJ Hall RC 1.00 2.50
162 Justin Forsett RC 1.25 3.00
163 Jaymar Johnson RC 1.00 2.50
164 Jacob Hester RC 1.00 2.50
165 Ali Highsmith RC 1.00 2.50
166 Sam Keller RC 1.00 2.50
167 Lance Leggett RC 1.50 4.00
168 Xavier Omon RC 1.00 2.50
169 Marcus Monk RC 1.25 3.00
170 Anthony Morelli RC 1.00 2.50
171 Marcus Smith RC 1.25 3.00
172 Allen Patrick RC 1.00 2.50
173 Kenny Phillips RC 1.00 2.50
174 Tyrell Johnson RC 1.00 2.50
175 Matt Flynn RC 1.00 2.50
176 Martin Rucker RC 1.00 2.50
177 Jordon Dizon RC 1.00 2.50
178 Owen Schmitt RC 1.00 2.50
179 Martellus Bennett RC 1.25 3.00
180 Terrence Wheatley RC 1.00 2.50
181 Terrell Thomas RC 1.00 2.50
182 Kyle Wright RC 1.00 2.50
183 Darius Reynaud RC 1.00 2.50
184 Chris Williams RC 1.00 2.50
185 Jeff Otah RC 1.00 2.50
186 Xavier Adibi RC 1.00 2.50
187 Jerod Mayo RC 1.50 4.00
188 Calais Campbell RC 1.25 3.00
189 Charles Godfrey RC 1.00 2.50
190 Reggie Smith RC 1.00 2.50
191 Pat Sims RC 1.25 3.00
192 Curtis Lofton RC 1.25 3.00
193 Tracy Porter RC 1.25 3.00
194 Patrick Lee RC 1.00 2.50
195 Cliff Avril RC 1.50 4.00
196 Trevor Laws RC 1.00 2.50
197 Lawrence Jackson RC 1.00 2.50
198 Antoine Cason RC 1.25 3.00
199 Chevis Jackson RC 1.00 2.50
200 Justin King RC 1.25 3.00

2008 Stadium Club First Day Issue

*VETS 1-100: 1X TO 2.5X BASIC CARDS
FIRST DAY/1499 ODDS 1:2 H, 1:7 R

2008 Stadium Club Photographer's Proofs Gold

*VETS 1-100: 3X TO 8X BASIC CARDS
*ROOKIES 101-200: .8X TO 2X BASIC CARDS
1-100 PP GOLD/50 ODDS 1:32H, 1:195R
101-200 PP GOLD/50 ODDS 1:32H, 1:335R

2008 Stadium Club Photographer's Proofs Platinum

UNPRICED PLATINUM 1/1 ODDS 1:940 HOB

2008 Stadium Club Photographer's Proofs Silver

*VETS 1-100: 2X TO 5X BASIC CARDS
*ROOKIES 101-200: .5X TO 1.2X BASIC CARDS
1-100 PP SLVR/199 ODDS 1:9H, 1:43R
101-200 PP SLVR/199 ODDS 1:9H, 1:75R

2008 Stadium Club Premiere Edition

*ROOKIES/50: .8X TO 2X BASIC RC/1799

2008 Stadium Club Special Edition

*ROOKIES: .4X TO 1X BASIC RC/1799

2008 Stadium Club Beam Team Autographs

GROUP A ODDS 1:452 H, 1:30,870 R
GROUP B ODDS 1:100 H, 1:6200 R
*GOLD/25: .5X TO 1.2X BASIC AUTO
BTAAG Anthony Gonzalez A 10.00 25.00
BTAAK Aaron Kampman A 40.00 80.00
BTAAW Andre Woodson B 10.00 25.00
BTABB Bernard Berrian A 10.00 25.00
BTABBR Brian Brohm B 10.00 25.00
BTABE Braylon Edwards A 10.00 25.00
BTACB Colt Brennan B 8.00 20.00
BTACH Chad Henne B 10.00 25.00
BTACL Chris Long B 5.00 12.00
BTADJ DeSean Jackson B 8.00 20.00
BTADM Darren McFadden B 25.00 60.00
BTAEM Eli Manning A 40.00 80.00
BTAFJ Felix Jones B 4.00 10.00
BTAGD Glenn Dorsey B 10.00 25.00
BTAJA Joseph Addai A 12.00 30.00
BTAJC Jamaal Charles B 8.00 20.00
BTAJF Joe Flacco B 15.00 40.00
BTAJH James Hardy B 10.00 25.00
BTAJS Jonathan Stewart B 20.00 50.00
BTAKW Kellen Winslow A 12.00 30.00
BTALS Limas Sweed B 4.00 10.00
BTAMH Mike Hart B 10.00 25.00
BTAMK Malcolm Kelly B 10.00 25.00
BTAMR Matt Ryan B 50.00 100.00
BTARM Rashard Mendenhall B 4.00 10.00
BTARR Ray Rice B 4.00 10.00
BTARW Reggie Wayne A 10.00 25.00
BTASS Steve Slaton B 6.00 15.00
BTAVY Vince Young A 15.00 40.00

2008 Stadium Club Beam Team Jerseys

JERSEY/99 ODDS 1:52 H, 1:503 R
*RETAIL: .3X TO .8X HOBBY/99
ONE SILVER PER SPECIAL RETAIL BOX
BTRAP Adrian Peterson 10.00 25.00
BTRBB Brian Brohm 1.25 3.00
BTRBR Ben Roethlisberger 6.00 15.00
BTRBU Brian Urlacher 6.00 15.00
BTRBW Brian Westbrook 4.00 10.00
BTRCH Chad Henne 1.50 4.00
BTRCL Chris Long 1.50 4.00
BTRDA Donnie Avery 5.00 12.00
BTRDM Darren McFadden 1.25 3.00
BTREM Eli Manning 5.00 12.00
BTRFJ Felix Jones 1.25 3.00
BTRFT Fred Taylor 4.00 10.00
BTRGD Glenn Dorsey 1.25 3.00
BTRJB John David Booty 1.25 3.00
BTRJL Jake Long 2.00 5.00
BTRJS Jonathan Stewart 2.00 5.00
BTRKO Kevin O'Connell 1.25 3.00
BTRLT LaDainian Tomlinson 6.00 15.00
BTRMB Marion Barber 4.00 10.00
BTRMK Malcolm Kelly 1.25 3.00
BTRMR Matt Ryan 4.00 10.00
BTRMS Michael Strahan 5.00 12.00
BTRPM Peyton Manning 15.00 40.00
BTRPR Philip Rivers 6.00 15.00
BTRRM Rashard Mendenhall 1.25 3.00
BTRTR Tony Romo 10.00 25.00

2008 Stadium Club Impact Relics

GROUP A/549 ODDS 1:39H, 1:375R
GROUP B/1349 ODDS 1:3H, 1:30R
*GOLD/50: .6X TO 1.5X BASIC JSY/1349
*GOLD/50: .6X TO 1.5X BASIC JSY/549
GOLD/50 ODDS 1:52 HOB, 1:505 RET
IRAC Andre Caldwell 1.50 4.00
IRAH Al Harris/1399 1.50 4.00
IRAS Asante Samuel 1.50 4.00
IRBB Brian Brohm 1.50 4.00
IRCH Chad Henne 2.00 5.00
IRCHJ Chad Johnson 1.50 4.00
IRCJ Chris Johnson 2.00 5.00
IRCP Carson Palmer/549 2.00 5.00
IRDJ DeSean Jackson 3.00 8.00
IRDM Darren McFadden 1.50 4.00
IRDR DeMeco Ryans 2.00 5.00
IRED Early Doucet 1.50 4.00
IRER Ed Reed 2.00 5.00
IRFJ Felix Jones 1.50 4.00
IRHD Harry Douglas 2.00 5.00
IRGE Greg Ellis 1.50 4.00
IRJB John David Booty 1.50 4.00
IRJC Jamaal Charles 2.50 6.00
IRJF Joe Flacco 3.00 8.00
IRJG Jeff Garcia 1.50 4.00
IRJH James Hardy 1.50 4.00
IRJL John Lynch 2.00 5.00
IRJLO Jake Long 2.50 6.00
IRJN Jerious Norwood/549 1.50 4.00
IRJR JaMarcus Russell/549 1.50 4.00
IRJS Jonathan Stewart 2.50 6.00
IRKO Kevin O'Connell 1.50 4.00
IRKS Kevin Smith 1.50 4.00
IRKW Kevin Williams 1.50 4.00
IRKWI Kellen Winslow 1.50 4.00
IRLN Lorenzo Neal 1.50 4.00
IRLS Limas Sweed 1.50 4.00
IRLT Lofa Tatupu/1399 1.50 4.00
IRLW LenDale White/549 1.50 4.00
IRMF Matt Forte 2.50 6.00
IRMK Malcolm Kelly 1.50 4.00
IRML Marshawn Lynch/549 2.00 5.00
IRMM Mario Manningham 1.50 4.00
IRMR Matt Ryan 5.00 12.00
IRMT Marcus Trufant 1.50 4.00
IRRL Ray Lewis 2.50 6.00
IRRM Rashard Mendenhall 1.50 4.00
IRRR Ray Rice 1.50 4.00
IRRW Roy Williams S 1.50 4.00
IRSA Shaun Alexander 1.50 4.00
IRSS Steve Slaton 1.50 4.00
IRTO Terrell Owens/549 2.00 5.00
IRVY Vince Young 1.50 4.00
IRWD Warrick Dunn 1.50 4.00

2008 Stadium Club Impact Relics Dual

DUAL/50 ODDS 1:52 HOB, 1:505 RET
UNPRICED GOLD/10 ODDS 1:280 HOB
DRBA R.Brown/J.Addai 2.00 5.00
DRBB C.Bailey/R.Barber 2.50 6.00
DRBD B.Brohm/H.Douglas 2.50 6.00
DRBDO D.Bowe/E.Doucet 2.50 6.00
DRBM R.Bush/D.McAllister 2.50 6.00
DRBME M.Barber/Mendenhall 2.00 5.00
DRBP L.Betts/C.Portis 2.00 5.00
DRCB B.Croyle/D.Bowe 2.50 6.00
DRCD J.Charles/G.Dorsey 3.00 8.00
DRCS A.Caldwell/J.Simpson 2.50 6.00
DRCSW J.Charles/L.Sweed 3.00 8.00
DRGD D.Garrard/M.Jones-Drew 2.00 5.00
DRHA Hasselbeck/Alexander 2.00 5.00
DRHF C.Henne/J.Flacco 4.00 10.00
DRHM C.Henne/Manningham 2.50 6.00
DRHE C.Henne/B.Edwards 2.50 6.00
DRHW A.Hawk/P.Willis 2.50 6.00
DRJD D.Jackson/E.Doucet 4.00 10.00
DRJF A.Johnson/L.Fitzgerald 2.50 6.00
DRJL D.Jackson/M.Lynch 4.00 10.00
DRJJ R.Johnson/C.Johnson 2.00 5.00
DRJJA S.Jackson/B.Jacobs 2.00 5.00
DRJS C.Johnson/K.Smith 2.50 6.00
DRJW B.Jackson/D.Wynn 2.50 6.00
DRJWA T.Jones/L.Washington 2.00 5.00
DRLB M.Leinart/J.Booty 2.00 5.00
DRLF J.Losman/M.Forte 3.00 8.00
DRLH J.Long/C.Henne 3.00 8.00
DRMJ D.McFadden/F.Jones 2.00 5.00
DRMM E.Manning/P.Manning 8.00 20.00
DRMS Mendenhall/J.Stewart 3.00 8.00
DROK G.Olsen/D.Keller 2.50 6.00
DRPE R.Parrish/L.Evans 2.50 6.00
DRPM A.Peterson/D.McFadden 3.00 8.00
DRPW T.Polamalu/R.Williams S 3.00 8.00
DRRB M.Ryan/B.Brohm 6.00 15.00
DRRJ R.Rice/F.Jones 2.00 5.00
DRRM M.Ryan/D.McFadden 6.00 15.00
DRRQ J.Russell/B.Quinn 2.00 5.00
DRRS A.Rodgers/A.Smith QB 6.00 15.00
DRSR S.Slaton/R.Rice 2.00 5.00
DRTM D.Thomas/M.Manningham 2.00 5.00
DRTP L.Tomlinson/A.Peterson 3.00 8.00
DRWO M.Williams/A.Okoye 2.50 6.00
DRWS D.Williams/J.Stewart 3.00 8.00
DRHWA S.Holmes/H.Ward 2.50 6.00

2008 Stadium Club Impact Relics Triple

TRIPLE/50 ODDS 1:52 HOB, 1:505 RET
UNPRICED GOLD/10 ODDS 1:280 HOB
TRBHF Brohm/Henne/Flacco 4.00 10.00
TRBMJ Brohm/Menden/Jackson 4.00 10.00
TRBMM Brady/Maroney/Moss 12.00 30.00
TRBSS Booty/Stewart/Sweed 6.00 15.00
TRBST Burress/Smith USC/Tmer 6.00 15.00
TRCCC Clemens/Coles/Cotchery 5.00 12.00
TRCSJ Charles/Stewart/Jackson 6.00 15.00
TRDAW Dorsey/Adams/M.Williams 5.00 12.00
TRDPW Dwkns/Polam/Will.S 6.00 15.00
TREPE Edwards/Parrish/Evans 6.00 15.00
TRFBB Fitzgrld/Boldin/Breaston 5.00 12.00
TRFHB Flacco/Henne/Brohm 4.00 10.00
TRFME Fitzgerald/Moss/Edwards 8.00 20.00
TRHAT Hassel/Alex/Trufant 5.00 12.00
TRHFB Henne/Flacco/Booty 4.00 10.00
TRHJH Henne/Jones/Hardy 2.50 6.00
TRHLM Henne/J.Long/Mannhm 6.00 15.00
TRHMD Hardy/Mannhm/Doucet 5.00 12.00
TRHWT Harris/Willis/Timmons 5.00 12.00
TRJCR Jones/Charles/Rice 3.00 8.00
TRJGG Johnson/Ginn/Gonzalez 6.00 15.00
TRJPR Jackson/Peterson/Rice 12.00 30.00
TRJRJ Jones/Rice/Johnson 2.50 6.00
TRJSF Johnson/K.Smith/Forte 3.00 8.00
TRKBC Kelly/Bradley/Clayton 5.00 12.00
TRKJH Kelly/Johnson/Holmes 5.00 12.00
TRKJS Kelly/Jackson/Sweed 6.00 15.00
TRKOD Keller/Olsen/Davis 5.00 12.00
TRKTJ Kelly/Thomas/Jackson 6.00 15.00
TRLTF Long/Thomas/Ferguson 5.00 12.00
TRLUB Lewis/Urlacher/Brooks 6.00 15.00
TRMBM Manning/Brady/Manning 15.00 40.00
TRMMS Menden/McFadd/Stewrt 3.00 8.00
TRMRR Manning/Rivers/Roeth 8.00 20.00
TRMWB McNbb/Westbrk/Brown 6.00 15.00
TRPBM Portis/Betts/Moss 5.00 12.00
TRPJH Palmer/Johnson/Housh 6.00 15.00
TRPLB Palmer/Leinart/Booty 8.00 20.00
TRPPM Portis/Parker/Maroney 6.00 15.00
TRRBH Ryan/Brohm/Henne 12.00 30.00
TRRBO Romo/Barber/Owens 12.00 30.00
TRRDA Russell/Doucet/Addai 6.00 15.00
TRRJJ Rodgers/Jones/Jenngs 12.00 30.00
TRRLD Ryan/Long/Dorsey 10.00 25.00
TRRMK Ryan/McFadden/Kelly 12.00 30.00
TRRPW Roeth/Parker/Ward 10.00 25.00
TRRRY Ryan/Russell/Young 10.00 25.00
TRSGG Shockey/Gates/Gnzalez 5.00 12.00
TRTPJ Taylor/Peterson/Jackson 12.00 30.00
TRWSD Williams/Smith/Delhmme 5.00 12.00

2008 Stadium Club Rookie Autographs

T10 GROUP A ODDS 1:190 H, 1:36,000 R
T10 GROUP B ODDS 1:35 H, 1:6600 R
T10 GROUP C ODDS 1:18 H, 1:4500 R
GROUP A ODDS 1:66 H, 1:4000 R
GROUP B ODDS 1:40 H, 1:2375 R
GROUP C ODDS 1:14 H, 1:790 R
GROUP D ODDS 1:10 H, 1:197 R
GROUP E ODDS 1:9 H, 1:495 R
UNPRICED PLATINUM/1 ODDS 1:1625
UNPRICED T10 PLATINUM/1 ODDS 1:8868
UNPRICED PRINT PLATE PRINT RUN 1
101 Matt Ryan T10 A 20.00 50.00
102 Brian Brohm A 6.00 15.00
103 Chad Henne B 4.00 10.00
104 Joe Flacco A 15.00 40.00
105 Andre Woodson B 2.50 6.00
106 John David Booty D 3.00 8.00
107 Josh Johnson D 3.00 8.00
108 Colt Brennan A 6.00 15.00
109 Dennis Dixon B 8.00 20.00
110 Erik Ainge C 3.00 8.00
111 Darren McFadden T10 A 8.00 20.00
112 Rashard Mendenhall A 3.00 8.00
113 Jonathan Stewart A 12.00 30.00
114 Felix Jones B 3.00 8.00
115 Jamaal Charles C 12.00 30.00
116 Ray Rice B 3.00 8.00
117 Chris Johnson E 4.00 10.00
118 Mike Hart C 3.00 8.00
119 Matt Forte E 12.00 30.00
120 Kevin Smith E 3.00 8.00
121 Steve Slaton C 3.00 8.00
122 Malcolm Kelly C 3.00 8.00
123 Limas Sweed B 3.00 8.00
124 DeSean Jackson C 6.00 15.00
125 James Hardy C 3.00 8.00
126 Mario Manningham D 6.00 15.00
127 Devin Thomas C 3.00 8.00
128 Early Doucet C 3.00 8.00
129 Andre Caldwell E 3.00 8.00
130 Jordy Nelson C 15.00 30.00
131 Eddie Royal D 3.00 8.00
132 Earl Bennett D 5.00 12.00
133 Fred Davis D 3.00 8.00
134 Dustin Keller C 3.00 8.00
135 John Carlson D 3.00 8.00
136 Chris Long T10 B 6.00 15.00
137 Jake Long T10 B 6.00 15.00
138 Glenn Dorsey T10 B 3.00 8.00
139 Sedrick Ellis T10 C 3.00 8.00
140 Vernon Gholston T10 C 3.00 8.00
141 Kevin O'Connell C 3.00 8.00
143 Keith Rivers T10 C 3.00 8.00
145 Derrick Harvey T10 C 3.00 8.00
149 Dominique Rodgers-Cromartie D 4.00 10.00
151 Sam Baker E 3.00 8.00
152 Adrian Arrington E 3.00 8.00
153 Donnie Avery C 4.00 10.00
154 Marcus Henry E 3.00 8.00
155 Dexter Jackson C 5.00 12.00
156 Jerome Simpson C 4.00 10.00
157 Keenan Burton D 3.00 8.00
158 Tashard Choice D 3.00 8.00
159 Harry Douglas D 4.00 10.00
160 Marcus Griffin D 3.00 8.00
161 DJ Hall D 3.00 8.00
162 Justin Forsett D 4.00 10.00
164 Jacob Hester D 3.00 8.00
167 Lance Leggett E 5.00 12.00
168 Xavier Omon E 3.00 8.00
169 Marcus Monk E 4.00 10.00
170 Anthony Morelli E 3.00 8.00
171 Marcus Smith E 4.00 10.00
172 Allen Patrick E 3.00 8.00
173 Kenny Phillips D 3.00 8.00
175 Matt Flynn D 3.00 8.00
176 Martin Rucker D 3.00 8.00
178 Owen Schmitt E 3.00 8.00
182 Kyle Wright E 3.00 8.00
183 Darius Reynaud D 3.00 8.00
187 Jerod Mayo T10 C 6.00 15.00

2008 Stadium Club Rookie Autographs Silver Holofoil

SLVR/50 T10 ODDS 1:191H, 1:75,000R
SLVR/50 ODDS 1:34H, 1:1950R
*GOLD/25: .5X TO 1.2X SILVER AU/50
101 Matt Ryan 40.00 80.00
102 Brian Brohm 5.00 12.00
103 Chad Henne 6.00 15.00
104 Joe Flacco 25.00 60.00
105 Andre Woodson 5.00 12.00
106 John David Booty 5.00 12.00
107 Josh Johnson 5.00 12.00
108 Colt Brennan 6.00 15.00
109 Dennis Dixon 5.00 12.00
110 Erik Ainge 5.00 12.00
111 Darren McFadden 5.00 12.00
112 Rashard Mendenhall 5.00 12.00
113 Jonathan Stewart 8.00 20.00
114 Felix Jones 5.00 12.00
115 Jamaal Charles 15.00 40.00
116 Ray Rice 5.00 12.00
117 Chris Johnson 6.00 15.00
118 Mike Hart 5.00 12.00
119 Matt Forte 8.00 20.00
120 Kevin Smith 5.00 12.00
121 Steve Slaton 5.00 12.00
122 Malcolm Kelly 5.00 12.00
123 Limas Sweed 5.00 12.00
124 DeSean Jackson 10.00 25.00
125 James Hardy 5.00 12.00
126 Mario Manningham 10.00 25.00
127 Devin Thomas 5.00 12.00
128 Early Doucet 5.00 12.00
129 Andre Caldwell 5.00 12.00
130 Jordy Nelson 12.00 30.00
131 Eddie Royal 5.00 12.00
132 Earl Bennett 8.00 20.00
133 Fred Davis 5.00 12.00
134 Dustin Keller 6.00 15.00
135 John Carlson 5.00 12.00
136 Chris Long 6.00 15.00
137 Jake Long 8.00 20.00
138 Glenn Dorsey 5.00 12.00
139 Sedrick Ellis 5.00 12.00
140 Vernon Gholston 5.00 12.00
141 Kevin O'Connell 5.00 12.00
143 Keith Rivers 5.00 12.00
145 Derrick Harvey 5.00 12.00
149 Dominique Rodgers-Cromartie 6.00 15.00
151 Sam Baker 5.00 12.00
152 Adrian Arrington 5.00 12.00
153 Donnie Avery 6.00 15.00
154 Marcus Henry 5.00 12.00
155 Dexter Jackson 8.00 20.00
156 Jerome Simpson 6.00 15.00
157 Keenan Burton 5.00 12.00
158 Tashard Choice 5.00 12.00
159 Harry Douglas 6.00 15.00
160 Marcus Griffin 5.00 12.00
161 DJ Hall 5.00 12.00
162 Justin Forsett 6.00 15.00
164 Jacob Hester 5.00 12.00
167 Lance Leggett 8.00 20.00
168 Xavier Omon 5.00 12.00
169 Marcus Monk 6.00 15.00
170 Anthony Morelli 5.00 12.00
171 Marcus Smith 6.00 15.00
172 Allen Patrick 5.00 12.00
173 Kenny Phillips 5.00 12.00
175 Matt Flynn 5.00 12.00
176 Martin Rucker 5.00 12.00
178 Owen Schmitt 5.00 12.00
182 Kyle Wright 5.00 12.00
183 Darius Reynaud 5.00 12.00
187 Jerod Mayo 8.00 20.00

2008 Stadium Club Super Teams

STATED ODDS 1:58 HOB
WIN CARDS GOOD FOR ROOKIE SET
1 Buffalo Bills 3.00 8.00
2 Miami Dolphins 3.00 8.00
3 New England Patriots 5.00 12.00
4 New York Jets 3.00 8.00
5 Baltimore Ravens WIN 10.00 25.00
6 Cincinnati Bengals 2.50 6.00
7 Cleveland Browns 2.50 6.00
8 Pittsburgh Steelers WIN 25.00 50.00
9 Houston Texans 2.50 6.00
10 Indianapolis Colts 6.00 15.00
11 Jacksonville Jaguars 3.00 8.00
12 Tennessee Titans 3.00 8.00
13 Denver Broncos 3.00 8.00
14 Kansas City Chiefs 2.50 6.00
15 Oakland Raiders 3.00 8.00
16 San Diego Chargers 4.00 10.00
17 Dallas Cowboys 6.00 15.00
18 New York Giants 4.00 10.00
19 Philadelphia Eagles WIN 10.00 25.00
20 Washington Redskins 3.00 8.00
21 Chicago Bears 3.00 8.00
22 Detroit Lions 2.50 6.00
23 Green Bay Packers 4.00 10.00
24 Minnesota Vikings 3.00 8.00
25 Atlanta Falcons 3.00 8.00
26 Carolina Panthers 3.00 8.00
27 New Orleans Saints 3.00 8.00
28 Tampa Bay Buccaneers 2.50 6.00
29 Arizona Cardinals WIN 10.00 25.00
30 San Francisco 49ers 2.50 6.00
31 Seattle Seahawks 3.00 8.00
32 St. Louis Rams 2.50 6.00

1991 Stadium Club Charter Member

This 50-card multi-sport standard-size set was sent to charter members in the Topps Stadium Club. The sports represented in the set are baseball (1-32), football (33-41), and hockey (42-50). The cards feature on the fronts full-bleed posed and action glossy color player photos. The player's name is shown in the light blue stripe that intersects the Stadium Club logo near the bottom of the picture. The words "Charter Member" are printed in gold foil lettering immediately below the stripe. The back design features a newspaper-like masthead (The Stadium Club Herald) complete with a headline announcing a major event in the player's season with copy below providing more information about the event. The cards are unnumbered and arranged below alphabetically within sports. Topps apparently made two printings of this set, which are most easily identifiable by the small asterisks on the bottom left of the card backs. The first printing cards have one asterisk, the second printing cards have two. The display box that contained the cards also included a Nolan Ryan bronze metallic card and a key chain. Very early members of the Stadium Club received a large size bronze metallic Nolan Ryan 1990 Topps card. It is valued below as well as the normal size Ryan metallic card. A third varation on the Ryan medallion has been found. This is another version of the 1991 Stadium Club charter member bronze medallion, except this one has a 24K logo on it. It is suspected that this might be a Home Shopping Newtork variety. No pricing is provided at this time for this piece due to lack of market information.

COMP.FACT SET (50) 6.00 15.00
33 Ottis Anderson .07 .20
Anderson& MVP of
Super Bowl XXV
34 Ottis Anderson .07 .20
Ottis The Giant
Reaches 10&000
35 Randall Cunningham .10 .30
36 Warren Moon .20 .50
37 Barry Sanders 1.00 2.50
38 Pete Stoyanovich .07 .20
39 Lawrence Taylor .20 .50
40 Derrick Thomas .20 .50
41 Richmond Webb .07 .20

1999 Stadium Club Chrome

Released as a 150-card set, the 1999 Stadium Club Chrome set parallels the earlier issue 1999 Stadium Club set in chrome version with updated rookie photography and traded information. The set was packaged in 24-pack boxes containing five cards each and carried a suggested retail price of $4.00.

COMPLETE SET (150) 25.00 60.00
1 Dan Marino .75 2.00
2 Andre Reed .40 1.00
3 Michael Westbrook .25 .60
4 Isaac Bruce .40 1.00
5 Curtis Martin .30 .75
6 Terrell Owens .30 .75
7 Warrick Dunn .25 .60
8 Jake Plummer .25 .60
9 Chad Brown .25 .60
10 Yancey Thigpen .25 .60
11 Keenan McCardell .30 .75
12 Shannon Sharpe .30 .75
13 Cameron Cleeland .25 .60
14 Mark Brunell .30 .75
15 Jamal Anderson .30 .75
16 Germane Crowell .25 .60
17 Rod Smith .30 .75
18 Cris Carter .40 1.00
19 Terrell Davis .30 .75
20 Tim Biakabutuka .30 .75
21 Jermaine Lewis .25 .60
22 Adrian Murrell .25 .60
23 Doug Flutie .40 1.00
24 Curtis Enis .25 .60
25 Skip Hicks .25 .60
26 Steve McNair .30 .75
27 Charles Woodson .40 1.00
28 Freddie Jones .25 .60
29 Warren Sapp .30 .75
30 Emmitt Smith .60 1.50
31 Reidel Anthony .25 .60
32 Tony Simmons .25 .60
33 Andre Hastings .25 .60
34 Byron Bam Morris .25 .60
35 Jimmy Smith .30 .75
36 Antonio Freeman .30 .75
37 Herman Moore .30 .75
38 Muhsin Muhammad .25 .60
39 Chris Chandler .30 .75
40 John Elway .60 1.50
41 Bobby Engram .25 .60
42 Keith Poole .25 .60
43 Mike Alstott .25 .60
44 Junior Seau .30 .75
45 Thurman Thomas .30 .75
46 Troy Aikman .50 1.25
47 Wesley Walls .30 .75
48 Robert Smith .25 .60
49 Elvis Grbac .25 .60
50 Ben Coates .30 .75
51 Bert Emanuel .30 .75
52 Jacquez Green .25 .60
53 Barry Sanders .60 1.50
54 James Jett .25 .60
55 Gary Brown .25 .60
56 Stephen Alexander .25 .60
57 Wayne Chrebet .25 .60
58 Drew Bledsoe .30 .75
59 Jake Reed .30 .75
60 Marvin Harrison .30 .75
61 Johnnie Morton .30 .75
62 Brett Favre .75 2.00
63 Charlie Batch .25 .60
64 Antowain Smith .25 .60
65 Ernie Mills .25 .60
66 Jeff Blake .30 .75
67 Curtis Conway .30 .75
68 Bruce Smith .30 .75
69 Peyton Manning 1.25 3.00
70 Tim Dwight .30 .75
71 O.J. McDuffie .30 .75
72 Jon Kitna .25 .60
73 Trent Dilfer .25 .60
74 Jerome Bettis .40 1.00
75 Dedric Ward .25 .60
76 Fred Taylor .25 .60
77 Ike Hilliard .25 .60
78 Frank Wycheck .30 .75
79 Eric Moulds .25 .60
80 Rob Moore .25 .60
81 Ed McCaffrey .30 .75
82 Carl Pickens .30 .75
83 Priest Holmes .25 .60
84 Terry Glenn .30 .75
85 Keyshawn Johnson .30 .75
86 Karim Abdul-Jabbar .25 .60
87 Ahman Green .30 .75
88 Duce Staley .25 .60
89 Vinny Testaverde .25 .60
90 Napoleon Kaufman .25 .60
91 Frank Sanders .25 .60
92 Steve Young .50 1.25
93 Darnay Scott .25 .60
94 Deion Sanders .30 .75
95 Corey Dillon .25 .60
96 Randall Cunningham .30 .75
97 Eddie George .30 .75
98 Derrick Alexander .25 .60
99 Mark Chmura .25 .60
100 Rickey Dudley .25 .60
101 Joey Galloway .30 .75
102 Ricky Proehl .25 .60
103 Natrone Means .30 .75
104 Dorsey Levens .30 .75
105 Andre Rison .30 .75
106 John Randle .40 1.00
107 Terance Mathis .25 .60
108 Rae Carruth .25 .60
109 Jerry Rice 1.00 2.50
110 Michael Irvin .40 1.00
111 Oronde Gadsden .25 .60
112 Jerome Pathon .25 .60
113 Ricky Watters .30 .75
114 J.J. Stokes .25 .60
115 Kordell Stewart .25 .60
116 Tim Brown .40 1.00
117 Tony Gonzalez .30 .75
118 Randy Moss .30 .75
119 Daunte Culpepper RC .60 1.50
120 Amos Zereoue RC .40 1.00
121 Champ Bailey RC .75 2.00
122 Peerless Price RC .40 1.00
123 Edgerrin James RC .60 1.50
124 Joe Germaine RC .50 1.25
125 David Boston RC .40 1.00
126 Kevin Faulk RC .40 1.00
127 Troy Edwards RC .40 1.00
128 Akili Smith RC .40 1.00
129 Kevin Johnson RC .50 1.25
130 Rob Konrad RC .40 1.00
131 Shaun King RC .40 1.00
132 James Johnson RC .40 1.00
133 Donovan McNabb RC 2.50 6.00
134 Torry Holt RC .75 2.00
135 Mike Cloud RC .40 1.00
136 Sedrick Irvin RC .40 1.00
137 Cade McNown RC .40 1.00
138 Ricky Williams RC .60 1.50
139 Karsten Bailey RC .40 1.00
140 Cecil Collins RC .40 1.00
141 Brock Huard RC .40 1.00
142 D'Wayne Bates RC .40 1.00
143 Tim Couch RC .50 1.25
144 Rocket Ismail .30 .75
145 Marshall Faulk .30 .75
146 Trent Green .25 .60
147 Tony Martin .30 .75
148 Jim Harbaugh .30 .75
149 Rich Gannon .30 .75
150 Brad Johnson .30 .75

1999 Stadium Club Chrome First Day

*STARS: 8X TO 20X HI COL.
*RCs: 3X TO 8X
STATED ODDS 1:59
STATED PRINT RUN 100 SER.#'d SETS

1999 Stadium Club Chrome First Day Refractors

*STARS: 15X TO 40X BASIC CARDS
*ROOKIES: 5X TO 12X
STATED ODDS 1:235
STATED PRINT RUN 25 SER.#'d SETS

1999 Stadium Club Chrome Refractors

COMPLETE SET (150) 150.00 300.00
*STARS: 2.5X TO 6X HI COL.
*RCs: .8X TO 2X
STATED ODDS 1:12

1999 Stadium Club Chrome Clear Shots

Randomly seeded in packs at the rate of one in 22, this 9-card set showcases nine of this year's top rookies on a clear card utilizing die-cut technology. Each card depicts the front of the featured player on the front of the card, and the back on the card back. A refractor version of this set was released also.

COMPLETE SET (9) 15.00 40.00
STATED ODDS 1:22
*REFRACTORS: 1X TO 2.5X HI COL.
REFRACTOR STATED ODDS 1:110
1 David Boston 1.50 4.00
2 Edgerrin James 5.00 12.00
3 Chris Claiborne 1.25 3.00
4 Torry Holt 3.00 8.00
5 Tim Couch 1.50 4.00
6 Donovan McNabb 4.00 10.00
7 Akili Smith 1.25 3.00
8 Champ Bailey 2.00 5.00
9 Troy Edwards 1.25 3.00

1999 Stadium Club Chrome Eyes of the Game

Randomly inserted in packs at the rate of one in 20, this 7-card set focuses on some of the NFL's most intense players. Cards are printed on a colored transparent card stock. A refractor version of this set was released also.

COMPLETE SET (7) 20.00 50.00
STATED ODDS 1:20
*REFRACTORS: 1X TO 2.5X HI COL.
REFRACTOR STATED ODDS 1:100
20 Tim Couch 1.00 2.50
21 Ricky Williams 1.50 4.00
22 Barry Sanders 6.00 15.00
23 Brett Favre 6.00 15.00
24 Terrell Davis 2.00 5.00
25 Peyton Manning 6.00 15.00
26 Randy Moss 5.00 12.00

1999 Stadium Club Chrome Never Compromise

Randomly seeded in packs at the rate of one in six, this 40-card set features 20 veterans and 20 rookies who play to their maximum potential week after week. Card backs carry a "NC" prefix. A refractor version of this set was also released.

COMPLETE SET (40) 75.00 150.00
STATED ODDS 1:6
*REFRACTORS: 1X TO 2.5X HI COL.
REFRACTOR STATED ODDS 1:30
NC1 Tim Couch 1.00 2.50
NC2 David Boston 1.00 2.50
NC3 Daunte Culpepper 4.00 10.00
NC4 Donovan McNabb 5.00 12.00
NC5 Ricky Williams 3.00 8.00
NC6 Troy Edwards 1.00 2.50
NC7 Akili Smith 1.00 2.50
NC8 Torry Holt 2.50 6.00
NC9 Cade McNown 1.00 2.50
NC10 Edgerrin James 4.00 10.00
NC11 Cecil Collins 1.00 2.50
NC12 Peerless Price 1.00 2.50
NC13 Kevin Johnson 1.00 2.50
NC14 Champ Bailey 1.50 4.00
NC15 Kevin Faulk 1.00 2.50
NC16 D'Wayne Bates 1.00 2.50
NC17 Shaun King 1.00 2.50
NC18 Sedrick Irvin 1.00 2.50
NC19 James Johnson 1.00 2.50
NC20 Rob Konrad 1.00 2.50
NC21 Randy Moss 6.00 15.00
NC22 Peyton Manning 8.00 20.00
NC23 Eddie George 1.50 4.00
NC24 Fred Taylor 2.50 6.00
NC25 Jamal Anderson 2.50 6.00
NC26 Joey Galloway 1.50 4.00
NC27 Terrell Davis 2.50 6.00
NC28 Keyshawn Johnson 1.50 4.00
NC29 Antonio Freeman 1.50 4.00
NC30 Jake Plummer 1.50 4.00
NC31 Steve Young 3.00 8.00
NC32 Barry Sanders 8.00 20.00
NC33 Dan Marino 8.00 20.00
NC34 Emmitt Smith 5.00 12.00
NC35 Brett Favre 8.00 20.00
NC36 Randall Cunningham 2.50 6.00
NC37 John Elway 8.00 20.00
NC38 Drew Bledsoe 3.00 8.00
NC39 Jerry Rice 5.00 12.00
NC40 Troy Aikman 5.00 12.00

1999 Stadium Club Chrome True Colors

Randomly inserted in packs at the rate of one in 120, this 10-card set features NFL players who perform best in clutch situations. A refractor version of this set was released also.

COMPLETE SET (10) 25.00 60.00
STATED ODDS 1:24
*REFRACTORS: 1X TO 2.5X BASIC INSERTS
REFRACTOR STATED ODDS 1:120
10 Doug Flutie 1.50 4.00
11 Steve Young 2.00 5.00
12 Jake Plummer 1.00 2.50
13 Jerry Rice 3.00 8.00
14 Randy Moss 4.00 10.00
15 Fred Taylor 1.50 4.00
16 Peyton Manning 5.00 12.00
17 Dan Marino 5.00 12.00
18 Brett Favre 5.00 12.00
19 Emmitt Smith 3.00 8.00

1991 Stadium Club Members Only

This 50-card multi-sport standard-size set was sent in three installments to members in the Topps Stadium Club. The first and second installments featured baseball players (card numbers 1-10 and 11-30), while the third spotlighted football (31-37) and hockey (38-50) players. The cards feature on the fronts full-bleed posed and action glossy color player photos. The player's name is shown in the light blue stripe that intersects the Stadium Club logo near the bottom of the picture. The words "Members Only" are printed in gold foil lettering immediately below the stripe. The back design features a newspaper-like masthead (The Stadium Club Herald) complete with a headline announcing a major event in the player's season with copy below providing more information about the event. The cards are unnumbered and arranged below alphabetically according to and within installments.

COMPLETE SET (50) 6.00 15.00
31 Art Monk .08 .25
32 Warren Moon .15 .40
33 Leonard Russell .07 .20
34 Mark Rypien .07 .20
35 Barry Sanders 1.00 2.50
36 Emmitt Smith 1.00 2.50
37 Tony Zendejas .07 .20

1992 Stadium Club Members Only

This 50-card standard-size set was sent to 1992 Stadium Club members in four installments. In addition to the Stadium Club cards, the first installment included one "Top Draft Picks of the '90s" card (as a bonus) and a randomly chosen "Master Photo" printed on 5" by 7" white card stock. The third and fourth installments included hockey and football players in addition to baseball players. The cards feature full-bleed glossy color player photos. The fronts of the regular cards have the words "Members Only" printed in gold foil at the bottom along with the player's name and the Stadium Club logo. The backs feature a stadium scene with the scoreboard displaying, in yellow neon, a career highlight. The cards are unnumbered and checklisted below alphabetically, with the two-player cards listed at the end.

COMPLETE SET (50) 12.00 30.00
37 Troy Aikman .50 1.25
38 Dale Carter .07 .20
39 Art Monk .07 .20
40 Frank Reich .07 .20
41 Emmitt Smith .75 2.00
42 Steve Young .40 1.00

1993 Stadium Club Members Only

This 59-card standard-size set was mailed out to Stadium Club Members in four separate mailings. Each box contained several sports. The fronts have full-bleed color action player photos with the words "Members Only" printed in gold foil at the bottom along with the player's name and the Stadium Club logo. On a multi-colored background, the horizontal backs carry player information and a computer generated drawing of a baseball player. The cards are unnumbered and checklisted below alphabetically according to sport as follows: baseball (1-28), basketball (29-44), football (45-53), and hockey (54-59).

COMPLETE SET (59) 10.00 20.00
45 Morten Andersen .07 .20
46 Jerome Bettis .30 .75
47 Steve Christie .07 .20
48 Jim Kelly .15 .40
49 Dan Marino 1.00 2.50
50 Sterling Sharpe .08 .25
51 Emmitt Smith .75 2.00
52 Dana Stubblefield .08 .25
53 Steve Young .40 1.00

1984 Stallions Team Sheets

This set was issued in one series totalling 6-different sheets of the USFL Birmingham Stallions. Each sheet includes black and white photos of eight or nine players and measure 8" by 10" with a white border.

COMPLETE SET (6) 10.00 25.00
1 Greg Anderson 2.00 5.00
Buddy Aydelette
Tom Banks
Mark Ba
2 Lester Dickey 2.00 5.00
Ron Frederick

Earl Gant
Charles G
3 Johnny Dirden 2.00 5.00
Mark Goodspeed
Lonnie Johnson
Syl
4 Michael Kincaid 2.00 5.00
Bob Lane
Reggie Lewis
Charles M
5 Mike Murphy 2.00 5.00
Scott Norwood
Pat Phenix
Mike Raine
6 Steve Stephens 2.00 5.00
Ken Talton
Michael Thomas
Emmuel

1963 Stancraft Playing Cards

This 54-card set, subtitled "Official NFL All-Time Greats," commemorates outstanding NFL players and was issued in conjunction with the opening of the Pro Football Hall of Fame in Canton, Ohio. It should be noted that several of the players in the set are not in the Pro Football Hall of Fame. The back of the cards was produced two different ways. One style has a checkerboard pattern, with the NFL logo in the middle and logos for the 14 NFL teams surrounding it against a red background; the other style has the 14 NFL team helmets floating on a green background. The set was issued in a plastic box which fit into a cardboard outer slip-case box. Apart from the aces and two jokers (featuring the NFL logo), the fronts of the other cards have a skillfully drawn picture (in brown ink) of the player, with his name, position, year(s), and team below the drawing. The set was also reportedly made in a pinochle format. We have checklisted this set in playing card order by suits and assigned numbers to Aces (1), Jacks (11), Queens (12), and Kings (13). Each card measures approximately 2 1/4" by 3 1/2" with rounded corners.

COMPLETE SET (54) 125.00 250.00
*GREEN BACKS: SAME PRICE
1C NFL Logo 1.50 3.00
1D NFL Logo 1.50 3.00
1H NFL Logo 1.50 3.00
1S NFL Logo 1.50 3.00
2C Johnny Blood McNally 2.00 4.00
2D Frankie Albert 1.50 3.00
2H Paul Hornung 5.00 10.00
2S Eddie LeBaron 2.00 4.00
3C Bobby Mitchell 3.00 6.00
3D Del Shofner 1.50 3.00
3H Johnny Unitas 7.50 15.00
3S Don Hutson 3.00 6.00
4C Billy Howton 1.50 3.00
4D Ollie Matson 3.00 6.00
4H Doak Walker 3.00 6.00
4S Clarke Hinkle 2.00 4.00
5C Fats Henry 2.00 4.00
5D Mike Ditka 6.00 12.00
5H Tom Fears 3.00 6.00
5S Charley Conerly 3.00 6.00
6C Tony Canadeo 2.50 5.00
6D Otto Graham 5.00 10.00
6H Jim Thorpe 7.50 15.00
6S Earl(Curly) Lambeau 1.50 3.00
7C Bulldog Turner 3.00 6.00
7D Chuck Bednarik 4.00 8.00
7H Gino Marchetti 3.00 6.00
7S Sid Luckman 4.00 8.00
8C Charley Trippi 3.00 6.00
8D Jim Taylor 4.00 8.00
8H Claude(Buddy) Young 1.50 3.00
8S Pete Pihos 2.50 5.00
9C Tommy Mason 1.50 3.00
9D Mel Hein 2.00 4.00
9H Jim Benton 1.50 3.00
9S Dante Lavelli 3.00 6.00
10C Dutch Clark 2.50 5.00
10D Eddie Price 1.50 3.00
10H Jim Brown 10.00 20.00
10S Norm Van Brocklin 4.00 8.00
11C Y.A. Tittle 4.00 8.00
11D Sonny Randle 1.50 3.00
11H George Halas 5.00 10.00
11S Cloyce Box 1.50 3.00
12C Lou Groza 3.00 6.00
12D Joe Perry 3.00 6.00
12H Sammy Baugh 5.00 10.00
12S Joe Schmidt 3.00 6.00
13C Bobby Layne 4.00 8.00
13D Bob Waterfield 4.00 8.00
13H Bill Dudley 2.50 5.00
13S Elroy Hirsch 3.00 6.00
NNO Joker (NFL Logo) 1.50 3.00
NNO Joker (NFL Logo) 1.50 3.00

1989 Star-Cal Decals

These decals were licensed by the NFL and NFL Players' Association. The first series features players from six NFL teams. The decals measure approximately 3" by 4 1/2" with rounded corners and a full-color action photo of the player. In the upper left corner, a silver logo with the words "First Edition 1989" distinguishes this series from future releases. As a bonus, each decal comes with a pennant-shaped miniature team banner decal in the player's team colors, with the team helmet and nickname on the banner. The decals are unnumbered and checklisted below alphabetically by player.

COMPLETE SET (54) 50.00 100.00
1 Raul Allegre .75 2.00
2 Carl Banks 1.25 3.00
3 Cornelius Bennett 1.25 3.00
4 Brian Blades 1.00 2.50
5 Kevin Butler .75 2.00
6 Harry Carson 1.25 3.00
7 Anthony Carter 1.25 3.00
8 Michael Carter .75 2.00
9 Shane Conlan .75 2.00
10 Roger Craig 1.50 4.00
11 Richard Dent 1.50 4.00
12 Chris Doleman 1.00 2.50
13 Tony Dorsett 2.50 6.00
14 Dave Duerson .75 2.00
15 Charles Haley 1.25 3.00
16 Dan Hampton 1.25 3.00
17 Al Harris .75 2.00
18 Mark Jackson 1.00 2.50
19 Vance Johnson 1.00 2.50
20 Steve Jordan 1.00 2.50
21 Clarence Kay .75 2.00
22 Jim Kelly 4.00 10.00
23 Tommy Kramer 1.25 3.00
24 Ronnie Lott 1.50 4.00
25 Lionel Manuel 1.00 2.50
26 Guy McIntyre .75 2.00
27 Steve McMichael 1.00 2.50
28 Karl Mecklenburg 1.25 3.00
29 Orson Mobley .75 2.00
30 Joe Montana 10.00 25.00
31 Joe Morris .75 2.00
32 Joe Nash .75 2.00
33 Ricky Nattiel .75 2.00
34 Chuck Nelson .75 2.00
35 Darrin Nelson .75 2.00
36 Karl Nelson .75 2.00
37 Scott Norwood .75 2.00
38 Bart Oates .75 2.00
39 Rufus Porter .75 2.00
40 Andre Reed 2.00 5.00
41 Phil Simms 1.50 4.00
42 Mike Singletary 1.50 4.00
43 Fred Smerlas .75 2.00
44 Bruce Smith 2.50 6.00
45 Kelly Stouffer .75 2.00
46 Scott Studwell .75 2.00
47 Matt Suhey .75 2.00
48 Steve Tasker 1.25 3.00
49 Keena Turner .75 2.00
50 John L. Williams 1.00 2.50
51 Wade Wilson 1.00 2.50
52 Sammy Winder .75 2.00
53 Tony Woods .75 2.00
54 Eric Wright 1.00 2.50

1990 Star-Cal Decals Prototypes

These prototype cards are unnumbered and are checklisted alphabetically. They were issued to promote the 1990 Star-Cal Decal set in their second year of issue.

COMPLETE SET (4) 2.00 5.00
1 Jeff Hostetler .30 .75
2 Mike Kenn .30 .75
3 Freeman McNeil .30 .75
4 Steve Young 1.20 3.00

1990 Star-Cal Decals

The 1990 Star-Cal decal set features six players from 12 of the most popular NFL teams and 36 NFL stars (most also represented in the team sets). The player decals measure approximately 3" by 4 1/2" and have on the fronts full-bleed color action player photos with rounded corners and a facsimile autograph. The player's name is printed on the lower left corner of the decal. The backs have instructions for applying the decals. Each player decal was issued with a pennant-shaped miniature team banner (3 1/2" by 2"), which displayed the team's helmet and name in the team's colors. The player decals are unnumbered and checklisted below according to player's name. The set is also known as the Grid-Star decal set. A few player decals (e.g., Steve Young) are known to exist in a variation with a serial number on their fronts. Also some decals vary slightly in autograph placement and the printing of his name in black or white at the lower left corner. Complete set price includes all variations.

COMPLETE SET (94) 75.00 150.00
1 Eric Allen .60 1.50
2A Marcus Allen 2.00 5.00
2B Marcus Allen 2.00 5.00
3 Flipper Anderson .60 1.50
4A Neal Anderson .60 1.50
4B Neal Anderson .60 1.50
5A Carl Banks .60 1.50
5B Carl Banks .60 1.50
6 Mark Bavaro .60 1.50
7 Cornelius Bennett .75 2.00
8 Brian Blades .60 1.50
9 Joey Browner .50 1.25
10 Keith Byars .60 1.50
11A Anthony Carter .60 1.50
11B Anthony Carter .60 1.50
12 Cris Carter 2.50 6.00
13 Michael Carter .50 1.25
14 Gary Clark .75 2.00
15 Mark Collins .50 1.25
16 Shane Conlan .50 1.25
17 Jim Covert .60 1.50
18A Roger Craig 1.00 2.50
18B Roger Craig 1.00 2.50
19 Richard Dent 1.00 2.50
20 Chris Doleman .60 1.50
21 Dave Duerson .50 1.25
22 Henry Ellard .75 2.00
23A John Elway 8.00 20.00
23B John Elway 10.00 25.00
24 Jim Everett .75 2.00
25 Mervyn Fernandez .50 1.25
26 Willie Gault .60 1.50
27 Bob Golic .60 1.50
28 Darrell Green 1.00 2.50
29 Kevin Greene .60 1.50
30 Charles Haley 1.00 2.50
31 Jay Hilgenberg .60 1.50
32 Pete Holohan .50 1.25
33 Kent Hull .50 1.25
34 Bobby Humphrey .60 1.50
35A Bo Jackson 1.50 4.00
35B Bo Jackson 1.50 4.00
36 Keith Jackson .75 2.00
37 Mark Jackson .60 1.50
38 Joe Jacoby .60 1.50
39 Vance Johnson .60 1.50
40 Jim Kelly 2.50 6.00
41 Bernie Kosar 1.00 2.50
42 Greg Kragen .50 1.25
43 Jeff Lageman .50 1.25
44 Pat Leahy .50 1.25
45 Howie Long 1.50 4.00
46A Ronnie Lott 1.25 3.00
46B Ronnie Lott 1.25 3.00
47 Kevin Mack .50 1.25
48 Charles Mann .50 1.25
49 Leonard Marshall .60 1.50
50 Clay Matthews .75 2.00
51 Erik McMillan .50 1.25
52 Karl Mecklenburg .60 1.50
53 Dave Meggett UER .60 1.50
54A Eric Metcalf .60 1.50
54B Eric Metcalf .60 1.50
55 Keith Millard .50 1.25
56 Frank Minnifield .50 1.25
57A Joe Montana 8.00 20.00
57B Joe Montana 10.00 25.00
57C Joe Montana 8.00 20.00
58 Joe Nash .50 1.25
59 Ken O'Brien .60 1.50
60 Rufus Porter .50 1.25
61 Andre Reed 1.25 3.00
62 Mark Rypien .75 2.00
63 Gerald Riggs .60 1.50
64 Mickey Shuler .50 1.25
65 Clyde Simmons .60 1.50
66A Phil Simms 1.00 2.50
66B Phil Simms 1.00 2.50
67A Mike Singletary 1.25 3.00
67B Mike Singletary 1.25 3.00
68 Jackie Slater .60 1.50
69 Bruce Smith 1.25 3.00
70A Kelly Stouffer .50 1.25
70B Kelly Stouffer .50 1.25
71 John Taylor .75 2.00
72 Lawyer Tillman .50 1.25
73 Al Toon .60 1.50
74A Herschel Walker .75 2.00
74B Herschel Walker .75 2.00
75 Reggie White 2.00 5.00
76A John L. Williams .60 1.50
76B John L. Williams .60 1.50
76C John L. Williams .60 1.50
77 Tony Woods .50 1.25
78 Gary Zimmerman .75 2.00

1988 Starline Prototypes

Issued as a prototype set for a release that never made it to market, these 4-cards carry a colored border and color player photo. Reportedly, just 300 complete sets were produced.

COMPLETE SET (4) 300.00 600.00
1 John Elway 75.00 150.00
2 Bernie Kosar 20.00 50.00
3 Joe Montana 100.00 200.00
4 Phil Simms 25.00 60.00

1928 Star Player Candy

This recently discovered set of cards is thought to have been issued by Dockman and Son's candy company since it closely resembles the 1928 Star Player Candy baseball card set. Based upon the players in the set, the year of issue is thought to be 1928 so it is possible that both the football and baseball players were packaged together. Red Grange is listed as Illinois instead of Professional so the true year of issue often comes under question. Each card is blankbacked and features a sepia colored photo of the player on the cardfront along with his name and either name of his university or the word "professional" (noted below) for those few players in the pros at the time. Each card measures roughly 2" by 3."

1 Russell Avery 150.00 300.00
2 Bullet Baker 150.00 300.00
3 Richard Black 150.00 300.00
4 E.J. Burke 150.00 300.00
5 Jack Chevigney 200.00 400.00
6 Fred Collins 200.00 400.00
7 A.C. Cornsweet 150.00 300.00
8 Jus Dart 150.00 300.00
9 Paddy Driscoll 1200.00 2000.00
10A Bruce Dumont 150.00 300.00
10B Bruce Dumont ERR 150.00 300.00
11 Fred Ellis 150.00 300.00
12 Benny Friedman 1200.00 2000.00
13 Gene Fritz 150.00 300.00
14 Walter Gebert 150.00 300.00
15 Louis Gilbert 150.00 300.00
16 Red Grange 1500.00 2500.00
17 Glen Harmeson 150.00 300.00
18 John Hazen 150.00 300.00
19 Gibson Holliday 150.00 300.00
20 Walt Holmer 150.00 300.00
21 John Karcis 150.00 300.00
22 Harry Lindblom 150.00 300.00
23 Jim McMillen UER 150.00 300.00
24 Hugh Mendenhall 150.00 300.00
25 Fred Miller 150.00 300.00
26 John Murrell 150.00 300.00
27 John Niemiec 150.00 300.00
28 A.J. Nowak 150.00 300.00
29 Irvine Phillips 150.00 300.00
30 E.H. Rose 150.00 300.00
31 Stanley Rosen 150.00 300.00
32 Paul Scull 150.00 300.00
33 J.W. Slagle 150.00 300.00
34 John Smith Ford. 150.00 300.00
35 John Smith Penn. 150.00 300.00
36 Euil Snitz Snider 150.00 300.00
37 M.E. Bud Sprague 150.00 300.00
38 Joe Sternaman 600.00 1000.00
39 Eddie Tryon 350.00 600.00
40 Rube Wagner 150.00 300.00
41 Saul Weislow 150.00 300.00
42 Ralph Welch 150.00 300.00
43 George Wilson 250.00 500.00

1959 Steelers San Giorgio Flipbooks

This set features members of the Pittsburgh Steelers printed on velum type paper stock created in a multi-image action sequence. The set is commonly referenced as the San Giorgio Macaroni Football Flipbooks. Members of the Philadelphia Eagles, Pittsburgh Steelers, and Washington Redskins were produced regionally with 15-players, reportedly, issued per team. Some players were produced in more than one sequence of poses with different captions and/or slightly different photos used. When the flipbooks are still in uncut form (which is most desirable), they measure approximately 5 3/4" by 3 9/16". The sheets are blank backed, in black and white, and provide 14-small numbered pages when cut apart. Collectors were encouraged to cut out each photo and stack them in such a way as to create a moving image of the player when flipped with the fingers. Any additions to this list are appreciated.

1 Darrel Brewster 90.00 150.00
2 Jack Butler 90.00 150.00
3 Gern Nagler 90.00 150.00
4 Tom Tracy 100.00 175.00

1961 Steelers Jay Publishing

This 12-card set features (approximately) 5" by 7" black-and-white player photos. The photos show players in traditional poses with the quarterback preparing to throw, the runner heading downfield, and the defenseman ready for the tackle. These cards were packaged 12 to a packet and originally sold for 25 cents. The backs are blank. The cards are unnumbered and checklisted below in alphabetical order.

COMPLETE SET (12) 75.00 150.00
1 Preston Carpenter 5.00 10.00
2 Dean Derby 5.00 10.00
3 Buddy Dial 5.00 10.00
4 John Henry Johnson 10.00 20.00
5 Bobby Layne 15.00 30.00
6 Gene Lipscomb 6.00 12.00
7 Bill Mack 5.00 10.00
8 Fred Mautino 5.00 10.00
9 Lou Michaels 5.00 10.00
10 Buddy Parker CO 5.00 10.00
11 Myron Pottios 5.00 10.00
12 Tom Tracy 5.00 10.00

1963 Steelers IDL

This unnumbered black and white card set (featuring the Pittsburgh Steelers) is complete at 26 cards. The cards feature an identifying logo of IDL Drug Store on the front left corner of the card. The cards measure approximately 4" by 5". Cards are blank backed and unnumbered and hence are ordered alphabetically in the checklist below.

COMPLETE SET (26) 125.00 250.00
1 Frank Atkinson 6.00 12.00
2 Jim Bradshaw 6.00 12.00
3 Ed Brown 6.00 12.00
4 John Burrell 6.00 12.00
5 Preston Carpenter 6.00 12.00
6 Lou Cordileone 6.00 12.00
7 Buddy Dial 6.00 12.00
8 Bob Ferguson 6.00 12.00
9 Glenn Glass 6.00 12.00
10 Dick Haley 6.00 12.00
11 Dick Hoak 7.50 15.00
12 John Henry Johnson 10.00 25.00
13 Brady Keys 6.00 12.00
14 Joe Krupa 6.00 12.00
15 Ray Lemek 6.00 12.00
16 Bill(Red) Mack 6.00 12.00
17 Lou Michaels 6.00 12.00
18 Bill Nelsen 6.00 12.00
19 Buzz Nutter 6.00 12.00
20 Myron Pottios 6.00 12.00
21 John Reger 6.00 12.00
22 Mike Sandusky 6.00 12.00
23 Ernie Stautner 10.00 25.00
24 George Tarasovic 6.00 12.00
25 Clendon Thomas 6.00 12.00
26 Tom Tracy 7.50 15.00

1963 Steelers McCarthy Postcards

This set of the Pittsburgh Steelers features posed player photos printed on postcard-size cards. Each was produced from photos taken by photographer J.D. McCarthy and likely distributed over a number of years. The cards are unnumbered and checklisted below in alphabetical order. Any additions to the checklist below are appreciated.

COMPLETE SET (3) 15.00 30.00
1 John Henry Johnson 7.50 15.00
2 Brady Keys 4.00 8.00
3 Buzz Nutter 4.00 8.00

1964 Steelers Emenee Electric Football

These sepia toned photos were sponsored by Emenee Electric Pro Football Game and KDKA TV and radio. Each includes a large photo of a Steelers player with an advertisement for the Emenee Football Game below the photo, as well as a mail in contest offer for fans to guess Steelers game yardage totals. The backs are blank and the photos have been arranged alphabetically below.

COMPLETE SET (9) 800.00 1400.00
1 Frank Atkinson 75.00 125.00
2 Gary Ballman 75.00 125.00
3 Ed Brown 90.00 150.00
4 Dick Hoak 75.00 125.00
5 Dan James 75.00 125.00
6 John Henry Johnson 100.00 175.00
7 Jim Kelly 75.00 125.00
8 Ray Lemek 75.00 125.00
9 Paul Martha 75.00 125.00
10 Buzz Nutter 75.00 125.00
11 Mike Sandusky 75.00 125.00

1965 Steelers Program Inserts

The Steelers issued these black and white player photos bound into game programs during the 1965-68 seasons. The 1965 version includes a large player photo along with bio information below the image on the front and another page of the program on the back.

1 Gary Ballman 3.00 8.00
2 Jim Bradshaw 3.00 8.00
3 Dan James 3.00 8.00
4 Ray Lemek 3.00 8.00

1966 Steelers Program Inserts

The Steelers issued these black and white player photos bound into home game programs during the 1965-68 seasons. The 1966 set was issued in two different styles. Version 1 follows the 1965 fomat and includes a large player photo along with bio information below the image on the front. Version two features a large player photo and bio as well as three circles intended to direct the collector to punch them out and insert the photos into a binder. Both versions have another page of the program on the back.

COMPLETE SET (12) 40.00 100.00
1 Gary Ballman 2 3.00 8.00
2 Charlie Bradshaw 1 3.00 8.00
3 John Campbell 1 3.00 8.00
4 Riley Gunnels 1 3.00 8.00
5 Chuck Hinton 1 3.00 8.00
6 Dick Hoak 2 3.00 8.00
7 Brady Keys 2 3.00 8.00
8 Ken Kortas 2 3.00 8.00
9 Ben McGee 1 3.00 8.00
10 Andy Russell 2 4.00 10.00
11 Bill Saul 1 3.00 8.00
12 Marv Woodson 2 3.00 8.00

1966 Steelers Team Issue

These photos were issued in the mid-1960s by the Pittsburgh Steelers. Each measures roughly 8" by 10", contains a black and white photo and was printed on glossy stock. The photos look nearly identical to the 1969 Team Issue set. The photo backs are blank and unnumbered.

COMPLETE SET (24) 100.00 200.00
1 Mike Clark 5.00 10.00
2 Dick Compton 5.00 10.00
3 Sam Davis G 5.00 10.00
4 Mike Haggerty 5.00 10.00
5 John Hilton 5.00 10.00
6 Chuck Hinton 5.00 10.00
7 Dick Hoak 5.00 10.00
8 Bob Hohn 5.00 10.00
9 Roy Jefferson 6.00 12.00
10 Ken Kortas 5.00 10.00
11 Ray Mansfield 5.00 10.00
12 Paul Martha 5.00 10.00
13 Ray May 5.00 10.00
14 Ben McGee 5.00 10.00
15 Bill Nelsen 6.00 12.00
16 Andy Russell 6.00 12.00
17 Bill Saul 5.00 10.00
18 Don Shy 5.00 10.00
19 Clendon Thomas 5.00 10.00
20 Bruce Van Dyke 5.00 10.00
21 Lloyd Voss 5.00 10.00
22 J.R. Wilburn 5.00 10.00
23 Marv Woodson 5.00 10.00
24 Coaching Staff 5.00 10.00

1967 Steelers Program Inserts

The Steelers issued these black and white player photos bound into home game programs during the 1965-68 seasons. The 1967 set was issued one, two or three per program and includes a large player photo along with bio information below the image on the front as well as three circles intended to direct the collector to punch them out and insert the photos into a binder. Each has another page of the program on the back.

COMPLETE SET (10) 40.00 80.00
1 John Baker 3.00 8.00
2 Jim Butler 3.00 8.00
3 Dick Compton 3.00 8.00
4 Larry Gagner 3.00 8.00
5 John Hilton 3.00 8.00
6 Ray Mansfield 3.00 8.00
7 Bill Saul 3.00 8.00
8 Clendon Thomas 3.00 8.00
9 J.R. Wilburn 3.00 8.00
10 Marv Woodson 3.00 8.00

1968 Steelers KDKA

The 1968 KDKA Pittsburgh Steelers card set contains 15 cards with horizontal poses of several players per card. The cards measure approximately 2 3/8" by 4 1/8". Each card depicts players of a particular position (defensive backs, tight ends, linebackers). The backs are essentially advertisements for radio station KDKA, the sponsor of the card set. The cards are unnumbered and hence are listed below alphabetically by position name for convenience.

COMPLETE SET (15) 75.00 150.00
1 Centers: 5.00 10.00
2 Coaches: 6.00 12.00
3 Defensive Backs: 5.00 10.00
4 Defensive Backs: 5.00 10.00
5 Defensive Linemen: 5.00 10.00
6 Flankers: 5.00 10.00
7 Fullbacks: 5.00 10.00
8 Guards: 5.00 10.00
9 Linebackers: 6.00 12.00
10 Quarterbacks: 5.00 10.00
11 Rookies: 5.00 10.00
12 Running Backs: 5.00 10.00
13 Split Ends: 5.00 10.00
14 Tackles: 5.00 10.00
15 Tight Ends: 5.00 10.00

1968 Steelers Program Inserts

The Steelers issued these black and white player photos bound into home game programs during the 1965-68 seasons. The 1968 set was issued one per program and includes a large player photo along with bio information below the image on the front as well as three circles intended to direct the collector to punch them out and insert the photos into a binder. Each has another page of the program on the back.

1 Roy Jefferson 3.00 8.00
2 Ben McGee 3.00 8.00

1968 Steelers Team Issue

These photos were issued around 1968 by the Pittsburgh Steelers. Each measures roughly 5" by 7" and contains a black and white photo printed on paper stock. The photo backs are blank and unnumbered.

COMPLETE SET (5) 25.00 50.00
1 Earl Gros 5.00 10.00
2 Paul Martha 5.00 10.00
3 Kent Nix 5.00 10.00
4 Andy Russell 6.00 12.00
5 Marv Woodson 5.00 10.00

1969 Steelers Team Issue

These photos were issued around 1969 by the Pittsburgh Steelers. Each measures roughly 8" by 10", contains a black and white photo and was printed on glossy stock. The photos look nearly identical to the 1966 Team Issue set. The photo backs are blank and unnumbered.

COMPLETE SET (6) 25.00 50.00
1 Earl Gros 5.00 10.00
2 Jerry Hillebrand 5.00 10.00
3 Gene Mingo 5.00 10.00
4 Dick Shiner 5.00 10.00
5 Bobby Walden 5.00 10.00
6 Erwin Williams 5.00 10.00

1972 Steelers Team Sheets

This set consists of eight 8" by 10" sheets that display eight glossy black-and-white player photos each. Each individual photo measures approximately 2" by 3". The player's name, number, and position are printed below the photo. A Steelers helmet icon appears in the lower left corner of the sheet. The backs are blank. The sheets are unnumbered and checklisted below alphabetically according to the player featured in the upper left corner.

COMPLETE SET (8) 75.00 150.00
1 Ralph Anderson 6.00 15.00
2 Jim Brumfield 7.50 20.00
3 Bud Carson CO 7.50 20.00
4 Jack Ham 7.50 20.00
5 Joe Greene 10.00 25.00
6 Chuck Noll CO 15.00 30.00
7 Dick Post 10.00 25.00
8 Mike Wagner 6.00 15.00

1973 Steelers Team Issue

The NFLPA worked with many teams in 1973 to issued photo packs to be sold at stadium concession stands. Each measures approximately 7" by 8-5/8" and features a color player photo with a blank back. A small sheet with a player checklist was included in each 6-photo pack which was also assigned a series number as follows: A (cards #1-6), B (cards #7-12), and C (cards #13-18).

COMPLETE SET (18) 60.00 120.00
1 Jim Clack 4.00 8.00
2 Henry Davis 4.00 8.00
3 Franco Harris 7.50 15.00
4 Ron Shanklin 4.00 8.00
5 Bruce Van Dyke 4.00 8.00
6 Dwight White 5.00 10.00
7 Terry Bradshaw 12.50 25.00
8 Larry Brown 4.00 8.00
9 Roy Gerela 4.00 8.00
10 L.C. Greenwood 6.00 12.00
11 Frank Lewis 4.00 8.00
12 Andy Russell 5.00 10.00
13 John Fuqua 5.00 10.00
14 Joe Greene 6.00 12.00
15 Jack Ham 6.00 12.00
16 Terry Hanratty 4.00 8.00
17 Ray Mansfield 4.00 8.00
18 Preston Pearson 5.00 10.00

1973 Steelers Team Issue Color

The NFLPA worked with many teams in 1973 to issued photo packs to be sold at stadium concession stands. Each measures approximately 7" by 8-5/8" and features a color player photo with a blank back. A small sheet with a player checklist was included in each 6-photo pack.

COMPLETE SET (6) 25.00 50.00
1 Jim Clack 4.00 8.00
2 Henry Davis 4.00 8.00
3 Franco Harris 7.50 15.00
4 Ron Shanklin 4.00 8.00
5 Bruce Van Dyke 4.00 8.00
6 Dwight White 5.00 10.00

1973 Steelers Team Sheets

This set consists of eight 8" by 10" sheets that display eight glossy black-and-white player photos each. Each individual photo on the sheets measures approximately 2" by 3". A Steelers helmet icon appears in the lower left corner of the sheet. The backs are blank. The sheets are unnumbered and checklisted below alphabetically according to the player featured in the upper left corner.

COMPLETE SET (8) 50.00 100.00
1 Ander./Clack/Davis/Kolb 6.00 12.00
Mansfield/Davis/Ham/Bernhardt
2 Edwards/Vincent/Dockery/Young 7.50 15.00
Harris/Fuqua/Russell/Davis
3 Hanratty/Gerela/Bradshaw 12.50 25.00
Gilliam/Bleier/Wagner/Shanklin/Pearson
4 Mullins/Greene/Holmes/White 6.00 12.00
Pear./Brown/McMakin/Webster
5 Noll/Carson/Fry/Hoak/Parilli 6.00 12.00
Perles/Riecke/Taylor/Uram/Widen.
6 Phares/Brad./Walden/Meyer
Lewis/Bankston/Blount/Rowser
7 Glenn Scolnik 5.00 10.00
James Thomas
Loren Toews
Gail Clark
Lee Nystrom
Nate Dorsey
Bracey Bonham
Tom Keating
8 Sten./Holmes/Furn./Van
Dyke/Henne./Greenwood/Curl/Gravelle 6.00 12.00

1974 Steelers Tribune-Review Posters

These posters (measuring roughly 14" by 21 1/2") were issued one per Greensburg Tribune-Review newspaper in 1974. Each includes a black and white photo of a Steelers' player on one side and another page from the newspaper on the back. We've listed them below in alphabetical order.

1 Mel Blount 7.50 15.00
2 Roy Gerela 5.00 10.00
3 Joe Greene 7.50 15.00
4 Jack Ham 7.50 15.00
5 Andy Russell 5.00 10.00
6 Ron Shanklin 5.00 10.00
7 Dwight White 6.00 12.00

1974 Steelers WTAE

These color 8" X 10" photos feature players of the Pittsburgh Steelers. The cards were sponsored by radio station WTAE and the cardbacks include player bio information. The cards may have been distributed by Arby's Restaurants as well. The set is thought to contain 14-different photos. Any additions to this checklist are appreciated.

1 Terry Bradshaw 75.00 125.00
2 Sam Davis 15.00 30.00
3 Glen Edwards 15.00 30.00
4 John Fuqua 25.00 40.00
5 Roy Gerela 15.00 30.00
6 Joe Gilliam 15.00 30.00
7 Joe Greene 35.00 60.00
8 Jack Ham 35.00 60.00
9 Terry Hanratty 25.00 40.00
10 Franco Harris 40.00 75.00
11 Ray Mansfield 15.00 30.00
12 Ron Shanklin 15.00 30.00
13 Mike Wagner 15.00 30.00

1976 Steelers Glasses

This set of glasses was issued for the Pittsburgh Steelers in 1976, licensed through MSA and sponsored by WTAE. Each features a black and white photo of a Steelers' player along with a gold and black stripe running above and below the photo. Any additions to the list below are appreciated. These glasses were available at the Isaly or Sweet William restaurants.

COMPLETE SET (7) 50.00 100.00
1 Rocky Bleier 6.00 12.00
2 Terry Bradshaw 15.00 30.00
3 Mel Blount 6.00 12.00
4 Joe Greene 7.50 15.00
5 Jack Ham 6.00 12.00
6 Jack Lambert 7.50 15.00
7 Andy Russell 5.00 10.00

1976 Steelers MSA Cups

This set of plastic cups was issued for the Pittsburgh Steelers in 1976 and licensed through MSA. Each features an artist's rendering of a Steelers' player wearing a black jersey. Some players also appeared in the nationally issued 1976 MSA Cups set with only slight differences in each. The unnumbered cups are listed below alphabetically.

COMPLETE SET (23) 100.00 200.00
1 Rocky Bleier 5.00 10.00
2 Mel Blount 5.00 10.00
3 Terry Bradshaw 10.00 20.00
4 Jim Clack 4.00 8.00
5 Sam Davis 4.00 8.00
6 Roy Gerela 4.00 8.00
7 Gordon Gravelle 4.00 8.00
8 Joe Greene 6.00 12.00
9 L.C. Greenwood 5.00 10.00
10 Randy Grossman 4.00 8.00
11 Jack Ham 5.00 10.00
12 Franco Harris 7.50 15.00
13 Marv Kellum 4.00 8.00
14 Jon Kolb 4.00 8.00
15 Jack Lambert 7.50 15.00
16 Ray Mansfield 4.00 8.00
17 Andy Russell 4.00 8.00
18 John Stallworth 6.00 12.00
19 Lynn Swann 7.50 15.00
20 J.T. Thomas 4.00 8.00
21 Loren Toews 4.00 8.00
22 Mike Wagner 4.00 8.00
23 Bobby Walden 4.00 8.00

1978 Steelers Team Issue

This set consists of 5" by 7" glossy black-and-white player photos. The player's jersey number, name, position (initials), and team name are printed in all caps below the photo. Each is blankbacked, unnumbered and checklisted below alphabetically.

1 Rocky Bleier 6.00 12.00
2 Mel Blount 6.00 12.00
3 Terry Bradshaw 12.50 25.00
4 Joe Greene 7.50 15.00
5 L.C. Greenwood 6.00 12.00
6 Jack Ham 7.50 15.00

1978 Steelers Team Sheets

This set consists of eight 10" by 8" sheets that display eight glossy black-and-white player photos each. Each photo measures approximately 2" by 3". The player's name, number, and position are printed below the photo. The sheets are blankbacked, unnumbered and checklisted below alphabetically according to the player featured in the upper left corner.

COMPLETE SET (8) 40.00 80.00
1 B Carr 6.00 12.00
Harr
Blou
Becker
Brz
Toew
Webs
Winst
2 Delo 5.00 10.00
Gains
Thorn
Moser
Reut
Terr
Lew
BWag
3 Fry 6.00 12.00
Furn
Beas
Pet
Dunn
Gree
FAnd
LRey
4 LaC 6.00 12.00
Kolb
Cole
SDav
Lamb
Ham
Cous
Hicks
5 Mull 6.00 12.00
Pure
Pinn
Green
Bana
Cour
DWhit
LBrow
6 Noll 10.00 20.00
Colq
Ger
Brad
Kruc
Stou
Blei
Dungy
7 Stall 7.50 15.00
Bell
Gross
Keys
JSmith
McC
Swa
Cunn
8 Wagner 6.00 12.00
R Scott
G Edward
AMaxson
RJohnson DB
LAnder

1979 Steelers McDonald's Glasses

McDonald's stores issued this set of glasses in the Pittsburgh area in 1979 following Super Bowl XIII. Each features a black and white photo of three different Steelers players with the McDonald's logo circling the bottom of the glass.

COMPLETE SET (4) 30.00 60.00
1 J.Banaszak 7.50 15.00
Sam Davis
Lambert
2 Bleier 7.50 15.00
Ham
Shell
3 Bradshaw 12.50 25.00
Greenwood
Webster
4 Greene 7.50 15.00
Stallworth
Wagner

1979 Steelers Notebook Pittsburgh Press

These small posters measure roughly 5 1/2" by 8" when properly cut. Each was issued in Pittsburgh Press newspapers in 1979 and includes a black and white photo of a Steelers' player or coach with extensive bio information on the front. The backs feature another page from the newspaper. We've listed them below in alphabetical order.

COMPLETE SET (56) 125.00 250.00
1 Anthony Anderson 3.00 6.00
2 Larry Anderson 3.00 6.00
3 Matt Bahr 3.00 6.00
4 John Banaszak 3.00 6.00
5 Tom Beasley 3.00 6.00
6 Theo Bell 3.00 6.00
7 Rocky Bleier 4.00 8.00
8 Mel Blount 5.00 10.00
9 Terry Bradshaw 10.00 20.00
10 Larry Brown 3.00 6.00
11 Robin Cole 3.00 6.00
12 Craig Colquitt 3.00 6.00
13 Steve Courson 3.00 6.00
14 Bennie Cunningham 3.00 6.00
15 Sam Davis 3.00 6.00
16 Tom Dornbrook 3.00 6.00
17 Rollie Dotsch CO 3.00 6.00
18 Gary Dunn 3.00 6.00
19 Steve Furness 3.00 6.00
20 Roy Gerela 3.00 6.00
21 Joe Greene 6.00 12.00
22 L.C. Greenwood 5.00 10.00
23 Randy Grossman 4.00 8.00
24 Jack Ham 5.00 10.00
25 Franco Harris 6.00 12.00
26 Greg Hawthorne 3.00 6.00
27 Dick Hoak CO 3.00 6.00
28 Ron Johnson 3.00 6.00
29 Jon Kolb 3.00 6.00
30 Mike Kruczek 3.00 6.00
31 Jack Lambert 6.00 12.00
32 Tom Moore CO 3.00 6.00
33 Rick Moser 3.00 6.00
34 Gerry Mullins 3.00 6.00
35 Chuck Noll CO 7.50 15.00
36 George Perles CO 3.00 6.00
37 Ted Peterson 3.00 6.00
38 Ray Pinney 3.00 6.00
39 Lou Riecke CO 3.00 6.00
40 Donnie Shell 4.00 8.00
41 Jim Smith 4.00 8.00
42 John Stallworth 6.00 12.00
43 Cliff Stoudt 4.00 8.00
44 Lynn Swann 7.50 15.00
45 Loren Toews 3.00 6.00
46 J.T. Thomas 3.00 6.00
47 Sidney Thornton 3.00 6.00
48 Paul Uram CO 3.00 6.00
49 Zack Valentine CO 3.00 6.00
50 Mike Wagner 3.00 6.00
51 Dick Walker CO 3.00 6.00
52 Mike Webster 5.00 10.00
53 Dwight White 4.00 8.00
54 Woody Widenhofer CO 3.00 6.00
55 Dennis Winston 3.00 6.00
56 Dwayne Woodruff 3.00 6.00

1979-80 Steelers Postcards

The Steelers released these postcards presumably in the late 1970s. The Bradshaw and Greene cards were printed by Coastal Printing and include a typical postcard format on the back with a color player photo on the front. The Swann card was printed by Ellie's and is slightly different in back design. Each measures roughly 6" by 9." The checklist below is thought to be incomplete.

COMPLETE SET (3) 20.00 40.00
1 Terry Bradshaw 10.00 20.00
2 Joe Greene 5.00 10.00
3 Lynn Swann 6.00 12.00

1980 Steelers McDonald's Glasses

McDonald's stores issued this set of glasses in the Pittsburgh area in 1980 following Super Bowl XIV. Each features a black and white photo of three different Steelers players with the McDonald's logo circling the bottom of the glass. The logos for the NFL Player's Association and MSA also appear.

COMPLETE SET (4) 17.50 35.00
1 Rocky Bleier 3.00 8.00
John Stallworth
Roy Winston
2 Mel Blount 3.00 8.00
Jon Kolb
Jack Lambert
3 Terry Bradshaw 6.00 15.00
Sam Davis
Jack Ham
4 Matt Bahr 3.00 8.00
Joe Greene
Sidney Thornton

1980 Steelers Pittsburgh Press Posters

These small posters (measuring roughly 13 1/2" by 21") were issued one per Pittsburgh Press newspaper in 1980. Each includes a color artist's rendering of a Steelers' player with a facsimile autograph below the image along with a copyright line and date. The backs feature a comics page from the newspaper. We've listed them below in alphabetical order.

COMPLETE SET (12) 50.00 100.00
1 Chris Bahr 2.50 6.00
2 Mel Blount 4.00 10.00
3 Terry Bradshaw 8.00 20.00
4 Sam Davis 2.50 6.00
5 Jack Ham 4.00 10.00
6 Franco Harris 5.00 12.00
7 Jon Kolb 2.50 6.00
8 Chuck Noll CO 4.00 10.00
9 Donnie Shell 3.00 8.00
10 John Stallworth 4.00 10.00
11 Lynn Swann 5.00 12.00
12 Mike Webster 3.00 8.00

1980-82 Steelers Boy Scouts

These standard sized cards were issued for the Boy Scouts and used as membership cards. Each was printed on thin stock and features a Steelers player on the front and Boy Scouts membership information on the back.

1 Rocky Bleier 20.00 40.00
2 Terry Bradshaw 1982 40.00 75.00
3 Franco Harris 25.00 50.00
4 John Stallworth 1981 20.00 40.00
5 Cliff Stoudt 1981 15.00 30.00
6 Lynn Swann 25.00 50.00
7 Mike Webster 1981 20.00 40.00

1981 Steelers Police

The 1981 Pittsburgh Steelers police set consists of 16 unnumbered cards which have been listed in the checklist below by the uniform number appearing on the fronts of the cards. The cards measure approximately 2 5/8" by 4 1/8". The set is sponsored by the local police department, the Pittsburgh Steelers, the Kiwanis Club, and Coca-Cola, the last three of which have their logos appearing on the backs of the cards. In addition, "Steelers' Tips" are featured on the back. Card backs have black printing with gold accent on white card stock. This set is very similar to the 1982 Police Steelers set; differences are noted parenthetically in the list below. The set also contains the only trading card of popular Steeler John Banaszak.

COMPLETE SET (16) 20.00 35.00
9 Matt Bahr .40 1.00
12 Terry Bradshaw 3.00 8.00
31 Donnie Shell .50 1.25
32 Franco Harris 2.00 5.00
47 Mel Blount 1.00 2.50
52 Mike Webster .60 1.50
57 Sam Davis .40 1.00
58 Jack Lambert 1.25 3.00
59 Jack Ham 1.00 2.50
64 Steve Furness .40 1.00
68 L.C. Greenwood .75 2.00
75 Joe Greene 1.25 3.00
76 John Banaszak 1.25 3.00
79 Larry Brown .40 1.00
82 John Stallworth 1.00 2.50
88 Lynn Swann 2.50 6.00

1982 Steelers McDonald's Glasses

McDonald's issued this set of four glasses as part of the Steelers' "50 Seasons" celebration. Each glass includes six current or former Steelers greats featured in a black and white photo. The glasses measure roughly 4 3/4" tall.

COMPLETE SET (4) 12.00 30.00
1 Gerry Mullins 3.00 8.00
Larry Brown
Jack lambert
Franco Harr
2 J.Greene 3.00 8.00
E.Nickel
Kolb
Bleier
Shell
Ham
3 Roy Gerela 3.00 8.00
Sam Davis
Mike Wagner

L.C. Greenwood
Mi
4 M.Blount 5.00 12.00
E.Stautner
T.Brad
A.Russ
Stallwort
Butler

1982 Steelers Police

The 16-card, 1982 Pittsburgh Steelers set is unnumbered, but has been listed in the checklist below by the player's uniform number which appears on the fronts of the cards. The cards measure 2 5/8" by 4 1/8". The backs of the cards feature Steelers' Tips, the Kiwanis logo, the Coca-Cola logo, and a Steelers helmet logo. The local police department sponsored this set, in addition to the organizations whose logos appear on the back. Card backs feature black print with gold trim. This set is very similar to the 1981 Police Steelers set; differences are noted parenthetically in the list below.

COMPLETE SET (16) 10.00 20.00
12 Terry Bradshaw 2.00 5.00
31 Donnie Shell .30 .75
32 Franco Harris 1.00 2.50
44 Frank Pollard .25 .60
47 Mel Blount .50 1.25
52 Mike Webster .40 1.00
58 Jack Lambert .75 2.00
59 Jack Ham .50 1.25
65 Tom Beasley 1.00 2.50
67 Gary Dunn .25 .60
74 Ray Pinney .25 .60
79 Larry Brown .25 .60
82 John Stallworth .50 1.25
88 Lynn Swann 1.25 3.00
89 Bennie Cunningham .25 .60
90 Bob Kohrs .25 .60

1982 Steelers Nu-Maid Butter Tubs

This set of butter cups or tubs was released by Nu-Maid and Miami Margarine in 1982 in the Pittsburgh area. Each tub includes color illustrations of the featured player and measures roughly 3 3/4" tall and 3" in diameter.

COMPLETE SET (6) 25.00 50.00
1 Mel Blount 3.00 8.00
2 L.C. Greenwood 3.00 8.00
3 Jack Ham 4.00 10.00
4 Franco Harris 6.00 15.00
5 John Stallworth 4.00 10.00
6 Mike Webster 2.50 6.00

1983 Steelers Police

This 17-card set features the Pittsburgh Steelers. Cards measure approximately 2 5/8" by 4 1/8" and read "1983" on the card backs. There was an error on the Chuck Noll ("Knoll") card, which was corrected. The set is considered complete with either one of the Noll variations. The set is unnumbered and hence is listed below ordered (and numbered) alphabetically by subject.

COMPLETE SET (16) 7.50 15.00
1 Walter Abercrombie .20 .50
2 Gary Anderson K .60 1.50
3 Mel Blount .40 1.00
4 Terry Bradshaw 1.50 4.00
5 Robin Cole .20 .50
6 Steve Courson .20 .50
7 Bennie Cunningham .20 .50
8 Franco Harris .75 2.00
9 Greg Hawthorne .20 .50
10 Jack Lambert .60 1.50
11A Chuck Noll CO ERR 1.50 4.00
11B Chuck Noll CO COR .40 1.00
12 Donnie Shell .25 .60
13 John Stallworth .50 1.25
14 Mike Webster .30 .75
15 Dwayne Woodruff .20 .50
16 Rick Woods .20 .50

1983 Steelers Team Issue

This set consists of team issued photos released in 1983. Each measures roughly 8" by 10" and includes black and white photos of the featured player or players printed on glossy stock. The top superstars on the team were given an entire sheet of photos for themselves, while the other players were grouped in traditional team sheet fashion with eight players to a page.

COMPLETE SET (5) 20.00 50.00
1 Walter Abercrombie 2.50 6.00
Gary Anderson K
Bennie Cunningham
Greg Hawthorne
Mel Blount
Dwayne Woodruff
Rick Woods
Gabe Rivera
2 Terry Bradshaw 8.00 20.00
3 Franco Harris 4.00 10.00
4 Jack Lambert 5.00 12.00
5 John Stallworth 3.00 8.00

1984 Steelers Police

This unnumbered set of 16 cards features players from the Pittsburgh Steelers. Cards measure 2 5/8" by 4 1/8". Card backs feature black printing on thin white card stock. The set was sponsored by McDonald's, Kiwanis, and local police departments. The players are listed below by uniform number. The set can be differentiated from other similar Steelers police sets by the presence of the Kiwanis logo on the card fronts.

COMPLETE SET (16) 5.00 10.00
1 Gary Anderson K .40 1.00
16 Mark Malone .25 .60
19 David Woodley .25 .60
30 Frank Pollard .20 .50
32 Franco Harris .75 2.00
34 Walter Abercrombie .20 .50
49 Dwayne Woodruff .20 .50
52 Mike Webster .40 1.00
57 Mike Merriweather .20 .50
58 Jack Lambert .50 1.25
67 Gary Dunn .20 .50
73 Craig Wolfley .20 .50
82 John Stallworth .50 1.25
83 Louis Lipps .25 .60
92 Keith Gary .20 .50
92 Keith Willis .20 .50

1985 Steelers Pittsburgh Press Pin-Ups

These small posters (measuring roughly 10" by 13") were issued one per Pittsburgh Press newspaper in 1985. Each includes a color artist's rendering of two member of the Steelers' with facsimile autographs of both. Each is numbered on the front and the backs feature another page from the newspaper.

COMPLETE SET (12) 50.00 100.00
1 M.Malone 4.00 10.00
D.Woodley
2 J.Stallworth 5.00 12.00
L.Lipps
3 W.Thompson 3.00 8.00
Erenberg
4 D.Shell 4.00 10.00
D.Woodruff
5 F.Pollard 4.00 10.00
W.Abercrombie
6 M.Webster 4.00 10.00
Cunningham
7 G.Dunn 3.00 8.00
D.Sims
8 J.Goodman 3.00 8.00
E.Nelson
9 R.Cole 3.00 8.00
D.Little
10 B.Hinkle 3.00 8.00
M.Merriweather
11 S.Campbell 3.00 8.00
G.Anderson
12 C.Noll CO 5.00 12.00
D.Rooney Pres.

1985 Steelers Police

This 16-card set of Pittsburgh Steelers is unnumbered except for uniform number. Cards measure approximately 2 5/8" by 4 1/8". The backs contain "Steeler Tips". The set was sponsored by Kiwanis, Giant Eagle, local Police Departments, and the Steelers. Card backs are written in black on white card stock. The 1985, 1986, and 1987 Police Steelers sets are identical except for the individual card differences noted parenthetically below.

COMPLETE SET (16) 5.00 10.00
1 Gary Anderson K .30 .75
16 Mark Malone .25 .60
21 Eric Williams S .20 .50
30 Frank Pollard .20 .50
31 Donnie Shell .30 .75
34 Walter Abercrombie .20 .50
49 Dwayne Woodruff .20 .50
50 David Little .20 .50
52 Mike Webster .40 1.00
53 Bryan Hinkle .20 .50
56 Robin Cole .20 .50
57 Mike Merriweather .20 .50
82 John Stallworth .60 1.50
83 Louis Lipps .25 .60
93 Keith Willis .20 .50
NNO Chuck Noll CO .60 1.50

1985 Steelers Stop'N'Go Cups

This set of 32-ounce cups was sponsored and distributed by Stop-n-Go stores in the Pittsburgh area. Each includes a picture of two-Steelers players and is numbered by both the series and cup number. Any additions to the list below are appreciated.

1-1 Jack Lambert 2.50 6.00
Louis Lipps
1-2 John Stallworth 2.50 6.00
Mike Webster

1986 Steelers Police

This 15-card set of Pittsburgh Steelers is unnumbered except for uniform number. Cards measure approximately 2 5/8" by 4 1/8". The backs contain "Steeler Tips". The set was sponsored by Kiwanis, Giant Eagle, local Police Departments, and the Steelers. Card backs are written in black on white card stock. The 1985, 1986, and 1987 Police Steelers sets are identical except for the individual card differences noted parenthetically below.

COMPLETE SET (15) 4.00 8.00
1 Gary Anderson K .30 .75
16 Mark Malone .25 .60
24 Rich Erenberg .20 .50
30 Frank Pollard .20 .50
31 Donnie Shell .30 .75
34 Walter Abercrombie .20 .50
49 Dwayne Woodruff .20 .50
52 Mike Webster .30 .75
53 Bryan Hinkle .20 .50
56 Robin Cole .20 .50
57 Mike Merriweather .20 .50
62 Tunch Ilkin .20 .50
64 Edmund Nelson .20 .50
67 Gary Dunn .20 .50
82 John Stallworth .50 1.25
83 Louis Lipps .25 .60

1987 Steelers Police

This 16-card set of Pittsburgh Steelers is unnumbered except for uniform number. Cards measure approximately 2 5/8" by 4 1/8". The backs contain "Steeler Tips". The set was sponsored by Kiwanis, Giant Eagle, local Police Departments, and the Steelers. The cards were given out by Pittsburgh area police officers one card per week. Card backs are written in black on white card stock. The 1985, 1986, and 1987 Police Steelers sets are identical except for the individual card differences noted parenthetically below.

COMPLETE SET (16) 4.00 8.00
1 Walter Abercrombie .20 .50
2 Gary Anderson K .25 .60
3 Bubby Brister .30 .75
4 Gary Dunn .20 .50
5 Preston Gothard .20 .50
6 Bryan Hinkle .20 .50
7 Earnest Jackson .25 .60
8 Louis Lipps .25 .60
9 Mark Malone .25 .60
10 Mike Merriweather .20 .50
11 Chuck Noll CO .40 1.00
12 John Rienstra .20 .50
13 Donnie Shell .30 .75
14 John Stallworth .50 1.25
15 Mike Webster .30 .75
16 Keith Willis .20 .50

1988 Steelers Police

The 1988 Police Pittsburgh Steelers set contains 16 player cards measuring approximately 2 5/8" by 4 1/8". The fronts show the players in uniform but not wearing helmets. The backs have definitions of football terms and safety tips. This unnumbered set is listed alphabetically below for convenience. The 1988 Police Steelers set is distinguishable from the 1985-87 Police Steelers sets by the Steelers helmet on back having three white diamonds instead of one white and two black diamonds.

COMPLETE SET (16) 4.00 8.00
1 Gary Anderson K .25 .60
2 Bubby Brister .30 .75
3 Thomas Everett .20 .50
4 Delton Hall .20 .50
5 Bryan Hinkle .20 .50
6 Tunch Ilkin .20 .50
7 Earnest Jackson .20 .50
8 Louis Lipps .25 .60
9 David Little .20 .50
10 Mike Merriweather .20 .50
11 Frank Pollard .20 .50
12 John Rienstra .20 .50
13 Mike Webster .40 1.00
14 Keith Willis .20 .50
15 Craig Wolfley .20 .50
16 Rod Woodson .75 2.00

1989 Steelers Police

The 1989 Police Pittsburgh Steelers set contains 16 cards measuring approximately 2 5/8" by 4 1/8". The fronts have white borders and color action photos; the vertically-oriented backs have safety tips. These cards were printed on very thin stock. The cards are unnumbered, so therefore are listed below according to uniform number. The card backs are subtitled "Steelers Tips '89". It has been reported that 175,000 cards of each player were given away by police officers in Western Pennsylvania.

COMPLETE SET (16) 4.00 8.00
1 Gary Anderson K .20 .50
6 Bubby Brister .20 .50
18 Harry Newsome .15 .40
24 Rodney Carter .15 .40
26 Rod Woodson .50 1.25
27 Thomas Everett .15 .40
33 Merril Hoge .15 .40
53 Bryan Hinkle .15 .40
54 Hardy Nickerson .30 .75
62 Tunch Ilkin .15 .40
C0 Dermontti Dawson .20 .50
74 Terry Long .15 .40
78 Tim Johnson .15 .40
83 Louis Lipps .20 .50
97 Aaron Jones .15 .40
98 Gerald Williams .15 .40

1990 Steelers McDonald's Glasses

McDonald's issued this set of four glasses to commemorate Steelers players in the Pro Football Hall of Fame. Each glass includes former Steelers greats featured in a black and white photo. The glasses measure roughly 6 3/8" tall and include sponsors logos by McDonald's, Diet Coke, and WPXI-TV.

COMPLETE SET (4) 8.00 20.00
1 Mel Blount 2.00 5.00
Jack Ham
Bobby Layne
2 Terry Bradshaw 3.20 8.00
Bill Dudley
John Henry Johnson
3 Joe Greene 2.00 5.00
Franco Harris
Johnny Blood McNally
4 Jack Lambert 2.00 5.00
Art Rooney
Ernie Stautner

1990 Steelers Police

This 16-card set, which measures approximately 2 5/8" by 4 1/8", was issued to promote safety in the Pittsburgh Area using members of the Pittsburgh Steelers to make safety tips. The fronts of the cards feature color portrait shots of the players surrounded by white borders. There are advertisements for the Giant Eagle shopping chain and the Kiwanis Club on the front along with the Steelers name on top of the photo and underneath the photo is the player's name and position. The back of the card features a safety tip. The back says the cards were sponsored by the local Kiwanis club, Giant Eagle, the local police departments, and the Pittsburgh Steelers. The set is checklisted below alphabetically.

COMPLETE SET (16) 4.00 8.00
1 Gary Anderson K .15 .40
2 Bubby Brister .30 .75
3 Thomas Everett .15 .40
4 Merril Hoge .15 .40
5 Tunch Ilkin .15 .40
6 Carnell Lake .20 .50
7 Louis Lipps .20 .50
8 David Little .15 .40
9 Greg Lloyd .40 1.00
10 Mike Mularkey .15 .40
11 Hardy Nickerson .20 .50
12 Chuck Noll CO .40 1.00
13 John Rienstra .15 .40
14 Keith Willis .15 .40
15 Rod Woodson .30 .75
16 Tim Worley .15 .40

1991 Steelers Police

This 16-card set was sponsored by the Kiwanis and Giant Eagle. The cards measure approximately 2 5/8" by 4 1/8". They were distributed by participating Pennsylvania police departments. The fronts feature color action player photos, with the team name at the top sandwiched between the two sponsor logos. Player information appears below the picture. On the card backs below a Steelers helmet, the backs have "Steelers Tips '91," which consist of anti-crime or anti-drug messages. The cards are unnumbered and checklisted below in alphabetical order.

COMPLETE SET (16) 4.00 8.00
1 Gary Anderson K .15 .40
2 Bubby Brister .20 .50
3 Dermontti Dawson .30 .75
4 Eric Green .20 .50
5 Bryan Hinkle .15 .40
6 Merril Hoge .20 .50
7 John Jackson T .15 .40
8 D.J. Johnson .15 .40
9 Carnell Lake .20 .50
10 Louis Lipps .20 .50
11 Greg Lloyd .30 .75
12 Mike Mularkey .15 .40
13 Chuck Noll CO .40 1.00
14 Dan Stryzinski .15 .40
15 Gerald Williams .15 .40
16 Rod Woodson .40 1.00

1992 Steelers Police

This 16-card set was sponsored by the Kiwanis Club and Giant Eagle, and it was distributed by local police departments. The cards measure approximately 2 5/8" by 4 3/16" and feature still color player photos on white card stock. Beneath the picture are the player's name, number, position, height, and weight. The team name and sponsor logos appear at the top. The backs are plain white with public service "Steelers Tips '92" printed within a black outline. The cards are unnumbered and checklisted below in alphabetical order.

COMPLETE SET (16) 4.00 8.00
1 Gary Anderson K .15 .40
2 Bubby Brister .20 .50
3 Bill Cowher CO 1.25 3.00
4 Dermontti Dawson .30 .75
5 Eric Green .20 .50
6 Carlton Haselrig .15 .40
7 Merril Hoge .15 .40
8 John Jackson T .15 .40
9 Carnell Lake .20 .50
10 Louis Lipps .20 .50
11 Greg Lloyd .30 .75
12 Neil O'Donnell .30 .75
13 Tom Ricketts .15 .40
14 Gerald Williams .15 .40
15 Jerrol Williams .15 .40
16 Rod Woodson .30 .75

1993 Steelers Police

Sponsored by the Pittsburgh Police Department, Kiwanis Club, and Giant Eagle, these 16 cards, when cut from the sheet, measure approximately 2 1/2" by 4". The fronts feature white-bordered color player action shots, with the player's name, uniform number, position, height, and weight appearing in black lettering within the bottom white margin. The team name appears in team color-coded lettering within the white margin above the photo, along with the Kiwanis and Giant Eagle logos. The white back has a large Steeler helmet logo at the top, followed below by the words "Steelers Tips '93," then the player's name, position, and highlight. The tip then appears, which contains a stay-in-school, anti-drug, or safety message. The Giant Eagle and Kiwanis logos at the bottom round out the card. The cards are unnumbered and checklisted below in alphabetical order.

COMPLETE SET (16) 3.00 6.00
1 Gary Anderson K .15 .40
2 Adrian Cooper .15 .40
3 Bill Cowher CO .40 1.00
4 Dermontti Dawson .25 .60
5 Donald Evans .15 .40
6 Eric Green .20 .50
7 Bryan Hinkle .15 .40
8 Merril Hoge .15 .40
9 Garry Howe .15 .40
10 Greg Lloyd .30 .75
11 Neil O'Donnell .20 .50
12 Jerry Olsavsky .15 .40
13 Leon Searcy .15 .40
14 Dwight Stone .15 .40
15 Gerald Williams .15 .40
16 Rod Woodson .30 .75

1995 Steelers Eat'n Park

This set of the Pittsburgh Steelers was issued in four strips of three peel-off player cards. Each sold for $.99 per strip. One strip was issued each week by Eat'n Park stores for four weeks. The fronts feature color action player cut-outs on a silver background with the player's name and position printed vertically on one side. The backs are blank. The cards are unnumbered and checklisted below according to the week number of the strip. A poster to house the set was also available for 99-cents.

COMPLETE SET (4) 4.00 10.00
1 Darren Perry .80 2.00
R.Woodson
G.Lloyd
2 Ray Seals .80 2.00
C.Lake
K.Greene
3 Derm.Dawson 1.00 2.50
E.Pegram
M.Bruener
4 Kord.Stewart 2.40 6.00
Y.Thigpen
N.O'Donnell

1995 Steelers Giant Eagle Proline/Coins

A set of nine coins and nine 1995 Classic ProLine series cards were issued as a promotion by the Pittsburgh Steelers and Giant Eagle Supermarkets in Pittsburgh. Each coin and card combo pack could be acquired for approximately $1.89 each at Giant Eagle Supermarkets in Pittsburgh. The program launch date was September 3, the duration was nine weeks, and the offer was valid while supplies lasted. The coin fronts display the player's face along with the player's name and team name. The backs carry the Steelers logo and the year '95-96. The coins are unnumbered and listed below alphabetically with a "CO" prefix. A colorful cardboard display featuring the Steelers defense was also produced to house the coins. The card fronts display full-bleed color action photos, with the player's name in a team color-coded diagonal stripe across the bottom. The back of every card carries a checklist for the set. We've numbered them below using a "CA" prefix on the card numbers.

COMP.CARD/COIN SET (18) 9.60 24.00
COMPLETE CARD SET (9) 4.80 12.00
COMPLETE COIN SET (9) 4.80 12.00
CA1 Kevin Greene .50 1.25
CA2 Franco Harris .60 1.50
CA3 Greg Lloyd .60 1.50
CA4 Joe Greene .60 1.50
CA5 Byron Bam Morris .50 1.25
CA6 Jack Lambert .60 1.50
CA7 Rod Woodson .60 1.50
CA8 Mel Blount .50 1.25
CA9 Bill Cowher CO .50 1.25
CO1 Mel Blount .50 1.25
CO2 Bill Cowher CO .50 1.25
CO3 Joe Greene .60 1.50
CO4 Kevin Greene .50 1.25
CO5 Franco Harris .60 1.50
CO6 Jack Lambert .60 1.50
CO7 Greg Lloyd .60 1.50
CO8 Byron Bam Morris .50 1.25
CO9 Rod Woodson .60 1.50
NNO Set Display Holder .80 2.00

1996 Steelers Kids Club

The Steelers sponsored this set featuring three top players and the head coach. Each card measures the standard size, is unnumbered, and features a black and yellow border.

COMPLETE SET (4) 2.00 5.00
1 Bill Cowher CO .40 1.00
2 Greg Lloyd .40 1.00
3 Kordell Stewart 1.20 3.00
4 Rod Woodson .40 1.00

1996 Steelers Team Issue

The Steelers issued these player photos in 1996. Each measures roughly 5" by 7" and features a black and white photo of a Steelers player with his uniform number, name, and position below the photo. The backs are blank and unnumbered. The 1996 release closely resembles the 1997 photos and are differentiated as noted below for like players.

1 Jerome Bettis 4.00 8.00
2 Chad Brown 2.50 5.00
3 Mark Bruener 2.00 4.00
4 Brentson Buckner 2.00 4.00
5 Dermontti Dawson 2.50 6.00
6 Deon Figures 2.00 4.00
7 Jason Gildon 2.50 5.00
8 Norm Johnson 2.00 4.00
9 Carnell Lake 2.50 5.00
10 Greg Lloyd 2.00 4.00
11 Jim Miller 2.50 5.00
12 Ernie Mills 2.00 4.00
13 Jerry Olsavsky 2.00 4.00
14 Erric Pegram 2.00 4.00
15 Ray Seals 2.00 4.00
16 Joel Steed 2.00 4.00
17 Kordell Stewart 4.00 8.00
18 Yancey Thigpen 2.00 4.00
19 Mike Tomczak 2.00 4.00
20 Willie Williams 2.00 4.00
21 Rod Woodson 2.50 5.00
22 Will Wolford 2.00 4.00

1997 Steelers Collector's Choice

Upper Deck released several team sets in 1997 in a blister pack wrapper. Each of the 14-cards in this set are very similar to the base Collector's Choice cards except for the card numbering on the cardback. A cover/checklist card was added featuring the team helmet.

COMPLETE SET (14) 1.20 3.00
PI1 Jerome Bettis .15 .40
PI2 Charles Johnson .08 .25
PI3 Mike Tomczak .05 .15
PI4 Levon Kirkland .05 .15
PI5 Carnell Lake .05 .15
PI6 Donnell Woolford .05 .15
PI7 Kordell Stewart .40 1.00
PI8 Greg Lloyd .08 .25
PI9 Will Blackwell .08 .25
PI10 George Jones .08 .25
PI11 J.B. Brown .05 .15
PI12 Darren Perry .05 .15
PI13 Mark Bruener .05 .15
PI14 Steelers Logo .05 .15
Checklist

1997 Steelers Eat'n Park Glasses

These set of glasses was released by Eat'n Park stores in 1997. Each glass features an artist's rendering of a member of the Steelers on one side with a short write-up of the player on the other side.

COMPLETE SET (4) 4.80 12.00
1 Jerome Bettis 2.00 5.00
2 Bill Cowher 1.20 3.00
3 Carnell Lake 1.20 3.00
4 Greg Lloyd 1.20 3.00

1997 Steelers Team Issue

The Steelers issued these player photos in 1997. Each measures roughly 5" by 7" and features a black and white photo of a Steelers player with his uniform number, name, and position below the photo. The backs are blank and unnumbered. The 1997 release closely resembles the 1996 photos and are differentiated as noted below for like players.

COMPLETE SET (20) 30.00 60.00
1 Jerome Bettis 4.00 8.00
2 Mark Bruener 2.00 4.00
3 Bill Cowher CO 2.00 4.00
4 Dermontti Dawson 2.50 6.00
5 Randy Fuller 2.00 4.00
6 John Jackson 2.00 4.00
7 Charles Johnson 2.00 4.00
8 Donta Jones 2.00 4.00
9 Levon Kirkland 2.00 4.00
10 Carnell Lake 2.50 5.00
11 Greg Lloyd 2.00 4.00
12 Fred McAfee 2.00 4.00
13 Jerry Olsavsky 2.00 4.00
14 Darren Perry 2.00 4.00
15 Kordell Stewart 4.00 8.00
16 Justin Strzelczyk 2.00 4.00
17 Yancey Thigpen 2.00 4.00
10 Mike Tomczak 2.00 4.00
19 Jon Witman 2.00 4.00
20 Will Wolford 2.00 4.00

1999 Steelers Tribune-Review Posters

These posters (measuring roughly 14" by 21 1/2") were issued one per Greensburg Tribune-Review newspaper in 1999. Each includes a color photo of a current or retired Steelers' player on one side and another page from the newspaper on the back. We've listed them below in alphabetical order.

1 Lethon Flowers 3.00 6.00
2 Donnie Shell 4.00 8.00

2000 Steelers Giant Eagle

This set was issued one card at a time to attendees of home game at Three Rivers Stadium during the 2000 Steelers regular season. Each card hightlights one "Three Rivers Greatest Moment" using a color action photo from a famous Steeler's event at the stadium. A Pin version of each cardfront was also produced and collectors would need to redeem one card at a Giant Eagle Store to get a pin. Reportedly, cards and pins #9 and #10 were short printed.

COMPLETE SET 12.50 25.00
*PINS: 1X TO 2X CARDS
1 December 23, 1972 2.00 4.00
2 December 30, 1978 3.00 5.00
3 January 14, 1996 1.25 3.00
4 January 6, 1980 2.00 4.00
5 September 24, 1978 1.25 3.00
6 January 6, 1980 2.00 4.00
7 December 27, 1975 1.25 3.00
8 October 26, 1997 3.00 5.00
9 December 30, 1978 4.00 8.00
10 January 7, 1979 3.00 5.00

2002 Steelers Post-Gazette

This set of oversized cards (roughly 4 1/2" by 6") was issued one card at a time for the Steelers 8-home games during the 2002 season. Each unnumbered card features a Steelers star on the front along with two small color photos of the player on the back, a brief bio, and the Pittsburgh Post-Gazette sponsor logo.

COMPLETE SET (6) 15.00 30.00
1 Jerome Bettis 2.50 6.00
2 Mark Bruener 1.25 3.00
3 Plaxico Burress 2.50 6.00
4 Jason Gildon 1.25 3.00
5 Joey Porter 1.50 4.00
6 Antwaan Randle El 4.00 10.00
7 Kordell Stewart 1.50 4.00
8 Hines Ward 2.50 6.00

2004 Steelers Beaver County Times Posters

These posters (measuring roughly 13 1/2" by 19") were issued one per Beaver County Times newspaper in 2004. Each includes a color photo of a Steeler's player on one side and another page from the newspaper on the back. We've listed them below in alphabetical order.

1 Jerome Bettis 5.00 10.00
2 Ben Roethlisberger 6.00 12.00
3 Joey Porter 3.00 6.00
4 Kimo Von Oelhoffen 3.00 6.00
5 Willie Williams 3.00 6.00

2005 Steelers Activa Medallions

COMPLETE SET (25) 30.00 80.00
1 Jerome Bettis 2.00 5.00
2 Alan Faneca 1.25 3.00
3 James Farrior 1.25 3.00
4 Larry Foote 1.25 3.00
5 Clark Haggans 1.25 3.00
6 Casey Hampton 1.25 3.00
7 Jeff Hartings 1.25 3.00
8 Chris Hope 1.25 3.00
9 Dan Kreider 1.25 3.00
10 Troy Polamalu 1.50 4.00
11 Joey Porter 1.25 3.00
12 Antwaan Randle El 1.50 4.00
13 Jeff Reed 1.25 3.00
14 Ben Roethlisberger 2.50 6.00
15 Kendall Simmons 1.25 3.00
16 Aaron Smith 1.25 3.00
17 Marvel Smith 1.25 3.00
18 Duce Staley 1.25 3.00
19 Max Starks 1.25 3.00
20 Deshea Townsend 1.25 3.00
21 Jerame Tuman 1.25 3.00
22 Kimo Von Oelhoffen 1.25 3.00
23 Hines Ward 1.50 4.00
24 Willie Williams 1.25 3.00
25 Steelers Logo 1.25 3.00

2006 Steelers Merrick Mint Quarters

COMPLETE SET (11) 60.00 100.00
1 Jerome Bettis 6.00 12.00
2 Tommy Maddox 5.00 10.00
3 Troy Polamalu 6.00 12.00
4 Joey Porter 5.00 10.00
5 Antwaan Randle El 5.00 10.00
6 Ben Roethlisberger 6.00 12.00
7 Duce Staley 5.00 10.00
8 DeShea Townsend 5.00 10.00
9 Hines Ward 5.00 10.00
10 Steelers black logo 5.00 10.00
11 Steelers throwback logo 5.00 10.00

2006 Steelers Topps

COMPLETE SET (12) 3.00 6.00
PIT1 Troy Polamalu .40 1.00
PIT2 Willie Parker .30 .75
PIT3 Heath Miller .25 .60
PIT4 Jerome Bettis .40 1.00
PIT5 Hines Ward .30 .75
PIT6 Ben Roethlisberger .50 1.25
PIT7 James Farrior .25 .60
PIT8 Cedrick Wilson .25 .60
PIT9 Joey Porter .25 .60
PIT10 Larry Foote .25 .60
PIT11 Santonio Holmes .30 .75
PIT12 Omar Jacobs .25 .60

2006 Steelers Topps Super Bowl XL

This boxed factory set was offered by Topps shortly after the Steelers Super Bowl victory in February 2006. Nearly every member of the team was featured in the set which carried an initial SRP of $19.95. One bonus jumbo (3 1/2" by 5") card was also included in every sealed set.

COMPLETE SET (55) 15.00 25.00
1 Jerome Bettis .50 1.25
2 Hines Ward .40 1.00
3 Heath Miller .40 1.00
4 James Farrior .30 .75
5 Ben Roethlisberger 2.00 5.00
6 Troy Polamalu .60 1.50
7 Willie Parker .60 1.50
8 Clark Haggans .30 .75
9 Antwaan Randle El .40 1.00
10 Charlie Batch .30 .75
11 Aaron Smith .30 .75
12 Casey Hampton .30 .75
13 Cedrick Wilson .30 .75
14 Ike Taylor .30 .75
15 Jeff Hartings .30 .75
16 Chris Hope .30 .75
17 Quincy Morgan .30 .75
18 Kimo von Oelhoffen .30 .75
19 Kendall Simmons .30 .75
20 DeShea Townsend .30 .75
21 Ricardo Colclough .30 .75
22 Jeff Reed .30 .75
23 Marvel Smith .30 .75
24 Larry Foote .30 .75
25 Joey Porter .30 .75
26 Tommy Maddox .30 .75
27 Chris Gardocki .30 .75
28 Verron Haynes .30 .75
29 Dan Kreider .30 .75
30 Tyrone Carter .30 .75
31 Duce Staley .40 1.00
32 Mike Logan .30 .75
33 Bryant McFadden .30 .75
34 Clint Kriewaldt .30 .75
35 Chris Hoke .30 .75
36 Jerame Tuman .30 .75
37 Chidi Iwuoma .30 .75
38 Brett Keisel .40 1.00
39 Pittsburgh Steelers Team .40 1.00
40 Willie Parker HL .50 1.25
41 Troy Polamalu HL .50 1.25
42 Ben Roethlisberger HL 1.00 2.50
43 Hines Ward HL .40 1.00
44 Jerome Bettis HL .50 1.25
45 Hines Ward HL .40 1.00
46 Cedrick Wilson HL .30 .75
47 Ben Roethlisberger HL 1.00 2.50
48 Joey Porter HL .30 .75
49 Ben Roethlisberger HL 1.00 2.50
50 Hines Ward HL .40 1.00
51 Ben Roethlisberger HL 1.00 2.50
52 Willie Parker HL .50 1.25
53 Antwaan Randle El HL .30 .75
54 Jerome Bettis HL .50 1.25
Hines Ward
55 Hines Ward MVP .40 1.00
JUM Pittsburgh Steelers Team Jumbo .75 2.00

2006 Steelers Upper Deck Super Bowl XL

This boxed factory set was offered by Upper Deck shortly after the Steelers Super Bowl victory in February 2006. Nearly every member of the team was featured in the set which carried an initial SRP of $19.95. One bonus jumbo (3 1/2" by 5") card was also included in every sealed set.

COMPLETE SET (51) 15.00 25.00
1 Charlie Batch .30 .75
2 Jerome Bettis .50 1.25
3 Tyrone Carter .30 .75
4 Ricardo Colclough .30 .75
5 Alan Faneca .30 .75
6 James Farrior .30 .75
7 Larry Foote .30 .75
8 Andre Frazier .30 .75
9 Chris Gardocki .30 .75
10 Clark Haggans .30 .75
11 Casey Hampton .30 .75
12 Chris Hope .30 .75
13 Jeff Hartings .30 .75
14 Verron Haynes .30 .75
15 Brett Keisel .40 1.00
16 Travis Kirschke .30 .75
17 Dan Kreider .30 .75
18 Clint Kriewaldt .30 .75
19 Mike Logan .30 .75
20 Tommy Maddox .30 .75
21 Bryant McFadden .30 .75
22 Heath Miller .40 1.00
23 Quincy Morgan .30 .75
24 Kimo von Oelhoffen .30 .75
25 Willie Parker .60 1.50
26 Troy Polamalu .60 1.50
27 Joey Porter .30 .75
28 Antwaan Randle El .40 1.00
29 Jeff Reed .30 .75
30 Ben Roethlisberger 2.00 5.00
31 Kendall Simmons .30 .75
32 Aaron Smith .30 .75
33 Marvel Smith .30 .75
34 Duce Staley .40 1.00
35 Max Starks .30 .75
36 Ike Taylor .30 .75
37 Deshea Townsend .30 .75
38 Hines Ward .40 1.00
39 Greg Warren .30 .75
40 Cedrick Wilson .30 .75
MM1 Ben Roethlisberger MM 1.00 2.50
MM2 Willie Parker MM .50 1.25
MM3 Antwaan Randle El MM .30 .75
MM4 Jerome Bettis MM .50 1.25
SH1 Willie Parker SH .50 1.25
SH2 Ben Roethlisberger SH 1.00 2.50
SH3 Troy Polamalu SH .50 1.25
SH4 Antwaan Randle El SH .30 .75
SH5 Jerome Bettis SH .50 1.25
MVP1 Hines Ward MVP .40 1.00
SBCC Super Bowl Champs Jumbo .75 2.00

2007 Steelers Playoff Promos

COMPLETE SET (6) 3.00 6.00
P1 Ben Roethlisberger .50 1.25
P2 Willie Parker .40 1.00
P3 Hines Ward .40 1.00
P4 Santonio Holmes .30 .75
P5 Troy Polamalu .50 1.25
P6 Matt Spaeth .50 1.25

2007 Steelers Topps

COMPLETE SET (12) 3.00 6.00
1 Willie Parker .50 1.25
2 Santonio Holmes .40 1.00
3 Heath Miller .40 1.00
4 Ben Roethlisberger .60 1.50
5 Hines Ward .50 1.25
6 Troy Polamalu .60 1.50
7 Nate Washington .40 1.00
8 James Farrior .40 1.00
9 Jeff Reed .40 1.00
10 Clark Haggans .40 1.00
11 Najeh Davenport .40 1.00
12 Lawrence Timmons .60 1.50

2008 Steelers Topps

COMPLETE SET (12) 4.00 8.00
1 Heath Miller .40 1.00
2 Willie Parker .50 1.25
3 Ben Roethlisberger .60 1.50
4 Santonio Holmes .40 1.00
5 Najeh Davenport .40 1.00
6 Hines Ward .50 1.25
7 Casey Hampton .40 1.00
8 Troy Polamalu .60 1.50
9 James Harrison 1.25 3.00
10 James Farrior .40 1.00
11 Rashard Mendenhall .40 1.00
12 Limas Sweed .40 1.00

2009 Steelers Breast Cancer Awareness

This three card set was issued at a Steelers game in 2009. Each unnumbered card was created by one of the three NFL licensed manufacturers and features the pink ribbon breast cancer awareness logo on the fronts.

COMPLETE SET (3) 2.50 6.00
1 Troy Polamalu Upper Deck 1.00 2.50
2 Ben Roethlisberger Topps 1.00 2.50
3 Hines Ward Panini .75 2.00

2009 Steelers Donruss Super Bowl XLIII

This set was issued at the Donruss/Playoff booth during the 2009 Super Bowl Card Show in Tampa, Florida. A complete set of Steelers and Cardinals was given to any collector that purchased a Score Super Bowl XLIII factory set at the booth during the show.

COMPLETE SET (9) 4.00 8.00
1 Ben Roethlisberger .60 1.50
2 Willie Parker .40 1.00
3 Mewelde Moore .40 1.00
4 Hines Ward .50 1.25
5 Santonio Holmes .40 1.00
6 Heath Miller .40 1.00
7 Limas Sweed .50 1.25
8 Troy Polamalu .60 1.50
9 James Harrison .60 1.50

2009 Steelers Public Opinion Posters

These large posters (measuring roughly 11 1/2" by 22 3/4") were issued one per Public Opinion newspaper in February 2009 the day of the Super Bowl and the day after. Each includes a color photo of a Steeler's player on one side and another page from the newspaper on the back. We've listed them below in alphabetical order.

2 Ben Roethlisberger 4.00 8.00
1 Santonio Holmes 2.50 5.00

2009 Steelers Upper Deck Super Bowl XLIII

COMP.FACT.SET (51) 7.50 15.00
1 Aaron Smith .25 .60
2 Ben Roethlisberger .40 1.00
3 Brett Keisel .30 .75
4 Bruce Davis .25 .60
5 Bryant McFadden .25 .60
6 Byron Leftwich .25 .60
7 Carey Davis .25 .60
8 Casey Hampton .25 .60
9 Chris Hoke .25 .60
10 Chris Kemoeatu .25 .60
11 Darnell Stapleton .25 .60
12 Deshea Townsend .25 .60
13 Gary Russell .25 .60
14 Hines Ward .30 .75
15 Ike Taylor .25 .60
16 James Farrior .25 .60
17 James Harrison .40 1.00
18 Jeff Reed .25 .60
19 Justin Hartwig .25 .60
20 Keyaron Fox .25 .60
21 LaMarr Woodley .25 .60
22 Larry Foote .25 .60
23 Lawrence Timmons .25 .60
24 Limas Sweed .30 .75
25 Matt Spaeth .25 .60
26 Max Starks .25 .60
27 Mewelde Moore .25 .60
28 Mitch Berger .25 .60
29 Nate Washington .25 .60
30 Nick Eason .25 .60
31 Orpheus Roye .25 .60
32 Ryan Clark .25 .60
33 Santonio Holmes .25 .60
34 Trai Essex .25 .60
35 Travis Kirschke .25 .60
36 Troy Polamalu .40 1.00
37 Tyrone Carter .25 .60
38 William Gay .25 .60
39 Willie Colon .25 .60
40 Willie Parker .25 .60
41 Troy Polamalu SH .40 1.00
42 Ben Roethlisberger SH .40 1.00
43 Willie Parker SH .25 .60
44 Mewelde Moore SH .25 .60
45 James Harrison SH .40 1.00
46 Santonio Holmes MM .25 .60
47 Ben Roethlisberger MM .40 1.00
48 James Harrison MM .40 1.00
49 Santonio Holmes MM .25 .60
50 Santonio Holmes SB MVP .25 .60
51 Pittsburgh Steelers Jumbo .75 2.00

2011 Steelers Panini Super Bowl XLV

This set was sold exclusively at the 2011 Super Bowl Card Show in Dallas. The cards feature the Super Bowl XLV logo on the fronts and the backs are numbered.

COMPLETE SET (9) 8.00 20.00
1 Troy Polamalu 1.25 3.00
2 Ben Roethlisberger 1.25 3.00
3 Hines Ward 1.00 2.50
4 James Harrison 1.00 2.50
5 LaMarr Woodley .75 2.00
6 Lawrence Timmons .75 2.00
7 Mike Wallace .75 2.00
8 Rashard Mendenhall .75 2.00
9 Emmanuel Sanders 1.25 3.00

1979 Stop'N'Go

The 1979 Stop 'N' Go Markets set contains 18 3-D cards. The cards measure approximately 2 1/8" by 3 1/4". They are numbered and contain both a 1979 National Football League Players Association copyright date and a Xograph (predecessor of Sportflics and Score) trademark registration on the back. The set shows a heavy emphasis on players from the two Texas teams, the Dallas Cowboys and Houston Oilers, as they were issued primarily in the south.

COMPLETE SET (18) 40.00 75.00
1 Gregg Bingham .60 1.50
2 Ken Burrough .75 2.00
3 Preston Pearson .75 2.00
4 Sam Cunningham .75 2.00
5 Robert Newhouse .75 2.00
6 Walter Payton 15.00 30.00
7 Robert Brazile .60 1.50
8 Rocky Bleier 2.00 4.00
9 Toni Fritsch .60 1.50
10 Jack Ham 2.00 4.00
11 Jay Saldi .60 1.50
12 Roger Staubach 12.00 20.00
13 Franco Harris 4.00 8.00
14 Otis Armstrong 1.50 3.00
15 Lyle Alzado 1.50 3.00
16 Billy Johnson .75 2.00
17 Elvin Bethea 1.50 3.00
18 Joe Greene 3.00 6.00

1980 Stop'N'Go

The 1980 Stop 'N' Go Markets football card set contains 48 3-D cards. The cards measure approximately 2 1/8" by 3 1/4". Although similar to the 1979 issue, the cards can easily be distinguished by the two stars surrounding the name plaque on the front of the 1980 set and the obvious copyright date on the respective backs. One card was given out with each soda fountain drink purchased through September at participating Stop'N'Go and Doty stores. While players from National Football League teams, other than those in Texas, are indeed contained in the set, the emphasis remains on the Cowboys and Oilers. Cards with a "Doty" logo on back are more difficult to find than the base Stop'N'Go.

COMPLETE SET (48) 25.00 40.00
*DOTY BACKS: 2.5X TO 6X
1 John Jefferson .40 1.00
2 Herb Scott .25 .60
3 Pat Donovan .25 .60
4 William Andrews .40 1.00
5 Frank Corral .25 .60
6 Fred Dryer .40 1.00
7 Franco Harris 2.50 6.00
8 Leon Gray .25 .60
9 Gregg Bingham .25 .60
10 Louie Kelcher .25 .60
11 Robert Newhouse .30 .75
12 Preston Pearson .40 1.00
13 Wallace Francis .30 .75
14 Pat Haden .40 1.00
15 Jim Youngblood .25 .60
16 Rocky Bleier .75 2.00
17 Gifford Nielsen .25 .60
18 Elvin Bethea .40 1.00
19 Charlie Joiner .75 2.00
20 Tony Hill .40 1.00
21 Drew Pearson .75 2.00
22 Alfred Jenkins .30 .75
23 Dave Elmendorf .25 .60
24 Jack Reynolds .30 .75
25 Joe Greene 1.50 4.00
26 Robert Brazile .25 .60
27 Mike Reinfeldt .25 .60
28 Bob Griese 2.50 6.00
29 Harold Carmichael .60 1.50
30 Ottis Anderson 1.25 3.00
31 Ahmad Rashad .75 2.00
32 Archie Manning .60 1.50
33 Ricky Bell .40 1.00
34 Jay Saldi .25 .60
35 Ken Burrough .30 .75
36 Don Woods .25 .60
37 Henry Childs .25 .60
38 Wilbur Jackson .25 .60

39 Steve DeBerg .40 1.00
40 Ron Jessie .30 .75
41 Mel Blount .75 2.00
42 Cliff Branch .75 2.00
43 Chuck Muncie .30 .75
44 Ken MacAfee .25 .60
45 Charle Young .30 .75
46 Cody Jones .25 .60
47 Jack Ham 1.00 2.50
48 Ray Guy .40 1.00

1997 Studio

The 1997 Studio football set was released in two-card packs with most cards being jumbo sized (roughly 8' by 10"). Only Quarterback Club members were included in the release. A 12-card Class of Distinction subset was included as well as three parallel and two insert sets.

COMPLETE SET (36) 7.50 20.00
1 Troy Aikman .75 2.00
2 Tony Banks .25 .60
3 Jeff Blake .25 .60
4 Drew Bledsoe .50 1.25
5 Mark Brunell .50 1.25
6 Kerry Collins .40 1.00
7 Trent Dilfer .40 1.00
8 John Elway 1.50 4.00
9 Brett Favre 1.50 4.00
10 Gus Frerotte .25 .60
11 Jeff George .25 .60
12 Neil O'Donnell .15 .40
13 Jim Harbaugh .25 .60
14 Michael Irvin .40 1.00
15 Dan Marino 1.50 4.00
16 Steve McNair .50 1.25
17 Rick Mirer .15 .40
18 Jerry Rice .75 2.00
19 Barry Sanders 1.25 3.00
20 Junior Seau .40 1.00
21 Heath Shuler .15 .40
22 Emmitt Smith 1.25 3.00
23 Kordell Stewart .40 1.00
24 Steve Young .50 1.25
25 Troy Aikman CD .40 1.00
26 Drew Bledsoe CD .25 .60
27 Mark Brunell CD .40 1.00
28 Kerry Collins CD .25 .60
29 John Elway CD .75 2.00
30 Brett Favre CD .75 2.00
31 Dan Marino CD .75 2.00
32 Jerry Rice CD .40 1.00
33 Barry Sanders CD .60 1.50
34 Emmitt Smith CD .60 1.50
35 Kordell Stewart CD .25 .60
36 Steve Young CD .40 1.00

1997 Studio Postcard Portraits

COMPLETE SET (36) 20.00 50.00
*PC PORTRAITS: .8X TO 2X BASIC CARDS

1997 Studio Press Proofs Gold

COMPLETE SET (36) 60.00 150.00
*GOLD STARS: 2.5X TO 6X BASIC CARDS
STATED PRINT RUN 1000 SERIAL #'d SETS

1997 Studio Press Proofs Silver

COMPLETE SET (36) 40.00 80.00
*SILVER STARS: 1.2X TO 3X BASIC CARDS
STATED PRINT RUN 4000 SETS

1997 Studio Red Zone Masterpieces

Randomly inserted in packs, this 24-card set features color action art work of superstar players printed on canvas card stock and measuring 8" by 10". Only 3500 of each card were produced and individually numbered.

COMPLETE SET (24) 50.00 120.00
STATED PRINT RUN 3500 SERIAL #'d SETS
1 Troy Aikman 4.00 10.00
2 Tony Banks 1.25 3.00
3 Jeff Blake 1.25 3.00
4 Drew Bledsoe 2.50 6.00
5 Mark Brunell 2.50 6.00
6 Kerry Collins 2.00 5.00
7 Trent Dilfer 2.00 5.00
8 John Elway 8.00 20.00
9 Brett Favre 8.00 20.00
10 Gus Frerotte 1.25 3.00
11 Jeff George 1.25 3.00
12 Elvis Grbac 1.25 3.00
13 Neil O'Donnell .75 2.00
14 Michael Irvin 2.00 5.00
15 Dan Marino 8.00 20.00
16 Steve McNair 2.50 6.00
17 Rick Mirer .75 2.00
18 Jerry Rice 4.00 10.00
19 Barry Sanders 6.00 15.00
20 Warren Moon 2.00 5.00
21 Heath Shuler .75 2.00
22 Emmitt Smith 6.00 15.00
23 Kordell Stewart 2.00 5.00
24 Steve Young 2.50 6.00

1997 Studio Stained Glass Stars

Randomly inserted in packs, this 24-card set features color action photos printed on 8" by 10" die-cut plastic with multi-color ink to give the appearance of stained glass. Only 1000 of each card were produced and individually numbered.

COMPLETE SET (24) 125.00 250.00
STATED PRINT RUN 1000 SERIAL #'d SETS
1 Troy Aikman 12.50 30.00
2 Tony Banks 4.00 10.00
3 Jeff Blake 4.00 10.00
4 Drew Bledsoe 8.00 20.00
5 Mark Brunell 8.00 20.00
6 Kerry Collins 6.00 15.00
7 Trent Dilfer 6.00 15.00
8 John Elway 25.00 60.00
9 Brett Favre 25.00 60.00
10 Gus Frerotte 4.00 10.00
11 Jeff George 4.00 10.00
12 Elvis Grbac 4.00 10.00
13 Jim Harbaugh 4.00 10.00
14 Michael Irvin 6.00 15.00
15 Dan Marino 25.00 60.00
16 Steve McNair 8.00 20.00
17 Rick Mirer 2.50 6.00
18 Jerry Rice 12.50 30.00
19 Barry Sanders 20.00 50.00
20 Junior Seau 6.00 15.00
21 Vinny Testaverde 4.00 10.00
22 Emmitt Smith 20.00 50.00
23 Kordell Stewart 6.00 15.00
24 Steve Young 8.00 20.00

1995 Summit

This is the first year of release for Summit and the 200 card set is billed as the series two Score set. The set came seven cards per pack with a suggested retail price of $1.99. Card fronts have a 24 paint white stock background with the player's name and helmet logo in gold foil at the bottom. Rookie Cards include Ki-Jana Carter, Kerry Collins, Joey Galloway, Curtis Martin, Steve McNair, Rashaan Salaam, Kordell Stewart, J.J. Stokes, Tamarick Vanover and Michael Westbrook. Three Promo cards were produced and listed at the end of our checklist.

COMPLETE SET (200) 7.50 20.00
1 Neil O'Donnell .07 .20
2 Jim Everett .02 .10
3 Craig Heyward .07 .20
4 Jeff Blake RC .40 1.00
5 Alvin Harper .02 .10
6 Heath Shuler .07 .20
7 Rodney Hampton .07 .20
8 Dave Krieg .02 .10
9 Mark Brunell .25 .60
10 Rob Moore .07 .20
11 Daryl Johnston .07 .20
12 Marcus Allen .15 .40
13 Terance Mathis .07 .20
14 Frank Reich .02 .10
15 Gus Frerotte .07 .20
16 John Elway .75 2.00
17 Amp Lee .02 .10
18 Chris Miller .02 .10
19 Leroy Hoard .02 .10
20 Stan Humphries .07 .20
21 Charlie Garner .15 .40
22 Jim Kelly .15 .40
23 Gary Brown .02 .10
24 Byron Bam Morris .02 .10
25 Edgar Bennett .07 .20
26 Erik Kramer .02 .10
27 Dan Marino .75 2.00
28 Michael Haynes .07 .20
29 Lake Dawson .07 .20
30 Ben Coates .07 .20
31 Michael Jackson .07 .20
32 Brett Favre .75 2.00
33 Calvin Williams .07 .20
34 Steve Young .30 .75
35 Troy Aikman .30 .75
36 Greg Hill .07 .20
37 Leonard Russell .02 .10
38 Jeff George .07 .20
39 Herschel Walker .07 .20
40 Eric Green .02 .10
41 Haywood Jeffires .02 .10
42 Terry Kirby .07 .20
43 Darnay Scott .07 .20
44 Tim Brown .15 .40
45 Brian Mitchell .02 .10
46 Desmond Howard .07 .20
47 Warren Moon .07 .20
48 Andre Reed .07 .20
49 Adrian Murrell .07 .20
50 Marshall Faulk .50 1.25
51 Lewis Tillman .02 .10
52 Don Beebe .02 .10
53 Jerome Bettis .15 .40
54 Brett Perriman .07 .20
55 Mario Bates .07 .20
56 Ronnie Harmon .02 .10
57 Isaac Bruce .25 .60
58 Jackie Harris .02 .10
59 Dexter Carter .02 .10
60 Charles Johnson .07 .20
61 Herman Moore .15 .40
62 Craig Erickson .02 .10
63 Tony Martin .07 .20
64 Emmitt Smith .60 1.50
65 Brent Jones .02 .10
66 Ricky Watters .07 .20
67 Henry Ellard .07 .20
68 Vinny Testaverde .07 .20
69 Mark Pike .02 .10
70 Curtis Conway .15 .40
71 Michael Irvin .15 .40
72 Jay Novacek .07 .20
73 Howard Cross .02 .10
74 Drew Bledsoe .25 .60
75 Steve Beuerlein .07 .20
76 Andre Rison .07 .20
77 Morten Andersen .02 .10
78 Trent Dilfer .15 .40
79 Cris Carter .15 .40
80 Natrone Means .07 .20
81 Bernie Parmalee .07 .20
82 Randall Cunningham .15 .40
83 Eric Metcalf .07 .20
84 Rick Mirer .07 .20
85 Mark Ingram .02 .10
86 David Klingler .07 .20
87 Kevin Williams .07 .20
88 Erric Pegram .07 .20
89 Keith Byars .02 .10
90 Sean Dawkins .07 .20
91 Chris Warren .07 .20
92 William Floyd .07 .20
93 Jeff Hostetler .07 .20
94 Carl Pickens .07 .20
95 Flipper Anderson .02 .10
96 Johnny Mitchell .02 .10
97 Larry Centers .07 .20
98 Shannon Sharpe .07 .20
99 Errict Rhett .07 .20
100 Fred Barnett .07 .20
101 Harold Green .02 .10
102 Scott Mitchell .07 .20
103 Jerry Rice .40 1.00
104 Shawn Jefferson .02 .10
105 Glyn Milburn .02 .10
106 Garrison Hearst .15 .40
107 John Taylor .02 .10
108 Keith Cash .02 .10
109 Robert Brooks .15 .40
110 Barry Sanders .60 1.50
111 Ernest Givins .02 .10
112 Steve Tasker .07 .20
113 Jeff Graham .02 .10
114 Chris Chandler .07 .20
115 Lorenzo Neal .02 .10
116 Bert Emanuel .15 .40
117 Mike Sherrard .02 .10
118 Harvey Williams .02 .10
119 Reggie Brooks .07 .20
120 Steve Walsh .02 .10
121 Leroy Thompson .02 .10
122 Dave Brown .07 .20
123 Lorenzo White .02 .10
124 Steve Bono .07 .20
125 Irving Fryar .07 .20
126 Jake Reed .07 .20
127 Boomer Esiason .07 .20
128 Rocket Ismail .07 .20
129 Vincent Brisby .02 .10
130 Robert Smith .15 .40
131 Anthony Miller .07 .20
132 Roosevelt Potts .02 .10
133 Dave Meggett .02 .10
134 Junior Seau CC .15 .40
135 Neil Smith CC .07 .20
136 Charles Haley CC .07 .20
137 Rod Woodson CC .07 .20
138 Deion Sanders CC .25 .60
139 Reggie White CC .15 .40
140 John Randle CC .07 .20
141 Greg Lloyd CC .07 .20
142 Cortez Kennedy CC .07 .20
143 Bruce Smith CC .15 .40
144 J.J. Stokes RC .15 .40
145 Kyle Brady RC .15 .40
146 Frank Sanders RC .15 .40
147 Michael Westbrook RC .15 .40
148 Rob Johnson RC .50 1.25
149 Tyrone Poole RC .15 .40
150 Lovell Pinkney RC .02 .10
151 Tyrone Wheatley RC .60 1.50
152 Steve McNair RC 1.50 4.00
153 Napoleon Kaufman RC .60 1.50
154 Tamarick Vanover RC .15 .40
155 Todd Collins RC .50 1.25
156 Kevin Carter RC .15 .40
157 Rodney Thomas RC .07 .20
158 Stoney Case RC .02 .10
159 Kordell Stewart RC .75 2.00
160 Tony Boselli RC .15 .40
161 Sherman Williams RC .02 .10
162 Christian Fauria RC .07 .20
163 Ray Zellars RC .07 .20
164 Ki-Jana Carter RC .15 .40
165 Terrell Fletcher RC .02 .10
166 Curtis Martin RC 1.50 4.00
167 Eric Zeier RC .15 .40
168 Joey Galloway RC .75 2.00
169 Warren Sapp RC .75 2.00
170 Kerry Collins RC .75 2.00
171 Mark Bruener RC .07 .20
172 Chris Sanders RC .07 .20
173 Rashaan Salaam RC .07 .20
174 Jerry Rice OW .20 .50
175 Marshall Faulk OW .25 .60
176 Drew Bledsoe OW .15 .40
177 Emmitt Smith OW .30 .75
178 Tim Brown OW .07 .20
179 Steve Young OW .15 .40
180 Barry Sanders OW .30 .75
181 Michael Irvin OW .07 .20
182 Dan Marino OW .40 1.00
183 Jeff George OW .07 .20
184 Chris Warren OW .07 .20
185 Herman Moore OW .15 .40
186 Andre Rison OW .07 .20
187 Byron Bam Morris OW .02 .10
188 Troy Aikman OW .20 .50
189 Jim Kelly OW .15 .40
190 John Elway OW .40 1.00
191 Cris Carter OW .15 .40
192 Shannon Sharpe OW .02 .10
193 Brett Favre OW .40 1.00
194 Drew Bledsoe CL .15 .40
195 John Elway CL .25 .60
196 Dan Marino CL .25 .60
197 Brett Favre CL .25 .60
198 Troy Aikman CL .15 .40
199 Steve Young CL .15 .40
200 Chase Program CL .07 .20
Rick Mirer
Napoleon Kaufman
Kevin Carter
Kyle Brady
Terrell Davis
P1 Emmitt Smith BS Promo .75 2.00
P34 Steve Young Promo .40 1.00
P74 Drew Bledsoe Promo .50 1.25

1995 Summit Ground Zero

COMPLETE SET (200) 60.00 120.00
*STARS: 3X TO 8X BASIC CARDS
*RCs: 1.5X TO 4X BASIC CARDS
STATED ODDS 1:7

1995 Summit Backfield Stars

Randomly inserted at a rate of one in 37 packs, this 20 card set features some of the league's best ball carriers. Card fronts contain a holographic gold foil background with the set name "Backfield Stars" on the left of the card against a black background. The player's name is located in white at the bottom of the front. Card backs are horizontal with a headshot of the player and a brief commentary.

COMPLETE SET (20) 25.00 60.00
STATED ODDS 1:37
1 Emmitt Smith 5.00 12.00
2 Marshall Faulk 4.00 10.00
3 Barry Sanders 5.00 12.00
4 Ricky Watters .60 1.50
5 Rodney Hampton .60 1.50
6 Chris Warren .60 1.50
7 Garrison Hearst 1.25 3.00
8 Tyrone Wheatley 3.00 6.00
9 Rashaan Salaam .30 .75
10 Natrone Means .60 1.50
11 Byron Bam Morris .30 .75
12 Jerome Bettis 1.25 3.00
13 Errict Rhett .60 1.50
14 William Floyd .60 1.50
15 Edgar Bennett .60 1.50
16 Marcus Allen 1.25 3.00
17 Mario Bates .60 1.50
18 Lorenzo White .30 .75
19 Gary Brown .30 .75
20 Craig Heyward .60 1.50

1995 Summit Rookie Summit

This 18 card set was randomly inserted at a rate of one in 23 packs and features some of the year's best draft picks. Card fronts contain a posed action shot of the rookie against a silver and blue foil background. The player's name, team and the card name "Rookie Summit" are located on the bottom of the card against a black background. Card backs also feature foil with the player's name and a brief commentary.

COMPLETE SET (18) 40.00 80.00
STATED ODDS 1:23
1 Kevin Carter 1.50 4.00
2 Sherman Williams .75 2.00
3 Kordell Stewart 2.00 5.00
4 Christian Fauria .75 2.00
5 J.J. Stokes 1.25 3.00
6 Joey Galloway 2.00 5.00
7 Michael Westbrook 1.50 4.00
8 James O. Stewart 1.50 4.00
9 Stoney Case .75 2.00
10 Kyle Brady .75 2.00
11 Terrell Fletcher .75 2.00
12 Todd Collins 3.00 8.00
13 Jimmy Oliver .75 2.00
14 Napoleon Kaufman 1.50 4.00
15 John Walsh .75 2.00
16 Kerry Collins 2.00 5.00
17 Ki-Jana Carter 1.25 3.00
18 Terrell Davis 3.00 8.00

1995 Summit Team Summit

This 12 card set was randomly inserted in packs at a rate of one in 91 and features some of the top players in the NFL. Card fronts contain a "Spectroetched" background, which features a combinatation of holographic foil and etching, with two player shots and the card name "Team Summit" along the left side. Card backs feature a headshot with the player's name and a brief commentary.

COMPLETE SET (12) 50.00 100.00
STATED ODDS 1:91
1 Dan Marino 8.00 20.00
2 Emmitt Smith 6.00 15.00
3 Drew Bledsoe 2.50 6.00
4 Troy Aikman 3.00 8.00
5 Byron Bam Morris .40 1.00
6 Steve Young 3.00 8.00
7 Randall Cunningham 1.50 4.00
8 Natrone Means .75 2.00
9 Barry Sanders 6.00 15.00
10 Brett Favre 8.00 20.00
11 Errict Rhett .75 2.00
12 Jerry Rice 4.00 10.00

1996 Summit

This standard-sized set of 200 cards was issued in seven-card packs. The cards have a picture of the player inside of a jagged oval with a black gridiron edging. There is gold foil stamping on the bottom which gives the players name and a gold foil helmet of his team. The backs have a picture of the player within a helmet, the card number, and a group of 1995 statistics.

COMPLETE SET (200) 12.00 30.00
1 Troy Aikman .50 1.25
2 Marshall Faulk .25 .60
3 Bruce Smith .08 .25
4 Jerome Bettis .20 .50
5 Bryan Cox .02 .10
6 Robert Brooks .20 .50
7 Dan Marino 1.00 2.50
8 Irving Fryar .08 .25
9 Jerry Rice .50 1.25
10 Ki-Jana Carter .08 .25
11 Herman Moore .08 .25
12 Derrick Thomas .20 .50
13 Curtis Martin .40 1.00
14 Jeff Hostetler .02 .10
15 Errict Rhett .08 .25
16 Emmitt Smith .75 2.00
17 Aaron Craver .02 .10
18 Kyle Brady .02 .10
19 Tony Martin .08 .25
20 Vinny Testaverde .08 .25
21 Charles Haley .08 .25
22 Rodney Thomas .02 .10
23 Jim Everett .02 .10
24 Brian Blades .02 .10
25 Frank Sanders .08 .25
26 Bryce Paup .02 .10
27 Anthony Miller .08 .25
28 Ken Dilger .08 .25
29 Orlando Thomas .02 .10
30 Rodney Hampton .08 .25
31 Ken Norton Jr. .02 .10
32 Darren Woodson .08 .25
33 Antonio Freeman .20 .50
34 Steve Bono .02 .10
35 Ben Coates .08 .25
36 Jeff George .08 .25
37 Curtis Conway .20 .50
38 Steve Atwater .02 .10
39 Fred Barnett .02 .10
40 Joey Galloway .20 .50
41 Jim Kelly .20 .50
42 Michael Irvin .20 .50
43 Steve Tasker .02 .10
44 Warren Moon .08 .25
45 Hugh Douglas .08 .25
46 Steve Walsh .02 .10
47 Kerry Collins .20 .50
48 Barry Sanders .75 2.00
49 Steve Young .40 1.00
50 Jim Harbaugh .08 .25
51 Tyrone Wheatley .08 .25
52 Boomer Esiason .08 .25
53 Deion Sanders .30 .75
54 Steve McNair .40 1.00
55 Willie McGinest .02 .10
56 Adrian Murrell .08 .25
57 Thurman Thomas .20 .50
58 John Elway 1.00 2.50
59 William Floyd .08 .25
60 Eric Zeier .02 .10
61 Dave Krieg .02 .10
62 Eric Bjornson .02 .10
63 Brett Favre 1.00 2.50
64 Derrick Alexander DE .02 .10
65 Charlie Garner .08 .25
66 Stan Humphries .08 .25
67 Bert Emanuel .08 .25
68 Scott Mitchell .08 .25
69 Quentin Coryatt .02 .10
70 Eric Green .02 .10
71 Jeff Graham .02 .10
72 Ernie Mills .02 .10
73 Trent Dilfer .20 .50
74 Sherman Williams .02 .10
75 Tamarick Vanover .08 .25
76 Drew Bledsoe .30 .75
77 Jay Novacek .02 .10
78 Edgar Bennett .08 .25
79 Tim Brown .20 .50
80 Greg Lloyd .08 .25
81 Darick Holmes .02 .10
82 Carl Pickens .08 .25
83 Flipper Anderson .02 .10
84 Bernie Kosar .02 .10
85 Dave Brown .02 .10
86 Calvin Williams .02 .10
87 Michael Westbrook .20 .50
88 Kevin Williams .02 .10
89 Chris Sanders .08 .25
90 Robert Smith .08 .25
91 Cris Carter .20 .50
92 Gus Frerotte .08 .25
93 Larry Centers .08 .25
94 Eric Metcalf .02 .10
95 Isaac Bruce .20 .50
96 Kordell Stewart .20 .50
97 Ricky Watters .08 .25
98 Terrell Fletcher .02 .10
99 Bernie Parmalee .02 .10
100 Harvey Williams .02 .10
101 Hardy Nickerson .02 .10
102 Jeff Blake .20 .50
103 Terry Allen .08 .25
104 Yancey Thigpen .08 .25
105 Greg Hill .08 .25
106 Chris Warren .08 .25
107 Terrell Davis .40 1.00
108 Mark Brunell .30 .75
109 Alvin Harper .02 .10
110 Marcus Allen .20 .50
111 Garrison Hearst .08 .25
112 Derek Loville .02 .10
113 Craig Heyward .02 .10
114 Kimble Anders .08 .25
115 O.J. McDuffie .08 .25
116 Junior Seau .20 .50
117 Terry Kirby .08 .25
118 Erric Pegram .02 .10
119 Rick Mirer .08 .25
120 Erik Kramer .02 .10
121 Brett Perriman .02 .10
122 Shawn Jefferson .02 .10
123 J.J. Stokes .20 .50
124 Kevin Greene .08 .25
125 Daryl Johnston .08 .25
126 Mark Chmura .08 .25
127 James O.Stewart .08 .25
128 Mario Bates .08 .25
129 Rodney Peete .02 .10
130 Quinn Early .02 .10
131 Shannon Sharpe .08 .25
132 Neil Smith .08 .25
133 Herschel Walker .08 .25
134 Aaron Bailey .02 .10
135 Rashaan Salaam .08 .25
136 Kevin Smith .02 .10
137 Sean Dawkins .02 .10
138 Jake Reed .08 .25
139 Neil O'Donnell .08 .25
140 Reggie White .20 .50
141 Vincent Brisby .02 .10
142 Napoleon Kaufman .20 .50
143 Brent Jones .02 .10
144 Mark Seay .02 .10
145 Heath Shuler .08 .25
146 Wayne Chrebet .30 .75
147 Leeland McElroy RC .08 .25
148 Tim Biakabutuka RC .20 .50
149 John Mobley RC .02 .10
150 Tony Brackens RC .20 .50
151 Danny Kanell RC .20 .50
152 Eddie Kennison RC .20 .50
153 Jonathan Ogden RC .50 1.25
154 Bobby Engram RC .20 .50
155 Chris Darkins RC .02 .10
156 Daryl Gardener RC .02 .10
157 Keyshawn Johnson RC .50 1.25
158 Mike Alstott RC .50 1.25
159 Simeon Rice RC .50 1.25
160 Eric Moulds RC .60 1.50
161 Stepfret Williams RC .08 .25
162 Eddie George RC .60 1.50
163 Duane Clemons RC .02 .10
164 Amani Toomer RC .50 1.25
165 Rickey Dudley RC .20 .50
166 Bobby Hoying RC .20 .50
167 Lawrence Phillips RC .20 .50
168 Willie Anderson RC .02 .10
169 Derrick Mayes RC .20 .50
170 Kevin Hardy RC .20 .50
171 Terry Glenn RC .50 1.25
172 Stephen Davis RC .75 2.00
173 Walt Harris RC .02 .10
174 Marvin Harrison RC 1.25 3.00
175 Karim Abdul-Jabbar RC .20 .50
176 Alex Molden RC .02 .10
177 Regan Upshaw RC .02 .10
178 Jerald Moore RC .08 .25
179 Alex Van Dyke RC .08 .25
180 Jeff Lewis RC .08 .25
181 Cedric Jones RC .02 .10
182 Jim Kelly QH .20 .50
183 Troy Aikman QH .25 .60
184 Jim Harbaugh QH .08 .25
185 Neil O'Donnell QH .08 .25
186 Steve Young QH .20 .50
187 Kerry Collins QH .20 .50
188 Scott Mitchell QH .02 .10
189 Drew Bledsoe QH .20 .50
190 Kordell Stewart QH .20 .50
191 Erik Kramer QH .02 .10
192 Brett Favre QH .50 1.25
193 Warren Moon QH .02 .10
194 Jeff Blake QH .08 .25
195 Mark Brunell QH .20 .50
196 John Elway QH .50 1.25
197 Emmitt Smith CL .20 .50
198 Dan Marino CL .25 .60
199 Brett Favre CL .25 .60
200 Jim Harbaugh CL .08 .25

1996 Summit Artist's Proofs

*AP STARS: 6X TO 15X BASIC CARDS
*AP RCs: 3X TO 8X BASIC CARDS

1996 Summit Ground Zero

COMPLETE SET (200) 125.00 250.00
*STARS: 3X TO 8X BASIC CARDS
*RCs: 1.5X TO 4X BASIC CARDS

1996 Summit Premium Stock

COMPLETE SET (200) 12.00 30.00
*PREMIUM STOCK: .4X TO 1X BASIC CARDS

1996 Summit Hit The Hole

This 16 card standard-sized set available in magazine packs features some of the top running backs in the NFL who are exceptionally good at picking a running hole in the defense.

COMPLETE SET (16) 60.00 150.00
RANDOM INSERTS IN MAGAZINE PACKS
1 Rashaan Salaam 1.25 3.00
2 Marshall Faulk 5.00 12.00
3 Ricky Watters 2.00 5.00
4 Leeland McElroy 1.25 3.00
5 Emmitt Smith 15.00 40.00
6 Eddie George 8.00 20.00
7 Curtis Martin 8.00 20.00
8 Lawrence Phillips 2.50 6.00
9 Darick Holmes .75 2.00
10 Barry Sanders 15.00 40.00
11 Karim Abdul-Jabbar 4.00 10.00
12 Errict Rhett 2.00 5.00
13 Terrell Davis 8.00 20.00
14 Chris Warren 2.00 5.00
15 Rodney Thomas .75 2.00
16 Tim Biakabutuka 2.50 6.00

1996 Summit Silver Foil

COMP.SILVER FOIL SET (200) 12.00 30.00
*SILVER FOILS: .4X TO 1X BASIC CARDS

1996 Summit Inspirations

Randomly inserted in packs at a rate of one in 17, this 18-card set features both rookie and veteran players talking about other NFL players who inspired them in their lives. The front of the card has a picture of the player in a ghosted blue background, with the player's name in the top left and the insert name on the bottom of the card. The back of the card contains another picture on a ghosted blue background, the player's commentary on the person who inspired them, their number within the set of 18, and the sequential #/8000.

COMPLETE SET (18) 25.00 60.00
STATED ODDS 1:17
STATED PRINT RUN 8000 SERIAL #'d SETS
1 Jim Harbaugh .75 2.00
2 Alex Van Dyke .30 .75
3 Mike Alstott 1.50 4.00
4 Jonathan Ogden 1.50 4.00
5 Brett Favre 8.00 20.00
6 Tony Brackens .60 1.50
7 Drew Bledsoe 2.50 6.00
8 Danny Kanell .60 1.50
9 Eric Moulds 2.00 5.00
10 John Elway 8.00 20.00
11 Eddie George 2.00 5.00
12 Karim Abdul-Jabbar .60 1.50
13 Tim Biakabutuka .60 1.50
14 Jeff Lewis .30 .75
15 Terry Glenn 1.50 4.00
16 Jeff Blake 1.50 4.00
17 Kevin Hardy .60 1.50
18 Bobby Engram .60 1.50

1996 Summit Third and Long

This 18 card standard-sized set features players that were dominant in third and long play situations. The rainbow foil fronts have a photo of the player over another ghosted photo, with both the player and insert name in the lower left hand corner of the card. The back of the card includes a serial number of 2000 sets produced, another player photo, a short career commentary on the player, and the card number. Mirage parallel versions of the cards were produced and released as part of a pack redemption program which expired on 3/31/97. Finally a "Promo" non-serial numbered version of each card was issued to promote the Summit product.

COMPLETE SET (18) 60.00 150.00
STATED PRINT RUN 2000
*MIRAGE REDEMPTIONS: .05X TO .1X
*MIRAGE PRIZE/600: .6X TO 1.5X
*PROMOS: .2X TO .5X BASIC INSERTS
1 Michael Irvin 2.00 5.00
2 Dan Marino 10.00 25.00
3 Keyshawn Johnson 2.50 6.00
4 Chris Warren 1.00 2.50
5 Rashaan Salaam 1.00 2.50
6 Brett Favre 10.00 25.00
7 Terry Glenn 2.50 6.00
8 Steve Young 4.00 10.00
9 Kerry Collins 2.00 5.00
10 Emmitt Smith 8.00 20.00
11 Marvin Harrison 6.00 15.00
12 Jerry Rice 5.00 12.00
13 John Elway 10.00 25.00
14 Drew Bledsoe 3.00 8.00
15 Eddie Kennison 1.00 2.50
16 Troy Aikman 5.00 12.00
17 Barry Sanders 8.00 20.00
18 Terrell Davis 4.00 10.00

1996 Summit Turf Team

This 16 card standard-sized set features the player's picture between a set of embossed goal posts. The player's name and set name are at the bottom of the card. The cardback has a picture of the player, along with a short biography. The cards are numbered with a "TT" prefix and individually numbered of 4000 sets produced.

COMPLETE SET (16) 50.00 125.00
STATED PRINT RUN 4000 SER.#'d SETS
*FOIL/500: .8X TO 2X BASIC INSERTS
FOILS: RAND.INS.IN PREMIUM STOCK
1 Emmitt Smith 6.00 15.00
2 Brett Favre 8.00 20.00
3 Curtis Martin 3.00 8.00
4 Steve Young 3.00 8.00
5 Kerry Collins 1.50 4.00
6 Barry Sanders 6.00 15.00
7 Dan Marino 8.00 20.00
8 Isaac Bruce 1.50 4.00
9 Troy Aikman 4.00 10.00
10 Marshall Faulk 2.00 5.00
11 Joey Galloway 1.50 4.00
12 Jeff Blake 1.50 4.00
13 Drew Bledsoe 2.50 6.00
14 John Elway 8.00 20.00
15 Jerry Rice 4.00 10.00
16 Michael Irvin 1.50 4.00

1976 Sunbeam NFL Die Cuts

This 28-card set features standard size cards. The cards are die-cut so that they can stand up when the perforation is popped. The team's helmet, team nickname, and a generic player drawing are pictured on each card front. The card back features a narrative about the team and the Sunbeam logo. The cards were printed on white or gray card stock. The cards are unnumbered and may be found with or without the Sunbeam logo on the white stock version. A header card was produced announcing the 1976 season. There was also a card saver book issued. All the prices below are for unpunched cards.

COMPLETE SET (29) 137.50 275.00
1 Atlanta Falcons 6.00 12.00
2 Baltimore Colts 6.00 12.00
3 Buffalo Bills 6.00 12.00
4 Chicago Bears 7.50 15.00
5 Cincinnati Bengals 6.00 12.00
6 Cleveland Browns 6.00 12.00
7 Dallas Cowboys 7.50 15.00
8 Denver Broncos 6.00 12.00
9 Detroit Lions 6.00 12.00
10 Green Bay Packers 7.50 15.00
11 Houston Oilers 6.00 12.00
12 Kansas City Chiefs 6.00 12.00
13 Los Angeles Rams 6.00 12.00
14 Miami Dolphins 7.50 15.00
15 Minnesota Vikings 7.50 15.00
16 New England Patriots 6.00 12.00
17 New Orleans Saints 6.00 12.00
18 New York Giants 6.00 12.00
19 New York Jets 6.00 12.00
20 Oakland Raiders 7.50 15.00
21 Philadelphia Eagles 6.00 12.00
22 Pittsburgh Steelers 7.50 15.00
23 St. Louis Cardinals 6.00 12.00
24 San Diego Chargers 6.00 12.00
25 San Francisco 49ers 7.50 15.00
26 Seattle Seahawks 6.00 12.00
27 Tampa Bay Buccaneers 6.00 12.00
28 Washington Redskins 7.50 15.00
NNO NFL Logo 7.50 15.00
NNO Saver Book 12.50 25.00

1976 Sunbeam NFL Pennant Stickers

This set of stickers was issued along with the logo cards and was intended to be pasted into the saver album. Each measures roughly 1 3/4" by 2 7/8" and includes the team's logo and name within a pennant shaped design. The backs feature the team's all-time record along with a Sunbeam ad.

COMPLETE SET (28) 137.50 275.00
1 Atlanta Falcons 6.00 12.00
2 Baltimore Colts 6.00 12.00
3 Buffalo Bills 6.00 12.00
4 Chicago Bears 7.50 15.00
5 Cincinnati Bengals 6.00 12.00
6 Cleveland Browns 7.50 15.00
7 Dallas Cowboys 7.50 15.00
8 Denver Broncos 6.00 12.00
9 Detroit Lions 6.00 12.00
10 Green Bay Packers 7.50 15.00
11 Houston Oilers 6.00 12.00
12 Kansas City Chiefs 6.00 12.00
13 Los Angeles Rams 6.00 12.00
14 Miami Dolphins 7.50 15.00
15 Minnesota Vikings 7.50 15.00
16 New England Patriots 6.00 12.00
17 New Orleans Saints 6.00 12.00
18 New York Giants 7.50 15.00
19 New York Jets 6.00 12.00
20 Oakland Raiders 7.50 15.00
21 Philadelphia Eagles 6.00 12.00
22 Pittsburgh Steelers 7.50 15.00
23 St. Louis Cardinals 6.00 12.00
24 San Diego Chargers 6.00 12.00
25 San Francisco 49ers 7.50 15.00
26 Seattle Seahawks 6.00 12.00
27 Tampa Bay Buccaneers 6.00 12.00
28 Washington Redskins 7.50 15.00

1972 Sunoco Stamps

In 1972, the Sun Oil Company issued a stamp set and two types of albums. Each stamp measures approximately 1 5/8" by 2 3/8" whereas the albums are approximately 10 3/8" by 10 15/16". The logo on the cover of the 56-page stamp album indicates "NFL Action '72". The other "deluxe" album contains 128 pages. Each team was represented with 12 offensive and 12 defensive player stamps. There are a total of 624 unnumbered stamps in the set, which made this stamp set the largest football set to date at that time. The albums indicate where each stamp is to be placed. The square for each player's stamp was marked by the player's number, name, position, height, weight, age, and college attended. When the album was issued, the back of the book included perforated sheets of stamps comprising more than one fourth of the set. The album also had sheets of tabs which were to be used for putting the stamps in the book, rather than licking the entire stamp. Each week of the promotion a purchase of gasoline yielded an additional nine-player perforated stamp sheet. The stamps and the album positions are unnumbered so the stamps are ordered and numbered below according to the team order in which they appear in the book. The team order is alphabetical. Since the same 144 stamps were included as an insert with each album; these 144 stamps are easier to find and are marked as DP's in the checklist below. The stamp set is considered in very good condition at best when glued in the album. There are a number of players appearing in this set in (or before) their Rookie Card year: Lyle Alzado, Mel Blount, Harold Carmichael, Dan Dierdorf, L.C. Greenwood, Jack Ham, Cliff Harris, Ted Hendricks, Charlie Joiner, Bob Kuechenberg, Larry Little, Archie Manning, Ray Perkins, Jim Plunkett, John Riggins, Art Shell, Steve Spurrier, Roger Staubach, Gene Upshaw, Jeff Van Note, and Jack Youngblood.

COMPLETE SET (624) 75.00 150.00
1 Ken Burrow .10 .20
2 Bill Sandeman .10 .20
3 Andy Maurer DP .08 .15
4 Jeff Van Note DP .13 .25
5 Malcolm Snider .10 .20
6 George Kunz .10 .20
7 Jim Mitchell TE .10 .20
8 Wes Chesson .10 .20
9 Bob Berry .10 .20
10 Dick Shiner .10 .20
11 Jim Butler .10 .20
12 Art Malone .10 .20
13 Claude Humphrey DP .13 .25
14 John Small DP .08 .15
15 Glen Condren .10 .20
16 John Zook .10 .20
17 Don Hansen .10 .20
18 Tommy Nobis .30 .60
19 Greg Brezina .10 .20
20 Ken Reaves .10 .20
21 Tom Hayes .10 .20
22 Tom McCauley DP .08 .15
23 Bill Bell K DP .08 .15
24 Billy Lothridge .10 .20
25 Eddie Hinton .10 .20
26 Bob Vogel DP .08 .15
27 Glenn Ressler .10 .20
28 Bill Curry DP .08 .15
29 John Williams G .10 .20
30 Dan Sullivan .10 .20
31 Tom Mitchell .10 .20
32 John Mackey .50 1.00
33 Ray Perkins .25 .50
34 Johnny Unitas 2.50 5.00
35 Tom Matte .15 .30
36 Norm Bulaich .10 .20
37 Bubba Smith DP .38 .75
38 Billy Newsome .10 .20
39 Fred Miller DP .08 .15
40 Roy Hilton .10 .20
41 Ray May DP .08 .15
42 Ted Hendricks .50 1.00
43 Charlie Stukes .10 .20
44 Rex Kern .10 .20
45 Jerry Logan .10 .20
46 Rick Volk .10 .20
47 David Lee .10 .20
48 Jim O'Brien .15 .30
49 J.D. Hill .15 .30
50 Willie Young Alcorn .10 .20
51 Jim Reilly T .10 .20
52 Bruce Jarvis DP .08 .15
53 Levert Carr .10 .20
54 Donnie Green DP .08 .15
55 Jan White DP .08 .15
56 Marlin Briscoe .10 .20
57 Dennis Shaw .15 .30
58 O.J. Simpson 2.00 4.00
59 Wayne Patrick .10 .20
60 John Leypoldt .10 .20
61 Al Cowlings .15 .30
62 Jim Dunaway DP .08 .15
63 Bob Tatarek .10 .20
64 Cal Snowden .10 .20
65 Paul Guidry .10 .20
66 Edgar Chandler .10 .20
67 Al Andrews DP .08 .15
68 Robert James .10 .20
69 Alvin Wyatt .10 .20
70 John Pitts DP .08 .15
71 Pete Richardson .10 .20
72 Spike Jones .10 .20
73 Dick Gordon .10 .20
74 Randy Jackson DP .08 .15
75 Glen Holloway .10 .20
76 Rich Coady DP .08 .15
77 Jim Cadile DP .08 .15
78 Steve Wright .10 .20
79 Bob Wallace .10 .20
80 George Farmer .10 .20
81 Bobby Douglass .15 .30
82 Don Shy .10 .20
83 Cyril Pinder .10 .20
84 Mac Percival .10 .20
85 Willie Holman .10 .20
86 George Seals DP .08 .15
87 Bill Staley .10 .20
88 Ed O'Bradovich DP .08 .15
89 Doug Buffone DP .08 .15
90 Dick Butkus 2.00 4.00
91 Ross Brupbacher .10 .20
92 Charlie Ford .10 .20
93 Joe Taylor .10 .20
94 Ron Smith .15 .30
95 Jerry Moore .10 .20
96 Bobby Joe Green .10 .20
97 Chip Myers .10 .20
98 Rufus Mayes DP .08 .15
99 Howard Fest .10 .20
100 Bob Johnson .15 .30
101 Pat Matson DP .08 .15
102 Vern Holland .10 .20
103 Bruce Coslet .15 .30
104 Bob Trumpy .20 .40
105 Virgil Carter .10 .20
106 Fred Willis .10 .20
107 Jess Phillips .10 .20
108 Horst Muhlmann .10 .20
109 Royce Berry .10 .20
110 Mike Reid DP .25 .50
111 Steve Chomyszak DP .08 .15
112 Ron Carpenter .10 .20
113 Al Beauchamp DP .08 .15
114 Bill Bergey .15 .30
115 Ken Avery .10 .20
116 Lemar Parrish .15 .30
117 Ken Riley .15 .30
118 Sandy Durko DP .08 .15
119 Dave Lewis .10 .20
120 Paul Robinson .10 .20
121 Fair Hooker .10 .20
122 Doug Dieken DP .08 .15
123 John Demarie .10 .20
124 Jim Copeland .10 .20
125 Gene Hickerson DP .10 .25
126 Bob McKay .10 .20
127 Milt Morin .10 .20
128 Frank Pitts .10 .20
129 Mike Phipps .15 .30
130 Leroy Kelly .50 1.00
131 Bo Scott .15 .30
132 Don Cockroft .10 .20
133 Ron Snidow .10 .20
134 Walter Johnson DP .08 .15
135 Jerry Sherk .15 .30
136 Jack Gregory .10 .20
137 Jim Houston DP .08 .15
138 Dale Lindsey .10 .20
139 Bill Andrews .10 .20
140 Clarence Scott .10 .20
141 Ernie Kellerman .10 .20
142 Walt Sumner .10 .20
143 Mike Howell DP .08 .15
144 Reece Morrison .10 .20
145 Bob Hayes .50 1.00
146 Ralph Neely .10 .20
147 John Niland DP .08 .15
148 Dave Manders .10 .20
149 Blaine Nye .10 .20
150 Rayfield Wright .10 .20
151 Billy Truax .10 .20
152 Lance Alworth 1.00 2.00
153 Roger Staubach 4.00 8.00
154 Duane Thomas .25 .50
155 Walt Garrison .15 .30
156 Mike Clark .10 .20
157 Larry Cole DP .08 .15
158 Jethro Pugh .10 .20
159 Bob Lilly .75 1.50
160 George Andrie .10 .20
161 Dave Edwards DP .08 .15
162 Lee Roy Jordan .38 .75
163 Chuck Howley .15 .30
164 Herb Adderley DP .38 .75
165 Mel Renfro .50 1.00
166 Cornell Green .15 .30
167 Cliff Harris DP .20 .40
168 Ron Widby .10 .20
169 Jerry Simmons .10 .20
170 Roger Shoals .10 .20
171 Larron Jackson .10 .20
172 George Goeddeke DP .08 .15
173 Mike Schnitker .10 .20
174 Mike Current .10 .20
175 Billy Masters .10 .20
176 Jack Gehrke .10 .20
177 Don Horn .10 .20
178 Floyd Little .30 .60

179 Bob Anderson .10 .20
180 Jim Turner DP .13 .25
181 Rich Jackson .10 .20
182 Paul Smith DP .08 .15
183 Dave Costa .10 .20
184 Lyle Alzado DP .38 .75
185 Olen Underwood .10 .20
186 Fred Forsberg DP .08 .15
187 Chip Myrtle .10 .20
188 Leroy Mitchell .10 .20
189 Bill Thompson DP .08 .15
190 Charlie Greer .10 .20
191 George Saimes .10 .20
192 Billy Van Heusen .10 .20
193 Earl McCullouch .15 .30
194 Jim Yarbrough .10 .20
195 Chuck Walton .10 .20
196 Ed Flanagan .10 .20
197 Frank Gallagher .10 .20
198 Rockne Freitas .10 .20
199 Charlie Sanders DP .10 .25
200 Larry Walton .10 .20
201 Greg Landry .20 .40
202 Altie Taylor .10 .20
203 Steve Owens .20 .40
204 Errol Mann DP .08 .15
205 Joe Robb .10 .20
206 Dick Evey .10 .20
207 Jerry Rush .10 .20
208 Larry Hand DP .08 .15
209 Paul Naumoff .10 .20
210 Mike Lucci .15 .30
211 Wayne Walker DP .13 .25
212 Lem Barney DP .38 .75
213 Dick LeBeau DP .08 .15
214 Mike Weger .10 .20
215 Wayne Rasmussen .10 .20
216 Herman Weaver .10 .20
217 John Spilis .10 .20
218 Francis Peay DP .08 .15
219 Bill Lueck .10 .20
220 Ken Bowman DP .08 .15
221 Gale Gillingham DP .08 .15
222 Dick Himes DP .08 .15
223 Rich McGeorge .10 .20
224 Carroll Dale .15 .30
225 Bart Starr 2.00 4.00
226 Scott Hunter .15 .30
227 John Brockington .15 .30
228 Dave Hampton .10 .20
229 Clarence Williams .10 .20
230 Mike McCoy DT .10 .20
231 Bob Brown DT .10 .20
232 Alden Roche .10 .20
233 Dave Robinson DP .13 .25
234 Jim Carter .10 .20
235 Fred Carr .10 .20
236 Ken Ellis .10 .20
237 Doug Hart .10 .20
238 Al Randolph .10 .20
239 Al Matthews .10 .20
240 Tim Webster .10 .20
241 Jim Beirne DP .08 .15
242 Bob Young .10 .20
243 Elbert Drungo .10 .20
244 Sam Walton .10 .20
245 Alvin Reed .10 .20
246 Charlie Joiner .75 1.50
247 Dan Pastorini .20 .40
248 Charley Johnson .15 .30
249 Lynn Dickey .15 .30
250 Woody Campbell .10 .20
251 Robert Holmes .10 .20
252 Mark Moseley .15 .30
253 Pat Holmes .10 .20
254 Mike Tilleman DP .08 .15
255 Leo Brooks .10 .20
256 Elvin Bethea .15 .30
257 George Webster .15 .30
258 Garland Boyette .10 .20
259 Ron Pritchard .10 .20
260 Zeke Moore DP .13 .25
261 Willie Alexander .10 .20
262 Ken Houston .50 1.00
263 John Charles DP .08 .15
264 Linzy Cole DP .08 .15
265 Elmo Wright .10 .20
266 Jim Tyrer DP .13 .25
267 Ed Budde .10 .20
268 Jack Rudnay DP .08 .15
269 Mo Moorman .10 .20
270 Dave Hill .10 .20
271 Morris Stroud .10 .20
272 Otis Taylor .20 .40
273 Len Dawson 1.00 2.00
274 Ed Podolak .15 .30
275 Wendell Hayes .15 .30
276 Jan Stenerud .38 .75
277 Marvin Upshaw DP .08 .15
278 Curley Culp .15 .30
279 Buck Buchanan .50 1.00
280 Aaron Brown .10 .20
281 Bobby Bell .50 1.00
282 Willie Lanier .50 1.00
283 Jim Lynch .10 .20
284 Jim Marsalis DP .08 .15
285 Emmitt Thomas .30 .75
286 Jim Kearney DP .08 .15
287 Johnny Robinson .15 .30
288 Jerrel Wilson DP .08 .15
289 Jack Snow .15 .30
290 Charlie Cowan .10 .20
291 Tom Mack DP .13 .25
292 Ken Iman .10 .20
293 Joe Scibelli .10 .20
294 Harry Schuh DP .08 .15
295 Bob Klein .10 .20
296 Lance Rentzel .15 .30
297 Roman Gabriel .25 .50
298 Les Josephson .15 .30
299 Willie Ellison .10 .20
300 David Ray .10 .20
301 Jack Youngblood .50 1.00
302 Merlin Olsen .50 1.00
303 Phil Olsen .15 .30
304 Coy Bacon .15 .30
305 Jim Purnell DP .08 .15
306 Marlin McKeever .10 .20
307 Isiah Robertson .15 .30
308 Jim Nettles DP .08 .15
309 Gene Howard DP .08 .15
310 Kermit Alexander .15 .30
311 Dave Elmendorf DP .08 .15
312 Pat Studstill .10 .20
313 Paul Warfield 1.00 2.00
314 Doug Crusan .10 .20
315 Bob Kuechenberg .15 .30
316 Bob DeMarco DP .08 .15
317 Larry Little .50 1.00
318 Norm Evans DP .13 .25
319 Marv Fleming DP .13 .25
320 Howard Twilley .15 .30
321 Bob Griese 1.25 2.50
322 Jim Kiick .20 .40
323 Larry Csonka 1.00 2.00
324 Garo Yepremian .15 .30
325 Jim Riley DP .08 .15
326 Manny Fernandez .15 .30
327 Bob Heinz DP .08 .15
328 Bill Stanfill .15 .30
329 Doug Swift .10 .20
330 Nick Buoniconti .38 .75
331 Mike Kolen .10 .20
332 Tim Foley .15 .30
333 Curtis Johnson .10 .20
334 Dick Anderson .15 .30
335 Jake Scott .20 .40
336 Larry Seiple .10 .20
337 Gene Washington Vik .15 .30
338 Grady Alderman .10 .20
339 Ed White DP .13 .25
340 Mick Tingelhoff DP .13 .25
341 Milt Sunde DP .08 .15
342 Ron Yary .15 .30
343 John Beasley .10 .20
344 John Henderson .10 .20
345 Fran Tarkenton 1.25 2.50
346 Clint Jones .10 .20
347 Dave Osborn .15 .30
348 Fred Cox .15 .30
349 Carl Eller DP .25 .50
350 Gary Larsen DP .08 .15
351 Alan Page .50 1.00
352 Jim Marshall .38 .75
353 Roy Winston .10 .20
354 Lonnie Warwick .10 .20
355 Wally Hilgenberg .10 .20
356 Bobby Bryant .10 .20
357 Ed Sharockman .10 .20
358 Charlie West .10 .20
359 Paul Krause .25 .50
360 Bob Lee .10 .20
361 Randy Vataha .10 .20
362 Mike Montler DP .08 .15
363 Halvor Hagen .10 .20
364 Jon Morris DP .08 .15
365 Len St. Jean .10 .20
366 Tom Neville .10 .20
367 Tom Beer .10 .20
368 Ron Sellers .10 .20
369 Jim Plunkett .63 1.25
370 Carl Garrett .15 .30
371 Jim Nance .15 .30
372 Charlie Gogolak .10 .20
373 Ike Lassiter DP .08 .15
374 Dave Rowe .10 .20
375 Julius Adams .10 .20
376 Dennis Wirgowski .10 .20
377 Ed Weisacosky .10 .20
378 Jim Cheyunski DP .08 .15
379 Steve Kiner .10 .20
380 Larry Carwell DP .08 .15
381 John Outlaw .10 .20
382 Rickie Harris .10 .20
383 Don Webb DP .08 .15
384 Tom Janik .10 .20
385 Al Dodd DP .08 .15
386 Don Morrison .10 .20
387 Jake Kupp .10 .20
388 John Didion .10 .20
389 Del Williams .10 .20
390 Glen Ray Hines .10 .20
391 Dave Parks DP .08 .15
392 Dan Abramowicz .15 .30
393 Archie Manning .63 1.25
394 Bob Gresham .10 .20
395 Virgil Robinson .10 .20
396 Charlie Durkee .10 .20
397 Richard Neal .10 .20
398 Bob Pollard DP .08 .15
399 Dave Long DP .08 .15
400 Joe Owens .10 .20
401 Carl Cunningham .10 .20
402 Jim Flanigan LB .10 .20
403 Wayne Colman .10 .20
404 D'Artagnan Martin DP .08 .15
405 Delles Howell .10 .20
406 Hugo Hollas .10 .20
407 Doug Wyatt DP .08 .15
408 Julian Fagan .10 .20
409 Don Herrmann .10 .20
410 Willie Young .10 .20
411 Bob Hyland .10 .20
412 Greg Larson DP .08 .15
413 Doug Van Horn .10 .20
414 Charlie Harper DP .08 .15
415 Bob Tucker .15 .30
416 Joe Morrison .15 .30
417 Randy Johnson .15 .30
418 Tucker Frederickson .15 .30
419 Ron Johnson .15 .30
420 Pete Gogolak .15 .30
421 Henry Reed .10 .20
422 Jim Kanicki DP .08 .15
423 Roland Lakes .10 .20
424 John Douglas DP .08 .15
425 Ron Hornsby DP .08 .15
426 Jim Files .10 .20
427 Willie Williams DP .08 .15
428 Otto Brown .10 .20
429 Scott Eaton .10 .20
430 Spider Lockhart .15 .30
431 Tom Blanchard .10 .20
432 Rocky Thompson .10 .20
433 Richard Caster .15 .30
434 Randy Rasmussen .10 .20
435 John Schmitt .10 .20
436 Dave Herman DP .08 .15
437 Winston Hill DP .08 .15
438 Pete Lammons .10 .20
439 Don Maynard 1.00 2.00
440 Joe Namath 4.00 8.00
441 Emerson Boozer .15 .30
442 John Riggins 1.25 2.50
443 George Nock .10 .20
444 Bobby Howfield .10 .20
445 Gerry Philbin .10 .20
446 John Little DT DP .08 .15
447 Chuck Hinton .10 .20
448 Mark Lomas .10 .20
449 Ralph Baker .10 .20
450 Al Atkinson DP .08 .15
451 Larry Grantham DP .08 .15
452 John Dockery .10 .20
453 Earlie Thomas DP .08 .15
454 Phil Wise .10 .20
455 W.K. Hicks .10 .20
456 Steve O'Neal .10 .20
457 Drew Buie .10 .20
458 Art Shell .50 1.00
459 Gene Upshaw .38 .75
460 Jim Otto DP .38 .75
461 George Buehler .10 .20
462 Bob Brown OT .15 .30
463 Raymond Chester .15 .30
464 Fred Biletnikoff 1.00 2.00
465 Daryle Lamonica .30 .60
466 Marv Hubbard .15 .30
467 Clarence Davis .10 .20
468 George Blanda 1.00 2.00
469 Tony Cline .10 .20
470 Art Thoms .10 .20
471 Tom Keating DP .08 .15
472 Ben Davidson .25 .50
473 Phil Villapiano .15 .30
474 Dan Conners DP .08 .15
475 Duane Benson DP .08 .15
476 Nemiah Wilson DP .08 .15
477 Willie Brown DP .38 .75
478 George Atkinson .10 .20
479 Jack Tatum .20 .40
480 Jerry DePoyster .10 .20
481 Harold Jackson .20 .40
482 Wade Key DP .08 .15
483 Henry Allison DP .08 .15
484 Mike Evans DP C .08 .15
485 Steve Smith T .10 .20
486 Harold Carmichael .50 1.00
487 Ben Hawkins .10 .20
488 Pete Liske .15 .30
489 Rick Arrington .10 .20
490 Lee Bouggess .10 .20
491 Tom Woodeshick .10 .20
492 Tom Dempsey .15 .30
493 Richard Harris .10 .20
494 Don Hultz .10 .20
495 Ernie Calloway .10 .20
496 Mel Tom DP .08 .15
497 Steve Zabel .10 .20
498 Tim Rossovich DP .08 .15
499 Ron Porter .10 .20
500 Al Nelson .10 .20
501 Nate Ramsey .10 .20
502 Leroy Keyes .15 .30
503 Bill Bradley .15 .30
504 Tom McNeill .10 .20
505 Dave Smith WR .10 .20
506 Jon Kolb .08 .15
507 Gerry Mullins .10 .20
508 Ray Mansfield DP .08 .15
509 Bruce Van Dyke DP .08 .15
510 John Brown DP .08 .15
511 Ron Shanklin .10 .20
512 Terry Bradshaw 3.00 6.00
513 Terry Hanratty .15 .30
514 Preston Pearson .20 .40
515 John Fuqua .15 .30
516 Roy Gerela .10 .20
517 L.C. Greenwood .38 .75
518 Joe Greene 1.00 2.00
519 Lloyd Voss DP .08 .15
520 Dwight White DP .13 .25
521 Jack Ham 1.25 2.50
522 Chuck Allen .10 .20
523 Brian Stenger .10 .20
524 Andy Russell .15 .30
525 John Rowser .10 .20
526 Mel Blount 1.00 2.00
527 Mike Wagner .15 .30
528 Bobby Walden .10 .20
529 Mel Gray .20 .40
530 Bob Reynolds .10 .20
531 Dan Dierdorf DP .38 .75
532 Wayne Mulligan .10 .20
533 Clyde Williams .10 .20
534 Ernie McMillan .10 .20
535 Jackie Smith .38 .75
536 John Gilliam DP .13 .25
537 Jim Hart .25 .50
538 Pete Beathard .15 .30
539 Johnny Roland .15 .30
540 Jim Bakken .15 .30
541 Ron Yankowski DP .08 .15
542 Fred Heron .10 .20
543 Bob Rowe .10 .20
544 Chuck Walker .10 .20
545 Larry Stallings .10 .20
546 Jamie Rivers DP .08 .15
547 Mike McGill .10 .20
548 Miller Farr .10 .20
549 Roger Wehrli .15 .30
550 Larry Willingham DP .08 .15
551 Larry Wilson .50 1.00
552 Chuck Latourette .10 .20
553 Billy Parks .10 .20
554 Terry Owens .15 .30
555 Doug Wilkerson .10 .20
556 Carl Mauck DP .08 .15
557 Walt Sweeney .10 .20
558 Russ Washington DP .08 .15
559 Pettis Norman .10 .20
560 Gary Garrison .15 .30
561 John Hadl .25 .50
562 Mike Montgomery .10 .20
563 Mike Garrett .15 .30
564 Dennis Partee DP .08 .15
565 Deacon Jones .50 1.00
566 Ron East DP .08 .15
567 Kevin Hardy .10 .20
568 Steve DeLong .10 .20
569 Rick Redman DP .08 .15
570 Bob Babich .10 .20
571 Pete Barnes .10 .20
572 Bob Howard .10 .20
573 Joe Beauchamp .10 .20
574 Bryant Salter .10 .20
575 Chris Fletcher .10 .20
576 Jerry LeVias .15 .30
577 Dick Witcher .10 .20
578 Len Rohde .10 .20
579 Randy Beisler .10 .20
580 Forrest Blue .10 .20
581 Woody Peoples .10 .20
582 Cas Banaszek .10 .20
583 Ted Kwalick .15 .30
584 Gene Washington 49er .15 .30
585 John Brodie .50 1.00
586 Ken Willard .15 .30
587 Vic Washington .10 .20
588 Bruce Gossett DP .08 .15
589 Tommy Hart .10 .20
590 Charlie Krueger .10 .20
591 Earl Edwards .10 .20
592 Cedrick Hardman DP .08 .15
593 Dave Wilcox DP .13 .25
594 Frank Nunley .10 .20
595 Skip Vanderbundt DP .08 .15
596 Jim Johnson DP .38 .75
597 Bruce Taylor .10 .20
598 Mel Phillips .10 .20
599 Roosevelt Taylor .15 .30
600 Steve Spurrier 2.00 4.00
601 Charley Taylor .50 1.00
602 Jim Snowden DP .08 .15
603 Ray Schoenke .10 .20
604 Len Hauss DP .08 .15
605 John Wilbur .10 .20
606 Walter Rock DP .08 .15
607 Jerry Smith .15 .30
608 Roy Jefferson .15 .30
609 Billy Kilmer .30 .60
610 Larry Brown .38 .75
611 Charlie Harraway .10 .20
612 Curt Knight .10 .20
613 Ron McDole .10 .20
614 Manny Sistrunk DP .13 .25
615 Diron Talbert .10 .20
616 Verlon Biggs DP .08 .15
617 Jack Pardee .20 .40
618 Myron Pottios .10 .20
619 Chris Hanburger .15 .30
620 Pat Fischer .15 .30
621 Mike Bass .10 .20
622 Richie Petitbon DP .13 .25
623 Brig Owens .10 .20
624 Mike Bragg .10 .20
NNO Album (64 pages) 5.00 10.00
NNO Deluxe Album 7.50 15.00

1972 Sunoco Stamps Update

The players listed below are those who are not explicitly listed in the 1972 Sunoco stamp album. They are otherwise indistinguishable from the 1972 Sunoco stamps listed immediately above. These unnumbered stamps are ordered below in team order and alphabetically within team. The stamps measure approximately 1 5/8" by 2 3/8" and were issued later in the year as part of complete team sheets. Uncut team sheets typically sell for $15-50 per team, except for the Bears and Raiders sheets which are the toughest to find. There are a number of players appearing in this set before their Rookie Card year: Cliff Branch, Jim Langer, and Bobby Moore (later known as Ahmad Rashad).

COMPLETE SET (82) 125.00 200.00
1 Clarence Ellis 1.50 4.00
2 Dave Hampton 1.50 4.00
3 Dennis Havig 1.25 3.00
4 John James 1.25 3.00
5 Joe Profit 1.25 3.00
6 Lonnie Hepburn 1.25 3.00
7 Dennis Nelson 1.25 3.00
8 Mike McBath 1.25 3.00
9 Walt Patulski 1.25 3.00
10 Bob Asher 10.00 20.00
11 Steve DeLong 10.00 20.00
12 Tony McGee 10.00 20.00
13 Jim Osborne 10.00 20.00
14 Jim Seymour 10.00 20.00
15 Tommy Casanova 1.50 4.00
16 Neal Craig 1.25 3.00
17 Essex Johnson 1.25 3.00
18 Sherman White 1.25 3.00
19 Bob Briggs 1.25 3.00
20 Thom Darden 1.25 3.00
21 Marv Bateman 1.25 3.00
22 Toni Fritsch 1.25 3.00
23 Calvin Hill 2.00 5.00
24 Pat Toomay 1.25 3.00
25 Pete Duranko 1.25 3.00
26 Marv Montgomery 1.25 3.00
27 Rod Sherman 1.25 3.00
28 Bob Kowalkowski 1.25 3.00
29 Jim Mitchell DT 1.25 3.00
30 Larry Woods 1.25 3.00
31 Willie Buchanon 1.50 4.00
32 Leland Glass 1.25 3.00
33 MacArthur Lane 1.50 4.00
34 Chester Marcol 1.25 3.00
35 Ron Widby 1.25 3.00
36 Ken Burrough 1.50 4.00
37 Calvin Hunt 1.25 3.00
38 Ron Saul 1.25 3.00
39 Greg Simpson 1.25 3.00
40 Mike Sensibaugh 1.50 4.00
41 Dave Chapple 1.25 3.00
42 Jim Langer 2.50 6.00
43 Mike Eischeid 1.25 3.00
44 John Gilliam 1.50 4.00
45 Ron Acks 1.25 3.00
46 Bob Gladieux 1.25 3.00
47 Honor Jackson 1.25 3.00
48 Reggie Rucker 1.50 4.00
49 Pat Studstill 1.25 3.00
50 Bob Windsor 1.25 3.00
51 Joe Federspiel 1.25 3.00
52 Bob Newland 1.25 3.00
53 Pete Athas 1.25 3.00
54 Charlie Evans 1.25 3.00
55 Jack Gregory 1.25 3.00
56 John Mendenhall 1.25 3.00
57 Ed Bell 1.25 3.00
58 John Elliott 1.25 3.00
59 Chris Farasopoulos 1.25 3.00
60 Bob Svihus 1.25 3.00
61 Steve Tannen 1.25 3.00
62 Cliff Branch 12.50 25.00
63 Gus Otto 10.00 20.00
64 Otis Sistrunk 10.00 20.00
65 Charlie Smith RB 10.00 20.00
66 John Reaves 1.25 3.00
67 Larry Watkins 1.25 3.00
68 Henry Davis 1.25 3.00
69 Ben McGee 1.25 3.00
70 Donny Anderson 2.00 5.00
71 Walker Gillette 1.25 3.00
72 Martin Imhoff 1.25 3.00
73 Bobby Moore 5.00 10.00
74 Norm Thompson 1.25 3.00
75 Lionel Aldridge 1.50 4.00
76 Dave Costa 1.25 3.00
77 Cid Edwards 1.25 3.00
78 Tim Rossovich 1.25 3.00
79 Dave Williams 1.25 3.00
80 Johnny Fuller 1.25 3.00
81 Terry Hermeling 1.25 3.00
82 Paul Laaveg 1.25 3.00

2001 Super Bowl XXXV Marino

This 5-card set was issued one card at a time at the 2001 NFL Experience Super Bowl Card Show in Tampa Florida. Each major card company produced one card as a wrapper redemption (for 5-wrappers) to be exchanged at their booth at the card show. Collector's Edge did not issue a card for the set. The Topps card was issued in a cello pack with one stick of gum.

COMPLETE SET (5) 35.00 50.00
COMMON CARD (1-6) 6.00 10.00
1 Dan Marino 8.00 12.00
Topps

2002 Super Bowl XXXVI Aikman

These five cards were issued at the 2002 Super Bowl Card Show in New Orleans as part of a wrapper redemption program. Each of the five NFL card manufacturers in attendance gave away one card of Troy Aikman in exchange for a number of card packs opened at their booths.

COMPLETE SET (5) 6.00 15.00
COMMON CARD (1-5) 1.25 3.00

2003 Super Bowl XXXVII Chargers

These 12-cards were issued at the 2003 Super Bowl Card Show in San Diego as part of a wrapper redemption program. Each of the five NFL card manufacturers in attendance gave away two cards in exchange for a number of card packs opened at their booths. Two additional cards were produced and given away by Sports Collector's Digest and Tuff Stuff magazines.

COMPLETE SET (12) 12.50 25.00
1 Drew Brees 1.50 4.00
2 LaDainian Tomlinson 1.50 4.00
3 Curtis Conway .60 1.50
Pacific
4 Junior Seau 1.00 2.50
Playoff
5 Quentin Jammer .40 1.00
Upper Deck
6 Tim Dwight .60 1.50
Tuff Stuff
7 Quentin Jammer .40 1.00
SCD
8 Drew Brees 1.50 4.00
9 Tim Dwight .60 1.50
Playoff
10 Junior Seau 1.00 2.50
Pacific
11 Curtis Conway .60 1.50
(Fleer
12 LaDainian Tomlinson 1.50 4.00

1992 Super Silhouettes

This 14-card set features plastic silhouettes of top players made from a material that clings to any smooth surface without adhesive and can be used over and over again. The image can be rolled up or folded in half essentially without destroying its original form. The silhouettes were distributed one to a package with the player's name, postion, and statistics printed on the back.

COMPLETE SET (14) 12.00 30.00
1 Dan Marino 2.40 6.00
2 Jim Kelly .80 2.00
3 John Elway 2.00 5.00
4 Lawrence Taylor .60 1.50
5 Bernie Kosar .40 1.00
6 Troy Aikman 1.20 3.00
7 Randall Cunningham .80 2.00
8 Mark Rypien .40 1.00
9 Chris Miller .40 1.00
10 Boomer Esiason .60 1.50
11 Warren Moon .60 1.50
12 Ronnie Lott .60 1.50
13 Jim Harbaugh .40 1.00
14 Barry Sanders 2.40 6.00

2005 Superstars Road to Forty Activa Medallions

COMPLETE SET (30) 30.00 60.00
1 Tom Brady 1.50 4.00
2 Randy Moss 1.25 3.00
3 Curtis Martin 1.25 3.00
4 Clinton Portis 1.25 3.00
5 Carson Palmer 1.25 3.00
6 Peyton Manning 1.50 4.00
7 Torry Holt 1.25 3.00
8 Ben Roethlisberger 2.00 5.00
9 Tiki Barber 1.25 3.00
10 Daunte Culpepper 1.25 3.00
11 Brett Favre 2.00 5.00
12 Roy Williams S 1.25 3.00
13 Tony Gonzalez 1.25 3.00
14 Terrell Owens 1.25 3.00
15 LaDainian Tomlinson 1.25 3.00
16 Michael Vick 1.50 4.00
17 Marvin Harrison 1.25 3.00
18 Takeo Spikes 1.00 2.50
19 Andre Johnson 1.00 2.50
20 Julius Peppers 1.00 2.50
21 Donovan McNabb 1.25 3.00
22 Priest Holmes 1.25 3.00
23 Ed Reed 1.00 2.50
24 Champ Bailey 1.00 2.50
25 Deuce Mcallister 1.00 2.50
26 Brian Urlacher 1.25 3.00
27 Hines Ward 1.25 3.00
28 Shaun Alexander 1.25 3.00
29 Jason Taylor 1.00 2.50
30 Ray Lewis 1.25 3.00

2002 Sweet Spot

Released in December 2002, this set features 90 veterans and 76 rookies. Rookies 91-150 were serial #'d to 1050, while rookies 151-166 were serial #'d to 550 or 125, and were also autographed. Please note some players were issed as redemption cards which expired 12/6/2005. Boxes contained 12 packs of 4 cards along with one oversized patch card box topper.

COMP.SET w/o SP's (90) 12.50 30.00
91-150 ROOKIE PRINT RUN 1050
1 Aaron Brooks .30 .75
2 Tim Couch .30 .75
3 Jon Kitna .30 .75
4 Brett Favre 1.00 2.50
5 Donovan McNabb .40 1.00
6 Jeff Garcia .30 .75
7 Michael Vick .40 1.00
8 Mark Brunell .40 1.00
9 Steve McNair .40 1.00
10 Kordell Stewart .30 .75
11 Drew Bledsoe .40 1.00
12 Tom Brady 4.00 10.00
13 Kurt Warner .40 1.00
14 Brian Griese .30 .75
15 Jim Miller .30 .75
16 Jake Plummer .30 .75
17 Quincy Carter .30 .75
18 Peyton Manning 1.25 3.00
19 Keyshawn Johnson .40 1.00
20 Travis Henry .30 .75
21 LaDainian Tomlinson .50 1.25
22 Emmitt Smith .75 2.00
23 Michael Bennett .30 .75
24 Duce Staley .30 .75
25 Thomas Jones .30 .75
26 Deuce McAllister .40 1.00
27 Eddie George .40 1.00
28 Marshall Faulk .40 1.00
29 Curtis Martin .40 1.00
30 Ahman Green .40 1.00
31 Priest Holmes .30 .75
32 Edgerrin James .40 1.00
33 Antowain Smith .40 1.00
34 Ricky Williams .40 1.00
35 Anthony Thomas .40 1.00
36 Jerome Bettis .50 1.25
37 Shaun Alexander .30 .75
38 Kerry Collins .30 .75
39 Drew Brees 1.00 2.50
40 Chris Redman .30 .75
41 Marc Bulger .30 .75
42 Jay Fiedler .40 1.00
43 Trent Green .30 .75
44 Daunte Culpepper .40 1.00
45 Rich Gannon .40 1.00
46 Rodney Peete .40 1.00
47 Vinny Testaverde .30 .75
48 Stephen Davis .30 .75
49 James Allen .30 .75
50 Tiki Barber .40 1.00
51 Ron Dayne .40 1.00
52 Ray Lewis .50 1.25
53 Corey Dillon .30 .75
54 Brian Urlacher .50 1.25
55 Junior Seau .40 1.00
56 Warrick Dunn .30 .75
57 Fred Taylor .30 .75
58 Jamal Lewis .40 1.00
59 Trent Dilfer .30 .75
60 James Stewart .30 .75
61 David Patten .30 .75
62 Eric Moulds .30 .75
63 Isaac Bruce .50 1.25
64 Troy Brown .30 .75
65 Terrell Owens .40 1.00
66 Moe Williams .30 .75
67 Joe Horn .30 .75
68 Az-Zahir Hakim .30 .75
69 Jimmy Smith .40 1.00
70 Michael Westbrook .30 .75
71 Olandis Gary .40 1.00
72 Chris Chambers .30 .75
73 Kevin Johnson .30 .75
74 Joey Galloway .40 1.00
75 Hines Ward .40 1.00
76 Garrison Hearst .30 .75
77 Wayne Chrebet .30 .75
78 Muhsin Muhammad .30 .75
79 Rod Gardner .30 .75
80 Jerry Rice 1.00 2.50
81 Tim Brown .50 1.25
82 Shannon Sharpe .40 1.00
83 Terry Glenn .40 1.00
84 Randy Moss .40 1.00
85 Corey Bradford .30 .75
86 Marty Booker .30 .75
87 Keenan McCardell .40 1.00
88 Marvin Harrison .40 1.00
89 David Boston .30 .75
90 Eddie Kennison .40 1.00
91 Tim Carter RC 1.50 4.00
92 Joey Harrington RC 1.25 3.00
93 Patrick Ramsey RC 1.50 4.00
94 David Garrard RC 1.50 4.00
95 Donte Stallworth RC 2.00 5.00
96 Reche Caldwell RC 1.50 4.00
97 William Green RC 1.50 4.00
98 Josh Reed RC 1.50 4.00
99 DeShaun Foster RC 2.00 5.00
100 Jeremy Shockey RC 2.00 5.00
101 Mike Williams RC 1.25 3.00
102 Daniel Graham RC 1.50 4.00
103 Josh McCown RC 2.00 5.00
104 Javon Walker RC 2.00 5.00
105 Travis Stephens RC 1.25 3.00
106 Marquise Walker RC 1.25 3.00
107 T.J. Duckett RC 1.25 3.00
108 Damien Anderson RC 1.25 3.00
109 Quentin Jammer RC 2.00 5.00
110 Bryan Thomas RC 1.25 3.00
111 Chad Hutchinson RC 1.25 3.00
112 Brian Westbrook RC 2.50 6.00
113 Lamar Gordon RC 1.50 4.00
114 Deion Branch RC 2.00 5.00
115 Ed Reed RC 8.00 20.00
116 Jonathan Wells RC 1.50 4.00
117 Phillip Buchanon RC 2.00 5.00
118 Wendell Bryant RC 1.25 3.00
119 Kurt Kittner RC 1.25 3.00
120 Randy McMichael RC 2.00 5.00
121 Brandon Doman RC 1.25 3.00
122 Adrian Peterson RC 1.50 4.00
123 Ricky Williams RC 1.50 4.00
124 Seth Burford RC 1.25 3.00
125 Shaun Hill RC 2.00 5.00
126 Anthony Weaver RC 1.25 3.00
127 Freddie Milons RC 1.25 3.00
128 Darrell Hill RC 1.25 3.00
129 Daryl Jones RC 1.25 3.00
130 Chester Taylor RC 2.00 5.00
131 Najeh Davenport RC 1.25 3.00
132 Jason McAddley RC 1.50 4.00
133 Preston Parsons RC 1.25 3.00
134 Michael Lewis RC 1.50 4.00
135 Mike Rumph RC 1.25 3.00
136 Lamont Thompson RC 1.50 4.00
137 Dwight Freeney RC 2.50 6.00
138 Napoleon Harris RC 1.50 4.00
139 Tank Williams RC 1.50 4.00
140 Lee Mays RC 1.25 3.00
141 Robert Thomas RC 1.25 3.00
142 Tellis Redmon RC 1.25 3.00
143 Alex Brown RC 2.00 5.00
144 Ryan Sims RC 2.00 5.00
145 Larry Tripplett RC 1.25 3.00
146 Quinn Gray RC 1.50 4.00
147 Jesse Chatman RC 1.25 3.00
148 Jamin Elliott RC 1.25 3.00
149 Ben Leber RC 1.25 3.00
150 Lito Sheppard RC 2.00 5.00
151 Antonio Bryant AU/550 RC 8.00 20.00
152 Rohan Davey AU/550 RC 8.00 20.00
153 Randy Fasani AU/550 RC 5.00 12.00
154 J.T. O'Sullivan AU/550 RC 6.00 15.00
155 Ron Johnson AU/550 RC 6.00 15.00
156 Maurice Morris AU/550 RC 6.00 15.00
157 Kahlil Hill AU/550 RC 5.00 12.00
158 Ant Randle El AU/550 RC 6.00 15.00
159 Cliff Russell AU/550 RC 5.00 12.00
160 Ladell Betts AU/550 RC 8.00 20.00
161 David Carr AU/125 RC 8.00 20.00
162 Andre Davis AU/125 RC 8.00 20.00
163 Julius Peppers AU/125 75.00 125.00
164 Ashley Lelie AU/125 RC 8.00 20.00
165 Jabar Gaffney AU/125 RC 8.00 20.00
166 Clinton Portis AU/125 RC 12.00 30.00

2002 Sweet Spot Gold Rookie Autographs

STATED PRINT RUN 25 SER.#'d SETS
151 Antonio Bryant 12.00 30.00
152 Rohan Davey 12.00 30.00
153 Randy Fasani 8.00 20.00
154 J.T. O'Sullivan 10.00 25.00
155 Ron Johnson
156 Maurice Morris 10.00 25.00
157 Kahlil Hill 8.00 20.00
158 Antwaan Randle El 15.00 40.00
159 Cliff Russell 8.00 20.00
160 Ladell Betts 12.00 30.00
161 David Carr 15.00 40.00
162 Andre Davis 8.00 20.00
163 Julius Peppers 40.00 100.00
164 Ashley Lelie 8.00 20.00
165 Jabar Gaffney 8.00 20.00
166 Clinton Portis 75.00 150.00

2002 Sweet Spot Hot Spots Football

Randomly inserted into packs, this cot featuroc premium football swatches produced in limited quantities. The print runs are noted below in our checklist. A parallel version of each card called "Official Hot Spots" was produced with the card being built around the "official" tag from the football which were cut up. Each of those was serial numbered between 3-24 copies.

STATED PRINT RUN 9-74
SERIAL #'d UNDER 20 NOT PRICED
UNPRICED OFFICIAL PRINT RUN 3-24
HSAG Ahman Green/21 10.00 25.00
HSBU Brian Urlacher/41 10.00 25.00
HSCP Chad Pennington/23 8.00 20.00
HSCR Chris Redman/32 6.00 15.00
HSCS Corey Simon/58 5.00 12.00
HSDB Drew Brees/41 20.00 50.00
HSDC Daunte Culpepper/44 8.00 20.00
HSDM Donovan McNabb/41 8.00 20.00
HSEJ Edgerrin James/44 8.00 20.00
HSLT LaDainian Tomlinson/32 10.00 25.00
HSMC Deuce McAllister/35 8.00 20.00
HSMV Michael Vick/21 10.00 25.00
HSPM Peyton Manning/74 30.00 80.00
HSPW Peter Warrick/23 8.00 20.00
HSQC Quincy Carter/29 8.00 20.00
HSRD Ron Dayne/21 10.00 25.00
HSRM Randy Moss/23 10.00 25.00
HSSA Shaun Alexander/44 6.00 15.00
HSSM Santana Moss/23 10.00 25.00
HSTJ Thomas Jones/21 8.00 20.00

2002 Sweet Spot Patches

Inserted one per box as a box topper, this set features patches glued onto cardboard that highlight the players name, jersey number, and position.

STATED ODDS ONE PER BOX
SWPAB Aaron Brooks 2.50 6.00
SWPAF Antonio Freeman 4.00 10.00
SWPAG Ahman Green 3.00 8.00
SWPAT Anthony Thomas 3.00 8.00
SWPBF Brett Favre 8.00 20.00
SWPBG Brian Griese 2.50 6.00
SWPBJ Brad Johnson 3.00 8.00
SWPBO David Boston 2.50 6.00
SWPBR Tom Brady 20.00 50.00
SWPBU Brian Urlacher 4.00 10.00
SWPCA David Carr SP 2.50 6.00
SWPCD Corey Dillon 2.50 6.00
SWPCM Curtis Martin 3.00 8.00
SWPDB Drew Bledsoe 3.00 8.00
SWPDC Daunte Culpepper 3.00 8.00
SWPDE Deuce McAllister 3.00 8.00
SWPDM Donovan McNabb 3.00 8.00
SWPDR Drew Brees 8.00 20.00
SWPEG Eddie George 3.00 8.00
SWPEJ Edgerrin James 3.00 8.00
SWPES Emmitt Smith 6.00 15.00
SWPJB Jerome Bettis 4.00 10.00
SWPJG Jeff Garcia 2.50 6.00
SWPJH Joey Harrington SP 2.50 6.00
SWPJP Jake Plummer 2.50 6.00
SWPJR Jerry Rice 8.00 20.00
SWPJS Jeremy Shockey SP 4.00 10.00
SWPKJ Keyshawn Johnson 3.00 8.00
SWPKS Kordell Stewart 2.50 6.00
SWPKW Kurt Warner 3.00 8.00
SWPLT LaDainian Tomlinson 4.00 10.00
SWPMB Mark Brunell 3.00 8.00
SWPMF Marshall Faulk 3.00 8.00
SWPMV Michael Vick 3.00 8.00
SWPPE Julius Peppers SP 6.00 15.00
SWPPM Peyton Manning 10.00 25.00
SWPPR Patrick Ramsey SP 3.00 8.00
SWPRG Rich Gannon 3.00 8.00
SWPRM Randy Moss 3.00 8.00
SWPRW Ricky Williams 3.00 8.00
SWPSA Shaun Alexander 2.50 6.00
SWPSD Stephen Davis 2.50 6.00
SWPSM Steve McNair 3.00 8.00
SWPSS Shannon Sharpe 3.00 8.00
SWPTB Tiki Barber 3.00 8.00
SWPTC Tim Couch 2.50 6.00
SWPTO Terrell Owens 3.00 8.00
SWPVT Vinny Testaverde 2.50 6.00
SWPWD Warrick Dunn 2.50 6.00
SWPWG William Green SP 3.00 8.00

2002 Sweet Spot Rookie Gallery Jersey

Inserted at a rate of 1:8, this set features jersey swatches from many of the NFL's top 2002 rookies. The five short-printed players were serial numbered to 350. In addition, there was a gold parallel set serial #'d to 100 or 50.

STATED ODDS 1:8
*GOLD/100: .6X TO 1.5X
*GOLD/50: .8X TO 2X
GOLD PRINT RUN 50-100
RGAB Antonio Bryant 3.00 8.00
RGAL Ashley Lelie 2.00 5.00
RGCP Clinton Portis 3.00 8.00
RGDC David Carr/350 2.00 5.00
RGDF DeShaun Foster 3.00 8.00
RGDS Donte Stallworth/350 3.00 8.00
RGEC Eric Crouch 3.00 8.00
RGEL Antwaan Randle El 2.50 6.00
RGJG Jabar Gaffney/350 2.00 5.00
RGJH Joey Harrington/350 2.00 5.00
RGJM Josh McCown 3.00 8.00
RGJR Josh Reed 2.50 6.00
RGJW Javon Walker 3.00 8.00
RGMM Maurice Morris 2.50 6.00
RGMW Marquise Walker 2.00 5.00
RGPR Patrick Ramsey/350 2.50 6.00
RGRC Reche Caldwell 2.50 6.00
RGRD Rohan Davey 3.00 8.00
RGTC Tim Carter 2.50 6.00
RGTJ T.J. Duckett 2.00 5.00
RGTS Travis Stephens 2.00 5.00
RGWG William Green 2.50 6.00

2002 Sweet Spot Sunday Stars Jerseys

Randomly inserted into packs, this set features authentic jersey swatches from top NFL superstars. In addition, a gold parallel was produced that was limited to 10-25 copies.

STATED PRINT RUN 150-250
*GOLD/25: 1X TO 2.5X BASIC JSY
GOLD PRINT RUN 10-25
SSAG Ahman Green/250 4.00 10.00
SSAT Anthony Thomas/250 4.00 10.00
SSBF Brett Favre/150 10.00 25.00
SSDC Daunte Culpepper/150 4.00 10.00
SSDM Donovan McNabb/150 4.00 10.00
SSEJ Edgerrin James/150 4.00 10.00
SSES Emmitt Smith/150 8.00 20.00
SSJB Jerome Bettis/250 5.00 12.00
SSJP Jake Plummer/250 3.00 8.00
SSJR Jerry Rice/150 10.00 25.00
SSKJ Keyshawn Johnson/250 4.00 10.00
SSKW Kurt Warner/150 4.00 10.00
SSLT LaDainian Tomlinson/250 5.00 12.00
SSMF Marshall Faulk/150 4.00 10.00
SSMV Michael Vick/150 4.00 10.00
SSPM Peyton Manning/250 12.00 30.00
SSRM Randy Moss/150 4.00 10.00
SSRW Ricky Williams/250 4.00 10.00
SSTB Tom Brady/250 25.00 60.00
SSTC Tim Couch/250 3.00 8.00

2002 Sweet Spot Sweet Impressions Autographs

Randomly inserted into packs, this set features authentic autographs from many of the NFL's top veterans and 2002 rookies signed on a simulated football swatch. In addition, a gold parallel was produced that was limited to 25 copies. Please note that some cards were issued as redemptions with an expiration date of 12/6/2005.

STATED PRINT RUN 50-450
*GOLD/25: .8X TO 2X BASIC AU/450
*GOLD/25: .6X TO 1.5X BASIC AU/50-100
SIAB Aaron Brooks/75 8.00 20.00
SIAS Antowain Smith/100 10.00 25.00
SIBR Drew Brees/50 40.00 80.00
SIDB Drew Bledsoe/450 12.00 30.00
SIDC Daunte Culpepper/50 12.00 30.00
SIER Ed Reed/450 25.00 50.00
SIFM Freddie Mitchell/450 6.00 15.00
SIGH Garrison Hearst/450 6.00 15.00
SIJB Jerome Bettis/450 30.00 60.00
SIJM Jim Miller/450 6.00 15.00
SIJP Jake Plummer/75 8.00 20.00
SIMB Michael Bennett/450 10.00 25.00
SIPM1 Peyton Manning/450 40.00 80.00
SIPM2 Peyton Manning/450 40.00 80.00
SIPM3 Peyton Manning/450 40.00 80.00
SIPM4 Peyton Manning/450 40.00 80.00
SISM Santana Moss/450 8.00 20.00
SISR Sage Rosenfels/450 8.00 20.00
SITC Tim Carter/450 8.00 20.00
SITG Tony Gonzalez/100 12.00 30.00

2003 Sweet Spot

Released in December of 2003, this set features 231 cards, consisting of 90 veterans, 126 rookies, and 15 Sunday Stars subset cards. Rookies 91-120 are serial numbered to 1500. The Sunday Stars subset (121-135) were inserted at a rate of 1:6, and are serial numbered to 100. Tier 1 rookies (136-185) are serial numbered to 675, Tier 2 rookies (186-210) are serial numbered to 300, and Tier 3 rookies (211-225) are serial numbered to 100. Rookies 226-231 are serial numbered to 250, and feature authentic player autographs on plastic helmet pieces embedded in card front. Please note that Byron Leftwich was issued as an exchange card in packs. The exchange deadline is 3/19/2007.

COMP.SET w/o SP's (90) 12.50 30.00
226-231 AU RC PRINT RUN 250
1 Chad Pennington .25 .60
2 Aaron Brooks .25 .60
3 Joey Harrington .25 .60
4 Brett Favre .75 2.00
5 Donovan McNabb .30 .75
6 Jeff Garcia .25 .60
7 Michael Vick .30 .75
8 David Carr .25 .60
9 Drew Brees .40 1.00
10 Trent Green .25 .60
11 Patrick Ramsey .30 .75
12 Tom Brady 1.50 4.00
13 Kurt Warner .30 .75
14 Brad Johnson .30 .75
15 Brian Griese .25 .60
16 Jake Plummer .25 .60
17 Drew Bledsoe .25 .60
18 Peyton Manning 1.00 2.50
19 Tim Couch .25 .60
20 Kordell Stewart .25 .60
21 Jay Fiedler .25 .60
22 Rich Gannon .30 .75
23 Josh McCown .30 .75
24 Matt Hasselbeck .25 .60
25 Tommy Maddox .25 .60
26 Rodney Peete .25 .60
27 Jake Delhomme .25 .60
28 Chris Redman .25 .60
29 Mark Brunell .25 .60
30 Marc Bulger .25 .60

31 Kelly Holcomb .25 .60
32 Chad Hutchinson .25 .60
33 Quincy Carter .25 .60
34 Steve McNair .30 .75
35 Marshall Faulk .30 .75
36 Deuce McAllister .30 .75
37 Emmitt Smith .60 1.50
38 LaDainian Tomlinson .40 1.00
39 Kevan Barlow .25 .60
40 Michael Bennett .25 .60
41 Shaun Alexander .25 .60
42 Edgerrin James .30 .75
43 Ricky Williams .30 .75
44 Priest Holmes .25 .60
45 Ahman Green .30 .75
46 Curtis Martin .30 .75
47 Anthony Thomas .30 .75
48 Travis Henry .25 .60
49 Jerome Bettis .40 1.00
50 Fred Taylor .25 .60
51 Corey Dillon .25 .60
52 Jamal Lewis .30 .75
53 William Green .25 .60
54 Brian Urlacher .40 1.00
55 Junior Seau .30 .75
56 Ray Lewis .40 1.00
57 Julius Peppers .40 1.00
58 Terrell Owens .30 .75
59 David Boston .25 .60
60 Isaac Bruce .40 1.00
61 Marvin Harrison .30 .75
62 Chris Chambers .25 .60
63 Chad Johnson .25 .60
64 Peter Warrick .25 .60
65 Peerless Price .25 .60
66 Antonio Bryant .25 .60
67 Laveranues Coles .25 .60
68 Rod Gardner .25 .60
69 Hines Ward .30 .75
70 Plaxico Burress .25 .60
71 Keyshawn Johnson .40 1.00
72 Jabar Gaffney .25 .60
73 Eric Moulds .25 .60
74 Santana Moss .30 .75
75 Koren Robinson .30 .75
76 Jimmy Smith .30 .75
77 Donte Stallworth .25 .60
78 Kevin Johnson .25 .60
79 Quincy Morgan .25 .60
80 Jerry Rice .75 2.00
81 Tim Brown .40 1.00
82 Rod Smith .30 .75
83 Ashley Lelie .25 .60
84 Randy Moss .30 .75
85 Torry Holt .30 .75
86 Troy Brown .25 .60
87 Donald Driver .30 .75
88 Todd Heap .25 .60
89 Tony Gonzalez .30 .75
90 Jeremy Shockey .25 .60
91 Casey Moore RC 1.50 4.00
92 Chris Crocker RC 2.00 5.00
93 Pisa Tinoisamoa RC 2.50 6.00
94 Nnamdi Asomugha RC 2.50 6.00
95 Tyler Brayton RC 2.00 5.00
96 Eddie Moore RC 1.50 4.00
97 Terrence Kiel RC 2.00 5.00
98 Casey Fitzsimmons RC 2.00 5.00
99 George Foster RC 1.50 4.00
100 J.J. Moses RC 1.50 4.00
101 Dan Klecko RC 2.00 5.00
102 Terry Pierce RC 1.50 4.00
103 Brad Pyatt RC 1.50 4.00
104 Boss Bailey RC 2.00 5.00
105 Michael Haynes RC 1.50 4.00
106 Jimmy Kennedy RC 2.00 5.00
107 Jerome McDougle RC 1.50 4.00
108 William Joseph RC 1.50 4.00
109 Visanthe Shiancoe RC 2.50 6.00
110 L.J. Smith RC 2.50 6.00
111 Avon Cobourne RC 1.50 4.00
112 Bennie Joppru RC 1.50 4.00
113 Ken Hamlin RC 2.50 6.00
114 Jeremi Johnson RC 1.50 4.00
115 Justin Griffith RC 2.00 5.00
116 Joffrey Reynolds RC 1.50 4.00
117 Kassim Osgood RC 2.50 6.00
118 Donald Lee RC 2.00 5.00
119 Denero Marriott RC 1.50 4.00
120 Jamal Burke RC 1.50 4.00
121 Michael Vick SS 3.00 8.00
122 Donovan McNabb SS 3.00 8.00
123 Jerry Rice SS 8.00 20.00
124 Brett Favre SS 8.00 20.00
125 Kurt Warner SS 3.00 8.00
126 Marshall Faulk SS 3.00 8.00
127 Ricky Williams SS 3.00 8.00
128 Emmitt Smith SS 6.00 15.00
129 Tom Brady SS 15.00 40.00
130 Randy Moss SS 3.00 8.00
131 LaDainian Tomlinson SS 4.00 10.00
132 Jeff Garcia SS 2.50 6.00
133 Brian Urlacher SS 4.00 10.00
134 Drew Bledsoe SS 3.00 8.00
135 Peyton Manning SS 10.00 25.00
136 Dave Ragone RC 2.00 5.00
137 Brian St.Pierre RC 2.00 5.00
138 Kliff Kingsbury RC 3.00 8.00
139 Marquel Blackwell RC 2.00 5.00
140 Brett Engemann RC 2.00 5.00
141 Kirk Farmer RC 2.50 6.00
142 Andrew Pinnock RC 2.50 6.00
143 Tony Romo RC 20.00 50.00
144 Nate Hybl RC 2.50 6.00
145 Ken Dorsey RC 2.50 6.00
146 Brock Forsey RC 2.50 6.00
147 Musa Smith RC 2.00 5.00
148 Domanick Davis RC 2.50 6.00
149 LaBrandon Toefield RC 2.00 5.00
150 B.J. Askew RC 2.50 6.00
151 Quentin Griffin RC 2.50 6.00
152 Ahmaad Galloway RC 2.50 6.00
153 Cecil Sapp RC 2.00 5.00
154 Justin Fargas RC 3.00 8.00
155 Sultan McCullough RC 2.00 5.00
156 Malaefou MacKenzie RC 2.00 5.00
157 Tom Lopienski RC 2.00 5.00
158 Lee Suggs RC 2.00 5.00
159 Richard Angulo RC 2.00 5.00
160 Dwone Hicks RC 2.00 5.00
161 Nate Burleson RC 2.50 6.00
162 Billy McMullen RC 2.00 5.00
163 David Tyree RC 2.50 6.00
164 Gerald Hayes RC 2.50 6.00
165 Anthony Adams RC 2.50 6.00
166 George Wrighster RC 2.00 5.00
167 Tyrone Calico RC 2.00 5.00
168 Shaun McDonald RC 2.50 6.00
169 Bobby Wade RC 2.50 6.00
170 Larry Johnson RC 2.50 6.00
171 Ryan Hoag RC 2.00 5.00
172 Doug Gabriel RC 2.50 6.00
173 Antonio Gates RC 15.00 40.00
174 Brandon Lloyd RC 3.00 8.00
175 Arnaz Battle RC 3.00 8.00
176 Kelley Washington RC 2.00 5.00
177 Antwone Savage RC 2.00 5.00
178 Keenan Howry RC 2.00 5.00
179 Adrian Madise RC 2.00 5.00
180 LaTarence Dunbar RC 2.00 5.00
181 Walter Young RC 2.00 5.00
182 Travaris Robinson RC 2.00 5.00
183 DeAndrew Rubin RC 2.00 5.00
184 Carl Ford RC 2.00 5.00
185 Zuriel Smith RC 2.00 5.00
186 Willie Ponder RC 2.50 6.00
187 Gibran Hamdan RC 2.50 6.00
188 Aaron Moorehead RC 3.00 8.00
189 Nick Barnett RC 4.00 10.00
190 Chris Brown RC 2.50 6.00
191 ReShard Lee RC 4.00 10.00
192 Anquan Boldin RC 4.00 10.00
193 Kevin Curtis RC 2.50 6.00
194 Taylor Jacobs RC 2.50 6.00
195 Sam Aiken RC 3.00 8.00
196 Aaron Walker RC 3.00 8.00
197 Mike Seidman RC 2.50 6.00
198 Jason Witten RC 10.00 25.00
199 Dallas Clark RC 4.00 10.00
200 Rashean Mathis RC 2.50 6.00
201 DeWayne Robertson RC 3.00 8.00
202 Johnathan Sullivan RC 2.50 6.00
203 Drayton Florence RC 4.00 10.00
204 Sammy Davis RC 3.00 8.00
205 Andre Woolfolk RC 2.50 6.00
206 Terence Newman RC 4.00 10.00
207 Mike Doss RC 4.00 10.00
208 Troy Polamalu RC 25.00 60.00
209 Terrell Suggs RC 3.00 8.00
210 Marcus Trufant RC 3.00 8.00
211 Seneca Wallace RC 4.00 10.00
212 Brooks Bollinger RC 4.00 10.00
213 Jason Gesser RC 4.00 10.00
214 Onterrio Smith RC 3.00 8.00
215 Artose Pinner RC 3.00 8.00
216 J.R. Tolver RC 4.00 10.00
217 Kerry Carter RC 3.00 8.00
218 Tony Hollings RC 4.00 10.00
219 Teyo Johnson RC 4.00 10.00
220 Bethel Johnson RC 3.00 8.00
221 Rex Grossman RC 4.00 10.00
222 Andre Johnson RC 15.00 40.00
223 Terrence Edwards RC 3.00 8.00
224 Willis McGahee RC 4.00 10.00
225 Charles Rogers RC 4.00 10.00
226 Chris Simms AU RC 6.00 15.00
227 Bryant Johnson AU RC 10.00 25.00
228 Byron Leftwich AU RC 8.00 20.00
229 Carson Palmer AU RC 20.00 50.00
230 Justin Gage AU RC 8.00 20.00
231 Kyle Boller AU RC 6.00 15.00

2003 Sweet Spot Gold

*ROOKIES 136-185: 1.5X TO 4X BASIC CARDS
*ROOKIES 186-210: 1.2X TO 3X BASIC CARDS
*ROOKIES 211-225: 1X TO 2.5X BASIC CARDS
*ROOK.AU 226-231: .8X TO 2X BASIC CARDS
STATED PRINT RUN 25 SER.#'d SETS
143 Tony Romo 100.00 200.00
173 Antonio Gates 100.00 200.00
208 Troy Polamalu 125.00 200.00

2003 Sweet Spot By the Letters Autographed 10x12

Randomly inserted in packs, this set consists of exchange cards issued in packs redeemable for an autographed 10x12 framed piece from the player named on the card. Print runs were provided by Upper Deck. The exchange deadline is 12/1/2006. There is a Gold parallel of this set that is not priced due to scarcity.

STATED PRINT RUN 5-49
UNPRICED GOLD PRINT RUN 1-5
SERIAL #'d UNDER 20 NOT PRICED
AB Anquan Boldin/43 25.00 60.00
AJ Andre Johnson/49 60.00 120.00
AP Artose Pinner/43 15.00 40.00
BJ Bethel Johnson/43 15.00 40.00
BL Byron Leftwich/43 20.00 50.00
BR Bryant Johnson/43 25.00 60.00
CB Chris Brown/43
CP Carson Palmer/43 100.00 200.00
DC Dallas Clark/43 25.00 60.00
DR Dave Ragone/43 15.00 40.00
JF Justin Fargas/42 25.00 60.00
KB Kyle Boller/40 15.00 40.00
KC Kevin Curtis/43 15.00 40.00
KK Kliff Kingsbury/43 25.00 60.00
KW Kelley Washington/44 15.00 40.00
LJ Larry Johnson/47 20.00 50.00
MS Musa Smith/43
MT Marcus Trufant/43 20.00 50.00
NB Nate Burleson/43 20.00 50.00
OS Onterrio Smith/43 15.00 40.00
RG Rex Grossman/43 20.00 50.00
RO DeWayne Robertson/24 20.00 50.00
SP Brian St.Pierre/45 15.00 40.00
SW Seneca Wallace/43 20.00 50.00
TC Tyrone Calico/44 15.00 40.00
TE Teyo Johnson/43 20.00 50.00
TJ Taylor Jacobs/43 15.00 40.00
TN Terence Newman/43 25.00 60.00
TS Terrell Suggs/43 30.00 80.00
WM Willis McGahee/43 75.00 150.00

2003 Sweet Spot Classics

Inserted at a rate of 1:4, this set features collectible patches on the card fronts in the shape of the team logo for the player pictured. A Numbers parallel of this set exists, and features collectible patches on the card fronts in the shape of the player's jersey number. Cards in the Numbers parallel set are serial numbered to 100. There is also a Gold parallel of this set, and features collectible patches on the card fronts in the shape of the team logo on a gold background. Gold patches are serial numbered to 25 and are not priced due to scarcity.

OVERALL CLASSICS ODDS 1:4
*NUMBER/100: .8X TO 2X BASIC INSERT
NUMBERS PRINT RUN 100 SER.#'d SETS
*GOLD/25: 1.2X TO 3X BASIC INSERT
GOLD PRINT RUN 25 SER.#'d SETS
PAB Aaron Brooks 2.50 6.00
PAG Ahman Green 3.00 8.00
PAJ Andre Johnson 4.00 10.00
PBE Bethel Johnson 2.50 6.00
PBF Brett Favre 8.00 20.00
PBJ Brad Johnson 3.00 8.00
PBL Byron Leftwich 2.00 5.00
PBR Drew Brees 4.00 10.00
PBU Brian Urlacher 4.00 10.00
PCP Chad Pennington 2.50 6.00
PCR Charles Rogers 2.50 6.00
PCS Chris Simms 2.50 6.00
PCU Daunte Culpepper 3.00 8.00
PDB Drew Bledsoe 3.00 8.00
PDC David Carr 2.50 6.00
PDM Donovan McNabb 3.00 8.00
PDU Deuce McAllister 3.00 8.00
PEG Eddie George 3.00 8.00
PEJ Edgerrin James 3.00 8.00
PES Emmitt Smith 6.00 15.00
PJG Jeff Garcia 2.50 6.00
PJH Joey Harrington 2.50 6.00
PJO Bryant Johnson 2.50 6.00
PJR Jerry Rice 8.00 20.00
PJS Jeremy Shockey 2.50 6.00
PKB Kyle Boller 2.50 6.00
PKW Kurt Warner 3.00 8.00
PLJ Larry Johnson 2.00 5.00
PLT LaDainian Tomlinson 4.00 10.00
PMF Marshall Faulk 3.00 8.00
PMV Michael Vick 3.00 8.00
PPH Priest Holmes 2.50 6.00
PPM Peyton Manning 10.00 25.00
PPO Clinton Portis 2.50 6.00
PRG Rex Grossman 2.00 5.00
PRM Randy Moss 3.00 8.00
PRW Ricky Williams 3.00 8.00
PSC Carson Palmer 3.00 8.00
PTB Tom Brady 15.00 40.00
PTJ Taylor Jacobs 2.50 6.00
PTO Terrell Owens 3.00 8.00
PWM Willis McGahee 2.00 5.00

2003 Sweet Spot Jerseys

This set feautres game worn jersey swatches of established NFL stars. Each card is serial numbered to 300. A Gold parallel of this set exists. Cards in the Jerseys Gold set feature gold highlights and are serial numbered to 25.

STATED PRINT RUN 300 SER.#'d SETS
*GOLD/25: 1X TO 2.5X BASIC JSY/300
GOLD PRINT RUN 25 SER.#'d SETS
OVERALL JSY ODDS 1:12
JCAB Aaron Brooks 2.50 6.00
JCBF Brett Favre 8.00 20.00
JCBG Brian Griese 2.50 6.00
JCBO David Boston 2.50 6.00
JCBU Brian Urlacher 4.00 10.00
JCCP Chad Pennington 2.50 6.00
JCDB Drew Brees 4.00 10.00
JCDC David Carr 2.50 6.00
JCDM Donovan McNabb 3.00 8.00
JCEG Eddie George 3.00 8.00
JCEJ Edgerrin James 3.00 8.00
JCES Emmitt Smith 6.00 15.00
JCJF Jay Fiedler 2.50 6.00
JCJG Jeff Garcia 2.50 6.00
JCJP Jake Plummer 2.50 6.00
JCJR Jerry Rice 8.00 20.00
JCJS Jeremy Shockey 2.50 6.00
JCKC Kerry Collins 2.50 6.00
JCKS Kordell Stewart 2.50 6.00
JCKW Kurt Warner 3.00 8.00
JCLC Laveranues Coles 2.50 6.00
JCLT LaDainian Tomlinson 4.00 10.00
JCMV Michael Vick 3.00 8.00
JCPM Peyton Manning 10.00 25.00
JCPO Clinton Portis 2.50 6.00
JCRG Rich Gannon 3.00 8.00
JCRL Ray Lewis 4.00 10.00
JCRM Randy Moss 3.00 8.00
JCSM Steve McNair 3.00 8.00
JCTB Tom Brady 10.00 25.00
JCTI Tim Brown 4.00 10.00
JCTO Terrell Owens 3.00 8.00
JCWD Warrick Dunn 2.50 6.00

2003 Sweet Spot Rookie Gallery Jersey

This set features jersey swatches of promising NFL rookies. Each card is serial numbered to 300. A Gold parallel of this set exists. Cards in the Jerseys Gold set feature gold highlights and are serial numbered to 25.

PRINT RUN 300 SERIAL #'d SETS
OVERALL JSY ODDS 1:12
RGAB Anquan Boldin 3.00 8.00
RGAJ Andre Johnson 5.00 12.00
RGAP Artose Pinner 2.00 5.00
RGBE Bethel Johnson 2.00 5.00
RGBJ Bryant Johnson 3.00 8.00
RGBL Byron Leftwich 2.50 6.00
RGCA Curt Anes 2.00 5.00
RGCB Chris Brown 2.00 5.00
RGCM Carl Morris 2.00 5.00
RGCP Carson Palmer 10.00 25.00
RGDC Dallas Clark 3.00 8.00
RGDR Dave Ragone 2.00 5.00
RGJF Justin Fargas 3.00 8.00
RGJG Justin Gage 2.50 6.00
RGKB Kyle Boller 2.00 5.00
RGKC Kevin Curtis 2.00 5.00
RGKK Kliff Kingsbury 3.00 8.00
RGKO Kassim Osgood 3.00 8.00
RGKW Kelley Washington 2.00 5.00
RGLJ Larry Johnson 2.50 6.00
RGMS Musa Smith 2.00 5.00
RGMT Marcus Trufant 2.50 6.00
RGNB Nate Burleson 2.50 6.00
RGOS Onterrio Smith 2.00 5.00
RGRG Rex Grossman 2.50 6.00
RGRO DeWayne Robertson 2.50 6.00
RGSP Brian St.Pierre 2.00 5.00
RGSW Seneca Wallace 2.50 6.00
RGTC Tyrone Calico 2.00 5.00
RGTE Teyo Johnson 2.50 6.00
RGTN Terence Newman 3.00 8.00
RGTP Troy Polamalu 30.00 80.00
RGTS Terrell Suggs 2.50 6.00
RGWM Willis McGahee 6.00 15.00
RGWY Walter Young 2.00 5.00

2003 Sweet Spot Rookie Gallery Jersey Gold

*GOLD/25: 1.2X TO 3X BASIC JSY
GOLD PRINT RUN 25 SER.#'d SETS
RGTP Troy Polamalu 75.00 150.00

2003 Sweet Spot Signatures

This set features authentic player autographs on plastic helmet pieces imbedded on the card fronts. Please note that D.Carr, M.Hasselbeck, P.Holmes, R.Moss, T.Bradshaw, and T.Owens were issued as exchange cards in packs. A Signatures Gold parallel exists. Signatures Gold feature gold highlights, and are serial numbred to 25. Some print runs were provided by Upper Deck and are marked with an * below.. The exchange deadline is 3/19/2007.

OVERALL SIGNATURES ODDS 1:24
*GOLD/25: .8X TO 2X BASIC AUTO
*GOLD/25: .5X TO 1.2X AUTO/60-100
*GOLD/25: .4X TO 1X AUTO/20
GOLD PRINT RUN 25 SER.#'d SETS
SSAB Aaron Brooks 8.00 20.00
SSAN Anquan Boldin/100* 12.00 30.00
SSBB Boss Bailey 10.00 25.00
SSBL Drew Bledsoe 25.00 50.00
SSBU Brian Urlacher 40.00 80.00
SSCJ Chad Johnson 8.00 20.00
SSCP Chad Pennington 8.00 20.00
SSDB Drew Brees 30.00 60.00
SSDC David Carr 8.00 20.00
SSDE Deuce McAllister/75* 20.00 50.00
SSDH Dwone Hicks 8.00 20.00
SSDM Donovan McNabb/99* 30.00 60.00
SSJB Jim Brown/75 75.00 135.00
SSJG Jeff Garcia 8.00 20.00
SSJM Joe Montana/60* 100.00 200.00
SSJR Jerry Rice/20* 150.00 300.00
SSLD LaTarence Dunbar 8.00 20.00
SSLS Lynn Swann 150.00 250.00
SSMH Matt Hasselbeck 8.00 20.00
SSMS Musa Smith 8.00 20.00
SSOS Onterrio Smith 8.00 20.00
SSPH Priest Holmes/450 6.00 15.00
SSPM Peyton Manning 60.00 120.00
SSPO Clinton Portis 8.00 20.00
SSRI John Riggins/75* 25.00 60.00
SSRW Ricky Williams/75* 30.00 60.00
SSSW Seneca Wallace 10.00 25.00
SSTA Troy Aikman 50.00 100.00
SSTB Terry Bradshaw/65* 60.00 120.00
SSTB Tim Brown/75* 40.00 80.00
SSTC Tyrone Calico 8.00 20.00
SSTG Trent Green 8.00 20.00
SSTO Terrell Owens 15.00 40.00

2004 Sweet Spot

Sweet Spot initially released in late-January 2005. The base set consists of 289-cards including 12-Legends serial numbered to 2499, 63-rookies numbered to 1299, 35-rookies numbered to 999, and 20-rookies numbered to 499. Additionally, 59-rookies were issued as autograph cards serial numbered between 125 and 699. Hobby boxes contained 12-packs of 4-cards and carried an S.R.P. of $9.99 per pack. Two parallel sets and a variety of autographed and jersey memorabilia inserts can be found seeded in packs.

COMP.SET w/o SP's (100) 15.00 30.00
176-210 ROOKIE PRINT RUN 999
211-230 ROOKIE PRINT RUN 499
1 Anquan Boldin .30 .75
2 Emmitt Smith .75 2.00
3 Josh McCown .40 1.00
4 Michael Vick .40 1.00
5 Warrick Dunn .30 .75
6 Peerless Price .30 .75
7 Jamal Lewis .40 1.00
8 Deion Sanders .40 1.00
9 Kyle Boller .30 .75
10 Drew Bledsoe .40 1.00
11 Travis Henry .30 .75
12 Eric Moulds .30 .75
13 Jake Delhomme .30 .75
14 Stephen Davis .30 .75
15 Julius Peppers .40 1.00
16 Thomas Jones .30 .75
17 Rex Grossman .30 .75
18 Brian Urlacher .50 1.25
19 Carson Palmer .40 1.00
20 Chad Johnson .30 .75
21 Rudi Johnson .30 .75
22 Jeff Garcia .30 .75
23 William Green .30 .75
24 Andre Davis .30 .75
25 Vinny Testaverde .30 .75
26 Eddie George .40 1.00
27 Keyshawn Johnson .40 1.00
28 Reuben Droughns .40 1.00
29 Jake Plummer .30 .75
30 Ashley Lelie .30 .75
31 Rod Smith .40 1.00
32 Joey Harrington .30 .75
33 Artose Pinner .30 .75
34 Az-Zahir Hakim .30 .75
35 Brett Favre 1.00 2.50
36 Javon Walker .30 .75
37 Ahman Green .40 1.00
38 Andre Johnson .40 1.00
39 David Carr .30 .75
40 Domanick Davis .30 .75
41 Peyton Manning 1.25 3.00
42 Edgerrin James .40 1.00
43 Marvin Harrison .40 1.00
44 Byron Leftwich .30 .75
45 Fred Taylor .30 .75
46 Jimmy Smith .40 1.00
47 Priest Holmes .30 .75
48 Trent Green .30 .75
49 Dante Hall .30 .75
50 Tony Gonzalez .40 1.00
51 Randy McMichael .30 .75
52 Jay Fiedler .30 .75
53 Chris Chambers .30 .75
54 Randy Moss .40 1.00
55 Daunte Culpepper .40 1.00
56 Onterrio Smith .30 .75
57 Tom Brady 2.00 5.00
58 Deion Branch .30 .75
59 Corey Dillon .30 .75
60 Deuce McAllister .40 1.00
61 Aaron Brooks .30 .75
62 Joe Horn .30 .75
63 Jeremy Shockey .30 .75
64 Tiki Barber .40 1.00
65 Michael Strahan .40 1.00
66 Curtis Martin .40 1.00
67 Chad Pennington .30 .75
68 Santana Moss .40 1.00
69 Charles Woodson .50 1.25
70 Kerry Collins .30 .75
71 Warren Sapp .40 1.00
72 Donovan McNabb .40 1.00
73 Brian Westbrook .30 .75
74 Terrell Owens .40 1.00
75 Hines Ward .40 1.00
76 Plaxico Burress .30 .75
77 Duce Staley .30 .75
78 LaDainian Tomlinson .50 1.25
79 Antonio Gates .50 1.25
80 Drew Brees .50 1.25
81 Eric Johnson .30 .75
82 Kevan Barlow .30 .75
83 Tim Rattay .30 .75
84 Matt Hasselbeck .30 .75
85 Shaun Alexander .30 .75
86 Jerry Rice 1.00 2.50
87 Marc Bulger .30 .75
88 Torry Holt .40 1.00
89 Marshall Faulk .40 1.00
90 Isaac Bruce .50 1.25
91 Brad Johnson .40 1.00
92 Derrick Brooks .30 .75
93 Joey Galloway .40 1.00
94 Steve McNair .40 1.00
95 Derrick Mason .30 .75
96 Chris Brown .30 .75
97 Clinton Portis .30 .75
98 Mark Brunell .40 1.00
99 Laveranues Coles .30 .75
100 LaVar Arrington .30 .75
101 Roger Staubach 2.00 5.00
102 Troy Aikman 2.00 5.00
103 John Elway 2.50 6.00
104 Barry Sanders 4.00 10.00
105 Fran Tarkenton 1.50 4.00
106 Archie Manning 1.25 3.00
107 Joe Namath 2.50 6.00
108 Ken Stabler 2.00 5.00
109 Howie Long 1.50 4.00
110 Kellen Winslow Sr. 1.50 4.00
111 Joe Montana 5.00 12.00
112 Joe Theismann 1.50 4.00
113 Darnell Dockett RC 3.00 8.00
114 Randy Starks RC 2.00 5.00
115 Rashad Baker RC 2.50 6.00
116 Tim Anderson RC 2.50 6.00
117 Darrion Scott RC 2.50 6.00
118 Courtney Watson RC 2.00 5.00
119 Gilbert Gardner RC 2.00 5.00
120 Marquis Cooper RC 2.00 5.00
121 Caleb Miller RC 2.00 5.00
122 Jeff Shoate RC 2.00 5.00
123 Keyaron Fox RC 2.50 6.00
124 Landon Johnson RC 2.00 5.00
125 Reggie Torbor RC 2.00 5.00
126 Demorrio Williams RC 3.00 8.00
127 Niko Koutouvides RC 2.00 5.00
128 Richard Seigler RC 2.00 5.00
129 Brandon Chillar RC 2.50 6.00
130 Nate Kaeding RC 2.50 6.00
131 Dave Ball RC 2.50 6.00
132 Josh Thomas RC 2.00 5.00
133 Josh Scobee RC 2.50 6.00
134 Wes Welker RC 10.00 25.00
135 Darrell McClover RC 2.00 5.00
136 Ben Utecht RC 2.50 6.00
137 Chris Snee RC 4.00 10.00
138 Jake Grove RC 2.00 5.00
139 Justin Smiley RC 2.50 6.00
140 Max Starks RC 2.50 6.00
141 Randall Gay RC 3.00 8.00
142 Charlie Anderson RC 2.00 5.00
143 Alain Kashama RC 2.00 5.00
144 Eric Edwards RC 2.00 5.00
145 Jacques Reeves RC 2.50 6.00
146 Jarrett Payton RC 2.50 6.00
147 Curtis Deloatch RC 2.00 5.00
148 Michael Gaines RC 2.00 5.00
149 Erik Jensen RC 2.00 5.00
150 Courtney Anderson RC 2.00 5.00
151 Bruce Thornton RC 2.00 5.00
152 Glenn Earl RC 2.00 5.00
153 Michael Waddell RC 2.00 5.00
154 J.R. Reed RC 2.00 5.00
155 Dwight Anderson RC 2.50 6.00
156 Von Hutchins RC 2.00 5.00
157 Travis LaBoy RC 2.50 6.00
158 Terry Johnson RC 2.00 5.00
159 Dwan Edwards RC 2.00 5.00
160 Colby Bockwoldt RC 2.00 5.00
161 Madieu Williams RC 2.00 5.00
162 Will Poole RC 3.00 8.00
163 Igor Olshansky RC 2.50 6.00
164 Michael Boulware RC 3.00 8.00
165 Shaun Phillips RC 2.50 6.00
166 Keith Smith RC 2.00 5.00
167 Will Smith RC 2.50 6.00
168 D.J. Williams RC 3.00 8.00
169 Derrick Strait RC 2.00 5.00
170 Karlos Dansby RC 2.50 6.00
171 Ricardo Colclough RC 2.00 5.00
172 Chad Lavalais RC 2.00 5.00
173 Teddy Lehman RC 2.00 5.00
174 Jim Sorgi RC 2.50 6.00
175 Bob Sanders RC 4.00 10.00
176 Sean Taylor RC 15.00 40.00
177 Marcus Tubbs RC 2.50 6.00
178 Daryl Smith RC 2.50 6.00
179 Bradlee Van Pelt RC 3.00 8.00
180 Shawntae Spencer RC 2.50 6.00
181 Nathan Vasher RC 4.00 10.00
182 Jared Allen RC 15.00 30.00
183 Rod Davis RC 2.50 6.00
184 Brian Jones RC 2.50 6.00
185 Will Allen RC 3.00 8.00
186 Antwan Odom RC 2.50 6.00
187 Vernon Carey RC 2.50 6.00
188 Mike Karney RC 3.00 8.00
189 Joey Thomas RC 2.50 6.00
190 Casey Bramlet RC 2.50 6.00
191 Keiwan Ratliff RC 2.50 6.00
192 Rich Gardner RC 3.00 8.00
193 Jason Babin RC 4.00 10.00
194 Dontarrious Thomas RC 3.00 8.00
195 Dexter Reid RC 2.50 6.00
196 Marquise Hill RC 2.50 6.00
197 Jonathan Smith RC 2.50 6.00
198 Larry Croom RC 2.50 6.00
199 Gibril Wilson RC 4.00 10.00
200 Erik Coleman RC 3.00 8.00
201 B.J. Sams RC 2.50 6.00
202 Bruce Perry RC 2.50 6.00
203 Brock Lesnar RC 20.00 40.00
204 Brandon Miree RC 2.50 6.00
205 Clarence Moore RC 2.50 6.00
206 Mark Jones RC 2.50 6.00
207 Patrick Crayton RC 4.00 10.00
208 Jeff Dugan RC 2.50 6.00
209 Sean Ryan RC 2.50 6.00
210 Sloan Thomas RC 3.00 8.00
211 Triandos Luke RC 3.00 8.00
212 Dexter Wynn RC 3.00 8.00
213 Matt Kranchick RC 4.00 10.00
214 Tim Euhus RC 3.00 8.00
215 Ryan Krause RC 3.00 8.00
216 Junior Siavii RC 3.00 8.00
217 Ran Carthon RC 3.00 8.00
218 Derrick Pope RC 4.00 10.00
219 Alex Lewis RC 3.00 8.00
220 Chris Cooley RC 4.00 10.00
221 Jamaar Taylor RC 3.00 8.00
222 Stuart Schweigert RC 4.00 10.00
223 Jason David RC 3.00 8.00
224 Maurice Mann RC 3.00 8.00
225 Robert Geathers RC 3.00 8.00
226 Matt Mauck RC 3.00 8.00
227 Jammal Lord RC 3.00 8.00
228 Travelle Wharton RC 3.00 8.00
229 D.J. Hackett RC 3.00 8.00
230 Thomas Tapeh RC 4.00 10.00
232 Ahmad Carroll AU/699 RC 6.00 15.00
233 Kenechi Udeze AU/699 RC 8.00 20.00
234 Tommie Harris AU/699 RC 8.00 20.00
235 Jonathan Vilma AU/699 RC 8.00 20.00
236 Vince Wilfork AU/699 RC 10.00 25.00
237 B.J. Symons AU/699 RC 6.00 15.00
238 B.J. Johnson AU/699 RC 6.00 15.00
239 Kris Wilson AU/699 RC 8.00 20.00
240 Josh Harris AU/699 RC 6.00 15.00
241 Troy Fleming AU/699 RC 6.00 15.00
242 J.Morant AU/699 RC 6.00 15.00
243 Craig Krenzel AU/699 RC 6.00 15.00
244 Q.Wilson AU/699 RC 6.00 15.00
245 P.K. Sam AU/699 RC 6.00 15.00
246 Michael Turner AU/699 RC 6.00 15.00
247 Carlos Francis AU/699 RC 6.00 15.00
248 Jared Lorenzen AU/699 RC 8.00 20.00
249 John Navarre AU/675 RC 6.00 15.00
250 Jeff Smoker AU/699 RC 8.00 20.00
251 Ernest Wilford AU/559 RC 8.00 20.00
252 M.Moore AU/699 RC 8.00 20.00
253 Chris Gamble AU/699 RC 6.00 15.00
254 Jerricho Cotchery AU/699 RC 8.00 20.00
255 Derrick Hamilton AU/699 RC 6.00 15.00
256 Samie Parker AU/699 RC 6.00 15.00
257 Cody Pickett AU/699 RC 6.00 15.00
259 Ben Hartsock AU/699 RC 6.00 15.00
260 Cedric Cobbs AU/699 RC 6.00 15.00
261 Matt Schaub AU/699 RC 6.00 15.00
262 Bernard Berrian AU/699 RC 6.00 15.00
263 Devard Darling AU/699 RC 6.00 15.00
264 Ben Watson AU/699 RC 8.00 20.00
265 Darius Watts AU/699 RC 6.00 15.00
266 DeAngelo Hall AU/399 RC 12.00 30.00
267 Ben Troupe AU/699 RC 6.00 15.00
268 Michael Jenkins AU/399 RC 8.00 20.00
269 Keary Colbert AU/699 RC 6.00 15.00
270 Robert Gallery AU/699 RC 8.00 20.00
271 Greg Jones AU/650 RC 6.00 15.00
272 Mic.Clayton AU/699 RC 8.00 20.00
273 Luke McCown AU/699 RC 6.00 15.00
274 R.Woods AU/699 RC 6.00 15.00
275 Reg.Williams AU/699 RC 6.00 15.00
276 D.Henderson AU/699 RC 6.00 15.00
277 Tatum Bell AU/699 RC 6.00 15.00
278 Lee Evans AU/350 RC 12.00 30.00
279 J.P. Losman AU/199 RC 10.00 25.00
280 Drew Henson AU/199 RC 10.00 25.00
281 K.Winslow AU/125 RC 10.00 25.00
282 Chris Perry AU/199 RC 10.00 25.00
283 Julius Jones AU/199 RC 10.00 25.00
284 S.Jackson AU/199 RC 15.00 40.00
285 Kevin Jones AU/199 RC 12.00 30.00
286 Roy Williams AU/149 RC 10.00 25.00
287 Roethlisbrgr AU/199 RC 75.00 150.00
288 Philip Rivers AU/199 RC 100.00 200.00
289 L.Fitzgerald AU/150 RC 40.00 100.00
290 Eli Manning AU/150 RC 60.00 125.00

2004 Sweet Spot Gold

*VETS: 4X TO 10X BASIC CARDS
*LEGENDS: 1X TO 2.5X BASIC CARDS
*ROOKIES 113-175: 1X TO 2.5X
*ROOKIES 176-210: .8X TO 2X
*ROOKIES 211-230: .6X TO 1.5X
STATED PRINT RUN 50 SER.#'d SETS

2004 Sweet Spot Silver

*VETS: 2.5X TO 6X BASIC CARDS
*LEGENDS: .6X TO 1.5X BASIC CARDS
*ROOKIES 113-175: .6X TO 1.5X
*ROOKIES 176-210: .5X TO 1.2X
*ROOKIES 211-230: .4X TO 1X BASE CARD HI
STATED PRINT RUN 100 SER.#'d SETS

2004 Sweet Spot Gold Rookie Autographs

STATED PRINT RUN 35-100
232 Ahmad Carroll 8.00 20.00
233 Kenechi Udeze 10.00 25.00
234 Tommie Harris 10.00 25.00
235 Jonathan Vilma 10.00 25.00
236 Vince Wilfork 12.00 30.00
237 B.J. Symons 8.00 20.00
238 B.J. Johnson 8.00 20.00
239 Kris Wilson 10.00 25.00
240 Josh Harris 8.00 20.00
241 Troy Fleming 8.00 20.00
242 Johnnie Morant 8.00 20.00
243 Craig Krenzel 8.00 20.00
244 Quincy Wilson 8.00 20.00
245 P.K. Sam 8.00 20.00
246 Michael Turner 8.00 20.00
247 Carlos Francis 8.00 20.00
248 Jared Lorenzen 10.00 25.00
249 John Navarre 8.00 20.00
250 Jeff Smoker 10.00 25.00
251 Ernest Wilford 10.00 25.00
252 Mewelde Moore 10.00 25.00
253 Chris Gamble 8.00 20.00
254 Jerricho Cotchery 10.00 25.00
255 Derrick Hamilton 8.00 20.00
256 Samie Parker 8.00 20.00
257 Cody Pickett 8.00 20.00
259 Ben Hartsock 8.00 20.00
260 Cedric Cobbs 8.00 20.00
261 Matt Schaub 8.00 20.00
262 Bernard Berrian 8.00 20.00
263 Devard Darling 8.00 20.00
264 Ben Watson 10.00 25.00
265 Darius Watts 8.00 20.00
266 DeAngelo Hall 12.00 30.00
267 Ben Troupe 8.00 20.00
268 Michael Jenkins 8.00 20.00
269 Keary Colbert 8.00 20.00
270 Robert Gallery 10.00 25.00
271 Greg Jones 8.00 20.00
272 Michael Clayton 10.00 25.00
273 Luke McCown 8.00 20.00
274 Rashaun Woods 8.00 20.00
275 Reggie Williams 8.00 20.00
276 Devery Henderson 8.00 20.00
277 Tatum Bell 8.00 20.00
278 Lee Evans 12.00 30.00
279 J.P. Losman 8.00 20.00
280 Drew Henson 8.00 20.00
281 Kellen Winslow/50 8.00 20.00
282 Chris Perry 8.00 20.00
283 Julius Jones 8.00 20.00
284 Steven Jackson 12.00 30.00
285 Kevin Jones 10.00 25.00
286 Roy Williams WR 8.00 20.00
287 Ben Roethlisberger 75.00 150.00
288 Philip Rivers 75.00 150.00
289 Larry Fitzgerald/35 60.00 150.00
290 Eli Manning/50 75.00 150.00

2004 Sweet Spot Signatures

STATED ODDS 1:24
*GOLD/100: .5X TO 1.2X BASIC AU
*GOLD/100: .4X TO 1X BASIC AU SP
GOLD PRINT RUN 100 SER.#'d SETS
SSAG Ahman Green 12.00 30.00
SSAP Alan Page 10.00 25.00
SSBF Brett Favre 125.00 250.00
SSBG Bob Griese 15.00 40.00
SSBP Bill Parcells 25.00 60.00
SSBS Barry Sanders SP 75.00 150.00
SSBW Brian Westbrook 10.00 25.00
SSCB Chris Brown 10.00 25.00
SSCH Charlie Joiner 10.00 25.00
SSCJ Chad Johnson 12.00 30.00
SSCP Chad Pennington 10.00 25.00
SSDA Dave Casper 10.00 25.00
SSDD Domanick Davis 10.00 25.00
SSDF Dan Fouts 20.00 50.00
SSDM Donovan McNabb 12.00 30.00
SSDP Drew Pearson 12.00 30.00
SSFT Fran Tarkenton 25.00 60.00
SSHL Howie Long 25.00 50.00
SSJA Jack Ham 15.00 40.00
SSJE John Elway SP 75.00 150.00
SSJG Jon Gruden 12.00 30.00
SSJJ Jimmy Johnson 15.00 40.00
SSJN Joe Namath SP 75.00 150.00
SSJO Joe Montana SP 100.00 200.00
SSJT Joe Theismann SP 25.00 50.00
SSKA Ken Anderson 8.00 20.00
SSKE Kellen Winslow Sr. 15.00 40.00
SSKS Ken Stabler 25.00 60.00
SSLD Len Dawson 15.00 40.00
SSLT LaDainian Tomlinson 25.00 60.00
SSMA Dan Marino SP 100.00 200.00
SSMC Mark Clayton 10.00 25.00
SSMV Michael Vick SP 15.00 40.00
SSPH Paul Hornung SP 20.00 50.00
SSPM Peyton Manning SP 75.00 125.00
SSRG Rex Grossman 8.00 20.00
SSRJ Rudi Johnson 10.00 25.00
SSRO Roy Williams S 10.00 25.00
SSRS Roger Staubach SP 75.00 150.00
SSRW Randy White 12.00 30.00
SSTA Troy Aikman 40.00 100.00

2004 Sweet Spot Sweet Panel Signatures

STATED PRINT RUN 80-100
*GOLD/25: .6X TO 1.5X BASIC AU
GOLD PRINT RUN 25 SER.#'d SETS
SPBL Byron Leftwich 10.00 25.00
SPBR Ben Roethlisberger 75.00 135.00
SPBS Bart Starr/80 75.00 150.00
SPCH Chris Perry 10.00 25.00
SPCP Chad Pennington 10.00 25.00
SPDD Domanick Davis 10.00 25.00
SPEM Eli Manning 90.00 150.00
SPFT Fran Tarkenton 20.00 50.00
SPHL Howie Long 30.00 60.00
SPJP J.P. Losman 10.00 25.00
SPJT Joe Theismann 15.00 40.00
SPKJ Kevin Jones 12.00 30.00
SPKW Kellen Winslow Jr. 10.00 25.00
SPMV Michael Vick 25.00 60.00
SPPH Paul Hornung 25.00 60.00
SPPM Peyton Manning 60.00 120.00
SPPR Philip Rivers 75.00 150.00
SPRJ Rudi Johnson 10.00 25.00
SPRO Roman Gabriel 10.00 25.00
SPTA Tatum Bell 10.00 25.00
SPZT Zach Thomas 12.00 30.00

2004 Sweet Spot Sweet Swatches

STATED ODDS 1:12
SWBR Ben Roethlisberger 12.00 30.00
SWBT Ben Troupe 2.00 5.00
SWBW Ben Watson 2.50 6.00
SWCC Cedric Cobbs 2.00 5.00
SWCP Chris Perry 2.00 5.00
SWDD Devard Darling 2.00 5.00
SWDE Devery Henderson 2.00 5.00
SWDH DeAngelo Hall 3.00 8.00
SWDW Darius Watts 2.00 5.00
SWEM Eli Manning 8.00 20.00
SWGJ Greg Jones 2.00 5.00
SWHA Derrick Hamilton 2.00 5.00
SWJJ Julius Jones 2.00 5.00
SWJP J.P. Losman 2.00 5.00
SWKC Keary Colbert 2.00 5.00
SWKJ Kevin Jones SP 2.50 6.00
SWKW Kellen Winslow Jr. 2.00 5.00
SWLE Lee Evans 3.00 8.00
SWLF Larry Fitzgerald 8.00 20.00
SWLM Luke McCown 2.00 5.00
SWMC Michael Clayton 2.50 6.00
SWMJ Michael Jenkins 2.00 5.00
SWMS Matt Schaub 2.00 5.00
SWPR Philip Rivers 8.00 20.00
SWRA Rashaun Woods 2.00 5.00
SWRG Robert Gallery 2.50 6.00
SWRO Roy Williams WR 2.00 5.00
SWRW Reggie Williams SP 2.00 5.00
SWSJ Steven Jackson 3.00 8.00
SWTB Tatum Bell 2.00 5.00

2005 Sweet Spot

This 302-card set was released in December, 2005. The set was issued in the hobby through four-card packs with an $9.99 SRP which came 12 packs to a box. Cards numbered 1-99 feature veterans in sequential order by team while the rest of the set features rookies. Cards numbered 243-284 were all signed by the player and those cards have stated print runs between 175 and 650 serial numbered sets. The other rookies have the following print runs: Cards numbered 101-142 was issued to a stated print run of 899 serial numbered sets while cards numbered 143-182 were issued to a stated print run of 699 serial nuimbered sets, cards numbered 183-222 was issued to a stated print run of 499 serial numbered sets, cards numbered 223-242 was issued to a stated print run of 299 serial numbered sets and cards numbered 285-302 were issued to a stated print run of 899 serial numbered sets. Some players did not return their signatures in time for pack out and those cards could be redeemed until December 9, 2008.

COMP.SET w/o RCs (100) 15.00 30.00
101-142 PRINT RUN 899 SER.#'d SETS
143-182 PRINT RUN 699 SER.#'d SETS
183-222 PRINT RUN 499 SER.#'d SETS
223-242 PRINT RUN 299 SER.#'d SETS
285-302 PRINT RUN 899 SER.#'d SETS
1 Larry Fitzgerald .40 1.00
2 Anquan Boldin .25 .60
3 Kurt Warner .30 .75
4 Michael Vick .30 .75
5 T.J. Duckett .25 .60
6 Peerless Price .25 .60
7 Todd Heap .25 .60
8 Jamal Lewis .30 .75
9 Kyle Boller .25 .60
10 Derrick Mason .25 .60
11 J.P. Losman .25 .60
12 Willis McGahee .25 .60
13 Lee Evans .30 .75
14 Eric Moulds .25 .60
15 Jake Delhomme .25 .60
16 Keary Colbert .25 .60
17 DeShaun Foster .30 .75
18 Brian Urlacher .40 1.00
19 Rex Grossman .25 .60
20 Muhsin Muhammad .25 .60
21 Carson Palmer .30 .75
22 Rudi Johnson .25 .60
23 Chad Johnson .25 .60
24 Julius Jones .25 .60
25 Keyshawn Johnson .30 .75
26 Drew Bledsoe .30 .75
27 Tatum Bell .25 .60
28 Jake Plummer .25 .60
29 Ashley Lelie .25 .60
30 Roy Williams WR .25 .60
31 Kevin Jones .25 .60
32 Joey Harrington .25 .60
33 Brett Favre .75 2.00
34 Ahman Green .30 .75
35 Javon Walker .25 .60
36 David Carr .25 .60
37 Andre Johnson .30 .75
38 Domanick Davis .25 .60
39 Peyton Manning 1.00 2.50
40 Reggie Wayne .30 .75
41 Edgerrin James .30 .75
42 Marvin Harrison .30 .75
43 Byron Leftwich .25 .60
44 Fred Taylor .25 .60
45 Jimmy Smith .30 .75
46 Priest Holmes .25 .60
47 Tony Gonzalez .30 .75
48 Trent Green .25 .60
49 A.J. Feeley .25 .60
50 Chris Chambers .25 .60
51 Randy McMichael .25 .60
52 Daunte Culpepper .30 .75
53 Michael Bennett .25 .60
54 Nate Burleson .25 .60
55 Tom Brady 1.50 4.00
56 Corey Dillon .25 .60
57 Deion Branch .25 .60
58 Richard Seymour .25 .60
59 Aaron Brooks .25 .60
60 Deuce McAllister .30 .75
61 Joe Horn .25 .60
62 Eli Manning .60 1.50
63 Jeremy Shockey .25 .60
64 Tiki Barber .30 .75
65 Chad Pennington .25 .60
66 Curtis Martin .30 .75
67 Laveranues Coles .25 .60
68 Kerry Collins .25 .60
69 LaMont Jordan .30 .75
70 Randy Moss .30 .75
71 Donovan McNabb .30 .75
72 Terrell Owens .30 .75
73 Jeremiah Trotter .25 .60
74 Brian Westbrook .25 .60
75 Ben Roethlisberger .60 1.50
76 Willie Parker .30 .75
77 Hines Ward .30 .75
78 Antwaan Randle El .25 .60
79 Drew Brees .40 1.00
80 LaDainian Tomlinson .40 1.00
81 Antonio Gates .40 1.00
82 Tim Rattay .25 .60
83 Brandon Lloyd .25 .60
84 Eric Johnson .25 .60
85 Shaun Alexander .25 .60
86 Darrell Jackson .25 .60
87 Matt Hasselbeck .25 .60
88 Marc Bulger .25 .60
89 Steven Jackson .25 .60
90 Marshall Faulk .30 .75
91 Torry Holt .30 .75
92 Joey Galloway .30 .75
93 Brian Griese .25 .60
94 Michael Clayton .25 .60
95 Steve McNair .30 .75
96 Drew Bennett .30 .75
97 Chris Brown .25 .60
98 Clinton Portis .25 .60
99 Patrick Ramsey .30 .75
100 Santana Moss .30 .75
101 Antonio Perkins RC 2.00 5.00
102 James Sanders RC 1.50 4.00
103 Justin Green RC 2.50 6.00
104 Andre Maddox RC 1.50 4.00
105 C.C. Brown RC 1.50 4.00
106 Michael Hawkins RC 1.50 4.00
107 Deandra Cobb RC 1.50 4.00
108 Nehemiah Broughton RC 2.00 5.00
109 Madison Hedgecock RC 2.50 6.00
110 Paris Warren RC 2.00 5.00
111 Chris Harris RC 1.50 4.00
112 Matt Cassel RC 1.50 4.00
113 Justin Beriault RC 1.50 4.00
114 Roydell Williams RC 2.00 5.00
115 Alex Barron RC 1.50 4.00
116 Jammal Brown RC 2.50 6.00
117 Bo Scaife RC 2.00 5.00
118 Patrick Estes RC 1.50 4.00

119 Elton Brown RC 1.50 4.00
120 Rasheed Marshall RC 2.00 5.00
121 Jovan Haye RC 1.50 4.00
122 Nick Collins RC 2.50 6.00
123 Travis Daniels RC 2.00 5.00
124 Reynaldo Hill RC 2.00 5.00
125 Billy Bajema RC 1.50 4.00
126 Jim Leonhard RC 2.00 5.00
127 Boomer Grigsby RC 2.50 6.00
128 Chauncey Davis RC 1.50 4.00
129 David McMillan RC 2.50 6.00
130 Alfred Fincher RC 2.00 5.00
131 Kelvin Hayden RC 2.00 5.00
132 Kevin Burnett RC 2.00 5.00
133 Jonathan Welsh RC 1.50 4.00
134 Stanley Wilson RC 2.00 5.00
135 Stanford Routt RC 2.00 5.00
136 Kerry Rhodes RC 2.00 5.00
137 Ellis Hobbs RC 2.50 6.00
138 Darrent Williams RC 2.50 6.00
139 Eric King RC 1.50 4.00
140 Domonique Foxworth RC 2.00 5.00
141 Anthony Bryant RC 2.00 5.00
142 Scott Starks RC 2.00 5.00
143 Marviel Underwood RC 2.00 5.00
144 Mike Montgomery RC 2.50 6.00
145 Kevin Vickerson RC 2.50 6.00
146 Jerome Carter RC 1.50 4.00
147 Jay Ratliff RC 6.00 15.00
148 Damien Nash RC 2.00 5.00
149 Noah Herron RC 1.50 4.00
150 Jonathan Fanene RC 2.50 6.00
151 Chase Lyman RC 1.50 4.00
152 Adam Seward RC 2.00 5.00
153 Michael Boley RC 2.50 6.00
154 Pat Thomas RC 1.50 4.00
155 Evan Mathis RC 1.50 4.00
156 Derrick Johnson CB RC 1.50 4.00
157 Tab Perry RC 1.50 4.00
158 Joel Dreessen RC 2.00 5.00
159 Daven Holly RC 1.50 4.00
160 Brandon Jones RC 2.00 5.00
161 Dan Buenning RC 2.50 6.00
162 Kurt Campbell RC 1.50 4.00
163 Kerry Wright RC 2.00 5.00
164 Matt McCoy RC 2.00 5.00
165 Dave Rayner RC 1.50 4.00
166 Kirk Morrison RC 2.50 6.00
167 Lofa Tatupu RC 2.00 5.00
168 Bryant McFadden RC 2.00 5.00
169 Corey Webster RC 2.00 5.00
170 Eric Green RC 1.50 4.00
171 Fabian Washington RC 1.50 4.00
172 Donte Nicholson RC 1.50 4.00
173 Vonta Leach RC 2.00 5.00
174 Ronald Bartell RC 2.00 5.00
175 Sean Considine RC 1.50 4.00
176 Oshiomogho Atogwe RC 2.00 5.00
177 Ryan Grant RC 8.00 20.00
178 James Butler RC 2.00 5.00
179 Paul Ernster RC 1.50 4.00
180 Duke Preston RC 2.00 5.00
181 Mike Nugent RC 2.00 5.00
182 Sione Pouha RC 1.50 4.00
183 Geoff Hangartner RC 3.00 8.00
184 Justin Geisinger RC 3.00 8.00
185 Chris Kemoeatu RC 3.00 8.00
186 Ryan Fitzpatrick RC 3.00 8.00
187 Lionel Gates RC 2.00 5.00
188 Brandon Jacobs RC 2.50 6.00
189 Alvin Pearman RC 2.00 5.00
190 J.R. Russell RC 2.00 5.00
191 Manuel White RC 2.50 6.00
192 Tyson Thompson RC 2.00 5.00
193 Chad Owens RC 2.00 5.00
194 Dante Ridgeway RC 2.00 5.00
195 Stephen Spach RC 2.00 5.00
196 Scott Mruczkowski RC 3.00 8.00
197 Chris Carr RC 2.00 5.00
198 Jonathan Babineaux RC 2.00 5.00
199 Will Whitticker RC 3.00 8.00
200 Luis Castillo RC 2.50 6.00
201 Matt Roth RC 2.00 5.00
202 Shaun Cody RC 2.50 6.00
203 Justin Tuck RC 2.50 6.00
204 Vincent Burns RC 2.00 5.00
205 DeMarcus Ware RC 6.00 15.00
206 Bill Swancutt RC 2.00 5.00
207 Darryl Blackstock RC 2.00 5.00
208 Brady Poppinga RC 3.00 8.00
209 Leroy Hill RC 3.00 8.00
210 Ryan Claridge RC 2.00 5.00
211 Odell Thurman RC 3.00 8.00
212 Barrett Ruud RC 2.50 6.00
213 Lance Mitchell RC 2.50 6.00
214 Trent Cole RC 3.00 8.00
215 Jerome Mathis RC 3.00 8.00
216 Brandon Browner RC 3.00 8.00
217 Justin Miller RC 2.00 5.00
218 Thomas Davis RC 2.00 5.00
219 Brodney Pool RC 2.50 6.00
220 Dylan Gandy RC 2.00 5.00
221 Josh Bullocks RC 2.50 6.00
222 Vincent Fuller RC 2.50 6.00
223 Jordan Beck RC 2.50 6.00
224 Claude Terrell RC 3.00 8.00
225 Adrian McPherson RC 2.00 5.00
226 Jerome Collins RC 2.50 6.00
227 Cedric Houston RC 3.00 8.00
228 Daniel Loper RC 3.00 8.00
229 Adam Bergen RC 2.00 5.00
230 Jeb Huckeba RC 2.50 6.00
231 Eric Moore RC 2.00 5.00
232 Dan Cody RC 2.00 5.00
233 Alex Smith TE RC 2.00 5.00
234 Travis Johnson RC 2.00 5.00
235 Ryan Riddle RC 2.00 5.00
236 Mike Patterson RC 2.00 5.00
237 Darrell Shropshire RC 2.00 5.00
238 David Pollack RC 2.00 5.00
239 Marcus Spears RC 2.00 5.00
240 Shawne Merriman RC 3.00 8.00
241 Channing Crowder RC 2.50 6.00
242 Derrick Johnson RC 2.50 6.00
243 Kyle Orton AU/199 RC 15.00 40.00
244 David Greene AU/650 RC 5.00 12.00
245 Derek Anderson AU/650 RC 6.00 15.00
246 Dan Orlovsky AU/650 RC 5.00 12.00
247 Eric Shelton AU/650 RC 5.00 12.00
248 Stefan LeFors AU/650 RC 5.00 12.00
249 Reggie Brown AU/650 RC 5.00 12.00
250 Andrew Walter AU/650 RC 5.00 12.00
251 Mark Bradley AU/650 RC 5.00 12.00
252 Courtney Roby AU/650 RC 5.00 12.00
253 Vincent Jackson AU/650 RC 8.00 20.00
254 Terrence Murphy AU/650 RC 5.00 12.00
255 Marion Barber AU/650 RC 5.00 12.00
256 Frank Gore AU/650 RC 10.00 25.00
257 Chris Henry AU/650 RC 6.00 15.00
258 Heath Miller AU/650 RC 12.00 30.00
259 J.J.Arrington AU/650 RC 6.00 15.00
260 Antrell Rolle AU/650 RC 8.00 20.00
261 Fred Gibson AU/650 RC 5.00 12.00
262 Charlie Frye AU/650 RC 5.00 12.00
263 Adam Jones AU/650 RC 5.00 12.00
264 Ciatrick Fason AU/650 RC 5.00 12.00
265 Roscoe Parrish AU/650 RC 5.00 12.00
266 Erasmus James AU/650 RC 5.00 12.00
267 Carlos Rogers AU/650 RC 8.00 20.00
268 Ryan Moats AU/650 RC 5.00 12.00
269 Marlin Jackson AU/650 RC 5.00 12.00
270 Darren Sproles AU/650 RC 8.00 20.00
271 Maurice Clarett AU/199 RC 6.00 15.00
272 Jason Campbell AU/199 RC 6.00 15.00
273 Vernand Morency AU/199 RC 6.00 15.00
274 M.Clayton AU/199 RC EX 6.00 15.00
275 Roddy White AU/650 RC 8.00 20.00
276 Williamson AU/199 RC 6.00 15.00
277 M.Williams AU/199 EXCH 8.00 20.00
278 B.Edwards AU/199 RC 6.00 15.00
279 Cedric Benson AU/199 RC 6.00 15.00
280 Cadillac Williams AU/199 RC 6.00 15.00
281 Ronnie Brown AU/199 RC 8.00 20.00
282 Matt Jones AU/199 RC 6.00 15.00
283 Alex Smith QB AU/175 RC 30.00 80.00
284 Aaron Rodgers AU/199 RC 175.00 300.00
285 Rian Wallace RC 2.00 5.00
286 Nick Speegle RC 1.50 4.00
287 Chris Spencer RC 2.50 6.00
288 Logan Mankins RC 2.50 6.00
289 David Baas RC 1.50 4.00
290 Michael Roos RC 1.50 4.00
291 Khalif Barnes RC 1.50 4.00
292 Matt Giordano RC 2.00 5.00
293 Rick Razzano RC 1.50 4.00
294 Trai Essex RC 2.50 6.00
295 Roy Manning RC 2.50 6.00
296 Gerald Sensabaugh RC 2.50 6.00
297 Nick Kaczur RC 3.00 8.00
298 Ray Willis RC 1.50 4.00
299 Jason Brown RC 2.00 5.00
300 Frank Omiyale RC 1.50 4.00
301 Fred Amey RC 1.50 4.00
302 Reggie Hodges RC 1.50 4.00

2005 Sweet Spot Gold Rookie Autographs

*SINGLES: .5X TO 1.2X BASIC AUTO/650
*SINGLES: .4X TO 1X BASIC AUTO/175/199
STATED PRINT RUN 100 SER.#'d SETS
284 Aaron Rodgers 200.00 400.00

2005 Sweet Spot Rookie Sweet Swatches

STATED ODDS 1:12
SRAJ Adam Jones 1.50 4.00
SRAN Antrel Rolle 2.50 6.00
SRAR Aaron Rodgers 20.00 50.00
SRAS Alex Smith QB 6.00 15.00
SRAW Andrew Walter 1.50 4.00
SRBE Braylon Edwards 1.50 4.00
SRCB Cedric Benson 1.50 4.00
SRCF Charlie Frye 1.50 4.00
SRCI Ciatrick Fason 1.50 4.00
SRCR Carlos Rogers 2.50 6.00
SRCW Cadillac Williams 1.50 4.00
SRES Eric Shelton 1.50 4.00
SRFG Frank Gore 3.00 8.00
SRJA J.J. Arrington 2.00 5.00
SRJC Jason Campbell 1.50 4.00
SRKO Kyle Orton 1.50 4.00
SRMB Mark Bradley 1.50 4.00
SRMC Mark Clayton 1.50 4.00
SRMJ Matt Jones 1.50 4.00
SRMO Maurice Clarett 1.50 4.00
SRMW Mike Williams 2.00 5.00
SRRB Ronnie Brown 2.00 5.00
SRRE Reggie Brown 1.50 4.00
SRRP Roscoe Parrish 1.50 4.00
SRRW Roddy White 2.50 6.00
SRSL Stefan LeFors 1.50 4.00
SRTM Terrence Murphy 1.50 4.00
SRTW Troy Williamson 1.50 4.00
SRVJ Vincent Jackson 2.50 6.00
SRVM Vernand Morency 1.50 4.00

2005 Sweet Spot Signatures

OVERALL AUTO ODDS 1:12
SSAB Anquan Boldin 12.00 30.00
SSAG Ahman Green SP 6.00 15.00
SSAM Adrian McPherson 6.00 15.00
SSAN Antonio Gates 12.00 30.00
SSAS Alex Smith TE 8.00 20.00
SSBF Brett Favre SP 100.00 200.00
SSBI Billy Kilmer 12.00 30.00
SSBJ Bo Jackson SP 50.00 100.00
SSBK Bernie Kosar 12.00 30.00
SSBR Ben Roethlisberger SP 75.00 150.00
SSBS Barry Sanders SP 75.00 150.00
SSCP Carson Palmer SP 30.00 60.00
SSDB Drew Bennett 6.00 15.00
SSDD Domanick Davis 6.00 15.00
SSDM Donovan McNabb SP 30.00 60.00
SSDO Don Maynard 8.00 20.00
SSDP David Pollack 6.00 15.00
SSDR Drew Bledsoe SP 30.00 60.00
SSEM Eli Manning SP 75.00 135.00
SSHA Herb Adderley 10.00 25.00
SSJF Joe Ferguson 8.00 20.00
SSJJ Julius Jones SP 12.00 30.00
SSJM Joe Montana 100.00 200.00
SSJP Jim Plunkett 12.00 30.00
SSKC Keary Colbert 6.00 15.00
SSLE Lee Evans 8.00 20.00
SSLJ Larry Johnson 12.00 30.00
SSMA Marcus Allen SP 20.00 40.00
SSMB Marc Bulger 12.00 30.00
SSMM Muhsin Muhammad 8.00 20.00
SSMV Michael Vick SP 15.00 40.00
SSNB Nate Burleson 6.00 15.00
SSPH Paul Hornung 25.00 50.00
SSPM Peyton Manning SP 75.00 125.00
SSRJ Rudi Johnson 8.00 20.00
SSRW Reggie Wayne 12.00 30.00
SSSJ Steven Jackson SP 15.00 40.00
SSTA Troy Aikman SP 50.00 80.00

2005 Sweet Spot Signatures Gold

*GOLD: .6X TO 1.5X BASIC AUTOS
*GOLD: .6X TO 1.5X SP AUTOS
GOLD PRINT RUN 50 SER.#'d SETS
SSBF Brett Favre 150.00 250.00
SSBJ Bo Jackson 75.00 150.00
SSBR Ben Roethlisberger/40 90.00 150.00
SSBS Barry Sanders 75.00 150.00
SSCP Carson Palmer 40.00 80.00
SSEM Eli Manning 90.00 150.00
SSJM Joe Montana 125.00 200.00
SSPM Peyton Manning 75.00 150.00
SSSJ Steven Jackson 20.00 50.00

2005 Sweet Spot Sweet Panel Dual Signatures

UNPRICED PRINT RUN 10 SER.#'d SETS

2005 Sweet Spot Sweet Panel Signatures

STATED PRINT RUN 50 SER.#'d SETS
UNPRICED GOLD PRINT RUN 15 SETS
SPAB Anquan Boldin 8.00 20.00
SPAD Anthony Davis 6.00 15.00
SPAJ Adam Jones 6.00 15.00
SPAN Antrel Rolle
SPAR Aaron Rodgers 350.00 500.00
SPAS Alex Smith QB 30.00 80.00
SPAW Andrew Walter 6.00 15.00
SPBE Braylon Edwards 6.00 15.00
SPCF Charlie Frye 6.00 15.00
SPCI Ciatrick Fason 6.00 15.00
SPCR Carlos Rogers 10.00 25.00
SPCW Cadillac Williams 6.00 15.00
SPDA Derek Anderson 8.00 20.00
SPDB Drew Bledsoe 10.00 25.00
SPDD Domanick Davis 8.00 20.00
SPDG David Greene 6.00 15.00
SPDO Dan Orlovsky 6.00 15.00
SPEJ Erasmus James 6.00 15.00
SPFG Fred Gibson 6.00 15.00
SPFR Frank Gore 12.00 30.00
SPHA Herb Adderley 12.00 30.00
SPJC Jason Campbell 6.00 15.00
SPJH Joe Horn 8.00 20.00
SPJJ Julius Jones 8.00 20.00
SPKO Kyle Orton 6.00 15.00
SPMA Mark Clayton 6.00 15.00
SPMC Maurice Clarett 6.00 15.00
SPMI Michael Clayton 6.00 15.00
SPMW Mike Williams 8.00 20.00
SPNB Nate Burleson 6.00 15.00
SPPM Peyton Manning 75.00 135.00
SPRB Ronnie Brown 8.00 20.00
SPRE Reggie Brown 6.00 15.00
SPRM Ryan Moats 8.00 20.00
SPRO Roddy White 10.00 25.00
SPRP Roscoe Parrish 6.00 15.00
SPRW Reggie Wayne 15.00 40.00
SPTW Troy Williamson 6.00 15.00
SPVJ Vincent Jackson 10.00 25.00
SPVM Vernand Morency 8.00 20.00

2005 Sweet Spot Sweet Swatches

STATED PRINT RUN 40 SER.#'d SETS
SWAB Anquan Boldin 3.00 8.00
SWAG Ahman Green 4.00 10.00
SWAL Ashley Lelie 3.00 8.00
SWAR Antwaan Randle El 3.00 8.00
SWBF Brett Favre 10.00 25.00
SWBL Byron Leftwich 3.00 8.00
SWBR Ben Roethlisberger 8.00 20.00
SWBU Brian Urlacher 5.00 12.00
SWBW Brian Westbrook 3.00 8.00
SWCL Clinton Portis 3.00 8.00
SWCM Curtis Martin 4.00 10.00
SWCP Carson Palmer 4.00 10.00
SWCW Charles Woodson 5.00 12.00
SWDB Drew Bledsoe 4.00 10.00
SWDC David Carr 3.00 8.00
SWDM Deuce McAllister 4.00 10.00
SWDO Donovan McNabb 4.00 10.00
SWDR Drew Brees 5.00 12.00
SWDU Daunte Culpepper 4.00 10.00
SWEJ Edgerrin James 4.00 10.00
SWEM Eli Manning 8.00 20.00
SWJB Jerome Bettis 8.00 20.00
SWJJ Julius Jones 3.00 8.00
SWJP Jerry Porter 3.00 8.00
SWJS Jeremy Shockey 3.00 8.00
SWLA Lavar Arrington 3.00 8.00
SWLC Laveranues Coles 3.00 8.00
SWLT LaDainian Tomlinson 5.00 12.00
SWMA Matt Hasselbeck 3.00 8.00
SWMB Marc Bulger 3.00 8.00
SWMF Marshall Faulk 4.00 10.00
SWMH Marvin Harrison 4.00 10.00
SWMV Michael Vick 4.00 10.00
SWPH Priest Holmes 3.00 8.00
SWPM Peyton Manning 12.00 30.00
SWRG Rex Grossman 3.00 8.00
SWRJ Rudi Johnson 3.00 8.00
SWRL Ray Lewis 5.00 12.00
SWRM Randy Moss 4.00 10.00
SWRW Roy Williams S 3.00 8.00
SWSA Shaun Alexander 3.00 8.00
SWSM Steve McNair 4.00 10.00

2006 Sweet Spot

This 242-card set was released in December, 2006. The set was issued into the hobby in four-card packs, with an $9.99 SRP, which came 12 packs to a box. Cards numbered 1-100 are veterans in team alphabetical order while cards numbered 101-242 feature rookies. In the rookie groupings; cards numbered 101-200 were issued to a stated print run of 699 serial numbered sets while cards 201-242 were signed by the player to stated print runs of between 199 and 899 serial numbered copies. We have notated the specific print run for those signed cards in our checklist.

COMP.SET w/o RC's (100) 15.00 40.00
101-200 ROOKIE PRINT RUN 699
101-200 AU ROOKIE PRINT RUN 199-899
1 Larry Fitzgerald .30 .75
2 Anquan Boldin .25 .60
3 Edgerrin James .30 .75
4 Kurt Warner .30 .75
5 Michael Vick .30 .75
6 Warrick Dunn .25 .60
7 Alge Crumpler .30 .75
8 Steve McNair .30 .75
9 Jamal Lewis .30 .75
10 Mark Clayton .25 .60
11 Willis McGahee .25 .60
12 Lee Evans .30 .75
13 J.P. Losman .30 .75
14 Jake Delhomme .25 .60
15 Steve Smith .40 1.00
16 DeShaun Foster .30 .75
17 Keyshawn Johnson .30 .75
18 Cedric Benson .25 .60
19 Brian Urlacher .40 1.00
20 Rex Grossman .25 .60
21 Carson Palmer .30 .75
22 Chad Johnson .25 .60
23 Rudi Johnson .25 .60
24 Charlie Frye .30 .75
25 Reuben Droughns .30 .75
26 Braylon Edwards .25 .60
27 Drew Bledsoe .30 .75
28 Julius Jones .25 .60
29 Terrell Owens .30 .75
30 Jake Plummer .25 .60
31 Tatum Bell .25 .60
32 Rod Smith .30 .75
33 Kevin Jones .25 .60
34 Roy Williams WR .25 .60
35 Jon Kitna .25 .60
36 Brett Favre .75 2.00
37 Donald Driver .30 .75
38 Ahman Green .30 .75
39A David Carr .25 .60
39B Alex Smith QB
40 Ron Dayne .30 .75
41 Andre Johnson .30 .75
42 Peyton Manning 1.00 2.50
43 Dominic Rhodes .25 .60
44 Reggie Wayne .30 .75
45 Marvin Harrison .30 .75
46 Byron Leftwich .25 .60
47 Greg Jones .25 .60
48 Matt Jones .25 .60
49 Trent Green .25 .60
50 Larry Johnson .25 .60
51 Tony Gonzalez .30 .75
52 Daunte Culpepper .30 .75
53 Ronnie Brown .30 .75
54 Chris Chambers .25 .60
55 Brad Johnson .30 .75
56 Chester Taylor .30 .75
57 Travis Taylor .25 .60
58 Tom Brady 1.25 3.00
59 Corey Dillon .25 .60
60 Doug Gabriel .25 .60
61 Drew Brees .40 1.00
62 Deuce McAllister .30 .75
63 Joe Horn .25 .60
64 Eli Manning .30 .75
65 Tiki Barber .30 .75
66 Plaxico Burress .25 .60
67 Jeremy Shockey .25 .60
68 Chad Pennington .25 .60
69 Laveranues Coles .25 .60
70 Justin McCareins .25 .60
71 Andrew Walter .25 .60
72 Randy Moss .30 .75
73 LaMont Jordan .30 .75
74 Donovan McNabb .30 .75
75 Brian Westbrook .25 .60
76 Reggie Brown .25 .60
77 Ben Roethlisberger .50 1.25
78 Willie Parker .30 .75
79 Hines Ward .30 .75
80 Philip Rivers .40 1.00
81 LaDainian Tomlinson .40 1.00
82 Antonio Gates .40 1.00
83 Alex Smith QB .30 .75
84 Frank Gore .30 .75
85 Antonio Bryant .25 .60
86 Matt Hasselbeck .25 .60
87 Shaun Alexander .25 .60
88 Nate Burleson .25 .60
89 Marc Bulger .25 .60
90 Steven Jackson .25 .60
91 Torry Holt .30 .75
92 Chris Simms .25 .60
93 Cadillac Williams .30 .75
94 Joey Galloway .30 .75
95 Kerry Collins .25 .60
96 Drew Bennett .30 .75
97 Chris Brown .25 .60
98 Mark Brunell .30 .75
99 Clinton Portis .25 .60
100 Santana Moss .30 .75
101 Abdul Hodge RC 2.00 5.00
102 Adam Jennings RC 2.50 6.00
103 Anthony Fasano RC 2.00 5.00
104 Anthony Schlegel RC 2.50 6.00
105 Anthony Smith RC 3.00 8.00
106 Antoine Bethea RC 3.00 8.00
107 Cortland Finnegan RC 3.00 8.00
108 Ben Obomanu RC 2.50 6.00
109 Bennie Brazell RC 2.50 6.00
110 Bernard Pollard RC 2.50 6.00
111 Bobby Carpenter RC 2.00 5.00
112 Brandon Marshall RC 4.00 10.00
113 Brodie Croyle RC 2.00 5.00
114 Brodrick Bunkley RC 2.50 6.00
115 Bruce Gradkowski RC 2.50 6.00
116 Calvin Lowry RC 3.00 8.00
117 Cedric Griffin RC 2.50 6.00
118 Dawan Landry RC 3.00 8.00
119 Chad Greenway RC 3.00 8.00
120 Charles Davis RC 2.50 6.00
121 Chris Gocong RC 2.50 6.00
122 Claude Wroten RC 2.00 5.00
123 Clint Ingram RC 3.00 8.00
124 Corey Bramlet RC 2.50 6.00
125 Cory Rodgers RC 2.00 5.00
126 D.J. Shockley RC 2.50 6.00
127 Danieal Manning RC 3.00 8.00
128 Daniel Bullocks RC 2.00 5.00
129 Darnell Bing RC 2.50 6.00
130 Darryl Tapp RC 2.50 6.00
131 David Anderson RC 2.50 6.00
132 David Kirtman RC 2.50 6.00
133 David Pittman RC 2.50 6.00
134 David Thomas RC 2.00 5.00
135 Davin Joseph RC 2.50 6.00
136 Delanie Walker RC 4.00 10.00
137 DeMeco Ryans RC 2.50 6.00
138 Devin Aromashodu RC 2.00 5.00
139 John Madsen RC 2.50 6.00
140 Donte Whitner RC 2.50 6.00
141 D'Qwell Jackson RC 2.00 5.00
142 Dusty Dvoracek RC 3.00 8.00
143 Elvis Dumervil RC 3.00 8.00
144 Eric Smith RC 2.50 6.00
145 Ernie Sims RC 2.00 5.00
146 Ethan Kilmer RC 2.50 6.00
147 Freddie Keiaho RC 2.50 6.00
148 Frostee Rucker RC 2.50 6.00
149 Gabe Watson RC 2.00 5.00
150 Garrett Mills RC 2.50 6.00
151 Gerris Wilkinson RC 2.00 5.00
152 Greg Lee RC 2.00 5.00
153 Haloti Ngata RC 2.50 6.00
154 Hank Baskett RC 2.00 5.00
155 Ingle Martin RC 2.50 6.00
156 Jamar Williams RC 2.50 6.00
157 James Anderson RC 2.00 5.00
158 Jason Allen RC 2.50 6.00
159 Jason Avant RC 2.00 5.00
160 Jason Pociask RC 2.50 6.00
161 Jeff King RC 2.50 6.00
162 Jeff Webb RC 2.50 6.00
163 Jeremy Bloom RC 2.00 5.00
164 Jimmy Williams RC 2.00 5.00
165 Joe Klopfenstein RC 2.00 5.00
166 John McCargo RC 2.00 5.00
167 Johnathan Joseph RC 2.50 6.00
168 Jon Alston RC 2.00 5.00
169 Jonathan Orr RC 2.50 6.00
170 Kamerion Wimbley RC 2.50 6.00
171 Kelly Jennings RC 2.50 6.00
172 Kevin McMahan RC 2.50 6.00
173 Ko Simpson RC 2.50 6.00
174 Lawrence Vickers RC 2.50 6.00
175 Leon Williams RC 2.50 6.00
176 Manny Lawson RC 2.50 6.00
177 Marcus Vick RC 2.00 5.00
178 Marques Colston RC 3.00 8.00
179 Marques Hagans RC 2.00 5.00
180 Mathias Kiwanuka RC 3.00 8.00
181 Mike Bell RC 2.00 5.00
182 Mike Hass RC 2.00 5.00
183 Nick Mangold RC 2.50 6.00
184 Owen Daniels RC 3.00 8.00
185 Quinn Sypniewski RC 2.50 6.00
186 Quinton Ganther RC 2.00 5.00
187 Richard Marshall RC 2.00 5.00
188 Rocky McIntosh RC 2.00 5.00
189 Roman Harper RC 2.50 6.00
190 Stephen Tulloch RC 2.50 6.00
191 Keith Ellison RC 2.50 6.00
192 Tamba Hali RC 3.00 8.00
193 Thomas Howard RC 2.00 5.00
194 Todd Watkins RC 2.00 5.00
195 Tony Scheffler RC 3.00 8.00
196 Troy Bergeron RC 2.50 6.00
197 Tye Hill RC 2.00 5.00
198 Wali Lundy RC 2.00 5.00
199 Willie Reid RC 2.50 6.00
200 Winston Justice RC 2.50 6.00
201 Jay Cutler AU/299 RC 12.00 30.00
202 Matt Leinart AU/199 RC 10.00 25.00
203 A.J. Hawk AU/299 RC 10.00 25.00
204 D.Williams AU/299 RC 12.00 30.00
205 Reggie Bush AU/199 RC 15.00 40.00
206 Santonio Holmes AU/299 RC 12.00 60.00
207 Vince Young AU/199 RC 12.00 30.00
208 Vernon Davis AU/499 RC 8.00 20.00
209 Joseph Addai AU/499 RC 6.00 15.00
210 Sinorice Moss AU/499 RC 6.00 15.00
211 Chad Jackson AU/899 RC 5.00 12.00
212 Laurence Maroney AU/499 RC 6.00 15.00
213 Michael Huff AU/499 RC 8.00 20.00
214 Mario Williams AU/499 RC 10.00 25.00
215 Brandon Williams AU/899 RC 5.00 12.00
216 Michael Robinson AU/899 RC 5.00 12.00
217 Devin Hester AU/899 RC 10.00 25.00
218 Reggie McNeal AU/899 RC 5.00 12.00
219 Travis Wilson AU/899 RC 5.00 12.00
220 Jerome Harrison AU/899 RC 5.00 12.00
221 Maurice Stovall AU/899 RC 5.00 12.00
222 Leonard Pope AU/899 RC 8.00 20.00
223 Antonio Cromartie AU/899 RC 6.00 15.00
224 Charlie Whitehurst AU/899 RC 5.00 12.00
225 Skyler Green AU/899 RC 5.00 12.00
226 Derek Hagan AU/899 RC 6.00 15.00
227 Jerious Norwood AU/899 RC 5.00 12.00
228 Maurice Drew AU/899 RC 15.00 40.00
229 Marcedes Lewis AU/899 RC 5.00 12.00
230 D'Brickashaw Ferguson AU/899 RC 5.00 12.00
231 Kellen Clemens AU/899 RC 5.00 12.00
232 Leon Washington AU/899 RC 5.00 12.00
233 Brad Smith AU/899 RC 6.00 15.00
234 Brian Calhoun AU/899 RC 5.00 12.00
235 Greg Jennings AU/899 RC 8.00 20.00
236 Will Blackmon AU/899 RC 5.00 12.00
237 Dominique Byrd AU/899 RC 5.00 12.00
238 Demetrius Williams AU/899 RC 5.00 12.00
239 P.J. Daniels AU/899 RC 5.00 12.00
240 Omar Jacobs AU/899 RC 5.00 12.00
241 LenDale White AU/899 RC 5.00 12.00
242 Tarvaris Jackson AU/899 RC 5.00 12.00

2006 Sweet Spot Gold Rookie Autographs

*GOLD/100: .5X TO 1.2X BASIC AU/899
*GOLD/50: .5X TO 1.2X BASIC AU/499
*GOLD/50: .4X TO 1X BASIC AU/199-299
GOLD STATED PRINT RUN 50-100

2006 Sweet Spot Signatures

AB Aaron Brooks 6.00 15.00
AF Anthony Fasano 5.00 12.00
AG Antonio Gates 10.00 25.00
BA Ronde Barber 10.00 25.00
BF Brett Favre SP 100.00 200.00
BG Bruce Gradkowski 6.00 15.00
BM Brandon Marshall 10.00 25.00
BR Ben Roethlisberger SP 60.00 120.00
CR Cory Rodgers 5.00 12.00
CW Cadillac Williams SP 10.00 25.00
DB Drew Bledsoe SP 15.00 30.00
DF DeShaun Foster 8.00 20.00
DG David Givens 8.00 20.00
DM Dan Marino SP 125.00 200.00
DS D.J. Shockley 6.00 15.00
DW Donte Whitner 6.00 15.00
EM Eli Manning SP 40.00 80.00
GM Garrett Mills 6.00 15.00
HA Mike Hass 5.00 12.00
IM Ingle Martin 6.00 15.00
JA Jason Avant 5.00 12.00
JE John Elway SP 75.00 150.00
JM Joe Montana SP 100.00 175.00
JO LaMont Jordan 8.00 20.00
JW Jeff Webb 6.00 15.00
LJ Larry Johnson SP 12.00 30.00
LT LaDainian Tomlinson SP 30.00 80.00
MH Marques Hagans 5.00 12.00
MV Michael Vick SP 15.00 40.00
NM Nat Moore 8.00 20.00
OR Jonathan Orr 6.00 15.00
PH Paul Hornung 15.00 40.00
PM Peyton Manning 60.00 120.00
RB Reggie Brown 5.00 12.00
RW Reggie Wayne 10.00 25.00
SM Stanley Morgan 10.00 25.00
SS Steve Smith SP 12.00 30.00
TA Lofa Tatupu 6.00 15.00
TH Tye Hill 5.00 12.00

2006 Sweet Spot Signatures Gold

*GOLD/100: .5X TO 1.2X BASIC AUTOS
*GOLD/50: .5X TO 1.2X BASIC AUTOS
GOLD PRINT RUN 50-100
BF Brett Favre 100.00 200.00
BR Ben Roethlisberger 60.00 100.00
DM Dan Marino 100.00 200.00
EM Eli Manning 50.00 100.00
JE John Elway 75.00 150.00
JM Joe Montana/50 100.00 200.00
LT LaDainian Tomlinson 60.00 120.00
PM Peyton Manning 60.00 120.00

2006 Sweet Spot Sweet Images 5x7

ONE PER BOX
SIAC Alge Crumpler 2.50 6.00
SIBD Brian Dawkins 3.00 8.00
SIBE Braylon Edwards 2.00 5.00
SIBF Brett Favre 6.00 15.00
SIBG Bob Griese 3.00 8.00
SIBR Ben Roethlisberger 4.00 10.00
SICB Cedric Benson 2.00 5.00
SICF Charlie Frye 2.50 6.00
SICP Carson Palmer 2.50 6.00
SICW Cadillac Williams 2.50 6.00
SIDB Drew Bledsoe 2.50 6.00
SIDM Deuce McAllister 2.50 6.00
SIEM Eli Manning 2.50 6.00
SIJJ Julius Jones 2.00 5.00
SIJT Joe Theismann 3.00 8.00
SIKO Kyle Orton 2.00 5.00
SIMB Marc Bulger 2.00 5.00
SIMC Mark Clayton 2.00 5.00
SIMV Michael Vick 2.50 6.00
SIMW Mike Williams 2.00 5.00
SIPM Peyton Manning 8.00 20.00
SIRB Reggie Brown 2.00 5.00
SIRO Ronnie Brown 2.50 6.00
SIRW Reggie Wayne 2.50 6.00
SITB Tiki Barber 2.50 6.00

2006 Sweet Spot Sweet Images 5x7 Autographs

SIAC Alge Crumpler SP
SIBD Brian Dawkins SP
SIBE Braylon Edwards 10.00 25.00
SIBF Brett Favre SP 125.00 200.00
SIBG Bob Griese 15.00 30.00
SIBR Ben Roethlisberger 50.00 100.00
SICB Cedric Benson 10.00 25.00
SICF Charlie Frye 10.00 25.00
SICP Carson Palmer SP
SICW Cadillac Williams SP 15.00 40.00
SIDB Drew Bledsoe 20.00 40.00
SIDM Deuce McAllister SP
SIEM Eli Manning SP
SIJJ Julius Jones SP 12.00 30.00
SIJT Joe Theismann 25.00 50.00
SIKO Kyle Orton 8.00 20.00
SIMB Marc Bulger SP 10.00 25.00
SIMC Mark Clayton 10.00 25.00
SIMV Michael Vick SP 25.00 60.00
SIMW Mike Williams 8.00 20.00
SIPM Peyton Manning 60.00 120.00
SIRB Reggie Brown 8.00 20.00
SIRO Ronnie Brown 15.00 30.00
SIRW Reggie Wayne SP 15.00 30.00
SITB Tiki Barber 20.00 40.00

2006 Sweet Spot Sweet Leather Signatures

LEATHER AU PRINT RUN 20
UNPRICED DUAL PRINT RUN 5
SLSAG Antonio Gates 15.00 40.00
SLSBC Brian Calhoun 8.00 20.00
SLSBE Braylon Edwards 10.00 25.00
SLSBL Byron Leftwich 10.00 25.00
SLSBU Reggie Bush 12.00 30.00
SLSCB Cedric Benson 10.00 25.00
SLSCS Chris Simms 10.00 25.00
SLSDB Drew Bennett 12.00 30.00
SLSDF DeShaun Foster 10.00 25.00
SLSDM Derrick Mason 10.00 25.00
SLSEM Eli Manning 30.00 60.00
SLSGM Garrett Mills 10.00 25.00
SLSJC Jay Cutler 10.00 25.00
SLSJJ Julius Jones 10.00 25.00
SLSJN Jerious Norwood 8.00 20.00
SLSJO LaMont Jordan 12.00 30.00
SLSKC Kevin Curtis 12.00 30.00
SLSLJ Larry Johnson 10.00 25.00
SLSLM Laurence Maroney 8.00 20.00
SLSLT LaDainian Tomlinson 30.00 60.00
SLSMB Marc Bulger 10.00 25.00
SLSML Matt Leinart 8.00 20.00
SLSMM Muhsin Muhammad 10.00 25.00
SLSMR Michael Robinson 8.00 20.00
SLSMW Mario Williams 12.00 30.00
SLSNB Nate Burleson 10.00 25.00
SLSPM Peyton Manning 60.00 120.00
SLSPR Philip Rivers 30.00 60.00
SLSRB Reggie Brown 10.00 25.00
SLSRW Reggie Wayne 12.00 30.00
SLSSH Santonio Holmes 10.00 25.00
SLSSS Steve Smith 15.00 40.00
SLSTA Lofa Tatupu 10.00 25.00
SLSTH T.J. Houshmandzadeh 10.00 25.00
SLSTJ Thomas Jones 10.00 25.00
SLSTW Travis Wilson 8.00 20.00
SLSVD Vernon Davis 10.00 25.00
SLSVY Vince Young 8.00 20.00
SLSWI Mike Williams 12.00 30.00
SLSWP Willie Parker 12.00 30.00
SLSWR Willie Reid 10.00 25.00

2006 Sweet Spot Sweet Pairings Jerseys Dual

SPDAM J.Avant/S.Moss 5.00 12.00
SPDAS J.Avant/M.Stovall 4.00 10.00
SPDBL R.Bush/M.Leinart 8.00 20.00
SPDBW R.Bush/L.White 8.00 20.00
SPDCD B.Calhoun/M.Drew 6.00 15.00
SPDCM J.Cutler/B.Marshall 10.00 25.00
SPDCW K.Clemens/L.Washington 6.00 15.00
SPDDC D.Hagan/C.Jackson 5.00 12.00
SPDDD D.Williams/D.Hagan 4.00 10.00
SPDDK D.Williams/K.Clemens 4.00 10.00
SPDDL V.Davis/M.Lewis 6.00 15.00
SPDDN M.Drew/J.Norwood 6.00 15.00
SPDDR V.Davis/M.Robinson 6.00 15.00
SPDHH A.Hawk/M.Huff 8.00 20.00
SPDHJ S.Holmes/O.Jacobs 6.00 15.00
SPDHW S.Holmes/T.Wilson 6.00 15.00
SPDHY M.Huff/V.Young 12.00 30.00
SPDJC T.Jackson/K.Clemens 5.00 12.00
SPDJH C.Jackson/S.Holmes 6.00 15.00
SPDJJ T.Jackson/O.Jacobs 5.00 12.00
SPDJM C.Jackson/S.Moss 5.00 12.00
SPDJW O.Jacobs/C.Whitehurst 4.00 10.00
SPDKD J.Klopfenstein/V.Davis 6.00 15.00
SPDLD M.Lewis/M.Drew 6.00 15.00
SPDLL L.Maroney/L.White 6.00 15.00
SPDLW M.Leinart/L.White 8.00 20.00
SPDLY M.Leinart/V.Young 10.00 25.00
SPDMM L.Maroney/S.Moss 6.00 15.00
SPDMW B.Marshall/B.Williams 5.00 12.00
SPDNW J.Norwood/L.Washington 6.00 15.00
SPDRS M.Robinson/M.Stovall 5.00 12.00
SPDRW M.Robinson/B.Williams 5.00 12.00
SPDTB T.Wilson/B.Marshall 5.00 12.00
SPDWB M.Williams/R.Bush 8.00 20.00
SPDWC B.Williams/B.Calhoun 4.00 10.00
SPDWH M.Williams/A.Hawk 8.00 20.00
SPDWJ C.Whitehurst/T.Jackson 5.00 12.00
SPDWM D.Williams/L.Maroney 10.00 25.00
SPDWN D.Williams/J.Norwood 10.00 25.00
SPDWS T.Wilson/M.Stovall 4.00 10.00
SPDYC V.Young/J.Cutler 15.00 30.00
SPDYW V.Young/L.White 12.00 30.00

2006 Sweet Spot Update Spokesmen Signatures

OVERALL AUTO ODDS 1:6
UNPRICED AU PRINT RUN 5-20

2007 Sweet Spot

This 141-card set was released in December, 2007. The set was issued into the hobby in six-card pack (boxes) with an $120 SRP. Cards numbered 1-100 feature veterans in alphabetical order by team with a stated print run of 625 serial numbered sets. Cards 101-142 feature signed Rookie Cards. Cards numbered 101-130 were issued to stated print runs between 755 and 799 serial numbered sets and cards 131-142 were issued to stated print runs between 299 and 399 serial numbered sets. A few players did not return their signatures in time for pack out and those cards could be exchanged until November 26, 2009. Card number 127 was never issued.

1-100 STATED PRINT RUN 625
101-130 AU RC PRINT RUN 755-799
131-142 AU RC PRINT RUN 299-399
1 Matt Leinart 1.50 4.00
2 Edgerrin James 2.00 5.00
3 Larry Fitzgerald 2.00 5.00
4 Anquan Boldin 1.50 4.00
5 Joey Galloway 2.00 5.00
6 Warrick Dunn 1.50 4.00
7 Alge Crumpler 2.00 5.00
8 Steve McNair 2.00 5.00
9 Willis McGahee 1.50 4.00
10 Mark Clayton 1.50 4.00
11 J.P. Losman 1.50 4.00
12 Aaron Schobel 1.50 4.00
13 Lee Evans 2.00 5.00
14 Jake Delhomme 1.50 4.00
15 DeAngelo Williams 1.50 4.00
16 Steve Smith 2.00 5.00
17 Rex Grossman 1.50 4.00
18 Cedric Benson 1.50 4.00
19 Brian Urlacher 2.50 6.00
20 Carson Palmer 2.00 5.00
21 Rudi Johnson 1.50 4.00
22 Chad Johnson 1.50 4.00
23 T.J. Houshmandzadeh 1.50 4.00
24 Charlie Frye 2.00 5.00
25 Kellen Winslow 1.50 4.00
26 Braylon Edwards 1.50 4.00
27 Tony Romo 3.00 8.00
28 Marion Barber 2.00 5.00
29 Terrell Owens 2.00 5.00
30 Jay Cutler 1.50 4.00
31 Travis Henry 2.00 5.00
32 Javon Walker 2.00 5.00
33 Jon Kitna 1.50 4.00
34 Roy Williams WR 1.50 4.00
35 Mike Furrey 2.00 5.00
36 Brett Favre 5.00 12.00
37 Donald Driver 2.00 5.00
38 Greg Jennings 1.50 4.00
39 Matt Schaub 1.50 4.00
40 Ahman Green 2.00 5.00
41 Andre Johnson 2.00 5.00
42 Peyton Manning 6.00 15.00
43 Joseph Addai 1.50 4.00
44 Marvin Harrison 2.00 5.00
45 Reggie Wayne 2.00 5.00
46 David Garrard 1.50 4.00
47 Maurice Jones-Drew 1.50 4.00
48 Fred Taylor 1.50 4.00
49 Brodie Croyle 2.00 5.00
50 Larry Johnson 1.50 4.00
51 Tony Gonzalez 2.00 5.00
52 Trent Green 1.50 4.00
53 Ronnie Brown 1.50 4.00
54 Chris Chambers 1.50 4.00
55 Tarvaris Jackson 1.50 4.00
56 Chester Taylor 1.50 4.00
57 Bobby Wade 1.50 4.00
58 Tom Brady 8.00 20.00
59 Laurence Maroney 2.00 5.00
60 Randy Moss 2.00 5.00
61 Drew Brees 2.50 6.00
62 Reggie Bush 1.50 4.00
63 Deuce McAllister 2.00 5.00
64 Marques Colston 1.50 4.00
65 Eli Manning 2.00 5.00
66 Brandon Jacobs 1.50 4.00
67 Plaxico Burress 1.50 4.00
68 Chad Pennington 1.50 4.00
69 Thomas Jones 1.50 4.00
70 Jerricho Cotchery 1.50 4.00
71 LaMont Jordan 2.00 5.00
72 Dominic Rhodes 1.50 4.00
73 Ronald Curry 1.50 4.00
74 Donovan McNabb 2.00 5.00
75 Brian Westbrook 1.50 4.00
76 Reggie Brown 1.50 4.00
77 Ben Roethlisberger 2.50 6.00
78 Willie Parker 2.00 5.00
79 Hines Ward 2.00 5.00
80 Philip Rivers 2.50 6.00
81 LaDainian Tomlinson 2.50 6.00
82 Antonio Gates 2.50 6.00
83 Alex Smith QB 2.00 5.00
84 Frank Gore 2.00 5.00
85 Darrell Jackson 1.50 4.00
86 Matt Hasselbeck 1.50 4.00
87 Shaun Alexander 1.50 4.00
88 Deion Branch 1.50 4.00
89 Marc Bulger 1.50 4.00
90 Steven Jackson 1.50 4.00
91 Torry Holt 2.00 5.00
92 Jeff Garcia 1.50 4.00
93 Cadillac Williams 2.00 5.00
94 Josh Bidwell 1.50 4.00
95 Vince Young 1.50 4.00
96 LenDale White 2.00 5.00
97 Brandon Jones 1.50 4.00
98 Jason Campbell 1.50 4.00
99 Clinton Portis 1.50 4.00
100 Santana Moss 2.00 5.00
101 Laurent Robinson AU RC 8.00 20.00
102 Trent Edwards AU RC 5.00 12.00
103 Dwayne Wright AU RC 5.00 12.00
104 Chris Leak AU RC 5.00 12.00
105 Garrett Wolfe AU RC 5.00 12.00
106 Greg Olsen AU/755 RC 8.00 20.00
107 Leon Hall AU RC 5.00 12.00
108 Kenny Irons AU RC 5.00 12.00
109 Joe Thomas AU RC 8.00 20.00
110 Isaiah Stanback AU RC 5.00 12.00
111 Drew Stanton AU RC 5.00 12.00
112 Brandon Jackson AU RC 5.00 12.00
113 Amobi Okoye AU RC 6.00 15.00
114 John Beck AU RC 5.00 12.00
115 Lorenzo Booker AU RC 6.00 15.00
116 Antonio Pittman AU RC 5.00 12.00
117 Steve Smith USC AU RC 5.00 12.00
118 Michael Bush AU RC 5.00 12.00
119 Zach Miller AU RC 5.00 12.00
120 Johnnie Lee Higgins AU RC 5.00 12.00
121 Tony Hunt AU RC 5.00 12.00
122 Gary Russell AU RC 6.00 15.00
123 Craig Buster Davis AU RC 5.00 12.00
124 Patrick Willis AU RC 8.00 20.00
125 Courtney Taylor AU RC 5.00 12.00
126 Brian Leonard AU RC 5.00 12.00
128 Paul Williams AU RC 5.00 12.00
129 Jordan Palmer AU RC 6.00 15.00
130 LaRon Landry AU RC 8.00 20.00
131 Marshawn Lynch AU/399 RC 20.00 50.00
132 Dwayne Jarrett AU/399 RC 8.00 20.00
133 Adrian Peterson AU/299 RC 75.00 150.00
134 Brady Quinn AU/399 RC 6.00 15.00
135 C.Johnson AU/299 RC 50.00 100.00
136 Anthony Gonzalez AU/399 RC 6.00 15.00
137 Dwayne Bowe AU/399 RC 6.00 15.00
138 Ted Ginn AU/399 RC 8.00 20.00
139 Sidney Rice AU/315 RC 8.00 20.00
140 Robert Meachem AU/399 RC 8.00 20.00
141 JaMarcus Russell AU/399 RC 6.00 15.00
142 Kevin Kolb AU/399 RC 8.00 20.00

2007 Sweet Spot Pigskin Signatures Dual

STATED PRINT RUN 50 SER.#'d SETS
AA A.Gonzalez/A.Pittman 15.00 40.00
AL A.Branch/L.Hall 10.00 25.00
BB R.Brown/D.Bennett 10.00 25.00
BH C.Bailey/D.Hughes 12.00 30.00
BV B.Marshall/V.Jackson 10.00 25.00
CM S.Chandler/Z.Miller 12.00 30.00
CS J.Campbell/D.Stanton 8.00 20.00
DB C.Davis/D.Bowe 15.00 40.00
DE D.Hughes/E.Wright 12.00 30.00
DY K.Darby/S.Young 12.00 30.00
GW M.Griffin/E.Weddle 12.00 30.00
HF Housh/J.Filani 12.00 30.00
HT P.Hornung/J.Theismann 40.00 100.00
II K.Irons/D.Irons 12.00 30.00
JE D.Jackson/L.Evans 12.00 30.00
KS K.Kolb/D.Stanton 10.00 25.00
LL L.Landry/J.Lynch 10.00 25.00
LZ C.Leak/J.Zabransky 12.00 30.00
MC R.McKnight/D.Clowney 12.00 30.00
MG Meriweather/M.Griffin 12.00 30.00
MW M.McCauley/E.Wright 12.00 30.00
PL Peterson/Lynch 75.00 150.00
QR B.Quinn/J.Russell 8.00 20.00
RJ S.Ric/Ch.Jhnsn 20.00 50.00
SA C.Stuckey/A.Allison 10.00 25.00
TP L.Timmons/P.Posluszny 12.00 30.00
WC P.Williams/D.Clowney 12.00 30.00
WM Wayne/P.Manning 60.00 120.00
ZN J.Zabransky/L.Naanee 12.00 30.00

2007 Sweet Spot Pigskin Signatures Bronze 49

BRONZE 49 PRINT RUN 49 SER.#'d SETS
*BRONZE/25: .5X TO 1.2X BRONZE/49
GOLD 1/1 TOO SCARCE TO PRICE
*RED 15: .6X TO 1.5X BRONZE/49
RED/5 TOO SCARCE TO PRICE
AA2 Aundrae Allison 6.00 15.00
AN Jamaal Anderson 8.00 20.00
AO Amobi Okoye 8.00 20.00
AP Antonio Pittman 6.00 15.00
BA2 Marion Barber 12.00 30.00
BE2 Drew Bennett 8.00 20.00
BN Brandon Jacobs 8.00 20.00
CB Champ Bailey 12.00 30.00
CD2 Craig Buster Davis 6.00 15.00
CJ Chad Johnson 8.00 20.00
CS2 Chansi Stuckey 8.00 20.00
DC David Clowney 6.00 15.00
DJ2 Dwayne Jarrett 8.00 20.00
DS2 Drew Stanton 6.00 15.00
FG Frank Gore 10.00 25.00
GO2 Greg Olsen 10.00 25.00
GW2 Garrett Wolfe 6.00 15.00
HO2 T.J. Houshmandzadeh 8.00 20.00
HU Tony Hunt 6.00 15.00
JB2 John Beck 6.00 15.00
JC Jerricho Cotchery 8.00 20.00
JH Johnnie Lee Higgins 6.00 15.00
JL2 John Lynch 12.00 30.00
JP2 Jordan Palmer 8.00 20.00
JT2 Joe Thomas 10.00 25.00
LE2 Lee Evans 10.00 25.00
LW LaMarr Woodley 12.00 30.00
MB2 Michael Bush 6.00 15.00
MC Marques Colston 8.00 20.00
MS Matt Schaub 8.00 20.00
PM2 Peyton Manning 75.00 120.00
PW Patrick Willis 10.00 25.00
RB Ronnie Brown 8.00 20.00
RN Reggie Nelson 6.00 15.00
RW2 Reggie Wayne 12.00 30.00
CI Mike Cinglotary 15.00 40.00

SS2 Steve Smith USC 6.00 15.00
TA Chester Taylor 8.00 20.00
TH Joe Theismann 15.00 40.00
WI Paul Williams 6.00 15.00
WP2 Willie Parker 10.00 25.00

2007 Sweet Spot Pigskin Signatures Green 99

GREEN 99 PRINT RUN 99 SER.#'d SETS
*GREEN 75: .4X TO 1X GREEN/99
GREEN 75 PRINT RUN 75 SER.#'d SETS
*GREEN 50: .5X TO 1.2X GREEN/99
GREEN 50 PRINT RUN 50 SER.#'d SETS
*BLUE 20: .6X TO 1.5X GREEN/99
BLUE 20 PRINT RUN 20 SER.#'d SETS
GREEN 1/1 TOO SCARCE TO PRICE
AA Aundrae Allison 5.00 12.00
BA Marion Barber 10.00 25.00
BB Bernard Berrian 6.00 15.00
BE Drew Bennett 6.00 15.00
BL Brian Leonard 5.00 12.00
BM Brandon Marshall 8.00 20.00
BR Reggie Brown 6.00 15.00
CD Craig Buster Davis 5.00 12.00
CH Chris Henry RB 5.00 12.00
CL Mark Clayton 6.00 15.00
CS Chansi Stuckey 6.00 15.00
DJ Dwayne Jarrett 6.00 15.00
DS Drew Stanton 5.00 12.00
DW Darius Walker 5.00 12.00
GJ Greg Jennings 10.00 25.00
GO Greg Olsen 8.00 20.00
GW Garrett Wolfe 5.00 12.00
HI Jason Hill 5.00 12.00
HO T.J. Houshmandzadeh 6.00 15.00
JA Darrell Jackson 6.00 15.00
JB John Beck 5.00 12.00
JJ Jacoby Jones 8.00 20.00
JL John Lynch 10.00 25.00
JO James Jones 5.00 12.00
JP Jordan Palmer 6.00 15.00
JT Joe Thomas 8.00 20.00
KI Kenny Irons 5.00 12.00
KS Kolby Smith 5.00 12.00
LB Lorenzo Booker 6.00 15.00
LE Lee Evans 8.00 20.00
LL LaRon Landry 8.00 20.00
MB Michael Bush 5.00 12.00
ME Brandon Meriweather 6.00 15.00
PM Peyton Manning 50.00 100.00
QM Quentin Moses 6.00 15.00
RO Jeff Rowe 5.00 12.00
RW Reggie Wayne 10.00 25.00
SS Steve Smith USC 5.00 12.00
TE Trent Edwards 5.00 12.00
WP Willie Parker 8.00 20.00
YF Yamon Figurs 5.00 12.00

2007 Sweet Spot Rookie Signatures Gold 15

*GOLD/29: 1X TO 2.5X BASE AU/755-799
*GOLD/29: .8X TO 2X BASE AU/315-399
GOLD 15 PRINT RUN 15 SER.#'d SETS
133 Adrian Peterson 200.00 400.00
135 Calvin Johnson 60.00 150.00

2007 Sweet Spot Rookie Signatures Gold 29

*GOLD/29: .8X TO 2X BASE AU/755-799
*GOLD/29: .6X TO 1.5X BASE AU/315-399
GOLD 29 PRINT RUN 29 SER.#'d SETS
GOLD/5 TOO SCARCE TO PRICE
GOLD 1/1 TOO SCARCE TO PRICE
133 Adrian Peterson 150.00 300.00
135 Calvin Johnson 75.00 135.00

2007 Sweet Spot Signatures Silver 25

SILVER 25 PRINT RUN 25 SER.#'d SETS
*SILVER/49: .3X TO .8X SILVER/25
SILVER 49 PRINT RUN 49 SER.#'d SETS
*SILVER/15: .5X TO 1.2X SILVER/25
SILVER 15 PRINT RUN 15 SER.#'d SETS
*GOLD 15: .5X TO 1.2X SILVER/25
GOLD 15 PRINT RUN 15 SER.#'d SETS
GOLD/5 TOO SCARCE TO PRICE
AP Adrian Peterson 175.00 300.00
BF Brett Favre 150.00 250.00
BQ Brady Quinn 10.00 25.00
BR2 Ronnie Brown 12.00 30.00
BU2 Michael Bush 10.00 25.00
CD2 Craig Buster Davis 10.00 25.00
CL2 Chris Leak 10.00 25.00
CT2 Chester Taylor 12.00 30.00
CW2 Cadillac Williams 15.00 40.00
DB Drew Brees 40.00 80.00
ES Emmitt Smith 175.00 300.00
GO2 Greg Olsen 15.00 40.00
GW2 Garrett Wolfe 10.00 25.00
JA2 Joseph Addai 12.00 30.00
JB2 John Beck 10.00 25.00
JC2 Jason Campbell 12.00 30.00
JJ2 Jacoby Jones 15.00 40.00
JN2 Jerious Norwood 12.00 30.00
JO2 James Jones 10.00 25.00
JR JaMarcus Russell 10.00 25.00
JT2 Joe Thomas 15.00 40.00
KI2 Kenny Irons 10.00 25.00
LE2 Lee Evans 15.00 40.00
LJ Larry Johnson 12.00 30.00
LL2 LaRon Landry 15.00 40.00
LR2 Laurent Robinson 15.00 40.00
MB2 Marion Barber 15.00 40.00
MG2 Michael Griffin 10.00 25.00
ML Matt Leinart 12.00 30.00
MS2 Matt Schaub 12.00 30.00
NA Joe Namath
PM2 Peyton Manning 100.00 200.00
RB Reggie Bush 12.00 30.00
RN2 Reggie Nelson 10.00 25.00
RO2 Jeff Rowe 10.00 25.00
RW2 Reggie Wayne 20.00 50.00
SS2 Steve Smith USC 20.00 50.00
TH2 T.J. Houshmandzadeh 12.00 30.00
TN2 Joe Theismann 25.00 60.00
VY Vince Young 12.00 30.00
WP2 Willie Parker 15.00 40.00

2007 Sweet Spot Signatures Silver 99

SILVER 99 PRINT RUN 99 SER.#'d SETS
*SILVER/75: .4X TO 1X SILVER/99
SILVER 75 PRINT RUN 75 SER.#'d SETS
*SILVER/50: .5X TO 1.2X SILVER/99
SILVER 50 PRINT RUN 50 SER.#'d SETS
*GOLD/20: .6X TO 1.5X SILVER/99
GOLD 20 PRINT RUN 20 SER.#'d SETS
GOLD/10 TOO SCARCE TO PRICE
SILVER 1/1 TOO SCARCE TO PRICE
AB Anquan Boldin 8.00 20.00
AG Anthony Gonzalez 6.00 15.00
BB Bernard Berrian 8.00 20.00
BM Brandon Meriweather 8.00 20.00
BR Ronnie Brown 8.00 20.00
BU Michael Bush 6.00 15.00
CD Craig Buster Davis 6.00 15.00
CT Chester Taylor 8.00 20.00
CW Cadillac Williams 10.00 25.00
DJ Dwayne Jarrett 8.00 20.00
FG Frank Gore 10.00 25.00
GO Greg Olsen 10.00 25.00
GW Garrett Wolfe 6.00 15.00
HU Daymeion Hughes 6.00 15.00
JA Joseph Addai 8.00 20.00
JB John Beck 6.00 15.00
JC Jason Campbell 8.00 20.00
JJ Jacoby Jones 6.00 15.00
JN Jerious Norwood 8.00 20.00
JO James Jones 6.00 15.00
JP Jordan Palmer 10.00 25.00

JT Joe Thomas 10.00 25.00
KI Kenny Irons 6.00 15.00
LE Lee Evans 10.00 25.00
LF Larry Fitzgerald 20.00 50.00
LL LaRon Landry 10.00 25.00
LN Legedu Naanee 8.00 20.00
LR Laurent Robinson 10.00 25.00
MB Marion Barber 10.00 25.00
MC Marques Colston 8.00 20.00
MG Michael Griffin 6.00 15.00
MS Matt Schaub 8.00 20.00
PM Peyton Manning 60.00 120.00
RN Reggie Nelson 6.00 15.00
RO Jeff Rowe 6.00 15.00
RW Reggie Wayne 12.00 30.00
SS Steve Smith USC 12.00 30.00
TH T.J. Houshmandzadeh 8.00 20.00
TN Joe Theismann 15.00 40.00
WP Willie Parker 10.00 25.00

2007 Sweet Spot Sweet Swatch Jersey

*PATCH/50: .8X TO 2X BASIC JSYs
PATCH PRINT RUN 50 SER.#'d SETS
SSAB Anquan Boldin 2.50 6.00
SSAC Alge Crumpler 3.00 8.00
SSAD Gaines Adams 2.50 6.00
SSAG Anthony Gonzalez 1.25 3.00
SSAG2 Anthony Gonzalez 1.25 3.00
SSAP Adrian Peterson 10.00 25.00
SSAP2 Adrian Peterson 10.00 25.00
SSAV Adam Vinatieri 4.00 10.00
SSBA Champ Bailey 4.00 10.00
SSBD Brian Dawkins 4.00 10.00
SSBE Drew Bennett 2.50 6.00
SSBF Brett Favre 6.00 15.00
SSBJ Brandon Jackson 1.25 3.00
SSBL Brian Leonard 2.50 6.00
SSBO Dwayne Bowe 1.25 3.00
SSBO2 Dwayne Bowe 1.25 3.00
SSBQ Brady Quinn 1.25 3.00
SSBQ2 Brady Quinn 1.25 3.00
SSBR Ronnie Brown 2.50 6.00
SSBU Brian Urlacher 4.00 10.00
SSCB Cedric Benson 2.50 6.00
SSCH Chris Henry RB 2.50 6.00
SSCJ Calvin Johnson 5.00 12.00
SSCJ2 Calvin Johnson 5.00 12.00
SSCL Michael Clayton 2.50 6.00
SSCP Carson Palmer 3.00 8.00
SSCT Chester Taylor 2.50 6.00
SSDB Deion Branch 2.50 6.00
SSDC Daunte Culpepper 3.00 8.00
SSDJ Dwayne Jarrett 1.50 4.00
SSDJ2 Dwayne Jarrett 1.50 4.00
SSDM Donovan McNabb 3.00 8.00
SSDS Drew Stanton 1.25 3.00
SSEM Eli Manning 3.00 8.00
SSGA Antonio Gates 4.00 10.00
SSGJ Greg Jennings 4.00 10.00
SSGL Terry Glenn 3.00 8.00
SSGR Trent Green 2.50 6.00
SSGW Garrett Wolfe 1.25 3.00
SSHE Todd Heap 2.50 6.00
SSHI Johnnie Lee Higgins 2.50 6.00
SSHO Joe Horn 2.50 6.00
SSHU Tony Hunt 2.50 6.00
SSHW Hines Ward 5.00 12.00
SSJA Brandon Jacobs 2.50 6.00
SSJB John Beck 1.25 3.00
SSJB2 John Beck 1.25 3.00
SSJH Jason Hill 2.50 6.00
SSJL Jamal Lewis 3.00 8.00
SSJN Jerious Norwood 2.50 6.00
SSJO Thomas Jones 2.50 6.00
SSJP Jerry Porter 3.00 8.00
SSJR JaMarcus Russell 1.25 3.00
SSJR2 JaMarcus Russell 1.25 3.00
SSJS Jeremy Shockey 2.50 6.00
SSJT Jason Taylor 3.00 8.00
SSJW Javon Walker 3.00 8.00
SSKI Kenny Irons 2.50 6.00
SSKK Kevin Kolb 1.50 4.00
SSKK2 Kevin Kolb 1.50 4.00
SSKW Kellen Winslow 2.50 6.00
SSLB Lorenzo Booker 2.50 6.00
SSLE Byron Leftwich 2.50 6.00
SSLJ Larry Johnson 2.50 6.00
SSLM Laurence Maroney 3.00 8.00
SSMA Marion Barber 5.00 12.00
SSMB Michael Bush 1.25 3.00
SSMC Mark Clayton 2.50 6.00
SSMJ Maurice Jones-Drew 2.50 6.00
SSML Marshawn Lynch 2.50 6.00
SSML2 Marshawn Lynch 2.50 6.00
SSOL Greg Olsen 2.00 5.00
SSPE Julius Peppers 3.00 8.00
SSPI Antonio Pittman 2.50 6.00
SSPM Peyton Manning 10.00 25.00
SSPW Patrick Willis 2.00 5.00
SSRB Reggie Bush 2.50 6.00
SSRG Rex Grossman 2.50 6.00
SSRM Robert Meachem 2.50 6.00
SSRM2 Robert Meachem 2.50 6.00
SSRO Roy Williams WR 2.50 6.00
SSRW Reggie Wayne 3.00 8.00
SSSR Sidney Rice 1.50 4.00
SSSS Steve Smith USC 2.50 6.00
SSSS2 Steve Smith USC 2.50 6.00
SSTB Tedy Bruschi 3.00 8.00
SSTE Trent Edwards 1.25 3.00
SSTE2 Trent Edwards 1.25 3.00
SSTG Ted Ginn Jr. 1.50 4.00
SSTG2 Ted Ginn Jr. 1.50 4.00
SSTH Joe Thomas 2.50 6.00
SSTJ T.J. Houshmandzadeh 2.50 6.00
SSTO Tom Brady 12.00 30.00
SSTS Troy Smith 1.25 3.00
SSTS2 Troy Smith 1.25 3.00
SSWD Warrick Dunn 2.50 6.00
SSWI Paul Williams 2.50 6.00
SSWM Willis McGahee 2.50 6.00
SSYF Yamon Figurs 2.50 6.00

2010 Sweet Spot

COMP.SET w/o AU's (100) 12.00 30.00
ROOKIE AUTO PRINT RUN 100-400
1 Peyton Manning .75 2.00
2 Tom Brady .75 2.00
3 Ben Roethlisberger .30 .75
4 Matt Ryan .25 .60
5 Matthew Stafford .25 .60
6 Mark Sanchez .20 .50
7 Chris Johnson .20 .50
8 Chad Henne .25 .60
9 LaDainian Tomlinson .30 .75
10 Eli Manning .25 .60
11 Rashard Mendenhall .20 .50
12 Knowshon Moreno .20 .50
13 Brandon Marshall .25 .60
14 Philip Rivers .30 .75
15 Vincent Jackson .20 .50
16 Percy Harvin .20 .50
17 Sidney Rice .20 .50
18 Mike Wallace .20 .50
19 Kevin Kolb .20 .50
20 Carson Palmer .25 .60
21 Cedric Benson .20 .50
22 Chad Johnson .20 .50
23 A.J. Hawk .20 .50
24 Tony Romo .25 .60
25 Josh Freeman .25 .60
26 Donovan McNabb [illegible]
27 Adrian Peterson .30 .75
28 Brett Favre 1.25 3.00
29 Santonio Holmes .20 .50
30 Steven Jackson .20 .50
31 Larry Fitzgerald .25 .60
32 Marion Barber .25 .60
33 DeAngelo Williams .20 .50
34 Alex Smith QB .25 .60
35 Aaron Rodgers .60 1.50
36 Elvis Dumervil .20 .50
37 Matt Schaub .20 .50
38 Frank Gore .25 .60
39 Steve Smith USC .20 .50
40 Troy Polamalu .30 .75
41 Joseph Addai .20 .50
42 Ronnie Brown .20 .50
43 Ricky Williams .25 .60
44 Ray Rice .20 .50
45 Matt Cassel .20 .50
46 Ryan Grant .25 .60
47 DeSean Jackson .25 .60
48 Josh Cribbs .20 .50
49 Jeremy Maclin .20 .50
50 Anquan Boldin .20 .50
51 Joe Flacco .25 .60
52 Matt Moore .20 .50
53 Andre Johnson .25 .60
54 Jonathan Stewart .20 .50
55 Felix Jones .20 .50
56 Jason Campbell .20 .50
57 Jamaal Charles .25 .60
58 Jay Cutler .20 .50
59 Darren McFadden .20 .50
60 Mario Manningham .20 .50
61 Devin Hester .25 .60
62 Drew Brees .30 .75
63 Wes Welker .25 .60
64 Hines Ward .25 .60
65 Maurice Jones-Drew .20 .50
66 Calvin Johnson .30 .75
67 Randy Moss .25 .60
68 Thomas Jones .20 .50
69 Michael Turner .20 .50
70 Vince Young .20 .50
71 Sean Weatherspoon RC .60 1.50
72 Taylor Price RC .60 1.50
73 Levi Brown RC .60 1.50
74 Zac Robinson RC .75 2.00
75 Jonathan Crompton RC .60 1.50
76 Joe Webb RC .60 1.50
77 Riley Cooper RC .60 1.50
78 Carlos Dunlap RC .60 1.50
79 Earl Thomas RC 1.50 4.00
80 Jevan Snead RC .60 1.50
81 Antonio Brown RC 5.00 12.00
82 Rob Gronkowski RC 2.00 5.00
83 Taylor Mays RC .60 1.50
84 David Reed RC .60 1.50
85 James Starks RC .75 2.00
86 Marcus Easley RC .60 1.50
87 Carlton Mitchell RC .60 1.50
88 Rusty Smith RC 1.00 2.50
89 Sean Lee RC 1.25 3.00
90 Mike Kafka RC .75 2.00
91 Jimmy Graham RC 1.50 4.00
92 John Skelton RC .75 2.00
93 Kareem Jackson RC .60 1.50
94 Emmanuel Sanders RC 1.00 2.50
95 Kerry Meier RC .75 2.00
96 Bryan Bulaga RC .60 1.50
97 Rolando McClain RC .60 1.50
98 Armanti Edwards RC .75 2.00
99 Jason Pierre-Paul RC 1.00 2.50
100 Jerry Hughes RC .60 1.50
101 Joe Haden AU/400 RC 8.00 20.00
102 Blair White AU/400 RC 5.00 12.00
103 Dem.Thomas AU/100 RC 20.00 50.00
105 Jimmy Clausen AU/100 RC 8.00 20.00
106 Keiland Williams AU/400 RC 6.00 15.00
107 Jahvid Best AU/100 RC 8.00 20.00
108 J.Dwyer AU/300 RC 5.00 12.00
109 Eric Berry AU/400 RC 8.00 20.00
110 Golden Tate AU/100 RC 10.00 25.00
111 Arrelious Benn AU/150 RC 8.00 20.00
112 Damian Williams AU/300 RC 5.00 12.00
113 Gerald McCoy AU/400 RC 5.00 12.00
115 N.Suh AU/400 RC 10.00 25.00
116 Brandon Spikes AU/400 RC 5.00 12.00
117 Bill Stull AU/350 RC 5.00 12.00
118 Ryan Mathews AU/300 RC 5.00 12.00
119 Sergio Kindle AU/400 RC 5.00 12.00
120 Russell Okung AU/350 RC 5.00 12.00
121 Daryll Clark AU/400 RC 8.00 20.00
122 D.Briscoe AU/350 RC 5.00 12.00
123 Max Hall AU/400 RC 8.00 20.00
124 Colt McCoy AU/100 RC 10.00 25.00
125 Dan LeFevour AU/150 RC 8.00 20.00
126 Jarrett Brown AU/150 RC 8.00 20.00
127 Sam Bradford AU/100 RC 25.00 50.00
128 Sean Canfield AU/100 RC 8.00 20.00
129 Tim Tebow AU/100 RC 50.00 100.00
130 Tony Pike AU/100 RC 8.00 20.00
131 Derrick Morgan AU/300 RC 5.00 12.00
132 Chris McGaha AU/400 RC 5.00 12.00
133 Brandon Minor AU/400 RC 8.00 20.00
134 Anthony Dixon AU/400 RC 6.00 15.00
135 Ben Tate AU/350 RC 5.00 12.00
136 Charles Scott AU/400 RC 5.00 12.00
137 Chris Brown AU/400 RC 8.00 20.00
138 C.J. Spiller AU/100 RC 8.00 20.00
139 Javarris James AU/300 RC 5.00 12.00
140 Andre Roberts AU/350 RC 6.00 15.00
141 M.Hardesty AU/400 RC 5.00 12.00
142 Toby Gerhart AU/300 RC 5.00 12.00
143 Joe McKnight AU/300 RC 5.00 12.00
144 Dennis Pitta AU/400 RC 5.00 12.00
145 Garrett Graham AU/350 RC 5.00 12.00
146 A.McCoy AU/300 RC 5.00 12.00
147 Ed Dickson AU/350 RC 5.00 12.00
148 J.Gresham AU/300 RC 5.00 12.00
149 Brandon LaFell AU/100 RC 12.00 30.00
150 Jeremy Williams AU/300 RC 5.00 12.00
151 Dez Bryant AU/100 RC 40.00 80.00
152 Eric Decker AU/400 RC 6.00 15.00
153 Jacoby Ford AU/300 RC 5.00 12.00
154 Jordan Shipley AU/300 RC 5.00 12.00
155 Mardy Gilyard AU/250 RC 5.00 12.00
156 Mike Williams AU/300 RC 5.00 12.00
157 L.Blount AU/300 RC 10.00 25.00
158 A.Hernandez AU/400 RC 12.00 30.00
159 D.McCluster AU/300 RC 6.00 15.00
160 B.Graham AU/400 RC 6.00 15.00

2010 Sweet Spot Rookie Signatures Variations

*VAR AU/350: .4X TO 1X BASE AU/400
*VAR AU/200-250: .5X TO 1.2X BASE/250-400
*VAR AU/100-150: .6X TO 1.5X BASE/250-400
*VAR AU/50-75: .5X TO 1.2X BASE/100-150
*VAR AU/50: .8X TO 2X BASIC AU/300
*VAR AU/25: .6X TO 1.5X BASIC AU/100-150
VARIATION PRINT RUN 25-350
127A Sam Bradford/50 40.00 80.00
127B Sam Bradford/25 40.00 100.00
129A Tim Tebow/50 60.00 120.00
129B Tim Tebow/25 75.00 200.00

2010 Sweet Spot Signatures

STATED PRINT RUN 10-400
SERIAL #'d UNDER 30 NOT PRICED
AM Archie Manning/75 30.00 80.00
CM Craig Morton/300 8.00 20.00
CO Christian Okoye/400 8.00 20.00
DJ Daryl Johnston/100 15.00 40.00
DS Donnie Shell/125 10.00 25.00
FG Frank Gore/75 [illegible]
GJ Greg Jennings/125 15.00 40.00
HC Harry Carson/125 10.00 25.00
JT Joe Theismann/100 15.00 40.00
JY Jack Youngblood/100 15.00 40.00
MA Mike Alstott/150 15.00 40.00
MO Herman Moore/200 10.00 25.00
MS Mike Singletary/125 20.00 50.00
PA Alan Page/100 15.00 40.00
PH Paul Hornung/75 20.00 50.00
RC Roger Craig/100 15.00 40.00
RG Roman Gabriel/125 12.00 30.00
RI Rocket Ismail/100 15.00 40.00
RO Antrel Rolle/100 10.00 25.00
RW Ricky Williams/75 25.00 60.00
RY Ron Yary/300 8.00 20.00
SI Billy Sims/300 12.00 30.00
SM Bubba Smith/100 12.00 30.00
SR Sidney Rice/150 12.00 30.00
SS Steve Smith USC/100 10.00 25.00
SY Steve Young/30 30.00 80.00
TR Tom Rathman/75 15.00 40.00

2010 Sweet Spot Signatures Variations

STATED PRINT RUN 3-125
SERIAL #'d UNDER 25 NOT PRICED
AM1 Archie Manning/50 40.00 80.00
AM2 Archie Manning/25 40.00 100.00
CM1 Craig Morton/100 10.00 25.00
CM2 Craig Morton/50 12.00 30.00
DJ1 Daryl Johnston/50 20.00 50.00
DJ2 Daryl Johnston/25 25.00 60.00
DS1 Donnie Shell/25 15.00 40.00
FG1 Frank Gore/50 20.00 50.00
FG2 Frank Gore/25 25.00 60.00
GJ1 Greg Jennings/25 25.00 60.00
HC1 Harry Carson/25 15.00 40.00
JT1 Joe Theismann/50 20.00 50.00
JT2 Joe Theismann/25 25.00 60.00
JY1 Jack Youngblood/50 20.00 50.00
JY2 Jack Youngblood/25 25.00 60.00
MA1 Mike Alstott/100 15.00 40.00
MO1 Herman Moore/125 10.00 25.00
MO2 Herman Moore/125 10.00 25.00
MS1 Mike Singletary/25 NCAA 20.00 50.00
PA1 Alan Page/50 20.00 50.00
PA2 Alan Page/25 25.00 60.00
PH1 Paul Hornung/50 20.00 50.00
PH2 Paul Hornung/25 30.00 80.00
RC1 Roger Craig/50 20.00 50.00
RC2 Roger Craig/25 25.00 60.00
RG1 Roman Gabriel/25 NCAA 15.00 40.00
RI1 Rocket Ismail/50 20.00 50.00
RI2 Rocket Ismail/25 25.00 60.00
RO1 Antrel Rolle/50 12.00 30.00
RO2 Antrel Rolle/25 15.00 40.00
RW1 Ricky Williams/50 25.00 60.00
RW2 Ricky Williams/25 30.00 80.00
RY1 Ron Yary/100 10.00 25.00
RY2 Ron Yary/50 12.00 30.00
SI1 Billy Sims/100 15.00 40.00
SI2 Billy Sims/50 20.00 50.00
SM1 Bubba Smith/50 15.00 40.00
SR1 Sidney Rice/25 NCAA 15.00 40.00
SS1 Steve Smith USC/50 12.00 30.00
SS2 Steve Smith USC/25 15.00 40.00
TR1 Tom Rathman/50 15.00 40.00
TR2 Tom Rathman/25 25.00 60.00

2010 Sweet Spot Sweet Swatches

ONE AUTO OR JSY CARD PER PACK
SSW1 A.J. Hawk 2.50 6.00
SSW2 Gale Sayers 6.00 15.00
SSW3 Albert Haynesworth 2.50 6.00
SSW4 Ben Roethlisberger 5.00 12.00
SSW5 Bo Jackson 8.00 20.00
SSW6 Brandon Pettigrew 2.50 6.00
SSW7 Brett Favre 8.00 20.00
SSW8 Tom Brady 15.00 40.00
SSW9 Calvin Johnson 6.00 15.00
SSW10 Carson Palmer 3.00 8.00
SSW11 Chad Henne 3.00 8.00
SSW12 Chad Pennington 2.50 6.00
SSW13 Chris Johnson 2.50 6.00
SSW14 Chris Wells 2.50 6.00
SSW15 Chris Wells 2.50 6.00
SSW16 Dan Marino 10.00 25.00
SSW17 Darren McFadden 2.50 6.00
SSW18 Darrius Heyward-Bey 3.00 8.00
SSW19 DeSean Jackson 3.00 8.00
SSW20 Donald Brown 2.50 6.00
SSW21 Donald Brown 2.50 6.00
SSW22 Donnie Avery 2.50 6.00
SSW23 Donovan McNabb 3.00 8.00
SSW24 Drew Brees 4.00 10.00
SSW25 Dwayne Bowe 3.00 8.00
SSW26 Felix Jones 2.50 6.00
SSW27 Frank Gore 3.00 8.00
SSW28 Fran Tarkenton 6.00 15.00
SSW29 Hakeem Nicks 2.50 6.00
SSW30 Hakeem Nicks 2.50 6.00
SSW31 Mike Singletary 5.00 12.00
SSW32 Randall Cunningham 5.00 12.00
SSW33 Jamaal Charles 3.00 8.00
SSW34 Peyton Manning 15.00 40.00
SSW35 Jay Cutler 2.50 6.00
SSW36 Jeremy Maclin 2.50 6.00
SSW37 Jeremy Maclin 2.50 6.00
SSW38 Jim Kelly 6.00 15.00
SSW39 John Elway 8.00 20.00
SSW40 Jonathan Stewart 2.50 6.00
SSW41 Josh Freeman 3.00 8.00
SSW42 Josh Freeman 3.00 8.00
SSW43 Kenny Britt 2.50 6.00
SSW44 Kevin Smith 2.50 6.00
SSW45 Knowshon Moreno 2.50 6.00
SSW46 Knowshon Moreno 2.50 6.00
SSW47 Michael Crabtree 2.50 6.00
SSW48 Adrian Peterson 4.00 10.00
SSW49 LeSean McCoy 4.00 10.00
SSW50 LeSean McCoy 4.00 10.00
SSW51 Mario Manningham 2.50 6.00
SSW52 Marion Barber 3.00 8.00
SSW53 Mark Sanchez 4.00 10.00
SSW54 Mark Sanchez 4.00 10.00
SSW55 Aaron Rodgers 8.00 20.00
SSW56 Matt Forte 2.50 6.00
SSW57 Matt Leinart 2.50 6.00
SSW58 Matt Ryan 3.00 8.00
SSW59 Matthew Stafford 3.00 8.00
SSW60 Matthew Stafford 3.00 8.00
SSW61 Michael Crabtree 2.50 6.00
SSW62 Mike Wallace 2.50 6.00
SSW63 Mike Wallace 2.50 6.00
SSW64 Mohamed Massaquoi 3.00 8.00
SSW65 Percy Harvin 2.50 6.00
SSW66 Rashard Mendenhall 2.50 6.00
SSW67 Rashard Mendenhall 2.50 6.00
SSW68 Mario Williams 3.00 8.00
SSW69 Ricky Williams 3.00 8.00
SSW70 Ronnie Brown 2.50 6.00
SSW71 Steve Young 8.00 20.00
SSW72 Troy Aikman 8.00 20.00
SSW73 Warren Moon 6.00 15.00
SSW74 Paul Hornung 6.00 15.00
SSW75 Patrick Willis 3.00 8.00
SSW76 Drew Bledsoe 5.00 12.00
SSW77 Joe Flacco 3.00 8.00

2011 Sweet Spot

1 Tyron Smith .60 1.50
2 Daniel Thomas .50 1.25
3 Greg Salas .50 1.25
4 Vai Taua .50 1.25
5 DeMarco Murray 1.00 2.50
6 Stevan Ridley .50 1.25
7 Bilal Powell .60 1.50
8 Colin McCarthy .60 1.50
9 Da'Quan Bowers .50 1.25
10 Mark Herzlich .50 1.25
11 Edmond Gates .50 1.25
12 Courtney Smith .50 1.25
13 Niles Paul .50 1.25
14 Stefen Wisniewski .75 2.00
15 Stephen Paea .50 1.25
16 Ras-I Dowling .50 1.25
17 Cameron Jordan .60 1.50
18 Allen Bailey .50 1.25
19 Nate Solder .50 1.25
20 Christian Ponder .50 1.25
21 Kendall Hunter .50 1.25
22 Dwayne Harris .50 1.25
23 Akeem Ayers .50 1.25
24 Bruce Carter .50 1.25
25 Tyrod Taylor 1.00 2.50
26 Prince Amukamara .50 1.25
27 Mario Fannin .60 1.50
28 Jordan Todman .50 1.25
29 Ronald Johnson .50 1.25
30 Greg Little .60 1.50
31 Cecil Shorts .50 1.25
32 Von Miller .75 2.00
33 Matt Szczur .75 2.00
34 Greg Jones .60 1.50
35 J.J. Watt 3.00 8.00
36 Noel Devine .75 2.00
37 Armon Binns .60 1.50
38 James Cleveland .50 1.25
39 Nick Fairley .50 1.25
40 Austin Pettis .50 1.25
41 Dane Sanzenbacher .50 1.25
42 Armando Allen .75 2.00
43 Brandon Saine .75 2.00
44 Ryan Kerrigan .60 1.50
45 John Clay .75 2.00
46 Kelvin Sheppard .50 1.25
47 Ryan Whalen .50 1.25
48 Lance Kendricks .50 1.25
49 Colin Kaepernick .75 2.00
50 Anthony Allen .50 1.25
51 Mike Pouncey .75 2.00
52 Pat Devlin .75 2.00
53 Nathan Enderle .50 1.25
54 Leonard Hankerson .50 1.25
55 Delone Carter .50 1.25
56 Marvin Austin .50 1.25
57 Jeff Maehl .50 1.25
58 Jerrel Jernigan .50 1.25
59 Vincent Brown .50 1.25
60 Andy Dalton 1.00 2.50
61 Roy Helu .50 1.25
62 Adrian Clayborn .50 1.25
63 Luke Stocker .50 1.25
64 Terrence Toliver .60 1.50
65 Anthony Castonzo .50 1.25
66 Jeremy Beal .60 1.50
67 Ross Homan .60 1.50
68 DeAndre McDaniel .50 1.25
69 Evan Royster .50 1.25
70 Tandon Doss .50 1.25
71 Aldon Smith .50 1.25
72 Cameron Heyward .60 1.50
73 Drake Nevis .50 1.25
74 Quan Sturdivant .60 1.50
75 Jamie Harper .50 1.25
76 Jeremy Kerley .75 2.00
77 Jake Locker .50 1.25
78 Ricky Stanzi .50 1.25
79 Titus Young .50 1.25
80 D.J. Williams .50 1.25
81 Benjamin Ijalana .60 1.50
82 Graig Cooper .60 1.50
83 Derrick Locke .60 1.50
84 Randall Cobb .75 2.00
85 Cam Newton 2.50 6.00
86 Mikel Leshoure .50 1.25
87 Justin Houston .60 1.50
88 Jacquizz Rodgers .50 1.25
89 Mark Ingram .75 2.00
90 Blaine Gabbert .50 1.25
91 Ryan Mallett .50 1.25
92 Kyle Rudolph .50 1.25
93 Julio Jones 1.50 4.00
94 Shane Vereen .60 1.50
95 Dion Lewis .60 1.50
96 Torrey Smith .50 1.25
97 A.J. Green 1.25 3.00
98 Jonathan Baldwin .50 1.25
99 Marcell Dareus .50 1.25
100 Ryan Williams .50 1.25
101 Terrelle Pryor .75 2.00

2011 Sweet Spot Autographs

1 Tyron Smith 10.00 25.00
2 Daniel Thomas 4.00 10.00
3 Greg Salas 4.00 10.00
4 Vai Taua 4.00 10.00
5 DeMarco Murray 8.00 20.00
6 Stevan Ridley 4.00 10.00
7 Bilal Powell 5.00 12.00
8 Colin McCarthy 5.00 12.00
9 Da'Quan Bowers 4.00 10.00
10 Mark Herzlich 4.00 10.00
11 Edmond Gates 4.00 10.00
12 Courtney Smith 4.00 10.00
13 Niles Paul 4.00 10.00
14 Stefen Wisniewski 6.00 15.00
15 Stephen Paea 4.00 10.00
16 Ras-I Dowling 4.00 10.00
17 Cameron Jordan 5.00 12.00
18 Allen Bailey 4.00 10.00
19 Nate Solder 4.00 10.00
20 Christian Ponder 4.00 10.00
21 Kendall Hunter 4.00 10.00
22 Dwayne Harris 4.00 10.00
23 Akeem Ayers 4.00 10.00
24 Bruce Carter 8.00 20.00
25 Tyrod Taylor 8.00 20.00
26 Prince Amukamara 8.00 20.00
27 Mario Fannin 5.00 12.00
28 Jordan Todman 4.00 10.00
29 Ronald Johnson 4.00 10.00
30 Greg Little 5.00 12.00
31 Cecil Shorts 4.00 10.00
32 Von Miller 15.00 40.00
33 Matt Szczur 6.00 15.00
34 Greg Jones 5.00 12.00
35 J.J. Watt 40.00 100.00
36 Noel Devine 6.00 15.00
37 Armon Binns 5.00 12.00
38 James Cleveland 5.00 12.00
40 Austin Pettis 4.00 10.00
41 Dane Sanzenbacher 8.00 20.00
42 Armando Allen 6.00 15.00
43 Brandon Saine 8.00 20.00
44 Ryan Kerrigan 5.00 12.00
45 John Clay 6.00 15.00
46 Kelvin Sheppard 4.00 10.00
47 Ryan Whalen [illegible]
48 Lance Kendricks 4.00 10.00
49 Colin Kaepernick 6.00 15.00
50 Anthony Allen 4.00 10.00
51 Mike Pouncey 8.00 20.00
52 Pat Devlin 6.00 15.00
53 Nathan Enderle 4.00 10.00
54 Leonard Hankerson 4.00 10.00
55 Delone Carter 4.00 10.00
57 Jeff Maehl 4.00 10.00
58 Jerrel Jernigan 4.00 10.00
59 Vincent Brown 8.00 20.00
60 Andy Dalton 8.00 20.00
61 Roy Helu 4.00 10.00
62 Adrian Clayborn 15.00 30.00
63 Luke Stocker 4.00 10.00
64 Terrence Toliver 5.00 12.00
65 Anthony Castonzo 4.00 10.00
66 Jeremy Beal 5.00 12.00
67 Ross Homan 5.00 12.00
68 DeAndre McDaniel 4.00 10.00
69 Evan Royster 4.00 10.00
70 Tandon Doss 4.00 10.00
71 Aldon Smith 4.00 10.00
72 Cameron Heyward 5.00 12.00
73 Drake Nevis 4.00 10.00
74 Quan Sturdivant 5.00 12.00
75 Jamie Harper 4.00 10.00
76 Jeremy Kerley 6.00 15.00
77 Jake Locker 4.00 10.00
78 Ricky Stanzi 4.00 10.00
79 Titus Young 4.00 10.00
80 D.J. Williams 4.00 10.00
81 Benjamin Ijalana 5.00 12.00
82 Graig Cooper 5.00 12.00
83 Derrick Locke 5.00 12.00
84 Randall Cobb 6.00 15.00
85 Cam Newton 30.00 80.00
86 Mikel Leshoure 4.00 10.00
87 Justin Houston 5.00 12.00
88 Jacquizz Rodgers 8.00 20.00
89 Mark Ingram 6.00 15.00
90 Blaine Gabbert 4.00 10.00
91 Ryan Mallett 4.00 10.00
92 Kyle Rudolph 4.00 10.00
93 Julio Jones 20.00 50.00
94 Shane Vereen 5.00 12.00
95 Dion Lewis 5.00 12.00
96 Torrey Smith 4.00 10.00
97 A.J. Green 20.00 50.00
98 Jonathan Baldwin 10.00 25.00
99 Marcell Dareus 4.00 10.00
100 Ryan Williams 15.00 40.00
101 Terrelle Pryor 6.00 15.00

2011 Sweet Spot Chris Mortensen Retro Report

AVERAGE ODDS 1:2
AUTOS TOO SCARCE TO PRICE
MR1 Charles White 1.00 2.50
MR2 Troy Aikman 2.00 5.00
MR3 Steve Largent 1.50 4.00
MR4 Earl Campbell 1.50 4.00
MR5 Floyd Little 1.00 2.50
MR6 John Elway 2.50 6.00
MR7 Bob Griese 1.50 4.00
MR8 Jack Ham 1.25 3.00
MR9 Barry Sanders 2.50 6.00
MR10 Thurman Thomas 1.25 3.00
MR11 Brian Bosworth 1.25 3.00
MR12 Greg Pruitt 1.00 2.50
MR13 Alan Page 1.00 2.50
MR14 Paul Hornung 1.50 4.00
MR15 Rocket Ismail 1.25 3.00
MR16 Tim Brown 1.50 4.00
MR17 Roman Gabriel 1.00 2.50
MR18 Kellen Winslow Sr. 1.25 3.00
MR19 Jerry Rice 2.50 6.00
MR20 Bernie Kosar 1.25 3.00
MR21 Jim Kelly 1.50 4.00
MR22 Steve Young 2.00 5.00
MR23 Doug Flutie 1.25 3.00
MR24 Bo Jackson 2.00 5.00
MR25 Chris Mortensen 1.00 2.50

2011 Sweet Spot Rivalries Dual Autographs

STATED PRINT RUN 5-99
EXCH EXPIRATION: 7/14/2013
RBC T.Brwn/A.Crtr/25 EXCH 30.00 60.00
RBM Bledsoe/Moon/25 EXCH 40.00 80.00
RCD R.Dowling/B.Carter/99 8.00 20.00
RCS B.Sims/R.Craig/99 12.00 30.00
RGC Griffin/A.Carter/25 40.00 80.00
RGK Winslow Sr/Sayers/25 30.00 60.00
RHM Murray/Hunter/99 10.00 25.00
RMP E.Metcalf/G.Pruitt/75 25.00 50.00
RPH C.Ponder/Hankerson/75 20.00 50.00
RPS Page/B.Smith/99 EXCH 15.00 30.00
RPY R.Yary/A.Page/99 20.00 40.00
RRJ G.Jones/E.Royster/99 20.00 40.00
RRS B.Saine/E.Royster/99 20.00 40.00
RSC A.Carter/C.Spielman/25 30.00 60.00
RSW K.Winslow Sr/B.Sims/75 12.00 30.00
RTS Sims/T.Thomas/25 40.00 80.00
RTW C.White/Thsmn/99 25.00 50.00
RWJ H.Walker/Bo/25 60.00 120.00
RYB R.Yary/G.Beban/25 30.00 60.00

2011 Sweet Spot Rookie Signatures

STATED PRINT RUN 199-599
EXCH EXPIRATION: 7/14/2013
RSAB Allen Bailey/599 4.00 10.00
RSAC Adrian Clayborn/599 4.00 10.00
RSAD Andy Dalton/199 12.00 30.00
RSAG A.J. Green/199 25.00 60.00
RSAP Austin Pettis/599 4.00 10.00
RSBA Jonathan Baldwin/199 6.00 15.00
RSBC Bruce Carter/599 4.00 10.00
RSBG Blaine Gabbert/275 5.00 12.00
RSBI Armon Binns/599 5.00 12.00
RSBS Brandon Saine/599 6.00 15.00
RSCH Cameron Heyward/599 5.00 12.00
RSCK Colin Kaepernick/599 6.00 15.00
RSCN Cam Newton/199 50.00 100.00
RSCP Christian Ponder/199 6.00 15.00
RSDH Dwayne Harris/599 4.00 10.00
RSDM DeMarco Murray/199 12.00 30.00
RSDS Dane Sanzenbacher/599 4.00 10.00
RSDT Daniel Thomas/199 6.00 15.00
RSER Evan Royster/199 6.00 15.00
RSGC Graig Cooper/599 5.00 12.00
RSGJ Greg Jones/599 5.00 12.00
RSGL Greg Little/199 8.00 20.00
RSGS Greg Salas/599 4.00 10.00
RSHE Roy Helu/599 4.00 10.00
RSJB Jeremy Beal/599 5.00 12.00
RSJC James Cleveland/599 4.00 10.00
RSJK Jeremy Kerley/599 6.00 15.00
RSJL Jake Locker/275 5.00 12.00
RSJO Julio Jones/199 20.00 50.00
RSKH Kendall Hunter/599 4.00 10.00
RSKS Kelvin Sheppard/599 4.00 10.00
RSLH Leonard Hankerson/599 4.00 10.00
RSMH Mark Herzlich/599 4.00 10.00
RSMI Mark Ingram/199 10.00 25.00
RSND Noel Devine/599 6.00 15.00
RSNE Nathan Enderle/599 EXCH 4.00 10.00
RSNP Niles Paul/599 4.00 10.00
RSPA Prince Amukamara/199 6.00 15.00
RSPD Pat Devlin/199 10.00 25.00
RSQS Quan Sturdivant/599 5.00 12.00
RSRD Ras-I Dowling/599 4.00 10.00
RSRH Ross Homan/599 5.00 12.00
RSRJ Ronald Johnson/599 4.00 10.00
RSRK Ryan Kerrigan/599 5.00 12.00
RSRM Ryan Mallett/199 6.00 15.00
RSRS Ricky Stanzi/599 [illegible]
RSRW Ryan Williams/199 15.00 40.00
RSSP Stephen Paea/599 4.00 10.00
RSTA Tyrod Taylor/599 8.00 20.00
RSTT Terrence Toliver/599 5.00 12.00
RSTY Titus Young/599 4.00 10.00
RSVB Vincent Brown/599 4.00 10.00
RSVM Von Miller/599 10.00 25.00

2011 Sweet Spot Rookie Signatures Variations

*VARIATION/299: .5X TO 1.2X BASIC AU/599
*VARIATION/75: .5X TO 1.2X BASIC AU/199-275
STATED PRINT RUN 75-299
RSAD Andy Dalton/75 15.00 40.00
RSCK Colin Kaepernick/299 8.00 20.00
RSCN Cam Newton/75 40.00 100.00

2011 Sweet Spot Todd McShay Scouting Report

AVERAGE ODDS 1:2
AUTOS TOO SCARCE TO PRICE
TM1 Jordan Todman .40 1.00
TM2 Jonathan Baldwin .40 1.00
TM3 Ryan Williams .40 1.00
TM4 Mikel Leshoure .40 1.00
TM5 Torrey Smith .40 1.00
TM6 Christian Ponder .40 1.00
TM7 Jake Locker .40 1.00
TM8 Kendall Hunter .40 1.00
TM9 Tandon Doss .40 1.00
TM10 Jacquizz Rodgers .40 1.00
TM11 DeMarco Murray .75 2.00
TM12 Daniel Thomas .40 1.00
TM13 Leonard Hankerson .40 1.00
TM14 Randall Cobb .60 1.50
TM15 Kyle Rudolph .40 1.00
TM16 Titus Young .40 1.00
TM17 Cam Newton 2.00 5.00
TM18 Shane Vereen .50 1.25
TM19 Greg Little .50 1.25
TM20 Ryan Mallett .40 1.00
TM21 A.J. Green 1.00 2.50
TM22 Blaine Gabbert .40 1.00
TM23 Julio Jones 1.25 3.00
TM24 Mark Ingram .60 1.50
TM25 Todd McShay .40 1.00

2011 Sweet Spot Ultimate Rookie Signatures

STATED ODDS 1:360
21 Ras-I Dowling 8.00 20.00
22 Prince Amukamara 8.00 20.00
23 Adrian Clayborn 8.00 20.00
24 Greg Jones 10.00 25.00
25 Jeremy Beal 10.00 25.00
26 Bruce Carter 8.00 20.00
27 Colin Kaepernick 12.00 30.00
28 Ricky Stanzi
29 Andy Dalton
30 Roy Helu 8.00 20.00
31 Cameron Jordan 10.00 25.00
32 Tyrod Taylor 15.00 40.00
33 James Cleveland 8.00 20.00
34 Ryan Kerrigan 10.00 25.00
35 Greg Salas 8.00 20.00
36 Jeremy Kerley 12.00 30.00
37 Leonard Hankerson 8.00 20.00
38 Dwayne Harris 8.00 20.00
39 Vincent Brown 8.00 20.00
40 Jerrel Jernigan 8.00 20.00

2011 Sweet Spot Veteran Signatures

STATED PRINT RUN 15-80
*VARIATION/30: .5X TO 1.2X BASIC AU/50
EXCH EXPIRATION: 7/14/2013
SSAC Anthony Carter/80 15.00 40.00
SSAG Archie Griffin/15 40.00 80.00
SSAP Adrian Peterson/15
SSBB Brian Bosworth/50 20.00 50.00
SSBC Billy Cannon/50 20.00 50.00
SSBG Bob Griese/15
SSBJ Bo Jackson/15
SSBK Bernie Kosar/50 15.00 40.00
SSBS Barry Sanders/15 125.00 250.00
SSCS Chris Spielman/50 12.00 30.00
SSCW Charles White/50 12.00 30.00
SSDB Drew Brees/15 50.00 100.00
SSDC Dave Casper/50 15.00 40.00
SSDL Daryle Lamonica/50 15.00 40.00
SSDM Dan Marino/15 125.00 250.00
SSDW Danny Wuerffel/50 20.00 50.00
SSEC Earl Campbell/50 30.00 60.00
SSEG Eddie George/15
SSEM Eric Metcalf/50 15.00 40.00
SSGB Gary Beban/80 12.00 30.00
SSGP Greg Pruitt/50 12.00 30.00
SSGS Gale Sayers/15
SSHW Herschel Walker/50 30.00 60.00
SSJC John Cappelletti/50 12.00 30.00
SSJE John Elway/15 EXCH
SSJH Jack Ham/15
SSJK Jim Kelly/15 40.00 80.00
SSJM Jim McMahon/80 15.00 40.00
SSJP Jim Plunkett/50 20.00 50.00
SSJT Joe Theismann/50 12.00 30.00
SSJW Jason White/50 12.00 30.00
SSKW Kellen Winslow Sr./80 15.00 40.00
SSLS Lee Roy Selmon/50 20.00 50.00
SSMO Chris Mortensen/80 15.00 40.00
SSPA Alan Page/50 12.00 30.00
SSPH Paul Hornung/50 20.00 50.00
SSRB Rocky Bleier/50 15.00 40.00
SSRD Ron Dayne/80 12.00 30.00
SSSI Billy Sims/50 12.00 30.00
SSSJ Steven Jackson/15
SSSM Bubba Smith/80 EXCH 15.00 40.00
SSSY Steve Young/25 30.00 80.00
SSTA Troy Aikman/15 EXCH 50.00 100.00
SSTB Tim Brown/15 40.00 80.00
SSTD Tony Dorsett/15 50.00 100.00
SSTM Todd McShay/80 15.00 40.00
SSTR Tom Rathman/50 12.00 30.00
SSTT Thurman Thomas/15
SSWM Warren Moon/50 25.00 50.00

1988 Swell Greats

The 1988 Swell Football Greats set contains 144 standard size cards. This set was issued in 10-card packs. Each card depicts a member of the Pro Football Hall of Fame. The fronts have blue borders and color photos. The backs are baby blue and contain each player's career highlights. This issue was distributed in wax packs of ten cards and also as a complete set. The factory-collated complete set cards are sometimes found with slight notches along the upper border; this does not seem to be the case with the cards taken from wax packs. After each player's name below is listed his year of induction into the Hall of Fame. The set includes the 1988 Pro Football Hall of Fame inductees.

COMPLETE SET (144) 12.50 25.00
1 Pete Rozelle 85 .06 .15
2 Joe Namath 85 .50 1.25
3 Frank Gatski 85 .04 .10
4 O.J. Simpson 85 .15 .40
5 Roger Staubach 85 .30 .75
6 Herb Adderley 80 .06 .15
7 Lance Alworth 78 .12 .30
8 Doug Atkins 82 .06 .15
9 Red Badgro .04 .10
10 Cliff Battles 68 .04 .10
11 Sammy Baugh 63 .25 .60
12 Raymond Berry 73 .12 .30
13 Charles W. Bidwill 67 .04 .10
14 Chuck Bednarik 67 .12 .30
15 Bert Bell 63 .04 .10
16 Bobby Bell 83 .06 .15
17 George Blanda 81 .12 .30
18 Jim Brown 71 .40 1.00
19 Paul Brown 67 [illegible]
20 Roosevelt Brown 75 .06 .15
21 Ray Flaherty 76 .04 .10
22 Len Ford 76 .06 .15

23 Dan Fortmann 65 .04 .10
24 Bill George 74 .06 .15
25 Art Donovan 68 .10 .25
26 Paddy Driscoll .04 .10
27 Jimmy Conzelman 64 .04 .10
28 Willie Davis 81 .06 .15
29 Dutch Clark 63 .06 .15
30 George Connor 75 .06 .15
31 Guy Chamberlin 65 .04 .10
32 Jack Christiansen 70 .06 .15
33 Tony Canadeo 74 .06 .15
34 Joe Carr 63 .04 .10
35 Willie Brown 84 .06 .15
36 Dick Butkus 79 .25 .60
37 Bill Dudley 66 .06 .15
38 Turk Edwards 69 .04 .10
39 Weeb Ewbank 78 .04 .10
40 Tom Fears 70 .06 .15
41 Otto Graham 65 .25 .60
42 Red Grange 63 .20 .50
43 Frank Gifford 77 .20 .50
44 Sid Gillman 83 .04 .10
45 Forrest Gregg 77 .06 .15
46 Lou Groza 74 .10 .25
47 Joe Guyon 66 .04 .10
48 George Halas 63 .12 .30
49 Ed Healey 64 .04 .10
50 Mel Hein 63 .04 .10
51 Fats Henry 63 .04 .10
52 Arnie Herber 66 .04 .10
53 Bill Hewitt 71 .04 .10
54 Clarke Hinkle 64 .04 .10
55 Elroy Hirsch 68 .10 .25
56 Robert(Cal) Hubbard 63 .04 .10
57 Sam Huff 82 .10 .25
58 Lamar Hunt 72 .04 .10
59 Don Hutson 63 .10 .25
60 Deacon Jones 80 .10 .25
61 Sonny Jurgensen 83 .10 .25
62 Walt Kiesling 66 .04 .10
63 Frank(Bruiser) Kinard 71 .04 .10
64 Curly Lambeau 62 .04 .10
65 Dick Lane .06 .15
66 Yale Lary 79 .06 .15
67 Dante Lavelli 75 .06 .15
68 Bobby Layne 67 .20 .50
69 Tuffy Leemans 78 .04 .10
70 Bob Lilly 80 .12 .30
71 Vince Lombardi 71 .20 .50
72 Sid Luckman 65 .12 .30
73 Link Lyman 64 .04 .10
74 Tim Mara 63 .04 .10
75 Gino Marchetti 72 .06 .15
76 Geo.Preston Marshall 63 .04 .10
77 Ollie Matson 72 .10 .25
78 George McAfee 66 .06 .15
79 Mike McCormack 84 .06 .15
80 Hugh McElhenny 70 .10 .25
81 Johnny Blood McNally 63 .04 .10
82 Mike Michalske 64 .04 .10
83 Wayne Millner 68 .04 .10
84 Bobby Mitchell 83 .10 .25
85 Ron Mix 79 .06 .15
86 Lenny Moore 75 .12 .30
87 Marion Motley 68 .10 .25
88 George Musso 82 .04 .10
89 Bronko Nagurski 63 .12 .30
90 Greasy Neale .04 .10
91 Ernie Nevers 63 .06 .15
92 Ray Nitschke 78 .12 .30
93 Leo Nomellini 69 .06 .15
94 Merlin Olsen 82 .10 .25
95 Jim Otto 80 .10 .25
96 Steve Owen 66 .04 .10
97 Clarence(Ace) Parker 72 .04 .10
98 Jim Parker 73 .06 .15
99 Joe Perry 69 .10 .25
100 Pete Pihos 70 .06 .15
101 Hugh(Shorty) Ray 66 .04 .10
102 Dan Reeves 67 .04 .10
103 Jim Ringo 81 .06 .15
104 Andy Robustelli 71 .06 .15
105 Art Rooney 64 UER .04 .10
106 Gale Sayers 77 .20 .50
107 Joe Schmidt 73 .06 .15
108 Bart Starr 77 .30 .75
109 Ernie Stautner 69 .10 .25
110 Ken Strong 67 .06 .15
111 Joe Stydahar 67 .04 .10
112 Charley Taylor 84 .06 .15
113 Jim Taylor 76 .10 .25
114 Jim Thorpe 63 .20 .50
115 Y.A. Tittle 71 .15 .40
116 George Trafton 64 .04 .10
117 Charley Trippi 68 .06 .15
118 Emlen Tunnell 67 .06 .15
119 Bulldog Turner .10 .25
120 Johnny Unitas 79 .30 .75
121 Norm Van Brocklin 71 .10 .25
122 Steve Van Buren 65 UER .10 .25
123 Paul Warfield 83 .10 .25
124 Bob Waterfield 65 .10 .25
125 Arnie Weinmeister 84 .04 .10
126 Bill Willis 77 .06 .15
127 Larry Wilson 78 .06 .15
128 Alex Wojciechowicz 68 .04 .10
129 Doak Walker 86 .10 .25
130 Willie Lanier 86 .06 .15
131 Paul Hornung 86 .15 .40
132 Ken Houston 86 .06 .15
133 Fran Tarkenton 86 .15 .40
134 Don Maynard 87 .10 .25
135 Larry Csonka 87 .12 .30
136 Joe Greene 87 .12 .30
137 Len Dawson 87 .12 .30
138 Gene Upshaw 87 .06 .15
139 Jim Langer 87 .06 .15
140 John Henry Johnson 87 .06 .15
141 Fred Biletnikoff 88 .12 .30
142 Mike Ditka 88 .25 .60
143 Jack Ham 88 .12 .30
144 Alan Page 88 .06 .15

1989 Swell Greats

The 1989 Swell Football Greats set contains 150 standard-size cards, depicting all Pro Football Hall of Famers. The fronts have white borders and vintage photos; the vertically oriented backs feature player profiles. The cards were available in ten-card wax packs.

COMPLETE SET (150) 12.50 25.00
1 Terry Bradshaw .30 .75
2 Bert Bell .04 .10
3 Joe Carr .04 .10
4 Dutch Clark .06 .15
5 Red Grange .20 .50
6 Fats Henry .04 .10
7 Mel Hein .04 .10
8 Robert(Cal) Hubbard .04 .10
9 George Halas .12 .30
10 Don Hutson .10 .25
11 Curly Lambeau .04 .10
12 Tim Mara .04 .10
13 Geo.Preston Marshall .04 .10
14 Johnny Blood McNally .04 .10
15 Bronko Nagurski .12 .30
16 Ernie Nevers .06 .15
17 Jim Thorpe .20 .50
18 Ed Healey .04 .10
19 Clarke Hinkle .04 .10
20 Link Lyman .04 .10
21 Mike Michalske .04 .10
22 George Trafton .04 .10
23 Guy Chamberlin .04 .10
24 Paddy Driscoll .04 .10
25 Dan Fortmann .04 .10
26 Otto Graham .25 .60
27A Sid Luckman ERR .12 .30
27B Sid Luckman COR .40 1.00
28 Steve Van Buren .10 .25
29 Bob Waterfield .10 .25
30 Bill Dudley .06 .15
31 Joe Guyon .04 .10
32 Arnie Herber .04 .10
33 Walt Kiesling .04 .10
34 Jimmy Conzelman .04 .10
35 Art Rooney .06 .15
36 Willie Wood .06 .15
37 Art Shell .10 .25
38 Sammy Baugh .25 .60
39 Mel Blount .10 .25
40 Lamar Hunt .04 .10
41 Norm Van Brocklin .10 .25
42 Y.A. Tittle .15 .40
43 Andy Robustelli .06 .15
44 Vince Lombardi .20 .50
45 Frank(Bruiser) Kinard .04 .10
46 Bill Hewitt .04 .10
47 Jim Brown .40 1.00
48 Pete Pihos .06 .15
49 Hugh McElhenny .10 .25
50 Tom Fears .06 .15
51 Jack Christiansen .06 .15
52 Ernie Stautner .10 .25
53 Joe Perry .10 .25
54 Leo Nomellini .06 .15
55 Greasy Neale .04 .10
56 Turk Edwards .04 .10
57 Alex Wojciechowicz .04 .10
58 Charley Trippi .06 .15
59 Marion Motley .10 .25
60 Wayne Millner .04 .10
61 Elroy Hirsch .10 .25
62 Art Donovan .10 .25
63 Cliff Battles .04 .10
64 Emlen Tunnell .06 .15
65 Joe Stydahar .04 .10
66 Ken Strong .06 .15
67 Dan Reeves OWN .04 .10
68 Bobby Layne .20 .50
69 Paul Brown .10 .25
70 Charles W. Bidwill UER .04 .10
71 Chuck Bednarik .12 .30
72 Bulldog Turner .10 .25
73 Hugh(Shorty) Ray .04 .10
74 Steve Owen .04 .10
75 George McAfee .06 .15
76 Forrest Gregg .06 .15
77 Frank Gifford .20 .50
78 Jim Taylor .10 .25
79 Len Ford .06 .15
80 Ray Flaherty .04 .10
81 Lenny Moore .12 .30
82 Dante Lavelli .06 .15
83 George Connor .06 .15
84 Roosevelt Brown .06 .15
85 Dick Lane .06 .15
86 Lou Groza .10 .25
87 Bill George .06 .15
88 Tony Canadeo .06 .15
89 Joe Schmidt .06 .15
90 Jim Parker .06 .15
91 Raymond Berry .12 .30
92 Clarence(Ace) Parker .04 .10
93 Ollie Matson .10 .25
94 Gino Marchetti .06 .15
95 Larry Wilson .06 .15
96 Ray Nitschke .12 .30
97 Tuffy Leemans .04 .10
98 Weeb Ewbank UER .04 .10
99 Lance Alworth .12 .30
100 Bill Willis .06 .15
101 Bart Starr .30 .75
102 Gale Sayers .20 .50
103 Herb Adderley .06 .15
104 Johnny Unitas .30 .75
105 Ron Mix .06 .15
106 Yale Lary .06 .15
107 Red Badgro .04 .10
108 Jim Otto .10 .25
109 Bob Lilly .12 .30
110 Deacon Jones .10 .25
111 Doug Atkins .06 .15
112 Jim Ringo .06 .15
113 Willie Davis .06 .15
114 George Blanda .12 .30
115 Bobby Bell .06 .15
116 Merlin Olsen .10 .25
117 George Musso .04 .10
118 Sam Huff .10 .25
119 Paul Warfield .10 .25
120 Bobby Mitchell .10 .25
121 Sonny Jurgensen .10 .25
122 Sid Gillman UER .04 .10
123 Arnie Weinmeister .04 .10
124 Charley Taylor .06 .15
125 Mike McCormack .06 .15
126 Willie Brown .06 .15
127 O.J. Simpson .20 .50
128 Pete Rozelle .06 .15
129 Joe Namath .50 1.25
130 Frank Gatski .04 .10
131 Willie Lanier .06 .15
132 Ken Houston .06 .15
133 Paul Hornung .15 .40
134 Roger Staubach .30 .75
135 Len Dawson .12 .30
136 Larry Csonka .12 .30
137 Doak Walker .10 .25
138 Fran Tarkenton .15 .40
139 Don Maynard .10 .25
140 Jim Langer .06 .15
141 John Henry Johnson .06 .15
142 Joe Greene .12 .30
143 Jack Ham .12 .30
144 Mike Ditka .25 .60
145 Alan Page .06 .15
146 Fred Biletnikoff .12 .30
147 Gene Upshaw .06 .15
148 Dick Butkus .25 .60
149 Checklist Card .04 .10
150 Checklist Card .04 .10

1990 Swell Greats

The 1990 Swell Greats set contains 160 standard size cards, depicting all Pro Football Hall of Famers. The fronts have color photos, with a white border and blue and yellow lines. As in previous sets, some cards of the older players are sepia-toned. In fact, in several cases the same photos were reused from the previous two years of Swell sets. The vertically-oriented backs feature player profiles. The cards were primarily available in the form of ten-card wax packs.

COMPLETE SET (160) 12.50 25.00
1 Terry Bradshaw .30 .75
2 Bert Bell .04 .10
3 Joe Carr .04 .10
4 Dutch Clark .05 .15
5 Red Grange .20 .50
6 Fats Henry .04 .10
7 Mel Hein .04 .10
8 Robert(Cal) Hubbard .04 .10
9 George Halas .10 .30
10 Don Hutson .08 .25
11 Curly Lambeau .04 .10
12 Tim Mara .04 .10
13 Geo.Preston Marshall .04 .10
14 Johnny Blood McNally .04 .10
15 Bronko Nagurski .10 .30
16 Ernie Nevers .05 .15
17 Jim Thorpe .20 .50
18 Ed Healey .04 .10
19 Clarke Hinkle .04 .10
20 Link Lyman .04 .10
21 Mike Michalske .04 .10
22 George Trafton .04 .10
23 Guy Chamberlin .04 .10
24 Paddy Discoll .04 .10
25 Dan Fortmann .04 .10
26 Otto Graham .25 .60
27 Sid Luckman .10 .30
28 Steve Van Buren .08 .25
29 Bob Waterfield .08 .25
30 Bill Dudley .05 .15
31 Joe Guyon .04 .10
32 Arnie Herber .04 .10
33 Walt Kiesling .04 .10
34 Jimmy Conzelman .04 .10
35 Art Rooney .05 .15
36 Willie Wood .05 .15
37 Art Shell .08 .25
38 Sammy Baugh .25 .60
39 Mel Blount .08 .25
40 Lamar Hunt .04 .10
41 Norm Van Brocklin .08 .25
42 Y.A. Tittle .15 .40
43 Andy Robustelli .05 .15
44 Vince Lombardi .20 .50
45 Frank(Bruiser) Kinard .04 .10
46 Bill Hewitt .04 .10
47 Jim Brown .40 1.00
48 Pete Pihos .05 .15
49 Hugh McElhenny .08 .25
50 Tom Fears .05 .15
51 Jack Christiansen .05 .15
52 Ernie Stautner .08 .25
53 Joe Perry .08 .25
54 Leo Nomellini .05 .15
55 Greasy Neale .04 .10
56 Turk Edwards .04 .10
57 Alex Wojciechowicz .04 .10
58 Charley Trippi .05 .15
59 Marion Motley .08 .25
60 Wayne Millner .04 .10
61 Elroy Hirsch .08 .25
62 Art Donovan .08 .25
63 Cliff Battles .04 .10
64 Emlen Tunnell .05 .15
65 Joe Stydahar .04 .10
66 Ken Strong .05 .15
67 Dan Reeves OWN .04 .10
68 Bobby Layne .20 .50
69 Paul Brown .08 .25
70 Charles W. Bidwill .04 .10
71 Chuck Bednarik .10 .30
72 Bulldog Turner .08 .25
73 Hugh(Shorty) Ray .04 .10
74 Steve Owen .04 .10
75 George McAfee .05 .15
76 Forrest Gregg .05 .15
77 Frank Gifford .20 .50
78 Jim Taylor .08 .25
79 Len Ford .05 .15
80 Ray Flaherty .04 .10
81 Lenny Moore .10 .30
82 Dante Lavelli .05 .15
83 George Connor .05 .15
84 Roosevelt Brown .05 .15
85 Dick Lane .05 .15
86 Lou Groza .08 .25
87 Bill George .05 .15
88 Tony Canadeo .05 .15
89 Joe Schmidt .05 .15
90 Jim Parker .05 .15
91 Raymond Berry .10 .30
92 Clarence(Ace) Parker .04 .10
93 Ollie Matson .08 .25
94 Gino Marchetti .05 .15
95 Larry Wilson .05 .15
96 Ray Nitschke .10 .30
97 Tuffy Leemans .04 .10
98 Weeb Ewbank .04 .10
99 Lance Alworth .10 .30
100 Bill Willis .05 .15
101 Bart Starr .30 .75
102 Gale Sayers .20 .50
103 Herb Adderley .05 .15
104 Johnny Unitas .30 .75
105 Ron Mix .05 .15
106 Yale Lary .05 .15
107 Red Badgro .04 .10
108 Jim Otto .08 .25
109 Bob Lilly .10 .30
110 Deacon Jones .08 .25
111 Doug Atkins .05 .15
112 Jim Ringo .05 .15
113 Willie Davis .05 .15
114 George Blanda .10 .30
115 Bobby Bell .05 .15
116 Merlin Olsen .08 .25
117 George Musso .04 .10
118 Sam Huff .08 .25
119 Paul Warfield .08 .25
120 Bobby Mitchell .08 .25
121 Sonny Jurgensen .08 .25
122 Sid Gillman .04 .10
123 Arnie Weinmeister .04 .10
124 Charley Taylor .05 .15
125 Mike McCormack .05 .15
126 Willie Brown .05 .15
127 O.J. Simpson .20 .50
128 Pete Rozelle .05 .15
129 Joe Namath .50 1.25
130 Frank Gatski .04 .10
131 Willie Lanier .05 .15
132 Ken Houston .05 .15
133 Paul Hornung .15 .40
134 Roger Staubach .30 .75
135 Len Dawson .10 .30
136 Larry Csonka .10 .30
137 Doak Walker .08 .25
138 Fran Tarkenton .15 .40
139 Don Maynard .08 .25
140 Jim Langer .05 .15
141 John Henry Johnson .05 .15
142 Joe Greene .10 .30
143 Jack Ham .10 .30
144 Mike Ditka .25 .60
145 Alan Page .05 .15
146 Fred Biletnikoff .10 .30
147 Gene Upshaw .05 .15
148 Dick Butkus .25 .60
149 Buck Buchanan .05 .15
150 Franco Harris .15 .40
151 Tom Landry .10 .30
152 Ted Hendricks .05 .15
153 Bob St. Clair .05 .15
154 Jack Lambert .15 .40
155 Bob Griese .10 .30
156 Admission coupon .04 .10
157 Enshrinement Day .04 .10
158 Hall of Fame .04 .10
159 Checklist 1/2 .04 .10
160 Checklist 3/4 .04 .10

2001 Tallahassee Thunder AF2

COMPLETE SET (26) 6.00 12.00
1 Andrae Brooks .20 .50
2 Monk Bonasorte GM .20 .50
3 Ernest Certain .20 .50
4 Kevin Cleveland .20 .50
5 James Dickerson .20 .50
6 Paul Ficaro .20 .50
7 Chris Hixson .20 .50
8 Lamonte Jackson .20 .50
9 Demarco Johnson .20 .50
10 Canary Knight .20 .50
11 Billy Luckie .20 .50
12 Gene McDowell CO .20 .50
13 Michael McKee .20 .50
14 Salofi Nua .20 .50
15 Mesiah Porter .20 .50
16 Kenton Rickerson .20 .50
17 Terrence Samuel .20 .50
18 Phil Setterquist .20 .50
19 Marvin Taylor .20 .50
20 Kerry Ware .20 .50
21 Larry Williams DS .20 .50
22 Asssitant Coaches .30 .75
Ricky Bell
Michael McClinton
23 Support Staff .20 .50
24 Lightning Girls .20 .50
25 Team Card .20 .50

1998 Tampa Bay Storm AFL

COMPLETE SET (27) 7.50 15.00
1 Stevie Thomas .30 .75
2 Ron Adams .30 .75
3 Les Barley .30 .75
4 Mel Agee .40 1.00
5 Terry Beauford .30 .75
6 Sylvester Bembery .30 .75
7 Andre Bowden .30 .75
8 Johnnie Harris .30 .75
9 Steve Roughton .30 .75
10 George LaFrance .30 .75
11 Tony Jones .30 .75
12 Cornell Parker .30 .75
13 Tracey Perkins .30 .75
14 Lynn Rowland .30 .75
15 Lawrence Samuels .30 .75
16 Tracy Sanders .30 .75
17 Bjorn Nittmo .30 .75
18 Wayne Williams .30 .75
19 Peter Tom Willis .40 1.00
20 Tony Woods .30 .75
21 Antoine Worthman .30 .75
22 Willie Wyatt .30 .75
23 Keo Coleman .30 .75
24 Robert Goff .30 .75
25 Alvoid Mays .30 .75
26 Nyle Wiren .30 .75
27 Tim Marcum CO .30 .75

1962 Tang Team Photos

Each team in the NFL is represented in this set of 10" by 8" white-bordered color team photos. The team logo is superimposed over the picture at the lower right, and all the players and team personnel are identified by rows in wider white border. The backs are completely blank and the paper stock is thin. While Tang is not specifically identified as the sponsor on the photos, advertising pieces exist to verify this fact. Originally, complete sets were available via mail for 50-cents each with one innerseal from a Tang drink mix jar. The team photos are listed below in alphabetical order. Beware reprints.

COMPLETE SET (14) 150.00 250.00
1 Baltimore Colts 12.00 20.00
2 Chicago Bears 15.00 25.00
3 Cleveland Browns 20.00 35.00
4 Dallas Cowboys 20.00 35.00
5 Detroit Lions 12.00 20.00
6 Green Bay Packers 25.00 40.00
7 Los Angeles Rams 12.00 20.00
8 Minnesota Vikings 15.00 25.00
9 New York Giants 12.00 20.00
10 Philadelphia Eagles 12.00 20.00
11 Pittsburgh Steelers 12.00 20.00
12 St. Louis Cardinals 12.00 20.00
13 San Francisco 49ers 15.00 25.00
14 Washington Redskins 20.00 35.00

1981 TCMA Greats

This 78-card standard-size set was put out by TCMA in 1981. The set features retired football players from the '50s and '60s. The cards are in the popular "pure card" format where there is nothing on the card front except the color photo of the subject inside a simple white border. The card backs provide a short narrative printed in black ink on white card stock. The TCMA copyright is located in the lower right corner. The cards are numbered on the back at the top inside a football; however, some cards can also be found without the card number inside the football.

COMPLETE SET (78) 25.00 50.00
*UNNUMBERED: 2X TO 5X BASIC CARDS
1 Alex Karras .40 1.00
2 Fran Tarkenton .75 2.00
3 Johnny Unitas 2.50 6.00
4 Bobby Layne .75 2.00
5 Roger Staubach 1.50 4.00
6 Joe Namath 2.50 6.00
7 1954 New York Giants .25 .60
8 Jim Brown 2.00 5.00
9 Ray Wietecha .20 .50
10 R.C. Owens .20 .50
11 Alex Webster .20 .50
12 Jim Otto UER .30 .75
13 Jim Taylor .60 1.50
14 Kyle Rote .25 .60
15 Roger Ellis .20 .50
16 Nick Pietrosante .20 .50
17 Milt Plum .20 .50
18 Eddie LeBaron .25 .60
19 Jimmy Patton .20 .50
20 Yale Lary .25 .60
21 Leo Nomellini .30 .75
22 John Olszewski .20 .50
23 Ernie Koy .20 .50
24 Bill Wade .20 .50
25 Billy Wells .20 .50
26 Ron Waller .20 .50
27 Pat Summerall .30 .75
28 Joe Schmidt .30 .75
29 Bob St.Clair .25 .60
30 Dick Lynch .20 .50
31 Tommy McDonald .30 .75
32 Earl Morrall .20 .50
33 Jim Martin .20 .50
34 Dick Modzelewski .20 .50
35 Dick LeBeau .20 .50
36 Dick Post .20 .50
37 Les Richter .20 .50
38 Andy Robustelli .30 .75
39 Pete Retzlaff .20 .50
40 Fred Biletnikoff .60 1.50
41 Timmy Brown .20 .50
42 Babe Parilli .20 .50
43 Lance Alworth .60 1.50
44 Sammy Baugh .75 2.00
45 Paul(Tank) Younger .20 .50
46 Chuck Bednarik .50 1.25
47 Art Donovan .50 1.25
48 Len Dawson .75 2.00
49 Don Maynard .50 1.25
50 Joe Morrison .20 .50
51 John Elliott .20 .50
52 Jim Ringo .30 .75
53 Max McGee .20 .50
54 Art Powell .20 .50
55 Galen Fiss .20 .50
56 Jack Stroud .20 .50
57 Bake Turner .20 .50
58 Mike McCormack .25 .60
59 L.G. Dupre .20 .50
60 Bill McPeak .20 .50
61 Art Spinney .20 .50
62 Fran Rogel .20 .50
63 Ollie Matson .40 1.00
64 Doak Walker .40 1.00
65 Lenny Moore .50 1.25
66 George Shaw and .20 .50
67 K.Rote .25 .60
Howell
Krouse
68 Andy Robustelli .30 .75
69 Tucker Frederickson .20 .50
70 Gino Marchetti .30 .75
71 Earl Morrall and .20 .50
72 Roosevelt Brown .25 .60
73 Howard Cassady .20 .50
74 Don Chandler .20 .50
75 Joe Childress .20 .50
76 Rick Casares .20 .50
77 Charley Conerly .40 1.00
78 1958 Giants QB's .25 .60

1987 TCMA Update CMC

In 1987 CMC (the successor to TCMA) produced this 12-card standard-size set updating the 1981 TCMA issue. In fact the first 78 numbered cards were reissued at this time as part of a 90-card set; only the new-issue cards are listed below. Instead of copyright TCMA 1981, these 12 cards indicate copyright CMC 1987.

COMPLETE SET (12) 75.00 125.00
79 Fred Dryer 4.00 10.00
80 Ed Marinaro 5.00 12.00
81 O.J. Simpson 10.00 25.00
82 Joe Theismann 8.00 20.00
83 Roman Gabriel 4.00 10.00
84 Terry Metcalf 4.00 10.00
85 Lyle Alzado 4.00 10.00
86 Jake Scott 4.00 10.00
87 Cliff Branch 6.00 15.00
88 Rocky Bleier 8.00 20.00
89 Cliff Harris 4.00 10.00
90 Archie Manning 6.00 15.00

1994 Ted Williams

The 1994 Ted Williams Roger Staubach's NFL Football Preview Edition consists of 90 standard-size cards. Only 5,000 twelve box cases were produced. The cards are checklisted according to teams. The series closes with three topical subsets: Chalkboard Legends (64-72), Golden Arms (73-81), and Dawning of a Legacy (82-90). Randomly inserted in foil packs were three special chase cards: Charles Barkley, Fred Dryer, and Ted Williams. Two promo cards were produced and are listed below. They carry different photos than the regular issue cards.

COMPLETE SET (90) 4.00 10.00
1 Roger Staubach .30 .75
2 Tony Dorsett .15 .40
3 Bob Lilly .07 .20
4 Art Donovan .07 .20
5 Bert Jones UER .02 .10
6 Johnny Unitas .20 .50
7 Jack Kemp .07 .20
8 O.J. Simpson .20 .50
9 Dick Butkus .20 .50
10 Gale Sayers .20 .50
11 Mike Singletary .02 .10
12 Bronko Nagurski .08 .20
13 Ken Anderson .02 .10
14 Otto Graham .16 .40
15 Lou Groza .07 .20
16 Marion Motley .02 .10
17 Floyd Little .02 .10
18 Haven Moses .02 .10
19 Lem Barney .02 .10
20 Dick(Night Train) Lane .02 .10
21 Bobby Layne .16 .40
22 Ray Nitschke .08 .20
23 Willie Wood .02 .10
24 Billy(White Shoes) .02 .10
25 Mike Bell .02 .10
26 Buck Buchanan .02 .10
27 Len Dawson .08 .20
28 Roman Gabriel .02 .10
29 LeRoy Irvin .02 .10
30 Deacon Jones .02 .10
31 Bob Waterfield .07 .20
32 Bob Griese .16 .40
33 Carl Eller .02 .10
34 Fran Tarkenton .16 .40
35 John Hannah .02 .10
36 Jim Plunkett .02 .10
37 Tom Dempsey .02 .10
38 Archie Manning .04 .10
39 Sam Huff .07 .20
40 Andy Robustelli .02 .10
41 Charley Conerly .02 .10
42 Don Maynard .07 .20
43 Matt Snell .02 .10
44 Wesley Walker .02 .10
45 George Blanda .07 .20
46 Ben Davidson .02 .10
47 Jim Otto .02 .10
48 Norm Van Brocklin .07 .20
49 Harold Carmichael .02 .10
50 Joe Greene .08 .20
51 L.C. Greenwood .07 .20
52 Jack Lambert .08 .20
53 Lance Alworth .08 .20
54 Dan Fouts .07 .20
55 John Brodie .07 .20
56 Steve Largent .16 .40
57 Jim Zorn .02 .10
58 Jim Hart .02 .10
59 Mel Gray .02 .10
60 Lee Roy Selmon .02 .05
61 Sonny Jurgensen .07 .20
62 Sammy Baugh .16 .40
63 Checklist UER .02 .10
64 George Allen CO .07 .20
65 George Halas CO .16 .40
66 Tom Landry CO .16 .40
67 Vince Lombardi CO .20 .50
68 John Madden CO .16 .40
69 Chuck Noll CO .07 .20
70 Don Shula CO .12 .30
71 Hank Stram CO .02 .10
72 Checklist .02 .10
73 Terry Bradshaw .30 .75
74 Len Dawson .08 .20
75 Dan Fouts .07 .20
76 Bart Starr .20 .50
77 Roger Staubach .30 .75
78 Fran Tarkenton .16 .40
79 Y.A. Tittle .16 .40
80 Johnny Unitas .20 .50
81 Checklist .02 .10
82 Brett Favre .60 1.50
83 Brett Favre .60 1.50
84 Brett Favre .60 1.50
85 Brett Favre .60 1.50
86 Neil O'Donnell .02 .10
87 Neil O'Donnell .02 .10
88 Neil O'Donnell .02 .10
89 Neil O'Donnell .02 .10
90 Checklist Card .02 .10
P1 Roger Staubach Promo .40 1.00
P73 Terry Bradshaw Promo .40 1.00
S32 O.J. Simpson AU/500 20.00 50.00
CB1 Charles Barkley .30 .75
CB1AU Charles Barkley AU 60.00 150.00
HM1 Fred Dryer .30 .75
TF1 Ted Williams .80 2.00
TF1AU Ted Williams AU/64 200.00 600.00

1994 Ted Williams Auckland Collection

Randomly inserted in hobby packs only, the nine-card standard-size set consists of an illustrated series by one of the country's foremost sports artists, Jim Auckland. The cards are printed on a special matte finish paper stock. The white bordered fronts have illustrations from noted sports artist, Jim Auckland. The red and white bordered backs have a ghosted multi-player illustration with a player summary. The cards are numbered on the back with an "AC" prefix.

COMPLETE SET (9) 10.00 25.00
AC1 Brett Favre 3.20 8.00
AC2 Vince Lombardi 1.60 4.00
AC3 Walter Payton 3.20 8.00
AC4 Phil Simms .80 2.00
AC5 Bart Starr 1.60 4.00
AC6 Roger Staubach 2.00 5.00
AC7 Jim Thorpe 1.20 3.00
AC8 Johnny Unitas 1.60 4.00
AC9 Checklist .60 1.50
AC6A Roger Staubach AU/500 40.00 80.00

1994 Ted Williams Etched In Stone Unitas

Randomly inserted in packs, this nine-card 1994 Ted Williams Etched in Stone standard-size set highlights the career of football legend Johnny Unitas. When all nine cards are placed in a protective card sheet, the words "Etched in Stone," a gold star, and a stone mallet become visible. The narrative format on the back chronicals Unitas' career beginning with college football. The cards are numbered on the back with an "ES" prefix.

COMPLETE SET (9) 4.00 10.00
COMMON CARD (ES1-ES9) .50 1.25

1994 Ted Williams Instant Replays

Randomly inserted in hobby packs only, this 17-card standard-size set highlights four of the greatest dynasties in NFL history. The four teams were distributed by region. The set is organized according to teams as follows: New York Giants (1-4), Green Bay Packers (5-8), Pittsburgh Steelers (9-12), and Oakland/L.A. Raiders (13-16). The cards are numbered on the back with an "IR" prefix.

COMPLETE SET (17) 8.00 20.00
IR1 Phil Simms .40 1.00
IR2 Y.A. Tittle .50 1.25
IR3 Sam Huff .50 1.25
IR4 Brad Van Pelt .30 .75
IR5 Brett Favre 2.40 6.00
IR6 Bart Starr 1.00 2.50
IR7 Paul Hornung .60 1.50
IR8 Ray Nitschke .50 1.25
IR9 Neil O'Donnell .40 1.00
IR10 Terry Bradshaw 1.00 2.50
IR11 Joe Greene .50 1.25
IR12 Jack Lambert .50 1.25
IR13 Jeff Hostetler .30 .75
IR14 Lyle Alzado .30 .75
IR15 Dave Casper .30 .75
IR16 Ken Stabler .60 1.50
IR17 Checklist Card .30 .75

1994 Ted Williams Path to Greatness

Randomly inserted into packs, this nine-card standard-size set features collegiate players who went on to successful NFL careers. . The player's collegiate football highlights are listed in narrative format. The cards are numbered on the back with a "PG" prefix.

COMPLETE SET (9) 5.00 12.00
PG1 Tony Dorsett .75 2.00
PG2 Red Grange .75 2.00
PG3 Bob Griese .50 1.25
PG4 Jeff Hostetler .20 .50
PG5 Neil O'Donnell .20 .50
PG6 Jim Plunkett .30 .75
PG7 O.J. Simpson .75 2.00
PG8 Roger Staubach 1.20 3.00
PG9 Checklist Card .20 .50
PG7A O.J. Simpson AU/500 30.00 60.00

1994 Ted Williams Walter Payton

Available only in jumbo packs sold in mass market retail outlets, this nine-card set spotlights the career of one of football's greatest running backs, Walter Payton. The standard size cards feature full-bleed color action shots. The photo has a striped finish effect somewhat similar to a Sportflic card, but with only a single photo exposure. The set title appears in the lower right corner. The borderless blue backs have a sun design at the top, with the title of the card appearing below Payton's name. Each card chronicles a specific time of Payton's career beginning with college, and including a card listing career statistics. The cards are numbered on the back with a "WP" prefix.

COMPLETE SET (9) 4.80 12.00
COMMON CARD (WP1-WP9) .60 1.50

1994 Ted Williams POG Cards

The 1994 Ted Williams POG's were inserted in every foil pack of the 1994 Ted Williams Roger Staubach football cards. A total of 18 POG cards with 34 different players and a checklist were produced. On a dark blue background, each POG or Milk Cap card contains two POG's, each measuring approximately 1 5/8" in diameter. The cards measure standard size. The fronts feature a head shot of the player in color or black and white with the player's name printed above or below the photo. The white backs are blank. The cards are numbered on the front.

COMPLETE SET (18) 2.50 6.00
1 Roger Staubach .75 2.00
Brett Favre
2 Roman Gabriel .07 .20
Lee Roy Jordan
3 Dan Fouts .08 .25
John Brodie
4 Terry Bradshaw .40 1.00
Bart Starr
5 O.J. Simpson .15 .40
Floyd Little
6 Pete Pihos .08 .25
Steve Largent
7 Dick Lane .07 .20
Carl Eller
8 Sam Huff .07 .20
Ben Davidson
9 Jack Lambert .08 .25
Jethro Pugh
10 Mike Singletary .10 .30
Harold Carmichael
11 Chuck Noll CO .10 .30
Bud Grant CO
12 John Madden CO .20 .50
Lyle Alzado
13 Walter Payton .50 1.25
Gale Sayers
14 Fred Dryer .07 .20
Ron Mix
15 Bob Griese .08 .25
Doug Williams
16 Tony Dorsett .30 .75
Red Grange
17 Sonny Jurgensen .07 .20
Jeff Hostetler
18 Checklist Card .07 .20

1994 Ted Williams Trade for Staubach

A special "Trade for Roger" card was randomly inserted in foil packs, at a rate of one per case in all 5,000 cases. Collectors received one of 5,000 nine-card sets by sending in the redemption card with 3.00 for postage and handling. The deadline for the redemption was April 15, 1994, and the redemption card itself was also returned to the collector with a validation stamp on it. The fronts feature a mix of full-bleed color or sepia-toned photos, with the player's name in silver foil along the left edge. The backs carry the card subtitle and summarize various highlights during his career.

COMPLETE SET (10) 4.80 12.00
COMMON CARD (TR1-TR9) .50 1.25
NNO Trade for Roger .50 1.25

2004 Tennessee Valley AFL

COMPLETE SET (30) 7.50 15.00
1 John Bradley .30 .75
2 Corl Bucknor .30 .75
3 Michael Caraway .30 .75
4 Ronney Daniels .40 1.00
5 Kelly Fields .30 .75
6 Marquis Floyd .30 .75
7 Henry Freeman .30 .75
8 Andy Fuller .30 .75
9 Calvin Hall .30 .75
10 Kyle Henderson .30 .75
11 Jerrian James .30 .75
12 Curtis Jeter .30 .75
13 Josh Kellett .30 .75
14 Tracy Kendall .30 .75
15 Dedric Maffett .30 .75
16 Travis McAlpine .30 .75
17 Joe Minucci .30 .75
18 Dave Morrill .30 .75
19 Chris Royle .30 .75
20 Matt Sauk .30 .75
21 Tanaka Scott .30 .75
22 Bryan Snyder .30 .75
23 Wes Stephens .30 .75
24 Alex Walls .30 .75
25 Deon White .30 .75
26 Ron Wilson .30 .75
27 Kevin Guy CO .30 .75
28 Dance Team .30 .75
29 Team Mascot .30 .75
30 Cover Card CL .30 .75

2007 Tennessee Valley Vipers AF2

COMPLETE SET (28) 6.00 12.00
1 Farouk Adelekan .20 .50
2 Anthony Andriano .20 .50
3 Joel Babb .20 .50
4 Travis Blanchard .20 .50
5 John Bradley .20 .50
6 Quentin Burrell .20 .50
7 Carlos Campbell .20 .50
8 Tony Colston .20 .50
9 John Cousins .20 .50
10 Gary Elliott .20 .50
11 Henry Freeman .20 .50
12 James Gibson .20 .50
13 Troy Graham .20 .50
14 Chris Gunn .20 .50
15 Victor Horn .20 .50
16 Lewis Howes .20 .50
17 Brandon Isaiah .20 .50
18 Matt Jirges .20 .50
19 Steven Lee .20 .50
20 Marcus Lindsey .20 .50
21 Chad Motte .20 .50
22 Frisner Nelson .20 .50
23 Calvin Ousby .20 .50
24 Shaheed Richardson .20 .50
25 Milt Theodosatos CO .20 .50
26 Jon Williams .20 .50
27 Vinnie The Viper (Mascot) .20 .50
28 Dream Team Dancers .20 .50

2008 Tennessee Valley Vipers AF2

COMPLETE SET (16) 5.00 10.00
1 Travis Blanchard .30 .75
2 Maurice Brown .30 .75
3 Demetrius Derico .30 .75
4 Kevin Eakin .30 .75
5 Gary Elliott .30 .75
6 Kelly Fields .30 .75
7 Terrance Ford .30 .75
8 Andy Fuller .30 .75
9 Andy Hall .30 .75
10 Jerrian James .30 .75
11 Rajohn Myles .30 .75
12 Alonzo Nix .30 .75
13 Eric Scott .30 .75
14 John Simmons .30 .75
15 Wes Stephens .30 .75
16 Matt Weber .30 .75

1960 Texans 7-Eleven

This set was issued by 7-11 convenience stores in the Dallas area in 1960. Each card measures the standard size 2 1/2" by 3 1/2" and was unnumbered. The fronts include a posed sepia toned photo of the player with no border. The player's name, position, and school are listed below the picture in small print. The font size used on three of the cards is about 50% larger: Boydston, Burford, and Haynes. On all cards but two, the team name is printed from bottom to top along the right or left hand sides. The exceptions are Ray Collins, which is missing the team altogether, and Cotton Davidson which was printed with the team name along the top. The backs include biographical information running the length of the card in typewriter style print. A Paul Miller card is rumored to exist and was once cataloged. We've removed the card from the checklist after years of research trying to verify its existence. Since the cards are unnumbered, they are listed below alphabetically.

COMPLETE SET (11) 2000.00 3000.00
1 Max Boydston 175.00 300.00
2 Mel Branch 175.00 300.00
3 Chris Burford 175.00 300.00
4 Ray Collins UER 175.00 300.00
5 Cotton Davidson 175.00 300.00
6 Abner Haynes 200.00 350.00
7 Sherrill Headrick 175.00 300.00
8 Bill Krisher 175.00 300.00
9 Johnny Robinson 175.00 300.00
10 Jack Spikes 175.00 300.00

1960 Texans Team Issue

These photos were issued around 1960 by the Dallas Texans. Each features a black and white player photo with the player's position, name and team name printed below the picture. They measure approximately 8" by 10 1/4" and include a brief player bio on the unnumbered cardbacks. Any additions to this list are welcomed.

COMPLETE SET (12) 75.00 150.00
1 Max Boydston 6.00 12.00
2 Mel Branch 6.00 12.00
3 Chris Burford 6.00 12.00
4 Cotton Davidson 6.00 12.00
5 Abner Haynes 10.00 20.00
6 Charlie Jackson 6.00 12.00
7 Curley Johnson 6.00 12.00
8 Paul Miller 6.00 12.00
9 Johnny Robinson 7.50 15.00
10 Jack Spikes 6.00 12.00
11 Hank Stram CO 12.50 25.00
12 Jim Swink 6.00 12.00

1962 Texans Team Issue

These photos were issued in 1962 by the Dallas Texans. Each features a black and white player photo with the player's facsimile autograph printed within the picture. They measure approximately 5" by 7" and were printed on thick blankbacked paper stock.

1 Chris Burford 6.00 12.00
2 Walt Corey 6.00 12.00
3 Bobby Hunt 6.00 12.00
4 Curtis McClinton 7.50 15.00
5 Curt Merz 6.00 12.00
6 Al Reynolds 6.00 12.00
8 Jim Tyrer 6.00 12.00
7 Smokey Stover 6.00 12.00

2002 Texans Upper Deck

This set was issued by Upper Deck to commemorate the Houston Texans first season. The 20-cards and jumbo Houston Texans Logo card were issued in a factory set box and sold through Texan's souvenir outlets.

COMPLETE SET (21) 15.00 30.00
HT1 Jermaine Lewis .75 2.00
HT2 Jabar Gaffney 1.25 3.00
HT3 Corey Bradford .75 2.00

HT4 James Allen .75 2.00
HT5 Jonathan Wells .75 2.00
HT6 David Carr 1.50 4.00
HT7 Rod Rutledge .50 1.25
HT8 Steve McKinney .50 1.25
HT9 Ryan Young .50 1.25
HT10 Tony Boselli .50 1.25
HT11 Gary Walker .50 1.25
HT12 Seth Payne .50 1.25
HT13 Kailee Wong .50 1.25
HT14 Charles Hill .50 1.25
HT15 Jamie Sharper .50 1.25
HT16 Jay Foreman .50 1.25
HT17 Aaron Glenn .50 1.25
HT18 Marcus Coleman .50 1.25
HT19 Matt Stevens .50 1.25
HT20 Kevin Williams .50 1.25
HT21 Houston Texans Jumbo .50 1.25

2004 Texans Super Bowl XXXVIII Promos

This set of 8-cards was released at the 2004 Super Bowl XXXVIII Card Show in Houston. Each card was released in exchange for a group of wrappers from card packs opened at the featured manufacturer's booth at the show. Four different cards were issued the weekend before the game and four others the weekend of the game. Each card was printed in a style unique to the card company, but all are numbered of 8-cards in the set on the backs.

COMPLETE SET (8) 10.00 20.00
1 Aaron Glenn Topps .75 2.00
2 Corey Bradford Playoff .75 2.00
3 Billy Miller Fleer .75 2.00
4 Dave Ragone Upper Deck 1.00 2.50
5 Andre Johnson Upper Deck 1.50 4.00
6 Jabar Gaffney Fleer 1.00 2.50
7 Domanick Davis Playoff 1.50 4.00
8 David Carr Topps 1.50 4.00

2006 Texans Topps

COMPLETE SET (12) 3.00 6.00
HOU1 Jerome Mathis .25 .60
HOU2 Andre Johnson .30 .75
HOU3 David Carr .25 .60
HOU4 Domanick Davis .25 .60
HOU5 Dunta Robinson .25 .60
HOU6 Vernand Morency .25 .60
HOU7 Jeb Putzier .25 .60
HOU8 Kris Brown .25 .60
HOU9 Jason Babin .25 .60
HOU10 Eric Moulds .25 .60
HOU11 Mario Williams .40 1.00
HOU12 DeMeco Ryans .30 .75

2007 Texans Topps

COMPLETE SET (12) 2.50 5.00
1 Andre Johnson .50 1.25
2 Owen Daniels .40 1.00
3 Ron Dayne .50 1.25
4 Ahman Green .50 1.25
5 Matt Schaub .40 1.00
6 Kevin Walter .50 1.25
7 Wali Lundy .40 1.00
8 Mario Williams .50 1.25
9 Dunta Robinson .40 1.00
10 DeMeco Ryans .50 1.25
11 Kris Brown .40 1.00
12 Amobi Okoye .50 1.25

2008 Texans Topps

COMPLETE SET (12) 2.50 5.00
1 Matt Schaub .40 1.00
2 Sage Rosenfels .40 1.00
3 Andre Johnson .50 1.25
4 Ron Dayne .40 1.00
5 Owen Daniels .40 1.00
6 Mario Williams .50 1.25
7 Chris Brown .40 1.00
8 Kevin Walter .50 1.25
9 Amobi Okoye .40 1.00
10 DeMeco Ryans .50 1.25
11 Steve Slaton .40 1.00
12 Xavier Adibi .40 1.00

1937 Thrilling Moments

Doughnut Company of America produced these cards and distributed them on the outside of doughnut boxes twelve per box. The cards were to be cut from the boxes and affixed to an album that housed the set. The set's full name is Thrilling Moments in the Lives of Famous Americans. Only seven athletes were included among 65-other famous non-sport American figures. Each blankbacked card measures roughly 1 7/8" by 2 7/8" when neatly trimmed. The set was produced in four different colored backgrounds: blue, green, orange, and yellow with each subject being printed in only one background color.

28 Red Grange FB 800.00 1200.00
55 Knute Rockne FB 800.00 1200.00

2005 Throwback Threads

This 229-card set was released in September, 2005. The set was issued in five-card packs with an $4 SRP which came 24 packs to a box. Cards numbered 1-150 feature veterans sequenced in team alphabetical order while cards numbered 151-229 featured members of the 2005 rookie class. Cards numbered 201-229 were issued with player-worn jersey swatches. Cards numbered 151-200 were issued to a stated print run of 999 serial numbered sets while cards numbered 201-229 were issued to stated odds of one in 15 hobby packs and one in 1337 retail packs.

COMP.SET w/o SP's (150) 10.00 25.00
151-200 ROOKIE PRINT RUN 999
ROOKIE JSY ODDS 1:15 HOB, 1:1337 RET
1 Anquan Boldin .20 .50
2 Bryant Johnson .20 .50
3 Josh McCown .25 .60
4 Larry Fitzgerald .30 .75
5 Michael Vick .25 .60
6 Warrick Dunn .20 .50
7 Peerless Price .20 .50
8 T.J. Duckett .20 .50
9 Alge Crumpler .25 .60
10 Jamal Lewis .25 .60
11 Kyle Boller .20 .50
12 Todd Heap .20 .50
13 Ray Lewis .30 .75
14 J.P. Losman .20 .50
15 Eric Moulds .20 .50
16 Josh Reed .20 .50
17 Lee Evans .25 .60
18 Willis McGahee .20 .50
19 DeShaun Foster .25 .60
20 Jake Delhomme .20 .50
21 Julius Peppers .25 .60
22 Muhsin Muhammad .20 .50
23 Stephen Davis .20 .50
24 Steve Smith .30 .75
25 Brian Urlacher .30 .75
26 David Terrell .20 .50
27 Rex Grossman .20 .50
28 Thomas Jones .20 .50
29 Carson Palmer .25 .60
30 Chad Johnson .20 .50
31 Peter Warrick .20 .50
32 Rudi Johnson .20 .50
33 Jeff Garcia .20 .50
34 Kelly Holcomb .20 .50
35 Kellen Winslow Jr. .20 .50
36 Lee Suggs .20 .50
37 William Green .20 .50
38 Julius Jones .20 .50
39 Drew Bledsoe .25 .60
40 Roy Williams S .20 .50
41 Keyshawn Johnson .25 .60
42 Terence Newman .20 .50
43 Ashley Lelie .20 .50
44 Rod Smith .25 .60
45 Tatum Bell .20 .50
46 Champ Bailey .25 .60
47 Darius Watts .20 .50
48 Jake Plummer .20 .50
49 Quentin Griffin .20 .50
50 Charles Rogers .20 .50
51 Joey Harrington .20 .50
52 Kevin Jones .20 .50
53 Roy Williams WR .20 .50
54 Ahman Green .25 .60
55 Brett Favre .60 1.50
56 Javon Walker .20 .50
57 Nick Barnett .20 .50
58 Robert Ferguson .20 .50
59 Andre Johnson .25 .60
60 David Carr .20 .50
61 Domanick Davis .20 .50
62 Dallas Clark .20 .50
63 Edgerrin James .25 .60
64 Marvin Harrison .25 .60
65 Peyton Manning .75 2.00
66 Reggie Wayne .25 .60
67 Byron Leftwich .20 .50
68 Jimmy Smith .25 .60
69 Fred Taylor .20 .50
70 Reggie Williams .20 .50
71 Dante Hall .20 .50
72 Priest Holmes .20 .50
73 Tony Gonzalez .25 .60
74 Trent Green .20 .50
75 Eddie Kennison .20 .50
76 Chris Chambers .20 .50
77 Junior Seau .25 .60
78 Randy McMichael .20 .50
79 Zach Thomas .25 .60
80 A.J. Feeley .20 .50
81 Daunte Culpepper .25 .60
82 Michael Bennett .20 .50
83 Nate Burleson .20 .50
84 Onterrio Smith .20 .50
85 Corey Dillon .20 .50
86 Bethel Johnson .20 .50
87 Deion Branch .20 .50
88 Tom Brady 1.25 3.00
89 Ty Law .30 .75
90 Aaron Brooks .20 .50
91 Deuce McAllister .25 .60
92 Joe Horn .20 .50
93 Donte Stallworth .20 .50
94 Eli Manning .50 1.25
95 Ike Hilliard .20 .50
96 Jeremy Shockey .20 .50
97 Michael Strahan .25 .60
98 Tiki Barber .25 .60
99 Anthony Becht .20 .50
100 Chad Pennington .20 .50
101 Curtis Martin .25 .60
102 John Abraham .20 .50
103 Justin McCareins .20 .50
104 Santana Moss .25 .60
105 Shaun Ellis .20 .50
106 Kerry Collins .20 .50
107 Randy Moss .25 .60
108 Jerry Porter .20 .50
109 Chad Lewis .20 .50
110 Donovan McNabb .25 .60
111 Freddie Mitchell .20 .50
112 Jevon Kearse .20 .50
113 Terrell Owens .25 .60
114 Brian Westbrook .20 .50
115 Antwaan Randle El .20 .50
116 Ben Roethlisberger .50 1.25
117 Duce Staley .20 .50
118 Hines Ward .25 .60
119 Jerome Bettis .30 .75
120 Plaxico Burress .20 .50
121 Antonio Gates .30 .75
122 Drew Brees .30 .75
123 LaDainian Tomlinson .30 .75
124 Kevan Barlow .20 .50
125 Brandon Lloyd .20 .50
126 Darrell Jackson .20 .50
127 Koren Robinson .20 .50
128 Matt Hasselbeck .20 .50
129 Shaun Alexander .20 .50
130 Marc Bulger .20 .50
131 Isaac Bruce .30 .75
132 Marshall Faulk .25 .60
133 Steven Jackson .20 .50
134 Torry Holt .25 .60
135 Michael Clayton .20 .50
136 Brian Griese .20 .50
137 Derrick Brooks .20 .50
138 Mike Alstott .20 .50
139 Chris Brown .20 .50
140 Derrick Mason .20 .50
141 Keith Bulluck .20 .50
142 Steve McNair .25 .60
143 Tyrone Calico .20 .50
144 Drew Bennett .25 .60
145 Clinton Portis .20 .50
146 LaVar Arrington .20 .50
147 Sean Taylor .30 .75
148 Patrick Ramsey .25 .60
149 Laveranues Coles .20 .50
150 Rod Gardner .20 .50
151 Cedric Benson RC 1.25 3.00
152 DeMarcus Ware RC 4.00 10.00
153 Shawne Merriman RC 2.00 5.00
154 Thomas Davis RC 1.25 3.00
155 Derrick Johnson RC 1.50 4.00
156 Travis Johnson RC 1.25 3.00
157 David Pollack RC 1.25 3.00
158 Erasmus James RC 1.25 3.00
159 Marcus Spears RC 1.25 3.00
160 Fabian Washington RC 1.25 3.00
161 Marlin Jackson RC 1.25 3.00
162 Heath Miller RC 2.50 6.00
163 Shaun Cody RC 1.50 4.00
164 Dan Cody RC 1.25 3.00
165 Justin Miller RC 1.25 3.00
166 Chris Henry RC 1.50 4.00
167 David Greene RC 1.25 3.00
168 Brandon Jones RC 1.50 4.00
169 Marion Barber RC 1.25 3.00
170 Brandon Jacobs RC 1.50 4.00
171 Jerome Mathis RC 2.00 5.00
172 Craphonso Thorpe RC 1.25 3.00
173 Alvin Pearman RC 1.25 3.00
174 Darren Sproles RC 2.00 5.00
175 Fred Gibson RC 1.25 3.00
176 Roydell Williams RC 1.50 4.00
177 Airese Currie RC 1.25 3.00
178 Damien Nash RC 1.50 4.00
179 Dan Orlovsky RC 1.25 3.00
180 Adrian McPherson RC 1.25 3.00
181 Larry Brackins RC 1.25 3.00
182 Rasheed Marshall RC 1.50 4.00
183 Cedric Houston RC 2.00 5.00
184 Chad Owens RC 1.25 3.00
185 Tab Perry RC 1.25 3.00
186 Dante Ridgeway RC 1.25 3.00
187 Craig Bragg RC 1.25 3.00
188 Deandra Cobb RC 1.25 3.00
189 Derek Anderson RC 1.50 4.00
190 Marcus Maxwell RC 1.25 3.00
191 Paris Warren RC 1.50 4.00
192 Aaron Rodgers RC 20.00 40.00
193 James Kilian RC 1.25 3.00
194 Matt Cassel RC 1.25 3.00
195 Mike Williams 1.50 4.00
196 Lionel Gates RC 1.25 3.00
197 Anthony Davis RC 1.25 3.00
198 Noah Herron RC 1.25 3.00
199 Ryan Fitzpatrick RC 2.00 5.00
200 J.R. Russell RC 1.25 3.00
201 Adam Jones JSY RC 2.00 5.00
202 Alex Smith QB JSY RC 6.00 15.00
203 Antrel Rolle JSY RC 3.00 8.00
204 Andrew Walter JSY RC 2.00 5.00
205 Braylon Edwards JSY RC 2.00 5.00
206 Cadillac Williams JSY RC 2.00 5.00
207 Carlos Rogers JSY RC 3.00 8.00
208 Charlie Frye JSY RC 2.00 5.00
209 Ciatrick Fason JSY RC 2.00 5.00
210 Courtney Roby JSY RC 2.00 5.00
211 Eric Shelton JSY RC 2.00 5.00
212 Frank Gore JSY RC 4.00 10.00
213 J.J. Arrington JSY RC 2.50 6.00
214 Kyle Orton JSY RC 2.00 5.00
215 Jason Campbell JSY RC 2.00 5.00
216 Mark Bradley JSY RC 2.00 5.00
217 Mark Clayton JSY RC 2.00 5.00
218 Matt Jones JSY RC 2.00 5.00
219 Maurice Clarett JSY 2.00 5.00
220 Reggie Brown JSY RC 2.00 5.00
221 Ronnie Brown JSY RC 2.50 6.00
222 Roddy White JSY RC 3.00 8.00
223 Ryan Moats JSY RC 2.00 5.00
224 Roscoe Parrish JSY RC 2.00 5.00
225 Stefan LeFors JSY RC 2.00 5.00
226 Terrence Murphy JSY RC 2.00 5.00
227 Troy Williamson JSY RC 2.00 5.00
228 Vernand Morency JSY RC 2.00 5.00
229 Vincent Jackson JSY RC 3.00 8.00

2005 Throwback Threads Bronze Holofoil

*VETERANS: 2X TO 5X BASIC CARDS
BRONZE VETS PRINT RUN 250 SER.#'d SETS
*ROOKIES: .6X TO 1.5X BASIC CARDS
BRONZE ROOKIE PRINT RUN 150 SER.#'d SETS

2005 Throwback Threads Gold Holofoil

*VETERANS: 4X TO 10X BASIC CARDS
GOLD VET PRINT RUN 99 SER.#'d SETS
*ROOKIES: 1.2X TO 3X BASIC CARDS
GOLD ROOKIE PRINT RUN 50 SER.#'d SETS

2005 Throwback Threads Green

*VETERANS: 3X TO 8X BASIC CARDS
ATOMIC GREEN VET PRINT RUN 175 SETS
*ROOKIES: .8X TO 2X BASIC CARDS
ATOMIC GREEN ROOKIE PRINT RUN 75 SETS
ATOMIC GREENS IN SPECIAL RETAIL BOXES

2005 Throwback Threads Platinum Holofoil

*VETERANS: 6X TO 15X BASIC CARDS
PLAT.VET PRINT RUN 50 SER.#'d SETS
*ROOKIES: 2X TO 5X BASIC CARDS
PLAT.ROOKIE PRINT RUN 25 SER.#'d SETS

2005 Throwback Threads Red

*VETERANS: 4X TO 10X BASIC CARDS
RED VETERAN PRINT RUN 150 SETS
*ROOKIES: X TO X BASIC CARDS
RED ROOKIES SER.#'d TO 10
REDS INSERTED IN SPECIAL RETAIL BOXES

2005 Throwback Threads Retail Foil Rookies

*ROOKIES: .4X TO 1X BASIC CARDS
FOIL RETAIL ROOKIES SER.#'d OF 999

2005 Throwback Threads Silver Holofoil

*VETERANS: 3X TO 8X BASIC CARDS
SILVER VET PRINT RUN 150 SER.#'d SETS
*ROOKIES: .8X TO 2X BASIC CARDS
SILVER ROOKIE PRINT RUN 99 SER.#'d SETS

2005 Throwback Threads Century Stars

STATED ODDS 1:24 HOB/RET
*BLUE: .8X TO 2X BASIC INSERTS
BLUE PRINT RUN 100 SER.#'d SETS
1 Brett Favre 2.50 6.00
2 Carson Palmer 1.00 2.50
3 Corey Dillon .75 2.00
4 Dan Marino 2.50 6.00
5 Deion Sanders 1.00 2.50
6 Donovan McNabb 1.00 2.50
7 Edgerrin James 1.00 2.50
8 Jeremy Shockey .75 2.00
9 Jerry Rice 2.50 6.00
10 Joe Montana 4.00 10.00
11 Joe Namath 2.00 5.00
12 Marc Bulger .75 2.00
13 Marcus Allen 1.25 3.00
14 Michael Irvin 1.25 3.00
15 Michael Strahan 1.00 2.50
16 Michael Vick 1.00 2.50
17 Peyton Manning 3.00 8.00
18 Priest Holmes .75 2.00
19 Randy Moss 1.00 2.50
20 Shaun Alexander .75 2.00
21 Steve Young 1.50 4.00
22 Terrell Owens 1.00 2.50
23 Tom Brady 5.00 12.00
24 Troy Aikman 1.50 4.00
25 Walter Payton 3.00 8.00

2005 Throwback Threads Century Stars Material

STATED PRINT RUN 100 SER.#'d SETS
*PRIME: 1X TO 2.5X BASIC JERSEYS
PRIME PRINT RUN 25 SER.#'d SETS
1 Brett Favre 8.00 20.00
2 Carson Palmer 3.00 8.00
3 Corey Dillon 2.50 6.00
4 Dan Marino 10.00 25.00
5 Deion Sanders 4.00 10.00
6 Donovan McNabb 3.00 8.00
7 Edgerrin James 3.00 8.00
8 Jeremy Shockey 2.50 6.00
9 Jerry Rice 8.00 20.00
10 Joe Montana 15.00 40.00
11 Joe Namath 8.00 20.00
12 Marc Bulger 2.50 6.00
13 Marcus Allen 5.00 12.00
14 Michael Irvin 5.00 12.00
15 Michael Strahan 3.00 8.00
16 Michael Vick 3.00 8.00
17 Peyton Manning 10.00 25.00
18 Priest Holmes 2.50 6.00
19 Randy Moss 3.00 8.00
20 Shaun Alexander 2.50 6.00
21 Steve Young 6.00 15.00
22 Terrell Owens 3.00 8.00
23 Tom Brady 15.00 40.00
24 Troy Aikman 6.00 15.00
25 Walter Payton 12.00 30.00

2005 Throwback Threads Dynasty

STATED ODDS 1:54 HOB/RET
*BLUE: 1X TO 2.5X BASIC INSERTS
BLUE PRINT RUN 100 SER.#'d SETS
1 J.Lewis/R.Lewis/P.Holmes 1.25 3.00
2 Payton/Singletary/Dent 4.00 10.00
3 Deion/Aikman/Irvin 2.00 5.00
4 Elway/T.Davis/R.Smith 2.50 6.00
5 M.Allen/Stabler/Upshaw 1.50 4.00
6 Brady/Dillon/T.Brown 2.00 5.00
7 Bradshaw/Harris/Greene 2.50 6.00
8 Montana/Rice/Craig 3.00 8.00
9 Warner/Faulk/Holt 1.00 2.50
10 B.Johnson/Alstott/Keyshawn 1.00 2.50

2005 Throwback Threads Dynasty Material

STATED PRINT RUN 50 SER.#'d SETS
UNPRICED PRIME PRINT RUN 5 SETS
1 J.Lewis/R.Lewis/P.Holmes 7.50 20.00
2 Payton/Singletary/Dent 40.00 80.00
3 Deion/Aikman/Irvin 15.00 40.00
4 Elway/T.Davis/R.Smith 15.00 40.00
5 M.Allen/Stabler/Upshaw 15.00 40.00
6 Brady/Dillon/T.Brown 15.00 40.00
7 Bradshaw/Harris/Greene 20.00 50.00
8 Montana/Rice/Craig 30.00 80.00
9 Warner/Faulk/Holt 6.00 15.00
10 B.Johnson/Alstott/Keyshawn 6.00 15.00

2005 Throwback Threads Footballs

STATED PRINT RUN 275 SER.#'d SETS
1 Anquan Boldin 2.50 6.00
6 Warrick Dunn 2.50 6.00
7 Peerless Price 2.50 6.00
9 Alge Crumpler 3.00 8.00
10 Jamal Lewis 3.00 8.00
13 Ray Lewis 4.00 10.00
15 Eric Moulds 2.50 6.00
22 Muhsin Muhammad 2.50 6.00
23 Stephen Davis 2.50 6.00
25 Brian Urlacher 4.00 10.00
26 David Terrell 2.50 6.00
28 Thomas Jones 2.50 6.00
31 Peter Warrick 2.50 6.00
32 Rudi Johnson 2.50 6.00
33 Jeff Garcia 2.50 6.00
39 Drew Bledsoe 3.00 8.00
41 Keyshawn Johnson 3.00 8.00
44 Rod Smith 3.00 8.00
46 Champ Bailey 3.00 8.00
48 Jake Plummer 2.50 6.00
60 David Carr 2.50 6.00
63 Edgerrin James 3.00 8.00
64 Marvin Harrison 3.00 8.00
65 Peyton Manning 10.00 25.00
68 Jimmy Smith 3.00 8.00
72 Priest Holmes 2.50 6.00
76 Chris Chambers 2.50 6.00
77 Junior Seau 3.00 8.00
79 Zach Thomas 3.00 8.00
81 Daunte Culpepper 3.00 8.00
85 Corey Dillon 2.50 6.00
88 Tom Brady 15.00 40.00
89 Ty Law 4.00 10.00
90 Aaron Brooks 2.50 6.00
92 Joe Horn 2.50 6.00
97 Michael Strahan 3.00 8.00
98 Tiki Barber 3.00 8.00
100 Chad Pennington 2.50 6.00
101 Curtis Martin 3.00 8.00
102 John Abraham 2.50 6.00
104 Santana Moss 3.00 8.00
106 Kerry Collins 2.50 6.00
107 Randy Moss 3.00 8.00
108 Jerry Porter 2.50 6.00
109 Chad Lewis 2.50 6.00
110 Donovan McNabb 3.00 8.00
111 Freddie Mitchell 2.50 6.00
113 Terrell Owens 3.00 8.00
117 Duce Staley 2.50 6.00
123 LaDainian Tomlinson 4.00 10.00
124 Kevan Barlow 2.50 6.00
128 Matt Hasselbeck 2.50 6.00
129 Shaun Alexander 2.50 6.00
132 Marshall Faulk 3.00 8.00
134 Torry Holt 3.00 8.00
136 Brian Griese 2.50 6.00
137 Derrick Brooks 2.50 6.00
138 Mike Alstott 2.50 6.00
140 Derrick Mason 2.50 6.00
142 Steve McNair 3.00 8.00
145 Clinton Portis 2.50 6.00
146 LaVar Arrington 2.50 6.00
149 Laveranues Coles 2.50 6.00
150 Rod Gardner 2.50 6.00

2005 Throwback Threads Generations

STATED ODDS 1:24 HOB/RET
*BLUE: .8X TO 2X BASIC INSERTS
BLUE PRINT RUN 100 SER.#'d SETS
1 T.Owens/A.Johnson 1.25 3.00
2 T.Bradshaw/B.Roethlisberger 4.00 10.00
3 B.Sanders/K.Jones 2.50 6.00
4 J.Elway/B.Favre 3.00 8.00
5 B.Jackson/J.Lewis 1.50 4.00
6 J.Namath/C.Pennington 1.50 4.00
7 I.Woods/R.Johnson 1.25 3.00
8 J.Montana/T.Brady 4.00 10.00
9 J.Rice/M.Harrison 2.00 5.00
10 D.Marino/P.Manning 3.00 8.00
11 F.Tarkenton/D.Culpepper 1.25 3.00
12 D.Sanders/C.Bailey 1.25 3.00
13 J.Riggins/C.Portis 1.25 3.00
14 G.Sayers/J.Jones 1.50 4.00
15 W.Payton/L.Tomlinson 4.00 10.00
16 M.Allen/P.Holmes 1.25 3.00
17 R.Cunningham/D.McNabb 1.50 4.00
18 S.Young/M.Vick 2.00 5.00
19 R.Moss/J.Walker 1.25 3.00
20 T.Aikman/E.Manning 2.50 6.00
21 S.McNair/B.Leftwich 1.25 3.00
22 E.Campbell/S.Jackson 1.25 3.00
23 E.James/S.Alexander 1.50 4.00
24 L.Evans/E.Moulds 1.00 2.50
25 T.Thomas/W.McGahee 1.25 3.00

2005 Throwback Threads Generations Material

STATED PRINT RUN 50 SER.#'d SETS
UNPRICED PRIME PRINT RUN 10 SETS
1 T.Owens/A.Johnson 7.50 20.00
2 T.Bradshaw/B.Roethlisberger 20.00 50.00
3 B.Sanders/K.Jones 20.00 50.00
4 J.Elway/B.Favre 15.00 40.00
5 B.Jackson/J.Lewis 12.50 30.00
6 J.Namath/C.Pennington 12.50 30.00
7 I.Woods/R.Johnson 6.00 15.00
8 J.Montana/T.Brady 40.00 80.00
9 J.Rice/M.Harrison 12.50 30.00
10 D.Marino/P.Manning 20.00 50.00
11 F.Tarkenton/D.Culpepper 10.00 25.00
12 D.Sanders/C.Bailey 7.50 20.00
13 J.Riggins/C.Portis 7.50 20.00
14 G.Sayers/J.Jones 12.50 30.00
15 W.Payton/L.Tomlinson 25.00 60.00
16 M.Allen/P.Holmes 10.00 25.00
17 R.Cunningham/D.McNabb 10.00 25.00
18 S.Young/M.Vick 15.00 40.00
19 R.Moss/J.Walker 7.50 20.00
20 T.Aikman/E.Manning 15.00 30.00
21 S.McNair/B.Leftwich 7.50 20.00
22 E.Campbell/S.Jackson 10.00 25.00
23 E.James/S.Alexander 10.00 25.00
24 L.Evans/E.Moulds 6.00 15.00
25 T.Thomas/W.McGahee 7.50 20.00

2005 Throwback Threads Gridiron Kings

STATED ODDS 1:12
*BRONZE/500: .5X TO 1.2X BASIC INSERTS
BRONZE PRINT RUN 500 SER.#'d SETS
*FRAMED BLK/25: 2.5X TO 6X BASIC INSERTS
FRAMED BLACK PRINT RUN 25 SER.#'d SETS
*FRAMED BLU/100: .8X TO 2X BASIC INSERTS
FRAMED BLUE PRINT RUN 100 SER.#'d SETS
*FRAMED GRN/50: 1.2X TO 3X BASIC INSERTS
FRAMED GREEN PRINT RUN 50 SER.#'d SETS
*FRAMED PLAT/10: 4X TO 10X BASIC INSERTS
UNPRICED FRAMED PLATINUM #'d TO 10
*FRAMED RED: .5X TO 1.2X BASIC INSERTS
*GOLD/100: .8X TO 2X BASIC INSERTS
GOLD PRINT RUN 100 SER.#'d SETS
*PLATINUM/20: 4X TO 10X BASIC INSERTS
PLATINUM PRINT RUN 10 SER.#'d SETS
*SILVER/250: .6X TO 1.5X BASIC INSERTS
SILVER PRINT RUN 250 SER.#'d SETS
1 Ben Roethlisberger 1.50 4.00
2 Brett Favre 2.00 5.00
3 Brian Urlacher 1.00 2.50
4 Byron Leftwich .60 1.50
5 Carson Palmer .75 2.00
6 Chad Pennington .60 1.50
7 Clinton Portis .60 1.50
8 Corey Dillon .60 1.50
9 Daunte Culpepper .75 2.00
10 David Carr .60 1.50
11 Donovan McNabb .75 2.00
12 Edgerrin James .75 2.00
13 Eli Manning 1.50 4.00
14 Jerry Rice 2.00 5.00
15 Julius Jones .60 1.50
16 Kevin Jones .60 1.50
17 LaDainian Tomlinson 1.00 2.50
18 LaVar Arrington .60 1.50
19 Michael Vick .75 2.00
20 Peyton Manning 2.50 6.00
21 Priest Holmes .60 1.50
22 Randy Moss .75 2.00
23 Shaun Alexander .60 1.50
24 Terrell Owens .75 2.00
25 Tom Brady 4.00 10.00

2005 Throwback Threads Gridiron Kings Dual Material

STATED PRINT RUN 75 SER.#'d SETS
*PRIME: 1X TO 2.5X BASIC JERSEYS
PRIME PRINT RUN 25 SER.#'d SETS
1 Ben Roethlisberger 8.00 20.00
2 Brett Favre 10.00 25.00
3 Brian Urlacher 5.00 12.00
4 Byron Leftwich 3.00 8.00
5 Carson Palmer 4.00 10.00
6 Chad Pennington 3.00 8.00
7 Clinton Portis 3.00 8.00
8 Corey Dillon 3.00 8.00
9 Daunte Culpepper 4.00 10.00
10 David Carr 3.00 8.00
11 Donovan McNabb 4.00 10.00
12 Edgerrin James 4.00 10.00
13 Eli Manning 8.00 20.00
14 Jerry Rice 10.00 25.00
15 Julius Jones 3.00 8.00
16 Kevin Jones 3.00 8.00
17 LaDainian Tomlinson 5.00 12.00
18 LaVar Arrington 3.00 8.00
19 Michael Vick 4.00 10.00
20 Peyton Manning 12.00 30.00
21 Priest Holmes 3.00 8.00
22 Randy Moss 4.00 10.00
23 Shaun Alexander 3.00 8.00
24 Terrell Owens 4.00 10.00
25 Tom Brady 20.00 50.00

2005 Throwback Threads Jerseys

1 Anquan Boldin 2.00 5.00
2 Bryant Johnson 2.00 5.00
3 Josh McCown 2.50 6.00
4 Larry Fitzgerald 3.00 8.00
5 Michael Vick 2.50 6.00
7 Peerless Price 2.00 5.00
8 T.J. Duckett 2.00 5.00
10 Jamal Lewis 2.50 6.00
11 Kyle Boller 2.00 5.00
12 Todd Heap 2.00 5.00
15 Eric Moulds 2.00 5.00
16 Josh Reed 2.00 5.00
17 Lee Evans 2.50 6.00
18 Willis McGahee 2.00 5.00
19 DeShaun Foster 2.50 6.00
20 Jake Delhomme 2.00 5.00
21 Julius Peppers 2.50 6.00
22 Muhsin Muhammad 2.00 5.00
23 Stephen Davis 2.00 5.00
25 Brian Urlacher 3.00 8.00
26 David Terrell 2.00 5.00
27 Rex Grossman 2.00 5.00
28 Thomas Jones 2.00 5.00
29 Carson Palmer 2.50 6.00
30 Chad Johnson 2.00 5.00
31 Peter Warrick 2.00 5.00
33 Jeff Garcia 2.00 5.00
34 Kelly Holcomb 2.00 5.00
36 Lee Suggs 2.00 5.00
37 William Green 2.00 5.00
38 Julius Jones 2.00 5.00
39 Drew Bledsoe 2.50 6.00
40 Roy Williams S 2.00 5.00
42 Terence Newman 2.00 5.00
43 Ashley Lelie 2.00 5.00
46 Champ Bailey 2.50 6.00
47 Darius Watts 2.00 5.00
48 Jake Plummer 2.00 5.00
49 Quentin Griffin 2.00 5.00
50 Charles Rogers 2.00 5.00
51 Joey Harrington 2.00 5.00
52 Kevin Jones 2.00 5.00
53 Roy Williams WR 2.00 5.00
54 Ahman Green 2.50 6.00
55 Brett Favre 6.00 15.00
56 Javon Walker 2.00 5.00
57 Nick Barnett 2.00 5.00
58 Robert Ferguson 2.00 5.00
59 Andre Johnson 2.50 6.00
60 David Carr 2.00 5.00
61 Domanick Davis 2.00 5.00
62 Dallas Clark 2.00 5.00
63 Edgerrin James 2.50 6.00
64 Marvin Harrison 2.50 6.00
65 Peyton Manning 8.00 20.00
66 Reggie Wayne 2.50 6.00
67 Byron Leftwich 2.00 5.00
68 Jimmy Smith 2.50 6.00
69 Fred Taylor 2.00 5.00
70 Reggie Williams 2.00 5.00
71 Dante Hall 2.00 5.00
72 Priest Holmes 2.00 5.00
73 Tony Gonzalez 2.50 6.00
74 Trent Green 2.00 5.00
76 Chris Chambers 2.00 5.00
77 Junior Seau 2.50 6.00
78 Randy McMichael 2.00 5.00
79 Zach Thomas 2.50 6.00
81 Daunte Culpepper 2.50 6.00
82 Michael Bennett 2.00 5.00
85 Corey Dillon 2.00 5.00
86 Bethel Johnson 2.00 5.00
88 Tom Brady 12.00 30.00
89 Ty Law 3.00 8.00
90 Aaron Brooks 2.00 5.00
91 Deuce McAllister 2.50 6.00
93 Donte Stallworth 2.00 5.00
94 Eli Manning 5.00 12.00
95 Ike Hilliard 2.00 5.00
96 Jeremy Shockey 2.00 5.00
97 Michael Strahan 2.50 6.00
98 Tiki Barber 2.50 6.00
99 Anthony Becht 2.00 5.00
100 Chad Pennington 2.00 5.00
101 Curtis Martin 2.50 6.00
102 John Abraham 2.00 5.00
103 Justin McCareins 2.00 5.00
104 Santana Moss 2.50 6.00
105 Shaun Ellis 2.00 5.00
107 Randy Moss 2.50 6.00
108 Jerry Porter 2.00 5.00
109 Chad Lewis 2.00 5.00
110 Donovan McNabb 2.50 6.00
111 Freddie Mitchell 2.00 5.00
112 Jevon Kearse 2.00 5.00
113 Terrell Owens 2.50 6.00
115 Antwaan Randle El 2.00 5.00
116 Ben Roethlisberger 5.00 12.00
117 Duce Staley 2.00 5.00
118 Hines Ward 2.50 6.00
119 Jerome Bettis 3.00 8.00
120 Plaxico Burress 2.00 6.00
121 Antonio Gates 3.00 8.00
122 Drew Brees 3.00 8.00
123 LaDainian Tomlinson 3.00 8.00
124 Kevan Barlow 2.00 5.00
126 Darrell Jackson 2.00 5.00
127 Koren Robinson 2.00 5.00
128 Matt Hasselbeck 2.00 5.00
129 Shaun Alexander 2.00 5.00
130 Marc Bulger 2.00 5.00
131 Isaac Bruce 3.00 8.00
132 Marshall Faulk 2.50 6.00
133 Steven Jackson 2.00 5.00
134 Torry Holt 2.50 6.00
138 Mike Alstott 2.00 5.00
139 Chris Brown 2.00 5.00
140 Derrick Mason 2.00 5.00
141 Keith Bulluck 2.00 5.00
142 Steve McNair 2.50 6.00
143 Tyrone Calico 2.00 5.00
144 Drew Bennett 2.50 6.00
147 Sean Taylor 10.00 25.00
148 Patrick Ramsey 2.50 6.00
149 Laveranues Coles 2.00 5.00
150 Rod Gardner 2.00 5.00

2005 Throwback Threads Jerseys Prime

*PRIME: 1.2X TO 3X BASIC JERSEYS
PRIME PRINT RUN 25 SER.#'d SETS
6 Warrick Dunn 6.00 15.00
13 Ray Lewis 10.00 25.00
24 Steve Smith 10.00 25.00
32 Rudi Johnson 6.00 15.00
41 Keyshawn Johnson 8.00 20.00
44 Rod Smith 8.00 20.00
114 Brian Westbrook 6.00 15.00
145 Clinton Portis 6.00 15.00
146 LaVar Arrington 6.00 15.00

2005 Throwback Threads Pig Pens Autographs

2 Ahman Green/50 12.50 30.00
3 Antonio Gates/150 7.50 20.00
4 Chris Brown/150 7.50 20.00
6 Domanick Davis/150 7.50 20.00
7 Michael Vick/50 30.00 60.00
8 Christian Okoye/200 7.50 20.00
9 Deacon Jones/100 10.00 25.00
10 Herschel Walker/200 10.00 25.00
11 Ickey Woods/200 6.00 15.00
12 Jim Brown/50 40.00 80.00
13 Joe Montana/50 75.00 150.00
14 Joe Namath/50 50.00 100.00
15 John Taylor/100 7.50 20.00

2005 Throwback Threads Player Timelines

STATED ODDS 1:24 HOB/RET
*BLUE: .8X TO 2X BASIC INSERTS
BLUE PRINT RUN 100 SER.#'d SETS
1 Ahman Green 1.00 2.50
2 Andre Johnson 1.00 2.50
3 Anquan Boldin .75 2.00
4 Barry Sanders 2.00 5.00
5 Carson Palmer 1.00 2.50
6 Clinton Portis .75 2.00
7 Corey Dillon .75 2.00
8 Curtis Martin 1.00 2.50
9 Drew Bledsoe 1.00 2.50
10 Duce Staley .75 2.00
11 Edgerrin James 1.00 2.50
12 Jeremy Shockey .75 2.00
13 Jerry Rice 2.50 6.00
14 Jevon Kearse .75 2.00
15 Joe Montana 4.00 10.00
16 Jake Plummer .75 2.00
17 Kellen Winslow Jr. .75 2.00
18 Keyshawn Johnson 1.00 2.50
19 Michael Vick 1.00 2.50
20 Priest Holmes .75 2.00
21 Reggie Wayne 1.00 2.50
22 Steven Jackson .75 2.00
23 Thomas Jones .75 2.00
24 Thurman Thomas 1.00 2.50
25 Trent Green .75 2.00

2005 Throwback Threads Player Timelines Dual Material

STATED PRINT RUN 250 SER.#'d SETS
*PRIME: 1X TO 2.5X BASIC JERSEYS
PRIME PRINT RUN 25 SER.#'d SETS
1 Ahman Green 3.00 8.00
2 Andre Johnson 3.00 8.00
3 Anquan Boldin 2.50 6.00
4 Barry Sanders 6.00 15.00
5 Carson Palmer 3.00 8.00
6 Clinton Portis 2.50 6.00
7 Corey Dillon 2.50 6.00
8 Curtis Martin 3.00 8.00
9 Drew Bledsoe 3.00 8.00
10 Duce Staley 2.50 6.00
11 Edgerrin James 3.00 8.00
12 Jeremy Shockey 2.50 6.00
13 Jerry Rice 8.00 20.00
14 Jevon Kearse 2.50 6.00
15 Joe Montana 12.00 30.00
16 Jake Plummer 2.50 6.00
17 Kellen Winslow Jr. 2.50 6.00
18 Keyshawn Johnson 3.00 8.00
19 Michael Vick 3.00 8.00
20 Priest Holmes 2.50 6.00
21 Reggie Wayne 3.00 8.00
22 Steven Jackson 2.50 6.00
23 Thomas Jones 2.50 6.00
24 Thurman Thomas 3.00 8.00
25 Trent Green 2.50 6.00

2005 Throwback Threads Rookie Hoggs

STATED PRINT RUN 750 SER.#'d SETS
*GOLD HOLO: .8X TO 2X BASIC INSERTS
GOLD HOLOFOIL PRINT RUN 100 SETS
1 Alex Smith QB 3.00 8.00
2 Ronnie Brown 1.00 2.50
3 Braylon Edwards .75 2.00
4 Cedric Benson .75 2.00
5 Cadillac Williams .75 2.00
6 Adam Jones .75 2.00
7 Troy Williamson .75 2.00
8 Carlos Rogers 1.25 3.00
9 Antrel Rolle 1.25 3.00
10 Mike Williams 1.00 2.50
11 DeMarcus Ware 2.50 6.00
12 Erasmus James .75 2.00
13 Matt Jones .75 2.00
14 Mark Clayton .75 2.00
15 Aaron Rodgers 10.00 25.00
16 Jason Campbell .75 2.00
17 Roddy White 1.25 3.00
18 Heath Miller 1.50 4.00
19 Reggie Brown .75 2.00
20 Mark Bradley .75 2.00
21 J.J. Arrington 1.00 2.50
22 Eric Shelton .75 2.00
23 Roscoe Parrish .75 2.00
24 Terrence Murphy .75 2.00
25 Vincent Jackson 1.25 3.00
26 Frank Gore 1.50 4.00
27 Charlie Frye .75 2.00
28 Courtney Roby .75 2.00
29 Andrew Walter .75 2.00
30 Vernand Morency 1.00 2.50
31 Ryan Moats 1.00 2.50
32 Maurice Clarett 1.00 2.50
33 Kyle Orton .75 2.00
34 Ciatrick Fason .75 2.00
35 Stefan LeFors .75 2.00

2005 Throwback Threads Rookie Hoggs Autographs

STATED PRINT RUN 150 SER.#'d SETS
1 Alex Smith QB 30.00 80.00
2 Ronnie Brown 6.00 15.00
3 Braylon Edwards 5.00 12.00
4 Cedric Benson 5.00 12.00
5 Cadillac Williams 5.00 12.00
6 Adam Jones 5.00 12.00
7 Troy Williamson 5.00 12.00
8 Carlos Rogers 8.00 20.00
9 Antrel Rolle 8.00 20.00
13 Matt Jones 5.00 12.00
14 Mark Clayton 5.00 12.00
15 Aaron Rodgers 175.00 300.00
16 Jason Campbell 5.00 12.00
17 Roddy White 8.00 20.00
19 Reggie Brown 5.00 12.00
20 Mark Bradley 5.00 12.00
21 J.J. Arrington 6.00 15.00
22 Eric Shelton 5.00 12.00
23 Roscoe Parrish 5.00 12.00
24 Terrence Murphy 5.00 12.00
25 Vincent Jackson 8.00 20.00
26 Frank Gore 15.00 40.00
27 Charlie Frye 5.00 12.00
28 Courtney Roby 5.00 12.00
29 Andrew Walter 5.00 12.00
30 Vernand Morency 5.00 12.00
31 Ryan Moats 5.00 12.00
32 Maurice Clarett 5.00 12.00
33 Kyle Orton 5.00 12.00
34 Ciatrick Fason 5.00 12.00
35 Stefan LeFors 5.00 12.00

2005 Throwback Threads Rookie Hoggs Autographs Hawaii

HAWAII/12 TOO SCARCE TO PRICE

2005 Throwback Threads Throwback Collection

STATED ODDS 1:24 HOB/RET
*BLUE: .8X TO 2X BASIC INSERTS
BLUE PRINT RUN 100 SER.#'d SETS
1 J.Campbell/A.Smith QB 3.00 8.00
2 C.Frye/A.Walter .75 2.00
3 K.Orton/S.LeFors .75 2.00
4 C.Williams/Ron.Brown 1.00 2.50
5 E.Shelton/J.J.Arrington 1.00 2.50
6 F.Gore/V.Morency 1.50 4.00
7 M.Clarett/R.Moats .75 2.00
8 C.Fason/B.Edwards .75 2.00
9 M.Jones/T.Williamson .75 2.00
10 M.Clayton/R.White 1.25 3.00
11 Re.Brown/M.Bradley .75 2.00
12 T.Murphy/R.Parrish .75 2.00
13 B.Edwards/V.Jackson 1.25 3.00
14 A.Jones/C.Roby .75 2.00
15 A.Rolle/C.Rogers 1.25 3.00
16 Frye/Campbell/A.Smith QB 4.00 10.00
17 K.Orton/A.Walter/S.LeFors 1.00 2.50
18 Cadillac/Arringtn/Ro.Brown 1.25 3.00
19 Gore/Shelton/Morency 2.00 5.00
20 M.Clarett/C.Fason/R.Moats 1.00 2.50
21 Wllmsn/Edwards/M.Jones 1.00 2.50
22 Re.Brown/Clayton/White 1.50 4.00
23 Murphy/Bradley/Parrish 1.00 2.50
24 Edwards/V.Jackson/Roby 1.50 4.00
25 A.Rolle/A.Jones/C.Rogers 1.50 4.00

2005 Throwback Threads Throwback Collection Material

1-15 DUAL PRINT RUN 150 SER.#'d SETS
16-25 TRIPLE PRINT RUN 100 SER.#'d SETS
*PRIME: 1X TO 2.5X BASIC JSY DUALS
*PRIME: .8X TO 2X BASIC JSY TRIPLES
PRIME PRINT RUN 25 SER.#'d SETS
1 J.Campbell/A.Smith QB 10.00 25.00
2 C.Frye/A.Walter 2.00 5.00
3 K.Orton/S.LeFors 2.00 5.00
4 C.Williams/Ron.Brown 10.00 25.00
5 E.Shelton/J.J.Arrington 2.50 6.00
6 F.Gore/V.Morency 4.00 10.00
7 M.Clarett/R.Moats 2.00 5.00
8 C.Fason/B.Edwards 2.00 5.00
9 M.Jones/T.Williamson 2.00 5.00
10 M.Clayton/R.White 3.00 8.00
11 Re.Brown/M.Bradley 2.00 5.00
12 T.Murphy/R.Parrish 2.00 5.00
13 B.Edwards/V.Jackson 3.00 8.00
14 A.Jones/C.Roby 2.00 5.00
15 A.Rolle/C.Rogers 3.00 8.00
16 Frye/Campbell/A.Smith QB 12.00 30.00
17 K.Orton/A.Walter/S.LeFors 2.50 6.00
18 Cadillac/Arringtn/Ro.Brown 10.00 25.00
19 Gore/Shelton/Morency 5.00 12.00
20 M.Clarett/C.Fason/R.Moats 2.50 6.00
21 Wllmsn/Edwards/M.Jones 2.50 6.00
22 Re.Brown/Clayton/White 4.00 10.00
23 Murphy/Bradley/Parrish 2.50 6.00
24 Edwards/V.Jackson/Roby 4.00 10.00
25 A.Rolle/A.Jones/C.Rogers 4.00 10.00

1988 Time Capsule John Reaves

This set of five-cards was produced by Time Capsule for John Reaves during his run for Florida House of Representatives in 1988. Each card features a red border, a black and white photo, and the exact same card back except for the card number.

COMPLETE SET (5) 3.00 6.00
COMMON CARD (1-5) .60 1.50

2011 Timeless Treasures

1-125 STATED PRINT RUN 499
ROOKIE AU PRINT RUN 99-499
EXCH EXPIRATION: 3/21/2013
1 Aaron Rodgers 3.00 8.00
2 Adrian Peterson 1.50 4.00
3 Ahmad Bradshaw 1.00 2.50
4 Andre Johnson 1.25 3.00
5 Anquan Boldin 1.00 2.50
6 Antonio Gates 1.00 2.50
7 Arian Foster 1.00 2.50
8 Beanie Wells 1.00 2.50
9 Ben Roethlisberger 1.50 4.00
10 Brandon Lloyd 1.00 2.50
11 Braylon Edwards 1.00 2.50
12 Calvin Johnson 1.50 4.00
13 Jordan Shipley 1.00 2.50
14 Cedric Benson 1.00 2.50
15 Chad Henne 1.25 3.00
16 Chad Ochocinco 1.00 2.50
17 Chris Cooley 1.00 2.50
18 Chris Johnson 1.00 2.50
19 Colt McCoy 1.00 2.50
20 Danny Amendola 1.25 3.00
21 Danny Woodhead 1.25 3.00
22 Darren McFadden 1.00 2.50
23 David Garrard 1.00 2.50
24 Davone Bess 1.00 2.50
25 DeAngelo Williams 1.00 2.50
26 DeSean Jackson 1.25 3.00
27 Devin Hester 1.25 3.00
28 Donald Driver 1.25 3.00
29 Donovan McNabb 1.25 3.00
30 Drew Brees 1.50 4.00
31 Dwayne Bowe 1.25 3.00
32 Eli Manning 1.25 3.00
33 Felix Jones 1.00 2.50

34 Frank Gore 1.25 3.00
35 Fred Jackson 1.00 2.50
36 Greg Jennings 1.00 2.50
37 Hakeem Nicks 1.00 2.50
38 Jahvid Best 1.00 2.50
39 Jamaal Charles 1.25 3.00
40 Jason Campbell 1.00 2.50
41 Jason Witten 1.25 3.00
42 Jay Cutler 1.00 2.50
43 Jeremy Maclin 1.00 2.50
44 Joe Flacco 1.25 3.00
45 John Carlson 1.00 2.50
46 Johnny Knox 1.00 2.50
47 Jonathan Stewart 1.00 2.50
48 Josh Cribbs 1.00 2.50
49 Josh Freeman 1.25 3.00
50 Justin Forsett 1.25 3.00
51 Kenny Britt 1.00 2.50
52 Knowshon Moreno 1.00 2.50
53 LaDainian Tomlinson 1.50 4.00
54 Larry Fitzgerald 1.25 3.00
55 LeGarrette Blount 1.25 3.00
56 LeSean McCoy 1.50 4.00
57 Marcedes Lewis 1.00 2.50
58 Mario Manningham 1.00 2.50
59 Mark Sanchez 1.00 2.50
60 Marques Colston 1.00 2.50
61 Matt Cassel 1.00 2.50
62 Matt Forte 1.00 2.50
63 Matt Ryan 1.25 3.00
64 Matt Schaub 1.00 2.50
65 Matthew Stafford 1.25 3.00
66 Maurice Jones-Drew 1.00 2.50
67 Michael Crabtree 1.00 2.50
68 Michael Turner 1.00 2.50
69 Michael Vick 1.25 3.00
70 Mike Tolbert 1.00 2.50
71 Mike Wallace 1.00 2.50
72 Mike Williams 1.25 3.00
73 Mike Williams USC 1.00 2.50
74 Miles Austin 1.00 2.50
75 Nate Washington 1.00 2.50
76 Percy Harvin 1.00 2.50
77 Peyton Hillis 1.00 2.50
78 Peyton Manning 3.00 8.00
79 Philip Rivers 1.50 4.00
80 Pierre Garcon 1.25 3.00
81 Rashard Mendenhall 1.00 2.50
82 Ray Rice 1.00 2.50
83 Reggie Bush 1.00 2.50
84 Reggie Wayne 1.25 3.00
85 Roddy White 1.00 2.50
86 Ronnie Brown 1.25 3.00
87 Ryan Fitzpatrick 1.00 2.50
88 Ryan Torain 1.00 2.50
89 Sam Bradford 1.00 2.50
90 Sidney Rice 1.00 2.50
91 Steve Breaston 1.00 2.50
92 Steve Johnson 1.00 2.50
93 Steve Smith 1.25 3.00
94 Steven Jackson 1.00 2.50
95 Tim Tebow 4.00 10.00
96 Tom Brady 4.00 10.00
97 Tony Romo 1.25 3.00
98 Vernon Davis 1.00 2.50
99 Wes Welker 1.25 3.00
100 Zach Miller 1.00 2.50
101 Barry Sanders 3.00 8.00
102 Bob Griese 2.00 5.00
103 Bob Hayes 2.00 5.00
104 Boomer Esiason 1.50 4.00
105 Brett Favre 4.00 10.00
106 Bruce Smith 1.50 4.00
107 Dan Fouts 1.50 4.00
108 Deion Sanders 1.50 4.00
109 Dick Butkus 2.50 6.00
110 Emmitt Smith 3.00 8.00
111 Forrest Gregg 1.25 3.00
112 Fran Tarkenton 2.00 5.00
113 Franco Harris 2.00 5.00
114 Jack Lambert 2.00 5.00
115 Joe Greene 2.00 5.00
116 Joe Montana 5.00 12.00
117 John Randle 1.50 4.00
118 Priest Holmes 1.25 3.00
119 Ron Mix 1.25 3.00
120 Shannon Sharpe 1.50 4.00
121 Steve Young 2.50 6.00
122 Thurman Thomas 1.50 4.00
123 Tony Dorsett 2.00 5.00
124 Walter Payton 4.00 10.00
125 Y.A. Tittle 2.00 5.00
126 A.J. Green AU/165 RC 15.00 40.00
127 Aaron Williams AU/163 RC 5.00 12.00
128 Adrian Clayborn AU/299 RC 4.00 10.00
129 Ahmad Black AU/463 RC 5.00 12.00
130 Akeem Ayers AU/297 RC 4.00 10.00
131 Aldon Smith AU/299 RC EXCH
132 Aldrick Robinson AU/297 RC 5.00 12.00
133 Alex Green AU/265 RC 4.00 10.00
134 Allen Bradford AU/299 RC 4.00 10.00
135 Andy Dalton AU/165 RC 10.00 25.00
136 Anthony Allen AU/299 RC 4.00 10.00
137 Anthony Castonzo AU/499 RC 4.00 10.00
138 Austin Pettis AU/265 RC 4.00 10.00
139 Bilal Powell AU/265 RC 5.00 12.00
140 Blaine Gabbert AU/165 RC 5.00 12.00
141 Brandon Harris AU/463 RC 4.00 10.00
142 Cam Newton AU/163 RC 30.00 80.00
143 Cameron Heyward AU/458 RC 5.00 12.00
144 Cameron Jordan AU/463 RC 5.00 12.00
145 Cecil Shorts AU/299 RC 4.00 10.00
146 Christian Ponder AU/163 RC 5.00 12.00
147 Clyde Gates AU/265 RC 4.00 10.00
148 Colin Kaepernick AU/165 RC 8.00 20.00
149 Corey Liuget AU/299 RC 4.00 10.00
150 D.J. Williams AU/299 RC 4.00 10.00
151 Daniel Thomas AU/265 RC 4.00 10.00
152 Da'Quan Bowers AU/463 RC 4.00 10.00
153 Da'Rel Scott AU/294 RC 4.00 10.00
154 Delone Carter AU/265 RC 4.00 10.00
155 DeMarco Murray AU/265 RC 8.00 20.00
156 Denarius Moore AU/264 RC 12.00 30.00
157 Dion Lewis AU/463 RC 5.00 12.00
158 Dwayne Harris AU/299 RC 4.00 10.00
159 Evan Royster AU/299 RC 4.00 10.00
160 Greg Jones AU/299 RC 5.00 12.00
161 Greg Little AU/165 RC 6.00 15.00
162 Greg McElroy AU/299 RC 6.00 15.00
163 Greg Salas AU/299 RC 4.00 10.00
164 J.J. Watt AU/299 RC 50.00 100.00
165 Jacquizz Rodgers AU/299 RC 4.00 10.00
166 Jake Locker AU/165 RC 5.00 12.00
167 Jamie Harper AU/265 RC 4.00 10.00
168 Jeremy Kerley AU/299 RC 6.00 15.00
169 Jerrel Jernigan AU/165 RC 5.00 12.00
170 Jimmy Smith AU/463 RC 4.00 10.00
171 Johnny White AU/463 RC 4.00 10.00
172 Jonathan Baldwin AU/265 RC 4.00 10.00
173 Jordan Cameron AU/299 RC 5.00 12.00
174 Jordan Todman AU/260 RC 4.00 10.00
175 Julio Jones AU/165 RC 20.00 50.00
176 Julius Thomas AU/298 RC 5.00 12.00
177 Justin Houston AU/463 RC 5.00 12.00
178 Kealoha Pilares AU/299 RC 4.00 10.00
179 Kendall Hunter AU/265 RC 4.00 10.00
180 Kris Durham AU/299 RC 4.00 10.00
181 Kyle Rudolph AU/265 RC 4.00 10.00
182 Lance Kendricks AU/299 RC 4.00 10.00
183 Leonard Hankerson AU/265 RC 4.00 10.00
184 Luke Stocker AU/463 RC 4.00 10.00
185 Marcell Dareus AU/265 RC 4.00 10.00
186 Marcus Cannon AU/490 RC 4.00 10.00
187 Mark Ingram AU/265 RC 6.00 15.00
188 Martez Wilson AU/299 RC 4.00 10.00
189 Mikel Leshoure AU/265 RC 4.00 10.00
190 Nathan Enderle AU/99 RC 5.00 12.00
191 Niles Paul AU/463 RC 4.00 10.00
192 Owen Marecic AU/99 RC EXCH 5.00 12.00
193 Phil Taylor AU/458 RC 4.00 10.00
194 Prince Amukamara AU/296 RC 4.00 10.00
195 Quinton Carter AU/299 RC 4.00 10.00
196 Rahim Moore AU/299 RC 4.00 10.00
197 Randall Cobb AU/265 RC 6.00 15.00
198 Ricky Stanzi AU/299 RC 4.00 10.00
199 Robert Housler AU/299 RC 4.00 10.00
200 Ronald Johnson AU/299 RC 4.00 10.00
201 Roy Helu AU/299 RC 4.00 10.00
202 Ryan Kerrigan AU/299 RC 8.00 20.00
203 Ryan Mallett AU/165 RC 5.00 12.00
204 Ryan Whalen AU/299 RC 4.00 10.00
205 Ryan Williams AU/165 RC 5.00 12.00
206 Scotty McKnight AU/299 RC 4.00 10.00
207 Shane Bannon AU/299 RC EXCH 4.00 10.00
208 Shane Vereen AU/265 RC 5.00 12.00
209 Stanley Havili AU/450 RC 4.00 10.00
210 Stephen Burton AU/297 RC 4.00 10.00
211 Stephen Paea AU/299 RC 5.00 12.00
212 Stevan Ridley AU/265 RC 4.00 10.00
213 T.J. Yates AU/299 RC 4.00 10.00
214 Taiwan Jones AU/265 RC 4.00 10.00
215 Tandon Doss AU/463 RC 4.00 10.00
216 Titus Young AU/265 RC 4.00 10.00
217 Torrey Smith AU/265 RC 4.00 10.00
218 Tyler Sash AU/290 RC 4.00 10.00
219 Tyrod Taylor AU/299 RC 8.00 20.00
220 Tyron Smith AU/299 RC 5.00 12.00
221 Vincent Brown AU/265 RC 4.00 10.00
222 Von Miller AU/265 RC 10.00 25.00

2011 Timeless Treasures Gold

*VETS 1-100: 1.2X TO 3X BASIC CARDS
*LEGENDS 101-125: 1X TO 2.5X BASIC CARDS
1-125 STATED PRINT RUN 49
UNPRICED ROOKIE AUTO PRINT RUN 10

2011 Timeless Treasures Silver

*1-100 VETS/99: .8X TO 2X BASIC CARDS
*101-125 LGND/99: .6X TO 1.5X BASIC CARDS
*ROOK.AU/25: .6X TO 1.5X BASIC AU/260-499
*ROOK.AU/25: .5X TO 1.2X BASIC AU/99-165
164 J.J. Watt AU 125.00 200.00

2011 Timeless Treasures All Time Leaders Materials

STATED PRINT RUN 25 SER.#'d SETS
1 Brett Favre 20.00 50.00
2 Emmitt Smith 15.00 40.00
3 Jerry Rice 15.00 40.00
4 Bruce Smith 8.00 20.00
5 George Blanda 8.00 20.00

2011 Timeless Treasures Autographs Gold

STATED PRINT RUN 4-25
EXCH EXPIRATION: 3/21/2013
3 Ahmad Bradshaw/15 15.00 40.00
4 Andre Johnson/15
5 Anquan Boldin/15 10.00 25.00
6 Antonio Gates/15
8 Beanie Wells/15
9 Ben Roethlisberger/15 50.00 100.00
11 Braylon Edwards/15 12.00 30.00
12 Calvin Johnson/15
15 Chad Henne/25
16 Chad Ochocinco/15
17 Chris Cooley/15 15.00 40.00
19 Colt McCoy/25 40.00 80.00
20 Danny Amendola/15 15.00 40.00
25 DeAngelo Williams/15 12.00 30.00
27 Devin Hester/15 15.00 40.00
28 Donald Driver/15
29 Donovan McNabb/15 12.00 30.00
32 Eli Manning/15 40.00 80.00
34 Frank Gore/15
36 Greg Jennings/15 10.00 25.00
38 Jahvid Best/25
39 Jamaal Charles/15
41 Jason Witten/20 15.00 40.00
42 Jay Cutler/15 30.00 60.00
43 Jeremy Maclin/15 12.00 30.00
44 Joe Flacco/15 12.00 30.00
49 Josh Freeman/15 15.00 40.00
51 Kenny Britt/15
52 Knowshon Moreno/15
53 LaDainian Tomlinson/15 15.00 40.00
54 Larry Fitzgerald/15 15.00 40.00
56 LeSean McCoy/15 15.00 40.00
60 Marques Colston/15 EXCH
62 Matt Forte/25 15.00 40.00
64 Matt Schaub/15 15.00 40.00
65 Matthew Stafford/25 30.00 60.00
66 Maurice Jones-Drew/15 10.00 25.00
67 Michael Crabtree/15
68 Michael Turner/15
69 Michael Vick/15 40.00 80.00
70 Mike Tolbert/25 15.00 40.00
71 Mike Wallace/15
73 Mike Williams/15
76 Percy Harvin/25 15.00 40.00
77 Peyton Hillis/25 10.00 25.00
78 Peyton Manning/15 90.00 150.00
83 Reggie Bush/15 25.00 50.00
84 Reggie Wayne/15 12.00 30.00
86 Ronnie Brown/15
88 Ryan Torain/25
90 Sidney Rice/25
93 Steve Smith/15
97 Tony Romo/15 30.00 60.00
101 Barry Sanders/25 60.00 120.00
102 Bob Griese/25 12.00 30.00
104 Boomer Esiason/25 12.00 30.00
106 Bruce Smith/25 12.00 30.00
108 Deion Sanders/25 30.00 60.00
109 Dick Butkus/25 30.00 60.00
110 Emmitt Smith/22 100.00 175.00
111 Forrest Gregg/25 15.00 40.00
112 Fran Tarkenton/25 15.00 40.00
113 Franco Harris/25 20.00 50.00
114 Jack Lambert/25 30.00 60.00
115 Joe Greene/25 20.00 50.00
116 Joe Montana/25 60.00 120.00
117 John Randle/25 15.00 40.00
119 Ron Mix/25 12.00 30.00
120 Shannon Sharpe/25
122 Thurman Thomas/25 15.00 40.00
123 Tony Dorsett/25 15.00 40.00
125 Y.A. Tittle/19

2011 Timeless Treasures Championship Season Materials

STATED PRINT RUN 30-100
*PRIME/25: .8X TO 2X BASIC JSY/100
*PRIME/25: .6X TO 1.5X BASIC JSY/30
1 Troy Aikman/100 8.00 20.00
2 Steve Young/100 8.00 20.00
4 Terrell Davis/30 6.00 15.00
5 John Elway/100 10.00 25.00
7 Tom Brady/100 12.00 30.00
8 Peyton Manning/100 10.00 25.00
9 Aaron Rodgers/100 8.00 20.00

2011 Timeless Treasures Championship Season Materials Autographs

STATED PRINT RUN 5-20
UNPRICED PRIME AU PRINT RUN 1-10
1 Troy Aikman EXCH
2 Steve Young 30.00 60.00
4 Terrell Davis 15.00 40.00
5 John Elway 75.00 150.00

2011 Timeless Treasures Championship Season Materials Combos

1 L.Groza/O.Graham/25 10.00 25.00

2011 Timeless Treasures Changing Stripes

STATED PRINT RUN 3-249
1 Anquan Boldin/149 4.00 10.00
2 Y.A. Tittle/20 15.00 40.00
3 Braylon Edwards/249 4.00 10.00
4 Brett Favre/249 12.00 30.00
5 Cedric Benson/100 5.00 12.00
6 Deion Sanders/65 12.00 30.00
7 Donovan McNabb/249 5.00 12.00
8 Eric Dickerson/249 6.00 15.00
9 Fran Tarkenton/99 10.00 25.00
10 Jay Cutler/249 4.00 10.00
12 Jerry Rice/249 10.00 25.00
13 Joe Montana/249 20.00 50.00
14 Joe Namath/249 10.00 25.00
15 John Riggins/3
16 Boomer Esiason/249 6.00 15.00
17 Kellen Winslow/249 5.00 12.00
18 Keyshawn Johnson/15 8.00 20.00
19 LaDainian Tomlinson/249 6.00 15.00
20 Marcus Allen/249 8.00 20.00
21 Michael Vick/249 5.00 12.00
22 Randall Cunningham/249 8.00 20.00
23 Randy Moss/220 5.00 12.00
24 Reggie White/35 12.00 30.00
25 Ricky Williams/249 5.00 12.00
26 Ronnie Lott/249 6.00 15.00
27 Santonio Holmes/40 6.00 15.00
28 Steve McNair/249 6.00 15.00
29 Thurman Thomas/125 6.00 15.00
30 Tony Dorsett/249 8.00 20.00
31 Tony Gonzalez/249 5.00 12.00

2011 Timeless Treasures Changing Stripes Prime

PRIME PRINT RUN 1-49
6 Deion Sanders/21 15.00 40.00
7 Donovan McNabb/49 10.00 25.00
8 Eric Dickerson/49 12.00 30.00
11 Jeremy Shockey/49 8.00 20.00
12 Jerry Rice/49 20.00 50.00
13 Joe Montana/49 40.00 100.00
16 Boomer Esiason/49 12.00 30.00
17 Kellen Winslow/49 10.00 25.00
18 Keyshawn Johnson/49 8.00 20.00
19 LaDainian Tomlinson/15 15.00 40.00
20 Marcus Allen/35 15.00 40.00
22 Randall Cunningham/49 15.00 40.00
23 Randy Moss/49 10.00 25.00
25 Ricky Williams/49 10.00 25.00
26 Ronnie Lott/40 12.00 30.00
27 Santonio Holmes/49 8.00 20.00
28 Steve McNair/49 12.00 30.00
29 Thurman Thomas/49 12.00 30.00
30 Tony Dorsett/49 15.00 40.00
31 Tony Gonzalez/49 10.00 25.00
32 Warren Moon/49 15.00 40.00

2011 Timeless Treasures Classic Cuts Materials

STATED PRINT RUN 1-25
2 Bulldog Turner/25 40.00 80.00
7 Johnny Unitas/25 250.00 400.00

2011 Timeless Treasures Game Day Souvenirs 1st Quarter

1ST QUARTER PRINT RUN 20-250
*1Q-4Q PRM/15-25: 1X TO 2.5X 1Q JSY/115-250
*1Q-4Q PRIME/15-25: .8X TO 2X 1Q JSY/80
*2ND-4TH QUARTER: .4X TO 1X 1ST QRTR
1 Felix Jones/190 2.50 6.00
2 Michael Vick/250 3.00 8.00
3 DeSean Jackson/250 3.00 8.00
4 Marques Colston/165 2.50 6.00
5 Eli Manning/185 3.00 8.00
6 Adrian Peterson/155 4.00 10.00
7 Matt Ryan/190 3.00 8.00
8 Roddy White/115 2.50 6.00
9 Ahmad Bradshaw/20 5.00 12.00
10 Sam Bradford/90 3.00 8.00
11 Steven Jackson/250 2.50 6.00
12 Mark Sanchez/200 2.50 6.00
13 Joe Flacco/250 3.00 8.00
14 Ray Rice/250 2.50 6.00
15 Brandon Lloyd/50 3.00 8.00
16 Maurice Jones-Drew/125 2.50 6.00
17 David Garrard/185 2.50 6.00
18 Chris Johnson/200 2.50 6.00
19 Knowshon Moreno/150 2.50 6.00
20 Matt Cassel/250 2.50 6.00
21 Jamaal Charles/164 3.00 8.00
22 Darren McFadden/180 2.50 6.00
23 Philip Rivers/190 4.00 10.00
24 Antonio Gates/170 2.50 6.00
25 Hakeem Nicks/80 3.00 8.00
26 Johnny Knox/50 3.00 8.00
27 Peyton Manning/250 8.00 20.00
28 Philip Rivers/75 5.00 12.00
29 Roddy White/99 3.00 8.00
30 Santonio Holmes/99 3.00 8.00
31 Jon Beason/75 3.00 8.00
32 Visanthe Shiancoe/99 4.00 10.00

2011 Timeless Treasures Game Day Souvenirs Combos

STATED PRINT RUN 50 SER.#'d SETS
*PRIME/25: .6X TO 1.5X BASIC COMBO/50
1 D.Jackson/M.Vick 5.00 12.00
2 J.Laurinaitis/S.Bradford 4.00 10.00
3 M.Floyd/P.Rivers 6.00 15.00
4 M.Sanchez/S.Greene 4.00 10.00
5 D.Garrard/M.Jones-Drew 4.00 10.00

2011 Timeless Treasures Hall of Fame

RANDOM INSERTS IN PACKS
8 Deion Sanders 2.00 5.00
9 Richard Dent 1.50 4.00
10 Marshall Faulk 2.00 5.00
11 Chris Hanburger 1.25 3.00
12 Les Richter 1.25 3.00
13 Shannon Sharpe 1.50 4.00
14 Ed Sabol 1.25 3.00

2011 Timeless Treasures Hall of Fame Autographs

RANDOM INSERTS IN PACKS
8 Deion Sanders 30.00 80.00
9 Richard Dent 25.00 60.00
10 Marshall Faulk 20.00 40.00
11 Chris Hanburger 20.00 40.00
13 Shannon Sharpe 40.00 80.00
14 Ed Sabol 60.00 100.00

2011 Timeless Treasures HOF Combo Materials

STATED PRINT RUN 25 SER.#'d SETS
1 Jim Brown/Y.A. Tittle 12.00 30.00
2 Dick Lane/Lou Groza 8.00 20.00
3 Otto Graham/Sid Luckman 12.00 30.00
4 Dan Fouts/Walter Payton
5 Deion Sanders/Marshall Faulk 12.00 30.00

2011 Timeless Treasures HOF Quad Materials

STATED PRINT RUN 5-25
2 Wlkr/Trkntn/Hrng/Lnr/25 40.00 80.00
3 Mynrd/Grne/Csnk/Dws/25 15.00 40.00
4 Grse/Bchn/Hrris/Lmbrt/25 15.00 40.00
5 E.Smth/Rce/Rndl/Jcksn/25

2011 Timeless Treasures HOF Triple Materials

STATED PRINT RUN 10-25
1 Starr/Gregg/Sayers/25 15.00 40.00
3 Grse/Bchnon/Harris/25
4 Sanders/Eller/Elway/25 15.00 40.00
5 Hyes/B.Smith/Wdsn/25

2011 Timeless Treasures Jerseys

STATED PRINT RUN 9-250
1 Aaron Rodgers/250 8.00 20.00
2 Adrian Peterson/250 4.00 10.00
3 Ahmad Bradshaw/99 3.00 8.00
4 Andre Johnson/199 3.00 8.00
5 Anquan Boldin/50 4.00 10.00
6 Antonio Gates/250 2.50 6.00
7 Arian Foster/250 2.50 6.00
8 Beanie Wells/250 2.50 6.00
9 Ben Roethlisberger/250 4.00 10.00
10 Brandon Lloyd/99 3.00 8.00
11 Braylon Edwards/250 2.50 6.00
12 Calvin Johnson/250 4.00 10.00
14 Cedric Benson/250 2.50 6.00
15 Chad Henne/50 5.00 12.00
16 Chad Ochocinco/99 3.00 8.00
17 Chris Cooley/250 2.50 6.00
18 Chris Johnson/250 2.50 6.00
19 Colt McCoy/99 3.00 8.00
21 Danny Woodhead/250 6.00 15.00
22 Darren McFadden/250 2.50 6.00
23 David Garrard/250 2.50 6.00
25 DeAngelo Williams/250 2.50 6.00
26 DeSean Jackson/250 3.00 8.00
27 Devin Hester/250 3.00 8.00
29 Donovan McNabb/250 3.00 8.00
30 Drew Brees/99 5.00 12.00
31 Dwayne Bowe/250 3.00 8.00
32 Eli Manning/250 3.00 8.00
33 Felix Jones/250 2.50 6.00
34 Frank Gore/250 3.00 8.00
35 Fred Jackson/250 6.00 15.00
37 Hakeem Nicks/35 4.00 10.00
38 Jahvid Best/250 2.50 6.00
39 Jamaal Charles/99 4.00 10.00
40 Jason Campbell/250 2.50 6.00
41 Jason Witten/250 4.00 10.00
42 Jay Cutler/250 2.50 6.00
43 Jeremy Maclin/250 2.50 6.00
44 Joe Flacco/250 3.00 8.00
46 Johnny Knox/250 2.50 6.00
47 Jonathan Stewart/99 3.00 8.00
48 Josh Cribbs/99 3.00 8.00
49 Josh Freeman/250 3.00 8.00
52 Knowshon Moreno/250 2.50 6.00
53 LaDainian Tomlinson/250 4.00 10.00
54 Larry Fitzgerald/99 5.00 12.00
56 LeSean McCoy/250 4.00 10.00
59 Mark Sanchez/250 2.50 6.00
60 Marques Colston/250 2.50 6.00
61 Matt Cassel/250 2.50 6.00
62 Matt Forte/250 2.50 6.00
63 Matt Ryan/250 3.00 8.00
64 Matt Schaub/250 2.50 6.00
65 Matthew Stafford/99 4.00 10.00
66 Maurice Jones-Drew/99 3.00 8.00
67 Michael Crabtree/250 2.50 6.00
68 Michael Turner/250 2.50 6.00
69 Michael Vick/250 3.00 8.00
71 Mike Wallace/250 4.00 10.00
74 Miles Austin/250 4.00 10.00
75 Nate Washington/250 2.50 6.00
76 Percy Harvin/250 2.50 6.00
77 Peyton Hillis/250 2.50 6.00
78 Peyton Manning/99 10.00 25.00
79 Philip Rivers/99 5.00 12.00
80 Pierre Garcon/250 3.00 8.00
81 Rashard Mendenhall/250 2.50 6.00
82 Ray Rice/250 2.50 6.00
83 Reggie Bush/250 2.50 6.00
84 Reggie Wayne/250 3.00 8.00
85 Roddy White/250 2.50 6.00
86 Ronnie Brown/250 3.00 8.00
87 Ryan Fitzpatrick/250 2.50 6.00
89 Sam Bradford/250 2.50 6.00
90 Sidney Rice/250 2.50 6.00
94 Steven Jackson/250 2.50 6.00
95 Tim Tebow/250 4.00 10.00
96 Tom Brady/250 8.00 20.00
97 Tony Romo/250 3.00 8.00
98 Vernon Davis/250 2.50 6.00
99 Wes Welker/250 3.00 8.00
101 Barry Sanders/99 12.00 30.00
102 Bob Griese/250 6.00 15.00
103 Bob Hayes/250 8.00 20.00
104 Boomer Esiason/250 5.00 12.00
105 Brett Favre/250 10.00 25.00
106 Bruce Smith/99 6.00 15.00
107 Dan Fouts/250 5.00 12.00
108 Deion Sanders/250 5.00 12.00
109 Dick Butkus/250 8.00 20.00
110 Emmitt Smith/250 10.00 25.00
111 Forrest Gregg/250 4.00 10.00
112 Fran Tarkenton/250 5.00 12.00
113 Franco Harris/250 6.00 15.00
114 Jack Lambert/250 8.00 20.00
115 Joe Greene/250 6.00 15.00
116 Joe Montana/250 8.00 20.00
117 John Randle/99 6.00 15.00
118 Priest Holmes/250 4.00 10.00
120 Shannon Sharpe/99 6.00 15.00
121 Steve Young/250 6.00 15.00
122 Thurman Thomas/250 5.00 12.00
123 Tony Dorsett/250 6.00 15.00
124 Walter Payton/250 12.00 30.00
125 Y.A. Tittle/99 8.00 20.00

2011 Timeless Treasures Jerseys Prime

*PRIME/25: 1X TO 2.5X BASIC JSY/199-250
*PRIME/20-25: .8X TO 2X BASIC JSY/99
*PRIME/25: .6X TO 1.5X BASIC JSY/35-50
STATED PRINT RUN 2-25
28 Donald Driver/18 8.00 20.00
93 Steve Smith/25 8.00 20.00

2011 Timeless Treasures Material Ink Jerseys

STATED PRINT RUN 15-35
*PRIME/25: .4X TO 1X BASIC AU/30-35
EXCH EXPIRATION: 3/21/2013
1 Darren McFadden/15
2 Tim Tebow/15 30.00 80.00
3 Ray Rice/15
4 Rashard Mendenhall/15
5 Percy Harvin/15
6 Jared Allen/35 30.00 80.00
7 DeSean Jackson/15 15.00 40.00
8 Hines Ward/15 30.00 60.00
9 Roddy White/15 10.00 25.00
10 Michael Vick/15
11 Josh Freeman/15
12 Steven Jackson/15 15.00 40.00
13 Hakeem Nicks/15 10.00 25.00
14 Aaron Rodgers/15 175.00 300.00
15 Miles Austin/15 15.00 40.00
16 London Fletcher/30 25.00 60.00
17 Nnamdi Asomugha/30 10.00 25.00
18 Felix Jones/15 10.00 25.00
19 Philip Rivers/15 25.00 60.00
20 Jonathan Stewart/15 10.00 25.00

2011 Timeless Treasures MVP Materials

STATED PRINT RUN 99 SER.#'d SETS
1 Steve McNair 6.00 15.00
2 Steve Young 8.00 20.00
3 Walter Payton 15.00 40.00

2011 Timeless Treasures Rookie Recruits Materials

STATED PRINT RUN 250 SER.#'d SETS
*PRIME/25: .8X TO 2X BASIC INSERTS
1 Andy Dalton 3.00 8.00
2 A.J. Green 4.00 10.00
3 Cam Newton 8.00 20.00
4 Taiwan Jones 1.50 4.00
5 DeMarco Murray 3.00 8.00
6 Torrey Smith 1.50 4.00
7 Shane Vereen 2.00 5.00
8 Stevan Ridley 1.50 4.00
9 Ryan Mallett 1.50 4.00
10 Austin Pettis 1.50 4.00
11 Mikel Leshoure 1.50 4.00
12 Titus Young 1.50 4.00
13 Christian Ponder 1.50 4.00
14 Kyle Rudolph 1.50 4.00
15 Jordan Todman 1.50 4.00
16 Vincent Brown 1.50 4.00
17 Von Miller 2.50 6.00
18 Jonathan Baldwin 1.50 4.00
19 Jake Locker 1.50 4.00
20 Jamie Harper 1.50 4.00
21 Mark Ingram 2.50 6.00
22 Leonard Hankerson 1.50 4.00
23 Jerrel Jernigan 1.50 4.00
24 Delone Carter 1.50 4.00
25 Blaine Gabbert 1.50 4.00
26 Julio Jones 5.00 12.00
27 Marcell Dareus 1.50 4.00
28 Ryan Williams 1.50 4.00
29 Clyde Gates 1.50 4.00
30 Daniel Thomas 1.50 4.00
31 Greg Little 2.00 5.00
32 Colin Kaepernick 2.50 6.00
33 Kendall Hunter 1.50 4.00
34 Alex Green 1.50 4.00
35 Randall Cobb 2.50 6.00
36 Bilal Powell 2.00 5.00

2011 Timeless Treasures Rookie Recruits Materials Autographs

STATED PRINT RUN 30-100
*PRIME/25: .6X TO 1.5X BASIC AU/100
1 Andy Dalton/100 10.00 25.00
2 A.J. Green/100 20.00 50.00
3 Cam Newton/30 75.00 150.00
4 Taiwan Jones/50
5 DeMarco Murray/100 10.00 25.00
6 Torrey Smith/100 5.00 12.00
7 Shane Vereen/100 6.00 15.00
8 Stevan Ridley/50 15.00 40.00
9 Ryan Mallett/100 5.00 12.00
10 Austin Pettis/100 5.00 12.00
11 Mikel Leshoure/100 5.00 12.00
12 Titus Young/100 5.00 12.00
13 Christian Ponder/100 5.00 12.00
14 Kyle Rudolph/100 5.00 12.00
15 Jordan Todman/100 5.00 12.00
16 Vincent Brown/100 5.00 12.00
17 Von Miller/100 12.00 30.00
18 Jonathan Baldwin/100 5.00 12.00
19 Jake Locker/100 5.00 12.00
20 Jamie Harper/100 5.00 12.00
21 Mark Ingram/100 8.00 20.00
22 Leonard Hankerson/100 5.00 12.00
23 Jerrel Jernigan/100 5.00 12.00
24 Delone Carter/100 5.00 12.00
25 Blaine Gabbert/100 5.00 12.00
26 Julio Jones/100 30.00 60.00
27 Marcell Dareus/100 5.00 12.00
28 Ryan Williams/100 5.00 12.00
29 Clyde Gates/100 5.00 12.00
30 Daniel Thomas/100 5.00 12.00
31 Greg Little/100 6.00 15.00
32 Colin Kaepernick/100 8.00 20.00
33 Kendall Hunter/50 5.00 12.00
34 Alex Green/50
35 Randall Cobb/100 8.00 20.00
36 Bilal Powell/100 6.00 15.00

2011 Timeless Treasures Rookie Year Materials

STATED PRINT RUN 10-99
1 Troy Aikman/99 10.00 25.00
2 Don Meredith/99 10.00 25.00
3 Doak Walker/99 15.00 40.00
5 Darren McFadden/99 3.00 8.00
8 C.J. Spiller/99 3.00 8.00
10 Sam Bradford/99 3.00 8.00
11 Ryan Mathews/99 4.00 10.00
12 Tim Tebow/99 5.00 12.00

2011 Timeless Treasures Rookie Year Materials Prime

*PRIME/25: .8X TO 2X BASIC JSY/99
PRIME STATED PRINT RUN 25
6 Darren Sproles 8.00 20.00
7 Curtis Martin 12.00 30.00
9 Calvin Johnson 10.00 25.00

2011 Timeless Treasures Significant Signatures

STATED PRINT RUN 31-100
1 Bo Jackson/35 40.00 80.00
2 Boyd Dowler/100 12.00 30.00
3 Charlie Joiner/35 10.00 25.00
4 Dan Fouts/35 12.00 30.00
5 Dave Casper/35 12.00 30.00
6 Deacon Jones/38 15.00 40.00
7 Doug Williams/37 15.00 40.00
8 Gale Sayers/37 15.00 40.00
9 Jack Youngblood/33 12.00 30.00
10 Jim Otto/37 12.00 30.00
11 Joe Greene/38 15.00 40.00
12 Ken Stabler/37 25.00 50.00
13 Len Dawson/37 15.00 40.00
14 Leroy Kelly/35 12.00 30.00
15 Marshall Faulk/35 25.00 50.00
16 Paul Hornung/31 15.00 40.00
17 Ronnie Lott/37 25.00 50.00
18 Steve Young/35 25.00 50.00
19 Warren Moon/37 15.00 40.00
20 Y.A. Tittle/37 15.00 40.00

2011 Timeless Treasures Statistical Champions Materials

STATED PRINT RUN 45-100
1 Walter Payton/100 12.00 30.00
2 Dan Fouts/100 5.00 12.00
3 John Riggins/100 6.00 15.00
4 Jerry Rice/100 10.00 25.00
5 Steve Young/100 8.00 20.00
7 Brett Favre/100 10.00 25.00
8 Peyton Manning/100 10.00 25.00
9 Marshall Faulk/100 5.00 12.00
11 Priest Holmes/100 4.00 10.00
13 Curtis Martin/45 6.00 15.00
14 Michael Vick/100 4.00 10.00
15 Tony Gonzalez/100 4.00 10.00
16 Drew Brees/100 5.00 12.00
17 Peyton Manning/100 10.00 25.00
19 Adrian Peterson/100 5.00 12.00
20 Vernon Davis/100 3.00 8.00
21 Philip Rivers/100 5.00 12.00
22 Roddy White/100 5.00 12.00
23 Dwayne Bowe/100 4.00 10.00
24 Brandon Lloyd/100 3.00 8.00
25 Arian Foster/100 3.00 8.00

2011 Timeless Treasures Statistical Champions Materials Prime

*PRIME/25: 1X TO 2.5X BASIC JSY/100
*PRIME/25: .8X TO 2X BASIC JSY/45
PRIME PRINT RUN 25 SER.#'d SETS
6 Terrell Davis 12.00 30.00
10 Ricky Williams 12.00 30.00
18 Terrell Owens 10.00 25.00

2011 Timeless Treasures Statistical Champions Materials Autographs

STATED PRINT RUN 10-15
2 Dan Fouts/15 30.00 60.00
3 John Riggins/15
4 Jerry Rice/15
5 Steve Young/15
7 Brett Favre/15 100.00 200.00
8 Peyton Manning/15
9 Marshall Faulk/15 25.00 50.00
11 Priest Holmes/15 10.00 25.00
13 Curtis Martin/15 40.00 80.00
14 Michael Vick/15 50.00 100.00
16 Drew Brees/15 60.00 120.00
17 Peyton Manning/15 60.00 120.00
19 Adrian Peterson/15 60.00 120.00
20 Vernon Davis/15
22 Roddy White/15 10.00 25.00
23 Dwayne Bowe/15
24 Brandon Lloyd/15 10.00 25.00
25 Arian Foster/15 40.00 80.00

2009 Time Warner Cable Posluszny

NNO Paul Posluszny 2.00 5.00

2005 Tinactin All-Madden Team 20th Anniversary

This set was distributed by Tinactin and features members of the 20th Anniversary of the All-Madden Team. The fronts feature the Tinactin logo and the backs were printed in black and white.

COMPLETE SET (3) 4.00 10.00
1 Troy Aikman 2.00 5.00
2 Marcus Allen 1.25 3.00
3 Jackie Slater 1.00 2.50

2001 Titanium

This 216 card set was issued in five card packs with a SRP of $19.99 per pack and were issued six packs to a box. Each pack contained one double sided jersey card. Cards numbered 145-216 feature rookies and were inserted at a stated rate of one in 31 and were also serial numbered to 75.

COMP.SET w/o SP's (144) 40.00 80.00
ROOKIE/75 ODDS 1:31 HOBBY
1 David Boston .30 .75
2 Thomas Jones .30 .75
3 Rob Moore .30 .75
4 Michael Pittman .40 1.00
5 Jake Plummer .30 .75
6 Jamal Anderson .40 1.00
7 Chris Chandler .40 1.00
8 Shawn Jefferson .30 .75
9 Terance Mathis .30 .75
10 Terry Allen .40 1.00
11 Jason Brookins UER RC .50 1.25
12 Elvis Grbac .40 1.00
13 Qadry Ismail .30 .75
14 Jamal Lewis .50 1.25
15 Ray Lewis .50 1.25
16 Shannon Sharpe .40 1.00
17 Shawn Bryson .30 .75
18 Rob Johnson .40 1.00
19 Sammy Morris .30 .75
20 Eric Moulds .30 .75
21 Peerless Price .30 .75
22 Tim Biakabutuka .30 .75
23 Patrick Jeffers .30 .75
24 Muhsin Muhammad .30 .75
25 James Allen .30 .75
26 Shane Matthews .30 .75
27 Marcus Robinson .40 1.00
28 Brian Urlacher .60 1.50
29 Corey Dillon .30 .75
30 Jon Kitna .30 .75
31 Akili Smith .30 .75
32 Peter Warrick .30 .75
33 Tim Couch .30 .75
34 Kevin Johnson .30 .75
35 Dennis Northcutt .30 .75
36 Joey Galloway .40 1.00
37 Rocket Ismail .40 1.00
38 Emmitt Smith .75 2.00
39 Mike Anderson .30 .75
40 Terrell Davis .40 1.00
41 Brian Griese .30 .75
42 Ed McCaffrey .40 1.00
43 Rod Smith .40 1.00
44 Charlie Batch .30 .75
45 Germane Crowell .30 .75
46 Herman Moore .30 .75
47 Johnnie Morton .40 1.00
48 James Stewart .30 .75
49 Brett Favre 1.00 2.50
50 Antonio Freeman .50 1.25
51 Ahman Green .40 1.00
52 Bill Schroeder .40 1.00
53 Marvin Harrison .40 1.00
54 Edgerrin James .40 1.00
55 Peyton Manning 1.25 3.00
56 Jerome Pathon .30 .75
57 Terrence Wilkins .30 .75
58 Mark Brunell .40 1.00
59 Keenan McCardell .40 1.00
60 Jimmy Smith .40 1.00
61 Fred Taylor .30 .75
62 Derrick Alexander .30 .75
63 Tony Gonzalez .40 1.00
64 Trent Green .30 .75
65 Priest Holmes .30 .75
66 Jay Fiedler .40 1.00
67 Oronde Gadsden .30 .75
68 James McKnight .30 .75
69 Lamar Smith .40 1.00
70 Zach Thomas .40 1.00
71 Cris Carter .50 1.25
72 Daunte Culpepper .40 1.00
73 Randy Moss .40 1.00
74 Drew Bledsoe .40 1.00
75 Troy Brown .30 .75
76 Charles Johnson .30 .75
77 J.R. Redmond .30 .75
78 Antowain Smith .40 1.00
79 Jeff Blake .40 1.00
80 Aaron Brooks .30 .75
81 Albert Connell .30 .75
82 Joe Horn .30 .75
83 Ricky Williams .40 1.00
84 Tiki Barber .40 1.00
85 Kerry Collins .30 .75
86 Ron Dayne .40 1.00
87 Ike Hilliard .30 .75
88 Amani Toomer .30 .75
89 Richie Anderson .30 .75
90 Wayne Chrebet .30 .75
91 Laveranues Coles .40 1.00
92 Curtis Martin .40 1.00
93 Chad Pennington UER .30 .75
94 Vinny Testaverde .30 .75
95 Tim Brown .50 1.25
96 Rich Gannon .40 1.00
97 Charlie Garner .40 1.00
98 Jerry Rice 1.00 2.50
99 Tyrone Wheatley .40 1.00
100 Charles Woodson .40 1.00
101 Donovan McNabb .40 1.00
102 Todd Pinkston .30 .75
103 Duce Staley .30 .75
104 James Thrash .40 1.00
105 Jerome Bettis .50 1.25
106 Plaxico Burress .30 .75
107 Tommy Maddox .30 .75
108 Bobby Shaw .30 .75
109 Kordell Stewart .30 .75
110 Hines Ward .40 1.00
111 Isaac Bruce .50 1.25
112 Marshall Faulk .40 1.00
113 Az-Zahir Hakim .30 .75
114 Torry Holt .40 1.00
115 Kurt Warner .75 2.00
116 Curtis Conway .40 1.00
117 Tim Dwight .40 1.00
118 Doug Flutie .40 1.00
119 Jeff Graham .30 .75
120 Jeff Garcia .30 .75
121 Garrison Hearst .40 1.00
122 Terrell Owens .40 1.00
123 J.J. Stokes .30 .75
124 Tai Streets .30 .75
125 Shaun Alexander .30 .75
126 Matt Hasselbeck .30 .75
127 Darrell Jackson .40 1.00
128 Ricky Watters .40 1.00
129 Mike Alstott .30 .75
130 Warrick Dunn .30 .75
131 Jacquez Green .30 .75
132 Brad Johnson .40 1.00
133 Keyshawn Johnson .40 1.00
134 Warren Sapp .40 1.00
135 Kevin Dyson .30 .75
136 Eddie George .50 1.25
137 Mike Green .30 .75
138 Jevon Kearse .30 .75
139 Derrick Mason .30 .75
140 Steve McNair .40 1.00
141 Champ Bailey .40 1.00
142 Tony Banks .30 .75
143 Stephen Davis .30 .75
144 Michael Westbrook .30 .75
145 Bill Gramatica JSY RC 5.00 12.00
146 Arnold Jackson JSY RC 5.00 12.00
147 Bobby Newcombe JSY RC 6.00 15.00
148 Marcel Shipp JSY RC 8.00 20.00
149 Quentin McCord JSY RC 6.00 15.00
150 Michael Vick JSY RC 12.00 30.00
151 Chris Barnes JSY RC 5.00 12.00
152 Todd Heap JSY RC 6.00 15.00
153 Reggie Germany JSY RC 5.00 12.00
154 Travis Henry JSY RC 6.00 15.00
155 Chris Taylor JSY RC 5.00 12.00
156 Dee Brown JSY RC 5.00 12.00
157 Dan Morgan JSY RC 6.00 15.00
158 Steve Smith JSY RC 15.00 40.00
159 Chris Weinke JSY RC 6.00 15.00
160 David Terrell JSY RC 6.00 15.00
161 Anthony Thomas JSY RC 8.00 20.00
162 Houshmandzadeh JSY RC 6.00 15.00
163 Chad Johnson JSY RC 8.00 20.00
164 Rudi Johnson JSY RC 8.00 20.00
165 James Jackson JSY RC 5.00 12.00
166 Andre King JSY RC 5.00 12.00
167 Quincy Morgan JSY RC 6.00 15.00
168 Quincy Carter JSY RC 6.00 15.00
169 Ken-Yon Rambo JSY RC 5.00 12.00
170 Kevin Kasper JSY RC 5.00 12.00
171 Scotty Anderson JSY RC 5.00 12.00
172 Mike McMahon JSY RC 6.00 15.00
173 Robert Ferguson JSY RC 8.00 20.00
174 David Martin JSY RC 5.00 12.00
175 Reggie Wayne JSY RC 10.00 25.00
176 Richmond Flowers JSY RC 5.00 12.00
177 Derrick Blaylock JSY RC 6.00 15.00
178 Snoop Minnis JSY RC 5.00 12.00
179 Chris Chambers JSY RC 5.00 12.00
180 Josh Heupel JSY RC 8.00 20.00
181 Travis Minor JSY RC 6.00 15.00
182 Michael Bennett JSY RC 6.00 15.00
183 Cedric James JSY RC 5.00 12.00
184 Deuce McAllister JSY RC 8.00 20.00
185 Onome Ojo JSY RC 5.00 12.00
186 Jonathan Carter JSY RC 5.00 12.00
187 Jesse Palmer JSY RC 6.00 15.00
188 LaMont Jordan JSY RC 8.00 20.00
189 Derek Combs JSY RC 5.00 12.00
190 Marques Tuiasosopo JSY RC 6.00 15.00
191 Correll Buckhalter JSY RC 6.00 15.00
192 Freddie Mitchell JSY RC 5.00 12.00
193 Adam Archuleta JSY RC 6.00 15.00
194 Francis St.Paul JSY RC 5.00 12.00
195 Drew Brees JSY RC 40.00 80.00
196 LaDain Tomlinson JSY RC 40.00 80.00
197 Kevan Barlow JSY RC 6.00 15.00
199 Cedrick Wilson JSY RC 6.00 15.00
200 Alex Bannister JSY RC 5.00 12.00
201 Koren Robinson JSY RC 6.00 15.00
202 Milton Wynn JSY RC 5.00 12.00
203 Dan Alexander JSY RC 6.00 15.00
204 Eddie Berlin JSY RC 5.00 12.00
205 Justin McCareins JSY RC 6.00 15.00
206 Rod Gardner JSY RC 6.00 15.00
207 Damerien McCants JSY RC 6.00 15.00
208 Sage Rosenfels JSY RC 6.00 15.00
209 Nick Goings JSY RC 8.00 20.00
210 Josh Booty JSY RC 6.00 15.00
211 Benjamin Gay JSY RC 6.00 15.00
212 Gerard Warren JSY RC 6.00 15.00
213 Jamal Reynolds JSY RC 5.00 12.00
214 Will Allen JSY RC 8.00 20.00
215 Santana Moss JSY RC 8.00 20.00
216 Andre Carter JSY RC 6.00 15.00

2001 Titanium Premiere Date

*VETERANS: 4X TO 10X BASIC CARDS
PREMIERE DATE/99 ODDS 1:7 HOBBY
STATED PRINT RUN 99 SER.#'d SETS

2001 Titanium Red

*VETERANS: 5X TO 12X BASIC CARDS
RED/58 ODDS 1:13 HOBBY
STATED PRINT RUN 58 SER.#'d SETS

2001 Titanium Retail

*RETAIL VETS 1-144: .25X TO .6X HOBBY
COMMON ROOKIE (145-216) .75 2.00
ROOKIE SEMISTARS 1.00 2.50
ROOKIE UNL.STARS 1.25 3.00
ROOKIE STATED ODDS 2:25
150 Michael Vick RC 2.00 5.00
158 Steve Smith RC 2.50 6.00
162 T.J. Houshmandzadeh RC 1.00 2.50
163 Chad Johnson RC 1.25 3.00
175 Reggie Wayne RC 1.50 4.00
179 Chris Chambers RC .75 2.00
184 Deuce McAllister RC 1.25 3.00
195 Drew Brees RC 5.00 12.00
196 LaDainian Tomlinson RC 4.00 10.00
215 Santana Moss RC 1.25 3.00

2001 Titanium Double Sided Jerseys

Issued one per pack, these 120-cards feature two swatches from players game-worn uniforms.

STATED ODDS ONE PER PACK
1 B.Newcombe/A.Jackson 3.00 8.00
2 M.Shipp/B.Gramatica 4.00 10.00
3 L.Jordan/R.Gardner 4.00 10.00
5 M.Vick/Q.Carter 6.00 15.00
7 R.Germany/T.Henry 3.00 8.00
8 D.Brown/S.Smith 8.00 20.00
10 D.Morgan/A.Archuleta 3.00 8.00
11 D.Terrell/A.Thomas 4.00 10.00
13 R.Johnson/J.Jackson 4.00 10.00
14 A.King/Q.Morgan 3.00 8.00
15 K.Kasper/R.Flowers 2.50 6.00
16 S.Anderson/M.McMahon 3.00 8.00
17 R.Ferguson/D.Martin 4.00 10.00

18 R.Wayne/F.Mitchell 5.00 12.00
19 D.Blaylock/S.Minnis 3.00 8.00
20 C.Chambers/T.Minor 3.00 8.00
21 M.Bennett/C.James 3.00 8.00
22 D.McAllister/O.Ojo 4.00 10.00
23 J.Carter/J.Palmer 3.00 8.00
24 D.Combs/K.Rambo 2.50 6.00
25 M.Tuiasosopo/S.Rosenfels 3.00 8.00
26 C.Buckhalter/D.Alexander 3.00 8.00
27 C.Taylor/D.McCants 3.00 8.00
28 F.St. Paul/M.Wynn 2.50 6.00
29 D.Brees/L.Tomlinson 15.00 40.00
30 K.Barlow/C.Wilson 3.00 8.00
31 A.Bannister/K.Robinson 3.00 8.00
32 E.Berlin/J.McCareins 3.00 8.00
33 N.Brown/C.Lewis 2.50 6.00
34 T.Hardy/D.Sloan 2.50 6.00
35 T.Mitchell/D.McKinley 2.50 6.00
36 B.Gilmore/Jer.Lewis 2.50 6.00
37 D.Boston/J.Smith 3.00 8.00
38 M.Jenkins/R.Soward 2.50 6.00
39 T.Jones/F.Taylor 2.50 6.00
40 F.Sanders/T.Owens 3.00 8.00
41 C.Gedney/F.Wycheck 2.50 6.00
42 C.Griesen/N.O'Donnell 3.00 8.00
43 J.German/S.Jefferson 2.50 6.00
44 R.Kelly/M.Smith 2.50 6.00
45 T.Martin/D.Alexander 3.00 8.00
46 J Anderson/C.Martin 3.00 8.00
47 Jam.Lewis/M.Anderson 4.00 10.00
48 S.Sharpe/T.Gonzalez 3.00 8.00
49 R.Lewis/B.Cox 4.00 10.00
50 E.Grbac/K.Collins 3.00 8.00
51 O.Ayanbadejo/C.Fuamatu 2.50 6.00
52 Ant.Smith/Sam.Morris 3.00 8.00
53 T.Thomas/J.Johnson 3.00 8.00
54 D.Hayes/C.Hetherington 2.50 6.00
55 I.Byrd/R.White 4.00 10.00
56 B.Hoover/S.Beuerlein 3.00 8.00
57 T.Biakabutuka/W.Floyd 2.50 6.00
58 S.Matthews/J.Miller 3.00 8.00
59 M.Robinson/J.Morton 3.00 8.00
60 D.White/Syl.Morris 3.00 8.00
61 B.Urlacher/Z.Thomas 12.00 30.00
62 C.Groce/N.Williams 2.50 6.00
63 C.Dillon/P.Warrick 2.50 6.00
64 D.Griffin/T.Mack 2.50 6.00
65 D.Farmer/C.Yeast 2.50 6.00
66 M.Battaglia/T.Spikes 2.50 6.00
67 D.Scott/B.Schroeder 3.00 8.00
68 K.Thompson/J.White 2.50 6.00
69 T.Couch/J.Plummer 2.50 6.00
70 K.Johnson/A.Freeman 4.00 10.00
71 D.Northcutt/K.McCardell 3.00 8.00
72 A.Shea/M.Edwards 2.50 6.00
73 R.Ismail/J.Tucker 3.00 8.00
74 T.Hambrick/D.Woodson 3.00 8.00
75 J.Garcia/W.Moon 4.00 10.00
76 W.McGarity/J.McKnight 2.50 6.00
77 E.Smith/E.George 6.00 15.00
78 D.Carswell/B.Chamberlain 2.50 6.00
79 T.Davis/B.Griese 3.00 8.00
81 E.McCaffrey/T.Holt 3.00 8.00
82 G.Crowell/H.Moore 2.50 6.00
83 L.Foster/A.Rossum 2.50 6.00
84 J.Stewart/Rob.Smith 2.50 6.00
85 C.Batch/S.McNair 3.00 8.00
86 H.Goodman/D.Parker 2.50 6.00
87 D.Levens/L.Smith 3.00 8.00
88 B.Favre/K.Warner 8.00 20.00
89 E.Green/J.Pathon 2.50 6.00
90 E.James/P.Manning 10.00 25.00
91 M.Harrison/A.Toomer 3.00 8.00
92 A.Johnson/S.Mack 2.50 6.00
93 M.Brunell/C.Chandler 3.00 8.00
94 S.Dawkins/D.Mayes 2.50 6.00
95 P.Holmes/C.Garner 3.00 8.00
96 K.Anders/M.Alstott 2.50 6.00
97 L.Shepherd/B.Emanuel 2.50 6.00
98 O.McDuffie/J.Stokes 2.50 6.00
99 C.Walsh/T.Walters 2.50 6.00
100 D.Culpepper/R.Moss 3.00 8.00
101 C.Carter/W.Chrebet 4.00 10.00
102 Char.Johnson/T.Small 2.50 6.00
103 D.Bledsoe/R.Gannon 3.00 8.00
104 D.Huard/B.Huard 3.00 8.00
105 J.Blake/C.Morton 3.00 8.00
106 W.Jackson/K.Dyson 2.50 6.00
107 R.Dayne/T.Barber 3.00 8.00
108 J.Sehorn/C.Woodson 4.00 10.00
109 R.Dixon/A.Hakim 2.50 6.00
110 C.Pennington/V.Testaverde 2.50 6.00
111 T.Brown/J.Rice 8.00 20.00
112 A.Rison/T.Streets 3.00 8.00
113 T.Wheatley/S.Alexander 3.00 8.00
114 D.McNabb/D.Staley 3.00 8.00
115 J.Bettis/K.Stewart 4.00 10.00
116 O.Pace/J.Watson 2.50 6.00
117 C.Conway/D.Flutie 3.00 8.00
118 F.Beasley/P.Smith 2.50 6.00
119 C.Fauria/I.Mili 2.50 6.00
120 D.Jackson/R.Watters 3.00 8.00
121 T.Dilfer/T.Banks 2.50 6.00
122 Rab.Abdullah/A.Stecker 2.50 6.00
123 D.Moore/E.Kinney 2.50 6.00
124 Y.Thigpen/R.Thomas 2.50 6.00
125 D.Sanders/C.Bailey 3.00 8.00

2001 Titanium Double Sided Jerseys Patches

Randomly inserted in packs, these 114 cards feature two swatches of game-worn uniform patches on the card.

COMMON CARD 6.00 15.00
SEMISTARS 8.00 20.00
UNLISTED STARS 10.00 25.00

2001 Titanium Monday Knights

Inserted at stated odds of one in 25, these 25 cards honor some of the leading offensive threats in football.

COMPLETE SET (25) 15.00 40.00
STATED ODDS 1:7
1 Emmitt Smith 1.25 3.00
2 Mike Anderson .50 1.25
3 Terrell Davis .60 1.50
4 Brian Griese .50 1.25
5 Rod Smith .60 1.50
6 Brett Favre 1.50 4.00
7 Antonio Freeman .75 2.00
8 Ahman Green .60 1.50
9 Edgerrin James .60 1.50
10 Peyton Manning 2.00 5.00
11 Mark Brunell .60 1.50
12 Jimmy Smith .60 1.50
13 Fred Taylor .50 1.25
14 Cris Carter .75 2.00
15 Daunte Culpepper .60 1.50
16 Randy Moss .60 1.50
17 Rich Gannon .60 1.50
18 Jerry Rice 1.50 4.00
19 Donovan McNabb .60 1.50
20 Duce Staley .60 1.50
21 Isaac Bruce .75 2.00
22 Marshall Faulk .60 1.50
23 Kurt Warner 1.25 3.00
24 Eddie George .75 2.00
25 Steve McNair .60 1.50

2001 Titanium Players Fantasy

Issued at stated odds of one in 7, these 25 cards feature rookies who were slated to play at key offensive positions during 2001. Each card was printed with gold foil highlights on the cardfronts. A silver foil version of each card was produced later and distributed to attendees of the 2002 Hawaii Trade Conference in Honolulu.

COMPLETE SET (25) 25.00 60.00
STATED ODDS 1:7
*SILVER/2000: .2X TO .5X GOLD
SILVER PRINT RUIN 2000 SER.#'d SETS
1 Michael Vick 1.50 4.00
2 Travis Henry .75 2.00
3 Chris Weinke .75 2.00
4 David Terrell .75 2.00
5 Anthony Thomas 1.00 2.50
6 Chad Johnson 1.00 2.50
7 James Jackson .60 1.50
8 Quincy Morgan .75 2.00
9 Quincy Carter .75 2.00
10 Kevin Kasper .60 1.50
11 Reggie Wayne 1.25 3.00
12 Snoop Minnis .60 1.50
13 Chris Chambers .60 1.50
14 Travis Minor .75 2.00
15 Michael Bennett .75 2.00
16 Deuce McAllister 1.00 2.50
17 Santana Moss 1.00 2.50
18 Marques Tuiasosopo .75 2.00
19 Correll Buckhalter .60 1.50
20 Freddie Mitchell .60 1.50
21 Drew Brees 4.00 10.00
22 LaDainian Tomlinson 3.00 8.00
23 Kevan Barlow .75 2.00
24 Koren Robinson .75 2.00
25 Rod Gardner .75 2.00

2001 Titanium Team

Inserted at stated odds of one in 25, these 25 cards feature players a team would want to build their franchise around.

COMPLETE SET (25) 60.00 120.00
STATED ODDS 1:25
1 Corey Dillon 1.00 2.50
2 Peter Warrick 1.00 2.50
3 Tim Couch 1.00 2.50
4 Emmitt Smith 2.50 6.00
5 Mike Anderson 1.00 2.50
6 Olandis Gary 1.00 2.50
7 Brian Griese 1.00 2.50
8 Brett Favre 3.00 8.00
9 Edgerrin James 1.25 3.00
10 Peyton Manning 4.00 10.00
11 Mark Brunell 1.25 3.00
12 Fred Taylor 1.00 2.50
13 Daunte Culpepper 1.25 3.00
14 Randy Moss 1.25 3.00
15 Drew Bledsoe 1.25 3.00
16 Aaron Brooks 1.00 2.50
17 Ricky Williams 1.25 3.00
18 Ron Dayne 1.25 3.00
19 Jerry Rice 3.00 8.00
20 Donovan McNabb 1.25 3.00
21 Marshall Faulk 1.25 3.00
22 Kurt Warner 2.50 6.00
23 Jeff Garcia 1.00 2.50
24 Eddie George 1.50 4.00
25 Steve McNair 1.25 3.00

2002 Titanium

Released in January, 2003, this set features 100 veterans and 75 rookies. The first 100-veteran player cards were printed with gold foil highlights. Each serial numbered rookie card includes two players; the rookie and a veteran player. Those cards also feature a jersey swatch of the veteran player and were inserted one per pack. Boxes contained 6 packs of 10 cards and cases contained 20 boxes.

COMP.SET w/o SP's (100) 30.00 60.00
1 David Boston .25 .60
2 Thomas Jones .25 .60
3 Jake Plummer .25 .60
4 Warrick Dunn .25 .60
5 Shawn Jefferson .25 .60
6 Michael Vick .30 .75
7 Jamal Lewis .30 .75
8 Chris Redman .25 .60
9 Travis Taylor .25 .60
10 Drew Bledsoe .30 .75
11 Travis Henry .25 .60
12 Eric Moulds .25 .60
13 Peerless Price .25 .60
14 Muhsin Muhammad .25 .60
15 Rodney Peete .30 .75
16 Lamar Smith .25 .60
17 Chris Weinke .25 .60
18 Marty Booker .25 .60
19 Jim Miller .25 .60
20 Anthony Thomas .30 .75
21 Corey Dillon .25 .60
22 Gus Frerotte .25 .60
23 Peter Warrick .25 .60
24 Tim Couch .25 .60
25 Kevin Johnson .25 .60
26 Jamel White .25 .60
27 Quincy Carter .25 .60
28 Joey Galloway .30 .75
29 Emmitt Smith .60 1.50
30 Olandis Gary .30 .75
31 Brian Griese .25 .60
32 Ed McCaffrey .30 .75
33 Rod Smith .30 .75
34 Mike McMahon .25 .60
35 Bill Schroeder .25 .60
36 James Stewart .25 .60
37 Brett Favre .75 2.00
38 Terry Glenn .30 .75
39 Ahman Green .30 .75
40 James Allen .25 .60
41 Corey Bradford .25 .60
42 Jermaine Lewis .25 .60
43 Marvin Harrison .30 .75
44 Edgerrin James .30 .75
45 Peyton Manning 1.00 2.50
46 Mark Brunell .30 .75
47 Jimmy Smith .30 .75
48 Fred Taylor .25 .60
49 Tony Gonzalez .30 .75
50 Trent Green .25 .60
51 Priest Holmes .25 .60
52 Chris Chambers .25 .60
53 Jay Fiedler .30 .75
54 Ricky Williams .30 .75
55 Michael Bennett .25 .60
56 Daunte Culpepper .30 .75
57 Randy Moss .30 .75
58 Tom Brady 2.00 5.00
59 Troy Brown .25 .60
60 Antowain Smith .30 .75
61 Aaron Brooks .25 .60
62 Joe Horn .25 .60
63 Deuce McAllister .30 .75
64 Tiki Barber .30 .75
65 Kerry Collins .25 .60
66 Amani Toomer .25 .60
67 Laveranues Coles .30 .75
68 Curtis Martin .30 .75
69 Vinny Testaverde .25 .60
70 Tim Brown .40 1.00
71 Rich Gannon .30 .75
72 Jerry Rice .75 2.00
73 Donovan McNabb .30 .75
74 Duce Staley .25 .60
75 James Thrash .30 .75
76 Jerome Bettis .40 1.00
77 Kordell Stewart .25 .60
78 Hines Ward .30 .75
79 Isaac Bruce .40 1.00
80 Marshall Faulk .30 .75
81 Torry Holt .30 .75
82 Kurt Warner .30 .75
83 Drew Brees .75 2.00
84 LaDainian Tomlinson .40 1.00
85 Jeff Garcia .25 .60
86 Garrison Hearst .25 .60
87 Terrell Owens .30 .75
88 Shaun Alexander .25 .60
89 Trent Dilfer .25 .60
90 Koren Robinson .25 .60
91 Brad Johnson .30 .75
92 Keyshawn Johnson .30 .75
93 Keenan McCardell .30 .75
94 Eddie George .30 .75
95 Derrick Mason .25 .60
96 Steve McNair .30 .75
97 Stephen Davis .25 .60
98 Rod Gardner .25 .60
99 Shane Matthews .25 .60
100 Derrius Thompson .25 .60
101 F.Jones/J.McAddley/1000 RC 2.50 6.00
102 Plummer/J.McCown/250 RC 4.00 10.00
103 VandenB/W.Bryant/1100 RC 4.00 10.00
104 T.Jones/C.Taylor/1100 RC 5.00 12.00
105 Gilmore/T.Carter/1100 RC 2.50 6.00
106 Vick/K.Kittner/300 RC 6.00 15.00
107 Stokley/R.Johnson/150 RC 4.00 10.00
108 Redma/J.Hunter/100 RC 2.50 6.00
109 Price/J.Reed/250 RC 3.00 8.00
110 Byrd/J.Peppers/250 RC 4.00 10.00
111 D.White/J.Elliott/250 RC 2.50 6.00
112 Abdullah/Peterson/1000 RC 2.50 6.00
113 Urlacher/N.Harris/500 RC 5.00 12.00
114 Westb/Thompson/1100 RC 3.00 8.00
115 Dillon/T.J.Duckett/750 RC 4.00 10.00
116 Spikes/Ry.Williams/500 RC 4.00 10.00
117 A.Smith/C.Nall/1000 RC 3.00 8.00
118 Couch/A.Davis/250 RC 4.00 10.00
119 J.White/T.Redmon/500 RC 2.50 6.00
120 Q.Carter/Hutchinson/100 RC 4.00 10.00
121 Hambrick/A.Bryant/250 RC 4.00 10.00
122 E.Smith/W.Green/500 RC 8.00 20.00
123 Glover/Henderson/1100 RC 4.00 10.00
124 O'Neal/M.Rumph/300 RC 2.50 6.00
125 Foster/Drummond/1100 RC 2.50 6.00
126 A.Green/N.Davenport/300 RC 4.00 10.00
127 Driver/J.Walker/150 RC 5.00 12.00
128 Favre/D.Carr/500 RC 10.00 25.00
129 J.Allen/J.Wells/300 RC 2.50 6.00
130 J.Lewis/J.Gaffney/200 RC 2.50 6.00
131 James/Ri.Williams/250 RC 5.00 12.00
132 Manning/D.Freeney/750 RC 8.00 20.00
133 Brunell/D.Garrard/500 RC 5.00 12.00
134 J.Smith/M.Walker/500 RC 2.50 6.00
135 Jackson/Boerigter/1100 RC 3.00 8.00
136 Richardson/O.Easy/300 RC 2.50 6.00
137 D.Clark/McMichael/1000 RC 3.00 8.00
138 Z.Thomas/R.Thomas/250 RC 3.00 8.00
139 C.Walsh/S.Hill/500 RC 3.00 8.00
140 Culpepper/Fasani/1000 RC 4.00 10.00
141 Kleinsasser/Baxter/1100 RC 4.00 10.00
142 R.Moss/Stallworth/500 RC 5.00 12.00
143 Chavos/Buchanon/1100 RC 2.50 6.00
144 Fauria/D.Graham/750 RC 2.50 6.00
145 D.Huard/R.Davey/300 RC 4.00 10.00
146 Hayes/D.Branch/500 RC 4.00 10.00
147 T.Smith/O'Sullivan/300 RC 2.50 6.00
148 J.Carter/D.Jones/300 RC 2.50 6.00
149 Dayne/J.Shockey/300 RC 4.00 10.00
150 Becht/B.Thomas/1100 RC 2.50 6.00
151 C.Martin/D.Hunter/250 RC 4.00 10.00
152 Rice/A.Lelie/750 RC 8.00 20.00
153 Ritchie/E.Stansbury/1100 RC 2.50 6.00
154 C.Martin/F.Milons/1100 RC 2.50 6.00
155 McNabb/Sheppard/1000 RC 5.00 12.00
156 Thrash/Westbrook/1000 RC 5.00 12.00
157 Bettis/V.Haynes/1000 RC 5.00 12.00
158 Stewart/A.Randle El/500 RC 4.00 10.00
159 M.Faulk/L.Gordon/300 RC 4.00 10.00
160 Warner/J.Harrington/500 RC 5.00 12.00
161 Brees/Q.Jammer/500 RC 6.00 15.00
162 McCrary/S.Burford/1100 RC 2.50 6.00
163 S.Alexndr/Caldwell/1000 RC 3.00 8.00
164 Tomlinson/C.Portis/500 RC 6.00 15.00
165 Garcia/B.Doman/200 RC 4.00 10.00
166 P.Smith/L.Mays/250 RC 2.50 6.00
167 Sh.Alexndr/Morris/500 RC 4.00 10.00
168 Pittman/T.Stephens/500 RC 3.00 8.00
169 Dilger/J.Stevens/750 RC 2.50 6.00
170 Kinney/J.Simon/500 RC 2.50 6.00
171 McNair/Haynesworth/500 RC 5.00 12.00
172 George/D.Foster/500 RC 4.00 10.00
173 J.Green/L.Betts/250 RC 6.00 15.00
174 Gardner/C.Russell/200 RC 2.50 6.00
175 S.Matthews/Ramsey/250 RC 3.00 8.00

2002 Titanium Blue

*1-100 VETS: .8X TO 2X BASIC CARDS
COMMON ROOKIE (101-175) .50 1.25
ROOKIE SEMISTARS .60 1.50
ROOKIE UNL.STARS .75 2.00
STATED PRINT RUN 325 SERIAL #'d SETS
104 T.Jones/C.Taylor .75 2.00
110 I.Byrd/J.Peppers 1.25 3.00
113 B.Urlacher/N.Harris .75 2.00
116 T.Spikes/Roy Williams .50 1.25
121 T.Hambrick/A.Bryant .75 2.00
122 E.Smith/W.Green 1.25 3.00
128 B.Favre/D.Carr 1.50 4.00
132 P.Manning/D.Freeney 2.00 5.00
133 M.Brunell/D.Garrard .60 1.50
139 C.Walsh/S.Hill .75 2.00
149 R.Dayne/J.Shockey .75 2.00
152 J.Rice/A.Lelie 1.50 4.00
155 D.McNabb/L.Sheppard .75 2.00
156 J.Thrash/B.Westbrook 1.00 2.50
161 D.Brees/Q.Jammer 1.50 4.00
164 L.Tomlinson/C.Portis .75 2.00

2002 Titanium Blue Jerseys

*BLUE/100-200: .8X TO 2X BASIC CARD
*BLUE/45-85: 1X TO 2.5X BASIC CARD
*BLUE/20: 1.5X TO 4X BASIC CARD
BLUE STATED PRINT RUN 20-200

2002 Titanium Red

*1-100 VETS: .8X TO 2X BASIC CARDS
COMMON ROOKIE (101-175) .50 1.25
ROOKIE SEMISTARS .60 1.50
ROOKIE UNL.STARS .75 2.00
STATED PRINT RUN 275 SER.#'d SETS
104 T.Jones/C.Taylor .75 2.00
110 I.Byrd/J.Peppers 1.25 3.00
113 B.Urlacher/N.Harris .75 2.00
116 T.Spikes/Roy Williams .50 1.25
121 T.Hambrick/A.Bryant .75 2.00
122 E.Smith/W.Green 1.25 3.00
128 B.Favre/D.Carr 1.50 4.00
132 P.Manning/D.Freeney 2.00 5.00
133 M.Brunell/D.Garrard .60 1.50
139 C.Walsh/S.Hill .75 2.00
149 R.Dayne/J.Shockey .75 2.00
152 J.Rice/A.Lelie 1.50 4.00
155 D.McNabb/L.Sheppard .75 2.00
156 J.Thrash/B.Westbrook 1.00 2.50
161 D.Brees/Q.Jammer 1.50 4.00
164 L.Tomlinson/C.Portis .75 2.00

2002 Titanium Retail

*RETAIL SILVER: .4X TO 1X BASE CARDS
COMMON ROOKIE (101-175) .25 .60
ROOKIE SEMISTARS .30 .75
ROOKIE UNL.STARS .40 1.00
RET.ROOKIES DO NOT CONTAIN JSYs
104 T.Jones/C.Taylor RC .40 1.00
110 I.Byrd/J.Peppers RC .60 1.50
113 B.Urlacher/N.Harris RC .40 1.00
116 T.Spikes/Ry.Williams RC .25 .60
121 T.Hambrick/A.Bryant RC .40 1.00
122 E.Smith/W.Green RC .60 1.50
128 B.Favre/D.Carr RC .75 2.00
132 P.Manning/D.Freeney RC 1.00 2.50
133 M.Brunell/D.Garrard RC .30 .75
139 C.Walsh/S.Hill RC .40 1.00
149 R.Dayne/J.Shockey RC .40 1.00
152 J.Rice/A.Lelie RC .75 2.00
155 D.McNabb/L.Sheppard RC .40 1.00
156 J.Thrash/B.Westbrook RC .50 1.25
161 D.Brees/Q.Jammer RC .75 2.00
164 Tomlinson/C.Portis RC .40 1.00

2002 Titanium High Capacity

Inserted at a rate of 1:7, this set highlights some of the NFL's most electrifying players.

COMPLETE SET (10) 12.00 30.00
STATED ODDS 1:7
1 Michael Vick .75 2.00
2 Anthony Thomas .75 2.00
3 Emmitt Smith 1.50 4.00
4 Brett Favre 2.00 5.00
5 Peyton Manning 2.50 6.00
6 Randy Moss .75 2.00
7 Tom Brady 5.00 12.00
8 Jerry Rice 2.00 5.00
9 Marshall Faulk .75 2.00
10 Kurt Warner .75 2.00

2002 Titanium Monday Knights

Inserted at a rate of 1:3, this set highlights 21 players who starred on Monday Night Football.

COMPLETE SET (21) 25.00 60.00
STATED ODDS 1:3
1 Jamal Lewis 1.00 2.50
2 Anthony Thomas 1.00 2.50
3 Brian Griese .75 2.00
4 Ashley Lelie .60 1.50
5 Clinton Portis 1.00 2.50
6 Brett Favre 2.50 6.00
7 Edgerrin James 1.00 2.50
8 Peyton Manning 3.00 8.00
9 Tom Brady 6.00 15.00
10 Curtis Martin 1.00 2.50
11 Jerry Rice 2.50 6.00
12 Donovan McNabb 1.00 2.50
13 Jerome Bettis 1.25 3.00
14 Antwaan Randle El 1.00 2.50
15 Marshall Faulk 1.00 2.50
16 Kurt Warner 1.00 2.50
17 Jeff Garcia .75 2.00
18 Terrell Owens 1.00 2.50
19 Shaun Alexander .60 1.50
20 Eddie George 1.00 2.50
21 Steve McNair 1.00 2.50

2002 Titanium Rookie Team

Inserted at a rate of 1:13, this set is composed of Pacific's pick for an All-Rookie team.

COMPLETE SET (10) 15.00 40.00
STATED ODDS 1:13
1 Josh Reed 1.25 3.00
2 DeShaun Foster 1.50 4.00
3 William Green 1.25 3.00
4 Antonio Bryant 1.50 4.00
5 Ashley Lelie 1.00 2.50
6 Clinton Portis 1.50 4.00
7 Joey Harrington 1.00 2.50
8 David Carr 1.00 2.50
9 Donte Stallworth 1.50 4.00
10 Antwaan Randle El 1.25 3.00

2002 Titanium Shadows

Inserted at a rate of 1:5, this set highlights nine NFL superstars. Each card has a small color action photo, along with a shadow shot in the background.

COMPLETE SET (9) 12.00 30.00
STATED ODDS 1:5
1 Michael Vick .75 2.00
2 Emmitt Smith 1.50 4.00
3 Joey Harrington .60 1.50
4 Brett Favre 2.00 5.00
5 David Carr .60 1.50
6 Randy Moss .75 2.00
7 Tom Brady 5.00 12.00
8 Jerry Rice 2.00 5.00
9 Kurt Warner .75 2.00

2001 Titanium Post Season

This 100 card set was issued in February, 2002. The cards were issued in two card packs which came 10 packs to a box. The card stock is a reproduction of Pacific's Prism Atomic release with Post Season Edition written on the card front.Packs included one jersey card and one base card per pack. Rookies were serial numbered on card back to 750 of each made. A patch variation of the jerseys were also produced with limited quantatites of each player serial numbered on card front.

1 Arnold Jackson RC .75 2.00
2 Marcel Shipp RC 1.25 3.00
3 Alge Crumpler RC 1.25 3.00
4 Quentin McCord RC 1.00 2.50
5 Michael Vick RC 2.00 5.00
6 Kenyon Hambrick RC .75 2.00
7 Todd Heap RC 1.00 2.50
8 Nate Clements RC 1.00 2.50
9 Reggie Germany RC .75 2.00
10 Travis Henry RC 1.00 2.50
11 Jarrod Cooper RC 1.00 2.50
12 Nick Goings RC 1.25 3.00
13 Dan Morgan RC 1.00 2.50
14 Steve Smith RC 2.50 6.00
15 Chris Weinke RC 1.00 2.50
16 David Terrell RC 1.00 2.50
17 Anthony Thomas RC 1.25 3.00
18 T.J. Houshmandzadeh RC 1.00 2.50
19 Chad Johnson RC 1.25 3.00
20 Rudi Johnson RC 1.25 3.00
21 Justin Smith RC 1.50 4.00
22 Josh Booty RC 1.00 2.50
23 Benjamin Gay RC 1.00 2.50
24 Anthony Henry RC 1.25 3.00
25 James Jackson RC .75 2.00
26 Andre King RC .75 2.00
27 Quincy Morgan RC 1.00 2.50
28 Gerrard Warren RC 1.00 2.50
29 Quincy Carter RC 1.00 2.50
30 Tony Dixon RC .75 2.00
31 Ken-Yon Rambo RC .75 2.00
32 Randal Williams RC .75 2.00
33 Kevin Kasper RC .75 2.00
34 Willie Middlebrooks RC 1.00 2.50
35 Scotty Anderson RC .75 2.00
36 Mike McMahon RC 1.00 2.50
37 Shaun Rogers RC 1.25 3.00
38 Stephen Trejo RC .75 2.00
39 Robert Ferguson RC 1.25 3.00
40 Bhawoh Jue RC 1.00 2.50
41 David Martin RC .75 2.00
42 Idrees Bashir RC .75 2.00
43 Dominic Rhodes RC 1.00 2.50
44 Reggie Wayne RC 1.50 4.00
45 Elvis Joseph RC .75 2.00
46 Marcus Stroud RC 1.00 2.50
47 Derrick Blaylock RC 1.00 2.50
48 Snoop Minnis RC .75 2.00
49 Chris Chambers RC .75 2.00
50 Travis Minor RC 1.00 2.50
51 Michael Bennett RC 1.00 2.50
52 Richard Seymour RC 1.25 3.00
53 Deuce McAllister RC 1.25 3.00
54 Onome Ojo RC .75 2.00
55 Will Allen RC 1.25 3.00
56 Jesse Palmer RC 1.00 2.50
57 Will Peterson RC 1.00 2.50
58 Jamie Henderson RC 1.00 2.50
59 LaMont Jordan RC 1.25 3.00
60 Tory Woodbury RC .75 2.00
61 Derrick Gibson RC .75 2.00
62 Marques Tuiasosopo RC 1.00 2.50
63 Correll Buckhalter RC .75 2.00
64 A.J. Feeley RC 1.00 2.50
65 Freddie Mitchell RC .75 2.00
66 Tim Baker RC .75 2.00
67 Kendrell Bell RC 1.25 3.00
68 Casey Hampton RC 1.25 3.00
69 Adam Archuleta RC 1.00 2.50
70 Damione Lewis RC 1.00 2.50
71 Brandon Manumaleuna RC 1.00 2.50
72 Ryan Pickett RC .75 2.00
73 Tommy Polley RC .75 2.00
74 Drew Brees RC 5.00 12.00
75 Robert Carswell RC .75 2.00
76 Tay Cody RC .75 2.00
77 LaDainian Tomlinson RC 4.00 10.00
78 Nate Turner RC .75 2.00
79 Kevan Barlow RC 1.00 2.50
80 Andre Carter RC 1.00 2.50
81 Vinny Sutherland RC .75 2.00
82 Cedrick Wilson RC 1.00 2.50
83 Jamie Winborn RC 1.00 2.50
84 Alex Bannister RC .75 2.00
85 Heath Evans RC 1.00 2.50
86 Ken Lucas RC 1.00 2.50
87 Koren Robinson RC 1.00 2.50
88 Jameel Cook RC 1.00 2.50
89 Dan Alexander RC 1.00 2.50
90 Drew Bennett RC 1.25 3.00
91 Eddie Berlin RC .75 2.00
92 Andre Dyson RC .75 2.00
93 Justin McCareins RC 1.00 2.50
94 Rod Gardner RC 1.00 2.50
95 Damerien McCants RC 1.00 2.50
96 Sage Rosenfels RC 1.00 2.50
97 Justin Skaggs RC .75 2.00
98 Fred Smoot RC 1.00 2.50
99 Stanley Stephens RC .75 2.00
100 Kenny Watson RC 1.25 3.00

2001 Titanium Post Season Jerseys

This 100 card set was issed at a rate of one per pack. Cards feature swatches of game used jerseys cut in a circle cutout on card front. Cards have a grey silhouette in the background with a color action shot on card front.

ONE PER PACK
1 David Boston 2.50 6.00
2 Chris Greisen 2.50 6.00
3 Thomas Jones 2.50 6.00
4 Rob Moore 2.50 6.00
5 Michael Pittman 3.00 8.00
6 Jake Plummer 2.50 6.00
7 Terance Mathis 2.50 6.00
8 Randall Cunningham 3.00 8.00
9 Jamal Lewis 4.00 10.00
10 Moe Williams 2.50 6.00
11 Kwame Cavil 2.50 6.00
12 Reggie Germany 2.50 6.00
13 Travis Henry 3.00 8.00
14 Rob Johnson 3.00 8.00
15 Eric Moulds 2.50 6.00
16 Dee Brown 2.50 6.00
17 Patrick Jeffers 2.50 6.00
18 Dan Morgan 3.00 8.00
19 Steve Smith 5.00 12.00
20 Chris Weinke 3.00 8.00
21 James Allen 2.50 6.00
22 Marlon Barnes 2.50 6.00
23 Macey Brooks 2.50 6.00
24 David Terrell 3.00 8.00
25 Anthony Thomas 4.00 10.00
26 Brian Urlacher 5.00 12.00
27 Corey Dillon 2.50 6.00
28 T.J. Houshmandzadeh 3.00 8.00
29 Chad Johnson 2.50 6.00
30 Curtis Keaton 2.50 6.00
31 Peter Warrick 2.50 6.00
32 Tim Couch 2.50 6.00
33 Rickey Dudley 2.50 6.00
34 Curtis Enis 2.50 6.00
35 James Jackson 2.50 6.00
36 Andre King 2.50 6.00
37 Quincy Morgan 3.00 8.00
38 Quincy Carter 3.00 8.00
39 Emmitt Smith 6.00 15.00
40 Mike Anderson 2.50 6.00
41 Olandis Gary 2.50 6.00
42 Brian Griese 2.50 6.00
43 Eddie Kennison 3.00 8.00
44 Ed McCaffrey 3.00 8.00
45 Brett Favre 8.00 20.00
46 Ahman Green 3.00 8.00
47 Marvin Harrison 3.00 8.00
48 Edgerrin James 3.00 8.00
49 Peyton Manning 10.00 25.00
50 Reggie Wayne 3.00 8.00
51 Mark Brunell 3.00 8.00
52 Fred Taylor 2.50 6.00
53 Trent Green 2.50 6.00
54 Chris Chambers 2.50 6.00
55 Josh Heupel 4.00 10.00
56 Ray Lucas 2.50 6.00
57 Travis Minor 3.00 8.00
58 Dedric Ward 2.50 6.00
59 Michael Bennett 3.00 8.00
60 Cris Carter 4.00 10.00
61 Daunte Culpepper 3.00 8.00
62 Randy Moss 3.00 8.00
63 Travis Prentice 2.50 6.00
64 David Patten 2.50 6.00
65 Deuce McAllister 4.00 10.00
66 Onome Ojo 2.50 6.00
67 Ricky Williams 3.00 8.00
68 Ron Dayne 3.00 8.00
69 Ike Hilliard 2.50 6.00
70 Wayne Chrebet 2.50 6.00
71 Curtis Martin 3.00 8.00
72 Tim Brown 4.00 10.00
73 Jerry Rice 8.00 20.00
74 Marques Tuiasosopo 3.00 8.00
75 Tyrone Wheatley 3.00 8.00
76 Donovan McNabb 3.00 8.00
77 Freddie Mitchell 2.50 6.00
78 Duce Staley 2.50 6.00
79 Adam Archuleta 3.00 8.00
80 Marshall Faulk 3.00 8.00
81 Kurt Warner 6.00 15.00
82 Aeneas Williams 2.50 6.00
83 Drew Brees 10.00 25.00
84 Tim Dwight 3.00 8.00
85 LaDainian Tomlinson 8.00 20.00
86 Jeff Garcia 2.50 6.00
87 Karsten Bailey 2.50 6.00
88 Alex Bannister 2.50 6.00
89 Bobby Engram 2.50 6.00
90 Matt Hasselbeck 2.50 6.00
91 Koren Robinson 3.00 8.00
92 Ricky Watters 3.00 8.00
93 Warrick Dunn 2.50 6.00
94 Keyshawn Johnson 3.00 8.00
95 Warren Sapp 3.00 8.00
96 Eddie George 4.00 10.00
97 Steve McNair 3.00 8.00
98 Michael Bates 2.50 6.00
99 Rod Gardner 3.00 8.00
100 Sage Rosenfels 3.00 8.00

2001 Titanium Post Season Jersey Patches

Randomly inserted in packs, This 100 card set features premium patches of game used jerseys. The cards have "Patch" written in gold foil on the fronts and are also serial numbered in gold on the fronts to varying quantities.

STATED PRINT RUN 8-386
SERIAL #'d UNDER 15 NOT PRICED
4 Rob Moore/28 8.00 20.00
5 Michael Pittman/45 8.00 20.00
6 Jake Plummer/30 8.00 20.00
7 Terance Mathis/60 6.00 15.00
8 Randall Cunningham/93 6.00 15.00
9 Jamal Lewis/62 10.00 25.00
10 Moe Williams/146 5.00 12.00
16 Dee Brown/203 4.00 10.00
17 Patrick Jeffers/77 5.00 12.00
18 Dan Morgan/50 8.00 20.00
19 Steve Smith/50 12.00 30.00
20 Chris Weinke/125 6.00 15.00
21 James Allen/129 5.00 12.00
22 Marlon Barnes/15 10.00 25.00
23 Macey Brooks/209 4.00 10.00
24 David Terrell/86 6.00 15.00
25 Anthony Thomas/75 8.00 20.00
27 Corey Dillon/161 4.00 10.00
28 T.J. Houshmandzadeh/116 6.00 15.00
29 Chad Johnson/111 5.00 12.00
30 Curtis Keaton/244 4.00 10.00
31 Peter Warrick/120 5.00 12.00
32 Tim Couch/113 5.00 12.00
33 Rickey Dudley/310 4.00 10.00
34 Curtis Enis/25 8.00 20.00
35 James Jackson/244 4.00 10.00
36 Andre King/224 4.00 10.00
37 Quincy Morgan/145 6.00 15.00
38 Quincy Carter/75 6.00 15.00
39 Emmitt Smith/75 12.00 30.00
40 Mike Anderson/116 5.00 12.00
41 Olandis Gary/75 5.00 12.00
42 Brian Griese/111 5.00 12.00
43 Eddie Kennison/50 8.00 20.00
44 Ed McCaffrey/23 10.00 25.00
45 Brett Favre/74 20.00 50.00
46 Ahman Green/41 8.00 20.00
47 Marvin Harrison/136 6.00 15.00
48 Edgerrin James/213 5.00 12.00
49 Peyton Manning/173 15.00 40.00
50 Reggie Wayne/75 6.00 15.00
51 Mark Brunell/50 8.00 20.00
52 Fred Taylor/24 8.00 20.00
53 Trent Green/50 6.00 15.00
54 Chris Chambers/75 5.00 12.00
55 Josh Heupel/117 8.00 20.00
57 Travis Minor/75 6.00 15.00
58 Dedric Ward/35 8.00 20.00
59 Michael Bennett/84 6.00 15.00
60 Cris Carter/100 8.00 20.00
61 Daunte Culpepper/71 8.00 20.00
62 Randy Moss/100 6.00 15.00
63 Travis Prentice/20 8.00 20.00
64 David Patten/69 6.00 15.00
65 Deuce McAllister/79 8.00 20.00
66 Onome Ojo/75 5.00 12.00
67 Ricky Williams/104 6.00 15.00
68 Ron Dayne/50 8.00 20.00
71 Curtis Martin/50 8.00 20.00
72 Tim Brown/50 10.00 25.00
73 Jerry Rice/50 20.00 50.00
74 Marques Tuiasosopo/158 5.00 12.00
76 Donovan McNabb/109 6.00 15.00
77 Freddie Mitchell/86 5.00 12.00
78 Duce Staley/173 4.00 10.00
79 Adam Archuleta/241 5.00 12.00
80 Marshall Faulk/84 6.00 15.00
81 Kurt Warner/115 12.00 30.00
82 Aeneas Williams/386 4.00 10.00
84 Tim Dwight/195 5.00 12.00
86 Jeff Garcia/210 4.00 10.00
87 Karsten Bailey/50 6.00 15.00
88 Alex Bannister/75 5.00 12.00
89 Bobby Engram/64 6.00 15.00
90 Matt Hasselbeck/15 10.00 25.00
91 Koren Robinson/87 6.00 15.00
93 Warrick Dunn/219 4.00 10.00
94 Keyshawn Johnson/50 8.00 20.00
95 Warren Sapp/219 5.00 12.00
96 Eddie George/87 8.00 20.00
97 Steve McNair/98 6.00 15.00
98 Michael Bates/127 5.00 12.00

2002 Titanium Post Season

Released in late-January 2003, this set is composed of 50 rookies, 28 rookie jerseys, and 47 veteran jerseys. The jerseys were serial #'d to 435, and the rookies were serial #'d to 699.

1-50 ROOKIE PRINT RUN 699
1 Damien Anderson RC 1.25 3.00
2 Preston Parsons RC 1.25 3.00
3 T.J. Duckett RC 1.25 3.00
4 Kurt Kittner RC 1.25 3.00
5 Javin Hunter RC 1.25 3.00
6 Ed Reed RC 8.00 20.00
7 Anthony Weaver RC 1.25 3.00
8 Coy Wire RC 1.50 4.00
9 Randy Fasani RC 1.25 3.00
10 Matt Schobel RC 1.50 4.00
11 Derek Ross RC 1.50 4.00
12 Chris Cash RC 1.25 3.00
13 Najeh Davenport RC 1.25 3.00
14 Tony Fisher RC 1.25 3.00
15 Craig Nall RC 1.50 4.00
16 Dwight Freeney RC 2.50 6.00
17 Larry Tripplett RC 1.25 3.00
18 Ricky Williams RC 1.50 4.00
19 Akin Ayodele RC 1.50 4.00
20 John Henderson RC 1.50 4.00
21 Randy McMichael RC 2.00 5.00
22 Shaun Hill RC 2.00 5.00
23 Deion Branch RC 2.00 5.00
24 Rohan Davey RC 2.00 5.00
25 David Givens RC 2.00 5.00
26 Daniel Graham RC 1.50 4.00
27 Charles Grant RC 2.00 5.00
28 J.T. O'Sullivan RC 1.50 4.00
29 Daryl Jones RC 1.25 3.00
30 Jeremy Shockey RC 2.00 5.00
31 Charles Stackhouse RC 1.25 3.00
32 Phillip Buchanon RC 2.00 5.00
33 Napoleon Harris RC 1.50 4.00
34 Larry Foote RC 2.50 6.00
35 Lee Mays RC 1.25 3.00
36 Travis Fisher RC 1.50 4.00
37 Robert Thomas RC 1.25 3.00
38 Seth Burford RC 1.25 3.00
39 Quentin Jammer RC 2.00 5.00
40 Ben Leber RC 1.25 3.00
41 Josh Norman RC 1.25 3.00
42 Brandon Doman RC 1.25 3.00
43 Jeff Kelly RC 1.25 3.00
44 Jerramy Stevens RC 2.00 5.00
45 Travis Stephens RC 1.25 3.00
46 Carlos Hall RC 1.25 3.00
47 Darrell Hill RC 1.25 3.00
48 John Simon RC 1.25 3.00
49 Tank Williams RC 1.50 4.00
50 Rock Cartwright RC 2.00 5.00
51 Josh McCown JSY RC 4.00 10.00
52 Ron Johnson JSY RC 3.00 8.00
53 Josh Reed JSY RC 3.00 8.00
54 DeShaun Foster JSY RC 4.00 10.00
55 Julius Peppers JSY RC 6.00 15.00
56 Andre Davis JSY RC 2.50 6.00
57 William Green JSY RC 3.00 8.00
58 Antonio Bryant JSY RC 4.00 10.00
59 Chad Hutchinson JSY RC 2.50 6.00
60 Roy Williams JSY RC 2.50 6.00
61 Ashley Lelie JSY RC 2.50 6.00
62 Clinton Portis JSY RC 4.00 10.00
63 Joey Harrington JSY RC 2.50 6.00
64 Javon Walker JSY RC 4.00 10.00
65 David Carr JSY RC 2.50 6.00
66 Jabar Gaffney JSY RC 2.50 6.00
67 Jonathan Wells JSY RC 3.00 8.00
68 David Garrard JSY RC 3.00 8.00
69 Donte Stallworth JSY RC 4.00 10.00
70 Tim Carter JSY RC 3.00 8.00
71 Brian Westbrook JSY RC 5.00 12.00
72 Antwaan Randle El JSY RC 3.00 8.00
73 Lamar Gordon JSY RC 3.00 8.00
74 Reche Caldwell JSY RC 3.00 8.00
75 Maurice Morris JSY RC 3.00 8.00
76 Ladell Betts JSY RC 4.00 10.00
77 Patrick Ramsey JSY RC 3.00 8.00
78 Cliff Russell JSY RC 2.50 6.00
79 David Boston JSY 3.00 8.00
80 Jamal Lewis JSY 4.00 10.00
81 Drew Bledsoe JSY 4.00 10.00
82 Eric Moulds JSY 3.00 8.00
83 Anthony Thomas JSY 4.00 10.00
84 Brian Urlacher JSY 5.00 12.00
85 Corey Dillon JSY 3.00 8.00
86 Tim Couch JSY 3.00 8.00
87 Quincy Carter JSY 3.00 8.00
88 Emmitt Smith JSY 8.00 20.00
89 Terrell Davis JSY 4.00 10.00
90 Brian Griese JSY 3.00 8.00
91 Ed McCaffrey JSY 4.00 10.00
92 Brett Favre JSY 10.00 25.00
93 Terry Glenn JSY 4.00 10.00
94 Ahman Green JSY 4.00 10.00
95 Corey Bradford JSY 3.00 8.00
96 Marvin Harrison JSY 4.00 10.00
97 Edgerrin James JSY 4.00 10.00
98 Peyton Manning JSY 12.00 30.00
99 Fred Taylor JSY 3.00 8.00
100 Trent Green JSY 3.00 8.00
101 Priest Holmes JSY 3.00 8.00
102 Chris Chambers JSY 3.00 8.00
103 Ricky Williams JSY 4.00 10.00
104 Derrick Alexander JSY 3.00 8.00
105 Michael Bennett JSY 3.00 8.00
106 Randy Moss JSY 4.00 10.00
107 Aaron Brooks JSY 3.00 8.00
108 Deuce McAllister JSY 4.00 10.00
109 Tiki Barber JSY 4.00 10.00
110 Curtis Martin JSY 4.00 10.00
111 Tim Brown JSY 5.00 12.00
112 Duce Staley JSY 3.00 8.00
113 Jerome Bettis JSY 5.00 12.00
114 Kordell Stewart JSY 3.00 8.00
115 Isaac Bruce JSY 5.00 12.00
116 Marshall Faulk JSY 4.00 10.00
117 Torry Holt JSY 4.00 10.00
118 Kurt Warner JSY 4.00 10.00
119 Drew Brees JSY 10.00 25.00
120 LaDainian Tomlinson JSY 5.00 12.00
121 Jeff Garcia JSY 3.00 8.00
122 Terrell Owens JSY 4.00 10.00
123 Shaun Alexander JSY 3.00 8.00
124 Eddie George JSY 4.00 10.00
125 Steve McNair JSY 4.00 10.00

1961 Titans Jay Publishing

This 12-card set features (approximately) 5" by 7" black-and-white player photos of the New York Titans, one of the original AFL teams who later became the New York Jets. The photos show players in traditional poses with the quarterback preparing to throw, the runner heading downfield, and the defenseman ready for the tackle. The player's name and the team name appear in the wider bottom border. These cards were packaged 12 to a packet and originally sold for 25 cents through various Jay Publishing products. The backs are blank. The cards are unnumbered and checklisted below in alphabetical order.

COMPLETE SET (12) 60.00 120.00
1 Al Dorow 5.00 10.00
2 Larry Grantham 5.00 10.00
3 Mike Hagler 5.00 10.00
4 Mike Hudock 5.00 10.00
5 Bob Jewett 5.00 10.00
6 Jack Klotz 5.00 10.00
7 Don Maynard 15.00 30.00
8 John McMullan 5.00 10.00
9 Bob Mischak 5.00 10.00
10 Art Powell 6.00 12.00
11 Bob Reifsnyder 5.00 10.00
12 Sid Youngelman 5.00 10.00

1999 Titans Coca-Cola Kroger

This set was originally distributed as a perforated uncut sheet. Each card includes a color player photo on the cardfront with a brief player bio on the back. The cards were sponsored by Coca-Cola and Kroger. Each card is unnumbered and listed alphabetically below.

COMPLETE SET (16) 5.00 12.00
1 Blaine Bishop .20 .50
2 Joe Bowden .20 .50
3 Al Del Greco .20 .50
4 Kevin Dyson .40 1.00
5 Jeff Fisher CO .20 .50
6 Eddie George 1.20 3.00
7 Craig Hentrich .20 .50
8 Jevon Kearse 1.20 3.00
9 Bruce Matthews .20 .50
10 Steve McNair .80 2.00
11 Lorenzo Neal .20 .50
12 Eddie Robinson .20 .50
13 Samari Rolle .20 .50
14 Yancey Thigpen .30 .75
15 Denard Walker .20 .50
16 Frank Wycheck .30 .75

2006 Titans Topps

COMPLETE SET (12) 5.00 8.00
TEN1 Chris Brown .25 .60
TEN2 Drew Bennett .30 .75
TEN3 David Givens .30 .75
TEN4 Courtney Roby .25 .60
TEN5 Erron Kinney .25 .60
TEN6 Adam Jones .25 .60
TEN7 Steve McNair .30 .75
TEN8 Billy Volek .25 .60
TEN9 Kyle Vanden Bosch .25 .60
TEN10 Travis Henry .25 .60
TEN11 Vince Young 2.00 5.00
TEN12 LenDale White .50 1.25

2007 Titans Topps

COMPLETE SET (12) 2.50 5.00
1 LenDale White .50 1.25
2 Vince Young .40 1.00
3 Bo Scaife .40 1.00
4 Brandon Jones .40 1.00
5 Michael Griffin .40 1.00
6 David Givens .40 1.00
7 Ben Troupe .40 1.00
8 Keith Bulluck .40 1.00
9 Kyle Vanden Bosch .40 1.00
10 Chris Hope .40 1.00
11 Rob Bironas .40 1.00
12 Chris Henry .40 1.00

2008 Titans Topps

COMPLETE SET (12) 3.00 6.00
1 LenDale White .40 1.00
2 Alge Crumpler .40 1.00
3 Vince Young .40 1.00
4 Albert Haynesworth .40 1.00
5 Kyle Vanden Bosch .40 1.00
6 Keith Bulluck .40 1.00
7 Rob Bironas .40 1.00
8 Bo Scaife .40 1.00

9 Justin Gage .40 1.00
10 Roydell Williams .40 1.00
11 Chris Johnson .50 1.25
12 Lavelle Hawkins .50 1.25

2009 Titans Tennessean

These cards feature members of the 2009 Titans and were sponsored by The Tennessean newspaper (noted at the top of the card). Each is standard size with the addition of a perforated coupon attached below the card for a discount off a purchase at the Titans Pro Shop.

COMPLETE SET (6) 4.00 8.00
1 Keith Bullock .40 1.00
2 Kerry Collins .50 1.25
3 Chris Johnson 1.00 2.50
4 Kevin Mawae .40 1.00
5 Kyle Vanden Bosch .50 1.25
6 Vince Young .60 1.50

2013 Titans NFL Draft Selections

COMPLETE SET (9) 5.00 10.00
1 Lavar Edwards .50 1.25
2 Zaviar Gooden .50 1.25
3 Justin Hunter .40 1.00
4 Brian Schwenke .40 1.00
5 Daimion Stafford .50 1.25
6 Chance Warmack .40 1.00
7 Khalid Wooten .40 1.00
8 Blidi Wreh-Wilson .50 1.25
9 Cover Card .40 1.00

2014 Titans Shoe Carnival

COMPLETE SET (12) 5.00 10.00
1 Jurrell Casey .30 .75
2 Michael Griffin .30 .75
3 Justin Hunter .30 .75
4 Taylor Lewan .30 .75
5 Dexter McCluster .40 1.00
6 Jason McCourty .30 .75
7 Derrick Morgan .40 1.00
8 Bishop Sankey .30 .75
9 Delanie Walker .30 .75
10 Chance Warmack .30 .75
11 Kendall Wright .30 .75
12 Titan True Cover Card .30 .75

2015 Titans Shoe Carnival

COMPLETE SET (11) 5.00 10.00
1 Jurrell Casey .30 .75
2 Michael Griffin .30 .75
3 Taylor Lewan .30 .75
4 Marcus Mariota 1.25 3.00
5 Jason McCourty .30 .75
6 Derrick Morgan .40 1.00
7 Brian Orakpo .30 .75
8 Delanie Walker .30 .75
9 Chance Warmack .30 .75
10 Avery Williamson .30 .75
11 Kendall Wright .30 .75

1995 Tombstone Pizza

Titled "Classic Quarterback Series," one card from this 12-card standard-size set was inserted in specially-marked packages of Tombstone Pizza. Each of the quarterbacks autographed 10,000 cards for random insertion. The entire set was available through a mail-in offer for three Tombstone pizza logos plus 1.00. The fronts display color action cutouts framed by borders that fade from dark brown to orange. The player's last name is printed in large block lettering across the top. In addition to biography, career statistics, and a color headshot, the backs carry a "Classic Quarterback Quote."

COMPLETE SET (12) 10.00 25.00
1 Ken Anderson .50 1.25
2 Terry Bradshaw 1.60 4.00
3 Len Dawson .60 1.50
4 Dan Fouts .60 1.50
5 Bob Griese .80 2.00
6 Billy Kilmer .50 1.25
7 Joe Namath 2.00 5.00
8 Jim Plunkett .50 1.25
9 Ken Stabler 1.00 2.50
10 Bart Starr 1.20 3.00
11 Joe Theismann .50 1.25
12 Johnny Unitas 1.20 3.00

1995 Tombstone Pizza Autographs

Titled "Classic Quarterback Series," one card from this 12-card standard-size set was inserted in specially-marked packages of Tombstone Pizza. Each quarterback autographed 10,000 cards for random insertion.

1 Ken Anderson 6.00 15.00
2 Terry Bradshaw 30.00 60.00
3 Len Dawson 10.00 25.00
4 Dan Fouts 12.00 30.00
5 Bob Griese 10.00 25.00
6 Billy Kilmer 6.00 15.00
7 Joe Namath 40.00 100.00
8 Jim Plunkett 6.00 15.00
9 Ken Stabler 15.00 40.00
10 Bart Starr 25.00 60.00
11 Joe Theismann 6.00 15.00
12 Johnny Unitas 100.00 175.00

1996 Tombstone Pizza Quarterback Club Caps

This "milk cap" set was produced for Tombstone Pizza by Pinnacle Brands. The caps were distributed as a complete player set of 14 in a punch-out type board measuring approximately 8-1/2" by 11" and as two-cap packs in selected Tombstone Pizza packages. The two-cap packs included one player cap and a team logo cap. Each cap has a 1-5/8" diameter and features a player in the Quarterback Club. A black plastic "slammer" was also included with the Player Board set.

COMP.PANEL SET (28) 8.80 22.00
COMP.PLAYER BOARD (14) 8.00 20.00
1 Steve Young .50 1.25
2 Emmitt Smith 1.00 2.50
3 Junior Seau .20 .50
4 Barry Sanders 1.20 3.00
5 Jerry Rice .60 1.50
6 Dan Marino 1.20 3.00
7 Jim Kelly .30 .75
8 Michael Irvin .30 .75
9 Brett Favre 1.20 3.00
10 Marshall Faulk .50 1.25
11 John Elway 1.20 3.00
12 Randall Cunningham .30 .75
13 Drew Bledsoe .60 1.50
14 Troy Aikman .60 1.50
1T San Francisco 49ers .07 .20
2T Dallas Cowboys .07 .20
3T San Diego Chargers .07 .20
4T Detroit Lions .07 .20
5T San Francisco 49ers .07 .20
6T Miami Dolphins .07 .20
7T Buffalo Bills .07 .20
8T Dallas Cowboys .07 .20
9T Green Bay Packers .07 .20
10T Indianapolis Colts .07 .20
11T Denver Broncos .07 .20
12T Philadelphia Eagles .07 .20
13T New England Patriots .07 .20
14T Dallas Cowboys .07 .20

1983 Tonka Figurines

These small figurines were issued by Tonka in small blister packages as well as separate packaging with a Tonka die-cast truck. Each statue is a generic posable figure produced in the uniform of one of the 28-NFL teams with most being produced in a white and black player version. A sheet of numbers was also included with each statue so that any jersey number could be created.

1 Atlanta Falcons 15.00 40.00
2 Baltimore Colts 15.00 40.00
3 Buffalo Bills 20.00 50.00
4 Chicago Bears 20.00 50.00
5 Cincinnati Bengals 15.00 40.00
6 Cleveland Browns 20.00 50.00
7 Dallas Cowboys 40.00 80.00
8 Denver Broncos 20.00 50.00
9 Detroit Lions 15.00 40.00
10 Green Bay Packers 40.00 80.00
11 Houston Oilers 15.00 40.00
12 Kansas City Chiefs 20.00 50.00
13 Los Angeles Raiders 40.00 80.00
14 Los Angeles Rams 15.00 40.00
15 Miami Dolphins 20.00 50.00
16 Minnesota Vikings 15.00 40.00
17 New England Patriots 15.00 40.00
18 New Orleans Saints 15.00 40.00
19 New York Giants 20.00 50.00
20 New York Jets 20.00 50.00
21 Philadelphia Eagles 15.00 40.00
22 Pittsburgh Steelers 40.00 80.00
23 St. Louis Cardinals 15.00 40.00
24 San Diego Chargers 15.00 40.00
25 San Francisco 49ers 20.00 50.00
26 Seattle Seahawks 15.00 40.00
27 Tampa Bay Buccaneers 15.00 40.00
28 Washington Redskins 40.00 80.00

1994 Tony's Pizza QB Cubes

These "Cubes" were actually part of the backs of Tony's Pizza boxes. The collector was to to cut the cube from the box and fold it into a square. Each cube features one NFL QB Club member, an "In the Zone" moment from his career, and a small piece of a Troy Aikman picture. The full Aikman picture could be seen when all 6-cubes were used to complete the puzzle.

COMPLETE SET (6) 30.00 60.00
1 Troy Aikman 5.00 10.00
2 Randall Cunningham 2.50 5.00
3 John Elway 7.50 15.00
4 Jim Kelly 3.00 6.00
5 Dan Marino 10.00 20.00
6 Steve Young 4.00 8.00

1949 Topps Felt Backs

The 1949 Topps Felt Backs set contains 100-cards with each measuring approximately 7/8" by 1 7/16". The cards are unnumbered and arranged in alphabetical order below. The cardbacks are made of felt and depict a college pennant. Twenty-five of the cards were produced with either a brown or yellow background on the cardfront. For years the yellow version was thought to be slightly more difficult to find, but in recent years it has become apparent that the brown background version is actually the most difficult to find. Sheets of 25 cards with the same color background are often found. For more than 30 years, the set had been cataloged as a 1950 release, but evidence began to build that suggested the actual year of release was 1949. The wrapper actually has the year 1949 printed on it, the player selection matches the 1949 college football season much better than 1950, and a recent advertising piece from the period mentions a mail-in offer that expired in December, 1949. Perhaps the cards were released in both 1949 and 1950, but certainly 1949 was the initial release year.

COMPLETE SET (100) 6000.00 8000.00
WRAPPER (1-CENT) 60.00 120.00
1 Lou Allen RC 35.00 60.00
2 Morris Bailey RC 35.00 60.00
3 George Bell RC 35.00 60.00
4 Lindy Berry HOR RC 35.00 60.00
5A Mike Boldin Brn RC 50.00 80.00
5B Mike Boldin Yel RC 35.00 60.00
6A Bernie Botula Brn RC 50.00 80.00
6B Bernie Botula Yel RC 35.00 60.00
7 Bob Bowlby RC 35.00 60.00
8 Bob Bucher RC 35.00 60.00
9A Al Burnett Brn RC 50.00 80.00
9B Al Burnett Yel RC 35.00 60.00
10 Don Burson RC 35.00 60.00
11 Paul Campbell 35.00 60.00
12 Herb Carey RC 35.00 60.00
13A Bimbo Cecconi Brn RC 50.00 80.00
13B Bimbo Cecconi Yel RC 35.00 60.00
14 Bill Chauncey RC 35.00 60.00
15 Dick Clark RC 35.00 60.00
16 Tom Coleman RC 35.00 60.00
17 Billy Conn RC 35.00 60.00
18 John Cox RC 35.00 60.00
19 Lou Creekmur RC 90.00 150.00
20 Richard Glen Davis RC 40.00 75.00
21 Warren Davis RC 35.00 60.00
22 Bob Deuber RC 35.00 60.00
23 Ray Dooney RC 35.00 60.00
24 Tom Dublinski RC 40.00 75.00
25 Jeff Fleischman RC 35.00 60.00
26 Jack Friedland RC 35.00 60.00
27 Bob Fuchs RC 35.00 60.00
28 Arnold Galiffa RC 40.00 75.00
29 Dick Gilman RC 35.00 60.00
30A Frank Gitschier Brn RC 50.00 80.00
30B Frank Gitschier Yel RC 35.00 60.00
31 Gene Glick 35.00 60.00
32 Bill Gregus RC 35.00 60.00
33 Harold Hagan RC 35.00 60.00
34 Charles Hall RC 35.00 60.00
35A Leon Hart Brn 100.00 175.00
35B Leon Hart Yel 90.00 150.00
36A Bob Hester Brn RC 50.00 80.00
36B Bob Hester Yel RC 35.00 60.00
37 George Hughes RC 35.00 60.00
38 Levi Jackson 40.00 75.00
39A Jack.Jensen Brn 125.00 200.00
39B Jack.Jensen Yel 100.00 175.00
40 Charlie Justice 90.00 150.00
41 Gary Kerkorian RC 35.00 60.00
42 Bernie Krueger RC 35.00 60.00
43 Bill Kuhn RC 35.00 60.00
44 Dean Laun RC 35.00 60.00
45 Chet Leach RC 35.00 60.00
46A Bobby Lee Brn RC 50.00 80.00
46B Bobby Lee Yel RC 35.00 60.00
47 Roger Lehew RC 35.00 60.00
48 Glenn Lippman RC 35.00 60.00
49 Melvin Lyle RC 35.00 60.00
50 Len Makowski RC 35.00 60.00
51A Al Malekoff Brn RC 50.00 80.00
51B Al Malekoff Yel RC 35.00 60.00
52A Jim Martin Brn 60.00 100.00
52B Jim Martin Yel 50.00 80.00
53 Frank Mataya RC 35.00 60.00
54A Ray Mathews Brn RC 60.00 100.00
54B Ray Mathews Yel RC 50.00 80.00
55A Dick McKissack Brn RC 50.00 80.00
55B Dick McKissack Yel RC 35.00 60.00
56 Frank Miller RC 35.00 60.00
57A John Miller Brn RC 50.00 80.00
57B John Miller Yel RC 35.00 60.00
58 Ed Modzelewski RC 40.00 75.00
59 Don Mouser RC 35.00 60.00
60 James Murphy RC 35.00 60.00
61A Ray Nagle Brn RC 50.00 80.00
61B Ray Nagle Yel RC 35.00 60.00
62 Leo Nomellini 200.00 350.00
63 James O'Day RC 35.00 60.00
64 Joe Paterno RC 1200.00 2000.00
65 Andy Pavich RC 35.00 60.00
66A Pete Perini Brn 50.00 80.00
66B Pete Perini Yel 35.00 60.00
67 Jim Powers RC 35.00 60.00
68 Dave Rakestraw RC 35.00 60.00
69 Herb Rich RC 35.00 60.00
70 Fran Rogel RC 35.00 60.00
71A Darrell Royal Brn RC 300.00 500.00
71B Darrell Royal Yel RC 250.00 400.00
72 Steve Sawle RC 35.00 60.00
73 Nick Sebek RC 35.00 60.00
74 Herb Seidell RC 35.00 60.00
75A Charles Shaw Brn RC 50.00 80.00
75B Charles Shaw Yel RC 35.00 60.00
76A Emil Sitko Brn RC 50.00 80.00
76B Emil Sitko Yel RC 35.00 60.00
77 Butch Songin RC 40.00 75.00
78A Mariano Stalloni Brn RC 50.00 80.00
78B Mariano Stalloni Yel RC 35.00 60.00
79 Ernie Stautner RC 175.00 300.00
80 Don Stehley RC 35.00 60.00
81 Gil Stevenson RC 35.00 60.00
82 Bishop Strickland RC 35.00 60.00
83 Harry Szulborski 35.00 60.00
84A Wally Teninga Brn RC 50.00 80.00
84B Wally Teninga Yel RC 35.00 60.00
85 Clayton Tonnemaker 35.00 60.00
86A Dan Towler Brn RC 125.00 200.00
86B Dan Towler Yel RC 100.00 175.00
87A Bert Turek Brn RC 50.00 80.00
87B Bert Turek Yel RC 35.00 60.00
88 Harry Ulinski RC 35.00 60.00
89 Leon Van Billingham RC 35.00 60.00
90 Langdon Viracola RC 35.00 60.00
91 Leo Wagner RC 35.00 60.00
92A Doak Walker Brn 350.00 500.00
92B Doak Walker Yel 250.00 400.00
93 Jim Ward RC 35.00 60.00
94 Art Weiner 35.00 60.00
95 Dick Weiss RC 35.00 60.00
96 Froggie Williams RC 35.00 60.00
97 Robert Wilson RC 35.00 60.00
98 Roger Red Wilson RC 35.00 60.00
99 Carl Wren RC 35.00 60.00
100A Pete Zinaich Brn RC 50.00 80.00
100B Pete Zinaich Yel RC 35.00 60.00

1951 Topps Magic

The 1951 Topps Magic football set was Topps' second major college football issue and featured 75 different players. The cards measure approximately 2 1/16" by 2 15/16" and were produced with a perforated edge along the bottom. Two different distinct perforation configurations have been found - one with a very tight pattern of dimples and the other with the dimples roughly 3/16" apart. The tight pattern version are usually found slightly diamond cut. Despite the perforation, the cards were issued as single cards and not as pairs in 1951. The fronts contain color portraits with the player's name, position and team nickname in a black box at the bottom. The backs contain a brief write-up, a black and white photo of the player's college or university within a 'scratch-off" section (unscratched cards still show the silver substance) which gives the answer to a football quiz. Cards with the scratch-off back intact are valued at 50 percent more than the prices listed below. Rookie Cards in this set include Marion Campbell, Vic Janowicz, Babe Parilli, Bert Rechichar, Bill Wade and George Young.

COMPLETE SET (75) 800.00 1200.00
*BACK UNSCRATCHED: 1.5X TO 2.5X
WRAPPER (1-CENT) 150.00 200.00
WRAPPER (5-CENT) 250.00 300.00
1 Jimmy Monahan RC 15.00 30.00
2 Bill Wade RC 30.00 50.00
3 Bill Reichardt RC 10.00 18.00
4 Babe Parilli RC 30.00 50.00
5 Billie Burkhalter RC 10.00 18.00
6 Ed Weber RC 10.00 18.00
7 Tom Scott RC 15.00 25.00
8 Frank Guthridge RC 10.00 18.00
9 John Karras 10.00 18.00
10 Vic Janowicz RC 100.00 175.00
11 Lloyd Hill RC 10.00 18.00
12 Jim Weatherall RC 15.00 25.00
13 Howard Hansen RC 10.00 18.00
14 Lou D'Achille RC 10.00 18.00
15 Johnny Turco RC 10.00 18.00
16 Jerrell Price RC 10.00 18.00
17 John Coatta RC 10.00 18.00
18 Bruce Patton RC 10.00 18.00
19 Marion Campbell RC 20.00 35.00
20 Blaine Earon RC 10.00 18.00
21 Dewey McConnell RC 10.00 18.00
22 Ray Beck RC 10.00 18.00
23 Jim Prewett RC 10.00 18.00
24 Bob Steele RC 10.00 18.00
25 Art Betts RC 10.00 18.00
26 Walt Trillhaase RC 10.00 18.00
27 Gil Bartosh RC 10.00 18.00
28 Bob Bestwick RC 10.00 18.00
29 Tom Rushing RC 10.00 18.00
30 Bert Rechichar RC 20.00 35.00
31 Bill Owens RC 10.00 18.00
32 Mike Goggins RC 10.00 18.00
33 John Petitbon RC 10.00 18.00
34 Byron Townsend RC 10.00 18.00
35 Ed Rotticci RC 10.00 18.00
36 Steve Wadiak RC 10.00 18.00
37 Bobby Marlow RC 15.00 25.00
38 Bill Fuchs RC 10.00 18.00
39 Ralph Staub RC 10.00 18.00
40 Bill Vesprini RC 10.00 18.00
41 Zack Jordan RC 10.00 18.00
42 Bob Smith RC 15.00 25.00
43 Charles Hanson RC 10.00 18.00
44 Glenn Smith RC 10.00 18.00
45 Armand Kitto RC 10.00 18.00
46 Vinnie Drake RC 10.00 18.00
47 Bill Putich RC 10.00 18.00
48 George Young RC 30.00 50.00
49 Don McRae RC 10.00 18.00
50 Frank Smith RC 10.00 18.00
51 Dick Hightower RC 10.00 18.00
52 Clyde Pickard RC 10.00 18.00
53 Bob Reynolds RC 15.00 25.00
54 Dick Gregory RC 10.00 18.00
55 Dale Samuels RC 10.00 18.00
56 Gale Galloway RC 10.00 18.00
57 Vic Pujo RC 10.00 18.00
58 Dave Waters RC 10.00 18.00
59 Joe Ernest RC 10.00 18.00
60 Elmer Costa RC 10.00 18.00
61 Nick Liotta RC 10.00 18.00
62 John Dottley RC 10.00 18.00
63 Hi Faubion RC 10.00 18.00
64 David Harr RC 10.00 18.00
65 Bill Matthews RC 10.00 18.00
66 Carroll McDonald RC 10.00 18.00
67 Dick Dewing RC 10.00 18.00
68 Joe Johnson RB RC 10.00 18.00
69 Arnold Burwitz RC 10.00 18.00
70 Ed Dobrowolski RC 10.00 18.00
71 Joe Dudeck RC 10.00 18.00
72 Johnny Bright RC 15.00 25.00
73 Harold Loehlein RC 10.00 18.00
74 Lawrence Hairston RC 10.00 18.00
75 Bob Carey RC 15.00 25.00

1955 Topps All American

Issued in one-card penny packs, nine-card nickel packs as well as 22-card cello packs, the 1955 Topps All-American set features 100-cards of college football greats from years past. The cards measure approximately 2 5/8" by 3 5/8". Card fronts contain a color player photo superimposed over a black and white action photo. The player's college logo is in one upper corner and an All-American logo is at the bottom with the player's name and position. The backs contain collegiate highlights and a cartoon. There are many numbers which were printed in lesser supply. These short-printed cards are denoted in the checklist below by SP. The key Rookie Cards in this set are Doc Blanchard, Tommy Harmon, Don Hutson, Ernie Nevers and Amos Alonzo Stagg. The Four Horsemen (Notre Dame backfield in 1924), Knute Rockne, Jim Thorpe, Red Grange and former Supreme Court Justice Whizzer White are also key cards. Wrongbacks can be found on some cards with the Amos A. Stagg card seemingly the most common of those wrongbacks. They are not cataloged below as error cards.

COMPLETE SET (100) 2800.00 3800.00
WRAPPER (1-CENT) 250.00 400.00
WRAPPER (5-CENT) 200.00 350.00
1 Herman Hickman RC 65.00 125.00
2 John Kimbrough RC 10.00 18.00
3 Ed Weir RC 10.00 18.00
4 Erny Pinckert RC 10.00 18.00
5 Bobby Grayson RC 10.00 18.00
6 Nile Kinnick UER RC 75.00 135.00
7 Andy Bershak RC 10.00 18.00
8 George Cafego RC 10.00 18.00
9 Tom Hamilton SP RC 20.00 30.00
10 Bill Dudley 25.00 40.00
11 Bobby Dodd SP RC 20.00 30.00
12 Otto Graham 100.00 200.00
13 Aaron Rosenberg 10.00 18.00
14A Gaynell Tinsley ERR RC 50.00 100.00
14B Gaynell Tinsley COR RC 15.00 25.00
15 Ed Kaw SP 20.00 30.00
16 Knute Rockne 175.00 275.00
17 Bob Reynolds 10.00 18.00
18 Pudge Heffelfinger SP RC 25.00 40.00
19 Bruce Smith 25.00 40.00
20 Sammy Baugh 125.00 200.00
21A W.White RC SP ERR 150.00 250.00
21B W.White RC SP COR 60.00 100.00
22 Brick Muller RC 10.00 18.00
23 Dick Kazmaier RC 15.00 25.00
24 Ken Strong 30.00 50.00
25 Casimir Myslinski SP RC 20.00 30.00
26 Larry Kelley SP RC 25.00 40.00
27 Red Grange UER 200.00 300.00
28 Mel Hein SP RC 60.00 100.00
29 Leo Nomellini SP 50.00 80.00
30 Wes Fesler RC 10.00 18.00
31 George Sauer Sr. RC 15.00 25.00
32 Hank Foldberg RC 10.00 18.00
33 Bob Higgins RC 10.00 18.00
34 Davey O'Brien RC 30.00 50.00
35 Tom Harmon SP RC 60.00 100.00
36 Turk Edwards SP 35.00 60.00
37 Jim Thorpe 275.00 400.00
38 Amos A. Stagg RC 40.00 75.00
39 Jerome Holland RC 15.00 25.00
40 Donn Moomaw RC 10.00 18.00
41 Joseph Alexander SP RC 20.00 30.00
42 Eddie Tryon SP RC 25.00 40.00
43 George Savitsky 10.00 18.00
44 Ed Garbisch RC 10.00 18.00
45 Elmer Oliphant RC 10.00 18.00
46 Arnold Lassman RC 10.00 18.00
47 Bo McMillin RC 15.00 25.00
48 Ed Widseth RC 10.00 18.00
49 Don Gordon Zimmerman RC 10.00 18.00
50 Ken Kavanaugh 15.00 25.00
51 Duane Purvis SP RC 20.00 30.00
52 Johnny Lujack 50.00 90.00
53 John F. Green RC 10.00 18.00
54 Edwin Dooley SP RC 20.00 30.00
55 Frank Merritt SP RC 20.00 30.00
56 Ernie Nevers RC 75.00 125.00
57 Vic Hanson SP RC 20.00 30.00
58 Ed Franco RC 10.00 18.00
59 Doc Blanchard RC 30.00 50.00
60 Dan Hill RC 10.00 18.00
61 Charles Brickley SP RC 20.00 30.00
62 Harry Newman RC 15.00 30.00
63 Charlie Justice 20.00 35.00
64 Benny Friedman RC 20.00 35.00
65 Joe Donchess SP RC 20.00 30.00
66 Bruiser Kinard RC 20.00 35.00
67 Frankie Albert 15.00 25.00
68 Four Horsemen SP RC 325.00 500.00
69 Frank Sinkwich RC 15.00 25.00
70 Bill Daddio RC 10.00 18.00
71 Bobby Wilson 10.00 18.00
72 Chub Peabody RC 10.00 18.00
73 Paul Governali RC 15.00 25.00
74 Gene McEver RC 10.00 18.00
75 Hugh Gallarneau RC 10.00 18.00
76 Angelo Bertelli RC 15.00 25.00
77 Bowden Wyatt SP RC 20.00 30.00
78 Jay Berwanger RC 20.00 35.00
79 Pug Lund RC 10.00 18.00
80 Bennie Oosterbaan RC 10.00 18.00
81 Cotton Warburton RC 10.00 18.00
82 Alex Wojciechowicz 20.00 35.00
83 Ted Coy SP RC 20.00 30.00
84 Ace Parker SP RC 30.00 60.00
85 Sid Luckman 60.00 120.00
86 Albie Booth SP RC 20.00 30.00
87 Adolph Schultz SP 20.00 30.00
88 Ralph Kercheval 10.00 18.00
89 Marshall Goldberg 18.00 30.00
90 Charlie O'Rourke RC 10.00 18.00
91 Bob Odell UER RC 10.00 18.00
92 Biggie Munn RC 10.00 18.00
93 Willie Heston SP RC 25.00 40.00
94 Joe Bernard SP RC 25.00 40.00
95 Chris Cagle SP RC 25.00 40.00
96 Bill Hollenback SP 25.00 40.00
97 Don Hutson SP RC 150.00 225.00
98 Beattie Feathers SP 60.00 100.00
99 Don Whitmire SP RC 25.00 40.00
100 Fats Henry SP RC 100.00 200.00

1956 Topps

The 1956 set of 120 player cards marks Topps' first standard NFL football card set since acquiring Bowman. The cards measure 2 5/8" by 3 5/8" and were issued in one-card penny packs, nickel packs and 15-card cello packs. The card fronts have a player photo superimposed over a solid color background. The team logo is an upper corner with the player's name, team name and position grouped in a box toward the bottom of the photo. The card backs were printed in red and black on gray card stock. Statistical information from the immediate past season and career totals are given at the bottom. Players from the Washington Redskins and the Chicago Cardinals were apparently produced in lesser quantities, as they are more difficult to find compared to the other teams. Some veteran collectors believe that cards of members of the Baltimore Colts, Chicago Bears, and Cleveland Browns may also be slightly more difficult to find as well. An unnumbered checklist card and six contest cards were also issued along with this set, although in much lesser quantities. The contest cards have advertisements on both sides for Bazooka Bubble Gum. Both sides have orange-red and blue type on an off-white background. The fronts of the contest cards feature an offer to win one of three prizes (basketball, football, or autographed baseball glove) in the Bazooka Bubble Gum football contest, and the rules governing the contest are listed on the back. Any eligible contestant (not over 15 years old) who mailed in (before November 19th) the correct scores to the two NFL football games listed on the front of that particular card and includes five one-cent Bazooka Bubble Gum wrappers or one nickel Bazooka wrapper with the entry received a choice of one of the three above-mentioned prizes. The cards are either numbered (1-3) or lettered (A-C). Some dealers have doubted the existence of Contest Card C. Any proof of this card would be greatly appreciated. There also exists a three-card advertising panel consis

COMPLETE SET (120) 1200.00 1800.00
WRAPPER (1-CENT) 200.00 250.00
WRAPPER (5-CENT) 60.00 100.00
1 Johnny Carson SP 40.00 80.00
2 Gordy Soltau 3.50 6.00
3 Frank Varrichione 3.50 6.00
4 Eddie Bell 3.50 6.00
5 Alex Webster RC 7.50 15.00
6 Norm Van Brocklin 18.00 30.00
7 Green Bay Packers 15.00 25.00
8 Lou Creekmur 7.50 15.00
9 Lou Groza 15.00 25.00
10 Tom Bienemann SP RC 15.00 25.00
11 George Blanda 30.00 50.00
12 Alan Ameche 6.00 12.00
13 Vic Janowicz SP 25.00 45.00
14 Dick Moegle 4.00 8.00
15 Fran Rogel 3.50 6.00
16 Harold Giancanelli 3.50 6.00
17 Emlen Tunnell 7.50 15.00
18 Tank Younger 6.00 12.00
19 Billy Howton 4.00 8.00
20 Jack Christiansen 7.50 15.00
21 Darrel Brewster 3.50 6.00
22 Chicago Cardinals SP 60.00 100.00
23 Ed Brown 4.00 8.00
24 Joe Campanella 3.50 6.00
25 Leon Heath SP 15.00 25.00
26 San Francisco 49ers 10.00 18.00
27 Dick Flanagan RC 3.50 6.00
28 Chuck Bednarik 15.00 25.00
29 Kyle Rote 6.00 12.00
30 Les Richter 4.00 8.00
31 Howard Ferguson 3.50 6.00
32 Dorne Dibble 3.50 6.00
33 Kenny Konz 3.50 6.00
34 Dave Mann SP RC 15.00 25.00
35 Rick Casares 6.00 12.00
36 Art Donovan 18.00 30.00
37 Chuck Drazenovich SP 15.00 25.00
38 Joe Arenas 3.50 6.00
39 Lynn Chandnois 3.50 6.00
40 Philadelphia Eagles 10.00 18.00
41 Roosevelt Brown RC 25.00 40.00
42 Tom Fears 15.00 25.00
43 Gary Knafelc RC 3.50 6.00
44 Joe Schmidt RC 35.00 60.00
45 Cleveland Browns 10.00 18.00
46 Len Teeuws SP RC 15.00 25.00
47 Bill George RC 25.00 40.00
48 Baltimore Colts 10.00 18.00
49 Eddie LeBaron SP 25.00 50.00
50 Hugh McElhenny 18.00 30.00
51 Ted Marchibroda 6.00 12.00
52 Adrian Burk 3.50 6.00
53 Frank Gifford 35.00 60.00
54 Charley Toogood 3.50 6.00
55 Tobin Rote 4.00 8.00
56 Bill Stits 3.50 6.00
57 Don Colo 3.50 6.00
58 Ollie Matson SP 35.00 60.00
59 Harlon Hill 4.00 8.00
60 Lenny Moore RC 75.00 125.00
61 Wash.Redskins SP 50.00 90.00
62 Billy Wilson 3.50 6.00
63 Pittsburgh Steelers 10.00 18.00
64 Bob Pellegrini RC 3.50 6.00
65 Ken MacAfee E 3.50 6.00
66 Willard Sherman RC 3.50 6.00
67 Roger Zatkoff 3.50 6.00
68 Dave Middleton RC 3.50 6.00
69 Ray Renfro 4.00 8.00
70 Don Stonesifer SP 15.00 25.00
71 Stan Jones RC 25.00 40.00
72 Jim Mutscheller RC 3.50 6.00
73 Volney Peters SP 15.00 25.00
74 Leo Nomellini 12.00 20.00
75 Ray Mathews 3.50 6.00
76 Dick Bielski 3.50 6.00
77 Charley Conerly 15.00 25.00
78 Elroy Hirsch 18.00 30.00
79 Bill Forester RC 4.00 8.00
80 Jim Doran RC 3.50 6.00
81 Fred Morrison 3.50 6.00
82 Jack Simmons SP 15.00 25.00
83 Bill McColl 3.50 6.00
84 Bert Rechichar 3.50 6.00
85 Joe Scudero SP RC 15.00 25.00
86 Y.A.Tittle 30.00 50.00
87 Ernie Stautner 12.00 20.00
88 Norm Willey 3.50 6.00
89 Bob Schnelker RC 3.50 6.00
90 Dan Towler 6.00 12.00
91 John Martinkovic 3.50 6.00
92 Detroit Lions 10.00 18.00
93 George Ratterman 4.00 8.00
94 Chuck Ulrich SP 15.00 25.00
95 Bobby Watkins 3.50 6.00
96 Buddy Young 6.00 12.00
97 Billy Wells SP RC 15.00 25.00
98 Bob Toneff 3.50 6.00
99 Bill McPeak 3.50 6.00
100 Bobby Thomason 3.50 6.00
101 Roosevelt Grier RC 30.00 50.00
102 Ron Waller RC 3.50 6.00
103 Bobby Dillon 3.50 6.00
104 Leon Hart 6.00 12.00
105 Mike McCormack 7.50 15.00
106 John Olszewski SP 15.00 25.00
107 Bill Wightkin 3.50 6.00
108 George Shaw RC 4.00 8.00
109 Dale Atkeson SP 15.00 25.00
110 Joe Perry 15.00 25.00
111 Dale Dodrill 3.50 6.00
112 Tom Scott 3.50 6.00
113 New York Giants 10.00 18.00
114 Los Angeles Rams 10.00 18.00
115 Al Carmichael 3.50 6.00
116 Bobby Layne 30.00 50.00
117 Ed Modzelewski 3.50 6.00
118 Lamar McHan RC SP 15.00 25.00
119 Chicago Bears 10.00 18.00
120 Billy Vessels RC 20.00 40.00
AD1 Advertising Panel 500.00 800.00
Lou Groza
Don Colo
Darrel Brewster
NNO Checklist SP NNO! 250.00 400.00
C1 Contest Card 1 ! 45.00 80.00
C2 Contest Card 2 ! 45.00 80.00
C3 Contest Card 3 ! 45.00 80.00
CA Contest Card A ! 50.00 90.00
CB Contest Card B ! 70.00 110.00

1957 Topps

The 1957 Topps football set contains 154 standard-size cards of NFL players. Cards were issued in penny, nickel and cello packs. Horizontally designed fronts have a close-up photo (with player name) on the left and an in-action pose (with position and team name) to the right. Both have solid color backgrounds. The card backs were printed in red and black on gray card stock. Backs are also divided in two with statistical information on one side and a cartoon on the other. The Rookie Cards of Johnny Unitas, Bart Starr, and Paul Hornung are included in this set. Other notable Rookie Cards in this set are Raymond Berry, Dick "Night Train" Lane, Tommy McDonald and Earl Morrall. The second series (89-154) is generally more difficult to obtain than the first series. A number of cards (22) from the second series are much easier to find than the other 44, making those double prints (DP). It's thought that the John Unitas Rookie card is among the 22-DPs. An unnumbered checklist card was also issued with this set. The checklist card was printed in red, yellow, and blue or in red, white, and blue; neither variety currently is recognized as having any additional premium value above the price listed below. There also were produced several three-card advertising panels consisting of the card fronts of three players with ad copy on the reverse of the top two cards and a player's cardback at the bottom. The complete set price below refers to the 154 numbered cards minus the unnumbered checklist card.

COMPLETE SET (154) 1600.00 2200.00
WRAPPER (1-CENT) 30.00 50.00
WRAPPER (5-CENT) 50.00 75.00
1 Eddie LeBaron 30.00 50.00
2 Pete Retzlaff RC 7.50 15.00
3 Mike McCormack 6.00 12.00
4 Lou Baldacci RC 2.50 4.00
5 Gino Marchetti 10.00 20.00
6 Leo Nomellini 10.00 20.00
7 Bobby Watkins 2.50 4.00
8 Dave Middleton 2.50 4.00
9 Bobby Dillon 2.50 4.00
10 Les Richter 3.50 6.00
11 Roosevelt Brown 10.00 20.00
12 Lavern Torgeson RC 2.50 4.00
13 Dick Bielski 2.50 4.00
14 Pat Summerall 10.00 20.00
15 Jack Butler RC 15.00 25.00
16 John Henry Johnson 7.50 15.00
17 Art Spinney 2.50 4.00
18 Bob St. Clair 6.00 12.00
19 Perry Jeter RC 2.50 4.00
20 Lou Creekmur 6.00 12.00
21 Dave Hanner 3.50 6.00
22 Norm Van Brocklin 18.00 30.00
23 Don Chandler RC 5.00 10.00
24 Al Dorow 2.50 4.00
25 Tom Scott 2.50 4.00
26 Ollie Matson 12.00 20.00
27 Fran Rogel 2.50 4.00
28 Lou Groza 15.00 25.00
29 Billy Vessels 3.50 6.00
30 Y.A.Tittle 25.00 40.00
31 George Blanda 25.00 40.00
32 Bobby Layne 25.00 40.00
33 Billy Howton 3.50 6.00
34 Bill Wade 5.00 10.00
35 Emlen Tunnell 7.50 15.00
36 Leo Elter RC 2.50 4.00
37 Clarence Peaks RC 3.50 6.00
38 Don Stonesifer 2.50 4.00
39 George Tarasovic 2.50 4.00
40 Darrel Brewster 2.50 4.00
41 Bert Rechichar 2.50 4.00
42 Billy Wilson 2.50 4.00
43 Ed Brown 3.50 6.00
44 Gene Gedman RC 2.50 4.00
45 Gary Knafelc 2.50 4.00
46 Elroy Hirsch 18.00 30.00
47 Don Heinrich 3.50 6.00
48 Gene Brito 2.50 4.00
49 Chuck Bednarik 15.00 25.00
50 Dave Mann 2.50 4.00
51 Bill McPeak 2.50 4.00
52 Kenny Konz 2.50 4.00
53 Alan Ameche 5.00 10.00
54 Gordy Soltau 2.50 4.00
55 Rick Casares 3.50 6.00
56 Charlie Ane 2.50 4.00
57 Al Carmichael 2.50 4.00
58A W.Sherman ERR no pos/team 175.00 300.00
58B Willard Sherman COR 2.50 4.00
58C W.Sherman ERR no team 125.00 200.00
59 Kyle Rote 5.00 10.00
60 Chuck Drazenovich 2.50 4.00
61 Bobby Walston 2.50 4.00
62 John Olszewski 2.50 4.00
63 Ray Mathews 2.50 4.00
64 Maurice Bassett 2.50 4.00
65 Art Donovan 15.00 25.00
66 Joe Arenas 2.50 4.00
67 Harlon Hill 3.50 6.00
68 Yale Lary 6.00 12.00
69 Bill Forester 3.50 6.00
70 Bob Boyd 2.50 4.00
71 Andy Robustelli 12.00 20.00
72 Sam Baker RC 3.50 6.00
73 Bob Pellegrini 2.50 4.00
74 Leo Sanford 2.50 4.00
75 Sid Watson RC 2.50 4.00
76 Ray Renfro 3.50 6.00
77 Carl Taseff UER 2.50 4.00
78 Clyde Conner RC 2.50 4.00
79 J.C. Caroline RC 2.50 4.00
80 Howard Cassady RC 7.50 15.00
81 Tobin Rote 3.50 6.00
82 Ron Waller 2.50 4.00
83 Jim Patton RC 3.50 6.00
84 Volney Peters 2.50 4.00
85 Dick Lane RC 35.00 60.00
86 Royce Womble 2.50 4.00
87 Duane Putnam RC 3.50 6.00
88 Frank Gifford 30.00 60.00
89 Steve Meilinger 5.00 10.00
90 Buck Lansford 5.00 10.00
91 Lindon Crow DP 4.00 8.00
92 Ernie Stautner DP 12.50 25.00
93 Preston Carpenter DP RC 4.00 8.00
94 Raymond Berry RC 75.00 150.00
95 Hugh McElhenny 18.00 30.00
96 Stan Jones 15.00 25.00
97 Dorne Dibble 5.00 10.00
98 Joe Scudero DP 4.00 8.00
99 Eddie Bell 5.00 10.00
100 Joe Childress DP RC 4.00 8.00
101 Elbert Nickel 6.00 12.00
102 Walt Michaels 6.00 12.00
103 Jim Mutscheller DP 4.00 8.00
104 Earl Morrall RC 35.00 60.00
105 Larry Strickland RC 5.00 10.00
106 Jack Christiansen 7.50 15.00
107 Fred Cone DP 4.00 8.00
108 Bud McFadin RC 6.00 12.00
109 Charley Conerly 18.00 30.00
110 Tom Runnels DP RC 4.00 8.00
111 Ken Keller DP RC 4.00 8.00
112 James Root RC 5.00 10.00
113 Ted Marchibroda DP 5.00 10.00
114 Don Paul DB 5.00 10.00
115 George Shaw 6.00 12.00
116 Dick Moegle 6.00 12.00
117 Don Bingham 5.00 10.00
118 Leon Hart 7.50 15.00
119 Bart Starr RC 400.00 750.00
120 Paul Miller DP RC 4.00 8.00
121 Alex Webster 6.00 12.00
122 Ray Wietecha DP 4.00 8.00
123 Johnny Carson 5.00 10.00
124 Tom. McDonald DP RC 25.00 40.00
125 Jerry Tubbs RC 6.00 12.00
126 Jack Scarbath 5.00 10.00
127 Ed Modzelewski DP 4.00 8.00
128 Lenny Moore 30.00 50.00
129 Joe Perry DP 15.00 25.00
130 Bill Wightkin 5.00 10.00
131 Jim Doran 5.00 10.00
132 Howard Ferguson UER 5.00 10.00
133 Tom Wilson RC 5.00 10.00
134 Dick James RC 5.00 10.00
135 Jimmy Harris RC 5.00 10.00
136 Chuck Ulrich 5.00 10.00
137 Lynn Chandnois 5.00 10.00
138 Johnny Unitas DP RC 300.00 450.00
139 Jim Ridlon DP RC 4.00 8.00
140 Zeke Bratkowski DP 5.00 10.00
141 Ray Krouse 5.00 10.00
142 John Martinkovic 5.00 10.00
143 Jim Cason DP RC 4.00 8.00
144 Ken MacAfee E 5.00 10.00
145 Sid Youngelman RC 6.00 12.00
146 Paul Larson RC 5.00 10.00
147 Len Ford 18.00 30.00
148 Bob Toneff DP 4.00 8.00
149 Ronnie Knox DP RC 4.00 8.00
150 Jim David RC 6.00 12.00
151 Paul Hornung RC 250.00 400.00
152 Tank Younger 7.50 15.00
153 Bill Svoboda DP RC 4.00 8.00
154 Fred Morrison 35.00 70.00
AD1 Al Dorow 400.00 700.00
Harlon Hill
Bert Rechich
AD2 B.Watkins 400.00 700.00
G.Marchetti
C.Peaks
AD3 M.McCormack 400.00 700.00
L.Elter
J.Caroline
CL1 Checklist Bazooka SP 500.00 750.00
CL2 Checklist Blony SP 500.00 750.00

1958 Topps

The 1958 Topps set of 132 standard-size cards contains NFL players. After a one-year interruption, team cards returned to the Topps lineup. The cards were issued in penny, nickel and cello packs. Card fronts have an oval player photo surrounded by a solid color that varies according to team. The player's name, position and team are at the bottom. The backs are easily distinguished from other years, as they are printed in bright red ink on white stock. The right-hand side has a trivia question with which the answer could be obtained by rubbing with a coin over the blank space. The left side has stats and highlights. The key Rookie Cards in this set are Jim Brown and Sonny Jurgensen. Topps also randomly inserted in packs a card with the words "Free Felt Initial" across the top. The horizontally oriented front pictures a boy in a red shirt and a girl in a blue shirt, with a large yellow "L" and "A" respectively on each of their shirts. The card back indicates an initial could be obtained by sending in three Bazooka or Blony wrappers and a self-addressed stamped envelope with the initial of choice printed on the front and back of the envelope. According to a note in the December 15th, 1958 issue of Sports Illustrated, 110 million cards were produced for this issue.

COMPLETE SET (132) 850.00 1250.00
WRAPPER (1-CENT) 35.00 60.00
WRAPPER (5-CENT) 75.00 125.00
1 Gene Filipski RC 7.50 15.00
2 Bobby Layne 20.00 35.00
3 Joe Schmidt 6.00 12.00
4 Bill Barnes RC 2.00 4.00
5 Milt Plum RC 5.00 10.00
6 Billy Howton UER 2.50 5.00
7 Howard Cassady 2.50 5.00
8 Jim Dooley 2.00 4.00
9 Cleveland Browns 3.00 6.00
10 Lenny Moore 15.00 30.00
11 Darrel Brewster 2.00 4.00
12 Alan Ameche 4.00 8.00
13 Jim David 2.00 4.00
14 Jim Mutscheller 2.00 4.00
15 Andy Robustelli 5.00 10.00
16 Gino Marchetti 6.00 12.00
17 Ray Renfro 2.50 5.00
18 Yale Lary 4.00 8.00
19 Gary Glick RC 2.00 4.00
20 Jon Arnett RC 4.00 8.00
21 Bob Boyd 2.00 4.00
22 Johnny Unitas UER 90.00 150.00
23 Zeke Bratkowski 2.50 5.00
24 Sid Youngelman UER 2.00 4.00
25 Leo Elter 2.00 4.00
26 Kenny Konz 2.00 4.00
27 Washington Redskins 3.00 6.00
28 Carl Brettschneider RC 2.00 4.00
29 Chicago Bears 3.00 6.00
30 Alex Webster 2.50 5.00
31 Al Carmichael 2.00 4.00
32 Bobby Dillon 2.00 4.00
33 Steve Meilinger 2.00 4.00
34 Sam Baker 2.00 4.00
35 Chuck Bednarik 7.50 15.00
36 Bert Vic Zucco RC 2.00 4.00
37 George Tarasovic 2.00 4.00
38 Bill Wade 4.00 8.00
39 Dick Stanfel 2.50 5.00
40 Jerry Norton 2.00 4.00
41 San Francisco 49ers 3.00 6.00
42 Emlen Tunnell 5.00 10.00
43 Jim Doran 2.00 4.00
44 Ted Marchibroda 4.00 8.00
45 Chet Hanulak 2.00 4.00
46 Dale Dodrill 2.00 4.00
47 Johnny Carson 2.00 4.00
48 Dick Deschaine RC 2.00 4.00
49 Billy Wells UER 2.00 4.00
50 Larry Morris RC 2.00 4.00
51 Jack McClairen RC 2.00 4.00
52 Lou Groza 7.50 15.00
53 Rick Casares 2.50 5.00
54 Don Chandler 2.50 5.00
55 Duane Putnam 2.00 4.00
56 Gary Knafelc 2.00 4.00
57 Earl Morrall 5.00 10.00
58 Ron Kramer RC 2.50 5.00
59 Mike McCormack 4.00 8.00
60 Gern Nagler 2.00 4.00
61 New York Giants 3.00 6.00
62 Jim Brown RC 350.00 500.00
63 Joe Marconi RC 2.00 4.00
64 R.C. Owens UER RC 2.50 5.00
65 Jimmy Carr RC 2.50 5.00
66 Bart Starr UER 90.00 150.00
67 Tom Wilson 2.00 4.00
68 Lamar McHan 2.00 4.00
69 Chicago Cardinals 3.00 6.00
70 Jack Christiansen 4.00 8.00
71 Don McIlhenny RC 2.00 4.00
72 Ron Waller 2.00 4.00
73 Frank Gifford 25.00 50.00
74 Bert Rechichar 2.00 4.00
75 John Henry Johnson 5.00 10.00
76 Jack Butler 4.00 8.00
77 Frank Varrichione 2.00 4.00
78 Ray Mathews 2.00 4.00
79 Marv Matuszak UER RC 2.00 4.00
80 Harlon Hill UER 2.00 4.00
81 Lou Creekmur 4.00 8.00
82 Woodley Lewis UER 2.00 4.00
83 Don Heinrich 2.00 4.00
84 Charley Conerly 7.50 15.00
85 Los Angeles Rams 3.00 6.00
86 Y.A.Tittle 18.00 30.00
87 Bobby Walston 2.00 4.00
88 Earl Putman RC 2.00 4.00
89 Leo Nomellini 7.50 15.00
90 Sonny Jurgensen RC 60.00 100.00
91 Don Paul DB 2.00 4.00
92 Paige Cothren RC 2.00 4.00
93 Joe Perry 7.50 15.00
94 Tobin Rote 2.50 5.00
95 Billy Wilson 2.00 4.00
96 Green Bay Packers 7.50 15.00
97 Lavern Torgeson 2.00 4.00
98 Milt Davis RC 2.00 4.00
99 Larry Strickland 2.00 4.00
100 Matt Hazeltine RC 2.50 5.00
101 Walt Yowarsky RC 2.00 4.00
102 Roosevelt Brown 4.00 8.00
103 Jim Ringo 5.00 10.00
104 Joe Krupa RC 2.00 4.00
105 Les Richter 2.50 5.00
106 Art Donovan 12.00 20.00
107 John Olszewski 2.00 4.00
108 Ken Keller 2.00 4.00
109 Philadelphia Eagles 3.00 6.00
110 Baltimore Colts 3.00 6.00
111 Dick Bielski 2.00 4.00
112 Eddie LeBaron 4.00 8.00
113 Gene Brito 2.00 4.00
114 Willie Galimore RC 5.00 10.00
115 Detroit Lions 3.00 6.00
116 Pittsburgh Steelers 3.00 6.00
117 L.G. Dupre 2.50 5.00
118 Babe Parilli 2.50 5.00
119 Bill George 5.00 10.00
120 Raymond Berry 25.00 40.00
121 Jim Podoley UER RC 2.00 4.00
122 Hugh McElhenny 7.50 15.00
123 Ed Brown 2.50 5.00
124 Dick Moegle 2.50 5.00
125 Tom Scott 2.00 4.00
126 Tommy McDonald 6.00 12.00
127 Ollie Matson 10.00 20.00

128 Preston Carpenter	2.00	4.00
129 George Blanda	18.00	30.00
130 Gordy Soltau	2.00	4.00
131 Dick Nolan RC	2.50	5.00
132 Don Bosseler RC	10.00	20.00
AD1 Ad Panel	450.00	700.00
Leo Nomellini		
Chet Hanulak		
Cardinals Team		
Gordy Soltau back		
NNO Free Felt Initial Card	15.00	25.00

1959 Topps

The 1959 Topps football set contains 176 standard-size cards which were issued in two series of 88. The cards were issued in penny, nickel and cello packs. The cello packs contained 12 cards at a cost of 10 cents per and were packed 36 to a box. Card fronts contain a player photo over a solid background. Beneath the photo, is the player's name in red and blue letters. Beneath the name are the player's position and team. The card backs were printed in gray on white card stock. Statistical information from the immediate past season and career totals are given on the reverse. Card backs include a scratch-off quiz. Team cards (with checklist backs) as well as team pennant cards are included in the set. The key Rookie Cards in this set are Sam Huff, Alex Karras, Jerry Kramer, Bobby Mitchell, Jim Parker and Jim Taylor. The Taylor card was supposed to portray the great Packers running back. Instead, the card depicts the Cardinals linebacker.

COMPLETE SET (176)	600.00	900.00
WRAPPER (1-CENT)	50.00	90.00
WRAPPER (1-CENT, REP)	50.00	80.00
WRAPPER (5-CENT)	75.00	125.00
1 Johnny Unitas	60.00	120.00
2 Gene Brito	1.50	3.00
3 Detroit Lions CL	3.00	6.00
4 Max McGee RC	15.00	30.00
5 Hugh McElhenny	7.50	15.00
6 Joe Schmidt	4.00	8.00
7 Kyle Rote	3.00	6.00
8 Clarence Peaks	1.50	3.00
9 Steelers Pennant	1.75	3.50
10 Jim Brown	90.00	150.00
11 Ray Mathews	1.50	3.00
12 Bobby Dillon	1.50	3.00
13 Joe Childress	1.50	3.00
14 Terry Barr RC	1.50	3.00
15 Del Shofner RC	2.00	4.00
16 Bob Pellegrini UER	1.50	3.00
17 Baltimore Colts CL	3.00	6.00
18 Preston Carpenter	1.50	3.00
19 Leo Nomellini	5.00	10.00
20 Frank Gifford	25.00	40.00
21 Charlie Ane	1.50	3.00
22 Jack Butler	2.50	6.00
23 Bart Starr	35.00	60.00
24 Cardinals Pennant	1.75	3.50
25 Bill Barnes	1.50	3.00
26 Walt Michaels	2.00	4.00
27 Clyde Conner UER	1.50	3.00
28 Paige Cothren	1.50	3.00
29 Roosevelt Grier	3.00	6.00
30 Alan Ameche	3.00	6.00
31 Philadelphia Eagles CL	3.00	6.00
32 Dick Nolan	2.00	4.00
33 R.C. Owens	2.00	4.00
34 Dale Dodrill	1.50	3.00
35 Gene Gedman	1.50	3.00
36 Gene Lipscomb RC	5.00	10.00
37 Ray Renfro	2.00	4.00
38 Browns Pennant	1.75	3.50
39 Bill Forester	2.00	4.00
40 Bobby Layne	15.00	25.00
41 Pat Summerall	5.00	10.00
42 Jerry Mertens RC	1.50	3.00
43 Steve Myhra RC	1.50	3.00
44 John Henry Johnson	4.00	8.00
45 Woodley Lewis UER	1.50	3.00
46 Green Bay Packers CL	5.00	10.00
47 Don Owens UER RC	1.50	3.00
48 Ed Beatty RC	1.50	3.00
49 Don Chandler	1.50	3.00
50 Ollie Matson	6.00	12.00
51 Sam Huff RC	30.00	50.00
52 Tom Miner RC	1.50	3.00
53 Giants Pennant	1.75	3.50
54 Kenny Konz	1.50	3.00
55 Raymond Berry	10.00	20.00
56 Howard Ferguson UER	1.50	3.00
57 Chuck Ulrich	1.50	3.00
58 Bob St.Clair	3.00	6.00
59 Don Burroughs RC	1.50	3.00
60 Lou Groza	7.50	15.00
61 San Francisco 49ers CL	3.00	6.00
62 Andy Nelson RC	1.50	3.00
63 Harold Bradley RC	1.50	3.00
64 Dave Hanner	2.00	4.00
65 Charley Conerly	6.00	12.00
66 Gene Cronin RC	1.50	3.00
67 Duane Putnam	1.50	3.00
68 Colts Pennant	1.75	3.50
69 Ernie Stautner	4.00	8.00
70 Jon Arnett	2.00	4.00
71 Ken Panfil RC	1.50	3.00
72 Matt Hazeltine	1.50	3.00
73 Harley Sewell	1.50	3.00
74 Mike McCormack	3.00	6.00
75 Jim Ringo	4.00	8.00
76 Los Angeles Rams CL	3.00	6.00
77 Bob Gain RC	1.50	3.00
78 Buzz Nutter RC	1.50	3.00
79 Jerry Norton	1.50	3.00
80 Joe Perry	6.00	12.00
81 Carl Brettschneider	1.50	3.00
82 Paul Hornung	30.00	60.00
83 Eagles Pennant	1.75	3.50
84 Les Richter	2.00	4.00
85 Howard Cassady	2.00	4.00
86 Art Donovan	7.50	15.00
87 Jim Patton	2.00	4.00
88 Pete Retzlaff	2.00	4.00
89 Jim Mutscheller	1.00	2.00
90 Zeke Bratkowski	1.50	3.00
91 Washington Redskins CL	2.00	4.00
92 Art Hunter	1.00	2.00
93 Gern Nagler	1.00	2.00
94 Chuck Weber RC	1.00	2.00
95 Lew Carpenter RC	1.50	3.00
96 Stan Jones	2.50	5.00
97 Ralph Guglielmi UER	1.50	3.00
98 Packers Pennant	2.00	4.00
99 Ray Wietecha	1.00	2.00
100 Lenny Moore	6.00	12.00
101 Jim Ray Smith UER RC	1.50	3.00
102 Abe Woodson RC	1.50	3.00
103 Alex Karras RC	25.00	40.00
104 Chicago Bears CL	2.00	4.00
105 John David Crow RC	6.00	12.00
106 Joe Fortunato RC	1.00	2.00
107 Babe Parilli	1.50	3.00
108 Proverb Jacobs RC	1.00	2.00
109 Gino Marchetti	4.00	8.00
110 Bill Wade	1.50	3.00
111 49ers Pennant	1.50	3.00
112 Karl Rubke RC	1.00	2.00
113 Dave Middleton UER	1.00	2.00
114 Roosevelt Brown	2.50	5.00
115 John Olszewski	1.00	2.00
116 Jerry Kramer RC	18.00	30.00
117 King Hill RC	1.50	3.00
118 Chicago Cardinals CL	2.00	4.00
119 Frank Varrichione	1.00	2.00
120 Rick Casares	1.50	3.00
121 George Strugar RC	1.00	2.00
122 Bill Glass RC	1.50	3.00
123 Don Bosseler	1.00	2.00
124 John Reger RC	1.00	2.00
125 Jim Ninowski RC	1.00	2.00
126 Rams Pennant	1.50	3.00
127 Willard Sherman	1.00	2.00
128 Bob Schnelker	1.00	2.00
129 Ollie Spencer RC	1.00	2.00
130 Y.A.Tittle	15.00	25.00
131 Yale Lary	2.50	5.00
132 Jim Parker RC	15.00	30.00
133 New York Giants CL	2.00	4.00
134 Jim Schrader RC	1.00	2.00
135 M.C. Reynolds RC	1.00	2.00
136 Mike Sandusky RC	1.00	2.00
137 Ed Brown	1.50	3.00
138 Al Barry RC	1.00	2.00
139 Lions Pennant	1.50	3.00
140 Bobby Mitchell RC	20.00	35.00
141 Larry Morris	1.00	2.00
142 Jim Phillips RC	1.50	3.00
143 Jim David	1.00	2.00
144 Joe Krupa	1.00	2.00
145 Willie Galimore	1.50	3.00
146 Pittsburgh Steelers CL	2.00	4.00
147 Andy Robustelli	4.00	8.00
148 Billy Wilson	1.00	2.00
149 Leo Sanford	1.00	2.00
150 Eddie LeBaron	2.50	5.00
151 Bill McColl	1.00	2.00
152 Buck Lansford UER	1.00	2.00
153 Bears Pennant	1.50	3.00
154 Leo Sugar RC	1.00	2.00
155 Jim Taylor UER RC	20.00	35.00
156 Lindon Crow	1.00	2.00
157 Jack McClairen	1.00	2.00
158 Vince Costello RC UER	1.00	2.00
159 Stan Wallace RC	1.00	2.00
160 Mel Triplett RC	1.00	2.00
161 Cleveland Browns CL	2.00	4.00
162 Dan Currie RC	2.00	4.00
163 L.G. Dupre UER	1.50	3.00
164 John Morrow UER RC	1.00	2.00
165 Jim Podoley	1.00	2.00
166 Bruce Bosley RC	1.00	2.00
167 Harlon Hill	1.00	2.00
168 Redskins Pennant	1.50	3.00
169 Junior Wren RC	1.00	2.00
170 Tobin Rote	1.50	3.00
171 Art Spinney	1.00	2.00
172 Chuck Drazenovich UER	1.00	2.00
173 Bobby Joe Conrad RC	1.50	3.00
174 Jesse Richardson RC	1.00	2.00
175 Sam Baker	1.00	2.00
176 Tom Tracy RC	4.00	8.00
AD1 Ad Panel	350.00	500.00
Bill Forrester		
Bobby Dillon		
Ernie Stautner		
Gene Cronin back		

1960 Topps

The 1960 Topps football set contains 132 standard-size cards. Card fronts have a "pure card" effect in that the player photo dominates the card. The only design on front is the player's name, team name and position within a football-shaped icon toward the bottom of the file. The card backs are printed in green on white card stock. Statistical information from the immediate past season and career totals are given on the reverse. The set marks the debut of the Dallas Cowboys into the NFL. The backs feature a "Football Funnies" scratch-off quiz; answer was revealed by rubbing with an edge of a coin. The team cards feature numerical checklist backs. The team cards that have the 67-132 checklist backs (card Nos. 60, 102, 112, 122, 132) all misspell 124 Don Bosseler as Bossler along with a number of other like errors. Several 3-card panel advertisement sheets were released to promote the set. Each features the cardfronts of three base cards with the sheet back including a Gene Cronin mock cardback and several Topps ads.

COMPLETE SET (132)	400.00	600.00
WRAPPER (1-CENT)	60.00	100.00
WRAPPER (1-CENT, REP)	250.00	400.00
WRAPPER (5-CENT)	50.00	80.00
1 Johnny Unitas	40.00	80.00
2 Alan Ameche	2.00	4.00
3 Lenny Moore	5.00	10.00
4 Raymond Berry	6.00	12.00
5 Jim Parker	4.00	8.00
6 George Preas RC	1.25	2.50
7 Art Spinney	1.25	2.50
8 Bill Pellington RC	1.50	3.00
9 Johnny Sample RC	1.50	3.00
10 Gene Lipscomb	1.50	3.00
11 Baltimore Colts	1.50	3.00
12 Ed Brown	1.50	3.00
13 Rick Casares	1.50	3.00
14 Willie Galimore	1.50	3.00
15 Jim Dooley	1.25	2.50
16 Harlon Hill UER	1.25	2.50
17 Stan Jones	2.00	4.00
18 Bill George	2.00	4.00
19 Erich Barnes RC	1.50	3.00
20 Doug Atkins	3.00	6.00
21 Chicago Bears	1.50	3.00
22 Milt Plum	1.50	3.00
23 Jim Brown	60.00	100.00
24 Sam Baker	1.25	2.50
25 Bobby Mitchell	5.00	10.00
26 Ray Renfro	1.50	3.00
27 Billy Howton	1.50	3.00
28 Jim Ray Smith	1.25	2.50
29 Jim Shofner RC	1.50	3.00
30 Bob Gain	1.25	2.50
31 Cleveland Browns	1.50	3.00
32 Don Heinrich	1.25	2.50
33 Ed Modzelewski UER	1.25	2.50
34 Fred Cone	1.25	2.50
35 L.G. Dupre	1.50	3.00
36 Dick Bielski	1.25	2.50
37 Charlie Ane UER	1.25	2.50
38 Jerry Tubbs	1.50	3.00
39 Doyle Nix RC	1.25	2.50
40 Ray Krouse	1.25	2.50
41 Earl Morrall	2.00	4.00
42 Howard Cassady	1.50	3.00
43 Dave Middleton	1.25	2.50
44 Jim Gibbons RC	1.50	3.00
45 Darris McCord RC	1.25	2.50
46 Joe Schmidt	3.00	6.00
47 Terry Barr	1.25	2.50
48 Yale Lary	2.00	4.00
49 Gil Mains RC	1.25	2.50
50 Detroit Lions	1.50	3.00
51 Bart Starr	30.00	50.00
52 Jim Taylor UER	4.00	8.00
53 Lew Carpenter	1.50	3.00
54 Paul Hornung	30.00	45.00
55 Max McGee	2.00	4.00
56 Forrest Gregg RC UER	25.00	40.00
57 Jim Ringo	2.50	5.00
58 Bill Forester	1.50	3.00
59 Dave Hanner	1.50	3.00
60 Green Bay Packers	4.00	8.00
61 Bill Wade	1.50	3.00
62 Frank Ryan RC	2.50	5.00
63 Ollie Matson	5.00	10.00
64 Jon Arnett	1.50	3.00
65 Del Shofner	1.50	3.00
66 Jim Phillips	1.25	2.50
67 Art Hunter	1.25	2.50
68 Les Richter	1.50	3.00
69 Lou Michaels RC	1.50	3.00
70 John Baker RC	1.25	2.50
71 Los Angeles Rams	1.50	3.00
72 Charley Conerly	4.00	8.00
73 Mel Triplett	1.25	2.50
74 Frank Gifford	20.00	35.00
75 Alex Webster	1.50	3.00
76 Bob Schnelker	1.25	2.50
77 Pat Summerall	4.00	8.00
78 Roosevelt Brown	2.00	4.00
79 Jim Patton	1.25	2.50
80 Sam Huff	10.00	20.00
81 Andy Robustelli	3.00	6.00
82 New York Giants	1.50	3.00
83 Clarence Peaks	1.25	2.50
84 Bill Barnes	1.25	2.50
85 Pete Retzlaff	1.50	3.00
86 Bobby Walston	1.25	2.50
87 Chuck Bednarik UER	4.00	8.00
88 Bob Pellegrini	1.25	2.50
89 Tom Brookshier RC	1.50	3.00
90 Marion Campbell	1.50	3.00
91 Jesse Richardson	1.25	2.50
92 Philadelphia Eagles	1.50	3.00
93 Bobby Layne	18.00	30.00
94 John Henry Johnson	3.00	6.00
95 Tom Tracy UER	1.50	3.00
96 Preston Carpenter	1.25	2.50
97 Frank Varrichione UER	1.25	2.50
98 John Nisby RC	1.25	2.50
99 Dean Derby RC	1.25	2.50
100 George Tarasovic	1.25	2.50
101 Ernie Stautner	2.50	5.00
102 Pittsburgh Steelers	1.50	3.00
103 King Hill	1.25	2.50
104 Mal Hammack RC	1.25	2.50
105 John David Crow	1.50	3.00
106 Bobby Joe Conrad	1.50	3.00
107 Woodley Lewis	1.25	2.50
108 Don Gillis RC	1.25	2.50
109 Carl Brettschneider	1.25	2.50
110 Leo Sugar	1.25	2.50
111 Frank Fuller RC	1.25	2.50
112 St. Louis Cardinals	1.50	3.00
113 Y.A.Tittle	18.00	30.00
114 Joe Perry	4.00	8.00
115 J.D.Smith RC	1.50	3.00
116 Hugh McElhenny	4.00	8.00
117 Billy Wilson	1.25	2.50
118 Bob St.Clair	2.00	4.00
119 Matt Hazeltine	1.25	2.50
120 Abe Woodson	1.25	2.50
121 Leo Nomellini	2.50	5.00
122 San Francisco 49ers	1.50	3.00
123 Ralph Guglielmi UER	1.25	2.50
124 Don Bosseler	1.25	2.50
125 John Olszewski	1.25	2.50
126 Bill Anderson UER RC	1.25	2.50
127 Joe Walton RC	1.50	3.00
128 Jim Schrader	1.25	2.50
129 Ralph Felton RC	1.25	2.50
130 Gary Glick	1.25	2.50
131 Bob Toneff	1.25	2.50
132 Redskins Team	18.00	30.00
AD1 Alan Ameche	200.00	350.00
Paul Hornung		
Tom Tracy		
AD2 Del Shofner	125.00	200.00
Milt Plum		
Jim Patton		
AD3 Bob St.Clair	125.00	200.00
Jim Shofner		
Gil Mains		
AD4 Tom Brookshier	125.00	200.00
Packers Team		
George Preas		
AD5 Jimmy Patton	500.00	800.00
Bobby Joe Conrad		
Sam Huff		

1960 Topps Metallic Stickers Inserts

This set of 33 metallic team emblem stickers was inserted with the 1960 Topps regular issue football set. The stickers are unnumbered and are ordered below alphabetically within type. NFL teams are listed first (1-13) followed by college teams (14-33). The stickers measure approximately 2 1/8" by 3 1/16". The sticker fronts are either silver, gold, or blue with a black border.

COMPLETE SET (33)	200.00	400.00
1 Baltimore Colts	7.50	15.00
2 Chicago Bears	12.50	25.00
3 Cleveland Browns	12.50	25.00
4 Dallas Cowboys	12.50	25.00
5 Detroit Lions	7.50	15.00
6 Green Bay Packers	15.00	30.00
7 Los Angeles Rams	7.50	15.00
8 New York Giants	7.50	15.00
9 Philadelphia Eagles	7.50	15.00
10 Pittsburgh Steelers	7.50	15.00
11 St. Louis Cardinals	7.50	15.00
12 San Francisco 49ers	12.50	25.00
13 Washington Redskins	12.50	25.00
14 Air Force Falcons	5.00	10.00
15 Army Cadets	5.00	10.00
16 California Golden Bears	5.00	10.00
17 Dartmouth Indians	5.00	10.00
18 Duke Blue Devils	5.00	10.00
19 LSU Tigers	7.50	15.00
20 Michigan Wolverines	10.00	20.00
21 Minnesota Golden Gophers	5.00	10.00
22 Mississippi Rebels	5.00	10.00
23 Navy Midshipmen	5.00	10.00
24 Notre Dame Fight.Irish	12.50	25.00
25 SMU Mustangs	5.00	10.00
26 USC Trojans	7.50	15.00
27 Syracuse Orangemen	5.00	10.00
28 Tennessee Volunteers	7.50	15.00
29 Texas Longhorns	7.50	15.00
30 UCLA Bruins	7.50	15.00
31 Washington Huskies	5.00	10.00
32 Wisconsin Badgers	5.00	10.00
33 Yale Bulldogs	5.00	10.00

1960 Topps Tattoos

This set was thought to have been distributed in 1960 like the corresponding baseball issue. It appears they were issued as a separate set by both Topps and O-Pee-Chee in Canada. Each is actually the inside surface of the outer wrapper (measuring roughly 1 9/16" by 3 1/2") in which the collector would apply the tatoo by moistening the skin and then pressing the tattoo to the moistened spot. The tattoos are unnumbered and where produced in color. Any additions to the list below are appreciated.

1 Bill Anderson	125.00	250.00
2 Jim Brown	350.00	600.00
3 Rick Casares	125.00	250.00
4 Howard Cassady	125.00	250.00
5 Frank Gifford	200.00	350.00
6 Paul Hornung	250.00	400.00
7 Bobby Layne	200.00	350.00
8 Y.A. Tittle	200.00	350.00
9 Johnny Unitas	350.00	600.00
10 Bill Wade	125.00	250.00
11 Chicago Bears	50.00	100.00
12 Cleveland Browns	40.00	80.00
13 Dallas Cowboys	125.00	200.00
14 Detroit Lions	40.00	80.00
15 Green Bay Packers	125.00	200.00
16 New York Giants	40.00	80.00
17 Pittsburgh Steelers	60.00	120.00
18 St.Louis Cardinals	40.00	80.00
19 San Francisco 49ers	40.00	80.00
20 Washington Redskins	90.00	150.00
21 Air Force	30.00	60.00
22 Army	30.00	60.00
23 Baylor	30.00	60.00
24 Boston College	30.00	60.00
25 California	30.00	60.00
26 Duke	30.00	60.00
27 Illinois	30.00	60.00
28 Indiana	30.00	60.00
29 Iowa	30.00	60.00
30 Kentucky	40.00	80.00
31 Michigan	50.00	100.00
32 Michigan State	30.00	60.00
33 Minnesota	30.00	60.00
34 Mississippi	30.00	60.00
35 Navy	30.00	60.00
36 Nebraska	40.00	80.00
37 Northwestern	30.00	60.00
38 Notre Dame	75.00	150.00
39 Oklahoma	40.00	80.00
40 Oregon	30.00	60.00
41 Oregon State	30.00	60.00
42 Penn State	50.00	100.00
43 Pennsylvania	30.00	60.00
44 Pittsburgh	30.00	60.00
45 Princeton	30.00	60.00
46 Rice	30.00	60.00
47 Rutgers	30.00	60.00
48 SMU	30.00	60.00
49 South Carolina	30.00	60.00
50 Stanford	30.00	60.00
51 TCU	30.00	60.00
52 Tennessee	40.00	80.00
53 Texas	40.00	80.00
54 UCLA	40.00	80.00
55 USC	40.00	80.00
56 Washington State	30.00	60.00
57 Wisconsin	30.00	60.00
58 Wyoming	30.00	50.00
59 Generic	15.00	30.00
Actual Kicking of Football		
60 Generic	15.00	30.00
Catching a Pass		
61 Generic	15.00	30.00
Chasing a fumble		
62 Generic	15.00	30.00
Defender is grabbing shirt		
63 Generic	15.00	30.00
Defender trying to block kick		
64 Generic	15.00	30.00
Kicking Follow Through		
65 Generic	15.00	30.00
Lateral		
66 Generic	15.00	30.00
Passer ready to throw		
67 Generic	15.00	30.00
Player #8 is charging		
68 Generic	15.00	30.00
Player yelling at Referee		
69 Generic	15.00	30.00
Profile view of Passer		
70 Generic	15.00	30.00
Receiver and Defender		
71 Generic	15.00	30.00
Runner being tackled		
72 Generic	15.00	30.00
Runner is falling down		
73 Generic	15.00	30.00
Runner is Fumbling		
74 Generic	15.00	30.00
Runner using stiff arm		
75 Generic	15.00	30.00
Runner with football		
76 Generic	15.00	30.00
Taking a snap on one knee		

1961 Topps

The 1961 Topps football set of 198 standard-size cards contains NFL players (1-132) and AFL players (133-197). The fronts are very similar to the Topps 1961 baseball issue with the player's name, team and position at beneath posed player photos. The card backs are printed in light blue on white card stock. Statistical information from the immediate past season and career totals are given on the reverse. A "coin-rub" picture was featured on the right of the reverse. Cards are essentially numbered in team order by league. There are three checklist cards in the set, numbers 67, 122, and 198. The key Rookie Cards in this set are John Brodie, Tom Flores, Henry Jordan, Don Maynard, and Jim Otto. A 3-card advertising panel was issued as well.

COMPLETE SET (198)	650.00	1000.00
WRAPPER (1-CENT)	250.00	400.00
WRAPPER (1-CENT, REP)	125.00	200.00
WRAPPER (5-CENT)	60.00	100.00
1 Johnny Unitas	50.00	100.00
2 Lenny Moore	6.00	12.00
3 Alan Ameche	2.00	4.00
4 Raymond Berry	6.00	12.00
5 Jim Mutscheller	1.25	2.50
6 Jim Parker	2.50	5.00
7 Gino Marchetti	3.00	6.00
8 Gene Lipscomb	2.00	4.00
9 Baltimore Colts	1.50	3.00
10 Bill Wade	1.50	3.00
11 Johnny Morris RC	3.00	6.00
12 Rick Casares	1.50	3.00
13 Harlon Hill	1.25	2.50
14 Stan Jones	2.00	4.00
15 Doug Atkins	2.50	5.00
16 Bill George	2.00	4.00
17 J.C. Caroline	1.25	2.50
18 Chicago Bears	1.50	3.00
19 Eddie LeBaron IA	1.50	3.00
20 Eddie LeBaron	1.50	3.00
21 Don McIlhenny	1.25	2.50
22 L.G. Dupre	1.50	3.00
23 Jim Doran	1.25	2.50
24 Billy Howton	1.50	3.00
25 Buzz Guy RC	1.25	2.50
26 Jack Patera RC	1.25	2.50
27 Tom Franckhauser RC	1.25	2.50
28 Cowboys Team	7.50	15.00
29 Jim Ninowski	1.25	2.50
30 Dan Lewis RC	1.25	2.50
31 Nick Pietrosante RC	1.50	3.00
32 Gail Cogdill RC	1.50	3.00
33 Jim Gibbons	1.25	2.50
34 Jim Martin	1.25	2.50
35 Alex Karras	7.50	15.00
36 Joe Schmidt	2.50	5.00
37 Detroit Lions	1.50	3.00
38 Paul Hornung IA	9.00	18.00
39 Bart Starr	25.00	40.00
40 Paul Hornung	25.00	40.00
41 Jim Taylor	20.00	35.00
42 Max McGee	2.00	4.00
43 Boyd Dowler RC	5.00	10.00
44 Jim Ringo	2.50	5.00
45 Hank Jordan RC	20.00	40.00
46 Bill Forester	1.50	3.00
47 Green Bay Packers	7.50	15.00
48 Frank Ryan	1.50	3.00
49 Jon Arnett	1.50	3.00
50 Ollie Matson	4.00	8.00
51 Jim Phillips	1.25	2.50
52 Del Shofner	1.50	3.00
53 Art Hunter	1.25	2.50
54 Gene Brito	1.25	2.50
55 Lindon Crow	1.25	2.50
56 Los Angeles Rams	1.50	3.00
57 Johnny Unitas IA	15.00	25.00
58 Y.A.Tittle	18.00	30.00
59 John Brodie RC	25.00	40.00
60 J.D. Smith	1.25	2.50
61 R.C. Owens	1.50	3.00
62 Clyde Conner	1.25	2.50
63 Bob St.Clair	2.00	4.00
64 Leo Nomellini	3.00	6.00
65 Abe Woodson	1.25	2.50
66 San Francisco 49ers	1.50	3.00
67 Checklist Card	25.00	40.00
68 Milt Plum	1.50	3.00
69 Ray Renfro	1.50	3.00
70 Bobby Mitchell	4.00	8.00
71 Jim Brown	75.00	125.00
72 Mike McCormack	2.00	4.00
73 Jim Ray Smith	1.25	2.50
74 Sam Baker	1.25	2.50
75 Walt Michaels	1.50	3.00
76 Cleveland Browns	1.50	3.00
77 Jim Brown IA	25.00	40.00
78 George Shaw	1.25	2.50
79 Hugh McElhenny	4.00	8.00
80 Clancy Osborne RC	1.25	2.50
81 Dave Middleton	1.25	2.50
82 Frank Youso RC	1.25	2.50
83 Don Joyce RC	1.25	2.50
84 Ed Culpepper RC	1.25	2.50
85 Charley Conerly	4.00	8.00
86 Mel Triplett	1.25	2.50
87 Kyle Rote	1.50	3.00
88 Roosevelt Brown	2.00	4.00
89 Ray Wietecha	1.25	2.50
90 Andy Robustelli	2.50	5.00
91 Sam Huff	4.00	8.00
92 Jim Patton	1.25	2.50
93 New York Giants	1.50	3.00
94 Charley Conerly IA	3.00	6.00
95 Sonny Jurgensen	15.00	25.00
96 Tommy McDonald	2.50	5.00
97 Bill Barnes	1.25	2.50
98 Bobby Walston	1.25	2.50
99 Pete Retzlaff	1.50	3.00
100 Jim McCusker RC	1.25	2.50
101 Chuck Bednarik	4.00	8.00
102 Tom Brookshier	1.50	3.00
103 Philadelphia Eagles	1.50	3.00
104 Bobby Layne	18.00	30.00
105 John Henry Johnson	2.00	4.00
106 Tom Tracy	1.50	3.00
107 Buddy Dial RC	1.25	2.50
108 Jimmy Orr RC	3.00	6.00
109 Mike Sandusky	1.25	2.50
110 John Reger	1.25	2.50
111 Junior Wren	1.25	2.50
112 Pittsburgh Steelers	1.50	3.00
113 Bobby Layne IA	5.00	10.00
114 John Roach RC	1.25	2.50
115 Sam Etcheverry RC	1.50	3.00
116 John David Crow	1.50	3.00
117 Mal Hammack	1.25	2.50
118 Sonny Randle RC	1.50	3.00
119 Leo Sugar	1.25	2.50
120 Jerry Norton	1.25	2.50
121 St. Louis Cardinals	1.50	3.00
122 Checklist Card	30.00	50.00
123 Ralph Guglielmi	1.25	2.50
124 Dick James	1.25	2.50
125 Don Bosseler	1.25	2.50
126 Joe Walton	1.25	2.50
127 Bill Anderson	1.25	2.50
128 Vince Promuto RC	1.25	2.50
129 Bob Toneff	1.25	2.50
130 John Paluck RC	1.25	2.50
131 Washington Redskins	1.50	3.00
132 Milt Plum IA !	1.25	2.50
133 Abner Haynes !	4.00	8.00
134 Mel Branch UER	2.00	4.00
135 Jerry Cornelison UER	1.50	3.00
136 Bill Krisher	1.50	3.00
137 Paul Miller	1.50	3.00
138 Jack Spikes	2.00	4.00
139 Johnny Robinson RC	4.00	8.00
140 Cotton Davidson RC	2.00	4.00
141 Dave Smith RB	1.50	3.00
142 Bill Groman	1.50	3.00
143 Rich Michael RC	1.50	3.00
144 Mike Dukes RC	1.50	3.00
145 George Blanda	15.00	25.00
146 Billy Cannon	3.00	6.00
147 Dennit Morris RC	1.50	3.00
148 Jacky Lee UER	2.00	4.00
149 Al Dorow	1.50	3.00
150 Don Maynard RC	25.00	50.00
151 Art Powell RC	4.00	8.00
152 Sid Youngelman	1.50	3.00
153 Bob Mischak RC	1.50	3.00
154 Larry Grantham	1.50	3.00
155 Tom Saidock	1.50	3.00
156 Roger Donnahoo RC	1.50	3.00
157 Laverne Torczon RC	1.50	3.00
158 Archie Matsos RC	2.00	4.00
159 Elbert Dubenion	2.00	4.00
160 Wray Carlton RC	2.00	4.00
161 Rich McCabe RC	1.50	3.00
162 Ken Rice RC	1.50	3.00
163 Art Baker RC	1.50	3.00
164 Tom Rychlec	1.50	3.00
165 Mack Yoho	1.50	3.00
166 Jack Kemp	35.00	60.00
167 Paul Lowe	3.00	6.00
168 Ron Mix	5.00	10.00
169 Paul Maguire UER	3.00	6.00
170 Volney Peters	1.50	3.00
171 Ernie Wright RC	2.00	4.00
172 Ron Nery RC	1.50	3.00
173 Dave Kocourek RC	2.00	4.00
174 Jim Colclough RC	1.50	3.00
175 Babe Parilli	2.00	4.00
176 Billy Lott	1.50	3.00
177 Fred Bruney	1.50	3.00
178 Ross O'Hanley RC	1.50	3.00
179 Walt Cudzik RC	1.50	3.00
180 Charley Leo	1.50	3.00
181 Bob Dee	1.50	3.00
182 Jim Otto RC	25.00	40.00
183 Eddie Macon RC	1.50	3.00
184 Dick Christy RC	1.50	3.00
185 Alan Miller RC	1.50	3.00
186 Tom Flores RC	10.00	20.00
187 Joe Cannavino RC	1.50	3.00
188 Don Manoukian	1.50	3.00
189 Bob Coolbaugh RC	1.50	3.00
190 Lionel Taylor RC	4.00	8.00
191 Bud McFadin	1.50	3.00
192 Goose Gonsoulin RC	3.00	6.00
193 Frank Tripucka	2.00	4.00
194 Gene Mingo RC	2.00	4.00
195 Eldon Danenhauer RC	1.50	3.00
196 Bob McNamara	1.50	3.00
197 Dave Rolle UER RC	1.50	3.00
198 Checklist UER	40.00	80.00
AD1 Advertising Panel	150.00	250.00
Jim Martin		
George Shaw		
Jim Ray Smith		
AD2 Advertising Panel	175.00	300.00
Alex Karras		
Charley Conerly IA		
Jon Arnett		

1961 Topps Flocked Stickers Inserts

This set of 48 flocked stickers was inserted with the 1961 Topps regular issue football set. The stickers are unnumbered and are ordered below alphabetically within type. NFL teams are listed first (1-15), followed by AFL teams (16-24), and college teams (25-48). The capital letters in the listing below signify the letter on the detachable tab. The stickers measure approximately 2" by 2 3/4" without the letter tab and 2" by 3 3/8" with the letter tab. The prices below are for the stickers with tabs intact; stickers without tabs would be considered VG-E at best. There are letter tab variations on 12 of the stickers as noted by the double letters below. The complete set price below considers the set complete with the 48 different distinct teams, i.e., not including all 60 different tab combinations.

COMPLETE SET (48)	500.00	800.00
1 NFL Emblem N	10.00	20.00
2 Baltimore Colts U	10.00	20.00
3 Chicago Bears H	10.00	20.00
4 Cleveland Browns I	10.00	20.00
5 Dallas Cowboys K	25.00	40.00
6 Detroit Lions E	10.00	20.00
7 Green Bay Packers A	25.00	40.00
8 Los Angeles Rams M	10.00	20.00
9 Minnesota Vikings R	10.00	20.00
10 New York Giants D	10.00	20.00
11 Philadelphia Eagles O	10.00	20.00
12 Pittsburgh Steelers S	12.50	25.00
13 San Francisco 49ers P	10.00	20.00
14 St. Louis Cardinals L	10.00	20.00
15 Washington Redskins J	12.50	25.00
16 AFL Emblem A/G	10.00	20.00
17 Boston Patriots F/T	10.00	20.00
18 Buffalo Bills I/M	10.00	20.00
19 Dallas Texans P/R	12.50	25.00
20 Denver Broncos G/I	12.50	25.00
21 Houston Oilers A/H	10.00	20.00
22 Oakland Raiders B/O	18.00	30.00
23 San Diego Chargers E/K	10.00	20.00
24 New York Titans D/E	10.00	20.00
25 Air Force Falcons V	7.50	15.00
26 Alabama Crimson Tide L	10.00	20.00
27 Arkansas Razorbacks A	7.50	15.00
28 Army Cadets G	7.50	15.00
29 Baylor Bears E	7.50	15.00
30 California Golden Bears T	7.50	15.00
31 Georgia Tech F	7.50	15.00
32 Illinois Fighting Illini C	7.50	15.00
33 Kansas Jayhawks J	7.50	15.00
34 Kentucky Wildcats R	7.50	15.00
35 Miami Hurricanes H	7.50	15.00
36 Michigan Wolverines W	15.00	25.00
37 Missouri Tigers B	7.50	15.00
38 Navy Midshipmen J/S	7.50	15.00
39 Oregon Ducks C/N	7.50	15.00
40 Penn State Nittany Lions Z	10.00	20.00
41 Pittsburgh Panthers G	7.50	15.00
42 Purdue Boilermakers B	7.50	15.00
43 USC Trojans Y	7.50	15.00
44 Stanford Indians L/O	7.50	15.00
45 TCU Horned Frogs C	7.50	15.00
46 Virginia Cavaliers S	7.50	15.00
47 Washington Huskies D	7.50	15.00
48 Washington St.Cougers M UER	7.50	15.00

1962 Topps

The 1962 Topps football set contains 176 black-bordered standard-size cards. In designing the 1962 set, Topps chose a horizontally oriented card front for the first time since 1957. Two photos include a small action photo to the left that is joined by the player's name, team name and position. An up-close photo to the right covers majority of the card. Black borders, which are prone to chipping, make it quite difficult to put together a set in top grades. The short-printed (SP) cards are indicated in the checklist below. The shortage is probably attributable to the fact that the set size is not the standard 132-card, single-sheet size; hence all cards were not printed in equal amounts. Cards are again organized numerically in team order. The last card within each team grouping was a "rookie prospect" for that team. Many of the black and white inset photos on the card fronts (especially those of the rookie prospects) are not the player pictured and described on the card. The key Rookie Cards in this set are Ernie Davis, Mike Ditka, Roman Gabriel, Bill Kilmer, Norm Snead and Fran Tarkenton.

COMPLETE SET (176)	1200.00	2000.00
WRAPPER (1-CENT)	175.00	250.00
WRAPPER (5-CENT,STARS)	25.00	50.00
WRAPPER (5-CENT,BUCKS)	25.00	40.00
1 Johnny Unitas	125.00	200.00
2 Lenny Moore	6.00	12.00
3 Alex Hawkins SP RC	5.00	10.00
4 Joe Perry	4.00	8.00
5 Raymond Berry SP	25.00	40.00
6 Steve Myhra	2.00	4.00
7 Tom Gilburg SP RC	4.00	8.00
8 Gino Marchetti	4.00	8.00
9 Bill Pellington	2.00	4.00
10 Andy Nelson	2.00	4.00
11 Wendell Harris SP RC	4.00	8.00
12 Baltimore Colts Team	3.00	6.00
13 Bill Wade SP	5.00	10.00
14 Willie Galimore	2.50	5.00
15 Johnny Morris SP	4.00	8.00
16 Rick Casares	2.50	5.00
17 Mike Ditka RC	175.00	300.00
18 Stan Jones	3.00	6.00
19 Roger LeClerc RC	2.00	4.00
20 Angelo Coia RC	2.00	4.00
21 Doug Atkins	4.00	8.00
22 Bill George	3.00	6.00
23 Richie Petitbon RC	2.50	5.00
24 Ronnie Bull SP RC	4.00	8.00
25 Chicago Bears Team	3.00	6.00
26 Howard Cassady	2.50	5.00
27 Ray Renfro SP	5.00	10.00
28 Jim Brown	100.00	175.00
29 Rich Kreitling RC	2.00	4.00
30 Jim Ray Smith	2.00	4.00
31 John Morrow	2.00	4.00
32 Lou Groza	7.50	15.00
33 Bob Gain	2.00	4.00
34 Bernie Parrish RC	2.00	4.00
35 Jim Shofner	2.00	4.00
36 Ernie Davis SP RC	90.00	150.00
37 Cleveland Browns Team	3.00	6.00
38 Eddie LeBaron	2.50	5.00
39 Don Meredith SP	60.00	100.00
40 J.W. Lockett SP RC	4.00	8.00
41 Don Perkins RC	7.50	15.00
42 Billy Howton	2.50	5.00
43 Dick Bielski	2.00	4.00
44 Mike Connelly RC	2.00	4.00
45 Jerry Tubbs SP	4.00	8.00
46 Don Bishop SP RC	4.00	8.00
47 Dick Moegle	2.00	4.00
48 Bobby Plummer SP RC	4.00	8.00
49 Dallas Cowboys Team	12.00	20.00
50 Milt Plum	2.50	5.00
51 Dan Lewis	2.00	4.00
52 Nick Pietrosante SP	4.00	8.00
53 Gail Cogdill	2.00	4.00
54 Jim Gibbons	2.00	4.00
55 Jim Martin	2.00	4.00
56 Yale Lary	3.00	6.00
57 Darris McCord	2.00	4.00
58 Alex Karras	15.00	25.00
59 Joe Schmidt	4.00	8.00
60 Dick Lane	3.00	6.00
61 John Lomakoski SP RC	4.00	8.00
62 Detroit Lions Team SP	10.00	18.00
63 Bart Starr SP	75.00	125.00
64 Paul Hornung SP	60.00	100.00
65 Tom Moore SP	6.00	12.00
66 Jim Taylor SP	30.00	50.00
67 Max McGee SP	6.00	15.00
68 Jim Ringo SP	7.50	15.00
69 Fuzzy Thurston SP RC	18.00	30.00
70 Forrest Gregg	4.00	8.00
71 Boyd Dowler	3.00	6.00
72 Hank Jordan SP	7.50	15.00
73 Bill Forester SP	5.00	10.00
74 Earl Gros SP RC	4.00	8.00
75 Green Bay Packers Team SP	25.00	40.00
76 Checklist SP	50.00	80.00
77 Zeke Bratkowski SP	5.00	10.00
78 Jon Arnett SP	5.00	10.00
79 Ollie Matson SP	20.00	35.00
80 Dick Bass SP	5.00	10.00
81 Jim Phillips	2.00	4.00
82 Carroll Dale RC	2.50	5.00
83 Frank Varrichione	2.00	4.00
84 Art Hunter	2.00	4.00
85 Danny Villanueva RC	2.00	4.00
86 Les Richter SP	4.00	8.00
87 Lindon Crow	2.00	4.00
88 Roman Gabriel SP RC	35.00	60.00
89 Los Angeles Rams Team SP	10.00	18.00
90 Fran Tarkenton SP RC	125.00	225.00
91 Jerry Reichow SP RC	4.00	8.00
92 Hugh McElhenny SP	18.00	30.00
93 Mel Triplett SP	4.00	8.00
94 Tommy Mason SP RC	6.00	12.00
95 Dave Middleton SP	4.00	8.00
96 Frank Youso SP	4.00	8.00
97 Mike Mercer SP RC	4.00	8.00
98 Rip Hawkins SP	4.00	8.00
99 Cliff Livingston SP RC	4.00	8.00
100 Roy Winston SP RC	4.00	8.00
101 Minnesota Vikings Team SP	15.00	25.00
102 Y.A.Tittle	25.00	40.00
103 Joe Walton	2.00	4.00
104 Frank Gifford	30.00	50.00
105 Alex Webster	2.50	5.00
106 Del Shofner	2.50	5.00
107 Don Chandler	2.00	4.00
108 Andy Robustelli	4.00	8.00
109 Jim Katcavage RC	2.50	5.00
110 Sam Huff SP	25.00	40.00
111 Erich Barnes	2.00	4.00
112 Jim Patton	2.00	4.00
113 Jerry Hillebrand SP RC	4.00	8.00
114 New York Giants Team	3.00	6.00
115 Sonny Jurgensen	25.00	40.00
116 Tommy McDonald	4.00	8.00
117 Ted Dean SP	4.00	8.00
118 Clarence Peaks	2.00	4.00
119 Bobby Walston	2.00	4.00
120 Pete Retzlaff SP	5.00	10.00
121 Jim Schrader SP	4.00	8.00
122 J.D. Smith T RC	2.00	4.00
123 King Hill	2.00	4.00
124 Maxie Baughan	2.50	5.00
125 Pete Case SP RC	4.00	8.00
126 Philadelphia Eagles Team	3.00	6.00
127 Bobby Layne UER	25.00	40.00
128 Tom Tracy	2.50	5.00
129 John Henry Johnson	3.00	6.00
130 Buddy Dial SP	5.00	10.00
131 Preston Carpenter	2.00	4.00
132 Lou Michaels SP	4.00	8.00
133 Gene Lipscomb SP	5.00	10.00
134 Ernie Stautner SP	12.00	20.00
135 John Reger SP	4.00	8.00
136 Myron Pottios RC	2.00	4.00
137 Bob Ferguson SP RC	4.00	8.00
138 Pittsburgh Steelers Team SP	10.00	18.00
139 Sam Etcheverry	2.50	5.00
140 John David Crow SP	5.00	10.00
141 Bobby Joe Conrad SP	5.00	10.00
142 Prentice Gautt SP RC	4.00	8.00
143 Frank Mestnik	2.00	4.00
144 Sonny Randle	2.50	5.00
145 Gerry Perry UER RC	2.00	4.00
146 Jerry Norton	2.00	4.00
147 Jimmy Hill RC	2.00	4.00
148 Bill Stacy	2.00	4.00
149 Fate Echols SP RC	4.00	8.00
150 St. Louis Cardinals Team	3.00	6.00
151 Billy Kilmer RC	25.00	40.00
152 John Brodie	10.00	18.00
153 J.D. Smith RB	2.50	5.00
154 C.R. Roberts SP RC	4.00	8.00
155 Monty Stickles	2.00	4.00
156 Clyde Conner UER	2.00	4.00
157 Bob St.Clair	3.00	6.00
158 Tommy Davis RC	2.00	4.00
159 Leo Nomellini	4.00	8.00
160 Matt Hazeltine	2.00	4.00
161 Abe Woodson	2.00	4.00
162 Dave Baker	2.00	4.00
163 San Francisco 49ers Team	3.00	6.00
164 Norm Snead SP RC	18.00	30.00
165 Dick James	2.50	5.00
166 Bobby Mitchell	4.00	8.00
167 Sam Horner RC	2.00	4.00
168 Bill Barnes	2.00	4.00
169 Bill Anderson	2.00	4.00
170 Fred Dugan	2.00	4.00
171 John Aveni SP RC	4.00	8.00
172 Bob Toneff	2.00	4.00
173 Jim Kerr RC	2.00	4.00
174 Leroy Jackson SP RC	4.00	8.00
175 Washington Redskins Team	5.00	10.00
176 Checklist	60.00	100.00

1962 Topps Bucks Inserts

The 1962 Topps Football Bucks set contains 48 cards and was issued as an insert into wax packs of the 1962 Topps regular issue of football cards. Printing was done with black and green ink on off-white (very thin) paper stock. Bucks are typically found with a fold crease in the middle as they were inserted in packs in that manner. These "football bucks" measure approximately 1 1/4" by 4 1/4". Mike Ditka and Fran Tarkenton appear in their Rookie Card year.

COMPLETE SET (48)	350.00	450.00
1 J.D. Smith	2.00	4.00
2 Bart Starr	15.00	30.00
3 Dick James	2.00	4.00
4 Alex Webster	2.50	5.00
5 Paul Hornung	10.00	20.00
6 John David Crow	2.50	5.00
7 Jim Brown	30.00	50.00
8 Don Perkins	2.50	5.00
9 Bobby Walston	2.00	4.00
10 Jim Phillips	2.00	4.00
11 Y.A. Tittle	7.50	15.00
12 Sonny Randle	2.00	4.00
13 Jerry Reichow	2.00	4.00
14 Yale Lary	3.00	6.00
15 Buddy Dial	2.50	5.00
16 Ray Renfro	2.50	5.00
17 Norm Snead	3.00	6.00
18 Leo Nomellini	3.00	6.00
19 Hugh McElhenny	5.00	10.00
20 Eddie LeBaron	2.50	5.00
21 Billy Howton	2.50	5.00
22 Bobby Mitchell	4.00	8.00
23 Nick Pietrosante	2.00	4.00

Card		
24 Johnny Unitas	20.00	40.00
25 Raymond Berry	5.00	10.00
26 Billy Kilmer	4.00	8.00
27 Lenny Moore	5.00	10.00
28 Tommy McDonald	3.00	6.00
29 Del Shofner	2.50	5.00
30 Jim Taylor	7.50	15.00
31 Joe Schmidt	4.00	8.00
32 Bill George	3.00	6.00
33 Fran Tarkenton	30.00	50.00
34 Willie Galimore	2.50	5.00
35 Bobby Layne	7.50	15.00
36 Max McGee	2.50	5.00
37 Jon Arnett	2.50	5.00
38 Lou Groza	6.00	12.00
39 Frank Varrichione	2.00	4.00
40 Milt Plum	2.50	5.00
41 Prentice Gautt	2.00	4.00
42 Bill Wade	2.50	5.00
43 Gino Marchetti	4.00	8.00
44 John Brodie	5.00	10.00
45 Sonny Jurgensen UER	7.50	15.00
46 Clarence Peaks	2.50	5.00
47 Mike Ditka	15.00	30.00
48 John Henry Johnson	4.00	8.00

1963 Topps

The 1963 Topps set contains 170 standard-size cards of NFL players grouped together by teams. The card backs are printed in light orange ink on white card stock. Statistical information from the immediate past season and career totals are given on the reverse. The illustrated trivia question on the reverse (of each card) could be answered by placing red cellophane paper (which was inserted into wax packs) over the card. The 76 cards indicated by SP below are in shorter supply than the others because the set size is not the standard 132-card, single-sheet size; hence, all cards were not printed in equal amounts. There also exists a three-card advertising panel consisting of card fronts of Charlie Johnson, John David Crow and Bobby Joe Conrad. The back of the latter two players contains ad copy and a Y.A. Tittle card back on Johnson. Interestingly, Y.A. Tittle was also used as the player featured on the full box of packs. Finally, many of the cards in the set were printed with color variations in the background of the player photo, thus resulting in one version of the photo that appears to have a purple tinted background while the other is a color corrected blue background. This is most evident on cards with a large portion of sky in the background of the photo. Most collectors feel that the "purple" sky version was generally printed in shorter supply, but the market has not yet clearly indicated any price differences thus far.

75100202

1963 Topps

Card		
COMPLETE SET (170)	850.00	1350.00
WRAPPER (1-CENT)	1000.00	1500.00
WRAPPER (5-CENT)	50.00	80.00
1 Johnny Unitas	75.00	135.00
2 Lenny Moore	4.00	8.00
3 Jimmy Orr	1.50	3.00
4 Raymond Berry	4.00	8.00
5 Jim Parker	2.50	5.00
6 Alex Sandusky	1.25	2.50
7 Dick Szymanski RC	1.25	2.50
8 Gino Marchetti	3.00	6.00
9 Billy Ray Smith RC	1.50	3.00
10 Bill Pellington	1.25	2.50
11 Bob Boyd DB RC	1.25	2.50
12 Baltimore Colts SP	5.00	10.00
13 Frank Ryan SP	4.00	8.00
14 Jim Brown SP	100.00	200.00
15 Ray Renfro SP	4.00	8.00
16 Rich Kreitling SP	3.50	6.00
17 Mike McCormack SP	5.00	10.00
18 Jim Ray Smith SP	3.50	6.00
19 Lou Groza SP	15.00	25.00
20 Bill Glass SP	3.50	6.00
21 Galen Fiss SP	3.50	6.00
22 Don Fleming SP RC	4.00	8.00
23 Bob Gain SP	3.50	6.00
24 Cleveland Browns SP	5.00	10.00
25 Milt Plum	1.50	3.00
26 Dan Lewis	1.25	2.50
27 Nick Pietrosante	1.25	2.50
28 Gail Cogdill	1.25	2.50
29 Harley Sewell	1.25	2.50
30 Jim Gibbons	1.25	2.50
31 Carl Brettschneider	1.25	2.50
32 Dick Lane	2.50	5.00
33 Yale Lary	2.50	5.00
34 Roger Brown RC	1.50	3.00
35 Joe Schmidt	3.00	6.00
36 Detroit Lions SP	5.00	10.00
37 Roman Gabriel	4.00	8.00
38 Zeke Bratkowski	1.50	3.00
39 Dick Bass	1.50	3.00
40 Jon Arnett	1.50	3.00
41 Jim Phillips	1.25	2.50
42 Frank Varrichione	1.25	2.50
43 Danny Villanueva	1.25	2.50
44 Deacon Jones RC	35.00	60.00
45 Lindon Crow	1.25	2.50
46 Marlin McKeever RC	1.25	2.50
47 Ed Meador RC	1.25	2.50
48 Los Angeles Rams	2.00	4.00
49 Y.A.Tittle SP	30.00	50.00
50 Del Shofner SP	3.50	6.00
51 Alex Webster SP	4.00	8.00
52 Phil King SP RC	3.50	6.00
53 Jack Stroud SP	3.50	6.00
54 Darrell Dess SP	3.50	6.00
55 Jim Katcavage SP	3.50	6.00
56 Roosevelt Grier SP	5.00	10.00
57 Erich Barnes SP	3.50	6.00
58 Jim Patton SP	3.50	6.00
59 Sam Huff SP	12.00	20.00
60 New York Giants	2.00	4.00
61 Bill Wade	1.50	3.00
62 Mike Ditka	35.00	60.00
63 Johnny Morris	1.25	2.50
64 Roger LeClerc	1.25	2.50
65 Roger Davis RC	1.25	2.50
66 Joe Marconi	1.25	2.50
67 Herman Lee RC	1.25	2.50
68 Doug Atkins	3.00	6.00
69 Joe Fortunato	1.25	2.50
70 Bill George	2.50	5.00
71 Richie Petitbon	1.50	3.00
72 Bears Team SP	5.00	10.00
73 Eddie LeBaron SP	5.00	10.00
74 Don Meredith SP	35.00	60.00
75 Don Perkins SP	5.00	10.00
76 Amos Marsh SP RC	3.50	6.00
77 Billy Howton SP	4.00	8.00
78 Andy Cvercko SP RC	3.50	6.00
79 Sam Baker SP	3.50	6.00
80 Jerry Tubbs SP	3.50	6.00
81 Don Bishop SP	3.50	6.00
82 Bob Lilly SP RC	100.00	175.00
83 Jerry Norton SP	3.50	6.00
84 Cowboys Team SP	12.00	20.00
85 Checklist 1	15.00	25.00
86 Bart Starr	40.00	75.00
87 Jim Taylor	18.00	30.00
88 Boyd Dowler	2.50	5.00
89 Forrest Gregg	3.00	6.00
90 Fuzzy Thurston	3.00	6.00
91 Jim Ringo	3.00	6.00
92 Ron Kramer	1.50	3.00
93 Hank Jordan	3.00	6.00
94 Bill Forester	1.50	3.00
95 Willie Wood RC	25.00	40.00
96 Ray Nitschke RC	90.00	150.00
97 Green Bay Packers	7.50	15.00
98 Fran Tarkenton	35.00	60.00
99 Tommy Mason	1.50	3.00
100 Mel Triplett	1.25	2.50
101 Jerry Reichow	1.25	2.50
102 Frank Youso	1.25	2.50
103 Hugh McElhenny	4.00	8.00
104 Gerald Huth RC	1.25	2.50
105 Ed Sharockman RC	1.25	2.50
106 Rip Hawkins	1.25	2.50
107 Jim Marshall RC	20.00	40.00
108 Jim Prestel RC	1.25	2.50
109 Minnesota Vikings	2.00	4.00
110 Sonny Jurgensen SP	15.00	25.00
111 Timmy Brown SP RC	5.00	10.00
112 Tommy McDonald SP	7.50	15.00
113 Clarence Peaks SP	3.50	6.00
114 Pete Retzlaff SP	4.00	8.00
115 Jim Schrader SP	3.50	6.00
116 Jim McCusker SP	3.50	6.00
117 Don Burroughs SP	3.50	6.00
118 Maxie Baughan SP	3.50	6.00
119 Riley Gunnels SP RC	3.50	6.00
120 Jimmy Carr SP	3.50	6.00
121 Philadelphia Eagles SP	5.00	10.00
122 Ed Brown SP	4.00	8.00
123 John H.Johnson SP	7.50	15.00
124 Buddy Dial SP	3.50	6.00
125 Bill Red Mack SP RC	3.50	6.00
126 Preston Carpenter SP	3.50	6.00
127 Ray Lemek SP RC	3.50	6.00
128 Buzz Nutter SP	3.50	6.00
129 Ernie Stautner SP	7.50	15.00
130 Lou Michaels SP	3.50	6.00
131 Clendon Thomas SP RC	3.50	6.00
132 Tom Bettis SP	3.50	6.00
133 Pittsburgh Steelers SP	5.00	10.00
134 John Brodie	4.00	8.00
135 J.D. Smith	1.25	2.50
136 Billy Kilmer	2.50	5.00
137 Bernie Casey RC	1.50	3.00
138 Tommy Davis	1.25	2.50
139 Ted Connolly RC	1.25	2.50
140 Bob St.Clair	2.50	5.00
141 Abe Woodson	1.25	2.50
142 Matt Hazeltine	1.25	2.50
143 Leo Nomellini	3.00	6.00
144 Dan Colchico RC	1.25	2.50
145 San Francisco 49ers SP	5.00	10.00
146 Charley Johnson RC	4.00	8.00
147 John David Crow	1.50	3.00
148 Bobby Joe Conrad	1.50	3.00
149 Sonny Randle	1.25	2.50
150 Prentice Gautt	1.25	2.50
151 Taz Anderson RC	1.25	2.50
152 Ernie McMillan RC	1.50	3.00
153 Jimmy Hill	1.25	2.50
154 Bill Koman RC	1.25	2.50
155 Larry Wilson RC	12.00	20.00
156 Don Owens	1.25	2.50
157 St. Louis Cardinals SP	5.00	10.00
158 Norm Snead SP	5.00	10.00
159 Bobby Mitchell SP	7.50	15.00
160 Bill Barnes SP	3.50	6.00
161 Fred Dugan SP	3.50	6.00
162 Don Bosseler SP	3.50	6.00
163 John Nisby SP	3.50	6.00
164 Riley Mattson SP RC	3.50	6.00
165 Bob Toneff SP	3.50	6.00
166 Rod Breedlove SP RC	3.50	6.00
167 Dick James SP	3.50	6.00
168 Claude Crabb SP RC	3.50	6.00
169 Washington Redskins SP	5.00	10.00
170 Checklist 2 UER	30.00	50.00
AD1 C.Johnson/Crow/Conrad AD	600.00	1000.00

1964 Topps

The 1964 Topps football set begins a run of four straight years that Topps issued cards of American Football League (AFL) player cards. The cards in this 176-card set measure the standard size and are grouped by teams. Because the cards were not printed on a standard 132-card sheet, some cards are printed in lesser quantities than others. These cards are marked in the checklist with SP for short print. Cards fronts feature white boders with tiny red stars outlining the photo. The player's name, team and position are in a black box beneath the photo. The backs of the cards contain the card number, vital statistics, a short biography, the player's record for the past year and his career, and a cartoon-illustrated question and answer section. The cards are organized alphabetically within teams. The key Rookie Cards in this set are Bobby Bell, Buck Buchanan, John Hadl, and Darylc Lamonica.

Card		
COMPLETE SET (176)	1000.00	1500.00
WRAPPER (1-CENT)	60.00	100.00
WRAPPER (5-CENT, PENN)	75.00	125.00
WRAP. (5-CENT, 8-CARD)	90.00	150.00
1 Tommy Addison SP	15.00	40.00
2 Houston Antwine RC	2.00	4.00
3 Nick Buoniconti	15.00	25.00
4 Ron Burton SP	5.00	10.00
5 Gino Cappelletti	2.50	5.00
6 Jim Colclough SP	3.00	6.00
7 Bob Dee SP	3.00	6.00
8 Larry Eisenhauer	2.00	4.00
9 Dick Felt SP	3.00	6.00
10 Larry Garron	2.00	4.00
11 Art Graham RC	2.00	4.00
12 Ron Hall DB RC	2.00	4.00
13 Charles Long	2.00	4.00
14 Don McKinnon RC	2.00	4.00
15 Don Oakes SP RC	3.00	6.00
16 Ross O'Hanley SP	3.00	6.00
17 Babe Parilli SP	5.00	10.00
18 Jesse Richardson SP	3.00	6.00
19 Jack Rudolph SP RC	3.00	6.00
20 Don Webb RC	2.00	4.00
21 Boston Patriots	3.00	6.00
22 Ray Abruzzese UER	2.00	4.00
23 Stew Barber RC	2.00	4.00
24 Dave Behrman RC	2.00	4.00
25 Al Bemiller RC	2.00	4.00
26 Elbert Dubenion SP	5.00	10.00
27 Jim Dunaway SP RC	3.00	6.00
28 Booker Edgerson SP	3.00	6.00
29 Cookie Gilchrist SP	15.00	25.00
30 Jack Kemp SP	50.00	100.00
31 Daryle Lamonica RC	35.00	60.00
32 Bill Miller	2.00	4.00
33 Herb Paterra RC	2.00	4.00
34 Ken Rice SP	3.00	6.00
35 Ed Rutkowski UER RC	2.00	4.00
36 George Saimes RC	2.00	4.00
37 Tom Sestak	2.00	4.00
38 Billy Shaw SP	7.50	15.00
39 Mike Stratton	2.50	5.00
40 Gene Sykes RC	2.00	4.00
41 John Tracey SP RC	3.00	6.00
42 Sid Youngelman SP	3.00	6.00
43 Buffalo Bills	3.00	6.00
44 Eldon Danenhauer SP	3.00	6.00
45 Jim Fraser SP	3.00	6.00
46 Chuck Gavin SP	3.00	6.00
47 Goose Gonsoulin SP	5.00	10.00
48 Ernie Barnes RC	2.00	4.00
49 Tom Janik RC	2.00	4.00
50 Billy Joe RC	2.50	5.00
51 Ike Lassiter RC	2.00	4.00
52 John McCormick SP RC	3.00	6.00
53 Bud McFadin SP	3.00	6.00
54 Gene Mingo SP	3.00	6.00
55 Charlie Mitchell RC	2.00	4.00
56 John Nocera SP RC	3.00	6.00
57 Tom Nomina RC	2.00	4.00
58 Harold Olson SP RC	3.00	6.00
59 Bob Scarpitto	2.00	4.00
60 John Sklopan RC	2.00	4.00
61 Mickey Slaughter RC	2.00	4.00
62 Don Stone	2.00	4.00
63 Jerry Sturm RC	2.00	4.00
64 Lionel Taylor SP	6.00	12.00
65 Broncos Team SP	10.00	20.00
66 Scott Appleton RC	2.00	4.00
67 Tony Banfield SP	3.00	6.00
68 George Blanda SP	40.00	80.00
69 Billy Cannon	3.00	6.00
70 Doug Cline SP	3.00	6.00
71 Gary Cutsinger SP RC	3.00	6.00
72 Willard Dewveall SP RC	3.00	6.00
73 Don Floyd SP	3.00	6.00
74 Freddy Glick SP RC	3.00	6.00
75 Charlie Hennigan SP	5.00	10.00
76 Ed Husmann SP	3.00	6.00
77 Bobby Jancik SP RC	3.00	6.00
78 Jacky Lee SP	5.00	10.00
79 Bob McLeod SP RC	3.00	6.00
80 Rich Michael SP	3.00	6.00
81 Larry Onesti RC	2.00	4.00
82 Checklist Card UER	30.00	60.00
83 Bob Schmidt SP RC	3.00	6.00
84 Walt Suggs SP RC	3.00	6.00
85 Bob Talamini SP	3.00	6.00
86 Charley Tolar SP	3.00	6.00
87 Don Trull RC	2.00	4.00
88 Houston Oilers	3.00	6.00
89 Fred Arbanas	2.00	4.00
90 Bobby Bell RC	25.00	40.00
91 Mel Branch SP	5.00	10.00
92 Buck Buchanan RC	25.00	40.00
93 Ed Budde RC	2.00	4.00
94 Chris Burford SP	5.00	10.00
95 Walt Corey RC	2.50	5.00
96 Len Dawson SP	40.00	75.00
97 Dave Grayson RC	2.00	4.00
98 Abner Haynes	3.00	6.00
99 Sherrill Headrick SP	5.00	10.00
100 E.J. Holub	2.00	4.00
101 Bobby Hunt RC	2.00	4.00
102 Frank Jackson SP	3.00	6.00
103 Curtis McClinton	2.50	5.00
104 Jerry Mays SP	5.00	10.00
105 Johnny Robinson SP	6.00	12.00
106 Jack Spikes SP	3.00	6.00
107 Smokey Stover SP RC	3.00	6.00
108 Jim Tyrer RC	5.00	10.00
109 Duane Wood SP RC	3.00	6.00
110 Kansas City Chiefs	3.00	6.00
111 Dick Christy SP	3.00	6.00
112 Dan Ficca SP RC	3.00	6.00
113 Larry Grantham	2.00	4.00
114 Curley Johnson SP	3.00	6.00
115 Gene Heeter RC	2.00	4.00
116 Jack Klotz RC	2.00	4.00
117 Pete Liske RC	2.50	5.00
118 Bob McAdam RC	2.00	4.00
119 Dee Mackey SP RC	3.00	6.00
120 Bill Mathis SP	5.00	10.00
121 Don Maynard	20.00	35.00
122 Dainard Paulson SP	3.00	6.00
123 Gerry Philbin RC	2.50	5.00
124 Mark Smolinski SP RC	3.00	6.00
125 Matt Snell RC	10.00	20.00
126 Mike Taliaferro RC	2.00	4.00
127 Bake Turner SP RC	5.00	10.00
128 Jeff Ware RC	2.00	4.00
129 Clyde Washington RC	2.00	4.00
130 Dick Wood RC	2.00	4.00
131 New York Jets	3.00	6.00
132 Dalva Allen SP	3.00	6.00
133 Dan Birdwell RC	2.00	4.00
134 Dave Costa RC	2.00	4.00
135 Dobie Craig RC	2.00	4.00
136 Clem Daniels	2.50	5.00
137 Cotton Davidson SP	5.00	10.00
138 Claude Gibson RC	2.00	4.00
139 Tom Flores SP	7.50	15.00
140 Wayne Hawkins SP	3.00	6.00
141 Ken Herock RC	2.00	4.00
142 Jon Jelacic SP RC	3.00	6.00
143 Joe Krakoski RC	2.00	4.00
144 Archie Matsos SP	3.00	6.00
145 Mike Mercer	2.00	4.00
146 Alan Miller SP	3.00	6.00
147 Bob Mischak SP	3.00	6.00
148 Jim Otto SP	18.00	30.00
149 Clancy Osborne SP	3.00	6.00
150 Art Powell SP	6.00	12.00
151 Bo Roberson	2.00	4.00
152 Fred Williamson SP	18.00	30.00
153 Oakland Raiders	3.00	6.00
154 Chuck Allen SP RC	5.00	10.00
155 Lance Alworth	30.00	50.00
156 George Blair RC	2.00	4.00
157 Earl Faison	2.00	4.00
158 Sam Gruneisen RC	2.00	4.00
159 John Hadl RC	25.00	40.00
160 Dick Harris SP	3.00	6.00
161 Emil Karas SP RC	3.00	6.00
162 Dave Kocourek SP	3.00	6.00
163 Ernie Ladd	4.00	8.00
164 Keith Lincoln	3.00	6.00
165 Paul Lowe SP	6.00	12.00
166 Charlie McNeil	2.00	4.00
167 Jacque MacKinnon SP RC	3.00	6.00
168 Ron Mix SP	10.00	20.00
169 Don Norton SP	3.00	6.00
170 Don Rogers SP RC	3.00	6.00
171 Tobin Rote SP	5.00	10.00
172 Henry Schmidt SP RC	3.00	6.00
173 Bud Whitehead RC	2.00	4.00
174 Ernie Wright SP	5.00	10.00
175 San Diego Chargers	3.00	6.00
176 Checklist SP UER	80.00	160.00
AD1 Advertising Panel	250.00	400.00
Larry Eisenhauer		
Bo Roberson		
K.C. Chiefs Team		

1964 Topps Pennant Stickers Inserts

This set of 24 pennant stickers was inserted into the 1964 Topps regular issue AFL set. These inserts are actually 2 1/8" by 4 1/2" glassine type peel-offs on gray backing. The pennants are unnumbered and are ordered below alphabetically within type. The stickers were folded in order to fit into the 1964 Topps wax packs, so they are virtually always found with a crease or fold.

Card		
COMPLETE SET (24)	750.00	1500.00
1 Boston Patriots	50.00	100.00
2 Buffalo Bills	50.00	100.00
3 Denver Broncos	60.00	120.00
4 Houston Oilers	50.00	100.00
5 Kansas City Chiefs	50.00	100.00
6 New York Jets	50.00	100.00
7 Oakland Raiders	60.00	120.00
8 San Diego Chargers	50.00	100.00
9 Air Force Falcons	30.00	60.00
10 Army Cadets	30.00	60.00
11 Dartmouth Indians	30.00	60.00
12 Duke Blue Devils	30.00	60.00
13 Michigan Wolverines	37.50	75.00
14 Minnesota Golden Gophers	30.00	60.00
15 Mississippi Rebels	30.00	60.00
16 Navy Midshipmen	30.00	60.00
17 Notre Dame Fight.Irish	75.00	150.00
18 SMU Mustangs	30.00	60.00
19 USC Trojans	30.00	60.00
20 Syracuse Orangemen	30.00	60.00
21 Texas Longhorns	30.00	60.00
22 Washington Huskies	30.00	60.00
23 Wisconsin Badgers	30.00	60.00
24 Yale Bulldogs	30.00	60.00

1965 Topps

The 1965 Topps football card set contains 176 oversized (2 1/2" by 4 11/16") cards of American Football League players. Colorful card fronts have a player photo over a solid color background. The team name is at the top with the player's name and position at the bottom. Horizontal backs contain highlights and statistics to the left with a cartoon pertaining to the player to the right. The cards are grouped together and numbered in basic alphabetical order by teams. Since this set was not printed in the standard fashion, many of the cards were printed in lesser quantities than others. These cards are marked in the checklist with SP for short print. This set is somewhat significant in that it contains the Rookie Card of Joe Namath. Other notable Rookie Cards in this set of Oakland Raiders stars Fred Biletnikoff, Willie Brown and Ben Davidson.

Card		
COMPLETE SET (176)	2500.00	4000.00
WRAPPER (5-CENT)	90.00	150.00
1 Tommy Addison SP	20.00	35.00
2 Houston Antwine SP	7.00	12.00
3 Nick Buoniconti SP	18.00	30.00
4 Ron Burton SP	10.00	20.00
5 Gino Cappelletti SP	10.00	20.00
6 Jim Colclough	3.50	7.00
7 Bob Dee SP	7.00	12.00
8 Larry Eisenhauer	3.50	7.00
9 J.D. Garrett RC	3.50	7.00
10 Larry Garron	3.50	7.00
11 Art Graham SP	7.00	12.00
12 Ron Hall DB	3.50	7.00
13 Charles Long	3.50	7.00
14 Jon Morris RC	5.00	10.00
15 Billy Neighbors SP	7.00	12.00
16 Ross O'Hanley	3.50	7.00
17 Babe Parilli SP	10.00	20.00
18 Tony Romeo SP RC	7.00	12.00
19 Jack Rudolph SP	7.00	12.00
20 Bob Schmidt	3.50	7.00
21 Don Webb SP	7.00	12.00
22 Jim Whalen SP RC	7.00	12.00
23 Stew Barber	3.50	7.00
24 Glenn Bass SP RC	7.00	12.00
25 Al Bemiller SP	7.00	12.00
26 Wray Carlton SP	7.00	12.00
27 Tom Day RC	3.50	7.00
28 Elbert Dubenion SP	7.50	15.00
29 Jim Dunaway	3.50	7.00
30 Pete Gogolak SP RC	10.00	20.00
31 Dick Hudson SP	7.00	12.00
32 Harry Jacobs SP	7.00	12.00
33 Billy Joe SP	7.50	15.00
34 Tom Keating SP RC	7.00	12.00
35 Jack Kemp SP	75.00	150.00
36 Daryle Lamonica SP	30.00	50.00
37 Paul Maguire SP	10.00	20.00
38 Ron McDole SP RC	7.00	12.00
39 George Saimes SP	7.00	12.00
40 Tom Sestak SP	7.00	12.00
41 Billy Shaw SP	10.00	20.00
42 Mike Stratton SP	7.00	12.00
43 John Tracey SP	7.00	12.00
44 Ernie Warlick	3.50	7.00
45 Odell Barry RC	3.50	7.00
46 Willie Brown SP RC	75.00	135.00
47 Gerry Bussell SP RC	7.00	12.00
48 Eldon Danenhauer SP	7.00	12.00
49 Al Denson SP RC	7.00	12.00
50 Hewritt Dixon SP RC	7.50	15.00
51 Cookie Gilchrist SP	18.00	30.00
52 Goose Gonsoulin SP	7.50	15.00
53 Abner Haynes SP	10.00	20.00
54 Jerry Hopkins RC	3.50	7.00
55 Ray Jacobs SP	7.00	12.00
56 Jacky Lee SP	7.50	15.00
57 John McCormick QB	3.50	7.00
58 Bob McCullough SP	7.00	12.00
59 John McGeever RC	3.50	7.00
60 Charlie Mitchell SP	7.00	12.00
61 Jim Perkins SP RC	7.00	12.00
62 Bob Scarpitto SP	7.00	12.00
63 Mickey Slaughter SP	7.00	12.00
64 Jerry Sturm SP	7.00	12.00
65 Lionel Taylor SP	10.00	20.00
66 Scott Appleton SP	7.00	12.00
67 Johnny Baker SP RC	7.00	12.00
68 Sonny Bishop SP RC	7.00	12.00
69 George Blanda SP	75.00	125.00
70 Sid Blanks SP RC	7.00	12.00
71 Ode Burrell SP RC	7.00	12.00
72 Doug Cline SP	7.00	12.00
73 Willard Dewveall	3.50	7.00
74 Larry Elkins RC	3.50	7.00
75 Don Floyd SP	7.00	12.00
76 Freddy Glick	3.50	7.00
77 Tom Goode SP RC	7.00	12.00
78 Charlie Hennigan SP	10.00	20.00
79 Ed Husmann	3.50	7.00
80 Bobby Jancik SP	7.00	12.00
81 Bud McFadin SP	7.00	12.00
82 Bob McLeod SP	7.00	12.00
83 Jim Norton SP	7.00	12.00
84 Walt Suggs	3.50	7.00
85 Bob Talamini	3.50	7.00
86 Charley Tolar SP	7.00	12.00
87 Checklist SP	100.00	175.00
88 Don Trull SP	7.00	12.00
89 Fred Arbanas SP	7.00	12.00
90 Pete Beathard SP RC	7.00	12.00
91 Bobby Bell SP	25.00	40.00
92 Mel Branch SP	7.00	12.00
93 Tommy Brooker SP RC	7.00	12.00
94 Buck Buchanan SP	20.00	35.00
95 Ed Budde SP	7.00	12.00
96 Chris Burford SP	7.00	12.00
97 Walt Corey	3.50	7.00
98 Jerry Cornelison	3.50	7.00
99 Len Dawson SP	60.00	100.00
100 Jon Gilliam SP RC	7.00	12.00
101 Sherrill Headrick SP UER	7.00	12.00
102 Dave Hill SP RC	7.00	12.00
103 E.J. Holub SP	7.00	12.00
104 Bobby Hunt SP	7.00	12.00
105 Frank Jackson SP	7.00	12.00
106 Jerry Mays	5.00	10.00
107 Curtis McClinton SP	7.50	15.00
108 Bobby Ply SP RC	7.00	12.00
109 Johnny Robinson SP	7.50	15.00
110 Jim Tyrer SP	7.00	12.00
111 Bill Baird SP RC	7.00	12.00
112 Ralph Baker SP RC	7.00	12.00
113 Sam DeLuca SP	7.00	12.00
114 Larry Grantham SP	7.50	15.00
115 Gene Heeter SP	7.00	12.00
116 Winston Hill SP RC	10.00	20.00
117 John Huarte SP RC	18.00	30.00
118 Cosmo Iacavazzi SP RC	7.00	12.00
119 Curley Johnson SP	7.00	12.00
120 Dee Mackey UER	3.50	7.00
121 Don Maynard	30.00	50.00
122 Joe Namath SP RC	1200.00	1800.00
123 Dainard Paulson	3.50	7.00
124 Gerry Philbin SP	7.00	12.00
125 Sherman Plunkett SP RC	7.50	15.00
126 Mark Smolinski	3.50	7.00
127 Matt Snell SP	18.00	30.00
128 Mike Taliaferro SP	7.00	12.00
129 Bake Turner SP	7.00	12.00
130 Clyde Washington SP	7.00	12.00
131 Verlon Biggs SP RC	7.00	12.00
132 Dalva Allen	3.50	7.00
133 Fred Biletnikoff SP RC	150.00	250.00
134 Billy Cannon SP	10.00	20.00
135 Dave Costa SP	7.00	12.00
136 Clem Daniels SP	7.50	15.00
137 Ben Davidson SP RC	35.00	60.00
138 Cotton Davidson SP	7.50	15.00
139 Tom Flores SP	10.00	20.00
140 Claude Gibson	3.50	7.00
141 Wayne Hawkins	3.50	7.00
142 Archie Matsos SP	7.00	12.00
143 Mike Mercer SP	7.00	12.00
144 Bob Mischak SP	7.00	12.00
145 Jim Otto	18.00	30.00
146 Art Powell UER	5.00	10.00
147 Warren Powers SP RC	7.00	12.00
148 Ken Rice SP	7.00	12.00
149 Bo Roberson SP	7.00	12.00
150 Harry Schuh RC	3.50	7.00
151 Larry Todd SP RC	7.00	12.00
152 Fred Williamson SP	15.00	30.00
153 J.R. Williamson RC	3.50	7.00
154 Chuck Allen	5.00	10.00
155 Lance Alworth	50.00	75.00
156 Frank Buncom RC	3.50	7.00
157 Steve DeLong SP RC	7.00	12.00
158 Earl Faison SP	7.50	15.00
159 Kenny Graham SP RC	7.00	12.00
160 George Gross SP RC	7.00	12.00
161 John Hadl SP	20.00	35.00
162 Emil Karas SP	7.00	12.00
163 Dave Kocourek SP	7.00	12.00
164 Ernie Ladd SP	10.00	20.00
165 Keith Lincoln SP	12.00	25.00
166 Paul Lowe SP	10.00	20.00
167 Jacque MacKinnon	3.50	7.00
168 Ron Mix	12.00	20.00
169 Don Norton SP	7.00	12.00
170 Bob Petrich RC	3.50	7.00
171 Rick Redman SP RC	7.00	12.00
172 Pat Shea RC	3.50	7.00
173 Walt Sweeney SP RC	7.50	15.00
174 Dick Westmoreland RC	3.50	7.00
175 Ernie Wright SP	10.00	20.00
176 Checklist SP	125.00	225.00

1965 Topps Magic Rub-Off Inserts

This set of 36 rub-off team emblems was inserted into packs of the 1965 Topps AFL regular football issue. They are very similar to the 1961 Topps Baseball Magic Rub-Offs. Each rub-off measures 2" by 3"; eight AFL teams and 28 college teams are featured. The rub-offs are unnumbered and, hence, are numbered below alphabetically within type, i.e., AFL teams 1-8 and college teams 9-36.

Card		
COMPLETE SET (36)	400.00	800.00
1 Boston Patriots	15.00	30.00
2 Buffalo Bills	15.00	30.00
3 Denver Broncos	20.00	40.00
4 Houston Oilers	15.00	30.00
5 Kansas City Chiefs	15.00	30.00
6 New York Jets	15.00	30.00
7 Oakland Raiders	20.00	40.00
8 San Diego Chargers	15.00	30.00
9 Alabama Crimson Tide	12.50	25.00
10 Air Force Falcons	10.00	20.00
11 Arkansas Razorbacks	10.00	20.00
12 Army Cadets	10.00	20.00
13 Boston College Eagles	10.00	20.00
14 Duke Blue Devils	10.00	20.00
15 Illinois Fighting Illini	10.00	20.00
16 Kansas Jayhawks	10.00	20.00
17 Kentucky Wildcats	10.00	20.00
18 Maryland Terrapins	10.00	20.00
19 Miami Hurricanes	10.00	20.00
20 Minnesota Golden Gophers	10.00	20.00
21 Mississippi Rebels	10.00	20.00
22 Navy Midshipmen	10.00	20.00
23 Nebraska Cornhuskers	10.00	20.00
24 Notre Dame Fight.Irish	20.00	40.00
25 Penn State Nittany Lions	12.50	25.00
26 Purdue Boilermakers	10.00	20.00
27 SMU Mustangs	10.00	20.00
28 USC Trojans	10.00	20.00
29 Stanford Indians	10.00	20.00
30 Syracuse Orangemen	10.00	20.00
31 TCU Horned Frogs	10.00	20.00
32 Texas Longhorns	10.00	20.00
33 Virginia Cavaliers	10.00	20.00
34 Washington Huskies	10.00	20.00
35 Wisconsin Badgers	10.00	20.00
36 Yale Bulldogs	10.00	20.00

1966 Topps

The 1966 Topps set of 132 standard-size cards contains AFL players grouped together and numbered alphabetically within teams. The set marks the debut into the AFL of the Miami Dolphins. Card fronts are horizontal with woodgrain borders. Such a border offers a challenge to locate cards in top grades. The player's name, team and position are within the border below the photo. The card backs are printed in black and pink on white card stock. In actuality, card number 15 is not a football card at all but a "Funny Ring" checklist card; nevertheless, it is considered part of the set and is now regarded as the toughest card in the set to find in mint condition. Funny Ring cards were inserted one per pack but measure only 2 1/2" by 3 3/8". Notable Rookie Cards in this set include Wendell Hayes, George Sauer Jr., Otis Taylor, and Jim Turner.

Card		
COMPLETE SET (132)	950.00	1500.00
WRAPPER (5-CENT)	30.00	60.00
1 Tommy Addison	10.00	20.00
2 Houston Antwine	3.00	5.00
3 Nick Buoniconti	5.00	10.00
4 Gino Cappelletti	4.00	8.00
5 Bob Dee	3.00	5.00
6 Larry Garron	3.00	5.00
7 Art Graham	3.00	5.00
8 Ron Hall DB	3.00	5.00
9 Charles Long	3.00	5.00
10 Jon Morris	3.00	5.00
11 Don Oakes	3.00	5.00
12 Babe Parilli	4.00	8.00
13 Don Webb	3.00	5.00
14 Jim Whalen	3.00	5.00
15 Funny Ring Checklist !	200.00	300.00
16 Stew Barber	3.00	5.00
17 Glenn Bass	3.00	5.00
18 Dave Behrman	3.00	5.00
19 Al Bemiller	3.00	5.00
20 Butch Byrd RC	4.00	8.00
21 Wray Carlton	3.00	5.00
22 Tom Day	3.00	5.00
23 Elbert Dubenion	4.00	8.00
24 Jim Dunaway	3.00	5.00
25 Dick Hudson	3.00	5.00
26 Jack Kemp	60.00	120.00
27 Daryle Lamonica	12.00	20.00
28 Tom Sestak	3.00	5.00
29 Billy Shaw	5.00	10.00
30 Mike Stratton	3.00	5.00
31 Eldon Danenhauer	3.00	5.00
32 Cookie Gilchrist	5.00	10.00
33 Goose Gonsoulin	4.00	8.00
34 Wendell Hayes RC	5.00	10.00
35 Abner Haynes	5.00	10.00
36 Jerry Hopkins	3.00	5.00
37 Ray Jacobs	3.00	5.00
38 Charlie Janerette RC	3.00	5.00
39 Ray Kubala RC	3.00	5.00
40 John McCormick QB	3.00	5.00
41 Leroy Moore RC	3.00	5.00
42 Bob Scarpitto	3.00	5.00
43 Mickey Slaughter	3.00	5.00
44 Jerry Sturm	3.00	5.00
45 Lionel Taylor	5.00	10.00
46 Scott Appleton	3.00	5.00
47 Johnny Baker	3.00	5.00
48 George Blanda	20.00	35.00
49 Sid Blanks	3.00	5.00
50 Danny Brabham RC	3.00	5.00
51 Ode Burrell	3.00	5.00
52 Gary Cutsinger	3.00	5.00
53 Larry Elkins	3.00	5.00
54 Don Floyd	3.00	5.00
55 Willie Frazier RC	4.00	8.00
56 Freddy Glick	3.00	5.00
57 Charlie Hennigan	4.00	8.00
58 Bobby Jancik	3.00	5.00
59 Rich Michael	3.00	5.00
60 Don Trull	3.00	5.00
61 Checklist	30.00	55.00
62 Fred Arbanas	3.00	5.00
63 Pete Beathard	3.00	5.00
64 Bobby Bell	5.00	10.00
65 Ed Budde	3.00	5.00
66 Chris Burford	3.00	5.00
67 Len Dawson	25.00	40.00
68 Jon Gilliam	3.00	5.00
69 Sherrill Headrick	3.00	5.00
70 E.J. Holub UER	3.00	5.00
71 Bobby Hunt	3.00	5.00
72 Curtis McClinton	4.00	8.00
73 Jerry Mays	3.00	5.00
74 Johnny Robinson	4.00	8.00
75 Otis Taylor RC	15.00	25.00
76 Tom Erlandson RC	4.00	8.00
77 Norm Evans RC	5.00	10.00
78 Tom Goode	4.00	8.00
79 Mike Hudock	4.00	8.00
80 Frank Jackson	4.00	8.00
81 Billy Joe	4.00	8.00
82 Dave Kocourek	4.00	8.00
83 Bo Roberson	4.00	8.00
84 Jack Spikes	4.00	8.00
85 Jim Warren RC	4.00	8.00
86 Willie West RC	4.00	8.00
87 Dick Westmoreland	4.00	8.00
88 Eddie Wilson RC	4.00	8.00
89 Dick Wood	4.00	8.00
90 Verlon Biggs	4.00	8.00
91 Sam DeLuca	3.00	5.00
92 Winston Hill	3.00	5.00
93 Dee Mackey	3.00	5.00
94 Bill Mathis	3.00	5.00
95 Don Maynard	18.00	30.00
96 Joe Namath	150.00	250.00
97 Dainard Paulson	3.00	5.00
98 Gerry Philbin	4.00	8.00
99 Sherman Plunkett	3.00	5.00
100 Paul Rochester	3.00	5.00
101 George Sauer Jr. RC	7.50	15.00
102 Matt Snell	5.00	10.00
103 Jim Turner RC	4.00	8.00
104 Fred Biletnikoff UER	30.00	50.00
105 Bill Budness RC	3.00	5.00
106 Billy Cannon	5.00	10.00
107 Clem Daniels	4.00	8.00
108 Ben Davidson	7.50	15.00
109 Cotton Davidson	4.00	8.00
110 Claude Gibson	3.00	5.00
111 Wayne Hawkins	3.00	5.00
112 Ken Herock	3.00	5.00
113 Bob Mischak	3.00	5.00
114 Gus Otto RC	3.00	5.00
115 Jim Otto	12.00	20.00
116 Art Powell	5.00	10.00
117 Harry Schuh	3.00	5.00
118 Chuck Allen	3.00	5.00
119 Lance Alworth	25.00	40.00
120 Frank Buncom	3.00	5.00
121 Steve DeLong	3.00	5.00
122 John Farris RC	3.00	5.00
123 Kenny Graham	3.00	5.00
124 Sam Gruneisen	3.00	5.00
125 John Hadl	5.00	10.00
126 Walt Sweeney	3.00	5.00
127 Keith Lincoln	5.00	10.00
128 Ron Mix	5.00	10.00
129 Don Norton	3.00	5.00
130 Pat Shea	3.00	5.00
131 Ernie Wright	5.00	10.00
132 Checklist	50.00	100.00

1967 Topps

The 1967 Topps set of 132 standard-size cards contains AFL players only, with players grouped together and numbered by teams. The cardfronts include an oval design player photo surrounded by a team color. The cardbacks are printed in black text with a dark yellow or gold colored background on white card stock. A question (with upside-down answer) is given on the bottom of the cardbacks. Additionally, some cards were also issued along with the "Win-A-Card" board game from Milton Bradley that included cards from the 1965 Topps Hot Rods and 1968 Topps baseball card sets. This version of the cards is somewhat difficult to distinguish, but are often found with a slight touch of the 1968 baseball set border on the front top or bottom edge as well as a brighter yellow card back instead of the darker yellow or gold color. Known cards issued in this version include: #2, 12, 13, 18, 22, 28, 30, 31, 32, 48, 49, 51, 58, 60, 67, 68, 71, 84, 86, 87, 88, 92, 95, 98, 103, 106, 110, 116, 117, 121, 124, 125, and 130.

Card		
COMPLETE SET (132)	400.00	700.00
WRAPPER (5-CENT)	30.00	60.00
1 John Huarte	10.00	18.00
2 Babe Parilli	2.00	4.00
3 Gino Cappelletti	2.00	4.00
4 Larry Garron	1.50	3.00
5 Tommy Addison	1.50	3.00
6 Jon Morris	1.50	3.00
7 Houston Antwine	1.50	3.00
8 Don Oakes	1.50	3.00
9 Larry Eisenhauer	1.50	3.00
10 Jim Hunt RC	1.50	3.00
11 Jim Whalen	1.50	3.00
12 Art Graham	1.50	3.00
13 Nick Buoniconti	3.00	6.00
14 Bob Dee	1.50	3.00
15 Keith Lincoln	3.00	6.00
16 Tom Flores	2.00	4.00
17 Art Powell	2.00	4.00
18 Stew Barber	1.50	3.00
19 Wray Carlton	1.50	3.00
20 Elbert Dubenion	2.00	4.00
21 Jim Dunaway	1.50	3.00
22 Dick Hudson	1.50	3.00
23 Harry Jacobs	1.50	3.00
24 Jack Kemp	40.00	80.00
25 Ron McDole	1.50	3.00
26 George Saimes	1.50	3.00
27 Tom Sestak	1.50	3.00
28 Billy Shaw	3.00	6.00
29 Mike Stratton	1.50	3.00
30 Nemiah Wilson RC	1.50	3.00
31 John McCormick QB	1.50	3.00
32 Rex Mirich RC	1.50	3.00
33 Dave Costa	1.50	3.00
34 Goose Gonsoulin	2.00	4.00
35 Abner Haynes	3.00	6.00
36 Wendell Hayes	2.00	4.00
37 Archie Matsos	1.50	3.00
38 John Bramlett RC	1.50	3.00
39 Jerry Sturm	1.50	3.00
40 Max Leetzow RC	1.50	3.00
41 Bob Scarpitto	1.50	3.00
42 Lionel Taylor	3.00	6.00
43 Al Denson	1.50	3.00
44 Miller Farr RC	1.50	3.00
45 Don Trull	1.50	3.00
46 Jacky Lee	2.00	4.00
47 Bobby Jancik	1.50	3.00
48 Ode Burrell	1.50	3.00
49 Larry Elkins	1.50	3.00
50 W.K. Hicks RC	1.50	3.00
51 Sid Blanks	1.50	3.00
52 Jim Norton	1.50	3.00
53 Bobby Maples RC	1.50	3.00
54 Bob Talamini	1.50	3.00
55 Walt Suggs	1.50	3.00
56 Gary Cutsinger	1.50	3.00
57 Danny Brabham	1.50	3.00
58 Ernie Ladd	3.00	6.00
59 Checklist	25.00	50.00
60 Pete Beathard	1.50	3.00
61 Len Dawson	18.00	30.00
62 Bobby Hunt	1.50	3.00
63 Bert Coan RC	1.50	3.00
64 Curtis McClinton	2.00	4.00
65 Johnny Robinson	2.00	4.00
66 E.J. Holub	1.50	3.00
67 Jerry Mays	1.50	3.00
68 Jim Tyrer	2.00	4.00
69 Bobby Bell	3.00	6.00
70 Fred Arbanas	1.50	3.00
71 Buck Buchanan	3.00	6.00
72 Chris Burford	1.50	3.00
73 Otis Taylor	3.00	6.00
74 Cookie Gilchrist	4.00	8.00
75 Earl Faison	1.50	3.00
76 George Wilson Jr. RC	2.00	4.00
77 Rick Norton RC	1.50	3.00
78 Frank Jackson	2.00	4.00
79 Joe Auer RC	1.50	3.00
80 Willie West	1.50	3.00
81 Jim Warren	1.50	3.00
82 Wahoo McDaniel RC	30.00	50.00
83 Ernie Park RC	1.50	3.00
84 Billy Neighbors	1.50	3.00
85 Norm Evans	2.00	4.00
86 Tom Nomina	1.50	3.00
87 Rich Zecher RC	1.50	3.00
88 Dave Kocourek	1.50	3.00
89 Bill Baird	1.50	3.00
90 Ralph Baker	1.50	3.00
91 Verlon Biggs	1.50	3.00
92 Sam DeLuca	1.50	3.00
93 Larry Grantham	2.00	4.00
94 Jim Harris RC	1.50	3.00
95 Winston Hill	1.50	3.00
96 Bill Mathis	1.50	3.00
97 Don Maynard	12.00	20.00
98 Joe Namath	75.00	150.00
99 Gerry Philbin	2.00	4.00
100 Paul Rochester	1.50	3.00
101 George Sauer Jr.	2.00	4.00
102 Matt Snell	3.00	6.00
103 Daryle Lamonica	5.00	10.00
104 Glenn Bass	1.50	3.00
105 Jim Otto	3.00	6.00
106 Fred Biletnikoff	18.00	30.00
107 Cotton Davidson	2.00	4.00
108 Larry Todd	1.50	3.00
109 Billy Cannon	3.00	6.00
110 Clem Daniels	2.00	4.00
111 Dave Grayson	1.50	3.00
112 Kent McCloughan UER RC	1.50	3.00
113 Bob Svihus RC	1.50	3.00
114 Ike Lassiter	1.50	3.00
115 Harry Schuh	1.50	3.00
116 Ben Davidson	4.00	8.00
117 Tom Day	1.50	3.00
118 Scott Appleton	1.50	3.00
119 Steve Tensi RC	1.50	3.00
120 John Hadl	3.00	6.00
121 Paul Lowe	2.00	4.00
122 Jim Allison RC	1.50	3.00
123 Lance Alworth	20.00	35.00
124 Jacque MacKinnon	1.50	3.00
125 Ron Mix	3.00	6.00
126 Bob Petrich	1.50	3.00
127 Howard Kindig RC	1.50	3.00
128 Steve DeLong	1.50	3.00
129 Chuck Allen	1.50	3.00
130 Frank Buncom	1.50	3.00
131 Speedy Duncan RC	2.50	5.00
132 Checklist	35.00	70.00

1967 Topps Comic Pennants

This set was issued as an insert with the 1967 Topps regular issue football cards as well as being issued separately. The stickers are standard size, and the backs are blank. The set can also be found in adhesive form with the pennant merely printed on card stock. They are numbered in the upper right corner, although reportedly they can also occasionally be found without numbers. Many of the cards feature sayings or depictions that are in poor taste, i.e., sick humor. Perhaps they were discontinued or recalled before the end of the season, which would explain their relative scarcity.

Card		
COMPLETE SET (31)	300.00	600.00
1 Navel Academy	10.00	25.00
2 City College	10.00	25.00
3 Notre Dame	20.00	40.00
4 Psychedelic State	10.00	25.00
5 Minneapolis Mini-skirts	10.00	25.00
6 School of Art	10.00	25.00
7 Washington	10.00	25.00
8 School of Hard Knocks	10.00	25.00
9 Alaska	10.00	25.00
10 Confused State	10.00	25.00
11 Yale Locks	10.00	25.00
12 University of	10.00	25.00
13 Down With Teachers	10.00	25.00
14 Cornell	10.00	25.00
15 Houston Oilers	10.00	25.00
16 Harvard	10.00	25.00
17 Diskotech	10.00	25.00
18 Dropout U.	10.00	25.00
19 Air Force	10.00	25.00
20 Nutstu U.	10.00	25.00
21 Michigan State Pen	10.00	25.00
22 Denver Broncos	15.00	30.00
23 Buffalo Bills	12.50	30.00
24 Army of Dropouts	10.00	25.00
25 Miami Dolphins	15.00	30.00
26 Kansas City (Has Too	10.00	25.00
27 Boston Patriots	10.00	25.00
28 (Fat People In) Oakland	15.00	30.00
29 (I'd Go) West (If You'd	10.00	25.00
30 New York Jets	12.50	30.00
31 San Diego Chargers	10.00	25.00

1968 Topps

The 1968 set marks the beginning of a 21-year run of Topps being the only major producer of football cards. The two-series set of 219 standard-size cards is Topps' first set in seven years (since 1961) to contain players from both leagues. The set marks the AFL debut of the Cincinnati Bengals. Card fronts feature the player photo over a solid background. A team logo is in an upper corner. The player's name, team name and position are in a colored cicular box at the bottom. Cards for players from the previous year's Super Bowl teams, the Green Bay Packers and the Oakland Raiders, are the only cards to contain horizontally designed fronts. In addition, these cards also have color boders at top and bottom and the player photo is superimposed over yellow tinted game action artwork. The backs have statistics and highlights as well as a rub-off cartoon at the bottom. The cards in the second series have blue printing on the back whereas the cards in the first series had green printing on the back. Card backs of some of the cards in the second series can be used to form a ten-card puzzle of Bart Starr (141, 148, 153, 155, 168, 172, 186, 197, 201, and 213) or Len Dawson (145, 146, 151, 152, 163, 166, 170, 195, 199, and 200). The set features the Rookie Cards of quarterbacks Bob Griese, Jim Hart, and Craig Morton, and (ex-Syracuse) running backs Floyd Little and Jim Nance. The second series (132-219) is slightly more difficult to obtain than the first series. This set was issued in five card wax packs which cost five cents and came 24 packs to a box.

COMPLETE SET (219) 350.00 550.00
WRAPPER (5-CENT, SER.1) 10.00 20.00
WRAPPER (5-CENT, SER.2) 20.00 30.00
1 Bart Starr 25.00 40.00
2 Dick Bass 1.00 2.00
3 Grady Alderman .75 1.50
4 Obert Logan .75 1.50
5 Ernie Koy RC 1.00 2.00
6 Don Hultz RC .75 1.50
7 Earl Gros .75 1.50
8 Jim Bakken .75 1.50
9 George Mira 1.00 2.00
10 Carl Kammerer RC .75 1.50
11 Willie Frazier .75 1.50
12 Kent McCloughan UER .75 1.50
13 George Sauer Jr. 1.00 2.00
14 Jack Clancy RC .75 1.50
15 Jim Tyrer 1.00 2.00
16 Bobby Maples .75 1.50
17 Bo Hickey RC .75 1.50
18 Frank Buncom .75 1.50
19 Keith Lincoln 1.00 2.00
20 Jim Whalen .75 1.50
21 Junior Coffey .75 1.50
22 Billy Ray Smith .75 1.50
23 Johnny Morris .75 1.50
24 Ernie Green .75 1.50
25 Don Meredith 15.00 25.00
26 Wayne Walker .75 1.50
27 Carroll Dale 1.00 2.00
28 Bernie Casey 1.00 2.00
29 Dave Osborn RC 1.00 2.00
30 Ray Poage .75 1.50
31 Homer Jones .75 1.50
32 Sam Baker .75 1.50
33 Bill Saul RC .75 1.50
34 Ken Willard 1.00 2.00
35 Bobby Mitchell 2.00 4.00
36 Gary Garrison RC 1.00 2.00
37 Billy Cannon 1.00 2.00
38 Ralph Baker .75 1.50
39 Howard Twilley RC 2.00 4.00
40 Wendell Hayes 1.00 2.00
41 Jim Norton .75 1.50
42 Tom Beer RC .75 1.50
43 Chris Burford .75 1.50
44 Stew Barber .75 1.50
45 Leroy Mitchell UER RC .75 1.50
46 Dan Grimm .75 1.50
47 Jerry Logan .75 1.50
48 Andy Livingston RC .75 1.50
49 Paul Warfield 7.50 15.00
50 Don Perkins 1.50 3.00
51 Ron Kramer .75 1.50
52 Bob Jeter RC 1.00 2.00
53 Les Josephson RC 1.00 2.00
54 Bobby Walden .75 1.50
55 Checklist 7.50 15.00
56 Walter Roberts .75 1.50
57 Henry Carr .75 1.50
58 Gary Ballman .75 1.50
59 J.R. Wilburn RC .75 1.50
60 Jim Hart RC 5.00 10.00
61 Jim Johnson 1.50 3.00
62 Chris Hanburger 1.00 2.00
63 John Hadl 1.50 3.00
64 Hewritt Dixon 1.00 2.00
65 Joe Namath 50.00 80.00
66 Jim Warren .75 1.50
67 Curtis McClinton 1.00 2.00
68 Bob Talamini .75 1.50
69 Steve Tensi .75 1.50
70 Dick Van Raaphorst UER RC .75 1.50
71 Art Powell 1.00 2.00
72 Jim Nance RC 2.00 4.00
73 Bob Riggle RC .75 1.50
74 John Mackey 2.50 5.00
75 Gale Sayers 25.00 40.00
76 Gene Hickerson 1.25 2.50
77 Dan Reeves 5.00 10.00
78 Tom Nowatzke .75 1.50
79 Elijah Pitts 1.50 3.00
80 Lamar Lundy 1.00 2.00
81 Paul Flatley .75 1.50
82 Dave Whitsell .75 1.50
83 Spider Lockhart 1.00 2.00
84 Dave Lloyd .75 1.50
85 Roy Jefferson 1.00 2.00
86 Jackie Smith 3.00 6.00
87 John David Crow 1.00 2.00
88 Sonny Jurgensen 3.00 6.00
89 Ron Mix 1.50 3.00
90 Clem Daniels 1.00 2.00
91 Cornell Gordon RC .75 1.50
92 Tom Goode .75 1.50
93 Bobby Bell 1.50 3.00
94 Walt Suggs .75 1.50
95 Eric Crabtree RC .75 1.50
96 Sherrill Headrick .75 1.50
97 Wray Carlton .75 1.50
98 Gino Cappelletti 1.00 2.00
99 Tommy McDonald 2.00 4.00
100 Johnny Unitas 25.00 40.00
101 Richie Petitbon .75 1.50
102 Erich Barnes .75 1.50
103 Bob Hayes 5.00 10.00
104 Milt Plum 1.00 2.00
105 Boyd Dowler 1.00 2.00
106 Ed Meador .75 1.50
107 Fred Cox .75 1.50
108 Steve Stonebreaker RC .75 1.50
109 Aaron Thomas .75 1.50
110 Norm Snead 1.00 2.00
111 Paul Martha RC .75 1.50
112 Jerry Stovall .75 1.50
113 Kay McFarland RC .75 1.50
114 Pat Richter .75 1.50
115 Rick Redman .75 1.50
116 Tom Keating .75 1.50
117 Matt Snell 1.00 2.00
118 Dick Westmoreland .75 1.50
119 Jerry Mays .75 1.50
120 Sid Blanks .75 1.50
121 Al Denson .75 1.50
122 Bobby Hunt .75 1.50
123 Mike Mercer .75 1.50
124 Nick Buoniconti 1.50 3.00
125 Ron Vanderkelen RC .75 1.50
126 Ordell Braase .75 1.50
127 Dick Butkus 30.00 50.00
128 Gary Collins 1.00 2.00
129 Mel Renfro 3.00 6.00
130 Alex Karras 2.50 5.00
131 Herb Adderley 2.50 5.00
132 Roman Gabriel 2.00 4.00
133 Bill Brown 1.25 2.50
134 Kent Kramer RC 1.00 2.00
135 Tucker Frederickson 1.25 2.50
136 Nate Ramsey 1.00 2.00
137 Marv Woodson RC 1.00 2.00
138 Ken Gray 1.00 2.00
139 John Brodie 2.50 5.00
140 Jerry Smith 1.00 2.00
141 Brad Hubbert RC 1.00 2.00
142 George Blanda 10.00 20.00
143 Pete Lammons RC 1.00 2.00
144 Doug Moreau RC 1.00 2.00
145 E.J. Holub 1.00 2.00
146 Ode Burrell 1.00 2.00
147 Bob Scarpitto 1.00 2.00
148 Andre White RC 1.00 2.00
149 Jack Kemp 30.00 50.00
150 Art Graham 1.00 2.00
151 Tommy Nobis 3.00 6.00
152 Willie Richardson RC 1.25 2.50
153 Jack Concannon 1.00 2.00
154 Bill Glass 1.00 2.00
155 Craig Morton RC 5.00 10.00
156 Pat Studstill 1.00 2.00
157 Ray Nitschke 5.00 10.00
158 Roger Brown 1.00 2.00
159 Joe Kapp RC 2.50 5.00
160 Jim Taylor 7.50 15.00
161 Fran Tarkenton 10.00 20.00
162 Mike Ditka 18.00 30.00
163 Andy Russell RC 4.00 8.00
164 Larry Wilson 2.00 4.00
165 Tommy Davis 1.00 2.00
166 Paul Krause 2.00 4.00
167 Speedy Duncan 1.00 2.00
168 Fred Biletnikoff 7.50 15.00
169 Don Maynard 5.00 10.00
170 Frank Emanuel RC 1.00 2.00
171 Len Dawson 7.50 15.00
172 Miller Farr 1.00 2.00
173 Floyd Little RC 12.50 25.00
174 Lonnie Wright RC 1.00 2.00
175 Paul Costa RC 1.00 2.00
176 Don Trull 1.00 2.00
177 Jerry Simmons RC 1.00 2.00
178 Tom Matte 1.25 2.50
179 Bennie McRae 1.00 2.00
180 Jim Kanicki RC 1.00 2.00
181 Bob Lilly 7.50 15.00
182 Tom Watkins 1.00 2.00
183 Jim Grabowski RC 3.00 6.00
184 Jack Snow RC 2.00 4.00
185 Gary Cuozzo RC 1.25 2.50
186 Billy Kilmer 2.00 4.00
187 Jim Katcavage 1.00 2.00
188 Floyd Peters 1.00 2.00
189 Bill Nelsen 1.25 2.50
190 Bobby Joe Conrad 1.25 2.50
191 Kermit Alexander 1.00 2.00
192 Charley Taylor UER 3.00 6.00
193 Lance Alworth 10.00 20.00
194 Daryle Lamonica 2.50 5.00
195 Al Atkinson RC 1.00 2.00
196 Bob Griese RC 60.00 100.00
197 Buck Buchanan 2.00 4.00
198 Pete Beathard 1.00 2.00
199 Nemiah Wilson 1.00 2.00
200 Ernie Wright 1.00 2.00
201 George Saimes 1.00 2.00
202 John Charles RC 1.00 2.00
203 Randy Johnson 1.00 2.00
204 Tony Lorick 1.00 2.00
205 Dick Evey 1.00 2.00
206 Leroy Kelly 5.00 10.00
207 Lee Roy Jordan 3.00 6.00
208 Jim Gibbons 1.00 2.00
209 Donny Anderson RC 2.00 4.00
210 Maxie Baughan 1.00 2.00
211 Joe Morrison 1.00 2.00
212 Jim Snowden RC 1.00 2.00
213 Lenny Lyles 1.00 2.00
214 Bobby Joe Green 1.00 2.00
215 Frank Ryan 1.25 2.50
216 Cornell Green 1.25 2.50
217 Karl Sweetan 1.00 2.00
218 Dave Williams RC 1.00 2.00
219A Checklist Green 10.00 18.00
219B Checklist Blue 12.00 20.00

1968 Topps Posters Inserts

The 1968 Topps Football Posters set contains 16 NFL and AFL players on paper stock; the cards (posters) measure approximately 5" by 7". The posters, folded twice for insertion into first series wax packs, are numbered on the obverse at the lower left hand corner. The backs of these posters are blank. Fold marks are normal and do not detract from the poster's condition. These posters are the same style as the 1967 Topps baseball

COMPLETE SET (16) 40.00 80.00
1 Johnny Unitas 10.00 20.00
2 Leroy Kelly 2.50 5.00
3 Bob Hayes 3.00 6.00
4 Bart Starr 7.50 15.00
5 Charley Taylor 2.50 5.00
6 Fran Tarkenton 5.00 10.00
7 Jim Bakken 1.50 3.00
8 Gale Sayers 6.00 12.00
9 Gary Cuozzo 1.50 3.00
10 Les Josephson 1.50 3.00
11 Jim Nance 1.50 3.00
12 Brad Hubbert 1.50 3.00
13 Keith Lincoln 1.50 3.00
14 Don Maynard 3.00 6.00
15 Len Dawson 4.00 8.00
16 Jack Clancy 1.50 3.00

1968 Topps Stand-Ups Inserts

The 22-card 1968 Topps Football Stand-Ups standard-size set is unnumbered but has been numbered alphabetically in the checklist below for your convenience. Values listed below are for complete cards; the value is greatly reduced if the backs are detached, and such a card can be considered fair to good at best. The cards were issued as an insert in second series packs of 1968 Topps football cards, one per pack.

COMPLETE SET (22) 150.00 250.00
1 Sid Blanks 3.00 6.00
2 John Brodie 6.00 12.00
3 Jack Concannon 3.00 6.00
4 Roman Gabriel 4.00 8.00
5 Art Graham 3.00 6.00
6 Jim Grabowski 3.00 6.00
7 John Hadl 4.00 8.00
8 Jim Hart 4.00 8.00
9 Homer Jones 3.00 6.00
10 Sonny Jurgensen 6.00 12.00
11 Alex Karras 5.00 10.00
12 Billy Kilmer 4.00 8.00
13 Daryle Lamonica 4.00 8.00
14 Floyd Little 4.00 8.00
15 Curtis McClinton 3.00 6.00
16 Don Meredith 20.00 40.00
17 Joe Namath 40.00 80.00
18 Bill Nelsen 3.50 7.00
19 Dave Osborn 3.00 6.00
20 Willie Richardson 3.00 6.00
21 Frank Ryan 3.50 7.00
22 Norm Snead 3.50 7.00

1968 Topps Test Teams

The 25-card set of team cards was issued as a stand alone wax pack (10-cents per pack) product with cloth patch/sticker inserts. The fronts provide a black and white picture of the team while the backs give the names of the players in the picture in red print on vanilla card stock. Due to their positioning within the pack, these test team cards are typically found with gum stains on the card backs. The cards measure approximately 2 1/2" by 4 11/16" and are numbered on the back.

COMPLETE SET (25) 1800.00 3000.00
WRAPPER (10-cent) 250.00 350.00
1 Green Bay Packers 100.00 175.00
2 New Orleans Saints 60.00 100.00
3 New York Jets 75.00 150.00
4 Miami Dolphins 100.00 175.00
5 Pittsburgh Steelers 75.00 125.00
6 Detroit Lions 50.00 100.00
7 Los Angeles Rams 50.00 100.00
8 Atlanta Falcons 50.00 100.00
9 New York Giants 75.00 125.00
10 Denver Broncos 175.00 300.00
11 Dallas Cowboys 250.00 400.00
12 Buffalo Bills 75.00 125.00
13 Cleveland Browns 75.00 125.00
14 San Francisco 49ers 75.00 125.00
15 Baltimore Colts 50.00 100.00
16 San Diego Chargers 50.00 100.00
17 Oakland Raiders 100.00 200.00
18 Houston Oilers 50.00 100.00
19 Minnesota Vikings 75.00 125.00
20 Washington Redskins 100.00 175.00
21 St. Louis Cardinals 50.00 100.00
22 Kansas City Chiefs 50.00 100.00
23 Boston Patriots 50.00 100.00
24 Chicago Bears 75.00 135.00
25 Philadelphia Eagles 50.00 100.00

1968 Topps Test Team Patches

These team emblem cloth patches/stickers were distributed as an insert with the 1968 Topps Test Teams: one sticker per 10 cent pack along with one test team. In fact according to the wrapper, these stickers were the featured item; however the hobby has deemed the team cards to be more collectible and hence more valuable than these rather bland, but scarce, logo stickers. The complete set of 44 patches consisted of team emblems, the letters A through Z, and the numbers 0 through 9. The letters and number patches contained two letters or numbers on each patch. The number patches are printed in black on a blue background, the letter patches are white on a red background, and the team emblems were done in the team colors. The stickers measure 2 1/2" by 3 1/2". The backs are blank.

COMPLETE SET (44) 1000.00 2000.00
1 1 and 2 6.00 12.00
2 3 and 4 6.00 12.00
3 5 and 6 6.00 12.00
4 7 and 8 6.00 12.00
5 9 and 0 6.00 12.00
6 A and B 6.00 12.00
7 C and D 6.00 12.00
8 E and F 6.00 12.00
9 G and H 6.00 12.00
10 I and W 6.00 12.00
11 J and X 6.00 12.00
12 Atlanta Falcons 30.00 60.00
13 Baltimore Colts 30.00 60.00
14 Chicago Bears 45.00 90.00
15 Cleveland Browns 30.00 60.00
16 Dallas Cowboys 100.00 175.00
17 Detroit Lions 30.00 60.00
18 Green Bay Packers 75.00 125.00
19 Los Angeles Rams 30.00 60.00
20 Minnesota Vikings 45.00 90.00
21 New Orleans Saints 30.00 60.00
22 New York Giants 45.00 90.00
23 K and L 6.00 12.00
24 M and O 6.00 12.00
25 N and P 6.00 12.00
26 Q and R 6.00 12.00
27 S and T 6.00 12.00
28 U and V 6.00 12.00
29 Y and Z 6.00 12.00
30 Philadelphia Eagles 30.00 60.00
31 Pittsburgh Steelers 45.00 90.00
32 St. Louis Cardinals 30.00 60.00
33 San Francisco 49ers 30.00 60.00
34 Washington Redskins 100.00 200.00
35 Boston Patriots 30.00 60.00
36 Buffalo Bills 30.00 60.00
37 Denver Broncos 67.50 135.00
38 Houston Oilers 30.00 60.00
39 Kansas City Chiefs 30.00 60.00
40 Miami Dolphins 75.00 150.00
41 New York Jets 30.00 60.00
42 Oakland Raiders 75.00 150.00
43 San Diego Chargers 30.00 60.00
44 Cincinnati Bengals 30.00 60.00

1969 Topps

The 1969 Topps set of 263 standard-size cards was issued in two series. First series cards (1-132) are borderless whereas the second series (133-263) cards have white borders. The lack of borders makes the first series especially difficult to find in mint condition. The checklist card (132) was obviously printed with each series as it is found in both styles (with and without borders). The set was issued in 12-card 10-cent packs. Though the borders differ, the fronts have otherwise consistent designs. A player photo is superimposed over a solid color background with the team logo, player's name, team name and position at the bottom. The backs of the cards are predominantly black, but with a green and white accent. Card backs of some of the cards in the second series can be used to form a ten-card puzzle of Fran Tarkenton (137, 145, 168, 174, 177, 194, 211, 219, 224, and 256). This set is distinctive in that it contains the late Brian Piccolo's only regular issue card. Another notable Rookie Card in this set is Larry Csonka.

COMPLETE SET (263) 350.00 550.00
WRAPPER (5-CENT) 15.00 30.00
1 Leroy Kelly 10.00 20.00
2 Paul Flatley .75 1.50
3 Jim Cadile RC .75 1.50
4 Erich Barnes .75 1.50
5 Willie Richardson .75 1.50
6 Bob Hayes 4.00 8.00
7 Bob Jeter .75 1.50
8 Jim Colclough .75 1.50
9 Sherrill Headrick .75 1.50
10 Jim Dunaway .75 1.50
11 Bill Munson 1.00 2.00
12 Jack Pardee 1.00 2.00
13 Jim Lindsey RC .75 1.50
14 Dave Whitsell .75 1.50
15 Tucker Frederickson .75 1.50
16 Alvin Haymond 1.00 2.00
17 Andy Russell 1.00 2.00
18 Tom Beer .75 1.50
19 Bobby Maples .75 1.50
20 Len Dawson 4.00 8.00
21 Willis Crenshaw .75 1.50
22 Tommy Davis .75 1.50
23 Rickie Harris .75 1.50
24 Jerry Simmons .75 1.50
25 Johnny Unitas 25.00 50.00
26 Brian Piccolo UER RC 50.00 80.00
27 Bob Matheson RC .75 1.50
28 Howard Twilley 1.00 2.00
29 Jim Turner 1.00 2.00
30 Pete Banaszak RC 1.00 2.00
31 Lance Rentzel RC 1.00 2.00
32 Bill Triplett .75 1.50
33 Boyd Dowler 1.00 2.00
34 Merlin Olsen 2.50 5.00
35 Joe Kapp 1.50 3.00
36 Dan Abramowicz RC 2.00 4.00
37 Spider Lockhart 1.00 2.00
38 Tom Day .75 1.50
39 Art Graham .75 1.50
40 Bob Cappadona RC .75 1.50
41 Gary Ballman .75 1.50
42 Clendon Thomas .75 1.50
43 Jackie Smith 2.00 4.00
44 Dave Wilcox 1.50 3.00
45 Jerry Smith .75 1.50
46 Dan Grimm .75 1.50
47 Tom Matte 1.00 2.00
48 John Stofa RC .75 1.50
49 Rex Mirich .75 1.50
50 Miller Farr .75 1.50
51 Gale Sayers 25.00 40.00
52 Bill Nelsen 1.00 2.00
53 Bob Lilly 3.00 6.00
54 Wayne Walker .75 1.50
55 Ray Nitschke 2.50 5.00
56 Ed Meador .75 1.50
57 Lonnie Warwick RC .75 1.50
58 Wendell Hayes .75 1.50
59 Dick Anderson RC 2.50 5.00
60 Don Maynard 3.00 6.00
61 Tony Lorick .75 1.50
62 Pete Gogolak .75 1.50
63 Nate Ramsey .75 1.50
64 Dick Shiner RC .75 1.50
65 Larry Wilson UER 1.50 3.00
66 Ken Willard 1.00 2.00
67 Charley Taylor 2.50 5.00
68 Billy Cannon 1.00 2.00
69 Lance Alworth 4.00 8.00
70 Jim Nance 1.00 2.00
71 Nick Rassas RC .75 1.50
72 Lenny Lyles .75 1.50
73 Bennie McRae .75 1.50
74 Bill Glass .75 1.50
75 Don Meredith 15.00 25.00
76 Dick LeBeau 1.00 2.50
77 Carroll Dale 1.00 2.00
78 Ron McDole .75 1.50
79 Charley King RC .75 1.50
80 Checklist UER 7.50 15.00
81 Dick Bass 1.00 2.00
82 Roy Winston .75 1.50
83 Don McCall RC .75 1.50
84 Jim Katcavage 1.00 2.00
85 Norm Snead 1.00 2.00
86 Earl Gros .75 1.50
87 Don Brumm RC .75 1.50
88 Sonny Bishop .75 1.50
89 Fred Arbanas .75 1.50
90 Karl Noonan RC .75 1.50
91 Dick Witcher RC .75 1.50
92 Vince Promuto .75 1.50
93 Tommy Nobis 2.00 4.00
94 Jerry Hill RC .75 1.50
95 Ed O'Bradovich RC .75 1.50
96 Ernie Kellerman RC .75 1.50
97 Chuck Howley 1.00 2.00
98 Hewritt Dixon .75 1.50
99 Ron Mix 1.50 3.00
100 Joe Namath 40.00 75.00
101 Billy Gambrell RC .75 1.50
102 Elijah Pitts 1.00 2.00
103 Billy Truax RC 1.00 2.00
104 Ed Sharockman .75 1.50
105 Doug Atkins 1.50 3.00
106 Greg Larson .75 1.50
107 Israel Lang RC .75 1.50
108 Houston Antwine .75 1.50
109 Paul Guidry RC .75 1.50
110 Al Denson .75 1.50
111 Roy Jefferson 1.00 2.00
112 Chuck Latourette RC .75 1.50
113 Jim Johnson 1.50 3.00
114 Bobby Mitchell 2.00 4.00
115 Randy Johnson .75 1.50
116 Lou Michaels .75 1.50
117 Rudy Kuechenberg RC .75 1.50
118 Walt Suggs .75 1.50
119 Goldie Sellers RC .75 1.50
120 Larry Csonka RC 40.00 75.00
121 Jim Houston .75 1.50
122 Craig Baynham RC .75 1.50
123 Alex Karras 2.50 5.00
124 Jim Grabowski 1.00 2.00
125 Roman Gabriel 1.50 3.00
126 Larry Bowie .75 1.50
127 Dave Parks 1.00 2.00
128 Ben Davidson 1.50 3.00
129 Steve DeLong .75 1.50
130 Fred Hill RC .75 1.50
131 Ernie Koy 1.00 2.00
132A Checklist no border 7.50 15.00
132B Checklist bordered 10.00 20.00
133 Dick Hoak 1.00 2.00
134 Larry Stallings RC 1.00 2.00
135 Clifton McNeil RC 1.00 2.00
136 Walter Rock 1.00 2.00
137 Billy Lothridge RC 1.00 2.00
138 Bob Vogel 1.00 2.00
139 Dick Butkus 25.00 40.00
140 Frank Ryan 1.25 2.50
141 Larry Garron 1.00 2.00
142 George Saimes 1.00 2.00
143 Frank Buncom 1.00 2.00
144 Don Perkins 1.25 2.50
145 Johnnie Robinson UER RC 1.00 2.00
146 Lee Roy Caffey 1.25 2.50
147 Bernie Casey 1.25 2.50
148 Billy Martin E 1.00 2.00
149 Gene Howard RC 1.00 2.00
150 Fran Tarkenton 10.00 20.00
151 Eric Crabtree 1.00 2.00
152 W.K. Hicks 1.00 2.00
153 Bobby Bell 2.00 4.00
154 Sam Baker 1.00 2.00
155 Marv Woodson 1.00 2.00
156 Dave Williams 1.00 2.00
157 Bruce Bosley UER 1.00 2.00
158 Carl Kammerer 1.00 2.00
159 Jim Burson RC 1.00 2.00
160 Roy Hilton RC 1.00 2.00
161 Bob Griese 15.00 25.00
162 Bob Talamini 1.00 2.00
163 Jim Otto 2.00 4.00
164 Ronnie Bull 1.00 2.00
165 Walter Johnson RC 1.00 2.00
166 Lee Roy Jordan 2.00 4.00
167 Mike Lucci 1.25 2.50
168 Willie Wood 2.00 4.00
169 Maxie Baughan 1.00 2.00
170 Bill Brown 1.25 2.50
171 John Hadl 2.00 4.00
172 Gino Cappelletti 1.25 2.50
173 George Butch Byrd 1.25 2.50
174 Steve Stonebreaker 1.00 2.00
175 Joe Morrison 1.00 2.00
176 Joe Scarpati 1.00 2.00
177 Bobby Walden 1.00 2.00
178 Roy Shivers 1.00 2.00
179 Kermit Alexander 1.00 2.00
180 Pat Richter 1.00 2.00
181 Pete Perreault RC 1.00 2.00
182 Pete Duranko RC 1.00 2.00
183 Leroy Mitchell 1.00 2.00
184 Jim Simon RC 1.00 2.00
185 Billy Ray Smith 1.00 2.00
186 Jack Concannon 1.00 2.00
187 Ben Davis RC 1.00 2.00
188 Mike Clark 1.00 2.00
189 Jim Gibbons 1.00 2.00
190 Dave Robinson 3.00 6.00
191 Otis Taylor 1.25 2.50
192 Nick Buoniconti 2.00 4.00
193 Matt Snell 1.25 2.50
194 Bruce Gossett 1.00 2.00
195 Mick Tingelhoff 1.25 2.50
196 Earl Leggett 1.00 2.00
197 Pete Case 1.00 2.00
198 Tom Woodeshick RC 1.00 2.00
199 Ken Kortas RC 1.00 2.00
200 Jim Hart 2.00 4.00
201 Fred Biletnikoff 5.00 10.00
202 Jacque MacKinnon 1.00 2.00
203 Jim Whalen 1.00 2.00
204 Matt Hazeltine 1.00 2.00
205 Charlie Gogolak 1.00 2.00
206 Ray Ogden RC 1.00 2.00
207 John Mackey 2.00 4.00
208 Roosevelt Taylor 1.00 2.00
209 Gene Hickerson 1.25 2.50
210 Dave Edwards RC 1.25 2.50
211 Tom Sestak 1.00 2.00
212 Ernie Wright 1.00 2.00
213 Dave Costa 1.00 2.00
214 Tom Vaughn RC 1.00 2.00
215 Bart Starr 25.00 40.00
216 Les Josephson 1.00 2.00
217 Fred Cox 1.00 2.00
218 Mike Tilleman RC 1.00 2.00
219 Darrell Dess 1.00 2.00
220 Dave Lloyd 1.00 2.00
221 Pete Beathard 1.00 2.00
222 Buck Buchanan 2.00 4.00
223 Frank Emanuel 1.00 2.00
224 Paul Martha 1.00 2.00
225 Johnny Roland 1.00 2.00
226 Gary Lewis 1.00 2.00
227 Sonny Jurgensen UER 3.00 6.00
228 Jim Butler 1.00 2.00
229 Mike Curtis RC 4.00 8.00
230 Richie Petitbon 1.00 2.00
231 George Sauer Jr. 1.25 2.50
232 George Blanda 10.00 20.00
233 Gary Garrison 1.00 2.00
234 Gary Collins 1.25 2.50
235 Craig Morton 2.00 4.00
236 Tom Nowatzke 1.00 2.00
237 Donny Anderson 1.25 2.50
238 Deacon Jones 2.00 4.00
239 Grady Alderman 1.00 2.00
240 Billy Kilmer 2.00 4.00
241 Mike Taliaferro 1.00 2.00
242 Stew Barber 1.00 2.00
243 Bobby Hunt 1.00 2.00
244 Homer Jones 1.00 2.00
245 Bob Brown OT 2.00 4.00
246 Bill Asbury 1.00 2.00
247 Charley Johnson 1.25 2.50
248 Chris Hanburger 1.25 2.50
249 John Brodie 3.00 6.00
250 Earl Morrall 1.25 2.50
251 Floyd Little 2.50 5.00
252 Jerrel Wilson RC 1.00 2.00
253 Jim Keyes RC 1.00 2.00
254 Mel Renfro 2.00 4.00
255 Herb Adderley 2.00 4.00
256 Jack Snow 1.25 2.50
257 Charlie Durkee RC 1.00 2.00
258 Charlie Harper RC 1.00 2.00
259 J.R. Wilburn 1.00 2.00
260 Charlie Krueger 1.00 2.00
261 Pete Jacques RC 1.00 2.00
262 Gerry Philbin 1.00 2.00
263 Daryle Lamonica 5.00 10.00

1969 Topps Four-in-One Inserts

The 1969 Topps Four-in-One set contains 66 cards (each measuring the standard size) with each card having four small (1" by 1 1/2") cardboard stamps on the front. Cards 27 and 28 are the same except for colors. The cards were issued as inserts to the 1969 Topps regular football card set. The cards are unnumbered, but have been numbered in the checklist below for convenience in alphabetical order by the player in the northwest quadrant of the card. Prices below are for complete cards; individual stamps are not priced. An album exists to house the stamps on these cards (see 1969 Topps Mini Albums). It is interesting to note that not all the players appearing in this set also appear in the 1969 Topps regular issue set especially since there are almost the same number of players in each set. Jack Kemp is included in this set but not in the regular 1969 Topps set. Bryan Piccolo also appears in his only Topps appearance other than the 1969 Topps regular issue set. There are 19 players in this set who do not appear in the regular issue 1969 Topps set; they are marked by asterisks in the list below.

COMPLETE SET (66) 150.00 300.00
1 Gale Sayers 6.00 12.00
2 Jim Allison * 1.75 3.50
3 Lance Alworth/Maynard 3.00 6.00
4 Fred Biletnikoff 3.00 6.00
5 Ralph Baker 2.50 5.00
6 Gary Ballman 1.75 3.50
7 Tom Beer 1.75 3.50
8 Sonny Bishop 1.75 3.50
9 Bruce Bosley 1.75 3.50
10 Larry Bowie 1.75 3.50
11 Nick Buoniconti 2.50 5.00
12 Jim Burson 1.75 3.50
13 Reg Carolan * 1.75 3.50
14 Bert Coan * 2.50 5.00
15 Joe Namath 15.00 30.00
16 Fran Tarkenton 5.00 10.00
17 Pete Gogolak 1.75 3.50
18 Bob Griese 5.00 10.00
19 Jim Hart 1.75 3.50
20 Alvin Haymond 1.75 3.50
21 Dick Butkus 6.00 12.00
22 Fred Hill 2.50 5.00
23 Dick Hoak 2.50 5.00
24 Jim Houston 1.75 3.50
25 Gene Howard 1.75 3.50
26 Brian Piccolo 12.50 25.00
27 C.Johnson R 1.75 3.50
Katcav
G.Lewis
Triplett W
28 C.Johnson W 1.75 3.50
Katcav
G.Lewis
Triplett R
29 Walter Johnson 1.75 3.50
30 Sonny Jurgensen 4.00 8.00
31 Bart Starr 7.50 15.00
32 Charley King 1.75 3.50
33 Daryle Lamonica 2.50 5.00
34 Bob Lilly/Brodie 3.00 6.00
35 Jim Lindsey 2.50 5.00
36 Billy Lothridge 2.50 5.00
37 Bobby Maples 1.75 3.50
38 Don Meredith 6.00 12.00
39 Rex Mirich 1.75 3.50
40 Leroy Mitchell 1.75 3.50
41 Larry Csonka 6.00 12.00
42 Bill Nelsen 1.75 3.50
43 Jim Otto 2.50 5.00
44 Jack Pardee 1.75 3.50
45 Richie Petitbon 1.75 3.50
46 Nick Rassas 2.50 5.00
47 Pat Richter 1.75 3.50
48 Johnny Roland 1.75 3.50
49 Alex Karras 3.00 6.00
50 Joe Scarpati 1.75 3.50
51 Tom Sestak 1.75 3.50
52 Bob Hayes 2.50 5.00
53 Jackie Smith/C.Taylor 3.00 6.00
54 Larry Stallings 2.50 5.00
55 Mike Stratton * 1.75 3.50
56 Len Dawson 3.00 6.00
57 Jack Kemp/Blanda 12.50 25.00
58 Clendon Thomas 1.75 3.50
59 Don Trull * 2.50 5.00
60 Johnny Unitas 7.50 15.00
61 Merlin Olsen 2.50 5.00
62 Willie West * 1.75 3.50
63 Jerrel Wilson 1.75 3.50
64 Larry Wilson 2.50 5.00
65 Willie Wood 2.50 5.00
66 Tom Woodeshick 2.50 5.00

1969 Topps Mini-Albums Inserts

The 1969 Topps Mini-Card Team Albums is a set of 26 small (2 1/2" by 3 1/2") booklets which were issued in conjunction with the 1969 Four-in-One inserts. Each of these booklets has eight pages and a game action photo on the front. Many of the cover photos were from games from the early 1960s. We've included the player's names when known. A picture of each player is contained in the album, over which the stamps from the Four-in-One inserts were to be pasted. In order to be mint, the album must have no stamps pasted in it. The booklets are printed in blue and black ink on thick white paper and are numbered on the last page of the album. The card numbering cooresponds to an alphabetical listing by team name within each league.

COMPLETE SET (26) 37.50 75.00
1 Atlanta Falcons 1.50 3.00
2 Baltimore Colts 3.00 6.00
3 Chicago Bears 1.50 3.00
4 Cleveland Browns 2.00 4.00
5 Dallas Cowboys 2.50 5.00
6 Detroit Lions 1.50 3.00
7 Green Bay Packers 3.00 6.00
8 Los Angeles Rams 1.50 3.00
9 Minnesota Vikings 1.50 3.00
10 New Orleans Saints 1.50 3.00
11 New York Giants 1.50 3.00
12 Philadelphia Eagles 2.00 4.00
13 Pittsburgh Steelers 2.00 4.00
14 St. Louis Cardinals 1.50 3.00
15 San Francisco 49ers 1.50 3.00
16 Washington Redskins 1.50 3.00
17 Boston Patriots 1.50 3.00
18 Buffalo Bills 2.00 4.00
19 Cincinnati Bengals 2.00 4.00
20 Denver Broncos 1.50 3.00
21 Houston Oilers 1.50 3.00
22 Kansas City Chiefs 3.00 6.00
23 Miami Dolphins 2.00 4.00
24 New York Jets 2.00 4.00
25 Oakland Raiders 2.50 5.00
26 San Diego Chargers 1.50 3.00

1970 Topps

The 1970 Topps football set contains 263 standard-size cards that were issued in two series. The second series (133-263) was printed in slightly lesser quantities than the first series. This set was issued in 10 count, 10 cent packs which came 24 packs to a box. Card fronts have an oval photo surrounded by tan borders. At the bottom of photo is a color banner that contains the player's name and team. A football at bottom right contain the player's position. The card backs are done in orange, purple, and white and are horizontally designed. Statistics, highlights and a player cartoon adorn the backs. In the second series, card backs of offensive and defensive linemen have a coin rub-off cartoon rather than a printed cartoon as seen on all the other cards in the set. O.J. Simpson's Rookie Card appears in this set. Other notable Rookie Cards in this set are Lem Barney, Bill Bergey, Larry Brown, Fred Dryer, Mike Garrett, Calvin Hill, Harold Jackson, Tom Mack, Alan Page, Bubba Smith, Jan Stenerud, Bob Trumpy, and both Gene Washingtons.

COMPLETE SET (263) 300.00 475.00
WRAPPER (10-CENT) 8.00 12.00
1 Len Dawson UER 12.00 20.00
2 Doug Hart RC .40 1.00
3 Verlon Biggs .40 1.00
4 Ralph Neely RC .60 1.50
5 Harmon Wages RC .40 1.00
6 Dan Conners RC .40 1.00
7 Gino Cappelletti .60 1.50
8 Erich Barnes .40 1.00
9 Checklist 5.00 10.00
10 Bob Griese 7.50 15.00
11 Ed Flanagan RC .40 1.00
12 George Seals RC .40 1.00
13 Harry Jacobs .40 1.00
14 Mike Haffner RC .40 1.00
15 Bob Vogel .40 1.00
16 Bill Peterson RC .40 1.00
17 Spider Lockhart .40 1.00
18 Billy Truax .40 1.00
19 Jim Beirne RC .40 1.00
20 Leroy Kelly 3.00 6.00
21 Dave Lloyd .40 1.00
22 Mike Tilleman .40 1.00
23 Gary Garrison .40 1.00
24 Larry Brown RC 4.00 12.00
25 Jan Stenerud RC 6.00 12.00
26 Rolf Krueger RC .40 1.00
27 Roland Lakes .40 1.00
28 Dick Hoak .40 1.00
29 Gene Washington Vik RC 1.25 2.50
30 Bart Starr 12.50 25.00
31 Dave Grayson .40 1.00
32 Jerry Rush RC .40 1.00
33 Len St. Jean RC .40 1.00
34 Randy Edmunds RC .40 1.00
35 Matt Snell .60 1.50
36 Paul Costa .40 1.00
37 Mike Pyle .40 1.00
38 Roy Hilton .40 1.00
39 Steve Tensi .40 1.00
40 Tommy Nobis 1.25 2.50
41 Pete Case .40 1.00
42 Andy Rice RC .40 1.00
43 Elvin Bethea RC 4.00 8.00
44 Jack Snow .60 1.50
45 Mel Renfro 1.25 2.50
46 Andy Livingston .40 1.00
47 Gary Ballman .40 1.00
48 Bob DeMarco .40 1.00
49 Steve DeLong .40 1.00
50 Daryle Lamonica 2.00 4.00
51 Jim Lynch RC .40 1.00
52 Mel Farr RC .40 1.00
53 Bob Long RC .40 1.00
54 John Elliott RC .40 1.00
55 Ray Nitschke 2.50 5.00
56 Jim Shorter .40 1.00
57 Dave Wilcox 1.25 2.50
58 Eric Crabtree .40 1.00
59 Alan Page RC 15.00 30.00
60 Jim Nance .60 1.50
61 Glen Ray Hines RC .40 1.00
62 John Mackey 1.25 2.50
63 Ron McDole .40 1.00
64 Tom Beier RC .40 1.00
65 Bill Nelsen .60 1.50
66 Paul Flatley .40 1.00
67 Sam Brunelli RC .40 1.00
68 Jack Pardee .60 1.50
69 Brig Owens .40 1.00
70 Gale Sayers 12.50 25.00
71 Lee Roy Jordan 1.25 2.50
72 Harold Jackson RC 2.50 5.00
73 John Hadl 1.25 2.50
74 Dave Parks .40 1.00
75 Lem Barney RC 7.50 15.00
76 Johnny Roland .40 1.00
77 Ed Budde .40 1.00
78 Ben McGee .40 1.00
79 Ken Bowman RC .40 1.00
80 Fran Tarkenton 7.50 15.00
81 Gene Washington 49er RC 2.50 5.00
82 Larry Grantham .40 1.00
83 Bill Brown .60 1.50
84 John Charles .40 1.00
85 Fred Biletnikoff 3.50 7.00
86 Royce Berry RC .40 1.00
87 Bob Lilly 2.50 5.00
88 Earl Morrall .60 1.50
89 Jerry LeVias RC .60 1.50
90 O.J. Simpson 40.00 80.00
91 Mike Howell RC .40 1.00
92 Ken Gray .40 1.00
93 Chris Hanburger .40 1.00
94 Larry Seiple RC .40 1.00
95 Rich Jackson RC .40 1.00
96 Rockne Freitas RC .40 1.00
97 Dick Post RC .60 1.50
98 Ben Hawkins RC .40 1.00
99 Ken Reaves RC .40 1.00
100 Roman Gabriel 1.25 2.50
101 Dave Rowe RC .40 1.00
102 Dave Robinson .75 2.00
103 Otis Taylor .60 1.50
104 Jim Turner .40 1.00
105 Joe Morrison .40 1.00
106 Dick Evey .40 1.00
107 Ray Mansfield RC .40 1.00
108 Grady Alderman .40 1.00
109 Bruce Gossett .40 1.00
110 Bob Trumpy RC 2.00 4.00
111 Jim Hunt .40 1.00
112 Larry Stallings .40 1.00
113A Lance Rentzel Red .60 1.50
113B Lance Rentzel Black .60 1.50
114 Bubba Smith RC 12.50 25.00
115 Norm Snead .60 1.50
116 Jim Otto 1.25 2.50
117 Bo Scott RC .40 1.00
118 Rick Redman .40 1.00
119 George Butch Byrd .40 1.00
120 George Webster RC .60 1.50
121 Chuck Walton RC .40 1.00
122 Dave Costa .40 1.00
123 Al Dodd RC .40 1.00
124 Len Hauss .40 1.00
125 Deacon Jones 1.25 2.50
126 Randy Johnson .40 1.00
127 Ralph Heck .40 1.00
128 Emerson Boozer RC .60 1.50
129 Johnny Robinson .60 1.50
130 John Brodie 2.50 5.00
131 Gale Gillingham RC .40 1.00
132 Checklist DP 3.00 6.00
133 Chuck Walker RC .50 1.25
134 Bennie McRae .50 1.25
135 Paul Warfield 3.50 7.00
136 Dan Darragh RC .50 1.25
137 Paul Robinson RC .50 1.25
138 Ed Philpott RC .50 1.25
139 Craig Morton 1.50 3.00
140 Tom Dempsey RC .75 2.00
141 Al Nelson RC .50 1.25
142 Tom Matte .75 2.00
143 Dick Schafrath .50 1.25
144 Willie Brown 2.00 4.00
145 Charley Taylor UER 2.50 5.00
146 John Huard RC .50 1.25
147 Dave Osborn .50 1.25
148 Gene Mingo .50 1.25
149 Larry Hand RC .50 1.25
150 Joe Namath 25.00 50.00
151 Tom Mack RC 5.00 10.00
152 Kenny Graham .50 1.25
153 Don Herrmann RC .50 1.25
154 Bobby Bell 1.50 3.00
155 Hoyle Granger RC .50 1.25
156 Claude Humphrey RC 12.00 20.00
157 Clifton McNeil .50 1.25
158 Mick Tingelhoff .75 2.00
159 Don Horn RC .50 1.25
160 Larry Wilson 1.50 3.00
161 Tom Neville RC .50 1.25
162 Larry Csonka 10.00 20.00
163 Doug Buffone RC .50 1.25
164 Cornell Green .75 2.00
165 Haven Moses RC .75 2.00
166 Billy Kilmer 1.50 3.00
167 Tim Rossovich RC .50 1.25
168 Bill Bergey RC 2.00 4.00
169 Gary Collins .75 2.00
170 Floyd Little 1.50 3.00
171 Tom Keating .50 1.25
172 Pat Fischer .50 1.25
173 Walt Sweeney .50 1.25
174 Greg Larson .50 1.25
175 Carl Eller 1.50 3.00
176 George Sauer Jr. .75 2.00
177 Jim Hart 1.50 3.00
178 Bob Brown OT 1.50 3.00
179 Mike Garrett RC .75 2.00
180 Johnny Unitas 15.00 25.00
181 Tom Regner RC .50 1.25
182 Bob Jeter .50 1.25
183 Gail Cogdill .50 1.25
184 Earl Gros .50 1.25
185 Dennis Partee RC .50 1.25
186 Charlie Krueger .50 1.25
187 Martin Baccaglio RC .50 1.25
188 Charles Long .50 1.25
189 Bob Hayes 3.00 6.00
190 Dick Butkus 12.50 25.00
191 Al Bemiller .50 1.25
192 Dick Westmoreland .50 1.25
193 Joe Scarpati .50 1.25
194 Ron Snidow RC .50 1.25
195 Earl McCullouch RC .50 1.25
196 Jake Kupp RC .50 1.25
197 Bob Lurtsema RC .50 1.25
198 Mike Current RC .50 1.25
199 Charlie Smith RB RC .50 1.25
200 Sonny Jurgensen 3.00 6.00
201 Mike Curtis .75 2.00
202 Aaron Brown RC .50 1.25
203 Richie Petitbon .50 1.25
204 Walt Suggs .50 1.25
205 Roy Jefferson .50 1.25
206 Russ Washington RC .50 1.25
207 Woody Peoples RC .50 1.25
208 Dave Williams .50 1.25
209 John Zook RC .50 1.25
210 Tom Woodeshick .50 1.25
211 Howard Fest RC .50 1.25
212 Jack Concannon .50 1.25
213 Jim Marshall 1.50 3.00
214 Jon Morris .50 1.25
215 Dan Abramowicz .75 2.00
216 Paul Martha .50 1.25
217 Ken Willard .50 1.25
218 Walter Rock .50 1.25
219 Garland Boyette .50 1.25
220 Buck Buchanan 1.50 3.00
221 Bill Munson .75 2.00
222 David Lee RC .50 1.25
223 Karl Noonan .50 1.25
224 Harry Schuh .50 1.25
225 Jackie Smith 1.50 3.00
226 Gerry Philbin .50 1.25
227 Ernie Koy .50 1.25
228 Chuck Howley .75 2.00
229 Billy Shaw 1.50 3.00
230 Jerry Hillebrand .50 1.25
231 Bill Thompson RC .75 2.00
232 Carroll Dale .75 2.00
233 Gene Hickerson 1.50 3.00
234 Jim Butler .50 1.25
235 Greg Cook RC .50 1.25
236 Lee Roy Caffey .50 1.25
237 Merlin Olsen 2.00 4.00
238 Fred Cox .50 1.25
239 Nate Ramsey .50 1.25
240 Lance Alworth 3.50 7.00
241 Chuck Hinton RC .50 1.25
242 Jerry Smith .50 1.25
243 Tony Baker FB RC .50 1.25
244 Nick Buoniconti 1.50 3.00
245 Jim Johnson 1.50 3.00
246 Willie Richardson .50 1.25
247 Fred Dryer RC 5.00 10.00
248 Bobby Maples .50 1.25
249 Alex Karras 2.00 4.00
250 Joe Kapp .75 2.00
251 Ben Davidson 1.50 3.00
252 Mike Stratton .50 1.25
253 Les Josephson .50 1.25

254 Don Maynard 3.00 6.00
255 Houston Antwine .50 1.25
256 Mac Percival RC .50 1.25
257 George Goeddeke RC .50 1.25
258 Homer Jones .50 1.25
259 Bob Berry RC .50 1.25
260A Calvin Hill Red RC 7.50 15.00
260B Calvin Hill Black RC 10.00 20.00
261 Willie Wood 1.50 3.00
262 Ed Weisacosky RC .50 1.25
263 Jim Tyrer 1.50 3.00

1970 Topps Glossy Inserts

The 1970 Topps Super Glossy football set features 33 full-color, thick-stock, glossy cards each measuring 2 1/4" by 3 1/4". The corners are rounded and the backs contain only the player's name, his position, his team and the card number. The set numbering follows the player's team location within league (NFC 1-20 and AFC 21-33). The cards are quite attractive and a favorite with collectors. The cards were inserted in 1970 Topps first series football wax packs. The key cards in the set are Joe Namath and O.J. Simpson, appearing in his Rookie Card year.

COMPLETE SET (33) 150.00 250.00
1 Tommy Nobis 3.00 6.00
2 Johnny Unitas 20.00 40.00
3 Tom Matte 2.50 5.00
4 Mac Percival 2.00 4.00
5 Leroy Kelly 3.00 6.00
6 Mel Renfro 3.00 6.00
7 Bob Hayes 3.00 6.00
8 Earl McCullouch 2.00 4.00
9 Bart Starr 15.00 30.00
10 Willie Wood 3.00 6.00
11 Jack Snow 2.00 4.00
12 Joe Kapp 2.50 5.00
13 Dave Osborn 2.00 4.00
14 Dan Abramowicz 2.00 4.00
15 Fran Tarkenton 10.00 20.00
16 Tom Woodeshick 2.00 4.00
17 Roy Jefferson 2.00 4.00
18 Jackie Smith 2.50 5.00
19 Jim Johnson 2.50 5.00
20 Sonny Jurgensen 5.00 10.00
21 Houston Antwine 2.00 4.00
22 O.J. Simpson 10.00 20.00
23 Greg Cook 2.00 4.00
24 Floyd Little 2.50 5.00
25 Rich Jackson 2.00 4.00
26 George Webster 2.00 4.00
27 Len Dawson 5.00 10.00
28 Bob Griese 7.50 15.00
29 Joe Namath 20.00 40.00
30 Matt Snell 2.50 5.00
31 Daryle Lamonica 3.00 6.00
32 Fred Biletnikoff 5.00 10.00
33 Dick Post 2.00 4.00

1970 Topps Posters Inserts

This insert set of 24 folded thin paper posters was issued with the 1970 Topps regular football card issue. The posters are approximately 8" by 10" and were inserted in wax packs along with the 1970 Topps regular issue (second series) football cards. The posters are blank backed.

COMPLETE SET (24) 60.00 100.00
1 Gale Sayers 7.50 15.00
2 Bobby Bell 2.00 4.00
3 Roman Gabriel 1.50 3.00
4 Jim Tyrer 1.25 2.50
5 Willie Brown 2.00 4.00
6 Carl Eller 1.50 3.00
7 Tom Mack 1.50 3.00
8 Deacon Jones 2.00 4.00
9 Johnny Robinson 1.25 2.50
10 Jan Stenerud 1.50 3.00
11 Dick Butkus 7.50 15.00
12 Lem Barney 2.00 4.00
13 David Lee 1.25 2.50
14 Larry Wilson 1.50 3.00
15 Gene Hickerson 1.25 3.00
16 Lance Alworth 4.00 8.00
17 Merlin Olsen 2.50 5.00
18 Bob Trumpy 1.50 3.00
19 Bob Lilly 3.00 6.00
20 Mick Tingelhoff SP 3.00 6.00
21 Calvin Hill 1.50 3.00
22 Paul Warfield 4.00 8.00
23 Chuck Howley 1.50 3.00
24 Bob Brown OT 1.50 3.00

1970 Topps Super

The 1970 Topps Super set contains 35 cards. The cards measure approximately 3 1/8" by 5 1/4". The backs of the cards are identical in format to the regular football issue of 1970. The cards were sold in packs of three with a stick of gum for a dime and are on very thick card stock. The last seven cards in the set were printed in smaller quantities, i.e., short printed; these seven are designated SP in the checklist below. The cards were printed in sheets of seven rows and nine columns or 63 cards; thus 28 cards were double printed and seven cards were single printed. In more recent years wrongbacks and uncut sheets of the cards have been uncovered as well as some featuring square corners instead of rounded.

COMPLETE SET (35) 125.00 250.00
WRAPPER (10-CENT) 10.00 20.00
1 Fran Tarkenton 6.00 12.00
2 Floyd Little 1.50 4.00
3 Bart Starr 12.50 25.00
4 Len Dawson 4.00 8.00
5 Dick Post 1.25 3.00
6 Sonny Jurgensen 4.00 8.00
7 Deacon Jones 2.00 5.00
8 Leroy Kelly 2.00 5.00
9 Larry Wilson 1.50 4.00
10 Greg Cook 1.25 3.00
11 Carl Eller 1.50 4.00
12 Lem Barney 2.00 5.00
13 Lance Alworth 5.00 10.00
14 Dick Butkus 7.50 15.00
15 Johnny Unitas 15.00 30.00
16 Roy Jefferson 1.25 3.00
17 Bobby Bell 2.00 5.00
18 John Brodie 3.00 6.00
19 Dan Abramowicz 1.25 3.00
20 Matt Snell 1.50 4.00
21 Tom Matte 1.25 3.00
22 Gale Sayers 7.50 15.00
23 Tom Woodeshick 1.25 3.00
24 O.J. Simpson 7.50 15.00
25 Roman Gabriel 1.50 4.00
26 Jim Nance 1.25 3.00
27 Joe Morrison 1.25 3.00
28 Calvin Hill 1.50 4.00
29 Tommy Nobis SP 3.00 6.00
30 Bob Hayes SP 4.00 8.00
31 Joe Kapp SP 2.00 4.00
32 Daryle Lamonica SP 3.00 6.00
33 Joe Namath SP 25.00 50.00
34 George Webster SP 2.00 4.00
35 Bob Griese SP 10.00 20.00

1971 Topps

The 1971 Topps set contains 263 standard-size cards issued in two series. The second series (133-263) was printed in slightly lesser quantities than the first series. Card have a player photo surrounded by either a red (AFC), blue (NFC) or blue and red (All-Pros) border. The player's name, team name, position and conference are within the bottom border. An animated cartoon-like player icon appears by the position listing at the bottom. The card backs are printed in black ink with a gold accent on gray card stock. The content includes highlights and, a first for Topps football cards, yearly statistics. A player cartoon is at the top. The first cards of two Steeler greats, Terry Bradshaw and Mean Joe Greene, appear in this set. Other notable Rookie Cards in this set are Hall of Famers Ken Houston and Willie Lanier.

COMPLETE SET (263) 300.00 500.00
WRAPPER (10-CENT) 10.00 20.00
1 Johnny Unitas 15.00 30.00
2 Jim Butler .40 1.00
3 Marty Schottenheimer RC 6.00 12.00
4 Joe O'Donnell RC .40 1.00
5 Tom Dempsey .50 1.25
6 Chuck Allen .40 1.00
7 Ernie Kellerman .40 1.00
8 Walt Garrison RC .75 2.00
9 Bill Van Heusen RC .40 1.00
10 Lance Alworth 4.00 8.00
11 Greg Landry RC .75 2.00
12 Larry Krause RC .40 1.00
13 Buck Buchanan .75 2.00
14 Roy Gerela RC .50 1.25
15 Clifton McNeil .40 1.00
16 Bob Brown OT .75 2.00
17 Lloyd Mumphord RC .40 1.00
18 Gary Cuozzo .40 1.00
19 Don Maynard 2.50 5.00
20 Larry Wilson .75 2.00
21 Charlie Smith RB .40 1.00
22 Ken Avery RC .40 1.00
23 Billy Walik RC .40 1.00
24 Jim Johnson .75 2.00
25 Dick Butkus 12.50 25.00
26 Charley Taylor UER 2.00 4.00
27 Checklist UER 4.00 12.00
28 Lionel Aldridge RC .40 1.00
29 Billy Lothridge .40 1.00
30 Terry Hanratty RC .50 1.25
31 Lee Roy Jordan .75 2.00
32 Rick Volk RC .40 1.00
33 Howard Kindig .40 1.00
34 Carl Garrett RC .40 1.00
35 Bobby Bell .75 2.00
36 Gene Hickerson .75 2.00
37 Dave Parks .40 1.00
38 Paul Martha .40 1.00
39 George Blanda 7.50 15.00
40 Tom Woodeshick .40 1.00
41 Alex Karras 1.50 3.00
42 Rick Redman .40 1.00
43 Zeke Moore RC .40 1.00
44 Jack Snow .50 1.25
45 Larry Csonka 7.50 15.00
46 Karl Kassulke RC .40 1.00
47 Jim Hart .75 2.00
48 Al Atkinson .40 1.00
49 Horst Muhlmann RC .40 1.00
50 Sonny Jurgensen 2.50 5.00
51 Ron Johnson RC .50 1.25
52 Cas Banaszek RC .40 1.00
53 Bubba Smith 4.00 8.00
54 Bobby Douglass RC .50 1.25
55 Willie Wood .75 2.00
56 Bake Turner .40 1.00
57 Mike Morgan LB RC .40 1.00
58 George Butch Byrd .50 1.25
59 Don Horn .40 1.00
60 Tommy Nobis .75 2.00
61 Jan Stenerud 2.00 4.00
62 Altie Taylor RC .40 1.00
63 Gary Pettigrew RC .40 1.00
64 Spike Jones RC .40 1.00
65 Duane Thomas RC .75 2.00
66 Marty Domres RC .40 1.00
67 Dick Anderson .50 1.25
68 Ken Iman RC .40 1.00
69 Miller Farr .40 1.00
70 Daryle Lamonica 1.50 3.00
71 Alan Page 6.00 12.00
72 Pat Matson RC .40 1.00
73 Emerson Boozer .40 1.00
74 Pat Fischer .40 1.00
75 Gary Collins .50 1.25
76 John Fuqua RC .50 1.25
77 Bruce Gossett .40 1.00
78 Ed O'Bradovich .40 1.00
79 Bob Tucker RC .50 1.25
80 Mike Curtis .50 1.25
81 Rich Jackson .40 1.00
82 Tom Janik .40 1.00
83 Gale Gillingham .40 1.00
84 Jim Mitchell TE RC .40 1.00
85 Charley Johnson .50 1.25
86 Edgar Chandler RC .40 1.00
87 Cyril Pinder RC .40 1.00
88 Johnny Robinson .50 1.25
89 Ralph Neely .40 1.00
90 Dan Abramowicz .40 1.00
91 Mercury Morris RC 5.00 10.00
92 Steve DeLong .40 1.00
93 Larry Stallings .40 1.00
94 Tom Mack .75 2.00
95 Hewritt Dixon .40 1.00
96 Fred Cox .40 1.00
97 Chris Hanburger .40 1.00
98 Gerry Philbin .40 1.00
99 Ernie Wright .40 1.00
100 John Brodie 2.00 4.00
101 Tucker Frederickson .40 1.00
102 Bobby Walden .40 1.00
103 Dick Gordon .40 1.00
104 Walter Johnson .40 1.00
105 Mike Lucci .50 1.25
106 Checklist DP 3.00 6.00
107 Ron Berger RC .40 1.00
108 Dan Sullivan RC .40 1.00
109 George Kunz RC .40 1.00
110 Floyd Little .75 2.00
111 Zeke Bratkowski .50 1.25
112 Haven Moses .50 1.25
113 Ken Houston RC 7.50 15.00
114 Willie Lanier RC 7.50 15.00
115 Larry Brown .75 2.00
116 Tim Rossovich .40 1.00
117 Errol Linden RC .40 1.00
118 Mel Renfro .75 2.00
119 Mike Garrett .40 1.00
120 Fran Tarkenton 7.50 15.00
121 Garo Yepremian RC .75 2.00
122 Glen Condren RC .40 1.00
123 Johnny Roland .40 1.00
124 Dave Herman .40 1.00
125 Merlin Olsen 1.50 3.00
126 Doug Buffone .40 1.00
127 Earl McCullouch .40 1.00
128 Spider Lockhart .40 1.00
129 Ken Willard .40 1.00
130 Gene Washington Vik .40 1.00
131 Mike Phipps RC .50 1.25
132 Andy Russell .50 1.25
133 Ray Nitschke 2.00 6.00
134 Jerry Logan .50 1.25
135 MacArthur Lane RC .60 1.50
136 Jim Turner .50 1.25
137 Kent McCloughan .50 1.25
138 Paul Guidry .50 1.25
139 Otis Taylor .60 1.50
140 Virgil Carter RC .50 1.25
141 Joe Dawkins RC .50 1.25
142 Steve Preece RC .50 1.25
143 Mike Bragg RC .50 1.25
144 Bob Lilly 2.50 5.00
145 Joe Kapp .60 1.50
146 Al Dodd .50 1.25
147 Nick Buoniconti 1.25 2.50
148 Speedy Duncan .50 1.25
149 Cedrick Hardman RC .50 1.25
150 Gale Sayers 15.00 30.00
151 Jim Otto 1.25 2.50
152 Billy Truax .50 1.25
153 John Elliott .50 1.25
154 Dick LeBeau 1.25 2.50
155 Bill Bergey .60 1.50
156 Terry Bradshaw RC ! 125.00 200.00
157 Leroy Kelly 3.00 6.00
158 Paul Krause 1.25 2.50
159 Ted Vactor RC .50 1.25
160 Bob Griese 7.50 15.00
161 Ernie McMillan .50 1.25
162 Donny Anderson .60 1.50
163 John Pitts RC .50 1.25
164 Dave Costa .50 1.25
165 Gene Washington 49er .60 1.50
166 John Zook .50 1.25
167 Pete Gogolak .50 1.25
168 Erich Barnes .50 1.25
169 Alvin Reed RC .50 1.25
170 Jim Nance .60 1.50
171 Craig Morton 1.25 2.50
172 Gary Garrison .50 1.25
173 Joe Scarpati .50 1.25
174 Adrian Young UER RC .50 1.25
175 John Mackey 1.25 2.50
176 Mac Percival .50 1.25
177 Preston Pearson RC 2.00 4.00
178 Fred Biletnikoff 4.00 8.00
179 Mike Battle RC .50 1.25
180 Len Dawson 4.00 8.00
181 Les Josephson .50 1.25
182 Royce Berry .50 1.25
183 Herman Weaver RC .50 1.25
184 Norm Snead .60 1.50
185 Sam Brunelli .50 1.25
186 Jim Kiick RC 2.50 5.00
187 Austin Denney RC .50 1.25
188 Roger Wehrli RC 7.50 15.00
189 Dave Wilcox 1.25 2.50
190 Bob Hayes 2.00 4.00
191 Joe Morrison .50 1.25
192 Manny Sistrunk RC .50 1.25
193 Don Cockroft RC .50 1.25
194 Lee Bouggess RC .50 1.25
195 Bob Berry .50 1.25
196 Ron Sellers RC .50 1.25
197 George Webster .50 1.25
198 Hoyle Granger .50 1.25
199 Bob Vogel .50 1.25
200 Bart Starr 10.00 25.00
201 Mike Mercer .50 1.25
202 Dave Smith WR .50 1.25
203 Lee Roy Caffey .50 1.25
204 Mick Tingelhoff .60 1.50
205 Matt Snell .60 1.50
206 Jim Tyrer .50 1.25
207 Willie Brown 1.25 2.50
208 Bob Johnson RC .50 1.25
209 Deacon Jones 1.25 2.50
210 Charlie Sanders RC 6.00 12.00
211 Jake Scott RC 3.00 6.00
212 Bob Anderson RC .50 1.25
213 Charlie Krueger .50 1.25
214 Jim Bakken .50 1.25
215 Harold Jackson .60 1.50
216 Bill Brundige RC .50 1.25
217 Calvin Hill 2.50 5.00
218 Claude Humphrey .60 1.50
219 Glen Ray Hines .50 1.25
220 Bill Nelsen .60 1.50
221 Roy Hilton .50 1.25
222 Don Herrmann .50 1.25
223 John Bramlett .50 1.25
224 Ken Ellis RC .50 1.25
225 Dave Osborn .60 1.50
226 Edd Hargett RC .50 1.25
227 Gene Mingo .50 1.25
228 Larry Grantham .50 1.25
229 Dick Post .50 1.25
230 Roman Gabriel 1.25 2.50
231 Mike Eischeid RC .50 1.25
232 Jim Lynch .50 1.25
233 Lemar Parrish RC .60 1.50
234 Cecil Turner RC .50 1.25
235 Dennis Shaw RC .50 1.25
236 Mel Farr .50 1.25
237 Curt Knight RC .50 1.25
238 Chuck Howley .60 1.50
239 Bruce Taylor RC .50 1.25
240 Jerry LeVias .50 1.25
241 Bob Lurtsema .50 1.25
242 Earl Morrall .60 1.50
243 Kermit Alexander .50 1.25
244 Jackie Smith 1.25 2.50
245 Joe Greene RC 35.00 60.00
246 Harmon Wages .50 1.25
247 Errol Mann .50 1.25
248 Mike McCoy DT RC .50 1.25
249 Milt Morin RC .50 1.25
250 Joe Namath 35.00 60.00
251 Jackie Burkett .50 1.25
252 Steve Chomyszak RC .50 1.25
253 Ed Sharockman .50 1.25
254 Robert Holmes RC .50 1.25
255 John Hadl 1.25 2.50
256 Cornell Gordon .50 1.25
257 Mark Moseley RC .60 1.50
258 Gus Otto .50 1.25
259 Mike Taliaferro .50 1.25
260 O.J.Simpson 12.50 25.00
261 Paul Warfield 4.00 8.00
262 Jack Concannon .50 1.25
263 Tom Matte 1.25 2.50

1971 Topps Game Inserts

The 1971 Topps Game cards were issued as inserts with the 1971 regular issue football cards. The cards measure 2 1/4" by 3 1/4" with rounded corners. The cards can be used for a table game of football. The 52 player cards in the set are numbered and have light blue backs. The 53rd card (actually unnumbered) is a field position/first down marker which is used in the table game. Six of the cards in the set were double printed and are marked as DP in the checklist below. The key card in the set is Terry Bradshaw, appearing in his Rookie Card year.

COMPLETE SET (53) 75.00 125.00
1 Dick Butkus DP 3.00 6.00
2 Bob Berry DP .30 .60
3 Joe Namath DP 6.00 12.00
4 Mike Curtis .30 .60
5 Jim Nance .30 .60
6 Ron Berger .30 .60
7 O.J. Simpson 7.50 15.00
8 Haven Moses .50 1.00
9 Tommy Nobis .50 1.00
10 Gale Sayers 6.00 12.00
11 Virgil Carter .30 .60
12 Andy Russell DP .30 .60
13 Bill Nelsen .30 .60
14 Gary Collins .30 .60
15 Duane Thomas .50 1.00
16 Bob Hayes 1.00 2.00
17 Floyd Little .50 1.00
18 Sam Brunelli .30 .60
19 Charlie Sanders .40 1.00
20 Mike Lucci .30 .60
21 Gene Washington 49er .50 1.00
22 Willie Wood 1.00 2.00
23 Jerry LeVias .30 .60
24 Charley Johnson .50 1.00
25 Len Dawson 2.00 4.00
26 Bobby Bell 1.00 2.00
27 Merlin Olsen 1.50 3.00
28 Roman Gabriel 1.00 2.00
29 Bob Griese 3.00 6.00
30 Larry Csonka 3.00 6.00
31 Dave Osborn .30 .60
32 Gene Washington Vik .30 .60
33 Dan Abramowicz .30 .60
34 Tom Dempsey .30 .60
35 Fran Tarkenton 4.00 8.00
36 Clifton McNeil .30 .60
37 Johnny Unitas 7.50 15.00
38 Matt Snell .50 1.00
39 Daryle Lamonica 1.00 2.00
40 Hewritt Dixon .30 .60
41 Tom Woodeshick DP .30 .60
42 Harold Jackson .50 1.00
43 Terry Bradshaw 12.50 25.00
44 Ken Avery .30 .60
45 MacArthur Lane .30 .60
46 Larry Wilson .50 1.00
47 John Hadl .50 1.00
48 Lance Alworth 2.00 4.00
49 John Brodie 1.50 3.00
50 Bart Starr DP 4.00 8.00
51 Sonny Jurgensen 2.50 5.00
52 Larry Brown .50 1.00
NNO Field Marker .30 .60

1971 Topps Posters Inserts

The 1971 Topps Football pin-up posters are a set of 32 paper inserts each folded twice for insertion into gum packs. The cards (small posters) measure 4 7/8" by 6 7/8". The lower left hand corner of the obverse contains the pin-up number while the back features a green simulated football field upon which a football card game could be played as well as the instructions to accompany the card insert game. Inexplicably the second half of the set seems to be somewhat more difficult to find.

COMPLETE SET (32) 50.00 100.00
1 Gene Washington 49er .75 1.50
2 Andy Russell .75 1.50
3 Harold Jackson .75 1.50
4 Joe Namath 7.50 15.00
5 Fran Tarkenton 2.00 4.00
6 Dave Osborn .50 1.00
7 Bob Griese 2.50 5.00
8 Roman Gabriel 1.00 2.00
9 Jerry LeVias .50 1.00
10 Bart Starr 6.00 12.00
11 Bob Hayes 1.50 3.00
12 Gale Sayers 4.00 8.00
13 O.J. Simpson 4.00 8.00
14 Sam Brunelli .50 1.00
15 Jim Nance .75 1.50
16 Bill Nelsen .50 1.00
17 Sonny Jurgensen 2.00 4.00
18 John Brodie 2.00 4.00
19 Lance Alworth 2.50 5.00
20 Larry Wilson 1.50 3.00
21 Daryle Lamonica 1.50 3.00
22 Dan Abramowicz 1.00 2.00
23 Gene Washington Vik 1.00 2.00
24 Bobby Bell 2.00 4.00
25 Merlin Olsen 2.00 4.00
26 Charlie Sanders 1.25 2.50
27 Virgil Carter 1.00 2.00
28 Dick Butkus 4.00 8.00
29 Johnny Unitas 7.50 15.00
30 Tommy Nobis 1.50 3.00
31 Floyd Little 1.50 3.00
32 Larry Brown 1.00 2.00

1972 Topps

The 1972 Topps set contains 351 standard size cards that were issued in three series. The third series (264-351) is considerably more difficult to obtain than cards in the first two series. Card fronts are either horizontal and vertical and contain player photos that are bordered by a color that, for the most part, is part of the player's team color scheme. Vertical photos have team names at the top and horizontal photos have team names to the left. In either case, the player's name and position are at the bottom of the photo. The card backs are printed in blue and green on gray card stock. The backs have yearly statistics and a cartoon. Subsets include league leaders (1-8), In-Action cards (119-132, 250-263, 338-351), 1971 Playoffs (133-139) and All-Pro (264-287). The key Rookie Cards in this set are Lyle Alzado, L.C. Greenwood, Ted Hendricks, Charlie Joiner, Larry Little, Archie Manning, Jim Plunkett, John Riggins, Steve Spurrier, Roger Staubach, and Gene Upshaw. The cards were isssued in 10 cents wax packs.

COMPLETE SET (351) 1500.00 2500.00
WRAPPER (10-CENT) 6.00 10.00
WRAPPER SER.3 (10-CENT) 15.00 20.00
1 L.Csonka/Litt/Hubb LL 2.00 4.00
2 NFC Rushing Leaders .25 .60
3 B.Griese/Dawson/Cart LL .75 2.00
4 R.Staubach/Lan/Kil LL 2.50 5.00
5 AFC Receiving Leaders .50 1.25
6 NFC Receiving Leaders .25 .60
7 Yepre/Stener/O'Brien LL .25 .60
8 NFC Scoring Leaders .25 .60
9 Jim Kiick .75 2.00
10 Otis Taylor .50 1.25
11 Bobby Joe Green .25 .60
12 Ken Ellis .25 .60
13 John Riggins RC 10.00 20.00
14 Dave Parks .25 .60
15 John Hadl .75 2.00
16 Ron Hornsby RC .25 .60
17 Chip Myers RC .25 .60
18 Billy Kilmer .75 2.00
19 Fred Hoaglin RC .25 .60
20 Carl Eller .75 2.00
21 Steve Zabel RC .25 .60
22 Vic Washington RC .25 .60
23 Len St. Jean .25 .60
24 Bill Thompson .25 .60
25 Steve Owens RC 1.25 3.00
26 Ken Burrough RC .50 1.25
27 Mike Clark .25 .60
28 Willie Brown .75 2.00
29 Checklist 1-132 3.00 6.00
30 Marlin Briscoe RC .25 .60
31 Jerry Logan .25 .60
32 Donny Anderson .50 1.25
33 Rich McGeorge RC .25 .60
34 Charlie Durkee .25 .60
35 Willie Lanier 2.00 4.00
36 Chris Farasopoulos RC .25 .60
37 Ron Shanklin RC .25 .60
38 Forrest Blue RC .25 .60
39 Ken Reaves .25 .60
40 Roman Gabriel .75 2.00
41 Mac Percival .25 .60
42 Lem Barney 1.50 3.00
43 Nick Buoniconti .75 2.00
44 Charlie Gogolak .25 .60
45 Bill Bradley RC .50 1.25
46 Joe Jones DE RC .25 .60
47 Dave Williams .25 .60
48 Pete Athas RC .25 .60
49 Virgil Carter .25 .60
50 Floyd Little .75 2.00
51 Curt Knight .25 .60
52 Bobby Maples .25 .60
53 Charlie West RC .25 .60
54 Marv Hubbard RC .50 1.25
55 Archie Manning RC 10.00 25.00
56 Jim O'Brien RC .50 1.25
57 Wayne Patrick RC .25 .60
58 Ken Bowman .25 .60
59 Roger Wehrli .50 1.25
60 Charlie Sanders .50 1.25
61 Jan Stenerud .75 2.00
62 Willie Ellison RC .25 .60
63 Walt Sweeney .25 .60
64 Ron Smith .25 .60
65 Jim Plunkett RC 10.00 20.00
66 Herb Adderley UER .75 2.00
67 Mike Reid RC .75 2.00
68 Richard Caster RC .50 1.25
69 Dave Wilcox .75 2.00
70 Leroy Kelly 1.50 3.00
71 Bob Lee RC .25 .60
72 Verlon Biggs .25 .60
73 Henry Allison RC .25 .60
74 Steve Ramsey RC .25 .60
75 Claude Humphrey .60 1.50
76 Bob Grim RC .25 .60
77 John Fuqua .50 1.25
78 Ken Houston 2.00 4.00
79 Checklist 133-263 DP 2.50 5.00
80 Bob Griese 4.00 8.00
81 Lance Rentzel .50 1.25
82 Ed Podolak RC .50 1.25
83 Ike Hill RC .25 .60
84 George Farmer RC .25 .60
85 John Brockington RC .75 2.00
86 Jim Otto .75 2.00
87 Richard Neal RC .25 .60
88 Jim Hart .75 2.00
89 Bob Babich RC .25 .60
90 Gene Washington 49er .50 1.25
91 John Zook .25 .60
92 Bobby Duhon RC .25 .60
93 Ted Hendricks RC 7.50 15.00
94 Rockne Freitas .25 .60
95 Larry Brown .75 2.00
96 Mike Phipps .50 1.25
97 Julius Adams RC .25 .60
98 Dick Anderson .50 1.25
99 Fred Willis RC .25 .60
100 Joe Namath 20.00 35.00
101 L.C. Greenwood RC 7.50 15.00
102 Mark Nordquist RC .25 .60
103 Robert Holmes .25 .60
104 Ron Yary RC 2.00 5.00
105 Bob Hayes 1.00 2.50
106 Lyle Alzado RC 7.50 15.00
107 Bob Berry .25 .60
108 Phil Villapiano RC .50 1.25
109 Dave Elmendorf RC .25 .60
110 Gale Sayers 10.00 20.00
111 Jim Tyrer .25 .60
112 Mel Gray RC .75 2.00
113 Gerry Philbin .25 .60
114 Bob James RC .25 .60
115 Garo Yepremian .50 1.25
116 Dave Robinson .50 1.25
117 Jeff Queen RC .25 .60
118 Norm Snead .50 1.25
119 Jim Nance IA .50 1.25
120 Terry Bradshaw IA 7.50 15.00
121 Jim Kiick IA .50 1.25
122 Roger Staubach IA 12.00 20.00
123 Bo Scott IA .25 .60
124 John Brodie IA .75 2.00
125 Rick Volk IA .25 .60
126 John Riggins IA 3.00 6.00
127 Bubba Smith IA .75 2.00
128 Roman Gabriel IA .50 1.25
129 Calvin Hill IA .50 1.25
130 Bill Nelsen IA .25 .60
131 Tom Matte IA .50 1.25
132 Bob Griese IA 2.00 4.00
133 AFC Semi-Final .50 1.25
134 NFC Semi-Final .50 1.25
135 AFC Semi-Final .50 1.25
136 NFC Semi-Final .50 1.25
137 AFC Title Game/Unitas 1.50 3.00
138 NFC Title Game/Bob Lilly .75 2.00
139 Super Bowl VI/Staubach 2.50 5.00
140 Larry Csonka 4.00 8.00
141 Rick Volk .30 .75
142 Roy Jefferson .50 1.25
143 Raymond Chester RC .50 1.25
144 Bobby Douglass .30 .75
145 Bob Lilly 2.50 5.00
146 Harold Jackson .50 1.25
147 Pete Gogolak .30 .75
148 Art Malone RC .30 .75
149 Ed Flanagan .30 .75
150 Terry Bradshaw 25.00 40.00
151 MacArthur Lane .50 1.25
152 Jack Snow .50 1.25
153 Al Beauchamp RC .30 .75
154 Bob Anderson .30 .75
155 Ted Kwalick RC .30 .75
156 Dan Pastorini RC 1.00 2.50
157 Emmitt Thomas RC 10.00 20.00
158 Randy Vataha RC .30 .75
159 Al Atkinson .30 .75
160 O.J. Simpson 7.50 15.00
161 Jackie Smith .75 2.00
162 Ernie Kellerman .30 .75
163 Dennis Partee .30 .75
164 Jake Kupp .30 .75
165 John Unitas 12.50 25.00
166 Clint Jones RC .30 .75
167 Paul Warfield 3.00 6.00
168 Roland McDole RC .30 .75
169 Daryle Lamonica .75 2.00
170 Dick Butkus 7.50 15.00
171 Jim Butler .30 .75
172 Mike McCoy .30 .75
173 Dave Smith WR .30 .75
174 Greg Landry .50 1.25
175 Tom Dempsey .50 1.25
176 John Charles .30 .75
177 Bobby Bell .75 2.00
178 Don Horn .30 .75
179 Bob Trumpy .75 2.00
180 Duane Thomas .50 1.25
181 Merlin Olsen 1.50 3.00
182 Dave Herman .30 .75
183 Jim Nance .50 1.25
184 Pete Beathard .30 .75
185 Bob Tucker .30 .75
186 Gene Upshaw RC 7.50 15.00
187 Bo Scott .30 .75
188 J.D. Hill RC .30 .75
189 Bruce Gossett .30 .75
190 Bubba Smith 2.00 4.00
191 Edd Hargett .30 .75
192 Gary Garrison .30 .75
193 Jake Scott .50 1.25
194 Fred Cox .30 .75
195 Sonny Jurgensen 2.00 4.00
196 Greg Brezina RC .30 .75
197 Ed O'Bradovich .30 .75
198 John Rowser RC .30 .75
199 Altie Taylor UER .30 .75
200 Roger Staubach RC 100.00 175.00
201 Leroy Keyes RC .30 .75
202 Garland Boyette .30 .75
203 Tom Beer .30 .75
204 Buck Buchanan .75 2.00
205 Larry Wilson .75 2.00
206 Scott Hunter RC .30 .75
207 Ron Johnson .30 .75
208 Sam Brunelli .30 .75
209 Deacon Jones .75 2.00
210 Fred Biletnikoff 3.00 6.00
211 Bill Nelsen .50 1.25
212 George Nock RC .30 .75
213 Dan Abramowicz .50 1.25
214 Irv Goode .30 .75
215 Isiah Robertson RC .50 1.25
216 Tom Matte .50 1.25
217 Pat Fischer .30 .75
218 Gene Washington Vik .30 .75
219 Paul Robinson .30 .75
220 John Brodie 2.00 4.00
221 Manny Fernandez RC .50 1.25
222 Errol Mann .30 .75
223 Dick Gordon .30 .75
224 Calvin Hill .75 2.00
225 Fran Tarkenton 6.00 12.00
226 Jim Turner .30 .75
227 Jim Mitchell .30 .75
228 Pete Liske .30 .75
229 Carl Garrett .30 .75
230 Joe Greene 10.00 20.00
231 Gale Gillingham .30 .75
232 Norm Bulaich RC .50 1.25
233 Spider Lockhart .30 .75
234 Ken Willard .30 .75
235 George Blanda 6.00 12.00
236 Wayne Mulligan RC .30 .75
237 Dave Lewis RC .30 .75
238 Dennis Shaw .30 .75
239 Fair Hooker RC .30 .75
240 Larry Little RC 7.50 15.00
241 Mike Garrett .30 .75
242 Glen Ray Hines .30 .75
243 Myron Pottios .30 .75
244 Charlie Joiner RC 10.00 20.00
245 Len Dawson 3.00 6.00
246 W.K. Hicks .30 .75
247 Les Josephson .30 .75
248 Lance Alworth UER 3.00 6.00
249 Frank Nunley RC .30 .75
250 Mel Farr IA .30 .75
251 Johnny Unitas IA 4.00 8.00
252 George Farmer IA .30 .75
253 Duane Thomas IA .50 1.25
254 John Hadl IA .75 2.00
255 Vic Washington IA .30 .75
256 Don Horn IA .30 .75
257 L.C. Greenwood IA .75 2.00
258 Bob Lee IA .30 .75
259 Larry Csonka IA 2.00 4.00
260 Mike McCoy IA .30 .75
261 Greg Landry IA .50 1.25
262 Ray May IA .30 .75
263 Bobby Douglass IA .30 .75
264 Charlie Sanders AP 15.00 30.00
265 Ron Yary AP 15.00 30.00
266 Rayfield Wright AP 20.00 40.00
267 Larry Little AP 20.00 35.00
268 John Niland AP 15.00 30.00
269 Forrest Blue AP 15.00 30.00
270 Otis Taylor AP 15.00 30.00
271 Paul Warfield AP 30.00 50.00
272 Bob Griese AP 40.00 70.00
273 John Brockington AP 15.00 30.00
274 Floyd Little AP 15.00 30.00
275 Garo Yepremian AP 15.00 30.00
276 Jerrel Wilson AP 10.00 18.00
277 Carl Eller AP 15.00 30.00
278 Bubba Smith AP 25.00 40.00
279 Alan Page AP 25.00 40.00
280 Bob Lilly AP 30.00 60.00
281 Ted Hendricks AP 30.00 50.00
282 Dave Wilcox AP 15.00 30.00
283 Willie Lanier AP 20.00 35.00
284 Jim Johnson AP 15.00 30.00
285 Willie Brown AP 20.00 35.00
286 Bill Bradley AP 15.00 30.00
287 Ken Houston AP 20.00 35.00
288 Mel Farr 10.00 18.00
289 Kermit Alexander 10.00 18.00
290 John Gilliam RC 15.00 30.00
291 Steve Spurrier RC 50.00 100.00
292 Walter Johnson 10.00 18.00
293 Jack Pardee 12.50 25.00
294 Checklist UER 50.00 80.00
295 Winston Hill 10.00 18.00
296 Hugo Hollas RC 10.00 18.00
297 Ray May RC 10.00 18.00
298 Jim Bakken 10.00 18.00
299 Larry Carwell RC 10.00 18.00
300 Alan Page 30.00 50.00
301 Walt Garrison 12.50 25.00
302 Mike Lucci 12.50 25.00
303 Nemiah Wilson 10.00 18.00
304 Carroll Dale 12.50 25.00
305 Jim Kanicki 10.00 18.00
306 Preston Pearson 15.00 30.00
307 Lemar Parrish 12.50 25.00
308 Earl Morrall 12.50 25.00
309 Tommy Nobis 12.50 25.00
310 Rich Jackson 10.00 18.00
311 Doug Cunningham RC 10.00 18.00
312 Jim Marsalis RC 10.00 18.00
313 Jim Beirne 10.00 18.00
314 Tom McNeill RC 10.00 18.00
315 Milt Morin 10.00 18.00
316 Rayfield Wright RC 30.00 50.00
317 Jerry LeVias 12.50 25.00
318 Travis Williams RC 12.50 25.00
319 Edgar Chandler 10.00 18.00
320 Bob Wallace RC 10.00 18.00
321 Delles Howell RC 10.00 18.00
322 Emerson Boozer 12.50 25.00
323 George Atkinson RC 12.50 25.00
324 Mike Montler RC 10.00 18.00
325 Randy Johnson 10.00 18.00
326 Mike Curtis UER 12.50 25.00
327 Miller Farr 10.00 18.00
328 Horst Muhlmann 10.00 18.00
329 John Niland RC 15.00 30.00
330 Andy Russell 15.00 30.00
331 Mercury Morris 25.00 40.00
332 Jim Johnson 15.00 30.00
333 Jerrel Wilson 10.00 18.00
334 Charley Taylor 25.00 40.00
335 Dick LeBeau 10.00 18.00
336 Jim Marshall 15.00 30.00
337 Tom Mack 15.00 30.00
338 Steve Spurrier IA 30.00 60.00
339 Floyd Little IA 12.50 25.00
340 Len Dawson IA 25.00 40.00
341 Dick Butkus IA 40.00 70.00
342 Larry Brown IA 12.50 25.00
343 Joe Namath IA 75.00 150.00
344 Jim Turner IA 10.00 18.00
345 Doug Cunningham IA 10.00 18.00
346 Edd Hargett IA 10.00 18.00
347 Steve Owens IA 10.00 18.00
348 George Blanda IA 30.00 50.00
349 Ed Podolak IA 10.00 18.00
350 Rich Jackson IA 10.00 18.00
351 Ken Willard IA 25.00 40.00

1973 Topps

The 1973 set marks the first of ten years in a row that Topps produced a 528-card football standard-size set issued in a single series. The fronts have the players name at the top and position and team name at the bottom. The player's first name and team name are in a color that corresponds to one of the colors in a small banner-like design that emanates from the photo. The card backs are printed in blue ink with a red background on gray card stock. Highlights and statistics are accompanied by a cartoon and trivia question and answer. The first six cards in the set are statistical league leader cards. Cards 133-139 show the results of the previous season's playoff games. Cards 265-267 are Kid Pictures (KP) showing the player in a boyhood photo. Rookie Cards include this set are Ken Anderson, Al Cowlings, Dan Dierdorf, Jack Ham, Franco Harris, Jim Langer, Art Shell, Ken Stabler, and Jack Youngblood. An uncut sheet of team checklist cards was also available via a mail-in offer on wax pack wrappers.

COMPLETE SET (528) 200.00 400.00
1 Simpson/L.Brown LL 3.00 8.00
2 Passing Leaders .40 1.00
3 Jackson/Biletnikoff LL .60 1.50
4 Scoring Leaders .25 .60
5 Interception Leaders .25 .60
6 Punting Leaders .25 .60
7 Bob Trumpy .60 1.50
8 Mel Tom RC .25 .60
9 Clarence Ellis RC .25 .60
10 John Niland .25 .60
11 Randy Jackson RC .25 .60
12 Greg Landry .60 1.50
13 Cid Edwards RC .25 .60
14 Phil Olsen RC .25 .60
15 Terry Bradshaw 15.00 25.00
16 Al Cowlings RC .60 1.50
17 Walker Gillette RC .25 .60
18 Bob Atkins RC .25 .60
19 Diron Talbert RC .25 .60
20 Jim Johnson .60 1.50
21 Howard Twilley .40 1.00
22 Dick Enderle RC .25 .60
23 Wayne Colman RC .25 .60
24 John Schmitt RC .25 .60
25 George Blanda 5.00 10.00
26 Milt Morin .25 .60
27 Mike Current .25 .60
28 Rex Kern RC .25 .60
29 MacArthur Lane .40 1.00
30 Alan Page 1.50 3.00
31 Randy Vataha .25 .60
32 Jim Kearney RC .25 .60
33 Steve Smith T RC .25 .60
34 Ken Anderson RC 7.50 15.00
35 Calvin Hill .60 1.50
36 Andy Maurer RC .25 .60
37 Joe Taylor RC .25 .60
38 Deacon Jones .60 1.50
39 Mike Weger RC .25 .60
40 Roy Gerela .40 1.00
41 Les Josephson .25 .60
42 Dave Washington RC .25 .60
43 Bill Curry RC .40 1.00
44 Fred Heron RC .25 .60
45 John Brodie 1.50 3.00
46 Roy Winston .25 .60
47 Mike Bragg .25 .60
48 Mercury Morris .60 1.50
49 Jim Files RC .25 .60
50 Gene Upshaw 1.50 3.00
51 Hugo Hollas .25 .60
52 Rod Sherman RC .25 .60
53 Ron Snidow .25 .60
54 Steve Tannen RC .25 .60
55 Jim Carter RC .25 .60
56 Lydell Mitchell RC .60 1.50
57 Jack Rudnay RC .25 .60
58 Halvor Hagen RC .25 .60
59 Tom Dempsey .40 1.00
60 Fran Tarkenton 5.00 10.00
61 Lance Alworth 2.50 5.00
62 Vern Holland RC .25 .60
63 Steve DeLong .25 .60
64 Art Malone .25 .60
65 Isiah Robertson .40 1.00
66 Jerry Rush .25 .60
67 Bryant Salter RC .25 .60
68 Checklist 1-132 2.50 5.00
69 J.D. Hill .25 .60
70 Forrest Blue .25 .60
71 Myron Pottios .25 .60
72 Norm Thompson RC .25 .60
73 Paul Robinson .25 .60
74 Larry Grantham .25 .60
75 Manny Fernandez .40 1.00
76 Kent Nix RC .25 .60
77 Art Shell RC 7.50 15.00
78 George Saimes .25 .60
79 Don Cockroft .25 .60
80 Bob Tucker .40 1.00
81 Don McCauley RC .25 .60
82 Bob Brown DT RC .25 .60
83 Larry Carwell .25 .60
84 Mo Moorman RC .25 .60
85 John Gilliam .40 1.00
86 Wade Key RC .25 .60
87 Ross Brupbacher RC .25 .60
88 Dave Lewis .25 .60
89 Franco Harris RC 25.00 50.00
90 Tom Mack .60 1.50
91 Mike Tilleman .25 .60
92 Carl Mauck RC .25 .60
93 Larry Hand .25 .60
94 Dave Foley RC .25 .60
95 Frank Nunley .25 .60
96 John Charles .25 .60
97 Jim Bakken .25 .60
98 Pat Fischer .40 1.00
99 Randy Rasmussen RC .25 .60
100 Larry Csonka 3.00 6.00
101 Mike Siani RC .25 .60
102 Tom Roussel RC .25 .60
103 Clarence Scott RC .40 1.00
104 Charley Johnson .40 1.00
105 Rick Volk .25 .60
106 Willie Young RC .25 .60
107 Emmitt Thomas .60 1.50
108 Jon Morris .25 .60
109 Clarence Williams RC .25 .60
110 Rayfield Wright .40 1.00
111 Norm Bulaich .25 .60
112 Mike Eischeid .25 .60
113 Speedy Thomas RC .25 .60
114 Glen Holloway RC .25 .60
115 Jack Ham RC 15.00 30.00
116 Jim Nettles RC .25 .60
117 Errol Mann .25 .60
118 John Mackey .60 1.50
119 George Kunz .25 .60
120 Bob James .25 .60
121 Garland Boyette .25 .60
122 Mel Phillips RC .25 .60
123 Johnny Roland .25 .60
124 Doug Swift RC .25 .60
125 Archie Manning 2.00 4.00
126 Dave Herman .25 .60
127 Carleton Oats RC .25 .60
128 Bill Van Heusen .25 .60
129 Rich Jackson .25 .60
130 Len Hauss .40 1.00
131 Billy Parks RC .25 .60
132 Ray May .25 .60
133 NFC Semi/R.Staubach 2.00 5.00
134 AFC Semi/Immac.Rec. 1.00 2.50
135 NFC Semi-Final .40 1.00
136 AFC Semi/L.Csonka .75 2.00
137 NFC Title Game/Kilmer .60 1.50
138 AFC Title Game .40 1.00
139 Super Bowl VII .60 1.50
140 Dwight White RC 2.00 5.00
141 Jim Marsalis .25 .60
142 Doug Van Horn RC .25 .60
143 Al Matthews RC .25 .60
144 Bob Windsor RC .25 .60
145 Dave Hampton RC .25 .60
146 Horst Muhlmann .25 .60
147 Wally Hilgenberg RC .25 .60
148 Ron Smith .25 .60

Card	Low	High
149 Coy Bacon RC	.40	1.00
150 Winston Hill	.25	.60
151 Ron Jessie RC	.40	1.00
152 Ken Iman	.25	.60
153 Ron Saul RC	.25	.60
154 Jim Braxton RC	.40	1.00
155 Bubba Smith	1.25	2.50
156 Gary Cuozzo	.40	1.00
157 Charlie Krueger	.40	1.00
158 Tim Foley RC	.40	1.00
159 Lee Roy Jordan	.60	1.50
160 Bob Brown OT	.60	1.50
161 Margene Adkins RC	.25	.60
162 Ron Widby RC	.25	.60
163 Jim Houston	.25	.60
164 Joe Dawkins	.25	.60
165 L.C. Greenwood	2.00	4.00
166 Richmond Flowers RC	.25	.60
167 Curley Culp RC	6.00	20.00
168 Len St. Jean	.25	.60
169 Walter Rock	.25	.60
170 Bill Bradley	.40	1.00
171 Ken Riley RC	.60	1.50
172 Rich Coady RC	.25	.60
173 Don Hansen RC	.25	.60
174 Lionel Aldridge	.25	.60
175 Don Maynard	2.00	4.00
176 Dave Osborn	.40	1.00
177 Jim Bailey	.25	.60
178 John Pitts	.25	.60
179 Dave Parks	.25	.60
180 Chester Marcol RC	.25	.60
181 Len Rohde RC	.25	.60
182 Jeff Staggs RC	.25	.60
183 Gene Hickerson	.60	1.25
184 Charlie Evans RC	.25	.60
185 Mel Renfro	.60	1.50
186 Marvin Upshaw RC	.25	.60
187 George Atkinson	.40	1.00
188 Norm Evans	.40	1.00
189 Steve Ramsey	.25	.60
190 Dave Chapple RC	.25	.60
191 Gerry Mullins RC	.25	.60
192 John Didion RC	.25	.60
193 Bob Gladieux RC	.25	.60
194 Don Hultz	.25	.60
195 Mike Lucci	.25	.60
196 John Wilbur RC	.25	.60
197 George Farmer	.25	.60
198 Tommy Casanova RC	.40	1.00
199 Russ Washington	.25	.60
200 Claude Humphrey	.60	1.50
201 Pat Hughes RC	.25	.60
202 Zeke Moore	.25	.60
203 Chip Glass RC	.25	.60
204 Glenn Ressler RC	.25	.60
205 Willie Ellison	.40	1.00
206 John Leypoldt RC	.25	.60
207 Johnny Fuller RC	.25	.60
208 Bill Hayhoe RC	.25	.60
209 Ed Bell RC	.25	.60
210 Willie Brown	.60	1.50
211 Carl Eller	.60	1.50
212 Mark Nordquist	.25	.60
213 Larry Willingham RC	.25	.60
214 Nick Buoniconti	.60	1.50
215 John Hadl	.60	1.50
216 Jethro Pugh RC	.60	1.50
217 Leroy Mitchell	.25	.60
218 Billy Newsome RC	.25	.60
219 John McMakin RC	.25	.60
220 Larry Brown	.60	1.50
221 Clarence Scott RC	.25	.60
222 Paul Naumoff RC	.25	.60
223 Ted Fritsch Jr. RC	.25	.60
224 Checklist 133-264	2.50	5.00
225 Dan Pastorini	.60	1.50
226 Joe Beauchamp UER RC	.25	.60
227 Pat Matson	.25	.60
228 Tony McGee DT RC	.25	.60
229 Mike Phipps	.40	1.00
230 Harold Jackson	.60	1.50
231 Willie Williams RC	.25	.60
232 Spike Jones	.25	.60
233 Jim Tyrer	.25	.60
234 Roy Hilton	.25	.60
235 Phil Villapiano	.40	1.00
236 Charley Taylor UER	1.50	3.00
237 Malcolm Snider RC	.25	.60
238 Vic Washington	.25	.60
239 Grady Alderman	.25	.60
240 Dick Anderson	.40	1.00
241 Ron Yankowski RC	.25	.60
242 Billy Masters RC	.25	.60
243 Herb Adderley	.60	1.50
244 David Ray RC	.25	.60
245 John Riggins	4.00	8.00
246 Mike Wagner RC	1.25	3.00
247 Don Morrison RC	.25	.60
248 Earl McCullouch	.25	.60
249 Dennis Wirgowski RC	.25	.60
250 Chris Hanburger	.40	1.00
251 Pat Sullivan RC	.60	1.50
252 Walt Sweeney	.25	.60
253 Willie Alexander RC	.25	.60
254 Doug Dressler RC	.25	.60
255 Walter Johnson	.25	.60
256 Ron Hornsby	.25	.60
257 Ben Hawkins	.25	.60
258 Donnie Green RC	.25	.60
259 Fred Hoaglin	.25	.60
260 Jerrel Wilson	.25	.60
261 Horace Jones	.25	.60
262 Woody Peoples	.25	.60
263 Jim Hill RC	.25	.60
264 John Fuqua	.25	.60
265 Donny Anderson KP	.40	1.00
266 Roman Gabriel KP	.60	1.50
267 Mike Garrett KP	.40	1.00
268 Rufus Mayes RC	.25	.60
269 Chip Myrtle RC	.25	.60
270 Bill Stanfill RC	.40	1.00
271 Clint Jones	.25	.60
272 Miller Farr	.25	.60
273 Harry Schuh	.25	.60
274 Bob Hayes	.75	2.00
275 Bobby Douglass	.40	1.00
276 Gus Hollomon RC	.25	.60
277 Del Williams RC	.25	.60
278 Julius Adams	.25	.60
279 Herman Weaver	.25	.60
280 Joe Greene	4.00	8.00
281 Wes Chesson RC	.25	.60
282 Charlie Harraway RC	.25	.60
283 Paul Guidry	.25	.60
284 Terry Owens RC	.25	.60
285 Jan Stenerud	.60	1.50
286 Pete Athas	.25	.60
287 Dale Lindsey RC	.25	.60
288 Jack Tatum RC	6.00	20.00
289 Floyd Little	.60	1.50
290 Bob Johnson	.25	.60
291 Tommy Hart RC	.25	.60
292 Tom Mitchell RC	.25	.60
293 Walt Patulski RC	.25	.60
294 Jim Skaggs	.25	.60
295 Bob Griese	3.00	6.00
296 Mike McCoy	.25	.60
297 Mel Gray	.40	1.00
298 Bobby Bryant RC	.25	.60
299 Blaine Nye RC	.25	.60
300 Dick Butkus	6.00	12.00
301 Charlie Cowan RC	.25	.60
302 Mark Lomas RC	.25	.60
303 Josh Ashton RC	.25	.60
304 Happy Feller RC	.25	.60
305 Ron Shanklin	.25	.60
306 Wayne Rasmussen	.25	.60
307 Jerry Smith	.25	.60
308 Ken Reaves	.25	.60
309 Ron East RC	.25	.60
310 Otis Taylor	.60	1.50
311 John Garlington RC	.25	.60
312 Lyle Alzado	2.00	4.00
313 Remi Prudhomme RC	.25	.60
314 Cornelius Johnson RC	.25	.60
315 Lemar Parrish	.40	1.00
316 Jim Kiick	.60	1.50
317 Steve Zabel	.25	.60
318 Alden Roche RC	.25	.60
319 Tom Blanchard RC	.25	.60
320 Fred Biletnikoff	2.00	4.00
321 Ralph Neely	.40	1.00
322 Dan Dierdorf RC	7.50	20.00
323 Richard Caster	.40	1.00
324 Gene Howard	.25	.60
325 Elvin Bethea	.60	1.50
326 Carl Garrett	.40	1.00
327 Ron Billingsley RC	.25	.60
328 Charlie West	.25	.60
329 Tom Neville	.25	.60
330 Ted Kwalick	.40	1.00
331 Rudy Redmond RC	.25	.60
332 Henry Davis RC	.25	.60
333 John Zook	.25	.60
334 Jim Turner	.25	.60
335 Len Dawson	2.50	5.00
336 Bob Chandler RC	.40	1.00
337 Al Beauchamp	.25	.60
338 Tom Matte	.40	1.00
339 Paul Laaveg RC	.25	.60
340 Ken Ellis	.25	.60
341 Jim Langer RC	6.00	12.00
342 Ron Porter	.25	.60
343 Jack Youngblood RC	7.50	15.00
344 Cornell Green	.60	1.50
345 Marv Hubbard	.40	1.00
346 Bruce Taylor	.25	.60
347 Sam Havrilak RC	.25	.60
348 Walt Sumner RC	.25	.60
349 Steve O'Neal RC	.25	.60
350 Ron Johnson	.40	1.00
351 Rockne Freitas	.25	.60
352 Larry Stallings	.25	.60
353 Jim Cadile	.25	.60
354 Ken Burrough	.40	1.00
355 Jim Plunkett	2.00	4.00
356 Dave Long RC	.25	.60
357 Ralph Anderson RC	.25	.60
358 Checklist 265-396	2.50	5.00
359 Gene Washington Vik	.40	1.00
360 Dave Wilcox	.60	1.50
361 Paul Smith RC	.25	.60
362 Alvin Wyatt RC	.25	.60
363 Charlie Smith RB	.25	.60
364 Royce Berry	.25	.60
365 Dave Elmendorf	.25	.60
366 Scott Hunter	.40	1.00
367 Bob Kuechenberg RC	1.25	3.00
368 Pete Gogolak	.25	.60
369 Dave Edwards	.25	.60
370 Lem Barney	1.25	2.50
371 Verlon Biggs	.25	.60
372 John Reaves RC	.25	.60
373 Ed Podolak	.40	1.00
374 Chris Farasopoulos	.25	.60
375 Gary Garrison	.25	.60
376 Tom Funchess RC	.25	.60
377 Bobby Joe Green	.25	.60
378 Don Brumm	.25	.60
379 Jim O'Brien	.25	.60
380 Paul Krause	.60	1.50
381 Leroy Kelly	1.25	2.50
382 Ray Mansfield	.25	.60
383 Dan Abramowicz	.40	1.00
384 John Outlaw RC	.25	.60
385 Tommy Nobis	.60	1.50
386 Tom Domres RC	.25	.60
387 Ken Willard	.25	.60
388 Mike Stratton	.25	.60
389 Fred Dryer	1.25	2.50
390 Jake Scott	.60	1.50
391 Rich Houston RC	.25	.60
392 Virgil Carter	.25	.60
393 Tody Smith RC	.25	.60
394 Ernie Calloway RC	.25	.60
395 Charlie Sanders	.60	1.50
396 Fred Willis	.25	.60
397 Curt Knight	.25	.60
398 Nemiah Wilson	.25	.60
399 Carroll Dale	.40	1.00
400 Joe Namath	18.00	35.00
401 Wayne Mulligan	.25	.60
402 Jim Harrison RC	.25	.60
403 Tim Rossovich	.25	.60
404 David Lee	.25	.60
405 Frank Pitts RC	.25	.60
406 Jim Marshall	.60	1.50
407 Bob Brown TE	.25	.60
408 John Rowser	.25	.60
409 Mike Montler	.25	.60
410 Willie Lanier	.60	1.50
411 Bill Bell K RC	.25	.60
412 Cedrick Hardman	.25	.60
413 Bob Anderson	.25	.60
414 Earl Morrall	.60	1.50
415 Ken Houston	.60	1.50
416 Jack Snow	.40	1.00
417 Dick Cunningham RC	.25	.60
418 Greg Larson	.25	.60
419 Mike Bass RC	.40	1.00
420 Mike Reid	.60	1.50
421 Walt Garrison	.60	1.50
422 Pete Liske	.25	.60
423 Jim Yarbrough RC	.25	.60
424 Rich McGeorge	.25	.60
425 Bobby Howfield RC	.25	.60
426 Pete Banaszak	.25	.60
427 Willie Holman RC	.25	.60
428 Dale Hackbart	.25	.60
429 Fair Hooker	.25	.60
430 Ted Hendricks	2.50	5.00
431 Mike Garrett	.40	1.00
432 Glen Ray Hines	.25	.60
433 Fred Cox	.25	.60
434 Bobby Walden	.25	.60
435 Bobby Bell	.60	1.50
436 Dave Rowe	.25	.60
437 Bob Berry	.25	.60
438 Bill Thompson	.25	.60
439 Jim Beirne	.25	.60
440 Larry Little	1.50	3.00
441 Rocky Thompson RC	.25	.60
442 Brig Owens	.25	.60
443 Richard Neal	.25	.60
444 Al Nelson	.25	.60
445 Chip Myers	.25	.60
446 Ken Bowman	.25	.60
447 Jim Purnell RC	.25	.60
448 Altie Taylor	.25	.60
449 Linzy Cole	.25	.60
450 Bob Lilly	2.50	5.00
451 Charlie Ford RC	.25	.60
452 Milt Sunde	.25	.60
453 Doug Wyatt RC	.25	.60
454 Don Nottingham RC	.40	1.00
455 John Unitas	7.50	15.00
456 Frank Lewis RC	.40	1.00
457 Roger Wehrli	.40	1.00
458 Jim Cheyunski RC	.25	.60
459 Jerry Sherk RC	.40	1.00
460 Gene Washington 49er	.40	1.00
461 Jim Otto	.60	1.50
462 Ed Budde	.25	.60
463 Jim Mitchell	.40	1.00
464 Emerson Boozer	.40	1.00
465 Garo Yepremian	.60	1.50
466 Pete Duranko	.25	.60
467 Charlie Joiner	4.00	8.00
468 Spider Lockhart	.40	1.00
469 Marty Domres	.25	.60
470 John Brockington	.60	1.50
471 Ed Flanagan	.25	.60
472 Roy Jefferson	.40	1.00
473 Julian Fagan RC	.25	.60
474 Bill Brown	.40	1.00
475 Roger Staubach	15.00	30.00
476 Jan White RC	.25	.60
477 Pat Holmes RC	.25	.60
478 Bob DeMarco	.25	.60
479 Merlin Olsen	1.25	2.50
480 Andy Russell	.60	1.50
481 Steve Spurrier	10.00	20.00
482 Nate Ramsey	.25	.60
483 Dennis Partee	.25	.60
484 Jerry Simmons	.25	.60
485 Donny Anderson	.60	1.50
486 Ralph Baker	.25	.60
487 Ken Stabler RC	35.00	60.00
488 Ernie McMillan	.25	.60
489 Ken Burrow RC	.25	.60
490 Jack Gregory RC	.25	.60
491 Larry Seiple	.40	1.00
492 Mick Tingelhoff	.40	1.00
493 Craig Morton	.60	1.50
494 Cecil Turner	.25	.60
495 Steve Owens	.60	1.50
496 Rickie Harris	.25	.60
497 Buck Buchanan	.60	1.50
498 Checklist 397-528	2.50	5.00
499 Billy Kilmer	.60	1.50
500 O.J. Simpson	7.50	15.00
501 Bruce Gossett	.25	.60
502 Art Thoms RC	.25	.60
503 Larry Kaminski RC	.25	.60
504 Larry Smith RB RC	.25	.60
505 Bruce Van Dyke RC	.25	.60
506 Alvin Reed	.25	.60
507 Delles Howell	.25	.60
508 Leroy Keyes	.25	.60
509 Bo Scott	.40	1.00
510 Ron Yary	.60	1.50
511 Paul Warfield	2.50	5.00
512 Mac Percival	.25	.60
513 Essex Johnson RC	.25	.60
514 Jackie Smith	.60	1.50
515 Norm Snead	.60	1.50
516 Charlie Stukes RC	.25	.60
517 Reggie Rucker RC	.40	1.00
518 Bill Sandeman UER RC	.25	.60
519 Mel Farr	.40	1.00
520 Raymond Chester	.40	1.00
521 Fred Carr RC	.40	1.00
522 Jerry LeVias	.40	1.00
523 Jim Strong RC	.25	.60
524 Roland McDole	.25	.60
525 Dennis Shaw	.25	.60
526 Dave Manders	.25	.60
527 Skip Vanderbundt RC	.25	.60
528 Mike Sensibaugh RC	.60	1.50

1973 Topps Team Checklists

The 1973 Topps Team Checklist set contains 26 checklist cards, one for each of the 26 NFL teams. The cards measure 2 1/2" by 3 1/2" and were inserted into regular issue 1973 Topps football wax packs. The fronts show action scenes at the top of the card and a Topps helmet with the team name at its immediate right. The bottom portion of the card contains the checklist, complete with boxes in which to place check marks. Uniform numbers and positions are also given with the player's name. The backs of the cards form puzzles of Joe Namath and Larry Brown. These unnumbered cards are numbered below for convenience in alphabetical order by team name. The cards can all be found with one or two asterisks on the front and in a blank backed version.

Card	Low	High
COMPLETE SET (26)	50.00	100.00
1 Atlanta Falcons	2.00	4.00
2 Baltimore Colts	2.00	4.00
3 Buffalo Bills	2.00	4.00
4 Chicago Bears	2.50	5.00
5 Cincinnati Bengals	2.00	4.00
6 Cleveland Browns	2.50	5.00
7 Dallas Cowboys	3.00	6.00
8 Denver Broncos	2.00	4.00
9 Detroit Lions	2.00	4.00
10 Green Bay Packers	2.50	5.00
11 Houston Oilers	2.00	4.00
12 Kansas City Chiefs	2.00	4.00
13 Los Angeles Rams	2.00	4.00
14 Miami Dolphins	2.50	5.00
15 Minnesota Vikings	2.50	5.00
16 New England Patriots	2.00	4.00
17 New Orleans Saints	2.00	4.00
18 New York Giants	2.00	4.00
19 New York Jets	2.00	4.00
20 Oakland Raiders	3.00	6.00
21 Philadelphia Eagles	2.00	4.00
22 Pittsburgh Steelers	2.50	5.00
23 St. Louis Cardinals	2.00	4.00
24 San Diego Chargers	2.00	4.00
25 San Francisco 49ers	2.50	5.00
26 Washington Redskins	2.50	5.00

1974 Topps

The 1974 Topps set contains 528 standard-size cards. Card fronts have photos that are bordered on either side by uprights of a goal post. The goal post has a different color depending upon the player's team. The team name is in a color bar at the bottom. The player's name and position are beneath the crossbar. The card backs are printed in blue and yellow on gray card stock and include statistics and highlights. The bottom of the back provides part of a simulated football game which could be played by drawing cards. Subsets inlcude All-Pro (121-144), league leaders (328-333) and post-season action (460-463). This set contains the Rookie Cards of Harold Carmichael, Chuck Foreman, Ray Guy, John Hannah, Bert Jones, Ed Marinaro, John Matuszak and Ahmad Rashad. An uncut sheet of team checklist cards was also available via a mail-in offer on wax pack wrappers. There are a number of cards with copyright variations. On cards 26, 129, 130, 156, 162, 219, 265-364, 367-422, and 424-528, there are two asterisks with the copyright line. The rest of the cards have one asterisk. Topps also printed a very similar (and very confusing) 50-card set for Parker Brothers in early 1974 as part of its Pro Draft football board game. The only players in this set (game) were offensive players (with an emphasis on the skill positions) that were among the first 132 cards in the 1974 Topps set. There are several notable differences between these Parker Brothers Pro Draft cards and the basic issue. Those cards ending with 1972 statistics on the back (unlike the basic issue which go through 1973) are Parker Brothers cards. Parker Brothers game cards can also be distinguished by the presence of two asterisks rather than one on the copyright line. However, as noted above, there are cards in the regular 1974 Topps set that do have two asterisks but are not Parker Brothers Pro Draft cards. In fact, variations 23A, 49A, 116A, 124A, 126A, and 127A listed in the checklist below were issued with a later

Card	Low	High
COMPLETE SET (528)	175.00	300.00
1 O.J.Simpson RB UER	10.00	20.00
2 Blaine Nye	.25	.60
3 Don Hansen	.25	.60
4 Ken Bowman	.25	.60
5 Carl Eller	.60	1.50
6 Jerry Smith	.25	.60
7 Ed Podolak	.25	.60
8 Mel Gray	.60	1.50
9 Pat Matson	.25	.60
10 Floyd Little	.60	1.50
11 Frank Pitts	.25	.60
12 Vern Den Herder RC	.40	1.00
13 John Fuqua	.40	1.00
14 Jack Tatum	.75	2.00
15 Winston Hill	.25	.60
16 John Beasley RC	.25	.60
17 David Lee	.25	.60
18 Rich Coady	.25	.60
19 Ken Willard	.25	.60
20 Coy Bacon	.40	1.00
21 Ben Hawkins	.25	.60
22 Paul Guidry	.25	.60
23 Norm Snead HOR	.40	1.00
24 Jim Yarbrough	.25	.60
25 Jack Reynolds RC	1.25	3.00
26 Josh Ashton	.25	.60
27 Donnie Green	.25	.60
28 Bob Hayes	.75	2.00
29 John Zook	.25	.60
30 Bobby Bryant	.25	.60
31 Scott Hunter	.40	1.00
32 Dan Dierdorf	3.00	6.00
33 Curt Knight	.25	.60
34 Elmo Wright RC	.25	.60
35 Essex Johnson	.25	.60
36 Walt Sumner	.25	.60
37 Marv Montgomery RC	.25	.60
38 Tim Foley	.40	1.00
39 Mike Siani	.25	.60
40 Joe Greene	3.00	6.00
41 Bobby Howfield	.25	.60
42 Del Williams	.25	.60
43 Don McCauley	.25	.60
44 Randy Jackson	.25	.60
45 Ron Smith	.25	.60
46 Gene Washington 49er	.40	1.00
47 Po James RC	.25	.60
48 Solomon Freelon RC	.25	.60
49 Bob Windsor HOR	.25	.60
50 John Hadl	.60	1.50
51 Greg Larson	.25	.60
52 Steve Owens	.40	1.00
53 Jim Cheyunski	.25	.60
54 Rayfield Wright	.40	1.00
55 Dave Hampton	.25	.60
56 Ron Widby	.25	.60
57 Milt Sunde	.25	.60
58 Billy Kilmer	.60	1.50
59 Bobby Bell	.60	1.50
60 Jim Bakken	.25	.60
61 Rufus Mayes	.25	.60
62 Vic Washington	.25	.60
63 Gene Washington Vik	.40	1.00
64 Clarence Scott	.25	.60
65 Gene Upshaw	.75	2.00
66 Larry Seiple	.40	1.00
67 John McMakin	.25	.60
68 Ralph Baker	.25	.60
69 Lydell Mitchell	.40	1.00
70 Archie Manning	1.25	2.50
71 George Farmer	.25	.60
72 Ron East	.25	.60
73 Al Nelson	.25	.60
74 Pat Hughes	.25	.60
75 Fred Willis	.25	.60
76 Larry Walton RC	.25	.60
77 Tom Neville	.25	.60
78 Ted Kwalick	.25	.60
79 Walt Patulski	.25	.60
80 John Niland	.25	.60
81 Ted Fritsch Jr.	.25	.60
82 Paul Krause	.60	1.50
83 Jack Snow	.40	1.00
84 Mike Bass	.25	.60
85 Jim Tyrer	.25	.60
86 Ron Yankowski	.25	.60
87 Mike Phipps	.40	1.00
88 Al Beauchamp	.25	.60
89 Riley Odoms RC	.60	1.50
90 MacArthur Lane	.25	.60
91 Art Thoms	.25	.60
92 Marlin Briscoe	.25	.60
93 Bruce Van Dyke	.25	.60
94 Tom Myers RC	.25	.60
95 Calvin Hill	.60	1.50
96 Bruce Laird RC	.25	.60
97 Tony McGee DT	.25	.60
98 Len Rohde	.25	.60
99 Tom McNeill	.25	.60
100 Delles Howell	.25	.60
101 Gary Garrison	.25	.60
102 Dan Goich RC	.25	.60
103 Len St. Jean	.25	.60
104 Zeke Moore	.25	.60
105 Ahmad Rashad RC	10.00	20.00
106 Mel Renfro	.60	1.50
107 Jim Mitchell	.25	.60
108 Ed Budde	.25	.60
109 Harry Schuh	.25	.60
110 Greg Pruitt RC	2.00	4.00
111 Ed Flanagan	.25	.60
112 Larry Stallings	.25	.60
113 Chuck Foreman RC	4.00	8.00
114 Royce Berry	.25	.60
115 Gale Gillingham	.25	.60
116 Charlie Johnson HOR	.60	1.50
117 Checklist 1-132 UER	2.00	4.00
118 Bill Butler RC	.25	.60
119 Roy Jefferson	.40	1.00
120 Bobby Douglass	.40	1.00
121 Harold Carmichael RC	6.00	12.00
122 George Kunz AP	.25	.60
123 Larry Little AP	.75	2.00
124 Forrest Blue AP	.25	.60
125 Ron Yary AP	.60	1.50
126 Tom Mack AP	.60	1.50
127 Bob Tucker AP	.40	1.00
128 Paul Warfield AP	2.00	4.00
129 Fran Tarkenton AP	5.00	10.00
130 O.J. Simpson AP	6.00	12.00
131 Larry Csonka AP	3.00	6.00
132 Bruce Gossett AP	.25	.60
133 Bill Stanfill AP	.40	1.00
134 Alan Page AP	1.25	2.50
135 Paul Smith AP	.25	.60
136 Claude Humphrey AP	.50	1.25
137 Jack Ham AP	5.00	10.00
138 Lee Roy Jordan AP	.60	1.50
139 Phil Villapiano AP	.40	1.00
140 Ken Ellis AP	.25	.60
141 Willie Brown AP	.60	1.50
142 Dick Anderson AP	.40	1.00
143 Bill Bradley AP	.40	1.00
144 Jerrel Wilson AP	.25	.60
145 Reggie Rucker	.40	1.00
146 Marty Domres	.25	.60
147 Bob Kowalkowski RC	.25	.60
148 John Matuszak RC	2.50	6.00
149 Mike Adamle RC	.40	1.00
150 Johnny Unitas	7.50	15.00
151 Charlie Ford	.25	.60
152 Bob Klein RC	.25	.60
153 Jim Merlo RC	.25	.60
154 Willie Young	.25	.60
155 Donny Anderson	.40	1.00
156 Brig Owens	.25	.60
157 Bruce Jarvis RC	.25	.60
158 Ron Carpenter RC	.25	.60
159 Don Cockroft	.25	.60
160 Tommy Nobis	.60	1.50
161 Craig Morton	.60	1.50
162 Jon Staggers RC	.25	.60
163 Mike Eischeid	.25	.60
164 Jerry Sisemore RC	.25	.60
165 Cedrick Hardman	.25	.60
166 Bill Thompson	.40	1.00
167 Jim Lynch	.40	1.00
168 Bob Moore RC	.25	.60
169 Glen Edwards RC	.25	.60
170 Mercury Morris	.60	1.50
171 Julius Adams	.25	.60
172 Cotton Speyrer RC	.25	.60
173 Bill Munson	.40	1.00
174 Benny Johnson	.25	.60
175 Burgess Owens RC	.25	.60
176 Cid Edwards	.25	.60
177 Doug Buffone	.25	.60
178 Charlie Cowan	.25	.60
179 Bob Newland RC	.25	.60
180 Ron Johnson	.40	1.00
181 Bob Rowe RC	.25	.60
182 Len Hauss	.25	.60
183 Joe DeLamielleure RC	6.00	12.00
184 Sherman White RC	.25	.60
185 Fair Hooker	.25	.60
186 Nick Mike-Mayer RC	.25	.60
187 Ralph Neely	.25	.60
188 Rich McGeorge	.25	.60
189 Ed Marinaro RC	1.50	4.00
190 Dave Wilcox	.60	1.50
191 Joe Owens RC	.25	.60
192 Bill Van Heusen	.25	.60
193 Jim Kearney	.25	.60
194 Otis Sistrunk RC	.60	1.50
195 Ron Shanklin	.25	.60
196 Bill Lenkaitis RC	.25	.60
197 Tom Drougas RC	.25	.60
198 Larry Hand	.25	.60
199 Mack Alston RC	.25	.60
200 Bob Griese	3.00	6.00
201 Earlie Thomas RC	.25	.60
202 Carl Gersbach RC	.25	.60
203 Jim Harrison	.25	.60
204 Jake Kupp	.25	.60
205 Merlin Olsen	.75	2.00
206 Spider Lockhart	.40	1.00
207 Walker Gillette	.25	.60
208 Verlon Biggs	.25	.60
209 Bob James	.25	.60
210 Bob Trumpy	.60	1.50
211 Jerry Sherk	.25	.60
212 Andy Maurer	.25	.60
213 Fred Carr	.25	.60
214 Mick Tingelhoff	.40	1.00
215 Steve Spurrier	7.50	15.00
216 Richard Harris RC	.25	.60
217 Charlie Greer RC	.25	.60
218 Buck Buchanan	.60	1.50
219 Ray Guy RC	10.00	20.00
220 Franco Harris	6.00	12.00
221 Darryl Stingley RC	.60	1.50
222 Rex Kern	.25	.60
223 Toni Fritsch RC	.40	1.00
224 Levi Johnson RC	.25	.60
225 Bob Kuechenberg	.40	1.00
226 Elvin Bethea	.60	1.50
227 Al Woodall RC	.40	1.00
228 Terry Owens	.25	.60
229 Bivian Lee RC	.25	.60
230 Dick Butkus	5.00	10.00
231 Jim Bertelsen RC	.40	1.00
232 John Mendenhall RC	.25	.60
233 Conrad Dobler RC	.60	1.50
234 J.D. Hill	.40	1.00
235 Ken Houston	.60	1.50
236 Dave Lewis	.25	.60
237 John Garlington	.25	.60
238 Bill Sandeman	.25	.60
239 Alden Roche	.25	.60
240 John Gilliam	.40	1.00
241 Bruce Taylor	.25	.60
242 Vern Winfield RC	.25	.60
243 Bobby Maples	.25	.60
244 Wendell Hayes	.25	.60
245 George Blanda	4.00	8.00
246 Dwight White	.40	1.00
247 Sandy Durko RC	.25	.60
248 Tom Mitchell	.25	.60
249 Chuck Walton	.25	.60
250 Bob Lilly	2.00	4.00
251 Doug Swift	.25	.60
252 Lynn Dickey RC	.60	1.50
253 Jerome Barkum RC	.25	.60
254 Clint Jones	.25	.60
255 Billy Newsome	.25	.60
256 Bob Asher RC	.25	.60
257 Joe Scibelli RC	.25	.60
258 Tom Blanchard	.25	.60
259 Norm Thompson	.25	.60
260 Larry Brown	.60	1.50
261 Paul Seymour RC	.25	.60
262 Checklist 133-264	2.00	4.00
263 Doug Dieken RC	.25	.60
264 Lemar Parrish	.40	1.00
265 Bob Lee UER	.25	.60
266 Bob Brown DT	.25	.60
267 Roy Winston	.25	.60
268 Randy Beisler RC	.25	.60
269 Joe Dawkins	.25	.60
270 Tom Dempsey	.40	1.00
271 Jack Rudnay	.25	.60
272 Art Shell	2.50	5.00
273 Mike Wagner	.40	1.00
274 Rick Cash RC	.25	.60
275 Greg Landry	.60	1.50
276 Glenn Ressler	.25	.60
277 Billy Joe DuPree RC	1.25	3.00
278 Norm Evans	.25	.60
279 Billy Parks	.25	.60
280 John Riggins	3.00	6.00
281 Lionel Aldridge	.25	.60
282 Steve O'Neal	.25	.60
283 Craig Clemons RC	.25	.60
284 Willie Williams	.25	.60
285 Isiah Robertson	.40	1.00
286 Dennis Shaw	.25	.60
287 Bill Brundige	.25	.60
288 John Leypoldt	.25	.60
289 John DeMarie RC	.25	.60
290 Mike Reid	.60	1.50
291 Greg Brezina	.25	.60
292 Willie Buchanon RC	.25	.60
293 Dave Osborn	.40	1.00
294 Mel Phillips	.25	.60
295 Haven Moses	.40	1.00
296 Wade Key	.25	.60
297 Marvin Upshaw	.25	.60
298 Ray Mansfield	.25	.60
299 Edgar Chandler	.25	.60
300 Marv Hubbard	.40	1.00
301 Herman Weaver	.25	.60
302 Jim Bailey	.25	.60
303 D.D. Lewis RC	.60	1.50
304 Ken Burrough	.40	1.00
305 Jake Scott	.60	1.50
306 Randy Rasmussen	.25	.60
307 Pettis Norman	.25	.60
308 Carl Johnson RC	.25	.60
309 Joe Taylor	.25	.60
310 Pete Gogolak	.25	.60
311 Tony Baker FB	.25	.60
312 John Richardson RC	.25	.60
313 Dave Robinson	.40	1.00
314 Reggie McKenzie RC	.60	1.50
315 Isaac Curtis RC	.60	1.50
316 Thom Darden RC	.25	.60
317 Ken Reaves	.25	.60
318 Malcolm Snider	.25	.60
319 Jeff Siemon RC	.40	1.00
320 Dan Abramowicz	.40	1.00
321 Lyle Alzado	.75	2.00
322 John Reaves	.25	.60
323 Morris Stroud RC	.25	.60
324 Bobby Walden	.25	.60
325 Randy Vataha	.25	.60
326 Nemiah Wilson	.25	.60
327 Paul Naumoff	.25	.60
328 O.J.Simpson/Brock. LL	1.50	3.00
329 R.Staubach/Stabler LL	2.50	5.00
330 Harold Carmichael/Wil LL	.60	1.50
331 Scoring Leaders	.40	1.00
332 Interception Leaders	.40	1.00
333 Punting Leaders	.40	1.00
334 Dennis Nelson RC	.25	.60
335 Walt Garrison	.40	1.00
336 Tody Smith	.25	.60
337 Ed Bell	.25	.60
338 Bryant Salter	.25	.60
339 Wayne Colman	.25	.60
340 Garo Yepremian	.40	1.00
341 Bob Newton RC	.25	.60
342 Vince Clements RC	.25	.60
343 Ken Iman	.25	.60
344 Jim Tolbert RC	.25	.60
345 Chris Hanburger	.40	1.00
346 Dave Foley	.25	.60
347 Tommy Casanova	.40	1.00
348 John James RC	.25	.60
349 Clarence Williams	.25	.60
350 Leroy Kelly	.60	1.50
351 Stu Voigt RC	.40	1.00
352 Skip Vanderbundt	.25	.60
353 Pete Duranko	.25	.60
354 John Outlaw	.25	.60
355 Jan Stenerud	.60	1.50
356 Barry Pearson RC	.25	.60
357 Brian Dowling RC	.25	.60
358 Dan Conners	.25	.60
359 Bob Bell RC	.25	.60
360 Rick Volk	.25	.60
361 Pat Toomay RC	.40	1.00
362 Bob Gresham RC	.25	.60
363 John Schmitt	.25	.60
364 Mel Rogers RC	.25	.60
365 Manny Fernandez	.40	1.00
366 Ernie Jackson RC	.25	.60
367 Gary Huff RC	.40	1.00
368 Bob Grim	.25	.60
369 Ernie McMillan	.25	.60
370 Dave Elmendorf	.25	.60
371 Mike Bragg	.25	.60
372 John Skorupan RC	.25	.60
373 Howard Fest	.25	.60
374 Jerry Tagge RC	.40	1.00
375 Art Malone	.25	.60
376 Bob Babich	.25	.60
377 Jim Marshall	.60	1.50
378 Bob Hoskins RC	.25	.60
379 Don Zimmerman RC	.25	.60
380 Ray May	.25	.60
381 Emmitt Thomas	.40	1.00
382 Terry Hanratty	.40	1.00
383 John Hannah RC	10.00	20.00
384 George Atkinson	.25	.60
385 Ted Hendricks	1.50	3.00
386 Jim O'Brien	.25	.60
387 Jethro Pugh	.40	1.00
388 Elbert Drungo RC	.25	.60
389 Richard Caster	.40	1.00
390 Deacon Jones	.60	1.50
391 Checklist 265-396	2.00	4.00
392 Jess Phillips RC	.25	.60
393 Garry Lyle UER RC	.25	.60
394 Jim Files	.25	.60
395 Jim Hart	.60	1.50
396 Dave Chapple	.25	.60
397 Jim Langer	.75	2.00
398 John Wilbur	.25	.60
399 Dwight Harrison RC	.25	.60
400 John Brockington	.40	1.00
401 Ken Anderson	3.00	6.00
402 Mike Tilleman	.25	.60
403 Charlie Hall RC	.25	.60
404 Tommy Hart	.25	.60
405 Norm Bulaich	.40	1.00
406 Jim Turner	.25	.60
407 Mo Moorman	.25	.60
408 Ralph Anderson	.25	.60
409 Jim Otto	.60	1.50
410 Andy Russell	.60	1.50
411 Glenn Doughty RC	.25	.60
412 Altie Taylor	.25	.60
413 Marv Bateman RC	.25	.60
414 Willie Alexander	.25	.60
415 Bill Zapalac RC	.25	.60
416 Russ Washington	.25	.60
417 Joe Federspiel RC	.25	.60
418 Craig Cotton RC	.25	.60
419 Randy Johnson	.25	.60
420 Harold Jackson	.60	1.50
421 Roger Wehrli	.40	1.00
422 Charlie Harraway	.25	.60
423 Spike Jones	.25	.60
424 Bob Johnson	.25	.60
425 Mike McCoy DT	.25	.60
426 Dennis Havig RC	.25	.60
427 Bob McKay RC	.25	.60
428 Steve Zabel	.25	.60
429 Horace Jones	.25	.60
430 Jim Johnson	.60	1.50
431 Roy Gerela	.40	1.00
432 Tom Graham RC	.25	.60
433 Curley Culp	1.00	2.50
434 Ken Mendenhall RC	.25	.60
435 Jim Plunkett	1.25	2.50
436 Julian Fagan	.25	.60
437 Mike Garrett	.40	1.00
438 Bobby Joe Green	.25	.60
439 Jack Gregory	.25	.60
440 Charlie Sanders	.40	1.00
441 Bill Curry	.40	1.00
442 Bob Pollard RC	.25	.60
443 David Ray	.25	.60
444 Terry Metcalf RC	1.50	3.00
445 Pat Fischer	.40	1.00
446 Bob Chandler	.40	1.00
447 Bill Bergey	.40	1.00
448 Walter Johnson	.25	.60
449 Charle Young RC	.60	1.50
450 Chester Marcol	.25	.60
451 Ken Stabler	10.00	20.00
452 Preston Pearson	.60	1.50
453 Mike Current	.25	.60
454 Ron Bolton RC	.25	.60
455 Mark Lomas	.25	.60
456 Raymond Chester	.40	1.00
457 Jerry LeVias	.40	1.00
458 Skip Butler RC	.25	.60
459 Mike Livingston RC	.25	.60
460 AFC Semi-Final	.40	1.00
461 NFC Semi/R.Staubach	2.00	4.00
462 Playoff Champs/Stabler	1.50	3.00
463 Super Bowl/Dolphins 24/Vikings 7/(Larry Csonka pictured)	.75	2.00
464 Wayne Mulligan	.25	.60
465 Horst Muhlmann	.25	.60
466 Milt Morin	.25	.60
467 Don Parish RC	.25	.60
468 Richard Neal	.25	.60
469 Ron Jessie	.40	1.00
470 Terry Bradshaw	12.50	25.00
471 Fred Dryer	.60	1.50
472 Jim Carter	.25	.60
473 Ken Burrow	.25	.60
474 Wally Chambers RC	.40	1.00
475 Dan Pastorini	.60	1.50
476 Don Morrison	.25	.60
477 Carl Mauck	.25	.60
478 Larry Cole RC	.40	1.00
479 Jim Kiick	.60	1.50
480 Willie Lanier	.60	1.50
481 Don Herrmann	.40	1.00
482 George Hunt RC	.25	.60
483 Bob Howard RC	.25	.60
484 Myron Pottios	.25	.60
485 Jackie Smith	.60	1.50
486 Vern Holland	.25	.60
487 Jim Braxton	.25	.60
488 Joe Reed RC	.25	.60
489 Wally Hilgenberg	.25	.60
490 Fred Biletnikoff	2.00	4.00
491 Bob DeMarco	.25	.60
492 Mark Nordquist	.25	.60
493 Larry Brooks RC	.25	.60
494 Pete Athas	.25	.60
495 Emerson Boozer	.40	1.00
496 L.C. Greenwood	.75	2.00
497 Rockne Freitas	.25	.60
498 Checklist 397-528 UER	2.00	4.00
499 Joe Schmiesing RC	.25	.60
500 Roger Staubach	12.50	25.00
501 Al Cowlings UER	.40	1.00
502 Sam Cunningham RC	.60	1.50
503 Dennis Partee	.25	.60
504 John Didion	.25	.60
505 Nick Buoniconti	.60	1.50
506 Carl Garrett	.40	1.00
507 Doug Van Horn	.25	.60
508 Jamie Rivers RC	.25	.60
509 Jack Youngblood	2.00	4.00
510 Charley Taylor UER	1.25	2.50
511 Ken Riley	.60	1.50
512 Joe Ferguson RC	1.25	3.00
513 Bill Lueck RC	.25	.60
514 Ray Brown DB RC	.25	.60
515 Fred Cox	.25	.60
516 Joe Jones	.25	.60
517 Larry Schreiber RC	.25	.60
518 Dennis Wirgowski	.25	.60
519 Leroy Mitchell	.25	.60
520 Otis Taylor	.60	1.50
521 Henry Davis	.25	.60
522 Bruce Barnes RC	.25	.60
523 Charlie Smith RB	.25	.60
524 Bert Jones RC	3.00	6.00
525 Lem Barney	.75	2.00
526 John Fitzgerald RC	.25	.60
527 Tom Funchess	.25	.60
528 Steve Tannen	.60	1.50

1974 Topps Parker Brothers Pro Draft

This 50-card standard-size set was printed by Topps for distribution by Parker Brothers in early 1974 as part of a football board game. The only players in this set (game) are offensive players (with an emphasis on the skill positions) and all come from the first 132 cards in the 1974 Topps football card set. The cards are very similar and often confused with the 1974 Topps regular issue football cards. There are several notable differences between these cards and the 1974 Topps regular issue: cards with 1972 statistics on the back (unlike the 1974 Topps regular issue) are indicated in the checklist below with an asterisk and cards with pose variations (different from the 1974 Topps) are noted as well parenthetically; these six pose variations are numbers 23, 49, 116, 124, 126, and 127. Parker Brothers game cards can also be distinguished by the presence of two asterisks rather than one on the copyright line. However, there are cards in the regular 1974 Topps set that do have two asterisks but are not Parker Brothers Pro Draft cards. Cards in the 1974 Topps regular set with two asterisks include 26, 129, 130, 156, 162, 219, 265-364, 367-422, and 424-528; the rest have only one asterisk. The Parker Brothers cards are skip-numbered with the number on the back corresponding to that player's number in the Topps regular issue.

Card	Low	High
COMPLETE SET (50)	62.50	125.00
4 Ken Bowman	.50	1.00
6 Jerry Smith *	1.00	2.00
7 Ed Podolak *	1.00	2.00
9 Pat Matson	.50	1.00
11 Frank Pitts *	1.00	2.00
15 Winston Hill	.50	1.00
18 Rich Coady *	1.00	2.00
19 Ken Willard *	1.25	2.50
21 Ben Hawkins *	1.00	2.00
23A Norm Snead *	2.00	5.00
23B Norm Snead *	2.00	5.00
24 Jim Yarbrough *	1.00	2.00
28 Bob Hayes *	2.50	5.00
32 Dan Dierdorf *	3.00	6.00
35 Essex Johnson *	1.00	2.00
39 Mike Siani	.50	1.00
42 Del Williams	.50	1.00
43 Don McCauley *	1.00	2.00
44 Randy Jackson *	1.00	2.00
46 Gene Washington 49er *	1.50	3.00
49A Bob Windsor *	1.50	3.00
49B Bob Windsor *	1.50	3.00
50 John Hadl *	2.00	4.00
52 Steve Owens *	2.00	4.00
54 Rayfield Wright *	1.00	2.00
57 Milt Sunde *	1.00	2.00
58 Billy Kilmer *	2.00	4.00
61 Rufus Mayes *	1.00	2.00
63 Gene Washington Vik *	1.25	2.50
65 Gene Upshaw	2.50	5.00
75 Fred Willis *	1.00	2.00
77 Tom Neville	.50	1.00
78 Ted Kwalick *	1.25	2.50
80 John Niland *	1.00	2.00
81 Ted Fritsch Jr.	.50	1.00
83 Jack Snow *	1.50	3.00
87 Mike Phipps *	1.50	3.00
90 MacArthur Lane *	1.50	3.00
95 Calvin Hill *	1.00	2.00
98 Len Rohde	.50	1.00
101 Gary Garrison *	1.00	2.00
103 Len St. Jean	.50	1.00
107 Jim Mitchell *	1.00	2.00
109 Harry Schuh	.50	1.00
110 Greg Pruitt *	2.00	4.00
111 Ed Flanagan	.50	1.00
113 Chuck Foreman *	2.00	4.00
116A Charlie Johnson *	2.00	5.00
116B Charlie Johnson *	2.00	5.00
119 Roy Jefferson *	1.25	2.50
124A Forrest Blue *	1.50	3.00
124B Forrest Blue *	1.50	3.00
126A Tom Mack *	4.00	8.00
126B Tom Mack *	4.00	8.00
127B Bob Tucker *	1.50	3.00
127A Bob Tucker *	1.50	3.00

1974 Topps Team Checklists

The 1974 Topps Team Checklist set contains 26 standard-size cards. The cards were inserted into regular issue 1974 Topps football wax packs. The Topps logo and team name appear at the top of the card, while the mid-portion of the card contains the actual checklist giving each player's card number, check-off box, name, uniform number, and position. The lower portion of the card contains an ad to obtain all 26 team checklists. A picture of a boy collector is shown in the lower right corner. The back of the card contains rules for a football game to be played with the 1974 Topps football cards. These unnumbered cards are numbered below for convenience in alphabetical order by team name. Twenty of the 26 checklist cards show players out of alphabetical order on the card front. The cards can all be found with one or two asterisks on the front. The set was also available directly from Topps as a mail-away offer as a pair of unperforated uncut sheets, which had blank backs. Measuring approximately 13 1/2" by 10 1/2", each sheet featured thirteen team checklist cards and an offer for a football action poster.

COMPLETE SET (26) 37.50 75.00
*BLANKBACKS: 2X TO 4X BASIC CARDS
1 Atlanta Falcons 1.50 3.00
2 Baltimore Colts 1.50 3.00
3 Buffalo Bills 1.50 3.00
4 Chicago Bears 2.00 4.00
5 Cincinnati Bengals 1.50 3.00
6 Cleveland Browns UER 1.50 3.00
7 Dallas Cowboys 2.50 5.00
8 Denver Broncos 1.50 3.00
9 Detroit Lions 1.50 3.00
10 Green Bay Packers 2.00 4.00
11 Houston Oilers 1.50 3.00
12 Kansas City Chiefs 1.50 3.00
13 Los Angeles Rams 1.50 3.00
14 Miami Dolphins 2.00 4.00
15 Minnesota Vikings 2.00 4.00
16 New England Patriots 1.50 3.00
17 New Orleans Saints 1.50 3.00
18 New York Giants 2.00 4.00
19 New York Jets 1.50 3.00
20 Oakland Raiders 2.50 5.00
21 Philadelphia Eagles 1.50 3.00
22 Pittsburgh Steelers 2.00 4.00
23 St. Louis Cardinals 1.50 3.00
24 San Diego Chargers 1.50 3.00
25 San Francisco 49ers 2.00 4.00
26 Washington Redskins UER 2.00 4.00

1975 Topps

The 1975 Topps football set contains 528 standard-size cards. Beneath a color photo, card fronts contain a banner with the team name. Both were done in a team color. To the right of the banner is a football helmet the includes the player's position. The player's name is at the bottom. Subsets include leaders (1-6), All-Pro (201-225), Record Breakers (351-356), Highlights (452-460) and playoffs (526-528). The card backs are printed in black ink with a green background on gray card stock and contain statistics and highlights. The key Rookie Cards in this set are Otis Armstrong, Rocky Bleier, Mel Blount, Cliff Branch, Dan Fouts, Cliff Harris, Drew Pearson, Lynn Swann and Charlie Waters. The set also includes Joe Theismann's first NFL card after having performed in the Canadian Football League. An uncut sheet of team checklist cards was also available via a mail-in offer wax pack wrappers.

COMPLETE SET (528) 175.00 300.00
1 McCutcheon Armstrong LL .60 1.50
2 Jurgensen K.Anderson LL .60 1.50
3 Receiving Leaders .60 1.50
4 Scoring Leaders .30 .75
5 Interception Leaders .30 .75
6 Punting Leaders .60 1.50
7 George Blanda HL 2.50 5.00
8 George Blanda 2.50 5.00
9 Ralph Baker .20 .50
10 Don Woods RC .20 .50
11 Bob Asher .20 .50
12 Mel Blount RC 10.00 20.00
13 Sam Cunningham .30 .75
14 Jackie Smith .60 1.50
15 Greg Landry .30 .75
16 Buck Buchanan .60 1.50
17 Haven Moses .30 .75
18 Clarence Ellis .20 .50
19 Jim Carter .20 .50
20 Charley Taylor UER .75 2.00
21 Jess Phillips .20 .50
22 Larry Seiple .20 .50
23 Doug Dieken .20 .50
24 Ron Saul .20 .50
25 Isaac Curtis .60 1.50
26 Gary Larsen RC .20 .50
27 Bruce Jarvis .20 .50
28 Steve Zabel .20 .50
29 John Mendenhall .20 .50
30 Rick Volk .20 .50
31 Checklist 1-132 2.00 4.00
32 Dan Abramowicz .30 .75
33 Bubba Smith .60 1.50
34 David Ray .20 .50
35 Dan Dierdorf 2.00 4.00
36 Randy Rasmussen .20 .50
37 Bob Howard .20 .50
38 Gary Huff .30 .75
39 Rocky Bleier RC 10.00 20.00
40 Mel Gray .30 .75
41 Tony McGee DT .20 .50
42 Larry Hand .20 .50
43 Wendell Hayes .20 .50
44 Doug Wilkerson RC .20 .50
45 Paul Smith .20 .50
46 Dave Robinson .40 1.00
47 Bivian Lee .20 .50
48 Jim Mandich RC .30 .75
49 Greg Pruitt .60 1.50
50 Dan Pastorini .60 1.50
51 Ron Pritchard RC .20 .50
52 Dan Conners .20 .50
53 Fred Cox .20 .50
54 Tony Greene RC .20 .50
55 Craig Morton .60 1.50
56 Jerry Sisemore .20 .50
57 Glenn Doughty .20 .50
58 Larry Schreiber .20 .50
59 Charlie Waters RC 2.00 4.00
60 Jack Youngblood .60 1.50
61 Bill Lenkaitis .20 .50
62 Greg Brezina .20 .50
63 Bob Pollard .20 .50
64 Mack Alston .20 .50
65 Drew Pearson RC 10.00 20.00
66 Charlie Stukes .20 .50
67 Emerson Boozer .30 .75
68 Dennis Partee .20 .50
69 Bob Newton .20 .50
70 Jack Tatum .60 1.50
71 Frank Lewis .20 .50
72 Bob Young RC .20 .50
73 Julius Adams .20 .50
74 Paul Naumoff .20 .50
75 Otis Taylor .60 1.50
76 Dave Hampton .20 .50
77 Mike Current .20 .50
78 Brig Owens .20 .50
79 Bobby Scott RC .20 .50
80 Harold Carmichael 1.50 3.00
81 Bill Stanfill .20 .50
82 Bob Babich .20 .50
83 Vic Washington .20 .50
84 Mick Tingelhoff .30 .75
85 Bob Trumpy .60 1.50
86 Earl Edwards RC .20 .50
87 Ron Hornsby .20 .50
88 Don McCauley .20 .50
89 Jim Johnson .60 1.50
90 Andy Russell .30 .75
91 Cornell Green .60 1.50
92 Charlie Cowan .20 .50
93 Jon Staggers .20 .50
94 Billy Newsome .20 .50
95 Willie Brown .60 1.50
96 Carl Mauck .20 .50
97 Doug Buffone .20 .50
98 Preston Pearson .30 .75
99 Jim Bakken .20 .50
100 Bob Griese 2.50 5.00
101 Bob Windsor .20 .50
102 Rockne Freitas .20 .50
103 Jim Marsalis .20 .50
104 Bill Thompson .30 .75
105 Ken Burrow .20 .50
106 Diron Talbert .20 .50
107 Joe Federspiel .20 .50
108 Norm Bulaich .30 .75
109 Bob DeMarco .20 .50
110 Tom Wittum RC .20 .50
111 Larry Hefner RC .20 .50
112 Tody Smith .20 .50
113 Stu Voigt .20 .50
114 Horst Muhlmann .20 .50
115 Ahmad Rashad 3.00 6.00
116 Joe Dawkins .20 .50
117 George Kunz .20 .50
118 D.D. Lewis .30 .75
119 Levi Johnson .20 .50
120 Len Dawson 2.00 4.00
121 Jim Bertelsen .20 .50
122 Ed Bell .20 .50
123 Art Thoms .20 .50
124 Joe Beauchamp .20 .50
125 Jack Ham 3.00 6.00
126 Carl Garrett .20 .50
127 Roger Finnie RC .20 .50
128 Howard Twilley .30 .75
129 Bruce Barnes .20 .50
130 Nate Wright RC .20 .50
131 Jerry Tagge .20 .50
132 Floyd Little .60 1.50
133 John Zook .20 .50
134 Len Hauss .20 .50
135 Archie Manning .60 1.50
136 Po James .20 .50
137 Walt Sumner .20 .50
138 Randy Beisler .20 .50
139 Willie Alexander .20 .50
140 Garo Yepremian .30 .75
141 Chip Myers .20 .50
142 Jim Braxton .20 .50
143 Doug Van Horn .20 .50
144 Stan White RC .20 .50
145 Roger Staubach 10.00 20.00
146 Herman Weaver .20 .50
147 Marvin Upshaw .20 .50
148 Bob Klein .20 .50
149 Earlie Thomas .20 .50
150 John Brockington .30 .75
151 Mike Siani .20 .50
152 Sam Davis RC .20 .50
153 Mike Wagner .30 .75
154 Larry Stallings .20 .50
155 Wally Chambers .20 .50
156 Randy Vataha .20 .50
157 Jim Marshall .60 1.50
158 Jim Turner .20 .50
159 Walt Sweeney .20 .50
160 Ken Anderson 2.00 4.00
161 Ray Brown .20 .50
162 John Didion .20 .50
163 Tom Dempsey .20 .50
164 Clarence Scott .20 .50
165 Gene Washington 49er .30 .75
166 Willie Rodgers RC .20 .50
167 Doug Swift .20 .50
168 Rufus Mayes .20 .50
169 Marv Bateman .20 .50
170 Lydell Mitchell .30 .75
171 Ron Smith .20 .50
172 Bill Munson .30 .75
173 Bob Grim .20 .50
174 Ed Budde .20 .50
175 Bob Lilly UER 2.00 4.00
176 Jim Youngblood RC .60 1.50
177 Steve Tannen .20 .50
178 Rich McGeorge .20 .50
179 Jim Tyrer .20 .50
180 Forrest Blue .20 .50
181 Jerry LeVias .30 .75
182 Joe Gilliam RC .60 1.50
183 Jim Otis RC .30 .75
184 Mel Tom .20 .50
185 Paul Seymour .20 .50
186 George Webster .20 .50
187 Pete Duranko .20 .50
188 Essex Johnson .20 .50
189 Bob Lee .30 .75
190 Gene Upshaw .60 1.50
191 Tom Myers .20 .50
192 Don Zimmerman .20 .50
193 John Garlington .20 .50
194 Skip Butler .20 .50
195 Tom Mitchell .20 .50
196 Jim Langer .60 1.50
197 Ron Carpenter .20 .50
198 Dave Foley .20 .50
199 Bert Jones .60 1.50
200 Larry Brown .30 .75
201 Biletnikoff C.Taylor AP .75 2.00
202 All Pro Tackles .20 .50
203 L.Little T.Mack AP .60 1.50
204 All Pro Centers .20 .50
205 Hannah Gillingham AP .60 1.50
206 Dan Dierdorf W.Hill AP .60 1.50
207 All Pro Tight Ends .30 .75
208 F.Tarkenton Stabler AP 2.00 4.00
209 Simpson McCutch. AP 1.50 3.00
210 All Pro Backs .30 .75
211 All Pro Receivers .30 .75
212 All Pro Kickers .20 .50
213 Youngblood Bethea AP .60 1.50
214 All Pro Tackles .30 .75
215 M.Olsen M.Reid AP .60 1.50
216 Carl Eller L.Alzado AP .60 1.50
217 Hendricks Villapiano AP .60 1.50
218 Willie Lanier Jordan AP .60 1.50
219 All Pro Linebackers .30 .75
220 All Pro Cornerbacks .20 .50
221 All Pro Cornerbacks .20 .50
222 K.Houston D.Anderson AP .30 .75
223 Cliff Harris J.Tatum AP .60 1.50
224 All Pro Punters .30 .75
225 All Pro Returners .30 .75
226 Ted Kwalick .20 .50
227 Spider Lockhart .30 .75
228 Mike Livingston .20 .50
229 Larry Cole .20 .50
230 Gary Garrison .20 .50
231 Larry Brooks .20 .50
232 Bobby Howfield .20 .50
233 Fred Carr .20 .50
234 Norm Evans .20 .50
235 Dwight White .30 .75
236 Conrad Dobler .30 .75
237 Garry Lyle .20 .50
238 Darryl Stingley .60 1.50
239 Tom Graham .20 .50
240 Chuck Foreman .60 1.50
241 Ken Riley .30 .75
242 Don Morrison .20 .50
243 Lynn Dickey .30 .75
244 Don Cockroft .20 .50
245 Claude Humphrey .40 1.00
246 John Skorupan .20 .50
247 Raymond Chester .30 .75
248 Cas Banaszek .20 .50
249 Art Malone .20 .50
250 Ed Flanagan .20 .50
251 Checklist 133-264 2.00 4.00
252 Nemiah Wilson .20 .50
253 Ron Jessie .20 .50
254 Jim Lynch .20 .50
255 Bob Tucker .30 .75
256 Terry Owens .20 .50
257 John Fitzgerald .20 .50
258 Jack Snow .30 .75
259 Garry Puetz RC .20 .50
260 Mike Phipps .30 .75
261 Al Matthews .20 .50
262 Bob Kuechenberg .20 .50
263 Ron Yankowski .20 .50
264 Ron Shanklin .20 .50
265 Bobby Douglass .30 .75
266 Josh Ashton .20 .50
267 Bill Van Heusen .20 .50
268 Jeff Siemon .20 .50
269 Bob Newland .20 .50
270 Gale Gillingham .20 .50
271 Zeke Moore .20 .50
272 Mike Tilleman .20 .50
273 John Leypoldt .20 .50
274 Ken Mendenhall .20 .50
275 Norm Snead .30 .75
276 Bill Bradley .30 .75
277 Jerry Smith .20 .50
278 Clarence Davis RC .20 .50
279 Jim Yarbrough .20 .50
280 Lemar Parrish .20 .50
281 Bobby Bell .60 1.50
282 Lynn Swann UER RC 30.00 60.00
283 John Hicks RC .20 .50
284 Coy Bacon .30 .75
285 Lee Roy Jordan .60 1.50
286 Willie Buchanon .20 .50
287 Al Woodall .20 .50
288 Reggie Rucker .30 .75
289 John Schmitt .20 .50
290 Carl Eller .60 1.50
291 Jake Scott .30 .75
292 Donny Anderson .30 .75
293 Charley Wade RC .20 .50
294 John Tanner RC .20 .50
295 Charley Johnson .30 .75
296 Tom Blanchard .20 .50
297 Curley Culp .75 2.00
298 Jeff Van Note RC .30 .75
299 Bob James .20 .50
300 Franco Harris 4.00 8.00
301 Tim Berra RC .30 .75
302 Bruce Gossett .20 .50
303 Verlon Biggs .20 .50
304 Bob Kowalkowski .20 .50
305 Marv Hubbard .20 .50
306 Ken Avery .20 .50
307 Mike Adamle .20 .50
308 Don Herrmann .20 .50
309 Chris Fletcherv RC .20 .50
310 Roman Gabriel .60 1.50
311 Billy Joe DuPree .60 1.50
312 Fred Dryer .60 1.50
313 John Riggins 2.50 5.00
314 Bob McKay .20 .50
315 Ted Hendricks .60 1.50
316 Bobby Bryant .20 .50
317 Don Nottingham .20 .50
318 John Hannah 2.00 4.00
319 Rich Coady .20 .50
320 Phil Villapiano .30 .75
321 Jim Plunkett .60 1.50
322 Lyle Alzado .60 1.50
323 Ernie Jackson .20 .50
324 Billy Parks .20 .50
325 Willie Lanier .60 1.50
326 John James .20 .50
327 Joe Ferguson .30 .75
328 Ernie Holmes RC 3.00 6.00
329 Bruce Laird .20 .50
330 Chester Marcol .20 .50
331 Dave Wilcox .60 1.50
332 Pat Fischer .30 .75
333 Steve Owens .30 .75
334 Royce Berry .20 .50
335 Russ Washington .20 .50
336 Walker Gillette .20 .50
337 Mark Nordquist .20 .50
338 James Harris RC 1.00 2.50
339 Warren Koegel RC .20 .50
340 Emmitt Thomas .30 .75
341 Walt Garrison .30 .75
342 Thom Darden .20 .50
343 Mike Eischeid .20 .50
344 Ernie McMillan .20 .50
345 Nick Buoniconti .60 1.50
346 George Farmer .20 .50
347 Sam Adams .20 .50
348 Larry Cipa RC .20 .50
349 Bob Moore .20 .50
350 Otis Armstrong RC .60 1.50
351 George Blanda RB 1.50 3.00
352 Fred Cox RB .30 .75
353 Tom Dempsey RB .30 .75
354 Ken Houston RB .60 1.50
355 O.J.Simpson RB 2.50 5.00
356 Ron Smith RB .30 .75
357 Bob Atkins .20 .50
358 Pat Sullivan .30 .75
359 Joe DeLamielleure 1.00 2.50
360 Lawrence McCutcheon RC .60 1.50
361 David Lee .20 .50
362 Mike McCoy DT .20 .50
363 Skip Vanderbundt .20 .50
364 Mark Moseley .30 .75
365 Lem Barney .60 1.50
366 Doug Dressler .20 .50
367 Dan Fouts RC 20.00 40.00
368 Bob Hyland RC .20 .50
369 John Outlaw .20 .50
370 Roy Gerela .20 .50
371 Isiah Robertson .30 .75
372 Jerome Barkum .20 .50
373 Ed Podolak .20 .50
374 Milt Morin .20 .50
375 John Niland .20 .50
376 Checklist 265-396 UER 2.00 4.00
377 Ken Iman .20 .50
378 Manny Fernandez .30 .75
379 Dave Gallagher RC .20 .50
380 Ken Stabler 7.50 15.00
381 Mack Herron RC .20 .50
382 Bill McClard RC .20 .50
383 Ray May .20 .50
384 Don Hansen .20 .50
385 Elvin Bethea .60 1.50
386 Joe Scibelli .20 .50
387 Neal Craig RC .20 .50
388 Marty Domres .20 .50
389 Ken Ellis .20 .50
390 Charle Young .30 .75
391 Tommy Hart .20 .50
392 Moses Denson RC .20 .50
393 Larry Walton .20 .50
394 Dave Green RC .20 .50
395 Ron Johnson .30 .75
396 Ed Bradley RC .20 .50
397 J.T. Thomas RC .20 .50
398 Jim Bailey .20 .50
399 Barry Pearson .20 .50
400 Fran Tarkenton 4.00 8.00
401 Jack Rudnay .20 .50
402 Rayfield Wright .30 .75
403 Roger Wehrli .40 1.00
404 Vern Den Herder .20 .50
405 Fred Biletnikoff 1.50 3.00
406 Ken Grandberry RC .20 .50
407 Bob Adams RC .20 .50
408 Jim Merlo .20 .50
409 John Pitts .20 .50
410 Dave Osborn .30 .75
411 Dennis Havig .20 .50
412 Bob Johnson .20 .50
413 Ken Burrough UER .30 .75
414 Jim Cheyunski .20 .50
415 MacArthur Lane .20 .50
416 Joe Theismann RC 12.50 25.00
417 Mike Boryla RC .20 .50
418 Bruce Taylor .20 .50
419 Chris Hanburger .30 .75
420 Tom Mack .60 1.50
421 Errol Mann .20 .50
422 Jack Gregory .20 .50
423 Harrison Davis RC .20 .50
424 Burgess Owens .20 .50
425 Joe Greene 2.50 5.00
426 Morris Stroud .20 .50
427 John DeMarie .20 .50
428 Mel Renfro .60 1.50
429 Cid Edwards .20 .50
430 Mike Reid .60 1.50
431 Jack Mildren RC .20 .50
432 Jerry Simmons .20 .50
433 Ron Yary .60 1.50
434 Howard Stevens RC .20 .50
435 Ray Guy .75 2.00
436 Tommy Nobis .60 1.50
437 Solomon Freelon .20 .50
438 J.D. Hill .30 .75
439 Toni Linhart RC .20 .50
440 Dick Anderson .30 .75
441 Guy Morriss RC .20 .50
442 Bob Hoskins .20 .50
443 John Hadl .60 1.50
444 Roy Jefferson .20 .50
445 Charlie Sanders .40 1.00
446 Pat Curran RC .20 .50
447 David Knight RC .20 .50
448 Bob Brown DT .20 .50
449 Pete Gogolak .20 .50
450 Terry Metcalf .60 1.50
451 Bill Bergey .60 1.50
452 Dan Abramowicz HL .30 .75
453 Otis Armstrong HL .30 .75
454 Cliff Branch HL .60 1.50
455 John James HL .20 .50
456 Lydell Mitchell HL .30 .75
457 Lemar Parrish HL .30 .75
458 Ken Stabler HL 2.50 5.00
459 Lynn Swann HL 4.00 8.00
460 Emmitt Thomas HL .20 .50
461 Terry Bradshaw 10.00 20.00
462 Jerrel Wilson .20 .50
463 Walter Johnson .20 .50
464 Golden Richards RC .30 .75
465 Tommy Casanova .30 .75
466 Randy Jackson .20 .50
467 Ron Bolton .20 .50
468 Joe Owens .20 .50
469 Wally Hilgenberg .20 .50
470 Riley Odoms .30 .75
471 Otis Sistrunk .30 .75
472 Eddie Ray RC .20 .50
473 Reggie McKenzie .30 .75
474 Elbert Drungo .20 .50
475 Mercury Morris .60 1.50
476 Dan Dickel RC .20 .50
477 Merritt Kersey RC .20 .50
478 Mike Holmes RC .20 .50
479 Clarence Williams .20 .50
480 Billy Kilmer .60 1.50
481 Altie Taylor .20 .50
482 Dave Elmendorf .20 .50
483 Bob Rowe .20 .50
484 Pete Athas .20 .50
485 Winston Hill .20 .50
486 Bo Matthews RC .20 .50
487 Earl Thomas RC .20 .50
488 Jan Stenerud .60 1.50
489 Steve Holden RC .20 .50
490 Cliff Harris RC 3.00 6.00
491 Boobie Clark RC .30 .75
492 Joe Taylor .20 .50
493 Tom Neville .20 .50
494 Wayne Colman .20 .50
495 Jim Mitchell .20 .50
496 Paul Krause .60 1.50
497 Jim Otto .60 1.50
498 John Rowser .20 .50
499 Larry Little .60 1.50
500 O.J. Simpson 5.00 10.00
501 John Dutton RC .60 1.50
502 Pat Hughes .20 .50
503 Malcolm Snider .20 .50
504 Fred Willis .20 .50
505 Harold Jackson .60 1.50
506 Mike Bragg .20 .50
507 Jerry Sherk .30 .75
508 Mirro Roder RC .20 .50
509 Tom Sullivan RC .20 .50
510 Jim Hart .60 1.50
511 Cedrick Hardman .20 .50
512 Blaine Nye .20 .50
513 Elmo Wright .20 .50
514 Herb Orvis RC .20 .50
515 Richard Caster .30 .75
516 Doug Kotar RC .20 .50
517 Checklist 397-528 2.00 4.00
518 Jesse Freitas RC .20 .50
519 Ken Houston .60 1.50
520 Alan Page .60 1.50
521 Tim Foley .30 .75
522 Bill Olds RC .20 .50
523 Bobby Maples .20 .50
524 Cliff Branch RC 7.50 15.00
525 Merlin Olsen .60 1.50
526 AFC Champs Brad. Harris 2.00 4.00
527 NFC Champs Foreman .60 1.50
528 Super Bowl IX Bradshaw 2.50 5.00

1975 Topps Team Checklists

The 1975 Topps Team Checklist set contains 26 standard-size cards, one for each of the 26 NFL teams. The front of the card has the 1975 schedule, while the back of the card contains the checklist, complete with boxes in which to place check marks. The player's position is also listed with his name. The set was only available directly from Topps as a send-off offer as an uncut sheet; the prices below apply equally to uncut sheets as they are frequently found in their original uncut condition. As for individual cards, thin card stock mkaes it a challenge to find these cards in top grades. These unnumbered cards are numbered below for convenience in alphabetical order by team name.

COMPLETE SET (26) 125.00 250.00
1 Atlanta Falcons 5.00 10.00
2 Baltimore Colts 5.00 10.00
3 Buffalo Bills 5.00 10.00
4 Chicago Bears 7.50 15.00
5 Cincinnati Bengals 5.00 10.00
6 Cleveland Browns 7.50 15.00
7 Dallas Cowboys 10.00 20.00
8 Denver Broncos 5.00 10.00
9 Detroit Lions 5.00 10.00
10 Green Bay Packers 7.50 15.00
11 Houston Oilers 5.00 10.00
12 Kansas City Chiefs 5.00 10.00
13 Los Angeles Rams 5.00 10.00
14 Miami Dolphins 7.50 15.00
15 Minnesota Vikings 7.50 15.00
16 New England Patriots 5.00 10.00
17 New York Giants 7.50 15.00
18 New York Jets 5.00 10.00
19 New Orleans Saints 5.00 10.00
20 Oakland Raiders 10.00 20.00
21 Philadelphia Eagles 5.00 10.00
22 Pittsburgh Steelers 7.50 15.00
23 St. Louis Cardinals 5.00 10.00
24 San Diego Chargers 5.00 10.00
25 San Francisco 49ers 7.50 15.00
26 Washington Redskins 7.50 15.00

1976 Topps

The 1976 Topps football set contains 528 standard-size cards including the first year cards of Seattle Seahawks and Tampa Bay Buccaneers. Underneath photos that are bordered by a team color, card fronts contain a team colored football at bottom left with the team name within. The player's name and position are also at the bottom. The card backs are printed in orange and blue on gray card stock and are horizontally designed. The content includes statistics, highlights and a trivia question with answer. Subsets include Record Breakers (1-8), league leaders (201-206), playoffs (331-333) and team checklist (451-478) cards. The key Rookie Card belongs to all-time rushing leader Walter Payton. Other Rookie Cards include Randy Gradishar, Ed Too Tall Jones, Jack Lambert, Harvey Martin, and Randy White. An uncut sheet of team checklist cards was also available via a mail-in offer on wax packs.

COMPLETE SET (528) 200.00 350.00
1 George Blanda RB 2.50 5.00
2 Neal Colzie RB .30 .75
3 Chuck Foreman RB .30 .75
4 Jim Marshall RB .30 .75
5 Terry Metcalf RB .30 .75
6 O.J.Simpson RB 1.50 3.00
7 Fran Tarkenton RB 1.50 3.00
8 Charley Taylor RB .60 1.50
9 Ernie Holmes .30 .75
10 Ken Anderson AP .60 1.50
11 Bobby Bryant .20 .50
12 Jerry Smith .30 .75
13 David Lee .20 .50
14 Robert Newhouse RC .60 1.50
15 Vern Den Herder .20 .50
16 John Hannah .60 1.50
17 J.D. Hill .30 .75
18 James Harris .30 .75
19 Willie Buchanon .20 .50
20 Charle Young .30 .75
21 Jim Yarbrough .20 .50
22 Ronnie Coleman RC .20 .50
23 Don Cockroft .20 .50
24 Willie Lanier .60 1.50
25 Fred Biletnikoff 1.50 3.00
26 Ron Yankowski .20 .50
27 Spider Lockhart .20 .50
28 Bob Johnson .20 .50
29 J.T. Thomas .20 .50
30 Ron Yary .60 1.50
31 Brad Dusek RC .20 .50
32 Raymond Chester .30 .75
33 Larry Little .60 1.50
34 Pat Leahy RC .60 1.50
35 Steve Bartkowski RC 2.00 4.00
36 Tom Myers .20 .50
37 Bill Van Heusen .20 .50
38 Russ Washington .20 .50
39 Tom Sullivan .20 .50
40 Curley Culp .75 2.00
41 Johnnie Gray RC .20 .50
42 Bob Klein .20 .50
43 Lem Barney .60 1.50
44 Harvey Martin RC 3.00 6.00
45 Reggie Rucker .30 .75
46 Neil Clabo RC .20 .50
47 Ray Hamilton RC .20 .50
48 Joe Ferguson .30 .75
49 Ed Podolak .20 .50
50 Ray Guy AP .60 1.50
51 Glen Edwards .20 .50
52 Jim LeClair RC .20 .50
53 Mike Barnes RC .20 .50
54 Nat Moore RC .60 1.50
55 Billy Kilmer .60 1.50
56 Larry Stallings .20 .50
57 Jack Gregory .20 .50
58 Steve Mike-Mayer RC .20 .50
59 Virgil Livers RC .20 .50
60 Jerry Sherk .30 .75
61 Guy Morriss .20 .50
62 Barty Smith .20 .50
63 Jerome Barkum .20 .50
64 Ira Gordon RC .20 .50
65 Paul Krause .60 1.50
66 John McMakin .20 .50
67 Checklist 1-132 1.50 3.00
68 Charlie Johnson UER .30 .75
69 Tommy Nobis .60 1.50
70 Lydell Mitchell .30 .75
71 Vern Holland .20 .50
72 Tim Foley .30 .75
73 Golden Richards .30 .75
74 Bryant Salter .20 .50
75 Terry Bradshaw 10.00 20.00
76 Ted Hendricks .60 1.50
77 Rich Saul RC .20 .50
78 John Smith RC .20 .50
79 Altie Taylor .20 .50
80 Cedrick Hardman .20 .50
81 Ken Payne RC .20 .50
82 Zeke Moore .20 .50
83 Alvin Maxson RC .20 .50
84 Wally Hilgenberg .20 .50
85 John Niland .20 .50
86 Mike Sensibaugh .20 .50
87 Ron Johnson .30 .75
88 Winston Hill .20 .50
89 Charlie Joiner 2.00 4.00
90 Roger Wehrli .30 .75
91 Mike Bragg .20 .50
92 Dan Dickel .20 .50
93 Earl Morrall .30 .75
94 Pat Toomay .20 .50
95 Gary Garrison .20 .50
96 Ken Geddes RC .20 .50
97 Mike Current .20 .50
98 Bob Avellini RC .30 .75
99 Dave Pureifory RC .20 .50
100 Franco Harris AP 4.00 8.00
101 Randy Logan RC .20 .50
102 John Fitzgerald .20 .50
103 Gregg Bingham RC .30 .75
104 Jim Plunkett .60 1.50
105 Carl Eller .60 1.50
106 Larry Walton .20 .50
107 Clarence Scott .20 .50
108 Skip Vanderbundt .20 .50
109 Boobie Clark .30 .75
110 Tom Mack .60 1.50
111 Bruce Laird .20 .50
112 Dave Dalby RC .20 .50
113 John Leypoldt .20 .50
114 Barry Pearson .20 .50
115 Larry Brown .30 .75
116 Jackie Smith .60 1.50
117 Pat Hughes .20 .50
118 Al Woodall .20 .50
119 John Zook .20 .50
120 Jake Scott .30 .75
121 Rich Glover RC .20 .50
122 Ernie Jackson .20 .50
123 Otis Armstrong .60 1.50
124 Bob Grim .20 .50
125 Jeff Siemon .30 .75
126 Harold Hart RC .20 .50
127 John DeMarie .20 .50
128 Dan Fouts 6.00 12.00
129 Jim Kearney .20 .50
130 John Dutton AP .30 .75
131 Calvin Hill .60 1.50
132 Toni Fritsch .20 .50
133 Ron Jessie .20 .50
134 Don Nottingham .20 .50
135 Lemar Parrish .20 .50
136 Russ Francis RC .60 1.50
137 Joe Reed .20 .50
138 C.L. Whittington RC .20 .50
139 Otis Sistrunk .30 .75
140 Lynn Swann AP 10.00 20.00
141 Jim Carter .20 .50
142 Mike Montler .20 .50
143 Walter Johnson .20 .50
144 Doug Kotar .20 .50
145 Roman Gabriel .60 1.50
146 Billy Newsome .20 .50
147 Ed Bradley .20 .50
148 Walter Payton RC 125.00 250.00
149 Johnny Fuller .20 .50
150 Alan Page AP .60 1.50
151 Frank Grant RC .20 .50
152 Dave Green .20 .50
153 Nelson Munsey RC .20 .50
154 Jim Mandich .20 .50
155 Lawrence McCutcheon .60 1.50
156 Steve Ramsey .20 .50
157 Ed Flanagan .20 .50
158 Randy White RC 10.00 20.00
159 Gerry Mullins .20 .50
160 Jan Stenerud AP .60 1.50
161 Steve Odom RC .20 .50
162 Roger Finnie .20 .50
163 Norm Snead .30 .75
164 Jeff Van Note .30 .75
165 Bill Bergey .60 1.50
166 Allen Carter RC .20 .50
167 Steve Holden .20 .50
168 Sherman White .20 .50
169 Bob Berry .20 .50
170 Ken Houston AP .60 1.50
171 Bill Olds .20 .50
172 Larry Seiple .20 .50
173 Cliff Branch 2.00 4.00
174 Reggie McKenzie .30 .75
175 Dan Pastorini .60 1.50
176 Paul Naumoff .20 .50
177 Checklist 133-264 1.50 3.00
178 Durwood Keeton RC .20 .50
179 Earl Thomas .20 .50
180 L.C. Greenwood AP .60 1.50
181 John Outlaw .20 .50
182 Frank Nunley .20 .50
183 Dave Jennings RC .30 .75
184 MacArthur Lane .20 .50
185 Chester Marcol .20 .50
186 J.J. Jones RC .20 .50
187 Tom DeLeone RC .20 .50
188 Steve Zabel .20 .50
189 Ken Johnson DT RC .20 .50
190 Rayfield Wright .30 .75
191 Brent McClanahan RC .20 .50
192 Pat Fischer .30 .75
193 Roger Carr RC .30 .75
194 Manny Fernandez .30 .75
195 Roy Gerela .20 .50
196 Dave Elmendorf .20 .50
197 Bob Kowalkowski .20 .50
198 Phil Villapiano .30 .75
199 Will Wynn RC .20 .50
200 Terry Metcalf .60 1.50
201 Tarkenton Anderson LL .75 2.00
202 Receiving Leaders .30 .75
203 O.J.Simpson J.Otis LL 1.25 2.50
204 Simpson Foreman LL 1.25 2.50
205 M.Blount P.Krause LL .60 1.50
206 Punting Leaders .30 .75
207 Ken Ellis .20 .50
208 Ron Saul .20 .50
209 Toni Linhart .20 .50
210 Jim Langer AP .60 1.50
211 Jeff Wright S RC .20 .50
212 Moses Denson .20 .50
213 Earl Edwards .20 .50
214 Walker Gillette .20 .50
215 Bob Trumpy .30 .75
216 Emmitt Thomas .30 .75
217 Lyle Alzado .60 1.50
218 Carl Garrett .30 .75
219 Van Green RC .20 .50
220 Jack Lambert AP RC 20.00 35.00
221 Spike Jones .20 .50
222 John Hadl .60 1.50
223 Billy Johnson RC .60 1.50
224 Tony McGee DT .20 .50
225 Preston Pearson .30 .75
226 Isiah Robertson .30 .75
227 Errol Mann .20 .50
228 Paul Seal RC .20 .50
229 Roland Harper RC .20 .50
230 Ed White RC .30 .75
231 Joe Theismann 3.00 6.00
232 Jim Cheyunski .20 .50
233 Bill Stanfill .30 .75
234 Marv Hubbard .20 .50
235 Tommy Casanova .30 .75
236 Bob Hyland .20 .50
237 Jesse Freitas .20 .50
238 Norm Thompson .20 .50
239 Charlie Smith WR .20 .50
240 John James .20 .50
241 Alden Roche .20 .50
242 Gordon Jolley RC .20 .50
243 Larry Ely RC .20 .50
244 Richard Caster .20 .50
245 Joe Greene 2.00 5.00
246 Larry Schreiber .20 .50
247 Terry Schmidt RC .20 .50
248 Jerrel Wilson .20 .50
249 Marty Domres .20 .50
250 Isaac Curtis .30 .75
251 Harold McLinton RC .20 .50
252 Fred Dryer .60 1.50
253 Bill Lenkaitis .20 .50
254 Don Hardeman RC .20 .50
255 Bob Griese 2.00 4.00
256 Oscar Roan RC .20 .50
257 Randy Gradishar RC 2.00 5.00
258 Bob Thomas RC .20 .50
259 Joe Owens .20 .50
260 Cliff Harris AP .60 1.50
261 Frank Lewis .20 .50
262 Mike McCoy .20 .50
263 Rickey Young RC .20 .50
264 Brian Kelley RC .20 .50
265 Charlie Sanders .30 .75
266 Jim Hart .60 1.50
267 Greg Gantt RC .20 .50
268 John Ward RC .20 .50
269 Al Beauchamp .20 .50
270 Jack Tatum .60 1.50
271 Jim Lash RC .20 .50
272 Diron Talbert .20 .50
273 Checklist 265-396 1.50 3.00
274 Steve Spurrier 3.00 8.00
275 Greg Pruitt .60 1.50
276 Jim Mitchell .20 .50
277 Jack Rudnay .20 .50
278 Freddie Solomon RC .30 .75
279 Frank LeMaster RC .20 .50
280 Wally Chambers .20 .50
281 Mike Collier RC .20 .50
282 Clarence Williams .20 .50
283 Mitch Hoopes RC .20 .50
284 Ron Bolton .20 .50
285 Harold Jackson .60 1.50
286 Greg Landry .30 .75
287 Tony Greene .20 .50
288 Howard Stevens .20 .50
289 Roy Jefferson .20 .50
290 Jim Bakken .20 .50
291 Doug Sutherland RC .20 .50
292 Marvin Cobb RC .20 .50
293 Mack Alston .20 .50
294 Rod McNeill RC .20 .50
295 Gene Upshaw .60 1.50
296 Dave Gallagher .20 .50
297 Larry Ball RC .20 .50
298 Ron Howard RC .20 .50
299 Don Strock RC .60 1.50
300 O.J. Simpson AP 4.00 8.00
301 Ray Mansfield .20 .50
302 Larry Marshall RC .20 .50
303 Dick Himes RC .20 .50
304 Ray Wersching RC .20 .50
305 John Riggins 2.00 4.00
306 Bob Parsons RC .20 .50
307 Ray Brown .20 .50
308 Len Dawson 1.50 3.00
309 Andy Maurer .20 .50
310 Jack Youngblood AP .60 1.50
311 Essex Johnson .20 .50
312 Stan White .20 .50
313 Drew Pearson 2.00 5.00
314 Rockne Freitas .20 .50
315 Mercury Morris .60 1.50
316 Willie Alexander .20 .50
317 Paul Warfield 1.50 3.00
318 Bob Chandler .30 .75
319 Bobby Walden .20 .50
320 Riley Odoms .30 .75
321 Mike Boryla .20 .50
322 Bruce Van Dyke .20 .50
323 Pete Banaszak .20 .50
324 Darryl Stingley .60 1.50
325 John Mendenhall .20 .50
326 Dan Dierdorf .75 2.00
327 Bruce Taylor .20 .50
328 Don McCauley .20 .50
329 John Reaves UER .20 .50
330 Chris Hanburger .30 .75
331 NFC Champs Staubach 1.50 3.00
332 AFC Champs F.Harris .75 2.00
333 Super Bowl X Bradshaw 1.25 2.50
334 Godwin Turk RC .20 .50
335 Dick Anderson .30 .75
336 Woody Green RC .20 .50
337 Pat Curran .20 .50
338 Council Rudolph RC .20 .50
339 Joe Lavender RC .20 .50
340 John Gilliam .30 .75
341 Steve Furness RC .30 .75
342 D.D. Lewis .30 .75
343 Duane Carrell RC .20 .50
344 Jon Morris .20 .50
345 John Brockington .30 .75
346 Mike Phipps .30 .75
347 Lyle Blackwood RC .20 .50
348 Julius Adams .20 .50
349 Terry Hermeling RC .20 .50
350 Rolland Lawrence AP RC .20 .50
351 Glenn Doughty .20 .50
352 Doug Swift .20 .50
353 Mike Strachan RC .20 .50
354 Craig Morton .60 1.50
355 George Blanda 2.50 5.00
356 Garry Puetz .20 .50
357 Carl Mauck .20 .50
358 Walt Patulski .20 .50
359 Stu Voigt .20 .50
360 Fred Carr .20 .50
361 Po James .20 .50
362 Otis Taylor .60 1.50
363 Jeff West RC .20 .50
364 Gary Huff .30 .75
365 Dwight White .30 .75
366 Dan Ryczek RC .20 .50
367 Jon Keyworth RC .20 .50
368 Mel Renfro .60 1.50
369 Bruce Coslet RC .60 1.50
370 Len Hauss .20 .50
371 Rick Volk .20 .50
372 Howard Twilley .30 .75
373 Cullen Bryant RC .30 .75
374 Bob Babich .20 .50
375 Herman Weaver .20 .50
376 Steve Grogan RC 1.25 3.00
377 Bubba Smith .60 1.50
378 Burgess Owens .20 .50
379 Al Matthews .20 .50
380 Art Shell .60 1.50
381 Larry Brown .20 .50
382 Horst Muhlmann .20 .50
383 Ahmad Rashad 1.25 2.50
384 Bobby Maples .20 .50
385 Jim Marshall .60 1.50
386 Joe Dawkins .20 .50
387 Dennis Partee .20 .50
388 Eddie McMillan RC .20 .50

389 Randy Johnson .20 .50
390 Bob Kuechenberg .20 .50
391 Rufus Mayes .20 .50
392 Lloyd Mumphord .20 .50
393 Ike Harris RC .20 .50
394 Dave Hampton .20 .50
395 Roger Staubach 10.00 20.00
396 Doug Buffone .20 .50
397 Howard Fest .20 .50
398 Wayne Mulligan .20 .50
399 Bill Bradley .30 .75
400 Chuck Foreman AP .60 1.50
401 Jack Snow .30 .75
402 Bob Howard .20 .50
403 John Matuszak .60 1.50
404 Bill Munson .30 .75
405 Andy Russell .30 .75
406 Skip Butler .20 .50
407 Hugh McKinnis RC .20 .50
408 Bob Penchion RC .20 .50
409 Mike Bass .20 .50
410 George Kunz .20 .50
411 Ron Pritchard .20 .50
412 Barry Smith RC .20 .50
413 Norm Bulaich .20 .50
414 Marv Bateman .20 .50
415 Ken Stabler 6.00 12.00
416 Conrad Dobler .30 .75
417 Bob Tucker .30 .75
418 Gene Washington 49er .30 .75
419 Ed Marinaro .60 1.50
420 Jack Ham AP 2.00 4.00
421 Jim Turner .20 .50
422 Chris Fletcher .20 .50
423 Carl Barzilauskas RC .20 .50
424 Robert Brazile RC 2.00 5.00
425 Harold Carmichael .75 2.00
426 Ron Jaworski RC 3.00 6.00
427 Ed Too Tall Jones RC 10.00 20.00
428 Larry McCarren RC .20 .50
429 Mike Thomas RC .20 .50
430 Joe DeLamielleure .60 1.50
431 Tom Blanchard .20 .50
432 Ron Carpenter .20 .50
433 Levi Johnson .20 .50
434 Sam Cunningham .30 .75
435 Garo Yepremian .30 .75
436 Mike Livingston .20 .50
437 Larry Csonka 2.00 4.00
438 Doug Dieken .30 .75
439 Bill Lueck .20 .50
440 Tom MacLeod RC .20 .50
441 Mick Tingelhoff .30 .75
442 Terry Hanratty .30 .75
443 Mike Siani .20 .50
444 Dwight Harrison .20 .50
445 Jim Otis .30 .75
446 Jack Reynolds .30 .75
447 Jean Fugett RC .30 .75
448 Dave Beverly RC .20 .50
449 Bernard Jackson RC .20 .50
450 Charley Taylor .75 2.00
451 Atlanta Falcons CL .75 2.00
452 Baltimore Colts CL .75 2.00
453 Buffalo Bills CL .75 2.00
454 Chicago Bears CL .75 2.00
455 Cincinnati Bengals CL .75 2.00
456 Cleveland Browns CL .75 2.00
457 Dallas Cowboys CL .75 2.00
458 Denver Broncos CL UER .75 2.00
459 Detroit Lions CL .75 2.00
460 Green Bay Packers CL .75 2.00
461 Houston Oilers CL .75 2.00
462 Kansas City Chiefs CL .75 2.00
463 Los Angeles Rams CL .75 2.00
464 Miami Dolphins CL .75 2.00
465 Minnesota Vikings CL .75 2.00
466 New England Patriots CL .75 2.00
467 New Orleans Saints CL .75 2.00
468 New York Giants CL .75 2.00
469 New York Jets CL .75 2.00
470 Oakland Raiders CL .75 2.00
471 Philadelphia Eagles CL .75 2.00
472 Pittsburgh Steelers CL .75 2.00
473 St. Louis Cardinals CL .75 2.00
474 San Diego Chargers CL .75 2.00
475 San Francisco 49ers CL .75 2.00
476 Seattle Seahawks CL .75 2.00
477 Tampa Bay Buccaneers CL .75 2.00
478 Washington Redskins CL .75 2.00
479 Fred Cox .20 .50
480 Mel Blount AP 3.00 6.00
481 John Bunting RC .30 .75
482 Ken Mendenhall .20 .50
483 Will Harrell RC .20 .50
484 Marlin Briscoe .20 .50
485 Archie Manning .60 1.50
486 Tody Smith .20 .50
487 George Hunt .20 .50
488 Roscoe Word RC .20 .50
489 Paul Seymour .20 .50
490 Lee Roy Jordan AP .60 1.50
491 Chip Myers .20 .50
492 Norm Evans .20 .50
493 Jim Bertelsen .20 .50
494 Mark Moseley .30 .75
495 George Buehler RC .20 .50
496 Charlie Hall .20 .50
497 Marvin Upshaw .20 .50
498 Tom Banks RC .20 .50
499 Randy Vataha .20 .50
500 Fran Tarkenton AP 3.00 6.00
501 Mike Wagner .30 .75
502 Art Malone .20 .50
503 Fred Cook RC .20 .50
504 Rich McGeorge .20 .50
505 Ken Burrough .30 .75
506 Nick Mike-Mayer .20 .50
507 Checklist 397-528 1.50 3.00
508 Steve Owens .30 .75
509 Brad Van Pelt RC .20 .50
510 Ken Riley .30 .75
511 Art Thoms .20 .50
512 Ed Bell .20 .50
513 Tom Wittum .20 .50
514 Jim Braxton .20 .50
515 Nick Buoniconti .60 1.50
516 Brian Sipe RC 2.50 6.00
517 Jim Lynch .20 .50
518 Prentice McCray RC .20 .50
519 Tom Dempsey .20 .50
520 Mel Gray .30 .75
521 Nate Wright .20 .50
522 Rocky Bleier 3.00 6.00
523 Dennis Johnson RC .20 .50
524 Jerry Sisemore .20 .50
525 Bert Jones .20 .50
526 Perry Smith RC .20 .50
527 Blaine Nye .20 .50
528 Bob Moore .60 1.50

1976 Topps Team Checklists

The 1976 Topps Team Checklist set contains 30 standard-size cards, one for each of the 28 NFL teams plus two checklist cards. The front of the card has the 1976 Topps checklist for that particular team, complete with boxes in which to place check marks. The set was only available directly from Topps as a send-off offer as an uncut sheet; the prices below apply equally to uncut sheets as they are frequently found in their original uncut condition. As for individual cards, thin card stock makes it a challenge to obtain singles in top grades. These unnumbered cards are numbered below for convenience in alphabetical order by team name.

COMPLETE SET (30) 62.50 125.00
1 Atlanta Falcons 2.50 5.00
2 Baltimore Colts 2.50 5.00
3 Buffalo Bills 2.50 5.00
4 Chicago Bears 2.50 5.00
5 Cincinnati Bengals 2.50 5.00
6 Cleveland Browns 2.50 5.00
7 Dallas Cowboys 5.00 10.00
8 Denver Broncos 2.50 5.00
9 Detroit Lions 2.50 5.00
10 Green Bay Packers 3.75 7.50
11 Houston Oilers 2.50 5.00
12 Kansas City Chiefs 2.50 5.00
13 Los Angeles Rams 2.50 5.00
14 Miami Dolphins 3.75 7.50
15 Minnesota Vikings 2.50 5.00
16 New England Patriots 2.50 5.00
17 New York Giants 2.50 5.00
18 New York Jets 2.50 5.00
19 New Orleans Saints 2.50 5.00
20 Oakland Raiders 5.00 10.00
21 Philadelphia Eagles 2.50 5.00
22 Pittsburgh Steelers 3.75 7.50
23 St. Louis Cardinals 2.50 5.00
24 San Diego Chargers 2.50 5.00
25 San Francisco 49ers 3.75 7.50
26 Seattle Seahawks 2.50 5.00
27 Tampa Bay Buccaneers 2.50 5.00
28 Washington Redskins 3.75 7.50
29 Checklist 1-132 2.50 5.00
30 Checklist 133-264 2.50 5.00

1977 Topps

The 1977 Topps football set contains 528 standard-size cards. Card fronts have a banner (with team name), the player's name and position at the top. Backs that rushed for 1,000 yards have a "1,000 Yarder" football logo on front. The card backs are printed in purple and black on gray card stock. The backs contain yearly statistics, highlights and a note on the player's college career. Subsets include league leaders (1-6), team checklist cards (201-208), Record Breakers (451-455) and playoffs (526-528). The key Rookie Card is Steve Largent. Other Rookie Cards include Harry Carson, Dave Casper, Archie Griffin, Mike Haynes, Ray Rhodes, Lee Roy Selmon, Mike Webster, Danny White and Jim Zorn. An uncut sheet of team checklist cards was also available via a mail-in offer on wax pack wrappers. A Mexican version of this set was produced. All text is in Spanish (front and back) and is quite a bit tougher to find than the basic issue.

COMPLETE SET (528) 125.00 250.00
1 K.Stabler/J.Harris LL 1.25 2.50
2 Drew Pearson/M.Lane LL .40 1.00
3 W.Payton/Simpson LL 5.00 10.00
4 Scoring Leaders .25 .60
5 Interception Leaders .25 .60
6 Punting Leaders .15 .40
7 Mike Phipps .25 .60
8 Rick Volk .15 .40
9 Steve Furness .25 .60
10 Isaac Curtis .25 .60
11 Nate Wright .25 .60
12 Jean Fugett .15 .40
13 Ken Mendenhall .15 .40
14 Sam Adams .15 .40
15 Charlie Waters .40 1.00
16 Bill Stanfill .15 .40
17 John Holland RC .15 .40
18 Pat Haden RC .75 2.00
19 Bob Young .15 .40
20 Wally Chambers .15 .40
21 Lawrence Gaines RC .15 .40
22 Larry McCarren .15 .40
23 Horst Muhlmann .15 .40
24 Phil Villapiano .25 .60
25 Greg Pruitt .25 .60
26 Ron Howard .15 .40
27 Craig Morton .40 1.00
28 Rufus Mayes .15 .40
29 Lee Roy Selmon UER RC 7.50 15.00
30 Ed White .25 .60
31 Harold McLinton .15 .40
32 Glenn Doughty .15 .40
33 Bob Kuechenberg .40 1.00
34 Duane Carrell .15 .40
35 Riley Odoms .15 .40
36 Bobby Scott .15 .40
37 Nick Mike-Mayer .15 .40
38 Bill Lenkaitis .15 .40
39 Roland Harper .25 .60
40 Tommy Hart .15 .40
41 Mike Sensibaugh .15 .40
42 Rusty Jackson RC .15 .40
43 Levi Johnson .15 .40
44 Mike McCoy .15 .40
45 Roger Staubach 10.00 20.00
46 Fred Cox .15 .40
47 Bob Babich .15 .40
48 Reggie McKenzie .25 .60
49 Dave Jennings .15 .40
50 Mike Haynes RC 4.00 10.00
51 Larry Brown .25 .60
52 Marvin Cobb .15 .40
53 Fred Cook .15 .40
54 Freddie Solomon .25 .60
55 John Riggins 1.25 2.50
56 John Bunting .25 .60
57 Ray Wersching .25 .60
58 Mike Livingston .15 .40
59 Billy Johnson .25 .60
60 Mike Wagner .15 .40
61 Waymond Bryant RC .15 .40
62 Jim Otis .25 .60
63 Ed Galigher RC .15 .40
64 Randy Vataha .15 .40
65 Jim Zorn RC 2.00 5.00
66 Jon Keyworth .15 .40
67 Checklist 1-132 .75 2.00
68 Henry Childs RC .15 .40
69 Thom Darden .15 .40
70 George Kunz .15 .40
71 Lenvil Elliott RC .15 .40
72 Curtis Johnson RC .15 .40
73 Doug Van Horn .15 .40
74 Joe Theismann 2.00 4.00
75 Dwight White .25 .60
76 Scott Laidlaw RC .15 .40
77 Monte Johnson RC .15 .40
78 Dave Beverly .15 .40
79 Jim Mitchell .15 .40
80 Jack Youngblood AP .40 1.00
81 Mel Gray .25 .60
82 Dwight Harrison .15 .40
83 John Hadl .25 .60
84 Matt Blair RC .40 1.00
85 Charlie Sanders .25 .60
86 Noah Jackson RC .15 .40
87 Ed Marinaro .25 .60
88 Bob Howard .15 .40
89 John McDaniel RC .15 .40
90 Dan Dierdorf AP .60 1.50
91 Mark Moseley .25 .60
92 Cleo Miller RC .15 .40
93 Andre Tillman RC .15 .40
94 Bruce Taylor .15 .40
95 Bert Jones .40 1.00
96 Anthony Davis RC .40 1.00
97 Don Goode RC .15 .40
98 Ray Rhodes RC 2.00 6.00
99 Mike Webster RC 6.00 12.00
100 O.J. Simpson AP 3.00 6.00
101 Doug Plank RC .15 .40
102 Efren Herrera RC .25 .60
103 Charlie Smith .15 .40
104 Carlos Brown RC .40 1.00
105 Jim Marshall .40 1.00
106 Paul Naumoff .15 .40
107 Walter White RC .15 .40
108 John Cappelletti RC 1.25 3.00
109 Chip Myers .15 .40
110 Ken Stabler AP 5.00 10.00
111 Joe Ehrmann RC .15 .40
112 Rick Engles RC .15 .40
113 Jack Dolbin RC .15 .40
114 Ron Bolton .15 .40
115 Mike Thomas .15 .40
116 Mike Fuller RC .15 .40
117 John Hill RC .15 .40
118 Richard Todd RC .40 1.00
119 Duriel Harris RC .40 1.00
120 John James .15 .40
121 Lionel Antoine RC .15 .40
122 John Skorupan .15 .40
123 Skip Butler .15 .40
124 Bob Tucker .15 .40
125 Paul Krause .40 1.00
126 Dave Hampton .15 .40
127 Tom Wittum .15 .40
128 Gary Huff .25 .60
129 Emmitt Thomas .25 .60
130 Drew Pearson AP .75 2.00
131 Ron Saul .15 .40
132 Steve Niehaus RC .15 .40
133 Fred Carr .40 1.00
134 Norm Bulaich .15 .40
135 Bob Trumpy .25 .60
136 Greg Landry .25 .60
137 George Buehler .15 .40
138 Reggie Rucker .25 .60
139 Julius Adams .15 .40
140 Jack Ham AP 1.25 2.50
141 Wayne Morris RC .15 .40
142 Marv Bateman .15 .40
143 Bobby Maples .15 .40
144 Harold Carmichael .40 1.00
145 Bob Avellini .25 .60
146 Harry Carson RC 2.50 5.00
147 Lawrence Pillers RC .15 .40
148 Ed Williams RC .15 .40
149 Dan Pastorini .25 .60
150 Ron Yary .40 1.00
151 Joe Lavender .15 .40
152 Pat McInally RC .25 .60
153 Lloyd Mumphord .15 .40
154 Cullen Bryant .25 .60
155 Willie Lanier .40 1.00
156 Gene Washington 49er .25 .60
157 Scott Hunter .15 .40
158 Jim Merlo .15 .40
159 Randy Grossman RC .25 .60
160 Blaine Nye .15 .40
161 Ike Harris .15 .40
162 Doug Dieken .15 .40
163 Guy Morriss .15 .40
164 Bob Parsons .15 .40
165 Steve Grogan .40 1.00
166 John Brockington .25 .60
167 Charlie Joiner 1.25 2.50
168 Ron Carpenter .15 .40
169 Jeff Wright .15 .40
170 Chris Hanburger .15 .40
171 Roosevelt Leaks RC .25 .60
172 Larry Little .40 1.00
173 John Matuszak .25 .60
174 Joe Ferguson .25 .60
175 Brad Van Pelt .25 .60
176 Dexter Bussey RC .25 .60
177 Steve Largent RC 20.00 40.00
178 Dewey Selmon RC .25 .60
179 Randy Gradishar .40 1.00
180 Mel Blount AP 1.50 3.00
181 Dan Neal RC .15 .40
182 Rich Szaro RC .15 .40
183 Mike Boryla .15 .40
184 Steve Jones RC .15 .40
185 Paul Warfield 1.25 2.50
186 Greg Buttle RC .15 .40
187 Rich McGeorge .15 .40
188 Leon Gray RC .25 .60
189 John Shinners RC .15 .40
190 Toni Linhart .15 .40
191 Robert Miller RC .15 .40
192 Jake Scott .15 .40
193 Jon Morris .15 .40
194 Randy Crowder RC .15 .40
195 Lynn Swann UER 10.00 18.00
196 Marsh White RC .15 .40
197 Rod Perry RC .40 1.00
198 Willie Hall RC .15 .40
199 Mike Hartenstine RC .15 .40
200 Jim Bakken .15 .40
201 Atlanta Falcons CL UER .50 1.25
202 Baltimore Colts CL .50 1.25
203 Buffalo Bills CL .50 1.25
204 Chicago Bears CL .50 1.25
205 Cincinnati Bengals CL .50 1.25
206 Cleveland Browns CL .50 1.25
207 Dallas Cowboys CL .50 1.25
208 Denver Broncos CL .50 1.25
209 Detroit Lions CL .50 1.25
210 Green Bay Packers CL .50 1.25
211 Houston Oilers CL .50 1.25
212 Kansas City Chiefs CL .50 1.25
213 Los Angeles Rams CL .50 1.25
214 Miami Dolphins CL .50 1.25
215 Minnesota Vikings CL .50 1.25
216 New England Patriots CL .50 1.25
217 New Orleans Saints CL .50 1.25
218 New York Giants CL .50 1.25
219 New York Jets CL .50 1.25
220 Oakland Raiders CL .50 1.25
221 Philadelphia Eagles CL .50 1.25
222 Pittsburgh Steelers CL .50 1.25
223 St. Louis Cardinals CL .50 1.25
224 San Diego Chargers CL .50 1.25
225 San Francisco 49ers CL .50 1.25
226 Seattle Seahawks CL .50 1.25
227 Tampa Bay Buccaneers CL .50 1.25
228 Washington Redskins CL .50 1.25
229 Sam Cunningham .25 .60
230 Alan Page AP .40 1.00
231 Eddie Brown S RC .15 .40
232 Stan White .15 .40
233 Vern Den Herder .15 .40
234 Clarence Davis .15 .40
235 Ken Anderson .40 1.00
236 Karl Chandler RC .15 .40
237 Will Harrell .15 .40
238 Clarence Scott .15 .40
239 Bo Rather RC .15 .40
240 Robert Brazile AP .25 .60
241 Bob Bell .15 .40
242 Rolland Lawrence .15 .40
243 Tom Sullivan .15 .40
244 Larry Brunson RC .15 .40
245 Terry Bradshaw 10.00 20.00
246 Rich Saul .15 .40
247 Cleveland Elam RC .15 .40
248 Don Woods .15 .40
249 Bruce Laird .15 .40
250 Coy Bacon .25 .60
251 Russ Francis .40 1.00
252 Jim Braxton .15 .40
253 Perry Smith .15 .40
254 Jerome Barkum .15 .40
255 Garo Yepremian .25 .60
256 Checklist 133-264 .75 2.00
257 Tony Galbreath RC .25 .60
258 Troy Archer RC .15 .40
259 Brian Sipe .40 1.00
260 Billy Joe DuPree AP .25 .60
261 Bobby Walden .15 .40
262 Larry Marshall .15 .40
263 Ted Fritsch Jr. .15 .40
264 Larry Hand .15 .40
265 Tom Mack .40 1.00
266 Ed Bradley .15 .40
267 Pat Leahy .25 .60
268 Louis Carter RC .15 .40
269 Archie Griffin RC 3.00 6.00
270 Art Shell AP .40 1.00
271 Stu Voigt .15 .40
272 Prentice McCray .15 .40
273 MacArthur Lane .15 .40
274 Dan Fouts 3.00 6.00
275 Charle Young .25 .60
276 Wilbur Jackson RC .15 .40
277 John Hicks .15 .40
278 Nat Moore .40 1.00
279 Virgil Livers .15 .40
280 Curley Culp .40 1.00
281 Rocky Bleier 1.25 2.50
282 John Zook .15 .40
283 Tom DeLeone .15 .40
284 Danny White RC 6.00 12.00
285 Otis Armstrong .25 .60
286 Larry Walton .15 .40
287 Jim Carter .15 .40
288 Don McCauley .15 .40
289 Frank Grant .15 .40
290 Roger Wehrli .25 .60
291 Mick Tingelhoff .25 .60
292 Bernard Jackson .15 .40
293 Tom Owen RC .15 .40
294 Mike Esposito RC .15 .40
295 Fred Biletnikoff 1.25 2.50
296 Revie Sorey RC .15 .40
297 John McMakin .15 .40
298 Dan Ryczek .15 .40
299 Wayne Moore RC .15 .40
300 Franco Harris AP 2.00 4.00
301 Rick Upchurch RC .40 1.00
302 Jim Stienke RC .15 .40
303 Charlie Davis RC .15 .40
304 Don Cockroft .15 .40
305 Ken Burrough .25 .60
306 Clark Gaines RC .15 .40
307 Bobby Douglass .15 .40
308 Ralph Perretta RC .15 .40
309 Wally Hilgenberg .15 .40
310 Monte Jackson AP RC .25 .60
311 Chris Bahr RC .25 .60
312 Jim Cheyunski .15 .40
313 Mike Patrick RC .15 .40
314 Ed Too Tall Jones 2.50 5.00
315 Bill Bradley .15 .40
316 Benny Malone RC .15 .40
317 Paul Seymour .15 .40
318 Jim Laslavic RC .15 .40
319 Frank Lewis .25 .60
320 Ray Guy AP .40 1.00
321 Allan Ellis RC .15 .40
322 Conrad Dobler .25 .60
323 Chester Marcol .15 .40
324 Doug Kotar .15 .40
325 Lemar Parrish .25 .60
326 Steve Holden .15 .40
327 Jeff Van Note .25 .60
328 Howard Stevens .15 .40
329 Brad Dusek .25 .60
330 Joe DeLamielleure .40 1.00
331 Jim Plunkett .40 1.00
332 Checklist 265-396 .75 2.00
333 Lou Piccone RC .15 .40
334 Ray Hamilton .15 .40
335 Jan Stenerud .40 1.00
336 Jeris White RC .15 .40
337 Sherman Smith RC .15 .40
338 Dave Green .15 .40
339 Terry Schmidt .15 .40
340 Sammie White RC .50 1.25
341 Jon Kolb RC .15 .40
342 Randy White 4.00 8.00
343 Bob Klein .15 .40
344 Bob Kowalkowski .15 .40
345 Terry Metcalf .25 .60
346 Joe Danelo RC .15 .40
347 Ken Payne .15 .40
348 Neal Craig .15 .40
349 Dennis Johnson .15 .40
350 Bill Bergey AP .25 .60
351 Raymond Chester .15 .40
352 Bob Matheson .15 .40
353 Mike Kadish RC .15 .40
354 Mark Van Eeghen RC .60 1.50
355 L.C. Greenwood .40 1.00
356 Sam Hunt RC .15 .40
357 Darrell Austin RC .15 .40
358 Jim Turner .15 .40
359 Ahmad Rashad .75 2.00
360 Walter Payton AP 15.00 40.00
361 Mark Arneson RC .15 .40
362 Jerrel Wilson .15 .40
363 Steve Bartkowski .40 1.00
364 John Watson RC .15 .40
365 Ken Riley .25 .60
366 Gregg Bingham .15 .40
367 Golden Richards .25 .60
368 Clyde Powers RC .15 .40
369 Diron Talbert .15 .40
370 Lydell Mitchell .25 .60
371 Bob Jackson RC .15 .40
372 Jim Mandich .15 .40
373 Frank LeMaster .15 .40
374 Benny Ricardo RC .15 .40
375 Lawrence McCutcheon .25 .60
376 Lynn Dickey .25 .60
377 Phil Wise RC .15 .40
378 Tony McGee .15 .40
379 Norm Thompson .15 .40
380 Dave Casper RC 2.00 5.00
381 Glen Edwards .15 .40
382 Bob Thomas .15 .40
383 Bob Chandler .25 .60
384 Rickey Young .25 .60
385 Carl Eller .40 1.00
386 Lyle Alzado .40 1.00
387 John Leypoldt .15 .40
388 Gordon Bell RC .15 .40
389 Mike Bragg .15 .40
390 Jim Langer AP .40 1.00
391 Vern Holland .15 .40
392 Nelson Munsey .15 .40
393 Mack Mitchell RC .15 .40
394 Tony Adams RC .15 .40
395 Preston Pearson .25 .60
396 Emanuel Zanders RC .15 .40
397 Vince Papale RC 8.00 20.00
398 Joe Fields RC .25 .60
399 Craig Clemons .15 .40
400 Fran Tarkenton AP 2.50 5.00
401 Andy Johnson RC .15 .40
402 Willie Buchanon .15 .40
403 Pat Curran .15 .40
404 Ray Jarvis RC .15 .40
405 Joe Greene 1.25 2.50
406 Bill Simpson RC .15 .40
407 Ronnie Coleman .15 .40
408 J.K. McKay RC .25 .60
409 Pat Fischer .25 .60
410 John Dutton .25 .60
411 Boobie Clark .15 .40
412 Pat Tilley RC .40 1.00
413 Don Strock .25 .60
414 Brian Kelley .15 .40
415 Gene Upshaw .40 1.00
416 Mike Montler .15 .40
417 Checklist 397-528 .75 2.00
418 John Gilliam .15 .40
419 Brent McClanahan .15 .40
420 Jerry Sherk .15 .40
421 Roy Gerela .15 .40
422 Tim Fox RC .25 .60
423 John Ebersole RC .15 .40
424 James Scott RC .15 .40
425 Delvin Williams RC .25 .60
426 Spike Jones .15 .40
427 Harvey Martin .40 1.00
428 Don Herrmann .15 .40
429 Calvin Hill .25 .60
430 Isiah Robertson .15 .40
431 Tony Greene .15 .40
432 Bob Johnson .15 .40
433 Lem Barney .40 1.00
434 Eric Torkelson RC .15 .40
435 John Mendenhall .15 .40
436 Larry Seiple .25 .60
437 Art Kuehn RC .15 .40
438 John Vella RC .15 .40
439 Greg Latta RC .15 .40
440 Roger Carr .25 .60
441 Doug Sutherland .15 .40
442 Mike Kruczek RC .15 .40
443 Steve Zabel .15 .40
444 Mike Pruitt RC .40 1.00
445 Harold Jackson .25 .60
446 George Jakowenko RC .15 .40
447 John Fitzgerald .15 .40
448 Carey Joyce RC .15 .40
449 Jim LeClair .15 .40
450 Ken Houston AP .40 1.00
451 Steve Grogan RB .25 .60
452 Jim Marshall RB .25 .60
453 O.J.Simpson RB 1.25 2.50
454 Fran Tarkenton RB 1.50 3.00
455 Jim Zorn RB .40 1.00
456 Robert Pratt RC .15 .40
457 Walker Gillette .15 .40
458 Charlie Hall .15 .40
459 Robert Newhouse .25 .60
460 John Hannah AP .40 1.00
461 Ken Reaves .15 .40
462 Herman Weaver .15 .40
463 James Harris .25 .60
464 Howard Twilley .25 .60
465 Jeff Siemon .25 .60
466 John Outlaw .15 .40
467 Chuck Muncie RC .40 1.00
468 Bob Moore .15 .40
469 Robert Woods RC .15 .40
470 Cliff Branch AP .75 2.00
471 Johnnie Gray .15 .40
472 Don Hardeman .15 .40
473 Steve Ramsey .15 .40
474 Steve Mike-Mayer .15 .40
475 Gary Garrison .15 .40
476 Walter Johnson .15 .40
477 Neil Clabo .15 .40
478 Len Hauss .15 .40
479 Darryl Stingley .25 .60
480 Jack Lambert AP 4.00 8.00
481 Mike Adamle .25 .60
482 David Lee .15 .40
483 Tom Mullen RC .15 .40
484 Claude Humphrey .15 .40
485 Jim Hart .40 1.00
486 Bobby Thompson RC .15 .40
487 Jack Rudnay .15 .40
488 Rich Sowells RC .15 .40
489 Reuben Gant RC .15 .40
490 Cliff Harris AP .40 1.00
491 Bob Brown DT .15 .40
492 Don Nottingham .15 .40
493 Ron Jessie .15 .40
494 Otis Sistrunk .25 .60
495 Billy Kilmer .25 .60
496 Oscar Roan .15 .40
497 Bill Van Heusen .15 .40
498 Randy Logan .15 .40
499 John Smith .15 .40
500 Chuck Foreman AP .25 .60
501 J.T. Thomas .15 .40
502 Steve Schubert RC .15 .40
503 Mike Barnes .15 .40
504 J.V. Cain RC .15 .40
505 Larry Csonka 1.50 3.00
506 Elvin Bethea .40 1.00
507 Ray Easterling RC .15 .40
508 Joe Reed .15 .40
509 Steve Odom .15 .40
510 Tommy Casanova .15 .40
511 Dave Dalby .15 .40
512 Richard Caster .15 .40
513 Fred Dryer .40 1.00
514 Jeff Kinney RC .15 .40
515 Bob Griese 1.50 3.00
516 Butch Johnson RC .40 1.00
517 Gerald Irons RC .15 .40
518 Don Calhoun RC .15 .40
519 Jack Gregory .15 .40
520 Tom Banks .15 .40
521 Bobby Bryant .15 .40
522 Reggie Harrison RC .15 .40
523 Terry Hermeling .15 .40
524 David Taylor RC .15 .40
525 Brian Baschnagel RC .25 .60
526 AFC Champ/Stabler .40 1.00
527 NFC Championship .25 .60
528 Super Bowl XI .60 1.50

1977 Topps Holsum Packers/Vikings

In 1977 Topps produced a set of 11 Green Bay Packers (1-11) and 11 Minnesota Vikings (12-22) for Holsum Bread for distribution in the general area of those teams. One card was packed inside each loaf of bread. Unfortunately, nowhere on the card is Holsum mentioned leading to frequent misclassification of this set. The cards are in color and are standard size. An uncut production sheet was offered in the 1989 Topps Archives auction. The personal data on the card back is printed in brown and orange.

COMPLETE SET (22) 25.00 50.00
1 Lynn Dickey 1.25 3.00
2 John Brockington 1.00 2.50
3 Will Harrell .75 2.00
4 Ken Payne .75 2.00
5 Rich McGeorge .75 2.00
6 Steve Odom .75 2.00
7 Jim Carter .75 2.00
8 Fred Carr .75 2.00
9 Willie Buchanon 1.00 2.50
10 Mike McCoy DT .75 2.00
11 Chester Marcol .75 2.00
12 Chuck Foreman 2.00 4.00
13 Ahmad Rashad 3.00 6.00
14 Sammie White 1.25 3.00
15 Stu Voigt .75 2.00
16 Fred Cox .75 2.00
17 Carl Eller 2.00 4.00
18 Alan Page 3.00 6.00
19 Jeff Siemon .75 2.00
20 Bobby Bryant .75 2.00
21 Paul Krause 1.25 3.00
22 Ron Yary 1.25 3.00

1977 Topps Mexican

The Mexican version of the 1977 Topps football series contains the same 528 players as the American issue. The cards were issued in 2-card packs with a stick of gum, or in scarcer four-card packs without gum. All text is in Spanish (front and back). Several cases of cards made their way into the organized hobby in the early 1990s. Since then, all cards have been discovered. However, some cards are considered to be tougher to obtain and are priced below at higher levels than otherwise might be expected. Some collectors also pursue the wrappers, which feature various NFL stars on them.

COMPLETE SET (528) 5000.00 10000.00
1 Passing Leaders SP 75.00 125.00
2 Drew Pearson 200.00 400.00
M.Lane LL SP
3 Rushing Leaders SP 300.00 600.00
4 Scoring Leaders SP 200.00 400.00
5 Interception Leaders SP 200.00 400.00
6 Punting Leaders 125.00 250.00
7 Mike Phipps 4.00 8.00
8 Rick Volk SP 150.00 300.00
9 Steve Furness 4.00 8.00
10 Isaac Curtis 4.00 8.00
11 Nate Wright 4.00 8.00
12 Jean Fugett 6.00 12.00
13 Ken Mendenhall 3.00 6.00
14 Sam Adams OL 3.00 6.00
15 Charlie Waters 5.00 10.00
16 Bill Stanfill SP 50.00 100.00
17 John Holland 3.00 6.00
18 Pat Haden 20.00 40.00
19 Bob Young 3.00 6.00
20 Wally Chambers SP 100.00 200.00
21 Lawrence Gaines SP 125.00 250.00
22 Larry McCarren 3.00 6.00
23 Horst Muhlmann 3.00 6.00
24 Phil Villapiano 4.00 8.00
25 Greg Pruitt 40.00 80.00
26 Ron Howard 6.00 12.00
27 Craig Morton 5.00 10.00
28 Rufus Mayes 3.00 6.00
29 Lee Roy Selmon UER 100.00 200.00
30 Ed White SP 75.00 150.00
31 Harold McLinton SP 50.00 100.00
32 Glenn Doughty 3.00 6.00
33 Bob Kuechenberg 3.00 6.00
34 Duane Carrell 3.00 6.00
35 Riley Odoms 3.00 6.00
36 Bobby Scott 3.00 6.00
37 Nick Mike-Mayer 3.00 6.00
38 Bill Lenkaitis 3.00 6.00
39 Roland Harper 3.00 6.00
40 Tommy Hart SP 100.00 200.00
41 Mike Sensibaugh 3.00 6.00
42 Rusty Jackson 3.00 6.00
43 Levi Johnson 3.00 6.00
44 Mike McCoy DT 6.00 12.00
45 Roger Staubach 75.00 150.00
46 Fred Cox 3.00 6.00
47 Bob Babich 3.00 6.00
48 Reggie McKenzie 3.00 6.00
49 Dave Jennings SP 50.00 100.00
50 Mike Haynes 12.50 25.00
51 Larry Brown 4.00 8.00
52 Marvin Cobb 3.00 6.00
53 Fred Cook 3.00 6.00
54 Freddie Solomon 6.00 12.00
55 John Riggins 25.00 50.00
56 John Bunting 3.00 6.00
57 Ray Wersching 3.00 6.00
58 Mike Livingston 3.00 6.00
59 Billy Johnson 40.00 80.00
60 Mike Wagner AP 6.00 12.00
61 Waymond Bryant 3.00 6.00
62 Jim Otis 3.00 6.00
63 Ed Galigher SP 50.00 100.00
64 Randy Vataha 3.00 6.00
65 Jim Zorn 15.00 30.00
66 Jon Keyworth SP 50.00 100.00
67 Checklist 1-132 4.00 8.00
68 Henry Childs 3.00 6.00
69 Thom Darden 3.00 6.00
70 George Kunz AP 3.00 6.00
71 Lenvil Elliott 3.00 6.00
72 Curtis Johnson 3.00 6.00
73 Doug Van Horn 3.00 6.00
74 Joe Theismann 20.00 40.00
75 Dwight White 4.00 8.00
76 Scott Laidlaw 3.00 6.00
77 Monte Johnson 3.00 6.00
78 Dave Beverly 3.00 6.00
79 Jim Mitchell TE 40.00 80.00
80 Jack Youngblood 7.50 15.00
81 Mel Gray 3.00 6.00
82 Dwight Harrison 3.00 6.00
83 John Hadl 4.00 8.00
84 Matt Blair 4.00 8.00
85 Charlie Sanders 4.00 8.00
86 Noah Jackson 3.00 6.00
87 Ed Marinaro 5.00 10.00
88 Bob Howard 3.00 6.00
89 John McDaniel SP 150.00 300.00
90 Dan Dierdorf 6.00 12.00
91 Mark Moseley 3.00 6.00
92 Cleo Miller 3.00 6.00
93 Andre Tillman 3.00 6.00
94 Bruce Taylor 3.00 6.00
95 Bert Jones 5.00 10.00
96 Anthony Davis 50.00 100.00
97 Don Goode 3.00 6.00
98 Ray Rhodes SP 150.00 300.00
99 Mike Webster SP 60.00 120.00
100 O.J. Simpson AP 50.00 100.00
101 Doug Plank 3.00 6.00
102 Efren Herrera 3.00 6.00
103 Charlie Smith WR SP 75.00 150.00
104 Carlos Brown 40.00 80.00
105 Jim Marshall 5.00 10.00
106 Paul Naumoff 6.00 12.00
107 Walter White 6.00 12.00
108 John Cappelletti 7.50 15.00
109 Chip Myers 3.00 6.00
110 Ken Stabler AP 100.00 200.00
111 Joe Ehrmann 3.00 6.00
112 Rick Engles 3.00 6.00
113 Jack Dolbin 3.00 6.00
114 Ron Bolton 3.00 6.00
115 Mike Thomas 3.00 6.00
116 Mike Fuller 3.00 6.00
117 John Hill 3.00 6.00
118 Richard Todd SP 60.00 120.00
119 Duriel Harris 3.00 6.00
120 John James AP 3.00 6.00
121 Lionel Antoine 3.00 6.00
122 John Skorupan 3.00 6.00
123 Skip Butler 3.00 6.00
124 Bob Tucker 3.00 6.00
125 Paul Krause 3.00 6.00
126 Dave Hampton SP 75.00 150.00
127 Tom Wittum 3.00 6.00
128 Gary Huff 3.00 6.00
129 Emmitt Thomas 3.00 6.00
130 Drew Pearson 12.50 25.00
131 Ron Saul 6.00 12.00
132 Steve Niehaus 3.00 6.00
133 Fred Carr 3.00 6.00
134 Norm Bulaich 3.00 6.00
135 Bob Trumpy 5.00 10.00
136 Greg Landry 4.00 8.00
137 George Buehler 3.00 6.00
138 Reggie Rucker 3.00 6.00
139 Julius Adams 3.00 6.00
140 Jack Ham 15.00 30.00
141 Wayne Morris 3.00 6.00
142 Marv Bateman 6.00 12.00
143 Bobby Maples 3.00 6.00
144 Harold Carmichael 5.00 10.00
145 Bob Avellini 3.00 6.00
146 Harry Carson 20.00 40.00
147 Lawrence Pillers SP 75.00 150.00
148 Ed Williams 3.00 6.00
149 Dan Pastorini 3.00 6.00
150 Ron Yary AP 5.00 10.00
151 Joe Lavender 3.00 6.00
152 Pat McInally 3.00 6.00
153 Lloyd Mumphord 3.00 6.00
154 Cullen Bryant 3.00 6.00
155 Willie Lanier 30.00 60.00
156 Gene Washington 49er 4.00 8.00
157 Scott Hunter 3.00 6.00
158 Jim Merlo 3.00 6.00
159 Randy Grossman 3.00 6.00
160 Blaine Nye AP 3.00 6.00
161 Ike Harris 3.00 6.00
162 Doug Dieken 3.00 6.00
163 Guy Morriss SP 50.00 100.00
164 Bob Parsons SP 50.00 100.00
165 Steve Grogan 40.00 80.00
166 John Brockington 3.00 6.00
167 Charlie Joiner 7.50 15.00
168 Ron Carpenter 40.00 80.00
169 Jeff Wright S 40.00 80.00
170 Chris Hanburger AP 4.00 8.00
171 Roosevelt Leaks 3.00 6.00
172 Larry Little 4.00 8.00
173 John Matuszak 7.50 15.00
174 Joe Ferguson 3.00 6.00
175 Brad Van Pelt 40.00 80.00
176 Dexter Bussey SP 150.00 300.00
177 Steve Largent 300.00 500.00
178 Dewey Selmon 4.00 8.00
179 Randy Gradishar 5.00 10.00
180 Mel Blount 20.00 35.00
181 Dan Neal 40.00 80.00
182 Rich Szaro SP 75.00 150.00
183 Mike Boryla 6.00 12.00
184 Steve Jones 3.00 6.00
185 Paul Warfield 20.00 35.00
186 Greg Buttle SP 75.00 150.00
187 Rich McGeorge 3.00 6.00
188 Leon Gray SP 75.00 150.00
189 John Shinners 3.00 6.00
190 Toni Linhart AP 3.00 6.00
191 Robert Miller 3.00 6.00
192 Jake Scott 3.00 6.00
193 Jon Morris 40.00 80.00
194 Randy Crowder 3.00 6.00
195 Lynn Swann 60.00 120.00
196 Marsh White 3.00 6.00
197 Rod Perry 3.00 6.00
198 Willie Hall 3.00 6.00
199 Mike Hartenstine 3.00 6.00
200 Jim Bakken AP 3.00 6.00
201 Atlanta Falcons UER 50.00 100.00
202 Baltimore Colts 4.00 8.00
203 Buffalo Bills 10.00 20.00
204 Chicago Bears 4.00 8.00
205 Cincinnati Bengals 4.00 8.00
206 Cleveland Browns 4.00 8.00
207 Dallas Cowboys SP 75.00 150.00
208 Denver Broncos 4.00 8.00
209 Detroit Lions 4.00 8.00
210 Green Bay Packers 4.00 8.00
211 Houston Oilers 4.00 8.00
212 Kansas City Chiefs 4.00 8.00
213 Los Angeles Rams SP 50.00 100.00
214 Miami Dolphins 4.00 8.00
215 Minnesota Vikings 4.00 8.00
216 New England Patriots 4.00 8.00
217 New Orleans Saints 10.00 20.00
218 New York Giants 4.00 8.00
219 New York Jets 4.00 8.00
220 Oakland Raiders 4.00 8.00
221 Philadelphia Eagles 4.00 8.00
222 Pittsburgh Steelers 4.00 8.00
223 St. Louis Cardinals 4.00 8.00
224 San Diego Chargers 4.00 8.00
225 San Francisco 49ers 4.00 8.00
226 Seattle Seahawks SP 50.00 100.00
227 Tampa Bay Buccaneers 4.00 8.00
228 Washington Redskins SP 75.00 150.00
229 Sam Cunningham 4.00 8.00
230 Alan Page 7.50 15.00
231 Eddie Brown S SP 125.00 250.00
232 Stan White 3.00 6.00
233 Vern Den Herder 3.00 6.00
234 Clarence Davis 3.00 6.00
235 Ken Anderson 10.00 20.00
236 Karl Chandler 6.00 12.00
237 Will Harrell SP 100.00 200.00
238 Clarence Scott 3.00 6.00
239 Bo Rather 3.00 6.00
240 Robert Brazile 3.00 6.00
241 Bob Bell 3.00 6.00
242 Rolland Lawrence 3.00 6.00
243 Tom Sullivan SP 50.00 100.00
244 Larry Brunson 3.00 6.00
245 Terry Bradshaw 65.00 125.00
246 Rich Saul 3.00 6.00
247 Cleveland Elam 3.00 6.00
248 Don Woods 3.00 6.00
249 Bruce Laird 3.00 6.00
250 Coy Bacon AP 3.00 6.00
251 Russ Francis 5.00 10.00
252 Jim Braxton 3.00 6.00
253 Perry Smith 30.00 60.00
254 Jerome Barkum 3.00 6.00
255 Garo Yepremian 3.00 6.00
256 Checklist 133-264 4.00 8.00
257 Tony Galbreath 3.00 6.00
258 Troy Archer 3.00 6.00
259 Brian Sipe 5.00 10.00
260 Billy Joe DuPree 10.00 20.00
261 Bobby Walden 3.00 6.00
262 Larry Marshall 3.00 6.00
263 Ted Fritsch Jr. 3.00 6.00
264 Larry Hand 3.00 6.00
265 Tom Mack SP 50.00 100.00
266 Ed Bradley 3.00 6.00
267 Pat Leahy 3.00 6.00
268 Louis Carter SP 50.00 100.00
269 Archie Griffin SP 150.00 300.00
270 Art Shell 6.00 12.00
271 Stu Voigt 3.00 6.00
272 Prentice McCray 3.00 6.00
273 MacArthur Lane 7.50 15.00
274 Dan Fouts 25.00 50.00
275 Charle Young 3.00 6.00
276 Wilbur Jackson 125.00 250.00
277 John Hicks 3.00 6.00
278 Nat Moore 3.00 6.00
279 Virgil Livers 3.00 6.00
280 Curley Culp AP 4.00 10.00
281 Rocky Bleier 15.00 30.00
282 John Zook 7.50 15.00
283 Tom DeLeone 3.00 6.00
284 Danny White SP 150.00 300.00
285 Otis Armstrong 4.00 8.00
286 Larry Walton 3.00 6.00
287 Jim Carter 3.00 6.00
288 Don McCauley 3.00 6.00
289 Frank Grant 7.50 15.00
290 Roger Wehrli AP 4.00 8.00
291 Mick Tingelhoff 10.00 20.00

292 Bernard Jackson 7.50 15.00
293 Tom Owen 6.00 12.00
294 Mike Esposito 3.00 6.00
295 Fred Biletnikoff SP 200.00 400.00
296 Revie Sorey 3.00 6.00
297 John McMakin 3.00 6.00
298 Dan Ryczek 3.00 6.00
299 Wayne Moore 7.50 15.00
300 Franco Harris AP 60.00 120.00
301 Rick Upchurch 4.00 8.00
302 Jim Stienke 3.00 6.00
303 Charlie Davis 3.00 6.00
304 Don Cockroft 3.00 6.00
305 Ken Burrough 3.00 6.00
306 Clark Gaines SP 75.00 150.00
307 Bobby Douglass 4.00 8.00
308 Ralph Perretta 3.00 6.00
309 Wally Hilgenberg 3.00 6.00
310 Monte Jackson 3.00 6.00
311 Chris Bahr 3.00 6.00
312 Jim Cheyunski 3.00 6.00
313 Mike Patrick 3.00 6.00
314 Ed Too Tall Jones 75.00 150.00
315 Bill Bradley 3.00 6.00
316 Benny Malone 3.00 6.00
317 Paul Seymour 3.00 6.00
318 Jim Laslavic 3.00 6.00
319 Frank Lewis 3.00 6.00
320 Ray Guy 40.00 80.00
321 Allan Ellis 3.00 6.00
322 Conrad Dobler 3.00 6.00
323 Chester Marcol 3.00 6.00
324 Doug Kotar 3.00 6.00
325 Lemar Parrish 3.00 6.00
326 Steve Holden 3.00 6.00
327 Jeff Van Note 4.00 8.00
328 Howard Stevens 3.00 6.00
329 Brad Dusek 3.00 6.00
330 Joe DeLamielleure AP 5.00 10.00
331 Jim Plunkett SP 100.00 200.00
332 Checklist 265-396 SP 100.00 200.00
333 Lou Piccone 3.00 6.00
334 Ray Hamilton 3.00 6.00
335 Jan Stenerud 5.00 10.00
336 Jeris White 3.00 6.00
337 Sherman Smith 4.00 8.00
338 Dave Green 3.00 6.00
339 Terry Schmidt 3.00 6.00
340 Sammie White 4.00 8.00
341 Jon Kolb 7.50 15.00
342 Randy White 25.00 50.00
343 Bob Klein 3.00 6.00
344 Bob Kowalkowski 6.00 12.00
345 Terry Metcalf 4.00 8.00
346 Joe Danelo 3.00 6.00
347 Ken Payne 3.00 6.00
348 Neal Craig 3.00 6.00
349 Dennis Johnson 3.00 6.00
350 Bill Bergey 7.50 15.00
351 Raymond Chester SP 75.00 150.00
352 Bob Matheson 4.00 8.00
353 Mike Kadish 3.00 6.00
354 Mark Van Eeghen 5.00 10.00
355 L.C.Greenwood 6.00 12.00
356 Sam Hunt 3.00 6.00
357 Darrell Austin 3.00 6.00
358 Jim Turner 3.00 6.00
359 Ahmad Rashad 10.00 20.00
360 Walter Payton AP 250.00 400.00
361 Mark Arneson 3.00 6.00
362 Jerrel Wilson 3.00 6.00
363 Steve Bartkowski 5.00 10.00
364 John Watson 3.00 6.00
365 Ken Riley 3.00 6.00
366 Gregg Bingham 30.00 60.00
367 Golden Richards 4.00 8.00
368 Clyde Powers 3.00 6.00
369 Diron Talbert 7.50 15.00
370 Lydell Mitchell 20.00 40.00
371 Bob Jackson 3.00 6.00
372 Jim Mandich SP 75.00 150.00
373 Frank LeMaster 30.00 60.00
374 Benny Ricardo SP 125.00 250.00
375 Lawrence McCutcheon 3.00 6.00
376 Lynn Dickey 4.00 8.00
377 Phil Wise 3.00 6.00
378 Tony McGee DT 3.00 6.00
379 Norm Thompson 3.00 6.00
380 Dave Casper 20.00 40.00
381 Glen Edwards 3.00 6.00
382 Bob Thomas 3.00 6.00
383 Bob Chandler 3.00 6.00
384 Rickey Young 3.00 6.00
385 Carl Eller 5.00 10.00
386 Lyle Alzado 5.00 10.00
387 John Leypoldt 3.00 6.00
388 Gordon Bell SP 125.00 250.00
389 Mike Bragg 3.00 6.00
390 Jim Langer 4.00 8.00
391 Vern Holland 3.00 6.00
392 Nelson Munsey 3.00 6.00
393 Mack Mitchell 3.00 6.00
394 Tony Adams 3.00 6.00
395 Preston Pearson 4.00 8.00
396 Emanuel Zanders 3.00 6.00
397 Vince Papale 12.50 25.00
398 Joe Fields 3.00 6.00
399 Craig Clemons 3.00 6.00
400 Fran Tarkenton AP 30.00 60.00
401 Andy Johnson 3.00 6.00
402 Willie Buchanon 7.50 15.00
403 Pat Curran 3.00 6.00
404 Ray Jarvis SP 125.00 250.00
405 Joe Greene 20.00 35.00
406 Bill Simpson 3.00 6.00
407 Ronnie Coleman 3.00 6.00
408 J.K. McKay 3.00 6.00
409 Pat Fischer 10.00 20.00
410 John Dutton AP 3.00 6.00
411 Boobie Clark 3.00 6.00
412 Pat Tilley 6.00 12.00
413 Don Strock SP 75.00 150.00
414 Brian Kelley 3.00 6.00
415 Gene Upshaw 7.50 15.00
416 Mike Montler 3.00 6.00
417 Checklist 397-528 SP 100.00 200.00
418 John Gilliam 3.00 6.00
419 Brent McClanahan 3.00 6.00
420 Jerry Sherk AP 3.00 6.00
421 Roy Gerela 3.00 6.00
422 Tim Fox 3.00 6.00
423 John Ebersole SP 75.00 150.00
424 James Scott SP 75.00 150.00
425 Delvin Williams 30.00 60.00
426 Spike Jones 30.00 60.00
427 Harvey Martin SP 50.00 100.00
428 Don Herrmann 3.00 6.00
429 Calvin Hill 5.00 10.00
430 Isiah Robertson AP 30.00 60.00
431 Tony Greene 3.00 6.00
432 Bob Johnson 3.00 6.00
433 Lem Barney SP 100.00 200.00
434 Eric Torkelson SP 125.00 250.00
435 John Mendenhall 3.00 6.00
436 Larry Seiple 3.00 6.00
437 Art Kuehn 3.00 6.00
438 John Vella 3.00 6.00
439 Greg Latta 3.00 6.00
440 Roger Carr AP 3.00 6.00
441 Doug Sutherland 3.00 6.00
442 Mike Kruczek 6.00 12.00
443 Steve Zabel 3.00 6.00
444 Mike Pruitt SP 125.00 250.00
445 Harold Jackson SP 75.00 150.00
446 George Jakowenko 3.00 6.00
447 John Fitzgerald 3.00 6.00
448 Carey Joyce 3.00 6.00
449 Jim LeClair 4.00 8.00
450 Ken Houston 5.00 10.00
451 Steve Grogan RB 5.00 10.00
452 Jim Marshall RB 5.00 10.00
453 O.J. Simpson RB 75.00 150.00
454 Fran Tarkenton RB 20.00 40.00
455 Jim Zorn RB 25.00 50.00
456 Robert Pratt 3.00 6.00
457 Walker Gillette 6.00 12.00
458 Charlie Hall 3.00 6.00
459 Robert Newhouse 4.00 8.00
460 John Hannah 5.00 10.00
461 Ken Reaves 3.00 6.00
462 Herman Weaver 3.00 6.00
463 James Harris 3.00 6.00
464 Howard Twilley 3.00 6.00
465 Jeff Siemon SP 75.00 150.00
466 John Outlaw 3.00 6.00
467 Chuck Muncie 5.00 10.00
468 Bob Moore 3.00 6.00
469 Robert Woods 3.00 6.00
470 Cliff Branch SP 125.00 250.00
471 Johnnie Gray 3.00 6.00
472 Don Hardeman 3.00 6.00
473 Steve Ramsey 3.00 6.00
474 Steve Mike-Mayer SP 75.00 150.00
475 Gary Garrison 4.00 8.00
476 Walter Johnson 3.00 6.00
477 Neil Clabo 6.00 12.00
478 Len Hauss 3.00 6.00
479 Darryl Stingley 4.00 8.00
480 Jack Lambert AP 40.00 80.00
481 Mike Adamle 4.00 8.00
482 David Lee 3.00 6.00
483 Tom Mullen 3.00 6.00
484 Claude Humphrey 3.00 6.00
485 Jim Hart 3.00 6.00
486 Bobby Thompson SP 100.00 200.00
487 Jack Rudnay 3.00 6.00
488 Rich Sowells SP 125.00 250.00
489 Reuben Gant SP 100.00 200.00
490 Cliff Harris 5.00 10.00
491 Bob Brown DT 3.00 6.00
492 Don Nottingham 6.00 12.00
493 Ron Jessie SP 75.00 150.00
494 Otis Sistrunk 12.50 25.00
495 Billy Kilmer 4.00 8.00
496 Oscar Roan 3.00 6.00
497 Bill Van Heusen 3.00 6.00
498 Randy Logan 30.00 60.00
499 John Smith 3.00 6.00
500 Chuck Foreman SP 60.00 120.00
501 J.T. Thomas 3.00 6.00
502 Steve Schubert 3.00 6.00
503 Mike Barnes 3.00 6.00
504 J.V. Cain 3.00 6.00
505 Larry Csonka 30.00 60.00
506 Elvin Bethea 5.00 10.00
507 Ray Easterling 3.00 6.00
508 Joe Reed 6.00 12.00
509 Steve Odom 3.00 6.00
510 Tommy Casanova AP 4.00 8.00
511 Dave Dalby 3.00 6.00
512 Richard Caster 3.00 6.00
513 Fred Dryer SP 100.00 200.00
514 Jeff Kinney 6.00 12.00
515 Bob Griese 25.00 50.00
516 Butch Johnson 3.00 6.00
517 Gerald Irons 3.00 6.00
518 Don Calhoun 3.00 6.00
519 Jack Gregory 3.00 6.00
520 Tom Banks AP 3.00 6.00
521 Bobby Bryant 3.00 6.00
522 Reggie Harrison 3.00 6.00
523 Terry Hermeling 3.00 6.00
524 David Taylor 3.00 6.00
525 Brian Baschnagel 3.00 6.00
526 AFC Championship 30.00 60.00
527 NFC Championship 30.00 60.00
528 Super Bowl XI SP 500.00 800.00

1977 Topps Team Checklists

The 1977 Topps Team Checklist set contains 30 standard-size cards. The 28 NFL teams as well as 2 regular checklists were printed in this set. The front of the card has the 1977 Topps checklist for that particular team, complete with boxes in which to place check marks. The set was only available directly from Topps as a send-off offer as an uncut sheet; the prices below apply equally to uncut sheets as they are frequently found in their original uncut condition. As for individual cards, thin white card (almost paper-thin) stock makes it a challenge to find singles in top grades. These unnumbered cards are numbered below for convenience in alphabetical order by team name.

COMPLETE SET (30) 55.00 110.00
1 Atlanta Falcons 2.50 5.00
2 Baltimore Colts 2.50 5.00
3 Buffalo Bills 2.50 5.00
4 Chicago Bears 3.75 7.50
5 Cincinnati Bengals 2.50 5.00
6 Cleveland Browns 2.50 5.00
7 Dallas Cowboys 5.00 10.00
8 Denver Broncos 2.50 5.00
9 Detroit Lions 2.50 5.00
10 Green Bay Packers 5.00 10.00
11 Houston Oilers 2.50 5.00
12 Kansas City Chiefs 2.50 5.00
13 Los Angeles Rams 2.50 5.00
14 Miami Dolphins 3.75 7.50
15 Minnesota Vikings 2.50 5.00
16 New England Patriots 2.50 5.00
17 New York Giants 2.50 5.00
18 New York Jets 2.50 5.00
19 New Orleans Saints 2.50 5.00
20 Oakland Raiders 3.75 7.50
21 Philadelphia Eagles 2.50 5.00
22 Pittsburgh Steelers 3.75 7.50
23 St. Louis Cardinals 2.50 5.00
24 San Diego Chargers 2.50 5.00
25 San Francisco 49ers 3.75 7.50
26 Seattle Seahawks 2.50 5.00
27 Tampa Bay Buccaneers 2.50 5.00
28 Washington Redskins 3.75 7.50
NNO1 Checklist 1-132 2.50 5.00
NNO2 Checklist 133-264 2.50 5.00

1978 Topps

The 1978 Topps football set contains 528 standard-size cards. Card fronts have a color border that runs up the left side and contains the team name. The player's name is at the top and his position is within a football at the bottom right of the photo. The card backs are printed in black and green on gray card stock and are horizontally designed. Statistics, highlights and a player fact cartton are included. Subsets include Highlights (1-6), playoffs (166-168), league leaders (331-336) and team leaders (501-528). Rookie Cards include Tony Dorsett, Randy Cross, Tom Jackson, Joe Klecko, Stanley Morgan, John Stallworth, Wesley Walker and Reggie Williams.

COMPLETE SET (528) 80.00 150.00
1 Gary Huff HL .40 1.00
2 Craig Morton HL .40 1.00
3 Walter Payton HL 3.00 8.00
4 O.J.Simpson HL .75 2.00
5 Fran Tarkenton HL .75 2.00
6 Bob Thomas HL .10 .30
7 Joe Pisarcik RC .20 .50
8 Skip Thomas RC .10 .30
9 Roosevelt Leaks .10 .30
10 Ken Houston AP .40 1.00
11 Tom Blanchard .10 .30
12 Jim Turner .10 .30
13 Tom DeLeone .10 .30
14 Jim LeClair .10 .30
15 Bob Avellini .20 .50
16 Tony McGee DT .10 .30
17 James Harris .20 .50
18 Terry Nelson RC .10 .30
19 Rocky Bleier .75 2.00
20 Joe DeLamielleure .40 1.00
21 Richard Caster .10 .30
22 A.J. Duhe RC .40 1.00
23 John Outlaw .10 .30
24 Danny White .50 1.25
25 Larry Csonka 1.00 2.50
26 David Hill RC .20 .50
27 Mark Arneson .10 .30
28 Jack Tatum .20 .50
29 Norm Thompson .10 .30
30 Sammie White .20 .50
31 Dennis Johnson .10 .30
32 Robin Earl RC .10 .30
33 Don Cockroft .10 .30
34 Bob Johnson .10 .30
35 John Hannah .40 1.00
36 Scott Hunter .10 .30
37 Ken Burrough .20 .50
38 Wilbur Jackson .20 .50
39 Rich McGeorge .10 .30
40 Lyle Alzado AP .40 1.00
41 John Ebersole .10 .30
42 Gary Green RC .10 .30
43 Art Kuehn .10 .30
44 Glen Edwards .20 .50
45 Lawrence McCutcheon .20 .50
46 Duriel Harris .10 .30
47 Rich Szaro .10 .30
48 Mike Washington RC .10 .30
49 Stan White .10 .30
50 Dave Casper AP .40 1.00
51 Len Hauss .10 .30
52 James Scott .10 .30
53 Brian Sipe .40 1.00
54 Gary Shirk RC .10 .30
55 Archie Griffin .40 1.00
56 Mike Patrick .10 .30
57 Mario Clark RC .10 .30
58 Jeff Siemon .10 .30
59 Steve Mike-Mayer .10 .30
60 Randy White AP 2.00 4.00
61 Darrell Austin .10 .30
62 Tom Sullivan .10 .30
63 Johnny Rodgers RC .40 1.00
64 Ken Reaves .10 .30
65 Terry Bradshaw 6.00 12.00
66 Fred Steinfort RC .10 .30
67 Curley Culp .40 1.00
68 Ted Hendricks .40 1.00
69 Raymond Chester .10 .30
70 Jim Langer AP .40 1.00
71 Calvin Hill .20 .50
72 Mike Hartenstine .10 .30
73 Gerald Irons .10 .30
74 Billy Brooks RC .20 .50
75 John Mendenhall .10 .30
76 Andy Johnson .10 .30
77 Tom Wittum .10 .30
78 Lynn Dickey .20 .50
79 Carl Eller .40 1.00
80 Tom Mack .40 1.00
81 Clark Gaines .10 .30
82 Lem Barney .40 1.00
83 Mike Montler .10 .30
84 Jon Kolb .10 .30
85 Bob Chandler .20 .50
86 Robert Newhouse .20 .50
87 Frank LeMaster .10 .30
88 Jeff West .10 .30
89 Lyle Blackwood .20 .50
90 Gene Upshaw AP .40 1.00
91 Frank Grant .10 .30
92 Tom Hicks RC .10 .30
93 Mike Pruitt .20 .50
94 Chris Bahr .10 .30
95 Russ Francis .20 .50
96 Norris Thomas RC .10 .30
97 Gary Barbaro RC .20 .50
98 Jim Merlo .10 .30
99 Karl Chandler .10 .30
100 Fran Tarkenton 1.50 4.00
101 Abdul Salaam RC .10 .30
102 Marv Kellum RC .10 .30
103 Herman Weaver .10 .30
104 Roy Gerela .10 .30
105 Harold Jackson .20 .50
106 Dewey Selmon .20 .50
107 Checklist 1-132 .40 1.00
108 Clarence Davis .10 .30
109 Robert Pratt .10 .30
110 Harvey Martin AP .40 1.00
111 Brad Dusek .10 .30
112 Greg Latta .10 .30
113 Tony Peters RC .10 .30
114 Jim Braxton .10 .30
115 Ken Riley .20 .50
116 Steve Nelson RC .10 .30
117 Rick Upchurch .20 .50
118 Spike Jones .10 .30
119 Doug Kotar .10 .30
120 Bob Griese AP 1.00 2.50
121 Burgess Owens .10 .30
122 Rolf Benirschke RC .20 .50
123 Haskel Stanback RC .10 .30
124 J.T. Thomas .10 .30
125 Ahmad Rashad .60 1.50
126 Rick Kane RC .10 .30
127 Elvin Bethea .40 1.00
128 Dave Dalby .10 .30
129 Mike Barnes .10 .30
130 Isiah Robertson .10 .30
131 Jim Plunkett .40 1.00
132 Allan Ellis .10 .30
133 Mike Bragg .10 .30
134 Bob Jackson .10 .30
135 Coy Bacon .10 .30
136 John Smith .10 .30
137 Chuck Muncie .20 .50
138 Johnnie Gray .10 .30
139 Jimmy Robinson RC .10 .30
140 Tom Banks .10 .30
141 Marvin Powell RC .10 .30
142 Jerrel Wilson .10 .30
143 Ron Howard .10 .30
144 Rob Lytle RC .20 .50
145 L.C. Greenwood .40 1.00
146 Morris Owens RC .10 .30
147 Joe Reed .10 .30
148 Mike Kadish .10 .30
149 Phil Villapiano .20 .50
150 Lydell Mitchell .20 .50
151 Randy Logan .10 .30
152 Mike Williams RC .10 .30
153 Jeff Van Note .20 .50
154 Steve Schubert .10 .30
155 Billy Kilmer .20 .50
156 Boobie Clark .10 .30
157 Charlie Hall .10 .30
158 Raymond Clayborn RC .40 1.00
159 Jack Gregory .10 .30
160 Cliff Harris AP .40 1.00
161 Joe Fields .10 .30
162 Don Nottingham .10 .30
163 Ed White .20 .50
164 Toni Fritsch .10 .30
165 Jack Lambert 2.00 4.00
166 NFC Champs/Staubach .60 1.50
167 AFC Champs/Lytle .20 .50
168 Super Bowl XII/Dorsett 1.50 3.00
169 Neal Colzie RC .10 .30
170 Cleveland Elam .10 .30
171 David Lee .10 .30
172 Jim Otis .10 .30
173 Archie Manning .40 1.00
174 Jim Carter .10 .30
175 Jean Fugett .10 .30
176 Willie Parker RC .10 .30
177 Haven Moses .20 .50
178 Horace King RC .10 .30
179 Bob Thomas .10 .30
180 Monte Jackson .10 .30
181 Steve Zabel .10 .30
182 John Fitzgerald .10 .30
183 Mike Livingston .10 .30
184 Larry Poole RC .10 .30
185 Isaac Curtis .20 .50
186 Chuck Ramsey RC .10 .30
187 Bob Klein .10 .30
188 Ray Rhodes .40 1.00
189 Otis Sistrunk .20 .50
190 Bill Bergey .20 .50
191 Sherman Smith .20 .50
192 Dave Green .10 .30
193 Carl Mauck .10 .30
194 Reggie Harrison .10 .30
195 Roger Carr .20 .50
196 Steve Bartkowski .40 1.00
197 Ray Wersching .10 .30
198 Willie Buchanon .10 .30
199 Neil Clabo .10 .30
200 Walter Payton UER 12.50 25.00
201 Sam Adams .10 .30
202 Larry Gordon RC .10 .30
203 Pat Tilley .20 .50
204 Mack Mitchell .10 .30
205 Ken Anderson .40 1.00
206 Scott Dierking RC .10 .30
207 Jack Rudnay .10 .30
208 Jim Stienke .10 .30
209 Bill Simpson .10 .30
210 Errol Mann .10 .30
211 Bucky Dilts RC .10 .30
212 Reuben Gant .10 .30
213 Thomas Henderson RC .60 1.50
214 Steve Furness .20 .50
215 John Riggins .75 2.00
216 Keith Krepfle RC .10 .30
217 Fred Dean RC 6.00 12.00
218 Emanuel Zanders .10 .30
219 Don Testerman RC .10 .30
220 George Kunz .10 .30
221 Darryl Stingley .20 .50
222 Ken Sanders RC .10 .30
223 Gary Huff .10 .30
224 Gregg Bingham .10 .30
225 Jerry Sherk .10 .30
226 Doug Plank .10 .30
227 Ed Taylor RC .10 .30
228 Emery Moorehead RC .10 .30
229 Reggie Williams RC .40 1.00
230 Claude Humphrey .10 .30
231 Randy Cross RC 1.25 3.00
232 Jim Hart .40 1.00
233 Bobby Bryant .10 .30
234 Larry Brown .10 .30
235 Mark Van Eeghen .20 .50
236 Terry Hermeling .10 .30
237 Steve Odom .10 .30
238 Jan Stenerud .40 1.00
239 Andre Tillman .10 .30
240 Tom Jackson RC 2.00 5.00
241 Ken Mendenhall .10 .30
242 Tim Fox .10 .30
243 Don Herrmann .10 .30
244 Eddie McMillan .10 .30
245 Greg Pruitt .20 .50
246 J.K. McKay .10 .30
247 Larry Keller RC .10 .30
248 Dave Jennings .20 .50
249 Bo Harris RC .10 .30
250 Revie Sorey .10 .30
251 Tony Greene .10 .30
252 Butch Johnson .20 .50
253 Paul Naumoff .10 .30
254 Rickey Young .20 .50
255 Dwight White .20 .50
256 Joe Lavender .10 .30
257 Checklist 133-264 .40 1.00
258 Ronnie Coleman .10 .30
259 Charlie Smith WR .10 .30
260 Ray Guy AP .40 1.00
261 David Taylor .10 .30
262 Bill Lenkaitis .10 .30
263 Jim Mitchell .10 .30
264 Delvin Williams .10 .30
265 Jack Youngblood .40 1.00
266 Chuck Crist RC .10 .30
267 Richard Todd .20 .50
268 Dave Logan RC .40 1.00
269 Rufus Mayes .10 .30
270 Brad Van Pelt .10 .30
271 Chester Marcol .10 .30
272 J.V. Cain .10 .30
273 Larry Seiple .10 .30
274 Brent McClanahan .10 .30
275 Mike Wagner .10 .30
276 Diron Talbert .10 .30
277 Brian Baschnagel .10 .30
278 Ed Podolak .10 .30
279 Don Goode .10 .30
280 John Dutton .20 .50
281 Don Calhoun .10 .30
282 Monte Johnson .10 .30
283 Ron Jessie .10 .30
284 Jon Morris .10 .30
285 Riley Odoms .10 .30
286 Marv Bateman .10 .30
287 Joe Klecko RC .40 1.00
288 Oliver Davis RC .10 .30
289 John McDaniel .10 .30
290 Roger Staubach 6.00 12.00
291 Brian Kelley .10 .30
292 Mike Hogan RC .10 .30
293 John Leypoldt .10 .30
294 Jack Novak RC .10 .30
295 Joe Greene .75 2.00
296 John Hill .10 .30
297 Danny Buggs RC .10 .30
298 Ted Albrecht RC .10 .30
299 Nelson Munsey .10 .30
300 Chuck Foreman .20 .50
301 Dan Pastorini .20 .50
302 Tommy Hart .10 .30
303 Dave Beverly .10 .30
304 Tony Reed RC .20 .50
305 Cliff Branch .60 1.50
306 Clarence Duren RC .10 .30
307 Randy Rasmussen .10 .30
308 Oscar Roan .10 .30
309 Lenvil Elliott .10 .30
310 Dan Dierdorf AP .40 1.00
311 Johnny Perkins RC .10 .30
312 Rafael Septien RC .20 .50
313 Terry Beeson RC .10 .30
314 Lee Roy Selmon .75 2.00
315 Tony Dorsett RC 25.00 40.00
316 Greg Landry .20 .50
317 Jake Scott .10 .30
318 Dan Peiffer RC .10 .30
319 John Bunting .20 .50
320 John Stallworth RC 10.00 20.00
321 Bob Howard .10 .30
322 Larry Little .40 1.00
323 Reggie McKenzie .20 .50
324 Duane Carrell .10 .30
325 Ed Simonini RC .10 .30
326 John Vella .10 .30
327 Wesley Walker RC 1.50 3.00
328 Jon Keyworth .10 .30
329 Ron Bolton .10 .30
330 Tommy Casanova .10 .30
331 R.Staubach/B.Griese LL 2.00 4.00
332 A.Rashad/Mitchell LL .40 1.00
333 W.Payton
VanEeghenLL 1.25 3.00
334 W.Payton
E.Mann LL 1.25 3.00
335 Interception Leaders .10 .30
336 Punting Leaders .20 .50
337 Robert Brazile .20 .50
338 Charlie Joiner .60 1.50
339 Joe Ferguson .20 .50
340 Bill Thompson .10 .30
341 Sam Cunningham .20 .50
342 Curtis Johnson .10 .30
343 Jim Marshall .40 1.00
344 Charlie Sanders .20 .50
345 Willie Hall .10 .30
346 Pat Haden .40 1.00
347 Jim Bakken .10 .30
348 Bruce Taylor .10 .30
349 Barty Smith .10 .30
350 Drew Pearson AP .60 1.50
351 Mike Webster 1.00 2.50
352 Bobby Hammond RC .10 .30
353 Dave Mays RC .10 .30
354 Pat McInally .10 .30
355 Toni Linhart .10 .30
356 Larry Hand .10 .30
357 Ted Fritsch Jr. .10 .30
358 Larry Marshall .10 .30
359 Waymond Bryant .10 .30
360 Louie Kelcher RC .20 .50
361 Stanley Morgan RC .75 2.00
362 Bruce Harper RC .20 .50
363 Bernard Jackson .10 .30
364 Walter White .10 .30
365 Ken Stabler 4.00 8.00
366 Fred Dryer .40 1.00
367 Ike Harris .10 .30
368 Norm Bulaich .10 .30
369 Merv Krakau RC .10 .30
370 John James .10 .30
371 Bennie Cunningham RC .10 .30
372 Doug Van Horn .10 .30
373 Thom Darden .10 .30
374 Eddie Edwards RC .10 .30
375 Mike Thomas .10 .30
376 Fred Cook .10 .30
377 Mike Phipps .20 .50
378 Paul Krause .40 1.00
379 Harold Carmichael .40 1.00
380 Mike Haynes AP .40 1.00
381 Wayne Morris .10 .30
382 Greg Buttle .10 .30
383 Jim Zorn .40 1.00
384 Jack Dolbin .10 .30
385 Charlie Waters .20 .50
386 Dan Ryczek .10 .30
387 Joe Washington RC .40 1.00
388 Checklist 265-396 .40 1.00
389 James Hunter RC .10 .30
390 Billy Johnson .20 .50
391 Jim Allen RC .10 .30
392 George Buehler .10 .30
393 Harry Carson .40 1.00
394 Cleo Miller .10 .30
395 Gary Burley RC .10 .30
396 Mark Moseley .20 .50
397 Virgil Livers .10 .30
398 Joe Ehrmann .10 .30
399 Freddie Solomon .10 .30
400 O.J. Simpson 2.00 4.00
401 Julius Adams .10 .30
402 Artimus Parker RC .10 .30
403 Gene Washington 49er .20 .50
404 Herman Edwards RC .20 .50
405 Craig Morton .40 1.00
406 Alan Page .40 1.00
407 Larry McCarren .10 .30
408 Tony Galbreath .20 .50
409 Roman Gabriel .40 1.00
410 Efren Herrera .10 .30
411 Jim Smith RC .40 1.00
412 Bill Bryant RC .10 .30
413 Doug Dickon .10 .30
414 Marvin Cobb .10 .30
415 Fred Biletnikoff .75 2.00
416 Joe Theismann 1.00 2.50
417 Roland Harper .10 .30
418 Derrel Luce RC .10 .30
419 Ralph Perretta .10 .30
420 Louis Wright RC .40 1.00
421 Prentice McCray .10 .30
422 Garry Puetz .10 .30
423 Alfred Jenkins RC .40 1.00
424 Paul Seymour .10 .30
425 Garo Yepremian .20 .50
426 Emmitt Thomas .20 .50
427 Dexter Bussey .10 .30
428 John Sanders RC .10 .30
429 Ed Too Tall Jones .75 2.00
430 Ron Yary .40 1.00
431 Frank Lewis .20 .50
432 Jerry Golsteyn RC .10 .30
433 Clarence Scott .10 .30
434 Pete Johnson RC .40 1.00
435 Charle Young .20 .50
436 Harold McLinton .10 .30
437 Noah Jackson .10 .30
438 Bruce Laird .10 .30
439 John Matuszak .20 .50
440 Nat Moore AP .20 .50
441 Leon Gray .10 .30
442 Jerome Barkum .10 .30
443 Steve Largent 6.00 12.00
444 John Zook .10 .30
445 Preston Pearson .20 .50
446 Conrad Dobler .20 .50
447 Wilbur Summers RC .10 .30
448 Lou Piccone .10 .30
449 Ron Jaworski .40 1.00
450 Jack Ham AP .60 1.50
451 Mick Tingelhoff .20 .50
452 Clyde Powers .10 .30
453 John Cappelletti .40 1.00
454 Dick Ambrose RC .10 .30
455 Lemar Parrish .10 .30
456 Ron Saul .10 .30
457 Bob Parsons .10 .30
458 Glenn Doughty .10 .30
459 Don Woods .10 .30
460 Art Shell AP .40 1.00
461 Sam Hunt .10 .30
462 Lawrence Pillers .10 .30
463 Henry Childs .10 .30
464 Roger Wehrli .20 .50
465 Otis Armstrong .20 .50
466 Bob Baumhower RC .75 2.00
467 Ray Jarvis .10 .30
468 Guy Morriss .10 .30
469 Matt Blair .20 .50
470 Billy Joe DuPree .20 .50
471 Roland Hooks RC .10 .30
472 Joe Danelo .10 .30
473 Reggie Rucker .20 .50
474 Vern Holland .10 .30
475 Mel Blount .60 1.50
476 Eddie Brown .10 .30
477 Bo Rather .10 .30
478 Don McCauley .10 .30
479 Glen Walker RC .10 .30
480 Randy Gradishar AP .40 1.00
481 Dave Rowe .10 .30
482 Pat Leahy .20 .50
483 Mike Fuller .10 .30
484 David Lewis RC .10 .30
485 Steve Grogan .40 1.00
486 Mel Gray .20 .50
487 Eddie Payton RC .20 .50
488 Checklist 397-528 .40 1.00
489 Stu Voigt .10 .30
490 Rolland Lawrence .10 .30
491 Nick Mike-Mayer .10 .30
492 Troy Archer .10 .30
493 Benny Malone .10 .30
494 Golden Richards .20 .50
495 Chris Hanburger .10 .30
496 Dwight Harrison .10 .30
497 Gary Fencik RC .40 1.00
498 Rich Saul .10 .30
499 Dan Fouts 2.00 4.00
500 Franco Harris AP 2.00 4.00
501 Atlanta Falcons TL .30 .75
502 Baltimore Colts TL .30 .75
503 Bills TL/O.J.Simpson .60 1.50
504 Bears TL/W.Payton .75 2.00
505 Bengals TL/Reg.Williams .30 .75
506 Cleveland Browns TL .30 .75
507 Cowboys TL/T.Dorsett 1.00 2.50
508 Denver Broncos TL .40 1.00
509 Detroit Lions TL .30 .75
510 Green Bay Packers TL .40 1.00
511 Houston Oilers TL .30 .75
512 Kansas City Chiefs TL .30 .75
513 Los Angeles Rams TL .30 .75
514 Miami Dolphins TL .40 1.00
515 Minnesota Vikings TL .30 .75
516 New England Patriots TL .30 .75
517 New Orleans Saints TL .30 .75
518 New York Giants TL .30 .75
519 Jets TL/Wesley Walker .30 .75
520 Oakland Raiders TL .40 1.00
521 Philadelphia Eagles TL .30 .75
522 Steelers TL/Harris/Blount .40 1.00
523 St.Louis Cardinals TL .30 .75
524 San Diego Chargers TL .40 1.00
525 San Francisco 49ers TL .30 .75
526 Seahawks TL/S.Largent .60 1.50
527 Tampa Bay Bucs TL .30 .75
528 Redskins TL/Ken Houston .40 1.00

1978 Topps Holsum

In 1978, Topps produced a set of 33 NFL full-color standard-size cards for Holsum Bread. One card was packed inside each loaf of bread. Unfortunately, nowhere on the card is Holsum mentioned, leading to frequent misclassification of this set. An uncut production sheet was offered in the 1989 Topps Archives auction. The personal data on the card back is printed in yellow and green. Each card can be found with either one or two asterisks on the copyright line.

COMPLETE SET (33) 150.00 300.00
1 Rolland Lawrence 2.00 4.00
2 Walter Payton 60.00 120.00
3 Lydell Mitchell 2.50 5.00
4 Joe DeLamielleure 3.50 6.00
5 Ken Anderson 5.00 10.00
6 Greg Pruitt 2.50 5.00
7 Harvey Martin 3.00 6.00
8 Tom Jackson 3.00 6.00
9 Chester Marcol 2.00 4.00
10 Jim Carter 2.00 4.00
11 Will Harrell 2.00 4.00
12 Greg Landry 2.50 5.00
13 Billy Johnson 2.50 5.00
14 Jan Stenerud 3.00 6.00
15 Lawrence McCutcheon 2.50 5.00
16 Bob Griese 12.50 25.00
17 Chuck Foreman 2.50 5.00
18 Sammie White 2.50 5.00
19 Jeff Siemon 2.00 4.00
20 Mike Haynes 4.00 8.00
21 Archie Manning 7.50 15.00
22 Brad Van Pelt 2.00 4.00
23 Richard Todd 2.50 5.00
24 Dave Casper 4.00 8.00
25 Bill Bergey 2.50 5.00
26 Franco Harris 12.50 25.00
27 Mel Gray 2.50 5.00
28 Louie Kelcher 2.00 4.00
29 O.J. Simpson 15.00 30.00
30 Jim Zorn 2.50 5.00
31 Lee Roy Selmon 4.00 8.00
32 Ken Houston 3.00 6.00
33 Checklist Card 10.00 20.00

1978 Topps Team Checklists

These cards are essentially a parallel to the base 1978 Topps team checklist subset cards. The set was only available directly from Topps as a send-off offer in uncut sheet form. The prices below apply equally to uncut sheets as they are frequently found in their original uncut condition. As for individual cards, thin white card (almost paper-thin) stock makes it a challenge to find singles in top grades.

COMPLETE SET (28) 62.50 125.00
501 Atlanta Falcons TL 2.00 4.00
502 Baltimore Colts TL 2.00 4.00
503 Bills TL
O.J.Simpson 4.00 8.00
504 Bears TL
Walter Payton 7.50 15.00
505 Bengals TL
Reg.Williams 2.00 4.00
506 Cleveland Browns TL 2.00 4.00
507 Cowboys TL
T.Dorsett 5.00 10.00
508 Denver Broncos TL 3.00 6.00
509 Detroit Lions TL 2.00 4.00
510 Green Bay Packers TL 3.00 6.00
511 Houston Oilers TL 2.00 4.00
512 Kansas City Chiefs TL 2.00 4.00
513 Los Angeles Rams TL 2.00 4.00
514 Miami Dolphins TL 3.00 6.00
515 Minnesota Vikings TL 3.00 6.00
516 New England Patriots TL 2.00 4.00
517 New Orleans Saints TL 2.00 4.00
518 New York Giants TL 2.00 4.00
519 Jets TL
Wesley Walker 2.00 4.00
520 Oakland Raiders TL 3.00 6.00
521 Philadelphia Eagles TL 3.00 6.00
522 Steelers TL
Harris
Blount 4.00 8.00
523 St.Louis Cardinals TL 2.00 4.00
524 San Diego Chargers TL 3.00 6.00
525 San Francisco 49ers TL 3.00 6.00
526 Seahawks TL
S.Largent 4.00 8.00
527 Tampa Bay Bucs TL 3.00 6.00
528 Redskins TL
Ken Houston 3.00 6.00

1979 Topps

The 1979 Topps football set contains 528 standard-size cards. The cardfronts have the player's name, team name and position at the top and the position is within a football that is part of a banner-like design. The backs contain yearly statistics, highlights and a player cartoon. Subsets include League Leaders (1-6), Playoffs (166-168) and Record Breakers (331-336). Team Leaders (TL) depict team leaders in various categories on front and a team checklist on back. An uncut sheet of the 28-Team Leaders cards along with two checklists was available via a wrapper mail order offer. The set features the first and only major issue cards of Earl Campbell. Other Rookie Cards include Steve DeBerg, James Lofton, Ozzie Newsome and Doug Williams. Finally, every card was printed on the standard dark colored gray card stock as well as a thinner cream colored card stock that is slightly more difficult to find.

COMPLETE SET (528) 75.00 150.00
*CREAM BACK: .4X TO 1X GRAY BACK
1 Staubach/Bradshaw LL 4.00 8.00
2 S.Largent/R.Young LL .40 1.00
3 E.Campbell/W.Payton LL 4.00 8.00
4 Scoring Leaders .10 .30
5 Interception Leaders .10 .30
6 Punting Leaders .10 .30
7 Johnny Perkins .10 .30
8 Charles Phillips RC .10 .30
9 Derrel Luce .10 .30
10 John Riggins .50 1.25
11 Chester Marcol .10 .30
12 Bernard Jackson .10 .30
13 Dave Logan .10 .30
14 Bo Harris .10 .30
15 Alan Page .40 1.00
16 John Smith .10 .30
17 Dwight McDonald RC .10 .30
18 John Cappelletti .20 .50
19 Steelers TL/Harris/Dungy 5.00 12.00
20A Bill Bergey AP .20 .50
(Eagles printed in pink on front)
20B Bill Bergey AP Red 1.25 3.00
21 Jerome Barkum .10 .30
22 Larry Csonka 1.00 2.50
23 Joe Ferguson .20 .50
24 Ed Too Tall Jones .50 1.25
25 Dave Jennings .20 .50
26 Horace King .10 .30
27 Steve Little RC .20 .50
28 Morris Bradshaw RC .10 .30
29 Joe Ehrmann .10 .30
30 Ahmad Rashad AP .40 1.00
31 Joe Lavender .10 .30
32 Dan Neal .10 .30
33 Johnny Evans RC .10 .30
34 Pete Johnson .20 .50
35 Mike Haynes AP .40 1.00
36 Tim Mazzetti RC .10 .30
37 Mike Barber RC .10 .30
38 49ers TL/O.J.Simpson .60 1.50
39 Bill Gregory RC .10 .30
40 Randy Gradishar AP .40 1.00
41 Richard Todd .20 .50
42 Henry Marshall .10 .30
43 John Hill .10 .30
44 Sidney Thornton RC .10 .30
45 Ron Jessie .10 .30
46 Bob Baumhower .20 .50
47 Johnnie Gray .10 .30
48 Doug Williams RC 3.00 6.00
49 Don McCauley .10 .30
50 Ray Guy AP .20 .50
51 Bob Klein .10 .30
52 Golden Richards .10 .30
53 Mark Miller QB RC .10 .30
54 John Sanders .10 .30
55 Gary Burley .10 .30
56 Steve Nelson .10 .30
57 Buffalo Bills TL .30 .75
58 Bobby Bryant .10 .30
59 Rick Kane .10 .30
60 Larry Little .40 1.00
61 Ted Fritsch Jr. .10 .30
62 Larry Mallory RC .10 .30
63 Marvin Powell .10 .30
64 Jim Hart .40 1.00
65 Joe Greene AP .60 1.50
66 Walter White .10 .30
67 Gregg Bingham .10 .30
68 Errol Mann .10 .30
69 Bruce Laird .10 .30
70 Drew Pearson .40 1.00
71 Steve Bartkowski .40 1.00
72 Ted Albrecht .10 .30
73 Charlie Hall .10 .30
74 Pat McInally .10 .30
75 Bubba Baker RC .40 1.00
76 New England Pats TL .30 .75
77 Steve DeBerg RC .75 2.00
78 John Yarno RC .10 .30
79 Stu Voigt .10 .30
80 Frank Corral AP RC .10 .30
81 Troy Archer .10 .30
82 Bruce Harper .10 .30
83 Tom Jackson .60 1.50
84 Larry Brown .20 .50
85A Wilbert Montgomery AP RC .40 1.00
85B Wilbert Montgomery AP Red 1.50 4.00
86 Butch Johnson .20 .50
87 Mike Kadish .10 .30
88 Ralph Perretta .10 .30
89 David Lee .10 .30
90 Mark Van Eeghen .20 .50
91 John McDaniel .10 .30
92 Gary Fencik .20 .50
93 Mack Mitchell .10 .30
94 Cincinnati Bengals TL/Jauron .40 1.00
95 Steve Grogan .40 1.00
96 Garo Yepremian .20 .50
97 Barty Smith .10 .30
98 Frank Reed RC .10 .30
99 Jim Clack RC .10 .30
100 Chuck Foreman .20 .50
101 Joe Klecko .40 1.00
102 Pat Tilley .20 .50
103 Conrad Dobler .20 .50
104 Craig Colquitt RC .10 .30
105 Dan Pastorini .20 .50
106 Rod Perry AP .10 .30
107 Nick Mike-Mayer .10 .30
108 John Matuszak .20 .50
109 David Taylor .10 .30
110 Billy Joe DuPree AP .20 .50
111 Harold McLinton .10 .30
112 Virgil Livers .10 .30
113 Cleveland Browns TL .30 .75
114 Checklist 1-132 .40 1.00
115 Ken Anderson .40 1.00
116 Bill Lenkaitis .10 .30
117 Bucky Dilts .10 .30
118 Tony Greene .10 .30
119 Bobby Hammond .10 .30
120 Nat Moore .20 .50
121 Pat Leahy AP .20 .50
122 James Harris .20 .50
123 Lee Roy Selmon .50 1.25
124 Bennie Cunningham .20 .50
125 Matt Blair AP .20 .50
126 Jim Allen .10 .30
127 Alfred Jenkins .20 .50
128 Arthur Whittington RC .10 .30
129 Norm Thompson .10 .30
130 Pat Haden .40 1.00

131 Freddie Solomon .10 .30
132 Bears TL/W.Payton .75 2.00
133 Mark Moseley .10 .30
134 Cleo Miller .10 .30
135 Ross Browner RC .20 .50
136 Don Calhoun .10 .30
137 David Whitehurst RC .10 .30
138 Terry Beeson .10 .30
139 Ken Stone RC .10 .30
140 Brad Van Pelt AP .10 .30
141 Wesley Walker AP .40 1.00
142 Jan Stenerud .40 1.00
143 Henry Childs .10 .30
144 Otis Armstrong .40 1.00
145 Dwight White .20 .50
146 Steve Wilson RC .10 .30
147 Tom Skladany RC .10 .30
148 Lou Piccone .10 .30
149 Monte Johnson .10 .30
150 Joe Washington .20 .50
151 Eagles TL/W.Montgomery .30 .75
152 Fred Dean .40 1.00
153 Rolland Lawrence .10 .30
154 Brian Baschnagel .10 .30
155 Joe Theismann .75 2.00
156 Marvin Cobb .10 .30
157 Dick Ambrose .10 .30
158 Mike Patrick .10 .30
159 Gary Shirk .10 .30
160 Tony Dorsett 6.00 12.00
161 Greg Buttle .10 .30
162 A.J. Duhe .20 .50
163 Mick Tingelhoff .20 .50
164 Ken Burrough .20 .50
165 Mike Wagner .10 .30
166 AFC Champs/F.Harris .40 1.00
167 NFC Championship .20 .50
168 Super Bowl XIII/Harris .50 1.25
169 Raiders TL/Ted Hendricks .40 1.00
170 O.J. Simpson 1.50 4.00
171 Doug Nettles RC .10 .30
172 Dan Dierdorf AP .40 1.00
173 Dave Beverly .10 .30
174 Jim Zorn .40 1.00
175 Mike Thomas .10 .30
176 John Outlaw .10 .30
177 Jim Turner .10 .30
178 Freddie Scott RC .10 .30
179 Mike Phipps .20 .50
180 Jack Youngblood AP .40 1.00
181 Sam Hunt .10 .30
182 Tony Hill RC .40 1.00
183 Gary Barbaro .10 .30
184 Archie Griffin .20 .50
185 Jerry Sherk .10 .30
186 Bobby Jackson RC .10 .30
187 Don Woods .10 .30
188 New York Giants TL .30 .75
189 Raymond Chester .10 .30
190 Joe DeLamielleure AP .40 1.00
191 Tony Galbreath .20 .50
192 Robert Brazile AP .20 .50
193 Neil O'Donoghue RC .10 .30
194 Mike Webster AP .40 1.00
195 Ed Simonini .10 .30
196 Benny Malone .10 .30
197 Tom Wittum .10 .30
198 Steve Largent AP 4.00 8.00
199 Tommy Hart .10 .30
200 Fran Tarkenton 1.50 3.00
201 Leon Gray AP .10 .30
202 Leroy Harris RC .10 .30
203 Eric Williams LB RC .10 .30
204 Thom Darden AP .10 .30
205 Ken Riley .20 .50
206 Clark Gaines .10 .30
207 Kansas City Chiefs TL .30 .75
208 Joe Danelo .10 .30
209 Glen Walker .10 .30
210 Art Shell .40 1.00
211 Jon Keyworth .10 .30
212 Herman Edwards .10 .30
213 John Fitzgerald .10 .30
214 Jim Smith .20 .50
215 Coy Bacon .20 .50
216 Dennis Johnson RBK RC .10 .30
217 John Jefferson RC 1.50 3.00
218 Gary Weaver RC .10 .30
219 Tom Blanchard .10 .30
220 Bert Jones .40 1.00
221 Stanley Morgan .40 1.00
222 James Hunter .10 .30
223 Jim O'Bradovich RC .10 .30
224 Carl Mauck .10 .30
225 Chris Bahr .10 .30
226 Jets TL/Wesley Walker .30 .75
227 Roland Harper .10 .30
228 Randy Dean RC .10 .30
229 Bob Jackson .10 .30
230 Sammie White .20 .50
231 Mike Dawson RC .10 .30
232 Checklist 133-264 .40 1.00
233 Ken MacAfee RC .10 .30
234 Jon Kolb AP .10 .30
235 Willie Hall .10 .30
236 Ron Saul AP .10 .30
237 Haskel Stanback .10 .30
238 Zenon Andrusyshyn RC .10 .30
239 Norris Thomas .10 .30
240 Rick Upchurch .20 .50
241 Robert Pratt .10 .30
242 Julius Adams .10 .30
243 Rich McGeorge .10 .30
244 Seahawks TL/S.Largent .50 1.25
245 Blair Bush RC .10 .30
246 Billy Johnson .20 .50
247 Randy Rasmussen .10 .30
248 Brian Kelley .10 .30
249 Mike Pruitt .20 .50
250 Harold Carmichael AP .40 1.00
251 Mike Hartenstine .10 .30
252 Robert Newhouse .20 .50
253 Gary Danielson RC .40 1.00
254 Mike Fuller .10 .30
255 L.C. Greenwood AP .40 1.00
256 Lemar Parrish .10 .30
257 Ike Harris .10 .30
258 Ricky Bell RC .40 1.00
259 Willie Parker C .10 .30
260 Gene Upshaw .40 1.00
261 Glenn Doughty .10 .30
262 Steve Zabel .10 .30
263 Atlanta Falcons TL .30 .75
264 Ray Wersching .10 .30
265 Lawrence McCutcheon .20 .50
266 Willie Buchanon AP .10 .30
267 Matt Robinson RC .10 .30
268 Reggie Rucker .20 .50
269 Doug Van Horn .10 .30
270 Lydell Mitchell .20 .50
271 Vern Holland .10 .30
272 Eason Ramson RC .10 .30
273 Steve Towle RC .10 .30
274 Jim Marshall .40 1.00
275 Mel Blount .50 1.25
276 Rob Kuziel RC .10 .30
277 James Scott .10 .30
278 Tony Reed .10 .30
279 Dave Green .10 .30
280 Toni Linhart .10 .30
281 Andy Johnson .10 .30
282 Los Angeles Rams TL .30 .75
283 Phil Villapiano .20 .50
284 Dexter Bussey .10 .30
285 Craig Morton .40 1.00
286 Guy Morriss .10 .30
287 Lawrence Pillers .10 .30
288 Gerald Irons .10 .30
289 Scott Perry RC .10 .30
290 Randy White AP .75 2.00
291 Jack Gregory .10 .30
292 Bob Chandler .10 .30
293 Rich Szaro .10 .30
294 Sherman Smith .10 .30
295 Tom Banks AP .10 .30
296 Revie Sorey AP .10 .30
297 Ricky Thompson RC .10 .30
298 Ron Yary .40 1.00
299 Lyle Blackwood .10 .30
300 Franco Harris 1.25 2.50
301 Oilers TL/E.Campbell 1.50 3.00
302 Scott Bull RC .10 .30
303 Dewey Selmon .20 .50
304 Jack Rudnay .10 .30
305 Fred Biletnikoff .75 2.00
306 Jeff West .10 .30
307 Shafer Suggs RC .10 .30
308 Ozzie Newsome RC 6.00 12.00
309 Boobie Clark .10 .30
310 James Lofton RC 6.00 15.00
311 Joe Pisarcik .10 .30
312 Bill Simpson AP .10 .30
313 Haven Moses .20 .50
314 Jim Merlo .10 .30
315 Preston Pearson .20 .50
316 Larry Tearry RC .10 .30
317 Tom Dempsey .10 .30
318 Greg Latta .10 .30
319 Redskins TL/John Riggins .60 1.50
320 Jack Ham AP .50 1.25
321 Harold Jackson .20 .50
322 George Roberts RC .10 .30
323 Ron Jaworski .40 1.00
324 Jim Otis .10 .30
325 Roger Carr .20 .50
326 Jack Tatum .20 .50
327 Derrick Gaffney RC .10 .30
328 Reggie Williams .40 1.00
329 Doug Dieken .10 .30
330 Efren Herrera .10 .30
331 Earl Campbell RB 3.00 6.00
332 Tony Galbreath RB .10 .30
333 Bruce Harper RB .10 .30
334 John James RB .10 .30
335 Walter Payton RB 1.50 4.00
336 Rickey Young RB .10 .30
337 Jeff Van Note .20 .50
338 Chargers TL/J.Jefferson .40 1.00
339 Stan Walters RC .10 .30
340 Louis Wright AP .20 .50
341 Horace Ivory RC .10 .30
342 Andre Tillman .10 .30
343 Greg Coleman RC .10 .30
344 Doug English AP RC .40 1.00
345 Ted Hendricks .40 1.00
346 Rich Saul .10 .30
347 Mel Gray .20 .50
348 Toni Fritsch .10 .30
349 Cornell Webster RC .10 .30
350 Ken Houston .40 1.00
351 Ron Johnson DB RC .20 .50
352 Doug Kotar .10 .30
353 Brian Sipe .40 1.00
354 Billy Brooks .10 .30
355 John Dutton .20 .50
356 Don Goode .10 .30
357 Detroit Lions TL .30 .75
358 Reuben Gant .10 .30
359 Bob Parsons .10 .30
360 Cliff Harris AP .40 1.00
361 Raymond Clayborn .20 .50
362 Scott Dierking .10 .30
363 Bill Bryan RC .10 .30
364 Mike Livingston .10 .30
365 Otis Sistrunk .20 .50
366 Charle Young .20 .50
367 Keith Wortman RC .10 .30
368 Checklist 265-396 .40 1.00
369 Mike Michel RC .10 .30
370 Delvin Williams AP .10 .30
371 Steve Furness .20 .50
372 Emery Moorehead .10 .30
373 Clarence Scott .10 .30
374 Rufus Mayes .10 .30
375 Chris Hanburger .10 .30
376 Baltimore Colts TL .30 .75
377 Bob Avellini .20 .50
378 Jeff Siemon .10 .30
379 Roland Hooks .10 .30
380 Russ Francis .20 .50
381 Roger Wehrli .20 .50
382 Joe Fields .10 .30
383 Archie Manning .40 1.00
384 Rob Lytle .10 .30
385 Thomas Henderson .20 .50
386 Morris Owens .10 .30
387 Dan Fouts 1.50 3.00
388 Chuck Crist .10 .30
389 Ed O'Neil RC .10 .30
390 Earl Campbell RC 15.00 30.00
391 Randy Grossman .10 .30
392 Monte Jackson .10 .30
393 John Mendenhall .10 .30
394 Miami Dolphins TL .40 1.00
395 Isaac Curtis .20 .50
396 Mike Bragg .10 .30
397 Doug Plank .10 .30
398 Mike Barnes .10 .30
399 Calvin Hill .20 .50
400 Roger Staubach AP 5.00 10.00
401 Doug Beaudoin RC .10 .30
402 Chuck Ramsey .10 .30
403 Mike Hogan .10 .30
404 Mario Clark .10 .30
405 Riley Odoms .10 .30
406 Carl Eller .40 1.00
407 Packers TL/J.Lofton .60 1.50
408 Mark Arneson .10 .30
409 Vince Ferragamo RC .40 1.00
410 Cleveland Elam .10 .30
411 Donnie Shell RC 1.50 4.00
412 Ray Rhodes .40 1.00
413 Don Cockroft .10 .30
414 Don Bass RC .20 .50
415 Cliff Branch .40 1.00
416 Diron Talbert .10 .30
417 Tom Hicks .10 .30
418 Roosevelt Leaks .10 .30
419 Charlie Joiner .40 1.00
420 Lyle Alzado AP .40 1.00
421 Sam Cunningham .20 .50
422 Larry Keller .10 .30
423 Jim Mitchell .10 .30
424 Randy Logan .10 .30
425 Jim Langer .40 1.00
426 Gary Green .10 .30
427 Luther Blue RC .10 .30
428 Dennis Johnson .10 .30
429 Danny White .40 1.00
430 Roy Gerela .10 .30
431 Jimmy Robinson .10 .30
432 Minnesota Vikings TL .30 .75
433 Oliver Davis .10 .30
434 Lenvil Elliott .10 .30
435 Willie Miller RC .10 .30
436 Brad Dusek .10 .30
437 Bob Thomas .10 .30
438 Ken Mendenhall .10 .30
439 Clarence Davis .10 .30
440 Bob Griese 1.00 2.50
441 Tony McGee .10 .30
442 Ed Taylor .10 .30
443 Ron Howard .10 .30
444 Wayne Morris .10 .30
445 Charlie Waters .20 .50
446 Rick Danmeier RC .10 .30
447 Paul Naumoff .10 .30
448 Keith Krepfle .10 .30
449 Rusty Jackson .10 .30
450 John Stallworth 2.00 4.00
451 New Orleans Saints TL .30 .75
452 Ron Mikolajczyk RC .10 .30
453 Fred Dryer .40 1.00
454 Jim LeClair .10 .30
455 Greg Pruitt .20 .50
456 Jake Scott .10 .30
457 Steve Schubert .10 .30
458 George Kunz .10 .30
459 Mike Williams .10 .30
460 Dave Casper AP .40 1.00
461 Sam Adams .10 .30
462 Abdul Salaam .10 .30
463 Terdell Middleton RC .20 .50
464 Mike Wood RC .10 .30
465 Bill Thompson AP .10 .30
466 Larry Gordon .10 .30
467 Benny Ricardo .10 .30
468 Reggie McKenzie .20 .50
469 Cowboys TL/T.Dorsett .60 1.50
470 Rickey Young .20 .50
471 Charlie Smith .10 .30
472 Al Dixon RC .10 .30
473 Tom DeLeone .10 .30
474 Louis Breeden RC .20 .50
475 Jack Lambert .75 2.00
476 Terry Hermeling .10 .30
477 J.K. McKay .10 .30
478 Stan White .10 .30
479 Terry Nelson .10 .30
480 Walter Payton AP 10.00 20.00
481 Dave Dalby .10 .30
482 Burgess Owens .10 .30
483 Rolf Benirschke .10 .30
484 Jack Dolbin .10 .30
485 John Hannah AP .40 1.00
486 Checklist 397-528 .40 1.00
487 Greg Landry .20 .50
488 St. Louis Cardinals TL .30 .75
489 Paul Krause .40 1.00
490 John James .10 .30
491 Merv Krakau .10 .30
492 Dan Doornink RC .10 .30
493 Curtis Johnson .10 .30
494 Rafael Septien .10 .30
495 Jean Fugett .10 .30
496 Frank LeMaster .10 .30
497 Allan Ellis .10 .30
498 Billy Waddy RC .20 .50
499 Hank Bauer RC .10 .30
500 Terry Bradshaw UER 5.00 10.00
501 Larry McCarren .10 .30
502 Fred Cook .10 .30
503 Chuck Muncie .20 .50
504 Herman Weaver .10 .30
505 Eddie Edwards .10 .30
506 Tony Peters .10 .30
507 Denver Broncos TL .30 .75
508 Jimbo Elrod RC .10 .30
509 David Hill .10 .30
510 Harvey Martin .20 .50
511 Terry Miller RC .20 .50
512 June Jones RC .20 .50
513 Randy Cross .40 1.00
514 Duriel Harris .10 .30
515 Harry Carson .40 1.00
516 Tim Fox .10 .30
517 John Zook .10 .30
518 Bob Tucker .10 .30
519 Kevin Long RC .10 .30
520 Ken Stabler 3.00 6.00
521 John Bunting .20 .50
522 Rocky Bleier .50 1.25
523 Noah Jackson .10 .30
524 Cliff Parsley RC .10 .30
525 Louie Kelcher AP .20 .50
526 Bucs TL/Ricky Bell .30 .75
527 Bob Brudzinski RC .10 .30
528 Danny Buggs .10 .30

1979 Topps Team Checklists

These cards are essentially a parallel to the base 1979 Topps team checklist subset cards. The set was only available directly from Topps as a send-off offer in uncut sheet form. The prices below apply equally to uncut sheets as they are frequently found in their original uncut condition. As for individual cards, thin white card (almost paper-thin) stock makes it a challenge to find singles in top grades.

COMPLETE SET (28) 62.50 125.00
19 Steelers TL 5.00 10.00
F.Harris
Dungy
38 49ers TL 4.00 8.00
O.J.Simpson
57 Buffalo Bills TL 2.00 4.00
76 New England Pats TL 2.00 4.00
94 Cincinnati Bengals TL 4.00 8.00
Jauron
113 Cleveland Browns TL 2.00 4.00
132 Bears TL 6.00 12.00
Walter Payton
151 Eagles TL 3.00 6.00
W.Montgomery
169 Raiders TL 4.00 8.00
Ted Hendricks
188 New York Giants TL 2.00 4.00
207 Kansas City Chiefs TL 2.00 4.00
226 Jets TL 2.00 4.00
Wesley Walker
244 Seahawks TL 4.00 8.00
S.Largent
263 Atlanta Falcons TL 2.00 4.00
282 Los Angeles Rams TL 2.00 4.00
301 Oilers TL 6.00 12.00
Earl Campbell
319 Redskins TL 4.00 8.00
John Riggins
338 Chargers TL 3.00 6.00
J.Jefferson
357 Detroit Lions TL 2.00 4.00
376 Baltimore Colts TL 2.00 4.00
394 Miami Dolphins TL 2.00 4.00
407 Packers TL 5.00 10.00
James Lofton
432 Minnesota Vikings TL 3.00 6.00
451 New Orleans Saints TL 2.00 4.00
469 Cowboys TL 5.00 10.00
Tony Dorsett
488 St. Louis Cardinals TL 2.00 4.00
507 Denver Broncos TL 3.00 6.00
526 Bucs TL 3.00 6.00
Ricky Bell

1980 Topps

The 1980 Topps football card set contains 528 standard-size cards of NFL players. The set was issued in 12-card packs along with a bubble gum slab. The fronts feature a football at the bottom of the photo. Within the football is the player's team and position. A bar with the player's name runs through the center of the football. The backs of the cards contain year-by-year and career statistics and a cartoon-illustrated fact section. Subsets include Record-Breakers (1-6), league leaders (331-336) and playoffs (492-494). Team Leader (TL) cards depict team statistical leaders on the front and a team checklist on the back. The key Rookie Cards in this set are Ottis Anderson, Clay Matthews, and Phil Simms.

COMPLETE SET (528) 40.00 75.00
1 Ottis Anderson RB .40 1.00
2 Harold Carmichael RB .40 1.00
3 Dan Fouts RB .40 1.00
4 Paul Krause RB .20 .50
5 Rick Upchurch RB .20 .50
6 Garo Yepremian RB .10 .25
7 Harold Jackson .20 .50
8 Mike Williams .10 .25
9 Calvin Hill .20 .50
10 Jack Ham AP .40 1.00
11 Dan Melville .10 .25
12 Matt Robinson .10 .25
13 Billy Campfield RC .10 .25
14 Phil Tabor RC .10 .25
15 Randy Hughes UER RC .10 .25
16 Andre Tillman .10 .25
17 Isaac Curtis .20 .50
18 Charley Hannah .10 .25
19 Redskins TL/J.Riggins .40 1.00
20 Jim Zorn .20 .50
21 Brian Baschnagel .10 .25
22 Jon Keyworth .10 .25
23 Phil Villapiano .10 .25
24 Richard Osborne .10 .25
25 Rich Saul AP .10 .25
26 Doug Beaudoin .10 .25
27 Cleveland Elam .10 .25
28 Charlie Joiner .40 1.00
29 Dick Ambrose .10 .25
30 Mike Reinfeldt RC .10 .25
31 Matt Bahr RC .40 1.00
32 Keith Krepfle .10 .25
33 Herb Scott .10 .25
34 Doug Kotar .10 .25
35 Bob Griese .60 1.50
36 Jerry Butler RC .40 1.00
37 Rolland Lawrence .10 .25
38 Gary Weaver .10 .25
39 Chiefs TL/J.T.Smith .20 .50
40 Chuck Muncie .20 .50
41 Mike Hartenstine .10 .25
42 Sammie White .20 .50
43 Ken Clark .10 .25
44 Clarence Harmon .10 .25
45 Bert Jones .40 1.00
46 Mike Washington .10 .25
47 Joe Fields .10 .25
48 Mike Wood .10 .25
49 Oliver Davis .10 .25
50 Stan Walters AP .10 .25
51 Riley Odoms .10 .25
52 Steve Pisarkiewicz .10 .25
53 Tony Hill .40 1.00
54 Scott Perry .10 .25
55 George Martin RC .10 .25
56 George Roberts .10 .25
57 Seahawks TL/S. Largent .40 1.00
58 Billy Johnson .20 .50
59 Reuben Gant .10 .25
60 Dennis Harrah RC .10 .25
61 Rocky Bleier .40 1.00
62 Sam Hunt .10 .25
63 Allan Ellis .10 .25
64 Ricky Thompson .10 .25
65 Ken Stabler 1.50 4.00
66 Dexter Bussey .10 .25
67 Ken Mendenhall .10 .25
68 Woodrow Lowe .10 .25
69 Thom Darden .10 .25
70 Randy White AP .60 1.50
71 Ken MacAfee .10 .25
72 Ron Jaworski .40 1.00
73 William Andrews RC .40 1.00
74 Jimmy Robinson .10 .25
75 Roger Wehrli AP .20 .50
76 Dolphins TL/L.Csonka .40 1.00
77 Jack Rudnay .10 .25
78 James Lofton .75 2.00
79 Robert Brazile .20 .50
80 Russ Francis .20 .50
81 Ricky Bell .40 1.00
82 Bob Avellini .20 .50
83 Bobby Jackson .10 .25
84 Mike Bragg .10 .25
85 Cliff Branch .40 1.00
86 Blair Bush .10 .25
87 Sherman Smith .10 .25
88 Glen Edwards .10 .25
89 Don Cockroft .10 .25
90 Louis Wright AP .20 .50
91 Randy Grossman .10 .25
92 Carl Hairston RC .40 1.00
93 Archie Manning .40 1.00
94 New York Giants TL .20 .50
95 Preston Pearson .20 .50
96 Rusty Chambers .10 .25
97 Greg Coleman .10 .25
98 Charle Young .10 .25
99 Matt Cavanaugh RC .20 .50
100 Jesse Baker .10 .25
101 Doug Plank .10 .25
102 Checklist 1-132 .30 .75
103 Luther Bradley RC .10 .25
104 Bob Kuziel .10 .25
105 Craig Morton .20 .50
106 Sherman White .10 .25
107 Jim Breech RC .20 .50
108 Hank Bauer .10 .25
109 Tom Blanchard .10 .25
110 Ozzie Newsome AP .75 2.00
111 Steve Furness .10 .25
112 Frank LeMaster .10 .25
113 Cowboys TL/T.Dorsett .40 1.00
114 Doug Van Horn .10 .25
115 Delvin Williams .10 .25
116 Lyle Blackwood .10 .25
117 Derrick Gaffney .10 .25
118 Cornell Webster .10 .25
119 Sam Cunningham .20 .50
120 Jim Youngblood AP .20 .50
121 Bob Thomas .10 .25
122 Jack Thompson RC .20 .50
123 Randy Cross .40 1.00
124 Karl Lorch RC .10 .25
125 Mel Gray .10 .25
126 John James .10 .25
127 Terdell Middleton .10 .25
128 Leroy Jones .10 .25
129 Tom DeLeone .10 .25
130 John Stallworth AP .60 1.50
131 Jimmie Giles RC .20 .50
132 Philadelphia Eagles TL .40 1.00
133 Gary Green .10 .25
134 John Dutton .20 .50
135 Harry Carson AP .40 1.00
136 Bob Kuechenberg .20 .50
137 Ike Harris .10 .25
138 Tommy Kramer RC .40 1.00
139 Sam Adams OL .10 .25
140 Doug English AP .20 .50
141 Steve Schubert .10 .25
142 Rusty Jackson .10 .25
143 Reese McCall .10 .25
144 Scott Dierking .10 .25
145 Ken Houston AP .40 1.00
146 Bob Martin .10 .25
147 Sam McCullum .10 .25
148 Tom Banks .10 .25
149 Willie Buchanon .10 .25
150 Greg Pruitt .20 .50
151 Denver Broncos TL .40 1.00
152 Don Smith RC .10 .25
153 Pete Johnson .20 .50
154 Charlie Smith WR .10 .25
155 Mel Blount .40 1.00
156 John Mendenhall .10 .25
157 Danny White .40 1.00
158 Jimmy Cefalo RC .20 .50
159 Richard Bishop AP .10 .25
160 Walter Payton AP 5.00 12.00
161 Dave Dalby .10 .25
162 Preston Dennard .10 .25
163 Johnnie Gray .10 .25
164 Russell Erxleben .10 .25
165 Toni Fritsch AP .10 .25
166 Terry Hermeling .10 .25
167 Roland Hooks .10 .25
168 Roger Carr .10 .25
169 San Diego Chargers TL .40 1.00
170 Ottis Anderson RC 1.50 4.00
171 Brian Sipe .40 1.00
172 Leonard Thompson .10 .25
173 Tony Reed .10 .25
174 Bob Tucker .10 .25
175 Joe Greene .40 1.00
176 Jack Dolbin .10 .25
177 Chuck Ramsey .10 .25
178 Paul Hofer .10 .25
179 Randy Logan .10 .25
180 David Lewis AP .10 .25
181 Duriel Harris .10 .25
182 June Jones .20 .50
183 Larry McCarren .10 .25
184 Ken Johnson RB .10 .25
185 Charlie Waters .20 .50
186 Noah Jackson .10 .25
187 Reggie Williams .20 .50
188 New England Patriots TL .20 .50
189 Carl Eller .40 1.00
190 Ed White AP .10 .25
191 Mario Clark .10 .25
192 Roosevelt Leaks .10 .25
193 Ted McKnight .10 .25
194 Danny Buggs .10 .25
195 Lester Hayes RC 1.50 4.00
196 Clarence Scott .10 .25
197 Saints TL/Wes Chandler .20 .50
198 Richard Caster .10 .25
199 Louie Giammona RC .10 .25
200 Terry Bradshaw 3.00 8.00
201 Ed Newman .10 .25
202 Fred Dryer .40 1.00
203 Dennis Franks .10 .25
204 Bob Breunig RC .20 .50
205 Alan Page .40 1.00
206 Earnest Gray RC .10 .25
207 Vikings TL/A.Rashad .40 1.00
208 Horace Ivory .10 .25
209 Isaac Hagins .10 .25
210 Gary Johnson AP .10 .25
211 Kevin Long .10 .25
212 Bill Thompson .10 .25
213 Don Bass .10 .25
214 George Starke RC .10 .25
215 Efren Herrera .10 .25
216 Theo Bell .10 .25
217 Monte Jackson .10 .25
218 Reggie McKenzie .10 .25
219 Bucky Dilts .10 .25
220 Lyle Alzado .40 1.00
221 Tim Foley .10 .25
222 Mark Arneson .10 .25
223 Fred Quillan .10 .25
224 Benny Ricardo .10 .25
225 Phil Simms RC 4.00 10.00
226 Bears TL/Walter Payton .50 1.25
227 Max Runager .10 .25
228 Barty Smith .10 .25
229 Jay Saldi .20 .50
230 John Hannah AP .40 1.00
231 Tim Wilson .10 .25
232 Jeff Van Note .10 .25
233 Henry Marshall .10 .25
234 Diron Talbert .10 .25
235 Garo Yepremian .20 .50
236 Larry Brown .10 .25
237 Clarence Williams RB RC .10 .25
238 Burgess Owens .10 .25
239 Vince Ferragamo .20 .50
240 Rickey Young .10 .25
241 Dave Logan .10 .25
242 Larry Gordon .10 .25
243 Terry Miller .10 .25
244 Baltimore Colts TL .40 1.00
245 Steve DeBerg .40 1.00
246 Checklist 133-264 .30 .75
247 Greg Latta .10 .25
248 Raymond Clayborn .20 .50
249 Jim Clack .10 .25
250 Drew Pearson .40 1.00
251 John Bunting .20 .50
252 Rob Lytle .10 .25
253 Jim Hart .40 1.00
254 John McDaniel .10 .25
255 Dave Pear AP .10 .25
256 Donnie Shell .40 1.00
257 Dan Doornink .10 .25
258 Wallace Francis RC .40 1.00
259 Dave Beverly .10 .25
260 Lee Roy Selmon AP .40 1.00
261 Doug Dieken .10 .25
262 Gary Davis RC .10 .25
263 Bob Rush .10 .25
264 Buffalo Bills TL .20 .50
265 Greg Landry .20 .50
266 Jan Stenerud .40 1.00
267 Tom Hicks .10 .25
268 Pat McInally .10 .25
269 Tim Fox .10 .25
270 Harvey Martin .20 .50
271 Dan Lloyd RC .10 .25
272 Mike Barber .10 .25
273 Wendell Tyler RC .40 1.00
274 Jeff Komlo RC .10 .25
275 Wes Chandler RC .40 1.00
276 Brad Dusek .10 .25
277 Charlie Johnson NT .10 .25
278 Dennis Swilley .10 .25
279 Johnny Evans .10 .25
280 Jack Lambert AP .60 1.50
281 Vern Den Herder .10 .25
282 Tampa Bay Bucs TL .40 1.00
283 Bob Klein .10 .25
284 Jim Turner .10 .25
285 Marvin Powell AP .20 .50
286 Aaron Kyle .10 .25
287 Dan Neal .10 .25
288 Wayne Morris .10 .25
289 Steve Bartkowski .20 .50
290 Dave Jennings AP .20 .50
291 John Smith .10 .25
292 Bill Gregory .10 .25
293 Frank Lewis .10 .25
294 Fred Cook .10 .25
295 David Hill AP .10 .25
296 Wade Key .10 .25
297 Sidney Thornton .10 .25
298 Charlie Hall .10 .25
299 Joe Lavender .10 .25
300 Tom Rafferty RC .10 .25
301 Mike Renfro RC .20 .50
302 Wilbur Jackson .20 .50
303 Packers TL/J.Lofton .40 1.00
304 Henry Childs .10 .25
305 Russ Washington AP .10 .25
306 Jim LeClair .10 .25
307 Tommy Hart .10 .25
308 Gary Barbaro .10 .25
309 Billy Taylor .10 .25
310 Ray Guy .20 .50
311 Don Hasselbeck RC .20 .50
312 Doug Williams .40 1.00
313 Nick Mike-Mayer .10 .25
314 Don McCauley .10 .25
315 Wesley Walker .40 1.00
316 Dan Dierdorf .40 1.00
317 Dave Brown DB RC .20 .50
318 Leroy Harris .10 .25
319 Steelers TL/Harris/Lambrt .40 1.00
320 Mark Moseley AP UER .10 .25
321 Mark Dennard .10 .25
322 Terry Nelson .10 .25
323 Tom Jackson .40 1.00
324 Rick Kane .10 .25
325 Jerry Sherk .10 .25
326 Ray Preston .10 .25
327 Golden Richards .10 .25
328 Randy Dean .10 .25
329 Rick Danmeier .10 .25
330 Tony Dorsett 2.50 6.00
331 R.Staubach/Fouts LL 1.25 3.00
332 Receiving Leaders .20 .50
333 Sacks Leaders .40 1.00
334 Scoring Leaders .40 1.00
335 Interception Leaders .40 1.00
336 Punting Leaders .40 1.00
337 Freddie Solomon .10 .25
338 Cincinnati Bengals TL/Jauron .40 1.00
339 Ken Stone .10 .25
340 Greg Buttle AP .10 .25
341 Bob Baumhower .20 .50
342 Billy Waddy .10 .25
343 Cliff Parsley .10 .25
344 Walter White .10 .25
345 Mike Thomas .10 .25
346 Neil O'Donoghue .10 .25
347 Freddie Scott .10 .25
348 Joe Ferguson .20 .50
349 Doug Nettles .10 .25
350 Mike Webster AP .40 1.00
351 Ron Saul .10 .25
352 Julius Adams .10 .25
353 Rafael Septien .10 .25
354 Cleo Miller .10 .25
355 Keith Simpson AP .10 .25
356 Johnny Perkins .10 .25
357 Jerry Sisemore .10 .25
358 Arthur Whittington .10 .25
359 Cardinals TL/Anderson .40 1.00
360 Rick Upchurch .20 .50
361 Kim Bokamper RC .10 .25
362 Roland Harper .10 .25
363 Pat Leahy .10 .25
364 Louis Breeden .10 .25
365 John Jefferson .40 1.00
366 Jerry Eckwood .10 .25
367 David Whitehurst .10 .25
368 Willie Parker C .10 .25
369 Ed Simonini .10 .25
370 Jack Youngblood AP .40 1.00
371 Don Warren RC .40 1.00
372 Andy Johnson .10 .25
373 D.D. Lewis .20 .50
374A Beasley Reece ERR RC .40 1.00
374B Beasley Reece COR RC .20 .50
375 L.C. Greenwood .40 1.00
376 Cleveland Browns TL .20 .50
377 Herman Edwards .10 .25
378 Rob Carpenter RC .10 .25
379 Herman Weaver .10 .25
380 Gary Fencik .10 .25
381 Don Strock .20 .50
382 Art Shell .40 1.00
383 Tim Mazzetti .10 .25
384 Bruce Harper .10 .25
385 Al (Bubba) Baker .20 .50
386 Conrad Dobler .10 .25
387 Stu Voigt .10 .25
388 Ken Anderson .40 1.00
389 Pat Tilley .10 .25
390 John Riggins .40 1.00
391 Checklist 265-396 .30 .75
392 Fred Dean .20 .50
393 Benny Barnes RC .10 .25
394 Los Angeles Rams TL .20 .50
395 Brad Van Pelt .10 .25
396 Eddie Hare .10 .25
397 John Sciarra RC .10 .25
398 Bob Jackson .10 .25
399 John Yarno .10 .25
400 Franco Harris AP .75 2.00
401 Ray Wersching .10 .25
402 Virgil Livers .10 .25
403 Raymond Chester .10 .25
404 Leon Gray .10 .25
405 Richard Todd .20 .50
406 Larry Little .40 1.00
407 Ted Fritsch Jr. .10 .25
408 Larry Mucker .10 .25
409 Jim Allen .10 .25
410 Randy Gradishar .40 1.00
411 Atlanta Falcons TL .40 1.00
412 Louie Kelcher .20 .50
413 Robert Newhouse .20 .50
414 Gary Shirk .10 .25
415 Mike Haynes AP .40 1.00
416 Craig Colquitt .10 .25
417 Lou Piccone .10 .25
418 Clay Matthews RC 1.50 4.00
419 Marvin Cobb .10 .25
420 Harold Carmichael AP .40 1.00
421 Uwe Von Schamann RC .20 .50
422 Mike Phipps .20 .50
423 Nolan Cromwell RC .40 1.00
424 Glenn Doughty .10 .25
425 Bob Young AP .10 .25
426 Tony Galbreath .10 .25
427 Luke Prestridge RC .10 .25
428 Terry Beeson .10 .25
429 Jack Tatum .20 .50
430 Lemar Parrish AP .10 .25
431 Chester Marcol .10 .25
432 Houston Oilers TL .40 1.00
433 John Fitzgerald .10 .25
434 Gary Jeter RC .20 .50
435 Steve Grogan .40 1.00
436 Jon Kolb UER .10 .25
437 Jim O'Bradovich UER .10 .25
438 Gerald Irons .10 .25
439 Jeff West .10 .25
440 Wilbert Montgomery .20 .50
441 Norris Thomas .10 .25
442 James Scott .10 .25
443 Curtis Brown .10 .25
444 Ken Fantetti .10 .25
445 Pat Haden .40 1.00
446 Carl Mauck .10 .25
447 Bruce Laird .10 .25
448 Otis Armstrong .10 .25
449 Gene Upshaw .40 1.00
450 Steve Largent AP 2.50 6.00
451 Benny Malone .10 .25
452 Steve Nelson .10 .25
453 Mark Cotney RC .10 .25
454 Joe Danelo .10 .25
455 Billy Joe DuPree .20 .50
456 Ron Johnson DB .10 .25
457 Archie Griffin .20 .50
458 Reggie Rucker .10 .25
459 Claude Humphrey .10 .25
460 Lydell Mitchell .20 .50
461 Steve Towle .10 .25
462 Revie Sorey .10 .25
463 Tom Skladany .10 .25
464 Clark Gaines .10 .25
465 Frank Corral .10 .25
466 Steve Fuller RC .20 .50
467 Ahmad Rashad AP .40 1.00
468 Oakland Raiders TL .40 1.00
469 Brian Peets .10 .25
470 Pat Donovan RC .20 .50
471 Ken Burrough .10 .25
472 Don Calhoun .10 .25
473 Bill Bryan .10 .25
474 Terry Jackson .10 .25
475 Joe Theismann .50 1.25
476 Jim Smith .20 .50
477 Joe DeLamielleure .40 1.00
478 Mike Pruitt AP .20 .50
479 Steve Mike-Mayer .10 .25
480 Bill Bergey .20 .50
481 Mike Fuller .10 .25
482 Bob Parsons .10 .25
483 Billy Brooks .10 .25
484 Jerome Barkum .10 .25
485 Larry Csonka .60 1.50
486 John Hill .10 .25
487 Mike Dawson .10 .25
488 Detroit Lions TL .20 .50
489 Ted Hendricks .40 1.00
490 Dan Pastorini .20 .50
491 Stanley Morgan .40 1.00
492 AFC Champs/Bleier .40 1.00
493 NFC Champs/Ferragamo .20 .50
494 Super Bowl XIV .40 1.00
495 Dwight White .20 .50
496 Haven Moses .10 .25
497 Guy Morriss .10 .25
498 Dewey Selmon .20 .50
499 Dave Butz RC .40 1.00
500 Chuck Foreman .20 .50
501 Chris Bahr .10 .25
502 Mark Miller QB .10 .25
503 Tony Greene .10 .25
504 Brian Kelley .10 .25
505 Joe Washington .20 .50
506 Butch Johnson .20 .50
507 New York Jets TL .20 .50
508 Steve Little .10 .25
509 Checklist 397-528 .30 .75
510 Mark Van Eeghen .10 .25
511 Gary Danielson .20 .50
512 Manu Tuiasosopo RC .10 .25
513 Paul Coffman RC .20 .50
514 Cullen Bryant .10 .25
515 Nat Moore .20 .50
516 Bill Lenkaitis .10 .25
517 Lynn Cain RC .10 .25
518 Gregg Bingham .10 .25
519 Ted Albrecht .10 .25
520 Dan Fouts AP .75 2.00
521 Bernard Jackson .10 .25
522 Coy Bacon .10 .25
523 Tony Franklin RC .20 .50
524 Bo Harris .10 .25
525 Bob Grupp AP .10 .25
526 San Francisco 49ers TL .40 1.00
527 Steve Wilson .10 .25
528 Bennie Cunningham .20 .50

1980 Topps Super

The 1980 Topps Superstar Photo Football set features 30 large (approximately 4 7/8" by 6 7/8") and very colorful cards. This set, a football counterpart to Topps' Superstar Photo Baseball set of the same year, is numbered and is printed on white stock. The cards in this set, sold over the counter without gum at retail establishments, could be individually chosen by the buyer.

COMPLETE SET (30) 7.50 15.00
1 Franco Harris .75 2.00
2 Bob Griese .75 2.00
3 Archie Manning .20 .50
4 Harold Carmichael .20 .50
5 Wesley Walker .20 .50
6 Richard Todd .15 .40
7 Dan Fouts .60 1.50
8 Ken Stabler 1.25 3.00
9 Jack Youngblood .20 .50
10 Jim Zorn .20 .50
11 Tony Dorsett 1.25 3.00
12 Lee Roy Selmon .30 .75
13 Russ Francis .15 .40
14 John Stallworth .30 .75
15 Terry Bradshaw 1.50 4.00
16 Joe Theismann .50 1.25
17 Ottis Anderson .30 .75
18 John Jefferson .30 .75
19 Jack Ham .30 .75
20 Joe Greene .40 1.00
21 Chuck Muncie .15 .40
22 Ron Jaworski .20 .50
23 John Hannah .20 .50
24 Randy Gradishar .15 .40
25 Jack Lambert .40 1.00
26 Ricky Bell .15 .40
27 Drew Pearson .30 .75
28 Rick Upchurch .15 .40
29 Brad Van Pelt .15 .40
30 Walter Payton 2.50 6.00

1980 Topps Team Checklists

These cards are essentially a parallel to the base 1980 Topps team checklist subset cards. The set was only available directly from Topps as a send-off offer in uncut sheet form. The prices below apply equally to uncut sheets as they are frequently found in their original uncut condition. As for individual cards, thin white card (almost paper-thin) stock makes it a challenge to find singles in top grades. We've cataloged the cards below for convenience in alphabetical order by team name.

COMPLETE SET (28) 50.00 100.00
19 Redskins TL 2.50 6.00
John Riggins
39 Chiefs TL 1.25 3.00
J.T.Smith
57 Seahawks TL 2.50 6.00
Steve Largent
76 Dolphins TL 2.50 6.00
Larry Csonka
94 New York Giants TL 1.25 3.00
113 Cowboys TL 3.00 8.00
Tony Dorsett
132 Philadelphia Eagles TL 1.50 4.00
151 Denver Broncos TL 1.50 4.00
169 San Diego Chargers TL 1.50 4.00
188 New England Patriots TL 1.25 3.00
197 Saints TL 1.25 3.00
Wes Chandler
207 Vikings TL 1.50 4.00
Ahmad Rashad
226 Bears TL 4.00 10.00
Walter Payton

Card	Low	High
244 Baltimore Colts TL	1.25	3.00
264 Buffalo Bills TL	1.25	3.00
282 Tampa Bay Bucs TL	1.50	4.00
303 Packers TL	1.50	4.00
James Lofton		
319 Steelers TL	2.50	6.00
Harris		
Lambrt		
338 Cincinnati Bengals TL	2.50	6.00
Jauron		
359 Cardinals TL	2.50	6.00
O.Anderson		
376 Cleveland Browns TL	1.25	3.00
394 Los Angeles Rams TL	1.50	4.00
411 Atlanta Falcons TL	1.50	4.00
432 Houston Oilers TL	1.50	4.00
468 Oakland Raiders TL	1.50	4.00
488 Detroit Lions TL	1.25	3.00
507 New York Jets TL	1.25	3.00
526 San Francisco 49ers TL	1.50	4.00

1981 Topps

The 1981 Topps football card set contains 528 standard-size cards. This set was issued in 15-card wax packs as well as rack packs and cello packs. The fronts have a pennant-like design at the bottom. This design includes the team name and the player's name. The player's position is also at the bottom. Horizontally designed backs contain year-by-year records, highlights and a cartoon. Super Action (SA) cards of top players are scattered throughout the set. Subsets include league leaders (1-6), Record Breakers (331-336) and playoffs (492-494). Team Leader (TL) cards feature statistical leaders on the front and a team checklist on the back. The key Rookie Card in this set is Joe Montana. Other Rookie Cards include Dwight Clark, Vince Evans, Dan Hampton, Art Monk, Eddie Murray, Billy Sims and Kellen Winslow.

Card	Low	High
COMPLETE SET (528)	75.00	150.00
1 Ron Jaworski	.40	1.00
B.Sipe LL		
2 K.Winslow	.40	1.00
Cooper LL		
3 Sack Leaders	.20	.50
4 Scoring Leaders	.10	.25
5 Interception Leaders	.20	.50
6 Punting Leaders	.10	.25
7 Don Calhoun	.10	.25
8 Jack Tatum	.20	.50
9 Reggie Rucker	.10	.25
10 Mike Webster AP	.40	1.00
11 Vince Evans RC	.40	1.00
12 Ottis Anderson SA	.40	1.00
13 Leroy Harris	.10	.25
14 Gordon King	.10	.25
15 Harvey Martin	.20	.50
16 Johnny Lam Jones RC	.20	.50
17 Ken Greene	.10	.25
18 Frank Lewis	.10	.25
19 Seahawks TL	.40	1.00
Largent		
20 Lester Hayes AP	.40	1.00
21 Uwe Von Schamann	.10	.25
22 Joe Washington	.10	.25
23 Louie Kelcher	.10	.25
24 Willie Miller	.10	.25
25 Steve Grogan	.40	1.00
26 John Hill	.10	.25
27 Stan White	.10	.25
28 William Andrews SA	.20	.50
29 Clarence Scott	.10	.25
30 Leon Gray AP	.10	.25
31 Craig Colquitt	.10	.25
32 Doug Williams	.40	1.00
33 Dob Dreunig	.20	.50
34 Billy Taylor	.10	.25
35 Harold Carmichael	.40	1.00
36 Ray Wersching	.10	.25
37 Dennis Johnson LB RC	.10	.25
38 Archie Griffin	.20	.50
39 Los Angeles Rams TL	.20	.50
40 Gary Fencik	.20	.50
41 Lynn Dickey	.10	.25
42 Steve Bartkowski SA	.20	.50
43 Art Shell	.40	1.00
44 Wilbur Jackson	.10	.25
45 Frank Corral	.10	.25
46 Ted McKnight	.10	.25
47 Joe Klecko	.20	.50
48 Dan Doornink	.10	.25
49 Doug Dieken	.10	.25
50 Jerry Robinson RC	.20	.50
51 Wallace Francis	.10	.25
52 Dave Preston RC	.10	.25
53 Jay Saldi	.10	.25
54 Rush Brown	.10	.25
55 Phil Simms	1.00	2.50
56 Nick Mike-Mayer	.10	.25
57 Redskins TL	.75	2.00
A.Monk		
58 Mike Renfro	.10	.25
59 Ted Brown SA	.10	.25
60 Steve Nelson	.10	.25
61 Sidney Thornton	.10	.25
62 Kent Hill	.10	.25
63 Don Bessillieu	.10	.25
64 Fred Cook	.10	.25
65 Raymond Chester	.10	.25
66 Rick Kane	.10	.25
67 Mike Fuller	.10	.25
68 Dewey Selmon	.20	.50
69 Charles White RC	.40	1.00
70 Jeff Van Note	.10	.25
71 Robert Newhouse	.20	.50
72 Roynell Young RC	.10	.25
73 Lynn Cain SA	.10	.25
74 Mike Friede	.10	.25
75 Earl Cooper RC	.10	.25
76 New Orleans Saints TL	.20	.50
77 Rick Danmeier	.10	.25
78 Darrol Ray RC	.10	.25
79 Gregg Bingham	.10	.25
80 John Hannah AP	.40	1.00
81 Jack Thompson	.20	.50
82 Rick Upchurch	.20	.50
83 Mike Butler	.10	.25
84 Don Warren	.10	.25
85 Mark Van Eeghen	.10	.25
86 J.T. Smith RC	.40	1.00
87 Herman Weaver	.10	.25
88 Terry Bradshaw SA	1.00	2.50
89 Charlie Hall	.10	.25
90 Donnie Shell	.40	1.00
91 Ike Harris	.10	.25
92 Charlie Johnson	.10	.25
93 Rickey Watts	.10	.25
94 New England Patriots TL	.40	1.00
95 Drew Pearson	.40	1.00
96 Neil O'Donoghue	.10	.25
97 Conrad Dobler	.10	.25
98 Jewerl Thomas RC	.10	.25
99 Mike Barber	.10	.25
100 Billy Sims AP RC	1.25	3.00
101 Vern Den Herder	.10	.25
102 Greg Landry	.20	.50
103 Joe Cribbs SA	.20	.50
104 Mark Murphy RC	.10	.25
105 Chuck Muncie	.20	.50
106 Alfred Jackson	.20	.50
107 Chris Bahr	.10	.25
108 Gordon Jones	.10	.25
109 Willie Harper RC	.10	.25
110 Dave Jennings	.10	.25
111 Bennie Cunningham	.10	.25
112 Jerry Sisemore	.10	.25
113 Cleveland Browns TL	.40	1.00
114 Rickey Young	.10	.25
115 Ken Anderson	.40	1.00
116 Randy Gradishar	.40	1.00
117 Eddie Lee Ivery RC	.10	.25
118 Wesley Walker	.40	1.00
119 Chuck Foreman	.20	.50
120 Nolan Cromwell UER	.20	.50
121 Curtis Dickey SA	.10	.25
122 Wayne Morris	.10	.25
123 Greg Stemrick	.10	.25
124 Coy Bacon	.10	.25
125 Jim Zorn	.20	.50
126 Henry Childs	.10	.25
127 Checklist 1-132	.40	1.00
128 Len Walterscheid	.10	.25
129 Johnny Evans	.10	.25
130 Gary Barbaro	.10	.25
131 Jim Smith	.10	.25
132 New York Jets TL	.20	.50
133 Curtis Brown	.10	.25
134 D.D. Lewis	.10	.25
135 Jim Plunkett	.40	1.00
136 Nat Moore	.20	.50
137 Don McCauley	.10	.25
138 Tony Dorsett SA	.40	1.00
139 Julius Adams	.10	.25
140 Ahmad Rashad AP	.40	1.00
141 Rich Saul	.10	.25
142 Ken Fantetti	.10	.25
143 Kenny Johnson	.10	.25
144 Clark Gaines	.10	.25
145 Mark Moseley	.10	.25
146 Vernon Perry RC	.10	.25
147 Jerry Eckwood	.10	.25
148 Freddie Solomon	.10	.25
149 Jerry Sherk	.10	.25
150 Kellen Winslow RC	3.00	8.00
151 Packers TL	.40	1.00
Lofton		
152 Ross Browner	.10	.25
153 Dan Fouts SA	.40	1.00
154 Woody Peoples	.10	.25
155 Jack Lambert	.50	1.25
156 Mike Dennis	.10	.25
157 Rafael Septien	.10	.25
158 Archie Manning	.40	1.00
159 Don Hasselbeck	.10	.25
160 Alan Page AP	.40	1.00
161 Arthur Whittington	.10	.25
162 Billy Waddy	.10	.25
163 Horace Belton	.10	.25
164 Luke Prestridge	.10	.25
165 Joe Theismann	.50	1.25
166 Morris Towns	.10	.25
167 Dave Brown	.10	.25
168 Ezra Johnson	.10	.25
169 Tampa Bay Bucs TL	.10	.25
170 Joe DeLamielleure	.40	1.00
171 Earnest Gray SA	.10	.25
172 Mike Thomas	.10	.25
173 Jim Haslett RC	.75	2.00
174 David Woodley RC	.20	.50
175 Al(Bubba) Baker	.20	.50
176 Nesby Glasgow RC	.10	.25
177 Pat Leahy	.10	.25
178 Tom Brahaney RC	.10	.25
179 Herman Edwards	.10	.25
180 Junior Miller AP RC	.10	.25
181 Richard Wood RC	.10	.25
182 Lenvil Elliott	.10	.25
183 Sammie White	.20	.50
184 Russell Erxleben	.10	.25
185 Ed Too Tall Jones	.50	1.25
186 Ray Guy SA	.20	.50
187 Haven Moses	.10	.25
188 New York Giants TL	.20	.50
189 David Whitehurst	.10	.25
190 John Jefferson AP	.40	1.00
191 Terry Beeson	.10	.25
192 Dan Ross RC	.20	.50
193 Dave Williams RB RC	.10	.25
194 Art Monk RC	6.00	15.00
195 Roger Wehrli	.20	.50
196 Ricky Feacher	.10	.25
197 Miami Dolphins TL	.40	1.00
198 Carl Roaches RC	.10	.25
199 Billy Campfield	.10	.25
200 Ted Hendricks AP	.40	1.00
201 Fred Smerlas RC	.40	1.00
202 Walter Payton SA	3.00	8.00
203 Luther Bradley	.10	.25
204 Herb Scott	.10	.25
205 Jack Youngblood	.40	1.00
206 Danny Pittman	.10	.25
207 Houston Oilers TL	.20	.50
208 Vagas Ferguson RC	.20	.50
209 Mark Dennard	.10	.25
210 Lemar Parrish	.10	.25
211 Bruce Harper	.10	.25
212 Ed Simonini	.10	.25
213 Nick Lowery RC	.40	1.00
214 Kevin House RC	.20	.50
215 Mike Kenn RC	.40	1.00
216 Joe Montana RC	50.00	100.00
217 Joe Senser	.10	.25
218 Lester Hayes SA	.20	.50
219 Gene Upshaw	.40	1.00
220 Franco Harris	.60	1.50
221 Ron Bolton	.10	.25
222 Charles Alexander RC	.20	.50
223 Matt Robinson	.10	.25
224 Ray Oldham	.10	.25
225 George Martin	.10	.25
226 Buffalo Bills TL	.40	1.00
227 Tony Franklin	.10	.25
228 George Cumby	.10	.25
229 Butch Johnson	.20	.50
230 Mike Haynes	.40	1.00
231 Rob Carpenter	.20	.50
232 Steve Fuller	.20	.50
233 John Sawyer	.10	.25
234 Kenny King SA	.10	.25
235 Jack Ham	.50	1.25
236 Jimmy Rogers RC	.10	.25
237 Bob Parsons	.10	.25
238 Marty Lyons RC	.40	1.00
239 Pat Tilley	.10	.25
240 Dennis Harrah	.10	.25
241 Thom Darden	.10	.25
242 Rolf Benirschke	.10	.25
243 Gerald Small	.10	.25
244 Atlanta Falcons TL	.40	1.00
245 Roger Carr	.10	.25
246 Sherman White	.10	.25
247 Ted Brown	.10	.25
248 Matt Cavanaugh	.20	.50
249 John Dutton	.10	.25
250 Bill Bergey AP	.20	.50
251 Jim Allen	.10	.25
252 Mike Nelms SA	.10	.25
253 Tom Blanchard	.10	.25
254 Ricky Thompson	.10	.25
255 John Matuszak	.20	.50
256 Randy Grossman	.10	.25
257 Ray Griffin RC	.10	.25
258 Lynn Cain	.10	.25
259 Checklist 133-264	.40	1.00
260 Mike Pruitt	.20	.50
261 Chris Ward RC	.10	.25
262 Fred Steinfort	.10	.25
263 James Owens RC	.10	.25
264 Bears TL	.60	1.50
Payton		
Hampton		
265 Dan Fouts	.60	1.50
266 Arnold Morgado	.10	.25
267 John Jefferson SA	.40	1.00
268 Bill Lenkaitis	.10	.25
269 James Jones	.10	.25
270 Brad Van Pelt	.10	.25
271 Steve Largent	1.25	2.50
272 Elvin Bethea	.40	1.00
273 Cullen Bryant	.10	.25
274 Gary Danielson	.20	.50
275 Tony Galbreath	.10	.25
276 Dave Butz	.10	.25
277 Steve Mike-Mayer	.10	.25
278 Ron Johnson	.10	.25
279 Tom DeLeone	.10	.25
280 Ron Jaworski	.40	1.00
281 Mel Gray	.10	.25
282 San Diego Chargers TL	.40	1.00
283 Mark Brammer RC	.10	.25
284 Alfred Jenkins SA	.20	.50
285 Greg Buttle	.10	.25
286 Randy Hughes	.10	.25
287 Delvin Williams	.10	.25
288 Brian Baschnagel	.10	.25
289 Gary Jeter	.10	.25
290 Stanley Morgan AP	.40	1.00
291 Gerry Ellis	.10	.25
292 Al Richardson	.10	.25
293 Jimmie Giles	.20	.50
294 Dave Jennings SA	.10	.25
295 Wilbert Montgomery	.20	.50
296 Dave Pureifory	.10	.25
297 Greg Hawthorne	.10	.25
298 Dick Ambrose	.10	.25
299 Terry Hermeling	.10	.25
300 Danny White	.40	1.00
301 Ken Burrough	.10	.25
302 Paul Hofer	.10	.25
303 Denver Broncos TL	.40	1.00
304 Eddie Payton	.20	.50
305 Isaac Curtis	.20	.50
306 Benny Ricardo	.10	.25
307 Riley Odoms	.10	.25
308 Bob Chandler	.10	.25
309 Larry Heater	.10	.25
310 Art Still AP RC	.40	1.00
311 Harold Jackson	.20	.50
312 Charlie Joiner SA	.40	1.00
313 Jeff Nixon	.10	.25
314 Aundra Thompson	.10	.25
315 Richard Todd	.20	.50
316 Dan Hampton RC	1.25	3.00
317 Doug Marsh	.10	.25
318 Louie Giammona	.10	.25
319 49ers TL	.40	1.00
Dwight Clark		
320 Manu Tuiasosopo	.10	.25
321 Rich Milot	.10	.25
322 Mike Guman RC	.10	.25
323 Bob Kuechenberg	.20	.50
324 Tom Skladany	.10	.25
325 Dave Logan	.10	.25
326 Bruce Laird	.10	.25
327 James Jones SA	.10	.25
328 Joe Danelo	.10	.25
329 Kenny King RC	.20	.50
330 Pat Donovan	.10	.25
331 Earl Cooper RB	.20	.50
332 John Jefferson RB	.40	1.00
333 Kenny King RB	.20	.50
334 Rod Martin RB	.20	.50
335 Jim Plunkett RB	.40	1.00
336 Bill Thompson RB	.20	.50
337 John Cappelletti	.20	.50
338 Lions TL	.40	1.00
Billy Sims		
339 Don Smith	.10	.25
340 Rod Perry	.10	.25
341 David Lewis	.10	.25
342 Mark Gastineau RC	.50	1.25
343 Steve Largent SA	.40	1.00
344 Charle Young	.10	.25
345 Toni Fritsch	.10	.25
346 Matt Blair	.20	.50
347 Don Bass	.10	.25
348 Jim Jensen RC	.20	.50
349 Karl Lorch	.10	.25
350 Brian Sipe AP	.20	.50
351 Theo Bell	.10	.25
352 Sam Adams	.10	.25
353 Paul Coffman	.10	.25
354 Eric Harris	.10	.25
355 Tony Hill	.20	.50
356 J.T. Turner	.10	.25
357 Frank LeMaster	.10	.25
358 Jim Jodat	.10	.25
359 Raiders TL	.40	1.00
Hendricks		
360 Joe Cribbs AP RC	.40	1.00
361 James Lofton SA	.40	1.00
362 Dexter Bussey	.10	.25
363 Bobby Jackson	.10	.25
364 Steve DeBerg	.40	1.00
365 Ottis Anderson	.40	1.00
366 Tom Myers	.10	.25
367 John James	.10	.25
368 Reese McCall	.10	.25
369 Jack Reynolds	.20	.50
370 Gary Johnson	.10	.25
371 Jimmy Cefalo	.10	.25
372 Horace Ivory	.10	.25
373 Garo Yepremian	.10	.25
374 Brian Kelley	.10	.25
375 Terry Bradshaw	3.00	8.00
376 Cowboys TL	.40	1.00
Tony Dorsett		
377 Randy Logan	.10	.25
378 Tim Wilson	.10	.25
379 Archie Manning SA	.40	1.00
380 Revie Sorey	.10	.25
381 Randy Holloway	.10	.25
382 Henry Lawrence	.10	.25
383 Pat McInally	.10	.25
384 Kevin Long	.10	.25
385 Louis Wright	.20	.50
386 Leonard Thompson	.10	.25
387 Jan Stenerud	.20	.50
388 Raymond Butler RC	.10	.25
389 Checklist 265-396	.40	1.00
390 Steve Bartkowski AP	.20	.50
391 Clarence Harmon	.10	.25
392 Wilbert Montgomery SA	.20	.50
393 Billy Joe DuPree	.20	.50
394 Kansas City Chiefs TL	.20	.50
395 Earnest Gray	.10	.25
396 Ray Hamilton	.10	.25
397 Brenard Wilson	.10	.25
398 Calvin Hill	.20	.50
399 Robin Cole	.10	.25
400 Walter Payton	6.00	15.00
401 Jim Hart	.40	1.00
402 Ron Yary	.20	.50
403 Cliff Branch	.40	1.00
404 Roland Hooks	.10	.25
405 Ken Stabler	1.25	3.00
406 Chuck Ramsey	.10	.25
407 Mike Nelms RC	.10	.25
408 Ron Jaworski SA	.20	.50
409 James Hunter	.10	.25
410 Lee Roy Selmon AP	.40	1.00
411 Baltimore Colts TL	.20	.50
412 Henry Marshall	.10	.25
413 Preston Pearson	.20	.50
414 Richard Bishop	.10	.25
415 Greg Pruitt	.20	.50
416 Matt Bahr	.20	.50
417 Tom Mullady	.10	.25
418 Glen Edwards	.10	.25
419 Sam McCullum	.10	.25
420 Stan Walters	.10	.25
421 George Roberts	.10	.25
422 Dwight Clark RC	2.00	5.00
423 Pat Thomas RC	.10	.25
424 Bruce Harper SA	.10	.25
425 Craig Morton	.20	.50
426 Derrick Gaffney	.10	.25
427 Pete Johnson	.10	.25
428 Wes Chandler	.40	1.00
429 Burgess Owens	.10	.25
430 James Lofton AP	.75	2.00
431 Tony Reed	.10	.25
432 Vikings TL	.40	1.00
A.Rashad		
433 Ron Springs RC	.20	.50
434 Tim Fox	.10	.25
435 Ozzie Newsome	.75	2.00
436 Steve Furness	.10	.25
437 Will Lewis	.10	.25
438 Mike Hartenstine	.10	.25
439 John Bunting	.10	.25
440 Eddie Murray RC	.40	1.00
441 Mike Pruitt SA	.20	.50
442 Larry Swider	.10	.25
443 Steve Freeman	.10	.25
444 Bruce Hardy RC	.10	.25
445 Pat Haden	.20	.50
446 Curtis Dickey RC	.10	.25
447 Doug Wilkerson	.10	.25
448 Alfred Jenkins	.20	.50
449 Dave Dalby	.10	.25
450 Robert Brazile	.10	.25
451 Bobby Hammond	.10	.25
452 Raymond Clayborn	.10	.25
453 Jim Miller P RC	.10	.25
454 Roy Simmons	.10	.25
455 Charlie Waters	.20	.50
456 Ricky Bell	.40	1.00
457 Ahmad Rashad SA	.40	1.00
458 Don Cockroft	.10	.25
459 Keith Krepfle	.10	.25
460 Marvin Powell	.10	.25
461 Tommy Kramer	.40	1.00
462 Jim LeClair	.10	.25
463 Freddie Scott	.10	.25
464 Rob Lytle	.10	.25
465 Johnnie Gray	.10	.25
466 Doug France RC	.10	.25
467 Carlos Carson RC	.20	.50
468 Cardinals TL	.40	1.00
O.Anderson		
469 Efren Herrera	.10	.25
470 Randy White AP	.50	1.25
471 Richard Caster	.10	.25
472 Andy Johnson	.10	.25
473 Billy Sims SA	.40	1.00
474 Joe Lavender	.10	.25
475 Harry Carson	.20	.50
476 John Stallworth	.50	1.25
477 Bob Thomas	.10	.25
478 Keith Wright RC	.10	.25
479 Ken Stone	.10	.25
480 Carl Hairston	.20	.50
481 Reggie McKenzie	.10	.25
482 Bob Griese	.60	1.50
483 Mike Bragg	.10	.25
484 Scott Dierking	.10	.25
485 David Hill	.10	.25
486 Brian Sipe SA	.20	.50
487 Rod Martin RC	.20	.50
488 Cincinnati Bengals TL	.20	.50
489 Preston Dennard	.10	.25
490 John Smith	.10	.25
491 Mike Reinfeldt	.10	.25
492 NFC Champs	.40	1.00
Jaworski		
493 AFC Champs	.40	1.00
Plunkett		
494 Super Bowl XV	.40	1.00
J.Plunkett		
495 Joe Greene	.50	1.25
496 Charlie Joiner	.40	1.00
497 Rolland Lawrence	.10	.25
498 Al(Bubba) Baker SA	.20	.50
499 Brad Dusek	.10	.25
500 Tony Dorsett	1.50	4.00
501 Robin Earl	.10	.25
502 Theotis Brown RC	.10	.25
503 Joe Ferguson	.20	.50
504 Beasley Reece	.10	.25
505 Lyle Alzado	.40	1.00
506 Tony Nathan RC	.40	1.00
507 Philadelphia Eagles TL	.20	.50
508 Herb Orvis	.10	.25
509 Clarence Williams	.10	.25
510 Ray Guy AP	.20	.50
511 Jeff Komlo	.10	.25
512 Freddie Solomon SA	.10	.25
513 Tim Mazzetti	.10	.25
514 Elvis Peacock RC	.10	.25
515 Russ Francis	.20	.50
516 Roland Harper	.10	.25
517 Checklist 397-528	.40	1.00
518 Billy Johnson	.20	.50
519 Dan Dierdorf	.40	1.00
520 Fred Dean	.20	.50
521 Jerry Butler	.10	.25
522 Ron Saul	.10	.25
523 Charlie Smith	.10	.25
524 Kellen Winslow SA	1.25	3.00
525 Bert Jones	.40	1.00
526 Steelers TL	.40	1.00
Fr.Harris		
527 Duriel Harris	.10	.25
528 William Andrews	.40	1.00

1981 Topps Team Checklists

These cards are essentially a parallel to the base 1981 Topps team checklist subset cards. The set was only available directly from Topps as a send-off offer in uncut sheet form. The prices below apply equally to uncut sheets as they are frequently found in their original uncut condition. As for individual cards, thin white card (almost paper-thin) stock makes it a challenge to find singles in top grades. We've cataloged the cards below for convenience in alphabetical order by team name.

Card	Low	High
COMPLETE SET (28)	40.00	100.00
19 Seahawks TL	2.00	5.00
Larg		
J.Green		
39 Los Angeles Rams TL	1.50	4.00
57 Redskins TL	2.00	5.00
Art Monk		
76 New Orleans Saints TL	1.50	4.00
94 New England Patriots TL	1.25	3.00
113 Cleveland Browns TL	1.50	4.00
132 New York Jets TL	1.25	3.00
151 Packers TL	2.00	5.00
James Lofton		
169 Tampa Bay Buccaneers TL	1.50	4.00
188 New York Giants TL	1.25	3.00
197 Miami Dolphins TL	1.50	4.00
207 Houston Oilers TL	1.25	3.00
226 Buffalo Bills TL	1.50	4.00
244 Atlanta Falcons TL	1.50	4.00
264 Bears TL	3.00	8.00
Payton		
Hampton		
282 San Diego Chargers TL	1.50	4.00
303 Denver Broncos TL	1.50	4.00
319 49ers TL	1.50	4.00
Dwight Clark		
338 Lions TL	1.50	4.00
Billy Sims		
359 Raiders TL	2.00	5.00
Ted Hendricks		
376 Cowboys TL	2.50	6.00
Tony Dorsett		
394 Kansas City Chiefs TL	1.25	3.00
411 Baltimore Colts TL	1.25	3.00
432 Vikings TL	1.50	4.00
Ahmad Rashad		
468 Cardinals TL	1.50	4.00
O.Anderson		
488 Cincinnati Bengals TL	1.25	3.00
507 Philadelphia Eagles TL	1.25	3.00
526 Steelers TL	2.00	5.00
Franco Harris		

1981 Topps Thirst Break

This is a 56-card set of individual wax paper gum wrappers, similar to a Bazooka Comic. These wrappers were issued in Thirst Break Orange Gum, which was reportedly distributed in Pennsylvania and Ohio. Each of these small gum wrappers has a comic-style image of a particular great moment in sports. As the checklist below shows, many different sports are represented in this set. The wrappers each measure approximately 2 9/16" by 1 5/8". The wrappers are numbered in small print at the top. The backs of the wrappers are blank. The "1981 Topps" copyright is at the bottom of each card. There was an orange and green outer wrapper that did not have player images.

Card	Low	High
COMPLETE SET (56)	60.00	150.00
29 Garo Yepremian	.40	1.00
30 Bert Jones	.75	2.00
31 Norm Van Brocklin	1.00	2.50
32 Fran Tarkenton	2.00	5.00
33 Johnny Unitas	2.00	5.00
36 Bart Starr	2.00	5.00
37 O.J. Simpson	.75	2.00
38 Jim Brown	2.00	5.00
Football Fact		
39 Jim Marshall	1.00	2.50
40 George Blanda	1.00	2.50
41 Jack Tatum	1.00	2.50
42 Jim Brown UER	2.00	5.00
48 Tom Dempsey	.60	1.50
49 Gale Sayers	1.60	4.00

1982 Topps

The 1982 Topps football set features 528 standard-size cards and marked a breakthrough of sorts. Wax packs contained 15 cards. Licensed by NFL Properties for the first time, Topps was able to use team logos within its photos. Previously, logos on helmets were airbrushed. Card fronts contained a team helmet at bottom left and the player's name and position within a color banner at bottom right. Horizontally designed backs featured yearly statistics and highlights. Subsets include Record Breakers (1-6), playoffs (7-9), league leaders (257-262) and brothers (263-270). In-Action (IA) cards of top players are scattered throughout the set. Team Leader (TL) cards feature statistical leaders on the front as well as a team checklist on the back. The set is organized in team order alphabetically by team within conference (and with players within teams in alphabetical order). Rookie Cards include James Brooks, Cris Collinsworth, Drew Hill, Ronnie Lott, Freeman McNeil, Anthony Munoz and Lawrence Taylor.

Card	Low	High
COMPLETE SET (528)	40.00	80.00
1 Ken Anderson RB	.40	1.00
2 Dan Fouts RB	.40	1.00
3 LeRoy Irvin RB	.10	.25
4 Stump Mitchell RB	.10	.25
5 George Rogers RB	.40	1.00
6 Dan Ross RB	.10	.25
7 AFC Champs	.40	1.00
K.Anderson		
8 NFC Champs	.40	1.00
E.Cooper		
9 Super Bowl XVI	.40	1.00
A.Munoz		
10 Baltimore Colts TL	.10	.25
11 Raymond Butler	.10	.25
12 Roger Carr	.10	.25
13 Curtis Dickey	.20	.50
14 Zachary Dixon	.10	.25
15 Nesby Glasgow	.10	.25
16 Bert Jones	.40	1.00
17 Bruce Laird	.10	.25
18 Reese McCall	.10	.25
19 Randy McMillan	.10	.25
20 Ed Simonini	.10	.25
21 Buffalo Bills TL	.20	.50
22 Mark Brammer	.10	.25
23 Curtis Brown	.10	.25
24 Jerry Butler	.10	.25
25 Mario Clark	.10	.25
26 Joe Cribbs	.20	.50
27 Joe Cribbs IA	.20	.50
28 Joe Ferguson	.20	.50
29 Jim Haslett	.40	1.00
30 Frank Lewis	.10	.25
31 Frank Lewis IA	.10	.25
32 Shane Nelson	.10	.25
33 Charles Romes	.10	.25
34 Bill Simpson	.10	.25
35 Fred Smerlas	.10	.25
36 Bengals TL	.20	.50
C.Collinswort		
37 Charles Alexander	.10	.25
38 Ken Anderson AP	.40	1.00
39 Ken Anderson IA	.40	1.00
40 Jim Breech	.10	.25
41 Jim Breech IA	.10	.25
42 Louis Breeden	.10	.25
43 Ross Browner	.10	.25
44 Cris Collinsworth RC	1.00	2.50
45 Cris Collinsworth IA	.40	1.00
46 Isaac Curtis	.10	.25
47 Pete Johnson	.10	.25
48 Pete Johnson IA	.10	.25
49 Steve Kreider	.10	.25
50 Pat McInally	.10	.25
51 Anthony Munoz RC	4.00	10.00
52 Dan Ross	.10	.25
53 David Verser RC	.10	.25
54 Reggie Williams	.20	.50
55 Browns TL	.20	.50
O.Newsome		
56 Lyle Alzado	.40	1.00
57 Dick Ambrose	.10	.25
58 Ron Bolton	.10	.25
59 Steve Cox	.10	.25
60 Joe DeLamielleure	.40	1.00
61 Tom DeLeone	.10	.25
62 Doug Dieken	.10	.25
63 Ricky Feacher	.10	.25
64 Don Goode	.10	.25
65 Robert L.Jackson RC	.10	.25
66 Dave Logan	.10	.25
67 Ozzie Newsome	.50	1.25
68 Ozzie Newsome IA	.40	1.00
69 Greg Pruitt	.20	.50
70 Mike Pruitt	.20	.50
71 Mike Pruitt IA	.20	.50
72 Reggie Rucker	.10	.25
73 Clarence Scott	.10	.25
74 Brian Sipe	.20	.50
75 Charles White	.20	.50
76 Denver Broncos TL	.20	.50
77 Rubin Carter RC	.10	.25
78 Steve Foley	.10	.25
79 Randy Gradishar	.20	.50
80 Tom Jackson	.40	1.00
81 Craig Morton	.20	.50
82 Craig Morton IA	.20	.50
83 Riley Odoms	.10	.25
84 Rick Parros	.10	.25
85 Dave Preston	.10	.25
86 Tony Reed	.10	.25
87 Bob Swenson RC	.10	.25
88 Bill Thompson	.10	.25
89 Rick Upchurch	.20	.50
90 Steve Watson RC	.20	.50
91 Steve Watson IA	.10	.25
92 Houston Oilers TL	.10	.25
93 Mike Barber	.10	.25
94 Elvin Bethea	.40	1.00
95 Gregg Bingham	.10	.25
96 Robert Brazile	.10	.25
97 Ken Burrough	.10	.25
98 Toni Fritsch	.10	.25
99 Leon Gray	.10	.25
100 Gifford Nielsen RC	.20	.50
101 Vernon Perry	.10	.25
102 Mike Reinfeldt	.10	.25
103 Mike Renfro	.10	.25
104 Carl Roaches	.10	.25
105 Ken Stabler	.75	2.00
106 Greg Stemrick	.08	.25
107 J.C. Wilson	.10	.25
108 Tim Wilson	.10	.25
109 Kansas City Chiefs TL	.10	.25
110 Gary Barbaro	.10	.25
111 Brad Budde RC	.10	.25
112 Joe Delaney AP RC	.40	1.00
113 Joe Delaney IA	.20	.50
114 Steve Fuller	.10	.25
115 Gary Green	.10	.25
116 James Hadnot	.10	.25
117 Eric Harris	.10	.25
118 Billy Jackson	.10	.25
119 Bill Kenney RC	.10	.25
120 Nick Lowery AP	.40	1.00
121 Nick Lowery IA	.20	.50
122 Henry Marshall	.10	.25
123 J.T. Smith	.20	.50
124 Art Still	.10	.25
125 Miami Dolphins TL	.20	.50
126 Bob Baumhower	.20	.50
127 Glenn Blackwood RC	.10	.25
128 Jimmy Cefalo	.10	.25
129 A.J. Duhe	.20	.50
130 Andra Franklin RC	.10	.25
131 Duriel Harris	.10	.25
132 Nat Moore	.20	.50
133 Tony Nathan	.20	.50
134 Ed Newman	.10	.25
135 Earnie Rhone	.10	.25
136 Don Strock	.10	.25
137 Tommy Vigorito	.10	.25
138 Uwe Von Schamann	.10	.25
139 Uwe Von Schamann IA	.10	.25
140 David Woodley	.20	.50
141 New England Pats TL	.20	.50
142 Julius Adams	.10	.25
143 Richard Bishop	.10	.25
144 Matt Cavanaugh	.10	.25
145 Raymond Clayborn	.10	.25
146 Tony Collins RC	.10	.25
147 Vagas Ferguson	.10	.25
148 Tim Fox	.10	.25
149 Steve Grogan	.20	.50
150 John Hannah AP	.40	1.00
151 John Hannah IA	.20	.50
152 Don Hasselbeck	.10	.25
153 Mike Haynes	.20	.50
154 Harold Jackson	.20	.50
155 Andy Johnson	.10	.25
156 Stanley Morgan	.20	.50
157 Stanley Morgan IA	.20	.50
158 Steve Nelson	.10	.25
159 Rod Shoate RC	.10	.25
160 Jets TL	.20	.50
F.McNeil		
161 Dan Alexander RC	.10	.25
162 Mike Augustyniak	.10	.25
163 Jerome Barkum	.10	.25
164 Greg Buttle	.10	.25
165 Scott Dierking	.10	.25
166 Joe Fields	.10	.25
167 Mark Gastineau AP	.20	.50
168 Mark Gastineau IA	.20	.50
169 Bruce Harper	.10	.25
170 Johnny Lam Jones	.10	.25
171 Joe Klecko AP	.20	.50
172 Joe Klecko IA	.20	.50
173 Pat Leahy	.20	.50
174 Pat Leahy IA	.10	.25
175 Marty Lyons	.20	.50
176 Freeman McNeil RC	.40	1.00
177 Marvin Powell	.10	.25
178 Chuck Ramsey	.10	.25
179 Darrol Ray	.10	.25
180 Abdul Salaam	.10	.25
181 Richard Todd	.20	.50
182 Richard Todd IA	.20	.50
183 Wesley Walker	.20	.50
184 Chris Ward	.10	.25
185 Oakland Raiders TL	.20	.50
186 Cliff Branch	.40	1.00
187 Bob Chandler	.10	.25
188 Ray Guy	.20	.50
189 Lester Hayes	.20	.50
190 Ted Hendricks AP	.40	1.00
191 Monte Jackson	.10	.25
192 Derrick Jensen	.10	.25
193 Kenny King	.10	.25
194 Rod Martin	.10	.25
195 John Matuszak	.20	.50
196 Matt Millen RC	.60	1.50
197 Derrick Ramsey	.10	.25
198 Art Shell	.40	1.00
199 Mark Van Eeghen	.10	.25
200 Arthur Whittington	.10	.25
201 Marc Wilson RC	.20	.50
202 Steelers TL	.40	1.00
Fr.Harris		
203 Mel Blount AP	.40	1.00
204 Terry Bradshaw	2.00	5.00
205 Terry Bradshaw IA	.75	2.00
206 Craig Colquitt	.10	.25
207 Bennie Cunningham	.10	.25
208 Russell Davis RC	.10	.25
209 Gary Dunn	.10	.25
210 Jack Ham	.40	1.00
211 Franco Harris	.50	1.25
212 Franco Harris IA	.40	1.00
213 Jack Lambert AP	.40	1.00
214 Jack Lambert IA	.40	1.00
215 Mark Malone RC	.40	1.00
216 Frank Pollard RC	.10	.25
217 Donnie Shell AP	.40	1.00
218 Jim Smith	.10	.25
219 John Stallworth	.40	1.00
220 John Stallworth IA	.40	1.00
221 David Trout	.10	.25
222 Mike Webster AP	.40	1.00
223 San Diego Chargers TL	.40	1.00
224 Rolf Benirschke	.10	.25
225 Rolf Benirschke IA	.10	.25
226 James Brooks RC	.40	1.00
227 Willie Buchanon	.10	.25
228 Wes Chandler	.40	1.00
229 Wes Chandler IA	.20	.50
230 Dan Fouts	.50	1.25
231 Dan Fouts IA	.40	1.00
232 Gary Johnson	.10	.25
233 Charlie Joiner	.40	1.00
234 Charlie Joiner IA	.40	1.00
235 Louie Kelcher	.10	.25
236 Chuck Muncie	.20	.50
237 Chuck Muncie IA	.10	.25
238 George Roberts	.10	.25
239 Ed White	.10	.25
240 Doug Wilkerson	.10	.25
241 Kellen Winslow AP	.75	2.00
242 Kellen Winslow IA	.40	1.00
243 Seahawks TL	.40	1.00
S.Largent		
244 Theotis Brown	.10	.25
245 Dan Doornink	.10	.25
246 John Harris RC	.10	.25
247 Efren Herrera	.10	.25
248 David Hughes	.10	.25
249 Steve Largent	.75	2.00
250 Steve Largent IA	.40	1.00
251 Sam McCullum	.10	.25
252 Sherman Smith	.10	.25
253 Manu Tuiasosopo	.10	.25
254 John Yarno	.10	.25
255 Jim Zorn	.20	.50
256 Jim Zorn IA	.20	.50
257 J.Montana	1.50	4.00
Anderson LL		
258 Kellen Winslow	.40	1.00
Clark LL		
259 QB Sack Leaders	.10	.25
260 Scoring Leaders	.20	.50
261 Interception Leaders	.20	.50
262 Punting Leaders	.10	.25
263 Brothers: Bahr	.10	.25
264 Brothers: Blackwood	.20	.50
265 Brothers: Brock	.10	.25
266 Brothers: Griffin	.20	.50
267 Brothers: Hannah	.40	1.00
268 Brothers: Jackson	.10	.25
269 Walter	.50	1.25
Eddie Payton		
270 Brothers: Selmon	.40	1.00
271 Atlanta Falcons TL	.20	.50
272 William Andrews	.20	.50
273 William Andrews IA	.20	.50
274 Steve Bartkowski	.20	.50
275 Steve Bartkowski IA	.20	.50
276 Bobby Butler RC	.10	.25
277 Lynn Cain	.10	.25
278 Wallace Francis	.10	.25
279 Alfred Jackson	.10	.25
280 John James	.10	.25
281 Alfred Jenkins	.10	.25
282 Alfred Jenkins IA	.10	.25
283 Kenny Johnson	.10	.25
284 Mike Kenn AP	.40	1.00
285 Fulton Kuykendall	.10	.25
286 Mick Luckhurst RC	.10	.25
287 Mick Luckhurst IA	.10	.25
288 Junior Miller	.10	.25
289 Al Richardson	.10	.25
290 R.C. Thielemann RC	.10	.25
291 Jeff Van Note	.10	.25
292 Bears TL	.40	1.00
Walter Payton		
293 Brian Baschnagel	.10	.25
294 Robin Earl	.10	.25
295 Vince Evans	.20	.50
296 Gary Fencik	.10	.25
297 Dan Hampton	.40	1.00
298 Noah Jackson	.10	.25
299 Ken Margerum	.10	.25
300 Jim Osborne	.10	.25
301 Bob Parsons	.10	.25
302 Walter Payton	4.00	10.00
303 Walter Payton IA	2.00	5.00
304 Revie Sorey	.10	.25
305 Matt Suhey RC	.60	1.50
306 Rickey Watts	.10	.25
307 Cowboys TL	.40	1.00
Dorsett		
308 Bob Breunig	.10	.25
309 Doug Cosbie RC	.10	.25
310 Pat Donovan	.10	.25
311 Tony Dorsett AP	.75	2.00
312 Tony Dorsett IA	.40	1.00
313 Michael Downs RC	.10	.25
314 Billy Joe DuPree	.20	.50
315 John Dutton	.10	.25
316 Tony Hill	.20	.50
317 Butch Johnson	.20	.50
318 Ed Too Tall Jones AP	.40	1.00
319 James Jones	.10	.25
320 Harvey Martin	.20	.50
321 Drew Pearson	.40	1.00
322 Herb Scott AP	.10	.25
323 Rafael Septien	.10	.25
324 Rafael Septien IA	.10	.25
325 Ron Springs	.20	.50
326 Dennis Thurman RC	.10	.25
327 Everson Walls RC	.40	1.00
328 Everson Walls IA	.40	1.00
329 Danny White	.40	1.00
330 Danny White IA	.20	.50
331 Randy White AP	.40	1.00
332 Randy White IA	.40	1.00
333 Detroit Lions TL	.20	.50
334 Jim Allen	.10	.25
335 Al(Bubba) Baker	.20	.50
336 Dexter Bussey	.10	.25
337 Doug English	.20	.50
338 Ken Fantetti	.10	.25
339 William Gay RC	.10	.25
340 David Hill	.10	.25
341 Eric Hipple RC	.10	.25
342 Rick Kane	.10	.25
343 Ed Murray	.40	1.00
344 Ed Murray IA	.20	.50
345 Ray Oldham	.10	.25
346 Dave Pureifory	.10	.25
347 Freddie Scott	.10	.25
348 Freddie Scott IA	.10	.25
349 Billy Sims AP	.40	1.00
350 Billy Sims IA	.40	1.00
351 Tom Skladany	.10	.25
352 Leonard Thompson	.10	.25
353 Stan White	.10	.25
354 Packers TL	.40	1.00
Lofton		
355 Paul Coffman	.10	.25
356 George Cumby	.10	.25
357 Lynn Dickey	.10	.25
358 Lynn Dickey IA	.10	.25
359 Gerry Ellis	.10	.25
360 Maurice Harvey	.10	.25
361 Harlan Huckleby	.10	.25
362 John Jefferson	.40	1.00
363 Mark Lee RC	.10	.25
364 James Lofton AP	.50	1.25
365 James Lofton IA	.40	1.00
366 Jan Stenerud	.20	.50
367 Jan Stenerud IA	.20	.50
368 Rich Wingo	.10	.25

1982 Topps

Card	Low	High
369 Los Angeles Rams TL	.20	.50
370 Frank Corral	.10	.25
371 Nolan Cromwell AP	.20	.50
372 Nolan Cromwell IA	.20	.50
373 Preston Dennard	.10	.25
374 Mike Fanning	.10	.25
375 Doug France	.10	.25
376 Mike Guman	.10	.25
377 Pat Haden	.20	.50
378 Dennis Harrah	.10	.25
379 Drew Hill RC	.40	1.00
380 LeRoy Irvin RC	.10	.25
381 Cody Jones	.10	.25
382 Rod Perry	.10	.25
383 Rich Saul	.10	.25
384 Pat Thomas	.10	.25
385 Wendell Tyler	.20	.50
386 Wendell Tyler IA	.20	.50
387 Billy Waddy	.10	.25
388 Jack Youngblood	.40	1.00
389 Minnesota Vikings TL	.10	.25
390 Matt Blair	.10	.25
391 Ted Brown	.10	.25
392 Ted Brown IA	.10	.25
393 Rick Danmeier	.10	.25
394 Tommy Kramer	.20	.50
395 Mark Mullaney	.10	.25
396 Eddie Payton	.10	.25
397 Ahmad Rashad	.40	1.00
398 Joe Senser	.10	.25
399 Joe Senser IA	.10	.25
400 Sammie White	.20	.50
401 Sammie White IA	.10	.25
402 Ron Yary	.40	1.00
403 Rickey Young	.10	.25
404 Saints TL	.30	.75
Ric.Jackson		
405 Russell Erxleben	.10	.25
406 Elois Grooms	.10	.25
407 Jack Holmes	.10	.25
408 Archie Manning	.40	1.00
409 Derland Moore RC	.10	.25
410 George Rogers RC	.40	1.00
411 George Rogers IA	.40	1.00
412 Toussaint Tyler	.10	.25
413 Dave Waymer RC	.10	.25
414 Wayne Wilson	.10	.25
415 New York Giants TL	.10	.25
416 Scott Brunner RC	.10	.25
417 Rob Carpenter	.10	.25
418 Harry Carson AP	.20	.50
419 Bill Currier	.10	.25
420 Joe Danelo	.10	.25
421 Joe Danelo IA	.10	.25
422 Mark Haynes RC	.10	.25
423 Terry Jackson	.10	.25
424 Dave Jennings	.10	.25
425 Gary Jeter	.10	.25
426 Brian Kelley	.10	.25
427 George Martin	.10	.25
428 Curtis McGriff	.10	.25
429 Bill Neill	.10	.25
430 Johnny Perkins	.10	.25
431 Beasley Reece	.10	.25
432 Gary Shirk	.10	.25
433 Phil Simms	1.00	1.50
434 Lawrence Taylor RC	8.00	20.00
435 Lawrence Taylor IA	4.00	10.00
436 Brad Van Pelt	.10	.25
437 Philadelphia Eagles TL	.20	.50
438 John Bunting	.10	.25
439 Billy Campfield	.10	.25
440 Harold Carmichael	.40	1.00
441 Harold Carmichael IA	.40	1.00
442 Herman Edwards	.10	.25
443 Tony Franklin	.10	.25
444 Tony Franklin IA	.10	.25
445 Carl Hairston	.10	.25
446 Dennis Harrison RC	.10	.25
447 Ron Jaworski	.40	1.00
448 Charlie Johnson	.10	.25
449 Keith Krepfle	.10	.25
450 Frank LeMaster	.10	.25
451 Randy Logan	.10	.25
452 Wilbert Montgomery	.20	.50
453 Wilbert Montgomery IA	.20	.50
454 Hubie Oliver	.10	.25
455 Jerry Robinson	.10	.25
456 Jerry Robinson IA	.10	.25
457 Jerry Sisemore	.10	.25
458 Charlie Smith	.10	.25
459 Stan Walters	.10	.25
460 Brenard Wilson	.10	.25
461 Roynell Young	.10	.25
462 Cardinals TL	.20	.50
O.Anderson		
463 Ottis Anderson	.40	1.00
464 Ottis Anderson IA	.40	1.00
465 Carl Birdsong	.10	.25
466 Rush Brown	.10	.25
467 Mel Gray	.20	.50
468 Ken Greene	.10	.25
469 Jim Hart	.40	1.00
470 E.J. Junior RC	.20	.50
471 Neil Lomax RC	.40	1.00
472 Stump Mitchell RC	.40	1.00
473 Wayne Morris	.10	.25
474 Neil O'Donoghue	.10	.25
475 Pat Tilley	.10	.25
476 Pat Tilley IA	.10	.25
477 49ers TL	.20	.50
Dwight Clark		
478 Dwight Clark	.40	1.00
479 Dwight Clark IA	.40	1.00
480 Earl Cooper	.10	.25
481 Randy Cross	.20	.50
482 Johnny Davis RC	.10	.25
483 Fred Dean	.20	.50
484 Fred Dean IA	.10	.25
485 Dwight Hicks RC	.40	1.00
486 Ronnie Lott RC	8.00	20.00
487 Ronnie Lott IA	2.50	6.00
488 Joe Montana AP	6.00	15.00
489 Joe Montana IA	5.00	12.00
490 Ricky Patton	.10	.25
491 Jack Reynolds	.20	.50
492 Freddie Solomon	.10	.25
493 Ray Wersching	.10	.25
494 Charle Young	.10	.25
495 Tampa Bay Bucs TL	.20	.50
496 Cedric Brown	.10	.25
497 Neal Colzie	.10	.25
498 Jerry Eckwood	.10	.25
499 Jimmie Giles	.20	.50
500 Hugh Green RC	.40	1.00
501 Kevin House	.10	.25
502 Kevin House IA	.10	.25
503 Cecil Johnson	.10	.25
504 James Owens	.10	.25
505 Lee Roy Selmon AP	.40	1.00
506 Mike Washington	.10	.25
507 James Wilder RC	.20	.50
508 Doug Williams	.20	.50
509 Redskins TL	.40	1.00
Monk		
510 Perry Brooks	.10	.25
511 Dave Butz	.20	.50
512 Wilbur Jackson	.10	.25
513 Joe Lavender	.10	.25
514 Terry Metcalf	.20	.50
515 Art Monk	1.25	3.00
516 Mark Moseley	.10	.25
517 Mark Murphy	.10	.25
518 Mike Nelms	.10	.25
519 Lemar Parrish	.10	.25
520 John Riggins	.40	1.00
521 Joe Theismann	.40	1.00
522 Ricky Thompson	.10	.25
523 Don Warren UER	.10	.25
524 Joe Washington	.20	.50
525 Checklist 1-132	.40	1.00
526 Checklist 133-264	.40	1.00
527 Checklist 265-396	.40	1.00
528 Checklist 397-528	.40	1.00

1982 Topps Team Checklists

These cards are essentially a parallel to the base 1982 Topps team checklist subset cards. The set was only available directly from Topps as a send-off offer in uncut sheet form. The prices below apply equally to uncut sheets as they are frequently found in their original uncut condition. As for individual cards, thin white card (almost paper-thin) stock makes it a challenge to find singles in top grades. We've cataloged the cards below for convenience in alphabetical order by team name.

Card	Low	High
COMPLETE SET (28)	40.00	100.00
10 Baltimore Colts TL	1.25	3.00
21 Buffalo Bills TL	1.50	4.00
36 Bengals TL	1.50	4.00
C.Collinswort		
55 Browns TL	1.50	4.00
Ozzie Newsome		
76 Denver Broncos TL	1.50	4.00
92 Houston Oilers TL	1.25	3.00
109 Kansas City Chiefs TL	1.25	3.00
125 Miami Dolphins TL	1.50	4.00
141 New England Pats TL	1.25	3.00
160 Jets TL	1.50	4.00
Freeman McNeil		
185 Oakland Raiders TL	1.50	4.00
202 Steelers TL	2.00	5.00
Franco Harris		
223 San Diego Chargers TL	1.50	4.00
243 Seahawks TL	2.00	5.00
S.Largent		
271 Atlanta Falcons TL	1.50	4.00
292 Bears TL	3.00	8.00
Walter Payton		
307 Cowboys TL	2.50	6.00
Tony Dorsett		
333 Detroit Lions TL	1.50	4.00
354 Packers TL	2.00	5.00
James Lofton		
369 Los Angeles Rams TL	1.50	4.00
389 Minnesota Vikings TL	1.25	3.00
404 Saints TL	1.50	4.00
Rickey Jackson		
415 New York Giants TL	1.25	3.00
437 Philadelphia Eagles TL	1.50	4.00
462 Cardinals TL	1.50	4.00
O.Anderson		
477 49ers TL	1.50	4.00
Dwight Clark		
495 Tampa Bay Bucs TL	1.50	4.00
509 Redskins TL	2.00	5.00
Art Monk		

1983 Topps

After issuing 528-card sets since 1973, Topps dropped to 396 standard-size cards for 1983. The set was printed on four sheets. As a result, there are 132 double-printed cards which are noted in the checklist below by DP. The card fronts contain the player's name and position at the bottom in a rectangular area that differs in color according to team. Team names are in block letters at the top of the cards. The backs of the cards contain yearly statistics and a "Personal Facts" section. All the text is printed over a faint white team helmet. Subsets include Record Breakers (1-9), playoffs (10-12) and league leaders (202-207). The Team Leader (TL) cards are distributed throughout the set as the first card of the team sequence. The design of these cards differs from previous years in that only one leader (usually the team's rushing leader) is pictured. The backs contain team scoring information from the previous season. The team numbering is arranged alphabetically within each conference (with players ordered alphabetically within team). Rookie Cards include Marcus Allen, Gary Anderson (K), Todd Christensen, Roy Green, Jim McMahon, and Mike Singletary.

Card	Low	High
COMPLETE SET (396)	30.00	60.00
1 Ken Anderson RB	.25	.60
2 Tony Dorsett RB	.25	.60
3 Dan Fouts RB	.25	.60
4 Joe Montana RB	1.50	3.00
5 Mark Moseley RB	.15	.40
6 Mike Nelms RB	.10	.25
7 Darrol Ray RB	.10	.25
8 John Riggins RB	.25	.60
9 Fulton Walker RB	.10	.25
10 NFC Champs/Riggins	.25	.60
11 AFC Championship	.15	.40
12 Super Bowl XVII/Riggins	.10	.25
13 Falcons TL/Andrews	.15	.40
14 William Andrews DP	.15	.40
15 Steve Bartkowski	.15	.40
16 Bobby Butler	.10	.25
17 Buddy Curry	.10	.25
18 Alfred Jackson DP	.10	.25
19 Alfred Jenkins	.10	.25
20 Kenny Johnson	.10	.25
21 Mike Kenn	.10	.25
22 Mick Luckhurst	.10	.25
23 Junior Miller	.10	.25
24 Al Richardson	.10	.25
25 Gerald Riggs DP RC	.15	.40
26 R.C. Thielemann	.10	.25
27 Jeff Van Note	.10	.25
28 Bears TL/W.Payton	.40	1.00
29 Brian Baschnagel	.10	.25
30 Dan Hampton PB	.25	.60
31 Mike Hartenstine	.10	.25
32 Noah Jackson	.10	.25
33 Jim McMahon RC	4.00	10.00
34 Emery Moorehead DP	.10	.25
35 Bob Parsons	.10	.25
36 Walter Payton	3.00	8.00
37 Terry Schmidt	.10	.25
38 Mike Singletary RC	4.00	10.00
39 Matt Suhey DP	.15	.40
40 Rickey Watts DP	.10	.25
41 Otis Wilson DP RC	.15	.40
42 Cowboys TL/T.Dorsett	.25	.60
43 Bob Breunig	.15	.40
44 Doug Cosbie	.10	.25
45 Pat Donovan	.10	.25
46 Tony Dorsett DP PB	.40	1.00
47 Tony Hill	.15	.40
48 Butch Johnson DP	.15	.40
49 Ed Jones DP PB	.25	.60
50 Harvey Martin DP	.15	.40
51 Drew Pearson	.25	.60
52 Rafael Septien	.10	.25
53 Ron Springs DP	.10	.25
54 Dennis Thurman	.10	.25
55 Everson Walls PB	.15	.40
56 Danny White DP PB	.25	.60
57 Randy White PB	.25	.60
58 Detroit Lions TL	.15	.40
59 Al(Bubba) Baker DP	.15	.40
60 Dexter Bussey DP	.10	.25
61 Gary Danielson DP	.10	.25
62 Keith Dorney DP	.10	.25
63 Doug English	.10	.25
64 Ken Fantetti DP	.10	.25
65 Alvin Hall DP	.10	.25
66 David Hill DP	.10	.25
67 Eric Hipple	.10	.25
68 Ed Murray DP	.15	.40
69 Freddie Scott	.10	.25
70 Billy Sims DP PB	.15	.40
71 Tom Skladany DP	.10	.25
72 Leonard Thompson DP	.10	.25
73 Bobby Watkins	.10	.25
74 Green Bay Packers TL	.10	.25
75 John Anderson	.10	.25
76 Paul Coffman	.10	.25
77 Lynn Dickey	.10	.25
78 Mike Douglass DP	.10	.25
79 Eddie Lee Ivery	.10	.25
80 John Jefferson DP PB	.25	.60
81 Ezra Johnson	.10	.25
82 Mark Lee	.10	.25
83 James Lofton PB	.25	.60
84 Larry McCarren	.10	.25
85 Jan Stenerud DP	.15	.40
86 Los Angeles Rams TL	.10	.25
87 Bill Bain DP RC	.10	.25
88 Nolan Cromwell	.15	.40
89 Preston Dennard	.10	.25
90 Vince Ferragamo DP	.15	.40
91 Mike Guman	.10	.25
92 Kent Hill	.10	.25
93 Mike Lansford DP RC	.10	.25
94 Rod Perry	.10	.25
95 Pat Thomas DP	.10	.25
96 Jack Youngblood	.25	.60
97 Minnesota Vikings TL	.10	.25
98 Matt Blair	.10	.25
99 Ted Brown	.10	.25
100 Greg Coleman	.10	.25
101 Randy Holloway	.10	.25
102 Tommy Kramer	.15	.40
103 Doug Martin DP RC	.10	.25
104 Mark Mullaney	.10	.25
105 Joe Senser	.10	.25
106 Willie Teal DP	.10	.25
107 Sammie White	.15	.40
108 Rickey Young	.10	.25
109 New Orleans Saints TL	.15	.40
110 Stan Brock RC	.10	.25
111 Bruce Clark RC	.10	.25
112 Russell Erxleben DP	.10	.25
113 Russell Gary	.10	.25
114 Jeff Groth DP	.10	.25
115 John Hill DP	.10	.25
116 Derland Moore	.10	.25
117 George Rogers PB	.15	.40
118 Ken Stabler	.60	1.50
119 Wayne Wilson	.10	.25
120 New York Giants TL	.10	.25
121 Scott Brunner	.10	.25
122 Rob Carpenter	.10	.25
123 Harry Carson PB	.15	.40
124 Joe Danelo DP	.10	.25
125 Earnest Gray	.10	.25
126 Mark Haynes DP	.15	.40
127 Terry Jackson	.10	.25
128 Dave Jennings	.10	.25
129 Brian Kelley	.10	.25
130 George Martin	.10	.25
131 Tom Mullady	.10	.25
132 Johnny Perkins	.10	.25
133 Lawrence Taylor PB	2.00	5.00
134 Brad Van Pelt	.10	.25
135 Butch Woolfolk DP RC	.10	.25
136 Philadelphia Eagles TL	.15	.40
137 Harold Carmichael	.25	.60
138 Herman Edwards	.10	.25
139 Tony Franklin DP	.10	.25
140 Carl Hairston DP	.10	.25
141 Dennis Harrison DP	.10	.25
142 Ron Jaworski DP	.15	.40
143 Frank LeMaster	.10	.25
144 Wilbert Montgomery DP	.15	.40
145 Guy Morriss	.10	.25
146 Jerry Robinson	.10	.25
147 Max Runager	.10	.25
148 Ron Smith DP RC	.10	.25
149 John Spagnola	.10	.25
150 Stan Walters DP	.10	.25
151 Roynell Young DP	.10	.25
152 Cardinals TL	.15	.40
O.Anderson		
153 Ottis Anderson	.25	.60
154 Carl Birdsong	.10	.25
155 Dan Dierdorf DP	.25	.60
156 Roy Green RC	.25	.60
157 Elois Grooms	.10	.25
158 Neil Lomax DP	.15	.40
159 Wayne Morris	.10	.25
160 Tootie Robbins RC	.10	.25
161 Luis Sharpe RC	.10	.25
162 Pat Tilley	.10	.25
163 San Francisco 49ers TL	.10	.25
164 Dwight Clark PB	.25	.60
165 Randy Cross	.15	.40
166 Russ Francis	.15	.40
167 Dwight Hicks	.10	.25
168 Ronnie Lott PB	1.25	2.50
169 Joe Montana DP	4.00	10.00
170 Jeff Moore	.10	.25
171 R.Nehemiah DP RC	.25	.60
172 Freddie Solomon	.10	.25
173 Ray Wersching DP	.10	.25
174 Tampa Bay Bucs TL	.10	.25
175 Cedric Brown	.10	.25
176 Bill Capece	.10	.25
177 Neal Colzie	.10	.25
178 Jimmie Giles	.10	.25
179 Hugh Green PB	.15	.40
180 Kevin House DP	.10	.25
181 James Owens	.10	.25
182 Lee Roy Selmon PB	.25	.60
183 Mike Washington	.10	.25
184 James Wilder	.10	.25
185 Doug Williams DP	.15	.40
186 Redskins TL/J.Riggins	.25	.60
187 Jeff Bostic DP RC	.40	1.00
188 Charlie Brown PB RC	.15	.40
189 Vernon Dean DP RC	.10	.25
190 Joe Jacoby RC	1.25	3.00
191 Dexter Manley RC	.15	.40
192 Rich Milot	.10	.25
193 Art Monk DP	.40	1.00
194 Mark Moseley DP	.10	.25
195 Mike Nelms	.10	.25
196 Neal Olkewicz DP	.10	.25
197 Tony Peters	.10	.25
198 John Riggins DP	.25	.60
199 Joe Theismann PB	.25	.60
200 Don Warren	.10	.25
201 Jeris White DP	.10	.25
202 Theismann/K.Anderson LL	.25	.60
203 Receiving Leaders	.15	.40
204 T.Dorsett/F.McNeil LL	.25	.60
205 M.Allen	.50	1.25
W.Tyler LL		
206 Interception Leaders	.15	.40
207 Punting Leaders	.10	.25
208 Baltimore Colts TL	.10	.25
209 Matt Bouza	.10	.25
210 Johnie Cooks DP RC	.10	.25
211 Curtis Dickey	.10	.25
212 Nesby Glasgow DP	.10	.25
213 Derrick Hatchett	.10	.25
214 Randy McMillan	.10	.25
215 Mike Pagel RC	.15	.40
216 Rohn Stark DP RC	.15	.40
217 Donnell Thompson DP RC	.10	.25
218 Leo Wisniewski DP	.10	.25
219 Buffalo Bills TL	.15	.40
220 Curtis Brown	.10	.25
221 Jerry Butler	.10	.25
222 Greg Cater DP	.10	.25
223 Joe Cribbs	.15	.40
224 Joe Ferguson	.15	.40
225 Roosevelt Leaks	.10	.25
226 Frank Lewis	.10	.25
227 Eugene Marve RC	.10	.25
228 Fred Smerlas DP PB	.10	.25
229 Ben Williams DP RC	.10	.25
230 Cincinnati Bengals TL	.10	.25
231 Charles Alexander	.10	.25
232 Ken Anderson DP PB	.25	.60
233 Jim Breech DP	.10	.25
234 Ross Browner	.10	.25
235 Cris Collinsworth DP PB	.25	.60
236 Isaac Curtis	.10	.25
237 Pete Johnson	.10	.25
238 Steve Kreider DP	.10	.25
239 Max Montoya DP RC	.10	.25
240 Anthony Munoz PB	.40	1.00
241 Ken Riley	.10	.25
242 Dan Ross	.10	.25
243 Reggie Williams	.15	.40
244 Cleveland Browns TL	.15	.40
245 Chip Banks DP RC	.15	.40
246 Tom Cousineau DP RC	.15	.40
247 Joe DeLamielleure DP	.15	.40
248 Doug Dieken DP	.10	.25
249 Hanford Dixon RC	.10	.25
250 Ricky Feacher DP	.10	.25
251 Lawrence Johnson DP	.10	.25
252 Dave Logan DP	.10	.25
253 Paul McDonald DP RC	.10	.25
254 Ozzie Newsome DP	.25	.60
255 Mike Pruitt	.15	.40
256 Clarence Scott DP	.10	.25
257 Brian Sipe DP	.15	.40
258 Dwight Walker DP	.10	.25
259 Charles White	.15	.40
260 Denver Broncos TL	.10	.25
261 Steve DeBerg DP	.15	.40
262 Randy Gradishar DP PB	.15	.40
263 Rulon Jones DP RC	.10	.25
264 Rich Karlis DP	.10	.25
265 Don Latimer	.10	.25
266 Rick Parros DP	.10	.25
267 Luke Prestridge	.10	.25
268 Rick Upchurch	.15	.40
269 Steve Watson DP	.10	.25
270 Gerald Willhite DP	.10	.25
271 Houston Oilers TL	.10	.25
272 Harold Bailey	.10	.25
273 Jesse Baker DP	.10	.25
274 Gregg Bingham DP	.10	.25
275 Robert Brazile DP	.10	.25
276 Donnie Craft	.10	.25
277 Daryl Hunt RC	.10	.25
278 Archie Manning DP	.15	.40
279 Gifford Nielsen	.10	.25
280 Mike Renfro	.10	.25
281 Carl Roaches DP	.10	.25
282 Kansas City Chiefs TL	.15	.40
283 Gary Barbaro	.10	.25
284 Joe Delaney	.10	.25
285 Jeff Gossett RC	.25	.60
286 Gary Green DP	.10	.25
287 Eric Harris DP	.10	.25
288 Billy Jackson DP	.10	.25
289 Bill Kenney DP	.10	.25
290 Nick Lowery	.25	.60
291 Henry Marshall	.10	.25
292 Art Still DP	.10	.25
293 Raiders TL	.75	2.00
M.Allen		
294 Marcus Allen DP RC	6.00	15.00
295 Lyle Alzado	.25	.60
296 Chris Bahr DP	.10	.25
297 Cliff Branch	.25	.60
298 Todd Christensen RC	.30	.75
299 Ray Guy	.15	.40
300 Frank Hawkins DP	.10	.25
301 Lester Hayes DP	.10	.25
302 Ted Hendricks DP PB	.25	.60
303 Kenny King DP	.10	.25
304 Rod Martin	.10	.25
305 Matt Millen DP	.25	.60
306 Burgess Owens	.10	.25
307 Jim Plunkett	.25	.60
308 Miami Dolphins TL	.15	.40
309 Bob Baumhower	.10	.25
310 Glenn Blackwood	.10	.25
311 Lyle Blackwood DP	.10	.25
312 A.J. Duhe	.10	.25
313 Andra Franklin	.10	.25
314 Duriel Harris	.10	.25
315 Bob Kuechenberg DP	.15	.40
316 Don McNeal RC	.10	.25
317 Tony Nathan	.15	.40
318 Ed Newman	.10	.25
319 Earnie Rhone DP	.10	.25
320 Joe Rose DP	.10	.25
321 Don Strock DP	.10	.25
322 Uwe Von Schamann	.10	.25
323 David Woodley DP	.15	.40
324 New England Pats TL	.10	.25
325 Julius Adams	.10	.25
326 Pete Brock	.10	.25
327 Rich Camarillo DP RC	.10	.25
328 Tony Collins DP	.10	.25
329 Steve Grogan	.15	.40
330 John Hannah PB	.25	.60
331 Don Hasselbeck	.10	.25
332 Mike Haynes	.15	.40
333 Roland James RC	.10	.25
334A Stanley Morgan ERR IL	.25	.60
334B Stanley Morgan COR	.15	.40
335 Steve Nelson	.10	.25
336 Kenneth Sims DP	.10	.25
337 Mark Van Eeghen	.15	.40
338 New York Jets TL	.15	.40
339 Greg Buttle	.10	.25
340 Joe Fields	.10	.25
341 Mark Gastineau DP	.15	.40
342 Bruce Harper	.10	.25
343 Bobby Jackson	.10	.25
344 Bobby Jones	.10	.25
345 Johnny Lam Jones DP	.10	.25
346 Joe Klecko	.15	.40
347 Marty Lyons	.10	.25
348 Freeman McNeil PB	.25	.60
349 Lance Mehl RC	.10	.25
350 Marvin Powell DP	.10	.25
351 Darrol Ray DP	.10	.25
352 Abdul Salaam	.10	.25
353 Richard Todd	.15	.40
354 Wesley Walker PB	.15	.40
355 Steelers TL/F.Harris	.25	.60
356 Gary Anderson DP RC	2.50	6.00
357 Mel Blount DP	.25	.60
358 Terry Bradshaw DP	.60	1.50
359 Larry Brown	.10	.25
360 Bennie Cunningham	.10	.25
361 Gary Dunn	.10	.25
362 Franco Harris	.30	.75
363 Jack Lambert PB	.25	.60
364 Frank Pollard	.10	.25
365 Donnie Shell	.15	.40
366 John Stallworth PB	.25	.60
367 Loren Toews	.10	.25
368 Mike Webster DP PB	.25	.60
369 Dwayne Woodruff RC	.10	.25
370 San Diego Chargers TL	.15	.40
371 Rolf Benirschke DP	.10	.25
372 James Brooks	.25	.60
373 Wes Chandler	.15	.40
374 Dan Fouts DP PB	.25	.60
375 Tim Fox	.10	.25
376 Gary Johnson	.10	.25
377 Charlie Joiner DP	.25	.60
378 Louie Kelcher	.10	.25
379 Chuck Muncie	.10	.25
380 Cliff Thrift	.10	.25
381 Doug Wilkerson	.10	.25
382 Kellen Winslow PB	.30	.75
383 Seattle Seahawks TL	.10	.25
384 Kenny Easley RC	.25	.60
385 Jacob Green RC	.15	.40
386 John Harris	.10	.25
387 Michael Jackson	.10	.25
388 Norm Johnson RC	.10	.25
389 Steve Largent	.50	1.25
390 Keith Simpson	.10	.25
391 Sherman Smith	.10	.25
392 Jeff West DP	.10	.25
393 Jim Zorn DP	.15	.40
394 Checklist 1-132	.25	.60
395 Checklist 133-264	.25	.60
396 Checklist 265-396	.25	.60

1983 Topps Sticker Inserts

The 1983 Topps Football Sticker Inserts come as a set of 33 full-sized cards and were issued as inserts to the 1983 Topps wax packs. They were printed in the USA, whereas the smaller stickers of the previous two years were printed in Italy. The player's name, number, position, and team are included in a plaque at the bottom of the front of the card. The backs are parts of three puzzles, distinguished by either a red (A), blue (B), or green (C) border, each showing a different action scene from the previous year's Super Bowl between the Washington Redskins and Miami Dolphins. The actual set numbering is alphabetical by player's name.

Card	Low	High
COMPLETE SET (33)	6.00	15.00
1 Marcus Allen	1.25	3.00
2 Ken Anderson	.25	.60
3 Ottis Anderson	.15	.40
4 William Andrews	.15	.40
5 Terry Bradshaw	.60	1.50
6 Wes Chandler	.10	.25
7 Dwight Clark	.15	.40
8 Cris Collinsworth	.15	.40
9 Joe Cribbs	.10	.25
10 Nolan Cromwell	.10	.25
11 Tony Dorsett	.60	1.50
12 Dan Fouts	.30	.75
13 Mark Gastineau	.10	.25
14 Jimmie Giles	.10	.25
15 Franco Harris	.30	.75
16 Ted Hendricks	.15	.40
17 Tony Hill	.10	.25
18 John Jefferson	.15	.40
19 James Lofton	.25	.60
20 Freeman McNeil	.10	.25
21 Joe Montana	2.50	6.00
22 Mark Moseley	.10	.25
23 Ozzie Newsome	.25	.60
24 Walter Payton	1.50	4.00
25 John Riggins	.30	.75
26 Billy Sims	.15	.40
27 John Stallworth	.25	.60
28 Lawrence Taylor	.40	1.00
29 Joe Theismann	.25	.60
30 Richard Todd	.10	.25
31 Wesley Walker	.10	.25
32 Danny White	.15	.40
33 Kellen Winslow	.25	.60

1984 Topps

The 1984 Topps football card set contains 396 standard-size cards. Wax packs have 15 cards inside. Card photos are bordered in different colors depending on the player's team. The team logo and team name are at the bottom with the player's name in a red bar at the top. Horizontally designed green tinted backs have yearly statistics, highlights and a cartoon. Subsets include Record Breakers (1-6), playoffs (7-9) and league leaders (202-207). Team Leader (TL) cards primarily feature the team's rushing leader. The backs contain team scoring information from the previous year. Instant Replay (IR) cards of top players are scattered throughout the set. Cards are numbered and alphabetically arranged within teams except for the Colts which moved from Baltimore to Indianapolis. The set features the Rookie Cards of Morten Andersen, Roger Craig, Eric Dickerson, John Elway, Willie Gault, Darrell Green, Rickey Jackson, Dave Krieg, Howie Long, Dan Marino, Andre Tippett and Curt Warner.

Card	Low	High
COMPLETE SET (396)	60.00	120.00
COMP.FACT.SET (396)	250.00	400.00
1 Eric Dickerson RB	.25	.60
2 Ali Haji-Sheikh RB	.15	.40
3 Franco Harris RB	.25	.60
4 Mark Moseley RB	.15	.40
5 John Riggins RB	.25	.60
6 Jan Stenerud RB	.15	.40
7 AFC Champs	.25	.60
M.Allen		
8 NFC Champs	.15	.40
Riggins		
9 Super Bowl XVIII	.25	.60
Allen UER		
10 Indianapolis Colts TL	.10	.25
11 Raul Allegre RC	.10	.25
12 Curtis Dickey	.15	.40
13 Ray Donaldson RC	.15	.40
14 Nesby Glasgow	.10	.25
15 Chris Hinton PB RC	.25	.60
16 Vernon Maxwell RC	.10	.25
17 Randy McMillan	.10	.25
18 Mike Pagel	.15	.40
19 Rohn Stark	.15	.40
20 Leo Wisniewski	.10	.25
21 Buffalo Bills TL	.15	.40
22 Jerry Butler	.10	.25
23 Joe Danelo	.10	.25
24 Joe Ferguson	.15	.40
25 Steve Freeman	.10	.25
26 Roosevelt Leaks	.15	.40
27 Frank Lewis	.10	.25
28 Eugene Marve	.10	.25
29 Booker Moore	.10	.25
30 Fred Smerlas	.10	.25
31 Ben Williams	.15	.40
32 Cincinnati Bengals TL	.15	.40
33 Charles Alexander	.10	.25
34 Ken Anderson	.25	.60
35 Ken Anderson IR	.25	.60
36 Jim Breech	.10	.25
37 Cris Collinsworth PB	.25	.60
38 Cris Collinsworth IR	.25	.60
39 Isaac Curtis	.15	.40
40 Eddie Edwards	.10	.25
41 Ray Horton RC	.10	.25
42 Pete Johnson	.15	.40
43 Steve Kreider	.10	.25
44 Max Montoya	.10	.25
45 Anthony Munoz PB	.25	.60
46 Reggie Williams	.15	.40
47 Cleveland Browns TL	.15	.40
48 Matt Bahr	.15	.40
49 Chip Banks PB	.10	.25
50 Tom Cousineau	.10	.25
51 Joe DeLamielleure	.25	.60
52 Doug Dieken	.10	.25
53 Bob Golic RC	.25	.60
54 Bobby Jones	.10	.25
55 Dave Logan	.10	.25
56 Clay Matthews	.25	.60
57 Paul McDonald	.10	.25
58 Ozzie Newsome	.25	.60
59 Ozzie Newsome IR	.25	.60
60 Mike Pruitt	.15	.40
61 Denver Broncos TL	.15	.40
62 Barney Chavous RC	.10	.25
63 John Elway RC	25.00	50.00
64 Steve Foley	.10	.25
65 Tom Jackson	.25	.60
66 Rich Karlis	.10	.25
67 Luke Prestridge	.10	.25
68 Zach Thomas WR	.10	.25
69 Rick Upchurch	.15	.40
70 Steve Watson	.15	.40
71 Sammy Winder RC	.15	.40
72 Louis Wright	.15	.40
73 Houston Oilers TL	.10	.25
74 Jesse Baker	.10	.25
75 Gregg Bingham	.10	.25
76 Robert Brazile	.15	.40
77 Steve Brown RC	.10	.25
78 Chris Dressel RC	.10	.25
79 Doug France	.10	.25
80 Florian Kempf RC	.10	.25
81 Carl Roaches	.15	.40
82 Tim Smith WR RC	.15	.40
83 Willie Tullis	.10	.25
84 Kansas City Chiefs TL	.10	.25
85 Mike Bell RC	.10	.25
86 Theotis Brown	.10	.25
87 Carlos Carson PB	.25	.60
88 Carlos Carson IR	.15	.40
89 Deron Cherry PB RC	.15	.40
90 Gary Green	.10	.25
91 Billy Jackson	.10	.25
92 Bill Kenney	.15	.40
93 Bill Kenney IR	.15	.40
94 Nick Lowery	.25	.60
95 Henry Marshall	.10	.25
96 Art Still	.10	.25
97 Los Angeles Raiders TL	.15	.40
98 Marcus Allen	2.00	5.00
99 Marcus Allen IR	1.00	2.50
100 Lyle Alzado	.15	.40
101 Lyle Alzado IR	.15	.40
102 Chris Bahr	.10	.25
103 Malcolm Barnwell RC	.10	.25
104 Cliff Branch	.25	.60
105 Todd Christensen PB	.25	.60
106 Todd Christensen IR	.25	.60
107 Ray Guy	.25	.60
108 Frank Hawkins	.10	.25
109 Lester Hayes	.15	.40
110 Ted Hendricks PB	.25	.60
111 Howie Long PB RC	6.00	15.00
112 Rod Martin	.15	.40
113 Vann McElroy RC	.10	.25
114 Jim Plunkett	.25	.60
115 Greg Pruitt PB	.15	.40
116 Dolphins TL	.25	.60
M.Duper		
117 Bob Baumhower	.10	.25
118 Doug Betters PB RC	.10	.25
119 A.J. Duhe	.10	.25
120 Mark Duper PB RC	.25	.60
121 Andra Franklin	.10	.25
122 William Judson RC	.10	.25
123 Dan Marino RC	25.00	50.00
124 Dan Marino IR	5.00	12.00
125 Nat Moore	.15	.40
126 Ed Newman	.10	.25
127 Reggie Roby RC	.15	.40
128 Gerald Small	.10	.25
129 Dwight Stephenson RC	2.00	5.00
130 Uwe Von Schamann	.10	.25
131 New England Pats TL	.10	.25
132 Rich Camarillo	.15	.40
133 Tony Collins	.15	.40
134 Tony Collins IR	.10	.25
135 Bob Cryder	.10	.25
136 Steve Grogan	.15	.40
137 John Hannah PB	.25	.60
138 Brian Holloway RC	.10	.25
139 Roland James	.10	.25
140 Stanley Morgan	.15	.40
141 Rick Sanford	.10	.25
142 Mosi Tatupu RC	.10	.25
143 Andre Tippett RC	2.50	6.00
144 New York Jets TL	.15	.40
145 Jerome Barkum	.10	.25
146 Mark Gastineau	.15	.40
147 Mark Gastineau IR	.15	.40
148 Bruce Harper	.10	.25
149 Johnny Lam Jones	.10	.25
150 Joe Klecko	.15	.40
151 Pat Leahy	.10	.25
152 Freeman McNeil	.15	.40
153 Lance Mehl	.10	.25
154 Marvin Powell	.15	.40
155 Darrol Ray UER	.10	.25
156 Pat Ryan RC	.10	.25
157 Kirk Springs	.10	.25
158 Wesley Walker	.15	.40
159 Steelers TL	.25	.60
F.Harris		
160 Walter Abercrombie RC	.15	.40
161 Gary Anderson K	.25	.60
162 Terry Bradshaw	.75	2.00
163 Craig Colquitt	.10	.25
164 Bennie Cunningham	.10	.25
165 Franco Harris	.25	.60
166 Franco Harris IR	.25	.60
167 Jack Lambert PB	.25	.60
168 Jack Lambert IR	.25	.60
169 Frank Pollard	.10	.25
170 Donnie Shell	.15	.40
171 Mike Webster PB	.15	.40
172 Keith Willis RC	.10	.25
173 Rick Woods	.10	.25
174 Chargers TL	.25	.60
K.Winslow		
175 Rolf Benirschke	.10	.25
176 James Brooks	.15	.40
177 Maury Buford	.10	.25
178 Wes Chandler	.15	.40
179 Dan Fouts PB	.30	.75
180 Dan Fouts IR	.25	.60
181 Charlie Joiner	.25	.60
182 Linden King	.10	.25
183 Chuck Muncie	.15	.40
184 Billy Ray Smith RC	.25	.60
185 Danny Walters RC	.10	.25
186 Kellen Winslow PB	.30	.75
187 Kellen Winslow IR	.25	.60
188 Seahawks TL	.25	.60
C.Warner		
189 Steve August	.10	.25
190 Dave Brown	.10	.25
191 Zachary Dixon	.10	.25
192 Kenny Easley	.15	.40
193 Jacob Green	.10	.25
194 Norm Johnson	.15	.40
195 Dave Krieg RC	.60	1.50
196 Steve Largent	.40	1.00
197 Steve Largent IR	.25	.60
198 Curt Warner PB RC	.25	.60
199 Curt Warner IR	.25	.60
200 Jeff West	.10	.25
201 Charlie Young	.10	.25
202 D.Marino	2.50	6.00
Bartkow. LL		
203 Receiving Leaders	.15	.40
204 Eric Dickerson	.25	.60
Warner LL		
205 Scoring Leaders	.10	.25
206 Interception Leaders	.10	.25
207 Punting Leaders	.10	.25
208 Atlanta Falcons TL	.15	.40
209 William Andrews	.15	.40
210 William Andrews IR	.15	.40
211 Stacey Bailey RC	.10	.25
212 Steve Bartkowski	.25	.60
213 Steve Bartkowski IR	.15	.40
214 Ralph Giacomarro	.10	.25
215 Billy Johnson	.15	.40
216 Mike Kenn	.15	.40
217 Mick Luckhurst	.10	.25
218 Gerald Riggs	.25	.60
219 R.C. Thielemann	.10	.25
220 Jeff Van Note	.15	.40
221 Bears TL	.30	.75
W.Payton		
222 Jim Covert RC	.25	.60
223 Leslie Frazier	.10	.25
224 Willie Gault RC	.25	.60
225 Mike Hartenstine	.10	.25
226 Noah Jackson UER	.10	.25
227 Jim McMahon	.50	1.25
228 Walter Payton PB	3.00	8.00
229 Walter Payton IR	.60	1.50
230 Mike Richardson RC	.10	.25
231 Terry Schmidt	.10	.25
232 Mike Singletary	.50	1.25
233 Matt Suhey	.15	.40
234 Bob Thomas	.10	.25
235 Cowboys TL	.25	.60
T.Dorsett		
236 Bob Breunig	.10	.25
237 Doug Cosbie	.15	.40
238 Tony Dorsett PB	.40	1.00
239 Tony Dorsett IR	.25	.60
240 John Dutton	.10	.25
241 Tony Hill	.15	.40
242 Ed Jones PB	.25	.60
243 Drew Pearson	.25	.60
244 Rafael Septien	.10	.25
245 Ron Springs	.15	.40
246 Dennis Thurman	.10	.25
247 Everson Walls PB	.10	.25
248 Danny White	.25	.60
249 Randy White PB	.25	.60
250 Detroit Lions TL	.15	.40
251 Jeff Chadwick RC	.15	.40
252 Garry Cobb RC	.10	.25
253 Doug English	.15	.40
254 William Gay	.10	.25
255 Eric Hipple	.15	.40
256 James Jones RC	.15	.40
257 Bruce McNorton	.10	.25
258 Eddie Murray	.15	.40
259 Ulysses Norris	.10	.25
260 Billy Sims	.25	.60
261 Billy Sims IR	.15	.40
262 Leonard Thompson	.10	.25
263 Packers TL	.25	.60
J.Lofton		
264 John Anderson	.10	.25
265 Paul Coffman	.15	.40
266 Lynn Dickey	.15	.40
267 Gerry Ellis	.10	.25
268 John Jefferson	.25	.60
269 John Jefferson IR	.25	.60
270 Ezra Johnson	.10	.25
271 Tim Lewis RC	.10	.25
272 James Lofton PB	.25	.60
273 James Lofton IR	.25	.60
274 Larry McCarren	.10	.25
275 Jan Stenerud	.15	.40
276 Rams TL	.25	.60
E.Dickerson		
277 Mike Barber	.10	.25
278 Jim Collins	.10	.25
279 Nolan Cromwell	.15	.40
280 Erik Dickerson RC	5.00	10.00
281 Eric Dickerson IR	.75	2.00
282 George Farmer	.10	.25
283 Vince Ferragamo	.15	.40
284 Kent Hill	.10	.25
285 John Misko	.10	.25
286 Jackie Slater PB RC	1.50	4.00
287 Jack Youngblood	.15	.40
288 Minnesota Vikings TL	.10	.25
289 Ted Brown	.15	.40
290 Greg Coleman	.10	.25
291 Steve Dils	.10	.25
292 Tony Galbreath	.10	.25
293 Tommy Kramer	.15	.40
294 Doug Martin	.10	.25
295 Darrin Nelson RC	.15	.40
296 Benny Ricardo	.10	.25
297 John Swain	.10	.25
298 John Turner	.10	.25
299 New Orleans Saints TL	.15	.40
300 Morten Andersen RC	.60	1.50
301 Russell Erxleben	.10	.25
302 Jeff Groth	.10	.25
303 Rickey Jackson RC	.75	2.00
304 Johnnie Poe RC	.10	.25
305 George Rogers	.15	.40
306 Richard Todd	.15	.40
307 Jim Wilks RC	.10	.25
308 Dave Wilson RC	.10	.25
309 Wayne Wilson	.10	.25
310 New York Giants TL	.10	.25
311 Leon Bright	.10	.25
312 Scott Brunner	.10	.25
313 Rob Carpenter	.10	.25
314 Harry Carson PB	.15	.40
315 Earnest Gray	.10	.25
316 Ali Haji-Sheikh RC	.10	.25
317 Mark Haynes	.15	.40
318 Dave Jennings	.10	.25
319 Brian Kelley	.10	.25
320 Phil Simms	.30	.75
321 Lawrence Taylor PB	1.25	3.00
322 Lawrence Taylor IR	.60	1.50
323 Brad Van Pelt	.10	.25
324 Butch Woolfolk	.10	.25
325 Eagles TL	.15	.40
M.Quick		
326 Harold Carmichael	.15	.40
327 Herman Edwards	.10	.25
328 Michael Haddix RC	.10	.25
329 Dennis Harrison	.10	.25
330 Ron Jaworski	.15	.40
331 Wilbert Montgomery	.15	.40
332 Hubie Oliver	.10	.25
333 Mike Quick PB RC	.25	.60
334 Jerry Robinson	.10	.25
335 Max Runager	.10	.25
336 Michael Williams	.10	.25
337 Cardinals TL	.15	.40
O.Anderson		
338 Ottis Anderson	.25	.60
339 Al (Bubba) Baker	.15	.40
340 Carl Birdsong	.10	.25
341 David Galloway	.10	.25
342 Roy Green PB	.15	.40
343 Roy Green IR	.15	.40
344 Curtis Greer RC	.10	.25
345 Neil Lomax	.15	.40
346 Doug Marsh	.10	.25

347 Stump Mitchell .15 .40
348 Lionel Washington RC .15 .40
349 49ers TL .15 .40
D.Clark
350 Dwaine Board .10 .25
351 Dwight Clark .25 .60
352 Dwight Clark IR .15 .40
353 Roger Craig RC 2.00 5.00
354 Fred Dean .15 .40
355 Fred Dean IR w .25 .60
Marino
356 Dwight Hicks .15 .40
357 Ronnie Lott PB .60 1.50
358 Joe Montana PB 4.00 10.00
359 Joe Montana IR 1.25 3.00
360 Freddie Solomon .10 .25
361 Wendell Tyler .10 .25
362 Ray Wersching .10 .25
363 Eric Wright RC .15 .40
364 Tampa Bay Bucs TL .10 .25
365 Gerald Carter .10 .25
366 Hugh Green .15 .40
367 Kevin House .15 .40
368 Michael Morton RC .10 .25
369 James Owens .10 .25
370 Booker Reese .10 .25
371 Lee Roy Selmon .25 .60
372 Jack Thompson .15 .40
373 James Wilder .15 .40
374 Steve Wilson .10 .25
375 Redskins TL .25 .60
J.Riggins
376 Jeff Bostic .10 .25
377 Charlie Brown .25 .60
378 Charlie Brown IR .15 .40
379 Dave Butz .15 .40
380 Darrell Green RC 5.00 12.00
381 Russ Grimm PB RC 1.50 4.00
382 Joe Jacoby PB .15 .40
383 Dexter Manley .15 .40
384 Art Monk .40 1.00
385 Mark Moseley .15 .40
386 Mark Murphy .10 .25
387 Mike Nelms .10 .25
388 John Riggins .25 .60
389 John Riggins IR .25 .60
390 Joe Theismann PB .25 .60
391 Joe Theismann IR .25 .60
392 Don Warren .15 .40
393 Joe Washington .15 .40
394 Checklist 1-132 .10 .60
395 Checklist 133-264 .10 .60
396 Checklist 265-396 .10 .60

1984 Topps Glossy Inserts

The 1984 Topps Glossy Inserts set contains 11 standard-size cards featuring an attractive blue border. They were issued as an insert with the 1984 Topps football regular issue rack packs. The player selection appears to be based on conference-leading performers from the previous season in the categories of rushing, passing, receiving, and sacks. The key card in the set is Dan Marino appearing in his Rookie Card year.

COMPLETE SET (11) 10.00 25.00
1 Curt Warner .30 .75
2 Eric Dickerson 1.25 3.00
3 Dan Marino 8.00 20.00
4 Steve Bartkowski .30 .75
5 Todd Christensen .30 .75
6 Roy Green .20 .50
7 Charlie Brown .20 .50
8 Earnest Gray .20 .50
9 Mark Gastineau .20 .50
10 Fred Dean .20 .50
11 Lawrence Taylor .60 1.50

1984 Topps Play Cards

Inserted one per 1984 Topps pack, this 27-card set measures the standard size. On a yellow background, the fronts describe what collectors could win and how to play the game. A team name and a number of yards gained appears on the fronts. Collectors needed to accumulate a total of 25 yards to trade for a group of five 1984 Topps Glossy Send-In cards. The backs carry the official rules. The cards are numbered on the front as "Play x of 27".

COMPLETE SET (27) 8.00 20.00
1 Houston Oilers .30 .75
2 Houston Oilers .30 .75
3 Cleveland Browns .30 .75
4 Cleveland Browns .30 .75
5 Cincinnati Bengals .30 .75
6 Pittsburgh Steelers .40 2.00
7 New Orleans Saints .40 1.00
8 New York Giants .30 .75
9 Washington Redskins .40 1.00
10 Green Bay Packers .30 .75
11 Atlanta Falcons .30 .75
12 Detroit Lions .30 .75
13 New England Patriots .30 .75
14 New York Jets .40 1.00
15 Buffalo Bills .30 .75
16 Kansas City Chiefs .30 .75
17 Miami Dolphins .40 1.00
18 San Diego Chargers .30 .75
19 Seattle Seahawks .30 .75
20 Seattle Seahawks .30 .75
21 Dallas Cowboys .60 1.50
22 St. Louis Cardinals .30 .75
23 Chicago Bears .30 .75
24 San Francisco 49ers .60 1.50
25 Philadelphia Eagles .30 1.00
26 Minnesota Vikings .30 1.00
27 Los Angeles Rams .40 2.00

1984 Topps Glossy Send-In

The 1984 Topps Glossy Send-In set contains 30 cards with each measuring approximately 2 1/2" by 3 1/2." Complete sets were available via a mail-away offer from Topps involving the 1984 Play cards.

COMPLETE SET (30) 10.00 25.00
1 Marcus Allen .75 2.00
2 John Riggins .30 .75
3 Walter Payton 3.00 8.00
4 Tony Dorsett .75 2.00
5 Franco Harris .30 .75
6 Curt Warner .15 .40
7 Eric Dickerson .30 .75
8 Mike Pruitt .15 .40
9 Ken Anderson .30 .75
10 Dan Fouts .30 .75
11 Terry Bradshaw 1.25 3.00
12 Joe Theismann .30 .75
13 Joe Montana 2.50 6.00
14 Danny White .20 .50
15 Kellen Winslow .30 .75
16 Wesley Walker .15 .40
17 Drew Pearson .30 .75
18 James Lofton .30 .75
19 Cris Collinsworth .15 .40
20 Dwight Clark .20 .50
21 Mark Gastineau .15 .40
22 Lawrence Taylor .40 1.00
23 Randy White .30 .75
24 Ed Too Tall Jones .30 .75
25 Jack Lambert .30 .75
26 Fred Dean .15 .40
27 Jan Stenerud .20 .50
28 Bruce Harper .15 .40
29 Todd Christensen .15 .40
30 Greg Pruitt .15 .40

1984 Topps USFL

The 1984 Topps USFL set contains 132 standard-size cards, which were available as a complete set housed in its own specially made box. Card fronts have the "Premier USFL Edition" logo at the top border. Beneath the player photo is the team helmet and the player's name, team and position in a yellow box. The backs have NFL and USFL statistics (rookies have collecge stats) and a team fact. The cards in the set are numbered in alphabetical team order (with players arranged alphabetically within teams). Popular Extended Rookie Cards are quarterbacks Jim Kelly and Steve Young. Herschel Walker and Reggie White are other notable XRC's. More players making their first professional card appearence include Gary Anderson, Anthony Carter, Bobby Hebert, Craig James, Vaughan Johnson, Gary Plummer and Ricky Sanders.

COMP.FACT.SET (132) 150.00 300.00
COMPLETE SET (132) 150.00 300.00
1 Luther Bradley .75 2.00
2 Frank Corral .75 2.00
3 Trumaine Johnson XRC .75 2.00
4 Greg Landry 1.00 2.50
5 Kit Lathrop XRC .75 2.00
6 Kevin Long .75 2.00
7 Tim Spencer .75 2.00
8 Stan White .75 2.00
9 Buddy Aydelette .75 2.00
10 Tom Banks .75 2.00
11 Fred Bohannon .75 2.00
12 Joe Cribbs 1.50 4.00
13 Joey Jones .75 2.00
14 Scott Norwood XRC 1.00 2.50
15 Jim Smith 1.00 2.50
16 Cliff Stoudt 1.50 4.00
17 Vince Evans 1.50 4.00
18 Vagas Ferguson .75 2.00
19 John Gillen .75 2.00
20 Kris Haines .75 2.00
21 Glenn Hyde .75 2.00
22 Mark Keel .75 2.00
23 Gary Lewis XRC .75 2.00
24 Doug Plank .75 2.00
25 Neil Balholm .75 2.00
26 David Dumars .75 2.00
27 David Martin XRC .75 2.00
28 Craig Penrose .75 2.00
29 Dave Stalls .75 2.00
30 Harry Sydney XRC .75 2.00
31 Vincent White .75 2.00
32 George Yarno .75 2.00
33 Kiki DeAyala XRC .75 2.00
34 Sam Harrell .75 2.00
35 Mike Hawkins .75 2.00
36 Jim Kelly XRC 30.00 60.00
37 Mark Rush .75 2.00
38 Ricky Sanders XRC 2.50 6.00
39 Paul Bergmann .75 2.00
40 Tom Dinkel .75 2.00
41 Wyatt Henderson .75 2.00
42 Vaughan Johnson XRC 1.00 2.50
43 Willie McClendon Geor. .75 2.00
44 Matt Robinson .75 2.00
45 George Achica .75 2.00
46 Mark Adickes XRC .75 2.00
47 Howard Carson XRC .75 2.00
48 Kevin Nelson .75 2.00
49 Jeff Partridge .75 2.00
50 Jo Jo Townsell 1.00 2.50
51 Eddie Weaver .75 2.00
52 Steve Young XRC 50.00 100.00
53 Derrick Crawford XRC .75 2.00
54 Walter Lewis .75 2.00
55 Phil McKinnely .75 2.00
56 Vic Minore .75 2.00
57 Gary Shirk .75 2.00
58 Reggie White XRC 30.00 60.00
59 Anthony Carter XRC 5.00 12.00
60 John Corker XRC .75 2.00
61 David Greenwood XRC .75 2.00
62 Bobby Hebert XRC 1.50 4.00
63 Derek Holloway .75 2.00
64 Ken Lacy .75 2.00
65 Tyrone McGriff XRC .75 2.00
66 Ray Pinney XRC .75 2.00
67 Gary Barbaro .75 2.00
68 Sam Bowers .75 2.00
69 Clarence Collins .75 2.00
70 Willie Harper .75 2.00
71 Jim LeClair .75 2.00
72 Bobby Leopold XRC .75 2.00
73 Brian Sipe 1.50 4.00
74 Herschel Walker XRC 12.00 30.00
75 Junior Ah You XRC .75 2.00
76 Marcus Dupree XRC 6.00 15.00
77 Marcus Marek XRC .75 2.00
78 Tim Mazzetti .75 2.00
79 Mike Robinson XRC .75 2.00
80 Dan Ross 1.50 4.00
81 Mark Schellen .75 2.00
82 Johnnie Walton .75 2.00
83 Gordon Banks .75 2.00
84 Fred Besana .75 2.00
85 Dave Browning .75 2.00
86 Eric Jordan .75 2.00
87 Frank Manumaleuga .75 2.00
88 Gary Plummer XRC 1.50 4.00
89 Stan Talley XRC .75 2.00
90 Arthur Whittington .75 2.00
91 Terry Beeson .75 2.00
92 Mel Gray 1.50 4.00
93 Mike Katolin .75 2.00
94 Dewey McClain .75 2.00
95 Sidney Thornton .75 2.00
96 Doug Williams 2.50 6.00
97 Kelvin Bryant XRC 1.50 4.00
98 John Bunting .75 2.00
99 Irv Eatman XRC 1.00 2.50
100 Scott Fitzkee .75 2.00
101 Chuck Fusina XRC .75 2.00
102 Sean Landeta XRC 1.00 2.50
103 David Trout .75 2.00
104 Scott Woerner XRC .75 2.00
105 Glenn Carano .75 2.00
106 Ron Crosby .75 2.00
107 Jerry Holmes .75 2.00
108 Bruce Huther .75 2.00
109 Mike Rozier XRC 1.50 4.00
110 Larry Swider .75 2.00
111 Danny Buggs .75 2.00
112 Putt Choate .75 2.00
113 Rich Garza .75 2.00
114 Joey Hackett .75 2.00
115 Rick Neuheisel XRC 1.50 4.00
116 Mike St. Clair .75 2.00
117 Gary Anderson XRC RB 1.50 4.00
118 Zenon Andrusyshyn .75 2.00
119 Doug Beaudoin .75 2.00
120 Mike Butler .75 2.00
121 Willie Gillespie .75 2.00
122 Fred Nordgren .75 2.00
123 John Reaves .75 2.00
124 Eric Truvillion XRC .75 2.00
125 Reggie Collier .75 2.00
126 Mike Guess .75 2.00
127 Mike Hohensee .75 2.00
128 Craig James XRC 3.00 8.00
129 Eric Robinson XRC .75 2.00
130 Billy Taylor .75 2.00
131 Joey Walters XRC .75 2.00
132 Checklist 1-132 1.00 2.50

1985 Topps

The 1985 Topps set contains 396 standard-size cards. Wax packs contained 15-cards. Horizontal card fronts have black borders that are prone to chipping. To the right is the player's name and team name. Vertical backs have highlights and statistics. Subsets include Record Breakers (1-6), playoffs (7-9) and league leaders (192-197). Team Leader (TL) cards feature an action photo on the front with a caption. The backs contain team scoring information from the previous year. The order of teams (alphabetically arranged by conference with players themselves alphabetically ordered within each team). The key Rookie Card in this set is Warren Moon (although he had already appeared in several JOGO CFL card issues). Other Rookie Cards include Carl Banks, Mark Clayton, Richard Dent, Henry Ellard, Irving Fryar, Louis Lipps, Steve McMichael, Mike Munchak and Darryl Talley.

COMPLETE SET (396) 25.00 50.00
COMP.FACT.SET (396) 30.00 60.00
1 Mark Clayton RB .20 .50
2 Eric Dickerson RB .20 .50
3 Charlie Joiner RB .20 .50
4 Dan Marino RB 2.50 6.00
5 Art Monk RB .20 .50
6 Walter Payton RB .40 1.00
7 NFC Champs .12 .30
Suhey
8 AFC Championship .12 .30
9 Super Bowl XIX .12 .30
10 Atlanta Falcons TL .08 .20
11 William Andrews .12 .30
12 Stacey Bailey .08 .20
13 Steve Bartkowski .20 .50
14 Rick Bryan RC .08 .20
15 Alfred Jackson .08 .20
16 Kenny Johnson .08 .20
17 Mike Kenn .08 .20
18 Mike Pitts RC .08 .20
19 Gerald Riggs .12 .30
20 Sylvester Stamps .08 .20
21 R.C. Thielemann .08 .20
22 Bears TL .30 .75
W.Payton
23 Todd Bell RC .08 .20
24 Richard Dent RC 2.00 5.00
25 Gary Fencik .12 .30
26 Dave Finzer .08 .20
27 Leslie Frazier .08 .20
28 Steve Fuller .12 .30
29 Willie Gault .20 .50
30 Dan Hampton AP .20 .50
31 Jim McMahon .30 .75
32 Steve McMichael RC .20 .50
33 Walter Payton AP 3.00 8.00
34 Mike Singletary .30 .75
35 Matt Suhey .08 .20
36 Bob Thomas .08 .20
37 Cowboys TL/Dorsett .20 .50
38 Bill Bates RC .40 1.00
39 Doug Cosbie .12 .30
40 Tony Dorsett .30 .75
41 Michael Downs .08 .20
42 Mike Hegman UER RC .08 .20
43 Tony Hill .12 .30
44 Gary Hogeboom RC .08 .20
45 Jim Jeffcoat RC .20 .50
46 Ed Too Tall Jones .20 .50
47 Mike Renfro .08 .20
48 Rafael Septien .08 .20
49 Dennis Thurman .08 .20
50 Everson Walls .12 .30
51 Danny White .20 .50
52 Randy White .20 .50
53 Detroit Lions TL .08 .20
54 Jeff Chadwick .08 .20
55 Mike Cofer RC .08 .20
56 Gary Danielson .08 .20
57 Keith Dorney .08 .20
58 Doug English .12 .30
59 William Gay .08 .20
60 Ken Jenkins .08 .20
61 James Jones .12 .30
62 Eddie Murray .12 .30
63 Billy Sims .20 .50
64 Leonard Thompson .08 .20
65 Bobby Watkins .08 .20
66 Green Bay Packers TL .12 .30
67 Paul Coffman .08 .20
68 Lynn Dickey .12 .30
69 Mike Douglass .08 .20
70 Tom Flynn RC .08 .20
71 Eddie Lee Ivery .08 .20
72 Ezra Johnson .08 .20
73 Mark Lee .08 .20
74 Tim Lewis .08 .20
75 James Lofton .20 .50
76 Bucky Scribner .08 .20
77 Rams TL .20 .50
Dickerson
78 Nolan Cromwell .12 .30
79 Eric Dickerson AP .50 1.25
80 Henry Ellard RC 1.00 2.50
81 Kent Hill .08 .20
82 LeRoy Irvin .12 .30
83 Jeff Kemp RC .12 .30
84 Mike Lansford .08 .20
85 Barry Redden .08 .20
86 Jackie Slater .20 .50
87 Doug Smith C RC .12 .30
88 Jack Youngblood .12 .30
89 Minnesota Vikings TL .08 .20
90 Alfred Anderson RC .08 .20
91 Ted Brown .12 .30
92 Greg Coleman .08 .20
93 Tommy Hannon .08 .20
94 Tommy Kramer .12 .30
95 Leo Lewis RC .12 .30
96 Doug Martin .08 .20
97 Darrin Nelson .12 .30
98 Jan Stenerud AP .12 .30
99 Sammie White .12 .30
100 New Orleans Saints TL .08 .20
101 Morten Andersen .20 .50
102 Hoby Brenner RC .12 .30
103 Bruce Clark .08 .20
104 Hokie Gajan .08 .20
105 Brian Hansen RC .08 .20
106 Rickey Jackson .30 .75
107 George Rogers .12 .30
108 Dave Wilson .08 .20
109 Tyrone Young .08 .20
110 New York Giants TL .08 .20
111 Carl Banks RC .40 1.00
112 Jim Burt RC .20 .50
113 Rob Carpenter .08 .20
114 Harry Carson .12 .30
115 Earnest Gray .08 .20
116 Ali Haji-Sheikh .08 .20
117 Mark Haynes .12 .30
118 Bobby Johnson .08 .20
119 Lionel Manuel RC .12 .30
120 Joe Morris RC .20 .50
121 Zeke Mowatt RC .12 .30
122 Jeff Rutledge RC .08 .20
123 Phil Simms .20 .50
124 Lawrence Taylor AP .60 1.50
125 Philadelphia Eagles TL .08 .20
126 Greg Brown .08 .20
127 Ray Ellis .08 .20
128 Dennis Harrison .08 .20
129 Wes Hopkins RC .12 .30
130 Mike Horan RC .08 .20
131 Kenny Jackson RC .08 .20
132 Ron Jaworski .12 .30
133 Paul McFadden .08 .20
134 Wilbert Montgomery .12 .30
135 Mike Quick .20 .50
136 John Spagnola .08 .20
137 St.Louis Cardinals TL .08 .20
138 Ottis Anderson .20 .50
139 Al(Bubba) Baker .12 .30
140 Roy Green .12 .30
141 Curtis Greer .08 .20
142 E.J. Junior AP .08 .20
143 Neil Lomax .12 .30
144 Stump Mitchell .12 .30
145 Neil O'Donoghue .08 .20
146 Pat Tilley .08 .20
147 Lionel Washington .08 .20
148 49ers TL .50 1.25
J.Montana
149 Dwaine Board .08 .20
150 Dwight Clark .20 .50
151 Roger Craig .40 1.00
152 Randy Cross .12 .30
153 Fred Dean .12 .30
154 Keith Fahnhorst RC .08 .20
155 Dwight Hicks .08 .20
156 Ronnie Lott .20 .50
157 Joe Montana 4.00 10.00
158 Renaldo Nehemiah .12 .30
159 Fred Quillan .08 .20
160 Jack Reynolds .08 .20
161 Freddie Solomon .08 .20
162 Keena Turner RC .08 .20
163 Wendell Tyler .08 .20
164 Ray Wersching .08 .20
165 Carlton Williamson .08 .20
166 Tampa Bay Bucs TL .12 .30
167 Gerald Carter .08 .20
168 Mark Cotney .08 .20
169 Steve DeBerg .20 .50
170 Sean Farrell RC .08 .20
171 Hugh Green .12 .30
172 Kevin House .12 .30
173 David Logan .08 .20
174 Michael Morton .08 .20
175 Lee Roy Selmon .20 .50
176 James Wilder .08 .20
177 Redskins TL .20 .50
J.Riggins
178 Charlie Brown .08 .20
179 Monte Coleman RC .12 .30
180 Vernon Dean .08 .20
181 Darrell Green .20 .50
182 Russ Grimm .30 .75
183 Joe Jacoby .12 .30
184 Dexter Manley .12 .30
185 Art Monk AP .20 .50
186 Mark Moseley .12 .30
187 Calvin Muhammad .08 .20
188 Mike Nelms .08 .20
189 John Riggins .20 .50
190 Joe Theismann .20 .50
191 Joe Washington .12 .30
192 D.Marino 4.00 10.00
Montana LL
193 Art Monk .12 .30
O.Newsome LL
194 E.Dickerson .20 .50
Jackson LL
195 Scoring Leaders .08 .20
196 Interception Leaders .08 .20
197 Punting Leaders .08 .20
198 Bills TL .08 .20
Greg Bell
199 Greg Bell RC .12 .30
200 Preston Dennard .08 .20
201 Joe Ferguson .12 .30
202 Byron Franklin .08 .20
203 Steve Freeman .08 .20
204 Jim Haslett .12 .30
205 Charles Romes .08 .20
206 Fred Smerlas .08 .20
207 Darryl Talley RC .20 .50
208 Van Williams .08 .20
209 Cincinnati Bengals TL .12 .30
210 Ken Anderson .20 .50
211 Jim Breech .08 .20
212 Louis Breeden .08 .20
213 James Brooks .12 .30
214 Ross Browner .12 .30
215 Eddie Edwards .08 .20
216 M.L. Harris .08 .20
217 Bobby Kemp .08 .20
218 Larry Kinnebrew RC .08 .20
219 Anthony Munoz AP .20 .50
220 Reggie Williams .12 .30
221 Cleveland Browns TL .08 .20
222 Matt Bahr .12 .30
223 Chip Banks .08 .20
224 Reggie Camp .08 .20
225 Tom Cousineau .08 .20
226 Joe DeLamielleure .20 .50
227 Ricky Feacher .08 .20
228 Boyce Green RC .08 .20
229 Al Gross .08 .20
230 Clay Matthews .20 .50
231 Paul McDonald .08 .20
232 Ozzie Newsome AP .20 .50
233 Mike Pruitt .12 .30
234 Don Rogers .08 .20
235 Broncos TL 1.00 2.50
J.Elway
236 Rubin Carter .08 .20
237 Barney Chavous .08 .20
238 John Elway 5.00 12.00
239 Steve Foley .08 .20
240 Mike Harden RC .08 .20
241 Tom Jackson .20 .50
242 Butch Johnson .08 .20
243 Rulon Jones .08 .20
244 Rich Karlis .08 .20
245 Steve Watson .12 .30
246 Gerald Willhite .08 .20
247 Sammy Winder .12 .30
248 Houston Oilers TL .08 .20
249 Jesse Baker .08 .20
250 Carter Hartwig RC .08 .20
251 Warren Moon RC 6.00 15.00
252 Larry Moriarty RC .08 .20
253 Mike Munchak RC 1.25 3.00
254 Carl Roaches .08 .20
255 Tim Smith .12 .30
256 Willie Tullis .08 .20
257 Jamie Williams RC .08 .20
258 Indianapolis Colts TL .08 .20
259 Raymond Butler .08 .20
260 Johnie Cooks .08 .20
261 Eugene Daniel RC .08 .20
262 Curtis Dickey .12 .30
263 Chris Hinton .12 .30
264 Vernon Maxwell .08 .20
265 Randy McMillan .08 .20
266 Art Schlichter RC .20 .50
267 Rohn Stark .12 .30
268 Leo Wisniewski .08 .20
269 Kansas City Chiefs TL .08 .20
270 Jim Arnold RC .08 .20
271 Mike Bell .08 .20
272 Todd Blackledge RC .12 .30
273 Carlos Carson .12 .30
274 Deron Cherry .12 .30
275 Herman Heard RC .08 .20
276 Bill Kenney .12 .30
277 Nick Lowery .20 .50
278 Bill Maas RC .08 .20
279 Henry Marshall .08 .20
280 Art Still .08 .20
281 Raiders TL .20 .50
M.Allen
282 Marcus Allen 1.00 2.50
283 Lyle Alzado .12 .30
284 Chris Bahr .08 .20
285 Malcolm Barnwell .08 .20
286 Cliff Branch .20 .50
287 Todd Christensen .20 .50
288 Ray Guy .20 .50
289 Lester Hayes .12 .30
290 Mike Haynes .12 .30
291 Henry Lawrence .08 .20
292 Howie Long .75 2.00
293 Rod Martin .12 .30
294 Vann McElroy .08 .20
295 Matt Millen .12 .30
296 Bill Pickel RC .08 .20
297 Jim Plunkett .20 .50
298 Dokie Williams RC .08 .20
299 Marc Wilson .12 .30
300 Dolphins TL .12 .30
Duper
301 Bob Baumhower .08 .20
302 Doug Betters .08 .20
303 Glenn Blackwood .12 .30
304 Lyle Blackwood .12 .30
305 Kim Bokamper .08 .20
306 Charles Bowser RC .08 .20
307 Jimmy Cefalo .08 .20
308 Mark Clayton AP RC .50 1.25
309 A.J. Duhe .08 .20
310 Mark Duper .20 .50
311 Andra Franklin .08 .20
312 Bruce Hardy .08 .20
313 Pete Johnson .12 .30
314 Dan Marino 5.00 12.00
315 Tony Nathan .12 .30
316 Ed Newman .08 .20
317 Reggie Roby AP .20 .50
318 Dwight Stephenson .40 1.00
319 Uwe Von Schamann .08 .20
320 New England Pats TL .08 .20
321 Raymond Clayborn .12 .30
322 Tony Collins .12 .30
323 Tony Eason RC .20 .50
324 Tony Franklin .08 .20
325 Irving Fryar RC 2.00 5.00
326 John Hannah AP .20 .50
327 Brian Holloway .08 .20
328 Craig James RC .50 1.25
329 Stanley Morgan .12 .30
330 Steve Nelson .08 .20
331 Derrick Ramsey .08 .20
332 Stephen Starring RC .12 .30
333 Mosi Tatupu .08 .20
334 Andre Tippett .20 .50
335 New York Jets TL .12 .30
336 Russell Carter RC .08 .20
337 Mark Gastineau .12 .30
338 Bruce Harper .08 .20
339 Bobby Humphery RC .08 .20
340 Johnny Lam Jones .08 .20
341 Joe Klecko .12 .30
342 Pat Leahy .08 .20
343 Marty Lyons .12 .30
344 Freeman McNeil .12 .30
345 Lance Mehl .08 .20
346 Ken O'Brien RC .20 .50
347 Marvin Powell .08 .20
348 Pat Ryan .08 .20
349 Mickey Shuler RC .08 .20
350 Wesley Walker .12 .30
351 Pittsburgh Steelers TL .12 .30
352 Walter Abercrombie .08 .20
353 Gary Anderson K .12 .30
354 Robin Cole .08 .20
355 Bennie Cunningham .08 .20
356 Rich Erenberg .08 .20
357 Jack Lambert .20 .50
358 Louis Lipps RC .20 .50
359 Mark Malone .12 .30
360 Mike Merriweather RC .08 .20
361 Frank Pollard .08 .20
362 Donnie Shell .12 .30
363 John Stallworth .20 .50
364 Sam Washington .08 .20
365 Mike Webster .12 .30
366 Dwayne Woodruff .08 .20
367 San Diego Chargers TL .08 .20
368 Rolf Benirschke .08 .20
369 Gill Byrd RC .20 .50
370 Wes Chandler .12 .30
371 Bobby Duckworth .08 .20
372 Dan Fouts .20 .50
373 Mike Green .08 .20
374 Pete Holohan RC .08 .20
375 Earnest Jackson RC .12 .30
376 Lionel James RC .12 .30
377 Charlie Joiner .20 .50
378 Billy Ray Smith .12 .30
379 Kellen Winslow .20 .50
380 Seattle Seahawks TL .12 .30
381 Dave Brown .08 .20
382 Jeff Bryant RC .08 .20
383 Dan Doornink .08 .20
384 Kenny Easley .12 .30
385 Jacob Green .12 .30
386 David Hughes .08 .20
387 Norm Johnson .08 .20
388 Dave Krieg .20 .50
389 Steve Largent .40 1.00
390 Joe Nash RC .08 .20
391 Daryl Turner RC .08 .20
392 Curt Warner .20 .50
393 Fredd Young RC .12 .30
394 Checklist 1-132 .20 .50
395 Checklist 133-264 .20 .50
396 Checklist 265-396 .20 .50

1985 Topps Box Bottoms

This 16-card set, which measures 2 1/2" by 3 1/2", was issued on the bottom of 1985 Topps wax pack boxes. The cards are in the same design as the 1985 Topps regular issues except they are bordered in red and have the words "Topps Superstars" printed in very small letters above the players' photos. Similar to the regular issue, these cards have a horizontal orientation. The backs of the cards are just like the regular card in that they have biographical and complete statistical information. The cards are arranged in alphabetical order and include such stars as Joe Montana and Walter Payton.

COMPLETE SET (16) 20.00 40.00
A Marcus Allen 1.25 3.00
B Ottis Anderson .60 1.50
C Mark Clayton .60 1.50
D Eric Dickerson .75 2.00
E Tony Dorsett 1.25 3.00
F Dan Fouts 1.00 2.50
G Mark Gastineau .60 1.50
H Charlie Joiner .75 2.00
I James Lofton .75 2.00
J Neil Lomax .60 1.50
K Dan Marino 4.00 10.00
L Art Monk .75 2.00
M Joe Montana 4.00 10.00
N Walter Payton 4.00 10.00
O John Stallworth 1.00 2.50
P Lawrence Taylor 1.00 2.50
PAN1 Allen/Anderson/Clayton/Dickerson 2.50 6.00
PAN2 Dorsett/Fouts/Gastineau/Joiner 2.50 6.00
PAN3 Lofton/Lomax/Marino/Monk 5.00 12.00
PAN4 Montana/Payton/Stallworth/Taylor 8.00 20.00

1985 Topps Glossy Inserts

This red-bordered glossy insert set was distributed with rack packs of the 1985 Topps football regular issue. The backs of the cards are printed in red and blue on white card stock but provide very little about the player other than the most basic information.

COMPLETE SET (11) 8.00 20.00
1 Mark Clayton .20 .50
2 Eric Dickerson .30 .75
3 John Elway 2.00 5.00
4 Mark Gastineau .20 .50
5 Ronnie Lott UER .30 .75
6 Dan Marino 2.00 5.00
7 Joe Montana 2.50 6.00
8 Walter Payton 1.25 3.00
9 John Riggins .30 .75
10 John Stallworth .30 .75
11 Lawrence Taylor .40 1.00

1985 Topps USFL

The 1985 Topps USFL set contains 132 football standard-size cards, which were available as a complete set housed in its own specially made box. The card fronts have a red border with a blue and white stripe in the middle. The USFL logo is at the top of the photo with the team name in red block letters in a white box at the bottom of the photo. Also toward the bottom of the photo, is the player's name and position within a yellow football. The card backs are printed in red and blue on white card stock. Card backs describe each player's highlights of the previous USFL season and have NFL and USFL statistics. The cards in the set are ordered numerically by team with players within teams also ordered alphabetically. The key Extended Rookie Cards in this set are Gary Clark, Doug Flutie, William Fuller and Sam Mills. Other key cards in the set include the second USFL cards of Jim Kelly, Herschel Walker, Reggie White, and Steve Young.

COMP.FACT.SET (132) 60.00 120.00
COMPLETE SET (132) 50.00 100.00
1 Case DeBruijn XRC .20 .50
2 Mike Katolin .20 .50
3 Bruce Laird .20 .50
4 Kit Lathrop .20 .50
5 Kevin Long .20 .50
6 Karl Lorch .20 .50
7 Dave Tipton DT RXR .20 .50
8 Doug Williams .75 2.00
9 Luis Zendejas XRC .20 .50
10 Kelvin Bryant .40 1.00
11 Willie Collier .20 .50
12 Irv Eatman .20 .50
13 Scott Fitzkee .20 .50
14 William Fuller XRC 1.25 3.00
15 Chuck Fusina .20 .50
16 Pete Kugler XRC .20 .50
17 Garcia Lane XRC .20 .50
18 Mike Lush XRC .20 .50
19 Sam Mills XRC 2.00 5.00
20 Buddy Aydelette .20 .50
21 Joe Cribbs .75 2.00
22 David Dumars .20 .50
23 Robin Earl .20 .50
24 Joey Jones .20 .50
25 Leon Perry RB .20 .50
26 Dave Pureifory .20 .50
27 Bill Roe .20 .50
28 Doug Smith DT XRC .75 2.00
29 Cliff Stoudt .40 1.00
30 Jeff Delaney .20 .50
31 Vince Evans .40 1.00
32 Leonard Harris XRC .20 .50
33 Bill Johnson RB .20 .50
34 Marc Lewis XRC .20 .50
35 David Martin .20 .50
36 Bruce Thornton XRC .20 .50
37 Craig Walls .20 .50
38 Vincent White .20 .50
39 Luther Bradley .20 .50
40 Pete Catan XRC .20 .50
41 Kiki DeAyala .20 .50
42 Toni Fritsch .20 .50
43 Sam Harrell .20 .50
44 Richard Johnson WR XRC .40 1.00
45 Jim Kelly 8.00 20.00
46 Gerald McNeil XRC .20 .50
47 Clarence Verdin XRC .75 2.00
48 Dale Walters .20 .50
49 Gary Clark XRC 2.50 6.00
50 Tom Dinkel .20 .50
51 Mike Edwards LB .20 .50
52 Brian Franco .20 .50
53 Bob Gruber .20 .50
54 Robbie Mahfouz .20 .50
55 Mike Rozier .75 2.00
56 Brian Sipe .40 1.00
57 J.T. Turner .20 .50
58 Howard Carson .20 .50
59 Wymon Henderson XRC .20 .50
60 Kevin Nelson .20 .50
61 Jeff Partridge .20 .50
62 Ben Rudolph .20 .50
63 Jo Jo Townsell .40 1.00
64 Eddie Weaver .20 .50
65 Steve Young 15.00 40.00
66 Tony Zendejas XRC .40 1.00
67 Mossy Cade .20 .50
68 Leonard Coleman XRC .20 .50
69 John Corker .20 .50
70 Derrick Crawford .20 .50
71 Art Kuehn .20 .50
72 Walter Lewis .20 .50
73 Tyrone McGriff .20 .50
74 Tim Spencer .40 1.00
75 Reggie White 8.00 20.00
76 Gizmo Williams XRC .75 2.00
77 Sam Bowers .20 .50
78 Maurice Carthon XRC .75 2.00
79 Clarence Collins .20 .50
80 Doug Flutie XRC 8.00 20.00
81 Freddie Gilbert DE .20 .50
82 Kerry Justin XRC .20 .50
83 Dave Lapham .20 .50
84 Rick Partridge .20 .50
85 Roger Ruzek XRC .40 1.00
86 Herschel Walker 3.00 8.00
87 Gordon Banks .20 .50
88 Monte Bennett .20 .50
89 Albert Bentley XRC .40 1.00
90 Novo Bojovic .20 .50
91 Dave Browning .20 .50
92 Anthony Carter .75 2.00
93 Bobby Hebert .75 2.00
94 Ray Pinney .20 .50
95 Stan Talley .20 .50
96 Ruben Vaughan .20 .50
97 Curtis Bledsoe .20 .50
98 Reggie Collier .20 .50
99 Jerry Doerger .20 .50
100 Jerry Golsteyn .20 .50
101 Bob Niziolek .20 .50
102 Joel Patten .20 .50
103 Ricky Simmons .20 .50
104 Joey Walters .20 .50
105 Marcus Dupree 4.00 10.00
106 Jeff Gossett .40 1.00
107 Frank Lockett .20 .50
108 Marcus Marek .20 .50
109 Kenny Neil .20 .50
110 Robert Pennywell .20 .50
111 Matt Robinson .20 .50
112 Dan Ross .40 1.00
113 Doug Woodward .20 .50
114 Danny Buggs .20 .50
115 Putt Choate .20 .50
116 Greg Fields .20 .50
117 Ken Hartley .20 .50
118 Nick Mike-Mayer .20 .50
119 Rick Neuheisel .75 2.00
120 Peter Raeford .20 .50
121 Gary Worthy .20 .50
122 Gary Anderson RB .40 1.00
123 Zenon Andrusyshyn .20 .50
124 Greg Boone .20 .50
125 Mike Butler .20 .50
126 Mike Clark .20 .50
127 Willie Gillespie .20 .50
128 James Harrell XRC .20 .50
129 Marvin Harvey XRC .20 .50
130 John Reaves .40 1.00
131 Eric Truvillion .20 .50
132 Checklist 1-132 .40 1.00

1985 Topps USFL Generals

Topps produced this nine-card panel for the New Jersey Generals of the USFL. The entire panel measures approximately 7 1/2" by 10 1/2" and the individual cards, when cut, measure the standard size. Card backs are printed in yellow and red on gray card stock. The panels were supposedly distributed to members of the Generals' Infantry Club, which was a fan club for youngsters. The values below are applicable also for uncut sheets as that is the most common way this set is seen.

COMPLETE SET (9) 10.00 25.00
1 Walt Michaels CO .75 2.00
2 Sam Bowers .50 1.25
3 Clarence Collins .50 1.25
4 Doug Flutie 6.00 15.00
5 Gregory Johnson .50 1.25
6 Jim LeClair .50 1.25
7 Bobby Leopold .50 1.25
8 Herschel Walker 3.00 8.00
9 Membership card .50 1.25

1986 Topps

The 1986 Topps football card set contains 396 standard-size cards. As if to resemble a football field, player photos are surrounded by green borders with white lines. The player's name, team name and position are at the bottom. Horizontally designed backs have yearly statistics and highlights. The copyright line on the back also includes a letter (A, B, C, or D) to indicate which sheet the card was cut from. Note that each card in the set was produced on two different sheets. This resulted in each card including one of two different letter designations on the back, thus creating a variation on each card. Subsets include Record Breakers (1-7) and league leaders (225-229). Team cards feature a distinctive yellow border on the front with the team's results and leaders (from the previous season) listed on the back. The set numbering is in order of 1984 finish. Rookie Cards in this set include Mark Bavaro, Ray Childress, Boomer Esiason, Bernie Kosar, Wilber Marshall, Karl Mecklenburg, William Perry, Andre Reed, Jerry Rice, Bruce Smith and Al Toon. In addition, Anthony Carter, Gary Clark, Bobby Hebert, Reggie White and Steve Young are Rookie Cards, although they had each appeared in a previous Topps USFL set.

COMPLETE SET (396) 50.00 100.00
COMP.FACT.SET (396) 150.00 225.00
1 Marcus Allen RB .30 .75
2 Eric Dickerson RB .20 .50
3 Lionel James RB .08 .20
4 Steve Largent RB .20 .50
5 George Martin RB .08 .20
6 Stephone Paige RB .08 .20
7 Walter Payton RB .30 .75
8 Super Bowl XX .12 .30
9 Bears TL .25 .60
W.Payton
10 Jim McMahon .20 .50
11 Walter Payton AP 4.00 10.00
12 Matt Suhey .08 .20
13 Willie Gault .12 .30
14 Dennis McKinnon RC .08 .20
15 Emery Moorehead .08 .20
16 Jim Covert AP .12 .30
17 Jay Hilgenberg RC .20 .50
18 Kevin Butler RC .12 .30
19 Richard Dent AP .30 .75
20 William Perry RC .60 1.50
21 Steve McMichael .20 .50
22 Dan Hampton .20 .50
23 Otis Wilson .08 .20
24 Mike Singletary .25 .60
25 Wilber Marshall RC .20 .50
26 Leslie Frazier .08 .20
27 Dave Duerson RC .08 .20
28 Gary Fencik .08 .20
29 Patriots TL .20 .50
30 Tony Eason .08 .20
31 Steve Grogan .12 .30
32 Craig James .20 .50
33 Tony Collins .08 .20
34 Irving Fryar .50 1.25
35 Brian Holloway .08 .20
36 John Hannah AP .20 .50
37 Tony Franklin .08 .20
38 Garin Veris RC .08 .20
39 Andre Tippett AP .20 .50
40 Steve Nelson .08 .20
41 Raymond Clayborn .08 .20
42 Fred Marion RC .08 .20
43 Rich Camarillo .08 .20
44 Dolphins TL .75 2.00
D.Marino
45 Dan Marino AP 3.00 8.00
46 Tony Nathan .12 .30
47 Ron Davenport RC .08 .20
48 Mark Duper .20 .50
49 Mark Clayton .20 .50
50 Nat Moore .12 .30
51 Bruce Hardy .08 .20
52 Roy Foster RC .08 .20
53 Dwight Stephenson .30 .75
54 Fuad Reveiz RC .12 .30
55 Bob Baumhower .08 .20
56 Mike Charles .08 .20
57 Hugh Green .12 .30
58 Glenn Blackwood .08 .20
59 Reggie Roby .12 .30
60 Raiders TL .20 .50
M.Allen
61 Marc Wilson .08 .20

62 Marcus Allen AP .60 1.50
63 Dokie Williams .08 .20
64 Todd Christensen .20 .50
65 Chris Bahr .08 .20
66 Fulton Walker .08 .20
67 Howie Long .50 1.25
68 Bill Pickel .08 .20
69 Ray Guy .20 .50
70 Greg Townsend RC .20 .50
71 Rod Martin .12 .30
72 Matt Millen .12 .30
73 Mike Haynes .12 .30
74 Lester Hayes .12 .30
75 Vann McElroy .08 .20
76 Rams TL .20 .50
Dickerson
77 Dieter Brock RC .12 .30
78 Eric Dickerson .30 .75
79 Henry Ellard .40 1.00
80 Ron Brown RC .12 .30
81 Tony Hunter RC .08 .20
82 Kent Hill AP .08 .20
83 Doug Smith .08 .20
84 Dennis Harrah .08 .20
85 Jackie Slater .20 .50
86 Mike Lansford .08 .20
87 Gary Jeter .08 .20
88 Mike Wilcher RC .08 .20
89 Jim Collins .08 .20
90 LeRoy Irvin .12 .30
91 Gary Green .08 .20
92 Nolan Cromwell .12 .30
93 Dale Hatcher RC .08 .20
94 Jets TL .12 .30
95 Ken O'Brien .20 .50
96 Freeman McNeil .12 .30
97 Tony Paige RC .08 .20
98 Johnny Lam Jones .08 .20
99 Wesley Walker .12 .30
100 Kurt Sohn .08 .20
101 Al Toon RC .20 .50
102 Mickey Shuler .08 .20
103 Marvin Powell .08 .20
104 Pat Leahy .08 .20
105 Mark Gastineau .12 .30
106 Joe Klecko .12 .30
107 Marty Lyons .08 .20
108 Lance Mehl .08 .20
109 Bobby Jackson .08 .20
110 Dave Jennings .08 .20
111 Broncos TL .12 .30
112 John Elway 3.00 8.00
113 Sammy Winder .12 .30
114 Gerald Willhite .08 .20
115 Steve Watson .08 .20
116 Vance Johnson RC .20 .50
117 Rich Karlis .08 .20
118 Rulon Jones .08 .20
119 Karl Mecklenburg AP RC .20 .50
120 Louis Wright .08 .20
121 Mike Harden .08 .20
122 Dennis Smith RC .20 .50
123 Steve Foley .08 .20
124 Cowboys TL .12 .30
125 Danny White .20 .50
126 Tony Dorsett .25 .60
127 Timmy Newsome RC .08 .20
128 Mike Renfro .08 .20
129 Tony Hill .12 .30
130 Doug Cosbie .12 .30
131 Rafael Septien .08 .20
132 Ed Too Tall Jones .20 .50
133 Randy White .20 .50
134 Jim Jeffcoat .20 .50
135 Everson Walls .12 .30
136 Dennis Thurman .08 .20
137 Giants TL .12 .30
138 Phil Simms .20 .50
139 Joe Morris .20 .50
140 George Adams RC .08 .20
141 Lionel Manuel .12 .30
142 Bobby Johnson .08 .20
143 Phil McConkey RC .12 .30
144 Mark Bavaro RC .20 .50
145 Zeke Mowatt .08 .20
146 Brad Benson RC .08 .20
147 Bart Oates RC .12 .30
148 Leonard Marshall RC .20 .50
149 Jim Burt .12 .30
150 George Martin .08 .20
151 Lawrence Taylor AP .50 1.25
152 Harry Carson AP .12 .30
153 Elvis Patterson RC .08 .20
154 Sean Landeta RC .12 .30
155 49ers TL .20 .50
Roger Craig
156 Joe Montana 4.00 10.00
157 Roger Craig .20 .50
158 Wendell Tyler .08 .20
159 Carl Monroe .08 .20
160 Dwight Clark .12 .30
161 Jerry Rice RC 25.00 50.00
162 Randy Cross .12 .30
163 Keith Fahnhorst .08 .20
164 Jeff Stover .08 .20
165 Michael Carter RC .08 .20
166 Dwaine Board .08 .20
167 Eric Wright .12 .30
168 Ronnie Lott .30 .75
169 Carlton Williamson .08 .20
170 Redskins TL .12 .30
171 Joe Theismann .20 .50
172 Jay Schroeder RC .20 .50
173 George Rogers .12 .30
174 Ken Jenkins .08 .20
175 Art Monk AP .20 .50
176 Gary Clark RC .75 2.00
177 Joe Jacoby .12 .30
178 Russ Grimm .20 .50
179 Mark Moseley .08 .20
180 Dexter Manley .12 .30
181 Charles Mann RC .20 .50
182 Vernon Dean .08 .20
183 Raphel Cherry RC .08 .20
184 Curtis Jordan .08 .20
185 Browns TL .20 .50
Kosar
186 Gary Danielson .12 .30
187 Bernie Kosar RC 2.00 5.00
188 Kevin Mack RC .20 .50
189 Earnest Byner RC .30 .75
190 Glen Young .08 .20
191 Ozzie Newsome .20 .50
192 Mike Baab .08 .20
193 Cody Risien .12 .30
194 Bob Golic .12 .30
195 Reggie Camp .08 .20
196 Chip Banks .12 .30
197 Tom Cousineau .08 .20
198 Frank Minnifield RC .08 .20
199 Al Gross .08 .20
200 Seahawks TL .12 .30
201 Dave Krieg .20 .50
202 Curt Warner .12 .30
203 Steve Largent AP .25 .60
204 Norm Johnson .08 .20
205 Daryl Turner .08 .20
206 Jacob Green .08 .20
207 Joe Nash .08 .20
208 Jeff Bryant .08 .20
209 Randy Edwards .08 .20
210 Fredd Young .08 .20
211 Kenny Easley .08 .20
212 John Harris .08 .20
213 Packers TL .08 .20
214 Lynn Dickey .12 .30
215 Gerry Ellis .08 .20
216 Eddie Lee Ivery .08 .20
217 Jessie Clark .08 .20
218 James Lofton .20 .50
219 Paul Coffman .08 .20
220 Alphonso Carreker RC .08 .20
221 Ezra Johnson .08 .20
222 Mike Douglass .08 .20
223 Tim Lewis .08 .20
224 Mark Murphy RC .08 .20
225 Joe Montana .40 1.00
K.O'Brien LL
226 Receiving Leaders .12 .30
227 Marcus Allen .20 .50
G.Riggs LL
228 Scoring Leaders .12 .30
229 Interception Leaders .08 .20
230 Chargers TL .20 .50
Dan Fouts
231 Dan Fouts .20 .50
232 Lionel James .08 .20
233 Gary Anderson RB RC .20 .50
234 Tim Spencer RC .12 .30
235 Wes Chandler .12 .30
236 Charlie Joiner .20 .50
237 Kellen Winslow .20 .50
238 Jim Lachey RC .20 .50
239 Bob Thomas .08 .20
240 Jeffery Dale .08 .20
241 Ralf Mojsiejenko .08 .20
242 Lions TL .08 .20
243 Eric Hipple .08 .20
244 Billy Sims .12 .30
245 James Jones .08 .20
246 Pete Mandley RC .08 .20
247 Leonard Thompson .08 .20
248 Lomas Brown RC .12 .30
249 Eddie Murray .12 .30
250 Curtis Green .08 .20
251 William Gay .08 .20
252 Jimmy Williams .08 .20
253 Bobby Watkins .08 .20
254 Bengals TL .20 .50
B.Esiason
255 Boomer Esiason RC 2.50 6.00
256 James Brooks .12 .30
257 Larry Kinnebrew .08 .20
258 Cris Collinsworth .12 .30
259 Mike Martin .08 .20
260 Eddie Brown RC .20 .50
261 Anthony Munoz .20 .50
262 Jim Breech .08 .20
263 Ross Browner .12 .30
264 Carl Zander .08 .20
265 James Griffin .08 .20
266 Robert Jackson .08 .20
267 Pat McInally .08 .20
268 Eagles TL .20 .50
269 Ron Jaworski .12 .30
270 Earnest Jackson .12 .30
271 Mike Quick .12 .30
272 John Spagnola .08 .20
273 Mark Dennard .08 .20
274 Paul McFadden .08 .20
275 Reggie White RC 6.00 15.00
276 Greg Brown .08 .20
277 Herman Edwards .08 .20
278 Roynell Young .08 .20
279 Wes Hopkins .08 .20
280 Steelers TL .12 .30
281 Mark Malone .12 .30
282 Frank Pollard .08 .20
283 Walter Abercrombie .08 .20
284 Louis Lipps .20 .50
285 John Stallworth .20 .50
286 Mike Webster .12 .30
287 Gary Anderson K .12 .30
288 Keith Willis .08 .20
289 Mike Merriweather .08 .20
290 Dwayne Woodruff .08 .20
291 Donnie Shell .12 .30
292 Vikings TL .12 .30
293 Tommy Kramer .12 .30
294 Darrin Nelson .08 .20
295 Ted Brown .12 .30
296 Buster Rhymes RC .08 .20
297 Anthony Carter RC .40 1.00
298 Steve Jordan RC .20 .50
299 Keith Millard RC .20 .50
300 Joey Browner RC .20 .50
301 John Turner .08 .20
302 Greg Coleman .08 .20
303 Chiefs TL .08 .20
304 Bill Kenney .08 .20
305 Herman Heard .08 .20
306 Stephone Paige RC .20 .50
307 Carlos Carson .12 .30
308 Nick Lowery .12 .30
309 Mike Bell .08 .20
310 Bill Maas .08 .20
311 Art Still .08 .20
312 Albert Lewis RC .20 .50
313 Deron Cherry AP .12 .30
314 Colts TL .08 .20
315 Mike Pagel .08 .20
316 Randy McMillan .08 .20
317 Albert Bentley RC .12 .30
318 George Wonsley RC .08 .20
319 Robbie Martin .08 .20
320 Pat Beach .08 .20
321 Chris Hinton .12 .30
322 Duane Bickett RC .20 .50
323 Eugene Daniel .08 .20
324 Cliff Odom RC .08 .20
325 Rohn Stark .12 .30
326 Cardinals TL .08 .20
327 Neil Lomax .12 .30
328 Stump Mitchell .12 .30
329 Ottis Anderson .20 .50
330 J.T. Smith .12 .30
331 Pat Tilley .08 .20
332 Roy Green .12 .30
333 Lance Smith RC .08 .20
334 Curtis Greer .08 .20
335 Freddie Joe Nunn RC .12 .30
336 E.J. Junior .12 .30
337 Lonnie Young RC .08 .20
338 Saints TL .08 .20
339 Bobby Hebert RC .20 .50
340 Dave Wilson .08 .20
341 Wayne Wilson .08 .20
342 Hoby Brenner .08 .20
343 Stan Brock .12 .30
344 Morten Andersen .20 .50
345 Bruce Clark .08 .20
346 Rickey Jackson .20 .50
347 Dave Waymer .08 .20
348 Brian Hansen .08 .20
349 Oilers TL .20 .50
W.Moon
350 Warren Moon 1.50 3.00
351 Mike Rozier RC .20 .50
352 Butch Woolfolk .08 .20
353 Drew Hill .20 .50
354 Willie Drewrey RC .08 .20
355 Tim Smith .12 .30
356 Mike Munchak .20 .50
357 Ray Childress RC .20 .50
358 Frank Bush .08 .20
359 Steve Brown .08 .20
360 Falcons TL .08 .20
361 David Archer RC .20 .50
362 Gerald Riggs .12 .30
363 William Andrews .12 .30
364 Billy Johnson .12 .30
365 Arthur Cox .08 .20
366 Mike Kenn .08 .20
367 Bill Fralic RC .12 .30
368 Mick Luckhurst .08 .20
369 Rick Bryan .08 .20
370 Bobby Butler .08 .20
371 Rick Donnelly RC .08 .20
372 Buccaneers TL .08 .20
373 Steve DeBerg .20 .50
374 Steve Young RC 8.00 20.00
375 James Wilder .08 .20
376 Kevin House .08 .20
377 Gerald Carter .08 .20
378 Jimmie Giles .12 .30
379 Sean Farrell .08 .20
380 Donald Igwebuike .08 .20
381 David Logan .08 .20
382 Jeremiah Castille RC .08 .20
383 Bills TL .08 .20
384 Bruce Mathison RC .08 .20
385 Joe Cribbs .12 .30
386 Greg Bell .12 .30
387 Jerry Butler .08 .20
388 Andre Reed RC 3.00 8.00
389 Bruce Smith RC 3.00 8.00
390 Fred Smerlas .08 .20
391 Darryl Talley .20 .50
392 Jim Haslett .12 .30
393 Charles Romes .08 .20
394 Checklist 1-132 .12 .30
395 Checklist 133-264 .12 .30
396 Checklist 265-396 .12 .30

1986 Topps Box Bottoms

This four-card set, which measures 2 1/2" by 3 1/2", features the four teams which participated in the Super Bowl and in the Conference Championships. This set is arranged in order of how the teams finished, with the Super Bowl Champion Bears being the first team listed. The fronts of the card feature a team photo and identification of all those players is pictured on the back of the card. The cards were issued one per wax box as the side panel of the box, not on the box bottom as was typical of similar sets.

COMPLETE SET (4) 4.00 10.00
A Chicago Bears 1.00 2.50
B New England Patriots .75 2.00
C Los Angeles Rams .75 2.00
D Miami Dolphins 1.50 4.00

1986 Topps 1000 Yard Club

This 26-card standard-size set was distributed as an insert with the 1986 Topps regular issue football wax packs. Players featured are all members of the 1000-yard club, having gained over 1000 yards rushing or receiving during the previous season. The cards are numbered on back according to decreasing order of yardage gained. Roger Craig (22) actually gained over 1000 yards both rushing and receiving. Card backs have orange and red printing on white card stock. The obverses have an ornate border design of green and yellow.

COMPLETE SET (26) 2.50 6.00
1 Marcus Allen .60 1.50
2 Gerald Riggs .10 .25
3 Walter Payton 1.00 2.50
4 Joe Morris .10 .25
5 Freeman McNeil .10 .25
6 Tony Dorsett .30 .75
7 James Wilder .10 .25
8 Steve Largent .40 1.00
9 Mike Quick .10 .25
10 Eric Dickerson .30 .75
11 Craig James .20 .50
12 Art Monk .20 .50
13 Wes Chandler .10 .25
14 Drew Hill .10 .25
15 James Lofton .20 .50
16 Louis Lipps .10 .25
17 Cris Collinsworth .10 .25
18 Tony Hill .10 .25
19 Kevin Mack .10 .25
20 Curt Warner .10 .25
21 George Rogers .10 .25
22 Roger Craig .20 .50
23 Earnest Jackson .10 .25
24 Lionel James .10 .25
25 Stump Mitchell .10 .25
26 Earnest Byner .10 .25

1987 Topps

The 1987 Topps set consists of 396 standard-size cards. Wax packs contained 15 cards as well as a 1,000 yard club card. For the first time, hobby factory sets were issued. Card fronts have the team and player name in banners at the top above the player photo. These banners are in the colors of the player's team. The backs have highlights and statistics within an outline of the NFL shield. To the left is biographical information. Subsets include Record Breakers (2-8) and league leaders (227-231). The set numbering is ordered by teams. Team cards feature an action photo on the front with the team's statistical leaders and week-by-week game results from the previous season on back. The copyright line on the back also includes a letter (A, B, C, or D) to indicate which sheet the card was cut from. Note that each card in the set was produced on two different sheets. This resulted in each card including one of two different letter designations on the back, thus creating a variation on each card. Rookie Cards include Bill Brooks, Keith Byars, Randall Cunningham, Kenneth Davis, Jim Everett, Doug Flutie, Ernest Givins, Charles Haley, Sean Jones, Eric Martin and Jim Kelly. Kelly and Flutie previously appeared in a USFL set.

COMPLETE SET (396) 15.00 40.00
COMP.FACT.SET (396) 50.00 80.00
1 Super Bowl XXI .12 .30
2 Todd Christensen RB .10 .25
3 Dave Jennings RB .12 .30
4 Charlie Joiner RB .12 .30
5 Steve Largent RB .15 .40
6 Dan Marino RB .50 1.25
7 Donnie Shell RB .10 .25
8 Phil Simms RB .12 .30
9 New York Giants TL .12 .30
10 Phil Simms .12 .30
11 Joe Morris AP .10 .25
12 Maurice Carthon RC .12 .30
13 Lee Rouson .07 .20
14 Bobby Johnson .07 .20
15 Lionel Manuel .07 .20
16 Phil McConkey .07 .20
17 Mark Bavaro AP .12 .30
18 Zeke Mowatt .07 .20
19 Raul Allegre .07 .20
20 Sean Landeta .07 .20
21 Brad Benson .07 .20
22 Jim Burt .07 .20
23 Leonard Marshall .07 .20
24 Carl Banks .07 .20
25 Harry Carson .07 .20
26 Lawrence Taylor AP .15 .40
27 Terry Kinard RC .12 .30
28 Pepper Johnson RC .12 .30
29 Erik Howard RC .12 .30
30 Broncos TL .07 .20
31 John Elway .50 1.25
32 Gerald Willhite .07 .20
33 Sammy Winder .10 .25
34 Ken Bell .07 .20
35 Steve Watson .07 .20
36 Rich Karlis .07 .20
37 Keith Bishop .07 .20
38 Rulon Jones .07 .20
39 Karl Mecklenburg AP .10 .25
40 Louis Wright .07 .20
41 Mike Harden .07 .20
42 Dennis Smith .10 .25
43 Bears TL/W.Payton .25 .60
44 Jim McMahon .10 .25
45 Doug Flutie RC 3.00 8.00
46 Walter Payton 2.00 5.00
47 Matt Suhey .10 .25
48 Willie Gault .10 .25
49 Dennis Gentry RC .12 .30
50 Kevin Butler .07 .20
51 Jim Covert .07 .20
52 Jay Hilgenberg .10 .25
53 Dan Hampton .12 .30
54 Steve McMichael .12 .30
55 William Perry .12 .30
56 Richard Dent .12 .30
57 Otis Wilson .07 .20
58 Mike Singletary .12 .30
59 Wilber Marshall .12 .30
60 Mike Richardson .07 .20
61 Dave Duerson .07 .20
62 Gary Fencik .07 .20
63 Redskins TL .10 .25
64 Jay Schroeder .10 .25
65 George Rogers .10 .25
66 Kelvin Bryant RC .15 .40
67 Ken Jenkins .07 .20
68 Gary Clark .12 .30
69 Art Monk .12 .30
70 Clint Didier RC .12 .30
71 Steve Cox .07 .20
72 Joe Jacoby .07 .20
73 Russ Grimm .07 .20
74 Charles Mann .07 .20
75 Dave Butz .07 .20
76 Dexter Manley .07 .20
77 Darrell Green AP .12 .30
78 Curtis Jordan .07 .20
79 Browns TL .07 .20
80 Bernie Kosar .12 .30
81 Curtis Dickey .07 .20
82 Kevin Mack .10 .25
83 Herman Fontenot .07 .20
84 Brian Brennan RC .12 .30
85 Ozzie Newsome .12 .30
86 Jeff Gossett .10 .25
87 Cody Risien .07 .20
88 Reggie Camp .07 .20
89 Bob Golic .07 .20
90 Carl Hairston .07 .20
91 Chip Banks .07 .20
92 Frank Minnifield .07 .20
93 Hanford Dixon .07 .20
94 Gerald McNeil RC .12 .30
95 Dave Puzzuoli .07 .20
96 Patriots TL .12 .30
97 Tony Eason .10 .25
98 Craig James .10 .25
99 Tony Collins .10 .25
100 Mosi Tatupu .07 .20
101 Stanley Morgan .10 .25
102 Irving Fryar .12 .30
103 Stephen Starring .07 .20
104 Tony Franklin .07 .20
105 Rich Camarillo .07 .20
106 Garin Veris .07 .20
107 Andre Tippett AP .10 .25
108 Don Blackmon .07 .20
109 Ronnie Lippett RC .12 .30
110 Raymond Clayborn .07 .20
111 49ers TL/R.Craig .10 .25
112 Joe Montana 2.50 6.00
113 Roger Craig .10 .25
114 Joe Cribbs .10 .25
115 Jerry Rice AP 2.50 6.00
116 Dwight Clark .10 .25
117 Ray Wersching .07 .20
118 Max Runager .07 .20
119 Jeff Stover .07 .20
120 Dwaine Board .07 .20
121 Tim McKyer RC .15 .40
122 Don Griffin RC .15 .40
123 Ronnie Lott AP .12 .30
124 Tom Holmoe .07 .20
125 Charles Haley RC .75 2.00
126 Jets TL .10 .25
127 Ken O'Brien .10 .25
128 Pat Ryan .07 .20
129 Freeman McNeil .10 .25
130 Johnny Hector RC .12 .30
131 Al Toon AP .12 .30
132 Wesley Walker .10 .25
133 Mickey Shuler .07 .20
134 Pat Leahy .07 .20
135 Mark Gastineau .10 .25
136 Joe Klecko .10 .25
137 Marty Lyons .07 .20
138 Bob Crable RC .12 .30
139 Lance Mehl .07 .20
140 Dave Jennings .12 .30
141 Harry Hamilton RC .12 .30
142 Lester Lyles .07 .20
143 Bobby Humphery UER .07 .20
144 Rams TL/E.Dickerson .25 .60
145 Jim Everett RC .40 1.00
146 Eric Dickerson AP .25 .60
147 Barry Redden .07 .20
148 Ron Brown .10 .25
149 Kevin House .07 .20
150 Henry Ellard .12 .30
151 Doug Smith .07 .20
152 Dennis Harrah .07 .20
153 Jackie Slater .10 .25
154 Gary Jeter .07 .20
155 Carl Ekern .07 .20
156 Mike Wilcher .07 .20
157 Jerry Gray RC .12 .30
158 LeRoy Irvin .07 .20
159 Nolan Cromwell .10 .25
160 Chiefs TL .07 .20
161 Bill Kenney .07 .20
162 Stephone Paige .10 .25
163 Henry Marshall .07 .20
164 Carlos Carson .07 .20
165 Nick Lowery .10 .25
166 Irv Eatman RC .12 .30
167 Brad Budde .07 .20
168 Art Still .07 .20
169 Bill Maas .07 .20
170 Lloyd Burruss RC .12 .30
171 Deron Cherry AP .07 .20
172 Seahawks TL .10 .25
173 Dave Krieg .12 .30
174 Curt Warner .10 .25
175 John L. Williams RC .20 .50
176 Bobby Joe Edmonds RC .15 .40
177 Steve Largent .15 .40
178 Bruce Scholtz .07 .20
179 Norm Johnson .07 .20
180 Jacob Green .07 .20
181 Fredd Young .07 .20
182 Dave Brown .07 .20
183 Kenny Easley .07 .20
184 Bengals TL .10 .25
185 Boomer Esiason
186 James Brooks .10 .25
187 Larry Kinnebrew .07 .20
188 Cris Collinsworth .10 .25
189 Eddie Brown .12 .30
190 Tim McGee RC .15 .40
191 Jim Breech .07 .20
192 Anthony Munoz .12 .30
193 Max Montoya .07 .20
194 Eddie Edwards .07 .20
195 Ross Browner .10 .25
196 Emanuel King .07 .20
197 Louis Breeden .07 .20
198 Vikings TL .07 .20
199 Tommy Kramer .10 .25
200 Darrin Nelson .07 .20
201 Allen Rice .07 .20
202 Anthony Carter
203 Leo Lewis .07 .20
204 Steve Jordan .12 .30
205 Chuck Nelson RC .12 .30
206 Greg Coleman .07 .20
207 Gary Zimmerman RC .75 2.00
208 Doug Martin .07 .20
209 Keith Millard .07 .20
210 Issiac Holt RC .12 .30
211 Joey Browner .10 .25
212 Rufus Bess .07 .20
213 Raiders TL/M.Allen .12 .30
214 Jim Plunkett .12 .30
215 Marcus Allen .12 .30
216 Napoleon McCallum RC .15 .40
217 Dokie Williams .07 .20
218 Todd Christensen .10 .25
219 Chris Bahr .07 .20
220 Howie Long .12 .30
221 Bill Pickel .07 .20
222 Sean Jones RC .20 .50
223 Lester Hayes .10 .25
224 Mike Haynes .10 .25
225 Vann McElroy .07 .20
226 Fulton Walker .07 .20
227 Dan Marino/T.Kramer LL .50 1.25
228 J.Rice/Christensen LL .50 1.25
229 Eric Dickerson/Warner LL .25 .60
230 Scoring Leaders .07 .20
231 Interception Leaders .12 .30
232 Dolphins TL .10 .25
233 Dan Marino AP 2.00 5.00
234 Lorenzo Hampton RC .12 .30
235 Tony Nathan .10 .25
236 Mark Duper .12 .30
237 Mark Clayton .12 .30
238 Nat Moore .10 .25
239 Bruce Hardy .07 .20
240 Reggie Roby .10 .25
241 Roy Foster .07 .20
242 Dwight Stephenson .12 .30
243 Hugh Green .07 .20
244 John Offerdahl RC .20 .50
245 Mark Brown .07 .20
246 Doug Betters .07 .20
247 Bob Baumhower .07 .20
248 Falcons TL .10 .25
249 David Archer .12 .30
250 Gerald Riggs .10 .25
251 William Andrews .10 .25
252 Charlie Brown .07 .20
253 Arthur Cox .07 .20
254 Rick Donnelly .07 .20
255 Bill Fralic AP .07 .20
256 Mike Gann RC .12 .30
257 Rick Bryan .07 .20
258 Bret Clark .07 .20
259 Mike Pitts .07 .20
260 Cowboys TL/T.Dorsett .12 .30
261 Danny White .12 .30
262 Steve Pelluer RC .12 .30
263 Tony Dorsett .12 .30
264 Herschel Walker RC .40 1.00
265 Timmy Newsome .07 .20
266 Tony Hill .10 .25
267 Mike Sherrard RC .20 .50
268 Jim Jeffcoat .12 .30
269 Ron Fellows .07 .20
270 Bill Bates .12 .30
271 Michael Downs .07 .20
272 Saints TL/B.Hebert .10 .25
273 Dave Wilson .07 .20
274 Rueben Mayes UER RC .12 .30
275 Hoby Brenner .07 .20
276 Eric Martin RC .12 .30
277 Morten Andersen
278 Brian Hansen .07 .20
279 Rickey Jackson .12 .30
280 Dave Waymer .07 .20
281 Bruce Clark .07 .20
282 James Geathers RC .15 .40
283 Steelers TL .10 .25
284 Mark Malone .10 .25
285 Earnest Jackson .07 .20
286 Walter Abercrombie .10 .25
287 Louis Lipps .10 .25
288 John Stallworth UER
289 Gary Anderson K .07 .20
290 Keith Willis .07 .20
291 Mike Merriweather .07 .20
292 Lupe Sanchez .07 .20
293 Donnie Shell .10 .25
294 Eagles TL/K.Byars .12 .30
295 Mike Reichenbach .07 .20
296 R.Cunningham RC 2.50 6.00
297 Keith Byars RC .20 .50
298 Mike Quick .10 .25
299 Kenny Jackson .07 .20
300 John Teltschik RC .12 .30
301 Reggie White AP .15 .40
302 Ken Clarke .07 .20
303 Greg Brown .07 .20
304 Roynell Young .07 .20
305 Andre Waters RC .20 .50
306 Oilers TL/W.Moon .12 .30
307 Warren Moon .12 .30
308 Mike Rozier .10 .25
309 Drew Hill .10 .25
310 Ernest Givins RC .20 .50
311 Lee Johnson RC .12 .30
312 Kent Hill .07 .20
313 Dean Steinkuhler RC .15 .40
314 Ray Childress .12 .30
315 John Grimsley RC .12 .30
316 Jesse Baker .07 .20
317 Lions TL .07 .20
318 Chuck Long RC .15 .40
319 James Jones .07 .20
320 Garry James .07 .20
321 Jeff Chadwick .07 .20
322 Leonard Thompson .07 .20
323 Pete Mandley .07 .20
324 Jimmie Giles .10 .25
325 Herman Hunter .07 .20
326 Keith Ferguson .07 .20
327 Devon Mitchell .07 .20
328 Cardinals TL .10 .25
329 Neil Lomax .10 .25
330 Stump Mitchell .07 .20
331 Earl Ferrell .07 .20
332 Vai Sikahema RC .15 .40
333 Ron Wolfley RC .12 .30
334 J.T. Smith .10 .25
335 Roy Green .10 .25
336 Al(Bubba) Baker .07 .20
337 Freddie Joe Nunn .07 .20
338 Cedric Mack RC .12 .30
339 Chargers TL .12 .30
340 Dan Fouts .10 .25
341 Gary Anderson RB UER .12 .30
342 Wes Chandler .10 .25
343 Kellen Winslow .12 .30
344 Ralf Mojsiejenko .07 .20
345 Rolf Benirschke .07 .20
346 Lee Williams RC .15 .40
347 Leslie O'Neal RC .40 1.00
348 Billy Ray Smith .10 .25
349 Gill Byrd .10 .25
350 Packers TL .07 .20
351 Randy Wright .07 .20
352 Kenneth Davis RC .20 .50
353 Corry Ellis .07 .20
354 James Lofton .12 .30
355 Phillip Epps RC .12 .30
356 Walter Stanley RC .12 .30
357 Eddie Lee Ivery .07 .20
358 Tim Harris RC .20 .50
359 Mark Lee UER .07 .20
360 Mossy Cade .07 .20
361 Bills TL/J.Kelly .50 1.25
362 Jim Kelly RC 4.00 10.00
363 Robb Riddick RC .12 .30
364 Greg Bell .07 .20
365 Andre Reed .15 .40
366 Pete Metzelaars RC .20 .50
367 Sean McNanie .07 .20
368 Fred Smerlas .07 .20
369 Bruce Smith .75 2.00
370 Darryl Talley .10 .25
371 Charles Romes .07 .20
372 Colts TL .07 .20
373 Jack Trudeau RC .15 .40
374 Gary Hogeboom .10 .25
375 Randy McMillan .07 .20
376 Albert Bentley .07 .20
377 Matt Bouza .07 .20
378 Bill Brooks RC .15 .40
379 Rohn Stark .07 .20
380 Chris Hinton .07 .20
381 Ray Donaldson .07 .20
382 Jon Hand RC .12 .30
383 Buccaneers TL .07 .20
384 Steve Young .50 1.25
385 James Wilder .07 .20
386 Frank Garcia .07 .20
387 Gerald Carter .07 .20
388 Phil Freeman .07 .20
389 Calvin Magee .07 .20
390 Donald Igwebuike .07 .20
391 David Logan .07 .20
392 Jeff Davis RC .12 .30
393 Chris Washington .07 .20
394 Checklist 1-132 .10 .25
395 Checklist 133-264 .10 .25
396 Checklist 265-396 .10 .25

1987 Topps Box Bottoms

This 16-card set, which measures the standard size, was issued on the bottom of 1987 Topps wax pack boxes. The cards are in the same design as the 1987 Topps regular issues except they are bordered in yellow. The backs of the cards are just like the regular card in that they have biographical and complete statistical information. The cards are arranged in alphabetical order and include such stars as Joe Montana, Walter Payton, and Jerry Rice.

COMPLETE SET (16) 15.00 30.00
A Mark Bavaro .40 1.00
B Todd Christensen .30 .75
C Eric Dickerson .40 1.00
D John Elway 2.50 6.00
E Rulon Jones .30 .75
F Dan Marino 2.50 6.00
G Karl Mecklenburg .30 .75
H Joe Montana 2.50 6.00
I Joe Morris .30 .75
J Walter Payton 2.00 5.00
K Jerry Rice 2.00 5.00
L Phil Simms .50 1.25
M Lawrence Taylor .50 1.25
N Al Toon .40 1.00
O Curt Warner .40 1.00
P Reggie White .60 1.50

1987 Topps 1000 Yard Club

This glossy insert set was included one per wax pack with the regular issue 1987 Topps football cards. The set features, in order of yards gained, all players achieving 1000 yards gained either rushing or receiving. Cards have a light blue border on front; backs are blue and black print on white card stock. The cards are standard size. Card backs detail statistically the game by game performance of the player in terms of yards gained against each opponent.

COMPLETE SET (24) 2.50 6.00
1 Eric Dickerson 1.00 2.50
2 Jerry Rice 2.00 5.00
3 Joe Morris .40 1.00
4 Stanley Morgan .40 1.00
5 Curt Warner .40 1.00
6 Rueben Mayes .30 .75
7 Walter Payton 1.00 2.50
8 Gerald Riggs .40 1.00
9 Mark Duper .50 1.25
10 Gary Clark .50 1.25
11 George Rogers .40 1.00
12 Al Toon .50 1.25
13 Todd Christensen .40 1.00
14 Mark Clayton .50 1.25
15 Bill Brooks .40 1.00
16 Drew Hill .40 1.00
17 James Brooks .40 1.00
18 Steve Largent .60 1.50
19 Art Monk .50 1.25
20 Ernest Givins .50 1.25
21 Cris Collinsworth .40 1.00
22 Wesley Walker .40 1.00
23 J.T. Smith .40 1.00
24 Mark Bavaro .50 1.25

1987 Topps American/UK

This mini-size version of 1987 football cards was distributed in the United Kingdom for British fans of American football. Cards measure only 2 1/8" by 3". The photos used are different from the regular issue Topps football cards, although the style is essentially the same. The card backs are colorful and feature a "Talking Football" section where a football term is explained. A collector box (with a complete set checklist on the side) is also available. The cards are arranged according to teams. Cards 76 through 87 are puzzle pieces, combining to show team action photos on their fronts and William "The Refrigerator" Perry on their backs.

COMPLETE SET (88) 25.00 60.00
1 Phil Simms .75 2.00
2 Joe Morris .30 .75
3 Mark Bavaro .30 .75
4 Sean Landeta .20 .50
5 Lawrence Taylor 1.00 2.50
6 John Elway 5.00 12.00
7 Sammy Winder .20 .50
8 Rulon Jones .20 .50
9 Karl Mecklenburg .30 .75
10 Walter Payton 4.00 10.00
11 Dennis Gentry .20 .50
12 Kevin Butler .20 .50
13 Jim Covert .20 .50
14 Richard Dent .40 1.00
15 Mike Singletary .75 2.00
16 Jay Schroeder .20 .50
17 George Rogers .30 .75
18 Gary Clark .40 1.00
19 Art Monk .75 2.00
20 Dexter Manley .20 .50
21 Darrell Green .50 1.25
22 Bernie Kosar .40 1.00
23 Cody Risien .20 .50
24 Hanford Dixon .20 .50
25 Tony Eason .30 .75
26 Stanley Morgan .30 .75
27 Tony Franklin .20 .50
28 Andre Tippett .30 .75
29 Joe Montana 5.00 12.00
30 Jerry Rice 4.00 10.00
31 Ronnie Lott .75 2.00
32 Ken O'Brien .30 .75
33 Freeman McNeil .30 .75
34 Al Toon .30 .75
35 Wesley Walker .30 .75
36 Eric Dickerson .60 1.50
37 Dennis Harrah .20 .50
38 Bill Maas .20 .50
39 Deron Cherry .20 .50
40 Curt Warner .30 .75
41 Bobby Joe Edmonds .20 .50
42 Steve Largent 1.25 3.00
43 Boomer Esiason 1.00 2.50
44 James Brooks .30 .75
45 Cris Collinsworth .40 1.00
46 Tim McGee .30 .75
47 Tommy Kramer .30 .75
48 Marcus Allen 1.50 4.00
49 Todd Christensen .30 .75
50 Sean Jones .30 .75
51 Dan Marino 5.00 12.00
52 Mark Duper .30 .75
53 Mark Clayton .30 .75
54 Dwight Stephenson .30 .75
55 Gerald Riggs .30 .75
56 Bill Fralic .20 .50
57 Tony Dorsett 1.25 3.00
58 Herschel Walker .60 1.50
59 Rueben Mayes .20 .50
60 Lupe Sanchez .20 .50
61 Reggie White 2.00 5.00
62 Warren Moon .75 2.00
63 Ernest Givins .40 1.00
64 Drew Hill .30 .75
65 Jeff Chadwick .20 .50
66 Herman Hunter .20 .50
67 Vai Sikahema .20 .50
68 J.T. Smith .20 .50
69 Dan Fouts .75 2.00
70 Lee Williams .20 .50
71 Randy Wright .20 .50
72 Jim Kelly 2.50 6.00
73 Bruce Smith 1.25 3.00
74 Bill Brooks .30 .75
75 Rohn Stark .20 .50
76 Team Action .20 .50
77 Team Action .20 .50
78 Team Action .20 .50
79 Team Action .20 .50
80 Team Action .20 .50
81 Team Action .20 .50
82 Team Action .20 .50
83 Team Action .20 .50
84 Team Action .20 .50
85 Team Action .20 .50
86 Team Action .20 .50
87 Team Action .20 .50
88 Checklist Card .20 .50

1988 Topps

This 396-card, standard-size set was issued in 15-card wax packs as well as in factory sets. The wax packs also included an 1,000 yard club card. Card fronts feature a team helmet, player's name and position beneath the player photo. The borders surrounding the photo are in the colors of the team. The backs have highlights and yearly statistics. The set is ordered by how the teams finished. The Team Leader (TL) cards show an action scene for each team. Potential young stars are also designated by Topps as "Super Rookies." Rookie Cards include Neal Anderson, Cornelius Bennett, Jerome Brown, Shane Conlan, Chris Doleman, Mel Gray, Kevin Greene, Bo Jackson, Mark Jackson, Seth Joyner, Tom Rathman, Clyde Simmons, Webster Slaughter, Pat Swilling and Vinny Testaverde.

COMPLETE SET (396) 10.00 25.00
COMP.FACT.SET (396) 15.00 30.00
1 Super Bowl XXII .08 .20
2 Vencie Glenn RB .06 .15
3 Steve Largent RB .15 .40
4 Joe Montana RB .30 .75
5 Walter Payton RB .15 .40
6 Jerry Rice RB .30 .75
7 Redskins TL .08 .20
8 Doug Williams .08 .20
9 George Rogers .08 .20
10 Kelvin Bryant .08 .20
11 Timmy Smith SR .08 .20
12 Art Monk .15 .40
13 Gary Clark .15 .40
14 Ricky Sanders RC .15 .40
15 Steve Cox .06 .15
16 Joe Jacoby .06 .15
17 Charles Mann .08 .20
18 Dave Butz .06 .15
19 Darrell Green .08 .20
20 Dexter Manley .06 .15
21 Barry Wilburn .06 .15
22 Broncos TL .06 .15
23 John Elway .75 2.00
24 Sammy Winder .06 .15
25 Vance Johnson .08 .20
26 Mark Jackson RC .15 .40
27 Ricky Nattiel RC .06 .15
28 Clarence Kay RC .06 .15
29 Rich Karlis .06 .15
30 Keith Bishop .06 .15
31 Mike Horan .06 .15
32 Rulon Jones .06 .15
33 Karl Mecklenburg .08 .20
34 Jim Ryan .06 .15
35 Mark Haynes .08 .20
36 Mike Harden .06 .15
37 49ers TL .15 .40
38 Joe Montana .75 2.00
39 Steve Young .40 1.00
40 Roger Craig .08 .20
41 Tom Rathman RC .15 .40
42 Joe Cribbs .08 .20
43 Jerry Rice .75 2.00
44 Mike Wilson RC .06 .15
45 Ron Heller TE RC .06 .15
46 Ray Wersching .06 .15
47 Michael Carter .06 .15
48 Dwaine Board .06 .15
49 Michael Walter RC .06 .15
50 Don Griffin .06 .15
51 Ronnie Lott .15 .40
52 Charles Haley .15 .40
53 Dana McLemore .06 .15
54 Saints TL .08 .20
55 Bobby Hebert .08 .20
56 Rueben Mayes .06 .15
57 Dalton Hilliard RC .06 .15
58 Eric Martin .08 .20
59 John Tice RC .06 .15
60 Brad Edelman .06 .15
61 Morten Andersen .08 .20
62 Brian Hansen .06 .15
63 Mel Gray RC .15 .40
64 Rickey Jackson .08 .20
65 Sam Mills RC .30 .75
66 Pat Swilling RC .15 .40
67 Dave Waymer .06 .15
68 Bears TL .08 .20
69 Jim McMahon .15 .40
70 Mike Tomczak RC .06 .15
71 Neal Anderson RC .15 .40
72 Willie Gault .08 .20
73 Dennis Gentry .06 .15
74 Dennis McKinnon .06 .15
75 Kevin Butler .06 .15
76 Jim Covert .06 .15
77 Jay Hilgenberg .06 .15
78 Steve McMichael .08 .20
79 William Perry .08 .20
80 Richard Dent .15 .40
81 Ron Rivera RC .06 .15
82 Mike Singletary .15 .40
83 Dan Hampton .15 .40
84 Dave Duerson .06 .15
85 Browns TL .08 .20
86 Bernie Kosar .15 .40
87 Earnest Byner .15 .40

88 Kevin Mack .08 .20
89 Webster Slaughter RC .15 .40
90 Gerald McNeil .06 .15
91 Brian Brennan .06 .15
92 Ozzie Newsome .15 .40
93 Cody Risien .06 .15
94 Bob Golic .06 .15
95 Carl Hairston .06 .15
96 Mike Johnson RC .06 .15
97 Clay Matthews .08 .20
98 Frank Minnifield .06 .15
99 Hanford Dixon .06 .15
100 Dave Puzzuoli .06 .15
101 Felix Wright RC .06 .15
102 Oilers TL .15 .40
Moon
103 Warren Moon .20 .50
104 Mike Rozier .06 .15
105 Alonzo Highsmith RC .08 .20
106 Drew Hill .08 .20
107 Ernest Givins .15 .40
108 Curtis Duncan RC .15 .40
109 Tony Zendejas RC .06 .15
110 Mike Munchak .15 .40
111 Kent Hill .06 .15
112 Ray Childress .08 .20
113 Al Smith RC .08 .20
114 Keith Bostic RC .06 .15
115 Jeff Donaldson .06 .15
116 Colts TL .15 .40
Dickerson
117 Jack Trudeau .06 .15
118 Eric Dickerson .15 .40
119 Albert Bentley .06 .15
120 Matt Bouza .06 .15
121 Bill Brooks .15 .40
122 Dean Biasucci RC .06 .15
123 Chris Hinton .06 .15
124 Ray Donaldson .06 .15
125 Ron Solt RC .06 .15
126 Donnell Thompson .06 .15
127 Barry Krauss RC .06 .15
128 Duane Bickett .06 .15
129 Mike Prior RC .06 .15
130 Seahawks TL .08 .20
131 Dave Krieg .08 .20
132 Curt Warner .08 .20
133 John L.Williams .15 .40
134 Bobby Joe Edmonds .06 .15
135 Steve Largent .15 .40
136 Raymond Butler .06 .15
137 Norm Johnson .06 .15
138 Ruben Rodriguez .06 .15
139 Blair Bush .06 .15
140 Jacob Green .06 .15
141 Joe Nash .06 .15
142 Jeff Bryant .06 .15
143 Fredd Young .06 .15
144 Brian Bosworth RC .60 1.50
145 Kenny Easley .06 .15
146 Vikings TL .08 .20
147 Wade Wilson RC .15 .40
148 Tommy Kramer .08 .20
149 Darrin Nelson .06 .15
150 D.J.Dozier RC .08 .20
151 Anthony Carter .08 .20
152 Leo Lewis .06 .15
153 Steve Jordan .08 .20
154 Gary Zimmerman .12 .30
155 Chuck Nelson .06 .15
156 Henry Thomas RC .15 .40
157 Chris Doleman RC .40 1.00
158 Scott Studwell RC .06 .15
159 Jesse Solomon RC .06 .15
160 Joey Browner .06 .15
161 Neal Guggemos .06 .15
162 Steelers TL .08 .20
163 Mark Malone .06 .15
164 Walter Abercrombie .06 .15
165 Earnest Jackson .06 .15
166 Frank Pollard .06 .15
167 Dwight Stone RC .08 .20
168 Gary Anderson K .06 .15
169 Harry Newsome RC .06 .15
170 Keith Willis .06 .15
171 Keith Gary RC .06 .15
172 David Little RC .08 .20
173 Mike Merriweather .06 .15
174 Dwayne Woodruff .06 .15
175 Patriots TL .15 .40
176 Steve Grogan .08 .20
177 Tony Eason .08 .20
178 Tony Collins .08 .20
179 Mosi Tatupu .06 .15
180 Stanley Morgan .08 .20
181 Irving Fryar .15 .40
182 Stephen Starring .06 .15
183 Tony Franklin .06 .15
184 Rich Camarillo .06 .15
185 Garin Veris .06 .15
186 Andre Tippett .08 .20
187 Ronnie Lippett .06 .15
188 Fred Marion .06 .15
189 Dolphins TL .30 .75
D.Marino
190 Dan Marino .75 2.00
191 Troy Stradford RC .08 .20
192 Lorenzo Hampton .06 .15
193 Mark Duper .08 .20
194 Mark Clayton .08 .20
195 Reggie Roby .08 .20
196 Dwight Stephenson .15 .40
197 T.J. Turner RC .06 .15
198 John Bosa RC .06 .15
199 Jackie Shipp RC .06 .15
200 John Offerdahl .08 .20
201 Mark Brown .06 .15
202 Paul Lankford .06 .15
203 Chargers TL .15 .40
204 Tim Spencer .06 .15
205 Gary Anderson RB .08 .20
206 Curtis Adams .06 .15
207 Lionel James .06 .15
208 Chip Banks .06 .15
209 Kellen Winslow .15 .40
210 Ralf Mojsiejenko .06 .15
211 Jim Lachey .08 .20
212 Lee Williams .06 .15
213 Billy Ray Smith .06 .15
214 Vencie Glenn RC .08 .20
215 J.Montana .20 .50
B.Kosar LL
216 Receiving Leaders .08 .20
217 Eric Dickerson .08 .20
C.White L
218 Jerry Rice .15 .40
J.Breech LL
219 Interception Leaders .06 .15
220 Bills TL .15 .40
Jim Kelly
221 Jim Kelly .30 .75
222 Ronnie Harmon RC .15 .40
223 Robb Riddick .06 .15
224 Andre Reed .15 .40
225 Chris Burkett RC .06 .15
226 Pete Metzelaars .15 .40
227 Bruce Smith .20 .50
228 Darryl Talley .08 .20
229 Eugene Marve .06 .15
230 Cornelius Bennett RC .30 .75
231 Mark Kelso RC .06 .15
232 Shane Conlan RC .15 .40
233 Eagles TL .15 .40
R.Cunningham
234 Randall Cunningham .40 1.00
235 Keith Byars .15 .40
236 Anthony Toney RC .06 .15
237 Mike Quick .08 .20
238 Kenny Jackson .06 .15
239 John Spagnola .06 .15
240 Paul McFadden .06 .15
241 Reggie White .25 .60
242 Ken Clarke .06 .15
243 Mike Pitts .06 .15
244 Clyde Simmons RC .15 .40
245 Seth Joyner RC .15 .40
246 Andre Waters .15 .40
247 Jerome Brown RC .15 .40
248 Cardinals TL .06 .15
249 Neil Lomax .08 .20
250 Stump Mitchell .06 .15
251 Earl Ferrell .06 .15
252 Vai Sikahema .06 .15
253 J.T. Smith .08 .20
254 Roy Green .08 .20
255 Robert Awalt RC .08 .20
256 Freddie Joe Nunn .06 .15
257 Leonard Smith RC .06 .15
258 Travis Curtis RC .06 .15
259 Cowboys TL .15 .40
H.Walker
260 Danny White .15 .40
261 Herschel Walker .15 .40
262 Tony Dorsett .15 .40
263 Doug Cosbie .06 .15
264 Roger Ruzek RC .08 .20
265 Darryl Clack .06 .15
266 Ed Too Tall Jones .15 .40
267 Jim Jeffcoat .06 .15
268 Everson Walls .06 .15
269 Bill Bates .08 .20
270 Michael Downs .06 .15
271 Giants TL .08 .20
272 Phil Simms .15 .40
273 Joe Morris .08 .20
274 Lee Rouson .06 .15
275 George Adams .06 .15
276 Lionel Manuel .06 .15
277 Mark Bavaro .08 .20
278 Raul Allegre .06 .15
279 Sean Landeta .06 .15
280 Erik Howard .06 .15
281 Leonard Marshall .08 .20
282 Carl Banks .08 .20
283 Pepper Johnson .08 .20
284 Harry Carson .08 .20
285 Lawrence Taylor .15 .40
286 Terry Kinard .06 .15
287 Rams TL .15 .40
Everett
288 Jim Everett .15 .40
289 Charles White .08 .20
290 Ron Brown .08 .20
291 Henry Ellard .15 .40
292 Mike Lansford .06 .15
293 Dale Hatcher .06 .15
294 Doug Smith .06 .15
295 Jackie Slater .08 .20
296 Jim Collins .06 .15
297 Jerry Gray .06 .15
298 LeRoy Irvin .06 .15
299 Nolan Cromwell .08 .20
300 Kevin Greene RC .50 1.25
301 Jets TL .08 .20
302 Ken O'Brien .08 .20
303 Freeman McNeil .08 .20
304 Johnny Hector .06 .15
305 Al Toon .08 .20
306 JoJo Townsell RC .08 .20
307 Mickey Shuler .06 .15
308 Pat Leahy .06 .15
309 Roger Vick .06 .15
310 Alex Gordon RC .06 .15
311 Troy Benson RC .06 .15
312 Bob Crable .06 .15
313 Harry Hamilton .06 .15
314 Packers TL .06 .15
315 Randy Wright .06 .15
316 Kenneth Davis .08 .20
317 Phillip Epps .06 .15
318 Walter Stanley .06 .15
319 Frankie Neal .06 .15
320 Don Bracken .06 .15
321 Brian Noble RC .08 .20
322 Johnny Holland RC .08 .20
323 Tim Harris .08 .20
324 Mark Murphy .06 .15
325 Raiders TL .20 .50
B.Jackson
326 Marc Wilson .06 .15
327 Bo Jackson RC 5.00 12.00
328 Marcus Allen .15 .40
329 James Lofton .15 .40
330 Todd Christensen .08 .20
331 Chris Bahr .06 .15
332 Stan Talley .06 .15
333 Howie Long .15 .40
334 Sean Jones .15 .40
335 Matt Millen .08 .20
336 Stacey Toran .06 .15
337 Vann McElroy .06 .15
338 Greg Townsend .08 .20
339 Bengals TL .15 .40
Esiason
340 Boomer Esiason .15 .40
341 Larry Kinnebrew .06 .15
342 Stanford Jennings RC .06 .15
343 Eddie Brown .08 .20
344 Jim Breech .06 .15
345 Anthony Munoz .15 .40
346 Scott Fulhage RC .06 .15
347 Tim Krumrie RC .06 .15
348 Reggie Williams .08 .20
349 David Fulcher RC .06 .15
350 Buccaneers TL .06 .15
351 Frank Garcia .06 .15
352 Vinny Testaverde RC 1.50 4.00
353 James Wilder .06 .15
354 Jeff Smith RBK .06 .15
355 Gerald Carter .06 .15
356 Calvin Magee .06 .15
357 Donald Igwebuike .06 .15
358 Ron Holmes RC .06 .15
359 Chris Washington .06 .15
360 Ervin Randle .06 .15
361 Chiefs TL .06 .15
362 Bill Kenney .06 .15
363 Christian Okoye RC .15 .40
364 Paul Palmer RC .06 .15
365 Stephone Paige .08 .20
366 Carlos Carson .06 .15
367 Kelly Goodburn RC .06 .15
368 Bill Maas .06 .15
369 Mike Bell .06 .15
370 Dino Hackett RC .06 .15
371 Deron Cherry .06 .15
372 Lions TL .06 .15
373 Chuck Long .08 .20
374 Garry James .06 .15
375 James Jones FB .06 .15
376 Pete Mandley .06 .15
377 Gary Lee RC .06 .15
378 Eddie Murray .06 .15
379 Jim Arnold .06 .15
380 Dennis Gibson RC .06 .15
381 Michael Cofer LB .06 .15
382 James Griffin .06 .15
383 Falcons TL .06 .15
384 Scott Campbell .06 .15
385 Gerald Riggs .08 .20
386 Floyd Dixon RC .06 .15
387 Rick Donnelly .06 .15
388 Bill Fralic .08 .20
389 Major Everett .06 .15
390 Mike Gann .06 .15
391 Tony Casillas RC .08 .20
392 Rick Bryan .06 .15
393 John Rade RC .06 .15
394 Checklist 1-132 .06 .15
395 Checklist 133-264 .06 .15
396 Checklist 265-396 .06 .15

1988 Topps Box Bottoms

This 16-card standard-size set was issued on the bottom of 1988 Topps wax pack boxes. These cards feature NFL players who had won major awards while in college and they are displayed two players per card. The back of the card features brief biographical blurbs about how the players won the awards while they were in school. The set includes cards of Cornelius Bennett, Bo Jackson, and Vinny Testaverde during their rookie years for cards.

COMPLETE SET (16) 4.00 10.00
A Vinny Testaverde .30 .75
B Dean Steinkuhler .20 .50
C George Rogers .20 .50
D Kenneth Sims .20 .50
E Cornelius Bennett .25 .60
F Bo Jackson .30 .75
Ruth
G Ross Browner .20 .50
H Doug Flutie 1.25 3.00
I Herschel Walker .30 .75
J Jim Plunkett .30 .75
K Charles White .20 .50
L Brad Budde .20 .50
M Marcus Allen .60 1.50
N Mike Rozier .20 .50
O Tony Dorsett .30 .75
P Checklist .20 .50

1988 Topps 1000 Yard Club

This glossy insert set was included one per wax pack with the regular issue 1988 Topps football cards. The set typically features, in order of yards gained, all players achieving 1000 yards gained either rushing or receiving. However, this year, due to the players' strike which shortened the 1987 season, Topps projected 1,000 yard seasons for those players selected as noted in the checklist below. Cards have a green inner border on the front; backs are red and black print on white card stock. The cards are standard size. Card backs detail statistically the game by game performance of the player in terms of yards gained against each opponent.

COMPLETE SET (28) 2.00 5.00
1 Charles White .08 .20
2 Eric Dickerson .25 .60
3 J.T. Smith .06 .20
4 Jerry Rice 1.00 2.50
5 Gary Clark .15 .40
6 Carlos Carson .06 .20
7 Drew Hill .06 .20
8 Curt Warner UER .15 .40
9 Al Toon .15 .40
10 Mike Rozier .06 .20
11 Ernest Givins .15 .40
12 Anthony Carter .15 .40
13 Rueben Mayes .06 .20
14 Steve Largent .25 .60
15 Herschel Walker .15 .40
16 James Lofton .25 .60
17 Gerald Riggs .06 .20
18 Mark Bavaro .06 .20
19 Roger Craig .15 .40
20 Webster Slaughter .06 .20
21 Henry Ellard .15 .40
22 Mike Quick .06 .20
23 Stump Mitchell .06 .20
24 Eric Martin .08 .20
25 Mark Clayton .15 .40
26 Chris Burkett .08 .20
27 Marcus Allen .50 1.00
28 Andre Reed .25 .60

1989 Topps

This 396-card standard-size set was issued in 15-card wax packs as well as in factory set form. The 15-card wax packs also included an 1,000 yard club card. Card fronts have color stripes across the border one-quarter of the way down the card. The player's name, team name and position are toward the bottom of the photo. Horizontally designed backs have yearly statistics and highlights. The card are team order according to their finish in 1988. The Team Leader cards have an action scene on the front and a recap of the team's previous season on the back. Rookie Cards include Eric Allen, Steve Beuerlein, Brian Blades, Tim Brown, Mark Carrier (WR), Cris Carter, Michael Irvin, Keith Jackson, Anthony Miller, Chris Miller, Jay Novacek, Michael Dean Perry, Mark Rypien, Sterling Sharpe, Chris Spielman, John Taylor, Thurman Thomas and Rod Woodson.

COMPLETE SET (396) 7.50 20.00
COMP.FACT.SET (396) 12.00 30.00
1 Super Bowl XXIII .20 .50
Montana
2 Tim Brown RB .20 .50
3 Eric Dickerson RB .06 .15
4 Steve Largent RB .10 .25
5 Dan Marino RB .30 .75
6 49ers TL .20 .50
Montana
7 Jerry Rice .60 1.50
8 Roger Craig .10 .25
9 Ronnie Lott .10 .25
10 Michael Carter .04 .10
11 Charles Haley .10 .25
12 Joe Montana .75 2.00
13 John Taylor RC .20 .50
14 Michael Walter .04 .10
15 Mike Cofer RC .04 .10
16 Tom Rathman .06 .15
17 Daniel Stubbs RC .04 .10
18 Keena Turner .04 .10
19 Tim McKyer .04 .10
20 Larry Roberts .04 .10
21 Jeff Fuller .04 .10
22 Bubba Paris RC .04 .10
23 Bengals Team UER .04 .10
24 Eddie Brown .04 .10
25 Boomer Esiason .10 .25
26 Tim Krumrie .04 .10
27 Ickey Woods RC .20 .50
28 Anthony Munoz .10 .25
29 Tim McGee .04 .10
30 Max Montoya .04 .10
31 David Grant .04 .10
32 Rodney Holman RC .04 .10
33 David Fulcher .04 .10
34 Jim Skow RC .04 .10
35 James Brooks .06 .15
36 Reggie Williams .04 .10
37 Eric Thomas RC .04 .10
38 Stanford Jennings .04 .10
39 Jim Breech .04 .10
40 Bills TL .10 .25
Jim Kelly
41 Shane Conlan .04 .10
42 Scott Norwood RC .04 .10
43 Cornelius Bennett .10 .25
44 Bruce Smith .10 .25
45 Thurman Thomas RC .50 1.25
46 Jim Kelly .20 .50
47 John Kidd .04 .10
48 Kent Hull RC .04 .10
49 Art Still .04 .10
50 Fred Smerlas .04 .10
51A Derrick Burroughs .04 .10
51B Derrick Burroughs .04 .10
52 Andre Reed .10 .25
53 Robb Riddick .04 .10
54 Chris Burkett .04 .10
55 Ronnie Harmon .04 .10
56 Mark Kelso UER .04 .10
57 Bears Team .04 .10
58 Mike Singletary .10 .25
59 Jay Hilgenberg UER .04 .10
60 Richard Dent .10 .25
61 Ron Rivera .04 .10
62 Jim McMahon .10 .25
63 Mike Tomczak .06 .15
64 Neal Anderson .10 .25
65 Dennis Gentry .04 .10
66 Dan Hampton .10 .25
67 David Tate .04 .10
68 Thomas Sanders RC .04 .10
69 Steve McMichael .06 .15
70 Dennis McKinnon .04 .10
71 Brad Muster RC .10 .25
72 Vestee Jackson RC .04 .10
73 Dave Duerson .04 .10
74 Vikings Team .04 .10
75 Joey Browner .06 .15
76 Carl Lee RC .04 .10
77 Gary Zimmerman .10 .25
78 Hassan Jones RC .04 .10
79 Anthony Carter .10 .25
80 Ray Berry RC .04 .10
81 Steve Jordan .04 .10
82 Issiac Holt .04 .10
83 Wade Wilson .06 .15
84 Chris Doleman .06 .15
85 Alfred Anderson .04 .10
86 Keith Millard .04 .10
87 Darrin Nelson .04 .10
88 D.J. Dozier .04 .10
89 Scott Studwell .04 .10
90 Oilers Team .04 .10
91 Bruce Matthews RC .30 .75
92 Curtis Duncan .04 .10
93 Warren Moon .10 .25
94 Johnny Meads RC .04 .10
95 Drew Hill .06 .15
96 Alonzo Highsmith .06 .15
97 Mike Munchak .10 .25
98 Mike Rozier .06 .15
99 Tony Zendejas .04 .10
100 Jeff Donaldson .04 .10
101 Ray Childress .06 .15
102 Sean Jones .04 .10
103 Ernest Givins .06 .15
104 William Fuller RC .10 .25
105 Allen Pinkett RC .04 .10
106 Eagles TL .04 .10
R.Cunningham
107 Keith Jackson RC .10 .25
108 Reggie White .10 .25
109 Clyde Simmons .06 .15
110 John Teltschik .04 .10
111 Wes Hopkins .06 .15
112 Keith Byars .06 .15
113 Jerome Brown .06 .15
114 Mike Quick .06 .15
115 Randall Cunningham .15 .40
116 Anthony Toney .04 .10
117 Ron Johnson WR .04 .10
118 Terry Hoage .04 .10
119 Seth Joyner .06 .15
120 Eric Allen RC .10 .25
121 Cris Carter RC .60 1.50
122 Rams Team .04 .10
123 Tom Newberry RC .04 .10
124 Pete Holohan .04 .10
125 Robert Delpino UER RC .04 .10
126 Carl Ekern .04 .10
127 Greg Bell .04 .10
128 Mike Lansford .04 .10
129 Jim Everett .10 .25
130 Mike Wilcher .04 .10
131 Jerry Gray .04 .10
132 Dale Hatcher .04 .10
133 Doug Smith .04 .10
134 Kevin Greene .10 .25
135 Jackie Slater .10 .25
136 Aaron Cox RC .04 .10
137 Henry Ellard .10 .25
138 Browns Team .04 .10
139 Frank Minnifield .04 .10
140 Webster Slaughter .06 .15
141 Bernie Kosar .10 .25
142 Charles Buchanan .04 .10
143 Clay Matthews .06 .15
144 Reggie Langhorne RC .10 .25
145 Hanford Dixon .04 .10
146 Brian Brennan .04 .10
147 Earnest Byner .06 .15
148 Michael Dean Perry RC .06 .15
149 Kevin Mack .06 .15
150 Matt Bahr .04 .10
151 Ozzie Newsome .10 .25
152 Saints Team .04 .10
153 Morten Andersen .06 .15
154 Pat Swilling .06 .15
155 Sam Mills .06 .15
156 Lonzell Hill .04 .10
157 Dalton Hilliard .04 .10
158 Craig Heyward RC .10 .25
159 Vaughan Johnson RC .06 .15
160 Rueben Mayes .04 .10
161 Gene Atkins RC .04 .10
162 Bobby Hebert .06 .15
163 Rickey Jackson .06 .15
164 Eric Martin .04 .10
165 Giants Team .04 .10
166 Lawrence Taylor .10 .25
167 Bart Oates .06 .15
168 Carl Banks .06 .15
169 Eric Moore RC .04 .10
170 Sheldon White RC .04 .10
171 Mark Collins RC .10 .25
172 Phil Simms .10 .25
173 Jim Burt .06 .15
174 Stephen Baker RC .10 .25
175 Mark Bavaro .06 .15
176 Pepper Johnson .06 .15
177 Lionel Manuel .06 .15
178 Joe Morris .06 .15
179 Jumbo Elliott RC .06 .15
180 Gary Reasons RC .04 .10
181 Seahawks Team .04 .10
182 Brian Blades RC .10 .25
183 Steve Largent .10 .25
184 Rufus Porter RC .04 .10
185 Ruben Rodriguez .04 .10
186 Curt Warner .06 .15
187 Paul Moyer .04 .10
188 Dave Krieg .06 .15
189 Jacob Green .06 .15
190 John L.Williams .06 .15
191 Eugene Robinson RC .10 .25
192 Brian Bosworth .10 .25
193 Patriots Team .04 .10
194 John Stephens RC .04 .10
195 Robert Perryman RC .04 .10
196 Andre Tippett .10 .25
197 Fred Marion .04 .10
198 Doug Flutie .40 1.00
199 Stanley Morgan .06 .15
200 Johnny Rembert RC .04 .10
201 Tony Eason .06 .15
202 Marvin Allen .04 .10
203 Raymond Clayborn .04 .10
204 Irving Fryar .10 .25
205 Colts Team .04 .10
206 Eric Dickerson .10 .25
207 Chris Hinton .04 .10
208 Duane Bickett .04 .10
209 Chris Chandler RC .40 1.00
210 Jon Hand .04 .10
211 Ray Donaldson .04 .10
212 Dean Biasucci .04 .10
213 Bill Brooks .06 .15
214 Chris Goode RC .04 .10
215 Clarence Verdin RC .04 .10
216 Albert Bentley .04 .10
217 Passing Leaders .06 .15
218 Receiving Leaders .06 .15
219 Eric Dickerson .06 .15
Walker LL
220 Scoring Leaders .04 .10
221 Interception Leaders .04 .10
222 Jets Team .04 .10
223 Erik McMillan RC .04 .10
224 James Hasty RC .04 .10
225 Al Toon .06 .15
226 John Booty RC .04 .10
227 Johnny Hector .04 .10
228 Ken O'Brien .06 .15
229 Marty Lyons .04 .10
230 Mickey Shuler .04 .10
231 Robin Cole .04 .10
232 Freeman McNeil .06 .15
233 Marion Barber RC .10 .25
234 Jo Jo Townsell .04 .10
235 Wesley Walker .06 .15
236 Roger Vick .04 .10
237 Pat Leahy .04 .10
238 Broncos TL .20 .50
Elway
239 Mike Horan .04 .10
240 Tony Dorsett .10 .25
241 John Elway .75 2.00
242 Mark Jackson .04 .10
243 Sammy Winder .04 .10
244 Rich Karlis .04 .10
245 Vance Johnson .04 .10
246 Steve Sewell RC .04 .10
247 Karl Mecklenburg UER .06 .15
248 Rulon Jones .04 .10
249 Simon Fletcher RC .04 .10
250 Redskins Team .06 .15
251 Chip Lohmiller RC .04 .10
252 Jamie Morris .06 .15
253 Mark Rypien UER RC .10 .25
254 Barry Wilburn .04 .10
255 Mark May RC .06 .15
256 Wilber Marshall .06 .15
257 Charles Mann .04 .10
258 Gary Clark .10 .25
259 Doug Williams .10 .25
260 Art Monk .10 .25
261 Kelvin Bryant .04 .10
262 Dexter Manley .06 .15
263 Ricky Sanders .06 .15
264 Raiders Team .10 .25
265 Tim Brown RC .60 1.50
266 Jay Schroeder .04 .10
267 Marcus Allen .10 .25
268 Mike Haynes .06 .15
269 Bo Jackson .12 .30
270 Steve Beuerlein RC .25 .60
271 Vann McElroy .04 .10
272 Willie Gault .06 .15
273 Howie Long .10 .25
274 Greg Townsend .04 .10
275 Mike Wise DE .04 .10
276 Cardinals Team .04 .10
277 Luis Sharpe .04 .10
278 Scott Dill .04 .10
279 Vai Sikahema .04 .10
280 Ron Wolfley .04 .10
281 David Galloway .04 .10
282 Jay Novacek RC .20 .50
283 Neil Lomax .06 .15
284 Robert Awalt .04 .10
285 Cedric Mack .04 .10
286 Freddie Joe Nunn .04 .10
287 J.T. Smith .06 .15
288 Stump Mitchell .06 .15
289 Roy Green .06 .15
290 Dolphins TL .20 .50
Marino
291 Jarvis Williams RC .04 .10
292 Troy Stradford .04 .10
293 Dan Marino .75 2.00
294 T.J. Turner .04 .10
295 John Offerdahl .04 .10
296 Ferrell Edmunds RC .04 .10
297 Scott Schwedes .04 .10
298 Lorenzo Hampton .04 .10
299 Jim C.Jensen RC .04 .10
300 Brian Sochia .04 .10
301 Reggie Roby .04 .10
302 Mark Clayton .06 .15
303 Chargers Team .04 .10
304 Lee Williams .04 .10
305 Gary Plummer RC .06 .15
306 Gary Anderson RB .04 .10
307 Gill Byrd .04 .10
308 Jamie Holland RC .04 .10
309 Billy Ray Smith .06 .15
310 Lionel James .04 .10
311 Mark Vlasic RC .04 .10
312 Curtis Adams .04 .10
313 Anthony Miller RC .10 .25
314 Steelers Team .04 .10
315 Bubby Brister RC .10 .25
316 David Little .04 .10
317 Tunch Ilkin RC .04 .10
318 Louis Lipps .06 .15
319 Warren Williams RC .04 .10
320 Dwight Stone .04 .10
321 Merril Hoge RC .10 .25
322 Thomas Everett RC .04 .10
323 Rod Woodson RC .40 1.00
324 Gary Anderson K .04 .10
325 Buccaneers Team .04 .10
326 Donnie Elder .04 .10
327 Vinny Testaverde .12 .30
328 Harry Hamilton .04 .10
329 James Wilder .04 .10
330 Lars Tate .04 .10
331 Mark Carrier RC .10 .25
332 Bruce Hill RC .04 .10
333 Paul Gruber RC .06 .15
334 Ricky Reynolds .04 .10
335 Eugene Marve .04 .10
336 Falcons Team .04 .10
337 Aundray Bruce RC .04 .10
338 John Rade .04 .10
339 Scott Case RC .04 .10
340 Robert Moore .04 .10
341 Chris Miller RC .10 .25
342 Gerald Riggs .06 .15
343 Gene Lang .04 .10
344 Marcus Cotton RC .04 .10
345 Rick Donnelly .04 .10
346 John Settle RC .04 .10
347 Bill Fralic .06 .15
348 Chiefs Team .04 .10
349 Steve DeBerg .06 .15
350 Mike Stensrud RC .04 .10
351 Dino Hackett .04 .10
352 Deron Cherry .04 .10
353 Christian Okoye .06 .15
354 Bill Maas .04 .10
355 Carlos Carson .06 .15
356 Albert Lewis .06 .15
357 Paul Palmer .04 .10
358 Nick Lowery .04 .10
359 Stephone Paige .06 .15
360 Lions Team .04 .10
361 Chris Spielman RC .10 .25
362 Jim Arnold .04 .10
363 Devon Mitchell .04 .10
364 Mike Cofer .04 .10
365 Bennie Blades RC .04 .10
366 James Jones FB .04 .10
367 Garry James .04 .10
368 Pete Mandley .04 .10
369 Keith Ferguson .04 .10
370 Dennis Gibson .04 .10
371 Packers Team UER .04 .10
372 Brent Fullwood RC .04 .10
373 Don Majkowski RC .10 .25
374 Tim Harris .04 .10
375 Keith Woodside RC .04 .10
376 Mark Murphy .04 .10
377 Dave Brown DB .04 .10
378 Perry Kemp RC .04 .10
379 Sterling Sharpe RC .30 .75
380 Chuck Cecil RC .06 .15
381 Walter Stanley .04 .10
382 Cowboys Team .04 .10
383 Michael Irvin RC 1.25 3.00
384 Bill Bates .06 .15
385 Herschel Walker .10 .25
386 Darryl Clack .04 .10
387 Danny Noonan RC .04 .10
388 Eugene Lockhart RC .04 .10
389 Ed Too Tall Jones .06 .15
390 Steve Pelluer .04 .10
391 Ray Alexander .04 .10
392 Nate Newton RC .10 .25
393 Garry Cobb .04 .10
394 Checklist 1-132 .04 .10
395 Checklist 133-264 .04 .10
396 Checklist 265-396 .04 .10

1989 Topps Box Bottoms

These cards were printed on the bottom of 1989 Topps wax pack boxes. This 16-card standard-size set features the NFL's offensive and defensive players of the week for each week in the 1989 season. Each card features two players on the front.

COMPLETE SET (16) 4.00 10.00
A Neal Anderson .20 .50
B Boomer Esiason .30 .75
C Wesley Walker .20 .50
D Jim Everett .20 .50
E Neil Lomax .20 .50
F Kelvin Bryant .20 .50
G Roger Craig .30 .75
H Dan Marino 1.25 3.00
I Drew Hill .20 .50
J Neil Lomax .30 .75
K Roy Green .20 .50
L Bobby Hebert .20 .50
M Ickey Woods .30 .75
N Louis Lipps .20 .50
O Curt Warner .20 .50
P Dave Krieg .30 .75

1989 Topps 1000 Yard Club

This glossy insert set was included one per wax pack with the regular issue 1989 Topps football cards. The set features, in order of yards gained, all players achieving 1000 yards gained either rushing or receiving. The cards are standard size. The card numbers are actually a ranking of each player's standing with respect to total yards gained in 1988. Card backs detail statistically the game by game performance of the player in terms of yards gained against each opponent.

COMPLETE SET (24) 2.00 6.00
1 Eric Dickerson .20 .50
2 Herschel Walker .12 .30
3 Roger Craig .12 .30
4 Henry Ellard .12 .30
5 Jerry Rice .75 2.00
6 Eddie Brown .06 .15
7 Anthony Carter .12 .30
8 Greg Bell .06 .15
9 John Stephens .06 .15
10 Ricky Sanders .06 .15
11 Drew Hill .06 .15
12 Mark Clayton .12 .30
13 Gary Anderson RB .06 .15
14 Neal Anderson .12 .30
15 Roy Green .06 .15
16 Eric Martin .06 .15
17 Joe Morris .06 .15
18 Al Toon .12 .30
19 Ickey Woods .06 .15
20 Bruce Hill .06 .15
21 Lionel Manuel .06 .15
22 Curt Warner .12 .30
23 John Settle .06 .15
24 Mike Rozier .06 .15

1989 Topps Traded

The 1989 Topps Traded set contains 132 standard-size cards featuring rookies and traded players in their new uniforms. The cards are nearly identical to the 1989 Topps regular issue football set, except this traded series was printed on white stock and was distributed only as a boxed set. The card are numbered with a "T" suffix. Rookie Cards include Troy Aikman, Marion Butts, Jim Harbaugh, Greg Lloyd, Dave Meggett, Eric Metcalf, Frank Reich, Andre Rison, Barry Sanders, Deion Sanders, Derrick Thomas, Steve Walsh and Lorenzo White.

COMP.FACT.SET (132) 6.00 15.00
1T Eric Ball RC .06 .15
2T Tony Mandarich RC .06 .15
3T Shawn Collins RC .06 .15
4T Ray Bentley RC .04 .10
5T Tony Casillas .06 .15
6T Al Del Greco RC .06 .15
7T Dan Saleaumua RC .06 .15
8T Keith Bishop .04 .10
9T Rodney Peete RC .20 .50
10T Lorenzo White RC .10 .25
11T Steve Smith RC .04 .10
12T Pete Mandley .04 .10
13T Mervyn Fernandez RC .04 .10
14T Flipper Anderson RC .10 .25
15T Louis Oliver RC .06 .15
16T Rick Fenney RC .04 .10
17T Gary Jeter .04 .10
18T Greg Cox RC .04 .10
19T Bubba McDowell RC .04 .10
20T Ron Heller .04 .10
21T Tim McDonald RC .06 .15
22T Jerrol Williams RC .04 .10
23T Marion Butts RC .10 .25
24T Steve Young .30 .75
25T Mike Merriweather .06 .15
26T Richard Johnson RC .04 .10
27T Gerald Riggs .06 .15
28T Dave Waymer .04 .10
29T Issiac Holt .04 .10
30T Deion Sanders RC .60 1.50
31T Todd Blackledge .06 .15
32T Jeff Cross RC .06 .15
33T Steve Wisniewski RC .10 .25
34T Ron Brown .04 .10
35T Rod Bernstine RC .06 .15
36T Jeff Uhlenhake RC .04 .10
37T Donnell Woolford RC .10 .25
38T Bob Gagliano RC .04 .10
39T Ezra Johnson .04 .10
40T Ron Jaworski .10 .25
41T Lawyer Tillman RC .06 .15
42T Lorenzo Lynch RC .04 .10
43T Mike Alexander .04 .10
44T Tim Worley RC .06 .15
45T Guy Bingham .04 .10
46T Cleveland Gary RC .06 .15
47T Danny Peebles .04 .10
48T Clarence Weathers RC .10 .25
49T Jeff Lageman RC .10 .25
50T Eric Metcalf RC .10 .25
51T Myron Guyton RC .06 .15
52T Steve Atwater RC .10 .25
53T John Fourcade RC .06 .15
54T Randall McDaniel RC .40 1.00
55T Al Noga RC .04 .10
56T Sammie Smith RC .06 .15
57T Jesse Solomon .04 .10
58T Greg Kragen RC .04 .10
59T Don Beebe RC .10 .25
60T Hart Lee Dykes RC .04 .10
61T Trace Armstrong RC .06 .15
62T Steve Pelluer .04 .10
63T Barry Krauss .04 .10
64T Kevin Murphy RC .04 .10
65T Steve Tasker RC .10 .25
66T Jessie Small RC .06 .15
67T Dave Meggett RC .10 .25
68T Dean Hamel .04 .10
69T Jim Covert .06 .15
70T Troy Aikman RC 2.00 5.00
71T Raul Allegre .04 .10
72T Chris Jacke RC .04 .10
73T Leslie O'Neal .06 .15
74T Keith Taylor RC .04 .10
75T Steve Walsh RC .10 .25
76T Tracy Rocker .04 .10
77T Robert Massey RC .04 .10
78T Bryan Wagner .04 .10
79T Steve DeOssie .06 .15
80T Carnell Lake RC .10 .25
81T Frank Reich RC .10 .25
82T Tyrone Braxton RC .06 .15
83T Barry Sanders RC 3.00 8.00
84T Pete Stoyanovich RC .06 .15
85T Paul Palmer .04 .10
86T Billy Joe Tolliver RC .06 .15
87T Eric Hill RC .04 .10
88T Gerald McNeil .04 .10
89T Bill Hawkins RC .04 .10
90T Derrick Thomas RC .50 1.25
91T Jim Harbaugh RC .30 .75
92T Brian Williams OL RC .04 .10
93T Jack Trudeau .04 .10
94T Leonard Smith .04 .10
95T Gary Hogeboom .04 .10
96T A.J.Johnson RC .04 .10
97T Jim McMahon .06 .15
98T David Williams RC .04 .10
99T Rohn Stark .04 .10
100T Sean Landeta .06 .15
101T Tim Johnson RC .06 .15
102T Andre Rison RC .30 .75
103T Earnest Byner .06 .15
104T Don McPherson RC .04 .10
105T Zefross Moss RC .04 .10
106T Frank Stams RC .04 .10
107T Courtney Hall RC .04 .10
108T Marc Logan RC .04 .10
109T James Lofton .10 .25
110T Lewis Tillman RC .06 .15
111T Irv Pankey RC .04 .10
112T Ralf Mojsiejenko .04 .10
113T Bobby Humphrey RC .06 .15
114T Chris Burkett .04 .10
115T Greg Lloyd RC .10 .25
116T Matt Millen .06 .15
117T Carl Zander .04 .10
118T Wayne Martin RC .10 .25
119T Mike Saxon .04 .10
120T Herschel Walker .10 .25
121T Andy Heck RC .04 .10
122T Mark Robinson RC .04 .10
123T Keith Van Horne RC .04 .10
124T Ricky Hunley .04 .10
125T Timm Rosenbach RC .06 .15
126T Steve Grogan .10 .25
127T Stephen Braggs RC .04 .10
128T Terry Long .04 .10
129T Evan Cooper .04 .10
130T Robert Lyles RC .04 .10
131T Mike Webster .10 .25
132T Checklist 1-132 .04 .10

1989 Topps American/UK

This 33-card standard-size set was sold in the United Kingdom as a boxed set. The style of the cards is very similar to the 1989 Topps regular issue set. The backs are different as this set was printed on white card stock. The checklist for the set is on the back of the box. The set is populated with name players that, presumably, would be recognizable in England.

COMP.FACT SET (33) 8.00 20.00
1 Anthony Carter .25 .60
2 Jim Kelly .40 1.00
3 Bernie Kosar .25 .60
4 John Elway 2.00 5.00
5 Andre Tippett .15 .40
6 Henry Ellard .25 .60
7 Eddie Brown .15 .40
8 Gary Anderson RB .15 .40
9 Eric Martin .15 .40
10 Ickey Woods .15 .40
11 Mike Singletary .30 .75
12 Phil Simms .30 .75
13 Brian Bosworth .15 .40
14 Mark Clayton .25 .60
15 Eric Dickerson .30 .75
16 John Stephens .15 .40
17 Neal Anderson .25 .60
18 Al Toon .15 .40
19 Lionel Manuel .15 .40
20 Joe Montana 2.50 6.00
21 Reggie White .40 1.00
22 Randall Cunningham .40 1.00
23 Lawrence Taylor .30 .75
24 Jim Everett .25 .60
25 Neil Lomax .15 .40
26 Herschel Walker .25 .60
27 Roger Craig .25 .60
28 Greg Bell .15 .40
29 Ricky Sanders .15 .40
30 Joe Morris .15 .40
31 Curt Warner .15 .40
32 Boomer Esiason .30 .75
33 Dan Marino 2.00 5.00

1989 Topps Football Talk

LJN Toys distributed this set of cards to be used with their Sportstalk record player. Each player card features a reprint of a previously issued card on the fronts with a 1989 Topps football card style cardback along with a clear plastic audio record attached. Two program cover cards were included from historic NFL games. The eight cards were packaged in two seperate blister packs of four cards. Note that there were two card #1's produced and no #4.

COMPLETE SET (8)	60.00	120.00
1A 1958 Championship Program	4.00	10.00
1B Joe Greene	8.00	20.00
2 Bob Lilly	6.00	15.00
3 Super Bowl III Program	5.00	12.00
5 Franco Harris	10.00	25.00
6 Gale Sayers	10.00	25.00
7 Johnny Unitas	12.00	30.00
8 Billy Kilmer	4.00	10.00

1990 Topps

Returning to 528 cards for the first time since 1982, these standard size cards were available in factory sets, fifteen card wax packs and cello packs. Each pack included a 1,000 Yard Club card. The cardbacks can be found with variations: the NFL Properties disclaimer is either present or absent from the back of each card. The cards are arranged in team order and the teams themselves are ordered according to their finish in the 1989 standings. Subsets include Record Breakers (1-5) and Team Action (501-528) cards. League Leader cards are scattered throughout the set. A few leader cards (28, 193, 229, and 431) as well as all of the Team Action cards can be found with or without the hashmarks on the bottom of the card. Topps also produced a Tiffany or glossy edition of the set.

COMPLETE SET (528)	10.00	25.00
COMP.FACT.SET (528)	12.50	30.00
*DISCLAIMER BACK: .4X TO 1X		
1 Joe Montana RB	.30	.75
2 Flipper Anderson RB	.04	.10
3 Troy Aikman RB	.20	.50
4 Kevin Butler RB	.04	.10
5 Super Bowl XXIV	.04	.10
6 Dexter Carter RC	.04	.10
7 Matt Millen	.06	.15
8 Jerry Rice	.40	1.00
9 Ronnie Lott	.06	.15
10 John Taylor	.06	.15
11 Guy McIntyre	.04	.10
12 Roger Craig	.06	.15
13 Joe Montana	.50	1.25
14 Brent Jones RC	.12	.30
15 Tom Rathman	.04	.10
16 Harris Barton	.04	.10
17 Charles Haley	.06	.15
18 Pierce Holt RC	.04	.10
19 Michael Carter	.04	.10
20 Chet Brooks	.04	.10
21 Eric Wright	.04	.10
22 Mike Cofer	.04	.10
23 Jim Fahnhorst	.04	.10
24 Keena Turner	.04	.10
25 Don Griffin	.04	.10
26 Kevin Fagan RC	.04	.10
27 Bubba Paris	.04	.10
28A B.Sanders/C.Okoye LL	.30	.75
28B B.Sanders/Okoye LL no HM	.20	.50
29 Steve Atwater	.04	.10
30 Tyrone Braxton	.04	.10
31 Ron Holmes	.04	.10
32 Bobby Humphrey	.04	.10
33 Greg Kragen	.04	.10
34 David Treadwell	.04	.10
35 Karl Mecklenburg	.04	.10
36 Dennis Smith	.04	.10
37 John Elway	.50	1.25
38 Vance Johnson	.04	.10
39 Simon Fletcher UER	.04	.10
40 Jim Juriga	.04	.10
41 Mark Jackson	.04	.10
42 Melvin Bratton RC	.04	.10
43 Wymon Henderson RC	.04	.10
44 Ken Bell	.04	.10
45 Sammy Winder	.04	.10
46 Alphonso Carreker	.04	.10
47 Orson Mobley RC	.04	.10
48 Rodney Hampton RC	.12	.30
49 Dave Meggett	.06	.15
50 Myron Guyton	.04	.10
51 Phil Simms	.06	.15
52 Lawrence Taylor	.12	.30
53 Carl Banks	.04	.10
54 Pepper Johnson	.04	.10
55 Leonard Marshall	.04	.10
56 Mark Collins	.04	.10
57 Erik Howard	.04	.10
58 Eric Dorsey RC	.04	.10
59 Ottis Anderson	.06	.15
60 Mark Bavaro	.04	.10
61 Odessa Turner RC	.04	.10
62 Gary Reasons	.04	.10
63 Maurice Carthon	.04	.10
64 Lionel Manuel	.04	.10
65 Sean Landeta	.04	.10
66 Perry Williams	.04	.10
67 Pat Terrell RC	.04	.10
68 Flipper Anderson	.04	.10
69 Jackie Slater	.04	.10
70 Tom Newberry	.04	.10
71 Jerry Gray	.04	.10
72 Henry Ellard	.06	.15
73 Doug Smith	.04	.10
74 Kevin Greene	.06	.15
75 Jim Everett	.06	.15
76 Mike Lansford	.04	.10
77 Greg Bell	.04	.10
78 Pete Holohan	.04	.10
79 Robert Delpino	.04	.10
80 Mike Wilcher	.04	.10
81 Mike Piel	.04	.10
82 Mel Owens	.04	.10
83 Michael Stewart RC	.04	.10
84 Ben Smith RC	.04	.10
85 Keith Jackson	.06	.15
86 Reggie White	.12	.30
87 Eric Allen	.04	.10
88 Jerome Brown	.04	.10
89 Robert Drummond	.04	.10
90 Anthony Toney	.04	.10
91 Keith Byars	.04	.10
92 Cris Carter	.30	.75
93 Randall Cunningham	.12	.30
94 Ron Johnson WR	.04	.10
95 Mike Quick	.04	.10
96 Clyde Simmons	.04	.10
97 Mike Pitts	.04	.10
98 Izel Jenkins RC	.04	.10
99 Seth Joyner	.06	.15
100 Mike Schad	.04	.10
101 Wes Hopkins	.04	.10
102 Kirk Lowdermilk	.04	.10
103 Rick Fenney	.04	.10
104 Randall McDaniel	.12	.30
105 Herschel Walker	.06	.15
106 Al Noga	.04	.10
107 Gary Zimmerman	.06	.15
108 Chris Doleman	.04	.10
109 Keith Millard	.04	.10
110 Carl Lee	.04	.10
111 Joey Browner	.04	.10
112 Steve Jordan	.04	.10
113 Reggie Rutland RC	.04	.10
114 Wade Wilson	.06	.15
115 Anthony Carter	.06	.15
116 Rich Karlis	.04	.10
117 Hassan Jones	.04	.10
118 Henry Thomas	.04	.10
119 Scott Studwell	.04	.10
120 Ralf Mojsiejenko	.04	.10
121 Earnest Byner	.04	.10
122 Gerald Riggs	.06	.15
123 Tracy Rocker	.04	.10
124 A.J. Johnson	.04	.10
125 Charles Mann	.04	.10
126 Art Monk	.06	.15
127 Ricky Sanders	.04	.10
128 Gary Clark	.12	.30
129 Jim Lachey	.04	.10
130 Martin Mayhew RC	.04	.10
131 Ravin Caldwell	.04	.10
132 Don Warren	.04	.10
133 Mark Rypien	.06	.15
134 Ed Simmons RC	.04	.10
135 Darryl Grant	.04	.10
136 Darrell Green	.06	.15
137 Chip Lohmiller	.04	.10
138 Tony Bennett RC	.12	.30
139 Tony Mandarich	.04	.10
140 Sterling Sharpe	.12	.30
141 Tim Harris	.04	.10
142 Don Majkowski	.04	.10
143 Rich Moran RC	.04	.10
144 Jeff Query	.04	.10
145 Brent Fullwood	.04	.10
146 Chris Jacke	.04	.10
147 Keith Woodside	.04	.10
148 Perry Kemp	.04	.10
149 Herman Fontenot	.04	.10
150 Dave Brown DB	.04	.10
151 Brian Noble	.04	.10
152 Johnny Holland	.04	.10
153 Mark Murphy	.04	.10
154 Bob Nelson NT	.04	.10
155 Darrell Thompson RC	.04	.10
156 Lawyer Tillman	.04	.10
157 Eric Metcalf	.12	.30
158 Webster Slaughter	.06	.15
159 Frank Minnifield	.04	.10
160 Brian Brennan	.04	.10
161 Thane Gash RC	.04	.10
162 Robert Banks DE	.04	.10
163 Bernie Kosar	.06	.15
164 David Grayson	.04	.10
165 Kevin Mack	.04	.10
166 Mike Johnson	.04	.10
167 Tim Manoa	.04	.10
168 Ozzie Newsome	.06	.15
169 Felix Wright	.04	.10
170A Al Baker Orng.	.06	.15
170B Al Baker Wht.	.06	.15
171 Reggie Langhorne	.04	.10
172 Clay Matthews	.06	.15
173 Andrew Stewart	.04	.10
174 Barry Foster RC	.12	.30
175 Tim Worley	.04	.10
176 Tim Johnson	.04	.10
177 Carnell Lake	.04	.10
178 Greg Lloyd	.12	.30
179 Rod Woodson	.12	.30
180 Tunch Ilkin	.04	.10
181 Dermontti Dawson	.08	.25
182 Gary Anderson K	.04	.10
183 Bubby Brister	.04	.10
184 Louis Lipps	.06	.15
185 Merril Hoge	.04	.10
186 Mike Mularkey	.04	.10
187 Derek Hill RC	.04	.10
188 Rodney Carter	.04	.10
189 Dwayne Woodruff	.04	.10
190 Keith Willis	.04	.10
191 Jerry Olsavsky	.04	.10
192 Mark Stock	.04	.10
193 Sacks Leaders	.04	.10
194 Leonard Smith	.04	.10
195 Darryl Talley	.04	.10
196 Mark Kelso	.04	.10
197 Kent Hull	.04	.10
198 Nate Odomes RC	.06	.15
199 Pete Metzelaars	.04	.10
200 Don Beebe	.06	.15
201 Ray Bentley	.04	.10
202 Steve Tasker	.06	.15
203 Scott Norwood	.04	.10
204 Andre Reed	.12	.30
205 Bruce Smith	.12	.30
206 Thurman Thomas	.12	.30
207 Jim Kelly	.12	.30
208 Cornelius Bennett	.06	.15
209 Shane Conlan	.04	.10
210 Larry Kinnebrew	.04	.10
211 Jeff Alm RC	.04	.10
212 Robert Lyles	.04	.10
213 Bubba McDowell	.04	.10
214 Mike Munchak	.06	.15
215 Bruce Matthews	.06	.15
216 Warren Moon	.12	.30
217 Drew Hill	.04	.10
218 Ray Childress	.04	.10
219 Steve Brown	.04	.10
220 Alonzo Highsmith	.04	.10
221 Allen Pinkett	.04	.10
222 Sean Jones	.06	.15
223 Johnny Meads	.04	.10
224 John Grimsley	.04	.10
225 Haywood Jeffires RC	.12	.30
226 Curtis Duncan	.04	.10
227 Greg Montgomery RC	.04	.10
228 Ernest Givins	.06	.15
229A Montana/Esiason LL	.30	.75
229B Montana/Esiason LL no HM	.20	.50
230 Robert Massey	.04	.10
231 John Fourcade	.04	.10
232 Dalton Hilliard	.04	.10
233 Vaughan Johnson	.04	.10
234 Hoby Brenner	.04	.10
235 Pat Swilling	.06	.15
236 Kevin Haverdink RC	.04	.10
237 Bobby Hebert	.04	.10
238 Sam Mills	.06	.15
239 Eric Martin	.04	.10
240 Lonzell Hill	.04	.10
241 Steve Trapilo	.04	.10
242 Rickey Jackson	.06	.15
243 Craig Heyward	.06	.15
244 Rueben Mayes	.04	.10
245 Morten Andersen	.04	.10
246 Percy Snow RC	.04	.10
247 Pete Mandley	.04	.10
248 Derrick Thomas	.12	.30
249 Dan Saleaumua	.04	.10
250 Todd McNair RC	.04	.10
251 Leonard Griffin RC	.04	.10
252 Jonathan Hayes	.04	.10
253 Christian Okoye	.04	.10
254 Albert Lewis	.04	.10
255 Nick Lowery	.04	.10
256 Kevin Ross	.04	.10
257 Steve DeBerg UER	.04	.10
258 Stephone Paige	.04	.10
259 James Saxon RC	.04	.10
260 Herman Heard	.04	.10
261 Deron Cherry	.04	.10
262 Dino Hackett	.04	.10
263 Neil Smith	.12	.30
264 Steve Pelluer	.04	.10
265 Eric Thomas	.04	.10
266 Eric Ball	.04	.10
267 Leon White	.04	.10
268 Tim Krumrie	.04	.10
269 Jason Buck	.04	.10
270 Boomer Esiason	.06	.15
271 Carl Zander	.04	.10
272 Eddie Brown	.04	.10
273 David Fulcher	.04	.10
274 Tim McGee	.04	.10
275 James Brooks	.06	.15
276 Rickey Dixon RC	.04	.10
277 Ickey Woods	.04	.10
278 Anthony Munoz	.06	.15
279 Rodney Holman	.04	.10
280 Mike Alexander	.04	.10
281 Mervyn Fernandez	.04	.10
282 Steve Wisniewski	.06	.15
283 Steve Smith	.04	.10
284 Howie Long	.12	.30
285 Bo Jackson	.15	.40
286 Mike Dyal RC	.04	.10
287 Thomas Benson RC	.04	.10
288 Willie Gault	.06	.15
289 Marcus Allen	.12	.30
290 Greg Townsend	.04	.10
291 Steve Beuerlein	.06	.15
292 Scott Davis	.04	.10
293 Eddie Anderson RC	.04	.10
294 Terry McDaniel	.04	.10
295 Tim Brown	.12	.30
296 Bob Golic	.04	.10
297 Jeff Jaeger RC	.04	.10
298 Jeff George RC	.30	.75
299 Chip Banks	.04	.10
300 Andre Rison UER	.12	.30
301 Rohn Stark	.04	.10
302 Keith Taylor	.04	.10
303 Jack Trudeau	.04	.10
304 Chris Hinton	.04	.10
305 Ray Donaldson	.04	.10
306 Jeff Herrod RC	.04	.10
307 Clarence Verdin	.04	.10
308 Jon Hand	.04	.10
309 Bill Brooks	.04	.10
310 Albert Bentley	.04	.10
311 Mike Prior	.04	.10
312 Pat Beach	.04	.10
313 Eugene Daniel	.04	.10
314 Duane Bickett	.04	.10
315 Dean Biasucci	.04	.10
316 Richmond Webb RC	.04	.10
317 Jeff Cross	.04	.10
318 Louis Oliver	.04	.10
319 Sammie Smith	.04	.10
320 Pete Stoyanovich	.04	.10
321 John Offerdahl	.04	.10
322 Ferrell Edmunds	.04	.10
323 Dan Marino	.50	1.25
324 Andre Brown	.04	.10
325 Reggie Roby	.04	.10
326 Jarvis Williams	.04	.10
327 Roy Foster	.04	.10
328 Mark Clayton	.06	.15
329 Brian Sochia	.04	.10
330 Mark Duper	.06	.15
331 T.J. Turner	.04	.10
332 Jeff Uhlenhake	.04	.10
333 Jim C.Jensen	.04	.10
334 Cortez Kennedy RC	.30	.75
335 Andy Heck	.04	.10
336 Rufus Porter	.04	.10
337 Brian Blades	.06	.15
338 Dave Krieg	.06	.15
339 John L. Williams	.04	.10
340 David Wyman	.04	.10
341 Paul Skansi RC	.04	.10
342 Eugene Robinson	.04	.10
343 Joe Nash	.04	.10
344 Jacob Green	.04	.10
345 Jeff Bryant	.04	.10
346 Ruben Rodriguez	.04	.10
347 Norm Johnson	.04	.10
348 Darren Comeaux RC	.04	.10
349 Andre Ware RC	.06	.15
350 Richard Johnson	.04	.10
351 Rodney Peete	.06	.15
352 Barry Sanders	.50	1.25
353 Chris Spielman	.12	.30
354 Eddie Murray	.04	.10
355 Jerry Ball	.04	.10
356 Mel Gray	.06	.15
357 Eric Williams RC	.04	.10
358 Robert Clark RC	.04	.10
359 Jason Phillips	.04	.10
360 Terry Taylor RC	.04	.10
361 Bennie Blades	.04	.10
362 Michael Cofer	.04	.10
363 Jim Arnold	.04	.10
364 Marc Spindler RC	.04	.10
365 Jim Covert	.04	.10
366 Jim Harbaugh	.12	.30
367 Neal Anderson	.06	.15
368 Mike Singletary	.06	.15
369 John Roper	.04	.10
370 Steve McMichael	.06	.15
371 Dennis Gentry	.04	.10
372 Brad Muster	.04	.10
373 Ron Morris	.04	.10
374 James Thornton	.04	.10
375 Kevin Butler	.04	.10
376 Richard Dent	.06	.15
377 Dan Hampton	.06	.15
378 Jay Hilgenberg	.04	.10
379 Donnell Woolford	.04	.10
380 Trace Armstrong	.04	.10
381 Junior Seau RC	.50	1.25
382 Rod Bernstine	.04	.10
383 Marion Butts	.06	.15
384 Burt Grossman	.04	.10
385 Darrin Nelson	.04	.10
386 Leslie O'Neal	.06	.15
387 Billy Joe Tolliver	.04	.10
388 Courtney Hall	.04	.10
389 Lee Williams	.04	.10
390 Anthony Miller	.12	.30
391 Gill Byrd	.04	.10
392 Wayne Walker WR	.04	.10
393 Billy Ray Smith	.04	.10
394 Vencie Glenn	.04	.10
395 Tim Spencer	.04	.10
396 Gary Plummer	.04	.10
397 Arthur Cox	.04	.10
398 Jamie Holland	.04	.10
399 Keith McCants RC	.04	.10
400 Kevin Murphy	.04	.10
401 Danny Peebles	.04	.10
402 Mark Robinson	.04	.10
403 Broderick Thomas	.04	.10
404 Ron Hall	.04	.10
405 Mark Carrier WR	.12	.30
406 Paul Gruber	.04	.10
407 Vinny Testaverde	.06	.15
408 Bruce Hill	.04	.10
409 Lars Tate	.04	.10
410 Harry Hamilton	.04	.10
411 Ricky Reynolds	.04	.10
412 Donald Igwebuike	.04	.10
413 Reuben Davis	.04	.10
414 William Howard	.04	.10
415 Winston Moss RC	.04	.10
416 Chris Singleton RC	.04	.10
417 Hart Lee Dykes	.04	.10
418 Steve Grogan	.06	.15
419 Bruce Armstrong	.04	.10
420 Robert Perryman	.04	.10
421 Andre Tippett	.04	.10
422 Sammy Martin	.04	.10
423 Stanley Morgan	.04	.10
424 Cedric Jones RC	.04	.10
425 Sean Farrell	.04	.10
426 Marc Wilson	.04	.10
427 John Stephens	.04	.10
428 Eric Sievers RC	.04	.10
429 Maurice Hurst RC	.04	.10
430 Johnny Rembert	.04	.10
431A J.Rice/A.Reed LL	.15	.40
431B Rice/A.Reed LL no HM	.15	.40
432 Eric Hill	.04	.10
433 Gary Hogeboom	.04	.10
434 Timm Rosenbach UER	.04	.10
435 Tim McDonald	.04	.10
436 Rich Camarillo	.04	.10
437 Luis Sharpe	.04	.10
438 J.T. Smith	.04	.10
439 Roy Green	.06	.15
440 Ernie Jones RC	.04	.10
441 Robert Awalt	.04	.10
442 Vai Sikahema	.04	.10
443 Joe Wolf	.04	.10
444 Stump Mitchell	.04	.10
445 David Galloway	.04	.10
446 Ron Wolfley	.04	.10
447 Freddie Joe Nunn	.04	.10
448 Blair Thomas RC	.06	.15
449 Jeff Lageman	.04	.10
450 Tony Eason	.04	.10
451 Erik McMillan	.04	.10
452 Jim Sweeney	.04	.10
453 Ken O'Brien	.04	.10
454 Johnny Hector	.04	.10
455 Jo Jo Townsell	.04	.10
456 Roger Vick	.04	.10
457 James Hasty	.04	.10
458 Dennis Byrd RC	.06	.15
459 Ron Stallworth	.04	.10
460 Mickey Shuler	.04	.10
461 Bobby Humphery	.04	.10
462 Kyle Clifton	.04	.10
463 Al Toon	.06	.15
464 Freeman McNeil	.04	.10
465 Pat Leahy	.04	.10
466 Scott Case	.04	.10
467 Shawn Collins	.04	.10
468 Floyd Dixon	.04	.10
469 Deion Sanders	.30	.75
470 Tony Casillas	.04	.10
471 Michael Haynes RC	.12	.30
472 Chris Miller	.12	.30
473 John Settle	.04	.10
474 Aundray Bruce	.04	.10
475 Gene Lang	.04	.10
476 Tim Gordon RC	.04	.10
477 Scott Fulhage	.04	.10
478 Bill Fralic	.04	.10
479 Jessie Tuggle RC	.04	.10
480 Marcus Cotton	.04	.10
481 Steve Walsh	.06	.15
482 Troy Aikman	.40	1.00
483 Ray Horton	.04	.10
484 Tony Tolbert RC	.06	.15
485 Steve Folsom	.04	.10
486 Ken Norton Jr. RC	.12	.30
487 Kelvin Martin RC	.04	.10
488 Jack Del Rio	.06	.15
489 Daryl Johnston RC	.40	1.00
490 Bill Bates	.06	.15
491 Jim Jeffcoat	.04	.10
492 Vince Albritton	.04	.10
493 Eugene Lockhart	.04	.10
494 Mike Saxon	.04	.10
495 James Dixon	.04	.10
496 Willie Broughton	.04	.10
497 Checklist 1-132	.04	.10
498 Checklist 133-264	.04	.10
499 Checklist 265-396	.04	.10
500 Checklist 397-528	.04	.10
501A Bears TL/Harbaugh	.06	.15
501B Bears TL/Harbaugh no HM	.06	.15
502A Bengals TL/Esiason	.04	.10
502B Bengals TL/Esiason no HM	.04	.10
503A Bills TL/Conlan	.04	.10
503B Bills TL/Conlan no HM	.04	.10
504A Broncos TL	.04	.10
504B Broncos TL no HM	.04	.10
505A Browns TL/Kosar	.04	.10
505B Browns TL/Kosar no HM	.04	.10
506A Buccaneers TL	.04	.10
506B Buccaneers TL no HM	.04	.10
507A Cardinals TL	.04	.10
507B Cardinals TL no HM	.04	.10
508A Chargers TL	.04	.10
508B Chargers TL no HM	.04	.10
509A Chiefs TL	.04	.10
509B Chiefs TL no HM	.04	.10
510A Colts TL	.04	.10
510B Colts TL no HM	.04	.10
511A Cowboys TL/Aikman	.15	.40
511B Cowboys TL/Aikman no HM	.15	.40
512A Dolphins TL	.04	.10
512B Dolphins TL no HM	.04	.10
513A Eagles TL	.04	.10
513B Eagles TL no HM	.04	.10
514A Falcons TL	.04	.10
514B Falcons TL no HM	.04	.10
515A 49ers TL/Montana/Craig	.15	.40
515B 49ers TL/Montana/Craig no HM	.15	.40
516A Giants TL/Simms	.04	.10
516B Giants TL/Simms no HM	.04	.10
517A Jets TL	.04	.10
517B Jets TL no HM	.04	.10
518A Lions TL	.04	.10
518B Lions TL no HM	.04	.10
519A Oilers TL/Moon	.06	.15
519B Oilers TL/Moon no HM	.06	.15
520A Packers TL/Majik	.04	.10
520B Packers TL/Majik no HM	.04	.10
521A Patriots TL	.04	.10
521B Patriots TL no HM	.04	.10
522A Raiders TL/Bo	.06	.15
522B Raiders TL/Bo no HM	.06	.15
523A Rams TL/Everatt	.04	.10
523B Rams TL/Everatt no HM	.04	.10
524A Redskins TL/Riggs	.04	.10
524B Redskins TL/Riggs no HM	.04	.10
525A Saints TL	.04	.10
525B Saints TL no HM	.04	.10
526A Seahawks TL	.04	.10
526B Seahawks TL no HM	.04	.10
527A Steelers TL	.04	.10
527B Steelers TL no HM	.04	.10
528A Vikings TL	.04	.10
528B Vikings TL no HM	.04	.10

1990 Topps Tiffany

COMP.FACT.SET (528)	50.00	100.00
*VETERANS: 6X TO 15X BASIC CARDS		
*ROOKIES: 3X TO 8X BASIC CARDS		

1990 Topps Box Bottoms

These cards were printed on the bottom of the 1990 Topps Wax Boxes. This 16-card standard-size set features the NFL's offensive and defensive player of the week for each week of the 1989 season. Each card features two players on the front and the back explains why they were the player of the week and what they did to earn the title. The cards are lettered rather than numbered. The set is checklisted in order of weeks of the season and is arranged alphabetically. The cards in this set were released in two distinct varieties; the NFL Properties disclaimer is either present or absent from the back of each card.

COMPLETE SET (16)	3.00	8.00
*DISCLAIMER BACK: .4X TO 1X		
A Jim Kelly David Grayson	.40	1.00
B Henry Ellard Derrick Thomas	.25	.60
C Joe Montana Vince Newsome	.75	2.00
D Bubby Brister Tim Harris	.15	.40
E Christian Okoye Keith Millard	.15	.40
F Warren Moon Jerome Brown	.25	.60
G John Elway Mike Merriweather	.75	2.00
H Webster Slaughter Pat Swilling	.15	.40
I Rich Karlis Lawrence Taylor	.25	.60
J Dan Marino Greg Kragen	.75	2.00
K Boomer Esiason Brent Williams	.15	.40
L Flipper Anderson Pierce Holt	.15	.40
M Richard Johnson David Fulcher	.15	.40
N John Taylor Mike Prior	.15	.40
O Mark Rypien Brett Faryniarz	.15	.40
P Greg Bell Chris Doleman	.15	.40

1990 Topps 1000 Yard Club

Topps, once again in 1990, issued a card set which honored the players in the NFL who gained more than 1,000 yards in the 1989 season. One of these cards were included in every 1990 wax pack. The cards in this set were released in two distinct varieties; the NFL Properties disclaimer is either present or absent from the back of each card. Additionally, each of those two versions can be found with one or two asterisks next to the copyright line on the backs creating a total of four variations for each card.

COMPLETE SET (30)	2.00	5.00
*DISCLAIMER BACK: .4X TO 1X		
ONE PER PACK		
1 Jerry Rice	.40	1.00
2 Christian Okoye	.02	.05
3 Barry Sanders	.50	1.25
4 Sterling Sharpe	.10	.25
5 Mark Carrier WR	.10	.25
6 Henry Ellard	.04	.10
7 Andre Reed	.10	.25
8 Neal Anderson	.04	.10
9 Dalton Hilliard	.02	.05
10 Anthony Miller	.10	.25
11 Thurman Thomas	.10	.25
12 James Brooks	.04	.10
13 Webster Slaughter	.04	.10
14 Gary Clark	.10	.25
15 Tim McGee	.02	.05
16 Art Monk	.04	.10
17 Bobby Humphrey	.02	.05
18 Flipper Anderson	.02	.05
19 Ricky Sanders	.02	.05
20 Greg Bell	.02	.05
21 Vance Johnson	.02	.05
22 Richard Johnson UER	.02	.05
23 Eric Martin	.02	.05
24 John Taylor	.04	.10
25 Mervyn Fernandez	.02	.05
26 Anthony Carter	.04	.10
27 Brian Blades	.04	.10
28 Roger Craig	.04	.10
29 Ottis Anderson	.04	.10
30 Mark Clayton	.04	.10

1990 Topps Traded

This 132-card standard-size set was released by Topps as an update to their regular issue set. The set features players who were traded after Topps printed their regular set and rookies who were not in the 1990 Topps football set. The set was issued in its own custom box and was distributed through the Topps hobby distribution system. The cards were printed on white card stock and are numbered on the back with a "T" suffix. Rookie Cards in the set inlcude Fred Barnett, Reggie Cobb, Harold Green, Stan Humphries, Johnny Johnson, Tony Martin, Terance Mathis, Rob Moore, Emmitt Smith and Calvin Williams.

COMP.FACT.SET (132)	6.00	15.00
1T Gerald McNeil	.02	.05
2T Andre Rison	.08	.25
3T Steve Walsh	.08	.25
4T Lorenzo White	.04	.10
5T Max Montoya	.02	.05
6T William Roberts RC	.02	.05
7T Alonzo Highsmith	.02	.05
8T Chris Hinton	.04	.10
9T Stanley Morgan	.04	.10
10T Mickey Shuler	.02	.05
11T Bobby Humphery	.02	.05
12T Gary Anderson RB	.02	.05
13T Mike Tomczak	.04	.10
14T Anthony Pleasant RC	.04	.10
15T Walter Stanley	.02	.05
16T Greg Bell	.02	.05
17T Tony Martin RC	.30	.75
18T Terry Kinard	.02	.05
19T Cris Carter	.20	.50
20T James Wilder	.02	.05
21T Jerry Kauric RC	.02	.05
22T Irving Fryar	.08	.25
23T Ken Harvey RC	.08	.25
24T James Williams DB RC	.02	.05
25T Ron Cox RC	.02	.05
26T Andre Ware	.08	.25
27T Emmitt Smith RC	4.00	10.00
28T Junior Seau	.30	.75
29T Mark Carrier RC DB	.08	.25
30T Rodney Hampton	.08	.25
31T Rob Moore RC	.20	.50
32T Bern Brostek RC	.02	.05
33T Dexter Carter	.04	.10
34T Blair Thomas	.04	.10
35T Harold Green RC	.08	.25
36T Darrell Thompson	.02	.05
37T Eric Green RC	.08	.25
38T Renaldo Turnbull RC	.08	.25
39T Leroy Hoard RC	.08	.25
40T Anthony Thompson RC	.04	.10
41T Jeff George	.08	.25
42T Alexander Wright RC	.02	.05
43T Richmond Webb	.02	.05
44T Cortez Kennedy	.20	.50
45T Ray Agnew RC	.02	.05
46T Percy Snow	.02	.05
47T Chris Singleton	.02	.05
48T James Francis RC	.04	.10
49T Tony Bennett	.04	.10
50T Reggie Cobb RC	.04	.10
51T Barry Foster	.08	.25
52T Ben Smith	.02	.05
53T Anthony Smith RC	.08	.25
54T Steve Christie RC	.02	.05
55T Johnny Bailey RC	.04	.10
56T Alan Grant RC	.02	.05
57T Eric Floyd RC	.02	.05
58T Robert Blackmon RC	.02	.05
59T Brent Williams	.02	.05
60T Raymond Clayborn	.02	.05
61T Dave Duerson	.02	.05
62T Derrick Fenner RC	.04	.10
63T Ken Willis	.02	.05
64T Brad Baxter RC	.04	.10
65T Tony Paige	.02	.05
66T Jay Schroeder	.02	.05
67T Jim Breech	.02	.05
68T Barry Word RC	.04	.10
69T Anthony Dilweg FTC	.02	.05
70T Rich Gannon RC	.75	2.00
71T Stan Humphries RC	.08	.25
72T Jay Novacek	.08	.25
73T Tommy Kane RC	.02	.05
74T Everson Walls	.02	.05
75T Mike Rozier	.04	.10
76T Robb Thomas RC	.02	.05
77T Terance Mathis RC	.30	.75
78T LeRoy Irvin	.02	.05
79T Jeff Donaldson	.02	.05
80T Ethan Horton RC	.04	.10
81T J.B.Brown RC	.02	.05
82T Joe Kelly	.02	.05
83T John Carney RC	.02	.05
84T Dan Stryzinski RC	.02	.05
85T John Kidd	.02	.05
86T Al Smith	.04	.10
87T Travis McNeal	.02	.05
88T Reyna Thompson RC	.02	.05
89T Rick Donnelly	.02	.05
90T Marv Cook RC	.04	.10
91T Mike Farr RC	.02	.05
92T Daniel Stubbs	.02	.05
93T Jeff Campbell RC	.02	.05
94T Tim McKyer	.02	.05
95T Ian Beckles RC	.02	.05
96T Lemuel Stinson	.02	.05
97T Frank Cornish	.02	.05
98T Riki Ellison	.02	.05
99T Jamie Mueller RC	.02	.05
100T Brian Hansen	.02	.05
101T Warren Powers RC	.02	.05
102T Howard Cross RC	.02	.05
103T Tim Grunhard RC	.02	.05
104T Johnny Johnson RC	.08	.25
105T Calvin Williams RC	.08	.25
106T Keith McCants	.02	.05
107T Lamar Lathon RC	.04	.10
108T Steve Broussard RC	.04	.10
109T Glenn Parker RC	.02	.05
110T Alton Montgomery RC	.02	.05
111T Jim McMahon	.04	.10
112T Aaron Wallace RC	.02	.05
113T Keith Sims RC	.02	.05
114T Ervin Randle	.02	.05
115T Walter Wilson	.02	.05
116T Terry Wooden RC	.02	.05
117T Bernard Clark	.02	.05
118T Tony Stargell RC	.02	.05
119T Jimmie Jones RC	.02	.05
120T Andre Collins RC	.04	.10
121T Ricky Proehl RC	.08	.25
122T Darion Conner RC	.04	.10
123T Jeff Rutledge	.02	.05
124T Heath Sherman RC	.04	.10
125T Tommie Agee RC	.02	.05
126T Tory Epps RC	.02	.05
127T Tommy Hodson RC	.02	.05
128T Jessie Hester RC	.02	.05
129T Alfred Oglesby RC	.02	.05
130T Chris Chandler	.08	.25
131T Fred Barnett RC	.08	.25
132T Checklist 1-132	.02	.05

1991 Topps

This 660-card standard size set marked Topps' largest football card set to date. Factory sets were issued once again. The design of the card front was the same as the football and hockey sets of that year. A team-colored border outlines the photo with the player's name and position appearing in the bottom border. The team name is at the bottom right of the photo. The backs contain highlights and statistics. Subsets include Highlights (2-7), league leaders (8-12) and team cards (628-655). The cards are arranged by team in order of 1991 finish. Rookie Cards include Ricky Ervins, Alvin Harper, Russell Maryland, Herman Moore, Eric Turner and Harvey Williams.

COMPLETE SET (660)	10.00	20.00
COMP.FACT.SET (660)	15.00	30.00
1 Super Bowl XXV	.04	.10
2 Roger Craig HL	.02	.15
3 Derrick Thomas HL	.02	.15
4 Pete Stoyanovich HL	.04	.10
5 Ottis Anderson HL	.02	.15
6 Jerry Rice HL	.20	.50
7 Warren Moon HL	.02	.15
8 W.Moon/J.Everett LL	.02	.15
9 B.Sanders/T.Thomas LL	.15	.40
10 J.Rice/H.Jeffires LL	.10	.30
11 M.Carrier DB/R.Johnson LL	.04	.10
12 D.Thomas/C.Haley LL	.02	.15
13 Jumbo Elliott	.04	.10
14 Leonard Marshall	.04	.10
15 William Roberts	.04	.10
16 Lawrence Taylor	.10	.25
17 Mark Ingram	.02	.15
18 Rodney Hampton	.10	.25
19 Carl Banks	.04	.10
20 Ottis Anderson	.02	.15
21 Mark Collins	.04	.10
22 Pepper Johnson	.04	.10
23 Dave Meggett	.02	.15
24 Reyna Thompson	.04	.10
25 Stephen Baker	.04	.10
26 Mike Fox	.04	.10
27 Maurice Carthon UER	.04	.10
28 Jeff Hostetler	.10	.25
29 Greg Jackson RC	.04	.10
30 Sean Landeta	.04	.10
31 Bart Oates	.04	.10
32 Phil Simms	.02	.15
33 Erik Howard	.04	.10
34 Myron Guyton	.04	.10
35 Mark Bavaro	.04	.10
36 Jarrod Bunch RC	.04	.10
37 Will Wolford	.04	.10
38 Ray Bentley	.04	.10
39 Nate Odomes	.04	.10
40 Scott Norwood	.01	.10
41 Darryl Talley	.01	.10
42 Carwell Gardner	.01	.10
43 James Lofton	.02	.15
44 Shane Conlan	.01	.10
45 Steve Tasker	.02	.15
46 James Williams	.01	.10
47 Kent Hull	.04	.10
48 Al Edwards	.04	.10
49 Frank Reich	.02	.15
50 Leon Seals	.04	.10
51 Keith McKeller	.04	.10
52 Thurman Thomas	.10	.25
53 Leonard Smith	.04	.10
54 Andre Reed	.02	.15
55 Kenneth Davis	.04	.10
56 Jeff Wright RC	.04	.10
57 Jamie Mueller	.04	.10
58 Jim Ritcher	.04	.10
59 Bruce Smith	.10	.25
60 Ted Washington RC	.04	.10
61 Guy McIntyre	.04	.10
62 Michael Carter	.04	.10
63 Pierce Holt	.04	.10
64 Darryl Pollard	.04	.10
65 Mike Sherrard	.04	.10
66 Dexter Carter	.04	.10
67 Bubba Paris	.04	.10
68 Harry Sydney	.04	.10
69 Tom Rathman	.04	.10
70 Jesse Sapolu	.04	.10
71 Mike Cofer	.04	.10
72 Keith DeLong	.04	.10
73 Joe Montana	.50	1.25
74 Bill Romanowski	.04	.10
75 John Taylor	.02	.15
76 Brent Jones	.10	.25
77 Harris Barton	.04	.10
78 Charles Haley	.06	.15
79 Eric Davis	.04	.10
80 Kevin Fagan	.04	.10
81 Jerry Rice	.30	.75
82 Dave Waymer	.04	.10
83 Todd Marinovich RC	.04	.10
84 Steve Smith	.04	.10
85 Tim Brown	.10	.25
86 Ethan Horton	.04	.10
87 Marcus Allen	.10	.25
88 Terry McDaniel	.04	.10
89 Thomas Benson	.04	.10
90 Roger Craig	.06	.15
91 Don Mosebar	.04	.10
92 Aaron Wallace	.04	.10
93 Eddie Anderson	.04	.10
94 Willie Gault	.06	.15
95 Howie Long	.10	.25
96 Jay Schroeder	.04	.10
97 Ronnie Lott	.06	.15
98 Bob Golic	.04	.10
99 Bo Jackson	.10	.30
100 Max Montoya	.04	.10
101 Scott Davis	.04	.10
102 Greg Townsend	.04	.10
103 Garry Lewis	.04	.10
104 Mervyn Fernandez	.04	.10
105 Steve Wisniewski UER	.04	.10
106 Jeff Jaeger	.04	.10
107 Nick Bell RC	.04	.10
108 Mark Dennis RC	.04	.10
109 Jarvis Williams	.04	.10
110 Mark Clayton	.06	.15
111 Harry Galbreath	.04	.10
112 Dan Marino	.50	1.25
113 Louis Oliver	.04	.10
114 Pete Stoyanovich	.04	.10
115 Ferrell Edmunds	.04	.10
116 Jeff Cross	.04	.10
117 Richmond Webb	.04	.10
118 Jim C. Jensen	.04	.10
119 Keith Sims	.04	.10
120 Mark Duper	.06	.15
121 Shawn Lee RC	.04	.10
122 Reggie Roby	.04	.10
123 Jeff Uhlenhake	.04	.10
124 Sammie Smith	.04	.10
125 John Offerdahl	.04	.10
126 Hugh Green	.04	.10
127 Tony Paige	.04	.10
128 David Griggs	.04	.10
129 J.B. Brown	.04	.10
130 Harvey Williams RC	.10	.25
131 John Alt	.04	.10
132 Albert Lewis	.04	.10
133 Robb Thomas	.04	.10
134 Neil Smith	.10	.25
135 Stephone Paige	.04	.10
136 Nick Lowery	.04	.10
137 Steve DeBerg	.04	.10
138 Rich Baldinger RC	.04	.10
139 Percy Snow	.04	.10
140 Kevin Porter	.04	.10
141 Chris Martin	.04	.10
142 Deron Cherry	.04	.10
143 Derrick Thomas	.10	.25
144 Tim Grunhard	.04	.10
145 Todd McNair	.04	.10
146 David Szott RC	.04	.10
147 Dan Saleaumua	.04	.10
148 Jonathan Hayes	.04	.10
149 Christian Okoye	.04	.10
150 Dino Hackett	.04	.10
151 Bryan Barker RC	.04	.10
152 Kevin Ross	.04	.10
153 Barry Word	.04	.10
154 Stan Thomas	.04	.10
155 Brad Muster	.04	.10
156 Donnell Woolford	.04	.10
157 Neal Anderson	.06	.15
158 Jim Covert	.04	.10
159 Jim Harbaugh	.10	.25
160 Shaun Gayle	.04	.10
161 William Perry	.06	.15
162 Ron Morris	.04	.10
163 Mark Bortz	.04	.10
164 James Thornton	.04	.10
165 Ron Rivera	.04	.10
166 Kevin Butler	.04	.10
167 Jay Hilgenberg	.04	.10
168 Peter Tom Willis	.04	.10
169 Johnny Bailey	.04	.10
170 Ron Cox	.04	.10
171 Keith Van Horne	.04	.10
172 Mark Carrier DB	.06	.15
173 Richard Dent	.06	.15
174 Wendell Davis	.04	.10
175 Trace Armstrong	.04	.10
176 Mike Singletary	.06	.15
177 Chris Zorich RC	.10	.25
178 Gerald Riggs	.04	.10
179 Jeff Bostic	.04	.10
180 Kurt Gouveia RC	.04	.10
181 Stan Humphries	.10	.25
182 Chip Lohmiller	.04	.10
183 Raleigh McKenzie RC	.04	.10
184 Alvin Walton	.04	.10
185 Earnest Byner	.04	.10
186 Markus Koch	.04	.10
187 Art Monk	.06	.15
188 Ed Simmons	.04	.10
189 Bobby Wilson RC	.04	.10
190 Charles Mann	.04	.10
191 Darrell Green	.04	.10
192 Mark Rypien	.06	.15
193 Ricky Sanders	.04	.10
194 Jim Lachey	.04	.10
195 Martin Mayhew	.04	.10
196 Gary Clark	.10	.25
197 Wilber Marshall	.04	.10
198 Darryl Grant	.04	.10
199 Don Warren	.04	.10
200 Ricky Ervins UER RC	.06	.15
201 Eric Allen	.04	.10
202 Anthony Toney	.04	.10

203 Ben Smith UER .04 .10
204 David Alexander .04 .10
205 Jerome Brown .04 .10
206 Mike Golic .04 .10
207 Roger Ruzek .04 .10
208 Andre Waters .04 .10
209 Fred Barnett .10 .25
210 Randall Cunningham .10 .25
211 Mike Schad .04 .10
212 Reggie White .10 .25
213 Mike Bellamy .04 .10
214 Jeff Feagles RC .04 .10
215 Wes Hopkins .04 .10
216 Clyde Simmons .04 .10
217 Keith Byars .04 .10
218 Seth Joyner .06 .15
219 Byron Evans .04 .10
220 Keith Jackson .06 .15
221 Calvin Williams .06 .15
222 Mike Dumas RC .04 .10
223 Ray Childress .04 .10
224 Ernest Givins .06 .15
225 Lamar Lathon .04 .10
226 Greg Montgomery .04 .10
227 Mike Munchak .06 .15
228 Al Smith .04 .10
229 Bubba McDowell .04 .10
230 Haywood Jeffires .06 .15
231 Drew Hill .04 .10
232 William Fuller .06 .15
233 Warren Moon .10 .25
234 Doug Smith DT RC .06 .15
235 Cris Dishman RC .04 .10
236 Teddy Garcia RC .04 .10
237 Richard Johnson CB RC .04 .10
238 Bruce Matthews .06 .15
239 Gerald McNeil .04 .10
240 Johnny Meads .04 .10
241 Curtis Duncan .04 .10
242 Sean Jones .06 .15
243 Lorenzo White .04 .10
244 Rob Carpenter RC .04 .10
245 Bruce Reimers .04 .10
246 Ickey Woods .04 .10
247 Lewis Billups .04 .10
248 Boomer Esiason .06 .15
249 Tim Krumrie .04 .10
250 David Fulcher .04 .10
251 Jim Breech .04 .10
252 Mitchell Price RC .04 .10
253 Carl Zander .04 .10
254 Barney Bussey RC .04 .10
255 Leon White .04 .10
256 Eddie Brown .04 .10
257 James Francis .04 .10
258 Harold Green .06 .15
259 Anthony Munoz .06 .15
260 James Brooks .06 .15
261 Kevin Walker UER RC .04 .10
262 Bruce Kozerski .04 .10
263 David Grant .04 .10
264 Tim McGee .04 .10
265 Rodney Holman .04 .10
266 Dan McGwire RC .04 .10
267 Andy Heck .04 .10
268 Dave Krieg .06 .15
269 David Wyman .04 .10
270 Robert Blackmon .04 .10
271 Grant Feasel .04 .10
272 Patrick Hunter RC .04 .10
273 Travis McNeal .04 .10
274 John L. Williams .04 .10
275 Tony Woods .04 .10
276 Derrick Fenner .04 .10
277 Jacob Green .04 .10
278 Brian Blades .06 .15
279 Eugene Robinson .04 .10
280 Terry Wooden .04 .10
281 Jeff Bryant .04 .10
282 Norm Johnson .04 .10
283 Joe Nash UER .04 .10
284 Rick Donnelly .04 .10
285 Chris Warren .10 .25
286 Tommy Kane .04 .10
287 Cortez Kennedy .10 .25
288 Ernie Mills RC .06 .15
289 Dermontti Dawson .06 .15
290 Tunch Ilkin .04 .10
291 Tim Worley .04 .10
292 David Little .04 .10
293 Gary Anderson K .04 .10
294 Chris Calloway .04 .10
295 Carnell Lake .04 .10
296 Dan Stryzinski .04 .10
297 Rod Woodson .10 .25
298 John Jackson T RC .04 .10
299 Bubby Brister .04 .10
300 Thomas Everett .04 .10
301 Merril Hoge .04 .10
302 Eric Green .04 .10
303 Greg Lloyd .10 .25
304 Gerald Williams .04 .10
305 Bryan Hinkle .04 .10
306 Keith Willis .04 .10
307 Louis Lipps .04 .10
308 Donald Evans .04 .10
309 D.J. Johnson .04 .10
310 Wesley Carroll RC .04 .10
311 Eric Martin .04 .10
312 Brett Maxie .04 .10
313 Rickey Jackson .04 .10
314 Robert Massey .04 .10
315 Pat Swilling .06 .15
316 Morten Andersen .04 .10
317 Toi Cook RC .04 .10
318 Sam Mills .04 .10
319 Steve Walsh .04 .10
320 Tommy Barnhardt RC .04 .10
321 Vince Buck .04 .10
322 Joel Hilgenberg .04 .10
323 Rueben Mayes .04 .10
324 Renaldo Turnbull .04 .10
325 Brett Perriman .10 .25
326 Vaughan Johnson .04 .10
327 Gill Fenerty .04 .10
328 Stan Brock .04 .10
329 Dalton Hilliard .04 .10
330 Hoby Brenner .04 .10
331 Craig Heyward .06 .15
332 Jon Hand .04 .10
333 Duane Bickett .04 .10
334 Jessie Hester .04 .10
335 Rohn Stark .04 .10
336 Zefross Moss .04 .10
337 Bill Brooks .04 .10
338 Clarence Verdin .04 .10
339 Mike Prior .04 .10
340 Chip Banks .04 .10
341 Dean Biasucci .04 .10
342 Ray Donaldson .04 .10
343 Jeff Herrod .04 .10
344 Donnell Thompson .04 .10
345 Chris Goode .04 .10
346 Eugene Daniel .04 .10
347 Pat Beach .04 .10
348 Keith Taylor .04 .10
349 Jeff George .10 .25
350 Tony Siragusa RC .20 .50
351 Randy Dixon .04 .10
352 Albert Bentley .04 .10
353 Russell Maryland RC .10 .25
354 Mike Saxon .04 .10
355 Godfrey Myles RC UER .04 .10
356 Mark Stepnoski RC .06 .15
357 James Washington RC .04 .10
358 Jay Novacek .10 .25
359 Kelvin Martin .04 .10
360 Emmitt Smith UER 1.00 2.50
361 Jim Jeffcoat .04 .10
362 Alexander Wright .04 .10
363 James Dixon UER .04 .10
364 Alonzo Highsmith .04 .10
365 Daniel Stubbs .04 .10
366 Jack Del Rio .06 .15
367 Mark Tuinei RC .04 .10
368 Michael Irvin .10 .25
369 John Gesek RC .04 .10
370 Ken Willis .04 .10
371 Troy Aikman .30 .75
372 Jimmie Jones .04 .10
373 Nate Newton .06 .15
374 Issiac Holt .04 .10
375 Alvin Harper RC .10 .25
376 Todd Kalis .04 .10
377 Wade Wilson .06 .15
378 Joey Browner .04 .10
379 Chris Doleman .04 .10
380 Hassan Jones .04 .10
381 Henry Thomas .04 .10
382 Darrell Fullington .04 .10
383 Steve Jordan .04 .10
384 Gary Zimmerman .06 .15
385 Ray Berry .04 .10
386 Cris Carter .20 .50
387 Mike Merriweather .04 .10
388 Carl Lee .04 .10
389 Keith Millard .04 .10
390 Reggie Rutland .04 .10
391 Anthony Carter .06 .15
392 Mark Dusbabek .04 .10
393 Kirk Lowdermilk .04 .10
394 Al Noga UER .04 .10
395 Herschel Walker .06 .15
396 Randall McDaniel .06 .15
397 Herman Moore RC .10 .25
398 Eddie Murray .04 .10
399 Lomas Brown .04 .10
400 Marc Spindler .04 .10
401 Bennie Blades .04 .10
402 Kevin Glover .04 .10
403 Aubrey Matthews RC .04 .10
404 Michael Cofer .04 .10
405 Robert Clark .04 .10
406 Eric Andolsek .04 .10
407 William White .04 .10
408 Rodney Peete .06 .15
409 Mel Gray .06 .15
410 Jim Arnold .04 .10
411 Jeff Campbell .04 .10
412 Chris Spielman .06 .15
413 Jerry Ball .04 .10
414 Dan Owens .04 .10
415 Barry Sanders .50 1.25
416 Andre Ware .06 .15
417 Stanley Richard RC .04 .10
418 Gill Byrd .04 .10
419 John Kidd .04 .10
420 Sam Seale .04 .10
421 Gary Plummer .04 .10
422 Anthony Miller .06 .15
423 Ronnie Harmon .04 .10
424 Frank Cornish .04 .10
425 Marion Butts .06 .15
426 Leo Goeas .04 .10
427 Junior Seau .10 .25
428 Courtney Hall .04 .10
429 Leslie O'Neal .06 .15
430 Martin Bayless .04 .10
431 John Carney .04 .10
432 Lee Williams .04 .10
433 Arthur Cox .04 .10
434 Burt Grossman .04 .10
435 Nate Lewis RC .04 .10
436 Rod Bernstine .04 .10
437 Henry Rolling RC .04 .10
438 Billy Joe Tolliver .04 .10
439 Vinnie Clark RC .04 .10
440 Brian Noble .04 .10
441 Charles Wilson .04 .10
442 Don Majkowski .04 .10
443 Tim Harris .04 .10
444 Scott Stephen RC .04 .10
445 Perry Kemp .04 .10
446 Darrell Thompson .04 .10
447 Chris Jacke .04 .10
448 Mark Murphy .04 .10
449 Ed West .04 .10
450 LeRoy Butler .06 .15
451 Keith Woodside .04 .10
452 Tony Bennett .06 .15
453 Mark Lee .04 .10
454 James Campen RC .04 .10
455 Robert Brown .04 .10
456 Sterling Sharpe .10 .25
457A T.Mandarich ERR Bronc. 1.00 2.50
457B T.Mandarich COR Packers .04 .10
458 Johnny Holland .04 .10
459 Matt Brock RC .04 .10
460A Esera Tuaolo ERR RC .04 .10
460B Esera Tuaolo COR RC .04 .10
460C Terance Mathis UER .10 .25
461 Freeman McNeil .04 .10
463 Rob Moore .10 .25
464 Darrell Davis RC .04 .10
465 Chris Burkett .04 .10
466 Jeff Criswell .04 .10
467 Tony Stargell .04 .10
468 Ken O'Brien .04 .10
469 Erik McMillan .04 .10
470 Jeff Lageman UER .04 .10
471 Pat Leahy .04 .10
472 Dennis Byrd .04 .10
473 Jim Sweeney .04 .10
474 Brad Baxter .04 .10
475 Joe Kelly .04 .10
476 Al Toon .06 .15
477 Joe Prokop .04 .10
478 Mark Boyer .04 .10
479 Kyle Clifton .04 .10
480 James Hasty .04 .10
481 Browning Nagle RC .04 .10
482 Gary Anderson RB .04 .10
483 Mark Carrier WR .10 .25
484 Ricky Reynolds .04 .10
485 Bruce Hill .04 .10
486 Steve Christie .04 .10
487 Paul Gruber .04 .10
488 Jesse Anderson .04 .10
489 Reggie Cobb .04 .10
490 Harry Hamilton .04 .10
491 Vinny Testaverde .06 .15
492 Mark Royals RC .04 .10
493 Keith McCants .04 .10
494 Ron Hall .04 .10
495 Ian Beckles .04 .10
496 Mark Robinson .04 .10
497 Reuben Davis .04 .10
498 Wayne Haddix .04 .10
499 Kevin Murphy .04 .10
500 Eugene Marve .04 .10
501 Broderick Thomas .04 .10
502 Eric Swann UER RC .10 .25
503 Ernie Jones .04 .10
504 Rich Camarillo .04 .10
505 Tim McDonald .04 .10
506 Freddie Joe Nunn .04 .10
507 Tim Jorden RC .04 .10
508 Johnny Johnson .04 .10
509 Eric Hill .04 .10
510 Derek Kennard .04 .10
511 Ricky Proehl .04 .10
512 Bill Lewis .04 .10
513 Roy Green .04 .10
514 Anthony Bell .04 .10
515 Timm Rosenbach .04 .10
516 Jim Wahler RC .04 .10
517 Anthony Thompson .04 .10
518 Ken Harvey .06 .15
519 Luis Sharpe .04 .10
520 Walter Reeves .04 .10
521 Lonnie Young .04 .10
522 Rod Saddler .04 .10
523 Todd Lyght RC .04 .10
524 Alvin Wright .04 .10
525 Flipper Anderson .04 .10
526 Jackie Slater .04 .10
527 Damone Johnson RC .04 .10
528 Cleveland Gary .04 .10
529 Mike Piel .04 .10
530 Buford McGee .04 .10
531 Michael Stewart .04 .10
532 Jim Everett .06 .15
533 Mike Wilcher .04 .10
534 Irv Pankey .04 .10
535 Bern Brostek .04 .10
536 Henry Ellard .06 .15
537 Doug Smith .04 .10
538 Larry Kelm .04 .10
539 Pat Terrell .04 .10
540 Tom Newberry .04 .10
541 Jerry Gray .04 .10
542 Kevin Greene .06 .15
543 Duval Love RC .04 .10
544 Frank Stams .04 .10
545 Mike Croel RC .04 .10
546 Mark Jackson .04 .10
547 Greg Kragen .04 .10
548 Karl Mecklenburg .04 .10
549 Simon Fletcher .04 .10
550 Bobby Humphrey .04 .10
551 Ken Lanier .04 .10
552 Vance Johnson .04 .10
553 Ron Holmes .04 .10
554 John Elway .50 1.25
555 Melvin Bratton .04 .10
556 Dennis Smith .04 .10
557 Ricky Nattiel .04 .10
558 Clarence Kay .04 .10
559 Michael Brooks .04 .10
560 Mike Horan .04 .10
561 Warren Powers .04 .10
562 Keith Kartz .04 .10
563 Shannon Sharpe .20 .50
564 Wymon Henderson .04 .10
565 Steve Atwater .04 .10
566 David Treadwell .04 .10
567 Bruce Pickens RC .04 .10
568 Jessie Tuggle .04 .10
569 Chris Hinton .04 .10
570 Keith Jones .04 .10
571 Bill Fralic .04 .10
572 Mike Rozier .04 .10
573 Scott Fulhage .04 .10
574 Floyd Dixon .04 .10
575 Andre Rison .06 .15
576 Darion Conner .04 .10
577 Brian Jordan .06 .15
578 Michael Haynes .10 .25
579 Oliver Barnett .04 .10
580 Shawn Collins .04 .10
581 Tim Green .04 .10
582 Deion Sanders .15 .40
583 Mike Kenn .04 .10
584 Mike Gann .04 .10
585 Chris Miller .06 .15
586 Tory Epps .04 .10
587 Steve Broussard .04 .10
588 Gary Wilkins .04 .10
589 Eric Turner RC .06 .15
590 Thane Gash .04 .10
591 Clay Matthews .06 .15
592 Mike Johnson .04 .10
593 Raymond Clayborn .04 .10
594 Leroy Hoard .06 .15
595 Reggie Langhorne .04 .10
596 Mike Baab .04 .10
597 Anthony Pleasant .04 .10
598 David Grayson .04 .10
599 Rob Burnett RC .06 .15
600 Frank Minnifield .04 .10
601 Gregg Rakoczy .04 .10
602 Eric Metcalf UER .10 .25
603 Paul Farren .04 .10
604 Brian Brennan .04 .10
605 Tony Jones T RC .04 .10
606 Stephen Braggs .04 .10
607 Kevin Mack .04 .10
608 Pat Harlow RC .04 .10
609 Marv Cook .04 .10
610 John Stephens .04 .10
611 Ed Reynolds .04 .10
612 Tim Goad .04 .10
613 Chris Singleton .04 .10
614 Bruce Armstrong .04 .10
615 Tommy Hodson .04 .10
616 Sammy Martin .04 .10
617 Andre Tippett .04 .10
618 Johnny Rembert .04 .10
619 Maurice Hurst .04 .10
620 Vincent Brown .04 .10
621 Ray Agnew .04 .10
622 Ronnie Lippett .04 .10
623 Greg McMurtry .04 .10
624 Brent Williams .04 .10
625 Jason Staurovsky .04 .10
626 Marvin Allen .04 .10
627 Hart Lee Dykes .04 .10
628 Falcons TL/Jones .04 .10
629 Bills TL/Wright .04 .10
630 Bears TL/Harbaugh .06 .15
631 Bengals TL .04 .10
632 Browns TL/Metcalf .04 .10
633 Cowboys TL/Martin .04 .10
634 Broncos TL/Sh.Sharpe .04 .10
635 Lions TL/Peete .04 .10
636 Packers TL/Majik .04 .10
637 Oilers TL/W.Moon .06 .15
638 Colts TL/Jeff George .04 .10
639 Chiefs TL/Okoye .04 .10
640 Raiders TL/M.Allen .06 .15
641 Rams TL/Everett .04 .10
642 Dolphins TL/Stoyanovich .04 .10
643 Vikings TL/Gannon .06 .15
644 Patriots TL/Stephens .04 .10
645 Saints TL/Fenerty .04 .10
646 Giants TL/Carthon .04 .10
647 Jets TL/Leahy .04 .10
648 Eagles TL/Cunningham .04 .10
649 Cardinals TL/Lewis .04 .10
650 Steelers TL/Brister .04 .10
651 Chargers TL/Friesz .04 .10
652 49ers TL/Carter .04 .10
653 Seahawks TL/Fenner .04 .10
654 Buccaneers TL/Cobb .04 .10
655 Redskins TL/Byner .04 .10
656 Checklist 1-132 .04 .10
657 Checklist 132-264 .04 .10
658 Checklist 265-396 .04 .10
659 Checklist 397-528 .04 .10
660 Checklist 529-660 .04 .10

1991 Topps 1000 Yard Club

This 18-card standard-size set was issued by Topps to celebrate rushers and receivers who compiled 1000 yards or more in a season. The words "1000 Yard Club" appear at the top of the card. The color action player photo has a top red border, a red and purple left border, and no borders on the right and bottom. The player's name is given in an orange stripe toward the bottom of the picture. In blue and pink on white, the backs feature the rushing or receiving record of the player. The cards were inserted one per wax pack and each was printed with either one or two asterisks on the copyright line on the backs.

COMPLETE SET (18) 2.00 5.00
ONE PER PACK
1 Jerry Rice .50 1.25
2 Barry Sanders .75 2.00
3 Thurman Thomas .15 .40
4 Henry Ellard .05 .15
5 Marion Butts .05 .15
6 Earnest Byner .02 .10
7 Andre Rison .05 .15
8 Bobby Humphrey .02 .10
9 Gary Clark .15 .40
10 Sterling Sharpe .15 .40
11 Flipper Anderson .02 .10
12 Neal Anderson .05 .15
13 Haywood Jeffires .05 .15
14 Stephone Paige .02 .10
15 Drew Hill .02 .10
16 Barry Word .02 .10
17 Anthony Carter .05 .15
18 James Brooks .05 .15

1992 Topps

The 1992 Topps football set was issued in three series and totaled 759 standard-size cards. The first and second series consisted of 330 cards and a high series of 99 cards was released late in the season. A factory set was issued for the first 660 cards and it included 20 Topps Gold cards. A separate high series factory set of 113 cards was issued. It included 10 Topps Gold cards and one four-card No. 1 Draft Picks set. .The key Rookie Cards in the set are Edgar Bennett, Steve Bono, Robert Brooks, Terrell Buckley, Quentin Coryatt, Steve Emtman, Amp Lee, Tommy Maddox, Carl Pickens and Tommy Vardell. Members of both NFL Properties and the NFL Players Association are included in the third series.

COMPLETE SET (759) 25.00 50.00
COMP.FACT.SET (680) 40.00 80.00
COMP.SERIES 1 (330) 10.00 20.00
COMP.SERIES 2 (330) 10.00 20.00
COMP.HIGH SER.(99) 5.00 10.00
COMP.FACT.HIGH SET (113) 5.00 12.00
1 Tim McGee .04 .10
2 Rich Camarillo .04 .10
3 Anthony Johnson .06 .15
4 Larry Kelm .04 .10
5 Irving Fryar .06 .15
6 Joey Browner .04 .10
7 Michael Walter .04 .10
8 Cortez Kennedy .06 .15
9 Reyna Thompson .04 .10
10 John Friesz .06 .15
11 Leroy Hoard .06 .15
12 Steve McMichael .06 .15
13 Marvin Washington .04 .10
14 Clyde Simmons .04 .10
15 Stephone Paige .04 .10
16 Mike Utley .06 .15
17 Tunch Ilkin .04 .10
18 Lawrence Dawsey .06 .15
19 Vance Johnson .04 .10
20 Bryce Paup .10 .25
21 Jeff Wright .04 .10
22 Gill Fenerty .04 .10
23 Lamar Lathon .04 .10
24 Danny Copeland .04 .10
25 Marcus Allen .10 .25
26 Tim Green .04 .10
27 Pete Stoyanovich .04 .10
28 Alvin Harper .06 .15
29 Roy Foster .04 .10
30 Eugene Daniel .04 .10
31 Luis Sharpe .04 .10
32 Terry Wooden .04 .10
33 Jim Breech .04 .10
34 Randy Hilliard RC .04 .10
35 Roman Phifer .04 .10
36 Erik Howard .04 .10
37 Chris Singleton .04 .10
38 Matt Stover .04 .10
39 Tim Irwin .04 .10
40 Karl Mecklenburg .04 .10
41 Joe Phillips .04 .10
42 Bill Jones RC .04 .10
43 Mark Carrier DB .04 .10
44 George Jamison .04 .10
45 Rob Taylor .04 .10
46 Jeff Jaeger .04 .10
47 Don Majkowski .04 .10
48 Al Edwards .04 .10
49 Curtis Duncan .04 .10
50 Sam Mills .04 .10
51 Terance Mathis .06 .15
52 Brian Mitchell .06 .15
53 Mike Pritchard .06 .15
54 Calvin Williams .06 .15
55 Hardy Nickerson .06 .15
56 Nate Newton .04 .10
57 Steve Wallace .04 .10
58 John Offerdahl .04 .10
59 Aeneas Williams .06 .15
60 Lee Johnson .04 .10
61 Ricardo McDonald RC .04 .10
62 David Richards .04 .10
63 Paul Gruber .04 .10
64 Greg McMurtry .04 .10
65 Jay Hilgenberg .04 .10
66 Tim Grunhard .04 .10
67 Dwayne White RC .04 .10
68 Don Beebe .04 .10
69 Simon Fletcher .04 .10
70 Warren Moon .10 .25
71 Chris Jacke .04 .10
72 Steve Wisniewski UER .04 .10
73 Mike Cofer .04 .10
74 Tim Johnson UER .04 .10
75 T.J. Turner .04 .10
76 Scott Case .04 .10
77 Michael Jackson .06 .15
78 Jon Hand .04 .10
79 Stan Brock .04 .10
80 Robert Blackmon .04 .10
81 D.J. Johnson .04 .10
82 Damone Johnson .04 .10
83 Marc Spindler .04 .10
84 Larry Brown DB .04 .10
85 Ray Berry .04 .10
86 Andre Waters .04 .10
87 Carlos Huerta .04 .10
88 Brad Muster .04 .10
89 Chuck Cecil .04 .10
90 Nick Lowery .04 .10
91 Cornelius Bennett .06 .15
92 Jessie Tuggle .04 .10
93 Mark Schlereth RC .04 .10
94 Vestee Jackson .04 .10
95 Eric Bieniemy .04 .10
96 Jeff Hostetler .06 .15
97 Ken Lanier .04 .10
98 Wayne Haddix .04 .10
99 Lorenzo White .04 .10
100 Mervyn Fernandez .04 .10
101 Brent Williams .04 .10
102 Ian Beckles .04 .10
103 Harris Barton .04 .10
104 Edgar Bennett RC .10 .25
105 Mike Pitts .04 .10
106 Fuad Reveiz .04 .10
107 Vernon Turner .04 .10
108 Tracy Hayworth RC .04 .10
109 Checklist 1-110 .04 .10
110 Tom Waddle .04 .10
111 Fred Stokes .04 .10
112 Howard Ballard .04 .10
113 David Szott .04 .10
114 Tim McKyer .04 .10
115 Kyle Clifton .04 .10
116 Tony Bennett .04 .10
117 Joel Hilgenberg .04 .10
118 Dwayne Harper .04 .10
119 Mike Baab .04 .10
120 Mark Clayton .06 .15
121 Eric Swann .06 .15
122 Neil O'Donnell .06 .15
123 Mike Munchak .06 .15
124 Howie Long .10 .25
125 John Elway .50 1.25
126 Joe Prokop .04 .10
127 Pepper Johnson .04 .10
128 Richard Dent .06 .15
129 Robert Porcher RC .10 .25
130 Earnest Byner .04 .10
131 Kent Hull .04 .10
132 Mike Merriweather .04 .10
133 Scott Fulhage .04 .10
134 Kevin Porter .04 .10
135 Tony Casillas .04 .10
136 Dean Biasucci .04 .10
137 Ben Smith .04 .10
138 Bruce Kozerski .04 .10
139 Jeff Campbell .04 .10
140 Kevin Greene .06 .15
141 Gary Plummer .04 .10
142 Vincent Brown .04 .10
143 Ron Hall .04 .10
144 Louie Aguiar RC .04 .10
145 Mark Duper .04 .10
146 Jesse Sapolu .04 .10
147 Jeff Gossett .04 .10
148 Brian Noble .04 .10
149 Derek Russell .04 .10
150 Carlton Bailey RC .04 .10
151 Kelly Goodburn .04 .10
152 Audray McMillian UER .04 .10
153 Neal Anderson .04 .10
154 Bill Maas .04 .10
155 Rickey Jackson .04 .10
156 Chris Miller .06 .15
157 Darren Comeaux .04 .10
158 David Williams .04 .10
159 Rich Gannon .10 .25
160 Kevin Mack .04 .10
161 Jim Arnold .04 .10
162 Reggie White .10 .25
163 Leonard Russell .06 .15
164 Doug Smith .04 .10
165 Tony Mandarich .04 .10
166 Greg Lloyd .06 .15
167 Jumbo Elliott .04 .10
168 Jonathan Hayes .04 .10
169 Jim Ritcher .04 .10
170 Mike Kenn .04 .10
171 James Washington .04 .10
172 Tim Harris .04 .10
173 James Thornton .04 .10
174 John Brandes RC .04 .10
175 Fred McAfee RC .04 .10
176 Henry Rolling .04 .10
177 Tony Paige .04 .10
178 Jay Schroeder .04 .10
179 Jeff Herrod .04 .10
180 Emmitt Smith .60 1.50
181 Wymon Henderson .04 .10
182 Rob Moore .06 .15
183 Robert Wilson .04 .10
184 Michael Zordich RC .04 .10
185 Jim Harbaugh .10 .25
186 Vince Workman .04 .10
187 Ernest Givins .06 .15
188 Herschel Walker .06 .15
189 Dan Fike .04 .10
190 Seth Joyner .04 .10
191 Steve Young .25 .60
192 Dennis Gibson .04 .10
193 Darryl Talley .04 .10
194 Emile Harry .04 .10
195 Bill Fralic .04 .10
196 Michael Stewart .04 .10
197 James Francis .04 .10
198 Jerome Henderson .04 .10
199 John L. Williams .04 .10
200 Rod Woodson .10 .25
201 Mike Farr .04 .10
202 Greg Montgomery .04 .10
203 Andre Collins .04 .10
204 Scott Miller .04 .10
205 Clay Matthews .06 .15
206 Ethan Horton .04 .10
207 Rich Miano .04 .10
208 Chris Mims RC .04 .10
209 Anthony Morgan .04 .10
210 Rodney Hampton .06 .15
211 Chris Hinton .04 .10
212 Esera Tuaolo .04 .10
213 Shane Conlan .04 .10
214 John Carney .04 .10
215 Kenny Walker .04 .10
216 Scott Radecic .04 .10
217 Chris Martin .04 .10
218 Checklist 111-220 UER .04 .10
219 Wesley Carroll .04 .10
220 Bill Romanowski .04 .10
221 Reggie Cobb .04 .10
222 Alfred Anderson .04 .10
223 Cleveland Gary .04 .10
224 Eddie Blake RC .04 .10
225 Chris Spielman .06 .15
226 John Roper .04 .10
227 George Thomas RC .04 .10
228 Jeff Faulkner .04 .10
229 Chip Lohmiller UER .04 .10
230 Hugh Millen .04 .10
231 Ray Horton .04 .10
232 James Campen .04 .10
233 Howard Cross .04 .10
234 Keith McKeller .04 .10
235 Dino Hackett .04 .10
236 Jerome Brown .04 .10
237 Andy Heck .04 .10
238 Rodney Holman .04 .10
239 Bruce Matthews .04 .10
240 Jeff Lageman .04 .10
241 Bobby Hebert .04 .10
242 Gary Anderson K .04 .10
243 Mark Bortz .04 .10
244 Rich Moran .04 .10
245 Jeff Uhlenhake .04 .10
246 Ricky Sanders .04 .10
247 Clarence Kay .04 .10
248 Ed King .04 .10
249 Eddie Anderson .04 .10
250 Amp Lee RC .04 .10
251 Norm Johnson .04 .10
252 Michael Carter .04 .10
253 Felix Wright .04 .10
254 Leon Seals .04 .10
255 Nate Lewis .04 .10
256 Kevin Call .04 .10
257 Darryl Henley .04 .10
258 Jon Vaughn .04 .10
259 Matt Bahr .04 .10
260 Johnny Johnson .04 .10
261 Ken Norton .06 .15
262 Wendell Davis .04 .10
263 Eugene Robinson .04 .10
264 David Treadwell .04 .10
265 Michael Haynes .06 .15
266 Robb Thomas .04 .10
267 Nate Odomes .04 .10
268 Martin Mayhew .04 .10
269 Perry Kemp .04 .10
270 Jerry Ball .04 .10
271 Tommy Vardell RC .04 .10
272 Ernie Mills .04 .10
273 Mo Lewis .04 .10
274 Roger Ruzek .04 .10
275 Steve Smith .04 .10
276 Bo Orlando RC .04 .10
277 Louis Oliver .04 .10
278 Toi Cook .04 .10
279 Eddie Brown .04 .10
280 Keith McCants .04 .10
281 Rob Burnett .04 .10
282 Keith DeLong .04 .10
283 Stan Thomas UER .04 .10
284 Robert Brown .04 .10
285 John Alt .04 .10
286 Randy Dixon .04 .10
287 Siran Stacy RC .04 .10
288 Ray Agnew .04 .10
289 Darion Conner .04 .10
290 Kirk Lowdermilk .04 .10
291 Greg Jackson .04 .10
292 Ken Harvey .04 .10
293 Jacob Green .04 .10
294 Mark Tuinei .04 .10
295 Mark Rypien .04 .10
296 Gerald Robinson RC .04 .10
297 Broderick Thompson .04 .10
298 Doug Widell .04 .10
299 Carwell Gardner .04 .10
300 Barry Sanders .50 1.25
301 Eric Metcalf .06 .15
302 Eric Thomas .04 .10
303 Terrell Buckley RC .04 .10
304 Byron Evans .04 .10
305 Johnny Hector .04 .10
306 Steve Broussard .04 .10
307 Gene Atkins .04 .10
308 Terry McDaniel .04 .10
309 Charles McRae .04 .10
310 Jim Lachey .04 .10
311 Pat Harlow .04 .10
312 Kevin Butler .04 .10
313 Scott Stephen .04 .10
314 Dermontti Dawson .06 .15
315 Johnny Meads .04 .10
316 Checklist 221-330 .04 .10
317 Aaron Craver .04 .10
318 Michael Brooks .04 .10
319 Guy McIntyre .04 .10
320 Thurman Thomas .10 .25
321 Courtney Hall .04 .10
322 Dan Saleaumua .04 .10
323 Vinson Smith RC .04 .10
324 Steve Jordan .04 .10
325 Walter Reeves .04 .10
326 Erik Kramer .06 .15
327 Duane Bickett .04 .10
328 Tom Newberry .04 .10
329 John Kasay .04 .10
330 Dave Meggett .06 .15
331 Kevin Ross .04 .10
332 Keith Hamilton RC .06 .15
333 Dwight Stone .04 .10
334 Mel Gray .06 .15
335 Harry Galbreath .04 .10
336 William Perry .06 .15
337 Brian Blades .06 .15
338 Randall McDaniel .06 .15
339 Pat Coleman RC .04 .10
340 Michael Irvin .10 .25
341 Checklist 331-440 .04 .10
342 Chris Mohr .04 .10
343 Greg Davis .04 .10
344 Dave Cadigan .04 .10
345 Art Monk .06 .15
346 Tim Goad .04 .10
347 Vinnie Clark .04 .10
348 David Fulcher .04 .10
349 Craig Heyward .06 .15
350 Ronnie Lott .06 .15
351 Dexter Carter .04 .10
352 Mark Jackson .04 .10
353 Brian Jordan .06 .15
354 Ray Donaldson .04 .10
355 Jim Price .04 .10
356 Rod Bernstine .04 .10
357 Tony Mayberry RC .04 .10
358 Richard Brown RC .04 .10
359 David Alexander .04 .10
360 Haywood Jeffires .06 .15
361 Henry Thomas .04 .10
362 Jeff Graham .10 .25
363 Don Warren .04 .10
364 Scott Davis .04 .10
365 Harlon Barnett .04 .10
366 Mark Collins .04 .10
367 Rick Tuten .04 .10
368 Lonnie Marts RC .04 .10
369 Dennis Smith .04 .10
370 Steve Tasker .06 .15
371 Robert Massey .04 .10
372 Ricky Reynolds .04 .10
373 Alvin Wright .04 .10
374 Kelvin Martin .04 .10
375 Vince Buck .04 .10
376 John Kidd .04 .10
377 William White .04 .10
378 Bryan Cox .06 .15
379 Jamie Dukes RC .04 .10
380 Anthony Munoz .06 .15
381 Mark Gunn RC .04 .10
382 Keith Henderson .04 .10
383 Charles Wilson .04 .10
384 Shawn McCarthy RC .04 .10
385 Ernie Jones .04 .10
386 Nick Bell .04 .10
387 Derrick Walker .04 .10
388 Mark Stepnoski .06 .15
389 Broderick Thomas .04 .10
390 Reggie Roby .04 .10
391 Bubba McDowell .04 .10
392 Eric Martin .04 .10
393 Toby Caston RC .04 .10
394 Bern Brostek .04 .10
395 Christian Okoye .04 .10
396 Frank Minnifield .04 .10
397 Mike Golic .04 .10
398 Grant Feasel .04 .10
399 Michael Ball .04 .10
400 Mike Croel .04 .10
401 Maury Buford .04 .10
402 Jeff Bostic UER .04 .10
403 Sean Landeta .04 .10
404 Terry Allen .10 .25
405 Donald Evans .04 .10
406 Don Mosebar .04 .10
407 D.J. Dozier .04 .10
408 Bruce Pickens .04 .10
409 Jim Dombrowski .04 .10
410 Deron Cherry .04 .10
411 Richard Johnson CB .04 .10
412 Alexander Wright .04 .10
413 Tom Rathman .04 .10
414 Mark Dennis .04 .10
415 Phil Hansen .04 .10
416 Lonnie Young .04 .10
417 Burt Grossman .04 .10
418 Tony Covington .04 .10
419 John Stephens .04 .10
420 Jim Everett .06 .15
421 Johnny Holland .04 .10
422 Mike Barber RC .04 .10
423 Carl Lee .04 .10
424 Craig Patterson RC .04 .10
425 Greg Townsend .04 .10
426 Brett Perriman .10 .25
427 Morten Andersen .04 .10
428 John Gesek .04 .10
429 Bryan Barker .04 .10
430 John Taylor .06 .15
431 Donnell Woolford .04 .10
432 Ron Holmes .04 .10
433 Lee Williams .04 .10
434 Alfred Oglesby .04 .10
435 Jarrod Bunch .04 .10
436 Carlton Haselrig RC .04 .10
437 Rufus Porter .04 .10
438 Rohn Stark .04 .10
439 Tony Jones T .04 .10
440 Andre Rison .06 .15
441 Eric Hill .04 .10
442 Jesse Solomon .04 .10
443 Jackie Slater .04 .10
444 Donnie Elder .04 .10
445 Brett Maxie .04 .10
446 Max Montoya .04 .10
447 Will Wolford .04 .10
448 Craig Taylor .04 .10
449 Jimmie Jones .04 .10
450 Anthony Carter .06 .15
451 Brian Bollinger RC .04 .10
452 Checklist 441-550 .04 .10
453 Brad Edwards .04 .10
454 Gene Chilton RC .04 .10
455 Eric Allen .04 .10
456 William Roberts .04 .10
457 Eric Green .04 .10
458 Irv Eatman .04 .10
459 Derrick Thomas .10 .25
460 Tommy Kane .04 .10
461 LeRoy Butler .04 .10
462 Oliver Barnett .04 .10
463 Anthony Smith .04 .10
464 Cris Dishman .04 .10
465 Pat Terrell .04 .10
466 Greg Kragen .04 .10
467 Rodney Peete .06 .15
468 Willie Drewrey .04 .10
469 Jim Wilks .04 .10
470 Vince Newsome .04 .10
471 Chris Gardocki .04 .10
472 Chris Chandler .10 .25
473 George Thornton .04 .10
474 Albert Lewis .04 .10
475 Kevin Glover .04 .10
476 Joe Bowden RC .04 .10
477 Harry Sydney .04 .10
478 Bob Golic .04 .10
479 Tony Zendejas .04 .10
480 Brad Baxter .04 .10
481 Steve Beuerlein .06 .15
482 Mark Higgs .04 .10
483 Drew Hill .04 .10
484 Bryan Millard .04 .10
485 Mark Kelso .04 .10
486 David Grant .04 .10
487 Gary Zimmerman .04 .10
488 Leonard Marshall .04 .10
489 Keith Jackson .06 .15
490 Sterling Sharpe .10 .25
491 Ferrell Edmunds .04 .10
492 Wilber Marshall .04 .10
493 Charles Haley .06 .15
494 Riki Ellison .04 .10
495 Bill Brooks .04 .10
496 Bill Hawkins .04 .10
497 Erik Williams .04 .10
498 Leon Searcy RC .04 .10
499 Mike Horan .04 .10
500 Pat Swilling .04 .10
501 Maurice Hurst .04 .10
502 William Fuller .04 .10
503 Tim Newton .04 .10
504 Lorenzo Lynch .04 .10
505 Tim Barnett .04 .10
506 Tom Thayer .04 .10
507 Chris Burkett .04 .10
508 Ronnie Harmon .04 .10
509 James Brooks .06 .15
510 Bennie Blades .04 .10
511 Roger Craig .06 .15
512 Tony Woods .04 .10
513 Greg Lewis .04 .10
514 Erric Pegram .06 .15
515 Elvis Patterson .04 .10
516 Jeff Cross .04 .10
517 Myron Guyton .04 .10
518 Jay Novacek .06 .15
519 Leo Barker RC .04 .10
520 Keith Byars .04 .10
521 Dalton Hilliard .04 .10
522 Ted Washington .04 .10
523 Dexter McNabb RC .04 .10
524 Frank Reich .06 .15
525 Henry Ellard .06 .15
526 Barry Foster .06 .15
527 Barry Word .04 .10
528 Gary Anderson RB .04 .10
529 Reggie Rutland .04 .10
530 Stephen Baker .04 .10
531 John Flannery .04 .10
532 Steve Wright .04 .10
533 Eric Sanders .04 .10
534 Bob Whitfield RC .04 .10
535 Gaston Green .04 .10
536 Anthony Pleasant .04 .10
537 Jeff Bryant .04 .10
538 Jarvis Williams .04 .10
539 Jim Morrissey .04 .10
540 Andre Tippett .04 .10
541 Gill Byrd .04 .10
542 Raleigh McKenzie .04 .10
543 Jim Sweeney .04 .10
544 David Lutz .04 .10
545 Wayne Martin .04 .10
546 Karl Wilson .04 .10
547 Pierce Holt .04 .10
548 Doug Smith .04 .10
549 Nolan Harrison RC .04 .10
550 Freddie Joe Nunn .04 .10

551 Eric Moore .04 .10
552 Cris Carter .20 .50
553 Kevin Gogan .04 .10
554 Harold Green .04 .10
555 Kenneth Davis .04 .10
556 Travis McNeal .04 .10
557 Jim C. Jensen .04 .10
558 Willie Green .04 .10
559 Scott Galbraith RC .04 .10
560 Louis Lipps .04 .10
561 Matt Brock .04 .10
562 Mike Prior .04 .10
563 Checklist 551-660 .04 .10
564 Robert Delpino .04 .10
565 Vinny Testaverde .06 .15
566 Willie Gault .06 .15
567 Quinn Early .06 .15
568 Eric Moten .04 .10
569 Lance Smith .04 .10
570 Darrell Green .04 .10
571 Moe Gardner .04 .10
572 Steve Atwater .04 .10
573 Ray Childress .04 .10
574 Dave Krieg .06 .15
575 Bruce Armstrong .04 .10
576 Fred Barnett .10 .25
577 Don Griffin .04 .10
578 David Brandon RC .04 .10
579 Robert Young .04 .10
580 Keith Van Horne .04 .10
581 Jeff Criswell .04 .10
582 Lewis Tillman .04 .10
583 Bubby Brister .04 .10
584 Aaron Wallace .04 .10
585 Chris Doleman .04 .10
586 Marty Carter RC .04 .10
587 Chris Warren .10 .25
588 David Griggs .04 .10
589 Darrell Thompson .04 .10
590 Marion Butts .04 .10
591 Scott Norwood .04 .10
592 Lomas Brown .04 .10
593 Daryl Johnston .10 .25
594 Alonzo Mitz RC .04 .10
595 Tommy Barnhardt .04 .10
596 Tim Jorden .04 .10
597 Neil Smith .10 .25
598 Todd Marinovich .04 .10
599 Sean Jones .04 .10
600 Clarence Verdin .04 .10
601 Trace Armstrong .04 .10
602 Steve Bono RC .10 .25
603 Mark Ingram .04 .10
604 Flipper Anderson .04 .10
605 James Jones DT .04 .10
606 Al Noga .04 .10
607 Rick Bryan .04 .10
608 Eugene Lockhart .04 .10
609 Charles Mann .04 .10
610 James Hasty .04 .10
611 Jeff Feagles .04 .10
612 Tim Brown .10 .25
613 David Little .04 .10
614 Keith Sims .04 .10
615 Kevin Murphy .04 .10
616 Ray Crockett .04 .10
617 Jim Jeffcoat .04 .10
618 Patrick Hunter .04 .10
619 Keith Kartz .04 .10
620 Peter Tom Willis .04 .10
621 Vaughan Johnson .04 .10
622 Shawn Jefferson .04 .10
623 Anthony Thompson .04 .10
624 John Rienstra .04 .10
625 Don Maggs .04 .10
626 Todd Lyght .04 .10
627 Brent Jones .06 .15
628 Todd McNair .04 .10
629 Winston Moss .04 .10
630 Mark Carrier WR .06 .15
631 Dan Owens .04 .10
632 Sammie Smith UER .04 .10
633 James Lofton .06 .15
634 Paul McJulien RC .04 .10
635 Tony Tolbert .04 .10
636 Carnell Lake .04 .10
637 Gary Clark .10 .25
638 Brian Washington .04 .10
639 Jessie Hester .04 .10
640 Doug Riesenberg .04 .10
641 Joe Walter RC .04 .10
642 John Rade .04 .10
643 Wes Hopkins .04 .10
644 Kelly Stouffer .04 .10
645 Marv Cook .04 .10
646 Ken Clarke .04 .10
647 Bobby Humphrey UER .04 .10
648 Tim McDonald .04 .10
649 Donald Frank RC .04 .10
650 Richmond Webb .04 .10
651 Lemuel Stinson .04 .10
652 Merton Hanks .06 .15
653 Frank Warren .04 .10
654 Thomas Benson .04 .10
655 Al Smith .04 .10
656 Steve DeBerg .04 .10
657 Jayice Pearson RC .04 .10
658 Joe Morris .04 .10
659 Fred Strickland .04 .10
660 Kelvin Pritchett .04 .10
661 Lewis Billups .04 .10
662 Todd Collins RC .04 .10
663 Corey Miller RC .04 .10
664 Levon Kirkland RC .04 .10
665 Jerry Rice .30 .75
666 Mike Lodish RC .04 .10
667 Chuck Smith RC .04 .10
668 Lance Olberding RC .04 .10
669 Kevin Smith RC .04 .10
670 Dale Carter RC .06 .15
671 Sean Gilbert RC .06 .15
672 Ken O'Brien .04 .10
673 Ricky Proehl .04 .10
674 Junior Seau .10 .25
675 Courtney Hawkins RC .06 .15
676 Eddie Robinson RC .04 .10
677 Tommy Jeter RC .04 .10
678 Jeff George .10 .25
679 Cary Conklin .04 .10
680 Rueben Mayes .04 .10
681 Sean Lumpkin RC .04 .10
682 Dan Marino .50 1.25
683 Ed McDaniel RC .04 .10
684 Greg Skrepenak RC .04 .10
685 Tracy Scroggins RC .04 .10
686 Tommy Maddox RC .75 2.00
687 Mike Singletary .06 .15
688 Patrick Rowe RC .04 .10
689 Phillippi Sparks RC .04 .10
690 Joel Steed RC .04 .10
691 Kevin Fagan .04 .10
692 Deion Sanders .20 .50
693 Bruce Smith .10 .25
694 David Klingler RC .04 .10
695 Clayton Holmes RC .04 .10
696 Brett Favre 2.50 6.00
697 Marc Boutte RC .04 .10
698 Dwayne Sabb RC .04 .10

700 Randall Cunningham .10 .25
701 Quentin Coryatt RC .04 .10
702 Bernie Kosar .06 .15
703 Vaughn Dunbar RC .04 .10
704 Browning Nagle .04 .10
705 Mark Wheeler RC .04 .10
706 Paul Siever RC .04 .10
707 Anthony Miller .06 .15
708 Corey Widmer RC .04 .10
709 Eric Dickerson .06 .15
710 Martin Bayless .04 .10
711 Jason Hanson RC .06 .15
712 Michael Dean Perry .06 .15
713 Billy Joe Tolliver UER .04 .10
714 Chad Hennings RC .06 .15
715 Bucky Richardson RC .04 .10
716 Steve Israel RC .04 .10
717 Robert Harris RC .04 .10
718 Timm Rosenbach .04 .10
719 Joe Montana .50 1.25
720 Derek Brown TE RC .04 .10
721 Robert Brooks RC .30 .75
722 Boomer Esiason .06 .15
723 Troy Auzenne RC .04 .10
724 John Fina RC .04 .10
725 Chris Crooms RC .04 .10
726 Eugene Chung RC .04 .10
727 Darren Woodson RC .10 .25
728 Leslie O'Neal .06 .15
729 Dan McGwire .04 .10
730 Al Toon .06 .15
731 Michael Brandon RC .04 .10
732 Steve DeOssie .04 .10
733 Jim Kelly .10 .25
734 Webster Slaughter .04 .10
735 Tony Smith RC .04 .10
736 Shane Collins RC .04 .10
737 Randal Hill .04 .10
738 Chris Holder RC .04 .10
739 Russell Maryland .04 .10
740 Carl Pickens RC .10 .25
741 Andre Reed .06 .15
742 Steve Emtman RC .04 .10
743 Carl Banks .04 .10
744 Troy Aikman .30 .75
745 Mark Royals .04 .10
746 J.J. Birden .04 .10
747 Michael Cofer .04 .10
748 Darryl Ashmore RC .04 .10
749 Dion Lambert RC .04 .10
750 Phil Simms .06 .15
751 Reggie E.White RC .04 .10
752 Harvey Williams .10 .25
753 Ty Detmer .10 .25
754 Tony Brooks RC .04 .10
755 Steve Christie .04 .10
756 Lawrence Taylor .10 .25
757 Merril Hoge .04 .10
758 Robert Jones RC .04 .10
759 Checklist 661-759 .04 .10

1992 Topps Gold

COMPLETE SET (759) 60.00 150.00
COMP.SERIES 1 (330) 20.00 50.00
COMP.SERIES 2 (330) 20.00 50.00
COMP.HI SERIES (99) 25.00 60.00
*VETERANS: 1.5X TO 4X BASIC CARDS
*ROOKIES: 1.2X TO 3X BASIC CARDS
ONE PER PACK/THREE PER RACK
TWENTY PER LO FACTORY SET
TEN PER HIGH FACTORY SET
109 Freeman McNeil .25 .60
218 David Daniels .25 .60
316 Chris Hakel .25 .60
341 Ottis Anderson .25 .60
452 Shawn Moore .25 .60
563 Mike Mooney .25 .60
759 Curtis Whitley .25 .60

1992 Topps No.1 Draft Picks

In addition to being individually inserted randomly in 1992 Topps high series packs, this four-card standard-size insert set was included in each 1992 Topps "High Series" factory set. It features the No. 1 draft pick for 1990, 1991 and 1992 as well as a card for Raghib "Rocket" Ismail, who many experts feel could have been the number 1 pick if he had entered the NFL draft. Inside white borders, the fronts display color action player photos. The words "No. 1 Draft Pick of the 90's" are printed above the picture, while the player's name and team name appear respectively in two short color bars at the bottom. On a football design, the backs carry a color close-up photo and biographical information.

COMPLETE SET (4) 1.50 4.00
RANDOM INSERTS IN HIGH SERIES PACKS
ONE SET PER HIGH SERIES FACTORY SET
1 Jeff George .60 1.50
2 Russell Maryland .40 1.00
3 Steve Emtman .40 1.00
4 Rocket Ismail .40 1.00

1992 Topps 1000 Yard Club

is 20-card standard-size set was issued to celebrate rushers and receivers who compiled 1000 yards or more in the 1991 season. These cards were issued three per jumbo pack. . A Gold foil parallel to the set was also issued as a random insert in factory sets.

COMPLETE SET (20) 6.00 15.00
*GOLDS: 1.5X TO 4X BASIC INSERTS
GOLDS RANDOM INSERTS IN FACT.SETS
1 Emmitt Smith 1.50 4.00
2 Barry Sanders 1.25 3.00
3 Michael Irvin .25 .60
4 Thurman Thomas .25 .60
5 Gary Clark .25 .60
6 Haywood Jeffires .08 .25
7 Michael Haynes .08 .25
8 Drew Hill .05 .15
9 Mark Duper .05 .15
10 James Lofton .08 .25
11 Rodney Hampton .08 .25
12 Mark Clayton .08 .25
13 Henry Ellard .08 .25
14 Art Monk .08 .25
15 Earnest Byner .05 .15
16 Gaston Green .05 .15
17 Christian Okoye .05 .15
18 Irving Fryar .08 .25
19 John Taylor .08 .25
20 Brian Blades .08 .25

1992 Topps Stadium of Stars

This 12-card standard-size set measures the standard size and features stars from different sports and entertainment. The cards have the same design as the regular 1992 Topps cards. The fronts feature color portraits with red and white inner borders and white outer borders. The star's name and the set name appear in two short color stripes respectively at the bottom. The backs carry a short biography and personal information. The cards are unnumbered and checklisted below in alphabetical order

COMPLETE SET (12) 5.00 12.00

1993 Topps

The 1993 Topps football set consists of 660 standard-size cards that were issued in two series of 330. Each pack contained 14 cards plus one Topps Gold card. Factory sets of 673 cards contain 10 Topps Gold cards and three Topps Black Gold cards. Subsets featured are Record Breakers (1-2), Franchise Players (82-90), Team Leaders (171-184, 261-274), League Leaders (216-220) and Field Generals (291-300). Thirty Draft Pick cards are scattered throughout the set. Rookie Cards include Jerome Bettis, Drew Bledsoe, Reggie Brooks, Dave Brown, Curtis Conway, Garrison Hearst, Qadry Ismail, O.J. McDuffie, Natrone Means, Rick Mirer, Ronald Moore, Robert Smith and Dana Stubblefield.

COMPLETE SET (660) 20.00 50.00
COMP.FACT.SET (673) 75.00 125.00
COMP.SERIES 1 (330) 8.00 20.00
COMP.SERIES 2 (330) 8.00 20.00
1 Art Monk RB .06 .15
2 Jerry Rice RB .20 .50
3 Stanley Richard .04 .10
4 Ron Hall .04 .10
5 Daryl Johnston .10 .25
6 Wendell Davis .04 .10
7 Vaughn Dunbar .04 .10
8 Mike Jones .04 .10
9 Anthony Johnson .06 .15
10 Chris Miller .06 .15
11 Kyle Clifton .04 .10
12 Curtis Conway RC .15 .40
13 Lionel Washington .04 .10
14 Reggie Johnson .04 .10
15 David Little .04 .10
16 Nick Lowery .04 .10
17 Darryl Williams .04 .10
18 Brent Jones .06 .15
19 Bruce Matthews .06 .15
20 Heath Sherman .04 .10
21 John Kasay UER .04 .10
22 Troy Drayton RC .06 .15
23 Eric Metcalf .06 .15
24 Andre Tippett .06 .15
25 Rodney Hampton .06 .15
26 Henry Jones .04 .10
27 Jim Everett .06 .15
28 Steve Jordan .04 .10
29 LeRoy Butler .04 .10
30 Troy Vincent .04 .10
31 Nate Lewis .04 .10
32 Rickey Jackson .06 .15
33 Darion Conner .04 .10
34 Tom Carter RC .06 .15
35 Jeff George .10 .25
36 Larry Centers RC .10 .25
37 Reggie Cobb .04 .10
38 Mike Saxon .04 .10
39 Brad Baxter .04 .10
40 Reggie White .10 .25
41 Haywood Jeffires .06 .15
42 Alfred Williams .04 .10
43 Aaron Wallace .04 .10
44 Tracy Simien .04 .10
45 Pat Harlow .04 .10
46 D.J. Johnson .04 .10
47 Don Griffin .04 .10
48 Flipper Anderson .06 .15
49 Keith Kartz .04 .10
50 Bernie Kosar .06 .15
51 Kent Hull .04 .10
52 Erik Howard .04 .10
53 Pierce Holt .04 .10
54 Dwayne Harper .04 .10
55 Bennie Blades .04 .10
56 Mark Duper .04 .10
57 Brian Noble .04 .10
58 Jeff Feagles .04 .10
59 Michael Haynes .06 .15
60 Junior Seau .10 .25
61 Gary Anderson RB .06 .15
62 Jon Hand .04 .10
63 Lin Elliott RC .04 .10
64 Dana Stubblefield RC .10 .25
65 Vaughan Johnson .04 .10
66 Mo Lewis .04 .10
67 Aeneas Williams .06 .15
68 David Fulcher .04 .10
69 Chip Lohmiller .04 .10
70 Greg Townsend .06 .15
71 Simon Fletcher .04 .10
72 Sean Salisbury .06 .10
73 Christian Okoye .06 .10
74 Jim Arnold .04 .05
75 Bruce Smith .10 .25
76 Fred Barnett .06 .10
77 Bill Romanowski .06 .10
78 Dermontti Dawson .06 .10
79 Bern Brostek .04 .05
80 Warren Moon .10 .25
81 Bill Fralic .04 .05
82 Lomas Brown FP .04 .05
83 Duane Bickett FP .04 .05
84 Neil Smith FP .06 .10
85 Reggie White FP .06 .10
86 Tim McDonald FP .04 .05
87 Leslie O'Neal FP .04 .10
88 Steve Young FP .15 .40
89 Paul Gruber FP .04 .10
90 Wilber Marshall FP .04 .10
91 Trace Armstrong .04 .10
92 Bobby Houston RC .04 .10
93 George Thornton .04 .10
94 Keith McCants .04 .10
95 Ricky Sanders .04 .10
96 Jackie Harris .04 .10
97 Todd Marinovich .04 .10
98 Henry Thomas .04 .10
99 Jeff Wright .04 .10
100 John Elway .60 1.50
101 Garrison Hearst RC .30 .75
102 Roy Foster .04 .10
103 David Lang .04 .10
104 Matt Stover .04 .10
105 Lawrence Taylor .10 .25
106 Pete Stoyanovich .04 .10
107 Jessie Tuggle .04 .10
108 William White .04 .10
109 Andy Harmon RC .06 .15
110 John L. Williams .04 .10
111 Jon Vaughn .04 .10
112 John Alt .04 .10
113 Chris Jacke .04 .10
114 Jim Breech .04 .10
115 Eric Martin .04 .10
116 Derrick Walker .04 .10
117 Ricky Ervins .04 .10
118 Roger Craig .06 .15
119 Jeff Gossett .04 .10

121 Bob Whitfield .04 .10
122 Alonzo Spellman .04 .10
123 David Klingler .04 .10
124 Tommy Maddox .10 .25
125 Robert Porcher .04 .10
126 Edgar Bennett .10 .25
127 Harvey Williams .06 .15
128 Dave Brown RC .10 .25
129 Johnny Mitchell .04 .10
130 Drew Bledsoe RC 1.00 2.50
131 Zefross Moss .04 .10
132 Nate Odomes .04 .10
133 Rufus Porter .04 .10
134 Jackie Slater .06 .15
135 Steve Young .30 .75
136 Chris Calloway .06 .15
137 Steve Atwater .06 .15
138 Mark Carrier DB .04 .10
139 Marvin Washington .04 .10
140 Barry Foster .06 .15
141 Ricky Reynolds .04 .10
142 Bubba McDowell .04 .10
143 Dan Footman RC .04 .10
144 Richmond Webb .04 .10
145 Mike Pritchard .06 .15
146 Chris Spielman .06 .15
147 Dave Krieg .06 .15
148 Nick Bell .04 .10
149 Vincent Brown .04 .10
150 Seth Joyner .04 .10
151 Tommy Kane .04 .10
152 Carlton Gray RC .04 .10
153 Harry Newsome .04 .10
154 Rohn Stark .04 .10
155 Shannon Sharpe .10 .25
156 Charles Haley .06 .15
157 Cornelius Bennett .06 .15
158 Doug Riesenberg .04 .10
159 Amp Lee .04 .10
160 Sterling Sharpe UER .10 .25
161 Alonzo Mitz .04 .10
162 Pat Terrell .04 .10
163 Mark Schlereth .04 .10
164 Gary Anderson K .04 .10
165 Quinn Early .06 .15
166 Jerome Bettis RC 2.50 5.00
167 Lawrence Dawsey .04 .10
168 Derrick Thomas .10 .25
169 Rodney Peete .04 .10
170 Jim Kelly .10 .25
171 Deion Sanders TL .10 .25
172 Richard Dent TL .04 .10
173 Emmitt Smith TL .30 .75
174 Barry Sanders TL .25 .60
175 Sterling Sharpe TL .06 .15
176 Cleveland Gary TL .04 .10
177 Terry Allen TL .06 .15
178 Vaughan Johnson TL .04 .10
179 Rodney Hampton TL .04 .10
180 Randall Cunningham TL .06 .15
181 Ricky Proehl TL .04 .10
182 Jerry Rice TL .20 .50
183 Reggie Cobb TL .04 .10
184 Earnest Byner TL .04 .10
185 Jeff Lageman .04 .10
186 Carlos Jenkins .04 .10
187 G.Hearst .15 .40
Dye
Moore
Cole.
188 Todd Lyght .04 .10
189 Carl Simpson RC .04 .10
190 Barry Sanders .50 1.25
191 Jim Harbaugh .10 .25
192 Roger Ruzek .04 .10
193 Brent Williams .04 .10
194 Chip Banks .04 .10
195 Mike Croel .04 .10
196 Marion Butts .06 .15
197 James Washington .04 .10
198 John Offerdahl .04 .10
199 Tom Rathman .06 .15
200 Joe Montana .60 1.50
201 Pepper Johnson .06 .15
202 Cris Dishman .04 .10
203 Adrian White RC .04 .10
204 Reggie Brooks RC .06 .15
205 Cortez Kennedy .06 .15
206 Robert Massey .04 .10
207 Toi Cook .04 .10
208 Harry Sydney .04 .10
209 Lincoln Kennedy RC .04 .10
210 Randall McDaniel .10 .25
211 Eugene Daniel .04 .10
212 Rob Burnett .04 .10
213 Steve Broussard .04 .10
214 Brian Washington .04 .10
215 Leonard Renfro RC .04 .10
216 Audray McMillian LL .04 .10
217 Sterling Sharpe .04 .10
Miller L
218 Clyde Simmons LL .04 .10
219 Emmitt Smith .15 .40
B.Foster LL
220 Steve Young .10 .25
W.Moon LL
221 Mel Gray .06 .15
222 Luis Sharpe .04 .10
223 Eric Moten .04 .10
224 Albert Lewis .04 .10
225 Alvin Harper .06 .15
226 Steve Wallace .04 .10
227 Mark Higgs .04 .10
228 Eugene Lockhart .04 .10
229 Sean Jones .04 .10
230 J.Lynch RC/Thom/DuBose .25 .60
231 Jimmy Williams .04 .10
232 Demetrius DuBose RC .04 .10
233 John Roper .04 .10
234 Keith Hamilton .04 .10
235 Donald Evans .04 .10
236 Kenneth Davis .06 .15
237 John Copeland RC .06 .15
238 Leonard Russell .06 .15
239 Ken Harvey .04 .10
240 Dale Carter .04 .10
241 Anthony Pleasant .04 .10
242 Darrell Green .06 .15
243 Natrone Means RC .10 .25
244 Rob Moore .06 .15
245 Chris Doleman .04 .10
246 J.B. Brown .04 .10
247 Ray Crockett .04 .10
248 John Taylor .06 .15
249 Russell Maryland .04 .10
250 Brett Favre .75 2.00
251 Carl Pickens .06 .15
252 Andy Heck .04 .10
253 Jerome Henderson .04 .10
254 Deion Sanders .20 .50
255 Steve Emtman .04 .10
256 Calvin Williams .06 .15
257 Sean Gilbert .06 .15
258 Don Beebe .04 .10
259 Robert Smith RC .50 1.25
260 Robert Blackmon .04 .10
261 Jim Kelly TL .06 .15
262 Harold Green TL UER .04 .10
263 Clay Matthews TL .04 .10
264 John Elway TL .30 .75
265 Warren Moon TL .06 .15
266 Jeff George TL .06 .15

268 Howie Long TL .04 .10
269 Dan Marino TL .30 .75
270 Jon Vaughn TL .04 .10
271 Chris Burkett TL .04 .10
272 Barry Foster TL .04 .10
273 Marion Butts TL .04 .10
274 Chris Warren TL .04 .10
275 M.Strahan RC/M.Buck. .75 2.00
276 Tony Casillas .04 .10
277 Jarrod Bunch .04 .10
278 Eric Green .04 .10
279 Stan Brock .04 .10
280 Chester McGlockton .06 .15
281 Ricky Watters .10 .25
282 Dan Saleaumua .04 .10
283 Rich Camarillo .04 .10
284 Cris Carter .10 .25
285 Rick Mirer RC .10 .25
286 Matt Brock .04 .10
287 Burt Grossman .04 .10
288 Andre Collins .04 .10
289 Mark Jackson .04 .10
290 Dan Marino .60 1.50
291 Cornelius Bennett FG .04 .10
292 Steve Atwater FG .04 .10
293 Bryan Cox FG .04 .10
294 Sam Mills FG .04 .10
295 Pepper Johnson FG .04 .10
296 Seth Joyner FG .04 .10
297 Chris Spielman FG .04 .10
298 Junior Seau FG .06 .15
299 Cortez Kennedy FG .04 .10
300 Broderick Thomas FG .04 .10
301 Todd McNair .04 .10
302 Nate Newton .06 .15
303 Michael Walter .04 .10
304 Clyde Simmons .04 .10
305 Ernie Mills .04 .10
306 Steve Wisniewski .04 .10
307 Coleman Rudolph RC .04 .10
308 Thurman Thomas .10 .25
309 Reggie Roby .04 .10
310 Eric Swann .06 .15
311 Mark Wheeler .04 .10
312 Jeff Herrod .04 .10
313 Leroy Hoard .06 .15
314 Patrick Bates RC .04 .10
315 Earnest Byner .04 .10
316 Dave Meggett .04 .10
317 George Teague RC .06 .15
318 Ray Childress .06 .15
319 Mike Kenn .04 .10
320 Jason Hanson .04 .10
321 Gary Clark .06 .15
322 Chris Gardocki .04 .10
323 Ken Norton .06 .15
324 Eric Curry RC .04 .10
325 Byron Evans .04 .10
326 O.J. McDuffie RC .10 .25
327 Dwight Stone .04 .10
328 Tommy Barnhardt .04 .10
329 Checklist 1-165 .04 .10
330 Checklist 166-329 .04 .10
331 Erik Williams .04 .10
332 Phil Hansen .04 .10
333 Martin Harrison RC .04 .10
334 Mark Ingram .04 .10
335 Mark Rypien .06 .15
336 Anthony Miller .06 .15
337 Antone Davis .04 .10
338 Mike Munchak .06 .15
339 Wayne Martin .04 .10
340 Joe Montana .60 1.50
341 Deon Figures RC .04 .10
342 Ed McDaniel .04 .10
343 Chris Burkett .04 .10
344 Tony Smith .04 .10
345 James Lofton .06 .15
346 Courtney Hawkins .04 .10
347 Dennis Smith .04 .10
348 Anthony Morgan .04 .10
349 Chris Goode .04 .10
350 Phil Simms .06 .15
351 Patrick Hunter .04 .10
352 Brett Perriman .10 .25
353 Corey Miller .04 .10
354 Harry Galbreath .04 .10
355 Mark Carrier WR .06 .15
356 Troy Drayton .06 .15
357 Greg Davis .04 .10
358 Tim Krumrie .04 .10
359 Tim McDonald .04 .10
360 Webster Slaughter .04 .10
361 Steve Christie .04 .10
362 Courtney Hall .04 .10
363 Charles Mann .04 .10
364 Vestee Jackson .04 .10
365 Robert Jones .04 .10
366 Rich Miano .04 .10
367 Morten Andersen .06 .15
368 Jeff Graham .06 .15
369 Martin Mayhew .04 .10
370 Anthony Carter .06 .15
371 Greg Kragen .04 .10
372 Ron Cox .04 .10
373 Perry Williams .04 .10
374 Willie Gault .06 .15
375 Chris Warren .06 .15
376 Reyna Thompson .04 .10
377 Bennie Thompson .04 .10
378 Kevin Mack .04 .10
379 Clarence Verdin .04 .10
380 Marc Boutte .04 .10
381 Marvin Jones RC .04 .10
382 Greg Jackson .04 .10
383 Steve Bono .06 .15
384 Terrell Buckley .04 .10
385 Garrison Hearst .10 .25
386 Mike Brim .04 .10
387 Jesse Sapolu .04 .10
388 Carl Lee .04 .10
389 Jeff Cross .04 .10
390 Karl Mecklenburg .06 .15
391 Chad Hennings .04 .10
392 Oliver Barnett .04 .10
393 Dalton Hilliard .04 .10
394 Broderick Thompson .04 .10
395 Rocket Ismail .06 .15
396 John Kidd .04 .10
397 Eddie Anderson .04 .10
398 Lamar Lathon .04 .10
399 Darren Perry .04 .10
400 Drew Bledsoe .50 1.25
401 Ferrell Edmunds .04 .10
402 Lomas Brown .04 .10
403 Drew Hill .06 .15
404 David Whitmore .04 .10
405 Mike Johnson .04 .10
406 Paul Gruber .04 .10
407 Kirk Lowdermilk .04 .10
408 Curtis Conway .10 .25
409 Bryce Paup .06 .15
410 Boomer Esiason .06 .15
411 Jay Schroeder .04 .10
412 Anthony Newman .04 .10
413 Ernie Jones .04 .10
414 Carlton Bailey .04 .10
415 Kenneth Gant .04 .10
416 Todd Scott .04 .10
417 Anthony Smith .04 .10
418 Erik McMillan .04 .10
419 Ronnie Harmon .04 .10

421 Wymon Henderson .04 .10
422 Carnell Lake .04 .10
423 Al Noga .04 .10
424 Curtis Duncan .04 .10
425 Mike Gann .04 .10
426 Eugene Robinson .06 .15
427 Scott Mersereau .04 .10
428 Chris Singleton .04 .10
429 Gerald Robinson .04 .10
430 Pat Swilling .06 .15
431 Ed McCaffrey .10 .25
432 Neal Anderson .06 .15
433 Joe Phillips .04 .10
434 Jerry Ball .04 .10
435 Tyronne Stowe .04 .10
436 Dana Stubblefield .10 .25
437 Eric Curry .04 .10
438 Derrick Fenner .04 .10
439 Mark Clayton .06 .15
440 Quentin Coryatt .06 .15
441 Willie Roaf RC .12 .30
442 Ernest Dye .04 .10
443 Jeff Jaeger .04 .10
444 Stan Humphries .06 .15
445 Johnny Johnson .04 .10
446 Larry Brown DB .04 .10
447 Kurt Gouveia .04 .10
448 Qadry Ismail RC .10 .25
449 Dan Footman .04 .10
450 Tom Waddle .04 .10
451 Kelvin Martin .04 .10
452 Kanavis McGhee .04 .10
453 Herman Moore .10 .25
454 Jesse Solomon .04 .10
455 Shane Conlan .04 .10
456 Joel Steed .04 .10
457 Charles Arbuckle .04 .10
458 Shane Dronett .04 .10
459 Steve Tasker .06 .15
460 Herschel Walker .06 .15
461 Willie Davis .10 .25
462 Al Smith .04 .10
463 O.J. McDuffie .10 .25
464 Kevin Fagan .04 .10
465 Hardy Nickerson .06 .15
466 Leonard Marshall .06 .15
467 John Baylor .04 .10
468 Jay Novacek .06 .15
469 Wayne Simmons RC .04 .10
470 Tommy Vardell .04 .10
471 Cleveland Gary .04 .10
472 Mark Collins .06 .15
473 Craig Heyward .06 .15
474 John Copeland UER .06 .15
475 Jeff Hostetler .06 .15
476 Brian Mitchell .06 .15
477 Natrone Means .10 .25
478 Brad Muster .04 .10
479 David Lutz .04 .10
480 Andre Rison .06 .15
481 Michael Zordich .04 .10
482 Jim McMahon .06 .15
483 Carlton Gray .04 .10
484 Chris Mohr .04 .10
485 Ernest Givins .06 .15
486 Tony Tolbert .04 .10
487 Vai Sikahema UER .04 .10
488 Larry Webster .04 .10
489 James Hasty .04 .10
490 Reggie White .10 .25
491 Reggie Rivers RC .04 .10
492 Roman Phifer .04 .10
493 Levon Kirkland .04 .10
494 Demetrius DuBose .04 .10
495 William Perry .06 .15
496 Clay Matthews .06 .15
497 Aaron Jones .04 .10
498 Jack Trudeau .04 .10
499 Michael Brooks .04 .10
500 Jerry Rice .40 1.00
501 Lonnie Marts .04 .10
502 Tim McGee .06 .15
503 Kelvin Pritchett .04 .10
504 Bobby Hebert .06 .15
505 Audray McMillian .04 .10
506 Chuck Cecil .04 .10
507 Leonard Renfro .04 .10
508 Ethan Horton .04 .10
509 Kevin Smith .06 .15
510 Louis Oliver .04 .10
511 John Stephens .04 .10
512 Browning Nagle .04 .10
513 Ricardo McDonald .04 .10
514 Leslie O'Neal .06 .15
515 Lorenzo White .04 .10
516 Thomas Smith RC .06 .15
517 Tony Woods .04 .10
518 Darryl Henley .04 .10
519 Robert Delpino .04 .10
520 Rod Woodson .10 .25
521 Phillippi Sparks .04 .10
522 Jessie Hester .04 .10
523 Shaun Gayle .04 .10
524 Brad Edwards .04 .10
525 Randall Cunningham .10 .25
526 Marv Cook .04 .10
527 Dennis Gibson .04 .10
528 Erric Pegram .06 .15
529 Terry McDaniel .04 .10
530 Troy Aikman .30 .75
531 Irving Fryar .06 .15
532 Blair Thomas .04 .10
533 Jim Wilks .04 .10
534 Michael Jackson .06 .15
535 Eric Davis .04 .10
536 James Campen .04 .10
537 Steve Beuerlein .06 .15
538 Robert Smith .20 .50
539 J.J. Birden .04 .10
540 Broderick Thomas .04 .10
541 Darryl Talley .04 .10
542 Russell Freeman RC .04 .10
543 David Alexander .04 .10
544 Chris Mims .04 .10
545 Coleman Rudolph .04 .10
546 Steve McMichael .06 .15
547 David Williams .04 .10
548 Chris Hinton .04 .10
549 Jim Jeffcoat .04 .10
550 Howie Long .10 .25
551 Roosevelt Potts RC .04 .10
552 Bryan Cox .04 .10
553 David Richards UER .04 .10
554 Reggie Brooks .06 .15
555 Neil O'Donnell .10 .25
556 Irv Smith RC .04 .10
557 Henry Ellard .06 .15
558 Steve DeBerg .06 .15
559 Jim Sweeney .04 .10
560 Harold Green .04 .10
561 Darrell Thompson .04 .10
562 Vinny Testaverde .06 .15
563 Bubby Brister .04 .10
564 Sean Landeta .06 .15
565 Neil Smith .10 .25
566 Craig Erickson .06 .15
567 Jim Ritcher .04 .10
568 Don Mosebar .04 .10
569 John Gesek .04 .10
570 Gary Plummer .04 .10
571 Norm Johnson .04 .10
572 Ron Heller .04 .10

574 Greg Montgomery .04 .10
575 Dana Hall .04 .10
576 Vencie Glenn .04 .10
577 Dean Biasucci .04 .10
578 Rod Bernstine UER .04 .10
579 Randal Hill .04 .10
580 Sam Mills .06 .15
581 Santana Dotson .06 .15
582 Greg Lloyd .06 .15
583 Eric Thomas .04 .10
584 Henry Rolling .04 .10
585 Tony Bennett .04 .10
586 Sheldon White .04 .10
587 Mark Kelso .06 .15
588 Marc Spindler .04 .10
589 Greg McMurtry .04 .10
590 Art Monk .06 .15
591 Marco Coleman .04 .10
592 Tony Jones .04 .10
593 Melvin Jenkins .04 .10
594 Kevin Ross .04 .10
595 William Fuller .04 .10
596 James Joseph .04 .10
597 Lamar McGriggs RC .04 .10
598 Gill Byrd .04 .10
599 Alexander Wright .04 .10
600 Rick Mirer .10 .25
601 Richard Dent .06 .15
602 Thomas Everett .04 .10
603 Jack Del Rio .06 .15
604 Jerome Bettis 1.00 2.50
605 Ronnie Lott .06 .15
606 Marty Carter .04 .10
607 Arthur Marshall RC .04 .10
608 Lee Johnson .04 .10
609 Bruce Armstrong .04 .10
610 Ricky Proehl .06 .15
611 Will Wolford .04 .10
612 Mike Prior .04 .10
613 George Jamison .04 .10
614 Gene Atkins .04 .10
615 Merril Hoge .06 .15
616 Desmond Howard .06 .15
617 Jarvis Williams .04 .10
618 Marcus Allen .10 .25
619 Gary Brown .04 .10
620 Bill Brooks .04 .10
621 Eric Allen .04 .10
622 Todd Kelly .04 .10
623 Michael Dean Perry .06 .15
624 David Braxton .04 .10
625 Mike Sherrard .04 .10
626 Jeff Bryant .04 .10
627 Eric Bieniemy .04 .10
628 Tim Brown .10 .25
629 Troy Auzenne .04 .10
630 Michael Irvin .10 .25
631 Maurice Hurst .04 .10
632 Duane Bickett .04 .10
633 George Teague .06 .15
634 Vince Workman .04 .10
635 Renaldo Turnbull .04 .10
636 Johnny Bailey .04 .10
637 Dan Williams RC .04 .10
638 James Thornton .04 .10
639 Terry Allen .10 .25
640 Kevin Greene .06 .15
641 Tony Zendejas .04 .10
642 Scott Kowalkowski RC .04 .10
643 Jeff Query UER .04 .10
644 Brian Blades .06 .15
645 Keith Jackson .06 .15
646 Monte Coleman .04 .10
647 Guy McIntyre .04 .10
648 Barry Word .04 .10
649 Steve Everitt RC .04 .10
650 Patrick Bates .04 .10
651 Marcus Robertson RC .04 .10
652 John Carney .04 .10
653 Derek Brown TE .04 .10
654 Carwell Gardner .04 .10
655 Moe Gardner .04 .10
656 Andre Ware .06 .15
657 Keith Van Horne .04 .10
658 Hugh Millen .04 .10
659 Checklist 330-495 .04 .10
660 Checklist 496-660 .04 .10

1993 Topps Gold

*GOLD STARS: 1.5X TO 4X BASIC CARDS
*GOLD RCs: 1X TO 2.5X BASIC CARDS
ONE PER PACK
329 Terance Mathis .40 1.00
330 John Wojciechowski .20 .50
659 Pat Chaffey .20 .50
660 Milton Mack .20 .50

1993 Topps Black Gold

One Topps Black Gold card was inserted in approximately every 72 packs of 1993 Topps football. Card numbers 1-22 were randomly inserted in first series wax packs while card numbers 23-44 were featured in second series packs. Collectors could obtain the set by collecting individual random insert cards or receive 11, 22, or 44 Black Gold cards through the mail by sending in special "Winner, You've Just Won" Exchange (EXCH) cards entitling the holder to receive Group A (1-11), Group B (12-22), or Groups A and B (1-22) in series one, or second series EXCH inserts entitled the holder to receive Group C (23-33), Group D (34-44), Groups C and D (23-44), or Groups A-D (1-44). Each of these EXCH card featured small thumbnail images of the cards he would receive. As a bonus for mailing in the EXCH cards, the collector received a special "winner" checklist back card to replace his EXCH card and a congratulatory letter notifying the collector that his/her name has been entered into a drawing for one of 500 uncut sheets of all 44 Topps Black Gold cards in a leatherette frame.

COMPLETE SET (44) 12.00 30.00
COMP.SERIES 1 SET (22) 4.00 10.00
COMP.SERIES 2 SET (22) 8.00 20.00
STATED ODDS 1:72H/R, 1:14JUM, 1:24RAK
THREE PER FACTORY SET
1 Kelvin Martin .15 .40
2 Audray McMillian .15 .40
3 Terry Allen .20 .50
4 Vai Sikahema .15 .40
5 Clyde Simmons .15 .40
6 Lorenzo White .15 .40
7 Michael Irvin .30 .75
8 Troy Aikman 1.00 2.50
9 Mark Kelso .15 .40
10 Cleveland Gary .15 .40
11 Greg Montgomery .15 .40
12 Jerry Rice 1.50 4.00
13 Rod Woodson .25 .60
14 Leslie O'Neal .20 .50
15 Harold Green .15 .40
16 Randall Cunningham .25 .60
17 Ricky Watters .25 .60
18 Andre Rison .20 .50
19 Eugene Robinson .15 .40
20 Wayne Martin .15 .40
21 Chris Warren .20 .50
22 Anthony Miller .20 .50
23 Steve Young .75 2.00
24 Tim Harris .15 .40
25 Emmitt Smith 2.00 5.00
26 Sterling Sharpe .25 .60
27 Henry Jones .15 .40
28 Warren Moon .25 .60
29 Barry Foster .20 .50
30 Dale Carter .15 .40
31 Mel Gray .20 .50

33 Dan Marino 2.00 5.00
34 Fred Barnett .20 .50
35 Deion Sanders .50 1.25
36 Simon Fletcher .15 .40
37 Donnell Woolford .15 .40
38 Reggie Cobb .15 .40
39 Brett Favre 2.50 6.00
40 Thurman Thomas .30 .75
41 Rodney Hampton .20 .50
42 Eric Martin .20 .50
43 Pete Stoyanovich .15 .40
44 Herschel Walker .20 .50
A1 Winner A 1-11 EXCH 2.00 5.00
A2 Winner A 1-11 Prize .20 .50
B1 Winner B 12-22 EXCH UER 2.00 5.00
B2 Winner B 12-22 Prize .20 .50
C1 Winner C 23-33 EXCH 2.00 5.00
C2 Winner C 23-33 Prize .20 .50
D1 Winner D 34-44 EXCH 2.00 5.00
D2 Winner D 34-44 Prize .20 .50
AB1 Winner AB 1-22 EXCH 3.00 8.00
AB2 Winner AB 1-22 Prize .40 1.00
CD1 Winner CD 23-44 EXCH 3.00 8.00
CD2 Winner CD 23-44 Prize .40 1.00

1993 Topps FantaSports

This was the first interactive fantasy sports game that incorporated single player trading cards as a key playing element. The set included 200 cards with each produced with a black border and gold foil highlights. The card backs carried graphs of the players' three-year performances on all FantaSports criteria, comparisons with other players in that position, and scouting reports. The cards were issued in set form to contestants who paid the $159 entry fee. Included were the cards, entry into the league, stat book, worksheets, and instructions. The person who earned the best 18-game NFL fantasy score won four tickets to Super Bowl XXVIII. The game was test-marketed in four cities (Houston, Kansas City, Buffalo, and Washington D.C.) and the cards were not offered at retail in those cities. The cards are numbered on the back arranged by position, quarterbacks (1-30), running backs (31-89), wide receivers (90-137), tight ends (138-150), kickers (151-162), punters (163-172), and defensive players (173-200).

COMPLETE SET (200) 100.00 200.00
1 Chris Miller .30 .75
2 Jim Kelly .40 1.00
3 Jim Harbaugh .30 .75
4 David Klingler .30 .75
5 Bernie Kosar .30 .75
6 Troy Aikman 6.00 15.00
7 John Elway 10.00 25.00
8 Tommy Maddox .40 1.00
9 Rodney Peete .30 .75
10 Andre Ware .20 .50
11 Brett Favre 10.00 25.00
12 Warren Moon .40 1.00
13 Jeff George .40 1.00
14 Dave Krieg .30 .75
15 Joe Montana 15.00 30.00
16 Todd Marinovich .20 .50
17 Jim Everett .30 .75
18 Dan Marino 10.00 25.00
19 Sean Salisbury .20 .50
20 Drew Bledsoe 4.00 10.00
21 Dave Brown .30 .75
22 Phil Simms .30 .75
23 Boomer Esiason .30 .75
24 Browning Nagle .20 .50
25 Randall Cunningham .40 1.00
26 Neil O'Donnell .30 .75
27 Stan Humphries .30 .75
28 Steve Young 4.80 12.00
29 Rick Mirer .40 1.00
30 Mark Rypien .30 .75
31 Kenneth Davis .20 .50
32 Thurman Thomas .80 2.00
33 Steve Broussard .20 .50
34 Neal Anderson .30 .75
35 Craig Heyward .20 .50
36 Derrick Fenner .20 .50
37 Harold Green .20 .50
38 Leroy Hoard .20 .50
39 Kevin Mack .20 .50
40 Eric Metcalf .30 .75
41 Tommy Vardell .20 .50
42 Daryl Johnston .30 .75
43 Emmitt Smith 10.00 25.00
44 Barry Sanders 8.00 20.00
45 Edgar Bennett .40 1.00
46 Lorenzo White .30 .75
47 Anthony Johnson .30 .75
48 Todd McNair .20 .50
49 Christian Okoye .20 .50
50 Harvey Williams .30 .75
51 Barry Word .20 .50
52 Nick Bell .20 .50
53 Eric Dickerson .30 .75
54 Jerome Bettis 4.00 10.00
55 Cleveland Gary .20 .50
56 Mark Higgs .20 .50
57 Tony Paige .20 .50
58 Terry Allen .30 .75
59 Roger Craig .30 .75
60 Robert Smith .40 1.00
61 Leonard Russell .30 .75
62 Jon Vaughn .20 .50
63 Vaughn Dunbar .20 .50
64 Dalton Hilliard .20 .50
65 Jarrod Bunch .20 .50
66 Rodney Hampton .30 .75
67 Dave Meggett .30 .75
68 Brad Baxter .20 .50
69 Heath Sherman .20 .50
70 Vai Sikahema .20 .50
71 Johnny Bailey .20 .50
72 Larry Centers .30 .75
73 Garrison Hearst 2.40 6.00
74 Barry Foster .30 .75
75 Eric Bieniemy .20 .50
76 Marion Butts .20 .50
77 Ronnie Harmon .20 .50
78 Natrone Means .30 .75
79 Amp Lee .20 .50
80 Tom Rathman .20 .50
81 Ricky Watters .30 .75
82 Chris Warren .30 .75
83 John L. Williams .20 .50
84 Gary Anderson RB .20 .50
85 Reggie Cobb .20 .50
86 Vince Workman .20 .50
87 Reggie Brooks .30 .75
88 Earnest Byner .20 .50
89 Ricky Ervins .20 .50
90 Michael Haynes .30 .75
91 Mike Pritchard .30 .75
92 Andre Rison .30 .75
93 Don Beebe .20 .50
94 Andre Reed .30 .75
95 Curtis Conway .30 .75
96 Wendell Davis .20 .50
97 Tom Waddle .20 .50
98 Carl Pickens .30 .75
99 Michael Jackson .30 .75
100 Alvin Harper .20 .50
101 Michael Irvin 1.20 3.00
102 Vance Johnson .20 .50
103 Mel Gray .20 .50
104 Sterling Sharpe .30 .75
105 Curtis Duncan .20 .50
106 Ernest Givins .30 .75
107 Haywood Jeffires .30 .75
108 Tim Brown 1.60 4.00
109 Willie Gault .20 .50
110 Flipper Anderson .20 .50
111 Henry Ellard .30 .75
112 Mark Duper .30 .75
113 O.J. McDuffie .40 1.00
114 Anthony Carter .30 .75
115 Cris Carter 2.40 6.00
116 Mike Farr .20 .50
117 Quinn Early .30 .75
118 Eric Martin .20 .50
119 Chris Calloway .20 .50
120 Mark Jackson .20 .50
121 Rob Moore .30 .75
122 Fred Barnett .30 .75
123 Calvin Williams .30 .75
124 Gary Clark .30 .75
125 Randal Hill .20 .50
126 Ricky Proehl .20 .50
127 Jeff Graham .30 .75
128 Ernie Mills .30 .75
129 Dwight Stone .20 .50
130 Nate Lewis .20 .50
131 Jerry Rice 6.00 15.00
132 John Taylor .30 .75
133 Tommy Kane .20 .50
134 Kelvin Martin .20 .50
135 Lawrence Dawsey .30 .75
136 Courtney Hawkins .30 .75
137 Art Monk .30 .75
138 Pete Metzelaars .20 .50
139 Jay Novacek .30 .75
140 Reggie Johnson .20 .50
141 Shannon Sharpe .30 .75
142 Jackie Harris .20 .50
143 Troy Drayton .30 .75
144 Keith Jackson .30 .75
145 Steve Jordan .20 .50
146 Johnny Mitchell .20 .50
147 Eric Green .30 .75
148 Derrick Walker .20 .50
149 Brent Jones .30 .75
150 Ron Hall .20 .50
151 Norm Johnson .20 .50
152 Jim Breech .20 .50
153 Matt Stover .20 .50
154 Lin Elliott .20 .50
155 Jason Hanson .20 .50
156 Chris Jacke .20 .50
157 Nick Lowery .20 .50
158 Pete Stoyanovich .20 .50
159 Roger Ruzek .20 .50
160 Gary Anderson K .20 .50
161 John Kasay .20 .50
162 Chip Lohmiller .20 .50
163 Chris Gardocki .20 .50
164 Mike Saxon .20 .50
165 Jim Arnold .20 .50
166 Rohn Stark .20 .50
167 Jeff Gossett .20 .50
168 Reggie Roby .20 .50
169 Harry Newsome .20 .50
170 Tommy Barnhardt .20 .50
171 Jeff Feagles .20 .50
172 Rich Camarillo .20 .50
173 Deion Sanders 4.00 10.00
174 Cornelius Bennett .30 .75
175 Mark Carrier DB .30 .75
176 Darryl Williams .20 .50
177 Michael Dean Perry .30 .75
178 Russell Maryland .30 .75
179 Steve Atwater .20 .50
180 Bennie Blades .20 .50
181 Reggie White .40 1.00
182 Cris Dishman .20 .50
183 Steve Emtman .20 .50
184 Derrick Thomas .40 1.00
185 Howie Long .40 1.00
186 Sean Gilbert .30 .75
187 John Offerdahl .20 .50
188 Chris Doleman .20 .50
189 Andre Tippett .20 .50
190 Sam Mills .20 .50
191 Lawrence Taylor .30 .75
192 James Hasty .20 .50
193 Clyde Simmons .20 .50
194 Eric Swann .30 .75
195 Greg Lloyd .20 .50
196 Junior Seau .40 1.00
197 Kevin Fagan .20 .50
198 Cortez Kennedy .30 .75
199 Broderick Thomas .20 .50
200 Darrell Green .30 .75

1993 Topps FantaSports Winners

Collectors who won weekly prizes in the Topps fantasy football league received one of these cards. The fantasy player whose team won a region for the year received a complete set. Reportedly, only 50-sets were produced. On a black card face with gray streaks radiating from the bottom, the front shows a color action player photo. The player's name is printed above the picture and "Fantastars '93" is printed vertically in the left border. The horizontal backs display week-by-week statistics, career highlights, and a second color action photo. The unnumbered cards are listed alphabetically below.

1 Boomer Esiason 35.00 60.00
2 Houston Oilers 25.00 40.00
3 Andre Rison 30.00 50.00
4 Jason Hanson 25.00 40.00
5 Troy Aikman 90.00 150.00
6 John Elway 125.00 200.00
7 Michael Irvin 35.00 60.00
8 Thurman Thomas 35.00 60.00
9 Emmitt Smith 150.00 250.00
10 Pittsburgh Steelers 30.00 50.00
11 Jerry Rice 90.00 150.00
12 Eric Green 25.00 40.00
13 Steve Young 75.00 125.00
14 Sterling Sharpe 30.00 50.00
14 Harold Alexander 25.00 40.00
15 Shannon Sharpe 30.00 50.00
15 Johnny Johnson 25.00 40.00
16 Jerome Bettis 35.00 60.00

1994 Topps

The 1994 Topps football set consists of 660 standard-size cards issued in two series of 330. Subsets include League Leaders (116-120), Tools of the Game (196-205/542-556), Career Active Leaders (272-275/470-476) and Measure of Greatness (316-319/611-615). Rookie Cards include Trent Dilfer, Bert Emanuel, Marshall Faulk, William Floyd, Greg Hill, Charles Johnson, Willie McGinest, Errict Rhett, Darnay Scott, Heath Shuler and Bryant Young. A nine-card promo sheet was produced to promote the set as was a three-card Special Effects promo sheet.

COMPLETE SET (660) 50.00 100.00
COMP.SERIES 1 (330) 20.00 50.00
COMP.SERIES 2 (330) 20.00 50.00
1 Emmitt Smith .60 1.50
2 Russell Copeland .01 .05
3 Jesse Sapolu .01 .05
4 David Szott .01 .05
5 Rodney Hampton .02 .10
6 Bubba McDowell .01 .05
7 Bryce Paup .02 .10
8 Winston Moss .01 .05
9 Brett Perriman .02 .10
10 Rod Woodson .02 .10
11 John Randle .02 .10
12 David Wyman .01 .05
13 Jeff Cross .01 .05
14 Richard Cooper .01 .05
15 Johnny Mitchell .01 .05
16 David Alexander .01 .05
17 Ronnie Harmon .01 .05
18 Tyronne Stowe UER .01 .05
19 Chris Zorich .01 .05
20 Rob Burnett .01 .05
21 Harold Alexander .01 .05
22 Rod Stephens .01 .05
23 Mark Wheeler .01 .05
24 Dwayne Sabb .01 .05
25 Troy Drayton .01 .05
26 Kurt Gouveia .01 .05
27 Warren Moon .08 .25
28 Jeff Query .01 .05
29 Chuck Levy RC .01 .05
30 Bruce Smith .08 .25
31 Doug Riesenberg .01 .05
32 Willie Drewrey .01 .05
33 Nate Newton UER .01 .05
34 James Jett .01 .05
35 George Teague .01 .05
36 Marc Spindler .01 .05
37 Jack Del Rio .01 .05
38 Dale Carter .01 .05
39 Steve Atwater .01 .05
40 Herschel Walker .02 .10
41 James Hasty .01 .05
42 Seth Joyner .01 .05
43 Keith Jackson .01 .05
44 Tommy Vardell .01 .05
45 Antonio Langham RC .02 .10
46 Derek Brown RBK .01 .05
47 John Wojciechowski .01 .05
48 Horace Copeland .01 .05
49 Luis Sharpe .01 .05
50 Pat Harlow .01 .05
51 David Palmer RC .08 .25
52 Tony Smith RB .01 .05
53 Tim Johnson .01 .05
54 Anthony Newman .01 .05
55 Terry Wooden .01 .05
56 Derrick Fenner .01 .05
57 Mike Fox .01 .05
58 Brad Hopkins .01 .05
59 Daryl Johnston UER .02 .10
60 Steve Young .30 .75
61 Scottie Graham RC .02 .10
62 Nolan Harrison .01 .05
63 David Richards .01 .05
64 Chris Mohr .01 .05
65 Hardy Nickerson .02 .10
66 Heath Sherman .01 .05
67 Irving Fryar .02 .10
68 Ray Buchanan UER .01 .05
69 Jay Taylor .01 .05
70 Shannon Sharpe .02 .10
71 Vinny Testaverde .02 .10
72 Renaldo Turnbull .01 .05
73 Dwight Stone .01 .05
74 Willie McGinest RC .08 .25
75 Darrell Green .01 .05
76 Kyle Clifton .01 .05
77 Leo Goeas .01 .05
78 Ken Ruettgers .01 .05
79 Craig Heyward .02 .10
80 Andre Rison .02 .10
81 Chris Mims .01 .05
82 Gary Clark .02 .10
83 Ricardo McDonald .01 .05
84 Patrick Hunter .01 .05
85 Bruce Matthews .01 .05
86 Russell Maryland .01 .05
87 Gary Anderson K .01 .05
88 Brad Edwards .01 .05
89 Carlton Bailey .01 .05
90 Qadry Ismail .08 .25
91 Terry McDaniel .01 .05
92 Willie Green .01 .05
93 Cornelius Bennett .02 .10
94 Paul Gruber .01 .05
95 Pete Stoyanovich .01 .05
96 Merton Hanks .02 .10
97 Tre Johnson RC .01 .05
98 Jonathan Hayes .01 .05
99 Jason Elam .02 .10
100 Jerome Bettis .20 .50
101 Ronnie Lott .02 .10
102 Maurice Hurst .01 .05
103 Kirk Lowdermilk .01 .05
104 Tony Jones T .01 .05
105 Steve Beuerlein .02 .10
106 Isaac Davis RC .01 .05
107 Vaughan Johnson .01 .05
108 Terrell Buckley .01 .05
109 Pierce Holt .01 .05
110 Alonzo Spellman .01 .05
111 Patrick Robinson .01 .05
112 Cortez Kennedy .02 .10
113 Kevin Williams WR .02 .10
114 Danny Copeland .01 .05
115 Chris Doleman .01 .05
116 Jerry Rice LL .20 .50
117 Neil Smith LL .02 .10
118 Emmitt Smith LL .30 .75
119 E.Robinson Odomes LL .01 .05
120 Steve Young LL .08 .25
121 Carnell Lake .01 .05
122 Ernest Givins UER .02 .10
123 Henry Jones .01 .05
124 Michael Brooks .01 .05
125 Jason Hanson .01 .05
126 Andy Harmon .01 .05
127 Errict Rhett RC .08 .25
128 Harris Barton .01 .05
129 Greg Robinson .01 .05
130 Derrick Thomas .08 .25
131 Keith Kartz .01 .05
132 Lincoln Kennedy .01 .05
133 Leslie O'Neal .01 .05
134 Tim Goad .01 .05
135 Rohn Stark .01 .05
136 O.J. McDuffie .08 .25
137 Donnell Woolford .01 .05
138 Jamir Miller RC .02 .10
139 Eric Thomas UER .01 .05
140 Willie Roaf .01 .05
141 Wayne Gandy RC .01 .05
142 Mike Brim .01 .05
143 Kelvin Martin .01 .05
144 Edgar Bennett .08 .25
145 Michael Dean Perry .02 .10
146 Shante Carver RC .01 .05
147 Jessie Armstead UER .01 .05
148 Mo Elewonibi .01 .05
149 Dana Stubblefield .02 .10
150 Cody Carlson .01 .05
151 Vencie Glenn .01 .05
152 Levon Kirkland .01 .05
153 Derrick Moore .01 .05
154 John Fina .01 .05
155 Jeff Hostetler .02 .10
156 Courtney Hawkins .01 .05
157 Todd Collins .01 .05
158 Neil Smith .02 .10
159 Simon Fletcher .01 .05
160 Dan Marino .75 2.00
161 Sam Adams RC .02 .10
162 Marvin Washington .01 .05
163 John Copeland .01 .05
164 Eugene Robinson .01 .05
165 Mark Carrier DB .01 .05
166 Mike Kenn .01 .05
167 Tyrone Hughes .02 .10
168 Darren Carrington .01 .05
169 Shane Conlan .01 .05
170 Ricky Proehl .01 .05
171 Jeff Herrod .01 .05
172 Mark Carrier WR .02 .10
173 George Koonce .01 .05
174 Desmond Howard .02 .10
175 Dave Meggett .01 .05
176 Charles Haley .02 .10
177 Steve Wisniewski .01 .05
178 Dermontti Dawson .02 .10
179 Tim McDonald .01 .05
180 Broderick Thomas .01 .05
181 Bernard Dafney .01 .05
182 Bo Orlando .01 .05
183 Andre Reed .02 .10
184 Randall Cunningham .08 .25
185 Chris Spielman .02 .10
186 Keith Byars .01 .05
187 Ben Coates .02 .10
188 Tracy Simien .01 .05
189 Carl Pickens .02 .10
190 Reggie White .08 .25
191 Norm Johnson .01 .05
192 Brian Washington .01 .05
193 Stan Humphries .02 .10
194 Fred Stokes .01 .05
195 Dan Williams .01 .05
196 John Elway TOG .30 .75
197 Eric Allen TOG .01 .05
198 Hardy Nickerson TOG .02 .10
199 Jerome Bettis TOG .08 .25
200 Troy Aikman TOG .20 .50
201 Thurman Thomas TOG .02 .10
202 Cornelius Bennett TOG UER .02 .10
203 Michael Irvin TOG .02 .10
204 Jim Kelly TOG .02 .10
205 Junior Seau TOG .02 .10
206 Heath Shuler UER RC .08 .25
207 Howard Cross UER .01 .05
208 Pat Swilling .01 .05
209 Pete Metzelaars .01 .05
210 Tony McGee .01 .05
211 Neil O'Donnell .08 .25
212 Eugene Chung .01 .05
213 J.B. Brown .01 .05
214 Marcus Allen .08 .25
215 Harry Newsome .01 .05
216 Greg Hill RC .08 .25
217 Ryan Yarborough .01 .05
218 Marty Carter .01 .05
219 Bern Brostek .01 .05
220 Boomer Esiason .02 .10
221 Vince Buck .01 .05
222 Jim Jeffcoat .01 .05
223 Bob Dahl .01 .05
224 Marion Butts .01 .05
225 Ronald Moore .01 .05
226 Robert Blackmon .01 .05
227 Curtis Conway .08 .25
228 Jon Hand .01 .05
229 Shane Dronett .01 .05
230 Erik Williams UER .01 .05
231 Dennis Brown .01 .05
232 Ray Childress .01 .05
233 Johnnie Morton RC .20 .50
234 Kent Hull .01 .05
235 John Elliott .01 .05
236 Ron Heller .01 .05
237 J.J. Birden .01 .05
238 Thomas Randolph RC .01 .05
239 Chip Lohmiller .01 .05
240 Tim Brown .08 .25
241 Steve Tovar .01 .05
242 Moe Gardner .01 .05
243 Vincent Brown .01 .05
244 Tony Zendejas .01 .05
245 Eric Allen .01 .05
246 Joe King RC .01 .05
247 Mo Lewis .01 .05
248 Rod Bernstine .01 .05
249 Tom Waddle .01 .05
250 Junior Seau .08 .25
251 Eric Metcalf .02 .10
252 Cris Carter .20 .50
253 Bill Hitchcock .01 .05
254 Zefross Moss .01 .05
255 Morten Andersen .01 .05
256 Keith Rucker RC .01 .05
257 Chris Jacke .01 .05
258 Richmond Webb .01 .05
259 Herman Moore .08 .25
260 Phil Simms .02 .10
261 Mark Tuinei .01 .05
262 Don Beebe .01 .05
263 Marc Logan .01 .05
264 Willie Davis .02 .10
265 David Klingler .01 .05
266 Martin Mayhew UER .01 .05
267 Mark Bavaro .01 .05
268 Greg Lloyd .02 .10
269 Al Del Greco .01 .05
270 Reggie Brooks .02 .10
271 Greg Townsend .01 .05
272 Rohn Stark CAL .01 .05
273 Marcus Allen CAL .02 .10
274 Ronnie Lott CAL .02 .10
275 Dan Marino CAL .30 .75
276 Sean Gilbert .01 .05
277 LeRoy Butler .01 .05
278 Troy Auzenne .01 .05
279 Eric Swann .02 .10
280 Quentin Coryatt .01 .05
281 Anthony Pleasant .01 .05
282 Brad Baxter .01 .05
283 Carl Lee .01 .05
284 Courtney Hall .01 .05
285 Quinn Early .02 .10
286 Eddie Robinson .01 .05
287 Marco Coleman .01 .05
288 Harold Green .01 .05
289 Santana Dotson .02 .10
290 Robert Porcher .01 .05
291 Joe Phillips .01 .05
292 Mark McMillian .01 .05
293 Eric Davis .01 .05
294 Mark Jackson .01 .05
295 Darryl Talley .01 .05
296 Curtis Duncan .01 .05
297 Bruce Armstrong .01 .05
298 Eric Hill .01 .05
299 Andre Collins .01 .05
300 Jay Novacek .02 .10
301 Roosevelt Potts .01 .05
302 Eric Martin .01 .05
303 Chris Warren .02 .10
304 Deral Boykin RC .01 .05
305 Jessie Tuggle .01 .05
306 Glyn Milburn .02 .10
307 Terry Obee .01 .05
308 Eric Turner .01 .05
309 Dewayne Washington RC .02 .10
310 Sterling Sharpe .02 .10
311 Jeff Gossett .01 .05
312 John Carney .01 .05
313 Aaron Glenn RC .08 .25
314 Nick Lowery .01 .05
315 Thurman Thomas .08 .25
316 Troy Aikman MG .20 .50
317 Thurman Thomas MG .02 .10
318 Michael Irvin MG .02 .10
319 Steve Beuerlein MG .02 .10
320 Jerry Rice .40 1.00
321 Alexander Wright .01 .06
322 Michael Bates .01 .05
323 Greg Davis .01 .05
324 Mark Bortz .01 .05
325 Kevin Greene .02 .10
326 Wayne Simmons .01 .05
327 Wayne Martin .01 .05
328 Michael Irvin UER .08 .25
329 Checklist Card .01 .05
330 Checklist Card .01 .05
331 Doug Pelfrey .01 .05
332 Myron Guyton .01 .05
333 Howard Ballard .01 .05
334 Ricky Ervins .01 .05
335 Steve Emtman .01 .05
336 Eric Curry .01 .05
337 Bert Emanuel RC .08 .25
338 Darryl Ashmore .01 .05
339 Stevon Moore .01 .05
340 Garrison Hearst .08 .25
341 Vance Johnson .01 .05
342 Anthony Johnson .02 .10
343 Merril Hoge .01 .05
344 William Thomas .01 .05
345 Scott Mitchell .02 .10
346 Jim Everett .02 .10
347 Ray Crockett .01 .05
348 Bryan Cox .01 .05
349 Charles Johnson RC .08 .25
350 Randall McDaniel .02 .10
351 Micheal Barrow .01 .05
352 Darrell Thompson .01 .05
353 Kevin Gogan .01 .05
354 Brad Daluiso .01 .05
355 Mark Collins .01 .05
356 Bryant Young RC .15 .40
357 Steve Christie .01 .05
358 Derek Kennard .01 .05
359 Jon Vaughn .01 .05
360 Drew Bledsoe 3X .30 .75
361 Randy Baldwin .01 .05
362 Kevin Ross .01 .05
363 Reuben Davis .01 .05
364 Chris Miller .01 .05
365 Tim McGee .01 .05
366 Tony Woods .01 .05
367 Dean Biasucci .01 .05
368 George Jamison .01 .05
369 Lorenzo Lynch .01 .05
370 Johnny Johnson .01 .05
371 Greg Kragen .01 .05
372 Vinson Smith .01 .05
373 Vince Workman .01 .05
374 Allen Aldridge .01 .05
375 Terry Kirby .08 .25
376 Mario Bates RC .08 .25
377 Dixon Edwards .01 .05
378 Leon Searcy .01 .05
379 Eric Guliford RC .01 .05
380 Gary Brown .01 .05
381 Phil Hansen .01 .05
382 Keith Hamilton .01 .05
383 John Alt .01 .05
384 John Taylor .02 .10
385 Reggie Cobb .01 .05
386 Rob Fredrickson RC .02 .10
387 Pepper Johnson .01 .05
388 Kevin Lee RC .01 .05
389 Stanley Richard .01 .05
390 Jackie Slater .01 .05
391 Darrick Brilz .01 .05
392 John Gesek .01 .05
393 Kelvin Pritchett .01 .05
394 Aeneas Williams .01 .05
395 Henry Ford .01 .05
396 Eric Mahlum .01 .05
397 Tom Rouen .01 .05
398 Vinnie Clark .01 .05
399 Jim Sweeney .01 .05
400 Troy Aikman UER .40 1.00
401 Toi Cook .01 .05
402 Dan Saleaumua .01 .05
403 Andy Heck .01 .05
404 Deon Figures .01 .05
405 Henry Thomas .01 .05
406 Glenn Montgomery .01 .05
407 Trent Dilfer RC .40 1.00
408 Eddie Murray .01 .05
409 Gene Atkins .01 .05
410 Mike Sherrard .01 .05
411 Don Mosebar .01 .05
412 Thomas Smith .01 .05
413 Ken Norton Jr. .02 .10
414 Robert Brooks .08 .25
415 Jeff Lageman .01 .05
416 Tony Siragusa .01 .05
417 Brian Blades .02 .10
418 Matt Stover .01 .05
419 Jesse Solomon .01 .05
420 Reggie Roby .01 .05
421 Shawn Jefferson .01 .05
422 Marc Boutte .01 .05
423 William White .01 .05
424 Clyde Simmons .01 .05
425 Anthony Miller .02 .10
426 Brent Jones .02 .10
427 Tim Grunhard .01 .05
428 Alfred Williams .01 .05
429 Roy Barker RC .01 .05
430 Dante Jones .01 .05
431 Leroy Thompson .01 .05
432 Marcus Robertson .01 .05
433 Thomas Lewis RC .02 .10
434 Sean Jones .01 .05
435 Michael Haynes .02 .10
436 Albert Lewis .01 .05
437 Tim Bowens RC .02 .10
438 Marvcus Patton .01 .05
439 Rich Miano .01 .05
440 Craig Erickson .01 .05
441 Larry Allen RC 1.25 3.00
442 Fernando Smith .01 .05
443 D.J. Johnson .01 .05
444 Leonard Russell .01 .05
445 Marshall Faulk RC 2.00 5.00
446 Najee Mustafaa .01 .05
447 Brian Hansen .01 .05
448 Isaac Bruce RC 2.00 4.00
449 Kevin Scott .01 .05
450 Natrone Means UER .08 .25
451 Tracy Rogers RC .01 .05
452 Mike Croel .01 .05
453 Anthony Edwards .01 .05
454 Brentson Buckner RC .01 .05
455 Tom Carter .01 .05
456 Burt Grossman .01 .05
457 Jimmy Spencer RC .01 .05
458 Rocket Ismail .02 .10
459 Fred Strickland .01 .05
460 Jeff Burris RC .02 .10
461 Adrian Hardy .01 .05
462 Lamar McGriggs .01 .05
463 Webster Slaughter .01 .05
464 Demetrius DuBose .01 .05
465 Dave Brown .02 .10
466 Kenneth Gant .01 .05
467 Erik Kramer .02 .10
468 Mark Ingram .01 .05
469 Roman Phifer .01 .05
470 Steve Young .20 .50
471 Nick Lowery .01 .05
472 Irving Fryar .02 .10
473 Art Monk .02 .10
474 Mel Gray .01 .06
475 Reggie White .08 .25
476 Eric Ball .01 .05
477 Dwayne Harper .01 .05
478 Will Shields .01 .05
479 Roger Harper .01 .05
480 Rick Mirer .08 .25
481 Vincent Brisby .02 .10
482 John Jurkovic RC .02 .10
483 Michael Jackson .02 .10
484 Ed Cunningham .01 .05
485 Brad Ottis .01 .05
486 Sterling Palmer RC .01 .05
487 Tony Bennett .01 .05
488 Mike Pritchard .01 .05
489 Bucky Brooks RC .01 .05
490 Troy Vincent .01 .05
491 Eric Green .01 .05
492 Van Malone .01 .05
493 Marcus Spears RC .01 .05
494 Brian Williams OL .01 .05
495 Robert Smith .08 .25
496 Haywood Jeffires .02 .10
497 Darrin Smith .01 .05
498 Tommy Barnhardt .01 .05
499 Anthony Smith .01 .05
500 Ricky Watters .02 .10
501 Antone Davis .01 .05
502 David Braxton .01 .05
503 Donnell Bennett RC .08 .25
504 Donald Evans .01 .05
505 Lewis Tillman .01 .05
506 Lance Smith .01 .05
507 Aaron Taylor .01 .05
508 Ricky Sanders .01 .05
509 Dennis Smith .01 .05
510 Barry Foster .01 .05
511 Stan Brock .01 .05
512 Henry Rolling .01 .05
513 Walter Reeves .01 .05
514 John Booty .01 .05
515 Kenneth Davis .01 .05
516 Cris Dishman .01 .05
517 Bill Lewis .01 .05
518 Jeff Bryant .01 .05
519 Brian Mitchell .01 .05
520 Joe Montana .75 2.00
521 Keith Sims .01 .05
522 Harry Colon .01 .05
523 Leon Lett .01 .05
524 Carlos Jenkins .01 .05
525 Victor Bailey .01 .05
526 Harvey Williams .02 .10
527 Irv Smith .01 .05
528 Jason Sehorn RC .15 .40
529 John Thierry RC .01 .05
530 Brett Favre .75 2.00
531 Sean Dawkins RC .08 .25
532 Erric Pegram .01 .05
533 Jimmy Williams .01 .05
534 Michael Timpson .01 .05
535 Flipper Anderson .01 .05
536 John Parrella .01 .05
537 Freddie Joe Nunn .01 .05
538 Doug Dawson .01 .05
539 Michael Stewart .01 .05
540 John Elway .75 2.00
541 Ronnie Lott .02 .10
542 Barry Sanders TOG .30 .75
543 Andre Reed TOG .02 .10
544 Deion Sanders TOG .08 .25
545 Dan Marino TOG .30 .75
546 Carlton Bailey TOG .01 .05
547 Emmitt Smith TOG .30 .75
548 Alvin Harper TOG .02 .10
549 Eric Metcalf TOG .02 .10
550 Jerry Rice TOG .20 .50
551 Derrick Thomas TOG .08 .25
552 Mark Collins TOG .01 .05
553 Eric Turner TOG .01 .05
554 Sterling Sharpe TOG .02 .10
555 Steve Young TOG .08 .25
556 Darnay Scott RC .20 .50
557 Joel Steed .01 .05
558 Dennis Gibson .01 .05
559 Charles Mincy .01 .05
560 Rickey Jackson .01 .05
561 Dave Cadigan .01 .05
562 Rick Tuten .01 .05
563 Miko Caldwell .01 .05
564 Todd Steussie RC .02 .10
565 Kevin Smith .01 .05
566 Arthur Marshall .01 .05
567 Aaron Wallace .01 .05
568 Calvin Williams .02 .10
569 Todd Kelly .01 .05
570 Barry Sanders .60 1.50
571 Shaun Gayle .01 .05
572 Will Wolford .01 .05
573 Ethan Horton .01 .05
574 Chris Slade .01 .05
575 Jeff Wright .01 .05
576 Toby Wright .01 .05
577 Lamar Thomas .01 .05
578 Chris Singleton .01 .05
579 Ed West .01 .05
580 Jeff George .08 .25
581 Kevin Mitchell .01 .05
582 Chad Brown .01 .05
583 Rich Camarillo .01 .05
584 Gary Zimmerman .01 .05
585 Randal Hill .01 .05
586 Keith Cash .01 .05
587 Sam Mills .01 .05
588 Shawn Lee .01 .05
589 Kent Graham .02 .10
590 Steve Everitt .01 .05
591 Rob Moore .02 .10
592 Kevin Mawae RC .08 .25
593 Jerry Ball .01 .05
594 Larry Brown DB .01 .05
595 Tim Krumrie .01 .05
596 Aubrey Beavers RC .01 .05
597 Chris Hinton .01 .05
598 Greg Montgomery .01 .05
599 Jimmie Jones .01 .05
600 Jim Kelly .08 .25
601 Joe Johnson RC .01 .05
602 Tim Irwin .01 .05
603 Steve Jackson .01 .05
604 James Williams RC .01 .05
605 Blair Thomas .01 .05
606 Danan Hughes .01 .05
607 Russell Freeman .01 .05
608 Andre Hastings .02 .10
609 Ken Harvey .01 .05
610 Jim Harbaugh .08 .25
611 Emmitt Smith MG .30 .75
612 Andre Rison MG .02 .10
613 Steve Young MG .08 .25
614 Anthony Miller MG .01 .05
615 Barry Sanders MG .30 .75
616 Bernie Kosar .02 .10
617 Chris Gardocki .01 .05
618 William Floyd RC .08 .25
619 Matt Brock .01 .05
620 Dan Wilkinson RC .02 .10
621 Tony Meola RC .02 .10
622 Tony Tolbert .01 .05
623 Mike Zandofsky .01 .05
624 William Fuller .01 .05
625 Steve Jordan .01 .05
626 Mike Johnson .01 .05
627 Ferrell Edmunds .01 .06
628 Gene Williams .01 .05
629 Willie Beamon .01 .05
630 Gerald Perry .01 .05
631 John Baylor .01 .05
632 Carwell Gardner .01 .05
633 Thomas Everett .01 .05
634 Lamar Lathon .01 .05
635 Michael Bankston .01 .05
636 Ray Crittenden RC .01 .05
637 Kimble Anders .02 .10
638 Robert Delpino .01 .05
639 Darren Perry .01 .05
640 Byron Evans .01 .05
641 Mark Higgs .01 .05
642 Lorenzo Neal .01 .05
643 Henry Ellard .02 .10
644 Trace Armstrong .01 .05
645 Greg McMurtry .01 .05
646 Steve McMichael .02 .10
647 Terance Mathis .02 .10
648 Eric Bieniemy .01 .05
649 Bobby Houston .01 .05
650 Alvin Harper .02 .10
651 James Folston RC .01 .05
652 Mel Gray .01 .05
653 Adrian Cooper .01 .05
654 Dexter Carter .01 .05
655 Don Griffin .01 .05
656 Corey Widmer .01 .05
657 Lee Johnson .01 .05
658 Nate Odomes .01 .05
659 Checklist Card .01 .05
660 Checklist Card .01 .05
P1 Promo Sheet 1.50 4.00
P2 Promo Sheet Special Effects 1.50 4.00

1994 Topps Special Effects

ETS: 3X TO 8X BASIC CARDS
*ROOKIES : 1.5X TO 4X BASIC RC
STATED ODDS 1:2 H/R, 2:1 RACK PACK

1994 Topps All-Pros

is 25-card standard-size set features NFL stars and introduces Topps "Spectralight Foil Cards," which are foil-backed, foil-stamped cards. All-Pro cards are randomly inserted at a rate of one in every 36 packs. The front has the player photo superimposed over a football field background. Horizontal backs have a player photo to the right and highlights to the left.

COMPLETE SET (25) 20.00 50.00
STATED ODDS 1:36 SERIES 2
1 Michael Irvin 1.25 2.50
2 Erik Williams .20 .50
3 Steve Wisniewski .20 .50
4 Dermontti Dawson .40 1.00
5 Nate Newton .20 .50
6 Harris Barton .20 .50
7 Shannon Sharpe .40 1.00
8 Jerry Rice 5.00 10.00
9 Troy Aikman 5.00 10.00
10 Barry Sanders 8.00 15.00
11 Jerome Bettis 2.50 5.00
12 Jason Hanson .20 .50
13 Eric Metcalf .40 1.00
14 Reggie White 1.25 2.50
15 Cortez Kennedy .40 1.00
16 Michael Dean Perry .40 1.00
17 Bruce Smith 1.25 2.50
18 Darryl Talley .20 .50
19 Hardy Nickerson .40 1.00
20 Derrick Thomas 1.25 2.50
21 Mark Collins .20 .50
22 Eric Allen .20 .50
23 Tim McDonald .20 .50
24 Marcus Robertson .20 .50
25 Greg Montgomery .20 .50

1994 Topps 1000/3000

ndomly inserted in first series packs at an approximate rate of one in 36, these 32 standard-size cards feature metallic fronts with color player action cutouts set on silver-bordered multicolored designs. The cards are numbered on the back as "X of 32." The first 20 cards are of running backs and wide receivers; the last 12 are quarterbacks.

COMPLETE SET (32) 25.00 60.00
STATED ODDS 1:36 SERIES 1
1 Jerry Rice 3.00 8.00
2 Chris Warren .30 .75
3 Leonard Russell .15 .40
4 Gary Brown .15 .40
5 Tim Brown .75 2.00
6 Eric Pegram .15 .40
7 Irving Fryar .30 .75
8 Anthony Miller .30 .75
9 Reggie Langhorne .15 .40
10 Thurman Thomas .75 2.00
11 Reggie Brooks .30 .75
12 Andre Rison .30 .75
13 Ronald Moore .15 .40
14 Michael Irvin .75 2.00
15 Barry Sanders 5.00 12.00
16 Cris Carter 1.50 4.00
17 Rodney Hampton .30 .75
18 Jerome Bettis 1.50 4.00
19 Sterling Sharpe .30 .75
20 Emmitt Smith 5.00 12.00
21 John Elway 6.00 15.00
22 Brett Favre 6.00 15.00
23 Jim Kelly .75 2.00
24 Warren Moon .75 2.00
25 Phil Simms .30 .75
26 Craig Erickson .15 .40
27 Neil O'Donnell .75 2.00
28 Steve Young 2.50 6.00
29 Steve Beuerlein .30 .75
30 Troy Aikman 3.00 8.00
31 Jeff Hostetler .30 .75
32 Boomer Esiason .30 .75

1995 Topps

This 468 card standard-size set was issued in two series, both in 13 count foil packs with a suggested retail price of $1.29. Similar to the '95 baseball issue, these cards feature color action photos with white borders on the front. Two subsets are included in this set: 1,000 Yard Club (1-29) and 3,000 Yard Club (30-41). Rookie Cards in this set include Ki-Jana Carter, Kerry Collins, Rashaan Salaam, J.J. Stokes and Michael Westbrook.

COMPLETE SET (468) 15.00 40.00
COMP.FACT.SET (478) 40.00 80.00
COMP.SERIES 1 (248) 8.00 20.00
COMP.SERIES 2 (220) 8.00 20.00
1 Barry Sanders TYC .30 .75
2 Chris Warren TYC .07 .20
3 Jerry Rice TYC .20 .50
4 Emmitt Smith TYC .30 .75
5 Henry Ellard TYC .07 .20
6 Natrone Means TYC .07 .20
7 Terance Mathis TYC .07 .20
8 Tim Brown TYC .07 .20

9 Andre Reed TYC .07 .20
10 Marshall Faulk TYC .25 .60
11 Irving Fryar TYC .07 .20
12 Cris Carter TYC .10 .30
13 Michael Irvin TYC .10 .30
14 Jake Reed TYC .07 .20
15 Ben Coates TYC .07 .20
16 Herman Moore TYC .10 .30
17 Carl Pickens TYC .07 .20
18 Fred Barnett TYC .07 .20
19 Sterling Sharpe TYC .07 .20
20 Anthony Miller TYC .07 .20
21 Thurman Thomas TYC .10 .30
22 Andre Rison TYC .07 .20
23 Brian Blades TYC .07 .20
24 Rodney Hampton TYC .07 .20
25 Terry Allen TYC .07 .20
26 Jerome Bettis TYC .10 .30
27 Errict Rhett TYC .07 .20
28 Rob Moore TYC .07 .20
29 Shannon Sharpe TYC .07 .20
30 Drew Bledsoe TYC .10 .30
31 Dan Marino TYC .40 1.00
32 Warren Moon TYC .07 .20
33 Steve Young TYC .15 .40
34 Brett Favre TYC .40 1.00
35 Jim Everett TYC .02 .10
36 Jeff George TYC .07 .20
37 John Elway TYC .40 1.00
38 Jeff Hostetler TYC .07 .20
39 Randall Cunningham TYC .10 .30
40 Stan Humphries TYC .07 .20
41 Jim Kelly TYC .10 .30
42 Tommy Barnhardt .02 .10
43 Bob Whitfield .02 .10
44 William Thomas .02 .10
45 Glyn Milburn .02 .10
46 Steve Christie .02 .10
47 Kevin Mawae .02 .10
48 Vencie Glenn .02 .10
49 Eric Curry .02 .10
50 Jeff Hostetler .07 .20
51 Tyronne Stowe .02 .10
52 Steve Jackson .02 .10
53 Ben Coleman .02 .10
54 Brad Baxter .02 .10
55 Darryl Williams .02 .10
56 Troy Drayton .02 .10
57 George Teague .02 .10
58 Calvin Williams .07 .20
59 Jeff Cross .02 .10
60 Leroy Hoard .02 .10
61 John Carney .02 .10
62 Daryl Johnston .07 .20
63 Jim Jeffcoat .02 .10
64 Matt Stover .02 .10
65 LeRoy Butler .02 .10
66 Curtis Conway .10 .30
67 O.J. McDuffie .10 .30
68 Robert Massey .02 .10
69 Ed McDaniel .02 .10
70 William Floyd .07 .20
71 Willie Davis .07 .20
72 William Roberts .02 .10
73 Chester McGlockton .07 .20
74 D.J. Johnson .02 .10
75 Rondell Jones .02 .10
76 Morten Andersen .02 .10
77 Glenn Parker .02 .10
78 William Fuller .02 .10
79 Ray Buchanan .02 .10
80 Maurice Hurst .02 .10
81 Wayne Gandy .02 .10
82 Marcus Turner .02 .10
83 Greg Davis .02 .10
84 Terry Wooden .02 .10
85 Thomas Everett .02 .10
86 Steve Broussard .02 .10
87 Tom Carter .02 .10
88 Glenn Montgomery .02 .10
89 Larry Allen .07 .20
90 Donnell Woolford .02 .10
91 John Alt .02 .10
92 Phil Hansen .02 .10
93 Seth Joyner .02 .10
94 Michael Brooks .02 .10
95 Randall McDaniel .05 .15
96 Tydus Winans .02 .10
97 Rob Fredrickson .02 .10
98 Ray Crockett .02 .10
99 Courtney Hall .02 .10
100 Merton Hanks .02 .10
101 Aaron Glenn .02 .10
102 Roosevelt Potts .02 .10
103 Leon Lett .02 .10
104 Jessie Tuggle .02 .10
105 Martin Mayhew .02 .10
106 Willie Roaf .02 .10
107 Todd Lyght .02 .10
108 Ernest Givins .02 .10
109 Tony McGee .02 .10
110 Barry Sanders .60 1.50
111 Dermontti Dawson .15 .40
112 Rick Tuten .02 .10
113 Vincent Brisby .02 .10
114 Charlie Garner .10 .30
115 Irving Fryar .07 .20
116 Stevon Moore .02 .10
117 Matt Darby .02 .10
118 Howard Cross .02 .10
119 John Gesek .02 .10
120 Jack Del Rio .02 .10
121 Marcus Allen .10 .30
122 Torrance Small .02 .10
123 Chris Mims .02 .10
124 Don Mosebar .02 .10
125 Carl Pickens .07 .20
126 Tom Rouen .02 .10
127 Garrison Hearst .10 .30
128 Charles Johnson .07 .20
129 Derek Brown RBK .02 .10
130 Troy Aikman .40 1.00
131 Troy Vincent .02 .10
132 Ken Ruettgers .02 .10
133 Michael Jackson .07 .20
134 Dennis Gibson .02 .10
135 Brett Perriman .07 .20
136 Jeff Graham .02 .10
137 Chad Brown .07 .20
138 Ken Norton Jr. .07 .20
139 Chris Slade .02 .10
140 Dave Brown .07 .20
141 Bert Emanuel .10 .30
142 Renaldo Turnbull .02 .10
143 Jim Harbaugh .07 .20
144 Micheal Barrow .02 .10
145 Vincent Brown .02 .10
146 Bryant Young .07 .20
147 Boomer Esiason .07 .20
148 Sean Gilbert .07 .20
149 Greg Truitt .02 .10
150 Rod Woodson .07 .20
151 Robert Porcher .02 .10
152 Joe Phillips .02 .10
153 Gary Zimmerman .02 .10
154 Bruce Smith .10 .30
155 Randall Cunningham .10 .30
156 Fred Strickland .02 .10
157 Derrick Alexander WR .10 .30
158 James Williams LB .02 .10
159 Scott Dill .02 .10
160 Tim Bowens .02 .10
161 Floyd Turner .02 .10
162 Ronnie Harmon .02 .10
163 Wayne Martin .02 .10
164 John Randle .07 .20
165 Larry Centers .07 .20
166 Larry Brown DB .02 .10
167 Albert Lewis .02 .10
168 Michael Strahan .10 .30
169 Reggie Brooks .07 .20
170 Craig Heyward .07 .20
171 Pat Harlow .02 .10
172 Eugene Robinson .02 .10
173 Shane Conlan .02 .10
174 Bennie Blades .02 .10
175 Neil O'Donnell .07 .20
176 Steve Tovar .02 .10
177 Donald Evans .02 .10
178 Brent Jones .02 .10
179 Ray Childress .02 .10
180 Reggie White .10 .30
181 David Alexander .02 .10
182 Greg Hill .07 .20
183 Vinny Testaverde .07 .20
184 Jeff Burris .02 .10
185 Hardy Nickerson .02 .10
186 Terry Kirby .07 .20
187 Kirk Lowdermilk .02 .10
188 Eric Swann .07 .20
189 Chris Zorich .02 .10
190 Simon Fletcher .02 .10
191 Qadry Ismail .07 .20
192 Heath Shuler .07 .20
193 Michael Haynes .07 .20
194 Mike Sherrard .02 .10
195 Nolan Harrison .02 .10
196 Marcus Robertson .02 .10
197 Kevin Williams WR .07 .20
198 Moe Gardner .02 .10
199 Rick Mirer .07 .20
200 Junior Seau .10 .30
201 Byron Bam Morris .02 .10
202 Willie McGinest .07 .20
203 Chris Spielman .07 .20
204 Darnay Scott .07 .20
205 Jesse Sapolu .02 .10
206 Marvin Washington .02 .10
207 Anthony Newman .02 .10
208 Cortez Kennedy .07 .20
209 Quentin Coryatt .07 .20
210 Neil Smith .07 .20
211 Keith Sims .02 .10
212 Sean Jones .02 .10
213 Tony Jones T .02 .10
214 Lewis Tillman .02 .10
215 Darren Woodson .07 .20
216 Jason Hanson .02 .10
217 John Taylor .02 .10
218 Shawn Lee .02 .10
219 Kevin Greene .07 .20
220 Jerry Rice .40 1.00
221 Ki-Jana Carter RC .10 .30
222 Tony Boselli RC .10 .30
223 Michael Westbrook RC .10 .30
224 Kerry Collins RC .75 2.00
225 Kevin Carter RC .10 .30
226 Kyle Brady RC .10 .30
227 J.J. Stokes RC .10 .30
228 Derrick Alexander DE RC .02 .10
229 Warren Sapp RC .60 1.50
230 Ruben Brown RC .10 .30
231 Hugh Douglas RC .10 .30
232 Luther Elliss RC .02 .10
233 Rashaan Salaam RC .07 .20
234 Tyrone Poole RC .10 .30
235 Korey Stringer RC .10 .30
236 Devin Bush RC .02 .10
237 Cory Raymer RC .02 .10
238 Zach Wiegert RC .02 .10
239 Ron Davis RC .02 .10
240 Todd Collins RC .50 1.25
241 Bobby Taylor RC .10 .30
242 Patrick Riley RC .02 .10
243 Scott Gragg .02 .10
244 Marvcus Patton .02 .10
245 Alvin Harper .02 .10
246 Ricky Watters .07 .20
247 Checklist 1 .02 .10
248 Checklist 2 .02 .10
249 Terance Mathis .07 .20
250 Mark Carrier DB .02 .10
251 Elijah Alexander .02 .10
252 George Koonce .02 .10
253 Tony Bennett .02 .10
254 Steve Wisniewski .02 .10
255 Bernie Parmalee .07 .20
256 Dwayne Sabb .02 .10
257 Lorenzo Neal .02 .10
258 Corey Miller .02 .10
259 Fred Barnett .07 .20
260 Greg Lloyd .07 .20
261 Robert Blackmon .02 .10
262 Ken Harvey .02 .10
263 Eric Hill .02 .10
264 Russell Copeland .02 .10
265 Jeff Blake RC .30 .75
266 Carl Banks .02 .10
267 Jay Novacek .07 .20
268 Mel Gray .02 .10
269 Kimble Anders .07 .20
270 Cris Carter .10 .30
271 Johnny Mitchell .02 .10
272 Shawn Jefferson .02 .10
273 Doug Brien .02 .10
274 Sean Landeta .02 .10
275 Scott Mitchell .07 .20
276 Charles Wilson .02 .10
277 Anthony Smith .02 .10
278 Anthony Miller .07 .20
279 Steve Walsh .02 .10
280 Drew Bledsoe .25 .60
281 Jamir Miller .02 .10
282 Robert Brooks .10 .30
283 Sean Lumpkin .02 .10
284 Bryan Cox .02 .10
285 Byron Evans .02 .10
286 Chris Doleman .02 .10
287 Anthony Pleasant .02 .10
288 Stephen Grant RC .02 .10
289 Doug Riesenberg .02 .10
290 Natrone Means .07 .20
291 Henry Thomas .02 .10
292 Mike Pritchard .02 .10
293 Courtney Hawkins .02 .10
294 Bill Bates .07 .20
295 Jerome Bettis .10 .30
296 Russell Maryland .02 .10
297 Stanley Richard .02 .10
298 William White .02 .10
299 Dan Wilkinson .07 .20
300 Steve Young .30 .75
301 Gary Brown .02 .10
302 Jake Reed .07 .20
303 Carlton Gray .02 .10
304 Levon Kirkland .02 .10
305 Shannon Sharpe .07 .20
306 Luis Sharpe .02 .10
307 Marshall Faulk .50 1.25
308 Stan Humphries .07 .20
309 Chris Calloway .02 .10
310 Tim Brown .10 .30
311 Steve Everitt .02 .10
312 Raymont Harris .02 .10
313 Tim McDonald .02 .10
314 Trent Dilfer .10 .20
315 Jim Everett .02 .10
316 Ray Crittenden .02 .10
317 Jim Kelly .10 .30
318 Andre Reed .07 .20
319 Chris Miller .02 .10
320 Bobby Houston .02 .10
321 Charles Haley .07 .20
322 James Francis .02 .10
323 Bernard Williams .02 .10
324 Michael Bates .02 .10
325 Brian Mitchell .02 .10
326 Mike Johnson .02 .10
327 Eric Bieniemy .02 .10
328 Aubrey Beavers .02 .10
329 Dale Carter .07 .20
330 Emmitt Smith .60 1.50
331 Darren Perry .02 .10
332 Marquez Pope .02 .10
333 Clyde Simmons .02 .10
334 Corey Croom .02 .10
335 Thomas Randolph .02 .10
336 Harvey Williams .02 .10
337 Michael Timpson .02 .10
338 Eugene Daniel .02 .10
339 Shane Dronett .02 .10
340 Eric Turner .02 .10
341 Eric Metcalf .07 .20
342 Leslie O'Neal .07 .20
343 Mark Wheeler .02 .10
344 Mark Pike .02 .10
345 Brett Favre .75 2.00
346 Johnny Bailey .02 .10
347 Henry Ellard .07 .20
348 Chris Gardocki .02 .10
349 Henry Jones .02 .10
350 Dan Marino .75 2.00
351 Lake Dawson .07 .20
352 Mark McMillian .02 .10
353 Deion Sanders .25 .60
354 Antonio London .02 .10
355 Cris Dishman .02 .10
356 Ricardo McDonald .02 .10
357 Dexter Carter .02 .10
358 Kevin Smith .02 .10
359 Yancey Thigpen RC .07 .20
360 Chris Warren .07 .20
361 Quinn Early .07 .20
362 John Mangum .02 .10
363 Santana Dotson .02 .10
364 Rocket Ismail .07 .20
365 Aeneas Williams .02 .10
366 Dan Williams .02 .10
367 Sean Dawkins .07 .20
368 Pepper Johnson .02 .10
369 Roman Phifer .02 .10
370 Rodney Hampton .07 .20
371 Darrell Green .02 .10
372 Michael Zordich .02 .10
373 Andre Coleman .02 .10
374 Wayne Simmons .02 .10
375 Michael Irvin .10 .30
376 Clay Matthews .07 .20
377 Dewayne Washington .07 .20
378 Keith Byars .02 .10
379 Todd Collins LB .10 .30
380 Mark Collins .02 .10
381 Joel Steed .02 .10
382 Bart Oates .02 .10
383 Al Smith .02 .10
384 Rafael Robinson .02 .10
385 Mo Lewis .02 .10
386 Aubrey Matthews .02 .10
387 Corey Sawyer .02 .10
388 Bucky Brooks .02 .10
389 Erik Kramer .02 .10
390 Tyrone Hughes .07 .20
391 Terry McDaniel .02 .10
392 Craig Erickson .02 .10
393 Mike Flores .02 .10
394 Harry Swayne .02 .10
395 Irving Spikes .07 .20
396 Lorenzo Lynch .02 .10
397 Antonio Langham .02 .10
398 Edgar Bennett .07 .20
399 Thomas Lewis .07 .20
400 John Elway .75 2.00
401 Jeff George .07 .20
402 Errict Rhett .07 .20
403 Bill Romanowski .02 .10
404 Alexander Wright .02 .10
405 Warren Moon .07 .20
406 Eddie Robinson .02 .10
407 John Copeland .02 .10
408 Robert Jones .02 .10
409 Steve Bono .07 .20
410 Cornelius Bennett .07 .20
411 Ben Coates .07 .20
412 Dana Stubblefield .07 .20
413 Darryl Talley .02 .10
414 Brian Blades .07 .20
415 Herman Moore .10 .30
416 Nick Lowery .02 .10
417 Donnell Bennett .07 .20
418 Van Malone .02 .10
419 Pete Stoyanovich .02 .10
420 Joe Montana .75 2.00
421 Steve Young .20 .50
422 Steve Young .20 .50
423 Steve Young .20 .50
424 Steve Young .20 .50
425 Steve Young .20 .50
426 Rod Stephens .02 .10
427 Ellis Johnson UER RC .02 .10
428 Kordell Stewart RC .50 1.25
429 James O. Stewart RC .40 1.00
430 Steve McNair RC 1.00 2.50
431 Brian DeMarco .07 .20
432 Matt O'Dwyer .02 .10
433 Lorenzo Styles RC .02 .10
434 Anthony Cook RC .02 .10
435 Jesse James .02 .10
436 Darryl Pounds RC .02 .10
437 Derrick Graham RC .02 .10
438 Vernon Turner .02 .10
439 Carlton Bailey .02 .10
440 Darion Conner .02 .10
441 Randy Baldwin .02 .10
442 Tim McKyer .02 .10
443 Sam Mills .07 .20
444 Bob Christian .02 .10
445 Steve Lofton .02 .10
446 Lamar Lathon .02 .10
447 Tony Smith RB .02 .10
448 Don Beebe .02 .10
449 Barry Foster .07 .20
450 Frank Reich .02 .10
451 Pete Metzelaars .02 .10
452 Reggie Cobb .02 .10
453 Jeff Lageman .02 .10
454 Derek Brown TE .02 .10
455 Desmond Howard .07 .20
456 Vinnie Clark .02 .10
457 Keith Goganious .02 .10
458 Shawn Bouwens .02 .10
459 Rob Johnson RC .30 .75
460 Steve Beuerlein .07 .20
461 Mark Brunell .25 .60
462 Harry Colon .02 .10
463 Chris Hudson .02 .10
464 Darren Carrington .02 .10
465 Ernest Givins .02 .10
466 Kelvin Pritchett .02 .10
467 Checklist (249-358) .02 .10
468 Checklist (358-468) .02 .10

1995 Topps Factory Jaguars

COMP.FACT.SET (473) 20.00 50.00
*SINGLES: .4X TO 1X BASE CARD HI

1995 Topps Factory Panthers

COMP.FACT.SET (473) 20.00 50.00
*SINGLES: .4X TO 1X BASE CARD HI

1995 Topps 1000/3000 Boosters

This 41 card standard-size set was randomly inserted into packs at a rate of one in 36. This set is a parallel to the first 41 cards in the 1995 Topps set which features players who ran or caught passes for 1,000 yards or threw for 3,000 yards in the 1994 season. These cards are printed on thicker stock than the regular issue cards and feature prismatic foil printing.

COMPLETE SET (41) 30.00 80.00
STATED ODDS 1:36H,1:18J,1:72 SR SER.1
1 Barry Sanders 4.00 10.00
2 Chris Warren .50 1.25
3 Jerry Rice 2.50 6.00
4 Emmitt Smith 4.00 10.00
5 Henry Ellard .50 1.25
6 Natrone Means .50 1.25
7 Terance Mathis .50 1.25
8 Tim Brown .75 2.00
9 Andre Reed .50 1.25
10 Marshall Faulk 3.00 8.00
11 Irving Fryar .50 1.25
12 Cris Carter .75 2.00
13 Michael Irvin .75 2.00
14 Jake Reed .50 1.25
15 Ben Coates .50 1.25
16 Herman Moore .75 2.00
17 Carl Pickens .50 1.25
18 Fred Barnett .50 1.25
19 Sterling Sharpe .50 1.25
20 Anthony Miller .50 1.25
21 Thurman Thomas .75 2.00
22 Andre Rison .50 1.25
23 Brian Blades .50 1.25
24 Rodney Hampton .50 1.25
25 Terry Allen .50 1.25
26 Jerome Bettis .75 2.00
27 Errict Rhett .50 1.25
28 Rob Moore .50 1.25
29 Shannon Sharpe .50 1.25
30 Drew Bledsoe 1.50 4.00
31 Dan Marino 5.00 12.00
32 Warren Moon .50 1.25
33 Steve Young 2.00 5.00
34 Brett Favre 5.00 12.00
35 Jim Everett .25 .60
36 Jeff George .50 1.25
37 John Elway 5.00 12.00
38 Jeff Hostetler .50 1.25
39 Randall Cunningham .75 2.00
40 Stan Humphries .50 1.25
41 Jim Kelly .75 2.00

1995 Topps Air Raid

This 10 card set was randomly inserted in series two retail packs at a rate of one in 24 packs and feature some of the NFL's best quarterback/wide receiver combinations. Card fronts feature the holographic "Power Matrix" technology with the title "Air Raid" in gold along the top of the card and a foil etched football shape in the background. Card backs are vertical with commentary and statistics on the two players. The are numbered with an "AR" prefix.

COMPLETE SET (10) 20.00 50.00
SER.2 STATED ODDS 1:20J,1:24R,1:48SP.RET
1 S.Young J.Rice 5.00 10.00
2 C.Carter W.Moon 2.50 5.00
3 T.Mathis J.George 1.50 3.00
4 D.Brown M.Sherrard 1.50 3.00
5 D.Bledsoe B.Coates 2.50 6.00
6 J.Elway Sh.Sharpe 6.00 15.00
7 J.Blake C.Pickens 2.50 5.00
8 D.Marino I.Fryar 6.00 15.00
9 F.Barnett Cunningham 1.50 3.00
10 T.Aikman M.Irvin 5.00 10.00

1995 Topps All-Pros

Randomly inserted at a rate of one in eight series two hobby packs, this 22 card set features some the the games best. Card fronts have an all silver foil background with stars and feature a shot of the player with his name, position and team at the bottom. Card backs are horizontal with the player's name and team and some statistical summary. Cards are numbered with an "AP" prefix.

COMPLETE SET (22) 20.00 50.00
SER.2 STATED ODDS 1:8 HOBBY
1 Jerry Rice 2.50 6.00
2 Lomas Brown .30 .75
3 Nate Newton .30 .75
4 Dermontti Dawson .60 1.50
5 Keith Sims .30 .75
6 Richmond Webb .30 .75
7 Shannon Sharpe .75 2.00
8 Michael Irvin .75 2.00
9 Steve Young 2.00 5.00
10 Barry Sanders 4.00 10.00
11 Marshall Faulk 3.00 8.00
12 Bruce Smith .75 2.00
13 Dana Stubblefield .30 .75
14 John Randle .50 1.25
15 Reggie White .75 2.00
16 Greg Lloyd .30 .75
17 Junior Seau .75 2.00
18 Cornelius Bennett .50 1.25
19 Rod Woodson .50 1.25
20 Deion Sanders 2.00 5.00
21 Darren Woodson .50 1.25
22 Merton Hanks .30 .75

1995 Topps Expansion Team Boosters

This 20 card set was randomly inserted in series two packs at a rate of one in 36 and is a parallel version of the expansion team subset in series two. The cards are printed on 28-point stock and feature a diffraction foil front.

COMPLETE SET (30) 25.00 60.00
SER.2 ODDS 1:36H/R,1:18J,1:72 SPEC.RET.
FIVE PER JAGUARS/PANTHERS FACT.SET
437 Derrick Graham .75 2.00
438 Vernon Turner .75 2.00
439 Carlton Bailey .75 2.00
440 Darion Conner .75 2.00
441 Randy Baldwin .75 2.00
442 Tim McKyer .75 2.00
443 Sam Mills .75 2.00
444 Bob Christian .75 2.00
445 Steve Lofton .75 2.00
446 Lamar Lathon .75 2.00
447 Tony Smith RB .75 2.00
448 Don Beebe 1.00 2.50
449 Barry Foster 1.00 2.50
450 Frank Reich 1.00 2.50
451 Pete Metzelaars .75 2.00
452 Reggie Cobb .75 2.00
453 Jeff Lageman .75 2.00
454 Derek Brown TE .75 2.00
455 Desmond Howard 1.00 2.50
456 Vinnie Clark .75 2.00
457 Keith Goganious .75 2.00
458 Shawn Bowens .75 2.00
459 Rob Johnson 1.50 4.00
460 Steve Beuerlein 1.00 2.50
461 Mark Brunell 6.00 15.00
462 Harry Colon .75 2.00
463 Chris Hudson .75 2.00
464 Darren Carrington .75 2.00
465 Ernest Givins .75 2.00
466 Kelvin Pritchett .75 2.00

1995 Topps Finest Boosters

This 22 card set was randomly inserted into series two packs at a rate of one in 36 and utilizes the same design as the 1995 Finest set with players not found in series one. Card fronts feature a blue background with white lightning. Card backs feature a headshot with biographical and statistical information. Cards are numbered with a "Booster" prefix. The set also has a refractor parallel, randomly inserted into packs at a rate of one in 36 hobby packs and one in 432 retail packs. These cards have a refractive foil front and the letter "R" located in black in the lower left corner.

COMPLETE SET (22) 40.00 80.00
STATED ODDS 1:36H/R,1:18J,1:72SR.SER.2
*REFRACTORS: 1.2X TO 3X BASIC INSERTS
STATED ODDS 1:36H,1:216J,1:432R SER.2
B166 Barry Sanders 4.00 10.00
B167 Bryant Young .50 1.25
B168 Boomer Esiason .50 1.25
B169 Terance Mathis .50 1.25
B170 Troy Aikman 2.50 6.00
B171 Junior Seau .75 2.00
B172 Rodney Hampton .50 1.25
B173 Jim Everett .25 .60
B174 Dan Marino 5.00 12.00
B175 Steve Young 2.00 5.00
B176 Cris Carter .75 2.00
B177 Eric Swann .50 1.25
B178 Rick Mirer .50 1.25
B179 Jerome Bettis .75 2.00
B180 Emmitt Smith 4.00 10.00
B181 Jim Kelly .75 2.00
B182 John Elway 5.00 12.00
B183 Dana Stubblefield .50 1.25
B184 Drew Bledsoe 1.50 4.00
B185 Jerry Rice 2.50 6.00
B186 Michael Irvin .75 2.00
B187 Bruce Smith .75 2.00

1995 Topps Florida Hot Bed

This 15 card set was randomly inserted into special retail packs at one per pack and features NFL stars who played for a college in the state of Florida. Card fronts feature a map shot of Florida in the background with the card name "Florida Hotbed" in orange at the top. The player's name and team are in gold foil at the bottom. Card backs feature a blue water background with a headshot and a brief commentary on the player's college and NFL information. Card backs are numbered with a "FH" prefix.

COMPLETE SET (15) 5.00 12.00
ONE PER SPECIAL RETAIL PACK
FH1 Deion Sanders 1.00 2.50
FH2 Brian Blades .30 .75
FH3 Errict Rhett .30 .75
FH4 Kevin Williams .30 .75
FH5 Cortez Kennedy .30 .75
FH6 Corey Sawyer .15 .40
FH7 Russell Maryland .15 .40
FH8 Emmitt Smith 2.50 6.00
FH9 Vinny Testaverde .30 .75
FH10 William Floyd .30 .75
FH11 Brett Perriman .30 .75
FH12 Nate Newton .15 .40
FH13 Jim Kelly .50 1.25
FH14 LeRoy Butler .15 .40
FH15 Michael Irvin .50 1.25

1995 Topps Hit List

This 20-card standard-size set was randomly inserted one in four foil packs. Leading defensive players are featured in this set. The fronts feature an action player photo. The words "Hit List" are in yellow lettering on the top while the player is identified in gold foil on the bottom of the card. The horizontal backs contain player information as well as a photo.

COMPLETE SET (20) 2.50 6.00
STATED ODDS 1:4
1 Pepper Johnson .15 .40
2 Elijah Alexander .15 .40
3 Joe Cain .15 .40
4 Andre Collins .15 .40
5 Chris Spielman .30 .75
6 Bryan Cox .15 .40
7 Ed McDaniel .15 .40
8 Jack Del Rio .15 .40
9 Jeff Herrod .15 .40
10 Greg Lloyd .30 .75
11 Reggie White .50 1.25
12 Robert Jones .15 .40
13 Eric Turner .15 .40
14 Vincent Brown .15 .40
15 Kevin Greene .30 .75
16 Bruce Smith .50 1.25
17 Hardy Nickerson UER .15 .40
18 Seth Joyner .15 .40
19 Darryl Talley .15 .40
20 Junior Seau .50 1.25

1995 Topps Mystery Finest

is 27-card standard-size set features leading NFL players. These cards were inserted at the rate of one in 36. A new twist to these cards is that to identify the player, the collector needed to peel off the protector to see what player they obtained out of the pack. This set features nine quarterbacks, running backs and receivers. An instant winner card for the complete set created and issued with clear Finest protectors was included one in 1980 packs. There is a refractor parallel to this set. These cards were included one in 36 hobby packs, but only one in 72 retail packs.

COMPLETE SET (27) 20.00 50.00
STATED ODDS 1:36H,1:12J,1:72SP RET SER.1
*REFRACTORS: .8X to 2X BASIC INSERTS
STATED ODDS 1:36H,1:216J,1:864R SER.1
1 Troy Aikman 2.00 5.00
2 Jerome Bettis .60 1.50
3 Drew Bledsoe 1.25 3.00
4 Tim Brown .60 1.50
5 Cris Carter .60 1.50
6 Henry Ellard .40 1.00
7 John Elway 4.00 10.00
8 Marshall Faulk 2.50 6.00
9 Brett Favre 4.00 10.00
10 Irving Fryar .40 1.00
11 Rodney Hampton .40 1.00
12 Stan Humphries .40 1.00
13 Michael Irvin .60 1.50
14 Jim Kelly .60 1.50
15 Dan Marino 4.00 10.00
16 Terance Mathis .40 1.00
17 Natrone Means .40 1.00
18 Warren Moon .40 1.00
19 Herman Moore .60 1.50
20 Andre Reed .40 1.00
21 Errict Rhett .40 1.00
22 Jerry Rice 2.00 5.00
23 Barry Sanders 3.00 8.00
24 Emmitt Smith 3.00 8.00
25 Chris Warren .40 1.00
26 Ricky Watters .40 1.00
27 Steve Young 1.50 4.00

1995 Topps Profiles

Randomly inserted into series 2 packs at a rate of one in 12, this 15 card set features a bordered silver foil background. Card fronts feature a shot of the player with his name in gold foil at the bottom and the card title "Profiles" running along the right. A headshot of Steve Young is also featured on the lower right side of each card. Card backs are horizontal with a headshot and a commentary on the player by Steve Young. Cards are numbered with a "PF" prefix.

COMPLETE SET (15) 15.00 30.00
STATED ODDS 1:12H/R,1:6J,1:24SR SER.2
1 Emmitt Smith 5.00 10.00
2 Chris Spielman .60 1.25
3 Rod Woodson .60 1.25
4 Deion Sanders 2.00 4.00
5 Junior Seau 1.00 2.00
6 Byron Evans .25 .60
7 Jerome Bettis 1.00 2.00
8 Charles Haley .60 1.25
9 Jerry Rice 3.00 6.00
10 Barry Sanders 5.00 10.00
11 Hardy Nickerson .25 .60
12 Natrone Means .60 1.25
13 Darren Woodson .60 1.25
14 Reggie White 1.00 2.00
15 Troy Aikman 3.00 6.00

1995 Topps Sensational Sophomores

is 10 card standard-size set was randomly inserted in retail packs at a rate of one in 24 and feature 10 of the hottest 1994 rookies. Using Dot Matrix technology, card fronts have a etched football along a blue foil background. The card title "Sensational Sophomores" is in red at the top left of the card and the player's name is in purple at the lower right. Card backs are vertical with a red background and a commentary on the player. Rookie season statistics are located at the bottom of the card.

COMPLETE SET (10) 7.50 20.00
STATED ODDS 1:9JUM, 1:48 SP RET SER.1
1 Marshall Faulk 3.00 8.00
2 Heath Shuler 1.25 2.50
3 Tim Bowens .50 1.25
4 Bryant Young .50 1.25
5 Dan Wilkinson .50 1.25
6 Errict Rhett .50 1.25
7 Andre Coleman .50 1.25
8 Aaron Glenn .50 1.25
9 Trent Dilfer 1.25 2.50
10 Byron Bam Morris .50 1.25

1995 Topps Yesteryear

is 15-card standard-size set features leading NFL players and were inserted at a rate of one in 72 hobby packs. These cards, featuring both early career and current photos, were printed using the "Finest" technology. Card backs feature a statistical summary that compares the players rookie year to the past season and a brief commentary.

COMPLETE SET (15) 12.00 30.00
SER.1 STATED ODDS 1:72 HOBBY
1 Stan Humphries .60 1.50
2 Dan Marino 6.00 15.00
3 Irving Fryar .60 1.50
4 Warren Moon .60 1.50
5 Steve Young 2.50 6.00
6 Kevin Greene .60 1.50
7 Jeff Hostetler .60 1.50
8 Jack Del Rio .30 .75
9 Reggie White 1.00 2.50
10 Jerry Rice 3.00 8.00
11 Bruce Smith 1.00 2.50
12 Rod Woodson .60 1.50
13 Deion Sanders 2.00 5.00
14 Barry Sanders 5.00 12.00
15 Brett Favre 6.00 15.00

1995 Topps NPD Promo

is card was distributed to provide collectors with an early look at a possible upcoming new release. However, the set was never issued. The card is similar in design to the 1995 D3 baseball lenticular motion cards on the front and the back carries a blueprint design with no card number.

1 Glyn Milburn 2.00 5.00

1996 Topps

e 1996 Topps set was issued in one series totaling 440 standard-size cards. The 11-card hobby and retail foil packs carried a suggested retail price of $1.29 each. The packs were issued in 12-box foil cases which contained 36 packs in a box. Jumbo packs were also issued, these packs were in 8 box cases with 12 boxes per case and 39 cards per pack. The set contained the topical subsets: 1000 Yard Club (121-136/241-263) and 3000 Yard Club (371-386). Rookie Cards include Tim Biakabutuka, Eddie George, Marvin Harrison, Keyshawn Johnson, Leeland McLeroy, Eric Moulds and Lawrence Phillips. Topps produced a special promo card for the 1996 National Sports Collector's Convention. It featured Joe Namath and Steve Young printed in Finest technology with a Refractor version as well.

COMPLETE SET (440) 20.00 40.00
COMP.FACT.SET (448) 35.00 60.00
COMP.CER.FACT.SET (445) 20.00 40.00
1 Troy Aikman .40 1.00
2 Kevin Greene .07 .20
3 Robert Brooks .10 .30
4 Eugene Daniel .02 .10
5 Rodney Peete .02 .10
6 James Hasty .02 .10
7 Tim McDonald .02 .10
8 Darick Holmes .02 .10
9 Morten Andersen .02 .10
10 Junior Seau .10 .30
11 Brett Perriman .02 .10
12 Eric Green .02 .10
13 Jim Flanigan .02 .10
14 Cortez Kennedy .02 .10
15 Orlando Thomas .02 .10
16 Anthony Miller .07 .20
17 Sean Gilbert .02 .10
18 Rob Fredrickson .02 .10
19 Willie Green .02 .10
20 Jeff Blake .10 .30
21 Trent Dilfer .10 .30
22 Chris Chandler .07 .20
23 Renaldo Turnbull .02 .10
24 Dave Meggett .02 .10
25 Heath Shuler .07 .20
26 Michael Jackson .07 .20
27 Thomas Randolph .02 .10
28 Keith Goganious .02 .10
29 Seth Joyner .02 .10
30 Wayne Chrebet .25 .60
31 Craig Newsome .02 .10
32 William Fuller .02 .10
33 Morton Hanks .02 .10
34 Dale Carter .02 .10
35 Quentin Coryatt .02 .10
36 Robert Jones .02 .10
37 Eric Metcalf .02 .10
38 Byron Bam Morris .02 .10
39 Bill Brooks .02 .10
40 Barry Sanders .60 1.50
41 Michael Haynes .02 .10
42 Joey Galloway .10 .30
43 Robert Smith .07 .20
44 John Thierry .02 .10
45 Bryan Cox .02 .10
46 Anthony Parker .02 .10
47 Harvey Williams .02 .10
48 Terrell Davis .30 .75
49 Darnay Scott .07 .20
50 Kerry Collins .10 .30
51 Cris Dishman .02 .10
52 Dwayne Harper .02 .10
53 Warren Sapp .02 .10
54 Will Moore .02 .10
55 Earnest Byner .02 .10
56 Aaron Glenn .02 .10
57 Michael Westbrook .10 .30
58 Vencie Glenn .02 .10
59 Rob Moore .07 .20
60 Mark Brunell .25 .60
61 Craig Heyward .02 .10
62 Eric Allen .02 .10
63 Bill Romanowski .02 .10
64 Dana Stubblefield .07 .20
65 Steve Bono .02 .10
66 George Koonce .02 .10
67 Larry Brown .02 .10
68 Warren Moon .07 .20
69 Erric Pegram .02 .10
70 Jim Kelly .10 .30
71 Jason Belser .02 .10
72 Henry Thomas .02 .10
73 Mark Carrier DB .02 .10
74 Terry Wooden .02 .10
75 Terry McDaniel .02 .10
76 O.J. McDuffie .07 .20
77 Dan Wilkinson .02 .10
78 Blake Brockermeyer .02 .10
79 Micheal Barrow .02 .10
80 Dave Brown .02 .10
81 Todd Lyght .02 .10
82 Henry Ellard .02 .10
83 Jeff Lageman .02 .10
84 Anthony Pleasant .02 .10
85 Aeneas Williams .02 .10
86 Vincent Brisby .02 .10
87 Terrell Fletcher .02 .10
88 Brad Baxter .02 .10
89 Shannon Sharpe .07 .20
90 Errict Rhett .07 .20
91 Michael Zordich .02 .10
92 Dan Saleaumua .02 .10
93 Devin Bush .02 .10
94 Wayne Simmons .02 .10
95 Tyrone Hughes .02 .10
96 John Randle .07 .20
97 Tony Tolbert .02 .10
98 Yancey Thigpen .07 .20
99 J.J. Stokes .10 .30
100 Marshall Faulk .15 .40
101 Barry Minter RC .02 .10
102 Glenn Foley .07 .20
103 Chester McGlockton .02 .10
104 Carlton Gray .02 .10
105 Terry Kirby .07 .20
106 Darryll Lewis .02 .10
107 Thomas Smith .02 .10
108 Mike Fox .02 .10
109 Antonio Langham .02 .10
110 Drew Bledsoe .25 .60
111 Troy Drayton .02 .10
112 Marvcus Patton .02 .10
113 Tyrone Wheatley .07 .20
114 Desmond Howard .07 .20
115 Johnny Mitchell .02 .10
116 Dave Krieg .02 .10
117 Natrone Means .07 .20
118 Herman Moore .07 .20
119 Darren Woodson .07 .20
120 Ricky Watters .07 .20
121 Emmitt Smith TYC .30 .75
122 Barry Sanders TYC .30 .75
123 Curtis Martin TYC .10 .30
124 Chris Warren TYC .07 .20
125 Terry Allen TYC .07 .20
126 Ricky Watters TYC .07 .20
127 Errict Rhett TYC .07 .20
128 Rodney Hampton TYC .02 .10
129 Terrell Davis TYC .10 .30
130 Harvey Williams TYC .02 .10
131 Craig Heyward TYC .02 .10
132 Marshall Faulk TYC .10 .30
133 Rashaan Salaam TYC .07 .20
134 Garrison Hearst TYC .07 .20
135 Edgar Bennett TYC .07 .20
136 Thurman Thomas TYC .07 .20
137 Brian Washington .02 .10
138 Derek Loville .02 .10
139 Curtis Conway .10 .30
140 Isaac Bruce .10 .30
141 Ricardo McDonald .02 .10
142 Bruce Armstrong .02 .10
143 Will Wolford .02 .10
144 Thurman Thomas .10 .30
145 Mel Gray .02 .10
146 Napoleon Kaufman .10 .30
147 Terry Allen .07 .20
148 Chris Calloway .02 .10
149 Harry Colon .02 .10
150 Pepper Johnson .02 .10
151 Marco Coleman .02 .10
152 Shawn Jefferson .02 .10
153 Larry Centers .07 .20
154 Lamar Lathon .02 .10
155 Mark Chmura .07 .20
156 Dermontti Dawson .08 .20
157 Alvin Harper .02 .10
158 Randall McDaniel .05 .15
159 Allen Aldridge .02 .10
160 Chris Warren .07 .20
161 Jessie Tuggle .02 .10
162 Sean Lumpkin .02 .10
163 Bobby Houston .02 .10
164 Dexter Carter .02 .10
165 Erik Kramer .02 .10
166 Brock Marion .02 .10
167 Toby Wright .02 .10
168 John Copeland .02 .10
169 Sean Dawkins .02 .10
170 Tim Brown .10 .30
171 Darion Conner .02 .10
172 Aaron Hayden RC .02 .10
173 Charlie Garner .07 .20
174 Anthony Cook .02 .10
175 Derrick Thomas .10 .30
176 Willie McGinest .02 .10
177 Thomas Lewis .02 .10
178 Sherman Williams .02 .10
179 Cornelius Bennett .02 .10
180 Frank Sanders .10 .30
181 Leroy Hoard .02 .10
182 Bernie Parmalee .02 .10
183 Sterling Palmer .02 .10
184 Kelvin Pritchett .02 .10
185 Kordell Stewart .10 .30
186 Brent Jones .02 .10
187 Robert Blackmon .02 .10
188 Adrian Murrell .07 .20
189 Edgar Bennett .07 .20
190 Rashaan Salaam .07 .20
191 Ellis Johnson .02 .10
192 Andre Coleman .02 .10

193 Will Shields .02 .10
194 Derrick Brooks .10 .30
195 Carl Pickens .07 .20
196 Carlton Bailey .02 .10
197 Terance Mathis .07 .20
198 Carlos Jenkins .02 .10
199 Derrick Alexander .02 .10
200 Deion Sanders .25 .60
201 Glyn Milburn .02 .10
202 Chris Sanders .07 .20
203 Rocket Ismail .02 .10
204 Fred Barnett .02 .10
205 Quinn Early .02 .10
206 Henry Jones .02 .10
207 Herschel Walker .07 .20
208 James Washington .02 .10
209 Lee Woodall .02 .10
210 Neil Smith .07 .20
211 Tony Bennett .02 .10
212 Ernie Mills .02 .10
213 Clyde Simmons .02 .10
214 Chris Slade .02 .10
215 Tony Boselli .02 .10
216 Ryan McNeil .02 .10
217 Rob Burnett .02 .10
218 Stan Humphries .07 .20
219 Rick Mirer .07 .20
220 Troy Vincent .02 .10
221 Sean Jones .02 .10
222 Marty Carter .02 .10
223 Boomer Esiason .07 .20
224 Charles Haley .07 .20
225 Sam Mills .02 .10
226 Greg Biekert .02 .10
227 Bryant Young .07 .20
228 Ken Dilger .07 .20
229 Levon Kirkland .02 .10
230 Brian Mitchell .02 .10
231 Hardy Nickerson .02 .10
232 Elvis Grbac .07 .20
233 Kurt Schulz .02 .10
234 Chris Doleman .02 .10
235 Tamarick Vanover .07 .20
236 Jesse Campbell .02 .10
237 William Thomas .02 .10
238 Shane Conlan .02 .10
239 Jason Elam .07 .20
240 Steve McNair .30 .75
241 Jerry Rice TYC .20 .50
242 Isaac Bruce TYC .10 .30
243 Herman Moore TYC .07 .20
244 Michael Irvin TYC .07 .20
245 Robert Brooks TYC .10 .30
246 Brett Perriman TYC .02 .10
247 Cris Carter TYC .10 .30
248 Tim Brown TYC .07 .20
249 Yancey Thigpen TYC .07 .20
250 Jeff Graham TYC .02 .10
251 Carl Pickens TYC .07 .20
252 Tony Martin TYC .02 .10
253 Eric Metcalf TYC .02 .10
254 Jake Reed TYC .07 .20
255 Quinn Early TYC .02 .10
256 Anthony Miller TYC .07 .20
257 Joey Galloway TYC .10 .30
258 Bert Emanuel TYC .07 .20
259 Terance Mathis TYC .02 .10
260 Curtis Conway TYC .07 .20
261 Henry Ellard TYC .02 .10
262 Mark Carrier TYC .02 .10
263 Brian Blades TYC .02 .10
264 William Roaf .02 .10
265 Ed McDaniel .02 .10
266 Nate Newton .02 .10
267 Brett Maxie .02 .10
268 Anthony Smith .02 .10
269 Mickey Washington .02 .10
270 Jerry Rice .40 1.00
271 Shaun Gayle .02 .10
272 Gilbert Brown RC .10 .30
273 Mark Bruener .02 .10
274 Eugene Robinson .02 .10
275 Marvin Washington .02 .10
276 Keith Sims .02 .10
277 Ashley Ambrose .02 .10
278 Garrison Hearst .07 .20
279 Donnell Woolford .02 .10
280 Cris Carter .10 .30
281 Curtis Martin .30 .75
282 Scott Mitchell .07 .20
283 Stevon Moore .02 .10
284 Roman Phifer .02 .10
285 Ken Harvey .02 .10
286 Rodney Hampton .07 .20
287 Willie Davis .02 .10
288 Yonel Jourdain .02 .10
289 Brian DeMarco .02 .10
290 Reggie White .10 .30
291 Kevin Williams .02 .10
292 Gary Plummer .02 .10
293 Terrance Shaw .02 .10
294 Calvin Williams .02 .10
295 Eddie Robinson .02 .10
296 Tony McGee .02 .10
297 Clay Matthews .02 .10
298 Joe Cain .02 .10
299 Tim McKyer .02 .10
300 Greg Lloyd .07 .20
301 Steve Wisniewski .02 .10
302 Ray Buchanan .02 .10
303 Lake Dawson .02 .10
304 Kevin Carter .02 .10
305 Phillippi Sparks .02 .10
306 Emmitt Smith .60 1.50
307 Ruben Brown .02 .10
308 Tom Carter .02 .10
309 William Floyd .07 .20
310 Jim Everett .02 .10
311 Vincent Brown .02 .10
312 Dennis Gibson .02 .10
313 Lorenzo Lynch .02 .10
314 Corey Harris .02 .10
315 James O.Stewart .07 .20
316 Kyle Brady .02 .10
317 Irving Fryar .07 .20
318 Jake Reed .07 .20
319 Vinny Testaverde .07 .20
320 John Elway .75 2.00
321 Tracy Scroggins .02 .10
322 Chris Spielman .02 .10
323 Horace Copeland .02 .10
324 Chris Zorich .02 .10
325 Mike Mamula .02 .10
326 Henry Ford .02 .10
327 Steve Walsh .02 .10
328 Stanley Richard .07 .20
329 Mike Jones .02 .10
330 Jim Harbaugh .07 .20
331 Darren Perry .02 .10
332 Ken Norton .02 .10
333 Kimble Anders .07 .20
334 Harold Green .02 .10
335 Tyrone Poole .02 .10
336 Mark Fields .02 .10
337 Darren Bennett .02 .10
338 Mike Sherrard .02 .10
339 Terry Ray RC .02 .10
340 Bruce Smith .07 .20
341 Daryl Johnston .07 .20
342 Vinnie Clark .02 .10
343 Mike Caldwell .02 .10
344 Vinson Smith .02 .10
345 Mo Lewis .02 .10
346 Brian Blades .02 .10
347 Rod Stephens .02 .10
348 David Palmer .02 .10
349 Blaine Bishop .02 .10
350 Jeff George .07 .20
351 George Teague .02 .10
352 Jeff Hostetler .02 .10
353 Michael Strahan .07 .20
354 Eric Davis .02 .10
355 Jerome Bettis .10 .30
356 Irv Smith .02 .10
357 Jeff Herrod .02 .10
358 Jay Novacek .02 .10
359 Bryce Paup .02 .10
360 Neil O'Donnell .07 .20
361 Eric Swann .02 .10
362 Corey Sawyer .02 .10
363 Ty Law .10 .30
364 Bo Orlando .02 .10
365 Marcus Allen .10 .30
366 Mark McMillian .02 .10
367 Mark Carrier WR .02 .10
368 Jackie Harris .02 .10
369 Steve Atwater .02 .10
370 Steve Young .30 .75
371 Brett Favre TYC .40 1.00
372 Scott Mitchell TYC .02 .10
373 Warren Moon TYC .02 .10
374 Jeff George TYC .07 .20
375 Jim Everett TYC .02 .10
376 John Elway TYC .40 1.00
377 Erik Kramer TYC .02 .10
378 Jeff Blake TYC .07 .20
379 Dan Marino TYC .40 1.00
380 Dave Krieg TYC .02 .10
381 Drew Bledsoe TYC .10 .30
382 Stan Humphries TYC .02 .10
383 Troy Aikman TYC .20 .50
384 Steve Young TYC .10 .30
385 Jim Kelly TYC .10 .30
386 Steve Bono TYC .02 .10
387 David Sloan .02 .10
388 Jeff Graham .02 .10
389 Hugh Douglas .07 .20
390 Dan Marino .75 2.00
391 Winston Moss .02 .10
392 Darrell Green .02 .10
393 Mark Stepnoski .02 .10
394 Bert Emanuel .07 .20
395 Eric Zeier .02 .10
396 Willie Jackson .07 .20
397 Qadry Ismail .07 .20
398 Michael Brooks .02 .10
399 D'Marco Farr .02 .10
400 Brett Favre .75 2.00
401 Carnell Lake .02 .10
402 Pat Swilling .02 .10
403 Stephen Grant .02 .10
404 Steve Tasker .02 .10
405 Ben Coates .07 .20
406 Steve Tovar .02 .10
407 Tony Martin .07 .20
408 Greg Hill .07 .20
409 Eric Guilford .02 .10
410 Michael Irvin .10 .30
411 Eric Hill .02 .10
412 Mario Bates .07 .20
413 Brian Stablein RC .02 .10
414 Marcus Jones RC .02 .10
415 Reggie Brown LB RC .02 .10
416 Lawrence Phillips RC .10 .30
417 Alex Van Dyke RC .07 .20
418 Daryl Gardener RC .02 .10
419 Mike Alstott RC .40 1.00
420 Kevin Hardy RC .10 .30
421 Rickey Dudley RC .10 .30
422 Jerome Woods RC .02 .10
423 Eric Moulds RC .50 1.25
424 Cedric Jones RC .02 .10
425 Simeon Rice RC .30 .75
426 Marvin Harrison RC 1.00 2.50
427 Tim Biakabutuka RC .10 .30
428 Duane Clemons RC .02 .10
429 Alex Molden RC .02 .10
430 Keyshawn Johnson RC .40 1.00
431 Willie Anderson RC .02 .10
432 John Mobley RC .02 .10
433 Leeland McElroy RC .07 .20
434 Regan Upshaw RC .02 .10
435 Eddie George RC .50 1.25
436 Jonathan Ogden RC .50 1.25
437 Eddie Kennison RC .10 .30
438 Jermane Mayberry RC .02 .10
439 Checklist 1 of 2 .02 .10
440 Checklist 2 of 2 .02 .10
P1 Joe Namath Promo 7.50 15.00
Steve Young
P1R Joe Namath Promo 10.00 20.00
Steve Young
(Refractor version)

1996 Topps Broadway's Reviews

Randomly inserted in packs at a rate of one in 12 hobby foil packs, one in eight retail, one in six special retail, or one in three jumbo packs, this 10-card standard-size horizontal set features Joe Namath comments about the leading active NFL quarterbacks. The cards are numbered with a "BR" prefix.

COMPLETE SET (10) 10.00 25.00
STATED ODDS 1:12H, 1:8R, 1:3J, 1:6 SP.RET
BR1 Kerry Collins .40 1.00
BR2 Drew Bledsoe 1.00 2.00
BR3 Jeff Blake .40 1.00
BR4 Brett Favre 3.00 6.00
BR5 Scott Mitchell .25 .60
BR6 Troy Aikman 1.50 3.00
BR7 Steve Young 1.25 2.50
BR8 Jim Harbaugh .25 .60
BR9 John Elway 3.00 6.00
BR10 Dan Marino 3.00 6.00

1996 Topps 40th Anniversary Retros

ndomly inserted in packs at a rate of one in 6 foil packs, one in 4 retail and special retail packs, and one per jumbo pack, this 40-card standard-size set has today's players featured in card designs used by Topps over their 40 years of producing professional football cards. The set is sequenced in order of the design used with the design year after the player's name.

COMPLETE SET (40) 25.00 60.00
STATED ODDS 1:6 HOB, 1:4 RET, 1:4 SP.RET
1 Jim Harbaugh 1956 .30 .75
2 Greg Lloyd 1957 .30 .75
3 Barry Sanders 1958 3.00 6.00
4 Merton Hanks 1959 .15 .40
5 Herman Moore 1960 .30 .75
6 Tim Brown 1961 .60 1.25
7 Brett Favre 1962 4.00 8.00
8 Cris Carter 1963 .60 1.25
9 Curtis Martin 1964 1.50 3.00
10 Bryce Paup 1965 .15 .40
11 Steve Bono 1966 .15 .40
12 Blaine Bishop 1967 .15 .40
13 Emmitt Smith 1968 3.00 6.00
14 Carnell Lake 1969 .15 .40
15 Marshall Faulk 1970 .75 1.50
16 Mike Morris 1971 .15 .40
17 Shannon Sharpe 1972 .30 .75
18 Steve Young 1973 1.50 3.00
19 Jeff George 1974 .30 .75
20 Junior Seau 1975 .60 1.25
21 Chris Warren 1976 .30 .75
22 Heath Shuler 1977 .30 .75
23 Jeff Blake 1978 .60 1.25
24 Reggie White 1979 .60 1.25
25 Jeff Hostetler 1980 .15 .40
26 Errict Rhett 1981 .30 .75
27 Rodney Hampton 1982 .30 .75
28 Jerry Rice 1983 2.00 4.00
29 Jim Everett 1984 .15 .40
30 Isaac Bruce 1985 .60 1.25
31 Dan Marino 1986 4.00 8.00
32 Marcus Allen 1987 .60 1.25
33 Erik Kramer 1988 .15 .40
34 John Elway 1989 4.00 8.00
35 Ricky Watters 1990 .30 .75
36 Troy Aikman 1991 2.00 4.00
37 Drew Bledsoe 1992 1.25 2.50
38 Scott Mitchell 1993 .30 .75
39 Rashaan Salaam 1994 .30 .75
40 Kerry Collins 1995 .60 1.25

1996 Topps Hobby Masters

ndomly inserted in hobby foil packs at a rate of one in 36 or in hobby jumbo packs at a rate of one in ten packs, this 20-card standard-size set features players voted by hobby dealers as guys they would like to see in a set. These cards are printed on 28-point full diffraction foil stock with a prismatic background. The cards are numbered with an "HM" prefix.

COMPLETE SET (20) 50.00 120.00
STATED ODDS 1:10 JUMBO
HM1 Brett Favre 8.00 20.00
HM2 Emmitt Smith 6.00 15.00
HM3 Drew Bledsoe 2.50 6.00
HM4 Marshall Faulk 1.50 4.00
HM5 Steve Young 3.00 8.00
HM6 Barry Sanders 6.00 15.00
HM7 Troy Aikman 4.00 10.00
HM8 Jerry Rice 4.00 10.00
HM9 Michael Irvin 1.25 3.00
HM10 Dan Marino 8.00 20.00
HM11 Chris Warren .75 2.00
HM12 Reggie White 1.25 3.00
HM13 Jeff Blake 1.25 3.00
HM14 Greg Lloyd .75 2.00
HM15 Curtis Martin 3.00 8.00
HM16 Junior Seau 1.25 3.00
HM17 Kerry Collins 1.25 3.00
HM18 Deion Sanders 2.50 6.00
HM19 Joey Galloway 1.25 3.00
HM20 John Elway 8.00 20.00

1996 Topps Namath Reprints

ndomly inserted in foil packs at a rate of one in 18, this 10-card standard-size set features reprints from Joe Namath's nine-year Topps card career. The cards are close to the same as the original cards except for the UV coating, the "Topps 40th anniversary" logo on front and 1996 copyright information on the back. Jumbo packs included the cards at 1:5 and four cards were issued per cereal box factory set. The 1965 Namath insert card was standard sized, while a second version of the 1965 Reprint inserted into Topps factory sets was original large sized. Topps also issued a serial numbered (of 4000) framed poster that featured reprints of all Namath Topps cards.

COMPLETE SET (10) 20.00 50.00
COMMON NAMATH (1-10) 2.50 6.00
NAM.ODDS 1:18H,1:12R,1:5J,1:12 SP.RET
1 Joe Namath 1965 4.00 8.00
NNO Joe Namath 1965 6.00 12.00
NNO Joe Namath Poster/4000 15.00 25.00

1996 Topps Turf Warriors

is insert set features top players with a felt "turf" finish to the cardfront. The cards were randomly inserted in hobby at 1:36, and retail packs at 1:24, and special 16-card retail packs at the rate of 1:18 packs.

COMPLETE SET (22) 75.00 125.00
TW1 Bryce Paup .50 1.25
TW2 Ben Coates 1.00 2.50
TW3 Jim Harbaugh 1.00 2.50
TW4 Brian Mitchell .50 1.25
TW5 Brett Favre 10.00 25.00
TW6 Junior Seau 1.50 4.00
TW7 Michael Irvin 1.50 4.00
TW8 Steve Young 4.00 10.00
TW9 Terry McDaniel .50 1.25
TW10 Curtis Martin 4.00 10.00
TW11 Greg Lloyd 1.00 2.50
TW12 Cris Carter 1.50 4.00
TW13 Emmitt Smith 8.00 20.00
TW14 Reggie White 1.50 4.00
TW15 Marshall Faulk 2.00 5.00
TW16 Jerry Rice 5.00 12.00
TW17 Shannon Sharpe 1.00 2.50
TW18 Dan Marino 10.00 25.00
TW19 Ken Norton .50 1.25
TW20 Barry Sanders 8.00 20.00
TW21 Neil Smith 1.00 2.50
TW22 Troy Aikman 5.00 12.00

1997 Topps

is 1997 Topps set was issued in one series totaling 415 cards and distributed in 11-card packs with a suggested retail of $1.29. The first 385 cards feature the veteran players. The final 30-cards feature 1997 draft picks and were inserted 1:3 packs on average, making them short prints. The fronts feature color action player photos in a three-sided white border with a team color top and side margin. A special spot matte and gloss finish complement the design. The backs carry a small color player photo and career statistics. The set contains a 30-card subset of the 1997 NFL Draft Picks (#386-415) pictured in their new NFL team uniforms. Promo cards were released to promote the set and can only be differentiated by the green colored border on the cardback instead of gold.

COMPLETE SET (415) 25.00 50.00
COMP.FACT.SET (424) 50.00 80.00
1 Brett Favre .75 2.00
2 Lawyer Milloy .12 .30
3 Tim Biakabutuka .12 .30
4 Clyde Simmons .08 .20
5 Deion Sanders .20 .50
6 Anthony Miller .08 .20
7 Marquez Pope .08 .20
8 Mike Tomczak .08 .20
9 William Thomas .08 .20
10 Marshall Faulk .25 .60
11 John Randle .12 .30
12 Jim Kelly .20 .50
13 Steve Bono .12 .30
14 Rod Stephens .08 .20
15 Stan Humphries .08 .20
16 Terrell Buckley .08 .20
17 Ki-Jana Carter .08 .20
18 Marcus Robertson .08 .20
19 Corey Harris .08 .20
20 Rashaan Salaam .08 .20
21 Rickey Dudley .12 .30
22 Jamir Miller .08 .20
23 Martin Mayhew .08 .20
24 Jason Sehorn .12 .30
25 Isaac Bruce .20 .50
26 Johnnie Morton .12 .30
27 Antonio Langham .08 .20
28 Cornelius Bennett .08 .20
29 Joe Johnson .08 .20
30 Keyshawn Johnson .20 .50
31 Willie Green .08 .20
32 Craig Newsome .08 .20
33 Brock Marion .08 .20
34 Corey Fuller .08 .20
35 Ben Coates .12 .30
36 Ty Detmer .12 .30
37 Charles Johnson .10 .30
38 Willie Jackson .08 .20
39 Tyronne Drakeford .08 .20
40 Gus Frerotte .08 .20
41 Robert Blackmon .08 .20
42 Andre Coleman .08 .20
43 Mario Bates .08 .20
44 Chris Calloway .08 .20
45 Terry McDaniel .07 .20
46 Anthony Davis .07 .20
47 Stanley Pritchett .07 .20
48 Ray Buchanan .07 .20
49 Chris Chandler .10 .30
50 Ashley Ambrose .08 .20
51 Tyrone Braxton .08 .20
52 Pepper Johnson .08 .20
53 Frank Sanders .10 .30
54 Clay Matthews .08 .20
55 Bruce Smith .10 .30
56 Jermaine Lewis .20 .50
57 Mark Carrier WR UER .08 .20
58 Jeff Graham .08 .20
59 Keith Lyle .08 .20
60 Trent Dilfer .20 .50
61 Trace Armstrong .08 .20
62 Jeff Herrod .08 .20
63 Tyrone Wheatley .10 .30
64 Torrance Small .08 .20
65 Chris Warren .10 .30
66 Terry Kirby .10 .30
67 Eric Pegram .08 .20
68 Sean Gilbert .08 .20
69 Greg Biekert .08 .20
70 Ricky Watters .10 .30
71 Chris Hudson .08 .20
72 Tamarick Vanover .10 .30
73 Orlando Thomas .08 .20
74 Jimmy Spencer .08 .20
75 John Mobley .08 .20
76 Henry Thomas .08 .20
77 Santana Dotson .08 .20
78 Boomer Esiason .12 .30
79 Bobby Hebert .08 .20
80 Kerry Collins .20 .50
81 Bobby Engram .12 .30
82 Kevin Smith .08 .20
83 Rick Mirer .08 .20
84 Ted Johnson .08 .20
85 Derrick Alexander WR .12 .30
86 Hugh Douglas .08 .20
87 Rodney Harrison RC .40 1.00
88 Roman Phifer .08 .20
89 Warren Moon .20 .50
90 Thurman Thomas .20 .50
91 Michael McCrary .08 .20
92 Dana Stubblefield .08 .20
93 Andre Hastings UER .08 .20
94 William Fuller .08 .20
95 Jeff Hostetler .08 .20
96 Danny Kanell .08 .20
97 Mark Fields .08 .20
98 Eddie Robinson .08 .20
99 Daryl Gardener .08 .20
100 Drew Bledsoe .25 .60
101 Winslow Oliver .08 .20
102 Raymont Harris .08 .20
103 LeShon Johnson .08 .20
104 Byron Bam Morris .08 .20
105 Herman Moore .12 .30
106 Keith Jackson .08 .20
107 Chris Penn .08 .20
108 Robert Griffith RC .08 .20
109 Jeff Burris .08 .20
110 Troy Aikman .40 1.00
111 Allen Aldridge .08 .20
112 Mel Gray .08 .20
113 Aaron Bailey .08 .20
114 Michael Strahan .12 .30
115 Adrian Murrell .12 .30
116 Chris Mims .08 .20
117 Robert Jones .08 .20
118 Derrick Brooks .20 .50
119 Tom Carter .08 .20
120 Carl Pickens .12 .30
121 Tony Brackens .08 .20
122 O.J. McDuffie .12 .30
123 Napoleon Kaufman .20 .50
124 Chris T. Jones .08 .20
125 Kordell Stewart .20 .50
126 Ray Zellars .08 .20
127 Jessie Tuggle .08 .20
128 Greg Kragen .08 .20
129 Brett Perriman .08 .20
130 Steve Young .25 .60
131 Willie Clay .08 .20
132 Kimble Anders .12 .30
133 Eugene Daniel .08 .20
134 Jevon Langford .08 .20
135 Shannon Sharpe .12 .30
136 Wayne Simmons .08 .20
137 Leeland McElroy .08 .20
138 Mike Caldwell .08 .20
139 Eric Moulds .20 .50
140 Eddie George .20 .50
141 Jamal Anderson .20 .50
142 Michael Timpson .08 .20
143 Tony Tolbert .08 .20
144 Robert Smith .12 .30
145 Mike Alstott .20 .50
146 Gary Jones .08 .20
147 Terrance Shaw .08 .20
148 Carlton Gray .08 .20
149 Kevin Carter .08 .20
150 Darrell Green .12 .30
151 David Dunn .08 .20
152 Ken Norton .08 .20
153 Chad Brown .08 .20
154 Pat Swilling .08 .20
155 Irving Fryar .12 .30
156 Michael Haynes .08 .20
157 Shawn Jefferson .08 .20
158 Stephen Grant .08 .20
159 James O.Stewart .12 .30
160 Derrick Thomas .20 .50
161 Tim Bowens .08 .20
162 Dixon Edwards .08 .20
163 Micheal Barrow .08 .20
164 Antonio Freeman .20 .50
165 Terrell Davis .25 .60
166 Henry Ellard .12 .30
167 Daryl Johnston .12 .30
168 Bryan Cox .08 .20
169 Chad Cota .08 .20
170 Vinny Testaverde .12 .30
171 Andre Reed .12 .30
172 Larry Centers .12 .30
173 Craig Heyward .08 .20
174 Glyn Milburn .08 .20
175 Hardy Nickerson .08 .20
176 Corey Miller .08 .20
177 Bobby Houston .08 .20
178 Marco Coleman .08 .20
179 Winston Moss .08 .20
180 Tony Banks .12 .30
181 Jeff Lageman .08 .20
182 Jason Belser .08 .20
183 James Jett .12 .30
184 Wayne Martin .08 .20
185 Dave Meggett .08 .20
186 Terrell Owens .25 .60
187 Willie Williams .08 .20
188 Eric Turner .08 .20
189 Chuck Smith .08 .20
190 Simeon Rice .12 .30
191 Kevin Greene .12 .30
192 Lance Johnstone .08 .20
193 Marty Carter .08 .20
194 Ricardo McDonald .08 .20
195 Michael Irvin .20 .50
196 George Koonce .08 .20
197 Robert Porcher .08 .20
198 Mark Collins .08 .20
199 Louis Oliver .08 .20
200 John Elway .75 2.00
201 Jake Reed .12 .30
202 Rodney Hampton .12 .30
203 Aaron Glenn .08 .20
204 Mike Mamula .08 .20
205 Terry Allen .20 .50
206 John Lynch .12 .30
207 Todd Lyght .08 .20
208 Dean Wells .08 .20
209 Aaron Hayden .08 .20
210 Blaine Bishop .08 .20
211 Bert Emanuel .12 .30
212 Mark Carrier DB UER .08 .20
213 Dale Carter .08 .20
214 Jimmy Smith .12 .30
215 Jim Harbaugh .12 .30
216 Jeff George .12 .30
217 Anthony Newman .08 .20
218 Ty Law .12 .30
219 Brent Jones .08 .20
220 Emmitt Smith .60 1.50
221 Bennie Blades .08 .20
222 Alfred Williams .08 .20
223 Eugene Robinson .08 .20
224 Fred Barnett .08 .20
225 Errict Rhett .08 .20
226 Leslie O'Neal .08 .20
227 Michael Sinclair .08 .20
228 Marcus Patton .08 .20
229 Darrien Gordon .08 .20
230 Jerome Bettis .20 .50
231 Troy Vincent .08 .20
232 Ray Mickens .08 .20
233 Lonnie Johnson .08 .20
234 Charles Way .08 .20
235 Chris Sanders .08 .20
236 Bracy Walker .08 .20
237 Dave Krieg UER .08 .20
238 Kent Graham .08 .20
239 Ray Lewis .30 .75
240 Cris Carter .20 .50
241 Elvis Grbac .12 .30
242 Eric Davis .08 .20
243 Harvey Williams .08 .20
244 Eric Allen .08 .20
245 Bryant Young .08 .20
246 Terrell Fletcher .08 .20
247 Darren Perry .08 .20
248 Ken Harvey .08 .20
249 Marvin Washington .08 .20
250 Marcus Allen .20 .50
251 Darrin Smith .08 .20
252 James Francis .08 .20
253 Michael Jackson .12 .30
254 Ryan McNeil .08 .20
255 Mark Chmura .12 .30
256 Keenan McCardell .12 .30
257 Tony Bennett .08 .20
258 Irving Spikes .08 .20
259 Jason Dunn .08 .20
260 Joey Galloway .12 .30
261 Eddie Kennison .12 .30
262 Lonnie Marts .08 .20
263 Thomas Lewis .08 .20
264 Tedy Bruschi .40 1.00
265 Steve Atwater .08 .20
266 Dorsey Levens .20 .50
267 Kurt Schulz .08 .20
268 Rob Moore .12 .30
269 Walt Harris .08 .20
270 Steve McNair .25 .60
271 Bill Romanowski .08 .20
272 Sean Dawkins .08 .20
273 Don Beebe .08 .20
274 Fernando Smith .08 .20
275 Willie McGinest .08 .20
276 Levon Kirkland .08 .20
277 Tony Martin .12 .30
278 Warren Sapp .12 .30
279 Lamar Smith .20 .50
280 Mark Brunell .25 .60
281 Jim Everett .08 .20
282 Victor Green .08 .20
283 Mike Jones .08 .20
284 Charlie Garner .12 .30
285 Karim Abdul-Jabbar .12 .30
286 Michael Westbrook .12 .30
287 Lawrence Phillips .08 .20
288 Amani Toomer .12 .30
289 Neil Smith .12 .30
290 Barry Sanders .60 1.50
291 Willie Davis .08 .20
292 Bo Orlando .08 .20
293 Alonzo Spellman .08 .20
294 Eric Hill .08 .20
295 Wesley Walls .12 .30
296 Todd Collins .08 .20
297 Stevon Moore .08 .20
298 Eric Metcalf .12 .30
299 Darren Woodson .08 .20
300 Jerry Rice .40 1.00
301 Scott Mitchell .12 .30
302 Ray Crockett .08 .20
303 Jim Schwantz UER RC .08 .20
304 Steve Tovar .08 .20
305 Terance Mathis .12 .30
306 Earnest Byner .08 .20
307 Chris Spielman .08 .20
308 Curtis Conway .12 .30
309 Cris Dishman .08 .20
310 Marvin Harrison .20 .50
311 Sam Mills .08 .20
312 Brent Alexander RC .08 .20
313 Shawn Wooden RC .08 .20
314 Dewayne Washington .08 .20
315 Terry Glenn .20 .50
316 Winfred Tubbs .08 .20
317 Dave Brown .08 .20
318 Neil O'Donnell .12 .30
319 Anthony Parker .08 .20
320 Junior Seau .20 .50
321 Brian Mitchell .08 .20
322 Regan Upshaw .08 .20
323 Darryl Williams .08 .20
324 Chris Doleman .08 .20
325 Rod Woodson .12 .30
326 Derrick Witherspoon .08 .20
327 Chester McGlockton .08 .20
328 Mickey Washington .08 .20
329 Greg Hill .08 .20
330 Reggie White .20 .50
331 John Copeland .08 .20
332 Doug Evans .08 .20
333 Lamar Lathon .08 .20
334 Mark Maddox .08 .20
335 Natrone Means .12 .30
336 Corey Widmer .08 .20
337 Terry Wooden .08 .20
338 Merton Hanks .08 .20
339 Cortez Kennedy .08 .20
340 Tyrone Hughes .08 .20
341 Tim Brown .20 .50
342 John Jurkovic .08 .20
343 Carnell Lake .08 .20
344 Stanley Richard .08 .20
345 Darryll Lewis .08 .20
346 Dan Wilkinson .08 .20
347 Broderick Thomas .08 .20
348 Brian Williams .08 .20
349 Eric Swann .08 .20
350 Dan Marino .75 2.00
351 Anthony Johnson .08 .20
352 Joe Cain .08 .20
353 Quinn Early .08 .20
354 Seth Joyner .08 .20
355 Garrison Hearst .12 .30
356 Edgar Bennett .12 .30
357 Brian Washington .08 .20
358 Kevin Hardy .08 .20
359 Quentin Coryatt .08 .20
360 Tim McDonald .08 .20
361 Brian Blades .08 .20
362 Courtney Hawkins .08 .20
363 Ray Farmer .08 .20
364 Jessie Armstead .08 .20
365 Curtis Martin .25 .60
366 Zach Thomas .20 .50
367 Frank Wycheck .12 .30
368 Darnay Scott .12 .30
369 Percy Ellsworth RC .08 .20
370 Desmond Howard .12 .30
371 Aeneas Williams .08 .20
372 Bryce Paup .08 .20
373 Michael Bates .08 .20
374 Brad Johnson .20 .50
375 Jeff Blake .12 .30
376 Donnell Woolford UER .08 .20
377 Mo Lewis .08 .20
378 Phillippi Sparks .08 .20
379 Michael Bankston .08 .20
380 LeRoy Butler .08 .20
381 Tyrone Poole .08 .20
382 Wayne Chrebet .20 .50
383 Chris Slade .08 .20
384 Checklist 1 (1-208) .08 .20
385 Checklist 2 (209-415) .08 .20
386 Will Blackwell SP RC .12 .30
387 Tom Knight SP RC .12 .30
388 Darnell Autry SP RC .20 .50
389 Bryant Westbrook SP RC .20 .50
390 David LaFleur RC SP .12 .30
391 Antowain Smith SP RC 1.00 2.50
392 Kevin Lockett SP RC .20 .50
393 Rae Carruth SP RC .12 .30
394 Renaldo Wynn SP RC .12 .30
395 Jim Druckenmiller SP RC .20 .50
396 Kenny Holmes SP RC .30 .75
397 Shawn Springs SP RC .20 .50
398 Troy Davis SP RC .20 .50
399 Dwayne Rudd SP RC .30 .75
400 Orlando Pace SP RC .30 .75
401 Byron Hanspard SP RC .20 .50
402 Corey Dillon SP RC 1.50 4.00
403 Walter Jones SP RC .50 1.25
404 Reidel Anthony SP RC .30 .75
405 Peter Boulware SP RC .30 .75
406 Reinard Wilson SP RC .30 .75
407 Pat Barnes SP RC .30 .75
408 Yatil Green SP RC .30 .75
409 Joey Kent SP RC .30 .75
410 Ike Hilliard SP RC .60 1.50
411 Jake Plummer SP RC 1.50 4.00
412 Darrell Russell SP RC .12 .30
413 James Farrior SP RC .30 .75
414 Tony Gonzalez SP RC 2.00 5.00
415 Warrick Dunn SP RC 1.25 3.00
P40 Gus Frerotte PROMO .10 .25
P170 Vinny Testaverde PROMO .10 .25
P240 Cris Carter PROMO .15 .40
P250 Marcus Allen PROMO .15 .40
P285 Karim Abdul-Jabbar PROMO .10 .25
P356 Edgar Bennett PROMO .10 .25

1997 Topps Minted in Canton

COMPLETE SET (415) 250.00 500.00
*STARS: 5X TO 12X BASIC CARDS
*RCs: 1.5X TO 3X BASIC CARDS
STATED ODDS 1:6

1997 Topps Autographs

pps randomly inserted a total of 12-signed cards for the 1997 base Topps product. This set features color player photos of 8-current NFL stars with an authentic signature on the fronts. Junior Seau was randomly seeded at the rate of 1:364 hobby and 1:100 jumbo packs, while the overall odds for all 8-cards was 1:218 hobby and 1:60 jumbo packs.

CURRENT PLAYER ODDS 1:218H,1:60J
SEAU ODDS 1:364 HOB, 1:100 JUM
1 Karim Abdul-Jabbar 10.00 25.00
2 Terrell Davis 15.00 40.00
3 Eddie George 12.50 30.00
4 Jim Harbaugh 8.00 20.00
5 Desmond Howard 8.00 20.00
6 Herman Moore 8.00 20.00
7 Junior Seau 20.00 40.00
8 Chris Warren 8.00 20.00

1997 Topps Career Best

ndomly inserted in packs at a rate of one in 16, this 5-card set features color player photos of five of the best NFL players in terms of career statistics.

COMPLETE SET (5) 15.00 40.00
1 Dan Marino 8.00 20.00
2 Marcus Allen 2.50 6.00
3 Marcus Allen 2.50 6.00
4 Reggie White 2.50 6.00
5 Jerry Rice 5.00 12.00

1997 Topps Hall Bound

ndomly inserted in hobby only packs at a rate of one in 36, and hobby jumbos at 1 in 8, this 15-card set recognizes some of the players whose game performances are Hall of Fame caliber and features embossed color player photos on die-cut mirrorboard. The backs carry player information.

COMPLETE SET (15) 40.00 100.00
STATED ODDS 1:36 HOB, 1:8 JUM
HB1 Jerry Rice 4.00 10.00
HB2 Rod Woodson 1.25 3.00
HB3 Marcus Allen 2.00 5.00
HB4 Reggie White 2.00 5.00
HB5 Emmitt Smith 6.00 15.00
HB6 Junior Seau 2.00 5.00
HB7 Troy Aikman 4.00 10.00
HB8 Bruce Smith 1.25 3.00
HB9 John Elway 8.00 20.00
HB10 Brett Favre 8.00 20.00
HB11 Thurman Thomas 2.00 5.00
HB12 Deion Sanders 2.00 5.00
HB13 Dan Marino 8.00 20.00
HB14 Steve Young 2.50 6.00
HB15 Barry Sanders 6.00 15.00

1997 Topps Hall of Fame Autographs

is set features color player photos of the 4-new entrants into the Pro Football Hall of Fame. Each card includes an authentic signature on the front and was randomly seeded into basic issue 1997 Topps packs.

HAYNES/WEBSTER ODDS 1:436H,1:120J
MARA ODDS 1:872 HOB,1:240 JUM
SHULA ODDS 1:290HOB,1:80 JUM
HF1 Mike Haynes 30.00 60.00
HF2 Don Shula 40.00 80.00
HF3 Wellington Mara 60.00 120.00
HF4 Mike Webster 100.00 200.00

1997 Topps High Octane

ndomly inserted in packs at a rate of one in 36, this 15-card set features color player photos of superstars and is printed using Uniluster technology. The backs carry player information.

COMPLETE SET (15) 40.00 100.00
STATED ODDS 1:36 HOB, 1:8 JUM
HO1 Brett Favre 8.00 20.00
HO2 Jerome Bettis 2.00 5.00
HO3 Jerry Rice 4.00 10.00
HO4 Junior Seau 2.00 5.00
HO5 Emmitt Smith 6.00 15.00
HO6 Herman Moore 1.25 3.00
HO7 Shannon Sharpe 1.25 3.00
HO8 Curtis Martin 2.50 6.00
HO9 Eddie George 2.00 5.00
HO10 Barry Sanders 6.00 15.00
HO11 John Elway 8.00 20.00
HO12 Steve Young 2.50 6.00
HO13 Drew Bledsoe 2.50 6.00
HO14 Troy Aikman 4.00 10.00
HO15 Dan Marino 8.00 20.00

1997 Topps Mystery Finest Bronze

is 20-card insert set features color player photos of Pro Bowl players covered by a solid black coating to hide the player's identity. The Bronze version (1:36 packs) is the most common and features the player in his team's away jersey printed with bronze foil highlights. The Silver (home jersey, 1:108 packs) and Gold (Pro Bowl jersey, 1:324 packs) parallels are distinguished by the use of the different foil color and jersey. Refractor versions of each of the three colors were also produced and inserted as follows: Bronze (1:144 packs), Silver (1:432 packs), and Gold (1:1296 packs).

COMPLETE SET (20) 25.00 60.00
*SINGLES: 2.5X TO 6X BASE CARD HI
BRONZE STATED ODDS 1:36 HOB, 1:8 JUM
*BRONZE REF: 1.2X TO 3X BASIC INSERTS
BRONZE REF.ODDS 1:144 HOB, 1:38 JUM
*GOLDS: 1.5X TO 4X BASIC INSERTS
GOLD STATED ODDS 1:324 HOB, 1:88 JUM
*GOLD REF: 5X TO 12 BASIC INSERTS
GOLD REF.ODDS 1:1296 HOB, 1:354 JUM
COMP.SILVER SET (20) 75.00 150.00
*SILVERS: .6X TO 1.5X BASIC INSERTS
SILVER STATED ODDS 1:108 HOB, 1:28 JUM
COMP.SILVER REF (20) 200.00 400.00
*SILVER REF: 2X TO 5X BASIC INSERTS
SILVER REF.ODDS 1:432 HOB, 1:116 JUM
M1 Barry Sanders 4.00 10.00
M2 Mark Brunell 1.50 4.00
M3 Terrell Davis 1.50 4.00
M4 Isaac Bruce 1.25 3.00
M5 Jerry Rice 2.50 6.00
M6 Drew Bledsoe 1.50 4.00
M7 Carl Pickens .75 2.00
M8 Steve Young 1.50 4.00
M9 Cris Carter 1.25 3.00
M10 John Elway 5.00 12.00
M11 Junior Seau 1.25 3.00
M12 Herman Moore .75 2.00
M13 Vinny Testaverde .75 2.00
M14 Jerome Bettis 1.25 3.00
M15 Troy Aikman 2.50 6.00
M16 Reggie White 1.25 3.00
M17 Kerry Collins 1.25 3.00
M18 Curtis Martin 1.50 4.00
M19 Shannon Sharpe .75 2.00
M20 Brett Favre 2.50 6.00

1997 Topps Season's Best

ndomly inserted in packs at a rate of one in 16, this 25-card set features color player photos of the best players in five different categories: rushing leaders, passing experts, receiving specialists, sack masters, and all-purpose yardage gainers. The backs carry player information. The set is divided into the following subsets: Air Command (1-5), Thunder and Lightning (6-10), Magicians (11-15), Demolition Men (16-20), Special Delivery (21-25).

COMPLETE SET (25) 25.00 60.00
STATED ODDS: 1:16 HOB, 1:4 JUM
1 Mark Brunell 1.50 4.00
2 Vinny Testaverde .75 2.00
3 Drew Bledsoe 1.50 4.00
4 Brett Favre 5.00 12.00
5 Jeff Blake .75 2.00
6 Barry Sanders 4.00 10.00
7 Terrell Davis 1.50 4.00
8 Jerome Bettis 1.25 3.00
9 Ricky Watters .75 2.00
10 Eddie George 1.25 3.00
11 Brian Mitchell .50 1.25
12 Tyrone Hughes .50 1.25
13 Eric Metcalf .75 2.00
14 Glyn Milburn .50 1.25
15 Ricky Watters .75 2.00
16 Kevin Greene .75 2.00
17 Lamar Lathon .50 1.25
18 Bruce Smith .75 2.00
19 Michael Sinclair UER .50 1.25
20 Derrick Thomas 1.25 3.00
21 Jerry Rice 2.50 6.00
22 Herman Moore .75 2.00
23 Carl Pickens .75 2.00
24 Cris Carter 1.25 3.00
25 Brett Perriman .50 1.25

1997 Topps Underclassmen

Randomly inserted in retail only packs at a rate of one in 24, this 10-card set features color player photos of some of the best second- and third-year players. The cards were printed on shimmering, diffraction foil-stamped mirrorboard.

COMPLETE SET (10) 15.00 40.00
STATED ODDS: 1:24 RET
U1 Kerry Collins 2.50 6.00
U2 Karim Abdul-Jabbar 1.50 4.00
U3 Simeon Rice 1.50 4.00
U4 Keyshawn Johnson 2.50 6.00
U5 Eddie George 2.50 6.00
U6 Eddie Kennison 1.50 4.00
U7 Terry Glenn 2.50 6.00
U8 Kevin Hardy 1.00 2.50
U9 Steve McNair 3.00 8.00
U10 Kordell Stewart 2.50 6.00

1997 Topps Hall of Fame Class of 1997

This five-card set was distributed at the 1997 induction ceremonies for the Pro Football Hall of Fame. Along with the set, two 1997 Topps promo cards were also distributed. Each card includes a photo of a 1997 inductee printed in the style of a Topps card from the past. A gold foil "Class of '97" logo is featured on the cardfronts and the Hall of Fame is pictured on the cardbacks. Versions of the cards were later included as signed inserts in Topps packs and unsigned inserts in Topps factory sets.

COMPLETE SET (5) 2.00 5.00
1 Mike Haynes .40 1.00
2 Don Shula .60 1.50
3 Wellington Mara .40 1.00
4 Mike Webster .40 1.00
NNO Header Card .40 1.00

1998 Topps Promos

This set of six cards was released to preview the upcoming regular issue Topps football set for 1998. Each card closely resembles its base set counterpart and can be differentiated by the unique card number.

COMPLETE SET (6) 4.00 10.00

PP1 Mike Alstott .30 .75
PP2 Eddie George .50 1.25
PP3 Brett Favre 1.20 3.00
PP4 Terrell Davis 1.00 2.50
PP5 Dan Marino 1.20 3.00
PP6 Junior Seau .20 .50

1998 Topps

e 1998 Topps series one was issued with a total of 360 standard size cards. The 11-card packs retail for $1.29 each. The fronts feature color game-action photography on 16 point stock. The backs carry complete career statistics and insightful text on the pictured player. The factory sets contained five assorted insert sets (not including the Giants Owner promo card).

COMPLETE SET (360) 30.00 60.00
COMP. FACT.SET (365) 40.00 80.00
1 Barry Sanders .60 1.50
2 Derrick Rodgers .07 .20
3 Chris Calloway .07 .20
4 Bruce Armstrong .07 .20
5 Horace Copeland .07 .20
6 Chad Brown .07 .20
7 Ken Harvey .07 .20
8 Levon Kirkland .07 .20
9 Glenn Foley .12 .30
10 Corey Dillon .20 .50
11 Sean Dawkins .07 .20
12 Curtis Conway .12 .30
13 Chris Chandler .12 .30
14 Kerry Collins .12 .30
15 Jonathan Ogden .07 .20
16 Sam Shade .07 .20
17 Vaughn Hebron .07 .20
18 Quentin Coryatt .07 .20
19 Jerris McPhail .07 .20
20 Warrick Dunn .20 .50
21 Wayne Martin .07 .20
22 Chad Lewis .10 .30
23 Danny Kanell .10 .30
24 Shawn Springs .07 .20
25 Emmitt Smith .60 1.50
26 Todd Lyght .07 .20
27 Donnie Edwards .07 .20
28 Charlie Jones .07 .20
29 Willie McGinest .07 .20
30 Steve Young .25 .60
31 Darrell Russell .07 .20
32 Gary Anderson .07 .20
33 Stanley Richard .07 .20
34 Leslie O'Neal .07 .20
35 Dermontti Dawson .15 .40
36 Jeff Brady .07 .20
37 Kimble Anders .10 .30
38 Glyn Milburn .07 .20
39 Greg Hill .07 .20
40 Freddie Jones .07 .20
41 Bobby Engram .12 .30
42 Aeneas Williams .07 .20
43 Antowain Smith .20 .50
44 Reggie White .20 .50
45 Rae Carruth .08 .20
46 Leon Johnson .07 .20
47 Bryant Young .07 .20
48 Jamie Asher .07 .20
49 Hardy Nickerson .07 .20
50 Jerome Bettis .20 .50
51 Michael Strahan .12 .30
52 John Randle .12 .30
53 Kevin Hardy .07 .20
54 Eric Bjornson .07 .20
55 Morten Andersen UER .08 .20
56 Larry Centers .07 .20
57 Bryce Paup .07 .20
58 John Mobley .07 .20
59 Michael Bates .08 .20
60 Tim Brown .20 .50
61 Doug Evans .07 .20
62 Will Shields .08 .20
63 Jeff Graham .07 .20
64 Tony Martin UER .07 .20
65 Steve Broussard .08 .20
66 Blaine Bishop .07 .20
67 Ernie Conwell .07 .20
68 Heath Shuler .07 .20
69 Eric Metcalf .07 .20
70 Terry Glenn .20 .50
71 James Hasty .07 .20
72 Robert Porcher .07 .20
73 Keenan McCardell .12 .30
74 Tyrone Hughes .07 .20
75 Troy Aikman .40 1.00
76 Peter Boulware .07 .20
77 Rob Johnson .10 .30
78 Erik Kramer .07 .20
79 Kevin Smith .07 .20
80 Andre Rison .12 .30
81 Jim Harbaugh .12 .30
82 Chris Hudson .07 .20
83 Ray Zellars .07 .20
84 Jeff George .12 .30
85 Willie Davis .07 .20
86 Jason Gildon .07 .20
87 Robert Brooks .12 .30
88 Chad Cota .07 .20
89 Simeon Rice .12 .30
90 Mark Brunell .20 .50
91 Jay Graham .07 .20
92 Scott Greene .07 .20
93 Jeff Blake .12 .30
94 Jason Belser .07 .20
95 Derrick Alexander DE .07 .20
96 Ty Law .12 .30
97 Charles Johnson .07 .20
98 James Jett .12 .30
99 Darrell Green .12 .30
100 Brett Favre .75 2.00
101 George Jones .07 .20
102 Derrick Mason .12 .30
103 Sam Adams .07 .20
104 Lawrence Phillips .07 .20
105 Randal Hill .07 .20
106 John Mangum .07 .20
107 Natrone Means .12 .30
108 Bill Romanowski .07 .20
109 Terance Mathis .12 .30
110 Bruce Smith .12 .30
111 Pete Mitchell .07 .20
112 Duane Clemons .07 .20
113 Willie Clay .07 .20
114 Eric Allen .07 .20
115 Troy Drayton .07 .20
116 Derrick Thomas .20 .50
117 Charles Way .07 .20
118 Wayne Chrebet .20 .50
119 Bobby Hoying .12 .30
120 Michael Jackson .07 .20
121 Gary Zimmerman .07 .20
122 Yancey Thigpen .07 .20
123 Dana Stubblefield .07 .20
124 Keith Lyle .07 .20
125 Marco Coleman .07 .20
126 Karl Williams .07 .20
127 Stephen Davis .07 .20
128 Chris Sanders .07 .20
129 Cris Dishman .07 .20
130 Jake Plummer .20 .50
131 Darryl Williams .07 .20
132 Merton Hanks .07 .20
133 Torrance Small .07 .20
134 Aaron Glenn .07 .20
135 Chester McGlockton .07 .20
136 William Thomas .07 .20
137 Kordell Stewart .20 .50
138 Jason Taylor .12 .30
139 Lake Dawson .07 .20
140 Carl Pickens .12 .30
141 Eugene Robinson .07 .20
142 Ed McCaffrey .12 .30
143 Lamar Lathon .07 .20
144 Ray Buchanan .07 .20
145 Thurman Thomas .20 .50
146 Andre Reed .12 .30
147 Wesley Walls .12 .30
148 Rob Moore .12 .30
149 Darren Woodson .07 .20
150 Eddie George .20 .50
151 Michael Irvin .20 .50
152 Johnnie Morton .12 .30
153 Ken Dilger .07 .20
154 Tony Boselli .07 .20
155 Randall McDaniel .07 .20
156 Mark Fields .07 .20
157 Phillippi Sparks .07 .20
158 Troy Davis .07 .20
159 Troy Vincent .07 .20
160 Cris Carter .20 .50
161 Amp Lee .07 .20
162 Will Blackwell .07 .20
163 Chad Scott .07 .20
164 Henry Ellard .12 .30
165 Robert Jones .07 .20
166 Garrison Hearst .20 .50
167 James McKnight .20 .50
168 Rodney Harrison .12 .30
169 Adrian Murrell .12 .30
170 Rod Smith WR .12 .30
171 Desmond Howard .12 .30
172 Ben Coates .12 .30
173 David Palmer .07 .20
174 Zach Thomas .20 .50
175 Dale Carter .07 .20
176 Mark Chmura .12 .30
177 Elvis Grbac .12 .30
178 Jason Hanson .07 .20
179 Walt Harris .07 .20
180 Ricky Watters .12 .30
181 Ray Lewis .20 .50
182 Lonnie Johnson .07 .20
183 Marvin Harrison .20 .50
184 Dorsey Levens .20 .50
185 Tony Gonzalez .20 .50
186 Andre Hastings .07 .20
187 Kevin Turner .07 .20
188 Mo Lewis .07 .20
189 Jason Sehorn .12 .30
190 Drew Bledsoe .30 .75
191 Michael Sinclair .07 .20
192 William Floyd .07 .20
193 Kenny Holmes .07 .20
194 Marvcus Patton .07 .20
195 Warren Sapp .12 .30
196 Junior Seau .20 .50
197 Ryan McNeil .07 .20
198 Tyrone Wheatley .12 .30
199 Robert Smith .20 .50
200 Terrell Davis .20 .50
201 Brett Perriman .07 .20
202 Tamarick Vanover .07 .20
203 Stephen Boyd .07 .20
204 Zack Crockett .07 .20
205 Sherman Williams .07 .20
206 Neil Smith .12 .30
207 Jermaine Lewis .12 .30
208 Kevin Williams .07 .20
209 Byron Hanspard .07 .20
210 Warren Moon .20 .50
211 Tony McGee .07 .20
212 Raymont Harris .07 .20
213 Eric Davis .07 .20
214 Darrien Gordon .07 .20
215 James Stewart .12 .30
216 Derrick Mayes .12 .30
217 Brad Johnson .20 .50
218 Karim Abdul-Jabbar UER .20 .50
219 Hugh Douglas .07 .20
220 Terry Allen .20 .50
221 Rhett Hall .07 .20
222 Terrell Fletcher .07 .20
223 Carnell Lake .07 .20
224 Darryll Lewis .07 .20
225 Chris Slade .07 .20
226 Michael Westbrook .12 .30
227 Willie Williams .07 .20
228 Tony Banks .12 .30
229 Keyshawn Johnson .20 .50
230 Mike Alstott .20 .50
231 Tiki Barber .20 .50
232 Jake Reed .12 .30
233 Eric Swann .07 .20
234 Eric Moulds .20 .50
235 Vinny Testaverde .12 .30
236 Jessie Tuggle .07 .20
237 Ryan Wetnight RC .07 .20
238 Tyrone Poole .07 .20
239 Bryant Westbrook .07 .20
240 Steve McNair .20 .50
241 Jimmy Smith .12 .30
242 Dewayne Washington .07 .20
243 Robert Harris .07 .20
244 Rod Woodson .12 .30
245 Reidel Anthony .12 .30
246 Jessie Armstead .07 .20
247 O.J. McDuffie .12 .30
248 Carlton Gray .07 .20
249 LeRoy Butler .07 .20
250 Jerry Rice .40 1.00
251 Frank Sanders .12 .30
252 Todd Collins .07 .20
253 Fred Lane .07 .20
254 David Dunn .07 .20
255 Micheal Barrow .07 .20
256 Luther Elliss .07 .20
257 Scott Mitchell .12 .30
258 Dave Meggett .07 .20
259 Rickey Dudley .07 .20
260 Isaac Bruce .20 .50
261 Henry Jones UER .12 .30
262 Leslie Shepherd .07 .20
263 Derrick Brooks .20 .50
264 Greg Lloyd .07 .20
265 Terrell Buckley .07 .20
266 Antonio Freeman .20 .50
267 Tony Brackens .07 .20
268 Mark McMillian .07 .20
269 Dexter Coakley .07 .20
270 Dan Marino .75 2.00
271 Bryan Cox .07 .20
272 Leeland McElroy .07 .20
273 Jeff Burris .07 .20
274 Eric Green .07 .20
275 Darnay Scott .12 .30
276 Greg Clark .07 .20
277 Mario Bates .12 .30
278 Eric Turner .07 .20
279 Neil O'Donnell .12 .30
280 Herman Moore .12 .30
281 Gary Brown .07 .20
282 Terrell Owens .20 .50
283 Frank Wycheck .07 .20
284 Trent Dilfer .20 .50
285 Curtis Martin .20 .50
286 Ricky Proehl .07 .20
287 Steve Atwater .07 .20
288 Aaron Bailey .07 .20
289 William Henderson .12 .30
290 Marcus Allen .20 .50
291 Tom Knight .07 .20
292 Quinn Early .07 .20
293 Michael McCrary .07 .20
294 Bert Emanuel .12 .30
295 Tom Carter .07 .20
296 Kevin Glover .07 .20
297 Marshall Faulk .25 .60
298 Harvey Williams .07 .20
299 Chris Warren .12 .30
300 John Elway .75 2.00
301 Eddie Kennison .12 .30
302 Gus Frerotte .07 .20
303 Regan Upshaw .07 .20
304 Kevin Gogan .07 .20
305 Napoleon Kaufman .20 .50
306 Charlie Garner .12 .30
307 Shawn Jefferson .07 .20
308 Tommy Vardell .07 .20
309 Mike Hollis .07 .20
310 Irving Fryar .12 .30
311 Shannon Sharpe .12 .30
312 Byron Bam Morris .07 .20
313 Jamal Anderson .20 .50
314 Chris Gedney .07 .20
315 Chris Spielman .07 .20
316 Derrick Alexander WR .12 .30
317 O.J. Santiago .08 .20
318 Anthony Miller .07 .20
319 Ki-Jana Carter .07 .20
320 Deion Sanders .20 .50
321 Joey Galloway .12 .30
322 J.J. Stokes .12 .30
323 Rodney Thomas .08 .20
324 John Lynch .12 .30
325 Mike Pritchard .08 .20
326 Terrance Shaw .08 .20
327 Ted Johnson .08 .20
328 Ashley Ambrose .08 .20
329 Checklist 1 .08 .20
330 Checklist 2 .08 .20
331 Jerome Pathon RC 1.00 2.50
332 Ryan Leaf RC 1.00 2.00
333 Duane Starks RC .50 1.25
334 Brian Simmons RC .75 2.00
335 Keith Brooking RC 1.00 2.50
336 Robert Edwards RC .75 2.00
337 Curtis Enis RC .50 1.25
338 John Avery RC .75 2.00
339 Fred Taylor RC 1.50 4.00
340 Germane Crowell RC .75 2.00
341 Hines Ward RC 4.00 10.00
342 Marcus Nash RC .50 1.25
343 Jacquez Green RC .75 2.00
344 Joe Jurevicius RC 1.00 2.50
345 Greg Ellis RC .50 1.25
346 Brian Griese RC 1.50 4.00
347 Tavian Banks RC .75 2.00
348 Robert Holcombe RC .75 2.00
349 Skip Hicks RC .75 1.25
350 Ahman Green RC 2.00 5.00
351 Takeo Spikes RC 1.00 2.50
352 Randy Moss RC 4.00 10.00
353 Andre Wadsworth RC .75 2.00
354 Jason Peter RC .50 1.25
355 Grant Wistrom RC .75 2.00
356 Charles Woodson RC 2.00 5.00
357 Kevin Dyson RC 1.00 2.50
358 Pat Johnson RC .75 2.00
359 Tim Dwight RC 1.00 2.50
360 Peyton Manning RC 8.00 20.00
P1 Robert Tisch 2.00 5.00

1998 Topps Autographs

Randomly inserted into hobby packs only at the rate of one in 260, this 15-card set features color player photos with the player's signature on the front. The Peyton Manning card was printed with either gold or bronze foil highlights on the front.

STATED ODDS 1:260 HOBBY
A1 Randy Moss 100.00 200.00
A2 Mike Alstott 10.00 25.00
A3 Jake Plummer 10.00 25.00
A4 Corey Dillon 5.00 12.00
A5 Kordell Stewart 10.00 25.00
A6 Eddie George 10.00 25.00
A7 Jason Sehorn 8.00 20.00
A8 Joey Galloway 8.00 20.00
A9 Ryan Leaf 6.00 15.00
A10B Peyton Manning Brnz 400.00 600.00
A10G Peyton Manning Gold 400.00 600.00
A11 Dwight Stephenson 15.00 40.00
A12 Anthony Munoz 15.00 40.00
A13 Mike Singletary 20.00 50.00
A14 Tommy McDonald 15.00 40.00
A15 Paul Krause 15.00 40.00

1998 Topps Generation 2000

ndomly inserted in packs at a rate of one in 18, this 15-card set features color action photos of top young players who are destined to leave a lasting impression on the field. The backs carry player information.

COMPLETE SET (15) 25.00 50.00
STATED ODDS 1:18H/R, 1:12RET.JUM.
GE1 Warrick Dunn 1.50 4.00
GE2 Tony Gonzalez 1.50 4.00
GE3 Corey Dillon 1.50 4.00
GE4 Antowain Smith 1.50 4.00
GE5 Mike Alstott 1.50 4.00
GE6 Kordell Stewart 1.50 4.00
GE7 Peter Boulware .60 1.50
GE8 Jake Plummer 1.50 4.00
GE9 Tiki Barber 1.50 4.00
GE10 Terrell Davis 1.50 4.00
GE11 Steve McNair 1.50 4.00
GE12 Curtis Martin 1.50 4.00
GE13 Napoleon Kaufman 1.50 4.00
GE14 Terrell Owens 1.50 4.00
GE15 Eddie George 1.50 4.00

1998 Topps Gridiron Gods

Randomly inserted in hobby packs at the rate of one in 36, this 15-card hobby exclusive set features color action photos of top players printed on cards with celestial uniluster technology.

COMPLETE SET (15) 40.00 80.00
STATED ODDS 1:36 HOBBY
G1 Barry Sanders 5.00 12.00
G2 Jerry Rice 3.00 8.00
G3 Herman Moore 1.00 2.50
G4 Drew Bledsoe 2.50 6.00
G5 Kordell Stewart 1.50 4.00
G6 Tim Brown 1.50 4.00
G7 Eddie George 1.50 4.00
G8 Dorsey Levens 1.50 4.00
G9 Warrick Dunn 1.50 4.00
G10 Brett Favre 6.00 15.00
G11 Terrell Davis 1.50 4.00
G12 Steve Young 2.00 5.00
G13 Jerome Bettis 1.50 4.00
G14 Mark Brunell 1.50 4.00
G15 John Elway 6.00 15.00

1998 Topps Hidden Gems

Randomly inserted in retail packs at a rate of one in 12, this 15-card retail-exclusive set features color action photos of top performers who have taken the game not only by surprise but by storm. The backs carry player information.

COMPLETE SET (15) 7.50 20.00
STATED ODDS 1:12RET,1:8RET.JUMBO
HG1 Andre Reed .40 1.00
HG2 Kevin Greene .40 1.00
HG3 Tony Martin .40 1.00
HG4 Shannon Sharpe .40 1.00
HG5 Terry Allen .60 1.50
HG6 Brett Favre 2.50 6.00
HG7 Ben Coates .40 1.00
HG8 Michael Sinclair .25 .60
HG9 Keenan McCardell .40 1.00
HG10 Brad Johnson .60 1.50
HG11 Mark Brunell .60 1.50
HG12 Dorsey Levens .60 1.50
HG13 Terrell Davis .60 1.50
HG14 Curtis Martin .60 1.50
HG15 Derrick Rodgers .25 .60

1998 Topps Measures of Greatness

Randomly inserted in packs at a rate of one in 36, this 15-card set features color player photos printed with Topps' micro dyna-etch technology.

COMPLETE SET (15) 40.00 80.00
STATED ODDS 1:36H/R, 1:24RET.JUM.
MG1 John Elway 6.00 15.00
MG2 Marcus Allen 1.50 4.00
MG3 Jerry Rice 3.00 8.00
MG4 Tim Brown 1.50 4.00
MG5 Warren Moon 1.50 4.00
MG6 Bruce Smith 1.00 2.50
MG7 Troy Aikman 3.00 8.00
MG8 Reggie White 1.50 4.00
MG9 Irving Fryar 1.00 2.50
MG10 Barry Sanders 5.00 12.00
MG11 Cris Carter 1.50 4.00
MG12 Emmitt Smith 5.00 12.00
MG13 Dan Marino 6.00 15.00
MG14 Rod Woodson 1.00 2.50
MG15 Brett Favre 6.00 15.00

1998 Topps Mystery Finest

Randomly inserted in packs at a rate of one in 36, this 20-card insert set remains a mystery until a player is revealed when the opaque black protector is peeled back. A Refractor parallel version was also produced and seeded in packs at the rate of 1:144.

COMPLETE SET (20) 75.00 150.00
STATED ODDS 1:36H/R, 1:24 RET.JUM.
*REFRACTORS: .8X TO 2X BASIC INSERTS
REFRACTOR STATED ODDS 1:144
M1 Steve Young 2.50 6.00
M2 Dan Marino 8.00 20.00
M3 Brett Favre 8.00 20.00
M4 Drew Bledsoe 3.00 8.00
M5 Mark Brunell 2.00 5.00
M6 Troy Aikman 4.00 10.00
M7 Kordell Stewart 2.00 5.00
M8 John Elway 5.00 12.00
M9 Barry Sanders 6.00 15.00
M10 Jerome Bettis 2.00 5.00
M11 Eddie George 2.00 5.00
M12 Emmitt Smith 6.00 15.00
M13 Curtis Martin 2.00 5.00
M14 Warrick Dunn 2.00 5.00
M15 Dorsey Levens 2.00 5.00
M16 Terrell Davis 2.00 5.00
M17 Herman Moore 1.25 3.00
M18 Jerry Rice 4.00 10.00
M19 Tim Brown 2.00 5.00
M20 Yancey Thigpen .75 2.00

1998 Topps Season's Best

Randomly inserted in packs at a rate of one in 12, this 30-card insert set was printed on prismatic foilboard. The set features statistical leaders in five categories: Power & Speed (1-5) are the rushing leaders, Gunslingers (6-10) are the passing experts, Prime Targets (11-15) are the receiving leaders, Heavy Hitters (16-20) are the sack leaders, and Quick Six (21-25) are the leaders in yards gained. In addition, there are five Career Best cards for each category.

COMPLETE SET (30) 30.00 60.00
STATED ODDS 1:12
1 Terrell Davis 1.00 2.50
2 Barry Sanders 3.00 8.00
3 Jerome Bettis 1.00 2.50
4 Dorsey Levens 1.00 2.50
5 Eddie George 1.00 2.50
6 Brett Favre 4.00 10.00
7 Mark Brunell 1.00 2.50
8 Jeff George .60 1.50
9 Steve Young 1.25 3.00
10 John Elway 4.00 10.00
11 Herman Moore .60 1.50
12 Rob Moore .60 1.50
13 Yancey Thigpen .40 1.00
14 Cris Carter 1.00 2.50
15 Tim Brown 1.00 2.50
16 Bruce Smith .60 1.50
17 Michael Sinclair .40 1.00
18 John Randle .60 1.50
19 Dana Stubblefield .40 1.00
20 Michael Strahan .60 1.50
21 Tamarick Vanover .40 1.00
22 Darrien Gordon .40 1.00
23 Michael Bates .40 1.00
24 David Meggett .40 1.00
25 Jermaine Lewis .60 1.50
26 Terrell Davis 1.00 2.50
27 Jerry Rice 2.00 5.00
28 Barry Sanders 3.00 8.00
29 John Randle .60 1.50
30 John Elway 4.00 10.00

1998 Topps Hall of Fame

This set was distributed at the Pro Football Hall of Fame in Canton, Ohio. Each card includes a photo of a 1998 inductee with a green colored border. The set is identical to the "Class of 98" version except for the lack of the gold foil logo on the cardfronts and the re-numbering.

COMPLETE SET (5) 4.00 10.00
11 Dwight Stephenson .75 2.00
12 Anthony Munoz 1.25 3.00
13 Mike Singletary 1.25 3.00
14 Tommy McDonald .75 2.00
15 Paul Krause .75 2.00

1998 Topps Hall of Fame Class of 1998

This set was distributed at the 1998 induction ceremonies for the Pro Football Hall of Fame. Along with the set, two 1998 Topps base cards were also distributed. Each card includes a photo of a 1998 inductee with a green colored border. A gold foil "Class of '98" logo is featured on the cardfronts and the Hall of Fame is pictured on the cardbacks.

COMPLETE SET (6) 4.00 10.00
HOF1 Dwight Stephenson 1.00 2.50
HOF2 Anthony Munoz 1.00 2.50
HOF3 Mike Singletary 1.25 3.00
HOF4 Tommy McDonald .75 2.00
HOF5 Paul Krause .75 2.00
NNO Cover Card .08 .25

1999 Topps Promos

This 6-card set was released at various Topps sponsored events and throuhg its dealer network to promote the 1999 football release. The cards look very similar to the base set except for the card numbering scheme.

COMPLETE SET (6) 2.00 5.00
PP1 Jamal Anderson .20 .50
PP2 Peyton Manning 1.60 4.00
PP3 Keenan McCardell .10 .30
PP4 Aeneas Williams .07 .20
PP5 Antowain Smith .20 .50
PP6 Andre Rison .10 .30

1999 Topps

e 1999 Topps set was issued in one series for a total of 357 cards. The set features color action player photos printed on 16 pt. stock. The set contains the 10-card Season Highlights subset plus five cards showcasing five of the players selected in the Cleveland Browns Expansion Draft. Also included in the set were 27 cards of the 1999 NFL Draft Picks. The backs carry player information and career statistics.

COMPLETE SET (357) 20.00 50.00
COMP.SET w/o SP's (330) 10.00 20.00
1 Terrell Davis .20 .50
2 Adrian Murrell .15 .40
3 Ernie Mills .15 .40
4 Jimmy Hitchcock .15 .40
5 Charlie Garner .20 .50
6 Blaine Bishop .15 .40
7 Junior Seau .20 .50
8 Andre Rison .20 .50
9 Jake Reed .20 .50
10 Cris Carter .25 .60
11 Torrance Small .15 .40
12 Ronald McKinnon .15 .40
13 Tyrone Davis .15 .40
14 Warren Moon .25 .60
15 Joe Johnson .15 .40
16 Bert Emanuel .20 .50
17 Brad Culpepper .15 .40
18 Henry Jones .15 .40
19 Jonathan Ogden .20 .50
20 Terrell Owens .20 .50
21 Derrick Mason .15 .40
22 Jon Ritchie .15 .40
23 Eric Metcalf .15 .40
24 Kevin Carter .15 .40
25 Fred Taylor .15 .40
26 DeWayne Washington .15 .40
27 William Thomas .15 .40
28 Rocket Ismail .20 .50
29 Jason Taylor .20 .50
30 Doug Flutie .25 .60
31 Michael Sinclair .15 .40
32 Yancey Thigpen .15 .40
33 Darnay Scott .15 .40
34 Amani Toomer .15 .40
35 Edgar Bennett .20 .50
36 LeRoy Butler .20 .50
37 Jessie Tuggle .15 .40
38 Andrew Glover .15 .40
39 Tim McDonald .15 .40
40 Marshall Faulk .20 .50
41 Ray Mickens .15 .40
42 Kimble Anders .15 .40
43 Trent Green .15 .40
44 Dermontti Dawson .20 .50
45 Greg Ellis .15 .40
46 Hugh Douglas .20 .50
47 Amp Lee .15 .40
48 Lamar Thomas .15 .40
49 Curtis Conway .20 .50
50 Emmitt Smith .40 1.00
51 Elvis Grbac .15 .40
52 Tony Simmons .15 .40
53 Darrin Smith .15 .40
54 Donovin Darius .15 .40
55 Corey Chavous .15 .40
56 Phillippi Sparks .15 .40
57 Luther Elliss .15 .40
58 Tim Dwight .20 .50
59 Andre Hastings .15 .40
60 Dan Marino .50 1.25
61 Micheal Barrow .15 .40
62 Corey Fuller .15 .40
63 Bill Romanowski .20 .50
64 Derrick Rodgers .15 .40
65 Natrone Means .20 .50
66 Peter Boulware .15 .40
67 Brian Mitchell .20 .50
68 Cornelius Bennett .20 .50
69 Dedric Ward .15 .40
70 Drew Bledsoe .20 .50
71 Freddie Jones .15 .40
72 Derrick Thomas .25 .60
73 Willie Davis .15 .40
74 Larry Centers .15 .40
75 Mark Brunell .20 .50
76 Chuck Smith .15 .40
77 Desmond Howard .20 .50
78 Sedrick Shaw .15 .40
79 Tiki Barber .20 .50
80 Curtis Martin .20 .50
81 Barry Minter .15 .40
82 Skip Hicks .15 .40
83 O.J. Santiago .15 .40
84 Ed McCaffrey .20 .50
85 Terrell Buckley .20 .50
86 Charlie Jones .15 .40
87 Pete Mitchell .15 .40
88 La'Roi Glover RC .25 .60
89 Eric Davis .15 .40
90 John Elway .40 1.00
91 Kavika Pittman .15 .40
92 Fred Lane .15 .40
93 Warren Sapp .20 .50
94 Lorenzo Bromell RC .15 .40
95 Lawyer Milloy .15 .40
96 Aeneas Williams .15 .40
97 Michael McCrary .15 .40
98 Rickey Dudley .15 .40
99 Bryce Paup .15 .40
100 Jamal Anderson .20 .50
101 D'Marco Farr .15 .40
102 Johnnie Morton .20 .50
103 Jeff Graham .15 .40
104 Sam Cowart .15 .40
105 Bryant Young .20 .50
106 Jermaine Lewis .15 .40
107 Chad Bratzke .15 .40
108 Jeff Burris .15 .40
109 Roell Preston .15 .40
110 Vinny Testaverde .15 .40
111 Ruben Brown .15 .40
112 Darryll Lewis .15 .40
113 Billy Davis .15 .40
114 Bryant Westbrook .15 .40
115 Stephen Alexander .15 .40
116 Terrell Fletcher .15 .40
117 Terry Glenn .20 .50
118 Rod Smith .20 .50
119 Carl Pickens .20 .50
120 Tim Brown .25 .60
121 Mikhael Ricks .15 .40
122 Jason Gildon .20 .50
123 Charles Way .15 .40
124 Rob Moore .15 .40
125 Jerome Bettis .25 .60
126 Kerry Collins .15 .40
127 Bruce Smith .20 .50
128 James Hasty .15 .40
129 Ken Norton Jr. .15 .40
130 Charles Woodson .25 .60
131 Tony McGee .15 .40
132 Kevin Turner .15 .40
133 Jerome Pathon .15 .40
134 Garrison Hearst .15 .40
135 Craig Newsome .15 .40
136 Hardy Nickerson .15 .40
137 Ray Lewis .25 .60
138 Derrick Alexander .15 .40
139 Phil Hansen .15 .40
140 Joey Galloway .20 .50
141 Oronde Gadsden .15 .40
142 Herman Moore .20 .50
143 Bobby Taylor .20 .50
144 Mario Bates .15 .40
145 Kevin Dyson .15 .40
146 Aaron Glenn .15 .40
147 Ed McDaniel .15 .40
148 Terry Allen .20 .50
149 Ike Hilliard .15 .40
150 Steve Young .30 .75
151 Eugene Robinson .20 .50
152 John Mobley .15 .40
153 Kevin Hardy .15 .40
154 Lance Johnstone .15 .40
155 Willie McGinest .20 .50
156 Gary Anderson .15 .40
157 Dexter Coakley .15 .40
158 Mark Fields .15 .40
159 Steve McNair .20 .50
160 Corey Dillon .15 .40
161 Zach Thomas .20 .50
162 Kent Graham .15 .40
163 Tony Parrish .15 .40
164 Sam Gash .15 .40
165 Kyle Brady .15 .40
166 Donnell Bennett .15 .40
167 Tony Martin .20 .50
168 Michael Bates .15 .40
169 Bobby Engram .15 .40
170 Jimmy Smith .20 .50
171 Vonnie Holliday .15 .40
172 Simeon Rice .15 .40
173 Kevin Greene .25 .60
174 Mike Alstott .15 .40
175 Eddie George .20 .50
176 Michael Jackson .15 .40
177 Neil O'Donnell .20 .50
178 Sean Dawkins .15 .40
179 Courtney Hawkins .15 .40
180 Michael Irvin .25 .60
181 Thurman Thomas .20 .50
182 Cam Cleeland .15 .40
183 Ellis Johnson .15 .40
184 Will Blackwell .15 .40
185 Ty Law .25 .60
186 Merton Hanks .15 .40
187 Dan Wilkinson .20 .50
188 Andre Wadsworth .15 .40
189 Troy Vincent .15 .40
190 Frank Sanders .15 .40
191 Stephen Boyd .15 .40
192 Jason Elam .15 .40
193 Kordell Stewart .15 .40
194 Ted Johnson .15 .40
195 Glyn Milburn .15 .40
196 Gary Brown .15 .40
197 Travis Hall .15 .40
198 John Randle .25 .60
199 Jay Riemersma .15 .40
200 Barry Sanders .40 1.00
201 Chris Spielman .20 .50
202 Rod Woodson .25 .60
203 Darrell Russell .15 .40
204 Tony Boselli .20 .50
205 Darren Woodson .20 .50
206 Muhsin Muhammad .15 .40
207 Jim Harbaugh .20 .50
208 Isaac Bruce .25 .60
209 Mo Lewis .15 .40
210 Dorsey Levens .20 .50
211 Frank Wycheck .20 .50
212 Napoleon Kaufman .15 .40
213 Walt Harris .15 .40
214 Leon Lett .15 .40
215 Karim Abdul-Jabbar .15 .40
216 Carnell Lake .20 .50
217 Byron Bam Morris .15 .40
218 John Avery .15 .40
219 Chris Slade .15 .40
220 Robert Smith .15 .40
221 Mike Pritchard .15 .40
222 Ty Detmer .15 .40
223 Randall Cunningham .20 .50
224 Alonzo Mayes .15 .40
225 Jake Plummer .15 .40
226 Derrick Mayes .15 .40
227 Jeff Brady .15 .40
228 John Lynch .20 .50
229 Steve Atwater .20 .50
230 Warrick Dunn .15 .40
231 Shawn Jefferson .15 .40
232 Erik Kramer .20 .50
233 Ken Dilger .15 .40
234 Ryan Leaf .20 .50
235 Ray Buchanan .15 .40
236 Kevin Williams .15 .40
237 Ricky Watters .20 .50
238 Dwayne Rudd .15 .40
239 Duce Staley .15 .40
240 Charlie Batch .15 .40
241 Tim Biakabutuka .20 .50
242 Tony Gonzalez .20 .50
243 Bryan Still .15 .40
244 Donnie Edwards .15 .40
245 Troy Aikman .30 .75
246 Tony Banks .20 .50
247 Curtis Enis .15 .40
248 Chris Chandler .20 .50
249 James Jett .15 .40
250 Brett Favre .50 1.25
251 Keith Poole .15 .40
252 Ricky Proehl .15 .40
253 Shannon Sharpe .20 .50
254 Robert Jones .15 .40
255 Chad Brown .15 .40
256 Ben Coates .20 .50
257 Jacquez Green .15 .40
258 Jessie Armstead .20 .50
259 Dale Carter .15 .40
260 Antowain Smith .15 .40
261 Mark Chmura .15 .40
262 Michael Westbrook .15 .40
263 Marvin Harrison .20 .50
264 Darrien Gordon .15 .40
265 Rodney Harrison .15 .40
266 Charles Johnson .15 .40
267 Roman Phifer .15 .40
268 Reidel Anthony .15 .40
269 Jerry Rice .60 1.50
270 Eric Moulds .15 .40
271 Robert Porcher .15 .40
272 Deion Sanders .20 .50
273 Germane Crowell .15 .40
274 Randy Moss .20 .50
275 Antonio Freeman .20 .50
276 Trent Dilfer .15 .40
277 Eric Turner .15 .40
278 Jeff George .15 .40
279 Levon Kirkland .15 .40
280 O.J. McDuffie .20 .50
281 Takeo Spikes .15 .40
282 Jim Flanigan .15 .40
283 Chris Warren .20 .50
284 J.J. Stokes .15 .40
285 Bryan Cox .20 .50
286 Sam Madison .15 .40
287 Priest Holmes .15 .40
288 Keenan McCardell .20 .50
289 Michael Strahan .20 .50
290 Robert Edwards .15 .40
291 Tommy Vardell .20 .50
292 Wayne Chrebet .15 .40
293 Chris Calloway .15 .40
294 Wesley Walls .20 .50
295 Derrick Brooks .25 .60
296 Trace Armstrong .15 .40
297 Brian Simmons .15 .40
298 Darrell Green .25 .60
299 Robert Brooks .20 .50
300 Peyton Manning .75 2.00
301 Dana Stubblefield .15 .40
302 Shawn Springs .15 .40
303 Leslie Shepherd .15 .40
304 Ken Harvey .15 .40
305 Jon Kitna .15 .40
306 Terance Mathis .15 .40
307 Andre Reed .25 .60
308 Jackie Harris .20 .50
309 Rich Gannon .20 .50
310 Keyshawn Johnson .20 .50
311 Victor Green .15 .40
312 Eric Allen .20 .50
313 Terry Fair .15 .40
314 Jason Elam SH .15 .40
315 Garrison Hearst SH .12 .30
316 Jake Plummer SH .12 .30
317 Randall Cunningham SH .15 .40
318 Randy Moss SH .15 .40
319 Jamal Anderson SH .15 .40
320 John Elway SH .30 .75
321 Doug Flutie SH .20 .50
322 Emmitt Smith SH .30 .75
323 Terrell Davis SH .15 .40
324 Jerris McPhail .15 .40
325 Damon Gibson .15 .40
326 Jim Pyne .15 .40
327 Antonio Langham .15 .40
328 Freddie Solomon .15 .40
329 Ricky Williams RC 1.00 2.50
330 Daunte Culpepper RC 1.00 2.50
331 Chris Claiborne RC .60 1.50
332 Amos Zereoue RC .60 1.50
333 Chris McAlister RC .60 1.50
334 Kevin Faulk RC .60 1.50
335 James Johnson RC .60 1.50
336 Mike Cloud RC .60 1.50
337 Jevon Kearse RC .75 2.00
338 Akili Smith RC .60 1.50
339 Edgerrin James RC 1.00 2.50
340 Cecil Collins RC .60 1.50
341 Donovan McNabb RC 3.00 8.00
342 Kevin Johnson RC .75 2.00
343 Torry Holt RC 1.25 3.00
344 Rob Konrad RC .60 1.50
345 Tim Couch RC .75 2.00
346 David Boston RC .60 1.50
347 Karsten Bailey RC .60 1.50
348 Troy Edwards RC .60 1.50
349 Sedrick Irvin RC .60 1.50
350 Shaun King RC .60 1.50
351 Peerless Price RC .60 1.50
352 Brock Huard RC .60 1.50
353 Cade McNown RC .60 1.50
354 Champ Bailey RC 1.25 3.00
355 D'Wayne Bates RC .60 1.50
356 Checklist Card .15 .40
357 Checklist Card .15 .40

1999 Topps Collection

COMP.FACT.SET (357) 20.00 50.00
*COLLECT.VETS: .3X TO 1X BASIC TOPPS
*COLLECT.ROOKIES: .3X TO .8X BASIC TOPPS

1999 Topps MVP Promotion

*1-328 VETS: 15X TO 40X BASIC CARDS
*314-324 SH: 20X TO 50X BASIC SH
*VET WINNER: 25X TO 60X BASIC CARDS
*329-355 ROOKIES: 4X TO 10X BASIC RC
*ROOKIE WINNER: 5X TO 12X BASIC RC
MVP STATED ODDS 1:253 H/R, 1:69 HTA
MVP STATED PRINT RUN 100 SETS

1999 Topps MVP Promotion Prizes

leased as a redemption offer, this 22-card set was redeemable by sending in one of the 17 winning 1999 Topps MVP Promotion cards. The set is printed on an all-foil card front and features some of the NFL's hottest players week to week, as the set parallels the 1999 NFL season from week one to week 17, and then carries from the beginning of the playoffs through the Super Bowl. The set finishes off with it's last card picturing 1999 MVP, Kurt Warner. Card backs carry an "MVP" prefix.

COMPLETE SET (22) 40.00 100.00
MVP1 Troy Aikman 4.00 10.00
MVP2 Drew Bledsoe 2.50 6.00
MVP3 Marvin Harrison 1.25 3.00
MVP4 Terry Glenn 1.25 3.00
MVP5 Isaac Bruce 1.25 3.00
MVP6 Marshall Faulk 2.00 5.00
MVP7 Tim Brown 1.25 3.00
MVP8 Edgerrin James 7.50 20.00
MVP9 Germane Crowell .60 1.50
MVP10 Jevon Kearse 2.00 5.00
MVP11 Jimmy Smith .60 1.50
MVP12 Jeff George .60 1.50
MVP13 Amani Toomer .60 1.50
MVP14 Corey Dillon 1.25 3.00
MVP15 Cade McNown 1.25 3.00
MVP16 Steve McNair 1.25 3.00
MVP17 Dorsey Levens 1.25 3.00
MVP18 Robert Smith 1.25 3.00
MVP19 Eddie George 1.25 3.00
MVP20 Ricky Proehl .60 1.50
MVP21 Kurt Warner 10.00 25.00
MVP22 Kurt Warner MVP 10.00 25.00

1999 Topps All Matrix

Randomly inserted into packs at the rate of one in 14, this 30-card set features color action player photos printed on stunning dot matrix technology. The set includes 10 Running Backs who hit the 1200 yard mark in 1998, 11 Quarterbacks who hit the 3000 yard mark, and nine Rookies from the 1999 Draft.

COMPLETE SET (30) 30.00 60.00
STATED ODDS 1:14 H/R, 1:9 JUM, 1:4 HTA
AM1 Fred Taylor 1.00 2.50
AM2 Ricky Watters .60 1.50

AM3 Curtis Martin 1.00 2.50
AM4 Eddie George 1.00 2.50
AM5 Marshall Faulk 1.25 3.00
AM6 Emmitt Smith 2.00 5.00
AM7 Barry Sanders 3.00 8.00
AM8 Garrison Hearst .60 1.50
AM9 Jamal Anderson 1.00 2.50
AM10 Terrell Davis 1.00 2.50
AM11 Chris Chandler .60 1.50
AM12 Steve McNair 1.00 2.50
AM13 Vinny Testaverde .60 1.50
AM14 Trent Green 1.00 2.50
AM15 Dan Marino 3.00 8.00
AM16 Drew Bledsoe 1.25 3.00
AM17 Randall Cunningham 1.00 2.50
AM18 Jake Plummer .60 1.50
AM19 Peyton Manning 3.00 8.00
AM20 Steve Young 1.25 3.00
AM21 Brett Favre 3.00 8.00
AM22 Tim Couch .75 2.00
AM23 Edgerrin James 2.50 6.00
AM24 David Boston .75 2.00
AM25 Akili Smith .60 1.50
AM26 Troy Edwards .60 1.50
AM27 Torry Holt 1.50 4.00
AM28 Donovan McNabb 3.00 8.00
AM29 Daunte Culpepper 2.50 6.00
AM30 Ricky Williams 1.25 3.00

1999 Topps Autographs

ndomly inserted into packs at the rate of one in 509, this 10-card set features color action photos signed by the pictured player along with the Topps "Certified Autograph Issue" logo.

STATED ODDS 1:509 HOB, 1:140 HTA
R.WILL.AUTO ODDS 1:18,372H,1:5057HTA
A1 Randy Moss 30.00 60.00
A2 Wayne Chrebet 8.00 20.00
A3 Tim Couch 8.00 20.00
A4 Joey Galloway 8.00 20.00
A5 Ricky Williams 25.00 50.00
A6 Doug Flutie 10.00 25.00
A7 Terrell Owens 12.00 30.00
A8 Marshall Faulk 15.00 40.00
A9 Rod Smith 12.00 30.00
A10 Dan Marino 50.00 100.00

1999 Topps Hall of Fame Autographs

Randomly inserted into packs at the rate of one in 1,832, this five-card set features autographed color action photos of the Class of 1999 Hall of Famers with the "Certified Autograph Issue" mark assuring the cards authenticity.

STATED ODDS 1:1832 HOB, 1:503 HTA
HOF1 Eric Dickerson 20.00 50.00
HOF2 Billy Shaw 20.00 50.00
HOF3 Lawrence Taylor 25.00 60.00
HOF4 Tom Mack 20.00 50.00
HOF5 Ozzie Newsome 20.00 50.00

1999 Topps Jumbos

Randomly inserted one per hobby box, this eight card set features color action player photos printed on large cards.

COMPLETE SET (8) 10.00 20.00
ONE PER HOBBY BOX
1 Barry Sanders 2.00 5.00
2 Randy Moss 1.50 4.00
3 Terrell Davis .60 1.50
4 Dan Marino 2.00 5.00
5 Fred Taylor .60 1.50
6 John Elway 2.00 5.00
7 Brett Favre 2.00 5.00
8 Peyton Manning 2.00 5.00

1999 Topps Mystery Chrome

Randomly inserted into packs at the rate of one in 36, this 20-card set features color action photos of 20 NFL superstars printed on Chrome Technology. The object is to guess the player pictured on the front. A Refractor parallel version of this set was also produced and inserted into packs at the rate of one in 144.

COMPLETE SET (20) 35.00 80.00
STATED ODDS 1:36 H/R, 1:24 JUM, 1:8 HTA
*REFRACTORS: 1X TO 2.5X BASIC INSERTS
REFRACT.STATED ODDS 1:144H/R, 1:32 HTA
M1 Terrell Davis 1.50 4.00
M2 Steve Young 2.00 5.00
M3 Fred Taylor 1.50 4.00
M4 Chris Claiborne .50 1.25
M5 Terrell Davis 1.50 4.00
M6 Randall Cunningham 1.50 4.00
M7 Charlie Batch 1.50 4.00
M8 Fred Taylor 1.50 4.00
M9 Vinny Testaverde 1.00 2.50
M10 Jamal Anderson 1.50 4.00
M11 Randy Moss 4.00 10.00
M12 Keyshawn Johnson 1.50 4.00
M13 Vinny Testaverde 1.00 2.50
M14 Chris Chandler 1.00 2.50
M15 Fred Taylor 1.50 4.00
M16 Ricky Williams 1.50 4.00
M17 Chris Chandler 1.00 2.50
M18 John Elway 5.00 12.00
M19 Randy Moss 4.00 10.00
M20 Troy Edwards .75 2.00

1999 Topps Picture Perfect

Randomly inserted into packs at the rate of one in 14, this 10-card set features color action player photos printed with "visual errors" on the card fronts.

COMPLETE SET (10) 10.00 25.00
STATED ODDS 1:14 H/R, 1:9 JUM, 1:4 HTA
P1 Steve Young .75 2.00
P2 Brett Favre 2.00 5.00
P3 Terrell Davis .60 1.50
P4 Peyton Manning 2.00 5.00
P5 Jake Plummer .40 1.00
P6 Fred Taylor .60 1.50
P7 Barry Sanders 2.00 5.00
P8 Dan Marino 2.00 5.00
P9 John Elway 2.00 5.00
P10 Randy Moss 1.50 4.00

1999 Topps Record Numbers Silver

ndomly inserted into packs at the rate of one in 18, this 10-card set features color action photos of ten NFL record holders printed on silver cards.

COMPLETE SET (10) 15.00 30.00
STATED ODDS 1:18 H/R, 1:8 JUM, 1:6 HTA
RN1 Randy Moss 2.00 5.00
RN2 Terrell Davis .75 2.00
RN3 Emmitt Smith 1.50 4.00
RN4 Barry Sanders 2.50 6.00
RN5 Dan Marino 2.50 6.00
RN6 Brett Favre 2.50 6.00
RN7 Doug Flutie .75 2.00
RN8 Jerry Rice 1.50 4.00
RN9 Peyton Manning 2.50 6.00
RN10 Jason Elam .30 .75

1999 Topps Record Numbers Gold

RN1 Randy Moss/17 100.00 250.00
RN2 Terrell Davis/56 20.00 50.00
RN3 Emmitt Smith/125 30.00 60.00
RN4 Barry Sanders/1000 20.00 40.00
RN5 Dan Marino/408 20.00 40.00
RN6 Brett Favre/30 75.00 200.00
RN7 Doug Flutie/3291 4.00 10.00
RN8 Jerry Rice/164 15.00 40.00
RN9 Peyton Manning/3739 7.50 20.00
RN10 Jason Elam/63 5.00 12.00

1999 Topps Season's Best

Randomly inserted into packs at the rate of one in 18, this 30-card set features color action photos of the most dominant players in six categories printed on metallic foilboard. The six categories and the positions they represent are: Bull Rushers--Running Backs, Rocket Launchers--Quarterbacks, Deep Threats--Wide Receivers, Power Packed--"Defensive Players, Strike Force--Special Teamers, and Career Best--the leading active player in each of the previous five categories.

COMPLETE SET (30) 25.00 60.00
STATED ODDS 1:18 H/R, 1:12 JUM, 1:6 HTA
SB1 Terrell Davis 1.00 2.50
SB2 Jamal Anderson 1.00 2.50
SB3 Garrison Hearst .60 1.50
SB4 Barry Sanders 3.00 8.00
SB5 Emmitt Smith 2.00 5.00
SB6 Randall Cunningham 1.00 2.50
SB7 Brett Favre 3.00 8.00
SB8 Steve Young 1.25 3.00
SB9 Jake Plummer .60 1.50
SB10 Peyton Manning 3.00 8.00
SB11 Antonio Freeman 1.00 2.50
SB12 Eric Moulds 1.00 2.50
SB13 Randy Moss 2.50 6.00
SB14 Rod Smith .60 1.50
SB15 Jimmy Smith .60 1.50
SB16 Michael Sinclair .40 1.00
SB17 Kevin Greene .40 1.00
SB18 Michael Strahan .60 1.50
SB19 Michael McCrary .40 1.00
SB20 Hugh Douglas .40 1.00
SB21 Deion Sanders 1.00 2.50
SB22 Terry Fair .40 1.00
SB23 Jacquez Green .40 1.00
SB24 Corey Harris .40 1.00
SB25 Tim Dwight 1.00 2.50
SB26 Dan Marino 3.00 8.00
SB27 Barry Sanders 3.00 8.00
SB28 Jerry Rice 2.00 5.00
SB29 Bruce Smith .60 1.50
SB30 Darrien Gordon .40 1.00

1999 Topps Hall of Fame

This set was distributed at various Topps sponsored events and through the Pro Football Hall of Fame. Each card includes a photo of a 1999 inductee printed in the style of the 1999 set except without the gold foil logo on the cardfront. The cards were not numbered and have been assigned numbers below alphabetically.

COMPLETE SET (5) 3.20 8.00
1 Eric Dickerson .80 2.00
2 Tom Mack .50 1.25
3 Ozzie Newsome .80 2.00
4 Billy Shaw .50 1.25
5 Lawrence Taylor .80 2.00

1999 Topps Hall of Fame Class of 1999

This set was distributed at various Topps sponsored events in 1999 including ceremonies for the Pro Football Hall of Fame. Each card includes a photo of a 1999 inductee printed in the style of the 1998 set except with a blue border instead of green. A gold foil "Class of '99" logo appears on the cardfronts.

COMPLETE SET (5) 3.00 8.00
HOF1 Eric Dickerson .80 2.00
HOF2 Tom Mack .60 1.50
HOF3 Lawrence Taylor 1.25 3.00
HOF4 Billy Shaw .60 1.50
HOF5 Ozzie Newsome .80 2.00

2000 Topps Promos

This 6-card set was released at various Topps sponsored events and through its dealer network to promote the 2000 football release. The cards look very similar to the base set except for the card numbering scheme.

COMPLETE SET (6) 2.00 5.00
PP1 Peyton Manning 1.00 2.50
PP2 Zach Thomas .30 .75
PP3 Eddie George .30 .75
PP4 Rocket Ismail .30 .75
PP5 Fred Taylor .25 .60
PP6 Shaun King .25 .60

2000 Topps

Released as a 400-card set, 2000 Topps features 320 veteran cards, 10 Season Highlights, 10 Millennium Men, 20 NFL Europe Prospects, and 40 Draft Pick Cards seeded at one in five for Hobby and Retail and one in one for HTA packs. Hobby and Retail were packaged in 36-pack boxes with packs containing 10 cards and carried a suggested retail price of $1.29; and HTA was packaged in 12-pack boxes with packs containing 45 cards and carried a suggested retail price of $5.00.

COMPLETE SET (400) 30.00 60.00
COMP.SET w/o SP's (360) 8.00 20.00
361-400 ROOKIE ODDS 1:5H/R,1:1HTA
SBMVP STATED ODDS 1:1287 HTA
1 Kurt Warner .40 1.00
2 Darrell Russell .15 .40
3 Tai Streets .15 .40
4 Bryant Young .15 .40
5 Kent Graham .15 .40
6 Shawn Jefferson .15 .40
7 Wesley Walls .15 .40
8 Jessie Armstead .15 .40
9 Dedric Ward .15 .40
10 Emmitt Smith .40 1.00
11 James Stewart .15 .40
12 Frank Sanders .15 .40
13 Ray Buchanan .15 .40
14 Olindo Mare .15 .40
15 Andre Reed .25 .60
16 Curtis Conway .20 .50
17 Patrick Jeffers .15 .40
18 Greg Hill .15 .40
19 John Unitas .60 1.50
20 Brett Favre .50 1.25
21 Jerome Pathon .15 .40
22 Jason Tucker .15 .40
23 Charles Johnson .15 .40
24 Brian Mitchell .15 .40
25 Billy Miller .15 .40
26 Jay Fiedler .20 .50
27 Marcus Pollard .15 .40
28 De'Mond Parker .15 .40
29 Leslie Shepherd .15 .40
30 Fred Taylor .15 .40
31 Michael Pittman .15 .40
32 Ricky Watters .20 .50
33 Derrick Brooks .15 .40
34 Junior Seau .20 .50
35 Troy Vincent .15 .40
36 Eric Allen .15 .40
37 Pete Mitchell .15 .40
38 Tony Simmons .15 .40
39 Az-Zahir Hakim .15 .40
40 Dan Marino .50 1.25
41 Mac Cody .15 .40
42 Scott Dreisbach .15 .40
43 Al Wilson .15 .40
44 Luther Broughton RC .15 .40
45 Wane McGarity .15 .40
46 Stephen Boyd .15 .40
47 Michael Strahan .20 .50
48 Chris Chandler .20 .50
49 Tony Martin .20 .50
50 Edgerrin James .20 .50
51 John Randle .25 .60
52 Warrick Dunn .15 .40
53 Elvis Grbac .15 .40
54 Champ Bailey .20 .50
55 Kyle Brady .15 .40
56 John Lynch .20 .50
57 Kevin Carter .15 .40
58 Mike Pritchard .15 .40
59 Deon Mitchell RC .15 .40
60 Randy Moss .20 .50
61 Jermaine Fazande .15 .40
62 Donovan McNabb .20 .50
63 Richard Huntley .15 .40
64 Rich Gannon .20 .50
65 Aaron Glenn .15 .40
66 Amani Toomer .15 .40
67 Andre Hastings .15 .40
68 Ricky Williams .20 .50
69 Sam Madison .15 .40
70 Drew Bledsoe .20 .50
71 Eric Moulds .15 .40
72 Justin Armour .15 .40
73 Jamal Anderson .20 .50
74 Mario Bates .15 .40
75 Sam Gash .15 .40
76 Macey Brooks .15 .40
77 Tremain Mack .15 .40
78 David LaFleur .15 .40
79 Dexter Coakley .15 .40
80 Cris Carter .25 .60
81 Byron Chamberlain .15 .40
82 David Sloan .15 .40
83 Mike Devlin RC .15 .40
84 Jimmy Smith .20 .50
85 Derrick Alexander .15 .40
86 Damon Huard .15 .40
87 Jake Reed .20 .50
88 Darrell Green .20 .50
89 Derrick Mason .15 .40
90 Curtis Martin .20 .50
91 Donnie Abraham .15 .40
92 D'Marco Farr .15 .40
93 Ahman Green .20 .50
94 Shane Matthews .15 .40
95 Torrance Small .15 .40
96 Duce Staley .15 .40
97 Jon Ritchie .15 .40
98 Victor Green .15 .40
99 Kerry Collins .15 .40
100 Peyton Manning .60 1.50
101 Ben Coates .15 .40
102 Thurman Thomas .20 .50
103 Cornelius Bennett .15 .40
104 Terance Mathis .15 .40
105 Adrian Murrell .15 .40
106 Donald Hayes .15 .40
107 Terry Kirby .15 .40
108 James Allen .15 .40
109 Ty Law .25 .60
110 Tim Brown .25 .60
111 Chad Bratzke .15 .40
112 Deion Sanders .20 .50
113 James Johnson .15 .40
114 Tony Richardson RC .15 .40
115 Tony Brackens .15 .40
116 Ken Dilger .15 .40
117 Albert Connell .15 .40
118 Neil O'Donnell .15 .40
119 Selucio Sanford EP RC .15 .40
120 Steve Young .30 .75
121 Tony Horne .15 .40
122 Charlie Rogers .15 .40
123 J.J. Stokes .20 .50
124 Kenny Bynum .15 .40
125 Jeff Graham .15 .40
126 Ike Hilliard .15 .40
127 Ray Lucas .15 .40
128 Terry Glenn .20 .50
129 Rickey Dudley .15 .40
130 Joey Galloway .20 .50
131 Brian Dawkins .25 .60
132 Rob Moore .15 .40
133 Bob Christian .15 .40
134 Anthony Wright RC .20 .50
135 Antowain Smith .20 .50
136 Kevin Johnson .15 .40
137 Scott Covington .15 .40
138 D'Wayne Bates .15 .40
139 Sam Cowart .15 .40
140 Isaac Bruce .25 .60
141 Tony McGee .15 .40
142 Dale Carter .15 .40
143 Matt Hasselbeck .15 .40
144 Torry Holt .20 .50
145 Daunte Culpepper .20 .50
146 Yatil Green .15 .40
147 Chris Howard .15 .40
148 Irving Fryar .20 .50
149 Derrick Mayes .15 .40
150 Warren Sapp .20 .50
151 Ricky Proehl .15 .40
152 Eric Kresser EP .15 .40
153 Jeff Garcia .15 .40
154 Freddie Jones .15 .40
155 Mike Cloud .15 .40
156 Wayne Chrebet .15 .40
157 Joe Montgomery .15 .40
158 Shannon Sharpe .20 .50
159 Eddie Kennison .15 .40
160 Eddie George .20 .50
161 Jay Riemersma .15 .40
162 Peter Boulware .15 .40
163 Aeneas Williams .15 .40
164 Jim Miller .15 .40
165 Jamir Miller .15 .40
166 Tim Biakabutuka .20 .50
167 Kordell Stewart .15 .40
168 Charlie Garner .20 .50
169 Germane Crowell .15 .40
170 Stephen Davis .15 .40
171 Jeff George .20 .50
172 Mark Brunell .20 .50
173 Stephen Alexander .15 .40
174 Mike Alstott .15 .40
175 Terry Allen .20 .50
176 Ed McCaffrey .20 .50
177 Bobby Engram .15 .40
178 Andre Cooper .15 .40
179 Kevin Faulk .15 .40
180 Errict Rhett .20 .50
181 Jammi German .15 .40
182 Oronde Gadsden .20 .50
183 Jevon Kearse .15 .40
184 Herman Moore .15 .40
185 Terrence Wilkins .15 .40
186 Rocket Ismail .20 .50
187 Patrick Johnson .15 .40
188 Simeon Rice .20 .50
189 Mo Lewis .15 .40
190 Qadry Ismail .15 .40
191 Terry Jackson .15 .40
192 Rashaan Shehee .15 .40
193 Charles Woodson .25 .60
194 Akili Smith .15 .40
195 Yancey Thigpen .15 .40
196 Michael Westbrook .15 .40
197 Donnell Bennett .15 .40
198 Sedrick Irvin .15 .40
199 Keenan McCardell .20 .50
200 Marshall Faulk .20 .50
201 Jeff Blake .20 .50
202 Rob Johnson .20 .50
203 Vinny Testaverde .15 .40
204 Andy Katzenmoyer .15 .40
205 Michael Basnight .15 .40
206 Lance Schulters .15 .40
207 Shaun King .15 .40
208 Bill Schroeder .20 .50
209 Skip Hicks .15 .40
210 Jake Plummer .15 .40
211 Leroy Hoard .15 .40
212 Reggie Barlow .15 .40
213 E.G. Green .15 .40
214 Fred Lane .15 .40
215 Antonio Freeman .20 .50
216 Grant Wistrom .15 .40
217 Kevin Dyson .20 .50
218 Mikhael Ricks .15 .40
219 Rod Woodson .25 .60
220 Tim Dwight .20 .50
221 Darnay Scott .20 .50
222 Curtis Enis .15 .40
223 Sean Bennett .15 .40
224 Napoleon Kaufman .20 .50
225 Jonathan Linton .15 .40
226 Jim Harbaugh .20 .50
227 Hardy Nickerson .15 .40
228 Todd Lyght .15 .40
229 Dorsey Levens .20 .50
230 Steve Beuerlein .20 .50
231 Marty Booker .15 .40
232 Andre Wadsworth .15 .40
233 James Hasty .15 .40
234 Shawn Bryson .15 .40
235 Larry Centers .15 .40
236 Charlie Batch .15 .40
237 Steve McNair .20 .50
238 Darrin Chiaverini .15 .40
239 Jerome Bettis .25 .60
240 Muhsin Muhammad .15 .40
241 Terrell Fletcher .15 .40
242 Jon Kitna .15 .40
243 Frank Wycheck .20 .50
244 Tony Gonzalez .20 .50
245 Ron Rivers .15 .40
246 Olandis Gary .20 .50
247 Jermaine Lewis .15 .40
248 Joe Jurevicius .15 .40
249 Richie Anderson .15 .40
250 Marcus Robinson .20 .50
251 Shawn Springs .15 .40
252 William Floyd .15 .40
253 Bobby Shaw RC .15 .40
254 Glyn Milburn .15 .40
255 Brian Griese .15 .40
256 Donnie Edwards .15 .40
257 Joe Horn .20 .50
258 Cameron Cleeland .15 .40
259 Glenn Foley .15 .40
260 Corey Dillon .15 .40
261 Troy Brown .15 .40
262 Stoney Case .15 .40
263 Kevin Williams .15 .40
264 London Fletcher RC .40 1.00
265 O.J. McDuffie .20 .50
266 Jonathan Quinn .15 .40
267 Trent Dilfer .15 .40
268 Dameyune Craig .15 .40
269 Terrell Owens .20 .50
270 Tim Couch .20 .50
271 Dameane Douglas .15 .40
272 Moses Moreno .15 .40
273 Bruce Smith .20 .50
274 Peerless Price .20 .50
275 Sam Games .15 .40
276 Natrone Means .20 .50
277 Na Brown .15 .40
278 Dave Moore .15 .40
279 Chris Sanders .15 .40
280 Troy Aikman .30 .75
281 Cecil Collins .15 .40
282 Matthew Hatchette .15 .40
283 Bill Romanowski .15 .40
284 Basil Mitchell .15 .40
285 Tony Banks .15 .40
286 Jake Delhomme RC .20 .50
287 Keyshawn Johnson .20 .50
288 Dexter McCleon .20 .50
289 Corey Bradford .15 .40
290 Terrell Davis .20 .50
291 Johnnie Morton .20 .50
292 Kevin Lockett .15 .40
293 Robert Smith .15 .40
294 Jeff Lewis .15 .40
295 Wali Rainer .15 .40
296 Troy Edwards .15 .40
297 Keith Poole .15 .40
298 Priest Holmes .15 .40
299 David Boston .15 .40
300 Marvin Harrison .20 .50
301 Levon Kirkland .15 .40
302 Robert Holcombe .15 .40
303 Autry Denson .15 .40
304 Kevin Hardy .15 .40
305 Rod Smith .20 .50
306 Robert Porcher .15 .40
307 Cade McNown .15 .40
308 Craig Yeast .15 .40
309 Doug Flutie .20 .50
310 Jerry Rice .60 1.50
311 Brad Johnson .20 .50
312 Tiki Barber .20 .50
313 Will Blackwell .15 .40
314 Sean Dawkins .15 .40
315 Jacquez Green .15 .40
316 Zach Thomas .20 .50
317 Gus Frerotte .15 .40
318 Chris Warren .15 .40
319 Carl Pickens .20 .50
320 Tyrone Wheatley HL .12 .30
321 Kurt Warner HL .30 .75
322 Dan Marino HL .40 1.00
323 Cris Carter HL .20 .50
324 Brett Favre HL .40 1.00
325 Marshall Faulk HL .15 .40
326 Jevon Kearse HL .12 .30
327 Edgerrin James HL .15 .40
328 Emmitt Smith HL .30 .75
329 Andre Reed HL .20 .50
330 K.Dyson .15 .40
F.Wycheck HL
331 Olindo Mare MM .12 .30
332 Marcus Coleman MM .12 .30
333 James Johnson MM .12 .30
334 Ray Lucas MM .12 .30
335 Dedric Ward MM .12 .30
336 Richie Cunningham MM .12 .30
337 James Hasty MM .12 .30
338 Sedrick Shaw MM .12 .30
339 Kurt Warner MM .30 .75
340 Marshall Faulk MM .15 .40
341 Brian Shay EP .15 .40
342 L.C. Stevens EP .15 .40
343 Corey Thomas EP .15 .40
344 Scott Milanovich EP .15 .40
345 Pat Barnes EP .15 .40
346 Danny Wuerffel EP .25 .60
347 Kevin Daft EP .15 .40
348 Ron Powlus EP RC .25 .60
349 Tony Graziani EP .20 .50
350 Norman Miller EP RC .15 .40
351 Cory Sauter EP .15 .40
352 Marcus Crandell EP RC .15 .40
353 Sean Morey EP RC .15 .40
354 Jeff Ogden EP .15 .40
355 Ted White EP .15 .40
356 Jim Kubiak EP RC .15 .40
357 Aaron Stecker EP RC .15 .40
358 Ronnie Powell EP .15 .40
359 Matt Lytle EP RC .15 .40
360 Kendrick Nord EP RC .15 .40
361 Tim Rattay RC .75 2.00
362 Rob Morris RC .75 2.00
363 Chris Samuels RC 1.00 2.50
364 Todd Husak RC .60 1.50
365 Ahmed Plummer RC .60 1.50
366 Frank Murphy RC .60 1.50
367 Michael Wiley RC .60 1.50
368 Giovanni Carmazzi RC .60 1.50
369 Anthony Becht RC .60 1.50
370 John Abraham RC 1.00 2.50
371 Shaun Alexander RC 1.00 2.50
372 Thomas Jones RC .75 2.00
373 Courtney Brown RC .75 2.00
374 Curtis Keaton RC .60 1.50
375 Jerry Porter RC 1.00 2.50
376 Corey Simon RC .75 2.00
377 Dez White RC .60 1.50
378 Jamal Lewis RC 1.00 2.50
379 Ron Dayne RC 1.00 2.50
380 R.Jay Soward RC .60 1.50
381 Tee Martin RC .60 1.50
382 Shaun Ellis RC .75 2.00
383 Brian Urlacher RC 3.00 8.00
384 Reuben Droughns RC .60 1.50
385 Travis Taylor RC .60 1.50
386 Plaxico Burress RC .75 2.00
387 Chad Pennington RC .75 2.00
388 Sylvester Morris RC .60 1.50
389 Ron Dugans RC .60 1.50
390 Joe Hamilton RC .60 1.50
391 Chris Redman RC .60 1.50
392 Trung Canidate RC .60 1.50
393 J.R. Redmond RC .60 1.50
394 Danny Farmer RC .60 1.50
395 Todd Pinkston RC .60 1.50
396 Dennis Northcutt RC .60 1.50
397 Laveranues Coles RC .75 2.00
398 Bubba Franks RC .60 1.50
399 Travis Prentice RC .60 1.50
400 Peter Warrick RC .60 1.50
SBMVP Kurt Warner FB AU 50.00 120.00
CL1 Checklist Card .02 .10
CL2 Checklist Card .02 .10

2000 Topps Collection

COMP.FACT.SET (400) 35.00 60.00
*VETS 1-360: .4X TO 1X BASIC TOPPS
*ROOKIES 361-400: .2X TO .5X BASIC TOPPS

2000 Topps MVP Promotion

ET 1-360: 15X TO 40X BASIC CARDS
*VET WIN: 20X TO 50X BASIC CARDS
*ROOKIES 361-400: 3X TO 8X
STATED ODDS 1:234 HOB, 1:52 HTA

2000 Topps MVP Promotion Prizes

COMPLETE SET (17) 40.00 80.00
MVP1 Duce Staley 1.25 3.00
MVP2 Tony Banks 1.25 3.00
MVP3 Elvis Grbac 1.25 3.00
MVP4 Curtis Martin 1.50 4.00
MVP5 Randy Moss 1.50 4.00
MVP6 Tim Brown 2.00 5.00
MVP7 Edgerrin James 1.50 4.00
MVP8 Corey Dillon 1.25 3.00
MVP9 Marshall Faulk 1.50 4.00
MVP10 Antonio Freeman 1.50 4.00
MVP11 Daunte Culpepper 1.50 4.00
MVP12 Fred Taylor 1.25 3.00
MVP13 Jamal Lewis 2.00 5.00
MVP14 Warrick Dunn 1.25 3.00
MVP15 Donovan McNabb 1.50 4.00
MVP16 Terrell Owens 1.50 4.00
MVP17 Peyton Manning 5.00 12.00

2000 Topps Autographs

ndomly inserted in packs at the rate of one in 1015 and HTA packs at one in 226, this 16-card set features authentic autographs of each pictured player. Some cards were issued via redemption cards which carried an expiration date of 2/28/2001.

STATED ODDS 1:1015 H/R, 1:226HTA
ANNOUNCED AUTO PRINT RUNS 250-700
CP Chad Pennington 8.00 20.00
EJ Edgerrin James 10.00 25.00
JK Jon Kitna 6.00 15.00
JS Jimmy Smith 8.00 20.00
KC Kevin Carter 6.00 15.00
KW Kurt Warner 30.00 60.00
MF Marshall Faulk 12.00 30.00
MH Marvin Harrison 10.00 25.00
PM Peyton Manning 50.00 100.00
PW Peter Warrick SP 15.00 40.00
RD Ron Dayne 10.00 25.00
SA Shaun Alexander 10.00 25.00
SD Stephen Davis 6.00 15.00
SM Sylvester Morris 6.00 15.00
TJ Thomas Jones 8.00 20.00
ZT Zach Thomas 12.00 30.00

2000 Topps Chrome Previews

ndomly inserted in packs at the rate of one in 18 and one in five HTA, this 20-card set features color action player photos printed using the technology created for the 2000 Topps Chrome set which was released later in the year. Card backs carry a "CP" prefix.

COMPLETE SET (20) 15.00 40.00
STATED ODDS 1:18 H/R, 1:5 HTA
CP1 Kurt Warner 1.00 2.50
CP2 Shaun King .40 1.00
CP3 Brad Johnson .50 1.25
CP4 Daunte Culpepper .50 1.25
CP5 Brett Favre 1.25 3.00
CP6 Eddie George .50 1.25
CP7 Dan Marino 1.25 3.00
CP8 Randy Moss .50 1.25
CP9 Troy Aikman .75 2.00
CP10 Peyton Manning 1.50 4.00
CP11 Fred Taylor .40 1.00
CP12 Ricky Williams .50 1.25
CP13 Jimmy Smith .50 1.25
CP14 Jerry Rice 1.50 4.00
CP15 Marshall Faulk .50 1.25
CP16 Marvin Harrison .50 1.25
CP17 Stephen Davis .40 1.00
CP18 Isaac Bruce .60 1.50
CP19 Emmitt Smith 1.00 2.50
CP20 Edgerrin James .50 1.25

2000 Topps Combos

Randomly inserted in Hobby/Retail packs at one in 12 and HTA packs at one in 4, this 10-card set pairs some of the NFL's players into a dominating duo with original painted artwork. Card backs carry a "TC" prefix.

COMPLETE SET (10) 6.00 15.00
STATED ODDS 1:12 H/R 1:4HTA
TC1 J.Unitas/P.Manning 1.50 4.00
TC2 C.Carter/R.Moss .60 1.50
TC3 R.Williams/E.James .50 1.25
TC4 M.Harrison/J.Smith .50 1.25
TC5 I.Bruce/J.Galloway .60 1.50
TC6 McN/Cou/Kng/Cul/A.Smi .40 1.00
TC7 S.Davis/F.Taylor .40 1.00
TC8 M.Faulk/E.George .50 1.25
TC9 E.Smith/T.Aikman 1.00 2.50
TC10 K.Warner/D.Marino 1.25 3.00

2000 Topps Hall of Fame Autographs

Randomly seeded in packs at one in 3551 and in HTA packs at one in 790, this 5-card set pays tribute to the 2000 Football Hall of Fame Class with autographed cards featuring the Topps "Genuine Issue" sticker of authenticity. Card backs carry an "HOF" prifix.

STATED ODDS 1:3551H/R, 1:790 HTA
HOF1 Joe Montana 60.00 150.00
HOF2 Howie Long 40.00 100.00
HOF3 Ronnie Lott 50.00 100.00
HOF4 Dan Rooney 100.00 200.00
HOF5 Dave Wilcox 25.00 60.00

2000 Topps Hobby Masters

Randomly inserted in HTA packs at the rate of one in five, this 10-card set features top NFL players on a 16-point holographic card stock. Each card can be found printed on two slightly different styles of foil stock: one with a circular or swirl pattern holographic background and the other with a tight checkerboard pattern holographic background.

COMPLETE SET (10) 10.00 25.00
*CIRCULAR HOLO: .4X TO 1X BASIC INSERTS
STATED ODDS 1:5 HTA
HM1 Kurt Warner 1.25 3.00
HM2 Ricky Williams .60 1.50
HM3 Eddie George .60 1.50
HM4 Dan Marino 1.50 4.00
HM5 Edgerrin James .60 1.50
HM6 Marshall Faulk .60 1.50
HM7 Emmitt Smith 1.25 3.00
HM8 Jerry Rice 2.00 5.00
HM9 Brett Favre 1.50 4.00
HM10 Randy Moss .60 1.50

2000 Topps Jumbos

ndomly inserted one per hobby box, this eight card set features color action player photos printed on jumbo cards.

COMPLETE SET (8) 6.00 15.00
ONE PER HOBBY BOX
1 Peyton Manning 1.25 3.00
2 Marshall Faulk .40 1.00
3 Dan Marino 1.00 2.50
4 Randy Moss .40 1.00
5 Kurt Warner .75 2.00
6 Eddie George .40 1.00
7 Brett Favre 1.00 2.50
8 Edgerrin James .40 1.00

2000 Topps Own the Game

ndomly inserted in packs at one in 12, this 30-card set captures the league's best players in four offensive categories: Passing Yards, Rushing Yards, Receiving Yards, and Touchdowns. Each card was printed with a silver foil prismatic technology on the background of the player image. The cardbacks carry an "OTG" prefix.

COMPLETE SET (30) 15.00 40.00
STATED ODDS 1:12 H/R, 1:4 HTA
OTG1 Steve Beuerlein .60 1.50
OTG2 Kurt Warner 1.25 3.00
OTG3 Peyton Manning 2.00 5.00
OTG4 Brett Favre 1.50 4.00
OTG5 Brad Johnson .60 1.50
OTG6 Edgerrin James .60 1.50
OTG7 Curtis Martin .60 1.50
OTG8 Stephen Davis .50 1.25
OTG9 Emmitt Smith 1.25 3.00
OTG10 Marshall Faulk .60 1.50
OTG11 Eddie George .60 1.50
OTG12 Duce Staley .50 1.25
OTG13 Charlie Garner .60 1.50
OTG14 Marvin Harrison .60 1.50
OTG15 Jimmy Smith .60 1.50
OTG16 Randy Moss .60 1.50
OTG17 Marcus Robinson .60 1.50
OTG18 Tim Brown .75 2.00
OTG19 Germane Crowell .50 1.25
OTG20 Muhsin Muhammad .50 1.25
OTG21 Cris Carter .75 2.00
OTG22 Michael Westbrook .50 1.25
OTG23 Amani Toomer .50 1.25
OTG24 Keyshawn Johnson .60 1.50
OTG25 Isaac Bruce .75 2.00
OTG26 Kurt Warner 1.25 3.00
OTG27 Stephen Davis .50 1.25
OTG28 Edgerrin James .60 1.50
OTG29 Cris Carter .75 2.00
OTG30 Marvin Harrison .60 1.50

2000 Topps Pro Bowl Jerseys

Randomly inserted in Hobby packs with overall odds of one in 271, this 24-card set features authentic Player-Worn Jersey swatches of some of the NFL's top Pro Bowlers. Each card features the Topps "Genuine Issue" sticker of authenticity. Card backs are numbered by the player's initials and position.

STATED ODDS 1:271 HOB, 1:60 HTA
BMOG Bruce Matthews 8.00 20.00
CCWR Cris Carter 8.00 20.00
CDRB Corey Dillon 5.00 12.00
DRIL Darrell Russell 5.00 12.00
EGRB Eddie George 6.00 15.00
ESRB Emmitt Smith 12.00 30.00
JAOL Jessie Armstead 5.00 12.00
KCDE Kevin Carter 5.00 12.00
KHOL Kevin Hardy 5.00 12.00
KJWR Keyshawn Johnson 6.00 15.00
KWQB Kurt Warner 12.00 30.00
MAFB Mike Alstott 5.00 12.00
MBQB Mark Brunell 6.00 15.00
MHWR Marvin Harrison 6.00 15.00
MMWR Muhsin Muhammad 5.00 12.00
MSDE Michael Strahan 6.00 15.00
OMPK Olindo Mare 5.00 12.00
RGQB Rich Gannon 6.00 15.00
RWFS Rod Woodson 8.00 20.00
SBQB Steve Beuerlein 6.00 15.00
TBDE Tony Brackens 5.00 12.00
TGTE Tony Gonzalez 6.00 15.00
WSIL Warren Sapp 6.00 15.00
ZTIL Zach Thomas 6.00 15.00

2000 Topps Rookie Premier Autographs

ndomly inserted in packs at the rate of one in 5761, this set features autographed cards with photos of the 2000 Rookie Photo Shoot. These cards were processed and autographed on site over the span of two days. Each card was hand serial numbered of 25.

STATED ODDS 1:5761 H, 1:1276 HTA
STATED PRINT RUN 25 SER.#'d SETS
AB Anthony Becht 25.00 60.00
BU Brian Urlacher 350.00 500.00
CB Courtney Brown 30.00 80.00
CK Curtis Keaton 25.00 60.00
CP Chad Pennington 30.00 80.00
CR Chris Redman 25.00 60.00
CS Corey Simon 30.00 80.00
DF Danny Farmer 25.00 60.00
DN Dennis Northcutt 25.00 60.00
DW Dez White 25.00 60.00
JH Joe Hamilton 25.00 60.00
JL Jamal Lewis 100.00 175.00
JP Jerry Porter 40.00 100.00
JR J.R. Redmond 25.00 60.00
LC Laveranues Coles 30.00 80.00
PB Plaxico Burress 60.00 120.00
PW Peter Warrick 25.00 60.00
RD Ron Dayne 40.00 100.00
SA Shaun Alexander 150.00 300.00
SM Sylvester Morris 25.00 60.00
TC Trung Canidate 25.00 60.00
TJ Thomas Jones 30.00 80.00
TM Tee Martin 25.00 60.00
TP Todd Pinkston 25.00 60.00
TT Travis Taylor 30.00 80.00
DFR Bubba Franks 25.00 60.00
RDR Reuben Droughns 25.00 60.00
RDU Ron Dugans 25.00 60.00
TPR Travis Prentice 25.00 60.00

2000 Topps Unitas Reprints

ndomly inserted in packs at one in 19, this 18-card set features reprints of Johnny U's Topps issue cards from 1957-1974. Some cards were newly created in the design of a then current Topps issue for years in which Unitas was not included in the original set. Chrome parallel cards were randomly inserted in packs as well as signed versions for all 18-cards.

COMPLETE SET (18) 25.00 60.00
COMMON CARD (R1-R18) 1.50 4.00
STATED ODDS 1:19 HOB, 1:4 HTA
*CHROME: .6X TO 1.5X BASIC INSERTS
CHROME ODDS 1:72 H, 1:20 HTA
R1 Johnny Unitas 1957 3.00 8.00

2000 Topps Unitas Reprints Autographs

ndomly inserted in packs at a rate of 1:13,678 hobby and 1:3048 HTA packs, this 18-card set parallels the base Johnny Unitas Reprints Insert set with an autographed version. Card fronts feature the "Topps Certified Autograph" stamp and backs feature the Topps "Genuine Issue" sticker.

COMMON CARD (R1-R18) 175.00 350.00
AUTO ODDS 1:13,678 H, 1:3048 HTA

2000 Topps Hall of Fame Class of 2000

This set was distributed by Topps at the 2000 Induction ceremories for the Pro Football Hall of Fame. Each card includes a photo of a 2000 inductee printed with a border textured like a football. A gold foil "Class of 2000" logo also appears on the cardfronts. The cards are unnumbered and listed below alphabetically.

COMPLETE SET (5) 10.00 20.00
HOF1 Joe Montana 4.00 10.00
HOF2 Howie Long 1.50 4.00
HOF3 Ronnie Lott 1.50 4.00
HOF4 Dan Rooney 1.25 3.00
HOF5 Dave Wilcox 1.25 3.00

2001 Topps Promos

is set of 6-cards was released to promote the 2001 Topps base brand football release. Each card appears to be a parallel to the base set except for the card numbering on the backs.

COMPLETE SET (6) 2.00 5.00
P1 Emmitt Smith .60 1.50
P2 Warrick Dunn .25 .60
P3 Jeff Garcia .25 .60
P4 Wayne Chrebet .25 .60
P5 Jason Taylor .40 1.00
P6 Tony Gonzalez .30 .75

2001 Topps

leased as a 385-card set, 2001 Topps features 310 veteran cards and 75 Draft Pick Cards Hobby and Retail were packaged in 36-pack boxes with packs containing 10 cards and carried a suggested retail price of $1.49; and HTA was packaged in 12-pack boxes with packs containing 45 cards and carried a suggested retail price of $5.00. This set included 3 no number checklists that were randomly inserted in packs.

COMPLETE SET (385) 25.00 50.00
1 Marshall Faulk .20 .50
2 Lawyer Milloy .15 .40
3 Rich Gannon .20 .50
4 Rod Smith .20 .50
5 David Boston .15 .40
6 Jeremy McDaniel .15 .40
7 Joey Galloway .20 .50
8 Ron Dixon .15 .40
9 Terrell Fletcher .15 .40
10 Deion Sanders .20 .50
11 Jevon Kearse .15 .40
12 Charles Woodson .25 .60
13 Brian Walker .15 .40
14 Mike Peterson .15 .40
15 Marcus Robinson .20 .50
16 Duane Starks .15 .40
17 KaRon Coleman .15 .40
18 Randy Moss .20 .50
19 Reggie Jones .15 .40
20 Derrick Brooks .15 .40
21 Eddie George .25 .60
22 Wayne Chrebet .15 .40
23 Kevin Hardy .15 .40
24 Bill Schroeder .20 .50
25 Doug Flutie .20 .50
26 Tim Dwight .20 .50
27 Eddie Kennison .20 .50
28 Reggie Kelly .15 .40
29 Ricky Watters .20 .50
30 Stephen Alexander .15 .40
31 Az-Zahir Hakim .15 .40
32 Henri Crockett .15 .40
33 Joe Horn .15 .40
34 Danny Farmer .15 .40
35 Shannon Sharpe .20 .50
36 Brad Hoover .20 .50
37 David Patten .15 .40
38 Kevin Faulk .15 .40
39 Freddie Jones .15 .40
40 Michael Westbrook .15 .40
41 Jacquez Green .15 .40
42 Torrance Small .15 .40
43 Terrence Wilkins .15 .40
44 Brett Favre .50 1.25
45 Tony Banks .15 .40
46 Johnnie Morton .20 .50
47 Jimmy Smith .20 .50
48 Jerry Rice .50 1.25
49 Jeff George .20 .50
50 Ray Lewis .25 .60
51 Joe Johnson .15 .40
52 Rocket Ismail .20 .50
53 Muhsin Muhammad .15 .40
54 Ken Dilger .15 .40
55 Ike Hilliard .15 .40
56 Joey Porter RC 1.25 3.00
57 Shaun Alexander .15 .40
58 Jeff Garcia .15 .40
59 Jay Fiedler .20 .50
60 Wane McGarity .15 .40
61 Steve Beuerlein .20 .50
62 Tywan Mitchell .15 .40
63 Travis Prentice .15 .40
64 Robert Griffith .15 .40
65 Napoleon Kaufman .15 .40
66 Randall Godfrey .15 .40
67 Junior Seau .20 .50
68 Willie Jackson .15 .40
69 Larry Foster .15 .40
70 Brandon Stokley .15 .40
71 Hugh Douglas .15 .40
72 James Thrash .20 .50
73 Vinny Testaverde .15 .40
74 Leslie Shepherd .15 .40
75 Terrell Davis .20 .50
76 Jake Plummer .15 .40
77 Corey Dillon .15 .40
78 Ron Dayne .20 .50
79 Brock Huard .15 .40
80 Todd Husak .15 .40
81 Richard Huntley .15 .40
82 Shaun Ellis .15 .40
83 Kyle Brady .15 .40
84 Corey Bradford .15 .40
85 Eric Moulds .15 .40
86 Brian Finneran .20 .50
87 Antonio Freeman .25 .60
88 Terry Glenn .20 .50
89 Tai Streets .15 .40
90 Chris Sanders .15 .40
91 Sylvester Morris .15 .40
92 Peter Warrick .15 .40
93 Chris Greisen .15 .40
94 Cade McNown .20 .50

95 Jerome Pathon .15 .40
96 John Randle .20 .50
97 Curtis Conway .20 .50
98 Keyshawn Johnson .20 .50
99 Trent Green .15 .40
100 Mike Anderson .15 .40
101 Jeff Blake .20 .50
102 Tee Martin .20 .50
103 Darrell Jackson .20 .50
104 Mark Brunell .20 .50
105 Charlie Batch .15 .40
106 Wesley Walls .15 .40
107 Edgerrin James .20 .50
108 Robert Wilson .15 .40
109 Donovan McNabb .20 .50
110 Champ Bailey .20 .50
111 Isaac Bruce .25 .60
112 Michael Strahan .20 .50
113 Donnie Edwards .15 .40
114 Randall Cunningham .20 .50
115 Germane Crowell .15 .40
116 Jermaine Lewis .15 .40
117 Dennis McKinley .15 .40
118 Ryan Leaf .15 .40
119 Samari Rolle .15 .40
120 Daunte Culpepper .20 .50
121 Tim Couch .15 .40
122 Greg Biekert .15 .40
123 Warrick Dunn .15 .40
124 Richie Anderson .15 .40
125 Trace Armstrong .15 .40
126 Bernardo Harris .15 .40
127 Kwame Cavil .15 .40
128 James Allen .15 .40
129 Anthony Becht .15 .40
130 Tiki Barber .20 .50
131 Brad Johnson .20 .50
132 Tyrone Wheatley .20 .50
133 Kurt Warner .40 1.00
134 Desmond Howard .20 .50
135 Thomas Jones .15 .40
136 Peyton Manning .60 1.50
137 Tony Richardson .15 .40
138 Chris Chandler .20 .50
139 Plaxico Burress .15 .40
140 J.R. Redmond .15 .40
141 Fred Taylor .15 .40
142 Akili Smith .15 .40
143 Sammy Morris .15 .40
144 Jessie Armstead .15 .40
145 Charlie Garner .20 .50
146 Steve McNair .20 .50
147 Charles Johnson .15 .40
148 Troy Aikman .30 .75
149 Kevin Johnson .15 .40
150 Brian Urlacher .30 .75
151 Travis Taylor .15 .40
152 Aaron Shea .15 .40
153 Mike Cloud .15 .40
154 Donald Driver .20 .50
155 Chad Pennington .15 .40
156 Troy Edwards .15 .40
157 Reidel Anthony .15 .40
158 Michael Bishop .20 .50
159 Mo Lewis .15 .40
160 Damon Huard .20 .50
161 James McKnight .15 .40
162 Craig Yeast .15 .40
163 Michael Pittman .20 .50
164 Robert Smith .15 .40
165 Terrelle Smith .15 .40
166 Jeremiah Trotter .15 .40
167 Amani Toomer .15 .40
168 JaJuan Dawson .15 .40
169 Tim Biakabutuka .15 .40
170 Oronde Gadsden .15 .40
171 Ray Lucas .15 .40
172 Jermaine Fazande .15 .40
173 Todd Bouman .15 .40
174 Frank Wycheck .15 .40
175 Hines Ward .20 .50
176 Ahman Green .20 .50
177 Kaseem Sinceno .15 .40
178 Jamal Anderson .20 .50
179 Jay Riemersma .15 .40
180 Jarious Jackson .15 .40
181 Andre Rison .20 .50
182 Jerome Bettis .25 .60
183 Blaine Bishop .15 .40
184 Dorsey Levens .20 .50
185 James Stewart .15 .40
186 Chad Lewis .15 .40
187 Justin Watson .15 .40
188 Warren Sapp .20 .50
189 Rod Woodson .25 .60
190 Ricky Williams .20 .50
191 Marty Booker .15 .40
192 MarTay Jenkins .15 .40
193 Peerless Price .15 .40
194 Tony Gonzalez .20 .50
195 Jon Kitna .15 .40
196 Stephen Davis .15 .40
197 Curtis Martin .20 .50
198 Matt Hasselbeck .15 .40
199 Pat Johnson .15 .40
200 Emmitt Smith .40 1.00
201 Doug Johnson .15 .40
202 Autry Denson .15 .40
203 Troy Brown .15 .40
204 Jeff Graham .15 .40
205 Corey Simon .15 .40
206 Jamel White .15 .40
207 Jeff Lewis .15 .40
208 Frank Sanders .15 .40
209 Al Wilson .15 .40
210 Jason Sehorn .20 .50
211 Shaun King .15 .40
212 Torry Holt .20 .50
213 Kordell Stewart .15 .40
214 Keenan McCardell .20 .50
215 Dedric Ward .15 .40
216 Michael Wiley .15 .40
217 Rob Johnson .20 .50
218 Jamal Lewis .25 .60
219 Herman Moore .15 .40
220 Ron Dugans .15 .40
221 Jason Taylor .25 .60
222 Charles Lee .15 .40
223 J.J. Stokes .15 .40
224 Albert Connell .15 .40
225 Keith Poole .15 .40
226 Elvis Grbac .20 .50
227 Shawn Jefferson .15 .40
228 Jackie Harris .20 .50
229 Derrick Alexander .15 .40
230 Darnell Autry .15 .40
231 Bobby Shaw .15 .40
232 Aaron Brooks .15 .40
233 Cris Carter .25 .60
234 Desmond Clark .15 .40
235 Spergon Wynn .15 .40
236 Qadry Ismail .15 .40
237 Sam Cowart .15 .40
238 Zach Thomas .20 .50
239 Drew Bledsoe .20 .50
240 Ronney Jenkins .15 .40
241 Keith Mitchell RC .15 .40
242 Laveranues Coles .20 .60
243 Marcus Pollard .15 .40
244 Darren Sharper .20 .50
245 Donald Hayes .15 .40
246 Brian Griese .15 .40
247 Frank Moreau .15 .40
248 Bruce Smith .20 .50
249 Fred Beasley .15 .40
250 Mike Alstott .15 .40
251 Trent Dilfer .15 .40
252 Terance Mathis .15 .40
253 Shawn Bryson .15 .40
254 Dennis Northcutt .15 .40
255 Brandon Bennett .15 .40
256 Stacey Mack .15 .40
257 Tim Brown .25 .60
258 Duce Staley .15 .40
259 Sean Dawkins .15 .40
260 Ricky Proehl .15 .40
261 Chris Fuamatu-ma'afala .15 .40
262 La'Roi Glover .15 .40
263 Bubba Franks .15 .40
264 Kevin Lockett .15 .40
265 Lamar Smith .20 .50
266 Priest Holmes .15 .40
267 Macey Brooks .15 .40
268 Anthony Wright .15 .40
269 Ed McCaffrey .20 .50
270 Joe Jurevicius .15 .40
271 Terrell Owens .20 .50
272 Tony Simmons .15 .40
273 Itula Mili .15 .40
274 Chad Morton .15 .40
275 Marvin Harrison .20 .50
276 Jason Gildon .15 .40
277 Derrick Mason .15 .40
278 Greg Clark .15 .40
279 Casey Crawford .15 .40
280 Kerry Collins .15 .40
281 Terrell Owens SH .15 .40
282 Marshall Faulk SH .15 .40
283 Mike Anderson SH .12 .30
284 Cris Carter SH .20 .50
285 Corey Dillon SH .12 .30
286 Daunte Culpepper LL .15 .40
287 Peyton Manning LL .50 1.25
288 Torry Holt LL .15 .40
289 Marvin Harrison LL .15 .40
290 Edgerrin James LL .15 .40
291 Takeo Spikes .15 .40
292 John Lynch .20 .50
293 Sam Madison .15 .40
294 Stephen Boyd .15 .40
295 Tony Siragusa .20 .50
296 Robert Porcher .15 .40
297 Donnell Bennett .15 .40
298 Hardy Nickerson .15 .40
299 Jonathan Quinn .15 .40
300 Rob Morris .15 .40
301 E.G. Green .15 .40
302 David Sloan .15 .40
303 Jason Tucker .15 .40
304 Darrin Chiaverini .15 .40
305 Wali Rainer .15 .40
306 Jerry Azumah .15 .40
307 Jonathan Linton .15 .40
308 Dameyune Craig .15 .40
309 Courtney Brown .15 .40
310 Jammi German .15 .40
311 Michael Vick RC 5.00 12.00
312 Jamar Fletcher RC .30 .75
313 Will Allen RC .50 1.25
314 Jamal Reynolds RC .30 .75
315 Quincy Morgan RC .40 1.00
316 Eric Kelly RC .30 .75
317 Michael Stone RC .30 .75
318 Rod Gardner RC .40 1.00
319 Ken-Yon Rambo RC .30 .75
320 Eric Westmoreland RC .30 .75
321 Steve Smith RC 1.00 2.50
322 George Layne RC .30 .75
323 Justin McCareins RC .40 1.00
324 Adam Archuleta RC .40 1.00
325 Justin Smith RC .60 1.50
326 David Terrell RC .40 1.00
327 Correll Buckhalter RC .30 .75
328 Drew Brees RC 15.00 40.00
329 Chris Barnes RC .30 .75
330 Santana Moss RC .50 1.25
331 Josh Heupel RC .50 1.25
332 Cedrick Wilson RC .40 1.00
333 Gerard Warren RC .40 1.00
334 Jamie Henderson RC .40 1.00
335 Onomo Ojo RC .30 .75
336 Marcus Stroud RC .40 1.00
337 Quincy Carter RC .40 1.00
338 Koren Robinson RC .40 1.00
339 Ryan Pickett RC .30 .75
340 Chad Johnson RC .50 1.25
341 Nate Clements RC .40 1.00
342 Jesse Palmer RC .40 1.00
343 Snoop Minnis RC .30 .75
344 Reggie Wayne RC .60 1.50
345 Kevin Kasper RC .30 .75
346 Will Peterson RC .40 1.00
347 Marques Tuiasosopo RC .40 1.00
348 Sage Rosenfels RC .40 1.00
349 Dan Alexander RC .40 1.00
350 LaDainian Tomlinson RC 6.00 12.00
351 Dan Morgan RC .40 1.00
352 Scotty Anderson RC .30 .75
353 Deuce McAllister RC .50 1.25
354 Todd Heap RC .40 1.00
355 Tony Dixon RC .30 .75
356 Chris Chambers RC .30 .75
357 Eddie Berlin RC .30 .75
358 Anthony Thomas RC .50 1.25
359 James Jackson RC .30 .75
360 Richard Seymour RC .50 1.25
361 Andre Carter RC .40 1.00
362 Bobby Newcombe RC .40 1.00
363 Robert Ferguson RC .50 1.25
364 Jonathan Carter RC .30 .75
365 Damione Lewis RC .40 1.00
366 Darnerien McCants RC .40 1.00
367 Tim Hasselbeck RC .40 1.00
368 Derrick Gibson RC .30 .75
369 Rudi Johnson RC .50 1.25
370 Alge Crumpler RC .50 1.25
371 Derrick Blaylock RC .40 1.00
372 Moran Norris RC .30 .75
373 Travis Minor RC .40 1.00
374 LaMont Jordan RC .50 1.25
375 Kevan Barlow RC .40 1.00
376 Freddie Mitchell RC .30 .75
377 Shaun Rogers RC .50 1.25
378 Tay Cody RC .30 .75
379 Travis Henry RC .40 1.00
380 Chris Weinke RC .40 1.00
381 Willie Middlebrooks RC .40 1.00
382 Rashard Casey RC .30 .75
383 Mike McMahon RC .40 1.00
384 Michael Bennett RC .40 1.00
385 Jabari Holloway RC .30 .75
CL1 Checklist .02 .10
CL2 Checklist .02 .10
CL3 Checklist .02 .10
SBMVP Ray Lewis FB AU 200.00 350.00

2001 Topps Collection

COMP.FACT.SET (385) 50.00 80.00
*VETS: .4X TO 1X BASIC CARDS
*ROOKIES: .4X TO 1X BASIC CARDS

2001 Topps MVP Promotion

*VETS 1-310: 8X TO 20X BASIC CARDS
*VETS WIN: 10X TO 25X BASIC CARDS
*ROOKIES 311-385: 4X TO 10X
STATED ODDS 1:186H, 1:41HTA JUMBOS
311 Michael Vick 40.00 80.00
328 Drew Brees 40.00 80.00
350 LaDainian Tomlinson 30.00 80.00

2001 Topps MVP Promotion Prizes

Issued by mail only to winners of the 2001 Topps MVP Promotion, this set highlights the 17 weekly winners, as chosen by Topps.

COMPLETE SET (17) 25.00 60.00
AVAILABLE ONLY VIA REDEMPTION
MVP1 Brian Griese 1.00 2.50
MVP2 Peyton Manning 4.00 10.00
MVP3 Kurt Warner 2.50 6.00
MVP4 Ricky Williams 1.25 3.00
MVP5 Terrell Owens 1.25 3.00
MVP6 David Patten 1.00 2.50
MVP7 Corey Dillon 1.00 2.50
MVP8 Ahman Green 1.25 3.00
MVP9 Shaun Alexander 1.00 2.50
MVP10 Randy Moss 1.25 3.00
MVP11 Jay Fiedler 1.25 3.00
MVP12 Steve McNair 1.25 3.00
MVP13 Todd Bouman 1.00 2.50
MVP14 Kordell Stewart 1.00 2.50
MVP15 Marshall Faulk 1.25 3.00
MVP16 Tim Couch 1.00 2.50
MVP17 Anthony Thomas 1.50 4.00

2001 Topps Autographs

Randomly inserted in packs at an overall rate of 1:322 hobby and 1:72 HTA, this autograph set featured some of the top players from the NFL and a few youngsters fresh from the 2001 NFL Draft. The insertion odds varied by groups of cards: group 1 odds 1:21,614, group 2 odds 1:12,763, group 3 odds 1:4268, group 4 odds 1:912, group 5 odds 1:1418, and group 6 odds 1:1063. We've included the group number for each card below after the player's name. Note that there were a few redemption cards inserted into packs that carried an expiration date of 6/30/2003.

GROUP 1 ODDS 1:21,614H, 1:4731HTA
GROUP 2 ODDS 1:12,763H, 1:2839HTA
GROUP 3 ODDS 1:4268H, 1:946HTA
GROUP 4 STATED ODDS 1:912H, 1:203HTA
GROUP 5 STATED ODDS 1:1418H, 1:315HTA
GROUP 6 STATED ODDS 1:1063H, 1:236HTA
OVERALL ODDS 1:322H, 1:72HTA JUMBOS
TABU Brian Urlacher 4 15.00 40.00
TACC Chris Chambers 4 5.00 12.00
TACJ Chad Johnson 6 8.00 20.00
TADB Drew Brees 3 75.00 135.00
TADC Daunte Culpepper 1 12.00 30.00
TADH Donald Hayes 4 5.00 12.00
TADJM Deuce McAllister 1 8.00 20.00
TADM Derrick Mason 4 5.00 12.00
TAEM Eric Moulds 4 5.00 12.00
TAES Emmitt Smith 2 75.00 150.00
TAJB Josh Booty 5 6.00 15.00
TAJH Joe Horn 4 5.00 12.00
TAJP Jesse Palmer 5 6.00 15.00
TAJS Jimmy Smith 4 6.00 15.00
TAJT James Thrash 6 6.00 15.00
TAKB Kevan Barlow 6 6.00 15.00
TAMV Michael Vick 1 60.00 120.00
TASM Santana Moss 3 8.00 20.00
TATM Travis Minor 5 6.00 15.00
TATW Terrence Wilkins 3 5.00 12.00

2001 Topps Combos

Issued at a stated rate of one in eight hobby packs and one in two HTA packs, this 19 card set featured a rookie and a young player. While this was supposed to be a 20 card set, card number TC20 was never issued.

COMPLETE SET (19) 12.50 30.00
STATED ODDS 1:8H, 1:2HTA JUMBOS
TC1 E.James/S.Moss .40 1.00
TC2 T.Holt/K.Robinson .60 1.50
TC3 J.Lewis/T.Henry .75 2.00
TC4 C.Martin/K.Barlow .60 1.50
TC5 C.Carter/K.Rambo .75 2.00
TC6 T.Aikman/F.Mitchell 1.00 2.50
TC7 B.Griese/D.Terrell .50 1.25
TC8 T.Wheatley/A.Thomas .75 2.00
TC9 W.Dunn/T.Minor .50 1.25
TC10 P.Warrick/S.Minnis .50 1.25
TC11 W.Sapp/D.Morgan .60 1.50
TC12 T.Gonzalez/A.Carter .60 1.50
TC13 A.Freeman/M.Vick .75 2.00
TC14 R.Dayne/M.Bennett .60 1.50
TC15 M.Alstott/D.Brees 2.00 5.00
TC16 A.Green/C.Buckhalter .60 1.50
TC17 B.Johnson/C.Weinke .60 1.50
TC18 E.Moulds/F.Smoot .50 1.25
TC19 R.Lewis/R.Wayne .60 1.50

2001 Topps Hall of Fame Autographs

Randomly inserted in packs at a rate of 1:9242 hobby/retail and 1:2049 hobby jumbos, this set featured autographs from the Hall of Fame Class of 2001 as well as Deacon Jones from the 1980 class.

STATED ODDS 1:9242H, 1:2049HTA JUMBOS
TADJ Deacon Jones 60.00 120.00
TAJS Jackie Slater 60.00 120.00
TAJY Jack Youngblood 60.00 120.00
TAML Marv Levy 100.00 200.00
TARY Ron Yary 60.00 120.00
TAMM Mike Munchak 100.00 200.00

2001 Topps Hobby Masters

Randomly inserted in packs at a rate of 1:3 HTA Jumbos. This 10-card set was only available in hobby jumbo packs and featured the 10 superstars from the NFL. The set design featured a holographic-prism background with an action pose from the player.

COMPLETE SET (10) 6.00 15.00
STATED ODDS 1:3 HTA JUMBOS
HM1 Jamal Lewis .75 2.00
HM2 Daunte Culpepper .60 1.50
HM3 Kurt Warner 1.25 3.00
HM4 Edgerrin James .60 1.50
HM5 Randy Moss .60 1.50
HM6 Eddie George .75 2.00
HM7 Mike Anderson .50 1.25
HM8 Peyton Manning 2.00 5.00
HM9 Marvin Harrison .60 1.50
HM10 Cris Carter .75 2.00

2001 Topps King of Kings Jerseys

Randomly inserted in packs at a rate of 1:580 hobby/retail and 1:129 HTA jumbos this 9-card set was highlighted with the featured player with a swatch of his jersey.

STATED ODDS 1:580 H, 1:129HTA JUMBOS
KCD Corey Dillon 2.50 6.00
KDM Dan Marino 8.00 20.00
KES Emmitt Smith 6.00 15.00
KFT Fred Taylor 2.50 6.00
KJR Jerry Rice 8.00 20.00
KPM Peyton Manning 10.00 25.00
KRM Randy Moss 3.00 8.00
KTO Terrell Owens 3.00 8.00
KWP Walter Payton 12.00 30.00

2001 Topps King of Kings Jerseys Golden

Randomly inserted in packs at a rate of 1:1051 HTA jumbos this set was highlighted by the featured players with a swatch of their jerseys.

STATED ODDS 1:1051 HTA JUMBOS
KGDT C.Dillon/F.Taylor 15.00 40.00
KGOR T.Owens/J.Rice 30.00 80.00
KGSP E.Smith/W.Payton 75.00 150.00

2001 Topps Own the Game

Randomly inserted in packs at a rate of 1:8 hobby/retail and 1:2 HTA jumbos, this 30-card set features 5 different subsets: All The Way, Ground Warriors, Perfect Spiral, Intimidators, and Showtime. The card designs featured a holographic foil background with the subset name on the front of the card.

COMPLETE SET (30) 15.00 40.00
STATED ODDS 1:8H, 1:2HTA JUMBOS
AW1 Marvin Harrison .50 1.25
AW2 Muhsin Muhammad .40 1.00
AW3 Torry Holt .50 1.25
AW4 Rod Smith .50 1.25
AW5 Randy Moss .50 1.25
AW6 Cris Carter .60 1.50
AW7 Ed McCaffrey .50 1.25
AW8 Isaac Bruce .60 1.50
AW9 Terrell Owens .50 1.25
AW10 Tony Gonzalez .50 1.25
GW1 Edgerrin James .50 1.25
GW2 Robert Smith .40 1.00
GW3 Marshall Faulk .50 1.25
GW4 Mike Anderson .40 1.00
GW5 Eddie George .60 1.50
GW6 Corey Dillon .40 1.00
GW7 Fred Taylor .40 1.00
PS1 Brian Griese .40 1.00
PS2 Peyton Manning 1.50 4.00
PS3 Jeff Garcia .40 1.00
PS4 Daunte Culpepper .50 1.25
PS5 Brett Favre 1.25 3.00
PS6 Kurt Warner 1.00 2.50
PS7 Donovan McNabb .50 1.25
TI1 La'Roi Glover .40 1.00
TI2 Darren Sharper .50 1.25
TI3 Mike Peterson .40 1.00
TS1 Derrick Mason .40 1.00
TS2 Az-Zahir Hakim .40 1.00
TS3 Jermaine Lewis .40 1.00

2001 Topps Pro Bowl Jerseys

Randomly inserted in packs at a rate of 1:425 hobby/retail and 1:95 HTA jumbos, this 12-card set features jersey swatches from the 2001 NFL Pro-Bowl. The card design features an action pose in the foregroud with the Pro-Bowl logo shadowed with light blue in the background.

STATED ODDS 1:425H, 1:95HTA JUMBOS
TPCG Charlie Garner 3.00 8.00
TPCL Chad Lewis 2.50 6.00
TPDM Derrick Mason 2.50 6.00
TPEM Eric Moulds 2.50 6.00
TPJG Jeff Garcia 2.50 6.00
TPJL John Lynch 3.00 8.00
TPJS Junior Seau 3.00 8.00
TPJT Jason Taylor 4.00 10.00
TPMA Mike Alstott 2.50 6.00
TPRG Rich Gannon 3.00 8.00
TPRL Ray Lewis 4.00 10.00
TPTH Torry Holt 3.00 8.00

2001 Topps Pro Bowl Jerseys Autographs

Randomly inserted in packs at a rate of 1:9437 hobby/retail and 1:2114 HTA jumbos, this 4-card set features jersey swatches from the 2001 NFL Pro-Bowl. The card design features an action pose in the foreground with the Pro-Bowl logo shadowed with light blue in the background, with the signature on the front.

STATED ODDS 1:9437H, 1:2114HTA JUMBOS
TPADC Daunte Culpepper 30.00 80.00
TPADM Derrick Mason 20.00 50.00
TPAEJ Edgerrin James 40.00 100.00

2001 Topps Rookie Premier Autographs

Randomly inserted in packs at a rate of 1:140 HTA jumbos, this set features the top rookies from the 2001 NFL Draft scheduled to appear at the Rookie Photo Shoot. The card design is similar to the base set with the exception of a white stripe across the base of the card for the signature. The cards were produced at the Rookie Photo Shoot and signed at the event for insertion into packs. Some cards also hit the market without the Topps authenticity hologram on the back. Chad Johnson is thought to be the toughest card to find in the set.

STATED ODDS 1:140HTA JUMBOS
RPAC Andre Carter 15.00 40.00
RPAT Anthony Thomas 20.00 50.00
RPCC Chris Chambers 15.00 40.00
RPCJ Chad Johnson SP 20.00 50.00
RPCW Chris Weinke 15.00 40.00
RPDB Drew Brees 1700.00 2500.00
RPDM Dan Morgan 15.00 40.00
RPDMC Deuce McAllister 20.00 50.00
RPDT David Terrell 15.00 40.00
RPDTM D.Terrell/S.Moss 60.00 150.00
RPDVB M.Vick/D.Brees 800.00 1500.00
RPFM Freddie Mitchell 12.00 30.00
RPJH Josh Heupel 20.00 50.00
RPJJ James Jackson 12.00 30.00
RPJP Jesse Palmer 15.00 40.00
RPJS Justin Smith 25.00 60.00
RPKB Kevan Barlow 15.00 40.00
RPKR Koren Robinson 15.00 40.00
RPLD Leonard Davis 20.00 50.00
RPLT LaDainian Tomlinson 200.00 400.00
RPMB Michael Bennett 15.00 40.00
RPMMC Mike McMahon 15.00 40.00
RPMT Marques Tuiasosopo 15.00 40.00
RPMV Michael Vick 100.00 200.00
RPQC Quincy Carter 15.00 40.00
RPQM Quincy Morgan 15.00 40.00
RPRF Robert Ferguson 20.00 50.00
RPRG Rod Gardner 15.00 40.00
RPRJ Rudi Johnson 20.00 50.00
RPRS Richard Seymour 20.00 50.00
RPRW Reggie Wayne 30.00 80.00
RPSM Santana Moss 20.00 50.00
RPSM Snoop Minnis 12.00 30.00
RPSR Sage Rosenfels 15.00 40.00
RPTH Travis Henry 15.00 40.00
RPTM Travis Minor 15.00 40.00
RPGW Gerard Warren 15.00 40.00

2001 Topps Rookie Reprint Jerseys

Randomly inserted in packs at a rate of 1:1159 hobby/retail and 1:258 HTA jumbos this 4-card set features the reprint of the rookie card for the featured player and a swatch of his jersey.

STATED ODDS 1:1159H, 1:258HTA JUMBOS
TODM Dan Marino 40.00 100.00
TOES Emmitt Smith 30.00 80.00
TOJR Jerry Rice 25.00 60.00
TOWP Walter Payton 40.00 100.00

2001 Topps Super Bowl Bunting

Issued at a stated rate of one in 485 retail jumbo packs and one in 968 retail packs, these six cards feature players from Super Bowl XXXV along with a swatch of event used bunting.

ODDS 1:485 RET.JUMBO 1:968 RETAIL
SBB1 Kerry Collins 12.00 30.00
SBB2 Trent Dilfer 15.00 40.00
SBB3 Ike Hilliard 15.00 40.00
SBB4 Shannon Sharpe 15.00 40.00
SBB5 Ron Dayne 20.00 50.00
SBB6 Jason Sehorn 15.00 40.00

2001 Topps Super Bowl Ticket Stubs

Randomly inserted in packs at a rate of 1:4702 hobby/retail and 1:1046HTA jumbos, this 6-card set features a piece of a Super Bowl XXXV ticket stub and highlights a player that participated in Super Bowl XXXV.

STATED ODDS 1:4702H, 1:1046HTA JUMBOS
LEWIS AU STATED ODDS 1:1380 HTA JUMBOS
1 Ron Dayne 50.00 100.00
2 Ron Dixon 25.00 60.00
3 Jamal Lewis 30.00 80.00
4 Jermaine Lewis 25.00 60.00
5 Ray Lewis 90.00 150.00
6 Brandon Stokley 30.00 80.00
7 Amani Toomer 25.00 60.00

2001 Topps Team Topps Legends Autographs

Randomly inserted in various 2001, 2002 and 2003 Topps products packs, this set featured actual autographs from NFL legends who have earned a spot on the "Team Topps" roster. Most players were produced with both a rookie reprint and final year reprint card and many were initially released via mail redemption cards. The redemptions carried an expiration date of 6/30/2003.

OVERALL GALLERY ODDS 1:310 H/R
OVERALL HERITAGE ODDS 1:282 H/R
OVERALL STADIUM ODDS 1:146 HOB/RET
OVERALL TOPPS ODDS 1:1597H/R,1:355HTA
TTF4 Tommy McDonald 68T 10.00 25.00
TTF6 Terry Metcalf 82T 5.00 12.00
TTF7 Art Donovan 59T 25.00 50.00
TTF9 Otis Sistrunk 79T 5.00 12.00
TTF10 Chuck Foreman 81T 5.00 12.00
TTF12 Don Maynard 73T 10.00 25.00
TTF13 Joe Namath 73T 60.00 120.00
TTF14 Charlie Joiner 87T 5.00 12.00
TTF16 Cliff Branch 85T 8.00 20.00
TTF19 Paul Hornung 57T 40.00 80.00
TTF20 Tom Dempsey 79T 5.00 12.00
TTF21 Billy Kilmer 78T 5.00 12.00
TTR1 Jim Brown 58T 125.00 200.00
TTR2 Dick Butkus 68T 40.00 80.00
TTR4 Tommy McDonald 57T 10.00 25.00
TTR5 John Hannah 74T 8.00 20.00
TTR6 Terry Metcalf 74T 5.00 12.00
TTR7 Art Donovan 56T 25.00 50.00
TTR9 Otis Sistrunk 74T 5.00 12.00
TTR10 Chuck Foreman 74T 5.00 12.00
TTR11 Sonny Jurgensen 58T 40.00 80.00
TTR12 Don Maynard 61T 10.00 25.00
TTR13 Joe Namath 65T 60.00 120.00
TTR14 Charlie Joiner 72T 8.00 20.00
TTR15 Mike Singletary 83T 15.00 40.00
TTR16 Cliff Branch 75T 8.00 20.00
TTR17 Johnny Unitas 57T 250.00 400.00
TTR18 Fred Biletnikoff 65T 20.00 40.00
TTR20 Tom Dempsey 70T 5.00 12.00
TTR21 Billy Kilmer 62T 5.00 12.00
TTR22 Barry Sanders 89TT 125.00 200.00
TTR23 Len Dawson 64T 20.00 40.00

2001 Topps Walter Payton Reprints

Randomly inserted in packs at a rate of 1:12 hobby/retail and 1:3 HTA jumbos, this 12-card set was a reprint of each of Walter Payton's regular issue base Topps card. The set fully resembles the originals with the exceptions of the high gloss coating and the gold-foil stamp.

COMPLETE SET (12) 15.00 40.00
COMMON CARD (WP1-WP12) 1.50 4.00
STATED ODDS 1:12H, 1:3HTA JUMBO

2001 Topps Hall of Fame Class of 2001

This set was distributed by Topps at the 2001 Induction ceremories for the Pro Football Hall of Fame. Each card includes a photo of a 2001 inductee printed in a very similar style to the 2001 Topps Hall of Fame Autographs inserts. A gold foil "Class of 2001" logo appears on the cardfronts. The cards are unnumbered and listed below alphabetically.

COMPLETE SET (7) 6.00 15.00
1 Nick Buoniconti 1.25 3.00
2 Marv Levy 1.25 3.00
3 Mike Munchak 1.00 2.50
4 Jackie Slater 1.00 2.50
5 Lynn Swann 2.00 5.00
6 Ron Yary 1.00 2.50
7 Jack Youngblood 1.25 3.00

2001 Topps Pro Bowl Promos

is set of 9-cards were issued on one unperforated sheet inside the 2001 Pro Bowl game program. The cards were printed on slick glossy thick stock and resemble the design of the 2000 Topps base set cards. The Pro Bowl logo appears on the cardfronts.

COMPLETE SET (9) 3.00 6.00
1 Peyton Manning .75 2.00
2 Donovan McNabb .25 .60
3 Marshall Faulk .25 .60
4 Randy Moss .25 .60
5 Edgerrin James .25 .60
6 Daunte Culpepper .25 .60
7 Jamal Lewis .30 .75
8 Jeff Garcia .20 .50
9 Warren Sapp .25 .60

2001 Topps Super Bowl XXXV Card Show

is 12-card set was issued one card at a time by completing the Treasure Hunt challenge at the Topps booth at the 2001 NFL Experience Super Bowl Card Show. Each card features a star player printed with an atomic refractor type design on the cardfront and a traditional cardback.

COMPLETE SET (12) 25.00 50.00
1 Peyton Manning 4.00 10.00
2 Donovan McNabb 1.25 3.00
3 Marshall Faulk 1.25 3.00
4 Jeff Garcia 1.00 2.50
5 Randy Moss 1.25 3.00
6 Fred Taylor 1.00 2.50
7 Robert Smith 1.00 2.50
8 Mike Anderson 1.00 2.50
9 Edgerrin James 1.25 3.00
10 Warren Sapp 1.25 3.00
11 Daunte Culpepper 1.25 3.00
12 Jamal Lewis 1.50 4.00

2002 Topps

is 385-card set was released in late June, 2002. This set contains 290 veteran cards, 20 Weekly Wrap-Up (291-310) and 75 rookies (311-385) . Boxes contained 36 packs of 10 cards with each pack having an $1.49 SRP. HTA packs were also produced for this product, each of those packs had an $5 SRP and came 12 packs per box and six boxes per case.

COMPLETE SET (385) 30.00 60.00
1 Kurt Warner .20 .50
2 Jeff Graham .15 .40
3 Todd Bouman .15 .40
4 Duce Staley .15 .40
5 Jon Kitna .15 .40
6 Shannon Sharpe .20 .50
7 Darrell Jackson .20 .50
8 Michael Pittman .20 .50
9 Tony Gonzalez .20 .50
10 Wayne Chrebet .15 .40
11 Jevon Kearse .15 .40
12 Bill Schroeder .15 .40
13 Jeremy McDaniel .15 .40
14 Todd Pinkston .15 .40
15 Maurice Smith .15 .40
16 Charlie Batch .15 .40
17 Olandis Gary .20 .50
18 Ron Dugans .15 .40
19 Brian Urlacher .25 .60
20 Amani Toomer .15 .40
21 Tim Couch .15 .40
22 Derrick Brooks .15 .40
23 Frank Sanders .15 .40
24 James Williams .15 .40
25 Lamar Smith .15 .40
26 Darrick Vaughn .15 .40
27 Cris Carter .25 .60
28 Roland Williams .15 .40
29 Bobby Shaw .15 .40
30 Jerome Pathon .15 .40
31 Rod Woodson .25 .60
32 Ronney Jenkins .15 .40
33 Chris Chandler .20 .50
34 Dez White .15 .40
35 Rod Smith .20 .50
36 Troy Brown .15 .40
37 JaJuan Dawson .15 .40
38 Reidel Anthony .15 .40
39 Mike Green .15 .40
40 Steve Smith .25 .60
41 Willie Jackson .15 .40
42 MarTay Jenkins .15 .40
43 Reggie Germany .15 .40
44 Desmond Howard .20 .50
45 Fred Taylor .15 .40
46 Scotty Anderson .15 .40
47 John Lynch .20 .50
48 Amos Zereoue .15 .40
49 Darnay Scott .20 .50
50 Anthony Thomas .20 .50
51 Jeff Garcia .15 .40
52 Charlie Garner .20 .50
53 Drew Bledsoe .20 .50
54 Donnie Edwards .15 .40
55 Corey Bradford .15 .40
56 Desmond Clark .15 .40
57 Courtney Brown .15 .40
58 Wesley Walls .20 .50
59 Chad Brown .15 .40
60 Shawn Jefferson .15 .40
61 Corey Dillon .15 .40
62 Johnnie Morton .20 .50
63 Marcus Pollard .15 .40
64 Jason Taylor .20 .50
65 Kevin Faulk .15 .40
66 Shane Matthews .15 .40
67 Hines Ward .20 .50
68 Garrison Hearst .15 .40
69 Trung Canidate .15 .40
70 Tony Banks .15 .40
71 Matt Hasselbeck .15 .40
72 Correll Buckhalter .15 .40
73 Ron Dayne .20 .50
74 Zach Thomas .20 .50
75 Emmitt Smith .40 1.00
76 Peter Warrick .15 .40
77 Rob Johnson .20 .50
78 Michael Strahan .20 .50
79 Ray Lewis .25 .60
80 Jamir Miller .15 .40
81 Brian Griese .15 .40
82 Stacey Mack .15 .40
83 Michael Bennett .15 .40
84 Ricky Williams .20 .50
85 Jamal Lewis .20 .50
86 Doug Flutie .20 .50
87 Jonathan Quinn .15 .40
88 Mike Alstott .15 .40
89 Samari Rolle .15 .40
90 LaMont Jordan .20 .50
91 Dominic Rhodes .15 .40
92 Quincy Carter .15 .40
93 Marcus Robinson .20 .50
94 Travis Henry .15 .40
95 Jason Brookins .15 .40
96 Nick Goings .15 .40
97 Brian Finneran .15 .40
98 Dorsey Levens .20 .50
99 Reggie Swinton .15 .40
100 Chris Chambers .15 .40
101 Kordell Stewart .15 .40
102 Tai Streets .15 .40
103 Chris Redman .15 .40
104 Jacquez Green .15 .40
105 Rod Gardner .15 .40
106 Kevin Kasper .15 .40
107 Anthony Henry .15 .40
108 Dan Morgan .15 .40
109 Ronald McKinnon .15 .40
110 Qadry Ismail .15 .40
111 Chad Johnson .15 .40
112 James Stewart .15 .40
113 Terrence Wilkins .15 .40
114 Joey Galloway .20 .50
115 Deuce McAllister .20 .50
116 Joe Jurevicius .15 .40
117 Tyrone Wheatley .20 .50
118 Jason Gildon .20 .50
119 LaDainian Tomlinson .25 .60
120 Grant Wistrom .15 .40
121 Eddie George .20 .50
122 Laveranues Coles .20 .50
123 Antowain Smith .20 .50
124 Larry Parker .15 .40
125 Bubba Franks .15 .40
126 Troy Hambrick .15 .40
127 Jamal Reynolds .15 .40
128 Doug Chapman .15 .40
129 Freddie Mitchell .15 .40
130 Tim Dwight .15 .40
131 Erron Kinney .15 .40
132 James Allen .15 .40
133 Eric Moulds .15 .40
134 Keenan McCardell .20 .50
135 David Sloan .15 .40
136 Dennis Northcutt .15 .40
137 Kevan Barlow .15 .40
138 Bobby Engram .15 .40
139 Champ Bailey .20 .50
140 Donald Hayes .15 .40
141 Brandon Bennett .15 .40
142 Deltha O'Neal .15 .40
143 James Jackson .15 .40
144 Shaun Rogers .15 .40
145 Joe Johnson .15 .40
146 Ricky Watters .20 .50
147 Warrick Dunn .15 .40
148 Steve McNair .20 .50
149 Marvin Harrison .20 .50
150 Kendrell Bell .15 .40
151 Jim Miller .15 .40
152 Terry Allen .20 .50
153 Jake Plummer .15 .40
154 James McKnight .15 .40
155 Curtis Martin .20 .50
156 Keyshawn Johnson .20 .50
157 Kevin Lockett .15 .40
158 Jeremiah Trotter .15 .40
159 Derrick Alexander .15 .40
160 Brandon Stokley .15 .40
161 J.J. Stokes .15 .40
162 Drew Bennett .20 .50
163 Drew Brees .50 1.25
164 Tim Brown .25 .60
165 Daunte Culpepper .20 .50
166 Rocket Ismail .20 .50
167 Alex Van Pelt .15 .40
168 Arnold Jackson .15 .40
169 Oronde Gadsden .15 .40
170 Isaac Bruce .25 .60
171 Warren Sapp .20 .50
172 Michael Westbrook .15 .40
173 John Abraham .20 .50
174 Jessie Armstead .15 .40
175 Brock Marion .15 .40
176 Brett Favre .50 1.25
177 Benjamin Gay .15 .40
178 Muhsin Muhammad .15 .40
179 Reggie Wayne .20 .50
180 Kailee Wong .15 .40
181 Rich Gannon .20 .50
182 Chris Fuamatu-Ma'afala .15 .40
183 Shaun Alexander .15 .40
184 Kevin Dyson .20 .50
185 Kwamie Lassiter .15 .40
186 Elvis Joseph .15 .40
187 Trent Dilfer .15 .40
188 Marty Booker .15 .40
189 Travis Taylor .15 .40
190 Michael Vick .20 .50
191 Mike McMahon .15 .40
192 Jay Fiedler .20 .50
193 Zack Bronson .15 .40
194 Derrick Mason .15 .40
195 Anthony Becht .15 .40
196 Ahman Green .20 .50
197 Alge Crumpler .20 .50
198 Thomas Jones .15 .40
199 Tiki Barber .20 .50
200 Donovan McNabb .20 .50
201 Andre Carter .15 .40
202 Stephen Davis .15 .40
203 Troy Edwards .15 .40
204 Lawyer Milloy .15 .40
205 Peyton Manning .60 1.50
206 James Farrior .15 .40
207 Gerard Warren .15 .40
208 Peerless Price .15 .40
209 Avion Black .15 .40
210 Marcellus Wiley .15 .40
211 Torry Holt .20 .50
212 A.J. Feeley .15 .40
213 Travis Minor .15 .40
214 Darren Sharper .15 .40
215 Jerry Porter .15 .40
216 Randall Cunningham .20 .50
217 Chris Weinke .15 .40
218 Mike Anderson .15 .40
219 Snoop Minnis .15 .40
220 David Martin .15 .40
221 Vinny Sutherland .15 .40
222 Ki-Jana Carter .20 .50
223 Kevin Swayne .15 .40
224 Mark Brunell .20 .50
225 Quincy Morgan .15 .40
226 David Terrell .15 .40
227 Terance Mathis .15 .40
228 Frank Wycheck .15 .40
229 Az-Zahir Hakim .15 .40
230 Freddie Jones .15 .40
231 Jerry Rice .50 1.25
232 Ike Hilliard .15 .40
233 Terrell Davis .20 .50
234 Shawn Bryson .15 .40
235 David Boston .15 .40
236 Edgerrin James .20 .50
237 Trent Green .15 .40
238 Charlie Rogers .15 .40
239 Vinny Testaverde .15 .40
240 Koren Robinson .15 .40
241 Ronde Barber .15 .40
242 Dwayne Carswell .15 .40
243 Dedric Ward .15 .40
244 Richard Huntley .15 .40
245 Jamal Anderson .20 .50
246 Ryan Leaf .15 .40
247 Priest Holmes .15 .40
248 Tom Brady 6.00 15.00
249 Charles Woodson .25 .60
250 Jerome Bettis .25 .60
251 Tommy Polley .15 .40
252 Anthony Wright .15 .40
253 Chad Pennington .15 .40
254 David Patten .15 .40
255 Antonio Freeman .25 .60
256 Jamel White .15 .40
257 Jermaine Lewis .15 .40
258 Aaron Brooks .15 .40
259 Ron Dixon .15 .40
260 James Thrash .20 .50
261 Junior Seau .20 .50
262 Byron Chamberlain .15 .40
263 Ed McCaffrey .20 .50
264 Nate Clements .15 .40
265 Tony Martin .20 .50
266 Germane Crowell .15 .40
267 Terrell Owens .20 .50
268 Marshall Faulk .20 .50
269 Dat Nguyen .15 .40
270 Elvis Grbac .15 .40
271 Dante Hall .15 .40
272 Sylvester Morris .15 .40
273 Mike Brown .15 .40
274 Kevin Johnson .15 .40
275 Jimmy Smith .20 .50
276 Randy Moss .20 .50
277 Kerry Collins .15 .40
278 Santana Moss .20 .50
279 Plaxico Burress .15 .40
280 Brad Johnson .20 .50
281 Curtis Conway .20 .50
282 Eric Johnson .15 .40
283 Joe Horn .15 .40
284 Peter Boulware .15 .40
285 Larry Foster .15 .40
286 Nate Jacquet .15 .40
287 Terry Glenn .20 .50
288 Jarious Jackson .15 .40
289 Hugh Douglas .15 .40
290 Chad Lewis .15 .40
291 Ahman Green WW .15 .40
292 Peyton Manning WW .50 1.25
293 Kurt Warner WW .15 .40
294 Daunte Culpepper WW .15 .40
295 Tom Brady WW 5.00 12.00
296 Rod Gardner WW .12 .30
297 Corey Dillon WW .12 .30
298 Priest Holmes WW .12 .30
299 Shaun Alexander WW .12 .30
300 Randy Moss WW .15 .40
301 Eric Moulds WW .12 .30
302 Brett Favre WW .40 1.00
303 Todd Bouman WW .12 .30
304 Dominic Rhodes WW .12 .30
305 Marvin Harrison WW .15 .40
306 Torry Holt WW .15 .40
307 Derrick Mason WW .12 .30
308 Jerry Rice WW .40 1.00
309 Donovan McNabb WW .15 .40
310 Marshall Faulk WW .15 .40
311 David Carr RC .30 .75
312 Quentin Jammer RC .50 1.25
313 Mike Williams RC .30 .75
314 Rocky Calmus RC .40 1.00
315 Travis Fisher RC .40 1.00
316 Dwight Freeney RC .60 1.50
317 Jeremy Shockey RC .50 1.25
318 Marquise Walker RC .30 .75
319 Eric Crouch RC .50 1.25
320 DeShaun Foster RC .50 1.25
321 Roy Williams RC .30 .75
322 Andre Davis RC .30 .75
323 Alex Brown RC .50 1.25
324 Michael Lewis RC .40 1.00
325 Terry Charles RC .30 .75
326 Clinton Portis RC .50 1.25
327 Dennis Johnson RC .30 .75
328 Lito Sheppard RC .50 1.25
329 Ryan Sims RC .50 1.25

330 Raonall Smith RC .30 .75
331 Albert Haynesworth RC .50 1.25
332 Eddie Freeman RC .30 .75
333 Levi Jones RC .30 .75
334 Josh McCown RC .50 1.25
335 Cliff Russell RC .30 .75
336 Maurice Morris RC .40 1.00
337 Antwaan Randle El RC .40 1.00
338 Ladell Betts RC .50 1.25
339 Daniel Graham RC .40 1.00
340 David Garrard RC .40 1.00
341 Antonio Bryant RC .50 1.25
342 Patrick Ramsey RC .40 1.00
343 Kelly Campbell RC .40 1.00
344 Will Overstreet RC .30 .75
345 Ryan Denney RC .30 .75
346 John Henderson RC .40 1.00
347 Freddie Milons RC .30 .75
348 Tim Carter RC .40 1.00
349 Kurt Kittner RC .30 .75
350 Joey Harrington RC .30 .75
351 Ricky Williams RC .40 1.00
352 Bryant McKinnie RC .30 .75
353 Ed Reed RC 2.00 5.00
354 Josh Reed RC .40 1.00
355 Seth Burford RC .30 .75
356 Javon Walker RC .50 1.25
357 Jamar Martin RC .40 1.00
358 Leonard Henry RC .30 .75
359 Julius Peppers RC .75 2.00
360 Jabar Gaffney RC .30 .75
361 Kalimba Edwards RC .40 1.00
362 Napoleon Harris RC .40 1.00
363 Ashley Lelie RC .30 .75
364 Anthony Weaver RC .30 .75
365 Bryan Thomas RC .30 .75
366 Wendell Bryant RC .30 .75
367 Damien Anderson RC .30 .75
368 Travis Stephens RC .30 .75
369 Rohan Davey RC .50 1.25
370 Mike Pearson RC .30 .75
371 Marc Colombo RC .30 .75
372 Phillip Buchanon RC .50 1.25
373 T.J. Duckett RC .30 .75
374 Ron Johnson RC .40 1.00
375 Larry Tripplett RC .30 .75
376 Randy Fasani RC .30 .75
377 Keyuo Craver RC .30 .75
378 Marquand Manuel RC .30 .75
379 Jonathan Wells RC .40 1.00
380 Reche Caldwell RC .40 1.00
381 Luke Staley RC .30 .75
382 Donte Stallworth RC .50 1.25
383 Levar Fisher RC .30 .75
384 Lamar Gordon RC .40 1.00
385 William Green RC .40 1.00
SBMVP Tom Brady FB AU/150 400.00 650.00
CL1 Checklist Card .02 .10
CL2 Checklist Card .02 .10
CL3 Checklist Card .02 .10
CL4 Checklist Card .02 .10

2002 Topps Collection

COMP.FACT.SET (385) 40.00 75.00
*VETS: .4X TO 1X BASE TOPPS
*ROOKIES: .4X TO 1X BASE TOPPS

2002 Topps MVP Promotion

*1-310 VETS: 10X TO 25X BASIC CARDS
*311-385 ROOKIES: 4X TO 10X
STATED ODDS 1:112 HOB, 1:87 RET
40 Steve Smith WIN 10.00 25.00
51 Jeff Garcia WIN 10.00 25.00
53 Drew Bledsoe WIN 10.00 25.00
84 Ricky Williams WIN 10.00 25.00
94 Travis Henry WIN 10.00 25.00
149 Marvin Harrison WIN 10.00 25.00
176 Brett Favre WIN 25.00 50.00
183 Shaun Alexander WIN 10.00 25.00
190 Michael Vick WIN 10.00 25.00
200 Donovan McNabb WIN 10.00 25.00
247 Priest Holmes WIN 10.00 25.00
248 Tom Brady WIN 15.00 40.00
253 Chad Pennington WIN 10.00 25.00
267 Terrell Owens WIN 10.00 25.00
268 Marshall Faulk WIN 10.00 25.00
279 Plaxico Burress WIN 10.00 25.00
317 Jeremy Shockey WIN 10.00 25.00

2002 Topps MVP Promotion Prizes

is set was issued in factory set form via a mail redemption program. Topps chose 17-players as their weekly "MVPs" during the 2002 NFL season. Collectors who held the MVP Promotion insert card for one fo the 17 could send that card to Topps in exchange for this set. Each card was printed on foil stock and mentions the week in which the player was honored by Topps.
COMPLETE SET (17) 20.00 50.00
MVP1 Priest Holmes .75 2.00
MVP2 Drew Bledsoe 1.00 2.50
MVP3 Tom Brady 6.00 15.00
MVP4 Shaun Alexander .75 2.00
MVP5 Brett Favre 2.50 6.00
MVP6 Travis Henry .75 2.00
MVP7 Marshall Faulk 1.00 2.50
MVP8 Terrell Owens 1.00 2.50
MVP9 Jeff Garcia .75 2.00
MVP10 Plaxico Burress .75 2.00
MVP11 Donovan McNabb 1.00 2.50
MVP12 Ricky Williams 1.00 2.50
MVP13 Michael Vick 1.00 2.50
MVP14 Steve Smith 1.25 3.00
MVP15 Marvin Harrison 1.00 2.50
MVP16 Kerry Collins .75 2.00
MVP17 Chad Pennington .75 2.00

2002 Topps Autographs

serted at a rate of 1:250 hobby packs, and 1:80 HTA jumbo packs, this set features authentic autographs from several of the NFL's best young players.
OVERALL ODDS 1:258 HOB, 1:80 HTA JUM
TAAT Anthony Thomas 6.00 15.00
TACC Chris Chambers 5.00 12.00
TADM Derrick Mason 5.00 12.00
TALT LaDainian Tomlinson 40.00 80.00
TARL Ray Lewis 30.00 60.00
TAWJ Willie Jackson 5.00 12.00

2002 Topps Hobby Masters

This 10-card insert set is a Hobby pack exclusive. The cards were inserted at the rate of 1:9 hobby packs and 1:3 HTA jumbo packs.
COMPLETE SET (10) 10.00 25.00
STATED ODDS 1:9 HOB, 1:3 HTA JUM
HM1 Kurt Warner .60 1.50
HM2 Tom Brady 4.00 10.00
HM3 Marshall Faulk .60 1.50
HM4 Marvin Harrison .60 1.50
HM5 Randy Moss .60 1.50
HM6 Jerome Bettis .75 2.00
HM7 Jerry Rice 1.50 4.00
HM8 Brett Favre 1.50 4.00
HM9 Donovan McNabb .60 1.50
HM10 Curtis Martin .60 1.50

2002 Topps King of Kings Super Bowl MVP Jerseys

is 4-card insert set features dual players on each card along with swatches of the players' jerseys. Cards were inserted 1:4069 hobby packs, and 1:3120 retail packs.
STATED ODDS 1:4069 HOB, 1:3120 RET
KDA T.Davis/M.Allen 25.00 60.00
KME J.Montana/J.Elway 40.00 100.00
KMJ J.Montana/J.Rice 40.00 100.00
KYR S.Young/J.Rice 25.00 60.00

2002 Topps King of Kings Super Bowl MVP Autographs

is set is a parallel of the King of Kings Super Bowl MVP's set. Each card is serial numbered to 25 and signed by both players.
STATED PRINT RUN 25 SER.#'d SETS
KDA T.Davis/M.Allen 100.00 200.00
KME J.Montana/J.Elway 350.00 600.00
KMJ J.Montana/J.Rice 300.00 500.00
KYR S.Young/J.Rice 250.00 400.00

2002 Topps Own The Game

This 30-card insert set spotlights the stat leaders in the QB, WR, RB, and defensive positions. The cards were inserted at the rate of 1:12 hobby packs and 1:4 HTA jumbo packs.
COMPLETE SET (30) 30.00 80.00
STATED ODDS 1:12 HOB, 1:4 HTA JUM
OG1 Kurt Warner 1.00 2.50
OG2 Peyton Manning 3.00 8.00
OG3 Jeff Garcia .75 2.00
OG4 Brett Favre 2.50 6.00
OG5 Donovan McNabb 1.00 2.50
OG6 Rich Gannon 1.00 2.50
OG7 Tom Brady 6.00 15.00
OG8 Aaron Brooks .75 2.00
OG9 Priest Holmes .75 2.00
OG10 Curtis Martin 1.00 2.50
OG11 Stephen Davis .75 2.00
OG12 Ahman Green 1.00 2.50
OG13 Marshall Faulk 1.00 2.50
OG14 Shaun Alexander .75 2.00
OG15 Corey Dillon .75 2.00
OG16 Ricky Williams 1.00 2.50
OG17 David Boston .75 2.00
OG18 Marvin Harrison 1.00 2.50
OG19 Terrell Owens 1.00 2.50
OG20 Jimmy Smith 1.00 2.50
OG21 Torry Holt 1.00 2.50
OG22 Rod Smith 1.00 2.50
OG23 Keyshawn Johnson 1.00 2.50
OG24 Troy Brown .75 2.00
OG25 Michael Strahan 1.00 2.50
OG26 Ronald McKinnon .75 2.00
OG27 Ray Lewis 1.25 3.00
OG28 Zach Thomas 1.00 2.50
OG29 Ronde Barber .75 2.00
OG30 Anthony Henry .75 2.00

2002 Topps Pro Bowl Jerseys

This 10-card insert set features player-used jerseys worn by 2002 Pro Bowl participants. Cards were inserted at a rate of 1:399 hobby packs, and 1:343 retail packs.
STATED ODDS 1:399 HOB, 1:343 RET
APJE Jason Elam 5.00 12.00
APJL Jermaine Lewis 5.00 12.00
APLM Lawyer Milloy 5.00 12.00
APMF Marshall Faulk 6.00 15.00
APPH Priest Holmes 5.00 12.00
APRL Ray Lewis 8.00 20.00
APRW Rod Woodson 8.00 20.00
APSA Sam Adams 5.00 12.00
APSS Shannon Sharpe 6.00 15.00
APTB Tom Brady 15.00 40.00

2002 Topps Ring of Honor

This 35-card insert set pays tribute to Super Bowl MVP's. The cards were inserted at a rate of 1:9 hobby packs and 1:3 HTA jumbo packs.
COMPLETE SET (36) 30.00 80.00
STATED ODDS 1:9 HOB/RET, 1:3 HTA JUM
BS1 Bart Starr 2.50 6.00
BS2 Bart Starr 2.50 6.00
CH5 Chuck Howley .75 2.00
DH31 Desmond Howard 1.00 2.50
DW22 Doug Williams 1.00 2.50
ES28 Emmitt Smith 2.00 5.00
FB11 Fred Biletnikoff 1.25 3.00
FH9 Franco Harris 1.25 3.00
JE33 John Elway 2.00 5.00
JM16 Joe Montana 4.00 10.00
JM19 Joe Montana 4.00 10.00
JM24 Joe Montana 4.00 10.00
JN3 Joe Namath 2.00 5.00
JP15 Jim Plunkett 1.00 2.50
JR17 John Riggins 1.00 2.50
JR23 Jerry Rice 2.50 6.00
JS7 Jake Scott .75 2.00
KW34 Kurt Warner 1.00 2.50
LB30 Larry Brown .75 2.00
LC8 Larry Csonka 1.25 3.00
LD4 Len Dawson 1.25 3.00
MA18 Marcus Allen 1.25 3.00
MR26 Mark Rypien 1.00 2.50
OA25 Ottis Anderson .75 2.00
PS21 Phil Simms 1.00 2.50
RD20 Richard Dent 1.00 2.50
RL35 Ray Lewis 1.25 3.00
RS6 Roger Staubach 1.50 4.00
RW12 Randy White 1.00 2.50
SY29 Steve Young 1.50 4.00
TA27 Troy Aikman 1.50 4.00
TB13 Terry Bradshaw 1.50 4.00
TB14 Terry Bradshaw 1.50 4.00
TB36 Tom Brady 6.00 15.00
TD32 Terrell Davis 1.00 2.50

2002 Topps Ring of Honor Autographs

is 35-card parallel insert pays tribute to Super Bowl MVP's. Each card features an authentic signature. These cards were inserted into hobby packs at a rate of 1:225, and in retail packs at a rate of 1:1056.
OVERALL HOB STATED ODDS 1:225
OVERALL RET STATED ODDS 1:1056
RHBS Bart Starr SB I 200.00 400.00
RHBS2 Bart Starr SB II 200.00 400.00
RHCH Chuck Howley 40.00 100.00
RHDH Desmond Howard SP 300.00 500.00
RHDW Doug Williams 75.00 150.00
RHES Emmitt Smith 300.00 450.00
RHFB Fred Biletnikoff 100.00 200.00
RHFH Franco Harris 100.00 200.00
RHJE John Elway 175.00 300.00
RHJM Joe Montana SB XVI 175.00 300.00
RHJM2 Joe Montana SB XIX 175.00 300.00
RHJM3 Joe Montana SB XXIV 175.00 300.00
RHJN Joe Namath 150.00 300.00
RHJP Jim Plunkett 75.00 150.00
RHJR Jerry Rice 200.00 350.00
RHJRI John Riggins 100.00 200.00
RHJS Jake Scott SP 300.00 600.00
RHKW Kurt Warner 100.00 200.00
RHLB Larry Brown 50.00 120.00
RHLC Larry Csonka 100.00 200.00
RHLD Len Dawson 75.00 150.00
RHMA Marcus Allen 100.00 200.00
RHMR Mark Rypien 75.00 150.00
RHOA Ottis Anderson 75.00 150.00
RHPS Phil Simms 75.00 150.00
RHRD Richard Dent 75.00 150.00
RHRL Ray Lewis 175.00 300.00
RHRS Roger Staubach 125.00 250.00
RHRW Randy White 40.00 100.00
RHSY Steve Young 125.00 225.00
RHTA Troy Aikman 150.00 250.00
RHTB Terry Bradshaw SB XIII 150.00 300.00
RHTBR Tom Brady SB XXXVI 600.00 1000.00
RHTB2 Terry Bradshaw SB XIV 150.00 300.00
RHTD Terrell Davis 75.00 150.00

2002 Topps Rookie Premier Autographs

ndomly inserted into packs, this set features cards containing authentic signatures from top rookies in the 2002 rookie class. The cards were actually prodcued and signed at the Rookie Photo Shoot. Each card inserted into packs included the Topps Authentic Hologram on the back. Please note that some cards were given to the players at the event missing the Hologram on the back.
*HOLOGRAM MISSING: .2X TO .5X
RPAB Antonio Bryant 25.00 60.00
RPAD Andre Davis 15.00 40.00
RPAL Ashley Lelie 15.00 40.00
RPAR Antwaan Randle El 20.00 50.00
RPCP Clinton Portis 40.00 100.00
RPCR Cliff Russell 15.00 40.00
RPDC David Carr
RPDCH D.Carr/J.Harrington
RPDF DeShaun Foster 25.00 60.00
RPDG Daniel Graham 20.00 50.00
RPDGA David Garrard 20.00 50.00
RPDGD W.Green/T.Duckett 20.00 50.00
RPDS Donte Stallworth 25.00 60.00
RPDSL D.Stallworth/A.Lelie 25.00 60.00
RPEC Eric Crouch 25.00 60.00
RPJG Jabar Gaffney 15.00 40.00
RPJH Joey Harrington 15.00 40.00
RPJM Josh McCown 25.00 60.00
RPJP Julius Peppers 90.00 150.00
RPJR Josh Reed 20.00 50.00
RPJS Jeremy Shockey 75.00 150.00
RPJW Javon Walker 25.00 60.00
RPLB Ladell Betts 25.00 60.00
RPMM Maurice Morris 20.00 50.00
RPMW Marquise Walker 15.00 40.00
RPMWI Mike Williams 15.00 40.00
RPPR Patrick Ramsey 20.00 50.00
RPQJ Quentin Jammer 25.00 60.00
RPRC Reche Caldwell 20.00 50.00
RPRD Rohan Davey 25.00 60.00
RPRJ Ron Johnson 20.00 50.00
RPRW Roy Williams 15.00 40.00
RPTC Tim Carter 20.00 50.00
RPTJD T.J. Duckett 15.00 40.00
RPTS Travis Stephens 15.00 40.00
RPWG William Green 20.00 50.00

2002 Topps Super Bowl Goal Posts

Inserted at a rate of 1:410 hobby packs, and 1:352 retail packs, this set features swatches of the goal posts from the most recent Super Bowl. The Adam Vinatieri autograph was inserted at a rate of 1:1621 hobby packs.
COMPLETE SET (10) 150.00 300.00
STATED ODDS 1:410 HOB, 1:352 RET
VINATIERI AUTO ODDS 1:1621H
SBG1 Tom Brady 150.00 300.00
SBG2 Kurt Warner 10.00 25.00
SBG3 Antowain Smith 10.00 25.00
SBG4 Marshall Faulk 10.00 25.00
SBG5 Troy Brown 8.00 20.00
SBG6 Adam Vinatieri 20.00 50.00
SBG7 David Patten 8.00 20.00
SBG8 Torry Holt 10.00 25.00
SBG9 Ty Law 12.00 30.00
SBG10 Isaac Bruce 12.00 30.00
SBGAV Adam Vinatieri AUTO 75.00 150.00

2002 Topps Super Tix

This 10-card insert set features authentic game-used ticket stubs. Cards were inserted at a rate of 1:929 hobby packs, and 1:636 retail packs.
STATED ODDS 1:929 HOB, 1:636 RET
SBT1 Tom Brady 40.00 80.00
SBT2 Kurt Warner 12.00 30.00
SBT3 Antowain Smith 12.00 30.00
SBT4 Marshall Faulk 12.00 30.00
SBT5 Troy Brown 10.00 25.00
SBT6 Az-Zahir Hakim 10.00 25.00
SBT7 David Patten 10.00 25.00
SBT8 Torry Holt 12.00 30.00
SBT9 Ty Law 15.00 40.00
SBT10 Isaac Bruce 15.00 40.00

2002 Topps Terry Bradshaw Reprints

This 14-card insert set honors Terry Bradshaw with reprint cards of his 14 Topps base cards from 1971-1984. The cards were inserted at the rate of 1:9 hobby packs and 1:3 HTA jumbo packs.
COMPLETE SET (14) 15.00 40.00
COMMON CARD (1-14) 1.50 4.00
STATED ODDS 1:9 HOB/RET, 1:3 HTA JUM
AU STATED ODDS 1:8406 HOB, 1:7225 RET
1AU Terry Bradshaw '71 AUTO 60.00 120.00

2002 Topps Hall of Fame Class of 2002

is set was produced by Topps at issued at the 2002 Induction ceremories for the Pro Football Hall of Fame. Each card includes a photo of a 2002 inductee printed with a gold colored border. A gold foil "Class of 2002" logo appears on the cardfronts as well. The cards are unnumbered and listed below alphabetically.
COMPLETE SET (5) 6.00 15.00
1 Geoege Allen 1.25 3.00
2 Dave Casper 1.25 3.00
3 Dan Hampton 1.25 3.00
4 Jim Kelly 2.00 5.00
5 John Stallworth 1.50 4.00

2002 Topps Pro Bowl Card Show

This set was distributed to dealers who participated in the 2002 Pro Bowl Card Show in Hawaii. The cards are essentially identical to the Super Bowl Card Show set but include the 2002 Pro Bowl logo on the front. A Refractor parallel set was also produced with reportedly only 50-sets made.
COMPLETE SET (18) 10.00 20.00
*REFRACTOR: 1.5X TO 4X BASIC CARDS
1 Edgerrin James .40 1.00
2 Randy Moss .40 1.00
3 Peyton Manning 1.25 3.00
4 Aaron Brooks .40 1.00
5 Brian Griese .30 .75
6 Daunte Culpepper .30 .75
7 Terrell Owens .30 .75
8 Donovan McNabb .40 1.00
9 Jerome Bettis .40 1.00
10 Anthony Thomas .40 1.00
11 Brett Favre 1.00 2.50
12 Marshall Faulk .40 1.00
13 Doug Flutie .40 1.00
14 Jeff Garcia .30 .75
15 Kurt Warner .40 1.00
16 Kevan Barlow .30 .75
17 LaDainian Tomlinson .50 1.25
18 Michael Vick .40 1.00

2002 Topps Pro Bowl Card Show Jumbos

Topps distributed these 6-cards at the 2002 Pro Bowl Card Show in Hawaii. Collectors could obtain one card at a time by completing various scavenger hunt type tasks as part of Topps' Treasure Hunt promotion. The cards are jumbo (roughly 3 1/4" by 4 1/5") sized versions of the basic Pro Bowl Card Show cards.
COMPLETE SET (6) 12.50 30.00
1 Anthony Thomas 1.50 4.00
2 Randy Moss 1.50 4.00
3 Marshall Faulk 1.50 4.00
4 LaDainian Tomlinson 2.00 5.00
5 Michael Vick 1.50 4.00
6 Donovan McNabb 1.50 4.00

2002 Topps Super Bowl XXXVI Card Show

is set was distributed directly to dealers who participated in the 2002 Super Bowl Card Show in New Orleans. Each card was printed on metallic foil card stock and included the Super Bowl XXXVI logo on the front. A reprint of the 1989 Topps Traded Troy Aikman card was distributed at the show via a wrapper redemption program. It is not considered part of the 18-card set. A Refractor parallel set was also produced with reportedly only 50-sets made.
COMPLETE SET (18) 10.00 20.00
*REFRACTORS: 2X TO 5X BASIC CARDS
1 Edgerrin James .40 1.00
2 Randy Moss .40 1.00
3 Peyton Manning 1.25 3.00
4 Ricky Williams .40 1.00
5 Aaron Brooks .30 .75
6 Brian Griese .30 .75
7 Ahman Green .40 1.00
8 Daunte Culpepper .40 1.00
9 Donovan McNabb .40 1.00
10 Anthony Thomas .40 1.00
11 Brett Favre 1.00 2.50
12 Marshall Faulk .40 1.00
13 Doug Flutie .40 1.00
14 Jeff Garcia .30 .75
15 Kurt Warner .40 1.00
16 Chris Weinke .30 .75
17 LaDainian Tomlinson .50 1.25
18 Michael Vick .40 1.00

2003 Topps

Released in July of 2003, this set consists of 385 cards, including 310 veterans and 75 rookies. Boxes contained 36 packs of 10 cards. SRP was $2.99. Stated odds for the Dexter Jackson SBMVP37 card were 1:13590 hobby packs, and 1:3926 HTA packs.
COMPLETE SET (385) 25.00 60.00
SBMVP37 ODDS 1:13,590HOB, 1:3926HTA
1 Michael Vick .20 .50
2 Wesley Walls .20 .50
3 Josh Reed .15 .40
4 Josh McCown .20 .50
5 James Stewart .15 .40
6 Deltha O'Neal .15 .40
7 Quincy Morgan .15 .40
8 Tony Fisher .15 .40
9 Corey Bradford .15 .40
10 Byron Chamberlain .15 .40
11 James McKnight .15 .40
12 Fred Taylor .15 .40
13 David Patten .15 .40
14 Jerome Bettis .25 .60
15 Jerry Porter .15 .40
16 Anthony Becht .15 .40
17 Steve McNair .20 .50
18 Stephen Davis .15 .40
19 Terrence Wilkins .15 .40
20 Jamie Martin .15 .40
21 Tai Streets .15 .40
22 Frank Wycheck .15 .40
23 Sammy Knight .15 .40
24 Marcus Pollard .15 .40
25 Jamie Sharper .15 .40
26 T.J. Houshmandzadeh .15 .40
27 Javin Hunter .15 .40
28 Alge Crumpler .20 .50
29 Chris Weinke .20 .50
30 David Terrell .15 .40
31 Troy Hambrick .15 .40
32 Bubba Franks .20 .50
33 Todd Bouman .15 .40
34 Trent Green .15 .40
35 Mark Brunell .20 .50
36 James Thrash .15 .40
37 Donnie Edwards .15 .40
38 Mike Alstott .15 .40
39 Bobby Engram .15 .40
40 Deuce McAllister .20 .50
41 Santana Moss .20 .50
42 Kordell Stewart .15 .40
43 Jason Taylor .20 .50
44 Corey Dillon .15 .40
45 Damien Anderson .15 .40
46 Rodney Peete .15 .40
47 Jeff Blake .20 .50
48 Mike McMahon .15 .40
49 Ed McCaffrey .20 .50
50 Priest Holmes .15 .40
51 Moe Williams .15 .40
52 Brian Dawkins .25 .60
53 Tim Brown .25 .60
54 Curtis Martin .20 .50
55 Charles Stackhouse .15 .40
56 Derrius Thompson .15 .40
57 John Simon .15 .40
58 Joe Jurevicius .20 .50
59 Jonathan Wells .15 .40
60 William Green .15 .40
61 Ken-Yon Rambo .15 .40
62 Frank Sanders .15 .40
63 Chester Taylor .20 .50
64 Keith Brooking .20 .50
65 Bill Schroeder .15 .40
66 Travis Minor .15 .40
67 Eric Parker RC .30 .75
68 Phillip Buchanon .15 .40
69 Amos Zereoue .15 .40
70 Warren Sapp .20 .50
71 Ladell Betts .15 .40
72 Lamar Gordon .15 .40
73 Koren Robinson .20 .50
74 Ron Dayne .20 .50
75 Donovan McNabb .20 .50
76 Edgerrin James .20 .50
77 Stacey Mack .15 .40
78 Justin Smith .20 .50
79 Kelly Holcomb .15 .40
80 Thomas Jones .15 .40
81 Randy McMichael .15 .40
82 Daunte Culpepper .20 .50
83 Tommy Maddox .15 .40
84 Tyrone Wheatley .20 .50
85 Kevin Dyson .15 .40
86 Rod Gardner .15 .40
87 Wayne Chrebet .15 .40
88 Marc Boerigter .15 .40
89 Darnay Scott .20 .50
90 T.J. Duckett .15 .40
91 Marcel Shipp .15 .40
92 Ross Tucker .15 .40
93 Drew Bledsoe .20 .50
94 Scotty Anderson .15 .40
95 Rod Smith .20 .50
96 Jim Kleinsasser .15 .40
97 Peyton Manning .60 1.50
98 Junior Seau .20 .50
99 Darrell Jackson .20 .50
100 Brett Favre .50 1.25
101 Ashley Lelie .15 .40
102 Jajuan Dawson .15 .40
103 Kyle Brady .15 .40
104 Kevin Faulk .15 .40
105 Jeremy Shockey .15 .40
106 Hines Ward .20 .50
107 Jeff Garcia .15 .40
108 Shane Matthews .15 .40
109 Jevon Kearse .15 .40
110 Eddie Kennison .15 .40
111 Quincy Carter .15 .40
112 Brian Urlacher .25 .60
113 Charlie Rogers .15 .40
114 Robert Ferguson .15 .40
115 Christian Fauria .15 .40
116 Brian Westbrook .15 .40
117 Antwaan Randle El .15 .40
118 Eddie George .20 .50
119 Derrick Brooks .15 .40
120 Isaac Bruce .25 .60
121 Joe Horn .15 .40
122 Jermaine Lewis .15 .40
123 Jon Kitna .15 .40
124 David Boston .15 .40
125 Todd Heap .15 .40
126 Lamar Smith .20 .50
127 Marcus Robinson .20 .50
128 Germane Crowell .15 .40
129 Kevin Johnson .15 .40
130 Cris Carter .25 .60
131 Drew Brees .25 .60
132 Champ Bailey .20 .50
133 Brian Finneran .15 .40
134 Mike Anderson .15 .40
135 Derek Ross .15 .40
136 Javon Walker .20 .50
137 D'Wayne Bates .15 .40
138 Chad Lewis .20 .50
139 Charlie Garner .20 .50
140 Laveranues Coles .15 .40
141 Ron Dixon .15 .40
142 Rob Johnson .20 .50
143 Shaun Alexander .15 .40
144 Kevan Barlow .15 .40
145 Aaron Brooks .15 .40
146 Jay Foreman .15 .40
147 Mike Peterson .15 .40
148 Brandon Bennett .15 .40
149 Jake Plummer .15 .40
150 Emmitt Smith .40 1.00
151 Mikhael Ricks .15 .40
152 Terry Glenn .20 .50
153 Michael Bennett .15 .40
154 Deion Branch .15 .40
155 Justin McCareins .15 .40
156 Keyshawn Johnson .25 .60
157 Marc Bulger .15 .40
158 Matt Hasselbeck .15 .40
159 Garrison Hearst .15 .40
160 Jamel White .15 .40
161 Doug Johnson .15 .40
162 Larry Centers .15 .40
163 Dee Brown .15 .40
164 Dez White .15 .40
165 Brian Griese .15 .40
166 Johnnie Morton .20 .50
167 Oronde Gadsden .15 .40
168 Chad Morton .15 .40
169 Rod Woodson .20 .50
170 Ricky Proehl .20 .50
171 Tim Dwight .15 .40
172 Patrick Ramsey .20 .50
173 Donald Driver .20 .50
174 Joey Harrington .15 .40
175 Ricky Williams .20 .50
176 David Givens .15 .40
177 Antonio Freeman .20 .50
178 Dwight Freeney .15 .40
179 Jabar Gaffney .15 .40
180 Leon Johnson .15 .40
181 Freddie Jones .15 .40
182 Ron Johnson .15 .40
183 Duce Staley .15 .40
184 Charles Woodson .25 .60
185 Trung Canidate .15 .40
186 Jerome Pathon .15 .40
187 Jimmy Smith .20 .50
188 Reggie Wayne .20 .50
189 Chad Johnson .15 .40
190 Steve Beuerlein .20 .50
191 Joey Galloway .20 .50
192 Chris Walsh .15 .40
193 Ty Law .25 .60
194 Ike Hilliard .15 .40
195 Curtis Conway .15 .40
196 Kenny Watson .15 .40
197 Brad Johnson .20 .50
198 Shawn Jefferson .15 .40
199 Jamal Lewis .20 .50
200 Terrell Owens .20 .50
201 Todd Pinkston .15 .40
202 Maurice Morris .16 .40
203 Dante Hall .15 .40
204 Jeremiah Trotter UER .20 .50
205 Keenan McCardell .20 .50
206 Antonio Bryant .15 .40
207 Trevor Gaylor .15 .40
208 Eric Moulds .15 .40
209 Jim Miller .15 .40
210 Kabeer Gbaja-Biamila .15 .40
211 James Mungro .15 .40
212 Troy Brown .15 .40
213 J.J. Stokes .15 .40
214 Rich Gannon .20 .50
215 Chad Pennington .15 .40
216 Michael Strahan .20 .50
217 David Garrard .15 .40
218 Chris Chambers .15 .40
219 Antowain Smith .20 .50
220 Olandis Gary .15 .40
221 Jason McAddley .15 .40
222 Brandon Stokley .15 .40
223 Derrick Alexander .15 .40
224 Hugh Douglas .15 .40
225 Danny Wuerffel .20 .50
226 Derrick Mason .15 .40
227 Michael Pittman .15 .40
228 Torry Holt .20 .50
229 Bobby Shaw .15 .40
230 Tony Gonzalez .20 .50
231 Ed Hartwell .15 .40
232 Kris Mangum RC .15 .40
233 Martay Jenkins .15 .40
234 Marty Booker .15 .40
235 London Fletcher .20 .50
236 Shannon Sharpe .20 .50
237 Zach Thomas .20 .50
238 Plaxico Burress .15 .40
239 Trent Dilfer .15 .40
240 Kurt Warner .20 .50
241 Vinny Testaverde .15 .40
242 Al Wilson .15 .40
243 Chris Redman .15 .40
244 Warrick Dunn .15 .40
245 Jay Fiedler .15 .40
246 A.J. Feeley .15 .40
247 LaMont Jordan .20 .50
248 Kerry Collins .15 .40
249 Michael Lewis .15 .40
250 Jerry Rice .50 1.25
251 Simeon Rice .15 .40
252 Reche Caldwell .15 .40
253 Randy Moss .20 .50
254 Az-Zahir Hakim .15 .40
255 Nate Wayne .15 .40
256 James Allen .15 .40
257 Qadry Ismail .15 .40
258 Tom Brady 1.00 2.50
259 Brian Kelly .15 .40
260 Ray Lucas .15 .40
261 Amani Toomer .15 .40
262 Travis Henry .15 .40
263 Chris Chandler .20 .50
264 Peter Warrick .15 .40
265 Ray Lewis .25 .60
266 Sam Cowart .15 .40
267 Donte Stallworth .15 .40
268 David Carr .15 .40
269 Andre Davis .15 .40
270 Jake Delhomme .15 .40
271 Travis Taylor .15 .40
272 Steve Smith .25 .60
273 Tiki Barber .20 .50
274 Chad Hutchinson .15 .40
275 Marshall Faulk .20 .50
276 Chris Claiborne .15 .40
277 Billy Miller .15 .40
278 Peerless Price .15 .40
279 Ed Reed .20 .50
280 Ahman Green .20 .50
281 Roy Williams .15 .40
282 Dennis Northcutt .15 .40
283 Julius Peppers .25 .60
284 John Davis .15 .40
285 LaDainian Tomlinson .25 .60
286 Muhsin Muhammad .15 .40
287 Tim Couch .15 .40
288 Clinton Portis .15 .40
289 Anthony Thomas .20 .50
290 Marvin Harrison .20 .50
291 Priest Holmes WW .12 .30
292 Drew Bledsoe WW .15 .40
293 Tom Brady WW .75 2.00
294 Shaun Alexander WW .12 .30
295 Brett Favre WW .40 1.00
296 Travis Henry WW .12 .30
297 Marshall Faulk WW .15 .40
298 Terrell Owens WW .15 .40
299 Jeff Garcia WW .12 .30
300 Plaxico Burress WW .12 .30
301 Donovan McNabb WW .15 .40
302 Ricky Williams WW .15 .40
303 Michael Vick WW .15 .40
304 Steve Smith WW .20 .50
305 Marvin Harrison WW .15 .40
306 Chad Pennington WW .12 .30
307 Jeremy Shockey WW .12 .30
308 Tommy Maddox WW .12 .30
309 Steve McNair WW .15 .40
310 Rich Gannon WW .15 .40
311 Carson Palmer RC .60 1.50
312 Keenan Howry RC .30 .75
313 Michael Haynes RC .30 .75
314 Terrell Suggs RC .40 1.00
315 Rashean Mathis RC .30 .75
316 Chris Kelsay RC .40 1.00
317 Brad Banks RC .40 1.00
318 Jordan Gross RC .30 .75
319 Lee Suggs RC .30 .75
320 Kliff Kingsbury RC .50 1.25
321 William Joseph RC .30 .75
322 Kelley Washington RC .30 .75
323 Jerome McDougle RC .30 .75
324 Osi Umenyiora RC .60 1.50
325 Chris Simms RC .30 .75
326 Alonzo Jackson RC .30 .75
327 L.J. Smith RC .50 1.25
328 Mike Doss RC .50 1.25
329 Bobby Wade RC .40 1.00
330 Ken Hamlin RC .50 1.25
331 Brandon Lloyd RC .50 1.25
332 Justin Fargas RC .50 1.25
333 DeWayne Robertson RC .40 1.00
334 Bryant Johnson RC .50 1.25
335 Boss Bailey RC .40 1.00
336 Onterrio Smith RC .30 .75
337 Doug Gabriel RC .40 1.00
338 Jimmy Kennedy RC .40 1.00
339 B.J. Askew RC .40 1.00
340 Taylor Jacobs RC .30 .75
341 Dallas Clark RC .50 1.25
342 DeWayne White RC .30 .75
343 Arnaz Battle RC .50 1.25
344 Kareem Kelly RC .30 .75
345 Terry Pierce RC .30 .75
346 Billy McMullen RC .30 .75
347 Talman Gardner RC .30 .75
348 Anquan Boldin RC .50 1.25
349 Travis Anglin RC .30 .75
350 Byron Leftwich RC .40 1.00
351 Marcus Trufant RC .40 1.00
352 Sam Aiken RC .40 1.00
353 LaBrandon Toefield RC .30 .75
354 J.R. Tolver RC .40 1.00
355 Charles Rogers RC .40 1.00
356 Chaun Thompson RC .30 .75
357 Chris Brown RC .30 .75
358 Justin Gage RC .40 1.00
359 Kevin Williams RC .50 1.25
360 Willis McGahee RC .40 1.00
361 Victor Hobson RC .30 .75
362 Brian St.Pierre RC .30 .75
363 Nate Burleson RC .40 1.00
364 Calvin Pace RC .30 .75
365 Larry Johnson RC .40 1.00
366 Andre Woolfolk RC .30 .75
367 Tyrone Calico RC .30 .75
368 Seneca Wallace RC .40 1.00
369 Domanick Davis RC .40 1.00
370 Rex Grossman RC .40 1.00
371 Artose Pinner RC .30 .75
372 Jason Witten RC 1.25 3.00
373 Bennie Joppru RC .30 .75
374 Bethel Johnson RC .30 .75
375 Kyle Boller RC .30 .75
376 Shaun McDonald RC .40 1.00
377 Musa Smith RC .30 .75
378 Ken Dorsey RC .40 1.00
379 Johnathan Sullivan RC .30 .75
380 Andre Johnson RC .75 2.00
381 Nick Barnett RC .50 1.25
382 Teyo Johnson RC .40 1.00
383 Terence Newman RC .50 1.25
384 Kevin Curtis RC .30 .75
385 Dave Ragone RC .30 .75
MVP Dex.Jackson FB AU/250 400.00 100.00
RH Dexter Jackson RH .75 2.00
RHA Dexter Jackson RH AU 100.00 200.00

2003 Topps Black

*VETS 1-310: 6X TO 15X BASIC CARDS
*ROOKIES 311-385: 5X TO 12X
STATED PRINT RUN 150 SER.#'d SETS
BLACK/150 ODDS 1:21HOB, 1:8HTA

2003 Topps Collection

MP.FACT SET (385) 30.00 50.00
*VETS 1-310: .4X TO 1X BASIC TOPPS
*ROOKIES 311-385: .4X TO 1X TOPPS

2003 Topps First Edition

ETS 1-310: 1.5X TO 4X BASIC CARDS
*ROOKIES 311-385: 1.2X TO 3X
FOUND ONLY IN FIRST EDITION BOXES

2003 Topps Gold

*VETS 1-310: 2X TO 5X BASIC CARDS
*ROOKIES 311-385: 1.5X TO 4X
STATED PRINT RUN 499 SER.#'d SETS
GOLD/499 ODDS 1:17HOB, 1:5HTA

2003 Topps Autographs

This set features authentic player autographs from many top NFL superstars. Please note that Andre Davis, Charles Rogers, Derrick Mason, Marcel Shipp, and Julian Peterson were only available in packs as exchange cards, with an expiration date of 6/30/2005.
GROUP A ODDS 1:11,293HOB, 1:3256HTA
GROUP B ODDS 1:8266HOB, 1:2383HTA
GROUP C ODDS 1:4334HOB, 1:1376HTA
GROUP D ODDS 1:1814HOB, 1:645HTA
GROUP E ODDS 1:684HOB, 1:191HTA
GROUP F ODDS 1:384HOB, 1:95HTA
TBL Byron Leftwich A 8.00 20.00
TCPA Carson Palmer A 30.00 80.00
TDD Donald Driver F 20.00 40.00
TDM Derrick Mason C 6.00 15.00
TDN Dennis Northcutt F 6.00 15.00
TJM James Mungro F 6.00 15.00
TJP Jerry Porter E 6.00 15.00
TJT Jason Taylor C 15.00 30.00
TLC Laveranues Coles E 6.00 15.00
TLJ Larry Johnson D 8.00 20.00
TMS Marcel Shipp F 6.00 15.00
TRL ReShard Lee E 10.00 25.00
TSS Steve Smith F 15.00 30.00
TTH Travis Henry D 6.00 15.00
TTM Tommy Maddox B 12.00 30.00

2003 Topps Fan Favorite Vintage Buy Backs

serted into packs at a rate of 1:189 hobby packs, and 1:54 HTA packs, this set features cards that Topps bought back on the secondary market, and embossed with a special "Topps Fan Favorite Vintage" stamp.
STATED ODDS 1:189HOB, 1:54HTA
1 Troy Aikman 89 3.00 8.00
2 Marcus Allen 87 2.00 5.00
3 Randall Cunningham 89 2.00 5.00
4 Eric Dickerson IR 84 2.00 5.00
5 Eric Dickerson 85 2.00 5.00
6 Eric Dickerson 89 2.00 5.00
7 Tony Dorsett 84 2.50 6.00
8 John Elway 89 5.00 12.00
9 Steve Largent 84 7.50 20.00
10 Steve Largent 86 6.00 15.00
11 Dan Marino 89 5.00 12.00
12 Joe Montana RB 88 10.00 20.00
13 Warren Moon 85 6.00 15.00
14 Warren Moon 89 2.00 5.00
15 Walter Payton RB 88 6.00 15.00
16 Deion Sanders 89 2.50 6.00
17 Lawrence Taylor 89 2.00 5.00
18 Reggie White 89 2.00 5.00
19 Steve Young 89 2.50 6.00

2003 Topps Game Breakers Relics

Inserted at a rate of 1:14318 hobby packs, and 1:4306 HTA packs, this set features authentic game worn jersey swatches.
STATED ODDS 1:14,318HOB, 1:4306HTA
GB1 Brad Johnson 25.00 60.00
GB3 Keenan McCardell 25.00 60.00
GB5 Rich Gannon 25.00 60.00
GB6 Jerry Porter 20.00 50.00
GB7 Eric Johnson 25.00 60.00
GB8 Jerry Rice 50.00 120.00
GB9 Derrick Brooks 20.00 50.00

2003 Topps Hall of Fame Autographs

Inserted at a rate of 1:13590 hobby packs, and 1:3926 HTA packs, this set features autographs from the Hall of Fame class of 2003.
STATED ODDS 1:13,590 HOB, 1:3926 HTA
HOFEB Elvin Bethea 150.00 300.00
HOFHS Hank Stram 150.00 300.00
HOFJD Joe DeLamielleure 150.00 300.00
HOFJL James Lofton 150.00 300.00
HOFMA Marcus Allen 200.00 400.00

2003 Topps Hobby Masters

MPLETE SET (10) 10.00 25.00
STATED ODDS 1:18HOB, 1:6HTA
HM1 Michael Vick .75 2.00
HM2 Priest Holmes .60 1.50
HM3 Brett Favre 2.00 5.00
HM4 LaDainian Tomlinson 1.00 2.50
HM5 Terrell Owens .75 2.00
HM6 Marshall Faulk .75 2.00
HM7 Donovan McNabb .75 2.00
HM8 Peyton Manning 2.50 6.00
HM9 Deuce McAllister .75 2.00
HM10 David Carr .60 1.50

2003 Topps Own the Game

COMPLETE SET (30) 15.00 40.00
STATED ODDS 1:12 HOB, HTA
OTG1 Brett Favre 2.00 5.00
OTG2 Rich Gannon .75 2.00
OTG3 Drew Bledsoe .75 2.00
OTG4 Michael Vick .75 2.00
OTG5 Steve Mcnair .75 2.00
OTG6 Tom Brady 4.00 10.00
OTG7 Chad Pennington .60 1.50
OTG8 Peyton Manning 2.50 6.00
OTG9 Donovan McNabb .75 2.00
OTG10 Ricky Williams .75 2.00
OTG11 LaDainian Tomlinson 1.00 2.50
OTG12 Priest Holmes .60 1.50
OTG13 Clinton Portis .60 1.50
OTG14 Travis Henry .60 1.50
OTG15 Deuce McAllister .75 2.00
OTG16 Marshall Faulk .75 2.00
OTG17 Jamal Lewis .75 2.00
OTG18 Marvin Harrison .75 2.00
OTG19 Randy Moss .75 2.00
OTG20 Amani Toomer .60 1.50
OTG21 Hines Ward .75 2.00
OTG22 Plaxico Burress .60 1.50
OTG23 Terrell Owens .75 2.00
OTG24 Eric Moulds .60 1.50
OTG25 Jerry Rice 2.00 5.00
OTG26 Jason Taylor .75 2.00
OTG27 Simeon Rice .60 1.50
OTG28 Zach Thomas .75 2.00
OTG29 Brian Urlacher 1.00 2.50
OTG30 Rod Woodson .75 2.00

2003 Topps Pro Bowl Jerseys

serted at a rate of 1:200 hobby packs, and 1:28 HTA packs, this set features swatches of Pro Bowl worn jerseys.
STATED ODDS 1:200HOB, 1:28HTA
APBF Bubba Franks 5.00 12.00
APBU Brian Urlacher 6.00 15.00
APHW Hines Ward 5.00 12.00
APJG Jeff Garcia 4.00 10.00
APJH Joe Horn 4.00 10.00
APJP Joey Porter 6.00 15.00
APJR Jerry Rice 12.00 30.00
APLT LaDainian Tomlinson 6.00 15.00
APMA Mike Alstott 4.00 10.00
APMH Marvin Harrison 5.00 12.00
APML Michael Lewis 4.00 10.00
APMS Michael Strahan 5.00 12.00
APRG Rich Gannon 5.00 12.00
APRW Ricky Williams 5.00 12.00
APTH Todd Heap 4.00 10.00

2003 Topps Record Breakers

COMPLETE SET (29) 20.00 50.00
STATED ODDS 1:6
RB1 Barry Sanders 1.50 4.00
RB2 Brett Favre 2.00 5.00
RB3 Brian Mitchell .60 1.50
RB4 Bruce Matthews .60 1.50
RB5 Clinton Portis .60 1.50
RB6 Corey Dillon .60 1.50
RB7 Dan Marino 2.00 5.00
RB8 Derrick Mason .60 1.50
RB9 Emmitt Smith 1.50 4.00
RB10 Jason Elam .60 1.50
RB11 Jason Taylor .75 2.00
RB12 Jerry Rice 2.00 5.00
RB13 Jimmy Smith .75 2.00
RB14 Terrell Owens .75 2.00
RB15 John Elway 1.50 4.00
RB16 LaDainian Tomlinson 1.00 2.50
RB17 Lawrence Taylor 1.00 2.50

RB18 Randy Moss .75 2.00
RB19 Marshall Faulk .75 2.00
RB20 Marvin Harrison .75 2.00
RB21 Michael Strahan .75 2.00
RB22 Peyton Manning 2.50 6.00
RB23 Priest Holmes .60 1.50
RB24 Rich Gannon .75 2.00
RB25 Ricky Williams .75 2.00
RB26 Rod Woodson .75 2.00
RB27 Jevon Kearse .60 1.50
RB28 Tim Brown 1.00 2.50
RB29 Chris McAlister .75 2.00

2003 Topps Record Breakers Autographs

is set features authentic player autographs from some of the NFL's best. Please note that Derrick Mason was issued in packs as an exchange card with an expiration date of 6/30/2005 but never signed for the set.

GROUP A ODDS 1:13,590HOB, 1:3926HTA
GROUP B ODDS 1:4070HOB, 1:1112HTA
GROUP C ODDS 1:22,908HOB, 1:6357HTA
GROUP D ODDS 1:17,059HOB, 1:4603HTA
RBBF Brett Favre A 125.00 250.00
RBBS Barry Sanders A 125.00 250.00
RBCP Clinton Portis C 12.00 30.00
RBDM Dan Marino A 150.00 300.00
RBJE John Elway B 75.00 150.00
RBJS Jimmy Smith B 15.00 40.00
RBJT Jason Taylor B 15.00 40.00
RBLTO LaDainian Tomlinson A 75.00 150.00
RBMH Marvin Harrison B 15.00 40.00
RBMS Michael Strahan A 15.00 40.00
RBPH Priest Holmes D 15.00 40.00
RBSY Steve Young B 50.00 100.00

2003 Topps Record Breakers Autographs Duals

serted at a rate of 1:5492 hobby packs, and 1:552 HTA packs, this set features two autographs from NFL superstars. Please note that card #RBDTP was issued in packs as an exchange card, with an expiration date of 6/30/2005. Finally, a number of Sanders/Smith duals have surfaced with a correct Barry Sanders autograph but not Emmitt Smith signature. A large number of these cards have also been seen with a forged Emmitt Smith autograph.

STATED ODDS 1:5492HOB, 1:552HTA
RBDEM J.Elway/D.Marino 300.00 550.00
RBDMS D.Mason/J.Smith 12.00 30.00
RBDSS B.Sanders/E.Smith 400.00 600.00
RBDST M.Strahan/J.Taylor 25.00 50.00

2003 Topps Record Breakers Jerseys

ch card features swatches of game worn jerseys. Group A was inserted at a rate of 1:22272 hobby packs, and 1:5803 HTA packs. Group B was inserted at a rate of 1:1354 hobby packs, and 1:147 HTA packs.

GROUP A ODDS 1:22,272HOB, 1:5803HTA
GROUP B ODDS 1:1354HOB, 1:147HTA
RBRBS Barry Sanders B 15.00 40.00
RBRDM Dan Marino B 15.00 40.00
RBRES Emmitt Smith B 15.00 40.00
RBRJE John Elway B 15.00 40.00
RBRJR Jerry Rice B 15.00 40.00
RBRKW Kurt Warner B 8.00 20.00
RBRLT LaDainian Tomlinson B 10.00 25.00
RBRMF Marshall Faulk B 8.00 20.00
RBRRW Ricky Williams B 8.00 20.00
RBRSY Steve Young B 12.00 30.00
RBRWP Walter Payton A 40.00 100.00

2003 Topps Record Breakers Jerseys Duals

ch card features two swatches of game worn jerseys. Group A was inserted at a rate of 1:4066 hobby packs, and 1:3814 HTA packs. Group B was inserted at a rate of 1:2344 hobby packs, and 1:602 HTA packs.

GROUP A ODDS 1:14066HOB, 1:3814HTA
GROUP B ODDS 1:2344HOB, 1:602HTA
RDRDT C.Dillon/L.Tomlinson B 20.00 50.00
RDRFW M.Faulk/R.Williams 15.00 40.00
RDRME D.Marino/J.Elway 50.00 120.00
RDRPS W.Payton/E.Smith A 100.00 200.00
RDRSP B.Sanders/W.Payton A 100.00 200.00
RDRSR E.Smith/J.Rice 30.00 80.00
RDRSS B.Sanders/E.Smith B 30.00 80.00
RDRYE S.Young/J.Elway 20.00 50.00

2003 Topps Rookie Premiere Autographs

Inserted at rate of 1:196 HTA packs for single autographs, and 1:1963 HTA packs for dual autographs, this set features cards produced and signed by 2003 rookies at the NFL Rookie Photo Shoot.

OVERALL STATED ODDS 1:196 TOPPS HTA
OVERALL DUAL ODDS 1:1963 TOPPS HTA
GROUP A ODDS 1:336,480 TOPPS CHROME
GROUP B ODDS 1:56,080 TOPPS CHROME
GROUP C ODDS 1:29,206 TOPPS CHROME
GROUP D ODDS 1:8628 TOPPS CHROME
GROUP E ODDS 1:1482 TOPPS CHROME
*HOLOGRAM MISSING: .2X TO .5X
RPAB Anquan Boldin E 20.00 50.00
RPAJ Andre Johnson C 125.00 200.00
RPAP Artose Pinner E 12.00 30.00
RPBJ Bethel Johnson E 12.00 30.00
RPBJ2 Bryant Johnson B
RPBL Byron Leftwich A 20.00 50.00
RPBS Brian St.Pierre E 12.00 30.00
RPCB Chris Brown E 12.00 30.00
RPCP Carson Palmer A 50.00 120.00
RPDC Dallas Clark E 25.00 60.00
RPDMJ McGahee/L.Johnson 30.00 80.00
RPDPL C.Palmer/B.Leftwich 50.00 120.00
RPDR Dave Ragone E 12.00 30.00
RPDRJ An.Jhnsn/Br.Jhnsn 40.00 100.00
RPDR2 DeWayne Robertson C 15.00 40.00
RPJF Justin Fargas E 20.00 50.00
RPKB Kyle Boller E 12.00 30.00
RPKC Kevin Curtis E 12.00 30.00
RPKK Kliff Kingsbury E 20.00 50.00
RPKW Kelley Washington E 12.00 30.00
RPLJ Larry Johnson B 20.00 50.00
RPMS Musa Smith D 12.00 30.00
RPMT Marcus Trufant E 15.00 40.00
RPNB Nate Burleson E 15.00 40.00
RPOS Onterrio Smith E 12.00 30.00
RPRG Rex Grossman D 15.00 40.00
RPSW Seneca Wallace E 15.00 40.00
RPTC Tyrone Calico D 12.00 30.00
RPTJ Taylor Jacobs E 12.00 30.00
RPTJ2 Teyo Johnson E 15.00 40.00
RPTN Terence Newman E 20.00 50.00
RPTS Terrell Suggs D 30.00 80.00
RPWM Willis McGahee A 30.00 80.00

2003 Topps Split the Uprights

Inserted at a rate of 1:3383 hobby packs, and 1:967 HTA packs, this set features swatches of goal post from Super Bowl XXXVII.

STATED ODDS 1:3383 HOB, 1:967 HTA
SU1 Martin Gramatica 15.00 40.00
SU2 Sebastian Janikowski 15.00 40.00

2003 Topps Super Tix

serted at a rate of 1:614 hobby packs, and 1:89 HTA packs, this set features swatches of game tickets.

STATED ODDS 1:614 HOB, 1:89 HTA
ST1 Brad Johnson 10.00 25.00
ST2 Rich Gannon 10.00 25.00
ST3 Keyshawn Johnson 12.00 30.00
ST4 Jerry Rice 30.00 60.00
ST5 Michael Pittman 8.00 20.00
ST6 Charlie Garner 10.00 25.00
ST7 Derrick Brooks 8.00 20.00
ST8 Jerry Porter 8.00 20.00
ST9 Warren Sapp 10.00 25.00
ST10 Tim Brown 12.00 30.00

2003 Topps Hall of Fame Class of 2003

This set was distributed by Topps at the 2003 Induction ceremories for the Pro Football Hall of Fame. Each card includes a photo of a 2003 inductee printed in a very similar style to the 2003 Topps Hall of Fame Autographs inserts. A gold foil "Class of 2003" logo appears on the cardfronts. The cards are unnumbered and listed below alphabetically.

COMPLETE SET (5) 6.00 15.00
1 Marcus Allen 2.50 6.00
2 Elvin Bethea 1.00 2.50
3 Joe DeLamielleure 1.00 2.50
4 James Lofton 1.25 3.00
5 Hank Stram 1.25 3.00

2003 Topps Pro Bowl Card Show

This set was distributed directly to dealers who participated in the 2003 Pro Bowl Card Show in Hawaii. Each card was printed on metallic foil card stock and included the Pro Bowl logo on the front. A Gold foil parallel set was also produced of the set.

COMPLETE SET (18) 15.00 30.00
*GOLD CARDS: 1.2X TO 3X SILVER
1 Brett Favre 1.50 4.00
2 Clinton Portis .50 1.25
3 David Carr .50 1.25
4 Deuce McAllister .60 1.50
5 Donovan McNabb .60 1.50
6 Donte Stallworth .50 1.25
7 Edgerrin James .60 1.50
8 Emmitt Smith 1.25 3.00
9 Joey Harrington .50 1.25
10 LaDainian Tomlinson .75 2.00
11 Marshall Faulk .60 1.50
12 Peyton Manning 2.00 5.00
13 Priest Holmes .50 1.25
14 Ricky Williams .60 1.50
15 Tom Brady 3.00 8.00
16 Jeff Ulbrich .50 1.25
17 Ashley Lelie .50 1.25
18 Chris Fuamatu-Ma'afala .60 1.50

2003 Topps Pro Bowl Card Show Jumbos

Topps distributed these 6-cards at the 2003 Pro Bowl Card Show in Hawaii. The cards are jumbo (roughly 3 1/4" by 4 1/5") sized versions of six of the basic Pro Bowl Card Show cards along with different card numbers.

COMPLETE SET (6) 15.00 30.00
1 Brett Favre 3.00 8.00
2 David Carr 1.00 2.50
3 LaDainian Tomlinson 1.50 4.00
4 Marshall Faulk 1.25 3.00
5 Priest Holmes 1.00 2.50
6 Tom Brady 6.00 15.00

2003 Topps Super Bowl XXXVII Card Show

This set was distributed directly to dealers who participated in the 2003 Super Bowl Card Show. Each card was printed on metallic foil card stock and included the Super Bowl XXXVII logo on the front. A Gold foil parallel set was also produced.

COMPLETE SET (18) 12.50 25.00
*GOLD CARDS: 1.5X TO 4X SILVERS
1 Brett Favre 1.25 3.00
2 Clinton Portis .40 1.00
3 David Carr .40 1.00
4 Deuce McAllister .50 1.25
5 Donovan McNabb .50 1.25
6 Donte Stallworth .40 1.00
7 Drew Bledsoe .50 1.25
8 Drew Brees .60 1.50
9 Edgerrin James .50 1.25
10 Emmitt Smith 1.00 2.50
11 Joey Harrington .40 1.00
12 LaDainian Tomlinson .60 1.50
13 Marshall Faulk .50 1.25
14 Michael Vick .50 1.25
15 Peyton Manning 1.50 4.00
16 Priest Holmes .40 1.00
17 Ricky Williams .50 1.25
18 Tom Brady 2.50 6.00

2004 Topps

pps initially released in mid-July 2004. The base set consists of 385-cards printed with silver foil highlights including 75-rookies. Hobby boxes contained 36-packs of 10-cards and carried an S.R.P. of $1.59 per pack. Two basic parallel sets and a variety of inserts can be found seeded in packs highlighted by the Premiere Prospects Autograph and Rookie Premiere Autograph inserts. Special First Edition packs included cards for one additional parallel set as did the gold foil Topps Collection factory sets.

COMPLETE SET (385) 30.00 60.00
RH38 STATED ODDS 1:36 H/HTA/R
RH38A ODDS 1:13,494H, 1:3895HTA
SBMVP ODDS 1:35,787H, 1:10,710HTA, 1:33,984R
1 Peyton Manning .60 1.50
2 Curtis Conway .20 .50
3 Tim Brown .25 .60
4 David Givens .15 .40
5 Dorsey Levens .20 .50
6 Jamal Robertson .15 .40
7 Doug Flutie .20 .50
8 Lamar Gordon .15 .40
9 Leonard Little .15 .40
10 Patrick Ramsey .20 .50
11 Justin McCareins .15 .40
12 Charles Lee .15 .40
13 Matt Hasselbeck .15 .40
14 Chris Chambers .15 .40
15 Derrick Blaylock .15 .40
16 Shannon Sharpe .20 .50
17 Bubba Franks .15 .40
18 London Fletcher .20 .50
19 Eric Moulds .15 .40
20 Anquan Boldin .15 .40
21 Brian Urlacher .25 .60
22 Stephen Davis .15 .40
23 Mikhael Ricks .15 .40
24 Jason Taylor .20 .50
25 Michael Vick .20 .50
26 Dante Hall .15 .40
27 Marcus Pollard .15 .40
28 Rick Mirer .15 .40
29 David Tyree .15 .40
30 Chad Pennington .15 .40
31 Kevan Barlow .15 .40
32 James Farrior .15 .40
33 James Thrash .15 .40
34 Darnerien McCants .15 .40
35 L.J. Smith .20 .50
36 Tommy Maddox .15 .40
37 Tedy Bruschi .20 .50
38 Moe Williams .15 .40
39 Todd Bouman .15 .40
40 Domanick Davis .15 .40
41 Dwight Freeney .15 .40
42 Kyle Brady .15 .40
43 LaVar Arrington .15 .40
44 Troy Hambrick .15 .40
45 Jake Plummer .15 .40
46 Freddie Jones .15 .40
47 Chester Taylor .20 .50
48 Willis McGahee .15 .40
49 Bobby Wade .20 .50
50 Steve McNair .20 .50
51 Joe Jurevicius .15 .40
52 Ladell Betts .15 .40
53 LaMont Jordan .20 .50
54 Kerry Collins .15 .40
55 Hines Ward .20 .50
56 Scott Fujita .15 .40
57 Kevin Johnson .15 .40
58 Troy Brown .15 .40
59 Jerome Pathon .15 .40
60 Andre Johnson .20 .50
61 DeShaun Foster .20 .50
62 Terrell Suggs .15 .40
63 Marcel Shipp .15 .40
64 Allen Rossum .15 .40
65 Kyle Boller .15 .40
66 Terence Newman .20 .50
67 Javon Walker .15 .40
68 Shawn Bryson .15 .40
69 Travis Minor .15 .40
70 Terrell Owens .20 .50
71 Kassim Osgood .15 .40
72 Bobby Engram .15 .40
73 Drew Bennett .20 .50
74 Rock Cartwright .15 .40
75 Ahman Green .20 .50
76 Steve Beuerlein .20 .50
77 Takeo Spikes .15 .40
78 Dez White .20 .50
79 Tim Couch .20 .50
80 Travis Henry .15 .40
81 T.J. Duckett .15 .40
82 LaBrandon Toefield .15 .40
83 Randy McMichael .15 .40
84 Jonathan Carter .15 .40
85 Jerry Rice .50 1.25
86 Maurice Morris .20 .50
87 Kurt Warner .20 .50
88 Josh Scobey .15 .40
89 Travis Taylor .15 .40
90 Fred Taylor .15 .40
91 Zach Thomas .20 .50
92 Kelly Campbell .15 .40
93 Tim Carter .15 .40
94 Marques Tuiasosopo .15 .40
95 Laveranues Coles .15 .40
96 Chris Brown .15 .40
97 Thomas Jones .15 .40
98 Dane Looker .15 .40
99 Ross Tucker .15 .40
100 Priest Holmes .15 .40
101 Troy Walters .15 .40
102 Jamie Sharper .15 .40
103 Quincy Morgan .15 .40
104 Aveion Cason .15 .40
105 Joey Galloway .20 .50
106 Bill Schroeder .15 .40
107 Tony Fisher .15 .40
108 Adewale Ogunleye .20 .50
109 Justin Fargas .20 .50
110 Daunte Culpepper .20 .50
111 Donnie Edwards .20 .50
112 Jed Weaver .15 .40
113 Arlen Harris .15 .40
114 Keenan McCardell .15 .40
115 Chad Johnson .15 .40
116 Marty Booker .15 .40
117 Anthony Wright .15 .40
118 Brian Finneran .15 .40
119 Robert Ferguson .15 .40
120 Ricky Williams .20 .50
121 Shaun Ellis .15 .40
122 Brian Westbrook .15 .40
123 Sam Cowart .15 .40
124 Tim Rattay .15 .40
125 LaDainian Tomlinson .25 .60
126 Simeon Rice .15 .40
127 Jason Witten .20 .50
128 Lee Suggs .20 .50
129 Keith Brooking .15 .40
130 Rex Grossman .15 .40
131 Kelley Washington .15 .40
132 Antonio Bryant .20 .50
133 Dallas Clark .15 .40
134 Stacey Mack .15 .40
135 Charles Rogers .15 .40
136 Donte' Stallworth .15 .40
137 Deion Branch .15 .40
138 Nate Burleson .20 .50
139 Ike Hilliard .15 .40
140 Randy Moss .20 .50
141 Michael Strahan .20 .50
142 John Abraham .15 .40
143 Tim Dwight .15 .40
144 Isaac Bruce .25 .60
145 Brad Johnson .20 .50
146 Trung Canidate .15 .40
147 Warrick Dunn .15 .40
148 Josh McCown .20 .50
149 Muhsin Muhammad .15 .40
150 Donovan McNabb .20 .50
151 Tai Streets .15 .40
152 Antonio Gates .25 .60
153 Antwaan Randle El .15 .40
154 Doug Jolley .15 .40
155 Shaun Alexander .15 .40
156 William Green .15 .40
157 Carson Palmer .20 .50
158 Quentin Griffin .15 .40
159 Az-Zahir Hakim .15 .40
160 Edgerrin James .20 .50
161 Gus Frerotte .15 .40
162 Brandon Lloyd .20 .50
163 Brian Griese .15 .40
164 Boo Williams .15 .40
165 Santana Moss .20 .50
166 Tyrone Wheatley .20 .50
167 Eric Parker .20 .50
168 Amos Zereoue .15 .40
169 Itula Mili .15 .40
170 Marshall Faulk .20 .50
171 Tyrone Calico .20 .50
172 Tim Hasselbeck .15 .40
173 Anthony Becht .15 .40
174 Larry Johnson .15 .40
175 Marvin Harrison .20 .50
176 Tony Gonzalez .20 .50
177 Wayne Chrebet .15 .40
178 Mike Barrow .15 .40
179 Bethel Johnson .15 .40
180 Deuce McAllister .20 .50
181 Drew Brees .25 .60
182 Teyo Johnson .15 .40
183 Garrison Hearst .15 .40
184 Todd Pinkston .15 .40
185 Jeff Garcia .15 .40
186 Darrell Jackson .20 .50
187 Billy Volek .15 .40
188 Ray Lewis .25 .60
189 Ricky Proehl .20 .50
190 Rudi Johnson .15 .40
191 Emmitt Smith .40 1.00
192 Cedrick Wilson .15 .40
193 Julius Peppers .20 .50
194 Peter Warrick .15 .40
195 Trent Green .15 .40
196 Derrius Thompson .15 .40
197 Onterrio Smith .15 .40
198 Jerome Bettis .25 .60
199 Keyshawn Johnson .20 .50
200 Jamal Lewis .20 .50
201 Alge Crumpler .20 .50
202 Justin Gage .20 .50
203 Mike Rucker .15 .40
204 Michael Bennett .15 .40
205 Jimmy Smith .20 .50
206 Ricky Williams TT .15 .40
207 Corey Bradford .15 .40
208 Jerry Porter .15 .40
209 Erron Kinney .15 .40
210 Marc Bulger .15 .40
211 Jeff Blake .20 .50
212 Terry Jones .15 .40
213 Kordell Stewart .15 .40
214 Andra Davis .15 .40
215 David Carr .15 .40
216 Nick Barnett .15 .40
217 Mark Brunell .20 .50
218 Daniel Graham .15 .40
219 Jim Kleinsasser .15 .40
220 Aaron Brooks .15 .40
221 Plaxico Burress .15 .40
222 Correll Buckhalter .15 .40
223 Jevon Kearse .15 .40
224 Michael Pittman .20 .50
225 Clinton Portis .15 .40
226 Corey Dillon .15 .40
227 Steve Smith .25 .60
228 David Thornton .15 .40
229 Eddie Kennison .20 .50
230 Amani Toomer .15 .40
231 Artose Pinner .15 .40
232 Kelly Holcomb .15 .40
233 Jay Fiedler .15 .40
234 Ernie Conwell .15 .40
235 Torry Holt .20 .50
236 Eddie George .20 .50
237 Jeremy Shockey .15 .40
238 Troy Edwards .15 .40
239 Antowain Smith .20 .50
240 Jon Kitna .15 .40
241 Bryant Johnson .15 .40
242 Todd Heap .15 .40
243 Doug Johnson .15 .40
244 Ashley Lelie .15 .40
245 Byron Leftwich .15 .40
246 Shawn Barber .15 .40
247 Duce Staley .15 .40
248 Rod Gardner .15 .40
249 Warren Sapp .20 .50
250 Brett Favre .50 1.25
251 Olandis Gary .15 .40
252 Reggie Wayne .20 .50
253 Billy Miller .15 .40
254 Johnnie Morton .20 .50
255 Joe Horn .15 .40
256 Curtis Martin .20 .50
257 Freddie Mitchell .15 .40
258 Charlie Garner .20 .50
259 Marcus Robinson .15 .40
260 Derrick Mason .15 .40
261 Bobby Shaw .15 .40
262 Desmond Clark .15 .40
263 James Jackson .15 .40
264 Josh Reed .15 .40
265 David Boston .15 .40
266 Drew Bledsoe .20 .50
267 Brock Forsey .15 .40
268 Dat Nguyen .15 .40
269 Mike Anderson .15 .40
270 Anthony Thomas .20 .50
271 Najeh Davenport .15 .40
272 Jabar Gaffney .15 .40
273 Tiki Barber .20 .50
274 Rich Gannon .20 .50
275 Tom Brady 1.00 2.50
276 Terry Glenn .20 .50
277 Dennis Northcutt .15 .40
278 A.J. Feeley .15 .40
279 Peerless Price .15 .40
280 Jake Delhomme .15 .40
281 Kevin Faulk .15 .40
282 Quincy Carter .15 .40
283 Andre' Davis .15 .40
284 Tony Hollings .15 .40
285 Joey Harrington .15 .40
286 Richie Anderson .15 .40
287 Donald Driver .20 .50
288 Koren Robinson .15 .40
289 Tony Banks .15 .40
290 Rod Smith .20 .50
291 Anquan Boldin WW .10 .25
292 Jamal Lewis WW .12 .30
293 Priest Holmes WW .10 .25
294 Peyton Manning WW .40 1.00
295 Marvin Harrison WW .12 .30
296 Steve McNair WW .12 .30
297 Travis Henry WW .10 .25
298 Torry Holt WW .12 .30
299 Tom Brady WW .60 1.50
300 Ahman Green WW .12 .30
301 Donovan McNabb WW .12 .30
302 Deuce McAllister WW .12 .30
303 Domanick Davis WW .10 .25
304 Clinton Portis WW .10 .25
305 Rudi Johnson WW .10 .25
306 Brett Favre WW .30 .75
307 LaDainian Tomlinson WW .15 .40
308 Steve Smith WW .15 .40
309 Edgerrin James WW .12 .30
310 Ty Law WW .15 .40
311 Ben Roethlisberger RC 6.00 15.00
312 Ahmad Carroll RC .40 1.00
313 Johnnie Morant RC .40 1.00
314 Greg Jones RC .40 1.00
315 Michael Clayton RC .50 1.25
316 Josh Harris RC .40 1.00
317 Tatum Bell RC .40 1.00
318 Robert Gallery RC .50 1.25
319 B.J. Symons RC .40 1.00
320 Roy Williams RC .40 1.00
321 DeAngelo Hall RC .60 1.50
322 Jeff Smoker RC .50 1.25
323 Lee Evans RC .60 1.50
324 Michael Jenkins RC .40 1.00
325 Steven Jackson RC .60 1.50
326 Will Smith RC .50 1.25
327 Vince Wilfork RC .60 1.50
328 Ben Troupe RC .40 1.00
329 Chris Gamble RC .40 1.00
330 Kevin Jones RC .50 1.25
331 Jonathan Vilma RC .50 1.25
332 Dontarrious Thomas RC .50 1.25
333 Michael Boulware RC .60 1.50
334 Mewelde Moore RC .50 1.25
335 Drew Henson RC .40 1.00
336 D.J. Williams RC .60 1.50
337 Ernest Wilford RC .50 1.25
338 John Navarre RC .40 1.00
339 Jerricho Cotchery RC .50 1.25
340 Derrick Hamilton RC .40 1.00
341 Carlos Francis RC .40 1.00
342 Ben Watson RC .50 1.25
343 Reggie Williams RC .40 1.00
344 Devard Darling RC .40 1.00
345 Chris Perry RC .40 1.00
346 Derrick Strait RC .40 1.00
347 Sean Taylor RC 2.50 6.00
348 Michael Turner RC .40 1.00
349 Keary Colbert RC .40 1.00
350 Eli Manning RC 5.00 12.00
351 Julius Jones RC .40 1.00
352 Jason Babin RC .60 1.50
353 Cody Pickett RC .40 1.00
354 Kenechi Udeze RC .50 1.25
355 Rashaun Woods RC .40 1.00
356 Matt Schaub RC .40 1.00
357 Tommie Harris RC .50 1.25
358 Dwan Edwards RC .40 1.00
359 Shawn Andrews RC .50 1.25
360 Larry Fitzgerald RC 1.50 4.00
361 P.K. Sam RC .40 1.00
362 Teddy Lehman RC .40 1.00
363 Darius Watts RC .40 1.00
364 D.J. Hackett RC .40 1.00
365 Cedric Cobbs RC .40 1.00
366 Antwan Odom RC .40 1.00
367 Marquise Hill RC .40 1.00
368 Luke McCown RC .40 1.00
369 Triandos Luke RC .40 1.00
370 Kellen Winslow RC .40 1.00
371 Derek Abney RC .40 1.00
372 Chris Cooley RC .50 1.25
373 Dunta Robinson RC .40 1.00
374 Sean Jones RC .40 1.00
375 Philip Rivers RC 1.25 3.00
376 Craig Krenzel RC .40 1.00
377 Daryl Smith RC .40 1.00
378 Samie Parker RC .40 1.00
379 Ben Hartsock RC .40 1.00
380 J.P. Losman RC .40 1.00
381 Karlos Dansby RC .50 1.25
382 Ricardo Colclough RC .40 1.00
383 Bernard Berrian RC .40 1.00
384 Junior Siavii RC .40 1.00
385 Devery Henderson RC .40 1.00
TB38 Tom Brady RH 2.50 6.00
RHTBR2 Tom Brady RH AU 350.00 600.00
SBMVP Tom Brady FB AU/99 350.00 600.00
SAMV M.Vick Mr. Exct AU 40.00 80.00

2004 Topps Black

*VETS: 5X TO 12X BASIC CARDS
*ROOKIES: 3X TO 8X BASIC CARDS
STATED ODDS 1:25 H/R, 1:6 HTA
STATED PRINT RUN 150 SER.#'d SETS

2004 Topps Collection

COMP.FACT SET (385) 40.00 70.00
*VETS: .4X TO 1X BASIC TOPPS
*ROOKIES: .4X TO 1X BASIC TOPPS

2004 Topps First Edition

COMPLETE SET (385) 75.00 150.00
*FIRST ED.VETS: 1.2X TO 3X BASIC CARDS
*FIRST EDITION ROOKIES: .8X TO 2X

2004 Topps Gold

*VET: 2X TO 5X BASIC CARDS
*ROOKIES: 1.5X TO 4X BASIC CARDS
STATED ODDS 1:18 H, 1:5 HTA, 1:15 R
STATED PRINT RUN 499 SER.#'d SETS

2004 Topps Autographs

GROUP A ODDS 1:8664H, 1:2472HTA, 1:7313R
GROUP B ODDS 1:6750H, 1:1890HTA, 1:5811R
GROUP C ODDS 1:3200H, 1:1212HTA, 1:5644R
GROUP D ODDS 1:3360H, 1:952HTA, 1:2913R
GROUP E ODDS 1:2230H, 1:636HTA, 1:1937R
GROUP F ODDS 1:983H, 1:280HTA, 1:859R
GROUP G ODDS 1:3724H, 1:1062HTA, 1:3234R
GROUP H ODDS 1:3346H, 1:952HTA, 1:2913R
GROUP I ODDS 1:1112H, 1:317HTA, 1:978R
TAG Ahman Green A 20.00 40.00
TBR Ben Roethlisberger B 50.00 120.00
TBS Brandon Stokley E 6.00 15.00
TCP Chad Pennington B 20.00 40.00
TCPE Chris Perry A 8.00 20.00
TCPI Cody Pickett H 6.00 15.00
TDD Domanick Davis E 6.00 15.00
TEM Eli Manning C 50.00 120.00
TGJ Greg Jones F 6.00 15.00
TKB Kevan Barlow D 6.00 15.00
TKJ Kevin Jones F 6.00 15.00
TLE Lee Evans G 10.00 25.00
TMC Michael Clayton I 8.00 20.00
TMS Matt Schaub I 6.00 15.00
TPM Peyton Manning A 75.00 150.00
TRW Roy Williams WR F 6.00 15.00
TRWI Reggie Williams F 6.00 15.00
TRWO Rashaun Woods C 6.00 15.00
TSJ Steven Jackson A 12.00 30.00

2004 Topps Game Breakers Relics

STATED ODDS 1:7035H, 1:1977HTA, 1:5997R
GB1 Deion Branch 15.00 40.00
GB2 Tom Brady 50.00 100.00
GB3 Steve Smith 25.00 60.00
GB4 Jake Delhomme 15.00 40.00
GB5 David Givens 15.00 40.00
GB6 Antowain Smith 20.00 50.00
GB7 DeShaun Foster 20.00 50.00
GB8 Muhsin Muhammad 15.00 40.00
GB9 Mike Vrabel 25.00 60.00
GB10 Ricky Proehl 20.00 50.00

2004 Topps Hall of Fame Autographs

STATED ODDS 1:17,513H, 1:4943HTA, 1:14,625R
HOFBB Bob Brown 100.00 200.00
HOFBS Barry Sanders 150.00 300.00
HOFCE Carl Eller 100.00 200.00
HOFJE John Elway 125.00 250.00

2004 Topps Hobby Masters

COMPLETE SET (10) 10.00 25.00
STATED ODDS 1:18 H/R, 1:6 HTA
HM1 Peyton Manning 2.00 5.00
HM2 Michael Vick .60 1.50
HM3 Steve McNair .60 1.50
HM4 Ricky Williams .60 1.50
HM5 Priest Holmes .50 1.25
HM6 Brett Favre 1.50 4.00
HM7 Clinton Portis .50 1.25
HM8 Donovan McNabb .60 1.50
HM9 Randy Moss .60 1.50
HM10 LaDainian Tomlinson .75 2.00

2004 Topps League Leaders Relics

STATED ODDS 1:538 H, 1:35 HTA
LLRJL Jamal Lewis 4.00 10.00
LLRMS Michael Strahan 4.00 10.00
LLRPM Peyton Manning 12.00 30.00
LLRRL Ray Lewis 5.00 12.00
LLRTH Torry Holt 4.00 10.00

2004 Topps Own the Game

COMPLETE SET (30) 20.00 50.00
STATED ODDS 1:12 H/HTA/R
OTG1 Brett Favre 2.00 5.00
OTG2 Donovan McNabb .75 2.00
OTG3 Trent Green .60 1.50
OTG4 Peyton Manning 2.50 6.00
OTG5 Matt Hasselbeck .60 1.50
OTG6 Jon Kitna .60 1.50
OTG7 Steve McNair .75 2.00
OTG8 Tom Brady 4.00 10.00
OTG9 Marc Bulger .60 1.50
OTG10 Jamal Lewis .75 2.00
OTG11 Deuce McAllister .75 2.00
OTG12 Ahman Green .75 2.00
OTG13 Stephen Davis .60 1.50
OTG14 Clinton Portis .60 1.50
OTG15 Priest Holmes .60 1.50
OTG16 LaDainian Tomlinson 1.00 2.50
OTG17 Fred Taylor .60 1.50
OTG18 Shaun Alexander .60 1.50
OTG19 Torry Holt .75 2.00
OTG20 Randy Moss .75 2.00
OTG21 Chad Johnson .60 1.50
OTG22 Anquan Boldin .60 1.50
OTG23 Laveranues Coles .60 1.50
OTG24 Derrick Mason .60 1.50
OTG25 Hines Ward .75 2.00
OTG26 Marvin Harrison .75 2.00
OTG27 Santana Moss .75 2.00
OTG28 Michael Strahan .75 2.00
OTG29 Ray Lewis 1.00 2.50
OTG30 Jamie Sharper .60 1.50

2004 Topps Premiere Prospects

COMPLETE SET (20) 15.00 30.00
STATED ODDS 1:6 H/HTA/R
PP1 Ben Roethlisberger 6.00 15.00
PP2 Chris Perry .40 1.00
PP3 Darius Watts .40 1.00
PP4 Devery Henderson .40 1.00
PP5 Eli Manning 6.00 15.00
PP6 Greg Jones .40 1.00
PP7 J.P. Losman .40 1.00
PP8 Julius Jones .40 1.00
PP9 Kellen Winslow .40 1.00
PP10 Kevin Jones .50 1.25
PP11 Larry Fitzgerald 1.50 4.00
PP12 Lee Evans .60 1.50
PP13 Michael Clayton .50 1.25
PP14 Michael Jenkins .40 1.00
PP15 Philip Rivers 1.25 3.00
PP16 Rashaun Woods .40 1.00
PP17 Reggie Williams .40 1.00
PP18 Roy Williams WR .40 1.00
PP19 Steven Jackson .60 1.50
PP20 Tatum Bell .40 1.00

2004 Topps Premiere Prospects Autographs

NGLE AU ODDS 1:3473H,1:996HTA,1:2913R
SINGLE PRINT RUN 100 SER.#'d SETS
DUAL AU ODDS 1:13,951H,1:4016HTA,1:11,622R
DUAL PRINT RUN 50 SER.#'d SETS
PPBR Ben Roethlisberger 150.00 250.00
PPCP Chris Perry 12.00 30.00
PPDFW Fitzgerald/Williams WR 75.00 150.00
PPDJJ S.Jackson/K.Jones 25.00 60.00
PPDMR Eli/Roethlisberger 200.00 400.00
PPDPJ C.Perry/G.Jones 15.00 40.00
PPDWW Re.Williams/Woods 15.00 40.00
PPEM Eli Manning 75.00 150.00
PPGJ Greg Jones 12.00 30.00
PPKJ Kevin Jones 15.00 40.00
PPLE Lee Evans 20.00 50.00
PPRW Roy Williams WR 12.00 30.00
PPRWI Reggie Williams 12.00 30.00
PPRWO Rashaun Woods 12.00 30.00
PPSJ Steven Jackson 20.00 50.00

2004 Topps Pro Bowl Jerseys

STATED ODDS 1:204 H, 1:34 HTA, 1:190 R
PBAG Ahman Green 5.00 12.00
PBBU Brian Urlacher 8.00 20.00
PBCB Champ Bailey 5.00 12.00
PBCJ Chad Johnson 4.00 10.00
PBHW Hines Ward 10.00 25.00
PBKB Keith Brooking 4.00 10.00
PBLA LaVar Arrington 6.00 15.00
PBMH Marvin Harrison 5.00 12.00
PBMS Michael Strahan 5.00 12.00
PBPH Priest Holmes 4.00 10.00
PBPM Peyton Manning 15.00 40.00
PBSM Steve McNair 5.00 12.00
PBTG Trent Green 4.00 10.00
PBTGO Tony Gonzalez 5.00 12.00
PBTH Torry Holt 5.00 12.00

2004 Topps Ring of Honor Coaches' Cuts

STATED ODDS 1:102,888 H, 1:25,704 HTA
UNPRICED COACHES' CUTS #'d TO 1

2004 Topps Rookie Premiere Autographs

SINGLE AUTO ODDS 1:890 H, 1:225 HTA
DUAL AUTO ODDS 1:1977 HTA
AUTO 1/1 STATED ODDS 1:4016 HTA
*HOLOGRAM MISSING: .2X TO .5X
RPBB Bernard Berrian 15.00 40.00
RPBR Ben Roethlisberger 200.00 400.00
RPBT Ben Troupe 15.00 40.00
RPBW Ben Watson 20.00 50.00
RPCC Cedric Cobbs 15.00 40.00
RPCP Chris Perry 15.00 40.00
RPDD Devard Darling 15.00 40.00
RPDEH DeAngelo Hall 25.00 60.00
RPDFW Fitzgerd/Williams WR 125.00 250.00
RPDHA Derrick Hamilton 15.00 40.00
RPDHE Devery Henderson 15.00 40.00
RPDJJ S.Jackson/K.Jones 25.00 60.00
RPDMR E.Manning/P.Rivers 200.00 400.00
RPDR Dunta Robinson 15.00 40.00
RPDW Darius Watts 15.00 40.00
RPEM Eli Manning 200.00 400.00
RPGJ Greg Jones 15.00 40.00
RPJJ Julius Jones 15.00 40.00
RPJPL J.P. Losman 15.00 40.00
RPKC Keary Colbert 15.00 40.00
RPKJ Kevin Jones 20.00 50.00
RPKW Kellen Winslow 15.00 40.00
RPLE Lee Evans 25.00 60.00
RPLF Larry Fitzgerald 75.00 200.00
RPLM Luke McCown 15.00 40.00
RPMC Michael Clayton 20.00 50.00
RPMJ Michael Jenkins 20.00 50.00
RPMM Mewelde Moore 20.00 50.00
RPMS Matt Schaub 15.00 40.00
RPPR Philip Rivers 75.00 150.00
RPRG Robert Gallery 20.00 50.00
RPRW Roy Williams WR 15.00 40.00
RPRWI Reggie Williams 15.00 40.00
RPRWO Rashaun Woods 15.00 40.00
RPSJ Steven Jackson 25.00 60.00
RPTB Tatum Bell 15.00 40.00

2004 Topps Super Tix

STATED ODDS 1:696 H, 1:199 HTA, 1:580 R
STATED ODDS 1:74,827H,1:21,420HTA,1:65,856R
ST1 Tom Brady 30.00 50.00
ST2 Jake Delhomme 8.00 20.00
ST3 Antowain Smith 10.00 25.00
ST4 Stephen Davis 8.00 20.00
ST5 Deion Branch 8.00 20.00
ST6 Steve Smith 12.00 30.00
ST7 Troy Brown 8.00 20.00
ST8 Muhsin Muhammad 8.00 20.00
ST9 Ty Law 12.00 30.00
ST10 Julius Peppers 10.00 25.00
STATB Tom Brady AU 800.00 1200.00

2004 Topps Hall of Fame Class of 2004

is set was produced by Topps and distributed at the 2004 Induction ceremonies for the Pro Football Hall of Fame. Each card includes a photo of a 2004 inductee printed in a very similar style to the 2004 Topps Hall of Fame Autographs inserts. A gold foil "Class of 2004" logo appears on the top of the cardfronts.

COMPLETE SET (4) 7.50 20.00
BB Bob Brown 1.25 3.00
BS Barry Sanders 3.00 8.00
CE Carl Eller 1.25 3.00
JE John Elway 3.00 8.00

2004 Topps Super Bowl XXXVIII Card Show

This set was distributed directly to dealers who participated in the 2004 Super Bowl Card Show in Houston. Each card was printed on metallic dufex card stock and included the Super Bowl XXXVIII logo on the front. A Gold foil parallel set was also produced.

COMPLETE SET (16) 15.00 25.00
*GOLDS: 1.2X TO 3X BASIC CARDS
1 David Carr .30 .75
2 Priest Holmes .30 .75
3 Jamal Lewis .40 1.00
4 Steve McNair .40 1.00
5 Ricky Williams .40 1.00
6 Ahman Green .40 1.00
7 LaDainian Tomlinson .50 1.25
8 Clinton Portis .30 .75
9 Peyton Manning 1.25 3.00
10 Michael Vick .40 1.00
11 Terrell Owens .40 1.00
12 Daunte Culpepper .40 1.00
13 Andre Johnson .60 1.50
14 Byron Leftwich .50 1.25
15 Anquan Boldin .50 1.25
16 Domanick Davis .50 1.25

2004 Topps Super Bowl XXXVIII Card Show Jumbos

is set was distributed by Topps one card at a time at the 2004 Super Bowl Card Show in Houston. Each card was printed on metallic dufex card stock and included the Super Bowl XXXVIII logo on the front. Each is essentially a jumbo (measuring roughly 3 1/4" by 5") version of five cards from the basic Super Bowl Card Show set.

COMPLETE SET (5) 20.00 35.00
1 Priest Holmes 2.50 6.00
2 Peyton Manning 3.00 8.00
3 Michael Vick 4.00 10.00
4 Byron Leftwich 4.00 10.00
5 Andre Johnson 2.50 6.00

2005 Topps Promos

These 6-cards were issued through Tuff Stuff magazine during the Fall 2005. Each card is a promo version of the player's basic Topps Rookie Card with a different card number on the back. The cards also were printed with flat silver ink on the front instead of the gold foil highlights found on basic 2005 Topps cards.

COMPLETE SET (6) 3.00 6.00
1 Alex Smith .75 2.00
2 Matt Jones .30 .75
3 Braylon Edwards .50 1.25
4 Ronnie Brown .40 1.00
6 Cadillac Williams .40 1.00

2005 Topps Throwbacks Promos

These 7-cards were issued exclusively through Beckett Football magazines during the Fall 2005. Except for Alex Smith, the cards were designed like an older Topps card of a rookie player not featured in that year's set. These "cards that never were" have a card number on the back that reads "XX of 7" and cardback text written to reflect the player's rookie season.

COMPLETE SET (7) 12.50 25.00
1 Alex Smith QB 3.00 6.00
2 Mike Williams WR 2.50 5.00
3 Priest Holmes 2.00 4.00
4 Brett Favre 3.00 6.00
5 Curtis Martin 2.00 4.00
6 Tom Brady 2.50 5.00
7 Cedric Benson 2.00 4.00

2005 Topps

MP.COWBOYS SET (445) 25.00 50.00
COMP.EAGLES SET (445) 25.00 50.00
COMP.FACT.SET (445) 25.00 50.00
COMP.PACKERS SET (445) 25.00 50.00
COMP.RAIDERS SET (445) 25.00 50.00
COMP.SB XL SET (445) 50.00 80.00
COMPLETE SET (440) 30.00 50.00
RH39 STATED ODDS 1:275 HOB/HTA/RET
RH39A 1:62,233H, 1:15,547HTA, 1:51,346R
SBMVP 1:27,629H, 1:7774HTA, 1:43,632R
UNPRICED PLATINUM PRINT RUN 1 SET
1 Brian Westbrook .15 .40
2 Tim Rattay .15 .40
3 Domanick Davis .15 .40
4 Lee Suggs .15 .40
5 Keith Brooking .15 .40
6 Rex Grossman .15 .40
7 Chad Johnson .15 .40
8 Willis McGahee .15 .40
9 Eli Manning .40 1.00
10 Tom Brady 1.00 2.50
11 Ray Lewis .25 .60
12 Terence Newman .15 .40
13 Daunte Culpepper .20 .50
14 Marvin Harrison .20 .50
15 Greg Jones .15 .40
16 Anquan Boldin .15 .40
17 Julius Peppers .20 .50
18 Kevin Jones .15 .40
19 Javon Walker .15 .40
20 Michael Lewis .15 .40
21 Jamaar Taylor .15 .40
22 Hines Ward .20 .50
23 Drew Brees .25 .60
24 Marcus Trufant .15 .40
25 Derrick Brooks .15 .40
26 Sean Taylor .25 .60
27 Derrius Thompson .15 .40
28 Nick Barnett .15 .40
29 Dante Hall .15 .40
30 Mike Cloud .15 .40
31 Jake Plummer .15 .40
32 Donte Stallworth .15 .40
33 Shaun Ellis .15 .40
34 Jeremy Shockey .15 .40
35 Teyo Johnson .15 .40
36 Adam Archuleta .15 .40
37 Darius Watts .15 .40
38 Michael Pittman .15 .40
39 Drew Bennett .20 .50
40 Aaron Stecker .15 .40
41 Artose Pinner .15 .40
42 Dane Looker .15 .40
43 Jeff Garcia .15 .40
44 Travis Taylor .15 .40
45 Najeh Davenport .15 .40
46 Walter Jones .15 .40
47 Donnie Edwards .15 .40
48 Terrell Owens .20 .50
49 Matt Birk .15 .40
50 Chris Baker .15 .40
51 Brandon Lloyd .15 .40
52 Marshall Faulk .20 .50
53 Jonathan Vilma .15 .40
54 Dallas Clark .15 .40
55 David Carr .15 .40
56 Jerricho Cotchery .15 .40
57 Deuce McAllister .20 .50
58 Donald Driver .20 .50
59 Jeff Smoker .15 .40
60 Champ Bailey .20 .50
61 Jason Witten .20 .50
62 T.J. Houshmandzadeh .15 .40
63 Jay Fiedler .15 .40
64 Philip Rivers .25 .60
65 Jake Delhomme .15 .40
66 Terrence McGee RC .20 .50
67 Chester Taylor .20 .50
68 Tommy Maddox .15 .40
69 Bryant Johnson .15 .40
70 Justin Gage .15 .40
71 Troy Hambrick .15 .40

72 Kerry Collins .15 .40
73 Jeb Putzier .15 .40
74 Keary Colbert .15 .40
75 Jason Elam .15 .40
76 Jerramy Stevens .20 .50
77 Clinton Portis .15 .40
78 Sam Aiken .15 .40
79 Trent Green .15 .40
80 Dat Nguyen .15 .40
81 Ladell Betts .15 .40
82 Peter Warrick .15 .40
83 Dominic Rhodes .15 .40
84 Jason Taylor .20 .50
85 Antwaan Randle El .15 .40
86 Michael Jenkins .15 .40
87 Adam Vinatieri .15 .40
88 Mark Brunell .20 .50
89 Brian Finneran .15 .40
90 Ernie Conwell .15 .40
91 Chad Pennington .15 .40
92 Dan Morgan .15 .40
93 Kelly Holcomb .15 .40
94 Ronde Barber .15 .40
95 Torry Holt .20 .50
96 Bubba Franks .15 .40
97 Keyshawn Johnson .20 .50
98 J.P. Losman .15 .40
99 Ed Reed .20 .50
100 Chris McAlister .15 .40
101 Jamie Sharper .15 .40
102 Chad Lewis .15 .40
103 Chris Brown .15 .40
104 Marc Boerigter .15 .40
105 Zach Thomas .20 .50
106 Byron Leftwich .15 .40
107 Tatum Bell .15 .40
108 Tai Streets .15 .40
109 Tory James .15 .40
110 Cedrick Wilson .15 .40
111 Darrell Jackson .15 .40
112 Ben Roethlisberger .40 1.00
113 Quentin Jammer .15 .40
114 Maurice Morris .15 .40
115 Simeon Rice .15 .40
116 Tyrone Calico .15 .40
117 Patrick Ramsey .20 .50
118 Marcus Robinson .15 .40
119 Reggie Wayne .20 .50
120 Kevin Faulk .15 .40
121 Nate Burleson .15 .40
122 Aaron Brooks .15 .40
123 Willie Roaf .15 .40
124 Fred Taylor .15 .40
125 Dwight Freeney .15 .40
126 Olin Kreutz .20 .50
127 Dunta Robinson .15 .40
128 Warren Sapp .20 .50
129 Chris Perry .15 .40
130 Desmond Clark .15 .40
131 Takeo Spikes .15 .40
132 B.J. Sams .15 .40
133 Bertrand Berry .15 .40
134 Drew Henson .15 .40
135 Robert Ferguson .15 .40
136 Julius Jones .15 .40
137 Jeremiah Trotter .15 .40
138 Chris Simms .15 .40
139 Damerien McCants .15 .40
140 Robert Gallery .15 .40
141 Michael Strahan .20 .50
142 Reggie Williams .15 .40
143 Tony Gonzalez .20 .50
144 Priest Holmes .15 .40
145 Luke McCown .15 .40
146 Allen Rossum .15 .40
147 Eric Moulds .15 .40
148 Jonathan Wells .15 .40
149 Randy McMichael .15 .40
150 John Abraham .15 .40
151 Doug Gabriel .15 .40
152 Tiki Barber .20 .50
153 Marcel Shipp .15 .40
154 LaDainian Tomlinson .25 .60
155 Richard Seymour .15 .40
156 Mike Vanderjagt .15 .40
157 Roy Williams WR .15 .40
158 William Green .15 .40
159 DeAngelo Hall .15 .40
160 Josh McCown .20 .50
161 Terrell Suggs .15 .40
162 Brian Dawkins .25 .60
163 Lee Evans .20 .50
164 Nick Goings .15 .40
165 Carson Palmer .20 .50
166 Charles Woodson .25 .60
167 Keenan McCardell .20 .50
168 Kevan Barlow .15 .40
169 Matt Hasselbeck .15 .40
170 Steven Jackson .15 .40
171 Ben Troupe .15 .40
172 Jamal Lewis .20 .50
173 Sammy Morris .15 .40
174 Troy Polamalu .25 .60
175 Donovan McNabb .20 .50
176 Curtis Martin .20 .50
177 David Givens .15 .40
178 Kenechi Udeze .15 .40
179 A.J. Feeley .15 .40
180 Eddie Kennison .15 .40
181 LaBrandon Toefield .15 .40
182 Jabar Gaffney .15 .40
183 Bethel Johnson .15 .40
184 Eddie Drummond .15 .40
185 Rod Smith .20 .50
186 La'Roi Glover .15 .40
187 Onterrio Smith .15 .40
188 Antonio Bryant .15 .40
189 Lee Mays .15 .40
190 Michael Vick .20 .50
191 Samie Parker .15 .40
192 London Fletcher .20 .50
193 DeShaun Foster .20 .50
194 Rashaun Woods .15 .40
195 Marc Bulger .15 .40
196 Adrian Peterson .15 .40
197 Justin McCareins .15 .40
198 Corey Dillon .15 .40
199 James Farrior .15 .40
200 Antonio Gates .25 .60
201 Todd Pinkston .15 .40
202 Randy Hymes .15 .40
203 Peyton Manning .60 1.50
204 Ahman Green .20 .50
205 Charles Rogers .15 .40
206 John Lynch .20 .50
207 Larry Fitzgerald .25 .60
208 Jonathan Ogden .20 .50
209 Michael Bennett .15 .40
210 DeWayne Robertson .15 .40
211 Justin Fargas .20 .50
212 Duce Staley .15 .40
213 Koren Robinson .15 .40
214 Billy Volek .15 .40
215 Laveranues Coles .15 .40
216 Michael Clayton .15 .40
217 Amani Toomer .15 .40
218 Thomas Jones .15 .40
219 Todd Heap .15 .40
220 Ken Lucas .15 .40
221 Donovin Darius .15 .40
222 Ashley Lelie .15 .40
223 Warrick Dunn .15 .40
224 Doug Jolley .15 .40
225 Jimmy Smith .20 .50
226 Quentin Griffin .15 .40
227 Isaac Bruce .25 .60
228 Ronald Curry .15 .40
229 Corey Bradford .15 .40
230 LaVar Arrington .15 .40
231 William Henderson .15 .40
232 Brandon Stokley .15 .40
233 Alge Crumpler .20 .50
234 Joe Horn .15 .40
235 Bernard Berrian .15 .40
236 Michael Boulware .15 .40
237 Brett Favre .50 1.25
238 Dennis Northcutt .15 .40
239 Muhsin Muhammad .15 .40
240 Shawn Springs .15 .40
241 Kelly Campbell .15 .40
242 Johnnie Morton .20 .50
243 Derrick Blaylock .15 .40
244 Chris Chambers .15 .40
245 Joey Harrington .15 .40
246 Brian Urlacher .25 .60
247 T.J. Duckett .15 .40
248 Quincy Morgan .15 .40
249 Darren Sharper .15 .40
250 L.J. Smith .20 .50
251 Steve McNair .20 .50
252 Eric Parker .15 .40
253 Jerome Bettis .25 .60
254 LaMont Jordan .20 .50
255 Tedy Bruschi .20 .50
256 Ernest Wilford .15 .40
257 Reuben Droughns .15 .40
258 Lito Sheppard .20 .50
259 Steve Smith .25 .60
260 Shaun Alexander .15 .40
261 Kevin Curtis .20 .50
262 Drew Bledsoe .20 .50
263 Derrick Mason .15 .40
264 Jevon Kearse .15 .40
265 Jerry Porter .15 .40
266 Edgerrin James .20 .50
267 Santana Moss .20 .50
268 Kyle Boller .15 .40
269 Travis Henry .15 .40
270 Stephen Davis .15 .40
271 Gibril Wilson .15 .40
272 Plaxico Burress .15 .40
273 Deion Branch .15 .40
274 Larry Johnson .15 .40
275 Rudi Johnson .15 .40
276 Andre Johnson .20 .50
277 David Akers .15 .40
278 Randy Moss .20 .50
279 Roy Williams S .15 .40
280 Antoine Winfield .20 .50
281 Antonio Pierce .15 .40
282 Keith Bulluck .15 .40
283 Correll Buckhalter .15 .40
284 Troy Vincent .20 .50
285 D.J. Williams .15 .40
286 Matt Schaub .20 .50
287 Clarence Moore .15 .40
288 Billy Miller .15 .40
289 Terrence Holt .15 .40
290 Tony Hollings .15 .40
291 E.J. Henderson .15 .40
292 Fred Smoot .15 .40
293 Patrick Crayton .15 .40
294 Mike Alstott .15 .40
295 Mewelde Moore .15 .40
296 Shawn Bryson .15 .40
297 David Garrard .15 .40
298 Kurt Warner .20 .50
299 Nate Clements .20 .50
300 Kellen Winslow .15 .40
301 Eric Johnson .15 .40
302 Peerless Price .15 .40
303 Joey Galloway .20 .50
304 Sebastian Janikowski .15 .40
305 Jason McAddley .15 .40
306 Chris Gamble .15 .40
307 Brian Griese .15 .40
308 Greg Lewis .20 .50
309 Wes Welker .20 .50
310 Jesse Chatman .15 .40
311 Curtis Martin LL .15 .40
312 Daunte Culpepper LL .15 .40
313 Muhsin Muhammad LL .12 .30
314 Shaun Alexander LL .12 .30
315 Trent Green LL .12 .30
316 Joe Horn LL .12 .30
317 Corey Dillon LL .12 .30
318 Peyton Manning LL .50 1.25
319 Javon Walker LL .12 .30
320 Edgerrin James LL .15 .40
321 Jake Scott GM .15 .40
322 John Elway GM .40 1.00
323 Dwight Clark GM .20 .50
324 Lawrence Taylor GM .25 .60
325 Joe Namath GM .40 1.00
326 Richard Dent GM .20 .50
327 Peyton Manning GM .60 1.50
328 Don Maynard GM .20 .50
329 Joe Greene GM .25 .60
330 Roger Staubach GM .30 .75
331 Daunte Culpepper AP .15 .40
332 Peyton Manning AP .50 1.25
333 Tiki Barber AP .15 .40
334 Antonio Gates AP .20 .50
335 Marvin Harrison AP .15 .40
336 Lito Sheppard AP .15 .40
337 LaDainian Tomlinson AP .20 .50
338 Muhsin Muhammad AP .12 .30
339 Allen Rossum AP .12 .30
340 Dwight Freeney AP .12 .30
341 Jerome Bettis AP .20 .50
342 Alge Crumpler AP .15 .40
343 Ed Reed AP .15 .40
344 Ronde Barber AP .12 .30
345 Takeo Spikes AP .12 .30
346 Rudi Johnson AP .12 .30
347 Adam Vinatieri AP .12 .30
348 Torry Holt AP .15 .40
349 Chad Johnson AP .12 .30
350 Brian Westbrook AP .12 .30
351 Michael Vick AP .15 .40
352 Tom Brady AP .75 2.00
353 Donovan McNabb AP .15 .40
354 Ahman Green AP .15 .40
355 Andre Johnson AP .15 .40
356 Drew Brees AP .20 .50
357 Hines Ward AP .15 .40
358 Deion Branch PH .12 .30
359 Philadelphia Eagles PH .15 .40
360 Tom Brady PH .75 2.00
361 Taylor Stubblefield RC .40 1.00
362 Dan Cody RC .40 1.00
363 Ryan Claridge RC .40 1.00
364 David Pollack RC .40 1.00
365 Craig Bragg RC .40 1.00
366 Alvin Pearman RC .40 1.00
367 Marcus Maxwell RC .40 1.00
368 Brock Berlin RC .40 1.00
369 Khalif Barnes RC .40 1.00
370 Eric King RC .40 1.00
371 Alex Smith TE RC .40 1.00
372 Dante Ridgeway RC .40 1.00
373 Shaun Cody RC .50 1.25
374 Donte Nicholson RC .40 1.00
375 DeMarcus Ware RC 1.25 3.00
376 Lionel Gates RC .40 1.00
377 Fabian Washington RC .40 1.00
378 Brandon Jacobs RC .50 1.25
379 Noah Herron RC .40 1.00
380 Derrick Johnson RC .50 1.25
381 J.R. Russell RC .40 1.00
382 Adrian McPherson RC .40 1.00
383 Marcus Spears RC .40 1.00
384 Justin Miller RC .40 1.00
385 Marion Barber RC .40 1.00
386 Anthony Davis RC .40 1.00
387 Chad Owens RC .40 1.00
388 Craphonso Thorpe RC .40 1.00
389 Travis Johnson RC .40 1.00
390 Erasmus James RC .40 1.00
391 Mike Patterson RC .40 1.00
392 Alphonso Hodge RC .40 1.00
393 Airese Currie RC .40 1.00
394 Justin Tuck RC .50 1.25
395 Dan Orlovsky RC .40 1.00
396 Thomas Davis RC .40 1.00
397 Derek Anderson RC .50 1.25
398 Matt Roth RC .40 1.00
399 Darryl Blackstock RC .40 1.00
400 Chris Henry RC .50 1.25
401 Rasheed Marshall RC .50 1.25
402 Anttaj Hawthorne RC .40 1.00
403 Bryant McFadden RC .50 1.25
404 Darren Sproles RC .60 1.50
405 Oshiomogho Atogwe RC .50 1.25
406 Fred Gibson RC .40 1.00
407 J.J. Arrington RC .50 1.25
408 Cedric Benson RC .40 1.00
409 Mark Bradley RC .40 1.00
410 Reggie Brown RC .40 1.00
411 Ronnie Brown RC .50 1.25
412 Jason Campbell RC .40 1.00
413 Maurice Clarett .40 1.00
414 Mark Clayton RC .40 1.00
415 Braylon Edwards RC .40 1.00
416 Ciatrick Fason RC .40 1.00
417 Charlie Frye RC .40 1.00
418 Frank Gore RC .75 2.00
419 David Greene RC .40 1.00
420 Vincent Jackson RC .60 1.50
421 Adam Jones RC .40 1.00
422 Matt Jones RC .40 1.00
423 Stefan LeFors RC .40 1.00
424 Heath Miller RC .75 2.00
425 Ryan Moats RC .40 1.00
426 Vernand Morency RC .40 1.00
427 Terrence Murphy RC .40 1.00
428 Kyle Orton RC .40 1.00
429 Roscoe Parrish RC .40 1.00
430 Courtney Roby RC .40 1.00
431 Aaron Rodgers RC 12.00 30.00
432 Carlos Rogers RC .60 1.50
433 Antrel Rolle RC .60 1.50
434 Eric Shelton RC .40 1.00
435 Alex Smith QB RC 1.50 4.00
436 Andrew Walter RC .40 1.00
437 Roddy White RC .60 1.50
438 Cadillac Williams RC .40 1.00
439 Mike Williams .50 1.25
440 Troy Williamson RC .40 1.00
RHDB Deion Branch RH 2.00 5.00
RHDBA Deion Branch RH AU 150.00 300.00
SBMVP D.Branch FB AU/200 50.00 100.00

2005 Topps Black

*VETERANS: 2.5X TO 6X BASIC CARDS
*ROOKIES: 1X TO 2.5X BASIC CARDS
STATED ODDS 1:6 H/R, 1:2 HTA

2005 Topps First Edition

ETERANS: 1.2X TO 3X BASIC CARDS
*ROOKIES: .8X TO 2X BASIC CARDS

2005 Topps Gold

*VETERANS: 12X TO 30X BASIC CARDS
*ROOKIES: 5X TO 12X BASIC CARDS
STATED ODDS 1:296H, 1:83HTA, 1:251R
STATED PRINT RUN 50 SER.#'d SETS
431 Aaron Rodgers 125.00 200.00

2005 Topps 50th Anniversary Rookies

*SINGLES: 5X TO 12X BASIC CARDS
STATED ODDS 1:1467H, 1:394HTA, 1:1238R
STATED PRINT RUN 50 SER.#'d SETS
431 Aaron Rodgers 125.00 200.00

2005 Topps 50th Anniversary Team Autographs

ATED ODDS 1:11,051 HOB, 1:2564 HTA
STATED PRINT RUN 50 SER.#'d SETS
TABF Brett Favre 200.00 400.00
TABS Barry Sanders 175.00 300.00
TACM Curtis Martin 100.00 200.00
TADM Dan Marino 200.00 400.00
TAEC Earl Campbell 75.00 150.00
TAED Eric Dickerson 75.00 150.00
TAES Emmitt Smith 200.00 400.00
TAGS Gale Sayers 125.00 250.00
TAJB Jim Brown 150.00 300.00
TAJE John Elway 150.00 300.00
TAJM Joe Montana 200.00 400.00
TAJN Joe Namath 125.00 250.00
TAJR Jerry Rice 150.00 300.00
TALM Lenny Moore 40.00 100.00
TALT Lawrence Taylor 75.00 150.00
TAMA Marcus Allen 125.00 250.00
TAMH Marvin Harrison 50.00 120.00
TAON Ozzie Newsome 75.00 150.00
TAPM Peyton Manning 150.00 300.00
TARL Ronnie Lott 100.00 200.00
TARS Roger Staubach 150.00 300.00
TASY Steve Young 75.00 150.00
TATB Terry Bradshaw 175.00 350.00
TATBR Tom Brady 250.00 400.00
TATD Tony Dorsett 100.00 200.00

2005 Topps Autographs

GROUP A 1:62,233H, 1:19,135HTA, 1:51,346R
GROUP B ODDS 1:9500H, 1:2795HTA, 1:9969R
GROUP C ODDS 1:3536H, 1:1050HTA, 1:3152R
GROUP D ODDS 1:3536H, 1:1050HTA, 1:3052R
GROUP E ODDS 1:1603H, 1:479HTA, 1:1400R
GROUP F ODDS 1:4041H, 1:1196HTA, 1:3491R
GROUP G ODDS 1:478H, 1:207HTA, 1:953R
GROUP H ODDS 1:1407H, 1:419HTA, 1:1238R
TAD Anthony Davis F 7.50 20.00
TAG Antonio Gates C 12.00 30.00
TAR Aaron Rodgers B 150.00 250.00
TAS Alex Smith QB C 25.00 60.00
TBE Braylon Edwards B 10.00 25.00
TCB Cedric Benson B 10.00 25.00
TCF Charlie Frye C 10.00 25.00
TCJ Chad Johnson C 10.00 25.00
TCW Cadillac Williams B 12.00 30.00
TDB Drew Bennett C 10.00 25.00
TDG David Greene D 10.00 25.00
TDJ Derrick Johnson G 10.00 25.00
TDM Damerien McCants G 6.00 15.00
TDO Dan Orlovsky E 10.00 25.00
TDS Donte Stallworth C 10.00 25.00
TFG Fred Gibson G 6.00 15.00
TJF Justin Fargas E 10.00 25.00
TJS Junior Siavii E 7.50 20.00
TJW Jason White D 10.00 25.00
TKG Kevin Garrett G 6.00 15.00
TKK Kevin Kasper G 7.50 20.00
TKO Kyle Orton E 10.00 25.00
TLW LeVar Woods E 6.00 15.00
TMC Mark Clayton B 10.00 25.00
TMH Marquise Hill H 6.00 15.00
TMJ Marlin Jackson E 10.00 25.00
TMR Montae Reagor G 7.50 20.00
TMV Michael Vick A 60.00 120.00
TMW Mike Williams B 10.00 25.00
TNW Nate Wayne G 6.00 15.00
TPM Peyton Manning A 150.00 250.00
TRB Ronnie Brown D 10.00 25.00
TRJ Rudi Johnson C 7.50 20.00
TSM Santana Moss C 10.00 25.00
TTM Terrence Murphy G 10.00 25.00
TTS Trent Smith H 6.00 15.00
TTW Troy Williamson F 10.00 25.00
TCBR Chris Brown D 7.50 20.00
TJJA J.J. Arrington E 10.00 25.00

2005 Topps Golden Anniversary Glistening Gold

COMPLETE SET (15) 12.50 30.00
GOLDEN ANNIV.OVERALL ODDS 1:6 H/R
GG1 Priest Holmes .75 2.00
GG2 Michael Vick 1.00 2.50
GG3 Hines Ward 1.00 2.50
GG4 Terrell Owens 1.00 2.50
GG5 Randy Moss 1.00 2.50
GG6 Marvin Harrison 1.00 2.50
GG7 LaDainian Tomlinson 1.25 3.00
GG8 Donovan McNabb 1.00 2.50
GG9 Daunte Culpepper 1.00 2.50
GG10 Ahman Green 1.00 2.50
GG11 Shaun Alexander .75 2.00
GG12 Edgerrin James 1.00 2.50
GG13 Torry Holt 1.00 2.50
GG14 Clinton Portis .75 2.00
GG15 Jamal Lewis 1.00 2.50

2005 Topps Golden Anniversary Golden Greats

COMPLETE SET (10) 12.50 25.00
GOLDEN ANNIVERSARY OVERALL ODDS 1:6
GA1 Joe Montana 3.00 8.00
GA2 Joe Namath 1.50 4.00
GA3 Earl Campbell 1.00 2.50
GA4 Lawrence Taylor 1.00 2.50
GA5 John Elway 1.50 4.00
GA6 Barry Sanders 1.50 4.00
GA7 Jim Brown 1.25 3.00
GA8 Gale Sayers 1.00 2.50
GA9 Tony Dorsett 1.00 2.50
GA10 Ronnie Lott .75 2.00

2005 Topps Golden Anniversary Gold Nuggets

MPLETE SET (10) 10.00 25.00
GOLDEN ANNIVERSARY OVERALL ODDS 1:6
GN1 Curtis Martin 1.00 2.50
GN2 Brett Favre 2.50 6.00
GN3 Jerome Bettis 1.25 3.00
GN4 Tom Brady 5.00 12.00
GN5 Ray Lewis 1.25 3.00
GN6 Marshall Faulk 1.00 2.50
GN7 Michael Strahan 1.00 2.50
GN8 Peyton Manning 3.00 8.00
GN9 Tony Gonzalez 1.00 2.50
GN10 Jonathan Ogden 1.00 2.50

2005 Topps Golden Anniversary Greats Autographs

EATS/STARS 1:11,051H, 1:2795HTA, 1:8487R
UNPRICED RED INK AUTO PRINT RUN 5
GAGBS Barry Sanders 125.00 250.00
GAGEC Earl Campbell 30.00 80.00
GAGGS Gale Sayers 60.00 120.00
GAGJB Jim Brown 75.00 150.00
GAGJE John Elway 125.00 250.00
GAGJM Joe Montana 125.00 250.00
GAGJN Joe Namath 75.00 150.00
GAGLT Lawrence Taylor 50.00 100.00
GAGRL Ronnie Lott 30.00 80.00
GAGTD Tony Dorsett 50.00 100.00

2005 Topps Golden Anniversary Hidden Gold

MPLETE SET (15) 15.00 30.00
GOLDEN ANNIVERSARY OVERALL ODDS 1:6
HG1 Nate Burleson .75 2.00
HG2 Julius Jones .75 2.00
HG3 Eli Manning 2.00 5.00
HG4 Kevin Jones .75 2.00
HG5 Lee Evans 1.00 2.50
HG6 Ben Roethlisberger 2.00 5.00
HG7 Willis McGahee .75 2.00
HG8 Dunta Robinson .75 2.00
HG9 Chris Brown .75 2.00
HG10 Roy Williams WR .75 2.00
HG11 Steven Jackson .75 2.00
HG12 Carson Palmer 1.00 2.50
HG13 Antonio Gates 1.25 3.00
HG14 Chris Gamble .75 2.00
HG15 LaMont Jordan 1.00 2.50

2005 Topps Golden Anniversary Prospects Autographs

STATED ODDS 1:7810H, 1:2325HTA, 1:6790R
UNPRICED RED INK AUTO PRINT RUN 5
GAPAG Antonio Gates 30.00 60.00
GAPAR Aaron Rodgers 200.00 400.00
GAPAS Alex Smith QB 30.00 80.00
GAPBE Braylon Edwards 25.00 60.00
GAPCBE Cedric Benson 20.00 50.00
GAPMW Mike Williams 15.00 40.00
GAPRB Ronnie Brown 60.00 120.00
GAPTW Troy Williamson 15.00 40.00

2005 Topps Golden Anniversary Stars Autographs

EATS/STARS 1:11,051H, 1:2795HTA, 1:8487R
UNPRICED RED INK AUTO PRINT RUN 5
GASBF Brett Favre 150.00 250.00
GASMH Marvin Harrison 30.00 80.00
GASMV Michael Vick 40.00 80.00
GASPM Peyton Manning 75.00 150.00
GASTB Tom Brady 150.00 250.00

2005 Topps Hall of Fame Autographs

DS 1:30,255H, 1:8464HTA, 1:43,632R
HOFDM Dan Marino 125.00 250.00
HOFSY Steve Young 30.00 80.00

2005 Topps Pro Bowl Jerseys

DS 1:539 H, 1:44 HTA, 1:1947 R
APAG Antonio Gates 6.00 15.00
APBB Bertrand Berry 5.00 12.00
APCB Champ Bailey 5.00 12.00
APDC Daunte Culpepper 6.00 15.00
APDM Dan Morgan 5.00 12.00
APER Ed Reed 6.00 15.00
APLT LaDainian Tomlinson 6.00 15.00
APMH Marvin Harrison 6.00 15.00
APPM Peyton Manning 10.00 25.00
APTB Tiki Barber 6.00 15.00

2005 Topps Rookie Premiere Autographs

NGLE AUTO ODDS 1:195 HTA
DUAL AUTO ODDS 1:16,584 HTA
QUAD AUTO ODDS 1:10,816 HTA
UNPRICED RED INK AUTO PRINT RUN 10
*HOLOGRAM MISSING: .2X TO .5X
RCBWA Clrt/Brn/Wll/JJ 60.00 150.00
RCWBR Cmbll/Wlms/Brn/Rgs 75.00 150.00
REJWC Edwrd/Jnes/Wlmsn/Clyt 50.00 100.00
RPAJ Adam Jones 12.00 30.00
RPARO Antrel Rolle 20.00 50.00
RPAS Alex Smith QB 50.00 100.00
RPAW Andrew Walter 12.00 30.00
RPBE Braylon Edwards 12.00 30.00
RPCF Ciatrick Fason 12.00 30.00
RPCFR Charlie Frye 12.00 30.00
RPCR Courtney Roby 12.00 30.00
RPCRO Carlos Rogers 20.00 50.00
RPCW Cadillac Williams 12.00 30.00
RPDBW Ron.Brown/C.Will. 75.00 150.00
RPDEJ B.Edwards/M.Jones 25.00 60.00
RPDEW Edwards/Williamson 25.00 60.00
RPDJW M.Jones/Ro.White 25.00 60.00
RPES Eric Shelton 12.00 30.00
RPFG Frank Gore 60.00 120.00
RPJC Jason Campbell 30.00 80.00
RPJJA J.J. Arrington 15.00 40.00
RPKO Kyle Orton 12.00 30.00
RPMB Mark Bradley 12.00 30.00
RPMC Maurice Clarett 12.00 30.00
RPMCL Mark Clayton 12.00 30.00
RPRB Ronnie Brown 15.00 40.00
RPRBR Reggie Brown 12.00 30.00
RPRM Ryan Moats 12.00 30.00
RPRP Roscoe Parrish 12.00 30.00
RPRW Roddy White 20.00 50.00
RPSL Stefan LeFors 12.00 30.00
RPTM Terrence Murphy 12.00 30.00
RPTW Troy Williamson 12.00 30.00
RPVJ Vincent Jackson 20.00 50.00
RPVM Vernand Morency 12.00 30.00
RSWCF A.Smt/Wltr/Camp/Frye 75.00 150.00
RWWEJ Wmsn/Wht/Edwds/Jns 25.00 60.00

2005 Topps Rookie Throwback Jerseys

DS 1:361 H, 1:27 HTA, 1367 R
RTAJ Adam Jones 3.00 8.00
RTARO Antrel Rolle 4.00 10.00
RTAS Alex Smith QB 10.00 25.00
RTBE Braylon Edwards 2.50 6.00
RTCR Carlos Rogers 4.00 10.00
RTCW Cadillac Williams 2.50 6.00
RTJC Jason Campbell 2.50 6.00
RTJJA J.J. Arrington 3.00 8.00
RTMC Maurice Clarett 3.00 8.00
RTMCL Mark Clayton 2.50 6.00
RTMJ Matt Jones
RTRB Ronnie Brown 3.00 8.00
RTRW Roddy White 4.00 10.00
RTTM Terrence Murphy 2.50 6.00
RTTW Troy Williamson 2.50 6.00

2005 Topps Super Tix

ATED ODDS 1:588 H, 1:138 HTA, 1:489 R
ST1 Deion Branch 10.00 25.00
ST2 Donovan McNabb 12.50 30.00
ST3 Corey Dillon 10.00 25.00
ST4 Brian Westbrook 6.00 15.00
ST5 Rodney Harrison 6.00 15.00
ST6 Terrell Owens 10.00 25.00
ST7 Mike Vrabel 6.00 15.00
ST8 Jeremiah Trotter 6.00 15.00
ST9 Tom Brady 20.00 40.00
ST10 Brian Dawkins 6.00 15.00
STADB Deion Branch AU 75.00 135.00

2005 Topps Factory Set Rookie Bonus

These cards were included as bonus inserts in the various versions of 2005 Topps factory sets that include the four team specific versions and the basic nationally issued factory set.

COMP.COWBOYS SET (5) 4.00 10.00
COMP.EAGLES SET (5) 3.00 8.00
COMP.PACKERS SET (5) 3.00 8.00
COMP.RAIDERS SET (5) 3.00 8.00
COMP.MULTI TEAM (5) 3.00 8.00
FIVE PER TOPPS FACTORY SET
C1 Kevin Burnett .75 2.00
C2 Chris Canty 1.00 2.50
C3 Justin Beriault .60 1.50
C4 Rob Petitti .60 1.50
C5 Jay Ratliff 3.00 8.00
E1 Matt McCoy .75 2.00
E2 Sean Considine .60 1.50
E3 Calvin Armstrong .60 1.50
E4 Trent Cole 1.00 2.50
E5 David Bergeron .60 1.50
P1 Nick Collins 1.00 2.50
P2 Marviel Underwood .75 2.00
P3 Brady Poppinga 1.00 2.50
P4 Mike Montgomery 1.00 2.50
P5 Kurt Campbell .60 1.50
R1 Stanford Routt .75 2.00
R2 Kirk Morrison 1.00 2.50
R3 Ryan Riddle .60 1.50
R4 Pete McMahon .60 1.50
R5 Maurice Washington .60 1.50
S1 Luis Castillo .75 2.00
S2 Zach Tuiasosopo .60 1.50
S3 Kevin Burnett .75 2.00
S4 Corey Webster .75 2.00
S5 Paris Warren .75 2.00
T1 Jerome Mathis 1.00 2.50
T2 Mike Nugent .75 2.00
T3 Tab Perry .60 1.50
T4 Ryan Fitzpatrick 1.00 2.50
T5 Channing Crowder .75 2.00

2005 Topps Throwbacks

COMPLETE SET (49) 40.00 80.00
STATED ODDS 1:6 HOB/RET
TB1 LaDainian Tomlinson 1.25 3.00
TB2 Marvin Harrison 1.00 2.50
TB3 Shaun Alexander .75 2.00
TB4 Peyton Manning 3.00 8.00
TB5 Trent Green .75 2.00
TB6 Randy Moss 1.00 2.50
TB7 Brett Favre 2.50 6.00
TB8 Ben Roethlisberger 2.00 5.00
TB9 Donovan McNabb 1.00 2.50
TB10 Tom Brady 5.00 12.00
TB11 Dwight Freeney .75 2.00
TB12 Dante Hall .75 2.00
TB13 Edgerrin James 1.00 2.50
TB14 Daunte Culpepper 1.00 2.50
TB15 Ray Lewis 1.25 3.00
TB16 Joe Horn .75 2.00
TB17 Terrell Owens 1.00 2.50
TB18 Muhsin Muhammad .75 2.00
TB19 Curtis Martin 1.00 2.50
TB20 Michael Vick 1.00 2.50
TB21 Antonio Gates 1.25 3.00
TB22 Deuce McAllister 1.00 2.50
TB23 Javon Walker .75 2.00
TB24 Tony Gonzalez 1.00 2.50
TB25 Corey Dillon .75 2.00
TB26 Tiki Barber 1.00 2.50
TB27 Jamal Lewis 1.00 2.50
TB28 Reggie Wayne 1.00 2.50
TB29 Priest Holmes .75 2.00
TB30 Chris Brown .75 2.00
TB31 Marc Bulger .75 2.00
TB32 Hines Ward 1.00 2.50
TB33 Chad Johnson .75 2.00
TB34 Ahman Green 1.00 2.50
TB35 Willis McGahee .75 2.00
TB36 Rudi Johnson .75 2.00
TB37 Drew Brees 1.25 3.00
TB38 Isaac Bruce 1.25 3.00
TB39 Ed Reed 1.00 2.50
TB40 Domanick Davis .75 2.00
TB41 Jake Delhomme .75 2.00
TB42 Clinton Portis .75 2.00
TB43 Drew Bennett 1.00 2.50
TB44 Fred Taylor .75 2.00
TB45 Eric Moulds .75 2.00
TB46 Torry Holt 1.00 2.50
TB47 Brian Westbrook .75 2.00
TB48 Jake Plummer .75 2.00
TB49 Champ Bailey 1.00 2.50

2005 Topps Tribute

E PER HOBBY BOX
STATED PRINT RUN 1199 SER.#'d SETS
1 Daunte Culpepper 2.00 5.00
2 Marvin Harrison 2.00 5.00
3 Shaun Alexander 1.50 4.00
4 Peyton Manning 6.00 15.00
5 Corey Dillon 1.50 4.00
6 Terrell Owens 2.00 5.00
7 Antonio Gates 2.50 6.00
8 Ed Reed 2.00 5.00
9 Donovan McNabb 2.00 5.00
10 Tom Brady 10.00 25.00
11 Ray Lewis 2.50 6.00
12 LaDainian Tomlinson 2.50 6.00
13 Edgerrin James 2.00 5.00
14 Torry Holt 2.00 5.00
15 Michael Vick 2.00 5.00
16 Dwight Freeney 1.50 4.00
17 Ben Roethlisberger 4.00 10.00
18 Curtis Martin 2.00 5.00
19 Muhsin Muhammad 1.50 4.00
20 Joe Horn 1.50 4.00
21 Brett Favre 5.00 12.00
22 Deuce McAllister 2.00 5.00
23 Ahman Green 2.00 5.00
24 Randy Moss 2.00 5.00
25 Trent Green 1.50 4.00
26 Tiki Barber 2.00 5.00
27 Jamal Lewis 2.00 5.00
28 Reggie Wayne 2.00 5.00
29 Priest Holmes 1.50 4.00
30 Chris Brown 1.50 4.00
31 Marc Bulger 1.50 4.00
32 Hines Ward 2.00 5.00
33 Chad Johnson 1.50 4.00
34 Willis McGahee 1.50 4.00
35 Javon Walker 1.50 4.00
36 Rudi Johnson 1.50 4.00
37 Drew Brees 2.50 6.00
38 Isaac Bruce 2.50 6.00
39 Tony Gonzalez 2.00 5.00
40 Domanick Davis 1.50 4.00
41 Jake Delhomme 1.50 4.00
42 Clinton Portis 1.50 4.00
43 Drew Bennett 2.00 5.00
44 Fred Taylor 1.50 4.00
45 Eric Moulds 1.50 4.00
46 Dante Hall 1.50 4.00
47 Brian Westbrook 1.50 4.00
48 Plaxico Burress 1.50 4.00
49 Jake Plummer 1.50 4.00
50 Champ Bailey 2.00 5.00

2005 Topps Hall of Fame Class of 2005

is set was produced by Topps and distributed at the 2005 Induction ceremories for the Pro Football Hall of Fame. Each card includes a photo of a 2005 inductee printed in a very similar style to the 2005 Topps Hall of Fame Autographs inserts. A gold foil "Class of 2005" logo appears on the top of the cardfronts and a Topps 50th Anniversary logo at the bottom.

COMPLETE SET (4) 7.50 20.00
BF Benny Friedman 1.25 3.00
DM Dan Marino 4.00 10.00
FP Fritz Pollard 1.25 3.00
SY Steve Young 2.00 5.00

2005 Topps Super Bowl XXXIX Card Show

is set was distributed directly to dealers who participated in the 2005 Super Bowl Card Show in Jacksonville. Each card was printed in the design of the basic issue 2004 Topps football release along with the Super Bowl XXXIX logo at the top of the cardfront. A Black bordered parallel set was also produced with each card serial numbered of 199

COMPLETE SET (18) 20.00 40.00
*BLACK: 1.2X TO 3X BASE CARD HI
BLACK PRINT RUN 199 SER.#'d SETS
1 Donovan McNabb 1.00 2.50
2 LaDainian Tomlinson .60 1.50
3 Randy Moss .75 2.00
4 Brett Favre 1.50 4.00
5 Tom Brady 1.00 2.50
6 Eli Manning 2.50 6.00
7 Priest Holmes .60 1.50
8 Daunte Culpepper .60 1.50
9 Fred Taylor .60 1.50
10 Michael Vick 1.25 3.00
11 Terrell Owens .60 1.50
12 Peyton Manning 1.00 2.50
13 Michael Clayton .60 1.50
14 Byron Leftwich .60 1.50
15 Roy Williams WR 1.25 3.00
16 Brett Favre 1.50 4.00
17 Jimmy Smith .50 1.25
18 Ben Roethlisberger 3.00 8.00

2005 Topps Super Bowl XXXIX Card Show Promos

is set was issued at the Topps booth at the Super Bowl XXXIX Card Show in Jacksonville. A compete set was given to anyone making a purchase while supplies lasted. Each card was printed in the basic 2004 Topps football set design along with the Super Bowl logo at the top. The cardbacks featured a foil serial number out of 1000-sets produced.

COMPLETE SET (6) 7.50 20.00
1 Byron Leftwich .75 2.00
2 Tom Brady 1.25 3.00
3 Eli Manning 2.00 5.00
4 Fred Taylor .60 1.50
5 Ben Roethlisberger 2.50 6.00
6 Donovan McNabb 1.00 2.50

2005 Topps Turn Back the Clock

rds from this set were issued during the 2005 NFL season directly to HTA hobby shop owners. Each card was produced in the design of the 1956 Topps football set to celebrate their 50th year as an NFL licensed trading card company. The first 5-cards in the set were issued in a pack with a retail price of just 5-cents to commemorate the first year pack price of 1956 Topps football. Each card thereafter was issued one-per week directly to hobby shops to be given to their customers who buy Topps products.

COMPLETE SET (22) 6.00 15.00
COMMON CARD .40 1.00
ISSUED ONE PER WEEK VIA HTA SHOPS
1 Joe Namath .50 1.25
2 Joe Montana 1.00 2.50
3 John Elway .50 1.25
4 Brett Favre .75 2.00
5 Peyton Manning 1.00 2.50
6 Tom Brady 1.50 4.00
7 Curtis Martin .30 .75
8 Terrell Owens .30 .75
9 Daunte Culpepper .30 .75
10 Randy Moss .30 .75
11 Ben Roethlisberger .60 1.50
12 LaDainian Tomlinson .40 1.00
13 Donovan McNabb .30 .75
14 Ronnie Brown .15 .40
15 Michael Vick .30 .75
16 Alex Smith QB .50 1.25
17 Eli Manning .60 1.50
18 Steven Jackson .25 .60
19 Edgerrin James .30 .75
20 Braylon Edwards .12 .30
21 Julius Jones .25 .60
22 Cadillac Williams .12 .30

2005 Topps Youth Football

COMPLETE SET (20) 3.00 8.00
1 Dwight Freeney .15 .40
2 Willis McGahee .15 .40
3 Carson Palmer .20 .50
4 David Carr .15 .40
5 Fred Taylor .15 .40
6 Tony Gonzalez .20 .50
7 Jason Taylor .20 .50
8 Tom Brady 1.00 2.50
9 Chad Pennington .15 .40
10 Ben Roethlisberger .40 1.00
11 Larry Fitzgerald .25 .60
12 Alge Crumpler .20 .50
13 Jake Delhomme .15 .40
14 Brian Urlacher .25 .60
15 Brett Favre .50 1.25
16 Deuce McAllister .20 .50
17 Tiki Barber .20 .50
18 Donovan McNabb .20 .50
19 Shaun Alexander .15 .40
20 Derrick Brooks .15 .40

2006 Topps

is 385-card set was released in August, 2006. The set was released in a myriad of forms. The hobby form consisted of 12-card packs, with an $1.99 SRP, which came 36 packs to a box. Cards numbered 1-278 feature veterans, while cards numbered 279-286 are a league leader subset, cards numbered 287- 307 feature all pros, while cards numbered 308-310 are post-season highlight cards. The set concludes with a rookie card subset (Cards numbered 311-385). A special card of Hines Ward (#RH40) was inserted into packs at a stated rate of one in 36.

COMP.FACT.SET (390) 25.00 50.00
COMP.GIANTS SET (390) 25.00 50.00
COMP.PACKERS SET (390) 25.00 50.00
COMP.PATRIOTS SET (390) 25.00 50.00
COMP.STEELERS SET (390) 25.00 50.00
COMP.TARGET FACT.(391) 30.00 50.00
COMPLETE SET (385) 25.00 50.00
RH40 ODDS 1:36
RH40 AUTO ODDS 1:28,000 HOB
SB MVP AUTO ODDS 1:60,000 HOB
UNPRICED PLATINUM SER.#'d TO 1
UNPRICED PRINT PLATES SER.#'d TO 1
1 Jonathan Vilma .15 .40
2 Mewelde Moore .15 .40
3 Shaun McDonald .15 .40
4 Marcus Pollard .15 .40
5 Marcus Robinson .15 .40
6 David Garrard .15 .40
7 Chris Gamble .15 .40
8 Rex Grossman .15 .40
9 Lee Suggs .15 .40
10 Steve McNair .20 .50
11 Chester Taylor .20 .50
12 Randy Moss .20 .50
13 Jeremy Shockey .15 .40
14 Tedy Bruschi .20 .50
15 Walter Jones .15 .40
16 Troy Polamalu .25 .60
17 Ladell Betts .15 .40
18 DeMarcus Ware .20 .50
19 Erron Kinney .15 .40
20 Trent Cole .15 .40
21 Charlie Adams .15 .40
22 Brandon Jacobs .15 .40
23 Nathan Vasher .15 .40
24 Shawne Merriman .20 .50
25 Drew Carter .15 .40
26 Clinton Portis .15 .40
27 Alex Brown .15 .40
28 Osi Umenyiora .15 .40
29 Willie Parker .20 .50
30 Lofa Tatupu .15 .40
31 Odell Thurman .15 .40
32 Scottie Vines .15 .40
33 Sam Gado .15 .40
34 Todd DeVoe .15 .40
35 Keith Brooking .15 .40
36 Eddie Kennison .15 .40
37 Mike Williams .15 .40
38 Adam Jones .15 .40
39 Charlie Frye .20 .50
40 Reggie Wayne .20 .50
41 Donte Stallworth .15 .40
42 Vincent Jackson .15 .40
43 Alex Smith QB .20 .50
44 Greg Lewis .15 .40
45 Billy Volek .15 .40
46 Domonique Foxworth .15 .40
47 Terrell Owens .20 .50
48 Josh McCown .15 .40
49 Simeon Rice .15 .40
50 Curtis Martin .20 .50
51 Peyton Manning .60 1.50
52 Nick Barnett .15 .40
53 Marion Barber .20 .50
54 Chris McAlister .15 .40
55 Jerramy Stevens .20 .50
56 Jerome Bettis .25 .60
57 Chris Brown .15 .40
58 LeRon McCoy .15 .40
59 John Abraham .15 .40
60 LaMont Jordan .20 .50
61 Jason Taylor .20 .50
62 Michael Clayton .15 .40
63 Jake Plummer .15 .40
64 Travis Taylor .15 .40
65 Samie Parker .15 .40
66 Carlos Rogers .15 .40
67 Kevin Faulk .15 .40
68 Alvin Pearman .15 .40
69 Derrick Johnson .15 .40
70 Cedric Benson .15 .40
71 J.P. Losman .20 .50
72 Julius Peppers .20 .50
73 DeAngelo Hall .15 .40
74 Joey Galloway .20 .50
75 Marcus Trufant .15 .40
76 Frisman Jackson .15 .40
77 Jason Campbell .15 .40
78 Ron Dayne .20 .50
79 Ashley Lelie .15 .40
80 Drew Bennett .20 .50
81 Brandon Lloyd .15 .40
82 Trent Dilfer .15 .40
83 Marty Booker .15 .40
84 Aaron Rodgers .60 1.50
85 Deltha O'Neal .15 .40
86 Jon Kitna .15 .40
87 Doug Gabriel .15 .40
88 Keenan McCardell .20 .50
89 Brian Griese .15 .40
90 Michael Jenkins .15 .40
91 Brian Westbrook .15 .40
92 Terrence Holt .15 .40
93 Justin Gage .15 .40
94 Shayne Graham .15 .40
95 D.J. Hackett .15 .40
96 Kevan Barlow .15 .40
97 Bob Sanders .20 .50
98 Charles Rogers .20 .50
99 Kevin Curtis .20 .50
100 LaDainian Tomlinson .25 .60
101 Plaxico Burress .15 .40

102 Kyle Boller .15 .40
103 Donald Driver .20 .50
104 Jerome Mathis .15 .40
105 Takeo Spikes .15 .40
106 Tony Gonzalez .20 .50
107 Keary Colbert .15 .40
108 Derrick Burgess .15 .40
109 T.J. Duckett .15 .40
110 Chris Chambers .15 .40
111 Cadillac Williams .20 .50
112 Jerricho Cotchery .15 .40
113 Ernest Wilford .15 .40
114 Torry Holt .20 .50
115 Corey Dillon .15 .40
116 Chris Simms .15 .40
117 Philip Rivers .25 .60
118 LaVar Arrington .15 .40
119 Andrew Walter .15 .40
120 Joe Jurevicius .15 .40
121 Kyle Vanden Bosch .15 .40
122 London Fletcher .20 .50
123 Deuce McAllister .20 .50
124 Cedrick Wilson .15 .40
125 Jason Witten .20 .50
126 Troy Williamson .15 .40
127 Dominic Rhodes .15 .40
128 Koren Robinson .15 .40
129 Eli Manning .20 .50
130 Brian Finneran .15 .40
131 Fabian Washington .15 .40
132 Michael Boulware .15 .40
133 Bernard Berrian .15 .40
134 Stephen Davis .15 .40
135 Reggie Brown .15 .40
136 Chad Johnson .15 .40
137 Ronnie Brown .20 .50
138 Amani Toomer .15 .40
139 Deion Branch .15 .40
140 Darren Sproles .25 .60
141 L.J. Smith .15 .40
142 Arnaz Battle .15 .40
143 Jerry Porter .15 .40
144 Terry Glenn .20 .50
145 Mike Vrabel .20 .50
146 Chad Pennington .15 .40
147 Allen Rossum .15 .40
148 Greg Jones .15 .40
149 Jake Delhomme .15 .40
150 Tom Brady .75 2.00
151 Neil Rackers .15 .40
152 Charles Woodson .25 .60
153 Carson Palmer .20 .50
154 Kerry Collins .15 .40
155 Brian Urlacher .25 .60
156 Kevin Jones .15 .40
157 Eric Parker .15 .40
158 Daniel Graham .15 .40
159 Dallas Clark .15 .40
160 Matt Schaub .15 .40
161 Drew Brees .25 .60
162 Andre Johnson .20 .50
163 Ray Lewis .25 .60
164 Cato June .20 .50
165 J.J. Arrington .15 .40
166 Warren Sapp .20 .50
167 T.J. Houshmandzadeh .15 .40
168 Donnie Edwards .15 .40
169 Thomas Jones .15 .40
170 Mark Clayton .15 .40
171 Kyle Orton .15 .40
172 Najeh Davenport .15 .40
173 Dan Morgan .15 .40
174 David Pollack .15 .40
175 D.J. Williams .15 .40
176 Julius Jones .15 .40
177 Roy Williams WR .15 .40
178 Willis McGahee .15 .40
179 Keyshawn Johnson .20 .50
180 Dennis Northcutt .15 .40
181 Courtney Roby .15 .40
182 Jonathan Ogden .20 .50
183 Kellen Winslow .15 .40
184 Matt Jones .15 .40
185 Robert Gallery .15 .40
186 Mike Anderson .15 .40
187 Frank Gore .20 .50
188 Jimmy Smith .20 .50
189 Antonio Pierce .15 .40
190 Todd Heap .15 .40
191 Champ Bailey .20 .50
192 Roddy White .15 .40
193 Rod Smith .20 .50
194 Brian Dawkins .25 .60
195 Larry Johnson .15 .40
196 Ed Reed .20 .50
197 Marc Bulger .15 .40
198 Zach Thomas .20 .50
199 Cedric Houston .15 .40
200 Brett Favre .50 1.25
201 Mark Brunell .20 .50
202 Edgerrin James .20 .50
203 Ronald Curry .15 .40
204 Antonio Gates .25 .60
205 Roscoe Parrish .15 .40
206 Steve Smith .25 .60
207 Reuben Droughns .20 .50
208 Michael Vick .20 .50
209 Chris Cooley .15 .40
210 Chris Perry .20 .50
211 Muhsin Muhammad .15 .40
212 Trent Green .15 .40
213 Matt Hasselbeck .15 .40
214 Ben Roethlisberger .30 .75
215 Tyrone Calico .15 .40
216 Jamal Lewis .20 .50
217 Antwaan Randle El .15 .40
218 Byron Leftwich .15 .40
219 Priest Holmes .15 .40
220 Anquan Boldin .15 .40
221 Drew Bledsoe .20 .50
222 Randy McMichael .15 .40
223 Tatum Bell .15 .40
224 Daunte Culpepper .20 .50
225 David Carr .15 .40
226 Mark Bradley .15 .40
227 Lee Evans .20 .50
228 Domanick Davis .15 .40
229 Robert Ferguson .15 .40
230 Peter Warrick .15 .40
231 Heath Miller .15 .40
232 Derrick Brooks .15 .40
233 Isaac Bruce .25 .60
234 Aaron Brooks .15 .40
235 Nate Burleson .15 .40
236 Braylon Edwards .15 .40
237 Ben Watson .15 .40
238 Hines Ward .20 .50
239 Shaun Alexander .15 .40
240 Kurt Warner .20 .50
241 Warrick Dunn .15 .40
242 Rodney Harrison .15 .40
243 Dante Hall .15 .40
244 Tiki Barber .20 .50
245 Santana Moss .20 .50
246 Fred Taylor .15 .40
247 Laveranues Coles .15 .40
248 Darren Sharper .15 .40
249 Brandon Stokley .15 .40
250 Alge Crumpler .20 .50
251 Derrick Mason .15 .40
252 Antonio Bryant .15 .40
253 Antrel Rolle .15 .40
254 Eric Moulds .15 .40
255 Bubba Franks .15 .40
256 Joe Horn .15 .40
257 Dunta Robinson .15 .40
258 Larry Fitzgerald .20 .50
259 Roy Williams S .15 .40
260 Javon Walker .20 .50
261 Alex Smith TE .15 .40
262 Travis Henry .15 .40
263 Luke McCown .15 .40
264 James Farrior .15 .40
265 Darrell Jackson .20 .50
266 Marvin Harrison .20 .50
267 Patrick Ramsey .20 .50
268 Ernie Conwell .15 .40
269 Ahman Green .20 .50
270 Ryan Moats .15 .40
271 Donovan McNabb .20 .50
272 Steven Jackson .15 .40
273 Ronde Barber .15 .40
274 Michael Strahan .20 .50
275 Dwight Freeney .15 .40
276 DeShaun Foster .20 .50
277 Terence Newman .15 .40
278 Rudi Johnson .15 .40
279 Shaun Alexander LL .10 .25
280 Tom Brady LL .50 1.25
281 Steve Smith LL .15 .40
282 Tiki Barber LL .12 .30
283 Trent Green LL .10 .25
284 Santana Moss LL .12 .30
285 Larry Johnson LL .10 .25
286 Brett Favre LL .30 .75
287 Chad Johnson AP .10 .25
288 Peyton Manning AP .40 1.00
289 Matt Hasselbeck AP .10 .25
290 Edgerrin James AP .12 .30
291 Shaun Alexander AP .10 .25
292 Larry Johnson AP .10 .25
293 Tiki Barber AP .12 .30
294 Marvin Harrison AP .12 .30
295 Santana Moss AP .12 .30
296 Chad Johnson AP .10 .25
297 Alge Crumpler AP .12 .30
298 LaDainian Tomlinson AP .15 .40
299 Derrick Brooks AP .10 .25
300 Antonio Gates AP .15 .40
301 Steve Smith AP .15 .40
302 Shawne Merriman AP .12 .30
303 Michael Vick AP .12 .30
304 Tony Gonzalez AP .12 .30
305 Jake Delhomme AP .10 .25
306 Steve McNair AP .12 .30
307 Larry Fitzgerald AP .12 .30
308 Ben Roethlisberger HL .20 .50
309 Seattle Seahawks HL .25 .60
310 Pittsburgh Steelers HL .25 .60
311 Tamba Hali RC .60 1.50
312 Haloti Ngata RC .50 1.25
313 Mike Hass RC .40 1.00
314 Manny Lawson RC .50 1.25
315 Reggie McNeal RC .40 1.00
316 Kelly Jennings RC .50 1.25
317 Jason Allen RC .50 1.25
318 Joe Klopfenstein RC .40 1.00
319 Willie Reid RC .50 1.25
320 Brad Smith RC .50 1.25
321 Bruce Gradkowski RC .50 1.25
322 Ashton Youboty RC .40 1.00
323 Abdul Hodge RC .40 1.00
324 P.J. Daniels RC .40 1.00
325 D'Qwell Jackson RC .40 1.00
326 Johnathan Joseph RC .50 1.25
327 Antonio Cromartie RC .50 1.25
328 Elvis Dumervil RC .60 1.50
329 Tye Hill RC .40 1.00
330 Mathias Kiwanuka RC .60 1.50
331 Leonard Pope RC .60 1.50
332 DeMeco Ryans RC .50 1.25
333 Brodrick Bunkley RC .50 1.25
334 Devin Hester RC .75 2.00
335 Thomas Howard RC .40 1.00
336 Cory Rodgers RC .40 1.00
337 Ernie Sims RC .40 1.00
338 Todd Watkins RC .40 1.00
339 Rocky McIntosh RC .40 1.00
340 Donte Whitner RC .50 1.25
341 Anthony Schlegel RC .50 1.25
342 Kamerion Wimbley RC .50 1.25
343 Wali Lundy RC .40 1.00
344 Bobby Carpenter RC .40 1.00
345 Jimmy Williams RC ERR .40 1.00
346 Michael Robinson RC .40 1.00
347 Brandon Williams RC .40 1.00
348 Skyler Green RC .40 1.00
349 Jerious Norwood RC .40 1.00
350 Travis Wilson RC .40 1.00
351 Mario Williams RC .60 1.50
352 Santonio Holmes RC .50 1.25
353 Vince Young RC .40 1.00
354 Matt Leinart RC .40 1.00
355 D'Brickashaw Ferguson RC .40 1.00
356 Michael Huff RC .50 1.25
357 Chad Greenway RC .60 1.50
358 Chad Jackson RC .40 1.00
359A Reggie Bush RC left .60 1.50
359B Reggie Bush RC right .60 1.50
360 A.J. Hawk RC .50 1.25
361 DeAngelo Williams RC .50 1.25
362 Derek Hagan RC .50 1.25
363 Vernon Davis RC .50 1.25
364 Joseph Addai RC .40 1.00
365 Jay Cutler RC .50 1.25
366 Jason Avant RC .40 1.00
367 Brian Calhoun RC .40 1.00
368 LenDale White RC .40 1.00
369 Greg Jennings RC .60 1.50
370 Charlie Whitehurst RC .40 1.00
371 Sinorice Moss RC .40 1.00
372 Maurice Stovall RC .40 1.00
373 Laurence Maroney RC .40 1.00
374 Brodie Croyle RC .40 1.00
375 Demetrius Williams RC .40 1.00
376 Jerome Harrison RC .40 1.00
377 Maurice Drew RC .60 1.50
378 Kellen Clemens RC .40 1.00
379 Marcedes Lewis RC .40 1.00
380 Leon Washington RC .40 1.00
381 Anthony Fasano RC .40 1.00
382 Jeremy Bloom RC .40 1.00
383 Omar Jacobs RC .40 1.00
384 Tarvaris Jackson RC .40 1.00
385 Brandon Marshall RC .75 2.00
RH40 Hines Ward RH 2.00 5.00
RHAU Hines Ward RH AU 100.00 200.00
SBMVP H.Ward FB AU/100 125.00 250.00

2006 Topps Black

ETS 1-310: 10X TO 25X BASIC CARDS
*ROOKIES 311-385: 4X TO 10X BASIC CARDS
BLACK/51 ODDS 1:134 HOB

2006 Topps Gold

ETERANS: 4X TO 10X BASIC CARDS
*ROOKIES: 1.5X TO 4X BASIC CARDS
GOLD/2006 ODDS: 1:12 HOB, 1:8 RACK

2006 Topps Special Edition Rookies

*ROOKIES: 1.2X TO 3X BASIC CARDS
STATED ODDS 1:10 HOB/RACK

2006 Topps All-Pro Relics

OUP A ODDS 1:1142
GROUP B ODDS 1:212
APAG Antonio Gates B 5.00 12.00
APRW Brian Waters B 3.00 8.00
APCC Chris Chambers B 4.00 10.00
APCJ Chad Johnson A 5.00 12.00
APDB Derrick Brooks B 4.00 10.00
APDF Dwight Freeney A 4.00 10.00
APDO Deltha O'Neal B 3.00 8.00
APEJ Edgerrin James B 5.00 12.00
APJD Jake Delhomme B 5.00 12.00
APJL John Lynch A 4.00 10.00
APJO Jonathan Ogden B 3.00 8.00
APJP Joey Porter B 5.00 12.00
APKB Keith Brooking B 3.00 8.00
APKV Kyle Vanden Bosch B 4.00 10.00
APLA Larry Allen B 4.00 10.00
APMH Matt Hasselbeck B 5.00 12.00
APMS Mack Strong B 3.00 8.00
APNV Nathan Vasher A 5.00 12.00
APPM Peyton Manning B 8.00 20.00
APSA Shaun Alexander B 6.00 15.00
APSH Steve Hutchinson B 3.00 8.00
APSS Steve Smith A 5.00 12.00
APTH Torry Holt B 4.00 10.00
APTL Ty Law B 3.00 8.00
APMST Michael Strahan B 3.00 8.00

2006 Topps Autographs

OUP A ODDS 1:12,500 H, 1:8300 RACK
GROUP B ODDS 1:4470 H, 1:2980 RACK
GROUP C ODDS 1:3100 H, 1:2600 RACK
GROUP D ODDS 1:3300 H, 1:2400 RACK
GROUP E ODDS 1:2900 H, 1:2100 RACK
GROUP F ODDS 1:5800 H, 1:4200 RACK
GROUP G ODDS 1:292 H, 1:330 RACK
TAH A.J. Hawk C 15.00 40.00
TBC Brian Calhoun G 8.00 20.00
TBG Bruce Gradkowski G 8.00 20.00
TBJ Brandon Jacobs C 10.00 25.00
TCJ Chad Jackson G 10.00 25.00
TCT Chester Taylor E 8.00 20.00
TCW Charlie Whitehurst E 10.00 25.00
TDH Devin Hester G 8.00 20.00
TDW DeAngelo Williams B 20.00 50.00
TFG Frank Gore D 10.00 25.00
TFW Frank Walker G 6.00 15.00
TGL Greg Lewis E 6.00 15.00
TJA Joseph Addai C 10.00 25.00
TJB Jeremy Bloom D 8.00 20.00
TJC Jay Cutler B 30.00 80.00
TJH Jerome Harrison D 8.00 20.00
TJJ Julius Jones C 10.00 25.00
TKC Kellen Clemens G 10.00 25.00
TLM Laurence Maroney F 8.00 20.00
TLT LaDainian Tomlinson A 30.00 60.00
TLW LenDale White B 10.00 25.00
TMB Marc Bulger C 8.00 20.00
TMD Maurice Drew G 12.00 30.00
TML Matt Leinart B 12.00 30.00
TMT Michael Turner G 10.00 25.00
TOJ Omar Jacobs G 8.00 20.00
TPM Peyton Manning A 75.00 150.00
TRB Reggie Bush B 10.00 25.00
TSH Santonio Holmes B 12.00 30.00
TSM Sinorice Moss B 10.00 25.00
TSS Steve Smith A 30.00 60.00
TVD Vernon Davis C 12.00 30.00
TVY Vince Young A 25.00 50.00
TBCR Brodie Croyle G 10.00 25.00
TCHA Cortez Hankton G 6.00 15.00
TJAR J.J. Arrington G 6.00 15.00
TSME Shawne Merriman A 10.00 25.00

2006 Topps EA Sports Madden

COMPLETE SET (20) 12.00 30.00
STATED ODDS 1:18 HOB
1 Shaun Alexander 1.00 2.50
2 Larry Johnson 1.00 2.50
3 LaDainian Tomlinson 1.50 4.00
4 Clinton Portis 1.00 2.50
5 Tiki Barber 1.25 3.00
6 Edgerrin James 1.25 3.00
7 Terrell Owens 1.25 3.00
8 Vince Young .50 1.25
9 Peyton Manning 4.00 10.00
10 Matt Leinart .50 1.25
11 Jay Cutler .60 1.50
12 Tony Gonzalez 1.25 3.00
13 Tom Brady 5.00 12.00
14 Jeremy Shockey 1.00 2.50
15 Steve Smith 1.50 4.00
16 Chad Johnson 1.00 2.50
17 Torry Holt 1.25 3.00
18 Marvin Harrison 1.25 3.00
19 Randy Moss 1.25 3.00
20 Reggie Bush .75 2.00

2006 Topps EA Sports Street 3

COMPLETE SET (24) 8.00 20.00
INSERTS IN VIDEO GAME PACKAGES
1 Chad Johnson .40 1.00
2 Champ Bailey .50 1.25
3 Tiki Barber .50 1.25
4 Tom Brady 2.00 5.00
5 Tedy Bruschi .50 1.25
6 Reggie Bush .40 1.00
7 Brett Favre 1.25 3.00
8 Antonio Gates .60 1.50
9 Edgerrin James .50 1.25
10 Larry Johnson .40 1.00
11 Matt Leinart .25 .60
12 Peyton Manning 1.50 4.00
13 Randy Moss .50 1.25
14 Terrell Owens .50 1.25
15 Julius Peppers .50 1.25
16 Troy Polamalu .60 1.50
17 Ben Roethlisberger .75 2.00
18 Michael Strahan .50 1.25
19 LaDainian Tomlinson .60 1.50
20 Mario Williams .40 1.00
21 Clinton Portis .40 1.00
22 Byron Leftwich .40 1.00
23 Brian Urlacher .60 1.50
24 Shaun Alexander .40 1.00

2006 Topps Factory Set Rookie Bonus

These cards were included as bonus inserts in the various versions of 2006 Topps factory sets which included the following: hobby, retail, Super Bowl XLI, Giants, Packers, Patriots, and Steelers. Each card was numbered in the style "1 of 5" on the backs. We've added prefixes to aid in cataloging.

COMP.HOBBY SET (5) 4.00 10.00
COMP.RETAIL SET (5) 4.00 10.00
COMP.GIANTS SET (5) 4.00 10.00
COMP.PACKER SET (5) 4.00 10.00
COMP.PATRIOT SET (5) 4.00 10.00
COMP.STEELER SET (5) 4.00 10.00
COMP.SUPER BOWL (5) 6.00 15.00
G1 Gerris Wilkinson .60 1.50
G2 Jai Lewis .75 2.00
G3 Barry Cofield 1.00 2.50
G4 Charlie Prepah .75 2.00
G5 Gerrick McPhearson .60 1.50
H1 Marques Hagans .60 1.50
H2 Devin Aromashodu .60 1.50
H3 Ingle Martin .75 2.00
H4 Andre Hall .75 2.00
H5 D.J. Shockley .75 2.00
R1 Jonathan Orr .75 2.00
R2 Cedric Humes .60 1.50
R3 Dominique Byrd .60 1.50
R4 Marcus Vick .60 1.50
R5 Drew Olson .60 1.50
S1 Cedric Humes .60 1.50
S2 Anthony Smith 1.00 2.50
S3 Orien Harris .75 2.00
S4 Charles Davis .75 2.00
S5 Willie Colon .60 1.50
PK1 Will Blackmon .60 1.50
PK2 Ingle Martin .75 2.00
PK3 Tony Moll .60 1.50
PK4 Jason Spitz 1.00 2.50
PK5 Chris Francies .75 2.00
PT1 David Thomas .60 1.50
PT2 Garrett Mills .75 2.00
PT3 Freddie Roach .75 2.00
PT4 Jeremy Mincey 1.00 2.50
PT5 Willie Andrews .75 2.00
SB1 Vince Young .25 .60
SB2 Matt Leinart .25 .60
SB3 Joseph Addai .25 .60
SB4 Jay Cutler .30 .75
SB5 Reggie Bush .40 1.00
SB6 Laurence Maroney .25 .60

2006 Topps Target Exclusive Factory Set Rookie Jerseys

Matt Leinart 8.00 20.00
2 Reggie Bush 5.00 12.00
3 Vince Young 8.00 20.00
5 Mario Williams 5.00 12.00

2006 Topps Game Breakers Super Bowl Pylons

STATED ODDS 1:37,500 HOB
GBAR Antwaan Randle El 50.00 100.00
GBBR Ben Roethlisberger 60.00 120.00
GBHW Hines Ward 60.00 100.00
GBJS Jerramy Stevens 20.00 40.00
GBMH Matt Hasselbeck 50.00 100.00
GBWP Willie Parker 60.00 100.00

2006 Topps Hall of Fame Autographs

FHC Harry Carson 125.00 250.00
HOFJM John Madden 300.00 500.00
HOFTA Troy Aikman 250.00 500.00
HOFWM Warren Moon 250.00 400.00
HOFRWR Rayfield Wright 150.00 250.00

2006 Topps Hall of Fame Tribute

COMPLETE SET (9) 5.00 12.00
STATED ODDS 1:6 RACK
UNPRICED CUT AUTOS SER.#'d 1-10
BN Bronko Nagurski .75 2.00
HC Harry Carson .60 1.50
JM John Madden .75 2.00
JT Jim Thorpe 1.00 2.50
RW Reggie White .75 2.00
SB Sammy Baugh .75 2.00
TA Troy Aikman 1.00 2.50
WM Warren Moon .60 1.50
RWR Rayfield Wright .60 1.50

2006 Topps Hall of Fame Tribute Cut Autographs

THORPE ODDS 1:1,612,656 HOBBY
BAUGH/NAGURSKI ODDS 1:150,000 HOBBY

2006 Topps Hobby Masters

COMPLETE SET (10) 6.00 15.00
STATED ODDS 1:18 HOB
HM1 LaDainian Tomlinson 1.00 2.50
HM2 Peyton Manning 2.50 6.00
HM3 Tom Brady 3.00 8.00
HM4 Brett Favre 2.00 5.00
HM5 Cadillac Williams .75 2.00
HM6 Ben Roethlisberger 1.25 3.00
HM7 Shaun Alexander .60 1.50
HM8 Michael Vick .75 2.00
HM9 Tiki Barber .75 2.00
HM10 Larry Johnson .60 1.50

2006 Topps NFL 8306

COMPLETE SET (10) 6.00 15.00
STATED ODDS 1:6 HOB/RACK
NFL1 John Elway 2.00 5.00
NFL2 Jim Kelly 1.00 2.50
NFL3 Eric Dickerson .60 1.50
NFL4 Dan Marino 2.50 6.00
NFL5 Reggie Bush .60 1.50
NFL6 Matt Leinart .40 1.00
NFL7 Vince Young .40 1.00
NFL8 Jay Cutler .50 1.25
NFL9 DeAngelo Williams .50 1.25
NFL10 LenDale White .60 1.50

2006 Topps NFL 8306 Autographs

AUTO/50 ODDS 1:18,800 H, 1:15,000 RACK
DM Dan Marino 125.00 250.00
DW DeAngelo Williams 12.00 30.00
ED Eric Dickerson 75.00 150.00
JC Jay Cutler 12.00 30.00
JE John Elway 60.00 120.00
JK Jim Kelly 75.00 150.00
LW LenDale White 10.00 25.00
ML Matt Leinart 10.00 25.00
RB Reggie Bush 15.00 40.00
VY Vince Young 10.00 25.00

2006 Topps NFL 8306 Autographs Dual

DUAL AU/25 ODDS 1:85,000 H,1:60,000 RACK
DB E.Dickerson/R.Bush 30.00 60.00
EL J.Elway/M.Leinart 60.00 120.00
EY J.Elway/V.Young 50.00 100.00
KC J.Kelly/J.Cutler 50.00 100.00
ML D.Marino/M.Leinart 125.00 250.00

2006 Topps NFL 8306 Relics

GROUP A ODDS 1:42,000 HOB
GROUP B ODDS 1:2350 HOB
8306RDM Dan Marino B 25.00 50.00
8306RDW DeAngelo Williams B 6.00 15.00
8306RED Eric Dickerson B 4.00 10.00
8306RJE John Elway A 15.00 40.00
8306RJK Jim Kelly B 8.00 20.00
8306RLW LenDale White B 6.00 15.00
8306RML Matt Leinart B 8.00 20.00
8306RRB Reggie Bush B 3.00 8.00
8306RVY Vince Young B 8.00 20.00

2006 Topps Own The Game

STATED ODDS 1:22 HOB, RACK
OTG1 Tom Brady 5.00 12.00
OTG2 Trent Green 1.00 2.50
OTG3 Shaun Alexander 1.00 2.50
OTG4 Tiki Barber 1.25 3.00
OTG5 Steve Smith 1.50 4.00
OTG6 Santana Moss 1.25 3.00
OTG7 Derrick Burgess 1.00 2.50
OTG8 Osi Umenyiora 1.00 2.50
OTG9 Brett Favre 3.00 8.00
OTG10 Larry Johnson 1.00 2.50
OTG11 Chad Johnson 1.00 2.50
OTG12 Carson Palmer 1.25 3.00
OTG13 Clinton Portis 1.00 2.50
OTG14 Larry Fitzgerald 1.25 3.00
OTG15 Eli Manning 1.25 3.00
OTG16 Edgerrin James 1.25 3.00
OTG17 Anquan Boldin 1.00 2.50
OTG18 Ty Law 1.50 4.00
OTG19 Deltha O'Neal 1.00 2.50
OTG20 Drew Brees 1.50 4.00
OTG21 LaDainian Tomlinson 1.50 4.00
OTG22 Marvin Harrison 1.25 3.00
OTG23 Corey Dillon 1.00 2.50
OTG24 Matt Hasselbeck 1.00 2.50
OTG25 Chris Chambers 1.00 2.50
OTG26 Jonathan Vilma 1.00 2.50
OTG27 Jake Delhomme 1.00 2.50
OTG28 Rudi Johnson 1.00 2.50
OTG29 Zach Thomas 1.25 3.00
OTG30 Hines Ward 1.25 3.00

2006 Topps Red Hot Rookies

INSERTS IN TARGET RETAIL PACKS
UNPRICED AU/10 ODDS 1:22,000 TARGET
1 Reggie Bush 1.25 3.00
2 Tamba Hali 1.25 3.00
3 A.J. Hawk 1.00 2.50
4 Santonio Holmes 1.00 2.50
5 Matt Leinart .75 2.00
6 Brodie Croyle .75 2.00
7 Derek Hagan 1.00 2.50
8 Chad Jackson .75 2.00
9 Vince Young .75 2.00
10 Sinorice Moss .75 2.00
11 DeAngelo Williams 1.00 2.50
12 Omar Jacobs .75 2.00
13 Jay Cutler 1.00 2.50
14 Laurence Maroney .75 2.00
15 LenDale White .75 2.00
16 Brian Calhoun .75 2.00

2006 Topps Red Hot Rookies Jerseys

JERSEY/199 ODDS 1:1260 TARGET
AH A.J. Hawk 8.00 20.00
DW DeAngelo Williams 8.00 20.00
LW LenDale White 6.00 15.00
ML Matt Leinart 10.00 25.00
RB Reggie Bush 3.00 8.00
VY Vince Young 10.00 25.00

2006 Topps Red Hot Rookies Jerseys Dual

DUAL JSY/50 ODDS 1:12,000 TARGET RETAIL
BL R.Bush/M.Leinart 4.00 10.00
WB D.Williams/R.Bush 4.00 10.00
YL V.Young/M.Leinart 15.00 40.00

2006 Topps Rookie Premiere Autographs

D INK TOO SCARCE TO PRICE
BEWARE FORGED AUTOGRAPHS
RPAH A.J. Hawk 10.00 25.00
RPBM Brandon Marshall 15.00 40.00
RPBW Brandon Williams 8.00 20.00
RPCJ Chad Jackson 8.00 20.00
RPCW Charlie Whitehurst 8.00 20.00
RPDH Derek Hagan 10.00 25.00
RPDW DeAngelo Williams 10.00 25.00
RPJK Joe Klopfenstein 8.00 20.00
RPJN Jerious Norwood 8.00 20.00
RPKC Kellen Clemens 8.00 20.00
RPLM Laurence Maroney 8.00 20.00
RPLW LenDale White 8.00 20.00
RPMD Maurice Drew 15.00 40.00
RPMH Michael Huff 10.00 25.00
RPML Matt Leinart 8.00 20.00
RPMR Michael Robinson 8.00 20.00
RPMS Maurice Stovall 8.00 20.00
RPMW Mario Williams 12.00 30.00
RPOJ Omar Jacobs 8.00 20.00
RPRB Reggie Bush 12.00 30.00
RPSH Santonio Holmes 10.00 25.00
RPSM Sinorice Moss 8.00 20.00
RPTJ Tarvaris Jackson 8.00 20.00
RPTW Travis Wilson 8.00 20.00
RPVD Vernon Davis 10.00 25.00
RPVY Vince Young 8.00 20.00
RPBCA Brian Calhoun 8.00 20.00
RPDEW Demetrius Williams 8.00 20.00
RPJAV Jason Avant 8.00 20.00
RPLWA Leon Washington 8.00 20.00
RPMLE Marcedes Lewis 8.00 20.00

2006 Topps Rookie Premiere Autographs Dual

RED INK TOO SCARCE TO PRICE
LWML L.White/M.Leinart 25.00 60.00
LWVY L.White/V.Young 40.00 100.00
MLVY M.Leinart/V.Young 40.00 100.00
MWRB Ma.Williams/R.Bush 30.00 60.00
RBLW R.Bush/L.White 30.00 60.00
RBML R.Bush/M.Leinart 30.00 60.00

2006 Topps Signature Series

G SERIES/50 ODDS 1:33,000 HOB
TAAH A.J. Hawk 50.00 100.00
TABF Brett Favre 125.00 250.00
TACJ Chad Johnson 30.00 80.00
TACM Curtis Martin 60.00 120.00
TADM Dan Marino 125.00 250.00
TADMN Donovan McNabb 50.00 100.00
TAEM Eli Manning 60.00 120.00
TAES Emmitt Smith 125.00 250.00
TAGS Gale Sayers 30.00 80.00
TAJB Jim Brown 60.00 120.00
TAJC Jay Cutler 50.00 100.00
TAJM Joe Montana 100.00 200.00
TAJN Joe Namath 75.00 135.00
TALT LaDainian Tomlinson 30.00 80.00
TAML Matt Leinart 30.00 80.00
TAMV Michael Vick 50.00 100.00
TAPM Peyton Manning 100.00 200.00
TARB Reggie Bush 20.00 50.00
TASH Santonio Holmes 30.00 80.00
TASM Shawne Merriman 30.00 80.00
TASS Steve Smith 50.00 100.00
TASY Steve Young 50.00 120.00
TATA Troy Aikman 60.00 120.00
TATB Tom Brady 150.00 300.00
TAVY Vince Young 50.00 100.00

2006 Topps Super Tix

ATED ODDS 1:1750 HOB
ST1 Ben Roethlisberger 25.00 60.00
ST2 Lofa Tatupu 8.00 20.00
ST3 Willie Parker 20.00 50.00
ST4 Darrell Jackson 8.00 20.00
ST5 Hines Ward 30.00 60.00
ST6 Matt Hasselbeck 10.00 25.00
ST7 Jerome Bettis 40.00 80.00
ST8 Shaun Alexander 10.00 25.00
ST9 Troy Polamalu 20.00 50.00
ST10 Joey Porter 20.00 50.00
STAHW Hines Ward AU 150.00 250.00

2006 Topps True Champions

INSERTS IN WAL-MART RETAIL PACKS
1 Walter Payton 3.00 8.00
2 Reggie Bush 2.50 6.00
3 Brett Favre 3.00 8.00
4 Adam Vinatieri 1.00 2.50
5 Troy Aikman 1.50 4.00
6 Johnny Unitas 2.50 6.00
7 Matt Leinart 2.00 5.00
8 Tom Brady 2.00 5.00
9 John Elway 2.50 6.00
10 Ray Lewis 1.00 2.50
11 Joe Namath 1.50 4.00
12 Vince Young 3.00 8.00
13 Marshall Faulk 1.00 2.50
14 Terry Bradshaw 2.00 5.00
15 Joe Montana 3.00 8.00
16 Emmitt Smith 2.50 6.00
17 LenDale White 2.00 5.00
18 Torry Holt 1.00 2.50

2006 Topps True Champions Jerseys

Y/199 INSERTS IN WAL-MART PACKS
JN Joe Namath 20.00 40.00
JU Johnny Unitas 25.00 50.00
ML Matt Leinart
RB Reggie Bush 4.00 10.00
VY Vince Young 12.00 30.00
WP Walter Payton 20.00 50.00

2006 Topps True Champions Jerseys Dual

DUALS/50 INSERTS IN WAL-MART PACKS
NY J.Namath/V.Young 40.00 80.00
PB W.Payton/R.Bush 6.00 15.00
UL J.Unitas/M.Leinart 40.00 80.00

2006 Topps Hall of Fame Class of 2006

This set was produced by Topps and distributed at the 2006 Induction ceremories for the Pro Football Hall of Fame. Each card includes a photo of a 2006 inductee printed with a gold foil "Class of 2006" logo on the top of the cardfronts. This version of the cards is nearly identical to the basic 2006 Topps Hall of Fame Tribute inserts except for the difference in the prefix used for the card numbering on the backs. The induction ceremony version has a prefix that reads "HOF" versus "HOFT" for the pack insert.

COMPLETE SET (6) 5.00 10.00
HOFHC Harry Carson .60 1.50
HOFJM John Madden .75 2.00
HOFTA Troy Aikman .60 1.50
HOFWM Warren Moon .60 1.50
HOFRWR Rayfield Wright .60 1.50
HOFRW Reggie White .75 2.00

2006 Topps Super Bowl XL Card Show

This set was distributed directly to dealers who participated in the 2006 Super Bowl Card Show. Each card was printed in the design of the basic issue 2005 Topps football release along with the Super Bowl XL logo on the cardfront. The basic cards were printed with gold foil highlights and were serial numbered to 1000. A Platinum foil parallel set was also produced with each card serial numbered to 199.

COMPLETE SET (16) 15.00 30.00
GOLD PRINT RUN 1000 SER.#'d SETS
*PLATINUM: .8X TO 2X BASIC GOLDS
PLATINUM PRINT RUN 199 SER.#'d SETS
1 Kevin Jones .50 1.25
2 Cadillac Williams .60 1.50
3 Peyton Manning 2.00 5.00
4 Mike Williams .50 1.25
5 Ben Roethlisberger 1.00 2.50
6 Larry Johnson .50 1.25
7 LaDainian Tomlinson .75 2.00
8 Tom Brady 2.50 6.00
9 Eli Manning .60 1.50
10 Brett Favre 1.50 4.00
11 Shaun Alexander .50 1.25
12 Michael Vick .60 1.50
13 Ronnie Brown .60 1.50
14 Edgerrin James .60 1.50
15 Tiki Barber .60 1.50
16 Carson Palmer .60 1.50

2006 Topps Super Bowl XL Card Show Promos

These 6-cards were issued at the 2006 Super Bowl Card Show and produced by Topps. Cards were available at the Topps booth each day of event in exchange for football card wrappers from Topps products. Each card includes the Super Bowl XL logo on the front.

COMPLETE SET (6) 6.00 12.00
1 Mike Williams .60 1.50
2 Peyton Manning 1.25 3.00
3 Shaun Alexander .60 1.50
4 LaDainian Tomlinson .75 2.00
5 Tom Brady 1.25 3.00
6 Ben Roethlisberger 2.50 6.00

2006 Topps Turn Back the Clock

Cards from this set were issued during the 2006 NFL season directly to HTA hobby shop owners. Each card was produced in the design of the 1957 Topps football set. The first 5-cards in the set were issued in a pack with a retail price of just 5-cents to commemorate the first year pack price of 1956 Topps football. Each card thereafter was issued one-per week directly to hobby shops to be given to their customers who buy Topps products.

COMPLETE SET (22) 6.00 15.00
ISSUED ONE PER WEEK VIA HTA SHOPS
1 Sinorice Moss .10 .25
2 Matt Leinart .10 .25
3 DeAngelo Williams .12 .30
4 Maurice Drew .15 .40
5 Laurence Maroney .10 .25
6 LenDale White .20 .50
7 Mario Williams .30 .75
8 Vernon Davis .25 .60
9 Reggie Bush .30 .75
10 Chad Jackson .20 .50
11 Tarvaris Jackson .20 .50
12 Michael Huff .25 .60
13 Brian Calhoun .20 .50
14 Santonio Holmes .25 .60
15 Jay Cutler .25 .60
16 Greg Jennings .30 .75
17 D'Brickashaw Ferguson .20 .50
18 Joseph Addai .20 .50
19 Derek Hagan .25 .60
20 Kellen Clemens .20 .50
21 Vince Young .20 .50
22 Marcedes Lewis .20 .50

2007 Topps

is 440-card set was released in August, 2007. The set was issued into the hobby in nine-card packs, with a $1.99 SRP, which came 36 packs to a box. This set includes the following subsets: Rookies (286-395), League Leaders (396-404, 429), Pro Bowl (405-424), Award Winners (425-427), Post-Season Heroes (428, 430-440). A special card to commemorate Super Bowl MVP Peyton Manning was inserted into both hobby and retail packs at a stated rate of one in 36.

COMP.FACT.SET (445) 25.00 50.00
COMP.BEARS SET (445) 25.00 50.00
COMP.CHARGER SET (445) 25.00 50.00
COMP.COLTS SET (445) 25.00 50.00
COMP.JETS SET (445) 25.00 50.00
COMP.SUPER BOWL (446) 25.00 50.00
COMPLETE SET (440) 25.00 50.00
MANNING RH ODDS 1:36 HOB/RET
MANNING RH AUTO ODDS 1:17,000
MANNING SBMVP ODDS 1:500,000
1 Matt Leinart .15 .40
2 Kurt Warner .20 .50
3 Matt Schaub .15 .40
4 Michael Vick .20 .50
5 Kyle Boller .15 .40
6 Steve McNair .20 .50
7 J.P. Losman .15 .40
8 Jake Delhomme .15 .40
9 Rex Grossman .15 .40
10 Brian Griese .15 .40
11 Carson Palmer .20 .50
12 Charlie Frye .20 .50
13 Drew Bledsoe .20 .50
14 Tony Romo .30 .75
15 Joey Harrington .20 .50
16 Jay Cutler .15 .40
17 Jon Kitna .15 .40
18 Aaron Rodgers .60 1.50
19 Brett Favre .50 1.25
20 David Carr .15 .40
21 Peyton Manning .60 1.50
22 David Garrard .15 .40
23 Byron Leftwich .15 .40
24 Trent Green .15 .40
25 Damon Huard .20 .50
26 Daunte Culpepper .20 .50
27 Tarvaris Jackson .15 .40
28 Tom Brady .75 2.00
29 Drew Brees .25 .60
30 Eli Manning .20 .50
31 Chad Pennington .15 .40
32 Andrew Walter .15 .40
33 Aaron Brooks .15 .40
34 Donovan McNabb .20 .50
35 Jeff Garcia .15 .40
36 Ben Roethlisberger .25 .60
37 Philip Rivers .25 .60
38 Alex Smith QB .20 .50
39 Matt Hasselbeck .15 .40
40 Seneca Wallace .15 .40
41 Marc Bulger .15 .40
42 Chris Simms .15 .40
43 Bruce Gradkowski .15 .40
44 Vince Young .15 .40
45 Jason Campbell .15 .40
46 Jared Lorenzen .15 .40
47 Mark Brunell .20 .50
48 J.J. Arrington .20 .50
49 Edgerrin James .20 .50
50 Jerious Norwood .15 .40
51 Warrick Dunn .15 .40
52 Mike Anderson .15 .40
53 Jamal Lewis .20 .50
54 Willis McGahee .15 .40
55 DeShaun Foster .20 .50
56 DeAngelo Williams .15 .40
57 Cedric Benson .15 .40
58 Thomas Jones .15 .40
59 Chris Perry .15 .40
60 Rudi Johnson .15 .40
61 Reuben Droughns .20 .50
62 Jerome Harrison .15 .40
63 Marion Barber .20 .50
64 Julius Jones .15 .40
65 Tatum Bell .15 .40
66 Mike Bell .20 .50
67 Kevin Jones .15 .40
68 Brian Calhoun .15 .40
69 Ahman Green .20 .50
70 Vernand Morency .20 .50
71 Ron Dayne .20 .50
72 Wali Lundy .15 .40
73 Dominic Rhodes .15 .40
74 Joseph Addai .15 .40
75 Fred Taylor .15 .40
76 Maurice Jones-Drew .15 .40
77 Larry Johnson .15 .40
78 Sammy Morris .15 .40
79 Ronnie Brown .15 .40
80 Mewelde Moore .15 .40
81 Chester Taylor .15 .40
82 Kevin Faulk .15 .40
83 Corey Dillon .15 .40
84 Laurence Maroney .20 .50
85 Deuce McAllister .20 .50
86 Reggie Bush .15 .40
87 Brandon Jacobs .15 .40
88 Anthony Thomas .15 .40
89 Cedric Houston .15 .40
90 Leon Washington .15 .40
91 Kevan Barlow .20 .50
92 LaMont Jordan .20 .50
93 Justin Fargas .15 .40
94 Brian Westbrook .15 .40
95 Correll Buckhalter .15 .40
96 Willie Parker .20 .50
97 Najeh Davenport .15 .40
98 LaDainian Tomlinson .25 .60
99 Darren Sproles .20 .50
100 Frank Gore .20 .50
101 Michael Robinson .20 .50
102 Shaun Alexander .15 .40
103 Maurice Morris .15 .40
104 Steven Jackson .15 .40
105 Stephen Davis .15 .40
106 Cadillac Williams .20 .50
107 Travis Henry .20 .50
108 LenDale White .20 .50
109 Ladell Betts .15 .40
110 Clinton Portis .15 .40
111 Michael Turner .15 .40
112 T.J. Duckett .15 .40
113 Anquan Boldin .15 .40
114 Larry Fitzgerald .20 .50
115 Bryant Johnson .15 .40
116 Michael Jenkins .15 .40
117 Ashley Lelie .20 .50
118 Roddy White .15 .40
119 Mark Clayton .15 .40
120 Derrick Mason .15 .40
121 Demetrius Williams .15 .40
122 Peerless Price .15 .40
123 Lee Evans .20 .50
124 Drew Carter .15 .40
125 Keyshawn Johnson .20 .50
126 Steve Smith .20 .50
127 Bernard Berrian .15 .40
128 Mark Bradley .15 .40
129 Muhsin Muhammad .15 .40
130 Chad Johnson .15 .40
131 T.J. Houshmandzadeh .15 .40
132 Chris Henry .15 .40
133 Joe Jurevicius .15 .40
134 Braylon Edwards .15 .40
135 Terrell Owens .20 .50
136 Terry Glenn .20 .50
137 Skyler Green .15 .40
138 Rod Smith .20 .50
139 Javon Walker .20 .50
140 Brandon Marshall .20 .50
141 Mike Furrey .20 .50
142 Mike Williams .15 .40
143 Roy Williams WR .15 .40
144 Donald Driver .20 .50
145 Greg Jennings .15 .40
146 Andre Johnson .20 .50
147 Eric Moulds .15 .40
148 Reggie Wayne .20 .50
149 Marvin Harrison .20 .50
150 Ernest Wilford .15 .40
151 Matt Jones .20 .50
152 Reggie Williams .20 .50
153 Eddie Kennison .15 .40
154 Samie Parker .15 .40
155 Marty Booker .15 .40
156 Chris Chambers .15 .40
157 Wes Welker .20 .50
158 Travis Taylor .15 .40
159 Troy Williamson .15 .40
160 Reche Caldwell .15 .40
161 Chad Jackson .15 .40
162 Devery Henderson .15 .40
163 Joe Horn .15 .40
164 Marques Colston .15 .40
165 Plaxico Burress .15 .40
166 Amani Toomer .15 .40
167 Sinorice Moss .20 .50
168 Jerricho Cotchery .15 .40
169 Laveranues Coles .15 .40
170 Randy Moss .20 .50
171 Ronald Curry .15 .40
172 Donte Stallworth .20 .50
173 Reggie Brown .15 .40
174 Hines Ward .20 .50
175 Nate Washington .15 .40
176 Santonio Holmes .15 .40
177 Keenan McCardell .15 .40

178 Eric Parker .15 .40
179 Arnaz Battle .15 .40
180 Antonio Bryant .15 .40
181 D.J. Hackett .15 .40
182 Deion Branch .15 .40
183 Darrell Jackson .15 .40
184 Kevin Curtis .15 .40
185 Torry Holt .20 .50
186 Isaac Bruce .25 .60
187 Michael Clayton .15 .40
188 Joey Galloway .20 .50
189 Drew Bennett .15 .40
190 Bobby Wade .15 .40
191 Antwaan Randle El .15 .40
192 Santana Moss .20 .50
193 Roscoe Parrish .15 .40
194 Leonard Pope .15 .40
195 Alge Crumpler .20 .50
196 Todd Heap .15 .40
197 Desmond Clark .15 .40
198 Kellen Winslow .15 .40
199 Jason Witten .20 .50
200 Marcus Pollard .15 .40
201 Bubba Franks .15 .40
202 Dallas Clark .20 .50
203 George Wrighster .15 .40
204 Tony Gonzalez .20 .50
205 Randy McMichael .15 .40
206 Jermaine Wiggins .15 .40
207 Ben Watson .15 .40
208 Ernie Conwell .15 .40
209 Jeremy Shockey .15 .40
210 L.J. Smith .15 .40
211 Heath Miller .15 .40
212 Antonio Gates .25 .60
213 Vernon Davis .15 .40
214 Jerramy Stevens .15 .40
215 Joe Klopfenstein .15 .40
216 Alex Smith TE .15 .40
217 Bo Scaife .15 .40
218 Anthony Fasano .15 .40
219 Chris Cooley .15 .40
220 Robbie Gould .15 .40
221 Adam Vinatieri .15 .40
222 Devin Hester .20 .50
223 Justin Miller .15 .40
224 Sean Taylor .25 .60
225 DeAngelo Hall .15 .40
226 Chris McAlister .15 .40
227 Nate Clements .15 .40
228 Chris Gamble .15 .40
229 Ricky Manning .15 .40
230 Charles Tillman .20 .50
231 Deltha O'Neal .15 .40
232 Terence Newman .15 .40
233 Champ Bailey .20 .50
234 Charles Woodson .25 .60
235 Dunta Robinson .15 .40
236 Rashean Mathis .15 .40
237 Antoine Winfield .15 .40
238 Asante Samuel .15 .40
239 Nnamdi Asomugha .15 .40
240 Lito Sheppard .15 .40
241 Walt Harris .15 .40
242 Tye Hill .15 .40
243 Ronde Barber .15 .40
244 Quentin Jammer .15 .40
245 Ed Reed .20 .50
246 Roy Williams S .15 .40
247 Troy Polamalu .25 .60
248 Brian Dawkins .25 .60
249 Terrell Suggs .15 .40
250 Aaron Schobel .15 .40
251 Julius Peppers .20 .50
252 Alex Brown .15 .40
253 Kamerion Wimbley .15 .40
254 DeMarcus Ware .20 .50
255 Elvis Dumervil .15 .40
256 Mario Williams .20 .50
257 Dwight Freeney .15 .40
258 Tamba Hali .15 .40
259 Jason Taylor .20 .50
260 Michael Strahan .20 .50
261 Aaron Kampman .20 .50
262 Derrick Burgess .15 .40
263 Leonard Little .15 .40
264 Ty Warren .15 .40
265 Warren Sapp .20 .50
266 Luis Castillo .15 .40
267 Keith Brooking .15 .40
268 Ray Lewis .25 .60
269 London Fletcher .20 .50
270 Brian Urlacher .25 .60
271 Ernie Sims .15 .40
272 A.J. Hawk .15 .40
273 DeMeco Ryans .20 .50
274 Cato June .15 .40
275 Derrick Johnson LB .15 .40
276 Zach Thomas .20 .50
277 Antonio Pierce .15 .40
278 Jonathan Vilma .15 .40
279 James Farrior .15 .40
280 Shawne Merriman .15 .40
281 Lofa Tatupu .15 .40
282 Derrick Brooks .15 .40
283 Jonathan Ogden .20 .50
284 Steve Hutchinson .20 .50
285 Walter Jones .15 .40
286 JaMarcus Russell RC .40 1.00
287 Brady Quinn RC .40 1.00
288 Drew Stanton RC .40 1.00
289 Troy Smith RC .40 1.00
290 Kevin Kolb RC .50 1.25
291 Trent Edwards RC .40 1.00
292 John Beck RC .40 1.00
293 Jordan Palmer RC .50 1.25
294 Chris Leak RC .40 1.00
295 Isaiah Stanback RC .40 1.00
296 Tyler Palko RC .60 1.50
297 Jared Zabransky RC .40 1.00
298 Jeff Rowe RC .40 1.00
299 Zac Taylor RC .50 1.25
300 Lester Ricard RC .50 1.25
301 Adrian Peterson RC 4.00 10.00
302 Marshawn Lynch RC .75 2.00
303 Brandon Jackson RC .40 1.00
304 Michael Bush RC .40 1.00
305 Kenny Irons RC .40 1.00
306 Antonio Pittman RC .40 1.00
307 Tony Hunt RC .40 1.00
308 Darius Walker RC .40 1.00
309 Dwayne Wright RC .40 1.00
310 Lorenzo Booker RC .50 1.25
311 Kenneth Darby RC .40 1.00
312 Chris Henry RC .40 1.00
313 Selvin Young RC .40 1.00
314 Brian Leonard RC .40 1.00
315 Ahmad Bradshaw RC .60 1.50
316 Gary Russell RC .50 1.25
317 Kolby Smith RC .40 1.00
318 Thomas Clayton RC .50 1.25
319 Garrett Wolfe RC .40 1.00
320 Calvin Johnson RC 1.25 3.00
321 Ted Ginn Jr. RC .50 1.25
322 Dwayne Jarrett RC .50 1.25
323 Dwayne Bowe RC .40 1.00
324 Sidney Rice RC .50 1.25
325 Robert Meachem RC .50 1.25
326 Anthony Gonzalez RC .40 1.00
327 Craig Buster Davis RC .40 1.00
328 Aundrae Allison RC .40 1.00
329 Chansi Stuckey RC .50 1.25
330 David Clowney RC .40 1.00
331 Steve Smith USC RC .40 1.00
332 Courtney Taylor RC .40 1.00
333 Paul Williams RC .40 1.00
334 Johnnie Lee Higgins RC .40 1.00
335 Rhema McKnight RC .40 1.00
336 Jason Hill RC .40 1.00
337 Dallas Baker RC .40 1.00
338 Greg Olsen RC .60 1.50
339 Yamon Figurs RC .40 1.00
340 Scott Chandler RC .60 1.50
341 Matt Spaeth RC .60 1.50
342 Ben Patrick RC .50 1.25
343 Clark Harris RC .50 1.25
344 Martrez Milner RC .40 1.00
345 Joe Newton RC .40 1.00
346 Alan Branch RC .40 1.00
347 Amobi Okoye RC .50 1.25
348 DeMarcus Tank Tyler RC .40 1.00
349 Justin Harrell RC .40 1.00
350 Brandon Mebane RC .50 1.25
351 Gaines Adams RC .50 1.25
352 Jamaal Anderson RC .50 1.25
353 Adam Carriker RC .40 1.00
354 Jarvis Moss RC .40 1.00
355 Charles Johnson RC .40 1.00
356 Anthony Spencer RC .50 1.25
357 Quentin Moses RC .40 1.00
358 LaMarr Woodley RC .75 2.00
359 Victor Abiamiri RC .40 1.00
360 Ray McDonald RC .50 1.25
361 Tim Crowder RC .50 1.25
362 Patrick Willis RC .60 1.50
363 Brandon Siler RC .40 1.00
364 David Harris RC .40 1.00
365 Buster Davis RC .50 1.25
366 Lawrence Timmons RC .60 1.50
367 Paul Posluszny RC .40 1.00
368 Jon Beason RC .40 1.00
369 Rufus Alexander RC .40 1.00
370 Earl Everett RC .40 1.00
371 Stewart Bradley RC .40 1.00
372 Prescott Burgess RC .40 1.00
373 Leon Hall RC .40 1.00
374 Darrelle Revis RC .50 1.25
375 Aaron Ross RC .40 1.00
376 Daymeion Hughes RC .40 1.00
377 Marcus McCauley RC .40 1.00
378 Chris Houston RC .40 1.00
379 Tanard Jackson RC .40 1.00
380 Jonathan Wade RC .40 1.00
381 Josh Wilson RC .50 1.25
382 Eric Wright RC .40 1.00
383 A.J. Davis RC .40 1.00
384 David Irons RC .40 1.00
385 LaRon Landry RC .60 1.50
386 Reggie Nelson RC .40 1.00
387 Michael Griffin RC .40 1.00
388 Brandon Meriweather RC .50 1.25
389 Eric Weddle RC .50 1.25
390 Aaron Rouse RC .40 1.00
391 Josh Gattis RC .40 1.00
392 Joe Thomas RC .60 1.50
393 Levi Brown RC .40 1.00
394 Tony Ugoh RC .40 1.00
395 Ryan Kalil RC .40 1.00
396 Peyton Manning LL .50 1.25
397 Marc Bulger LL .12 .30
398 LaDainian Tomlinson LL .20 .50
399 Larry Johnson LL .12 .30
400 Frank Gore LL .15 .40
401 Chad Johnson LL .12 .30
402 Marvin Harrison LL .15 .40
403 Reggie Wayne LL .15 .40
404 LaDainian Tomlinson LL .20 .50
405 Peyton Manning PB .50 1.25
406 Marvin Harrison PB .15 .40
407 LaDainian Tomlinson PB .20 .50
408 Reggie Wayne PB .15 .40
409 Antonio Gates PB .20 .50
410 Jeff Saturday PB .12 .30
411 Jason Taylor PB .15 .40
412 Shawne Merriman PB .12 .30
413 Champ Bailey PB .15 .40
414 Troy Polamalu PB .20 .50
415 Drew Brees PB .20 .50
416 Frank Gore PB .15 .40
417 Tony Gonzalez PB .15 .40
418 Steve Smith PB .15 .40
419 Walter Jones PB .12 .30
420 Devin Hester PB .15 .40
421 Julius Peppers PB .15 .40
422 Tony Romo PB .25 .60
423 Ronde Barber PB .12 .30
424 Larry Johnson PB .12 .30
425 LaDainian Tomlinson MVP .20 .50
426 Vince Young OROY .12 .30
427 DeMeco Ryans DROY .15 .40
428 Reggie Wayne PSH .15 .40
429 Drew Brees LL .20 .50
430 Asante Samuel PSH .12 .30
431 New Orleans Saints PSH .20 .50
432 Reggie Bush PSH .12 .30
433 Peyton Manning PSH .50 1.25
434 Robbie Gould PSH .12 .30
435 T.Jones/C.Benson PSH .12 .30
436 Joseph Addai PSH .12 .30
437 Marlin Jackson PSH .12 .30
438 Colts Defense PSH .12 .30
439 Adam Vinatieri PSH .12 .30
440 Devin Hester PSH .15 .40
CL1 Checklist 1 .06 .15
CL2 Checklist 2 .06 .15
CL3 Checklist 3 .06 .15
RH41 Peyton Manning RH 2.50 6.00
RH41A Peyton Manning RH AU 250.00 350.00
SBMVP P.Manning MVP FB/25 125.00 200.00

2007 Topps Copper

*VETS: 3X TO 8X BASIC CARDS
*ROOKIES: 1X TO 2.5X BASIC CARDS
COPPER/2007 ODDS 1:7 HOB, 1:9 RET

2007 Topps First Edition

*VETS: 5X TO 12X BASIC CARDS
*ROOKIES 286-395: 1.5X TO 4X
STATED ODDS 1:36 HOB

2007 Topps Gold

*VETS: 10X TO 25X BASIC CARDS
*ROOKIES 286-395: 4X TO 10X
GOLD/52 ODDS 1:76 HOB

2007 Topps Platinum

UNPRICED PLAT 1/1 ODDS 1:15,000 HOB

2007 Topps All Pro Relics

ATED ODDS 1:326 H, 1:410 R
UNPRICED IN THE NAME ODDS 1:32,800 HOB
*PATCH/99: 1.2X TO 3X BASIC INSERTS
PATCH/99 ODDS 1:3082 HOB
AG Antonio Gates 4.00 10.00
CB Champ Bailey 4.00 10.00
CP Carson Palmer 7.50 20.00
DB Drew Brees 7.50 20.00
DH Devin Hester 7.50 20.00
FG Frank Gore 5.00 12.00
JP Julius Peppers 4.00 10.00
JS Jeff Saturday 4.00 10.00
JT Jason Taylor 4.00 10.00
LJ Larry Johnson 6.00 15.00
LT LaDainian Tomlinson
MH Marvin Harrison 6.00 15.00
PM Peyton Manning 12.50 30.00
RB Ronde Barber 4.00 10.00
RW Reggie Wayne 5.00 12.00
SM Shawne Merriman 5.00 12.00
SS Steve Smith 4.00 10.00
TG Tony Gonzalez 4.00 10.00
TP Troy Polamalu 10.00 25.00
TR Tony Romo 12.50 30.00
WJ Walter Jones 4.00 10.00

2007 Topps All Pro Team

MPLETE SET (12) 10.00 25.00
ONE PER RACK PACK
1 Drew Brees 1.25 3.00
2 Peyton Manning 3.00 8.00
3 Marc Bulger .75 2.00
4 LaDainian Tomlinson 1.25 3.00
5 Larry Johnson .75 2.00
6 Frank Gore 1.00 2.50
7 Chad Johnson .75 2.00
8 Marvin Harrison 1.00 2.50
9 Roy Williams WR .75 2.00
10 Shawne Merriman .75 2.00
11 Champ Bailey 1.00 2.50
12 Zach Thomas 1.00 2.50

2007 Topps Brett Favre Collection

MMON CARD (BF1-BF200) 1.25 3.00
STATED ODDS 1:6 HOB

2007 Topps Brett Favre Collection Autographs

AUTO/18-39 ODDS 1:75,000 H,1:40,000 R
BFA1 Brett Favre/18 100.00 200.00
BFA2 Brett Favre/19 100.00 200.00
BFA3 Brett Favre/33 100.00 200.00
BFA4 Brett Favre/38 100.00 200.00
BFA5 Brett Favre/39 100.00 200.00
BFA6 Brett Favre/35 100.00 200.00
BFA7 Brett Favre/18 100.00 200.00

2007 Topps Factory Set Rookie Bonus

These cards were included as bonus inserts in the various versions of 2007 Topps factory sets which included the following: hobby, Super Bowl XLII, Bears, Colts, Chargers, and Jets. Each card was numbered in the style "1 of 5" on the backs except for the hobby (111-115) and retail factory set players (those were numbered 116-120). We've added prefixes to aid in cataloging.

COMP.HOBBY SET (5) 3.00 8.00
COMP.BEARS SET (5) 3.00 8.00
COMP.CHARGER SET (5) 3.00 8.00
COMP.COLTS SET (5) 3.00 8.00
COMP.JETS SET (5) 3.00 8.00
COMP.RETAIL SET (5) 3.00 8.00
COMP.SUPER BOWL (6) 5.00 12.00
B1 Dan Bazuin .60 1.50
B2 Michael Okwo .60 1.50
B3 Kevin Payne .50 1.25
B4 Drisan James .60 1.50
B5 Trumaine McBride .60 1.50
C1 Roy Hall .75 2.00
C2 Brannon Condren .50 1.25
C3 Clint Session .60 1.50
C4 Michael Coe .50 1.25
C5 Keyunta Dawson .60 1.50
CH1 Anthony Waters .60 1.50
CH2 Legedu Naanee .60 1.50
CH3 Brandon Siler .50 1.25
CH4 Jarrett Hicks .60 1.50
CH5 Sonny Shackelford .50 1.25
J1 Jacob Bender .50 1.25
J2 James Ihedigbo .50 1.25
J3 Brett Ratliff .75 2.00
J4 Kyle Steffes .50 1.25
J5 Jesse Pellot .50 1.25
SB1 JaMarcus Russell .25 .60
SB2 Adrian Peterson .75 2.00
SB3 Brady Quinn .25 .60
SB4 Ted Ginn .30 .75
SB5 Marshawn Lynch .50 1.25
SB6 Calvin Johnson .75 2.00
111 James Jones .50 1.25
112 Steve Breaston .50 1.25
113 Jacoby Jones .50 1.25
114 Ryne Robinson .60 1.50
115 Chris Davis .50 1.25
116 Leâ•™Ron McClain .75 2.00
117 Joel Filani .50 1.25
118 Gerald Alexander .50 1.25
119 Justise Hairston .60 1.50
120 Nate Ilaoa .60 1.50

2007 Topps Game Breakers Super Bowl Pylons

PYLON/50 ODDS 1:15,000H, 1:30,000R
GBADH Devin Hester 75.00 150.00
GBADR Dominic Rhodes 60.00 120.00
GBAKH Kelvin Hayden 50.00 100.00
GBAMM Muhsin Muhammad
GBAPM Peyton Manning 75.00 150.00
GBARW Reggie Wayne 50.00 100.00

2007 Topps Generation Now

STATED ODDS 1:4 HOB
UNPRICED AU ODDS 1:160,000 HOB
AS1 Alex Smith QB .60 1.50
AS2 Alex Smith QB .60 1.50
AS3 Alex Smith QB .60 1.50
AS4 Alex Smith QB .60 1.50
BJ1 Brandon Jacobs .50 1.25
BJ2 Brandon Jacobs .50 1.25
BJ3 Brandon Jacobs .50 1.25
BJ4 Brandon Jacobs .50 1.25
BR1 Ben Roethlisberger .75 2.00
BR2 Ben Roethlisberger .75 2.00
BR3 Ben Roethlisberger .75 2.00
BR4 Ben Roethlisberger .75 2.00
CW1 Cadillac Williams .60 1.50
CW2 Cadillac Williams .60 1.50
CW3 Cadillac Williams .60 1.50
CW4 Cadillac Williams .60 1.50
DH1 Devin Hester .60 1.50
DH2 Devin Hester .60 1.50
DH3 Devin Hester .60 1.50
DH4 Devin Hester .60 1.50
DW1 DeAngelo Williams .50 1.25
DW2 DeAngelo Williams .50 1.25
DW3 DeAngelo Williams .50 1.25
DW4 DeAngelo Williams .50 1.25
EM1 Eli Manning .60 1.50
EM2 Eli Manning .60 1.50
EM3 Eli Manning .60 1.50
EM4 Eli Manning .60 1.50
FG1 Frank Gore .60 1.50
FG2 Frank Gore .60 1.50
FG3 Frank Gore .60 1.50
FG4 Frank Gore .60 1.50
GJ1 Greg Jennings .50 1.25
GJ2 Greg Jennings .50 1.25
GJ3 Greg Jennings .50 1.25
GJ4 Greg Jennings .50 1.25
JA1 Joseph Addai .50 1.25
JA2 Joseph Addai .50 1.25
JA3 Joseph Addai .50 1.25
JA4 Joseph Addai .50 1.25
JC1 Jay Cutler .50 1.25
JC2 Jay Cutler .50 1.25
JC3 Jay Cutler .50 1.25
JC4 Jay Cutler .50 1.25
JCO1 Jerricho Cotchery .50 1.25
JCO2 Jerricho Cotchery .50 1.25
JCO3 Jerricho Cotchery .50 1.25
JCO4 Jerricho Cotchery .50 1.25
JL1 J.P. Losman .50 1.25
JL2 J.P. Losman .50 1.25
JL3 J.P. Losman .50 1.25
JL4 J.P. Losman .50 1.25
KJ1 Kevin Jones .50 1.25
KJ2 Kevin Jones .50 1.25
KJ3 Kevin Jones .50 1.25
KJ4 Kevin Jones .50 1.25
LE1 Lee Evans .60 1.50
LE2 Lee Evans .60 1.50
LE3 Lee Evans .60 1.50
LE4 Lee Evans .60 1.50
LF1 Larry Fitzgerald .60 1.50
LF2 Larry Fitzgerald .60 1.50
LF3 Larry Fitzgerald .60 1.50
LF4 Larry Fitzgerald .60 1.50
LM1 Laurence Maroney .60 1.50
LM2 Laurence Maroney .60 1.50
LM3 Laurence Maroney .60 1.50
LM4 Laurence Maroney .60 1.50
MC1 Marques Colston .50 1.25
MC2 Marques Colston .50 1.25
MC3 Marques Colston .50 1.25
MC4 Marques Colston .50 1.25
MJ1 Maurice Jones-Drew .50 1.25
MJ2 Maurice Jones-Drew .50 1.25
MJ3 Maurice Jones-Drew .50 1.25
MJ4 Maurice Jones-Drew .50 1.25
ML1 Matt Leinart .50 1.25
ML2 Matt Leinart .50 1.25
ML3 Matt Leinart .50 1.25
ML4 Matt Leinart .50 1.25
PR1 Philip Rivers .75 2.00
PR2 Philip Rivers .75 2.00
PR3 Philip Rivers .75 2.00
PR4 Philip Rivers .75 2.00
RB1 Reggie Bush .50 1.25
RB2 Reggie Bush .50 1.25
RB3 Reggie Bush .50 1.25
RB4 Reggie Bush .50 1.25
RW1 Roy Williams WR .50 1.25
RW2 Roy Williams WR .50 1.25
RW3 Roy Williams WR .50 1.25
RW4 Roy Williams WR .50 1.25
SJ1 Steven Jackson .50 1.25
SJ2 Steven Jackson .50 1.25
SJ3 Steven Jackson .50 1.25
SJ4 Steven Jackson .50 1.25
VY1 Vince Young .50 1.25
VY2 Vince Young .50 1.25
VY3 Vince Young .50 1.25
VY4 Vince Young .50 1.25

2007 Topps Hall of Fame Class of 2007

COMPLETE SET (6) 4.00 10.00
STATED ODDS 1:12 HOB/RET
HOFBM1 Bruce Matthews White 1.00 2.50
HOFCS Charlie Sanders 1.00 2.50
HOFGH Gene Hickerson 1.00 2.50
HOFMI Michael Irvin 1.25 3.00
HOFRW Roger Wehrli 1.00 2.50
HOFTT Thurman Thomas 1.25 3.00
HOFBM2 Bruce Matthews Blue 1.00 2.50

2007 Topps Hall of Fame Autographs

ODDS 1:50,700 HOB, 1:40,000 RET
HOFABM Bruce Matthews 100.00 200.00
HOFACS Charlie Sanders 100.00 200.00
HOFAMI Michael Irvin 150.00 300.00
HOFATT Thurman Thomas 200.00 350.00

2007 Topps Hobby Masters

STATED ODDS 1:9 HOB
HMCJ Chad Johnson .60 1.50
HMCP Carson Palmer .75 2.00
HMLJ Larry Johnson .60 1.50
HMLT LaDainian Tomlinson 1.00 2.50
HMMV Michael Vick .75 2.00
HMPM Peyton Manning 2.50 6.00
HMSA Shaun Alexander .60 1.50
HMSJ Stoven Jackson .60 1.50
HMSS Steve Smith .75 2.00
HMTB Tom Brady 3.00 8.00

2007 Topps League Leaders Relics

GROUP A ODDS 1:4300 H, 1:5700 R
GROUP B ODDS 1:1172 H, 1:1525 R
LLRAJ Andre Johnson 4.00 10.00
LLRCB Champ Bailey 5.00 12.00
LLRCJ Chad Johnson 6.00 15.00
LLRCP Carson Palmer 6.00 15.00
LLRDB Drew Brees 5.00 12.00
LLRJK Jon Kitna
LLRLJ Larry Johnson 12.00 30.00
LLRLJ2 Larry Johnson 12.00 30.00
LLRLT LaDainian Tomlinson 12.00 30.00
LLRLT2 LaDainian Tomlinson 12.00 30.00
LLRMH Marvin Harrison 5.00 12.00
LLRPM Peyton Manning 15.00 40.00
LLRPM2 Peyton Manning 15.00 40.00
LLRSM Shawne Merriman 8.00 20.00
LLRTO Terrell Owens 8.00 20.00

2007 Topps LT Touchdown Tribute

COMPLETE SET (31) 20.00 50.00
COMMON CARD 1.00 2.50
ODDS 1:4 TARGET RETAIL

2007 Topps Own The Game

COMPLETE SET (30) 25.00 60.00
STATED ODDS 1:9 HOB/RET
OTGAK Aaron Kampman 1.25 3.00
OTGAS Aaron Schobel 1.00 2.50
OTGASA Asante Samuel 1.00 2.50
OTGCB Champ Bailey 1.25 3.00
OTGCJ Chad Johnson 1.00 2.50
OTGCP Carson Palmer 1.25 3.00
OTGDB Drew Brees 1.50 4.00
OTGDB2 Drew Brees 1.50 4.00
OTGDH Devin Hester 1.25 3.00
OTGDR DeMeco Ryans 1.25 3.00
OTGFG Frank Gore 1.25 3.00
OTGJM Justin Miller 1.00 2.50
OTGLF London Fletcher 1.25 3.00
OTGLJ Larry Johnson 1.00 2.50
OTGLJ2 Larry Johnson 1.00 2.50
OTGLT LaDainian Tomlinson 1.50 4.00
OTGLT2 LaDainian Tomlinson 1.50 4.00
OTGMB Marc Bulger 1.00 2.50
OTGMBA Marion Barber 1.50 4.00
OTGMH Marvin Harrison 1.25 3.00
OTGMH2 Marvin Harrison 1.25 3.00
OTGPM Peyton Manning 4.00 10.00
OTGPM2 Peyton Manning 4.00 10.00
OTGRG Robbie Gould 1.00 2.50
OTGRM Rashean Mathis 1.00 2.50
OTGRW Roy Williams WR 1.00 2.50
OTGSM Shawne Merriman 1.00 2.50
OTGTH Torry Holt 1.25 3.00
OTGTO Terrell Owens 1.25 3.00
OTGZT Zach Thomas 1.25 3.00

2007 Topps Performance Highlights Autographs

OUP A ODDS 1:50,000H, 1:40,000R
GROUP B ODDS 1:40,000H, 1:20,000R
GROUP C/D ODDS 1:2500H, 1:5500R
GROUP E ODDS 1:3381 H, 1:5500 R
GROUP F ODDS 1:849 H, 1:2500 R
THAAP Adrian Peterson A 75.00 150.00
THAAP Antonio Pittman F 4.00 10.00
THABJ Brandon Jackson E 4.00 10.00
THABL Brian Leonard F 4.00 10.00
THABQ Brady Quinn A
THACJ Calvin Johnson A 75.00 150.00
THACJ Chad Johnson B 25.00 50.00
THADB Drew Brees A 50.00 100.00
THADB Dwayne Bowe C 4.00 10.00
THADJ Dwayne Jarrett C 5.00 12.00
THADS Drew Stanton C 4.00 10.00
THADT Drew Tate F 5.00 12.00
THAFG Frank Gore B 15.00 40.00
THAIS Isaiah Stanback F 4.00 10.00
THAJH Justise Hairston F 5.00 12.00
THAJP Jordan Palmer F 5.00 12.00
THAJR JaMarcus Russell A 12.00 30.00
THAJZ Jared Zabransky F 4.00 10.00
THAKI Kenny Irons C 4.00 10.00
THAKK Kevin Kolb D 5.00 12.00
THALG Luke Getsy F 6.00 15.00
THALJ Larry Johnson B 12.00 30.00
THALN Legedu Naanee F 5.00 12.00
THALT LaDainian Tomlinson A
THAMB Michael Bush D 4.00 10.00
THAML Marshawn Lynch B
THAML Matt Leinart B
THARB Reggie Bush A 75.00 150.00
THARM Robert Meachem C 5.00 12.00
THARR Ryne Robinson F 5.00 12.00
THASJ Steven Jackson B 15.00 40.00
THASM Shawne Merriman B 30.00 60.00
THASR Sidney Rice C 10.00 25.00
THASS Steve Smith USC D 4.00 10.00
THASY Selvin Young F 8.00 20.00
THATB Tom Brady A 125.00 200.00
THATE Trent Edwards E 4.00 10.00
THATG Ted Ginn Jr. C 10.00 25.00
THATH Tony Hunt D 4.00 10.00
THATP Tyler Palko F 6.00 15.00
THATS Troy Smith C 4.00 10.00
THAVY Vince Young A
THAWP Willie Parker B

2007 Topps Performance Highlights Relics

GROUP A ODDS 1:8266 H, 1:12,000 R
GROUP B ODDS 1:1400 H, 1:1800 R
THRCJ Chad Johnson B 5.00 12.00
THRLJ Larry Johnson A 6.00 15.00
THRLT LaDainian Tomlinson A
THRMH Marvin Harrison B 5.00 12.00
THRML Matt Leinart B 6.00 15.00
THRPM Peyton Manning A 10.00 25.00
THRRB Reggie Bush B 10.00 25.00
THRSJ Steven Jackson B 5.00 12.00
THRTB Tom Brady B 6.00 15.00
THRVY Vince Young B 7.50 20.00

2007 Topps Red Hot Rookies

RANDOM INSERTS IN WAL-MART PACKS
1 JaMarcus Russell .60 1.50
2 Calvin Johnson 2.00 5.00
3 Adrian Peterson 2.00 5.00
4 Ted Ginn .75 2.00
5 Marshawn Lynch 1.25 3.00
6 Brady Quinn .60 1.50
7 Dwayne Bowe .60 1.50
8 Robert Meachem .75 2.00
9 Dwayne Jarrett .75 2.00
10 Greg Olsen 1.00 2.50
11 Anthony Gonzalez .60 1.50
12 Kevin Kolb .75 2.00
13 John Beck .60 1.50
14 Drew Stanton .60 1.50
15 Sidney Rice .75 2.00

2007 Topps Red Hot Rookies Autographs

RANDOM INSERTS IN WAL-MART PACKS
1 JaMarcus Russell 30.00 80.00
2 Ted Ginn Jr. 20.00 50.00
3 Marshawn Lynch 25.00 60.00
4 Brady Quinn 5.00 12.00
5 Dwayne Jarrett 12.00 30.00
6 Greg Olsen 20.00 40.00

2007 Topps Red Hot Rookies Jerseys

RANDOM INSERTS IN WAL-MART BLASTER
1 JaMarcus Russell 1.50 4.00
3 Adrian Peterson 5.00 12.00
2 Calvin Johnson 5.00 12.00
4 Ted Ginn 2.00 5.00
5 Marshawn Lynch 3.00 8.00
6 Brady Quinn 1.50 4.00
7 Dwayne Bowe 1.50 4.00
8 Robert Meachem 2.00 5.00
9 Dwayne Jarrett 2.00 5.00
10 Greg Olsen 2.50 6.00
11 Anthony Gonzalez 1.50 4.00
12 Kevin Kolb 2.00 5.00
13 John Beck 1.50 4.00
14 Drew Stanton 1.50 4.00
15 Sidney Rice 2.00 5.00

2007 Topps Rookie Fantasy Challenge

COMPLETE SET (20) 12.50 30.00
STATED ODDS 1.9 HOB
1 JaMarcus Russell .50 1.25
2 Adrian Peterson 1.50 4.00
3 Marshawn Lynch 1.00 2.50
4 Brandon Jackson .50 1.25
5 Calvin Johnson 1.50 4.00
6 Dwayne Bowe .50 1.25
7 Drew Stanton .50 1.25
8 Chris Henry .50 1.25
9 Robert Meachem .60 1.50
10 Craig Buster Davis .50 1.25
11 LaRon Landry .75 2.00
12 Patrick Willis .75 2.00
13 Lawrence Timmons .75 2.00
14 Anthony Gonzalez .50 1.25
15 Kevin Kolb .60 1.50
16 Jason Hill .50 1.25
17 Sidney Rice .60 1.50
18 Dwayne Jarrett .60 1.50
19 Kenny Irons .50 1.25
20 Lorenzo Booker .60 1.50

2007 Topps Rookie Premiere Autographs

RANDOM INSERTS IN PACKS
RED INK TOO SCARCE TO PRICE
AG Anthony Gonzalez 10.00 25.00
AP Adrian Peterson 75.00 150.00
AP Antonio Pittman 10.00 25.00
BJ Brandon Jackson 10.00 25.00
BL Brian Leonard 10.00 25.00
BQ Brady Quinn 10.00 25.00
CH Chris Henry 10.00 25.00
CJ Calvin Johnson 40.00 80.00
DB Dwayne Bowe 10.00 25.00
DJ Dwayne Jarrett 12.00 30.00
DS Drew Stanton 10.00 25.00
GA Gaines Adams 12.00 30.00
GO Greg Olsen 15.00 40.00
GW Garrett Wolfe 10.00 25.00
JB John Beck 10.00 25.00
JH Jason Hill 10.00 25.00
JR JaMarcus Russell 10.00 25.00
JT Joe Thomas 12.00 30.00
KI Kenny Irons 10.00 25.00
KK Kevin Kolb 12.00 30.00
LB Lorenzo Booker 12.00 30.00
MB Michael Bush 10.00 25.00
ML Marshawn Lynch 30.00 80.00
PW Patrick Willis 20.00 50.00
PW Paul Williams 10.00 25.00
RM Robert Meachem 12.00 30.00
SR Sidney Rice 12.00 30.00
SS Steve Smith 10.00 25.00
TE Trent Edwards 10.00 25.00
TG Ted Ginn Jr. 12.00 30.00
TH Tony Hunt 10.00 25.00
TS Troy Smith 10.00 25.00
YF Yamon Figurs 10.00 25.00
JLH Johnnie Lee Higgins 10.00 25.00

2007 Topps Rookie Premiere Autographs Duals

RANDOM INSERTS IN PACKS
RED INK TOO SCARCE TO PRICE
JS D.Jarrett/S.Smith USC 25.00 60.00
PJ A.Peterson/C.Johnson 100.00 200.00
PL A.Peterson/M.Lynch 75.00 150.00
RJ J.Russell/C.Johnson 30.00 80.00
RQ J.Russell/B.Quinn 12.00 30.00

2007 Topps Rookie Premiere Autographs Quads

RANDOM INSERTS IN PACKS
RED INK TOO SCARCE TO PRICE
JBGM Jhnsn/Bowe/Ginn/Meac 50.00 120.00
JGLP Jhnsn/Ginn/Lynch/Ptrsn 100.00 200.00
RQPJ Russ/Quinn/Ptrsn/Jhnsn 75.00 150.00
RQSB Russ/Quinn/Stant/Beck 20.00 50.00
SGGP T.Smith/Ginn/Gonz/Pittm 30.00 80.00

2007 Topps Running Back Royalty

MPLETE SET (10) 6.00 15.00
STATED ODDS 1:12 HOB/RET
TA L.Tomlinson/M.Allen 1.00 2.50
TB L.Tomlinson/J.Brown 1.25 3.00
TC L.Tomlinson/E.Campbell 1.00 2.50
TD L.Tomlinson/E.Dickerson 1.00 2.50
TF L.Tomlinson/M.Faulk 1.00 2.50
TP L.Tomlinson/W.Payton 2.00 5.00
TS L.Tomlinson/B.Sanders 1.50 4.00
TDO L.Tomlinson/T.Dorsett 1.00 2.50
TSA L.Tomlinson/G.Sayers 1.00 2.50
TSM L.Tomlinson/E.Smith 1.50 4.00

2007 Topps Running Back Royalty Autographs

AUTO/50 ODDS 1:20,000H, 1:17,000R
BS Barry Sanders 75.00 150.00
EC Earl Campbell 40.00 80.00
ED Eric Dickerson 30.00 80.00
ES Emmitt Smith 125.00 200.00
GS Gale Sayers 50.00 100.00
JB Jim Brown 60.00 120.00
LT LaDainian Tomlinson 60.00 120.00
MA Marcus Allen 40.00 80.00
MF Marshall Faulk 40.00 80.00
TD Tony Dorsett 40.00 80.00

2007 Topps Running Back Royalty Autographs Dual

AL AU/25 ODDS 1:44,600H, 1:40,000R
TA Tomlinson/M.Allen 100.00 200.00
TB Tomlinson/J.Brown 125.00 250.00
TC Tomlinson/E.Campbell 100.00 200.00
TD Tomlinson/E.Dickerson 100.00 200.00
TDO Tomlinson/T.Dorsett 100.00 200.00
TF Tomlinson/M.Faulk 100.00 200.00
TS Tomlinson/B.Sanders 150.00 300.00
TSA Tomlinson/G.Sayers 100.00 200.00
TSM Tomlinson/E.Smith 200.00 400.00

2007 Topps Signature Series

SIG SERIES/50 ODDS 1:85,000
SSBF Brett Favre 150.00 300.00
SSBQ Brady Quinn 20.00 50.00
SSBS Barry Sanders 100.00 200.00
SSDB Drew Brees 50.00 100.00
SSDM Dan Marino 125.00 250.00
SSEC Earl Campbell 30.00 80.00
SSES Emmitt Smith 125.00 250.00
SSFG Frank Gore 25.00 50.00
SSGS Gale Sayers 40.00 100.00
SSJB Jim Brown 60.00 120.00
SSJM Joe Montana 125.00 250.00
SSJN Joe Namath 60.00 120.00
SSJR Jerry Rice 100.00 200.00
SSJRU JaMarcus Russell 25.00 60.00
SSLJ Larry Johnson 25.00 60.00
SSLT LaDainian Tomlinson 40.00 100.00
SSMA Marcus Allen 50.00 100.00
SSMF Marshall Faulk 30.00 80.00
SSML Matt Leinart 30.00 80.00
SSRB Reggie Bush 30.00 80.00
SSSA Shaun Alexander 25.00 50.00
SSSJ Steven Jackson 25.00 50.00
SSTB Tom Brady 175.00 300.00
SSTR Tony Romo 75.00 150.00
SSVY Vince Young 25.00 60.00

2007 Topps Stat Breakers Super Bowl Footballs

UNPRICED FB/10 ODDS 1:155,000 HOB

2007 Topps Target Exclusive Factory Set Rookie Jerseys

TWO PER TARGET FACTORY SET
1 Brady Quinn 1.25 3.00
2 Calvin Johnson 4.00 10.00
3 Adrian Peterson 4.00 10.00
4 Dwayne Jarrett 1.50 4.00
5 JaMarcus Russell 1.25 3.00
6 Troy Smith 1.25 3.00

2007 Topps Retail Stars

This set of 12-cards was sold as a retail blister pack complete set through mass retail outlets. The cards are essentially the same as base 2007 Topps cards except that each has been re-numbered on the back.

COMPLETE SET (12) 4.00 8.00
1 Peyton Manning 1.00 2.50
2 Brett Favre .75 2.00
3 Reggie Bush .25 .60
4 Vince Young .25 .60
5 Michael Vick .30 .75
6 Ben Roethlisberger .40 1.00
7 Tom Brady 1.25 3.00
8 Brian Urlacher .40 1.00
9 LaDainian Tomlinson .40 1.00
10 Carson Palmer .30 .75
11 Tony Romo .50 1.25
12 Donovan McNabb .30 .75

2007 Topps Super Bowl XLI Card Show

This set was distributed directly to dealers who participated in the 2007 Super Bowl Card Show in Miami. Each card was serial numbered to 1000, printed in the design of the basic issue 2006 Topps football release, and featured a Super Bowl XLI logo at the top of the cardfront. A Black bordered parallel set was also produced with each card serial numbered of 199.

2007 Topps Super Bowl XLI Card Show

COMPLETE SET (16) 15.00 30.00
*BLACK BORDER/199: .8X TO 2X
1 Jason Taylor .60 1.50
2 Larry Johnson .50 1.25
3 Peyton Manning 2.00 5.00
4 Ronnie Brown .50 1.25
5 LaDainian Tomlinson .75 2.00
6 Tom Brady 2.50 6.00
7 Brian Urlacher .75 2.00
8 Frank Gore .60 1.50
9 Philip Rivers .75 2.00
10 Brett Favre 1.50 4.00
11 Tiki Barber .60 1.50
12 Marques Colston .50 1.25
13 Dan Marino 1.50 4.00
14 Reggie Bush .50 1.25
15 Vince Young .50 1.25
16 Matt Leinart .50 1.25

2007 Topps Turn Back The Clock

rds from this set were issued during the 2007 NFL season directly to HTA hobby shop owners. Each card was produced in the design of the 1958 Topps football set. Five cards in the set (#1, 7, 8, 9, 15) were issued in a pack with a retail price of just 5-cents to commemorate the first year pack price of 1956 Topps football. Each card thereafter was issued one-per week directly to hobby shops to be given to their customers who buy Topps products.

COMPLETE SET (22) 5.00 12.00
1 Brady Quinn .10 .25
2 Ted Ginn Jr. .25 .60
3 Greg Olsen .30 .75
4 Vince Young .20 .50
5 Joseph Addai .20 .50
6 Robert Meachem .25 .60
7 JaMarcus Russell .10 .25
8 Calvin Johnson .30 .75
9 Adrian Peterson .30 .75
10 LaDainian Tomlinson .30 .75
11 Frank Gore .25 .60
12 Steven Jackson .20 .50
13 Peyton Manning .75 2.00
14 Reggie Bush .20 .50
15 Marshawn Lynch .20 .50
16 Joe Montana 1.00 2.50
17 Joe Namath .40 1.00
18 Dan Marino .60 1.50
19 Jerry Rice .60 1.50
20 Barry Sanders .50 1.25
21 Roger Staubach .40 1.00
22 Jim Brown .40 1.00

2008 Topps

MP.FACT.SET (445) 30.00 50.00
COMP.COWBOY SET (445) 40.00 60.00
COMP.GIANTS SET (445) 30.00 50.00
COMP.PACKER SET (445) 30.00 50.00
COMP.PATRIOT SET (445) 30.00 50.00
COMPLETE SET (440) 25.00 50.00
BASE CARD VARIATION ODDS 1:1722 H/R
ELI RH ODDS 1:36
ELI RH AUTO ODDS 1:40,000
ELI SB FB/99 ODDS 1:12,175
ELI SB FB AU ODDS 1:180,000
UNPRICED PRINT PLATE 1/1 ODDS 1:910
1 Drew Brees .25 .60
2 Jon Kitna .15 .40
3 Tom Brady .75 2.00
4 Chad Pennington .15 .40
5 Steve McNair .20 .50
6 Josh McCown .15 .40
7 Matt Hasselbeck .15 .40
8 David Garrard .15 .40
9 Jay Cutler .15 .40
10 Matt Schaub .15 .40
11 Daunte Culpepper .20 .50
12 Kellen Clemens .15 .40
13 John Beck .15 .40
14 Trent Edwards .15 .40
15 Brodie Croyle .20 .50
16 Trent Dilfer .15 .40
17 Chris Redman .15 .40
18 Peyton Manning .60 1.50
19 Carson Palmer .20 .50
20 Ben Roethlisberger .25 .60
21 Eli Manning .20 .50
22 Tony Romo .20 .50
23 Donovan McNabb .20 .50
24 Joey Harrington .15 .40
25 Jeff Garcia .15 .40
26 Derek Anderson .15 .40
27 Rex Grossman .15 .40
28 Kyle Boller .15 .40
29 Sage Rosenfels .15 .40
30 JaMarcus Russell .15 .40
31 Gus Frerotte .15 .40
32 Luke McCown .15 .40
33 Marc Bulger .15 .40
34A Brett Favre .50 1.25
34B Brett Favre Lombardi 150.00 300.00
34C B.Favre Tractor Packers 75.00 150.00
34D Brett Favre Jets 6.00 15.00
35 Philip Rivers .25 .60
36 Vince Young .15 .40
37 Kurt Warner .20 .50
38 Cleo Lemon .15 .40
39 Damon Huard .15 .40
40 Jason Campbell .15 .40
41 Brian Griese .15 .40
42 Tarvaris Jackson .15 .40
43 J.P. Losman .15 .40
44 Troy Smith .20 .50
45 Brady Quinn .15 .40
46 Trent Green .15 .40
47 Quinn Gray .15 .40
48 Alex Smith QB .20 .50
49 Todd Collins .15 .40
50 Matt Moore .15 .40
51 A.J. Feeley .15 .40
52 Matt Leinart .15 .40
53 Jake Delhomme .15 .40
54 Steven Jackson .15 .40
55 Willie Parker .20 .50
56 Derrick Ward .15 .40
57 Julius Jones .15 .40
58 DeShaun Foster .15 .40
59 Shaun Alexander .15 .40
60 Reggie Bush .15 .40
61 Clinton Portis .15 .40
62 Ron Dayne .15 .40
63 Maurice Jones-Drew .15 .40
64 Warrick Dunn .15 .40
65 Adrian Peterson .25 .60
66 Brian Leonard .15 .40
67 Jerious Norwood .15 .40
68 Thomas Jones .15 .40
69 LaDainian Tomlinson .25 .60
70 Cedric Benson .15 .40
71 Marion Barber .15 .40
72 Brian Westbrook .15 .40
73 LenDale White .15 .40
74 Ronnie Brown .15 .40
75 Travis Henry .15 .40
76 Kenny Watson .15 .40
77 Fred Taylor .15 .40
78 Ryan Grant .20 .50
79 Marshawn Lynch .20 .50
80 Selvin Young .15 .40
81 Joseph Addai .15 .40
82 Laurence Maroney .20 .50
83 Brandon Jacobs .15 .40
84 Willis McGahee .15 .40
85 Frank Gore .20 .50
86 Edgerrin James .20 .50
87 Kevin Jones .15 .40
88 DeAngelo Williams .15 .40
89 Jamal Lewis .20 .50
90 Chester Taylor .15 .40
91 Earnest Graham .15 .40
92 Justin Fargas .15 .40
93 Kolby Smith .15 .40
94 Maurice Morris .15 .40
95 Larry Johnson .15 .40
96 LaMont Jordan .20 .50
97 Kenton Keith .15 .40
98 Jesse Chatman .15 .40
99 Adrian Peterson Bears .15 .40
100 Najeh Davenport .15 .40
101 Rudi Johnson .15 .40
102 Chris Brown .15 .40
103 Aaron Stecker .15 .40
104 Sammy Morris .15 .40
105A Leon Washington .15 .40
105B B.Favre Tractor Jets/500 25.00 60.00
106 T.J. Duckett .15 .40
107 Ladell Betts .15 .40
108 Michael Turner .15 .40
109 Correll Buckhalter .15 .40
110 Ahmad Bradshaw .15 .40
111 Greg Jennings .15 .40
112 Torry Holt .20 .50

113 T.J. Houshmandzadeh .15 .40
114 Jerricho Cotchery .15 .40
115 Derrick Mason .15 .40
116 Kevin Curtis .15 .40
117 Kevin Walter .20 .50
118 Joey Galloway .20 .50
119 Anquan Boldin .15 .40
120 Santonio Holmes .15 .40
121 Lee Evans .20 .50
122 Dwayne Bowe .20 .50
123 Laurent Robinson .15 .40
124 Wes Welker .20 .50
125 Roy Williams WR .15 .40
126 Randy Moss .20 .50
127 Plaxico Burress .15 .40
128 Terrell Owens .20 .50
129 Andre Johnson .20 .50
130 Roddy White .15 .40
131 Brandon Marshall .20 .50
132 Donald Driver .20 .50
133 Hines Ward .20 .50
134 Ike Hilliard .15 .40
135 James Jones .15 .40
136 Calvin Johnson .25 .60
137 Marques Colston .15 .40
138 Reggie Wayne .20 .50
139 Chad Johnson .15 .40
140 Amani Toomer .15 .40
141 Bernard Berrian .15 .40
142 Steve Smith .20 .50
143 Larry Fitzgerald .20 .50
144 Chris Chambers .15 .40
145 Braylon Edwards .15 .40
146 David Patten .15 .40
147 Bobby Engram .15 .40
148 Shaun McDonald .15 .40
149 Anthony Gonzalez .15 .40
150 Sidney Rice .15 .40
151 Santana Moss .15 .40
152 Reggie Brown .15 .40
153 Justin Gage .15 .40
154 Isaac Bruce .25 .60
155 Antwaan Randle El .15 .40
156 Roydell Williams .15 .40
157 Ronald Curry .15 .40
158 Jerry Porter .15 .40
159 Patrick Crayton .20 .50
160 Donte Stallworth .15 .40
161 Nate Burleson .15 .40
162 Mike Furrey .20 .50
163 Deion Branch .15 .40
164 Bobby Wade .15 .40
165 Laveranues Coles .15 .40
166 Brandon Stokley .15 .40
167 Reggie Williams .20 .50
168 Vincent Jackson .15 .40
169 Joe Jurevicius .15 .40
170 Dennis Northcutt .15 .40
171 Arnaz Battle .15 .40
172 Steve Smith USC .20 .50
173 Ted Ginn Jr. .15 .40
174 Antonio Gates .20 .50
175 Chris Cooley .15 .40
176 Owen Daniels .15 .40
177 Kellen Winslow .15 .40
178 Tony Gonzalez .20 .50
179 Jason Witten .20 .50
180 Greg Olsen .20 .50
181 Jeremy Shockey .15 .40
182 Dallas Clark .15 .40
183 Donald Lee .20 .50
184 Heath Miller .15 .40
185 Tony Scheffler .15 .40
186 Desmond Clark .15 .40
187 Vernon Davis .15 .40
188 Alge Crumpler .15 .40
189 Zach Miller .15 .40
190 Randy McMichael .15 .40
191 Bo Scaife .15 .40
192 Chris Baker .15 .40
193 Jeff King .15 .40
194 Marcedes Lewis .15 .40
195 Ben Watson .15 .40
196 Albert Haynesworth .15 .40
197 Kevin Williams .15 .40
198 Pat Williams .15 .40
199 Tommie Harris .15 .40
200 Darnell Dockett .15 .40
201 Vince Wilfork .15 .40
202 Jamal Williams .15 .40
203 Casey Hampton .15 .40
204 Amobi Okoye .15 .40
205 Patrick Kerney .15 .40
206 Gaines Adams .15 .40
207 Osi Umenyiora .15 .40
208 Mario Williams .20 .50
209 Jared Allen .15 .40
210 Trent Cole .15 .40
211 Aaron Kampman .20 .50
212 Kyle Vanden Bosch .15 .40
213 Elvis Dumervil .15 .40
214 Jason Taylor .20 .50
215 Aaron Schobel .15 .40
216 Andre Carter .15 .40
217 John Abraham .15 .40
218 Justin Tuck .15 .40
219 Michael Strahan .20 .50
220 Kabeer Gbaja-Biamila .15 .40
221 Adewale Ogunleye .15 .40
222 Julius Peppers .20 .50
223 Tamba Hali .15 .40
224 Luis Castillo .15 .40
225 Jon Beason .15 .40
226 D.J. Williams .15 .40
227 Ernie Sims .15 .40
228 DeMarcus Ware .20 .50
229 Nick Barnett .15 .40
230 Patrick Willis .20 .50
231 Mike Vrabel .15 .40
232 Shawne Merriman .15 .40
233 Greg Ellis .15 .40
234 Thomas Howard .15 .40
235 Brian Urlacher .25 .60
236 Keith Bulluck .15 .40
237 London Fletcher .20 .50
238 DeMeco Ryans .20 .50
239 David Harris .15 .40
240 Angelo Crowell .15 .40
241 James Harrison RC 1.50 4.00
242 Julian Peterson .15 .40
243 Lance Briggs .20 .50
244 Lofa Tatupu .15 .40
245 Ray Lewis .25 .60
246 Shaun Phillips .15 .40
247 Antonio Pierce .15 .40
248 Antonio Cromartie .15 .40
249 Marcus Trufant .15 .40
250 Asante Samuel .15 .40
251 Anthony Henry .15 .40
252 Leigh Bodden .15 .40
253 Antrel Rolle .15 .40
254 Roderick Hood .15 .40
255 DeAngelo Hall .15 .40
256 Dre Bly .15 .40
257 Leon Hall .15 .40
258 Ronde Barber .15 .40
259 Al Harris .15 .40
260 Terence Newman .15 .40
261 Champ Bailey .20 .50
262 Aaron Ross .15 .40
263 Bob Sanders .20 .50
264 Reggie Nelson .15 .40
265 Marvin Harrison .20 .50
266 Ed Reed .20 .50
267 O.J. Atogwe .15 .40
268 Ken Hamlin .15 .40
269 Kerry Rhodes .15 .40
270 Clinton Hart .15 .40
271 Atari Bigby .15 .40
272 Sean Jones .15 .40
273 Darren Sharper .15 .40
274 Roy Williams S .15 .40
275 Troy Polamalu .25 .60
276 John Lynch .20 .50
277 Antoine Bethea .15 .40
278 LaRon Landry .20 .50
279 Walter Jones .15 .40
280 Jonathan Ogden .20 .50
281 Joe Thomas .20 .50
282 Nick Folk .15 .40
283 Rob Bironas .15 .40
284 Devin Hester .20 .50
285 Josh Cribbs .15 .40
286 Tom Brady LL .60 1.50
287 Drew Brees LL .20 .50
288 Tony Romo LL .15 .40
289 LaDainian Tomlinson LL .20 .50
290 Adrian Peterson LL .20 .50
291 Brian Westbrook LL .12 .30
292 Reggie Wayne LL .15 .40
293 Randy Moss LL .15 .40
294 Chad Johnson LL .12 .30
295 Randy Moss LL .15 .40
296 Matt Hasselbeck PB .12 .30
297 Tony Romo PB .15 .40
298 Adrian Peterson PB .20 .50
299 Marion Barber PB .12 .30
300 Brian Westbrook PB .12 .30
301 Larry Fitzgerald PB .15 .40
302 Terrell Owens PB .15 .40
303 Osi Umenyiora PB .15 .40
304 Lofa Tatupu PB .12 .30
305 Jason Witten PB .15 .40
306 Torry Holt PB .15 .40
307 Donald Driver PB .15 .40
308 Peyton Manning PB .50 1.25
309 Ben Roethlisberger PB .20 .50
310 Joseph Addai PB .12 .30
311 Reggie Wayne PB .15 .40
312 Braylon Edwards PB .12 .30
313 Devin Hester PB .15 .40
314 Champ Bailey PB .15 .40
315 Ed Reed PB .15 .40
316 Eli Manning PSH .15 .40
317 David Tyree PSH .12 .30
318 Plaxico Burress PSH .12 .30
319 Lawrence Tynes PSH .15 .40
320 Patriots Defense PSH .15 .40
321 R.W. McQuarters PSH .15 .40
322 Ryan Grant PSH .15 .40
323 Philip Rivers PSH .20 .50
324 David Garrard PSH .12 .30
325 Laurence Maroney PSH .15 .40
326 Seattle Seahawks PSH .12 .30
327 San Diego Chargers PSH .15 .40
328 Tom Brady MVP .60 1.50
329 Adrian Peterson OROY .20 .50
330 Patrick Willis DROY .15 .40
331 Matt Ryan RC 1.25 3.00
331B Matt Ryan No Helm 30.00 80.00
332 Brian Brohm RC .40 1.00
332B Brian Brohm No Helm 12.00 30.00
333 Andre Woodson RC .40 1.00
334 Chad Henne RC .50 1.25
335 Joe Flacco RC .75 2.00
336 John David Booty RC .40 1.00
337 Colt Brennan RC .50 1.25
338 Dennis Dixon RC .40 1.00
339 Erik Ainge RC .40 1.00
340 Josh Johnson RC .40 1.00
341 Kevin O'Connell RC .40 1.00
342 Matt Flynn RC .40 1.00
343 Sam Keller RC .40 1.00
344 Harry Douglas RC .50 1.25
345 Anthony Morelli RC .40 1.00
346 Darren McFadden RC .40 1.00
346B Darren McFadden FB 25.00 50.00
347 Rashard Mendenhall RC .40 1.00
347B Rashard Mendenhall FB 8.00 15.00
348 Jonathan Stewart RC .60 1.50
348B Jonathan Stewart No Helm 25.00 50.00
349 Felix Jones RC .40 1.00
350 Jamaal Charles RC .60 1.50
351 Chris Johnson RC .50 1.25
352 Ray Rice RC .40 1.00
353 Mike Hart RC .40 1.00
354 Kevin Smith RC .40 1.00
355 Steve Slaton RC .40 1.00
356 Matt Forte RC .60 1.50
357 Tashard Choice RC .40 1.00
358 D.Rodgers-Cromartie RC .50 1.25
359 Cory Boyd RC .40 1.00
360 Allen Patrick RC .40 1.00
361 Thomas Brown RC .40 1.00
362 Justin Forsett RC .50 1.25
363 DeSean Jackson RC .75 2.00
364 Malcolm Kelly RC .40 1.00
365 Limas Sweed RC UER 362 .40 1.00
366 Mario Manningham RC .40 1.00
367 James Hardy RC .40 1.00
368 Early Doucet RC .40 1.00
369 Donnie Avery RC .50 1.25
370 Dexter Jackson RC .60 1.50
371 Devin Thomas RC .40 1.00
372 Jordy Nelson RC 1.25 3.00
373 Keenan Burton RC .40 1.00
374 Chris Williams RC .40 1.00
375 Earl Bennett RC .60 1.50
376 Jerome Simpson RC .50 1.25
377 Andre Caldwell RC .40 1.00
378 Josh Morgan RC .40 1.00
379 Fred Davis RC .40 1.00
380 John Carlson RC .40 1.00
381 Martellus Bennett RC .50 1.25
382 Martin Rucker RC .40 1.00
383 Jermichael Finley RC .40 1.00
384 Dustin Keller RC .50 1.25
385 Jacob Tamme RC .50 1.25
386 Kellen Davis RC .40 1.00
387 Jake Long RC .60 1.50
388 Sam Baker RC .40 1.00
389 Jeff Otah RC .40 1.00
390 Owen Schmitt RC .40 1.00
391 Chevis Jackson RC .40 1.00
392 Jacob Hester RC .40 1.00
393 Glenn Dorsey RC .40 1.00
394 Sedrick Ellis RC .40 1.00
395 Kentwan Balmer RC .40 1.00
396 Pat Sims RC .50 1.25
397 Marcus Harrison RC .40 1.00
398 Dre Moore RC .40 1.00
399 Red Bryant RC .40 1.00
400 Trevor Laws RC .40 1.00
401 Chris Long RC .50 1.25
402 Vernon Gholston RC .40 1.00
403 Derrick Harvey RC .40 1.00
404 Calais Campbell RC .50 1.25
405 Terrence Wheatley RC .40 1.00
406 Phillip Merling RC .40 1.00
407 Chris Ellis RC .40 1.00
408 Lawrence Jackson RC .40 1.00
409 Dan Connor RC .40 1.00
410 Curtis Lofton RC .50 1.25
411 Jerod Mayo RC .60 1.50
412 Tavares Gooden RC .40 1.00
413 Beau Bell RC .50 1.25
414 Philip Wheeler RC .50 1.25
415 Vince Hall RC .40 1.00
416 Jonathan Goff RC .40 1.00
417 Keith Rivers RC .40 1.00
418 Ali Highsmith RC .40 1.00
419 Xavier Adibi RC .40 1.00
420 Erin Henderson RC .50 1.25
421 Bruce Davis RC .50 1.25
422 Jordon Dizon RC .40 1.00
423 Shawn Crable RC .40 1.00
424 Geno Hayes RC .40 1.00
425 Mike Jenkins RC .40 1.00
426 Aqib Talib RC .60 1.50
427 Leodis McKelvin RC .50 1.25
428 Terrell Thomas RC .40 1.00
429 Reggie Smith RC .40 1.00
430 Antoine Cason RC .50 1.25
431 Patrick Lee RC .40 1.00
432 Tracy Porter RC .50 1.25
433 Kenny Phillips RC .40 1.00
434 Simeon Castille RC .40 1.00
435 Eddie Royal RC .40 1.00
436 Thomas DeCoud RC .40 1.00
437 Marcus Griffin RC .40 1.00
438 Charles Godfrey RC .40 1.00
439 Tyrell Johnson RC .40 1.00
440 Jamar Adams RC .40 1.00
RH42 Eli Manning RH 2.00 5.00
RHA42 Eli Manning RH AU 60.00 125.00
SBAEM Eli Manning FB AU/50 150.00 300.00
SBEM Eli Manning FB/99 30.00 80.00

2008 Topps Black

*VETS 1-330: 10X TO 25X BASIC CARDS
*ROOKIES 331-440: 4X TO 10X BASIC CARDS
BLACK/53 STATED ODDS 1:62
241 James Harrison 25.00 60.00

2008 Topps Gold Border

*VETS 1-330: 3X TO 8X BASIC CARDS
*ROOKIES 331-440: 1.2X TO 3X BASIC CARDS
GOLD BORDER/2008 ODDS 1:7H, 1:8R

2008 Topps Gold Foil

ETS 1-330: 1.5X TO 4X BASIC CARDS
*ROOKIES 331-440: .6X TO 1.5X BASIC CARDS

2008 Topps Platinum

UNPRICED PLATINUM 1/1 ODDS 1:12,000H

2008 Topps All-Stars

MPLETE SET (12) 4.00 6.00
1 Peyton Manning .75 2.00
2 Randy Moss .25 .60
3 Devin Hester .25 .60
4 Brett Favre .60 1.50
5 Adrian Peterson .30 .75
6 Ben Roethlisberger .30 .75
7 Tom Brady 1.00 2.50
8 Derek Anderson .20 .50
9 LaDainian Tomlinson .30 .75
10 Darren McFadden .20 .50
11 Tony Romo .25 .60
12 Eli Manning .25 .60

2008 Topps Brett Favre Collection

MMON CARD 1.25 3.00
STATED ODDS 1:6 H/R

2008 Topps Brett Favre Collection Autographs

MMON CARD 100.00 200.00
FAVRE AU/13-32 ODDS 1:38,173

2008 Topps Dynasties

ATED ODDS 1:4 H/R
DYNAV Adam Vinatieri .60 1.50
DYNBB Bill Bates .60 1.50
DYNBJ Brent Jones .75 2.00
DYNCH Charles Haley 1.00 2.50
DYNDB Deion Branch .60 1.50
DYNDC Dwight Clark .75 2.00
DYNDS Deion Sanders 1.00 2.50
DYNDSH Donnie Shell .75 2.00
DYNDWH Dwight White .75 2.00
DYNES Emmitt Smith 1.50 4.00
DYNES2 Emmitt Smith 1.50 4.00
DYNFH Franco Harris 1.00 2.50
DYNFH2 Franco Harris 1.00 2.50
DYNJG Joe Greene 1.00 2.50
DYNJM Joe Montana 3.00 8.00
DYNJM2 Joe Montana 3.00 8.00
DYNJM3 Joe Montana 3.00 8.00
DYNJN Jay Novacek .75 2.00
DYNJR Jerry Rice 2.00 5.00
DYNJR2 Jerry Rice 2.00 5.00
DYNJT John Taylor .75 2.00
DYNKT Keena Turner .60 1.50
DYNLG L.C. Greenwood .75 2.00
DYNLL Leon Lett .60 1.50
DYNLM Lawyer Milloy .60 1.50
DYNMB Mel Blount .75 2.00
DYNRB Rocky Bleier .75 2.00
DYNRC Randy Cross .75 2.00
DYNRCR Roger Craig .75 2.00
DYNRL Ronnie Lott .75 2.00
DYNTA Troy Aikman 1.25 3.00
DYNTA2 Troy Aikman 1.25 3.00
DYNTB Tom Brady 3.00 8.00
DYNTB2 Tom Brady 3.00 8.00
DYNTBR Terry Bradshaw 1.25 3.00
DYNTBR2 Terry Bradshaw 1.25 3.00
DYNTJ Ted Johnson .60 1.50
DYNTL Ty Law .60 1.50
DYNTR Tom Rathman .75 2.00

2008 Topps Dynasties Autographs

GROUP A/25-100 ODDS 1:6482H, 1:20,734R
GROUP B/200 ODDS 1:9200 H, 1:28,754 R
GROUP C/500 ODDS 1:2350 H, 1:10,200 R
DYNARL Ronnie Lott/50 30.00 60.00
DYNAAV Adam Vinatieri/100 40.00 80.00
DYNABB Bill Bates/500 8.00 20.00
DYNABJ Brent Jones/200 8.00 20.00
DYNACH Charles Haley/200 10.00 25.00
DYNADB Deion Branch/100 12.50 30.00
DYNADC Dwight Clark/100 20.00 40.00
DYNADS Deion Sanders/25 60.00 120.00
DYNADSH Donnie Shell/500 12.50 30.00
DYNADWH Dwight White/100 35.00 60.00
DYNAES Emmitt Smith/25 100.00 200.00
DYNAES2 Emmitt Smith/25 100.00 200.00
DYNAFH Franco Harris/25 50.00 100.00
DYNAFH2 Franco Harris/25 50.00 100.00
DYNAJG Joe Greene/50 20.00 50.00
DYNAJM Joe Montana/25 90.00 175.00
DYNAJM2 Joe Montana/25 90.00 175.00
DYNAJM3 Joe Montana/25 90.00 175.00
DYNAJN Jay Novacek/100 20.00 40.00
DYNAJR Jerry Rice/25 125.00 200.00
DYNAJR2 Jerry Rice/25 125.00 200.00
DYNAJT John Taylor/200 10.00 25.00
DYNAKT Keena Turner/500 10.00 25.00
DYNALG L.C. Greenwood/100 20.00 40.00
DYNALL Leon Lett/100 12.50 30.00
DYNALM Lawyer Milloy/500 6.00 15.00
DYNARB Rocky Bleier/200 15.00 40.00
DYNARC Randy Cross/100 10.00 25.00
DYNARCR Roger Craig/50 30.00 60.00
DYNATA Troy Aikman/25 60.00 120.00
DYNATA2 Troy Aikman/25 60.00 120.00
DYNATB Tom Brady/25 150.00 300.00
DYNATB2 Tom Brady/25 150.00 300.00
DYNATBR Terry Bradshaw/25 90.00 175.00
DYNATBR2 Terry Bradshaw/25 90.00 175.00
DYNATL Ty Law/200 12.00 30.00
DYNATR Tom Rathman/500 10.00 25.00

2008 Topps Dynasties Jerseys

NASTIES JSY/99 ODDS 1:2428
JM Joe Montana 15.00 40.00
SY Steve Young 15.00 40.00
TA Troy Aikman 15.00 40.00
TB Terry Bradshaw 15.00 40.00
TBR Tom Brady 10.00 25.00

2008 Topps Dynasties Jerseys Autographs

Y AUTO/25 ODDS 1:180,000
JM Joe Montana
SY Steve Young
TA Troy Aikman 75.00 150.00
TB Terry Bradshaw 100.00 200.00
TBR Tom Brady 175.00 300.00

2008 Topps Factory Set Rookie Bonus

COMP.HOBBY SET (5) 3.00 8.00
COMP.RETAIL SET (5) 3.00 8.00
COMP.COWBOY SET (5) 5.00 12.00
COMP.GIANTS SET (5) 3.00 8.00
COMP.PACKER SET (5) 3.00 8.00
COMP.PATRIOT SET (5) 3.00 8.00
H1 Marcus Smith .60 1.50
H2 Marcus Henry .50 1.25
H3 Ryan Torain .60 1.50
H4 Chauncey Washington .60 1.50
H5 Darius Reynaud .50 1.25
R1 Kyle Wright .50 1.25
R2 Adrian Arrington .50 1.25
R2 DJ Hall .50 1.25
R4 Lance Leggett .75 2.00
R5 Marcus Monk .60 1.50
DC1 Orlando Scandrick .50 1.25
DC2 Erik Walden .50 1.25
DC3 Danny Amendola 4.00 10.00
DC4 Mark Bradford .50 1.25
DC5 Keon Lattimore .60 1.50
GBP1 Jeremy Thompson .50 1.25
GBP2 Josh Sitton .75 2.00
GBP3 Breno Giacomini .50 1.25
GBP4 Brett Swain .50 1.25
GBP5 Kregg Lumpkin .75 2.00
NEP1 Jonathan Wilhite .50 1.25
NEP2 Matt Slater .75 2.00
NEP3 Bo Ruud .60 1.50
NEP4 Mark Dillard .50 1.25
NEP5 Casey Tyler .50 1.25
NYG1 Bryan Kehl .50 1.25
NYG2 Robert Henderson .50 1.25
NYG3 DJ Hall .50 1.25
NYG4 Taurean Rhetta .50 1.25
NYG5 Willie Copeland .50 1.25

2008 Topps Game Breakers Super Bowl Pylons

PYLON/50 ODDS 1:4040
GBDT David Tyree UER 20.00 40.00
GBEM Eli Manning UER 40.00 80.00
GBLM Laurence Maroney UER 12.50 30.00
GBPB Plaxico Burress UER 30.00 60.00
GBRM Randy Moss UER 20.00 50.00
GBTB Tom Brady UER 40.00 80.00

2008 Topps Hall of Fame Class of 2008

MPLETE SET (6) 4.00 10.00
STATED ODDS 1:12 H/R
HOFAM Art Monk 1.00 2.50
HOFAT Andre Tippett .75 2.00
HOFDG Darrell Green 1.00 2.50
HOFET Emmitt Thomas .75 2.00
HOFFD Fred Dean .75 2.00
HOFGZ Gary Zimmerman .75 2.00

2008 Topps Hall of Fame Autographs

STATED ODDS 1:31,068
HOFAAM Art Monk 150.00 300.00
HOFAAT Andre Tippett 75.00 200.00
HOFADD Fred Dean 60.00 150.00
HOFADG Darrell Green 60.00 150.00
HOFAET Emmitt Thomas 125.00 250.00
HOFAGZ Gary Zimmerman 125.00 250.00

2008 Topps League Leaders Relics

GROUP A ODDS 1:298
GROUP B ODDS 1:248
LLRAC Antonio Cromartie B 3.00 8.00
LLRAP Adrian Peterson A 10.00 25.00
LLRDB Drew Brees A 3.00 8.00
LLRJA Jared Allen B 2.00 5.00
LLRLT LaDainian Tomlinson Yds A 3.00 8.00
LLRLT2 LaDainian Tomlinson TDs A 3.00 8.00
LLRPW Patrick Willis B 3.00 8.00
LLRRW Reggie Wayne A 3.00 8.00
LLRTB Tom Brady A 6.00 15.00
LLRTB2 Tom Brady A 6.00 15.00
LLRTR Tony Romo A 8.00 20.00
LLRWW Wes Welker B 4.00 10.00

2008 Topps Armed Forces Fans of the Game

MPLETE SET (11) 3.00 8.00
STATED ODDS 1:6 H/R
AFFJL TBD .40 1.00
AFFMM TBD .40 1.00
AFFSR TBD .40 1.00
AFFMH TBD .40 1.00
AFFPL TBD .40 1.00
AFFRL TBD .40 1.00
AFFGB TBD .40 1.00
AFFCA TBD .40 1.00
AFFTW TBD .40 1.00
AFFJC TBD .40 1.00
AFFWT TBD .40 1.00

2008 Topps Honor Roll

MPLETE SET (9) 4.00 10.00
STATED ODDS 1:9 H/R
HRAD Art Donovan .60 1.50
HRCB Chuck Bednarik .75 2.00
HRGM Gino Marchetti .60 1.50
HRJM Johnny Blood McNally .60 1.50
HRLG Lou Groza .75 2.00
HRNB Norm Van Brocklin .75 2.00
HRRB Rocky Bleier .75 2.00
HRRS Roger Staubach 1.25 3.00
HRTF Tom Fears .60 1.50

2008 Topps Honor Roll Relic Patches

STATED ODDS 1:186
AD 101st Airborne Division 10.00 25.00
BA Blue Angels 10.00 25.00
CA 1st Cavalry 10.00 25.00
FF F-16 Fighting Falcon 10.00 25.00
IF Operation Iraqi Freedom Patch 10.00 25.00
MC Marines Eagle, Globe and Anchor 10.00 25.00
MR 7th Marine Regiment 10.00 25.00
MS Spade 10.00 25.00
NE 158th Fighter Wing 10.00 25.00
NI US Naval Intelligence 10.00 25.00
NS The Only Easy Day Was Yesterday 10.00 25.00
SO 82nd Airborne Division 10.00 25.00
TB Thunderbirds 10.00 25.00

2008 Topps Honor Roll Mini Medals

ATED ODDS 1:2715
HRRAD Art Donovan 20.00 50.00
HRRCB Chuck Bednarik 20.00 50.00
HRRGM Gino Marchetti 20.00 50.00
HRRJM Johnny Blood McNally 20.00 50.00
HRRLG Lou Groza 20.00 50.00
HRRNB Norm Van Brocklin 20.00 50.00
HRRRB Rocky Bleier 60.00 120.00
HRRRB2 Rocky Bleier 60.00 120.00
HRRRS Roger Staubach 75.00 150.00
HRRTF Tom Fears 20.00 50.00

2008 Topps Own The Game

COMPLETE SET (30) 10.00 25.00
STATED ODDS 1:9 H/R
OTGAC Antonio Cromartie .60 1.50
OTGAP Adrian Peterson 1.00 2.50
OTGAP2 Adrian Peterson 1.00 2.50
OTGBE Braylon Edwards .60 1.50
OTGBR Ben Roethlisberger 1.00 2.50
OTGBW Brian Westbrook .60 1.50
OTGCJ Chad Johnson .60 1.50
OTGDB Drew Brees 1.00 2.50
OTGDH Devin Hester .75 2.00
OTGDW D.J. Williams .60 1.50
OTGER Ed Reed .75 2.00
OTGJA Joseph Addai .60 1.50
OTGJAL Jared Allen .60 1.50
OTGJB Jon Beason .60 1.50
OTGLT LaDainian Tomlinson 1.00 2.50
OTGLT2 LaDainian Tomlinson 1.00 2.50
OTGLW Leon Washington .60 1.50
OTGMW Mario Williams .75 2.00
OTGOA O.J. Atogwe .60 1.50
OTGPK Patrick Kerney .60 1.50
OTGPW Patrick Willis .75 2.00
OTGRB Rob Bironas .60 1.50
OTGRM Randy Moss .75 2.00
OTGRM2 Randy Moss .75 2.00
OTGRW Reggie Wayne .75 2.00
OTGTB Tom Brady 3.00 8.00
OTGTB2 Tom Brady 3.00 8.00
OTGTO Terrell Owens .75 2.00
OTGTR Tony Romo .75 2.00
OTGTR2 Tony Romo .75 2.00

2008 Topps Performance Highlights Autographs

OUP A ODDS 1:7500 H, 1:23,090 R
GROUP B ODDS 1:4200 H, 1:13,500 R
GROUP C ODDS 1:4600 H, 1:14,500 R
GROUP D ODDS 1:482 H, 1:1165 R
THAAA Adrian Arrington 2.50 6.00
THAAC Andre Caldwell 2.50 6.00
THAAM Anthony Morelli 4.00 10.00
THAAP Allen Patrick 2.50 6.00
THAAW Andre Woodson 4.00 10.00
THABB Brian Brohm 6.00 15.00
THABF Brett Favre 150.00 250.00
THACH Chad Henne 4.00 10.00
THADA Derek Anderson 15.00 30.00
THADB Drew Brees 30.00 60.00
THADF De'Cody Fagg 3.00 8.00
THADJ DeSean Jackson 6.00 15.00
THADM Darren McFadden 15.00 40.00
THAFJ Felix Jones 4.00 10.00
THAHD Harry Douglas 3.00 8.00
THAJC Jamaal Charles 5.00 12.00
THAJF Joe Flacco 20.00 50.00
THAJS Jonathan Stewart 6.00 15.00
THAKB Keenan Burton 2.50 6.00
THAKW Kellen Winslow 10.00 25.00
THALL Lance Leggett 4.00 10.00
THALS Limas Sweed 10.00 25.00
THAMB Marion Barber 20.00 40.00
THAMF Matt Forte 12.00 30.00
THAMG Marcus Griffin 3.00 8.00
THAMK Malcolm Kelly 3.00 8.00
THAML Marshawn Lynch 20.00 40.00
THAMM Mario Manningham 3.00 8.00
THAMMO Marcus Monk 3.00 8.00
THAMR Matt Ryan 20.00 50.00
THAPM Peyton Manning 75.00 150.00
THAPW Patrick Willis 10.00 25.00
THARM Rashard Mendenhall 4.00 10.00
THARR Ray Rice 3.00 8.00
THAWW Wes Welker 20.00 40.00

2008 Topps Performance Highlights Relics

THRAG Antonio Gates A 3.00 8.00
THRBF Brett Favre A 8.00 20.00
THRBJ Brandon Jacobs B 2.50 6.00
THRDB Drew Brees A 4.00 10.00
THRDH Devin Hester B 3.00 8.00
THRML Marshawn Lynch B 3.00 8.00
THRPW Patrick Willis B 3.00 8.00
THRTH T.J. Houshmandzadeh B 2.50 6.00

2008 Topps Pro Bowl Jerseys

STATED ODDS 1:99
*PATCH/99: .6X TO 1.5X BASIC JSYs
PATCH/99 STATED ODDS 1:1214
UNPRICED IN THE NAME PRINT RUN 1
APRAP Adrian Peterson 5.00 12.00
APRBE Braylon Edwards 3.00 8.00
APRDH Devin Hester 4.00 10.00
APRJA Joseph Addai 3.00 8.00
APRLF Larry Fitzgerald 4.00 10.00
APRMB Marion Barber 3.00 8.00
APRPM Peyton Manning 12.00 30.00
APRRW Reggie Wayne 4.00 10.00
APRTO Terrell Owens 4.00 10.00
APRTR Tony Romo 4.00 10.00

2008 Topps Red Hot Rookies

RANDOM INSERTS IN WAL-MART PACKS
1 Matt Ryan 2.00 5.00
2 Joe Flacco 1.25 3.00
3 Brian Brohm .60 1.50
4 Chad Henne .75 2.00
5 Darren McFadden .60 1.50
6 Jonathan Stewart 1.00 2.50
7 Felix Jones .60 1.50
8 Rashard Mendenhall .60 1.50
9 Chris Johnson .75 2.00
10 Ray Rice .60 1.50
11 Donnie Avery .75 2.00
12 Devin Thomas .60 1.50
13 DeSean Jackson 1.25 3.00
14 Malcolm Kelly .60 1.50
15 Limas Sweed .60 1.50

2008 Topps Retail Game Jerseys

ONE PER SPECIAL RETAIL BOX
AC Antonio Cromartie 2.50 6.00
ACA Andre Caldwell 2.50 6.00
AF Alan Faneca 3.00 8.00
AG Andre Gurode 2.50 6.00
AGO Anthony Gonzalez 2.50 6.00
AJ Andre Johnson 3.00 8.00
AK Aaron Kampman 4.00 10.00
BA Brendon Ayanbadejo 2.50 6.00
BM Brian Moorman 2.50 6.00
BR Ben Roethlisberger 4.00 10.00
BW Brian Waters 2.50 6.00
CB Champ Bailey 3.00 8.00
CB2 Champ Bailey 3.00 8.00
CH Casey Hampton 2.50 6.00
CJ Chris Johnson 2.00 5.00
CP Chad Pennington 2.50 6.00
CS Chris Samuels 2.50 6.00
CS2 Chris Samuels 2.50 6.00
DBO Dwayne Bowe 3.00 8.00
DB Derrick Burgess 2.50 6.00
DJ Dwayne Jarrett 3.00 8.00
DK Dustin Keller 3.00 8.00
DM Derrick Mason 2.50 6.00
DT Devin Thomas 1.50 4.00
DW DeMarcus Ware 3.00 8.00
ED Early Doucet 1.50 4.00
FA Flozell Adams 2.50 6.00
GO Greg Olsen 3.00 8.00
HM Hank Milligan 2.50 6.00
JB John Beck 2.50 6.00
JC Josh Cribbs 5.00 12.00
JD Jake Delhomme 2.50 6.00
JDB John David Booty 1.50 4.00
JL J.P. Losman 2.50 6.00
JN Jordy Nelson 5.00 12.00
JT Joe Thomas 3.00 8.00
JW Jamal Williams 2.50 6.00
JW2 Jason Witten 3.00 8.00
KC Kellen Clemens 2.50 6.00
KD Kris Dielman 2.50 6.00
KK Kevin Kolb 2.50 6.00
KS Kevin Smith 1.50 4.00
KV Kyle Vanden Bosch 2.50 6.00
KW Kevin Williams 2.50 6.00
LA Larry Allen 4.00 10.00
LB LeCharles Bentley 2.50 6.00
LBO Lorenzo Booker 2.50 6.00
LD Leonard Davis 2.50 6.00
LJ LaMont Jordan 3.00 8.00
LN Lorenzo Neal 2.50 6.00
LS Limas Sweed 1.50 4.00
LT Lofa Tatupu 2.50 6.00
MB Matt Birk 2.50 6.00
MH Matt Hasselbeck 2.50 6.00
MK Malcolm Kelly 1.50 4.00
ML Marshawn Lynch 3.00 8.00
MMA Mario Manningham 1.50 4.00
MM2 Marcus McNeill 2.50 6.00
MS Marcus Stroud 2.50 6.00
MW Mike Wahle 2.50 6.00
OP Orlando Pace 2.50 6.00
OU Osi Umenyiora 2.50 6.00
PWIL Patrick Willis 3.00 8.00
PWI Paul Williams 2.50 6.00
PW Pat Williams 2.50 6.00
RJ Rudi Johnson 2.50 6.00
RR Ray Rice 1.50 4.00
RW1 Roy Williams S wht 2.50 6.00
RW2 Roy Williams S PB 2.50 6.00
SM Shawne Merriman 2.50 6.00
SM2 Shawne Merriman PB 2.50 6.00
SS Steve Slaton 1.50 4.00
SS Steve Smith USC 3.00 8.00
TE Trent Edwards 2.50 6.00
TGI Ted Ginn 2.50 6.00
TGL Tarik Glenn 2.50 6.00
TG Tony Gonzalez in hat 3.00 8.00
TGO Tony Gonzalez in helmet 3.00 8.00
TH Tony Hunt 3.00 8.00
TP Troy Polamalu 6.00 15.00
TR Tony Romo 3.00 8.00
TS Terrell Suggs 2.50 6.00
TSM Troy Smith 3.00 8.00
VD Vernon Davis 2.50 6.00
WA Willie Anderson 2.50 6.00
WJ Walter Jones 2.50 6.00
WJ2 Walter Jones PB 2.50 6.00

2008 Topps Retro Rookies

STATED ODDS 1:4 RETAIL
*COLOR/50: 1X TO 2.5X BASIC INSERTS
COLOR/50 ODDS 1:835 RETAIL
*SEPIA/199: .6X TO 1.5X BASIC INSERTS
SEPIA/199 ODDS 1:210 RETAIL
1 Matt Ryan 2.00 5.00
2 Joe Flacco 1.25 3.00
3 Brian Brohm .60 1.50
4 Chad Henne .75 2.00
5 Darren McFadden .60 1.50
6 Jonathan Stewart 1.00 2.50
7 Felix Jones .60 1.50
8 Rashard Mendenhall .60 1.50
9 Chris Johnson .75 2.00
10 Ray Rice .60 1.50
11 Donnie Avery .75 2.00
12 Devin Thomas .60 1.50
13 DeSean Jackson 1.25 3.00
14 Malcolm Kelly .60 1.50
15 Limas Sweed .60 1.50

2008 Topps Rookie Premiere Autographs

RED INK TOO SCARCE TO PRICE
RPAAW Andre Woodson 10.00 25.00
RPABB Brian Brohm 10.00 25.00
RPACH Chad Henne 12.00 30.00
RPACJ Chris Johnson 12.00 30.00
RPADA Donnie Avery 12.00 30.00
RPADD Dennis Dixon 10.00 25.00
RPADJ DeSean Jackson 15.00 40.00
RPADJA Dexter Jackson 15.00 40.00
RPADK Dustin Keller 12.00 30.00
RPADM Darren McFadden 15.00 40.00
RPADT Devin Thomas 10.00 25.00
RPAEB Earl Bennett 15.00 40.00
RPAED Early Doucet 10.00 25.00
RPAER Eddie Royal 10.00 25.00
RPAFJ Felix Jones 10.00 25.00
RPAHD Harry Douglas 12.00 30.00
RPAJB John David Booty 10.00 25.00
RPAJC Jamaal Charles 15.00 40.00
RPAJF Joe Flacco 20.00 50.00
RPAJH James Hardy 10.00 25.00
RPAJL Jake Long 15.00 40.00
RPAJN Jordy Nelson 15.00 40.00
RPAJS Jonathan Stewart 15.00 40.00
RPAJSI Jerome Simpson 12.00 30.00
RPAKO Kevin O'Connell 10.00 25.00
RPAKS Kevin Smith 10.00 25.00
RPALS Limas Sweed 10.00 25.00
RPAMF Matt Forte 15.00 40.00
RPAMK Malcolm Kelly 10.00 25.00
RPAMM Mario Manningham 10.00 25.00
RPAMR Matt Ryan 30.00 80.00
RPARM Rashard Mendenhall 10.00 25.00
RPARR Ray Rice 10.00 25.00
RPASS Steve Slaton 10.00 25.00

2008 Topps Rookie Premiere Autographs Dual

RED INK TOO SCARCE TO PRICE
FR J.Flacco/R.Rice 25.00 60.00
MJ D.McFadden/F.Jones 25.00 80.00
RB M.Ryan/B.Brohm 30.00 80.00
RM M.Ryan/D.McFadden 75.00 150.00
SM J.Stewart/R.Mendenhall 25.00 60.00

2008 Topps Rookie Premiere Autographs Quads

RED INK TOO SCARCE TO PRICE
JMTK Jksn/Mnghm/Thms/Klly 6.00 15.00
JRCS Jhnsn/Rce/Chrls/Sltn 60.00 150.00
MSJM McFad/Stwrt/Jns/Mndn 50.00 100.00
RFBH Ryan/Flac/Brhm/Hnne 60.00 125.00
RFMS Ryan/Flac/McFad/Stwrt 60.00 125.00

2008 Topps Rookie Premiere Jersey

GROUP A ODDS 1:247 BOW.HOB
GROUP B ODDS 1:520 BOW.HOB
GROUP C ODDS 1:371 BOW.HOB
GROUP D ODDS 1:325 BOW.HOB
*CHR.PATCH/25: .8X TO 2X BASIC JSY
CHROME PATCH/25 ODDS 1:2320 BOW.CHR
RPRBB Brian Brohm A 2.00 5.00
RPRCH Chad Henne C 2.50 6.00
RPRDA Donnie Avery C 2.50 6.00
RPRDM Darren McFadden A 2.00 5.00
RPRFJ Felix Jones B 2.00 5.00
RPRJF Joe Flacco C 4.00 10.00
RPRJH James Hardy C 2.00 5.00
RPRJS Jonathan Stewart A 6.00 15.00
RPRLS Limas Sweed A 2.00 5.00
RPRMK Malcolm Kelly A 2.00 5.00
RPRMR Matt Ryan A 10.00 25.00
RPRRM Rashard Mendenhall A 2.00 5.00
RPRRR Ray Rice B 2.00 5.00

2008 Topps Rookie Premiere Jersey Autographs

JSY AU/25 ODDS 1:2950 BOW, 1:5000 BOW.CHR
UNPRICED REFRAC/10 ODDS 1:2750 BOW.CHR
RPARBB Brian Brohm
RPARCH Chad Henne 8.00 20.00
RPARDA Donnie Avery
RPARDM Darren McFadden 6.00 15.00
RPARFJ Felix Jones
RPARJF Joe Flacco 50.00 100.00
RPARJH James Hardy
RPARJS Jonathan Stewart
RPARLS Limas Sweed
RPARMK Malcolm Kelly
RPARMR Matt Ryan 100.00 200.00
RPARRM Rashard Mendenhall 6.00 15.00
RPARRR Ray Rice 6.00 15.00

2008 Topps Signature Series

AUTO/50 ODDS 1:60,622 TOPPS
SSAP Adrian Peterson 60.00 120.00
SSBB Brian Brohm
SSBE Braylon Edwards 40.00 80.00
SSBS Bart Starr 100.00 175.00
SSDA Derek Anderson 30.00 60.00
SSDB Dwayne Bowe 30.00 60.00
SSDBR Drew Brees 40.00 80.00
SSDM Dan Marino 90.00 150.00
SSDMC Darren McFadden 6.00 15.00
SSEM Eli Manning 60.00 120.00
SSES Emmitt Smith 90.00 150.00
SSJB Jim Brown 60.00 120.00
SSJM Joe Montana 90.00 150.00
SSJR Jerry Rice 90.00 150.00
SSLT LaDainian Tomlinson 50.00 100.00
SSML Marshawn Lynch 40.00 80.00
SSMR Matt Ryan 100.00 175.00
SSPM Peyton Manning 90.00 150.00
SSRW Reggie Wayne 40.00 80.00
SSSJ Steven Jackson 40.00 80.00
SSTD Tony Dorsett 50.00 100.00
SSTT Thurman Thomas 40.00 80.00
SSTY Y.A. Tittle 40.00 80.00
SSVY Vince Young 40.00 80.00
SSWP Willie Parker 50.00 100.00

2008 Topps Stat Breakers Super Bowl Footballs

FB/40 ODDS 1:5400
SBAB Ahmad Bradshaw UER 20.00 40.00
SBEM Eli Manning UER 40.00 100.00
SBJT Justin Tuck UER 25.00 50.00
SBPB Plaxico Burress UER 25.00 50.00
SBTB Tom Brady UER 40.00 80.00
SBWW Wes Welker UER 30.00 60.00

2008 Topps Super Bowl XLII Card Show

MPLETE SET (16) 12.50 25.00
MAROON BORDER PRINT RUN 1000
*BLACK BORDER/199: .8X TO 2X
1 Tom Brady 2.00 5.00
2 Brett Favre 1.25 3.00
3 Tony Romo .50 1.25
4 Peyton Manning 1.50 4.00
5 Vince Young .40 1.00
6 Willie Parker .50 1.25
7 Larry Fitzgerald .50 1.25
8 Willis McGahee .40 1.00
9 Frank Gore .50 1.25
10 Adrian Peterson .60 1.50
11 LaDainian Tomlinson .60 1.50
12 Randy Moss .50 1.25
13 Chad Johnson .40 1.00
14 Plaxico Burress .40 1.00
15 Calvin Johnson .60 1.50
16 Dwayne Bowe .50 1.25

2008 Topps Super Bowl XLII Card Show Promos

COMPLETE SET (6) 5.00 10.00
MAROON BORDER PRINT RUN 1000
*BLACK BORDER/199: .8X TO 2X
1 Tom Brady 2.00 5.00
2 Peyton Manning 1.50 4.00
3 Adrian Peterson .60 1.50
4 LaDainian Tomlinson .60 1.50
5 Tony Romo .50 1.25
6 Randy Moss .50 1.25

2008 Topps Tom Brady Tribute

COMPLETE SET (16) 10.00 25.00
COMMON CARD (TB1-TB16) .75 2.00
RANDOM INSERTS IN TARGET PACKS

2008 Topps Topps Chrome Gold Refractor Inserts

Brett Favre 6.00 15.00
298 Adrian Peterson 2.00 5.00
346 Darren McFadden 4.00 10.00

2008 Topps Turn Back the Clock

CK P ODDS 1:9 HOB/RET
P ISSUED IN PACKS, S ISSUED AT SHOPS
1 Matt Ryan S .60 1.50
2 Rashard Mendenhall S .20 .50
3 Eli Manning S .40 1.00
4 Tony Romo S .40 1.00
5 Eric Dickerson S .50 1.25
6 Felix Jones S .20 .50
7 Malcolm Kelly P .30 .75
8 Brian Westbrook S .30 .75
9 Tom Brady P 2.50 6.00
10 Barry Sanders S 1.00 2.50
11 Dan Marino P 2.00 5.00
12 Brian Brohm S .20 .50
13 Darren McFadden P .30 .75
14 Ben Roethlisberger S .50 1.25
15 Adrian Peterson P .75 2.00
16 Tony Dorsett S .60 1.50
17 Gale Sayers P 1.00 2.50
18 Jonathan Stewart S .30 .75
19 Joe Flacco P .60 1.50
24 DeSean Jackson S .40 1.00
21 Randy Moss P .60 1.50
22 John Elway S 1.00 2.50
23 Terry Bradshaw P 1.25 3.00
20 LaDainian Tomlinson S .50 1.25

25 Ray Rice P .30 .75
26 Peyton Manning S 1.25 3.00
27 Willie Parker P .60 1.50
28 Troy Aikman S .75 2.00
29 Vince Lombardi P 1.50 4.00
30 Limas Sweed S .20 .50
31 Drew Brees P .75 2.00
32 Jamal Lewis S .40 1.00
33 Brett Favre P 1.50 4.00
34 Emmitt Smith S 1.00 2.50
35 Carson Palmer P .60 1.50
36 Reggie Wayne S .40 1.00
37 Joe Namath P 1.25 3.00
38 Chad Johnson S .30 .75
39 Larry Fitzgerald P .60 1.50
40 Terrell Owens P .60 1.50

2009 Topps

COMPLETE SET (440) 25.00 50.00
COMP.FACT.SET (445) 40.00 80.00
BASE SP ODDS 1:410 HOB
HOLMES RH ODDS 1:36
HOLMES RH AUTO ODDS 1:61,000
1 Hines Ward .20 .50
2 Ryan Torain .15 .40
3 Harry Douglas .15 .40
4 James Jones .15 .40
5 Willis McGahee .15 .40
6 Owen Daniels .15 .40
7 Peyton Hillis .20 .50
8 Hank Baskett .15 .40
9 Leonard Davis .15 .40
10 Peyton Manning .60 1.50
11 Shawne Merriman .15 .40
12 Laurence Maroney .20 .50
13 Chris Hope .15 .40
14 Joe Thomas .20 .50
15 Marshawn Lynch .20 .50
16 Kevin Williams .15 .40
17 London Fletcher .20 .50
18 Jason Campbell .15 .40
19 Antonio Bryant .15 .40
20 LaDainian Tomlinson .25 .60
21 Marc Bulger .15 .40
22 Vernon Davis .15 .40
23 Justin Tuck .15 .40
24 Deuce McAllister .20 .50
25 T.J. Houshmandzadeh .15 .40
26 Bernard Berrian .15 .40
27 Ryan Grant .20 .50
28 Tashard Choice .15 .40
29 Michael Jenkins .15 .40
30 Brian Dawkins .15 .40
31 Michael Turner .15 .40
32 Anquan Boldin .15 .40
33 Justin Gage .15 .40
34 Michael Bush .15 .40
35 Braylon Edwards .15 .40
36 Rashard Mendenhall .15 .40
37 Leon Washington .15 .40
38 Ricky Williams .20 .50
39 Rashean Mathis .15 .40
40 Ray Lewis .25 .60
41 Josh Cribbs .15 .40
42 James Hardy .20 .50
43 Joe Flacco .20 .50
44 Terrell Suggs .15 .40
45 Jay Cutler .15 .40
46 Glenn Holt .15 .40
47 D.J. Williams .15 .40
48 Andre Davis .15 .40
49 Dwayne Bowe .20 .50
50 DeAngelo Williams .15 .40
51 Wes Welker .20 .50
52 Willie Parker .15 .40
53 Dominique Rodgers-Cromartie .15 .40
54A Tony Romo .20 .50
54B Tony Romo SP golf 15.00 40.00
55 Steve Slaton .15 .40
56 Jason Witten .20 .50
57 Terence Newman .15 .40
58 Jeff Garcia .15 .40
59 Barrett Ruud .15 .40
60 Andre Johnson .20 .50
61 Jordy Nelson .20 .50
62 Davone Bess .15 .40
63 Jacob Hester .15 .40
64 Jason Avant .15 .40
65 Joseph Addai .15 .40
66 Dennis Northcutt .15 .40
67 Maurice Morris .15 .40
68 Shaun Hill .15 .40
69 Dustin Keller .15 .40
70 Antonio Gates .20 .50
71 BenJarvus Green-Ellis RC 1.25 3.00
72 Brent Celek .15 .40
73 Ray Rice .15 .40
74 Vince Young .15 .40
75 Maurice Jones-Drew .15 .40
76 Devery Henderson .15 .40
77 Domenik Hixon .15 .40
78 Mike Walker .20 .50
79 Miles Austin .15 .40
80 DeMarcus Ware .20 .50
81 Jordan Gross .15 .40
82 Chris Samuels .20 .50
83 Jay Ratliff .25 .60
84 Pat Williams .15 .40
85 Tony Gonzalez .20 .50
86 Andre Gurode .15 .40
87 Nick Mangold .15 .40
88 Bobby Engram .15 .40
89 Osi Umenyiora .15 .40
90 Brian Westbrook .15 .40
91 Jason Peters .15 .40
92 Shaun Rogers .15 .40
93 Kris Jenkins .15 .40
94 Kevin Mawae .15 .40
95 Ronnie Brown .15 .40
96 Joey Galloway .20 .50
97 Chris Snee .15 .40
98 Nick Collins .15 .40
99 Adrian Wilson .15 .40
100 Reggie Wayne .20 .50
101 Kellen Clemens .15 .40
102 LaRon Landry .15 .40
103 Walter Jones .15 .40
104 Josh Morgan .15 .40
105 Joey Porter .20 .50
106 Martellus Bennett .15 .40
107 Kirk Morrison .15 .40
108 Bradie James .15 .40
109 Le'Ron McClain .20 .50
110A Adrian Peterson .25 .60
110B A.Peterson SP Red Shirt 25.00 50.00
111 Trent Edwards .15 .40
112 Carson Palmer .20 .50
113 Jamal Lewis .20 .50
114 Champ Bailey .20 .50
115A Tom Brady .75 2.00
115B T.Brady SP No helm 40.00 80.00
116 Dominic Rhodes .15 .40
117 David Garrard .15 .40
118 Jamaal Charles .20 .50
119 Fred Taylor .15 .40
120 Matt Leinart .15 .40
121 Ted Ginn .15 .40
122 Sammy Morris .15 .40
123 Jerricho Cotchery .15 .40
124 JaMarcus Russell .15 .40
125 Thomas Jones .15 .40
126 Mewelde Moore .15 .40
127 Philip Rivers .25 .60
128 Antonio Cromartie .15 .40
129 Bo Scaife .15 .40
130 Jonathan Vilma .15 .40
131 Kurt Warner .20 .50
132 Steve Breaston .20 .50
133 Roddy White .15 .40
134 Jake Delhomme .15 .40
135 Darren McFadden .25 .60
136 Muhsin Muhammad .15 .40
137 Greg Olsen .20 .50
138 Felix Jones .15 .40
139 Ernie Sims .15 .40
140 Ed Reed .20 .50
141 Aaron Rodgers .50 1.25
142 Donald Lee .15 .40
143 Visanthe Shiancoe .20 .50
144 Drew Brees .25 .60
145A Ben Roethlisberger .25 .60
145B Roethlisbrger SP Trophy 30.00 60.00
146 Jason David .15 .40
147 Samari Rolle .15 .40
148 Brandon Jacobs .15 .40
149 DeSean Jackson .20 .50
150 Brady Quinn .15 .40
151 Isaac Bruce .25 .60
152 Matt Hasselbeck .15 .40
153 Lofa Tatupu .15 .40
154 Oshiomogho Atogwe .15 .40
155 Troy Polamalu .25 .60
156 Marvin Harrison .20 .50
157 Roscoe Parrish .15 .40
158 Paul Posluszny .15 .40
159 Eli Manning .20 .50
160 Randy Moss .20 .50
161 Earnest Graham .15 .40
162 Derrick Brooks .15 .40
163 Chris Cooley .15 .40
164 Antwaan Randle El .15 .40
165 Santonio Holmes .15 .40
166 Ronde Barber .15 .40
167 Donnie Avery .15 .40
168 Nate Clements .15 .40
169 Kevin Boss .15 .40
170 Jon Beason .15 .40
171 Jeremy Shockey .15 .40
172 Antoine Winfield .15 .40
173 Charles Woodson .25 .60
174 Terrell Owens .20 .50
175 Chris Johnson .15 .40
176 Charles Tillman .20 .50
177 Julius Peppers .20 .50
178 John Abraham .15 .40
179 Karlos Dansby .15 .40
180 Steve Smith USC .20 .50
181 Edgerrin James .20 .50
182 Cortland Finnegan .15 .40
183 Keith Bulluck .15 .40
184 Stephen Cooper RC .20 .50
185 LenDale White .15 .40
186 Vincent Jackson .15 .40
187 LaMarr Woodley .15 .40
188 Nnamdi Asomugha .15 .40
189 Calvin Pace .15 .40
190 Kellen Winslow Jr. .15 .40
191 Brandon Meriweather .15 .40
192 Matt Cassel .15 .40
193 Greg Camarillo .20 .50
194 Jarrad Page .15 .40
195 Tim Hightower .15 .40
196 Larry Johnson .15 .40
197 Matt Jones .20 .50
198 Bob Sanders .20 .50
199 Dwight Freeney .15 40
200 Brandon Marshall .20 .50
201 Mario Williams .20 .50
202 Tony Scheffler .15 .40
203 D'Qwell Jackson .15 .40
204 Keith Rivers .15 .40
205 Larry Fitzgerald .20 .50
206 Chad Ochocinco .15 .40
207 Fred Jackson .20 .50
208 Bart Scott .15 .40
209 Todd Heap .15 .40
210 Clinton Portis .15 .40
211 Santana Moss .20 .50
212 Aqib Talib .15 .40
213 Warrick Dunn .15 .40
214 Torry Holt .20 .50
215 Matt Ryan .20 .50
216 Julius Jones .15 .40
217 Patrick Willis .20 .50
218 Correll Buckhalter .15 .40
219 Derrick Ward .15 .40
220 Steven Jackson .15 .40
221 Pierre Thomas .15 .40
222 Tarvaris Jackson .20 .50
223 Donald Driver .20 .50
224 Devin Hester .20 .50
225 Jonathan Stewart .15 .40
226 Steve Smith .20 .50
227 Jerious Norwood .15 .40
228 Albert Haynesworth .15 .40
229 Darren Sproles .20 .50
230 Frank Gore .20 .50
231 James Harrison .25 .60
232 Zach Miller .15 .40
233 Darrelle Revis .15 .40
234 Richard Seymour .15 .40
235 Matt Forte .15 .40
236 Ellis Hobbs .15 .40
237 Anthony Fasano .15 .40
238 Chad Pennington .15 .40
239 Tyler Thigpen .15 .40
240 Donovan McNabb .20 .50
241 Robert Mathis .15 .40
242 Kevin Walter .20 .50
243 Matt Schaub .15 .40
244 Brandon McDonald .15 .40
245 Marion Barber .20 .50
246 Cedric Benson .15 .40
247 Lee Evans .20 .50
248 Derrick Mason .15 .40
249 Eddie Royal .15 .40
250 Reggie Bush .15 .40
251 Dallas Clark .15 .40
252 Anthony Gonzalez .15 .40
253 Derrick Johnson .15 .40
254 Jerod Mayo .20 .50
255 Kevin Smith .15 .40
256 Laveranues Coles .15 .40
257 Gibril Wilson .15 .40
258 Justin Fargas .15 .40
259 Lance Briggs .20 .50
260 Greg Jennings .15 .40
261 Kyle Orton .15 .40
262 Michael Griffin .15 .40
263 Kerry Collins .15 .40
264 Chris Chambers .15 .40
265 Jared Allen .15 .40
266 Heath Miller .15 .40
267 James Farrior .15 .40
268 John Carlson .20 .50
269 J.T. O'Sullivan .15 .40
270 Calvin Johnson .25 .60
271 Asante Samuel .15 .40
272 Ahmad Bradshaw .15 .40
273 Trent Cole .15 .40
274 Lance Moore .15 .40
275 Marques Colston .15 .40
276 Chester Taylor .15 .40
277 Aaron Kampman .20 .50
278 Derrick Harvey .15 .40
279 Brian Urlacher .25 .60
280 Roy Williams WR .15 .40
281 Drew Brees LL .20 .50
282 Kurt Warner LL .15 .40
283 Jay Cutler LL .12 .30
284 Adrian Peterson LL .20 .50
285 Michael Turner LL .12 .30
286 DeAngelo Williams LL .12 .30
287 Andre Johnson LL .15 .40
288 Larry Fitzgerald LL .15 .40
289 Steve Smith LL .15 .40
290 Drew Brees PB .20 .50
291 Adrian Peterson PB .20 .50
292 Larry Fitzgerald PB .15 .40
293 Anquan Boldin PB .12 .30
294 Steve Smith PB .15 .40
295 Jason Witten PB .15 .40
296 DeMarcus Ware PB .15 .40
297 Jon Beason PB .12 .30
298 James Harrison PB .20 .50
299 Michael Turner PB .12 .30
300 Peyton Manning PB .50 1.25
301 Eli Manning PB .15 .40
302 Thomas Jones PB .12 .30
303 Andre Johnson PB .15 .40
304 Brandon Marshall PB .15 .40
305 Reggie Wayne PB .15 .40
306 Tony Gonzalez PB .15 .40
307 Ray Lewis PB .20 .50
308 Darrelle Revis PB .12 .30
309 Joey Porter PB .15 .40
310 Donovan McNabb PH .15 .40
311 Joe Flacco PH .15 .40
312 Larry Fitzgerald PH .15 .40
313 Darren Sproles PH .15 .40
314 Ed Reed PH .15 .40
315 Kurt Warner PH .15 .40
316 Willie Parker PH .12 .30
317 Asante Samuel PH .12 .30
318 Troy Polamalu PH .20 .50
319 Larry Fitzgerald PH .15 .40
320 Santonio Holmes PH .12 .30
321 Peyton Manning MVP .50 1.25
322 James Harrison D-POY .20 .50
323 Matt Ryan O-ROY .15 .40
324 Jerod Mayo D-ROY .15 .40
325 Jonathan Stewart CC/DeAngelo Williams .12 .30
326 Ed Reed CC/Ray Lewis .20 .50
327 LenDale White CC/Chris Johnson .12 .30
328 Thomas Jones CC/Leon Washington .12 .30
329 Ben Roethlisberger CC/Willie Parker .20 .50
330 DeAngelo Williams LL .12 .30
331 Aaron Brown RC .40 1.00
332 B.J. Raji RC .50 1.25
333 Aaron Maybin RC .50 1.25
334 Alphonso Smith RC .40 1.00
335 Hakeem Nicks RC .50 1.25
336 Andre Smith RC .40 1.00
337 Andy Levitre RC .50 1.25
338 Asher Allen RC .40 1.00
339 Austin Collie RC .40 1.00
340A Aaron Curry RC .60 1.50
340B A.Curry SP FB in hand 15.00 30.00
341 Brandon Gibson RC .50 1.25
342 Michael Oher RC .60 1.50
343 Brandon Tate RC .50 1.25
344 Brandon Underwood RC .40 1.00
345 Javon Ringer RC .40 1.00
346 Brian Hartline RC .60 1.50
347 Brian Orakpo RC .50 1.25
348 Mike Wallace RC .60 1.50
349 Brooks Foster RC .40 1.00
350 Brian Cushing RC .40 1.00
351 Chase Coffman RC .40 1.00
352 Darius Butler RC .50 1.25
353 Clay Matthews RC 1.50 4.00
354 Clint Sintim RC .40 1.00
355 Kenny Britt RC .60 1.50
356 Patrick Turner RC .40 1.00
357 Courtney Greene RC .40 1.00
358 Curtis Painter RC .40 1.00
359 D.J. Moore RC .50 1.25
360 Chris Wells RC .40 1.00
361A Darrius Heyward-Bey RC .60 1.50
361B Heywrd-By SP FB in hands 8.00 20.00
361C D.Heyward-Bey RET .40 1.00
362 Demetrius Byrd RC .50 1.25
363 Deon Butler RC .40 1.00
364 Derrick Williams RC .40 1.00
365 Pat White RC .50 1.25
366 Duke Robinson RC .40 1.00
367 Eben Britton RC .50 1.25
368 Eugene Monroe RC .40 1.00
369 Everette Brown RC .40 1.00
370A Donald Brown RC .40 1.00
370B D.Brown SP No helm 8.00 20.00
370C Donald Brown RET .25 .60
371 Gartrell Johnson RC .40 1.00
372 Glen Coffee RC .40 1.00
373 Andre Brown RC .50 1.25
374 James Casey RC .50 1.25
375A Percy Harvin RC .40 1.00
375B P.Harvin SP No helm 5.00 12.00
375C Percy Harvin RET .25 .60
376 Roy Miller RC .40 1.00
377 Jamon Meredith RC .40 1.00
378 Jared Cook RC .50 1.25
379 Jarett Dillard RC .40 1.00
380A Jeremy Maclin RC .50 1.25
380B J.Maclin SP FB in hand 15.00 40.00
381 Jason Williams RC .50 1.25
382 Javarris Williams RC .50 1.25
383 Cedric Peerman RC .40 1.00
384 Jason Smith RC .40 1.00
385 Fili Moala RC .40 1.00
386 Rey Maualuga RC .60 1.50
387 Travis Beckum RC .40 1.00
388 Juaquin Iglesias RC .40 1.00
389 Connor Barwin RC .50 1.25
390A Knowshon Moreno RC .40 1.00
390B K.Moreno SP Cutting 6.00 15.00
391 Kenny McKinley RC .40 1.00
392 Kevin Ellison RC .40 1.00
393 Larry English RC .50 1.25
394 Marko Mitchell RC .40 1.00
395 Louis Delmas RC .50 1.25
396 Shonn Greene RC .40 1.00
397 Malcolm Jenkins RC .40 1.00
398 Manuel Johnson RC .40 1.00
399 Marcus Freeman RC .40 1.00
400 LeSean McCoy RC 1.00 2.50
401 Zack Follett RC .40 1.00
402 Shawn Nelson RC .40 1.00
403 Rashad Jennings RC .50 1.25
404 Michael Hamlin RC .40 1.00
405 Michael Johnson RC .40 1.00
406 Brandon Pettigrew RC .40 1.00
407 Mike Goodson RC .50 1.25
408 Mike Mickens RC .40 1.00
409 Mike Teel RC .40 1.00
410 Mike Thomas RC .40 1.00
411 Brian Robiskie RC .40 1.00
412 Mohamed Massaquoi RC .40 1.00
413 Nate Davis RC .40 1.00
414 Patrick Chung RC .40 1.00
415 Cornelius Ingram RC .40 1.00
416 James Davis RC .40 1.00
417 Peria Jerry RC .40 1.00
418 Phil Loadholt RC .50 1.25
419 Ramses Barden RC .40 1.00
420A Michael Crabtree RC .60 1.50
420B M.Crabtree SP No helm 20.00 50.00
421 Rashad Johnson RC .40 1.00
422 Johnny Knox RC .50 1.25
423 Rhett Bomar RC .40 1.00
424 Robert Ayers RC .40 1.00
425 James Laurinaitis RC .40 1.00
426 Sammie Stroughter RC .40 1.00
427 Scott McKillop RC .40 1.00
428 Sean Smith RC .40 1.00
429 Sen'Derrick Marks RC .40 1.00
430A Matthew Stafford RC 2.00 5.00
430B M.Stafford SP No helm 15.00 40.00
430C Matthew Stafford RET 1.25 3.00
431 Louis Murphy RC .40 1.00
432 Stephen McGee RC .40 1.00
433 Tiquan Underwood RC .40 1.00
434 Tom Brandstater RC .50 1.25
435A Josh Freeman RC .40 1.00
435B J.Freeman SP No helm 6.00 15.00
436 Tyson Jackson RC .40 1.00
437 Victor Harris RC .50 1.25
438 Vontae Davis RC .40 1.00
439 William Moore RC .40 1.00
440A Mark Sanchez RC .40 1.00
440B M.Sanchez SP w/helmet 25.00 50.00
440C Mark Sanchez RET .25 .60
441 Barack Obama SP 25.00 50.00
CL1 Checklist 1 .05 .15
CL2 Checklist 2 .05 .15
CL3 Checklist 3 .05 .15
CL4 Checklist 4 .05 .15
RH43 Santonio Holmes RH .60 1.50
RH43A Santonio Holmes RH AU 75.00 200.00

2009 Topps Black

*VETS 1-330: 10X TO 25X BASIC CARDS
*ROOKIES 331-440: 3X TO 8X BASIC CARDS
BLACK/54 ODDS 1:42 HOB
71 BenJarvus Green-Ellis 12.00 30.00
430 Matthew Stafford 30.00 80.00

2009 Topps Gold

*VETS 1-330: 3X TO 8X BASIC CARDS
*ROOKIES 331-440: 1X TO 2.5X BASIC CARDS
GOLD/2009 ODDS 1:3

2009 Topps Career Best Autographs

OUP A ODDS 1:5700 HOB
GROUP B ODDS 1:1485 HOB
GROUP C ODDS 1:421 HOB
AB Ahmad Bradshaw A 4.00 10.00
AF Anthony Fasano C 4.00 10.00
AP Adrian Peterson A 60.00 120.00
BF Brett Favre A 125.00 250.00
BM Brandon Marshall A 6.00 15.00
CJ Chris Johnson C 4.00 10.00
CW Chris Wells A 20.00 40.00
DA Donnie Avery B 4.00 10.00
DB Donald Brown A 10.00 25.00
DB1 Drew Brees A 30.00 60.00
DH Devin Hester B 5.00 12.00
DJ DeSean Jackson B 5.00 12.00
DT Devin Thomas B 4.00 10.00
DW DeAngelo Williams A 15.00 40.00
EB Earl Bennett C 5.00 12.00
EM Eli Manning A 75.00 150.00
ER Eddie Royal B 4.00 10.00
HN Hakeem Nicks C 4.00 10.00
JA1 Joseph Addai A 4.00 10.00
JA2 Jason Avant B 4.00 10.00
JC Jay Cutler A 60.00 120.00
JF Joe Flacco A 15.00 40.00
JH Jacob Hester C 4.00 10.00
JH2 James Hardy B 5.00 12.00
JM Jeremy Maclin A 12.00 30.00
JM2 Josh Morgan B 4.00 10.00
JN Jordy Nelson C 10.00 25.00
JR Javon Ringer C 3.00 8.00
JS Jonathan Stewart A 15.00 40.00
JS2 Jerome Simpson B 4.00 10.00
KM Knowshon Moreno A 15.00 40.00
LM LeSean McCoy B 12.50 25.00
LT LaDainian Tomlinson A 40.00 80.00
MB Marion Barber A 12.00 30.00
MC Michael Crabtree A 40.00 100.00
MC1 Marques Colston A 10.00 25.00
MH Mike Hart C 5.00 12.00
MR Matt Ryan A 50.00 100.00
MS Mark Sanchez A 50.00 100.00
MS2 Matthew Stafford A 50.00 100.00
PC Patrick Crayton C 4.00 10.00
PH Percy Harvin C 3.00 8.00
PM Peyton Manning A 75.00 150.00
RR Ray Rice A 4.00 10.00
SG Shonn Greene C 3.00 8.00
SS Steve Slaton B 4.00 10.00
SS2 Steve Smith B 5.00 12.00
TC Tashard Choice C 3.00 8.00
TJ Tarvaris Jackson B 5.00 12.00

2009 Topps Career Best Dual Autographs

DUAL AUTO/25 ODDS 1:24,000 HOB
BM T.Brady/R.Moss 250.00 400.00
BR M.Barber/T.Romo 60.00 100.00
CM M.Crabtree/J.Maclin 40.00 100.00
EM J.Elway/D.Marino 150.00 250.00
HB D.Hester/E.Bennett 20.00 50.00
JC F.Jones/T.Choice 20.00 50.00
JM B.Jackson/D.McFadden 30.00 80.00
JW C.Johnson/L.White 20.00 50.00
MB D.Marino/D.Brees 100.00 200.00
MM P.Manning/E.Manning 150.00 250.00
PT A.Peterson/L.Tomlinson 125.00 250.00
SS M.Stafford/M.Sanchez 150.00 300.00
SWH S.Slaton/P.White 20.00 50.00
WJ B.Westbrook/D.Jackson 20.00 50.00
SW J.Stewart/D.Williams 20.00 50.00

2009 Topps Career Best Dual Jerseys

STATED ODDS 1:3000 HOB
BR1 M.Barber/T.Romo 6.00 15.00
BR2 D.Brees/M.Ryan 10.00 25.00
FB L.Fitzgerald/A.Boldin 6.00 15.00
HF D.Hester/M.Forte 6.00 15.00
JA S.Jackson/D.Avery
JS A.Johnson/S.Slaton 6.00 15.00
JW C.Johnson/L.White
MJ D.McNabb/D.Jackson 6.00 15.00
MR B.Marshall/E.Royal
PT A.Peterson/L.Tomlinson 8.00 20.00
RH Roethlisberger/S.Holmes
RJ A.Rodgers/G.Jennings
RL E.Reed/R.Lewis 12.00 30.00
WS D.Williams/J.Stewart

2009 Topps Career Best Jerseys

OUP A ODDS 1:137 HOB
GROUP B ODDS 1:97 HOB
*PLATINUM: .5X TO 1.2X BASIC JSY
AB1 Anquan Boldin A 2.50 6.00
AB2 Andre Brown B 2.50 6.00
AG Anthony Gonzalez A 2.50 6.00
BC Brian Cushing B 2.00 5.00
BG Brandon Gibson B 3.00 8.00
BM Brandon Marshall A 3.00 8.00
BP Brandon Pettigrew B 2.00 5.00
BR Brian Robiskie B 2.00 5.00
BU Brian Urlacher A 4.00 10.00
CJ Calvin Johnson A 4.00 10.00
CM Clay Matthews B 8.00 20.00
CP Cedric Peerman B 2.00 5.00
DA Donnie Avery A 2.50 6.00
DB Dwayne Bowe A 3.00 8.00
DK Dustin Keller A 2.50 6.00
DM Darren McFadden A 4.00 10.00
DW DeAngelo Williams A 2.50 6.00
ER Eddie Royal A 2.50 6.00
GJ Greg Jennings A 2.50 6.00
JC Jerricho Cotchery A 2.50 6.00
JD James Davis B 2.00 5.00
JF Joe Flacco A 3.00 8.00
JI Juaquin Iglesias B 4.00 10.00
LT LaDainian Tomlinson A 4.00 10.00
MF Matt Forte A 2.50 6.00
PW Pat White B 2.50 6.00
RB1 Ramses Barden B 2.00 5.00
RB2 Rhett Bomar B 2.00 5.00
RJ Rashad Jennings B 2.50 6.00
RL Ray Lewis A 5.00 12.00
RM Rey Maualuga B 4.00 10.00
RW Roddy White A 2.50 6.00
SJ Steven Jackson A 2.50 6.00
SM Shawne Merriman A 2.50 6.00
SS Steve Slaton A 2.50 6.00
WM William Moore B 3.00 8.00

2009 Topps Career Best Jerseys Autographs

Y AUTO/50 ODDS 1:25,000 HOB
AP Adrian Peterson 100.00 200.00
CJ Chris Johnson
DB Drew Brees 40.00 80.00
FG Frank Gore 15.00 40.00
LT LaDainian Tomlinson
MR Matt Ryan 60.00 120.00
PM Peyton Manning 90.00 150.00
RW Reggie Wayne 15.00 40.00
SJ Steven Jackson 15.00 40.00
SS Steve Slaton

2009 Topps Cheerleaders

COMPLETE SET (15) 4.00 10.00
STATED ODDS 1:9 HOB
C1 Tara .40 1.25
C2 Amanda .40 1.25
C3 Kelli .40 1.25
C4 Emily C. .40 1.25
C5 Kayla S. .40 1.25
C6 Laurie .40 1.25
C7 TaJonda .40 1.25
C8 Amanda .40 1.25
C9 Samantha .40 1.25
C10 Amy .40 1.25
C11 Fabiola .40 1.25
C12 Johanna .40 1.25
C13 Bibiana .40 1.25
C14 Monica .40 1.25
C15 Tiffany .40 1.25

2009 Topps Chicle

Card from this insert were released across both hobby and retail packs, as well as special retail cereal style boxes. Cereal box exclusives included: #1, 5, 8, 14, 21, 24, 30, 31, 35, 40, 42, 46, 55, 59, 66, 71, 73, 74, 75, 76, 83, 89, 90, 93.

COMPLETE SET (100) 50.00 80.00
STATED ODDS 1:6 HOB, 1:1 CEREAL
1 Brian Westbrook .40 1.00
2 Eli Manning .50 1.25
3 Thomas Jones .40 1.00
4 Brandon Marshall .50 1.25
5 Tony Gonzalez .50 1.25
6 Jay Cutler .40 1.00
7 Darren McFadden .60 1.50
8 Steven Jackson .40 1.00
9 Hines Ward .50 1.25
10 Frank Gore .50 1.25
11 Kurt Warner .50 1.25
12 Aaron Rodgers 1.25 3.00
13 Philip Rivers .60 1.50
14 Adrian Peterson .60 1.50
15 Clinton Portis .40 1.00
16 Michael Turner .40 1.00
17 DeAngelo Williams .40 1.00
18 Larry Fitzgerald .50 1.25
19 Steve Smith .50 1.25
20 Andre Johnson .50 1.25
21 Calvin Johnson .60 1.50
22 Roddy White .40 1.00
23 Ed Reed .50 1.25
24 Troy Polamalu .60 1.50
25 Willie Parker .40 1.00
26 Steve Slaton .40 1.00
27 Matt Forte .40 1.00
28 Chris Johnson .40 1.00
29 Ryan Grant .50 1.25
30 Drew Brees .60 1.50
31 LaDainian Tomlinson .60 1.50
32 Brandon Jacobs .40 1.00
33 Marshawn Lynch .50 1.25
34 Kevin Smith .40 1.00
35 Jamal Lewis .50 1.25
36 Ronnie Brown .40 1.00
37 Matthew Stafford 2.00 5.00
38 Donovan McNabb .50 1.25
39 DeSean Jackson .50 1.25
40 Peyton Manning 1.50 4.00
41 Marion Barber .50 1.25
42 Tony Romo .50 1.25
43 Jonathan Stewart .40 1.00
44 Maurice Jones-Drew .40 1.00
45 Warrick Dunn .40 1.00
46 LenDale White .40 1.00
47 Willis McGahee .40 1.00
48 Joseph Addai .40 1.00
49 Reggie Bush .40 1.00
50 Tim Hightower .40 1.00
51 Darren Sproles .50 1.25
52 T.J. Houshmandzadeh .40 1.00
53 Eddie Royal .40 1.00
54 Anquan Boldin .40 1.00
55 Dwayne Bowe .50 1.25
56 Antonio Bryant .40 1.00
57 Chris Cooley .40 1.00
58 Reggie Wayne .50 1.25
59 Jason Witten .50 1.25
60 Greg Jennings .40 1.00
61 Derrick Mason .40 1.00
62 Santana Moss .50 1.25
63 Randy Moss .50 1.25
64 Terrell Owens .50 1.25
65 Torry Holt .50 1.25
66 Jerricho Cotchery .40 1.00
67 Donald Driver .50 1.25
68 Laveranues Coles .40 1.00
69 Trent Edwards .40 1.00
70 Antonio Gates .50 1.25
71 Ted Ginn .40 1.00
72 John Carlson .50 1.25
73 Vincent Jackson .40 1.00
74 Lee Evans .50 1.25
75 Wes Welker .50 1.25
76 Ben Roethlisberger .60 1.50
77 LeSean McCoy 1.00 2.50
78 Braylon Edwards .40 1.00
79 Kevin Walter .50 1.25
80 Santonio Holmes .40 1.00
81 Chris Wells .40 1.00
82 Donnie Avery .40 1.00
83 Devin Hester .50 1.25
84 Anthony Gonzalez .40 1.00
85 Matt Ryan .50 1.25
86 Joe Flacco .50 1.25
87 Michael Crabtree .60 1.50
88 Ray Lewis .60 1.50
89 Joey Porter .50 1.25
90 Darrius Heyward-Bey .60 1.50
91 DeMarcus Ware .50 1.25
92 Hakeem Nicks .50 1.25
93 Jon Beason .40 1.00
94 Knowshon Moreno .40 1.00
95 Mark Sanchez .40 1.00
96 Aaron Curry .60 1.50
97 Brian Orakpo .50 1.25
98 Jeremy Maclin .50 1.25
99 Percy Harvin .40 1.00
100 Josh Freeman .40 1.00

2009 Topps Letter Patch Autographs

TOTAL PRINT RUNS 10-20 PER PLAYER
DHB Darrius Heyward-Bey

2009 Topps Factory Set Rookie Bonus

MPLETE SET (5) 6.00 15.00
1-5 INSERTS IN HOBBY FACTORY SETS
1 Matthew Stafford HOB 1.25 3.00
2 Mark Sanchez HOB .25 .60
3 Michael Crabtree HOB .40 1.00
4 Knowshon Moreno HOB .25 .60
5 Chris Wells HOB .25 .60

2009 Topps Target Exclusive Factory Set Patches

TWO PER TARGET EXCLUSIVE FACTORY SET
AP Adrian Peterson 07 Draft 1.50 4.00
KM Knowshon Moreno 09 Draft .40 1.00
PM Peyton Manning 98 Draft 4.00 10.00
TB Tom Brady 00 Draft 5.00 12.00
MS1 Mark Sanchez 09 Draft .40 1.00
MS2 Matthew Stafford 09 Draft 2.00 5.00

2009 Topps Flashback

MPLETE SET (15) 6.00 15.00
STATED ODDS 1:6 HOB
FB1 Frank Tripucka .50 1.25
FB2 Jack Kemp .60 1.50
FB3 George Blanda .60 1.50
FB4 Abner Haynes .50 1.25
FB5 Billy Cannon .50 1.25
FB6 Paul Lowe .50 1.25
FB7 Don Maynard .60 1.50
FB8 Bill Groman .50 1.25
FB9 Jim Marshall .50 1.25
FB10 Larry Grantham .50 1.25
FB11 Tom Flores .50 1.25
FB12 Babe Parilli .50 1.25
FB13 Lionel Taylor .50 1.25
FB14 Paul Maguire .50 1.25
FB15 Wahoo McDaniel .50 1.25

2009 Topps Letter Patch

OUP A ODDS 1:3900 HOB
GROUP B ODDS 1:414 HOB
GROUP C ODDS 1:975 HOB
AC Andre Caldwell C 5.00 12.00
AP Adrian Peterson B 8.00 20.00
AT Aqib Talib B 5.00 12.00
BR Ben Roethlisberger B 8.00 20.00
CB Colt Brennan B 6.00 15.00
DD Dennis Dixon A 5.00 12.00
DM Dan Marino B 30.00 60.00
DT Devin Thomas B 5.00 12.00
FJ Felix Jones B 5.00 12.00
JE John Elway C 15.00 40.00
JF Joe Flacco B 6.00 15.00
JH Jacob Hester B 5.00 12.00
JH Joe Montana C 20.00 50.00
JN Jordy Nelson B 6.00 15.00
JS Jonathan Stewart A 5.00 12.00
LF Larry Fitzgerald B 10.00 25.00
MF Matt Forte A 10.00 25.00
MR Matt Ryan B 6.00 15.00
PM Peyton Manning B 15.00 40.00
SS Steve Slaton B 5.00 12.00
TB Tom Brady B 15.00 40.00
TD Tony Dorsett B 8.00 20.00
TR Tony Romo A 6.00 15.00
RM1 Rashard Mendenhall B 8.00 20.00
RM2 Randy Moss A 6.00 15.00

2009 Topps Postseason Patches

ONE PER RETAIL BLASTER BOX
PPR1 Terry Bradshaw SB XIV 12.00 30.00
PPR2 Terry Bradshaw SB XIII 12.00 30.00
PPR3 Terry Bradshaw SB X 12.00 30.00
PPR4 Terry Bradshaw SB IX 12.00 30.00
PPR5 Tony Dorsett SB XII 6.00 15.00
PPR6 Tony Dorsett SB XIII 6.00 15.00
PPR7 Tony Dorsett PB 1981 6.00 15.00
PPR8 Tony Dorsett PB 1983 6.00 15.00
PPR9 Joe Montana SB XXIV 25.00 60.00
PPR10 Joe Montana SB XXIII 25.00 60.00
PPR11 Joe Montana SB XIX 25.00 60.00
PPR12 Joe Montana SB XVI 25.00 60.00
PPR13 Eric Dickerson PB 1983 6.00 15.00
PPR14 Eric Dickerson PB 1984 6.00 15.00
PPR15 Eric Dickerson PB 1986 6.00 15.00
PPR16 Eric Dickerson PB 1988 6.00 15.00
PPR17 Earl Campbell PB 1980 8.00 20.00
PPR18 Earl Campbell PB 1981 8.00 20.00
PPR19 Earl Campbell PB 1983 8.00 20.00
PPR20 John Elway SB XXXIII 12.00 30.00
PPR21 John Elway SB XXXII 12.00 30.00
PPR22 John Elway SB XXIV 12.00 30.00
PPR23 John Elway SB XXI 12.00 30.00
PPR24 Dan Marino PB 1984 12.00 30.00
PPR25 Dan Marino PB 1985 12.00 30.00
PPR26 Dan Marino PB 1986 12.00 30.00
PPR27 Dan Marino SB XIX 12.00 30.00
PPR28 Peyton Manning SB XLI 20.00 50.00
PPR29 Peyton Manning PB 2005 20.00 50.00
PPR30 Peyton Manning PB 2007 20.00 50.00
PPR31 Tom Brady SB XXXVI 25.00 60.00
PPR32 Tom Brady SB XXXVIII 25.00 60.00
PPR33 Tom Brady SB XXXIX 25.00 60.00
PPR34 Eli Manning SB XLII 6.00 15.00
PPR35 Ray Lewis SB XXXV 12.00 30.00
PPR36 Ben Roethlisberger SB XL 8.00 20.00
PPR37 Ben Roethlisberger SB XLIII 8.00 20.00
PPR38 Larry Fitzgerald PB 2009 6.00 15.00
PPR39 Adrian Peterson PB 2008 8.00 20.00
PPR40 Randy Moss PB 2007 6.00 15.00
PPR41 LaDainian Tomlinson PB 2006 8.00 20.00
PPR42 LaDainian Tomlinson PB 2007 8.00 20.00
PPR43 Kurt Warner SB XXXV 6.00 15.00
PPR44 Hines Ward SB XL 6.00 15.00
PPR45 Drew Brees 8.00 20.00
PPR46 Chris Wells 1.50 4.00
PPR47 Percy Harvin 1.50 4.00
PPR48 Jeremy Maclin 2.00 5.00
PPR49 Matthew Stafford 8.00 20.00
PPR50 Mark Sanchez 1.50 4.00

2009 Topps Rookie Premiere Autographs

RED INK TOO SCARCE TO PRICE
AB Andre Brown 6.00 15.00
AC Aaron Curry 8.00 20.00
BP Brandon Pettigrew 5.00 12.00
BR Brian Robiskie 5.00 12.00
CW Chris Wells 5.00 12.00
DB Deon Butler 5.00 12.00
DBR Donald Brown 5.00 12.00
DH Darrius Heyward-Bey 8.00 20.00
DW Derrick Williams 5.00 12.00
GC Glen Coffee 5.00 12.00
HN Hakeem Nicks 6.00 15.00
JF Josh Freeman 5.00 12.00
JI Juaquin Iglesias 5.00 12.00
JM Jeremy Maclin 6.00 15.00
JR Javon Ringer 5.00 12.00
JS Jason Smith 5.00 12.00
KB Kenny Britt 8.00 20.00
KM Knowshon Moreno 5.00 12.00
LM LeSean McCoy 12.00 30.00
MC Michael Crabtree 8.00 20.00
MM Mohamed Massaquoi 5.00 12.00
MS Mark Sanchez 12.00 30.00
MST Matthew Stafford 30.00 80.00
MT Mike Thomas 5.00 12.00
MW Mike Wallace 8.00 20.00
ND Nate Davis 5.00 12.00
PH Percy Harvin 5.00 12.00
PT Patrick Turner 5.00 12.00
PW Pat White 6.00 15.00
RB Ramses Barden 5.00 12.00
RMB Rhett Bomar 5.00 12.00
SG Shonn Greene 5.00 12.00
SM Stephen McGee 5.00 12.00
TJ Tyson Jackson 5.00 12.00

2009 Topps Rookie Premiere Autographs Dual

D INK TOO SCARCE TO PRICE
BM D.Brwn red/McCoy blu 30.00 80.00
CH M.Crabtree/Heyward-Bey 20.00 80.00
MH J.Maclin/P.Harvin 40.00 80.00
MW K.Moreno/C.Wells 40.00 100.00
SS M.Stafford/M.Sanchez 75.00 150.00

2009 Topps Rookie Premiere Autographs Quads

D INK TOO SCARCE TO PRICE
BWGM Brwn/Wlls/Grne/McCy 75.00 150.00
CHMH Crbtr/Hyrd-By/Mcln/Hrvn 20.00 50.00
MWBM Mrno/Wlls/Brwn/McCy 75.00 150.00
SSCM Stffrd/Snchz/Crbtr/Mcln 60.00 120.00
SSFW Snchz/Stffrd/Frmn/Whte 150.00 300.00

2009 Topps Target Exclusive Allen and Ginter

is insert set was issued exclusively in Target Stores retail feeder boxes. The print run apparently was very low as the singles are typically difficult to find. It appears that the Stafford, Crabtree, and Roethlisberger cards were issued in short supply while the E;way, Ryan, Sanchez cards appear to be double printed.

STATED ODDS 1:4 TARGET PACKS
AG1 Earl Campbell 6.00 15.00
AG2 Matthew Stafford SP 20.00 40.00
AG3 Peyton Manning 12.00 30.00
AG4 Chris Johnson 3.00 8.00
AG5 John Elway DP 10.00 25.00
AG6 Mark Sanchez DP 1.50 4.00
AG7 Adrian Peterson 5.00 12.00
AG8 Matt Ryan DP 4.00 10.00
AG9 Ben Roethlisberger SP 12.00 30.00
AG10 Terry Bradshaw 6.00 15.00
AG11 Michael Crabtree SP 6.00 15.00
AG12 Bo Jackson 6.00 15.00
AG13 Gale Sayers 5.00 12.00
AG14 Chris Wells 1.25 3.00
AG15 Dan Marino 10.00 25.00

2009 Topps Topps Town Silver

MPLETE SET (25) 4.00 10.00
ONE TOPPSTOWN PER PACK
*GOLD: .8X TO 2X SILVER
TTT1 Donovan McNabb .25 .60
TTT2 Eli Manning .25 .60
TTT3 Aaron Rodgers .60 1.50
TTT4 Peyton Manning .75 2.00
TTT5 Jay Cutler .20 .50
TTT6 Joe Flacco .25 .60
TTT7 Kurt Warner .25 .60
TTT8 Philip Rivers .30 .75
TTT9 Matt Ryan .25 .60
TTT10 Tony Romo .25 .60
TTT11 Matt Hasselbeck .20 .50
TTT12 Jason Campbell .20 .50
TTT13 Trent Edwards .20 .50
TTT14 Brady Quinn .20 .50
TTT15 Matt Schaub .20 .50
TTT16 Matt Cassel .20 .50
TTT17 Tom Brady 1.00 2.50
TTT18 Drew Brees .30 .75
TTT19 Ben Roethlisberger .30 .75
TTT20 Kerry Collins .20 .50
TTT21 JaMarcus Russell .20 .50
TTT22 Chad Pennington .20 .50
TTT23 David Garrard .20 .50
TTT24 Kyle Orton .20 .50
TTT25 Carson Palmer .25 .60

2009 Topps Wal-Mart Exclusive All Americans

ATED ODDS 1:4 WAL-MART PACKS
AC Aaron Curry 1.00 2.50
AM Aaron Maybin .75 2.00
BO Brian Orakpo .75 2.00
CW Chris Wells .60 1.50
DB Donald Brown .60 1.50
DW Derrick Williams .60 1.50
JM Jeremy Maclin .75 2.00
JR Javon Ringer .60 1.50
JS Jason Smith .60 1.50
KB Kenny Britt 1.00 2.50
KM Knowshon Moreno .60 1.50
MC Michael Crabtree 1.00 2.50
MS Matthew Stafford 3.00 8.00
PH Percy Harvin .60 1.50
RM Rey Maualuga 1.00 2.50

2009 Topps Wal-Mart Exclusive Factory Set Gold Refractors

W1 Peyton Manning 2.00 5.00
W2 Tom Brady 2.00 5.00

2010 Topps

COMPLETE SET (440) 25.00 50.00
COMP.FACT.SET (445) 30.00 60.00
COMP.SUPER BOWL (445) 50.00 80.00
ONE ROOKIE CARD PER PACK
DREW BREES RH ODDS 1:36
1 Peyton Manning .60 1.50
2 Kareem Jackson RC .30 .75
3 Malcolm Kelly .15 .40
4 Tim Hightower .15 .40
5 Derrick Ward .15 .40
6 Marques Colston .15 .40
7 Heath Miller .15 .40
8 Mike Wallace .15 .40
9 Carlos Dunlap RC .30 .75
10 Adrian Peterson .25 .60
11 DeMarcus Ware .20 .50
12 Jairus Byrd .20 .50
13 George Wilson .15 .40
14 Kevin Smith .15 .40
15 Hightower/Fitzgerald TC .15 .40
16 Matt Ryan TC .15 .40
17 Jeremy Shockey .15 .40
18 Jay Ratliff AP .20 .50
19 Rennie Curran RC .30 .75
20 Randy Moss .20 .50
21 Jermichael Finley .15 .40
22 Matt Ryan .20 .50
23 Jason Pierre-Paul RC .50 1.25
24 D.Revis/R.Moss CM .15 .40
25 Ray Lewis AP .25 .60
26 Will Smith .15 .40
27 Bryan Bulaga RC .30 .75
28 Sergio Kindle RC .30 .75
29 Michael Turner .15 .40
30 Tom Brady .60 1.50
31 Dwayne Bowe .20 .50
32 Amari Spievey RC .30 .75
33 Koa Misi RC .40 1.00
34 Louis Murphy .15 .40
35 M.Cassel/J.Charles TC .15 .40
36 Asante Samuel .15 .40
37 DeMeco Ryans .15 .40
38 Anthony Gonzalez .15 .40
39 Mario Manningham .15 .40
40 Chris Johnson .15 .40
41 Charles Woodson AP .25 .60

42 Roddy White .15 .40
43 Nate Burleson .15 .40
44A Mike Williams RC .30 .75
44B M.Williams SP Helmet 6.00 15.00
45 Steve Smith .20 .50
46 Major Wright RC .30 .75
47 Jacoby Jones .15 .40
48 Nick Collins .15 .40
49 Chad Greenway .15 .40
50 Andre Johnson .20 .50
51 Bob Sanders .20 .50
52 Akwasi Owusu-Ansah RC .30 .75
53 Knowshon Moreno .15 .40
54 Darrius Heyward-Bey .20 .50
55 Jason Avant .15 .40
56 J.Johnson/K.Winslow TC .12 .30
57 Ed Dickson RC .30 .75
58 Taylor Price RC .30 .75
59 Osi Umenyiora .15 .40
60 Brett Favre 1.00 2.50
61 Antonio Bryant .15 .40
62 Jason Witten .20 .50
63 Richard Seymour .15 .40
64 Jermaine Gresham RC .30 .75
65 Nick Barnett .15 .40
66 M.Forte/J.Cutler TC .12 .30
67 Joey Porter .15 .40
68 Tyvon Branch .15 .40
69 Brandon Spikes RC .30 .75
70 Maurice Jones-Drew .15 .40
71 Sheldon Brown .15 .40
72 Damian Williams RC .30 .75
73 DeSean Jackson TC .20 .50
74 Ernie Sims .15 .40
75 Javier Arenas RC .30 .75
76 Donald Driver .20 .50
77 DeMarcus Ware AP .20 .50
78 Andre Johnson AP .20 .50
79 P.Manning/Addai TC .50 1.25
80 Larry Fitzgerald .20 .50
81 Jared Odrick RC .40 1.00
82 Dustin Keller .15 .40
83 Deon Butler .15 .40
84 Willie Parker .15 .40
85 Brandon Ghee RC .30 .75
86 Yeremiah Bell .15 .40
87 Chris Cooley .15 .40
88 Brian Cushing .15 .40
89 Leon Washington .15 .40
90 Steven Jackson .15 .40
91 Sean Canfield RC .30 .75
92 Brandon Flowers .15 .40
93 Russell Okung RC .30 .75
94 T.J. Houshmandzadeh .15 .40
95 Devin Hester .20 .50
96 Aaron Hernandez RC .30 .75
97 M.Sanchez/S.Greene TC .12 .30
98 Lee Evans .20 .50
99 Tony Gonzalez .20 .50
100 Drew Brees .25 .60
101A Arrelious Benn RC .30 .75
101B A.Benn SP Catch 3.00 8.00
102 Louis Delmas .15 .40
103 Adrian Peterson AP .25 .60
104 Brandon Jacobs .15 .40
105 F.Jackson/L.Evans TC .15 .40
106 Troy Polamalu .25 .60
107 Sean Lee RC .60 1.50
108 Brandon Meriweather .15 .40
109A Jordan Shipley RC .30 .75
109B J.Shipley SP No helm 3.00 8.00
110 Wes Welker .20 .50
111 Michael Jenkins .15 .40
112 Marshawn Lynch .20 .50
113 Clay Matthews .25 .60
114 Mike Bell .15 .40
115 Hakeem Nicks .15 .40
116 E.Manning/B.Jacobs TC .15 .40
117 M.Stafford/K.Smith TC .15 .40
118 Curtis Lofton .15 .40
119 Maurice Jones-Drew TC .12 .30
120 Thomas Jones .15 .40
121 Darryl Sharpton RC .30 .75
122 Marcus Easley RC .30 .75
123 Taylor Mays RC .30 .75
124 Jon Beason .15 .40
125 Jonathan Vilma .15 .40
126 Felix Jones .15 .40
127 Maurkice Pouncey RC .40 1.00
128 Thomas DeCoud .15 .40
129 Dwight Freeney AP .15 .40
130 Dwight Freeney .15 .40
131 Donald Brown .15 .40
132A Montario Hardesty RC .30 .75
132B M.Hardesty SP Leaping 6.00 15.00
133 Chris Johnson AP .15 .40
134 Visanthe Shiancoe .20 .50
135 Brandon Gibson .15 .40
136 Darren Sharper .15 .40
137 D.Brees/M.Colston TC .20 .50
138 Linval Joseph RC .30 .75
139 John Conner RC .30 .75
140 Matt Schaub .15 .40
141 Greg Jennings .15 .40
142 David Reed RC .30 .75
143 Nate Kaeding AP .15 .40
144 Peyton Manning MVP .60 1.50
145 Brandon Pettigrew .15 .40
146 C.Portis/S.Moss TC .15 .40
147A Joe McKnight RC .30 .75
147B J.McKnight SP Leaping 8.00 20.00
148A Rob Gronkowski RC 1.00 2.50
148B R.Gronkowski SP Leaping 10.00 25.00
149 Levi Brown RC .30 .75
150 Aaron Rodgers .50 1.25
151 Patrick Willis .20 .50
152 Calvin Johnson .25 .60
153 Kenny Britt .15 .40
154 Roscoe Parrish .15 .40
155 Karlos Dansby .15 .40
156 Sean Weatherspoon RC .30 .75
157 Earl Thomas RC .75 2.00
158 Rashad Jennings .15 .40
159 Jermaine Cunningham RC .30 .75
160 Ray Lewis .25 .60
161 Mike Thomas .20 .50
162 Aqib Talib .15 .40
163 Ahmad Bradshaw .15 .40
164 Donnie Avery .15 .40
165 Cortland Finnegan .15 .40
166 Elvis Dumervil .15 .40
167A C.J. Spiller RC .30 .75
167B C.J. Spiller SP Catch 8.00 20.00
168 Tony Pike RC .30 .75
169 Joe Haden RC .50 1.25
170 LaDainian Tomlinson .25 .60
171 J.Stewart/S.Smith TC .15 .40
172 Brandon Graham RC .40 1.00
173 Anthony Davis RC .40 1.00
174 Devin Aromashodu .15 .40
175 Steve Slaton .15 .40
176 Chris Wells .15 .40
177 Brian Urlacher .25 .60
178 Willis McGahee .15 .40
179 Ted Ginn .15 .40
180 Reggie Wayne .20 .50
181 Adrian Wilson .15 .40
182 Johnathan Joseph .15 .40
183 Matthew Stafford .20 .50
184 C.Palmer/C.Ochocinco TC .15 .40
185 David Harris .15 .40
186 Vince Young .15 .40
187 Torry Holt .20 .50
188 B.Favre/A.Peterson TC .40 1.00
189 Kevin Kolb .15 .40
190 Brandon Marshall .20 .50
191 Braylon Edwards .15 .40
192 Carlton Mitchell RC .30 .75
193 Nnamdi Asomugha .15 .40
194A Colt McCoy RC .40 1.00
194B C.McCoy SP No helm 15.00 40.00
194C C.McCoy FS Helmt w/crwd .30 .75
195 Walter McFadden RC .40 1.00
196 Brian Robiskie .15 .40
197 Myron Rolle RC .30 .75
198 Shonn Greene .15 .40
199 Jamaal Charles .20 .50
200 Tony Romo .20 .50
201 K.Orton/K.Moreno TC .12 .30
202 Santana Moss .20 .50
203A Toby Gerhart RC .30 .75
203B T.Gerhart SP Leaping 3.00 8.00
204 James Harrison .25 .60
205 Stephen Cooper .15 .40
206 Brian Cushing ROY .15 .40
207 Zach Miller .15 .40
208 Ed Reed .20 .50
209 Chaz Schilens .15 .40
210 Chad Ochocinco .15 .40
211 Paul Posluszny .15 .40
212 Cadillac Williams .15 .40
213 Joe Webb RC .30 .75
214 Vince Wilfork .15 .40
215 Terrence Cody RC .30 .75
216 Rivers/Gates/Jackson TC .20 .50
217 Darren Sharper AP .15 .40
218 Davone Bess .15 .40
219 Laurence Maroney .15 .40
220 Dallas Clark .15 .40
221A Jimmy Clausen RC .30 .75
221B J.Clausen SP Passing 10.00 25.00
221C J.Clausen FS No FB .25 .60
221D J.Clausen FS Drop back .25 .60
222 Michael Crabtree .15 .40
223 DeSean Jackson .20 .50
224 Jerome Harrison .15 .40
225 Trent Williams RC .40 1.00
226 E.Manning/T.Romo CM .15 .40
227 Mike Iupati RC .50 1.25
228 Jerry Hughes RC .30 .75
229 Adrian Wilson AP .15 .40
230 Ray Rice .15 .40
231 Julius Jones .15 .40
232 Brent Celek .15 .40
233 Darnell Dockett .15 .40
234 Greg Olsen .20 .50
235 John Skelton RC .40 1.00
236 Darren Sproles .20 .50
237 Donte Stallworth .15 .40
238 Todd Heap .15 .40
239 Percy Harvin .15 .40
240 Ryan Grant .20 .50
241 Devery Henderson .15 .40
242 Riley Cooper RC .30 .75
243 Jared Allen .15 .40
244 Mike Kafka RC .40 1.00
245 T.J. Ward RC .50 1.25
246 LeSean McCoy .25 .60
247 Ronnie Brown TC .12 .30
248A Dexter McCluster RC .40 1.00
248B D.McCluster SP No Helm 4.00 10.00
249 David Garrard .15 .40
250 Philip Rivers .25 .60
251 Sidney Rice .15 .40
252 LaMarr Woodley .15 .40
253 Malcom Floyd .15 .40
254A Emmanuel Sanders RC .50 1.25
254B E.Sanders SP Leaping 5.00 12.00
255 Ronnie Brown .15 .40
256 Trent Cole .15 .40
257 Frank Gore .20 .50
258 Eric Decker RC .40 1.00
259 Chester Taylor .15 .40
260 Cedric Benson .15 .40
261 Justin Tuck .15 .40
262 Arian Foster .20 .50
263 Dan Williams RC .30 .75
264 Mardy Gilyard RC .30 .75
265 Jimmy Graham RC .75 2.00
266 Jay Cutler .15 .40
267 Ray Lewis TC .20 .50
268A Jahvid Best RC .30 .75
268B J.Best SP Two arms up 3.00 8.00
268C J.Best FS One arm up .25 .60
269 Austin Collie .15 .40
270 Steve Smith USC .15 .40
271 Jacoby Ford RC .30 .75
272 Jerod Mayo .20 .50
273 Antwaan Randle El .15 .40
274 Josh Morgan .20 .50
275A Demaryius Thomas RC .75 2.00
275B D.Thomas SP No helm 8.00 20.00
276 Nate Washington .15 .40
277 Rashard Mendenhall .15 .40
278 Chris Cook RC .30 .75
279 Josh Freeman .20 .50
280 Ben Roethlisberger .25 .60
281 Favre vs. Packers CM .40 1.00
282 Aaron Curry .20 .50
283 James Laurinaitis .20 .50
284 Shaun Phillips .15 .40
285 Kevin Thomas RC .40 1.00
286 Kellen Winslow .15 .40
287 Ryan Clady AP .15 .40
288 Pierre Garcon .20 .50
289 Darrelle Revis .15 .40
290 Jonathan Stewart .15 .40
291 Leon Hall .15 .40
292 Matt Cassel .15 .40
293 Earl Bennett .20 .50
294 Everson Griffen RC .30 .75
295 Devin McCourty RC .40 1.00
296 Anquan Boldin .15 .40
297 Jonathan Crompton RC .30 .75
298 Zac Robinson RC .40 1.00
299 Barrett Ruud .15 .40
300A Sam Bradford RC 3.00 8.00
300B S.Bradford SP Takng snap 40.00 80.00
300C S.Bradford FS Rolling out 4.00 10.00
300D S.Bradford FS Pass w/field 4.00 10.00
301 Chad Henne .20 .50
302 Clinton Portis .15 .40
303 Matt Leinart .15 .40
304 Dominique Rodgers-Cromartie .15 .40
305 Bradie James .15 .40
306 Julius Peppers .20 .50
307 Anthony Dixon RC .30 .75
308 Lance Moore .15 .40
309 Pierre Thomas .15 .40
310 Joseph Addai .15 .40
311 Santonio Holmes .15 .40
312 Jerricho Cotchery .15 .40
313 Rashean Mathis .15 .40
314 Anthony McCoy RC .30 .75
315A Armanti Edwards RC .40 1.00
315B A.Edwards SP Leaping 4.00 10.00
316 Marion Barber .20 .50
317 Dallas Clark AP .15 .40
318 Jason Campbell .15 .40
319 Jahri Evans AP RC .15 .40
320 Hines Ward .20 .50
321 M.Schaub/A.Johnson TC .15 .40
322 Ricky Williams .20 .50
323 Early Doucet .15 .40
324 Joe Thomas AP .15 .40
325 Julian Edelman .25 .60
326 Jerome Murphy RC .40 1.00
327 London Fletcher .20 .50
328 Dezmon Briscoe RC .30 .75
329 Vernon Davis .15 .40
330 Joe Flacco .20 .50
331 Steve Breaston .15 .40
332 F.Gore/A.Smith TC .15 .40
333 Percy Harvin ROY .15 .40
334 James Davis .15 .40
335 LaRon Landry .15 .40
336 Alex Smith QB .20 .50
337 David Hawthorne .25 .60
338 Michael Bush .15 .40
339 Bernard Scott .15 .40
340 Vincent Jackson .15 .40
341 Peyton Manning AP .60 1.50
342 Matt Hasselbeck .15 .40
343 Josh Cribbs AP .15 .40
344 Nate Allen RC .50 1.25
345 D.J. Williams .15 .40
346 Super Bowl Champions .25 .60
347 T.Brady/R.Moss TC .50 1.25
348 James Starks RC .40 1.00
349 Charles Brown RC .30 .75
350 Donovan McNabb .20 .50
351 Chad Jones RC .30 .75
352 Kyle Orton .15 .40
353 Steven Jackson TC .12 .30
354 Laurent Robinson .15 .40
355 V.Young/C.Johnson TC .12 .30
356A Brandon LaFell RC .50 1.25
356B B.LaFell SP Catching 5.00 12.00
357 Elvis Dumervil AP .15 .40
358 Darren McFadden .15 .40
359 John Carlson .15 .40
360A Ndamukong Suh RC .60 1.50
360B N.Suh SP No helmet 6.00 15.00
361 Jeremy Maclin .15 .40
362 Derrick Morgan RC .30 .75
363 Patrick Robinson RC .40 1.00
364A Jonathan Dwyer RC .30 .75
364B J.Dwyer SP Running 3.00 8.00
365 Larry Johnson .15 .40
366 Justin Forsett .20 .50
367 Morgan Burnett RC UER .40 1.00
368 Roy Williams WR .15 .40
369 T.Polamalu/J.Flacco CM .20 .50
370 Carson Palmer .20 .50
371 Ed Wang RC .50 1.25
372 Nick Mangold AP .15 .40
373 Kevin Boss .15 .40
374 Reggie Brown .15 .40
375 Matt Forte .15 .40
376 Robert Meachem .15 .40
377 J.Cribbs/Massaquoi TC .15 .40
378 Rodgers/Jennings TC .40 1.00
379 Kirk Morrison .15 .40
380 Antonio Gates .20 .50
381 Torell Troup RC .30 .75
382 Kevin Williams AP .15 .40
383 Jabar Gaffney .15 .40
384 Jake Long .15 .40
385 Hasselbeck/J.Jones TC .12 .30
386 Jerious Norwood .15 .40
387 Tyson Alualu RC .30 .75
388 Daryl Washington RC .30 .75
389 Ben Watson .15 .40
390 Reggie Bush .15 .40
391 Mike Sims-Walker .15 .40
392 Chris Chambers .15 .40
393 Haloti Ngata .15 .40
394 DeAngelo Williams .15 .40
395A Eric Berry RC .50 1.25
395B E.Berry SP Ball in hand 5.00 12.00
396 Fred Jackson .20 .50
397 Pat Angerer RC .30 .75
398A Golden Tate RC .40 1.00
398B Golden Tate SP No helm 4.00 10.00
399 Kyle Wilson RC .30 .75
400 Eli Manning .20 .50
401 Darrelle Revis AP .15 .40
402 Stephen Tulloch .15 .40
403A Ryan Mathews RC .30 .75
403B R.Mathews SP Catching 10.00 25.00
403C R.Mathews FS Pointing .25 .60
404 Jared Allen AP .15 .40
405 Patrick Willis AP .20 .50
406 Johnny Knox .15 .40
407 Tashard Choice .15 .40
408 Steve Hutchinson AP .15 .40
409 Anthony Becht .15 .40
410 Gerald McCoy RC .30 .75
411 Wes Welker AP .20 .50
412 2010 Rookie Premiere CL .60 1.50
413 Leonard Weaver AP .15 .40
414 Eddie Royal .15 .40
415 Lamarr Houston RC .40 1.00
416A Ben Tate RC .30 .75
416B Ben Tate SP No helm 3.00 8.00
417 Shane Lechler AP .15 .40
418 Brian Dawkins .15 .40
419 T.Romo/M.Barber TC .15 .40
420 Mark Sanchez .15 .40
421 James Jones .15 .40
422 Kevin Walter .20 .50
423 Andre Roberts RC .40 1.00
424 Charles Scott RC .30 .75
425A Dez Bryant RC .75 2.00
425B Dez Bryant SP Goalpost 15.00 40.00
425C Dez Bryant FS Running .60 1.50
426 Glen Coffee .15 .40
427 Mohamed Massaquoi .20 .50
428 Rolando McClain RC .30 .75
429 Dan LeFevour RC .30 .75
430 Terrell Owens .20 .50
431 Phillip Dillard RC .30 .75
432 Rodger Saffold RC .30 .75
433 Devin Thomas .15 .40
434 Derrick Mason .15 .40
435 Miles Austin .15 .40
436 Oshiomogho Atogwe .15 .40
437 Pittsburgh Steelers TC .20 .50
438 Bernard Berrian .15 .40
439 Chaz Schilens TC .15 .40
440A Tim Tebow RC 5.00 10.00
440B Tim Tebow SP Pointing 40.00 80.00
440C T.Tebow FS Pass w/ball 6.00 12.00
440D T.Tebow FS Pass w/o ball 6.00 12.00
RH44DB Drew Brees RH .60 1.50

2010 Topps Black

ETS/55: 10X TO 25X BASIC CARDS
*ROOKIES/55: 5X TO 12X BASIC CARDS
BLACK/55 STATED ODDS 1:70 HOB

2010 Topps Blue

*VETS/349: 5X TO 12X BASIC CARDS
*ROOKIE/349: 2X TO 5X BASIC CARDS
WAL-MART BLUE PRINT RUN 349

2010 Topps Gold

ETS: 3X TO 8X BASIC CARDS
*ROOKIES: 1.2X TO 3X BASIC CARDS
GOLD/2010 ODDS 1:5 HOB, 1:10 RET
60 Brett Favre 5.00 12.00

2010 Topps 1952 Bowman

COMPLETE SET (50) 15.00 40.00
STATED ODDS 1:3 HOB/RET
*TAN BACK/52: 3X TO 8X BASIC INSERTS
TAN BACK/52 ODDS 1:2700 HOB/RET
52B1 Peyton Manning 1.50 4.00
52B2 Elvis Dumervil .40 1.00
52B3 Ronnie Brown .40 1.00
52B4 Golden Tate .30 .75
52B5 Beanie Wells .40 1.00
52B6 Aaron Rodgers 1.25 3.00
52B7 Matt Schaub .40 1.00
52B8 Frank Gore .50 1.25
52B9 Tim Tebow .75 2.00
52B10 Chris Johnson .40 1.00
52B11 Brandon Marshall .50 1.25
52B12 Philip Rivers .60 1.50
52B13 DeAngelo Williams .40 1.00
52B14 Ryan Grant .50 1.25
52B15 Dez Bryant .60 1.50
52B16 Knowshon Moreno .40 1.00
52B17 Jahvid Best .25 .60
52B18 Randy Moss .50 1.25
52B19 Dexter McCluster .30 .75
52B20 Adrian Peterson .60 1.50
52B21 Maurice Jones-Drew .40 1.00
52B22 Colt McCoy .30 .75
52B23 C.J. Spiller .25 .60
52B24 Sidney Rice .40 1.00
52B25 Greg Jennings .40 1.00
52B26 Joe McKnight .25 .60
52B27 Ben Tate .25 .60
52B28 Sam Bradford .30 .75
52B29 Jimmy Clausen .25 .60
52B30 Larry Fitzgerald .50 1.25
52B31 Steven Jackson .40 1.00
52B32 Jon Beason .40 1.00
52B33 DeSean Jackson .50 1.25
52B34 Toby Gerhart .25 .60
52B35 Michael Turner .40 1.00
52B36 Ryan Mathews .25 .60
52B37 Montario Hardesty .25 .60
52B38 Ray Rice .40 1.00
52B39 Arrelious Benn .25 .60
52B40 Andre Johnson .50 1.25
52B41 Eric Berry .40 1.00
52B42 Calvin Johnson .60 1.50
52B43 Tom Brady 1.50 4.00
52B44 Reggie Wayne .50 1.25
52B45 Miles Austin .40 1.00
52B46 Rashard Mendenhall .40 1.00
52B47 Darrelle Revis .40 1.00
52B48 Jamaal Charles .50 1.25
52B49 Demaryius Thomas .60 1.50
52B50 Drew Brees .60 1.50

2010 Topps Anniversary Reprints

MPLETE SET (20) 8.00 20.00
STATED ODDS 1:9 HOB/RET
1 Drew Brees .75 2.00
2 Tom Brady 2.00 5.00
3 Eric Dickerson .75 2.00
4 Tony Dorsett 1.00 2.50
5 John Elway 1.50 4.00
6 Larry Fitzgerald .60 1.50
7 Frank Gore .60 1.50
8 Steven Jackson .50 1.25
9 Andre Johnson .60 1.50
10 Chris Johnson .50 1.25
11 Ray Lewis .75 2.00
12 Peyton Manning 2.00 5.00
13 Dan Marino 2.00 5.00
14 Joe Montana 3.00 8.00
15 Randy Moss .60 1.50
16 Adrian Peterson .75 2.00
17 Troy Polamalu .75 2.00
18 Aaron Rodgers 1.50 4.00
19 Gale Sayers 1.00 2.50
20 Reggie Wayne .60 1.50

2010 Topps Draft 75th Anniversary

MPLETE SET (50) 15.00 40.00
STATED ODDS 1:6 HOB/RET
75DA1 Joe Montana 2.50 6.00
75DA2 Ray Lewis .75 2.00
75DA3 Tom Brady 2.00 5.00
75DA4 Sam Bradford .40 1.00
75DA5 Dexter McCluster .40 1.00
75DA6 Randy Moss .60 1.50
75DA7 Adrian Peterson .75 2.00
75DA8 C.J. Spiller .30 .75
75DA9 Mark Sanchez .50 1.25
75DA10 Ben Tate .30 .75
75DA11 LaDainian Tomlinson .75 2.00
75DA12 Tim Tebow 3.00 8.00
75DA13 Patrick Willis .60 1.50
75DA14 Demaryius Thomas .75 2.00
75DA15 Peyton Manning 2.00 5.00
75DA16 Brandon Marshall .60 1.50
75DA17 Cadillac Williams .50 1.25
75DA18 Gale Sayers .75 2.00
75DA19 Jimmy Clausen .30 .75
75DA20 Dan Marino 1.50 4.00
75DA21 Rashard Mendenhall .50 1.25
75DA22 Brian Cushing .50 1.25
75DA23 Vince Young .50 1.25
75DA24 Matt Ryan .60 1.50
75DA25 Brett Favre 1.50 4.00
75DA26 Jamaal Charles .60 1.50
75DA27 Ray Rice .50 1.25
75DA28 Reggie Wayne .60 1.50
75DA29 John Elway 1.25 3.00
75DA30 Emmitt Smith 1.25 3.00
75DA31 Matt Leinart .50 1.25
75DA32 Frank Gore .60 1.50
75DA33 Eli Manning .60 1.50
75DA34 Golden Tate .40 1.00
75DA35 Eric Berry .50 1.25
75DA36 DeSean Jackson .60 1.50
75DA37 Jahvid Best .30 .75
75DA38 Philip Rivers .75 2.00
75DA39 Dez Bryant .75 2.00
75DA40 Troy Aikman 1.00 2.50
75DA41 DeAngelo Williams .50 1.25
75DA42 Tony Dorsett .75 2.00
75DA43 Ryan Mathews .30 .75
75DA44 Steven Jackson .50 1.25
75DA45 Eric Dickerson .60 1.50
75DA46 Shonn Greene .50 1.25
75DA47 Percy Harvin .50 1.25
75DA48 Colt McCoy .40 1.00
75DA49 Jim Brown 1.00 2.50
75DA50 Brian Westbrook .50 1.25

2010 Topps Gridiron Giveaway

MPLETE SET (10) 12.00 30.00
STATED ODDS 1:6 HOB
GG1 Joe Montana 1.25 3.00
GG2 Drew Brees 1.25 3.00
GG3 Ray Lewis 1.25 3.00
GG4 Gale Sayers 1.25 3.00
GG5 John Elway 1.25 3.00
GG6 Peyton Manning 1.25 3.00
GG7 Tony Dorsett 1.25 3.00
GG8 Tom Brady 1.25 3.00
GG9 Eric Dickerson 1.25 3.00
GG10 Dan Marino 1.25 3.00

2010 Topps Gridiron Lineage

MPLETE SET (20) 6.00 15.00
STATED ODDS 1:4 HOB/RET
GLAR T.Aikman/T.Romo 1.00 2.50
GLBP J.Brown/A.Peterson .75 2.00
GLDA E.Dickerson/J.Addai .50 1.25
GLDB B.Dawkins/E.Berry .40 1.00
GLDJ E.Dickerson/S.Jackson .50 1.25
GLDM T.Dorsett/L.McCoy .60 1.50
GLET J.Elway/T.Tebow 2.50 6.00
GLJB C.Johnson/J.Best .25 .60
GLMB D.Marino/D.Brees 1.25 3.00
GLMC J.Montana/J.Clausen 1.25 3.00
GLMT B.Marshall/D.Thomas .60 1.50
GLNS J.Namath/M.Sanchez .75 2.00
GLPH A.Peterson/P.Harvin .60 1.50
GLSF G.Sayers/M.Forte .60 1.50
GLST E.Smith/L.Tomlinson 1.00 2.50
GLTM L.Tomlinson/R.Mathews 1.00 2.50
GLTS T.Thomas/C.Spiller .30 .75
GLWM P.Willis/R.McClain .30 .75
GLMBR R.Moss/D.Bryant 1.00 2.50
GLMOB J.Montana/T.Brady 2.00 5.00

2010 Topps Gridiron Lineage Autographs

AL AU/25 ODDS 1:17,000H, 1:48,000R
GLDAAR T.Aikman/T.Romo 75.00 150.00
GLDABP J.Brown/A.Peterson 125.00 200.00
GLDADA E.Dickerson/J.Addai 25.00 60.00
GLDADJ E.Dickerson/S.Jackson 50.00 100.00
GLDADM T.Dorsett/L.McCoy 25.00 60.00
GLDAET J.Elway/T.Tebow 150.00 300.00
GLDAHM P.Harvin/D.McCluster 30.00 80.00
GLDAMC J.Montana/J.Clausen 100.00 200.00
GLDAMT B.Marshall/D.Thomas 50.00 100.00
GLDAPH A.Peterson/P.Harvin 60.00 120.00
GLDASD J.Stewart/J.Dwyer 25.00 60.00
GLDASJ E.Smith/F.Jones 125.00 200.00
GLDAST E.Smith/L.Tomlinson 125.00 200.00
GLDATS T.Thomas/C.Spiller 75.00 135.00
GLDAWM P.Willis/R.McClain 25.00 60.00

2010 Topps Gridiron Lineage Relics

DUAL JSY/50 ODDS 1:20,000H, 1:22,000R
GLRDJ E.Dickerson/S.Jackson 8.00 20.00
GLRET J.Elway/T.Tebow 30.00 80.00
GLRFR B.Favre/A.Rodgers 60.00 120.00
GLRMB L.Tomlinson/R.Mathews 20.00 40.00
GLRMC J.Montana/J.Clausen 30.00 60.00
GLRNS B.Dawkins/E.Berry 20.00 40.00
GLRRC S.Smith/G.Tate 8.00 20.00
GLRSF G.Sayers/M.Forte 12.00 30.00
GLRSJ C.Johnson/J.Best 15.00 40.00
GLRMBR R.Moss/D.Bryant 15.00 40.00

2010 Topps Peak Performance

COMPLETE SET (50) 10.00 25.00
STATED ODDS 1:4 HOB/RET
PP1 Sam Bradford .30 .75
PP2 Tim Tebow .75 2.00
PP3 C.J. Spiller .25 .60
PP4 Ryan Mathews .25 .60
PP5 Dez Bryant .60 1.50
PP6 Peyton Manning 1.50 4.00
PP7 Tom Brady 1.50 4.00
PP8 Brandon Marshall .50 1.25
PP9 Ray Rice .40 1.00
PP10 Reggie Wayne .50 1.25
PP11 Adrian Peterson .60 1.50
PP12 Steven Jackson .40 1.00
PP13 Eric Dickerson .50 1.25
PP14 Tony Dorsett .60 1.50
PP15 Frank Gore .50 1.25
PP16 Eli Manning .50 1.25
PP17 Kellen Winslow .40 1.00
PP18 Marques Colston .40 1.00
PP19 Joseph Addai .40 1.00
PP20 DeSean Jackson .50 1.25
PP21 Joe Flacco .50 1.25
PP22 Toby Gerhart .25 .60
PP23 Arrelious Benn .25 .60
PP24 Demaryius Thomas .60 1.50
PP25 Jamaal Charles .50 1.25
PP26 Jonathan Dwyer .25 .60
PP27 Mike Williams .25 .60
PP28 Dexter McCluster .30 .75
PP29 Jerod Mayo .50 1.25
PP30 Jerome Harrison .40 1.00
PP31 Jonathan Stewart .40 1.00
PP32 Mike Sims-Walker .40 1.00
PP33 John Elway 1.00 2.50
PP34 Dan Marino 1.25 3.00
PP35 Brett Favre 1.25 3.00
PP36 Jahvid Best .25 .60
PP37 Calvin Johnson .60 1.50
PP38 Darren McFadden .40 1.00
PP39 Rashard Mendenhall .40 1.00
PP40 Sidney Rice .40 1.00
PP41 DeMarcus Ware .50 1.25
PP42 Felix Jones .40 1.00
PP43 Michael Crabtree .40 1.00
PP44 Brian Dawkins .40 1.00
PP45 Dallas Clark .40 1.00
PP46 Golden Tate .30 .75
PP47 Joe McKnight .25 .60
PP48 Montario Hardesty .25 .60
PP49 Jimmy Clausen .25 .60
PP50 Colt McCoy .30 .75

2010 Topps Peak Performance Autographs

GROUP A ODDS 1:1465 H, 1:4200 R
GROUP B ODDS 1:247 H, 1:735 R
PPAAB Arrelious Benn 3.00 8.00
PPAABR Ahmad Bradshaw 3.00 8.00
PPAAD Anthony Dixon 3.00 8.00
PPAAE Armanti Edwards 4.00 10.00
PPAAH Aaron Hernandez 6.00 15.00
PPAAR Andre Roberts 4.00 10.00
PPABF Brett Favre A 175.00 300.00
PPABM Brandon Marshall A 20.00 40.00
PPABT Ben Tate 3.00 8.00
PPACH Chad Henne 4.00 10.00
PPACM Carlton Mitchell 3.00 8.00
PPACS Charles Scott 3.00 8.00
PPACT Chester Taylor 3.00 8.00
PPADA Donnie Avery 3.00 8.00
PPADAM Darren McFadden 8.00 20.00
PPADBR Dezmon Briscoe 3.00 8.00
PPADD Dennis Dixon 3.00 8.00
PPADH David Harris 3.00 8.00
PPADJ DeSean Jackson 6.00 15.00
PPADM Dan Marino A 40.00 100.00
PPADMC Dexter McCluster 4.00 10.00
PPADR David Reed 3.00 8.00
PPADT Demaryius Thomas 8.00 20.00
PPAEM Eli Manning A 40.00 80.00
PPAES Emmanuel Sanders 5.00 12.00
PPAEW Ed Wang 5.00 12.00
PPAFD Fred Davis 3.00 8.00
PPAFG Frank Gore 8.00 20.00
PPAJA Joseph Addai 3.00 8.00
PPAJAF Jacoby Ford 3.00 8.00
PPAJC Jamaal Charles 8.00 20.00
PPAJD Jonathan Dwyer 3.00 8.00
PPAJDA James Davis 3.00 8.00
PPAJE John Elway A 75.00 150.00
PPAJF Joe Flacco 15.00 40.00
PPAJFO Justin Forsett 4.00 10.00
PPAJH Jerome Harrison 3.00 8.00
PPAJJ James Jones 3.00 8.00
PPAJM Joe McKnight 3.00 8.00
PPAJMA Jerod Mayo 4.00 10.00
PPAJN Jordy Nelson 12.50 25.00
PPAJS James Starks 4.00 10.00
PPAJSK John Skelton 4.00 10.00
PPAJST Jonathan Stewart A 6.00 15.00
PPAJW Joe Webb 3.00 8.00
PPAKW Kellen Winslow 3.00 8.00
PPAMC Marques Colston 3.00 8.00
PPAME Marcus Easley 3.00 8.00
PPAMG Mardy Gilyard 3.00 8.00
PPAMJ Michael Jenkins 3.00 8.00
PPAMM Mohamed Massaquoi 4.00 10.00
PPAMR Myron Rolle 3.00 8.00
PPAMSW Mike Sims-Walker 3.00 8.00
PPAMW Mike Williams 3.00 8.00
PPANB Nate Burleson 3.00 8.00
PPAPM Peyton Manning A 50.00 100.00
PPARC Riley Cooper 3.00 8.00
PPARW Reggie Wayne A 12.00 30.00
PPASB Sam Bradford 25.00 60.00
PPASS Steve Slaton 3.00 8.00
PPATC Tashard Choice 3.00 8.00
PPATG Toby Gerhart 6.00 15.00
PPATP Taylor Price 3.00 8.00
PPATT Tim Tebow 30.00 60.00

2010 Topps Peak Performance Relics

GROUP A ODDS 1:265 H, 1:1730 R
GROUP B ODDS 1:141 H, 1:908 R
GROUP B ODDS 1:91 H, 1:589
PPRAB Arrelious Benn 1.50 4.00
PPRAJH A.J. Hawk 2.50 6.00
PPRAR Aaron Rodgers 8.00 20.00
PPRBD Brian Dawkins 2.50 6.00
PPRBM Brandon Marshall 3.00 8.00
PPRBT Ben Tate 1.50 4.00
PPRCC Chris Cooley 4.00 10.00
PPRCJO Chris Johnson 2.50 6.00
PPRCM Colt McCoy 2.00 5.00
PPRDB Dez Bryant 5.00 12.00
PPRDC Dallas Clark 2.50 6.00
PPRDG David Garrard 2.50 6.00
PPRDH David Harris 2.50 6.00
PPRDM Dexter McCluster 3.00 8.00
PPRDMA Derrick Mason 2.50 6.00
PPRDMC Darren McFadden 2.50 6.00
PPRER Eddie Royal 2.50 6.00
PPRFJ Felix Jones 2.50 6.00
PPRGT Golden Tate 3.00 8.00
PPRJB Jahvid Best 4.00 10.00
PPRJC Jimmy Clausen 1.50 4.00
PPRJCU Jay Cutler 2.50 6.00
PPRJD Jonathan Dwyer 1.50 4.00
PPRJJ James Jones 2.50 6.00
PPRJM Joe McKnight 1.50 4.00
PPRKK Kevin Kolb 2.50 6.00
PPRKW Kellen Winslow 2.50 6.00
PPRLE Lee Evans 3.00 8.00
PPRLM Laurence Maroney 2.50 6.00
PPRME Marcus Easley 2.50 6.00
PPRMH Montario Hardesty 1.50 4.00
PPRML Matt Leinart 2.50 6.00
PPRMR Matt Ryan 3.00 8.00
PPRRL Ray Lewis 5.00 12.00
PPRRM Rashard Mendenhall 2.50 6.00
PPRRW Ricky Williams 3.00 8.00
PPRRWA Reggie Wayne 3.00 8.00
PPRSB Sam Bradford 6.00 15.00
PPRSBR Steve Breaston 2.50 6.00
PPRSR Sidney Rice 2.50 6.00
PPRSS Steve Slaton 2.50 6.00
PPRSSM Steve Smith 3.00 8.00
PPRTB Tom Brady 8.00 20.00
PPRTP Taylor Price 1.50 4.00
PPRTT Tim Tebow 6.00 15.00

2010 Topps Peak Performance Relics Autographs

JSY AU/50 ODDS 1:15,000 HOB
PPARAG Antonio Gates 20.00 50.00
PPARAP Adrian Peterson 75.00 150.00
PPARBM Brandon Marshall 25.00 50.00
PPARDB Dez Bryant 40.00 100.00
PPARED Eric Dickerson 40.00 80.00
PPARFJ Felix Jones 20.00 40.00
PPARPM Peyton Manning 90.00 150.00
PPARRM Ryan Mathews 8.00 20.00
PPARRR Ray Rice 20.00 50.00
PPARRW Reggie Wayne 20.00 40.00
PPARSB Sam Bradford 60.00 120.00
PPARSJ Steven Jackson 30.00 60.00
PPARTD Tony Dorsett 40.00 80.00
PPARTT Tim Tebow 50.00 100.00
PPARCJS C.J. Spiller 8.00 20.00

2010 Topps Peak Performance Relics Jumbo

JUMBO/20 ODDS 1:18,000 HOB
PPJR1 Tim Tebow 12.00 30.00
PPJR2 Ryan Mathews 4.00 10.00
PPJR3 Dez Bryant 10.00 25.00
PPJR4 C.J. Spiller 4.00 10.00
PPJR5 Jimmy Clausen 4.00 10.00
PPJR6 Santana Moss 12.00 30.00
PPJR7 Jahvid Best 4.00 10.00
PPJR8 Jonathan Dwyer 4.00 10.00
PPJR9 Roddy White 10.00 25.00
PPJR10 Brandon Marshall 12.00 30.00
PPJR11 Ray Rice 10.00 25.00
PPJR12 Chris Johnson 20.00 50.00
PPJR13 Golden Tate 5.00 12.00
PPJR14 Steven Jackson 10.00 25.00
PPJR15 Maurice Jones-Drew 10.00 25.00
PPJR16 Reggie Bush 10.00 25.00
PPJR17 Colt McCoy 5.00 12.00
PPJR18 Calvin Johnson 15.00 40.00
PPJR19 Montario Hardesty 4.00 10.00
PPJR20 Jamaal Charles 12.00 30.00

2010 Topps Rookie Premiere Autographs

AUTO/90 ODDS 1:750 HOB
RPAAB Arrelious Benn 10.00 25.00
RPAAE Armanti Edwards 12.00 30.00
RPAAR Andre Roberts 10.00 25.00
RPABL Brandon LaFell 12.00 30.00
RPABT Ben Tate 10.00 25.00
RPACM Colt McCoy 12.00 30.00
RPADB Dez Bryant 60.00 120.00
RPADM Dexter McCluster 12.00 30.00
RPADT Demaryius Thomas 25.00 60.00
RPADW Damian Williams 10.00 25.00
RPAEB Eric Berry 25.00 60.00
RPAED Eric Decker 12.00 30.00
RPAES Emmanuel Sanders 15.00 40.00
RPAGM Gerald McCoy 10.00 25.00
RPAGT Golden Tate 12.00 30.00
RPAJB Jahvid Best 10.00 25.00
RPAJC Jimmy Clausen 10.00 25.00
RPAJD Jonathan Dwyer 10.00 25.00
RPAJG Jermaine Gresham 10.00 25.00
RPAJM Joe McKnight 10.00 25.00
RPAJS Jordan Shipley 10.00 25.00
RPAME Marcus Easley 10.00 25.00
RPAMG Mardy Gilyard 10.00 25.00
RPAMH Montario Hardesty 10.00 25.00
RPAMK Mike Kafka 12.00 30.00
RPAMW Mike Williams 10.00 25.00
RPANS Ndamukong Suh 40.00 80.00
RPARG Rob Gronkowski 75.00 150.00
RPARM Rolando McClain 10.00 25.00
RPARM Ryan Mathews 10.00 25.00
RPASB Sam Bradford 30.00 80.00
RPATG Toby Gerhart 10.00 25.00
RPATP Taylor Price 10.00 25.00
RPATT Tim Tebow 50.00 120.00
RPACJS C.J. Spiller 10.00 25.00

2010 Topps Rookie Premiere Autographs Dual

DUAL AU/25 ODDS 1:18,000 HOB
RPDABC S.Bradford/J.Clausen 40.00 80.00
RPDABD J.Best/McCluster 25.00 60.00
RPDABT D.Bryant/D.Thomas 75.00 150.00
RPDASM C.Spiller/R.Mathews 25.00 60.00
RPDATM T.Tebow/C.McCoy 75.00 150.00

2010 Topps Rookie Redemption

COMPLETE SET (17) 8.00 20.00
ISSUED VIA MAIL REDEMPTION
GR1 Jahvid Best .40 1.00
GR2 Demaryius Thomas 1.00 2.50
GR3 C.J. Spiller .40 1.00
GR4 Sam Bradford .50 1.25
GR5 Max Hall .60 1.50
GR6 Chris Ivory 1.00 2.50
GR7 Jordan Shipley .40 1.00
GR8 LeGarrette Blount .75 2.00
GR9 Colt McCoy .50 1.25
GR10 Rob Gronkowski 1.25 3.00
GR11 Mike Williams .40 1.00
GR12 Toby Gerhart .40 1.00
GR13 Javarris James .40 1.00
GR14 Arrelious Benn .40 1.00
GR15 Tim Tebow 1.25 3.00
GR16 Ryan Mathews .40 1.00
GR17 Joe McKnight .40 1.00

2010 Topps Rookie Red Zone Autographs

RED ZONE STATED PRINT RUN 93-100
RZRAAB Arrelious Benn/100 8.00 20.00
RZRAAE Armanti Edwards/100 10.00 25.00
RZRAAR Andre Roberts/100 10.00 25.00
RZRABL Brandon LaFell/100 12.00 30.00
RZRABT Ben Tate/100 8.00 20.00
RZRACM Colt McCoy/100 10.00 25.00
RZRADB Dez Bryant/100 20.00 50.00
RZRADM Dexter McCluster/100 10.00 25.00
RZRADT Demaryius Thomas/100 20.00 50.00
RZRADW Damian Williams/100 8.00 20.00
RZRAEB Eric Berry/100 12.00 30.00
RZRAED Eric Decker/100 10.00 25.00
RZRAES Emmanuel Sanders/100 12.00 30.00
RZRAGM Gerald McCoy/99 8.00 20.00
RZRAGT Golden Tate/100 10.00 25.00
RZRAJB Jahvid Best/100 8.00 20.00
RZRAJC Jimmy Clausen/100 8.00 20.00
RZRAJD Jonathan Dwyer/93 8.00 20.00
RZRAJG Jermaine Gresham/100 8.00 20.00
RZRAJM Joe McKnight/100 8.00 20.00
RZRAJS Jordan Shipley/100 8.00 20.00
RZRAME Marcus Easley/100 8.00 20.00
RZRAMG Mardy Gilyard/98 8.00 20.00
RZRAMH Montario Hardesty/100 8.00 20.00
RZRAMK Mike Kafka/100 10.00 25.00
RZRAMW Mike Williams/100 8.00 20.00
RZRANS Ndamukong Suh/100 15.00 40.00
RZRARG Rob Gronkowski/100 40.00 80.00
RZRARM Rolando McClain/100 8.00 20.00
RZRARM Ryan Mathews/100 8.00 20.00
RZRASB Sam Bradford/100 25.00 50.00
RZRATG Toby Gerhart/100 8.00 20.00
RZRATP Taylor Price/100 8.00 20.00
RZRATT Tim Tebow/100 40.00 100.00
RZRACJS C.J. Spiller/100 8.00 20.00

2010 Topps Super Bowl Highlights

COMPLETE SET (5) 2.50 6.00
ONE SET PER TOPPS SB FACTORY
SB1 Drew Brees .60 1.50
SB2 Santonio Holmes .40 1.00
SB3 David Tyree .40 1.00
SB4 Tom Brady 1.50 4.00
SB5 Adam Vinatieri .40 1.00

2010 Topps Target Exclusive Factory Set Patches

TWO PER TARGET EXCLUSIVE FACTORY SET
TRGT1 Sam Bradford 6.00 15.00
TRGT2 Peyton Manning 6.00 15.00
TRGT3 Tim Tebow 7.50 20.00
TRGT4 Drew Brees 6.00 15.00
TRGT5 Jimmy Clausen 2.00 5.00
TRGT6 Tom Brady 6.00 15.00

2010 Topps Throwback Patch

ONE PER RETAIL BLASTER BOX
LPC1 Santana Moss 4.00 10.00
LPC2 LeSean McCoy 5.00 12.00
LPC3 Ryan Grant 4.00 10.00
LPC4 Reggie Wayne 4.00 10.00
LPC5 Sam Bradford 2.00 5.00
LPC6 Randy Moss 4.00 10.00
LPC7 Darrelle Revis 3.00 8.00
LPC8 Brian Urlacher 5.00 12.00
LPC9 Mark Sanchez 3.00 8.00
LPC10 Steven Jackson 3.00 8.00
LPC11 Kenny Britt 4.00 10.00
LPC12 Mike Williams 5.00 12.00
LPC13 T.J. Houshmandzadeh 3.00 8.00
LPC14 Cedric Benson 3.00 8.00
LPC15 Montario Hardesty 3.00 8.00
LPC16 C.J. Spiller 1.50 4.00
LPC17 Chris Wells 3.00 8.00
LPC18 Brandon Jacobs 3.00 8.00
LPC19 Joe McKnight 4.00 10.00
LPC20 Knowshon Moreno 3.00 8.00
LPC21 Marques Colston 3.00 8.00
LPC22 Jahvid Best 6.00 15.00
LPC23 Peyton Manning 12.00 30.00
LPC24 Drew Brees 6.00 15.00
LPC25 Greg Jennings 3.00 8.00
LPC26 Pierre Thomas 3.00 8.00
LPC27 Colt McCoy 6.00 15.00
LPC28 Ryan Mathews 1.50 4.00
LPC29 Demaryius Thomas 4.00 10.00
LPC30 Larry Fitzgerald 4.00 10.00
LPC31 Matt Forte 3.00 8.00
LPC32 Jonathan Dwyer 5.00 12.00
LPC33 Matthew Stafford 4.00 10.00
LPC34 Vincent Jackson 3.00 8.00
LPC35 Rashard Mendenhall 5.00 12.00
LPC36 Tim Tebow 5.00 12.00
LPC37 Tom Brady 12.00 30.00
LPC38 Donovan McNabb 4.00 10.00
LPC39 Tony Romo 8.00 20.00
LPC40 Eli Manning 4.00 10.00
LPC41 Fred Jackson 4.00 10.00

LPC42 Aaron Rodgers 8.00 20.00
LPC43 Arrelious Benn 4.00 10.00
LPC44 Troy Polamalu 5.00 12.00
LPC45 Dez Bryant 4.00 10.00
LPC46 Golden Tate 5.00 12.00
LPC47 Chad Ochocinco 3.00 8.00
LPC48 Philip Rivers 6.00 15.00
LPC49 Chris Johnson 6.00 15.00
LPC50 DeSean Jackson 4.00 10.00

2011 Topps

COMP.FACT.HOBBY (485) 30.00 55.00
COMP.FACT.RETAIL (485) 30.00 55.00
COMP.FACT.SPCL RET (486) 40.00 60.00
COMP.SET w/o SP's (440) 25.00 50.00
ONE ROOKIE PER PACK
RH EXCH EXPIRATION: 7/31/2014
1A Aaron Rodgers .40 1.00
1B Aaron Rodgers TB SP 20.00 50.00
2 S.Bradford/S.Jackson TC .12 .30
3 Ben Watson .15 .40
4 Reggie Bush .15 .40
5 Lance Briggs .20 .50
6A Kyle Rudolph RC .30 .75
6B Kyle Rudolph SP 3.00 8.00
7 Vincent Brown RC .30 .75
8 Blair White .15 .40
9 Antonio Brown .25 .60
10A Larry Fitzgerald wht .20 .50
10B L.Fitzgerald SP red 8.00 20.00
11A Leonard Hankerson RC .30 .75
11B Leonard Hankerson SP 10.00 25.00
12 Demaryius Thomas .25 .60
13 Brian Cushing .15 .40
14 Tyrod Taylor RC .60 1.50
15 Brandon Harris RC .30 .75
16 Colt McCoy .15 .40
17 T.Tebow/B.Lloyd TC .20 .50
18 M.Schaub/A.Foster TC .12 .30
19A Titus Young RC .30 .75
19B Titus Young SP 3.00 8.00
20 Eli Manning .20 .50
21 Jermaine Gresham .15 .40
22 Austin Collie .15 .40
23 Brandon Meriweather .15 .40
24 Jake Long .15 .40
25 Steve Smith .20 .50
26 Robert Mathis .15 .40
27 Phil Taylor RC .30 .75
28 Sanchez/Holmes/Edwards TC .12 .30
29 Brooks Reed RC .40 1.00
30 Maurice Jones-Drew .15 .40
31 Knowshon Moreno .15 .40
32 Brent Celek .15 .40
33 Jonathan Stewart .15 .40
34 David Harris .15 .40
35 J.Freeman/L.Blount TC .15 .40
36 Devin Hester .20 .50
37 Seyi Ajirotutu .15 .40
38 Mike Tolbert .15 .40
39 DeAngelo Williams .15 .40
40 Greg Jennings .15 .40
41 Akeem Ayers RC .30 .75
42 M.Vick/L.McCoy TC .20 .50
43 Danny Watkins RC .30 .75
44 Davone Bess .15 .40
45 Elvis Dumervil .15 .40
46 Dion Lewis RC .40 1.00
47 Derrick Johnson .15 .40
48 Vonta Leach .15 .40
49 DeMeco Ryans .15 .40
50 Josh Freeman .20 .50
51 Rob Housler RC .30 .75
52 J.Campbell/McFadden TC .12 .30
53 J.Flacco/A.Boldin TC .15 .40
54 Sam Bradford ROY .15 .40
55 Da'Rel Scott RC .30 .75
56 Mike Thomas .20 .50
57 BenJarvus Green-Ellis .15 .40
58 Prince Amukamara RC .30 .75
59 Cameron Wake .20 .50
60A Chris Johnson .15 .40
60B Chris Johnson SP wht 6.00 15.00
61 Anthony Armstrong .20 .50
62 Terrell Suggs .15 .40
63 Vernon Davis .15 .40
64 Dwayne Bowe .20 .50
65 Billy Cundiff .15 .40
66 Jay Ratliff .20 .50
67 David Gettis .15 .40
68 Beanie Wells .15 .40
69 Tyron Smith RC .40 1.00
70A Andy Dalton RC .60 1.50
70B A.Dalton SP in air 10.00 25.00
71 Alex Smith QB .20 .50
72 Jacquizz Rodgers RC .30 .75
73 Aaron Williams RC .30 .75
74 T.J. Yates RC .30 .75
75 Percy Harvin .15 .40
76 Donald Brown .15 .40
77 Mike Goodson .15 .40
78 Roy Williams WR .15 .40
79 Keith Brooking .15 .40
80 Calvin Johnson .25 .60
81 Steve Smith USC .15 .40
82 Anthony Allen RC .30 .75
83 Kevin Boss .15 .40
84 A.Rodgers/J.Nelson TC .30 .75
85A Troy Polamalu .25 .60
85B T.Polamalu SP vert 10.00 25.00
86 Matthew Stafford .20 .50
87 Asante Samuel .15 .40
88 David Garrard .15 .40
89 Chris Long .15 .40
90 Ben Roethlisberger .25 .60
91 Adrian Wilson .15 .40
92 Dexter McCluster .15 .40
93 Tramon Williams .15 .40
94 Pierre Thomas .15 .40
95 Jeremy Kerley RC .50 1.25
96 Lofa Tatupu .15 .40
97 Brandon LaFell .15 .40
98 Zach Miller .15 .40
99 Ryan Torain .15 .40
100A Drew Brees .25 .60
100B Drew Brees SP 10.00 25.00
101 Tandon Doss RC .30 .75
102 Chris Clemons .15 .40
103 Karlos Dansby .15 .40
104 Ndamukong Suh ROY .20 .50
105 Brandon Pettigrew .15 .40
106 Lee Evans .20 .50
107 Marvin Austin RC .30 .75
108 Delone Carter RC .30 .75
109 Jermichael Finley .15 .40
110 Sam Bradford .15 .40
111 Michael Crabtree .15 .40
112 Nathan Enderle RC .30 .75
113 James Starks .15 .40
114 Darren Sproles .20 .50
115 Malcom Floyd .15 .40
116 Fred Jackson .15 .40
117 Chris Johnson TC .12 .30
118 Felix Jones .15 .40
119 Atlanta Falcons TC .15 .40
120 Frank Gore .20 .50
121 Bernard Scott .15 .40
122 C.Ochocinco/R.Kelly TC .12 .30
123 Brian Dawkins .15 .40
124 Nnamdi Asomugha .15 .40
125 S.Johnson/F.Jackson TC .12 .30
126A DeMarco Murray RC .60 1.50
126B D.Murray SP left 6.00 15.00
127 Ryan Whalen RC .30 .75
128 T.J. Ward .15 .40
129 Lawrence Timmons .15 .40
130 Dez Bryant .25 .60
131 Hines Ward .20 .50
132 Julius Thomas RC .40 1.00
133 Ryan Fitzpatrick .15 .40
134 Ricky Stanzi RC .30 .75
135 Brian Hartline .20 .50
136 Brandon Marshall .20 .50
137 Hasselbeck/M.Lynch TC .15 .40
138 James Harrison .20 .50
139 James Jones .15 .40
140 Jay Cutler .15 .40
141 LaMarr Woodley .15 .40
142 Brad Smith .15 .40
143 Bilal Powell RC .40 1.00
144 Danny Amendola .20 .50
145 Jason Campbell .15 .40
146 Dontay Moch RC .30 .75
147 Michael Bush .15 .40
148 Nate Washington .15 .40
149A Randall Cobb RC .50 1.25
149B R.Cobb SP run 8.00 20.00
150 Mark Sanchez .15 .40
151A A.J. Green RC .75 2.00
151B A.J. Green SP fwd 8.00 20.00
151C A.J. Green FS catch .60 1.50
152 Julius Peppers .20 .50
153 Curtis Lofton .15 .40
154 Vince Wilfork .15 .40
155 Kendall Hunter RC .30 .75
156 D.Brees/L.Moore TC .20 .50
157 Rashad Jennings .15 .40
158 Aaron Hernandez .20 .50
159 Donovan McNabb .20 .50
160A Blaine Gabbert RC .30 .75
160B Blaine Gabbert SP run 10.00 25.00
160C Blaine Gabbert FS pass .25 .60
161 Ronnie Brown .20 .50
162 Mario Manningham .15 .40
163 M.Austin/Williams WR TC .12 .30
164 Ray Rice .15 .40
165 Edmond Gates RC .30 .75
166 Vince Young .15 .40
167 Champ Bailey .20 .50
168 Ovie Mughelli .15 .40
169 Mike Pouncey RC .50 1.25
170 Jason Witten .20 .50
171 Brian Urlacher .25 .60
172 Derek Sherrod RC .30 .75
173 Jacoby Jones .15 .40
174 Thomas Jones .15 .40
175 Todd Heap .15 .40
176 Osi Umenyiora .15 .40
177 Ahmad Bradshaw .15 .40
178 Aldon Smith RC .30 .75
179 Kevin Kolb .15 .40
180 Peyton Hillis .15 .40
181 Corey Liuget RC .30 .75
182 Earl Thomas .20 .50
183 Ray Lewis .25 .60
184 Wes Welker .20 .50
185 Stephen Tulloch .15 .40
186 Jerricho Cotchery .15 .40
187 2011 Rookie Premiere .60 1.50
188 Kris Durham RC .30 .75
189 Jahvid Best .15 .40
190 Miles Austin .15 .40
191 Dwight Freeney .15 .40
192 Emmanuel Sanders .25 .60
193 Alex Green RC .30 .75
194 Delon Branch .15 .40
195 Jahri Evans .15 .40
196 Luke Stocker RC .30 .75
197 Steve Breaston .15 .40
198 Jimmy Graham .25 .60
199 J.Stewart/J.Shockey TC .12 .30
200A Cam Newton RC 1.50 4.00
200B C.Newton SP field 30.00 60.00
200C Cam Newton FS 1.25 3.00
201 Brandon Gibson .15 .40
202 Paul Posluszny .15 .40
203 A.J. Hawk .15 .40
204 Tom Brady RB .60 1.50
205 John Kuhn .25 .60
206 Carson Palmer .20 .50
207 Kenny Britt .15 .40
208 Logan Mankins .15 .40
209 Visanthe Shiancoe .20 .50
210 Tim Tebow .25 .60
211 Chris Ivory .20 .50
212 Nate Solder RC .30 .75
213 Gabe Carimi RC .40 1.00
214 Curtis Brown RC .30 .75
215 Denarius Moore RC .30 .75
216 T.Polamalu/I.Taylor TC .20 .50
217 Anquan Boldin RB .15 .40
218 DeAngelo Hall .15 .40
219 Nick Fairley RC .30 .75
220 Michael Turner .15 .40
221 Jacob Tamme .15 .40
222 Darren McFadden .15 .40
223 Haloti Ngata .15 .40
224 Brandon Jackson .15 .40
225 B.J. Raji .15 .40
226 D.Bess/Pennington TC .15 .40
227 Anquan Boldin .15 .40
228 Ryan Kerrigan RC .40 1.00
229 Quinton Carter RC .30 .75
230 Rashard Mendenhall .15 .40
231 Danny Woodhead .20 .50
232 P.Rivers/A.Gates TC .20 .50
233 Chris Snee .15 .40
234 Devin McCourty .15 .40
235A Jerrel Jernigan RC .30 .75
235B J.Jernigan SP leap 6.00 15.00
236 Mohamed Massaquoi .15 .40
237 Trent Cole .15 .40
238A Christian Ponder RC .30 .75
238B C.Ponder SP pass 8.00 20.00
239 Brandon Tate .15 .40
240 Tom Brady MVP .60 1.50
241 Joe Flacco .20 .50
242A Jon Baldwin RC .30 .75
242B Jon Baldwin SP 8.00 20.00
243 Jerod Mayo .15 .40
244 Arrelious Benn .15 .40
245 Marcedes Lewis .15 .40
246 Donald Driver .20 .50
247 Rodgers/Matthews SB .30 .75
248 Joseph Addai .15 .40
249 Roy Helu RC .30 .75
250A Andre Johnson .20 .50
250B Andre Johnson SP red 10.00 25.00
251 Justin Houston RC .40 1.00
252 Takeo Spikes .15 .40
253 Tony Moeaki .15 .40
254 J.Peppers/H.Melton TC .15 .40
255 Chad Henne .20 .50
256 Marcell Dareus RC .30 .75
257 Eric Berry .20 .50
258 Randy Moss .20 .50
259 Lee Smith RC .40 1.00
260A Roddy White .15 .40
260B Roddy White SP wht 6.00 15.00
261 Charles Johnson .15 .40
262 Justin Smith .15 .40
263 Josh Cribbs .15 .40
264 Shane Lechler .15 .40
265 Brandon Lloyd .15 .40
266 Dustin Keller .20 .50
267 Patrick Peterson RC .60 1.50
268 DeSean Jackson .20 .50
269 John Abraham .15 .40
270A Philip Rivers .25 .60
270B Philip Rivers SP blu 10.00 25.00
271 Robert Quinn RC .30 .75
272 Terrell Owens .20 .50
273 LeGarrette Blount .20 .50
274A Torrey Smith RC .30 .75
274B Torrey Smith SP 8.00 20.00
275 James Carpenter RC .40 1.00
276 Kris Dielman .15 .40
277 Muhammad Wilkerson RC .30 .75
278 Ben Obomanu .15 .40
279 Nick Collins .15 .40
280A Antonio Gates .15 .40
(horizontal format)
280B Antonio Gates SP vert 6.00 15.00
281 Tim Hightower .15 .40
282 Matt Schaub .15 .40
283 Mario Williams .15 .40
284 Antrel Rolle .15 .40
285 Joe Thomas .15 .40
286 Sam Bradford RB .15 .40
287 Santana Moss .20 .50
288 A.Smith QB/V.Davis TC .15 .40
289 A.Peterson/Shiancoe TC .20 .50
290 LaDainian Tomlinson .25 .60
291 Greg Olsen .20 .50
292 Niles Paul RC .30 .75
293 Tamba Hali .15 .40
294 Jon Beason .15 .40
295 Shaun Hill .15 .40
296 LaRon Landry .15 .40
297 Jordan Shipley .15 .40
298 Ricky Williams .20 .50
299 Cameron Heyward RC .40 1.00
300A Peyton Manning .50 1.25
300B P.Manning SP blu 20.00 40.00
301 Derrick Mason .15 .40
302 Joe Haden .15 .40
303 Steve Johnson .15 .40
304 Eddie Royal .15 .40
305 Brent Grimes .15 .40
306 Kevin Walter .15 .40
307 Cortland Finnegan .15 .40
308 Chris Cooley .15 .40
309 Danario Alexander .15 .40
310 Ndamukong Suh .20 .50
311 Ras-I Dowling RC .30 .75
312 Jacoby Ford .20 .50
313 Taiwan Jones RC .30 .75
314 Mike Williams USC .15 .40
315 Sidney Rice .15 .40
316 C.J. Spiller .15 .40
317 Matt Cassel TC .12 .30
318 Matt Cassel .15 .40
319 Chad Ochocinco .15 .40
320 Santonio Holmes .15 .40
321A Greg Little RC .40 1.00
321B G.Little SP one-arm 6.00 15.00
322 Tony Gonzalez RB .20 .50
323 Shaun Phillips .15 .40
324 Lance Moore .15 .40
325 Jordan Todman RC .30 .75
326 Allen Bradford RC .30 .75
327 P.Hillis/L.Vickers TC .12 .30
328 Jerome Simpson .15 .40
329 Nick Mangold .15 .40
330A Arian Foster wht .15 .40
330B A.Foster SP blu 6.00 15.00
331 J.J. Watt RC 1.50 4.00
332 Mike Sims-Walker .20 .50
333 Johnny Knox .15 .40
334 Patrick Willis .20 .50
335 Carlos Dunlap .15 .40
336 Marshawn Lynch .20 .50
337 Anthony Castonzo RC .30 .75
338 Kyle Orton .15 .40
339 Cedric Benson .15 .40
340 Hakeem Nicks .15 .40
341 Braylon Edwards .15 .40
342 Jimmy Smith RC .30 .75
343 London Fletcher .20 .50
344 Jeremy Shockey .15 .40
345 Jonathan Vilma .15 .40
346 T.Brady/Woodhead TC .50 1.25
347 Brandon Jacobs .15 .40
348 Allen Bailey RC .30 .75
349 Cameron Jordan RC .40 1.00
350A Julio Jones RC 1.00 2.50
350B J.Jones SP fwd 10.00 25.00
350C J.Jones FS left .75 2.00
351 Greg McElroy RC .50 1.25
352 Pierre Garcon .20 .50
353 Nate Burleson .15 .40
354 Dallas Clark .15 .40
355 Evan Royster RC .30 .75
356 Justin Tuck .15 .40
357 Martez Wilson RC .30 .75
358 Robert Meachem .15 .40
359 Andre Gurode .15 .40
360 Tony Romo .20 .50
361 James Laurinaitis .15 .40
362 Adrian Clayborn RC .30 .75
363 Donte Whitner .15 .40
364 Jason Snelling .15 .40
365 Kealoha Pilares RC .30 .75
366A Daniel Thomas RC .30 .75
366B D.Thomas SP left 6.00 15.00
367 Jabaal Sheard RC .30 .75
368 P.Manning/D.Brown TC .40 1.00
369 Casey Matthews RC .30 .75
370 LeSean McCoy .25 .60
371 Shonn Greene .15 .40
372 Louis Murphy .15 .40
373 Greg Salas RC .30 .75
374 Kellen Winslow .15 .40
375 Fitzgrld/Komar/Brstn TC .15 .40
376 Jared Allen .15 .40
377 Brian Orakpo .20 .50
378 Virgil Green RC .30 .75
379 Matt Forte .15 .40
380A Jamaal Charles red .20 .50
380B Jamaal Charles SP wht 6.00 15.00
381 Heath Miller .15 .40
382A Jamie Harper RC .30 .75
382B J.Harper SP stands 5.00 12.00
383 Mike Williams .20 .50
384 Chad Greenway .20 .50
385 Cecil Shorts RC .30 .75
386 Dwayne Harris RC .30 .75
387 Charles Woodson .25 .60
388 B.Orakpo/L.Fletcher TC .15 .40
389 Rob Gronkowski .25 .60
390 Reggie Wayne .20 .50
391 John Carlson .15 .40
392 Clay Matthews .25 .60
393 Jason Babin .15 .40
394 Jeremy Maclin .15 .40
395A Ryan Williams RC .30 .75
395B R.Williams SP catch 3.00 8.00
396 Austin Pettis RC .30 .75
397 Da'Quan Bowers RC .30 .75
398 Joe Webb .15 .40
399 Johnny White RC .30 .75
400A Tom Brady red .60 1.50
400B Tom Brady SP blu 25.00 60.00
401 Jones-Drew/Garrard/Miller TC .12 .30
402A Shane Vereen RC .40 1.00
402B S.Vereen SP leap 4.00 10.00
403 Jordy Nelson .20 .50
404 Bruce Carter RC .30 .75
405 Marques Colston .15 .40
406 Jabar Gaffney .15 .40
407 J.Tuck/Umenyiora TC .15 .40
408 Ed Reed .20 .50
409 D.J. Williams RC .30 .75
410A Adrian Peterson wht .25 .60
410B Adrian Peterson SP purpl 10.00 25.00
411 Willis McGahee .15 .40
412 Ronald Johnson RC .30 .75
413A Colin Kaepernick RC .50 1.25
413B C.Kaepernick SP hold 5.00 12.00
414 Steven Jackson .15 .40
415 DeMarcus Ware .20 .50
416 Darnell Dockett .15 .40
*417 Tony Gonzalez .20 .50
418 Aldrick Robinson RC .40 1.00
419 Darrelle Revis .15 .40
420 Matt Ryan .20 .50
421 Lance Kendricks RC .30 .75
422 Ryan Mathews .20 .50
423 Richard Seymour .15 .40
424A Mikel Leshoure RC .30 .75
424B M.Leshoure SP catch 3.00 8.00
425 Jordan Cameron RC .40 1.00
426A Mark Ingram RC .50 1.25
426B M.Ingram SP right 5.00 12.00
426C M.Ingram FS both .40 1.00
427A Von Miller RC .50 1.25
427B V.Miller SP no ball 5.00 12.00
428 Owen Daniels .15 .40
429 Christian Ballard RC .30 .75
430A Jake Locker RC .30 .75
430B J.Locker SP run 3.00 8.00
431 Vincent Jackson .15 .40
432 Stevan Ridley RC .30 .75
433 Jimmy Clausen .15 .40
434 Rahim Moore RC .30 .75
435 Matt Hasselbeck .15 .40
436 Mike Wallace .15 .40
437 Stephen Paea RC .30 .75
438A Ryan Mallett RC .30 .75
438B R.Mallett SP pass 3.00 8.00
439 N.Suh/C.Houston TC .15 .40
440A Michael Vick wht .20 .50
440B M.Vick SP grn 15.00 30.00
RH45 Aaron Rodgers RH AU EXCH 250.00 450.00

2011 Topps Black

*VETS/55: 10X TO 25X BASIC CARDS
*ROOKIES/55: 5X TO 12X BASIC RC
STATED PRINT RUN 55 SER.#'d SETS
200 Cam Newton 50.00 120.00

2011 Topps Gold

ETS/2011: 3X TO 8X BASIC CARDS
*ROOKIES/2011: 1.5X TO 4X BASIC RC
GOLD/2011 ODDS 1:10

2011 Topps Red

*VETS/77: 6X TO 15X BASIC CARDS
*ROOKIES/77: 3X TO 8X BASIC RC
FIVE RED/77 PER HOBBY FACTORY SET

2011 Topps 1950 Bowman

MPLETE SET (144) 50.00 100.00
STATED ODDS 1:3
*SILVER/50: 3X TO 8X BASIC INSERTS
1 Ndamukong Suh .50 1.25
2 Calvin Johnson .60 1.50
3 Ray Lewis .60 1.50
4 Ray Rice .40 1.00
5 Joe Flacco .50 1.25
6 Colt McCoy .40 1.00
7 Peyton Hillis .40 1.00
8 Greg Little .30 .75
9 Clay Matthews .60 1.50
10 Aaron Rodgers 1.00 2.50
11 A.J. Hawk .40 1.00
12 Dallas Clark .40 1.00
13 Peyton Manning 1.25 3.00
14 Reggie Wayne .50 1.25
15 Sam Bradford .40 1.00
16 Austin Pettis .25 .60
17 Steven Jackson .40 1.00
18 Ben Roethlisberger .60 1.50
19 Mike Wallace .40 1.00
20 Rashard Mendenhall .40 1.00
21 Chris Wells .40 1.00
22 Larry Fitzgerald .50 1.25
23 DeSean Jackson .50 1.25
24 LeSean McCoy .60 1.50
25 Michael Vick .50 1.25
26 Matt Forte .40 1.00
27 Julius Peppers .50 1.25
28 Greg Olsen .50 1.25
29 Santana Moss .50 1.25
30 Chris Cooley .40 1.00
31 Leonard Hankerson .25 .60
32 Ahmad Bradshaw .40 1.00
33 Eli Manning .50 1.25
34 Frank Gore .50 1.25
35 Michael Crabtree .40 1.00
36 Vernon Davis .40 1.00
37 Jahvid Best .40 1.00
38 Brandon Pettigrew .40 1.00
39 Matthew Stafford .50 1.25
40 Matt Ryan .50 1.25
41 Michael Turner .40 1.00
42 Roddy White .40 1.00
43 Ben Watson .40 1.00
44 Mohamed Massaquoi .40 1.00
45 Jason Avant .40 1.00
46 Alex Green .25 .60
47 Charles Woodson .60 1.50
48 Shonn Greene .40 1.00
49 Dustin Keller .50 1.25
50 Mark Sanchez .40 1.00
51 Eric Berry .50 1.25
52 Dwayne Bowe .50 1.25
53 Jamaal Charles .50 1.25
54 Troy Polamalu .60 1.50
55 Emmanuel Sanders .60 1.50
56 DeAngelo Williams .40 1.00
57 Jonathan Stewart .40 1.00
58 Jeremy Shockey .40 1.00
59 Knowshon Moreno .40 1.00
60 Tim Tebow .60 1.50
61 Jabar Gaffney .40 1.00
62 C.J. Spiller .40 1.00
63 Lee Evans .50 1.25
64 Brandon Marshall .50 1.25
65 Ronnie Brown .50 1.25
66 Jake Long .40 1.00
67 Hakeem Nicks .40 1.00
68 Mario Manningham .40 1.00
69 Steve Smith USC .40 1.00
70 Darren McFadden .40 1.00
71 Rolando McClain .40 1.00
72 Jason Witten .50 1.25
73 DeMarco Murray .50 1.25
74 Felix Jones .40 1.00
75 Dez Bryant .60 1.50
76 Cecil Shorts .25 .60
77 David Garrard .40 1.00
78 Mike Thomas .50 1.25
79 Maurice Jones-Drew .40 1.00
80 Adrian Peterson .60 1.50
81 Toby Gerhart .50 1.25
82 Christian Ponder .25 .60
83 Andy Dalton .50 1.25
84 Jermaine Gresham .40 1.00
85 Jon Baldwin .25 .60
86 Ricky Stanzi .25 .60
87 Devery Henderson .40 1.00
88 Drew Brees .60 1.50
89 Arian Foster .40 1.00
90 Andre Johnson .50 1.25
91 Mario Williams .40 1.00
92 Patrick Peterson .50 1.25
93 Ryan Williams .25 .60
94 Jordan Shipley .40 1.00
95 A.J. Green .60 1.50
96 Jamie Harper .25 .60
97 Chris Johnson .40 1.00
98 Kenny Britt .40 1.00
99 Jake Locker .25 .60
100 Philip Rivers .60 1.50
101 Antonio Gates .40 1.00
102 Jordan Todman .25 .60
103 Joe McKnight .50 1.25
104 Bilal Powell .40 1.00
105 Santonio Holmes .40 1.00
106 Ryan Mathews .50 1.25
107 Vincent Brown .40 1.00
108 Stevan Ridley .25 .60
109 Ryan Mallett .25 .60
110 Tom Brady 1.50 4.00
111 Mikel Leshoure .25 .60
112 Titus Young .25 .60
113 Torrey Smith .25 .60
114 Delone Carter .25 .60
115 Percy Harvin .40 1.00
116 Kyle Rudolph .25 .60
117 Sidney Rice .40 1.00
118 Marshawn Lynch .50 1.25
119 Randall Cobb .40 1.00
120 Greg Jennings .40 1.00
121 Jerrel Jernigan .25 .60
122 Prince Amukamara .25 .60
123 Colin Kaepernick .40 1.00
124 Kendall Hunter .25 .60
125 Mike Williams .50 1.25
126 Josh Freeman .50 1.25
127 Julio Jones .75 2.00
128 Jacquizz Rodgers .25 .60
129 Marcell Dareus .25 .60
130 Blaine Gabbert .25 .60
131 Marcedes Lewis .40 1.00
132 Shane Vereen .30 .75
133 Rob Gronkowski .60 1.50
134 Daniel Thomas .25 .60
135 Edmond Gates .25 .60
136 Kellen Winslow .40 1.00
137 Cadillac Williams .40 1.00
138 Von Miller .40 1.00
139 Reggie Bush .40 1.00
140 Mark Ingram .40 1.00
141 LaDainian Tomlinson .60 1.50
142 Braylon Edwards .40 1.00
143 Taiwan Jones .25 .60
144 Cam Newton 1.25 3.00

2011 Topps End Zone Icons Patches

ONE PER SPECIAL BLASTER BOX
1 Tom Brady 12.00 30.00
2 Nick Collins 3.00 8.00
3 Braylon Edwards 3.00 8.00
4 Nate Burleson 3.00 8.00
5 Chris Johnson 3.00 8.00
6 Mike Thomas 4.00 10.00
7 Steve Johnson 3.00 8.00
8 Eli Manning 4.00 10.00
9 Mikel Leshoure 2.00 5.00
10 Larry Fitzgerald 4.00 10.00
11 LeSean McCoy 5.00 12.00
12 Rashard Mendenhall 3.00 8.00
13 Brandon Lloyd 3.00 8.00
14 Ricky Williams 4.00 10.00
15 Reggie Wayne 4.00 10.00
16 Peyton Hillis 3.00 8.00
17 Matt Cassel 3.00 8.00
18 Michael Crabtree 3.00 8.00
19 Darren McFadden 3.00 8.00
20 Drew Brees 5.00 12.00
21 Mark Ingram 3.00 8.00
22 Steve Smith 4.00 10.00
23 Rob Gronkowski 5.00 12.00
24 Felix Jones 3.00 8.00
25 Andre Johnson 4.00 10.00
26 Mike Williams 4.00 10.00
27 Greg Olsen 4.00 10.00
28 Jordy Nelson 4.00 10.00
29 Brandon Jacobs 3.00 8.00
30 Michael Vick 4.00 10.00
31 Jon Baldwin 2.00 5.00
32 Dominique Rodgers-Cromartie 3.00 8.00
33 Vernon Davis 3.00 8.00
34 Percy Harvin 3.00 8.00
35 LaDainian Tomlinson 5.00 12.00
36 Steven Jackson 3.00 8.00
37 Peyton Manning 10.00 25.00
38 Marcedes Lewis 3.00 8.00
39 Philip Rivers 5.00 12.00
40 A.J. Green 5.00 12.00
41 DeAngelo Hall 3.00 8.00
42 Jake Locker 2.00 5.00
43 Terrell Owens 4.00 10.00
44 LaMarr Woodley 3.00 8.00
45 Roddy White 3.00 8.00
46 Ryan Williams 2.00 5.00
47 Danny Woodhead 4.00 10.00
48 Mark Sanchez 3.00 8.00
49 Brent Celek 3.00 8.00
50 Aaron Rodgers 8.00 20.00
51 Antonio Gates 3.00 8.00
52 Matt Hasselbeck 3.00 8.00
53 Anquan Boldin 3.00 8.00
54 Randall Cobb 3.00 8.00
55 DeSean Jackson 4.00 10.00
56 Hakeem Nicks 3.00 8.00
57 Matt Forte 3.00 8.00
58 Zach Miller 3.00 8.00
59 Daniel Thomas 2.00 5.00
60 Blaine Gabbert 2.00 5.00
61 Kyle Rudolph 2.00 5.00
62 Greg Jennings 3.00 8.00
63 Mike Wallace 3.00 8.00
64 Mohamed Massaquoi 3.00 8.00
65 Maurice Jones-Drew 3.00 8.00
66 Miles Austin 3.00 8.00
67 Brandon Pettigrew 3.00 8.00
68 Pierre Garcon 4.00 10.00
69 Christian Ponder 2.00 5.00
70 Arian Foster 3.00 8.00
71 Lee Evans 4.00 10.00
72 Sam Bradford 3.00 8.00
73 Reggie Bush 3.00 8.00
74 Taylor Mays 3.00 8.00
75 Julio Jones 6.00 15.00
76 Cedric Benson 3.00 8.00
77 Santana Moss 4.00 10.00
78 Knowshon Moreno 3.00 8.00
79 Hines Ward 4.00 10.00
80 Tony Romo 4.00 10.00
81 Andy Dalton 4.00 10.00
82 Devin Hester 4.00 10.00
83 Malcom Floyd 3.00 8.00
85 Matt Ryan 4.00 10.00
86 Wes Welker 4.00 10.00
87 Tim Hightower 3.00 8.00
88 Kenny Britt 3.00 8.00
89 Ahmad Bradshaw 3.00 8.00
90 Adrian Peterson 5.00 12.00
91 Darrius Heyward-Bey 3.00 8.00
92 Ryan Mallett 2.00 5.00
93 Ray Rice 3.00 8.00
94 B.J. Raji 3.00 8.00
95 Jamaal Charles 4.00 10.00
06 Tim Tobow 6.00 12.00
97 Calvin Johnson 5.00 12.00
98 Marion Barber 3.00 8.00
99 Davone Bess 3.00 8.00
100 Cam Newton 12.00 30.00

2011 Topps Faces of the Franchise

STATED ODDS 1:4
BJ S.Bradford/S.Jackson .40 1.00
BW D.Bryant/J.Witten .60 1.50
FO M.Forte/G.Olsen .50 1.25
FW J.Freeman/M.Williams .50 1.25
JM D.Jackson/L.McCoy .60 1.50
MA D.McFadden/M.Allen .60 1.50
MB B.Marshall/D.Bess .50 1.25
MW P.Manning/R.Wayne 1.25 3.00
NS J.Namath/M.Sanchez .75 2.00
NW C.Newton/D.Williams 1.25 3.00
PH A.Peterson/P.Harvin .60 1.50
RF A.Rodgers/B.Favre 1.25 3.00
RJ A.Rodgers/G.Jennings 1.00 2.50
RP Roethlisbrgr/Polamalu .60 1.50
RW M.Ryan/R.White .50 1.25
SD C.Spiller/M.Dareus .25 .60
SF N.Suh/N.Fairley .30 .75
UP B.Urlacher/J.Peppers .60 1.50
WJ R.White/J.Jones .75 2.00
GJD B.Gabbert/Jones-Drew .25 .60

2011 Topps Faces of the Franchise Autographs

AL AUTO ODDS 1:20,840 RET
BJ S.Bradford/S.Jackson
BW D.Bryant/J.Witten 30.00 60.00
FO M.Forte/G.Olsen 25.00 50.00
FW J.Freeman/M.Williams 40.00 80.00
HG P.Harvin/C.Greenway 50.00 100.00
JM D.Jackson/L.McCoy 25.00 50.00
JN G.Jennings/J.Nelson
ML B.Marshall/J.Long
NS J.Namath/M.Sanchez 60.00 120.00
NW C.Newton/D.Williams 100.00 175.00
RW M.Ryan/R.White 40.00 80.00
SD C.Spiller/M.Dareus 30.00 60.00
SF N.Suh/N.Fairley 15.00 40.00
WJ R.White/J.Jones 50.00 100.00
GJD B.Gabbert/Jones-Drew 25.00 60.00

2011 Topps Faces of the Franchise Relics

DUAL RELIC/50 ODDS 1:23,250 RET
FO M.Forte/G.Olsen 10.00 25.00
MA D.McFadden/M.Allen 12.00 30.00
MW P.Manning/R.Wayne 20.00 50.00
NW C.Newton/D.Williams 15.00 40.00
RF A.Rodgers/B.Favre 30.00 60.00
RP Roethlisbrgr/Polamalu 10.00 25.00
RW M.Ryan/R.White 8.00 20.00
UP B.Urlacher/J.Peppers 8.00 20.00
WJ R.White/J.Jones 10.00 25.00
GJD B.Gabbert/Jones-Drew 3.00 8.00

2011 Topps Game Day

MPLETE SET (50) 10.00 25.00
STATED ODDS 1:4
GDAG A.J. Green .40 1.00
GDAP Adrian Peterson .40 1.00
GDBF Brett Favre .75 2.00
GDBG Blaine Gabbert .15 .40
GDBL Brandon Lloyd .25 .60
GDBR Ben Roethlisberger .40 1.00
GDCJ Calvin Johnson .40 1.00
GDCM Colt McCoy .25 .60
GDCN Cam Newton .75 2.00
GDCW Charles Woodson .40 1.00
GDDB Dwayne Bowe .30 .75
GDDBR Drew Brees .40 1.00
GDDM Dan Marino .75 2.00
GDEM Eli Manning .30 .75
GDER Ed Reed .30 .75
GDFB Fred Biletnikoff .40 1.00
GDFG Frank Gore .30 .75
GDGJ Greg Jennings .25 .60
GDHN Hakeem Nicks .25 .60
GDJA Jared Allen .25 .60
GDJB Jerome Bettis .40 1.00
GDJBE Jahvid Best .25 .60
GDJC Jamaal Charles .30 .75
GDJF Joe Flacco .30 .75
GDJJ Julio Jones .50 1.25
GDJN Joe Namath .50 1.25
GDJW Jason Witten .30 .75
GDLF Larry Fitzgerald .30 .75
GDMA Miles Austin .25 .60
GDMF Matt Forte .25 .60
GDMI Mark Ingram .25 .60
GDMJD Maurice Jones-Drew .25 .60
GDMR Matt Ryan .30 .75
GDMV Michael Vick .30 .75
GDNA Nnamdi Asomugha .25 .60
GDNS Ndamukong Suh .30 .75
GDPH Percy Harvin .25 .60
GDPM Peyton Manning .75 2.00
GDPW Patrick Willis .30 .75
GDRL Ray Lewis .40 1.00
GDRM Rashard Mendenhall .25 .60
GDRW Roddy White .25 .60
GDSB Sam Bradford .25 .60
GDSG Shonn Greene .25 .60
GDSH Santonio Holmes .25 .60
GDSM Santana Moss .30 .75
GDTA Troy Aikman .50 1.25
GDTG Tony Gonzalez .30 .75
GDTP Troy Polamalu .40 1.00
GDTR Tony Romo .30 .75

2011 Topps Game Day Autographs

OUP A ODDS 1:10,340
GROUP B ODDS 1:2433
GROUP C ODDS 1:1061
GDAAG A.J. Green 15.00 30.00
GDAAH Aaron Hernandez 6.00 15.00
GDAAP Austin Pettis 2.50 6.00
GDABF Brett Favre 75.00 150.00
GDABP Bilal Powell 3.00 8.00
GDACG Chad Greenway 4.00 10.00
GDACK Colin Kaepernick 4.00 10.00
GDACM Colt McCoy 12.00 30.00
GDADB Drew Brees 50.00 100.00
GDAEB Eric Berry 5.00 12.00
GDAED Early Doucet 3.00 8.00
GDAER Ed Reed 20.00 40.00
GDAES Emmanuel Sanders 5.00 12.00
GDAFB Fred Biletnikoff 10.00 25.00
GDAFJ Fred Jackson 20.00 40.00
GDAGJ Greg Jennings 3.00 8.00
GDAHN Hakeem Nicks 6.00 15.00
GDAJB Jerome Bettis 30.00 60.00
GDAJC James Casey 3.00 8.00
GDAJJ James Jones 3.00 8.00
GDAJN Joe Namath 40.00 80.00
GDAJS James Starks 3.00 8.00
GDAJT Jordan Todman 2.50 6.00
GDAJW Joe Webb 5.00 12.00
GDAKH Kendall Hunter 2.50 6.00
GDAKR Kyle Rudolph 2.50 6.00
GDALH Leonard Hankerson 5.00 12.00
GDAMF Matt Forte 6.00 15.00
GDAMJ Malcolm Jenkins 4.00 10.00
GDANS Ndamukong Suh 15.00 30.00
GDARC Randall Cobb 4.00 10.00
GDARG Rob Gronkowski 20.00 40.00
GDARJ Rashad Jennings 3.00 8.00
GDARM Rashard Mendenhall 6.00 15.00
GDARW Roddy White 6.00 15.00
GDACD Cam Dradford 20.00 50.00
GDASG Shonn Greene 6.00 15.00
GDASH Santonio Holmes 8.00 20.00
GDATY Titus Young 2.50 6.00
GDAVJ Vincent Jackson 8.00 20.00
GDAVM Von Miller 6.00 15.00
GDABFL Brandon Flowers 3.00 8.00
GDAERO Eddie Royal 3.00 8.00
GDAJBE Jahvid Best 6.00 15.00
GDAJJO Julio Jones 15.00 30.00
GDAJNE Jordy Nelson 10.00 25.00
GDAJSM Jimmy Smith 2.50 6.00
GDAJWI Jason Witten 15.00 30.00
GDAKRI Keith Rivers 3.00 8.00
GDAMJE Michael Jenkins 3.00 8.00

2011 Topps Game Day Relics

GROUP A ODDS 1:444
GROUP B ODDS 1:1273
GDRAB Anquan Boldin 2.50 6.00
GDRAG A.J. Green 4.00 10.00
GDRAJH A.J. Hawk 2.50 6.00
GDRAS Asante Samuel 4.00 10.00
GDRBC Brent Celek 2.50 6.00
GDRBG Blaine Gabbert 1.50 4.00
GDRBJ Brandon Jacobs 2.50 6.00
GDRBL Brandon Lloyd 2.50 6.00
GDRBR Ben Roethlisberger 5.00 12.00
GDRCG Chad Greenway 4.00 10.00
GDRCJ Calvin Johnson 4.00 10.00
GDRCN Cam Newton 8.00 20.00
GDRCW Charles Woodson 6.00 15.00
GDRDB Dwayne Bowe 3.00 8.00
GDRDK Dustin Keller 3.00 8.00
GDRDM Dan Marino 10.00 25.00
GDRED Early Doucet 2.50 6.00
GDREM Eli Manning 3.00 8.00
GDRGO Greg Olsen 3.00 8.00
GDRJA Jared Allen 4.00 10.00
GDRJC Jamaal Charles 3.00 8.00
GDRJF Joe Flacco 3.00 8.00
GDRJJ Julio Jones 5.00 12.00
GDRJK Jake Locker 1.50 4.00
GDRKB Kenny Britt 2.50 6.00
GDRKR Kyle Rudolph 1.50 4.00
GDRLF Larry Fitzgerald 3.00 8.00
GDRMA Miles Austin 4.00 10.00
GDRMC Michael Crabtree 2.50 6.00
GDRMCA Matt Cassel 2.50 6.00
GDRMF Matt Forte 2.50 6.00
GDRMI Mark Ingram 2.50 6.00
GDRMJD Maurice Jones-Drew 2.50 6.00
GDRML Mikel Leshoure 1.50 4.00
GDRMV Michael Vick 3.00 8.00
GDRNA Nnamdi Asomugha 4.00 10.00
GDRPM Peyton Manning 8.00 20.00
GDRPW Patrick Willis 3.00 8.00
GDRRB Ronnie Brown 3.00 8.00
GDRRL Ray Lewis 5.00 12.00
GDRRW Ryan Williams 1.50 4.00
GDRSJ Steven Jackson 2.50 6.00
GDRSM Santana Moss 3.00 8.00
GDRSR Sidney Rice 2.50 6.00
GDRTA Troy Aikman 6.00 15.00
GDRTG Tony Gonzalez 3.00 8.00
GDRTP Troy Polamalu 4.00 10.00
GDRTR Tony Romo 3.00 8.00
GDRVJ Vincent Jackson 4.00 10.00
GDRVM Von Miller 2.50 6.00

2011 Topps Game Day Relics Jumbos

STATED PRINT RUN 20 SER.#'d SETS
GDJRAB Anquan Boldin 6.00 15.00
GDJRAP Adrian Peterson 10.00 25.00
GDJRBC Brent Celek 6.00 15.00
GDJRBJ Brandon Jacobs 6.00 15.00
GDJRBL Brandon Lloyd 6.00 15.00
GDJRCB Cedric Benson 10.00 25.00
GDJRDB Dwayne Bowe 8.00 20.00
GDJRJA John Abraham 8.00 20.00
GDJRJAL Jared Allen 12.00 30.00
GDJRJC Jamaal Charles 8.00 20.00
GDJRJF Joe Flacco 8.00 20.00
GDJRKB Kenny Britt 10.00 25.00
GDJRMA Miles Austin 12.00 30.00
GDJRMC Michael Crabtree 6.00 15.00
GDJRMCA Matt Cassel 6.00 15.00
GDJRMF Matt Forte 6.00 15.00
GDJRRB Ronnie Brown 8.00 20.00
GDJRRL Ray Lewis 12.00 30.00
GDJRTG Tony Gonzalez 8.00 20.00
GDJRWW Wes Welker 12.00 30.00

2011 Topps Game Day Relics Autographs

STATED PRINT RUN 50 SER.#'d SETS
GDARAP Adrian Peterson 50.00 100.00
GDARBF Brandon Flowers 12.00 30.00
GDARCB Champ Bailey 15.00 40.00
GDARCG Chad Greenway 25.00 50.00
GDARER Ed Reed 15.00 40.00
GDARFJ Fred Jackson 40.00 80.00
GDARGJ Greg Jennings 12.00 30.00
GDARGO Greg Olsen 15.00 40.00
GDARHN Hakeem Nicks 12.00 30.00
GDARJN Jordy Nelson 15.00 40.00
GDARKR Keith Rivers 6.00 15.00
GDARMR Matt Ryan 15.00 40.00
GDARPH Percy Harvin 12.00 30.00
GDARRW Roddy White 12.00 30.00
GDARVJ Vincent Jackson 12.00 30.00

2011 Topps Rookie Autographs

STATED ODDS 1:12,175
6 Kyle Rudolph 6.00 15.00
7 Vincent Brown 10.00 25.00
11 Leonard Hankerson 6.00 15.00
19 Titus Young 6.00 15.00
70 Andy Dalton 25.00 60.00
108 Delone Carter 6.00 15.00
126 DeMarco Murray 12.00 30.00
143 Bilal Powell 10.00 25.00
149 Randall Cobb 10.00 25.00
151 A.J. Green 40.00 100.00
155 Kendall Hunter 6.00 15.00
160 Blaine Gabbert 6.00 15.00
193 Alex Green 15.00 40.00
200 Cam Newton 150.00 300.00
235 Jerrel Jernigan 6.00 15.00
238 Christian Ponder 6.00 15.00
242 Jon Baldwin 12.00 30.00
256 Marcell Dareus 40.00 80.00
274 Torrey Smith 6.00 15.00
313 Taiwan Jones 6.00 15.00
321 Greg Little 8.00 20.00
325 Jordan Todman 12.00 30.00
350 Julio Jones 75.00 150.00
366 Daniel Thomas 6.00 15.00
382 Jamie Harper 12.00 30.00
395 Ryan Williams
390 Austin Pettis 12.00 30.00

402 Shane Vereen 8.00 20.00
413 Colin Kaepernick 10.00 25.00
424 Mikel Leshoure 6.00 15.00
426 Mark Ingram 10.00 25.00
427 Von Miller 12.00 30.00
430 Jake Locker 40.00 100.00
432 Stevan Ridley 6.00 15.00
438 Ryan Mallett 6.00 15.00

2011 Topps Rookie NFL Shield

ONE PER SPECIAL RETAIL FACTORY SET
LPR1 Cam Newton 6.00 15.00
LPR2 Jake Locker 1.25 3.00
LPR3 Julio Jones 4.00 10.00
LPR4 Mark Ingram 2.00 5.00

2011 Topps Rookie Patch

HRPAD Andy Dalton 5.00 12.00
HRPAG A.J. Green 6.00 15.00
HRPAGR Alex Green 2.50 6.00
HRPBG Blaine Gabbert 2.50 6.00
HRPBP Bilal Powell 3.00 8.00
HRPCK Colin Kaepernick 4.00 10.00
HRPCN Cam Newton 15.00 40.00
HRPCP Christian Ponder 2.50 6.00
HRPCP Austin Pettis 2.50 6.00
HRPDM Delone Carter 2.50 6.00
HRPDM DeMarco Murray 5.00 12.00
HRPGL Daniel Thomas 2.50 6.00
HRPGL Greg Little 3.00 8.00
HRPJH Jon Baldwin 2.50 6.00
HRPJH Jamie Harper 2.50 6.00
HRPJJE Jerrel Jernigan 2.50 6.00
HRPJL Jake Locker 10.00 25.00
HRPJL Julio Jones 8.00 20.00
HRPKH Jordan Todman 2.50 6.00
HRPKH Kendall Hunter 2.50 6.00
HRPKR Kyle Rudolph 2.50 6.00
HRPLH Leonard Hankerson 2.50 6.00
HRPMD Marcell Dareus 2.50 6.00
HRPMI Mark Ingram 4.00 10.00
HRPML Mikel Leshoure 2.50 6.00
HRPRC Randall Cobb 4.00 10.00
HRPRM Ryan Mallett 2.50 6.00
HRPRW Ryan Williams 2.50 6.00
HRPSR Stevan Ridley 2.50 6.00
HRPSV Shane Vereen 3.00 8.00
HRPTJ Taiwan Jones 2.50 6.00
HRPTS Torrey Smith 2.50 6.00
HRPTY Titus Young 6.00 15.00
HRPVB Vincent Brown 4.00 10.00
HRPVM Von Miller 4.00 10.00

2011 Topps Rookie Premiere Autographs

STATED PRINT RUN 90 SER.#'d SETS
RPAD Andy Dalton 15.00 40.00
RPAG Alex Green 10.00 25.00
RPAJG A.J. Green 50.00 120.00
RPAP Austin Pettis 10.00 25.00
RPBG Blaine Gabbert 10.00 25.00
RPBP Bilal Powell 12.00 30.00
RPCK Colin Kaepernick 15.00 40.00
RPCN Cam Newton 125.00 250.00
RPCP Christian Ponder 12.00 30.00
RPDC Delone Carter 10.00 25.00
RPDM DeMarco Murray 20.00 50.00
RPDT Daniel Thomas 10.00 25.00
RPEG Edmond Gates 10.00 25.00
RPGL Greg Little 12.00 30.00
RPJB Jon Baldwin 30.00 60.00
RPJH Jamie Harper 10.00 25.00
RPJJ Julio Jones 40.00 100.00
RPJJE Jerrel Jernigan 10.00 25.00
RPJL Jake Locker 10.00 25.00
RPJT Jordan Todman 10.00 25.00
RPKH Kendall Hunter 10.00 25.00
RPKR Kyle Rudolph 10.00 25.00
RPLH Leonard Hankerson 10.00 25.00
RPMD Marcell Dareus 10.00 25.00
RPMI Mark Ingram 15.00 40.00
RPML Mikel Leshoure 10.00 25.00
RPRC Randall Cobb 15.00 40.00
RPRM Ryan Mallett 10.00 25.00
RPRW Ryan Williams 10.00 25.00
RPSR Stevan Ridley 10.00 25.00
RPSV Shane Vereen 12.00 30.00
RPTJ Taiwan Jones 10.00 25.00
RPTS Torrey Smith 10.00 25.00
RPTY Titus Young 10.00 25.00
RPVB Vincent Brown 10.00 25.00
RPVM Von Miller 25.00 60.00

2011 Topps Rookie Premiere Autographs Dual

ATED PRINT RUN 25 SER.#'d SETS
DG A.Dalton/A.Green 60.00 120.00
GJ A.Green/J.Jones 60.00 120.00
GN B.Gabbert/C.Newton 125.00 250.00
IL M.Ingram/M.Leshoure 12.00 30.00
LY M.Leshoure/T.Young 40.00 80.00

2011 Topps Rookie Red Zone Autographs

ATED PRINT RUN 100 SER.#'d SETS
RZRAAD Andy Dalton 12.00 30.00
RZRAAG Alex Green 8.00 20.00
RZRAAJG A.J. Green 25.00 60.00
RZRAAP Austin Pettis 8.00 20.00
RZRABG Blaine Gabbert 8.00 20.00
RZRABP Bilal Powell 10.00 25.00
RZRACK Colin Kaepernick 12.00 30.00
RZRACN Cam Newton 75.00 150.00
RZRACP Christian Ponder 8.00 20.00
RZRADC Delone Carter 8.00 20.00
RZRADM DeMarco Murray 15.00 40.00
RZRADT Daniel Thomas 8.00 20.00
RZRAEG Edmond Gates 8.00 20.00
RZRAGL Greg Little 10.00 25.00
RZRAJB Jon Baldwin 25.00 50.00
RZRAJH Jamie Harper 8.00 20.00
RZRAJJ Julio Jones 25.00 60.00
RZRAJJE Jerrel Jernigan 8.00 20.00
RZRAJL Jake Locker 8.00 20.00
RZRAJT Jordan Todman 8.00 20.00
RZRAKH Kendall Hunter 8.00 20.00
RZRAKR Kyle Rudolph 8.00 20.00
RZRALH Leonard Hankerson 8.00 20.00
RZRAMD Marcell Dareus 8.00 20.00
RZRAMI Mark Ingram 12.00 30.00
RZRAML Mikel Leshoure 8.00 20.00
RZRARC Randall Cobb 12.00 30.00
RZRARM Ryan Mallett 8.00 20.00
RZRARW Ryan Williams 8.00 20.00
RZRASR Stevan Ridley 8.00 20.00
RZRASV Shane Vereen 10.00 25.00
RZRATJ Taiwan Jones 8.00 20.00
RZRATS Torrey Smith 8.00 20.00
RZRATY Titus Young 8.00 20.00
RZRAVB Vincent Brown 12.00 30.00
RZRAVM Von Miller 20.00 50.00

2011 Topps Rookie Refractors

ONE PER SPECIAL RETAIL BOX
TMB1 Cam Newton 2.50 6.00
TMB2 Blaine Gabbert .50 1.25

2011 Topps Super Bowl Legends

ATED ODDS 1:6
SBLI Bart Starr 1.00 2.50
SBLII Bart Starr 1.00 2.50
SBLIII Joe Namath .75 2.00
SBLIV Len Dawson .60 1.50
SBLV Chuck Howley .40 1.00
SBLVI Roger Staubach .75 2.00
SBLIX Franco Harris .60 1.50
SBLXI Fred Biletnikoff .60 1.50
SBLXIII Terry Bradshaw .75 2.00
SBLXIV Terry Bradshaw .75 2.00
SBLXV Jim Plunkett .50 1.25
SBLXL Hines Ward .60 1.50
SBLXVI Joe Montana 1.50 4.00
SBLXVIII Marcus Allen .60 1.50
SBLXIX Joe Montana 1.50 4.00
SBLXX Richard Dent .40 1.00
SBLXXI Phil Simms .50 1.25
SBLXXIII Jerry Rice 1.00 2.50
SBLXXIV Joe Montana 1.50 4.00
SBLXXV Ottis Anderson .40 1.00
SBLXXVII Troy Aikman .75 2.00
SBLXXVIII Emmitt Smith 1.00 2.50
SBLXXIX Steve Young .75 2.00
SBLXXX Larry Brown .40 1.00
SBLXXXIII John Elway 1.00 2.50
SBLXXXIV Kurt Warner .50 1.25
SBLXXXV Ray Lewis .60 1.50
SBLXXXVI Tom Brady 1.50 4.00
SBLXXXVIII Tom Brady 1.50 4.00
SBLXXXIX Deion Branch .40 1.00
SBLXLI Peyton Manning 1.25 3.00
SBLXLII Eli Manning .50 1.25
SBLXLIII Santonio Holmes .40 1.00
SBLXLIV Drew Brees .60 1.50
SBLXLV Aaron Rodgers 1.00 2.50

2011 Topps Super Bowl Legends Autographs

AUTO/25 ODDS 1:17,600
EXCH EXPIRATION: 7/31/2014
SBAI Bart Starr 125.00 200.00
SBAII Bart Starr 125.00 200.00
SBAIII Joe Namath 75.00 150.00
SBAIV Len Dawson 40.00 80.00
SBAV Chuck Howley 20.00 40.00
SBAVI Roger Staubach 75.00 150.00
SBAIX Franco Harris 40.00 80.00
SBAXI Fred Biletnikoff 25.00 60.00
SBAXIII Terry Bradshaw 100.00 175.00
SBAXIV Terry Bradshaw 100.00 175.00
SBAXV Jim Plunkett 25.00 60.00
SBAXVI Joe Montana 100.00 200.00
SBAXVIII Marcus Allen 40.00 80.00
SBAXIX Joe Montana 100.00 200.00
SBAXX Richard Dent 50.00 100.00
SBAXXI Phil Simms 25.00 50.00
SBAXXIII Jerry Rice 100.00 175.00
SBAXXIV Joe Montana 100.00 200.00
SBAXXV Ottis Anderson 20.00 40.00
SBAXXVII Troy Aikman 50.00 100.00
SBAXXVIII Emmitt Smith 100.00 175.00
SBAXXIX Steve Young 50.00 100.00
SBAXXX Larry Brown 25.00 60.00
SBAXXXIII John Elway 125.00 200.00
SBAXXXIV Kurt Warner EXCH 50.00 100.00
SBAXXXV Ray Lewis 75.00 135.00
SBAXXXIX Deion Branch 25.00 50.00
SBAXL Hines Ward 75.00 150.00
SBAXLI Peyton Manning 100.00 175.00
SBAXLIII Santonio Holmes 25.00 50.00
SBAXLIV Drew Brees 60.00 120.00
SBAXLV Aaron Rodgers 175.00 300.00

2011 Topps Super Bowl Legends Coins Pewter

PEWTER/75 STATED ODDS 1:3100
*BRONZE/50: .6X TO 1.5X PEWTER/75
*SILVER/25: .8X TO 2X PEWTER/75
SBLCI Bart Starr 12.00 30.00
SBLCII Bart Starr 12.00 30.00
SBLCIII Joe Namath 10.00 25.00
SBLCIV Len Dawson 10.00 25.00
SBLCVI Roger Staubach 10.00 25.00
SBLCIX Franco Harris 8.00 20.00
SBLCXI Fred Biletnikoff 8.00 20.00
SBLCXIII Terry Bradshaw 10.00 25.00
SBLCXIV Terry Bradshaw 10.00 25.00
SBLCXV Jim Plunkett 8.00 20.00
SBLCXVI Joe Montana 20.00 50.00
SBLCXVIII Marcus Allen 10.00 25.00
SBLCXIX Joe Montana 20.00 50.00
SBLCXXI Phil Simms 6.00 15.00
SBLCXXIV Joe Montana 20.00 50.00
SBLCXXVII Troy Aikman 8.00 20.00
SBLCXXVIII Emmitt Smith 12.00 30.00
SBLCXXIX Steve Young 10.00 25.00
SBLCXXXIII John Elway 15.00 40.00
SBLCXXXV Ray Lewis 12.00 30.00
SBLCXXXVI Tom Brady 20.00 50.00
SBLCXXXVIII Tom Brady 20.00 50.00
SBLCXXXIX Deion Branch 5.00 12.00
SBLCXL Hines Ward 8.00 20.00
SBLCXLI Peyton Manning 15.00 40.00
SBLCXLII Eli Manning 6.00 15.00
SBLCXLIII Santonio Holmes 8.00 20.00
SBLCXLIV Drew Brees 8.00 20.00
SBLCXLV Aaron Rodgers 12.00 30.00

2011 Topps Super Bowl Legends Giveaway

RANDOM INSERTS IN PACKS
SBLG1 Joe Namath 1.25 3.00
SBLG2 Terry Bradshaw 1.25 3.00
SBLG3 Joe Montana 1.25 3.00
SBLG4 Jerry Rice 1.25 3.00
SBLG5 Emmitt Smith 1.25 3.00
SBLG6 John Elway 1.25 3.00
SBLG7 Tom Brady 1.25 3.00
SBLG8 Peyton Manning 1.25 3.00
SBLG9 Drew Brees 1.25 3.00
SBLG10 Aaron Rodgers 1.25 3.00

2011 Topps Super Bowl Legends Giveaway Die Cut

ISSUED VIA MAIL REDEMPTION
*GOLD/99: .6X TO 1.5X BASIC CARD
1 Joe Namath 6.00 15.00
2 Terry Bradshaw 6.00 15.00
3 Joe Montana 12.00 30.00
4 Jerry Rice 8.00 20.00
5 Emmitt Smith 8.00 20.00
6 John Elway 8.00 20.00
7 Tom Brady 12.00 30.00
8 Peyton Manning 10.00 25.00
9 Drew Brees 5.00 12.00
10 Aaron Rodgers 15.00 40.00
11 Bart Starr 8.00 20.00
12 Bart Starr 8.00 20.00
13 Len Dawson 5.00 12.00
14 Chuck Howley 3.00 8.00
15 Roger Staubach 6.00 15.00
16 Franco Harris 5.00 12.00
17 Fred Biletnikoff 5.00 12.00
18 Terry Bradshaw 6.00 15.00
19 Jim Plunkett 4.00 10.00
20 Joe Montana 12.00 30.00
21 Marcus Allen 5.00 12.00
22 Richard Dent 3.00 8.00
23 Phil Simms 4.00 10.00
24 Joe Montana 12.00 30.00
25 Ottis Anderson 3.00 8.00
26 Troy Aikman 6.00 15.00
27 Steve Young 6.00 15.00
28 Larry Brown 3.00 8.00
29 Kurt Warner 4.00 10.00
30 Ray Lewis 5.00 12.00
31 Tom Brady 12.00 30.00
32 Deion Branch 3.00 8.00
33 Hines Ward 4.00 10.00
34 Eli Manning 4.00 10.00
35 Santonio Holmes 3.00 8.00
36 Greg Jennings 3.00 8.00
37 Clay Matthews 5.00 12.00
38 Jordy Nelson 4.00 10.00
39 Marques Colston 3.00 8.00
40 Terry Bradshaw 6.00 15.00
41 Hines Ward 4.00 10.00
42 Ben Roethlisberger 5.00 12.00
43 Steve Smith USC 3.00 8.00
44 Justin Tuck 3.00 8.00
45 Reggie Wayne 4.00 10.00
46 Joseph Addai 3.00 8.00
47 Jerome Bettis 5.00 12.00
48 Troy Polamalu 5.00 12.00
49 Tom Brady 12.00 30.00
50 Deion Branch 3.00 8.00
51 Terry Bradshaw 6.00 15.00
52 John Elway 8.00 20.00
53 Troy Aikman 6.00 15.00
54 Emmitt Smith 8.00 20.00
55 Jerry Rice 8.00 20.00
56 Troy Aikman 6.00 15.00
57 Emmitt Smith 8.00 20.00
58 Art Monk 5.00 12.00
59 Ronnie Lott 4.00 10.00
60 Jerry Rice 8.00 20.00
61 Ronnie Lott 4.00 10.00
62 Joe Montana 12.00 30.00
63 Art Monk 5.00 12.00
64 Ronnie Lott 4.00 10.00
65 Jim Plunkett 4.00 10.00
66 Howie Long 5.00 12.00
67 Ronnie Lott 4.00 10.00
68 Franco Harris 5.00 12.00
69 Franco Harris 5.00 12.00
70 Roger Staubach 6.00 15.00
71 Tony Dorsett 5.00 12.00
72 Ken Stabler 5.00 12.00
73 Franco Harris 5.00 12.00
74 James Harrison 4.00 10.00
75 Adam Vinatieri 3.00 8.00

2011 Topps Super Bowl Legends Giveaway Die Cut Autographs

SB1 Joe Namath 100.00 175.00

2011 Topps Super Bowl Legends Jerseys

JERSEY/45 ODDS 1:8860
*GOLD/35: .4X TO 1X BASIC JSY/45
*HOLOFOIL/15: .6X TO 1.5X BASIC JSY/45
SBRIII Joe Namath 12.00 30.00
SBRVI Roger Staubach 12.00 30.00
SBRIX Franco Harris
SBRXI Fred Biletnikoff 10.00 25.00
SBRXIII Terry Bradshaw 12.00 30.00
SBRXIV Terry Bradshaw 12.00 30.00
SBRXV Jim Plunkett 8.00 20.00
SBRXVI Joe Montana 15.00 40.00
SBRXVIII Marcus Allen 10.00 25.00
SBRXIX Joe Montana 15.00 40.00
SBRXXI Phil Simms 8.00 20.00
SBRXXIII Jerry Rice 12.00 30.00
SBRXXIV Joe Montana 15.00 40.00
SBRXXVII Troy Aikman 12.00 30.00
SBRXXVIII Emmitt Smith 15.00 40.00
SBRXXIX Steve Young 12.00 30.00
SBRXXXIII John Elway 15.00 40.00
SBRXXXIV Kurt Warner 8.00 20.00
SBRXXXV Ray Lewis 12.00 30.00
SBRXXXVI Tom Brady 25.00 60.00
SBRXXXVIII Tom Brady 25.00 60.00
SBRXL Hines Ward 12.00 30.00
SBRXLI Peyton Manning 15.00 40.00
SBRXLII Eli Manning 8.00 20.00
SBRXLIII Santonio Holmes 10.00 25.00
SBRXLIV Drew Brees 10.00 25.00
SBRXLV Aaron Rodgers 15.00 40.00

2011 Topps Super Bowl Legends Logo Stamps

GO STAMP/100 ODDS 1:980
*PLAYER STAMP/100: .4X TO 1X LOGO/100
*RING/137: .4X TO 1X LOGO STAMP/100
*SB PATCH/50: .5X TO 1.2X LOGO STAMP/100
SBLSI Bart Starr 12.00 30.00
SBLSII Bart Starr 12.00 30.00
SBLSIII Joe Namath 10.00 25.00
SBLSIV Len Dawson 8.00 20.00
SBLSV Chuck Howley 5.00 12.00
SBLSVI Roger Staubach 10.00 25.00
SBLSIX Franco Harris 8.00 20.00
SBLSXI Fred Biletnikoff 8.00 20.00
SBLSXIII Terry Bradshaw 10.00 25.00
SBLSXIV Terry Bradshaw 10.00 25.00
SBLSXV Jim Plunkett 6.00 15.00
SBLSXVI Joe Montana 12.00 30.00
SBLSXVIII Marcus Allen 8.00 20.00
SBLSXIX Joe Montana 12.00 30.00
SBLSXX Richard Dent 8.00 20.00
SBLSXXI Phil Simms 6.00 15.00
SBLSXXIII Jerry Rice 12.00 30.00
SBLSXXIV Joe Montana 12.00 30.00
SBLSXXV Ottis Anderson 5.00 12.00
SBLSXXVII Troy Aikman 10.00 25.00
SBLSXXVIII Emmitt Smith 12.00 30.00
SBLSXXIX Steve Young 10.00 25.00
SBLSXXX Larry Brown 5.00 12.00
SBLSXXXIII John Elway 12.00 30.00
SBLSXXXIV Kurt Warner 6.00 15.00
SBLSXXXV Ray Lewis 12.00 30.00
SBLSXXXVI Tom Brady 20.00 50.00
SBLSXXXVIII Tom Brady 20.00 50.00
SBLSXXXIX Deion Branch 5.00 12.00
SBLSXL Hines Ward 8.00 20.00
SBLSXLI Peyton Manning 15.00 40.00
SBLSXLII Eli Manning 6.00 15.00
SBLSXLIII Santonio Holmes 8.00 20.00
SBLSXLIV Drew Brees 10.00 25.00
SBLSXLV Aaron Rodgers 20.00 50.00

2011 Topps Super Bowl Legends Venue Relics

VENUE RELIC/100 ODDS 1:14,500
SBVRII Bart Starr Seat 12.00 30.00
SBVRIII Joe Namath Seat 12.00 30.00
SBVRV Chuck Howley Seat 8.00 20.00
SBVRXIII Terry Bradshaw Seat 10.00 25.00
SBVRXV Jim Plunkett Turf 8.00 20.00
SBVRXX Richard Dent Turf 8.00 20.00
SBVRXXIV Joe Montana Turf 15.00 40.00
SBVRXXXVI Tom Brady Pylon 15.00 40.00
SBVRXXXIX Deion Branch Pylon 10.00 25.00
SBVRXLV Aaron Rodgers Pylon 15.00 40.00

2011 Topps Topps Town

ATED ODDS 1:6
TT1 Aaron Rodgers .50 1.25
TT2 Adrian Peterson .30 .75
TT3 Andre Johnson .25 .60
TT4 Mark Ingram .25 .60
TT5 Michael Vick .25 .60
TT6 Chris Johnson .20 .50
TT7 Tom Brady .75 2.00
TT8 Jake Locker .15 .40
TT9 Roddy White .20 .50
TT10 Drew Brees .30 .75
TT11 Arian Foster .20 .50
TT12 Calvin Johnson .30 .75
TT13 Matt Schaub .20 .50
TT14 Peyton Manning .60 1.50
TT15 Maurice Jones-Drew .20 .50
TT16 Antonio Gates .20 .50
TT17 Torrey Smith .15 .40
TT18 Hakeem Nicks .20 .50
TT19 Philip Rivers .30 .75
TT20 A.J. Green .40 1.00
TT21 Ray Rice .20 .50
TT22 Greg Jennings .20 .50
TT23 Josh Freeman .25 .60
TT24 Christian Ponder .15 .40
TT25 Jamaal Charles .25 .60
TT26 Mike Wallace .20 .50
TT27 Jerrel Jernigan .15 .40
TT28 Reggie Wayne .25 .60
TT29 Matt Ryan .25 .60
TT30 Blaine Gabbert .15 .40
TT31 Rashard Mendenhall .20 .50
TT32 Ryan Mallett .15 .40
TT33 Larry Fitzgerald .25 .60
TT34 Darren McFadden .20 .50
TT35 Mikel Leshoure .15 .40
TT36 Joe Flacco .25 .60
TT37 Kyle Rudolph .15 .40
TT38 LeSean McCoy .30 .75
TT39 Julio Jones .50 1.25
TT40 Dwayne Bowe .25 .60
TT41 Andy Dalton .30 .75
TT42 DeSean Jackson .25 .60
TT43 Sam Bradford .20 .50
TT44 Michael Turner .20 .50
TT45 Ryan Williams .15 .40
TT46 Wes Welker .25 .60
TT47 Matt Forte .20 .50
TT48 Greg Little .20 .50
TT49 Jason Witten .25 .60
TT50 Cam Newton .75 2.00

2011 Topps Super Bowl XLV

This set was issued exclusively at the 2011 Super Bowl Card Show in Dallas via a wrapper redemption program. Each card features the Super Bowl logo at the top with Cowboys Stadium at the bottom.

COMPLETE SET (7) 20.00 40.00
SBWR1 Tom Brady 6.00 15.00
SBWR2 Drew Brees 2.50 6.00
SBWR3 Michael Vick 2.00 5.00
SBWR4 Miles Austin 1.50 4.00
SBWR5 Sam Bradford 1.50 4.00
SBWR6 Dez Bryant 2.50 6.00
SBWR7 Tony Romo 2.00 5.00

2012 Topps

MPLETE SET (440) 25.00 50.00
COMP.FACT.HOBBY (445) 35.00 50.00
COMP.FACT.RETAIL (445) 35.00 55.00
COMP.FACT.SB47 (445) 35.00 50.00
VETERAN SP ODDS 1:335 HOB
ROOKIE SP ODDS 1:410 HOB
1A Aaron Rodgers .40 1.00
1B Aaron Rodgers SP 15.00 30.00
2 Jahvid Best .15 .40
3A Brandon Weeden RC .25 .60
3B Brandon Weeden SP 3.00 8.00
4 Colt McCoy .20 .50
5 John Kuhn .15 .40
6 Robert Turbin RC .25 .60
7 Rashard Mendenhall .15 .40
8 Eric Weddle .15 .40
9 C.J. Spiller .15 .40
10 Troy Polamalu .25 .60
11 Earl Thomas .20 .50
12 Owen Daniels .15 .40
13 Bears/Ctler/Frte .12 .30
14 T.Y. Hilton RC .50 1.25
15 Harrison Smith RC .25 .60
16 Brian Cushing .15 .40
17 Brandon Lloyd .15 .40
18A Alshon Jeffery RC .50 1.25
18B Alshon Jeffery SP 6.00 15.00
19 T.J. Yates .15 .40
20 Andre Johnson .20 .50
21 Eric LeGrand RC .25 .60
22 Melvin Ingram RC .25 .60
23 Charles Johnson .15 .40
24 Jason Avant .15 .40
25 Ray Lewis .25 .60
26 Antonio Gates .20 .50
27 Adrian Wilson .15 .40
28 DeVier Posey RC .25 .60
29 Titus Young .15 .40
30 Patrick Willis .20 .50
31 Sean Lee .25 .60
32 David DeCastro RC .25 .60
33 Eric Decker .15 .40
34 Jeremy Maclin .15 .40
35 Justin Smith .15 .40
36 Ed Dickson .15 .40
37 T.J. Graham RC .25 .60
38 Johnathan Joseph .15 .40
39 Reggie Wayne .20 .50
40 Dwayne Bowe .20 .50
41 Tamba Hali .15 .40
42 Vick Ballard RC .30 .75
43 Giants/E.Manning .15 .40
44 Bruce Irvin RC .30 .75
45 Dennis Pitta .15 .40
46 Malcom Floyd .15 .40
47 Mark Barron RC .25 .60
48 Ryan Lindley RC .25 .60
49 Eric Berry .20 .50
50A Tim Tebow Jets .25 .60
50B Tim Tebow Broncos SP 8.00 20.00
51 Gerell Robinson RC .25 .60
52A Alex Smith white .20 .50
52B Alex Smith red SP 6.00 15.00
53 Jermichael Finley .15 .40
54 Kevin Kolb .15 .40
55 Roy Helu .15 .40
56 Bills/B.Smith .12 .30
57 Anquan Boldin .15 .40
58A Dwayne Allen RC .25 .60
58B Dwayne Allen SP 3.00 8.00
59 Daniel Thomas .15 .40
60 Darren McFadden .15 .40
61 Brandon Gibson .15 .40
62 Steve Johnson .20 .50
63 Nick Toon RC .25 .60
64 Andy Lee .15 .40
65 Marvin McNutt RC .25 .60
66 Jerod Mayo .15 .40
67 Donald Brown .15 .40
68 Dolphins/Lng/Henne .12 .30
69 Dez Bryant .25 .60
70A Rob Gronkowski .25 .60
70B Rob Gronkowski SP 8.00 20.00
71 Nnamdi Asomugha .15 .40
72 Bucs/Frman/Wnslw .15 .40
73 Rookie Premiere .75 2.00
74 Doug Baldwin .25 .60
75 Carson Palmer .20 .50
76 Chandler Jones RC .25 .60
77A Ryan Broyles RC .25 .60
77B Ryan Broyles SP 6.00 15.00
78 Joe Flacco .20 .50
79 Fletcher Cox RC .40 1.00
80 Chris Johnson .15 .40
81 Chiefs/Cassel/Albert .12 .30
82A DeMarco Murray .20 .50
82B DeMarco Murray SP 8.00 20.00
83 Kendall Reyes RC .25 .60
84 Pierre Garcon .20 .50
85 Joe Adams RC .25 .60
86 Sebastian Janikowski .20 .50
87 Joe Haden .15 .40
88 Dexter McCluster .15 .40
89 Michael Brockers RC .25 .60
90 Jason Pierre-Paul .15 .40
91A Michael Floyd RC .25 .60
91B Michael Floyd SP 8.00 20.00
92 Chandler Harnish RC .25 .60
93 Jason Peters .15 .40
94 Sidney Rice .15 .40
95 Rishard Matthews RC .25 .60
96 Devery Henderson .15 .40
97 Jared Crick RC .25 .60
98 Jon Baldwin .15 .40
99 Robert Meachem .15 .40
100A Drew Brees white .25 .60
100B Drew Brees blk SP 10.00 25.00
101 Chargers/Cason/Jammer .12 .30
102 Jaguars/Gbbrt/J-Drw .12 .30
103 Damian Williams .15 .40
104 Travis Benjamin RC .25 .60
105 Knowshon Moreno .15 .40
106 Mark Ingram .20 .50
107 Matt Schaub .15 .40
108 Brent Celek .15 .40
109 Heath Miller .15 .40
110 Darrelle Revis .15 .40
111 Drew Brees POY .25 .60
112A A.J. Jenkins RC .25 .60
112B A.J. Jenkins SP 3.00 8.00
113 Dallas Clark .15 .40
114 Jabaal Sheard .15 .40
115A Stephen Hill RC .25 .60
115B Stephen Hill SP 3.00 8.00
116 Jake Ballard .15 .40
117 Early Doucet .15 .40
118 Denarius Moore .15 .40
119 Arrelious Benn .15 .40
120A Maurice Jones-Drew wht .15 .40
120B Maurice Jones-Drew teal SP 5.00 12.00
121 Marcedes Lewis .15 .40
122 Jared Cook .15 .40
123 Robert Mathis .15 .40
124 Sean Weatherspoon .15 .40
125 Mike Wallace .15 .40
126 Quinton Coples RC .25 .60
127 DeSean Jackson .20 .50
128 Trent Cole .15 .40
129 Pat Angerer .15 .40
130A Hakeem Nicks .15 .40
130B Hakeem Nicks SP 5.00 12.00
131 Tavon Wilson RC .30 .75
132A Coby Fleener RC .25 .60
132B Coby Fleener SP 3.00 8.00
133 Fred Jackson .20 .50
134A Ryan Tannehill RC .40 1.00
134B Ryan Tannehill SP 8.00 20.00
135 Jay Cutler .15 .40
136 Josh Freeman .20 .50
137 Jermaine Gresham .15 .40
138 Matt Cassel .15 .40
139 Jerel Worthy RC .25 .60
140A Andrew Luck RC 4.00 10.00
140B A.Luck SP rabbit foot 150.00 250.00
140C A.Luck SP scrmblng 60.00 120.00
140D A.Luck FS twisting 6.00 15.00
141 Cam Newton ROY .25 .60
142 Darrius Heyward-Bey .15 .40
143 Steven Jackson .15 .40
144 John Abraham .15 .40
145 Saints/D.Brees .20 .50
146 Cyrus Gray RC .25 .60
147 Lions/Tulloch .12 .30
148 Von Miller ROY .20 .50
149 Michael Egnew RC .25 .60
150A Larry Fitzgerald .20 .50
150B Larry Fitzgerald SP 6.00 15.00
151A Mohamed Sanu RC .40 1.00
151B Mohamed Sanu SP 5.00 12.00
152 Matt Ryan .20 .50
153 Santana Moss .20 .50
154 Stephon Gilmore RC .30 .75
155 Paul Posluszny .15 .40
156 Whitney Mercilus RC .25 .60
157 Kam Chancellor RC .50 1.25
158 B.J. Raji .20 .50
159 Steelers/Roethlis .20 .50
160 Mark Sanchez .15 .40
161 Seahawks/Lynch/Rice .15 .40
162 LaMarr Woodley .15 .40
163 Packers/Rdgrs/Strks .30 .75
164A Vernon Davis .15 .40
164B Vernon Davis SP 5.00 12.00
165A Russell Wilson RC 2.00 5.00
165B R.Wilson SP field 30.00 80.00
166 Falcons/Ryan/White .15 .40
167 Christian Ponder .15 .40
168 Kyle Arrington .15 .40
169 Percy Harvin .15 .40
170 Ben Roethlisberger .25 .60
171 Vince Wilfork .15 .40
172 Carlos Rogers .15 .40
173 Michael Bush .15 .40
174 Nick Barnett .15 .40
175 Ed Reed .20 .50
176 John Skelton .15 .40
177 Aaron Rodgers MVP .40 1.00
178 Santonio Holmes .15 .40
179 Casey Hayward RC .25 .60
180A Ray Rice purple .15 .40
180B Ray Rice white SP 5.00 12.00
181 Chris Clemons .15 .40
182 Isaac Redman .25 .60
183 Ryan Grant .15 .40
184 Brandon Jacobs .15 .40
185A LaMichael James RC .25 .60
185B LaMichael James SP 8.00 20.00
186A Nick Foles RC .60 1.50
186B Nick Foles SP 8.00 20.00
187 Torrey Smith .15 .40
188 Brooks Reed .15 .40
189 Haloti Ngata .15 .40
190 DeMarcus Ware .25 .60
191 Connor Barwin .15 .40
192 Jake Locker .25 .60
193 Kevin Zeitler RC .25 .60
194 Julio Jones .25 .60
195 Keshawn Martin RC .30 .75
196 Curtis Lofton .15 .40
197 Ryan Fitzpatrick .15 .40
198 Joe Thomas .15 .40
199 Tommy Streeter RC .25 .60
200 Adrian Peterson .25 .60
201 Peyton Hillis .15 .40
202 Marvin Jones RC .25 .60
203 Julius Peppers .20 .50
204A Doug Martin RC .40 1.00
204B D.Martin SP forward 5.00 12.00
204C D.Martin FS cutting .50 1.25
205 Greg Jennings .15 .40
206 George Iloka RC .25 .60
207 Plaxico Burress .15 .40
208 Alfonzo Dennard RC .25 .60
209 Jahri Evans .15 .40
210A LeSean McCoy .25 .60
210B LeSean McCoy SP 8.00 20.00
211 Randall Cobb .20 .50
212 Courtney Upshaw RC .30 .75
213 Asante Samuel .20 .50
214A Bernard Pierce RC .25 .60
214B Bernard Pierce SP 3.00 8.00
215 Marques Colston .15 .40
216 Bengals/Gresham .15 .40
217 Stevan Ridley .15 .40
218 Tim Hightower .15 .40
219 Osi Umenyiora .15 .40
220A Wes Welker .20 .50
220B Wes Welker SP 6.00 15.00
221 Don Tate .15 .40
222 Janoris Jenkins RC .30 .75
223A Antonio Brown yell .25 .60
223B Antonio Brown blk SP 8.00 20.00
224 Jamaal Charles .20 .50
225A Matthew Stafford .20 .50
225B Matthew Stafford SP 6.00 15.00
226 Jonathan Martin RC .25 .60
227 Lance Briggs .20 .50
228 Brandon Boykin RC .30 .75
229 Vinny Curry RC .30 .75
230 Frank Gore .20 .50
231 Aldon Smith .15 .40
232 Steve Breaston .15 .40
233 Chris Long .15 .40
234 Davone Bess .15 .40
235 J.J. Watt .25 .60
236 Mychal Kendricks RC .40 1.00
237A Demaryius Thomas .25 .60
237B Demaryius Thomas SP 8.00 20.00
238 Rams/Laurinaitus/Long/Chamberlain .12 .30
239 Jake Bequette RC .40 1.00
240A Justin Blackmon RC .25 .60
240B J.Blackmon SP standing 3.00 8.00
240C J.Blackmon FS leap .30 .75
241 James Anderson .15 .40
242 Lamar Miller RC .40 1.00
243 Peter Konz RC .25 .60
244 Andre Carter .15 .40
245 Devon Wylie RC .25 .60
246 Blaine Gabbert .15 .40
247 Leonard Hankerson .15 .40
248 Bernard Scott .15 .40
249 James Jones .20 .50
250A Cam Newton .25 .60
250B Cam Newton SP 8.00 20.00
251 Willis McGahee .15 .40
252 Jarius Wright RC .25 .60
253 Akeem Ayers .15 .40
254 Ravens/Rice .12 .30
255 David Nelson .15 .40
256 Jordan White RC .30 .75
257 Lavonte David RC .40 1.00
258 Randy Moss .20 .50
259 Cardinals/Heap/Roberts .15 .40
260 Matt Forte .15 .40
261 Dustin Keller .15 .40
262 Kellen Winslow .15 .40
263 LeGarrette Blount .20 .50
264 Johnny Knox .15 .40
265A Reggie Bush .15 .40
265B Reggie Bush SP 5.00 12.00
266 Devon Still RC .30 .75
267 Felix Jones .15 .40
268 Nate Burleson .12 .30
269 Nick Mangold .15 .40
270 Philip Rivers .25 .60
271 Austin Collie .15 .40
272 DeAngelo Williams .15 .40
273 Nate Washington .15 .40
274 Maurkice Pouncey .20 .50
275 Andy Dalton .20 .50
276 Matt Moore .15 .40
277 Matt Flynn .15 .40
278 Juron Criner RC .25 .60
279A Brian Quick RC .25 .60
279B Brian Quick SP 3.00 8.00
280A Jimmy Graham .25 .60
280B Jimmy Graham SP 8.00 20.00
281 Lance Moore .15 .40
282 Panthers/Nwtn/Stwrt .25 .60
283 Ronnie Hillman RC .25 .60
284 Derrick Johnson .15 .40
285 Dontari Poe RC .25 .60
286 Brandon Thompson RC .30 .75
287 Shea McClellin RC .30 .75
288 Patrick Peterson .15 .40
289A David Wilson RC .25 .60
289B David Wilson SP 3.00 8.00
290 Roddy White .15 .40
291 Toby Gerhart .15 .40
292 James Starks .15 .40
293 Brandon Pettigrew .15 .40
294 Fred Davis .15 .40
295 D'Qwell Jackson .15 .40
296 Geno Atkins RC .25 .60
297 Charles Tillman .20 .50
298 Ahmad Bradshaw .15 .40
299 James Harrison .20 .50
300A Eli Manning blue .20 .50
300B Eli Manning white SP 6.00 15.00
301 Mike Williams .20 .50
302 Shane Lechler .15 .40
303 Devin Hester .20 .50
304 LaDainian Tomlinson .25 .60
305 Jason Babin .15 .40
306 Mario Williams .15 .40
307 Tarvaris Jackson .15 .40
308 Michael Turner .15 .40
309 Antwan Barnes .15 .40
310 Ndamukong Suh .20 .50
311 Raiders/C.Palmer .15 .40
312 Greg Olsen .20 .50
313 Terrell Suggs POY .15 .40
314A Rueben Randle RC .25 .60
314B Rueben Randle SP 6.00 15.00
315 Mike Tolbert .15 .40
316 Brandon Browner .15 .40
317 Jerome Simpson .15 .40
318 Dwight Bentley RC .30 .75
319 Matt Kalil RC .25 .60
320A A.J. Green black .25 .60
320B A.J. Green orange SP 8.00 20.00
321 Kenny Britt .15 .40
322 Dont'a Hightower RC .40 1.00
323 Aaron Hernandez .20 .50
324 Broncos/Prater/Paxton .20 .50
325 Von Miller .20 .50
326 Kirk Cousins RC 1.00 2.50
327 Jabar Gaffney .15 .40
328 Colts/Freeney/Mathis .12 .30
329 Brian Urlacher .25 .60
330 Michael Vick .20 .50
331 Elvis Dumervil .15 .40
332 Nick Perry RC .30 .75
333 Laurent Robinson .15 .40
334 BenJarvus Green-Ellis .20 .50
335 Michael Crabtree .15 .40
336 Kendall Hunter .20 .50
337 Dre Kirkpatrick RC .25 .60
338 Anthony Fasano .15 .40
339 Billy Winn RC .40 1.00
340A Robert Griffin III RC .30 .75
340B R.Griffin III SP scrmblng 4.00 10.00
340C R.Griffin III FS leapng 2.00 5.00
341 Deion Branch .15 .40
342 Pierre Thomas .15 .40
343 49ers/V.Davis/O-Line .15 .40
344 James Laurinaitis .15 .40
345 Riley Reiff RC .25 .60
346 Eagles/McCoy/Cooper .20 .50
347 Matt Hasselbeck .15 .40
348 Clay Matthews .25 .60
349 Chris Ivory .25 .60
350 Peyton Manning .50 1.25
351 Jackie Battle .15 .40
352 Greg Little .15 .40
353 Dwight Freeney .15 .40
354 Chris Houston .15 .40
355 Morris Claiborne RC .25 .60
356 Terrance Ganaway RC .30 .75
357 Chris Givens RC .25 .60
358 Kevin Smith .15 .40
359 Cliff Avril .15 .40
360A Arian Foster white .20 .50
360B Arian Foster blue SP 6.00 15.00
361 London Fletcher .20 .50
362 Andre Branch RC .25 .60
363 Zach Brown RC .25 .60
364 Antonio Allen RC .25 .60
365A Brock Osweiler RC .25 .60
365B Brock Osweiler SP 3.00 8.00
366 Markelle Martin RC .30 .75
367 Greg Childs RC .25 .60
368 Orson Charles RC .25 .60
369 Chris Rainey RC .25 .60
370 Sam Bradford .15 .40
371 Vontae Davis .15 .40
372A Marshawn Lynch white .20 .50
372B Marshawn Lynch blue SP 6.00 15.00
373 Justin Tuck .15 .40
374A Steve Smith .20 .50
374B Steve Smith SP 6.00 15.00
375 Tony Gonzalez .20 .50
376A Darren Sproles .20 .50
376B Darren Sproles SP 8.00 20.00
377 Kellen Moore RC .30 .75
378A Kendall Wright RC .25 .60
378B Kendall Wright SP 3.00 8.00
379 Jason Hill .15 .40
380A Trent Richardson RC .25 .60
380B T.Richardson SP ctch 3.00 8.00
380C T.Richardson FS fwd .30 .75
381 Champ Bailey .20 .50
382 David Akers .15 .40
383 Carlos Dunlap .15 .40
384 Brandon LaFell .15 .40
385 Miles Austin .15 .40
386 Jonathan Stewart .15 .40
387 Beanie Wells .15 .40
388 Vikings/Ptrsn/Rdlph .20 .50
389 Mike Thomas .20 .50
390 Charles Woodson .25 .60
391 Redskins/Fletcher/Orakpo .15 .40
392 Shonn Greene .15 .40
393 Tramon Williams .15 .40
394 Brian Orakpo .20 .50
395 Texans/Foster .15 .40
396 Adrian Clayborn .15 .40
397 Cedric Benson .15 .40
398 Ryan Mathews .20 .50
399A Isaiah Pead RC .25 .60
399B Isaiah Pead SP 3.00 8.00
400A Calvin Johnson blue .25 .60
400B Calvin Johnson white SP 8.00 20.00
401 Mike Adams RC .25 .60
402 Josh Cribbs .15 .40
403 Cowboys/Bryant/Witten .20 .50
404 David Harris .15 .40
405 Richard Seymour .15 .40
406 Ryan Kerrigan .15 .40
407 Kelechi Osemele RC .25 .60
408 Marcell Dareus .15 .40
409 Patriots/Gronk/Welker .25 .60
410 Tony Romo .20 .50
411 NaVorro Bowman .20 .50
412 Titans/Locker .20 .50
413 Aaron Corp RC .25 .60
414 Cam Johnson RC .40 1.00
415 Dashon Goldson .15 .40
416 Jordy Nelson .20 .50
417 Chad Greenway .20 .50
418 Browns/McCoy .15 .40
419 Derek Wolfe RC .30 .75
420A Jared Allen .15 .40
420B Jared Allen SP 5.00 12.00
421 Vincent Jackson .15 .40
422 Giants Champs/Eli .15 .40
423 Scott Chandler .15 .40
424 Carl Nicks .15 .40
425 Terrell Suggs .15 .40
426 Mario Manningham .15 .40
427 Brandon Taylor RC .25 .60
428 Rex Grossman .15 .40
429 Dan Herron RC .25 .60
430A Victor Cruz blue .20 .50
430B Victor Cruz white SP 6.00 15.00
431 Andre Roberts .20 .50
432 Cordy Glenn RC .30 .75
433 Luke Kuechly RC .60 1.50
434 Jason Witten .20 .50
435 David Garrard .15 .40
436 Vonta Leach .15 .40
437 Cortland Finnegan .15 .40
438 Brandon Marshall .20 .50
439 Jets/S.Holmes .12 .30
440A Tom Brady white .60 1.50
440B Tom Brady blue SP 20.00 50.00
RH46 Eli Manning RH .50 1.25

2012 Topps Black

*VETS/57: 10X TO 25X BASIC CARDS
*ROOKIES/57: 6X TO 15X BASIC RC
BLACK/57 ODDS 1:69 HOB
134 Ryan Tannehill 6.00 15.00
140 Andrew Luck 100.00 200.00
165 Russell Wilson 50.00 100.00

2012 Topps Camo

*VETS/399: 5X TO 12X BASIC CARDS
*ROOKIES/399: 3X TO 8X BASIC RC
CAMO/399 ODDS 1:60 HOB
140 Andrew Luck 30.00 80.00
165 Russell Wilson 15.00 40.00

2012 Topps Gold

ETS/2012: 2.5X TO 6X BASIC CARDS
*ROOKIES/2012: 1.5X TO 4X BASIC RC
GOLD/2012 ODDS 1:12 HOB
134 Ryan Tannehill 1.50 4.00
140 Andrew Luck 15.00 40.00
165 Russell Wilson 10.00 25.00

2012 Topps Orange

ETS/86: 6X TO 15X BASIC CARDS
*ROOKIES/86: 4X TO 10X BASIC RC
ORANGE/86 FOUR PER HOBBY FACTORY SET
140 Andrew Luck 30.00 80.00
165 Russell Wilson 20.00 50.00

2012 Topps Pink

*VETS/399: 5X TO 12X BASIC CARDS
*ROOKIES/399: 3X TO 8X BASIC RC
PINK/399 STATED ODDS 1:60 HOB
134 Ryan Tannehill 3.00 8.00
140 Andrew Luck 30.00 80.00
165 Russell Wilson 15.00 40.00

2012 Topps 1957 Green

EACH HAS TWO CARDS OF EQUAL VALUE
RANDOM INSERTS IN PACKS
*BLUE WAL-MART: .5X TO 1.2X GREEN
*RED TARGET: .5X TO 1.2X GREEN
1 Andrew Luck 6.00 15.00
2 Andrew Luck 6.00 15.00
3 Robert Griffin III .75 2.00
4 Robert Griffin III .75 2.00
5 Trent Richardson .60 1.50
6 Trent Richardson .60 1.50
7 Ryan Tannehill 1.00 2.50
8 Ryan Tannehill 1.00 2.50
9 Justin Blackmon .60 1.50
10 Justin Blackmon .60 1.50
11 Stephen Hill .60 1.50
12 Rueben Randle .60 1.50
13 Michael Floyd .60 1.50
14 Michael Floyd .60 1.50
15 Kendall Wright .60 1.50
16 Kendall Wright .60 1.50
17 Brandon Weeden .60 1.50
18 Brandon Weeden .60 1.50
19 Coby Fleener .60 1.50
20 Coby Fleener .60 1.50
21 David Wilson .60 1.50

22 David Wilson .60 1.50
23 Lamar Miller 1.00 2.50
24 Lamar Miller 1.00 2.50
25 Doug Martin 1.00 2.50
26 Doug Martin 1.00 2.50
27 Brock Osweiler .60 1.50
28 Brock Osweiler .60 1.50
29 Rueben Randle .60 1.50
30 Stephen Hill .60 1.50

2012 Topps 1965 Mini

MPLETE SET (141) 60.00 120.00
STATED ODDS 1:3 HOB
1 Cam Newton .60 1.50
2 Brandon Jacobs .40 1.00
3 Jamaal Charles .50 1.25
4 Hakeem Nicks .40 1.00
5 Michael Turner .40 1.00
6 Tarvaris Jackson .40 1.00
7 Jeremy Maclin .40 1.00
8 Terrell Suggs .40 1.00
9 Nick Mangold .40 1.00
10 LeSean McCoy .60 1.50
11 Carson Palmer .50 1.25
12 Pat Angerer .40 1.00
13 Fred Jackson .50 1.25
14 Andy Dalton .50 1.25
15 Mark Ingram .50 1.25
16 Miles Austin .40 1.00
17 Joe Thomas .40 1.00
18 Kevin Kolb .40 1.00
19 Leonard Hankerson .40 1.00
20 Drew Brees .60 1.50
21 Ryan Fitzpatrick .40 1.00
22 Titus Young .40 1.00
23 Ed Reed .50 1.25
24 DeSean Jackson .50 1.25
25 Michael Vick .50 1.25
26 Pierre Thomas .40 1.00
27 Doug Baldwin .60 1.50
28 Jared Allen .40 1.00
29 Osi Umenyiora .40 1.00
30 Rob Gronkowski .60 1.50
31 Willis McGahee .40 1.00
32 Frank Gore .50 1.25
33 Matt Ryan .50 1.25
34 Cedric Benson .40 1.00
35 Jason Babin .40 1.00
36 Early Doucet .40 1.00
37 Devery Henderson .40 1.00
38 Kenny Britt .40 1.00
39 Ryan Grant .40 1.00
40 Adrian Peterson .60 1.50
41 Toby Gerhart .40 1.00
42 Brandon Marshall .50 1.25
43 Mike Wallace .40 1.00
44 Darrius Heyward-Bey .40 1.00
45 Sean Lee .60 1.50
46 Dallas Clark .40 1.00
47 Marcedes Lewis .40 1.00
48 Steve Johnson .50 1.25
49 Jake Locker .60 1.50
50 Tom Brady 1.50 4.00
51 Jason Witten .50 1.25
52 Tim Tebow .60 1.50
53 Darren Sproles .50 1.25
54 Elvis Dumervil .40 1.00
55 Sam Bradford .40 1.00
56 Jermichael Finley .40 1.00
57 Troy Polamalu .60 1.50
58 Devin Hester .50 1.25
59 Christian Ponder .40 1.00
60 Calvin Johnson .60 1.50
61 Greg Jennings .40 1.00
62 Mark Sanchez .40 1.00
63 Anquan Boldin .40 1.00
64 Donald Brown .40 1.00
65 Paul Posluszny .40 1.00
66 Marcell Dareus .40 1.00
67 Josh Freeman .50 1.25
68 Jon Baldwin .40 1.00
69 Patrick Peterson .40 1.00
70 Ray Rice .40 1.00
71 Marques Colston .40 1.00
72 Colt McCoy .50 1.25
73 Ryan Mathews .50 1.25
74 Nnamdi Asomugha .40 1.00
75 Arian Foster .50 1.25
76 Stevan Ridley .40 1.00
77 John Kuhn .40 1.00
78 David Akers .40 1.00
79 Chris Johnson .40 1.00
80 Larry Fitzgerald .50 1.25
81 Greg Little .40 1.00
82 Dustin Keller .40 1.00
83 Antonio Brown .60 1.50
84 Antonio Gates .50 1.25
85 Julio Jones .60 1.50
86 Malcom Floyd .40 1.00
87 Matt Schaub .40 1.00
88 Daniel Thomas .40 1.00
89 Marshawn Lynch .50 1.25
90 Ben Roethlisberger .60 1.50
91 DeMarcus Ware .60 1.50
92 Randall Cobb .50 1.25
93 Alex Smith .50 1.25
94 Jordy Nelson .50 1.25
95 Joe Flacco .50 1.25
96 Julius Peppers .50 1.25
97 Aaron Hernandez .50 1.25
98 Jason Pierre-Paul .40 1.00
99 Peyton Hillis .40 1.00
100 Eli Manning .50 1.25
101 Vernon Davis .40 1.00
102 Demaryius Thomas .60 1.50
103 Von Miller .50 1.25
104 Torrey Smith .40 1.00
105 Rashard Mendenhall .40 1.00
106 Ahmad Bradshaw .40 1.00
107 Heath Miller .40 1.00
108 Victor Cruz .50 1.25
109 Matthew Stafford .50 1.25
110 Maurice Jones-Drew .40 1.00
111 Matt Forte .40 1.00
112 Matt Moore .40 1.00
113 Blaine Gabbert .40 1.00
114 Darren McFadden .40 1.00
115 Kendall Hunter .50 1.25
116 Steven Jackson .40 1.00
117 Reggie Bush .40 1.00
118 Charles Tillman .50 1.25
119 B.J. Raji .40 1.00
120 Aaron Rodgers 1.00 2.50
121 Knowshon Moreno .40 1.00
122 Joe Namath 2.00 5.00
123 Santana Moss .50 1.25
124 Darrelle Revis .40 1.00
125 Andre Johnson .50 1.25
126 Beanie Wells .40 1.00
127 Eric Decker .40 1.00
128 DeMarco Murray .50 1.25
129 Percy Harvin .40 1.00
130 Jimmy Graham .60 1.50
131 Santonio Holmes .40 1.00
132 Robert Mathis .40 1.00
133 Mario Manningham .40 1.00
134 Dez Bryant .60 1.50
135 Patrick Willis .50 1.25
136 A.J. Green .60 1.50
137 Jermaine Gresham .40 1.00
138 Jay Cutler .40 1.00
139 Wes Welker .50 1.25
140 Philip Rivers .60 1.50
141 Peyton Manning 1.25 3.00

2012 Topps 1965 Mini Autographs

STATED ODDS 1:1650 HOB
142 Ryan Tannehill 20.00 50.00
143 Nick Foles 30.00 80.00
144 Michael Floyd 12.00 30.00
145 Kendall Wright 12.00 30.00
146 Brandon Weeden 30.00 80.00
147 Michael Egnew 12.00 30.00
148 David Wilson 12.00 30.00
149 Lamar Miller 20.00 50.00
150 Andrew Luck 300.00 500.00
151 Brock Osweiler 12.00 30.00
152 Russell Wilson 200.00 350.00
153 A.J. Jenkins 30.00 60.00
154 Chris Givens 12.00 30.00
154 Alshon Jeffery 25.00 60.00
155 Mohamed Sanu 20.00 50.00
156 Rueben Randle 30.00 60.00
157 Nick Toon 12.00 30.00
158 Isaiah Pead 12.00 30.00
159 Doug Martin 20.00 50.00
160 Robert Griffin III 40.00 80.00
161 LaMichael James 30.00 80.00
162 Brian Quick 12.00 30.00
163 Robert Turbin 10.00 25.00
164 DeVier Posey 12.00 30.00
165 Bernard Pierce EXCH 12.00 30.00
167 Coby Fleener 12.00 30.00
168 Jarius Wright 12.00 30.00
169 Dwayne Allen 20.00 50.00
170 Trent Richardson 25.00 60.00
171 Stephen Hill 12.00 30.00
172 Ryan Broyles 12.00 30.00
173 Joe Adams 12.00 30.00
174 Ronnie Hillman 12.00 30.00
175 Justin Blackmon 12.00 30.00
176 T.J. Graham 12.00 30.00

2012 Topps 1984 Autographs

AUTO/100 ODDS 1:1650 HOB
1 Andrew Luck 200.00 400.00
2 Kendall Wright 10.00 25.00
3 Michael Floyd 10.00 25.00
4 Nick Foles 25.00 60.00
5 Brandon Weeden 20.00 50.00
6 Lamar Miller 15.00 40.00
7 David Wilson 10.00 25.00
8 Dwayne Allen 10.00 25.00
9 Brock Osweiler 10.00 25.00
10 Robert Griffin III 40.00 80.00
11 Nick Toon 10.00 25.00
12 Rueben Randle 10.00 25.00
13 Mohamed Sanu 15.00 40.00
14 Russell Wilson 150.00 250.00
15 DeVier Posey 10.00 25.00
16 A.J. Jenkins 10.00 25.00
17 Isaiah Pead 10.00 25.00
19 Brian Quick 10.00 25.00
20 Trent Richardson 25.00 60.00
21 LaMichael James 10.00 25.00
22 Doug Martin 15.00 40.00
23 Bernard Pierce EXCH 10.00 25.00
24 Robert Turbin 10.00 25.00
25 Ryan Tannehill 15.00 40.00
26 Coby Fleener 10.00 25.00
27 Chris Givens 10.00 25.00
28 Stephen Hill 10.00 25.00
29 T.J. Graham 10.00 25.00
30 Justin Blackmon 10.00 25.00
31 Ryan Broyles 10.00 25.00
32 Joe Adams 10.00 25.00
33 Ronnie Hillman 10.00 25.00
34 Michael Egnew 10.00 25.00
35 Jarius Wright 10.00 25.00
36 Alshon Jeffery 20.00 50.00

2012 Topps AstroTurf NFLPA Collegiate Bowl Autographs

STATED ODDS 1:121 BOWMAN HOB
92 Jacory Harris 4.00 10.00
30 Patrick Witt 4.00 10.00
77 Bo Levi Mitchell 4.00 10.00

2012 Topps Continuity Autographs

STATED PRINT RUN 100 SER.#'d SETS
AL Andrew Luck 125.00 250.00
RG Robert Griffin III 20.00 50.00

2012 Topps Factory Set Patch

TLPAL Andrew Luck 8.00 20.00
TLPRG Robert Griffin III 6.00 15.00

2012 Topps Field General Medals

STATED PRINT RUN 50 SER.#'d SETS
NFGAD Andy Dalton 15.00 40.00
NFGAR Aaron Rodgers 40.00 80.00
NFGBR Ben Roethlisberger 30.00 60.00
NFGCN Cam Newton 30.00 60.00
NFGCP Carson Palmer 15.00 40.00
NFGDB Drew Brees 30.00 60.00
NFGEM Eli Manning 30.00 60.00
NFGJC Jay Cutler 12.00 30.00
NFGJF Josh Freeman 12.00 30.00
NFGJFL Joe Flacco 15.00 40.00
NFGMR Matt Ryan 15.00 40.00
NFGMS Matthew Stafford 15.00 40.00
NFGMSA Mark Sanchez 12.00 30.00
NFGMSC Matt Schaub 12.00 30.00
NFGMV Michael Vick 15.00 40.00
NFGPM Peyton Manning 50.00 100.00
NFGPR Philip Rivers 12.00 30.00
NFGSB Sam Bradford 12.00 30.00
NFGTB Tom Brady 40.00 80.00
NFGTR Tony Romo 15.00 40.00

2012 Topps Game Time Giveaway Die Cut

ISSUED VIA MAIL REDEMPTION
*GOLD/99: 1X TO 2.5X SILVER
1 Robert Griffin III 1.50 4.00
2 Rob Gronkowski 3.00 8.00
3 Isaiah Pead 1.25 3.00
4 Doug Martin 2.00 5.00
5 Aaron Rodgers 5.00 12.00
6 Bernard Pierce 1.25 3.00
7 Calvin Johnson 3.00 8.00
8 Ryan Broyles 1.25 3.00
9 Brandon Weeden 1.25 3.00
10 Dan Marino 6.00 15.00
11 Nick Toon 1.25 3.00
12 Arian Foster 2.50 6.00
13 Rueben Randle 1.25 3.00
14 LaMichael James 1.25 3.00
15 Jim Brown 4.00 10.00
16 Russell Wilson 10.00 25.00
17 Patrick Willis 2.50 6.00
18 Ray Rice 2.00 5.00
19 Nick Foles 3.00 8.00
20 Tom Brady 8.00 20.00
21 Matthew Stafford 2.50 6.00
22 David Wilson 1.25 3.00
23 Kendall Wright 1.25 3.00
24 Michael Floyd 1.25 3.00
25 Jerry Rice 5.00 12.00
26 Tony Romo 2.50 6.00
27 Frank Gore 2.50 6.00
28 Alshon Jeffery 2.50 6.00
29 Brock Osweiler 1.25 3.00
30 Emmitt Smith 5.00 12.00
31 Maurice Jones-Drew 2.00 5.00
32 Adrian Peterson 5.00 12.00
33 Michael Vick 2.50 6.00
34 Stephen Hill 1.25 3.00
35 Drew Brees 3.00 8.00
36 Mark Sanchez 2.00 5.00
37 Jeremy Maclin 2.00 5.00
38 Cam Newton 3.00 8.00
39 Justin Blackmon 1.25 3.00
40 Eli Manning 2.50 6.00
41 Mohamed Sanu 2.00 5.00
42 LeSean McCoy 3.00 8.00
43 Jimmy Graham 3.00 8.00
44 Trent Richardson 1.25 3.00
45 Terry Bradshaw 4.00 10.00
46 Lamar Miller 2.00 5.00
47 Brian Quick 1.25 3.00
48 Ryan Tannehill 2.00 5.00
49 Coby Fleener 1.25 3.00
50 Andrew Luck 12.00 30.00

2012 Topps Game Time Giveaway Die Cut Autographs

STATED PRINT RUN 25 SER.#'d SETS
1 Robert Griffin III 25.00 60.00
4 Doug Martin 20.00 50.00
9 Brandon Weeden 25.00 60.00
22 David Wilson 12.00 30.00
23 Kendall Wright 12.00 30.00
24 Michael Floyd 12.00 30.00
39 Justin Blackmon 12.00 30.00
44 Trent Richardson 40.00 100.00
48 Ryan Tannehill 20.00 50.00
50 Andrew Luck 150.00 300.00

2012 Topps NFL Captains Patches

RANDOM INSERTS IN PACKS
*PINK/99: .8X TO 2X BASIC PATCH
NCPAJ Andre Johnson 5.00 12.00
NCPAJH A.J. Hawk 4.00 10.00
NCPAR Aaron Rodgers 10.00 25.00
NCPAW Adrian Wilson 4.00 10.00
NCPBD Brian Dawkins 4.00 10.00
NCPCB Champ Bailey 5.00 12.00
NCPCW Charles Woodson 6.00 15.00
NCPDB Drew Brees 10.00 25.00
NCPDH DeAngelo Hall 4.00 10.00
NCPDM Darren McFadden 4.00 10.00
NCPDR Darrelle Revis 4.00 10.00
NCPDW DeMarcus Ware 6.00 15.00
NCPEM Eli Manning 10.00 25.00
NCPFJ Fred Jackson 5.00 12.00
NCPJB Jon Beason 4.00 10.00
NCPJC Jay Cutler 4.00 10.00
NCPJF Josh Freeman 5.00 12.00
NCPJL Jake Long 4.00 10.00
NCPJP Julius Peppers 6.00 15.00
NCPJW Jason Witten 5.00 12.00
NCPLF Larry Fitzgerald 5.00 12.00
NCPMH Matt Hasselbeck 4.00 10.00
NCPMJD Maurice Jones-Drew 4.00 10.00
NCPML Marcedes Lewis 4.00 10.00
NCPMS Mark Sanchez 4.00 10.00
NCPMSC Matt Schaub 6.00 15.00
NCPMST Matthew Stafford 5.00 12.00
NCPPM Peyton Manning 12.00 30.00
NCPRF Ryan Fitzpatrick 4.00 10.00
NCPRS Richard Seymour 4.00 10.00
NCPSJ Steven Jackson 4.00 10.00
NCPSM Santana Moss 5.00 12.00
NCPSS Steve Smith 5.00 12.00
NCPTR Tony Romo 5.00 12.00
NCPWM Willis McGahee 4.00 10.00

2012 Topps NFL MVPs

MVP/50 ODDS 1:7000 HOB
LMVPAR Aaron Rodgers 15.00 40.00
LMVPBS Bart Starr 15.00 40.00
LMVPDM Dan Marino 30.00 60.00
LMVPJE John Elway 15.00 40.00
LMVPBF1 Brett Favre 20.00 50.00
LMVPBF2 Brett Favre 20.00 50.00
LMVPBF3 Brett Favre 20.00 50.00
LMVPJM1 Joe Montana 25.00 60.00
LMVPJM2 Joe Montana 25.00 60.00
LMVPKW1 Kurt Warner 1996 UER 8.00 20.00
LMVPKW2 Kurt Warner 2001 8.00 20.00
LMVPPM1 Peyton Manning 20.00 50.00
LMVPPM2 Peyton Manning 20.00 50.00
LMVPPM3 Peyton Manning 20.00 50.00
LMVPPM4 Peyton Manning 20.00 50.00
LMVPSY1 Steve Young 12.00 30.00
LMVPSY2 Steve Young 12.00 30.00
LMVPTBR Terry Bradshaw 15.00 40.00
LMVPYAT Y.A. Tittle 10.00 25.00
LMVPTBR1 Tom Brady 25.00 60.00
LMVPTBR2 Tom Brady 25.00 60.00

2012 Topps Paramount Pairs

MPLETE SET (22) 5.00 12.00
STATED ODDS 1:4 HOB
PABB D.Bryant/J.Blackmon .20 .50
PABD C.Benson/A.Dalton .25 .60
PABJA L.Blount/L.James .15 .40
PABP A.Bradshaw/J.Pierre-Paul .20 .50
PABR Blackmon/Richardson .12 .30
PACS M.Colston/D.Sproles .25 .60
PACT M.Colston/P.Thomas .20 .50
PAEP J.Elway/J.Plunkett .50 1.25
PAFJ R.Fitzpatrick/S.Johnson .25 .60
PAGM F.Gore/L.Miller .20 .50
PAGW R.Griffin III/K. Wright .15 .40
PAHG P.Harvin/J.Gaffney .20 .50
PAJW V.Jackson/M.Williams .25 .60
PALE A.Luck/J.Elway 1.25 3.00
PALF R.Lewis/J.Flacco .30 .75
PALG A.Luck/R.Griffin III 2.50 6.00
PALP A.Luck/J.Plunkett 1.00 2.50
PALW B.Lloyd/W.Welker .25 .60
PAMM W.McGahee/L.Miller .20 .50
PARJ S.Rice/A.Jeffery .25 .60
PATG R.Tannehill/C.Gray .20 .50
PAWBL B.Weeden/J.Blackmon .12 .30

2012 Topps Paramount Pairs Autographs

AU PAIRS/25 ODDS 1:20,500 HOB
PAABB D.Bryant/J.Blackmon 50.00 100.00
PAABJ L.Blount/L.James
PAABP A.Bradshaw/Pierre-Paul 30.00 60.00
PAABR J.Blackmon/Richardson 25.00 60.00
PAACS M.Colston/D.Sproles 25.00 50.00
PAAEP J.Elway/Jim Plunkett 60.00 120.00
PAAGM F.Gore/Lamar Miller
PAAGW R.Griffin III/K.Wright 40.00 80.00
PAAHG P.Harvin/Jabar Gaffney 12.00 30.00
PAAJW V.Jackson/M.Williams
PAALE A.Luck/John Elway 200.00 350.00
PAALG A.Luck/R.Griffin III 150.00 300.00
PAALP A.Luck/Jim Plunkett 125.00 200.00
PAAMM W.McGahee/L.Miller
PAARJ S.Rice/Alshon Jeffery
PAATG R.Tannehill/Cyrus Gray
PAAWBL B.Weeden/J.Blackmon

2012 Topps Paramount Pairs Relics

RELIC PAIRS/50 ODDS 1:11,900 HOB
PARBD C.Benson/A.Dalton 6.00 15.00
PARBR Blackmon/Richardson 3.00 8.00
PARCT M.Colston/P.Thomas 5.00 12.00
PARFJ Fitzpatrick/S.Johnson 6.00 15.00
PARGW R.Griffin III/K.Wright 15.00 40.00
PARLF R.Lewis/J.Flacco
PARLG A.Luck/R.Griffin III 25.00 60.00
PARLW B.Lloyd/W.Welker 10.00 25.00
PARNC H.Nicks/V.Cruz 15.00 40.00
PARTR M.Turner/M.Ryan 6.00 15.00

2012 Topps Prolific Playmakers

MPLETE SET (50) 8.00 20.00
STATED ODDS 1:4 HOB
PPAB Anquan Boldin .30 .75
PPABR Ahmad Bradshaw .30 .75
PPAD Andy Dalton .40 1.00
PPAF Arian Foster .40 1.00
PPAJG A.J. Green .50 1.25
PPAL Andrew Luck 2.00 5.00
PPANB Antonio Brown .50 1.25
PPBL Brandon Lloyd .30 .75
PPBM Brandon Marshall .40 1.00
PPCB Cedric Benson .30 .75
PPCF Coby Fleener .20 .50
PPDB Dwayne Bowe .40 1.00
PPDEB Dez Bryant .50 1.25
PPDMO Denarius Moore .30 .75
PPDS Darren Sproles .40 1.00
PPFG Frank Gore .40 1.00
PPJA Jared Allen .30 .75
PPJB Jahvid Best .30 .75
PPJBL Justin Blackmon .20 .50
PPJF Joe Flacco .40 1.00
PPJG Jabar Gaffney .30 .75
PPJGR Jimmy Graham .50 1.25
PPJPP Jason Pierre-Paul .30 .75
PPKK Kevin Kolb .30 .75
PPLB LeGarrette Blount .40 1.00
PPLF Larry Fitzgerald .40 1.00
PPLK Luke Kuechly .50 1.25
PPLR Laurent Robinson .30 .75
PPMA Miles Austin .30 .75
PPMC Marques Colston .30 .75
PPMF Matt Forte .30 .75
PPMI Mark Ingram .40 1.00
PPMJD Maurice Jones-Drew .30 .75
PPMK Matt Kalil .20 .50
PPML Marshawn Lynch .40 1.00
PPMWI Mike Williams .40 1.00
PPPH Percy Harvin .30 .75
PPPHI Peyton Hillis .30 .75
PPPW Patrick Willis .40 1.00
PPRF Ryan Fitzpatrick .30 .75
PPRG Robert Griffin III .25 .60
PPRH Ronnie Hillman .20 .50
PPRL Ray Lewis .50 1.25
PPSG Shonn Greene .30 .75
PPSJ Steven Jackson .30 .75
PPSR Sidney Rice .30 .75
PPTR Trent Richardson .20 .50
PPVC Victor Cruz .40 1.00
PPVJ Vincent Jackson .30 .75
PPWM Willis McGahee .30 .75

2012 Topps Prolific Playmakers Autographs

STATED ODDS 1:550 HOB
PPAAB Ahmad Bradshaw 4.00 10.00
PPAABR Antonio Brown 15.00 30.00
PPAAJG A.J. Green SP 12.50 25.00
PPAAL Andrew Luck SP 125.00 200.00
PPACF Coby Fleener 4.00 10.00
PPACM Colt McCoy 5.00 12.00
PPADB Dez Bryant 15.00 40.00
PPADM Denarius Moore 4.00 10.00
PPADS Darren Sproles 6.00 15.00
PPADST Devon Still 4.00 10.00
PPAFG Frank Gore SP 8.00 20.00
PPAGJ Greg Jennings 4.00 10.00
PPAJBL Justin Blackmon SP 4.00 10.00
PPAJF Jermichael Finley 4.00 10.00
PPAJG Jimmy Graham 8.00 20.00
PPAJGA Jabar Gaffney 4.00 10.00
PPAJPP Jason Pierre-Paul 4.00 10.00
PPAJW Jerel Worthy 5.00 12.00
PPAKK Kevin Kolb SP 4.00 10.00
PPALB LeGarrette Blount 5.00 12.00
PPALK Luke Kuechly 8.00 20.00
PPALR Laurent Robinson 4.00 10.00
PPAMC Marques Colston SP 8.00 20.00
PPAMF Matt Forte SP 10.00 25.00
PPAMK Matt Kalil 4.00 10.00
PPAML Marshawn Lynch 20.00 40.00
PPAMWI Mike Williams 4.00 10.00
PPANT Nick Toon 4.00 10.00
PPAPG Pierre Garcon 6.00 15.00
PPAPH Percy Harvin 6.00 15.00
PPAPW Patrick Willis 8.00 20.00
PPARG Robert Griffin III SP 30.00 80.00
PPARH Ronnie Hillman 4.00 10.00
PPART Robert Turbin 4.00 10.00
PPASR Sidney Rice 4.00 10.00
PPATR Trent Richardson SP 15.00 40.00
PPAVJ Vincent Jackson 4.00 10.00
PPAWM Willis McGahee 4.00 10.00

2012 Topps Prolific Playmakers Relics

STATED ODDS 1:50 HOB
PPRAB Anquan Boldin 2.50 6.00
PPRAD Andy Dalton 3.00 8.00
PPRAF Arian Foster 3.00 8.00
PPRBL Brandon Lloyd 2.50 6.00
PPRBM Brandon Marshall 3.00 8.00
PPRBT Ben Tate 2.50 6.00
PPRCB Cedric Benson 2.50 6.00
PPRCM Colt McCoy 3.00 8.00
PPRCP Carson Palmer 3.00 8.00
PPRDB Dwayne Bowe 3.00 8.00
PPRDBR Dez Bryant 5.00 12.00
PPRDM Darren McFadden 2.50 6.00
PPRHN Hakeem Nicks 2.50 6.00
PPRJA Jared Allen 2.50 6.00
PPRJB Jahvid Best 2.50 6.00
PPRJF Joe Flacco 3.00 8.00
PPRJFO Jacoby Ford 2.50 6.00
PPRLF Larry Fitzgerald 3.00 8.00
PPRMA Miles Austin 2.50 6.00
PPRMC Marques Colston 2.50 6.00
PPRMI Mark Ingram 3.00 8.00
PPRMJD Maurice Jones-Drew 2.50 6.00
PPRMR Matt Ryan 3.00 8.00
PPRMT Michael Turner 2.50 6.00
PPRMW Mike Wallace 2.50 6.00
PPRNS Ndamukong Suh 3.00 8.00
PPRPH Peyton Hillis 2.50 6.00
PPRRF Ryan Fitzpatrick 2.50 6.00
PPRRL Ray Lewis 4.00 10.00
PPRRM Ryan Mathews 3.00 8.00
PPRRW Roddy White 2.50 6.00
PPRSG Shonn Greene 2.50 6.00
PPRSJ Steven Jackson 2.50 6.00
PPRTT Tim Tebow 6.00 15.00
PPRVC Victor Cruz 5.00 12.00
PPRVJ Vincent Jackson 2.50 6.00

2012 Topps Prolific Playmakers Relics Autographs

RELIC AU/50 ODDS 1:2610 HOB
PPARAB Ahmad Bradshaw 10.00 25.00
PPARAP Adrian Peterson 40.00 80.00
PPARDS Darren Sproles 15.00 40.00
PPARFJ Fred Jackson 12.00 30.00
PPARJM Jeremy Maclin 10.00 25.00
PPARMS Matt Schaub 10.00 25.00
PPARMSA Mark Sanchez 15.00 40.00
PPARMV Michael Vick 25.00 50.00
PPARPB Plaxico Burress 10.00 25.00
PPARPH Percy Harvin 10.00 25.00
PPARRH Roy Helu 10.00 25.00
PPARSB Sam Bradford 30.00 60.00
PPARWM Willis McGahee 10.00 25.00

2012 Topps Prolific Playmakers Relics Jumbo

JUMBO/20 ODDS 1:4244 HOB
PPJRAD Andy Dalton 6.00 15.00
PPJRBL Brandon Lloyd 5.00 12.00
PPJRCB Cedric Benson 5.00 12.00
PPJRJA Jared Allen 8.00 20.00
PPJRJB Jahvid Best 5.00 12.00
PPJRJF Joe Flacco 6.00 16.00
PPJRMC Marques Colston 5.00 12.00
PPJRMW Mike Wallace 8.00 20.00
PPJRNS Ndamukong Suh 6.00 15.00
PPJRRF Ryan Fitzpatrick 5.00 12.00
PPJRRL Ray Lewis 8.00 20.00
PPJRRM Ryan Mathews 6.00 15.00
PPJRRW Roddy White 5.00 12.00
PPJRSG Shonn Greene 5.00 12.00
PPJRVJ Vincent Jackson 5.00 12.00

2012 Topps QB Immortals

COMPLETE SET (19) 5.00 12.00
STATED ODDS 1:6 HOB
QIBG Bob Griese .40 1.00
QIBS Bart Starr .60 1.50
QIDF Dan Fouts .30 .75
QIDM Dan Marino .75 2.00
QIJE John Elway .60 1.50
QIJK Jim Kelly .40 1.00
QIJM Joe Montana 1.00 2.50
QIJN Joe Namath .60 1.50
QIJP Jim Plunkett .30 .75
QIKW Kurt Warner .30 .75
QILD Len Dawson .40 1.00
QIPS Phil Simms .30 .75
QIRS Roger Staubach .50 1.25
QISJ Sonny Jurgensen .30 .75
QISY Steve Young .50 1.25
QITA Troy Aikman .50 1.25
QITB Terry Bradshaw .50 1.25
QIWM Warren Moon .40 1.00
QIYAT Y.A. Tittle .40 1.00

2012 Topps QB Immortals Autographs

AUTO/25 ODDS 1:14,750 HOB
*SILVER/15: .5X TO 1.2X BASIC AU/25
QIABF Brett Favre 75.00 150.00
QIABG Bob Griese 25.00 50.00
QIABS Bart Starr 60.00 120.00
QIADF Dan Fouts
QIADM Dan Marino 60.00 120.00
QIAJE John Elway 60.00 120.00
QIAJK Jim Kelly 30.00 60.00
QIAJM Joe Montana 60.00 120.00
QIAJN Joe Namath 50.00 100.00
QIAJP Jim Plunkett
QIAKW Kurt Warner
QIALD Len Dawson 30.00 60.00
QIAPS Phil Simms 30.00 60.00
QIARS Roger Staubach 40.00 80.00
QIASY Steve Young
QIATA Troy Aikman 30.00 60.00
QIATB Terry Bradshaw 60.00 120.00
QIAWM Warren Moon 25.00 50.00
QIAYAT Y.A. Tittle 25.00 50.00

2012 Topps QB Immortals Plaques

PLAQUE/50 ODDS 1:5050 HOB
QIPBF Brett Favre 30.00 80.00
QIPBG Bob Griese 15.00 40.00
QIPBS Bart Starr 20.00 50.00
QIPDF Dan Fouts 20.00 50.00
QIPDM Dan Marino 30.00 80.00
QIPJE John Elway 25.00 60.00
QIPJK Jim Kelly 20.00 50.00
QIPJM Joe Montana 40.00 100.00
QIPJN Joe Namath 30.00 80.00
QIPJP Jim Plunkett 15.00 40.00
QIPKW Kurt Warner 20.00 50.00
QIPLD Len Dawson 15.00 40.00
QIPPS Phil Simms 15.00 40.00
QIPRS Roger Staubach 15.00 40.00
QIPTB Terry Bradshaw 20.00 50.00
QIPWM Warren Moon 15.00 40.00
QIPYAT Y.A. Tittle 15.00 40.00

2012 Topps QB Immortals Relics

RELIC/50 ODDS 1:7500 HOB
*GOLD/15: .6X TO 1.5X BASIC JSY/50
*SILVER/25: .5X TO 1.2X BASIC JSY/50
QIRBF Brett Favre 15.00 40.00
QIRDM Dan Marino 15.00 40.00
QIRJE John Elway 12.00 30.00
QIRJM Joe Montana 20.00 50.00
QIRJN Joe Namath 20.00 50.00
QIRKW Kurt Warner 6.00 15.00
QIRSY Steve Young 10.00 25.00

2012 Topps Quarterback Milestones Medallions Touchdowns Bronze

TD BRONZE/75 ODDS 1:3400 HOB
*GOLD/25: .6X TO 1.5X BRONZE/75
*SILVER/50: .5X TO 1.2X BRONZE/75
QMTBF Brett Favre 20.00 50.00
QMTBG Bob Griese 10.00 25.00
QMTDB Drew Brees 12.00 30.00
QMTDF Dan Fouts 8.00 20.00
QMTDM Dan Marino 20.00 50.00
QMTEM Eli Manning 8.00 20.00
QMTJE John Elway 15.00 40.00
QMTJK Jim Kelly 10.00 25.00
QMTJM Joe Montana 25.00 60.00
QMTKW Kurt Warner 8.00 20.00
QMTLD Len Dawson 10.00 25.00
QMTMH Matt Hasselbeck 6.00 15.00
QMTPM Peyton Manning 20.00 50.00
QMTPS Phil Simms 8.00 20.00
QMTSY Steve Young 12.00 30.00
QMTTB Terry Bradshaw 15.00 40.00
QMTWM Warren Moon 10.00 25.00
QMTDMC Donovan McNabb 8.00 20.00
QMTTBR Tom Brady 25.00 60.00
QMTYAT Y.A. Tittle 10.00 25.00

2012 Topps Quarterback Milestones Medallions Wins Bronze

BRONZE/75 ODDS 1:2800 HOB
*GOLD/25: .6X TO 1.5X BRONZE/75
*SILVER/50: .5X TO 1.2X BRONZE/75
QMWBF Brett Favre 20.00 50.00
QMWBG Bob Griese 10.00 25.00
QMWBR Ben Roethlisberger 12.00 30.00
QMWBS Bart Starr 15.00 40.00
QMWDB Drew Brees 12.00 30.00
QMWDF Dan Fouts 8.00 20.00
QMWDM Dan Marino 20.00 50.00
QMWEM Eli Manning 8.00 20.00
QMWJE John Elway 15.00 40.00
QMWJK Jim Kelly 10.00 25.00
QMWJM Joe Montana 25.00 60.00
QMWJP Jim Plunkett 8.00 20.00
QMWLD Len Dawson 10.00 25.00
QMWMH Matt Hasselbeck 6.00 15.00
QMWPM Peyton Manning 20.00 50.00
QMWPS Phil Simms 8.00 20.00
QMWRS Roger Staubach 12.00 30.00
QMWSY Steve Young 12.00 30.00
QMWTA Troy Aikman 12.00 30.00
QMWTB Terry Bradshaw 15.00 40.00
QMWWM Warren Moon 10.00 25.00
QMWDMC Donovan McNabb 8.00 20.00
QMWTBR Tom Brady 25.00 60.00
QMWYAT Y.A. Tittle 10.00 25.00

2012 Topps Quarterback Milestones Medallions Yardage Bronze

YARDS BRONZE/75 ODDS 1:3450 HOB
*GOLD/25: .6X TO 1.5X BRONZE/75
*SILVER/50: .5X TO 1.2X BRONZE/75
QMPBF Brett Favre 20.00 50.00
QMPDB Drew Brees 12.00 30.00
QMPDF Dan Fouts 8.00 20.00
QMPDM Dan Marino 15.00 40.00
QMPEM Eli Manning 8.00 20.00
QMPJE John Elway 15.00 40.00
QMPJK Jim Kelly 10.00 25.00
QMPJM Joe Montana 25.00 60.00
QMPKW Kurt Warner 8.00 20.00
QMPLD Len Dawson 10.00 25.00
QMPMH Matt Hasselbeck 6.00 15.00
QMPPM Peyton Manning 20.00 50.00
QMPPS Phil Simms 8.00 20.00
QMPSY Steve Young 12.00 30.00
QMPTA Troy Aikman 12.00 30.00
QMPTB Terry Bradshaw 15.00 40.00
QMPWM Warren Moon 10.00 25.00
QMPDMC Donovan McNabb 8.00 20.00
QMPTBR Tom Brady 25.00 60.00
QMPYAT Y.A. Tittle 10.00 25.00

2012 Topps Rookie Autographs

ROOKIE AU ODDS 1:1650 HOB
3 Brandon Weeden SP 30.00 80.00
6 Robert Turbin 4.00 10.00
14 T.Y. Hilton SP 12.00 30.00
18 Alshon Jeffery SP 15.00 40.00
28 DeVier Posey SP 6.00 15.00
37 T.J. Graham SP 6.00 15.00
58 Dwayne Allen 6.00 15.00
63 Nick Toon 4.00 10.00
77 Ryan Broyles SP
85 Joe Adams SP 6.00 15.00
91 Michael Floyd SP 6.00 15.00
112 A.J. Jenkins SP 6.00 15.00
115 Stephen Hill SP 12.00 30.00
132 Coby Fleener 5.00 12.00
134 Ryan Tannehill SP 40.00 80.00
140 Andrew Luck SP 250.00 400.00
146 Cyrus Gray SP 6.00 15.00
149 Michael Egnew SP
151 Mohamed Sanu SP 12.00 30.00
165 Russell Wilson SP 150.00 300.00
185 LaMichael James SP 6.00 15.00
186 Nick Foles SP 15.00 40.00
204 Doug Martin SP 10.00 25.00
214 Bernard Pierce SP EXCH 6.00 15.00
240 Justin Blackmon SP 15.00 40.00
242 Lamar Miller SP 12.00 30.00
252 Jarius Wright SP
279 Brian Quick SP
283 Ronnie Hillman 4.00 10.00
289 David Wilson SP
314 Rueben Randle SP 6.00 15.00
326 Kirk Cousins SP 25.00 60.00
340 Robert Griffin III SP 30.00 80.00
357 Chris Givens SP 6.00 15.00
365 Brock Osweiler SP 6.00 15.00
378 Kendall Wright SP 15.00 40.00
380 Trent Richardson SP 30.00 80.00
399 Isaiah Pead SP 6.00 15.00

2012 Topps Rookie Patch

RPAJ Alshon Jeffery 5.00 12.00
RPAL Andrew Luck 15.00 30.00
RPBO Brock Osweiler 2.50 6.00
RPBP Bernard Pierce 2.50 6.00
RPBQ Brian Quick 2.50 6.00
RPBW Brandon Weeden 2.50 6.00
RPCF Coby Fleener 2.50 6.00
RPDM Doug Martin 4.00 10.00
RPDP DeVier Posey 2.50 6.00
RPDW David Wilson 2.50 6.00
RPIP Isaiah Pead 2.50 6.00
RPJA Joe Adams 2.50 6.00
RPJB Justin Blackmon 2.50 6.00
RPJW Jarius Wright 2.50 6.00
RPKW Kendall Wright 2.50 6.00
RPLJ LaMichael James 2.50 6.00
RPLM Lamar Miller 4.00 10.00
RPME Michael Egnew 4.00 10.00
RPMF Michael Floyd 5.00 12.00
RPMS Mohamed Sanu 4.00 10.00
RPNF Nick Foles 6.00 15.00
RPNT Nick Toon 2.50 6.00
RPRB Ryan Broyles 2.50 6.00
RPRG Robert Griffin III 8.00 20.00
RPRH Ronnie Hillman 2.50 6.00
RPRR Rueben Randle 2.50 6.00
RPRT Ryan Tannehill 4.00 10.00
RPRW Russell Wilson 8.00 20.00
RPSH Stephen Hill 2.50 6.00
RPTG T.J. Graham 2.50 6.00
RPTR Trent Richardson 6.00 15.00
RPAJJ A.J. Jenkins 2.50 6.00
RPCGI Chris Givens 2.50 6.00

2012 Topps Rookie Premiere Autographs

AUTO/90 ODDS 1:535 HOB
RPAAJ Alshon Jeffery 20.00 50.00
RPAAJJ A.J. Jenkins 10.00 25.00
RPAAL Andrew Luck 250.00 400.00
RPABO Brock Osweiler 10.00 25.00
RPABP Bernard Pierce 10.00 25.00
RPABQ Brian Quick 15.00 40.00
RPABW Brandon Weeden 10.00 25.00
RPACF Coby Fleener 10.00 25.00
RPACGI Chris Givens 10.00 25.00
RPADA Dwayne Allen 12.00 30.00
RPADM Doug Martin 15.00 40.00
RPADP DeVier Posey 12.00 30.00
RPADW David Wilson 10.00 25.00
RPAIP Isaiah Pead 10.00 25.00
RPAJA Joe Adams 12.00 30.00
RPAJB Justin Blackmon 15.00 40.00
RPAJW Jarius Wright 12.00 30.00
RPAKW Kendall Wright 15.00 40.00
RPALJ LaMichael James 10.00 25.00
RPALM Lamar Miller 15.00 40.00
RPAME Michael Egnew 10.00 25.00
RPAMF Michael Floyd 40.00 80.00
RPAMS Mohamed Sanu 15.00 40.00
RPANF Nick Foles 25.00 60.00
RPANT Nick Toon 10.00 25.00
RPARB Ryan Broyles 10.00 25.00
RPARG Robert Griffin III 40.00 100.00
RPARH Ronnie Hillman 10.00 25.00
RPARR Rueben Randle 10.00 25.00
RPART Ryan Tannehill 15.00 40.00
RPARTU Robert Turbin 10.00 25.00
RPARW Russell Wilson 150.00 250.00
RPASH Stephen Hill 10.00 25.00
RPATG T.J. Graham 10.00 25.00
RPATR Trent Richardson 25.00 60.00

2012 Topps Rookie Premiere Autographs Dual

DUAL AU/25 ODDS 1:13,720 HOB
RPDABR Blackmon/Richardson
RPDAGW R.Griffin III/K.Wright 60.00 120.00
RPDALG A.Luck/R.Griffin III
RPDARH R.Randle/S.Hill 20.00 40.00
RPDAWB B.Weeden/Blackmon

2012 Topps Rookie Refractors

ONE PER SPECIAL VALUE PACK
TFHMAL Andrew Luck 8.00 20.00
TFHMRG Robert Griffin III 3.00 8.00

2012 Topps Rookie Relic Jumbos

RJRAJ Alshon Jeffery 4.00 10.00
RJRAJJ A.J. Jenkins 2.00 5.00
RJRAL Andrew Luck 15.00 40.00
RJRBP Bernard Pierce 2.00 5.00
RJRBQ Brian Quick 2.00 5.00
RJRBW Brandon Weeden 2.00 5.00
RJRCF Coby Fleener 2.00 5.00
RJRCGI Chris Givens 2.00 5.00
RJRDA Dwayne Allen 2.00 5.00
RJRDM Doug Martin 3.00 8.00
RJRDP DeVier Posey 2.00 5.00
RJRDW David Wilson 2.00 5.00
RJRIP Isaiah Pead 2.00 5.00
RJRJA Joe Adams 2.00 5.00
RJRJB Justin Blackmon 2.00 5.00
RJRJW Jarius Wright 2.00 5.00
RJRKW Kendall Wright 2.00 5.00
RJRLJ LaMichael James 2.00 5.00
RJRLM Lamar Miller 3.00 8.00
RJRME Michael Egnew 2.00 5.00
RJRMF Michael Floyd 4.00 10.00
RJRMS Mohamed Sanu 3.00 8.00
RJRNF Nick Foles 5.00 12.00
RJRNT Nick Toon 2.00 5.00
RJRPBO Brock Osweiler 2.00 5.00
RJRRB Ryan Broyles 2.00 5.00
RJRRG Robert Griffin III 2.50 6.00
RJRRH Ronnie Hillman 2.00 5.00
RJRRR Rueben Randle 2.00 5.00
RJRRT Ryan Tannehill 3.00 8.00
RJRRTU Robert Turbin 2.00 5.00
RJRRW Russell Wilson 8.00 20.00
RJRSH Stephen Hill 2.00 5.00
RJRTG T.J. Graham 2.00 5.00
RJRTR Trent Richardson 2.00 5.00

2012 Topps Rookie Reprint

COMPLETE SET (21) 6.00 15.00
STATED ODDS 1:6 HOB
63 John Elway 84 .60 1.50
65 Jim Plunkett 72 .30 .75
90 Sonny Jurgensen 58 .30 .75
119 Bart Starr 57 .60 1.50
122 Joe Namath 65 .75 2.00
123 Dan Marino 84 .75 2.00
156 Terry Bradshaw 71 .50 1.25
196 Bob Griese 68 .40 1.00
200 Roger Staubach 72 .50 1.25
216 Joe Montana 81 1.00 2.50
225 Phil Simms 80 .30 .75
251 Warren Moon 85 .40 1.00
311 Michael Vick 01 .30 .75
328 Drew Brees 01 .50 1.25
350 Eli Manning 04 .30 .75
360 Peyton Manning 98 1.00 2.50
362 Jim Kelly 87 .40 1.00
367 Dan Fouts 75 .30 .75
374 Steve Young 86 .50 1.25
430 Matthew Stafford 09 .50 1.25
431 Aaron Rodgers 05 .75 2.00

2012 Topps Rookie Reprint Autographs

AUTO/25 ODDS 1:16,600 HOB
63 John Elway 84 125.00 200.00
65 Jim Kelly 72 30.00 60.00
119 Bart Starr 57 125.00 200.00
122 Joe Namath 65 90.00 150.00
123 Dan Fouts 75 30.00 60.00
156 Terry Bradshaw 71 125.00 200.00
196 Bob Griese 68 50.00 100.00
200 Roger Staubach 72
216 Joe Montana 81 100.00 200.00
225 Phil Simms 80 30.00 60.00
251 Warren Moon 85 50.00 100.00
311 Michael Vick 01 40.00 80.00
328 Drew Brees 01 100.00 175.00
362 Jim Plunkett 72 30.00 60.00
367 Dan Marino 84 200.00 350.00
374 Steve Young 86 90.00 150.00
430 Matthew Stafford 09 50.00 100.00
431 Aaron Rodgers 05 175.00 300.00

2012 Topps Rookie Reprint Relics

RELIC/25 ODDS 1:11,900 HOB
63 John Elway 84 40.00 80.00
122 Joe Namath 65 60.00 120.00
216 Joe Montana 81 40.00 80.00
311 Michael Vick 01 6.00 15.00
350 Eli Manning 04 6.00 15.00
367 Dan Marino 84 40.00 80.00
374 Steve Young 86 10.00 25.00

2012 Topps Super Bowl MVPs

MVP/46 ODDS 1:6750 HOB
SBMVPAR Aaron Rodgers 40.00 80.00
SBMVPDB Drew Brees 25.00 50.00
SBMVPJE John Elway 15.00 40.00
SBMVPJN Joe Namath 15.00 40.00
SBMVPJP Jim Plunkett 8.00 20.00
SBMVPKW Kurt Warner 8.00 20.00
SBMVPLD Len Dawson 12.00 30.00
SBMVPPM Peyton Manning 20.00 50.00
SBMVPPS Phil Simms 8.00 20.00
SBMVPRS Roger Staubach 12.00 30.00
SBMVPSY Steve Young 12.00 30.00
SBMVPTA Troy Aikman 12.00 30.00
SBMVPBS1 Bart Starr 15.00 40.00
SBMVPBS2 Bart Starr 15.00 40.00
SBMVPEM1 Eli Manning 25.00 50.00
SBMVPEM2 Eli Manning 25.00 50.00
SBMVPJM1 Joe Montana 25.00 60.00
SBMVPJM2 Joe Montana 25.00 60.00
SBMVPJM3 Joe Montana 25.00 60.00
SBMVPTB1 Terry Bradshaw 15.00 40.00
SBMVPTB2 Terry Bradshaw 15.00 40.00
SBMVPTBR1 Tom Brady 30.00 60.00
SBMVPTBR2 Tom Brady 30.00 60.00

2012 Topps Under Armour High School All-America Autographs

UAAC Amari Cooper/265 30.00 60.00
UAAP Andrus Peat/272 5.00 12.00
UADF Dante Fowler Jr./285 8.00 20.00
UAEG Eddie Goldman/280 4.00 10.00
UAJW Jameis Winston/259 50.00 100.00
UALC Landon Collins/152 8.00 20.00
UAMB Malcom Brown/250 5.00 12.00
UANA Nelson Agholor/110 15.00 30.00
UAPW P.J. Williams/285 4.00 10.00

2012 Topps Super Bowl XLVII MVPs

COMPLETE SET (5) 3.00 8.00
INSERTED IN SUPER BOWL FACTORY SET
SDHBF Brett Favre SBXXXI 1.00 2.50
SDHJM Joe Montana SBXXIV 1.25 3.00
SDHJP Jim Plunkett XV .40 1.00
SDHRS Roger Staubach SBXII .60 1.50
SDHTB Tom Brady SBXXXVI 1.25 3.00

2012 Topps Super Bowl XLVII Patches

AL Andrew Luck 25.00 60.00
DB Drew Brees 15.00 40.00
EM Eli Manning 10.00 25.00
PM Peyton Manning 15.00 40.00
RG Robert Griffin III 3.00 8.00

2012 Topps Super Bowl XLVII Rookies

SBWRAL Andrew Luck 2.50 6.00
SBWRRG Robert Griffin III .30 .75

2013 Topps

COMPLETE SET (440) 25.00 40.00
COMP.FACT HOBBY (445) 35.00 50.00
COMP.FACT RETAIL (441) 35.00 60.00
VETERAN SP ODDS 1:189 HOB
ROOKIE SP ODDS 1:227 HOB
1A Adrian Peterson AP .25 .60
1B Adrian Peterson SP 5.00 12.00
2 Devin McCourty .15 .40
3 Leonard Hankerson .15 .40
4 Jacquizz Rodgers .20 .50
5 Jordan Rodgers RC .30 .75
6 Jacob Tamme .15 .40
7 Joel Dreessen .15 .40
8 Antonio Brown .25 .60
9 Ronnie Hillman .15 .40
10 Aldon Smith .15 .40
11A Manti Te'o RC .30 .75
11B Manti Te'o SP catch 2.50 6.00
11C Manti Te'o FS run .40 1.00
12 Heath Miller .15 .40

13 Star Lotulelei RC .30 .75
14 Joe Haden .15 .40
15 Harry Douglas .15 .40
16 Saints/Drew Brees .20 .50
17 Vontaze Burfict .15 .40
18 Danario Alexander .15 .40
19 Casey Hayward .15 .40
20A Matt Ryan white jsy .20 .50
20B Matt Ryan SP red jsy 4.00 10.00
21 Matt Scott RC .25 .60
22 Andrew Hawkins .15 .40
23 Ravens SB/Flacco .15 .40
24 Browns/Weed/Rchrdsn .12 .30
25 Richard Sherman .25 .60
26 Robert Quinn .20 .50
27 T.J. McDonald RC .25 .60
28 Duane Brown .15 .40
29 Mike Iupati .15 .40
30 Marshawn Lynch .20 .50
31 Travis Kelce RC .60 1.50
32 Brad Sorensen RC .25 .60
33 Zach Miller .15 .40
34 Darren McFadden .20 .50
35 Luke Joeckel RC .25 .60
36 Bears/Bennett/Marshall/Jennings .15 .40
37A Andre Ellington RC .25 .60
37B A.Ellington SP lft hnd 2.00 5.00
38 Brandon LaFell .15 .40
39 D.J. Hayden RC .25 .60
40A Anquan Boldin red .15 .40
40B Anquan Boldin SP wht 5.00 12.00
41 Carlos Dunlap .15 .40
42 Broncos/Decker/Thomas/Moreno .15 .40
43A Mike Glennon RC .25 .60
43B M.Glennon SP no bll 2.00 5.00
44 Zac Dysert RC .25 .60
45 Andre Roberts .15 .40
46 Patrick Peterson .15 .40
47 Harrison Smith .15 .40
48 Chad Greenway .20 .50
49 Dee Milliner RC .25 .60
50A Andrew Luck pass .40 1.00
50B A.Luck SP arms up 8.00 20.00
51A D.Thomas catching .20 .50
51B D.Thomas SP leaping 5.00 12.00
52 Jonathan Cyprien RC .25 .60
53 Cecil Shorts .15 .40
54 Jay Cutler .15 .40
55 Panthers huddle/Newton .20 .50
56 Jamar Taylor RC .25 .60
57 Vonta Leach .15 .40
58 John Jenkins RC .25 .60
59 Khaseem Greene RC .25 .60
60 Darrelle Revis .15 .40
61A Montee Ball RC .25 .60
61B Montee Ball SP catch 4.00 10.00
62 Andy Dalton .20 .50
63 D.J. Swearinger RC .25 .60
64 Derrick Johnson .15 .40
65 Kyle Long RC .30 .75
66 Eric Weddle .15 .40
67 Leodis McKelvin .15 .40
68 Dashon Goldson .15 .40
69 Daryl Richardson .15 .40
70A Alfred Morris spike .15 .40
70B Alfred Morris SP run 3.00 8.00
71 Cameron Jordan .15 .40
72 Jairus Byrd .15 .40
73 Stephen Hill .15 .40
74A Stepfan Taylor RC .25 .60
74B S.Taylor SP squatting 4.00 10.00
75 Jamaal Charles .20 .50
76 Michael Vick .20 .50
77 Ace Sanders RC .25 .60
78 Tavarres King RC .25 .60
79 Brooks Reed .15 .40
80 Ray Rice .15 .40
81 Bruce Irvin .15 .40
82 Jonathan Dwyer .15 .40
83 Sylvester Williams RC .25 .60
84 Seahawks/Wilson/Lynch .40 1.00
85 Charles Tillman .20 .50
86 Mark Barron .20 .50
87 Johnathan Joseph .15 .40
88 Alex Okafor RC .25 .60
89 Ronde Barber .15 .40
90 Julius Peppers .20 .50
91 Cliff Avril .15 .40
92 Steve Smith .20 .50
93 Sidney Rice .15 .40
94 Morris Claiborne .15 .40
95 Stevie Brown RC .25 .60
96 Johnathan Hankins RC .25 .60
97 Lions/Stafford/Johnson .20 .50
98 Cowboys/Romo/Murray .20 .50
99 J.J. Watt POY .20 .50
100A Tom Brady horizontal .60 1.50
100B Tom Brady SP vertical 12.00 30.00
101 Jerrell Freeman RC .25 .60
102 Xavier Rhodes RC .25 .60
103 Max Unger .15 .40
104 DeMeco Ryans .15 .40
105 Steelers/Roeth/Pncey .20 .50
106 Jets/Cromartie/Harris/Lankster .12 .30
107 D.J. Fluker RC .25 .60
108 Darius Reynaud .15 .40
109 Owen Daniels .15 .40
110 Greg Jennings .15 .40
111 Stevan Ridley .15 .40
112A Tavon Austin RC .30 .75
112B T.Austin SP abv head 8.00 20.00
112C T.Austin FS run .40 1.00
113 Chiefs/Johnson/Daniels/Siler .12 .30
114 Joseph Randle RC .25 .60
115 Michael Floyd .15 .40
116 Brandon Browner .15 .40
117 Adrian Peterson MVP .25 .60
118 Malcom Floyd .15 .40
119 49ers/Kprnck/Crbtr .15 .40
120A Ed Reed pointing .20 .50
120B Ed Reed SP running 4.00 10.00
121 Vince Wilfork .15 .40
122 Mikel Leshoure .15 .40
123 Lamarr Houston .15 .40
124 Kerwynn Williams RC .25 .60
125A C.J. Spiller black glv .15 .40
125B C.Spiller SP pink glv 3.00 8.00
126A Geno Smith RC .25 .60
126B Geno Smith SP run 2.00 5.00
126C Geno Smith FS scrmb .30 .75
127 Anthony Spencer .15 .40
128 Haloti Ngata .15 .40
129 Jared Allen .15 .40
130A Doug Martin leaping .20 .50
130B D.Martin SP run fwd 4.00 10.00
131 Darius Butler .15 .40
132 Charles Johnson .15 .40
133 Denard Robinson RC .25 .60
134 Brandon Spikes .15 .40
135 Eric Reid RC .30 .75
136 Kenjon Barner RC .25 .60
137 David Harris .15 .40
138 Kam Chancellor .30 .75
139 Chad Henne .15 .40
140 Brandon Marshall .20 .50
141 Lamar Miller .15 .40
142 Danny Amendola .20 .50
143 Ezekiel Ansah RC .25 .60
144 Jahri Evans .15 .40
145A J.Franklin RC .25 .60
145B J.Franklin SP catch 4.00 10.00
146 Brian Orakpo .20 .50
147 Rex Burkhead RC .30 .75
148 Shane Vereen .20 .50
149 Redskins/RG3/Morris .12 .30
150A Robert Griffin III white .15 .40
150B R.Griffin III SP yellow 3.00 8.00
151 Dwayne Bowe .20 .50
152 Brian Cushing .15 .40
153 Jason McCourty .15 .40
154 Rookie Premiere .10 .25
155A DeAndre Hopkins RC .60 1.50
155B D.Hopkins SP ball in lft 6.00 15.00
156 Kawann Short RC .25 .60
157 Bernard Pierce .15 .40
158 Jamie Collins RC .25 .60
159A Ryan Nassib RC .25 .60
159B R.Nassib SP fcmsk 4.00 10.00
160A Trent Richardson white .15 .40
160B T.Richardson SP brwn 3.00 8.00
161 Lavonte David .15 .40
162 Daryl Washington .15 .40
163 Fred Davis .15 .40
164 Davone Bess .15 .40
165 Alshon Jeffery .20 .50
166 Terrell Suggs .15 .40
167 Raiders/Janikowski/Branch .12 .30
168 Derron Sproles .20 .50
169 Vikings/Petersn/Crlsn .20 .50
170 Michael Crabtree .15 .40
171 Tamba Hali .15 .40
172 Johnthan Banks RC .25 .60
173 Cornellius Carradine RC .25 .60
174 BenJarvus Green-Ellis .20 .50
175A J.J. Watt red jsy .20 .50
175B J.J. Watt SP blue jsy 4.00 10.00
176 DeSean Jackson .20 .50
177 Chris Clemons .15 .40
178 Damontre Moore RC .25 .60
179 Marques Colston .15 .40
180 Troy Polamalu .25 .60
181 Nate Washington .15 .40
182 Victor Cruz .20 .50
183 Dion Jordan RC .25 .60
184 Desmond Trufant RC .25 .60
185 Chris Long .15 .40
186 Brent Celek .15 .40
187 Ryan Clady .15 .40
188 Asante Samuel .15 .40
189 Jonathan Stewart .15 .40
190 Reggie Wayne .20 .50
191 Rams/Jenkins/Laurinaitis .15 .40
192 Mike Gillislee RC .25 .60
193 Marcedes Lewis .15 .40
194 DeMarcus Ware .25 .60
195 Jordy Nelson .20 .50
196 Fred Jackson .20 .50
197 Torrey Smith .15 .40
198 Josh Gordon .15 .40
199 Michael Bush .15 .40
200A Peyton Manning blue jsy .50 1.25
200B P.Manning SP ornge jsy 10.00 25.00
201 Sheldon Richardson RC .25 .60
202 Stedman Bailey RC .25 .60
203 Eric Decker .15 .40
204 Nate Burleson .15 .40
205 Muhammad Wilkerson .15 .40
206 Ravens/Flacco/Rice .15 .40
207 Coby Fleener .15 .40
208 Margus Hunt RC .25 .60
209 Jarvis Jones RC .25 .60
210A Rob Gronkowski red jsy .25 .60
210B R.Gronkowski SP blu jsy 5.00 12.00
211 Tyrann Mathieu RC .40 1.00
212 Ryan Swope RC .25 .60
213 NaVorro Bowman .20 .50
214 Chris Johnson .15 .40
215A EJ Manuel RC .25 .60
215B E.Manuel SP passing 8.00 20.00
215C EJ Manuel FS scrmb .30 .75
216 Janoris Jenkins .15 .40
217 DeMarco Murray .20 .50
218 B.J. Raji .15 .40
219 Dexter McCluster .20 .50
220 Philip Rivers .25 .60
221A Clay Matthews celebrt .25 .60
221B C.Matthews SP kneel 8.00 20.00
222 T.J. Graham .15 .40
223 Matt Forte .15 .40
224 Vance McDonald RC .30 .75
225 Luke Kuechly .20 .50
226 Cameron Wake .15 .40
227 Arthur Brown RC .25 .60
228 James Jones .15 .40
229 Lance Briggs .20 .50
230A Arian Foster wht jsy .20 .50
230B A.Foster SP blue jsy 4.00 10.00
231 Ndamukong Suh .20 .50
232 Paul Posluszny .15 .40
233 Russell Allen .15 .40
234 Jarius Wright .15 .40
235 Justin Pugh RC .25 .60
236 Bengals/Dalton/Green .20 .50
237 Dolphins/Tanne/Fasano .15 .40
238 Jermaine Gresham .20 .50
239 Marquise Goodwin RC .25 .60
240 Maurice Jones-Drew .15 .40
241 Sam Bradford .15 .40
242 Tyler Bray RC .25 .60
243 Rueben Randle .15 .40
244 Brandon Weeden .15 .40
245A Matt Barkley RC .25 .60
245B M.Barkley SP stands 6.00 15.00
246 David Wilson .15 .40
247 Mike Williams .20 .50
248A Justin Hunter RC .25 .60
248B J.Hunter SP FB in hnd 5.00 12.00
249 Travis Frederick RC .25 .60
250A Calvin Johnson tackled .25 .60
250B C.Johnson SP leaping 5.00 12.00
251 Dennis Pitta .15 .40
252 Chris Givens .15 .40
253 Brandon Carr .15 .40
254 Mohamed Sanu .15 .40
255 Ryan Broyles .20 .50
256 Falcons/Jones/White .20 .50
257 Sharrif Floyd RC .25 .60
258 Kyle Rudolph .15 .40
259 Josh Boyce RC .25 .60
260 Frank Gore .20 .50
261 Geno Atkins .15 .40
262 Robert Turbin .15 .40
263 Kenny Britt .15 .40
264 Kenny Vaccaro RC .25 .60
265 Pierre Garcon .20 .50
266 Bobby Wagner .15 .40
267 Justin Tuck .15 .40
268 Matthew Stafford .20 .50
269 Theo Riddick RC .25 .60
270A Julio Jones ball in left .25 .60
270B J.Jones SP FB in rght 5.00 12.00
271 Cobi Hamilton RC .25 .60
272 Quinton Patton RC .25 .60
273 Denarius Moore .15 .40
274 Jonathan Cooper RC .25 .60
275 Steven Jackson .15 .40
276 Daniel Thomas .15 .40
277 Nick Foles .20 .50
278 Miguel Maysonet RC .25 .60
279 Scott Chandler .15 .40
280A Russell Wilson blu jsy .50 1.25
280B R.Wilson SP wht jsy 10.00 25.00
281A Robert Woods RC .40 1.00
281B R.Woods SP running 3.00 8.00
282 Barkevious Mingo RC .25 .60
283 Vick Ballard .15 .40
284 Tony Romo .20 .50
285 Mario Manningham .15 .40
286 Dwayne Allen .15 .40
287 T.Y. Hilton .20 .50
288 Markus Wheaton RC .25 .60
289 Brandon Myers .20 .50
290 Von Miller .20 .50
291 DeAngelo Williams .15 .40
292 Jason Pierre-Paul .15 .40
293 Shaun Phillips .15 .40
294 Christine Michael RC .25 .60
295 Thomas DeCoud .15 .40
296 Willis McGahee .15 .40
297 A.J. Hawk .15 .40
298 Blair Walsh .15 .40
299 Ryan Williams .15 .40
300 Aaron Rodgers .40 1.00
301 Bilal Powell .15 .40
302 T.J. Ward .15 .40
303 Chandler Jones .15 .40
304 Tim Jennings .15 .40
305 Rey Maualuga .15 .40
306 Golden Tate .15 .40
307 Cortland Finnegan .15 .40
308 Kendall Wright .15 .40
309 Texans/Foster/Schaub .15 .40
310 Ben Roethlisberger .25 .60
311 Vontae Davis .15 .40
312 Justin Blackmon .15 .40
313 Mario Williams .15 .40
314A Marcus Lattimore RC .25 .60
314B M.Lattimore SP stands 2.00 5.00
315 Vernon Davis .15 .40
316 Tim Tebow .20 .50
317A Jordan Reed RC .40 1.00
317B J.Reed SP catch 3.00 8.00
318 Adrian Clayborn .15 .40
319 Earl Thomas .20 .50
320 Eli Manning .20 .50
321 Mark Ingram .20 .50
322 Knile Davis RC .25 .60
323 Buccaneers/Martin/Clark .15 .40
324 Bryce Brown .20 .50
325 Roddy White .15 .40
326 Andy Lee .15 .40
327 Hakeem Nicks .15 .40
328 Christian Ponder .15 .40
329 Thomas Davis .15 .40
330 Jimmy Graham .25 .60
331 Blidi Wreh-Wilson RC .30 .75
332A Tyler Wilson RC .25 .60
332B T.Wilson SP run 5.00 12.00
333 Giants/Tuck .12 .30
334 Luke Kuechly ROY .20 .50
335 Shawn Williams RC .25 .60
336A Colin Kaepernick passing .20 .50
336B C.Kaepernick SP flexing 15.00 30.00
337 William Moore .15 .40
338 Robert Griffin III ROY .15 .40
339 Knowshon Moreno .15 .40
340A Wes Welker orng jsy .20 .50
340B Wes Welker SP blu jsy 4.00 10.00
341 Santana Moss .20 .50
342 Ryan Kerrigan .15 .40
343 Carson Palmer .20 .50
344 James Laurinaitis .20 .50
345 Jeremy Maclin .15 .40
346 Bills/Dareus/Williams/Anderson .12 .30
347 Jeremy Kerley .15 .40
348 Jermichael Finley .15 .40
349 Nick Fairley .15 .40
350 Tony Gonzalez .20 .50
351 Ryan Tannehill .20 .50
352 Cardinals/Peterson/Lenon .12 .30
353 Alec Ogletree RC .25 .60
354 Andre Brown .20 .50
355 Curtis Lofton .15 .40
356 Jaguars/Henne/Shorts/Blackmon .12 .30
357 Bacarri Rambo RC .30 .75
358A Giovani Bernard RC .25 .60
358B G.Bernard SP leaping 2.00 5.00
359 Antonio Cromartie .15 .40
360 Champ Bailey .20 .50
361 Packers/Rodgers .30 .75
362 Antonio Gates .20 .50
363 Kiko Alonso RC .30 .75
364 Trent Cole .15 .40
365 Brandon Pettigrew .15 .40
366 Robert Mathis .15 .40
367 Alex Smith .20 .50
368 Eric Fisher RC .25 .60
369 Patriots/Brady/Gronk .50 1.25
370 LeSean McCoy .25 .60
371 Lawrence Timmons .15 .40
372 Matt Elam RC .25 .60
373A Aaron Hernandez .20 .50
373B Brian Banks FS RC .25 .60
374 Santonio Holmes .15 .40
375A Dez Bryant catch .25 .60
375B Dez Bryant SP run 5.00 12.00
376 David Amerson RC .25 .60
377 Elvis Dumervil .15 .40
378 Darius Slay RC .25 .60
379 Chance Warmack RC .25 .60
380 Patrick Willis .20 .50
381 Lance Kendricks .15 .40
382 Brian Hartline .15 .40
383 Greg Olsen .20 .50
384A Zach Ertz RC .50 1.25
384B Z.Ertz SP arms out 4.00 10.00
385 Jacoby Jones .15 .40
386A Cordarrelle Patterson RC .25 .60
386B C.Patterson SP running 2.00 5.00
387 Kenny Stills RC .25 .60
388 London Fletcher .20 .50
389 Ryan Mathews .20 .50
390 Cam Newton .25 .60
391 Reggie Bush .15 .40
392 Brian Urlacher .25 .60
393 Mike Wallace .15 .40
394 Lance Moore .15 .40
395 Gavin Escobar RC .25 .60
396 Kroy Biermann RC .30 .75
397 Titans/C.Johnson .12 .30
398A Jason Witten blu jsy .20 .50
398B J.Witten SP wht jsy 4.00 10.00
399 Josh Freeman .20 .50
400A Drew Brees blk jsy .25 .60
400B D.Brees SP wht jsy 6.00 15.00
401 Eric Berry .20 .50
402A Aaron Dobson RC .25 .60
402B A.Dobson SP rht hnd 8.00 20.00
403A Le'Veon Bell RC .75 2.00
403B L.Bell SP left hand 6.00 15.00
404 Bjoern Werner RC .25 .60
405 Marcel Reece .15 .40
406A Eddie Lacy RC .25 .60
406B E.Lacy SP rght hnd 2.00 5.00
406C Eddie Lacy FS .30 .75
407A Tyler Eifert RC .25 .60
407B T.Eifert SP point 2.00 5.00
408A Osi Umenyiora .15 .40
408B Michael Crabtree SP 3.00 8.00
409 Malcolm Jenkins .15 .40
410A Andre Johnson both .15 .40
410B A.Johnson SP left 3.00 8.00
411 Mark Sanchez .15 .40
412 Kevin Minter RC .25 .60
413 Miles Austin .15 .40
414 Lane Johnson RC .30 .75
415A Randall Cobb left .20 .50
415B R.Cobb SP right 5.00 12.00
416 Jake Locker .20 .50
417 D'Qwell Jackson .15 .40
418 Mike Tolbert .15 .40
419 Zach Brown .15 .40
420 A.J. Green .25 .60
421 Chris Harper RC .25 .60
422 Jon Bostic RC .25 .60
423 Datone Jones RC .25 .60
424 Jerod Mayo .20 .50
425 Percy Harvin .15 .40
426 Matt Schaub .15 .40
427 Michael Johnson .15 .40
428 Terrance Williams RC .25 .60
429 Colts/Luck/Wayne .30 .75
430A Larry Fitzgerald blk glv .20 .50
430B L.Fitzgerald SP pink glv 4.00 10.00
431 Chargers/Rivers/Alexander .20 .50
432 Eagles/Vick .15 .40
433 Landry Jones RC .25 .60
434 Zac Stacy RC .25 .60
435A Keenan Allen RC .50 1.25
435B Keenan Allen SP catch 4.00 10.00
436 Steve Johnson .20 .50
437 Justin Smith .15 .40
438 Jawan Jamison RC .25 .60
439 Vincent Jackson .15 .40
440A J.Flacco prpl jsy .20 .50
440B J.Flacco SP wht jsy 4.00 10.00
BWSP Brent Williams SP 30.00 60.00
SPTT T.Tebow/T.Brady SP 25.00 60.00

2013 Topps Black

*VETS/58: 8X TO 20X BASIC CARDS
*ROOKIES/58: 5X TO 12X BASIC RC
BLACK/58 ODDS 1:69 HOBBY

2013 Topps Camo

*VETS/399: 3X TO 8X BASIC CARDS
*ROOKIES/399: 2X TO 5X BASIC RC
CAMO/399 ODDS 1:48 HOBBY

2013 Topps Gold

*VETS/2013: 2X TO 5X BASIC CARDS
*ROOKIES/2013: 1.2X TO 3X BASIC RC
GOLD/2013 ODDS 1:11 HOB

2013 Topps Pink

ETS/399: 3X TO 8X BASIC CARDS
*ROOKIES/399: 2X TO 5X BASIC RC
PINK/399 ODDS 1:48 HOBBY

2013 Topps 1000 Yard Club

ATED ODDS 1:4 HOBBY
1 Adrian Peterson .50 1.25
2 Calvin Johnson .50 1.25
3 Alfred Morris .30 .75
4 Andre Johnson .30 .75
5 Marshawn Lynch .40 1.00
6 Jamaal Charles .40 1.00
7 Brandon Marshall .40 1.00
8 Doug Martin .40 1.00
9 Demaryius Thomas .40 1.00
10 Arian Foster .40 1.00
11 Vincent Jackson .30 .75
12 Dez Bryant .50 1.25
13 Reggie Wayne .40 1.00
14 Wes Welker .40 1.00
15 Roddy White .30 .75
16 A.J. Green .50 1.25
17 Stevan Ridley .30 .75
18 C.J. Spiller .30 .75
19 Chris Johnson .30 .75
20 Frank Gore .40 1.00
21 Julio Jones .50 1.25
22 Steve Smith .40 1.00
23 Marques Colston .30 .75
24 Ray Rice .30 .75
25 Michael Crabtree .30 .75
26 Matt Forte .30 .75
27 BenJarvus Green-Ellis .40 1.00
28 Victor Cruz .40 1.00
29 Brian Hartline .30 .75
30 Eric Decker .30 .75
31 Shonn Greene .30 .75
32 Steve Johnson .40 1.00
33 Steven Jackson .30 .75
34 Lance Moore .30 .75
35 Jason Witten .40 1.00

2013 Topps 1959 Mini Autographs

STATED ODDS 1:1445 HOB
1 Keenan Allen 10.00 25.00
2 Geno Smith 5.00 12.00
3 Matt Barkley 5.00 12.00
4 Cordarrelle Patterson 5.00 12.00
5 Mike Glennon 5.00 12.00
6 Zach Ertz 10.00 25.00
7 DeAndre Hopkins 12.00 30.00
8 Eddie Lacy 5.00 12.00
9 Tyler Eifert 5.00 12.00
10 Tavon Austin 6.00 15.00
11 Tyler Wilson 5.00 12.00
12 Robert Woods 8.00 20.00
13 Quinton Patton 5.00 12.00
14 Ryan Nassib 5.00 12.00
15 Terrance Williams 5.00 12.00
16 Markus Wheaton 5.00 12.00
17 Aaron Dobson 5.00 12.00
18 Giovani Bernard 5.00 12.00
19 EJ Manuel 5.00 12.00
20 Justin Hunter 5.00 12.00
21 Joseph Randle 5.00 12.00
22 Le'Veon Bell 25.00 50.00
23 Montee Ball 5.00 12.00
24 Marcus Lattimore 5.00 12.00
25 Andre Ellington 5.00 12.00
26 Stepfan Taylor 5.00 12.00
27 Jordan Reed 8.00 20.00
28 Landry Jones 5.00 12.00
29 Mike Gillislee 5.00 12.00
30 Kenny Stills 5.00 12.00
31 Denard Robinson 5.00 12.00
32 Marquise Goodwin 5.00 12.00
33 Manti Te'o 6.00 15.00
34 Vance McDonald 6.00 15.00
35 Gavin Escobar 5.00 12.00
36 Johnathan Franklin 5.00 12.00
37 Stedman Bailey 5.00 12.00
38 Knile Davis 5.00 12.00
39 Christine Michael 20.00 50.00
41 Dion Jordan 5.00 12.00

2013 Topps 1959 Mini

MPLETE SET (99) 30.00 60.00
STATED ODDS 1:3 HOBBY
1 Trent Richardson .40 1.00
2 Dwayne Bowe .50 1.25
3 Drew Brees .60 1.50
4 Adrian Peterson .60 1.50
5 Cam Newton .60 1.50
6 Philip Rivers .60 1.50
7 Sidney Rice .40 1.00
8 Jason Witten .50 1.25
9 Barry Sanders 1.00 2.50
10 Christian Ponder .40 1.00
11 Steve Smith .50 1.25
12 Michael Vick .50 1.25
13 Aldon Smith .40 1.00
14 Emmitt Smith 1.00 2.50
15 Justin Smith .40 1.00
16 Jacoby Jones .40 1.00
17 Marshawn Lynch .50 1.25
18 Julio Jones .60 1.50
19 Andy Dalton .50 1.25
20 Eric Weddle .40 1.00
21 Jared Allen .40 1.00
22 Josh Freeman .50 1.25
23 James Laurinaitis .50 1.25
24 Santana Moss .50 1.25
25 Chris Johnson .40 1.00
26 NaVorro Bowman .50 1.25
27 LeSean McCoy .60 1.50
28 Tony Romo .50 1.25
29 Terrell Suggs .40 1.00
30 Ndamukong Suh .50 1.25
31 Jake Locker .50 1.25
32 Russell Wilson 1.25 3.00
33 Earl Thomas .50 1.25
34 Reggie Wayne .50 1.25
35 Patrick Peterson .40 1.00
36 Mark Sanchez .40 1.00
37 Jimmy Graham .60 1.50
38 Richard Sherman .60 1.50
39 London Fletcher .50 1.25
40 Jerry Rice 1.00 2.50
41 Michael Crabtree .40 1.00
42 Rob Gronkowski .60 1.50
43 Eli Manning .50 1.25
44 Eric Decker .40 1.00
45 Matt Forte .40 1.00
46 Peyton Manning 1.25 3.00
47 Aaron Rodgers .75 2.00
48 Colin Kaepernick .50 1.25
49 Robert Mathis .40 1.00
50 Andrew Luck 1.00 2.50
51 Cameron Wake .40 1.00
52 Willis McGahee .40 1.00
53 Ray Rice .40 1.00
54 Ronde Barber .40 1.00
55 Tim Tebow .50 1.25
56 Julius Peppers .50 1.25
57 Victor Cruz .50 1.25
58 Chris Long .40 1.00
59 Dan Marino 1.25 3.00
60 DeSean Jackson .50 1.25
61 Patrick Willis .50 1.25
62 J.J. Watt .50 1.25
63 Joe Montana 1.50 4.00
64 Matt Ryan .50 1.25
65 Vince Wilfork .40 1.00
66 Jay Cutler .40 1.00
67 Sam Bradford .40 1.00
68 Hakeem Nicks .40 1.00
69 Frank Gore .50 1.25
70 Jason Pierre-Paul .40 1.00
71 Calvin Johnson .60 1.50
72 Dez Bryant .60 1.50
73 Tom Brady 1.50 4.00
74 Andre Johnson .40 1.00
76 Von Miller .50 1.25
77 Antonio Cromartie .40 1.00
78 Doug Martin .50 1.25
79 Charles Tillman .50 1.25
80 DeMarco Murray .50 1.25
81 Roddy White .40 1.00
82 Troy Polamalu .60 1.50
83 Joe Flacco .50 1.25
84 Ryan Tannehill .50 1.25
85 Vernon Davis .40 1.00
86 Jamaal Charles .50 1.25
87 Brandon Spikes .40 1.00
88 A.J. Green .60 1.50
89 Randall Cobb .50 1.25
90 Arian Foster .50 1.25
91 Luke Kuechly .50 1.25
92 Demaryius Thomas .50 1.25
93 Tony Gonzalez .50 1.25
94 C.J. Spiller .40 1.00
95 Darren McFadden .50 1.25
96 Robert Griffin III .40 1.00
97 Antonio Brown .60 1.50
98 Brandon Marshall .50 1.25
99 Ben Roethlisberger .60 1.50
100 Clay Matthews .60 1.50

2013 Topps 1965 Mini Autographs

STATED ODDS 1:1445 HOBBY
1 Keenan Allen 10.00 25.00
2 Geno Smith 5.00 12.00
3 Matt Barkley 5.00 12.00
4 Cordarrelle Patterson 5.00 12.00
5 Mike Glennon 5.00 12.00
6 Zach Ertz 10.00 25.00
7 DeAndre Hopkins 12.00 30.00
8 Eddie Lacy 5.00 12.00
9 Tyler Eifert 5.00 12.00
10 Tavon Austin 6.00 15.00
11 Tyler Wilson 5.00 12.00
12 Robert Woods 8.00 20.00
13 Quinton Patton 5.00 12.00
14 Ryan Nassib 5.00 12.00
15 Terrance Williams 5.00 12.00
16 Markus Wheaton 5.00 12.00
17 Aaron Dobson 5.00 12.00
18 Giovani Bernard 5.00 12.00
19 EJ Manuel 5.00 12.00
20 Justin Hunter 5.00 12.00
21 Joseph Randle 5.00 12.00
22 Le'Veon Bell 25.00 50.00
23 Montee Ball 5.00 12.00
24 Marcus Lattimore 5.00 12.00
25 Andre Ellington 5.00 12.00
26 Stepfan Taylor 5.00 12.00
27 Jordan Reed 8.00 20.00
28 Landry Jones 5.00 12.00
29 Mike Gillislee 5.00 12.00
30 Kenny Stills 5.00 12.00
31 Denard Robinson 5.00 12.00
32 Marquise Goodwin 5.00 12.00
33 Manti Te'o 6.00 15.00
34 Vance McDonald 6.00 15.00
35 Gavin Escobar 5.00 12.00
36 Johnathan Franklin 5.00 12.00
37 Stedman Bailey 5.00 12.00
38 Knile Davis 5.00 12.00
39 Christine Michael 15.00 40.00
41 Dion Jordan 5.00 12.00

2013 Topps 1969 Green

*BLUE WAL-MART: .5X TO 1.2X GREEN
*RED TARGET: .5X TO 1.2X GREEN
EACH HAS TWO CARDS OF EQUAL VALUE
1 Matt Barkley .60 1.50
2 Matt Barkley .60 1.50
3 Geno Smith .60 1.50
4 Geno Smith .60 1.50
5 Mike Glennon .60 1.50
6 Mike Glennon .60 1.50
7 Keenan Allen 1.25 3.00
8 Keenan Allen 1.25 3.00
9 Cordarrelle Patterson .60 1.50
10 Cordarrelle Patterson .60 1.50
11 DeAndre Hopkins 1.50 4.00
12 DeAndre Hopkins 1.50 4.00
13 Eddie Lacy .60 1.50
14 Eddie Lacy .60 1.50
15 Giovani Bernard .60 1.50
16 Giovani Bernard .60 1.50
17 Montee Ball .60 1.50
18 Montee Ball .60 1.50
19 Robert Woods 1.00 2.50
20 Robert Woods 1.00 2.50
21 Tyler Eifert .60 1.50
22 Tyler Eifert .60 1.50
23 Manti Te'o .75 2.00
24 Manti Te'o .75 2.00
25 Tavon Austin .75 2.00
26 Tavon Austin .75 2.00
27 EJ Manuel .60 1.50
28 EJ Manuel .60 1.50
29 Justin Hunter .60 1.50
30 Justin Hunter .60 1.50

2013 Topps 1986 Autographs

1986 AU/140 ODDS 1:795 HOB
1 Keenan Allen 10.00 25.00
2 Geno Smith 5.00 12.00
3 Matt Barkley 5.00 12.00
4 Cordarrelle Patterson 5.00 12.00
5 Mike Glennon 5.00 12.00
6 Zach Ertz 10.00 25.00
7 DeAndre Hopkins 12.00 30.00
8 Eddie Lacy 5.00 12.00
9 Tyler Eifert 5.00 12.00
10 Tavon Austin 6.00 15.00
11 Tyler Wilson 5.00 12.00
12 Robert Woods 8.00 20.00
13 Quinton Patton 5.00 12.00
14 Ryan Nassib 5.00 12.00
15 Terrance Williams 5.00 12.00
16 Markus Wheaton 5.00 12.00
17 Aaron Dobson 5.00 12.00
18 Giovani Bernard 5.00 12.00
19 EJ Manuel 5.00 12.00
20 Justin Hunter 5.00 12.00
21 Joseph Randle 5.00 12.00
22 Le'Veon Bell 25.00 50.00
23 Montee Ball 5.00 12.00
24 Marcus Lattimore 5.00 12.00
25 Andre Ellington 5.00 12.00
26 Stepfan Taylor 5.00 12.00
27 Jordan Reed 8.00 20.00
28 Landry Jones 10.00 25.00
29 Mike Gillislee 5.00 12.00
30 Kenny Stills 5.00 12.00
31 Denard Robinson 5.00 12.00
32 Marquise Goodwin 5.00 12.00
33 Manti Te'o 6.00 15.00
34 Vance McDonald 6.00 15.00
35 Gavin Escobar 5.00 12.00
36 Johnathan Franklin 5.00 12.00
37 Stedman Bailey 5.00 12.00
38 Knile Davis 5.00 12.00
39 Christine Michael 10.00 25.00
41 Dion Jordan 5.00 12.00

2013 Topps 4000 Yard Club

STATED ODDS 1:6 HOBBY
1 Drew Brees .50 1.25
2 Matthew Stafford .40 1.00
3 Tony Romo .40 1.00
4 Tom Brady 1.25 3.00
5 Matt Ryan .40 1.00
6 Peyton Manning 1.00 2.50
7 Andrew Luck .75 2.00
8 Aaron Rodgers .75 2.00
9 Josh Freeman .40 1.00
10 Carson Palmer .40 1.00

2013 Topps All Pro Team

ALL PRO TEAM/99 ODDS 1:3310 HOB
APTAP Adrian Peterson 12.00 30.00
APTAS Aldon Smith 10.00 25.00
APTBM Brandon Marshall 10.00 25.00
APTCJ Calvin Johnson 10.00 25.00
APTCM Clay Matthews 12.00 30.00
APTCT Charles Tillman 10.00 25.00
APTCW Cameron Wake 6.00 15.00
APTET Earl Thomas 8.00 20.00
APTGA Geno Atkins 10.00 25.00
APTJB Jairus Byrd 6.00 15.00
APTJJW J.J. Watt 12.00 30.00
APTJS Justin Smith 6.00 15.00
APTJST Joe Staley 6.00 15.00
APTMI Mike Iupati 6.00 15.00
APTML Marshawn Lynch 8.00 20.00
APTMU Max Unger 6.00 15.00
APTMY Marshal Yanda 6.00 15.00
APTPM Peyton Manning 15.00 40.00
APTRC Ryan Clady 6.00 15.00
APTRS Richard Sherman 8.00 20.00
APTTG Tony Gonzalez 8.00 20.00
APTVM Von Miller 8.00 20.00

2013 Topps All Star Rookies

ALL STAR ROOKIE/99 ODDS 1:4868 HOB
ASRAL Andrew Luck 25.00 50.00
ASRAM Alfred Morris 6.00 15.00
ASRBW Bobby Wagner 6.00 15.00
ASRCJ Chandler Jones 6.00 15.00
ASRDA Dwayne Allen 6.00 15.00
ASRDM Doug Martin 8.00 20.00
ASRJB Justin Blackmon 6.00 15.00
ASRJG Josh Gordon 6.00 15.00
ASRJJ Janoris Jenkins 6.00 15.00
ASRLK Luke Kuechly 10.00 25.00
ASRMK Matt Kalil 6.00 15.00
ASRRG Robert Griffin III 6.00 15.00
ASRRW Russell Wilson 20.00 50.00
ASRTR Trent Richardson 6.00 15.00
ASRTYH T.Y. Hilton 8.00 20.00

2013 Topps Autographs

VETERAN AU ODDS 1:2868 HOBBY
ROOKIE AU ODDS 1:4550 HOBBY
EXCH EXPIRATION: 7/31/2016
EACH HAS TWO CARDS OF EQUAL VALUE
11A Manti Te'o 5.00 12.00
11B Manti Te'o 5.00 12.00
30A Marshawn Lynch 20.00 50.00
30B Marshawn Lynch 20.00 50.00
35A Luke Joeckel 6.00 15.00
37A Andre Ellington 6.00 15.00
43A Mike Glennon 4.00 10.00
43B Mike Glennon 4.00 10.00
44A Zac Dysert 4.00 10.00
46A Patrick Peterson 10.00 25.00
46B Patrick Peterson 10.00 25.00
50A Andrew Luck 75.00 125.00
50B Andrew Luck 75.00 125.00
51A Demaryius Thomas 8.00 20.00
51B Demaryius Thomas 8.00 20.00
61A Montee Ball 4.00 10.00
61B Montee Ball 4.00 10.00
70A Alfred Morris 6.00 15.00
70B Alfred Morris 6.00 15.00
74A Stepfan Taylor 4.00 10.00
74B Stepfan Taylor 4.00 10.00
75A Jamaal Charles 8.00 20.00
75B Jamaal Charles 8.00 20.00
78B Tavarres King 4.00 10.00
80A Ray Rice 6.00 15.00
80B Ray Rice 12.00 30.00
88A Alex Okafor 4.00 10.00
92A Steve Smith 12.00 30.00
92B Steve Smith 10.00 25.00
112A Tavon Austin 5.00 12.00
112B Tavon Austin 5.00 12.00
126A Geno Smith passing 4.00 10.00
126B Geno Smith running 4.00 10.00
128A Haloti Ngata 6.00 15.00
128B Haloti Ngata 6.00 15.00
130A Doug Martin 15.00 40.00
130B Doug Martin 15.00 40.00
133A Denard Robinson 4.00 10.00
133B Denard Robinson 4.00 10.00
136A Kenjon Barner 4.00 10.00
136B Kenjon Barner 4.00 10.00
143A Ezekiel Ansah 4.00 10.00
143B Ezekiel Ansah 4.00 10.00
145A Johnathan Franklin 4.00 10.00
145B Johnathan Franklin 4.00 10.00
148A Shane Vereen 6.00 15.00
148B Shane Vereen 6.00 15.00
150A Robert Griffin III 75.00 125.00
150B Robert Griffin III 60.00 120.00
155A DeAndre Hopkins 10.00 25.00
155B DeAndre Hopkins 10.00 25.00
159A Ryan Nassib 4.00 10.00
159B Ryan Nassib 4.00 10.00
160A Trent Richardson 12.00 30.00
160B Trent Richardson 12.00 30.00
170A Michael Crabtree 6.00 15.00
170B Michael Crabtree 6.00 15.00
174A BenJarvus Green-Ellis 6.00 15.00
174B BenJarvus Green-Ellis 6.00 15.00
183B Dion Jordan 4.00 10.00
186A Brent Celek 6.00 15.00
186B Brent Celek 6.00 15.00
192A Mike Gillislee 4.00 10.00
198A Josh Gordon 6.00 15.00
198B Josh Gordon 6.00 15.00
202A Stedman Bailey 8.00 20.00
202B Stedman Bailey 8.00 20.00
209A Jarvis Jones 4.00 10.00
209B Jarvis Jones 4.00 10.00
210A Rob Gronkowski 15.00 30.00
210B Rob Gronkowski 15.00 30.00
214A Chris Johnson 15.00 30.00
214B Chris Johnson 15.00 30.00
215A EJ Manuel 4.00 10.00
215B EJ Manuel 4.00 10.00
230A Arian Foster 15.00 30.00
230B Arian Foster 15.00 30.00
242A Tyler Bray 4.00 10.00
242B Tyler Bray 4.00 10.00
245A Matt Barkley 10.00 25.00
245B Matt Barkley 10.00 25.00
248A Justin Hunter 10.00 25.00
248B Justin Hunter 10.00 25.00
260A Frank Gore 10.00 25.00
260B Frank Gore 10.00 25.00
265A Pierre Garcon 8.00 20.00
265B Pierre Garcon 8.00 20.00
268A Matthew Stafford 20.00 40.00
268B Matthew Stafford 20.00 40.00
270A Julio Jones 20.00 40.00
270B Julio Jones 20.00 40.00
280A Russell Wilson 60.00 100.00
280B Russell Wilson 60.00 100.00
281A Robert Woods 6.00 15.00
281B Robert Woods 6.00 15.00
282A Barkevious Mingo 6.00 15.00
282B Barkevious Mingo 6.00 15.00
287A T.Y. Hilton 8.00 20.00
287B T.Y. Hilton 8.00 20.00
289A Brandon Myers 5.00 12.00
289B Brandon Myers 5.00 12.00
290A Reggie Wayne 15.00 30.00
290B Reggie Wayne 15.00 30.00
292A Jason Pierre-Paul 6.00 15.00
292B Jason Pierre-Paul 6.00 15.00
294B Christine Michael 10.00 25.00
306A Golden Tate 6.00 15.00
306B Golden Tate 10.00 25.00
314A Marcus Lattimore 4.00 10.00
314B Marcus Lattimore 4.00 10.00
317A Jordan Reed 6.00 15.00
317B Jordan Reed 6.00 15.00
325A Roddy White 6.00 15.00
325B Roddy White 6.00 15.00
330A Jimmy Graham 10.00 25.00
330B Jimmy Graham 12.00 30.00
332A Tyler Wilson 12.00 30.00
332B Tyler Wilson 12.00 30.00
348A Jermichael Finley 6.00 15.00
348B Jermichael Finley 6.00 15.00
351A Ryan Tannehill 25.00 50.00
351B Ryan Tannehill 25.00 50.00
353A Alec Ogletree 4.00 10.00
358A Giovani Bernard 4.00 10.00
358B Giovani Bernard 4.00 10.00
382A Brian Hartline 6.00 15.00
382B Brian Hartline 6.00 15.00
384A Zach Ertz 8.00 20.00
384B Zach Ertz 8.00 20.00
386A Cordarrelle Patterson 4.00 10.00
386B Cordarrelle Patterson 4.00 10.00
387B Kenny Stills 4.00 10.00
402B Aaron Dobson 4.00 10.00
403B Le'Veon Bell 25.00 50.00
406A Eddie Lacy 4.00 10.00
406B Eddie Lacy 4.00 10.00
407A Tyler Eifert 4.00 10.00
407B Tyler Eifert 4.00 10.00
435A Keenan Allen 8.00 20.00
435B Keenan Allen 8.00 20.00

2013 Topps Factory Set Patch

ONE PER RETAIL FACTORY SET
AP Adrian Peterson LEG 2.50 6.00
AR Aaron Rodgers LEG 4.00 10.00
EM EJ Manuel NFL 1.25 3.00
GS Geno Smith NFL 1.25 3.00
PM Peyton Manning LEG 5.00 12.00
TA Tavon Austin NFL 1.50 4.00

2013 Topps Future Legends

STATED ODDS 1:4 HOBBY
FLAD Andy Dalton .40 1.00
FLAJG A.J. Green .50 1.25
FLAL Andrew Luck .75 2.00
FLAM Alfred Morris .30 .75
FLAS Aldon Smith .30 .75
FLCJS C.J. Spiller .30 .75
FLCK Colin Kaepernick .40 1.00
FLCN Cam Newton .50 1.25
FLCP Cordarrelle Patterson .25 .60
FLDB Dez Bryant .50 1.25
FLDH DeAndre Hopkins .60 1.50
FLDM Doug Martin .40 1.00
FLDMI Dee Milliner .25 .60
FLDT Demaryius Thomas .40 1.00
FLEL Eddie Lacy .25 .60
FLET Earl Thomas .40 1.00
FLGB Giovani Bernard .25 .60
FLGS Geno Smith .25 .60
FLJG Jimmy Graham .50 1.25
FLJJ Julio Jones .50 1.25
FLJJE Janoris Jenkins .30 .75
FLJJW J.J. Watt .40 1.00
FLJPP Jason Pierre-Paul .30 .75
FLKA Keenan Allen .50 1.25
FLLK Luke Kuechly .40 1.00
FLMB Matt Barkley .25 .60
FLNB NaVorro Bowman .40 1.00
FLPP Patrick Peterson .30 .75
FLRG Rob Gronkowski .50 1.25
FLRG3 Robert Griffin III .30 .75
FLRS Richard Sherman .50 1.25
FLRT Ryan Tannehill .40 1.00
FLRW Russell Wilson 1.00 2.50
FLSB Sam Bradford .30 .75
FLTA Tavon Austin .30 .75
FLTE Tyler Eifert .25 .60
FLTR Trent Richardson .30 .75
FLVC Victor Cruz .40 1.00
FLVM Von Miller .40 1.00

2013 Topps Gridiron Legends

ATED ODDS 1:6 HOBBY
GLAR Andre Reed .50 1.25
GLBF Brett Favre 1.25 3.00
GLBJ Bo Jackson .75 2.00
GLBS Barry Sanders 1.00 2.50
GLBSM Bruce Smith .50 1.25
GLCM Curtis Martin .50 1.25
GLDM Dan Marino 1.25 3.00
GLDS Deion Sanders .50 1.25
GLED Eric Dickerson .50 1.25
GLES Emmitt Smith 1.00 2.50
GLJB Jerome Bettis .60 1.50

GLJE John Elway 1.00 2.50
GLJG Joe Greene .60 1.50
GLJK Jim Kelly .60 1.50
GLJM Joe Montana 1.50 4.00
GLJR Jerry Rice 1.00 2.50
GLKW Kurt Warner .50 1.25
GLLT Lawrence Taylor .60 1.50
GLLTO LaDainian Tomlinson .50 1.25
GLMA Marcus Allen .60 1.50
GLMF Marshall Faulk .50 1.25
GLRC Roger Craig .50 1.25
GLRL Ronnie Lott .50 1.25
GLRW Rod Woodson .50 1.25
GLSL Steve Largent .60 1.50
GLSY Steve Young .75 2.00
GLTA Troy Aikman .75 2.00
GLTD Terrell Davis .50 1.25
GLTT Thurman Thomas .50 1.25
GLWM Warren Moon .60 1.50

2013 Topps Gridiron Legends Busts Bronze

BRONZE PRINT RUN 75 SER.#'d SETS
*GOLD/25: .6X TO 1.5X BRONZE/75
*SILVER/50: .5X TO 1.2X BRONZE/75
GLBAR Andre Reed 8.00 20.00
GLBBF Brett Favre 20.00 50.00
GLBBJ Bo Jackson 12.00 30.00
GLBBS Barry Sanders 15.00 40.00
GLBBSM Bruce Smith 8.00 20.00
GLBCM Curtis Martin 8.00 20.00
GLBDM Dan Marino 20.00 50.00
GLBDS Deion Sanders 8.00 20.00
GLBED Eric Dickerson 10.00 25.00
GLBES Emmitt Smith 15.00 40.00
GLBHL Howie Long 12.00 30.00
GLBJB Jerome Bettis 12.00 30.00
GLBJE John Elway 15.00 40.00
GLBJG Joe Greene 12.00 30.00
GLBJK Jim Kelly 10.00 25.00
GLBJM Joe Montana 15.00 40.00
GLBJR Jerry Rice 12.00 30.00
GLBKW Kurt Warner 12.00 30.00
GLBLTO LaDainian Tomlinson 10.00 25.00
GLBMA Marcus Allen 10.00 25.00
GLBMF Marshall Faulk 8.00 20.00
GLBRC Roger Craig 8.00 20.00
GLBRCU Randall Cunningham 8.00 20.00
GLBRL Ronnie Lott 8.00 20.00
GLBSY Steve Young 12.00 30.00
GLBTA Troy Aikman 12.00 30.00
GLBTD Terrell Davis 12.00 30.00
GLBTT Thurman Thomas 8.00 20.00
GLBWM Warren Moon 10.00 25.00

2013 Topps Gridiron Legends Rings Bronze

*BRONZE/75: .4X TO 1X BRONZE BUST/75
*GOLD/25: .6X TO 1.5X BRONZE/75
*SILVER/50: .5X TO 1.2X BRONZE/75

2013 Topps Jumbo Relics

MBO JSY/20 ODDS 1:4384 HOB
TJRAE Andre Ellington 3.00 8.00
TJRAJG A.J. Green 8.00 20.00
TJRAL Andrew Luck 12.00 30.00
TJRAM Alfred Morris 8.00 20.00
TJRCN Cam Newton 8.00 20.00
TJRCP Cordarrelle Patterson 3.00 8.00
TJRDH DeAndre Hopkins 6.00 15.00
TJRDM DeMarco Murray 6.00 15.00
TJREL Eddie Lacy 3.00 8.00
TJRGS Geno Smith 3.00 8.00
TJRJJ Julio Jones 8.00 20.00
TJRKA Keenan Allen 6.00 15.00
TJRMB Matt Barkley 3.00 8.00
TJRMT Manti Te'o 8.00 20.00
TJRRG Robert Griffin III 5.00 12.00
TJRRT Ryan Tannehill 6.00 15.00
TJRRW Russell Wilson 10.00 25.00
TJRSR Stevan Ridley 5.00 12.00
TJRTA Tavon Austin 4.00 10.00
TJRTE Tyler Eifert 8.00 20.00

2013 Topps Legendary Achievement Medals Bronze

*BRONZE/75: .4X TO 1X BRONZE BUST/75
*GOLD/25: .6X TO 1.5X BRONZE/75
*SILVER/50: .5X TO 1.2X BRONZE/75

2013 Topps Legendary Captains Patches

*CAPT PATCH/99: .3X TO .8X BRONZE BUST/75
CAPT PATCH/99 ODDS 1:2434 HOB

2013 Topps Legendary Club Coins Bronze

BRONZE STATED PRINT RUN 75
*GOLD/25: .6X TO 1.5X BRONZE/75
*SILVER/50: .5X TO 1.2X BRONZE/75
LCAB Anquan Boldin 6.00 15.00
LCAJ Andre Johnson 6.00 15.00
LCAP Adrian Peterson 10.00 25.00
LCAR Andre Reed 8.00 20.00
LCARO Aaron Rodgers 15.00 40.00
LCBF Brett Favre 20.00 50.00
LCBS Barry Sanders 15.00 40.00
LCCJ Calvin Johnson 10.00 25.00
LCCM Curtis Martin 8.00 20.00
LCDB Drew Brees 10.00 25.00
LCDM Dan Marino 20.00 50.00
LCED Eric Dickerson 10.00 25.00
LCES Emmitt Smith 15.00 40.00
LCJB Jerome Bettis 15.00 40.00
LCJBR Jim Brown 12.00 30.00
LCJR Jerry Rice 15.00 40.00
LCKW Kurt Warner 12.00 30.00
LCLF Larry Fitzgerald 8.00 20.00
LCLTO LaDainian Tomlinson 10.00 25.00
LCMA Marcus Allen 10.00 25.00
LCMF Marshall Faulk 8.00 20.00
LCPM Peyton Manning 20.00 50.00
LCRC Roger Craig 8.00 20.00
LCSJ Steven Jackson 6.00 15.00
LCSY Steve Young 12.00 30.00
LCTBR Tom Brady 25.00 60.00
LCTD Terrell Davis 12.00 30.00
LCTT Thurman Thomas 8.00 20.00
LCWM Warren Moon 10.00 25.00

2013 Topps Legendary Moments

LEG.MOMENT/99 ODDS 1:2434 HOB
LMAR Andre Reed 6.00 15.00
LMBF Brett Favre 25.00 50.00
LMBJ Bo Jackson 10.00 25.00
LMBS Barry Sanders 12.00 30.00
LMBSM Bruce Smith 6.00 15.00
LMCM Curtis Martin 6.00 15.00
LMDM Dan Marino 25.00 50.00
LMDS Deion Sanders 6.00 15.00
LMED Eric Dickerson 6.00 15.00
LMES Emmitt Smith 12.00 30.00
LMHL Howie Long 8.00 20.00
LMJB Jerome Bettis 8.00 20.00
LMJE John Elway 12.00 30.00
LMJG Joe Greene 8.00 20.00
LMJK Jim Kelly 8.00 20.00
LMJM Joe Montana 30.00 60.00
LMJR Jerry Rice 12.00 30.00
LMKW Kurt Warner 6.00 15.00
LMLTO LaDainian Tomlinson 8.00 20.00
LMMA Marcus Allen 8.00 20.00
LMMF Marshall Faulk 6.00 15.00
LMRC Roger Craig 6.00 15.00
LMRCU Randall Cunningham 8.00 20.00
LMRL Ronnie Lott 6.00 15.00
LMSY Steve Young 10.00 25.00
LMTA Troy Aikman 10.00 25.00
LMTD Terrell Davis 6.00 15.00
LMTT Thurman Thomas 6.00 15.00
LMWM Warren Moon 8.00 20.00

2013 Topps Legends In The Making

ATED ODDS 1:6 HOBBY
LMAB Anquan Boldin .30 .75
LMAF Arian Foster .40 1.00
LMAG Antonio Gates .40 1.00
LMAJ Andre Johnson .30 .75
LMAP Adrian Peterson .50 1.25
LMAR Aaron Rodgers .75 2.00
LMBM Brandon Marshall .40 1.00
LMBR Ben Roethlisberger .50 1.25
LMCJ Calvin Johnson .50 1.25
LMDB Drew Brees .50 1.25
LMDR Darrelle Revis .30 .75
LMDW DeMarcus Ware .50 1.25
LMEM Eli Manning .40 1.00
LMER Ed Reed .40 1.00
LMFG Frank Gore .40 1.00
LMJA Jared Allen .30 .75
LMJF Joe Flacco .40 1.00
LMJW Jason Witten .40 1.00
LMLF Larry Fitzgerald .40 1.00
LMMJD Maurice Jones-Drew .30 .75
LMML Marshawn Lynch .40 1.00
LMPM Peyton Manning 1.00 2.50
LMPW Patrick Willis .40 1.00
LMRW Reggie Wayne .40 1.00
LMRWH Roddy White .30 .75
LMSJ Steven Jackson .30 .75
LMTB Tom Brady 1.25 3.00
LMTG Tony Gonzalez .40 1.00
LMTP Troy Polamalu .50 1.25
LMWW Wes Welker .40 1.00

2013 Topps Orange

*VETS/82: 6X TO 15X BASIC CARDS
*ROOKIES/82: 4X TO 10X BASIC RC
ORANGE/82 FOUR PER HOBBY FACTORY SET

2013 Topps NFL Captains Patches Camo

CAMO PATCH/99 ODDS 1:2143 HOB
*PINK/99: .4X TO 1X CAMO/99
NCPAD Andy Dalton 6.00 15.00
NCPAJ Andre Johnson 8.00 20.00
NCPAL Andrew Luck 12.00 30.00
NCPAR Aaron Rodgers 20.00 40.00
NCPCB Champ Bailey 6.00 15.00
NCPCJ Calvin Johnson 8.00 20.00
NCPCM Clay Matthews 12.00 30.00
NCPDB Drew Brees 12.00 30.00
NCPDM Darren McFadden 6.00 15.00
NCPDW DeMarcus Ware 8.00 20.00
NCPEM Eli Manning 12.00 30.00
NCPFJ Fred Jackson 6.00 15.00
NCPJC Jay Cutler 5.00 12.00
NCPJF Josh Freeman 6.00 15.00
NCPJJ James Jones 5.00 12.00
NCPJJW J.J. Watt 12.00 30.00
NCPJL James Laurinaitis 6.00 15.00
NCPJLO Jake Locker 6.00 15.00
NCPJP Julius Peppers 8.00 20.00
NCPJT Joe Thomas 8.00 20.00
NCPJTU Justin Tuck 6.00 15.00
NCPJW Jason Witten 6.00 15.00
NCPLF Larry Fitzgerald 8.00 20.00
NCPLFL London Fletcher 6.00 15.00
NCPMR Matt Ryan 6.00 15.00
NCPMS Matthew Stafford 6.00 15.00
NCPMSC Matt Schaub 5.00 12.00
NCPPM Peyton Manning 25.00 60.00
NCPRG Robert Griffin III 5.00 12.00
NCPRW Reggie Wayne 6.00 15.00
NCPSB Sam Bradford 5.00 12.00
NCPSS Steve Smith 6.00 15.00
NCPTR Tony Romo 6.00 15.00
NCPVJ Vincent Jackson 5.00 12.00

2013 Topps Relics

STATED ODDS 1:51 HOBBY
TRAD Andy Dalton 3.00 8.00
TRAE Andre Ellington 1.50 4.00
TRAG Antonio Gates 3.00 8.00
TRAJG A.J. Green 4.00 10.00
TRAL Andrew Luck 6.00 15.00
TRAM Alfred Morris 2.50 6.00
TRBO Brian Orakpo 3.00 8.00
TRCF Coby Fleener 2.50 6.00
TRCJS C.J. Spiller 2.50 6.00
TRCK Colin Kaepernick 6.00 15.00
TRCN Cam Newton 4.00 10.00
TRCP Cordarrelle Patterson 1.50 4.00
TRCW Cameron Wake 2.50 6.00
TRDB Dez Bryant 4.00 10.00
TRDH DeAndre Hopkins 4.00 10.00
TRDJ DeSean Jackson 3.00 8.00
TRDM Doug Martin 3.00 8.00
TRDR Denard Robinson 1.50 4.00
TRDT Demaryius Thomas 3.00 8.00
TREJM EJ Manuel 1.50 4.00
TREL Eddie Lacy 1.50 4.00
TRET Earl Thomas 3.00 8.00
TRFJ Fred Jackson 3.00 8.00
TRGB Giovani Bernard 1.50 4.00
TRGS Geno Smith 1.50 4.00
TRJB Justin Blackmon 2.50 6.00
TRJC Jay Cutler 2.50 6.00
TRJCH Jamaal Charles 3.00 8.00
TRJD Jonathan Dwyer 2.50 6.00
TRJG Jermaine Gresham 3.00 8.00
TRJGO Josh Gordon 2.50 6.00
TRJJ Julio Jones 4.00 10.00
TRJL James Laurinaitis 3.00 8.00
TRKA Keenan Allen 3.00 8.00
TRKW Kendall Wright 2.50 6.00
TRMA Miles Austin 2.50 6.00
TRMB Matt Barkley 4.00 10.00
TRMG Mike Glennon 1.50 4.00
TRMJD Maurice Jones-Drew 2.50 6.00
TRMT Manti Te'o 4.00 10.00
TRMW Mike Williams 3.00 8.00
TRRG Robert Griffin III 2.50 6.00
TRRT Ryan Tannehill 3.00 8.00
TRRW Russell Wilson 8.00 20.00
TRSJ Steve Johnson 3.00 8.00
TRTA Tavon Austin 2.00 5.00
TRTE Tyler Eifert 3.00 8.00
TRTR Trent Richardson 2.50 6.00
TRTRO Tony Romo 3.00 8.00
TRZE Zach Ertz 3.00 8.00

2013 Topps Relics Autographs

JSY AU/50 ODDS 1:2338 HOB
*GOLD PATCH/50: .5X TO 1.2X JSY AU/50
TARAF Arian Foster 15.00 30.00
TARAL Andrew Luck 75.00 150.00
TARAM Alfred Morris 6.00 15.00
TARBC Brent Celek 6.00 15.00
TARBH Brian Hartline 6.00 15.00
TARCS Cecil Shorts 6.00 15.00
TARDT Demaryius Thomas 10.00 25.00
TARHN Haloti Ngata 10.00 25.00
TARJG Josh Gordon 12.00 30.00
TARJL James Laurinaitis 8.00 20.00
TARLM LeSean McCoy 10.00 25.00
TARML Mikel Leshoure 6.00 15.00
TARPP Patrick Peterson 15.00 40.00
TARSJ Steve Johnson 8.00 20.00
TARTR Trent Richardson 12.00 30.00

2013 Topps Ribbons Camo Team Logo

*CAMO NFL/99: .5X TO 1.2X CAMO TEAM
*PINK NFL/99: .5X TO 1.2X CAMO TEAM
*PINK TEAM: .4X TO 1X CAMO TEAM
PRAF Arian Foster 4.00 10.00
PRAG Antonio Gates 4.00 10.00
PRAJ Andre Johnson 5.00 12.00
PRAJG A.J. Green 5.00 12.00
PRAL Andrew Luck 10.00 25.00
PRAM Alfred Morris 3.00 8.00
PRAP Adrian Peterson 5.00 12.00
PRAR Aaron Rodgers 12.00 30.00
PRBM Brandon Marshall 4.00 10.00
PRBO Brian Orakpo 4.00 10.00
PRBR Ben Roethlisberger 10.00 25.00
PRCJ Calvin Johnson 5.00 12.00
PRCJO Chris Johnson 3.00 8.00
PRCJS C.J. Spiller 3.00 8.00
PRCK Colin Kaepernick 4.00 10.00
PRCM Clay Matthews 8.00 20.00
PRCN Cam Newton 5.00 12.00
PRCP Carson Palmer 4.00 10.00
PRDB Drew Brees 10.00 25.00
PRDJ DeSean Jackson 4.00 10.00
PRDM Darren McFadden 4.00 10.00
PRDMA Doug Martin 4.00 10.00
PRDW Demarcus Ware 5.00 12.00
PREM Eli Manning 10.00 25.00
PRER Ed Reed 4.00 10.00
PRFG Frank Gore 4.00 10.00
PRFJ Fred Jackson 4.00 10.00
PRJA Jared Allen 3.00 8.00
PRJC Jamaal Charles 5.00 12.00
PRJF Joe Flacco 4.00 10.00
PRJG Jimmy Graham 5.00 12.00
PRJJ Julio Jones 5.00 12.00
PRJJW J.J. Watt 8.00 20.00
PRJL James Laurinaitis 4.00 10.00
PRJPP Jason Pierre-Paul 3.00 8.00
PRLF Larry Fitzgerald 5.00 12.00
PRLM LeSean McCoy 5.00 12.00
PRMF Matt Forte 3.00 8.00
PRMJD Maurice Jones-Drew 3.00 8.00
PRML Marshawn Lynch 6.00 15.00
PRMR Matt Ryan 4.00 10.00
PRMS Matthew Stafford 5.00 12.00
PRNM Nick Mangold 3.00 8.00
PRPM Peyton Manning 15.00 40.00
PRPR Philip Rivers 5.00 12.00
PRPW Patrick Willis 5.00 12.00
PRRG Rob Gronkowski 8.00 20.00
PRRG3 Robert Griffin III 3.00 8.00
PRRT Ryan Tannehill 8.00 20.00
PRRW Roddy White 3.00 8.00
PRRWA Reggie Wayne 4.00 10.00
PRRWI Russell Wilson 10.00 25.00
PRSB Sam Bradford 3.00 8.00
PRTB Tom Brady 12.00 30.00
PRTP Troy Polamalu 5.00 12.00
PRTR Trent Richardson 3.00 8.00
PRTRO Tony Romo 4.00 10.00
PRTS Torrey Smith 3.00 8.00
PRVC Victor Cruz 4.00 10.00
PRVD Vernon Davis 3.00 8.00
PRVJ Vincent Jackson 3.00 8.00
PRVM Von Miller 4.00 10.00
PRWW Wes Welker 6.00 15.00

2013 Topps Road To Victory Redemption

STATED ODDS 1:5300 HOB
1 Arizona Cardinals 3.00 8.00
2 Atlanta Falcons 4.00 10.00
3 Baltimore Ravens 4.00 10.00
4 Buffalo Bills 3.00 8.00
5 Carolina Panthers 3.00 8.00
6 Chicago Bears 4.00 10.00
7 Cincinnati Bengals 4.00 10.00
8 Cleveland Browns 3.00 8.00
9 Dallas Cowboys 4.00 10.00
10 Denver Broncos WIN 20.00 50.00
11 Detroit Lions 3.00 8.00
12 Green Bay Packers 6.00 15.00
13 Houston Texans 3.00 8.00
14 Indianapolis Colts 5.00 12.00
15 Jacksonville Jaguars 3.00 8.00
16 Kansas City Chiefs 4.00 10.00
17 Miami Dolphins 3.00 8.00
18 Minnesota Vikings 3.00 8.00
19 New England Patriots 5.00 12.00
20 New Orleans Saints 4.00 10.00
21 New York Giants 3.00 8.00
22 New York Jets 4.00 10.00
23 Oakland Raiders 3.00 8.00
24 Philadelphia Eagles 3.00 8.00
25 Pittsburgh Steelers 4.00 10.00
26 San Diego Chargers 4.00 10.00
27 San Francisco 49ers 5.00 12.00
28 Seattle Seahawks WIN 20.00 50.00
29 St. Louis Rams 3.00 8.00
30 Tampa Bay Buccaneers 3.00 8.00
31 Tennessee Titans 3.00 8.00
32 Washington Redskins 3.00 8.00

2013 Topps Rookie Legends Gold

EGACY GOLD/99: 5X TO 12X BASIC RC
LEGEND GOLD/99 ODDS 1:271 HOB

2013 Topps Rookie Patch

RPAD Aaron Dobson 1.50 4.00
RPAE Andre Ellington 1.50 4.00
RPCM Christine Michael 1.50 4.00
RPCP Cordarrelle Patterson 1.50 4.00
RPDH DeAndre Hopkins 4.00 10.00
RPDRO Denard Robinson 1.50 4.00
RPEJM EJ Manuel 1.50 4.00
RPEL Eddie Lacy 1.50 4.00
RPGB Giovani Bernard 1.50 4.00
RPGE Gavin Escobar 1.50 4.00
RPGS Geno Smith 1.50 4.00
RPJF Johnathan Franklin 1.50 4.00
RPJH Justin Hunter 1.50 4.00
RPKA Keenan Allen 3.00 8.00
RPKS Kenny Stills 1.50 4.00
RPLB Le'Veon Bell 5.00 12.00
RPLJ Landry Jones 1.50 4.00
RPMB Matt Barkley 1.50 4.00
RPMBA Montee Ball 1.50 4.00
RPMG Mike Glennon 1.50 4.00
RPMGI Mike Gillislee 1.50 4.00
RPMGO Marquise Goodwin 1.50 4.00
RPML Marcus Lattimore 1.50 4.00
RPMT Manti Te'o 2.00 5.00
RPMW Markus Wheaton 1.50 4.00
RPQP Quinton Patton 1.50 4.00
RPRN Ryan Nassib 1.50 4.00
RPRW Robert Woods 2.50 6.00
RPSB Stedman Bailey 1.50 4.00
RPST Stepfan Taylor 1.50 4.00
RPTA Tavon Austin 2.00 5.00
RPTE Tyler Eifert 1.50 4.00
RPTW Tyler Wilson 1.50 4.00
RPTWI Terrance Williams 1.50 4.00
RPZE Zach Ertz 3.00 8.00

2013 Topps Rookie Premiere Autographs

RP AUTO/90 ODDS 1:542 HOB
RPAAD Aaron Dobson 8.00 20.00
RPAAE Andre Ellington 8.00 20.00
RPACM Christine Michael 8.00 20.00
RPACP Cordarrelle Patterson 8.00 20.00
RPADH DeAndre Hopkins 15.00 40.00
RPADJ Dion Jordan 8.00 20.00
RPADRO Denard Robinson 8.00 20.00
RPAEJM EJ Manuel 8.00 20.00
RPAEL Eddie Lacy 40.00 100.00
RPAGB Giovani Bernard 8.00 20.00
RPAGE Gavin Escobar 8.00 20.00
RPAGS Geno Smith 8.00 20.00
RPAJF Johnathan Franklin 8.00 20.00
RPAJH Justin Hunter 8.00 20.00
RPAJR Joseph Randle 8.00 20.00
RPAJRE Jordan Reed 12.00 30.00
RPAKA Keenan Allen 15.00 40.00
RPAKD Knile Davis 8.00 20.00
RPAKS Kenny Stills 8.00 20.00
RPALB Le'Veon Bell 20.00 50.00
RPALJ Landry Jones 8.00 20.00
RPAMB Matt Barkley 20.00 50.00
RPAMBA Montee Ball 8.00 20.00
RPAMG Mike Glennon 8.00 20.00
RPAMGI Mike Gillislee 8.00 20.00
RPAMGO Marquise Goodwin 8.00 20.00
RPAML Marcus Lattimore 20.00 50.00
RPAMT Manti Te'o 10.00 25.00
RPAMW Markus Wheaton 8.00 20.00
RPAQP Quinton Patton 8.00 20.00
RPARN Ryan Nassib 8.00 20.00
RPARW Robert Woods 12.00 30.00
RPASB Stedman Bailey 8.00 20.00
RPAST Stepfan Taylor 8.00 20.00
RPATA Tavon Austin 10.00 25.00
RPATE Tyler Eifert 8.00 20.00
RPATW Tyler Wilson 8.00 20.00
RPATWI Terrance Williams 8.00 20.00
RPAVM Vance McDonald 10.00 25.00
RPAZE Zach Ertz 15.00 40.00

2013 Topps Rookie Premiere Autographs Dual

DUAL AU/25 ODDS 1:14,000 HOB
RPDABW R.Woods/M.Barkley 40.00 80.00
RPDALB M.Ball/E.Lacy 40.00 100.00
RPDAMS E.Manuel/G.Smith 15.00 40.00
RPDAPH J.Hunter/C.Patterson 15.00 40.00
RPDASA T.Austin/G.Smith 8.00 20.00

2013 Topps Rookie Refractors

INSERTED IN HOLIDAY RETAIL BOXES
MBCCP Cordarrelle Patterson .50 1.25
MBCDH DeAndre Hopkins 1.25 3.00
MBCDR Denard Robinson .50 1.25
MBCEL Eddie Lacy .50 1.25
MBCEM EJ Manuel .50 1.25
MBCGS Geno Smith .50 1.25
MBCMB Montee Ball .50 1.25
MBCMT Manti Te'o .60 1.50
MBCTA Tavon Austin .60 1.50
MBCMBA Matt Barkley .50 1.25

2013 Topps Rookie Relic Jumbos

RJRAD Aaron Dobson 1.25 3.00
RJRAE Andre Ellington 1.25 3.00
RJRCM Christine Michael 1.25 3.00
RJRCP Cordarrelle Patterson 1.25 3.00
RJRDH DeAndre Hopkins 3.00 8.00
RJRDRO Denard Robinson 1.25 3.00
RJREJM EJ Manuel 1.25 3.00
RJREL Eddie Lacy 1.25 3.00
RJRGB Giovani Bernard 1.25 3.00
RJRGE Gavin Escobar 1.25 3.00
RJRGS Geno Smith 1.25 3.00
RJRJH Justin Hunter 1.25 3.00
RJRJR Joseph Randle 1.25 3.00
RJRJRE Jordan Reed 2.50 6.00
RJRKA Keenan Allen 2.50 6.00
RJRKD Knile Davis 1.25 3.00
RJRKS Kenny Stills 1.25 3.00
RJRLB Le'Veon Bell 4.00 10.00
RJRLJ Landry Jones 1.25 3.00
RJRMB Matt Barkley 1.25 3.00
RJRMBA Montee Ball 1.25 3.00
RJRMG Mike Glennon 1.25 3.00
RJRMGO Marquise Goodwin 1.25 3.00
RJRML Marcus Lattimore 1.25 3.00
RJRMT Manti Te'o 1.50 4.00
RJRMW Markus Wheaton 1.25 3.00
RJRQP Quinton Patton 1.25 3.00
RJRRW Robert Woods 2.00 5.00
RJRSB Stedman Bailey 1.25 3.00
RJRTA Tavon Austin 1.50 4.00
RJRTE Tyler Eifert 1.25 3.00
RJRTW Tyler Wilson 1.25 3.00
RJRTWI Terrance Williams 1.25 3.00
RJRVM Vance McDonald 1.50 4.00
RJRZE Zach Ertz 2.50 6.00

2013 Topps Signatures

STATED ODDS 1:3400 HOBBY
EXCH EXPIRATION: 7/31/2016
TAAL Andrew Luck 75.00 125.00
TAAR Andre Roberts 4.00 10.00
TABC Brent Celek 4.00 10.00
TABG BenJarvus Green-Ellis 5.00 12.00
TABH Brian Hartline 4.00 10.00
TABM Brandon Myers 4.00 10.00
TABMI Barkevious Mingo 3.00 8.00
TABP Brandon Pettigrew 4.00 10.00
TACS Cecil Shorts 4.00 10.00
TADA Danario Alexander 4.00 10.00
TADAM Danny Amendola EXCH 10.00 25.00
TADB Drew Brees 30.00 80.00
TADM Dee Milliner 3.00 8.00
TADR Da'Rick Rogers 3.00 8.00
TAEA Ezekiel Ansah 3.00 8.00
TAEF Eric Fisher 3.00 8.00
TAEL Eddie Lacy EXCH 3.00 8.00
TAEM EJ Manuel 3.00 8.00
TAET Earl Thomas 10.00 25.00
TAGS Geno Smith 3.00 8.00
TAGT Golden Tate
TAJC Jamaal Charles 10.00 25.00
TAJG Jermaine Gresham 5.00 12.00
TAJK Jeremy Kerley 4.00 10.00
TAJN Jordy Nelson 8.00 20.00
TAJPP Jason Pierre-Paul
TAJR Jacquizz Rodgers 4.00 10.00
TAJRE Jordan Reed 5.00 12.00
TAKA Keenan Allen 6.00 15.00
TAKB Kroy Biermann 4.00 10.00
TAKBA Kenjon Barner 3.00 8.00
TAKS Kenny Stills 3.00 8.00
TALJO Landry Jones 3.00 8.00
TALM Lance Moore 6.00 15.00
TAMB Matt Barkley 3.00 8.00
TAMBA Montee Ball 3.00 8.00
TAMC Michael Crabtree 6.00 15.00
TAMG Mike Gillislee 3.00 8.00
TAML Marshawn Lynch 25.00 50.00
TAMLA Marcus Lattimore 3.00 8.00
TAMLE Mikel Leshoure 4.00 10.00
TAMR Marcel Reece 3.00 8.00
TAMS Matthew Stafford 25.00 50.00
TANB NaVorro Bowman 12.00 30.00
TAPP Patrick Peterson 8.00 20.00
TARG Robert Griffin III 15.00 40.00
TASJ Steve Johnson 5.00 12.00
TASR Stevan Ridley 4.00 10.00
TASV Shane Vereen 5.00 12.00
TATA Tavon Austin
TATE Tyler Eifert 6.00 15.00
TAVW Vince Wilfork 6.00 15.00
TAZD Zac Dysert 3.00 8.00

2013 Topps Truly Legendary Autographs Rainbow Silver

STATED PRINT RUN 20 SER.#'d SETS
*SILVER/30: .3X TO .8X RAINBOW/20
TLAAR Andre Reed EXCH 40.00 80.00
TLABF Brett Favre 125.00 250.00
TLABJ Bo Jackson 60.00 120.00
TLABS Barry Sanders
TLABSM Bruce Smith 25.00 60.00
TLACM Curtis Martin 25.00 60.00
TLADM Dan Marino 100.00 200.00
TLADS Deion Sanders 30.00 80.00
TLAED Eric Dickerson 20.00 50.00
TLAES Emmitt Smith 100.00 200.00
TLAHL Howie Long EXCH 25.00 60.00
TLAJB Jerome Bettis 50.00 125.00
TLAJE John Elway 60.00 120.00
TLAJG Joe Greene 40.00 80.00
TLAJK Jim Kelly EXCH 25.00 60.00
TLAJM Joe Montana 100.00 200.00
TLAJR Jerry Rice 100.00 175.00
TLAKW Kurt Warner 50.00 100.00
TLALT Lawrence Taylor 25.00 60.00
TLALTO LaDainian Tomlinson 20.00 50.00
TLAMA Marcus Allen 40.00 80.00
TLAMF Marshall Faulk 20.00 50.00
TLARCU Randall Cunningham 25.00 60.00
TLARL Ronnie Lott 50.00 100.00
TLASL Steve Largent 25.00 60.00
TLASY Steve Young 60.00 120.00
TLATA Troy Aikman 60.00 120.00
TLATD Terrell Davis 15.00 40.00
TLATT Thurman Thomas 15.00 40.00
TLAWM Warren Moon 25.00 60.00

2013 Topps NFLPA Collegiate Bowl Autographs

DS 1:22 BOW.HOB, 1:79 BOW.RET
2 D.J. Monroe 2.50 6.00
3 David Allen 2.50 6.00
5 Taylor Knowles 2.50 6.00
6 Jeff Tuel 2.50 6.00
7 Jordan Cowart 3.00 8.00
8 Norman White 2.50 6.00
9 Andrew Abbott 2.50 6.00
10 Damien Holmes 2.50 6.00
11 Sean Stanley 3.00 8.00
12 Herman Lathers 6.00 15.00
13 Michael James 5.00 12.00
14 Darius Smith 2.50 6.00
15 Vaughn Telemaque 3.00 8.00
16 Samuel McGuffie 2.50 6.00
17 Luke Willson 4.00 10.00
18 Jordan Rodgers 5.00 12.00
19 Bruce Taylor 3.00 8.00
20 Michael Zordich 4.00 10.00
21 Lloyd Morrison Jr. 2.50 6.00
22 Gregory Jenkins 2.50 6.00
24 Richard Samuel 3.00 8.00
25 Evan Jacobsen 2.50 6.00
26 Andre Kates 2.50 6.00
27 Uona Kaveinga 3.00 8.00
29 Devan Avery 2.50 6.00
30 William Compton 10.00 25.00
31 Benjamin Cotton 8.00 20.00
33 Dominique Battle 2.50 6.00
34 Drew Frey 2.50 6.00
35 Ryan Seymour 2.50 6.00
36 Jeff Nady 2.50 6.00
37 Stephen Warner 2.50 6.00
38 Myles White 4.00 10.00
39 Tristan Okpalaugo 3.00 8.00
40 Marcus Malbrough 2.50 6.00
41 Adam Yates 2.50 6.00
42 Demetrius McCray 2.50 6.00
43 Brian Slay 2.50 6.00
45 Jacob Johnson 2.50 6.00
46 Burton Scott 4.00 10.00
48 Jamal-Rashad Patterson 2.50 6.00
50 Daniel Zychlinski 2.50 6.00
51 Darius Barnes 2.50 6.00
52 Jeremy Coleman 2.50 6.00
53 Marcus Cromartie 2.50 6.00
54 Alfred Diller 2.50 6.00
55 Deon Goggins 2.50 6.00
56 Jakar Hamilton 2.50 6.00
57 Duron Harmon 3.00 8.00
58 Caylin Hauptmann 2.50 6.00
59 Richard Helepiko 2.50 6.00
60 Kemal Ishmael 3.00 8.00
61 Scott Kovanda 2.50 6.00
62 Alex Kupper 2.50 6.00
63 Trevor Marrongelli 2.50 6.00
64 Jonathan Mathis 2.50 6.00
65 Nathan Palmer 4.00 10.00
66 Kevin Saia 2.50 6.00
67 Orwin Smith 2.50 6.00
68 J.J. Swain 2.50 6.00
69 Ryan Higgins 3.00 8.00
70 Mario Benavides 2.50 6.00
71 Xavier Boyce 2.50 6.00
72 Brodrick Brown 2.50 6.00
73 Donovan Carter 2.50 6.00
74 Allen Chapman 2.50 6.00
75 Dayne Crist 3.00 8.00
76 Joaquenssi Eugene 2.50 6.00
78 Templeton Hardy 2.50 6.00
79 Byron Jerideau 2.50 6.00
80 Peter Massaro 2.50 6.00
82 Shane McCardell 2.50 6.00
83 Craig McIntosh 2.50 6.00
86 Mike Purcell 2.50 6.00
87 Kyle Quinn 2.50 6.00
88 Drew Schaefer 2.50 6.00
89 Marsalis Teague 3.00 8.00
91 Josh Williams 4.00 10.00
92 Duane Zlatnik 2.50 6.00
93 James Nelson 2.50 6.00
94 Kevin Norrell 2.50 6.00
95 Kentrell Harris 2.50 6.00
97 Quincy McDuffie 2.50 6.00
98 Eric Stephens Jr. 2.50 6.00
99 Alex Debniak 2.50 6.00
102 Ryan Mad Dog Mattos/100 3.00 8.00

2014 Topps

COMPLETE SET (440) 20.00 40.00
COMP.HOBBY FACT.(445) 35.00 50.00
COMP.RETAIL FACT.(445) 35.00 50.00
VETERAN SP ODDS 1:86 HOB
ROOKIE SP ODDS 1:155 HOB
GTW STATED ODDS 1:6500 HOB
1A Jeremy Kerley .15 .40
1B Drew Brees SP 6.00 15.00
2A T.Y. Hilton .20 .50
2B Victor Cruz SP 3.00 8.00
3A Brandon Carr .15 .40
3B Rob Gronkowski SP 4.00 10.00
4A Kyle Rudolph .15 .40
4B Peyton Manning SP 8.00 20.00
5A Matthew Stafford .20 .50
5B DeSean Jackson SP 3.00 8.00
6A Patriots/Brady .30 .75
6B Alshon Jeffery SP 3.00 8.00
7A Jordy Nelson .20 .50
7B Demaryius Thomas SP 3.00 8.00
8A Ryan Broyles .15 .40
8B Matthew Stafford SP 3.00 8.00
9A Julius Thomas .15 .40
9B Julius Thomas SP 2.50 6.00
10A Coby Fleener .15 .40
10B Tony Romo SP 3.00 8.00
11A A.J. Green .25 .60
11B Kiko Alonso SP 2.50 6.00
12A Emmanuel Sanders .20 .50
12B Jay Cutler SP 2.50 6.00
13A Sean Lee .20 .50
13B Ray Rice SP 2.50 6.00
14A Zach Ertz .20 .50
14B Kenny Stills SP 2.50 6.00
15A Mohamed Sanu .15 .40
15B Andre Johnson SP 3.00 8.00
16A Kenny Vaccaro .15 .40
16B Nick Foles SP 3.00 8.00
17A DeSean Jackson .20 .50
17B Colin Kaepernick SP 6.00 15.00
18A Antoine Bethea .15 .40
18B Zac Stacy SP 2.50 6.00
19A Ace Sanders .15 .40
19B Giovani Bernard SP 2.50 6.00
20A Cameron Jordan .15 .40
20B Ben Roethlisberger SP 6.00 15.00
21A Nick Foles .20 .50
21B Philip Rivers SP 4.00 10.00
22A Victor Cruz .20 .50
22B Richard Sherman SP 8.00 20.00
23A Captain Munnerlyn .15 .40
23B EJ Manuel SP 2.50 6.00
24A Charles Tillman .20 .50
24B T.Y. Hilton SP 3.00 8.00
25A James Jones .15 .40
25B Matt Ryan SP 3.00 8.00
26A Brandon Pettigrew .15 .40
26B Tamba Hali SP 2.50 6.00
27A Matt Ryan .20 .50
27B Robert Quinn SP 3.00 8.00
28A Santonio Holmes .15 .40
28B Vernon Davis SP 2.50 6.00
29A Sheldon Richardson .15 .40
29B Ryan Mathews SP 3.00 8.00
30A Maurice Jones-Drew .15 .40
30B Cam Newton SP 4.00 10.00
31A Jay Cutler .15 .40
31B Antonio Brown SP 4.00 10.00
32A Russell Wilson .40 1.00
32B Adrian Peterson SP 4.00 10.00
33A Peyton Manning .50 1.25
33B J.J. Watt SP 4.00 10.00
34A Frank Gore .20 .50
34B LeSean McCoy SP 4.00 10.00
35A Johnny Hekker RC .15 .40
35B NaVorro Bowman SP 3.00 8.00
36A Cordarrelle Patterson .15 .40
36B Ndamukong Suh SP 3.00 8.00
37A Peyton Manning POY .50 1.25
37B Tom Brady SP 10.00 25.00
38A Kansas City Chiefs .20 .50
38B Andrew Luck SP 5.00 12.00
39A Pittsburgh Steelers .25 .60
39B Josh Gordon SP 2.50 6.00
40A Calais Campbell .15 .40
40B Luke Kuechly SP 3.00 8.00
41A Tyrann Mathieu .20 .50
41B Jimmy Graham SP 4.00 10.00
42A Steven Jackson .15 .40
42B Calvin Johnson SP 4.00 10.00
43A Jimmy Smith .15 .40
43B Jason Witten SP 3.00 8.00
44A EJ Manuel .15 .40
44B Andy Dalton SP 3.00 8.00
45A Cam Newton .25 .60
45B Patrick Willis SP 3.00 8.00
46A Domata Peko RC .15 .40
46B Eddie Lacy SP 2.50 6.00
47A DeMarco Murray .20 .50
47B Dez Bryant SP 4.00 10.00
48A Dez Bryant .25 .60
48B Alfred Morris SP 2.50 6.00
49A Jason Witten .20 .50
49B Keenan Allen SP 3.00 8.00
50A A.J. Hawk .15 .40
50B Le'Veon Bell SP 3.00 8.00
51A Adrian Peterson .25 .60
51B Randall Cobb SP 3.00 8.00
52A Tom Brady .60 1.50
52B Michael Crabtree SP 4.00 10.00
53A Drew Brees .25 .60
53B Tavon Austin SP 2.50 6.00
54A Pierre Thomas .15 .40
54B Eric Berry SP 3.00 8.00
55A Darren Sproles .20 .50
55B Mike Glennon SP 3.00 8.00
56A Marques Colston .15 .40
56B Alex Smith SP 3.00 8.00
57A David Wilson .15 .40
57B Arian Foster SP 3.00 8.00
58A Stephen Hill .15 .40
58B Sheldon Richardson SP 2.50 6.00
59A Matt McGloin .20 .50
59B Patrick Peterson SP 2.50 6.00
60A Antonio Gates .15 .40
60B Darrelle Revis SP 2.50 6.00
61A Manti Te'o .20 .50
61B Cordarrelle Patterson SP 2.50 6.00
62A Michael Crabtree .15 .40
62B Jamaal Charles SP 3.00 8.00
63A Sidney Rice .15 .40
63B A.J. Green SP 4.00 10.00
64A Jake Long .15 .40
64B Marshawn Lynch SP 3.00 8.00
65A Mike Glennon .20 .50
65B Russell Wilson SP 6.00 15.00
66A Brian Orakpo .15 .40
66B Aaron Rodgers SP 10.00 25.00
67A J.J. Watt .25 .60
67B Reggie Bush SP 2.50 6.00
68A Minnesota Vikings .25 .60
68B Roddy White SP 2.50 6.00
69A Andrew Luck .30 .75
69B Malcolm Smith SP 4.00 10.00
70 Brian Robison .15 .40
71 Robert Quinn .20 .50
72 Perry Riley Jr. .15 .40
73 San Diego Chargers .20 .50
74 Chris Givens .15 .40
75 Mario Williams .15 .40
76 Morris Claiborne .15 .40
77 Ryan Tannehill .20 .50
78 Le'Veon Bell .20 .50
79 B.J. Raji .15 .40
80 Nate Burleson .15 .40
81 Donald Brown .15 .40
82 Brian Hoyer .15 .40
83 Brandon Marshall .15 .40
84 DeMarcus Ware .20 .50
85 C.J. Spiller .15 .40
86 Joique Bell .15 .40
87 Darren McFadden .15 .40
88 Rookie Premiere .15 .40
89 Justin Hunter .15 .40
90 Vincent Jackson .15 .40
91 Anquan Boldin .15 .40
92 Eric Decker .15 .40
93 Vontaze Burfict .15 .40
94 Miami Dolphins .15 .40
95 Kyle Long .15 .40
96 Zac Stacy .15 .40
97 Andre Johnson .20 .50
98 Ryan Succop .15 .40
99 New Orleans Saints .25 .60
100 Daryl Richardson .15 .40
101 Baltimore Ravens .15 .40
102 Torrey Smith .15 .40
103 Jason Campbell .15 .40
104 Darrelle Revis .15 .40
105 Tennessee Titans .15 .40
106 Golden Tate .20 .50
107 Joe Haden .15 .40
108 Oakland Raiders .15 .40
109 Percy Harvin .15 .40
110 Buffalo Bills .20 .50
111 Wesley Woodyard .15 .40
112 Cameron Wake .15 .40
113 Garrett Graham .15 .40
114 Evan Mathis .15 .40
115 Clay Matthews .25 .60
116 Washington Redskins .15 .40
117 Alex Smith .20 .50
118 Brooks Reed .15 .40
119 Lavonte David .15 .40
120 Marvin Jones .15 .40
121 LeSean McCoy .25 .60
122 Dominique Rodgers-Cromartie .15 .40
123 Michael Vick .20 .50
124 Leonard Hankerson .15 .40
125 Kendall Wright .15 .40
126 Geno Atkins .15 .40
127 Sheldon Richardson ROY .15 .40
128 Stephen Gostkowski .20 .50
129 Charles Clay .15 .40
130 Philadelphia Eagles .20 .50
131 DeAngelo Williams .15 .40
132 Matt Prater .25 .60
133 Nick Fairley .15 .40
134 Theo Riddick .15 .40
135 Julio Jones .25 .60
136 Jason Pierre-Paul .15 .40
137 Stevan Ridley .15 .40
138 Nate Washington .15 .40
139 Terrell Suggs .15 .40
140 Steve Smith .20 .50
141 Colin Kaepernick .20 .50
142 Ronnie Hillman .15 .40
143 Scott Chandler .15 .40
144 Shane Vereen .20 .50
145 Doug Martin .20 .50
146 Carolina Panthers .25 .60
147 Kirk Cousins .25 .60
148 Julian Edelman .25 .60
149 DeAndre Hopkins .20 .50
150 Jairus Byrd .15 .40
151 Martellus Bennett .15 .40
152 Pierre Garcon .20 .50
153 Jarrett Boykin .15 .40
154 Brian Hartline .15 .40
155 Heath Miller .15 .40
156 Reggie Bush .15 .40
157 Derrick Coleman .15 .40
158 St. Louis Rams .20 .50
159 Greg Olsen .20 .50
160 Matt Kalil .15 .40
161 Aaron Dobson .15 .40
162 Troy Polamalu .25 .60
163 Joseph Fauria .15 .40
164 Kenny Stills .15 .40
165 Rod Streater .15 .40
166 Chicago Bears .20 .50
167 Randall Cobb .20 .50
168 Bobby Rainey .15 .40
169 Jermaine Gresham .15 .40
170 Mike Tolbert .15 .40
171 Sebastian Janikowski .15 .40
172 Aaron Rodgers .50 1.25
173 Matt Forte .15 .40
174 Peyton Manning MVP .50 1.25
175 Carson Palmer .20 .50
176 Von Miller .20 .50
177 Wes Welker .20 .50
178 Daniel Thomas .15 .40
179 Eli Manning .20 .50
180 Malcom Floyd .15 .40
181 Jamaal Charles .20 .50
182 P.Manning/D.Thomas .30 .75
183 Eddie Lacy ROY .15 .40
184 Shea McClellin .20 .50
185 Dion Jordan .15 .40
186 Justin Tucker .15 .40
187 Gerald McCoy .15 .40
188 Andre Brown .15 .40
189 Bernard Pierce .15 .40
190 Tyler Eifert .20 .50
191 San Francisco 49ers .20 .50
192 Roddy White .15 .40
193 Indianapolis Colts .25 .60
194 Ted Ginn .15 .40
195 Robert Mathis .15 .40
196 NaVorro Bowman .20 .50
197 Jake Locker .20 .50
198 Denarius Moore .15 .40
199 Janoris Jenkins .15 .40
200 Desmond Trufant .15 .40
201 Calvin Johnson .25 .60
202 Harrison Smith .15 .40
203 Matt Flynn .15 .40
204 Seattle Seahawks .20 .50
Marshawn Lynch
205 Greg Hardy .15 .40
206 Eric Weddle .15 .40
207 Lance Briggs .20 .50
208 James Laurinaitis .20 .50
209 Jason Peters .15 .40
210 Andre Roberts .15 .40
211 Philip Rivers .25 .60
212 New York Giants .20 .50
213 Detroit Lions .25 .60
214 Lardarius Webb .15 .40
215 Brandon LaFell .15 .40
216 D.J. Swearinger .20 .50
217 Jared Allen .15 .40
218 Lamar Miller .15 .40
219 Paul Kruger .15 .40
220 Josh Gordon .15 .40
221 A.Rodgers/J.Nelson .30 .75
222 Andre Ellington .15 .40
223 Jordan Cameron .15 .40
224 Case Keenum .20 .50
225 Demaryius Thomas .20 .50
226 Tampa Bay Buccaneers .15 .40
227 Haloti Ngata .15 .40
228 Vernon Davis .15 .40
229 Alterraun Verner .15 .40
230 Bobby Wagner .15 .40
231 Eddie Lacy .15 .40
232 Sam Bradford .15 .40
233 Brent Celek .15 .40
234 Jimmy Graham .25 .60
235 Ben Tate .15 .40
236 New York Jets .15 .40
237 Matt Schaub .15 .40
238 Star Lotulelei .15 .40
239 Muhammad Wilkerson .15 .40
240 Jacoby Jones .15 .40
241 Eric Fisher .15 .40
242 Arian Foster .20 .50
243 Alshon Jeffery .20 .50
244 Nick Perry .15 .40
245 Ray Rice .15 .40
246 Ndamukong Suh .20 .50
247 Robert Griffin III .15 .40
248 Eric Berry .20 .50
249 Joel Dreessen .15 .40
250 Terrelle Pryor .15 .40
251 Cincinnati Bengals .25 .60
252 BenJarvus Green-Ellis .20 .50
253 Champ Bailey .20 .50
254 Eric Reid .20 .50
255 Marshawn Lynch .20 .50
256 Bruce Irvin .15 .40
257 Seahawks Super Bowl .25 .60
258 Rob Gronkowski .25 .60
259 Richard Sherman .25 .60
260 Mike Wallace .15 .40
261 Mike Williams .20 .50
262 Patrick Willis .20 .50
263 Dennis Pitta .15 .40
264 Ben Roethlisberger .25 .60
265 Fred Jackson .20 .50
266 Christian Ponder .15 .40

267 Justin Tuck .15 .40
268 Cleveland Browns .15 .40
269 Paul Worrilow .15 .40
270 Kiko Alonso .15 .40
271 Dallas Cowboys .25 .60
272 Luke Kuechly POY .20 .50
273 Trent Richardson .15 .40
274 Tony Romo .20 .50
275 Patrick Peterson .15 .40
276 Julius Peppers .20 .50
277 Chris Johnson .15 .40
278 Andy Dalton .20 .50
279 Bilal Powell .15 .40
280 Ryan Mathews .20 .50
281 Cecil Shorts .15 .40
282 Brian Cushing .15 .40
283 Earl Thomas .20 .50
284 Dwayne Bowe .20 .50
285 Giovani Bernard .15 .40
286 Luke Kuechly .20 .50
287 Harry Douglas .15 .40
288 Rey Maualuga .15 .40
289 Greg Jennings .15 .40
290 Antrel Rolle .15 .40
291 Jordan Reed .15 .40
292 Brandon Myers .20 .50
293 Antonio Brown .25 .60
294 Tamba Hali .15 .40
295 Tavon Austin .15 .40
296 Steven Hauschka RC .50 1.25
297 Carlos Dunlap .15 .40
298 Arizona Cardinals .20 .50
299 Jacksonville Jaguars .15 .40
300 Keenan Allen .20 .50
301 Joe Flacco .20 .50
302 Larry Fitzgerald .20 .50
303 Alec Ogletree .15 .40
304 Malcolm Smith RC .25 .60
305 Knowshon Moreno .15 .40
306 Montee Ball .15 .40
307 Miles Austin .15 .40
308 Joe Thomas .15 .40
309 Ed Dickson .15 .40
310 Chandler Jones .15 .40
311 Charles Johnson .15 .40
312 Alfred Morris .15 .40
313 Danny Amendola .20 .50
314 Atlanta Falcons .15 .40
315 Ryan Kalil .15 .40
316 Kenbrell Thompkins .15 .40
317 Sam Shields .25 .60
318 Terrance Williams .15 .40
319 Michael Floyd .15 .40
320 Ed Reed .20 .50
321 Geno Smith .15 .40
322 Ezekiel Ansah .15 .40
323 Brett Keisel .15 .40
324 Louis Vasquez .15 .40
325 Antonio Cromartie .15 .40
326 Reggie Wayne .20 .50
327 Houston Texans .15 .40
328 Owen Daniels .15 .40
329 Steve Johnson .20 .50
330 Justin Blackmon .15 .40
331 Prince Amukamara .15 .40
332 Ha Ha Clinton-Dix RC .30 .75
333 Jordan Lynch RC .30 .75
334 Arthur Lynch RC .25 .60
335 Calvin Pryor RC .25 .60
336 Louis Nix RC .25 .60
337A Davante Adams RC .40 1.00
337B Davante Adams SP 2.50 6.00
338 Lache Seastrunk RC .25 .60
339 Cody Latimer RC .30 .75
340A Eric Ebron RC .30 .75
340B Eric Ebron SP 2.00 5.00
341A De'Anthony Thomas RC .25 .60
341B De'Anthony Thomas SP 1.50 4.00
342 Austin Seferian-Jenkins RC .25 .60
343 Kyle Van Noy RC .30 .75
344 Bruce Ellington RC .25 .60
345 Jake Matthews RC .25 .60
346 Connor Shaw RC .25 .60
347 Tom Savage RC .25 .60
348 Ryan Shazier RC .40 1.00
349 Trent Murphy RC .25 .60
350 Henry Josey RC .25 .60
351 Silas Redd RC .30 .75
352A Robert Herron RC .25 .60
352B Robert Herron SP 1.50 4.00
353A Tajh Boyd RC .25 .60
353B Tajh Boyd SP 1.50 4.00
354A Brandin Cooks RC .40 1.00
354B Brandin Cooks SP 2.50 6.00
355A Odell Beckham Jr. RC .60 1.50
355B Odell Beckham Jr. SP 15.00 30.00
356A Jadeveon Clowney RC .30 .75
356B Jadeveon Clowney SP 2.00 5.00
357 Cody Hoffman RC .25 .60
358 Taylor Lewan RC .25 .60
359A Zach Mettenberger RC .25 .60
359B Zach Mettenberger SP 1.50 4.00
360A Bishop Sankey RC .25 .60
360B Bishop Sankey SP 1.50 4.00
361 Will Sutton RC .30 .75
362 Marcus Roberson RC .30 .75
363 Dion Bailey RC .25 .60
364 Logan Thomas RC .25 .60
365A Ka'Deem Carey RC .25 .60
365B Ka'Deem Carey SP 1.50 4.00
366 Bradley Roby RC .25 .60
367A Teddy Bridgewater RC .40 1.00
367B Teddy Bridgewater SP 2.50 6.00
368A Stephen Morris RC .25 .60
368B Stephen Morris SP 1.50 4.00
369 Jason Verrett RC .25 .60
370A Andre Williams RC .25 .60
370B Andre Williams SP 1.50 4.00
371A Jeremy Hill RC .30 .75
371B Jeremy Hill SP 2.00 5.00
372 Tyler Gaffney RC .25 .60
373A Khalil Mack RC 1.00 2.50
373B Khalil Mack SP 6.00 15.00
374A Blake Bortles RC .30 .75
374B Blake Bortles SP 2.00 5.00
375A Allen Robinson RC .40 1.00
375B Allen Robinson SP 2.50 6.00
376A Darqueze Dennard RC .30 .75
376B Darqueze Dennard SP 2.00 5.00
377 Dri Archer RC .25 .60
378 C.J. Mosley RC .30 .75
379 Devonta Freeman RC .40 1.00
380 Loucheiz Purifoy RC .25 .60
381 A.J. McCarron RC .25 .60
382 Xavier Grimble RC .30 .75
383A Carlos Hyde RC .30 .75
383B Carlos Hyde SP 2.00 5.00
384 Terrance West RC .25 .60
385 David Fales RC .25 .60
386 Jeff Janis RC .25 .60
387A Mike Evans RC .60 1.50
387B Mike Evans SP 4.00 10.00
388 Kevin Norwood RC .25 .60
389A Michael Sam RC .25 .60
389B Michael Sam SP 1.50 4.00
390 Donte Bucannon RC .25 .60
391 Kony Ealy RC .30 .75
392 Storm Johnson RC .25 .60
393 Jeff Mathews RC .30 .75
394A Jarvis Landry RC .50 1.25
394B Jarvis Landry SP 3.00 8.00
395 Timmy Jernigan RC .25 .60
396 Shaquelle Evans RC .25 .60
397A Devin Street RC .25 .60
397B Devin Street SP 1.50 4.00
398 LaDarius Perkins RC .25 .60
399A C.J. Fiedorowicz RC .25 .60
399B C.J. Fiedorowicz SP 1.50 4.00
400 Ra'Shede Hageman RC .25 .60
401A Paul Richardson RC .30 .75
401B Paul Richardson SP 2.00 5.00
402 Marion Grice RC .25 .60
403 Pierre Desir RC .25 .60
404 Scott Crichton RC .25 .60
405 George Atkinson III RC .25 .60
406 Zack Martin RC .30 .75
407 Josh Huff RC .30 .75
408A Jordan Matthews RC .40 1.00
408B Jordan Matthews SP 2.50 6.00
409A Kelvin Benjamin RC .40 1.00
409B Kelvin Benjamin SP 2.50 6.00
410 Damien Williams RC .25 .60
411 Mike Davis RC .25 .60
412 Cyrus Kouandjio RC .30 .75
413 Anthony Barr RC .25 .60
414 Aaron Murray RC .25 .60
415 Jalen Saunders RC .25 .60
416 Stephon Tuitt RC .40 1.00
417A Greg Robinson RC .25 .60
417B Greg Robinson SP 1.50 4.00
418 Yawin Smallwood RC .25 .60
419A Martavis Bryant RC .30 .75
419B Martavis Bryant SP 2.00 5.00
420 Antone Exum RC .25 .60
421 Charles Sims RC .25 .60
422A Tre Mason RC .25 .60
422B Tre Mason SP 1.50 4.00
423 Jared Abbrederis RC .25 .60
424A Aaron Donald RC .60 1.50
424B Aaron Donald SP 4.00 10.00
425 Caraun Reid RC .30 .75
426 Justin Gilbert RC .25 .60
427 Donte Moncrief RC .25 .60
428A Troy Niklas RC .25 .60
428B Troy Niklas SP 1.50 4.00
429A Johnny Manziel RC .40 1.00
429B Johnny Manziel SP 2.50 6.00
430 Kareem Martin RC .25 .60
431A Marqise Lee RC .30 .75
431B Marqise Lee SP 2.00 5.00
432A Jimmy Garoppolo RC 2.00 5.00
432B Jimmy Garoppolo SP 12.00 30.00
433 Brandon Coleman RC .25 .60
434A Sammy Watkins RC .40 1.00
434B Sammy Watkins SP 2.50 6.00
435 Craig Loston RC .25 .60
436 Aaron Colvin RC .25 .60
437 Ahmad Dixon RC .25 .60
438A Derek Carr RC 1.50 4.00
438B Derek Carr SP 10.00 25.00
439A Jace Amaro RC .25 .60
439B Jace Amaro SP 1.50 4.00
440 Ryan Grant RC .25 .60
442B Jordan Lynch SP 2.00 5.00
GTW JD golden ticket winner 4.00 10.00

2014 Topps Black

*VETS/59: 6X TO 15X BASIC CARDS
*ROOKIES/59: 4X TO 10X BASIC CARDS

2014 Topps Camo

*VETS/399: 2.5X TO 6X BASIC CARDS
*ROOKIES/399: 1.5X TO 4X BASIC CARDS

2014 Topps Gold

*VETS/2014: 1.5X TO 4X BASIC CARDS
*ROOKIES/2014: 1X TO 2.5X BASIC CARDS
355 Odell Beckham Jr. 8.00 20.00

2014 Topps Orange

*VETS/90: 5X TO 12X BASIC CARDS
*ROOKIES/90: 3X TO 8X BASIC RC

2014 Topps Pink

*VETS/499: 2X TO 5X BASIC CARDS
*ROOKIES/499: 1.2X TO 3X BASIC CARDS

2014 Topps 1000 Yard Club

COMPLETE SET (37) 6.00 15.00
STATED ODDS 1:4 HOBBY
1 Jimmy Graham .50 1.25
2 Torrey Smith .30 .75
3 Andre Johnson .40 1.00
4 Jamaal Charles .40 1.00
5 Matt Forte .30 .75
6 Anquan Boldin .30 .75
7 Julian Edelman .50 1.25
8 Calvin Johnson .50 1.25
9 A.J. Green .50 1.25
10 Knowshon Moreno .30 .75
11 Chris Johnson .30 .75
12 Vincent Jackson .30 .75
13 Harry Douglas .30 .75
14 Jordy Nelson .40 1.00
15 Ryan Mathews .40 1.00
16 DeMarco Murray .40 1.00
17 Reggie Bush .30 .75
18 LeSean McCoy .50 1.25
19 Alfred Morris .30 .75
20 Adrian Peterson .50 1.25
21 Kendall Wright .30 .75
22 Josh Gordon .30 .75
23 DeSean Jackson .40 1.00
24 Eddie Lacy .30 .75
25 Demaryius Thomas .40 1.00
26 Antonio Brown .50 1.25
27 Brian Hartline .30 .75
28 Pierre Garcon .40 1.00
29 Marshawn Lynch .40 1.00
30 Michael Floyd .30 .75
31 Keenan Allen .40 1.00
32 Dez Bryant .50 1.25
33 Alshon Jeffery .40 1.00
34 Brandon Marshall .30 .75
35 Eric Decker .30 .75
36 T.Y. Hilton .40 1.00
37 Frank Gore .40 1.00

2014 Topps 1963 Mini

COMPLETE SET (132) 60.00 120.00
STATED ODDS 1:3 HOBBY
200 Alshon Jeffery .50 1.25
201 Reggie Bush .40 1.00
202 Kendall Wright .40 1.00
203 Jordan Matthews .60 1.50
204 Darrelle Revis .40 1.00
205 Denarius Moore .40 1.00
206 Mike Davis .40 1.00
207 EJ Manuel .40 1.00
208 Tom Brady 1.50 4.00
209 Andre Johnson .50 1.25
210 Matt Forte .40 1.00
211 Derek Carr 2.50 6.00
212 Troy Polamalu .60 1.50
213 Jimmy Garoppolo 3.00 8.00
214 Eddie Lacy .40 1.00
215 Odell Beckham Jr. 1.00 2.50
216 Calvin Johnson .60 1.50
217 Deion Sanders .50 1.25
218 Demaryius Thomas .50 1.25
219 Tony Romo .50 1.25
221 Aaron Murray .40 1.00
222 Austin Seferian-Jenkins .40 1.00
223 Manti Te'o .50 1.25
224 Drew Brees .60 1.50
225 Bishop Sankey .40 1.00
226 Zach Mettenberger .40 1.00
227 Josh Gordon .40 1.00
228 Marcus Allen .60 1.50
229 Lache Seastrunk .40 1.00
230 Jadeveon Clowney .50 1.25
231 Carlos Hyde .50 1.25
232 Doug Martin .50 1.25
233 Teddy Bridgewater .60 1.50
234 Reggie Wayne .50 1.25
235 Marqise Lee .50 1.25
236 Wes Welker .50 1.25
237 Larry Fitzgerald .50 1.25
238 Nick Foles .50 1.25
239 Patrick Peterson .40 1.00
240 Jamaal Charles .50 1.25
241 Charles Sims .40 1.00
242 Philip Rivers .60 1.50
243 Jimmy Graham .60 1.50
244 Tavon Austin .40 1.00
245 Aaron Rodgers 1.25 3.00
246 Peyton Manning 1.25 3.00
247 Bo Jackson .75 2.00
248 Robert Griffin III .40 1.00
249 Torrey Smith .40 1.00
250 Andrew Luck .75 2.00
251 Martavis Bryant .50 1.25
252 Mike Wallace .40 1.00
253 Jarvis Landry .75 2.00
254 Jason Witten .50 1.25
255 Eli Manning .50 1.25
256 Eric Ebron .50 1.25
257 Brandon Marshall .40 1.00
258 Johnny Manziel .60 1.50
259 Ndamukong Suh .50 1.25
260 Pierre Garcon .50 1.25
261 Carson Palmer .50 1.25
262 Dez Bryant .60 1.50
263 Brett Favre 1.25 3.00
264 Jeremy Hill .50 1.25
265 Troy Aikman .75 2.00
266 Colin Kaepernick .50 1.25
267 Victor Cruz .50 1.25
268 Patrick Willis .50 1.25
269 Paul Richardson .50 1.25
270 Ben Roethlisberger .60 1.50
271 Blake Bortles .50 1.25
272 Joe Flacco .50 1.25
273 David Fales .40 1.00
274 Kelvin Benjamin .60 1.50
275 Jay Cutler .40 1.00
276 Jace Amaro .40 1.00
277 Vernon Davis .40 1.00
278 Jared Abbrederis .40 1.00
279 A.J. Green .60 1.50
280 Kiko Alonso .40 1.00
281 Robert Quinn .50 1.25
282 DeSean Jackson .50 1.25
283 Sammy Watkins .60 1.50
285 Alfred Morris .40 1.00
286 Marshawn Lynch .50 1.25
287 Roddy White .40 1.00
288 Von Miller .50 1.25
289 Terrell Suggs .40 1.00
290 Steve Young .75 2.00
291 Luke Kuechly .50 1.25
292 Devonta Freeman .60 1.50
293 Antonio Brown .60 1.50
294 Donte Moncrief .40 1.00
295 Ryan Tannehill .50 1.25
296 Ka'Deem Carey .40 1.00
297 Allen Robinson .60 1.50
298 Barry Sanders 1.00 2.50
299 Frank Gore .50 1.25
300 Clay Matthews .60 1.50
301 Adrian Peterson .60 1.50
302 A.J. McCarron .40 1.00
303 Cam Newton .60 1.50
304 Geno Smith .40 1.00
305 Keenan Allen .50 1.25
306 LaDainian Tomlinson .50 1.25
307 Zac Stacy .40 1.00
308 Rob Gronkowski .60 1.50
309 Russell Wilson 1.00 2.50
310 Julio Jones .60 1.50
311 Jake Locker .50 1.25
312 Joe Montana 1.50 4.00
313 Richard Sherman .60 1.50
314 Tajh Boyd .40 1.00
315 LeSean McCoy .60 1.50
316 Matt Ryan .50 1.25
317 Giovani Bernard .40 1.00
318 J.J. Watt .60 1.50
319 Earl Thomas .50 1.25
320 Mike Evans 1.00 2.50
321 Michael Crabtree .40 1.00
322 Tre Mason .40 1.00
323 Andre Williams .40 1.00
324 Brandin Cooks .60 1.50
325 Eric Berry .50 1.25
326 Cecil Shorts .40 1.00
327 Mike Glennon .50 1.25
328 Lawrence Taylor .60 1.50
329 Davante Adams .60 1.50
330 Matthew Stafford .50 1.25
331 Cordarrelle Patterson .40 1.00
337 Terrance West .40 1.00
338 Robert Herron .40 1.00

2014 Topps '63 Mini Autographs

201 Jordan Matthews 5.00 12.00
202 Carlos Hyde 4.00 10.00
203 Tajh Boyd 3.00 8.00
204 Mike Evans 8.00 20.00
205 A.J. McCarron 3.00 8.00
207 Brandin Cooks 5.00 12.00
208 Ka'Deem Carey 3.00 8.00
211 Austin Seferian-Jenkins 3.00 8.00
212 Teddy Bridgewater 12.00 30.00
214 Derek Carr 15.00 40.00
215 Bishop Sankey 3.00 8.00
216 Blake Bortles 4.00 10.00
217 Davante Adams 5.00 12.00
218 Aaron Murray 3.00 8.00
219 Jarvis Landry 6.00 15.00
220 Jimmy Garoppolo 30.00 60.00
221 Kelvin Benjamin 6.00 15.00
222 Allen Robinson 5.00 12.00
223 Sammy Watkins 20.00 40.00
225 Charles Sims 3.00 8.00
226 Marqise Lee 4.00 10.00
227 Jace Amaro 6.00 15.00
228 Tre Mason 10.00 25.00
230 Odell Beckham Jr. 40.00 80.00
231 Jadeveon Clowney 4.00 10.00
232 Eric Ebron 4.00 10.00
234 Johnny Manziel 5.00 12.00
237 Donte Moncrief 3.00 8.00
239 Andre Williams 3.00 8.00
240 Jeremy Hill 10.00 25.00
243 Devonta Freeman 5.00 12.00
247 Terrance West 3.00 8.00
252 De'Anthony Thomas 3.00 8.00
254 Logan Thomas 3.00 8.00
257 Tom Savage 3.00 8.00
261 Michael Sam 3.00 8.00
262 Khalil Mack 50.00 400.00

2014 Topps 1965 Autographs

101 Jimmy Garoppolo 50.00 100.00
102 Ka'Deem Carey 3.00 8.00
103 Teddy Bridgewater 12.00 30.00
105 Sammy Watkins 20.00 40.00
106 Eric Ebron 4.00 10.00
107 Davante Adams 5.00 12.00
108 Carlos Hyde 4.00 10.00
109 Kelvin Benjamin 15.00 30.00
110 Allen Robinson 5.00 12.00
111 Jarvis Landry 6.00 15.00
112 Tajh Boyd 3.00 8.00
113 Derek Carr 25.00 50.00
115 Odell Beckham Jr. 40.00 80.00
117 Brandin Cooks 5.00 12.00
118 Johnny Manziel 15.00 40.00
119 Austin Seferian-Jenkins 3.00 8.00
120 Jordan Matthews 5.00 12.00
123 A.J. McCarron 3.00 8.00
124 Mike Evans 8.00 20.00
125 Marqise Lee 4.00 10.00
128 Tre Mason 10.00 25.00
129 Jadeveon Clowney 4.00 10.00
130 Bishop Sankey 3.00 8.00
133 Blake Bortles 30.00 60.00
134 Aaron Murray 3.00 8.00
135 Jace Amaro 6.00 15.00
138 Donte Moncrief 3.00 8.00
142 Jeremy Hill 10.00 25.00
144 Andre Williams 3.00 8.00
146 Devonta Freeman 10.00 25.00
148 Terrance West 3.00 8.00
151 De'Anthony Thomas 3.00 8.00
153 Logan Thomas 3.00 8.00
156 Tom Savage 3.00 8.00
159 Michael Sam 3.00 8.00
160 Khalil Mack 50.00 100.00

2014 Topps 1985 Autographs

302 Jadeveon Clowney 4.00 10.00
304 Johnny Manziel 15.00 40.00
308 Andre Williams 3.00 8.00
310 Marqise Lee 4.00 10.00
312 Austin Seferian-Jenkins 3.00 8.00
314 Jordan Matthews 5.00 12.00
315 Eric Ebron 4.00 10.00
316 Tre Mason 10.00 25.00
318 Jimmy Garoppolo 50.00 100.00
319 Kelvin Benjamin 15.00 30.00
320 Jarvis Landry 6.00 15.00
321 Jace Amaro EXCH 6.00 15.00
322 Carlos Hyde 4.00 10.00
323 Allen Robinson 5.00 12.00
324 Davante Adams 5.00 12.00
325 Odell Beckham Jr. EXCH 40.00 80.00
326 Bishop Sankey 3.00 8.00
327 Brandin Cooks 5.00 12.00
329 Ka'Deem Carey 3.00 8.00
333 Devonta Freeman 10.00 25.00
334 Charles Sims 3.00 8.00
337 Teddy Bridgewater 12.00 30.00
339 Blake Bortles 30.00 60.00
341 Sammy Watkins 20.00 40.00
342 A.J. McCarron 3.00 8.00
343 Mike Evans 8.00 20.00
345 Derek Carr 25.00 50.00
346 Tajh Boyd 3.00 8.00
348 Aaron Murray 3.00 8.00
352 Tom Savage 3.00 8.00
353 Khalil Mack 30.00 60.00
356 Dri Archer 3.00 8.00
357 Michael Sam 3.00 8.00
359 Cody Latimer 4.00 10.00
386 Logan Thomas 3.00 8.00

2014 Topps 4000 Yard Club

COMPLETE SET (9) 3.00 8.00
STATED ODDS 1:6 HOBBY
1 Andy Dalton .40 1.00
2 Matt Ryan .40 1.00
3 Peyton Manning 1.00 2.50
4 Carson Palmer .40 1.00
5 Philip Rivers .50 1.25
6 Drew Brees .50 1.25
7 Ben Roethlisberger .50 1.25
8 Tom Brady 1.25 3.00
9 Matthew Stafford .40 1.00

2014 Topps All Pro Team

AP TEAM/99 ODDS 1:6000 HOBBY
APTCJ Calvin Johnson 8.00 20.00
APTCP Cordarrelle Patterson 5.00 12.00
APTDR Darrelle Revis 5.00 12.00
APTDT Demaryius Thomas 6.00 15.00
APTEB Eric Berry 6.00 15.00
APTET Earl Thomas 6.00 15.00
APTJC Jamaal Charles 10.00 25.00
APTJG Jimmy Graham 8.00 20.00
APTJS Joe Staley 6.00 15.00
APTJW J.J. Watt 8.00 20.00
APTLK Luke Kuechly 6.00 15.00
APTLM LeSean McCoy 8.00 20.00
APTLV Louis Vasquez 5.00 12.00
APTMP Mike Pouncey 5.00 12.00
APTMR Matt Prater 8.00 20.00
APTMT Mike Tolbert 5.00 12.00
APTNB NaVorro Bowman 6.00 15.00
APTNS Ndamukong Suh 8.00 20.00
APTPC Pat McAfee 6.00 15.00
APTPM Peyton Manning 15.00 40.00
APTRQ Robert Quinn 6.00 15.00
APTRS Richard Sherman 10.00 25.00

2014 Topps All Star Rookies

AS ROOKIES/99 ODDS 1:3025
ASRAD Aaron Dobson 6.00 15.00
ASRAE Andre Ellington 6.00 15.00
ASRCP Cordarrelle Patterson 6.00 15.00
ASREL Eddie Lacy 6.00 15.00
ASREM EJ Manuel 6.00 15.00
ASRGB Giovani Bernard 6.00 15.00
ASRGS Geno Smith 6.00 15.00
ASRJR Jordan Reed 6.00 15.00
ASRKA Keenan Allen 8.00 20.00
ASRKD Knile Davis 6.00 15.00
ASRLB Le'Veon Bell 8.00 20.00
ASRMG Mike Glennon 8.00 20.00
ASRSB Stedman Bailey 6.00 15.00
ASRTA Tavon Austin 6.00 15.00
ASRTW Terrance Williams 6.00 15.00
ASRZE Zach Ertz 8.00 20.00
ASRZS Zac Stacy 6.00 15.00

2014 Topps Autographs

VET STATED ODDS 1:2100 HOB
ROOKIE STATED ODDS 1:2070 HOB
EACH HAS TWO CARDS OF EQUAL VALUE
EXCH EXPIRATION: 7/31/2017
2A T.Y. Hilton 8.00 20.00
17A DeSean Jackson 8.00 20.00
21A Nick Foles 25.00 50.00
22A Victor Cruz 20.00 50.00
36A Cordarrelle Patterson 12.00 30.00
44A EJ Manuel 6.00 15.00
49A Jason Witten
52A Tom Brady 250.00 400.00
53A Drew Brees 40.00 80.00
62A Michael Crabtree 6.00 15.00
65A Mike Glennon 8.00 20.00
78A Le'Veon Bell 8.00 20.00
96A Zac Stacy 6.00 15.00
97A Andre Johnson 8.00 20.00
121A LeSean McCoy 10.00 25.00
156A Reggie Bush 12.00 30.00
164A Kenny Stills 6.00 15.00
167A Randall Cobb 8.00 20.00
181A Jamaal Charles 10.00 25.00
192A Roddy White 10.00 25.00
196A NaVorro Bowman 10.00 25.00
220A Josh Gordon
231A Eddie Lacy EXCH 30.00 60.00
243A Alshon Jeffery 8.00 20.00
246A Ndamukong Suh 8.00 20.00
248A Eric Berry 10.00 25.00
258A Rob Gronkowski 12.00 30.00
270A Kiko Alonso
275A Patrick Peterson 6.00 15.00
280A Ryan Mathews
286A Luke Kuechly 25.00 50.00
293A Antonio Brown 10.00 25.00
295A Tavon Austin
300A Keenan Allen 10.00 25.00
312A Alfred Morris 10.00 25.00
333A Jordan Lynch 5.00 12.00
337A Davante Adams 12.00 30.00
340A Eric Ebron 5.00 12.00
341A De'Anthony Thomas 4.00 10.00
353A Tajh Boyd 4.00 10.00
354A Brandin Cooks 6.00 15.00
355A Odell Beckham Jr. 60.00 100.00
356A Jadeveon Clowney 5.00 12.00
359A Zach Mettenberger 4.00 10.00
360A Bishop Sankey 4.00 10.00
365A Ka'Deem Carey 4.00 10.00
367A Teddy Bridgewater 12.00 30.00
368A Stephen Morris 4.00 10.00
370A Andre Williams 4.00 10.00
371A Jeremy Hill 5.00 12.00
373A Khalil Mack 10.00 25.00
374A Blake Bortles 5.00 12.00
375A Allen Robinson 6.00 15.00
376A Darqueze Dennard 5.00 12.00
383A Carlos Hyde 5.00 12.00
387A Mike Evans 10.00 25.00
394A Jarvis Landry 8.00 20.00
399A C.J. Fiedorowicz 4.00 10.00
408A Jordan Matthews 6.00 15.00
409A Kelvin Benjamin 6.00 15.00
417A Greg Robinson 4.00 10.00
419A Martavis Bryant 5.00 12.00
422A Tre Mason 4.00 10.00
424A Aaron Donald 10.00 25.00
429A Johnny Manziel 6.00 15.00
431A Marqise Lee 5.00 12.00
432A Jimmy Garoppolo 40.00 80.00
434A Sammy Watkins 6.00 15.00
438A Derek Carr 25.00 50.00
439A Jace Amaro 4.00 10.00

2014 Topps Defensive Club Bronze

BRONZE/75 ODDS 1:6700 HOB
*GOLD/25: .6X TO 1.5X BRONZE/75
*SILVER/50: .5X TO 1.2X BRONZE/75
TDCBS Bruce Smith 5.00 12.00
TDCCT Charles Tillman 6.00 15.00
TDCDR Darrelle Revis 4.00 10.00
TDCDS Deion Sanders 5.00 12.00
TDCDW DeMarcus Ware 5.00 12.00
TDCET Earl Thomas 5.00 12.00
TDCHL Howie Long 8.00 20.00
TDCJL James Laurinaitis 5.00 12.00
TDCJM Jerod Mayo 4.00 10.00
TDCJW J.J. Watt 8.00 20.00
TDCLK Luke Kuechly 8.00 20.00
TDCLT Lawrence Taylor 25.00 50.00
TDCNB NaVorro Bowman 5.00 12.00
TDCRL Ronnie Lott 5.00 12.00
TDCRS Richard Sherman 8.00 20.00

2014 Topps Factory Set Jerseys

1 Jadeveon Clowney 2.00 5.00
2 Sammy Watkins 2.50 6.00
3 Teddy Bridgewater 6.00 15.00
4 Blake Bortles 6.00 15.00
5 Marqise Lee 2.00 5.00
6 Eric Ebron 2.00 5.00

2014 Topps Factory Set Quad Jerseys

1 Andre Williams 2.50 6.00

2014 Topps Factory Set Triple Jerseys

1 Bishop Sankey 2.00 5.00
2 Charles Sims 2.00 5.00
3 Tom Savage 2.00 5.00
4 Paul Richardson 2.50 6.00
5 A.J. McCarron 2.00 5.00

2014 Topps Fantasy Focus

COMPLETE SET (55) 8.00 20.00
STATED ODDS 1:6 HOBBY
FFAB Antonio Brown .50 1.25
FFAD Andy Dalton .40 1.00
FFAG A.J. Green .50 1.25
FFAJ Alshon Jeffery .40 1.00
FFAL Andrew Luck .60 1.50
FFAP Adrian Peterson .50 1.25
FFAR Aaron Rodgers 1.00 2.50
FFBM Brandon Marshall .30 .75
FFBR Ben Roethlisberger .50 1.25
FFCJ Calvin Johnson .50 1.25
FFCK Colin Kaepernick .40 1.00
FFCN Cam Newton .50 1.25
FFDB Drew Brees .50 1.25
FFDJ DeSean Jackson .40 1.00
FFDM DeMarco Murray .40 1.00
FFDT Demaryius Thomas .40 1.00
FFED Eric Decker .30 .75
FFEL Eddie Lacy .30 .75
FFGB Giovani Bernard .30 .75
FFJC Jamaal Charles .40 1.00
FFJE Julian Edelman .50 1.25
FFJG Josh Gordon .30 .75
FFJN Jordy Nelson .40 1.00
FFJT Julius Thomas .30 .75
FFJW Jason Witten .40 1.00
FFKA Keenan Allen .40 1.00
FFKM Knowshon Moreno .30 .75
FFLF Larry Fitzgerald .40 1.00
FFLK Luke Kuechly .40 1.00
FFLM LeSean McCoy .50 1.25
FFMC Marques Colston .30 .75
FFMF Matt Forte .30 .75
FFML Marshawn Lynch .40 1.00
FFMR Matt Ryan .40 1.00
FFMS Matthew Stafford .40 1.00
FFNB NaVorro Bowman .40 1.00
FFNF Nick Foles .40 1.00
FFPG Pierre Garcon .40 1.00
FFPM Peyton Manning 1.00 2.50
FFPR Philip Rivers .50 1.25
FFRB Reggie Bush .30 .75
FFRM Ryan Mathews .40 1.00
FFRW Russell Wilson .75 2.00
FFTB Tom Brady 1.25 3.00
FFTH T.Y. Hilton .40 1.00
FFTR Tony Romo .40 1.00
FFVD Vernon Davis .30 .75
FFVJ Vincent Jackson .30 .75
FFZS Zac Stacy .30 .75
FFABO Anquan Boldin .30 .75
FFAJO Andre Johnson .40 1.00
FFDBR Dez Bryant .50 1.25
FFJCA Jordan Cameron .30 .75
FFJGR Jimmy Graham .50 1.25
FFJWA J.J. Watt .50 1.25

2014 Topps Fantasy Stock Watch Autographs

NFLFFAB Antonio Brown 10.00 25.00
NFLFFAE Andre Ellington 6.00 15.00
NFLFFCP Cordarrelle Patterson 15.00 40.00
NFLFFEL Eddie Lacy EXCH 6.00 15.00
NFLFFJC Jamaal Charles 8.00 20.00
NFLFFJE Julian Edelman 10.00 25.00
NFLFFJG Josh Gordon
NFLFFJJ Julio Jones 15.00 40.00
NFLFFJT Julius Thomas 10.00 25.00
NFLFFKA Keenan Allen 10.00 25.00
NFLFFKS Kenny Stills 6.00 15.00
NFLFFKW Kendall Wright 10.00 25.00
NFLFFMC Michael Crabtree 6.00 15.00
NFLFFMS Matthew Stafford 15.00 30.00
NFLFFNF Nick Foles 15.00 40.00
NFLFFPG Pierre Garcon 8.00 20.00
NFLFFRM Ryan Mathews 8.00 20.00
NFLFFTA Tavon Austin
NFLFFZS Zac Stacy
NFLFFTYH T.Y. Hilton 8.00 20.00

2014 Topps Fantasy Strategies

COMPLETE SET (35) 6.00 15.00
STATED ODDS 1:6 HOBBY
FFSAG A.J. Green .50 1.25
FFSAJ Alshon Jeffery .40 1.00
FFSAL Andrew Luck .60 1.50
FFSAM Alfred Morris .30 .75
FFSAR Aaron Rodgers 1.00 2.50
FFSBM Brandon Marshall .30 .75
FFSCJ Calvin Johnson .50 1.25
FFSCK Colin Kaepernick .40 1.00
FFSCN Cam Newton .50 1.25
FFSDA Doug Martin .40 1.00
FFSDB Drew Brees .50 1.25
FFSDJ DeSean Jackson .40 1.00
FFSDM DeMarco Murray .40 1.00
FFSDR Dez Bryant .50 1.25
FFSDT Demaryius Thomas .40 1.00
FFSED Eric Decker .30 .75
FFSGB Giovani Bernard .30 .75
FFSGO Greg Olsen .40 1.00
FFSJC Jordan Cameron .30 .75
FFSJG Jimmy Graham .50 1.25
FFSJW Jason Witten .40 1.00
FFSLB Le'Veon Bell .40 1.00
FFSLF Larry Fitzgerald .40 1.00
FFSMF Matt Forte .30 .75
FFSMR Matt Ryan .40 1.00
FFSPH Percy Harvin .30 .75
FFSRB Reggie Bush .30 .75
FFSRG Rob Gronkowski .50 1.25
FFSRR Ray Rice .30 .75
FFSRW Russell Wilson .75 2.00
FFSTB Tom Brady 1.25 3.00
FFSVC Victor Cruz .40 1.00
FFSVD Vernon Davis .30 .75
FFSVJ Vincent Jackson .30 .75
FFSWW Wes Welker .40 1.00

2014 Topps Greatness Unleashed

COMPLETE SET (65) 12.00 30.00
STATED ODDS 1:4 HOBBY
GUAB Antonio Brown .50 1.25
GUAG Antonio Gates .30 .75
GUAJ Alshon Jeffery .40 1.00
GUAL Andrew Luck .60 1.50
GUAP Adrian Peterson .50 1.25
GUAR Aaron Rodgers 1.00 2.50
GUAS Aldon Smith .30 .75
GUBM Brandon Marshall .30 .75
GUCJ Calvin Johnson .50 1.25
GUCK Colin Kaepernick .40 1.00
GUCM Clay Matthews .50 1.25
GUCN Cam Newton .50 1.25
GUCP Cordarrelle Patterson .30 .75
GUDB Drew Brees .50 1.25
GUDJ DeSean Jackson .40 1.00
GUDR Darrelle Revis .30 .75
GUDT Demaryius Thomas .40 1.00
GUEB Eric Berry .40 1.00
GUEL Eddie Lacy .30 .75
GUET Earl Thomas .40 1.00
GUFG Frank Gore .40 1.00
GUJC Jamaal Charles .40 1.00
GUJF Joe Flacco .40 1.00
GUJG Jimmy Graham .50 1.25
GUJJ Julio Jones .50 1.25
GUJW J.J. Watt .50 1.25
GUKA Keenan Allen .40 1.00
GUKM Knowshon Moreno .30 .75
GUKW Kendall Wright .30 .75
GULF Larry Fitzgerald .40 1.00
GULK Luke Kuechly .40 1.00
GULM LeSean McCoy .50 1.25
GUMF Matt Forte .30 .75
GUML Marshawn Lynch .40 1.00
GUMS Matthew Stafford .40 1.00
GUMW Muhammad Wilkerson .30 .75
GUNB NaVorro Bowman .40 1.00
GUNF Nick Foles .40 1.00
GUNS Ndamukong Suh .40 1.00
GUPG Pierre Garcon .40 1.00
GUPH Percy Harvin .30 .75
GUPM Peyton Manning 1.00 2.50
GUPP Patrick Peterson .30 .75
GUPR Philip Rivers .50 1.25
GUPW Patrick Willis .40 1.00
GURB Reggie Bush .30 .75
GURG Robert Griffin III .30 .75
GURM Robert Mathis .30 .75
GURS Richard Sherman .50 1.25
GURT Ryan Tannehill .40 1.00
GURW Russell Wilson .75 2.00
GUTB Tom Brady 1.25 3.00
GUTP Troy Polamalu .50 1.25
GUTS Torrey Smith .30 .75
GUVC Victor Cruz .40 1.00
GUVD Vernon Davis .30 .75
GUVJ Vincent Jackson .30 .75
GUVM Von Miller .40 1.00
GUWW Wes Welker .40 1.00
GUZS Zac Stacy .30 .75
GUAJG A.J. Green .50 1.25
GUAJO Andre Johnson .40 1.00
GUJGO Josh Gordon .30 .75
GURGR Rob Gronkowski .50 1.25
GURWA Reggie Wayne .40 1.00

2014 Topps Kickoff Coins

*BCA/50: .6X TO 1.5X BASIC COIN
*MILITARY/99: .5X TO 1.2X BASIC COIN
NFLKCAA Antonio Gates 3.00 8.00
NFLKCAG A.J. Green 5.00 12.00
NFLKCAL Andrew Luck 6.00 15.00
NFLKCAP Adrian Peterson 5.00 12.00
NFLKCAR Aaron Rodgers 10.00 25.00
NFLKCBM Brandon Marshall 3.00 8.00
NFLKCBR Ben Roethlisberger 8.00 20.00
NFLKCCJ Calvin Johnson 6.00 15.00
NFLKCCK Colin Kaepernick 4.00 10.00
NFLKCCN Cam Newton 5.00 12.00
NFLKCCS Cecil Shorts 3.00 8.00
NFLKCDB Drew Brees 6.00 15.00
NFLKCDM Denarius Moore 4.00 10.00
NFLKCEA EJ Manuel 3.00 8.00
NFLKCEM Eli Manning 6.00 15.00
NFLKCJC Jamaal Charles 4.00 10.00
NFLKCJF Joe Flacco 5.00 12.00
NFLKCJG Josh Gordon 3.00 8.00
NFLKCJL James Laurinaitis 4.00 10.00
NFLKCJW J.J. Watt 8.00 20.00
NFLKCKW Kendall Wright 4.00 10.00
NFLKCLF Larry Fitzgerald 4.00 10.00
NFLKCLM LeSean McCoy 5.00 12.00
NFLKCMR Matt Ryan 4.00 10.00
NFLKCMW Muhammad Wilkerson 4.00 10.00
NFLKCPM Peyton Manning 10.00 25.00
NFLKCRG Robert Griffin III 3.00 8.00
NFLKCRT Ryan Tannehill 4.00 10.00
NFLKCRW Russell Wilson 12.00 30.00
NFLKCTB Tom Brady 12.00 30.00
NFLKCTR Tony Romo 6.00 15.00
NFLKCVJ Vincent Jackson 3.00 8.00

2014 Topps Mega Chrome Rookies

COMPLETE SET (6) 4.00 10.00
ONE PER TOPPS MEGA BOX
1 Jadeveon Clowney .20 .50
2 Johnny Manziel .25 .60
3 Blake Bortles .20 .50
4 Sammy Watkins .25 .60
5 Teddy Bridgewater .25 .60
6 Derek Carr 1.00 2.50

2014 Topps NFL Captains Patches

PATCH/99 ODDS 1:3600 HOB
*CAMO/50: .5X TO 1.2X BASIC PATCH/99
*PINK/25: .6X TO 1.5X BASIC PATCH/99
NCPAD Andy Dalton 5.00 12.00
NCPAL Andrew Luck 10.00 25.00
NCPAS Alex Smith 5.00 12.00
NCPCJ Calvin Johnson 6.00 15.00
NCPCN Cam Newton 6.00 15.00
NCPDB Drew Brees 6.00 15.00
NCPDJ D'Qwell Jackson 4.00 10.00
NCPEM Eli Manning 5.00 12.00
NCPEW Eric Weddle 4.00 10.00
NCPFJ Fred Jackson 5.00 12.00
NCPJL Jake Locker 5.00 12.00
NCPJP Julius Peppers 5.00 12.00
NCPJW J.J. Watt 6.00 15.00
NCPLF Larry Fitzgerald 6.00 15.00
NCPLH Lamarr Houston 5.00 12.00
NCPPM Peyton Manning 15.00 40.00
NCPRG Robert Griffin III 4.00 10.00
NCPRW Russell Wilson 10.00 25.00
NCPSB Sam Bradford 4.00 10.00
NCPTR Tony Romo 5.00 12.00
NCPVJ Vincent Jackson 4.00 10.00

2014 Topps Play 60 Community Mentors

COMMON CARD 1.25 3.00
1 Alan Ball 1.25 3.00
2 Kelvin Beachum 1.25 3.00
3 Martellus Bennett 1.25 3.00
4 Matt Bosher 1.25 3.00
5 David Bruton 1.25 3.00
6 Morgan Burnett 1.25 3.00
7 Calais Campbell 1.25 3.00
8 Johnny Hekker 1.25 3.00
9 Fred Jackson 1.50 4.00
10 Vincent Jackson 1.25 3.00
11 Luke Kuechly 1.50 4.00
12 Adrian Peterson 2.00 5.00
13 Dontari Poe 1.25 3.00
14 DeMeco Ryans 1.25 3.00
15 Torrey Smith 1.25 3.00

2014 Topps Play 60 Super Kids

STATED ODDS 1:36 HOBBY
1 Thomas Brown 1.25 3.00
2 Dylan Browning 1.25 3.00
3 Noelle Cain 1.25 3.00
4 Caroline Callahan 1.25 3.00
5 Xiang Chi 1.25 3.00
6 Hayley Dewitt 1.25 3.00
7 Daniel Dorantes 1.25 3.00
8 Alexander Duncan 1.25 3.00
9 Austin Gardner 1.25 3.00
10 Jeremy Gaudet 1.25 3.00
11 Evan Grossman 1.25 3.00
12 Camren Hedgespeth 1.25 3.00
13 Wesley Hill 1.25 3.00
14 Zackery Koroskenyi 1.25 3.00
15 Zach Lebovitz 1.25 3.00
16 Kenneth Lorenzo 1.25 3.00
17 Hans Mueller 1.25 3.00
18 Cole Mullenix 1.25 3.00
19 Daniel Oberlin 1.25 3.00
20 Finn Papenfus 1.25 3.00
21 Destiny Regalia 1.25 3.00
22 Sara Rogers 1.25 3.00
23 Trenton Rumley 1.25 3.00
24 Domenic Scalese 1.25 3.00
25 Emily Shaffer 1.25 3.00
26 Caleb Tate 1.25 3.00
27 Dean Upholzer 1.25 3.00
28 Maison Vigil 1.25 3.00
29 Aden Walls 1.25 3.00
30 Colin Wanek 1.25 3.00
31 Jackson Wotruba 1.25 3.00

2014 Topps Power Players

PP1 Ed Dickson .30 .75
PP2 Dez Bryant .50 1.25
PP3 Patrick Willis .40 1.00
PP4 DeSean Jackson .40 1.00
PP5 Bruce Ellington .30 .75
PP6 Darrelle Revis .30 .75
PP7 Darren Sproles .40 1.00
PP8 Mike Glennon .40 1.00
PP9 Jeff Mathews .40 1.00
PP10 Marqise Lee .40 1.00
PP11 Garrett Graham .30 .75
PP12 Alex Smith .40 1.00
PP13 Tom Brady 1.25 3.00
PP14 Stephen Hill .30 .75
PP15 Devonta Freeman .50 1.25
PP16 Storm Johnson .30 .75
PP17 Mohamed Sanu .30 .75
PP18 Eric Berry .40 1.00
PP19 Cordarrelle Patterson .30 .75
PP20 Frank Gore .40 1.00
PP21 Martavis Bryant .40 1.00
PP22 Josh Gordon .30 .75
PP23 Percy Harvin .30 .75
PP24 Pierre Garcon .40 1.00
PP25 Dennis Pitta .30 .75
PP26 A.J. Green .50 1.25
PP27 Prince Amukamara .30 .75
PP28 Vincent Jackson .30 .75
PP29 Andre Ellington .30 .75
PP30 Torrey Smith .30 .75
PP31 Mike Tolbert .30 .75
PP32 Aaron Dobson .30 .75
PP33 Jeremy Kerley .30 .75
PP34 Doug Martin .40 1.00
PP35 Allen Robinson .50 1.25
PP36 Darren McFadden .30 .75
PP37 Maurice Jones-Drew .30 .75
PP38 LeSean McCoy .50 1.25
PP39 Carlos Hyde .40 1.00
PP40 Kenbrell Thompkins .30 .75
PP41 Eli Manning .40 1.00
PP42 Arthur Lynch .30 .75
PP43 Stephen Morris .30 .75
PP44 Case Keenum .40 1.00
PP45 Antonio Brown .50 1.25
PP46 Andre Williams .30 .75
PP47 Cody Hoffman .30 .75
PP48 Xavier Grimble .40 1.00
PP49 Andy Dalton .40 1.00
PP50 Jordan Cameron .30 .75
PP51 Kendall Wright .30 .75
PP52 Blake Bortles .40 1.00
PP53 Donte Moncrief .30 .75
PP54 Carson Palmer .40 1.00
PP55 Dwayne Bowe .40 1.00
PP56 Brandon Myers .40 1.00
PP57 Brent Celek .30 .75
PP58 Derek Carr 2.00 5.00
PP59 Jacoby Jones .30 .75
PP60 Kiko Alonso .30 .75
PP61 Jason Witten .40 1.00
PP62 Arian Foster .40 1.00
PP63 Greg Jennings .30 .75
PP64 Shane Vereen .40 1.00
PP65 Ray Rice .30 .75
PP66 Julius Thomas .30 .75
PP67 Matthew Stafford .40 1.00
PP68 Dri Archer .30 .75
PP69 Mike Davis .30 .75
PP70 Teddy Bridgewater .50 1.25
PP71 Patrick Peterson .30 .75

PP72 Morris Claiborne .30 .75
PP73 Ben Roethlisberger .50 1.25
PP74 Matt Ryan .40 1.00
PP75 Justin Blackmon .30 .75
PP76 Tamba Hali .30 .75
PP77 Kenny Stills .30 .75
PP78 Paul Richardson .40 1.00
PP79 Tony Romo .40 1.00
PP80 Jeremy Hill .40 1.00
PP81 Harry Douglas .30 .75
PP82 Calvin Johnson .50 1.25
PP83 Danny Amendola .40 1.00
PP84 Michael Crabtree .30 .75
PP85 Larry Fitzgerald .40 1.00
PP86 Ndamukong Suh .40 1.00
PP87 Reggie Bush .30 .75
PP88 Zach Ertz .40 1.00
PP89 Henry Josey .30 .75
PP90 Josh Huff .40 1.00
PP91 Marion Grice .30 .75
PP92 Shaquelle Evans .30 .75
PP93 Ace Sanders .30 .75
PP94 Muhammad Wilkerson .30 .75
PP95 Donald Brown .30 .75
PP96 Davante Adams .50 1.25
PP97 BenJarvus Green-Ellis .40 1.00
PP98 Jordy Nelson .40 1.00
PP99 Jamaal Charles .40 1.00
PP100 Jason Pierre-Paul .30 .75
PP101 De'Anthony Thomas .30 .75
PP102 Troy Niklas .30 .75
PP103 Alshon Jeffery .40 1.00
PP104 Charles Clay .30 .75
PP105 Kyle Rudolph .30 .75
PP106 Eric Decker .30 .75
PP107 Austin Seferian-Jenkins .30 .75
PP108 Kelvin Benjamin .50 1.25
PP109 Lache Seastrunk .30 .75
PP110 Aaron Rodgers 1.00 2.50
PP111 DeAndre Hopkins .40 1.00
PP112 Alfred Morris .30 .75
PP113 Jarvis Landry .60 1.50
PP114 Heath Miller .30 .75
PP115 Jermaine Gresham .30 .75
PP116 Malcolm Smith .50 1.25
PP117 Brandin Cooks .50 1.25
PP118 Khalil Mack 1.25 3.00
PP119 Eddie Lacy .30 .75
PP120 EJ Manuel .30 .75
PP121 Luke Kuechly .40 1.00
PP122 Julian Edelman .50 1.25
PP123 Vernon Davis .30 .75
PP124 Fred Jackson .40 1.00
PP125 Keenan Allen .40 1.00
PP126 Connor Shaw .30 .75
PP127 Jimmy Garoppolo 2.50 6.00
PP128 Reggie Wayne .40 1.00
PP129 C.J. Spiller .30 .75
PP130 Wes Welker .40 1.00
PP131 Adrian Peterson .50 1.25
PP132 Jordan Reed .30 .75
PP133 Bishop Sankey .30 .75
PP134 C.J. Fiedorowicz .30 .75
PP135 Tre Mason .30 .75
PP136 Richard Sherman .50 1.25
PP137 Tavon Austin .30 .75
PP138 Cody Latimer .40 1.00
PP139 Eric Ebron .40 1.00
PP140 Jeff Janis .30 .75
PP141 Jared Abbrederis .30 .75
PP142 Robert Herron .30 .75
PP143 Jadeveon Clowney .40 1.00
PP144 Trent Richardson .30 .75
PP145 Robert Griffin III .30 .75
PP146 Tyler Gaffney .30 .75
PP147 Ryan Mathews .40 1.00
PP148 Roddy White .30 .75
PP149 Andrew Luck .60 1.50
PP150 Rod Streater .30 .75
PP151 David Fales .30 .75
PP152 Jace Amaro .30 .75
PP153 Michael Floyd .30 .75
PP154 Julio Jones .50 1.25
PP155 Steven Jackson .30 .75
PP156 Joe Flacco .40 1.00
PP157 Steve Johnson .40 1.00
PP158 Cam Newton .50 1.25
PP159 Brandon Marshall .30 .75
PP160 Jay Cutler .30 .75
PP161 Matt Forte .30 .75
PP162 Giovani Bernard .30 .75
PP163 Marvin Jones .30 .75
PP164 Joe Haden .30 .75
PP165 Paul Kruger .30 .75
PP166 Demaryius Thomas .40 1.00
PP167 Montee Ball .30 .75
PP168 Peyton Manning 1.00 2.50
PP169 Brandon Pettigrew .30 .75
PP170 Jarrett Boykin .30 .75
PP171 Randall Cobb .40 1.00
PP172 Andre Johnson .40 1.00
PP173 J.J. Watt .50 1.25
PP174 Coby Fleener .30 .75
PP175 T.Y. Hilton .40 1.00
PP176 Cecil Shorts .30 .75
PP177 Ryan Tannehill .40 1.00
PP178 Rob Gronkowski .50 1.25
PP179 Stevan Ridley .30 .75
PP180 Jimmy Graham .50 1.25
PP181 Pierre Thomas .30 .75
PP182 David Wilson .30 .75
PP183 Victor Cruz .40 1.00
PP184 Bilal Powell .30 .75
PP185 Geno Smith .30 .75
PP186 Sheldon Richardson .30 .75
PP187 Denarius Moore .30 .75
PP188 Justin Tuck .30 .75
PP189 Nick Foles .40 1.00
PP190 Antonio Gates .30 .75
PP191 Philip Rivers .50 1.25
PP192 Anquan Boldin .30 .75
PP193 NaVorro Bowman .40 1.00
PP194 Marshawn Lynch .40 1.00
PP195 Russell Wilson .75 2.00
PP196 Robert Quinn .40 1.00
PP197 Zac Stacy .30 .75
PP198 Aaron Murray .30 .75
PP199 A.J. McCarron .30 .75
PP200 Brandon Coleman .30 .75
PP201 Charles Sims .30 .75
PP202 Jalen Saunders .30 .75
PP203 Johnny Manziel .50 1.25
PP204 Jordan Matthews .50 1.25
PP205 Ka'Deem Carey .30 .75
PP206 Kevin Norwood .30 .75
PP207 Logan Thomas .30 .75
PP208 Mike Evans .75 2.00
PP209 Odell Beckham Jr. .75 2.00
PP210 Ryan Grant .30 .75
PP211 Sammy Watkins .50 1.25
PP212 Silas Redd .40 1.00
PP213 Tajh Boyd .30 .75
PP214 Terrance West .30 .75
PP215 Tom Savage .30 .75
PP216 Zach Mettenberger .30 .75
PP217 Justin Gilbert .30 .75
PP218 Drew Brees .50 1.25
PP219 Colin Kaepernick .40 1.00
PP220 Le'Veon Bell .40 1.00

2014 Topps Punt Pass and Kick Champions

STATED ODDS 1:36 HOBBY
1 Luke Adams 1.25 3.00
2 Jason Alani 1.25 3.00
3 Madison Bradley 1.25 3.00
4 Kadyn Camper 1.25 3.00
5 Davis Dalton 1.25 3.00
6 Marco Damiani 1.25 3.00
7 Destinee Dugas 1.25 3.00
8 Alisa Fallon 1.25 3.00
9 Curtis Flannick 1.25 3.00
10 Alex Folz 1.25 3.00
11 Nicholas Hooley 1.25 3.00
12 Nalukea Kamakea 1.25 3.00
13 Nathan Kern 1.25 3.00
14 Kaya Kline 1.25 3.00
15 Bailey Kortan 1.25 3.00
16 Carter Lind 1.25 3.00
17 Sebastian Lippman 1.25 3.00
18 Reece Macrae 1.25 3.00
19 Luke Martin 1.25 3.00
20 Lalelei Mataafa 1.25 3.00
21 Jayla Medeiros 1.25 3.00
22 Dakota Moberg 1.25 3.00
23 McKenna Murphy 1.25 3.00
24 Kloie Oguntodu 1.25 3.00
25 Eryn Puett 1.25 3.00
26 Katie Rahilly 1.25 3.00
27 Hunter Renner 1.25 3.00
28 Julia Roland 1.25 3.00
29 Sophia Saucerman 1.25 3.00
30 Kaylynn Spurgin 1.25 3.00
31 Nathan Tewell 1.25 3.00
32 Noah Wanzek 1.25 3.00
33 Jaxxon Warren 1.25 3.00
34 Tyler Warren 1.25 3.00
35 Nicholas Williams 1.25 3.00
36 Isabella Winston 1.25 3.00
37 Samantha Woods 1.25 3.00
38 Kamden Wright 1.25 3.00

2014 Topps Quarterback Club Bronze

BRONZE/75 ODDS 1:5030 HOB
*GOLD/25: .6X TO 1.5X BRONZE/75
*SILVER/50: .5X TO 1.2X BRONZE/75
TQCAL Andrew Luck 8.00 20.00
TQCAR Aaron Rodgers 12.00 30.00
TQCBF Brett Favre 12.00 30.00
TQCBR Ben Roethlisberger 12.00 30.00
TQCCK Colin Kaepernick 5.00 12.00
TQCCN Cam Newton 6.00 15.00
TQCDB Drew Brees 10.00 25.00
TQCDM Dan Marino 20.00 40.00
TQCEM Eli Manning 8.00 20.00
TQCJE John Elway 10.00 25.00
TQCJM Joe Montana 25.00 50.00
TQCKW Kurt Warner 8.00 20.00
TQCMS Matthew Stafford 5.00 12.00
TQCPM Peyton Manning 40.00 80.00
TQCRG Robert Griffin III 4.00 10.00
TQCRW Russell Wilson 10.00 25.00
TQCSY Steve Young 10.00 25.00
TQCTA Troy Aikman 10.00 25.00
TQCTB Tom Brady 12.00 30.00
TQCTR Tony Romo 5.00 12.00

2014 Topps Relics

STATED ODDS 1:47 HOBBY
TRAB Antonio Brown 6.00 15.00
TRAF Arian Foster 2.50 6.00
TRAJ Alshon Jeffery 2.50 6.00
TRAL Andrew Luck 10.00 25.00
TRAM A.J. McCarron 1.25 3.00
TRBB Blake Bortles 1.50 4.00
TRBC Brandin Cooks 2.00 5.00
TRCA Cordarrelle Patterson 2.00 5.00
TRCB Champ Bailey 2.50 6.00
TRCH Carlos Hyde 1.50 4.00
TRCJ Charles Johnson 2.00 5.00
TRCN Cam Newton 3.00 8.00
TRCP C.J. Spiller 2.00 5.00
TRCS Charles Sims 1.25 3.00
TRDB Dez Bryant 3.00 8.00
TRDC Derek Carr 4.00 10.00
TRDJ DeSean Jackson 2.50 6.00
TRDM DeMarco Murray 2.50 6.00
TREB Eric Berry 2.50 6.00
TREE Eric Ebron 1.50 4.00
TREL Eddie Lacy 2.00 5.00
TREM EJ Manuel 2.00 5.00
TRHN Haloti Ngata 2.00 5.00
TRJA Jordan Matthews 2.00 5.00
TRJC Jadeveon Clowney 1.50 4.00
TRJH Jamaal Charles 2.50 6.00
TRJJ Julio Jones 3.00 8.00
TRJM Johnny Manziel 2.00 5.00
TRJR Jace Amaro 1.25 3.00
TRJS Jonathan Stewart 2.00 5.00
TRKB Kelvin Benjamin 2.00 5.00
TRKC Ka'Deem Carey 1.25 3.00
TRLF Larry Fitzgerald 2.50 6.00
TRMC Marques Colston 2.00 5.00
TRME Mike Evans 4.00 10.00
TRMF Matt Forte 2.00 5.00
TRML Marqise Lee 4.00 10.00
TRMW Mike Wallace 2.00 5.00
TRNF Nick Foles 2.50 6.00
TRNM Nick Mangold 2.00 5.00
TROB Odell Beckham Jr. 3.00 8.00
TROU Osi Umenyiora 2.00 5.00
TRRC Randall Cobb 2.50 6.00
TRRG Robert Griffin III 2.00 5.00
TRRR Rob Gronkowski 3.00 8.00
TRSW Sammy Watkins 2.00 5.00
TRTA Tavon Austin 2.00 5.00
TRTB Teddy Bridgewater 2.00 5.00
TRTM Tre Mason 1.25 3.00
TRZM Zach Mettenberger 1.25 3.00

2014 Topps Relics Autographs

RELIC AU/50 ODDS 1:1315 HOB
TARAF Arian Foster 8.00 20.00
TARAG Antonio Gates 6.00 15.00
TARAJ Alshon Jeffery
TARAR A.J. Green 15.00 40.00
TARBH Brian Hartline 6.00 15.00
TARCP Cordarrelle Patterson 12.00 30.00
TARDJ DeSean Jackson 10.00 25.00
TAREA EJ Manuel 6.00 15.00
TAREL Eddie Lacy 6.00 15.00
TAREM Eli Manning 40.00 80.00
TARGB Giovani Bernard 6.00 15.00
TARGS Geno Smith 6.00 15.00
TARJG Josh Gordon 6.00 15.00
TARJK Jeremy Kerley 6.00 15.00
TARKA Keenan Allen
TARKS Kenny Stills 6.00 15.00
TARKW Kendall Wright
TARMB Montee Ball 6.00 15.00
TARMF Matt Forte 15.00 40.00
TARMS Matthew Stafford 15.00 40.00
TARPM Peyton Manning 125.00 200.00
TARRB Reggie Bush 12.00 30.00
TARRM Ryan Mathews 6.00 15.00
TARRW Robert Woods 8.00 20.00
TARVC Victor Cruz EXCH 8.00 20.00

2014 Topps Rookie Jumbo Relics

RJRAR Allen Robinson 2.00 5.00
RJRAW Andre Williams 1.25 3.00
RJRBB Blake Bortles 1.50 4.00
RJRBC Brandin Cooks 2.00 5.00
RJRBS Bishop Sankey 1.25 3.00
RJRCH Carlos Hyde 1.50 4.00
RJRDA Davante Adams 2.00 5.00
RJRDC Derek Carr 6.00 15.00
RJRDF Devonta Freeman 2.00 5.00
RJRDM Donte Moncrief 1.25 3.00
RJRDT De'Anthony Thomas 1.25 3.00
RJREE Eric Ebron 1.50 4.00
RJRJC Jadeveon Clowney 1.50 4.00
RJRJG Jimmy Garoppolo 5.00 12.00
RJRJH Jeremy Hill 1.50 4.00
RJRJL Jarvis Landry 2.50 6.00
RJRJM Johnny Manziel 2.00 5.00
RJRKB Kelvin Benjamin 2.00 5.00
RJRKC Ka'Deem Carey 1.25 3.00
RJRKM Khalil Mack 5.00 12.00
RJRLT Logan Thomas 1.25 3.00
RJRME Mike Evans 3.00 8.00
RJRML Marqise Lee 1.50 4.00
RJRMS Michael Sam 1.25 3.00
RJROB Odell Beckham Jr. 12.00 30.00
RJRPR Paul Richardson 1.50 4.00
RJRSW Sammy Watkins 2.00 5.00
RJRTB Tajh Boyd 1.25 3.00
RJRTM Tre Mason 1.25 3.00
RJRTW Terrance West 1.25 3.00
RJRASJ Austin Seferian-Jenkins 1.25 3.00
RJRCLA Cody Latimer 1.50 4.00
RJRCSI Charles Sims 1.25 3.00
RJRJMA Jordan Matthews 2.00 5.00
RJRTBR Teddy Bridgewater 2.00 5.00

2014 Topps Rookie Patch

TRPAR Allen Robinson 2.50 6.00
TRPAW Andre Williams 1.50 4.00
TRPBB Blake Bortles 2.00 5.00
TRPBC Brandin Cooks 2.50 6.00
TRPBS Bishop Sankey 1.50 4.00
TRPCH Carlos Hyde 2.00 5.00
TRPCL Cody Latimer 2.00 5.00
TRPCS Charles Sims 1.50 4.00
TRPDA Davante Adams 2.50 6.00
TRPDC Derek Carr 10.00 25.00
TRPDF Devonta Freeman 2.50 6.00
TRPDM Donte Moncrief 1.50 4.00
TRPDT De'Anthony Thomas 1.50 4.00
TRPEE Eric Ebron 2.00 5.00
TRPJC Jadeveon Clowney 2.00 5.00
TRPJG Jimmy Garoppolo 12.00 30.00
TRPJH Jeremy Hill 2.00 5.00
TRPJL Jarvis Landry 3.00 8.00
TRPJM Johnny Manziel 2.50 6.00
TRPKB Kelvin Benjamin 2.50 6.00
TRPKC Ka'Deem Carey 1.50 4.00
TRPKM Khalil Mack 6.00 15.00
TRPME Mike Evans 4.00 10.00
TRPML Marqise Lee 2.00 5.00
TRPMS Michael Sam 1.50 4.00
TRPOB Odell Beckham Jr. 4.00 10.00
TRPPR Paul Richardson 2.00 5.00
TRPSW Sammy Watkins 2.50 6.00
TRPTB Tajh Boyd 1.50 4.00
TRPTM Tre Mason 1.50 4.00
TRPTW Terrance West 1.50 4.00
TRPASJ Austin Seferian-Jenkins 1.50 4.00
TRPDAR Dri Archer 1.50 4.00
TRPJMA Jordan Matthews 2.50 6.00
TRPTBR Teddy Bridgewater 2.50 6.00

2014 Topps Rookie Patch Autographs Jumbo

RAJJAR Allen Robinson 12.00 30.00
RAJJAW Andre Williams 8.00 20.00
RAJJBB Blake Bortles 10.00 25.00
RAJJBC Brandin Cooks 12.00 30.00
RAJJBS Bishop Sankey 8.00 20.00
RAJJCH Carlos Hyde 10.00 25.00
RAJJCL Cody Latimer 10.00 25.00
RAJJDA Davante Adams 12.00 30.00
RAJJDC Derek Carr 50.00 125.00
RAJJDM Donte Moncrief 8.00 20.00
RAJJDT De'Anthony Thomas 8.00 20.00
RAJJEE Eric Ebron 10.00 25.00
RAJJJA Jace Amaro 8.00 20.00
RAJJJC Jadeveon Clowney 10.00 25.00
RAJJJG Jimmy Garoppolo 60.00 150.00
RAJJJH Jeremy Hill 10.00 25.00
RAJJJL Jarvis Landry 15.00 40.00
RAJJJM Johnny Manziel 12.00 30.00
RAJJKB Kelvin Benjamin 12.00 30.00
RAJJKC Ka'Deem Carey 8.00 20.00
RAJJKM Khalil Mack 30.00 80.00
RAJJME Mike Evans 20.00 50.00
RAJJML Marqise Lee 10.00 25.00
RAJJOB Odell Beckham Jr. 20.00 50.00
RAJJPR Paul Richardson 10.00 25.00
RAJJSW Sammy Watkins 12.00 30.00
RAJJTB Tajh Boyd 8.00 20.00
RAJJTM Tre Mason 8.00 20.00
RAJJTS Tom Savage 8.00 20.00
RAJJTW Terrance West 8.00 20.00
RAJJZM Zach Mettenberger 8.00 20.00
RAJJASJ Austin Seferian-Jenkins 8.00 20.00
RAJJDFE Devonta Freeman 12.00 30.00
RAJJJMA Jordan Matthews 12.00 30.00
RAJJTBR Teddy Bridgewater 12.00 30.00

2014 Topps Rookie Premiere Autographs

PREM.AU/90 ODDS 1:522 HOBBY
RPAAC A.J. McCarron 20.00 50.00
RPAAM Aaron Murray 6.00 15.00
RPAAR Allen Robinson 10.00 25.00
RPAAS Austin Seferian-Jenkins 6.00 15.00
RPABB Blake Bortles 8.00 20.00
RPABC Brandin Cooks 10.00 25.00
RPABS Bishop Sankey 6.00 15.00
RPACH Carlos Hyde 8.00 20.00
RPACL Cody Latimer 8.00 20.00
RPACS Charles Sims 6.00 15.00
RPADA Davante Adams 10.00 25.00
RPADC Derek Carr 40.00 100.00
RPAEE Eric Ebron 10.00 25.00
RPAJA Jace Amaro 6.00 15.00
RPAJC Jadeveon Clowney 8.00 20.00
RPAJG Jimmy Garoppolo 40.00 80.00
RPAJH Jeremy Hill 8.00 20.00
RPAJL Jarvis Landry 12.00 30.00
RPAJM Johnny Manziel 10.00 25.00
RPAJT Jordan Matthews 10.00 25.00
RPAKB Kelvin Benjamin 10.00 25.00
RPAKC Ka'Deem Carey 6.00 15.00
RPAKM Khalil Mack 15.00 40.00
RPALT Logan Thomas 6.00 15.00
RPAME Mike Evans 15.00 40.00
RPAML Marqise Lee 8.00 20.00
RPAMS Michael Sam 6.00 15.00
RPAOB Odell Beckham Jr. 50.00 100.00
RPASW Sammy Watkins 10.00 25.00
RPATB Teddy Bridgewater 10.00 25.00
RPATM Tre Mason 20.00 50.00
RPATO Tajh Boyd 6.00 15.00
RPATS Tom Savage 6.00 15.00
RPADAR Dri Archer 6.00 15.00
RPADFR Devonta Freeman 10.00 25.00

2014 Topps Rookie Premiere Autographs Dual

RPDABC B.Bortles/D.Carr 40.00 100.00
RPDABL O.Beckham Jr./J.Landry 75.00 150.00
RPDALW S.Watkins/M.Lee 20.00 50.00
RPDAMB T.Bridgewater/J.Manziel
RPDAMH T.Mason/C.Hyde 12.00 30.00

2014 Topps Running Back Club Bronze

BRONZE/75 ODDS 1:5030 HOB
*GOLD/25: .6X TO 1.5X BRONZE/75
*SILVER/50: .5X TO 1.2X BRONZE/75
TRBCAM Alfred Morris 4.00 10.00
TRBCAP Adrian Peterson 8.00 15.00
TRBCBS Barry Sanders 10.00 25.00
TRBCCJ Chris Johnson 4.00 10.00
TRBCCM Curtis Martin 5.00 12.00
TRBCDM Doug Martin 5.00 12.00
TRBCED Eric Dickerson 6.00 15.00
TRBCEL Eddie Lacy 4.00 10.00
TRBCFG Frank Gore 5.00 12.00
TRBCGB Giovani Bernard 4.00 10.00
TRBCJC Jamaal Charles 6.00 15.00
TRBCKM Knowshon Moreno 4.00 10.00
TRBCLM LeSean McCoy 6.00 15.00
TRBCLT LaDainian Tomlinson 6.00 15.00
TRBCMA Marcus Allen 8.00 20.00
TRBCMF Marshall Faulk 8.00 20.00
TRBCML Marshawn Lynch 6.00 15.00
TRBCMO Matt Forte 8.00 20.00
TRBCRB Reggie Bush 4.00 10.00
TRBCZS Zac Stacy 4.00 10.00

2014 Topps Signatures

STATED ODDS 1:2100 HOB
TAAB Anthony Barr 2.50 6.00
TAAE Andre Ellington 3.00 8.00
TAAM Aaron Murray 2.50 6.00
TAAP Adrian Peterson SP 40.00 80.00
TABB Blake Bortles 3.00 8.00
TABF Brett Favre SP 100.00 175.00
TABM Barkevious Mingo 3.00 8.00
TABS Barry Sanders SP 75.00 125.00
TACH Carlos Hyde 3.00 8.00
TACM C.J. Mosley 3.00 8.00
TACS Charles Sims 2.50 6.00
TADA Danny Amendola 4.00 10.00
TADB Drew Brees SP 40.00 80.00
TADD Darqueze Dennard 3.00 8.00
TADM Donte Moncrief 2.50 6.00
TADS Deion Sanders SP 30.00 60.00
TAEE Eric Ebron 3.00 8.00
TAET Earl Thomas 12.00 30.00
TAGO Greg Olsen 4.00 10.00
TAHC Ha Ha Clinton-Dix 3.00 8.00
TAJA Jordan Matthews 4.00 10.00
TAJC Jadeveon Clowney 3.00 8.00
TAJE Jordan Cameron 3.00 8.00
TAJG Jimmy Garoppolo 25.00 50.00
TAJH Jeremy Hill 3.00 8.00
TAJK Jeremy Kerley 3.00 8.00
TAJL Jordan Lynch 3.00 8.00
TAJM Johnny Manziel SP
TAJN Jordy Nelson 6.00 15.00
TAJO Julius Thomas 3.00 8.00
TAJR Jordan Reed 3.00 8.00
TAJT Jake Matthews 2.50 6.00
TAMD Mike Davis 2.50 6.00
TAME Matt Elam 3.00 8.00
TAMG Mike Glennon 4.00 10.00
TAML Marqise Lee SP 3.00 8.00
TAMT Manti Te'o 4.00 10.00
TAMY Marshawn Lynch 15.00 30.00
TAOB Odell Beckham Jr. SP 40.00 80.00
TAPM Peyton Manning SP 125.00 200.00
TAPW Paul Worrilow 4.00 10.00
TARB Reggie Bush SP
TARW Rod Woodson SP 20.00 40.00
TASV Shane Vereen 4.00 10.00
TASW Sammy Watkins SP 25.00 50.00
TATB Teddy Bridgewater SP 30.00 60.00
TATM Tyrann Mathieu 3.00 8.00
TATO Tajh Boyd 2.50 6.00
TATW Terrance West 2.50 6.00
TAXR Xavier Rhodes 3.00 8.00

2015 Topps Under Armour High School All-America

UACW Christian Wilkins 5.00 10.00
UADR Drew Richmond 7.50 15.00
UAKM Kyler Murray 100.00 200.00
UAKT Kevin Toliver 5.00 10.00
UAPL Paul Lucas 5.00 10.00
UASJ Sterling Jenkins 5.00 10.00
UASJ Soso Jamabo 6.00 15.00

2014 Topps Wal-Mart Purple

*TARGET: .4X TO 1X WAL-MART
1 Justin Gilbert 1.25 3.00
2 Dion Bailey 1.25 3.00
3 Tyler Gaffney 1.25 3.00
4 Andre Williams 1.25 3.00
5 C.J. Fiedorowicz 1.25 3.00
6 Bishop Sankey 1.25 3.00
7 Josh Huff 1.50 4.00
8 Jarvis Landry 2.50 6.00
9 De'Anthony Thomas 1.25 3.00
10 Henry Josey 1.25 3.00
11 Khalil Mack 5.00 12.00
12 Terrance West 1.25 3.00
13 Antone Exum 1.25 3.00
14 Brandon Coleman 1.25 3.00
15 Jared Abbrederis 1.25 3.00
16 Sammy Watkins 2.00 5.00
17 Troy Niklas 1.25 3.00
18 Ryan Shazier 2.00 5.00
19 Cody Hoffman 1.25 3.00
20 Lache Seastrunk 1.25 3.00
21 Calvin Pryor 1.25 3.00
22 Stephon Tuitt 2.00 5.00
23 Cyrus Kouandjio 1.50 4.00
24 Arthur Lynch 1.25 3.00
25 Jalen Saunders 1.25 3.00
26 Louis Nix 1.25 3.00
27 George Atkinson III 1.25 3.00
28 Loucheiz Purifoy 1.25 3.00
29 Aaron Donald 3.00 8.00
30 Connor Shaw 1.25 3.00
31 Brandin Cooks 2.00 5.00
32 LaDarius Perkins 1.25 3.00
33 Jake Matthews 1.25 3.00
34 Ra'Shede Hageman 1.25 3.00
35 Kony Ealy 1.50 4.00
36 Paul Richardson 1.50 4.00
37 David Fales 1.25 3.00
38 Ka'Deem Carey 1.25 3.00
39 Zach Mettenberger 1.25 3.00
40 Aaron Colvin 1.25 3.00
41 Devonta Freeman 2.00 5.00
42 Silas Redd 1.50 4.00
43 Shaquelle Evans 1.25 3.00
44 Taylor Lewan 1.25 3.00
45 Scott Crichton 1.25 3.00
46 Jason Verrett 1.25 3.00
47 Dri Archer 1.25 3.00
48 Ha Ha Clinton-Dix 1.50 4.00
49 Craig Loston 1.25 3.00
50 Marqise Lee 1.50 4.00
51 Teddy Bridgewater 2.00 5.00
52 Deone Bucannon 1.25 3.00
53 Anthony Barr 1.25 3.00
54 Greg Robinson 1.25 3.00
55 Logan Thomas 1.25 3.00
56 Jeff Janis 1.25 3.00
57 Michael Sam 1.25 3.00
58 Derek Carr 8.00 20.00
59 Jimmy Garoppolo 10.00 25.00
60 Will Sutton 1.50 4.00
61 Jace Amaro 1.25 3.00
62 Eric Ebron 1.50 4.00
63 Stephen Morris 1.25 3.00
64 Pierre Desir 1.25 3.00
65 Aaron Murray 1.25 3.00
66 Ahmad Dixon 1.25 3.00
67 Carlos Hyde 1.50 4.00
68 Kevin Norwood 1.25 3.00
69 Allen Robinson 2.00 5.00
70 Xavier Grimble 1.50 4.00
71 Storm Johnson 1.25 3.00
72 A.J. McCarron 1.25 3.00
73 Jordan Matthews 2.00 5.00
74 C.J. Mosley 1.50 4.00
75 Jeremy Hill 1.50 4.00
76 Marcus Roberson 1.50 4.00
77 Cody Latimer 1.50 4.00
78 Johnny Manziel 2.00 5.00
79 Donte Moncrief 1.25 3.00
80 Charles Sims 1.25 3.00
81 Kelvin Benjamin 2.00 5.00
82 Yawin Smallwood 1.25 3.00
83 Austin Seferian-Jenkins 1.25 3.00
84 Mike Davis 1.25 3.00
85 Bruce Ellington 1.25 3.00
86 Johnny Manziel 2.00 5.00
87 Trent Murphy 1.25 3.00
88 Damien Williams 1.25 3.00
89 Davante Adams 2.00 5.00
90 Devin Street 1.25 3.00
91 Ryan Grant 1.25 3.00
92 Darqueze Dennard 1.50 4.00
93 Martavis Bryant 1.50 4.00
94 Odell Beckham Jr. 3.00 8.00
95 Jeff Mathews 1.50 4.00
96 Jadeveon Clowney 1.50 4.00
97 Mike Evans 3.00 8.00
98 Jordan Lynch 1.50 4.00
99 Tajh Boyd 1.25 3.00
100 Zack Martin 1.50 4.00
101 Tom Savage 1.25 3.00
102 Kareem Martin 1.25 3.00
103 Bradley Roby 1.25 3.00
104 Caraun Reid 1.50 4.00
105 Robert Herron 1.25 3.00
106 Blake Bortles 1.50 4.00
107 Kyle Van Noy 1.50 4.00
108 Timmy Jernigan 1.25 3.00
109 Marion Grice 1.25 3.00
110 Tre Mason 1.25 3.00

2014 Topps Wide Receivers Club Bronze

BRONZE/75 ODDS 1:5030 HOB
*GOLD/25: .6X TO 1.5X BRONZE/75
*SILVER/50: .5X TO 1.2X BRONZE/75
TWRCAB Antonio Brown 6.00 15.00
TWRCAG A.J. Green 6.00 15.00
TWRCAJ Alshon Jeffery 5.00 12.00
TWRCAL Anquan Boldin 4.00 10.00
TWRCAO Andre Johnson 5.00 12.00
TWRCAR Andre Reed 5.00 12.00
TWRCBM Brandon Marshall 6.00 15.00
TWRCCJ Calvin Johnson 8.00 20.00
TWRCDB Dez Bryant 6.00 15.00
TWRCDJ DeSean Jackson 5.00 12.00
TWRCDT Demaryius Thomas 5.00 12.00
TWRCJG Josh Gordon 4.00 10.00
TWRCJJ Julio Jones 6.00 15.00
TWRCJN Jordy Nelson 5.00 12.00
TWRCJR Jerry Rice 10.00 25.00
TWRCKA Keenan Allen 5.00 12.00
TWRCLF Larry Fitzgerald 5.00 12.00
TWRCPG Pierre Garcon 5.00 12.00
TWRCRH Roddy White 4.00 10.00
TWRCRW Reggie Wayne 5.00 12.00
TWRCSL Steve Largent 8.00 20.00
TWRCTS Torrey Smith 4.00 10.00
TWRCVC Victor Cruz 5.00 12.00
TWRCVJ Vincent Jackson 4.00 10.00
TWRCWW Wes Welker 5.00 12.00

2014 Topps 5x7 '63 Topps

COMPLETE SET (30) 40.00 60.00
208 Tom Brady 2.50 6.00
211 Derek Carr 2.00 5.00
214 Eddie Lacy .60 1.50
215 Odell Beckham Jr. .75 2.00
216 Calvin Johnson 1.00 2.50
217 Deion Sanders .75 2.00
224 Drew Brees 1.00 2.50
230 Jadeveon Clowney .40 1.00
233 Teddy Bridgewater .50 1.25
235 Aaron Rodgers 2.00 5.00
246 Peyton Manning 2.00 5.00
247 Bo Jackson 1.25 3.00
258 Johnny Manziel .50 1.25
262 Dez Bryant 1.00 2.50
264 Brett Favre 2.00 5.00
265 Troy Aikman 1.25 3.00
266 Colin Kaepernick .75 2.00
271 Blake Bortles .40 1.00
274 Kelvin Benjamin .50 1.25
283 Sammy Watkins .50 1.25
286 Marshawn Lynch .75 2.00
290 Steve Young 1.25 3.00
298 Barry Sanders 1.50 4.00
303 Cam Newton 1.00 2.50
308 Rob Gronkowski 1.00 2.50
309 Russell Wilson 1.50 4.00
312 Joe Montana 2.50 6.00
313 Richard Sherman 1.00 2.50
318 J.J. Watt 1.00 2.50
320 Mike Evans .75 2.00

2014 Topps 5x7 1000 Yard Club Receiving

COMPLETE SET (13) 35.00 50.00
1 Josh Gordon 1.00 2.50
2 Antonio Brown 1.50 4.00
3 Calvin Johnson 1.50 4.00
4 Demaryius Thomas 1.25 3.00
5 A.J. Green 1.50 4.00
6 Alshon Jeffery 1.25 3.00
7 Andre Johnson 1.25 3.00
8 Pierre Garcon 1.25 3.00
9 DeSean Jackson 1.25 3.00
10 Jordy Nelson 1.25 3.00
11 Brandon Marshall 1.00 2.50
12 Eric Decker 1.00 2.50
13 Dez Bryant 1.50 4.00
14 Vincent Jackson 1.00 2.50
15 Jimmy Graham 1.50 4.00
16 Anquan Boldin 1.00 2.50
17 Torrey Smith 1.00 2.50
18 T.Y. Hilton 1.25 3.00

2014 Topps 5x7 1000 Yard Club Rushing

COMPLETE SET (13) 18.00 30.00
1 LeSean McCoy 1.50 4.00
2 Matt Forte 1.00 2.50
3 Jamaal Charles 1.25 3.00
4 Alfred Morris 1.00 2.50
5 Adrian Peterson 1.50 4.00
6 Marshawn Lynch 1.25 3.00
7 Ryan Mathews 1.25 3.00
8 Eddie Lacy 1.00 2.50
9 Frank Gore 1.25 3.00
10 DeMarco Murray 1.25 3.00
11 Chris Johnson 1.00 2.50
12 Knowshon Moreno 1.00 2.50
13 Reggie Bush 1.00 2.50

2014 Topps 5x7 4000-Yard Club Passers

COMPLETE SET (9) 15.00 25.00
1 Andy Dalton 1.00 2.50
2 Matt Ryan 1.00 2.50
3 Peyton Manning 2.50 6.00
4 Carson Palmer 1.00 2.50
5 Philip Rivers 1.25 3.00
6 Drew Brees 1.25 3.00
7 Ben Roethlisberger 1.25 3.00
8 Tom Brady 3.00 8.00
9 Matthew Stafford 1.00 2.50

2014 Topps 5x7 Top Rookies

COMPLETE SET (29) 50.00 80.00
332 Ha Ha Clinton-Dix .60 1.50
337 Davante Adams .75 2.00
339 Cody Latimer .60 1.50
340 Eric Ebron .60 1.50
354 Brandin Cooks .75 2.00
355 Odell Beckham Jr. 1.25 3.00
356 Jadeveon Clowney .60 1.50
359 Zach Mettenberger .50 1.25
360 Bishop Sankey .50 1.25
367 Teddy Bridgewater .75 2.00
370 Andre Williams .50 1.25
371 Jeremy Hill .60 1.50
373 Khalil Mack 2.00 5.00
374 Blake Bortles .60 1.50
383 Carlos Hyde .60 1.50
384 Terrance West .50 1.25
387 Mike Evans 1.25 3.00
394 Jarvis Landry 1.00 2.50
406 Zack Martin .60 1.50
408 Jordan Matthews .75 2.00
409 Kelvin Benjamin .75 2.00
413 Anthony Barr .50 1.25
417 Greg Robinson .50 1.25
419 Martavis Bryant .60 1.50
422 Tre Mason .50 1.25
429 Johnny Manziel .75 2.00
432 Jimmy Garoppolo 4.00 10.00
438 Derek Carr 3.00 8.00
439 Jace Amaro .50 1.25

2015 Topps

COMP.HOBBY FACTORY (505) 35.00 50.00
COMP.RETAIL FACTORY (505) 35.00 50.00
COMP.SET w/o SP's (500) 25.00 40.00
1A Aaron Rodgers .50 1.25
1B Aaron Rodgers SP 8.00 20.00
1C Brett Favre SP 15.00 30.00
2 Michael Floyd .15 .40
3A Jordy Nelson .20 .50
3B Jordy Nelson SP 3.00 8.00
4A Joseph Randle .15 .40
4B Roger Staubach SP 5.00 12.00
5 Demaryius Thomas .20 .50
6 A.J. Green .25 .60
7 Joique Bell .15 .40
8 Jermaine Gresham .20 .50
9 Joe Flacco .20 .50
10A Eddie Lacy holding ball .15 .40
10B Eddie Lacy SP 2.50 6.00
11A Clay Matthews tackling .25 .60
11B Clay Matthews SP 4.00 10.00
12 John Brown .20 .50
13 Steven Jackson .15 .40
14 Julius Peppers .20 .50
15A Matt Forte .15 .40
15B Matt Forte SP 2.50 6.00
15C Gale Sayers SP 4.00 10.00
16 Giovani Bernard .15 .40
17 Andrew Hawkins .15 .40
18 Terrance Williams .15 .40
19 Robert Turbin .15 .40
20A Randall Cobb .20 .50
20B Randall Cobb SP 3.00 8.00
21 Aqib Talib .15 .40
22 Ryan Fitzpatrick .15 .40
23 Montee Ball .15 .40
24A Tony Romo blue jersey .20 .50
24B Tony Romo SP white jersey 3.00 8.00
25A Kelvin Benjamin .20 .50
25B Kelvin Benjamin 3.00 8.00
26 James Starks .15 .40
27 Golden Tate .15 .40
28 Jason Witten .20 .50
29 Kyle Fuller .15 .40
30A Cam Newton .25 .60
30B Cam Newton SP 4.00 10.00
30C Braylon Beam SP 6.00 15.00
31 Tyler Eifert .20 .50
32 Jordan Cameron .15 .40
33 Luke Kuechly .20 .50
34 Cole Beasley .25 .60
35A Dez Bryant .25 .60
35B Dez Bryant SP 4.00 10.00
36 Ronnie Hillman .15 .40
37 Antone Smith .20 .50
38 Larry Fitzgerald .20 .50
39 Rolando McClain .15 .40
40A DeMarco Murray .20 .50
40B DeMarco Murray SP 3.00 8.00
41 Justin Forsett .20 .50
42 Carson Palmer .20 .50
43 Jonathan Stewart .15 .40
44A Troy Polamalu .25 .60
44B Troy Polamalu SP 6.00 15.00
44C Ronnie Lott SP 3.00 8.00
45 Patrick Peterson .15 .40
46 Julius Thomas .15 .40
47 Andy Dalton .20 .50
48 Marvin Jones .15 .40
49 Fred Jackson .20 .50
50A Matt Ryan .20 .50
50B Matt Ryan SP 3.00 8.00
51 Devonta Freeman .20 .50
52 Mohamed Sanu .15 .40
53 Ha Ha Clinton-Dix .15 .40
54 Brandon Marshall .15 .40
55A Julio Jones .25 .60
55B Deion Sanders SP 3.00 8.00
56 Johnny Manziel .20 .50
57 Devon Still .25 .60
58 Owen Daniels .15 .40
59 Alfred Blue .15 .40
60 Jeremy Hill .15 .40
61 Kiko Alonso .15 .40
62 Robert Woods .20 .50
63 Mason Crosby .15 .40
64 Torrey Smith .15 .40
65A Alshon Jeffery .20 .50
65B Alshon Jeffery SP 3.00 8.00
66 DeMarcus Ware .20 .50
67 Steve Smith .20 .50
68 Justin Hunter .15 .40
69 Reggie Bush .15 .40
70A Calvin Johnson .25 .60
70B Barry Sanders SP 6.00 15.00
71 Terrance West .15 .40
72 C.J. Mosley .25 .60
73 EJ Manuel .15 .40
74 Isaiah Crowell .15 .40
75A Arian Foster .20 .50
75B Arian Foster SP 3.00 8.00
75C Earl Campbell SP 4.00 10.00
76 Terrell Suggs .15 .40
77 Roddy White .15 .40
78 Emmanuel Sanders .20 .50
79 Von Miller .20 .50
80A Peyton Manning .50 1.25
80B Peyton Manning SP 8.00 20.00
80C John Elway SP 6.00 15.00
81 Devin Hester .20 .50
82 Greg Olsen .20 .50
83 Terrance Knighton .15 .40
84 Knowshon Moreno .15 .40
85 Ndamukong Suh .20 .50
86 Andre Ellington .15 .40
87 Mario Williams .15 .40
88 Martellus Bennett .15 .40
89 Tyrann Mathieu .20 .50
90A Matthew Stafford .20 .50
90B Matthew Stafford SP 3.00 8.00
91 Lorenzo Taliaferro .15 .40
92 Jay Cutler .15 .40
93 Zach Martin .15 .40
94 Theo Riddick .15 .40
95A Sammy Watkins .20 .50
95B Sammy Watkins SP 3.00 8.00
96 Stepfan Taylor .15 .40
97 Eric Ebron .15 .40
98 Dan Bailey .15 .40
99 Vontaze Burfict .15 .40
100 Joe Haden .15 .40
101 Ahmad Bradshaw .15 .40
102 Charles Clay .15 .40
103 Tim Wright .15 .40
104 Brandon LaFell .15 .40
105A Jamaal Charles .20 .50
105B Jamaal Charles SP 3.00 8.00
106 DeAndre Hopkins .20 .50
107 Darren McFadden .15 .40
108 Riley Cooper .20 .50
109 Dwayne Bowe .20 .50
110A Jimmy Graham .25 .60
110B Jimmy Graham SP 4.00 10.00
111 Danny Woodhead .20 .50
112 Andre Johnson .20 .50
113 Blake Bortles .15 .40
114 Mike Pouncey .15 .40
115A J.J. Watt SP .25 .60
115B J.J. Watt 4.00 10.00
116 Reggie Wayne .20 .50
117 Johnathan Hankins .15 .40
118 Travis Kelce .25 .60
119 Jadeveon Clowney .15 .40
120A Odell Beckham Jr. .25 .60
120B Odell Beckham Jr. SP 4.00 10.00
120C Jerry Rice SP 6.00 15.00
121 Andre Williams .15 .40
122 Anthony Barr .15 .40
123 Doug Martin .20 .50
124 Jarvis Landry .20 .50
125A Tom Brady .60 1.50
125B Tom Brady SP 10.00 25.00
126 Allen Hurns .15 .40
127 Nick Foles .20 .50
128 Victor Cruz .20 .50
129 Dontari Poe .15 .40
130A Ben Roethlisberger .25 .60
130B Ben Roethlisberger SP 6.00 15.00
130C Terry Bradshaw SP 12.00 30.00
131 Darrelle Revis .15 .40
132 Alex Smith .20 .50
133 Chris Ivory .20 .50
134 Marqise Lee .15 .40
135 Jordan Matthews .20 .50
136 Pierre Thomas .15 .40
137 Antrel Rolle .15 .40
138 De'Anthony Thomas .15 .40
139 Dwayne Allen .15 .40
140 Latavius Murray .15 .40
141 Tavon Austin .15 .40
142 Mark Sanchez .15 .40
143 Cordarrelle Patterson .15 .40
144 Allen Robinson .20 .50
145 Khalil Mack .25 .60
146 Geno Smith .15 .40
147 Darren Sproles .20 .50
148 Lamar Miller .15 .40
149 Clay Harbor .15 .40
150A Drew Brees .25 .60
150B Drew Brees SP 4.00 10.00
151 Prince Amukamara .15 .40
152 Nick Mangold .15 .40
153 Denard Robinson .15 .40
154 Robert Quinn .20 .50
155A Eli Manning .20 .50
155B Eli Manning SP 3.00 8.00
156 Brandin Cooks .20 .50
157 Malcolm Butler .25 .60
158 Xavier Rhodes .15 .40
159 Mychal Rivera .15 .40
160A Andrew Luck .30 .75
160B Andrew Luck SP 10.00 25.00
161 Travaris Cadet RC .15 .40
162 Percy Harvin .15 .40
163 Andre Holmes .20 .50
164 Stephen Gostkowski .20 .50
165 Sheldon Richardson .15 .40
166 Chandler Jones .15 .40
167 Marques Colston .15 .40
168 C.J. Spiller .15 .40
169 Vontae Davis .15 .40
170 Julian Edelman .25 .60
171 Coby Fleener .15 .40
172 Knile Davis .15 .40
173 Shane Vereen .20 .50
174 Matt Asiata .15 .40
175A Rob Gronkowski .25 .60
175B Rob Gronkowski SP 4.00 10.00
176 Muhammad Wilkerson .15 .40
177 Chris Johnson .15 .40
178 Jace Amaro .15 .40
179 Jeremy Kerley .15 .40
180 Cameron Wake .15 .40
181 Pierre Garcon .20 .50
182 T.Y. Hilton .20 .50
182B T.Y. Hilton SP 3.00 8.00
183 Eric Decker .15 .40
184 Rashad Jennings .15 .40
185A LeSean McCoy .25 .60
185B LeSean McCoy SP 4.00 10.00
186A Jason Pierre-Paul .15 .40
186B Lawrence Taylor SP 4.00 10.00
187 Larry Donnell .15 .40
188 Mike Wallace .15 .40
189 Mark Ingram .20 .50
190 Derek Carr .25 .60
191 Christine Michael .15 .40
192 Kenny Stills .15 .40
193 Adam Vinatieri .15 .40
194 Rueben Randle .15 .40
195 Teddy Bridgewater .20 .50
196 Jerick McKinnon .15 .40
197 Jeremy Maclin .15 .40
198A Ryan Tannehill .20 .50
198B Dan Marino SP 8.00 20.00
199 Zach Ertz .20 .50
200 Eric Berry .20 .50
201 Aaron Donald .25 .60
202 Kendall Wright .15 .40
203 Martavis Bryant .15 .40
204 Vincent Jackson .15 .40
205A Mike Evans .20 .50
205B Mike Evans SP 3.00 8.00
206A Marshawn Lynch .20 .50
206B Marshawn Lynch SP 3.00 8.00
206C Terrell Davis 3.00 8.00
207 Keenan Allen .20 .50
208A Alfred Morris .15 .40
208B Alfred Morris SP 2.50 6.00
209A Richard Sherman .25 .60
209B Richard Sherman SP 4.00 10.00
210A Philip Rivers .25 .60
210B Philip Rivers SP 5.00 12.00
211 Heath Miller .15 .40
212A Patrick Willis .20 .50
212B Mike Singletary SP 4.00 10.00
213 Eric Weddle .15 .40
214 Anquan Boldin .15 .40
215 Antonio Gates .15 .40
216 Delanie Walker .15 .40
217 Markus Wheaton .15 .40
218 Davante Adams .20 .50

219 Robert Griffin III .15 .40
220A C.J. Anderson .20 .50
220B Marshawn Lynch wht 3.00 8.00
221 Zach Mettenberger .15 .40
222 Vernon Davis .15 .40
223 DeSean Jackson .20 .50
224 Donte Moncrief .20 .50
225A Le'Veon Bell .20 .50
225B Le'Veon Bell SP 3.00 8.00
225C Bo Jackson SP 5.00 12.00
226 Bishop Sankey .15 .40
227 Jason Verrett .15 .40
228A Adrian Peterson .25 .60
228B Adrian Peterson SP 4.00 10.00
229A Tre Mason .20 .50
229B Marshall Faulk SP 3.00 8.00
229C Eric Dickerson SP 3.00 8.00
230A Frank Gore .20 .50
230B Frank Gore SP 3.00 8.00
230C Steve Young SP 5.00 12.00
230D Colin Kaepernick SP 3.00 8.00
231 Kam Chancellor .25 .60
232 Doug Baldwin .20 .50
233 LeGarrette Blount .20 .50
234 Carlos Hyde .15 .40
235A Russell Wilson .30 .75
235B Russell Wilson SP 5.00 12.00
236 Branden Oliver .20 .50
237 Michael Crabtree .15 .40
238 Colin Kaepernick .20 .50
239 Earl Thomas .20 .50
240A Antonio Brown .25 .60
240B Antonio Brown SP 4.00 10.00
241 Detroit Lions .20 .50
Matt Stafford
Calvin Johnson
242 New Orleans Saints .20 .50
Drew Brees
Jimmy Graham
243 Dez Bryant AP .20 .50
244 Carolina Panthers .20 .50
Cam Newton
Jerricho Cotchery
245 DeMarco Murray AP .15 .40
246 Atlanta Falcons .15 .40
Matt Ryan
247 Buffalo Bills .15 .40
Sammy Watkins
248 Cleveland Browns .12 .30
Glenn Winston
249 Jacksonville Jaguars .12 .30
Marqise Lee
Allen Hurns
250 Chicago Bears .15 .40
Matt Forte
Alshon Jeffery
251 St. Louis Rams .12 .30
Chris Long
Tavon Austin
252 Aaron Rodgers AP .40 1.00
253 Ndamukong Suh AP .15 .40
254 Indianapolis Colts .25 .60
Andrew Luck
T.Y. Hilton
255 Philadelphia Eagles .20 .50
Jordan Matthews
LeSean McCoy
256 Houston Texans .12 .30
Mike Mohamed
Jumal Rolle
257 Miami Dolphins .15 .40
Lamar Miller
Ryan Tannehill
258 Luke Kuechly AP .15 .40
259 Le'Veon Bell AP .15 .40
260 Zack Martin AP .12 .30
261 New York Giants .20 .50
Odell Beckham Jr.
262 Pittsburgh Steelers .20 .50
Le'Veon Bell
Antonio Brown
263 Rob Gronkowski AP .20 .50
264 Patriots/Brady/Gronk .30 .75
265 J.J. Watt AP .20 .50
266 Packers/Rdgrs/Nlsn .30 .75
267 Arizona Cardinals .15 .40
Carson Palmer
Larry Fitzgerald
268 Maurkice Pouncey AP .12 .30
269 Antonio Brown AP .20 .50
270 Broncos/Mann/Thm .30 .75
271 Elvis Dumervil AP .12 .30
272 Tyron Smith AP .12 .30
273 Marshal Yanda AP RC .25 .60
274 Washington Redskins .12 .30
Alfred Morris
Niles Paul
275 Baltimore Ravens .15 .40
Justin Forsett
Torrey Smith
276 Seattle Seahawks .20 .50
Richard Sherman
277 New York Jets .15 .40
Chris Ivory
278 Cincinnati Bengals .15 .40
Andy Dalton
Jeremy Hill
279 Dallas Cowboys .15 .40
Tony Romo
Jason Witten
280 Adam Jones AP .12 .30
281 Marcell Dareus AP .12 .30
282 Pat McAfee AP RC .25 .60
283 Tampa Bay Buccaneers .15 .40
Louis Murphy
Mike Evans
284 John Kuhn AP .12 .30
285 Bobby Wagner AP .12 .30
286 San Diego Chargers .20 .50
Keenan Allen
Philip Rivers
287 Richard Sherman AP .20 .50
288 Eric Weddle AP .12 .30
289 Mario Williams AP .12 .30
290 Kansas City Chiefs .15 .40
Albert Wilson
Jamaal Charles
291 Oakland Raiders .20 .50
Derek Carr
292 Minnesota Vikings .15 .40
Teddy Bridgewater
Charles Johnson
293 San Francisco 49ers .15 .40
Colin Kaepernick
Carlos Hyde
294 Darrelle Revis AP .12 .30
295 Joe Thomas AP .12 .30
296 Adam Vinatieri AP .12 .30
297 Justin Houston AP .12 .30
298 Earl Thomas AP .15 .40
299 Tennessee Titans .12 .30
Bishop Sankey
300 DeMarco Murray POY .15 .40
301 J.J. Watt POY .20 .50
302 Patriots Champs/Brady .30 .75
303 Aaron Rodgers MVP .40 1.00
304 Odell Beckham Jr. ROY .20 .50
305 Aaron Donald ROY .20 .50
306 DeMarco Murray FS .15 .40
307 Jimmy Graham FS .20 .50
308 Tom Brady FS .50 1.25
309 Aaron Rodgers FS .40 1.00
310 Odell Beckham Jr. FS [illegible]
311 Ben Roethlisberger FS .20 .50
312 Rob Gronkowski FS .20 .50
313 Dez Bryant FS .20 .50
314 Le'Veon Bell FS .15 .40
315 Calvin Johnson FS .20 .50
316 Matthew Stafford FS .15 .40
317 Peyton Manning FS .40 1.00
318 Demaryius Thomas FS .15 .40
319 Jordy Nelson FS .15 .40
320 LeSean McCoy FS .20 .50
321 Andrew Luck FS .25 .60
322 Jamaal Charles FS .15 .40
323 Eddie Lacy FS .12 .30
324 Russell Wilson FS .25 .60
325 Matt Forte FS .12 .30
326 Antonio Brown FS .20 .50
327 Julio Jones FS .20 .50
328 Drew Brees FS .20 .50
329 Adrian Peterson FS .20 .50
330 Marshawn Lynch FS .15 .40
331 J.J. Watt T60 .20 .50
332 LeSean McCoy T60 .20 .50
333 Kam Chancellor T60 .20 .50
334 DeSean Jackson T60 .15 .40
335 Matthew Stafford T60 .15 .40
336 Dez Bryant T60 .20 .50
337 Earl Thomas T60 .15 .40
338 Drew Brees T60 .20 .50
339 T.Y. Hilton T60 .15 .40
340 DeMarco Murray T60 .15 .40
341 Terrell Suggs T60 .12 .30
342 Adrian Peterson T60 .20 .50
343 Julio Jones T60 .20 .50
344 Richard Sherman T60 .20 .50
345 Eddie Lacy T60 .12 .30
346 C.J. Anderson T60 .15 .40
347 Cam Newton T60 .20 .50
348 Jimmy Graham T60 .20 .50
349 Randall Cobb T60 .15 .40
350 Jamaal Charles T60 .15 .40
351 Tom Brady T60 .50 1.25
352 Matt Ryan T60 .15 .40
353 Ben Roethlisberger T60 .20 .50
354 Frank Gore T60 .15 .40
355 Alshon Jeffery T60 .15 .40
356 Patrick Peterson T60 .12 .30
357 Aaron Rodgers T60 .40 1.00
358 Antonio Brown T60 .20 .50
359 Peyton Manning T60 .40 1.00
360 Joe Flacco T60 .15 .40
361 Mario Williams T60 .12 .30
362 Colin Kaepernick T60 .15 .40
363 Calvin Johnson T60 .20 .50
364 Ndamukong Suh T60 .15 .40
365 A.J. Green T60 .20 .50
366 Russell Wilson T60 .25 .60
367 Kelvin Benjamin T60 .15 .40
368 Le'Veon Bell T60 .15 .40
369 Arian Foster T60 .15 .40
370 Jeremy Hill T60 .12 .30
371 Jordy Nelson T60 .15 .40
372 Matt Forte T60 .12 .30
373 Brandon Marshall T60 .12 .30
374 Darrelle Revis T60 .12 .30
375 Andrew Luck T60 .25 .60
376 Justin Houston T60 .12 .30
377 Mike Evans T60 .15 .40
378 Demaryius Thomas T60 .15 .40
379 Marshawn Lynch T60 .15 .40
380 Antonio Gates T60 .12 .30
381 Sammy Watkins T60 .15 .40
382 Tony Romo T60 .15 .40
383 Odell Beckham Jr. T60 .20 .50
384 Eli Manning T60 .15 .40
385 Rob Gronkowski T60 .20 .50
386 Philip Rivers T60 .20 .50
387 Luke Kuechly T60 .15 .40
388 Alfred Morris T60 .12 .30
389 Larry Fitzgerald T60 .15 .40
390 Clay Matthews T60 .20 .50
391A DeVante Parker RC .40 1.00
391B DeVante Parker SP 2.50 6.00
392 Vic Beasley RC .30 .75
393 Michael Bennett RC .25 .60
394 Alex Carter RC .25 .60
395 Paul Dawson RC .30 .75
396 Ereck Flowers RC .30 .75
397 Benardrick McKinney RC .25 .60
398A Nelson Agholor RC .30 .75
398B Nelson Agholor SP 2.00 5.00
399A Chris Conley RC .25 .60
399B Chris Conley SP 1.50 4.00
400 Rookie Premiere .50 1.25
401A Kevin White RC .30 .75
401B Kevin White SP 4.00 10.00
402A Maxx Williams RC .25 .60
402B Maxx Williams SP 1.50 4.00
403 Levi Norwood RC .25 .60
404 Deontay Greenberry RC .25 .60
405 P.J. Williams RC .30 .75
406A Devin Smith RC .25 .60
406B Devin Smith SP 1.50 4.00
407A Sammie Coates RC .30 .75
407B Sammie Coates SP 2.00 5.00
408 Nate Orchard RC .25 .60
409A Breshad Perriman RC .25 .60
409B Breshad Perriman SP 1.50 4.00
410A Javorius Allen RC .30 .75
410B Javorius Allen SP 2.00 5.00
411 Cody Fajardo RC .30 .75
412 D'Joun Smith RC .40 1.00
413 Clive Walford RC .25 .60
414A Phillip Dorsett RC .25 .60
414B Phillip Dorsett SP 1.50 4.00
415 Dominique Brown RC .25 .60
416 Ben Koyack RC .40 1.00
417 Byron Jones RC .40 1.00
418A Devin Funchess RC .40 1.00
418B Devin Funchess SP 2.50 6.00
419 Nick O'Leary RC .25 .60
420 Owamagbe Odighizuwa RC .30 .75
421 Trae Waynes RC .25 .60
422A Todd Gurley RC 1.00 2.50
422B Todd Gurley SP 6.00 15.00
422C Todd Gurley FS 1.25 3.00
423A Melvin Gordon RC .60 1.50
423B Melvin Gordon SP 8.00 20.00
423C Melvin Gordon FS .75 2.00
424 Landon Collins RC .30 .75
425 T.J. Clemmings RC .25 .60
426 Karlos Williams RC .25 .60
427 Shaq Thompson RC .30 .75
428 Tre McBride RC .25 .60
429A Marcus Mariota RC 1.00 2.50
429B Marcus Mariota SP 12.00 30.00
429C Marcus Mariota FS 1.25 3.00
430A T.J. Yeldon RC .25 .60
430B T.J. Yeldon SP 1.50 4.00
431 Eddie Goldman RC .25 .60
432A David Cobb RC .25 .60
432B David Cobb SP 1.50 4.00
433A Jay Ajayi RC .40 1.00
433B Jay Ajayi SP 2.50 6.00
434 Eric Kendricks RC .25 .60
435 D.J. Humphries RC .25 .60
436 Kevin Johnson RC .25 .60
437 Bo Wallace RC .25 .60
438 Marcus Murphy RC .25 .60
439 Eli Harold RC .25 .60
440 Carl Davis RC .30 .75
441 Malcolm Brown RC .30 .75
442A Garrett Grayson RC .25 .60
442B Garrett Grayson SP [illegible]
443 Danielle Hunter RC .30 .75
444 Dante Fowler Jr. RC .40 1.00
445A Jaelen Strong RC .30 .75
445B Jaelen Strong SP 2.00 5.00
446A Ty Montgomery RC .25 .60
446B Ty Montgomery SP 1.50 4.00
447A Brett Hundley RC .25 .60
447B Brett Hundley SP 1.50 4.00
448A Duke Johnson RC .40 1.00
448B Duke Johnson SP 2.50 6.00
449 Dres Anderson RC .25 .60
450A Mike Davis RC .25 .60
450B Mike Davis SP 1.50 4.00
451A Amari Cooper RC .75 2.00
451B Amari Cooper SP 8.00 20.00
451C Amari Cooper FS 1.00 2.50
452A Stefon Diggs RC .60 1.50
452B Stefon Diggs SP 4.00 10.00
453 Joey Iosefa RC .50 1.25
454 La'el Collins RC .30 .75
455 Lorenzo Mauldin RC .25 .60
456 Kenny Bell RC .40 1.00
457 Brandon Scherff RC .40 1.00
458 Dezmin Lewis RC .25 .60
459A Bryce Petty RC .25 .60
459B Bryce Petty SP 1.50 4.00
460 Antwan Goodley RC .25 .60
461 Jesse James RC .30 .75
462A Tyler Lockett RC .40 1.00
462B Tyler Lockett SP 2.50 6.00
463 Marcus Peters RC .40 1.00
464 Cameron Artis-Payne RC .25 .60
465 Jeff Heuerman RC .30 .75
466 Terrence Magee RC .40 1.00
467 Damarious Randall RC .30 .75
468 Shane Carden RC .25 .60
469A Justin Hardy RC .25 .60
469B Justin Hardy SP 1.50 4.00
470 Jalen Collins RC .25 .60
471A Jeremy Langford RC .25 .60
471B Jeremy Langford SP 1.50 4.00
472 Tyler Kroft RC .30 .75
473A David Johnson RC .60 1.50
473B David Johnson SP 4.00 10.00
474A Vince Mayle RC .30 .75
474B Vince Mayle SP 2.00 5.00
475 Shane Ray RC .25 .60
476A Matt Jones RC .25 .60
476B Matt Jones SP 1.50 4.00
477A Dorial Green-Beckham RC .25 .60
477B Dorial Green-Beckham SP 1.50 4.00
478 Jordan Phillips RC .25 .60
479A Leonard Williams RC .25 .60
479B Leonard Williams SP 1.50 4.00
480 Tony Lippett RC .25 .60
481 Mario Alford Jr. RC .25 .60
482 Senquez Golson RC .25 .60
483 Josh Harper RC .25 .60
484 Austin Hill RC .25 .60
485 Andrus Peat RC .25 .60
486 Randy Gregory RC .25 .60
487 Denzel Perryman RC .25 .60
488 Kenny Hilliard RC .25 .60
489 Alvin Dupree RC .30 .75
490A Tevin Coleman RC .30 .75
490B Tevin Coleman SP 2.00 5.00
491 Kaelin Clay RC .25 .60
492 Danny Shelton RC .25 .60
493 Keith Mumphery RC .25 .60
494A Jamison Crowder RC .30 .75
494B Jamison Crowder SP 2.00 5.00
495A Rashad Greene RC .25 .60
495B Rashad Greene SP 1.50 4.00
496 Cedric Ogbuehi RC .25 .60
497A Ameer Abdullah RC .40 1.00
497B Ameer Abdullah SP 2.50 6.00
498 Josh Robinson RC .25 .60
499A Sean Mannion RC .25 .60
499B Sean Mannion SP 1.50 4.00
500A Jameis Winston RC .60 1.50
500B Jameis Winston SP 10.00 25.00
500C Jameis Winston FS .75 2.00

2015 Topps 60th Anniversary Factory Set

COMPLETE SET (500) 35.00 50.00
*VETS: .4X TO 1X BASIC CARDS
*ROOKIES: .4X TO 1X BASIC CARDS

2015 Topps 60th Anniversary Red

*VETS/60: 6X TO 15X BASIC CARDS
*ROOKIES/60: 4X TO 10X BASIC CARDS

2015 Topps Camo

*VETS/399: 2.5X TO 6X BASIC CARDS
*ROOKIES/399: 1.5X TO 4X BASIC CARDS

2015 Topps Gold

*VETS/2014: 1.5X TO 4X BASIC CARDS
*ROOKIES/2014: 1X TO 2.5X BASIC CARDS

2015 Topps Orange

*VETS/75: 5X TO 12X BASIC CARDS
*ROOKIES/75: 3X TO 8X BASIC RC

2015 Topps Pink

*VETS/499: 2X TO 5X BASIC CARDS
*ROOKIES/499: 1.2X TO 3X BASIC CARDS

2015 Topps Super Bowl 50 Parallel

*VETS: .4X TO 1X BASIC CARDS
*ROOKIES: .4X TO 1X BASIC CARDS

2015 Topps Toys R Us Purple Border

*VETS: 3X TO 8X BASIC CARDS
*ROOKIES: 2X TO 5X BASIC CARDS

2015 Topps 1000 Yard Club

1KYCAB Antonio Brown .50 1.25
1KYCAF Arian Foster .40 1.00
1KYCAG A.J. Green .50 1.25
1KYCAJ Alshon Jeffery .40 1.00
1KYCAM Alfred Morris .30 .75
1KYCCJ Calvin Johnson .50 1.25
1KYCDB Dez Bryant .50 1.25
1KYCDH DeAndre Hopkins .40 1.00
1KYCDJ DeSean Jackson .40 1.00
1KYCDM DeMarco Murray .40 1.00
1KYCDT Demaryius Thomas .40 1.00
1KYCEL Eddie Lacy .30 .75
1KYCES Emmanuel Sanders .40 1.00
1KYCFG Frank Gore .40 1.00
1KYCGO Greg Olsen .40 1.00
1KYCGT Golden Tate .30 .75
1KYCJC Jamaal Charles .40 1.00
1KYCJF Justin Forsett .40 1.00
1KYCJH Jeremy Hill .30 .75
1KYCJJ Julio Jones .50 1.25
1KYCJM Jeremy Maclin .30 .75
1KYCJN Jordy Nelson .40 1.00
1KYCKB Kelvin Benjamin .40 1.00
1KYCLB Le'Veon Bell .40 1.00
1KYCLM LeSean McCoy .50 1.25
1KYCME Mike Evans .40 1.00
1KYCMF Matt Forte .30 .75
1KYCML Marshawn Lynch .40 1.00
1KYCOB Odell Beckham Jr. .50 1.25
1KYCRC Randall Cobb .40 1.00
1KYCRG Rob Gronkowski .50 1.25
1KYCSS Steve Smith .40 1.00
1KYCTH T.Y. Hilton .40 1.00
1KYCVJ Vincent Jackson .30 .75
1KYCABO Anquan Boldin .30 .75
1KYCLMI Lamar Miller .30 .75

2015 Topps '63 Mini Autographs

63AAA Ameer Abdullah/100 10.00 25.00
63ABH Brett Hundley/75 15.00 40.00
63ABP Bryce Petty/250 3.00 8.00
63ABPE Breshad Perriman/75
63ACC Chris Conley/250 3.00 8.00
63ADC David Cobb/200 3.00 8.00
63ADF Devin Funchess/75 10.00 25.00
63ADFO Dante Fowler Jr./250 5.00 12.00
63ADJ Duke Johnson/100 10.00 25.00
63ADJO David Johnson/250 10.00 25.00
63ADP DeVante Parker/25
63ADS Devin Smith/100 6.00 15.00
63AJA Jay Ajayi/100 10.00 25.00
63AJC Jamison Crowder/250 4.00 10.00
63AJHA Justin Hardy/250 3.00 8.00
63AJL Jeremy Langford/250 3.00 8.00
63AJS Jaelen Strong/75 8.00 20.00
63AJW Jameis Winston/25 75.00 150.00
63AKW Kevin White/25 30.00 60.00
63ALW Leonard Williams/200 3.00 8.00
63AMD Mike Davis/250
63AMG Melvin Gordon 15.00 40.00
63AMJ Matt Jones/250 10.00 25.00
63AMM Marcus Mariota/25 100.00 200.00
63AMW Maxx Williams/250 3.00 8.00
63ANA Nelson Agholor/25 12.00 30.00
63APD Phillip Dorsett/75 6.00 15.00
63ARG Rashad Greene/250 3.00 8.00
63ASC Sammie Coates/250 4.00 10.00
63ASD Stefon Diggs/250 8.00 20.00
63ASM Sean Mannion/200 3.00 8.00
63ATC Tevin Coleman/200 4.00 10.00
63ATG Todd Gurley/25 50.00 100.00
63ATL Tyler Lockett/250 5.00 12.00
63ATM Ty Montgomery/200 3.00 8.00
63ATY T.J. Yeldon/100 6.00 15.00
63AVM Vince Mayle/250 3.00 8.00

2015 Topps '76 Autographs

76AAA Ameer Abdullah/100 5.00 12.00
76AAC Amari Cooper/25 125.00 250.00
76ABH Brett Hundley/75 25.00 50.00
76ABP Bryce Petty/250 2.50 6.00
76ABPE Breshad Perriman/75 4.00 10.00
76ACC Chris Conley/250 2.50 6.00
76ADC David Cobb/200 2.50 6.00
76ADF Devin Funchess/75 6.00 15.00
76ADFO Dante Fowler Jr./250 4.00 10.00
76ADG Dorial Green-Beckham/100 10.00 25.00
76ADJ Duke Johnson/100 5.00 12.00
76ADJO David Johnson/250 8.00 20.00
76ADP DeVante Parker/25 15.00 40.00
76ADS Devin Smith/100 3.00 8.00
76AJA Jay Ajayi/100 10.00 25.00
76AJAL Javorius Allen/250 3.00 8.00
76AJC Jamison Crowder/250 3.00 8.00
76AJHA Justin Hardy/250 2.50 6.00
76AJL Jeremy Langford/250 2.50 6.00
76AJS Jaelen Strong/75 5.00 12.00
76AJW Jameis Winston/25 150.00 300.00
76AKB Kenny Bell/250 4.00 10.00
76AKW Kevin White/25 30.00 60.00
76AKWI Karlos Williams/250 2.50 6.00
76ALW Leonard Williams/200 2.50 6.00
76AMD Mike Davis/250 2.50 6.00
76AMG Melvin Gordon/25 15.00 40.00
76AMJ Matt Jones/250 10.00 25.00
76AMM Marcus Mariota/25 100.00 200.00
76AMW Maxx Williams/250 2.50 6.00
76ANA Nelson Agholor/25 15.00 40.00
76APD Phillip Dorsett/75 15.00 40.00
76ARG Rashad Greene/250 2.50 6.00
76ASC Sammie Coates/250 3.00 8.00
76ASD Stefon Diggs/250 6.00 15.00
76ASM Sean Mannion/200 2.50 6.00
76ATC Tevin Coleman/200 3.00 8.00
76ATG Todd Gurley/25 50.00 100.00
76ATL Tyler Lockett/250 4.00 10.00
76ATM Ty Montgomery/200 2.50 6.00
76ATY T.J. Yeldon/100 3.00 8.00
76AVM Vince Mayle/250 3.00 8.00

2015 Topps '87 Autographs

87AAA Ameer Abdullah/100 5.00 12.00
87AAC Amari Cooper/25 125.00 250.00
87ABH Brett Hundley/75 25.00 50.00
87ABP Bryce Petty/250 2.50 6.00
87ABPE Breshad Perriman/75 4.00 10.00
87ACC Chris Conley/250 2.50 6.00
87ADC David Cobb/200 2.50 6.00
87ADF Devin Funchess/75 6.00 15.00
87ADFO Dante Fowler Jr./250 4.00 10.00
87ADG Dorial Green-Beckham/100 10.00 25.00
87ADJ Duke Johnson/100 5.00 12.00
87ADJO David Johnson/250 8.00 20.00
87ADP DeVante Parker/25 15.00 40.00
87ADS Devin Smith/100 3.00 8.00
87AJA Jay Ajayi/100 10.00 25.00
87AJAL Javorius Allen/250 3.00 8.00
87AJC Jamison Crowder/250 3.00 8.00
87AJHA Justin Hardy/250 2.50 6.00
87AJL Jeremy Langford/250 2.50 6.00
87AJS Jaelen Strong/75 5.00 12.00
87AJW Jameis Winston/25 150.00 300.00
87AKB Kenny Bell/250 4.00 10.00
87AKW Kevin White/25 30.00 60.00
87ALW Leonard Williams/200 2.50 6.00
87AMD Mike Davis/250 2.50 6.00
87AMG Melvin Gordon/25 15.00 40.00
87AMJ Matt Jones/250 10.00 25.00
87AMM Marcus Mariota/25 100.00 200.00
87AMW Maxx Williams/250 2.50 6.00
87ANA Nelson Agholor/25 15.00 40.00
87APD Phillip Dorsett/75 15.00 40.00
87ARG Rashad Greene/250 2.50 6.00
87ASC Sammie Coates/250 3.00 8.00
87ASD Stefon Diggs/250 6.00 15.00
87ASM Sean Mannion/200 2.50 6.00
87ATC Tevin Coleman/200 3.00 8.00
87ATG Todd Gurley/25 50.00 100.00
87ATL Tyler Lockett/250 4.00 10.00
87ATM Ty Montgomery/200 2.50 6.00
87ATY T.J. Yeldon/100 3.00 8.00
87AVM Vince Mayle/250 3.00 8.00

2015 Topps 4000 Yard Club

4KYCAL Andrew Luck .60 1.50
4KYCAR Aaron Rodgers 1.00 2.50
4KYCBR Ben Roethlisberger .50 1.25
4KYCDB Drew Brees .50 1.25
4KYCEM Eli Manning .40 1.00
4KYCMR Matt Ryan .40 1.00
4KYCMS Matthew Stafford .40 1.00
4KYCPM Peyton Manning 1.00 2.50
4KYCPR Philip Rivers .50 1.25
4KYCRT Ryan Tannehill .40 1.00
4KYCTB Tom Brady 1.25 3.00

2015 Topps 60th Anniversary Throwbacks

T60AA Ameer Abdullah .50 1.25
T60AB Antonio Brown .50 1.25
T60AC Amari Cooper 1.00 2.50
T60AF Arian Foster .40 1.00
T60AG A.J. Green .50 1.25
T60AGA Antonio Gates .30 .75
T60AJ Alshon Jeffery .40 1.00
T60AL Andrew Luck .60 1.50
T60AM Alfred Morris .30 .75
T60AP Adrian Peterson .60 1.25
T60AR Aaron Rodgers 1.00 2.50
T60BF Brett Favre 1.00 2.50
T60BH Brett Hundley .30 .75
T60BJ Bo Jackson .60 1.50
T60BM Brandon Marshall .30 .75
[illegible]
T60BR Ben Roethlisberger .50 1.25
T60BS Barry Sanders .75 2.00
T60CA C.J. Anderson .40 1.00
T60CJ Calvin Johnson .50 1.25
T60CK Colin Kaepernick .40 1.00
T60CM Clay Matthews .50 1.25
T60CN Cam Newton .50 1.25
T60DB Drew Brees .50 1.25
T60DBR Dez Bryant .50 1.25
T60DC David Cobb .30 .75
T60DF Devin Funchess .50 1.25
T60DG Dorial Green-Beckham .30 .75
T60DJO Duke Johnson .50 1.25
T60DM DeMarco Murray .40 1.00
T60DMA Dan Marino 1.00 2.50
T60DP DeVante Parker .50 1.25
T60DS Deion Sanders .40 1.00
T60DSM Devin Smith .30 .75
T60DT Demaryius Thomas .40 1.00
T60EC Earl Campbell .50 1.25
T60ED Eric Dickerson .40 1.00
T60EL Eddie Lacy .30 .75
T60EM Eli Manning .40 1.00
T60ES Emmitt Smith .75 2.00
T60GG Garrett Grayson .30 .75
T60GS Gale Sayers .50 1.25
T60JA Jay Ajayi .50 1.25
T60JC Jamaal Charles .40 1.00
T60JE Julian Edelman .50 1.25
T60JEL John Elway .75 2.00
T60JF Joe Flacco .40 1.00
T60JG Jimmy Graham .50 1.25
T60JJ Julio Jones .50 1.25
T60JM Jeremy Maclin .30 .75
T60JN Jordy Nelson .40 1.00
T60JR Jerry Rice .75 2.00
T60JW J.J. Watt .50 1.25
T60JWI Jameis Winston .75 2.00
T60KB Kelvin Benjamin .40 1.00
T60KW Kevin White .40 1.00
T60KWA Kurt Warner .40 1.00
T60LB Le'Veon Bell .40 1.00
T60LF Larry Fitzgerald .40 1.00
T60LM LeSean McCoy .50 1.25
T60LT Lawrence Taylor .50 1.25
T60LW Leonard Williams .30 .75
T60MD Mike Davis .30 .75
T60ME Mike Evans .40 1.00
T60MF Matt Forte .30 .75
T60MFA Marshall Faulk .40 1.00
T60MG Melvin Gordon .75 2.00
T60ML Marshawn Lynch .40 1.00
T60MM Marcus Mariota 1.25 3.00
T60MR Matt Ryan .40 1.00
T60MS Matthew Stafford .40 1.00
T60MW Maxx Williams .30 .75
T60NA Nelson Agholor .40 1.00
T60OB Odell Beckham Jr. .50 1.25
T60PD Phillip Dorsett .30 .75
T60PH Paul Hornung .50 1.25
T60PM Peyton Manning 1.00 2.50
T60PR Philip Rivers .50 1.25
T60RC Randall Cobb .40 1.00
T60RG Rob Gronkowski .50 1.25
T60RGR Robert Griffin III .30 .75
T60RS Richard Sherman .50 1.25
T60RST Roger Staubach .60 1.50
T60RT Ryan Tannehill .40 1.00
T60RW Russell Wilson .60 1.50
T60SC Sammie Coates .40 1.00
T60SL Steve Largent .50 1.25
T60SW Sammy Watkins .40 1.00
T60SY Steve Young .60 1.50
T60TB1 Tom Brady 1.25 3.00
T60TB2 Tim Brown .50 1.25
T60TBRA Terry Bradshaw .60 1.50
T60TC Tevin Coleman .40 1.00
T60TD Terrell Davis .40 1.00
T60TDO Tony Dorsett .50 1.25
T60TG Todd Gurley 1.25 3.00
T60TH T.Y. Hilton .40 1.00
T60TL Tyler Lockett .50 1.25
T60TP Troy Polamalu .50 1.25
T60TY T.J. Yeldon .30 .75

2015 Topps 60th Anniversary Autographs

T60AAB Antonio Brown
T60AAJ Alshon Jeffery
T60AAL Andrew Luck/15 200.00 300.00
T60AAM Alfred Morris/35 12.00 30.00
T60ABF Brett Favre
T60ABJ Bo Jackson/25 90.00 150.00
T60ABS Barry Sanders/15 40.00 100.00
T60ACM Clay Matthews/25 40.00 100.00
T60ADB Drew Brees/15 150.00 250.00
T60ADM Dan Marino/15 200.00 300.00
T60ADMU DeMarco Murray/35 15.00 40.00
T60ADS Deion Sanders/25 75.00 125.00
T60AEC Earl Campbell
T60AED Eric Dickerson/25 75.00 150.00
T60AEL Eddie Lacy/35 40.00 80.00
T60AEM Eli Manning/15 50.00 100.00
T60AES Emmitt Smith/15
T60AGS Gale Sayers/35 20.00 50.00
T60AJE John Elway/15 300.00 500.00
T60AJH Jeremy Hill/35 30.00 60.00
T60AJNE Jordy Nelson/35 40.00 80.00
T60AJR Jerry Rice/15
T60AKB Kelvin Benjamin/25 15.00 40.00
T60AKW Kurt Warner/25 75.00 150.00
T60ALT Lawrence Taylor/25 60.00 125.00
T60AME Mike Evans 20.00 40.00
T60AMF Matt Forte
T60AMFA Marshall Faulk
T60AML Marshawn Lynch/35 100.00 200.00
T60AMR Matt Ryan
T60AMST Matthew Stafford/25 90.00 150.00
T60AOB Odell Beckham Jr./35 40.00 80.00
T60APH Paul Hornung
T60APM Peyton Manning
T60ARC Randall Cobb/35 15.00 40.00
T60ARG Rob Gronkowski
T60ARS Roger Staubach/15
T60ARSH Richard Sherman/25 75.00 150.00
T60ART Ryan Tannehill/35 75.00 150.00
T60ARW Russell Wilson/15 150.00 250.00
T60ASL Steve Largent/25 20.00 50.00
T60ASW Sammy Watkins/25 40.00 80.00
T60ASY Steve Young/15 75.00 150.00
T60ATBRA Terry Bradshaw/25 150.00 250.00
T60ATBRO Tim Brown/25 50.00 100.00
T60ATD Terrell Davis/25 40.00 100.00
T60ATDO Tony Dorsett/25 50.00 100.00
T60ATED Teddy Bridgewater/25 100.00 200.00
T60ATH T.Y. Hilton
T60ATP Troy Polamalu/35 100.00 200.00
T60RARJ Ron Jaworski 15.00 40.00

2015 Topps 60th Anniversary Medallions Silver

*GOLD/25: .5X TO 1.2X SILVER/50
T60RAB Antonio Brown 20.00 40.00
T60RAF Arian Foster 8.00 20.00
T60RAJG A.J. Green 10.00 25.00
T60RAL Andrew Luck 12.00 30.00
T60RAP Adrian Peterson 12.00 30.00
T60RAR Aaron Rodgers 25.00 50.00
T60RBF Brett Favre
T60RBJ Bo Jackson
T60RBR Ben Roethlisberger 10.00 25.00
T60RBSA Barry Sanders
T60RCJ Calvin Johnson 10.00 25.00
T60RCK Colin Kaepernick 8.00 20.00
T60RCM Clay Matthews 10.00 25.00
T60RCN Cam Newton 10.00 25.00
T60RDB Drew Brees 10.00 25.00
T60RDBR Dez Bryant
T60RDM DeMarco Murray 8.00 20.00
T60RDMA Dan Marino 20.00 50.00
T60RDS Deion Sanders 8.00 20.00
T60RDT Demaryius Thomas 8.00 20.00
T60RED Eric Dickerson 8.00 20.00
T60REL Eddie Lacy 12.00 30.00
T60REM Eli Manning 12.00 30.00
T60RES Emmitt Smith 15.00 40.00
T60RGS Gale Sayers
T60RJBE Jerome Bettis 10.00 25.00
T60RJC Jamaal Charles 8.00 20.00
T60RJE John Elway
T60RJGR Jimmy Graham 10.00 25.00
T60RJJ Julio Jones 10.00 25.00
T60RJJW J.J. Watt 10.00 25.00
T60RJN Jordy Nelson 8.00 20.00
T60RJR Jerry Rice 25.00 50.00
T60RKB Kelvin Benjamin 8.00 20.00
T60RKW Kurt Warner 8.00 20.00
T60RLB Le'Veon Bell 15.00 40.00
T60RLM LeSean McCoy 10.00 25.00
T60RLT Lawrence Taylor 10.00 25.00
T60RMA Marcus Allen 10.00 25.00
T60RME Mike Evans 8.00 20.00
T60RMF Matt Forte 6.00 15.00
T60RMFA Marshall Faulk 15.00 40.00
T60RML Marshawn Lynch 15.00 40.00
T60RMR Matt Ryan 8.00 20.00
T60RMS Matthew Stafford 8.00 20.00
T60RMSI Mike Singletary 10.00 25.00
T60ROBJ Odell Beckham Jr. 10.00 25.00
T60RPM Peyton Manning 15.00 40.00
T60RPR Philip Rivers 10.00 25.00
T60RRG Rob Gronkowski 20.00 40.00
T60RRS Richard Sherman 10.00 25.00
T60RRST Roger Staubach 12.00 30.00
T60RRW Russell Wilson 12.00 30.00
T60RSW Sammy Watkins 8.00 20.00
T60RSY Steve Young 12.00 30.00
T60RTB Tom Brady 25.00 60.00
T60RTBR Terry Bradshaw
T60RTD Terrell Davis 8.00 20.00
T60RTP Troy Polamalu 15.00 40.00
T60RTR Tony Romo 12.00 30.00

2015 Topps All Time Fantasy Legends

ATFLAB Antonio Brown .40 1.00
ATFLAF Arian Foster .30 .75
ATFLAG Antonio Gates .25 .60
ATFLAL Andrew Luck .50 1.25
ATFLAP Adrian Peterson .40 1.00
ATFLAR Aaron Rodgers .75 2.00
ATFLBF Brett Favre .75 2.00
ATFLBJ Bo Jackson .50 1.25
ATFLBS Barry Sanders .60 1.50
ATFLCJ Calvin Johnson .40 1.00
ATFLCM Curtis Martin .30 .75
ATFLDB Drew Brees .40 1.00
ATFLDM Dan Marino .75 2.00
ATFLDT Demaryius Thomas .30 .75
ATFLEC Earl Campbell .40 1.00
ATFLED Eric Dickerson .30 .75
ATFLEG Eddie George .30 .75
ATFLEM Eli Manning .30 .75
ATFLES Emmitt Smith .60 1.50
ATFLGS Gale Sayers .40 1.00
ATFLJB Jerome Bettis .40 1.00
ATFLJE John Elway .60 1.50
ATFLJG Jimmy Graham .40 1.00
ATFLJK Jim Kelly .40 1.00
ATFLJR Jerry Rice .60 1.50
ATFLKW Kurt Warner .30 .75
ATFLLB Le'Veon Bell .30 .75
ATFLLD Len Dawson .40 1.00
ATFLLF Larry Fitzgerald .30 .75
ATFLLT LaDainian Tomlinson .30 .75
ATFLMA Marcus Allen .40 1.00
ATFLMD Mike Ditka .40 1.00
ATFLMF Marshall Faulk .30 .75
ATFLML Marshawn Lynch .30 .75
ATFLPH Paul Hornung .40 1.00
ATFLPM Peyton Manning .75 2.00
ATFLPS Phil Simms .30 .75
ATFLRG Rob Gronkowski .40 1.00
ATFLRS Roger Staubach .50 1.25
ATFLSL Steve Largent .40 1.00
ATFLSY Steve Young .50 1.25
ATFLTB Terry Bradshaw .50 1.25
ATFLTD Terrell Davis .30 .75
ATFLWM Warren Moon .40 1.00
ATFLJNE Jordy Nelson .30 .75
ATFLJRI John Riggins .30 .75
ATFLMFO Matt Forte .25 .60
ATFLTBR Tim Brown .40 1.00
ATFLTDO Tony Dorsett .40 1.00
ATFLTBRA Tom Brady 1.00 2.50

2015 Topps Autographs

1 Brett Favre
3A Jordy Nelson
3B Jordy Nelson
4 Roger Staubach 125.00 200.00
6 A.J. Green 12.00 30.00
10A Eddie Lacy 20.00 50.00
10B Eddie Lacy 20.00 50.00
11A Clay Matthews 40.00 80.00
11B Clay Matthews 40.00 80.00
15A Matt Forte 6.00 15.00
15B Matt Forte 6.00 15.00
15C Gale Sayers 25.00 50.00
16 Giovani Bernard 6.00 15.00
20A Randall Cobb 12.00 30.00
20B Randall Cobb 12.00 30.00
25 Kelvin Benjamin 8.00 20.00
33 Luke Kuechly 12.00 30.00
40 Emmitt Smith
40A DeMarco Murray 8.00 20.00
40B DeMarco Murray 8.00 20.00
44 Ronnie Lott
50 Matt Ryan 12.00 30.00
55 Deion Sanders 20.00 40.00
60 Jeremy Hill
65A Alshon Jeffery 8.00 20.00
65B Alshon Jeffery 8.00 20.00
70 Barry Sanders
74 Isaiah Crowell 6.00 15.00
75 Earl Campbell 20.00 40.00
80 Peyton Manning
82 Greg Olsen 8.00 20.00
90 Matthew Stafford
95A Sammy Watkins 8.00 20.00
95B Sammy Watkins 8.00 20.00
105A Jamaal Charles
105B Jamaal Charles
106 DeAndre Hopkins
118 Travis Kelce 10.00 25.00
120A Odell Beckham Jr. 40.00 80.00
120B Odell Beckham Jr. 40.00 80.00
120C Jerry Rice
130 Terry Bradshaw
135 Jordan Matthews 8.00 20.00
150 Drew Brees
155A Eli Manning
155B Eli Manning
156 Brandin Cooks 8.00 20.00
160 Andrew Luck
181 Pierre Garcon 8.00 20.00
182 T.Y. Hilton 8.00 20.00
184 Rashad Jennings 6.00 15.00
186 Lawrence Taylor 20.00 40.00
190 Derek Carr 10.00 25.00
195 Teddy Bridgewater
198A Ryan Tannehill 8.00 20.00
198B Dan Marino 75.00 150.00
205A Mike Evans 8.00 20.00
205B Mike Evans 8.00 20.00
206A Marshawn Lynch 40.00 80.00
206B Terrell Davis 8.00 20.00
208 Alfred Morris 12.00 30.00
209 Richard Sherman
212 Mike Singletary 20.00 40.00
220 C.J. Anderson
225 Bo Jackson
229 Marshall Faulk 12.00 30.00
230 Steve Young
235 Russell Wilson
239 Earl Thomas
240A Antonio Brown 20.00 40.00
240B Antonio Brown 20.00 40.00
391A DeVante Parker 12.00 30.00
391B DeVante Parker 12.00 30.00
398A Nelson Agholor 5.00 12.00
398B Nelson Agholor 5.00 12.00
399A Chris Conley 4.00 10.00
399B Chris Conley 4.00 10.00
401A Kevin White 20.00 50.00
401B Kevin White 20.00 50.00
402A Maxx Williams 4.00 10.00
402B Maxx Williams 4.00 10.00
406A Devin Smith
406B Devin Smith
407A Sammie Coates 10.00 25.00
407B Sammie Coates 10.00 25.00
409 Breshad Perriman 4.00 10.00
413A Clive Walford 4.00 10.00
413B Clive Walford 4.00 10.00
414 Phillip Dorsett 4.00 10.00
416A Ben Koyack 6.00 15.00
416B Ben Koyack 6.00 15.00
418 Devin Funchess 6.00 15.00
422A Todd Gurley 25.00 50.00
422B Todd Gurley 25.00 50.00
423A Melvin Gordon 20.00 50.00
423B Melvin Gordon 20.00 50.00
426 Karlos Williams 4.00 10.00
428 Tre McBride 5.00 12.00
429A Marcus Mariota 60.00 125.00
429B Marcus Mariota 60.00 125.00
430A T.J. Yeldon 4.00 10.00
430B T.J. Yeldon 4.00 10.00
432A David Cobb 4.00 10.00
432B David Cobb 4.00 10.00
433A Jay Ajayi 12.00 30.00
433B Jay Ajayi 12.00 30.00
444A Dante Fowler Jr. 6.00 15.00
444B Dante Fowler Jr. 6.00 15.00
445 Jaelen Strong 5.00 12.00
446 Ty Montgomery 4.00 10.00
447A Brett Hundley 4.00 10.00
447B Brett Hundley 4.00 10.00
448A Duke Johnson 6.00 15.00
448B Duke Johnson 6.00 15.00
450A Mike Davis 4.00 10.00
450B Mike Davis 4.00 10.00
451A Amari Cooper
451B Amari Cooper
452A Stefon Diggs 10.00 25.00
452B Stefon Diggs 10.00 25.00
454A Jameis Winston 75.00 125.00
454B Jameis Winston 75.00 125.00
456 Kenny Bell 6.00 15.00
459A Bryce Petty 4.00 10.00
459B Bryce Petty 4.00 10.00
461 Jesse James 5.00 12.00
462A Tyler Lockett 6.00 15.00
462B Tyler Lockett 6.00 15.00
464A Cameron Artis-Payne 4.00 10.00
464B Cameron Artis-Payne 4.00 10.00
465 Jeff Heuerman 5.00 12.00
469A Justin Hardy 6.00 15.00
469B Justin Hardy 6.00 15.00
471A Jeremy Langford 4.00 10.00
471B Jeremy Langford 4.00 10.00
473A David Johnson 10.00 25.00
473B David Johnson 10.00 25.00
474A Vince Mayle 5.00 12.00
474B Vince Mayle 5.00 12.00
477A Dorial Green-Beckham
477B Dorial Green-Beckham
490A Tevin Coleman 5.00 12.00
490B Tevin Coleman 5.00 12.00
494A Jamison Crowder 5.00 12.00
494B Jamison Crowder 5.00 12.00
495A Rashad Greene 4.00 10.00
495B Rashad Greene 4.00 10.00
497A Ameer Abdullah 6.00 15.00
497B Ameer Abdullah 6.00 15.00
499A Sean Mannion 4.00 10.00
499B Sean Mannion 4.00 10.00

2015 Topps Fantasy Focus

FFAB Antonio Brown .50 1.25
FFAF Arian Foster .40 1.00
FFAG A.J. Green .50 1.25
FFAJ Alshon Jeffery .40 1.00
FFAL Andrew Luck .60 1.50
FFAM Alfred Morris .30 .75
FFAP Adrian Peterson .50 1.25
FFAR Aaron Rodgers 1.00 2.50
FFBR Ben Roethlisberger .50 1.25
FFCA C.J. Anderson .40 1.00
FFCH Carlos Hyde .30 .75
FFCJ Calvin Johnson .50 1.25
FFCK Colin Kaepernick .40 1.00
FFDB Dez Bryant .50 1.25
FFDH DeAndre Hopkins .40 1.00
FFDJ DeSean Jackson .40 1.00
FFDM DeMarco Murray .40 1.00
FFDT Demaryius Thomas .40 1.00
FFEL Eddie Lacy .30 .75
FFEM Eli Manning .40 1.00
FFES Emmanuel Sanders .40 1.00
FFFG Frank Gore .40 1.00
FFJC Jamaal Charles .40 1.00
FFJG Jimmy Graham .50 1.25
FFJH Jeremy Hill .30 .75
FFJJ Julio Jones .50 1.25
FFJM Jeremy Maclin .30 .75
FFJN Jordy Nelson .40 1.00
FFKB Kelvin Benjamin .40 1.00
FFLB Le'Veon Bell .40 1.00
FFLM LeSean McCoy .50 1.25
FFME Mike Evans .40 1.00
FFMF Matt Forte .30 .75
FFMI Mark Ingram .40 1.00
FFML Marshawn Lynch .40 1.00
FFMR Matt Ryan .40 1.00
FFMS Matthew Stafford .40 1.00
FFOB Odell Beckham Jr. .50 1.25
FFPM Peyton Manning 1.00 2.50
FFPR Philip Rivers .50 1.25
FFRC Randall Cobb .40 1.00
FFRG Rob Gronkowski .50 1.25
FFRT Ryan Tannehill .40 1.00
FFSW Sammy Watkins .40 1.00
FFTB Tom Brady 1.25 3.00
FFTH T.Y. Hilton .40 1.00
FFTR Tony Romo .40 1.00
FFDBR Drew Brees .50 1.25
FFLMI Lamar Miller .30 .75
FFTBR Teddy Bridgewater .40 1.00

2015 Topps NFL Captains Patches
*CAMO/50: .5X TO 1.2X BASIC PATCH/99
*PINK/25: .6X TO 1.5X BASIC PATCH/99
CPAD Andy Dalton 5.00 12.00
CPAR Aaron Rodgers 12.00 30.00
CPCN Cam Newton 6.00 15.00
CPCP Carson Palmer 5.00 12.00
CPDB Drew Brees 8.00 20.00
CPDT Demaryius Thomas 5.00 12.00
CPEM Eli Manning 10.00 25.00
CPFJ Fred Jackson 5.00 12.00
CPGM Gerald McCoy 4.00 10.00
CPJN Jordy Nelson 10.00 25.00
CPJW Jason Witten 5.00 12.00
CPKC Kam Chancellor 10.00 25.00
CPLK Luke Kuechly 10.00 25.00
CPMR Matt Ryan 10.00 25.00
CPPM Peyton Manning 12.00 30.00
CPPR Philip Rivers 6.00 15.00
CPRT Ryan Tannehill 8.00 20.00
CPRW Russell Wilson 8.00 20.00
CPTR Tony Romo 5.00 12.00
CPRWH Roddy White 4.00 10.00

2015 Topps Past and Present Performers
PPPAD C.Anderson/T.Davis .40 1.00
PPPBB L.Bell/J.Bettis .50 1.25
PPPBSM D.Bryant/E.Smith .75 2.00
PPPBTA O.Beckham/L.Taylor .50 1.25
PPPCB D.Carr/T.Brown .50 1.25
PPPCJ A.Cooper/B.Jackson 1.00 2.50
PPPFS M.Forte/G.Sayers .50 1.25
PPPGT M.Gordon/L.Tomlinson .75 2.00
PPPGW A.Green/I.Woods .50 1.25
PPPHW J.Hill/I.Woods .30 .75
PPPJS C.Johnson/B.Sanders .75 2.00
PPPKY C.Kaepernick/S.Young .60 1.50
PPPLF E.Lacy/B.Favre 1.00 2.50
PPPME P.Manning/J.Elway 1.00 2.50
PPPMF T.Mason/M.Faulk .40 1.00
PPPMR A.Morris/J.Riggins .40 1.00
PPPMS T.Romo/E.Smith .75 2.00
PPPMSI E.Manning/P.Simms .40 1.00
PPPNH J.Nelson/P.Hornung .50 1.25
PPPPG T.Polamalu/J.Greene .50 1.25
PPPPW T.Polamalu/R.Woodson .50 1.25
PPPRB B.Rthlsbrgr/T.Bradshaw .60 1.50
PPPRF A.Rodgers/B.Favre 1.00 2.50
PPPRH A.Rodgers/P.Hornung 1.00 2.50
PPPROST T.Romo/R.Staubach .60 1.50
PPPSD A.Smith/L.Dawson .50 1.25
PPPSS M.Stafford/B.Sanders .75 2.00
PPPTM R.Tannehill/D.Marino 1.00 2.50
PPPWK S.Watkins/J.Kelly .50 1.25
PPPWL R.Wilson/S.Largent .60 1.50

2015 Topps Presidential Celebration
PC1 Jimmy Carter 4.00 10.00
PC2 George H.W. Bush 4.00 10.00
PC3 Barack Obama 4.00 10.00
PC4 Barack Obama 4.00 10.00
PC5 Bill Clinton 4.00 10.00
PC6 George W. Bush 4.00 10.00
PC7 George W. Bush 4.00 10.00
PC8 George W. Bush 4.00 10.00
PC9 George W. Bush 4.00 10.00
PC10 Barack Obama 4.00 10.00
PC11 Barack Obama 4.00 10.00
PC12 Barack Obama 4.00 10.00
PC13 Barack Obama 4.00 10.00
PC14 Barack Obama 4.00 10.00

2015 Topps Quarterback Club Bronze
*SILVER/50: .5X TO 1.2X BRONZE/75
*GOLD/25: .6X TO 1.5X BRONZE/75
QBFCAL Andrew Luck 10.00 25.00
QBFCAR Aaron Rodgers 15.00 40.00
QBFCBR Ben Roethlisberger 10.00 25.00
QBFCCK Colin Kaepernick 6.00 15.00
QBFCCN Cam Newton 8.00 20.00
QBFCDB Drew Brees 10.00 25.00
QBFCDC Derek Carr 8.00 20.00
QBFCEM Eli Manning 6.00 15.00
QBFCJC Jay Cutler 5.00 12.00
QBFCJF Joe Flacco 6.00 15.00
QBFCMR Matt Ryan 6.00 15.00
QBFCMS Matthew Stafford 6.00 15.00
QBFCPM Peyton Manning 15.00 40.00
QBFCPR Philip Rivers 8.00 20.00
QBFCRG Robert Griffin III 5.00 12.00
QBFCRT Ryan Tannehill 6.00 15.00
QBFCRW Russell Wilson 10.00 25.00
QBFCTB Tom Brady 20.00 50.00
QBFCTR Tony Romo 6.00 15.00
QBFCTBR Teddy Bridgewater 6.00 15.00

2015 Topps Relics
TRAA Ameer Abdullah 2.00 5.00
TRAC Amari Cooper 4.00 10.00
TRAG Antonio Gates 2.00 5.00
TRAJ Alshon Jeffery 2.50 6.00
TRAL Andrew Luck 4.00 10.00
TRBB Blake Bortles 2.00 5.00
TRBC Brandin Cooks 2.50 6.00
TRCH Carlos Hyde 2.00 5.00
TRCN Cam Newton 3.00 8.00
TRDA Davante Adams 2.50 6.00
TRDB Drew Brees 3.00 8.00
TRDC Derek Carr 3.00 8.00
TRDH DeAndre Hopkins 2.50 6.00
TRDP DeVante Parker 2.00 5.00
TREL Eddie Lacy 2.00 5.00
TRET Earl Thomas 2.50 6.00
TRGB Giovani Bernard 2.00 5.00
TRJC Jadeveon Clowney 2.00 5.00
TRJH Jeremy Hill 2.00 5.00
TRJJ Julio Jones 3.00 8.00
TRJL Jarvis Landry 2.50 6.00
TRJM Johnny Manziel 2.50 6.00
TRJW Jameis Winston 3.00 8.00
TRKB Kelvin Benjamin 2.50 6.00
TRLB Le'Veon Bell 2.50 6.00
TRLM Lamar Miller 2.00 5.00
TRME Mike Evans 2.50 6.00
TRMG Melvin Gordon 3.00 8.00
TRMM Marcus Mariota 6.00 15.00
TRNA Nelson Agholor 1.50 4.00
TROB Odell Beckham Jr. 3.00 8.00
TRPW Patrick Willis 2.50 6.00
TRRC Randall Cobb 2.50 6.00
TRRG Robert Griffin III 2.00 5.00
TRRT Ryan Tannehill 2.50 6.00
TRRW Russell Wilson 4.00 10.00
TRSW Sammy Watkins 2.50 6.00
TRTB Teddy Bridgewater 2.50 6.00
TRTG Todd Gurley 5.00 12.00
TRTH T.Y. Hilton 2.50 6.00
TRTM Tre Mason 2.50 6.00
TRTY T.J. Yeldon 1.25 3.00
TRAGR A.J. Green 3.00 8.00
TRDGB Dorial Green-Beckham 1.25 3.00
TRDTH Demaryius Thomas 2.50 6.00
TRJCH Jamaal Charles 2.50 6.00
TRJMA Jordan Matthews 2.50 6.00
TRKWH Kevin White 1.50 4.00
TRRGR Rob Gronkowski 3.00 8.00
TRRWH Roddy White 2.00 5.00

2015 Topps Relics Autographs
TARAB Antonio Brown/25 25.00 50.00
TARAG A.J. Green/25 15.00 30.00
TARAL Andrew Luck
TARCM Clay Matthews/50 40.00 80.00
TARDC Derek Carr/50 10.00 25.00
TARDH DeAndre Hopkins/50 8.00 20.00
TARDMO Donte Moncrief/50 15.00 30.00
TAREL Eddie Lacy/50 20.00 40.00
TAREM Eli Manning
TARGS Gale Sayers/50 20.00 40.00
TARJC Jamaal Charles/50 15.00 30.00
TARJE John Elway
TARJH Jeremy Hill/50 6.00 15.00
TARJHA Joe Haden/50 10.00 25.00
TARJMA Jordan Matthews
TARKB Kelvin Benjamin/50 8.00 20.00
TARLMI Lamar Miller/50 6.00 15.00
TARMB Martavis Bryant/50 15.00 30.00
TARME Mike Evans/50 8.00 20.00
TARMI Mark Ingram/50 10.00 25.00
TARML Marshawn Lynch/50 30.00 60.00
TARMR Matt Ryan/25 12.00 30.00
TARMS Mike Singletary/50 10.00 25.00
TAROBJ Odell Beckham Jr./50 40.00 80.00
TARRC Randall Cobb/50 10.00 25.00
TARRT Ryan Tannehill/50 12.00 30.00
TARSW Sammy Watkins/50
TARTB Tim Brown/35 20.00 50.00
TARTYH T.Y. Hilton/50

2015 Topps Rookie Jumbo Relics
RJRAA Ameer Abdullah 2.50 6.00
RJRAC Amari Cooper 5.00 12.00
RJRBH Brett Hundley 1.50 4.00
RJRBP Bryce Petty 1.50 4.00
RJRCC Chris Conley 1.50 4.00
RJRDC David Cobb 1.50 4.00
RJRDG Dorial Green-Beckham 1.50 4.00
RJRDJ Duke Johnson 2.50 6.00
RJRDP DeVante Parker 2.50 6.00
RJRDS Devin Smith 1.50 4.00
RJRGG Garrett Grayson 1.50 4.00
RJRJA Jay Ajayi 2.50 6.00
RJRJC Jamison Crowder 2.00 5.00
RJRJL Jeremy Langford 1.50 4.00
RJRJS Jaelen Strong 2.00 5.00
RJRJW Jameis Winston 8.00 20.00
RJRKW Kevin White
RJRLW Leonard Williams 1.50 4.00
RJRMD Mike Davis 1.50 4.00
RJRMG Melvin Gordon 4.00 10.00
RJRMJ Matt Jones 1.50 4.00
RJRMM Marcus Mariota 6.00 15.00
RJRMW Maxx Williams 1.50 4.00
RJRNA Nelson Agholor 2.00 5.00
RJRPD Phillip Dorsett 1.50 4.00
RJRRG Rashad Greene 1.50 4.00
RJRSC Sammie Coates 2.00 5.00
RJRSD Stefon Diggs 4.00 10.00
RJRSM Sean Mannion 1.50 4.00
RJRTC Tevin Coleman 2.00 5.00
RJRTG Todd Gurley
RJRTL Tyler Lockett 2.50 6.00
RJRTM Ty Montgomery 1.50 4.00
RJRTY T.J. Yeldon 1.50 4.00
RJRVM Vince Mayle 2.00 5.00
RJRBPE Breshad Perriman 1.50 4.00
RJRDJO David Johnson 4.00 10.00
RJRJAL Javorius Allen 2.00 5.00
RJRJHA Justin Hardy 1.50 4.00

2015 Topps Rookie Patch
TRPAA Ameer Abdullah 2.50 6.00
TRPAC Amari Cooper 5.00 12.00
TRPBH Brett Hundley 1.50 4.00
TRPBP Bryce Petty 1.50 4.00
TRPCC Chris Conley 1.50 4.00
TRPDC David Cobb 1.50 4.00
TRPDG Dorial Green-Beckham 1.50 4.00
TRPDJ Duke Johnson 2.50 6.00
TRPDP DeVante Parker 2.50 6.00
TRPDS Devin Smith 1.50 4.00
TRPGG Garrett Grayson 1.50 4.00
TRPJA Jay Ajayi 2.50 6.00
TRPJC Jamison Crowder 2.00 5.00
TRPJL Jeremy Langford 1.50 4.00
TRPJS Jaelen Strong 2.00 5.00
TRPJW Jameis Winston 8.00 20.00
TRPKW Kevin White 6.00 15.00
TRPLW Leonard Williams 1.50 4.00
TRPMD Mike Davis 1.50 4.00
TRPMG Melvin Gordon 4.00 10.00
TRPMJ Matt Jones 1.50 4.00
TRPMM Marcus Mariota 6.00 15.00
TRPMW Maxx Williams 1.50 4.00
TRPNA Nelson Agholor 2.00 5.00
TRPPD Phillip Dorsett 1.50 4.00
TRPRG Rashad Greene 1.50 4.00
TRPSC Sammie Coates 2.00 5.00
TRPSD Stefon Diggs 4.00 10.00
TRPSM Sean Mannion 1.50 4.00
TRPTC Tevin Coleman 2.00 5.00
TRPTG Todd Gurley 6.00 15.00
TRPTL Tyler Lockett 2.50 6.00
TRPTM Ty Montgomery 1.50 4.00
TRPTY T.J. Yeldon 1.50 4.00
TRPVM Vince Mayle 2.00 5.00
TRPBPE Breshad Perriman 1.50 4.00
TRPDJO David Johnson 4.00 10.00
TRPJAL Javorius Allen 2.00 5.00
TRPJHA Justin Hardy 1.50 4.00

2015 Topps Rookie Patch Autographs Jumbo
RPAAA Ameer Abdullah 8.00 20.00
RPAAC Amari Cooper 40.00 80.00
RPABH Brett Hundley 5.00 12.00
RPABP Bryce Petty 5.00 12.00
RPABPE Breshad Perriman 5.00 12.00
RPACC Chris Conley 5.00 12.00
RPADC David Cobb 5.00 12.00
RPADGB Dorial Green-Beckham 5.00 12.00
RPADJ David Johnson 12.00 30.00
RPADJU Duke Johnson 8.00 20.00
RPADPA DeVante Parker 8.00 20.00
RPADS Devin Smith 5.00 12.00
RPAJA Jay Ajayi 12.00 30.00
RPAJAL Javorius Allen 6.00 15.00
RPAJC Jamison Crowder 6.00 15.00
RPAJH Justin Hardy 5.00 12.00
RPAJL Jeremy Langford 5.00 12.00
RPAJS Jaelen Strong 6.00 15.00
RPAJW Jameis Winston 75.00 150.00
RPAKW Karlos Williams 5.00 12.00
RPAKWH Kevin White 12.00 30.00
RPALW Leonard Williams 5.00 12.00
RPAMD Mike Davis 5.00 12.00
RPAMG Melvin Gordon 20.00 50.00
RPAMM Marcus Mariota 100.00 200.00
RPAMW Maxx Williams 5.00 12.00
RPANA Nelson Agholor 6.00 15.00
RPAPD Phillip Dorsett 5.00 12.00
RPARG Rashad Greene
RPASCO Sammie Coates 25.00 50.00
RPASD Stefon Diggs 12.00 30.00
RPASM Sean Mannion 5.00 12.00
RPATC Tevin Coleman 6.00 15.00
RPATG Todd Gurley 30.00 60.00
RPATLO Tyler Lockett 8.00 20.00
RPATY T.J. Yeldon 5.00 12.00
RPAVM Vince Mayle 6.00 15.00
RPATMO Ty Montgomery 5.00 12.00

2015 Topps Rookie Premiere Autographs
RPAAA Ameer Abdullah/75 10.00 25.00
RPAAC Amari Cooper/25 90.00 150.00
RPABH Brett Hundley/25 30.00 60.00
RPABP Bryce Petty/150 5.00 12.00
RPABPE Breshad Perriman/50 8.00 20.00
RPACC Chris Conley/150 5.00 12.00
RPADC David Cobb/150 5.00 12.00
RPADG Dorial Green-Beckham/50 15.00 40.00
RPADJ Duke Johnson/75 10.00 25.00
RPADJO David Johnson/75 15.00 40.00
RPADP DeVante Parker/25 15.00 40.00
RPADS Devin Smith/75 6.00 15.00
RPAJAL Javorius Allen/150 6.00 15.00
RPAJC Jamison Crowder/150 6.00 15.00
RPAJHA Justin Hardy/150 5.00 12.00
RPAJL Jeremy Langford/150 5.00 12.00
RPAJS Jaelen Strong/25 12.00 30.00
RPAJW Jameis Winston/25 200.00 300.00
RPAKW Kevin White/25 30.00 80.00
RPAKWI Karlos Williams/150 5.00 12.00
RPALW Leonard Williams/75 6.00 15.00
RPAMD Mike Davis/150 5.00 12.00
RPAMG Melvin Gordon/25 25.00 60.00
RPAMJ Matt Jones/150 5.00 12.00
RPAMM Marcus Mariota/25 150.00 300.00
RPAMW Maxx Williams/150 5.00 12.00
RPANA Nelson Agholor/25 12.00 30.00
RPAPD Phillip Dorsett/50 8.00 20.00
RPARG Rashad Greene/150 6.00 15.00
RPASC Sammie Coates/150 6.00 15.00
RPASD Stefon Diggs/150 12.00 30.00
RPASM Sean Mannion/75 6.00 15.00
RPATC Tevin Coleman/150 6.00 15.00
RPATG Todd Gurley/25 50.00 100.00
RPATL Tyler Lockett/150 8.00 20.00
RPATM Ty Montgomery/75 6.00 15.00
RPATY T.J. Yeldon/75 6.00 15.00
RPAVM Vince Mayle/150 6.00 15.00

2015 Topps Running Back Club Bronze
*SILVER/50: .5X TO 1.2X BRONZE/75
*GOLD/25: .6X TO 1.5X BRONZE/75
RBFCAF Arian Foster 6.00 15.00
RBFCAM Alfred Morris 5.00 12.00
RBFCAP Adrian Peterson 12.00 30.00
RBFCCA C.J. Anderson 6.00 15.00
RBFCCH Carlos Hyde 5.00 12.00
RBFCDM DeMarco Murray 6.00 15.00
RBFCEL Eddie Lacy 5.00 12.00
RBFCFG Frank Gore 6.00 15.00
RBFCGB Giovani Bernard 5.00 12.00
RBFCJB Joique Bell 5.00 12.00
RBFCJC Jamaal Charles 6.00 15.00
RBFCJH Jeremy Hill 5.00 12.00
RBFCLB Le'Veon Bell 6.00 15.00
RBFCLM LeSean McCoy 8.00 20.00
RBFCMF Matt Forte 5.00 12.00
RBFCMI Mark Ingram 6.00 15.00
RBFCML Marshawn Lynch 15.00 40.00
RBFCTM Tre Mason 6.00 15.00
RBFCLMI Lamar Miller 5.00 12.00
RBFCLMU Latavius Murray 5.00 12.00

2015 Topps Signatures
TAAA Ameer Abdullah 10.00 25.00
TAAC Amari Cooper
TAAJ Alshon Jeffery 4.00 10.00
TAAL Andrew Luck
TAARO Allen Robinson 4.00 10.00
TABC Brandin Cooks 6.00 15.00
TABH Brett Hundley
TABP Bryce Petty 2.50 6.00
TABPE Breshad Perriman
TABS Bishop Sankey 3.00 8.00
TABSA Barry Sanders 75.00 125.00
TACA C.J. Anderson
TACAP Cameron Artis-Payne 2.50 6.00
TACCO Chris Conley 2.50 6.00
TADA Davante Adams
TADC David Cobb 4.00 10.00
TADGB Dorial Green-Beckham 2.50 6.00
TADJ David Johnson 6.00 15.00
TADJO Duke Johnson 4.00 10.00
TADM Donte Moncrief 4.00 10.00
TADMU DeMarco Murray 30.00 60.00
TADP DeVante Parker 20.00 40.00
TADS Devin Smith 2.50 6.00
TAEB Eric Berry 20.00 40.00
TAEL Eddie Lacy 15.00 30.00
TAEM Eli Manning
TAES Emmanuel Sanders 8.00 20.00
TAGO Greg Olsen 4.00 10.00
TAIC Isaiah Crowell 3.00 8.00
TAJAJ Jay Ajayi 8.00 20.00
TAJBE Joique Bell 3.00 8.00
TAJH Jeremy Hill
TAJHA Joe Haden 3.00 8.00
TAJLA Jeremy Langford 2.50 6.00
TAJMA Jordan Matthews 4.00 10.00
TAJMAN Johnny Manziel 30.00 60.00
TAJR Jordan Reed 3.00 8.00
TAJW Jameis Winston
TAKB Kelvin Benjamin 4.00 10.00
TAKBE Kenny Bell 4.00 10.00
TAKS Kenny Stills 6.00 15.00
TAKW Kevin White
TAKWI Karlos Williams 2.50 6.00
TALK Luke Kuechly 30.00 60.00
TAMB Martavis Bryant 3.00 8.00
TAMD Mike Davis 2.50 6.00
TAMG Melvin Gordon 15.00 40.00
TAMI Mark Ingram 6.00 15.00
TAML Marqise Lee 3.00 8.00
TAMM Marcus Mariota 50.00 100.00
TAMR Matt Ryan 20.00 40.00
TAMS Mike Singletary 10.00 25.00
TANA Nelson Agholor 3.00 8.00
TAOB Odell Beckham Jr. 30.00 60.00
TAPD Phillip Dorsett 2.50 6.00
TAPG Pierre Garcon 4.00 10.00
TAPM Peyton Manning 100.00 200.00
TARCR Roger Craig 4.00 10.00
TARG Rashad Greene 2.50 6.00
TASC Sammie Coates 6.00 15.00
TASD Stefon Diggs 6.00 15.00
TATC Tevin Coleman
TATG Todd Gurley 25.00 50.00
TATK Travis Kelce 5.00 12.00
TATLO Tyler Lockett 4.00 10.00
TATY T.J. Yeldon 2.50 6.00

2015 Topps Super Bowl Coins
*SILVER/99: .5X TO 1.2X BASIC COIN
*GOLD/50: .6X TO 1.5X BASIC COIN
NFLSBC1 SUPER BOWL I 6.00 15.00
NFLSBC2 SUPER BOWL II 6.00 15.00
NFLSBC3 SUPER BOWL III 6.00 15.00
NFLSBC4 SUPER BOWL IV 6.00 15.00
NFLSBC5 SUPER BOWL V 6.00 15.00
NFLSBC6 SUPER BOWL VI 6.00 15.00
NFLSBC7 SUPER BOWL VII 6.00 15.00
NFLSBC8 SUPER BOWL VIII 6.00 15.00
NFLSBC9 SUPER BOWL IX 6.00 15.00
NFLSBC10 SUPER BOWL X 6.00 15.00
NFLSBC11 SUPER BOWL XI 6.00 15.00
NFLSBC12 SUPER BOWL XII 6.00 15.00
NFLSBC13 SUPER BOWL XIII 6.00 15.00
NFLSBC14 SUPER BOWL XIV 6.00 15.00
NFLSBC15 SUPER BOWL XV 6.00 15.00
NFLSBC16 SUPER BOWL XVI 6.00 15.00
NFLSBC17 SUPER BOWL XVII 6.00 15.00
NFLSBC18 SUPER BOWL XVIII 6.00 15.00
NFLSBC19 SUPER BOWL XIX 6.00 15.00
NFLSBC20 SUPER BOWL XX 6.00 15.00
NFLSBC21 SUPER BOWL XXI 6.00 15.00
NFLSBC22 SUPER BOWL XXII 6.00 15.00
NFLSBC23 SUPER BOWL XXIII 6.00 15.00
NFLSBC24 SUPER BOWL XXIV 6.00 15.00
NFLSBC25 SUPER BOWL XXV 6.00 15.00
NFLSBC26 SUPER BOWL XXVI 6.00 15.00
NFLSBC27 SUPER BOWL XXVII 6.00 15.00
NFLSBC28 SUPER BOWL XXVIII 6.00 15.00
NFLSBC29 SUPER BOWL XXIX 6.00 15.00
NFLSBC30 SUPER BOWL XXX 6.00 15.00
NFLSBC31 SUPER BOWL XXXI 6.00 15.00
NFLSBC32 SUPER BOWL XXXII 6.00 15.00
NFLSBC33 SUPER BOWL XXXIII 6.00 15.00
NFLSBC34 SUPER BOWL XXXIV 6.00 15.00
NFLSBC35 SUPER BOWL XXXV 6.00 15.00
NFLSBC36 SUPER BOWL XXXVI 6.00 15.00
NFLSBC37 SUPER BOWL XXXVII 6.00 15.00
NFLSBC38 SUPER BOWL XXXVIII 6.00 15.00
NFLSBC39 SUPER BOWL XXXIX 6.00 15.00
NFLSBC40 SUPER BOWL XL 6.00 15.00
NFLSBC41 SUPER BOWL XLI 6.00 15.00
NFLSBC42 SUPER BOWL XLII 6.00 15.00
NFLSBC43 SUPER BOWL XLIII 6.00 15.00
NFLSBC44 SUPER BOWL XLIV 6.00 15.00
NFLSBC45 SUPER BOWL XLV 6.00 15.00
NFLSBC46 SUPER BOWL XLVI 6.00 15.00
NFLSBC47 SUPER BOWL XLVII 6.00 15.00
NFLSBC48 SUPER BOWL XLVIII 6.00 15.00
NFLSBC49 SUPER BOWL XLIX 6.00 15.00

2015 Topps Wide Receivers Club Bronze
*SILVER/50: .5X TO 1.2X BRONZE/75
*GOLD/25: .6X TO 1.5X BRONZE/75
WRFCAB Antonio Brown 10.00 25.00
WRFCAG A.J. Green 8.00 20.00
WRFCAJ Alshon Jeffery 6.00 15.00
WRFCBC Brandin Cooks 6.00 15.00
WRFCBM Brandon Marshall 5.00 12.00
WRFCCJ Calvin Johnson 8.00 20.00
WRFCDB Dez Bryant 8.00 20.00
WRFCDH DeAndre Hopkins 6.00 15.00
WRFCDJ DeSean Jackson 6.00 15.00
WRFCDT Demaryius Thomas 6.00 15.00
WRFCES Emmanuel Sanders 6.00 15.00
WRFCGT Golden Tate 5.00 12.00
WRFCJE Julian Edelman 8.00 20.00
WRFCJJ Julio Jones 8.00 20.00
WRFCJM Jeremy Maclin 5.00 12.00
WRFCJN Jordy Nelson 12.00 30.00
WRFCKB Kelvin Benjamin 6.00 15.00
WRFCLF Larry Fitzgerald 6.00 15.00
WRFCME Mike Evans 6.00 15.00
WRFCOB Odell Beckham Jr. 8.00 20.00
WRFCRC Randall Cobb 6.00 15.00
WRFCSS Steve Smith 6.00 15.00
WRFCSW Sammy Watkins 6.00 15.00
WRFCTH T.Y. Hilton 6.00 15.00
WRFCJMA Jordan Matthews 6.00 15.00

1998 Topps Action Flats Kickoff Edition
The 1998 Topps Action Flats set was issued in one series with a total of 8-statues/cards. The single-card/action figures retail for $2.99 each. The action figures are miniature plastic flat-sculpted silhouettes of NFL superstars. The accompanying 1998 Topps card features the player in the same pose as the action figure with a gold foil Action Flats logo and new card number.
COMPLETE SET (8) 7.50 15.00
K1 Troy Aikman 1.00 2.50
K2 Brett Favre 1.25 3.00
K3 John Elway 1.25 3.00
K4 Dan Marino 1.25 3.00
K5 Peyton Manning 2.50 6.00
K6 Ryan Leaf .75 2.00
K7 Barry Sanders 1.25 3.00
K8 Jerry Rice 1.00 2.50

1999 Topps Action Flats
This set was issued in one series with a total of 12-statues and cards. The package with one card and an action figures originally retailed for $2.99. The action figures are miniature plastic flat-sculpted silhouettes of NFL superstars. The accompanying 1999 Topps card features the player in the same pose as the action figure with a gold foil Action Flats logo and new card number.
COMPLETE SET (12) 10.00 20.00
1 Jamal Anderson .60 1.50
2 Jerome Bettis .60 1.50
3 Mark Brunell .80 2.00
4 Terrell Davis 1.20 3.00
5 Doug Flutie .80 2.00
6 Eddie George .80 2.00
7 Keyshawn Johnson .60 1.50
8 Randy Moss 1.60 4.00
9 Jako Plummer .60 1.50
10 Emmitt Smith 1.20 3.00
11 Fred Taylor .75 2.00
12 Steve Young .80 2.00

2003 Topps All American
Released in early June of 2003, this set contains 150 cards including 100 veterans and 50 rookies. The rookies were inserted at a rate of 1:4. Each pack contained 6 cards, including one Foil parallel. Boxes contained 20 packs. Each case held 8 boxes. Pack SRP was $4.00
COMPLETE SET (150) 50.00 100.00
COMP.SET w/o SP's (100) 10.00 25.00
ROOKIE STATED ODDS 1:4
1 Marvin Harrison .30 .75
2 Tiki Barber .30 .75
3 Jamal Lewis .30 .75
4 Tim Couch .25 .60
5 Michael Bennett .25 .60
6 Brad Johnson .30 .75
7 Garrison Hearst .25 .60
8 Plaxico Burress .25 .60
9 Rod Gardner .25 .60
10 Charlie Garner .30 .75
11 Chad Pennington .25 .60
12 Brian Griese .25 .60
13 Julius Peppers .40 1.00
14 David Boston .25 .60
15 Anthony Thomas .30 .75
16 Ahman Green .30 .75
17 Fred Taylor .25 .60
18 Joe Horn .25 .60
19 Joey Galloway .30 .75
20 Eddie George .30 .75
21 Jeff Garcia .25 .60
22 Hines Ward .30 .75
23 Kurt Warner .30 .75
24 Marty Booker .25 .60
25 Joey Harrington .25 .60
26 Jay Fiedler .25 .60
27 Troy Brown .25 .60
28 David Carr .25 .60
29 Eric Moulds .25 .60
30 Michael Vick .30 .75
31 Keyshawn Johnson .40 1.00
32 Torry Holt .30 .75
33 LaDainian Tomlinson .40 1.00
34 Duce Staley .25 .60
35 Curtis Martin .30 .75
36 Stephen Davis .25 .60
37 Jim Miller .25 .60
38 Travis Taylor .25 .60
39 Jimmy Smith .30 .75
40 Trent Green .25 .60
41 Tom Brady 1.50 4.00
42 Randy Moss .30 .75
43 Clinton Portis .25 .60
44 Emmitt Smith .60 1.50
45 Steve McNair .30 .75
46 Shaun Alexander .25 .60
47 Jerome Bettis .40 1.00
48 Rich Gannon .30 .75
49 William Green .25 .60
50 Priest Holmes .25 .60
51 James Stewart .25 .60
52 Warrick Dunn .25 .60
53 Jake Plummer .25 .60
54 Antowain Smith .30 .75
55 Peyton Manning 1.00 2.50
56 Deuce McAllister .30 .75
57 Jeremy Shockey .25 .60
58 Darrell Jackson .30 .75
59 Derrick Mason .25 .60
60 Terrell Owens .30 .75
61 Laveranues Coles .25 .60
62 Amani Toomer .25 .60
63 Tony Gonzalez .30 .75
64 Corey Bradford .25 .60
65 Donald Driver .30 .75
66 Rod Smith .30 .75
67 Chad Johnson .25 .60
68 Travis Henry .25 .60
69 Mark Brunell .30 .75
70 Edgerrin James .30 .75
71 Jerry Rice .75 2.00
72 Aaron Brooks .25 .60
73 Marshall Faulk .30 .75
74 Curtis Conway .25 .60
75 Tommy Maddox .25 .60
76 Isaac Bruce .40 1.00
77 Matt Hasselbeck .25 .60
78 Muhsin Muhammad .25 .60
79 Drew Bledsoe .30 .75
80 Ricky Williams .30 .75
81 Daunte Culpepper .30 .75
82 Chad Hutchinson .25 .60
83 Brian Urlacher .40 1.00
84 Drew Brees .40 1.00
85 Corey Dillon .25 .60
86 Chris Chambers .25 .60
87 Peerless Price .25 .60
88 Kerry Collins .25 .60
89 Donovan McNabb .30 .75
90 Brett Favre .75 2.00
91 Patrick Ramsey .30 .75
92 T.J. Duckett .25 .60
93 Derrick Brooks .25 .60
94 Jon Kitna .25 .60
95 Jerry Porter .25 .60
96 Todd Pinkston .25 .60
97 Tai Streets .25 .60
98 Ray Lewis .40 1.00
99 Michael Pittman .25 .60
100 Brian Finneran .25 .60
101 Carson Palmer RC 1.50 4.00
102 Terrell Suggs RC 1.00 2.50
103 Boss Bailey RC 1.00 2.50
104 Justin Gage RC 1.00 2.50
105 Bobby Wade RC 1.00 2.50
106 Larry Johnson RC 1.00 2.50
107 Ken Dorsey RC 1.00 2.50
108 Quentin Griffin RC 1.00 2.50
109 Musa Smith RC .75 2.00
110 Chris Simms RC .75 2.00
111 Michael Haynes RC .75 2.00
112 Charles Rogers RC 1.00 2.50
113 Kliff Kingsbury RC 1.25 3.00
114 Jerome McDougle RC .75 2.00
115 ReShard Lee RC 1.25 3.00
116 Chris Brown RC .75 2.00
117 Bryant Johnson RC 1.25 3.00
118 Teyo Johnson RC 1.00 2.50
119 Talman Gardner RC .75 2.00
120 Brian St.Pierre RC .75 2.00
121 Onterrio Smith RC .75 2.00
122 Marcus Trufant RC 1.00 2.50
123 Earnest Graham RC 1.25 3.00
124 Kareem Kelly RC .75 2.00
125 Jason Witten RC 3.00 8.00
126 Brandon Lloyd RC 1.25 3.00
127 Anquan Boldin RC 1.25 3.00
128 Lee Suggs RC .75 2.00
129 Terry Pierce RC .75 2.00
130 Dallas Clark RC 1.25 3.00
131 Kelley Washington RC .75 2.00
132 Seneca Wallace RC 1.00 2.50
133 Domanick Davis RC 1.00 2.50
134 Terrence Edwards RC .75 2.00
135 Dave Ragone RC .75 2.00
136 Andre Johnson RC 2.00 5.00
137 Taylor Jacobs RC .75 2.00
138 Kyle Boller RC .75 2.00
139 Willis McGahee RC 1.00 2.50
140 Byron Leftwich RC 1.00 2.50
141 Sam Aiken RC 1.00 2.50
142 Bennie Joppru RC .75 2.00
143 Justin Fargas RC 1.25 3.00
144 Avon Cobourne RC .75 2.00
145 Rex Grossman RC 1.00 2.50
146 LaBrandon Toefield RC .75 2.00
147 Tyrone Calico RC .75 2.00
148 Brad Banks RC 1.00 2.50
149 Terence Newman RC 1.25 3.00
150 Jimmy Kennedy RC 1.00 2.50

2003 Topps All American Foil
*VETS 1-100: 1X TO 2.5X BASIC CARDS
VETERAN ODDS: ONE PER PACK
*ROOKIES 101-150: .6X TO 1.5X
ROOKIE STATED ODDS 1:30

2003 Topps All American Foil Gold
*VETS 1-100: 5X TO 12X BASIC CARDS
*ROOKIES 101-150: 3X TO 8X
FOIL GOLD/55 ODDS 1:90
STATED PRINT RUN 55 SER.#'d SETS

2003 Topps All American Autographs
Inserted at various odds, this set features authentic player autographs on a horizontal card. Please note that some cards were issued as redemptions with an expiration date of 6/30/2005.
GROUP A STATED ODDS 1:856
GROUP B STATED ODDS 1:2007
GROUP C STATED ODDS 1:997
GROUP D STATED ODDS 1:1198
GROUP E STATED ODDS 1:598
GROUP F STATED ODDS 1:460
GROUP G STATED ODDS 1:332
GROUP H STATED ODDS 1:315
GROUP I STATED ODDS 1:28
AAAC Avon Cobourne G 5.00 12.00
AAAJ Andre Johnson C 12.00 30.00
AABBE Brad Banks D 6.00 15.00
AABJ Bryant Johnson A 10.00 25.00
AABL Byron Leftwich C 6.00 15.00
AABM Billy McMullen I 5.00 12.00
AACB Chris Brown A 6.00 15.00
AACP Carson Palmer A 25.00 60.00
AACS Chris Simms A 15.00 40.00
AAEG Earnest Graham I 8.00 20.00
AAJF Justin Fargas I 8.00 20.00
AAJT Jason Thomas D 5.00 12.00
AAKB Kyle Boller B 5.00 12.00
AAKD Ken Dorsey A 8.00 20.00
AAKKE Kareem Kelly I 5.00 12.00
AAKW Kelley Washington E 5.00 12.00
AALJ Larry Johnson C 10.00 25.00
AALT LaBrandon Toefield I 5.00 12.00
AAOS Onterrio Smith I 5.00 12.00
AAQG Quentin Griffin H 6.00 15.00
AARG Rex Grossman A 12.00 30.00
AASW Seneca Wallace I 6.00 15.00
AATC Tyrone Calico I 5.00 12.00
AATG Talman Gardner I 5.00 12.00
AATJ Taylor Jacobs E 5.00 12.00
AAWM Willis McGahee F 6.00 15.00

2003 Topps All American Campus Connection Autographs
Inserted at rate of 1:1208, this set features cards with two autographs from players share an alma mater. Each card was serial numbered to 100. Some cards were issued in packs via a mail redemption card that carried an expiration date of June 30, 2005.
STATED ODDS 1:1208
STATED PRINT RUN 100 SER.#'d SETS
CCHS P.Holmes/C.Simms 20.00 50.00
CCMD K.Dorsey/S.Moss 15.00 40.00
CCPD C.Portis/K.Dorsey 20.00 50.00
CCZC A.Zereoue/A.Cobourne 12.00 30.00

2003 Topps All American Conference Call Autographs
Inserted at a rate of 1:1208, this set features cards with two autographs from players who competed against each other in their college conferences. Each card was serial numbered to 100. Some cards were issued in packs via a mail redemption card that carried an expiration date of June 30, 2005.
STATED ODDS 1:1208
STATED PRINT RUN 100 SER.#'d SETS
CCABP C.Palmer/K.Boller 15.00 40.00
CCACM McGahee/Cobourne 20.00 50.00
CCAGB C.Brown/Q.Griffin 15.00 40.00
CCASM W.McGahee/L.Suggs 15.00 40.00

2003 Topps All American Fabric of America
Inserted at various odds, this set features Senior Bowl jersey swatches from several of the NFL's top rookie players.
GROUP A STATED ODDS 1:61
GROUP B STATED ODDS 1:59
GROUP C STATED ODDS 1:166
GROUP D STATED ODDS 1:63
GROUP E STATED ODDS 1:25
GROUP F STATED ODDS 1:136
FAAC Angelo Crowell A 3.00 8.00
FAAP Artose Pinner E 2.50 6.00
FAAW Andre Woolfolk E 2.50 6.00
FAAWA Aaron Walker A 3.00 8.00
FABJA Bradie James D 4.00 10.00
FABJO Bennie Joppru F 2.50 6.00
FABN Bruce Nelson A 2.50 6.00
FABW Brett Williams A 2.50 6.00
FACK Chris Kelsay C 3.00 8.00
FACP Carson Palmer E 7.50 20.00
FACS Chris Simms D 2.50 6.00
FADD Domanick Davis E 3.00 8.00
FADG Doug Gabriel E 3.00 8.00
FADR Dave Ragone B 2.50 6.00
FAEG Earnest Graham A 4.00 10.00
FAES Eric Steinbach B 2.50 6.00
FAJB Julian Battle E 3.00 8.00
FAJG DeJuan Groce F 4.00 10.00
FAJGR Justin Griffith E 3.00 8.00
FAJJ Jarret Johnson D 3.00 8.00
FAJM Jerome McDougle D 2.50 6.00
FAJS Jon Stinchcomb A 3.00 8.00
FAKG Kevin Garrett A 2.50 6.00
FAKK Kliff Kingsbury C 4.00 10.00
FAKW Kevin Williams B 4.00 10.00
FAMH Michael Haynes B 2.50 6.00
FAMT Marcus Trufant E 3.00 8.00
FAMW Matt Wilhelm D 3.00 8.00
FARM Rashean Mathis B 2.50 6.00
FASA Sam Aiken E 3.00 8.00
FATBC Tully Banta-Cain A 4.00 10.00
FATC Tyrone Calico E 2.50 6.00
FATG Talman Gardner A 2.50 6.00
FATJ Taylor Jacobs B 2.50 6.00
FATW Ty Warren E 3.00 8.00
FAVH Victor Hobson E 2.50 6.00
FAVM Vincent Manuwai A 2.50 6.00

2003 Topps All American Jersey Backs
Inserted at a rate of 1:2762, this set features oversize jersey swatches that cover almost the entire card. Cards contain game worn jerseys from the 2002 Senior Bowl. Each card is serial #'d to 25.
STATED ODDS 1:2762
STATED PRINT RUN 25 SER.#'d SETS
JBBJ Bryant Johnson 12.00 30.00
JBCP Carson Palmer 20.00 50.00
JBCS Chris Simms 8.00 20.00
JBDR Dave Ragone 8.00 20.00
JBJF Justin Fargas 12.00 30.00
JBKK Kliff Kingsbury 12.00 30.00
JBLJ Larry Johnson 10.00 25.00
JBTG Talman Gardner 8.00 20.00
JBTJ Taylor Jacobs 8.00 20.00

2005 Topps All American
This 91-card set was released in November, 2005. The set was issued through the hobby in six-card packs with an $5 SRP which came 24 packs to a box.
COMPLETE SET (91) 15.00 40.00
UNPRICED PRINT PLATE PRINT RUN 1 SET
ES5 STATED ODDS 1:1220 HOB/RET
ES5C STATED ODDS 1:27,245 HOB/RET
1 Dan Fouts .40 1.00
2 Kellen Winslow .40 1.00
3 Marty Lyons .50 1.25
4 Alan Page .30 .75
5 Carl Eller .30 .75
6 Jake Scott .30 .75
7 William Perry .30 .75
8 Joe Montana 1.50 4.00
9 Fred Biletnikoff .50 1.25
10 Dave Casper .30 .75
11 Earl Campbell .50 1.25
12 Mark May .30 .75
13 Joe Greene .50 1.25
14 Ozzie Newsome .40 1.00
15 Joe Namath .75 2.00
16 Ted Hendricks .30 .75
17 Lawrence Taylor .50 1.25
18 Randy Gradishar .40 1.00
19 Reggie McKenzie .30 .75
20 Dave Foley .50 1.25
21 Mike Montler ERR .30 .75
22 Merlin Olsen .30 .75
23 John David Crow .30 .75
24 Paul Hornung .50 1.25
25 Jim Brown .60 1.50
26 Bob Lilly .40 1.00
27 Mel Renfro .30 .75
28 Dick Butkus .60 1.50
29 Roger Staubach .60 1.50
30 Gale Sayers .50 1.25
31 Bob Griese .50 1.25
32 Dick Anderson .30 .75
33 Jim Plunkett .40 1.00
34 Johnny Rodgers .50 1.25
35 Ed Marinaro .30 .75
36 Greg Pruitt .50 1.25
37 Johnny Musso .50 1.25
38 Johnny Majors .40 1.00
39 Bert Jones .30 .75
40 Steve Bartkowski .40 1.00
41 John Cappelletti .40 1.00
42 Archie Griffin .50 1.25
43 Randy White .40 1.00
44 Tommy Kramer .30 .75
45 Mike Singletary .50 1.25
46 Tony Dorsett .50 1.25
47 Tony Franklin .30 .75
48 John Jefferson .30 .75
49 Billy Sims .50 1.25
50 Charles White .40 1.00
51 Herschel Walker .50 1.25
52 Ronnie Lott .40 1.00
53 Anthony Carter .30 .75
54 Jim McMahon .50 1.25
55 Marcus Allen .50 1.25
56 John Elway .75 2.00
57 Mike Rozier .50 1.25
58 Irving Fryar .50 1.25
59 Bo Jackson .60 1.50
60 Eric Dickerson .40 1.00
61 Kenny Easley .30 .75
62 Bruce Matthews .30 .75
63 Alex Karras .40 1.00
64 Bubba Smith .30 .75
65 Chuck Long .40 1.00
66 Lorenzo White .30 .75
67 Cris Carter .50 1.25
68 Brad Muster .30 .75
69 D.J. Dozier .40 1.00
70 Craig Heyward .30 .75
71 Chris Spielman .50 1.25
72 Chuck Cecil .30 .75
73 Hart Lee Dykes .30 .75
74 Tony Mandarich .30 .75
75 Barry Sanders .75 2.00
76 Troy Aikman .60 1.50
77 Andre Ware .30 .75
78 Desmond Howard .50 1.25
79 Gino Torretta .30 .75
80 Charlie Ward .30 .75
81 Danny Wuerffel .40 1.00
82 Tommie Frazier .50 1.25
83 Ty Detmer .30 .75
84 Wendell Davis .30 .75
85 Jay Novacek .40 1.00
86 Keith Byars .40 1.00
87 Steve Spurrier .50 1.25
88 Earl Morrall .40 1.00
89 Anthony Davis .30 .75
90 Brad Van Pelt .30 .75
91 Roland James .30 .75
ES5 Elvis Presley Shirt/500 50.00 100.00
ES5C Elvis Shirt Chr/25 125.00 200.00

2005 Topps All American Chrome
*SINGLES: 2X TO 5X BASIC CARDS
CHROME/555 STATED ODDS 1:12
UNPRICED XFRACTOR PRINT RUN 5 SETS

2005 Topps All American Chrome Refractor
*SINGLES: 5X TO 12X BASIC CARDS
CHROME REFRACTOR/55 ODDS 1:121
78 Desmond Howard 10.00 25.00

2005 Topps All American Chrome Xfractor
UNPRICED XFRACTOR/5 ODDS 1:1328

2005 Topps All American Gold Chrome
*SINGLES: 2X TO 5X BASIC CARDS
GOLD CHROME/555 STATED ODDS 1:12
UNPRICED GOLD XFRACT.PRINT RUN 5 SETS

2005 Topps All American Gold Chrome Refractor
*SINGLES: 5X TO 12X BASIC CARDS
GOLD CHROME REFRACT/55 ODDS 1:121

2005 Topps All American Gold Chrome Xfractor
UNPRICED XFRACTOR/5 ODDS 1:1328

2005 Topps All American Autographs
UNPRICED GROUP A/4 ODDS 1:58,000 H
GROUP B/19 ODDS 1:2000 H, 1:6024 R
GROUP C/44 ODDS 1:642 H, 1:3917 R
GROUP D/69 ODDS 1:5800 H, 1:9792 R
GROUP E/144 ODDS 1:1115 H, 1:305 R
GROUP F/194 ODDS 1:99 H, 1:280 R
GROUP G ODDS 1:2231 H, 1:1958 R
GROUP H ODDS 1:574 H, 1:593 R
GROUP I ODDS 1:71 H, 1:72 R
GROUP J ODDS 1:82 H, 1:122 R
GROUP K ODDS 1:57 H, 1:164 R
TOPPS ANNOUNCED PRINT RUNS BELOW
AJMA Johnny Majors J 12.50 30.00
AAC Anthony Carter/194* 12.00 30.00
AAD Anthony Davis J 10.00 25.00
AAG Archie Griffin/144* 30.00 60.00
AAK Alex Karras I 12.50 30.00
AAP Alan Page/194* 25.00 50.00
AAW Andre Ware/194* 15.00 30.00
ABG Bob Griese/144* 25.00 50.00
ABJ Bert Jones I 10.00 25.00
ABL Bob Lilly/144* 25.00 60.00
ABM Brad Muster J 6.00 15.00
ABMA Bruce Matthews/144* 15.00 40.00
ABOJ Bo Jackson/69* 75.00 135.00
ABS Bubba Smith/144* 25.00 50.00
ABSA Barry Sanders/4*
ABSI Billy Sims/144* 25.00 50.00
ABVP Brad Van Pelt I 7.50 20.00
ACC Cris Carter/144* 30.00 60.00
ACCE Chuck Cecil K 6.00 15.00
ACE Carl Eller/194* 15.00 40.00
ACH Craig Heyward J 10.00 25.00
ACL Chuck Long/194* 25.00 60.00
ACS Chris Spielman/194* 25.00 50.00
ACW Charles White I 8.00 20.00
ACWA Charlie Ward/144* 20.00 40.00
ADA Dick Anderson/144* 25.00 50.00
ADB Dick Butkus/144* 60.00 120.00
ADC Dave Casper H 10.00 25.00
ADD D.J. Dozier I 7.50 20.00
ADF Dan Fouts/44* 50.00 100.00
ADFO Dave Foley/194* 15.00 30.00
ADH Desmond Howard/144* 25.00 50.00
ADW Danny Wuerffel I 12.00 30.00
AEC Earl Campbell/44* 60.00 120.00
AED Eric Dickerson/44* 60.00 120.00
AEM Earl Morrall K 10.00 25.00
AEMA Ed Marinaro I 6.00 20.00
AFB Fred Biletnikoff/144* 20.00 50.00
AGP Greg Pruitt I 8.00 20.00
AGS Gale Sayers/19* 150.00 250.00
AGT Gino Torretta/194* 15.00 40.00
AHLD Hart Lee Dykes I 6.00 15.00
AHW Herschel Walker/144* 40.00 80.00
AIR Irving Fryar/144* 20.00 50.00
AJB Jim Brown/19* 250.00 400.00
AJC John Cappelletti K 10.00 25.00
AJDC John David Crow K 12.00 30.00
AJE John Elway/19* 250.00 450.00
AJG Joe Greene/144* 40.00 75.00
AJJ John Jefferson I 7.50 20.00
AJM Joe Montana/19* 350.00 500.00
AJMC Jim McMahon/144* 20.00 50.00
AJMU Johnny Musso J 10.00 25.00
AJN Joe Namath/19* 250.00 400.00
AJNO Jay Novacek/194* 15.00 40.00
AJP Jim Plunkett/194* 20.00 50.00
AJR Johnny Rodgers I 10.00 25.00
AJS Jake Scott/44* 50.00 100.00
AKB Keith Byars/194* 15.00 40.00
AKE Kenny Easley J 6.00 15.00
AKW Kellen Winslow/44* 30.00 80.00
ALT Lawrence Taylor/44* 60.00 120.00
ALW Lorenzo White/194* 15.00 30.00
AMA Marcus Allen/19* 150.00 250.00
AML Marty Lyons/194* 15.00 40.00
AMM Mark May/194* 15.00 30.00
AMMO Mike Montler ERR/194* 15.00 30.00
AMO Merlin Olsen H 20.00 50.00
AMR Mel Renfro I 10.00 25.00
AMRO Mike Rozier/144* 15.00 40.00
AMS Mike Singletary/144* 25.00 50.00
AON Ozzie Newsome G 10.00 25.00
APH Paul Hornung/44* 50.00 100.00
ARG Randy Gradishar/194* 15.00 40.00

ARJ Roland James I 6.00 15.00
ARL Ronnie Lott/44* 60.00 120.00
ARM Reggie McKenzie/194* 15.00 30.00
ARS Roger Staubach/19* 175.00 300.00
ARW Randy White/144* 25.00 50.00
ASB Steve Bartkowski I 8.00 20.00
ASS Steve Spurrier/144* 40.00 80.00
ATA Troy Aikman/19* 175.00 300.00
ATD Tony Dorsett/19* 125.00 200.00
ATF Tony Franklin I 6.00 15.00
ATFR Tommie Frazier I 12.50 30.00
ATH Ted Hendricks/44* 40.00 80.00
ATK Tommy Kramer I 8.00 20.00
ATM Tony Mandarich/194* 15.00 30.00
ATYD Ty Detmer I 6.00 15.00
AWD Wendell Davis I 6.00 20.00
AWP William Perry H 12.50 30.00

2005 Topps All American Autographs Chrome Refractors

*CHROME REF/55: .6X TO 1.5X BASIC AUTOS
*CHROME REF/55: .5X TO 1.2X AUTO/144/194
*CHROME REF/55: .5X TO 1.2X AUTO/44
GROUP A/5 ODDS 1:12,429 H, 1:17,311 R
GROUP B/55 ODDS 1:63 H, 1:282 R
SERIAL #'d TO 5 TOO SCARCE TO PRICE

2005 Topps All American College Co-Signers

CO-SIGNER/25 ODDS 1:5612 H, 4896 R
AABJ Bo Jackson/J.Brown 150.00 250.00
AABS G.Sayers/J.Brown 125.00 250.00
AAMA J.Montana/T.Aikman 200.00 350.00
AAME J.Montana/J.Elway 200.00 400.00
AASD B.Sanders/T.Dorsett 150.00 250.00

2006 Topps Allen and Ginter

This 350-card set was release in August, 2006. The set was issued in seven-card hobby packs with an $4 SRP. Those packs came 24 to a box and there were 12 boxes in a case. In addition, there were also six-card retail packs issued and those packs came 24 packs to a box and 20 boxes to a case. There were some subsets included in this set including Rookies (251-265); Retired Greats (266-290); Managers (291-300); Modern Personalities (301-314); Reprinted Allen and Ginters (316-319); Famous People of the Past (326-349).`

COMPLETE SET (350) 60.00 120.00
COMP.SET w/o SP's (300) 15.00 40.00
SP STATED ODDS 1:2 HOBBY, 1:2 RETAIL
SP CL: 5/15/25/35/45/50-59/65/85/105/115
SP CL: 125/135/145/150-159/165/175/185
SP CL: 205/215/235/245/251/255-256/265
SP CL: 285/295/305/315/325/335/345
FRAMED ORIGINALS ODDS 1:3227 H, 1:3227 R
314 Jim Thorpe .25 .60

2006 Topps Allen and Ginter Mini

*MINI 1-350: 1X TO 2.5X BASIC
*MINI 1-350: 1X TO 2.5X BASIC RC's
APPX.15 MINIS PER 24-CT SEALED BOX
*MINI SP 1-350: .6X TO 1.5X BASIC SP
*MINI SP 1-350: .6X TO 1.5X BASIC SP RC's
MINI SP ODDS 1:13 H, 1:13 R
COMMON CARD (351-375) 20.00 50.00
SEMISTARS 351-375 30.00 60.00
UNLISTED STARS 351-375 30.00 60.00
351-375 RANDOM WITHIN RIP CARDS
OVERALL PLATE ODDS 1:865 H, 1:865 R
PLATE PRINT RUN 1 SET PER COLOR
BLACK-CYAN-MAGENTA-YELLOW ISSUED
NO PLATE PRICING DUE TO SCARCITY

2006 Topps Allen and Ginter Mini A and G Back

*A & G BACK: 2X TO 5X BASIC
*A & G BACK: 1.5X TO 4X BASIC RC's
STATED ODDS 1:5 H, 1:5 R
*A & G BACK SP: 1X TO 2.5X BASIC SP
*A & G BACK SP: 1X TO 2.5X BASIC SP RC's
SP STATED ODDS 1:65 H, 1:65 R

2006 Topps Allen and Ginter Mini Black

*BLACK: 4X TO 10X BASIC
*BLACK: 2.5X TO 6X BASIC RC's
STATED ODDS 1:10 H, 1:10 R
*BLACK SP: 1.5X TO 4X BASIC SP
*BLACK SP: 1.5X TO 4X BASIC SP RC's
SP STATED ODDS 1:130 H, 1:130 R

2006 Topps Allen and Ginter Mini No Card Number

*NO NBR: 6X TO 15X BASIC
*NO NBR: 4X TO 10X BASIC RC's
*NO NBR: 2X TO 5X BASIC SP
*NO NBR: 2X TO 5X BASIC SP RC's
STATED ODDS 1:60 H, 1:168 R
STATED PRINT RUN 50 SETS
CARDS ARE NOT SERIAL-NUMBERED
PRINT RUN INFO PROVIDED BY TOPPS

2006 Topps Allen and Ginter National Promos

COMPLETE SET (8) 15.00 30.00
*MINIS: .6X TO 1.5X BASE CARDS
NCC1 Matt Leinart 1.50 4.00
NCC3 LenDale White 1.25 3.00
NCC5 Reggie Bush 2.50 6.00

2007 Topps Allen and Ginter National Mini Promos

NCC1 Brady Quinn 1.50 4.00
NCC2 Joe Thomas .60 1.50
NCC3 Ted Ginn Jr. .75 2.00

2007 Topps Allen and Ginter National Promos

NCC1 Brady Quinn 1.50 4.00
NCC2 Joe Thomas .60 1.50
NCC3 Ted Ginn Jr. .75 2.00

2008 Topps Allen and Ginter

COMP.SET w/o FUKU.(350) 30.00 60.00
COMP.SET w/o SPs (300) 15.00 40.00
COMMON CARD (1-300) .15 .40
COMMON RC (1-300) .40 1.00
COMMON SP (301-350) 1.25 3.00
SP STATED ODDS 1:2 HOBBY
FRAMED ORIG.ODDS 1:26,500 HOBBY
187 Les Miles .25 .60

2008 Topps Allen and Ginter Mini

INI 1-300: .75X TO 2X BASIC
*MINI 1-300 RC: .5X TO 1.2X BASIC RC's
APPX. ONE MINI PER PACK
*MINI SP 300-350: .75X TO 2X BASIC SP
MINI SP ODDS 1:13 HOBBY
351-390 RANDOM WITHIN RIP CARDS
OVERALL PLATE ODDS 1:961 HOBBY
PLATE PRINT RUN 1 SET PER COLOR
BLACK-CYAN-MAGENTA-YELLOW ISSUED
NO PLATE PRICING DUE TO SCARCITY

2008 Topps Allen and Ginter Mini A and G Back

*A & G BACK: 1X TO 2.5X BASIC
*A & G BACK RCs: .6X TO 1.5X BASIC RCs
STATED ODDS 1:5 HOBBY
*A & G BACK SP: 1X TO 2.5X BASIC SP
SP STATED ODDS 1:65 HOBBY

2008 Topps Allen and Ginter Mini Black

LACK: 1.5X TO 4X BASIC
*BLACK RCs: .75X TO 2X BASIC RCs
STATED ODDS 1:10 HOBBY
*BLACK SP: 1.2X TO 3X BASIC SP
SP STATED ODDS 1:130 HOBBY

2008 Topps Allen and Ginter Mini No Card Number

*NO NBR: 10X TO 25X BASIC
*NO NBR RCs: 4X TO 10X BASIC RCs
*NO NBR: 1.5X TO 4X BASIC SP
STATED ODDS 1:151 HOBBY
STATED PRINT RUN 50 SETS
CARDS ARE NOT SERIAL-NUMBERED
PRINT RUN INFO PROVIDED BY TOPPS

2008 Topps Allen and Ginter Autographs

GROUP A ODDS 1:277 HOBBY
GROUP B ODDS 1:256 HOBBY
GROUP C ODDS 1:135 HOBBY
GRP A PRINT RUNS B/W 90-240 COPIES PER
CARDS ARE NOT SERIAL-NUMBERED
PRINT RUNS PROVIDED BY TOPPS
EXCHANGE DEADLINE 7/31/2010
LM Les Miles A/190 * 15.00 40.00

2008 Topps Allen and Ginter Relics

GROUP A ODDS 1:280 HOBBY
GROUP B ODDS 1:71 HOBBY
GROUP C ODDS 1:20 HOBBY
RELIC AU ODDS 1:26,431 HOBBY
GROUP A B/W 100-250 COPIES PER
CARDS ARE NOT SERIAL NUMBERED
PRINT RUN INFO PROVIDED BY TOPPS
LM Les Miles A/250 * 10.00 25.00

2008 Topps Allen and Ginter National Convention

COMPLETE SET (7) 8.00 20.00
5 Johnny Unitas 2.50 6.00

2010 Topps Allen and Ginter

COMPLETE SET (350) 60.00 120.00
COMP.SET w/o SPs (300) 15.00 40.00
COMMON CARD (1-300) .15 .40
COMMON RC (1-300) .40 1.00
COMMON SP (301-350) 1.25 3.00
SP STATED ODDS 1:2 HOBBY
287 Drew Brees .40 1.00

2010 Topps Allen and Ginter Mini

INI 1-300: .75X TO 2X BASIC
*MINI 1-300 RC: .5X TO 1.2X BASIC RC's
APPX. ONE MINI PER PACK
*MINI SP 301-350: .5X TO 1.2X BASIC SP
MINI SP ODDS 1:13 HOBBY
COMMON CARD (351-400) 6.00 15.00
351-400 RANDOM WITHIN RIP CARDS
STRASBURG 401 ISSUED IN PACKS
OVERALL PLATE ODDS 1:799 HOBBY

2010 Topps Allen and Ginter Mini A and G Back

*A & G BACK: 1X TO 2.5X BASIC
*A & G BACK RCs: .6X TO 1.5X BASIC RCs
STATED ODDS 1:5 HOBBY
*A & G BACK SP: .6X TO 1.5X BASIC SP
SP STATED ODDS 1:65 HOBBY

2010 Topps Allen and Ginter Mini Black

*BLACK: 2X TO 5X BASIC
*BLACK RCs: .75X TO 2X BASIC RCs
STATED ODDS 1:10 HOBBY
*BLACK SP: .75X TO 2X BASIC SP
SP STATED ODDS 1:130 HOBBY

2010 Topps Allen and Ginter Mini No Card Number

*NO NBR: 8X TO 20X BASIC
*NO NBR RCs: 3X TO 8X BASIC RCs
*NO NBR SP: 1.2X TO 3X BASIC SP
STATED ODDS 1:140 HOBBY

2010 Topps Allen and Ginter Autographs

STATED ODDS 1:HOBBY
ASTERISK EQUALS PARTIAL EXCHANGE
DBR Drew Brees 60.00 120.00

2010 Topps Allen and Ginter Relics

ATED ODDS 1:11 HOBBY
DBR Drew Brees 10.00 25.00

2011 Topps Allen and Ginter

MPLETE SET (350) 50.00 100.00
COMP.SET w/o SP's (300) 12.50 30.00
COMMON CARD (1-300) .15 .40
COMMON RC (1-300) .40 1.00
COMMON SP (301-350) 1.25 3.00
SP ODDS 1:2 HOBBY
3 Lou Holtz .15 .40
238 Rudy Ruettiger .15 .40

2011 Topps Allen and Ginter Glossy

ISSUED VIA TOPPS ONLINE STORE
STATED PRINT RUN 999 SER.#'d SETS
3 Lou Holtz .75 2.00
238 Rudy Ruettiger .75 2.00

2011 Topps Allen and Ginter Mini

INI 1-300: .75X TO 2X BASIC
*MINI 1-300 RC: .5X TO 1.2X BASIC RC's
*MINI SP 301-350: .5X TO 1.2X BASIC SP
MINI SP ODDS 1:13 HOBBY
COMMON CARD (351-400) 10.00 25.00
351-400 RANDOM WITHIN RIP CARDS
STATED PLATE ODDS 1:751 HOBBY
PLATE PRINT RUN 1 SET PER COLOR
BLACK-CYAN-MAGENTA-YELLOW ISSUED
NO PLATE PRICING DUE TO SCARCITY

2011 Topps Allen and Ginter Mini A and G Back

*A & G BACK: 1X TO 2.5X BASIC
*A & G BACK RCs: .6X TO 1.5X BASIC RCs
A & G BACK ODDS 1:5 HOBBY
*A & G BACK SP: .6X TO 1.5X BASIC SP
A & G BACK SP ODDS 1:65 HOBBY

2011 Topps Allen and Ginter Mini Black

*BLACK: 2X TO 5X BASIC
*BLACK RCs: .75X TO 2X BASIC RCs
BLACK ODDS 1:10 HOBBY
BLACK SP ODDS 1:130 HOBBY
*BLACK SP: .75X TO 2X BASIC SP

2011 Topps Allen and Ginter Mini No Card Number

*NO NBR: 8X TO 20X BASIC
*NO NBR RCs: 3X TO 8X BASIC RCs
*NO NBR SP: 1.2X TO 3X BASIC SP
STATED ODDS 1:142 HOBBY

2011 Topps Allen and Ginter Autographs

ATED ODDS 1:68 HOBBY
DUAL AUTO ODDS 1:56,000 HOBBY
EXCHANGE DEADLINE 6/30/2014
LH Lou Holtz 25.00 80.00
RRU Rudy Ruettiger 10.00 25.00

2011 Topps Allen and Ginter Code Cards

*MINI 1-300: 1.5X TO 4X BASIC
*MINI 1-300 RC: .75X TO 2X BASIC RC's
OVERALL CODE ODDS 1:8 HOBBY

2011 Topps Allen and Ginter Relics

STATED ODDS 1:10 HOBBY
EXCHANGE DEADLINE 6/30/2014
LHO Lou Holtz 20.00 50.00
RRU Rudy Ruettiger 12.00 30.00

2012 Topps Allen and Ginter

COMPLETE SET (350) 30.00 60.00
COMP.SET w/o SP's (300) 15.00 40.00
SP ODDS 1:2 HOBBY
36 Kirk Herbstreit .15 .40
184 Ara Parseghian .25 .60
220 James Brown .15 .40

2012 Topps Allen and Ginter Mini

*MINI 1-300: .75X TO 2X BASIC
*MINI 1-300 RC: .5X TO 1.2X BASIC RC's
*MINI SP 301-350: .5X TO 1.2X BASIC SP
MINI SP ODDS 1:13 HOBBY
351-400 RANDOM WITHIN RIP CARDS
STATED PLATE ODDS 1:564 HOBBY
PLATE PRINT RUN 1 SET PER COLOR
NO PLATE PRICING DUE TO SCARCITY

2012 Topps Allen and Ginter Mini A and G Back

*A & G BACK: 1X TO 2.5X BASIC
*A & G BACK RCs: .6X TO 1.5X BASIC RCs
A & G BACK ODDS 1:5 HOBBY
*A & G BACK SP: .6X TO 1.5X BASIC SP
A & G BACK SP ODDS 1:65 HOBBY

2012 Topps Allen and Ginter Mini Black

*BLACK: 1.5X TO 4X BASIC
*BLACK RCs: .6X TO 1.5X BASIC RCs
BLACK ODDS 1:10 HOBBY
*BLACK SP: 1X TO 2.5X BASIC SP
BLACK SP ODDS 1:130 HOBBY

2012 Topps Allen and Ginter Mini Gold Border

*GOLD: .5X TO 1.2X BASIC
*GOLD RCs: .5X TO 1.2X BASIC RCs
COMMON SP (301-350) .40 1.00
SP SEMIS .60 1.50
SP UNLISTED 1.00 2.50

2012 Topps Allen and Ginter Mini No Card Number

*NO NBR: 5X TO 12X BASIC
*NO NBR RCs: 2X TO 5X BASIC RCs
*NO NBR SP: 1.2X TO 3X BASIC SP
STATED ODDS 1:111 HOBBY
ANNC'D PRINT RUN OF 50 SETS

2012 Topps Allen and Ginter Autographs

STATED ODDS 1:51 HOBBY
EXCHANGE DEADELINE 06/30/2015
APA Ara Parseghian 15.00 40.00
JBR James Brown 10.00 25.00
KH Kirk Herbstreit 10.00 25.00

2012 Topps Allen and Ginter Relics

STATED ODDS 1:10 HOBBY
EXCHANGE DEADELINE 06/30/2015
JBR James Brown 6.00 15.00
KH Kirk Herbstreit 4.00 10.00

2013 Topps Allen and Ginter

COMPLETE SET (350) 20.00 50.00
COMP.SET w/o SP's (300) 12.00 30.00
SP ODDS 1:2 HOBBY
131 Brian Kelly .40 1.00
244 Nick Saban .40 1.00
255 Bobby Bowden .40 1.00
278 Mike McCarthy .40 1.00

2013 Topps Allen and Ginter Mini

INI 1-300: .75X TO 2X BASIC
*MINI 1-300 RC: .5X TO 1.2X BASIC RC's
*MINI SP 301-350: .5X TO 1.2X BASIC SP
MINI SP ODDS 1:13 HOBBY
351-400 RANDOM WITHIN RIP CARDS
STATED PLATE ODDS 1:594 HOBBY
PLATE PRINT RUN 1 SET PER COLOR
BLACK-CYAN-MAGENTA-YELLOW ISSUED
NO PLATE PRICING DUE TO SCARCITY

2013 Topps Allen and Ginter Mini A and G Back

& G BACK: 1X TO 2.5X BASIC
*A & G BACK RCs: .6X TO 1.5X BASIC RCs
A & G BACK ODDS 1:5 HOBBY
*A & G BACK SP: .6X TO 1.5X BASIC SP
A & G BACK SP ODDS 1:65 HOBBY

2013 Topps Allen and Ginter Mini Black

LACK: 1.5X TO 4X BASIC
*BLACK RCs: 1X TO 2.5X BASIC RCs
BLACK ODDS 1:10 HOBBY
*BLACK SP: 1X TO 2.5X BASIC SP
BLACK SP ODDS 1:130 HOBBY

2013 Topps Allen and Ginter Mini No Card Number

*NO NBR: 4X TO 10X BASIC
*NO NBR RCs: 2.5X TO 6X BASIC RCs
*NO NBR SP: 1.2X TO 3X BASIC SP
STATED ODDS 1:102 HOBBY
ANNC'D PRINT RUN OF 50 SETS

2013 Topps Allen and Ginter Autographs

STATED ODDS 1:49 HOBBY
EXCHANGE DEADLINE 07/31/2016
BB Bobby Bowden 15.00 40.00
BK Brian Kelly 6.00 15.00
MMC Mike McCarthy 30.00 80.00
NS Nick Saban 100.00 250.00

2013 Topps Allen and Ginter Autographs Red Ink

STATED ODDS 1:931 HOBBY
PRINT RUNS B/WN 10-409 SER.#'d SETS
NO PRICING ON MOST DUE TO SCARCITY
EXCHANGE DEADLINE 07/31/2013

2013 Topps Allen and Ginter Framed Mini Relics

VERSION A ODDS 1:29 HOBBY
VERSION B ODDS 1:27 HOBBY
BBW Bobby Bowden 4.00 10.00
BK Brian Kelly 4.00 10.00
MMC Mike McCarthy 6.00 15.00
NS Nick Saban 12.00 30.00

2014 Topps Allen and Ginter

COMPLETE SET (350) 25.00 60.00
COMP.SET w/o SP's (300) 12.00 30.00
SP ODDS 1:2 HOBBY
262 Mike Pereira .15 .40

2014 Topps Allen and Ginter Framed Mini Autographs

STATED ODDS 1:52 HOBBY
EXCHANGE DEADLINE 6/30/2017
AGAMPE Mike Pereira 8.00 20.00

2014 Topps Allen and Ginter Mini

*MINI 1-300: 1X TO 2.5X BASIC
*MINI 1-300 RC: .6X TO 1.5X BASIC RCs
*MINI SP 301-350: .6X TO 1.5X BASIC SP
MINI SP ODDS 1:13 HOBBY
351-400 RANDOM WITHIN RIP CARDS
STATED PLATE ODDS 1:412 HOBBY
PLATE PRINT RUN 1 SET PER COLOR
BLACK-CYAN-MAGENTA-YELLOW ISSUED
NO PLATE PRICING DUE TO SCARCITY

2014 Topps Allen and Ginter Mini A and G Back

*A & G BACK: 1.2X TO 3X BASIC
*A & G BACK RCs: .75X TO 2X BASIC RCs
A & G BACK ODDS 1:5 HOBBY
*A & G BACK SP: .75X TO 2X BASIC SP
A & G BACK SP ODDS 1:65 HOBBY

2014 Topps Allen and Ginter Mini Black

*BLACK: 2X TO 5X BASIC
*BLACK RCs: 1.2X TO 3X BASIC RCs
BLACK ODDS 1:10 HOBBY
*BLACK SP: 1.2X TO 3X BASIC SP
BLACK SP ODDS 1:130 HOBBY

2014 Topps Allen and Ginter Mini Gold

*GOLD: 1.5X TO 4X BASIC
*GOLD RCs: 1X TO 2.5X BASIC RCs
*GOLD SP: 1X TO 2.5X BASIC SP
RANDOM INSERTS IN BACKS

2014 Topps Allen and Ginter Mini No Card Number

*NO NBR: 5X TO 12X BASIC
*NO NBR RCs: 3X TO 8X BASIC RCs
*NO NBR SP: 1.2X TO 3X BASIC SP
STATED ODDS 1:64 HOBBY
ANNC'D PRINT RUN OF 50 SETS

2014 Topps Allen and Ginter Mini Red

*RED: 12X TO 30X BASIC
*RED RCs: 8X TO 20X BASIC RCs
*RED SP: 5X TO 12X BASIC SP
STATED PRINT RUN 33 SER.#'d SETS

2014 Topps Allen and Ginter National Convention Mini

NCCSJB Jim Brown 2.50 6.00
NCCSJC Jordan Cameron 2.50 6.00
NCCSJC Jadeveon Clowney 2.50 6.00
NCCSJM Johnny Manziel 5.00 12.00

2015 Topps Allen and Ginter

COMPLETE SET (350) 30.00 80.00
ORIGINAL BUYBACK ODDS 1:7958 HOBBY
ORIG.BUYBACK PRINT RUN 1 SER.#'d SET
185 Gus Malzahn .15 .40
268 Jimbo Fisher .15 .40

2015 Topps Allen and Ginter Mini

*MINI 1-300: 1X TO 2.5X BASIC
*MINI 1-300 RC: .5X TO 1.2X BASIC RCs
*MINI SP 301-350: .6X TO 1.5X BASIC
MINI SP ODDS 1:13 HOBBY
351-400 RANDOM WITHIN RIP CARDS
STATED PLATE ODDS 1:495 HOBBY
PLATE PRINT RUN 1 SET PER COLOR
BLACK-CYAN-MAGENTA-YELLOW ISSUED
NO PLATE PRICING DUE TO SCARCITY

2015 Topps Allen and Ginter Mini A and G Back

*MINI AG 1-300: 1.2X TO 3X BASIC
*MINI AG 1-300 RC: .6X TO 1.5X BASIC RCs
*MINI AG SP 301-350: .75X TO 2X BASIC
MINI AG ODDS 1:5 HOBBY
MINI AG SP ODDS 1:65 HOBBY

2015 Topps Allen and Ginter Mini Black

*MINI BLK 1-300: 2X TO 5X BASIC
*MINI BLK 1-300 RC: 1X TO 2.5X BASIC RCs
*MINI BLK SP 301-350: 1.2X TO 3X BASIC
MINI BLK ODDS 1:10 HOBBY
MINI BLK SP ODDS 1:130 HOBBY

2015 Topps Allen and Ginter Mini Flag Back

*MINI FLAG: 5X TO 12X BASIC
*MINI FLAG RC: 2.5X TO 6X BASIC RCs
MINI FLAG ODDS 1:157 HOBBY
STATED PRINT RUN 25 SER.#'d SETS

2015 Topps Allen and Ginter Mini No Card Number

*MINI NNO: 6X TO 15X BASIC
*MINI NNO RC: 3X TO 8X BASIC RCs
MINI NNO ODDS 1:79 HOBBY
ANNCD PRINT RUN OF 50 COPIES EACH

2015 Topps Allen and Ginter Mini Red

*MINI RED: 5X TO 12X BASIC
*MINI RED RC: 2.5X TO 6X BASIC RCs
MINI RED ODDS 1:12 HOBBY BOXES
STATED PRINT RUN 40 SER.#'d SETS

2015 Topps Allen and Ginter Framed Mini Autographs

STATED ODDS 1:54 HOBBY
EXCHANGE DEADLINE 6/30/2018
AGAGM Gus Malzahn 12.00 30.00
AGAJF Jimbo Fisher 8.00 20.00

2009 Topps American Heritage

COMPLETE SET (150) 50.00 100.00
COMP.SET w/o SP's (125) 12.50 25.00
SP STATED ODDS 1:4
87 Joe Namath .40 1.00

2009 Topps American Heritage Chrome

MPLETE SET (100) 25.00 50.00
STATED ODDS 1:2 H, 1:7 R
PRINT RUN 1776 SER. #'d SETS
*CHROME: .8X TO 2X BASE

2009 Topps American Heritage Chrome Refractors

COMPLETE SET (100)
STATED ODDS 1:53 H, 1:100 R
PRINT RUN 76 SER. #'d SETS
*REFRACTOR: 10X TO 25X BASE

2009 Topps American Heritage Relics

OUP A ODDS 1:282 H, 1:1200 R
GROUP B ODDS 1:228 H, 1:925 R
GROUP C ODDS 1:33 H, 1:135 R
GROUP D ODDS 1:195 H, 1:825 R
NO PRICING ON PRINT RUN OF 10 OR LESS
JN Joe Namath Wall B 12.50 25.00

2009 Topps American Heritage Heroes Heroes of Sport

COMPLETE SET (25) 12.50 25.00
STATED ODDS 1:4
*GOLD/199: 3X TO 8X BASIC INSERTS
*PLATINUM/25: 5X TO 12X BASIC INSERTS
HS9 Tony Dorsett .40 1.00
HS13 Dan Marino .60 1.50
HS21 Jim Brown .60 1.50

2009 Topps American Heritage Heroes Heroes of Sport Relics

STATED ODDS 1:234
HSR6 Jim Brown Jsy 10.00 25.00
HSR13 Dan Marino Jsy 20.00 50.00
HSR15 Terry Bradshaw Jsy 10.00 25.00

1994 Topps Archives 1956

Topps reprinted all 274 standard-size cards in the original 1956 and 1957 sets. The 1956 reprint set contained 120 standard-siez cards, not including the unnumbered checklist card which was not reprinted. The suggested retail for a 12-card pack was 2.00. Factual and grammatical errors in the original cards were not changed in reprints. The fronts feature action player cutouts on bright color backgrounds. The backs were printed in red and black on gray card stock.

COMPLETE SET (120) 8.00 20.00
1 Johnny Carson .02 .10
2 Gordy Soltau .02 .10
3 Frank Varrichione .02 .10
4 Eddie Bell .02 .10
5 Alex Webster .07 .20
6 Norm Van Brocklin .80 2.00
7 Green Bay Packers .10 .30
8 Lou Creekmur .07 .20
9 Lou Groza .60 1.50
10 Tom Bienemann .02 .10
11 George Blanda .50 1.25
12 Alan Ameche .15 .40
13 Vic Janowicz .15 .40
14 Dick Moegle .07 .20
15 Fran Rogel .02 .10
16 Harold Giancanelli .02 .10
17 Emlen Tunnell .25 .60
18 Paul(Tank) Younger .10 .30
19 Billy Howton .07 .20
20 Jack Christiansen .30 .75
21 Darrel Brewster .02 .10
22 Chicago Cardinals .10 .30
23 Ed Brown .07 .20
24 Joe Campanella .02 .10
25 Leon Heath .02 .10
26 San Francisco 49ers .10 .30
27 Dick Flanagan .02 .10
28 Chuck Bednarik .50 1.25
29 Kyle Rote .25 .60
30 Les Richter .07 .20
31 Howard Ferguson .02 .10
32 Dorne Dibble .02 .10
33 Kenny Konz .02 .10
34 Dave Mann .02 .10
35 Rick Casares .07 .20
36 Art Donovan .40 1.00
37 Chuck Drazenovich .02 .10
38 Joe Arenas .02 .10
39 Lynn Chandnois .02 .10
40 Philadelphia Eagles .10 .30
41 Roosevelt Brown .25 .60
42 Tom Fears .30 .75
43 Gary Knafelc .02 .10
44 Joe Schmidt .40 1.00
45 Cleveland Browns .25 .60
46 Len Teeuws .02 .10
47 Bill George .25 .60
48 Baltimore Colts .10 .30
49 Eddie LeBaron .15 .40
50 Hugh McElhenny .50 1.25
51 Ted Marchibroda .07 .20
52 Adrian Burk .02 .10
53 Frank Gifford 1.00 2.50
54 Charley Toogood .02 .10
55 Tobin Rote .07 .20
56 Bill Stits .02 .10
57 Don Colo .02 .10
58 Ollie Matson .50 1.25
59 Harlon Hill .02 .10
60 Lenny Moore .80 2.00
61 Washington Redskins .10 .30
62 Billy Wilson .07 .20
63 Pittsburgh Steelers .10 .30
64 Bob Pellegrini .02 .10
65 Ken MacAfee E .07 .20
66 Willard Sherman .02 .10
67 Roger Zatkoff .02 .10
68 Dave Middleton .02 .10
69 Ray Renfro .07 .20
70 Don Stonesifer .02 .10
71 Stan Jones .25 .60
72 Jim Mutscheller .02 .10
73 Volney Peters .02 .10
74 Leo Nomellini .30 .75
75 Ray Mathews .02 .10
76 Dick Bielski .02 .10
77 Charley Conerly .50 1.25
78 Elroy Hirsch .50 1.25
79 Bill Forester .07 .20
80 Jim Doran .02 .10
81 Fred Morrison .02 .10
82 Jack Simmons .02 .10
83 Bill McColl .02 .10
84 Bert Rechichar .02 .10
85 Joe Scudero .02 .10
86 Y.A. Tittle 1.00 2.50
87 Ernie Stautner .40 1.00
88 Norm Willey .02 .10
89 Bob Schnelker .02 .10
90 Dan Towler .10 .30
91 John Martinkovic .02 .10
92 Detroit Lions .10 .30
93 George Ratterman .02 .10
94 Chuck Ulrich .02 .10
95 Bobby Watkins .02 .10
96 Buddy Young .10 .30
97 Billy Wells .02 .10
98 Bob Toneff .02 .10
99 Bill McPeak .02 .10
100 Bobby Thomason .02 .10
101 Roosevelt Grier .25 .60
102 Ron Waller .02 .10
103 Bobby Dillon .02 .10
104 Leon Hart .10 .30
105 Mike McCormack .25 .60
106 John Olszewski .02 .10
107 Bill Wightkin .02 .10
108 George Shaw .07 .20
109 Dale Atkeson .02 .10
110 Joe Perry .50 1.25
111 Dale Dodrill .02 .10
112 Tom Scott .02 .10
113 New York Giants .12 .30
114 Los Angeles Rams .10 .30
115 Al Carmichael .02 .10
116 Bobby Layne 1.00 2.50
117 Ed Modzelewski .07 .20
118 Lamar McHan .02 .10
119 Chicago Bears .10 .30
120 Billy Vessels .20 .50

1994 Topps Archives 1956 Gold

COMPLETE SET (120) 20.00 50.00
*GOLD CARDS: .8X TO 2X BASIC CARDS

1994 Topps Archives 1957

Topps reprinted all 274 cards in the original 1956 and 1957 sets. The 1957 reprint set contained 154 standard-size cards, not including the unnumbered checklist card which was not reprinted. The suggested retail for a 12-card pack was 2.00. Factual and grammatical errors in the original cards were not changed in reprints. The fronts feature action player cutouts on bright color backgrounds. The backs were printed in red and black on gray card stock.

COMPLETE SET (154) 8.00 20.00
1 Eddie LeBaron .10 .30
2 Pete Retzlaff .07 .20
3 Mike McCormack .20 .50
4 Lou Baldacci .02 .10
5 Gino Marchetti .40 1.00
6 Leo Nomellini .30 .75
7 Bobby Watkins .02 .10
8 Dave Middleton .02 .10
9 Bobby Dillon .02 .10
10 Les Richter .07 .20
11 Roosevelt Brown .20 .50
12 Lavern Torgeson .02 .10
13 Dick Bielski .02 .10
14 Pat Summerall .40 1.00
15 Jack Butler .02 .10
16 John Henry Johnson .30 .75
17 Art Spinney .02 .10
18 Bob St. Clair .20 .50
19 Perry Jeter .02 .10
20 Lou Creekmur .10 .30
21 Dave Hanner .02 .10
22 Norm Van Brocklin .60 1.50
23 Don Chandler .02 .10
24 Al Dorow .02 .10
25 Tom Scott .02 .10
26 Ollie Matson .50 1.25
27 Fran Rogel .02 .10
28 Lou Groza .60 1.50
29 Billy Vessels .07 .20
30 Y.A. Tittle .80 2.00
31 George Blanda .60 1.50
32 Bobby Layne .80 2.00
33 Billy Howton .07 .20
34 Bill Wade .07 .20
35 Emlen Tunnell .30 .75
36 Leo Elter .02 .10
37 Clarence Peaks .07 .20
38 Don Stonesifer .02 .10
39 George Tarasovic .02 .10
40 Darrel Brewster .02 .10
41 Bert Rechichar .02 .10
42 Billy Wilson .07 .20
43 Ed Brown .07 .20
44 Gene Gedman .02 .10
45 Gary Knafelc .02 .10
46 Elroy Hirsch .50 1.25
47 Don Heinrich .02 .10
48 Gene Brito .02 .10
49 Chuck Bednarik .40 1.00
50 Dave Mann .02 .10
51 Bill McPeak .02 .10
52 Kenny Konz .02 .10
53 Alan Ameche .15 .40
54 Gordy Soltau .02 .10
55 Rick Casares .10 .30
56 Charlie Ane .02 .10
57 Al Carmichael .02 .10
58 Willard Sherman .02 .10
59 Kyle Rote .20 .50
60 Chuck Drazenovich .02 .10
61 Bobby Walston .02 .10
62 John Olszewski .02 .10
63 Ray Mathews .02 .10
64 Maurice Bassett .02 .10
65 Art Donovan .40 1.00
66 Joe Arenas .02 .10
67 Harlon Hill .02 .10
68 Yale Lary .25 .60
69 Bill Forester .07 .20
70 Bob Boyd .02 .10
71 Andy Robustelli .40 1.00
72 Sam Baker .07 .20
73 Bob Pellegrini .02 .10
74 Leo Sanford .02 .10
75 Sid Watson .02 .10
76 Ray Renfro .07 .20
77 Carl Taseff .02 .10
78 Clyde Conner .02 .10
79 J.C. Caroline .02 .10
80 Howard Cassady .10 .30
81 Tobin Rote .07 .20
82 Ron Waller .02 .10
83 Jim Patton .07 .20
84 Volney Peters .02 .10
85 Dick Lane .25 .60
86 Royce Womble .02 .10
87 Duane Putnam .02 .10
88 Frank Gifford .80 2.00
89 Steve Meilinger .02 .10
90 Buck Lansford .02 .10
91 Lindon Crow .02 .10
92 Ernie Stautner .30 .75
93 Preston Carpenter .07 .20
94 Raymond Berry .60 1.50
95 Hugh McElhenny .50 1.25
96 Stan Jones .20 .50
97 Dorne Dibble .02 .10
98 Joe Scudero .02 .10
99 Eddie Bell .02 .10
100 Joe Childress .02 .10
101 Elbert Nickel .02 .10
102 Walt Michaels .07 .20
103 Jim Mutscheller .02 .10
104 Earl Morrall .15 .40
105 Larry Strickland .02 .10
106 Jack Christiansen .30 .75
107 Fred Cone .02 .10
108 Bud McFadin .02 .10
109 Charley Conerly .50 1.25
110 Tom Runnels .02 .10
111 Ken Keller .02 .10
112 James Root .02 .10
113 Ted Marchibroda .10 .30
114 Don Paul DB .02 .10
115 George Shaw .07 .20
116 Dick Moegle .07 .20
117 Don Bingham .02 .10
118 Leon Hart .07 .20
119 Bart Starr 1.60 4.00
120 Paul Miller .02 .10
121 Alex Webster .07 .20
122 Ray Wietecha .02 .10
123 Johnny Carson .02 .10
124 Tommy McDonald .10 .30
125 Jerry Tubbs .02 .10
126 Jack Scarbath .02 .10
127 Ed Modzelewski .02 .10
128 Lenny Moore .50 1.25
129 Joe Perry .50 1.25
130 Bill Wightkin .02 .10
131 Jim Doran .02 .10
132 Howard Ferguson UER .02 .10
133 Tom Wilson .02 .10
134 Dick James .02 .10
135 Jimmy Harris .02 .10
136 Chuck Ulrich .02 .10
137 Lynn Chandnois .02 .10
138 Johnny Unitas 1.60 4.00
139 Jim Ridlon .02 .10
140 Zeke Bratkowski .07 .20
141 Ray Krouse .02 .10
142 John Martinkovic .02 .10
143 Jim Cason .02 .10
144 Ken MacAfee E .07 .20
145 Sid Youngelman .02 .10
146 Paul Larson .02 .10
147 Len Ford .40 1.00
148 Bob Toneff .02 .10
149 Ronnie Knox .02 .10
150 Jim David .02 .10
151 Paul Hornung 1.20 3.00
152 Paul(Tank) Younger .10 .30
153 Bill Svoboda .02 .10
154 Fred Morrison .10 .30

1994 Topps Archives 1957 Gold

COMPLETE SET (154) 20.00 50.00
*GOLD CARDS: .8X TO 2X BASIC CARDS

2001 Topps Archives Previews

Issued as five card packs in the 2001 Topps Collection factory sets, these 10 cards were used to preview the new brand Topps Archive product.

COMPLETE SET (10) 6.00 15.00
1 Daunte Culpepper .50 1.25
2 Peyton Manning 1.25 3.00
3 Jerry Rice 1.00 2.50
4 Donovan McNabb .60 1.50
5 Emmitt Smith 1.00 2.50
6 Randy Moss 1.00 2.50
7 Eddie George .50 1.25
8 Cris Carter .50 1.25
9 Tim Brown .50 1.25
10 Edgerrin James .60 1.50

2001 Topps Archives

is 177 card set was issued in eight-card packs with a SRP of $4. The set was split up into three parts: Cards numbered one through 86 were issued in the players Rookie Card style, cards numbered 87 through 92 were issued in the style of the 1955 All-American set while cards numbered 93 through 179 were issued in the style of the players final card.

COMPLETE SET (178) 30.00 80.00
1 Warren Moon 85 .75 2.00
2 Alan Ameche 56 .50 1.25
3 Art Donovan 56 .50 1.25
4 Jackie Slater 84 .50 1.25
5 Bart Starr 57 1.50 4.00
6 Billy Howton 56 .50 1.25
7 Jack Youngblood 73 .50 1.25
8 Billy Kilmer 62 .60 1.50
9 Billy Sims 81 .60 1.50
10 Bo Jackson 88 1.00 2.50
11 Bob Griese 68 .75 2.00
12 Boomer Esiason 86 .60 1.50
13 Charley Conerly 56 .50 1.25
14 Charlie Joiner 72 .50 1.25
15 Christian Okoye 88 .50 1.25
16 Chuck Bednarik 56 .60 1.50
17 Cliff Branch 75 .50 1.25
18 Dan Fouts 75 .60 1.50
19 Dan Marino 84 1.50 4.00
20 Dave Casper 77 .50 1.25
21 Deacon Jones 63 .60 1.50
22 Dick Lane 57 .50 1.25
23 Don Maynard 61 .60 1.50
24 Doug Williams 79 .60 1.50
25 Barry Sanders 89 1.25 3.00
26 Bubba Smith 70 .50 1.25
27 Ed Too Tall Jones 76 .50 1.25
28 Chuck Foreman 74 .50 1.25
29 Elroy Hirsch 56 .60 1.50
30 Eric Dickerson 84 .60 1.50
31 Harold Carmichael 74 .50 1.25
32 Frank Gifford 56 .75 2.00
33 Fred Biletnikoff 65 .75 2.00
34 Gale Sayers 68 .75 2.00
35 John Brodie 61 .50 1.25
36 Henry Ellard 85 .50 1.25
37 Jack Lambert 76 .75 2.00
38 Jim Brown 58 1.00 2.50
39 James Lofton 79 .50 1.25
40 Joe Montana 81 2.50 6.00
41 Joe Namath 65 1.25 3.00
42 Joe Theismann 75 .75 2.00
43 Tommy McDonald 57 .50 1.25
44 John Elway 84 1.25 3.00
45 John Riggins 72 .60 1.50
46 Johnny Unitas 57 1.50 4.00
47 Kellen Winslow 81 .60 1.50
48 Ken Anderson 73 .60 1.50
49 Ken Stabler 73 1.00 2.50
50 Drew Pearson 75 .60 1.50
51 Lawrence Taylor 82 .75 2.00
52 Len Dawson 64 .75 2.00
53 Lenny Moore 56 .50 1.25
54 Lester Hayes 80 .50 1.25
55 Troy Aikman 89 1.00 2.50
56 Mark Clayton 85 .50 1.25
57 John Taylor 89 .50 1.25
58 Norm Van Brocklin 56 .60 1.50
59 Gene Upshaw 72 .50 1.25
60 Otis Sistrunk 74 .50 1.25
61 Ottis Anderson 80 .50 1.25
62 Ozzie Newsome 79 .60 1.50
63 Paul Hornung 57 .75 2.00
64 Phil Simms 80 .60 1.50
65 Raymond Berry 57 .60 1.50
66 Roger Staubach 72 1.00 2.50
67 Ronnie Lott 82 .60 1.50
68 Roosevelt Brown 56 .50 1.25
69 Roosevelt Grier 56 .50 1.25
70 Sonny Jurgensen 58 .75 2.00
71 Marcus Allen 83 .75 2.00
72 Steve Grogan 76 .50 1.25
73 Roger Craig 84 .60 1.50
74 Ted Hendricks 72 .50 1.25
75 Jim Plunkett 72 .60 1.50
76 Terry Metcalf 74 .50 1.25
77 Tom Dempsey 70 .50 1.25
78 Tom Fears 56 .50 1.25
79 Tony Dorsett 78 .75 2.00
80 Walter Payton 76 2.00 5.00
81 Y.A. Tittle 56 .75 2.00
82 William Perry 86 .50 1.25
83 Steve Young 86 1.00 2.50
84 Rodney Hampton 90 .50 1.25
85 Jim Kelly 87 .75 2.00
86 Gino Marchetti 57 .50 1.25
87 Sid Luckman 55 .60 1.50
88 Sammy Baugh 55 1.00 2.50
89 Red Grange 55 1.25 3.00
90 Otto Graham 55 .75 2.00
91 Knute Rockne 55 1.25 3.00
92 Jim Thorpe 55 1.25 3.00
93 Don Maynard 73 .40 1.00
94 Barry Sanders 99 .75 2.00
95 Joe Theismann 86 .50 1.25
96 John Riggins 85 .40 1.00
97 William Perry 93 .30 .75
98 Jim Brown 62 .60 1.50
99 Chuck Bednarik 61 .40 1.00
100 Warren Moon 99 .50 1.25
101 Frank Gifford 62 .50 1.25
102 Billy Sims 86 .40 1.00
103 Doug Williams 89 .40 1.00
104 Lester Hayes 87 .30 .75
105 Jim Plunkett 87 .40 1.00
106 Dan Marino 00 1.00 2.50
107 Jack Youngblood 85 .30 .75
108 Tom Dempsey 79 .30 .75
109 Otis Sistrunk 79 .30 .75
110 Gale Sayers 72 .50 1.25
111 Billy Howton 62 .30 .75
112 Chuck Foreman 81 .30 .75
113 Jim Kelly 97 .50 1.25
114 Norm Van Brocklin 57 .40 1.00
115 Tommy McDonald 68 .30 .75
116 John Brodie 73 .30 .75
117 Art Donovan 59 .30 .75
118 Ted Hendricks 84 .30 .75
119 Henry Ellard 98 .30 .75
120 Bart Starr 71 1.00 2.50
121 Bo Jackson 91 .60 1.50
122 Tom Fears 56 .30 .75
123 Drew Pearson 84 .40 1.00
124 Ronnie Lott 94 .40 1.00
125 Terry Metcalf 82 .30 .75
126 Lenny Moore 63 .30 .75
127 Raymond Berry 63 .40 1.00
128 John Elway 99 .75 2.00
129 Steve Grogan 90 .30 .75
130 Roger Craig 93 .40 1.00
131 Bob Griese 81 .50 1.25
132 Johnny Unitas 74 1.00 2.50
133 Cliff Branch 85 .30 .75
134 Billy Kilmer 78 .40 1.00
135 Boomer Esiason 97 .40 1.00
136 Fred Biletnikoff 79 .50 1.25
137 Marcus Allen 95 .50 1.25
138 Paul Hornung 62 .50 1.25
139 Kellen Winslow 88 .40 1.00
140 Joe Namath 73 .75 2.00
141 Jackie Slater 94 .30 .75
142 John Taylor 95 .30 .75
143 Phil Simms 94 .40 1.00
144 Ken Stabler 83 .60 1.50
145 Dave Casper 79 .30 .75
146 Dan Fouts 87 .40 1.00
147 Dick Lane 63 .30 .75
148 Alan Ameche 61 .30 .75
149 Sonny Jurgensen 72 .50 1.25
150 Harold Carmichael 84 .30 .75
151 Ed Too Tall Jones 89 .30 .75
152 Lawrence Taylor 93 .50 1.25
153 Ken Anderson 85 .40 1.00
154 Deacon Jones 74 .40 1.00
155 Ozzie Newsome 90 .40 1.00
156 Steve Young 00 .60 1.50
157 Charlie Joiner 87 .30 .75
158 Tony Dorsett 89 .50 1.25
159 Christian Okoye 93 .30 .75

160 Charley Conerly 61 .30 .75
161 Elroy Hirsch 57 .40 1.00
162 Len Dawson 76 .50 1.25
163 Jack Lambert 85 .50 1.25
164 Mark Clayton 93 .30 .75
165 Y.A. Tittle 63 .50 1.25
166 Troy Aikman 01 .60 1.50
167 Roger Staubach 79 .60 1.50
168 Roosevelt Grier 63 .30 .75
169 Gino Marchetti 63 .30 .75
170 Walter Payton 87 1.25 3.00
171 Rodney Hampton 97 .30 .75
172 Eric Dickerson 92 .40 1.00
173 Ottis Anderson 91 .30 .75
174 James Lofton 93 .30 .75
175 Bubba Smith 76 .30 .75
176 Roosevelt Brown 61 .30 .75
177 Gene Upshaw 81 .30 .75
178 Joe Montana 95 1.50 4.00
NNO Checklist .07 .20

2001 Topps Archives Relic Seats

sued at an overall rate of one per nine packs, these 16 cards feature retired players along with a piece of a stadium seat from the stadium where they became famous. The odds of pulling a specific card ranged anywhere from one in 27 to one in 81.

COMPLETE SET (16) 75.00 200.00
GROUP A STATED ODDS 1:81
GROUP B STATED ODDS 1:32
GROUP C, D STATED ODDS 1:27
OVERALL STATED ODDS 1:9
ASBS Bubba Smith 5.00 12.00
ASBST Bart Starr 12.50 30.00
ASCB Chuck Bednarik 6.00 15.00
ASCO Christian Okoye 5.00 12.00
ASED Eric Dickerson 6.00 15.00
ASFG Frank Gifford 7.50 20.00
ASJB Jim Brown 10.00 25.00
ASJU Johnny Unitas 12.50 30.00
ASKA Ken Anderson 6.00 15.00
ASLD Len Dawson 10.00 25.00
ASLM Lenny Moore 6.00 15.00
ASMA Marcus Allen 7.50 20.00
ASPH Paul Hornung 7.50 20.00
ASRB Raymond Berry 6.00 15.00
ASSB Sammy Baugh 10.00 25.00
ASSJ Sonny Jurgensen 7.50 20.00

2001 Topps Archives Rookie Reprint Autographs

sued at an overall rate of one in 19 packs, these cards feature player's signatures on a reprint of their Rookie Card. The chances of pulling a specific card ranged from one in 35 to one in 10,000. A few players did not return their card in time for inclusion in this product and those cards were redeemable until October 30, 2003.

GROUP A STATED ODDS 1:10000
GROUP B STATED ODDS 1:1238
GROUP C STATED ODDS 1:2245
GROUP D STATED ODDS 1:4126
GROUP E STATED ODDS 1:1177
GROUP F STATED ODDS 1:330
GROUP G STATED ODDS 1:1653
GROUP H STATED ODDS 1:1102
GROUP I STATED ODDS 1:198
GROUP J STATED ODDS 1:35
GROUP K STATED ODDS 1:110
GROUP L STATED ODDS 1:309
OVERALL STATED ODDS 1:19
AABG Bob Griese C 25.00 60.00
AABK Billy Kilmer 10.00 25.00
AABS Barry Sanders C 125.00 250.00
AABSI Billy Sims J 12.00 30.00
AABSM Bubba Smith J 12.00 30.00
AACB Cliff Branch 12.00 30.00
AACBE Chuck Bednarik J 12.00 30.00
AACO Christian Okoye K 10.00 25.00
AADB Dick Butkus D 25.00 60.00
AADC Dave Casper J 12.00 30.00
AADF Dan Fouts F 30.00 50.00
AADJ Deacon Jones J 15.00 40.00
AADMA Don Maynard L 10.00 25.00
AADW Doug Williams I 12.00 30.00
AAED Eric Dickerson F 35.00 60.00
AAEJ Ed Too Tall Jones J 15.00 40.00
AAFG Frank Gifford E 40.00 80.00
AAGM Gino Marchetti I 12.00 30.00
AAGS Gale Sayers F 25.00 60.00
AAHE Henry Ellard I 10.00 25.00
AAJB Jim Brown B
AAJH John Hannah 10.00 25.00
AAJM Joe Montana B 400.00 600.00
AAJN Joe Namath A 150.00 300.00
AAJR John Riggins G 30.00 90.00
AAJU Johnny Unitas H 250.00 400.00
AAKA Ken Anderson J 12.00 30.00
AAKW Kellen Winslow F 15.00 40.00
AALD Len Dawson E 20.00 50.00
AALH Lester Hayes J 12.00 30.00
AALT Lawrence Taylor B 60.00 120.00
AAMA Marcus Allen B 40.00 100.00
AAMC Mark Clayton K 12.00 30.00
AAOA Ottis Anderson J 10.00 25.00
AAON Ozzie Newsome F 12.00 30.00
AARB Roosevelt Brown J 12.00 30.00
AARBE Raymond Berry I 12.00 30.00
AARG Roosevelt Grier J 12.00 30.00
AARH Rodney Hampton J 10.00 25.00
AARS Roger Staubach F 100.00 200.00
AASG Steve Grogan J 12.00 30.00
AATD Tom Dempsey 10.00 25.00
AATH Ted Hendricks K 10.00 25.00
AAWP William Perry J 12.00 30.00
AAYT Y.A. Tittle I 25.00 50.00

2001 Topps Archives Reserve

MPLETE SET (94) 30.00 60.00
1 Warren Moon 85 1.25 3.00
2 Alan Ameche 56 .75 2.00
3 Art Donovan 56 .75 2.00
4 Jackie Slater 84 .75 2.00
5 Bart Starr 57 2.50 6.00
6 Billy Howton 56 .75 2.00
7 Jack Youngblood 73 .75 2.00
8 Billy Kilmer 62 1.00 2.50
9 Billy Sims 81 1.00 2.50
10 Bo Jackson 88 1.50 4.00
11 Bob Griese 68 1.25 3.00
12 Boomer Esiason 86 1.00 2.50
13 Charley Conerly 56 .75 2.00
14 Charlie Joiner 72 .75 2.00
15 Christian Okoye 88 .75 2.00
16 Chuck Bednarik 56 1.00 2.50
17 Cliff Branch 75 .75 2.00
18 Dan Fouts 75 1.00 2.50
19 Dan Marino 84 2.50 6.00
20 Dave Casper 77 .75 2.00
21 Deacon Jones 63 1.00 2.50
22 Dick Lane 57 .75 2.00
23 Don Maynard 61 1.00 2.50
24 Doug Williams 79 1.00 2.50
25 Barry Sanders 89 4.00 10.00
26 Bubba Smith 70 .75 2.00
27 Ed Too Tall Jones 76 .75 2.00
28 Chuck Foreman 74 .75 2.00
29 Elroy Hirsch 56 1.00 2.50
30 Eric Dickerson 84 1.00 2.50
31 Harold Carmichael 74 .75 2.00
32 Frank Gifford 56 1.25 3.00
33 Fred Biletnikoff 65 1.25 3.00
34 Gale Sayers 68 1.25 3.00
35 John Brodie 61 .75 2.00
36 Henry Ellard 85 .75 2.00
37 Jack Lambert 76 1.25 3.00
38 Jim Brown 58 1.50 4.00
39 James Lofton 79 .75 2.00
40 Joe Montana 81 4.00 10.00
41 Joe Namath 65 2.00 5.00
42 Joe Theismann 75 1.25 3.00
43 Tommy McDonald 57 .75 2.00
44 John Elway 84 2.00 5.00
45 John Riggins 72 1.00 2.50
46 Johnny Unitas 57 2.50 6.00
47 Kellen Winslow 81 1.00 2.50
48 Ken Anderson 73 1.00 2.50
49 Ken Stabler 73 1.50 4.00
50 Drew Pearson 75 1.00 2.50
51 Lawrence Taylor 82 1.25 3.00
52 Len Dawson 64 1.25 3.00
53 Lenny Moore 56 .75 2.00
54 Lester Hayes 80 .75 2.00
55 Troy Aikman 89 1.50 4.00
56 Mark Clayton 85 .75 2.00
57 John Taylor 89 .75 2.00
58 Norm Van Brocklin 56 1.00 2.50
59 Gene Upshaw 72 .75 2.00
60 Otis Sistrunk 74 .75 2.00
61 Ottis Anderson 80 .75 2.00
62 Ozzie Newsome 79 1.00 2.50
63 Paul Hornung 57 1.25 3.00
64 Phil Simms 80 1.00 2.50
65 Raymond Berry 57 1.00 2.50
66 Roger Staubach 72 1.50 4.00
67 Ronnie Lott 82 1.00 2.50
68 Roosevelt Brown 56 .75 2.00
69 Roosevelt Grier 56 .75 2.00
70 Sonny Jurgensen 58 1.25 3.00
71 Marcus Allen 83 1.25 3.00
72 Steve Grogan 76 .75 2.00
73 Roger Craig 84 1.00 2.50
74 Ted Hendricks 72 .75 2.00
75 Jim Plunkett 72 1.00 2.50
76 Terry Metcalf 74 .75 2.00
77 Tom Dempsey 70 .75 2.00
78 Tom Fears 56 .75 2.00
79 Tony Dorsett 78 1.25 3.00
80 Walter Payton 76 3.00 8.00
81 Y.A. Tittle 56 1.25 3.00
82 William Perry 86 .75 2.00
83 Steve Young 86 1.50 4.00
84 Rodney Hampton 90 .75 2.00
85 Jim Kelly 87 1.25 3.00
86 Gino Marchetti 57 .75 2.00
87 Sid Luckman 55 1.00 2.50
88 Sammy Baugh 55 1.50 4.00
89 Red Grange 55 2.00 5.00
90 Otto Graham 55 1.25 3.00
91 Mike Singletary 83 1.25 3.00
92 Dick Butkus 68 1.50 4.00
93 John Hannah 74 .75 2.00
94 Derrick Thomas 89 1.25 3.00

2001 Topps Archives Reserve Jerseys

Randomly inserted in packs, these 12 cards feature jersey swatches of retired NFL stars.

GROUP A STATED ODDS 1:8.5
GROUP B STATED ODDS 1:12
OVERALL STATED ODDS 1:3.3
ARRAT Al Toon 5.00 12.00
ARRBE Boomer Esiason 6.00 15.00
ARRBS Barry Sanders 12.50 30.00
ARRDM Dan Marino 12.00 30.00
ARRDT Derrick Thomas 12.00 30.00
ARRJE John Elway 15.00 40.00
ARRJK Jim Kelly 10.00 25.00
ARRJM Joe Montana 15.00 40.00
ARRLT Lawrence Taylor 10.00 25.00
ARRMA Marcus Allen 8.00 20.00
ARRPS Phil Simms 8.00 20.00
ARRSY Steve Young 8.00 20.00

2001 Topps Archives Reserve Mini Helmet Autographs

Issued as box-toppers, these signed mini-helmets were issued one per box and feature 21 of the NFL's all-time leading players. Each helmet included the Topps Hologram seal of authenticity.

ONE PER BOX
1 Marcus Allen 30.00 60.00
2 Ottis Anderson 15.00 30.00
3 Jim Brown 75.00 125.00
4 Mark Clayton 15.00 30.00
5 Roger Craig 20.00 40.00
6 Eric Dickerson 20.00 40.00
8 Lester Hayes 15.00 30.00
9 Ed Too Tall Jones 20.00 40.00
10 Dan Marino 125.00 200.00
11 Don Maynard 15.00 30.00
12 Tommy McDonald 15.00 30.00
13 Terry Metcalf 15.00 30.00
14 Joe Montana 100.00 175.00
15 Joe Namath 90.00 150.00
16 Christian Okoye 15.00 30.00
17 Drew Pearson 15.00 30.00
18 Jim Plunkett 20.00 40.00
19 Mike Singletary 20.00 40.00
20 Lawrence Taylor 40.00 80.00
21 Doug Williams 20.00 40.00

2001 Topps Archives Reserve Rookie Reprint Autographs

serted one per box, these 31 cards feature leading NFL players who autographed their rookie reprint cards. The cards were printed using the Refractor printing technology.

ONE PER BOX
ARABK Billy Kilmer 10.00 25.00
ARABS Barry Sanders 100.00 200.00
ARACB Cliff Branch 10.00 25.00
ARACF Chuck Foreman 7.50 20.00
ARACJ Charlie Joiner 7.50 20.00
ARADB Dick Butkus 25.00 60.00
ARADC Dave Casper 10.00 25.00
ARADJ Deacon Jones 12.00 30.00
ARADM Don Maynard 10.00 25.00
ARADW Doug Williams 12.00 30.00
ARAED Eric Dickerson 30.00 60.00
ARAEJ Ed Too Tall Jones 20.00 40.00
ARAFG Frank Gifford 35.00 60.00
ARAHE Henry Ellard 7.50 20.00
ARAJH John Hannah 10.00 25.00
ARAJM Joe Montana 150.00 350.00
ARAJN Joe Namath 125.00 250.00
ARAJR John Riggins 30.00 60.00
ARAJU Johnny Unitas 250.00 400.00
ARALD Len Dawson 20.00 50.00
ARALH Lester Hayes 12.00 30.00
ARALT Lawrence Taylor 40.00 100.00
ARAMA Marcus Allen 50.00 100.00
ARAMC Mark Clayton 7.50 20.00
ARAON Ozzie Newsome 12.00 30.00
ARARB Raymond Berry 12.00 30.00
ARARH Rodney Hampton 7.50 20.00
ARATD Tom Dempsey 7.50 20.00
ARATH Ted Hendricks 7.50 20.00
ARATM Terry Metcalf 7.50 20.00
ARAWP William Perry 7.50 20.00

2013 Topps Archives

COMPLETE SET (240) 75.00 150.00
COMP.SET w/o SP's (200) 20.00 40.00
B PHOTO VARIATION ODDS 1:384 HOB
1A Andrew Luck White 1.50 4.00
1B Andrew Luck Blue SP 15.00 40.00
2 Ryan Williams .20 .50
3 Matt Ryan .25 .60
4 Jermichael Finley .20 .50
5 Maurice Jones-Drew .20 .50
6 Dez Bryant .30 .75
7 Josh Gordon .20 .50
8 Jonathan Stewart .20 .50
9 Jason Pierre-Paul .20 .50
10 Jim Kelly .30 .75
11 Charles Woodson .30 .75
12 Tom Brady .75 2.00
13 Jared Allen .20 .50
14 Roddy White .20 .50
15 Antonio Gates .25 .60
16 Harrison Smith .20 .50
17 Carson Palmer .25 .60
18 Steve Johnson .25 .60
19A R.Wilson both hands 1.00 2.50
19B R.Wilson one hand SP 20.00 40.00
20 Randy Moss .25 .60
21 Darrelle Revis .20 .50
22 BenJarvus Green-Ellis .25 .60
23 Marques Colston .20 .50
24 David Wilson .20 .50
25 Dan Marino .60 1.50
26 Willis McGahee .20 .50
27 LaMichael James .20 .50
28 Ben Roethlisberger .30 .75
29 Miles Austin .20 .50
30 Drew Brees .30 .75
31 Michael Floyd .20 .50
32 J.J. Watt .25 .60
33 LeSean McCoy .30 .75
34 Mark Barron .25 .60
35 Kurt Warner .25 .60
36 Matt Forte .20 .50
37 Mike Williams .25 .60
38 Travis Benjamin .20 .50
39 Dwayne Bowe .25 .60
40 John Elway .50 1.25
41 Stevan Ridley .20 .50
42 Dontari Poe .20 .50
43 Chris Long .20 .50
44 Mikel Leshoure .20 .50
45 Ray Lewis .30 .75
46 Coby Fleener .20 .50
47 Kenny Britt .20 .50
48 Fred Davis .20 .50
49 Kendall Wright .20 .50
50 Joe Montana .75 2.00
51A J.Blackmon cutting .30 .75
51B J.Blackmon stiff arm SP 10.00 25.00
52 Kevin Kolb .20 .50
53 Michael Turner .20 .50
54 Malcom Floyd .20 .50
55 Steve Young .40 1.00
56 Lamar Miller .20 .50
57 Isaac Redman .30 .75
58 Mark Sanchez .20 .50
59 Vick Ballard .20 .50
60 Ed Reed .25 .60
61 Patrick Willis .25 .60
62 Andy Dalton .25 .60
63 Jay Cutler .20 .50
64 Luke Kuechly .25 .60
65 Y.A. Tittle .30 .75
66 Jason Witten .25 .60
67 Blaine Gabbert .20 .50
68 Stephen Hill .20 .50
69 Troy Polamalu .30 .75
70 Jerry Rice .50 1.25
71 Chris Rainey .20 .50
72 Jeremy Maclin .20 .50
73 Greg Jennings .20 .50
74 DeAngelo Williams .20 .50
75A T.Richardson both hnds .30 .75
75B T.Richardson one hand SP 12.00 30.00
76 Tim Tebow .25 .60
77 Torrey Smith .20 .50
78 Brian Quick .20 .50
79 Matt Schaub .20 .50
80 Peyton Manning .60 1.50
81 T.Y. Hilton .25 .60
82 Mark Ingram .25 .60
83 Tony Romo .25 .60
84 Reggie Wayne .25 .60
85 Len Dawson .30 .75
86 Chandler Jones .20 .50
87 Victor Cruz .25 .60
88 Ryan Fitzpatrick .20 .50
89 Reggie Bush .20 .50
90 Adrian Peterson .30 .75
91 Brandon Pettigrew .20 .50
92A B.Weeden white .30 .75
92B B.Weeden brown SP 10.00 25.00
93 Sidney Rice .20 .50
94 Sam Bradford .20 .50
95 Troy Aikman .40 1.00
96 Chris Johnson .20 .50
97 Mychal Kendricks .20 .50
98 Wes Welker .25 .60
99 Pierre Garcon .25 .60
100 Arian Foster .25 .60
101A Doug Martin red .40 1.00
101B Doug Martin orange SP 20.00 40.00
102 Beanie Wells .20 .50
103 Julio Jones .30 .75
104 Eric Decker .20 .50
105 Marshawn Lynch .25 .60
106 A.J. Jenkins .20 .50
107 Santonio Holmes .20 .50
108 Anquan Boldin .20 .50
109 Matt Kalil .20 .50
110 Bart Starr .50 1.25
111 Ben Tate .20 .50
112 Cyrus Gray .20 .50
113 Matt Cassel .20 .50
114 DeMarco Murray .25 .60
115 Eli Manning .25 .60
116 Fred Jackson .25 .60
117 Rashard Mendenhall .20 .50
118 Alshon Jeffery .25 .60
119 Darren Sproles .25 .60
120 Emmitt Smith .50 1.25
121 Juron Criner .20 .50
122 Christian Ponder .20 .50
123 D'Qwell Jackson .20 .50
124 Clay Matthews .30 .75
125 Calvin Johnson .30 .75
126 Mike Wallace .20 .50
127 Steve Smith .25 .60
128 Isaiah Pead .20 .50
129 Davone Bess .20 .50
130 Brett Favre .60 1.50
131 Michael Vick .25 .60
132 Brock Osweiler .25 .60
133 Ryan Mathews .25 .60
134 Donald Brown .20 .50
135 Brandon Marshall .25 .60
136 Frank Gore .25 .60
137 Dont'a Hightower .20 .50
138 Von Miller .25 .60
139 Rob Gronkowski .30 .75
140 Joe Namath .40 1.00
141 Darrius Heyward-Bey .20 .50
142 Matthew Stafford .25 .60
143 Keshawn Martin .20 .50
144 Steven Jackson .20 .50
145 Roger Staubach .40 1.00
146A A.Morris left arm .30 .75
146B A.Morris right arm SP 3.00 8.00
147 Josh Freeman .25 .60
148 A.J. Green .30 .75
149 Jake Locker .25 .60
150A Robert Griffin III white .30 .75
150B Robert Griffin III red SP 3.00 8.00
151A Ryan Tannehill white .40 1.00
151B R.Tannehill green SP 10.00 25.00
152 Antonio Brown .30 .75
153 Brian Orakpo .25 .60
154 Bernard Pierce .20 .50
155 Larry Fitzgerald .25 .60
156 Philip Rivers .30 .75
157 Jordy Nelson .25 .60
158 T.J. Graham .20 .50
159 Alex Smith .25 .60
160 Warren Moon .30 .75
161 DeSean Jackson .25 .60
162 Joe Adams .20 .50
163 Greg Little .20 .50
164 Ahmad Bradshaw .20 .50
165 Tony Gonzalez .25 .60
166 Mohamed Sanu .20 .50
167 Julius Peppers .25 .60
168 Shonn Greene .20 .50
169 Andre Johnson .20 .50
170 Cam Newton .30 .75
171 Ronnie Hillman .20 .50
172 C.J. Spiller .20 .50
173 Jamaal Charles .25 .60
174 Ryan Broyles .25 .60
175 Aaron Rodgers .50 1.25
176 Joe Flacco .25 .60
177 Hakeem Nicks .20 .50
178 DeVier Posey .20 .50
179 Brian Urlacher .30 .75
180 Terry Bradshaw .40 1.00
181 Percy Harvin .20 .50
182 Dwayne Allen .20 .50
183 Demaryius Thomas .25 .60
184 Aaron Hernandez .25 .60
185 Phil Simms .25 .60
186 Michael Egnew .20 .50
187 Laurent Robinson .20 .50
188 Titus Young .20 .50
189 Jarius Wright .20 .50
190 Jim Plunkett .25 .60
191 DeMarcus Ware .30 .75
192 Jimmy Graham .30 .75
193 Rueben Randle .20 .50
194 Darren McFadden .25 .60
195 Dan Fouts .25 .60
196 Nick Foles .25 .60
197 Vincent Jackson .20 .50
198 Vernon Davis .20 .50
199A Robert Turbin flexing .30 .75
199B Robert Turbin run SP 8.00 20.00
200 Ray Rice .20 .50
201 Flipper Anderson 1.25 3.00
202 Steve Bartkowski 1.50 4.00
203 Don Beebe 1.25 3.00
204 Anthony Carter 1.25 3.00
205 Wayne Chrebet 1.25 3.00
206 Gary Clark 1.25 3.00
207 Mark Clayton 1.25 3.00
208 Ben Coates 1.25 3.00
209 Vinny Testaverde 1.25 3.00
210 Willie Gault 1.25 3.00
211 Ernest Givins 1.25 3.00
212 Merril Hoge 1.25 3.00
213 Haywood Jeffires 1.25 3.00
214 Billy Johnson 1.25 3.00
215 Ed Too Tall Jones 1.25 3.00
216 Rodney Hampton 1.25 3.00
217 Louis Lipps 1.25 3.00
218 Rocket Ismail 1.50 4.00
219 Ed McCaffrey 1.25 3.00
220 Stump Mitchell 1.25 3.00
221 Mercury Morris 1.25 3.00
222 Christian Okoye 1.25 3.00
223 Vince Papale 1.50 4.00
224 William Perry 1.25 3.00
225 Mike Rozier 1.25 3.00
226 Al Toon 1.25 3.00
227 Wesley Walker 1.25 3.00
228 Ickey Woods 1.25 3.00
229 Eric Allen 1.25 3.00
230 William Andrews 1.25 3.00
231 Cornelius Bennett 1.25 3.00
232 Harold Carmichael 1.25 3.00
233 Mike Golic 1.25 3.00
234 Brent Jones 1.25 3.00
235 Seth Joyner 1.25 3.00
236 Kevin Mack 1.25 3.00
237 Chuck Muncie 1.25 3.00
238 Vai Sikahema 1.25 3.00
230 Clyde Simmons 1.25 3.00
240 Curt Warner 1.25 3.00

2013 Topps Archives Gold

*GOLD: 4X TO 10X BASIC CARDS
STATED ODDS 1:12 HOB
B PHOTO VARIATIONS NOT PRICED
1A Andrew Luck White 15.00 40.00
1B Andrew Luck Blue SP 50.00 120.00
19A R.Wilson both hands 10.00 25.00
25 Dan Marino 12.00 30.00
50 Joe Montana 12.00 30.00
51B J.Blackmon stiff arm SP 20.00 50.00
120 Emmitt Smith 6.00 15.00
145 Roger Staubach 5.00 12.00
180 Terry Bradshaw 5.00 12.00

2013 Topps Archives 1000 Yard Club

MPLETE SET (25) 20.00 40.00
STATED ODDS 1:8 RACK PACK
1 A.J. Green 1.00 2.50
2 Adrian Peterson 1.00 2.50
3 Ahmad Bradshaw .60 1.50
4 Andre Johnson .60 1.50
5 Arian Foster .75 2.00
6 Brandon Lloyd .60 1.50
7 Calvin Johnson 1.00 2.50
8 Chris Johnson .60 1.50
9 Emmitt Smith 1.50 4.00
10 Frank Gore .75 2.00
11 Jamaal Charles .75 2.00
12 Jerry Rice 1.50 4.00
13 Larry Fitzgerald .75 2.00
14 LeSean McCoy 1.00 2.50
15 Matt Forte .60 1.50
16 Maurice Jones-Drew .60 1.50
17 Mike Wallace .60 1.50
18 Randy Moss .75 2.00
19 Reggie Wayne .75 2.00
20 Ryan Mathews .75 2.00
21 Santana Moss .75 2.00
22 Steven Jackson .60 1.50
23 Victor Cruz .75 2.00
24 Wes Welker .75 2.00
25 Willis McGahee .60 1.50

2013 Topps Archives 1962 Jerseys

62RAF Arian Foster
62RAG Antonio Gates
62RAJ Alshon Jeffery 5.00 12.00
62RAJG A.J. Green 6.00 15.00
62RAJJ A.J. Jenkins 4.00 10.00
62RAJO Andre Johnson 3.00 8.00
62RAI Andrew Luck 12.00 30.00
62RBG Blaine Gabbert 4.00 10.00
62RBP Bernard Pierce 4.00 10.00
62RBQ Brian Quick 4.00 10.00
62RBW Brandon Weeden 4.00 10.00
62RCN Cam Newton
62RDB Drew Brees 6.00 15.00
62RDBO Dwayne Bowe 15.00 40.00
62RDBR Dez Bryant 8.00 20.00
62RDM Doug Martin 6.00 15.00
62RDMU DeMarco Murray 6.00 15.00
62RDP DeVier Posey 4.00 10.00
62RDR Darrelle Revis 4.00 10.00
62RDW David Wilson 4.00 10.00
62REM Eli Manning SP 10.00 25.00
62RIP Isaiah Pead 4.00 10.00
62RJA Joe Adams 4.00 10.00
62RJB Justin Blackmon 4.00 10.00
62RJC Jamaal Charles 8.00 20.00
62RJCU Jay Cutler 6.00 15.00
62RJG Jimmy Graham 6.00 15.00
62RJJ Julio Jones 6.00 15.00
62RKW Kendall Wright 4.00 10.00
62RLF Larry Fitzgerald 5.00 12.00
62RLJ LaMichael James 4.00 10.00
62RLM Lamar Miller 6.00 15.00
62RME Michael Egnew 4.00 10.00
62RMF Michael Floyd 4.00 10.00
62RMFO Matt Forte 12.00 30.00
62RMI Mark Ingram 5.00 12.00
62RMJD Maurice Jones-Drew 4.00 10.00
62RMS Mohamed Sanu 4.00 10.00
62RNF Nick Foles 5.00 12.00
62RRB Ryan Broyles 4.00 10.00
62RRG Rob Gronkowski 8.00 20.00
62RRG3 Robert Griffin III 4.00 10.00
62RRL Ray Lewis 6.00 15.00
62RRR Rueben Randle 4.00 10.00
62RRT Ryan Tannehill 10.00 25.00
62RRTU Robert Turbin 4.00 10.00
62RRW Russell Wilson 10.00 25.00
62RSH Stephen Hill 4.00 10.00
62RSJ Steve Johnson
62RTB Tom Brady SP 12.50 25.00
62RTG T.J. Graham 4.00 10.00
62RTR Trent Richardson 4.00 10.00
62RTRO Tony Romo 8.00 20.00
62RTS Torrey Smith 4.00 10.00
62RTYH T.Y. Hilton 5.00 12.00

2013 Topps Archives 1965 Autographs

65TBABO Brock Osweiler 30.00 80.00
65TBABQ Brian Quick 20.00 50.00
65TBADM Doug Martin 30.00 80.00
65TBAJ Alshon Jeffery 25.00 60.00
65TBAJB Justin Blackmon 25.00 60.00
65TBAJG Josh Gordon 30.00 80.00
65TBAJJ A.J. Jenkins 25.00 60.00
65TBAL Andrew Luck 150.00 300.00
65TBAM Alfred Morris 25.00 60.00
65TBART Ryan Tannehill 50.00 100.00
65TBBW Brandon Weeden 20.00 50.00
65TBDW David Wilson 25.00 60.00
65TBIP Isaiah Pead 20.00 50.00
65TBKW Kendall Wright
65TBLJ LaMichael James 25.00 60.00
65TBLM Lamar Miller 25.00 60.00
65TBMF Michael Floyd 25.00 60.00
65TBRG Robert Griffin III 25.00 60.00
65TBSH Stephen Hill 25.00 60.00
65TBTR Trent Richardson 25.00 60.00

2013 Topps Archives 1968 Stand-Ups

MPLETE SET (15) 25.00 50.00
STATED ODDS 1:12
68SUAL Andrew Luck 2.00 5.00
68SUDB Drew Brees 1.25 3.00
68SUEM Eli Manning 1.00 2.50
68SUJA Jared Allen .75 2.00
68SUJB Justin Blackmon .75 2.00
68SUJG Jimmy Graham 1.25 3.00
68SULF Larry Fitzgerald 1.00 2.50
68SUMF Marshawn Lynch 1.00 2.50
68SUPM Peyton Manning 2.50 6.00
68SURG Robert Griffin III .75 2.00
68SUSY Steve Young 1.50 4.00
68SUTA Troy Aikman 1.50 4.00
68SUTR Trent Richardson .75 2.00
68SUWW Wes Welker 1.00 2.50
68SUJBR Jim Brown 1.50 4.00

2013 Topps Archives 1970 Glossy

ATED ODDS 1:6 HOB
1 Aaron Rodgers 2.00 5.00
2 Alshon Jeffery 1.00 2.50
3 Andrew Luck 2.00 5.00
4 Arian Foster 1.00 2.50
5 Calvin Johnson 1.25 3.00
6 Cam Newton 1.25 3.00
7 Darren McFadden 1.00 2.50
8 Doug Martin 1.00 2.50
9 Drew Brees 1.25 3.00
10 Jason Pierre-Paul .75 2.00
11 Joe Montana 3.00 8.00
12 Joe Namath 1.50 4.00
13 John Elway 2.00 5.00
14 Julio Jones 1.25 3.00
15 Justin Blackmon .75 2.00
16 Kurt Warner 1.00 2.50
17 Matt Forte .75 2.00
18 Ray Rice .75 2.00
19 Ray Lewis 1.25 3.00
20 Reggie Bush .75 2.00
21 Rob Gronkowski 1.25 3.00
22 Robert Griffin III .75 2.00
23 Tom Brady 3.00 8.00
24 Tony Romo 1.00 2.50
25 Troy Polamalu 1.25 3.00

2013 Topps Archives 1981 Super Action

STATED ODDS 1:100
81SAAJ Alshon Jeffery 8.00 20.00
81SAAJJ A.J. Jenkins 8.00 20.00
81SAAL Andrew Luck 25.00 50.00
81SAAM Alfred Morris 6.00 15.00
81SABO Brock Osweiler 8.00 20.00
81SABQ Brian Quick 6.00 15.00
81SABW Brandon Weeden 6.00 15.00
81SADM Doug Martin 12.00 30.00
81SADW David Wilson 6.00 15.00
81SAIP Isaiah Pead 6.00 15.00
81SAJB Justin Blackmon 10.00 25.00
81SAJG Josh Gordon 6.00 15.00
81SAKW Kendall Wright 6.00 15.00
81SALM Lamar Miller 6.00 15.00
81SAMF Michael Floyd 6.00 15.00
81SAMS Mohamed Sanu 6.00 15.00
81SARB Ryan Broyles 8.00 20.00
81SARG Robert Griffin III 6.00 15.00
81SARH Ronnie Hillman 6.00 15.00
81SARR Rueben Randle 15.00 40.00
81SART Ryan Tannehill 12.00 30.00
81SARTU Robert Turbin 6.00 15.00
81SASH Stephen Hill 6.00 15.00
81SATR Trent Richardson 12.00 30.00

2013 Topps Archives 1988 Mini Autographs

EXCH EXPIRATION: 5/31/2016
88MAJ Alshon Jeffery 25.00 60.00
88MAJJ A.J. Jenkins 20.00 50.00
88MAL Andrew Luck 150.00 250.00
88MAM Alfred Morris 20.00 50.00
88MBO Brock Osweiler 25.00 60.00
88MBQ Brian Quick 20.00 50.00
88MBW Brandon Weeden 20.00 50.00
88MDM Doug Martin 25.00 60.00
88MDW David Wilson 20.00 50.00
88MIP Isaiah Pead 20.00 50.00
88MJB Justin Blackmon 20.00 50.00
88MJG Josh Gordon 20.00 50.00
88MKW Kendall Wright 20.00 50.00
88MLJ LaMichael James EXCH 20.00 50.00
88MLM Lamar Miller 30.00 80.00
88MMF Michael Floyd 20.00 50.00
88MMS Mohamed Sanu 20.00 50.00
88MRB Ryan Broyles 12.00 30.00
88MRG Robert Griffin III 20.00 50.00
88MRH Ronnie Hillman 20.00 60.00
88MRR Rueben Randle 20.00 50.00
88MRT Ryan Tannehill 50.00 100.00
88MRTU Robert Turbin 20.00 50.00
88MSH Stephen Hill 20.00 50.00
88MTR Trent Richardson 20.00 50.00

2013 Topps Archives Box Bottoms

AF Arian Foster .25 .60
AL Andrew Luck .75 2.00
AM Alfred Morris .30 .75
AP Adrian Peterson .30 .75
AR Aaron Rodgers .50 1.25
BW Brandon Weeden .30 .75
DB Drew Brees .30 .75
DM Doug Martin .40 1.00
EM Eli Manning .25 .60
PM Peyton Manning .60 1.50
RG Robert Griffin III .30 .75
RR Ray Rice .20 .50
RT Ryan Tannehill .40 1.00
RW Russell Wilson 1.00 2.50
TB Tom Brady .75 2.00
TR Trent Richardson .30 .75
PAN1 Brees/Fstr/Wilsn/Morris 1.50 4.00
PAN2 Eli/RGIII/Rdgrs/Wden 2.00 5.00
PAN3 Mnng/Brdy/Luck/Tnnhll 2.00 5.00
PAN4 Ptrsn/Rce/Rchdsn/Mrtn 1.50 4.00

2013 Topps Archives Fan Favorite Autographs

TWO PER HOBBY BOX
EXCH EXPIRATION: 5/31/2016
FFAAC Anthony Carter 8.00 20.00
FFAAT Al Toon 6.00 15.00
FFABB Bubby Brister 8.00 20.00
FFABC Ben Coates 6.00 15.00
FFABG Bob Golic 6.00 15.00
FFABJ Billy Johnson 6.00 15.00
FFABJO Brent Jones 6.00 15.00
FFABS Brian Sipe 10.00 25.00
FFACB Cornelius Bennett 6.00 15.00
FFACM Chuck Muncie 10.00 25.00
FFACO Christian Okoye 6.00 15.00
FFACS Clyde Simmons 6.00 15.00
FFACW Curt Warner 8.00 20.00
FFADB Don Beebe 8.00 20.00
FFADK Dave Krieg 8.00 20.00
FFADPL Doug Plank 10.00 25.00
FFAEA Eric Allen EXCH 6.00 15.00
FFAEG Ernest Givins 6.00 15.00
FFAEJ Ed Too Tall Jones 8.00 20.00
FFAEM Ed McCaffrey 8.00 20.00
FFAGC Gary Clark 8.00 20.00
FFAHC Harold Carmichael 8.00 20.00
FFAHJ Haywood Jeffires 6.00 15.00
FFAHM Herman Moore 6.00 15.00
FFAJLW John L. Williams 6.00 15.00
FFAJW Ickey Woods 8.00 20.00
FFAJZ Jim Zorn 8.00 20.00
FFAKA Ken Anderson 10.00 25.00
FFAKM Kevin Mack 8.00 20.00
FFAKME Karl Mecklenburg 8.00 20.00
FFALB Leroy Butler 8.00 20.00
FFALJ Lionel James 6.00 15.00
FFALL Louis Lipps 8.00 20.00
FFAMC Mark Clayton 8.00 20.00
FFAMD Mark Duper 8.00 20.00
FFAMG Mike Golic 8.00 20.00
FFAMH Merril Hoge 10.00 25.00
FFAMM Mercury Morris EXCH 10.00 25.00
FFAMQ Mike Quick 6.00 15.00
FFAMR Mike Rozier 6.00 15.00
FFANL Neil Lomax 6.00 15.00
FFARH Rodney Hampton 6.00 15.00
FFARI Rocket Ismail 8.00 20.00
FFASB Steve Bartkowski 6.00 15.00
FFASJ Seth Joyner 6.00 15.00
FFASM Stump Mitchell 6.00 15.00
FFATR Tom Rathman 6.00 15.00
FFAVP Vince Papale 10.00 25.00
FFAVS Vai Sikahema 6.00 15.00
FFAVT Vinny Testaverde 8.00 20.00
FFAWM Willie McGinest 6.00 15.00
FFAWC Wayne Chrebet 6.00 15.00
FFAWFA Flipper Anderson 6.00 15.00
FFAWG Willie Gault 8.00 20.00
FFAWP William Perry EXCH 10.00 25.00
FFAWW Wesley Walker 6.00 15.00

2013 Topps Archives Mayo

STATED ODDS 1:40
MAJ Alshon Jeffery 2.00 5.00
MAJJ A.J. Jenkins 1.50 4.00
MAL Andrew Luck 4.00 10.00
MAM Alfred Morris 1.50 4.00
MBO Brock Osweiler 2.00 5.00
MBQ Brian Quick 1.50 4.00
MBW Brandon Weeden 1.50 4.00
MDM Doug Martin 2.00 5.00
MDW David Wilson 1.50 4.00
MIP Isaiah Pead 1.50 4.00
MJB Justin Blackmon 1.50 4.00
MJG Josh Gordon 1.50 4.00
MKW Kendall Wright 1.50 4.00
MLJ LaMichael James 1.50 4.00
MLM Lamar Miller 1.50 4.00
MMF Michael Floyd 1.50 4.00
MMS Mohamed Sanu 1.50 4.00
MRB Ryan Broyles 2.00 5.00
MRG Robert Griffin III 1.50 4.00
MRH Ronnie Hillman 1.50 4.00
MRR Rueben Randle 1.50 4.00
MRT Robert Turbin 1.50 4.00
MRT Ryan Tannehill 2.00 5.00
MSH Stephen Hill 1.50 4.00
MTR Trent Richardson 1.50 4.00

2013 Topps Archives Rookie Autographs

UNPRICED ODDS 1:2769 HOB
EXCH EXPIRATION: 5/31/2016
CP Cordarrelle Patterson EXCH 8.00 20.00
EL Eddie Lacy EXCH 8.00 20.00
MB1 Montee Ball EXCH 8.00 20.00
MB2 Matt Barkley EXCH 40.00 80.00
ML Marcus Lattimore 8.00 20.00
MT Manti Te'o 10.00 25.00
NNO Mystery Player EXCH 90.00 150.00

2010 Topps Attax

John Abraham .12 .30
2 Joseph Addai .12 .30
3 Jared Allen .12 .30
4 Nnamdi Asomugha .12 .30
5 Oshiomogho Atogwe .12 .30
6 Miles Austin .12 .30
7 Donnie Avery .12 .30
8 Jordan Babineaux .12 .30
9 Champ Bailey .15 .40
10 Nick Barnett .12 .30
11 Jon Beason .12 .30
12 Yeremiah Bell .12 .30
13 Arrelious Benn RC .40 1.00
14 Cedric Benson .12 .30
15 Eric Berry RC .60 1.50
16 Jahvid Best RC .40 1.00
17 Anquan Boldin .12 .30
18 Dwayne Bowe .15 .40
19 Sam Bradford RC .50 1.25
20 Stewart Bradley .12 .30
21 Tom Brady .50 1.25
22 Tyvon Branch .12 .30
23 Drew Brees .20 .50
24 Lance Briggs .15 .40
25 Kenny Britt .12 .30
26 Keith Brooking .12 .30
27 Milo Brown .12 .30
28 Ronnie Brown .12 .30
29 Sheldon Brown .12 .30
30 Dez Bryant RC 1.00 2.50
31 Keith Bulluck .12 .30
32 Reggie Bush .12 .30
33 Darius Butler .12 .30
34 Jairus Byrd .15 .40
35 Calais Campbell .12 .30
36 Matt Cassel .12 .30
37 Brent Celek .12 .30
38 Jamaal Charles .15 .40
39 Dallas Clark .12 .30
40 Jimmy Clausen RC .40 1.00
41 Nate Clements .12 .30
42 Trent Cole .12 .30
43 Nick Collins .12 .30
44 Marques Colston .12 .30
45 Stephen Cooper .12 .30
46 Michael Crabtree .12 .30
47 Antonio Cromartie .12 .30
48 Aaron Curry .15 .40
49 Brian Cushing .12 .30
50 Jay Cutler .12 .30
51 Karlos Dansby .12 .30
52 Vernon Davis .12 .30
53 Vontae Davis .12 .30
54 Brian Dawkins .12 .30
55 Louis Delmas .12 .30
56 Darnell Dockett .12 .30
57 Donald Driver .15 .40
58 Elvis Dumervil .12 .30
59 Jonathan Dwyer .40 1.00
60 Braylon Edwards .12 .30
61 Shaun Ellis .12 .30
62 James Farrior .12 .30
63 Brett Favre 1.50 4.00
64 Cortland Finnegan .12 .30
65 Larry Fitzgerald .15 .40
66 Joe Flacco .15 .40
67 London Fletcher .15 .40
68 Brandon Flowers .12 .30
69 Matt Forte .12 .30
70 Josh Freeman .15 .40
71 Dwight Freeney .12 .30
72 Chris Gamble .12 .30
73 Pierre Garcon .15 .40
74 David Garrard .12 .30
75 Antonio Gates .15 .40
76 Tony Gonzalez .15 .40
77 Frank Gore .15 .40
78 Ryan Grant .15 .40
79 Shonn Greene .12 .30
80 Chad Greenway .12 .30
81 Cedric Griffin .12 .30
82 Leon Hall .12 .30
83 Casey Hampton .12 .30
84 David Harris .12 .30
85 James Harrison .20 .50
86 Percy Harvin .12 .30
87 Matt Hasselbeck .12 .30
88 A.J. Hawk .12 .30
89 David Hawthorne RC .60 1.50
90 Geno Hayes .12 .30
91 Chad Henne .15 .40
92 Devin Hester .15 .40
93 Santonio Holmes .12 .30
94 Chris Hope .12 .30
95 T.J. Houshmandzadeh .12 .30
96 DeSean Jackson .15 .40
97 Steven Jackson .12 .30
98 Vincent Jackson .12 .30
99 Brandon Jacobs .12 .30
100 Bradie James .12 .30
101 Malcolm Jenkins .12 .30
102 Mike Jenkins .12 .30
103 Greg Jennings .12 .30
104 Andre Johnson .15 .40
105 Calvin Johnson .20 .50
106 Chris Johnson .12 .30
107 Dhani Jones .12 .30
108 Felix Jones .12 .30
109 Maurice Jones-Drew .12 .30
110 Johnathan Joseph .12 .30
111 Kevin Kolb .12 .30
112 LaRon Landry .12 .30
113 James Laurinaitis .15 .40
114 Ray Lewis .20 .50
115 Curtis Lofton .12 .30
116 Chris Long .12 .30
117 Jeremy Maclin .12 .30
118 Eli Manning .15 .40
119 Peyton Manning .50 1.25
120 Brandon Marshall .15 .40
121 Derrick Mason .12 .30
122 Mohamed Massaquoi .15 .40
123 Ryan Mathews RC .40 1.00
124 Robert Mathis .12 .30
125 Clay Matthews .20 .50
126 Rey Maualuga .12 .30
127 Jerod Mayo .15 .40
128 Dexter McCluster RC .50 1.25
129 Colt McCoy RC .50 1.25
130 LeSean McCoy .20 .50
131 Darren McFadden .12 .30
132 Donovan McNabb .15 .40
133 Rashard Mendenhall .12 .30
134 Brandon Meriweather .12 .30
135 Shawne Merriman .12 .30
136 Knowshon Moreno .12 .30
137 Kirk Morrison .12 .30
138 Randy Moss .15 .40
139 Santana Moss .15 .40
140 Terence Newman .12 .30
141 Hakeem Nicks .12 .30
142 Chad Ochocinco .12 .30
143 Brian Orakpo .12 .30
144 Kyle Orton .12 .30
145 Terrell Owens .15 .40
146 Carson Palmer .15 .40
147 Julius Peppers .15 .40
148 Adrian Peterson .20 .50
149 Julian Peterson .12 .30
150 Mike Peterson .12 .30
151 Kenny Phillips .12 .30
152 Shaun Phillips .12 .30
153 Troy Polamalu .20 .50
154 Joey Porter .12 .30
155 Clinton Portis .12 .30
156 Paul Posluszny .12 .30
157 Ed Reed .15 .40
158 Darrelle Revis .12 .30
159 Ray Rice .12 .30
160 Sidney Rice .12 .30
161 Philip Rivers .20 .50
162 Aaron Rodgers .40 1.00
163 Dominque Rodgers-Cromartie .12 .30
164 Ben Roethlisberger .20 .50
165 Antrel Rolle .12 .30
166 Tony Romo .15 .40
167 Barrett Ruud .12 .30
168 Matt Ryan .15 .40
169 DeMeco Ryans .12 .30
170 Asante Samuel .12 .30
171 Mark Sanchez .12 .30
172 Matt Schaub .12 .30
173 Aaron Schobel .12 .30
174 Bart Scott .12 .30
175 Clint Session .12 .30
176 Darren Sharper .12 .30
177 Ernie Sims .12 .30
178 Mike Sims-Walker .12 .30
179 Steve Slaton .12 .30
180 Alex Smith QB .15 .40

181 Sean Smith .12 .30
182 Steve Smith .15 .40
183 Steve Smith USC .12 .30
184 Will Smith .12 .30
185 C.J. Spiller RC .40 1.00
186 Matthew Stafford .15 .40
187 Terrell Suggs .12 .30
188 Ndamukong Suh RC .75 2.00
189 Aqib Talib .12 .30
190 Golden Tate RC .50 1.25
191 Tim Tebow RC 1.25 3.00
192 Demaryius Thomas RC 1.00 2.50
193 Charles Tillman .15 .40
194 Justin Tuck .12 .30
195 Stephen Tulloch .12 .30
196 Michael Turner .12 .30
197 Osi Umenyiora .12 .30
198 Brian Urlacher .20 .50
199 Jonathan Vilma .12 .30
200 Mike Wallace .12 .30
201 Hines Ward .15 .40
202 DeMarcus Ware .15 .40
203 Reggie Wayne .15 .40
204 Wes Welker .15 .40
205 Chris Wells .12 .30
206 Roddy White .12 .30
207 Vince Wilfork .12 .30
208 Cadillac Williams .12 .30
209 D.J. Williams .12 .30
210 DeAngelo Williams .12 .30
211 Demorrio Williams .12 .30
212 Kevin Williams .12 .30
213 Mario Williams .15 .40
214 Patrick Willis .15 .40
215 Adrian Wilson .12 .30
216 Kellen Winslow .12 .30
217 Jason Witten .15 .40
218 LaMarr Woodley .12 .30
219 Charles Woodson .20 .50
220 Vince Young .12 .30

2010 Topps Attax Code Cards

COMPLETE SET (50) 20.00 40.00
ONE FOIL OR CODE CARD PER BOOSTER
ONE CODE CARD PER 2010 TOPPS
1 Jared Allen .40 1.00
2 Nnamdi Asomugha .40 1.00
3 Oshiomogho Atogwe .40 1.00
4 Miles Austin .40 1.00
5 Jon Beason .40 1.00
6 Cedric Benson .40 1.00
7 Tom Brady 1.50 4.00
8 Drew Brees .60 1.50
9 Brian Dawkins .40 1.00
10 Brett Favre 3.00 8.00
11 Larry Fitzgerald .50 1.25
12 Dwight Freeney .40 1.00
13 Antonio Gates .50 1.25
14 Frank Gore .50 1.25
15 David Harris .40 1.00
16 James Harrison .60 1.50
17 DeSean Jackson .50 1.25
18 Steven Jackson .40 1.00
19 Andre Johnson .50 1.25
20 Calvin Johnson .60 1.50
21 Chris Johnson .40 1.00
22 Maurice Jones-Drew .40 1.00
23 James Laurinaitis .50 1.25
24 Ray Lewis .60 1.50
25 Peyton Manning 1.50 4.00
26 Brandon Marshall .50 1.25
27 Jerod Mayo .50 1.25
28 Rashard Mendenhall .40 1.00
29 Randy Moss .50 1.25
30 Julius Peppers .50 1.25
31 Adrian Peterson .60 1.50
32 Troy Polamalu .60 1.50
33 Ed Reed .50 1.25
34 Darrelle Revis .40 1.00
35 Ray Rice .40 1.00
36 Philip Rivers .60 1.50
37 Aaron Rodgers 1.25 3.00
38 DeMeco Ryans .40 1.00
39 Asante Samuel .40 1.00
40 Matt Schaub .40 1.00
41 Darren Sharper .40 1.00
42 Michael Turner .40 1.00
43 Osi Umenyiora .40 1.00
44 Brian Urlacher .60 1.50
45 Jonathan Vilma .40 1.00
46 DeMarcus Ware .50 1.25
47 Reggie Wayne .50 1.25
48 D.J. Williams .40 1.00
49 Patrick Willis .50 1.25
50 Adrian Wilson .40 1.00

2010 Topps Attax Legends Foil

COMPLETE SET (4) 10.00 25.00
ONE FOIL OR CODE CARD PER BOOSTER
1 John Elway 3.00 8.00
2 Ronnie Lott 1.50 4.00
3 Dan Marino 4.00 10.00
4 Emmitt Smith 3.00 8.00

2010 Topps Attax Red Zone

MPLETE SET (70) 30.00 60.00
ONE FOIL OR CODE CARD PER BOOSTER
1 Joseph Addai .50 1.25
2 Oshiomogho Atogwe .50 1.25
3 Miles Austin .50 1.25
4 Champ Bailey .60 1.50
5 Cedric Benson .50 1.25
6 Eric Berry .60 1.50
7 Sam Bradford .50 1.25
8 Lance Briggs UER .60 1.50
9 Ronnie Brown .50 1.25
10 Dez Bryant 1.00 2.50
11 Jairus Byrd .60 1.50
12 Jamaal Charles .60 1.50
13 Dallas Clark .50 1.25
14 Trent Cole .50 1.25
15 Nick Collins .50 1.25
16 Marques Colston .50 1.25
17 Michael Crabtree .50 1.25
18 Aaron Curry .60 1.50
19 Brian Cushing .50 1.25
20 Karlos Dansby .50 1.25
21 Louis Delmas .50 1.25
22 Elvis Dumervil .50 1.25
23 Brett Favre 1.50 4.00
24 Joe Flacco .60 1.50
25 David Garrard .50 1.25
26 Antonio Gates .60 1.50
27 Ryan Grant .60 1.50
28 Shonn Greene .50 1.25
29 David Harris .50 1.25
30 Percy Harvin .50 1.25
31 A.J. Hawk .50 1.25
32 T.J. Houshmandzadeh .50 1.25
33 DeSean Jackson .60 1.50
34 Vincent Jackson .50 1.25
35 Brandon Jacobs .50 1.25
36 Greg Jennings .50 1.25
37 Calvin Johnson .75 2.00
38 James Laurinaitis .60 1.50
39 Robert Mathis .50 1.25
40 Clay Matthews .75 2.00
41 Rey Maualuga .50 1.25
42 Jerod Mayo .60 1.50
43 LeSean McCoy .75 2.00
44 Rashard Mendenhall .50 1.25
45 Brandon Meriweather .50 1.25
46 Knowshon Moreno .50 1.25
47 Terence Newman .50 1.25
48 Hakeem Nicks .50 1.25
49 Julius Peppers .60 1.50
50 Joey Porter .50 1.25
51 Ray Rice .50 1.25
52 Sidney Rice .50 1.25
53 Philip Rivers .75 2.00
54 Dominque Rodgers-Cromartie .50 1.25
55 Antrel Rolle .50 1.25
56 Tony Romo .60 1.50
57 Barrett Ruud .50 1.25
58 Matt Ryan .60 1.50
59 DeMeco Ryans .50 1.25
60 Steve Smith .60 1.50
61 C.J. Spiller .40 1.00
62 Ndamukong Suh .75 2.00
63 Aqib Talib .50 1.25
64 Michael Turner .50 1.25
65 Osi Umenyiora .50 1.25
66 Chris Wells .50 1.25
67 Roddy White .50 1.25
68 D.J. Williams .50 1.25
69 DeAngelo Williams .50 1.25
70 Mario Williams .60 1.50
71 Adrian Wilson .50 1.25
72 LaMarr Woodley .50 1.25
73 Charles Woodson .75 2.00

2010 Topps Attax Signed Stars Rookie Autographs

ATED ODDS 1:1393 B/J
1 Jahvid Best 8.00 20.00
2 Sam Bradford 75.00 135.00
3 Dez Bryant 50.00 100.00
4 Jimmy Clausen 15.00 40.00
5 Ryan Mathews 15.00 40.00
6 Colt McCoy 25.00 60.00
7 C.J. Spiller 15.00 40.00
8 Golden Tate 12.00 30.00
9 Tim Tebow 60.00 120.00

2010 Topps Attax Superstars

COMPLETE SET (30) 20.00 40.00
ONE FOIL OR CODE CARD PER BOOSTER
1 Jared Allen .60 1.50
2 Nnamdi Asomugha .60 1.50
3 Jon Beason .60 1.50
4 Tom Brady 2.50 6.00
5 Drew Brees 1.00 2.50
6 Brian Dawkins .60 1.50
7 Larry Fitzgerald .75 2.00
8 Dwight Freeney .60 1.50
9 Frank Gore .75 2.00
10 James Harrison 1.00 2.50
11 Steven Jackson .60 1.50
12 Andre Johnson .75 2.00
13 Chris Johnson .60 1.50
14 Maurice Jones-Drew .60 1.50
15 Ray Lewis 1.00 2.50
16 Peyton Manning 2.50 6.00
17 Brandon Marshall .75 2.00
18 Randy Moss .75 2.00
19 Adrian Peterson 1.00 2.50
20 Ed Reed .75 2.00
21 Darrelle Revis .60 1.50
22 Aaron Rodgers 2.00 5.00
23 Asante Samuel .60 1.50
24 Matt Schaub .60 1.50
25 Darren Sharper .60 1.50
26 Brian Urlacher 1.00 2.50
27 Jonathan Vilma .60 1.50
28 DeMarcus Ware .75 2.00
29 Reggie Wayne .75 2.00
30 Patrick Willis .75 2.00

1996 Topps Chrome

e 1996 Topps Chrome set was issued in one series totalling 165 cards. The 4-card packs had a suggested retail of $3.00 each. These standard-sized cards are the same as the regular 1996 set except for numbering and the chrome foil treatment.

COMPLETE SET (165) 40.00 100.00
1 Troy Aikman 1.00 2.50
2 Kevin Greene .20 .50
3 Robert Brooks .40 1.00
4 Junior Seau .40 1.00
5 Brett Perriman .07 .20
6 Cortez Kennedy .07 .20
7 Orlando Thomas .07 .20
8 Anthony Miller .20 .50
9 Jeff Blake .40 1.00
10 Trent Dilfer .40 1.00
11 Heath Shuler .20 .50
12 Michael Jackson .20 .50
13 Merton Hanks .07 .20
14 Dale Carter .07 .20
15 Eric Metcalf .07 .20
16 Barry Sanders 1.50 4.00
17 Joey Galloway .40 1.00
18 Bryan Cox .07 .20
19 Harvey Williams .07 .20
20 Terrell Davis .60 1.50
21 Darnay Scott .20 .50
22 Kerry Collins .40 1.00
23 Warren Sapp .07 .20
24 Michael Westbrook .40 1.00
25 Mark Brunell .60 1.50
26 Craig Heyward .07 .20
27 Eric Allen .07 .20
28 Dana Stubblefield .20 .50
29 Steve Bono .07 .20
30 Larry Brown .07 .20
31 Warren Moon .20 .50
32 Jim Kelly .40 1.00
33 Terry McDaniel .07 .20
34 Dan Wilkinson .07 .20
35 Dave Brown .07 .20
36 Todd Lyght .07 .20
37 Aeneas Williams .07 .20
38 Shannon Sharpe .20 .50
39 Errict Rhett .20 .50
40 Yancey Thigpen .20 .50
41 J.J. Stokes .40 1.00
42 Marshall Faulk .50 1.25
43 Chester McGlockton .07 .20
44 Darryll Lewis .07 .20
45 Drew Bledsoe .60 1.50
46 Tyrone Wheatley .20 .50
47 Herman Moore .20 .50
48 Darren Woodson .20 .50
49 Ricky Watters .20 .50
50 Emmitt Smith TYC .60 1.50
51 Barry Sanders TYC .60 1.50
52 Curtis Martin TYC .40 1.00
53 Chris Warren TYC .20 .50
54 Errict Rhett TYC .20 .50
55 Rodney Hampton TYC .07 .20
56 Terrell Davis TYC .40 1.00
57 Marshall Faulk TYC .40 1.00
58 Rashaan Salaam TYC .20 .50
59 Curtis Conway .40 1.00
60 Isaac Bruce .40 1.00
61 Thurman Thomas .40 1.00
62 Terry Allen .20 .50
63 Lamar Lathon .07 .20
64 Mark Chmura .20 .50
65 Chris Warren .20 .50
66 Jessie Tuggle .07 .20
67 Erik Kramer .07 .20
68 Tim Brown .40 1.00
69 Derrick Thomas .40 1.00
70 Willie McGinest .07 .20
71 Frank Sanders .20 .50
72 Bernie Parmalee .07 .20
73 Kordell Stewart .40 1.00
74 Brent Jones .07 .20
75 Edgar Bennett .20 .50
76 Rashaan Salaam .20 .50
77 Carl Pickens .20 .50
78 Terance Mathis .07 .20
79 Deion Sanders .50 1.25
80 Glyn Milburn .07 .20
81 Lee Woodall .07 .20
82 Neil Smith .20 .50
83 Stan Humphries .20 .50
84 Rick Mirer .20 .50
85 Troy Vincent .07 .20
86 Sam Mills .07 .20
87 Brian Mitchell .07 .20
88 Hardy Nickerson .07 .20
89 Tamarick Vanover .20 .50
90 Steve McNair .60 1.50
91 Jerry Rice TYC .40 1.00
92 Isaac Bruce TYC .40 1.00
93 Herman Moore TYC .20 .50
94 Cris Carter TYC .40 1.00
95 Tim Brown TYC .20 .50
96 Carl Pickens TYC .20 .50
97 Joey Galloway TYC .40 1.00
98 Jerry Rice 1.00 2.50
99 Cris Carter .40 1.00
100 Curtis Martin .60 1.50
101 Scott Mitchell .20 .50
102 Ken Harvey .07 .20
103 Rodney Hampton .20 .50
104 Reggie White .40 1.00
105 Eddie Robinson .07 .20
106 Greg Lloyd .20 .50
107 Phillippi Sparks .07 .20
108 Emmitt Smith 1.50 4.00
109 Tom Carter .07 .20
110 Jim Everett .07 .20
111 James O.Stewart .20 .50
112 Kyle Brady .07 .20
113 Irving Fryar .20 .50
114 Vinny Testaverde .20 .50
115 John Elway 2.00 5.00
116 Chris Spielman .07 .20
117 Mike Mamula .07 .20
118 Jim Harbaugh .20 .50
119 Ken Norton .07 .20
120 Bruce Smith .20 .50
121 Daryl Johnston .20 .50
122 Blaine Bishop .07 .20
123 Jeff George .20 .50
124 Jeff Hostetler .07 .20
125 Jerome Bettis .40 1.00
126 Jay Novacek .07 .20
127 Bryce Paup .07 .20
128 Neil O'Donnell .20 .50
129 Marcus Allen .40 1.00
130 Steve Young .60 1.50
131 Brett Favre TYC .75 2.00
132 Scott Mitchell TYC .07 .20
133 John Elway TYC .75 2.00
134 Jeff Blake TYC .20 .50
135 Dan Marino TYC .75 2.00
136 Drew Bledsoe TYC .40 1.00
137 Troy Aikman TYC .40 1.00
138 Steve Young TYC .40 1.00
139 Jim Kelly TYC .40 1.00
140 Jeff Graham .07 .20
141 Hugh Douglas .20 .50
142 Dan Marino 2.00 5.00
143 Darrell Green .07 .20
144 Eric Zeier .07 .20
145 Brett Favre 2.00 5.00
146 Carnell Lake .07 .20
147 Ben Coates .20 .50
148 Tony Martin .20 .50
149 Michael Irvin .40 1.00
150 Lawrence Phillips RC .40 1.00
151 Alex Van Dyke RC .60 1.50
152 Kevin Hardy RC .60 1.50
153 Rickey Dudley RC .75 2.00
154 Eric Moulds RC 4.00 10.00
155 Simeon Rice RC 1.50 4.00
156 Marvin Harrison RC 7.50 20.00
157 Tim Biakabutuka RC 1.50 4.00
158 Duane Clemons RC .40 1.00
159 Keyshawn Johnson RC 5.00 12.00
160 John Mobley RC .60 1.50
161 Leeland McElroy RC .60 1.50
162 Eddie George RC 6.00 12.00
163 Jonathan Ogden RC 2.00 5.00
164 Eddie Kennison RC 2.00 5.00
165 Checklist .07 .20

1996 Topps Chrome Refractors

*REF.STARS: 2X TO 5X BASIC CARDS
*UNLISTED REF.RCs: .8X TO 2X
REF.STATED ODDS 1:12
156 Marvin Harrison 25.00 60.00

1996 Topps Chrome 40th Anniversary Retros

ndomly inserted in packs at a rate of one in 8, this 40-card standard-sized chrome foil set has a current player set in the design of an earlier Topps football issue. The year of the design is listed after the player below.

COMPLETE SET (40) 60.00 120.00
STATED ODDS 1:8
*REFRACTORS: .75X TO 2X BASIC INSERTS
REF.STATED ODDS 1:24
1 Jim Harbaugh 1956 .60 1.50
2 Greg Lloyd 1957 .60 1.50
3 Barry Sanders 1958 5.00 12.00
4 Merton Hanks 1959 .25 .60
5 Herman Moore 1960 .60 1.50
6 Tim Brown 1961 1.25 3.00
7 Brett Favre 1962 6.00 15.00
8 Cris Carter 1963 1.25 3.00
9 Curtis Martin 1964 2.00 5.00
10 Bryce Paup 1965 .25 .60
11 Steve Bono 1966 .25 .60
12 Blaine Bishop 1967 .25 .60
13 Emmitt Smith 1968 5.00 12.00
14 Carnell Lake 1969 .25 .60
15 Marshall Faulk 1970 1.50 4.00
16 Mike Morris 1971 .25 .60
17 Shannon Sharpe 1972 .60 1.50
18 Steve Young 1973 2.00 5.00
19 Jeff George 1974 .60 1.50
20 Junior Seau 1975 1.25 3.00
21 Chris Warren 1976 .60 1.50
22 Heath Shuler 1977 .60 1.50
23 Jeff Blake 1978 1.25 3.00
24 Reggie White 1979 1.25 3.00
25 Jeff Hostetler 1980 .25 .60
26 Errict Rhett 1981 .60 1.50
27 Rodney Hampton 1982 .60 1.50
28 Jerry Rice 1983 3.00 8.00
29 Jim Everett 1984 .25 .60
30 Isaac Bruce 1985 1.25 3.00
31 Dan Marino 1986 6.00 15.00
32 Marcus Allen 1987 1.25 3.00
33 Erik Kramer 1988 .25 .60
34 John Elway 1989 6.00 15.00
35 Ricky Watters 1990 .60 1.50
36 Troy Aikman 1991 3.00 8.00
37 Drew Bledsoe 1992 2.00 5.00
38 Scott Mitchell 1993 .60 1.50
39 Rashaan Salaam 1994 .60 1.50
40 Kerry Collins 1995 1.25 3.00

1996 Topps Chrome Tide Turners

Randomly inserted in packs at a rate of one in 12, this 15-card standard-sized chrome foil set features players whose exploits can turn the tide of a game. The front of the cards have a wave over which the player is superimposed with his name and the insert name at the bottom of the card.

COMPLETE SET (15) 20.00 50.00
STATED ODDS 1:12
*REFRACT: 1X TO 2.5X BASIC INSERTS
REF.STATED ODDS 1:48
TT1 Rashaan Salaam .60 1.50
TT2 Warren Moon .60 1.50
TT3 Marshall Faulk 1.50 4.00
TT4 Jeff Blake 1.25 3.00
TT5 Curtis Martin 2.00 5.00
TT6 Eric Metcalf .25 .60
TT7 Errict Rhett .60 1.50
TT8 Scott Mitchell .60 1.50
TT9 Ricky Watters .60 1.50
TT10 Jerry Rice 3.00 8.00
TT11 Emmitt Smith 5.00 12.00
TT12 Erik Kramer .25 .60
TT13 Jim Harbaugh .60 1.50
TT14 Barry Sanders 5.00 12.00
TT15 John Elway 6.00 15.00

1997 Topps Chrome

e 1997 Topps Chrome set was issued in one series totalling 165 cards and was distributed in four-card packs with a suggested retail price of $3. The fronts feature color action player photos printed with Chromium technology. The backs carry player information.

COMPLETE SET (165) 30.00 60.00
1 Brett Favre 2.50 6.00
2 Tim Biakabutuka .40 1.00
3 Deion Sanders .60 1.50
4 Marshall Faulk .75 2.00
5 John Randle .40 1.00
6 Stan Humphries .40 1.00
7 Ki-Jana Carter .25 .60
8 Rashaan Salaam .25 .60
9 Rickey Dudley .40 1.00
10 Isaac Bruce .60 1.50
11 Keyshawn Johnson .60 1.50
12 Ben Coates .40 1.00
13 Ty Detmer .40 1.00
14 Gus Frerotte .25 .60
15 Mario Bates .25 .60
16 Chris Calloway .25 .60
17 Frank Sanders .40 1.00
18 Bruce Smith .40 1.00
19 Jeff Graham .25 .60
20 Trent Dilfer .60 1.50
21 Tyrone Wheatley .40 1.00
22 Chris Warren .40 1.00
23 Terry Kirby .40 1.00
24 Tony Gonzalez RC 4.00 10.00
25 Ricky Watters .40 1.00
26 Tamarick Vanover .40 1.00
27 Kerry Collins .60 1.50
28 Bobby Engram .40 1.00
29 Derrick Alexander WR .40 1.00
30 Hugh Douglas .25 .60
31 Thurman Thomas .60 1.50
32 Drew Bledsoe .75 2.00
33 LeShon Johnson .25 .60
34 Byron Bam Morris .25 .60
35 Herman Moore .40 1.00
36 Troy Aikman 1.25 3.00
37 Mel Gray .25 .60
38 Adrian Murrell .40 1.00
39 Carl Pickens .40 1.00
40 Tony Brackens .25 .60
41 O.J. McDuffie .40 1.00
42 Napoleon Kaufman .60 1.50
43 Chris T. Jones .25 .60
44 Kordell Stewart .60 1.50
45 Steve Young .75 2.00
46 Shannon Sharpe .40 1.00
47 Leeland McElroy .25 .60
48 Eric Moulds .60 1.50
49 Eddie George .60 1.50
50 Jamal Anderson .60 1.50
51 Robert Smith .40 1.00
52 Mike Alstott .60 1.50
53 Darrell Green .40 1.00
54 Irving Fryar .40 1.00
55 Derrick Thomas .60 1.50
56 Antonio Freeman .60 1.50
57 Terrell Davis .75 2.00
58 Henry Ellard .25 .60
59 Daryl Johnston .40 1.00
60 Bryan Cox .25 .60
61 Vinny Testaverde .40 1.00
62 Andre Reed .40 1.00
63 Larry Centers .40 1.00
64 Hardy Nickerson .25 .60
65 Tony Banks .40 1.00
66 Dave Meggett .25 .60
67 Simeon Rice .40 1.00
68 Warrick Dunn RC 3.00 8.00
69 Michael Irvin .60 1.50
70 John Elway 2.50 6.00
71 Jake Reed .40 1.00
72 Rodney Hampton .40 1.00
73 Aaron Glenn .25 .60
74 Terry Allen .60 1.50
75 Blaine Bishop .25 .60
76 Bert Emanuel .40 1.00
77 Mark Carrier WR .25 .60
78 Jimmy Smith .40 1.00
79 Jim Harbaugh .40 1.00
80 Brent Jones .40 1.00
81 Emmitt Smith 2.00 5.00
82 Fred Barnett .25 .60
83 Errict Rhett .25 .60
84 Michael Sinclair .25 .60
85 Jerome Bettis .60 1.50
86 Chris Sanders .25 .60
87 Kent Graham .25 .60
88 Cris Carter .60 1.50
89 Harvey Williams .25 .60
90 Eric Allen .25 .60
91 Bryant Young .25 .60
92 Marcus Allen .60 1.50
93 Michael Jackson .40 1.00
94 Mark Chmura .40 1.00
95 Keenan McCardell .40 1.00
96 Joey Galloway .40 1.00
97 Eddie Kennison .40 1.00
98 Steve Atwater .25 .60
99 Dorsey Levens .60 1.50
100 Rob Moore .40 1.00
101 Steve McNair .75 2.00
102 Sean Dawkins .25 .60
103 Don Beebe .25 .60
104 Willie McGinest .25 .60
105 Tony Martin .40 1.00
106 Mark Brunell .75 2.00
107 Karim Abdul-Jabbar .60 1.50
108 Michael Westbrook .40 1.00
109 Lawrence Phillips .25 .60
110 Barry Sanders 2.00 5.00
111 Willie Davis .25 .60
112 Wesley Walls .40 1.00
113 Todd Collins .25 .60
114 Jerry Rice 1.25 3.00
115 Scott Mitchell .40 1.00
116 Terance Mathis .40 1.00
117 Chris Spielman .25 .60
118 Curtis Conway .40 1.00
119 Marvin Harrison .60 1.50
120 Terry Glenn .60 1.50
121 Dave Brown .25 .60
122 Neil O'Donnell .40 1.00
123 Junior Seau .60 1.50
124 Reggie White .60 1.50
125 Lamar Lathon .25 .60
126 Natrone Means .40 1.00
127 Tim Brown .60 1.50
128 Eric Swann .25 .60
129 Dan Marino 2.50 6.00
130 Anthony Johnson .25 .60
131 Edgar Bennett .40 1.00
132 Kevin Hardy .25 .60
133 Brian Blades .25 .60
134 Curtis Martin .75 2.00
135 Zach Thomas .60 1.50
136 Darnay Scott .40 1.00
137 Desmond Howard .40 1.00
138 Aeneas Williams .25 .60
139 Bryce Paup .25 .60
140 Brad Johnson .60 1.50
141 Jeff Blake .40 1.00
142 Wayne Chrebet .60 1.50
143 Will Blackwell RC .50 1.25
144 Tom Knight RC .25 .60
145 Darnell Autry RC .40 1.00
146 Bryant Westbrook RC .25 .60
147 David LaFleur RC .30 .75
148 Antowain Smith RC 2.50 6.00
149 Rae Carruth RC .30 .75
150 Jim Druckenmiller RC .40 1.00
151 Shawn Springs RC .30 .75
152 Troy Davis RC .50 1.25
153 Orlando Pace RC .75 2.00
154 Byron Hanspard RC .50 1.25
155 Corey Dillon RC 4.00 10.00
156 Reidel Anthony RC .75 2.00
157 Peter Boulware RC .75 2.00
158 Reinard Wilson RC .50 1.25
159 Pat Barnes RC .75 2.00
160 Joey Kent RC .75 2.00
161 Ike Hilliard RC 1.25 3.00
162 Jake Plummer RC 3.00 8.00
163 Darrell Russell RC .30 .75
164 Checklist Card .25 .60
165 Checklist Card .25 .60

1997 Topps Chrome Refractors

MPLETE SET (165) 300.00 800.00
*STARS: 2X TO 5X BASIC CARDS
*RC'S: 1.2X TO 3X BASIC CARDS
STATED ODDS 1:12
24 Tony Gonzalez 20.00 50.00
68 Warrick Dunn 15.00 40.00
148 Antowain Smith 12.00 30.00
155 Corey Dillon 20.00 50.00
162 Jake Plummer 15.00 40.00

1997 Topps Chrome Career Best

ndomly inserted in packs, this five-card set features color player photos of five of the best NFL players in terms of career statistics printed with Chromium technology.

COMPLETE SET (5) 30.00 60.00
*REFRACTORS: 1X TO 2X BASIC INSERTS
1 Dan Marino 12.50 30.00
2 Marcus Allen 3.00 8.00
3 Marcus Allen 3.00 8.00
4 Reggie White 3.00 8.00
5 Jerry Rice 6.00 15.00

1997 Topps Chrome Draft Year

ndomly inserted in packs at the rate of one in 48, this 15-card set features double-sided chromium cards with color photos of two players from the last 15 rookie drafts.

COMPLETE SET (15) 75.00 150.00
STATED ODDS 1:48
*REFRACTORS: 1X TO 2X HI COL.
REFRACTOR STATED ODDS 1:144
DR1 D.Marino J.Elway 12.50 30.00
DR2 R.White S.Young 5.00 12.00
DR3 B.Smith J.Rice 6.00 15.00
DR4 R.Harmon P.Swilling 2.00 5.00
DR5 Harbaugh Testaverde 2.00 5.00
DR6 M.Irvin T.Brown 3.00 8.00
DR7 T.Aikman B.Sanders 10.00 25.00
DR8 E.Smith J.Seau 10.00 25.00
DR9 B.Favre R.Watters 10.00 25.00
DR10 C.Pickens J.Blake 3.00 8.00
DR11 M.Brunell D.Bledsoe 4.00 10.00
DR12 M.Faulk I.Bruce 4.00 10.00
DR13 T.Davis C.Martin 7.50 20.00
DR14 E.George T.Glenn 3.00 8.00
DR15 I.Hilliard S.Springs 3.00 8.00

1997 Topps Chrome Season's Best

ndomly inserted in packs at the rate of one in 12, this 25-card set features color action photos of players who lead the league in certain statistics. The set contains the topical subsets: Air Command (1-5), Thunder and Lightning (6-10), Magicians (11-15), Demolition Men (16-20), and Special Delivery (21-25).

COMPLETE SET (25) 50.00 100.00
STATED ODDS 1:12
*REFRACTORS: 1X TO 2X HI COL.
REFRACTOR STATED ODDS 1:36
1 Mark Brunell 2.50 6.00
2 Vinny Testaverde 1.25 3.00
3 Drew Bledsoe 2.50 6.00
4 Brett Favre 8.00 20.00
5 Jeff Blake 1.25 3.00
6 Barry Sanders 6.00 15.00
7 Terrell Davis 2.50 6.00
8 Jerome Bettis 2.00 5.00
9 Ricky Watters 1.25 3.00
10 Eddie George 2.00 5.00
11 Brian Mitchell .75 2.00
12 Tyrone Hughes .75 2.00
13 Eric Metcalf 1.25 3.00
14 Glyn Milburn .75 2.00
15 Ricky Watters 1.25 3.00
16 Kevin Greene 1.25 3.00
17 Lamar Lathon .75 2.00
18 Bruce Smith 1.25 3.00
19 Michael Sinclair .75 2.00
20 Derrick Thomas 2.00 5.00
21 Jerry Rice 4.00 10.00
22 Herman Moore 1.25 3.00
23 Carl Pickens 1.25 3.00
24 Cris Carter 2.00 5.00
25 Brett Perriman .75 2.00

1997 Topps Chrome Underclassmen

ndomly inserted in packs at the rate of one in eight, this 10-card set featues action color photos of the top second and third year players.

COMPLETE SET (10) 12.00 30.00
STATED ODDS 1:16
*REFRACTORS: 1X TO 2X BASIC INSERTS
REFRACTOR STATED ODDS 1:48
U1 Kerry Collins 2.00 5.00
U2 Karim Abdul-Jabbar 2.00 6.00
U3 Simeon Rice 1.25 3.00
U4 Keyshawn Johnson 2.00 5.00
U5 Eddie George 2.00 5.00
U6 Eddie Kennison 1.25 3.00
U7 Terry Glenn 2.00 5.00
U8 Kevin Hardy .75 2.00
U9 Steve McNair 2.50 6.00
U10 Kordell Stewart 2.00 5.00

1998 Topps Chrome

e 1998 Topps Chrome set was issued in one series totalling 165 cards. The four-card packs retail for $3.00 each. The cards feature action color player photos printed with chromium technology.

COMPLETE SET (165) 50.00 120.00
1 Barry Sanders .60 1.50
2 Duane Starks RC .75 2.00
3 J.J. Stokes .30 .75
4 Joey Galloway .30 .75
5 Deion Sanders .30 .75
6 Anthony Miller .25 .60
7 Jamal Anderson .30 .75
8 Shannon Sharpe .30 .75
9 Irving Fryar .30 .75
10 Curtis Martin .30 .75
11 Shawn Jefferson .25 .60
12 Charlie Garner .30 .75
13 Robert Edwards RC 1.00 2.50
14 Napoleon Kaufman .25 .60
15 Gus Frerotte .25 .60
16 John Elway .60 1.50
17 Jerome Pathon RC 1.00 2.50
18 Marshall Faulk .30 .75
19 Michael McCrary .25 .60
20 Marcus Allen .40 1.00
21 Trent Dilfer .30 .75
22 Frank Wycheck .30 .75
23 Terrell Owens .30 .75
24 Herman Moore .30 .75
25 Neil O'Donnell .30 .75
26 Darnay Scott .30 .75
27 Keith Brooking RC 1.25 3.00
28 Eric Green .25 .60
29 Dan Marino .75 2.00
30 Antonio Freeman .40 1.00
31 Tony Martin .30 .75
32 Isaac Bruce .40 1.00
33 Rickey Dudley .25 .60
34 Scott Mitchell .30 .75
35 Randy Moss RC 6.00 15.00
36 Fred Lane .25 .60
37 Frank Sanders .25 .60
38 Jerry Rice 1.00 2.50
39 O.J. McDuffie .30 .75
40 Jessie Armstead .25 .60
41 Reidel Anthony .25 .60
42 Steve McNair .30 .75
43 Jake Reed .30 .75
44 Charles Woodson RC 3.00 8.00
45 Tiki Barber .30 .75
46 Mike Alstott .25 .60
47 Keyshawn Johnson .30 .75
48 Tony Banks .30 .75
49 Michael Westbrook .30 .75
50 Chris Slade .25 .60
51 Terry Allen .30 .75
52 Karim Abdul-Jabbar .25 .60
53 Brad Johnson .30 .75
54 Tony McGee .25 .60
55 Kevin Dyson RC 1.00 2.50
56 Warren Moon .40 1.00
57 Byron Hanspard .25 .60
58 Jermaine Lewis .25 .60
59 Neil Smith .30 .75
60 Tamarick Vanover .25 .60
61 Terrell Davis .30 .75
62 Robert Smith .25 .60
63 Junior Seau .30 .75
64 Warren Sapp .30 .75
65 Michael Sinclair .25 .60
66 Ryan Leaf RC 1.00 2.50
67 Drew Bledsoe .30 .75
68 Jason Sehorn .30 .75
69 Andre Hastings .25 .60
70 Tony Gonzalez .30 .75
71 Dorsey Levens .30 .75
72 Ray Lewis .40 1.00
73 Grant Wistrom RC .75 2.00
74 Elvis Grbac .30 .75
75 Mark Chmura .25 .60
76 Zach Thomas .30 .75
77 Ben Coates .30 .75
78 Rod Smith WR .30 .75
79 Andre Wadsworth RC 1.25 3.00
80 Garrison Hearst .25 .60
81 Will Blackwell .25 .60
82 Cris Carter .40 1.00
83 Mark Fields .25 .60
84 Ken Dilger .25 .60
85 Johnnie Morton .30 .75
86 Michael Irvin .40 1.00
87 Eddie George .30 .75
88 Rob Moore .25 .60
89 Takeo Spikes RC 1.00 2.50
90 Wesley Walls .30 .75
91 Andre Reed .40 1.00
92 Thurman Thomas .30 .75
93 Ed McCaffrey .30 .75
94 Carl Pickens .30 .75
95 Jason Taylor .30 .75
96 Kordell Stewart .25 .60
97 Greg Ellis RC 1.00 2.50
98 Aaron Glenn .25 .60
99 Jake Plummer .25 .60
100 Checklist .25 .60
101 Chris Sanders .25 .60
102 Michael Jackson .25 .60
103 Bobby Hoying .30 .75
104 Wayne Chrebet .25 .60
105 Charles Way .25 .60
106 Derrick Thomas .40 1.00
107 Troy Drayton .25 .60
108 Robert Holcombe RC .75 2.00
109 Pete Mitchell .25 .60
110 Bruce Smith .30 .75
111 Terance Mathis .25 .60
112 Lawrence Phillips .30 .75
113 Brett Favre .75 2.00
114 Darrell Green .40 1.00
115 Charles Johnson .25 .60
116 Jeff Blake .30 .75
117 Mark Brunell .30 .75
118 Simeon Rice .30 .75
119 Robert Brooks .30 .75
120 Jacquez Green RC 1.00 2.50
121 Willie Davis .25 .60
122 Jeff George .30 .75
123 Andre Rison .30 .75
124 Erik Kramer .25 .60
125 Peter Boulware .25 .60
126 Marcus Nash RC .75 2.00
127 Troy Aikman .50 1.25
128 Keenan McCardell .30 .75
129 Bryant Westbrook .25 .60
130 Terry Glenn .30 .75
131 Blaine Bishop .25 .60
132 Tim Brown .40 1.00
133 Brian Griese RC 1.50 4.00
134 John Mobley .25 .60
135 Larry Centers .25 .60
136 Eric Bjornson .25 .60
137 Kevin Hardy .25 .60
138 John Randle .40 1.00
139 Michael Strahan .30 .75
140 Jerome Bettis .40 1.00
141 Rae Carruth .25 .60
142 Reggie White .40 1.00
143 Antowain Smith .30 .75
144 Aeneas Williams .25 .60
145 Bobby Engram .25 .60
146 Germane Crowell RC .75 2.00
147 Freddie Jones .25 .60
148 Kimble Anders .25 .60
149 Steve Young .50 1.25
150 Willie McGinest .25 .60
151 Emmitt Smith .60 1.50
152 Fred Taylor RC 1.50 4.00
153 Danny Kanell .25 .60
154 Warrick Dunn .25 .60
155 Kerry Collins .25 .60
156 Chris Chandler .30 .75
157 Curtis Conway .30 .75
158 Curtis Enis RC 1.00 2.50
159 Corey Dillon .25 .60
160 Glenn Foley .25 .60
161 Marvin Harrison .30 .75
162 Chad Brown .25 .60
163 Derrick Rodgers .25 .60
164 Levon Kirkland .25 .60
165 Peyton Manning RC 25.00 60.00

1998 Topps Chrome Refractors

ETS: 4X TO 10X BASIC CARDS
*ROOKIE STARS: 1.2X TO 3X
STATED ODDS 1:12
165 Peyton Manning 125.00 200.00

1998 Topps Chrome Hidden Gems

ndomly inserted in packs at a rate of one in 12, this 15-card set features color player photos printed using mirrorboard technology. A Refractor parallel version of the set was also produced with an insertion rate of one in 24 packs.

COMPLETE SET (15) 15.00 30.00
STATED ODDS 1:12
*REFRACTORS: .6X TO 1.5X BASIC INSERTS
REFRACTOR ODDS 1:24
HG1 Andre Reed .75 2.00
HG2 Kevin Greene .75 2.00
HG3 Tony Martin .75 2.00
HG4 Shannon Sharpe .75 2.00
HG5 Terry Allen 1.25 3.00
HG6 Brett Favre 5.00 12.00
HG7 Ben Coates .75 2.00
HG8 Michael Sinclair .50 1.25
HG9 Keenan McCardell .75 2.00
HG10 Brad Johnson 1.25 3.00
HG11 Mark Brunell 1.25 3.00
HG12 Dorsey Levens 1.25 3.00
HG13 Terrell Davis 1.25 3.00
HG14 Curtis Martin 1.25 3.00
HG15 Derrick Rodgers .50 1.25

1998 Topps Chrome Measures of Greatness

ndomly inserted in packs at a rate of one in 12, this 15-card set features color action photos of players who are headed for the NFL Hall of Fame printed using micro dyna-etch technology. A refractor version of this set was also produced with an insertion rate of 1:48 packs.

COMPLETE SET (15) 30.00 60.00
STATED ODDS 1:12
*REFRACTORS: 1X TO 2.5X BASIC INSERTS
REFRACTOR ODDS 1:48
MG1 John Elway 5.00 12.00
MG2 Marcus Allen 1.25 3.00
MG3 Jerry Rice 2.50 6.00
MG4 Tim Brown 1.25 3.00
MG5 Warren Moon 1.25 3.00
MG6 Bruce Smith .75 2.00
MG7 Troy Aikman 2.50 6.00
MG8 Reggie White 1.25 3.00
MG9 Irving Fryar .75 2.00
MG10 Barry Sanders 4.00 10.00
MG11 Cris Carter 1.25 3.00
MG12 Emmitt Smith 4.00 10.00
MG13 Dan Marino 5.00 12.00
MG14 Rod Woodson .75 2.00
MG15 Brett Favre 5.00 12.00

1998 Topps Chrome Season's Best

ndomly inserted in packs at a rate of one in 8, this 30-card set features statistical league leaders in five categories: Power & Speed are the rushing leaders, Gunslingers are the hottest quarterbacks, Prime Targets are the leading receivers, Heavy Hitters are leaders of the sack, and Quick Six are the leaders in yards gained. In addition, there are five Career Best cards for each category. A refractive version of this set was also produced with an insertion rate of 1:24 packs.

COMPLETE SET (30) 30.00 80.00
STATED ODDS 1:8
*REFRACTORS: .6X TO 1.5X BASIC INSERTS
REFRACTOR ODDS 1:24
1 Terrell Davis 1.25 3.00
2 Barry Sanders 4.00 10.00
3 Jerome Bettis 1.25 3.00
4 Dorsey Levens 1.25 3.00
5 Eddie George 1.25 3.00
6 Brett Favre 5.00 12.00
7 Mark Brunell 1.25 3.00
8 Jeff George .75 2.00
9 Steve Young 1.50 4.00
10 John Elway 5.00 12.00
11 Herman Moore .75 2.00
12 Rob Moore .75 2.00
13 Yancey Thigpen .75 2.00
14 Cris Carter 1.25 3.00
15 Tim Brown 1.25 3.00
16 Bruce Smith .75 2.00
17 Michael Sinclair .50 1.25
18 John Randle .75 2.00
19 Dana Stubblefield .50 1.25
20 Michael Strahan .75 2.00
21 Tamarick Vanover .50 1.25
22 Darrien Gordon .50 1.25
23 Michael Bates .50 1.25
24 David Meggett .50 1.25
25 Jermaine Lewis .75 2.00
26 Terrell Davis 1.25 3.00
27 Jerry Rice 2.50 6.00
28 Barry Sanders 4.00 10.00
29 John Randle .75 2.00
30 John Elway 5.00 12.00

1999 Topps Chrome

e 1999 Topps Chrome set was released as a 165 card color action shot with an all chromium card front. Key rookies within the set include Tim Couch, Ricky Williams, and Cade McNown.

COMPLETE SET (165) 60.00 150.00
COMP.SET w/o SP's (135) 25.00 50.00
1 Randy Moss .30 .75
2 Keyshawn Johnson .30 .75
3 Priest Holmes .25 .60
4 Warren Moon .40 1.00
5 Joey Galloway .30 .75
6 Zach Thomas .30 .75
7 Cam Cleeland .25 .60
8 Jim Harbaugh .30 .75
9 Napoleon Kaufman .25 .60
10 Fred Taylor .25 .60
11 Mark Brunell .30 .75
12 Shannon Sharpe .30 .75
13 Jacquez Green .25 .60
14 Adrian Murrell .25 .60
15 Cris Carter .40 1.00
16 Jerome Pathon .25 .60
17 Drew Bledsoe .30 .75
18 Curtis Martin .30 .75
19 Johnnie Morton .30 .75
20 Doug Flutie .40 1.00
21 Carl Pickens .30 .75
22 Jerome Bettis .40 1.00
23 Derrick Alexander .25 .60

24 Antowain Smith	.25	.60
25 Barry Sanders	.60	1.50
26 Reidel Anthony	.25	.60
27 Wayne Chrebet	.25	.60
28 Terance Mathis	.25	.60
29 Shawn Springs	.25	.60
30 Emmitt Smith	.60	1.50
31 Robert Smith	.25	.60
32 Charles Johnson	.25	.60
33 Mike Alstott	.25	.60
34 Ike Hilliard	.25	.60
35 Ricky Watters	.30	.75
36 Charles Woodson	.40	1.00
37 Rod Smith	.30	.75
38 Pete Mitchell	.25	.60
39 Derrick Thomas	.40	1.00
40 Dan Marino	.75	2.00
41 Darnay Scott	.25	.60
42 Jake Reed	.30	.75
43 Chris Chandler	.30	.75
44 Dorsey Levens	.30	.75
45 Kordell Stewart	.25	.60
46 Eddie George	.30	.75
47 Corey Dillon	.25	.60
48 Rich Gannon	.30	.75
49 Chris Spielman	.30	.75
50 Jerry Rice	1.00	2.50
51 Trent Dilfer	.25	.60
52 Mark Chmura	.25	.60
53 Jimmy Smith	.30	.75
54 Isaac Bruce	.40	1.00
55 Karim Abdul-Jabbar	.25	.60
56 Sedrick Shaw	.25	.60
57 Jake Plummer	.25	.60
58 Tony Gonzalez	.30	.75
59 Ben Coates	.30	.75
60 John Elway	.60	1.50
61 Bruce Smith	.30	.75
62 Tim Brown	.40	1.00
63 Tim Dwight	.30	.75
64 Yancey Thigpen	.25	.60
65 Terrell Owens	.30	.75
66 Kyle Brady	.25	.60
67 Tony Martin	.30	.75
68 Michael Strahan	.30	.75
69 Deion Sanders	.30	.75
70 Steve Young	.50	1.25
71 Dale Carter	.25	.60
72 Ty Law	.40	1.00
73 Frank Wycheck	.30	.75
74 Marshall Faulk	.30	.75
75 Vinny Testaverde	.25	.60
76 Chad Brown	.25	.60
77 Natrone Means	.30	.75
78 Bert Emanuel	.30	.75
79 Kerry Collins	.25	.60
80 Randall Cunningham	.30	.75
81 Garrison Hearst	.25	.60
82 Curtis Enis	.25	.60
83 Steve Atwater	.30	.75
84 Kevin Greene	.40	1.00
85 Steve McNair	.30	.75
86 Andre Reed	.40	1.00
87 J.J. Stokes	.25	.60
88 Eric Moulds	.25	.60
89 Marvin Harrison	.30	.75
90 Troy Aikman	.50	1.25
91 Herman Moore	.30	.75
92 Michael Irvin	.40	1.00
93 Frank Sanders	.25	.60
94 Duce Staley	.25	.60
95 James Jett	.25	.60
96 Ricky Proehl	.25	.60
97 Andre Rison	.30	.75
98 Leslie Shepherd	.25	.60
99 Trent Green	.25	.60
100 Terrell Davis	.30	.75
101 Freddie Jones	.25	.60
102 Skip Hicks	.25	.60
103 Jeff Graham	.25	.60
104 Rob Moore	.25	.60
105 Torrance Small	.25	.60
106 Antonio Freeman	.30	.75
107 Robert Brooks	.30	.75
108 Jon Kitna	.25	.60
109 Curtis Conway	.30	.75
110 Brett Favre	.75	2.00
111 Warrick Dunn	.25	.60
112 Elvis Grbac	.25	.60
113 Corey Fuller	.25	.60
114 Rickey Dudley	.25	.60
115 Jamal Anderson	.30	.75
116 Terry Glenn	.30	.75
117 Rocket Ismail	.30	.75
118 John Randle	.40	1.00
119 Chris Calloway	.25	.60
120 Peyton Manning	1.25	3.00
121 Keenan McCardell	.30	.75
122 O.J. McDuffie	.30	.75
123 Ed McCaffrey	.30	.75
124 Charlie Batch	.25	.60
125 Jason Elam SH	.25	.60
126 Randy Moss SH	.25	.60
127 John Elway SH	.50	1.25
128 Emmitt Smith SH	.50	1.25
129 Terrell Davis SH	.25	.60
130 Jerris McPhail	.25	.60
131 Damon Gibson	.25	.60
132 Jim Pyne	.25	.60
133 Antonio Langham	.25	.60
134 Freddie Solomon	.25	.60
135 Ricky Williams RC	2.00	5.00
136 Daunte Culpepper RC	2.00	5.00
137 Chris Claiborne RC	1.25	3.00
138 Amos Zereoue RC	1.25	3.00
139 Chris McAlister RC	1.25	3.00
140 Kevin Faulk RC	1.25	3.00
141 James Johnson RC	1.25	3.00
142 Mike Cloud RC	1.25	3.00
143 Jevon Kearse RC	1.50	4.00
144 Akili Smith RC	1.25	3.00
145 Edgerrin James RC	2.00	5.00
146 Cecil Collins RC	1.25	3.00
147 Donovan McNabb RC	8.00	20.00
148 Kevin Johnson RC	1.50	4.00
149 Torry Holt RC	2.50	6.00
150 Rob Konrad RC	1.25	3.00
151 Tim Couch RC	1.50	4.00
152 David Boston RC	1.25	3.00
153 Karsten Bailey RC	1.25	3.00
154 Troy Edwards RC	1.25	3.00
155 Sedrick Irvin RC	1.25	3.00
156 Shaun King RC	1.25	3.00
157 Peerless Price RC	1.25	3.00
158 Brock Huard RC	1.25	3.00
159 Cade McNown RC	1.25	3.00
160 Champ Bailey RC	2.50	6.00
161 D'Wayne Bates RC	1.25	3.00
162 Joe Germaine RC	1.50	4.00
163 Andy Katzenmoyer RC	1.50	4.00
164 Antoine Winfield RC	1.25	3.00
165 Checklist Card	.25	.60

1999 Topps Chrome Refractors

EF.VETS: 2.5X TO 6X BASIC CARDS
REFRACTOR VETERANS ODDS 1:12
REFRACTOR ROOKIES ODDS 1:32

1999 Topps Chrome All-Etch

Randomly inserted in packs at a rate of 1 in 24 packs, this 30 card insert set features 3 levels which are shown on card front. They are 1,200 yard club, 3000 yard club, and 99 rookie rush. Cards are done with color action photo.

COMPLETE SET (30)	100.00	200.00

STATED ODDS 1:24
*REF.STARS: 1.2X TO 3X BASIC INSERTS
*REF.ROOKIES: .8X TO 2X BASIC INSERTS
REFRACTOR STATED ODDS 1:120

AE1 Fred Taylor	2.00	5.00
AE2 Ricky Watters	1.25	3.00
AE3 Curtis Martin	2.00	5.00
AE4 Eddie George	2.00	5.00
AE5 Marshall Faulk	2.50	6.00
AE6 Emmitt Smith	4.00	10.00
AE7 Barry Sanders	6.00	15.00
AE8 Garrison Hearst	1.25	3.00
AE9 Jamal Anderson	2.00	5.00
AE10 Terrell Davis	2.00	5.00
AE11 Chris Chandler	1.25	3.00
AE12 Steve McNair	2.00	5.00
AE13 Vinny Testaverde	1.25	3.00
AE14 Trent Green	2.00	5.00
AE15 Dan Marino	6.00	15.00
AE16 Drew Bledsoe	2.50	6.00
AE17 Randall Cunningham	2.00	5.00
AE18 Jake Plummer	1.25	3.00
AE19 Peyton Manning	6.00	15.00
AE20 Steve Young	2.50	6.00
AE21 Brett Favre	6.00	15.00
AE22 Tim Couch	.60	1.50
AE23 Edgerrin James	2.50	6.00
AE24 David Boston	.60	1.50
AE25 Akili Smith	.50	1.25
AE26 Troy Edwards	.50	1.25
AE27 Torry Holt	2.00	5.00
AE28 Donovan McNabb	3.00	8.00
AE29 Daunte Culpepper	3.00	8.00
AE30 Ricky Williams	1.25	3.00

1999 Topps Chrome Hall of Fame

This 30 card insert set was inserted at a rate 1 in 29 packs and features key rookies such as Daunte Culpepper and Tim Couch as well as veteran stars Terrell Davis and Barry Sanders. Set features players who could soon be members of Pro Football Hall of Fame.

COMPLETE SET (30)	50.00	120.00

STATED ODDS 1:29
*REF.STARS: 2.5X TO 6X BASIC INSERTS
*REF.ROOKIES: 2X TO 5X BASIC INSERTS
REFRACTOR PRINT RUN 100 SERIAL #'d SETS

H1 Akili Smith	.50	1.25
H2 Troy Edwards	.50	1.25
H3 Donovan McNabb	3.00	8.00
H4 Cade McNown	.50	1.25
H5 Ricky Williams	1.25	3.00
H6 David Boston	.60	1.50
H7 Daunte Culpepper	3.00	8.00
H8 Edgerrin James	2.50	6.00
H9 Torry Holt	2.00	5.00
H10 Tim Couch	.60	1.50
H11 Terrell Davis	2.00	5.00
H12 Fred Taylor	2.00	5.00
H13 Antonio Freeman	2.00	5.00
H14 Jamal Anderson	2.00	5.00
H15 Randy Moss	5.00	12.00
H16 Joey Galloway	1.25	3.00
H17 Eddie George	2.00	5.00
H18 Jake Plummer	1.25	3.00
H19 Curtis Martin	2.00	5.00
H20 Peyton Manning	6.00	15.00
H21 Barry Sanders	6.00	15.00
H22 Steve Young	2.50	6.00
H23 Cris Carter	2.00	5.00
H24 Emmitt Smith	4.00	10.00
H25 John Elway	6.00	15.00
H26 Drew Bledsoe	2.50	6.00
H27 Troy Aikman	4.00	10.00
H28 Brett Favre	6.00	15.00
H29 Jerry Rice	4.00	10.00
H30 Dan Marino	6.00	15.00

1999 Topps Chrome Record Numbers

ndomly inserted in packs at a rate of 1 in 72 packs, This 10 card insert set features top NFL record setting statistics shown on the card front. Cards are color action shots done on a silver Background. Stars include Dan Marino and Bret Favre.

COMPLETE SET (10)	40.00	80.00

STATED ODDS 1:72
REFRACTORS: 1.2X TO 3X BASIC INSERTS
REFRACTOR STATED ODDS 1:360

RN1 Randy Moss	5.00	12.00
RN2 Terrell Davis	2.00	5.00
RN3 Emmitt Smith	4.00	10.00
RN4 Barry Sanders	6.00	15.00
RN5 Dan Marino	6.00	15.00
RN6 Brett Favre	6.00	15.00
RN7 Doug Flutie	2.00	5.00
RN8 Jerry Rice	4.00	10.00
RN9 Peyton Manning	6.00	15.00
RN10 Jason Elam	.75	2.00

1999 Topps Chrome Season's Best

Randomly inserted in packs at a rate of 1 in 24 cards this 30 card insert set features key veteran players such as Dan Marino and Jake Plummer done on a metallic foil showcasing the active career leader for each particluar stat shown on the card front.

COMPLETE SET (30)	50.00	100.00

STATED ODDS: 1:24
*REFRACTORS: 1.2X TO 3X BASIC INSERTS
REFRACTOR STATED ODDS 1:120

SB1 Terrell Davis	1.50	4.00
SB2 Jamal Anderson	1.50	4.00
SB3 Garrison Hearst	1.00	2.50
SB4 Barry Sanders	5.00	12.00
SB5 Emmitt Smith	3.00	8.00
SB6 Randall Cunningham	1.50	4.00
SB7 Brett Favre	5.00	12.00
SB8 Steve Young	2.00	5.00
SB9 Jake Plummer	1.00	2.50
SB10 Peyton Manning	5.00	12.00
SB11 Antonio Freeman	1.50	4.00
SB12 Eric Moulds	1.50	4.00
SB13 Randy Moss	4.00	10.00
SB14 Rod Smith	1.00	2.50
SB15 Jimmy Smith	1.00	2.50
SB16 Michael Sinclair	.60	1.50
SB17 Kevin Greene	.60	1.50
SB18 Michael Strahan	1.00	2.50
SB19 Michael McCrary	.60	1.50
SB20 Hugh Douglas	.60	1.50
SB21 Deion Sanders	1.50	4.00
SB22 Terry Fair	1.00	2.50
SB23 Jacquez Green	.60	1.50
SB24 Corey Harris	.60	1.50
SB25 Tim Dwight	1.50	4.00
SB26 Dan Marino	5.00	12.00
SB27 Barry Sanders	5.00	12.00
SB28 Jerry Rice	3.00	8.00
SB29 Bruce Smith	1.00	2.50
SB30 Darrien Gordon	.60	1.50

2000 Topps Chrome

Released as a 270-card set, the Topps Chrome card design parallels the regular Topps set with cards enhanced by foil card stock. Rookie cards are sequentially numbered to 1650. Chrome was packaged in 24-pack boxes with packs containing four cards and carried a suggested retail price of $3.00.

COMPLETE SET (270)	250.00	500.00
COMP.SET w/o SP's (180)	25.00	50.00

181-190/231-270 ROOKIE PRINT RUN 1650

1 Daunte Culpepper	.40	1.00
2 Troy Edwards	.30	.75
3 Terrell Owens	.40	1.00
4 Ricky Proehl	.30	.75
5 Shaun King	.30	.75
6 Jeff George	.40	1.00
7 Champ Bailey	.40	1.00
8 Amani Toomer	.30	.75
9 Stephen Boyd	.30	.75
10 Thurman Thomas	.40	1.00
11 Patrick Jeffers	.30	.75
12 Jake Plummer	.30	.75
13 Peter Boulware	.30	.75
14 Darrin Chiaverini	.30	.75
15 Olandis Gary	.40	1.00
16 Peyton Manning	1.25	3.00
17 Joe Horn	.40	1.00
18 Wayne Chrebet	.30	.75
19 Freddie Jones	.30	.75
20 Kurt Warner	.75	2.00
21 Mike Alstott	.30	.75
22 Stephen Davis	.30	.75
23 Tim Brown	.50	1.25
24 Damon Huard	.30	.75
25 Terry Glenn	.40	1.00
26 Ricky Williams	.40	1.00
27 Tim Dwight	.40	1.00
28 Jay Riemersma	.30	.75
29 Carl Pickens	.40	1.00
30 Brett Favre	1.00	2.50
31 Oronde Gadsden	.40	1.00
32 Steve McNair	.40	1.00
33 Michael Pittman	.30	.75
34 Emmitt Smith	.75	2.00
35 Mark Brunell	.40	1.00
36 Ed McCaffrey	.40	1.00
37 Tyrone Wheatley	.30	.75
38 Sean Dawkins	.30	.75
39 Jevon Kearse	.30	.75
40 Tai Streets	.30	.75
41 Keyshawn Johnson	.40	1.00
42 Germane Crowell	.30	.75
43 Yatil Green	.30	.75
44 Anthony Wright RC	.40	1.00
45 Jerry Rice	1.25	3.00
46 Az-Zahir Hakim	.30	.75
47 Stephen Alexander	.30	.75
48 Zach Thomas	.40	1.00
49 Tony Simmons	.30	.75
50 Jessie Armstead	.30	.75
51 Kordell Stewart	.30	.75
52 Cade McNown	.30	.75
53 Tony Gonzalez	.40	1.00
54 John Randle	.50	1.25
55 Donovan McNabb	.40	1.00
56 Warrick Dunn	.30	.75
57 Dorsey Levens	.40	1.00
58 Errict Rhett	.40	1.00
59 Priest Holmes	.30	.75
60 Terrell Davis	.40	1.00
61 Natrone Means	.40	1.00
62 Brad Johnson	.40	1.00
63 Rickey Dudley	.30	.75
64 Billy Miller	.30	.75
65 Randy Moss	.40	1.00
66 Joe Montgomery	.30	.75
67 Johnnie Morton	.40	1.00
68 Peerless Price	.40	1.00
69 Rocket Ismail	.40	1.00
70 David Boston	.30	.75
71 Fred Taylor	.30	.75
72 Jermaine Fazande	.30	.75
73 Elvis Grbac	.30	.75
74 Derrick Mayes	.30	.75
75 Yancey Thigpen	.30	.75
76 Ike Hilliard	.30	.75
77 Muhsin Muhammad	.30	.75
78 Shawn Jefferson	.30	.75
79 Rod Smith	.40	1.00
80 Darnay Scott	.40	1.00
81 Cam Cleeland	.30	.75
82 Steve Young	.60	1.50
83 E.G. Green	.30	.75
84 Robert Smith	.30	.75
85 Jermaine Lewis	.30	.75
86 Tim Biakabutuka	.40	1.00
87 Jerome Pathon	.30	.75
88 Kent Graham	.30	.75
89 Bruce Smith	.40	1.00
90 Isaac Bruce	.50	1.25
91 Curtis Enis	.30	.75
92 D'Marco Farr	.30	.75
93 Keith Poole	.30	.75
94 Troy Aikman	.60	1.50
95 Rich Gannon	.40	1.00
96 Michael Westbrook	.30	.75
97 Albert Connell	.30	.75
98 James Johnson	.30	.75
99 Jeff Blake	.40	1.00
100 Joey Galloway	.40	1.00
101 Rob Moore	.30	.75
102 Chris Chandler	.40	1.00
103 Fred Lane	.30	.75
104 Eddie Kennison	.30	.75
105 Kevin Hardy	.30	.75
106 Napoleon Kaufman	.40	1.00
107 Kevin Dyson	.40	1.00
108 Keenan McCardell	.40	1.00
109 Drew Bledsoe	.40	1.00
110 Kevin Johnson	.30	.75
111 Terance Mathis	.30	.75
112 Gus Frerotte	.30	.75
113 Matthew Hatchette	.30	.75
114 Herman Moore	.30	.75
115 Curtis Martin	.40	1.00
116 Jacquez Green	.30	.75
117 Jake Reed	.40	1.00
118 Antonio Freeman	.40	1.00
119 Jim Miller	.30	.75
120 Frank Sanders	.30	.75
121 Brian Griese	.30	.75
122 Troy Brown	.30	.75
123 Jeff Graham	.30	.75
124 Marshall Faulk	.40	1.00
125 Vinny Testaverde	.30	.75
126 Frank Wycheck	.40	1.00
127 Kerry Collins	.30	.75
128 Jay Fiedler	.40	1.00
129 Cris Carter	.50	1.25
130 Jason Tucker	.30	.75
131 Antowain Smith	.40	1.00
132 Tony Banks	.30	.75
133 Terrence Wilkins	.30	.75
134 Tony Martin	.40	1.00
135 Richard Huntley	.30	.75
136 J.J. Stokes	.40	1.00
137 Ricky Watters	.40	1.00
138 Pete Mitchell	.30	.75
139 Jimmy Smith	.40	1.00
140 Doug Flutie	.40	1.00
141 Corey Bradford	.30	.75
142 Curtis Conway	.40	1.00
143 Moses Moreno	.30	.75
144 Torry Holt	.40	1.00
145 Warren Sapp	.40	1.00
146 Duce Staley	.30	.75
147 Mikhael Ricks	.30	.75
148 Edgerrin James	.40	1.00
149 Charlie Batch	.30	.75
150 Rob Johnson	.40	1.00
151 Jamal Anderson	.40	1.00
152 Tim Couch	.40	1.00
153 O.J. McDuffie	.40	1.00
154 Charles Woodson	.50	1.25
155 Jake Delhomme RC	.40	1.00
156 Eddie George	.40	1.00
157 Jim Harbaugh	.40	1.00
158 Jon Kitna	.30	.75
159 Derrick Alexander	.30	.75
160 Marvin Harrison	.40	1.00
161 James Stewart	.30	.75
162 Qadry Ismail	.30	.75
163 Wesley Walls	.30	.75
164 Steve Beuerlein	.40	1.00
165 Marcus Robinson	.40	1.00
166 Bill Schroeder	.40	1.00
167 Charles Johnson	.30	.75
168 Charlie Garner	.40	1.00
169 Eric Moulds	.30	.75
170 Jerome Bettis	.50	1.25
171 Tai Streets	.30	.75
172 Akili Smith	.30	.75
173 Jonathan Linton	.30	.75
174 Corey Dillon	.30	.75
175 Junior Seau	.40	1.00
176 Jonathan Quinn	.30	.75
177 Bobby Engram	.30	.75
178 Shannon Sharpe	.40	1.00
179 Michael Basnight	.30	.75
180 Sedrick Irvin	.30	.75
181 Sammy Morris RC	3.00	8.00
182 Ron Dixon RC	3.00	8.00
183 Trevor Gaylor RC	3.00	8.00
184 Chris Cole RC	4.00	10.00
185 Deltha O'Neal RC	3.00	8.00
186 Sebastian Janikowski RC	5.00	12.00
187 Kwame Cavil RC	3.00	8.00
188 Chad Morton RC	4.00	10.00
189 Terrelle Smith RC	3.00	8.00
190 Frank Moreau RC	3.00	8.00
191 Kurt Warner HL	.60	1.50
192 Dan Marino HL	.75	2.00
193 Cris Carter HL	.40	1.00
194 Brett Favre HL	.75	2.00
195 Marshall Faulk HL	.30	.75
196 Jevon Kearse HL	.25	.60
197 Edgerrin James HL	.30	.75
198 Emmitt Smith HL	.60	1.50
199 Andre Reed HL	.40	1.00
200 K.Dyson F.Wycheck HL	.30	.75
201 Olindo Mare MM	.30	.75
202 Marcus Coleman MM	.30	.75
203 James Johnson MM	.30	.75
204 Ray Lucas MM	.30	.75
205 Dedric Ward MM	.30	.75
206 Richie Cunningham MM	.30	.75
207 James Hasty MM	.30	.75
208 Sedrick Shaw MM	.30	.75
209 Kurt Warner MM	.60	1.50
210 Marshall Faulk MM	.30	.75
211 Brian Shay EP	.30	.75
212 L.C. Stevens EP	.30	.75
213 Corey Thomas EP	.30	.75
214 Scott Milanovich EP	.30	.75
215 Pat Barnes EP	.30	.75
216 Danny Wuerffel EP	.50	1.25
217 Kevin Daft EP	.30	.75
218 Ron Powlus EP RC	.50	1.25
219 Eric Kresser EP	.30	.75
220 Norman Miller EP RC	.30	.75
221 Cory Sauter EP	.30	.75
222 Marcus Crandell EP RC	.30	.75
223 Sean Morey EP RC	.30	.75
224 Jeff Ogden EP	.30	.75
225 Ted White EP	.30	.75
226 Jim Kubiak EP RC	.30	.75
227 Aaron Stecker EP RC	.30	.75
228 Ronnie Powell EP	.30	.75
229 Matt Lytle EP RC	.30	.75
230 Kendrick Nord EP RC	.30	.75
231 Tim Rattay RC	4.00	10.00
232 Rob Morris RC	4.00	10.00
233 Chris Samuels RC	5.00	12.00
234 Todd Husak RC	3.00	8.00
235 Ahmed Plummer RC	3.00	8.00
236 Frank Murphy RC	3.00	8.00
237 Michael Wiley RC	3.00	8.00
238 Giovanni Carmazzi RC	3.00	8.00
239 Anthony Becht RC	3.00	8.00
240 John Abraham RC	5.00	12.00
241 Shaun Alexander RC	5.00	12.00
242 Thomas Jones RC	4.00	10.00
243 Courtney Brown RC	4.00	10.00
244 Curtis Keaton RC	3.00	8.00
245 Jerry Porter RC	5.00	12.00
246 Corey Simon RC	4.00	10.00
247 Dez White RC	3.00	8.00
248 Jamal Lewis RC	5.00	12.00
249 Ron Dayne RC	5.00	12.00
250 R.Jay Soward RC	3.00	8.00
251 Tee Martin RC	3.00	8.00
252 Shaun Ellis RC	4.00	10.00
253 Brian Urlacher RC	15.00	40.00
254 Reuben Droughns RC	3.00	8.00
255 Travis Taylor RC	3.00	8.00
256 Plaxico Burress RC	4.00	10.00
257 Chad Pennington RC	4.00	10.00
258 Sylvester Morris RC	3.00	8.00
259 Ron Dugans RC	3.00	8.00
260 Joe Hamilton RC	3.00	8.00
261 Chris Redman RC	3.00	8.00
262 Trung Canidate RC	3.00	8.00
263 J.R. Redmond RC	3.00	8.00
264 Danny Farmer RC	3.00	8.00
265 Todd Pinkston RC	3.00	8.00
266 Dennis Northcutt RC	3.00	8.00
267 Laveranues Coles RC	4.00	10.00
268 Bubba Franks RC	3.00	8.00
269 Travis Prentice RC	3.00	8.00
270 Peter Warrick RC	3.00	8.00

2000 Topps Chrome Refractors

*VETS: 2.5X TO 6X BASIC CARDS
VETERAN REFRACTOR ODDS 1:12
*ROOKIES: .6X TO 1.5X BASIC CARDS
ROOKIE STATED PRINT RUN 150

2000 Topps Chrome Combos

Randomly inserted in packs at the rate of one in 20, this 10-card set pairs some of the NFL's players into a dominating duo with original painted artwork. Card backs carry a "TC" prefix.

COMPLETE SET (10)	15.00	30.00

STATED ODDS 1:20
*REFRACTOR: 1.2X TO 3X BASIC INSERTS
REFRACTOR STATED ODDS 1:200

TC1 J.Unitas/P.Manning	2.50	6.00
TC2 C.Carter/R.Moss	1.00	2.50
TC3 R.Williams/E.James	.75	2.00
TC4 M.Harrison/J.Smith	.75	2.00
TC5 I.Bruce/J.Galloway	1.00	2.50
TC6 McN/Cou/Kng/Cul/A.Smi	.60	1.50
TC7 S.Davis/F.Taylor	.60	1.50
TC8 M.Faulk/E.George	.75	2.00
TC9 E.Smith/T.Aikman	1.50	4.00
TC10 K.Warner/D.Marino	2.00	5.00

2000 Topps Chrome Own the Game

Randomly inserted in packs at one in 12, this 30-card set captures the league's best players in four offensive categories: Passing Yards, Rushing Yards, Receiving Yards, and Touchdowns. Each card was printed with a slightly sculpted flat silver foil background on the cardfronts. The cardbacks carry an "OTG" prefix

COMPLETE SET (30)	30.00	60.00

STATED ODDS 1:12
*REFRACTOR: 1.2X TO 3X BASIC INSERTS
REFRACTOR STATED ODDS 1:120

OTG1 Steve Beuerlein	.50	1.25
OTG2 Kurt Warner	1.00	2.50
OTG3 Peyton Manning	1.50	4.00
OTG4 Brett Favre	1.25	3.00
OTG5 Brad Johnson	.50	1.25
OTG6 Edgerrin James	.50	1.25
OTG7 Curtis Martin	.50	1.25
OTG8 Stephen Davis	.40	1.00
OTG9 Emmitt Smith	1.00	2.50
OTG10 Marshall Faulk	.50	1.25
OTG11 Eddie George	.50	1.25
OTG12 Duce Staley	.40	1.00
OTG13 Charlie Garner	.50	1.25
OTG14 Marvin Harrison	.50	1.25
OTG15 Jimmy Smith	.50	1.25
OTG16 Randy Moss	.50	1.25
OTG17 Marcus Robinson	.50	1.25
OTG18 Tim Brown	.60	1.50
OTG19 Germane Crowell	.40	1.00
OTG20 Muhsin Muhammad	.40	1.00
OTG21 Cris Carter	.60	1.50
OTG22 Michael Westbrook	.40	1.00
OTG23 Amani Toomer	.40	1.00
OTG24 Keyshawn Johnson	.50	1.25
OTG25 Isaac Bruce	.60	1.50
OTG26 Kurt Warner	1.00	2.50
OTG27 Stephen Davis	.40	1.00
OTG28 Edgerrin James	.50	1.25
OTG29 Cris Carter	.60	1.50
OTG30 Marvin Harrison	.50	1.25

2000 Topps Chrome Preseason Picks

Randomly inserted in packs at the rate of one in 22, this 31-card set spotlights each of the NFL teams with a standout player on the front of the card and a montage of teammates on the back.

COMPLETE SET (31)	40.00	80.00

STATED ODDS 1:22 HOBBY
*REFRACTORS: 1.2X TO 3X BASIC INSERTS
REFRACTOR ODDS 1:220 HOB

P1 Jake Plummer	.40	1.00
P2 Troy Aikman	.75	2.00
P3 Kerry Collins	.40	1.00
P4 Donovan McNabb	.50	1.25
P5 Stephen Davis	.40	1.00
P6 McNown/Robinson/Enis/Engram	.50	1.25
P7 Charlie Batch	.40	1.00
P8 Brett Favre	1.25	3.00
P9 Randy Moss	.50	1.25
P10 Shaun King	.40	1.00
P11 Tim Couch	.50	1.25
P12 Jamal Anderson	.50	1.25
P13 Steve Beuerlein	.50	1.25
P14 Ricky Williams	.50	1.25
P15 Kurt Warner	1.00	2.50
P16 Jerry Rice	1.50	4.00
P17 Eric Moulds	.40	1.00
P18 Peyton Manning	1.50	4.00
P19 Zach Thomas	.50	1.25
P20 Drew Bledsoe	.50	1.25
P21 Curtis Martin	.50	1.25
P22 Tony Banks	.40	1.00
P23 Akili Smith	.40	1.00
P24 Jimmy Smith	.50	1.25
P25 Jerome Bettis	.60	1.50
P26 Eddie George	.50	1.25
P27 Terrell Davis	.50	1.25
P28 Tony Gonzalez	.50	1.25
P29 Tim Brown	.60	1.50
P30 Junior Seau	.50	1.25
P31 Jon Kitna	.40	1.00

2000 Topps Chrome Unitas Reprints Refractors

ndomly inserted in packs at the rate of one in 14, this 18-card set features reprints of Johnny U's 14 base Topps cards as well as four other designs. Each card is enhanced with the rainbow holofoil refractor effect and carries the word "Refractor" on the card back.

COMPLETE SET (18)	40.00	100.00
COMMON CARD (R1-R18)	2.50	6.00

STATED ODDS 1:14

R1 Johnny Unitas 1957	4.00	10.00

2001 Topps Chrome

Topps released its Chrome set in August of 2001 as a 320-card set. The set was made up of 210 veterans and 110 short printed rookies. The rookies were serial numbered to 999 and were only available as refractors. The set looked identical to the base Topps set with the chromium technology.

COMP.SET w/o SP's (210)	20.00	50.00

ROOKIE/999 STATED ODDS 1:12

1 Randy Moss	.40	1.00
2 Desmond Howard	.40	1.00
3 Shawn Bryson	.30	.75
4 Lamar Smith	.40	1.00
5 Peter Warrick	.30	.75
6 Hines Ward	.40	1.00
7 J.R. Redmond	.30	.75
8 Reidel Anthony	.30	.75
9 Rich Gannon	.40	1.00
10 Ed McCaffrey	.40	1.00
11 Jamel White	.30	.75
12 Michael Pittman	.40	1.00
13 Rob Johnson	.40	1.00
14 Tim Couch	.30	.75
15 Stephen Alexander	.30	.75
16 Ricky Watters	.40	1.00
17 Kerry Collins	.30	.75
18 Ricky Williams	.40	1.00
19 Joey Galloway	.40	1.00
20 Chris Chandler	.40	1.00
21 Marty Booker	.30	.75
22 Mark Brunell	.40	1.00
23 Antonio Freeman	.50	1.25
24 Richie Anderson	.30	.75
25 Amani Toomer	.30	.75
26 Trent Green	.30	.75
27 Terrell Fletcher	.30	.75
28 Kevin Lockett	.30	.75
29 Ron Dixon	.30	.75
30 Charlie Batch	.30	.75
31 Oronde Gadsden	.30	.75
32 Dorsey Levens	.40	1.00
33 Jamal Lewis	.50	1.25
34 Craig Yeast	.30	.75
35 Muhsin Muhammad	.30	.75
36 Willie Jackson	.30	.75
37 Isaac Bruce	.50	1.25
38 Frank Wycheck	.30	.75
39 Troy Brown	.30	.75
40 Anthony Wright	.30	.75
41 Zach Thomas	.40	1.00
42 Qadry Ismail	.30	.75
43 Jake Plummer	.30	.75
44 Keenan McCardell	.40	1.00
45 Charles Johnson	.30	.75
46 Brett Favre	1.00	2.50
47 Jacquez Green	.30	.75
48 Matt Hasselbeck	.30	.75
49 Tiki Barber	.40	1.00
50 Jeff Garcia	.30	.75
51 Shawn Jefferson	.30	.75
52 Kevin Johnson	.30	.75
53 Terrence Wilkins	.30	.75
54 Mike Anderson	.30	.75
55 Tim Brown	.50	1.25
56 Champ Bailey	.40	1.00
57 Jimmy Smith	.40	1.00
58 Trent Dilfer	.30	.75
59 James Allen	.30	.75
60 David Boston	.30	.75
61 Jeremiah Trotter	.30	.75
62 Freddie Jones	.30	.75
63 Deion Sanders	.40	1.00
64 Darrell Jackson	.40	1.00
65 David Patten	.30	.75
66 Jeremy McDaniel	.30	.75
67 Jay Fiedler	.40	1.00
68 Chad Lewis	.30	.75
69 Rocket Ismail	.40	1.00
70 Cade McNown	.40	1.00
71 Jevon Kearse	.30	.75
72 Jermaine Fazande	.30	.75
73 Junior Seau	.40	1.00
74 Rod Smith	.40	1.00
75 Jermaine Lewis	.30	.75
76 Dennis Northcutt	.30	.75
77 Charlie Garner	.40	1.00
78 Charles Woodson	.50	1.25
79 Wayne Chrebet	.30	.75
80 Ahman Green	.40	1.00
81 Donald Hayes	.30	.75
82 Terance Mathis	.30	.75
83 Warrick Dunn	.30	.75
84 Chris Sanders	.30	.75
85 Albert Connell	.30	.75
86 Robert Griffith	.30	.75
87 Germane Crowell	.30	.75
88 Tony Banks	.30	.75
89 Travis Taylor	.30	.75
90 Akili Smith	.30	.75
91 Michael Westbrook	.30	.75
92 Doug Flutie	.40	1.00
93 Ike Hilliard	.30	.75
94 Terry Glenn	.40	1.00
95 Leslie Shepherd	.30	.75
96 Az-Zahir Hakim	.30	.75
97 La'Roi Glover	.30	.75
98 Peyton Manning	1.25	3.00
99 Jackie Harris	.40	1.00
100 Edgerrin James	.40	1.00
101 Peerless Price	.30	.75
102 Jamal Anderson	.40	1.00
103 Keyshawn Johnson	.40	1.00
104 Derrick Mason	.30	.75
105 J.J. Stokes	.30	.75
106 Kevin Faulk	.30	.75
107 Tony Richardson	.30	.75
108 James Stewart	.30	.75
109 Tim Biakabutuka	.30	.75
110 Jon Kitna	.30	.75
111 Thomas Jones	.30	.75
112 Steve McNair	.40	1.00
113 Sean Dawkins	.30	.75
114 Jerome Bettis	.50	1.25
115 Donovan McNabb	.40	1.00
116 Bill Schroeder	.40	1.00
117 Rod Woodson	.50	1.25
118 James McKnight	.30	.75
119 Daunte Culpepper	.40	1.00
120 Todd Husak	.30	.75
121 Shaun King	.30	.75
122 Tyrone Wheatley	.40	1.00
123 Curtis Martin	.40	1.00
124 Terrell Davis	.40	1.00
125 Steve Beuerlein	.40	1.00
126 Brad Johnson	.40	1.00
127 Joe Horn	.30	.75
128 Fred Taylor	.30	.75
129 Brian Urlacher	.60	1.50
130 Ray Lewis	.50	1.25
131 Marshall Faulk	.40	1.00
132 Curtis Conway	.40	1.00
133 Jason Sehorn	.40	1.00
134 Jerome Pathon	.30	.75
135 Derrick Alexander	.30	.75
136 Jerry Rice	1.00	2.50
137 Jeff George	.40	1.00
138 Johnnie Morton	.40	1.00
139 Eric Moulds	.30	.75
140 Duce Staley	.30	.75
141 Vinny Testaverde	.30	.75
142 Eddie George	.50	1.25
143 Shaun Alexander	.30	.75
144 Drew Bledsoe	.40	1.00
145 Emmitt Smith	.75	2.00
146 Marvin Harrison	.40	1.00
147 Frank Sanders	.30	.75
148 Aaron Shea	.30	.75
149 Cris Carter	.50	1.25
150 Tony Gonzalez	.40	1.00
151 Marcus Robinson	.40	1.00
152 Danny Farmer	.30	.75
153 Warren Sapp	.40	1.00
154 Kurt Warner	.75	2.00
155 Jessie Armstead	.30	.75
156 Lawyer Milloy	.30	.75
157 Brian Griese	.30	.75
158 Jason Taylor	.50	1.25
159 Jeff Lewis	.30	.75
160 Travis Prentice	.30	.75
161 Tim Dwight	.40	1.00
162 Kyle Brady	.30	.75
163 Bubba Franks	.30	.75
164 James Thrash	.40	1.00
165 Bobby Shaw	.30	.75
166 Ron Dayne	.40	1.00
167 Mike Alstott	.30	.75
168 Bruce Smith	.40	1.00
169 Jeff Graham	.30	.75
170 Jeff Blake	.40	1.00
171 Laveranues Coles	.40	1.00
172 Herman Moore	.30	.75
173 Shannon Sharpe	.40	1.00
174 Corey Dillon	.30	.75
175 Ken Dilger	.30	.75
176 Eddie Kennison	.40	1.00
177 Andre Rison	.40	1.00
178 Stephen Davis	.30	.75
179 Torry Holt	.40	1.00
180 Samari Rolle	.30	.75
181 Michael Strahan	.40	1.00
182 Plaxico Burress	.30	.75
183 Darnell Autry	.30	.75
184 Wesley Walls	.30	.75
185 Elvis Grbac	.40	1.00
186 Marcus Pollard	.30	.75
187 Keith Poole	.30	.75
188 Ryan Leaf	.30	.75
189 Terrell Owens	.40	1.00
190 Dedric Ward	.30	.75
191 Donald Driver	.40	1.00
192 Larry Foster	.30	.75
193 Priest Holmes	.30	.75
194 Sammy Morris	.30	.75
195 Reggie Jones	.30	.75
196 Kordell Stewart	.30	.75
197 Sylvester Morris	.30	.75
198 Aaron Brooks	.30	.75
199 Tai Streets	.30	.75
200 Chad Pennington	.30	.75
201 Terrell Owens SH	.40	1.00
202 Marshall Faulk SH	.40	1.00
203 Mike Anderson SH	.30	.75
204 Cris Carter SH	.50	1.25
205 Corey Dillon SH	.30	.75
206 Daunte Culpepper SH	.40	1.00
207 Peyton Manning SH	1.75	4.00
208 Torry Holt SH	.40	1.00
209 Marvin Harrison SH	.40	1.00
210 Edgerrin James SH	.40	1.00
211 Sam Madison	.30	.75
212 Jonathan Quinn	.30	.75
213 Rob Morris	.30	.75
214 E.G. Green	.30	.75
215 David Sloan	.30	.75
216 Jason Tucker	.30	.75
217 Wali Rainer	.30	.75
218 Jerry Azumah	.30	.75
219 Dameyune Craig	.30	.75
220 Jammi German	.30	.75
221 LaDainian Tomlinson RC	150.00	300.00
222 Quincy Morgan RC	5.00	12.00
223 Steve Smith RC	15.00	30.00
224 Santana Moss RC	6.00	15.00
225 Koren Robinson RC	5.00	12.00
226 Kevin Kasper RC	4.00	10.00
227 Jamie Henderson RC	5.00	12.00
228 Adam Archuleta RC	5.00	12.00
229 Drew Brees RC	900.00	1500.00
230 Michael Stone RC	4.00	10.00
231 Jamar Fletcher RC	4.00	10.00
232 Eric Westmoreland RC	4.00	10.00
233 Chris Barnes RC	4.00	10.00
234 Gerard Warren RC	5.00	12.00
235 Snoop Minnis RC	4.00	10.00
236 Chris Chambers RC	4.00	10.00
237 Damerien McCants RC	5.00	12.00
238 Kevan Barlow RC	5.00	12.00
239 Mike McMahon RC	5.00	12.00
240 Jabari Holloway RC	4.00	10.00
241 Travis Henry RC	5.00	12.00
242 Derrick Blaylock RC	5.00	12.00
243 Tim Hasselbeck RC	5.00	12.00
244 Andre Carter RC	5.00	12.00
245 Sage Rosenfels RC	5.00	12.00
246 Cedrick Wilson RC	5.00	12.00
247 Scotty Anderson RC	4.00	10.00
248 Ken-Yon Rambo RC	4.00	10.00
249 Marques Tuiasosopo RC	5.00	12.00
250 Reggie Wayne RC	60.00	100.00
251 Onomo Ojo RC	4.00	10.00
252 James Jackson RC	4.00	10.00
253 Moran Norris RC	4.00	10.00
254 Rashard Casey RC	4.00	10.00
255 Rudi Johnson RC	6.00	15.00
256 Willie Middlebrooks RC	5.00	12.00
257 Freddie Mitchell RC	4.00	10.00
258 Deuce McAllister RC	6.00	15.00
259 Chad Johnson RC	6.00	15.00
260 David Terrell RC	5.00	12.00
261 Jamal Reynolds RC	4.00	10.00
262 Michael Vick RC	20.00	50.00
263 Marcus Stroud RC	5.00	12.00
264 Dan Alexander RC	5.00	12.00
265 Jonathan Carter RC	4.00	10.00
266 Bobby Newcombe RC	5.00	12.00
267 Eddie Berlin RC	4.00	10.00
268 LaMont Jordan RC	6.00	15.00
269 Michael Bennett RC	5.00	12.00
270 Shaun Rogers RC	6.00	15.00
271 Travis Minor RC	5.00	12.00
272 Jesse Palmer RC	5.00	12.00
273 Derrick Gibson RC	4.00	10.00
274 Chris Weinke RC	5.00	12.00
275 Nate Clements RC	5.00	12.00
276 Eric Kelly RC	4.00	10.00
277 Justin Smith RC	8.00	20.00
278 Ryan Pickett RC	4.00	10.00
279 Anthony Thomas RC	6.00	15.00
280 Will Allen RC	6.00	15.00
281 Quincy Carter RC	5.00	12.00
282 Richard Seymour RC	8.00	20.00
283 Dan Morgan RC	5.00	12.00
284 Tay Cody RC	4.00	10.00
285 Alge Crumpler RC	6.00	15.00
286 Robert Ferguson RC	6.00	15.00
287 Will Peterson RC	5.00	12.00
288 Tony Dixon RC	4.00	10.00
289 Correll Buckhalter RC	4.00	10.00
290 Rod Gardner RC	5.00	12.00
291 Justin McCareins RC	5.00	12.00
292 Josh Heupel RC	6.00	15.00
293 Todd Heap RC	8.00	20.00
294 Damione Lewis RC	5.00	12.00
295 George Layne RC	4.00	10.00
296 Jamie Winborn RC	5.00	12.00
297 Billy Baber RC	4.00	10.00
298 T.J. Houshmandzadeh RC	5.00	12.00
299 Aaron Schobel RC	6.00	15.00
300 Gary Baxter RC	4.00	10.00
301 DeLawrence Grant RC	4.00	10.00
302 Morlon Greenwood RC	4.00	10.00
303 Shad Meier RC	4.00	10.00
304 Torrance Marshall RC	4.00	10.00
305 David Martin RC	4.00	10.00
306 Anthony Henry RC	6.00	15.00
307 Derrick Burgess RC	6.00	15.00
308 Andre Dyson RC	4.00	10.00
309 Ryan Helming RC	4.00	10.00
310 Fred Smoot RC	5.00	12.00
311 Arther Love RC	4.00	10.00
312 John Capel RC	4.00	10.00
313 Brandon Spoon RC	5.00	12.00
314 Karon Riley RC	4.00	10.00
315 Andre King RC	4.00	10.00
316 Quentin McCord RC	5.00	12.00
317 Zeke Moreno RC	5.00	12.00
318 Francis St. Paul RC	4.00	10.00
319 Richmond Flowers RC	4.00	10.00
320 Derek Combs RC	4.00	10.00

2001 Topps Chrome Refractors

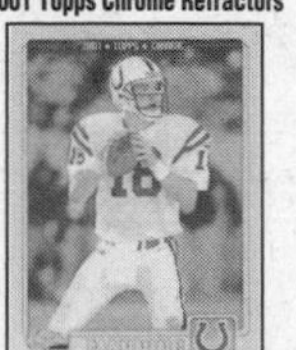

*VETS/999: 2X TO 5X BASIC CARDS
*ROOKIES/100: 1X TO 2.5X
VETERAN/999 STATED ODDS 1:6
ROOKIE/100 STATED ODDS 1:125

221 LaDainian Tomlinson	300.00	600.00
229 Drew Brees	3500.00	5000.00
250 Reggie Wayne	75.00	150.00
262 Michael Vick	60.00	150.00

2001 Topps Chrome Combos

Combos were inserted in packs of 2001 Topps Chrome at a rate of 1:12. The 19-card set featured the refractor technology with each card marked "Refractor" on the back.The cards highlighted NFL players who played for the same colleges.

COMPLETE SET (19) 15.00 40.00
STATED ODDS 1:12
TC1 E.James/S.Moss .50 1.25
TC2 T.Holt/K.Robinson .75 2.00
TC3 J.Lewis/T.Henry 1.00 2.50
TC4 C.Martin/K.Barlow .75 2.00
TC5 C.Carter/K.Rambo 1.00 2.50
TC6 T.Aikman/F.Mitchell 1.25 3.00
TC7 B.Griese/D.Terrell .60 1.50
TC8 T.Wheatley/A.Thomas 1.00 2.50
TC9 W.Dunn/T.Minor .60 1.50
TC10 P.Warrick/S.Minnis .60 1.50
TC11 W.Sapp/D.Morgan .75 2.00
TC12 T.Gonzalez/A.Carter .75 2.00
TC13 A.Freeman/M.Vick 1.00 2.50
TC14 R.Dayne/M.Bennett .75 2.00
TC15 M.Alstott/D.Brees 12.00 30.00
TC16 A.Green/C.Buckhalter .75 2.00
TC17 B.Johnson/C.Weinke .75 2.00
TC18 E.Moulds/F.Smoot .60 1.50
TC19 R.Lewis/R.Wayne .75 2.00

2001 Topps Chrome King of Kings Jerseys

e King of Kings set was inserted in packs of 2001 Topps Chrome. Please note that the cards had various serial numbers, and Randy Moss at the time of release was issued as an exchange card. The overall stated odds was 1:734.

GROUP 1 ODDS 1:17766H
GROUP 2 ODDS 1:4890H
GROUP 3 ODDS 1:8094H
GROUP 4 ODDS 1:4834H
GROUP 5 ODDS 1:2194H
GROUP 6 ODDS 1:3215H
JSY/75-375 OVERALL ODDS 1:734H
KCD Corey Dillon/375 4.00 10.00
KDM Dan Marino/125 12.00 30.00
KES Emmitt Smith/150 10.00 25.00
KFT Fred Taylor/250 4.00 10.00
KJR Jerry Rice/125 12.00 30.00
KTO Terrell Owens/275 5.00 12.00
KWP Walter Payton/75 20.00 50.00

2001 Topps Chrome Own the Game

n the Game had 5 different sets that were released in 2001 Topps Chrome. The overall odds for any of these sets was 1:16. The 10-card Award Winners sets carried an 'AW' prefix for the card numbering. The 7-card Ground Warrior sets carried a 'GW' prefix for the card numbering. The 7-card Perfect Spiral sets carried a 'PS' prefix for the card numbering. The 3-card Intimidators sets carried a 'TI' prefix for the card numbering. The 3-card Showtime sets carried a 'TS' prefix for the card numbering. All of the card designs were available only with the refractor technology.

COMPLETE SET (10) 25.00 60.00
STATED ODDS 1:16
AW1 Marvin Harrison .75 2.00
AW2 Muhsin Muhammad .60 1.50
AW3 Torry Holt .75 2.00
AW4 Rod Smith .75 2.00
AW5 Randy Moss .75 2.00
AW6 Cris Carter 1.00 2.50
AW7 Ed McCaffrey .75 2.00
AW8 Isaac Bruce 1.00 2.50
AW9 Terrell Owens .75 2.00
AW10 Tony Gonzalez .75 2.00
GW1 Edgerrin James .75 2.00
GW2 Robert Smith .60 1.50
GW3 Marshall Faulk .75 2.00
GW4 Mike Anderson .60 1.50
GW5 Eddie George 1.00 2.50
GW6 Corey Dillon .60 1.50
GW7 Fred Taylor .60 1.50
PS1 Brian Griese .60 1.50
PS2 Peyton Manning 2.50 6.00
PS3 Jeff Garcia .60 1.50
PS4 Daunte Culpepper .75 2.00
PS5 Brett Favre 2.00 5.00
PS6 Kurt Warner 1.50 4.00
PS7 Donovan McNabb .75 2.00
TI1 La'Roi Glover .60 1.50
TI2 Darren Sharper .75 2.00
TI3 Mike Peterson .60 1.50
TS1 Derrick Mason .60 1.50
TS2 Az-Zahir Hakim .60 1.50
TS3 Jermaine Lewis .60 1.50

2001 Topps Chrome Pro Bowl Jerseys

o Bowl Jersey cards were randomly inserted into packs of 2001 Topps Chrome at an overall rate of 1:299. The serial numbering varried from player to player, therefore an overall rate was given. Each card featured a jersey swatch from the player's Pro Bowl jersey. The cards carried a 'TP' prefix for the card numbering.

GROUP 1 ODDS 1:4834H
GROUP 2 ODDS 1:1863H
GROUP 3 ODDS 1:1072H
GROUP 4 ODDS 1:602H
JSY/250-400 OVERALL ODDS 1:299H
TPCL Chad Lewis/400 4.00 10.00
TPDM Derrick Mason/400 4.00 10.00
TPEM Eric Moulds/375 4.00 10.00
TPJG Jeff Garcia/250 4.00 10.00
TPJL John Lynch/325 5.00 12.00
TPJS Junior Seau/375 5.00 12.00
TPJT Jason Taylor/400 6.00 15.00
TPMA Mike Alstott/400 4.00 10.00
TPRG Rich Gannon/325 5.00 12.00
TPRL Ray Lewis/375 6.00 15.00
TPTH Torry Holt/400 5.00 12.00

2001 Topps Chrome Rookie Reprint Jerseys

okie Reprint Jerseys were randomly inserted into packs of 2001 Topps Chrome at an overall rate of 1:2729. The cards were serial numbered to 75, 100, 125, and 150 depending on the player. The cards used the refractor technology and carried a 'TO' prefix for the card numbering.

GROUP 1 ODDS 1:16766H
GROUP 2 ODDS 1:12354H
GROUP 3 ODDS 1:9780H
GROUP 4 ODDS 1:8094H
JSY/75-150 OVERALL ODDS 1:2729H
TODM Dan Marino/125 40.00 100.00
TOES Emmitt Smith/150 40.00 100.00
TOJR Jerry Rice/100 40.00 100.00
TOWP Walter Payton/75 30.00 80.00

2001 Topps Chrome Walter Payton Reprints Refractors

e Walter Payton Reprints are the same as the Topps set of these with the exception of the chromium and refractor technology. The odds for these were 1:20 packs and were only found in 2001 Topps Chrome. The set also featured a jersey swatch that was cut into the shape of a 34 on the front of the card, and the design was that of the 1976 rookie. The stated odds for pulling the jersey was 1:1204.

COMPLETE SET (12) 25.00 60.00
COMMON CARD (1-12) 3.00 8.00
STATED ODDS 1:20
JSY STATED ODDS 1:1204
JSY FEATURES 34 DIECUT SWATCH
WPR Walter Payton JSY 40.00 100.00

2002 Topps Chrome

leased in mid-August 2002, this 265-card set includes 165 veterans and 100 rookies. The rookies were inserted at a rate of 1:3. Boxes contained 24 packs of four cards. S.R.P. was $3.00 per pack.

COMPLETE SET (265) 100.00 200.00
COMP.SET w/o SP's (165) 20.00 50.00
166-265 ROOKIE ODDS 1:3 HOB/RET
1 Anthony Thomas .40 1.00
2 Jake Plummer .30 .75
3 Maurice Smith .30 .75
4 Jamal Lewis .40 1.00
5 Ray Lewis .50 1.25
6 Alex Van Pelt .30 .75
7 Chris Weinke .30 .75
8 Corey Dillon .30 .75
9 Quincy Morgan .30 .75
10 Rocket Ismail .40 1.00
11 Brian Griese .30 .75
12 Johnnie Morton .40 1.00
13 Edgerrin James .40 1.00
14 Keenan McCardell .40 1.00
15 Travis Minor .30 .75
16 Sylvester Morris .30 .75
17 Randy Moss .40 1.00
18 Drew Bledsoe .40 1.00
19 Willie Jackson .30 .75
20 Michael Strahan .40 1.00
21 Santana Moss .40 1.00
22 Duce Staley .30 .75
23 Kendrell Bell .30 .75
24 LaDainian Tomlinson .50 1.25
25 Terrell Owens .40 1.00
26 Shaun Alexander .30 .75
27 Trung Canidate .30 .75
28 Mike Alstott .30 .75
29 Kevin Dyson .40 1.00
30 Rod Gardner .30 .75
31 David Boston .30 .75
32 Michael Vick .40 1.00
33 Qadry Ismail .30 .75
34 Peerless Price .30 .75
35 Rob Johnson .40 1.00
36 Marcus Robinson .40 1.00
37 Peter Warrick .30 .75
38 Kevin Johnson .30 .75
39 Ed McCaffrey .40 1.00
40 Shaun Rogers .30 .75
41 Marvin Harrison .40 1.00
42 Priest Holmes .30 .75
43 Oronde Gadsden .30 .75
44 Terry Glenn .40 1.00
45 Ike Hilliard .30 .75
46 Charles Woodson .50 1.25
47 Freddie Mitchell .30 .75
48 Drew Brees 1.00 2.50
49 Jeff Garcia .30 .75
50 Kurt Warner .40 1.00
51 Keyshawn Johnson .40 1.00
52 Jevon Kearse .30 .75
53 Stephen Davis .30 .75
54 Shannon Sharpe .40 1.00
55 Eric Moulds .30 .75
56 Muhsin Muhammad .30 .75
57 Brian Urlacher .50 1.25
58 Chad Johnson .30 .75
59 Tim Couch .30 .75
60 Mike Anderson .30 .75
61 James Stewart .30 .75
62 Corey Bradford .30 .75
63 Reggie Wayne .40 1.00
64 Mark Brunell .40 1.00
65 Trent Green .30 .75
66 Zach Thomas .40 1.00
67 Michael Bennett .30 .75
68 Troy Brown .30 .75
69 Amani Toomer .30 .75
70 Curtis Martin .40 1.00
71 Tim Brown .50 1.25
72 Correll Buckhalter .30 .75
73 Kordell Stewart .30 .75
74 Junior Seau .40 1.00
75 Kevan Barlow .30 .75
76 Matt Hasselbeck .30 .75
77 Marshall Faulk .40 1.00
78 Warren Sapp .40 1.00
79 Frank Wycheck .30 .75
80 Michael Westbrook .30 .75
81 Travis Henry .30 .75
82 David Terrell .30 .75
83 Jon Kitna .30 .75
84 James Jackson .30 .75
85 Joey Galloway .40 1.00
86 Rod Smith .40 1.00
87 Germane Crowell .30 .75
88 Bill Schroeder .30 .75
89 Dominic Rhodes .30 .75
90 Fred Taylor .30 .75
91 Snoop Minnis .30 .75
92 Chris Chambers .30 .75
93 Daunte Culpepper .40 1.00
94 Deuce McAllister .40 1.00
95 Kerry Collins .30 .75
96 John Abraham .40 1.00
97 Rich Gannon .40 1.00
98 Tiki Barber .40 1.00
99 Hines Ward .40 1.00
100 Tom Brady 20.00 50.00
101 Tim Dwight .30 .75
102 Garrison Hearst .30 .75
103 Darrell Jackson .40 1.00
104 Isaac Bruce .50 1.25
105 Brad Johnson .40 1.00
106 Steve McNair .40 1.00
107 Champ Bailey .40 1.00
108 Emmitt Smith .75 2.00
109 Mike McMahon .30 .75
110 Terrell Davis .40 1.00
111 Antonio Freeman .50 1.25
112 Jimmy Smith .40 1.00
113 Tony Gonzalez .40 1.00
114 Jay Fiedler .40 1.00
115 Cris Carter .50 1.25
116 David Patten .30 .75
117 Joe Horn .30 .75
118 Laveranues Coles .40 1.00
119 Charlie Garner .40 1.00
120 Donovan McNabb .40 1.00
121 Jerome Bettis .50 1.25
122 Curtis Conway .40 1.00
123 Az-Zahir Hakim .30 .75
124 Warrick Dunn .30 .75
125 Eddie George .40 1.00
126 Quincy Carter .30 .75
127 Ahman Green .40 1.00
128 Peyton Manning 1.25 3.00
129 James McKnight .30 .75
130 Antowain Smith .40 1.00
131 Ricky Williams .40 1.00
132 Chad Pennington .30 .75
133 Jerry Rice 1.00 2.50
134 Todd Pinkston .30 .75
135 Plaxico Burress .30 .75
136 Doug Flutie .40 1.00
137 Koren Robinson .30 .75
138 Torry Holt .40 1.00
139 Aaron Brooks .30 .75
140 Ron Dayne .40 1.00
141 Vinny Testaverde .30 .75
142 Brett Favre 1.00 2.50
143 James Thrash .40 1.00
144 Wayne Chrebet .30 .75
145 Derrick Mason .30 .75
146 Ahman Green WW .30 .75
147 Peyton Manning WW 1.00 2.50
148 Kurt Warner WW .30 .75
149 Daunte Culpepper WW .30 .75
150 Tom Brady WW 10.00 25.00
151 Rod Gardner WW .25 .60
152 Corey Dillon WW .25 .60
153 Priest Holmes WW .25 .60
154 Shaun Alexander WW .25 .60
155 Randy Moss WW .30 .75
156 Eric Moulds WW .25 .60
157 Brett Favre WW .75 2.00
158 Todd Bouman WW .25 .60
159 Dominic Rhodes WW .25 .60
160 Marvin Harrison WW .30 .75
161 Torry Holt WW .30 .75
162 Derrick Mason WW .25 .60
163 Jerry Rice WW .75 2.00
164 Donovan McNabb WW .30 .75
165 Marshall Faulk WW .30 .75
166 David Carr RC 2.00 5.00
167 Quentin Jammer RC 3.00 8.00
168 Mike Williams RC 2.00 5.00
169 Rocky Calmus RC 2.50 6.00
170 Travis Fisher RC 2.50 6.00
171 Dwight Freeney RC 4.00 10.00
172 Jeremy Shockey RC 3.00 8.00
173 Marquise Walker RC 2.00 5.00
174 Eric Crouch RC 3.00 8.00
175 DeShaun Foster RC 4.00 10.00
176 Roy Williams RC 2.00 5.00
177 Andre Davis RC 2.00 5.00
178 Alex Brown RC 3.00 8.00
179 Michael Lewis RC 2.50 6.00
180 Terry Charles RC 2.00 5.00
181 Clinton Portis RC 3.00 8.00
182 Dennis Johnson RC 2.00 5.00
183 Lito Sheppard RC 3.00 8.00
184 Ryan Sims RC 3.00 8.00
185 Raonall Smith RC 2.00 5.00
186 Albert Haynesworth RC 3.00 8.00
187 Eddie Freeman RC 2.00 5.00
188 Levi Jones RC 2.00 5.00
189 Josh McCown RC 3.00 8.00
190 Cliff Russell RC 2.00 5.00
191 Maurice Morris RC 2.50 6.00
192 Antwaan Randle El RC 2.50 6.00
193 Ladell Betts RC 3.00 8.00
194 Daniel Graham RC 2.50 6.00
195 David Garrard RC 2.50 6.00
196 Antonio Bryant RC 3.00 8.00
197 Patrick Ramsey RC 2.50 6.00
198 Kelly Campbell RC 2.50 6.00
199 Will Overstreet RC 2.00 5.00
200 Ryan Denney RC 2.00 5.00
201 John Henderson RC 2.50 6.00
202 Freddie Milons RC 2.00 5.00
203 Tim Carter RC 2.50 6.00
204 Kurt Kittner RC 2.00 5.00
205 Joey Harrington RC 2.00 5.00
206 Ricky Williams RC 2.50 6.00
207 Bryant McKinnie RC 2.00 5.00
208 Ed Reed RC 6.00 15.00
209 Josh Reed RC 2.50 6.00
210 Seth Burford RC 2.00 5.00
211 Javon Walker RC 3.00 8.00
212 Jamar Martin RC 2.50 6.00
213 Leonard Henry RC 2.00 5.00
214 Julius Peppers RC 5.00 12.00
215 Jabar Gaffney RC 2.00 5.00
216 Kalimba Edwards RC 2.50 6.00
217 Napoleon Harris RC 2.50 6.00
218 Ashley Lelie RC 2.00 5.00
219 Anthony Weaver RC 2.00 5.00
220 Bryan Thomas RC 2.00 5.00
221 Wendell Bryant RC 2.00 5.00
222 Damien Anderson RC 2.00 5.00
223 Travis Stephens RC 2.00 5.00
224 Rohan Davey RC 3.00 8.00
225 Mike Pearson RC 2.00 5.00
226 Marc Colombo RC 2.00 5.00
227 Phillip Buchanon RC 3.00 8.00
228 T.J. Duckett RC 2.00 5.00
229 Ron Johnson RC 2.50 6.00
230 Larry Tripplett RC 2.00 5.00
231 Randy Fasani RC 2.00 5.00
232 Keyuo Craver RC 2.00 5.00
233 Marquand Manuel RC 2.00 5.00
234 Jonathan Wells RC 2.50 6.00
235 Reche Caldwell RC 2.50 6.00
236 Luke Staley RC 2.00 5.00
237 Donte Stallworth RC 3.00 8.00
238 Levar Fisher RC 2.00 5.00
239 Lamar Gordon RC 2.50 6.00
240 William Green RC 2.50 6.00
241 Dusty Bonner RC 2.00 5.00
242 Craig Nall RC 2.50 6.00
243 Eric McCoo RC 2.00 5.00
244 David Thornton RC 2.00 5.00
245 Terry Jones RC 2.00 5.00
246 Lee Mays RC 2.00 5.00
247 Bryan Fletcher RC 2.00 5.00
248 Verron Haynes RC 2.00 5.00
249 Zak Kustok RC 2.00 5.00
250 Chad Hutchinson RC 2.00 5.00
251 Andra Davis RC 2.00 5.00
252 Wes Pate RC 2.00 5.00
253 Jon McGraw RC 2.00 5.00
254 Howard Green RC 2.00 5.00
255 Daryl Jones RC 2.00 5.00
256 David Priestley RC 2.00 5.00
257 Marques Anderson RC 2.50 6.00
258 Roosevelt Williams RC 2.00 5.00
259 Major Applewhite RC 3.00 8.00
260 Ronald Curry RC 2.00 5.00
261 Adrian Peterson RC 2.50 6.00
262 Tellis Redmon RC 2.00 5.00
263 Chester Taylor RC 3.00 8.00
264 Deion Branch RC 3.00 8.00
265 Tank Williams RC 2.50 6.00

2002 Topps Chrome Refractors

*VETS 1-165: 3X TO 8X BASIC CARDS
1-165 VET/599 ODDS 1:11 HOB/RET
1-165 STATED PRINT RUN 599 SER.#'d SETS
*ROOKIES 166-265: 1.2X TO 3X
166-265 ROOK/100 ODDS 1:109 HOB, 1:110 RET
166-265 STATED PRINT RUN 100 SER.#'d SETS

2002 Topps Chrome Gridiron Badges Jerseys

This 22-card insert set features game-worn jerseys swatches with various serial numbering. Cards were inserted 1:382 hobby packs, and 1:384 retail packs.

OVERALL ODDS 1:382 HOB, 1:384 RET
GBBF Brett Favre/200 12.00 30.00
GBCM Curtis Martin/200 5.00 12.00
GBDB David Boston/200 4.00 10.00
GBDC David Carr/50 5.00 12.00
GBDF Doug Flutie/100 5.00 12.00
GBDFO DeShaun Foster/100 6.00 15.00
GBDM Dan Marino/200 15.00 40.00
GBJG Jeff Garcia/100 4.00 10.00
GBJR Jerry Rice/150 12.00 30.00
GBKS Kordell Stewart/100 4.00 10.00
GBKW Kurt Warner/200 5.00 12.00
GBLT LaDainian Tomlinson/50 8.00 20.00
GBMF Marshall Faulk/50 6.00 15.00
GBMH Marvin Harrison/200 5.00 12.00
GBMS Michael Strahan/200 5.00 12.00
GBMW Marquise Walker/50 5.00 12.00
GBRL Ray Lewis/200 10.00 25.00
GBSY Steve Young/100 10.00 25.00
GBTB Tom Brady/200 30.00 80.00
GBTBR Tim Brown/100 6.00 15.00
GBTO Terrell Owens/100 5.00 12.00

2002 Topps Chrome King of Kings Super Bowl MVP Jerseys

This set features cards with dual players and dual memorabilia swatches. Cards were inserted at a rate of 1:3643 hobby packs, and 1:3760 retail packs.

OVERALL ODDS 1:3643 HOB, 1:3760 RET
ALL CARDS FEATURE REFRACTOR FRONTS
KDA T.Davis/M.Allen 25.00 60.00
KME J.Montana/J.Elway 150.00 250.00
KMR J.Montana/J.Rice 175.00 350.00
KYR S.Young/J.Rice 50.00 120.00

2002 Topps Chrome Own the Game

Inserted in packs at a rate of 1:8, this 30-card insert set highlights top NFL players. There is also a refractor parallel which was inserted 1:364 hobby packs and 1:365 retail packs.

STATED ODDDS 1:8 HOB/RET
*REFRACT/100: 1X TO 2.5X BASIC INSERT
REFRACTOR/100 ODDS 1:364 H, 1:365 R
REFRACTOR PRINT RUN 100 SER.#'d SETS
OG1 Kurt Warner .60 1.50
OG2 Peyton Manning 2.00 5.00
OG3 Jeff Garcia .50 1.25
OG4 Brett Favre 1.50 4.00
OG5 Donovan McNabb .60 1.50
OG6 Rich Gannon .60 1.50
OG7 Tom Brady 4.00 10.00
OG8 Aaron Brooks .50 1.25
OG9 Priest Holmes .50 1.25
OG10 Curtis Martin .60 1.50
OG11 Stephen Davis .50 1.25
OG12 Ahman Green .60 1.50
OG13 Marshall Faulk .60 1.50
OG14 Shaun Alexander .50 1.25
OG15 Corey Dillon .50 1.25
OG16 Ricky Williams .60 1.50
OG17 David Boston .50 1.25
OG18 Marvin Harrison .60 1.50
OG19 Terrell Owens .60 1.50
OG20 Jimmy Smith .60 1.50
OG21 Torry Holt .60 1.50
OG22 Rod Smith .60 1.50
OG23 Keyshawn Johnson .60 1.50
OG24 Troy Brown .50 1.25
OG25 Michael Strahan .60 1.50
OG26 Ronald McKinnon .50 1.25
OG27 Ray Lewis .75 2.00
OG28 Zach Thomas .60 1.50
OG29 Ronde Barber .50 1.25
OG30 Anthony Henry .50 1.25

2002 Topps Chrome Pro Bowl Jerseys

serted at a rate of 1:109 hobby and 1:110 retail, these cards feature authentic Pro Bowl jersey swatches.

STATED ODDS 1:109 HOB, 1:110 RET
PPAW Aeneas Williams 2.50 6.00
PPBD Brian Dawkins 4.00 10.00
PPDO Deltha O'Neal 2.50 6.00
PPJM Jamir Miller 2.50 6.00
PPLC Larry Centers 2.50 6.00
PPLG La'Roi Glover 2.50 6.00
PPRB Ruben Brown 2.50 6.00
PPRH Rodney Harrison 2.50 6.00
PPRP Robert Porcher 2.50 6.00
PPSK Sammy Knight 2.50 6.00

2002 Topps Chrome Ring of Honor

Inserted at a rate of 1:8 hobby/retail packs, this set salutes Super Bowl MVP's. There is also a refractor parallel available that is serial #'d to 100 and inserted 1:312 packs. Please note that Dexter Jackson was only available in packs of 2003 Topps Chrome.

STATED ODDS 1:8 HOB/RET
*REF/100: 2X TO 5X BASIC INSERTS
REFRACTOR/100 STATED ODDS 1:312
REFRACTOR PRINT RUN 100 SER.#'d SETS
BS1 Bart Starr 1.50 4.00
BS2 Bart Starr 1.50 4.00
CH5 Chuck Howley .50 1.25
DH31 Desmond Howard .60 1.50
DJ37 Dexter Jackson .75 2.00
DW22 Doug Williams .60 1.50
ES28 Emmitt Smith 1.25 3.00
FB11 Fred Biletnikoff .75 2.00
FH9 Franco Harris .75 2.00
JE33 John Elway 1.25 3.00
JM16 Joe Montana 2.50 6.00
JM19 Joe Montana 2.50 6.00
JM24 Joe Montana 2.50 6.00
JN3 Joe Namath 1.25 3.00
JP15 Jim Plunkett .60 1.50
JR17 John Riggins .60 1.50
JR23 Jerry Rice 1.50 4.00
JS7 Jake Scott .50 1.25
KW34 Kurt Warner .60 1.50
LB30 Larry Brown .50 1.25
LC8 Larry Csonka .75 2.00
LD4 Len Dawson .75 2.00
MA18 Marcus Allen .75 2.00
MR26 Mark Rypien .60 1.50
OA25 Ottis Anderson .50 1.25
PS21 Phil Simms .60 1.50
RD20 Richard Dent .60 1.50
RL35 Ray Lewis .75 2.00
RS6 Roger Staubach 1.00 2.50
SY29 Steve Young 1.00 2.50
TA27 Troy Aikman 1.00 2.50
TB13 Terry Bradshaw 1.00 2.50
TB14 Terry Bradshaw 1.00 2.50
TB36 Tom Brady 4.00 10.00
TD32 Terrell Davis .60 1.50
WM12 Randy White .60 1.50

2002 Topps Chrome Super Bowl Goal Posts

is 10-card insert set offers pieces from the Super Bowl XXXVI game-winning goal post. They were inserted at a rate of 1:437. Please note that all cards feature a refractor like front.

STATED ODDS 1:437 HOB, 1:437 RET
ALL CARDS FEATURE REFRACTOR FRONTS
SBG1 Tom Brady 50.00 80.00
SBG2 Kurt Warner 12.00 30.00
SBG3 Antowain Smith 12.00 30.00
SBG4 Marshall Faulk 12.00 30.00
SBG5 Troy Brown 10.00 25.00
SBG6 Adam Vinatieri 35.00 60.00
SBG7 David Patten 10.00 25.00
SBG8 Torry Holt 12.00 30.00
SBG9 Ty Law 15.00 40.00
SBG10 Isaac Bruce 15.00 40.00

2002 Topps Chrome Terry Bradshaw Reprints

is 14-card insert set honors Terry Bradshaw's 14 year NFL reign. These cards were inserted at a rate of 1:12. There was also a refractor parallel that was #'d/100, and a black bordered refractor parallel #'d to 25. The refractors were inserted at a rate of 1:780 hobby packs and 1:783 retail packs. The black bordered refractors were inserted 1:3119 hobby packs, and 1:3223 retail packs.

COMPLETE SET (14) 20.00 50.00
STATED ODDS 1:12 HOB/RET
*REFRACT/100: 1.2X TO 3X BASIC INSERT
REFRACTOR/100 ODDS 1:780 HOB, 1:783 RET
REFRACTOR PRINT RUN 100 SER.#'d SETS
*BLK.BORDER REFR/25: 3X TO 8X
BLACK BORD.REF/25.ODDS 1:3119 HOB, 1:3223 RET
BLK.BORDER PRINT RUN 25 SER.#'d SETS

2003 Topps Chrome

Released in September of 2003, this set consists of 275 cards including 165 veterans and 110 rookies. The rookies were inserted at a rate of 1:3. The URB1 card was inserted at a rate of 1:28040. Boxes contained 24 packs of 4 cards. Each box also contained one Xfractor parallel card, which was included in a silver foil pack, and was packaged in a hard plastic holder. Pack SRP was $3.

COMPLETE SET (275) 100.00 200.00
COMP.SET w/o SP's (165) 15.00 40.00
ROOKIE 166-275 ODDS 1:3
1 Michael Vick .40 1.00
2 Josh Reed .30 .75
3 James Stewart .30 .75
4 Quincy Morgan .30 .75
5 Corey Bradford .30 .75
6 Fred Taylor .30 .75
7 David Patten .30 .75
8 Jerome Bettis .50 1.25
9 Jerry Porter .30 .75
10 Steve McNair .40 1.00
11 Stephen Davis .30 .75
12 Frank Wycheck .30 .75
13 Marcus Pollard .30 .75
14 David Terrell .30 .75
15 Bubba Franks .40 1.00
16 Trent Green .30 .75
17 Mark Brunell .40 1.00
18 James Thrash .30 .75
19 Mike Alstott .30 .75
20 Deuce McAllister .40 1.00
21 Santana Moss .40 1.00
22 Jason Taylor .40 1.00
23 Corey Dillon .30 .75
24 Jeff Blake .40 1.00
25 Ed McCaffrey .40 1.00
26 Priest Holmes .30 .75
27 Tim Brown .50 1.25
28 Curtis Martin .40 1.00
29 Derrius Thompson .30 .75
30 Jonathan Wells .30 .75
31 William Green .30 .75
32 Bill Schroeder .30 .75
33 Amos Zereoue .30 .75
34 Warren Sapp .40 1.00
35 Koren Robinson .40 1.00
36 Donovan McNabb .40 1.00
37 Edgerrin James .40 1.00
38 Kelly Holcomb .30 .75
39 Daunte Culpepper .40 1.00
40 Tommy Maddox .30 .75
41 Rod Gardner .30 .75
42 T.J. Duckett .30 .75
43 Drew Bledsoe .40 1.00
44 Rod Smith .40 1.00
45 Peyton Manning 1.25 3.00
46 Darrell Jackson .40 1.00
47 Brett Favre 1.00 2.50
48 Ashley Lelie .30 .75
49 Jeremy Shockey .30 .75
50 Hines Ward .40 1.00
51 Jeff Garcia .30 .75
52 Eddie Kennison .30 .75
53 Brian Urlacher .50 1.25
54 Antwaan Randle El .30 .75
55 Eddie George .40 1.00
56 Derrick Brooks .30 .75
57 Isaac Bruce .50 1.25
58 Joe Horn .30 .75
59 Jon Kitna .30 .75
60 David Boston .30 .75
61 Todd Heap .30 .75
62 Lamar Smith .40 1.00
63 Germane Crowell .30 .75
64 Kevin Johnson .30 .75
65 Drew Brees .50 1.25
66 Chad Lewis .40 1.00
67 Charlie Garner .40 1.00
68 Laveranues Coles .30 .75
69 Shaun Alexander .30 .75
70 Kevan Barlow .30 .75
71 Aaron Brooks .30 .75
72 Jake Plummer .30 .75
73 Emmitt Smith .75 2.00
74 Terry Glenn .40 1.00
75 Michael Bennett .30 .75
76 Deion Branch .30 .75
77 Keyshawn Johnson .50 1.25
78 Marc Bulger .30 .75
79 Matt Hasselbeck .30 .75
80 Garrison Hearst .30 .75
81 Brian Griese .30 .75
82 Johnnie Morton .40 1.00
83 Patrick Ramsey .40 1.00
84 Donald Driver .40 1.00
85 Joey Harrington .30 .75
86 Ricky Williams .40 1.00
87 Jabar Gaffney .30 .75
88 Duce Staley .30 .75
89 Jimmy Smith .40 1.00
90 Reggie Wayne .40 1.00
91 Chad Johnson .30 .75
92 Steve Beuerlein .40 1.00
93 Joey Galloway .40 1.00
94 Curtis Conway .30 .75
95 Brad Johnson .40 1.00
96 Jamal Lewis .40 1.00
97 Terrell Owens .40 1.00
98 Todd Pinkston .30 .75
99 Keenan McCardell .40 1.00
100 Antonio Bryant .30 .75
101 Eric Moulds .30 .75
102 Jim Miller .30 .75
103 Troy Brown .30 .75
104 Rich Gannon .40 1.00
105 Chad Pennington .30 .75
106 Michael Strahan .40 1.00
107 Chris Chambers .30 .75
108 Antowain Smith .40 1.00
109 Derrick Mason .30 .75
110 Michael Pittman .30 .75
111 Torry Holt .40 1.00
112 Tony Gonzalez .40 1.00
113 Marty Booker .30 .75
114 Shannon Sharpe .40 1.00
115 Zach Thomas .40 1.00
116 Plaxico Burress .30 .75
117 Kurt Warner .40 1.00
118 Warrick Dunn .30 .75
119 Jay Fiedler .30 .75
120 LaMont Jordan .40 1.00
121 Kerry Collins .30 .75
122 Jerry Rice 1.00 2.50
123 Randy Moss .40 1.00
124 Tom Brady 2.00 5.00
125 Amani Toomer .30 .75
126 Travis Henry .30 .75
127 Chris Chandler .40 1.00
128 Ray Lewis .50 1.25
129 Donte Stallworth .30 .75
130 David Carr .30 .75
131 Andre Davis .30 .75
132 Travis Taylor .30 .75
133 Steve Smith .50 1.25
134 Tiki Barber .40 1.00
135 Chad Hutchinson .30 .75
136 Marshall Faulk .40 1.00
137 Peerless Price .30 .75
138 Ahman Green .40 1.00
139 Julius Peppers .50 1.25
140 LaDainian Tomlinson .50 1.25
141 Muhsin Muhammad .30 .75
142 Tim Couch .30 .75
143 Clinton Portis .30 .75
144 Anthony Thomas .40 1.00
145 Marvin Harrison .40 1.00
146 Priest Holmes WW .25 .60
147 Drew Bledsoe WW .30 .75
148 Tom Brady WW 1.50 4.00
149 Shaun Alexander WW .25 .60
150 Brett Favre WW .75 2.00
151 Travis Henry WW .25 .60
152 Marshall Faulk WW .30 .75
153 Terrell Owens WW .30 .75
154 Jeff Garcia WW .25 .60
155 Plaxico Burress WW .25 .60
156 Donovan McNabb WW .30 .75
157 Ricky Williams WW .30 .75
158 Michael Vick WW .30 .75
159 Steve Smith WW .40 1.00
160 Marvin Harrison WW .30 .75
161 Chad Pennington WW .25 .60
162 Jeremy Shockey WW .25 .60
163 Tommy Maddox WW .25 .60
164 Steve McNair WW .30 .75
165 Rich Gannon WW .30 .75
166 Carson Palmer RC 2.50 6.00
167 J.R. Tolver RC 1.50 4.00
168 Michael Haynes RC 1.25 3.00
169 Terrell Suggs RC 1.50 4.00
170 Rashean Mathis RC 1.25 3.00
171 Chris Kelsay RC 1.50 4.00
172 Brad Banks RC 1.50 4.00
173 Jordan Gross RC 1.25 3.00
174 Lee Suggs RC 1.25 3.00
175 Kliff Kingsbury RC 2.00 5.00
176 William Joseph RC 1.25 3.00
177 Kelley Washington RC 1.25 3.00
178 Jerome McDougle RC 1.25 3.00
179 Keenan Howry RC 1.25 3.00
180 Chris Simms RC 1.25 3.00
181 Alonzo Jackson RC 1.25 3.00
182 L.J. Smith RC 2.00 5.00
183 Mike Doss RC 2.00 5.00
184 Bobby Wade RC 1.50 4.00
185 Ken Hamlin RC 2.00 5.00
186 Brandon Lloyd RC 2.00 5.00
187 Justin Fargas RC 2.00 5.00
188 DeWayne Robertson RC 1.50 4.00
189 Bryant Johnson RC 2.00 5.00
190 Boss Bailey RC 1.50 4.00
191 Onterrio Smith RC 1.25 3.00
192 Doug Gabriel RC 1.50 4.00
193 Jimmy Kennedy RC 1.50 4.00
194 B.J. Askew RC 1.50 4.00
195 Taylor Jacobs RC 1.25 3.00
196 Dallas Clark RC 2.00 5.00
197 DeWayne White RC 1.25 3.00
198 Arnaz Battle RC 2.00 5.00
199 Kareem Kelly RC 1.25 3.00
200 Talman Gardner RC 1.25 3.00
201 Billy McMullen RC 1.25 3.00
202 Travis Anglin RC 1.25 3.00
203 Anquan Boldin RC 2.00 5.00
204 Osi Umenyiora RC 2.50 6.00
205 Byron Leftwich RC 1.50 4.00
206 Marcus Trufant RC 1.50 4.00
207 Sam Aiken RC 1.50 4.00
208 LaBrandon Toefield RC 1.25 3.00
209 Terry Pierce RC 1.25 3.00
210 Charles Rogers RC 1.50 4.00
211 Chaun Thompson RC 1.25 3.00
212 Chris Brown RC 1.25 3.00
213 Justin Gage RC 1.50 4.00
214 Kevin Williams RC 2.00 5.00
215 Willis McGahee RC 1.50 4.00
216 Victor Hobson RC 1.25 3.00
217 Brian St.Pierre RC 1.25 3.00
218 Nate Burleson RC 1.50 4.00
219 Calvin Pace RC 1.25 3.00
220 Larry Johnson RC 2.50 6.00
221 Andre Woolfolk RC 1.25 3.00
222 Tyrone Calico RC 1.25 3.00
223 Seneca Wallace RC 1.50 4.00
224 Domanick Davis RC 1.50 4.00
225 Rex Grossman RC 1.50 4.00
226 Artose Pinner RC 1.25 3.00
227 Jason Witten RC 10.00 20.00
228 Bennie Joppru RC 1.25 3.00
229 Bethel Johnson RC 1.25 3.00
230 Kyle Boller RC 1.25 3.00
231 Shaun McDonald RC 1.50 4.00
232 Musa Smith RC 1.25 3.00
233 Ken Dorsey RC 1.50 4.00
234 Johnathan Sullivan RC 1.25 3.00
235 Andre Johnson RC 6.00 15.00
236 Nick Barnett RC 2.00 5.00
237 Teyo Johnson RC 1.50 4.00
238 Terence Newman RC 2.00 5.00
239 Kevin Curtis RC 1.25 3.00
240 Dave Ragone RC 1.25 3.00
241 Ty Warren RC 1.50 4.00
242 Walter Young RC 1.25 3.00
243 Kevin Walter RC 3.00 8.00
244 Carl Ford RC 1.25 3.00
245 Cecil Sapp RC 1.25 3.00
246 Sultan McCullough RC 1.25 3.00
247 Eugene Wilson RC 2.00 5.00
248 Ricky Manning RC 1.50 4.00
249 Andrew Williams RC 1.25 3.00
250 Juston Wood RC 1.25 3.00
251 Cory Redding RC 1.50 4.00
252 Charles Tillman RC 6.00 15.00
253 Terrence Edwards RC 1.25 3.00
254 Adrian Madise RC 1.25 3.00
255 David Kircus RC 1.50 4.00
256 Zuriel Smith RC 1.25 3.00
257 Earnest Graham RC 2.00 5.00
258 Ronald Bellamy RC 1.50 4.00
259 John Anderson RC 1.25 3.00
260 David Tyree RC 1.50 4.00
261 Malaefou MacKenzie RC 1.25 3.00
262 Ahmaad Galloway RC 1.50 4.00
263 Brooks Bollinger RC 1.50 4.00
264 Gibran Hamdan RC 1.25 3.00
265 Taco Wallace RC 1.25 3.00
266 LaTarence Dunbar RC 1.25 3.00
267 Justin Griffith RC 1.50 4.00
268 Bradie James RC 2.00 5.00
269 Danny Curley RC 1.25 3.00
270 Kenny Peterson RC 1.50 4.00
271 DeAndrew Rubin RC 1.25 3.00
272 Ryan Hoag RC 1.25 3.00
273 Rien Long RC 1.25 3.00
274 Troy Polamalu RC 15.00 40.00
275 Terrence Holt RC 1.50 4.00
URB1 E.Smth/Pytn/B.Sndrs/25 200.00 350.00

2003 Topps Chrome Black Refractors

*VETS 1-165: 2.5X TO 6X BASIC CARDS
1-165 VETERAN/599 ODDS 1:12
STATED PRINT RUN 599 SER.#'d SETS
*ROOKIES 166-275: 2X TO 5X
166-275 ROOKIE/100 ODDS 1:108
ROOKIES PRINT RUN 100 SER.#'d SETS
274 Troy Polamalu 150.00 250.00

2003 Topps Chrome Gold Xfractors

ETS 1-165: 4X TO 10X BASIC CARDS
*ROOKIES 166-275: 1.5X TO 4X
GOLD XFRACT/101: ONE PER HOB BOX
STATED PRINT RUN 101 SER.#'d SETS
274 Troy Polamalu 150.00 250.00

2003 Topps Chrome Gridiron Badges Jerseys

serted at a rate of 1:674, this set features authentic game worn jersey swatches. Each card is serial numbered to 75.

JERSEY/75 ODDS 1:674
GBBF Bubba Franks 6.00 15.00
GBBU Brian Urlacher 8.00 20.00
GBCB Champ Bailey 6.00 15.00
GBCD Corey Dillon 5.00 12.00
GBDB Drew Bledsoe 6.00 15.00
GBEM Eric Moulds 5.00 12.00
GBES Emmitt Smith 12.00 30.00
GBHW Hines Ward 6.00 15.00
GBJA John Abraham 6.00 15.00
GBJG Jeff Garcia 5.00 12.00
GBJH Joe Horn 5.00 12.00
GBJL John Lynch 6.00 15.00
GBJR Jerry Rice 15.00 40.00
CBJS Jeremy Shockey 5.00 12.00
GBJT Jason Taylor 6.00 15.00
GBMF Marshall Faulk 6.00 15.00
GBMH Marvin Harrison 6.00 15.00
GBMS Michael Strahan 6.00 15.00
GBPM Peyton Manning 20.00 50.00
GBRG Rich Gannon 6.00 15.00
GBRW Ricky Williams 6.00 15.00
GBRWO Rod Woodson 6.00 15.00
GBTD Todd Heap 5.00 12.00
GBTO Terrell Owens 6.00 15.00

2003 Topps Chrome Pro Bowl Jerseys

serted at a rate of 1:84, this set features jersey swatches worn at the 2002 Pro Bowl game in Hawaii.

STATED ODDS 1:84
PBCB Champ Bailey 3.00 8.00
PBDB Drew Bledsoe 3.00 8.00
PBEM Eric Moulds 2.50 6.00
PBJL John Lynch 3.00 8.00
PBJP Julian Peterson 2.50 6.00
PBJS Jeremy Shockey 2.50 6.00
PBJT Jason Taylor 6.00 15.00
PBLG La'Roi Glover 2.50 6.00
PBMF Marshall Faulk 3.00 8.00
PBPM Peyton Manning 10.00 25.00
PBRW Rod Woodson 4.00 10.00
PBTL Ty Law 4.00 10.00

2003 Topps Chrome Record Breakers

MPLETE SET (29) 20.00 50.00
STATED ODDS 1:8
*REFRACTOR/100: 1.5X TO 4X
REFRACTOR/100 ODDS 1:408
REFRACTOR PRINT RUN 100 SER.#'d SETS
RB1 Barry Sanders 2.00 5.00
RB2 Brett Favre 2.50 6.00
RB3 Brian Mitchell .75 2.00
RB4 Bruce Matthews .75 2.00
RB5 Clinton Portis .75 2.00
RB6 Corey Dillon .75 2.00
RB7 Dan Marino 2.50 6.00
RB8 Derrick Mason .75 2.00
RB9 Emmitt Smith 2.00 5.00
RB10 Jason Elam .75 2.00
RB11 Jason Taylor 1.00 2.50
RB12 Jerry Rice 2.50 6.00
RB13 Jimmy Smith 1.00 2.50
RB14 Terrell Owens 1.00 2.50
RB15 John Elway 2.00 5.00
RB16 LaDainian Tomlinson 1.25 3.00
RB17 Lawrence Taylor 1.25 3.00
RB18 Randy Moss 1.00 2.50
RB19 Marshall Faulk 1.00 2.50
RB20 Marvin Harrison 1.00 2.50
RB21 Michael Strahan 1.00 2.50
RB22 Peyton Manning 3.00 8.00
RB23 Priest Holmes .75 2.00
RB24 Rich Gannon 1.00 2.50
RB25 Ricky Williams 1.00 2.50
RB26 Rod Woodson 1.00 2.50
RB27 Jevon Kearse .75 2.00
RB28 Tim Brown 1.25 3.00
RB29 Chris McAlister 1.00 2.50

2003 Topps Chrome Record Breakers Jerseys

Inserted at a rate of 1:1467, this set features authentic game worn jersey swatches. Each card is serial numbered to 75.

JERSEY/75 STATED ODDS 1:1467
STATED PRINT RUN 75 SER.#'d SETS
RBRBS Barry Sanders 12.00 30.00
RBRDM Dan Marino 25.00 60.00
RBRES Emmitt Smith 12.00 30.00
RBRJE John Elway 20.00 50.00
RBRJR Jerry Rice 15.00 40.00
RBRKW Kurt Warner 6.00 15.00
RBRLT LaDainian Tomlinson 8.00 20.00
RBRMF Marshall Faulk 6.00 15.00
RBRRW Ricky Williams 6.00 15.00
RBRSY Steve Young 15.00 40.00
RBRWP Walter Payton 50.00 120.00

2003 Topps Chrome Record Breakers Jerseys Duals

Inserted at a rate of 1:6425, this set features two swatches of authentic game worn jerseys. Each card is serial numbered to 25.

STATED ODDS 1:6425
STATED PRINT RUN 25 SER.#'d SETS
RDRDT C.Dillon/L.Tomlinson 20.00 50.00
RDRFW M.Faulk/R.Williams 15.00 40.00
RDRME D.Marino/J.Elway 60.00 150.00
RDRPS W.Payton/E.Smith 75.00 150.00
RDRSP B.Sanders/W.Payton 60.00 120.00
RDRSR E.Smith/J.Rice 50.00 120.00
RDRSS B.Sanders/E.Smith 50.00 120.00
RDRYE S.Young/J.Elway 50.00 120.00

2004 Topps Chrome

pps Chrome initially released in mid-September 2004. The base set consists of 275-cards including 110-rookies. Hobby boxes contained 24-packs of 8-cards and carried an S.R.P. of $3 per pack. Three very popular parallel sets and a variety of inserts can be found seeded in packs highlighted by the Premium Performers Autographed Jersey inserts.

COMPLETE SET (275) 100.00 200.00
COMP.SET w/o SP's (165) 12.50 30.00
ROOKIE STATED ODDS 1:2
1 Peyton Manning 1.25 3.00
2 Patrick Ramsey .40 1.00
3 Justin McCareins .30 .75
4 Matt Hasselbeck .30 .75
5 Chris Chambers .30 .75
6 Bubba Franks .30 .75
7 Eric Moulds .30 .75
8 Anquan Boldin .30 .75
9 Brian Urlacher .50 1.25
10 Stephen Davis .30 .75
11 Michael Vick .40 1.00
12 Dante Hall .30 .75
13 Chad Pennington .30 .75
14 Kevan Barlow .30 .75
15 Tommy Maddox .30 .75
16 Domanick Davis .30 .75
17 Dwight Freeney .30 .75
18 LaVar Arrington .30 .75
19 Troy Hambrick .30 .75
20 Jake Plummer .30 .75
21 Willis McGahee .30 .75
22 Steve McNair .40 1.00

23 Kerry Collins .30 .75
24 Hines Ward .40 1.00
25 Terrell Owens .40 1.00
26 Jerome Pathon .30 .75
27 Andre Johnson .40 1.00
28 DeShaun Foster .40 1.00
29 Terrell Suggs .30 .75
30 Marcel Shipp .30 .75
31 Kyle Boller .30 .75
32 Javon Walker .30 .75
33 Ahman Green .40 1.00
34 Travis Henry .30 .75
35 Randy McMichael .30 .75
36 Jerry Rice 1.00 2.50
37 Travis Taylor .30 .75
38 Fred Taylor .30 .75
39 Zach Thomas .40 1.00
40 Marques Tuiasosopo .30 .75
41 Laveranues Coles .30 .75
42 Thomas Jones .30 .75
43 Jamie Sharper .30 .75
44 Quincy Morgan .30 .75
45 Troy Brown .30 .75
46 Joey Galloway .40 1.00
47 Justin Fargas .40 1.00
48 Daunte Culpepper .40 1.00
49 Keenan McCardell .30 .75
50 Priest Holmes .30 .75
51 Chad Johnson .30 .75
52 Marty Booker .30 .75
53 Tim Rattay .30 .75
54 Brian Westbrook .30 .75
55 Ricky Williams .40 1.00
56 Lee Suggs .40 1.00
57 Keith Brooking .30 .75
58 Rex Grossman .30 .75
59 Dallas Clark .30 .75
60 Charles Rogers .30 .75
61 Donte' Stallworth .30 .75
62 Deion Branch .30 .75
63 Ike Hilliard .30 .75
64 Michael Strahan .40 1.00
65 Randy Moss .40 1.00
66 Isaac Bruce .50 1.25
67 Brad Johnson .40 1.00
68 Warrick Dunn .30 .75
69 Josh McCown .40 1.00
70 Donovan McNabb .40 1.00
71 Shaun Alexander .30 .75
72 William Green .30 .75
73 Carson Palmer .40 1.00
74 Quentin Griffin .30 .75
75 LaDainian Tomlinson .50 1.25
76 Edgerrin James .40 1.00
77 Santana Moss .40 1.00
78 Marshall Faulk .40 1.00
79 Tyrone Calico .40 1.00
80 Marvin Harrison .40 1.00
81 Tony Gonzalez .40 1.00
82 Deuce McAllister .40 1.00
83 Drew Brees .50 1.25
84 Todd Pinkston .30 .75
85 Jeff Garcia .30 .75
86 Darrell Jackson .40 1.00
87 Ray Lewis .50 1.25
88 Billy Volek .30 .75
89 Rudi Johnson .30 .75
90 Julius Peppers .40 1.00
91 Peter Warrick .30 .75
92 Trent Green .30 .75
93 Onterrio Smith .30 .75
94 Jerome Bettis .50 1.25
95 Keyshawn Johnson .40 1.00
96 Jamal Lewis .40 1.00
97 Alge Crumpler .40 1.00
98 Michael Bennett .30 .75
99 Jimmy Smith .40 1.00
100 Brett Favre 1.00 2.50
101 Jerry Porter .30 .75
102 Marc Bulger .30 .75
103 David Carr .30 .75
104 Mark Brunell .40 1.00
105 Aaron Brooks .30 .75
106 Plaxico Burress .30 .75
107 Correll Buckhalter .30 .75
108 Jevon Kearse .30 .75
109 Michael Pittman .40 1.00
110 Clinton Portis .30 .75
111 Corey Dillon .30 .75
112 Steve Smith .50 1.25
113 Eddie Kennison .40 1.00
114 Amani Toomer .30 .75
115 Kelly Holcomb .30 .75
116 Torry Holt .40 1.00
117 Eddie George .40 1.00
118 Jeremy Shockey .30 .75
119 Jon Kitna .30 .75
120 Todd Heap .30 .75
121 Ashley Lelie .30 .75
122 Byron Leftwich .30 .75
123 Duce Staley .30 .75
124 Rod Gardner .30 .75
125 Tom Brady 2.00 5.00
126 Reggie Wayne .40 1.00
127 Joe Horn .30 .75
128 Curtis Martin .40 1.00
129 Charlie Garner .40 1.00
130 Derrick Mason .30 .75
131 Marcus Robinson .30 .75
132 David Boston .30 .75
133 Drew Bledsoe .40 1.00
134 Anthony Thomas .40 1.00
135 Tiki Barber .40 1.00
136 Terry Glenn .40 1.00
137 A.J. Feeley .30 .75
138 Peerless Price .30 .75
139 Jake Delhomme .30 .75
140 Kevin Faulk .30 .75
141 Quincy Carter .30 .75
142 Joey Harrington .30 .75
143 Donald Driver .40 1.00
144 Koren Robinson .30 .75
145 Rod Smith .40 1.00
146 Anquan Boldin WW .15 .40
147 Jamal Lewis WW .20 .50
148 Priest Holmes WW .15 .40
149 Peyton Manning WW .60 1.50
150 Marvin Harrison WW .20 .50
151 Steve McNair WW .20 .50
152 Travis Henry WW .15 .40
153 Torry Holt WW .20 .50
154 Tom Brady WW 1.00 2.50
155 Ahman Green WW .20 .50
156 Donovan McNabb WW .20 .50
157 Deuce McAllister WW .20 .50
158 Domanick Davis WW .15 .40
159 Clinton Portis WW .15 .40
160 Rudi Johnson WW .15 .40
161 Brett Favre WW .50 1.25
162 LaDainian Tomlinson WW .25 .60
163 Steve Smith WW .25 .60
164 Edgerrin James WW .20 .50
165 Ty Law WW .25 .60
166 Ben Roethlisberger RC 30.00 60.00
167 Ahmad Carroll RC 1.25 3.00
168 Johnnie Morant RC 1.25 3.00
169 Greg Jones RC 1.25 3.00
170 Michael Clayton RC 1.50 4.00
171 Josh Harris RC 1.25 3.00
172 Tatum Bell RC 1.25 3.00
173 Robert Gallery RC 1.50 4.00
174 B.J. Symons RC 1.25 3.00
175 Roy Williams RC 1.25 3.00
176 DeAngelo Hall RC 2.00 5.00
177 Jeff Smoker RC 1.50 4.00
178 Lee Evans RC 2.00 5.00
179 Michael Jenkins RC 1.25 3.00
180 Steven Jackson RC 2.00 5.00
181 Will Smith RC 1.50 4.00
182 Vince Wilfork RC 2.00 5.00
183 Ben Troupe RC 1.25 3.00
184 Chris Gamble RC 1.25 3.00
185 Kevin Jones RC 1.50 4.00
186 Jonathan Vilma RC 1.50 4.00
187 Dontarrious Thomas RC 1.50 4.00
188 Michael Boulware RC 2.00 5.00
189 Mewelde Moore RC 1.50 4.00
190 Drew Henson RC 1.25 3.00
191 D.J. Williams RC 2.00 5.00
192 Ernest Wilford RC 1.50 4.00
193 John Navarre RC 1.25 3.00
194 Jerricho Cotchery RC 1.50 4.00
195 Derrick Hamilton RC 1.25 3.00
196 Carlos Francis RC 1.25 3.00
197 Ben Watson RC 1.50 4.00
198 Reggie Williams RC 1.25 3.00
199 Devard Darling RC 1.25 3.00
200 Chris Perry RC 1.25 3.00
201 Derrick Strait RC 1.25 3.00
202 Sean Taylor RC 8.00 20.00
203 Michael Turner RC 1.25 3.00
204 Keary Colbert RC 1.25 3.00
205 Eli Manning RC 12.00 30.00
206 Julius Jones RC 1.25 3.00
207 Jason Babin RC 2.00 5.00
208 Cody Pickett RC 1.25 3.00
209 Kenechi Udeze RC 1.50 4.00
210 Rashaun Woods RC 1.25 3.00
211 Matt Schaub RC 1.25 3.00
212 Tommie Harris RC 1.50 4.00
213 Dwan Edwards RC 1.25 3.00
214 Shawn Andrews RC 1.50 4.00
215 Larry Fitzgerald RC 5.00 12.00
216 P.K. Sam RC 1.25 3.00
217 Teddy Lehman RC 1.25 3.00
218 Darius Watts RC 1.25 3.00
219 D.J. Hackett RC 1.25 3.00
220 Cedric Cobbs RC 1.25 3.00
221 Antwan Odom RC 1.25 3.00
222 Marquise Hill RC 1.25 3.00
223 Luke McCown RC 1.25 3.00
224 Triandos Luke RC 1.25 3.00
225 Kellen Winslow RC 1.25 3.00
226 Derek Abney RC 1.25 3.00
227 Chris Cooley RC 1.50 4.00
228 Dunta Robinson RC 1.25 3.00
229 Sean Jones RC 1.25 3.00
230 Philip Rivers RC 4.00 10.00
231 Craig Krenzel RC 1.25 3.00
232 Daryl Smith RC 1.25 3.00
233 Samie Parker RC 1.25 3.00
234 Ben Hartsock RC 1.25 3.00
235 J.P. Losman RC 1.25 3.00
236 Karlos Dansby RC 1.50 4.00
237 Ricardo Colclough RC 1.25 3.00
238 Bernard Berrian RC 1.25 3.00
239 Junior Siavii RC 1.25 3.00
240 Devery Henderson RC 1.25 3.00
241 Adimchinobe Echemandu RC 1.50 4.00
242 Patrick Crayton RC 2.00 5.00
243 Marcus Tubbs RC 1.25 3.00
244 Jamaar Taylor RC 1.25 3.00
245 Andy Hall RC 1.25 3.00
246 Darnell Dockett RC 2.00 5.00
247 Darrion Scott RC 1.50 4.00
248 Jim Sorgi RC 1.50 4.00
249 Jeff Dugan RC 1.25 3.00
250 Ryan Krause RC 1.25 3.00
251 Nate Lawrie RC 1.25 3.00
252 Casey Bramlet RC 1.25 3.00
253 Donnell Washington RC 1.50 4.00
254 Jonathan Smith RC 1.25 3.00
255 Tank Johnson RC 1.25 3.00
256 Keith Smith RC 1.25 3.00
257 Brandon Miree RC 1.25 3.00
258 Michael Gaines RC 1.25 3.00
259 Keiwan Ratliff RC 1.25 3.00
260 Stuart Schweigert RC 1.50 4.00
261 Derrick Ward RC 2.00 5.00
262 Matt Ware RC 2.00 5.00
263 Tim Anderson RC 1.50 4.00
264 Bradlee Van Pelt RC 1.50 4.00
265 Shawntae Spencer RC 1.25 3.00
266 Joey Thomas RC 1.25 3.00
267 Maurice Mann RC 1.25 3.00
268 Tim Euhus RC 1.25 3.00
269 Matt Mauck RC 1.25 3.00
270 Sloan Thomas RC 1.50 4.00
271 Jeris McIntyre RC 1.25 3.00
272 Randy Starks RC 1.25 3.00
273 Clarence Moore RC 1.25 3.00
274 Drew Carter RC 1.50 4.00
275 Sean Ryan RC 1.25 3.00
RH38 Tom Brady RH 2.00 5.00

2004 Topps Chrome Black Refractors

*VETS: 5X TO 12X BASIC CARDS
*ROOKIES: 2X TO 5X BASIC CARDS
BLACK REF/100 ODDS 1:45 HOB, 1:46 RET
STATED PRINT RUN 100 SER.#'d SETS
166 Ben Roethlisberger 100.00 200.00
205 Eli Manning 100.00 200.00

2004 Topps Chrome Gold Xfractors

OOKIES: 1.2X TO 3X BASIC CARDS
ONE PER HOBBY BOX
STATED PRINT RUN 279 SER.#'d SETS
166 Ben Roethlisberger 40.00 100.00
170AU Michael Clayton AU/250 15.00 40.00
172 Tatum Bell AU/250 10.00 25.00
186 Jonathan Vilma AU/250 12.50 30.00
203 Michael Turner AU/250 15.00 40.00
205 Eli Manning 40.00 100.00
216 P.K. Sam AU/250 12.50 30.00

2004 Topps Chrome Refractors

*VETS: 2.5X TO 6X BASIC CARDS
*ROOKIES: .8X TO 2X BASIC CARDS
STATED ODDS 1:6 HOB/RET
RH38 STATED ODDS 1:12,581H, 1:13,248R
166 Ben Roethlisberger 75.00 150.00
205 Eli Manning 25.00 60.00
RH38 Tom Brady RH/100 15.00 40.00

2004 Topps Chrome Gridiron Badges Jerseys

ATED ODDS 1:1707 HOB, 1:1816 RET
STATED PRINT RUN 50 SER.#'d SETS
GBAB Anquan Boldin 5.00 12.00
GBAG Ahman Green 6.00 15.00
GBBU Brian Urlacher 8.00 20.00
GBCJ Chad Johnson 5.00 12.00
GBHW Hines Ward 6.00 15.00
GBJL Jamal Lewis 6.00 15.00
GBLA LaVar Arrington 8.00 20.00
GBMH Marvin Harrison 6.00 15.00
GBPH Priest Holmes 5.00 12.00
GBPM Peyton Manning 20.00 50.00
GBRL Ray Lewis 8.00 20.00
GBSM Steve McNair 6.00 15.00
GBTH Torry Holt 6.00 15.00

2004 Topps Chrome Premiere Prospects

MPLETE SET (20) 25.00 50.00
STATED ODDS 1:6 HOB/RET
*REFRACTOR/100: 2X TO 5X BASIC INSERTS
REFRACTOR STATED ODDS 1:627H, 1:629R
REFRACTOR PRINT RUN 100 SER.#'d SETS
PP1 Ben Roethlisberger 5.00 12.00
PP2 Chris Perry .60 1.50
PP3 Darius Watts .60 1.50
PP4 Devery Henderson .60 1.50
PP5 Eli Manning 5.00 12.00
PP6 Greg Jones .60 1.50
PP7 J.P. Losman .60 1.50
PP8 Julius Jones .60 1.50
PP9 Kellen Winslow .60 1.50
PP10 Kevin Jones .75 2.00
PP11 Larry Fitzgerald 2.50 6.00
PP12 Lee Evans 1.00 2.50
PP13 Michael Clayton .75 2.00
PP14 Michael Jenkins .60 1.50
PP15 Philip Rivers 2.00 5.00
PP16 Rashaun Woods .60 1.50
PP17 Reggie Williams .60 1.50
PP18 Roy Williams WR .60 1.50
PP19 Steven Jackson 1.00 2.50
PP20 Tatum Bell .60 1.50

2004 Topps Chrome Premium Performers Jersey Autographs

GROUP A/50 ODDS 1:25,611 H, 1:27,648 R
GROUP B/100 ODDS 1:3187 H, 1:3170 R
UNPRICED GOLD/10 1:27,581H, 1:32,496R
PPCP Chad Pennington/50 20.00 50.00
PPEM Eli Manning/100 100.00 200.00
PPMV Michael Vick/100 30.00 60.00
PPPM Peyton Manning/100 75.00 150.00
PPRW Roy Williams WR/100 20.00 50.00

2004 Topps Chrome Pro Bowl Jerseys

OUP A STATED ODDS 1:1260H, 1:1273R
GROUP B STATED ODDS 1:965 H, 1:984 R
GROUP C STATED ODDS 1:89 H, 1:89 R
AB Anquan Boldin C 3.00 8.00
AO Adewale Ogunleye C 4.00 10.00
CB Champ Bailey B 5.00 12.00
DF Dwight Freeney C 3.00 8.00
DH Dante Hall C 3.00 8.00
JL Jamal Lewis C 4.00 10.00
KB Keith Brooking B 4.00 10.00
LL Leonard Little B 4.00 10.00
RL Ray Lewis C 5.00 12.00
SD Stephen Davis C 3.00 8.00
SE Shaun Ellis B 4.00 10.00
TH Todd Heap C 3.00 8.00
TL Ty Law A 5.00 12.00
ZT Zach Thomas C 4.00 10.00

2005 Topps Chrome

is 275-card set was released in September, 2005. The set was issued through the hobby in four-card packs with an $3 SRP which came 24 packs to a box. Cards numbered 1-145 featured veterans, while cards 146-155 are a league leader subset and cards numbered 156-165 is a golden moment subset. This set concludes with a rookie subset (166-275). The rookie cards were issued at a stated rate of one in two hobby or retail packs.

COMPLETE SET (275) 75.00 150.00
COMP.SET w/o RC's (165) 12.50 30.00
ROOKIE STATED ODDS 1:2 HOB/RET
RH STATED ODDS 1:288 HOB/RET
RH REFRACT.ODDS 1:17,884 H, 1:22,080 R
1 Deuce McAllister .30 .75
2 Sean Taylor .40 1.00
3 Koren Robinson .25 .60
4 Tiki Barber .30 .75
5 LaDainian Tomlinson .40 1.00
6 Lee Evans .30 .75
7 Aaron Brooks .25 .60
8 LaMont Jordan .30 .75
9 Dante Hall .25 .60
10 Daunte Culpepper .30 .75
11 Thomas Jones .25 .60
12 Warrick Dunn .25 .60
13 Willis McGahee .25 .60
14 Ed Reed .30 .75
15 Derrick Mason .25 .60
16 Jason Witten .30 .75
17 Chad Johnson .25 .60
18 Amani Toomer .25 .60
19 Joey Harrington .25 .60
20 Brian Urlacher .40 1.00
21 Brian Westbrook .25 .60
22 Matt Hasselbeck .25 .60
23 Michael Vick .30 .75
24 Kevin Jones .25 .60
25 Julius Peppers .30 .75
26 Michael Clayton .25 .60
27 Javon Walker .25 .60
28 Santana Moss .30 .75
29 Travis Henry .25 .60
30 Stephen Davis .25 .60
31 Larry Johnson .25 .60
32 Terrell Owens .30 .75
33 Ray Lewis .40 1.00
34 Jake Plummer .25 .60
35 Philip Rivers .40 1.00
36 Eli Manning .60 1.50
37 Tedy Bruschi .30 .75
38 Adam Vinatieri .25 .60
39 J.P. Losman .25 .60
40 Zach Thomas .30 .75
41 Deion Branch .25 .60
42 Andre Johnson .30 .75
43 Marshall Faulk .30 .75
44 Bertrand Berry .25 .60
45 Terrell Suggs .25 .60
46 Tom Brady 1.50 4.00
47 Ashley Lelie .25 .60
48 Jonathan Wells .25 .60
49 Randy McMichael .25 .60
50 Charles Rogers .25 .60
51 Larry Fitzgerald .40 1.00
52 Hines Ward .30 .75
53 Jason Taylor .30 .75
54 Ronde Barber .25 .60
55 T.J. Houshmandzadeh .25 .60
56 Keary Colbert .25 .60
57 DeAngelo Hall .25 .60
58 Chris Brown .25 .60
59 Chris Perry .25 .60
60 Steven Jackson .25 .60
61 Kyle Boller .25 .60
62 Rudi Johnson .25 .60
63 Roy Williams S .25 .60
64 Onterrio Smith .25 .60
65 Roy Williams WR .25 .60
66 Jerry Porter .25 .60
67 Edgerrin James .30 .75
68 Randy Moss .30 .75
69 Brian Griese .25 .60
70 Donovan McNabb .30 .75
71 Joe Horn .25 .60
72 Muhsin Muhammad .25 .60
73 Johnnie Morton .30 .75
74 Chad Pennington .25 .60
75 Torry Holt .30 .75
76 Marc Bulger .25 .60
77 Duce Staley .25 .60
78 Todd Heap .25 .60
79 Lee Suggs .25 .60
80 Patrick Ramsey .30 .75
81 Drew Bennett .30 .75
82 Michael Strahan .30 .75
83 Priest Holmes .25 .60
84 DeShaun Foster .30 .75
85 Corey Dillon .25 .60
86 Antonio Gates .40 1.00
87 Trent Green .25 .60
88 Brandon Stokley .25 .60
89 Alge Crumpler .30 .75
90 Keyshawn Johnson .30 .75
91 Byron Leftwich .25 .60
92 Dunta Robinson .25 .60
93 Ben Roethlisberger .60 1.50
94 Rod Smith .30 .75
95 Robert Gallery .25 .60
96 Tony Gonzalez .30 .75
97 Steve McNair .30 .75
98 Jeremy Shockey .25 .60
99 Dominic Rhodes .25 .60
100 Michael Jenkins .25 .60
101 Jake Delhomme .25 .60
102 Jerome Bettis .40 1.00
103 Jevon Kearse .25 .60
104 Plaxico Burress .25 .60
105 Dwight Freeney .25 .60
106 Marcus Robinson .25 .60
107 Rex Grossman .25 .60
108 Drew Henson .25 .60
109 Julius Jones .25 .60
110 Jamal Lewis .30 .75
111 Justin McCareins .25 .60
112 Billy Volek .25 .60
113 Curtis Martin .30 .75
114 Tatum Bell .25 .60
115 Domanick Davis .25 .60
116 Marvin Harrison .30 .75
117 Anquan Boldin .25 .60
118 Jimmy Smith .30 .75
119 Drew Brees .40 1.00
120 Donte Stallworth .25 .60
121 Nate Burleson .25 .60
122 Fred Taylor .25 .60
123 Takeo Spikes .25 .60
124 Jonathan Ogden .30 .75
125 Michael Bennett .25 .60
126 Clinton Portis .25 .60
127 Ahman Green .30 .75
128 Drew Bledsoe .30 .75
129 Darrell Jackson .25 .60
130 Jonathan Vilma .25 .60
131 David Carr .25 .60
132 Champ Bailey .30 .75
133 Derrick Blaylock .25 .60
134 T.J. Duckett .25 .60
135 Shaun Alexander .25 .60
136 Peyton Manning 1.00 2.50
137 Isaac Bruce .40 1.00
138 LaVar Arrington .25 .60
139 Brett Favre .75 2.00
140 Allen Rossum .25 .60
141 Eric Moulds .25 .60
142 Carson Palmer .30 .75
143 Laveranues Coles .25 .60
144 Chester Taylor .30 .75
145 Reggie Wayne .30 .75
146 Curtis Martin LL .25 .60
147 Daunte Culpepper LL .25 .60
148 Muhsin Muhammad LL .20 .50
149 Shaun Alexander LL .20 .50
150 Trent Green LL .20 .50
151 Joe Horn LL .20 .50
152 Corey Dillon LL .20 .50
153 Peyton Manning LL .75 2.00
154 Javon Walker LL .20 .50
155 Edgerrin James LL .25 .60
156 Jake Scott GM .20 .50
157 John Elway GM .50 1.25
158 Dwight Clark GM .25 .60
159 Lawrence Taylor GM .30 .75
160 Joe Namath GM .50 1.25
161 Richard Dent GM .25 .60
162 Peyton Manning GM .75 2.00
163 Don Maynard GM .25 .60
164 Joe Greene GM .30 .75
165 Roger Staubach GM .40 1.00
166 J.J. Arrington RC 1.50 4.00
167 Cedric Benson RC 1.25 3.00
168 Mark Bradley RC 1.25 3.00
169 Reggie Brown RC 1.25 3.00
170 Ronnie Brown RC 1.50 4.00
171 Jason Campbell RC 1.25 3.00
172 Maurice Clarett 1.25 3.00
173 Mark Clayton RC 1.25 3.00
174 Braylon Edwards RC 1.25 3.00
175 Ciatrick Fason RC 1.25 3.00
176 Charlie Frye RC 1.25 3.00
177 Frank Gore RC 2.50 6.00
178 David Greene RC 1.25 3.00
179 Vincent Jackson RC 2.00 5.00
180 Adam Jones RC 1.25 3.00
181 Matt Jones RC 1.25 3.00
182 Stefan LeFors RC 1.25 3.00
183 Heath Miller RC 2.50 6.00
184 Ryan Moats RC 1.25 3.00
185 Vernand Morency RC 1.25 3.00
186 Terrence Murphy RC 1.25 3.00
187 Kyle Orton RC 1.25 3.00
188 Roscoe Parrish RC 1.25 3.00
189 Courtney Roby RC 1.25 3.00
190 Aaron Rodgers RC 100.00 200.00
191 Carlos Rogers RC 2.00 5.00
192 Antrel Rolle RC 2.00 5.00
193 Eric Shelton RC 1.25 3.00
194 Alex Smith QB RC 4.00 10.00
195 Andrew Walter RC 1.25 3.00
196 Roddy White RC 2.00 5.00
197 Cadillac Williams RC 1.25 3.00
198 Mike Williams 1.50 4.00
199 Troy Williamson RC 1.25 3.00
200 Taylor Stubblefield RC 1.25 3.00
201 Dan Cody RC 1.25 3.00
202 David Pollack RC 1.25 3.00
203 Craig Bragg RC 1.25 3.00
204 Alvin Pearman RC 1.25 3.00
205 Marcus Maxwell RC 1.25 3.00
206 Brock Berlin RC 1.25 3.00
207 Khalif Barnes RC 1.25 3.00
208 Eric King RC 1.25 3.00
209 Alex Smith TE RC 1.25 3.00
210 Dante Ridgeway RC 1.25 3.00
211 Shaun Cody RC 1.50 4.00
212 Donte Nicholson RC 1.25 3.00
213 DeMarcus Ware RC 4.00 10.00
214 Lionel Gates RC 1.25 3.00
215 Fabian Washington RC 1.25 3.00
216 Brandon Jacobs RC 1.50 4.00
217 Noah Herron RC 1.25 3.00
218 Derrick Johnson RC 1.50 4.00
219 J.R. Russell RC 1.25 3.00
220 Adrian McPherson RC 1.25 3.00
221 Marcus Spears RC 1.25 3.00
222 Justin Miller RC 1.25 3.00
223 Marion Barber RC 1.25 3.00
224 Anthony Davis RC 1.25 3.00
225 Chad Owens RC 1.25 3.00
226 Craphonso Thorpe RC 1.25 3.00
227 Travis Johnson RC 1.25 3.00
228 Erasmus James RC 1.25 3.00
229 Mike Patterson RC 1.25 3.00
230 Airese Currie RC 1.25 3.00
231 Justin Tuck RC 1.50 4.00
232 Dan Orlovsky RC 1.25 3.00
233 Thomas Davis RC 1.25 3.00
234 Derek Anderson RC 1.50 4.00
235 Matt Roth RC 1.25 3.00
236 Chris Henry RC 1.50 4.00
237 Rasheed Marshall RC 1.50 4.00
238 Bryant McFadden RC 1.50 4.00
239 Darren Sproles RC 2.00 5.00
240 Fred Gibson RC 1.25 3.00
241 Barrett Ruud RC 1.50 4.00
242 Kelvin Hayden RC 1.50 4.00
243 Ryan Fitzpatrick RC 2.00 5.00
244 Patrick Estes RC 1.25 3.00
245 Zach Tuiasosopo RC 1.25 3.00
246 Luis Castillo RC 1.50 4.00
247 Lance Mitchell RC 1.50 4.00
248 Ronald Bartell RC 1.50 4.00
249 Jerome Mathis RC 2.00 5.00
250 Marlin Jackson RC 1.25 3.00
251 James Kilian RC 1.25 3.00
252 Roydell Williams RC 1.50 4.00
253 Joel Dreessen RC 1.50 4.00
254 Paris Warren RC 1.50 4.00
255 Dustin Fox RC 1.50 4.00
256 Ellis Hobbs RC 2.00 5.00
257 Mike Nugent RC 1.50 4.00
258 Channing Crowder RC 1.50 4.00
259 Kerry Rhodes RC 1.50 4.00
260 Jerome Collins RC 1.50 4.00
261 Stanford Routt RC 1.50 4.00
262 Madison Hedgecock RC 2.00 5.00
263 Rian Wallace RC 1.50 4.00
264 Larry Brackins RC 1.25 3.00
265 Manuel White RC 1.50 4.00
266 Corey Webster RC 1.50 4.00
267 Eric Moore RC 1.25 3.00
268 Kirk Morrison RC 2.00 5.00
269 Atiyyah Ellison RC 1.25 3.00
270 Travis Daniels RC 1.50 4.00
271 Boomer Grigsby RC 2.00 5.00
272 Alex Barron RC 1.25 3.00
273 Tab Perry RC 1.25 3.00
274 Cedric Houston RC 2.00 5.00
275 Kevin Burnett RC 1.50 4.00
RH39 Deion Branch RH 2.00 5.00
RH39R Deion Branch RHR/100 6.00 15.00

2005 Topps Chrome Black Refractors

*VETS/100: 5X TO 12X BASIC CARDS
*ROOKIES/100: 2X TO 5X BASIC RC
STATED ODDS 1:66 HOB/RET
STATED PRINT RUN 100 SER.#'d SETS
190 Aaron Rodgers 300.00 500.00

2005 Topps Chrome 50th Anniversary Retro Rookie Refractors

*RETRO GOLD/50: 4X TO 10X BASIC RC
STATED ODDS 1:724 HOB, 1:727 RET
STATED PRINT RUN 50 SER.#'d SETS
190 Aaron Rodgers 350.00 600.00

2005 Topps Chrome Gold Xfractors

*GOLD XFRACT/399: 1.2X TO 3X BASIC RC
ONE PER HOBBY BOX
STATED PRINT RUN 399 SER.#'d SETS
183 Heath Miller AU 20.00 50.00
185 Vernand Morency AU 12.50 30.00
190 Aaron Rodgers AU 800.00 1500.00
198 Mike Williams AU 20.00 50.00

2005 Topps Chrome Refractors

*VETERANS: 2.5X TO 6X BASIC CARDS
*ROOKIES: .8X TO 2X BASIC CARDS
STATED ODDS 1:6 HOB/RET

2005 Topps Chrome Golden Anniversary Glistening Gold

COMPLETE SET (15) 15.00 30.00
GOLDEN ANNIV. OVERALL ODDS 1:6
*REFRACTORS: 1.5X TO 4X BASIC INSERTS
GOLDEN ANN. REFRACTOR ODDS 1:364
REFRACTOR PRINT RUN 100 SER.#'d SETS
GG1 Priest Holmes .75 2.00
GG2 Michael Vick 1.00 2.50
GG3 Hines Ward 1.00 2.50
GG4 Terrell Owens 1.00 2.50
GG5 Randy Moss 1.00 2.50
GG6 Marvin Harrison 1.00 2.50
GG7 LaDainian Tomlinson 1.25 3.00
GG8 Donovan McNabb 1.00 2.50
GG9 Daunte Culpepper 1.00 2.50
GG10 Ahman Green 1.00 2.50
GG11 Shaun Alexander .75 2.00
GG12 Edgerrin James 1.00 2.50
GG13 Torry Holt 1.00 2.50
GG14 Clinton Portis .75 2.00
GG15 Jamal Lewis 1.00 2.50

2005 Topps Chrome Golden Anniversary Gold Nuggets

COMPLETE SET (10) 10.00 25.00
GOLDEN ANNIV. OVERALL ODDS 1:6
*REFRACTORS: 1.5X TO 4X BASIC INSERTS
GOLDEN ANN. REFRACTOR ODDS 1:364
REFRACTOR PRINT RUN 100 SER.#'d SETS
GN1 Curtis Martin 1.00 2.50
GN2 Brett Favre 2.50 6.00
GN3 Jerome Bettis 1.25 3.00
GN4 Tom Brady 5.00 12.00
GN5 Ray Lewis 1.25 3.00
GN6 Marshall Faulk 1.00 2.50
GN7 Michael Strahan 1.00 2.50
GN8 Peyton Manning 3.00 8.00
GN9 Tony Gonzalez 1.00 2.50
GN10 Jonathan Ogden 1.00 2.50

2005 Topps Chrome Golden Anniversary Golden Greats

COMPLETE SET (10) 15.00 30.00
GOLDEN ANNIV. OVERALL ODDS 1:6
*REFRACTORS: 1.5X TO 4X BASIC INSERTS
GOLDEN ANN. REFRACTOR ODDS 1:364
REFRACTOR PRINT RUN 100 SER.#'d SETS
GA1 Joe Montana 5.00 12.00
GA2 Joe Namath 2.50 6.00
GA3 Earl Campbell 1.50 4.00
GA4 Lawrence Taylor 1.50 4.00
GA5 John Elway 2.50 6.00
GA6 Barry Sanders 2.50 6.00
GA7 Jim Brown 2.00 5.00
GA8 Gale Sayers 1.50 4.00
GA9 Tony Dorsett 1.50 4.00
GA10 Ronnie Lott 1.25 3.00

2005 Topps Chrome Golden Anniversary Hidden Gold

COMPLETE SET (15) 15.00 30.00
GOLDEN ANNIV. OVERALL ODDS 1:6
*REFRACTORS: 1.5X TO 4X BASIC INSERTS
GOLDEN ANN. REFRACTOR ODDS 1:364
REFRACTOR PRINT RUN 100 SER.#'d SETS
HG1 Nate Burleson .75 2.00
HG2 Julius Jones .75 2.00
HG3 Eli Manning 2.00 5.00
HG4 Kevin Jones .75 2.00
HG5 Lee Evans 1.00 2.50
HG6 Ben Roethlisberger 2.00 5.00
HG7 Willis McGahee .75 2.00
HG8 Dunta Robinson .75 2.00
HG9 Chris Brown .75 2.00
HG10 Roy Williams WR .75 2.00
HG11 Steven Jackson .75 2.00
HG12 Carson Palmer 1.00 2.50
HG13 Antonio Gates 1.25 3.00
HG14 Chris Gamble .75 2.00
HG15 LaMont Jordan 1.00 2.50

2005 Topps Chrome Gridiron Badges Jerseys

GROUP A/50 ODDS 1:7409 H, 1:8544 R
GROUP B/100 ODDS 1:1075 H, 1:1132 R
GBAG Antonio Gates/100 8.00 20.00
GBAGR Ahman Green/100 6.00 15.00
GBAV Adam Vinatieri/50 6.00 15.00
GBCB Champ Bailey/100 6.00 15.00
GBCJ Chad Johnson/100 5.00 12.00
GBDB Drew Brees/100 8.00 20.00
GBDC Daunte Culpepper/100 6.00 15.00
GBDF Dwight Freeney/100 5.00 12.00
GBDM Donovan McNabb/100 6.00 15.00
GBJP Julius Peppers/100 6.00 15.00
GBJW Javon Walker/100 5.00 12.00
GBJWI Jason Witten/100 6.00 15.00
GBLA Larry Allen/100 8.00 20.00
GBLT LaDainian Tomlinson/50 10.00 25.00
GBMC Mark Clayton/50 6.00 15.00
GBMM Muhsin Muhammad/100 5.00 12.00
GBMV Michael Vick/50 8.00 20.00
GBPM Peyton Manning/100 20.00 50.00
GBRW Roy Williams S/50 6.00 15.00
GBTB Tom Brady/100 30.00 80.00
GBTBA Tiki Barber/100 6.00 15.00
GBTG Tony Gonzalez/100 6.00 15.00

2005 Topps Chrome Premium Performers Jersey Autographs

STATED ODDS 1:7740 H, 1:8544 R
STATED PRINT RUN 40 SER.#'d SETS
UNPRICED GOLD REFRACT.SER.#'d TO 10
PPBF Brett Favre 175.00 300.00
PPBS Barry Sanders 125.00 250.00
PPES Emmitt Smith 150.00 300.00
PPJR Jerry Rice 125.00 250.00
PPPM Peyton Manning 150.00 300.00
PPTB Tom Brady 175.00 300.00

2005 Topps Chrome Pro Bowl Jerseys

GROUP A ODDS 1:754 HOB/RET
GROUP B ODDS 1:258 HOB/RET
GROUP C ODDS 1:226 HOB/RET
GROUP D ODDS 1:335 HOB/RET
PBPAG Ahman Green B 5.00 12.00
PBPDM Donovan McNabb D 6.00 15.00
PBPJF James Farrior C 5.00 12.00
PBPJP Joey Porter B 6.00 15.00
PBPJT Jason Taylor A 3.00 8.00
PBPJW Jason Witten C 4.00 10.00
PBPJWA Javon Walker B 4.00 10.00
PBPKB Keith Brooking B 3.00 8.00
PBPKM Kevin Mawae C 3.00 8.00
PBPLA Larry Allen D 4.00 10.00
PBPMV Michael Vick C 7.50 20.00
PBPNC Nate Clements A 4.00 10.00
PBPRW Roy Williams S C 5.00 12.00
PBPSR Shaun Rogers D 3.00 8.00
PBPTR Tony Richardson B 4.00 10.00

2005 Topps Chrome Throwbacks

MPLETE SET (49) 40.00 80.00
STATED ODDS 1:6 HOB/RET
*REFRACTORS: 1.5X TO 4X BASIC INSERTS
REFRACTOR ODDS 1:369 HOB, 1:371 RET
REFRACTOR PRINT RUN 100 SER.#'d SETS
TB1 LaDainian Tomlinson 1.25 3.00
TB2 Marvin Harrison 1.00 2.50
TB3 Shaun Alexander .75 2.00
TB4 Peyton Manning 3.00 8.00
TB5 Trent Green .75 2.00
TB6 Randy Moss 1.00 2.50
TB7 Brett Favre 2.50 6.00
TB8 Ben Roethlisberger 2.00 5.00
TB9 Donovan McNabb 1.00 2.50
TB10 Tom Brady 5.00 12.00
TB11 Dwight Freeney .75 2.00
TB12 Dante Hall .75 2.00
TB13 Edgerrin James 1.00 2.50
TB14 Daunte Culpepper 1.00 2.50
TB15 Ray Lewis 1.25 3.00
TB16 Joe Horn .75 2.00
TB17 Terrell Owens 1.00 2.50
TB18 Muhsin Muhammad .75 2.00
TB19 Curtis Martin 1.00 2.50
TB20 Michael Vick 1.00 2.50
TB21 Antonio Gates 1.25 3.00
TB22 Deuce McAllister 1.00 2.50
TB23 Javon Walker .75 2.00
TB24 Tony Gonzalez 1.00 2.50
TB25 Corey Dillon .75 2.00
TB26 Tiki Barber 1.00 2.50
TB27 Jamal Lewis 1.00 2.50
TB28 Reggie Wayne 1.00 2.50
TB29 Priest Holmes .75 2.00
TB30 Chris Brown .75 2.00
TB31 Marc Bulger .75 2.00
TB32 Hines Ward 1.00 2.50
TB33 Chad Johnson .75 2.00
TB34 Ahman Green 1.00 2.50
TB35 Willis McGahee .75 2.00
TB36 Rudi Johnson .75 2.00
TB37 Drew Brees 1.25 3.00
TB38 Isaac Bruce 1.25 3.00
TB39 Ed Reed 1.00 2.50
TB40 Domanick Davis .75 2.00
TB41 Jake Delhomme .75 2.00
TB42 Clinton Portis .75 2.00
TB43 Drew Bennett 1.00 2.50
TB44 Fred Taylor .75 2.00
TB45 Eric Moulds .75 2.00
TB46 Torry Holt 1.00 2.50
TB47 Brian Westbrook .75 2.00
TB48 Jake Plummer .75 2.00
TB49 Champ Bailey 1.00 2.50

2006 Topps Chrome

This 270-card set was released in August, 2006. The set was issued into the hobby in four-cards packs which came 24 to a box. The first 165 cards in the set feature veterans while cards numbered 166-270 feature 2006 rookies. The rookies were inserted into packs at a stated rate of one in two. Similar to the basic topps set, a special card of Super Bowl XL hero Hines Ward (#RH40) was produced and that card was inserted at a stated rate of one in 36.

COMPLETE SET (270) 50.00 100.00
COMP.SET w/o RC's (165) 12.00 30.00
ROOKIE STATED ODDS 1:2
RH40 STATED ODDS 1:36
1 Jonathan Vilma .25 .60
2 Chester Taylor .30 .75
3 Troy Polamalu .40 1.00
4 Nathan Vasher .25 .60
5 Clinton Portis .25 .60
6 Willie Parker .30 .75
7 Lofa Tatupu .25 .60
8 Peyton Manning 1.00 2.50
9 LaMont Jordan .30 .75
10 Jason Taylor .30 .75
11 Travis Taylor .25 .60
12 Derrick Johnson .25 .60
13 Jason Campbell .25 .60
14 Aaron Rodgers 1.00 2.50
15 Deltha O'Neal .25 .60
16 LaDainian Tomlinson .40 1.00
17 Keary Colbert .25 .60
18 Chris Chambers .25 .60
19 Chris Simms .25 .60
20 Troy Williamson .25 .60
21 Chad Johnson .25 .60
22 Jake Delhomme .25 .60
23 Willis McGahee .25 .60
24 Roddy White .25 .60
25 Rod Smith .30 .75
26 Zach Thomas .30 .75
27 Antonio Gates .40 1.00
28 Michael Vick .30 .75
29 Antwaan Randle El .25 .60
30 Drew Bledsoe .30 .75
31 Randy McMichael .25 .60
32 Heath Miller .25 .60
33 Fred Taylor .25 .60
34 Alge Crumpler .30 .75
35 Roy Williams S .25 .60
36 Ryan Moats .25 .60
37 Dwight Freeney .25 .60
38 Jeremy Shockey .25 .60
39 Shawne Merriman .30 .75
40 Charlie Frye .30 .75
41 Reggie Wayne .30 .75
42 Alex Smith QB .30 .75
43 Jerome Bettis .40 1.00
44 Chris Brown .25 .60
45 Michael Clayton .25 .60
46 Carlos Rogers .25 .60
47 DeAngelo Hall .25 .60
48 Drew Bennett .30 .75
49 Brandon Lloyd .25 .60
50 Corey Dillon .25 .60
51 Eli Manning .30 .75
52 Jerry Porter .25 .60
53 Carson Palmer .30 .75
54 Kevin Jones .25 .60
55 Andre Johnson .30 .75
56 Ray Lewis .40 1.00
57 Kyle Orton .25 .60
58 Julius Jones .25 .60
59 Roy Williams WR .25 .60
60 Jonathan Ogden .30 .75
61 Antonio Pierce .25 .60
62 Larry Johnson .25 .60
63 Muhsin Muhammad .25 .60
64 Trent Green .25 .60
65 Tatum Bell .25 .60
66 Lee Evans .30 .75
67 Braylon Edwards .25 .60
68 Hines Ward .30 .75
69 Warrick Dunn .25 .60
70 Antonio Bryant .25 .60
71 Mewelde Moore .25 .60
72 Samkon Gado .25 .60
73 Mike Williams .25 .60
74 Marion Barber .40 1.00
75 Samie Parker .25 .60
76 Julius Peppers .30 .75
77 Brian Westbrook .25 .60
78 Kevan Barlow .25 .60
79 Kyle Boller .25 .60
80 Donnie Edwards .25 .60
81 Courtney Roby .25 .60
82 Marc Bulger .25 .60
83 Steve Smith .40 1.00
84 Ben Roethlisberger .50 1.25
85 Byron Leftwich .25 .60
86 Isaac Bruce .40 1.00
87 Kurt Warner .30 .75
88 Tiki Barber .30 .75
89 Derrick Mason .25 .60
90 Joe Horn .25 .60
91 Donovan McNabb .30 .75
92 DeShaun Foster .30 .75
93 Rex Grossman .25 .60
94 Randy Moss .30 .75
95 Tedy Bruschi .30 .75
96 Tony Gonzalez .30 .75
97 Cadillac Williams .30 .75
98 Torry Holt .30 .75
99 Philip Rivers .40 1.00
100 Deuce McAllister .30 .75
101 Jason Witten .30 .75
102 Reggie Brown .25 .60
103 Ronnie Brown .30 .75
104 Deion Branch .25 .60
105 Terry Glenn .30 .75
106 Tom Brady 1.25 3.00
107 Dallas Clark .25 .60
108 Mark Clayton .25 .60
109 D.J. Williams .25 .60
110 Matt Jones .25 .60
111 Ed Reed .30 .75
112 Reuben Droughns .30 .75
113 Matt Hasselbeck .25 .60
114 Anquan Boldin .25 .60
115 David Carr .25 .60
116 Domanick Davis .25 .60
117 Nate Burleson .25 .60
118 Shaun Alexander .25 .60
119 Dante Hall .25 .60
120 Santana Moss .30 .75
121 Brandon Stokley .25 .60
122 Larry Fitzgerald .30 .75
123 Marvin Harrison .30 .75
124 Steve McNair .30 .75
125 Osi Umenyiora .25 .60
126 Odell Thurman .25 .60
127 Josh McCown .25 .60
128 Curtis Martin .30 .75
129 Jake Plummer .25 .60
130 Cedric Benson .25 .60
131 J.P. Losman .30 .75
132 Joey Galloway .30 .75
133 Brian Griese .25 .60
134 Plaxico Burress .25 .60
135 Brian Urlacher .40 1.00
136 T.J. Houshmandzadeh .25 .60
137 Todd Heap .25 .60
138 Champ Bailey .30 .75
139 Mark Brunell .30 .75
140 Chris Cooley .25 .60
141 Priest Holmes .25 .60
142 Aaron Brooks .25 .60
143 Steven Jackson .25 .60
144 Michael Strahan .30 .75
145 Rudi Johnson .25 .60
146 Terrell Owens .30 .75
147 John Abraham .25 .60
148 Jon Kitna .25 .60
149 LaVar Arrington .25 .60
150 Joe Jurevicius .25 .60
151 Dominic Rhodes .25 .60
152 Chad Pennington .25 .60
153 Charles Woodson .40 1.00
154 Kerry Collins .25 .60
155 Drew Brees .40 1.00
156 Keyshawn Johnson .30 .75
157 Mike Anderson .25 .60
158 Jimmy Smith .30 .75
159 Brett Favre .75 2.00
160 Edgerrin James .30 .75
161 Jamal Lewis .30 .75
162 Daunte Culpepper .30 .75
163 Eric Moulds .25 .60
164 Patrick Ramsey .30 .75
165 Ahman Green .30 .75
166 Kamerion Wimbley RC 1.50 4.00
167 Bobby Carpenter RC 1.25 3.00
168 Abdul Hodge RC 1.25 3.00
169 P.J. Daniels RC 1.25 3.00
170 D'Qwell Jackson RC 1.25 3.00
171 Johnathan Joseph RC 1.50 4.00
172 Antonio Cromartie RC 1.50 4.00
173 Elvis Dumervil RC 2.00 5.00
174 Tamba Hali RC 2.00 5.00
175 Derek Hagan RC 1.50 4.00
176 Haloti Ngata RC 1.50 4.00
177 Manny Lawson RC 1.50 4.00
178 Kelly Jennings RC 1.50 4.00
179 Jason Allen RC 1.50 4.00
180 Mathias Kiwanuka RC 2.00 5.00
181 Marques Hagans RC 1.25 3.00
182 Devin Aromashodu RC 1.25 3.00
183 Brandon Johnson RC 1.50 4.00
184 Ingle Martin RC 1.50 4.00
185 Claude Wroten RC 1.25 3.00
186 Tye Hill RC 1.25 3.00
187 Ashton Youboty RC 1.25 3.00
188 DeMeco Ryans RC 1.50 4.00
189 Brodrick Bunkley RC 1.50 4.00
190 Thomas Howard RC 1.25 3.00
191 Ernie Sims RC 1.25 3.00

192 Rocky McIntosh RC 1.25 3.00
193 Donte Whitner RC 1.50 4.00
194 Anthony Schlegel RC 1.50 4.00
195 Jimmy Williams RC 1.25 3.00
196 Brett Basanez RC 2.00 5.00
197 Ben Obomanu RC 1.50 4.00
198 Jonathan Orr RC 1.50 4.00
199 Andre Hall RC 1.50 4.00
200 James Anderson RC 1.25 3.00
201 Darnell Bing RC 1.50 4.00
202 Jovon Bouknight RC 1.50 4.00
203 Gabe Watson RC 1.25 3.00
204 Garrett Mills RC 1.50 4.00
205 Jeff Webb RC 1.50 4.00
206 Kevin McMahan RC 1.50 4.00
207 D.J. Shockley RC 1.50 4.00
208 A.J. Nicholson RC 1.25 3.00
209 Cedric Humes RC 1.25 3.00
210 Winston Justice RC 1.50 4.00
211 Lawrence Vickers RC 1.50 4.00
212 Daniel Bullocks RC 1.25 3.00
213 Tim Day RC 1.50 4.00
214 Ko Simpson RC 1.50 4.00
215 Dusty Dvoracek RC 2.00 5.00
216 Davin Joseph RC 1.50 4.00
217 Dominique Byrd RC 1.25 3.00
218 Marcus Vick RC 1.25 3.00
219 John McCargo RC 1.25 3.00
220 Danieal Manning RC 2.00 5.00
221 Reggie Bush RC 2.00 5.00
222 A.J. Hawk RC 1.50 4.00
223 Vince Young RC 1.25 3.00
224 Matt Leinart RC 1.25 3.00
225 Kellen Clemens RC 1.25 3.00
226 Sinorice Moss RC 1.25 3.00
227 Laurence Maroney RC 1.25 3.00
228 DeAngelo Williams RC 1.50 4.00
229 Jay Cutler RC 1.50 4.00
230 LenDale White RC 1.25 3.00
231 Leonard Pope RC 2.00 5.00
232 Chad Greenway RC 2.00 5.00
233 Chad Jackson RC 1.25 3.00
234 Vernon Davis RC 1.50 4.00
235 Todd Watkins RC 1.25 3.00
236 David Thomas RC 1.25 3.00
237 Marcedes Lewis RC 1.25 3.00
238 Leon Washington RC 1.25 3.00
239 Will Blackmon RC 1.25 3.00
240 Michael Huff RC 1.50 4.00
241 Jerious Norwood RC 1.25 3.00
242 Reggie McNeal RC 1.25 3.00
243 Wali Lundy RC 1.25 3.00
244 Santonio Holmes RC 1.50 4.00
245 Jerome Harrison RC 1.25 3.00
246 Bruce Gradkowski RC 1.50 4.00
247 Maurice Drew RC 2.00 5.00
248 Brandon Williams RC 1.25 3.00
249 Anthony Fasano RC 1.25 3.00
250 Omar Jacobs RC 1.25 3.00
251 Domenik Hixon RC 2.00 5.00
252 Devin Hester RC 2.50 6.00
253 Maurice Stovall RC 1.25 3.00
254 Tarvaris Jackson RC 1.25 3.00
255 Michael Robinson RC 1.25 3.00
256 Mario Williams RC 2.00 5.00
257 Jason Avant RC 1.25 3.00
258 Brian Calhoun RC 1.25 3.00
259 Skyler Green RC 1.25 3.00
260 Greg Jennings RC 2.00 5.00
261 Charlie Whitehurst RC 1.25 3.00
262 Mike Hass RC 1.25 3.00
263 Brandon Marshall RC 2.50 6.00
264 Drew Olson RC 1.25 3.00
265 Demetrius Williams RC 1.25 3.00
266 Travis Wilson RC 1.25 3.00
267 Joe Klopfenstein RC 1.25 3.00
268 Joseph Addai RC 1.25 3.00
269 Brad Smith RC 1.50 4.00
270 Willie Reid RC 1.50 4.00
RH40 Hines Ward RH 2.50 6.00

2006 Topps Chrome Black Refractors

*VETS 1-165: 4X TO 10X BASIC CARDS
*ROOKIES 166-270: 1.2X TO 3X BASIC CARDS
1-165 VET/199 ODDS 1:76H, 1:80R
166-270 ROOKIE/199 ODDS 1:227H, 1:242R
ALL ROOKIES HAVE SPECIAL EDITION LOGO

2006 Topps Chrome Blue

ETS 1-165: 8X TO 20X BASIC CARDS
*ROOKIES 166-220: 2X TO 5X
1-220/50 ODDS 1:227 HOB, 1:240 RET
COMMON AUTO 10.00 25.00
AUTO SEMISTARS 12.00 30.00
AUTO UNL.STARS 15.00 40.00
221-270 ROOK.AU/50 ODDS 1:994H, 1:1100R
222 A.J. Hawk AU 40.00 100.00
223 Vince Young AU 40.00 100.00
224 Matt Leinart AU 30.00 60.00
228 DeAngelo Williams AU 50.00 100.00
229 Jay Cutler AU 12.00 30.00
234 Vernon Davis AU 12.00 30.00
244 Santonio Holmes AU 30.00 80.00
247 Maurice Drew AU 50.00 120.00
252 Devin Hester AU 20.00 50.00
256 Mario Williams AU 25.00 60.00
260 Greg Jennings AU 15.00 40.00

2006 Topps Chrome Red Refractors

*VETS 1-165: 4X TO 10X BASIC CARDS
*ROOKIES 166-270: 2.5X TO 6X
ONE PER HOBBY BOX
1-165 PRINT RUN 259 SER.#'d SETS
166-270 PRINT RUN 25 SER.#'d SETS
221 Reggie Bush 40.00 80.00
223 Vince Young 20.00 50.00
224 Matt Leinart 30.00 80.00
229 Jay Cutler 60.00 150.00

2006 Topps Chrome Refractors

*VETS 1-165: 2.5X TO 6X BASIC CARDS
*ROOKIES 166-270: .8X TO 2X BASIC CARDS
1-165 VET STATED ODDS 1:4 H, 1:6 R
166-270 ROOKIE ODDS 1:12 HOB/RET
ALL ROOKIES HAVE SPECIAL EDITION LOGO
RH40 Hines Ward RH/100 8.00 20.00

2006 Topps Chrome Special Edition Rookies

*SE ROOKIE: .5X TO 1.2X BASIC CARDS
STATED ODDS 1:6 HOB/RET

2006 Topps Chrome Rookie Autographs

OUP A ODDS 1:850 H, 1:875 R
GROUP B ODDS 1:639 H, 1:450 R
GROUP C ODDS 1:400 H, 1:310 R
GROUP D ODDS 1:28 H, 1:72 R
UNPRICED PRINT.PLATES #'d TO 1
221 Reggie Bush A 20.00 40.00
222 A.J. Hawk A 15.00 40.00
223 Vince Young A 4.00 10.00
224 Matt Leinart A 8.00 20.00
225 Kellen Clemens D 4.00 10.00
226 Sinorice Moss A 12.00 30.00
227 Laurence Maroney B 5.00 12.00
228 DeAngelo Williams A 15.00 40.00
229 Jay Cutler A 5.00 12.00
230 LenDale White A 6.00 15.00
231 Leonard Pope D 6.00 15.00
232 Chad Greenway D 6.00 15.00
233 Chad Jackson C 4.00 10.00
234 Vernon Davis A 5.00 12.00
235 Todd Watkins D 4.00 10.00
236 David Thomas D 4.00 10.00
237 Marcedes Lewis D 4.00 10.00
238 Leon Washington D 6.00 15.00
239 Will Blackmon D 4.00 10.00
240 Michael Huff B 6.00 15.00
241 Jerious Norwood D 4.00 10.00
242 Reggie McNeal D 4.00 10.00
243 Wali Lundy D 4.00 10.00
244 Santonio Holmes A 10.00 25.00
245 Jerome Harrison D 4.00 10.00
246 Bruce Gradkowski D 5.00 12.00
247 Maurice Drew D 6.00 15.00
248 Brandon Williams D 4.00 10.00
249 Anthony Fasano D 4.00 10.00
250 Omar Jacobs B 5.00 12.00
251 Domenik Hixon D 6.00 15.00
252 Devin Hester D 8.00 20.00
253 Maurice Stovall D 4.00 10.00
254 Tarvaris Jackson D 4.00 10.00
255 Michael Robinson D 4.00 10.00
256 Mario Williams B 15.00 40.00
257 Jason Avant D 4.00 10.00
258 Brian Calhoun D 4.00 10.00
259 Skyler Green D 4.00 10.00
260 Greg Jennings D 6.00 15.00
261 Charlie Whitehurst C 4.00 10.00
262 Mike Hass C 4.00 10.00
263 Brandon Marshall D 10.00 25.00
264 Drew Olson D 4.00 10.00
265 Demetrius Williams C 4.00 10.00
266 Travis Wilson D 4.00 10.00
267 Joe Klopfenstein D 4.00 10.00
268 Joseph Addai B 6.00 15.00
269 Brad Smith C 5.00 12.00
270 Willie Reid D 5.00 12.00

2006 Topps Chrome Hall of Fame Tribute

MPLETE SET (9) 6.00 15.00
STATED ODDS 1:12 HOB/RET
*REFRACTOR: 4X TO 10X BASIC INSERTS
REFRACTOR/100 ODDS 1:2600H, 1:3100R
BN Bronko Nagurski 1.25 3.00
HC Harry Carson 1.00 2.50
JM John Madden 1.25 3.00
JT Jim Thorpe 1.50 4.00
RW Reggie White 1.25 3.00
SB Sammy Baugh 1.25 3.00
TA Troy Aikman 1.50 4.00
WM Warren Moon 1.00 2.50
RWR Rayfield Wright 1.00 2.50

2006 Topps Chrome NFL 8306

ATED ODDS 1:12 HOB/RET
*VET REF/100: 1.5X TO 4X BASIC INSERTS
*ROOK.REF/100: 2X TO 5X BASIC INSERTS
REFRACTOR/100 ODDS 1:2500H, 1:2635R
NFL1 John Elway 2.50 6.00
NFL2 Jim Kelly 1.25 3.00
NFL3 Eric Dickerson .75 2.00
NFL4 Dan Marino 3.00 8.00
NFL5 Reggie Bush .60 1.50
NFL6 Matt Leinart .40 1.00
NFL7 Vince Young .40 1.00
NFL8 Jay Cutler .50 1.25
NFL9 DeAngelo Williams .50 1.25
NFL10 LenDale White .40 1.00

2006 Topps Chrome Own The Game

COMPLETE SET (30) 10.00 25.00
STATED ODDS 1:6 HOB/RET
*REFRACTOR: 2X TO 5X BASIC INSERTS
REFRACTOR/100 ODDS 1:850H, 1:865R
OTG1 Tom Brady 3.00 8.00
OTG2 Trent Green .60 1.50
OTG3 Shaun Alexander .60 1.50
OTG4 Tiki Barber .75 2.00
OTG5 Steve Smith 1.00 2.50
OTG6 Santana Moss .75 2.00
OTG7 Derrick Burgess .60 1.50
OTG8 Osi Umenyiora .60 1.50
OTG9 Brett Favre 2.00 5.00
OTG10 Larry Johnson .60 1.50
OTG11 Chad Johnson .60 1.50
OTG12 Carson Palmer .75 2.00
OTG13 Clinton Portis .60 1.50
OTG14 Larry Fitzgerald .75 2.00
OTG15 Eli Manning .75 2.00
OTG16 Edgerrin James .75 2.00
OTG17 Anquan Boldin .60 1.50
OTG18 Ty Law 1.00 2.50
OTG19 Deltha O'Neal .60 1.50
OTG20 Drew Brees 1.00 2.50
OTG21 LaDainian Tomlinson 1.00 2.50
OTG22 Marvin Harrison .75 2.00
OTG23 Corey Dillon .60 1.50
OTG24 Matt Hasselbeck .60 1.50
OTG25 Chris Chambers .60 1.50
OTG26 Jonathan Vilma .60 1.50
OTG27 Jake Delhomme .60 1.50
OTG28 Rudi Johnson .60 1.50
OTG29 Zach Thomas .75 2.00
OTG30 Hines Ward .75 2.00

2007 Topps Chrome

This 265-card set was released in August, 2007. The set was issued into the hobby in four-card packs, with a $2.99 SRP, which came 24 packs to a box. Cards numbered 1-165 feature veterans while cards numbered 166-265 feature 2007 NFL rookies. Those Rookie Cards were inserted into packs at a stated rate of one in two hobby or retail packs. In addition, just as in the regular Topps set, a special card to honor Super Bowl MVP Peyton Manning was created and that card was inserted into packs at a stated rate of one in 24.

COMPLETE SET (265) 60.00 150.00
COMP.SET w/o RC's (165) 12.50 30.00
ROOKIE STATED ODDS 1:2 H/R
MANNING RH ODDS 1:24
MANNING RH REF ODDS 1:12,565
MANN.RH WHITE REF ODDS 1:25,000
TC1 Matt Leinart .25 .60
TC2 J.P. Losman .25 .60
TC3 Carson Palmer .30 .75
TC4 Jay Cutler .25 .60
TC5 Peyton Manning 1.00 2.50
TC6 Tom Brady 1.25 3.00
TC7 Chad Pennington .25 .60
TC8 Philip Rivers .40 1.00
TC9 Marc Bulger .25 .60
TC10 Edgerrin James .30 .75
TC11 Willis McGahee .25 .60
TC12 Thomas Jones .25 .60
TC13 Marion Barber .30 .75
TC14 Fred Taylor .25 .60
TC15 Chester Taylor .25 .60
TC16 Reggie Bush .25 .60
TC17 Willie Parker .30 .75
TC18 Shaun Alexander .25 .60
TC19 LenDale White .30 .75
TC20 Larry Fitzgerald .30 .75
TC21 Lee Evans .30 .75
TC22 Muhsin Muhammad .25 .60
TC23 Rod Smith .30 .75
TC24 Andre Johnson .30 .75
TC25 Matt Jones .30 .75
TC26 Devery Henderson .25 .60
TC27 Plaxico Burress .25 .60
TC28 Randy Moss .30 .75
TC29 Santonio Holmes .25 .60
TC30 Torry Holt .30 .75
TC31 Antwaan Randle El .25 .60
TC32 Todd Heap .25 .60
TC33 Tony Gonzalez .30 .75
TC34 Heath Miller .25 .60
TC35 Alex Smith TE .25 .60
TC36 Champ Bailey .30 .75
TC37 Roy Williams S .25 .60
TC38 Julius Peppers .30 .75
TC39 Jason Taylor .30 .75
TC40 Brian Urlacher .40 1.00
TC41 Marc Bulger LL .20 .50
TC42 Frank Gore LL .25 .60
TC43 Reggie Wayne LL .25 .60
TC44 Peyton Manning PB .75 2.00
TC45 Reggie Wayne PB .25 .60
TC46 Jason Taylor PB .25 .60
TC47 Troy Polamalu PB .30 .75
TC48 Tony Gonzalez PB .25 .60
TC49 Devin Hester PB .25 .60
TC50 LaDainian Tomlinson MVP .30 .75
TC51 Reggie Wayne PSH .25 .60
TC52 New Orleans Saints PSH .30 .75
TC53 Peyton Manning PSH .75 2.00
TC54 T.Jones/C.Benson PSH .20 .50
TC55 Colts Defense PSH .20 .50
TC56 Steve McNair .30 .75
TC57 Rex Grossman .25 .60
TC58 Tony Romo .50 1.25
TC59 David Carr .25 .60
TC60 Tarvaris Jackson .25 .60
TC61 Eli Manning .30 .75
TC62 Ben Roethlisberger .40 1.00
TC63 Matt Hasselbeck .25 .60
TC64 Jason Campbell .25 .60
TC65 Warrick Dunn .25 .60
TC66 Jamal Lewis .30 .75
TC67 Cedric Benson .25 .60
TC68 Reuben Droughns .30 .75
TC69 Joseph Addai .25 .60
TC70 Ronnie Brown .25 .60
TC71 Deuce McAllister .30 .75
TC72 Brian Westbrook .25 .60
TC73 Frank Gore .30 .75
TC74 Cadillac Williams .30 .75
TC75 Anquan Boldin .25 .60
TC76 Mark Clayton .25 .60
TC77 Bernard Berrian .25 .60
TC78 Braylon Edwards .25 .60
TC79 Donald Driver .30 .75
TC80 Marvin Harrison .30 .75
TC81 Troy Williamson .25 .60
TC82 Marques Colston .25 .60
TC83 Laveranues Coles .25 .60
TC84 Hines Ward .30 .75
TC85 Deion Branch .25 .60
TC86 Alge Crumpler .30 .75
TC87 Kellen Winslow .25 .60
TC88 Dallas Clark .30 .75
TC89 L.J. Smith .25 .60
TC90 Vernon Davis .25 .60
TC91 Sean Taylor .40 1.00
TC92 Ronde Barber .25 .60
TC93 Brian Dawkins .40 1.00
TC94 Dwight Freeney .25 .60
TC95 Ray Lewis .40 1.00
TC96 Peyton Manning LL .75 2.00
TC97 Larry Johnson LL .20 .50
TC98 Marvin Harrison LL .25 .60
TC99 LaDainian Tomlinson PB .30 .75
TC100 Jeff Saturday PB .20 .50
TC101 Champ Bailey PB .25 .60
TC102 Frank Gore PB .25 .60
TC103 Walter Jones PB .20 .50
TC104 Tony Romo PB .40 1.00
TC105 Ronde Barber PB .20 .50
TC106 Larry Johnson PB .20 .50
TC107 Vince Young OROY .20 .50
TC108 Asante Samuel PSH .20 .50
TC109 Marlin Jackson PSH .20 .50
TC110 Devin Hester PSH .25 .60
TC111 Michael Vick SP 30.00 60.00
TC112 Jake Delhomme .25 .60
TC113 Charlie Frye .30 .75
TC114 Brett Favre .75 2.00
TC115 Trent Green .25 .60
TC116 Drew Brees .40 1.00
TC117 Donovan McNabb .30 .75
TC118 Alex Smith QB .30 .75
TC119 Vince Young .25 .60
TC120 DeAngelo Williams .25 .60
TC121 Rudi Johnson .25 .60
TC122 Julius Jones .25 .60
TC123 Larry Johnson .25 .60
TC124 Laurence Maroney .30 .75
TC125 Brandon Jacobs .25 .60
TC126 LaDainian Tomlinson .40 1.00
TC127 Steven Jackson .25 .60
TC128 Clinton Portis .25 .60
TC129 Michael Jenkins .25 .60
TC130 Steve Smith .30 .75
TC131 Chad Johnson .25 .60
TC132 Roy Williams WR .25 .60
TC133 Reggie Wayne .30 .75
TC134 Reggie Williams .30 .75
TC135 Chris Chambers .25 .60
TC136 Sinorice Moss .30 .75
TC137 Reggie Brown .25 .60
TC138 Arnaz Battle .25 .60
TC139 Michael Clayton .25 .60
TC140 Santana Moss .30 .75
TC141 Desmond Clark .25 .60
TC142 Jeremy Shockey .25 .60
TC143 Antonio Gates .40 1.00
TC144 Chris Cooley .25 .60
TC145 Devin Hester .30 .75
TC146 Asante Samuel .25 .60
TC147 Troy Polamalu .40 1.00
TC148 DeMarcus Ware .30 .75
TC149 Michael Strahan .30 .75
TC150 A.J. Hawk .25 .60
TC151 LaDainian Tomlinson LL .30 .75
TC152 Chad Johnson LL .20 .50
TC153 LaDainian Tomlinson LL .30 .75
TC154 Marvin Harrison PB .25 .60
TC155 Antonio Gates PB .30 .75
TC156 Shawne Merriman PB .20 .50
TC157 Drew Brees PB .30 .75
TC158 Steve Smith PB .25 .60
TC159 Julius Peppers PB .25 .60
TC160 DeMeco Ryans DROY .25 .60
TC161 Drew Brees PSH .30 .75
TC162 Reggie Bush PSH .20 .50
TC163 Robbie Gould PSH .20 .50
TC164 Joseph Addai PSH .20 .50
TC165 Adam Vinatieri PSH .20 .50
TC166 JaMarcus Russell RC 1.00 2.50
TC167 Brady Quinn RC 1.00 2.50
TC168 Drew Stanton RC 1.00 2.50
TC169 Troy Smith RC 1.00 2.50
TC170 Kevin Kolb RC 1.25 3.00
TC171 Trent Edwards RC 1.00 2.50
TC172 John Beck RC 1.00 2.50
TC173 Jordan Palmer RC 1.25 3.00
TC174 Chris Leak RC 1.00 2.50
TC175 Isaiah Stanback RC 1.00 2.50
TC176 Tyler Palko RC 1.50 4.00
TC177 Jared Zabransky RC 1.00 2.50
TC178 Jeff Rowe RC 1.00 2.50
TC179 Zac Taylor RC 1.25 3.00
TC180 Lester Ricard RC 1.25 3.00
TC181 Adrian Peterson RC 12.00 30.00
TC182 Marshawn Lynch RC 5.00 12.00
TC183 Brandon Jackson RC 1.00 2.50
TC184 Michael Bush RC 1.00 2.50
TC185 Kenny Irons RC 1.00 2.50
TC186 Antonio Pittman RC 1.00 2.50
TC187 Tony Hunt RC 1.00 2.50
TC188 Darius Walker RC 1.00 2.50
TC189 Dwayne Wright RC 1.00 2.50
TC190 Lorenzo Booker RC 1.25 3.00
TC191 Kenneth Darby RC 1.00 2.50
TC192 Chris Henry RB RC 1.00 2.50
TC193 Selvin Young RC 1.00 2.50
TC194 Brian Leonard RC 1.00 2.50
TC195 Ahmad Bradshaw RC 1.50 4.00
TC196 Gary Russell RC 1.25 3.00
TC197 Kolby Smith RC 1.00 2.50
TC198 Thomas Clayton RC 1.25 3.00
TC199 Garrett Wolfe RC 1.00 2.50
TC200 Calvin Johnson RC 8.00 20.00
TC201 Ted Ginn Jr. RC 1.25 3.00
TC202 Dwayne Jarrett RC 1.25 3.00
TC203 Dwayne Bowe RC 1.00 2.50
TC204 Sidney Rice RC 1.25 3.00
TC205 Robert Meachem RC 1.25 3.00
TC206 Anthony Gonzalez RC 1.00 2.50
TC207 Craig Buster Davis RC 1.00 2.50
TC208 Aundrae Allison RC 1.00 2.50
TC209 Chansi Stuckey RC 1.25 3.00
TC210 David Clowney RC 1.00 2.50
TC211 Steve Smith USC RC 1.00 2.50
TC212 Courtney Taylor RC 1.00 2.50
TC213 Paul Williams RC 1.00 2.50
TC214 Johnnie Lee Higgins RC 1.00 2.50
TC215 Rhema McKnight RC 1.00 2.50
TC216 Jason Hill RC 1.00 2.50
TC217 Dallas Baker RC 1.00 2.50
TC218 Greg Olsen RC 1.50 4.00
TC219 Yamon Figurs RC 1.00 2.50
TC220 Scott Chandler RC 1.50 4.00
TC221 Matt Spaeth RC 1.50 4.00
TC222 Ben Patrick RC 1.25 3.00
TC223 Clark Harris RC 1.25 3.00
TC224 Martrez Milner RC 1.00 2.50
TC225 Alan Branch RC 1.00 2.50
TC226 Amobi Okoye RC 1.25 3.00
TC227 DeMarcus Tank Tyler RC 1.00 2.50
TC228 Justin Harrell RC 1.00 2.50
TC229 Gaines Adams RC 1.25 3.00
TC230 Jamaal Anderson RC 1.25 3.00
TC231 Adam Carriker RC 1.00 2.50
TC232 Jarvis Moss RC 1.00 2.50
TC233 Charles Johnson RC 1.00 2.50
TC234 Anthony Spencer RC 1.25 3.00
TC235 Quentin Moses RC 1.00 2.50
TC236 LaMarr Woodley RC 2.00 5.00
TC237 Victor Abiamiri RC 1.00 2.50
TC238 Ray McDonald RC 1.25 3.00
TC239 Tim Crowder RC 1.25 3.00
TC240 Patrick Willis RC 1.50 4.00
TC241 David Harris RC 1.00 2.50
TC242 Buster Davis RC 1.25 3.00
TC243 Lawrence Timmons RC 1.50 4.00
TC244 Paul Posluszny RC 1.00 2.50
TC245 Jon Beason RC 1.00 2.50
TC246 Rufus Alexander RC 1.00 2.50
TC247 Prescott Burgess RC 1.00 2.50
TC248 Leon Hall RC 1.00 2.50
TC249 Darrelle Revis RC 1.25 3.00
TC250 Aaron Ross RC 1.00 2.50
TC251 Daymeion Hughes RC 1.00 2.50
TC252 Marcus McCauley RC 1.00 2.50
TC253 Chris Houston RC 1.00 2.50
TC254 Tanard Jackson RC 1.00 2.50
TC255 Jonathan Wade RC 1.00 2.50
TC256 Josh Wilson RC 1.25 3.00
TC257 Eric Wright RC 1.00 2.50
TC258 David Irons RC 1.00 2.50
TC259 Laron Landry RC 1.50 4.00
TC260 Reggie Nelson RC 1.00 2.50
TC261 Michael Griffin RC 1.00 2.50
TC262 Brandon Meriweather RC 1.25 3.00
TC263 Eric Weddle RC 1.25 3.00
TC264 Joe Thomas RC 1.50 4.00
TC265 Levi Brown RC 1.00 2.50
RH41 Peyton Manning RH 2.00 5.00

2007 Topps Chrome Blue Refractors

*VETS 1-165: 2.5X TO 6X BASIC CARDS
*ROOKIES 166-265: 1X TO 2.5X
STATED ODDS 1:6 RETAIL
TC111 Michael Vick SP 125.00 250.00
RH41 Peyton Manning RH/50 20.00 50.00

2007 Topps Chrome Red Refractors Uncirculated

ETS 1-165: 5X TO 12X BASIC CARDS
*ROOKIES 166-265: 1.5X TO 4X
RED REF/139 ONE PER HOBBY BOX
TC181 Adrian Peterson 75.00 150.00
TC200 Calvin Johnson 60.00 120.00
RH41 Peyton Manning RH/10 60.00 120.00

2007 Topps Chrome Refractors

*VETS 1-165: 2X TO 5X BASIC CARDS
*ROOKIES 166-265: .8X TO 2X
STATED ODDS 1:3 HOB/RET
TC111 Michael Vick SP 100.00 200.00
RH41 Peyton Manning RH/199 15.00 40.00

2007 Topps Chrome White Refractors

*VETERANS 1-165: 3X TO 8X BASIC CARDS
*ROOKIES 166-265: 1X TO 2.5X
WHITE REF/869 ODDS 1:6 H, 1:24 R
RH41 Peyton Manning RH/100 20.00 50.00

2007 Topps Chrome Xfractors

TS 1-165: 3X TO 8X BASIC CARDS
*ROOKIES 166-265: 1X TO 2.5X
STATED ODDS 1:3 RETAIL
TC181 Adrian Peterson 20.00 50.00

2007 Topps Chrome Brett Favre Collection

COMMON CARD (1-200) 2.00 5.00
STATED ODDS 1:4 HOB, 1:6 RET
*BLUE REF/50: 2.5X TO 6X BASIC INSERTS
BLUE REFRACTOR/50 ODDS 1:149 RET
*REF/199: 1X TO 2.5X BASIC INSERTS
REFRACT/199 ODDS 1:63 H/R
*WHITE REF/100: 1.5X TO 4X BASIC INSERTS
WHITE REF/100 ODDS 1:125 H/R
*RED REF UNC/10: 6X TO 15X BASIC INSERTS
*SUPERFRACT/1: 12X TO 30X BASIC INSERTS
RED REFRACTORS UNCIRCULATED PRINT RUN 10 SER.#'d SETS

2007 Topps Chrome LaDainian Tomlinson

COMMON CARD 1.00 2.50
STATED ODDS 1:12 HOB/RET
*BLUE REFRACT: 1.2X TO 3X BASIC INSERTS
BLUE REFRACTOR ODDS 1:963 RET
*REF/199: 1.2X TO 3X BASIC INSERTS
REFRACTOR/199 ODDS 1:405 H/R
*WHITE REF/100: 1.5X TO 4X BASIC INSERTS
WHITE REF/100 ODDS 1:806 H/R
*RED REF UNC/10: 6X TO 15X BASIC INSERTS
RED REFRACTORS UNCIRCULATED PRINT RUN 10 SER.#'d SETS
UNPRICED SUPERFRACTORS #'d TO 1
UNPRICED AUTOGRAPHS #'d TO 1

2007 Topps Chrome Rookie Autographs

OUP A ODDS 1:8816 H, 1:12,288 R
GROUP B ODDS 1:2380 H, 1:3072 R
GROUP C ODDS 1:240 H, 1:650 R
GROUP D ODDS 1:450 H, 1:1100 R
GROUP E ODDS 1:2017 H, 1:3500 R
GROUP F ODDS 1:153 H, 1:1500 R
GROUP G ODDS 1:43 H, 1:76 R
GROUP H ODDS 1:285 H, 1:338 R
GOLD SUPERFRACTORS UNCIRCULATED PRINT RUN 10 SER.#'d SETS
UNPRICED PRINTING PLATES #'d TO1
UNPRICED SUPERFRACTORS #'d TO1
TC166 JaMarcus Russell A 12.00 30.00
TC167 Brady Quinn B 5.00 12.00
TC168 Drew Stanton E 4.00 10.00
TC169 Troy Smith B 6.00 15.00
TC170 Kevin Kolb C 8.00 20.00
TC171 Trent Edwards F 4.00 10.00
TC172 John Beck D 4.00 10.00
TC174 Chris Leak D 4.00 10.00
TC175 Isaiah Stanback H 4.00 10.00
TC176 Tyler Palko G 6.00 15.00
TC181 Adrian Peterson A 150.00 300.00
TC182 Marshawn Lynch B 20.00 40.00
TC183 Brandon Jackson D 4.00 10.00
TC184 Michael Bush C 4.00 10.00
TC185 Kenny Irons A 12.00 30.00
TC186 Antonio Pittman C 4.00 10.00
TC187 Tony Hunt G 4.00 10.00
TC189 Dwayne Wright H 4.00 10.00
TC190 Lorenzo Booker D 5.00 12.00
TC192 Chris Henry G 4.00 10.00
TC193 Selvin Young G 4.00 10.00
TC196 Gary Russell G 5.00 12.00
TC198 Thomas Clayton G 5.00 12.00
TC199 Garrett Wolfe G 4.00 10.00
TC200 Calvin Johnson A 75.00 150.00
TC201 Ted Ginn Jr. B 8.00 20.00
TC202 Dwayne Jarrett C 5.00 12.00
TC203 Dwayne Bowe C 4.00 10.00
TC204 Sidney Rice C 5.00 12.00
TC205 Robert Meachem C 5.00 12.00
TC206 Anthony Gonzalez F 4.00 10.00
TC207 Craig Buster Davis C 4.00 10.00
TC208 Aundrae Allison G 4.00 10.00
TC209 Chansi Stuckey G 5.00 12.00
TC213 Paul Williams G 4.00 10.00
TC214 Johnnie Lee Higgins H 4.00 10.00
TC216 Jason Hill G 4.00 10.00
TC217 Dallas Baker G 4.00 10.00
TC218 Greg Olsen C 6.00 15.00
TC226 Amobi Okoye G 5.00 12.00
TC229 Gaines Adams G 5.00 12.00
TC230 Jamaal Anderson F 5.00 12.00
TC231 Adam Carriker F 4.00 10.00
TC240 Patrick Willis G 6.00 15.00
TC243 Lawrence Timmons G 6.00 15.00
TC244 Paul Posluszny H 4.00 10.00
TC248 Leon Hall G 4.00 10.00
TC250 Aaron Ross G 4.00 10.00
TC258 David Irons F 4.00 10.00
TC259 Laron Landry G 6.00 15.00

2007 Topps Chrome Rookie Autographs Refractors

EFRACT/50: .6X TO 1.5X BASIC GROUP B
*REFRACT/50: .8X TO 2X BASIC GROUP C-G
*REFRACT/25: .5X TO 1.2X BASIC GROUP A
REFRACTORS PRINT RUN 25-50
TC181 Adrian Peterson/25 400.00 700.00
TC200 Calvin Johnson/25 200.00 350.00

2007 Topps Chrome Running Back Royalty

COMPLETE SET (10) 6.00 15.00
STATED ODDS 1:12 HOB/RET
*BLUE REFRACT: 1X TO 2.5X BASIC INSERTS
BLUE REFRACTOR ODDS 1:2987 RET
*REFRACT/199: 1X TO 2.5X BASIC INSERTS
REFRACTOR/199 ODDS 1:1256 H/R
*WHITE REF/100: 1.5X TO 4X BASIC INSERTS
WHITE REFRACT/100 ODDS 1:2500 H/R
*RED REF UNCIRC/10: 8X TO 20X BASIC INSERTS
RED REFRACT.UNCIRCULATED PRINT RUN 10
UNPRICED SUPERFRACTORS SER.#'d TO 1
TA L.Tomlinson/M.Allen 1.00 2.50
TB L.Tomlinson/J.Brown 1.25 3.00
TC L.Tomlinson/E.Campbell 1.00 2.50
TD L.Tomlinson/E.Dickerson 1.00 2.50
TF L.Tomlinson/M.Faulk 1.00 2.50
TP L.Tomlinson/W.Payton 2.00 5.00
TS L.Tomlinson/B.Sanders 1.50 4.00
TDO L.Tomlinson/T.Dorsett 1.00 2.50
TSA L.Tomlinson/G.Sayers 1.00 2.50
TSM L.Tomlinson/E.Smith 1.50 4.00

2008 Topps Chrome

This set was released on August 20, 2008. The base set consists of 275 cards. Cards 1-165 feature veterans, and cards 166-275 are rookies.

COMPLETE SET (275) 25.00 60.00
COMP.SET w/o RC's (165) 12.50 30.00
ONE ROOKIE PER PACK
UNPRICED PRINT.PLATE PRINT RUN 1
UNPRICED SUPERFRACTOR PRINT RUN 1
TC1 Drew Brees .40 1.00
TC2 Jon Kitna .25 .60
TC3 Tom Brady 1.25 3.00
TC4 Chad Pennington .25 .60
TC5 Matt Hasselbeck .25 .60
TC6 David Garrard .25 .60
TC7 Jay Cutler .25 .60
TC8 Matt Schaub .25 .60
TC9 Trent Edwards .25 .60
TC10 Peyton Manning 1.00 2.50
TC11 Carson Palmer .30 .75
TC12 Ben Roethlisberger .40 1.00
TC13 Eli Manning .30 .75
TC14 Tony Romo .30 .75
TC15 Donovan McNabb .30 .75
TC16 Joey Harrington .25 .60
TC17 Jeff Garcia .25 .60
TC18 Derek Anderson .25 .60
TC19 Kyle Boller .25 .60
TC20 Sage Rosenfels .25 .60
TC21 Marc Bulger .25 .60
TC22 Brett Favre .75 2.00
TC23 Philip Rivers .40 1.00
TC24 Vince Young .25 .60
TC25 Kurt Warner .30 .75
TC26 Cleo Lemon .25 .60
TC27 Damon Huard .25 .60
TC28 Jason Campbell .25 .60
TC29 Brian Griese .25 .60
TC30 Tarvaris Jackson .25 .60
TC31 Steven Jackson .25 .60
TC32 Willie Parker .30 .75
TC33 DeShaun Foster .25 .60
TC34 Shaun Alexander .25 .60
TC35 Clinton Portis .25 .60
TC36 Ron Dayne .25 .60
TC37 Maurice Jones-Drew .25 .60
TC38 Warrick Dunn .25 .60
TC39 Adrian Peterson .40 1.00
TC40 Thomas Jones .25 .60
TC41 LaDainian Tomlinson .40 1.00
TC42 Marion Barber .25 .60
TC43 Brian Westbrook .25 .60
TC44 LenDale White .25 .60
TC45 Kenny Watson .25 .60
TC46 Fred Taylor .25 .60
TC47 Ryan Grant .30 .75
TC48 Marshawn Lynch .30 .75
TC49 Selvin Young .25 .60
TC50 Joseph Addai .25 .60
TC51 Laurence Maroney .30 .75
TC52 Brandon Jacobs .25 .60
TC53 Willis McGahee .25 .60
TC54 Frank Gore .30 .75
TC55 Edgerrin James .30 .75
TC56 DeAngelo Williams .25 .60
TC57 Jamal Lewis .30 .75
TC58 Chester Taylor .25 .60
TC59 Earnest Graham .25 .60
TC60 Justin Fargas .25 .60
TC61 Greg Jennings .25 .60
TC62 Torry Holt .30 .75
TC63 T.J. Houshmandzadeh .25 .60
TC64 Jerricho Cotchery .25 .60
TC65 Derrick Mason .25 .60
TC66 Kevin Curtis .25 .60
TC67 Joey Galloway .30 .75
TC68 Anquan Boldin .25 .60
TC69 Santonio Holmes .25 .60
TC70 Lee Evans .30 .75
TC71 Dwayne Bowe .30 .75
TC72 Wes Welker .30 .75
TC73 Roy Williams WR .25 .60
TC74 Randy Moss .30 .75
TC75 Plaxico Burress .25 .60
TC76 Terrell Owens .30 .75
TC77 Andre Johnson .30 .75
TC78 Roddy White .25 .60
TC79 Brandon Marshall .30 .75
TC80 Donald Driver .30 .75
TC81 Marques Colston .25 .60
TC82 Reggie Wayne .30 .75
TC83 Chad Johnson .25 .60
TC84 Bernard Berrian .25 .60
TC85 Steve Smith .30 .75
TC86 Larry Fitzgerald .30 .75
TC87 Braylon Edwards .25 .60
TC88 Bobby Engram .25 .60
TC89 Shaun McDonald .25 .60
TC90 Santana Moss .25 .60
TC91 Antonio Gates .30 .75
TC92 Chris Cooley .25 .60
TC93 Owen Daniels .25 .60
TC94 Kellen Winslow .25 .60
TC95 Tony Gonzalez .30 .75
TC96 Jason Witten .30 .75
TC97 Jeremy Shockey .25 .60
TC98 Dallas Clark .25 .60
TC99 Donald Lee .30 .75
TC100 Heath Miller .25 .60
TC101 Tony Scheffler .25 .60
TC102 Desmond Clark .25 .60
TC103 Vernon Davis .25 .60
TC104 Alge Crumpler .25 .60
TC105 Zach Miller .25 .60
TC106 Patrick Kerney .25 .60
TC107 Osi Umenyiora .25 .60
TC108 Mario Williams .30 .75
TC109 Jared Allen .25 .60
TC110 Michael Strahan .30 .75
TC111 Ernie Sims .25 .60
TC112 DeMarcus Ware .30 .75
TC113 Patrick Willis .30 .75
TC114 Shawne Merriman .25 .60
TC115 Brian Urlacher .40 1.00
TC116 Ray Lewis .40 1.00
TC117 Antonio Cromartie .25 .60
TC118 Champ Bailey .30 .75
TC119 Bob Sanders .30 .75
TC120 Ed Reed .30 .75
TC121 Tom Brady LL 1.00 2.50
TC122 Drew Brees LL .30 .75
TC123 Tony Romo LL .25 .60
TC124 LaDainian Tomlinson LL .30 .75
TC125 Adrian Peterson LL .30 .75
TC126 Brian Westbrook LL .20 .50
TC127 Reggie Wayne LL .25 .60
TC128 Randy Moss LL .25 .60
TC129 Chad Johnson LL .20 .50
TC130 Randy Moss LL .25 .60
TC131 Matt Hasselbeck AP .20 .50
TC132 Tony Romo AP .25 .60
TC133 Adrian Peterson AP .30 .75
TC134 Marion Barber AP .20 .50
TC135 Brian Westbrook AP .20 .50
TC136 Larry Fitzgerald AP .25 .60
TC137 Terrell Owens AP .25 .60
TC138 Osi Umenyiora AP .20 .50
TC139 Lofa Tatupu AP .20 .50
TC140 Jason Witten AP .25 .60
TC141 Torry Holt AP .25 .60
TC142 Donald Driver AP .25 .60
TC143 Peyton Manning AP .75 2.00
TC144 Ben Roethlisberger AP .30 .75
TC145 Joseph Addai AP .20 .50
TC146 Reggie Wayne AP .25 .60
TC147 Braylon Edwards AP .20 .50
TC148 Devin Hester AP .25 .60
TC149 Champ Bailey AP .25 .60
TC150 Ed Reed AP .25 .60
TC151 Eli Manning PSH .25 .60
TC152 David Tyree PSH .20 .50
TC153 Plaxico Burress PSH .20 .50
TC154 Lawrence Tynes PSH .20 .50
TC155 Patriots defense PSH .25 .60
TC156 R.W. McQuarters PSH .20 .50
TC157 Ryan Grant PSH .25 .60
TC158 Philip Rivers PSH .30 .75
TC159 David Garrard PSH .20 .50
TC160 Laurence Maroney PSH .25 .60
TC161 Seahawks PSH .20 .50
TC162 Chargers defense PSH .20 .50
TC163 Tom Brady MVP 1.00 2.50
TC164 Adrian Peterson OROY .30 .75
TC165 Patrick Willis DROY .25 .60
TC166 Matt Ryan RC 4.00 10.00
TC167 Brian Brohm RC .75 2.00
TC168 Andre Woodson RC .75 2.00
TC169 Chad Henne RC 1.00 2.50
TC170 Joe Flacco RC 1.50 4.00
TC171 John David Booty RC .75 2.00
TC172 Colt Brennan RC 1.00 2.50
TC173 Dennis Dixon RC .75 2.00
TC174 Erik Ainge RC .75 2.00
TC175 Josh Johnson RC .75 2.00
TC176 Kevin O'Connell RC .75 2.00
TC177 Matt Flynn RC .75 2.00
TC178 Sam Keller RC .75 2.00
TC179 Harry Douglas RC 1.00 2.50
TC180 Anthony Morelli RC .75 2.00
TC181 Darren McFadden RC .75 2.00
TC182 Rashard Mendenhall RC .75 2.00
TC183 Jonathan Stewart RC 1.25 3.00
TC184 Felix Jones RC .75 2.00
TC185 Jamaal Charles RC 1.25 3.00
TC186 Chris Johnson RC 1.00 [illegible]
TC187 Ray Rice RC .75 2.00
TC188 Mike Hart RC .75 2.00
TC189 Kevin Smith RC .75 2.00
TC190 Steve Slaton RC .75 2.00
TC191 Matt Forte RC 1.25 3.00
TC192 Tashard Choice RC .75 2.00
TC193 D.Rodgers-Cromartie RC 1.00 2.50
TC194 Cory Boyd RC .75 2.00
TC195 Allen Patrick RC .75 2.00
TC196 Thomas Brown RC .75 2.00
TC197 Justin Forsett RC 1.00 2.50
TC198 DeSean Jackson RC 1.50 4.00
TC199 Malcolm Kelly RC .75 2.00
TC200 Limas Sweed RC .75 2.00
TC201 Mario Manningham RC .75 2.00
TC202 James Hardy RC .75 2.00
TC203 Early Doucet RC .75 2.00
TC204 Donnie Avery RC 1.00 2.50
TC205 Dexter Jackson RC 1.25 3.00
TC206 Devin Thomas RC .75 2.00
TC207 Jordy Nelson RC 2.50 6.00
TC208 Keenan Burton RC .75 2.00
TC209 Chris Williams RC .75 2.00
TC210 Earl Bennett RC 1.25 3.00
TC211 Jerome Simpson RC 1.00 2.50
TC212 Andre Caldwell RC .75 2.00
TC213 Josh Morgan RC .75 2.00
TC214 Fred Davis RC .75 2.00
TC215 John Carlson RC .75 2.00
TC216 Martellus Bennett RC 1.00 2.50
TC217 Martin Rucker RC .75 2.00
TC218 Jermichael Finley RC .75 2.00
TC219 Dustin Keller RC 1.00 2.50
TC220 Jacob Tamme RC 1.00 2.50
TC221 Kellen Davis RC .75 2.00
TC222 Jake Long RC 1.25 3.00
TC223 Sam Baker RC .75 2.00
TC224 Jeff Otah RC .75 2.00
TC225 Owen Schmitt RC .75 2.00
TC226 Chevis Jackson RC .75 2.00
TC227 Jacob Hester RC .75 2.00
TC228 Glenn Dorsey RC .75 2.00
TC229 Sedrick Ellis RC .75 2.00
TC230 Kentwan Balmer RC .75 2.00
TC231 Pat Sims RC 1.00 2.50
TC232 Marcus Harrison RC .75 2.00
TC233 Dre Moore RC .75 2.00
TC234 Red Bryant RC .75 2.00
TC235 Trevor Laws RC .75 2.00
TC236 Chris Long RC 1.00 2.50
TC237 Vernon Gholston RC .75 2.00
TC238 Derrick Harvey RC .75 2.00
TC239 Calais Campbell RC 1.00 2.50
TC240 Terrence Wheatley RC .75 2.00
TC241 Phillip Merling RC .75 2.00
TC242 Chris Ellis RC .75 2.00
TC243 Lawrence Jackson RC .75 2.00
TC244 Dan Connor RC .75 2.00
TC245 Curtis Lofton RC 1.00 2.50
TC246 Jerod Mayo RC 1.25 3.00
TC247 Tavares Gooden RC .75 2.00
TC248 Beau Bell RC 1.00 2.50
TC249 Philip Wheeler RC 1.00 2.50
TC250 Vince Hall RC .75 2.00
TC251 Jonathan Goff RC .75 2.00
TC252 Keith Rivers RC .75 2.00
TC253 Ali Highsmith RC .75 2.00
TC254 Xavier Adibi RC .75 2.00
TC255 Erin Henderson RC 1.00 2.50
TC256 Bruce Davis RC 1.00 2.50
TC257 Jordon Dizon RC .75 2.00
TC258 Shawn Crable RC .75 2.00
TC259 Geno Hayes RC .75 2.00
TC260 Mike Jenkins RC .75 2.00
TC261 Aqib Talib RC 1.25 3.00
TC262 Leodis McKelvin RC 1.00 2.50
TC263 Terrell Thomas RC .75 2.00
TC264 Reggie Smith RC .75 2.00
TC265 Antoine Cason RC 1.00 2.50
TC266 Patrick Lee RC .75 2.00
TC267 Tracy Porter RC 1.00 2.50
TC268 Kenny Phillips RC .75 2.00
TC269 Simeon Castille RC .75 2.00
TC270 Eddie Royal RC .75 2.00
TC271 Thomas DeCoud RC .75 2.00
TC272 Marcus Griffin RC .75 2.00
TC273 Charles Godfrey RC .75 2.00
TC274 Tyrell Johnson RC .75 2.00
TC275 Jamar Adams RC .75 2.00
RH42 Eli Manning RH .75 2.00

2008 Topps Chrome Blue Refractors

*BLUE REF VETS: 3X TO 8X BASIC CARDS
*BLUE REF ROOKIES: 1X TO 2.5X
RANDOM INSERTS IN RETAIL PACKS
RH Eli Manning RH/100 2.50 6.00

2008 Topps Chrome Copper Refractors

ETS 1-165: 2.5X TO 6X BASIC CARDS
*ROOKIES 166-275: .8X TO 2X BASIC CARDS
COPPER REF/425 ODDS 1:22 HOB

2008 Topps Chrome Gold Refractors

*VETS 1-165: 4X TO 10X BASIC CARDS
*ROOKIES 166-275: 2X TO 5X BASIC CARDS
GOLD REF/199 ISSUED AS HOBBY BOX TOPPER
TC177 Matt Flynn 4.00 10.00

2008 Topps Chrome Red Refractors

*VETS 1-165: 8X TO 20X BASIC CARDS
*ROOKIES 166-275: 3X TO 8X BASIC CARDS
RED REFRACTOR/25 ODDS 1:196 HOB
TC177 Matt Flynn 6.00 15.00

2008 Topps Chrome Refractors

ETS 1-165: 1.5X TO 4X BASIC CARDS
*ROOKIES 166-275: .6X TO 1.5X BASIC CARDS
STATED ODDS 1:3
RH Eli Manning RH/199 5.00 12.00

2008 Topps Chrome Xfractors

*VETS: 1.5X TO 4X BASIC CARDS
*ROOKIES: .6X TO 1.5X BASIC CARDS
RANDOM INSERTS IN RETAIL PACKS

2008 Topps Chrome Brett Favre Collection

MMON CARD (BF201-BF442) 1.25 3.00
STATED ODDS 1:4 HOB
*BLUE REFRACT/50: 3X TO 8X BASIC INSERTS
BLUE REF/50 INSERTED IN RETAIL PACKS
*REFRACT/199: 1X TO 2.5X BASIC INSERTS
REFRACTOR/199 ODDS 1:58 HOB
*RED REFRACT/10: 6X TO 15X BASIC INSERTS
RED REFRACTOR/10 ODDS 1:1158 HOB
UNPRICED SUPERFRACTOR PRINT RUN 1
*WHITE REFRACT/100: 2X TO 5X BASIC INSERTS
WHITE REFRACT/100 ODDS 1:114 HOB

2008 Topps Chrome Dynasties

MPLETE SET (39) 15.00 40.00
STATED ODDS 1:6 HOB
*REFRACTOR/199: 1X TO 2.5X BASIC INSERTS
REFRACTOR/199 ODDS 1: HOB 1:304
*BLUE REF/50: 2X TO 5X BASIC INSERTS
BLUE REFRACTOR PRINT RUN 50
*RED REFRACT/10: 5X TO 12X BASIC INSERTS
RED REFRACTOR/10 ODDS 1:6089 HOB
UNPRICED SUPERFRACTOR/1 ODDS 1:29,400
*WHITE REFRACT/100: 1.5X TO 4X BASIC INSERTS
WHITE REFRACTOR/100 ODDS 1:[illegible] HOB
DYNAV Adam Vinatieri .60 1.25
DYNBB Bill Bates .50 1.25
DYNBJ Brent Jones .60 1.50
DYNCH Charles Haley .75 2.00
DYNDB Deion Branch .50 1.25
DYNDC Dwight Clark [illegible]

DYNDS Deion Sanders .75 2.00
DYNDSH Donnie Shell .60 1.50
DYNDWH Dwight White .60 1.50
DYNES Emmitt Smith 1.25 3.00
DYNES2 Emmitt Smith 1.25 3.00
DYNFH Franco Harris .75 2.00
DYNFH2 Franco Harris .75 2.00
DYNJG Joe Greene .75 2.00
DYNJM Joe Montana 2.50 6.00
DYNJM2 Joe Montana 2.50 6.00
DYNJM3 Joe Montana 2.50 6.00
DYNJN Jay Novacek .60 1.50
DYNJR Jerry Rice 1.50 4.00
DYNJR2 Jerry Rice 1.50 4.00
DYNJT John Taylor .60 1.50
DYNKT Keena Turner .50 1.25
DYNLG L.C. Greenwood .60 1.50
DYNLL Leon Lett .50 1.25
DYNLM Lawyer Milloy .50 1.25
DYNMB Mel Blount .60 1.50
DYNRB Rocky Bleier .60 1.50
DYNRC Randy Cross .60 1.50
DYNRCR Roger Craig .60 1.50
DYNRL Ronnie Lott .60 1.50
DYNTA Troy Aikman 1.00 2.50
DYNTA2 Troy Aikman 1.00 2.50
DYNTB Tom Brady 2.50 6.00
DYNTB2 Tom Brady 2.50 6.00
DYNTBR Terry Bradshaw 1.00 2.50
DYNTBR2 Terry Bradshaw 1.00 2.50
DYNTJ Ted Johnson .50 1.25
DYNTL Ty Law .50 1.25
DYNTR Tom Rathman .60 1.50

2008 Topps Chrome Hall of Fame

MPLETE SET (6) 3.00 8.00
STATED ODDS 1:8
*REFRACTOR/199: 1.5X TO 4X BASIC INSERTS
REFRACTOR/199 ODDS 1:304 HOB
*WHITE REFRACT/100: 2X TO 5X BASIC INSERTS
WHITE REFRACTOR/100 ODDS 1.608 HOB
*RED REFRACT/10: 8X TO 20X BASIC INSERTS
RED REFRACTOR/10 ODDS 1:6089 HOB
UNPRICED SUPERFRACT/1 ODDS 1:29,400
*GOLD REF/50: 2.5X TO 6X BASIC INSERTS
HOFAM Art Monk 1.25 3.00
HOFAT Andre Tippett 1.00 2.50
HOFDG Darrell Green 1.25 3.00
HOFET Emmitt Thomas 1.00 2.50
HOFFD Fred Dean 1.00 2.50
HOFGZ Gary Zimmerman 1.00 2.50

2008 Topps Chrome Honor Roll

COMPLETE SET (9) 4.00 10.00
STATED ODDS 1:6 HOB
HRAD Art Donovan .50 1.25
HRCB Chuck Bednarik .60 1.50
HRGM Gino Marchetti .50 1.25
HRJM Johnny Blood McNally .50 1.25
HRLG Lou Groza .60 1.50
HRNB Norm Van Brocklin .60 1.50
HRRB Rocky Bleier .60 1.50
HRRS Roger Staubach 1.00 2.50
HRTF Tom Fears .50 1.25

2008 Topps Chrome Honor Roll Relic Patches

STATED ODDS 1:4135 HOB
AD 101st Airborne Division 15.00 40.00
AD2 82nd Airborne Division 15.00 40.00
BA Blue Angels 15.00 40.00
CA 1st Cavalry 15.00 40.00
FF F-16 Fighting Falcon 15.00 40.00
IF Operation Iraqi Freedom Patch 15.00 40.00
MC Marine Corps Eagle, Globe and Anchor 25.00 60.00
MR 7th Marine Regiment 15.00 40.00
MS Semper Fidelis 15.00 40.00
NE 158th Fighter Wing Operation Noble Eagle 15.00 40.00
NI United States Naval Intelligence 15.00 40.00
NS The Only Easy Day Was Yesterday 15.00 40.00
TB Thunderbirds 15.00 40.00

2008 Topps Chrome Rookie Autographs

GROUP A ODDS 1:862 HOB
GROUP B ODDS 1:143 HOB
GROUP C ODDS 1:458 HOB
GROUP D ODDS 1:191 HOB
GROUP E ODDS 1:42 HOB
UNPRICED GOLD REFRACTOR #'d TO 10
UNPRICED PRINT.PLATE PRINT RUN 1
TC166 Matt Ryan A 100.00 200.00
TC167 Brian Brohm A 10.00 25.00
TC168 Andre Woodson A 6.00 15.00
TC169 Chad Henne B 8.00 20.00
TC170 Joe Flacco A 25.00 50.00
TC171 John David Booty D 4.00 10.00
TC172 Colt Brennan A 8.00 20.00
TC173 Dennis Dixon B 10.00 25.00
TC174 Erik Ainge B 4.00 10.00
TC175 Josh Johnson E 4.00 10.00
TC176 Kevin O'Connell B 4.00 10.00
TC177 Matt Flynn E 8.00 20.00
TC179 Harry Douglas E 5.00 12.00
TC180 Anthony Morelli E 5.00 12.00
TC181 Darren McFadden A 20.00 50.00
TC182 Rashard Mendenhall A 6.00 15.00
TC183 Jonathan Stewart A 15.00 40.00
TC184 Felix Jones B 6.00 15.00
TC185 Jamaal Charles B 15.00 40.00
TC186 Chris Johnson E 5.00 12.00
TC187 Ray Rice B 6.00 15.00
TC188 Mike Hart B 4.00 10.00
TC189 Kevin Smith D 4.00 10.00
TC190 Steve Slaton B 4.00 10.00
TC191 Matt Forte E 12.00 30.00
TC192 Tashard Choice E 4.00 10.00
TC193 Dominique Rodgers-Cromartie D 5.00 12.00
TC195 Allen Patrick E 4.00 10.00
TC197 Justin Forsett E 5.00 12.00
TC198 DeSean Jackson B 12.00 30.00
TC199 Malcolm Kelly B 4.00 10.00
TC200 Limas Sweed B 4.00 10.00
TC201 Mario Manningham D 8.00 20.00
TC202 James Hardy B 4.00 10.00
TC203 Early Doucet B 4.00 10.00
TC204 Donnie Avery B 5.00 12.00
TC205 Dexter Jackson B 6.00 15.00
TC206 Devin Thomas B 4.00 10.00
TC207 Jordy Nelson B 15.00 40.00
TC208 Keenan Burton E 4.00 10.00
TC210 Earl Bennett E 6.00 15.00
TC211 Jerome Simpson B 5.00 12.00
TC212 Andre Caldwell E 4.00 10.00
TC214 Fred Davis E 4.00 10.00
TC219 Dustin Keller B 5.00 12.00
TC222 Jake Long B 6.00 15.00
TC225 Owen Schmitt E 4.00 10.00
TC227 Jacob Hester C 4.00 10.00
TC228 Glenn Dorsey B 4.00 10.00
TC236 Chris Long B 5.00 12.00
TC237 Vernon Gholston B 4.00 10.00
TC238 Derrick Harvey C 4.00 10.00
TC244 Dan Connor C 4.00 10.00
TC252 Keith Rivers C 4.00 10.00
TC253 Ali Highsmith E 4.00 10.00
TC260 Mike Jenkins E 4.00 10.00
TC261 Aqib Talib C 6.00 15.00
TC268 Kenny Phillips D 4.00 10.00
TC270 Eddie Royal D 4.00 10.00
TC272 Marcus Griffin E 4.00 10.00

2008 Topps Chrome Rookie Autographs Refractors

*REFRACTOR/50: .6X TO 1.5X BASIC AUTO
REFRACTOR/50 ODDS 1:584H
TC166 Matt Ryan 200.00 400.00
TC170 Joe Flacco 40.00 80.00

2008 Topps Chrome Rookie Autographs Patch

TCH AUTO/25 ODDS 1:1655 HOB
TC166 Matt Ryan 200.00 400.00
TC167 Brian Brohm 15.00 40.00
TC169 Chad Henne 20.00 50.00
TC170 Joe Flacco 150.00 250.00
TC171 John David Booty 15.00 40.00
TC176 Kevin O'Connell 12.00 30.00
TC179 Harry Douglas 20.00 50.00
TC181 Darren McFadden 75.00 150.00
TC182 Rashard Mendenhall 15.00 40.00
TC183 Jonathan Stewart 60.00 120.00
TC184 Felix Jones 15.00 40.00
TC185 Jamaal Charles 60.00 100.00
TC186 Chris Johnson 20.00 50.00
TC187 Ray Rice 15.00 40.00
TC189 Kevin Smith 15.00 40.00
TC190 Steve Slaton 15.00 40.00
TC191 Matt Forte 60.00 120.00
TC198 DeSean Jackson 60.00 120.00
TC199 Malcolm Kelly 15.00 40.00
TC200 Limas Sweed 15.00 40.00
TC201 Mario Manningham 25.00 60.00
TC202 James Hardy 15.00 40.00
TC203 Early Doucet 15.00 40.00
TC204 Donnie Avery 20.00 50.00
TC205 Dexter Jackson 25.00 60.00
TC206 Devin Thomas 12.00 30.00
TC207 Jordy Nelson 50.00 100.00
TC210 Earl Bennett 25.00 60.00
TC211 Jerome Simpson 15.00 40.00
TC212 Andre Caldwell 15.00 40.00
TC219 Dustin Keller 20.00 50.00
TC222 Jake Long 25.00 60.00
TC228 Glenn Dorsey 15.00 40.00
TC270 Eddie Royal 15.00 40.00

2008 Topps Chrome Tom Brady Tribute Autographs

UNPRICED BRADY AUTO PRINT RUN 1

2009 Topps Chrome

MPLETE SET (220) 75.00 150.00
COMP.SET w/o RC's (110) 8.00 20.00
ROOKIE STATED ODDS 1:2
SP STATED ODDS 1:325 HOB
TC1 Santana Moss .25 .60
TC2 Vernon Davis .20 .50
TC3 Philip Rivers .30 .75
TC4 Santonio Holmes .20 .50
TC5 Jamarcus Russell .20 .50
TC6 Thomas Jones .20 .50
TC7 Randy Moss .25 .60
TC8 Tyler Thigpen .20 .50
TC9 Maurice Jones-Drew .20 .50
TC10 Calvin Johnson .30 .75
TC11 Champ Bailey .25 .60
TC12 Felix Jones .20 .50
TC13 Brady Quinn .20 .50
TC14 Carson Palmer .25 .60
TC15 Marshawn Lynch .25 .60
TC16 Ed Reed .25 .60
TC17 Tim Hightower .20 .50
TC18 Karlos Dansby .20 .50
TC19 Chris Cooley .20 .50
TC20 Donnie Avery .20 .50
TC21 John Carlson .25 .60
TC22 Hines Ward .25 .60
TC23 DeSean Jackson .25 .60
TC24 Justin Tuck .20 .50
TC25 Marques Colston .20 .50
TC26A D.Brees back in view .30 .75
TC26B D.Brees facing SP 10.00 25.00
TC27 Wes Welker .25 .60
TC28A Adrian Peterson wht .30 .75
TC28B Adrian Peterson prple SP 25.00 50.00
TC29 David Garrard .20 .50
TC30 Greg Jennings .20 .50
TC31 Kevin Smith .20 .50
TC32 Marion Barber .25 .60
TC33 Keith Rivers .20 .50
TC34 Devin Hester .25 .60
TC35 Trent Edwards .20 .50
TC36 Kurt Warner .25 .60
TC37 Clinton Portis .20 .50
TC38 LenDale White .20 .50
TC39 Chris Johnson .20 .50
TC40 Antonio Bryant .20 .50
TC41 Matt Hasselbeck .20 .50
TC42 Frank Gore .25 .60
TC43 Antonio Gates .25 .60
TC44 Troy Polamalu .30 .75
TC45 Brian Westbrook .20 .50
TC46 Steve Smith .25 .60
TC47 Darrelle Revis .20 .50
TC48 Kevin Boss .20 .50
TC49 Jeremy Shockey .20 .50
TC50 Tarvaris Jackson .25 .60
TC51 Ted Ginn Jr. .20 .50
TC52 Dwayne Bowe .25 .60
TC53 Bob Sanders .25 .60
TC54 Reggie Wayne .25 .60
TC55 DeMarcus Ware .25 .60
TC56A T.Romo in tunnel .25 .60
TC56B T.Romo passing SP 12.00 30.00
TC57 Matt Forte .20 .50
TC58 Jonathan Stewart .20 .50
TC59 Roddy White .20 .50
TC60 Anquan Boldin .20 .50
TC61 Kerry Collins .20 .50
TC62 Steven Jackson .20 .50
TC63 Darren Sproles .25 .60
TC64 Willie Parker .20 .50
TC65 Asante Samuel .20 .50
TC66 Donovan McNabb .25 .60
TC67 Jerricho Cotchery .20 .50
TC68 Brandon Jacobs .20 .50
TC69 Jerod Mayo .25 .60
TC70A T.Brady passing 1.00 2.50
TC70B T.Brady drop back SP 20.00 40.00
TC71 Jared Allen .20 .50
TC72 Ronnie Brown .20 .50
TC73 Tony Gonzalez .25 .60
TC74A Andre Johnson wht .25 .60
TC74B Andre Johnson blu SP 8.00 20.00
TC75A A.Rodgers passing .60 1.50
TC75B A.Rodgers jogging SP 20.00 40.00
TC76 Eddie Royal .20 .50
TC77 Terrell Owens .25 .60
TC78 Kellen Winslow Jr. .20 .50
TC79 Chad Ochocinco .20 .50
TC80 DeAngelo Williams .20 .50
TC81 Joe Flacco .25 .60
TC82 Michael Turner .20 .50
TC83 Larry Fitzgerald .25 .60
TC84 Keith Bulluck .20 .50
TC85 Aqib Talib .20 .50
TC86 Patrick Willis .25 .60
TC87 LaDainian Tomlinson .30 .75
TC88 Ben Roethlisberger .30 .75
TC89 Darren McFadden .30 .75
TC90 Leon Washington .20 .50
TC91 Eli Manning .25 .60
TC92 Reggie Bush .20 .50
TC93 Chad Pennington .20 .50
TC94 Joey Porter .25 .60
TC95 Anthony Gonzalez .20 .50
TC96A Peyton Manning blu .75 2.00
TC96B Peyton Manning wht SP 20.00 40.00
TC97 Matt Schaub .20 .50
TC98 Steve Slaton .20 .50
TC99 Aaron Kampman .25 .60
TC100 Ernie Sims .20 .50
TC101 Brandon Marshall .25 .60
TC102 Jay Cutler .20 .50
TC103 Jason Witten .25 .60
TC104 Braylon Edwards .20 .50
TC105 T.J. Houshmandzadeh .20 .50
TC106 Brian Urlacher .30 .75
TC107 Julius Peppers .25 .60
TC108 Willis McGahee .20 .50
TC109 Ray Lewis .30 .75
TC110 Matt Ryan .25 .60
TC111 Aaron Brown RC 1.00 2.50
TC112 B.J. Raji RC 1.00 2.50
TC113 Aaron Maybin RC 1.00 2.50
TC114 Alphonso Smith RC .75 2.00
TC115 Hakeem Nicks RC 1.00 2.50
TC116 Andre Smith RC .75 2.00
TC117 Andy Levitre RC 1.00 2.50
TC118 Asher Allen RC .75 2.00
TC119 Austin Collie RC .75 2.00
TC120 Aaron Curry RC 1.25 3.00
TC121 Brandon Gibson RC 1.00 2.50
TC122 Michael Oher RC 1.25 3.00
TC123 Brandon Tate RC 1.00 2.50
TC124 Brandon Underwood RC .75 2.00
TC125 Javon Ringer RC .75 2.00
TC126 Brian Hartline RC 1.25 3.00
TC127 Brian Orakpo RC 1.00 2.50
TC128 Mike Wallace RC 1.25 3.00
TC129 Brooks Foster RC .75 2.00
TC130 Brian Cushing RC .75 2.00
TC131 Chase Coffman RC .75 2.00
TC132 Darius Butler RC 1.00 2.50
TC133 Clay Matthews RC 4.00 10.00
TC134 Clint Sintim RC .75 2.00
TC135 Kenny Britt RC 1.25 3.00
TC136 Patrick Turner RC .75 2.00
TC137 Courtney Greene RC .75 2.00
TC138 Curtis Painter RC .75 2.00
TC139 D.J. Moore RC 1.00 2.50
TC140 Chris Wells RC .75 2.00
TC141 Darrius Heyward-Bey RC 1.25 3.00
TC142 Demetrius Byrd RC 1.00 2.50
TC143 Deon Butler RC .75 2.00
TC144 Derrick Williams RC .75 2.00
TC145A Pat White scrmblng RC 1.00 2.50
TC145B Pat White passing SP 12.00 30.00
TC146 Duke Robinson RC .75 2.00
TC147 Eben Britton RC 1.00 2.50
TC148 Eugene Monroe RC .75 2.00
TC149 Everette Brown RC .75 2.00
TC150 Donald Brown RC .75 2.00
TC151 Gartrell Johnson RC .75 2.00
TC152 Glen Coffee RC .75 2.00
TC153 Andre Brown RC 1.00 2.50
TC154 James Casey RC 1.00 2.50
TC155 Percy Harvin RC .75 2.00
TC156 Roy Miller RC .75 2.00
TC157 Jamon Meredith RC .75 2.00
TC158 Jared Cook RC 1.00 2.50
TC159 Jarett Dillard RC .75 2.00
TC160 Jeremy Maclin RC 1.00 2.50
TC161 Jason Williams RC 1.00 2.50
TC162 Javarris Williams RC 1.00 2.50
TC163 Cedric Peerman RC .75 2.00
TC164 Jason Smith RC .75 2.00
TC165 Fili Moala RC .75 2.00
TC166 Rey Maualuga RC 1.25 3.00
TC167 Travis Beckum RC .75 2.00
TC168 Juaquin Iglesias RC .75 2.00
TC169 Connor Barwin RC 1.00 2.50
TC170 Knowshon Moreno RC .75 2.00
TC171 Kenny McKinley RC .75 2.00
TC172 Kevin Ellison RC .75 2.00
TC173 Larry English RC 1.00 2.50
TC174 Marko Mitchell RC .75 2.00
TC175 Louis Delmas RC 1.00 2.50
TC176 Shonn Greene RC .75 2.00
TC177 Malcolm Jenkins RC .75 2.00
TC178 Manuel Johnson RC .75 2.00
TC179 Marcus Freeman RC .75 2.00
TC180 LeSean McCoy RC 2.00 5.00
TC181 Zack Follett RC .75 2.00
TC182 Shawn Nelson RC .75 2.00
TC183 Rashad Jennings RC 1.00 2.50
TC184 Michael Hamlin RC .75 2.00
TC185 Michael Johnson RC .75 2.00
TC186 Brandon Pettigrew RC .75 2.00
TC187 Mike Goodson RC 1.00 2.50
TC188 Mike Mickens RC .75 2.00
TC189 Mike Teel RC .75 2.00
TC190 Mike Thomas RC .75 2.00
TC191 Brian Robiskie RC .75 2.00
TC192 Mohamed Massaquoi RC .75 2.00
TC193 Nate Davis RC .75 2.00
TC194 Patrick Chung RC .75 2.00
TC195 Cornelius Ingram RC .75 2.00
TC196 James Davis RC .75 2.00
TC197 Peria Jerry RC .75 2.00
TC198 Phil Loadholt RC 1.00 2.50
TC199 Ramses Barden RC .75 2.00
TC200A Michael Crabtree RC 1.25 3.00
TC200B M.Crabtree ball in air SP 15.00 30.00
TC201 Rashad Johnson RC .75 2.00
TC202 Johnny Knox RC 1.00 2.50
TC203 Rhett Bomar RC .75 2.00
TC204 Robert Ayers RC .75 2.00
TC205 James Laurinaitis RC .75 2.00
TC206 Sammie Stroughter RC .75 2.00
TC207 Scott McKillop RC .75 2.00
TC208 Sean Smith RC .75 2.00
TC209 Sen'Derrick Marks RC .75 2.00
TC210 Matthew Stafford RC 4.00 10.00
TC211 Louis Murphy RC .75 2.00
TC212 Stephen McGee RC .75 2.00
TC213 Tiquan Underwood RC .75 2.00
TC214 Tom Brandstater RC 1.00 2.50
TC215 Josh Freeman RC .75 2.00
TC216 Tyson Jackson RC .75 2.00
TC217 Victor Harris RC 1.00 2.50
TC218 Vontae Davis RC .75 2.00
TC219 William Moore RC .75 2.00
TC220A Mark Sanchez RC .75 2.00
TC220B Mark Sanchez w/hlmt SP 30.00 60.00
RHC43 Santonio Holmes RH .75 2.00

2009 Topps Chrome Copper Refractors

ETS: 3X TO 8X BASIC CARDS
*ROOKIES: .8X TO 2X BASIC CARDS
COPPER REF/649 ODDS 1:12 HOB

2009 Topps Chrome Blue Refractors

*VETS: 5X TO 12X BASIC CARDS
*ROOKIES: 1.2X TO 3X BASIC CARDS
RANDOM INSERTS IN RETAIL PACKS
RH Santonio Holmes RH/100 5.00 12.00

2009 Topps Chrome Red Refractors

*VETS: 15X TO 40X BASIC CARDS
*ROOKIES: 3X TO 8X BASIC CARDS
RED REF/25 ODDS 1:138 HOB
TC10 Calvin Johnson 15.00 40.00
TC210 Matthew Stafford 40.00 100.00

2009 Topps Chrome Refractors

ETS: 2.5X TO 6X BASIC CARDS
*ROOKIES: .6X TO 1.5X BASIC CARDS
REFRACTOR STATED ODDS 1:3 HOB
RH Santonio Holmes RH/199 4.00 10.00

2009 Topps Chrome Xfractors

ETS: 2.5X TO 6X BASIC CARDS
*ROOKIES: .6X TO 1.5X BASIC CARDS
RANDOM INSERTS IN RETAIL PACKS

2009 Topps Chrome Cheerleaders

COMPLETE SET (15) 5.00 12.00
OVERALL STATED ODDS 1:8
*REFRACT/199: 4X TO 10X BASIC INSERTS
*BLUE REF/50: 6X TO 15X BASIC INSERTS
*WHITE REF/100: 5X TO 12X BASIC INSERTS
TCC1 Tara .50 1.50
TCC2 Amanda .50 1.50
TCC3 Kelli .50 1.50
TCC4 Emily C. .50 1.50
TCC5 Kayla S. .50 1.50
TCC6 Laurie .50 1.50
TCC7 TaJonda .50 1.50
TCC8 Amanda .50 1.50
TCC9 Samantha .50 1.50
TCC10 Amy .50 1.50
TCC11 Fabiola .50 1.50
TCC12 Johanna .50 1.50
TCC13 Bibiana .50 1.50
TCC14 Monica .50 1.50
TCC15 Tiffany .50 1.50

2009 Topps Chrome Chicle

COMPLETE SET (25) 8.00 20.00
OVERALL ODDS 1:4 HOB
*REFRACT/199: 1.5X TO 4X BASIC INSERTS
*BLUE REF/50: 2.5X TO 6X BASIC INSERTS
*WHITE REF/100: 2X TO 5X BASIC INSERTS
C1 Brian Westbrook .30 .75
C5 Tony Gonzalez .40 1.00
C8 Steven Jackson .30 .75
C14 Adrian Peterson .50 1.25
C21 Calvin Johnson .50 1.25
C24 Troy Polamalu .50 1.25
C30 Drew Brees .50 1.25
C31 LaDainian Tomlinson .50 1.25
C35 Jamal Lewis .40 1.00
C40 Peyton Manning 1.25 3.00
C42 Tony Romo .40 1.00
C46 LenDale White .30 .75
C55 Dwayne Bowe .40 1.00
C59 Jason Witten .40 1.00
C66 Jerricho Cotchery .30 .75
C71 Ted Ginn Jr. .30 .75
C73 Vincent Jackson .30 .75
C74 Lee Evans .40 1.00
C75 Wes Welker .40 1.00
C76 Ben Roethlisberger .50 1.25
C79 Kevin Walter .40 1.00
C83 Devin Hester .40 1.00
C89 Joey Porter .40 1.00
C90 Darrius Heyward-Bey .40 1.00
C93 Jon Beason .30 .75

2009 Topps Chrome Rookie Autographs

OUP A ODDS 1:7000 HOB
GROUP B ODDS 1:507 HOB
GROUP C ODDS 1:220 HOB
GROUP D ODDS 1:115 HOB
GROUP E ODDS 1:146 HOB
GROUP F ODDS 1:60 HOB
EXCH EXPIRATION: 8/31/2012
TC115 Hakeem Nicks D 5.00 12.00
TC120 Aaron Curry D 6.00 15.00
TC125 Javon Ringer F 4.00 10.00
TC127 Brian Orakpo E 5.00 12.00
TC130 Brian Cushing D 4.00 10.00
TC131 Chase Coffman E 4.00 10.00
TC135 Kenny Britt C 6.00 15.00
TC136 Patrick Turner F 4.00 10.00
TC140 Chris Wells C 4.00 10.00
TC141 Darrius Heyward-Bey B 8.00 20.00
TC142 Demetrius Byrd A 12.00 30.00
TC144 Derrick Williams C 4.00 10.00
TC145 Pat White C 5.00 12.00
TC150 Donald Brown C 4.00 10.00
TC151 Gartrell Johnson F 4.00 10.00
TC152 Glen Coffee F 4.00 10.00
TC153 Andre Brown F 5.00 12.00
TC154 James Casey E 5.00 12.00
TC155 Percy Harvin D 10.00 25.00
TC158 Jared Cook D 5.00 12.00
TC160 Jeremy Maclin C 5.00 12.00
TC163 Cedric Peerman E 4.00 10.00
TC166 Rey Maualuga E 6.00 15.00
TC168 Juaquin Iglesias F 4.00 10.00
TC171 Knowshon Moreno B 4.00 10.00
TC176 Shonn Greene F 4.00 10.00
TC177 Malcolm Jenkins D 4.00 10.00
TC181 LeSean McCoy D 10.00 25.00
TC183 Rashad Jennings F 5.00 12.00
TC185 Michael Johnson F 4.00 10.00
TC186 Brandon Pettigrew C 4.00 10.00
TC191 Brian Robiskie D 4.00 10.00
TC192 Mohamed Massaquoi F 4.00 10.00
TC193 Nate Davis F 4.00 10.00
TC195 Cornelius Ingram D 4.00 10.00
TC196 James Davis C 4.00 10.00
TC199 Ramses Barden D 4.00 10.00
TC200 Michael Crabtree B 6.00 15.00
TC202 Johnny Knox F 5.00 12.00
TC203 Rhett Bomar F 4.00 10.00
TC205 James Laurinaitis E 4.00 10.00
TC210 Matthew Stafford B 100.00 200.00
TC212 Stephen McGee E 4.00 10.00
TC213 Tiquan Underwood F 4.00 10.00
TC214 Tom Brandstater D 5.00 12.00
TC215 Josh Freeman B 12.00 30.00
TC220 Mark Sanchez B 25.00 60.00

2009 Topps Chrome Rookie Autographs Black Refractors

*BLACK REF/25: 1X TO 2.5X BASIC AU
BLACK REF/25 ODDS 1:788 HOB
TC210 Matthew Stafford 200.00 400.00

2009 Topps Chrome Rookie Autographs Patch

PATCH AU/25 ODDS 1:1130 HOB
ARPAB Andre Brown 15.00 40.00
ARPAC Aaron Curry 20.00 50.00
ARPBP Brandon Pettigrew 12.00 30.00
ARPBR Brian Robiskie 12.00 30.00
ARPCW Chris Wells 12.00 30.00
ARPDB Donald Brown 12.00 30.00
ARPDH Darrius Heyward-Bey 20.00 50.00
ARPGC Glen Coffee 12.00 30.00
ARPHN Hakeem Nicks 15.00 40.00
ARPJF Josh Freeman 40.00 100.00
ARPJI Juaquin Iglesias 12.00 30.00
ARPJM Jeremy Maclin 15.00 40.00
ARPJR Javon Ringer 12.00 30.00
ARPKB Kenny Britt 20.00 50.00
ARPKM Knowshon Moreno 12.00 30.00
ARPLM LeSean McCoy 90.00 150.00
ARPMC Michael Crabtree 20.00 50.00
ARPMM Mohamed Massaquoi 12.00 30.00
ARPMS Mark Sanchez 50.00 120.00
ARPND Nate Davis 12.00 30.00
ARPPH Percy Harvin 30.00 80.00
ARPPT Patrick Turner 12.00 30.00
ARPPW Pat White 15.00 40.00
ARPRB Ramses Barden 12.00 30.00
ARPSG Shonn Greene 12.00 30.00
ARPSM Stephen McGee 12.00 30.00
ARPJMS Matthew Stafford 200.00 400.00
ARPRMB Rhett Bomar 12.00 30.00

2010 Topps Chrome

COMP.SET w/o SP's (220) 20.00 50.00
C1 Adrian Peterson .30 .75
C2 Sidney Rice .20 .50
C3A Jahvid Best run RC .50 1.25
C3B Jahvid Best catch SP 4.00 10.00
C4 Terrell Owens .25 .60
C5 Brandon Marshall .25 .60
C6 Philip Rivers .30 .75
C7 Vernon Davis .20 .50
C8 Percy Harvin .20 .50
C9 Jamaal Charles .25 .60
C10 Donovan McNabb .25 .60
C11A Golden Tate helm RC .60 1.50
C11B Golden Tate no helm SP 5.00 12.00
C12 Myron Rolle RC .50 1.25
C13A Dexter McCluster helm RC .60 1.50
C13B Dexter McCluster no helm SP 5.00 12.00
C14 Morgan Burnett RC .60 1.50
C15 Jason Witten .25 .60
C16A Jonathan Dwyer rght RC .50 1.25
C16B Jonathan Dwyer left SP 4.00 10.00
C17 Dezmon Briscoe RC .50 1.25
C18 Brian Urlacher .30 .75
C19 DeAngelo Williams .20 .50
C20 Tony Romo .25 .60
C21 Charles Scott RC .50 1.25
C22 Linval Joseph RC .50 1.25
C23 Ed Wang RC .75 2.00
C24 Tony Gonzalez .25 .60
C25 Darren McFadden .20 .50
C26 Matt Forte .20 .50
C27 Kenny Britt .20 .50
C28 Anthony Dixon RC .50 1.25
C29 Chad Jones RC .50 1.25
C30 Troy Polamalu .30 .75
C31 Taylor Mays RC .50 1.25
C32 Devin McCourty RC .60 1.50
C33 Matthew Stafford .25 .60
C34 London Fletcher .25 .60
C35 Darren Sproles .25 .60
C36 Dan LeFevour RC .50 1.25
C37 Michael Turner .20 .50
C38 Sean Lee RC 1.00 2.50
C39 Nnamdi Asomugha .20 .50
C40 Andre Johnson .25 .60
C41 Ryan Grant .25 .60
C42 Donald Driver .25 .60
C43 Eli Manning .25 .60
C44A Mike Williams no hlm RC .50 1.25
C44B Mike Williams helm SP 4.00 10.00
C45 Anquan Boldin .20 .50
C46A Ben Tate helm RC 1.00 2.50
C46B Ben Tate no helm SP 4.00 10.00
C47 Andre Roberts RC .60 1.50
C48 Kareem Jackson RC .50 1.25
C49 Zac Robinson RC .60 1.50
C50 Peyton Manning .75 2.00
C51A Brandon LaFell run RC .75 2.00
C51B Brandon LaFell catch SP 6.00 15.00
C52 Santana Moss .25 .60
C53 Russell Okung RC .50 1.25
C54 Julius Peppers .25 .60
C55 Hines Ward .25 .60
C56 Brandon Graham RC .60 1.50
C57 Steve Smith .25 .60
C58 Mike Iupati RC .75 2.00
C59 Joe Flacco .25 .60
C60A Dez Bryant RC 1.25 3.00
C60B Dez Bryant SP 30.00 60.00
C61 Rashard Mendenhall .20 .50
C62 James Harrison .30 .75
C63 Wes Welker .25 .60
C64 Jerod Mayo .25 .60
C65 Carlos Dunlap RC .50 1.25
C66 Taylor Price RC .50 1.25
C67 Jimmy Graham RC 1.25 3.00
C68 Walter McFadden RC .60 1.50
C69 Patrick Robinson RC .60 1.50
C70A Colt McCoy helm RC .60 1.50
C70B Colt McCoy no hlm SP 10.00 25.00
C71 Marion Barber .25 .60
C72 Tyson Alualu RC .50 1.25
C73 Chris Cook RC .50 1.25
C74 Joe Webb RC .50 1.25
C75 Brian Dawkins .20 .50
C76 Greg Jennings .20 .50
C77 Jonathan Stewart .20 .50
C78 Ronnie Brown .20 .50
C79 Willis McGahee .20 .50
C80 Tom Brady .75 2.00
C81 Clinton Portis .20 .50
C82 Jerry Hughes RC .50 1.25
C83 Knowshon Moreno .20 .50
C84 David Reed RC .50 1.25
C85 Brandon Spikes RC .50 1.25
C86 Joe Haden RC .75 2.00
C87 Aaron Hernandez RC .50 1.25
C88 Terrence Cody RC .50 1.25
C89 Felix Jones .20 .50
C90 Brett Favre .60 1.50
C91 Carson Palmer .25 .60
C92 Jay Cutler .20 .50
C93 Carlton Mitchell RC .50 1.25
C94 DeSean Jackson .25 .60
C95 LeSean McCoy .30 .75
C96 John Conner RC .50 1.25
C97 Charles Brown RC .50 1.25
C98 Eric Decker RC .60 1.50
C99 Brandon Ghee RC .50 1.25
C100A Tim Tebow leap RC 1.50 4.00
C100B Tim Tebow point SP 20.00 50.00
C101 Darren Sharper .20 .50
C102 Trent Williams RC .60 1.50
C103 Riley Cooper RC .50 1.25
C104 Brian Cushing .20 .50
C105 Miles Austin .20 .50
C106A Emmanuel Sanders RC .75 2.00
C106B Emmanuel Sanders SP 6.00 15.00
C107 Jermaine Gresham RC .50 1.25
C108 Vincent Jackson .20 .50
C109 Jermaine Cunningham RC .50 1.25
C110A Demaryius Thomas RC 1.75 5.00
C110B Demaryius Thomas SP 10.00 25.00
C111 Pierre Thomas .20 .50
C112A R.Gronkowski run RC 4.00 10.00
C112B R.Gronkowski ctch SP 10.00 25.00
C113 Major Wright RC .50 1.25
C114 Anthony Davis RC .60 1.50
C115 Darrelle Revis .20 .50
C116 Ray Lewis .30 .75
C117 Daryl Washington RC .50 1.25
C118 Kyle Wilson RC .50 1.25
C119 Koa Misi RC .60 1.50
C120A C.J. Spiller RC .50 1.25
C120B C.J. Spiller SP 4.00 10.00
C121 Pat Angerer RC .50 1.25
C122 Cadillac Williams .20 .50
C123 DeMarcus Ware UER 11 .25 .60
C124 Aaron Rodgers .60 1.50
C125 Dan Williams RC .50 1.25
C126 Dallas Clark .20 .50
C127 Santonio Holmes .20 .50
C128 Michael Crabtree .20 .50
C129 Bryan Bulaga RC .50 1.25
C130A Jimmy Clausen point RC .50 1.25
C130B Jimmy Clausen pass SP 4.00 10.00
C131 Chad Ochocinco .20 .50
C132 Ben Roethlisberger .30 .75
C133 Steve Smith USC .20 .50
C134 Everson Griffen RC .50 1.25
C135 Earl Thomas RC 1.50 4.00
C136A Armanti Edwards RC .60 1.50
C136B Armanti Edwards SP 5.00 12.00
C137 Kevin Kolb .20 .50
C138 Akwasi Owusu-Ansah RC .50 1.25
C139 Mike Kafka RC .60 1.50
C140A Ryan Mathews run RC .50 1.25
C140B Ryan Mathews catch SP 4.00 10.00
C141 T.J. Houshmandzadeh .20 .50
C142 Chris Cooley .20 .50
C143 Randy Moss .25 .60
C144 Rodger Saffold RC .50 1.25
C145 Maurice Jones-Drew .20 .50
C146 Jonathan Vilma .20 .50
C147 Matt Schaub .20 .50
C148 Jacoby Ford RC .50 1.25
C149 T.J. Ward RC .75 2.00
C150A Sam Bradford run RC 2.50 6.00
C150B Sam Bradford snap SP 40.00 80.00
C151 Joey Porter .20 .50
C152 Ray Rice .20 .50
C153 James Starks RC .60 1.50
C154 Joseph Addai .20 .50
C155 Matt Hasselbeck .20 .50
C156 Antonio Gates .25 .60
C157 Mardy Gilyard RC .50 1.25
C158 Jerome Murphy RC .60 1.50
C159A Joe McKnight catch RC .50 1.25
C159B Joe McKnight jump SP 6.00 15.00
C160A Ndamukong Suh RC 1.00 2.50
C160B Ndamukong Suh SP 15.00 40.00
C161 Marcus Easley RC .50 1.25
C162 Marques Colston .20 .50
C163 Torell Troup RC .50 1.25
C164 Amari Spievey RC .50 1.25
C165 Sergio Kindle RC .50 1.25
C166 Jonathan Crompton RC .50 1.25
C167 James Laurinaitis .25 .60
C168A Montario Hardesty run RC .50 1.25
C168B Montario Hardesty jump SP 4.00 10.00
C169 Frank Gore .25 .60
C170 Gerald McCoy RC .50 1.25
C171 Sean Weatherspoon RC .50 1.25
C172 Damian Williams RC .50 1.25
C173 Reggie Bush .20 .50
C174 Kellen Winslow .20 .50
C175 Tony Pike RC .50 1.25
C176 Reggie Wayne .25 .60
C177 Dwayne Bowe .25 .60
C178 Brandon Jacobs .20 .50
C179 Levi Brown RC .50 1.25
C180 Larry Fitzgerald .25 .60
C181 Cedric Benson .20 .50
C182 Patrick Willis .25 .60
C183 Maurkice Pouncey RC .60 1.50
C184 Sean Canfield RC .50 1.25
C185 Ed Dickson RC .50 1.25
C186A Arrelious Benn RC .50 1.25
C186B Arrelious Benn SP 4.00 10.00
C187 Matt Ryan .25 .60
C188 Jared Odrick RC .60 1.50
C189 Phillip Dillard RC .50 1.25
C190 Steven Jackson .20 .50
C191 Jeremy Maclin .20 .50
C192 Ed Reed .25 .60
C193 Calvin Johnson .30 .75
C194 Chris Wells .20 .50
C195A Eric Berry catch RC .75 2.00
C195B Eric Berry leap SP 6.00 15.00
C196 Shonn Greene .20 .50
C197 Rennie Curran RC .50 1.25
C198 Javier Arenas RC .50 1.25
C199 Kevin Thomas UER RC .60 1.50
C200 Chris Johnson .20 .50
C201 Jason Pierre-Paul RC .75 2.00
C202 Jared Allen .20 .50
C203 Steve Slaton .20 .50
C204 Lamarr Houston RC .60 1.50
C205 Anthony McCoy RC .50 1.25
C206 Mark Sanchez .20 .50
C207 Derrick Morgan RC .50 1.25
C208A Jordan Shipley helm RC .50 1.25
C208B Jordan Shipley no helm SP 4.00 10.00
C209 Dwight Freeney .20 .50
C210 LaDainian Tomlinson .30 .75
C211 Matt Cassel .20 .50
C212 Rolando McClain RC .50 1.25
C213 Nate Allen RC .75 2.00
C214 Thomas Jones .20 .50
C215 Darryl Sharpton RC .50 1.25
C216A Toby Gerhart cut RC .50 1.25
C216B Toby Gerhart leap SP 4.00 10.00
C217 Jon Beason .20 .50
C218 John Skelton RC .60 1.50
C219 D.J. Williams .20 .50
C220 Drew Brees .30 .75

2010 Topps Chrome Blue Refractors

*VETS: 6X TO 15X BASIC CARDS
*ROOKIES: 2.5X TO 6X BASIC CARDS
BLUE/199 STATED ODDS 1:52

2010 Topps Chrome Gold Refractors

*VETS: 10X TO 25X BASIC CARDS
*ROOKIES: 4X TO 10X BASIC CARDS
GOLD/50 STATED ODDS 1:208
C100 Tim Tebow 30.00 80.00
C150 Sam Bradford 30.00 80.00

2010 Topps Chrome Orange Refractors

*VETS: 3X TO 8X BASIC CARDS
*ROOKIES: 1.2X TO 3X BASIC CARDS
RANDOM INSERTS IN RETAIL PACKS

2010 Topps Chrome Purple Refractors

*VETS: 4X TO 10X BASIC CARDS
*ROOKIES: 1.5X TO 4X BASIC CARDS
RETAIL INSERT PRINT RUN 555

2010 Topps Chrome Red Refractors

*VETS: 12X TO 30X BASIC CARDS
*ROOKIES: 5X TO 12X BASIC CARDS
RED REFRACTOR/25 ODDS 1:204
C100 Tim Tebow 40.00 100.00
C150 Sam Bradford 50.00 120.00

2010 Topps Chrome Refractors

*VETS: 2X TO 5X BASIC CARDS
*ROOKIES: .8X TO 2X BASIC CARDS
STATED ODDS 1:3 HOB/RET

2010 Topps Chrome Xfractors

*VETS: 3X TO 8X BASIC CARDS
*ROOKIES: 1.2X TO 3X BASIC CARDS
STATED ODDS 1:3 RETAIL

2010 Topps Chrome Anniversary Reprints

EFRACT/99: 1X TO 2.5X BASIC INSERTS
1 Jim Brown 1.50 4.00
2 Eric Dickerson 1.00 2.50
3 Tony Dorsett 1.25 3.00
4 John Elway 2.00 5.00
5 Frank Gore .75 2.00
6 Steven Jackson .60 1.50
7 Chad Johnson .60 1.50
8 Felix Jones .60 1.50
9 Ray Lewis 1.00 2.50
10 Eli Manning .75 2.00
11 Peyton Manning 2.50 6.00
12 Dan Marino 2.50 6.00
13 Brandon Marshall .75 2.00
14 LeSean McCoy 1.00 2.50
15 Joe Montana 4.00 10.00
16 Adrian Peterson 1.00 2.50
17 Mark Sanchez .60 1.50
18 Gale Sayers 1.25 3.00
19 LaDainian Tomlinson 1.00 2.50
20 Reggie Wayne .75 2.00

2010 Topps Chrome Gridiron Lineage

EFRACT/99: 1.2X TO 3X BASIC INSERTS
CGLAR T.Aikman/T.Romo 1.25 3.00
CGLBL D.Bowe/B.LaFell .75 2.00
CGLDA E.Dickerson/J.Addai .60 1.50
CGLDJ E.Dickerson/S.Jackson .60 1.50
CGLDM T.Dorsett/L.McCoy .75 2.00
CGLET J.Elway/T.Tebow 3.00 8.00
CGLGG A.Gates/J.Gresham .60 1.50
CGLGS A.Gonzalez/J.Shipley .30 .75
CGLHM P.Harvin/D.McCluster .40 1.00
CGLMC J.Montana/J.Clausen 1.50 4.00
CGLMT B.Marshall/D.Thomas .75 2.00
CGLNS J.Namath/M.Sanchez 1.00 2.50
CGLPB A.Peterson/J.Best .50 1.25
CGLPH A.Peterson/P.Harvin .75 2.00
CGLSD J.Stewart/J.Dwyer .30 .75
CGLSJ E.Smith/F.Jones 1.25 3.00
CGLST E.Smith/L.Tomlinson 1.25 3.00
CGLTM L.Tomlinson/R.Mathews .50 1.25
CGLTS T.Thomas/C.Spiller .40 1.00
CGLWM P.Willis/R.McClain .40 1.00

2010 Topps Chrome Retail Exclusive Rookie Refractors

INSERTS IN SPECIAL RETAIL BOXES
TMB1 Sam Bradford .60 1.50
TMB2 Jimmy Clausen .50 1.25

2010 Topps Chrome Rookie Autographs

GROUP A ODDS 1:200 HOB
GROUP B ODDS 1:31 HOB
C3 Jahvid Best A 5.00 12.00
C13 Dexter McCluster B 4.00 10.00
C16 Jonathan Dwyer B 4.00 10.00
C17 Dezmon Briscoe B 3.00 8.00
C23 Ed Wang B 5.00 12.00
C36 Dan LeFevour B 3.00 8.00
C46 Ben Tate B 3.00 8.00
C47 Andre Roberts B 4.00 10.00
C49 Zac Robinson B 4.00 10.00
C51 Brandon LaFell B 5.00 12.00
C60 Dez Bryant A 25.00 60.00
C66 Taylor Price B 3.00 8.00
C70 Colt McCoy A 6.00 15.00
C74 Joe Webb B 3.00 8.00
C84 David Reed B 3.00 8.00
C87 Aaron Hernandez B 12.00 30.00
C98 Eric Decker B 4.00 10.00
C100 Tim Tebow A 40.00 80.00
C103 Riley Cooper B 6.00 15.00
C106 Emmanuel Sanders A 5.00 12.00
C110 Demaryius Thomas A 20.00 50.00
C112 Rob Gronkowski B 60.00 120.00
C120 C.J. Spiller A 5.00 12.00
C130 Jimmy Clausen A 5.00 12.00
C135 Earl Thomas B 15.00 40.00
C136 Armanti Edwards B 4.00 10.00
C139 Mike Kafka B 4.00 10.00
C140 Ryan Mathews A 5.00 12.00
C148 Jacoby Ford B 3.00 8.00
C150 Sam Bradford A 6.00 15.00
C159 Joe McKnight A 5.00 12.00
C160 Ndamukong Suh A 15.00 40.00
C161 Marcus Easley B 3.00 8.00
C168 Montario Hardesty B 3.00 8.00
C170 Gerald McCoy B 3.00 8.00
C172 Damian Williams B 3.00 8.00
C175 Tony Pike B 3.00 8.00
C186 Arrelious Benn B 3.00 8.00
C208 Jordan Shipley B 3.00 8.00
C218 John Skelton B 4.00 10.00

2010 Topps Chrome Rookie Autographs Black Refractors

*BLACK REF/25: 1X TO 2.5X BASIC GRP A
*BLACK REF/25: 1.5X TO 4X BASIC GRP B
BLACK REFRCTOR PRINT RUN 25
C60 Dez Bryant 100.00 200.00
C100 Tim Tebow 150.00 300.00
C112 Rob Gronkowski 150.00 300.00
C140 Ryan Mathews 12.00 30.00
C160 Ndamukong Suh 50.00 120.00

2010 Topps Chrome Rookie Autographs Refractors

*REFRACT/50: .6X TO 1.5X BASIC GRP A
*REFRACT/50: 1X TO 2.5X BASIC GRP B
REFRACTOR AU PRINT RUN 50
C60 Dez Bryant 60.00 125.00
C100 Tim Tebow 75.00 200.00
C112 Rob Gronkowski 60.00 120.00
C150 Sam Bradford 10.00 25.00

2010 Topps Chrome Rookie Autographs Dual

STATED PRINT RUN 25 SER.#'d SETS
CDRA1 C.McCoy/M.Hardesty 30.00 80.00
CDRA2 T.Tebow/A.Hernandez 75.00 150.00
CDRA3 S.Bradford/J.Clausen 25.00 50.00
CDRA4 C.Spiller/R.Mathews 100.00 175.00
CDRA5 D.Bryant/D.Thomas 50.00 100.00

2010 Topps Chrome Rookie Autographs Patch

PATCH AU/25 ODDS 1:1561 HOB
C3 Jahvid Best 12.00 30.00
C11 Golden Tate 15.00 40.00
C13 Dexter McCluster 15.00 40.00
C16 Jonathan Dwyer 25.00 60.00
C46 Ben Tate 12.00 30.00
C47 Andre Roberts 30.00 60.00
C51 Brandon LaFell 20.00 50.00
C60 Dez Bryant 100.00 200.00
C70 Colt McCoy 40.00 100.00
C86 Joe Haden 20.00 50.00
C98 Eric Decker 15.00 40.00
C100 Tim Tebow 150.00 300.00
C106 Emmanuel Sanders 20.00 50.00
C107 Jermaine Gresham 12.00 30.00
C110 Demaryius Thomas 75.00 135.00
C112 Rob Gronkowski 125.00 200.00
C120 C.J. Spiller 12.00 30.00
C130 Jimmy Clausen 12.00 30.00
C136 Armanti Edwards 15.00 40.00
C140 Ryan Mathews 12.00 30.00
C150 Sam Bradford 15.00 40.00
C159 Joe McKnight 12.00 30.00
C160 Ndamukong Suh 60.00 120.00
C168 Montario Hardesty 12.00 30.00
C170 Gerald McCoy 12.00 30.00
C172 Damian Williams 12.00 30.00
C186 Arrelious Benn 12.00 30.00
C195 Eric Berry 20.00 50.00
C208 Jordan Shipley 12.00 30.00
C212 Rolando McClain 12.00 30.00
C216 Toby Gerhart 12.00 30.00

2011 Topps Chrome

COMP.SET w/o SP's (220) 30.00 80.00
ROOKIE SP ODDS 1:330 HOB
1A Cam Newton RC 4.00 10.00
1B Cam Newton SP 40.00 80.00
2 Ray Lewis .30 .75
3 Rob Housler RC .50 1.25
4 Matthew Stafford .25 .60
5 Gabe Carimi RC .60 1.50
6 Prince Amukamara RC .50 1.25

7 Beanie Wells .20 .50
8 Calvin Johnson .30 .75
9 Ryan Kerrigan RC .60 1.50
10 Arian Foster .20 .50
11 Ryan Torain .20 .50
12 Eli Manning .25 .60
13 Lance Kendricks RC .50 1.25
14 Adrian Clayborn RC .50 1.25
15 Darrelle Revis .20 .50
16 Percy Harvin .20 .50
17 Santana Moss .25 .60
18 Marshawn Lynch .25 .60
19 Lee Smith RC .60 1.50
20 Tom Brady .75 2.00
21 Matt Schaub .20 .50
22 Edmond Gates RC .50 1.25
23 Steve Smith .25 .60
24 Nathan Enderle RC .50 1.25
25A Colin Kaepernick RC .75 2.00
25B Colin Kaepernick SP 6.00 15.00
26 Tyrod Taylor RC 1.00 2.50
27 Patrick Willis .25 .60
28 Peyton Hillis .20 .50
29 Antonio Gates .20 .50
30 Chris Johnson .20 .50
31 Virgil Green RC .50 1.25
32 Da'Rel Scott RC .50 1.25
33 Denarius Moore RC .50 1.25
34 Sam Bradford .20 .50
35 Johnny White RC .50 1.25
36 Jason Witten .25 .60
37 Aldon Smith RC .50 1.25
38 Tyron Smith RC 1.00 2.50
39 Cameron Jordan RC .60 1.50
40 Maurice Jones-Drew .20 .50
41 Derrick Mason .20 .50
42 Vincent Brown RC .50 1.25
43 Felix Jones .20 .50
44 Rahim Moore RC .50 1.25
45 Kenny Britt .20 .50
46 Curtis Brown RC .50 1.25
47 Luke Stocker RC .50 1.25
48 Derek Sherrod RC .50 1.25
49 Brandon Pettigrew .20 .50
50A Mark Ingram RC .75 2.00
50B Mark Ingram SP 6.00 15.00
51A Andy Dalton RC 1.00 2.50
51B Andy Dalton SP 20.00 40.00
52 James Harrison .25 .60
53 Ricky Stanzi RC .50 1.25
54 Joseph Addai .20 .50
55A Blaine Gabbert RC .50 1.25
55B Blaine Gabbert SP 4.00 10.00
56 Jeremy Kerley RC .75 2.00
57 Chad Ochocinco .20 .50
58 Jordan Cameron RC .60 1.50
59 Brandon Marshall .25 .60
60 Andre Johnson .25 .60
61 Taiwan Jones RC .50 1.25
62 Kendall Hunter RC .50 1.25
63 Jimmy Smith RC .50 1.25
64 LeSean McCoy .30 .75
65 D.J. Williams RC .50 1.25
66 Mike Pouncey RC .75 2.00
67 Greg Jennings .20 .50
68 Owen Daniels .20 .50
69 Darren McFadden .20 .50
70 Michael Vick .25 .60
71A Ryan Williams RC .50 1.25
71B Ryan Williams SP 4.00 10.00
72 Da'Quan Bowers RC .50 1.25
73 Jamaal Charles .25 .60
74A Mikel Leshoure RC .50 1.25
74B Mikel Leshoure SP 4.00 10.00
75 Ronnie Brown .25 .60
76 Jimmy Graham .30 .75
77 Jermichael Finley .20 .50
78 DeSean Jackson .25 .60
79 Brian Urlacher .30 .75
80 Larry Fitzgerald .25 .60
81 Hakeem Nicks .20 .50
82 Evan Royster RC .50 1.25
83 Matt Forte .20 .50
84 Sidney Rice .20 .50
85 Hines Ward .25 .60
86 Greg McElroy RC .75 2.00
87 Tony Gonzalez .25 .60
88A Greg Little RC .60 1.50
88B Greg Little SP 5.00 12.00
89 Kris Durham RC .50 1.25
90 Philip Rivers .30 .75
91 Dez Bryant .30 .75
92 Julius Thomas RC .60 1.50
93A Randall Cobb RC .75 2.00
93B Randall Cobb SP 6.00 15.00
94 Niles Paul RC .50 1.25
95 Joe Flacco .25 .60
96 C.J. Spiller .20 .50
97A Torrey Smith RC .50 1.25
97B Torrey Smith SP 4.00 10.00
98 Wes Welker .25 .60
99 Dwayne Bowe .25 .60
100 Aaron Rodgers .50 1.25
101 Randy Moss .25 .60
102 Brooks Reed RC .60 1.50
103 Ryan Mathews .25 .60
104 J.J. Watt RC 2.50 6.00
105 Dallas Clark .20 .50
106 Delone Carter RC .50 1.25
107 Matt Cassel .20 .50
108 Knowshon Moreno .20 .50
109 Ras-I Dowling RC .50 1.25
110 Peyton Manning .60 1.50
111A Leonard Hankerson RC .50 1.25
111B Leonard Hankerson SP 4.00 10.00
112 Corey Liuget RC .50 1.25
113 Dontay Moch RC .50 1.25
114 Reggie Wayne .25 .60
115 Justin Houston RC .60 1.50
116 Greg Salas RC .50 1.25
117 Cameron Heyward RC .60 1.50
118 Anthony Allen RC .50 1.25
119 Anquan Boldin .20 .50
120 Ben Roethlisberger .30 .75
121 Santonio Holmes .20 .50
122A Ryan Mallett RC .50 1.25
122B Ryan Mallett SP 4.00 10.00
123A Jon Baldwin RC .50 1.25
123B Jon Baldwin SP 4.00 10.00
124 Marcell Dareus RC .50 1.25
125 Jabaal Sheard RC .50 1.25
126 Phil Taylor RC .50 1.25
127 Danny Watkins RC .50 1.25
128 Bilal Powell RC .60 1.50
129 Martez Wilson RC .50 1.25
130 Drew Brees .30 .75
131A Julio Jones RC 1.50 4.00
131B Julio Jones SP 12.00 30.00
132 Rob Gronkowski .30 .75
133 Mike Wallace .20 .50
134 Kellen Winslow .20 .50
135 Jordan Todman RC .50 1.25
136A Daniel Thomas RC .50 1.25
136B Daniel Thomas SP 4.00 10.00
137A Titus Young RC .50 1.25
137B Titus Young SP 4.00 10.00
138 Braylon Edwards .20 .50
139 Malcom Floyd .20 .50
140 Matt Ryan .25 .60
141 Jay Cutler .20 .50
142 Jeremy Maclin .20 .50
143 LaDainian Tomlinson .30 .75
144 Allen Bailey RC .50 1.25
145 Dwayne Harris RC .50 1.25
146 Mike Williams .25 .60
147 Steve Johnson .20 .50
148 Tim Tebow .30 .75
149 Alex Green RC .50 1.25
150A A.J. Green RC 1.25 3.00
150B A.J. Green SP 10.00 25.00
151 Quinton Carter RC .50 1.25
152 Cedric Benson .20 .50
153 Julius Peppers .25 .60
154 Marques Colston .20 .50
155 Clay Matthews .30 .75
156 Aaron Williams RC .50 1.25
157 Vincent Jackson .20 .50
158 Ed Reed .25 .60
159 T.J. Yates RC .50 1.25
160 Tony Romo .25 .60
161 DeAngelo Williams .20 .50
162 Brandon Lloyd .20 .50
163 Jacquizz Rodgers RC .50 1.25
164 James Carpenter RC .60 1.50
165A Christian Ponder RC .50 1.25
165B Christian Ponder SP 4.00 10.00
166 Akeem Ayers RC .50 1.25
167 Christian Ballard RC .50 1.25
168 Dion Lewis RC .60 1.50
169 Ryan Whalen RC .50 1.25
170 Mark Sanchez .20 .50
171 Marvin Austin RC .50 1.25
172 Deion Branch .20 .50
173A DeMarco Murray RC 1.00 2.50
173B DeMarco Murray SP 8.00 20.00
174 Tandon Doss RC .50 1.25
175 Bruce Carter RC .50 1.25
176 Chris Cooley .20 .50
177 Josh Freeman .25 .60
178 Robert Quinn RC .50 1.25
179 DeMarcus Ware .25 .60
180 Troy Polamalu .30 .75
181A Jamie Harper RC .50 1.25
181B Jamie Harper SP 4.00 10.00
182 Brandon Harris RC .50 1.25
183 Jonathan Stewart .20 .50
184A Shane Vereen RC .60 1.50
184B Shane Vereen SP 5.00 12.00
185A Jake Locker RC .50 1.25
185B Jake Locker SP 4.00 10.00
186 Brandon Jacobs .20 .50
187 Shonn Greene .20 .50
188 Jordan Shipley .20 .50
189 Casey Matthews RC .50 1.25
190 Michael Turner .20 .50
191A Jerrel Jernigan RC .50 1.25
191B Jerrel Jernigan SP 4.00 10.00
192 Muhammad Wilkerson RC .50 1.25
193 Stevan Ridley RC .50 1.25
194 Kealoha Pilares RC .50 1.25
195 Miles Austin .20 .50
196 Cecil Shorts RC .50 1.25
197 Jahvid Best .20 .50
198 Donovan McNabb .25 .60
199 Vernon Davis .20 .50
200 Steven Jackson .20 .50
201 Frank Gore .25 .60
202 Pierre Garcon .25 .60
203A Kyle Rudolph RC .50 1.25
203B Kyle Rudolph SP 4.00 10.00
204 Ronald Johnson RC .50 1.25
205 Aldrick Robinson RC .60 1.50
206 Roy Helu RC .50 1.25
207 Ahmad Bradshaw .20 .50
208 Austin Pettis RC .50 1.25
209 Roddy White .20 .50
210 Ray Rice .20 .50
211 Patrick Peterson RC 1.00 2.50
212A Von Miller RC .75 2.00
212B Von Miller SP 6.00 15.00
213 Anthony Castonzo RC .50 1.25
214 Carson Palmer .25 .60
215 Nate Solder RC .50 1.25
216 Stephen Paea RC .50 1.25
217 Nick Fairley RC .50 1.25
218 Rashard Mendenhall .20 .50
219 Allen Bradford RC .50 1.25
220 Adrian Peterson .30 .75

2011 Topps Chrome Black Refractors

ETS/299: 5X TO 12X BASIC CARDS
*ROOKIES/299: 2X TO 5X BASIC CARDS
BLACK REF/299 ODDS 1:30 HOB

2011 Topps Chrome Blue Refractors

*VETS/199: 6X TO 15X BASIC CARDS
*ROOKIES/199: 2.5X TO 6X BASIC CARDS
BLUE REF/199 ODDS 1:47
104 J.J. Watt 25.00 50.00

2011 Topps Chrome Crystal Atomic Refractors

ETS/139: 8X TO 20X BASIC CARDS
*ROOKIES/139: 3X TO 8X BASIC CARDS
CRYSTAL ATOMIC/139 ODDS 1:24 HOB

2011 Topps Chrome Gold Refractors

*VETS/50: 10X TO 25X BASIC CARDS
*ROOKIES/50: 4X TO 10X BASIC CARDS
1 Cam Newton 75.00 150.00
25 Colin Kaepernick 8.00 20.00
51 Andy Dalton 20.00 50.00

2011 Topps Chrome Orange Refractors

*VETS: 3X TO 8X BASIC CARDS
*ROOKIES: 1.2X TO 3X BASIC CARDS

2011 Topps Chrome Purple Refractors

*VETS/499: 4X TO 10X BASIC CARDS
*ROOKIES/499: 1.5X TO 4X BASIC CARDS

2011 Topps Chrome Red Refractors

*VETS/25: 12X TO 30X BASIC CARDS
*ROOKIES/25: 6X TO 15X BASIC CARDS
1 Cam Newton 125.00 250.00
51 Andy Dalton 50.00 100.00
150 A.J. Green 40.00 80.00

2011 Topps Chrome Refractors

ETS: 2.5X TO 6X BASIC CARDS
*ROOKIES: 1X TO 2.5X BASIC CARDS

2011 Topps Chrome Sepia Refractors

ETS/99: 6X TO 15X BASIC CARDS
*ROOKIES/99: 2.5X TO 6X BASIC CARDS
1 Cam Newton 50.00 120.00
25 Colin Kaepernick 5.00 12.00

2011 Topps Chrome Xfractors

*VETS: 3X TO 8X BASIC CARDS
*ROOKIES: 1.2X TO 3X BASIC CARDS

2011 Topps Chrome Finest Freshman

MPLETE SET (36) 12.00 30.00
STATED ODDS 1:6 HOB
*ATOMIC REF/50: 3X TO 8X BASIC INSERTS
*GOLD REF/75: 2.5X TO 6X BASIC INSERTS
*REFRACT/99: 2X TO 5X BASIC INSERTS
FFAD Andy Dalton .75 2.00
FFAG Alex Green .40 1.00
FFAJG A.J. Green 1.00 2.50
FFAP Austin Pettis .40 1.00
FFBG Blaine Gabbert .40 1.00
FFBP Bilal Powell .50 1.25
FFCK Colin Kaepernick .60 1.50
FFCM Cam Newton 2.00 5.00
FFCP Christian Ponder .40 1.00
FFDC Dolono Cortor .40 1.00
FFDM DeMarco Murray .75 2.00
FFDT Daniel Thomas .40 1.00
FFEG Edmond Gates .40 1.00
FFGL Greg Little .50 1.25
FFJB Jon Baldwin .40 1.00
FFJH Jamie Harper .40 1.00
FFJJ Julio Jones 1.25 3.00
FFJJE Jerrel Jernigan .40 1.00
FFJL Jake Locker .40 1.00
FFJT Jordan Todman .40 1.00
FFKH Kendall Hunter .40 1.00
FFKR Kyle Rudolph .40 1.00
FFLH Leonard Hankerson .40 1.00
FFMD Marcell Dareus .40 1.00
FFMI Mark Ingram .60 1.50
FFML Mikel Leshoure .40 1.00
FFRC Randall Cobb .60 1.50
FFRM Ryan Mallett .40 1.00
FFRW Ryan Williams .40 1.00
FFSR Stevan Ridley .40 1.00
FFSV Shane Vereen .50 1.25
FFTJ Taiwan Jones .40 1.00
FFTS Torrey Smith .40 1.00
FFTY Titus Young .40 1.00
FFVB Vincent Brown .40 1.00
FFVM Von Miller .60 1.50

2011 Topps Chrome Rookie Autographs

OUP A ODDS 1:502 HOB
GROUP B ODDS 1:153 HOB
GROUP C ODDS 1:50 HOB
EXCH EXPIRATION: 10/31/2014
1 Cam Newton A 125.00 200.00
9 Ryan Kerrigan C 4.00 10.00
13 Lance Kendricks 3.00 8.00
22 Edmond Gates C 3.00 8.00
25 Colin Kaepernick A 40.00 80.00
37 Aldon Smith C 3.00 8.00
42 Vincent Brown C 3.00 8.00
50 Mark Ingram A 12.00 30.00
51 Andy Dalton A 15.00 40.00
55 Blaine Gabbert A 5.00 12.00
61 Taiwan Jones C 3.00 8.00
62 Kendall Hunter C 6.00 15.00
65 D.J. Williams B 3.00 8.00
71 Ryan Williams A 8.00 20.00
74 Mikel Leshoure B 6.00 15.00
86 Greg McElroy C 5.00 12.00
88 Greg Little B 6.00 15.00
93 Randall Cobb B 5.00 12.00
97 Torrey Smith B 3.00 8.00
106 Delone Carter C 3.00 8.00
111 Leonard Hankerson B 3.00 8.00
116 Greg Salas C 3.00 8.00
122 Ryan Mallett A 5.00 12.00
123 Jon Baldwin B 8.00 20.00
124 Marcell Dareus B 3.00 8.00
128 Bilal Powell C 4.00 10.00
135 Jordan Todman C 3.00 8.00
136 Daniel Thomas C 3.00 8.00
137 Titus Young B 3.00 8.00
145 Dwayne Harris B 6.00 15.00
149 Alex Green C 5.00 12.00
150 A.J. Green A 40.00 80.00
165 Christian Ponder A 6.00 15.00
166 Akeem Ayers C 3.00 8.00
168 Dion Lewis C 4.00 10.00
173 DeMarco Murray C 6.00 15.00
181 Jamie Harper C 3.00 8.00
184 Shane Vereen C 4.00 10.00
185 Jake Locker A 5.00 12.00
191 Jerrel Jernigan C 4.00 10.00
193 Stevan Ridley C 3.00 8.00
203 Kyle Rudolph C 3.00 8.00
204 Ronald Johnson C 3.00 8.00
208 Austin Pettis C 3.00 8.00
212 Von Miller B 8.00 20.00

2011 Topps Chrome Rookie Autographs Black Refractors

*BLK REF/25: 1.2X TO 3X BASE AU GRP A
*BLK REF/25: 1.5X TO 4X BASE AU GRP B-C
BLACK REF/25 ODDS 1:836 HOB
1 Cam Newton 300.00 600.00
25 Colin Kaepernick 125.00 250.00
51 Andy Dalton 100.00 200.00
173 DeMarco Murray 30.00 80.00

2011 Topps Chrome Rookie Autographs Crystal Atomic Refractors

*ATOM.REF/50: .8X TO 2X BASE AU GRP A
*ATOM.REF/50: 1X TO 2.5X BASE AU GRP B-C
ATOMIC REF/50 ODDS 1:341 HOB
1 Cam Newton 250.00 500.00
25 Colin Kaepernick 75.00 150.00
173 DeMarco Murray 20.00 50.00

2011 Topps Chrome Rookie Autographs Refractors

*REF/99: .6X TO 1.5X BASE AU GRP A
*REF/99: .8X TO 2X BASE AU GRP B-C
REFRACTOR/99 ODDS 1:462 HOB
1 Cam Newton 150.00 300.00
25 Colin Kaepernick 60.00 125.00
165 Christian Ponder 8.00 20.00
173 DeMarco Murray 15.00 40.00
185 Jake Locker 8.00 20.00

2011 Topps Chrome Rookie Autographs Refractors Variations

*UNNUMBERED REF: .4X TO 1X REF AU/99
UNNUMBERED REF ODDS 1:572 HOB
1 Cam Newton 200.00 350.00
25 Colin Kaepernick 40.00 100.00
131 Julio Jones 100.00 175.00
173 DeMarco Murray 12.00 30.00

2011 Topps Chrome Rookie Autographs Dual

DUAL AUTO/25 ODDS 1:16,500 HOB
CDRA1 C.Newton/J.Locker 50.00 100.00
CDRA2 A.Green/J.Jones 60.00 120.00
CDRA3 M.Ingram/J.Jones 75.00 150.00
CDRA4 B.Gabbert/C.Ponder 12.00 30.00
CDRA5 A.Green/J.Baldwin 40.00 80.00

2011 Topps Chrome Rookie Autographs Patch

PATCH AU/25 ODDS 1:795 HOB
AD Andy Dalton 100.00 200.00
AG Alex Green 12.00 30.00
AJG A.J. Green 100.00 200.00
AP Austin Pettis 12.00 30.00
BG Blaine Gabbert 12.00 30.00
BP Bilal Powell 15.00 40.00
CK Colin Kaepernick 100.00 200.00
CN Cam Newton 150.00 300.00
CP Christian Ponder 12.00 30.00
DC Delone Carter 12.00 30.00
DM DeMarco Murray 25.00 60.00
DT Daniel Thomas 12.00 30.00
EG Edmond Gates 12.00 30.00
GL Greg Little 15.00 40.00
JB Jon Baldwin 30.00 80.00
JH Leonard Hankerson 12.00 30.00
JH Jamie Harper 12.00 30.00
JJ Julio Jones 100.00 175.00
JJE Jerrel Jernigan 12.00 30.00
JL Jake Locker 12.00 30.00
JT Jordan Todman 12.00 30.00
KH Kendall Hunter 25.00 60.00
KR Kyle Rudolph 25.00 60.00
MD Marcell Dareus 12.00 30.00
MI Mark Ingram 100.00 175.00
ML Mikel Leshoure 12.00 30.00
RC Randall Cobb EXCH 20.00 60.00
RM Ryan Mallett 12.00 30.00
RW Ryan Williams 12.00 30.00
SR Stevan Ridley 12.00 30.00
SV Shane Vereen 15.00 40.00
TJ Taiwan Jones 12.00 30.00
TS Torrey Smith 12.00 30.00
TY Titus Young 12.00 30.00
VB Vincent Brown 12.00 30.00
VM Von Miller 30.00 80.00

2011 Topps Chrome Rookie Recognition

COMPLETE SET (36) 20.00 50.00
STATED ODDS 1:12 HOB
RRAD Andy Dalton 1.00 2.50
RRAG Alex Green .50 1.25
RRAJG A.J. Green 1.25 3.00
RRAP Austin Pettis .60 1.50
RRBG Blaine Gabbert .50 1.25
RRBP Bilal Powell .60 1.50
RRCK Colin Kaepernick .75 2.00
RRCM Cam Newton 2.50 6.00
RRCP Christian Ponder .50 1.25
RRDC Delone Carter .50 1.25
RRDM DeMarco Murray 1.00 2.50
RRDT Daniel Thomas .50 1.25
RREG Edmond Gates .50 1.25
RRGL Greg Little .60 1.50
RRJB Jon Baldwin .50 1.25
RRJH Jamie Harper .60 1.50
RRJJ Julio Jones 1.50 4.00
RRJJE Jerrel Jernigan .50 1.25
RRJL Jake Locker .50 1.25
RRJT Jordan Todman .50 1.25
RRKH Kendall Hunter .50 1.25
RRKR Kyle Rudolph .50 1.25
RRLH Leonard Hankerson .50 1.25
RRMD Marcell Dareus .50 1.25
RRMI Mark Ingram .75 2.00
RRML Mikel Leshoure .50 1.25
RRRC Randall Cobb .75 2.00
RRRM Ryan Mallett .50 1.25
RRRW Ryan Williams .50 1.25
RRSR Stevan Ridley .50 1.25
RRSV Shane Vereen .60 1.50
RRTJ Taiwan Jones .50 1.25
RRTS Torrey Smith .50 1.25
RRTY Titus Young .50 1.25
RRVB Vincent Brown .50 1.25
RRVM Von Miller .75 2.00

2011 Topps Chrome Rookie Recognition Autographs

STATED ODDS 1:818 HOB
RRAAD Andy Dalton EXCH 30.00 60.00
RRAAG Alex Green
RRAAJG A.J. Green 40.00 100.00
RRAAP Austin Pettis 5.00 12.00
RRABG Blaine Gabbert 5.00 12.00
RRABP Bilal Powell 6.00 15.00
RRACK Colin Kaepernick 40.00 80.00
RRACM Cam Newton 150.00 300.00
RRACP Christian Ponder 5.00 12.00
RRADC Delone Carter 5.00 12.00
RRADM DeMarco Murray 10.00 25.00
RRADT Daniel Thomas 5.00 12.00
RRAEG Edmond Gates 5.00 12.00
RRAGL Greg Little 10.00 25.00
RRAJB Jon Baldwin 20.00 40.00
RRAJH Jamie Harper 5.00 12.00
RRAJJ Julio Jones
RRAJJE Jerrel Jernigan 5.00 12.00
RRAJL Jake Locker 5.00 12.00
RRAJT Jordan Todman 5.00 12.00
RRAKH Kendall Hunter 10.00 25.00
RRAKR Kyle Rudolph 5.00 12.00
RRALH Leonard Hankerson 5.00 12.00
RRAMI Mark Ingram 8.00 20.00
RRAML Mikel Leshoure 5.00 12.00
RRARC Randall Cobb 8.00 20.00
RRARM Ryan Mallett 5.00 12.00
RRARW Ryan Williams 12.00 30.00
RRASR Stevan Ridley 5.00 12.00
RRASV Shane Vereen 6.00 15.00
RRATJ Taiwan Jones 10.00 25.00
RRATS Torrey Smith 5.00 12.00
RRATY Titus Young 5.00 12.00
RRAVB Vincent Brown 5.00 12.00
RRAVM Von Miller 12.00 30.00

2011 Topps Chrome Superlative Rookies

STATED ODDS 1:24 HOB
*BLUE REF/50: 1.5X TO 4X BASIC INSERTS
SRAD Andy Dalton 1.50 4.00
SRAG Alex Green .75 2.00
SRAJG A.J. Green 2.00 5.00
SRAP Austin Pettis .75 2.00
SRBG Blaine Gabbert .75 2.00
SRBP Bilal Powell 1.00 2.50
SRCK Colin Kaepernick 1.25 3.00
SRCM Cam Newton 4.00 10.00
SRCP Christian Ponder .75 2.00
SRDC Delone Carter .75 2.00
SRDM DeMarco Murray 1.50 4.00
SRDT Daniel Thomas .75 2.00
SREG Edmond Gates .75 2.00
SRGL Greg Little 1.00 2.50
SRJB Jon Baldwin .75 2.00
SRJH Jamie Harper .75 2.00
SRJJ Julio Jones 2.50 6.00
SRJJE Jerrel Jernigan .75 2.00
SRJL Jake Locker .75 2.00
SRJT Jordan Todman .75 2.00
SRKH Kendall Hunter .75 2.00
SRKR Kyle Rudolph .75 2.00
SRLH Leonard Hankerson .75 2.00
SRMD Marcell Dareus .75 2.00
SRMI Mark Ingram 1.25 3.00
SRML Mikel Leshoure .75 2.00
SRRC Randall Cobb 1.25 3.00
SRRM Ryan Mallett .75 2.00
SRRW Ryan Williams .75 2.00
SRSR Stevan Ridley .75 2.00
SRSV Shane Vereen 1.00 2.50
SRTJ Taiwan Jones .75 2.00
SRTS Torrey Smith .75 2.00
SRTY Titus Young .75 2.00
SRVB Vincent Brown .75 2.00
SRVM Von Miller 1.25 3.00

2011 Topps Chrome Superlative Rookies Red Refractors

*RED REF/25: 2.6X TO 6X BASIC INSERTS
RED REF/25 ODDS 1:2360 HOB
SRCK Colin Kaepernick 8.00 20.00
SRCM Cam Newton 100.00 175.00

2012 Topps Chrome

COMP.SET w/o SP's (220) 30.00 60.00
1A Andrew Luck RC pass 15.00 30.00
1B Andrew Luck SP drop 75.00 135.00
2 Michael Egnew RC .50 1.25
3 Devon Still RC .60 1.50
4 Riley Reiff RC .50 1.25
5 Robert Mathis .20 .50
6 Percy Harvin .20 .50
7 Jay Cutler .20 .50
8 Brian Orakpo .25 .60
9 Doug Baldwin .30 .75
10 Derek Wolfe RC .60 1.50
11 Jared Crick RC .50 1.25
12 Rob Gronkowski .30 .75
13A Justin Blackmon RC cut .50 1.25
13B J.Blackmon SP frwrd 3.00 8.00
14 Miles Austin .20 .50
15 Alfonzo Dennard RC .50 1.25
16 Keshawn Martin RC .60 1.50
17A Dwayne Allen RC hlmt .50 1.25
17B D.Allen SP no hlmt 3.00 8.00
18 Frank Gore .25 .60
19 Marques Colston .20 .50
20 Cam Newton .30 .75
21 DeMarco Murray .25 .60
22 Von Miller .25 .60
23A T.Rchardson RC cut .50 1.25
23B T.Richardson SP frwrd 3.00 8.00
24 Vernon Davis .20 .50
25 Roddy White .20 .50
26 Stephon Gilmore RC .60 1.50
27 Kellen Moore RC .60 1.50
28 Dre Kirkpatrick RC .50 1.25
29 Mark Barron RC .50 1.25
30 Philip Rivers .30 .75
31 Ndamukong Suh .25 .60
32 Randy Moss .25 .60
33 Darrelle Revis .20 .50
34 Matt Schaub .20 .50
35 Dez Bryant .30 .75
36 Brandon Boykin RC .60 1.50
37 Dwayne Bowe .25 .60
38 Lamar Miller RC .75 2.00
39 Maurice Jones-Drew .20 .50
40A Russell Wilson RC stnds 8.00 20.00
40B R.Wilson SP grn bckgrnd 40.00 80.00
41 Greg Childs RC .50 1.25
42 Jake Bequette RC .75 2.00
43 Travis Benjamin RC .50 1.25
44 Chris Johnson .20 .50
45 Luke Kuechly RC 1.25 3.00
46 Matt Hasselbeck .20 .50
47 T.J. Graham RC .50 1.25
48 Jonathan Martin RC .50 1.25
49 Cyrus Gray RC .50 1.25
50 Aaron Rodgers .50 1.25
51 Ray Rice .20 .50
52 Torrey Smith .20 .50
53 Chris Rainey RC .50 1.25
54 Brandon Marshall .25 .60
55 Blaine Gabbert .20 .50
56 Chandler Harnish RC .50 1.25
57 Michael Brockers RC .50 1.25
58 Charles Woodson .30 .75
59 Jeremy Maclin .20 .50
60 Aaron Corp RC .50 1.25
61 Marvin McNutt RC .50 1.25
62A Alshon Jeffery RC ctch 2.00 5.00
62B Alshon Jeffery SP run 6.00 15.00
63 Tony Romo .25 .60
64 Jermichael Finley .20 .50
65 Brandon Taylor RC .50 1.25
66 Josh Cribbs .20 .50
67 Casey Hayward RC .50 1.25
68 Robert Turbin RC .50 1.25
69 Matt Forte .20 .50
70A Rueben Randle RC cut .50 1.25
70B R.Randle SP leap 3.00 8.00
71 Courtney Upshaw RC .60 1.50
72 Cordy Glenn RC .60 1.50
73 Jimmy Graham .30 .75
74 Steve Johnson .25 .60
75 Reggie Bush .20 .50
76 Jason Pierre-Paul .20 .50
77 Harrison Smith RC .50 1.25
78 LeSean McCoy .30 .75
79A B.Weeden RC frwrd .50 1.25
79B B.Weeden SP sideways 3.00 8.00
80 Patrick Willis .25 .60
81 Tommy Streeter RC .50 1.25
82 Fletcher Cox RC .75 2.00
83 Anquan Boldin .20 .50
84 Mike Williams .25 .60
85 A.J. Green .30 .75
86 Daniel Thomas .20 .50
87 Steven Jackson .20 .50
88 Alex Smith .25 .60
89 Orson Charles RC .50 1.25
90 Dwight Bentley RC .60 1.50
91 Matt Ryan .25 .60
92 DeSean Jackson .25 .60
93 Jerel Worthy RC .50 1.25
94 Dontari Poe RC .50 1.25
95 Sam Bradford .20 .50
96 Peter Konz RC .50 1.25
97 Ahmad Bradshaw .20 .50
98A Mohamed Sanu RC cut .75 2.00
98B Mohamed Sanu SP leap 5.00 12.00
99A Brian Quick RC leap .50 1.25
99B Brian Quick SP cut 3.00 8.00
100 Drew Brees .30 .75
101 Antonio Allen RC .50 1.25
102 Tamba Hali .20 .50
103 Eli Manning .25 .60
104 Andre Branch RC .50 1.25
105 Ryan Lindley RC .50 1.25
106 Antonio Brown .30 .75
107 Darren McFadden .20 .50
108 Matt Kalil RC .50 1.25
109A Ryan Tannehill RC w/FB .75 2.00
109B Ryan Tannehill SP no FB 5.00 12.00
110 Jon Baldwin .20 .50
111 Whitney Mercilus RC .50 1.25
112 Aaron Hernandez .25 .60
113 Dan Herron RC .50 1.25
114 DeVier Posey RC .50 1.25
115 Calvin Johnson .30 .75
116 Kendall Reyes RC .50 1.25
117 Ryan Mathews .25 .60
118 Devon Wylie RC .50 1.25
119 Mark Sanchez .20 .50
120 Michael Vick .25 .60
121 Ray Lewis .30 .75
122 Quinton Coples RC .50 1.25
123 Shea McClellin RC .60 1.50
124 Santonio Holmes .20 .50
125 Troy Polamalu .30 .75
126 Matthew Stafford .25 .60
127 LeGarrette Blount .25 .60
128 Janoris Jenkins RC .60 1.50
129 Wes Welker .25 .60
130 Michael Turner .20 .50
131 Vinny Curry RC .60 1.50
132 Marshawn Lynch .25 .60
133 Joe Adams RC .50 1.25
134 DeMarcus Ware .30 .75
135 Jake Locker .30 .75
136 Darren Sproles .25 .60
137 Tavon Wilson RC .60 1.50
138 David DeCastro RC .50 1.25
139 Ryan Fitzpatrick .20 .50
140 Chandler Jones RC .50 1.25
141 Larry Fitzgerald .25 .60
142 Chris Givens RC .50 1.25
143 Brandon Thompson RC .60 1.50
144 Clay Matthews .30 .75
145 Josh Freeman .25 .60
146 Kirk Cousins RC 2.00 5.00
147A Doug Martin RC catch .75 2.00
147B Doug Martin SP run 5.00 12.00
148 Melvin Ingram RC .50 1.25
149 Jordan White RC .60 1.50
150 Willis McGahee .20 .50
151 Dwight Freeney .20 .50
152 Zach Brown RC .50 1.25
153A Nick Foles RC pass 1.25 3.00
153B N.Foles SP drop back 8.00 20.00
154 Jared Allen .20 .50
155 Andre Johnson .25 .60
156A A.J. Jenkins RC run .50 1.25
156B A.J. Jenkins SP Hsmn 3.00 8.00
157 Greg Jennings .20 .50
158 Adrian Peterson .30 .75
159 Cam Johnson RC .75 2.00
160 Hakeem Nicks .20 .50
161 Peyton Manning .60 1.50
162 Carson Palmer .25 .60
163 Markelle Martin RC .60 1.50
164 Andy Dalton .25 .60
165 Joe Flacco .25 .60
166A M.Floyd RC team nme .50 1.25
166B M.Floyd SP no tm nme 3.00 8.00
167 Fred Jackson .25 .60
168 T.Y. Hilton RC 1.00 2.50
169 Vick Ballard RC .60 1.50
170 Mike Wallace .20 .50
171 Mark Ingram .25 .60
172 Eric LeGrand RC .50 1.25
173 Terrance Ganaway RC .60 1.50
174 Beanie Wells .20 .50
175A Stephen Hill RC cut .50 1.25
175B Stephen Hill SP Hsmn 3.00 8.00
176 Bruce Irvin RC .60 1.50
177 Kelechi Osemele RC .50 1.25
178 Terrell Suggs .20 .50
179 Jordy Nelson .25 .60
180 Tim Tebow .30 .75
181 Mario Williams .20 .50
182 Ben Roethlisberger .30 .75
183 Christian Ponder .20 .50
184 Tim Hightower .20 .50
185 Nick Perry RC .60 1.50
186A R.Broyles RC bth hnds .50 1.25
186B R.Broyles SP one hnd 3.00 8.00
187 Morris Claiborne RC .50 1.25
188 Steve Smith .25 .60
189A D.Wilson RC one hnd .50 1.25
189B D.Wilson SP both hnds 3.00 8.00
190 Reggie Wayne .25 .60
191A L.James RC stnds .50 1.25
191B L.James SP grn bckgrn 3.00 8.00
192 Ronnie Hillman RC .50 1.25
193 Nick Toon RC .50 1.25
194 Marvin Jones RC .50 1.25
195 Juron Criner RC .50 1.25
196 Billy Winn RC .75 2.00
197 Mike Adams RC .50 1.25
198 Lavonte David RC .75 2.00
199 Vincent Jackson .20 .50
200A R.Griffin III RC maroon .60 1.50
200B R.Griffin III SP white 4.00 10.00
201 Earl Thomas .25 .60
202A Isaiah Pead RC cut .50 1.25
202B Isaiah Pead SP leap 3.00 8.00
203 Jarius Wright RC .50 1.25
204 Rishard Matthews RC .50 1.25
205 George Iloka RC .50 1.25
206 Arian Foster .25 .60
207 Kevin Zeitler RC .50 1.25
208 Antonio Gates .25 .60
209A C.Fleener RC catch .50 1.25
209B C.Fleener SP cuttng 3.00 8.00
210A B.Osweiler RC fwd .50 1.25
210B B.Osweiler SP right 3.00 8.00
211 Mychal Kendricks RC .75 2.00
212A K.Wright RC FB in hands .50 1.25
212B K.Wright SP no FB 3.00 8.00
213A B.Pierce RC catch .50 1.25
213B B.Pierce SP run fwd 3.00 8.00
214 Gerell Robinson RC .50 1.25
215 D'Qwell Jackson .20 .50
216 Victor Cruz .25 .60
217 Julio Jones .30 .75
218 Roy Helu .20 .50
219 Dont'a Hightower RC .75 2.00
220 Tom Brady .75 2.00

2012 Topps Chrome Black Refractors

*VETS/299: 4X TO 10X BASIC CARDS
*ROOKIES/299: 1.5X TO 4X BASIC CARDS
STATED PRINT RUN 299 SER.#'d SETS
1 Andrew Luck 50.00 120.00
40 Russell Wilson 30.00 80.00

2012 Topps Chrome Blue Refractors

*VETS/199: 5X TO 12X BASIC CARDS
*ROOKIES/199: 2X TO 5X BASIC CARDS
STATED PRINT RUN 199 SER.#'d SETS
1 Andrew Luck 125.00 200.00
40 Russell Wilson 50.00 100.00

2012 Topps Chrome Camo Refractors

*VETS/499: 3X TO 8X BASIC CARDS
*ROOKIES/499: 1.2X TO 3X BASIC CARDS
STATED PRINT RUN 499 SER.#'d SETS
1 Andrew Luck 50.00 120.00
40 Russell Wilson 30.00 60.00

2012 Topps Chrome Gold Refractors

*VETS/50: 10X TO 25X BASIC CARDS
*ROOKIES/50: 4X TO 10X BASIC CARDS
STATED PRINT RUN 50 SER.#'d SETS
1 Andrew Luck 250.00 500.00
40 Russell Wilson 125.00 200.00

2012 Topps Chrome Orange Refractors

*VETS: 2X TO 5X BASIC CARDS
*ROOKIES: .8X TO 2X BASIC CARDS
INSERTS IN RETAIL RACK PACKS
200 Robert Griffin III 1.25 3.00

2012 Topps Chrome Pink Refractors

*VETS/399: 3X TO 8X BASIC CARDS
*ROOKIES/399: 1.2X TO 3X BASIC CARDS
STATED PRINT RUN 399 SER.#'d SETS
1 Andrew Luck 50.00 120.00
40 Russell Wilson 20.00 50.00

2012 Topps Chrome Prism Refractors

ETS/216: 4X TO 10X BASIC CARDS
*ROOKIES/216: 1.5X TO 4X BASIC CARDS
STATED PRINT RUN 216 SER.#'d SETS
1 Andrew Luck 100.00 200.00
40 Russell Wilson 30.00 80.00

2012 Topps Chrome Purple Refractors

*VETS/499: 3X TO 8X BASIC CARDS
*ROOKIES/499: 1.2X TO 3X BASIC CARDS
PURPLE/499 INSERTED IN RETAIL PACKS
1 Andrew Luck 50.00 120.00
40 Russell Wilson 20.00 50.00

2012 Topps Chrome Red Refractors

*VETS/25: 12X TO 30X BASIC CARDS
*ROOKIES/25: 5X TO 12X BASIC CARDS
STATED PRINT RUN 25 SER.#'d SETS
1 Andrew Luck 500.00 1000.00
40 Russell Wilson 200.00 350.00

2012 Topps Chrome Refractors

ETS: 1.5X TO 4X BASIC CARDS
*ROOKIES: .6X TO 1.5X BASIC RC
*ROOKIE SP: .6X TO 1.5X RC SP
RANDOM INSERTS IN PACKS
1B Andrew Luck SP drop 125.00 200.00

2012 Topps Chrome Sepia Refractors

*VETS/99: 6X TO 15X BASIC CARDS
*ROOKIES/99: 2.5X TO 6X BASIC CARDS
STATED PRINT RUN 99 SER.#'d SETS
1 Andrew Luck 100.00 200.00
40 Russell Wilson 60.00 120.00

2012 Topps Chrome Xfractors

*VETS: 2X TO 5X BASIC CARDS
*ROOKIES: .8X TO 2X BASIC CARDS
RANDOM INSERTS IN PACKS
1 Andrew Luck 30.00 60.00

2012 Topps Chrome 1957

COMPLETE SET (30) 15.00 40.00
*REFRACT/99: 1.5X TO 4X BASIC INSERTS
1 Andrew Luck 8.00 20.00
2 Andrew Luck 8.00 20.00
3 Robert Griffin III .50 1.25
4 Robert Griffin III .50 1.25
5 Trent Richardson .40 1.00
6 Trent Richardson .40 1.00
7 Ryan Tannehill .60 1.50
8 Ryan Tannehill .60 1.50
9 Justin Blackmon .40 1.00
10 Justin Blackmon .40 1.00
11 Rueben Randle .40 1.00
12 Rueben Randle .40 1.00
13 Michael Floyd .40 1.00
14 Michael Floyd .40 1.00
15 Kendall Wright .40 1.00
16 Kendall Wright .40 1.00
17 Brandon Weeden .40 1.00
18 Brandon Weeden .40 1.00
19 Coby Fleener .40 1.00
20 Coby Fleener .40 1.00
21 David Wilson .40 1.00
22 David Wilson .40 1.00
23 Lamar Miller .60 1.50
24 Lamar Miller .60 1.50
25 Doug Martin .60 1.50
26 Doug Martin .60 1.50
27 Brock Osweiler .40 1.00
28 Brock Osweiler .40 1.00
29 Stephen Hill .40 1.00
30 Stephen Hill .40 1.00

2012 Topps Chrome 1957 Refractors Autographs

EXCH EXPIRATION: 10/31/2015
EXCH HAS TWO CARDS EQUAL VALUE
1 Andrew Luck 250.00 500.00
3 Robert Griffin III 40.00 80.00
5 Trent Richardson 30.00 80.00
7 Ryan Tannehill 10.00 25.00
9 Justin Blackmon 6.00 15.00
11 Rueben Randle 6.00 15.00
13 Michael Floyd 20.00 50.00
15 Kendall Wright 6.00 15.00
17 Brandon Weeden 6.00 15.00
19 Coby Fleener 6.00 15.00
21 David Wilson 6.00 15.00
23 Lamar Miller 10.00 25.00
25 Doug Martin 15.00 40.00
27 Brock Osweiler 6.00 15.00
29 Stephen Hill 12.00 30.00

2012 Topps Chrome 1965

COMPLETE SET (35) 30.00 80.00
*REFRACT/99: 1.5X TO 4X BASIC INSERTS
1 Andrew Luck 6.00 15.00
2 Ryan Tannehill .75 2.00
3 Nick Foles 1.25 3.00
4 Michael Floyd .50 1.25
5 Kendall Wright .50 1.25
6 Brandon Weeden .50 1.25
7 Michael Egnew .50 1.25
8 David Wilson .50 1.25
9 Lamar Miller .75 2.00
10 Robert Griffin III .60 1.50
11 Brock Osweiler .50 1.25
12 Russell Wilson 5.00 12.00
13 A.J. Jenkins .50 1.25
14 Chris Givens .50 1.25
15 Mohamed Sanu .75 2.00
16 Rueben Randle .50 1.25
17 Nick Toon .50 1.25
18 Isaiah Pead .50 1.25
19 Doug Martin .75 2.00
20 Trent Richardson .50 1.25
21 LaMichael James .50 1.25
22 Brian Quick .50 1.25
23 Robert Turbin .50 1.25
24 DeVier Posey .50 1.25
25 Bernard Pierce .50 1.25
26 Alshon Jeffery 1.00 2.50
27 Coby Fleener .50 1.25
28 Jarius Wright .50 1.25
29 Dwayne Allen .50 1.25
30 Justin Blackmon .50 1.25
31 Stephen Hill .50 1.25
32 Ryan Broyles .50 1.25
33 Joe Adams .50 1.25
34 Ronnie Hillman .50 1.25
35 T.J. Graham .50 1.25

2012 Topps Chrome 1965 Prism Refractors

*PRISM REF/50: 3X TO 8X BASIC INSERTS
1 Andrew Luck 75.00 150.00
12 Russell Wilson 40.00 100.00

2012 Topps Chrome 1965 Red Refractors

*RED REF/75: 2.5X TO 6X BASIC INSERTS
1 Andrew Luck 60.00 120.00

2012 Topps Chrome 1965 Refractors Autographs

STATED PRINT RUN 15 SER.#'d SETS
EXCH EXPIRATION: 10/31/2015
1 Andrew Luck 600.00 1000.00
2 Ryan Tannehill 15.00 40.00
3 Nick Foles 25.00 60.00
4 Michael Floyd 40.00 80.00
5 Kendall Wright 10.00 25.00
6 Brandon Weeden 30.00 80.00
7 Michael Egnew 10.00 25.00
8 David Wilson 10.00 25.00
9 Lamar Miller 40.00 80.00
10 Robert Griffin III 75.00 150.00
11 Brock Osweiler 10.00 25.00
12 Russell Wilson 250.00 400.00
13 A.J. Jenkins 10.00 25.00
14 Chris Givens EXCH 10.00 25.00
15 Mohamed Sanu 15.00 40.00
16 Rueben Randle 10.00 25.00
17 Nick Toon EXCH 10.00 25.00
18 Isaiah Pead EXCH 25.00 50.00
19 Doug Martin 15.00 40.00
20 Trent Richardson 60.00 120.00
21 LaMichael James 10.00 25.00
22 Brian Quick 10.00 25.00
23 Robert Turbin 10.00 25.00
24 DeVier Posey 15.00 40.00
25 Bernard Pierce
26 Alshon Jeffery 20.00 50.00
27 Coby Fleener 10.00 25.00
28 Jarius Wright 10.00 25.00
29 Dwayne Allen
30 Justin Blackmon 10.00 25.00
31 Stephen Hill 30.00 60.00
32 Ryan Broyles 10.00 25.00
33 Joe Adams 10.00 25.00
34 Ronnie Hillman 10.00 25.00
35 T.J. Graham 10.00 25.00

2012 Topps Chrome 1984

COMPLETE SET (35) 20.00 50.00
*REFRACT/99: 2X TO 5X BASIC INSERTS
1 Andrew Luck 5.00 12.00
2 Kendall Wright .40 1.00
3 Michael Floyd .40 1.00
4 Nick Foles 1.00 2.50
5 Brandon Weeden .40 1.00
6 Lamar Miller .60 1.50
7 David Wilson .40 1.00
8 Dwayne Allen .40 1.00
9 Brock Osweiler .40 1.00
10 Robert Griffin III .50 1.25
11 Nick Toon .40 1.00
12 Rueben Randle .40 1.00
13 Mohamed Sanu .60 1.50
14 Russell Wilson 5.00 12.00
15 DeVier Posey .40 1.00

16 A.J. Jenkins .40 1.00
17 Isaiah Pead .40 1.00
18 Alshon Jeffery .75 2.00
19 Brian Quick .40 1.00
20 Trent Richardson .40 1.00
21 LaMichael James .40 1.00
22 Doug Martin .60 1.50
23 Bernard Pierce .40 1.00
24 Robert Turbin .40 1.00
25 Ryan Tannehill .60 1.50
26 Coby Fleener .40 1.00
27 Chris Givens .40 1.00
28 Stephen Hill .40 1.00
29 T.J. Graham .40 1.00
30 Justin Blackmon .40 1.00
31 Ryan Broyles .40 1.00
32 Joe Adams .40 1.00
33 Ronnie Hillman .40 1.00
34 Michael Egnew .40 1.00
35 Jarius Wright .40 1.00

2012 Topps Chrome 1984 Gold Refractors

*GOLD REF/75: 2.5X TO 6X BASIC INSERTS
1 Andrew Luck 75.00 150.00
14 Russell Wilson 60.00 120.00

2012 Topps Chrome 1984 Prism Refractors

*PRISM REF/50: 3X TO 8X BASIC INSERTS
1 Andrew Luck 100.00 200.00

2012 Topps Chrome 1984 Refractors Autographs

STATED PRINT RUN 15 SER.#'d SETS
EXCH EXPIRATION: 10/31/2015
1 Andrew Luck 800.00 1200.00
2 Kendall Wright 12.00 30.00
3 Michael Floyd EXCH 12.00 30.00
4 Nick Foles 30.00 80.00
5 Brandon Weeden 40.00 100.00
6 Lamar Miller 50.00 100.00
7 David Wilson 12.00 30.00
8 Dwayne Allen 12.00 30.00
9 Brock Osweiler 12.00 30.00
10 Robert Griffin III 75.00 150.00
11 Nick Toon EXCH 12.00 30.00
12 Rueben Randle 12.00 30.00
13 Mohamed Sanu 20.00 50.00
14 Russell Wilson 350.00 600.00
15 DeVier Posey 20.00 50.00
16 A.J. Jenkins 12.00 30.00
17 Isaiah Pead EXCH 12.00 30.00
18 Alshon Jeffery 50.00 100.00
19 Brian Quick 30.00 60.00
20 Trent Richardson 60.00 120.00
21 LaMichael James EXCH 12.00 30.00
22 Doug Martin 20.00 50.00
23 Bernard Pierce
24 Robert Turbin 40.00 80.00
25 Ryan Tannehill 20.00 50.00
26 Coby Fleener 12.00 30.00
27 Chris Givens EXCH 20.00 50.00
28 Stephen Hill EXCH 40.00 80.00
29 T.J. Graham 12.00 30.00
30 Justin Blackmon 12.00 30.00
31 Ryan Broyles 12.00 30.00
32 Joe Adams 12.00 30.00
33 Ronnie Hillman EXCH 12.00 30.00
34 Michael Egnew 12.00 30.00
35 Jarius Wright 12.00 30.00

2012 Topps Chrome Blue Wave Refractors Autographs

ISSUED VIA MAIL REDEMPTION
BWAAM Alfred Morris 5.00 12.00

2012 Topps Chrome Blue Wave Refractors

*BLUE WAVE REF: 3X TO 8X BASIC RC
ISSUED VIA MAIL REDEMPTION
BW1 Andrew Luck 75.00 150.00
BW60 Andrew Luck 75.00 150.00

2012 Topps Chrome Dual Rookie Autographs

STATED PRINT RUN 30 SER.#'d SETS
DRAGW K.Wright/R.Griffin III 40.00 80.00
DRALF C.Fleener/A.Luck 175.00 300.00
DRALG R.Griffin III/A.Luck 250.00 500.00
DRARW B.Weeden/T.Richardson 25.00 60.00
DRAWB J.Blackmon/B.Woodon 25.00 60.00

2012 Topps Chrome Red Zone Rookies Refractors

LUE REF/50: 1.2X TO 3X BASIC INSERTS
RZDC1 Andrew Luck 8.00 20.00
RZDC2 Kendall Wright .75 2.00
RZDC3 Michael Floyd .75 2.00
RZDC4 Nick Foles 2.00 5.00
RZDC5 Brandon Weeden .75 2.00
RZDC6 Lamar Miller 1.25 3.00
RZDC7 David Wilson .75 2.00
RZDC8 Dwayne Allen .75 2.00
RZDC9 Brock Osweiler .75 2.00
RZDC10 Robert Griffin III 1.00 2.50
RZDC11 Nick Toon .75 2.00
RZDC12 Rueben Randle .75 2.00
RZDC13 Mohamed Sanu 1.25 3.00
RZDC14 Russell Wilson 8.00 20.00
RZDC15 DeVier Posey .75 2.00
RZDC16 A.J. Jenkins .75 2.00
RZDC17 Isaiah Pead .75 2.00
RZDC18 Alshon Jeffery 1.50 4.00
RZDC19 Brian Quick .75 2.00
RZDC20 Trent Richardson .75 2.00
RZDC21 LaMichael James .75 2.00
RZDC22 Doug Martin 1.25 3.00
RZDC23 Bernard Pierce .75 2.00
RZDC24 Robert Turbin .75 2.00
RZDC25 Ryan Tannehill 1.25 3.00
RZDC26 Coby Fleener .75 2.00
RZDC27 Chris Givens .75 2.00
RZDC28 Stephen Hill .75 2.00
RZDC29 T.J. Graham .75 2.00
RZDC30 Justin Blackmon .75 2.00
RZDC31 Ryan Broyles .75 2.00
RZDC32 Joe Adams .75 2.00
RZDC33 Ronnie Hillman .75 2.00
RZDC34 Michael Egnew .75 2.00
RZDC35 Jarius Wright .75 2.00

2012 Topps Chrome Red Zone Rookies Gold Refractors

*GOLD REF/25: 2.5X TO 6X BASIC INSERTS
RZDC1 Andrew Luck 75.00 150.00
RZDC10 Robert Griffin III 40.00 80.00

2012 Topps Chrome Rookie Autographs

CH EXPIRATION: 10/31/2015
1 Andrew Luck SP 450.00 800.00
2 Michael Egnew 3.00 8.00
13 Justin Blackmon SP 4.00 10.00
17 Dwayne Allen 8.00 20.00
23 Trent Richardson SP 15.00 40.00
28 Dre Kirkpatrick 6.00 15.00
29 Mark Barron 10.00 25.00
38 Lamar Miller 5.00 12.00
40 Russell Wilson 75.00 150.00
41 Greg Childs 3.00 8.00
43 Travis Benjamin 3.00 8.00
45 Luke Kuechly 25.00 50.00
47 T.J. Graham 3.00 8.00
49 Cyrus Gray 3.00 8.00
53 Chris Rainey 3.00 8.00
62 Alshon Jeffery 15.00 30.00
68 Robert Turbin 3.00 8.00
70 Rueben Randle 6.00 15.00
79 Brandon Weeden SP 8.00 20.00
94 Dontari Poe 3.00 8.00
98 Mohamed Sanu 5.00 12.00
99 Brian Quick 6.00 15.00
108 Matt Kalil 6.00 15.00
109 Ryan Tannehill SP 5.00 12.00
114 DeVier Posey 3.00 8.00
133 Joe Adams 3.00 8.00
147 Doug Martin 6.00 15.00
153 Nick Foles 25.00 50.00
156 A.J. Jenkins 3.00 8.00
166 Michael Floyd SP 12.00 30.00
168 T.Y. Hilton 12.00 30.00
175 Stephen Hill EXCH 3.00 8.00
186 Ryan Broyles 3.00 8.00
189 David Wilson 3.00 8.00
191 LaMichael James SP 8.00 20.00
192 Ronnie Hillman 3.00 8.00
193 Nick Toon 3.00 8.00
195 Juron Criner 3.00 8.00
200 Robert Griffin III SP 40.00 100.00
202 Isaiah Pead 3.00 8.00
203 Jarius Wright 3.00 8.00
209 Coby Fleener 3.00 8.00
210 Brock Osweiler 3.00 8.00
212 Kendall Wright 3.00 8.00
213 Bernard Pierce 6.00 15.00

2012 Topps Chrome Rookie Autographs Black Refractors

*BLACK REF/25: 1.2X TO 3X BASIC AUTO
*BLACK REF/25: 1X TO 2.5X BASIC AU SP
1 Andrew Luck 700.00 1000.00
23 Trent Richardson 30.00 80.00
40 Russell Wilson 200.00 400.00
147 Doug Martin 25.00 60.00

2012 Topps Chrome Rookie Autographs Camo Refractors

*CAMO/105: .8X TO 2X BASIC AUTO
40 Russell Wilson 175.00 350.00

2012 Topps Chrome Rookie Autographs Pink Refractors

*PINK/75: 1X TO 2.5X BASIC AUTO
*PINK/75: .8X TO 2X BASIC AU SP
1 Andrew Luck 350.00 600.00
23 Trent Richardson 25.00 60.00
40 Russell Wilson 250.00 500.00
147 Doug Martin 20.00 50.00

2012 Topps Chrome Rookie Autographs Prism Refractors

*PRISM/50: 1X TO 2.5X BASIC AUTO
*PRISM/50: .8X TO 2X BASIC AU SP
1 Andrew Luck 400.00 700.00
23 Trent Richardson 25.00 60.00
40 Russell Wilson 200.00 400.00
147 Doug Martin 12.00 30.00

2012 Topps Chrome Rookie Autographs Refractors

*REFRACTOR/178: .6X TO 1.5X BASIC AUTO
*REFRACTOR/178: .5X TO 1.2X BASIC AU SP
STATED PRINT RUN 178 SER.#'d SETS
EXCH EXPIRATION: 10/31/2015
40 Russell Wilson 150.00 300.00

2012 Topps Chrome Rookie Autographs Refractors Variations

*UNNUMBERED REF: .8X TO 2X BASIC AU
*UNNUMBERED REF: .6X TO 1.5X BASIC AU SP
1 Andrew Luck 300.00 450.00
13 Justin Blackmon 6.00 15.00
23 Trent Richardson 30.00 80.00
40 Russell Wilson 100.00 200.00
200 Robert Griffin III 100.00 200.00

2012 Topps Chrome Rookie Autographs Patches

STATED PRINT RUN 50 SER.#'d SETS
RAPAJ Alshon Jeffery 15.00 40.00
RAPAJE A.J. Jenkins 8.00 20.00
RAPAL Andrew Luck 300.00 500.00
RAPBP Bernard Pierce 8.00 20.00
RAPBQ Brian Quick 8.00 20.00
RAPBW Brandon Weeden 8.00 20.00
RAPCF Coby Fleener 8.00 20.00
RAPDA Dwayne Allen 8.00 20.00
RAPDM Doug Martin 20.00 50.00
RAPDP DeVier Posey 8.00 20.00
RAPGC Greg Childs 8.00 20.00
RAPIP Isaiah Pead 8.00 20.00
RAPJA Joe Adams 8.00 20.00
RAPJB Justin Blackmon 8.00 20.00
RAPJC Juron Criner 8.00 20.00
RAPJW Jarius Wright 8.00 20.00
RAPKW Kendall Wright 8.00 20.00
RAPLJ LaMichael James 8.00 20.00
RAPLM Lamar Miller 12.00 30.00
RAPME Michael Egnew 8.00 20.00
RAPMF Michael Floyd 20.00 50.00
RAPMS Mohamed Sanu 12.00 30.00
RAPNT Nick Toon 8.00 20.00
RAPRB Ryan Broyles 8.00 20.00
RAPRH Ronnie Hillman 8.00 20.00
RAPRR Rueben Randle 8.00 20.00
RAPRT Robert Turbin 8.00 20.00
RAPRW Russell Wilson 175.00 300.00
RAPSH Stephen Hill 8.00 20.00
RAPTG T.J. Graham 8.00 20.00
RAPTHI T.Y. Hilton 40.00 80.00
RAPTR Trent Richardson 50.00 120.00

2012 Topps Chrome Rookie Relics

*BLACK REF/25: .8X TO 2X BASIC JSY
*PURPLE REF/75: .6X TO 1.5X BASIC JSY
*REF/150: .5X TO 1.2X BASIC JSY
*XFRACTOR/99: .6X TO 1.5X BASIC JSY
RR1 Andrew Luck 12.00 30.00
RR2 Chris Givens 1.25 3.00
RR3 Brock Osweiler 1.25 3.00
RR4 Brandon Weeden 1.25 3.00
RR5 Nick Foles 3.00 8.00
RR6 Isaiah Pead 1.25 3.00
RR8 Lamar Miller 2.00 5.00
RR9 Doug Martin 2.00 5.00
RR10 Trent Richardson 1.25 3.00
RR11 LaMichael James 1.25 3.00
RR12 Bernard Pierce 1.25 3.00
RR13 Ronnie Hillman 1.25 3.00
RR14 Nick Toon 1.25 3.00
RR15 Michael Floyd 1.25 3.00
RR16 Michael Egnew 1.25 3.00
RR17 Jarius Wright 1.25 3.00
RR18 Mohamed Sanu 2.00 5.00
RR19 Rueben Randle 1.25 3.00
RR20 Justin Blackmon 1.25 3.00
RR21 Stephen Hill 1.25 3.00
RR22 Brian Quick 1.25 3.00
RR23 Joe Adams 1.25 3.00
RR24 Dwayne Allen 1.25 3.00
RR25 Coby Fleener 1.25 3.00
RR26 Russell Wilson 15.00 30.00
RR27 Robert Turbin 1.25 3.00
RR28 A.J. Jenkins 1.25 3.00
RR29 DeVier Posey 1.25 3.00
RR30 Ryan Tannehill 2.00 5.00
RR31 Ryan Broyles 1.25 3.00
RR32 T.J. Graham 1.25 3.00
RR33 Kendall Wright 1.25 3.00
RR34 Alshon Jeffery 2.50 6.00
RR35 T.Y. Hilton 2.50 6.00
RR37 Greg Childs 1.25 3.00
RR39 Juron Criner 1.25 3.00
RR40 Robert Griffin III 1.50 4.00

2012 Topps Chrome Rookie Reprint

*REFRACT/99: 3X TO 8X BASIC INSERTS
63 John Elway 1984 1.00 2.50
65 Jim Plunkett 1972 .50 1.25
90 Fran Tarkenton 1962 .60 1.50
90 Sonny Jurgensen 1958 .50 1.25
119 Bart Starr 1957 1.00 2.50
122 Joe Namath 1965 1.25 3.00
123 Dan Marino 1984 1.25 3.00
156 Terry Bradshaw 1971 .75 2.00
196 Bob Griese 1968 .60 1.50
200 Roger Staubach 1972 .75 2.00
216 Joe Montana 1981 1.50 4.00
225 Phil Simms 1980 .50 1.25
251 Warren Moon 1985 .60 1.50
311 Michael Vick 2001 .50 1.25
328 Drew Brees 2001 .75 2.00
362 Jim Kelly 1987 .60 1.50
367 Dan Fouts 1975 .50 1.25
374 Steve Young 1986 .75 2.00
430 Matthew Stafford 2009 .50 1.25
431 Aaron Rodgers 2005 1.25 3.00
487 Ken Stabler 1973 .60 1.50

2012 Topps Chrome Rookie Reprint Refractors Autographs

EXCH EXPIRATION: 10/31/2015
63 John Elway 1984 125.00 200.00
65 Jim Plunkett 1972 25.00 50.00
90 Fran Tarkenton 1962
90 Sonny Jurgensen 1958 25.00 50.00
119 Bart Starr 1957
122 Joe Namath 1965 100.00 175.00
123 Dan Marino 1984 200.00 350.00
156 Terry Bradshaw 1971
196 Bob Griese 1968 30.00 60.00
200 Roger Staubach 1972 50.00 120.00
216 Joe Montana 1981 150.00 250.00
225 Phil Simms 1980
251 Warren Moon 1985
311 Michael Vick 2001 30.00 80.00
328 Drew Brees 2001 75.00 150.00
362 Jim Kelly 1987 40.00 80.00
367 Dan Fouts 1975 30.00 60.00
374 Steve Young 1986 50.00 100.00
430 Matthew Stafford 2009 50.00 100.00
431 Aaron Rodgers 2005
487 Ken Stabler 1973 30.00 60.00

2012 Topps Chrome Triple Rookie Autographs

STATED PRINT RUN 15
TRALGT Tnnhill/RG3/Luck/15 400.00 800.00

2013 Topps Chrome

MP. SET w/o SP's (220) 15.00 40.00
1A Peyton Manning .60 1.50
1B Peyton Manning SP 20.00 40.00
2A Larry Fitzgerald .25 .60
2B Larry Fitzgerald SP 4.00 10.00
3A Robert Woods RC .60 1.50
3B Robert Woods SP 4.00 10.00
4 Tyrann Mathieu RC .60 1.50
5 Zac Dysert RC .40 1.00
6 Marshawn Lynch .25 .60
7 Gavin Escobar RC .40 1.00
8 Rex Burkhead RC .50 1.25
9 D.J. Swearinger RC .40 1.00
10 Chris Harper RC .40 1.00
11A Montee Ball RC .40 1.00
11B Montee Ball SP 2.50 6.00
12 Patrick Willis .25 .60
13 Miguel Maysonet RC .40 1.00
14A Keenan Allen RC .75 2.00
14B Keenan Allen SP 5.00 12.00
15 LeSean McCoy .30 .75
16 D.J. Hayden RC .40 1.00
17 Ezekiel Ansah RC .40 1.00
18A Justin Hunter RC .40 1.00
18B Justin Hunter SP 2.50 6.00
19A Cordarrelle Patterson RC .40 1.00
19B Cordarrelle Patterson SP 2.50 6.00
20 Hakeem Nicks .20 .50
21A Geno Smith RC .40 1.00
21B Geno Smith SP 2.50 6.00
22 Alex Smith .25 .60
23 DeMarco Murray .25 .60
24A Matt Ryan .25 .60
24B Matt Ryan SP 4.00 10.00
25A Drew Brees .30 .75
25B Drew Brees SP 6.00 15.00
26 Victor Cruz .25 .60
27 Brian Banks RC .40 1.00
28 Jamie Collins RC .40 1.00
29 Joseph Randle RC .40 1.00
30A Tyler Eifert RC .40 1.00
30B Tyler Eifert SP 2.50 6.00
31 Jarvis Jones RC .40 1.00
32A Julio Jones .30 .75
32B Julio Jones SP 5.00 12.00
33 Andy Dalton .25 .60
34A Ed Reed .25 .60
34B Ed Reed SP 4.00 10.00
35A Rob Gronkowski .30 .75
35B Rob Gronkowski SP 6.00 15.00
36 Christian Ponder .20 .50
37 Johnathan Cyprien RC .40 1.00
38 Danny Amendola .25 .60
39A C.J. Spiller .20 .50
39B C.J. Spiller SP 3.00 8.00
40 Tyler Bray RC .40 1.00
41A Ryan Nassib RC .40 1.00
41B Ryan Nassib SP 2.50 6.00
42A Demaryius Thomas .25 .60
42B Demaryius Thomas SP 4.00 10.00
43 Percy Harvin .20 .50
44 Carson Palmer .25 .60
45A EJ Manuel RC .40 1.00
45B EJ Manuel SP 10.00 25.00
46 Reggie Bush .20 .50
47 Bjoern Werner RC .40 1.00
48 Cecil Shorts .20 .50
49 Justin Pugh RC .40 1.00
50A Tom Brady .75 2.00
50B Tom Brady SP 12.00 30.00
51 Antonio Gates .25 .60
52 Ben Roethlisberger .30 .75
53 Brandon Weeden .20 .50
54A Stepfan Taylor RC .40 1.00
54B Stepfan Taylor SP 4.00 10.00
55 Ryan Swope RC .40 1.00
56 Jake Locker .25 .60
57 Darren Sproles .25 .60
58 Jared Allen .20 .50
59 Champ Bailey .25 .60
60 Charles Tillman .25 .60
61 Jairus Byrd .20 .50
62 Kyle Long RC .50 1.25
63A Manti Te'o RC .50 1.25
63B Manti Te'o SP 3.00 8.00
64 Arthur Brown RC .40 1.00
65A Aaron Dobson RC .40 1.00
65B Aaron Dobson SP 2.50 6.00
66 David Amerson RC .40 1.00
67 Brad Sorensen RC .40 1.00
68 Sharrif Floyd RC .40 1.00
69 Von Miller .25 .60
70A Arian Foster .25 .60
70B Arian Foster SP 4.00 10.00
71 Santonio Holmes .20 .50
72 Antonio Cromartie .20 .50
73 Luke Kuechly .25 .60
74 Shawn Williams RC .40 1.00
75A Andrew Luck .50 1.25
75B Andrew Luck SP 8.00 20.00
76A Zach Ertz RC .75 2.00
76B Zach Ertz SP 5.00 12.00
77 Earl Thomas .25 .60
78 Darren McFadden .25 .60
79 Ace Sanders RC .40 1.00
80 Knile Davis RC .40 1.00
81A Jordan Reed RC .60 1.50
81B Jordan Reed SP 4.00 10.00
82A Joe Flacco .25 .60
82B Joe Flacco SP 4.00 10.00
83 Ray Rice .20 .50
84 Philip Rivers .30 .75
85A Andre Johnson .20 .50
85B Andre Johnson SP 5.00 12.00
86 Kenny Vaccaro RC .40 1.00
87 Blidi Wreh-Wilson RC .50 1.25
88 Lane Johnson RC .50 1.25
89 David Wilson .20 .50
90 Zac Stacy RC .40 1.00
91 Jacoby Jones .20 .50
92 Cornellius Carradine RC .40 1.00
93 Theo Riddick RC .40 1.00
94 Markus Wheaton RC .40 1.00
95A Dez Bryant .30 .75
95B Dez Bryant SP 5.00 12.00
96A Giovani Bernard RC .40 1.00
96B Giovani Bernard SP 2.50 6.00
97 Eric Decker .20 .50
98 Landry Jones RC .40 1.00
99 Kerwynn Williams RC .40 1.00
100A Adrian Peterson .30 .75
100B Adrian Peterson SP 5.00 12.00
101 Terrance Williams RC .40 1.00
102 Dashon Goldson .20 .50
103 Jason Pierre-Paul .20 .50
104 Roddy White .20 .50
105 Eli Manning .25 .60
106 Barkevious Mingo RC .40 1.00
107A Clay Matthews .30 .75
107B Clay Matthews SP 6.00 15.00
108A Wes Welker .25 .60
108B Wes Welker SP 6.00 15.00
109 Margus Hunt RC .40 1.00
110 Josh Freeman .25 .60
111A Tyler Wilson RC .40 1.00
111B Tyler Wilson SP 2.50 6.00
112 Khaseem Greene RC .40 1.00
113 Patrick Peterson .20 .50
114 Denard Robinson RC .40 1.00
115 London Fletcher .25 .60
116 Jimmy Graham .30 .75
117A Tavon Austin RC .50 1.25
117B Tavon Austin SP 3.00 8.00
118 Travis Kelce RC 1.00 2.50
119 Xavier Rhodes RC .40 1.00
120 Jonathan Cooper RC .40 1.00
121 Dion Jordan RC .40 1.00
122 Antonio Brown .30 .75
123 Troy Polamalu .30 .75
124 T.J. McDonald RC .40 1.00
125A Robert Griffin III .20 .50
125B Robert Griffin III SP 3.00 8.00
126 Desmond Trufant RC .40 1.00
127 Chance Warmack RC .40 1.00
128 Johnthan Banks RC .40 1.00
129A Anquan Boldin .20 .50
129B Anquan Boldin SP 3.00 8.00
130 Jay Cutler .20 .50
131A Eddie Lacy RC .40 1.00
131B Eddie Lacy SP 2.50 6.00
132 Jordan Rodgers RC .50 1.25
133 Matt Forte .20 .50
134 D.J. Fluker RC .40 1.00
135 Jawan Jamison RC .40 1.00
136 Aldon Smith .20 .50
137 Luke Joeckel RC .40 1.00
138 Kiko Alonso RC .50 1.25
139 Eric Reid RC .50 1.25
140 Matthew Stafford .25 .60
141 Reggie Wayne .25 .60
142 Brandon Marshall .25 .60
143 DeSean Jackson .25 .60
144 Steve Smith .25 .60
145 Sylvester Williams RC .40 1.00
146 Mike Gillislee RC .40 1.00
147 Cam Newton .30 .75
148A Doug Martin .25 .60
148B Doug Martin SP 4.00 10.00
149 Matt Schaub .20 .50
150 Aaron Rodgers .50 1.25
151 John Jenkins RC .40 1.00
152 Josh Boyce RC .40 1.00
153 Matt Scott RC .40 1.00
154A DeAndre Hopkins RC 1.00 2.50
154B DeAndre Hopkins SP 6.00 15.00
155 Mike Wallace .20 .50
156 Richard Sherman .30 .75
157 Travis Frederick RC .40 1.00
158 Cobi Hamilton RC .40 1.00
159A J.J. Watt .25 .60
159B J.J. Watt SP 4.00 10.00
160 Darrelle Revis .20 .50
161 Stevan Ridley .20 .50
162A Matt Barkley RC .40 1.00
162B Matt Barkley SP 2.50 6.00
163 Stedman Bailey RC .40 1.00
164A Trent Richardson .20 .50
164B Trent Richardson SP 3.00 8.00
165 Star Lotulelei RC .50 1.25
166 Eric Fisher RC .40 1.00
167 Darius Slay RC .40 1.00
168 Michael Vick .25 .60
169 Tavarres King RC .40 1.00
170A Marcus Lattimore RC .40 1.00
170B Marcus Lattimore SP 2.50 6.00
171A Randall Cobb .25 .60
171B Randall Cobb SP 5.00 12.00
172 Jamar Taylor RC .40 1.00
173 Justin Blackmon .20 .50
174 Kawann Short RC .40 1.00
175A Russell Wilson .60 1.50
175B Russell Wilson SP 10.00 25.00
176 Ryan Tannehill .25 .60
177 Cameron Wake .20 .50
178 Kenjon Barner RC .40 1.00
179A Michael Crabtree .20 .50
179B Michael Crabtree SP 3.00 8.00
180 Tony Gonzalez .25 .60
181 Quinton Patton RC .40 1.00
182 Elvis Dumervil .20 .50
183 Alec Ogletree RC .40 1.00
184 Chris Johnson .20 .50
185 Datone Jones RC .40 1.00
186 Christine Michael RC .40 1.00
187 NaVorro Bowman .25 .60
188 Vance McDonald RC .50 1.25
189 Jon Bostic RC .40 1.00
190 Damontre Moore RC .40 1.00
191 Steven Jackson .20 .50
192 Jamaal Charles .25 .60
193 Torrey Smith .20 .50
194 Kenny Stills RC .40 1.00
195A Jason Witten .25 .60
195B Jason Witten SP 4.00 10.00
196 Tony Romo .25 .60
197 Marquise Goodwin RC .40 1.00
198A Le'Veon Bell RC 1.25 3.00
198B Le'Veon Bell SP 8.00 20.00
199 Dee Milliner RC .40 1.00
200A Calvin Johnson .30 .75
200B Calvin Johnson SP 8.00 20.00
201 Frank Gore .25 .60
202 Sheldon Richardson RC .40 1.00
203 Sam Bradford .20 .50
204 Vincent Jackson .20 .50
205A Andre Ellington RC .40 1.00
205B Andre Ellington SP 2.50 6.00
206 Kevin Minter RC .40 1.00
207 Matt Elam RC .40 1.00
208 Bacarri Rambo RC .50 1.25
209 Johnathan Hankins RC .40 1.00
210 Chris Long .20 .50
211 Alex Okafor RC .40 1.00
212 Dwayne Bowe .25 .60
213 A.J. Green .30 .75
214 Brian Orakpo .25 .60
215 Maurice Jones-Drew .20 .50
216A Alfred Morris .20 .50
216B Alfred Morris SP 3.00 8.00
217A Johnathan Franklin RC .40 1.00
217B Johnathan Franklin SP 5.00 12.00
218A Mike Glennon RC .40 1.00
218B Mike Glennon SP 8.00 20.00
219 Greg Jennings .20 .50
220A Colin Kaepernick .25 .60
220B Colin Kaepernick SP 20.00 40.00

2013 Topps Chrome Black Refractors

ETS/299: 4X TO 10X BASIC CARDS
*ROOKIES/299: 2X TO 5X BASIC RC
175 Russell Wilson 10.00 25.00

2013 Topps Chrome Blue Refractors

*VETS/199: 4X TO 10X BASIC CARDS
*ROOKIES/199: 2X TO 5X BASIC RC
75 Andrew Luck 12.00 30.00
175 Russell Wilson 10.00 25.00

2013 Topps Chrome Blue Wave Refractors

ETS: 1.5X TO 4X BASIC CARDS
*ROOKIES: .8X TO 2X BASIC RC

2013 Topps Chrome Camo Refractors

*VETS/499: 3X TO 8X BASIC CARDS
*ROOKIES/499: 1.5X TO 4X BASIC RC
75 Andrew Luck 10.00 25.00
175 Russell Wilson 6.00 15.00

2013 Topps Chrome Gold Refractors

*VETS/50: 12X TO 30X BASIC CARDS
*ROOKIES/50: 6X TO 15X BASIC RC

2013 Topps Chrome Orange Refractors

*VETS: 1.5X TO 4X BASIC CARDS
*ROOKIES: .8X TO 2X BASIC RC
THREE PER RETAIL VALUE PACK
75 Andrew Luck 10.00 25.00

2013 Topps Chrome Pink Refractors

*VETS/399: 3X TO 8X BASIC CARDS
*ROOKIES/399: 1.5X TO 4X BASIC RC
75 Andrew Luck 10.00 25.00
175 Russell Wilson 8.00 20.00

2013 Topps Chrome Prism Refractors

*VETS: 3X TO 8X BASIC CARDS
*ROOKIES: 1.5X TO 4X BASIC RC
75 Andrew Luck 6.00 15.00

2013 Topps Chrome Prism Refractors 260

*VETS/260: 4X TO 10X BASIC CARDS
*ROOKIES/260: 2X TO 5X BASIC RC

2013 Topps Chrome Purple Refractors

*VETS/499: 2.5X TO 6X BASIC CARDS
*ROOKIES/499: 1.2X TO 3X BASIC RC
75 Andrew Luck 8.00 20.00
175 Russell Wilson 6.00 15.00

2013 Topps Chrome Red Refractors

*VETS/25: 15X TO 40X BASIC CARDS
*ROOKIES/25: 8X TO 20X BASIC RC
1 Peyton Manning 60.00 120.00
45 EJ Manuel 40.00 80.00
131 Eddie Lacy 8.00 20.00

2013 Topps Chrome Refractors

ETS: 1.2X TO 3X BASIC CARDS
*ROOKIES: .6X TO 1.5X BASIC CARDS

2013 Topps Chrome Sepia Refractors

*VETS/99: 5X TO 12X BASIC CARDS
*ROOKIES/99: 2.5X TO 6X BASIC RC
175 Russell Wilson 15.00 40.00

2013 Topps Chrome Xfractors

*VETS: 1.5X TO 4X BASIC CARDS
*ROOKIES: .8X TO 2X BASIC RC

2013 Topps Chrome 1000 Yard Club

*RED REF/99: .6X TO 1.5X BASIC INSERTS
1 Adrian Peterson 3.00 8.00
2 Calvin Johnson 3.00 8.00
3 Alfred Morris 2.00 5.00
4 Andre Johnson 2.00 5.00
5 Marshawn Lynch 2.50 6.00
6 Brandon Marshall 2.50 6.00
7 Doug Martin 2.50 6.00
8 Demaryius Thomas 2.50 6.00
9 Arian Foster 2.50 6.00
10 Dez Bryant 3.00 8.00
11 Reggie Wayne 2.50 6.00
12 Roddy White 2.00 5.00
13 A.J. Green 3.00 8.00
14 Chris Johnson 2.00 5.00
15 Frank Gore 2.50 6.00
16 Steve Johnson 2.50 6.00
17 Steve Smith 2.50 6.00
18 Ray Rice 2.00 5.00
19 Michael Crabtree 2.00 5.00
20 Matt Forte 2.00 5.00
21 Victor Cruz 2.50 6.00

2013 Topps Chrome 1000 Yard Club Red Refractor Autographs

EXCH EXPIRATION: 11/30/2016
1 Adrian Peterson 75.00 125.00
2 Calvin Johnson
3 Alfred Morris EXCH 12.00 30.00
4 Andre Johnson
5 Marshawn Lynch 15.00 40.00
6 Brandon Marshall
7 Doug Martin EXCH 15.00 40.00
8 Demaryius Thomas EXCH 20.00 50.00
9 Arian Foster 15.00 40.00
10 Dez Bryant
11 Reggie Wayne 30.00 60.00
12 Roddy White
13 A.J. Green 30.00 80.00
14 Chris Johnson 12.00 30.00
15 Frank Gore 15.00 40.00
16 Steve Johnson
17 Steve Smith 15.00 40.00
18 Ray Rice 12.00 30.00
19 Michael Crabtree 12.00 30.00
20 Matt Forte
21 Victor Cruz

2013 Topps Chrome 1959 Minis

RISM REF/50: 2.5X TO 6X BASIC INSERTS
*RED REF/75: 2X TO 5X BASIC INSERTS
*REFRACT/99: 1.5X TO 4X BASIC INSERTS
1 Keenan Allen .75 2.00
2 Geno Smith .40 1.00
3 Matt Barkley .40 1.00
4 Cordarrelle Patterson .40 1.00
5 Mike Glennon .40 1.00
6 Zach Ertz .75 2.00
7 DeAndre Hopkins 1.00 2.50
8 Eddie Lacy .40 1.00
9 Tyler Eifert .40 1.00
10 Tavon Austin .50 1.25
11 Tyler Wilson .40 1.00
12 Robert Woods .60 1.50
13 Quinton Patton .40 1.00
14 Ryan Nassib .40 1.00
15 Terrance Williams .40 1.00
16 Markus Wheaton .40 1.00
17 Aaron Dobson .40 1.00
18 Giovani Bernard .40 1.00
19 EJ Manuel .40 1.00
20 Justin Hunter .40 1.00
21 Joseph Randle .40 1.00
22 Montee Ball .40 1.00
23 Dion Jordan .40 1.00
24 Andre Ellington .40 1.00
25 Stepfan Taylor .40 1.00
26 Jordan Reed .60 1.50
27 Landry Jones .40 1.00
28 Manti Te'o .50 1.25
29 Johnathan Franklin .40 1.00
30 Stedman Bailey .40 1.00
31 Christine Michael .40 1.00
32 Le'Veon Bell 1.25 3.00
33 Denard Robinson .40 1.00
34 Marquise Goodwin .40 1.00
35 Kenny Stills .40 1.00

2013 Topps Chrome 1959 Minis Autographs

1 Keenan Allen 50.00 100.00
2 Geno Smith 10.00 25.00
3 Matt Barkley 20.00 50.00
4 Cordarrelle Patterson
5 Mike Glennon 10.00 25.00
6 Zach Ertz 20.00 50.00
7 DeAndre Hopkins 40.00 80.00
8 Eddie Lacy 10.00 25.00
9 Tyler Eifert 10.00 25.00
10 Tavon Austin 20.00 50.00
11 Tyler Wilson
12 Robert Woods EXCH 15.00 40.00
13 Quinton Patton 10.00 25.00
14 Ryan Nassib 25.00 50.00
15 Terrance Williams 10.00 25.00
16 Markus Wheaton
17 Aaron Dobson 40.00 80.00
18 Giovani Bernard 10.00 25.00
19 EJ Manuel
20 Justin Hunter 10.00 25.00
21 Joseph Randle EXCH 10.00 25.00
22 Montee Ball 10.00 25.00
23 Dion Jordan
24 Andre Ellington 40.00 80.00
25 Stepfan Taylor 10.00 25.00
26 Jordan Reed
27 Landry Jones 25.00 50.00
28 Manti Te'o 12.00 30.00
29 Johnathan Franklin 10.00 25.00
30 Stedman Bailey 10.00 25.00
31 Christine Michael 30.00 60.00
32 Le'Veon Bell
33 Denard Robinson
34 Marquise Goodwin
35 Kenny Stills 50.00 100.00

2013 Topps Chrome 1965

EFRACT/99: 1.2X TO 3X BASIC INSERTS
1 Keenan Allen 1.00 2.50
2 Geno Smith .50 1.25
3 Matt Barkley .50 1.25
4 Cordarrelle Patterson .50 1.25
5 Mike Glennon .50 1.25
6 Zach Ertz 1.00 2.50
7 DeAndre Hopkins 1.25 3.00
8 Eddie Lacy .50 1.25
9 Tyler Eifert .50 1.25
10 Tavon Austin .60 1.50
11 Robert Woods .75 2.00
12 Quinton Patton .50 1.25
13 Terrance Williams .50 1.25
14 Aaron Dobson .50 1.25
15 Giovani Bernard .50 1.25
16 EJ Manuel .50 1.25
17 Justin Hunter .50 1.25
18 Montee Ball .50 1.25
19 Andre Ellington .50 1.25
20 Jordan Reed .75 2.00
21 Landry Jones .50 1.25
22 Manti Te'o .60 1.50
23 Gavin Escobar .50 1.25
24 Johnathan Franklin .50 1.25
25 Dion Jordan .50 1.25
26 Stedman Bailey .50 1.25
27 Christine Michael .50 1.25
28 Marcus Lattimore .50 1.25
29 Denard Robinson .50 1.25
30 Le'Veon Bell 1.50 4.00

2013 Topps Chrome 1965 Autographs

1 Keenan Allen 40.00 80.00
2 Geno Smith
3 Matt Barkley 10.00 25.00
4 Cordarrelle Patterson 10.00 25.00
5 Mike Glennon 10.00 25.00
6 Zach Ertz 20.00 50.00
7 DeAndre Hopkins 25.00 50.00
8 Eddie Lacy 10.00 25.00
9 Tyler Eifert 10.00 25.00
10 Tavon Austin 20.00 50.00
11 Robert Woods EXCH 15.00 40.00
12 Quinton Patton 10.00 25.00
13 Terrance Williams 10.00 25.00
14 Aaron Dobson
15 Giovani Bernard 10.00 25.00
16 EJ Manuel
17 Justin Hunter 10.00 25.00
18 Montee Ball 10.00 25.00
19 Andre Ellington 10.00 25.00
20 Jordan Reed 15.00 40.00
21 Landry Jones 10.00 25.00
22 Manti Te'o 25.00 60.00
23 Gavin Escobar EXCH 10.00 25.00
24 Johnathan Franklin 10.00 25.00
25 Dion Jordan 10.00 25.00
26 Stedman Bailey 10.00 25.00
27 Christine Michael 40.00 100.00
28 Marcus Lattimore 10.00 25.00
29 Denard Robinson 10.00 25.00
30 Le'Veon Bell 40.00 80.00

2013 Topps Chrome 1969

*REFRACT/99: 2X TO 5X BASIC INSERTS
1 Cordarrelle Patterson .40 1.00
2 DeAndre Hopkins 1.00 2.50
3 EJ Manuel .40 1.00
4 Eddie Lacy .40 1.00
5 Geno Smith .40 1.00
6 Giovani Bernard .40 1.00
7 Justin Hunter .40 1.00
8 Keenan Allen .75 2.00
9 Manti Te'o .50 1.25
10 Matt Barkley .40 1.00
11 Mike Glennon .40 1.00
12 Montee Ball .40 1.00
13 Robert Woods .60 1.50
14 Tavon Austin .50 1.25
15 Tyler Eifert .40 1.00
16 Andre Ellington .40 1.00
17 Luke Joeckel .40 1.00
18 Ryan Nassib .40 1.00
19 Tyler Wilson .40 1.00
20 Stepfan Taylor .40 1.00
21 Marquise Goodwin .40 1.00
22 Terrance Williams .40 1.00
23 Johnathan Franklin .40 1.00
24 Denard Robinson .40 1.00
25 Aaron Dobson .40 1.00
26 Zach Ertz .75 2.00
27 Marcus Lattimore .40 1.00
28 Le'Veon Bell 1.25 3.00
29 Markus Wheaton .40 1.00
30 Quinton Patton .40 1.00

2013 Topps Chrome 1969 Autographs

1 Cordarrelle Patterson 6.00 15.00
2 DeAndre Hopkins 15.00 40.00
3 EJ Manuel 6.00 15.00
4 Eddie Lacy 6.00 15.00
5 Geno Smith 6.00 15.00
6 Giovani Bernard 6.00 15.00
7 Justin Hunter 6.00 15.00
8 Keenan Allen 25.00 60.00
9 Manti Te'o 8.00 20.00
10 Matt Barkley 6.00 15.00
11 Mike Glennon 6.00 15.00
12 Montee Ball 6.00 15.00
13 Robert Woods EXCH 10.00 25.00
14 Tavon Austin 8.00 20.00
15 Tyler Eifert 6.00 15.00
16 Andre Ellington 6.00 15.00
17 Luke Joeckel 6.00 15.00
18 Ryan Nassib 12.00 30.00
19 Tyler Wilson 6.00 15.00
20 Stepfan Taylor 6.00 15.00
21 Marquise Goodwin 6.00 15.00
22 Terrance Williams 6.00 15.00
23 Johnathan Franklin 6.00 15.00
24 Denard Robinson 12.00 30.00
25 Aaron Dobson 6.00 15.00
26 Zach Ertz 12.00 30.00
27 Marcus Lattimore 6.00 15.00
28 Le'Veon Bell 30.00 60.00
29 Markus Wheaton 6.00 15.00
30 Quinton Patton 6.00 15.00

2013 Topps Chrome 1986

COMPLETE SET (35) 12.00 30.00
*GOLD REF/75: 2.5X TO 6X BASIC INSERTS
*PRISM REF/50: 2.5X TO 6X BASIC INSERTS
*REFRACT/99: 2X TO 5X BASIC INSERTS
1 Keenan Allen .75 2.00
2 Geno Smith .40 1.00
3 Matt Barkley .40 1.00
4 Cordarrelle Patterson .40 1.00
5 Mike Glennon .40 1.00
6 Zach Ertz .75 2.00
7 DeAndre Hopkins 1.00 2.50
8 Eddie Lacy .40 1.00
9 Tyler Eifert .40 1.00
10 Tavon Austin .50 1.25
11 Tyler Wilson .40 1.00
12 Robert Woods .60 1.50
13 Ryan Nassib .40 1.00
14 Terrance Williams .40 1.00
15 Markus Wheaton .40 1.00
16 Aaron Dobson .40 1.00
17 Giovani Bernard .40 1.00
18 EJ Manuel .40 1.00
19 Justin Hunter .40 1.00
20 Montee Ball .40 1.00
21 Dion Jordan .40 1.00
22 Andre Ellington .40 1.00
23 Stepfan Taylor .40 1.00
24 Manti Te'o .50 1.25
25 Gavin Escobar .40 1.00
26 Johnathan Franklin .40 1.00
27 Stedman Bailey .40 1.00
28 Marcus Lattimore .40 1.00
29 Le'Veon Bell 1.25 3.00
30 Mike Gillislee .40 1.00
31 Kenny Stills .40 1.00
32 Denard Robinson .40 1.00
33 Marquise Goodwin .40 1.00
34 Vance McDonald .50 1.25
35 Knile Davis .40 1.00

2013 Topps Chrome 1986 Autographs

1 Keenan Allen 40.00 80.00
2 Geno Smith 10.00 25.00
3 Matt Barkley 20.00 50.00
4 Cordarrelle Patterson
5 Mike Glennon 10.00 25.00
6 Zach Ertz 20.00 50.00
7 DeAndre Hopkins 40.00 80.00
8 Eddie Lacy 10.00 25.00
9 Tyler Eifert 10.00 25.00
10 Tavon Austin 12.00 30.00
11 Tyler Wilson 10.00 25.00
12 Robert Woods 15.00 40.00
13 Ryan Nassib 30.00 60.00
14 Terrance Williams 10.00 25.00
15 Markus Wheaton 10.00 25.00
16 Aaron Dobson 40.00 80.00
17 Giovani Bernard 10.00 25.00
18 EJ Manuel 40.00 80.00
19 Justin Hunter 20.00 50.00
20 Montee Ball 10.00 25.00
21 Dion Jordan 10.00 25.00
22 Andre Ellington 40.00 80.00
23 Stepfan Taylor 10.00 25.00
24 Manti Te'o 12.00 30.00
25 Gavin Escobar
26 Johnathan Franklin 10.00 25.00
27 Stedman Bailey 10.00 25.00
28 Marcus Lattimore 10.00 25.00
29 Le'Veon Bell 60.00 120.00
30 Mike Gillislee 10.00 25.00
31 Kenny Stills 50.00 100.00
32 Denard Robinson 10.00 25.00
33 Marquise Goodwin 10.00 25.00
34 Vance McDonald 12.00 30.00
35 Knile Davis 30.00 60.00

2013 Topps Chrome 4000 Yard Club

*RED REF/99: .8X TO 2X BASIC INSERTS
1 Drew Brees 2.50 6.00
2 Matthew Stafford 2.00 5.00
3 Tony Romo 2.00 5.00
4 Tom Brady 6.00 15.00
5 Matt Ryan 2.00 5.00
6 Peyton Manning 5.00 12.00
7 Andrew Luck 4.00 10.00
8 Aaron Rodgers 4.00 10.00
9 Josh Freeman 2.00 5.00

2013 Topps Chrome 4000 Yard Club Red Refractor Autographs

1 Drew Brees 30.00 60.00
2 Matthew Stafford 20.00 50.00
3 Tony Romo
4 Tom Brady
5 Matt Ryan 15.00 40.00
6 Peyton Manning 100.00 200.00
7 Andrew Luck 50.00 100.00
8 Aaron Rodgers
9 Josh Freeman 15.00 40.00

2013 Topps Chrome Dual Rookie Autographs

EXCH EXPIRATION: 11/30/2016
DRAAB S.Bailey/T.Austin 10.00 25.00
DRAHP J.Hunter/C.Patterson 8.00 20.00
DRALF J.Franklin/E.Lacy 8.00 20.00
DRAMB E.Manuel/G.Bernard 8.00 20.00
DRASM G.Smith/D.Milliner 8.00 20.00

2013 Topps Chrome Rookie Autographs

CH EXPIRATION: 11/30/2016
*BLUE/50: 1X TO 2.5X BASIC AU
*CAMO/99: .8X TO 2X BASIC AU
*PINK/75: 1X TO 2.5X BASIC AU
*REFRACT/150: .6X TO 1.5X BASIC AU
*REF VARIATION: .8X TO 2X BASIC AU

3 Robert Woods/600 5.00 12.00
4 Tyrann Mathieu/447 5.00 12.00
7 Gavin Escobar/600 3.00 8.00
10 Chris Harper/600 3.00 8.00
11 Montee Ball/600 3.00 8.00
13 Miguel Maysonet/600 3.00 8.00
14 Keenan Allen/600 6.00 15.00
16 D.J. Hayden/600 3.00 8.00
17 Ezekiel Ansah/600 3.00 8.00
18 Justin Hunter/600 3.00 8.00
19 Cordarrelle Patterson/447 3.00 8.00
21 Geno Smith/447 3.00 8.00
29 Joseph Randle/600 3.00 8.00
30 Tyler Eifert/600 3.00 8.00
31 Jarvis Jones/600 3.00 8.00
41 Ryan Nassib/600 3.00 8.00
45 EJ Manuel/447 3.00 8.00
47 Bjoern Werner/600 3.00 8.00
54 Stepfan Taylor/600 3.00 8.00
55 Ryan Swope/600 3.00 8.00
63 Manti Te'o/447 4.00 10.00
65 Aaron Dobson/600 3.00 8.00
76 Zach Ertz/600 6.00 15.00
79 Ace Sanders/600 3.00 8.00
81 Jordan Reed/600 5.00 12.00
86 Kenny Vaccaro/600 3.00 8.00
94 Markus Wheaton/600 3.00 8.00
96 Giovani Bernard/600 3.00 8.00
98 Landry Jones/600 3.00 8.00
101 Terrance Williams/600 3.00 8.00
106 Barkevious Mingo/600 3.00 8.00
111 Tyler Wilson/600 3.00 8.00
114 Denard Robinson/600 3.00 8.00
117 Tavon Austin/447 4.00 10.00
121 Dion Jordan/600 3.00 8.00
131 Eddie Lacy/600 3.00 8.00
137 Luke Joeckel EXCH 3.00 8.00
146 Mike Gillislee/600 3.00 8.00
152 Josh Boyce/600 3.00 8.00
154 DeAndre Hopkins/447 25.00 50.00
162 Matt Barkley/447 3.00 8.00
163 Stedman Bailey/600 3.00 8.00
166 Eric Fisher/447 3.00 8.00
169 Tavarres King/600 3.00 8.00
170 Marcus Lattimore/600 3.00 8.00
178 Kenjon Barner/600 3.00 8.00
181 Quinton Patton/600 3.00 8.00
186 Christine Michael/600 3.00 8.00
188 Vance McDonald/600 4.00 10.00
194 Kenny Stills/600 3.00 8.00
197 Marquise Goodwin/600 3.00 8.00
198 Le'Veon Bell/600 30.00 60.00
199 Dee Milliner/600 3.00 8.00
205 Andre Ellington/600 6.00 15.00
207 Matt Elam/600 3.00 8.00
217 Johnathan Franklin/600 3.00 8.00
218 Mike Glennon/447 3.00 8.00
221 Da'Rick Rogers/600 3.00 8.00
222 Conner Vernon/600 3.00 8.00
223 Dion Sims/600 3.00 8.00

2013 Topps Chrome Rookie Autographs Black Refractors

*BLACK/25: 1.2X TO 3X BASIC AU
45 EJ Manuel 40.00 80.00
117 Tavon Austin 12.00 30.00
131 Eddie Lacy 10.00 25.00
198 Le'Veon Bell 100.00 200.00

2013 Topps Chrome Rookie Autographs Patches

RAPAD Aaron Dobson 8.00 20.00
RAPAE Andre Ellington 15.00 40.00
RAPCM Christine Michael 8.00 20.00
RAPCP Cordarrelle Patterson 8.00 20.00
RAPDH DeAndre Hopkins 20.00 50.00
RAPDJ Dion Jordan 8.00 20.00
RAPDR Denard Robinson 8.00 20.00
RAPGB Giovani Bernard 8.00 20.00
RAPGE Gavin Escobar 8.00 20.00
RAPGS Geno Smith 8.00 20.00
RAPJF Johnathan Franklin 8.00 20.00
RAPJH Justin Hunter 8.00 20.00
RAPJR Joseph Randle 8.00 20.00
RAPKA Keenan Allen 15.00 40.00
RAPKD Knile Davis 8.00 20.00
RAPKS Kenny Stills 8.00 20.00
RAPLB Le'Veon Bell 25.00 60.00
RAPLJ Landry Jones 8.00 20.00
RAPMB Matt Barkley 8.00 20.00
RAPML Marcus Lattimore 8.00 20.00
RAPMT Manti Te'o 10.00 25.00
RAPMW Markus Wheaton 8.00 20.00
RAPQP Quinton Patton 8.00 20.00
RAPRN Ryan Nassib 8.00 20.00
RAPRW Robert Woods EXCH 12.00 30.00
RAPSB Stedman Bailey 8.00 20.00
RAPST Stepfan Taylor 8.00 20.00
RAPTA Tavon Austin 10.00 25.00
RAPTE Tyler Eifert 12.00 30.00
RAPTW Tyler Wilson 8.00 20.00
RAPVM Vance McDonald 10.00 25.00
RAPZE Zach Ertz 15.00 40.00
RAPEJM EJ Manuel 8.00 20.00
RAPJRE Jordan Reed 12.00 30.00
RAPMBA Montee Ball 8.00 20.00
RAPMGI Mike Gillislee 8.00 20.00
RAPMGO Marquise Goodwin 8.00 20.00
RAPTWI Terrance Williams 8.00 20.00

2013 Topps Chrome Rookie Die Cuts

LUE REF/50: 1.5X TO 4X BASIC INSERTS
*RED REF/25: 2X TO 5X BASIC INSERTS
*REFRACT: .6X TO 1.5X BASIC INSERTS
RDCAD Aaron Dobson .50 1.25
RDCAE Andre Ellington .50 1.25
RDCCP Cordarrelle Patterson .50 1.25
RDCDH DeAndre Hopkins 1.25 3.00
RDCDJ Dion Jordan .50 1.25
RDCDR Denard Robinson .50 1.25
RDCEJM EJ Manuel .50 1.25
RDCEL Eddie Lacy .50 1.25
RDCGB Giovani Bernard .50 1.25
RDCGE Gavin Escobar .50 1.25
RDCGS Geno Smith .50 1.25
RDCJF Johnathan Franklin .50 1.25
RDCJH Justin Hunter .50 1.25
RDCJR Joseph Randle .50 1.25
RDCJRE Jordan Reed .75 2.00
RDCKA Keenan Allen 1.00 2.50
RDCKS Kenny Stills .50 1.25
RDCLB Le'Veon Bell 1.50 4.00
RDCMB Matt Barkley .50 1.25
RDCMBA Montee Ball .50 1.25
RDCMG Mike Glennon .50 1.25
RDCMGI Mike Gillislee .50 1.25
RDCMGO Marquise Goodwin .50 1.25
RDCMT Manti Te'o .60 1.50
RDCMW Markus Wheaton .50 1.25
RDCQP Quinton Patton .50 1.25
RDCRN Ryan Nassib .50 1.25
RDCRW Robert Woods .75 2.00
RDCSB Stedman Bailey .50 1.25
RDCST Stepfan Taylor .50 1.25
RDCTA Tavon Austin .60 1.50
RDCTE Tyler Eifert .50 1.25
RDCTW Tyler Wilson .50 1.25
RDCTWI Terrance Williams .50 1.25
RDCZE Zach Ertz 1.00 2.50

2013 Topps Chrome Rookie Die Cuts Autographs

RDCAD Aaron Dobson 40.00 80.00
RDCAE Andre Ellington 40.00 80.00
RDCCP Cordarrelle Patterson 10.00 25.00
RDCDH DeAndre Hopkins
RDCDJ Dion Jordan 10.00 25.00
RDCDR Denard Robinson 10.00 25.00
RDCEL Eddie Lacy 10.00 25.00
RDCGB Giovani Bernard 10.00 25.00
RDCGE Gavin Escobar
RDCGS Geno Smith 10.00 25.00
RDCJF Johnathan Franklin 10.00 25.00
RDCJH Justin Hunter 10.00 25.00
RDCJR Joseph Randle EXCH 10.00 25.00
RDCKA Keenan Allen 50.00 100.00
RDCKS Kenny Stills 50.00 100.00
RDCLB Le'Veon Bell 60.00 120.00
RDCMB Matt Barkley 10.00 25.00
RDCMG Mike Glennon 10.00 25.00
RDCMT Manti Te'o 12.00 30.00
RDCMW Markus Wheaton 10.00 25.00
RDCQP Quinton Patton 10.00 25.00
RDCRN Ryan Nassib 25.00 50.00
RDCRW Robert Woods EXCH 15.00 40.00
RDCSB Stedman Bailey 10.00 25.00
RDCST Stepfan Taylor 10.00 25.00
RDCTA Tavon Austin 12.00 30.00
RDCTE Tyler Eifert 10.00 25.00
RDCTW Tyler Wilson 10.00 25.00
RDCZE Zach Ertz 20.00 50.00
RDCEJM EJ Manuel 40.00 80.00
RDCJRE Jordan Reed 15.00 40.00
RDCMBA Montee Ball 10.00 25.00
RDCMGI Mike Gillislee 10.00 25.00
RDCMGO Marquise Goodwin 10.00 25.00
RDCTWI Terrance Williams 10.00 25.00

2013 Topps Chrome Rookie Relics

*BLACK/25: 1X TO 2.5X BASIC JSY
*GOLD/10: 1.2X TO 3X BASIC JSY
*PURPLE/75: .6X TO 1.5X BASIC JSY
*REFRACT/150: .5X TO 1.2X BASIC JSY
*XFRACT/99: .6X TO 1.5X BASIC JSY
RRAD Aaron Dobson 1.25 3.00
RRAE Andre Ellington 1.25 3.00
RRCM Christine Michael 1.25 3.00
RRCP Cordarrelle Patterson 1.25 3.00
RRDH DeAndre Hopkins 3.00 8.00
RRDJ Dion Jordan 1.25 3.00
RRDR Denard Robinson 1.25 3.00
RREJM EJ Manuel 1.25 3.00
RREL Eddie Lacy 1.25 3.00
RRGB Giovani Bernard 1.25 3.00
RRGE Gavin Escobar 1.25 3.00
RRGS Geno Smith 1.25 3.00
RRJF Johnathan Franklin 1.25 3.00
RRJH Justin Hunter 1.25 3.00
RRJR Joseph Randle 1.25 3.00
RRJRE Jordan Reed 2.00 5.00
RRKA Keenan Allen 2.50 6.00
RRKD Knile Davis 1.25 3.00
RRKS Kenny Stills 1.25 3.00
RRLB Le'Veon Bell 3.00 8.00
RRLJ Landry Jones 1.25 3.00
RRMB Matt Barkley 1.25 3.00
RRMBA Montee Ball 1.25 3.00
RRMG Mike Glennon 1.25 3.00
RRMGI Mike Gillislee 1.25 3.00
RRMGO Marquise Goodwin 1.25 3.00
RRML Marcus Lattimore 1.25 3.00
RRMT Manti Te'o 1.50 4.00
RRMW Markus Wheaton 1.25 3.00
RRQP Quinton Patton 1.25 3.00
RRRN Ryan Nassib 1.25 3.00
RRRW Robert Woods 2.00 5.00
RRSB Stedman Bailey 1.25 3.00
RRST Stepfan Taylor 1.25 3.00
RRTA Tavon Austin 1.50 4.00
RRTE Tyler Eifert 1.25 3.00
RRTW Tyler Wilson 1.25 3.00
RRTWI Terrance Williams 1.25 3.00
RRVM Vance McDonald 1.50 4.00
RRZE Zach Ertz 2.50 6.00

2013 Topps Chrome Triple Rookie Autographs

TRAMAB Manl/Brnrd/Aust 25.00 60.00

2014 Topps Chrome

Frank Gore .25 .60
2 Cecil Shorts .20 .50
3 Justin Tuck .20 .50
4 Jordan Reed .20 .50
5 Demaryius Thomas .25 .60
6 Joe Flacco .25 .60
7 Randall Cobb .25 .60
8 Patrick Willis .25 .60
9A Antonio Brown .30 .75
9B Antonio Brown SP 4.00 10.00
10 Clay Matthews .30 .75
11 EJ Manuel .20 .50
12 Julius Thomas .20 .50
13 Dominique Rodgers-Cromartie .20 .50
14 Reggie Wayne .25 .60
15 Darrelle Revis .20 .50
16 Pierre Thomas .20 .50
17A Drew Brees .30 .75
17B Drew Brees SP 4.00 10.00
18 Pierre Garcon .25 .60
19 Kendall Wright .20 .50
20 NaVorro Bowman .25 .60
21 Tamba Hali .20 .50
22 DeSean Jackson .25 .60
23 Ryan Tannehill .25 .60
24 Greg Hardy .20 .50
25 Brandon Marshall .20 .50
26 Wes Welker .25 .60
27 C.J. Spiller .20 .50
28 Geno Smith .20 .50
29 J.J. Watt .30 .75
30 Troy Polamalu .30 .75
31 Vincent Jackson .20 .50
32A Michael Crabtree .20 .50
32B Michael Crabtree SP 2.50 6.00
33A Alshon Jeffery .25 .60
33B Alshon Jeffery SP 3.00 8.00
34 Zach Ertz .25 .60
35 Mike Glennon .25 .60
36 T.Y. Hilton .25 .60
37 Terrell Suggs .20 .50
38 Ndamukong Suh .25 .60
39 Patrick Peterson .20 .50
40 DeAndre Hopkins .25 .60
41 Cameron Jordan .20 .50
42A Peyton Manning .60 1.50
42B Peyton Manning SP 12.00 30.00
43 Ryan Mathews .25 .60
44 Eric Berry .25 .60
45A A.J. Green .30 .75
45B A.J. Green SP 4.00 10.00
46 Matt Forte .20 .50
47A Andrew Luck .40 1.00
47B Andrew Luck SP 5.00 12.00
48 Ace Sanders .20 .50
49 Jason Pierre-Paul .20 .50
50A Le'Veon Bell .25 .60
50B Le'Veon Bell SP 3.00 8.00
51 Mario Williams .20 .50
52A Alfred Morris .20 .50
52B Alfred Morris SP 2.50 6.00
53 Sheldon Richardson .20 .50
54 Alex Smith .25 .60
55 Josh Gordon .20 .50
56A Colin Kaepernick .25 .60
56B Colin Kaepernick SP 3.00 8.00
57 Tavon Austin .20 .50
58 Jay Cutler .20 .50
59 Percy Harvin .20 .50
60A Victor Cruz .25 .60
60B Victor Cruz SP 3.00 8.00
61A Marshawn Lynch .25 .60
61B Marshawn Lynch SP 3.00 8.00
62A Tom Brady .75 2.00
62B Tom Brady SP 10.00 25.00
63A Giovani Bernard .20 .50
63B Giovani Bernard SP 2.50 6.00
64A LeSean McCoy .30 .75
64B LeSean McCoy SP 4.00 10.00
65 Kiko Alonso .20 .50
66 Montee Ball .20 .50
67A Jimmy Graham .30 .75
67B Jimmy Graham SP 4.00 10.00
68 Mike Wallace .20 .50
69 Jordan Cameron .20 .50
70 Muhammad Wilkerson .20 .50
71A Reggie Bush .20 .50
71B Reggie Bush SP 2.50 6.00
72A Jamaal Charles .25 .60
72B Jamaal Charles SP 3.00 8.00
73 Matthew Stafford .25 .60
74 Robert Quinn .25 .60
75 Denarius Moore .20 .50
76 Larry Fitzgerald .25 .60
77 Tony Romo .25 .60
78A Dez Bryant .30 .75
78B Dez Bryant SP 4.00 10.00
79 Torrey Smith .20 .50
80 Robert Mathis .20 .50
81 Brian Hartline .20 .50
82A Rob Gronkowski .30 .75
82B Rob Gronkowski SP 4.00 10.00
83A Aaron Rodgers .60 1.50
83B Aaron Rodgers SP 8.00 20.00
84 Cordarrelle Patterson .20 .50
85 Andy Dalton .25 .60
86 Vontaze Burfict .20 .50
87 Luke Kuechly .25 .60
88 Julio Jones .30 .75
89A Adrian Peterson .30 .75
89B Adrian Peterson SP 4.00 10.00
90 Sean Lee .25 .60
91A Philip Rivers .30 .75
91B Philip Rivers SP 4.00 10.00
92 Anquan Boldin .20 .50
93 Eli Manning .25 .60
94 Matt Ryan .25 .60
95 Earl Thomas .25 .60
96 Robert Griffin III .20 .50
97A Richard Sherman .30 .75
97B Richard Sherman SP 6.00 15.00
98A Calvin Johnson .30 .75
98B Calvin Johnson SP 4.00 10.00
99A Roddy White .20 .50
99B Roddy White SP 2.50 6.00
100 Jordy Nelson .25 .60
101 Andre Johnson .25 .60
102A Russell Wilson .50 1.25
102B Russell Wilson SP 6.00 15.00
103A Cam Newton .30 .75
103B Cam Newton SP 4.00 10.00
104 Keenan Allen .25 .60
105 Julian Edelman .30 .75
106A Eddie Lacy .20 .50
106B Eddie Lacy SP 2.50 6.00
107 Arian Foster .25 .60
108 Von Miller .25 .60
109A Nick Foles .25 .60
109B Nick Foles SP 3.00 8.00
110 DeMarco Murray .25 .60
111 Craig Loston RC .30 .75
112 Henry Josey RC .30 .75
113 Jeff Mathews RC .40 1.00
114A Davante Adams RC .50 1.25
114B Davante Adams SP 3.00 8.00
115A Derek Carr RC 2.50 6.00
115B Derek Carr SP 12.00 30.00
116 Bruce Ellington RC .30 .75
117A Odell Beckham Jr. RC 4.00 10.00
117B Odell Beckham Jr. SP 15.00 40.00
118 Mike Davis RC .30 .75
119 Cyrus Kouandjio RC .40 1.00
120A Jadeveon Clowney RC .40 1.00
120B Jadeveon Clowney SP 2.50 6.00
121 Josh Huff RC .40 1.00
122 Marion Grice RC .30 .75
123 Cody Hoffman RC .30 .75
124A Kelvin Benjamin RC .50 1.25
124B Kelvin Benjamin SP 3.00 8.00
125A Jeremy Hill RC .40 1.00
125B Jeremy Hill SP 2.50 6.00
126A Marqise Lee RC .40 1.00
126B Marqise Lee SP 2.50 6.00
127 Devin Street RC .30 .75
128 Yawin Smallwood RC .30 .75
129 Aaron Murray RC .30 .75
130 Jared Abbrederis RC .30 .75
131 C.J. Fiedorowicz RC .30 .75
132 Shaquelle Evans RC .30 .75
133 Martavis Bryant RC .40 1.00
134 Storm Johnson RC .30 .75
135 Greg Robinson RC .30 .75
136 Ahmad Dixon RC .30 .75
137 Loucheiz Purifoy RC .30 .75
138A Sammy Watkins RC .50 1.25
138B Sammy Watkins SP 3.00 8.00
139 Tom Savage RC .30 .75
140 Kony Ealy RC .40 1.00
141A Tajh Boyd RC .30 .75
141B Tajh Boyd SP 2.00 5.00
142 Kevin Norwood RC .40 1.00
143 LaDarius Perkins RC .30 .75
144 A.J. McCarron RC .30 .75
145 Jalen Saunders RC .30 .75
146 Connor Shaw RC .30 .75
147 Brandon Coleman RC .30 .75
148 George Atkinson III RC .30 .75
149A Brandin Cooks RC .50 1.25
149B Brandin Cooks SP 3.00 8.00
150A Jimmy Garoppolo RC 2.50 6.00
150B Jimmy Garoppolo SP 15.00 40.00
151 Logan Thomas RC .30 .75
152 Justin Gilbert RC .30 .75
153 Louis Nix RC .30 .75
154 Andre Williams RC .30 .75
155A De'Anthony Thomas RC .30 .75
155B De'Anthony Thomas SP 2.00 5.00
156 Xavier Grimble RC .40 1.00
157 Calvin Pryor RC .30 .75
158A Carlos Hyde RC .40 1.00
158B Carlos Hyde SP 2.50 6.00
159 Ha Ha Clinton-Dix RC .40 1.00
160 Jerick McKinnon RC .40 1.00
161 Anthony Barr RC .30 .75
162 Kareem Martin RC .30 .75
163A Bishop Sankey RC .30 .75
163B Bishop Sankey SP 2.00 5.00
164A Tre Mason RC .30 .75
164B Tre Mason SP 2.00 5.00
165 Ryan Grant RC .30 .75
166 Ra'Shede Hageman RC .30 .75
167 Stephen Morris RC .30 .75
168 David Fales RC .30 .75
169A Johnny Manziel RC .50 1.25
169B Johnny Manziel SP 3.00 8.00
170 Will Sutton RC .40 1.00
171 Arthur Lynch RC .30 .75
172A Allen Robinson RC .50 1.25
172B Allen Robinson SP 3.00 8.00
173A Teddy Bridgewater RC .50 1.25
173B Teddy Bridgewater SP 3.00 8.00
174A Michael Sam RC .30 .75
174B Michael Sam SP 2.00 5.00
175 Aaron Donald RC .75 2.00
176 Scott Crichton RC .30 .75
177A Jarvis Landry RC .60 1.50
177B Jarvis Landry SP 4.00 10.00
178 Austin Seferian-Jenkins RC .30 .75
179 Lache Seastrunk RC .30 .75
180 Taylor Lewan RC .30 .75
181 Jordan Lynch RC .40 1.00
182 Troy Niklas RC .30 .75
183 Antone Exum RC .30 .75
184 Khalil Mack RC 1.25 3.00
185A Mike Evans RC .75 2.00
185B Mike Evans SP 5.00 12.00
186 Deone Bucannon RC .30 .75
187A Blake Bortles RC .40 1.00
187B Blake Bortles SP 2.50 6.00
188 Ka'Deem Carey RC .30 .75
189 Pierre Desir RC .30 .75
190 Marcus Roberson RC .40 1.00
191 Charles Sims UER RC .30 .75
192 Jeff Janis RC .30 .75
193 Jace Amaro RC .30 .75
194 Silas Redd RC .40 1.00
195 Jason Verrett RC .30 .75
196 Tyler Gaffney RC .30 .75
197 Donte Moncrief RC .30 .75
198 Timmy Jernigan RC .30 .75
199 Jake Matthews RC .30 .75
200 Robert Herron RC .30 .75
201 Aaron Colvin RC .30 .75
202 Terrance West RC .30 .75
203 C.J. Mosley RC .40 1.00
204 Darqueze Dennard RC .40 1.00
205 Kyle Van Noy RC .40 1.00
206 Zach Mettenberger RC .30 .75
207 Zack Martin RC .40 1.00
208 Dion Bailey RC .30 .75
209 Bradley Roby RC .30 .75
210 Stephon Tuitt RC .50 1.25
211 Cody Latimer RC .40 1.00
212A Jordan Matthews RC .50 1.25
212B Jordan Matthews SP 3.00 8.00
213A Eric Ebron RC .40 1.00
213B Eric Ebron SP 2.50 6.00
214 Dri Archer RC .30 .75
215 Caraun Reid RC .40 1.00
216 Devonta Freeman RC .50 1.25
217 Trent Murphy RC .30 .75
218 Ryan Shazier RC .50 1.25
219A Paul Richardson RC .40 1.00
219B Paul Richardson SP 2.50 6.00
220 Damien Williams RC .30 .75

2014 Topps Chrome Black Refractors

*1-110 VETS/299: 3X TO 8X BASIC CARDS
*110-220 ROOKIE/299: 2X TO 5X BASIC RC

2014 Topps Chrome Blue Refractors

*1-110 VETS/199: 3X TO 8X BASIC CARDS
*110-220 ROOKIE/199: 2X TO 5X BASIC RC

2014 Topps Chrome Blue Wave Refractors

*1-110 VETS: 3X TO 5X BASIC CARDS
*110-220 ROOKIE: 1.2X TO 3X BASIC RC

2014 Topps Chrome Camo Refractors

*1-110 VETS/499: 2.5X TO 6X BASIC CARDS
*110-220 ROOKIE/499: 1.5X TO 4X RC

2014 Topps Chrome Gold Refractors

*1-110 VETS/50: 6X TO 15X BASIC CARDS
*110-220 ROOKIE/50: 4X TO 10X BASIC RC
117 Odell Beckham Jr. 100.00 200.00

2014 Topps Chrome Green Refractors

*1-110 VETS: 1.5X TO 4X BASIC CARDS
*110-220 ROOKIE: 1X TO 2.5X BASIC RC

2014 Topps Chrome Orange Refractors

*1-110 VETS: 1.5X TO 4X BASIC CARDS
*110-220 ROOKIE: 1X TO 2.5X BASIC RC

2014 Topps Chrome Pink Refractors

*1-110 VETS/399: 2.5X TO 6X BASIC CARDS
*ROOKIES/399: 1.5X TO 4X BASIC RC

2014 Topps Chrome Pulsar Refractors

*1-110 VETS: 2X TO 5X BASIC CARDS
*110-220 ROOKIE: 1.2X TO 3X BASIC RC

2014 Topps Chrome Purple Refractors

*1-110 VETS: 2X TO 5X BASIC CARDS
*110-220 ROOKIE: 1.2X TO 3X BASIC RC

2014 Topps Chrome Red Refractors

*1-110 VETS/25: 15X TO 40X BASIC CARDS
*110-220 ROOKIE/25: 10X TO 25X BASIC RC
117 Odell Beckham Jr. 150.00 250.00

2014 Topps Chrome Refractors

*1-110 VETS: 1.2X TO 3X BASIC CARDS
*110-220 ROOKIE: .8X TO 2X BASIC RC

2014 Topps Chrome Sepia Refractors

*1-110 VETS/99: 5X TO 12X BASIC CARDS
*110-220 ROOKIE/99: 3X TO 8X BASIC RC

2014 Topps Chrome Xfractors

*1-110 VETS: 1.5X TO 4X BASIC CARDS
*110-220 ROOKIE: 1X TO 2.5X BASIC RC

2014 Topps Chrome 1000 Yard Club

*BLUE WAVE/25: .6X TO 1.5X BASIC INSERTS
*RED REF/99: .5X TO 1.2X BASIC INSERTS
1 Jordy Nelson 1.50 4.00
2 Jimmy Graham 2.00 5.00
3 Dez Bryant 2.00 5.00
4 Calvin Johnson 2.00 5.00
5 Julian Edelman 2.00 5.00
6 Andre Johnson 1.50 4.00
7 Adrian Peterson 2.00 5.00
8 Alfred Morris 1.25 3.00
9 Josh Gordon 1.25 3.00
10 Eddie Lacy 1.25 3.00
11 Frank Gore 1.50 4.00
12 Jamaal Charles 1.50 4.00
13 T.Y. Hilton 1.50 4.00
14 Knowshon Moreno 1.25 3.00
15 Antonio Brown 2.00 5.00
16 A.J. Green 2.00 5.00
17 LeSean McCoy 2.00 5.00
18 Reggie Bush 1.25 3.00
19 Marshawn Lynch 1.50 4.00
20 Demaryius Thomas 1.50 4.00
21 Alshon Jeffery 1.50 4.00
22 DeMarco Murray 1.50 4.00

2014 Topps Chrome 1000 Yard Club Red Refractor Autographs

1 Jordy Nelson/75 25.00 50.00
8 Alfred Morris/75
9 Josh Gordon/25 20.00 50.00
10 Eddie Lacy/75 10.00 25.00
11 Frank Gore/25 15.00 40.00
13 T.Y. Hilton/75 12.00 30.00
17 LeSean McCoy/25
18 Reggie Bush/25 12.00 30.00
19 Marshawn Lynch/25 50.00 100.00
21 Alshon Jeffery/75 12.00 30.00

2014 Topps Chrome 1963 Minis

*PULSA DC/50: 2.5X TO 6X BASIC INSERTS
*REFRACT/99: 1.2X TO 3X BASIC INSERTS
1 Marqise Lee .40 1.00
2 Tre Mason .30 .75
3 Jordan Matthews .50 1.25
4 Odell Beckham Jr. .75 2.00
5 Michael Sam .30 .75
6 Kelvin Benjamin .50 1.25
7 Derek Carr 2.00 5.00
8 Jimmy Garoppolo 1.50 4.00
9 Ka'Deem Carey .30 .75
10 Jace Amaro .30 .75
11 Terrance West .30 .75
12 Tajh Boyd .30 .75
13 Aaron Murray .30 .75
14 De'Anthony Thomas .30 .75
15 Davante Adams .50 1.25
16 Jeremy Hill .40 1.00
17 Jadeveon Clowney .40 1.00
18 Austin Seferian-Jenkins .30 .75
19 A.J. McCarron .30 .75
20 Sammy Watkins .50 1.25
21 Mike Evans .75 2.00
22 Teddy Bridgewater .50 1.25
23 Paul Richardson .40 1.00
24 Donte Moncrief .30 .75
25 Brandin Cooks .50 1.25
26 Johnny Manziel .50 1.25
27 Eric Ebron .40 1.00
28 Jarvis Landry .60 1.50
29 Andre Williams .30 .75
30 Blake Bortles .40 1.00
31 Logan Thomas .30 .75
32 Tom Savage .30 .75
33 Bishop Sankey .30 .75
34 Carlos Hyde .40 1.00
35 Allen Robinson .50 1.25
36 Martavis Bryant .40 1.00
37 Charles Sims .30 .75
38 Jared Abbrederis .30 .75
39 Zach Mettenberger .30 .75
40 David Fales .30 .75
41 Devonta Freeman .50 1.25
42 James White .60 1.50
43 Robert Herron .30 .75
44 Bruce Ellington .30 .75
45 Cody Latimer .40 1.00

2014 Topps Chrome 1963 Minis Refractor Autographs

EXCH EXPIRATION: 10/31/2017
1 Marqise Lee
2 Tre Mason 6.00 15.00
3 Jordan Matthews 15.00 40.00
4 Odell Beckham Jr. 125.00 250.00
6 Kelvin Benjamin EXCH 10.00 25.00
7 Derek Carr 90.00 150.00
8 Jimmy Garoppolo 50.00 100.00
9 Ka'Deem Carey 6.00 15.00
11 Terrance West 12.00 30.00
13 Aaron Murray EXCH 6.00 15.00
15 Davante Adams 10.00 25.00
16 Jeremy Hill 8.00 20.00
17 Jadeveon Clowney 8.00 20.00
18 Austin Seferian-Jenkins
19 A.J. McCarron EXCH 6.00 15.00
20 Sammy Watkins 60.00 120.00
21 Mike Evans 30.00 60.00
22 Teddy Bridgewater 10.00 25.00
23 Paul Richardson 8.00 20.00
24 Donte Moncrief
25 Brandin Cooks 10.00 25.00
26 Johnny Manziel 10.00 25.00
27 Eric Ebron
28 Jarvis Landry 12.00 30.00
29 Andre Williams
30 Blake Bortles EXCH 8.00 20.00
31 Logan Thomas 6.00 15.00
32 Tom Savage
33 Bishop Sankey EXCH 6.00 15.00
34 Carlos Hyde EXCH 20.00 50.00
35 Allen Robinson EXCH 12.00 30.00
39 Zach Mettenberger EXCH 6.00 15.00
41 Devonta Freeman
42 James White 12.00 30.00
45 Cody Latimer

2014 Topps Chrome 1965

*REFRACT/99: 1.2X TO 3X BASIC INSERTS
TB1 Jace Amaro .40 1.00
TB2 Allen Robinson .60 1.50
TB3 A.J. McCarron .40 1.00
TB4 Tajh Boyd .40 1.00
TB5 Aaron Murray .40 1.00
TB6 Andre Williams .40 1.00
TB7 Terrance West .40 1.00
TB8 Tre Mason .40 1.00
TB9 Jimmy Garoppolo 3.00 8.00
TB10 Jarvis Landry .75 2.00
TB11 Jadeveon Clowney .50 1.25
TB12 Johnny Manziel .60 1.50
TB13 Teddy Bridgewater .60 1.50
TB14 Blake Bortles .50 1.25
TB15 Carlos Hyde .50 1.25
TB16 Davante Adams .60 1.50
TB17 Bishop Sankey .40 1.00
TB18 Paul Richardson .50 1.25
TB19 De'Anthony Thomas .30 .75
TB20 Kelvin Benjamin .60 1.50
TB21 Sammy Watkins .60 1.50
TB22 Mike Evans 1.00 2.50
TB23 Derek Carr 2.50 6.00
TB24 Eric Ebron .50 1.25
TB25 Marqise Lee .50 1.25
TB26 Odell Beckham Jr. 1.00 2.50
TB27 Brandin Cooks .60 1.50
TB28 Ka'Deem Carey .40 1.00
TB29 Austin Seferian-Jenkins .40 1.00
TB30 Jordan Matthews .60 1.50
TB31 Tom Savage .40 1.00
TB32 Michael Sam .40 1.00
TB33 Jeremy Hill .50 1.25
TB34 Donte Moncrief .40 1.00
TB35 Cody Latimer .50 1.25
TB36 Devonta Freeman .60 1.50
TB37 James White .75 2.00
TB38 Josh Huff .50 1.25
TB39 Charles Sims .40 1.00
TB40 Zach Mettenberger .40 1.00

2014 Topps Chrome 1965 Autographs

TB2 Allen Robinson
TB3 A.J. McCarron
TB5 Aaron Murray
TB6 Andre Williams
TB7 Terrance West
TB11 Jadeveon Clowney
TB12 Johnny Manziel
TB13 Teddy Bridgewater
TB14 Blake Bortles 8.00 20.00
TB15 Carlos Hyde 20.00 50.00
TB16 Davante Adams
TB17 Bishop Sankey EXCH
TB18 Paul Richardson
TB20 Kelvin Benjamin
TB21 Sammy Watkins
TB22 Mike Evans
TB23 Derek Carr
TB24 Eric Ebron
TB26 Odell Beckham Jr.
TB27 Brandin Cooks
TB28 Ka'Deem Carey
TB29 Austin Seferian-Jenkins
TB30 Jordan Matthews
TB31 Tom Savage
TB33 Jeremy Hill
TB35 Cody Latimer
TB36 Devonta Freeman
TB37 James White
TB39 Charles Sims
TB40 Zach Mettenberger

2014 Topps Chrome 1985

COMPLETE SET (40) 15.00 40.00
*GOLD REF/75: 2.5X TO 6X BASIC INSERTS
*PULSAR REF/50: 3X TO 8X BASIC INSERTS
*REFRACT/99: 2X TO 5X BASIC INSERTS
1 Tom Savage .30 .75
2 Khalil Mack 1.25 3.00
3 Jimmy Garoppolo 2.50 6.00
4 Jarvis Landry .60 1.50
5 Davante Adams .50 1.25
6 Teddy Bridgewater .50 1.25
7 Tre Mason .30 .75
8 Jordan Matthews 1.00 2.50
9 Paul Richardson .40 1.00
10 Allen Robinson .50 1.25
11 Bishop Sankey .30 .75
12 Mike Evans .75 2.00
13 Eric Ebron .40 1.00
14 Michael Sam .30 .75
15 Odell Beckham Jr. .75 2.00
16 Jadeveon Clowney .40 1.00
17 Tajh Boyd .30 .75
18 Derek Carr 2.00 5.00
19 Carlos Hyde .40 1.00
20 Blake Bortles .40 1.00
21 Marqise Lee .40 1.00
22 A.J. McCarron .30 .75
23 Jace Amaro .30 .75
24 Logan Thomas .30 .75
25 Aaron Murray .30 .75
26 Johnny Manziel .50 1.25
27 Ka'Deem Carey .30 .75
28 Cody Latimer .40 1.00
29 Sammy Watkins .50 1.25
30 Charles Sims .30 .75
31 Brandin Cooks .50 1.25
32 Dri Archer .30 .75
33 Kelvin Benjamin .50 1.25
34 Austin Seferian-Jenkins .30 .75
35 Devonta Freeman .50 1.25
36 Jeremy Hill .40 1.00
37 Donte Moncrief .30 .75
38 Andre Williams .30 .75
39 De'Anthony Thomas .30 .75
40 Zach Mettenberger .30 .75

2014 Topps Chrome 1985 Refractor Autographs

1 Tom Savage
3 Jimmy Garoppolo
4 Jarvis Landry
5 Davante Adams
6 Teddy Bridgewater
7 Tre Mason EXCH
8 Jordan Matthews
9 Paul Richardson
10 Allen Robinson
11 Bishop Sankey
12 Mike Evans
13 Eric Ebron
15 Odell Beckham Jr. 125.00 250.00
16 Jadeveon Clowney
18 Derek Carr
19 Carlos Hyde 20.00 50.00
20 Blake Bortles
21 Marqise Lee
22 A.J. McCarron
23 Jace Amaro
24 Logan Thomas
25 Aaron Murray
26 Johnny Manziel
27 Ka'Deem Carey
28 Cody Latimer
29 Sammy Watkins
30 Charles Sims
31 Brandin Cooks
32 Dri Archer
33 Kelvin Benjamin
34 Austin Seferian-Jenkins
35 Devonta Freeman
36 Jeremy Hill
38 Andre Williams
40 Zach Mettenberger

2014 Topps Chrome 4000 Yard Club

*BLUE WAVE/25: .8X TO 2X BASIC INSERTS
*RED REF/99: .6X TO 1.5X BASIC INSERTS
1 Tom Brady 5.00 12.00
2 Drew Brees 2.00 5.00
3 Andy Dalton 1.50 4.00
4 Ben Roethlisberger 2.00 5.00
5 Matt Ryan 1.50 4.00
6 Peyton Manning 5.00 12.00
7 Philip Rivers 2.00 5.00
8 Matthew Stafford 1.50 4.00

2014 Topps Chrome Dual Rookie Autographs

DRABM J.Manziel/T.Bridgewater 10.00 25.00
DRACB D.Carr/B.Bortles 60.00 120.00
DRALB J.Landry/O.Beckham Jr. 100.00 175.00
DRAWE S.Watkins/M.Evans 50.00 100.00
DRAWL M.Lee/S.Watkins 40.00 80.00

2014 Topps Chrome Fantasy Focus

*REFRACT/99: 1.2X TO 3X BASIC INSERTS
FFAB Antonio Brown .60 1.50
FFAG A.J. Green .60 1.50
FFAJ Alshon Jeffery .50 1.25
FFAL Andrew Luck .75 2.00
FFAP Adrian Peterson .60 1.50
FFAR Aaron Rodgers 1.25 3.00
FFBM Brandon Marshall .40 1.00
FFCJ Calvin Johnson .60 1.50
FFCK Colin Kaepernick .50 1.25
FFCN Cam Newton .60 1.50
FFDB Drew Brees .60 1.50
FFDM DeMarco Murray .50 1.25
FFDR Dez Bryant .60 1.50
FFDT Demaryius Thomas .50 1.25
FFEL Eddie Lacy .40 1.00
FFJC Jamaal Charles .50 1.25
FFJN Jordy Nelson .50 1.25
FFJR Jimmy Graham .60 1.50
FFJT Julius Thomas .40 1.00
FFJW Jason Witten .50 1.25
FFLM LeSean McCoy .60 1.50
FFMF Matt Forte .40 1.00
FFML Marshawn Lynch .50 1.25
FFMS Matthew Stafford .50 1.25
FFPM Peyton Manning 1.25 3.00
FFRB Reggie Bush .40 1.00
FFRW Russell Wilson 1.00 2.50
FFTB Tom Brady 1.50 4.00
FFTR Tony Romo .50 1.25
FFVD Vernon Davis .40 1.00

2014 Topps Chrome Rookie Autographs

112 Henry Josey 2.50 6.00
114 Davante Adams 12.00 30.00
115 Derek Carr SP 100.00 200.00
116 Bruce Ellington 2.50 6.00
117 Odell Beckham Jr. 40.00 80.00
118 Mike Davis 2.50 6.00
120 Jadeveon Clowney SP 3.00 8.00
122 Marion Grice 2.50 6.00
123 Cody Hoffman 2.50 6.00
124 Kelvin Benjamin 6.00 15.00
125 Jeremy Hill 3.00 8.00
129 Aaron Murray 2.50 6.00
130 Jared Abbrederis 2.50 6.00
131 C.J. Fiedorowicz 2.50 6.00
132 Shaquelle Evans 2.50 6.00
133 Martavis Bryant SP 10.00 25.00
134 Storm Johnson 2.50 6.00
138 Sammy Watkins 1.00 25.00
139 Tom Savage 2.50 6.00
140 Kony Ealy 3.00 8.00
142 Kevin Norwood 2.50 6.00
144 A.J. McCarron SP 2.50 6.00
146 Connor Shaw 2.50 6.00
147 Brandon Coleman 2.50 6.00
149 Brandin Cooks 4.00 10.00
150 Jimmy Garoppolo 50.00 100.00
151 Logan Thomas 2.50 6.00
154 Andre Williams 2.50 6.00
158 Carlos Hyde SP 12.00 30.00
159 Ha Ha Clinton-Dix 3.00 8.00
160 Jerick McKinnon 3.00 8.00
161 Anthony Barr 2.50 6.00
163 Bishop Sankey 6.00 15.00
164 Tre Mason SP
167 Stephen Morris 2.50 6.00
168 David Fales 2.50 6.00
169 Johnny Manziel SP 15.00 40.00
171 Arthur Lynch 2.50 6.00
172 Allen Robinson 4.00 10.00
173 Teddy Bridgewater SP 8.00 20.00
175 Aaron Donald 12.00 30.00
176 Scott Crichton 2.50 6.00
177 Jarvis Landry 12.00 30.00
178 Austin Seferian-Jenkins 2.50 6.00
179 Lache Seastrunk 2.50 6.00
181 Jordan Lynch 3.00 8.00
182 Troy Niklas 2.50 6.00
185 Mike Evans 20.00 50.00
187 Blake Bortles SP 3.00 8.00
188 Ka'Deem Carey 2.50 6.00
189 Pierre Desir 2.50 6.00
191 Charles Sims 2.50 6.00
192 Jeff Janis 5.00 12.00
195 Jason Verrett 2.50 6.00
199 Jake Matthews 2.50 6.00
200 Robert Herron 2.50 6.00
202 Terrance West 2.50 6.00
203 C.J. Mosley 4.00 10.00
204 Darqueze Dennard 3.00 8.00
206 Zach Mettenberger 2.50 6.00
209 Bradley Roby 2.50 6.00
211 Cody Latimer 3.00 8.00
212 Jordan Matthews 4.00 10.00
213 Eric Ebron SP 3.00 8.00
216 Devonta Freeman 10.00 25.00
219 Paul Richardson 3.00 8.00
220 Damien Williams 2.50 6.00
221 Trey Millard 3.00 8.00
222 James White 5.00 12.00
223 Michael Campanaro 2.50 6.00
224 Garrett Gilbert 2.50 6.00
225 Isaiah Crowell 3.00 8.00
226 John Brown 4.00 10.00

2014 Topps Chrome Rookie Autographs Black Refractors

*BLACK REF/25: 1.2X TO 3X BASIC AU
115 Derek Carr 150.00 250.00
117 Odell Beckham Jr. 150.00 300.00
150 Jimmy Garoppolo 400.00 800.00
173 Teddy Bridgewater 25.00 60.00
185 Mike Evans 100.00 200.00
225 Isaiah Crowell 10.00 25.00

2014 Topps Chrome Rookie Autographs Camo Refractors

*CAMO REF/99: .6X TO 1.5X BASIC AU
115 Derek Carr 125.00 250.00
117 Odell Beckham Jr. 100.00 200.00
150 Jimmy Garoppolo 125.00 250.00

2014 Topps Chrome Rookie Autographs Pink Refractors

*PINK REF/75: .6X TO 1.5X BASIC AU
115 Derek Carr 125.00 250.00
117 Odell Beckham Jr. 100.00 200.00
150 Jimmy Garoppolo 125.00 250.00

2014 Topps Chrome Rookie Autographs Refractors

*REFRACT/150: .5X TO 1.2X BASIC AU
117 Odell Beckham Jr. 60.00 125.00
150 Jimmy Garoppolo 150.00 250.00

2014 Topps Chrome Rookie Autographs Variations

*REF VAR/75: .6X TO 1.5X BASIC INSERTS
115 Derek Carr 125.00 250.00
117 Odell Beckham Jr. 100.00 200.00
150 Jimmy Garoppolo 200.00 400.00
169 Johnny Manziel 6.00 15.00
177 Jarvis Landry 40.00 80.00

2014 Topps Chrome Rookie Autographs Patches

EXCH EXPIRATION: 10/31/2017
RAPAM A.J. McCarron 8.00 20.00
RAPAR Allen Robinson 12.00 30.00
RAPASP Austin Seferian-Jenkins 8.00 20.00
RAPAU Aaron Murray 8.00 20.00
RAPAW Andre Williams 8.00 20.00
RAPBB Blake Bortles 10.00 25.00
RAPBC Brandin Cooks 12.00 30.00
RAPBS Bishop Sankey 8.00 20.00
RAPCH Carlos Hyde EXCH 40.00 80.00
RAPCL Cody Latimer
RAPCS Charles Sims 8.00 20.00
RAPDA Davante Adams 12.00 30.00
RAPDAR Dri Archer 8.00 20.00
RAPDC Derek Carr 100.00 200.00
RAPDFR Devonta Freeman 30.00 80.00
RAPDM Donte Moncrief 8.00 20.00
RAPEE Eric Ebron 10.00 25.00
RAPJC Jadeveon Clowney 10.00 25.00
RAPJG Jimmy Garoppolo 150.00 250.00
RAPJH Jeremy Hill 10.00 25.00
RAPJM Jordan Matthews 12.00 30.00
RAPJN Jarvis Landry 20.00 50.00
RAPJR Jace Amaro 8.00 20.00
RAPJZ Johnny Manziel 15.00 40.00
RAPKB Kelvin Benjamin 20.00 50.00
RAPKC Ka'Deem Carey 8.00 20.00
RAPLT Logan Thomas 8.00 20.00
RAPMB Martavis Bryant EXCH 12.00 30.00
RAPME Mike Evans 30.00 60.00
RAPML Marqise Lee 10.00 25.00
RAPMS Michael Sam 8.00 20.00
RAPOB Odell Beckham Jr. 100.00 200.00
RAPPR Paul Richardson 15.00 40.00
RAPSW Sammy Watkins 30.00 80.00
RAPTB Tajh Boyd 8.00 20.00
RAPTI Teddy Bridgewater 15.00 40.00
RAPTM Tre Mason EXCH 25.00 50.00
RAPTS Tom Savage 8.00 20.00
RAPTW Terrance West 8.00 20.00
RAPZM Zach Mettenberger 8.00 20.00

2014 Topps Chrome Rookie Die Cuts

*BLUE WAVE/50: 2X TO 5X BASIC INSERTS
*RED REF/25: 3X TO 8X BASIC INSERTS
CRDCAM A.J. McCarron .40 1.00
CRDCAR Allen Robinson .60 1.50
CRDCAS Austin Seferian-Jenkins .40 1.00
CRDCAW Andre Williams .40 1.00
CRDCBB Blake Bortles .50 1.25
CRDCBC Brandin Cooks .60 1.50
CRDCBS Bishop Sankey .40 1.00
CRDCCH Carlos Hyde .50 1.25
CRDCCL Cody Latimer .50 1.25
CRDCCS Charles Sims .40 1.00
CRDCDA Davante Adams .60 1.50
CRDCDC Derek Carr 2.50 6.00
CRDCDF Devonta Freeman .60 1.50

CRDCDM Donte Moncrief .40 1.00
CRDCDT De'Anthony Thomas .40 1.00
CRDCEE Eric Ebron .50 1.25
CRDCJA Jace Amaro .40 1.00
CRDCJC Jadeveon Clowney .50 1.25
CRDCJG Jimmy Garoppolo 3.00 8.00
CRDCJH Jeremy Hill .50 1.25
CRDCJL Jarvis Landry .75 2.00
CRDCJM Johnny Manziel .60 1.50
CRDCKB Kelvin Benjamin .60 1.50
CRDCKC Ka'Deem Carey .40 1.00
CRDCLT Logan Thomas .40 1.00
CRDCME Mike Evans 1.00 2.50
CRDCML Marqise Lee .50 1.25
CRDCMS Michael Sam .40 1.00
CRDCOB Odell Beckham Jr. 1.00 2.50
CRDCPR Paul Richardson .50 1.25
CRDCSW Sammy Watkins .60 1.50
CRDCTB Teddy Bridgewater .60 1.50
CRDCTM Tre Mason .40 1.00
CRDCTS Tom Savage .40 1.00
CRDCTW Terrance West .40 1.00
CRDCZM Zach Mettenberger .40 1.00
CRDCAMU Aaron Murray .40 1.00
CRDCDFA David Fales .40 1.00
CRDCJMA Jordan Matthews .60 1.50
CRDCTBO Tajh Boyd .40 1.00

2014 Topps Chrome Rookie Die Cuts Autographs

CRDCAM A.J. McCarron 10.00 25.00
CRDCAMU Aaron Murray 10.00 25.00
CRDCAR Allen Robinson 15.00 40.00
CRDCAS Austin Seferian-Jenkins 10.00 25.00
CRDCAW Andre Williams 30.00 60.00
CRDCBB Blake Bortles 12.00 30.00
CRDCBC Brandin Cooks 40.00 80.00
CRDCBS Bishop Sankey 10.00 25.00
CRDCCH Carlos Hyde 30.00 80.00
CRDCCL Cody Latimer 12.00 30.00
CRDCCS Charles Sims 10.00 25.00
CRDCDA Davante Adams 15.00 40.00
CRDCDC Derek Carr 125.00 200.00
CRDCDF Devonta Freeman 60.00 120.00
CRDCDFA David Fales
CRDCEE Eric Ebron 12.00 30.00
CRDCJC Jadeveon Clowney 12.00 30.00
CRDCJG Jimmy Garoppolo 60.00 120.00
CRDCJH Jeremy Hill 12.00 30.00
CRDCJL Jarvis Landry 20.00 50.00
CRDCJM Johnny Manziel 15.00 40.00
CRDCJMA Jordan Matthews 15.00 40.00
CRDCKB Kelvin Benjamin 15.00 40.00
CRDCKC Ka'Deem Carey 10.00 25.00
CRDCLT Logan Thomas 10.00 25.00
CRDCME Mike Evans 60.00 120.00
CRDCML Marqise Lee 12.00 30.00
CRDCOB Odell Beckham Jr. 125.00 250.00
CRDCPR Paul Richardson 25.00 50.00
CRDCSW Sammy Watkins 25.00 50.00
CRDCTB Teddy Bridgewater 50.00 100.00
CRDCTM Tre Mason 30.00 60.00
CRDCTS Tom Savage 10.00 25.00
CRDCTW Terrance West 10.00 25.00
CRDCZM Zach Mettenberger 10.00 25.00

2014 Topps Chrome Rookie Relics

*BLACK REF/25: 1.2X TO 3X BASIC JSY
*GOLD REF/10: 2X TO 5X BASIC JSY
*PURP.REF/75: .6X TO 1.5X BASIC JSY
*REFRACT/150: .5X TO 1.2X BASIC JSY
*XFRACTOR/99: .6X TO 1.5X BASIC JSY
RRAM A.J. McCarron 1.25 3.00
RRAR Allen Robinson 2.00 5.00
RRAS Austin Seferian-Jenkins 1.25 3.00
RRAU Aaron Murray 1.25 3.00
RRAW Andre Williams 1.25 3.00
RRBB Blake Bortles 1.50 4.00
RRBC Brandin Cooks 2.00 5.00
RRBS Bishop Sankey 1.25 3.00
RRCH Carlos Hyde 1.50 4.00
RRCL Cody Latimer 1.50 4.00
RRCS Charles Sims 1.25 3.00
RRDA Davante Adams 2.00 5.00
RRDC Derek Carr 4.00 10.00
RRDF Devonta Freeman 2.00 5.00
RRDM Donte Moncrief 1.25 3.00
RRDR Dri Archer 1.25 3.00
RRDT De'Anthony Thomas 1.25 3.00
RREE Eric Ebron 1.50 4.00
RRJA Johnny Manziel 2.00 5.00
RRJC Jadeveon Clowney 1.50 4.00
RRJG Jimmy Garoppolo 10.00 25.00
RRJH Jeremy Hill 1.50 4.00
RRJL Jarvis Landry 2.50 6.00
RRJM Jordan Matthews 2.00 5.00
RRJR Jace Amaro 1.25 3.00
RRJU Josh Huff 1.50 4.00
RRKB Kelvin Benjamin 2.00 5.00
RRKC Ka'Deem Carey 1.25 3.00
RRKM Khalil Mack 5.00 12.00
RRLT Logan Thomas 1.25 3.00
RRME Mike Evans 3.00 8.00
RRML Marqise Lee 1.50 4.00
RROB Odell Beckham Jr. 8.00 20.00
RRPR Paul Richardson 1.50 4.00
RRSW Sammy Watkins 2.00 5.00
RRTB Teddy Bridgewater 2.00 5.00
RRTM Tre Mason 1.25 3.00
RRTO Tajh Boyd 1.25 3.00
RRTS Tom Savage 1.25 3.00
RRTW Terrance West 1.25 3.00

2014 Topps Chrome Triple Rookie Autographs

TRAMBB Brtls/Brdgwtr/Mnzl 20.00 50.00

2015 Topps Chrome

1 Marshawn Lynch .25 .60
2A Aaron Rodgers .60 1.50
2B Brett Favre SP 12.00 30.00
3 Robert Griffin III .20 .50
4A Sammy Watkins .25 .60
4B Sammy Watkins SP 3.00 8.00
5A Calvin Johnson .30 .75
5B Jerry Rice SP 6.00 15.00
6A Andrew Luck .40 1.00
6B Roger Staubach SP 8.00 20.00
7A Jamaal Charles .25 .60
7B Jamaal Charles SP 3.00 8.00
8 Le'Veon Bell .25 .60
9A Richard Sherman .30 .75
9B Richard Sherman SP
10 Rob Gronkowski .30 .75
11 Percy Harvin .20 .50
12A Drew Brees .30 .75
12B Drew Brees SP 4.00 10.00
13A Antonio Brown .30 .75
13B Antonio Brown SP 4.00 10.00
14 Demaryius Thomas .25 .60
15A Russell Wilson .40 1.00
15B Russell Wilson SP 5.00 12.00
16 Dez Bryant .30 .75
17 Julio Jones .30 .75
18A Odell Beckham Jr. .30 .75
18B Odell Beckham Jr. SP 4.00 10.00
19A Eddie Lacy .20 .50
19B Eddie Lacy SP 12.00 30.00
20 Cam Newton .30 .75
21A Jordy Nelson .25 .60
21B Jordy Nelson SP 3.00 8.00
22 Ndamukong Suh .25 .60
23A DeMarco Murray .25 .60
23B Eric Dickerson SP 3.00 8.00
24 Adrian Peterson .30 .75
25 Jimmy Graham .30 .75
26A Luke Kuechly .25 .60
26B Mike Singletary SP 4.00 10.00
27 LeSean McCoy .30 .75
28 A.J. Green .30 .75
29 Earl Thomas .25 .60
30A Ben Roethlisberger .30 .75
30B Terry Bradshaw SP 5.00 12.00
31 Terrell Suggs .20 .50
32A Matt Forte .20 .50
32B Matt Forte SP
33 Mario Williams .20 .50
34A Randall Cobb .25 .60
34B Randall Cobb SP 3.00 8.00
35 Patrick Peterson .20 .50
36 Philip Rivers .30 .75
37 Kam Chancellor .30 .75
38A Arian Foster .25 .60
38B Earl Campbell SP 4.00 10.00
39 Darrelle Revis .20 .50
40A Matthew Stafford .25 .60
40B Matthew Stafford SP 3.00 8.00
40C Barry Sanders SP 6.00 15.00
41A Alshon Jeffery .25 .60
41B Alshon Jeffery SP 3.00 8.00
42 Jeremy Hill .20 .50
43 T.Y. Hilton .25 .60
44A Tony Romo .25 .60
44B Emmitt Smith SP 6.00 15.00
45A Clay Matthews .30 .75
45B Clay Matthews SP 4.00 10.00
46A Mike Evans .25 .60
46B Mike Evans SP 3.00 8.00
47 Kelvin Benjamin .25 .60
48A C.J. Anderson .25 .60
48B Terrell Davis SP 3.00 8.00
49 Brandon Marshall .20 .50
50 Tom Brady .75 2.00
51A Matt Ryan .25 .60
51B Matt Ryan SP 3.00 8.00
52 DeSean Jackson .25 .60
53 Frank Gore .25 .60
54 Joe Flacco .25 .60
55A Eli Manning .25 .60
55B Eli Manning SP 3.00 8.00
56A Colin Kaepernick .25 .60
56B Steve Young SP 5.00 12.00
57 Alfred Morris .20 .50
58 Larry Fitzgerald .25 .60
59 Justin Houston .20 .50
60 Antonio Gates .20 .50
61 Emmanuel Sanders .25 .60
62 Mark Ingram .25 .60
63 Lamar Miller .20 .50
64 Carlos Hyde .20 .50
65 Julian Edelman .30 .75
66 Vontae Davis .20 .50
67A Patrick Willis .25 .60
67B Ronnie Lott SP 3.00 8.00
68 Bobby Wagner .20 .50
69 Giovani Bernard .20 .50
70A Troy Polamalu .30 .75
70B Troy Polamalu SP 4.00 10.00
71 Eric Berry .25 .60
72 Golden Tate .20 .50
73 Jeremy Maclin .20 .50
74 Nick Foles .25 .60
75 J.J. Watt .30 .75
76A Ryan Tannehill .25 .60
76B Dan Marino SP 10.00 25.00
77 Jay Cutler .20 .50
78 C.J. Spiller .20 .50
79 Teddy Bridgewater .25 .60
80 Blake Bortles .20 .50
81 Alex Smith .25 .60
82A Tre Mason .25 .60
82B Marshall Faulk SP 3.00 8.00
83 Joique Bell .20 .50
84 Steve Smith .25 .60
85 Jadeveon Clowney .20 .50
86 Travis Kelce .30 .75
87 Greg Olsen .25 .60
88 Jason Witten .25 .60
89A Latavius Murray .20 .50
89B Bo Jackson SP 5.00 12.00
90 Jonathan Stewart .20 .50
91 Carson Palmer .25 .60
92 Derek Carr .30 .75
93 Andy Dalton .25 .60
94 Devonta Freeman .25 .60
95 Brandin Cooks .25 .60
96 Andre Johnson .25 .60
97 Jordan Matthews .25 .60
98 Vincent Jackson .20 .50
99 Eric Decker .20 .50
100A Peyton Manning .60 1.50
100B Peyton Manning SP 8.00 20.00
100C John Elway SP 6.00 15.00
101 Vic Beasley RC .40 1.00
102A Brett Hundley RC .30 .75
102B Brett Hundley SP 8.00 20.00
103A DeVante Parker RC .50 1.25
103B DeVante Parker SP 2.50 6.00
104 Trae Waynes RC .30 .75
105A Melvin Gordon RC .75 2.00
105B Melvin Gordon SP 4.00 10.00
106A Dorial Green-Beckham RC .30 .75
106B Dorial Green-Beckham SP 1.50 4.00
107A Devin Funchess RC .50 1.25
107B Devin Funchess SP 2.50 6.00
108A Jaelen Strong RC .40 1.00
108B Jaelen Strong SP 2.00 5.00
109 P.J. Williams RC .40 1.00
110A Todd Gurley RC 1.25 3.00
110B Todd Gurley SP 15.00 40.00
111A Ameer Abdullah RC .50 1.25
111B Ameer Abdullah SP 2.50 6.00
112 Michael Bennett RC .30 .75
113A Sammie Coates RC .40 1.00
113B Sammie Coates SP 2.00 5.00
114 Randy Gregory RC .30 .75
115A Amari Cooper RC 1.00 2.50
115B Amari Cooper SP 15.00 40.00
116 Shaq Thompson RC .40 1.00
117 Brandon Scherff RC .50 1.25
118 Landon Collins RC .40 1.00
119 Ty Montgomery RC .30 .75
120A Jay Ajayi RC .50 1.25
120B Jay Ajayi SP 2.50 6.00
121A Tevin Coleman RC .40 1.00
121B Tevin Coleman SP 2.00 5.00
122 Shane Ray RC .30 .75
123 Josh Harper RC .30 .75
124 Marcus Peters RC .50 1.25
125A Kevin White RC .40 1.00
125B Kevin White SP 2.00 5.00
126 Dezmin Lewis RC .30 .75
127 Dante Fowler Jr. RC .50 1.25
128 Terrence Magee RC .50 1.25
129 Kenny Bell RC .50 1.25
130 Leonard Williams RC .30 .75
131 Danny Shelton RC .30 .75
132 Benardrick McKinney RC .30 .75
133 Andrus Peat RC .30 .75
134 Cedric Ogbuehi RC .30 .75
135 La'el Collins RC .40 1.00
136 Ereck Flowers RC .40 1.00
137A Bryce Petty RC .30 .75
137B Bryce Petty SP 6.00 15.00
138A T.J. Yeldon RC .30 .75
138B T.J. Yeldon SP 1.50 4.00
139 Mike Davis RC .30 .75
140A Duke Johnson RC .50 1.25
140B Duke Johnson SP 2.50 6.00
141 Karlos Williams RC .30 .75
142 Jeremy Langford RC .30 .75
143 Marcus Murphy RC .30 .75
144 Nick O'Leary RC .30 .75
145 Ben Koyack RC .50 1.25
146A Nelson Agholor RC .40 1.00
146B Nelson Agholor SP 2.00 5.00
147 Rashad Greene RC .30 .75
148 Stefon Diggs RC .75 2.00
149 Justin Hardy RC .30 .75
150A Marcus Mariota RC 1.25 3.00
150B Marcus Mariota SP 20.00 50.00
151A Garrett Grayson RC .30 .75
151B Garrett Grayson SP 6.00 15.00
152 Javorius Allen RC .40 1.00
153 Matt Jones RC .30 .75
154 David Cobb RC .30 .75
155 Austin Hill RC .30 .75
156 Clive Walford RC .30 .75
157 Alvin Dupree RC .40 1.00
158 Eli Harold RC .30 .75
159 Chris Conley RC .30 .75
160 Eddie Goldman RC .30 .75
161 Alex Carter RC .30 .75
162 Jalen Collins RC .30 .75
163 T.J. Clemmings RC .30 .75
164 Nate Orchard RC .30 .75
165A Maxx Williams RC .30 .75
165B Maxx Williams SP 1.50 4.00
166 Tony Lippett RC .30 .75
167 Cameron Artis-Payne RC .30 .75
168 Vince Mayle RC .40 1.00
169 Dres Anderson RC .30 .75
170A Phillip Dorsett RC .30 .75
170B Phillip Dorsett SP 1.50 4.00
171 Shane Carden RC .30 .75
172 Jamison Crowder RC .40 1.00
173 Danielle Hunter RC .40 1.00
174 Lorenzo Mauldin RC .30 .75
175 Paul Dawson RC .40 1.00
176 Owamagbe Odighizuwa RC .40 1.00
177 David Johnson RC .75 2.00
178A Tyler Lockett RC .50 1.25
178B Tyler Lockett SP 2.50 6.00
179 Dominique Brown RC .30 .75
180 Kevin Johnson RC .30 .75
181 Eric Kendricks RC .30 .75
182 Sean Mannion RC .30 .75
183 Denzel Perryman RC .30 .75
184 Malcolm Brown RC .40 1.00
185 Jeff Heuerman RC .40 1.00
186 Antwan Goodley RC .30 .75
187 Deontay Greenberry RC .30 .75
188 Bo Wallace RC .30 .75
189 Levi Norwood RC .30 .75
190 Tyler Kroft RC .40 1.00
191 Senquez Golson RC .30 .75
192 D'Joun Smith RC .50 1.25
193 Jesse James RC .40 1.00
194A Devin Smith RC .30 .75
194B Devin Smith SP 1.50 4.00
195 Carl Davis RC .40 1.00
196 Tre McBride RC .30 .75
197A Breshad Perriman RC .30 .75
197B Breshad Perriman SP 1.50 4.00
198 Josh Robinson RC .30 .75
199 Cody Fajardo RC .40 1.00
200A Jameis Winston RC .75 2.00
200B Jameis Winston SP 15.00 40.00

2015 Topps Chrome Black Refractors

*1 100 VETS/299: 3X TO 8X BASIC CARDS
*101-200 ROOKIE/299: 2X TO 5X BASIC RC
110 Todd Gurley 6.00 15.00
115 Amari Cooper 15.00 30.00
150 Marcus Mariota 8.00 20.00
200 Jameis Winston 15.00 30.00

2015 Topps Chrome Blue Refractors

*VETS/199: X TO X BASIC CARDS
*ROOK/199: X TO X BASIC CARDS
110 Todd Gurley 6.00 15.00
115 Amari Cooper 20.00 40.00
150 Marcus Mariota 15.00 40.00
200 Jameis Winston 15.00 30.00

2015 Topps Chrome Blue Wave Refractors

*1-100 VETS: 3X TO 5X BASIC CARDS
*101-200 ROOKIE: 1.2X TO 3X BASIC RC

2015 Topps Chrome Camo Refractors

*1-101 VETS/499: 2.5X TO 6X BASIC CARDS
*101-200 ROOKIE/499: 1.5X TO 4X RC
110 Todd Gurley 5.00 12.00
150 Marcus Mariota 20.00 40.00
200 Jameis Winston 10.00 25.00

2015 Topps Chrome Diamond

*1-100 VETS: 3X TO 5X BASIC CARDS
*101-200 ROOKIE: 1.2X TO 3X BASIC RC
110 Todd Gurley 4.00 10.00
150 Marcus Mariota 20.00 40.00
200 Jameis Winston 10.00 25.00

2015 Topps Chrome Gold Refractors

*1-100 VETS/50: 6X TO 15X BASIC CARDS
*101-200 ROOKIE/50: 4X TO 10X BASIC RC
110 Todd Gurley 20.00 50.00
115 Amari Cooper 60.00 100.00
150 Marcus Mariota 50.00 100.00
200 Jameis Winston 75.00 125.00

2015 Topps Chrome Green Refractors

*1-100 VETS: 1.5X TO 4X BASIC CARDS
*101-200 ROOKIE: 1X TO 2.5X BASIC RC

2015 Topps Chrome Orange Refractors

*ORANGE REFRACTOR: 1.2X TO 3X BASIC RC

2015 Topps Chrome Pink Refractors

*1-100 VETS/399: 2.5X TO 6X BASIC CARDS
*101-200 ROOKIE/399: 1.5X TO 4X RC
110 Todd Gurley 15.00 30.00
150 Marcus Mariota 20.00 40.00
200 Jameis Winston 10.00 25.00

2015 Topps Chrome Pulsar Refractors

*1-100 VETS: 2X TO 5X BASIC CARDS
*100-290 ROOKIE: 1.2X TO 3X BASIC RC
150 Marcus Mariota 15.00 30.00

2015 Topps Chrome Purple Refractors

*1-100 VETS: 3X TO 5X BASIC CARDS
*101-200 ROOKIE: 1.2X TO 3X BASIC RC

2015 Topps Chrome Red Refractors

*1-100 VETS/25: 15X TO 40X BASIC CARDS
*101-200 ROOKIE/25: 10X TO 25X BASIC RC
200 Jameis Winston 125.00 200.00

2015 Topps Chrome Refractors

*1-100 VETS: 1.2X TO 3X BASIC CARDS
*100-200 ROOKIE: .8X TO 2X BASIC RC

2015 Topps Chrome Sepia Refractors

*1-100 VETS/99: 5X TO 12X BASIC CARDS
*101-200 ROOKIE/99: 3X TO 8X BASIC RC
110 Todd Gurley 40.00 80.00
115 Amari Cooper 25.00 50.00
150 Marcus Mariota 40.00 80.00
200 Jameis Winston 30.00 60.00

2015 Topps Chrome Xfractors

*1-110 VETS: 1.5X TO 4X BASIC CARDS
*110-220 ROOKIE: 1X TO 2.5X BASIC RC

2015 Topps Chrome '76

*REFRACTOR/99: 1.2X TO 3X BASIC INSERTS
*PULSAR/50: 1.5X TO 4X BASIC INSERTS
76AA Ameer Abdullah .60 1.50
76AC Amari Cooper 1.25 3.00
76BH Brett Hundley .40 1.00
76BP Breshad Perriman .40 1.00
76BPE Bryce Petty .40 1.00
76CC Chris Conley .40 1.00
76DC David Cobb .40 1.00
76DF Devin Funchess .60 1.50
76DG Dorial Green-Beckham .40 1.00
76DJ Duke Johnson .60 1.50
76DJO David Johnson 1.00 2.50
76DP DeVante Parker .60 1.50
76DS Devin Smith .40 1.00
76JA Jay Ajayi .60 1.50
76JAL Javorius Allen .50 1.25
76JL Jeremy Langford .40 1.00
76JS Jaelen Strong .50 1.25
76JW Jameis Winston 1.00 2.50
76KW Kevin White .50 1.25
76LW Leonard Williams .40 1.00
76MD Mike Davis .40 1.00
76MG Melvin Gordon 1.00 2.50
76MJ Matt Jones .40 1.00
76MM Marcus Mariota 1.50 4.00
76MW Maxx Williams .40 1.00
76NA Nelson Agholor .50 1.25
76PD Phillip Dorsett .40 1.00
76SC Sammie Coates .50 1.25
76SD Stefon Diggs 1.00 2.50
76SM Sean Mannion .40 1.00
76TC Tevin Coleman .50 1.25
76TG Todd Gurley 1.50 4.00
76TL Tyler Lockett .60 1.50
76TM Ty Montgomery .40 1.00
76TY T.J. Yeldon .40 1.00

2015 Topps Chrome '76 Pulsar Refractors

*PULSAR/50: 1.5X TO 4X BASIC INSERTS
76MM Marcus Mariota 50.00 100.00
76TG Todd Gurley 40.00 80.00

2015 Topps Chrome '76 Autographs

76AAA Ameer Abdullah/15 20.00 50.00
76AAC Amari Cooper/15
76ABH Brett Hundley 10.00 25.00
76ABP Breshad Perriman 10.00 25.00
76ABPE Bryce Petty
76ACC Chris Conley 10.00 25.00
76ADC David Cobb 10.00 25.00
76ADF Devin Funchess 40.00 80.00
76ADG Dorial Green-Beckham 10.00 25.00
76ADJ Duke Johnson 15.00 40.00
76ADJO David Johnson 50.00 100.00
76ADP DeVante Parker 40.00 80.00
76ADS Devin Smith
76AJA Jay Ajayi 15.00 40.00
76AJS Jaelen Strong
76AJW Jameis Winston
76AKW Kevin White
76AMD Mike Davis 10.00 25.00
76AMG Melvin Gordon 25.00 60.00
76AMJ Matt Jones 10.00 25.00
76AMM Marcus Mariota
76AMW Maxx Williams 10.00 25.00
76ANA Nelson Agholor 12.00 30.00
76APD Phillip Dorsett
76ASC Sammie Coates 12.00 30.00
76ATG Todd Gurley 300.00 500.00
76ATL Tyler Lockett 15.00 40.00
76ATM Ty Montgomery 10.00 25.00
76ATY T.J. Yeldon

2015 Topps Chrome '89

*GOLD/75. 1.2X TO 3X BASIC INSERTS
*PULSAR/50: 1.5X TO 4X BASIC INSERTS
89AA Ameer Abdullah .60 1.50
89AC Amari Cooper 1.25 3.00
89BH Brett Hundley .40 1.00
89BP Breshad Perriman .40 1.00
89BPE Bryce Petty .40 1.00
89CC Chris Conley .40 1.00
89DC David Cobb .40 1.00
89DF Devin Funchess .60 1.50
89DG Dorial Green-Beckham .40 1.00
89DJ Duke Johnson .60 1.50
89DJO David Johnson 1.00 2.50
89DP DeVante Parker .60 1.50
89DS Devin Smith .40 1.00
89JA Jay Ajayi .60 1.50
89JAL Javorius Allen .50 1.25
89JL Jeremy Langford .40 1.00
89JS Jaelen Strong .50 1.25
89JW Jameis Winston 1.00 2.50
89KW Kevin White .50 1.25
89LW Leonard Williams .40 1.00
89MD Mike Davis .40 1.00
89MG Melvin Gordon 1.00 2.50
89MJ Matt Jones .40 1.00
89MM Marcus Mariota 1.50 4.00
89MW Maxx Williams .40 1.00
89NA Nelson Agholor .50 1.25
89PD Phillip Dorsett .40 1.00
89SC Sammie Coates .50 1.25
89SD Stefon Diggs 1.00 2.50
89SM Sean Mannion .40 1.00
89TC Tevin Coleman .50 1.25
89TG Todd Gurley 1.50 4.00
89TL Tyler Lockett .60 1.50
89TM Ty Montgomery .40 1.00
89TY T.J. Yeldon .40 1.00

2015 Topps Chrome '89 Pulsar Refractors

*PULSAR/50: 1.5X TO 4X BASIC INSERTS
89MM Marcus Mariota 60.00 100.00
89TG Todd Gurley 25.00 50.00

2015 Topps Chrome 60th Anniversary

T60AB Antonio Brown .60 1.50
T60AC Amari Cooper 1.25 3.00
T60AG A.J. Green .60 1.50
T60AJ Alshon Jeffery .50 1.25
T60AL Andrew Luck .75 2.00
T60AP Adrian Peterson .60 1.50
T60AR Aaron Rodgers 1.25 3.00
T60BF Brett Favre 1.25 3.00
T60BJ Bo Jackson .75 2.00
T60BR Ben Roethlisberger .60 1.50
T60BS Barry Sanders 1.00 2.50
T60CJ Calvin Johnson .60 1.50
T60CK Colin Kaepernick .50 1.25
T60CM Clay Matthews .60 1.50
T60CN Cam Newton .60 1.50
T60DB Drew Brees .60 1.50
T60DBR Dez Bryant .60 1.50
T60DM Dan Marino 1.25 3.00
T60DMU DeMarco Murray .50 1.25
T60DS Deion Sanders .50 1.25
T60DT Demaryius Thomas .50 1.25
T60EC Earl Campbell .60 1.50
T60ED Eric Dickerson .50 1.25
T60EL Eddie Lacy .40 1.00
T60EM Eli Manning .50 1.25
T60ES Emmitt Smith 1.00 2.50
T60GS Gale Sayers .60 1.50
T60JE John Elway 1.00 2.50
T60JF Joe Flacco .50 1.25
T60JR Jerry Rice 1.00 2.50
T60JW J.J. Watt .60 1.50
T60JWI Jameis Winston 1.00 2.50
T60KB Kelvin Benjamin .50 1.25
T60KW Kurt Warner .50 1.25
T60KWH Kevin White .50 1.25
T60LB Le'Veon Bell .50 1.25
T60LT Lawrence Taylor .60 1.50
T60ME Mike Evans .50 1.25
T60MF Marshall Faulk .50 1.25
T60ML Marshawn Lynch .50 1.25
T60MM Marcus Mariota 1.50 4.00
T60MR Matt Ryan .50 1.25
T60OB Odell Beckham Jr. .60 1.50
T60PM Peyton Manning 1.25 3.00
T60RC Randall Cobb .50 1.25
T60RG Robert Griffin III .40 1.00
T60RGR Rob Gronkowski .60 1.50
T60RS Roger Staubach .75 2.00
T60RT Ryan Tannehill .50 1.25
T60RW Russell Wilson .75 2.00
T60SL Steve Largent .60 1.50
T60SW Sammy Watkins .50 1.25
T60SY Steve Young .75 2.00
T60TB Tim Brown .60 1.50
T60TBRA Tom Brady 1.50 4.00
T60TD Terrell Davis .50 1.25
T60TDO Tony Dorsett .60 1.50
T60TEBR Terry Bradshaw .75 2.00
T60TG Todd Gurley 1.50 4.00
T60TP Troy Polamalu .60 1.50

2015 Topps Chrome 60th Anniversary Relics

*REFRACTORS/150: .5X TO 1.2X BASIC JSY
*PURPLE/75: .6X TO 1.5X BASIC JSY
*GOLD/25: 1X TO 2.5X BASIC JSY
T60RAA Ameer Abdullah 2.00 5.00
T60RAC Amari Cooper 4.00 10.00
T60RBH Brett Hundley 1.25 3.00
T60RBPE Bryce Petty 1.25 3.00
T60RDC David Cobb 1.25 3.00
T60RDF Devin Funchess 2.00 5.00
T60RDG Dorial Green-Beckham 1.25 3.00
T60RDJ Duke Johnson 2.00 5.00
T60RDJO David Johnson 3.00 8.00
T60RDP DeVante Parker 2.00 5.00
T60RDS Devin Smith 1.25 3.00
T60RGG Garrett Grayson 1.25 3.00
T60RJA Jay Ajayi 2.00 5.00
T60RJS Jaelen Strong 1.50 4.00
T60RJW Jameis Winston 5.00 12.00
T60RKW Kevin White 1.50 4.00
T60RLW Leonard Williams 1.25 3.00
T60RMD Mike Davis 1.25 3.00
T60RMG Melvin Gordon 3.00 8.00
T60RMM Marcus Mariota 5.00 12.00
T60RMW Maxx Williams 1.25 3.00
T60RNA Nelson Agholor 1.50 4.00
T60RPD Phillip Dorsett 1.25 3.00
T60RRG Rashad Greene 1.25 3.00
T60RSC Sammie Coates 1.50 4.00
T60RTC Tevin Coleman 1.50 4.00
T60RTG Todd Gurley 6.00 15.00
T60RTL Tyler Lockett 2.00 5.00
T60RTM Ty Montgomery 1.25 3.00
T60RTY T.J. Yeldon 1.25 3.00

2015 Topps Chrome 60th Anniversary Rookies

T60RCAA Ameer Abdullah .75 2.00
T60RCAC Amari Cooper 1.50 4.00
T60RCBH Brett Hundley .50 1.25
T60RCBPE Bryce Petty .50 1.25
T60RCDC David Cobb .50 1.25
T60RCDF Devin Funchess .75 2.00
T60RCDG Dorial Green-Beckham .50 1.25
T60RCDJ Duke Johnson .75 2.00
T60RCDJO David Johnson 1.25 3.00
T60RCDP DeVante Parker .75 2.00
T60RCDS Devin Smith .50 1.25
T60RCGG Garrett Grayson .50 1.25
T60RCJA Jay Ajayi .75 2.00
T60RCJS Jaelen Strong .60 1.50
T60RCJW Jameis Winston 1.25 3.00
T60RCKW Kevin White .60 1.50
T60RCLW Leonard Williams .50 1.25
T60RCMD Mike Davis .50 1.25
T60RCMG Melvin Gordon 1.25 3.00
T60RCMM Marcus Mariota 2.00 5.00
T60RCMW Maxx Williams .50 1.25
T60RCNA Nelson Agholor .60 1.50
T60RCPD Phillip Dorsett .50 1.25
T60RCRG Rashad Greene .50 1.25
T60RCSC Sammie Coates .60 1.50
T60RCTC Tevin Coleman .60 1.50
T60RCTG Todd Gurley 2.00 5.00
T60RCTL Tyler Lockett .75 2.00
T60RCTM Ty Montgomery .50 1.25
T60RCTY T.J. Yeldon .50 1.25

2015 Topps Chrome All Time 1000 Yard Club

AT1KAB Antonio Brown 2.00 5.00
AT1KAG A.J. Green 2.00 5.00
AT1KAM Alfred Morris 1.25 3.00
AT1KAP Adrian Peterson 2.00 5.00
AT1KBJ Bo Jackson 2.50 6.00
AT1KBS Barry Sanders 3.00 8.00
AT1KCJ Calvin Johnson 2.00 5.00
AT1KCM Curtis Martin 1.50 4.00
AT1KEC Earl Campbell 2.00 5.00
AT1KED Eric Dickerson 1.50 4.00
AT1KEG Eddie George 1.50 4.00
AT1KEL Eddie Lacy 1.25 3.00
AT1KES Emmitt Smith 3.00 8.00
AT1KGS Gale Sayers 2.00 5.00
AT1KJC Jamaal Charles 1.50 4.00
AT1KJH Jeremy Hill 1.25 3.00
AT1KJN Jordy Nelson 1.50 4.00
AT1KKB Kelvin Benjamin 1.50 4.00
AT1KLB Le'Veon Bell 1.50 4.00
AT1KLT LaDainian Tomlinson 1.50 4.00
AT1KMA Marcus Allen 2.00 5.00
AT1KME Mike Evans 1.50 4.00
AT1KMF Matt Forte 1.25 3.00
AT1KML Marshawn Lynch 1.50 4.00
AT1KOB Odell Beckham Jr. 2.00 5.00
AT1KPH Paul Hornung 2.00 5.00
AT1KRC Randall Cobb 1.50 4.00
AT1KRG Rob Gronkowski 2.00 5.00
AT1KSL Steve Largent 2.00 5.00
AT1KTB Tim Brown 2.00 5.00
AT1KTD Terrell Davis 1.50 4.00
AT1KESA Emmanuel Sanders 1.50 4.00
AT1KJRI Jerry Rice 3.00 8.00
AT1KMFA Marshall Faulk 1.50 4.00
AT1KTDO Tony Dorsett 2.00 5.00

2015 Topps Chrome All Time 4000 Yard Club

AT4KAL Andrew Luck 2.50 6.00
AT4KAR Aaron Rodgers 4.00 10.00
AT4KBF Brett Favre 4.00 10.00
AT4KDB Drew Brees 2.00 5.00
AT4KDM Dan Marino 4.00 10.00
AT4KEM Eli Manning 1.50 4.00
AT4KJE John Elway 3.00 8.00
AT4KKW Kurt Warner 1.50 4.00
AT4KMR Matt Ryan 1.50 4.00
AT4KMS Matthew Stafford 1.50 4.00
AT4KPM Peyton Manning 4.00 10.00
AT4KPS Phil Simms 1.50 4.00
AT4KSY Steve Young 2.50 6.00
AT4KTB Tom Brady 5.00 12.00
AT4KWM Warren Moon 2.00 5.00

2015 Topps Chrome Rookie Autographs

101 Vic Beasley 3.00 8.00
102 Brett Hundley SP 8.00 20.00
104 Trae Waynes 2.50 6.00
105 Melvin Gordon SP 10.00 25.00
106 Dorial Green-Beckham SP 2.50 6.00
107 Devin Funchess SP 4.00 10.00
108 Jaelen Strong 3.00 8.00
110 Todd Gurley SP 60.00 125.00
111 Ameer Abdullah 4.00 10.00
113 Sammie Coates 3.00 8.00
115 Amari Cooper SP 30.00 60.00
116 Shaq Thompson 3.00 8.00
118 Landon Collins 3.00 8.00
119 Ty Montgomery 6.00 15.00
120 Jay Ajayi 12.00 30.00
123 Josh Harper 2.50 6.00
124 Marcus Peters 4.00 10.00
125 Kevin White SP 3.00 8.00
126 Dezmin Lewis 2.50 6.00
127 Dante Fowler Jr. SP 4.00 10.00
128 Terrence Magee 4.00 10.00
130 Leonard Williams SP
137 Bryce Petty 2.50 6.00
138 T.J. Yeldon 2.50 6.00
139 Mike Davis 2.50 6.00
140 Duke Johnson 4.00 10.00
141 Karlos Williams 2.50 6.00
142 Jeremy Langford 2.50 6.00
143 Marcus Murphy 2.50 6.00
145 Ben Koyack 4.00 10.00
146 Nelson Agholor 3.00 8.00
147 Rashad Greene 2.50 6.00
149 Justin Hardy 2.50 6.00
150 Marcus Mariota SP
153 Matt Jones 2.50 6.00
154 David Cobb 2.50 6.00
155 Austin Hill 2.50 6.00
156 Clive Walford 2.50 6.00
157 Alvin Dupree 3.00 8.00
159 Chris Conley 2.50 6.00
160 Eddie Goldman 2.50 6.00
165 Maxx Williams 2.50 6.00
166 Tony Lippett 2.50 6.00
167 Cameron Artis-Payne 2.50 6.00
168 Vince Mayle 3.00 8.00
169 Dres Anderson 2.50 6.00
170 Phillip Dorsett 2.50 6.00
175 Paul Dawson 3.00 8.00
177 David Johnson 12.00 30.00
178 Tyler Lockett 4.00 10.00
179 Dominique Brown 2.50 6.00
181 Eric Kendricks 2.50 6.00
184 Malcolm Brown 3.00 8.00
186 Antwan Goodley 2.50 6.00
187 Deontay Greenberry 2.50 6.00
189 Levi Norwood 2.50 6.00
190 Tyler Kroft 3.00 8.00
193 Jesse James 3.00 8.00
194 Devin Smith 2.50 6.00
196 Tre McBride 2.50 6.00
197 Breshad Perriman 2.50 6.00
198 Josh Robinson 2.50 6.00
200 Jameis Winston SP 50.00 100.00
201 Byron Jones 4.00 10.00
205 J.J. Nelson

2015 Topps Chrome Rookie Autographs Black Refractors

*BLACK/25: 1.2X TO 3X BASIC AU
110 Todd Gurley 250.00 350.00
200 Jameis Winston 150.00 300.00

2015 Topps Chrome Rookie Autographs Blue Refractors

*BLUE/50: .8X TO 2X BASIC AU
110 Todd Gurley 150.00 300.00
150 Marcus Mariota 50.00 125.00

2015 Topps Chrome Rookie Autographs Camo Refractors

*CAMO/99: .6X TO 1.5X BASIC AU
110 Todd Gurley 150.00 250.00
150 Marcus Mariota 40.00 100.00
200 Jameis Winston 75.00 150.00

2015 Topps Chrome Rookie Autographs Hot Box Sepia Gold Refractors

*HOT BOX GOLD/50-65: .8X TO 2X BASIC AU
*HOT BOX GOLD/100: .6X TO 1.5X BASIC AU
*HOT BOX GOLD/150: .5X TO 1.2X BASIC AU
110 Todd Gurley/50 125.00 250.00
150 Marcus Mariota/100 40.00 100.00
200 Jameis Winston/100 75.00 150.00

2015 Topps Chrome Rookie Autographs Pink Refractors

*PINK/75: .6X TO 1.5X BASIC AU
110 Todd Gurley 150.00 250.00
150 Marcus Mariota 40.00 100.00

2015 Topps Chrome Rookie Autographs Refractors

*REFRACTOR/150: .5X TO 1.2X BASIC AU
110 Todd Gurley 60.00 125.00
150 Marcus Mariota 40.00 80.00
200 Jameis Winston 60.00 125.00

2015 Topps Chrome Rookie Autographs Variations

105 Melvin Gordon/25
106 Dorial Green-Beckham 30.00 60.00
110 Todd Gurley/25 150.00 250.00
111 Ameer Abdullah 30.00 60.00
115 Amari Cooper/25
125 Kevin White/25
137 Bryce Petty/25 25.00 60.00
138 T.J. Yeldon 4.00 10.00
146 Nelson Agholor 5.00 12.00
150 Marcus Mariota 100.00 200.00
170 Phillip Dorsett 4.00 10.00
197 Breshad Perriman
200 Jameis Winston 75.00 150.00

2015 Topps Chrome Rookie Autographs Patches

RAPAA Ameer Abdullah/75 10.00 25.00
RAPAC Amari Cooper/75 40.00 80.00
RAPBH Brett Hundley/25 10.00 25.00
RAPBP Breshad Perriman/50 8.00 20.00
RAPBPE Bryce Petty/75 6.00 15.00
RAPCC Chris Conley/25 10.00 25.00
RAPDC David Cobb/50 8.00 20.00
RAPDF Devin Funchess/25 15.00 40.00
RAPDG Dorial Green-Beckham/75 6.00 15.00
RAPDJ Duke Johnson/25 15.00 40.00
RAPDJO David Johnson/50 40.00 80.00
RAPDP DeVante Parker/25 15.00 40.00
RAPDS Devin Smith/50 8.00 20.00
RAPJA Jay Ajayi/50 12.00 30.00
RAPJHA Justin Hardy/50 8.00 20.00
RAPJL Jeremy Langford/25 40.00 80.00
RAPJS Jaelen Strong/25 12.00 30.00
RAPJW Jameis Winston/75 40.00 80.00
RAPKW Kevin White/75 30.00 60.00
RAPKWI Karlos Williams/50 15.00 40.00
RAPLW Leonard Williams/50 12.00 30.00
RAPMD Mike Davis/25 10.00 25.00
RAPMG Melvin Gordon/75 15.00 40.00
RAPMJ Matt Jones
RAPMM Marcus Mariota/75 60.00 125.00
RAPMW Maxx Williams/50 8.00 20.00
RAPNA Nelson Agholor/50 10.00 25.00
RAPPD Phillip Dorsett/50 8.00 20.00
RAPRG Rashad Greene/50 8.00 20.00
RAPSC Sammie Coates/50 10.00 25.00
RAPTG Todd Gurley/75 60.00 125.00
RAPTM Ty Montgomery/25 10.00 25.00
RAPTY T.J. Yeldon/75 6.00 15.00
RAPVM Vince Mayle/50 10.00 25.00

2015 Topps Chrome Rookie Relics

TCRRAA Ameer Abdullah 2.00 5.00
TCRRAC Amari Cooper 4.00 10.00
TCRRBH Brett Hundley 1.25 3.00
TCRRBP Breshad Perriman 1.25 3.00
TCRRBPE Bryce Petty 1.25 3.00
TCRRCC Chris Conley 1.25 3.00
TCRRDC David Cobb 1.25 3.00
TCRRDF Devin Funchess 2.00 5.00
TCRRDG Dorial Green-Beckham 1.25 3.00
TCRRDJ Duke Johnson 2.00 5.00
TCRRDJO David Johnson 3.00 8.00
TCRRDP DeVante Parker 2.00 5.00
TCRRDS Devin Smith 1.25 3.00
TCRRGG Garrett Grayson 1.25 3.00
TCRRJA Jay Ajayi 2.00 5.00
TCRRJAL Javorius Allen 1.50 4.00
TCRRJC Jamison Crowder 1.50 4.00
TCRRJHA Justin Hardy 1.25 3.00
TCRRJL Jeremy Langford 1.25 3.00
TCRRJS Jaelen Strong 1.50 4.00
TCRRJW Jameis Winston 5.00 12.00
TCRRKW Kevin White 4.00 10.00
TCRRLW Leonard Williams 1.25 3.00
TCRRMD Mike Davis 1.25 3.00
TCRRMG Melvin Gordon 3.00 8.00
TCRRMJ Matt Jones 1.25 3.00
TCRRMM Marcus Mariota 5.00 12.00
TCRRMW Maxx Williams 1.25 3.00
TCRRNA Nelson Agholor 1.50 4.00
TCRRPD Phillip Dorsett 1.25 3.00
TCRRRG Rashad Greene 1.25 3.00
TCRRSC Sammie Coates 1.50 4.00
TCRRSD Stefon Diggs 3.00 8.00
TCRRSM Sean Mannion 1.25 3.00
TCRRTC Tevin Coleman 1.50 4.00
TCRRTG Todd Gurley 5.00 12.00
TCRRTL Tyler Lockett 4.00 10.00
TCRRTM Ty Montgomery 1.25 3.00
TCRRTY T.J. Yeldon 1.25 3.00
TCRRVM Vince Mayle 1.50 4.00

2015 Topps Chrome Super Bowl 50 Die Cuts

*REFRACTOR/99: 1.5X TO 4X BASIC INSERTS
*PULSAR/50: 2.5X TO 6X BASIC INSERTS
SBDCAR Aaron Rodgers 2.00 5.00
SBDCBF Brett Favre 2.00 5.00
SBDCBR Ben Roethlisberger 1.00 2.50
SBDCCM Clay Matthews 1.00 2.50
SBDCDB Drew Brees 1.00 2.50
SBDCDS Deion Sanders .75 2.00
SBDCEM Eli Manning .75 2.00
SBDCES Emmitt Smith 1.50 4.00
SBDCJB Jerome Bettis 1.00 2.50
SBDCJE John Elway 1.50 4.00
SBDCJF Joe Flacco .75 2.00
SBDCJG Joe Greene 1.00 2.50
SBDCJN Jordy Nelson .75 2.00
SBDCJR John Riggins .75 2.00
SBDCKW Kurt Warner .75 2.00
SBDCLD Len Dawson 1.00 2.50
SBDCLT Lawrence Taylor 1.00 2.50
SBDCMA Marcus Allen 1.00 2.50
SBDCMF Marshall Faulk .75 2.00
SBDCML Marshawn Lynch .75 2.00
SBDCMS Mike Singletary 1.00 2.50
SBDCPH Paul Hornung 1.00 2.50
SBDCPM Peyton Manning 2.00 5.00
SBDCPS Phil Simms .75 2.00
SBDCRG Rob Gronkowski 1.00 2.50
SBDCRL Ronnie Lott .75 2.00
SBDCRS Richard Sherman 1.00 2.50
SBDCRW Russell Wilson 1.25 3.00
SBDCSY Steve Young 1.25 3.00
SBDCTB Tom Brady 2.50 6.00
SBDCTD Tony Dorsett 1.00 2.50
SBDCJRI Jerry Rice 1.50 4.00
SBDCRST Roger Staubach 1.25 3.00
SBDCTBR Terry Bradshaw 1.25 3.00
SBDCTDA Terrell Davis .75 2.00

2014 Topps Chrome Mini

COMP.SET w/o SP's (220) 15.00 40.00
1 Frank Gore .25 .60
2 Cecil Shorts .20 .50
3 Justin Tuck .20 .50
4 Jordan Reed .20 .50
5 Demaryius Thomas .25 .60
6 Joe Flacco .25 .60
7 Randall Cobb .25 .60
8 Patrick Willis .25 .60
9A Antonio Brown .30 .75
9B Antonio Brown SP 4.00 10.00
10 Clay Matthews .30 .75
11 EJ Manuel .20 .50
12 Julius Thomas .20 .50
13 Dominique Rodgers-Cromartie .20 .50
14 Reggie Wayne .25 .60
15 Darrelle Revis .20 .50
16 Pierre Thomas .20 .50
17A Drew Brees .30 .75
17B Drew Brees SP 3.00 8.00
18 Pierre Garcon .25 .60
19 Kendall Wright .20 .50
20 NaVorro Bowman .25 .60
21 Tamba Hali .20 .50
22 DeSean Jackson .25 .60
23 Ryan Tannehill .25 .60
24 Isa Abdul-Quddus RC .20 .50
25 Brandon Marshall .20 .50
26 Wes Welker .25 .60
27 C.J. Spiller .20 .50
28 Geno Smith .20 .50
29 J.J. Watt .30 .75
30 Troy Polamalu .30 .75
31 Vincent Jackson .20 .50
32A Michael Crabtree .20 .50
32B Michael Crabtree SP 2.50 6.00
33A Alshon Jeffery .25 .60
33B Alshon Jeffery SP 3.00 8.00
34 Zach Ertz .25 .60
35 Mike Glennon .25 .60
36 T.Y. Hilton .25 .60
37 Terrell Suggs .20 .50
38 Ndamukong Suh .25 .60
39 Patrick Peterson .20 .50
40 DeAndre Hopkins .25 .60
41 Cameron Jordan .20 .50
42A Peyton Manning .60 1.50
42B Peyton Manning SP 12.00 30.00
43 Ryan Mathews .25 .60
44 Eric Berry .25 .60
45A A.J. Green .30 .75
45B A.J. Green SP 4.00 10.00
46 Matt Forte .20 .50
47A Andrew Luck .40 1.00
47B Andrew Luck SP 5.00 12.00
48 Ace Sanders .20 .50
49 Jason Pierre-Paul .20 .50
50A Le'Veon Bell .25 .60
50B Le'Veon Bell SP 3.00 8.00
51 Mario Williams .20 .50
52A Alfred Morris .20 .50
52B Alfred Morris SP 2.50 6.00
53 Sheldon Richardson .20 .50
54 Alex Smith .25 .60
55 Josh Gordon .20 .50
56A Colin Kaepernick .25 .60
56B Colin Kaepernick SP 3.00 8.00
57 Tavon Austin .20 .50
58 Jay Cutler .20 .50
59 Percy Harvin .20 .50
60A Victor Cruz .25 .60

60B Victor Cruz SP 3.00 8.00
61A Marshawn Lynch .25 .60
61B Marshawn Lynch SP 3.00 8.00
62A Tom Brady .75 2.00
62B Tom Brady SP 10.00 25.00
63A Giovani Bernard .20 .50
63B Giovani Bernard SP 2.50 6.00
64A LeSean McCoy .30 .75
64B LeSean McCoy SP 4.00 10.00
65 Kiko Alonso .20 .50
66 Montee Ball .20 .50
67A Jimmy Graham .30 .75
67B Jimmy Graham SP 4.00 10.00
68 Mike Wallace .20 .50
69 Jordan Cameron .20 .50
70 Muhammad Wilkerson .20 .50
71A Reggie Bush .20 .50
71B Reggie Bush SP 2.50 6.00
72A Jamaal Charles .25 .60
72B Jamaal Charles SP 3.00 8.00
73 Matthew Stafford .25 .60
74 Robert Quinn .25 .60
75 Denarius Moore .20 .50
76 Larry Fitzgerald .25 .60
77 Tony Romo .25 .60
78A Dez Bryant .30 .75
78B Dez Bryant SP 4.00 10.00
79 Torrey Smith .20 .50
80 Robert Mathis .20 .50
81 Brian Hartline .20 .50
82A Rob Gronkowski .30 .75
82B Rob Gronkowski SP 4.00 10.00
83A Aaron Rodgers .60 1.50
83B Aaron Rodgers SP 8.00 20.00
84 Cordarrelle Patterson .20 .50
85 Andy Dalton .25 .60
86 Vontaze Burfict .20 .50
87 Luke Kuechly .25 .60
88 Julio Jones .30 .75
89A Brian Hoyer .20 .50
89B Adrian Peterson SP 4.00 10.00
90 Sean Lee .25 .60
91A Philip Rivers .30 .75
91B Philip Rivers SP 4.00 10.00
92 Anquan Boldin .20 .50
93 Eli Manning .25 .60
94 Matt Ryan .25 .60
95 Earl Thomas .25 .60
96 Robert Griffin III .20 .50
97A Richard Sherman .30 .75
97B Richard Sherman SP 6.00 15.00
98A Calvin Johnson .30 .75
98B Calvin Johnson SP 4.00 10.00
99A Roddy White .20 .50
99B Roddy White SP 2.50 6.00
100 Jordy Nelson .25 .60
101 Andre Johnson .25 .60
102A Russell Wilson .50 1.25
102B Russell Wilson SP 6.00 15.00
103A Cam Newton .30 .75
103B Cam Newton SP 4.00 10.00
104 Keenan Allen .25 .60
105 Julian Edelman .30 .75
106A Eddie Lacy .20 .50
106B Eddie Lacy SP 2.50 6.00
107 Arian Foster .25 .60
108 Von Miller .25 .60
109A Nick Foles .25 .60
109B Nick Foles SP 3.00 8.00
110 DeMarco Murray .25 .60
111 Craig Loston RC .30 .75
112 Henry Josey RC .30 .75
113 Jeff Mathews RC .40 1.00
114A Davante Adams RC .50 1.25
114B Davante Adams SP 3.00 8.00
115A Derek Carr RC 2.00 5.00
115B Derek Carr SP 12.00 30.00
116 Bruce Ellington RC .30 .75
117A Odell Beckham Jr. RC 3.00 8.00
117B Odell Beckham Jr. SP 25.00 50.00
118 Mike Davis RC .30 .75
119 Cyrus Kouandjio RC .40 1.00
120A Jadeveon Clowney RC .40 1.00
120B Jadeveon Clowney SP 2.50 6.00
121 Josh Huff RC .40 1.00
122 Marion Grice RC .30 .75
123 Cody Hoffman RC .30 .75
124A Kelvin Benjamin RC .50 1.25
124B Kelvin Benjamin SP 3.00 8.00
125A Jeremy Hill RC .40 1.00
125B Jeremy Hill SP 2.50 6.00
126A Marqise Lee RC .40 1.00
126B Marqise Lee SP 2.50 6.00
127 Devin Street RC .30 .75
128 Yawin Smallwood RC .30 .75
129 Aaron Murray RC .30 .75
130 Jared Abbrederis RC .30 .75
131 C.J. Fiedorowicz RC .30 .75
132 Shaquelle Evans RC .30 .75
133 Martavis Bryant RC .40 1.00
134 Storm Johnson RC .30 .75
135 Greg Robinson RC .30 .75
136 Ahmad Dixon RC .30 .75
137 Loucheiz Purifoy RC .30 .75
138A Sammy Watkins RC .50 1.25
138B Sammy Watkins SP 3.00 8.00
139 Tom Savage RC .30 .75
140 Kony Ealy RC .40 1.00
141A Tajh Boyd RC .30 .75
141B Tajh Boyd SP 2.00 5.00
142 Kevin Norwood RC .30 .75
143 LaDarius Perkins RC .30 .75
144 A.J. McCarron RC .30 .75
145 Jalen Saunders RC .30 .75
146 Connor Shaw RC .30 .75
147 Brandon Coleman RC .30 .75
148 George Atkinson III RC .30 .75
149A Brandin Cooks RC .50 1.25
149B Brandin Cooks SP 3.00 8.00
150A Jimmy Garoppolo RC 2.50 6.00
150B Jimmy Garoppolo SP 15.00 40.00
151 Logan Thomas RC .30 .75
152 Justin Gilbert RC .30 .75
153 Louis Nix RC .30 .75
154 Andre Williams RC .30 .75
155A De'Anthony Thomas RC .30 .75
155B De'Anthony Thomas SP 2.00 5.00
156 Xavier Grimble RC .40 1.00
157 Calvin Pryor RC .30 .75
158A Carlos Hyde RC .40 1.00
158B Carlos Hyde SP 2.50 6.00
159 Ha Ha Clinton-Dix .40 1.00
160 Jerick McKinnon RC .40 1.00
161 Anthony Barr RC .30 .75
162 Kareem Martin RC .30 .75
163A Bishop Sankey RC .30 .75
163B Bishop Sankey SP 2.00 5.00
164A Tre Mason RC .30 .75
164B Tre Mason SP 2.00 5.00
165 Ryan Grant RC .30 .75
166 Ra'Shede Hageman RC .30 .75
167 Stephen Morris RC .30 .75
168 David Fales RC .30 .75
169A Johnny Manziel RC .50 1.25
169B Johnny Manziel SP 3.00 8.00
170 Will Sutton RC .40 1.00
171 Arthur Lynch RC .30 .75
172A Allen Robinson RC .50 1.25
172B Allen Robinson SP 3.00 8.00
173A Teddy Bridgewater RC .50 1.25
173B Teddy Bridgewater SP 3.00 8.00
174A Michael Sam RC .30 .75
174B Michael Sam SP .30 .75
175 Aaron Donald RC .75 2.00
176 Scott Crichton RC .30 .75
177A Jarvis Landry RC .60 1.50
177B Jarvis Landry SP 4.00 10.00
178 Austin Seferian-Jenkins RC .30 .75
179 Lache Seastrunk RC .30 .75
180 Taylor Lewan RC .30 .75
181 Jordan Lynch RC .40 1.00
182 Troy Niklas RC .30 .75
183 Antone Exum RC .30 .75
184 Khalil Mack RC 1.25 3.00
185A Mike Evans RC .75 2.00
185B Mike Evans SP 5.00 12.00
186 Deone Bucannon RC .30 .75
187A Blake Bortles RC .40 1.00
187B Blake Bortles SP 2.50 6.00
188 Ka'Deem Carey RC .30 .75
189 Pierre Desir RC .30 .75
190 Marcus Roberson RC .40 1.00
191 Charles Sims UER RC .30 .75
192 Jeff Janis RC .30 .75
193 Jace Amaro RC .30 .75
194 Silas Redd RC .40 1.00
195 Jason Verrett RC .30 .75
196 Tyler Gaffney RC .30 .75
197 Donte Moncrief RC .30 .75
198 Timmy Jernigan RC .30 .75
199 Jake Matthews RC .30 .75
200 Robert Herron RC .30 .75
201 Aaron Colvin RC .30 .75
202 Terrance West RC .30 .75
203 C.J. Mosley RC .40 1.00
204 Darqueze Dennard RC .40 1.00
205 Kyle Van Noy RC .40 1.00
206 Zach Mettenberger RC .30 .75
207 Zack Martin RC .40 1.00
208 Dion Bailey RC .30 .75
209 Bradley Roby RC .30 .75
210 Stephon Tuitt RC .50 1.25
211 Cody Latimer RC .40 1.00
212A Jordan Matthews RC .50 1.25
212B Jordan Matthews SP 3.00 8.00
213A Eric Ebron RC .40 1.00
213B Eric Ebron SP 2.50 6.00
214 Dri Archer RC .30 .75
216 Devonta Freeman RC .50 1.25
217 Trent Murphy RC .30 .75
218 Ryan Shazier RC .50 1.25
219A Paul Richardson RC .40 1.00
219B Paul Richardson SP 2.50 6.00
220 Damien Williams RC .30 .75
221 Lorenzo Taliaferro RC .30 .75

2014 Topps Chrome Mini Black Refractors

*1-110 VETS/15: 12X TO 30X BASIC CHROME
*111-220 ROOK/15: 8X TO 20X CHROME RC
117 Odell Beckham Jr. 100.00 175.00

2014 Topps Chrome Mini Camo Refractors

*1-110 VETS/99: 4X TO 10X BASIC CHROME
*111-220 ROOK/99: 2.5X TO 6X CHROME RC

2014 Topps Chrome Mini Gold Refractors

*1-110 VETS/10: 12X TO 30X BASIC CHROME
*111-220 ROOK/10: 8X TO 20X CHROME RC
117 Odell Beckham Jr. 125.00 200.00

2014 Topps Chrome Mini Pink Refractors

*1-110 VETS/25: 10X TO 25X BASIC CHROME
*111-220 ROOK/25: 6X TO 15X CHROME RC
117 Odell Beckham Jr. 50.00 100.00

2014 Topps Chrome Mini Pulsar Refractors

*1-110 VETS/102: 4X TO 10X BASIC CHROME
*111-220 ROOK/102: 2.5X TO 6X CHROME RC

2014 Topps Chrome Mini Refractors

*1-110 VETS: 1.2X TO 3X BASIC CARDS
*111-220 ROOKIES: .8X TO 2X BASIC RC
STATED ODDS 1:8 HOB

2014 Topps Chrome Mini 1000 Yard Club

*BLUE WAVE/25: .8X TO 2X BASIC INSERTS
*RED REF/60: .6X TO 1.5X BASIC INSERTS
1 Jordy Nelson 1.50 4.00
2 Jimmy Graham 2.00 5.00
3 Dez Bryant 2.00 5.00
4 Calvin Johnson 2.00 5.00
5 Julian Edelman 2.00 5.00
6 Andre Johnson 1.50 4.00
7 Adrian Peterson 2.00 5.00
8 Alfred Morris 1.25 3.00
9 Josh Gordon 1.25 3.00
10 Eddie Lacy 1.25 3.00
11 Frank Gore 1.50 4.00
12 Jamaal Charles 1.50 4.00
13 T.Y. Hilton 1.50 4.00
14 Knowshon Moreno 1.25 3.00
15 Antonio Brown 2.00 5.00
16 A.J. Green 2.00 5.00
17 LeSean McCoy 2.00 5.00
18 Reggie Bush 1.25 3.00
19 Marshawn Lynch 1.50 4.00
20 Demaryius Thomas 1.50 4.00
21 Alshon Jeffery 1.50 4.00
22 DeMarco Murray 1.50 4.00

2014 Topps Chrome Mini 1985

*PULSAR REF/25: 3X TO 8X BASIC INSERTS
*REFRACT/50: 2.5X TO 6X BASIC INSERTS
1 Tom Savage .30 .75
2 Khalil Mack 1.25 3.00
3 Jimmy Garoppolo 2.50 6.00
4 Jarvis Landry .60 1.50
5 Davante Adams .50 1.25
6 Teddy Bridgewater .50 1.25
7 Tre Mason .30 .75
8 Jordan Matthews .50 1.25
9 Paul Richardson .40 1.00
10 Allen Robinson .50 1.25
11 Bishop Sankey .30 .75
12 Mike Evans .75 2.00
13 Eric Ebron .40 1.00
14 Michael Sam .30 .75
15 Odell Beckham Jr. .75 2.00
16 Jadeveon Clowney .40 1.00
17 Tajh Boyd .30 .75
18 Derek Carr 2.00 5.00
19 Carlos Hyde .40 1.00
20 Blake Bortles .40 1.00
21 Marqise Lee .40 1.00
22 A.J. McCarron .30 .75
23 Jace Amaro .30 .75
24 Logan Thomas .30 .75
25 Aaron Murray .30 .75
26 Johnny Manziel .50 1.25
27 Ka'Deem Carey .30 .75
28 Cody Latimer .40 1.00
29 Sammy Watkins .50 1.25
30 Charles Sims .30 .75
31 Brandin Cooks .50 1.25
32 Dri Archer .30 .75
33 Kelvin Benjamin .50 1.25
34 Austin Seferian-Jenkins .30 .75
35 Devonta Freeman .50 1.25
36 Jeremy Hill .40 1.00
37 Donte Moncrief .30 .75
38 Andre Williams .30 .75
39 De'Anthony Thomas .30 .75
40 Zach Mettenberger .30 .75

2014 Topps Chrome Mini 1985 Autographs

EXCH EXPIRATION: 7/31/2017
1 Tom Savage
3 Jimmy Garoppolo 150.00 250.00
4 Jarvis Landry
5 Davante Adams
6 Teddy Bridgewater 12.00 30.00
7 Tre Mason
8 Jordan Matthews 30.00 60.00
9 Paul Richardson
10 Allen Robinson 12.00 30.00
11 Bishop Sankey
12 Mike Evans
13 Eric Ebron 10.00 25.00
15 Odell Beckham Jr. EXCH 150.00 250.00
16 Jadeveon Clowney
17 Tajh Boyd
18 Derek Carr
19 Carlos Hyde 20.00 50.00
20 Blake Bortles 10.00 25.00
21 Marqise Lee 10.00 25.00
22 A.J. McCarron 8.00 20.00
23 Jace Amaro EXCH 15.00 40.00
24 Logan Thomas 8.00 20.00
25 Aaron Murray 8.00 20.00
26 Johnny Manziel
27 Ka'Deem Carey
28 Cody Latimer
29 Sammy Watkins
30 Charles Sims 8.00 20.00
31 Brandin Cooks
32 Dri Archer 8.00 20.00
33 Kelvin Benjamin EXCH 20.00 50.00
34 Austin Seferian-Jenkins
35 Devonta Freeman 50.00 100.00
36 Jeremy Hill
37 Donte Moncrief
38 Andre Williams

2014 Topps Chrome Mini 4000 Yard Club

*BLUE WAVE/25: .8X TO 2X BASIC INSERTS
*RED REF/210: .5X TO 1.2X BASIC INSERTS
1 Tom Brady 5.00 12.00
2 Drew Brees 2.00 5.00
3 Andy Dalton 1.50 4.00
4 Ben Roethlisberger 2.00 5.00
5 Matt Ryan 1.50 4.00
6 Peyton Manning 4.00 10.00
7 Philip Rivers 2.00 5.00
8 Matthew Stafford 1.50 4.00

2014 Topps Chrome Mini 4000 Yard Club Autographs

1 Tom Brady
2 Drew Brees
8 Matthew Stafford 30.00 60.00

2014 Topps Chrome Mini Fantasy Focus

*REFRACT/50: 2X TO 5X BASIC INSERTS
FFAB Antonio Brown .60 1.50
FFAG A.J. Green .60 1.50
FFAJ Alshon Jeffery .50 1.25
FFAL Andrew Luck .75 2.00
FFAP Adrian Peterson .60 1.50
FFAR Aaron Rodgers 1.25 3.00
FFBM Brandon Marshall .40 1.00
FFCJ Calvin Johnson .60 1.50
FFCK Colin Kaepernick .50 1.25
FFCN Cam Newton .60 1.50
FFDB Drew Brees .60 1.50
FFDM DeMarco Murray .50 1.25
FFDR Dez Bryant .60 1.50
FFDT Demaryius Thomas .50 1.25
FFEL Eddie Lacy .40 1.00
FFJC Jamaal Charles .50 1.25
FFJG Jimmy Graham .60 1.50
FFJN Jordy Nelson .50 1.25
FFJT Julius Thomas .40 1.00
FFJW Jason Witten .50 1.25
FFLM Lesean McCoy .60 1.50
FFMF Matt Forte .40 1.00
FFML Marshawn Lynch .50 1.25
FFMS Matthew Stafford .50 1.25
FFPM Peyton Manning 1.25 3.00
FFRB Reggie Bush .40 1.00
FFRW Russell Wilson 1.00 2.50
FFTB Tom Brady 1.50 4.00
FFTR Tony Romo .50 1.25
FFVD Vernon Davis .40 1.00

2014 Topps Chrome Mini Rookie Autographs

114 Davante Adams 10.00 25.00
115 Derek Carr 40.00 80.00
116 Bruce Ellington 2.50 6.00
117 Odell Beckham Jr. 40.00 80.00
120 Jadeveon Clowney 3.00 8.00
124 Kelvin Benjamin 4.00 10.00
125 Jeremy Hill 3.00 8.00
129 Aaron Murray 2.50 6.00
130 Jared Abbrederis 6.00 15.00
131 C.J. Fiedorowicz 2.50 6.00
133 Martavis Bryant 3.00 8.00
138 Sammy Watkins 4.00 10.00
141 Tajh Boyd 2.50 6.00
150 Jimmy Garoppolo 75.00 150.00
151 Logan Thomas 2.50 6.00
154 Andre Williams 2.50 6.00
155 De'Anthony Thomas 2.50 6.00
158 Carlos Hyde 3.00 8.00
163 Bishop Sankey 2.50 6.00
164 Tre Mason 2.50 6.00
168 David Fales 2.50 6.00
169 Johnny Manziel 10.00 25.00
173 Teddy Bridgewater 8.00 20.00
182 Troy Niklas 2.50 6.00
185 Mike Evans 10.00 25.00
187 Blake Bortles
188 Ka'Deem Carey 2.50 6.00
193 Jace Amaro 2.50 6.00
197 Donte Moncrief 2.50 6.00
200 Robert Herron 2.50 6.00
202 Terrance West 2.50 6.00
203 Lorenzo Taliaferro 2.50 6.00
206 Zach Mettenberger 2.50 6.00
211 Cody Latimer 3.00 8.00
212 Jordan Matthews 4.00 10.00
213 Eric Ebron 8.00 20.00
216 Devonta Freeman 12.00 30.00
221 Lorenzo Taliaferro 2.50 6.00
222 James White 5.00 12.00

2014 Topps Chrome Mini Rookie Autographs Black Refractors

*BLACK REF/25: .8X TO 2X BASIC AUTO
117 Odell Beckham Jr. 75.00 150.00

2014 Topps Chrome Mini Rookie Autographs Camo Refractors

*CAMO REF/99: .6X TO 1.5X BASIC AUTO
115 Derek Carr
117 Odell Beckham Jr.

2014 Topps Chrome Mini Rookie Autographs Pink Refractors

*PINK AU/75: .6X TO 1.5X BASIC AU
115 Derek Carr 60.00 100.00
117 Odell Beckham Jr. 60.00 100.00

2014 Topps Chrome Mini Rookie Autographs Refractors

*REFRACT/150: .5X TO 1.2X BASIC AUTO
*REFRACT/75: .6X TO 1.5X BASIC AUTO
117 Odell Beckham Jr.

2014 Topps Chrome Mini Rookie Die Cuts

*BLUE WAVE/25: 2X TO 5X BASIC INSERTS
*RED REF/25: 3X TO 8X BASIC INSERTS
CRDCAM A.J. McCarron .40 1.00
CRDCAR Allen Robinson .60 1.50
CRDCAS Austin Seferian-Jenkins .40 1.00
CRDCAW Andre Williams .40 1.00
CRDCBB Blake Bortles .50 1.25
CRDCBC Brandin Cooks .60 1.50
CRDCBS Bishop Sankey .40 1.00
CRDCCH Carlos Hyde .50 1.25
CRDCCL Cody Latimer .50 1.25
CRDCCS Charles Sims .40 1.00
CRDCDA Davante Adams .60 1.50
CRDCDC Derek Carr 2.50 6.00
CRDCDF Devonta Freeman .60 1.50
CRDCDM Donte Moncrief .40 1.00
CRDCDT De'Anthony Thomas .40 1.00
CRDCEE Eric Ebron .50 1.25
CRDCJA Jace Amaro .40 1.00
CRDCJC Jadeveon Clowney .50 1.25
CRDCJG Jimmy Garoppolo 3.00 8.00
CRDCJH Jeremy Hill .50 1.25
CRDCJL Jarvis Landry .75 2.00
CRDCJM Johnny Manziel .60 1.50
CRDCKB Kelvin Benjamin .60 1.50
CRDCKC Ka'Deem Carey .40 1.00
CRDCLT Logan Thomas .40 1.00
CRDCME Mike Evans 1.00 2.50
CRDCML Marqise Lee .50 1.25
CRDCMS Michael Sam .40 1.00
CRDCOB Odell Beckham Jr. 1.00 2.50
CRDCPR Paul Richardson .50 1.25
CRDCSW Sammy Watkins .60 1.50
CRDCTB Teddy Bridgewater .60 1.50
CRDCTM Tre Mason .40 1.00
CRDCTS Tom Savage .40 1.00
CRDCTW Terrance West .40 1.00
CRDCZM Zach Mettenberger .40 1.00
CRDCAMU Aaron Murray .40 1.00
CRDCDFA David Fales .40 1.00
CRDCJMA Jordan Matthews .60 1.50
CRDCTBO Tajh Boyd .40 1.00

2015 Topps Chrome Mini

1 Marshawn Lynch .25 .60
2A Aaron Rodgers .60 1.50
2B Brett Favre SP 10.00 25.00
3 Robert Griffin III .20 .50
4A Sammy Watkins .25 .60
4B Sammy Watkins SP 2.50 6.00
5A Calvin Johnson .30 .75
5B Jerry Rice SP 5.00 12.00
6A Andrew Luck .40 1.00
6B Roger Staubach SP 6.00 15.00
7A Jamaal Charles .25 .60
7B Jamaal Charles SP 2.50 6.00
8 Le'Veon Bell .25 .60
9A Richard Sherman .30 .75
9B Richard Sherman SP
10 Rob Gronkowski .30 .75
11 Percy Harvin .20 .50
12A Drew Brees .30 .75
12B Drew Brees SP 3.00 8.00
13A Antonio Brown .30 .75
13B Antonio Brown SP 3.00 8.00
14 Demaryius Thomas .25 .60
15A Russell Wilson .40 1.00
15B Russell Wilson SP 4.00 10.00
16 Dez Bryant .30 .75
17 Julio Jones .30 .75
18A Odell Beckham Jr. .30 .75
18B Odell Beckham Jr. SP 3.00 8.00
19A Eddie Lacy .20 .50
19B Eddie Lacy SP
20 Cam Newton .30 .75
21A Jordy Nelson .25 .60
21B Jordy Nelson SP 2.50 6.00
22 Ndamukong Suh .25 .60
23A DeMarco Murray .25 .60
23B Eric Dickerson SP 2.50 6.00
24 Adrian Peterson .30 .75
25 Jimmy Graham .30 .75
26A Luke Kuechly .25 .60
26B Mike Singletary SP 3.00 8.00
27 LeSean McCoy .30 .75
28 A.J. Green .30 .75
29 Earl Thomas .25 .60
30A Ben Roethlisberger .30 .75
30B Terry Bradshaw SP 4.00 10.00
31 Terrell Suggs .20 .50
32A Matt Forte .20 .50
32B Matt Forte SP 2.00 5.00
33 Mario Williams .20 .50
34A Randall Cobb .25 .60
34B Randall Cobb SP 2.50 6.00
35 Patrick Peterson .20 .50
36 Philip Rivers .30 .75
37 Kam Chancellor .30 .75
38A Arian Foster .25 .60
38B Earl Campbell SP 3.00 8.00
39 Darrelle Revis .20 .50
40A Matthew Stafford .25 .60
40B Matthew Stafford SP 2.50 6.00
40C Barry Sanders SP
41A Alshon Jeffery .25 .60
41B Alshon Jeffery SP 2.50 6.00
42 Jeremy Hill .20 .50
43 T.Y. Hilton .25 .60
44A Tony Romo .25 .60
44B Emmitt Smith SP 5.00 12.00
45A Clay Matthews .30 .75
45B Clay Matthews SP 3.00 8.00
46A Mike Evans .25 .60
46B Mike Evans SP 2.50 6.00
47 Kelvin Benjamin .25 .60
48A C.J. Anderson .25 .60
48B Terrell Davis SP 2.50 6.00
49 Brandon Marshall .20 .50
50 Tom Brady .75 2.00
51A Matt Ryan .25 .60
51B Matt Ryan SP 2.50 6.00
52 DeSean Jackson .25 .60
53 Frank Gore .25 .60
54 Joe Flacco .25 .60
55A Eli Manning .25 .60
55B Eli Manning SP 2.50 6.00
56A Colin Kaepernick .25 .60
56B Steve Young SP 4.00 10.00
57 Alfred Morris .20 .50
58 Larry Fitzgerald .25 .60
59 Justin Houston .20 .50
60 Antonio Gates .20 .50
61 Emmanuel Sanders .25 .60
62 Mark Ingram .25 .60
63 Lamar Miller .20 .50
64 Carlos Hyde .20 .50
65 Julian Edelman .30 .75
66 Vontae Davis .20 .50
67A Patrick Willis .25 .60
67B Ronnie Lott SP 2.50 6.00
68 Bobby Wagner .20 .50
69 Giovani Bernard .20 .50
70A Troy Polamalu .30 .75
70B Troy Polamalu SP 3.00 8.00
71 Eric Berry .25 .60
72 Golden Tate .20 .50
73 Jeremy Maclin .20 .50
74 Nick Foles .25 .60
75 J.J. Watt .30 .75
76 Ryan Tannehill .25 .60
76B Dan Marino SP 8.00 20.00
77 Jay Cutler .20 .50
78 C.J. Spiller .20 .50
79 Teddy Bridgewater .25 .60
80 Blake Bortles .20 .50
81 Alex Smith .25 .60
82A Tre Mason .25 .60
82B Marshall Faulk SP 2.50 6.00
83 Joique Bell .20 .50
84 Steve Smith .25 .60
85 Jadeveon Clowney .20 .50
86 Travis Kelce .30 .75
87 Greg Olsen .25 .60
88 Jason Witten .25 .60
89A Latavius Murray .20 .50
89B Bo Jackson SP 4.00 10.00
90 Jonathan Stewart .20 .50
91 Carson Palmer .25 .60
92 Derek Carr .30 .75
93 Andy Dalton .25 .60
94 Devonta Freeman .25 .60
95 Brandin Cooks .25 .60
96 Andre Johnson .25 .60
97 Jordan Matthews .25 .60
98 Vincent Jackson .20 .50
99 Eric Decker .20 .50
100A Peyton Manning .60 1.50
100B Peyton Manning SP 6.00 15.00
100C John Elway SP
101 Vic Beasley RC .40 1.00
102A Brett Hundley RC .30 .75
102B Brett Hundley SP 6.00 15.00
103A DeVante Parker RC .50 1.25
103B DeVante Parker SP 2.00 5.00
104 Trae Waynes RC .30 .75
105A Melvin Gordon RC .75 2.00
105B Melvin Gordon SP 3.00 8.00
106A Dorial Green-Beckham RC .30 .75
106B Dorial Green-Beckham SP 1.25 3.00
107A Devin Funchess RC .50 1.25
107B Devin Funchess SP 2.00 5.00
108A Jaelen Strong RC .40 1.00
108B Jaelen Strong SP 1.50 4.00
109 P.J. Williams RC .40 1.00
110A Todd Gurley RC 1.25 3.00
110B Todd Gurley SP 10.00 25.00
111A Ameer Abdullah RC .50 1.25
111B Ameer Abdullah SP 2.00 5.00
112 Michael Bennett RC .30 .75
113A Sammie Coates RC .40 1.00
113B Sammie Coates SP 1.50 4.00
114 Randy Gregory RC .30 .75
115A Amari Cooper RC 1.00 2.50
115B Amari Cooper SP 12.00 30.00
116 Shaq Thompson RC .40 1.00
117 Brandon Scherff RC .50 1.25
118 Landon Collins RC .40 1.00
119 Ty Montgomery RC .30 .75
120A Jay Ajayi RC .50 1.25
120B Jay Ajayi SP 2.00 5.00
121A Tevin Coleman RC .40 1.00
121B Tevin Coleman SP 1.50 4.00
122 Shane Ray RC .30 .75
123 Josh Harper RC .30 .75
124 Marcus Peters RC .50 1.25
125A Kevin White RC .40 1.00
125B Kevin White SP 1.50 4.00
126 Dezmin Lewis RC .30 .75
127 Dante Fowler Jr. RC .50 1.25
128 Terrence Magee RC .50 1.25
129 Kenny Bell RC .50 1.25
130 Leonard Williams RC .30 .75
131 Danny Shelton RC .30 .75
132 Benardrick McKinney RC .30 .75
133 Andrus Peat RC .30 .75
134 Cedric Ogbuehi RC .30 .75
135 La'el Collins RC .40 1.00
136 Ereck Flowers RC .40 1.00
137A Bryce Petty RC .30 .75
137B Bryce Petty SP 5.00 12.00
138A T.J. Yeldon RC .30 .75
138B T.J. Yeldon SP 1.25 3.00
139 Mike Davis RC .30 .75
140A Duke Johnson RC .50 1.25
140B Duke Johnson SP 2.00 5.00
141 Karlos Williams RC .30 .75
142 Jeremy Langford RC .30 .75
143 Marcus Murphy RC .30 .75
144 Nick O'Leary RC .30 .75
145 Ben Koyack RC .50 1.25
146A Nelson Agholor RC .40 1.00
146B Nelson Agholor SP 1.50 4.00
147 Rashad Greene RC .30 .75
148 Stefon Diggs RC .75 2.00
149 Justin Hardy RC .30 .75
150A Marcus Mariota RC 1.25 3.00
150B Marcus Mariota SP 15.00 40.00
151A Garrett Grayson RC .30 .75
151B Garrett Grayson SP 5.00 12.00
152 Javorius Allen RC .40 1.00
153 Matt Jones RC .30 .75
154 David Cobb RC .30 .75
155 Austin Hill RC .30 .75
156 Clive Walford RC .30 .75
157 Alvin Dupree RC .40 1.00
158 Eli Harold RC .30 .75
159 Chris Conley RC .30 .75
160 Eddie Goldman RC .30 .75
161 Alex Carter RC .30 .75
162 Jalen Collins RC .30 .75
163 T.J. Clemmings RC .30 .75
164 Nate Orchard RC .30 .75
165A Maxx Williams RC .30 .75
165B Maxx Williams SP 1.25 3.00
166 Tony Lippett RC .30 .75
167 Cameron Artis-Payne RC .30 .75
168 Vince Mayle RC .40 1.00
169 Dres Anderson RC .30 .75
170A Phillip Dorsett RC .30 .75
170B Phillip Dorsett SP 1.25 3.00
171 Shane Carden RC .30 .75
172 Jamison Crowder RC .40 1.00
173 Danielle Hunter RC .40 1.00
174 Lorenzo Mauldin RC .30 .75
175 Paul Dawson RC .40 1.00
176 Owamagbe Odighizuwa RC .40 1.00
177 David Johnson RC .75 2.00
178A Tyler Lockett RC .50 1.25
178B Tyler Lockett SP 2.00 5.00
179 Dominique Brown RC .30 .75
180 Kevin Johnson RC .30 .75
181 Eric Kendricks RC .30 .75
182 Sean Mannion RC .30 .75
183 Denzel Perryman RC .30 .75
184 Malcolm Brown RC .40 1.00
185 Jeff Heuerman RC .40 1.00
186 Antwan Goodley RC .30 .75
187 Deontay Greenberry RC .30 .75
188 Bo Wallace RC .30 .75
189 Levi Norwood RC .30 .75
190 Tyler Kroft RC .40 1.00
191 Senquez Golson RC .30 .75
192 D'Joun Smith RC .50 1.25
193 Jesse James RC .40 1.00
194A Devin Smith RC .30 .75
194B Devin Smith SP 1.25 3.00
195 Carl Davis RC .40 1.00
196 Tre McBride RC .30 .75
197A Breshad Perriman RC .30 .75
197B Breshad Perriman SP 1.25 3.00
198 Josh Robinson RC .30 .75
199 Cody Fajardo RC .40 1.00
200A Jameis Winston RC .75 2.00
200B Jameis Winston SP 12.00 30.00

2015 Topps Chrome Mini Black Refractors

*1-110 VETS/15: 12X TO 30X BASIC CHROME
*111-220 ROOK/15: 8X TO 20X CHROME RC

2015 Topps Chrome Mini Blue Refractors

*1-100 VETS: 3X TO 8X BASIC CARDS
*100-290 ROOKIE: 2X TO 5X BASIC RC

2015 Topps Chrome Mini Camo Refractors

*1-100 VETS/99: 4X TO 10X BASIC CARDS
*101-200 ROOKIE/99: 2.5X TO 6X BASIC RC

2015 Topps Chrome Mini Diamond Refractors

*1-100 VETS: 1.5X TO 4X BASIC CARDS
*100-290 ROOKIE: 1X TO 2.5X BASIC RC

2015 Topps Chrome Mini Green Refractors

*1-100 VETS: 2.5X TO 6X BASIC CARDS
*100-290 ROOKIE: 1.5X TO 4X BASIC RC

2015 Topps Chrome Mini Pink Refractors

*1-110 VETS/25: 10X TO 25X BASIC CHROME
*111-220 ROOK/25: 6X TO 15X CHROME RC

2015 Topps Chrome Mini Pulsar Refractors

*1-100 VETS: 2X TO 5X BASIC CARDS
*100-290 ROOKIE: 1.2X TO 3X BASIC RC

2015 Topps Chrome Mini Purple Refractors

*1-100 VETS: 4X TO 10X BASIC CARDS
*101-200 ROOKIE: 2.5X TO 6X BASIC RC

2015 Topps Chrome Mini Refractors

*1-100 VETS: 1.2X TO 3X BASIC CARDS
*100-200 ROOKIE: .8X TO 2X BASIC RC

2015 Topps Chrome Mini Sepia Refractors

*1-100 VETS: 1.5X TO 4X BASIC CARDS
*100-290 ROOKIE: 1X TO 2.5X BASIC RC

2015 Topps Chrome Mini '76

*PULSAR/25: 2.5X TO 6X BASIC INSERTS
T76AA Ameer Abdullah .60 1.50
T76AC Amari Cooper 1.25 3.00
T76BH Brett Hundley .40 1.00
T76BP Bryce Petty .40 1.00
T76BP Breshad Perriman .40 1.00
T76CC Chris Conley .40 1.00
T76DC David Cobb .40 1.00
T76DF Devin Funchess .60 1.50
T76DP DeVante Parker .60 1.50
T76DS Devin Smith .40 1.00
T76JL Jeremy Langford .40 1.00
T76JS Jaelen Strong .50 1.25
T76JW Jameis Winston 1.00 2.50
T76KW Kevin White .50 1.25
T76LW Leonard Williams .40 1.00
T76MD Mike Davis .40 1.00
T76MG Melvin Gordon 1.00 2.50
T76MJ Matt Jones .40 1.00
T76MM Marcus Mariota 1.50 4.00
T76MW Maxx Williams .40 1.00
T76NA Nelson Agholor .50 1.25
T76PD Phillip Dorsett .40 1.00
T76SC Sammie Coates .50 1.25
T76SD Stefon Diggs 1.00 2.50
T76SM Sean Mannion .40 1.00
T76TC Tevin Coleman .50 1.25
T76TG Todd Gurley 1.50 4.00
T76TL Tyler Lockett .60 1.50
T76TM Ty Montgomery .40 1.00
T76TY T.J. Yeldon .40 1.00
T76DAJ David Johnson 1.00 2.50
T76DGB Dorial Green-Beckham .40 1.00
T76DUJ Duke Johnson .60 1.50
T76JAJ Jay Ajayi .60 1.50
T76JAL Javorius Allen .50 1.25

2015 Topps Chrome Mini '76 Autographs

76AAA Ameer Abdullah/25 10.00 25.00
76AAC Amari Cooper
76ABH Brett Hundley
76ABP Breshad Perriman
76ABP Bryce Petty/35 6.00 15.00
76ADF Devin Funchess/25 40.00 80.00
76ADGB Dorial Green-Beckham
76ADS Devin Smith/25 6.00 15.00
76AJL Jeremy Langford
76AJS Jaelen Strong/25 10.00 25.00
76AJW Jameis Winston
76AKW Kevin White
76ALW Leonard Williams/25 6.00 15.00
76AMD Mike Davis/35 6.00 15.00
76AMG Melvin Gordon/15 30.00 80.00
76AMJ Matt Jones
76AMM Marcus Mariota
76AMW Maxx Williams
76ANA Nelson Agholor/25 8.00 20.00
76APD Phillip Dorsett
76ATC Tevin Coleman/25 8.00 20.00
76ATG Todd Gurley/15 100.00 175.00
76ATY T.J. Yeldon

2015 Topps Chrome Mini 1989

*GOLD/50: 2X TO 5X BASIC INSERTS
*PULSAR/25: 2.5X TO 6X BASIC INSERTS
T89AA Ameer Abdullah .60 1.50
T89AC Amari Cooper 1.25 3.00
T89BH Brett Hundley .40 1.00
T89BP Bryce Petty .40 1.00
T89BP Breshad Perriman .40 1.00
T89CC Chris Conley .40 1.00
T89DC David Cobb .40 1.00
T89DF Devin Funchess .60 1.50
T89DJ Duke Johnson .60 1.50
T89DJ David Johnson 1.00 2.50
T89DP DeVante Parker .60 1.50
T89DS Devin Smith .40 1.00
T89JL Jeremy Langford .40 1.00
T89JS Jaelen Strong .50 1.25
T89JW Jameis Winston 1.00 2.50
T89KW Kevin White .50 1.25
T89LW Leonard Williams .40 1.00
T89MD Mike Davis .40 1.00
T89MG Melvin Gordon 1.00 2.50
T89MJ Matt Jones .40 1.00
T89MM Marcus Mariota 1.50 4.00
T89MW Maxx Williams .40 1.00
T89NA Nelson Agholor .50 1.25
T89PD Phillip Dorsett .40 1.00
T89SC Sammie Coates .50 1.25
T89SD Stefon Diggs 1.00 2.50
T89SM Sean Mannion .40 1.00
T89TC Tevin Coleman .50 1.25
T89TG Todd Gurley 1.50 4.00
T89TL Tyler Lockett .60 1.50
T89TM Ty Montgomery .40 1.00
T89TY T.J. Yeldon .40 1.00
T89DGB Dorial Green-Beckham .40 1.00
T89JAJ Jay Ajayi .60 1.50
T89JAL Javorius Allen .50 1.25

2015 Topps Chrome Mini '89 Autographs

89AAA Ameer Abdullah
89AAC Amari Cooper
89ABH Brett Hundley/40 5.00 12.00
89ABP Breshad Perriman
89ABP Bryce Petty/40 5.00 12.00
89ADF Devin Funchess/25 40.00 80.00
89ADGB Dorial Green-Beckham
89ADS Devin Smith
89AJS Jaelen Strong/40 6.00 15.00
89AJW Jameis Winston
89AKW Kevin White
89ALW Leonard Williams
89AMD Mike Davis
89AMG Melvin Gordon
89AMJ Matt Jones/40 5.00 12.00
89AMM Marcus Mariota
89AMW Maxx Williams/40 5.00 12.00
89ANA Nelson Agholor
89APD Phillip Dorsett/25 6.00 15.00
89ATC Tevin Coleman
89ATG Todd Gurley
89ATY T.J. Yeldon/25 12.00 30.00

2015 Topps Chrome Mini 60th Anniversary

*REFRACTORS/50: 2X TO 5X BASIC INSERTS
*PULSAR/25: 2.5X TO 6X BASIC INSERTS
T60AB Antonio Brown .60 1.50
T60AC Amari Cooper 1.25 3.00
T60AG A.J. Green .60 1.50
T60AJ Alshon Jeffery .50 1.25
T60AL Andrew Luck .75 2.00
T60AP Adrian Peterson .60 1.50
T60AR Aaron Rodgers 1.25 3.00
T60BF Brett Favre 1.25 3.00
T60BJ Bo Jackson .75 2.00
T60BR Ben Roethlisberger .60 1.50
T60BS Barry Sanders 1.00 2.50
T60CJ Calvin Johnson .60 1.50
T60CK Colin Kaepernick .50 1.25
T60CM Clay Matthews .60 1.50
T60CN Cam Newton .60 1.50
T60DB Drew Brees .60 1.50
T60DB Dez Bryant .60 1.50
T60DM Dan Marino 1.25 3.00
T60DM DeMarco Murray .50 1.25
T60DS Deion Sanders .50 1.25
T60DT Demaryius Thomas .50 1.25
T60EC Earl Campbell .60 1.50
T60ED Eric Dickerson .50 1.25
T60EL Eddie Lacy .40 1.00
T60EM Eli Manning .50 1.25
T60ES Emmitt Smith 1.00 2.50
T60GS Gale Sayers .60 1.50
T60JE John Elway 1.00 2.50
T60JF Joe Flacco .50 1.25
T60JR Jerry Rice 1.00 2.50
T60JW J.J. Watt .60 1.50
T60JW Jameis Winston 1.00 2.50
T60KB Kelvin Benjamin .50 1.25
T60KW Kevin White .50 1.25
T60KW Kurt Warner .50 1.25
T60LB Le'Veon Bell .50 1.25
T60LT Lawrence Taylor .60 1.50
T60ME Mike Evans .50 1.25
T60MF Marshall Faulk .50 1.25
T60ML Marshawn Lynch .50 1.25
T60MM Marcus Mariota 1.50 4.00
T60MR Matt Ryan .50 1.25
T60OB Odell Beckham Jr. .60 1.50
T60PM Peyton Manning 1.25 3.00
T60RC Randall Cobb .50 1.25
T60RG Rob Gronkowski .60 1.50
T60RG Robert Griffin III .40 1.00
T60RS Roger Staubach .75 2.00
T60RT Ryan Tannehill .50 1.25
T60RW Russell Wilson .75 2.00
T60SL Steve Largent .60 1.50
T60SW Sammy Watkins .50 1.25
T60SY Steve Young .75 2.00
T60TB Tom Brady 1.50 4.00
T60TB Terry Bradshaw .75 2.00
T60TB Tim Brown .60 1.50
T60TD Terrell Davis .50 1.25
T60TD Tony Dorsett .60 1.50
T60TG Todd Gurley 1.50 4.00
T60TP Troy Polamalu .60 1.50

2015 Topps Chrome Mini Rookie Autographs Refractors

*CAMO/75: .5X TO 1.2X BASIC AU
*PINK/50: .6X TO 1.5X BASIC AU
101 Vic Beasley 3.00 8.00
102 Brett Hundley
104 Trae Waynes 2.50 6.00
105 Melvin Gordon 10.00 25.00
107 Devin Funchess 4.00 10.00
108 Jaelen Strong 3.00 8.00
110 Todd Gurley 25.00 60.00
111 Ameer Abdullah
115 Amari Cooper
118 Landon Collins 3.00 8.00
122 Shane Ray 2.50 6.00
123 Josh Harper 2.50 6.00
129 Kenny Bell 4.00 10.00
130 Leonard Williams
137 Bryce Petty 2.50 6.00
139 Mike Davis 2.50 6.00
142 Jeremy Langford 2.50 6.00
143 Marcus Murphy 2.50 6.00
145 Ben Koyack 4.00 10.00
146 Nelson Agholor 3.00 8.00
147 Rashad Greene 2.50 6.00
149 Justin Hardy 2.50 6.00
153 Matt Jones
155 Austin Hill 2.50 6.00
156 Clive Walford 2.50 6.00
157 Alvin Dupree
161 Alex Carter 2.50 6.00
166 Tony Lippett 2.50 6.00
167 Cameron Artis-Payne 2.50 6.00
168 Vince Mayle 3.00 8.00
169 Dres Anderson 2.50 6.00
177 David Johnson 20.00 40.00
184 Malcolm Brown 3.00 8.00
186 Antwan Goodley 2.50 6.00
187 Deontay Greenberry 2.50 6.00
189 Levi Norwood 2.50 6.00
190 Tyler Kroft 3.00 8.00
194 Devin Smith 2.50 6.00
196 Tre McBride 2.50 6.00
198 Josh Robinson 2.50 6.00

2015 Topps Chrome Mini Rookie Autographs Black Refractors

*BLACK/25: 1X TO 2.5X BASIC AU
110 Todd Gurley 75.00 150.00
111 Ameer Abdullah 10.00 25.00
157 Alvin Dupree 12.00 30.00
200 Jameis Winston 125.00 250.00

2015 Topps Chrome Mini Rookie Autographs Blue Refractors

*BLUE/35: .8X TO 2X BASIC AU
110 Todd Gurley UER 60.00 125.00
111 Ameer Abdullah 8.00 20.00
115 Amari Cooper 40.00 80.00
150 Marcus Mariota 30.00 80.00
200 Jameis Winston 100.00 200.00

2015 Topps Chrome Mini Rookie Autographs Pulsar Refractors

*PULSAR/15: 1.2X TO 3X BASIC AU
110 Todd Gurley 100.00 200.00
111 Ameer Abdullah 12.00 30.00
157 Alvin Dupree 15.00 40.00
200 Jameis Winston 150.00 300.00

2007 Topps Co-Signers

This 100-card set was released in November, 2007. The set was issued into the hobby in six-card packs, with a $10 SRP, which came 12 packs to a box. The set contains veteran players (1-35); retired greats (36-50) and 2007 NFL

rookies (51-100). The Rookie Cards were issued to a stated print run of 2249 serial numbered cards and were inserted into packs at a stated rate of one in three.
COMP.SET w/o RC's (50) 8.00 20.00
ROOKIE/2249 ODDS 1:3
UNPRICED PRINT PLATE/1 ODDS 1:838
1 Peyton Manning 1.25 3.00
2 Brett Favre 1.00 2.50
3 Carson Palmer .40 1.00
4 Tom Brady 1.50 4.00
5 Eli Manning .40 1.00
6 Philip Rivers .50 1.25
7 Matt Leinart .30 .75
8 Vince Young .30 .75
9 Jay Cutler .30 .75
10 Ben Roethlisberger .50 1.25
11 Drew Brees .50 1.25
12 LaDainian Tomlinson .50 1.25
13 Larry Johnson .30 .75
14 Frank Gore .40 1.00
15 Steven Jackson .30 .75
16 Willie Parker .40 1.00
17 Rudi Johnson .30 .75
18 Thomas Jones .30 .75
19 Edgerrin James .40 1.00
20 Julius Jones .30 .75
21 Joseph Addai .30 .75
22 Maurice Jones-Drew .30 .75
23 Shaun Alexander .30 .75
24 Laurence Maroney .40 1.00
25 Cedric Benson .30 .75
26 Reggie Bush .30 .75
27 Chad Johnson .30 .75
28 Marvin Harrison .40 1.00
29 Steve Smith .40 1.00
30 Randy Moss .40 1.00
31 Terrell Owens .40 1.00
32 Andre Johnson .40 1.00
33 Greg Jennings .30 .75
34 Marques Colston .30 .75
35 Jerricho Cotchery .30 .75
36 Troy Aikman .75 2.00
37 Terry Bradshaw .75 2.00
38 John Elway 1.00 2.50
39 Roger Staubach .75 2.00
40 Dan Marino 1.25 3.00
41 Joe Namath .75 2.00
42 Joe Montana 2.00 5.00
43 Paul Hornung .60 1.50
44 Emmitt Smith 1.00 2.50
45 Jim Brown .75 2.00
46 Barry Sanders 1.00 2.50
47 Marcus Allen .60 1.50
48 Tony Dorsett .60 1.50
49 Fred Biletnikoff .60 1.50
50 Jerry Rice 1.25 3.00
51 JaMarcus Russell RC .75 2.00
52 John Beck RC .75 2.00
53 Trent Edwards RC .75 2.00
54 Chris Leak RC .75 2.00
55 Brady Quinn RC .75 2.00
56 Jeff Rowe RC .75 2.00
57 Troy Smith RC .75 2.00
58 Kevin Kolb RC 1.00 2.50
59 Drew Stanton RC .75 2.00
60 Jordan Palmer RC 1.00 2.50
61 Luke Getsy RC 1.25 3.00
62 Brian Leonard RC .75 2.00
63 Lorenzo Booker RC 1.00 2.50
64 Michael Bush RC .75 2.00
65 Chris Henry RC .75 2.00
66 Tony Hunt RC .75 2.00
67 Kenny Irons RC .75 2.00
68 Brandon Jackson RC .75 2.00
69 Marshawn Lynch RC 1.50 4.00
70 Adrian Peterson RC 2.50 6.00
71 Garrett Wolfe RC .75 2.00
72 Antonio Pittman RC .75 2.00
73 Kolby Smith RC .75 2.00
74 Greg Olsen RC 1.25 3.00
75 Zach Miller RC .75 2.00
76 Dwayne Bowe RC .75 2.00
77 Steve Breaston RC .75 2.00
78 David Clowney RC .75 2.00
79 Craig Buster Davis RC .75 2.00
80 Chris Davis RC .75 2.00
81 Yamon Figurs RC .75 2.00
82 Ted Ginn RC 1.00 2.50
83 Anthony Gonzalez RC .75 2.00
84 Jason Hill RC .75 2.00
85 Dwayne Jarrett RC 1.00 2.50
86 Calvin Johnson RC 2.50 6.00
87 Robert Meachem RC 1.00 2.50
88 Sidney Rice RC 1.00 2.50
89 Steve Smith RC .75 2.00
90 Mike Walker RC 1.25 3.00
91 Roy Hall RC 1.25 3.00
92 Dallas Baker RC .75 2.00
93 Johnnie Lee Higgins RC .75 2.00
94 Ryne Robinson RC 1.00 2.50
95 Chansi Stuckey RC 1.00 2.50
96 Gaines Adams RC 1.00 2.50
97 Adam Carriker RC .75 2.00
98 Paul Posluszny RC .75 2.00
99 Patrick Willis RC 1.25 3.00
100 LaRon Landry RC 1.25 3.00

2007 Topps Co-Signers Changing Faces Gold Red

GOLD RED PRINT RUN 399 SER.#'d SETS
*GOLD BLUE/349: .4X TO 1X GOLD RED/399
GOLD BLUE/349 ODDS 1:5
*GOLD GREEN/249: .5X TO 1.2X GOLD RED/399
GOLD GREEN/249 ODDS 1:7
*HOLOGOLD BLUE/25: 2X TO 5X GOLD RED/399
HOLOGOLD BLUE/25 ODDS 1:68
UNPRICED HOLOGOLD GREEN/1 ODDS 1:676
*HOLOGOLD RED/50: 1X TO 2.5X GOLD RED/399
HOLOGOLD RED/50 ODDS 1:34
*HOLOSLVR BLUE/99: .8X TO 2X GOLD RED/399
HOLOSILVER BLUE/99 ODDS 1:17
*HLSLVR GREEN/75: .8X TO 2X GOLD RED/399
HOLOSILVER GREEN/75 1:23
*HLSLVR RED/150: .6X TO 1.5X GOLD RED/399
HOLOSILVER RED/150 ODDS 1:12
1A P.Manning/M.Harrison 3.00 8.00
1B P.Manning/A.Gonzalez 3.00 8.00
2A B.Favre/P.Hornung 2.50 6.00
2B B.Favre/B.Jackson 2.50 6.00
3A Carson Palmer 1.00 2.50
Chad Johnson
3B Carson Palmer 1.00 2.50
Jeff Rowe
4A T.Brady/R.Moss 5.00 12.00
4B T.Brady/S.Breaston 4.00 10.00
5A E.Manning/P.Manning 2.50 6.00
5B E.Manning/S.Smith USC 1.00 2.50
6A P.Rivers/Tomlinson 1.25 3.00
6B Philip Rivers 1.25 3.00
Craig Buster Davis
7A M.Leinart/E.James 1.00 2.50
7B M.Leinart/S.Breaston .75 2.00
8A V.Young/J.Elway 2.50 6.00
8B V.Young/C.Henry .75 2.00
9A J.Cutler/J.Elway 3.00 8.00
9B J.Cutler/C.Leak .75 2.00
10A Roethlisberger/Bradshaw 1.50 4.00
10B Roethlisberger/D.Baker 1.25 3.00
11A D.Brees/R.Bush 1.25 3.00
11B Drew Brees 1.25 3.00
Robert Meachem
12A L.Tomlinson/B.Sanders 1.50 4.00
12B L.Tomlinson/C.Davis 1.25 3.00
13A Larry Johnson 1.25 3.00
Marcus Allen
13B Larry Johnson .60 1.50
Kolby Smith
14A F.Gore/J.Montana 4.00 10.00
14B Frank Gore 1.00 2.50
Jason Hill
15A Steven Jackson .75 2.00
Shaun Alexander
15B Steven Jackson .75 2.00
Brian Leonard
16A W.Parker/Roethlisberger 1.25 3.00
16B Willie Parker 1.00 2.50
Dallas Baker
17A Rudi Johnson 1.00 2.50
Carson Palmer
17B Rudi Johnson .75 2.00
Kenny Irons
18A Thomas Jones .75 2.00
Jerricho Cotchery
18B Thomas Jones 1.00 2.50
Chansi Stuckey
19A E.James/M.Leinart 1.00 2.50
19B Edgerrin James 1.00 2.50
Steve Breaston
20A J.Jones/E.Smith 1.50 4.00
20B J.Jones/B.Quinn .50 1.25
21A J.Addai/P.Manning 3.00 8.00
21B J.Addai/R.Hall 1.25 3.00
22A Maurice Jones-Drew 1.00 2.50
Laurence Maroney
22B Maurice Jones-Drew 1.25 3.00
Mike Walker
23A Shaun Alexander .75 2.00
Larry Johnson
23B Shaun Alexander .75 2.00
Kenny Irons
24A L.Maroney/T.Brady 3.00 8.00
24B Laurence Maroney 1.00 2.50
Tony Hunt
25A C.Benson/V.Young .60 1.50
25B Cedric Benson .75 2.00
Garrett Wolfe
26A R.Bush/D.Brees 1.25 3.00
26B R.Bush/A.Pittman .75 2.00
27A Chad Johnson .75 2.00
Rudi Johnson
27B Chad Johnson .75 2.00
Jeff Rowe
28A M.Harrison/J.Addai 1.00 2.50
28B M.Harrison/A.Gonzalez 1.00 2.50
29A S.Smith/J.Rice 2.00 5.00
29B S.Smith/D.Jarrett 1.00 2.50
30A Randy Moss 1.00 2.50
Laurence Maroney
30B R.Moss/C.Johnson 1.50 4.00
31A Terrell Owens 1.25 3.00
Troy Aikman
31B Terrell Owens .60 1.50
Ted Ginn Jr.
32A Andre Johnson 1.25 3.00
Fred Biletnikoff
32B A.Johnson/G.Olsen 1.25 3.00
33A G.Jennings/B.Favre 2.00 5.00
33B Greg Jennings .75 2.00
David Clowney
34A M.Colston/R.Bush .60 1.50
34B Marques Colston 1.00 2.50
Robert Meachem
35A Jerricho Cotchery .75 2.00
Thomas Jones
35B Jerricho Cotchery 1.00 2.50
Chansi Stuckey
36A T.Aikman/E.Smith 2.00 5.00
36B T.Aikman/B.Quinn 1.00 2.50
37A T.Bradshaw/W.Parker 1.50 4.00
37B T.Bradshaw/D.Baker 1.50 4.00
38A J.Elway/J.Cutler 2.50 6.00
38B J.Elway/T.Edwards 1.50 4.00
39A R.Staubach/T.Aikman 2.00 5.00
39B R.Staubach/J.Russell 1.00 2.50
40A D.Marino/J.Elway 3.00 8.00
40B D.Marino/J.Beck 2.50 6.00
41A J.Namath/J.Cotchery 1.50 4.00
41B J.Namath/C.Stuckey 1.50 4.00
42A J.Montana/J.Rice 6.00 15.00
42B J.Montana/L.Getsy 5.00 12.00
43A Paul Hornung 1.25 3.00
Greg Jennings
43B P.Hornung/B.Jackson 1.25 3.00
44A E.Smith/T.Dorsett 2.00 5.00
44B E.Smith/C.Leak 2.00 5.00
45A J.Brown/Tomlinson 1.50 4.00
45B J.Brown/B.Quinn 1.25 3.00
46A B.Sanders/E.Smith 2.00 5.00
46B B.Sanders/C.Johnson 1.50 4.00
47A Marcus Allen 1.25 3.00
Fred Biletnikoff
47B Marcus Allen 1.00 2.50
Michael Bush
48A T.Dorsett/R.Staubach 1.50 4.00
48B T.Dorsett/A.Peterson 1.50 4.00
49A Fred Biletnikoff 1.25 3.00
Marcus Allen
49B Fred Biletnikoff 1.25 3.00
Johnnie Lee Higgins
50A J.Rice/F.Gore 2.50 6.00
50B J.Rice/J.Hill 2.50 6.00
51A J.Russell/M.Bush .60 1.50
51B J.Russell/J.Addai .60 1.50
52A J.Beck/L.Booker .75 2.00
52B J.Beck/J.Cutler .60 1.50
53A T.Edwards/M.Lynch 1.25 3.00
53B T.Edwards/M.Leinart .60 1.50
54A Chris Leak .60 1.50
Garrett Wolfe
54B Chris Leak .60 1.50
Cedric Benson
55A B.Quinn/J.Russell .60 1.50
55B B.Quinn/P.Manning 2.50 6.00
56A Jeff Rowe .60 1.50
Kenny Irons
56B Jeff Rowe .60 1.50
Chad Johnson
57A T.Smith/Y.Figurs .60 1.50
57B T.Smith/V.Young .60 1.50
58A K.Kolb/T.Hunt .75 2.00
58B K.Kolb/Roethlisberger 1.00 2.50
59A D.Stanton/C.Johnson 1.50 4.00
59B D.Stanton/D.Brees 1.00 2.50
60A J.Palmer/L.Landry 1.00 2.50
60B Jordan Palmer .75 2.00
Carson Palmer
61A Luke Getsy 1.00 2.50
Jason Hill
61B Luke Getsy 1.00 2.50
Frank Gore
62A Brian Leonard .60 1.50
Adam Carriker
62B Brian Leonard .60 1.50
Steven Jackson
63A L.Booker/T.Ginn Jr. .60 1.50
63B Lorenzo Booker .75 2.00
Laurence Maroney
64A M.Bush/Z.Miller .60 1.50
64B M.Bush/M.Jones-Drew .60 1.50
65A Chris Henry .60 1.50
Chris Davis
65B C.Henry/V.Young .50 1.25
66A T.Hunt/K.Kolb .75 2.00
66B Tony Hunt .60 1.50
Larry Johnson
67A Kenny Irons .60 1.50
Jeff Rowe
67B Kenny Irons .75 2.00
Carson Palmer
68A B.Jackson/D.Clowney .60 1.50
68B B.Jackson/G.Jennings .60 1.50
69A M.Lynch/P.Posluszny 1.25 3.00
69B M.Lynch/J.Addai 1.25 3.00
70A A.Peterson/S.Rice 2.00 5.00
70B A.Peterson/Tomlinson 2.00 5.00
71A G.Wolfe/G.Olsen 1.00 2.50
71B Garrett Wolfe .60 1.50
Cedric Benson
72A Antonio Pittman .75 2.00
Robert Meachem
72B Antonio Pittman 1.00 2.50
Drew Brees
73A K.Smith/D.Bowe .50 1.25
73B K.Smith/L.Johnson .60 1.50
74A G.Olsen/C.Leak 1.00 2.50
74B G.Olsen/C.Benson 1.00 2.50
75A Zach Miller .60 1.50
Johnnie Lee Higgins
75B Zach Miller .75 2.00
Randy Moss
76A D.Bowe/K.Smith .60 1.50
76B D.Bowe/L.Johnson .60 1.50
77A S.Breaston/C.Davis .60 1.50
77B Steve Breaston .75 2.00
Edgerrin James
78A D.Clowney/B.Jackson .60 1.50
78B D.Clowney/B.Favre 2.00 5.00
79A C.Davis/D.Bowe .50 1.25
79B C.Davis/Tomlinson 1.00 2.50
80A Chris Davis .60 1.50
Chris Henry
80B C.Davis/V.Young .50 1.25
81A Y.Figurs/T.Smith .60 1.50
81B Yamon Figurs .75 2.00
Steve Smith
82A T.Ginn Jr./J.Beck .60 1.50
82B T.Ginn Jr./R.Moss .75 2.00
83A A.Gonzalez/R.Hall 1.00 2.50
83B A.Gonzalez/M.Harrison .75 2.00
84A J.Hill/P.Willis .75 2.00
84B Jason Hill .75 2.00
Frank Gore
85A D.Jarrett/R.Robinson .75 2.00
85B D.Jarrett/S.Smith .75 2.00
86A C.Johnson/D.Stanton 2.00 5.00
86B C.Johnson/T.Owens 2.00 5.00
87A Robert Meachem .75 2.00
Antonio Pittman
87B R.Meachem/R.Bush .60 1.50
88A S.Rice/A.Peterson 1.50 4.00
88B S.Rice/A.Johnson .75 2.00
89A S.Smith USC/D.Jarrett .75 2.00
89B S.Smith USC/E.Mann .75 2.00
90A Mike Walker 1.00 2.50
Dallas Baker
90B Mike Walker 1.00 2.50
Maurice Jones-Drew
91A R.Hall/A.Gonzalez .75 2.00
91B Roy Hall 1.00 2.50
Marvin Harrison
92A Dallas Baker .60 1.50
Steve Breaston
92B Dallas Baker .75 2.00
Willie Parker
93A J.Higgins/J.Russell .50 1.25
93B Johnnie Lee Higgins .60 1.50
Greg Jennings
94A R.Robinson/D.Jarrett .75 2.00
94B Ryne Robinson .75 2.00
Steve Smith
95A Stuckey/S.Smith USC .75 2.00
95B Chansi Stuckey .75 2.00
Jerricho Cotchery
96A Gaines Adams .75 2.00
Chansi Stuckey
96B Gaines Adams .75 2.00
Andre Johnson
97A Adam Carriker .60 1.50
Brian Leonard
97B Adam Carriker .60 1.50
Steven Jackson
98A P.Posluszny/T.Edwards .50 1.25
98B P.Posluszny/L.Johnson .60 1.50
99A P.Willis/L.Getsy 1.00 2.50
99B P.Willis/F.Gore 1.00 2.50
100A L.Landry/J.Palmer 1.00 2.50
100B L.Landry/J.Addai 1.00 2.50

2007 Topps Co-Signers Co-Signer Autographs

GROUP A/20 ODDS 1:886
GROUP B/25 ODDS 1:13,842
GROUP C/50 ODDS 1:1378
GROUP D/75 ODDS 1:4548
GROUP E/100 ODDS 1:1702
GROUP F/200 ODDS 1:846
GROUP G/250 ODDS 1:677
GROUP H ODDS 1:675
GROUP I ODDS 1:562
GROUP J ODDS 1:449
GROUP K ODDS 1:374
GROUP L ODDS 1:364
GROUP M ODDS 1:112
GROUP N ODDS 1:269
GROUP O ODDS 1:112
GROUP P ODDS 1:56
GROUP Q ODDS 1:45
TOPPS ANNOUNCED SOME PRINT RUNS
UNPRICED HOLOGOLD/1 ODDS 1:6774
UNPRICED HOLOSILVER/10 ODDS 1:674
UNPRICED PRINT PLATE/1 ODDS 1:1684
AB M.Alstott/D.Brooks E/100 25.00 50.00
AS Aikman/Staubach A/20 100.00 200.00
BB D.Branch/M.Bush D/75 6.00 15.00
BC D.Brees/M.Colston C/50 50.00 100.00
BH Bradshaw/F.Harris A/20 100.00 200.00
BHA A.Branch/L.Hall M 5.00 12.00
BJ B.Jackson/C.Henry M 5.00 12.00
BM T.Brady/Montana A/20 300.00 500.00
BP T.Brown/J.Plunkett A/20 30.00 80.00
BS R.Bush/B.Sanders A/20 100.00 200.00
CB R.Curry/M.Bush H 5.00 12.00
CC J.Cotchery/Colston F/200 8.00 20.00
CJ D.Clowney/B.Jackson O 5.00 12.00
DL C.Davis/L.Landry Q 8.00 20.00
DS Dickerson/B.Sanders A/20 100.00 200.00
FJ Y.Figurs/Jac.Jones Q 5.00 12.00
FS B.Favre/B.Starr A/20 250.00 400.00
GC F.Gore/T.Clayton F/200 8.00 20.00
GG J.Galloway/T.Ginn G/250 8.00 20.00
GJ F.Gore/L.Johnson A/20 12.00 30.00
GT Tar.Glenn/J.Thomas L 8.00 20.00
HH D.Hall/L.Hall C/50 6.00 15.00
HI D.Hall/D.Irons C/50 6.00 15.00
HP T.Hunt/Posluszny O 5.00 12.00
HW Hutchinson/W.Jones K 10.00 25.00
JA S.Jackson/Alexander A/20 12.00 30.00
JH Jennings/Holmes C/50 10.00 25.00
JJ Ju.Jones/T.Jones C/50 8.00 20.00
JJO Jac.Jones/Jam.Jones P 5.00 12.00
JP R.Jaworski/V.Papale E/100 25.00 60.00
KH B.Kassell/D.Harris N 5.00 12.00
KT J.Kelly/T.Thomas A/20 75.00 150.00
MC Meachem/Colston G/250 8.00 20.00
MH P.Manning/Harrison A/20 100.00 200.00
MN D.Marino/J.Namath A/20 125.00 250.00
MR J.Montana/J.Rice A/20 175.00 300.00
NE J.Namath/J.Elway A/20 100.00 200.00
PH A.Pittman/T.Hunt P 5.00 12.00
RS T.Romo/I.Stanback J 20.00 50.00
SB G.Sayers/B.Sanders A/20 100.00 200.00
SC C.Stuckey/J.Cotchery I 6.00 15.00
SD E.Smith/T.Dorsett A/20 150.00 300.00
SDA B.Starr/L.Dawson A/20 75.00 150.00
SJ S.Smith USC/Jarrett B/25 10.00 25.00
TB Tomlinson/R.Bush A/20 50.00 120.00
TL D.Tate/B.Leonard Q 6.00 15.00
WH L.Woodley/D.Harris P 10.00 25.00
WP K.Williams/Posluszny M 5.00 12.00
YM S.Young/J.Montana A/20 125.00 250.00
YT V.Young/Tomlinson A/20 20.00 50.00

2007 Topps Co-Signers Co-Signer Autographs Gold

*GOLD/25: .75X TO 1.5X BASE AU GROUP E-Q
*GOLD/25: .6X TO 1.2X BASE AU GROUP C-D
*GOLD/25: .5X TO 1X BASE AU GROUP A-B
GOLD/25 ODDS 1:281
BM T.Brady/Montana 250.00 400.00
BS R.Bush/B.Sanders 125.00 250.00
FS B.Favre/B.Starr 250.00 400.00
MH P.Manning/Harrison 150.00 250.00
MN D.Marino/J.Namath 150.00 250.00
MR J.Montana/J.Rice 175.00 300.00
SD E.Smith/T.Dorsett 150.00 300.00
YM S.Young/J.Montana 125.00 250.00

2007 Topps Co-Signers Rookie Autographs

OUP A/25 ODDS 1:4682
GROUP B/50 ODDS 1:6921
GROUP C/100 ODDS 1:3425
GROUP D/150 ODDS 1:188
GROUP E/250 ODDS 1:169
GROUP F ODDS 1:84
GROUP G ODDS 1:374
GROUP H ODDS 1:48
GROUP I ODDS 1:32
TOPPS ANNOUNCED SOME PRINT RUNS
UNPRICED PRINT PLATE/1 ODDS 1:3387
AC Adam Carriker D 4.00 10.00
AG Anthony Gonzalez D 4.00 10.00
AP Adrian Peterson A 100.00 200.00
API Antonio Pittman F 3.00 8.00
BJ Brandon Jackson E 4.00 10.00
BL Brian Leonard E 4.00 10.00
BQ Brady Quinn B 6.00 15.00
CD Craig Buster Davis H 3.00 8.00
CDA Chris Davis F 3.00 8.00
CH Chris Henry F 3.00 8.00
CJ Calvin Johnson A 60.00 100.00
CL Chris Leak F 3.00 8.00
CS Chansi Stuckey H 4.00 10.00
DB Dwayne Bowe D 15.00 40.00
DBA Dallas Baker I 3.00 8.00
DC David Clowney H 3.00 8.00
DJ Dwayne Jarrett D 5.00 12.00
DS Drew Stanton D 4.00 10.00
GO Greg Olsen D 6.00 15.00
GS Gaines Adams F 4.00 10.00
GW Garrett Wolfe F 3.00 8.00
JB John Beck F 3.00 8.00
JH Jason Hill H 3.00 8.00
JHI Johnnie Lee Higgins I 3.00 8.00
JP Jordan Palmer I 4.00 10.00
JR JaMarcus Russell A 15.00 40.00
JRO Jeff Rowe H 3.00 8.00
KK Kevin Kolb D 5.00 12.00
KS Kolby Smith H 3.00 8.00
LB Lorenzo Booker E 5.00 12.00
LL LaRon Landry E 6.00 15.00
MB Michael Bush D 4.00 10.00
ML Marshawn Lynch C 20.00 40.00
MW Mike Walker I 5.00 12.00
PP Paul Posluszny F 3.00 8.00
PW Patrick Willis E 6.00 15.00
RH Roy Hall H 5.00 12.00
RM Robert Meachem D 5.00 12.00
RR Ryne Robinson I 4.00 10.00
SB Steve Breaston I 3.00 8.00
SR Sidney Rice D 5.00 12.00
SS Steve Smith E 4.00 10.00
TE Trent Edwards E 4.00 10.00
TG Ted Ginn D 5.00 12.00
TH Tony Hunt E 4.00 10.00
TS Troy Smith D 4.00 10.00
YF Yamon Figurs I 3.00 8.00
ZM Zach Miller G 3.00 8.00

2007 Topps Co-Signers Rookie Autographs Gold

*GOLD/25: .8X TO 2X BASE AU GROUP F-I
*GOLD/25: .6X TO 1.5X BASE AU GROUP D-E
GOLD GROUP A/10 ODDS 1:12,735
GOLD GROUP B/25 ODDS 1:312
UNPRICED HOLOGOLD/1 ODDS 1:6921
UNPRICED HOLOSILVER GRP A ODDS 1:22,741
UNPRICED HOLOSILVER GRP B/10 ODDS 1:749
AP Adrian Peterson/10 200.00 350.00
BQ Brady Quinn/25 10.00 25.00
CJ Calvin Johnson/10 75.00 150.00
JR JaMarcus Russell/10 25.00 60.00
ML Marshawn Lynch/25 25.00 60.00

2007 Topps Co-Signers Rookie Co-Signer Autographs

GROUP A/10 ODDS 1:12,735
GROUP B/25 ODDS 1:936
GROUP C/50 ODDS 1:982
UNPRICED GOLD/10 ODDS 1:1349
UNPRICED HOLOGOLD/1 ODDS 1:13,842
UNPRICED HOLOSILVER/5 ODDS 1:2698
UNPRICED PRINT PLATES/1 ODDS 1:3387
SER.#'d UNDER 10 NOT PRICED
AA G.Adams/J.Anderson/25 10.00 25.00
BB L.Booker/J.Beck/25 10.00 25.00
BD D.Bowe/C.Davis/50 5.00 12.00
BM D.Bowe/R.Meachem/25 10.00 25.00
BS M.Bush/K.Smith/25 8.00 20.00
DW C.Davis/P.Williams/25 8.00 20.00
GJ T.Ginn/D.Jarrett/50 6.00 15.00
HH L.Hall/D.Harris/25 8.00 20.00
HW C.Henry/P.Williams/25 8.00 20.00
JT B.Jackson/Z.Taylor/25 10.00 25.00
KH K.Kolb/T.Hunt/25 10.00 25.00
LO C.Leak/G.Olsen/50 8.00 20.00
MW R.McKnight/D.Walker/25 8.00 20.00
OM G.Olsen/Z.Miller/25 12.00 30.00
PH A.Pittman/T.Hunt/25 8.00 20.00
QT B.Quinn/J.Thomas/25 12.00 30.00
RR R.Robinson/L.Robinson/25 12.00 30.00
SE D.Stanton/T.Edwards/50 5.00 12.00
SG T.Smith/T.Ginn/50 6.00 15.00
TW L.Timmons/P.Willis/50 8.00 20.00
WB L.Woodley/A.Branch/25 15.00 40.00
WL D.Wright/M.Lynch/50 10.00 25.00

2007 Topps Co-Signers Tri-Signer Autographs

GROUP A/15 ODDS 1:8163
GROUP B/20 ODDS 1:2211
GROUP C/150 ODDS 1:2258
GROUP D/175 ODDS 1:1941
GROUP E/200 ODDS 1:846
UNPRICED GOLD/10 ODDS 1:2242
UNPRICED HOLOGOLD/1 ODDS 1:22,741
UNPRICED HOLOSILVER/5 ODDS 1:4484
UNPRICED PRINT PLATES/1 ODDS 1:5685
AWL Adams/Willis/Landry/150 15.00 40.00
BIL Bker/K.Irons/Leonard/20 30.00 60.00
BMB Brdshw/Montana/Brady/20 400.00 600.00
BMD Bowe/Meach/C.Dvis/175 15.00 40.00
BSS Brown/B.Sndrs/Emmitt/20 300.00 500.00
DDA Dorsett/Dickrsn/Allen/20
DFJ Dckrsn/Faulk/S.Jcksn/20 50.00 120.00
HJH Hnry/Br.Jcksn/Hunt/200 15.00 40.00
JGJ C.Jhnsn/Ginn/Jarrett/15 50.00 100.00
JTA LJ/Tomlinson/Sh.Alex/20 40.00 100.00
LPB Lynch/Ptrsn/M.Bush/15 200.00 400.00
MEN Marino/Elway/Namath/20 250.00 400.00
PTP Pslszny/Timm/Willis/200 15.00 40.00
RQS Russell/Quinn/Stanton/15
SDP Starr/Dawson/Plunkett/20 125.00 250.00

2001 Topps Debut

This 175-card base set features 100 veterans and 75 short-printed rookies. Cards 101-110 are rookie autographs and serial numbered to 499, 111-150 are rookie game-worn jersey cards and serial numbered to 999, and 151-175 are rookies and serial numbered to 1499. No rookies had more than one version of their cards.
COMP.SET w/o SP's (100) 7.50 20.00
1 Marshall Faulk .25 .60
2 Ricky Watters .25 .60
3 Bill Schroeder .25 .60
4 Muhsin Muhammad .20 .50
5 Peter Warrick .20 .50
6 Marvin Harrison .25 .60
7 Stephen Davis .20 .50
8 Cris Carter .30 .75
9 Charlie Batch .20 .50
10 David Boston .20 .50
11 Ike Hilliard .20 .50
12 Steve McNair .25 .60
13 Kordell Stewart .20 .50
14 Travis Prentice .20 .50
15 Sammy Morris .20 .50
16 Vinny Testaverde .20 .50
17 Tyrone Wheatley .25 .60
18 Jeff Garcia .20 .50
19 Brett Favre .60 1.50
20 Jake Plummer .20 .50
21 Cade McNown .25 .60
22 Rob Johnson .25 .60
23 Tim Couch .20 .50
24 Jerome Bettis .30 .75
25 Ricky Williams .25 .60
26 Darrell Jackson .25 .60
27 Troy Brown .20 .50
28 Jamal Lewis .30 .75
29 Isaac Bruce .30 .75
30 Lamar Smith .25 .60
31 Qadry Ismail .20 .50
32 Elvis Grbac .25 .60
33 Shaun Alexander .20 .50
34 Peyton Manning .75 2.00
35 Curtis Martin .25 .60
36 Jamal Anderson .25 .60
37 Mark Brunell .25 .60
38 Emmitt Smith .50 1.25
39 Chad Lewis .20 .50
40 Randy Moss .25 .60
41 Kurt Warner .50 1.25
42 Terrence Wilkins .20 .50
43 Corey Dillon .20 .50
44 Brian Griese .20 .50
45 Jon Kitna .20 .50
46 Eric Moulds .20 .50
47 Steve Beuerlein .25 .60
48 James Allen .20 .50
49 Amani Toomer .20 .50
50 Daunte Culpepper .25 .60
51 Michael Pittman .25 .60
52 Warrick Dunn .20 .50
53 Terrell Owens .25 .60
54 Donald Hayes .20 .50
55 Keenan McCardell .25 .60
56 Tony Gonzalez .25 .60
57 Freddie Jones .20 .50
58 Charlie Garner .25 .60
59 Shawn Jefferson .20 .50
60 Brian Urlacher .40 1.00
61 Donovan McNabb .25 .60
62 Az-Zahir Hakim .20 .50
63 James Thrash .25 .60
64 Hines Ward .25 .60
65 Shawn Bryson .20 .50
66 Wayne Chrebet .20 .50
67 Kevin Johnson .20 .50
68 Eddie George .30 .75
69 Derrick Alexander .20 .50
70 Tim Brown .30 .75
71 Jay Fiedler .25 .60
72 Aaron Brooks .20 .50
73 Torry Holt .25 .60
74 Edgerrin James .25 .60
75 Shannon Sharpe .25 .60
76 Oronde Gadsden .20 .50
77 Rod Smith .25 .60
78 Rich Gannon .25 .60
79 Fred Taylor .20 .50
80 Derrick Mason .20 .50
81 Joe Horn .20 .50
82 Robert Smith .20 .50
83 James Stewart .20 .50
84 Jeff George .25 .60
85 Troy Aikman .40 1.00
86 Charles Johnson .20 .50
87 Ahman Green .25 .60
88 Shaun King .20 .50
89 Ray Lewis .30 .75
90 Trent Dilfer .20 .50
91 Drew Bledsoe .25 .60
92 Jimmy Smith .25 .60
93 Ed McCaffrey .25 .60
94 Kerry Collins .20 .50
95 Terry Glenn .25 .60
96 Ron Dayne .25 .60
97 Keyshawn Johnson .25 .60
98 Antonio Freeman .30 .75
99 Tiki Barber .25 .60
100 Mike Anderson .20 .50
101 Drew Brees AU RC 250.00 500.00
102 Chris Weinke AU RC 6.00 15.00
103 LaDain.Tomlinson AU RC 30.00 80.00
104 Michael Bennett AU RC 6.00 15.00
105 Anthony Thomas AU RC 8.00 20.00
106 LaMont Jordan AU RC 8.00 20.00
107 David Terrell AU RC 6.00 15.00
108 Michael Vick AU RC 12.00 30.00
109 Deuce McAllister AU RC 8.00 20.00
110 James Jackson AU RC 5.00 12.00
111 Mike McMahon JSY RC 5.00 12.00
112 Cedrick Wilson JSY RC 5.00 12.00
113 Ken Lucas JSY RC 5.00 12.00
114 Fred Smoot JSY RC 5.00 12.00
115 Alge Crumpler JSY RC 6.00 15.00
116 Sage Rosenfels JSY RC 5.00 12.00
117 Rashard Casey JSY RC 4.00 10.00
118 David Allen JSY RC 4.00 10.00
119 Bobby Newcombe JSY RC 5.00 12.00
120 Jesse Palmer JSY RC 5.00 12.00
121 Tommy Polley JSY RC 4.00 10.00
122 Kevan Barlow JSY RC 5.00 12.00
123 Scotty Anderson JSY RC 4.00 10.00
124 Travis Minor JSY RC 5.00 12.00
125 Snoop Minnis JSY RC 4.00 10.00
126 Moran Norris JSY RC 4.00 10.00
127 Alex Lincoln JSY RC 4.00 10.00
128 Chad Johnson JSY RC 6.00 15.00
129 Boo Williams JSY RC 4.00 10.00
130 Brian Natkin JSY RC 4.00 10.00
131 Orlando Huff JSY RC 4.00 10.00
132 Derrick Gibson JSY RC 4.00 10.00
133 Tony Driver JSY RC 5.00 12.00
134 Torrance Marshall JSY RC 4.00 10.00
135 Alex Bannister JSY RC 4.00 10.00
136 Morlon Greenwood JSY RC 4.00 10.00
137 Ennis Davis JSY RC 4.00 10.00
138 Mike Cerimele JSY RC 4.00 10.00
139 David Rivers JSY RC 4.00 10.00
140 Dustin McClintock JSY RC 5.00 12.00
141 Tay Cody JSY RC 4.00 10.00
142 Arther Love JSY RC 4.00 10.00
143 Sly Johnson JSY RC 4.00 10.00
144 Dan Alexander JSY RC 5.00 12.00
145 Will Allen JSY RC 6.00 15.00
146 Andre Dyson JSY RC 4.00 10.00
147 Margin Hooks JSY RC 4.00 10.00
148 Adam Archuleta JSY RC 5.00 12.00
149 Sedrick Hodge JSY RC 4.00 10.00
150 Kendrell Bell JSY RC 6.00 15.00
151 Reggie Wayne RC 2.50 6.00
152 Rod Gardner RC 1.50 4.00
153 Chris Chambers RC 1.25 3.00
154 Jamal Reynolds RC 1.25 3.00
155 Ben Hamilton RC 1.25 3.00
156 Dan Morgan RC 1.50 4.00
157 Quincy Morgan RC 1.50 4.00
158 Travis Henry RC 1.50 4.00
159 Ken-Yon Rambo RC 1.25 3.00
160 Josh Heupel RC 2.00 5.00
161 Marcus Stroud RC 1.50 4.00
162 Marques Tuiasosopo RC 1.50 4.00
163 Reggie Germany RC 1.25 3.00
164 Robert Ferguson RC 2.00 5.00
165 Jabari Holloway RC 1.25 3.00
166 Ben Leard RC 1.25 3.00
167 Bhawoh Jue RC 1.50 4.00
168 Freddie Mitchell RC 1.25 3.00
169 Vinny Sutherland RC 1.25 3.00
170 Jeff Backus RC 1.25 3.00
171 Correll Buckhalter RC 1.25 3.00
172 Mario Fatafehi RC 1.25 3.00
173 Rudi Johnson RC 2.00 5.00
174 Koren Robinson RC 1.50 4.00
175 Santana Moss RC 2.00 5.00

2002 Topps Debut

is 200-card set contains 150 veterans and 50 rookies. Cards 151-155 are rookie autographs, cards 156-160 are rookie jersey cards, and both groups of cards are serial #'d to 1499. Rookies 161-200 were inserted at a rate of 1:3. Boxes contained 24 packs of 5 cards. SRP was $2.99
COMP.SET w/o SP's (150) 10.00 25.00
1 Kurt Warner .25 .60
2 James Thrash .25 .60
3 Aaron Brooks .20 .50
4 Mark Brunell .25 .60
5 Mike Anderson .20 .50
6 Benjamin Gay .20 .50
7 Marvin Harrison .25 .60
8 Randy Moss .25 .60
9 Ron Dayne .25 .60
10 Tim Brown .30 .75
11 Vinny Testaverde .20 .50
12 Mike Alstott .20 .50
13 Tony Banks .20 .50
14 Plaxico Burress .20 .50
15 Chris Chambers .20 .50
16 Brett Favre .60 1.50
17 Quincy Carter .20 .50
18 Brian Urlacher .30 .75
19 Byron Chamberlain .20 .50
20 Tony Gonzalez .25 .60
21 Troy Brown .20 .50
22 Drew Brees .60 1.50
23 Koren Robinson .20 .50
24 Donald Hayes .20 .50
25 Michael Vick .25 .60
26 Travis Taylor .20 .50
27 Peerless Price .20 .50
28 Chad Johnson .20 .50
29 Tim Couch .20 .50
30 Edgerrin James .25 .60
31 Willie Jackson .20 .50
32 Hines Ward .25 .60
33 Terrell Owens .25 .60
34 Eddie George .25 .60
35 Michael Westbrook .20 .50
36 Kerry Collins .20 .50
37 Terrell Davis .25 .60
38 Marcus Robinson .25 .60
39 Charlie Batch .20 .50
40 Jake Plummer .20 .50
41 Qadry Ismail .20 .50
42 Snoop Minnis .20 .50
43 Jimmy Smith .25 .60
44 Charlie Garner .25 .60
45 Jeff Graham .20 .50
46 Torry Holt .25 .60
47 Kevin Dyson .25 .60
48 Maurice Smith .20 .50
49 Muhsin Muhammad .20 .50
50 Curtis Martin .25 .60
51 Todd Pinkston .20 .50
52 Matt Hasselbeck .20 .50
53 Corey Dillon .20 .50
54 Michael Pittman .25 .60
55 Antonio Freeman .30 .75
56 Oronde Gadsden .20 .50
57 Tiki Barber .25 .60
58 Isaac Bruce .30 .75
59 Rod Gardner .20 .50
60 Derrick Mason .20 .50
61 Joe Horn .20 .50
62 Antowain Smith .25 .60
63 Johnnie Morton .25 .60
64 Kevin Johnson .20 .50
65 Nick Goings .20 .50
66 Jason Brookins .20 .50
67 Travis Henry .20 .50
68 Brian Griese .20 .50
69 Priest Holmes .20 .50
70 Daunte Culpepper .25 .60
71 Amani Toomer .20 .50
72 Rich Gannon .25 .60
73 Correll Buckhalter .20 .50
74 Kevan Barlow .20 .50
75 Stephen Davis .20 .50
76 Keenan McCardell .25 .60
77 Jon Kitna .20 .50
78 Eric Moulds .20 .50
79 Dez White .20 .50
80 Rocket Ismail .25 .60
81 Dominic Rhodes .20 .50
82 Lamar Smith .20 .50
83 David Patten .20 .50
84 Duce Staley .20 .50
85 Curtis Conway .25 .60
86 Kordell Stewart .20 .50
87 Brad Johnson .25 .60
88 Wayne Chrebet .20 .50
89 Michael Bennett .20 .50
90 Quincy Morgan .20 .50
91 Steve Smith .30 .75
92 David Boston .20 .50
93 Shannon Sharpe .25 .60
94 Mike McMahon .20 .50
95 Stacey Mack .20 .50
96 Santana Moss .25 .60
97 Jeff Garcia .20 .50
98 Keyshawn Johnson .25 .60
99 Rod Smith .25 .60
100 Jerome Bettis .30 .75
101 LaDainian Tomlinson .30 .75
102 Warrick Dunn .20 .50
103 Ray Lewis .30 .75
104 Chris Chandler .25 .60
105 Jim Miller .20 .50
106 Ahman Green .25 .60
107 Jay Fiedler .25 .60
108 Tom Brady 1.50 4.00
109 Michael Strahan .25 .60
110 James Jackson .20 .50
111 Rob Johnson .25 .60
112 Elvis Grbac .20 .50
113 Troy Hambrick .20 .50
114 Corey Bradford .20 .50
115 Trent Green .20 .50
116 Cris Carter .30 .75
117 Chris Fuamatu-Ma'afala .20 .50
118 Chris Weinke .20 .50
119 MarTay Jenkins .20 .50
120 Laveranues Coles .25 .60
121 Donovan McNabb .25 .60
122 Jerry Rice .60 1.50
123 Garrison Hearst .20 .50
124 Steve McNair .25 .60
125 Trung Canidate .20 .50
126 Doug Flutie .25 .60
127 Ricky Williams .25 .60
128 Peyton Manning .75 2.00
129 Kevin Kasper .20 .50
130 Emmitt Smith .50 1.25
131 Peter Warrick .20 .50
132 Anthony Thomas .25 .60
133 Ike Hilliard .20 .50
134 Kendrell Bell .20 .50
135 Shaun Alexander .20 .50
136 Wesley Walls .25 .60
137 Gerard Warren .20 .50
138 James Stewart .20 .50
139 Drew Bledsoe .25 .60
140 Fred Taylor .20 .50
141 Marshall Faulk .25 .60
142 Marcus Pollard .20 .50
143 Bill Schroeder .20 .50
144 Marty Booker .20 .50
145 Amos Zereoue .20 .50
146 Darrell Jackson .25 .60
147 Brian Finneran .20 .50
148 Alex Van Pelt .20 .50
149 Andre Carter .20 .50
150 Joey Galloway .25 .60
151 Joey Harrington AU RC 4.00 10.00
152 Andre Davis AU RC 4.00 10.00
153 Eric Crouch AU RC 6.00 15.00
154 Kelly Campbell AU RC 5.00 12.00
155 Ron Johnson AU RC 5.00 12.00
156 David Carr JSY RC 3.00 8.00
157 Kurt Kittner JSY RC 3.00 8.00
158 Javon Walker JSY RC 5.00 12.00
159 DeShaun Foster JSY RC 5.00 12.00
160 Lamar Gordon JSY RC 4.00 10.00
161 Antwaan Randle El RC 1.00 2.50
162 Clinton Portis RC 1.25 3.00
163 Luke Staley RC .75 2.00
164 Daniel Graham RC 1.00 2.50
165 Ashley Lelie RC .75 2.00
166 Ladell Betts RC 1.25 3.00
167 Rocky Calmus RC 1.00 2.50
168 Ryan Sims RC 1.25 3.00
169 Jeremy Shockey RC 1.25 3.00
170 Damien Anderson RC .75 2.00
171 Bryant McKinnie RC .75 2.00
172 Kahlil Hill RC .75 2.00
173 John Henderson RC 1.00 2.50
174 Donte Stallworth RC 1.25 3.00
175 Kalimba Edwards RC 1.00 2.50
176 Freddie Milons RC .75 2.00
177 Antonio Bryant RC 1.25 3.00
178 Cliff Russell RC .75 2.00
179 T.J. Duckett RC .75 2.00
180 Roy Williams RC .75 2.00
181 Patrick Ramsey RC 1.00 2.50
182 Josh Reed RC 1.00 2.50
183 Wendell Bryant RC .75 2.00
184 Jabar Gaffney RC .75 2.00
185 Napoleon Harris RC 1.00 2.50
186 Adrian Peterson RC 1.00 2.50
187 David Garrard RC 1.00 2.50
188 Levar Fisher RC .75 2.00
189 Quentin Jammer RC 1.25 3.00
190 Anthony Weaver RC .75 2.00
191 Dwight Freeney RC 1.50 4.00
192 Reche Caldwell RC 1.00 2.50
193 Larry Tripplett RC .75 2.00
194 Rohan Davey RC 1.25 3.00
195 Marquise Walker RC .75 2.00
196 William Green RC 1.00 2.50
197 Tracey Wistrom RC 1.00 2.50
198 Alan Harper RC .75 2.00
199 Lito Sheppard RC 1.25 3.00
200 Albert Haynesworth RC 1.25 3.00

2002 Topps Debut Red

*VETS 1/150: 3X TO 8X BASIC CARDS
*151-155 ROOKIE AU: 1X TO 2.5X
151-155 ROOKIE AU ODDS 1:642
*156-160 ROOKIE JSY: 1X TO 2.5X
156-160 ROOKIE JSY ODDS 1:645
*161-200 ROOKIES: 1.2X TO 3X
161-200 ROOKIE ODDS 1:17
STATED PRINT RUN 199 SER.#'d SETS

2002 Topps Debut All-Star Materials

This 23-card insert set is standard size and features future NFL stars with pieces of their game-worn Senior Bowl jerseys. The set is randomly inserted at an average of 2 per hobby box.
STATED ODDS 1:14
*GOLD: 1.2X TO 3X BASIC INSERTS
GOLD STATED ODDS 1:525
GOLD STATED PRINT RUN 25 SER.#'d SETS
AMAA Akin Ayodele 2.50 6.00
AMAD Andra Davis 2.00 5.00
AMAP Adrian Peterson 2.50 6.00
AMAR Antwaan Randle El 2.50 6.00
AMAW Anthony Weaver 2.00 5.00
AMBF Bryan Fletcher 2.00 5.00
AMBT Bryan Thomas 2.00 5.00

AMBW Brian Westbrook	4.00	10.00
AMCH Chris Hope	3.00	8.00
AMCR Cliff Russell	2.00	5.00
AMDG David Garrard	2.50	6.00
AMDGR Daniel Graham	2.50	6.00
AMFM Freddie Milons	2.00	5.00
AMJMC Jason McAddley	2.50	6.00
AMKC Kenyon Coleman	2.00	5.00
AMMW Marquise Walker	2.00	5.00
AMNH Napoleon Harris	2.50	6.00
AMPR Patrick Ramsey	2.50	6.00
AMRC Rocky Calmus	2.50	6.00
AMRD Rohan Davey	3.00	8.00
AMRJ Ron Johnson	2.50	6.00
AMRS Ryan Sims	3.00	8.00
AMTW Tracey Wistrom	2.50	6.00

2002 Topps Debut Collegiate Classics

This 19-card set features collegiate standouts who now play in the NFL. Cards were inserted at a rate of 1:12.

COMPLETE SET (19)	15.00	40.00
STATED ODDS 1:12		
1 Randy Moss	.75	2.00
2 Antonio Bryant	1.00	2.50
3 David Carr	.60	1.50
4 William Green	.75	2.00
5 Eric Crouch	1.00	2.50
6 Jabar Gaffney	.60	1.50
7 Andre Davis	.60	1.50
8 Joey Harrington	.60	1.50
9 T.J. Duckett	.60	1.50
10 Josh Reed	.75	2.00
11 DeShaun Foster	1.00	2.50
12 Kurt Kittner	.60	1.50
13 Marquise Walker	.60	1.50
14 Clinton Portis	1.00	2.50
15 Woody Dantzler	.75	2.00
16 David Boston	.60	1.50
17 Donovan McNabb	.75	2.00
18 Peyton Manning	2.50	6.00
19 Keyshawn Johnson	.75	2.00

2002 Topps Debut Dynamite Debuts

Inserted at a rate of 1:6, this set features standout rookies from the 2001 season.

COMPLETE SET (20)	12.00	30.00
STATED ODDS 1:8		
DD1 Anthony Thomas	.75	2.00
DD2 Kendrell Bell	.60	1.50
DD3 LaDainian Tomlinson	1.00	2.50
DD4 Chris Chambers	.60	1.50
DD5 Travis Henry	.60	1.50
DD6 Chris Weinke	.60	1.50
DD7 Koren Robinson	.60	1.50
DD8 James Jackson	.60	1.50
DD9 Dominic Rhodes	.60	1.50
DD10 Michael Bennett	.60	1.50
DD11 Correll Buckhalter	.60	1.50
DD12 Rod Gardner	.60	1.50
DD13 Kevan Barlow	.60	1.50
DD14 Michael Vick	.75	2.00
DD15 Mike Anderson	.60	1.50
DD16 Brian Urlacher	1.00	2.50
DD17 Jamal Lewis	.75	2.00
DD18 Ron Dayne	.75	2.00
DD19 Darrell Jackson	.75	2.00
DD20 Sylvester Morris	.60	1.50

2002 Topps Debut Heads of Class Jerseys

This 5-card set contains dual player cards featuring two swatches of game used memorabilia. Cards were inserted at a rate of 1:281. There was also a gold parallel version which was serial #'d to 25 and inserted into packs at a rate of 1:2297.

STATED ODDS 1:281		
*GOLD/25: 1X TO 2.5X BASIC DUAL		
GOLD/25 STATED ODDS 1:2297		
GOLD STATED PRINT RUN 25 SER.#'d SETS		
HCDO S.Davis/T.Owens	6.00	15.00
HCFD A.Freeman/T.Davis	8.00	20.00
HCJT K.Johnson/Z.Thomas	6.00	15.00
HCSD W.Sapp/T.Davis	6.00	15.00
HCTB L.Tomlinson/D.Brees	15.00	40.00

2015 Topps Definitive Collection

DC1 Marcus Mariota JSY AU RC	75.00	150.00
DC2 Jameis Winston JSY AU RC	250.00	400.00
DC3 Amari Cooper JSY AU RC	50.00	100.00
DC4 DeVante Parker JSY AU RC	12.00	30.00
DC5 Kevin White JSY AU RC	10.00	25.00
DC6 Melvin Gordon JSY AU RC	20.00	50.00
DC7 Dorial Green-Beckham JSY AU RC EXCH	8.00	20.00
DC8 Jaelen Strong JSY AU RC	10.00	25.00
DC9 Brett Hundley JSY AU RC	8.00	20.00
DC10 Devin Funchess JSY AU RC	12.00	30.00
DC11 Todd Gurley JSY AU RC	50.00	100.00
DC12 Sammie Coates JSY AU RC	10.00	25.00
DC13 Maxx Williams JSY AU RC	8.00	20.00
DC14 Ameer Abdullah JSY AU RC	12.00	30.00
DC15 Ty Montgomery JSY AU RC	8.00	20.00
DC16 Tevin Coleman JSY AU RC	10.00	25.00
DC17 Duke Johnson JSY AU RC	12.00	30.00
DC18 Jay Ajayi JSY AU RC	12.00	30.00
DC19 Nelson Agholor JSY AU RC	10.00	25.00
DC20 T.J. Yeldon JSY AU RC	8.00	20.00
DC21 Justin Hardy JSY AU RC	8.00	20.00
DC22 Mike Davis JSY AU RC	8.00	20.00
DC23 Rashad Greene JSY AU RC	8.00	20.00
DC24 Tyler Lockett JSY AU RC EXCH	25.00	60.00
DC25 Bryce Petty JSY AU RC	8.00	20.00
DC26 David Cobb JSY AU RC	8.00	20.00
DC27 Jeremy Langford JSY AU RC	8.00	20.00
DC28 Karlos Williams JSY AU RC	8.00	20.00
DC29 Phillip Dorsett JSY AU RC	8.00	20.00
DC30 Matt Jones JSY AU RC	8.00	20.00
DC31 Devin Smith JSY AU RC	8.00	20.00
DC32 Chris Conley JSY AU RC	8.00	20.00
DC33 Jamison Crowder JSY AU RC	10.00	25.00
DC34 Leonard Williams JSY AU RC	8.00	20.00
DC35 David Johnson JSY AU RC	30.00	60.00
DC36 Sean Mannion JSY AU RC	8.00	20.00
DC37 Breshad Perriman JSY AU RC	8.00	20.00
DC39 Clive Walford JSY AU RC	8.00	20.00
DC40 Javorius Allen JSY AU RC	30.00	60.00
DC43 Josh Robinson JSY AU RC	8.00	20.00

2015 Topps Definitive Collection Green

*GREEN/25: .5X TO 1.2X BASIC JSY AU/50		
DC1 Marcus Mariota JSY AU	150.00	300.00

2015 Topps Definitive Collection Framed Rookie Autograph Patches

FRAPAA Ameer Abdullah		
FRAPAC Amari Cooper	60.00	125.00
FRAPBH Brett Hundley	10.00	25.00
FRAPBP Breshad Perriman	10.00	25.00
FRAPBPE Bryce Petty		
FRAPCC Chris Conley	10.00	25.00
FRAPDF Devin Funchess	15.00	40.00
FRAPDG Dorial Green-Beckham	10.00	25.00
FRAPDJ David Johnson	60.00	120.00
FRAPDJO Duke Johnson	15.00	40.00
FRAPDP DeVante Parker	60.00	120.00
FRAPDS Devin Smith	10.00	25.00
FRAPJA Jay Ajayi		
FRAPJAL Javorius Allen	12.00	30.00
FRAPJH Justin Hardy	10.00	25.00
FRAPJL Jeremy Langford	10.00	25.00
FRAPJS Jaelen Strong	12.00	30.00
FRAPJW Jameis Winston	250.00	400.00
FRAPKW Karlos Williams	10.00	25.00
FRAPKWH Kevin White	60.00	120.00
FRAPLW Leonard Williams	10.00	25.00
FRAPMD Mike Davis	10.00	25.00
FRAPMG Melvin Gordon	25.00	60.00
FRAPMJ Matt Jones		
FRAPMM Marcus Mariota	150.00	300.00
FRAPMW Maxx Williams	10.00	25.00
FRAPNA Nelson Agholor		
FRAPPD Phillip Dorsett	10.00	25.00
FRAPSC Sammie Coates	12.00	30.00
FRAPSM Sean Mannion	10.00	25.00
FRAPTC Tevin Coleman	12.00	30.00
FRAPTG Todd Gurley	75.00	150.00
FRAPTL Tyler Lockett	15.00	40.00
FRAPTM Ty Montgomery	10.00	25.00
FRAPTY T.J. Yeldon	10.00	25.00

2015 Topps Definitive Collection Framed Rookie Autographs

FRAAA Ameer Abdullah	10.00	25.00
FRAAC Amari Cooper	50.00	100.00
FRABH Brett Hundley	6.00	15.00
FRABP Breshad Perriman	6.00	15.00
FRABPE Bryce Petty	6.00	15.00
FRACC Chris Conley	6.00	15.00
FRADF Devin Funchess	10.00	25.00
FRADG Dorial Green-Beckham	6.00	15.00
FRADJ Duke Johnson	10.00	25.00
FRADP DeVante Parker	25.00	50.00
FRAJA Jay Ajayi	10.00	25.00
FRAJL Jeremy Langford		
FRAJW Jameis Winston	125.00	250.00
FRAKW Karlos Williams	6.00	15.00
FRAKWH Kevin White	50.00	100.00
FRAMG Melvin Gordon	15.00	40.00
FRAMJ Matt Jones	6.00	15.00
FRAMM Marcus Mariota	100.00	200.00
FRANA Nelson Agholor	8.00	20.00
FRAPD Phillip Dorsett	6.00	15.00
FRATC Tevin Coleman	8.00	20.00
FRATG Todd Gurley	90.00	150.00
FRATL Tyler Lockett	50.00	100.00
FRATM Ty Montgomery	6.00	15.00
FRATY T.J. Yeldon	6.00	15.00

2015 Topps Definitive Collection Helmet Collection

DHCAC Amari Cooper/26	40.00	80.00
DHCBP Breshad Perriman/36	20.00	40.00
DHCDP DeVante Parker/40	12.00	30.00
DHCJW Jameis Winston/51	40.00	80.00
DHCKWH Kevin White/16	25.00	50.00
DHCMG Melvin Gordon/16		
DHCMM Marcus Mariota/38	20.00	50.00
DHCNA Nelson Agholor/36	20.00	40.00
DHCPD Phillip Dorsett/20	5.00	12.00
DHCTG Todd Gurley/55	12.00	30.00

2015 Topps Definitive Collection Jumbo Patch Collection

*BLUE/25: .5X TO 1.2X BASIC JSY/40-60		
JPCAA Ameer Abdullah/60	5.00	12.00
JPCAC Amari Cooper/60	10.00	25.00
JPCAJ Alshon Jeffery/40	4.00	10.00
JPCAL Andrew Luck/40	6.00	15.00
JPCBH Brett Hundley/60	3.00	8.00
JPCBPR Breshad Perriman/50	3.00	8.00
JPCCM Clay Matthews/40	5.00	12.00
JPCCN Cam Newton/40	5.00	12.00
JPCDAJ David Johnson/50	8.00	20.00
JPCDC Derek Carr/40	5.00	12.00
JPCDF Devin Funchess/50	5.00	12.00
JPCDG Dorial Green-Beckham/60	3.00	8.00
JPCDH DeAndre Hopkins/40	4.00	10.00
JPCDM DeMarco Murray/40	4.00	10.00
JPCDP DeVante Parker/60	5.00	12.00
JPCDT Demaryius Thomas/40	4.00	10.00
JPCDUJ Duke Johnson/40	5.00	12.00
JPCEL Eddie Lacy/40	3.00	8.00
JPCGG Garrett Grayson/50	3.00	8.00
JPCJC Jamaal Charles/40	4.00	10.00
JPCJH Jeremy Hill/40	3.00	8.00
JPCJJ Julio Jones/40	5.00	12.00
JPCJLA Jeremy Langford/50	3.00	8.00
JPCJLN Jarvis Landry/40	4.00	10.00
JPCJM Jordan Matthews/40	4.00	10.00
JPCJW Jameis Winston/60	15.00	40.00
JPCKB Kelvin Benjamin/40	4.00	10.00
JPCKWH Kevin White/60	8.00	20.00
JPCKWI Karlos Williams/50	3.00	8.00
JPCLB Le'Veon Bell/40	12.00	30.00
JPCME Mike Evans/40	4.00	10.00
JPCMG Melvin Gordon/60	8.00	20.00
JPCMJ Matt Jones/60	3.00	8.00
JPCMM Marcus Mariota/60	12.00	30.00
JPCMS Matthew Stafford/40	4.00	10.00
JPCNA Nelson Agholor/60	4.00	10.00
JPCOB Odell Beckham Jr./40	5.00	12.00
JPCPD Phillip Dorsett/60	3.00	8.00
JPCRG Rob Gronkowski/40	15.00	40.00
JPCRT Ryan Tannehill/40	4.00	10.00
JPCRW Russell Wilson/40	6.00	15.00
JPCSM Sean Mannion/50	3.00	8.00
JPCSW Sammy Watkins/40	4.00	10.00
JPCTB Teddy Bridgewater/40	10.00	25.00
JPCTC Tevin Coleman		
JPCTG Todd Gurley/60	12.00	30.00
JPCTH T.Y. Hilton/40	4.00	10.00
JPCTL Tyler Lockett/60	5.00	12.00
JPCTM Ty Montgomery/50	3.00	8.00
JPCTY T.J. Yeldon/60	3.00	8.00

2015 Topps Definitive Collection Rookie Autographs

DRAAA Ameer Abdullah/99	6.00	15.00
DRAAC Amari Cooper/50 EXCH	40.00	80.00
DRABH Brett Hundley/75		
DRABP Breshad Perriman/99	4.00	10.00
DRABPE Bryce Petty/99	4.00	10.00
DRACA Cameron Artis-Payne/99	4.00	10.00
DRACC Chris Conley/99	4.00	10.00
DRACW Clive Walford/99	4.00	10.00
DRADC David Cobb/99	4.00	10.00
DRADF Devin Funchess/75	6.00	15.00
DRADFJ Dante Fowler Jr./99	6.00	15.00
DRADG Dorial Green-Beckham/99 EXCH	4.00	10.00
DRADJ David Johnson/99	15.00	30.00
DRADJO Duke Johnson/99	6.00	15.00
DRADP DeVante Parker/50	8.00	20.00
DRADS Devin Smith/99	4.00	10.00
DRAJA Jay Ajayi/99	6.00	15.00
DRAJAL Javorius Allen/99	5.00	12.00
DRAJC Jamison Crowder/99	5.00	12.00
DRAJH Justin Hardy/99	4.00	10.00
DRAJJ Jesse James/99	5.00	12.00
DRAJR Josh Robinson/99	4.00	10.00
DRAJS Jaelen Strong/75	5.00	12.00
DRAJW Jameis Winston/50	50.00	100.00
DRAKW Karlos Williams/99	4.00	10.00
DRAKWH Kevin White/50	6.00	15.00
DRAMD Mike Davis/99	4.00	10.00
DRAMG Melvin Gordon/50	12.00	30.00
DRAMJ Matt Jones/99	4.00	10.00
DRAMM Marcus Mariota/50	60.00	125.00
DRAMW Maxx Williams/50 EXCH	5.00	12.00
DRANA Nelson Agholor/75	5.00	12.00
DRAPD Phillip Dorsett/99	4.00	10.00
DRARG Rashad Greene/99	4.00	10.00
DRASC Sammie Coates/99	5.00	12.00
DRATC Tevin Coleman/99	5.00	12.00
DRATG Todd Gurley/50	30.00	60.00
DRATL Tyler Lockett/99 EXCH	6.00	15.00
DRATM Ty Montgomery/99	4.00	10.00
DRATY T.J. Yeldon/99	4.00	10.00

2015 Topps Definitive Collection Rookie Autographs Green

DRABH Brett Hundley	20.00	50.00
DRAJW Jameis Winston	100.00	200.00
DRATG Todd Gurley	30.00	80.00

2015 Topps Diamond Autographs

AA1 Ameer Abdullah RC	40.00	80.00
AA2 Ameer Abdullah RC	40.00	80.00
AA3 Ameer Abdullah RC	40.00	80.00
AA4 Ameer Abdullah RC	40.00	80.00
AA5 Ameer Abdullah RC	40.00	80.00
AA6 Ameer Abdullah RC	40.00	80.00
AA7 Ameer Abdullah RC	40.00	80.00
AA8 Ameer Abdullah RC	40.00	80.00
AA9 Ameer Abdullah RC	40.00	80.00
AB1 Antonio Brown	50.00	100.00
AB2 Antonio Brown	50.00	100.00
AB3 Antonio Brown	50.00	100.00
AB4 Antonio Brown	50.00	100.00
AB5 Antonio Brown	50.00	100.00
AB6 Antonio Brown	50.00	100.00
AC1 Amari Cooper RC	30.00	80.00
AC2 Amari Cooper RC	30.00	80.00
AC3 Amari Cooper RC	30.00	80.00
AC4 Amari Cooper RC	30.00	80.00
AC5 Amari Cooper RC	30.00	80.00
AC6 Amari Cooper RC	30.00	80.00
AC7 Amari Cooper RC	30.00	80.00
AC8 Amari Cooper RC	30.00	80.00
AC9 Amari Cooper RC	30.00	80.00
AJ1 Alshon Jeffery	15.00	40.00
AJ2 Alshon Jeffery	15.00	40.00
AJ3 Alshon Jeffery	15.00	40.00
AJ4 Alshon Jeffery	15.00	40.00
AJ5 Alshon Jeffery	15.00	40.00
AJ6 Alshon Jeffery	15.00	40.00
AJ7 Alshon Jeffery	15.00	40.00
AJ8 Alshon Jeffery	15.00	40.00
AR1 Aaron Rodgers	200.00	350.00
AR2 Aaron Rodgers	200.00	350.00
AR3 Aaron Rodgers	200.00	350.00
AR4 Aaron Rodgers	200.00	350.00
AR5 Aaron Rodgers	200.00	350.00
BF1 Brett Favre	100.00	200.00
BF2 Brett Favre	100.00	200.00
BF3 Brett Favre	100.00	200.00
BH1 Brett Hundley RC	20.00	50.00
BH2 Brett Hundley RC	20.00	50.00
BH3 Brett Hundley RC	20.00	50.00
BH4 Brett Hundley RC	20.00	50.00
BH5 Brett Hundley RC	20.00	50.00
BH6 Brett Hundley RC	20.00	50.00
BH7 Brett Hundley RC	20.00	50.00
BH8 Brett Hundley RC	20.00	50.00
BH9 Brett Hundley RC	20.00	50.00
BP1 Bryce Petty RC	15.00	40.00
BP2 Bryce Petty RC	15.00	40.00
BP3 Bryce Petty RC	15.00	40.00
BP4 Bryce Petty RC	15.00	40.00
BP5 Bryce Petty RC	15.00	40.00
BP6 Bryce Petty RC	15.00	40.00
BP7 Bryce Petty RC	15.00	40.00
BP8 Bryce Petty RC	15.00	40.00
BP9 Bryce Petty RC	15.00	40.00
BPE1 Breshad Perriman RC	12.00	30.00
BPE2 Breshad Perriman RC	12.00	30.00
BPE3 Breshad Perriman RC	12.00	30.00
BPE4 Breshad Perriman RC	12.00	30.00
BPE5 Breshad Perriman RC	12.00	30.00
BPE6 Breshad Perriman RC	12.00	30.00
BPE7 Breshad Perriman RC	12.00	30.00
BPE8 Breshad Perriman RC	12.00	30.00
BPE9 Breshad Perriman RC	12.00	30.00
CA1 C.J. Anderson	12.00	30.00
CA2 C.J. Anderson	12.00	30.00
CA3 C.J. Anderson	12.00	30.00
CA4 C.J. Anderson	12.00	30.00
CA5 C.J. Anderson	12.00	30.00
CA6 C.J. Anderson	12.00	30.00
CA7 C.J. Anderson	12.00	30.00
CA8 C.J. Anderson	12.00	30.00
CA9 C.J. Anderson	12.00	30.00
CC1 Chris Conley RC	12.00	30.00
CC2 Chris Conley RC	12.00	30.00
CC3 Chris Conley RC	12.00	30.00
CC4 Chris Conley RC	12.00	30.00
CC5 Chris Conley RC	12.00	30.00
CC6 Chris Conley RC	12.00	30.00
CC7 Chris Conley RC	12.00	30.00
CC8 Chris Conley RC	12.00	30.00
CC9 Chris Conley RC	12.00	30.00
CM1 Clay Matthews	40.00	80.00
CM2 Clay Matthews	40.00	80.00
CM3 Clay Matthews	40.00	80.00
CM4 Clay Matthews	40.00	80.00
CM5 Clay Matthews	40.00	80.00
DB1 Drew Brees	50.00	100.00
DB2 Drew Brees	50.00	100.00
DB3 Drew Brees	50.00	100.00
DB4 Drew Brees	50.00	100.00
DC1 David Cobb RC	12.00	30.00
DC2 David Cobb RC	12.00	30.00
DC3 David Cobb RC	12.00	30.00
DC4 David Cobb RC	12.00	30.00
DC5 David Cobb RC	12.00	30.00
DC6 David Cobb RC	12.00	30.00
DC7 David Cobb RC	12.00	30.00
DC8 David Cobb RC	12.00	30.00
DC9 David Cobb RC	12.00	30.00
DF1 Devin Funchess RC	20.00	50.00
DF2 Devin Funchess RC	20.00	50.00
DF3 Devin Funchess RC	20.00	50.00
DF4 Devin Funchess RC	20.00	50.00
DF5 Devin Funchess RC	20.00	50.00
DF6 Devin Funchess RC	20.00	50.00
DF7 Devin Funchess RC	20.00	50.00
DF8 Devin Funchess RC	20.00	50.00
DF9 Devin Funchess RC	20.00	50.00
DGB1 Dorial Green-Beckham RC	15.00	40.00
DGB2 Dorial Green-Beckham RC	15.00	40.00
DGB3 Dorial Green-Beckham RC	15.00	40.00
DGB4 Dorial Green-Beckham RC	15.00	40.00
DGB5 Dorial Green-Beckham RC	15.00	40.00
DGB6 Dorial Green-Beckham RC	15.00	40.00
DGB7 Dorial Green-Beckham RC	15.00	40.00
DGB8 Dorial Green-Beckham RC	15.00	40.00
DGB9 Dorial Green-Beckham RC	15.00	40.00
DJ1 David Johnson RC	30.00	60.00
DJ2 David Johnson RC	30.00	60.00
DJ3 David Johnson RC	30.00	60.00
DJ4 David Johnson RC	30.00	60.00
DJ5 David Johnson RC	30.00	60.00
DJ6 David Johnson RC	30.00	60.00
DJ7 David Johnson RC	30.00	60.00
DJ8 David Johnson RC	30.00	60.00
DJ9 David Johnson RC	30.00	60.00
DJO1 Duke Johnson RC	12.00	30.00
DJO2 Duke Johnson RC	12.00	30.00
DJO3 Duke Johnson RC	12.00	30.00
DJO4 Duke Johnson RC	12.00	30.00
DJO5 Duke Johnson RC	12.00	30.00
DJO6 Duke Johnson RC	12.00	30.00
DJO7 Duke Johnson RC	12.00	30.00
DJO8 Duke Johnson RC	12.00	30.00
DJO9 Duke Johnson RC	12.00	30.00
DM1 DeMarco Murray	15.00	40.00
DM2 DeMarco Murray	15.00	40.00
DM3 DeMarco Murray	15.00	40.00
DM4 DeMarco Murray	15.00	40.00
DM5 DeMarco Murray	15.00	40.00
DM6 DeMarco Murray	15.00	40.00
DM7 DeMarco Murray	15.00	40.00
DM8 DeMarco Murray	15.00	40.00
DM9 DeMarco Murray	15.00	40.00
DMA1 Dan Marino		
DMA2 Dan Marino		
DMA3 Dan Marino		
DMA4 Dan Marino		
DMA5 Dan Marino		
DMA6 Dan Marino		
DP1 DeVante Parker RC	15.00	40.00
DP2 DeVante Parker RC	15.00	40.00
DP3 DeVante Parker RC	15.00	40.00
DP4 DeVante Parker RC	15.00	40.00
DP5 DeVante Parker RC	15.00	40.00
DP6 DeVante Parker RC	15.00	40.00
DP7 DeVante Parker RC	15.00	40.00
DP8 DeVante Parker RC	15.00	40.00
DP9 DeVante Parker RC	15.00	40.00
DS1 Devin Smith RC	12.00	30.00
DS2 Devin Smith RC	12.00	30.00
DS3 Devin Smith RC	12.00	30.00
DS4 Devin Smith RC	12.00	30.00
DS5 Devin Smith RC	12.00	30.00
DS6 Devin Smith RC	12.00	30.00
DS7 Devin Smith RC	12.00	30.00
DS8 Devin Smith RC	12.00	30.00
DS9 Devin Smith RC	12.00	30.00
EG1 Eddie George	40.00	80.00
EG2 Eddie George	40.00	80.00
EG3 Eddie George	40.00	80.00
EG4 Eddie George	40.00	80.00
EG5 Eddie George	40.00	80.00
EG6 Eddie George	40.00	80.00
EL1 Eddie Lacy	25.00	50.00
EL2 Eddie Lacy	25.00	50.00
EL3 Eddie Lacy	25.00	50.00
EL4 Eddie Lacy	25.00	50.00
EL5 Eddie Lacy	25.00	50.00
EL6 Eddie Lacy	25.00	50.00
EL7 Eddie Lacy	25.00	50.00
EL8 Eddie Lacy	25.00	50.00
EL9 Eddie Lacy	25.00	50.00
EM1 Eli Manning	75.00	150.00
EM2 Eli Manning	75.00	150.00
EM3 Eli Manning	75.00	150.00
EM4 Eli Manning	75.00	150.00
ES1 Emmitt Smith		
ES2 Emmitt Smith		
ES3 Emmitt Smith		
GS1 Gale Sayers	30.00	60.00
GS2 Gale Sayers	30.00	60.00
GS3 Gale Sayers	30.00	60.00
GS4 Gale Sayers	30.00	60.00
GS5 Gale Sayers	30.00	60.00
GS6 Gale Sayers	30.00	60.00
HL1 Howie Long	40.00	80.00
HL2 Howie Long	40.00	80.00
HL3 Howie Long	40.00	80.00
HL4 Howie Long	40.00	80.00
HL5 Howie Long	40.00	80.00
HL6 Howie Long	40.00	80.00
HW1 Hines Ward		
HW2 Hines Ward		
HW3 Hines Ward		
HW4 Hines Ward		
HW5 Hines Ward		
HW6 Hines Ward		
IW1 Ickey Woods	12.00	30.00
IW2 Ickey Woods	12.00	30.00
IW3 Ickey Woods	12.00	30.00
IW4 Ickey Woods	12.00	30.00
IW5 Ickey Woods	12.00	30.00
IW6 Ickey Woods	12.00	30.00
IW7 Ickey Woods	12.00	30.00
IW8 Ickey Woods	12.00	30.00
IW9 Ickey Woods	12.00	30.00
JA1 Javorius Allen RC	12.00	30.00
JA2 Javorius Allen RC	12.00	30.00
JA3 Javorius Allen RC	12.00	30.00
JA4 Javorius Allen RC	12.00	30.00
JA5 Javorius Allen RC	12.00	30.00
JA6 Javorius Allen RC	12.00	30.00
JA7 Javorius Allen RC	12.00	30.00
JA8 Javorius Allen RC	12.00	30.00
JA9 Javorius Allen RC	12.00	30.00
JAJ1 Jay Ajayi RC	12.00	30.00
JAJ2 Jay Ajayi RC	12.00	30.00
JAJ3 Jay Ajayi RC	12.00	30.00
JAJ4 Jay Ajayi RC	12.00	30.00
JAJ5 Jay Ajayi RC	12.00	30.00
JAJ6 Jay Ajayi RC	12.00	30.00
JAJ7 Jay Ajayi RC	12.00	30.00
JAJ8 Jay Ajayi RC	12.00	30.00
JAJ9 Jay Ajayi RC	12.00	30.00
JC1 Jamison Crowder RC	15.00	40.00
JC2 Jamison Crowder RC	15.00	40.00
JC3 Jamison Crowder RC	15.00	40.00
JC4 Jamison Crowder RC	15.00	40.00
JC5 Jamison Crowder RC	15.00	40.00
JC6 Jamison Crowder RC	15.00	40.00
JC7 Jamison Crowder RC	15.00	40.00
JC8 Jamison Crowder RC	15.00	40.00
JC9 Jamison Crowder RC	15.00	40.00
JG1 Joe Greene	40.00	80.00
JG2 Joe Greene	40.00	80.00
JG3 Joe Greene	40.00	80.00
JG4 Joe Greene	40.00	80.00
JG5 Joe Greene	40.00	80.00
JG6 Joe Greene	40.00	80.00
JH1 Justin Hardy RC	15.00	40.00
JH2 Justin Hardy RC	15.00	40.00
JH3 Justin Hardy RC	15.00	40.00
JH4 Justin Hardy RC	15.00	40.00
JH5 Justin Hardy RC	15.00	40.00
JH6 Justin Hardy RC	15.00	40.00
JH7 Justin Hardy RC	15.00	40.00
JH8 Justin Hardy RC	15.00	40.00
JH9 Justin Hardy RC	15.00	40.00
JHI1 Jeremy Hill	15.00	40.00
JHI2 Jeremy Hill	15.00	40.00
JHI3 Jeremy Hill	15.00	40.00
JHI4 Jeremy Hill	15.00	40.00
JHI5 Jeremy Hill	15.00	40.00
JHI6 Jeremy Hill	15.00	40.00
JHI7 Jeremy Hill	15.00	40.00
JHI8 Jeremy Hill	15.00	40.00
JHI9 Jeremy Hill	15.00	40.00
JK1 Jim Kelly	40.00	80.00
JK2 Jim Kelly	40.00	80.00
JK3 Jim Kelly	40.00	80.00
JL1 Jeremy Langford RC	20.00	50.00
JL2 Jeremy Langford RC	20.00	50.00
JL3 Jeremy Langford RC	20.00	50.00
JL4 Jeremy Langford RC	20.00	50.00
JL5 Jeremy Langford RC	20.00	50.00
JL6 Jeremy Langford RC	20.00	50.00
JL7 Jeremy Langford RC	20.00	50.00
JL8 Jeremy Langford RC	20.00	50.00
JL9 Jeremy Langford RC	20.00	50.00
JN1 Jordy Nelson	30.00	60.00
JN2 Jordy Nelson	30.00	60.00
JN3 Jordy Nelson	30.00	60.00
JN4 Jordy Nelson	30.00	60.00
JN5 Jordy Nelson	30.00	60.00
JN6 Jordy Nelson	30.00	60.00
JN7 Jordy Nelson	30.00	60.00
JN8 Jordy Nelson	30.00	60.00
JN9 Jordy Nelson	30.00	60.00
JS1 Jaelen Strong RC	12.00	30.00
JS2 Jaelen Strong RC	12.00	30.00
JS3 Jaelen Strong RC	12.00	30.00
JS4 Jaelen Strong RC	12.00	30.00
JS5 Jaelen Strong RC	12.00	30.00
JS6 Jaelen Strong RC	12.00	30.00
JS7 Jaelen Strong RC	12.00	30.00
JS8 Jaelen Strong RC	12.00	30.00
JS9 Jaelen Strong RC	12.00	30.00
JW1 Jameis Winston RC	90.00	150.00
JW2 Jameis Winston RC	90.00	150.00
JW3 Jameis Winston RC	90.00	150.00
JW4 Jameis Winston RC	90.00	150.00
JW5 Jameis Winston RC	90.00	150.00
JWI1 J.J. Watt	60.00	120.00
JWI2 J.J. Watt	60.00	120.00
JWI3 J.J. Watt	60.00	120.00
JWI4 J.J. Watt	60.00	120.00
KB1 Kelvin Benjamin	15.00	40.00
KB2 Kelvin Benjamin	15.00	40.00
KB3 Kelvin Benjamin	15.00	40.00
KB4 Kelvin Benjamin	15.00	40.00
KB5 Kelvin Benjamin	15.00	40.00
KW1 Karlos Williams RC	20.00	50.00
KW2 Karlos Williams RC	20.00	50.00
KW3 Karlos Williams RC	20.00	50.00
KW4 Karlos Williams RC	20.00	50.00
KW5 Karlos Williams RC	20.00	50.00
KW6 Karlos Williams RC	20.00	50.00
KW7 Karlos Williams RC	20.00	50.00
KW8 Karlos Williams RC	20.00	50.00
KW9 Karlos Williams RC	20.00	50.00
KWA1 Kurt Warner		
KWA2 Kurt Warner		
KWA3 Kurt Warner		
KWA4 Kurt Warner		
KWA5 Kurt Warner		
KWH1 Kevin White RC	30.00	60.00
KWH2 Kevin White RC	30.00	60.00
KWH3 Kevin White RC	30.00	60.00
KWH4 Kevin White RC	30.00	60.00
KWH5 Kevin White RC	30.00	60.00
KWH6 Kevin White RC	30.00	60.00
KWH7 Kevin White RC	30.00	60.00
KWH8 Kevin White RC	30.00	60.00
KWH9 Kevin White RC	30.00	60.00
LD1 Len Dawson	15.00	40.00
LD2 Len Dawson	15.00	40.00
LD3 Len Dawson	15.00	40.00
LD4 Len Dawson	15.00	40.00
LD5 Len Dawson	15.00	40.00
LD6 Len Dawson	15.00	40.00
LD7 Len Dawson	15.00	40.00
LD8 Len Dawson	15.00	40.00
LK1 Luke Kuechly	60.00	120.00
LK2 Luke Kuechly	60.00	120.00
LK3 Luke Kuechly	60.00	120.00
LK4 Luke Kuechly	60.00	120.00
LT1 Lawrence Taylor	50.00	100.00
LT2 Lawrence Taylor	50.00	100.00
LT3 Lawrence Taylor	50.00	100.00
LT4 Lawrence Taylor	50.00	100.00
LTO1 LaDainian Tomlinson		
LTO2 LaDainian Tomlinson		
LTO3 LaDainian Tomlinson		
LW1 Leonard Williams RC	12.00	30.00
LW2 Leonard Williams RC	12.00	30.00
LW3 Leonard Williams RC	12.00	30.00
LW4 Leonard Williams RC	12.00	30.00
LW5 Leonard Williams RC	12.00	30.00
LW6 Leonard Williams RC	12.00	30.00
LW7 Leonard Williams RC	12.00	30.00
LW8 Leonard Williams RC	12.00	30.00
LW9 Leonard Williams RC	12.00	30.00
MD1 Mike Davis RC	12.00	30.00
MD2 Mike Davis RC	12.00	30.00
MD3 Mike Davis RC	12.00	30.00
MD4 Mike Davis RC	12.00	30.00
MD5 Mike Davis RC	12.00	30.00
MD6 Mike Davis RC	12.00	30.00
MD7 Mike Davis RC	12.00	30.00
MD8 Mike Davis RC	12.00	30.00
MD9 Mike Davis RC	12.00	30.00
MDI1 Mike Ditka	30.00	60.00
MDI2 Mike Ditka	30.00	60.00
MDI3 Mike Ditka	30.00	60.00
MDI4 Mike Ditka	30.00	60.00
MDI5 Mike Ditka	30.00	60.00
MDI6 Mike Ditka	30.00	60.00
ME1 Mike Evans	15.00	40.00
ME2 Mike Evans	15.00	40.00
ME3 Mike Evans	15.00	40.00
ME4 Mike Evans	15.00	40.00
ME5 Mike Evans	15.00	40.00
ME6 Mike Evans	15.00	40.00
ME7 Mike Evans	15.00	40.00
ME8 Mike Evans	15.00	40.00
ME9 Mike Evans	15.00	40.00
MF1 Matt Forte	15.00	40.00
MF2 Matt Forte	15.00	40.00
MF3 Matt Forte	15.00	40.00
MF4 Matt Forte	15.00	40.00
MF5 Matt Forte	15.00	40.00
MF6 Matt Forte	15.00	40.00
MF7 Matt Forte	15.00	40.00
MF8 Matt Forte	15.00	40.00
MG1 Melvin Gordon RC	30.00	60.00
MG2 Melvin Gordon RC	30.00	60.00
MG3 Melvin Gordon RC	30.00	60.00
MG4 Melvin Gordon RC	30.00	60.00
MG5 Melvin Gordon RC	30.00	60.00
MG6 Melvin Gordon RC	30.00	60.00
MG7 Melvin Gordon RC	30.00	60.00
MG8 Melvin Gordon RC	30.00	60.00
MG9 Melvin Gordon RC	30.00	60.00
MJ1 Matt Jones RC	15.00	40.00
MJ2 Matt Jones RC	15.00	40.00
MJ3 Matt Jones RC	15.00	40.00
MJ4 Matt Jones RC	15.00	40.00
MJ5 Matt Jones RC	15.00	40.00
MJ6 Matt Jones RC	15.00	40.00
MJ7 Matt Jones RC	15.00	40.00
MJ8 Matt Jones RC	15.00	40.00
MJ9 Matt Jones RC	15.00	40.00
ML1 Marshawn Lynch	30.00	60.00
ML2 Marshawn Lynch	30.00	60.00
ML3 Marshawn Lynch	30.00	60.00
ML4 Marshawn Lynch	30.00	60.00
ML5 Marshawn Lynch	30.00	60.00
MM1 Marcus Mariota RC	75.00	150.00
MM2 Marcus Mariota RC	75.00	150.00
MM3 Marcus Mariota RC	75.00	150.00
MM4 Marcus Mariota RC	75.00	150.00
MM5 Marcus Mariota RC	75.00	150.00
MR1 Matt Ryan	40.00	80.00
MR2 Matt Ryan	40.00	80.00
MR3 Matt Ryan	40.00	80.00
MR4 Matt Ryan	40.00	80.00
MR5 Matt Ryan	40.00	80.00
MR6 Matt Ryan	40.00	80.00
MR7 Matt Ryan	40.00	80.00
MR8 Matt Ryan	40.00	80.00
MS1 Mike Singletary	12.00	30.00
MS2 Mike Singletary	12.00	30.00
MS3 Mike Singletary	12.00	30.00
MS4 Mike Singletary	12.00	30.00
MS5 Mike Singletary	12.00	30.00
MS6 Mike Singletary	12.00	30.00
MW1 Maxx Williams RC	12.00	30.00
MW2 Maxx Williams RC	12.00	30.00
MW3 Maxx Williams RC	12.00	30.00
MW4 Maxx Williams RC	12.00	30.00
MW5 Maxx Williams RC	12.00	30.00
MW6 Maxx Williams RC	12.00	30.00
MW7 Maxx Williams RC	12.00	30.00
MW8 Maxx Williams RC	12.00	30.00
MW9 Maxx Williams RC	12.00	30.00
NA1 Nelson Agholor RC	15.00	40.00
NA2 Nelson Agholor RC	15.00	40.00
NA3 Nelson Agholor RC	15.00	40.00
NA4 Nelson Agholor RC	15.00	40.00
NA5 Nelson Agholor RC	15.00	40.00
NA7 Nelson Agholor RC	15.00	40.00
NA8 Nelson Agholor RC	15.00	40.00
NA9 Nelson Agholor RC	15.00	40.00
PD1 Phillip Dorsett RC	15.00	40.00
PD2 Phillip Dorsett RC	15.00	40.00
PD3 Phillip Dorsett RC	15.00	40.00
PD4 Phillip Dorsett RC	15.00	40.00
PD5 Phillip Dorsett RC	15.00	40.00
PD6 Phillip Dorsett RC	15.00	40.00
PD7 Phillip Dorsett RC	15.00	40.00
PD8 Phillip Dorsett RC	15.00	40.00
PD9 Phillip Dorsett RC	15.00	40.00
PH1 Paul Hornung	20.00	50.00
PH2 Paul Hornung	20.00	50.00
PH3 Paul Hornung	20.00	50.00
PH4 Paul Hornung	20.00	50.00
PH5 Paul Hornung	20.00	50.00
PH6 Paul Hornung	20.00	50.00
PM1 Peyton Manning	150.00	250.00
PM2 Peyton Manning	150.00	250.00
PM3 Peyton Manning	150.00	250.00
PM4 Peyton Manning	150.00	250.00
PM5 Peyton Manning	150.00	250.00
PM6 Peyton Manning	150.00	250.00
PS1 Phil Simms	30.00	60.00
PS2 Phil Simms	30.00	60.00
PS3 Phil Simms	30.00	60.00
PS4 Phil Simms	30.00	60.00
PS5 Phil Simms	30.00	60.00
PS6 Phil Simms	30.00	60.00
RG1 Rashad Greene RC	15.00	40.00
RG2 Rashad Greene RC	15.00	40.00
RG3 Rashad Greene RC	15.00	40.00
RG4 Rashad Greene RC	15.00	40.00
RG5 Rashad Greene RC	15.00	40.00
RG6 Rashad Greene RC	15.00	40.00
RG7 Rashad Greene RC	15.00	40.00
RG8 Rashad Greene RC	15.00	40.00
RG9 Rashad Greene RC	15.00	40.00
RL1 Ronnie Lott	40.00	80.00
RL2 Ronnie Lott	40.00	80.00
RL3 Ronnie Lott	40.00	80.00
RL4 Ronnie Lott	40.00	80.00
RL5 Ronnie Lott	40.00	80.00
RL6 Ronnie Lott	40.00	80.00
RS1 Roger Staubach	50.00	100.00
RS2 Roger Staubach	50.00	100.00
RS3 Roger Staubach	50.00	100.00
RT1 Ryan Tannehill	15.00	40.00
RT2 Ryan Tannehill	15.00	40.00
RT3 Ryan Tannehill	15.00	40.00
RT4 Ryan Tannehill	15.00	40.00
RT5 Ryan Tannehill	15.00	40.00
RT6 Ryan Tannehill	15.00	40.00
RT7 Ryan Tannehill	15.00	40.00
RT8 Ryan Tannehill	15.00	40.00
RT9 Ryan Tannehill	15.00	40.00
SC1 Sammie Coates RC	15.00	40.00
SC2 Sammie Coates RC	15.00	40.00
SC3 Sammie Coates RC	15.00	40.00
SC4 Sammie Coates RC	15.00	40.00
SC5 Sammie Coates RC	15.00	40.00
SC6 Sammie Coates RC	15.00	40.00
SC7 Sammie Coates RC	15.00	40.00
SC8 Sammie Coates RC	15.00	40.00
SC9 Sammie Coates RC	15.00	40.00
SM1 Sean Mannion RC	15.00	40.00
SM2 Sean Mannion RC	15.00	40.00
SM3 Sean Mannion RC	15.00	40.00
SM4 Sean Mannion RC	15.00	40.00
SM5 Sean Mannion RC	15.00	40.00
SM6 Sean Mannion RC	15.00	40.00
SM7 Sean Mannion RC	15.00	40.00
SM8 Sean Mannion RC	15.00	40.00
SM9 Sean Mannion RC	15.00	40.00
SW1 Sammy Watkins	20.00	50.00
SW2 Sammy Watkins	20.00	50.00
SW3 Sammy Watkins	20.00	50.00
SW4 Sammy Watkins	20.00	50.00
SY1 Steve Young		
SY2 Steve Young		
SY3 Steve Young		
TB1 Tim Brown	30.00	60.00
TB2 Tim Brown	30.00	60.00
TB3 Tim Brown	30.00	60.00
TB4 Tim Brown	30.00	60.00
TB5 Tim Brown	30.00	60.00
TB6 Tim Brown	30.00	60.00
TC1 Tevin Coleman RC	12.00	30.00
TC2 Tevin Coleman RC	12.00	30.00
TC3 Tevin Coleman RC	12.00	30.00
TC4 Tevin Coleman RC	12.00	30.00
TC5 Tevin Coleman RC	12.00	30.00
TC6 Tevin Coleman RC	12.00	30.00
TC7 Tevin Coleman RC	12.00	30.00
TC8 Tevin Coleman RC	12.00	30.00
TC9 Tevin Coleman RC	12.00	30.00
TD1 Terrell Davis	30.00	60.00
TD2 Terrell Davis	30.00	60.00
TD3 Terrell Davis	30.00	60.00
TD4 Terrell Davis	30.00	60.00
TD5 Terrell Davis	30.00	60.00
TD6 Terrell Davis	30.00	60.00
TG1 Todd Gurley RC EXCH	50.00	100.00
TG2 Todd Gurley RC EXCH	50.00	100.00
TG3 Todd Gurley RC EXCH	50.00	100.00
TG4 Todd Gurley RC EXCH	50.00	100.00
TG5 Todd Gurley RC EXCH	50.00	100.00
TG6 Todd Gurley RC EXCH	50.00	100.00
TG7 Todd Gurley RC EXCH	50.00	100.00
TG8 Todd Gurley RC EXCH	50.00	100.00
TG9 Todd Gurley RC EXCH	50.00	100.00
TJY1 T.J. Yeldon RC	20.00	50.00
TJY2 T.J. Yeldon RC	20.00	50.00
TJY3 T.J. Yeldon RC	20.00	50.00
TJY4 T.J. Yeldon RC	20.00	50.00
TJY5 T.J. Yeldon RC	20.00	50.00
TJY6 T.J. Yeldon RC	20.00	50.00
TJY7 T.J. Yeldon RC	20.00	50.00
TJY8 T.J. Yeldon RC	20.00	50.00
TJY9 T.J. Yeldon RC	20.00	50.00
TL1 Tyler Lockett RC	30.00	60.00
TL2 Tyler Lockett RC	30.00	60.00
TL3 Tyler Lockett RC	30.00	60.00
TL4 Tyler Lockett RC	30.00	60.00
TL5 Tyler Lockett RC	30.00	60.00
TL6 Tyler Lockett RC	30.00	60.00
TL7 Tyler Lockett RC	30.00	60.00
TL8 Tyler Lockett RC	30.00	60.00
TL9 Tyler Lockett RC	30.00	60.00
TM1 Ty Montgomery RC	20.00	50.00
TM2 Ty Montgomery RC	20.00	50.00
TM3 Ty Montgomery RC	20.00	50.00
TM4 Ty Montgomery RC	20.00	50.00
TM5 Ty Montgomery RC	20.00	50.00
TM6 Ty Montgomery RC	20.00	50.00
TM7 Ty Montgomery RC	20.00	50.00
TM8 Ty Montgomery RC	20.00	50.00
TM9 Ty Montgomery RC	20.00	50.00
WM1 Warren Moon	30.00	60.00
WM2 Warren Moon	30.00	60.00
WM3 Warren Moon	30.00	60.00
WM4 Warren Moon	30.00	60.00
WM5 Warren Moon	30.00	60.00
WM6 Warren Moon	30.00	60.00

2015 Topps Diamond Autographs Blue Ink

*BLUE/5: X TO X BASIC AU/10		
JW1 Jameis Winston	100.00	200.00

2015 Topps Diamond Patch Autographs

DAPCAB Antonio Brown EXCH	40.00	80.00
DAPCAG A.J. Green/75	15.00	40.00
DAPCAJ Alshon Jeffery/150	15.00	40.00
DAPCAL Andrew Luck		
DAPCBJ Bo Jackson EXCH	40.00	80.00
DAPCBS Barry Sanders/25	100.00	200.00
DAPCCA C.J. Anderson EXCH	15.00	40.00
DAPCDC Dwight Clark/50	15.00	40.00
DAPCDM Dan Marino EXCH		
DAPCDMU DeMarco Murray/50	15.00	40.00
DAPCEG Eddie George EXCH	40.00	80.00
DAPCEL Eddie Lacy/150	15.00	40.00
DAPCEM Eli Manning		
DAPCGS Gale Sayers EXCH	30.00	60.00
DAPCHW Hines Ward/50	40.00	80.00
DAPCJB Jerome Bettis/25	50.00	100.00
DAPCJC Jamaal Charles EXCH	20.00	50.00
DAPCJE John Elway EXCH		
DAPCJH Jeremy Hill EXCH	15.00	40.00
DAPCJK Jim Kelly/50	50.00	100.00
DAPCJM Jordan Matthews/75	15.00	40.00
DAPCJN Jordy Nelson/75	20.00	40.00
DAPCJR Jerry Rice		
DAPCJRI John Riggins/50	25.00	50.00
DAPCKB Kelvin Benjamin		
DAPCLK Luke Kuechly EXCH		
DAPCLT LaDainian Tomlinson EXCH		
DAPCMA Marcus Allen EXCH	15.00	40.00
DAPCME Mike Evans/150	15.00	40.00
DAPCMF Matt Forte EXCH	15.00	40.00
DAPCML Marshawn Lynch EXCH		
DAPCMR Matt Ryan/25		
DAPCMS Matthew Stafford EXCH	20.00	50.00
DAPCMSI Mike Singletary EXCH	20.00	50.00
DAPCPH Paul Hornung EXCH	20.00	50.00
DAPCPS Phil Simms EXCH	20.00	50.00
DAPCRSH Richard Sherman EXCH	30.00	60.00
DAPCRT Ryan Tannehill EXCH	20.00	50.00
DAPCRW Russell Wilson EXCH	100.00	200.00
DAPCSW Sammy Watkins EXCH		
DAPCTB Terry Bradshaw EXCH		
DAPCTBR Tim Brown/50		
DAPCTD Tony Dorsett/25	30.00	60.00
DAPCTDA Terrell Davis/50	30.00	60.00

2015 Topps Diamond Rookie Jumbo Patch Autographs

RAJPAA Ameer Abdullah/95	15.00	40.00
RAJPAC Amari Cooper/75	15.00	40.00
RAJPBH Brett Hundley/75	15.00	40.00
RAJPBP Breshad Perriman/75	12.00	30.00
RAJPBPE Bryce Petty/150	10.00	25.00
RAJPCA Cameron Artis-Payne/125	10.00	25.00
RAJPCC Chris Conley EXCH	10.00	25.00
RAJPCW Clive Walford/150	8.00	20.00
RAJPDC David Cobb EXCH	8.00	20.00
RAJPDF Devin Funchess	8.00	20.00
RAJPDG Dorial Green-Beckham/95	12.00	30.00
RAJPDJ Duke Johnson/125	10.00	25.00
RAJPDJO David Johnson/150	30.00	60.00
RAJPDP DeVante Parker EXCH	15.00	40.00
RAJPDS Devin Smith/125	8.00	20.00
RAJPJA Jay Ajayi/125	10.00	25.00
RAJPJAL Javorius Allen EXCH	8.00	20.00
RAJPJC Jamison Crowder/150	15.00	40.00
RAJPJH Justin Hardy/150	10.00	25.00
RAJPJJ Jesse James/150	10.00	25.00
RAJPJL Jeremy Langford/125	12.00	30.00
RAJPJR Josh Robinson/150	8.00	20.00
RAJPJS Jaelen Strong EXCH	10.00	25.00
RAJPJW Jameis Winston		
RAJPKB Kenny Bell/150	8.00	20.00
RAJPKW Kevin White/85	25.00	50.00
RAJPKWI Karlos Williams/150	15.00	40.00
RAJPLW Leonard Williams/150	8.00	20.00
RAJPMD Mike Davis/150	8.00	20.00
RAJPMG Melvin Gordon/75	20.00	40.00
RAJPMJ Matt Jones EXCH	12.00	30.00
RAJPMM Marcus Mariota EXCH		
RAJPMW Maxx Williams/125	8.00	20.00
RAJPNA Nelson Agholor/75	10.00	25.00
RAJPPD Phillip Dorsett EXCH	12.00	30.00
RAJPRG Rashad Greene/150	8.00	20.00
RAJPSC Sammie Coates EXCH	12.00	30.00
RAJPSM Sean Mannion EXCH	10.00	25.00
RAJPSR Shane Ray EXCH	12.00	30.00
RAJPTC Tevin Coleman/125	10.00	25.00
RAJPTG Todd Gurley EXCH	30.00	80.00
RAJPTL Tyler Lockett EXCH	25.00	50.00
RAJPTM Ty Montgomery/125	10.00	25.00
RAJPTY T.J. Yeldon EXCH	15.00	40.00

2003 Topps Draft Picks and Prospects

This 165-card set was released in May, 2003. This set was issued in five card packs with a $3 SRP. The packs came 24 to a box and 10 boxes to a case. Cards numbered 1-110 featured veterans while cards 111-165 featured rookies.

COMPLETE SET (165)	25.00	50.00
1 Priest Holmes	.20	.50
2 Tommy Maddox	.20	.50
3 Donald Driver	.25	.60
4 Drew Bledsoe	.25	.60
5 Tiki Barber	.25	.60
6 Terrell Owens	.25	.60
7 Rich Gannon	.20	.50
8 Isaac Bruce	.30	.75
9 Stephen Davis	.20	.50
10 Peyton Manning	.75	2.00
11 Tony Gonzalez	.25	.60
12 Marty Booker	.20	.50
13 Warrick Dunn	.20	.50
14 Jimmy Smith	.25	.60
15 Troy Brown	.20	.50
16 Jerry Rice	.60	1.50
17 Curtis Conway	.20	.50
18 Kurt Warner	.25	.60
19 Steve McNair	.25	.60
20 Edgerrin James	.25	.60
21 Aaron Brooks	.25	.60
22 Joey Galloway	.25	.60
23 Peerless Price	.25	.60
24 Torry Holt	.25	.60
25 Derrick Mason	.20	.50
26 Curtis Martin	.25	.60
27 Daunte Culpepper	.25	.60
28 Ahman Green	.25	.60
29 Tim Couch	.20	.50
30 Ricky Williams	.25	.60
31 Darrell Jackson	.25	.60
32 Keyshawn Johnson	.30	.75
33 Jeff Garcia	.25	.60
34 Charlie Garner	.25	.60
35 Randy Moss	.25	.60
36 Rod Smith	.25	.60
37 Jamal Lewis	.25	.60
38 Corey Dillon	.20	.50
39 Marvin Harrison	.20	.50
40 Joe Horn	.20	.50
41 Laveranues Coles	.25	.60
42 Hines Ward	.25	.60
43 Brad Johnson	.25	.60
44 Eddie George	.25	.60
45 Donovan McNabb	.25	.60
46 Marshall Faulk	.25	.60
47 Amani Toomer	.20	.50
48 Trent Green	.20	.50
49 Emmitt Smith	.50	1.25
50 Brett Favre	.60	1.50
51 Brian Griese	.20	.50
52 Eric Moulds	.20	.50
53 Plaxico Burress	.20	.50
54 Fred Taylor	.20	.50
55 Tom Brady	1.25	3.00
56 Michael Vick	.25	.60
57 Andre Davis	.20	.50
58 Chris Chambers	.20	.50
59 Javon Walker	.25	.60
60 Marc Bulger	.20	.50

61 LaDainian Tomlinson .30 .75
62 Chad Pennington .20 .50
63 Marc Boerigter .20 .50
64 Rod Gardner .20 .50
65 DeShaun Foster .25 .60
66 Chris Redman .20 .50
67 Chad Hutchinson .20 .50
68 Deion Branch .20 .50
69 Jeremy Shockey .20 .50
70 Shaun Alexander .20 .50
71 Derrius Thompson .20 .50
72 A.J. Feeley .20 .50
73 Reggie Wayne .25 .60
74 William Green .20 .50
75 Julius Peppers .30 .75
76 Travis Henry .20 .50
77 Marcel Shipp .20 .50
78 Michael Bennett .20 .50
79 Maurice Morris .20 .50
80 Josh Reed .20 .50
81 David Terrell .20 .50
82 Drew Brees .30 .75
83 Jonathan Wells .20 .50
84 Anthony Thomas .25 .60
85 Quincy Morgan .20 .50
86 Jerry Porter .20 .50
87 Ron Johnson .20 .50
88 Najeh Davenport .20 .50
89 Lamar Gordon .20 .50
90 Joey Harrington .20 .50
91 Donte Stallworth .20 .50
92 Kenny Watson .20 .50
93 LaMont Jordan .25 .60
94 Antonio Bryant .20 .50
95 Steve Smith .30 .75
96 T.J. Duckett .20 .50
97 Patrick Ramsey .25 .60
98 Santana Moss .25 .60
99 Chad Johnson .20 .50
100 Clinton Portis .20 .50
101 Reche Caldwell .20 .50
102 Kevan Barlow .20 .50
103 Deuce McAllister .25 .60
104 Koren Robinson .25 .60
105 Todd Heap .20 .50
106 Jabar Gaffney .20 .50
107 Randy McMichael .20 .50
108 Dwight Freeney .20 .50
109 Antwaan Randle El .20 .50
110 David Carr .20 .50
111 Carson Palmer RC .75 2.00
112 Dahrran Diedrick RC .40 1.00
113 Kyle Boller RC .40 1.00
114 Terrell Suggs RC .50 1.25
115 Rien Long RC .40 1.00
116 Justin Gage RC .50 1.25
117 William Joseph RC .40 1.00
118 Chris Simms RC .40 1.00
119 Avon Cobourne RC .40 1.00
120 Victor Hobson RC .40 1.00
121 Jason Gesser RC .50 1.25
122 Ronald Bellamy RC .50 1.25
123 Terence Newman RC .60 1.50
124 Terrence Edwards RC .40 1.00
125 Sultan McCullough RC .40 1.00
126 Kareem Kelly RC .40 1.00
127 Jason Witten RC 1.50 4.00
128 Mike Doss RC .60 1.50
129 Seneca Wallace RC .50 1.25
130 Chris Brown RC .40 1.00
131 Larry Johnson RC .50 1.25
132 Taylor Jacobs RC .40 1.00
133 Jerome McDougle RC .40 1.00
134 Kelley Washington RC .40 1.00
135 Brad Banks RC .50 1.25
136 DeWayne White RC .40 1.00
137 LaBrandon Toefield RC .40 1.00
138 Brian St.Pierre RC .40 1.00
139 Kindal Moorehead RC .50 1.25
140 Willis McGahee RC .50 1.25
141 Jimmy Kennedy RC .50 1.25
142 Talman Gardner RC .40 1.00
143 Chris Kelsay RC .50 1.25
144 Cory Redding RC .50 1.25
145 Dave Ragone RC .40 1.00
146 Earnest Graham RC .60 1.50
147 Andre Johnson RC 1.00 2.50
148 Boss Bailey RC .50 1.25
149 Sam Aiken RC .50 1.25
150 Byron Leftwich RC .50 1.25
151 Teyo Johnson RC .50 1.25
152 Quentin Griffin RC .50 1.25
153 Justin Fargas RC .60 1.50
154 Bradie James RC .60 1.50
155 Andre Woolfolk RC .40 1.00
156 Marcus Trufant RC .50 1.25
157 Ken Dorsey RC .50 1.25
158 Onterrio Smith RC .40 1.00
159 Bryant Johnson RC .60 1.50
160 Charles Rogers RC .50 1.25
161 Kliff Kingsbury RC .60 1.50
162 Michael Haynes RC .40 1.00
163 Bennie Joppru RC .40 1.00
164 Brandon Lloyd RC .60 1.50
165 Jarret Johnson RC .50 1.25

2003 Topps Draft Picks and Prospects Chrome

*VETS 1-110: .8X TO 2X BASIC CARDS
*ROOKIES 111-165: 1.2X TO 3X
ONE CHROME PER PACK

2003 Topps Draft Picks and Prospects Chrome Gold Refractors

*VETS 1-110: 2X TO 5X BASIC CARDS
*ROOKIES 111-165: 3X TO 8X
STATED ODDS 1:4

2003 Topps Draft Picks and Prospects Class Marks Autographs

serted at a overall stated rate of one in 44, these cards feature authentic autographs of some leading 2003 NFL rookies. These cards were signed as part of eight different groups and we have notated what group the players belong to (as well as the odds) in our checklist. A few players did not return their autograph in time for inclusion and those exchange cards could be redeemed until May 31, 2005.

GROUP A STATED ODDS 1:7647
GROUP B STATED ODDS 1:826
GROUP C STATED ODDS 1:4904
GROUP D STATED ODDS 1:1825
GROUP E STATED ODDS 1:839
GROUP F STATED ODDS 1:559
GROUP G STATED ODDS 1:93
OVERALL AUTOGRAPH ODDS 1:44
*SILVER/100: .8X TO 2X BASIC AU/D-G
*SILVER/100: .6X TO 1.5X BASIC AU/A-C
CMAC Avon Cobourne G 4.00 10.00
CMAJ Andre Johnson B 12.00 30.00
CMBJ Bryant Johnson C 8.00 20.00
CMBL Byron Leftwich A 15.00 40.00
CMCB Chris Brown B 5.00 12.00
CMCP Carson Palmer A 12.00 30.00
CMJT Jason Thomas B 5.00 12.00
CMKB Kyle Boller B 5.00 12.00
CMKD Ken Dorsey B 6.00 15.00
CMKKE Kareem Kelly G 4.00 10.00
CMKW Kelley Washington D 4.00 10.00
CMLJ Larry Johnson B 6.00 15.00
CMLS Lee Suggs B 5.00 12.00
CMLT LaBrandon Toefield G 4.00 10.00
CMMB Marquel Blackwell B 5.00 12.00
CMOS Onterrio Smith E 4.00 10.00
CMQB Quentin Griffin G 5.00 12.00
CMSW Seneca Wallace G 5.00 12.00
CMTG Talman Gardner G 4.00 10.00
CMTJ Taylor Jacobs D 4.00 10.00
CMWM Willis McGahee F 5.00 12.00

2003 Topps Draft Picks and Prospects Classmate Cuts

Issued at a stated rate of one in 1951, these five cards feature players who were teammates in college. Each of these cards were issued to a stated print run of 75 serial numbered sets and feature jersey swatches for both players.

STATED PRINT RUN 75 SER.#'d SETS
STATED ODDS 1:1951
*FOIL/25: .6X TO 1.5X BASIC DUAL/75
FOIL STATED ODDS 1:5854
FOIL PRINT RUN 25 SER.#'d SETS
CCDCW K.Curtis/K.Washington 6.00 15.00
CCDDG K.Dorsey/J.Gesser 8.00 20.00
CCDFJ J.Fargas/L.Johnson 10.00 25.00
CCDJL B.Johnson/B.Lloyd 10.00 25.00
CCDRB D.Ragone/K.Boller 6.00 15.00

2003 Topps Draft Picks and Prospects Collegiate Cuts

serted at different rates depending on which group the card belonged to, these 23 cards feature game used memorabilia of the featured player. We have notated both the odds information as well as what group the card belongs to in our checklist.

GROUP A STATED ODDS 1:811
GROUP B STATED ODDS 1:135
GROUP C STATED ODDS 1:487
GROUP D STATED ODDS 1:90
GROUP E STATED ODDS 1:192
GROUP F STATED ODDS 1:98
GROUP G STATED ODDS 1:90
GROUP H STATED ODDS 1:292
*FOIL: .6X TO 1.5X BASIC JSY
FOIL STATED ODDS 1:96
*PATCH/75: 1X TO 2.5X BASIC JSY
PATCH/75 STATED ODDS 1:427
PATCH PRINT RUN 75 SER.#'d SETS
*FOIL PATCH/25: 1.2X TO 3X BASIC JSY
FOIL PATCH PRINT RUN 25
CCAJ Andre Johnson B 6.00 15.00
CCBJ Bryant Johnson C 4.00 10.00
CCBLL Brandon Lloyd B 4.00 10.00
CCDC Dallas Clark B 4.00 10.00
CCDR Dave Ragone F 2.50 6.00
CCJF Justin Fargas D 4.00 10.00
CCJG Justin Gage D 3.00 8.00
CCJGE Jason Gesser E 3.00 8.00
CCJJ Jarret Johnson D 3.00 8.00
CCJW Jason Witten G 10.00 25.00
CCKB Kyle Boller H 2.50 6.00
CCKC Kevin Curtis F 2.50 6.00
CCKD Ken Dorsey B 3.00 8.00
CCKK Kliff Kingsbury A 5.00 12.00
CCKM Kindal Moorhead G 3.00 8.00
CCKW Kelley Washington D 2.50 6.00
CCLJ Larry Johnson F 6.00 15.00
CCRL ReShard Lee D 4.00 10.00
CCSW Seneca Wallace G 3.00 8.00
CCTC Tyrone Calico F 2.50 6.00
CCTE Terrence Edwards G 2.50 6.00
CCTS Terrell Suggs E 3.00 8.00
CCWM Willis McGahee B 3.00 8.00

2003 Topps Draft Picks and Prospects Pen Pals Autographs

Inserted at a stated rate of one in 1979, these five cards feature two players with something in common as they begin their NFL career. Each of these cards were issued to a stated print run of 75 serial numbered sets. Andre Johnson did not return his card in time for pack-out and the exchange card could be redeemed until May 31, 2005.

STATED ODDS 1:1979
STATED PRINT RUN 75 SER.#'d SETS
*FOIL/25: .5X TO 1.2X BASIC DUAL/75
FOIL STATED ODDS 1:6180
FOIL PRINT RUN 25 SER.#'d SETS
PPDS K.Dorsey/C.Simms 12.00 30.00
PPJM L.Johnson/W.McGahee 12.00 30.00
PPLP B.Leftwich/C.Palmer 25.00 60.00
PPSS L.Suggs/O.Smith 10.00 25.00

2004 Topps Draft Picks and Prospects

Topps Draft Picks and Prospects released in May of 2004 making it Topps' first football card release of the year. The base set consists of 165-cards including 110-veterans and prospects and 55-rookies. Note that Mike Williams made an apearance in this product although he was declared ineligible for the NFL Draft. Hobby boxes contained 24-packs of 5-cards with an SRP of $3 per pack. Two parallel sets and a variety of game-used inserts can be found seeded in packs highlighted by the Class Marks (rookie) Autographs and the triple signed Mannings Legacy card

COMPLETE SET (165) 40.00 80.00
1 Steve McNair .30 .75
2 Stephen Davis .25 .60
3 Chris Chambers .25 .60
4 Curtis Martin .30 .75
5 Shaun Alexander .25 .60
6 Jon Kitna .25 .60
7 Jimmy Smith .30 .75
8 Travis Henry .25 .60
9 Torry Holt .30 .75
10 Jamal Lewis .30 .75
11 Clinton Portis .25 .60
12 Aaron Brooks .25 .60
13 Plaxico Burress .25 .60
14 Trent Green .25 .60
15 Chad Johnson .25 .60
16 Jake Delhomme .25 .60
17 David Boston .25 .60
18 Joe Horn .25 .60
19 Ahman Green .30 .75
20 Fred Taylor .25 .60
21 Terrell Owens .30 .75
22 Brad Johnson .30 .75
23 Laveranues Coles .25 .60
24 Ricky Williams .30 .75
25 Peyton Manning 1.00 2.50
26 Hines Ward .30 .75
27 Matt Hasselbeck .25 .60
28 Marshall Faulk .30 .75
29 Tony Gonzalez .30 .75
30 Marvin Harrison .30 .75
31 Eric Moulds .25 .60
32 Chad Pennington .25 .60
33 Jerry Porter .25 .60
34 Jeff Garcia .25 .60
35 Derrick Mason .25 .60
36 Anthony Thomas .30 .75
37 Drew Bledsoe .30 .75
38 Jake Plummer .25 .60
39 Tiki Barber .30 .75
40 Brett Favre .75 2.00
41 Joey Harrington .25 .60
42 Daunte Culpepper .30 .75
43 LaVar Arrington .25 .60
44 Santana Moss .30 .75
45 David Carr .25 .60
46 Randy Moss .30 .75
47 LaDainian Tomlinson .40 1.00
48 Deuce McAllister .30 .75
49 Amani Toomer .25 .60
50 Donovan McNabb .30 .75
51 Priest Holmes .25 .60
52 Corey Dillon .25 .60
53 Tom Brady 1.50 4.00
54 Edgerrin James .30 .75
55 Michael Vick .30 .75
56 Anquan Boldin .25 .60
57 Robert Ferguson .25 .60
58 Onterrio Smith .25 .60
59 Marques Tuiasosopo .25 .60
60 Rudi Johnson .25 .60
61 Alge Crumpler .30 .75
62 Antonio Bryant .30 .75
63 LaMont Jordan .30 .75
64 Lamar Gordon .25 .60
65 Tim Rattay .25 .60
66 Antwaan Randle El .25 .60
67 Ladell Betts .25 .60
68 LaBrandon Toefield .25 .60
69 Ashley Lelie .25 .60
70 Marc Bulger .25 .60
71 Reggie Wayne .30 .75
72 William Green .25 .60
73 Josh Reed .25 .60
74 T.J. Duckett .25 .60
75 Andre Johnson .30 .75
76 Deion Branch .25 .60
77 Tyrone Calico .30 .75
78 Jeremy Shockey .25 .60
79 Najeh Davenport .25 .60
80 Byron Leftwich .25 .60
81 Correll Buckhalter .25 .60
82 Justin McCareins .25 .60
83 Carson Palmer .30 .75
84 Bryant Johnson .25 .60
85 Patrick Ramsey .30 .75
86 Justin Fargas .30 .75
87 Dallas Clark .25 .60
88 Kelly Campbell .25 .60
89 DeShaun Foster .30 .75
90 Charles Rogers .25 .60
91 Donte' Stallworth .25 .60
92 Dante Hall .25 .60
93 Randy McMichael .25 .60
94 Marcel Shipp .25 .60
95 Kyle Boller .25 .60
96 Steve Smith .40 1.00
97 Brian Westbrook .25 .60
98 Kevan Barlow .25 .60
99 Darnerien McCants .25 .60
100 Domanick Davis .25 .60
101 Andre' Davis .25 .60
102 Nate Burleson .30 .75
103 Larry Johnson .25 .60
104 Drew Brees .40 1.00
105 Koren Robinson .25 .60
106 Quincy Carter .25 .60
107 Javon Walker .25 .60
108 Willis McGahee .25 .60
109 Chris Simms .25 .60
110 Rex Grossman .25 .60
111 Steven Jackson RC .75 2.00
112 Greg Jones RC .50 1.25
113 Brandon Everage RC .50 1.25
114 DeAngelo Hall RC .75 2.00
115 Talum Bell RC .50 1.25
116 B.J. Symons RC .50 1.25
117 Michael Clayton RC .60 1.50
118 Jared Lorenzen RC .60 1.50
119 Josh Harris RC .50 1.25
120 Roy Williams RC .50 1.25
121 Mewelde Moore RC .60 1.50
122 Jeff Smoker RC .60 1.50
123 Lee Evans RC .75 2.00
124 Michael Jenkins RC .50 1.25
125 Drew Henson RC .50 1.25
126 Ben Watson RC .60 1.50
127 Jerricho Cotchery RC .60 1.50
128 Ben Troupe RC .50 1.25
129 Chris Gamble RC .50 1.25
130 Kevin Jones RC .60 1.50
131 Cody Pickett RC .50 1.25
132 J.P. Losman RC .50 1.25
133 Michael Boulware RC .75 2.00
134 Julius Jones RC .50 1.25
135 Keary Colbert RC .50 1.25
136 Vince Wilfork RC .75 2.00
137 Ernest Wilford RC .60 1.50
138 John Navarre RC .50 1.25
139 D.J. Williams RC .75 2.00
140 Larry Fitzgerald RC 2.00 5.00
141 Quincy Wilson RC .50 1.25
142 James Newson RC .75 2.00
143 Reggie Williams RC .50 1.25
144 Devard Darling RC .50 1.25
145 Chris Perry RC .50 1.25
146 Derrick Strait RC .50 1.25
147 Teddy Lehman RC .50 1.25
148 Michael Turner RC .50 1.25
149 Will Smith RC .60 1.50
150 Eli Manning RC 8.00 20.00
151 Cedric Cobbs RC .50 1.25
152 Ell Roberson UER RC .75 2.00
153 Matt Schaub RC .50 1.25
154 Derrick Knight RC .50 1.25
155 Rashaun Woods RC .50 1.25
156 Jonathan Vilma RC .60 1.50
157 Tommie Harris RC .60 1.50
158 Dwan Edwards RC .50 1.25
159 Will Poole RC .75 2.00
160 Mike Williams RC .60 1.50
161 Philip Rivers RC 1.50 4.00
162 Sean Taylor RC 3.00 8.00
163 Darius Watts RC .50 1.25
164 Casey Clausen RC .60 1.50
165 Ben Roethlisberger RC 8.00 20.00

2004 Topps Draft Picks and Prospects Chrome

COMPLETE SET (165) 75.00 150.00
*VETS: .8X TO 2X BASIC CARDS
*ROOKIES: .6X TO 1.5X BASIC CARDS
STATED ODDS 1:1

2004 Topps Draft Picks and Prospects Gold Chrome

ETS: 3X TO 8X BASIC CARDS
*ROOKIES: 2.5X TO 6X BASIC CARDS
STATED ODDS 1:12 H/R

2004 Topps Draft Picks and Prospects Big Dog Relics

OUP A STATED ODDS 1:207H, 1:204R
GROUP B STATED ODDS 1:275H, 1:272R
GROUP C STATED ODDS 1:158H, 1:155R
GROUP D STATED ODDS 1:259H, 1:239R
GROUP E STATED ODDS 1:242H, 1:236R
GROUP F STATED ODDS 1:68H, 1:49R
GROUP G STATED ODDS 1:161H, 1:156R
GROUP H STATED ODDS 1:99H, 1:97R
*SILVER: .6X TO 1.5X BASIC INSERTS
SILVER STATED ODDS 1:245H, 1:175R
SILVER PRINT RUN 100 SER.#'d SETS
UNPRICED SLVR PATCH ODDS 1:574H, 1:541R
BDAS Antonio Smith F 4.00 10.00
BDBE Brandon Everage G 3.00 8.00
BDBH Bryan Hickman F 3.00 8.00
BDBM Bobby McCray F 3.00 8.00
BDBW Ben Watson E 4.00 10.00
BDCC Cedric Cobbs C 3.00 8.00
BDCCO Chris Cooley H 4.00 10.00
BDCP Cody Pickett A 3.00 8.00
BDCW Courtney Watson F 3.00 8.00
BDDC Darrell Campbell G 3.00 8.00
BDDE Dwan Edwards H 3.00 8.00
BDDH Devery Henderson H 3.00 8.00
BDDM DeMarco McNeil F 3.00 8.00
BDDS Derrick Strait E 3.00 8.00
BDDSM Daryl Smith F 3.00 8.00
BDDT Dontarrious Thomas F 4.00 10.00
BDDW Demorrio Williams F 5.00 12.00
BDEW Ernest Wilford A 4.00 10.00
BDGJ Greg Jones A 3.00 8.00
BDJC Jerricho Cotchery D 4.00 10.00
BDJH Josh Harris B 3.00 8.00
BDJJ Julius Jones B 3.00 8.00
BDJM Johnnie Morant F 3.00 8.00
BDJN John Navarre D 3.00 8.00
BDJNE James Newson E 5.00 12.00
BDJPL J.P. Losman C 3.00 8.00
BDKC Keary Colbert C 3.00 8.00
BDKF Keyaron Fox F 4.00 10.00
BDKW Kris Wilson F 4.00 10.00
BDMB Michael Boulware G 5.00 12.00
BDMBR Maurice Brown F 3.00 8.00
BDMJ Michael Jenkins A 3.00 8.00
BDMM Mewelde Moore C 4.00 10.00
BDMS Matt Schaub C 3.00 8.00
BDMT Michael Turner B 3.00 8.00
BDNK Niko Koutouvides H 3.00 8.00
BDPR Philip Rivers A 12.00 30.00
BDRL Rodney Leisle H 3.00 8.00
BDTB Tatum Bell D 3.00 8.00
BDTL Teddy Lehman G 3.00 8.00
BDTLU Triandos Luke H 3.00 8.00

2004 Topps Draft Picks and Prospects Class Marks Autographs

OUP A STATED ODDS 1:5702H, 1:5561R
GROUP B STATED ODDS 1:1026H, 1:1029R
GROUP C STATED ODDS 1:457H/R
GROUP D STATED ODDS 1:165H, 1:325R
GROUP E STATED ODDS 1:97H, 1:273R
GROUP F STATED ODDS 1:421H/R
CMBR Ben Roethlisberger B 60.00 120.00
CMCC Cedric Cobbs E 6.00 15.00
CMCP Chris Perry C 6.00 15.00
CMCPI Cody Pickett C 6.00 15.00
CMEM Eli Manning A 40.00 100.00
CMEW Ernest Wilford D 8.00 20.00
CMGJ Greg Jones B 6.00 15.00
CMJC Jerricho Cotchery D 8.00 20.00
CMKJ Kevin Jones E 8.00 20.00
CMLE Lee Evans D 10.00 25.00
CMLF Larry Fitzgerald A 50.00 80.00
CMMC Michael Clayton E 8.00 20.00
CMMJ Michael Jenkins D 6.00 15.00
CMMS Matt Schaub C 10.00 25.00
CMPR Philip Rivers B 25.00 60.00
CMRW Roy Williams WR C 6.00 15.00
CMRWI Reggie Williams E 6.00 15.00
CMRWO Rashaun Woods B 6.00 15.00
CMSJ Steven Jackson A 12.00 30.00
CMTB Tatum Bell F 6.00 15.00

2004 Topps Draft Picks and Prospects Class Marks Autographs Silver

LVER/50 ODDS 1:847 H, 1:824 R
SILVER PRINT RUN 50 SER.#'d SETS
CMBR Ben Roethlisberger 75.00 150.00
CMCC Cedric Cobbs 8.00 20.00
CMCP Chris Perry 8.00 20.00
CMCPI Cody Pickett 8.00 20.00
CMEM Eli Manning 50.00 120.00
CMEW Ernest Wilford 10.00 25.00
CMGJ Greg Jones 8.00 20.00
CMJC Jerricho Cotchery 10.00 25.00
CMKJ Kevin Jones 10.00 25.00
CMLE Lee Evans 12.00 30.00
CMLF Larry Fitzgerald 60.00 100.00
CMMC Michael Clayton 10.00 25.00
CMMJ Michael Jenkins 8.00 20.00
CMMS Matt Schaub 12.00 30.00
CMPR Philip Rivers 30.00 80.00
CMRW Roy Williams WR 8.00 20.00
CMRWO Rashaun Woods 8.00 20.00
CMSJ Steven Jackson 12.00 30.00
CMTB Tatum Bell 8.00 20.00

2004 Topps Draft Picks and Prospects Old School Dual Relics

ATED ODDS 1:846H, 1:820R
OSBJ A.Boldin/Gr.Jones 5.00 12.00
OSDP C.Dillon/C.Pickett 8.00 20.00
OSDW An.Davis/E.Wilford 6.00 15.00
OSGJ E.George/M.Jenkins 6.00 15.00
OSHR T.Holt/P.Rivers 30.00 50.00

2004 Topps Draft Picks and Prospects Quarterback Legacy Autographs

NGLE AUTO ODDS 1:2753H, 1:2780R
TRIPLE SILVER ODDS 1:16,630H, 1:46,320R
TRIPLE GOLD 1/1 STATED ODDS 1:399,120
QBS Archie/Peyt/Eli Silver/50 300.00 500.00
QBAM Archie Manning/100 25.00 40.00
QBEM Eli Manning/100 30.00 60.00
QBPM Peyton Manning/100 40.00 100.00

2005 Topps Draft Picks and Prospects

pps Draft Picks and Prospects initially released in late-May 2005 as Toppsâ€™ first football product of the year. The base set consists of 170-cards including 55-rookies issued one per pack and five autographed draft picks cards. Hobby boxes contained 14-packs of 5-cards and carried an S.R.P. of $2.99 per pack. Four parallel sets and a variety of inserts can be found seeded in packs highlighted by the Class Marks Autographs and Double Feature Dual Autographs inserts.

COMP.SET w/o AU's (165) 15.00 40.00
COMP.SET w/o RC's (110) 10.00 25.00
ONE ROOKIE PER PACK
DRAFT PICK AUTO ODDS 1:1179H, 1:1182R
UNPRICED GOLD SUPERFRACTORS #'d TO 1
UNPRICED PRINTING PLATES #'d TO 1
1 Marvin Harrison .30 .75
2 Rudi Johnson .25 .60
3 Matt Hasselbeck .25 .60
4 Plaxico Burress .25 .60
5 Chad Pennington .25 .60
6 Jamal Lewis .30 .75
7 Terrell Owens .30 .75
8 LaDainian Tomlinson .40 1.00
9 Tiki Barber .30 .75
10 Dante Hall .25 .60
11 Peyton Manning 1.00 2.50
12 Marshall Faulk .30 .75
13 Donovan McNabb .30 .75
14 Randy Moss .30 .75
15 Muhsin Muhammad .25 .60
16 Deuce McAllister .30 .75
17 Fred Taylor .25 .60
18 Jake Plummer .25 .60
19 Javon Walker .25 .60
20 Tony Gonzalez .30 .75
21 Michael Vick .30 .75
22 Brett Favre .75 2.00
23 Joe Horn .25 .60
24 Jeremy Shockey .25 .60
25 Laveranues Coles .25 .60
26 Trent Green .25 .60
27 Alge Crumpler .30 .75
28 Curtis Martin .30 .75
29 Torry Holt .30 .75
30 Daunte Culpepper .30 .75
31 Aaron Brooks .25 .60
32 Priest Holmes .25 .60
33 Eric Moulds .25 .60
34 Jerome Bettis .40 1.00
35 David Carr .25 .60
36 Chad Johnson .25 .60
37 Ahman Green .30 .75
38 Clinton Portis .25 .60
39 Drew Brees .40 1.00
40 Darrell Jackson .25 .60
41 Corey Dillon .25 .60
42 Reggie Wayne .30 .75
43 Shaun Alexander .25 .60
44 Hines Ward .30 .75
45 Tom Brady 1.50 4.00
46 Isaac Bruce .40 1.00
47 Byron Leftwich .25 .60
48 Chris Chambers .25 .60
49 Marc Bulger .25 .60
50 Edgerrin James .30 .75
51 Jake Delhomme .25 .60
52 Koren Robinson .25 .60
53 Brian Westbrook .25 .60
54 Reuben Droughns .25 .60
55 Joey Harrington .25 .60
56 Eli Manning .60 1.50
57 Julius Jones .25 .60
58 Nick Goings .25 .60
59 T.J. Houshmandzadeh .25 .60
60 Ben Roethlisberger .60 1.50
61 Charles Rogers .25 .60
62 Billy Volek .25 .60
63 Drew Henson .25 .60
64 Andre Johnson .30 .75
65 Carson Palmer .30 .75
66 Anquan Boldin .25 .60
67 Lee Suggs .25 .60
68 Jerry Porter .25 .60
69 J.P. Losman .25 .60
70 Nate Burleson .25 .60
71 Lee Evans .30 .75
72 Tatum Bell .25 .60
73 Chester Taylor .30 .75
74 Philip Rivers .40 1.00
75 Rex Grossman .25 .60
76 Willis McGahee .25 .60
77 Antonio Gates .40 1.00
78 Steven Jackson .25 .60
79 Roy Williams WR .25 .60
80 Chris Simms .25 .60
81 Najeh Davenport .25 .60
82 Kevin Jones .25 .60
83 Jason Witten .30 .75
84 Brandon Lloyd .25 .60
85 Larry Johnson .25 .60
86 Ronald Curry .25 .60
87 Chris Brown .25 .60
88 Kyle Boller .25 .60
89 Chris Perry .25 .60
90 Keary Colbert .25 .60
91 Sean Taylor .40 1.00
92 Greg Jones .25 .60
93 Larry Fitzgerald .40 1.00
94 Michael Clayton .25 .60
95 Mewelde Moore .25 .60
96 Drew Bennett .30 .75
97 Reggie Williams .25 .60
98 Quentin Griffin .25 .60
99 Josh McCown .30 .75
100 Santana Moss .30 .75
101 Kellen Winslow .25 .60
102 Michael Jenkins .25 .60
103 Dunta Robinson .25 .60
104 Luke McCown .25 .60
105 Brandon Stokley .25 .60
106 Derrick Blaylock .25 .60
107 Ernest Wilford .25 .60
108 Domanick Davis .25 .60
109 Jonathan Vilma .25 .60
110 Dwight Freeney .25 .60
111 Alex Smith QB AU RC 20.00 50.00
112 Derrick Johnson AU RC 10.00 25.00
113 Charlie Frye AU RC 10.00 25.00
114 Ronnie Brown AU RC 12.00 30.00
115 Mike Williams AU 10.00 25.00
116 Erasmus James RC .50 1.25
117 Alex Smith TE RC .50 1.25
118 Dan Orlovsky RC .50 1.25
119 Eric Shelton RC .50 1.25
120 Reggie Brown RC .50 1.25
121 Carlos Rogers RC .75 2.00
122 Dan Cody RC .50 1.25
123 J.J. Arrington RC .60 1.50
124 Travis Johnson RC .50 1.25
125 Antrel Rolle RC .75 2.00
126 Andrew Walter RC .50 1.25
127 Craphonso Thorpe RC .50 1.25
128 Bryan Randall RC .60 1.50
129 Anttaj Hawthorne RC .50 1.25
130 David Pollack RC .50 1.25
131 Heath Miller RC 1.00 2.50
132 Charles Frederick RC .50 1.25
133 Anthony Davis RC .50 1.25
134 Chris Rix RC .60 1.50
135 T.A. McLendon RC .50 1.25
136 David Greene RC .50 1.25
137 Timmy Chang RC .50 1.25
138 Marcus Spears RC .50 1.25
139 Airese Currie RC .50 1.25
140 Chris Henry RC .60 1.50
141 Josh Davis RC .50 1.25
142 Jason Campbell RC .50 1.25
143 Barrett Ruud RC .60 1.50
144 Courtney Roby RC .50 1.25
145 Mike Patterson RC .50 1.25
146 Jason White RC .75 2.00
147 Fred Gibson RC .50 1.25
148 Marion Barber RC .50 1.25
149 Braylon Edwards RC .50 1.25
150 Cadillac Williams RC .50 1.25
151 Kyle Orton RC .50 1.25
152 Aaron Rodgers RC 7.50 15.00
153 Alvin Pearman RC .50 1.25
154 Stefan LeFors RC .50 1.25
155 Marlin Jackson RC .50 1.25
156 Taylor Stubblefield RC .50 1.25
157 Ciatrick Fason RC .50 1.25
158 Kay-Jay Harris RC .50 1.25
159 Frank Gore RC 1.00 2.50
160 Vernand Morency RC .60 1.50
161 Adam Jones RC .50 1.25
162 Troy Williamson RC .50 1.25
163 Roddy White RC .75 2.00
164 Thomas Davis RC .50 1.25
165 Mark Clayton RC .50 1.25
166 Craig Bragg RC .50 1.25
167 Noah Herron RC .50 1.25
168 Darren Sproles RC .75 2.00
169 Terrence Murphy RC .50 1.25
170 Walter Reyes RC .50 1.25

2005 Topps Draft Picks and Prospects Chrome

MPLETE SET (165) 60.00 120.00
*VETERANS: 1X TO 2.5X BASIC CARDS
*ROOKIES: .8X TO 2X BASIC CARDS
ONE PER PACK

2005 Topps Draft Picks and Prospects Chrome Black Refractors

ETERANS: 8X TO 20X BASIC CARDS
*ROOKIES: 5X TO 12X BASIC CARDS
STATED ODDS 1:284 HOB, 1:285 RET
STATED PRINT RUN 25 SER.#'d SETS
152 Aaron Rodgers 150.00 250.00

2005 Topps Draft Picks and Prospects Chrome Gold Refractors

ETERANS: 5X TO 12X BASIC CARDS
*ROOKIES: 3X TO 8X BASIC CARDS
STATED ODDS 1:35 HOB, 1:36 RET
STATED PRINT RUN 199 SER.#'d SETS

2005 Topps Draft Picks and Prospects Class Marks Autographs

OUP A ODDS 1:555 HOB, 1:556 RET
GROUP B ODDS 1:227 HOB/RET
GROUP C ODDS 1:778 HOB, 1:768 RET
GROUP D ODDS 1:173 HOB/RET
GROUP E ODDS 1:240 HOB, 1:219 RET
GROUP F ODDS 1:68 HOB, 1:80 RET
GOLD STATED ODDS 1:5241 HOB/RET
UNPRICED GOLD PRINT RUN 10 SETS
UNPRICED PRINT PLATE PRINT RUN 1 SET
RAINBOW STATED ODDS 1:22,990 HOB
UNPRICED RAINBOW PRINT RUN 1 SET
CMAD Anthony Davis B 5.00 12.00
CMAR Aaron Rodgers A 175.00 300.00
CMAW Andrew Walter A 5.00 12.00
CMBE Braylon Edwards A 12.00 30.00
CMCB Cedric Benson A 12.00 30.00
CMCF Charles Frederick F 5.00 12.00
CMCH Chris Henry D 6.00 15.00
CMCHO Cedric Houston F 8.00 20.00
CMCR Chris Rix D 6.00 15.00
CMCT Craphonso Thorpe B 5.00 12.00
CMCW Cadillac Williams A 5.00 12.00
CMDC Dan Cody A 5.00 12.00
CMDG David Greene B 5.00 12.00
CMES Eric Shelton E 5.00 12.00
CMFG Fred Gibson F 5.00 12.00
CMJA J.J. Arrington E 6.00 15.00
CMJC Jason Campbell A 5.00 12.00
CMJW Jason White A 8.00 20.00
CMKO Kyle Orton B 15.00 40.00
CMMB Marion Barber F 5.00 12.00
CMMC Mark Clayton A 5.00 12.00
CMMJ Marlin Jackson D 5.00 12.00
CMRBR Reggie Brown B 5.00 12.00
CMTAM T.A. McLendon C 5.00 12.00
CMWR Walter Reyes F 5.00 12.00

2005 Topps Draft Picks and Prospects Class Marks Autographs Silver

SILVER/50 ODDS 1:940 HOB, 1:942 RET
SILVER PRINT RUN 50 SER.#'d SETS
CMAD Anthony Davis 8.00 20.00
CMAR Aaron Rodgers 175.00 350.00
CMAW Andrew Walter 8.00 20.00
CMBE Braylon Edwards 8.00 20.00
CMCB Cedric Benson 15.00 40.00
CMCF Charles Frederick 8.00 20.00
CMCH Chris Henry 10.00 25.00
CMCHO Cedric Houston 12.00 30.00
CMCR Chris Rix 10.00 25.00
CMCT Craphonso Thorpe 8.00 20.00
CMCW Cadillac Williams 8.00 20.00
CMDC Dan Cody 8.00 20.00
CMDG David Greene 8.00 20.00
CMES Eric Shelton 8.00 20.00
CMFG Fred Gibson 8.00 20.00
CMJA J.J. Arrington 10.00 25.00
CMJC Jason Campbell 8.00 20.00
CMJW Jason White 12.00 30.00
CMKO Kyle Orton 20.00 50.00
CMMB Marion Barber 8.00 20.00
CMMC Mark Clayton 8.00 20.00
CMMJ Marlin Jackson 8.00 20.00
CMRBR Reggie Brown 8.00 20.00
CMTAM T.A. McLendon 8.00 20.00
CMWR Walter Reyes 8.00 20.00

2005 Topps Draft Picks and Prospects Double Feature Dual Autographs

ATED ODDS 1:5108 HOB, 1:4702 RET
BW C.Benson/C.Williams 30.00 80.00
EC B.Edwards/Ma.Clayton 20.00 50.00
EW B.Edwards/M.Williams 20.00 50.00
SR A.Smith QB/A.Rodgers 150.00 250.00
WB C.Williams/R.Brown 50.00 120.00

2005 Topps Draft Picks and Prospects Senior Standout Jersey

OUP A ODDS 1:1304 HOB, 1:1309
GROUP B ODDS 1:275 HOB/RET
GROUP C ODDS 1:188 HOB/RET
GROUP D ODDS 1:171 HOB/RET
GROUP E ODDS 1:869 HOB, 1:874
GROUP F ODDS 1:270 HOB/RET
GROUP G ODDS 1:535 HOB/RET
GROUP H ODDS 1:245 HOB/RET
GROUP I ODDS 1:470 HOB/RET
GROUP J ODDS 1:107 HOB, 1:103 RET
GROUP K ODDS 1:250 HOB, 1:185 RET
GROUP L ODDS 1:385 HOB, 1:379 RET
GROUP M ODDS 1:356 HOB/RET
UNPRICED GOLD PRINT RUN 10 SETS
UNPRICED PRINT PLATE PRINT RUN 1 SET
*SILVER: .6X TO 1.5X GROUP A-B JSYs
*SILVER: .8X TO 2X GROUP C-M JSYs
SILVER ODDS 1:1207 HOB, 1:1181 RET
SILVER PRINT RUN 50 SER.#'d SETS
SSAR Antrel Rolle SB A 5.00 12.00
SSAR2 Antrel Rolle Mia G 4.00 10.00
SSAS Alex Smith TE F 2.50 6.00
SSBJ Brandon Jones C 3.00 8.00
SSBR Barrett Ruud L 3.00 8.00
SSCF Charlie Frye C 2.50 6.00
SSCH Cedric Houston C 4.00 10.00
SSCR Carlos Rogers SB D 4.00 10.00
SSCR2 Carlos Rogers Aub J 4.00 10.00
SSCT Craphonso Thorpe C 2.50 6.00
SSCW Cadillac Williams Aub J 2.50 6.00
SSCW2 Cadillac Williams SB D 2.50 6.00
SSDG David Greene D 2.50 6.00
SSDS Darren Sproles E 4.00 10.00
SSFG Fred Gibson D 2.50 6.00
SSFGO Frank Gore M 6.00 15.00
SSJA J.J. Arrington D 3.00 8.00
SSJC Jason Campbell B 3.00 8.00
SSKO Kyle Orton K 2.50 6.00
SSMC Mark Clayton H 2.50 6.00
SSMJ Marlin Jackson H 2.50 6.00
SSMS Marcus Spears LSU K 2.50 6.00
SSMS2 Marcus Spears SB B 3.00 8.00
SSRB Reggie Brown C 2.50 6.00
SSRBR Ronnie Brown I 10.00 25.00
SSSC Shaun Cody F 3.00 8.00
SSSCU Sonny Cumbie I 2.50 6.00
SSTS Taylor Stubblefield J 2.50 6.00
SSVJ Vincent Jackson J 4.00 10.00
SSMSC Morgan Scalley J 2.50 6.00

2005 Topps Draft Picks and Prospects Senior Standout Jersey Autographs

LVER STATED ODDS 1:2398 HOB/RET
SILVER PRINT RUN 50 SER.#'d SETS
GOLD STATED ODDS 1:13,457 HOB/RET
UNPRICED GOLD PRINT RUN 10 SETS
RAINBOW STATED ODDS 1:61,307 HOB
RAINBOW PRINT RUN 1 SER.#'d SETS
SSAAR Antrel Rolle 20.00 50.00
SSACF Charlie Frye 20.00 50.00
SSACW Cadillac Williams 20.00 50.00
SSADG David Greene 15.00 40.00
SSAJA J.J. Arrington 15.00 40.00
SSAJC Jason Campbell 40.00 80.00
SSAKO Kyle Orton 25.00 50.00
SSAMC Mark Clayton 15.00 40.00
SSARB Reggie Brown 20.00 50.00
SSARBR Ronnie Brown 40.00 100.00

2006 Topps Draft Picks and Prospects

is 175-card set was released in May, 2006. The set was issued into the hobby in five-card packs, with an $3 SRP, which came 24 packs to a box. The first 109 cards in this set are veterans while the rest of the set features 2006 NFL rookies. The overall odds of finding a rookie was stated to be one per pack. The final 10 cards (#166-175(in the set were all signed by the rookie. Those signed rookie cards were issued to a stated print run of 199 serial numbered copies and those cards were inserted into packs at a stated rate of one in 1282.

COMP.SET w/o SP's (165) 12.50 30.00
COMP.SET w/o RC's (110) 6.00 15.00
ONE ROOKIE CARD PER PACK
166-175 ROOKIE AU/199 ODDS 1:1282
UNPRICED PRINT PLATES SER.#'d TO 1
1 Plaxico Burress .25 .60
2 Ahman Green .30 .75
3 Domanick Davis .25 .60
4 Andre Johnson .30 .75
5 Donovan McNabb .30 .75
6 Marvin Harrison .30 .75
7 Michael Vick .30 .75
8 Priest Holmes .25 .60
9 Torry Holt .30 .75
10 Marc Bulger .25 .60
11 Ben Roethlisberger .50 1.25
12 Larry Fitzgerald .30 .75
13 Peyton Manning 1.00 2.50
14 Chris Perry .30 .75
15 Antonio Gates .40 1.00
16 Eli Manning .30 .75
17 Brett Favre .75 2.00
18 Reggie Brown .25 .60
19 Curtis Martin .30 .75
20 Charlie Frye .30 .75
21 Tom Brady 1.25 3.00
22 Cadillac Williams .30 .75
23 Trent Green .25 .60
24 Matt Jones .25 .60
25 Anquan Boldin .25 .60
26 Larry Johnson .25 .60
27 Rudi Johnson .25 .60
28 Marion Barber .30 .75
29 Jake Delhomme .25 .60
30 Philip Rivers .40 1.00
31 Fred Taylor .25 .60
32 Frank Gore .30 .75
33 Shaun Alexander .25 .60
34 Chris Simms .25 .60
35 LaDainian Tomlinson .40 1.00
36 Troy Williamson .25 .60
37 Clinton Portis .25 .60
38 Kyle Orton .25 .60
39 Tony Gonzalez .30 .75
40 Mark Clayton .25 .60
41 Steve Smith .40 1.00
42 Heath Miller .25 .60
43 Warrick Dunn .25 .60
44 Alex Smith TE .25 .60
45 Chris Brown .25 .60
46 Billy Volek .25 .60
47 Tiki Barber .30 .75
48 Julius Jones .25 .60
49 Drew Bledsoe .30 .75
50 Charles Rogers .30 .75
51 Jake Plummer .25 .60
52 Greg Jones .25 .60
53 Chad Johnson .25 .60
54 Braylon Edwards .25 .60
55 Carson Palmer .30 .75
56 Scottie Vines .25 .60
57 Keary Colbert .25 .60
58 Alex Smith QB .30 .75
59 Roy Williams WR .25 .60
60 Roddy White .25 .60
61 Willis McGahee .25 .60
62 Michael Clayton .25 .60
63 Edgerrin James .30 .75
64 Aaron Rodgers 1.00 2.50
65 Byron Leftwich .25 .60
66 Tatum Bell .25 .60
67 Daunte Culpepper .30 .75
68 Chris Henry .25 .60
69 Corey Dillon .25 .60
70 Ronnie Brown .30 .75
71 Kevin Jones .25 .60
72 J.P. Losman .30 .75
73 Steven Jackson .25 .60
74 Mike Williams .25 .60
75 Jeremy Shockey .30 .75
76 DeMarcus Ware .30 .75
77 LaMont Jordan .30 .75
78 Cedric Benson .25 .60
79 Ricky Williams .25 .60
80 Brandon Jones .25 .60
81 Brian Westbrook .25 .60
82 Willie Parker .30 .75
83 Hines Ward .30 .75
84 Ernest Wilford .25 .60
85 Matt Hasselbeck .25 .60
86 Jason Campbell .25 .60
87 Joey Galloway .30 .75
88 Odell Thurman .25 .60
89 Santana Moss .30 .75
90 Courtney Roby .25 .60
91 Deuce McAllister .30 .75
92 Derrick Johnson .25 .60
93 Drew Brees .40 1.00
94 Michael Jenkins .25 .60
95 Jerome Bettis .40 1.00
96 Osi Umenyiora .25 .60
97 Reggie Wayne .30 .75
98 Ryan Moats .25 .60
99 Randy Moss .30 .75
100 Samie Parker .25 .60
101 Mark Bradley .25 .60
102 Samkon Gado .25 .60
103 Matt Schaub .25 .60
104 Shaun McDonald .25 .60
105 D.J. Hackett .25 .60
106 Mewelde Moore .25 .60
107 Chester Taylor .30 .75
108 Greg Lewis .25 .60
109 Chris Cooley .25 .60
110 Todd DeVoe RC .25 .60
111 Joel Klopfenstein RC .60 1.50
112 Devin Hester RC 1.25 3.00
113 Brad Smith RC .75 2.00
114 Jason Avant RC .60 1.50
115 Michael Robinson RC .60 1.50
116 Kellen Clemens RC .60 1.50
117 Anthony Fasano RC .60 1.50
118 Leon Washington RC .60 1.50
119 Laurence Maroney RC .60 1.50
120 Martin Nance RC .60 1.50
121 Demetrius Williams RC .60 1.50
122 A.J. Nicholson RC .60 1.50
123 Jimmy Williams RC .60 1.50
124 Michael Huff RC .75 2.00
125 Chad Jackson RC .60 1.50
126 Mike Hass RC .60 1.50
127 Brodie Croyle RC .60 1.50
128 Jerome Harrison RC .60 1.50
129 Hank Baskett RC .60 1.50
130 Santonio Holmes RC .75 2.00
131 Chad Greenway RC 1.00 2.50
132 Mario Williams RC 1.00 2.50
133 Charlie Whitehurst RC .60 1.50

134 Darrell Hackney RC .75 2.00
135 DeMeco Ryans RC .75 2.00
136 Mathias Kiwanuka RC 1.00 2.50
137 Omar Jacobs RC .60 1.50
138 Bruce Gradkowski RC .75 2.00
139 Drew Olson RC .60 1.50
140 Maurice Stovall RC .60 1.50
141 Greg Jennings RC 1.00 2.50
142 D'Brickashaw Ferguson RC .60 1.50
143 Manny Lawson RC .75 2.00
144 Tamba Hali RC 1.00 2.50
145 Vernon Davis RC .75 2.00
146 Greg Lee RC .60 1.50
147 Dominique Byrd RC .60 1.50
148 Leonard Pope RC 1.00 2.50
149 Bobby Carpenter RC .60 1.50
150 Haloti Ngata RC .75 2.00
151 Marcedes Lewis RC .60 1.50
152 Ernie Sims RC .60 1.50
153 Ashton Youboty RC .60 1.50
154 D.J. Shockley RC .75 2.00
155 Paul Pinegar RC .60 1.50
156 Maurice Drew RC 1.00 2.50
157 Jeremy Bloom RC .60 1.50
158 Cory Rodgers RC .60 1.50
159 Abdul Hodge RC .60 1.50
160 Tye Hill RC .60 1.50
161 D'Qwell Jackson RC .60 1.50
162 Jonathan Orr RC .75 2.00
163 Antonio Cromartie RC .75 2.00
164 Todd Watkins RC .60 1.50
165 Gerald Riggs RC .75 2.00
166 Matt Leinart AU RC 8.00 20.00
167 Reggie Bush AU RC 12.00 30.00
168 DeAngelo Williams AU RC 10.00 25.00
169 A.J. Hawk AU RC 20.00 50.00
170 Vince Young AU RC 8.00 20.00
171 Derek Hagan AU RC 10.00 25.00
172 Joseph Addai AU RC 8.00 20.00
173 Jay Cutler AU RC 10.00 25.00
174 Sinorice Moss AU RC 8.00 20.00
175 LenDale White AU RC 8.00 20.00
RBML R.Bush/Leinart AU/25 40.00 80.00

2006 Topps Draft Picks and Prospects Chrome Black

COMPLETE SET (165) 60.00 120.00
*VETS 1-110: 1X TO 2.5X BASIC CARDS
*ROOKIES 111-165: .6X TO 1.5X
OVERALL CHROME PARALLEL ODDS 1:1

2006 Topps Draft Picks and Prospects Chrome Black Refractors

*VETS 1-110: 1.5X TO 4X BASIC CARDS
*ROOKIES 111-165: 1X TO 2.5X BASIC CARDS
STATED ODDS 1:4

2006 Topps Draft Picks and Prospects Chrome Bronze

*VETS 1-110: 3X TO 8X BASIC CARDS
*ROOKIES 111-165: 2X TO 5X BASIC CARDS
BRONZE/449 STATED ODDS 1:31

2006 Topps Draft Picks and Prospects Chrome Bronze Refractors

*VETS 1-110: 4X TO 10X BASIC CARDS
*ROOKIES 111-165: 2.5X TO 6X BASIC CARDS
BRONZE REF/299 STATED ODDS 1:52

2006 Topps Draft Picks and Prospects Chrome Gold

*VETS 1-110: 8X TO 20X BASIC CARDS
*ROOKIES 111-165: 6X TO 15X BASIC CARDS
GOLD/25 STATED ODDS 1:617

2006 Topps Draft Picks and Prospects Chrome Gold Refractors

PRICED GOLD REF PRINT RUN 1 SET

2006 Topps Draft Picks and Prospects Chrome Silver

ETS 1-110: 5X TO 12X BASIC CARDS
*ROOKIES 111-165: 4X TO 10X BASIC CARDS
SILVER/199 STATED ODDS 1:78

2006 Topps Draft Picks and Prospects Chrome Silver Refractors

*VETS 1-110: 6X TO 15X BASIC CARDS
*ROOKIES 111-165: 5X TO 12X BASIC CARDS
SILVER REF/99 STATED ODDS 1:156

2006 Topps Draft Picks and Prospects Class Marks Autographs

GROUP A ODDS 1:4275
GROUP B ODDS 1:1664
GROUP C ODDS 1:385
GROUP D ODDS 1:1275
GROUP E ODDS 1:278
GROUP F ODDS 1:93
UNPRICED GOLD/10 ODDS 1:9000
UNPRICED HOLOFOIL/1 ODDS 1:60,206
UNPRICED PRINT PLATES SER.#'d TO 1
*SILVER/50: .8X TO 2X AU GRP B-F
*SILVER/50: .6X TO 1.5X AU GRP A
SILVER/50 STATED ODDS 1:1185
CMBB Brett Basanez F 6.00 15.00
CMBC Brian Calhoun B 4.00 10.00
CMBG Bruce Gradkowski D 5.00 12.00
CMCG Chad Greenway F 6.00 15.00
CMCJ Chad Jackson C 4.00 10.00
CMCR Cory Rodgers F 4.00 10.00
CMCW Charlie Whitehurst C 4.00 10.00
CMDH Derek Hagan B 5.00 12.00
CMDM DonTrell Moore F 5.00 12.00
CMDO Drew Olson E 4.00 10.00
CMDS D.J. Shockley E 5.00 12.00
CMDW DeAngelo Williams A 12.00 30.00
CMDW Demetrius Williams C 4.00 10.00
CMGJ Greg Jennings F 6.00 15.00
CMGL Greg Lee F 4.00 10.00
CMGR Gerald Riggs F 5.00 12.00
CMJA Jason Avant D 4.00 10.00
CMJB Jeremy Bloom C 4.00 10.00
CMJC Jay Cutler A 5.00 12.00
CMJH Jerome Harrison E 4.00 10.00
CMLM Laurence Maroney B 4.00 10.00
CMLW Leon Washington 4.00 10.00
CMMD Maurice Drew C 12.00 30.00
CMML Matt Leinart A 12.00 30.00
CMMN Martin Nance E 4.00 10.00
CMMR Michael Robinson E 4.00 10.00
CMMS Maurice Stovall F 4.00 10.00
CMOJ Omar Jacobs C 4.00 10.00
CMPP Paul Pinegar C 4.00 10.00
CMRB Reggie Bush A 6.00 15.00
CMRM Reggie McNeal F 4.00 10.00
CMSH Santonio Holmes B 12.00 30.00
CMSM Sinorice Moss B 4.00 10.00
CMTW Todd Watkins E 4.00 10.00
CMTW Travis Wilson F 4.00 10.00
CMVD Vernon Davis C 5.00 12.00
CMVY Vince Young A 4.00 10.00
CMAMH Mike Hass C 4.00 10.00
CMBCR Brodie Croyle C 4.00 10.00
CMDHA Darrell Hackney C 5.00 12.00
CMDHE Devin Hester C 8.00 20.00
CMJAD Joseph Addai B 4.00 10.00
CMLEW LenDale White A 8.00 20.00

2006 Topps Draft Picks and Prospects First and Ten Autographs

RST AND TEN AUTO/50 ODDS 1:4900
UNPRICED DUAL AUTO/10 ODDS 1:32,000
UNPRICED DUAL GLD AU ODDS 1:1,400,000
BJ Bo Jackson 40.00 80.00
EC Earl Campbell 25.00 50.00
EM Eli Manning 50.00 100.00
JE John Elway 75.00 150.00
JP Jim Plunkett 25.00 50.00
MV Michael Vick 25.00 50.00
PH Paul Hornung 25.00 50.00
PM Peyton Manning 60.00 120.00
RB Reggie Bush 12.00 30.00
TA Troy Aikman 50.00 100.00
TB Terry Bradshaw 50.00 100.00

2006 Topps Draft Picks and Prospects Senior Standout Jersey

OUP A ODDS 1:251
GROUP B ODDS 1:212
GROUP C ODDS 1:797
GROUP D ODDS 1:309
GROUP E ODDS 1:233
GROUP F ODDS 1:457
GROUP G ODDS 1:149
GROUP H ODDS 1:413
UNPRICED GOLD/10 ODDS 1:8000
UNPRICED HOLOFOIL/1 ODDS 1:49,700
*SILVER: .6X TO 1.5X BASIC INSERTS
SILVER/50 STATED ODDS 1:1120
UNPRICED PRINT PLATES SER.#'d TO 1
SSAH Andre Hall D 2.50 6.00
SSAM Anthony Mix E 2.50 6.00
SSAP Anwar Phillips A 2.50 6.00
SSBB Broderick Bunkley G 2.50 6.00
SSBC Brodie Croyle D 2.00 5.00
SSCG Chad Greenway G 3.00 8.00
SSDA Devin Aromashodu E 2.00 5.00
SSDB Dominique Byrd E 2.00 5.00
SSDD Dusty Dvoracek G 3.00 8.00
SSDF D'Brickashaw Ferguson H 2.00 5.00
SSDJ D'Qwell Jackson B 2.00 5.00
SSDM DeMario Minter B 2.50 6.00
SSDR DeMeco Ryans D 2.50 6.00
SSDS D.J. Shockley E 2.50 6.00
SSDW DeAngelo Williams B 2.50 6.00
SSED Elvis Dumervil F 3.00 8.00
SSEW Eric Winston H 2.00 5.00
SSGM Garrett Mills C 2.50 6.00
SSHB Hank Baskett D 2.00 5.00
SSJA Joseph Addai A 2.00 5.00
SSJC Jay Cutler E 2.50 6.00
SSJH Jerome Harrison E 2.00 5.00
SSJK Joe Klopfenstein G 2.00 5.00
SSJM Jesse Mahelona H 2.50 6.00
SSJN Jerious Norwood A 2.00 5.00
SSLW Lawrence Vickers E 2.50 6.00
SSMB Mike Bell E 2.00 5.00
SSMK Mathias Kiwanuka G 3.00 8.00
SSML Manny Lawson G 2.50 6.00
SSMN Martin Nance A 2.00 5.00
SSMR Michael Robinson E 2.00 5.00
SSMS Maurice Stovall E 2.00 5.00
SSOH Orien Harris F 2.50 6.00
SSSG Skyler Green A 2.00 5.00
SSSH Spencer Havner F 2.50 6.00
SSSM Sinorice Moss A 2.00 5.00
SSTH Tye Hill B 2.00 5.00
SSTW Terrence Whitehead E 2.50 6.00
SSTJ T.J. Williams G 3.00 8.00
SSWB Will Blackmon B 2.00 5.00
SSAHO Abdul Hodge C 2.00 5.00
SSDEW Demetrius Williams B 2.00 5.00
SSDH1 Darrell Hackney E 2.50 6.00
SSDH2 Derek Hagan A 2.50 6.00
SSJAV Jason Avant B 2.00 5.00
SSMLE Marcedes Lewis G 2.00 5.00
SSTHA Tamba Hali G 3.00 8.00
SSTHO Thomas Howard D 2.00 5.00
SSTRW Travis Wilson B 2.00 5.00

2006 Topps Draft Picks and Prospects Senior Standout Jersey Autographs Silver

SILVER/50 STATED ODDS 1:5150
UNPRICED HOLOFOIL/1 ODDS 1:1,400,000
UNPRICED GOLD/10 ODDS 1:37,000
SSADF D'Brickashaw Ferguson 15.00 40.00
SSADS D.J. Shockley 12.50 30.00
SSADW DeAngelo Williams 25.00 60.00
SSAJA Joseph Addai 30.00 80.00
SSAJC Jay Cutler 60.00 120.00
SSAMN Martin Nance 15.00 30.00
SSAMR Michael Robinson 15.00 40.00
SSAMS Maurice Stovall 15.00 40.00
SSASM Sinorice Moss 15.00 40.00
SSADHA Derek Hagan 15.00 40.00

2006 Topps Draft Picks and Prospects Upperclassmen Jersey

GROUP A ODDS 1:3408
GROUP B ODDS 1:2690
GROUP C ODDS 1:1157
GROUP D ODDS 1:200
GROUP E ODDS 1:269
GROUP F ODDS 1:607
GROUP G ODDS 1:850
GROUP H ODDS 1:797
GROUP I ODDS 1:1459
GROUP J ODDS 1:1380
GROUP K ODDS 1:207
GROUP L ODDS 1:378
GROUP M ODDS 1:114
*SILVER: .6X TO 1.5X BASIC INSERTS
SILVER/50 STATED ODDS 1:1175
UNPRICED PRINT PLATES SER.#'d TO 1
UCAJ Andre Johnson M 2.50 6.00
UCAL Ashley Lelie D 2.00 5.00
UCAM Amani Toomer E 2.00 5.00
UCBL Byron Leftwich L 2.00 5.00
UCBR Ben Roethlisberger K 4.00 10.00
UCBU Brian Urlacher H 3.00 8.00
UCCB Cedric Benson E 2.00 5.00
UCCC Chris Chambers D 2.00 5.00
UCCD Corey Dillon K 2.00 5.00
UCCJ Chad Johnson D 2.00 5.00
UCCM Curtis Martin D 2.50 6.00
UCCP Clinton Portis E 2.00 5.00
UCCS Chris Simms G 2.00 5.00
UCCW Cadillac Williams D 2.50 6.00
UCDB Drew Brees D 3.00 8.00
UCDD Domanick Davis 2.00 5.00
UCDF DeShaun Foster I 2.50 6.00
UCDH DeAngelo Hall C 2.00 5.00
UCDM Deuce McAllister K 2.50 6.00
UCEM Eric Moulds K 2.00 5.00
UCHW Hines Ward K 2.50 6.00
UCIB Isaac Bruce M 3.00 8.00
UCJB Jerome Bettis M 3.00 8.00
UCJS Jeremy Shockey D 2.00 5.00
UCJT Jason Taylor F 2.50 6.00
UCLA LaVar Arrington F 2.00 5.00
UCLT LaDainian Tomlinson D 3.00 8.00
UCMH Marvin Harrison M 2.50 6.00
UCPH Priest Holmes M 2.00 5.00
UCRM Randy Moss C 2.50 6.00
UCSA Shaun Alexander A 2.00 5.00
UCSD Stephen Davis J 2.00 5.00
UCSJ Steven Jackson E 2.00 5.00
UCSM Santana Moss E 2.50 6.00
UCTB Tatum Bell M 2.00 5.00
UCTG Tony Gonzalez F 2.50 6.00
UCTH Torry Holt L 2.50 6.00
UCTS Terrell Suggs G 2.00 5.00
UCWD Warrick Dunn K 2.00 5.00
UCWM Willis McGahee B 2.00 5.00
UCZT Zach Thomas D 2.50 6.00
UCARE Antwaan Randle El D 2.00 5.00
UCCBA Champ Bailey D 2.50 6.00
UCDBR Drew Brees L 3.00 8.00
UCTBA Tiki Barber E 2.50 6.00
UCTBE Tom Brady M 10.00 25.00
UCTGR Trent Green H 2.00 5.00
UCTHE Todd Heap E 2.00 5.00

2007 Topps Draft Picks and Prospects

is 155-card set was released in May, 2007. The set was issued into the hobby in five-card packs, with a $3 SRP, which came 24 packs to a box. Cards numbered 1-100 feature veterans while cards numbered 101-155 feature 2007 NFL rookies.

COMPLETE SET (155) 20.00 50.00
1 Donovan McNabb .30 .75
2 Larry Johnson .25 .60
3 Willis McGahee .25 .60
4 Tom Brady 1.25 3.00
5 Anquan Boldin .25 .60
6 Steve Smith .30 .75
7 Philip Rivers .40 1.00
8 LaDainian Tomlinson .40 1.00
9 Reuben Droughns .30 .75
10 Julius Jones .25 .60
11 Drew Brees .40 1.00
12 Chad Johnson .25 .60
13 Ronnie Brown .25 .60
14 Brett Favre .75 2.00
15 J.P. Losman .25 .60
16 Clinton Portis .25 .60
17 Edgerrin James .30 .75
18 Andre Johnson .30 .75
19 Fred Taylor .25 .60
20 Marc Bulger .25 .60
21 Peyton Manning 1.00 2.50
22 Reggie Wayne .30 .75
23 Hines Ward .30 .75
24 Michael Vick .30 .75
25 Santana Moss .30 .75
26 Torry Holt .30 .75
27 Jake Delhomme .25 .60
28 Brian Westbrook .25 .60
29 Tony Gonzalez .30 .75
30 Larry Fitzgerald .30 .75
31 Matt Hasselbeck .25 .60
32 Kevin Jones .25 .60
33 Willie Parker .30 .75
34 Jeremy Shockey .25 .60
35 Marvin Harrison .30 .75
36 Warrick Dunn .25 .60
37 Ahman Green .30 .75
38 Ben Roethlisberger .40 1.00
39 Randy Moss .30 .75
40 Rudi Johnson .25 .60
41 Carson Palmer .30 .75
42 Trent Green .25 .60
43 Plaxico Burress .25 .60
44 Steven Jackson .25 .60
45 Deuce McAllister .30 .75
46 Antonio Gates .40 1.00
47 Cadillac Williams .30 .75
48 Eli Manning .30 .75
49 Rex Grossman .25 .60
50 Shaun Alexander .25 .60
51 DeAngelo Williams .25 .60
52 Joseph Addai .25 .60
53 Vince Young .25 .60
54 Matt Leinart .25 .60
55 Sinorice Moss .30 .75
56 Matt Jones .30 .75
57 Tony Romo .50 1.25
58 Jay Cutler .25 .60
59 Marques Colston .25 .60
60 Vernon Davis .25 .60
61 Cedric Benson .25 .60
62 Mario Williams .30 .75
63 Hank Baskett .30 .75
64 Alex Smith QB .30 .75
65 Jason Campbell .25 .60
66 Mike Furrey .30 .75
67 Greg Jennings .25 .60
68 Laurence Maroney .30 .75
69 Charlie Frye .30 .75
70 Michael Robinson .30 .75
71 Michael Huff .30 .75
72 A.J. Hawk .25 .60
73 Marion Barber .40 1.00
74 Santonio Holmes .25 .60
75 Kellen Winslow .25 .60
76 Reggie Bush .25 .60
77 Charlie Whitehurst .25 .60
78 Brad Smith .25 .60
79 Leon Washington .25 .60
80 Wali Lundy .25 .60
81 Owen Daniels .25 .60
82 Devin Hester .30 .75
83 Chad Jackson .25 .60
84 Braylon Edwards .25 .60
85 Bruce Gradkowski .25 .60
86 Tarvaris Jackson .25 .60
87 Derek Hagan .25 .60
88 Mike Bell .30 .75
89 Frank Gore .30 .75
90 LenDale White .30 .75
91 Chris Henry .25 .60
92 Kellen Clemens .25 .60
93 Nate Washington .25 .60
94 Jerious Norwood .25 .60
95 Maurice Jones-Drew .25 .60
96 Mark Clayton .25 .60
97 Jason Avant .25 .60
98 Mathias Kiwanuka .25 .60
99 Brandon Jacobs .25 .60
100 Chris Cooley .25 .60
101 Brady Quinn RC .60 1.50
102 Michael Bush RC .60 1.50
103 Leon Hall RC .60 1.50
104 Jason Hill RC .60 1.50
105 Patrick Willis RC 1.00 2.50
106 Brian Leonard RC .60 1.50
107 Gaines Adams RC .75 2.00
108 Kenneth Darby RC .60 1.50
109 Marcus McCauley RC .60 1.50
110 Paul Posluszny RC .60 1.50
111 Drew Stanton RC .60 1.50
112 Troy Smith RC .60 1.50
113 Garrett Wolfe RC .60 1.50
114 Chris Leak RC .60 1.50
115 Joe Thomas RC 1.00 2.50
116 Paul Williams RC .60 1.50
117 LaRon Landry RC 1.00 2.50
118 Aundrae Allison RC .60 1.50
119 Kenny Irons RC .60 1.50
120 Kevin Kolb RC .75 2.00
121 Tyler Palko RC 1.00 2.50
122 Steve Smith USC RC .60 1.50
123 Steve Breaston RC .60 1.50
124 Tyrone Moss RC .60 1.50
125 LaMarr Woodley RC 1.25 3.00
126 Brandon Meriweather RC .75 2.00
127 Rhema McKnight RC .60 1.50
128 Daymeion Hughes RC .60 1.50
129 Jared Zabransky RC .60 1.50
130 Chansi Stuckey RC .75 2.00
131 Amobi Okoye RC .75 2.00
132 Calvin Johnson RC 2.00 5.00
133 Marshawn Lynch RC 1.25 3.00
134 Ted Ginn Jr. RC .75 2.00
135 Adrian Peterson RC 2.00 5.00
136 Dwayne Jarrett RC .75 2.00
137 Greg Olsen RC 1.00 2.50
138 Adam Carriker RC .60 1.50
139 Darius Walker RC .60 1.50
140 Robert Meachem RC .75 2.00
141 Jordan Palmer RC .75 2.00
142 JaMarcus Russell RC .60 1.50
143 DeShawn Wynn RC .60 1.50
144 Zach Miller RC .60 1.50
145 Lorenzo Booker RC .75 2.00
146 Selvin Young RC .60 1.50
147 Courtney Lewis RC .75 2.00
148 Tony Hunt RC .60 1.50
149 Dwayne Bowe RC .60 1.50
150 Aaron Ross RC .60 1.50
151 Antonio Pittman RC .60 1.50
152 Anthony Gonzalez RC .60 1.50
153 John Beck RC .60 1.50
154 Sidney Rice RC .75 2.00
155 Lawrence Timmons RC 1.00 2.50

2007 Topps Draft Picks and Prospects Chrome Black

*VETS 1-100: 1X TO 2.5X BASIC CARDS
*ROOKIES 101-155: .5X TO 1.2X
OVERALL CHROME ODDS ONE PER PACK

2007 Topps Draft Picks and Prospects Chrome Bronze

*VETS 1-100: 1.2X TO 3X BASIC CARDS
*ROOKIES 101-155: .6X TO 1.5X
STATED ODDS 1:6

2007 Topps Draft Picks and Prospects Chrome Gold

*VETS 1-100: 4X TO 10X BASIC CARDS
*ROOKIES 101-155: 2X TO 5X BASIC CARDS
GOLD/99 ODDS 1:145

2007 Topps Draft Picks and Prospects Chrome Silver

*VETS 1-100: 2.5X TO 6X BASIC CARDS
*ROOKIES 101-155: 1.2X TO 3X BASIC CARDS
SILVER/299 ODDS 1:48

2007 Topps Draft Picks and Prospects Chrome Black Refractors

*VETS 1-100: 2X TO 5X BASIC CARDS
*ROOKIES 101-155: 1X TO 2.5X BASIC CARDS
STATED ODDS 1:12

2007 Topps Draft Picks and Prospects Chrome Bronze Refractors

ETS 1-100: 2.5X TO 6X BASIC CARDS
*ROOKIES 101-155: 1.2X TO 3X BASIC CARDS
BRONZE REFRACTOR/250 ODDS 1:58

2007 Topps Draft Picks and Prospects Chrome Gold Refractors

*VETS 1-100: 8X TO 20X BASIC CARDS
*ROOKIES 101-155: 4X TO 10X BASIC CARDS
GOLD REFRACTOR/25 ODDS 1:577

2007 Topps Draft Picks and Prospects Chrome Silver Refractors

*VETS 1-100: 4X TO 10X BASIC CARDS
*ROOKIES 101-155: 2X TO 5X BASIC CARDS
SILVER REFRACTOR/125 ODDS 1:115

2007 Topps Draft Picks and Prospects All-Star Alumni Autographs

SINGLE AUTO/50 ODDS 1:4900
AP Adrian Peterson 75.00 150.00
BQ Brady Quinn 12.00 30.00
CJ Calvin Johnson 75.00 150.00
DJ Dwayne Jarrett 15.00 40.00
JM Joe Montana 75.00 150.00
ML Matt Leinart 12.00 30.00
RB Reggie Bush 12.00 30.00
TB Tim Brown 20.00 50.00
TG Ted Ginn Jr. 15.00 40.00
VY Vince Young 12.00 30.00

2007 Topps Draft Picks and Prospects All-Star Alumni Autographs Dual

DUAL AUTO/25 ODDS 1:19,000
BJ R.Bush/D.Jarrett 100.00 200.00
BM T.Brown/J.Montana 125.00 250.00
LB M.Leinart/R.Bush 100.00 200.00
QM B.Quinn/J.Montana 150.00 300.00
SG T.Smith/T.Ginn Jr. 50.00 120.00
SP B.Sims/A.Peterson 200.00 400.00

2007 Topps Draft Picks and Prospects Class Marks Autographs

GROUP A ODDS 1:3470
GROUP B ODDS 1:1440
GROUP C ODDS 1:1985
GROUP D ODDS 1:520
GROUP E ODDS 1:164
GROUP F ODDS 1:155
UNPRICED HOLOFOIL/10 ODDS 1:5690
AA Aundrae Allison E 4.00 10.00
AO Amobi Okoye B 6.00 15.00
AP1 Adrian Peterson A 75.00 150.00
AP2 Antonio Pittman B 5.00 12.00
BL Brian Leonard E 4.00 10.00
BQ Brady Quinn A 6.00 15.00
CLE Chris Leak D 4.00 10.00
CS Chansi Stuckey E 5.00 12.00
DB Dwayne Bowe B 5.00 12.00
DC David Clowney D 4.00 10.00
DJ Dwayne Jarrett A 8.00 20.00
DS Drew Stanton B 5.00 12.00
DW Darius Walker E 4.00 10.00
GA Gaines Adams E 5.00 12.00
GO Greg Olsen B 8.00 20.00
GW Garrett Wolfe F 4.00 10.00
JH Jason Hill F 4.00 10.00
JP Jordan Palmer C 5.00 12.00
JR JaMarcus Russell A 6.00 15.00
JZ Jared Zabransky C 4.00 10.00
KD Kenneth Darby E 4.00 10.00
KI Kenny Irons B 5.00 12.00
KK Kevin Kolb B 6.00 15.00
LH Leon Hall B 5.00 12.00
LL Laron Landry D 6.00 15.00
LT Lawrence Timmons D 6.00 15.00
LW LaMarr Woodley C 8.00 20.00
MB Michael Bush B 5.00 12.00
ML Marshawn Lynch A 15.00 40.00
PP Paul Posluszny D 4.00 10.00
PW Paul Williams F 4.00 10.00
RM Rhema McKnight F 4.00 10.00
RME Robert Meachem B 6.00 15.00
SB Steve Breaston F 4.00 10.00
SR Sidney Rice B 6.00 15.00
SS Steve Smith USC E 4.00 10.00
TG Ted Ginn Jr. A 8.00 20.00
TH Tony Hunt E 4.00 10.00
TP Tyler Palko F 6.00 15.00
TS Troy Smith A 12.00 30.00

2007 Topps Draft Picks and Prospects Class Marks Autographs Gold

*GOLD/25: .75X TO 1.5X BASE AU GRP A
*GOLD/25: .8X TO 2X BASE AU GRP B
*GOLD/25: 1X TO 2.5X BASE AU GRP C-F
GOLD/25 ODDS 1:2300
AP1 Adrian Peterson 125.00 250.00
BQ Brady Quinn 10.00 25.00

2007 Topps Draft Picks and Prospects Class Marks Autographs Silver

*SILVER/75: .4X TO 1X BASE AU GRP A
*SILVER/75: .5X TO 1.2X BASE AU GRP B
*SILVER/75: .6X TO 1.5X BASE AU GRP C-F
SILVER/75 ODDS 1:810
AP1 Adrian Peterson 75.00 150.00

2007 Topps Draft Picks and Prospects Class of 2006 Unsigned

HR.BLACK: .5X TO 1.2X BASIC INSERTS
*CHR.BLACK REF: .8X TO 2X BASIC INSERTS
*CHR.BRONZE: .6X TO 1.5X BASIC INSERTS
*CHR.BRONZE REF/250: 1.2X TO 3X
*CHR.GOLD/99: 2X TO 5X BASIC INSERTS
*CHR.GOLD REF/25: 4X TO 10X BASIC INSERTS
*CHR.SILVER/299: 1X TO 2.5X BASIC INSERTS
*CHR.SILVER REF/125: 1.5X TO 4X
166 Matt Leinart 1.00 2.50
167 Reggie Bush 1.00 2.50
170 Vince Young 1.00 2.50
172 Joseph Addai 1.00 2.50
173 Jay Cutler 1.00 2.50

2007 Topps Draft Picks and Prospects Rookie Autographs

AUTO/100 STATED ODDS 1:610
101 Brady Quinn 8.00 20.00
102 Michael Bush 8.00 20.00
103 Leon Hall 8.00 20.00
104 Jason Hill 8.00 20.00
106 Brian Leonard 8.00 20.00
107 Gaines Adams 10.00 25.00
108 Kenneth Darby 8.00 20.00
110 Paul Posluszny 8.00 20.00
111 Drew Stanton 8.00 20.00
112 Troy Smith 8.00 20.00
116 Paul Williams 8.00 20.00
118 Aundrae Allison 8.00 20.00
119 Kenny Irons 8.00 20.00
120 Kevin Kolb 10.00 25.00
122 Steve Smith USC 8.00 20.00
123 Steve Breaston 8.00 20.00
127 Rhema McKnight 8.00 20.00
130 Chansi Stuckey 10.00 25.00
132 Calvin Johnson 75.00 150.00
133 Marshawn Lynch 15.00 40.00
134 Ted Ginn Jr. 10.00 25.00
135 Adrian Peterson 100.00 200.00
136 Dwayne Jarrett 10.00 25.00
142 JaMarcus Russell 8.00 20.00
147 Courtney Lewis 10.00 25.00

2007 Topps Draft Picks and Prospects Senior Standout Jersey

ATED ODDS 1:23
*GOLD/25: 1X TO 2.5X BASIC JSYs
UNPRICED HOLOFOIL SER.#'d TO 10
*PRIME/99: .6X TO 1.5X BASIC JSYs
*SILVER/75: .6X TO 1.5X BASIC JSYs
AA Aundrae Allison 3.00 8.00
AC Adam Carriker 3.00 8.00
AO Amobi Okoye 4.00 10.00
AR Aaron Ross 3.00 8.00
AS Anthony Spencer 4.00 10.00
BD Buster Davis 4.00 10.00
BL Brian Leonard 3.00 8.00
BM Brandon Myles 4.00 10.00
BME Brandon Meriweather 4.00 10.00
BP Ben Patrick 4.00 10.00
CD Chris Davis 3.00 8.00
CL Chris Leak 5.00 12.00
CS Chansi Stuckey 4.00 10.00
CT Courtney Taylor 3.00 8.00
DB Dallas Baker 3.00 8.00
DBO Dwayne Bowe 3.00 8.00
DC David Clowney 3.00 8.00
DH David Harris 3.00 8.00
DI David Irons 3.00 8.00
DS Drew Stanton 3.00 8.00
DT DeMarcus Tank Tyler 3.00 8.00
EE Earl Everett 3.00 8.00
EW Eric Weddle 4.00 10.00
HB H.B. Blades 3.00 8.00
JG Josh Gattis 3.00 8.00
JH Johnnie Lee Higgins 3.00 8.00
JHL Jason Hill 3.00 8.00
JN Joe Newton 3.00 8.00
JP Jordan Palmer 4.00 10.00
JW Josh Wilson 4.00 10.00
JWI Jonathan Wade 3.00 8.00
KD Kenneth Darby 3.00 8.00
KI Kenny Irons 3.00 8.00
KK Kevin Kolb 4.00 10.00
KS Kolby Smith 3.00 8.00
LB Levi Brown 3.00 8.00
LB Lorenzo Booker 4.00 10.00
LH Leon Hall 3.00 8.00
LM Le'Ron McClain 5.00 12.00
MG Michael Griffin 3.00 8.00
MM Marcus McCauley 3.00 8.00
MM Martrez Milner 3.00 8.00
PB Prescott Burgess 3.00 8.00
PP Paul Posluszny 3.00 8.00
PW Patrick Willis 5.00 12.00
PWI Paul Williams 3.00 8.00
QM Quentin Moses 3.00 8.00
QP Quinn Pitcock 4.00 10.00
RK Ryan Kalil 3.00 8.00
RM Rhema McKnight 3.00 8.00
RMC Ray McDonald 4.00 10.00
SC Scott Chandler 5.00 12.00
TC Tim Crowder 4.00 10.00
TCL Thomas Clayton 4.00 10.00
TH Tony Hunt 3.00 8.00
TJ Tanard Jackson 3.00 8.00
TP Tyler Palko 5.00 12.00
TT Tony Taylor 4.00 10.00
VA Victor Abiamiri 3.00 8.00

2007 Topps Draft Picks and Prospects Senior Standout Jersey Combos

STATED PRINT RUN 199 SER.#'d SETS
*PRIME/49: 1X TO 2.5X BASIC JSYs
*SILVER/35: .8X TO 2X BASIC JSYs
UNPRICED GOLD SERIAL #'d TO 10
UNPRICED HOLOFOIL SERIAL #'d TO 5
AH A.Allison/J.Hill 3.00 8.00
BB D.Baker/D.Bowe 3.00 8.00
BD L.Booker/C.Davis 4.00 10.00
CC A.Carriker/T.Crowder 4.00 10.00
DM K.Darby/L.McClain 5.00 12.00
GW J.Gattis/J.Wilson 4.00 10.00
HB L.Hall/P.Burgess 3.00 8.00
IT K.Irons/C.Taylor 3.00 8.00
IW K.Irons/J.Wade 3.00 8.00
LC B.Leonard/T.Clayton 4.00 10.00
MCM R.McKnight/B.Myles 4.00 10.00
ME R.McDonald/E.Everett 4.00 10.00
MM M.Milner/Q.Moses 3.00 8.00
NC J.Newton/S.Chandler 5.00 12.00
PB T.Palko/H.Blades 5.00 12.00
PH J.Palmer/J.Higgins 4.00 10.00
PHU P.Posluszny/T.Hunt 3.00 8.00
RG A.Ross/M.Griffin 3.00 8.00
SC C.Stuckey/D.Clowney 4.00 10.00
SK D.Stanton/K.Kolb 4.00 10.00
SO K.Smith/A.Okoye 4.00 10.00
TB D.Tyler/L.Brown 3.00 8.00
WM P.Williams/M.McCuley 3.00 8.00
WME P.Willis/B.Meriweather 5.00 12.00

2007 Topps Draft Picks and Prospects Senior Standout Jersey Autographs Silver

LVER/75 STATED ODDS 1:912
*GOLD/25: .5X TO 1.2X SILVER AUTO/75
UNPRICED HOLOFOIL/10 ODDS 1:9200
AA Aundrae Allison 10.00 25.00
AO Amobi Okoye 12.00 30.00
BL Brian Leonard 10.00 25.00
CL Chris Leak 10.00 25.00
CS Chansi Stuckey 12.00 30.00
CT Courtney Taylor 10.00 25.00
DB Dallas Baker 10.00 25.00
DC David Clowney 10.00 25.00
DS Drew Stanton 10.00 25.00
JH Jason Hill 10.00 25.00
JH Johnnie Lee Higgins 10.00 25.00
JP Jordan Palmer 12.00 30.00
KD Kenneth Darby 10.00 25.00
KI Kenny Irons 10.00 25.00
KK Kevin Kolb 12.00 30.00
KS Kolby Smith 10.00 25.00
LB Lorenzo Booker 12.00 30.00
LH Leon Hall 10.00 25.00
PP Paul Posluszny 10.00 25.00
PW Paul Williams 10.00 25.00
RM Rhema McKnight 10.00 25.00
TC Thomas Clayton 12.00 30.00
TH Tony Hunt 10.00 25.00
TP Tyler Palko 15.00 40.00

2007 Topps Draft Picks And Prospects Upperclassmen Jersey

GROUP A ODDS 1:220
GROUP B ODDS 1:330
GROUP C ODDS 1:288
*SILVER/50: .6X TO 1.5X BASIC JSYs
AJ Andre Johnson A 4.00 10.00
BW Brian Westbrook A 3.00 8.00
CJ Chad Johnson C 3.00 8.00
CT Chester Taylor A 3.00 8.00
CW Cadillac Williams A 4.00 10.00
DB Drew Brees A 5.00 12.00
DW DeAngelo Williams B 3.00 8.00
FG Frank Gore A 4.00 10.00
JS Jeremy Shockey B 3.00 8.00
LJ Larry Johnson C 3.00 8.00
LM Laurence Maroney A 4.00 10.00
MV Michael Vick B 4.00 10.00
RJ Rudi Johnson B 3.00 8.00
SJ Steven Jackson C 3.00 8.00
TB Tom Brady C 15.00 40.00

2007 Topps Exclusive Rookies

MP.FACTORY SET (31) 15.00 25.00
COMPLETE SET (30) 6.00 12.00
1 JaMarcus Russell .30 .75
2 Calvin Johnson 1.00 2.50
3 Adrian Peterson 1.00 2.50
4 Ted Ginn .40 1.00
5 Marshawn Lynch .60 1.50
6 Brady Quinn .30 .75
7 Dwayne Bowe .30 .75
8 Robert Meachem .40 1.00
9 Greg Olsen .50 1.25
10 Brandon Jackson .30 .75
11 Anthony Gonzalez .30 .75
12 Kevin Kolb .40 1.00
13 John Beck .30 .75
14 Drew Stanton .30 .75
15 Sidney Rice .40 1.00
16 Dwayne Jarrett .40 1.00
17 Chris Henry .30 .75
18 Steve Smith .30 .75
19 Brian Leonard .30 .75
20 Lorenzo Booker .40 1.00
21 Jason Hill .30 .75
22 Paul Williams .30 .75
23 Tony Hunt .30 .75
24 Trent Edwards .30 .75
25 Johnnie Lee Higgins .30 .75
26 Joe Thomas .50 1.25
27 Gaines Adams .40 1.00
28 Patrick Willis .50 1.25
29 Troy Smith .30 .75
30 Michael Bush .30 .75

2007 Topps Exclusive Rookies Jerseys

ONE PER FACTORY SET
1 JaMarcus Russell 1.25 3.00
2 Calvin Johnson 4.00 10.00
3 Adrian Peterson 4.00 10.00
4 Ted Ginn 1.50 4.00
5 Marshawn Lynch 2.50 6.00
6 Brady Quinn 1.25 3.00
7 Dwayne Bowe 1.25 3.00
8 Robert Meachem 1.50 4.00
9 Greg Olsen 2.00 5.00
10 Brandon Jackson 1.25 3.00
11 Anthony Gonzalez 1.25 3.00
12 Kevin Kolb 1.50 4.00
13 John Beck 1.25 3.00
14 Drew Stanton 1.25 3.00
15 Sidney Rice 1.50 4.00
16 Dwayne Jarrett 1.50 4.00
17 Chris Henry 1.25 3.00
18 Steve Smith 1.25 3.00
19 Brian Leonard 1.25 3.00
20 Lorenzo Booker 1.50 4.00
21 Jason Hill 1.25 3.00
22 Paul Williams 1.25 3.00
23 Tony Hunt 1.25 3.00
24 Trent Edwards 1.25 3.00
25 Johnnie Lee Higgins 2.00 5.00
26 Joe Thomas 2.00 5.00
27 Gaines Adams 1.50 4.00
28 Patrick Willis 2.00 5.00
29 Troy Smith 1.25 3.00
30 Michael Bush 1.25 3.00

2004 Topps Fan Favorites

Topps Fan Favorites was initially released in early March 2005 making it Toppsâ€™ final football product of the 2004 NFL season. The base set consists entirely of retired players grouped thematically in famous offensive and defensive units of the past. Hobby boxes contained 24-packs of 6-cards and carried an S.R.P. of $5 per pack. Two parallel sets can be found seeded in packs as well as one of the more popular Autograph insert sets of the season.

COMPLETE SET (85) 20.00 50.00
1 Alan Page .40 1.00
2 Abdul Salaam .40 1.00
3 Bob Baumhower .40 1.00
4 Bob Brudzinski .40 1.00
5 Billy Johnson .40 1.00
6 Cliff Branch .40 1.00
7 Carl Banks .40 1.00
8 Charles Bowser .40 1.00
9 Clint Didier .40 1.00
10 Carl Eller .40 1.00
11 Charlie Joiner .40 1.00
12 Dick Anderson .40 1.00
13 Doug Betters .40 1.00
14 Dave Casper .40 1.00
15 Dwight Clark .50 1.25
16 Dan Fouts .50 1.25
17 Dave Foley .40 1.00
18 Donnie Green .40 1.00
19 Deacon Jones .50 1.25
20 Don Maynard .50 1.25
21 Dan Pastorini .40 1.00
22 Drew Pearson .50 1.25
23 Dwight White .40 1.00
24 Emerson Boozer .40 1.00
25 Earl Campbell .60 1.50
26 Ernie Holmes .50 1.25
27 Fred Biletnikoff .60 1.50
28 Glenn Blackwood .40 1.00
29 Gary Larsen .40 1.00
30 Greg Lloyd .50 1.25
31 George Martin .40 1.00
32 Gene Upshaw .40 1.00
33 Harry Carson .40 1.00
34 Harold Jackson .40 1.00
35 Hugh McElhenny .40 1.00
36 Jeff Bostic .40 1.00
37 Jim Burt .40 1.00
38 Joe Greene .60 1.50
39 John Hannah .40 1.00
40 John Henry Johnson .40 1.00
41 Joe Jacoby .40 1.00
42 Jim Kiick .40 1.00
43 Joe Klecko .40 1.00
44 Joe Delamielleure .40 1.00
45 Joe Montana 2.00 5.00
46 Jim Marshall .40 1.00
47 Joe Namath 1.00 2.50
48 Jake Scott .40 1.00
49 John Taylor .40 1.00
50 Kim Bokamper .40 1.00
51 Kevin Greene .60 1.50
52 Karl Mecklenburg .40 1.00
53 Ken Stabler .75 2.00
54 Kellen Winslow .60 1.50
55 Lyle Blackwood .40 1.00
56 Larry Csonka .60 1.50
57 L.C. Greenwood .40 1.00
58 Lamar Lundy .40 1.00
59 Leonard Marshall .40 1.00
60 Lawrence Taylor .60 1.50
61 Mark Clayton .40 1.00
62 Mark Duper .40 1.00
63 Manny Fernandez .40 1.00
64 Mark Gastineau .40 1.00
65 Marty Lyons .40 1.00
66 Mark May .40 1.00
67 Mike Montler .40 1.00
68 Merlin Olsen .40 1.00
69 Matt Snell .40 1.00
70 Ozzie Newsome .50 1.25
71 Otis Sistrunk .40 1.00
72 Phil Villapiano UER .40 1.00
73 Roger Craig .60 1.50
74 Richard Dent .40 1.00
75 Randy Gradishar .40 1.00
76 Russ Grimm .40 1.00
77 Reggie McKenzie .40 1.00
78 Roosevelt Grier .40 1.00
79 Roger Staubach .75 2.00
80 Steve Grogan .40 1.00
81 Stanley Morgan .40 1.00
82 Tony Dorsett .60 1.50
83 Ted Hendricks .40 1.00
84 Tony Hill .40 1.00
85 Y.A. Tittle .60 1.50

2004 Topps Fan Favorites Chrome

*CHROME/499: 3X TO 8X BASIC CARDS
STATED ODDS 1:14 H/R
STATED PRINT RUN 499 SER.#'d SETS

2004 Topps Fan Favorites Chrome Refractors

HR.REF/99: 5X TO 12X BASIC CARDS
STATED ODDS 1:74 HOB, 1:123 RET
STATED PRINT RUN 99 SER.#'d SETS

2004 Topps Fan Favorites Autographs

OUP A ODDS 1:5362 H, 1:6144 R
GROUP B ODDS 1:2289 H, 1:2458 R
GROUP C ODDS 1:1014 H, 1:1024 R
GROUP D ODDS 1:3754 H, 1:4096 R
GROUP E ODDS 1:3412 H, 1:3520 R
GROUP F ODDS 1:140 H, 1:141 R
GROUP G ODDS 1:2208 H, 1:2261 R
GROUP H ODDS 1:22 H, 1:193 R
GROUP I ODDS 1:168 H/R
GROUP J ODDS 1:1188 H, 1:1229 R
GROUP K ODDS 1:1031 H, 1:1039 R
GROUP L ODDS 1:500 H, 1:503 R
GROUP M ODDS 1:67 H, 1:66 R
ANNOUNCED PRINT RUNS BELOW
UNPRICED NOTATIONS PRINT RUN 10 SETS
AP Alan Page K 12.00 30.00
AS Abdul Salaam M 8.00 20.00
BB Bob Baumhower H 12.00 30.00
BBR Bob Brudzinski H 15.00 40.00
BJ Billy Johnson M 8.00 20.00
CB Cliff Branch H 8.00 20.00
CBA Carl Banks F 12.00 30.00
CBO Charles Bowser H 6.00 15.00
CBR Charlie Brown H 8.00 20.00
CD Clint Didier F 8.00 20.00
CE Carl Eller L 12.00 30.00
CJ Charlie Joiner M 8.00 20.00
DA Dick Anderson F 8.00 20.00
DB Doug Betters H 8.00 20.00
DC Dave Casper/90* C 30.00 60.00
DCL Dwight Clark F 12.00 30.00
DF Dan Fouts/190* E 20.00 50.00
DFO Dave Foley F 8.00 20.00
DG Donnie Green H 8.00 20.00
DH Dan Hampton I 8.00 20.00
DJ Deacon Jones/90* C 40.00 80.00
DM Don Maynard/170* D 15.00 40.00
DP Dan Pastorini H 8.00 20.00
DPE Drew Pearson M 12.00 30.00
DW Dwight White H 40.00 80.00
EB Emerson Boozer H 15.00 40.00
EC Earl Campbell/90* C 50.00 100.00
EH Ernie Holmes H 40.00 80.00
FB Fred Biletnikoff/70* B 40.00 100.00
GB Glenn Blackwood H 8.00 20.00
GF Gary Fencik M 8.00 20.00
GL Gary Larsen M 8.00 20.00
GLL Greg Lloyd F 25.00 50.00
GM George Martin H 8.00 20.00
GU Gene Upshaw F 30.00 50.00
HC Harry Carson F 15.00 40.00
HJ Harold Jackson M 8.00 20.00
HM Hugh McElhenny H 8.00 20.00
JB Jeff Bostic H 8.00 20.00
JBU Jim Burt H 12.00 30.00
JG Joe Greene/70* B 100.00 200.00
JH John Hannah I 8.00 20.00
JHJ John Henry Johnson H 15.00 40.00
JJ Joe Jacoby H 8.00 20.00
JKI Jim Kiick G 20.00 50.00
JKL Joe Klecko L 12.00 30.00
JL Joe Delamielleure H 8.00 20.00
JM Joe Montana/90* C 75.00 150.00
JMA Jim Marshall M 12.00 30.00
JN Joe Namath/40* A 100.00 200.00
JS Jake Scott/90* C 75.00 150.00
JT John Taylor F 10.00 25.00
KB Kim Bokamper H 8.00 20.00
KG Kevin Greene F 25.00 60.00
KM Karl Mecklenburg H 12.00 30.00
KS Ken Stabler F 25.00 50.00
KW Kellen Winslow F 12.00 30.00
LB Lyle Blackwood H 8.00 20.00
LC Larry Csonka/90* C 40.00 80.00
LCG L.C. Greenwood H 20.00 50.00
LL Lamar Lundy I 15.00 40.00
LM Leonard Marshall I 8.00 20.00
LT Lawrence Taylor/90* C 40.00 80.00
MC Mark Clayton I 10.00 25.00
MD Mark Duper I 12.00 30.00
MF Manny Fernandez F 15.00 40.00

MG Mark Gastineau H 15.00 40.00
MJ Mark Jackson M 8.00 20.00
ML Marty Lyons M 8.00 20.00
MM Mark May F 20.00 40.00
MMO Mike Montler F 12.00 30.00
MO Merlin Olsen I 15.00 40.00
MS Matt Snell H 8.00 20.00
ON Ozzie Newsome/90* C 25.00 60.00
OS Otis Sistrunk H 8.00 20.00
PV Phil Villapiano H 8.00 20.00
RC Roger Craig F 12.00 30.00
RD Richard Dent I 8.00 20.00
RG Randy Gradishar F 8.00 20.00
RGR Russ Grimm I 20.00 40.00
RM Reggie McKenzie F 8.00 20.00
RN Ricky Nattiel M 8.00 20.00
ROG Roosevelt Grier H 12.00 30.00
RS Roger Staubach/40* A 90.00 150.00
SG Steve Grogan J 8.00 20.00
SM Stanley Morgan M 8.00 20.00
TD Tony Dorsett/40* A 50.00 120.00
TH Ted Hendricks F 10.00 25.00
THI Tony Hill H 8.00 20.00
VJ Vance Johnson M 8.00 20.00
WP William Perry M 8.00 20.00
YAT Y.A. Tittle/70* B 40.00 80.00

2004 Topps Fan Favorites Buy Back Autographs

Y. A. TITTLE
QUARTERBACK SAN FRANCISCO 49ERS

STATED ODDS 1:4692 H, 1:4200 R
NOT PRICED DUE TO SCARCITY
FB Fred Biletnikoff 71T
JG Joe Greene 81T
DM1 Don Maynard 64T
DM3 Don Maynard 67T
DM2 Don Maynard 66T
DM4 Don Maynard 68T
HM1 Hugh McElhenny 58T
HM2 Hugh McElhenny 60T
HM3 Hugh McElhenny 62T
KS1 Ken Stabler 75T
KS2 Ken Stabler HL 75T
KS3 Ken Stabler 76T
YT1 Y.A.Tittle 59T
YT2 Y.A.Tittle 60T

2004 Topps Fan Favorites Co-Signers

STATED ODDS 1:2288 H, 1:2148 R
ANNOUNCED PRINT RUN 50 SETS
CODC M.Duper/M.Clayton 50.00 100.00
COFW Fouts/K.Winslow 60.00 120.00
COKG J.Klecko/M.Gastineau 50.00 100.00
CONM J.Namath/D.Maynard 125.00 200.00
COPE A.Page/C.Eller 50.00 100.00
COSD Staubach/Dorsett 125.00 200.00

2004 Topps Fan Favorites Jumbos

COMPLETE SET (10) 40.00 80.00
ONE PER BOX
1 Joiner/Fouts/Winslow 3.00 8.00
2 Prsn/Stabch/Drstt/Hll 6.00 15.00
3 Jones/Lundy/Olsen/Grier 2.50 6.00
4 M.Clayton/M.Duper 2.00 5.00
5 McElh/Johnson/Tittle 3.00 8.00
6 Salm/Klcko/Gast/Lyns 2.00 5.00
7 Page/Eller/Lrsn/Marshall 2.00 5.00
8 Brnch/Cspr/Bilet/Stbler 5.00 12.00
9 Mayn/Bzer/Nmth/Snell 6.00 15.00
10 Whte/Hlms/Grne/Grnwd 3.00 8.00

2015 Topps Field Access

*BLUE: .5X TO 1.2X BASIC CARDS
*GOLD/99: .6X TO 1.5X BASIC CARDS
*GREEN/50: .8X TO 2X BASIC CARDS
*PURPLE/25: 1.2X TO 3X BASIC CARDS
1 Tom Brady 1.50 4.00
2 Jadeveon Clowney .40 1.00
3 Connor Shaw .40 1.00
4 Terrance West .40 1.00
5 Rob Gronkowski .60 1.50
6 Richard Rodgers .50 1.25
7 Storm Johnson .40 1.00
8 Malcolm Brown RC .40 1.00
9 Eli Harold RC .30 .75
10 Sammy Watkins .50 1.25
11 Jared Abbrederis .40 1.00
12 Bishop Sankey .40 1.00
13 C.J. Mosley .60 1.50
14 Jordan Reed .40 1.00
15 Allen Hurns .40 1.00
16 Kirk Cousins .60 1.50
17 Riley Cooper .50 1.25
18 Zach Mettenberger .40 1.00
19 Aaron Murray .40 1.00
20 Mike Evans .50 1.25
21 Tavon Austin .40 1.00
22 Andre Williams .40 1.00
23 Levi Norwood RC .30 .75
24 Charles Clay .40 1.00
25 Eric Berry .50 1.25
26 Charles Sims .40 1.00
27 Ka'Deem Carey .40 1.00
28 Connor Shaw .40 1.00
29 Rueben Randle .40 1.00
30 Allen Robinson .50 1.25
31 Christion Jones RC .30 .75
32 Kaelin Clay RC .30 .75
33 Xavier Cooper RC .30 .75
34 Trey Flowers RC .50 1.25
35 Marcus Peters RC .50 1.25
36 J.J. Nelson RC .30 .75
37 Eddie Goldman RC .30 .75
38 Austin Hill RC .30 .75
39 Mike Davis RC .30 .75
40 Ifo Ekpre-Olomu RC .30 .75
41 Chris Harper RC .40 1.00
42 Henry Anderson RC .40 1.00
43 Deontay Greenberry RC .30 .75
44 Dres Anderson RC .30 .75
45 Bishop Sankey .40 1.00
46 Silas Redd .40 1.00
47 Eric Ebron .40 1.00
48 Eric Ebron .40 1.00
49 Rueben Randle .40 1.00
50 Eli Manning .50 1.25
51 Titus Davis .50 1.25
52 Devin Smith RC .30 .75
53 Jordan Matthews .50 1.25
54 Jordan Matthews .50 1.25
55 Nelson Agholor RC .40 1.00
56 Nelson Agholor RC .40 1.00
57 Dezmin Lewis RC .30 .75
58 Ben Koyack RC .50 1.25
59 Allen Robinson .50 1.25
60 Jeremy Hill .40 1.00
61 Blake Bortles .40 1.00
62 Tom Savage .40 1.00
63 Austin Seferian-Jenkins .40 1.00
64 Nate Orchard RC .30 .75
65 Jadeveon Clowney .40 1.00
66 Brandin Cooks .50 1.25
67 Michael Campanaro .40 1.00
68 Dominique Brown .40 1.00
69 Allen Robinson .50 1.25
70 Ameer Abdullah RC .50 1.25
71 Andrus Peat RC .30 .75
72 Dennis Pitta .40 1.00
73 Vic Beasley .50 1.25
74 Jason Verrett .40 1.00
75 C.J. Anderson .50 1.25
76 Eric Ebron .40 1.00
77 Danny Shelton RC .30 .75
78 T.J. Clemmings RC .30 .75
79 Kenny Bell RC .50 1.25
80 Eli Manning .50 1.25
81 Roddy White .40 1.00
82 Jimmy Clausen .40 1.00
83 Tyler Kroft .50 1.25
84 Austin Seferian-Jenkins .40 1.00
85 Kevin White RC .40 1.00
86 Damontre Moore .40 1.00
87 Ha Ha Clinton-Dix .40 1.00
88 Kelvin Benjamin .50 1.25
89 Rashad Jennings .40 1.00
90 Marcus Mariota RC 1.25 3.00
91 Travis Kelce .60 1.50
92 Devin Gardner RC .50 1.25
93 Gerald Christian RC .40 1.00
94 Mario Alford .40 1.00
95 Richard Rodgers .50 1.25
96 James White .50 1.25
97 Robert Mathis .40 1.00
98 Alex Carter RC .30 .75
99 Donte Moncrief RC .40 1.00
100 Jameis Winston RC .75 2.00
101 Martavis Bryant .40 1.00
102 Melvin Gordon RC .75 2.00
103 Brandon Scherff RC .50 1.25
104 Jace Amaro .40 1.00
105 Jeremy Langford RC .30 .75
106 Shane Carden RC .30 .75
107 Kenny Stills .40 1.00
108 Justin Hardy RC .30 .75
109 Nick Foles .50 1.25
110 DeAndre Hopkins .50 1.25
111 Victor Cruz .50 1.25
112 Jaelen Strong RC .40 1.00
113 Nelson Agholor RC .40 1.00
114 Troy Niklas .40 1.00
115 Greg Olsen .50 1.25
116 Cameron Artis-Payne RC .30 .75
117 Isaiah Crowell .40 1.00
118 Kenny Britt .40 1.00
119 Antrel Rolle .40 1.00
120 Todd Gurley RC 1.25 3.00
121 Teddy Bridgewater .50 1.25
122 Josh Harper RC .30 .75
123 Zac Stacy .40 1.00
124 Dorial Green-Beckham RC .30 .75
125 Luke Kuechly .50 1.25
126 Matthew Stafford .50 1.25
127 Alshon Jeffery .50 1.25
128 Brandon Marshall .40 1.00
129 T.J. Yeldon RC .30 .75
130 Johnny Manziel .50 1.25
131 Rashad Greene RC .30 .75
132 Lamar Miller .40 1.00
133 T.Y. Hilton .50 1.25
134 Brett Hundley RC .30 .75
135 Andrew Luck .75 2.00
136 J.J. Watt .60 1.50
137 Reggie Bush .40 1.00
138 Matt Jones RC .30 .75
139 Amari Cooper RC 1.00 2.50
140 Davante Adams .50 1.25
141 Devin Funchess RC .50 1.25
142 Jarvis Landry RC .40 1.00
143 Russell Wilson .75 2.00
144 Clive Walford RC .30 .75
145 Karlos Williams RC .30 .75
146 Duke Johnson RC .50 1.25
147 A.J. Green .60 1.50
148 Tyler Lockett RC .50 1.25
149 David Johnson RC .75 2.00
150 Peyton Manning 1.25 3.00
151 Jay Ajayi RC .50 1.25
152 Aaron Rodgers 1.25 3.00
153 Drew Brees .60 1.50
154 Alex Smith .50 1.25
155 Cam Newton .60 1.50
156 Antonio Brown .60 1.50
157 Calvin Johnson .60 1.50
158 Emmanuel Sanders .50 1.25
159 Eddie Lacy .40 1.00
160 Ka'Deem Carey .40 1.00
161 Matt Ryan .50 1.25
162 Clay Matthews .60 1.50
163 Derek Carr .60 1.50
164 John Elway 1.00 2.50
165 Emmitt Smith 1.00 2.50
166 Dan Marino 1.25 3.00
167 Brett Favre 1.25 3.00
168 Jerry Rice 1.00 2.50
169 Darrelle Revis .40 1.00
170 Aaron Donald .60 1.50
171 Steve Smith .50 1.25
172 Adrian Peterson .60 1.50
173 Arian Foster .50 1.25
174 Tony Romo .50 1.25
175 Barry Sanders 1.00 2.50
176 Chris Ivory .50 1.25
177 Marvin Jones .40 1.00
178 Robert Woods .50 1.25
179 Pierre Thomas .40 1.00
180 Adam Vinatieri .40 1.00
181 Manti Te'o .50 1.25
182 Jimmy Garoppolo .75 2.00
183 Jimmy Garoppolo .75 2.00
184 EJ Manuel .40 1.00
185 Golden Tate .40 1.00
186 Ezekiel Ansah .40 1.00
187 C.J. Spiller .40 1.00
188 EJ Manuel .40 1.00
189 Dion Lewis .40 1.00
190 Eric Fisher .40 1.00
191 Tim Tebow .50 1.25
192 Damian Williams .40 1.00
193 Brian Hoyer .40 1.00
194 Ezekiel Ansah .40 1.00
195 Terrance Williams .40 1.00
196 Tyler Eifert .50 1.25
197 Jonathan Hankins .40 1.00
198 Barkevious Mingo .40 1.00
199 Terrance Williams .40 1.00
200 Odell Beckham Jr. .60 1.50

2015 Topps Field Access Adrenaline Rush

*BLUE/99: .6X TO 1.5X BASIC INSERTS
*GOLD/75: .6X TO 1.5X BASIC INSERTS
*GREEN/50: .8X TO 2X BASIC INSERTS
*PURPLE/25: 1X TO 2.5X BASIC INSERTS
ARAAA Ameer Abdullah .60 1.50
ARAAC Amari Cooper 1.25 3.00
ARAAL Andrew Luck 1.00 2.50
ARAAM Alfred Morris .50 1.25
ARAAP Adrian Peterson .75 2.00
ARACM Clay Matthews .75 2.00
ARADC Dwight Clark .60 1.50
ARADF Devin Funchess .60 1.50
ARADH DeAndre Hopkins .60 1.50
ARAEB Eric Berry .60 1.50
ARAEL Eddie Lacy .50 1.25
ARAEM Eli Manning .60 1.50
ARAES Emmanuel Sanders .60 1.50
ARAFH Franco Harris 1.00 2.50
ARAGO Greg Olsen .60 1.50
ARAJC Jadeveon Clowney .50 1.25
ARAJH Jeremy Hill .50 1.25
ARAJR Jerry Rice 1.50 4.00
ARAJW Jameis Winston 1.00 2.50
ARALD Len Dawson 1.00 2.50
ARALT LaDainian Tomlinson .75 2.00
ARAME Mike Evans .60 1.50
ARAMG Melvin Gordon 1.00 2.50
ARAMI Mark Ingram .60 1.50
ARAMM Marcus Mariota 1.50 4.00
ARAMR Matt Ryan .60 1.50
ARAMS Mike Singletary 1.00 2.50
ARANA Nelson Agholor .50 1.25
ARAPM Peyton Manning 1.50 4.00
ARAPS Phil Simms .75 2.00
ARARC Randall Cobb .60 1.50
ARARL Ronnie Lott .75 2.00
ARARW Roddy White .50 1.25
ARASW Sammy Watkins .60 1.50
ARATB Tim Brown 1.00 2.50
ARATD Tony Dorsett 1.00 2.50
ARATG Todd Gurley 1.50 4.00
ARATH T.Y. Hilton .60 1.50
ARATK Travis Kelce .75 2.00
ARATY T.J. Yeldon .40 1.00
ARAVC Victor Cruz .60 1.50
ARABSA Barry Sanders 1.50 4.00
ARAJCH Jamaal Charles .60 1.50
ARAJRI John Riggins .75 2.00
ARAKWA Kurt Warner .75 2.00
ARALTA Lawrence Taylor 1.00 2.50
ARAMST Matthew Stafford .60 1.50
ARARSH Richard Sherman .75 2.00
ARATBR Tom Brady 2.00 5.00
ARATBRA Terry Bradshaw 1.25 3.00

2015 Topps Field Access All Access

*BLUE/99: .6X TO 1.5X BASIC INSERTS
*GOLD/75: .6X TO 1.5X BASIC INSERTS
*GREEN/50: .8X TO 2X BASIC INSERTS
*PURPLE/25: 1X TO 2.5X BASIC INSERTS
AAAAC Amari Cooper 1.25 3.00
AAAAG A.J. Green .75 2.00
AAAAM Alfred Morris .50 1.25
AAAAP Adrian Peterson .75 2.00
AAABF Brett Favre 2.00 5.00
AAABM Brandon Marshall .50 1.25
AAABS Barry Sanders 1.50 4.00
AAADM Dan Marino 2.00 5.00
AAADS Devin Smith .40 1.00
AAAED Eric Dickerson .75 2.00
AAAEL Eddie Lacy .50 1.25
AAAEM Eli Manning .60 1.50
AAAES Emmitt Smith 1.50 4.00
AAAET Earl Thomas .75 2.00
AAAGO Greg Olsen .60 1.50
AAAGS Gale Sayers 1.00 2.50
AAAHL Howie Long 1.00 2.50
AAAHW Hines Ward .75 2.00
AAAJC Jadeveon Clowney .50 1.25
AAAJE John Elway 1.50 4.00
AAAJM Jordan Matthews .60 1.50
AAAJR Jerry Rice 1.50 4.00
AAAKW Kevin White .50 1.25
AAALT LaDainian Tomlinson .75 2.00
AAAMG Melvin Gordon 1.00 2.50
AAAMM Marcus Mariota 1.50 4.00
AAAMR Matt Ryan .60 1.50
AAAMS Matthew Stafford .60 1.50
AAANA Nelson Agholor .50 1.25
AAAPM Peyton Manning 1.50 4.00
AAARC Randall Cobb .60 1.50
AAARG Rob Gronkowski .75 2.00
AAARL Ronnie Lott .75 2.00
AAASW Sammy Watkins .60 1.50
AAASY Steve Young 1.25 3.00
AAATB Tim Brown 1.00 2.50
AAATD Tony Dorsett 1.00 2.50
AAATG Todd Gurley 1.50 4.00
AAATK Travis Kelce .75 2.00
AAATY T.J. Yeldon .40 1.00
AAAVC Victor Cruz .60 1.50
AAABRA Tom Brady 2.00 5.00
AAADMU Demarco Murray .60 1.50
AAADSA Deion Sanders .75 2.00
AAAESA Emmanuel Sanders .60 1.50
AAAJBR John Brown .60 1.50
AAALTA Lawrence Taylor 1.00 2.50
AAARSH Richard Sherman .75 2.00
AAATBR Terry Bradshaw 1.25 3.00
AAATBRI Teddy Bridgewater .60 1.50

2015 Topps Field Access Autographs

2 Jadeveon Clowney 2.50 6.00
3 Connor Shaw 2.50 6.00
4 Terrance West 2.50 6.00
6 Richard Rodgers 3.00 8.00
7 Storm Johnson 2.50 6.00
8 Malcolm Brown 3.00 8.00
9 Eli Harold 2.50 6.00
10 Sammy Watkins 3.00 8.00
11 Jared Abbrederis 2.50 6.00
12 Bishop Sankey 2.50 6.00
13 C.J. Mosley 4.00 10.00
14 Jordan Reed 2.50 6.00
15 Allen Hurns 2.50 6.00
16 Kirk Cousins 10.00 25.00
17 Riley Cooper 3.00 8.00
18 Zach Mettenberger 2.50 6.00
19 Aaron Murray 2.50 6.00
20 Mike Evans 3.00 8.00
21 Tavon Austin 2.50 6.00
22 Andre Williams 2.50 6.00
23 Levi Norwood 2.50 6.00
24 Charles Clay 2.50 6.00
25 Eric Berry 6.00 15.00
26 Charles Sims 2.50 6.00
27 Ka'Deem Carey 2.50 6.00
28 Connor Shaw 2.50 6.00
29 Rueben Randle 2.50 6.00
30 Allen Robinson 3.00 8.00
31 Christion Jones 2.50 6.00
32 Kaelin Clay 2.50 6.00
33 Xavier Cooper 2.50 6.00
34 Trey Flowers 4.00 10.00
35 Marcus Peters 4.00 10.00
36 J.J. Nelson 2.50 6.00
37 Eddie Goldman 2.50 6.00
38 Austin Hill 2.50 6.00
39 Mike Davis 2.50 6.00
40 Ifo Ekpre-Olomu 2.50 6.00
41 Chris Harper 3.00 8.00
42 Henry Anderson 3.00 8.00
43 Deontay Greenberry 2.50 6.00
44 Dres Anderson 2.50 6.00
45 Bishop Sankey 2.50 6.00
46 Silas Redd 2.50 6.00
47 Eric Ebron 2.50 6.00
48 Eric Ebron 2.50 6.00
49 Rueben Randle 2.50 6.00
50 Eli Manning 20.00 40.00
51 Titus Davis 3.00 8.00
52 Devin Smith 6.00 15.00
53 Jordan Matthews 3.00 8.00
54 Jordan Matthews 3.00 8.00
55 Nelson Agholor 3.00 8.00
56 Nelson Agholor 3.00 8.00
57 Dezmin Lewis 2.50 6.00
58 Ben Koyack 4.00 10.00
59 Allen Robinson 3.00 8.00
60 Jeremy Hill 2.50 6.00
61 Blake Bortles 10.00 25.00
62 Tom Savage 2.50 6.00
63 Austin Seferian-Jenkins 2.50 6.00
64 Nate Orchard 2.50 6.00
65 Jadeveon Clowney 2.50 6.00
66 Brandin Cooks 3.00 8.00
67 Michael Campanaro 2.50 6.00
68 Dominique Brown 2.50 6.00
69 Allen Robinson 3.00 8.00
70 Ameer Abdullah 4.00 10.00
71 Andrus Peat 2.50 6.00
72 Dennis Pitta 2.50 6.00
73 Vic Beasley 3.00 8.00
74 Jason Verrett 2.50 6.00
75 C.J. Anderson 3.00 8.00
76 Eric Ebron 2.50 6.00
77 Danny Shelton 2.50 6.00
78 T.J. Clemmings 2.50 6.00
79 Kenny Bell 4.00 10.00
80 Eli Manning 20.00 40.00
81 Roddy White 2.50 6.00
82 Jimmy Clausen 2.50 6.00
83 Tyler Kroft 3.00 8.00
84 Austin Seferian-Jenkins 2.50 6.00
85 Kevin White 3.00 8.00
86 Damontre Moore 2.50 6.00
87 Ha Ha Clinton-Dix
88 Kelvin Benjamin 6.00 15.00
89 Rashad Jennings 2.50 6.00
90 Marcus Mariota 25.00 60.00
91 Travis Kelce 4.00 10.00
92 Devin Gardner 4.00 10.00
93 Gerald Christian 3.00 8.00
94 Mario Alford Jr. 2.50 6.00
95 Richard Rodgers 3.00 8.00
96 James White 3.00 8.00
97 Robert Mathis 2.50 6.00
98 Alex Carter 2.50 6.00
99 Donte Moncrief 3.00 8.00
100 Jameis Winston 25.00 60.00
101 Martavis Bryant 6.00 15.00
102 Melvin Gordon 6.00 15.00
103 Brandon Scherff 4.00 10.00
104 Jace Amaro 2.50 6.00
105 Jeremy Langford 2.50 6.00
106 Shane Carden 2.50 6.00
107 Kenny Stills 2.50 6.00
108 Justin Hardy 2.50 6.00
109 Nick Foles 3.00 8.00
110 DeAndre Hopkins
111 Victor Cruz 3.00 8.00
112 Jaelen Strong 3.00 8.00
113 Nelson Agholor 3.00 8.00
114 Troy Niklas 2.50 6.00
115 Greg Olsen 3.00 8.00
116 Cameron Artis-Payne 2.50 6.00
117 Isaiah Crowell 2.50 6.00
118 Kenny Britt 2.50 6.00
119 Antrel Rolle 10.00 25.00
120 Todd Gurley 15.00 40.00
121 Teddy Bridgewater 10.00 25.00
122 Josh Harper 2.50 6.00
123 Zac Stacy 2.50 6.00
124 Dorial Green-Beckham
125 Luke Kuechly 12.00 30.00
126 Matthew Stafford 10.00 25.00
127 Alshon Jeffery 3.00 8.00
128 Brandon Marshall
129 T.J. Yeldon
130 Johnny Manziel
131 Rashad Greene 2.50 6.00
132 Lamar Miller 2.50 6.00
133 T.Y. Hilton 3.00 8.00
134 Brett Hundley
135 Andrew Luck 40.00 80.00
136 J.J. Watt
137 Reggie Bush 2.50 6.00
138 Matt Jones 2.50 6.00
139 Amari Cooper 40.00 80.00
140 Davante Adams 3.00 8.00
141 Devin Funchess 4.00 10.00
142 Jarvis Landry 3.00 8.00
143 Russell Wilson 20.00 50.00
144 Clive Walford 2.50 6.00
145 Karlos Williams
146 Duke Johnson 4.00 10.00
148 Tyler Lockett
149 David Johnson
150 Peyton Manning 90.00 150.00
151 Jay Ajayi 4.00 10.00
152 Aaron Rodgers
153 Drew Brees 40.00 80.00
154 Alex Smith 3.00 8.00
160 Ka'Deem Carey 2.50 6.00
162 Clay Matthews
163 Derek Carr
164 John Elway
165 Emmitt Smith
166 Dan Marino
167 Brett Favre
168 Jerry Rice
169 Darrelle Revis 2.50 6.00
170 Aaron Donald 4.00 10.00
172 Adrian Peterson
173 Arian Foster 3.00 8.00
174 Tony Romo 20.00 40.00
175 Barry Sanders 50.00 100.00
176 Chris Ivory 3.00 8.00
177 Marvin Jones 2.50 6.00
179 Pierre Thomas 2.50 6.00
180 Adam Vinatieri 8.00 20.00
181 Manti Te'o 3.00 8.00
182 Jimmy Garoppolo 30.00 60.00
183 Jimmy Garoppolo 30.00 60.00
184 EJ Manuel 2.50 6.00
185 Golden Tate 2.50 6.00
186 Ezekiel Ansah 2.50 6.00
187 C.J. Spiller 2.50 6.00
188 EJ Manuel 2.50 6.00
189 Dion Lewis 2.50 6.00
190 Eric Fisher 2.50 6.00
192 Damian Williams 2.50 6.00
194 Ezekiel Ansah 2.50 6.00
195 Terrance Williams 2.50 6.00
196 Tyler Eifert 3.00 8.00
197 Jonathan Hankins 2.50 6.00
198 Barkevious Mingo 2.50 6.00
199 Terrance Williams 2.50 6.00

2015 Topps Field Access Autographs Gold

*GOLD/99: .5X TO 1.2X BASIC AU
100 Jameis Winston 40.00 80.00

2015 Topps Field Access Autographs Green

*GREEN/50: .6X TO 1.5X BASIC AU
100 Jameis Winston 50.00 100.00
172 Adrian Peterson 40.00 80.00

2015 Topps Field Access Autographs Purple

*PURPLE/25: .8X TO 2X BASIC AU
175 Barry Sanders 90.00 150.00

2014 Topps Fire

COMPLETE SET (150) 20.00 40.00
1 Emmitt Smith .60 1.50
2 Luke Kuechly .30 .75
3 Mike Wallace .25 .60
4 Julius Thomas .25 .60
5 Rod Woodson .30 .75
6 Colin Kaepernick .30 .75
7 Marshall Faulk .30 .75
8 C.J. Spiller .25 .60
9 Cordarrelle Patterson .25 .60
10 Demaryius Thomas .30 .75
11 DeMarco Murray .30 .75
12 Vincent Jackson .25 .60
13 Vernon Davis .25 .60
14 John Elway .60 1.50
15 Andre Johnson .30 .75
16 Percy Harvin .25 .60
17 EJ Manuel .25 .60
18 Eric Dickerson .30 .75
19 Ronnie Lott .30 .75
20 LeSean McCoy .40 1.00
21 Arian Foster .30 .75
22 Richard Sherman .40 1.00
23 Deion Sanders .30 .75
24 Andrew Luck .50 1.25
25 Andre Ellington .25 .60
26 Cam Newton .40 1.00
27 Rob Gronkowski .40 1.00
28 Jake Locker .30 .75
29 Montee Ball .25 .60
30 Ryan Tannehill .30 .75
31 Pierre Garcon .30 .75
32 Dan Marino .75 2.00
33 Randall Cobb .30 .75
34 Geno Smith .25 .60
35 DeSean Jackson .30 .75
36 Steve Young .50 1.25
37 Michael Floyd .25 .60
38 Troy Aikman .50 1.25
39 Philip Rivers .40 1.00
40 Eli Manning .30 .75
41 Zac Stacy .25 .60
42 Nick Foles .30 .75
43 Barry Sanders .60 1.50
44 T.Y. Hilton .30 .75
45 Ndamukong Suh .30 .75
46 Russell Wilson .60 1.50
47 Ben Roethlisberger .40 1.00
48 Jerome Bettis .40 1.00
49 Michael Crabtree .25 .60
50 Jimmy Graham .40 1.00
51 Larry Fitzgerald .30 .75
52 Eddie Lacy .25 .60
53 Jason Pierre-Paul .25 .60
54 Brett Favre .75 2.00
55 Robert Griffin III .25 .60
56 Patrick Willis .30 .75
57 Giovani Bernard .25 .60
58 Clay Matthews .40 1.00
59 Marshawn Lynch .30 .75
60 Jordan Cameron .25 .60
61 Joe Namath .50 1.25
62 Jordan Reed .25 .60
63 Matthew Stafford .30 .75
64 Matt Forte .25 .60
65 Bo Jackson .50 1.25
66 Brandon Marshall .25 .60
67 Tom Brady 1.00 2.50
68 Frank Gore .30 .75
69 Dez Bryant .40 1.00
70 Alshon Jeffery .30 .75
71 Jason Witten .30 .75
72 Peyton Manning .75 2.00
73 Drew Brees .40 1.00
74 Aaron Rodgers .75 2.00
75 Darrelle Revis .25 .60
76 Troy Polamalu .40 1.00
77 Doug Martin .30 .75
78 Keenan Allen .30 .75
79 Alfred Morris .25 .60
80 Jay Cutler .25 .60
81 Von Miller .30 .75
82 Reggie Bush .25 .60
83 Joe Flacco .30 .75
84 Antonio Brown .40 1.00
85 Earl Thomas .30 .75
86 Jordy Nelson .30 .75
87 Ryan Mathews .30 .75
88 Calvin Johnson .40 1.00
89 Julio Jones .40 1.00
90 Terry Bradshaw .50 1.25
91 Wes Welker .30 .75
92 Tony Romo .30 .75
93 Matt Ryan .30 .75
94 Chris Johnson .25 .60
95 Reggie Wayne .30 .75
96 A.J. Green .40 1.00
97 Victor Cruz .30 .75
98 J.J. Watt .40 1.00
99 Jamaal Charles .30 .75
100 Le'Veon Bell .30 .75
106 Tom Savage RC .30 .75
107 Andre Williams RC .30 .75
108 Logan Thomas RC .30 .75
109 Ha Ha Clinton-Dix RC .40 1.00
110 Martavis Bryant RC .40 1.00
111 Paul Richardson RC .40 1.00
112 Jadeveon Clowney RC .40 1.00
113 Terrance West RC .30 .75
114 Blake Bortles RC .40 1.00
115 Jimmy Garoppolo RC 2.50 6.00
116 Cody Latimer RC .40 1.00
117 Zach Mettenberger RC .30 .75
118 Anthony Barr RC .30 .75
119 Odell Beckham Jr. RC 4.00 10.00
120 Bruce Ellington RC .30 .75
121 Aaron Murray RC .30 .75
122 A.J. McCarron RC .30 .75
123 Kevin Norwood RC .30 .75
124 Sammy Watkins RC .50 1.25
125 Austin Seferian-Jenkins RC .30 .75
126 Marqise Lee RC .40 1.00
127 Donte Moncrief RC .30 .75
128 Teddy Bridgewater RC .50 1.25
129 Allen Hurns RC .40 1.00
130 Jerick McKinnon RC .40 1.00
131 John Brown RC .50 1.25
132 Brandin Cooks RC .50 1.25
133 Jeremy Hill RC .40 1.00
134 Robert Herron RC .30 .75
135 Jordan Matthews RC .50 1.25
136 Charles Sims RC .30 .75
137 Allen Robinson RC .50 1.25
138 Isaiah Crowell RC .40 1.00
139 James White RC .60 1.50
140 Ka'Deem Carey RC .30 .75
141 Silas Redd RC .40 1.00
142 Bishop Sankey RC .30 .75
143 Johnny Manziel RC .50 1.25
144 Troy Niklas RC .30 .75
145 Davante Adams RC .50 1.25
146 Jarvis Landry RC .60 1.50
147 Devonta Freeman RC .50 1.25
148 Kelvin Benjamin RC .50 1.25
149 Eric Ebron RC .40 1.00
150 David Fales RC .30 .75
151 Carlos Hyde RC .40 1.00
152 Tre Mason RC .30 .75
153 Mike Evans RC .75 2.00
154 Derek Carr RC 2.00 5.00
155 Josh Huff RC .40 1.00

2014 Topps Fire Blue

*VETS/299: 1.5X TO 4X BASIC CARDS
*ROOKIES/299: 1X TO 2.5X BASIC CARDS
STATED BLUE ODDS 1:21 HOBBY

2014 Topps Fire Flame

*VETS: 1X TO 2.5X BASIC CARDS
*ROOKIES: .6X TO 1.5X BASIC CARDS

2014 Topps Fire Gold

*VETS/50: 2.5X TO 6X BASIC CARDS
*ROOKIES/50: 1.5X TO 4X BASIC CARDS
STATED GOLD ODDS 1:124 HOBBY

2014 Topps Fire Green

*VETS/99: 2.5X TO 6X BASIC CARDS
*ROOKIES/99: 1.5X TO 4X BASIC CARDS
STATED GREEN ODDS 1:63 HOBBY

2014 Topps Fire Onyx

*VETS/25: 5X TO 12X BASIC CARDS
*ROOKIES/25: 4X TO 10X BASIC CARDS
STATED ONYX ODDS 1:247 HOBBY
119 Odell Beckham Jr. 60.00 120.00

2014 Topps Fire Purple

*VETS/499: 1.25X TO 3X BASIC CARDS
*ROOKIES/499: .75X TO 2X BASIC CARDS
STATED PURPLE ODDS 1:13 HOBBY

2014 Topps Fire Wood

*VETS/25: 5X TO 12X BASIC CARDS
*ROOKIES/25: 4X TO 10X BASIC CARDS
STATED WOOD ODDS 1:240 HOBBY
119 Odell Beckham Jr. 90.00 150.00

2014 Topps Fire Autographs

STATED ODDS 1:60
FAAB Anthony Barr 2.00 5.00
FAAH Allen Hurns 2.50 6.00
FAAMU Aaron Murray 2.00 5.00
FAAR Allen Robinson 3.00 8.00
FAAS Austin Seferian-Jenkins
FABB Blake Bortles
FABC Brandin Cooks 3.00 8.00
FABO Branden Oliver 3.00 8.00
FABS Bishop Sankey 2.00 5.00
FACF C.J. Fiedorowicz
FACH Carlos Hyde EXCH 2.50 6.00
FACM Clay Matthews 40.00 80.00
FACS Charles Sims 2.00 5.00
FADA Davante Adams EXCH 8.00 20.00
FADB Drew Brees
FADC Derek Carr 20.00 40.00
FADF David Fales 2.00 5.00
FADFR Devonta Freeman EXCH 8.00 20.00
FADM Donte Moncrief 2.00 5.00
FAEE Eric Ebron
FAEL Eddie Lacy 5.00 12.00
FAHC Ha Ha Clinton-Dix 2.50 6.00
FAIC Isaiah Crowell 2.50 6.00
FAJC Jadeveon Clowney
FAJG Jimmy Garoppolo 10.00 25.00
FAJH Jeremy Hill 2.50 6.00
FAJL Jarvis Landry EXCH 4.00 10.00
FAJM Jordan Matthews 3.00 8.00
FAJN Jordy Nelson
FAJW James White 4.00 10.00
FAKB Kelvin Benjamin
FAKC Ka'Deem Carey 2.00 5.00
FAKN Kevin Norwood 2.00 5.00
FALT Logan Thomas 2.00 5.00
FALTA Lorenzo Taliaferro 2.00 5.00
FAMB Montee Ball 5.00 12.00
FAME Mike Evans
FAML Marshawn Lynch
FAMLE Marqise Lee
FAOB Odell Beckham Jr. 30.00 60.00
FAPR Paul Richardson EXCH 2.50 6.00
FARG Rob Gronkowski/25 30.00 60.00
FASR Silas Redd 2.50 6.00
FASW Sammy Watkins
FATB Teddy Bridgewater 3.00 8.00
FATM Tre Mason EXCH 2.00 5.00
FATS Tom Savage
FATW Terrance West 2.00 5.00
FAZM Zach Mettenberger 2.00 5.00

2014 Topps Fire Autographs Dual

STATED PRINT RUN 25 SER.#'d SETS
EXCH EXPIRATION: 12/31/2017
DABC K.Benjamin/B.Cooks 30.00 60.00
DABL C.Latimer/M.Ball
DABP Patterson/Bridgewtr EXCH 20.00 50.00
DABW A.Williams/O.Beckham Jr. 40.00 100.00
DAES M.Evans/C.Sims 25.00 50.00
DAFC K.Carey/D.Fales
DALA E.Lacy/D.Adams EXCH 40.00 80.00
DAMS B.Sankey/T.Mason
DAWE S.Watkins/M.Evans 30.00 80.00
DAESE A.Seferian-Jen/E.Ebron

2014 Topps Fire Autographs Triple

STATED PRINT RUN 15 SER.#'d SETS
TABPM Brdgwtr/McKnn/Pttrsn 25.00 60.00
TABWE Bnjmn/Wtkns/Evns 60.00 120.00
TAESS SfrnJnkns/Sms/Evns
TAMBB Brdgwtr/Mnzl/Brtls
TASMH Msn/Snky/Hyde

2014 Topps Fire Combo Patches

STATED COMBO ODDS 1:485 HOBBY
DCPAB D.Archer/L.Bell 4.00 10.00
DCPAM T.Mason/T.Austin 3.00 8.00
DCPBE M.Evans/K.Benjamin 8.00 20.00
DCPBG G.Bernard/A.Green 10.00 25.00
DCPBL C.Latimer/M.Ball 4.00 10.00
DCPBM T.Bridgewater/J.Manziel 5.00 12.00
DCPBN K.Benjamin/C.Newton 5.00 12.00
DCPBP T.Bridgewater/C.Patterson 5.00 12.00
DCPBW A.Williams/O.Beckham Jr. 8.00 20.00
DCPCG J.Garoppolo/D.Carr 25.00 60.00
DCPCS J.Clowney/T.Savage 4.00 10.00
DCPEM J.Manziel/M.Evans 8.00 20.00
DCPES C.Sims/M.Evans 8.00 20.00
DCPEW M.Evans/S.Watkins 8.00 20.00
DCPFM N.Foles/L.McCoy 10.00 25.00
DCPGK C.Kaepernick/F.Gore 8.00 20.00
DCPHM J.Matthews/J.Huff 5.00 12.00
DCPLR A.Rodgers/E.Lacy 30.00 60.00
DCPLT J.Landry/R.Tannehill 6.00 15.00
DCPMS T.Mason/B.Sankey 3.00 8.00
DCPMT D.Thomas/A.Murray 3.00 8.00
DCPMW E.Manuel/S.Watkins 5.00 12.00
DCPRB T.Romo/D.Bryant 20.00 40.00
DCPWL R.Wilson/A.Luck 15.00 40.00
DCPBLE M.Lee/B.Bortles 4.00 10.00
DCPBMA J.Manziel/B.Bortles 5.00 12.00
DCPCMA K.Mack/D.Carr 20.00 50.00
DCPHMA T.Mason/C.Hyde 4.00 10.00
DCPHMC A.McCarron/J.Hill 4.00 10.00
DCPMSA Z.Mettenberger/B.Sankey 3.00 8.00

2014 Topps Fire Competitive Fire

STATED ODDS 1:10 HOBBY
CFAR T.Aikman/T.Romo 1.25 3.00
CFAS T.Aikman/E.Smith 1.50 4.00
CFBG T.Brady/R.Gronkowski 2.50 6.00
CFBGR J.Graham/D.Brees 1.00 2.50
CFCW J.Clowney/J.Watt 1.00 2.50
CFEM J.Elway/P.Manning 2.00 5.00
CFFM J.Manziel/B.Favre 2.50 6.00
CFFR B.Favre/A.Rodgers 3.00 8.00
CFGM A.Morris/R.Griffin III .60 1.50
CFMB D.Bryant/D.Murray 1.00 2.50
CFMBR P.Manning/D.Brees 2.00 5.00
CFMC E.Manning/V.Cruz .75 2.00
CFMCU R.Cunningham/L.McCoy 1.00 2.50
CFME D.Marino/J.Elway 2.00 5.00
CFMJ B.Marshall/A.Jeffery .75 2.00
CFML P.Manning/A.Luck 2.50 6.00
CFMM E.Manning/P.Manning 2.00 5.00
CFMN J.Manziel/J.Namath 2.50 6.00
CFMT D.Marino/R.Tannehill 2.00 5.00
CFNB K.Benjamin/C.Newton 2.00 5.00
CFPR T.Polamalu/B.Roethlisberger 1.00 2.50
CFRJ J.Jones/M.Ryan 1.00 2.50
CFRN A.Rodgers/J.Nelson 2.00 5.00
CFSC M.Crabtree/R.Sherman 1.00 2.50
CFSJ B.Sanders/C.Johnson 1.50 4.00
CFSJO C.Johnson/M.Stafford 1.00 2.50
CFSS D.Sanders/R.Sherman 1.50 4.00
CFWK C.Kaepernick/R.Wilson 1.50 4.00
CFWL M.Lynch/R.Wilson 1.50 4.00
CFWM P.Willis/C.Matthews 1.00 2.50

2014 Topps Fire Forged By Fire Die Cut

STATED ODDS 1:10 HOBBY
FFAM A.J. McCarron .60 1.50
FFAMU Aaron Murray .60 1.50
FFAS Austin Seferian-Jenkins .60 1.50
FFAW Andre Williams .60 1.50
FFBB Blake Bortles .75 2.00
FFBC Brandin Cooks 1.00 2.50
FFBS Bishop Sankey .60 1.50
FFCH Carlos Hyde .75 2.00
FFCL Cody Latimer .75 2.00
FFCS Charles Sims .60 1.50
FFDA Davante Adams 1.00 2.50
FFDC Derek Carr 4.00 10.00
FFDF Devonta Freeman 1.00 2.50
FFDM Donte Moncrief .60 1.50
FFDT De'Anthony Thomas .60 1.50
FFEE Eric Ebron .75 2.00
FFJC Jadeveon Clowney .75 2.00
FFJG Jimmy Garoppolo 5.00 12.00
FFJH Jeremy Hill .75 2.00
FFJL Jarvis Landry 1.25 3.00
FFJM Jordan Matthews 1.00 2.50
FFJMA Johnny Manziel 1.00 2.50
FFJMC Jerick McKinnon .75 2.00
FFKB Kelvin Benjamin 1.00 2.50
FFKC Ka'Deem Carey .60 1.50
FFLT Logan Thomas .60 1.50
FFME Mike Evans 1.50 4.00
FFML Marqise Lee .75 2.00
FFOB Odell Beckham Jr. 1.50 4.00
FFPR Paul Richardson .75 2.00
FFSW Sammy Watkins 1.00 2.50
FFTB Teddy Bridgewater 1.00 2.50
FFTM Tre Mason .60 1.50
FFTS Tom Savage .60 1.50
FFTW Terrance West .60 1.50

2014 Topps Fire Jumbo Patches

FJPAL Andrew Luck 20.00 40.00
FJPAM A.J. McCarron
FJPAW Andre Williams 4.00 10.00
FJPBB Blake Bortles
FJPBC Brandin Cooks 6.00 15.00
FJPBS Bishop Sankey 4.00 10.00
FJPCH Carlos Hyde
FJPCN Cam Newton 6.00 15.00
FJPDC Derek Carr 25.00 60.00
FJPEE Eric Ebron 5.00 12.00
FJPEM Eli Manning 5.00 12.00
FJPJC Jadeveon Clowney
FJPJG Jimmy Garoppolo 10.00 25.00
FJPJM Johnny Manziel
FJPJMA Jordan Matthews
FJPKB Kelvin Benjamin
FJPME Mike Evans
FJPML Marqise Lee 5.00 12.00
FJPOB Odell Beckham Jr.
FJPPR Paul Richardson 5.00 12.00
FJPRW Russell Wilson 20.00 40.00
FJPSW Sammy Watkins 20.00 50.00
FJPTB Teddy Bridgewater 6.00 15.00
FJPTM Tre Mason
FJPTW Terrance West 4.00 10.00

2014 Topps Fire Out of This World Rookies

STATED ODDS 1:5 HOBBY
*RED/43: 1X TO 2.5X BASIC INSERTS
OOWAS Austin Seferian-Jenkins .50 1.25
OOWBB Blake Bortles .60 1.50
OOWBC Brandin Cooks .75 2.00
OOWBS Bishop Sankey .50 1.25
OOWCH Carlos Hyde .60 1.50
OOWCL Cody Latimer .60 1.50
OOWDA Davante Adams .75 2.00
OOWDC Derek Carr 3.00 8.00
OOWDF Devonta Freeman .75 2.00
OOWEE Eric Ebron .60 1.50
OOWJC Jadeveon Clowney .60 1.50
OOWJH Jeremy Hill .60 1.50
OOWJL Jarvis Landry 1.00 2.50
OOWJM Johnny Manziel .75 2.00
OOWJMA Jordan Matthews .75 2.00
OOWKB Kelvin Benjamin .75 2.00
OOWKC Ka'Deem Carey .50 1.25
OOWME Mike Evans 1.25 3.00
OOWML Marqise Lee .60 1.50
OOWOB Odell Beckham Jr. 1.25 3.00
OOWSW Sammy Watkins .75 2.00
OOWTB Teddy Bridgewater .75 2.00
OOWTM Tre Mason .50 1.25
OOWTS Tom Savage .50 1.25
OOWTW Terrance West .50 1.25

2014 Topps Fire Relics

*GREEN/75: .5X TO 1.2X BASIC JSY
*GOLD/50: .6X TO 1.5X BASIC JSY
*ONYX/25: .75X TO 2X BASIC JSY
FRAL Andrew Luck 4.00 10.00
FRAM A.J. McCarron 1.25 3.00
FRAMU Aaron Murray 1.25 3.00
FRAR Allen Robinson 2.00 5.00
FRAS Austin Seferian-Jenkins 1.25 3.00
FRAW Andre Williams 1.25 3.00
FRBB Blake Bortles 1.50 4.00
FRBC Brandin Cooks 2.00 5.00
FRBS Bishop Sankey 1.25 3.00
FRCH Carlos Hyde 1.50 4.00
FRCL Cody Latimer 1.50 4.00
FRCN Cam Newton 3.00 8.00
FRCS Charles Sims 1.25 3.00
FRDA Davante Adams 2.00 5.00
FRDAR Dri Archer 1.25 3.00
FRDC Derek Carr 8.00 20.00
FRDF Devonta Freeman 2.00 5.00
FRDM Donte Moncrief 1.25 3.00
FRDT De'Anthony Thomas 1.25 3.00
FREE Eric Ebron 1.50 4.00
FREL Eddie Lacy 2.00 5.00
FREM Eli Manning 2.50 6.00
FRFG Frank Gore 2.50 6.00
FRGB Giovani Bernard 2.00 5.00
FRJC Jadeveon Clowney 1.50 4.00
FRJG Jimmy Garoppolo 3.00 8.00
FRJH Jeremy Hill 1.50 4.00
FRJJ Julio Jones 3.00 8.00
FRJL Jarvis Landry 2.50 6.00
FRJM Johnny Manziel 2.00 5.00
FRJMA Jordan Matthews 2.00 5.00
FRKB Kelvin Benjamin 4.00 10.00
FRKC Ka'Deem Carey 1.25 3.00
FRLB Le'Veon Bell 2.50 6.00
FRLM LeSean McCoy 3.00 8.00
FRLT Logan Thomas 1.25 3.00
FRMB Montee Ball 2.00 5.00
FRME Mike Evans 3.00 8.00
FRML Marqise Lee 1.50 4.00
FRNF Nick Foles 2.50 6.00
FROB Odell Beckham Jr. 6.00 15.00
FRPR Paul Richardson 1.50 4.00
FRRG Robert Griffin III 2.00 5.00
FRRT Ryan Tannehill 2.50 6.00
FRRW Russell Wilson 5.00 12.00
FRSW Sammy Watkins 2.00 5.00
FRTB Teddy Bridgewater 2.00 5.00

FRTM Tre Mason 1.25 3.00
FRTS Tom Savage 1.25 3.00
FRTW Terrance West 1.25 3.00

2014 Topps Fire Ring of Fire

STATED ODDS 1:20 HOBBY
ROFBF Brett Favre 2.50 6.00
ROFDB Drew Brees 1.25 3.00
ROFDS Deion Sanders 1.00 2.50
ROFJB Jerome Bettis 1.25 3.00
ROFJE John Elway 2.00 5.00
ROFRW Russell Wilson 2.00 5.00
ROFSY Steve Young 1.50 4.00
ROFTA Troy Aikman 1.50 4.00
ROFTB Tom Brady 3.00 8.00
ROFTBR Terry Bradshaw 1.50 4.00

2014 Topps Fire Rookie Autograph Patches

STATED PATCH ODDS 1:28 HOBBY
EXCH EXPIRATION: 12/31/2017
FRAPAM A.J. McCarron EXCH 3.00 8.00
FRAPAMU Aaron Murray/300 3.00 8.00
FRAPAR Allen Robinson/500 5.00 12.00
FRAPAS Austin Seferian-Jenkins/100 6.00 15.00
FRAPAW Andre Williams/500 3.00 8.00
FRAPBB Blake Bortles/50 6.00 15.00
FRAPBC Brandin Cooks/100 6.00 15.00
FRAPBS Bishop Sankey/500 3.00 8.00
FRAPCH Carlos Hyde EXCH 8.00 20.00
FRAPCL Cody Latimer EXCH 4.00 10.00
FRAPCS Charles Sims/200 3.00 8.00
FRAPDA Davante Adams/500 5.00 12.00
FRAPDAR Dri Archer/500 3.00 8.00
FRAPDC Derek Carr/50 40.00 80.00
FRAPDF Devonta Freeman EXCH 12.00 30.00
FRAPDM Donte Moncrief/500 3.00 8.00
FRAPEE Eric Ebron/50 6.00 15.00
FRAPJC Jadeveon Clowney/50 6.00 15.00
FRAPJG Jimmy Garoppolo/100 40.00 80.00
FRAPJH Jeremy Hill/100 5.00 12.00
FRAPJL Jarvis Landry EXCH 6.00 15.00
FRAPJM Johnny Manziel/50 8.00 20.00
FRAPJM Jordan Matthews/100 6.00 15.00
FRAPJMC Jerick McKinnon/100 5.00 12.00
FRAPJW James White/500 6.00 15.00
FRAPKB Kelvin Benjamin/100 15.00 30.00
FRAPKC Ka'Deem Carey/500 3.00 8.00
FRAPLT Logan Thomas/500 3.00 8.00
FRAPMB Martavis Bryant/500 4.00 10.00
FRAPME Mike Evans/50 15.00 40.00
FRAPML Marqise Lee/500 4.00 10.00
FRAPOB Odell Beckham Jr./50 40.00 80.00
FRAPPR Paul Richardson EXCH 4.00 10.00
FRAPRH Robert Herron/500 3.00 8.00
FRAPRR Richard Rodgers/500 5.00 12.00
FRAPSW Sammy Watkins/50 8.00 20.00
FRAPTB Teddy Bridgewater
FRAPTM Tre Mason EXCH 3.00 8.00
FRAPTW Terrance West/500 3.00 8.00
FRAPZM Zach Mettenberger/500 3.00 8.00

2014 Topps Fire Rookie Autographs

STATED ODDS 1:25
106 Tom Savage
107 Andre Williams 2.00 5.00
108 Logan Thomas 2.00 5.00
109 Ha Ha Clinton-Dix 2.50 6.00
110 Martavis Bryant EXCH 2.50 6.00
111 Paul Richardson
113 Terrance West 2.00 5.00
115 Jimmy Garoppolo 25.00 50.00
117 Zach Mettenberger 2.00 5.00
120 Bruce Ellington 2.00 5.00
121 Aaron Murray 2.00 5.00
125 Austin Seferian-Jenkins 2.00 5.00
126 Marqise Lee 2.50 6.00
127 Donte Moncrief 2.00 5.00
129 Allen Hurns 2.50 6.00
130 Jerick McKinnon 2.50 6.00
131 John Brown 3.00 8.00
132 Brandin Cooks 3.00 8.00
133 Jeremy Hill 2.50 6.00
134 Isaiah Crowell 2.50 6.00
135 Jordan Matthews 3.00 8.00
136 Charles Sims 2.00 5.00
137 Allen Robinson 3.00 8.00
139 James White 4.00 10.00
140 Ka'Deem Carey 2.00 5.00
142 Bishop Sankey 2.00 5.00
148 Kelvin Benjamin 3.00 8.00
149 Eric Ebron
150 David Fales 2.00 5.00
152 Tre Mason
156 Anthony Barr 2.00 5.00
157 Troy Niklas 2.00 5.00
158 Silas Redd 2.50 6.00
160 Robert Herron 2.00 5.00
162 Kevin Norwood 2.00 5.00

2014 Topps Fire Rookie Autographs Gold

*GOLD/50: .8X TO 2X BASIC AU
GOLD/50 STATED ODDS 1:189
119 Odell Beckham Jr. 50.00 100.00
124 Sammy Watkins 6.00 15.00
128 Teddy Bridgewater 25.00 60.00
154 Derek Carr 30.00 60.00

2014 Topps Fire Rookie Autographs Green

*GREEN/75: .6X TO 1.5X BASIC AU
GREEN/75 STATED ODDS 1:114
106 Tom Savage 3.00 8.00
148 Kelvin Benjamin 5.00 12.00

2014 Topps Fire Rookie Autographs Onyx

*ONYX/25: 1X TO 2.5X BASIC AU
ONYX/25 STATED ODDS 1:265
EXCH EXPIRATION: 12/31/2017
112 Jadeveon Clowney
114 Blake Bortles 6.00 15.00
115 Jimmy Garoppolo 60.00 125.00
119 Odell Beckham Jr. 60.00 125.00
122 A.J. McCarron EXCH 5.00 12.00
128 Teddy Bridgewater 30.00 80.00
143 Johnny Manziel 8.00 20.00
153 Mike Evans 25.00 60.00
154 Derek Carr 40.00 80.00

2014 Topps Fire 5x7 Competitive Fire

COMPLETE SET (29) 35.00 60.00
CFAR Troy Aikman 1.00 2.50
Tony Romo
CFAS Troy Aikman 1.25 3.00
Emmitt Smith
CFBG Tom Brady 2.00 5.00
Rob Gronkowski
CFCW Jadeveon Clowney .75 2.00
J.J. Watt
CFEM John Elway 1.50 4.00
Peyton Manning
CFFM Brett Favre 1.50 4.00
Johnny Manziel
CFGB Jimmy Graham .75 2.00
Drew Brees
CFMC Eli Manning .60 1.50
Victor Cruz
CFMC LeSean McCoy .75 2.00
Randall Cunningham
CFME Dan Marino 1.50 4.00
John Elway
CFMG Alfred Morris .50 1.25
Robert Griffin III
CFMJ Brandon Marshall .60 1.50
Alshon Jeffery
CFML Peyton Manning 1.50 4.00
Andrew Luck
CFMM Peyton Manning 1.50 4.00
Eli Manning
CFMT Dan Marino 1.50 4.00
Ryan Tannehill
CFNB Cam Newton .75 2.00
Kelvin Benjamin
CFPR Troy Polamalu .75 2.00
Ben Roethlisberger
CFRJ Matt Ryan .75 2.00
Julio Jones
CFRN Aaron Rodgers 1.50 4.00
Jordy Nelson
CFSC Richard Sherman .75 2.00
Michael Crabtree
CFSS Deion Sanders .75 2.00
Richard Sherman
CFWK Russell Wilson 1.25 3.00
Colin Kaepernick
CFWL Russell Wilson 1.25 3.00
Marshawn Lynch
CFWM Patrick Willis .75 2.00
Clay Matthews
CFMB1 Peyton Manning 1.50 4.00
Drew Brees
CFMB2 DeMarco Murray .75 2.00
Dez Bryant
CFNMN Johnny Manziel 1.00 2.50
Joe Namath
CFSJ1 Barry Sanders 1.25 3.00
Calvin Johnson
CFSJ2 Matthew Stafford .75 2.00
Calvin Johnson

2014 Topps Fire 5x7 Out of This World

COMPLETE SET (24) 40.00 60.00
ASJ Austin Seferian-Jenkins .50 1.25
BB Blake Bortles .60 1.50
BC Brandin Cooks .75 2.00
BS Bishop Sankey .50 1.25
CH Carlos Hyde .60 1.50
CL Cody Latimer .60 1.50
DA Davante Adams .75 2.00
DC Derek Carr 3.00 8.00
DF Devonta Freeman .75 2.00
EE Eric Ebron .60 1.50
JC Jadeveon Clowney .60 1.50
JL Jarvis Landry 1.00 2.50
JM Johnny Manziel .75 2.00
JM Jordan Matthews .75 2.00
KB Kelvin Benjamin .75 2.00
KC Ka'Deem Carey .50 1.25
ME Mike Evans 1.25 3.00
ML Marqise Lee .60 1.50
OB Odell Beckham Jr. 1.25 3.00
SW Sammy Watkins .75 2.00
TB Teddy Bridgewater .75 2.00
TM Tre Mason .50 1.25
TS Tom Savage .50 1.25
TW Terrance West .50 1.25

2014 Topps Fire 5x7 Ring of Fire

COMPLETE SET (10) 18.00 30.00
ROFBF Brett Favre 2.00 5.00
ROFDB Drew Brees 1.00 2.50
ROFDS Deion Sanders .75 2.00
ROFJB Jerome Bettis 1.00 2.50
ROFJE John Elway 1.50 4.00
ROFRW Russell Wilson 1.50 4.00
ROFSY Steve Young 1.25 3.00
ROFTA Troy Aikman 1.25 3.00
ROFTB Tom Brady 2.50 6.00
ROFTB2 Terry Bradshaw 1.25 3.00

2015 Topps Fire

1A Calvin Johnson .40 1.00
1B Jameis Winston RC .75 2.00
2A Tim Brown .40 1.00
2B Alvin Dupree RC .40 1.00
3A Aaron Rodgers .75 2.00
3B Amari Cooper RC 1.00 2.50
4A Sammy Watkins .30 .75
4B Clive Walford RC .30 .75
5A Emmanuel Sanders .30 .75
5B Jamison Crowder RC .40 1.00
6A Jamaal Charles .30 .75
6B Brett Hundley RC .30 .75
7A Matt Ryan .30 .75
7B Vince Mayle RC .40 1.00
8A Eric Dickerson .30 .75
8B Trae Waynes RC .30 .75
9A Antonio Gates .25 .60
9B Ty Montgomery RC .30 .75
10A Terrell Suggs .25 .60
10B Marcus Mariota RC 1.25 3.00
11A Terry Bradshaw .50 1.25
11B Devin Funchess RC .50 1.25
12A Ben Roethlisberger .40 1.00
12B Kevin White RC .40 1.00
13A Le'Veon Bell .30 .75
13B Chris Conley RC .30 .75
14A Jimmy Graham .40 1.00
14B DeVante Parker RC .50 1.25
15A Sam Bradford .25 .60
15B Vic Beasley RC .40 1.00
16A A.J. Green .40 1.00
16B Todd Gurley RC 1.25 3.00
17A Dan Marino .75 2.00
17B Breshad Perriman RC .30 .75
18A Tony Dorsett .40 1.00
18B Jesse James RC .40 1.00
19A Philip Rivers .40 1.00
19B Eric Kendricks RC .30 .75
20A Rob Gronkowski .40 1.00
20B David Cobb RC .30 .75
21A Julio Jones .40 1.00
21B T.J. Yeldon RC .30 .75
22A Adrian Peterson .40 1.00
22B Tyler Lockett RC .50 1.25
23A J.J. Watt .40 1.00
23B Dorial Green-Beckham RC .30 .75
24A Larry Fitzgerald .30 .75
24B Leonard Williams RC .30 .75
25A Ronnie Lott .30 .75
25B Jeremy Langford RC .30 .75
26A Lawrence Taylor .40 1.00
26B Cameron Artis-Payne RC .30 .75
27A Marshawn Lynch .30 .75
27B Rashad Greene RC .30 .75
28A Drew Brees .40 1.00
28B Sammie Coates RC .40 1.00
29A Jerry Rice .60 1.50
29B Phillip Dorsett RC .30 .75
30A Golden Tate .25 .60
30B Devin Smith RC .30 .75
31A Eddie George .30 .75
31B Javorius Allen RC .40 1.00
32A Steve Young .50 1.25
32B Nelson Agholor RC .40 1.00
33A Phil Simms .30 .75
33B Justin Hardy RC .30 .75
34A Andrew Luck .50 1.25
34B Josh Robinson RC .30 .75
35A Joe Flacco .30 .75
35B Bryce Petty RC .30 .75
36A Mark Ingram .30 .75
36B Deontay Greenberry RC .30 .75
37A Odell Beckham Jr. .40 1.00
37B Tony Lippett RC .30 .75
38A Roger Staubach .50 1.25
38B Melvin Gordon RC .75 2.00
39A Marshall Faulk .30 .75
39B Sean Mannion RC .30 .75
40A Dez Bryant .40 1.00
40B David Johnson RC .75 2.00
41A Brandon Marshall .25 .60
41B Dres Anderson RC .30 .75
42A Kurt Warner .30 .75
42B Ameer Abdullah RC .50 1.25
43A Clay Matthews .40 1.00
43B Duke Johnson RC .50 1.25
44A Ryan Tannehill .30 .75
44B Josh Harper RC .30 .75
45A Matthew Stafford .30 .75
45B Tre McBride RC .30 .75
46A Eddie Lacy .25 .60
46B Mike Davis RC .30 .75
47A Luke Kuechly .30 .75
47B Maxx Williams RC .30 .75
48A Earl Campbell .40 1.00
48B Tevin Coleman RC .40 1.00
49A Ndamukong Suh .30 .75
49B Jaelen Strong RC .40 1.00
50A Peyton Manning .75 2.00
50B Jay Ajayi RC .50 1.25
51 Russell Wilson .50 1.25
52 Jeremy Hill .25 .60
53 Jeremy Maclin .25 .60
54 Jordy Nelson .30 .75
55 Antonio Brown .40 1.00
56 Troy Polamalu .40 1.00
57 John Elway .60 1.50
58 Jarvis Landry .30 .75
59 Matt Forte .25 .60
60 DeMarco Murray .30 .75
61 Tony Romo .30 .75
62 Deion Sanders .30 .75
63 DeSean Jackson .30 .75
64 Mike Evans .30 .75
65 Marcus Allen .40 1.00
66 Jordan Matthews .30 .75
67 Lamar Miller .25 .60
68 Alfred Morris .25 .60
69 Barry Sanders .60 1.50
70 Jerome Bettis .40 1.00
71 Earl Thomas .30 .75
72 Gale Sayers .40 1.00
73 Derek Carr .40 1.00
74 Travis Kelce .40 1.00
75 Greg Olsen .30 .75
76 Colin Kaepernick .30 .75
77 Arian Foster .30 .75
78 Kelvin Benjamin .30 .75
79 Richard Sherman .40 1.00
80 Joique Bell .25 .60
81 Bo Jackson .50 1.25
82 Randall Cobb .30 .75
83 LeSean McCoy .40 1.00
84 T.Y. Hilton .30 .75
85 Warren Moon .40 1.00
86 Robert Griffin III .25 .60
87 Demaryius Thomas .30 .75
88 Eli Manning .30 .75
89 Kam Chancellor .40 1.00
90 Teddy Bridgewater .30 .75
91 Frank Gore .30 .75
92 Brett Favre .75 2.00
93 C.J. Anderson .30 .75
94 Terrell Davis .30 .75
95 Alshon Jeffery .30 .75
96 Mike Singletary .40 1.00
97 Davante Adams .30 .75
98 Cam Newton .40 1.00
99 Emmitt Smith .60 1.50
100 Tom Brady 1.00 2.50

2015 Topps Fire Blue

*VETS/99: 2.5X TO 6X BASIC CARDS
*ROOKIES/99: 1.5X TO 4X BASIC CARDS
STATED BLUE ODDS 1:73 HOBBY

2015 Topps Fire Flame

*VETS: 1X TO 2.5X BASIC CARDS
*ROOKIES: .6X TO 1.5X BASIC CARDS

2015 Topps Fire Gold

*VETS/299: 1.5X TO 4X BASIC CARDS
*ROOKIES/299: 1X TO 2.5X BASIC CARDS

2015 Topps Fire Green

*VETS/199: 2X TO 5X BASIC CARDS
*ROOKIES/199: 1.2X TO 3X BASIC CARDS
STATED GREEN ODDS 1:37 HOBBY

2015 Topps Fire Magenta

*VETS/25: 5X TO 12X BASIC CARDS
*ROOKIES/25: 4X TO 10X BASIC CARDS
STATED MAGENTA ODDS 1:289 HOBBY

2015 Topps Fire Onyx

*VETS/25: 5X TO 12X BASIC CARDS
*ROOKIES/25: 4X TO 10X BASIC CARDS
STATED ODDS 1:240 HOBBY

2015 Topps Fire Orange

*VETS/499: 1.25X TO 3X BASIC CARDS
*ROOKIES/499: .75X TO 2X BASIC CARDS
STATED ORANGE ODDS 1:15 HOBBY

2015 Topps Fire Purple

*VETS/50: 2.5X TO 6X BASIC CARDS
*ROOKIES/50: 1.5X TO 4X BASIC CARDS
STATED PURPLE ODDS 1:146 HOBBY

2015 Topps Fire Silver

*VETS: .8X TO 2X BASIC CARDS
*ROOKIES: .5X TO 1.2X BASIC CARDS
INSERTED ONE PER HOBBY PACK

2015 Topps Fire Fired Up

STATED ODDS 1:20 HOBBY
FIUAB Antonio Brown 1.25 3.00
FIUAL Andrew Luck 1.50 4.00
FIUAP Adrian Peterson 1.25 3.00
FIUCJ Calvin Johnson 1.25 3.00
FIUCM Clay Matthews 1.25 3.00
FIUCN Cam Newton 1.25 3.00
FIUDB Dez Bryant 1.25 3.00
FIUJW J.J. Watt 1.25 3.00
FIULB Le'Veon Bell 1.00 2.50
FIUML Marshawn Lynch 1.00 2.50
FIURG Rob Gronkowski 1.25 3.00
FIURS Richard Sherman 1.25 3.00
FIUTB Tom Brady 3.00 8.00

2015 Topps Fire Forces of Nature

STATED ODDS 1:10 HOBBY
FONAB Antonio Brown 1.00 2.50
FONAC Amari Cooper 1.25 3.00
FONAL Andrew Luck 1.25 3.00
FONAP Adrian Peterson 1.00 2.50
FONAR Aaron Rodgers 2.00 5.00
FONBF Brett Favre 2.00 5.00
FONBJ Bo Jackson 1.25 3.00
FONBR Ben Roethlisberger 1.00 2.50
FONCJ Calvin Johnson 1.00 2.50
FONCK Colin Kaepernick .75 2.00
FONCM Clay Matthews 1.00 2.50
FONCN Cam Newton 1.00 2.50
FONDBE Drew Brees 1.00 2.50
FONDBY Dez Bryant 1.00 2.50
FONDM Dan Marino 2.00 5.00
FONEL Eddie Lacy .60 1.50
FONEM Eli Manning .75 2.00
FONES Emmitt Smith 1.50 4.00
FONJC Jamaal Charles .75 2.00
FONJE John Elway 1.50 4.00
FONJR Jerry Rice 1.50 4.00
FONJWA J.J. Watt 1.00 2.50
FONJWI Jameis Winston 1.00 2.50
FONKW Kevin White .50 1.25
FONLB Le'Veon Bell .75 2.00
FONLT LaDainian Tomlinson .75 2.00
FONMG Melvin Gordon 1.00 2.50
FONMM Marcus Mariota 1.50 4.00
FONMS Matthew Stafford .75 2.00
FONOB Odell Beckham Jr. 1.00 2.50
FONPM Peyton Manning 2.00 5.00
FONRG Rob Gronkowski 1.00 2.50
FONTB Tom Brady 2.50 6.00
FONTG Todd Gurley 1.50 4.00
FONTR Tony Romo .75 2.00

2015 Topps Fire Into the Wild

STATED ODDS 1:4 HOBBY
ITWAG A.J. Green .60 1.50
ITWAJ Alshon Jeffery .50 1.25
ITWAL Andrew Luck .75 2.00
ITWBS Barry Sanders 1.00 2.50
ITWCJ Calvin Johnson .60 1.50
ITWCN Cam Newton .60 1.50
ITWDF Devonta Freeman .50 1.25
ITWDH DeAndre Hopkins .50 1.25
ITWDMU DeMarco Murray .50 1.25
ITWDS Deion Sanders .50 1.25
ITWDT DeMaryius Thomas .50 1.25
ITWFG Frank Gore .50 1.25
ITWJE John Elway 1.00 2.50
ITWJG Jimmy Graham .60 1.50
ITWJH Jeremy Hill .40 1.00
ITWJJ Julio Jones .60 1.50
ITWJW J.J. Watt .60 1.50
ITWKB Kelvin Benjamin .50 1.25
ITWKWH Kevin White .50 1.25
ITWLM LeSean McCoy .60 1.50
ITWMFO Matt Forte .40 1.00
ITWML Marshawn Lynch .50 1.25
ITWMR Matt Ryan .50 1.25
ITWMST Matthew Stafford .50 1.25
ITWNA Nelson Agholor .50 1.25
ITWPM Peyton Manning 1.25 3.00
ITWRS Richard Sherman .60 1.50
ITWRW Russell Wilson .75 2.00
ITWSW Sammy Watkins .50 1.25
ITWTT Tyrod Taylor .50 1.25

2015 Topps Fire Jumbo Relics

*YELLOW/125: .5X TO 1.2X BASIC JSY
*GREEN/99: .6X TO 1.5X BASIC JSY
*BLUE/75: .6X TO 1.5X BASIC JSY
*PURPLE/50: .75X TO 2X BASIC JSY
*MAGENTA/25: 1X TO 2.5X BASIC JSY
FJRAA Ameer Abdullah 2.00 5.00
FJRAC Amari Cooper 4.00 10.00
FJRAG A.J. Green 3.00 8.00
FJRAL Andrew Luck 4.00 10.00
FJRBB Blake Bortles 2.00 5.00
FJRBH Brett Hundley 1.25 3.00
FJRBP Breshad Perriman 1.25 3.00
FJRBPT Bryce Petty 1.25 3.00
FJRCC Chris Conley 1.25 3.00
FJRCK Colin Kaepernick 2.50 6.00
FJRCN Cam Newton 3.00 8.00
FJRDB Drew Brees 3.00 8.00
FJRDC Derek Carr 3.00 8.00
FJRDF Devin Funchess 2.00 5.00
FJRDG Dorial Green-Beckham 1.25 3.00
FJRDJ Duke Johnson 2.00 5.00
FJRDM DeMarco Murray 2.50 6.00
FJRDP DeVante Parker 2.00 5.00
FJRDS Devin Smith 1.25 3.00
FJRDT Demaryius Thomas 2.50 6.00
FJREL Eddie Lacy 2.00 5.00
FJRGG Garrett Grayson 1.25 3.00
FJRJA Javorius Allen 1.50 4.00
FJRJAJ Jay Ajayi 2.00 5.00
FJRJC Jamaal Charles 2.50 6.00
FJRJJ Julio Jones 3.00 8.00
FJRJL Jeremy Langford 1.25 3.00
FJRJW Jameis Winston 5.00 12.00
FJRKB Kelvin Benjamin 2.50 6.00
FJRKW Kevin White 1.50 4.00
FJRLB Le'Veon Bell 2.50 6.00
FJRMD Mike Davis 1.25 3.00
FJRMG Melvin Gordon 3.00 8.00
FJRMJ Matt Jones 1.25 3.00
FJRMM Marcus Mariota 5.00 12.00
FJRMS Matthew Stafford 2.50 6.00
FJRMW Maxx Williams 1.25 3.00
FJRNA Nelson Agholor 1.50 4.00
FJROB Odell Beckham Jr. 3.00 8.00
FJRPD Phillip Dorsett 1.25 3.00
FJRRT Ryan Tannehill 2.50 6.00
FJRRW Russell Wilson 4.00 10.00
FJRSC Sammie Coates 1.50 4.00
FJRSD Stefon Diggs 3.00 8.00
FJRSM Sean Mannion 1.25 3.00
FJRSW Sammy Watkins 2.50 6.00
FJRTB Teddy Bridgewater 2.50 6.00
FJRTC Tevin Coleman 1.50 4.00
FJRTG Todd Gurley 5.00 12.00
FJRTL Tyler Lockett 2.00 5.00
FJRTM Ty Montgomery 1.25 3.00
FJRTY T.J. Yeldon 1.25 3.00

2015 Topps Fire Rookie Autograph Patches

*PATCH AU/400-500: .25X TO .6X BLUE/75
*PATCH AU/150-231: .3X TO .8X BLUE/75
*PATCH AU/91-100: .4X TO 1X BLUE/75

2015 Topps Fire Rookie Autograph Patches Blue

FRAPAA Ameer Abdullah 6.00 15.00
FRAPAC Amari Cooper 30.00 60.00
FRAPBH Brett Hundley 4.00 10.00
FRAPBP Breshad Perriman 4.00 10.00
FRAPBPT Bryce Petty 4.00 10.00
FRAPCA Cameron Artis-Payne 4.00 10.00
FRAPCC Chris Conley 4.00 10.00
FRAPDAJ David Johnson 15.00 40.00
FRAPDC David Cobb 4.00 10.00
FRAPDF Devin Funchess 6.00 15.00
FRAPDFJ Dante Fowler Jr. 6.00 15.00
FRAPDG Dorial Green-Beckham 4.00 10.00
FRAPDJ Duke Johnson 6.00 15.00
FRAPDP DeVante Parker
FRAPDS Devin Smith
FRAPJAJ Jay Ajayi 6.00 15.00
FRAPJC Jamison Crowder 5.00 12.00
FRAPJH Justin Hardy 4.00 10.00
FRAPJL Jeremy Langford 4.00 10.00
FRAPJS Jaelen Strong 5.00 12.00
FRAPJW Jameis Winston 50.00 100.00
FRAPKW Kevin White 5.00 12.00
FRAPKWI Karlos Williams 6.00 15.00
FRAPMD Mike Davis 4.00 10.00
FRAPMG Melvin Gordon
FRAPMJ Matt Jones 4.00 10.00
FRAPMM Marcus Mariota 40.00 80.00
FRAPNA Nelson Agholor 5.00 12.00
FRAPPD Phillip Dorsett 4.00 10.00
FRAPRG Rashad Greene 4.00 10.00
FRAPSD Stefon Diggs 10.00 25.00
FRAPSM Sean Mannion 4.00 10.00
FRAPTC Tevin Coleman 5.00 12.00
FRAPTG Todd Gurley 25.00 60.00
FRAPTL Tyler Lockett 6.00 15.00
FRAPTM Ty Montgomory 4.00 10.00
FRAPTY T.J. Yeldon

2015 Topps Fire Rookie Autograph Patches Magenta

*MAGENTA/25: .6X TO 1.5X BLUE/75
FRAPJW Jameis Winston

2015 Topps Fire Rookie Autograph Patches Purple

*PURPLE/50: .5X TO 1.2X BLUE/75
FRAPJW Jameis Winston

2015 Topps Fire Transcendent Touchdowns

STATED ODDS 1:5 HOBBY
*BLUE/99: 1X TO 2.5X BASIC INSERTS
*PURPLE/50: 1.2X TO 3X BASIC INSERTS
*MAGENTA/25: 2X TO 5X BASIC INSERTS
TTAP Adrian Peterson .75 2.00
TTBJ Bo Jackson 1.00 2.50
TTBS Barry Sanders 1.25 3.00
TTCJ Calvin Johnson .75 2.00
TTCK Colin Kaepernick .60 1.50
TTDH Devin Hester .60 1.50
TTDM Dan Marino 1.50 4.00
TTDS Deion Sanders .60 1.50
TTES Emmitt Smith 1.25 3.00
TTFH Franco Harris .75 2.00
TTJED Julian Edelman .75 2.00
TTJEL John Elway 1.25 3.00
TTJH James Harrison .60 1.50
TTJN Jordy Nelson .60 1.50
TTJR Jerry Rice 1.25 3.00
TTJW J.J. Watt .75 2.00
TTLT LaDainian Tomlinson .60 1.50
TTML Marshawn Lynch .60 1.50
TTMM Marcus Mariota 1.25 3.00
TTOB Odell Beckham Jr. .75 2.00
TTPM Peyton Manning 1.50 4.00
TTRG Rob Gronkowski .75 2.00
TTRS Roger Staubach 1.00 2.50
TTSY Steve Young 1.00 2.50
TTTD Terrell Davis .60 1.50

2010 Topps Five Star

1-150 VET/LEGEND PRINT RUN 79
151-180 ROOKIE JSY AU PRINT RUN 50-90
1 Peyton Manning 15.00 40.00
2 Franco Harris 6.00 15.00
3 Rashard Mendenhall 3.00 8.00
4 Roger Staubach 6.00 15.00
5 BenJarvus Green-Ellis 5.00 12.00
6 Michael Turner 3.00 8.00
7 Joe Flacco 4.00 10.00
8 Dallas Clark 3.00 8.00
9 Tony Dorsett 5.00 12.00
10 Adrian Peterson 5.00 12.00
11 LeSean McCoy 5.00 12.00
12 Eli Manning 4.00 10.00
13 Patrick Willis 4.00 10.00
14 Calvin Johnson 5.00 12.00
15 Brandon Pettigrew 3.00 8.00
16 Chris Cooley 3.00 8.00
17 Percy Harvin 3.00 8.00
18 Jerome Bettis 10.00 25.00
19 Peyton Hillis 4.00 10.00
20 Brandon Marshall 4.00 10.00
21 Matt Forte 3.00 8.00
22 Jon Beason 3.00 8.00
23 Cris Carter 8.00 20.00
24 DeAngelo Hall 3.00 8.00
25 Dwayne Bowe 4.00 10.00
26 Matthew Stafford 4.00 10.00
27 Fred Jackson 4.00 10.00
28 Danny Woodhead 30.00 60.00
29 Jermichael Finley 3.00 8.00
30 Chris Johnson 3.00 8.00
31 Randy Moss 4.00 10.00
32 Thomas Jones 3.00 8.00
33 Dwight Freeney 3.00 8.00
34 Ed Reed 4.00 10.00
35 Steve Smith USC 3.00 8.00
36 Jay Cutler 3.00 8.00
37 Jerod Mayo 4.00 10.00
38 Frank Gore 4.00 10.00
39 Ronnie Brown 3.00 8.00
40 Jim Brown 5.00 12.00
41 Ray Lewis 5.00 12.00
42 Felix Jones 3.00 8.00
43 Tim Hightower 3.00 8.00
44 Braylon Edwards 3.00 8.00
45 Terrell Owens 4.00 10.00
46 Hines Ward 5.00 12.00
47 Darrelle Revis 3.00 8.00
48 Chad Henne 4.00 10.00
49 Joseph Addai 3.00 8.00
50 Drew Brees 6.00 15.00
51 Jared Allen 3.00 8.00
52 Jason Witten 4.00 10.00
53 Andre Johnson 4.00 10.00
54 Mike Tolbert 4.00 10.00
55 Santana Moss 4.00 10.00
56 Ricky Williams 4.00 10.00
57 Miles Austin 3.00 8.00
58 Jeremy Maclin 3.00 8.00
59 Tony Romo 4.00 10.00
60 Dan Marino 20.00 50.00
61 Beanie Wells 3.00 8.00
62 Jabar Gaffney 3.00 8.00
63 Carson Palmer 4.00 10.00
64 Clay Matthews 6.00 15.00
65 Dustin Keller 3.00 8.00
66 Michael Vick 4.00 10.00
67 Matt Cassel 3.00 8.00
68 Ray Rice 3.00 8.00
69 Greg Jennings 3.00 8.00
70 Larry Fitzgerald 4.00 10.00
71 Wes Welker 4.00 10.00
72 Hakeem Nicks 3.00 8.00
73 Johnny Knox 3.00 8.00
74 Knowshon Moreno 3.00 8.00
75 Eric Dickerson 4.00 10.00
76 Julius Peppers 4.00 10.00
77 Davone Bess 3.00 8.00
78 Kellen Winslow 3.00 8.00
79 Kyle Orton 3.00 8.00
80 Joe Namath 6.00 15.00
81 DeMeco Ryans 3.00 8.00
82 Pierre Garcon 4.00 10.00
83 Junior Seau 4.00 10.00
84 Donovan McNabb 4.00 10.00
85 Howie Long 5.00 12.00
86 Lance Moore 3.00 8.00
87 Louis Murphy 3.00 8.00
88 Matt Ryan 4.00 10.00
89 Josh Freeman 5.00 12.00
90 Tom Brady 20.00 50.00
91 Sidney Rice 5.00 12.00
92 Malcom Floyd 3.00 8.00
93 Antonio Gates 4.00 10.00
94 Marion Barber 4.00 10.00
95 Lee Evans 4.00 10.00
96 Kenny Britt 3.00 8.00
97 Philip Rivers 5.00 12.00
98 Troy Polamalu 5.00 12.00
99 Reggie Wayne 4.00 10.00
100 Aaron Rodgers 30.00 60.00
101 Brian Urlacher 5.00 12.00
102 Ahmad Bradshaw 3.00 8.00
103 Steve Young 8.00 20.00
104 Troy Aikman 6.00 15.00
105 DeSean Jackson 4.00 10.00
106 Pierre Thomas 3.00 8.00
107 Jamaal Charles 4.00 10.00
108 Anquan Boldin 3.00 8.00
109 Thurman Thomas 4.00 10.00
110 LaDainian Tomlinson 5.00 12.00
111 Clinton Portis 3.00 8.00
112 Mario Manningham 3.00 8.00
113 Brett Favre 20.00 50.00
114 Kevin Kolb 3.00 8.00
115 Zach Miller 3.00 8.00
116 Mario Williams 4.00 10.00
117 Matt Schaub 3.00 8.00
118 Marques Colston 3.00 8.00
119 Vince Young 3.00 8.00
120 Joe Montana 15.00 40.00
121 Michael Crabtree 3.00 8.00
122 Mark Sanchez 3.00 8.00
123 Austin Collie 3.00 8.00
124 Mike Wallace 3.00 8.00
125 Osi Umenyiora 3.00 8.00
126 Paul Posluszny 5.00 12.00
127 Art Monk 8.00 20.00
128 Brandon Lloyd 3.00 8.00
129 Eddie Royal 3.00 8.00
130 Arian Foster 4.00 10.00
131 Steven Jackson 3.00 8.00
132 Vernon Davis 3.00 8.00
133 Roddy White 3.00 8.00
134 Chad Ochocinco 3.00 8.00
135 DeAngelo Williams 3.00 8.00
136 Steve Breaston 3.00 8.00
137 Shonn Greene 3.00 8.00
138 Darren McFadden 3.00 8.00
139 Ryan Torain 3.00 8.00
140 Maurice Jones-Drew 3.00 8.00
141 Steve Johnson 4.00 10.00
142 Ronnie Lott 4.00 10.00
143 Steve Smith 4.00 10.00
144 Emmitt Smith 12.00 30.00
145 Tony Gonzalez 4.00 10.00
146 DeMarcus Ware 4.00 10.00
147 Cedric Benson 3.00 8.00
148 Gale Sayers 5.00 12.00
149 Santonio Holmes 3.00 8.00
150 John Elway 12.00 30.00
151 E.Sanders JSY AU/90 RC 12.00 30.00
152 A.Roberts JSY AU/90 RC 10.00 25.00
153 Taylor Price JSY AU/90 RC 8.00 20.00
154 Mardy Gilyard JSY AU/90 RC 8.00 20.00
155 D.Williams JSY AU/90 RC 8.00 20.00
156 A.Edwards JSY AU/90 RC 10.00 25.00
157 J.Dwyer JSY AU/90 RC 8.00 20.00
158 B.LaFell JSY AU/90 RC 12.00 30.00
159 J.Shipley JSY AU/90 RC 8.00 20.00
160 Colt McCoy JSY AU/50 RC 10.00 25.00
161 R.Gronkowski JSY AU/90 RC 40.00 80.00
162 A.Benn JSY AU/75 RC 8.00 20.00
163 Toby Gerhart JSY AU/75 RC 8.00 20.00
164 M.Hardesty JSY AU/90 RC 8.00 20.00
166 Ben Tate JSY AU/75 RC 8.00 20.00
167 Golden Tate JSY AU/90 RC 10.00 25.00
168 J.Gresham JSY AU/90 RC 8.00 20.00
169 G.McCoy JSY AU/75 RC 8.00 20.00
170 Sam Bradford JSY AU/50 RC 10.00 25.00
171 N.Suh JSY AU/50 RC 25.00 60.00
172 Jahvid Best JSY AU/50 RC 8.00 20.00
173 D.Thomas JSY AU/50 RC 20.00 50.00
174 R.Mathews JSY AU/50 RC 8.00 20.00
175 C.J. Spiller JSY AU/50 RC 8.00 20.00
176 Mike Kafka JSY AU/60 RC 10.00 25.00
177 Eric Decker JSY AU/90 RC 10.00 25.00
178 M.Easley JSY AU/75 RC 8.00 20.00
179 Eric Berry JSY AU/75 RC 12.00 30.00
180 Tim Tebow JSY AU/50 RC 40.00 100.00
189 J.Clausen JSY AU/90 RC 8.00 20.00
RHA Drew Brees RH AU/50 125.00 200.00

2010 Topps Five Star Jumbo Jerseys

JUMBO JERSEY PRINT RUN 40-65
*PATCH/20: .5X TO 1.2X JMBO JSY VET
*PATCH/20: .4X TO 1X JMBO JSY LGND
*PATCH/20: .5X TO 1.2X JMBO JSY ROOK
JJRAB Arrelious Benn/40 3.00 8.00
JJRAE Armanti Edwards/40 4.00 10.00
JJRAG Antonio Gates/40 6.00 15.00
JJRAP Adrian Peterson/40 15.00 40.00
JJRBL Brandon LaFell/40 5.00 12.00
JJRBT Ben Tate/40 3.00 8.00
JJRCJ Calvin Johnson/40 10.00 25.00
JJRCJO Chris Johnson/40 5.00 12.00
JJRCJS C.J. Spiller/40 3.00 8.00
JJRCM Colt McCoy/40 4.00 10.00
JJRDB Dez Bryant/40 8.00 20.00
JJRDJ DeSean Jackson/65 6.00 15.00
JJRDM Dan Marino/40 30.00 80.00
JJRDMC Dexter McCluster/40 4.00 10.00
JJRDR Darrelle Revis/40 5.00 12.00
JJRDT Demaryius Thomas/40 8.00 20.00
JJREB Eric Berry/40 5.00 12.00
JJRES Emmanuel Sanders/40 5.00 12.00
JJRFH Franco Harris/40 15.00 40.00
JJRGM Gerald McCoy/40 3.00 8.00
JJRGT Golden Tate/40 4.00 10.00
JJRJB Jahvid Best/40 3.00 8.00
JJRJC Jimmy Clausen/40 3.00 8.00
JJRJD Jonathan Dwyer/40 3.00 8.00
JJRJG Jermaine Gresham/40 3.00 8.00
JJRJM Joe Montana/40 50.00 125.00
JJRJMC Joe McKnight/40 3.00 8.00
JJRJS Jordan Shipley/40 3.00 8.00
JJRLF Larry Fitzgerald/40 6.00 15.00
JJRLT LaDainian Tomlinson/40 8.00 20.00
JJRMG Mardy Gilyard/40 3.00 8.00
JJRMH Montario Hardesty/40 3.00 8.00
JJRMJD Maurice Jones-Drew/40 5.00 12.00
JJRMS Mark Sanchez/40 5.00 12.00
JJRMW Mike Williams/40 3.00 8.00
JJRNS Ndamukong Suh/40 6.00 15.00
JJRPR Philip Rivers/40 10.00 25.00
JJRRG Rob Gronkowski/40 10.00 25.00
JJRRL Ray Lewis/40 10.00 25.00
JJRRM Randy Moss/40 6.00 15.00
JJRRMA Ryan Mathews/40 3.00 8.00
JJRRMC Rolando McClain/40 3.00 8.00
JJRRR Ray Rice/65 5.00 12.00
JJRRS Roger Staubach/40 20.00 50.00
JJRSB Sam Bradford/40 4.00 10.00
JJRSJ Steven Jackson/40 5.00 12.00
JJRSY Steve Young/40 20.00 40.00
JJRTG Toby Gerhart/40 3.00 8.00
JJRTP Taylor Price/40 3.00 8.00
JJRTT Tim Tebow/40 15.00 40.00

2010 Topps Five Star Rookie Autographed Patch Gold

*AU GLD/40: .4X TO 1X BASIC JSY AU
STATED PRINT RUN 40 SER.#'d SETS
180 Tim Tebow JSY AU 30.00 80.00

2010 Topps Five Star Rookie Autographed Patch Platinum

*AU PLAT/20: .5X TO 1.2X JSY AU RC
STATED PRINT RUN 20 SER.#'d SETS

2010 Topps Five Star Rookie Autographed Triple Patch Silver

TRIPLE SILVER AU PRINT RUN 20-25
*QUAD SLV AU/20-25: .4X TO 1X TRP/20-25
3RAB Arrelious Benn/25 10.00 25.00
3RAE Armanti Edwards/25 12.00 30.00
3RAR Andre Roberts/25 12.00 30.00
3RBL Brandon LaFell/25 15.00 40.00
3RBT Ben Tate/25 10.00 25.00
3RCJS C.J. Spiller/20 10.00 25.00
3RCM Colt McCoy/20 12.00 30.00
3RDT Demaryius Thomas/25 25.00 60.00
3RDW Damian Williams/25 10.00 25.00
3REB Eric Berry/25 20.00 50.00
3RED Eric Decker/25 12.00 30.00
3RES Emmanuel Sanders/25 15.00 40.00
3RGM Gerald McCoy/25 10.00 25.00
3RGT Golden Tate/25 12.00 30.00
3RJB Jahvid Best/25 10.00 25.00
3RJC Jimmy Clausen/25 10.00 25.00
3RJD Jonathan Dwyer/25 10.00 25.00
3RJG Jermaine Gresham/25 10.00 25.00
3RJS Jordan Shipley/25 10.00 25.00
3RME Marcus Easley/25 10.00 25.00
3RMG Mardy Gilyard/25 10.00 25.00
3RMH Montario Hardesty/25 10.00 25.00
3RMK Mike Kafka/25 12.00 30.00
3RNS Ndamukong Suh/20 40.00 100.00
3RRG Rob Gronkowski/25 75.00 150.00
3RRM Ryan Mathews/20 10.00 25.00
3RSB Sam Bradford/20 75.00 150.00
3RTG Toby Gerhart/25 10.00 25.00
3RTP Taylor Price/25 10.00 25.00
3RTT Tim Tebow/20 100.00 200.00

2010 Topps Five Star Rookie Autographs Gold

OKIE GOLD AUTO PRINT RUN 50-100
AAB Arrelious Benn/100 6.00 15.00
AAE Armanti Edwards/100 8.00 20.00
ABL Brandon LaFell/100 10.00 25.00
ABT Ben Tate/100 6.00 15.00
ACI Chris Ivory/100 15.00 40.00
ACJS C.J. Spiller/100 6.00 15.00
ACM Colt McCoy/100 8.00 20.00
ADT Demaryius Thomas/75 15.00 40.00
ADW Damian Williams/100 6.00 15.00
AEB Eric Berry/75 10.00 25.00
AED Eric Decker/100 8.00 20.00
AES Emmanuel Sanders/100 10.00 25.00
AET Earl Thomas/100 25.00 50.00
AGM Gerald McCoy/75 6.00 15.00
AGT Golden Tate/100 8.00 20.00
AJB Jahvid Best/75 6.00 15.00
AJC Jimmy Clausen/100 6.00 15.00
AJD Jonathan Dwyer/100 6.00 15.00
AJG Jermaine Gresham/75 6.00 15.00
AJPP Jason Pierre-Paul/50 10.00 25.00
AJS Jordan Shipley/100 6.00 15.00
AMG Mardy Gilyard/100 8.00 20.00
AMH Montario Hardesty/100 6.00 15.00
ANS Ndamukong Suh/75 30.00 80.00
ARG Rob Gronkowski/100 30.00 60.00
ARM Ryan Mathews/100 6.00 15.00
ASB Sam Bradford/100 25.00 50.00
ASW Sean Weatherspoon/75 6.00 15.00
ATG Toby Gerhart/100 6.00 15.00
ATT Tim Tebow/100 50.00 120.00

2010 Topps Five Star Rookie Quotable Autographs

ROOKIE QUOTE AU PRINT RUN 15
EXCH EXPIRATION: 2/28/2014
AAB Arrelious Benn 15.00 40.00
AAE Armanti Edwards 20.00 50.00
ABL Brandon LaFell 25.00 60.00
ABT Ben Tate 15.00 40.00
ACI Chris Ivory 40.00 100.00
ACJS C.J. Spiller 15.00 40.00
ACM Colt McCoy 50.00 120.00
ADT Demaryius Thomas 75.00 135.00
ADW Damian Williams 15.00 40.00
AEB Eric Berry 25.00 60.00
AED Eric Decker 20.00 50.00
AES Emmanuel Sanders 25.00 60.00
AET Earl Thomas 40.00 100.00
AGM Gerald McCoy 15.00 40.00
AGT Golden Tate 20.00 50.00
AJB Jahvid Best 15.00 40.00
AJC Jimmy Clausen 15.00 40.00
AJD Jonathan Dwyer 15.00 40.00
AJG Jermaine Gresham 15.00 40.00
AJPP Jason Pierre-Paul 25.00 60.00
AJS Jordan Shipley 15.00 40.00
AMG Mardy Gilyard 15.00 40.00
AMH Montario Hardesty 15.00 40.00
ANS Ndamukong Suh 75.00 150.00
ARG Rob Gronkowski 75.00 150.00
ARM Ryan Mathews 15.00 40.00
ASB Sam Bradford EXCH 100.00 200.00
ASW Sean Weatherspoon 15.00 40.00
ATG Toby Gerhart 15.00 40.00
ATT Tim Tebow 200.00 400.00

2010 Topps Five Star Veteran Autographed Patch Gold

LD PATCH AU PRINT RUN 30
*PLATINUM/15: .5X TO 1.2X GOLD AU/30
*SILVER/50-60: .3X TO .8X GOLD AU/30
*SILVER/35: .4X TO 1X GOLD AU/30
SPAM Art Monk 40.00 80.00
SPBM Brandon Marshall 15.00 40.00
SPCP Clinton Portis 12.00 30.00
SPDB Drew Brees 60.00 120.00
SPDR Darrelle Revis 20.00 50.00
SPER Ed Reed 50.00 100.00
SPFG Frank Gore 15.00 40.00
SPFJ Felix Jones 12.00 30.00
SPHL Howie Long 40.00 80.00
SPJB Jerome Bettis 50.00 120.00
SPJS Junior Seau 30.00 60.00
SPJW Jason Witten 30.00 60.00
SPLM LeSean McCoy 20.00 50.00
SPMF Matt Forte 12.00 30.00
SPRL Ronnie Lott 25.00 60.00
SPRM Rashard Mendenhall 12.00 30.00
SPRR Ray Rice 12.00 30.00
SPTO Terrell Owens 15.00 40.00
SPVJ Vincent Jackson 12.00 30.00

2010 Topps Five Star Veteran Autographed Triple Patch Silver

SILVER PATCH AU PRINT RUN 20
EXCH EXPIRATION: 2/28/2014
SBAM Art Monk 60.00 120.00
SBAP Adrian Peterson 100.00 200.00
SBBF Brett Favre 175.00 300.00
SBCO Chad Ochocinco 25.00 60.00
SBCP Clinton Portis 25.00 60.00
SBDB Drew Brees 100.00 175.00
SBDR Darrelle Revis 25.00 60.00
SBEM Eli Manning 90.00 150.00
SBES Emmitt Smith 150.00 250.00
SBFG Frank Gore 30.00 80.00
SBGJ Greg Jennings 30.00 80.00
SBHL Howie Long 30.00 80.00
SBJB Jerome Bettis 100.00 200.00
SBJE John Elway 150.00 250.00
SBJN Joe Namath 75.00 150.00
SBJS Junior Seau 40.00 100.00
SBKM Knowshon Moreno 25.00 60.00
SBLT LaDainian Tomlinson 40.00 100.00
SBMR Matt Ryan 30.00 80.00
SBMS Mark Sanchez 40.00 100.00
SBPM Peyton Manning 150.00 250.00
SBRL Ronnie Lott 75.00 135.00
SBRM Rashard Mendenhall 15.00 40.00
SBRR Ray Rice 25.00 60.00
SBRW Roddy White 25.00 60.00

SBSY Steve Young	75.00	150.00
SBTO Terrell Owens	30.00	80.00
SBTR Tony Romo	30.00	80.00
SBVJ Vincent Jackson	25.00	60.00
SBMST Matthew Stafford	60.00	120.00

2010 Topps Five Star Veteran Autographs Gold

GOLD AU STATED PRINT RUN 35
*PLATINUM/20: .5X TO 1.2X GOLD AU/35
*SILVER/50: .3X TO .8X GOLD AU/35
*SILVER/40: .4X TO 1X GOLD AU/35
EXCH EXPIRATION: 2/28/2014

SAM Art Monk	30.00	60.00
SBM Brandon Marshall	12.00	30.00
SBW Beanie Wells	10.00	25.00
SCP Clinton Portis	10.00	25.00
SDB Drew Brees	50.00	100.00
SDR Darrelle Revis	20.00	50.00
SER Ed Reed	25.00	60.00
SHL Howie Long	25.00	50.00
SJB Jim Brown	50.00	100.00
SJS Junior Seau	25.00	50.00
SJW Jason Witten	15.00	40.00
SLM LeSean McCoy	15.00	40.00
SMF Matt Forte	10.00	25.00
SMS Mark Sanchez	20.00	50.00
SMST Matthew Stafford	30.00	60.00
SRM Rashard Mendenhall	15.00	40.00
SRR Ray Rice	10.00	25.00
SRW Roddy White	15.00	40.00
SSH Santonio Holmes	10.00	25.00
SSY Steve Young	40.00	80.00
SVJ Vincent Jackson	10.00	25.00

2010 Topps Five Star Veteran Quotable Autographs

EXCH EXPIRATION: 2/28/2014

2011 Topps Five Star

1-150 STATED PRINT RUN 129
ROOKIE JSY AU PRINT RUN 65-199
EXCH EXPIRATION: 2/28/2015

1 Bart Starr	8.00	20.00
2 Jermaine Gresham	3.00	8.00
3 Ben Roethlisberger	5.00	12.00
4 Jim Plunkett	4.00	10.00
5 Dez Bryant	5.00	12.00
6 Greg Jennings	3.00	8.00
7 Charles Woodson	6.00	15.00
8 Antonio Gates	3.00	8.00
9 Richard Dent	3.00	8.00
10 Larry Fitzgerald	4.00	10.00
11 Rob Gronkowski	5.00	12.00
12 James Starks	3.00	8.00
13 Jermichael Finley	3.00	8.00
14 Tim Hightower	3.00	8.00
15 Anquan Boldin	3.00	8.00
16 BenJarvus Green-Ellis	3.00	8.00
17 Ndamukong Suh	4.00	10.00
18 Deion Branch	3.00	8.00
19 Sam Bradford	3.00	8.00
20 Arian Foster	3.00	8.00
21 Kenny Britt	3.00	8.00
22 Ray Lewis	5.00	12.00
23 Darren McFadden	3.00	8.00
24 Owen Daniels	3.00	8.00
25 Patrick Willis	4.00	10.00
26 Joe Flacco	4.00	10.00
27 Brandon Lloyd	3.00	8.00
28 Frank Gore	4.00	10.00
29 Jeremy Maclin	3.00	8.00
30 Andre Johnson	4.00	10.00
31 Brandon Marshall	4.00	10.00
32 LeGarrette Blount	4.00	10.00
33 Hines Ward	4.00	10.00
34 Eli Manning	6.00	15.00
35 Nate Burleson	3.00	8.00
36 Tony Romo	6.00	15.00
37 Mike Thomas	4.00	10.00
38 Vernon Davis	3.00	8.00
39 Santana Moss	4.00	10.00
40 Michael Vick	4.00	10.00
41 Mike Wallace	3.00	8.00
42 Ryan Torain	3.00	8.00
43 Ed Reed	4.00	10.00
44 Robert Meachem	3.00	8.00
45 Devery Henderson	3.00	8.00
46 Colt McCoy	3.00	8.00
47 Dallas Clark	3.00	8.00
48 Rashard Mendenhall	3.00	8.00
49 Jason Pierre-Paul	3.00	8.00
50 Terry Bradshaw	6.00	15.00
51 Joseph Addai	3.00	8.00
52 Plaxico Burress	3.00	8.00
53 Tony Gonzalez	4.00	10.00
54 Troy Polamalu	5.00	12.00
55 Clay Matthews	6.00	15.00
56 Pierre Thomas	3.00	8.00
57 Santonio Holmes	3.00	8.00
58 Fred Davis	3.00	8.00
59 Steven Jackson	3.00	8.00
60 Adrian Peterson	5.00	12.00
61 Cedric Benson	3.00	8.00
62 Brandon Jacobs	3.00	8.00
63 Matt Schaub	3.00	8.00
64 Maurice Jones-Drew	3.00	8.00
65 Darrius Heyward-Bey	3.00	8.00
66 Greg Olsen	4.00	10.00
67 Jamaal Charles	4.00	10.00
68 Kurt Warner	4.00	10.00
69 Ryan Grant	3.00	8.00
70 Joe Namath	6.00	15.00
71 Hakeem Nicks	3.00	8.00
72 LaDainian Tomlinson	5.00	12.00
73 Matthew Stafford	4.00	10.00
74 Chris Johnson	3.00	8.00
75 Reggie Bush	3.00	8.00
76 Darrelle Revis	3.00	8.00
77 Jordy Nelson	5.00	12.00
78 Devin Hester	4.00	10.00
79 Matt Cassel	3.00	8.00
80 Jerry Rice	8.00	20.00
81 Mark Sanchez	3.00	8.00
82 Jimmy Graham	5.00	12.00
83 Jared Allen	5.00	12.00
84 Steve Johnson	3.00	8.00
85 Eric Decker	3.00	8.00
86 Phil Simms	4.00	10.00
87 Michael Crabtree	3.00	8.00
88 Fred Jackson	3.00	8.00
89 Beanie Wells	3.00	8.00
90 Dan Marino	10.00	25.00
91 Malcom Floyd	3.00	8.00
92 Kevin Kolb	3.00	8.00
93 Mike Tolbert	3.00	8.00
94 Tarvaris Jackson	3.00	8.00
95 Davone Bess	3.00	8.00
96 Percy Harvin	3.00	8.00
97 Jason Witten	4.00	10.00
98 Carson Palmer	4.00	10.00
99 Marques Colston	3.00	8.00
100 Joe Montana	12.00	30.00
101 Matt Hasselbeck	3.00	8.00
102 Felix Jones	3.00	8.00
103 Aaron Hernandez	4.00	10.00
104 Ryan Fitzpatrick	3.00	8.00
105 Chuck Howley	3.00	8.00
106 Steve Breaston	3.00	8.00
107 Mario Manningham	3.00	8.00
108 Michael Turner	3.00	8.00
109 Dustin Keller	4.00	10.00
110 Peyton Hillis	3.00	8.00
111 Tom Brady	15.00	30.00
112 Ahmad Bradshaw	3.00	8.00
113 Mike Williams	4.00	10.00
114 Jahvid Best	3.00	8.00
115 Victor Cruz	4.00	10.00
116 Dwayne Bowe	4.00	10.00
117 Jay Cutler	3.00	8.00
118 Shonn Greene	3.00	8.00
119 Brandon Pettigrew	3.00	8.00
120 Roddy White	3.00	8.00
121 Wes Welker	4.00	10.00
122 Calvin Johnson	5.00	12.00
123 Vincent Jackson	3.00	8.00
124 Josh Freeman	4.00	10.00
125 Matt Forte	3.00	8.00
126 DeMarcus Ware	4.00	10.00
127 Jonathan Stewart	3.00	8.00
128 Matt Ryan	4.00	10.00
129 Nate Washington	3.00	8.00
130 Peyton Manning	12.50	25.00
131 Miles Austin	3.00	8.00
132 LeSean McCoy	5.00	12.00
133 Alex Smith QB	4.00	10.00
134 Marshawn Lynch	4.00	10.00
135 DeSean Jackson	4.00	10.00
136 DeAngelo Williams	3.00	8.00
137 Reggie Wayne	4.00	10.00
138 Ray Rice	3.00	8.00
139 Kellen Winslow Jr.	3.00	8.00
140 Drew Brees	6.00	15.00
141 Tim Tebow	5.00	12.00
142 Knowshon Moreno	3.00	8.00
143 Sidney Rice	3.00	8.00
144 Philip Rivers	5.00	12.00
145 Ryan Mathews	4.00	10.00
146 Willis McGahee	3.00	8.00
147 Steve Smith WR	4.00	10.00
148 Pierre Garcon	4.00	10.00
149 Darren Sproles	4.00	10.00
150 Aaron Rodgers	15.00	30.00
151 D.Thomas JSY AU/120 RC	8.00	20.00
152 J.Baldwin JSY AU/75 RC	8.00	20.00
153 C.Ponder JSY AU/65 RC	8.00	20.00
154 A.Green JSY AU/175 RC	8.00	20.00
155 B.Gabbert JSY AU/65 RC	8.00	20.00
156 J.Todman JSY AU/199 RC	8.00	20.00
157 K.Hunter JSY AU/199 RC	15.00	40.00
158 B.Powell JSY AU/175 RC	10.00	25.00
159 G.Little JSY AU/65 RC	10.00	25.00
160 M.Ingram JSY AU/65 RC	12.00	30.00
161 A.Dalton JSY AU/75 RC	25.00	60.00
162 D.Carter JSY AU/175 RC	8.00	20.00
163 A.Pettis JSY AU/199 RC	8.00	20.00
164 J.Locker JSY AU/75 RC	8.00	20.00
165 K.Rudolph JSY AU/120 RC	8.00	20.00
166 J.Jernigan JSY AU/120 RC	8.00	20.00
167 R.Mallett JSY AU/65 RC	8.00	20.00
168 V.Brown JSY AU/199 RC	8.00	20.00
169 J.Harper JSY AU/199 RC	8.00	20.00
170 C.Newton JSY AU/199 RC	60.00	125.00
171 V.Miller JSY AU/65 RC	20.00	50.00
172 D.Murray JSY AU/130 RC	15.00	40.00
173 R.Williams JSY AU/75 RC	8.00	20.00
174 S.Ridley JSY AU/99 RC	8.00	20.00
175 T.Smith JSY AU/75 RC	8.00	20.00
176 M.Leshoure JSY AU/75 RC	20.00	50.00
177 T.Young JSY AU/75 RC	20.00	50.00
178 R.Cobb JSY AU/99 RC	12.00	30.00
179 M.Dareus JSY AU/75 RC	15.00	40.00
180 A.Green JSY AU/65 RC	50.00	100.00
181 C.Kaepernick JSY AU/65 RC	60.00	120.00
182 L.Hankerson JSY AU/99 RC	12.00	30.00
183 S.Vereen JSY AU/130 RC	10.00	25.00

2011 Topps Five Star Dual Patches

STATED PRINT RUN 15 SER.#'d SETS

FSDPBC D.Bowe/J.Charles	15.00	40.00
FSDPBS J.Baldwin/T.Smith	5.00	12.00
FSDPCG R.Cobb/A.Green	8.00	20.00
FSDPDP A.Dalton/C.Ponder	10.00	25.00
FSDPGD A.J. Green/A.Dalton	12.00	30.00
FSDPGJ A.J. Green/J.Jones	15.00	40.00
FSDPGL B.Gabbert/J.Locker	5.00	12.00
FSDPGN B.Gabbert/C.Newton	25.00	60.00
FSDPGP B.Gabbert/C.Ponder	5.00	12.00
FSDPID M.Ingram/M.Dareus	8.00	20.00
FSDPIJ M.Ingram/J.Jones	15.00	40.00
FSDPIL M.Ingram/M.Leshoure	8.00	20.00
FSDPJD J.Jones/M.Dareus	12.00	30.00
FSDPKH C.Kaepernick/K.Hunter	8.00	20.00
FSDPLD J.Locker/A.Dalton	10.00	25.00
FSDPLG G.Little/A.J. Green	12.00	30.00
FSDPLH J.Locker/J.Harper	5.00	12.00
FSDPLM J.Locker/R.Mallett	5.00	12.00
FSDPMD V.Miller/M.Dareus	8.00	20.00
FSDPMR R.Mallett/S.Ridley	5.00	12.00
FSDPMV R.Mallett/S.Vereen	6.00	15.00
FSDPNI C.Newton/M.Ingram	20.00	50.00
FSDPNJ C.Newton/J.Jones	30.00	80.00
FSDPRJ M.Ryan/J.Jones	20.00	50.00
FSDPRP K.Rudolph/C.Ponder	5.00	12.00
FSDPVR S.Vereen/S.Ridley	6.00	15.00
FSDPWL R.Williams/M.Leshoure	12.00	30.00
FSDPYP T.Young/A.Pettis	12.00	30.00

2011 Topps Five Star Dual Rookie Autographed Patch

STATED PRINT RUN 15 SER.#'d SETS
EXCH EXPIRATION: 2/28/2015

FSFDAPBS J. Baldwin/T.Smith	12.00	30.00
FSFDAPCAJ C.Newton/A.Green	200.00	400.00
FSFDAPCG R.Cobb/A.Green	20.00	50.00
FSFDAPCY R.Cobb/T.Young	20.00	50.00
FSFDAPDG Dalton/A.Green EXCH	150.00	250.00
FSFDAPDM M.Dareus/V.Miller	30.00	80.00
FSFDAPGL B.Gabbert/J.Locker	12.00	30.00
FSFDAPHC Harper/D.Carter	12.00	30.00
FSFDAPHJ Hankerson/Jernigan	12.00	30.00
FSFDAPHS Hankerson/T.Smith	12.00	30.00
FSFDAPIL M.Ingram/M.Leshoure	20.00	50.00
FSFDAPKH Kaepernick/Hunter	20.00	50.00
FSFDAPLH G.Little/L.Hankerson	15.00	40.00
FSFDAPLHA J.Locker/J.Harper	12.00	30.00
FSFDAPLS G.Little/T.Smith	15.00	40.00
FSFDAPLY M.Leshoure/T.Young	12.00	30.00
FSFDAPMH D.Murray/K.Hunter	25.00	60.00
FSFDAPMR R.Mallett/S.Ridley	12.00	30.00
FSFDAPMT D.Murray/D.Thomas	25.00	60.00
FSFDAPMV R.Mallett/S.Vereen	15.00	40.00
FSFDAPNG C.Newton/B.Gabbert	100.00	200.00
FSFDAPNI C.Newton/M.Ingram	75.00	150.00
FSFDAPPR C.Ponder/K.Rudolph	60.00	120.00
FSFDAPSG T.Smith/A.J. Green	30.00	80.00
FSFDAPTB J.Todman/V.Brown	12.00	30.00
FSFDAPTG D.Thomas/E.Gates	12.00	30.00
FSFDAPTP D.Thomas/B.Powell	15.00	40.00
FSFDAPVR S.Vereen/S.Ridley	15.00	40.00
FSFDAPWH R.Williams/K.Hunter	40.00	80.00
FSFDAPYP T.Young/A.Pettis	12.00	30.00

2011 Topps Five Star Dual Rookie Autographs

STATED PRINT RUN 20 SER.#'d SETS
EXCH EXPIRATION: 2/28/2015

FSFDABB J.Baldwin/V.Brown	10.00	25.00
FSFDABJ J.Baldwin/T.Jones	10.00	25.00
FSFDABS J.Baldwin/T.Smith	10.00	25.00
FSFDACG R.Cobb/A.Green	15.00	40.00
FSFDACT D.Carter/J.Todman	10.00	25.00
FSFDACY R.Cobb/T.Young	15.00	40.00
FSFDADG A.Dalton/A.J. Green	60.00	125.00
FSFDADM M.Dareus/V.Miller	25.00	60.00
FSFDAGL B.Gabbert/J.Locker	10.00	25.00
FSFDAGS A.J. Green/T.Smith	25.00	60.00
FSFDAHC J.Harper/D.Carter	10.00	25.00
FSFDAHJ Hankerson/Jernigan	10.00	25.00
FSFDAHS Hankerson/T.Smith	10.00	25.00
FSFDAID M.Ingram/M.Dareus	15.00	40.00
FSFDAIR M.Ingram/S.Ridley	15.00	40.00
FSFDAJP J.Jernigan/B.Powell	12.00	30.00
FSFDAKG Kaepernick/A.Green	15.00	40.00
FSFDAKH Kaepernick/Hunter	15.00	40.00
FSFDAKW Kaepernick/Williams	15.00	40.00
FSFDALG M.Leshoure/A.Green	12.00	30.00
FSFDALH G.Little/Hankerson	20.00	50.00
FSFDALS G.Little/T.Smith	12.00	30.00
FSFDALY Leshoure/T.Young	25.00	60.00
FSFDAMH D.Murray/K.Hunter	20.00	50.00
FSFDAMR R.Mallett/S.Ridley	10.00	25.00
FSFDAMT Murray/D.Thomas	20.00	50.00
FSFDAMV R.Mallett/S.Vereen	12.00	30.00
FSFDANG Newton/B.Gabbert	40.00	80.00
FSFDANI C.Newton/M.Ingram	40.00	80.00
FSFDAPG B.Powell/E.Gates	12.00	30.00
FSFDAPR Ponder/K.Rudolph	40.00	100.00
FSFDASG T.Smith/A.J. Green	25.00	60.00
FSFDATB J.Todman/V.Brown	10.00	25.00
FSFDATG D.Thomas/E.Gates	10.00	25.00
FSFDATJ J.Todman/T.Jones	10.00	25.00
FSFDATP D.Thomas/B.Powell	12.00	30.00
FSFDAVP S.Vereen/B.Powell	12.00	30.00
FSFDAVR S.Vereen/S.Ridley	12.00	30.00
FSFDAWH R.Williams/K.Hunter	10.00	25.00
FSFDAWL R.Williams/Leshoure	10.00	25.00
FSFDAYP T.Young/A.Pettis	15.00	40.00
FSFDACAJ C.Newton/A.Green	100.00	250.00
FSFDAGLI A.J. Green/G.Little	25.00	60.00
FSFDALHA J.Locker/J.Harper	10.00	25.00
FSFDAPRI B.Powell/S.Ridley	12.00	30.00

2011 Topps Five Star Patches

STATED PRINT RUN 40 SER.#'d SETS
*JUMBO JSY/88: .3X TO .8X PATCH/40

FSPAD Andy Dalton	6.00	15.00
FSPAF Arian Foster	12.00	30.00
FSPAGA Antonio Gates	6.00	15.00
FSPAJG A.J. Green	8.00	20.00
FSPAP Adrian Peterson	10.00	25.00
FSPAR Aaron Rodgers	25.00	50.00
FSPBG Blaine Gabbert	3.00	8.00
FSPBP Bilal Powell	4.00	10.00
FSPCB Cedric Benson	6.00	15.00
FSPCK Colin Kaepernick	5.00	12.00
FSPCN Cam Newton	15.00	40.00
FSPCP Christian Ponder	3.00	8.00
FSPDB Dwayne Bowe	6.00	15.00
FSPDC Delone Carter	3.00	8.00
FSPDH Devin Hester	8.00	20.00
FSPDMU DeMarco Murray	6.00	15.00
FSPDT Daniel Thomas	3.00	8.00
FSPDW DeAngelo Williams	6.00	15.00
FSPGL Greg Little	4.00	10.00
FSPHN Hakeem Nicks	6.00	15.00
FSPHW Hines Ward	10.00	25.00
FSPJB Jonathan Baldwin	3.00	8.00
FSPJC Jamaal Charles	8.00	20.00
FSPJE John Elway	15.00	40.00
FSPJJ Julio Jones	8.00	20.00
FSPJJE Jerrel Jernigan	3.00	8.00
FSPJL Jake Locker	3.00	8.00
FSPKH Kendall Hunter	6.00	15.00
FSPKR Kyle Rudolph	3.00	8.00
FSPLF Larry Fitzgerald	8.00	20.00
FSPLH Leonard Hankerson	5.00	12.00
FSPMD Marcell Dareus	3.00	8.00
FSPMI Mark Ingram	5.00	12.00
FSPML Mikel Leshoure	6.00	15.00
FSPMR Matt Ryan	8.00	20.00
FSPMS Mark Sanchez	8.00	20.00
FSPMV Michael Vick	8.00	20.00
FSPRC Randall Cobb	5.00	12.00
FSPRL Ray Lewis	12.00	30.00
FSPRM Ryan Mallett	3.00	8.00
FSPRW Ryan Williams	3.00	8.00
FSPSR Stevan Ridley	3.00	8.00
FSPSV Shane Vereen	4.00	10.00
FSPTR Tony Romo	8.00	20.00
FSPTS Torrey Smith	3.00	8.00
FSPTY Titus Young	3.00	8.00
FSPVM Von Miller	5.00	12.00

2011 Topps Five Star Rookie Autographed Patch Gold

*GOLD AU/55: .5X TO 1.2X BASIC JSY AU
STATED PRINT RUN 55 SER.#'d SETS

170 Cam Newton	100.00	200.00
181 Colin Kaepernick	15.00	40.00

2011 Topps Five Star Rookie Autographed Patch Rainbow

*RAINBOW AU/25: .6X TO 1.5X BASIC JSY AU
STATED PRINT RUN 25 SER.#'d SETS

170 Cam Newton	150.00	300.00
172 DeMarco Murray	25.00	60.00

2011 Topps Five Star Rookie Autographed Quad Jersey

QUAD JSY AU PRINT RUN 35-95
*QUAD GOLD/15: .5X TO 1.2X QUAD AU
*TRIPLE AU/30-50: .4X TO 1X QUAD AU
*TRIPLE GLD/15: .5X TO 1.2X QUAD AU
EXCH EXPIRATION: 2/28/2015

FSFA4AD Andy Dalton/35	25.00	50.00
FSFA4AJG A.J. Green/35	30.00	80.00
FSFA4BG Blaine Gabbert/35	10.00	25.00
FSFA4BP Bilal Powell/35	12.00	30.00
FSFA4CK Colin Kaepernick/35	15.00	40.00
FSFA4CN Cam Newton/50	100.00	200.00
FSFA4CP Christian Ponder/35	15.00	40.00
FSFA4DC Delone Carter/35	10.00	25.00
FSFA4DM DeMarco Murray/35	20.00	50.00
FSFA4DT Daniel Thomas/35	10.00	25.00
FSFA4GL Greg Little/35	12.00	30.00
FSFA4JB Jonathan Baldwin/35	10.00	25.00
FSFA4JJE Jerrel Jernigan/35	10.00	25.00
FSFA4JL Jake Locker/35	10.00	25.00
FSFA4JT Jordan Todman/35	10.00	25.00
FSFA4KR Kyle Rudolph/35	15.00	40.00
FSFA4LH Leonard Hankerson/35	10.00	25.00
FSFA4MD Marcell Dareus/35	10.00	25.00
FSFA4MI Mark Ingram/35	15.00	40.00
FSFA4ML Mikel Leshoure/35	25.00	60.00
FSFA4RC Randall Cobb/50	15.00	40.00
FSFA4RM Ryan Mallett/35	10.00	25.00
FSFA4RW Ryan Williams/35	10.00	25.00
FSFA4SR Stevan Ridley/35	10.00	25.00
FSFA4SV Shane Vereen/35	12.00	30.00
FSFA4TJ Taiwan Jones/95	12.00	30.00
FSFA4TS Torrey Smith/50	10.00	25.00
FSFA4TY Titus Young/35	10.00	25.00
FSFA4VM Von Miller/35	25.00	60.00

2011 Topps Five Star Rookie Autographs

STATED PRINT RUN 55-199
EXCH EXPIRATION: 2/28/2015

FSFAAD Andy Dalton/55	15.00	40.00
FSFAAGR Alex Green/190	5.00	12.00
FSFAAJG A.J. Green/165	20.00	50.00
FSFAAP Austin Pettis/199	5.00	12.00
FSFABG Blaine Gabbert/110	5.00	12.00
FSFABP Bilal Powell/199	6.00	15.00
FSFACK Colin Kaepernick/90	8.00	20.00
FSFACN Cam Newton/110	50.00	100.00
FSFACP Christian Ponder/90	5.00	12.00
FSFADC Delone Carter/199	5.00	12.00
FSFADM DeMarco Murray/199	10.00	25.00
FSFADT Daniel Thomas/199	5.00	12.00
FSFAGL Greg Little/175	6.00	15.00
FSFAJB Jonathan Baldwin/165	5.00	12.00
FSFAJH Jamie Harper/199	6.00	15.00
FSFAJJE Jerrel Jernigan/175	5.00	12.00
FSFAJL Jake Locker/110	5.00	12.00
FSFAJT Jordan Todman/175	5.00	12.00
FSFAKH Kendall Hunter/190	10.00	25.00
FSFAKR Kyle Rudolph/199	10.00	25.00
FSFALH Leonard Hankerson/165	5.00	12.00
FSFAMD Marcell Dareus/155	5.00	12.00
FSFAMI Mark Ingram/55	8.00	20.00
FSFAML Mikel Leshoure/145	10.00	25.00
FSFARC Randall Cobb/160	8.00	20.00
FSFARH Roy Helu/110	12.00	30.00
FSFARM Ryan Mallett/90	5.00	12.00
FSFARW Ryan Williams/155	5.00	12.00
FSFASR Stevan Ridley/199	5.00	12.00
FSFASV Shane Vereen/199	6.00	15.00
FSFATJ Taiwan Jones/199	5.00	12.00
FSFATP Terrelle Pryor/110	8.00	20.00
FSFATS Torrey Smith/160	5.00	12.00
FSFATY Titus Young/145	5.00	12.00
FSFAVB Vincent Brown/199	5.00	12.00
FSFAVM Von Miller/165	12.00	30.00

2011 Topps Five Star Rookie Quotable Autographs

STATED PRINT RUN 25 SER.#'d SETS

FSFQAAD Andy Dalton	75.00	150.00
FSFQAAJG A.J. Green	75.00	150.00
FSFQABG Blaine Gabbert	20.00	50.00
FSFQABP Bilal Powell	25.00	60.00
FSFQACK Colin Kaepernick	30.00	80.00
FSFQACN Cam Newton	200.00	400.00
FSFQACP Christian Ponder	60.00	150.00
FSFQADC Delone Carter	20.00	50.00
FSFQADM DeMarco Murray	40.00	100.00
FSFQADT Daniel Thomas	20.00	50.00
FSFQAGL Greg Little	25.00	60.00
FSFQAJB Jonathan Baldwin	20.00	50.00
FSFQAJJE Jerrel Jernigan	20.00	50.00
FSFQAJL Jake Locker	40.00	100.00
FSFQAKH Kendall Hunter	20.00	50.00
FSFQAKR Kyle Rudolph	25.00	60.00
FSFQALH Leonard Hankerson	30.00	80.00
FSFQAMD Marcell Dareus	20.00	50.00
FSFQAMI Mark Ingram	30.00	80.00
FSFQARC Randall Cobb	30.00	80.00
FSFQARM Ryan Mallett	20.00	50.00
FSFQARW Ryan Williams	20.00	50.00
FSFQASR Stevan Ridley	20.00	50.00
FSFQASV Shane Vereen	20.00	50.00
FSFQATJ Taiwan Jones	20.00	50.00
FSFQATS Torrey Smith	20.00	50.00
FSFQATY Titus Young	20.00	50.00
FSFQAVM Von Miller	50.00	120.00

2011 Topps Five Star Super Bowl MVP Autograph

SBMVPAR Aaron Rodgers	200.00	400.00

2011 Topps Five Star Super Bowl MVP Relics

STATED PRINT RUN 16-20

SBMVPAR Aaron Rodgers FB/20	250.00	500.00
SBMVPRAR Aaron Rodgers Pylon/16	250.00	500.00

2011 Topps Five Star Veteran Autographed Patch

PATCH AUTO PRINT RUN 50-99
*GOLD/40: .5X TO 1.2X PATCH AU/50-99
*RAINBOW/25: .6X TO 1.5X PATCH AU/50-99
EXCH EXPIRATION: 2/28/2015

FSSPAG Antonio Gates/90	12.00	30.00
FSSPAR Aaron Rodgers/70	125.00	250.00
FSSPCB Champ Bailey/50	30.00	60.00
FSSPDB Dwayne Bowe/99	12.00	30.00
FSSPDM Darren McFadden/99	12.00	30.00
FSSPDR Darrelle Revis/99	12.00	30.00
FSSPHW Hines Ward/99	50.00	100.00
FSSPJC Jamaal Charles/70	15.00	40.00
FSSPJR Jerry Rice/50	125.00	200.00
FSSPKN Knowshon Moreno/99	12.00	30.00
FSSPKW Kurt Warner/50	40.00	80.00
FSSPLM LeSean McCoy EXCH	20.00	50.00
FSSPMA Miles Austin EXCH	20.00	50.00
FSSPMJ Maurice Jones-Drew/99	12.00	30.00
FSSPMS Mark Sanchez EXCH	15.00	40.00
FSSPMT Michael Turner/50	12.00	30.00
FSSPMV Michael Vick/50	15.00	40.00
FSSPPW Patrick Willis/70	25.00	60.00
FSSPRL Ray Lewis/50	60.00	120.00
FSSPTB Terry Bradshaw/50	75.00	150.00

2011 Topps Five Star Veteran Autographed Triple Jersey

STATED PRINT RUN 25-35
*GOLD/10: .5X TO 1.2X TRIP.JSY AU/25-35

FSSBAG Antonio Gates/35	15.00	40.00
FSSBAR Aaron Rodgers/35	200.00	350.00
FSSBCB Champ Bailey/35	30.00	60.00
FSSBDB Dwayne Bowe/35	15.00	40.00
FSSBDM Dan Marino/25	150.00	250.00
FSSBDMC Darren McFadden/35	25.00	60.00
FSSBDR Darrelle Revis/35	15.00	40.00
FSSBHW Hines Ward/35	50.00	100.00
FSSBJC Jamaal Charles/35	20.00	50.00
FSSBJM Joe Montana/25	150.00	250.00
FSSBJN Joe Namath/25	125.00	200.00
FSSBJR Jerry Rice/25	125.00	200.00
FSSBKM Knowshon Moreno/35	15.00	40.00
FSSBKW Kurt Warner/35	50.00	100.00
FSSBLM LeSean McCoy EXCH	25.00	60.00
FSSBMA Miles Austin EXCH	25.00	60.00
FSSBMS Mark Sanchez EXCH	15.00	40.00
FSSBMT Michael Turner/35	15.00	40.00
FSSBMV Michael Vick/35	40.00	100.00
FSSBPM Peyton Manning/25	125.00	200.00
FSSBPW Patrick Willis/35	20.00	50.00
FSSBRL Ray Lewis/35	75.00	150.00
FSSBSG Shonn Greene/35	15.00	40.00
FSSBSM Santana Moss/35	20.00	50.00
FSSBTR Tony Romo/35	50.00	100.00
FSSBVD Vernon Davis/35	20.00	50.00

2011 Topps Five Star Veteran Autographs

STATED PRINT RUN 10-190
*GOLD/25: .6X TO 1.5X BASIC AU/150-190
*GOLD/25: .5X TO 1.2X BASIC AU/35-70
*RAINBOW/15: .6X TO 1.5X BASIC AU/150-190
*RAINBOW/15: .5X TO 1.X BASIC AU/35-70
EXCH EXPIRATION: 2/28/2015

FSSAF Arian Foster/190	12.00	30.00
FSSBS Bart Starr/50	75.00	150.00
FSSCB Champ Bailey/70	20.00	40.00
FSSCH Chuck Howley/50	12.00	30.00
FSSDM Dan Marino/40	100.00	200.00
FSSJC Jamaal Charles/60	12.00	30.00
FSSJM Joe Montana/40	100.00	200.00
FSSJMA Jeremy Maclin/190	6.00	15.00
FSSJN Joe Namath/40	60.00	120.00
FSSJR Jerry Rice/35	75.00	150.00
FSSKW Kurt Warner/150	30.00	60.00
FSSKWI Kellen Winslow Jr./150	6.00	15.00
FSSLM LeSean McCoy	30.00	60.00
FSSMC Marques Colston/150	10.00	25.00
FSSMJ Maurice Jones-Drew/50	12.00	30.00
FSSMT Michael Turner/35	12.00	30.00
FSSMW Mike Wallace/190	15.00	40.00
FSSPH Peyton Hillis/150	10.00	25.00
FSSPM Peyton Manning/40	75.00	150.00
FSSPS Phil Simms/60	25.00	50.00
FSSPW Patrick Willis/60	15.00	40.00
FSSRD Richard Dent/150	15.00	30.00
FSSSG Shonn Greene/150	6.00	15.00
FSSSM Santana Moss/150	8.00	20.00
FSSTB Terry Bradshaw/60	60.00	120.00
FSSVD Vernon Davis/190	12.00	30.00

2012 Topps Five Star

1-150 VETERAN PRINT RUN 139
ROOKIE JSY AU PRINT RUN 50-300
EXCH EXPIRATION: 4/30/2016

1 Eli Manning	5.00	12.00
2 Randy Moss	3.00	8.00
3 Jimmy Graham	4.00	10.00
4 Jeremy Maclin	2.50	6.00
5 Heath Miller	2.50	6.00
6 Ryan Williams	2.50	6.00
7 Percy Harvin	2.50	6.00
8 Matt Schaub	2.50	6.00
9 Arian Foster	3.00	8.00
10 Joe Montana	10.00	25.00
11 Titus Young	2.50	6.00
12 Hakeem Nicks	2.50	6.00
13 Marques Colston	2.50	6.00
14 Mark Ingram	3.00	8.00
15 Danny Amendola	3.00	8.00
16 Mikel Leshoure	2.50	6.00
17 Aaron Hernandez	3.00	8.00
18 Victor Cruz	3.00	8.00
19 John Skelton	2.50	6.00
20 Terry Bradshaw	6.00	15.00
21 Reggie Wayne	3.00	8.00
22 Laurent Robinson	2.50	6.00
23 Jared Allen	2.50	6.00
24 Patrick Willis	3.00	8.00
25 Jim Kelly	4.00	10.00
26 Matt Ryan	3.00	8.00
27 Darren Sproles	3.00	8.00
28 Frank Gore	3.00	8.00
29 Stevan Ridley	2.50	6.00
30 John Elway	6.00	15.00
31 Brandon Marshall	3.00	8.00
32 Chris Long	2.50	6.00
33 Philip Rivers	4.00	10.00
34 Von Miller	3.00	8.00
35 Michael Turner	2.50	6.00
36 Julio Jones	4.00	10.00
37 Troy Polamalu	4.00	10.00
38 Brian Urlacher	4.00	10.00
39 Torrey Smith	2.50	6.00
40 Steve Young	5.00	12.00
41 Joique Bell	3.00	8.00
42 Jordy Nelson	3.00	8.00
43 Anquan Boldin	2.50	6.00
44 Larry Fitzgerald	3.00	8.00
45 Michael Bush	2.50	6.00
46 Rashard Mendenhall	2.50	6.00
47 Malcom Floyd	2.50	6.00
48 Mark Sanchez	2.50	6.00
49 A.J. Green	4.00	10.00
50 Joe Namath	6.00	15.00
51 Jermichael Finley	2.50	6.00
52 Greg Jennings	4.00	10.00
53 Darrius Heyward-Bay	2.50	6.00
54 Clay Matthews	4.00	10.00
55 Fred Jackson	3.00	8.00
56 C.J. Spiller	2.50	6.00
57 Miles Austin	2.50	6.00
58 Fred Davis	2.50	6.00
59 Michael Vick	3.00	8.00
60 Aaron Rodgers	10.00	25.00
61 Matt Cassel	2.50	6.00
62 Andre Roberts	3.00	8.00
63 Ray Rice	2.50	6.00
64 D'Qwell Jackson	2.50	6.00
65 Jamaal Charles	3.00	8.00
66 Tony Romo	3.00	8.00
67 Brian Hartline	3.00	8.00
68 DeMarco Murray	3.00	8.00
69 Sam Bradford	2.50	6.00
70 Emmitt Smith	8.00	20.00
71 Darren McFadden	2.50	6.00
72 Steve Smith	3.00	8.00
73 Wes Welker	3.00	8.00
74 Santonio Holmes	2.50	6.00
75 Brett Favre	12.00	30.00
76 Demaryius Thomas	4.00	10.00
77 DeSean Jackson	3.00	8.00
78 Brandon Pettigrew	2.50	6.00
79 Dwayne Bowe	3.00	8.00
80 Dan Marino	10.00	25.00
81 Marshawn Lynch	3.00	8.00
82 Antonio Brown	4.00	10.00
83 Charles Woodson	5.00	12.00
84 Carson Palmer	3.00	8.00
85 Ben Roethlisberger	5.00	12.00
86 Tony Gonzalez	3.00	8.00
87 Steve Johnson	3.00	8.00
88 Andre Johnson	3.00	8.00
89 Matt Forte	2.50	6.00
90 Cam Newton	4.00	10.00
91 Ryan Fitzpatrick	2.50	6.00
92 Adrian Peterson	6.00	15.00
93 Steven Jackson	2.50	6.00
94 Rob Gronkowski	4.00	10.00
95 Cedric Benson	2.50	6.00
96 DeMarcus Ware	4.00	10.00
97 Alex Smith	3.00	8.00
98 Shonn Greene	2.50	6.00
99 BenJarvus Green-Ellis	3.00	8.00
100 Jim Brown	5.00	12.00
101 Dennis Pitta	2.50	6.00
102 Andy Dalton	3.00	8.00
103 James Jones	3.00	8.00
104 Chris Johnson	2.50	6.00
105 Mike Williams	3.00	8.00
106 Isaac Redman	4.00	10.00
107 Joe Flacco	3.00	8.00
108 Vernon Davis	2.50	6.00
109 Kyle Rudolph	2.50	6.00
110 Warren Moon	4.00	10.00
111 Charles Tillman	3.00	8.00
112 Willis McGahee	2.50	6.00
113 Reggie Bush	2.50	6.00
114 Jake Locker	4.00	10.00
115 Jay Cutler	4.00	10.00
116 Felix Jones	2.50	6.00
117 Jonathan Stewart	2.50	6.00
118 Vincent Jackson	2.50	6.00
119 Denarius Moore	2.50	6.00
120 Peyton Manning	10.00	25.00
121 Roddy White	2.50	6.00
122 Matthew Stafford	3.00	8.00
123 Calvin Johnson	4.00	10.00
124 Ryan Mathews	3.00	8.00
125 Tom Brady	8.00	20.00
126 Sidney Rice	2.50	6.00
127 Ray Lewis	4.00	10.00
128 Josh Freeman	3.00	8.00
129 Tim Tebow	4.00	10.00
130 Drew Brees	5.00	12.00
131 LeSean McCoy	4.00	10.00
132 Antonio Gates	3.00	8.00
133 Dez Bryant	4.00	10.00
134 Davone Bess	2.50	6.00
135 Maurice Jones-Drew	2.50	6.00
136 Ahmad Bradshaw	2.50	6.00
137 Blaine Gabbert	2.50	6.00
138 Julius Peppers	3.00	8.00
139 Mike Wallace	2.50	6.00
140 Dan Fouts	3.00	8.00
141 Golden Tate	2.50	6.00
142 Ed Reed	3.00	8.00
143 Randall Cobb	3.00	8.00
144 J.J. Watt	4.00	10.00
145 Eric Decker	2.50	6.00
146 Christian Ponder	2.50	6.00
147 Jason Witten	3.00	8.00
148 DeAngelo Williams	2.50	6.00
149 Jason Pierre-Paul	2.50	6.00
150 Jerry Rice	6.00	15.00
151 Tannehill JSY AU/50 RC	10.00	25.00
152 B.Weeden JSY AU/50 RC	6.00	15.00
153 M.Floyd JSY AU/50 RC	6.00	15.00
155 K. Wright JSY AU/50 RC	6.00	15.00
156 B.Osweiler JSY AU/50 RC	6.00	15.00
157 S.Hill JSY AU/50 RC	6.00	15.00
158 A.Jenkins JSY AU/50 RC	6.00	15.00
159 R.Wilson JSY AU/50 RC	125.00	200.00
160 Griffin III JSY AU/50 RC EX	20.00	50.00
161 A.Jeffery JSY AU/50 RC	12.00	30.00
162 Isaiah Pead JSY AU/50 RC	6.00	15.00
163 Lamar Miller JSY AU/50 RC	20.00	50.00
164 B.Quick JSY AU/50 RC	6.00	15.00
165 Doug Martin JSY AU/50 RC	10.00	25.00
166 L.James JSY AU/50 RC	6.00	15.00
167 M.Sanu JSY AU/50 RC	10.00	25.00
168 R.Randle JSY AU/100 RC	6.00	15.00
169 J.Gordon JSY AU/100 RC	15.00	40.00
170 A.Luck JSY AU/50 RC	150.00	250.00
171 R.Broyles JSY AU/100 RC	6.00	15.00
172 Nick Foles JSY AU/100 RC	30.00	60.00
173 D.Posey JSY AU/100 RC	6.00	15.00
174 T.Y. Hilton JSY AU/100 RC	15.00	40.00
175 J.Blackmon JSY AU/50 RC	6.00	15.00
176 A.Morris JSY AU/100 RC	6.00	15.00
177 C.Fleener JSY AU/300 RC	5.00	12.00
178 Kirkpatrick JSY AU/300 RC	5.00	12.00
180 Richardson JSY AU/50 RC	6.00	15.00
181 R.Hillman JSY AU/300 RC	5.00	12.00
182 R.Turbin JSY AU/300 RC	5.00	12.00
183 M.Egnew JSY AU/300 RC	5.00	12.00
184 T. Graham JSY AU/300 RC	5.00	12.00
185 J.Wright JSY AU/300 RC	6.00	15.00
188 V.Ballard JSY AU/50 RC	8.00	20.00
190 D.Allen JSY AU/300 RC	5.00	12.00
SBMVPA Eli Manning SB JSY/16	125.00	250.00
LMVPAR Aaron Rodgers AU EXCH	175.00	300.00
SBMVPB Eli Manning SB FB/20	125.00	250.00

2012 Topps Five Star Rookie Autographed Patch Gold

*GOLD/55: .6X TO 1.5X BASE JSY AU/300
*GOLD/55: .5X TO 1.2X BASE JSY AU/50-100

159 Russell Wilson JSY AU	100.00	200.00
170 Andrew Luck JSY AU	300.00	500.00

2012 Topps Five Star Rookie Autographed Patch Rainbow

*RAINBOW/25: .8X TO 2X JSY AU/300
*RAINBOW/25: .6X TO 1.5X JSY AU/50-100

159 Russell Wilson JSY AU	250.00	400.00
170 Andrew Luck JSY AU	400.00	700.00
176 Alfred Morris JSY AU	10.00	25.00

2012 Topps Five Star Veteran Autographed Triple Jersey

EXCH EXPIRATION: 4/30/2016

FSSBAH Aaron Hernandez	20.00	50.00
FSSBAR Aaron Rodgers	150.00	250.00
FSSBBF Brett Favre	150.00	250.00
FSSBDB Dwayne Bowe	20.00	50.00
FSSBDM Dan Marino EXCH	75.00	150.00
FSSBDS Darren Sproles	20.00	50.00
FSSBES Emmitt Smith	125.00	225.00
FSSBFJ Fred Jackson	20.00	50.00
FSSBJE John Elway	100.00	200.00
FSSBJG Jimmy Graham EXCH	25.00	60.00
FSSBJM Joe Montana	125.00	200.00
FSSBJN Joe Namath EXCH	60.00	120.00
FSSBMF Matt Forte	15.00	40.00
FSSBMR Matt Ryan	40.00	80.00
FSSBMS Matthew Stafford	40.00	80.00
FSSBMV Michael Vick	25.00	60.00
FSSBMW Mike Wallace	15.00	40.00
FSSBRG Rob Gronkowski	30.00	60.00
FSSBRW Roddy White	15.00	40.00
FSSBSR Sidney Rice	15.00	40.00
FSSBSS Steve Smith	20.00	50.00
FSSBTR Tony Romo	40.00	80.00
FSSBTS Torrey Smith	15.00	40.00
FSSBVC Victor Cruz	20.00	50.00
FSSBVM Von Miller	20.00	50.00
FSSBWM Willis McGahee	15.00	40.00
FSSBAJG A.J. Green	25.00	60.00
FSSBDMC Darren McFadden	15.00	40.00
FSSBMJD Maurice Jones-Drew	15.00	40.00
FSSBMSC Matt Schaub	20.00	50.00

2012 Topps Five Star Dual Patches

FSDPBF J.Blackmon/M.Floyd	5.00	12.00
FSDPBP I.Pead/S.Bradford	5.00	12.00
FSDPBW K.Wright/J.Blackmon	5.00	12.00
FSDPCJ J.Cutler/A.Jeffery	10.00	25.00
FSDPDS A.Dalton/M.Sanu	12.00	30.00
FSDPFA D.Allen/C.Fleener	6.00	15.00
FSDPFG R.Fitzpatrick/T.Graham	5.00	12.00
FSDPFH T.Hilton/C.Fleener	10.00	25.00
FSDPFQ M.Floyd/B.Quick	8.00	20.00
FSDPGB B.Gabbert/J.Blackmon	5.00	12.00
FSDPGL R.Griffin III/A.Luck	30.00	80.00
FSDPGW R.Griffin III/K.Wright	30.00	80.00
FSDPHP R.Hillman/B.Pierce	5.00	12.00
FSDPIR T.Richardson/M.Ingram	6.00	15.00
FSDPJJ L.James/A.Jenkins	5.00	12.00
FSDPKH D.Hightower/L.Kuechly	12.00	30.00
FSDPLB A.Luck/J.Blackmon	30.00	80.00
FSDPLF C.Fleener/A.Luck	20.00	50.00
FSDPNA C.Newton/J.Adams	12.00	30.00
FSDPOF N.Foles/B.Osweiler	12.00	30.00
FSDPQJ B.Quick/A.Jeffery		
FSDPQP I.Pead/B.Quick	5.00	12.00
FSDPRM T.Richardson/D.Martin	8.00	20.00
FSDPRW T.Richardson/B.Weeden	5.00	12.00
FSDPSH S.Hill/M.Sanchez	5.00	12.00
FSDPSR T.Smith/R.Randle	5.00	12.00
FSDPTB J.Blackmon/R.Tannehill	8.00	20.00
FSDPTM R.Tannehill/L.Miller	8.00	20.00
FSDPWO B.Weeden/B.Osweiler	5.00	12.00
FSDPWT R.Turbin/R.Wilson	30.00	80.00

2012 Topps Five Star Dual Rookie Autographed Patch

FSFDAPBF M.Floyd/J.Blackmon	12.00	30.00
FSFDAPBJ A.Jeffery/R.Broyles	25.00	60.00
FSFDAPBQ B.Quick/J.Blackmon	12.00	30.00
FSFDAPBW Blackmon/K.Wright	12.00	30.00
FSFDAPFA D.Allen/C.Fleener	12.00	30.00
FSFDAPGB Blackmon/RG3 EX	75.00	150.00
FSFDAPGR RG3/Richardson EX	75.00	150.00
FSFDAPGW R.Griffin/K.Wright	75.00	150.00
FSFDAPJS M.Sanu/A.Jeffery	30.00	60.00
FSFDAPLB A.Luck/J.Blackmon	100.00	200.00
FSFDAPLF C.Fleener/A.Luck		
FSFDAPLG R.Griffin/A.Luck	100.00	200.00
FSFDAPLR T.Rchrdsn/A.Luck	100.00	200.00
FSFDAPMW D.Wilson/D.Martin	20.00	50.00
FSFDAPOH Osweiler/Hillman EX	12.00	30.00
FSFDAPQP B.Quick/I.Pead	15.00	40.00
FSFDAPRB Blackmn/Richardsn	40.00	100.00
FSFDAPRH R.Randle/S.Hill	15.00	40.00
FSFDAPRW D.Wilson/R.Randle	12.00	30.00
FSFDAPRWI Richardson/Wilson	12.00	30.00
FSFDAPTE Tannehill/M.Egnew	20.00	50.00
FSFDAPTH S.Hill/N.Toon	25.00	50.00
FSFDAPTM L.Miller/R.Tannehill	20.00	50.00
FSFDAPTO Tannehill/Oswlr EX	20.00	50.00
FSFDAPWB Blackmon/Weeden	30.00	60.00
FSFDAPWJ K.Wright/A.Jeffery	40.00	80.00
FSFDAPWJE A.Jenkins/K.Wright	30.00	60.00
FSFDAPWR Richardson/Weeden	40.00	100.00
FSFDAPWT R.Wilson/N.Toon	100.00	200.00
FSFDAPWTU R.Wilson/R.Turbin	100.00	200.00

2012 Topps Five Star Dual Rookie Autographs

FSFDABF M.Floyd/J.Blackmon	10.00	25.00
FSFDABQ B.Quick/J.Blackmon	10.00	25.00
FSFDABW K.Wright/J.Blackmon	10.00	25.00
FSFDAFA C.Fleener/D.Allen	10.00	25.00
FSFDAGB RG3/Blackmon EX	50.00	100.00
FSFDAGR Richardson/RG3 EX	60.00	120.00
FSFDAGW K.Wright/R.Griffin III	60.00	120.00
FSFDAJS M.Sanu/A.Jeffery	20.00	50.00
FSFDALB A.Luck/J.Blackmon	100.00	200.00
FSFDALF A.Luck/C.Fleener	100.00	200.00
FSFDALG A.Luck/R.Griffin III	100.00	200.00
FSFDALR Richardson/A.Luck	100.00	200.00
FSFDAMW D.Wilson/D.Martin	15.00	40.00
FSFDAOH Osweiler/Hillman	10.00	25.00
FSFDAQP I.Pead/B.Quick	12.00	30.00
FSFDARB Blackmon/Richardson	10.00	25.00
FSFDARW R.Randle/D.Wilson	10.00	25.00
FSFDATH N.Toon/S.Hill	10.00	25.00
FSFDATM L.Miller/R.Tannehill	15.00	40.00
FSFDATO Tannehill/Osweiler EX	15.00	40.00
FSFDAWB B.Weeden/J.Blackmon	10.00	25.00
FSFDAWJ K.Wright/A.Jeffery	20.00	50.00
FSFDAWR Weeden/Richardson	25.00	60.00
FSFDAWT R.Wilson/N.Toon	75.00	150.00
FSFDARWI Wilson/Richardson	10.00	25.00
FSFDAWTU R.Wilson/R.Turbin	100.00	175.00

2012 Topps Five Star Jumbo Jerseys

OLD/25: .6X TO 1.5X BASIC JSY/89

FSJJRAB Anquan Boldin	4.00	10.00
FSJJRAD Andy Dalton	8.00	20.00
FSJJRAF Arian Foster	5.00	12.00
FSJJRAG Antonio Gates	5.00	12.00
FSJJRAJ Alshon Jeffery	5.00	12.00
FSJJRAJG A.J. Green	6.00	15.00
FSJJRAJH A.J. Hawk	4.00	10.00
FSJJRAJJ A.J. Jenkins	2.50	6.00
FSJJRAL Andrew Luck	25.00	50.00
FSJJRBG Blaine Gabbert	4.00	10.00
FSJJRBO Brock Osweiler	2.50	6.00
FSJJRBQ Brian Quick	2.50	6.00
FSJJRBU Brian Urlacher	6.00	15.00
FSJJRBW Brandon Weeden	5.00	12.00
FSJJRCF Coby Fleener	2.50	6.00
FSJJRDA Dwayne Allen	2.50	6.00
FSJJRDB Dez Bryant	6.00	15.00
FSJJRDM Doug Martin	4.00	10.00
FSJJRED Eric Decker	4.00	10.00
FSJJRIP Isaiah Pead	2.50	6.00
FSJJRJA Joe Adams	4.00	10.00
FSJJRJB Justin Blackmon	2.50	6.00
FSJJRJC Jay Cutler	4.00	10.00
FSJJRJG Jimmy Graham	6.00	15.00
FSJJRJJ Julio Jones	6.00	15.00
FSJJRJW Jarius Wright	2.50	6.00
FSJJRKW Kendall Wright	2.50	6.00
FSJJRLJ LaMichael James	6.00	15.00
FSJJRLM Lamar Miller	4.00	10.00
FSJJRME Michael Egnew	4.00	10.00
FSJJRMF Matt Forte	6.00	15.00
FSJJRMFL Michael Floyd	2.50	6.00
FSJJRMS Mohamed Sanu	4.00	10.00
FSJJRNF Nick Foles	6.00	15.00
FSJJRNT Nick Toon	4.00	10.00
FSJJRRB Ryan Broyles	2.50	6.00
FSJJRRBU Reggie Bush	4.00	10.00
FSJJRRG Robert Griffin III	3.00	8.00
FSJJRRH Ronnie Hillman	2.50	6.00
FSJJRRR Rueben Randle	2.50	6.00
FSJJRRT Ryan Tannehill	4.00	10.00
FSJJRRTU Robert Turbin	2.50	6.00
FSJJRRWI Russell Wilson	15.00	40.00
FSJJRSB Sam Bradford	5.00	12.00
FSJJRSH Stephen Hill	2.50	6.00
FSJJRTG Tony Gonzalez	6.00	15.00
FSJJRTJG T.J. Graham	4.00	10.00
FSJJRTR Trent Richardson	6.00	15.00
FSJJRTYH T.Y. Hilton	5.00	12.00

2012 Topps Five Star Rookie Autographed Quad Jersey

*QUAD JSY/40: .4X TO 1X TRIPLE/42
*GOLD/15: .6X TO 1.5X QUAD JSY/40

FSFA4AL Andrew Luck	250.00	400.00
FSFA4DM Doug Martin	12.00	30.00
FSFA4RG Robert Griffin III EXCH	40.00	100.00
FSFA4RT Ryan Tannehill	12.00	30.00
FSFA4RW Russell Wilson	200.00	350.00
FSFA4TR Trent Richardson	8.00	20.00

2012 Topps Five Star Rookie Autographed Triple Jersey

*GOLD/15: .6X TO 1.5X TRIPLE JSY/42

FSFA3AJ Alshon Jeffery	20.00	50.00
FSFA3AJJ A.J. Jenkins	8.00	20.00
FSFA3AL Andrew Luck	150.00	300.00
FSFA3AM Alfred Morris	8.00	20.00
FSFA3BO Brock Osweiler	8.00	20.00
FSFA3BQ Brian Quick	8.00	20.00
FSFA3BW Brandon Weeden	8.00	20.00
FSFA3CF Coby Fleener	8.00	20.00
FSFA3DA Dwayne Allen	8.00	20.00
FSFA3DM Doug Martin	12.00	30.00
FSFA3IP Isaiah Pead	8.00	20.00
FSFA3JB Justin Blackmon	8.00	20.00
FSFA3JG Josh Gordon	20.00	50.00
FSFA3KW Kendall Wright	8.00	20.00
FSFA3LJ LaMichael James	8.00	20.00
FSFA3LM Lamar Miller	12.00	30.00
FSFA3MF Michael Floyd	8.00	20.00
FSFA3MS Mohamed Sanu	12.00	30.00
FSFA3NF Nick Foles	20.00	50.00
FSFA3NT Nick Toon	8.00	20.00
FSFA3RB Ryan Broyles	8.00	20.00
FSFA3RG Robert Griffin III	30.00	80.00
FSFA3RH Ronnie Hillman	8.00	20.00
FSFA3RR Rueben Randle	8.00	20.00
FSFA3RT Ryan Tannehill	12.00	30.00
FSFA3RTU Robert Turbin	8.00	20.00
FSFA3RW Russell Wilson	100.00	200.00
FSFA3SH Stephen Hill	8.00	20.00
FSFA3TJG T.J. Graham	8.00	20.00
FSFA3TR Trent Richardson	12.00	30.00

2012 Topps Five Star Rookie Autographs

CH EXPIRATION: 4/30/2016

FSFAAJ Alshon Jeffery/150	15.00	40.00
FSFAAL Andrew Luck/100	175.00	300.00
FSFAAM Alfred Morris/150	4.00	10.00
FSFABO Brock Osweiler/100	4.00	10.00
FSFABQ Brian Quick/150	4.00	10.00
FSFABW Brandon Weeden/100	4.00	10.00
FSFACF Coby Fleener/200	4.00	10.00
FSFACJ Chandler Jones/150	4.00	10.00
FSFADM Doug Martin/150	8.00	20.00
FSFADP DeVier Posey/200	4.00	10.00
FSFADW David Wilson/100	4.00	10.00
FSFAJB Justin Blackmon/100	4.00	10.00
FSFAJC Juron Criner/200	6.00	15.00
FSFAJG Josh Gordon/150	10.00	25.00
FSFAJW Jarius Wright/200	4.00	10.00
FSFAKW Kendall Wright/200	4.00	10.00
FSFALJ LaMichael James/150	4.00	10.00
FSFALK Luke Kuechly/150	30.00	60.00
FSFAME Michael Egnew/200	4.00	10.00
FSFAMF Michael Floyd/100	4.00	10.00
FSFAMS Mohamed Sanu/150	6.00	15.00
FSFANF Nick Foles/150	10.00	25.00
FSFANT Nick Toon/200	4.00	10.00
FSFARB Ryan Broyles/150	4.00	10.00
FSFARG Robert Griffin III/100	25.00	60.00
FSFARR Rueben Randle/150	4.00	10.00
FSFART Ryan Tannehill/100	6.00	15.00

FSFARTU Robert Turbin/200 8.00 20.00
FSFARW Russell Wilson/150 100.00 200.00
FSFASH Stephen Hill/150 4.00 10.00
FSFATB Travis Benjamin/200 4.00 10.00
FSFATJG T.J. Graham/200 4.00 10.00
FSFATR Trent Richardson/100 4.00 10.00
FSFATYH T.Y. Hilton/200 8.00 20.00
FSFAVB Vick Ballard/200 5.00 12.00

2012 Topps Five Star Rookie Autographs Rainbow

*RAINBOW/25: .6X TO 1.5X AU/100-200
FSFAAL Andrew Luck 200.00 400.00
FSFAAM Alfred Morris 6.00 15.00
FSFART Ryan Tannehill 10.00 25.00
FSFARW Russell Wilson 150.00 250.00

2012 Topps Five Star Rookie Quotable Autographs

FSFQAAJ Alshon Jeffery 20.00 50.00
FSFQAAJJ A.J. Jenkins 10.00 25.00
FSFQAAL Andrew Luck 500.00 800.00
FSFQAAM Alfred Morris 10.00 25.00
FSFQABO Brock Osweiler 10.00 25.00
FSFQABQ Brian Quick 10.00 25.00
FSFQABW Brandon Weeden 10.00 25.00
FSFQACF Coby Fleener 10.00 25.00
FSFQADA Dwayne Allen 10.00 25.00
FSFQADM Doug Martin 15.00 40.00
FSFQADW David Wilson 10.00 25.00
FSFQAIP Isaiah Pead 20.00 50.00
FSFQAJB Justin Blackmon 10.00 25.00
FSFQAJG Josh Gordon 25.00 60.00
FSFQAKW Kendall Wright 10.00 25.00
FSFQALJ LaMichael James 10.00 25.00
FSFQALM Lamar Miller 40.00 80.00
FSFQAMF Michael Floyd 10.00 25.00
FSFQAMS Mohamed Sanu 15.00 40.00
FSFQANF Nick Foles 25.00 60.00
FSFQANT Nick Toon 15.00 40.00
FSFQARB Ryan Broyles 10.00 25.00
FSFQARG Robert Griffin III 40.00 80.00
FSFQARH Ronnie Hillman 10.00 25.00
FSFQARR Rueben Randle 10.00 25.00
FSFQART Ryan Tannehill 15.00 40.00
FSFQARTU Robert Turbin 30.00 60.00
FSFQARW Russell Wilson 250.00 400.00
FSFQASH Stephen Hill 10.00 25.00
FSFQATR Trent Richardson 25.00 60.00

2012 Topps Five Star Veteran Autographed Patch

*GOLD/40: .5X TO 1.2X BASIC AU/75
*RAINBOW/25: .6X TO 1.5X BASIC AU/75
FSSPAH Aaron Hernandez 12.00 30.00
FSSPAP Adrian Peterson 50.00 100.00
FSSPDB Dwayne Bowe 10.00 25.00
FSSPDM Dan Marino 60.00 120.00
FSSPDMU DeMarco Murray 15.00 40.00
FSSPGJ Greg Jennings 10.00 25.00
FSSPHN Hakeem Nicks 10.00 25.00
FSSPJR Jerry Rice 75.00 150.00
FSSPLM LeSean McCoy 15.00 40.00
FSSPMJD Maurice Jones-Drew 10.00 25.00
FSSPMR Matt Ryan 20.00 50.00
FSSPMT Michael Turner 10.00 25.00
FSSPRM Rashard Mendenhall 10.00 25.00
FSSPSS Steve Smith 12.00 30.00
FSSPSY Steve Young 60.00 120.00
FSSPTR Tony Romo 40.00 80.00
FSSPTS Torrey Smith 10.00 25.00
FSSPVC Victor Cruz 12.00 30.00
FSSPVM Von Miller 12.00 30.00
FSSPWM Willis McGahee 10.00 25.00

2012 Topps Five Star Veteran Autographs

*GOLD/25: .6X TO 1.5X BASIC AU/200
*GOLD/25: .5X TO 1.2X BASIC AU/85
*RAINBOW/15: .6X TO 1.5X BASIC AU/200
*RAINBOW/15: .5X TO 1.2X BASIC AU/85
EXCH EXPIRATION: 4/30/2016
FSSAH Aaron Hernandez/200 10.00 25.00
FSSAP Adrian Peterson/85 75.00 125.00
FSSBF Brett Favre/85 100.00 200.00
FSSBS Bart Starr/85 75.00 125.00
FSSBSA Barry Sanders/85 75.00 135.00
FSSCB Cedric Benson/200 6.00 15.00
FSSCH Chuck Howley/85 10.00 25.00
FSSDB Dwayne Bowe/85 8.00 20.00
FSSDF Dan Fouts/85 25.00 60.00
FSSJB Jim Brown/85 40.00 80.00
FSSJF Jermichael Finley/85 8.00 20.00
FSSJG Jimmy Graham/200 EXCH 10.00 25.00
FSSJK Jim Kelly/85 25.00 60.00
FSSJM Joe Montana/85 75.00 150.00
FSSJP Jim Plunkett/200 EXCH 10.00 25.00
FSSKW Kurt Warner/85 30.00 60.00
FSSMS Matthew Stafford/85 20.00 40.00
FSSRW Roddy White/200 6.00 15.00
FSSSH Santonio Holmes/85 6.00 15.00
FSSSR Sidney Rice/200 6.00 15.00
FSSTB Terry Bradshaw/85 40.00 80.00
FSSTS Torrey Smith/200 8.00 20.00
FSSVC Victor Cruz/200 12.00 30.00
FSSWM Warren Moon/85 15.00 40.00
FSSWMC Willis McGahee/85 8.00 20.00

2012 Topps Five Star Club

STATED PRINT RUN 50 SER.#'d SETS
FSC6 Robert Griffin III 15.00 40.00
FSC7 Andrew Luck 75.00 150.00
FSC8 Trent Richardson 8.00 20.00
FSC9 Justin Blackmon 8.00 20.00
FSC10 Ryan Tannehill 10.00 25.00

2013 Topps Five Star

ATED PRINT RUN 208
101-45 ROOKIE JSY AU PRINT RUN 94
EXCH EXPIRATION: 4/30/2017
1 Rob Gronkowski 2.50 6.00
2 Vincent Jackson 1.50 4.00
3 Elvis Dumervil 1.50 4.00
4 Bo Jackson 4.00 10.00
5 Adrian Peterson 2.50 6.00
6 Deion Sanders 4.00 10.00
7 C.J. Spiller 1.50 4.00
8 Matt Forte 1.50 4.00
9 Curtis Martin 2.00 5.00
10 Eli Manning 2.00 5.00
11 Marcus Allen 2.50 6.00
12 Arian Foster 2.00 5.00
13 Frank Gore 2.00 5.00
14 Wes Welker 2.00 5.00
15 Matt Ryan 2.00 5.00
16 Geno Atkins 1.50 4.00
17 Marshawn Lynch 2.00 5.00
18 Aaron Rodgers 4.00 10.00
19 Steve Largent 2.50 6.00
20 Ed Reed 2.00 5.00
21 A.J. Green 2.50 6.00
22 Julio Jones 2.50 6.00
23 Maurice Jones-Drew 1.50 4.00
24 Alfred Morris 1.50 4.00
25 Andrew Luck 4.00 10.00
26 Colin Kaepernick 2.00 5.00
27 Chris Johnson 1.50 4.00
28 Darren McFadden 2.00 5.00
29 Patrick Willis 2.00 5.00
30 Joe Montana 6.00 15.00
31 Eric Dickerson 2.00 5.00
32 Luke Kuechly 2.00 5.00
33 Von Miller 2.00 5.00
34 Bruce Smith 2.00 5.00
35 Carson Palmer 2.00 5.00
36 Michael Vick 2.00 5.00
37 Randall Cobb 2.00 5.00
38 Ray Rice 1.50 4.00
39 Troy Aikman 3.00 8.00
40 Jerry Rice 4.00 10.00
41 Earl Thomas 2.00 5.00
42 Doug Martin 2.00 5.00
43 Cam Newton 2.50 6.00
44 Joe Flacco 2.00 5.00
45 Jason Witten 2.00 5.00
46 Mike Wallace 1.50 4.00
47 LeSean McCoy 2.50 6.00
48 T.Y. Hilton 2.00 5.00
49 Drew Brees 2.50 6.00
50 Demaryius Thomas 2.00 5.00
51 J.J. Watt 2.00 5.00
52 Dwayne Bowe 2.00 5.00
53 Roddy White 1.50 4.00
54 Patrick Peterson 1.50 4.00
55 Matthew Stafford 2.00 5.00
56 Jay Cutler 1.50 4.00
57 Clay Matthews 2.50 6.00
58 Dez Bryant 2.50 6.00
59 Andy Dalton 2.00 5.00
60 Peyton Manning 5.00 12.00
61 Dan Marino 5.00 12.00
62 Darrelle Revis 1.50 4.00
63 Charles Tillman 2.00 5.00
64 Robert Griffin III 1.50 4.00
65 Sam Bradford 1.50 4.00
66 Kurt Warner 2.00 5.00
67 Warren Moon 2.50 6.00
68 Russell Wilson 8.00 20.00
69 Ryan Tannehill 2.00 5.00
70 Aldon Smith 1.50 4.00
71 Ben Roethlisberger 2.50 6.00
72 Jamaal Charles 2.00 5.00
73 Troy Polamalu 2.50 6.00
74 Brett Favre 6.00 15.00
75 LaDainian Tomlinson 2.00 5.00
76 Victor Cruz 2.00 5.00
77 DeMarcus Ware 2.50 6.00
78 Antonio Cromartie 1.50 4.00
79 Andre Johnson 1.50 4.00
80 Jimmy Graham 2.50 6.00
81 Richard Sherman 3.00 8.00
82 Marshall Faulk 2.00 5.00
83 Larry Fitzgerald 4.00 10.00
84 Steve Young 3.00 8.00
85 Calvin Johnson 4.00 10.00
86 Reggie Bush 1.50 4.00
87 Trent Richardson 1.50 4.00
88 Reggie Wayne 2.00 5.00
89 Chris Long 1.50 4.00
90 Tom Brady 5.00 12.00
91 Barry Sanders 4.00 10.00
92 Steve Smith 2.00 5.00
93 Tony Romo 2.00 5.00
94 Lawrence Taylor 2.50 6.00
95 Steven Jackson 1.50 4.00
96 John Elway 4.00 10.00
97 Terrell Suggs 1.50 4.00
98 Philip Rivers 2.50 6.00
99 Jared Allen 1.50 4.00
100 Brandon Marshall 2.00 5.00
101 Geno Smith JSY AU RC 5.00 12.00
102 EJ Manuel JSY AU RC 12.00 30.00
103 Matt Barkley JSY AU RC 8.00 20.00
104 Tavon Austin JSY AU RC 6.00 15.00
105 D.Hopkins JSY AU RC 10.00 25.00
106 C.Patterson JSY AU RC 5.00 12.00
107 Mike Glennon JSY AU RC 5.00 12.00
108 Manti Te'o JSY AU RC 6.00 15.00
109 Justin Hunter JSY AU RC 10.00 25.00
110 Dion Jordan JSY AU RC 5.00 12.00
112 Ryan Nassib JSY AU RC 5.00 12.00
113 Giovani Bernard JSY AU RC 8.00 20.00
114 Le'Veon Bell JSY AU RC 30.00 60.00
115 Robert Woods JSY AU RC 8.00 20.00
116 Eddie Lacy JSY AU RC 5.00 12.00
117 Aaron Dobson JSY AU RC 5.00 12.00
118 Tyler Eifert JSY AU RC 10.00 25.00
119 Montee Ball JSY AU RC 5.00 12.00
120 C.Michael JSY AU RC 5.00 12.00
121 Zach Ertz JSY AU RC 10.00 25.00
123 M.Wheaton JSY AU RC 5.00 12.00
124 Joseph Randle JSY AU RC 5.00 12.00
125 Landry Jones JSY AU RC 5.00 12.00
126 J.Franklin JSY AU RC 5.00 12.00
127 Stepfan Taylor JSY AU RC 5.00 12.00
128 Keenan Allen JSY AU RC 10.00 25.00
129 Quinton Patton JSY AU RC 5.00 12.00
130 Andre Ellington JSY AU RC 10.00 25.00
131 Gavin Escobar JSY AU RC 5.00 12.00
132 Stedman Bailey JSY AU RC 5.00 12.00
133 M.Lattimore JSY AU RC 5.00 12.00
134 Kenny Stills JSY AU RC 5.00 12.00
135 D.Robinson JSY AU RC 5.00 12.00
136 M.Goodwin JSY AU RC 5.00 12.00
137 V.McDonald JSY AU RC 6.00 15.00
138 Knile Davis JSY AU RC 5.00 12.00
139 Jordan Reed JSY AU RC 8.00 20.00
140 Mike Gillislee JSY AU RC
142 Ansah JSY AU RC EXCH 5.00 12.00
144 Josh Boyce JSY AU RC 5.00 12.00
145 Kenjon Barner JSY AU RC 5.00 12.00
SBMVPAJF J.Flacco SB MVP/50 40.00 100.00

2013 Topps Five Star Rookie Autographed Patch Gold

*GOLD/55: .5X TO 1.2X BASIC JSY AU/94
116 Eddie Lacy JSY AU 6.00 15.00

2013 Topps Five Star Rookie Autographed Patch Rainbow

*RAINBOW/25: .6X TO 1.5X BASIC JSY AU/94
116 Eddie Lacy JSY AU 8.00 20.00

2013 Topps Five Star Dual Rookie Autographs

STATED PRINT RUN 20
FSFDAAB S.Bailey/T.Austin
FSFDABB M.Ball/G.Bernard 8.00 20.00
FSFDABD M.Ball/K.Davis 25.00 50.00
FSFDABL L.Bell/E.Lacy EXCH 50.00 100.00
FSFDABW R.Woods/M.Barkley 12.00 30.00
FSFDACJ J.Hunter/Patterson 8.00 20.00
FSFDAEE T.Eifert/Z.Ertz 15.00 40.00
FSFDAGE G.Bernard/E.Lacy 40.00 80.00
FSFDAGW T.Wilson/M.Glennon
FSFDAJG M.Gillislee/D.Jordan
FSFDAJT D.Jordan/M.Te'o
FSFDALF E.Lacy/J.Franklin 25.00 60.00
FSFDALM L.Bell/Wheaton EXCH 30.00 60.00
FSFDAMB E.Manuel/M.Barkley
FSFDAME McDonald/Escobar
FSFDAMH D.Hayden/D.Milliner
FSFDAML Lattimore/C.Michael 8.00 20.00
FSFDAMS G.Smith/E.Manuel 8.00 20.00
FSFDAMW Woods/Manuel EXCH 12.00 30.00
FSFDANJ L.Jones/R.Nassib
FSFDAPH D.Hopkins/Patterson 40.00 80.00
FSFDARS Robinson/A.Sanders 8.00 20.00
FSFDASA S.Taylor/A.Ellington 20.00 40.00
FSFDASG M.Glennon/G.Smith
FSFDATE M.Te'o/T.Eifert 10.00 25.00
FSFDAWD A.Dobson/R.Woods 12.00 30.00

2013 Topps Five Star Jumbo Jerseys

STATED PRINT RUN 87 SER.#'d SETS
FSJJRAD Aaron Dobson 1.50 4.00
FSJJRAG Antonio Gates 4.00 10.00
FSJJRAJG A.J. Green 5.00 12.00
FSJJRAL Andrew Luck 8.00 20.00
FSJJRAP Adrian Peterson 5.00 12.00
FSJJRCP Cordarrelle Patterson 1.50 4.00
FSJJRDB Dez Bryant 8.00 20.00
FSJJRDH DeAndre Hopkins 4.00 10.00
FSJJRDM Darren McFadden 4.00 10.00
FSJJRDR Denard Robinson 1.50 4.00
FSJJRED Eric Decker 3.00 8.00
FSJJREJM EJ Manuel 1.50 4.00
FSJJREL Eddie Lacy 1.50 4.00
FSJJRGB Giovani Bernard 1.50 4.00
FSJJRGE Gavin Escobar 1.50 4.00
FSJJRGS Geno Smith 1.50 4.00
FSJJRJC Jay Cutler 3.00 8.00
FSJJRJF Joe Flacco 4.00 10.00
FSJJRJH Justin Hunter 1.50 4.00
FSJJRJJ Julio Jones 5.00 12.00
FSJJRJR Joseph Randle 1.50 4.00
FSJJRKA Keenan Allen 3.00 8.00
FSJJRLB Le'Veon Bell 6.00 15.00
FSJJRLF Larry Fitzgerald 4.00 10.00
FSJJRMA Miles Austin 3.00 8.00
FSJJRMB Matt Barkley 1.50 4.00
FSJJRMBA Montee Ball 1.50 4.00
FSJJRMF Matt Forte 6.00 15.00
FSJJRMG Mike Glennon 1.50 4.00
FSJJRMJD Maurice Jones-Drew 5.00 12.00
FSJJRML Marcus Lattimore 1.50 4.00
FSJJRMS Matt Schaub 3.00 8.00
FSJJRMT Manti Te'o 2.00 5.00
FSJJRMV Michael Vick 4.00 10.00
FSJJRMW Markus Wheaton 1.50 4.00
FSJJRRG Robert Griffin III 3.00 8.00
FSJJRRR Ray Rice 3.00 8.00
FSJJRRT Ryan Tannehill 4.00 10.00
FSJJRRW Robert Woods 2.50 6.00
FSJJRRWH Roddy White 3.00 8.00
FSJJRRWI Russell Wilson 10.00 25.00
FSJJRSB Sam Bradford 3.00 8.00
FSJJRST Stepfan Taylor 1.50 4.00
FSJJRTA Tavon Austin 2.00 5.00
FSJJRTE Tyler Eifert 1.50 4.00
FSJJRTR Tony Romo 4.00 10.00
FSJJRTS Torrey Smith 3.00 8.00
FSJJRTW Terrance Williams 1.50 4.00
FSJJRVM Von Miller 4.00 10.00
FSJJRZE Zach Ertz 3.00 8.00

2013 Topps Five Star Rookie Autographed Triple Jersey

STATED PRINT RUN 38
*TRIPLE GOLD/15: .5X TO 1.2X TRIPLE/38
*QUAD/38: .4X TO 1X TRIPLE/38
*QUAD GOLD/15: .6X TO 1.5X TRIPLE/38
FSFA3AD Aaron Dobson 8.00 20.00
FSFA3AE Andre Ellington 12.00 30.00
FSFA3CP Cordarrelle Patterson 8.00 20.00
FSFA3DH DeAndre Hopkins 15.00 40.00
FSFA3DR Denard Robinson 8.00 20.00
FSFA3EJM EJ Manuel 15.00 40.00
FSFA3EL Eddie Lacy 8.00 20.00
FSFA3GB Giovani Bernard 8.00 20.00
FSFA3GE Gavin Escobar 8.00 20.00
FSFA3GS Geno Smith 8.00 20.00
FSFA3JF Johnathan Franklin 8.00 20.00
FSFA3JH Justin Hunter 15.00 40.00
FSFA3JR Jordan Reed 12.00 30.00
FSFA3KA Keenan Allen 20.00 50.00
FSFA3KS Kenny Stills 8.00 20.00
FSFA3LB Le'Veon Bell 25.00 60.00
FSFA3MB Matt Barkley 15.00 40.00
FSFA3MBA Montee Ball 8.00 20.00
FSFA3MG Mike Glennon 8.00 20.00
FSFA3ML Marcus Lattimore 8.00 20.00
FSFA3MT Manti Te'o 10.00 25.00
FSFA3MW Markus Wheaton 8.00 20.00
FSFA3RW Robert Woods 12.00 30.00
FSFA3SB Stedman Bailey 8.00 20.00
FSFA3ST Stepfan Taylor 8.00 20.00
FSFA3TA Tavon Austin 10.00 25.00
FSFA3TE Tyler Eifert 8.00 20.00
FSFA3TW Tyler Wilson 8.00 20.00
FSFA3TWI Terrance Williams 8.00 20.00
FSFA3ZE Zach Ertz 15.00 40.00

2013 Topps Five Star Rookie Autographs

STATED PRINT RUN 130 SER.#'d SETS
FSFAAD Aaron Dobson 4.00 10.00
FSFAAE Andre Ellington 8.00 20.00
FSFACM Christine Michael 10.00 25.00
FSFACP Cordarrelle Patterson 4.00 10.00
FSFADH DeAndre Hopkins 8.00 20.00
FSFADJ Dion Jordan 4.00 10.00
FSFADR Denard Robinson 4.00 10.00
FSFAEF Eric Fisher 4.00 10.00
FSFAEJM EJ Manuel 4.00 10.00
FSFAEL Eddie Lacy 4.00 10.00
FSFAGB Giovani Bernard 4.00 10.00
FSFAGE Gavin Escobar 6.00 15.00
FSFAGS Geno Smith 4.00 10.00
FSFAJF Johnathan Franklin 4.00 10.00
FSFAJH Justin Hunter 8.00 20.00
FSFAJR Joseph Randle 4.00 10.00
FSFAJRE Jordan Reed 5.00 12.00
FSFAKA Keenan Allen 8.00 20.00
FSFAKD Knile Davis 4.00 10.00
FSFAKS Kenny Stills 4.00 10.00
FSFAKT Kenbrell Thompkins 6.00 15.00
FSFALB Le'Veon Bell 12.00 30.00
FSFALJ Landry Jones 4.00 10.00
FSFAMBA Montee Ball 4.00 10.00
FSFAMG Mike Glennon 4.00 10.00
FSFAMGI Mike Gillislee 4.00 10.00
FSFAMGO Marquise Goodwin 4.00 10.00
FSFAML Marcus Lattimore 4.00 10.00
FSFAMT Manti Te'o 5.00 12.00
FSFAMW Markus Wheaton 4.00 10.00
FSFAQP Quinton Patton 4.00 10.00
FSFARN Ryan Nassib 4.00 10.00
FSFARW Robert Woods 6.00 15.00
FSFASB Stedman Bailey 4.00 10.00
FSFAST Stepfan Taylor 4.00 10.00
FSFATA Tavon Austin 5.00 12.00
FSFATE Tyler Eifert 8.00 20.00
FSFATM Tyrann Mathieu 6.00 15.00
FSFAVM Vance McDonald 5.00 12.00
FSFAZE Zach Ertz 8.00 20.00

2013 Topps Five Star Rookie Autographs Rainbow

*RAINBOW/25: .6X TO 1.5X BASIC AU/130

2013 Topps Five Star Rookie Quotable Autographs

*QUOTABLE/25: 1X TO 2.5X BASIC AU/130
FSFQAEL Eddie Lacy 10.00 25.00

2013 Topps Five Star Signature Book Autographs Patch

STATED PRINT RUN 38
FSSBAG Antonio Gates 15.00 40.00
FSSBAJG A.J. Green 20.00 50.00
FSSBAP Adrian Peterson 100.00 175.00
FSSBBH Brian Hartline 12.00 30.00
FSSBCJ Chris Johnson 12.00 30.00
FSSBCJS C.J. Spiller 12.00 30.00
FSSBDB Drew Brees 60.00 120.00
FSSBDM Dan Marino 75.00 150.00
FSSBDMC Darren McFadden 15.00 40.00
FSSBDS Deion Sanders 50.00 100.00
FSSBEM Eli Manning 50.00 100.00
FSSBFG Frank Gore 20.00 50.00
FSSBJC Jamaal Charles 15.00 40.00
FSSBJE John Elway 75.00 150.00
FSSBJF Joe Flacco 20.00 50.00
FSSBJM Joe Montana 90.00 150.00
FSSBJW Jason Witten 15.00 40.00
FSSBKW Kurt Warner
FSSBLM LeSean McCoy 20.00 50.00
FSSBLT LaDainian Tomlinson 30.00 60.00
FSSBMF Marshall Faulk 25.00 60.00
FSSBMFO Matt Forte 20.00 50.00
FSSBMJD Maurice Jones-Drew 12.00 30.00
FSSBMR Matt Ryan 20.00 50.00
FSSBPM Peyton Manning
FSSBRC Randall Cobb 30.00 60.00
FSSBRW Reggie Wayne 20.00 50.00
FSSBSJ Steve Johnson EXCH 15.00 40.00
FSSBSR Stevan Ridley
FSSBSV Shane Vereen 15.00 40.00
FSSBSY Steve Young 50.00 100.00
FSSBVJ Vincent Jackson 12.00 30.00

2013 Topps Five Star Veteran Autographed Patch

STATED PRINT RUN 75 SER.#'d SETS
*GOLD/40: .4X TO 1X PATCH AU/75
*RAINBOW/25: .5X TO 1.2X PATCH AU/75
FSSPAG Antonio Gates 12.00 30.00
FSSPAJG A.J. Green 15.00 40.00
FSSPAL Andrew Luck 90.00 150.00
FSSPAP Adrian Peterson 50.00 100.00
FSSPAR Aaron Rodgers 150.00 250.00
FSSPBH Brian Hartline 10.00 25.00
FSSPDB Drew Brees 50.00 100.00
FSSPDM Darren McFadden 12.00 30.00
FSSPED Eric Dickerson 25.00 50.00
FSSPEM Eli Manning 50.00 100.00
FSSPFG Frank Gore 15.00 40.00
FSSPJC Jamaal Charles 12.00 30.00
FSSPJW Jason Witten 20.00 50.00
FSSPLM LeSean McCoy 15.00 40.00
FSSPLT LaDainian Tomlinson 25.00 60.00
FSSPMF Marshall Faulk 25.00 50.00
FSSPMFO Matt Forte 15.00 40.00
FSSPMR Matt Ryan 15.00 40.00
FSSPRW Reggie Wayne 12.00 30.00
FSSPVJ Vincent Jackson 10.00 25.00

2013 Topps Five Star Veteran Autographs

STATED PRINT RUN 115 SER.#'d SETS
*GOLD/25: .5X TO 1.2X BASIC AU/115
*RAINBOW/15: .6X TO 1.5X AU/115
FSSAJG A.J. Green 12.00 30.00
FSSAR Andre Reed 12.00 30.00
FSSBJ Bo Jackson 40.00 100.00
FSSBS Barry Sanders 60.00 120.00
FSSBSM Bruce Smith 15.00 40.00
FSSCM Curtis Martin 25.00 50.00
FSSDB Drew Brees 40.00 80.00
FSSDS Deion Sanders 40.00 80.00
FSSED Eric Dickerson 15.00 40.00
FSSHL Howie Long 15.00 40.00
FSSJB Jerome Bettis 50.00 100.00
FSSJC Jamaal Charles 12.00 30.00
FSSLT Lawrence Taylor 25.00 50.00
FSSMA Marcus Allen 25.00 50.00
FSSMF Matt Forte
FSSMJD Maurice Jones-Drew 8.00 20.00
FSSML Marshawn Lynch 30.00 60.00
FSSMS Matthew Stafford 15.00 40.00
FSSPM Peyton Manning 100.00 200.00
FSSRC Randall Cobb 12.00 30.00
FSSRL Ronnie Lott 12.00 30.00
FSSROC Roger Craig 12.00 30.00
FSSSL Steve Largent 15.00 40.00
FSSSY Steve Young 40.00 80.00
FSSVJ Vincent Jackson 8.00 20.00
FSSWM Warren Moon 15.00 40.00

2014 Topps Five Star Autographs

FSAAB Antonio Brown 20.00 40.00
FSAAJ Alshon Jeffery 6.00 15.00
FSAAJG A.J. Green 8.00 20.00
FSAAL Andrew Luck SP
FSAAM Aaron Murray 4.00 10.00
FSAAMC A.J. McCarron 4.00 10.00
FSAAMO Alfred Morris 8.00 20.00
FSAAR Aaron Rodgers SP EXCH
FSAARO Allen Robinson 6.00 15.00
FSAASJ Austin Seferian-Jenkins 4.00 10.00
FSAAW Andre Williams 4.00 10.00
FSABB Blake Bortles SP
FSABC Brandin Cooks 6.00 15.00
FSABF Brett Favre SP 100.00 175.00
FSABJ Bo Jackson SP
FSABM Brandon Marshall 20.00 40.00
FSABS Bishop Sankey 4.00 10.00
FSABSA Barry Sanders SP 75.00 135.00
FSACH Carlos Hyde 5.00 12.00
FSACL Cody Latimer 5.00 12.00
FSACM Curtis Martin SP
FSACMA Clay Matthews SP
FSACS Charles Sims 4.00 10.00
FSADA Dri Archer 4.00 10.00
FSADAD Davante Adams 6.00 15.00
FSADB Drew Brees 30.00 60.00
FSADC Derek Carr 75.00 150.00
FSADF Devonta Freeman 6.00 15.00
FSADM Dan Marino SP
FSADMA Doug Martin 6.00 15.00
FSADMO Donte Moncrief 4.00 10.00
FSAEC Earl Campbell 20.00 40.00
FSAED Eric Dickerson SP
FSAEE Eric Ebron 5.00 12.00
FSAEL Eddie Lacy 5.00 12.00
FSAEM Eli Manning SP 20.00 50.00
FSAES Emmitt Smith SP 90.00 150.00
FSAFG Frank Gore 12.00 30.00
FSAGS Gale Sayers 12.00 30.00
FSAIC Isaiah Crowell 5.00 12.00
FSAJA Jace Amaro 4.00 10.00
FSAJB Jerome Bettis 40.00 80.00
FSAJBRO John Brown 6.00 15.00
FSAJC Jadeveon Clowney EXCH 5.00 12.00
FSAJCA Jordan Cameron 5.00 12.00
FSAJCH Jamaal Charles 10.00 25.00
FSAJE John Elway SP 50.00 100.00
FSAJG Jimmy Garoppolo 60.00 125.00
FSAJH Jeremy Hill 5.00 12.00
FSAJJ Julio Jones 25.00 50.00
FSAJL Jarvis Landry 8.00 20.00
FSAJM Johnny Manziel 10.00 25.00
FSAJMA Jordan Matthews 6.00 15.00
FSAJMAC Jeremy Maclin 5.00 12.00
FSAJMC Jerick McKinnon 5.00 12.00
FSAJN Joe Namath 60.00 125.00
FSAJNE Jordy Nelson 6.00 15.00
FSAJR John Riggins 20.00 50.00
FSAJT Julius Thomas 5.00 12.00
FSAJW James White 8.00 20.00
FSAKB Kelvin Benjamin 6.00 15.00
FSAKC Ka'Deem Carey 4.00 10.00
FSALM LeSean McCoy SP
FSALT Lawrence Taylor SP
FSALTA Lorenzo Taliaferro 4.00 10.00
FSALTH Logan Thomas 4.00 10.00
FSAMA Marcus Allen SP 12.00 30.00
FSAME Mike Evans 10.00 25.00
FSAMF Marshall Faulk SP
FSAMFL Michael Floyd 5.00 12.00
FSAMFO Matt Forte 5.00 12.00
FSAML Marshawn Lynch EXCH 25.00 50.00
FSAMLE Marqise Lee 5.00 12.00
FSAMSI Mike Singletary 15.00 40.00
FSAMST Matthew Stafford SP
FSANF Nick Foles SP
FSAOBJ Odell Beckham Jr. 50.00 100.00
FSAPG Pierre Garcon 6.00 15.00
FSAPM Peyton Manning SP 100.00 175.00
FSAPR Paul Richardson 6.00 15.00
FSARB Reggie Bush 5.00 12.00
FSARC Roger Craig 8.00 20.00
FSARG Rob Gronkowski 12.00 30.00
FSARJ Rashad Jennings 5.00 12.00
FSARL Ronnie Lott 12.00 30.00
FSARMA Ryan Mathews 6.00 15.00
FSARW Russell Wilson SP 75.00 125.00
FSARWA Reggie Wayne 10.00 25.00
FSARWH Roddy White 5.00 12.00
FSASW Sammy Watkins 6.00 15.00
FSASY Steve Young SP
FSATB Teddy Bridgewater SP 20.00 50.00
FSATBR Terry Bradshaw SP
FSATBRA Tom Brady SP 350.00 600.00
FSATM Tre Mason 4.00 10.00
FSATP Troy Polamalu SP 50.00 100.00
FSATS Tom Savage 4.00 10.00
FSATW Terrance West 4.00 10.00
FSATYH T.Y. Hilton 10.00 25.00
FSAVC Victor Cruz 6.00 15.00
FSAVJ Vincent Jackson 5.00 12.00
FSAWM Warren Moon 10.00 25.00
FSAZM Zach Mettenberger 4.00 10.00

2014 Topps Five Star Autographs Rainbow

*VETS/25: .6X TO 1.5X BASIC AUTO
*ROOKIES/25: .6X TO 1.5X BASIC AUTO
FSAAL Andrew Luck 150.00 250.00
FSAAR Aaron Rodgers EXCH 150.00 300.00
FSABB Blake Bortles 8.00 20.00
FSABF Brett Favre 150.00 250.00
FSACMA Clay Matthews 40.00 80.00
FSALT Lawrence Taylor 150.00 250.00
FSAMF Marshall Faulk 30.00 60.00
FSAPM Peyton Manning 100.00 200.00
FSATB Teddy Bridgewater 30.00 80.00
FSATBRA Tom Brady EXCH 350.00 600.00

2014 Topps Five Star Four Piece Signature Book Autographs

STATED PRINT RUN 49 SER.#'d SETS
FSSBBB Blake Bortles 10.00 25.00
FSSBJC Jamaal Charles 20.00 50.00
FSSBJJ Julio Jones EXCH 25.00 60.00
FSSBJM Johnny Manziel 12.00 30.00
FSSBJN Joe Namath 75.00 125.00
FSSBME Mike Evans 20.00 50.00
FSSBMF Matt Forte 15.00 40.00
FSSBRW Roddy White 30.00 60.00
FSSBTB Teddy Bridgewater 12.00 30.00
FSSBJCL Jadeveon Clowney

2014 Topps Five Star Golden Graphs

FSGGAJ Alshon Jeffery 15.00 40.00
FSGGAR Aaron Rodgers
FSGGBC Brandin Cooks 10.00 25.00
FSGGBJ Bo Jackson/30 40.00 80.00
FSGGCM Clay Matthews EXCH
FSGGDB Drew Brees
FSGGDC Derek Carr 75.00 150.00
FSGGDS Deion Sanders 40.00 80.00
FSGGED Eric Dickerson 15.00 40.00
FSGGEE Eric Ebron 8.00 20.00
FSGGGS Gale Sayers 15.00 40.00
FSGGJC Jadeveon Clowney EXCH
FSGGJCH Jamaal Charles 15.00 40.00
FSGGJM Johnny Manziel
FSGGKB Kelvin Benjamin 10.00 25.00
FSGGME Mike Evans 15.00 40.00
FSGGMF Marshall Faulk 12.00 30.00
FSGGOB Odell Beckham Jr. 50.00 100.00
FSGGRB Reggie Bush 12.00 30.00
FSGGRG Rob Gronkowski 40.00 80.00
FSGGRL Ronnie Lott 20.00 50.00
FSGGSW Sammy Watkins 10.00 25.00
FSGGSY Steve Young
FSGGTB Teddy Bridgewater
FSGGTBR Terry Bradshaw
FSGGTP Troy Polamalu 60.00 120.00

2014 Topps Five Star Golden Graphs Blue

*BLUE/20: .5X TO 1.2X BASE AU/60
*BLUE/20: .4X TO 1X BASE AU/30
FSGGOB Odell Beckham Jr. 60.00 125.00

2014 Topps Five Star Golden Graphs Green

FSGGDS Deion Sanders 40.00 100.00
FSGGJM Johnny Manziel 15.00 40.00
FSGGTP Troy Polamalu 100.00 200.00

2014 Topps Five Star Golden Graphs Purple

*PURPLE/25: .5X TO 1.2X BASIC AU/60
*PURPLE/25: .4X TO 1X BASIC AU/30
FSGGRG Rob Gronkowski 40.00 100.00
FSGGRL Ronnie Lott

2014 Topps Five Star Jumbo Patch Autographs

STATED PRINT RUN 35 SER.#'d SETS
FSAJPAJ Alshon Jeffery 20.00 50.00
FSAJPAM A.J. McCarron 6.00 15.00
FSAJPBB Blake Bortles 10.00 25.00
FSAJPBC Brandin Cooks 12.00 30.00
FSAJPBS Bishop Sankey
FSAJPCL Cody Latimer 10.00 25.00
FSAJPDC Derek Carr 100.00 200.00
FSAJPEE Eric Ebron 10.00 25.00
FSAJPJC Jamaal Charles
FSAJPJCL Jadeveon Clowney EXCH 10.00 25.00
FSAJPJG Jimmy Garoppolo 100.00 200.00
FSAJPJJ Julio Jones 25.00 60.00
FSAJPJM Johnny Manziel 12.00 30.00
FSAJPKB Kelvin Benjamin 15.00 40.00
FSAJPME Mike Evans
FSAJPOB Odell Beckham Jr. 60.00 125.00
FSAJPTB Teddy Bridgewater 12.00 30.00
FSAJPVC Victor Cruz 20.00 50.00

2014 Topps Five Star Legend Patches

STATED PRINT RUN 25 SER.#'d SETS
FSLRBS Barry Sanders
FSLRCM Curtis Martin 6.00 15.00
FSLRDB Drew Brees 8.00 20.00
FSLRDM Dan Marino
FSLREC Earl Campbell 8.00 20.00
FSLRED Eric Dickerson
FSLRES Emmitt Smith
FSLRGS Gale Sayers
FSLRJN Joe Namath
FSLRMA Marcus Allen 8.00 20.00
FSLRMAL Marcus Allen 8.00 20.00
FSLRMF Marshall Faulk 6.00 15.00
FSLRMS Mike Singletary
FSLRPM Peyton Manning 15.00 40.00
FSLRSY Steve Young 10.00 25.00
FSLRTB Terry Bradshaw 10.00 25.00
FSLRTBR Tom Brady

2014 Topps Five Star Signature Book Jumbo Jersey Autographs

STATED PRINT RUN 49 SER.#'d SETS
FSAJRBAJ Alshon Jeffery
FSAJRBBB Blake Bortles 8.00 20.00
FSAJRBJC Jadeveon Clowney EXCH
FSAJRBJCH Jamaal Charles 15.00 40.00
FSAJRBJM Johnny Manziel 10.00 25.00
FSAJRBME Mike Evans 15.00 40.00
FSAJRBRB Reggie Bush
FSAJRBTB Teddy Bridgewater 10.00 25.00

2014 Topps Five Star Silver Signatures

STATED PRINT RUN 50-60
FSSSAJ Alshon Jeffery 15.00 40.00
FSSSAL Andrew Luck
FSSSBB Blake Bortles 8.00 20.00
FSSSBC Brandin Cooks 10.00 25.00
FSSSBJ Bo Jackson
FSSSDC Derek Carr 75.00 150.00
FSSSDS Deion Sanders
FSSSEE Eric Ebron 8.00 20.00
FSSSEM Eli Manning/50 30.00 80.00
FSSSES Emmitt Smith
FSSSGS Gale Sayers 15.00 40.00
FSSSJC Jadeveon Clowney EXCH 8.00 20.00
FSSSKB Kelvin Benjamin 10.00 25.00
FSSSLT Lawrence Taylor
FSSSME Mike Evans 15.00 40.00
FSSSML Marshawn Lynch EXCH 50.00 100.00
FSSSMS Matthew Stafford
FSSSNF Nick Foles 15.00 40.00
FSSSOB Odell Beckham Jr. 50.00 100.00
FSSSRB Reggie Bush
FSSSRG Rob Gronkowski 20.00 50.00
FSSSRL Ronnie Lott 12.00 30.00
FSSSRW Russell Wilson
FSSSSW Sammy Watkins 10.00 25.00
FSSSTB Teddy Bridgewater
FSSSVC Victor Cruz 15.00 40.00

2014 Topps Five Star Silver Signatures Blue

*BLUE/20: .5X TO 1.2X BASIC SILV SIG
FSSSBJ Bo Jackson 40.00 80.00

2014 Topps Five Star Silver Signatures Green

*GREEN/15: .6X TO 1.5X BASIC SILV SIG
FSSSBB Blake Bortles 12.00 30.00
FSSSBJ Bo Jackson 50.00 100.00
FSSSDS Deion Sanders 30.00 60.00
FSSSTB Teddy Bridgewater 15.00 40.00

2014 Topps Five Star Silver Signatures Purple

*PURPLE/25: .5X TO 1.2X BASIC SILV SIG
FSSSBB Blake Bortles 10.00 25.00
FSSSDS Deion Sanders 15.00 40.00
FSSSOB Odell Beckham Jr. 75.00 150.00

1997 Topps Gallery

The 1997 Topps Gallery set was issued in one series totalling 135 cards and was distributed in six-card packs with a suggested retail price of $3. The fonts feature color photos of young stars, future stars, and veterans with bright colored frame-like borders and printed on 24 pt. card stock. Randomly inserted into packs was a "John Elway Feel the Power Instant Win" card. Every card was a winner, but the prize was unknown until the card was redeemed. Prizes included: a Pro Bowl/Super Bowl trip, trips to the Super Bowl, John Elway autographs, free packs of trading cards.

COMPLETE SET (135) 12.50 30.00
1 Orlando Pace RC .25 .60
2 Darrell Russell RC .10 .30
3 Shawn Springs RC .20 .50
4 Peter Boulware RC .25 .60
5 Bryant Westbrook RC .10 .30
6 Walter Jones RC .40 1.00
7 Ike Hilliard RC .75 2.00
8 James Farrior RC .25 .60
9 Tom Knight RC .10 .30
10 Warrick Dunn RC 2.00 5.00
11 Tony Gonzalez RC 2.50 6.00
12 Reinard Wilson RC .20 .50
13 Yatil Green RC .20 .50
14 Reidel Anthony RC .25 .60
15 Kenny Holmes RC .25 .60
16 Dwayne Rudd RC .25 .60
17 Renaldo Wynn RC .10 .30
18 David LaFleur RC .40 1.00
19 Antowain Smith RC 1.50 4.00
20 Jim Druckenmiller RC .20 .50
21 Rae Carruth RC .10 .30
22 Byron Hanspard RC .20 .50
23 Jake Plummer RC 2.50 6.00
24 Corey Dillon RC 2.50 6.00
25 Darnell Autry RC .20 .50
26 Kevin Lockett RC .20 .50
27 Troy Davis RC .20 .50
28 Mike Alstott .25 .60
29 Napoleon Kaufman .25 .60
30 Terrell Davis .30 .75
31 Byron Bam Morris .10 .30
32 Dana Stubblefield .10 .30
33 Ki-Jana Carter .10 .30
34 Hugh Douglas .10 .30
35 Natrone Means .20 .50
36 Marshall Faulk .30 .75
37 Tyrone Wheatley .20 .50
38 Tony Banks .20 .50
39 Marvin Harrison .25 .60
40 Eddie George .25 .60
41 Eddie Kennison .20 .50
42 Ray Mickens .10 .30
43 Mike Mamula .10 .30
44 Tamarick Vanover .20 .50
45 Rashaan Salaam .10 .30
46 Trent Dilfer .25 .60
47 John Mobley .10 .30
48 Gus Frerotte .10 .30
49 Isaac Bruce .25 .60
50 Mark Brunell .30 .75
51 Jamal Anderson .25 .60
52 Keyshawn Johnson .25 .60
53 Curtis Conway .20 .50
54 Zach Thomas .25 .60
55 Simeon Rice .20 .50
56 Lawrence Phillips .10 .30
57 Ty Detmer .20 .50
58 Bobby Engram .20 .50
59 Joey Galloway .20 .50
60 Curtis Martin .30 .75
61 Kevin Hardy .10 .30
62 Eric Moulds .25 .60
63 Michael Westbrook .20 .50
64 Robert Smith .20 .50
65 Karim Abdul-Jabbar .25 .60
66 Errict Rhett .10 .30
67 Ray Lewis .40 1.00
68 Terry Glenn .25 .60
69 Leeland McElroy .10 .30
70 Kerry Collins .25 .60
71 Steve McNair .30 .75
72 Kordell Stewart .25 .60
73 Terry Allen .25 .60
74 Michael Irvin .25 .60
75 John Elway 1.00 2.50
76 Lamar Lathon .10 .30
77 Rob Moore .20 .50
78 Irving Fryar .20 .50
79 Jim Everett .10 .30
80 Steve Young .30 .75
81 Bryan Cox .10 .30
82 Dale Carter .10 .30
83 Chris Warren .20 .50
84 Shannon Sharpe .20 .50
85 Reggie White .25 .60
86 Deion Sanders .25 .60
87 Hardy Nickerson .10 .30
88 Edgar Bennett .20 .50
89 Kent Graham .10 .30
90 Dan Marino 1.00 2.50
91 Kevin Greene .20 .50
92 Derrick Thomas .25 .60
93 Carl Pickens .20 .50
94 Neil O'Donnell .20 .50
95 Drew Bledsoe .30 .75
96 Michael Haynes .10 .30
97 Tony Martin .20 .50
98 Scott Mitchell .20 .50
99 Rodney Hampton .20 .50
100 Brett Favre 1.00 2.50
101 Darrell Green .20 .50
102 Rod Woodson .20 .50
103 Chris Spielman .10 .30
104 Jake Reed .20 .50
105 Jerry Rice .50 1.25
106 Jeff Hostetler .10 .30
107 Anthony Johnson .10 .30
108 Keenan McCardell .20 .50
109 Ben Coates .20 .50
110 Emmitt Smith .75 2.00
111 LeRoy Butler .10 .30
112 Steve Atwater .10 .30
113 Ricky Watters .20 .50
114 Jim Harbaugh .20 .50
115 Marcus Allen .25 .60
116 Levon Kirkland .10 .30
117 Jessie Tuggle .10 .30
118 Ken Norton .10 .30
119 Thurman Thomas .25 .60
120 Junior Seau .25 .60
121 Tim Brown .25 .60
122 Michael Jackson .20 .50
123 Eric Metcalf .20 .50
124 Herman Moore .20 .50
125 Bruce Smith .20 .50
126 Cris Carter .25 .60
127 Dave Brown .10 .30
128 Jeff Blake .20 .50
129 Robert Blackmon .10 .30
130 Barry Sanders .75 2.00
131 Blaine Bishop .10 .30
132 Jerome Bettis .25 .60
133 Stan Humphries .20 .50
134 Vinny Testaverde .20 .50
135 Troy Aikman .50 1.25
P54 Zach Thomas Promo .40 1.00

1997 Topps Gallery Player's Private Issue

COMPLETE SET (135) 1000.00 2000.00
*STARS: 8X TO 20X HI COLUMN
*RCs: 2.5X TO 6X HI
STATED ODDS 1:12
STATED PRINT RUN 250 #'d SETS

1997 Topps Gallery Critics Choice

Randomly inserted in packs at a rate of one in 24, this 20-card set features action photos of some of the most talented NFL players of today as picked by selected critics. The cards were printed on silver foil embossed card stock.

COMPLETE SET (20) 60.00 120.00
STATED ODDS 1:24
CC1 Barry Sanders 6.00 15.00
CC2 Jeff Blake 1.50 4.00
CC3 Vinny Testaverde 1.50 4.00
CC4 Ricky Watters 1.50 4.00
CC5 John Elway 8.00 20.00
CC6 Drew Bledsoe 2.50 6.00
CC7 Kordell Stewart 2.00 5.00
CC8 Mark Brunell 2.50 6.00
CC9 Troy Aikman 4.00 10.00
CC10 Brett Favre 8.00 20.00
CC11 Kevin Hardy 1.00 2.50
CC12 Shannon Sharpe 1.50 4.00
CC13 Emmitt Smith 6.00 15.00
CC14 Rob Moore 1.50 4.00
CC15 Eddie George 2.00 5.00
CC16 Herman Moore 1.50 4.00
CC17 Terry Glenn 2.00 5.00
CC18 Jim Harbaugh 1.50 4.00
CC19 Terrell Davis 2.50 6.00
CC20 Junior Seau 2.00 5.00

1997 Topps Gallery Gallery of Heroes

Randomly inserted in packs at a rate of one in 36, this 15-card set features color player images on luminous backgrounds that capture the color and light of stained glass.

COMPLETE SET (15) 100.00 200.00
STATED ODDS 1:36
GH1 Desmond Howard 3.00 8.00
GH2 Marcus Allen 2.00 5.00
GH3 Kerry Collins 2.00 5.00
GH4 Troy Aikman 7.50 20.00
GH5 Jerry Rice 7.50 20.00
GH6 Drew Bledsoe 6.00 15.00
GH7 John Elway 15.00 40.00
GH8 Mark Brunell 6.00 15.00
GH9 Junior Seau 2.00 5.00
GH10 Brett Favre 15.00 40.00
GH11 Dan Marino 15.00 40.00
GH12 Barry Sanders 12.50 30.00
GH13 Reggie White 2.00 5.00
GH14 Emmitt Smith 12.50 30.00
GH15 Steve Young 6.00 15.00

1997 Topps Gallery Peter Max Serigraphs

Randomly inserted in packs at a rate of one in 24, this 10-card set features art work of ten current Pro Football legends by renowned artist Peter Max. Max also signed a special version of each card that were inserted as well at the rate of 1:1200.

COMPLETE SET (10) 50.00 100.00
STATED ODDS 1:24
PM1 Brett Favre 5.00 12.00
PM2 Jerry Rice 5.00 12.00
PM3 Emmitt Smith 4.00 10.00
PM4 John Elway 8.00 20.00
PM5 Barry Sanders 4.00 10.00
PM6 Reggie White 2.50 6.00
PM7 Steve Young 4.00 10.00
PM8 Troy Aikman 3.00 8.00
PM9 Drew Bledsoe 2.00 5.00
PM10 Dan Marino 8.00 20.00

1997 Topps Gallery Peter Max Serigraphs Max Signatures

RANDOM INSERTS IN PACKS
PM1 Brett Favre 175.00 350.00
PM2 Jerry Rice 175.00 350.00
PM3 Emmitt Smith 175.00 350.00
PM4 John Elway 175.00 350.00
PM5 Barry Sanders 175.00 350.00
PM6 Reggie White 175.00 350.00
PM7 Steve Young 175.00 350.00
PM8 Troy Aikman 175.00 350.00
PM9 Drew Bledsoe 175.00 350.00
PM10 Dan Marino 175.00 350.00

1997 Topps Gallery Photo Gallery

Randomly inserted in packs at a rate of one in 24, this 15-card set features up-close photographs of NFL stars with customized designs and double foil stamping.

COMPLETE SET (15) 75.00 150.00
STATED ODDS 1:24
PG1 Eddie George 2.00 5.00
PG2 Drew Bledsoe 2.50 6.00
PG3 Brett Favre 8.00 20.00

PG4 Emmitt Smith 6.00 15.00
PG5 Dan Marino 8.00 20.00
PG6 Terrell Davis 2.50 6.00
PG7 Kevin Greene 1.50 4.00
PG8 Troy Aikman 4.00 10.00
PG9 Curtis Martin 2.50 6.00
PG10 Barry Sanders 6.00 15.00
PG11 Junior Seau 2.00 5.00
PG12 Deion Sanders 2.00 5.00
PG13 Steve Young 2.50 6.00
PG14 Reggie White 2.00 5.00
PG15 Jerry Rice 4.00 10.00

2000 Topps Gallery

Released as a 175-card set, 2000 Topps Gallery is comprised of 125 base veteran cards, 25 Apprentices which feature rookies from the 2000 draft, 13 Artisans which feature young stars, and 12 Masters which picture top NFL veterans. Either one subset or Rookie Card was included in each pack. Gallery was packaged in 24-pack boxes where packs contained six cards and carried a suggested retail price of $3.00.

COMPLETE SET (175) 20.00 50.00
COMP.SET w/o SP's (125) 7.50 20.00
UNPRICED PRESS PLATE PRINT RUN 1
1 Marshall Faulk .25 .60
2 Kordell Stewart .20 .50
3 Priest Holmes .20 .50
4 James Johnson .20 .50
5 Charlie Garner .25 .60
6 Jeff Blake .25 .60
7 Joey Galloway .25 .60
8 Terrell Davis .25 .60
9 Jerome Bettis .30 .75
10 Bobby Engram .20 .50
11 Muhsin Muhammad .20 .50
12 Marcus Robinson .25 .60
13 Kerry Collins .20 .50
14 Jake Plummer .20 .50
15 J.J. Stokes .25 .60
16 Tim Couch .25 .60
17 Napoleon Kaufman .25 .60
18 Az-Zahir Hakim .20 .50
19 Jimmy Smith .25 .60
20 Eddie George .25 .60
21 Jacquez Green .20 .50
22 Champ Bailey .25 .60
23 Wesley Walls .20 .50
24 Eric Moulds .20 .50
25 Corey Dillon .20 .50
26 Freddie Jones .20 .50
27 Jevon Kearse .20 .50
28 Ray Lucas .20 .50
29 Germane Crowell .20 .50
30 Randy Moss .25 .60
31 Patrick Jeffers .20 .50
32 Zach Thomas .25 .60
33 Shannon Sharpe .25 .60
34 Derrick Mayes .20 .50
35 Antonio Freeman .25 .60
36 Terance Mathis .20 .50
37 Herman Moore .20 .50
38 Tony Banks .20 .50
39 Jerry Rice .75 2.00
40 Troy Aikman .40 1.00
41 Rickey Dudley .20 .50
42 Troy Edwards .20 .50
43 Curtis Martin .25 .60
44 Eddie Kennison .20 .50
45 Mark Brunell .25 .60
46 Shaun King .20 .50
47 Duce Staley .20 .50
48 Damay Scott .25 .60
49 Sean Dawkins .20 .50
50 Edgerrin James .25 .60
51 Olandis Gary .25 .60
52 Peerless Price .25 .60
53 Akili Smith .20 .50
54 Charlie Batch .20 .50
55 Tim Biakabutuka .25 .60
56 Rob Moore .20 .50
57 Keenan McCardell .25 .60
58 Dan Marino .60 1.50
59 Tony Gonzalez .25 .60
60 Stephen Davis .20 .50
61 Ricky Watters .25 .60
62 Frank Wycheck .25 .60
63 Kevin Johnson .20 .50
64 Isaac Bruce .30 .75
65 Andre Reed .30 .75
66 Jamal Anderson .25 .60
67 Dorsey Levens .25 .60
68 Rocket Ismail .25 .60
69 Albert Connell .20 .50
70 Brett Favre .60 1.50
71 Wayne Chrebet .20 .50
72 Jon Kitna .20 .50
73 Brian Griese .20 .50
74 Rob Johnson .25 .60
75 Qadry Ismail .20 .50
76 Derrick Alexander .20 .50
77 Tim Dwight .25 .60
78 Ike Hilliard .20 .50
79 Frank Sanders .20 .50
80 Fred Taylor .20 .50
81 Robert Smith .20 .50
82 Vinny Testaverde .20 .50
83 Steve Young .40 1.00
84 Tyrone Wheatley .20 .50
85 Mikhael Ricks .20 .50
86 Tony Martin .25 .60
87 Carl Pickens .25 .60
88 Warrick Dunn .20 .50
89 Emmitt Smith .50 1.25
90 Keyshawn Johnson .25 .60
91 James Stewart .20 .50
92 Doug Flutie .25 .60
93 Torry Holt .25 .60
94 Jeff Graham .20 .50
95 Steve McNair .25 .60
96 Errict Rhett .25 .60
97 Terrell Owens .25 .60
98 Terry Glenn .25 .60
99 Steve Beuerlein .25 .60
100 Kurt Warner .50 1.25
101 Jeff George .25 .60
102 Deion Sanders .25 .60
103 Johnnie Morton .25 .60
104 Antowain Smith .25 .60
105 O.J. McDuffie .25 .60
106 Rod Smith .25 .60
107 Jim Harbaugh .25 .60
108 Marvin Harrison .25 .60
109 Curtis Enis .20 .50
110 Drew Bledsoe .25 .60
111 Mike Alstott .20 .50
112 Amani Toomer .20 .50
113 Elvis Grbac .20 .50
114 Tim Brown .30 .75
115 Cris Carter .30 .75
116 Donovan McNabb .25 .60
117 Chris Chandler .25 .60
118 Kevin Dyson .25 .60
119 Rich Gannon .25 .60
120 Ricky Williams .25 .60
121 Brad Johnson .25 .60
122 Cade McNown .20 .50
123 Ed McCaffrey .25 .60
124 Michael Westbrook .20 .50
125 Peyton Manning .75 2.00
126 Brett Favre MAS .75 2.00
127 Emmitt Smith MAS .60 1.50
128 Tim Brown MAS .40 1.00
129 Troy Aikman MAS .50 1.25
130 Jimmy Smith MAS .30 .75
131 Dan Marino MAS .75 2.00
132 Cris Carter MAS .40 1.00
133 Jerry Rice MAS 1.00 2.50
134 Steve Young MAS .50 1.25
135 Marshall Faulk MAS .30 .75
136 Eddie George MAS .30 .75
137 Drew Bledsoe MAS .30 .75
138 Randy Moss ART .30 .75
139 Germane Crowell ART .25 .60
140 Akili Smith ART .25 .60
141 Tim Couch ART .30 .75
142 Marcus Robinson ART .30 .75
143 Daunte Culpepper ART .30 .75
144 Jevon Kearse ART .25 .60
145 Edgerrin James ART .30 .75
146 Tony Gonzalez ART .30 .75
147 Cade McNown ART .25 .60
148 Fred Taylor ART .25 .60
149 Donovan McNabb ART .30 .75
150 Ricky Williams ART .30 .75
151 Jamal Lewis RC .60 1.50
152 Tee Martin RC .40 1.00
153 Plaxico Burress RC .50 1.25
154 Chad Pennington RC .50 1.25
155 Curtis Keaton RC .40 1.00
156 Thomas Jones RC .50 1.25
157 Courtney Brown RC .50 1.25
158 Ron Dayne RC .60 1.50
159 Shaun Alexander RC .60 1.50
160 Travis Taylor RC .40 1.00
161 Sylvester Morris RC .40 1.00
162 Giovanni Carmazzi RC .40 1.00
163 Laveranues Coles RC .50 1.25
164 Chris Redman RC .40 1.00
165 Bubba Franks RC .40 1.00
166 R.Jay Soward RC .40 1.00
167 Reuben Droughns RC .40 1.00
168 Todd Pinkston RC .40 1.00
169 Trung Canidate RC .40 1.00
170 Danny Farmer RC .40 1.00
171 Ron Dugans RC .40 1.00
172 Dennis Northcutt RC .40 1.00
173 J.R. Redmond RC .40 1.00
174 Travis Prentice RC .40 1.00
175 Peter Warrick RC .40 1.00

2000 Topps Gallery Player's Private Issue

*VETS 1-125: 2.5X TO 6X BASIC CARDS
*SUBSET 126-150: 2X TO 5X
*ROOKIES 151-175: 1.5X TO 4X
PRIVATE ISSUE/250 ODDS 1:16H
STATED PRINT RUN 250 SER.#'d SETS

2000 Topps Gallery Autographs

Randomly inserted in packs, this 6-card set features authentic player autographs coupled with action player photos. Each card carried the "Topps Authentic Autograph" stamp. Peter Warrick was released via mail redemption that carried an expiration date of 5/03/2001.

GROUP A STATED ODDS 1:236H
GROUP B STATED ODDS 1:2849H
OVERALL STATED ODDS 1:218H
JK Jon Kitna 5.00 12.00
JL Jamal Lewis 12.50 30.00
MF Marshall Faulk 20.00 50.00
PW Peter Warrick 8.00 20.00
SM Sylvester Morris 5.00 12.00
TJ Thomas Jones 6.00 15.00
ZT Zach Thomas 6.00 15.00

2000 Topps Gallery Exhibitions

Randomly inserted in packs at the rate of one in 18, this 15-card set features top players on a canvas card stock. Card backs carry a "GE" prefix.

COMPLETE SET (15) 15.00 40.00
STATED ODDS 1:32H
GE1 Marshall Faulk .75 2.00
GE2 Muhsin Muhammad .60 1.50
GE3 Marvin Harrison .75 2.00
GE4 Stephen Davis .60 1.50
GE5 Eddie George .75 2.00
GE6 Antonio Freeman .75 2.00
GE7 Isaac Bruce 1.00 2.50
GE8 Jovon Kearse .60 1.50
GE9 Curtis Martin .75 2.00
GE10 Troy Aikman 1.25 3.00
GE11 Jimmy Smith .75 2.00
GE12 Edgerrin James .75 2.00
GE13 Randy Moss .75 2.00
GE14 Steve Beuerlein .75 2.00
GE15 Kurt Warner 1.50 4.00

2000 Topps Gallery Gallery of Heroes

ndomly inserted in packs at the rate of one in 24, this 10-card set features full color action shots on a die-cut transparent colored plastic card stock that resemble stained glass. Card backs carry a "GH" prefix.

COMPLETE SET (10) 15.00 40.00
STATED ODDS 1:24H
GH1 Emmitt Smith 1.50 4.00
GH2 Troy Aikman 1.25 3.00
GH3 Brett Favre 2.00 5.00
GH4 Edgerrin James .75 2.00
GH5 Peyton Manning 2.50 6.00
GH6 Randy Moss .75 2.00
GH7 Marshall Faulk .75 2.00
GH8 Jerry Rice 2.50 6.00
GH9 Kurt Warner 1.50 4.00
GH10 Eddie George .75 2.00

2000 Topps Gallery Heritage

ndomly inserted in packs at the rate of one in 12, this 10-card set places today's players on the 1956 card design. Card backs carry an "H" prefix. A Proof set was also produced and seeded at a rate of one in 48. Finally a serial numbered Artist's Signed version was also released via a mail in exchange contest.

COMPLETE SET (10) 15.00 40.00
STATED ODDS 1:12H
*PROOF: .6X TO 1.5X BASIC INSERT
PROOFS STATED ODDS 1:48H
*ART.SIGN/175: 2.5X TO 6X BASIC INSERT
H1 Marshall Faulk .50 1.25
H2 Troy Aikman .75 2.00
H3 Randy Moss .50 1.25
H4 Brett Favre 1.25 3.00
H5 Jerry Rice 1.50 4.00
H6 Dan Marino 1.25 3.00
H7 Peyton Manning 1.50 4.00
H8 Emmitt Smith 1.00 2.50
H9 Edgerrin James .50 1.25
H10 Kurt Warner 1.00 2.50

2000 Topps Gallery Proof Positive

ndomly inserted in packs at the rate of one in 48, this 10-card set features dual-player positive and negative photography on a clear plastic card stock. Card backs carry a "P" prefix.

COMPLETE SET (10) 15.00 40.00
STATED ODDS 1:48H
P1 D.Marino 2.50 6.00
K.Warner
P2 E.George 1.00 2.50
R.Williams
P3 J.Rice 3.00 8.00
K.Johnson
P4 B.Smith 1.00 2.50
J.Kearse
P5 M.Faulk 1.00 2.50
E.James
P6 M.Harrison 1.00 2.50
M.Robinson
P7 E.Smith 2.00 5.00
S.Davis
P8 I.Bruce 1.25 3.00
R.Moss
P9 S.Young 1.50 4.00
M.Brunell
P10 D.Bledsoe 3.00 8.00
P.Manning

2001 Topps Gallery

pps Gallery was released in mid-August of 2001. The set design was a hand painted theme. This 145-card set included 140 base cards along with five short printed cards. There were 40 rookies and 100 veterans in the base set and the five short printed legends cards which were highlighted with a copper-foil along the nameplate. Please note the Joe Namath legends card was available in both a hobby and retail version.

COMPLETE SET (145) 30.00 80.00
COMP.SET w/o SP's (100) 10.00 25.00
1 Donovan McNabb .25 .60
2 Jamal Anderson .25 .60
3 Steve McNair .25 .60
4 Peyton Manning .75 2.00
5 Curtis Martin .25 .60
6 Joey Galloway .25 .60
7 Daunte Culpepper .25 .60
8 Corey Dillon .20 .50
9 Brad Johnson .25 .60
10 Doug Flutie .25 .60
11 Jerome Bettis .30 .75
12 Elvis Grbac .25 .60
13 Aaron Brooks .20 .50
14 Ray Lewis .30 .75
15 Tim Dwight .25 .60
16 Robert Smith .20 .50
17 Jake Plummer .20 .50
18 Jay Fiedler .25 .60
19 Fred Taylor .20 .50
20 Jerry Rice .60 1.50
21 Shaun King .20 .50
22 Cade McNown .25 .60
23 Drew Bledsoe .25 .60
24 Ricky Watters .25 .60
25 Muhsin Muhammad .20 .50
26 Shawn Jefferson .20 .50
27 Tiki Barber .25 .60
28 Derrick Alexander .20 .50
29 Stephen Davis .20 .50
30 James Stewart .20 .50
31 Terrell Owens .25 .60
32 Ed McCaffrey .25 .60
33 Jeff Graham .20 .50
34 Jamal Lewis .30 .75
35 Edgerrin James .25 .60
36 Tim Couch .20 .50
37 Marshall Faulk .25 .60
38 Ike Hilliard .20 .50
39 Ahman Green .25 .60
40 Tim Biakabutuka .20 .50
41 Akili Smith .20 .50
42 David Boston .20 .50
43 Eddie George .30 .75
44 Hines Ward .25 .60
45 Chad Lewis .20 .50
46 Brian Urlacher .40 1.00
47 Eric Moulds .20 .50
48 Ricky Williams .25 .60
49 Warrick Dunn .20 .50
50 Kerry Collins .20 .50
51 Isaac Bruce .30 .75
52 Jimmy Smith .25 .60
53 Emmitt Smith .50 1.25
54 Cris Carter .30 .75
55 Jeff Garcia .20 .50
56 Mike Anderson .20 .50
57 Lamar Smith .25 .60
58 Brett Favre .60 1.50
59 Steve Beuerlein .25 .60
60 Terry Glenn .25 .60
61 Tyrone Wheatley .25 .60
62 Charlie Batch .20 .50
63 Chris Chandler .25 .60
64 Sylvester Morris .20 .50
65 Joe Horn .20 .50
66 Kevin Johnson .20 .50
67 Rob Johnson .25 .60
68 Jeff George .25 .60
69 Keyshawn Johnson .25 .60
70 Wayne Chrebet .20 .50
71 Randy Moss .25 .60
72 Marvin Harrison .25 .60
73 Peter Warrick .20 .50
74 Darrell Jackson .25 .60
75 Derrick Mason .20 .50
76 Oronde Gadsden .20 .50
77 Charles Johnson .20 .50
78 James Allen .20 .50
79 Torry Holt .25 .60
80 Troy Brown .20 .50
81 Amani Toomer .20 .50
82 Junior Seau .25 .60
83 Troy Aikman .40 1.00
84 Mark Brunell .25 .60
85 Brian Griese .20 .50
86 Charlie Garner .25 .60
87 Rich Gannon .25 .60
88 Jeff Blake .25 .60
89 Donald Hayes .20 .50
90 Germane Crowell .20 .50
91 Tony Gonzalez .25 .60
92 Jon Kitna .20 .50
93 Vinny Testaverde .20 .50
94 Kordell Stewart .20 .50
95 Keenan McCardell .25 .60
96 Kurt Warner .50 1.25
97 Bill Schroeder .25 .60
98 Rod Smith .25 .60
99 Tim Brown .30 .75
100 Trent Dilfer .20 .50
101 Michael Vick RC 1.00 2.50
102 Koren Robinson RC .50 1.25
103 LaDainian Tomlinson RC 2.00 5.00
104 Todd Heap RC .50 1.25
105 Correll Buckhalter RC .40 1.00
106 Freddie Mitchell RC .40 1.00
107 Josh Booty RC .50 1.25
108 Chris Chambers RC .40 1.00
109 Chris Weinke RC .50 1.25
110 Steve Smith RC 1.25 3.00
111 Travis Minor RC .50 1.25
112 Ken-Yon Rambo RC .40 1.00
113 Marques Tuiasosopo RC .50 1.25
114 Bobby Newcombe RC .50 1.25
115 Drew Brees RC 10.00 25.00
116 LaMont Jordan RC .60 1.50
117 Dan Morgan RC .50 1.25
118 Reggie Wayne RC .75 2.00
119 Dan Alexander RC .50 1.25
120 Alge Crumpler RC .60 1.50
121 Robert Ferguson RC .60 1.50
122 Rod Gardner RC .50 1.25
123 Mike McMahon RC .50 1.25
124 Kevan Barlow RC .50 1.25
125 Snoop Minnis RC .40 1.00
126 Sage Rosenfels RC .50 1.25
127 Jesse Palmer RC .50 1.25
128 Michael Bennett RC .50 1.25
129 Rudi Johnson RC .60 1.50
130 Deuce McAllister RC .60 1.50
131 Santana Moss RC .60 1.50
132 Josh Heupel RC .60 1.50
133 Quincy Morgan RC .50 1.25
134 Quincy Carter RC .50 1.25
135 Anthony Thomas RC .60 1.50
136 James Jackson RC .40 1.00
137 Kevin Kasper RC .40 1.00
138 Alex Bannister RC .40 1.00
139 David Terrell RC .50 1.25
140 Chad Johnson RC .60 1.50
141 Walter Payton 1.50 4.00
142 Bart Starr 1.25 3.00
143 Sonny Jurgensen .60 1.50
144 Jim Brown .75 2.00
145A Joe Namath HTA 4.00 10.00
145B Joe Namath RETAIL 6.00 15.00
CL Checklist Card .05 .15
NNO Joe Namath Bucks 1.50 4.00

2001 Topps Gallery Autographs

e autographs were randomly inserted in packs of 2001 Topps Gallery with various odds depending on which group the player was in. The overall odds of an autograph was 1:84. Please note the group listing is noted next to the player below, and also note that Eddie George was released as an exchange card at the time of this product's release.

GROUP A ODDS 1:669HTA
GROUP B ODDS 1:502HTA
GROUP C ODDS 1:668HTA
GROUP D ODDS 1:250HTA
GROUP E ODDS 1:334HTA
OVERALL ODDS 1:84
AB Aaron Brooks E 5.00 12.00
DC Daunte Culpepper A 15.00 40.00
EG Eddie George A 15.00 40.00
JG Jeff Garcia B 8.00 20.00
JL Jamal Lewis B 8.00 20.00
MA Mike Anderson C 5.00 12.00
TB Tim Brown A 20.00 40.00
TD Tim Dwight D 6.00 15.00
WC Wayne Chrebet D 5.00 12.00

2001 Topps Gallery Heritage

Heritage was inserted into packs of 2001 Topps Gallery at a rate of 1.12. This 9-card set featured stars from the NFL's past and present, in these retro styled inserts. The cards carried a 'GH' prefix for the card number. The card design is that of the 1958 Topps set which included 4 players from this set.

COMPLETE SET (9) 7.50 20.00
STATED ODDS 1:12
GH1 Johnny Unitas 1.50 4.00
GH2 Bart Starr 1.50 4.00
GH3 Y.A. Tittle 1.00 2.50
GH4 Chuck Bednarik .60 1.50
GH5 Randy Moss 1.25 3.00
GH6 Jerry Rice 1.25 3.00
GH7 Peyton Manning 1.50 4.00
GH8 Brett Favre 2.00 5.00
GH9 Marshall Faulk .75 2.00

2001 Topps Gallery Heritage Relics

ritage Relics were randomly inserted in packs of 2001 Topps Gallery at a rate of 1:211. Each card from this 5-card set featured a jersey swatch unless noted in the player description below. The cards carried a 'GR' prefix for the card numbers.

STATED ODDS 1:211
GRBF Brett Favre 6.00 15.00
GRBS Bart Starr Seat 6.00 15.00
GRFG Frank Gifford Seat 3.00 8.00
GRJR Jerry Rice 6.00 15.00
GRRM Randy Moss 2.50 6.00

2001 Topps Gallery Heritage Relics Autographs

Heritage Relics were randomly inserted in packs of 2001 Topps Gallery at a rate of 1:4166. Each card from this 5-card set featured a jersey swatch, unless noted in the player description below, along with an autograph. The cards carried a 'GRA' prefix for the card numbers.

STATED ODDS 1:4166
GRABF Brett Favre 125.00 250.00
GRABS Bart Starr Seat 150.00 250.00
GRAFG Frank Gifford Seat 40.00 80.00
GRAJR Jerry Rice
GRARM Randy Moss

2001 Topps Gallery Originals Relics

e Originals Relics were inserted in packs of 2001 Topps Gallery with various odds, depending on which group the player's in. The overall stated odds for this set was 1:50. This 10-card set featured 5 rookies and 5 veterans. Each card carried a 'GO' prefix for the card numbering.

GROUP A ODDS 1:685HTA
GROUP B ODDS 1:668HTA
GROUP C ODDS 1:557HTA
GROUP D ODDS 1:501HTA
GROUP E ODDS 1:76HTA
OVERALL ODDS 1:50
GOCC Cris Carter 3.00 8.00
GOCD Corey Dillon 2.00 5.00
GOCJ Chad Johnson 3.00 8.00
GODA Dan Alexander 2.50 6.00
GOKB Kevan Barlow 2.50 6.00
GOKW Kurt Warner 5.00 12.00
GOPM Peyton Manning 8.00 20.00
GORC Rashard Casey 2.00 5.00
GORG Rod Gardner 2.50 6.00
GOWS Warren Sapp 2.50 6.00

2001 Topps Gallery Star Gallery

Star Gallery inserts were found in packs of 2001 Topps Gallery at a rate of 1:8. This 10-card set featured some of the top players from the NFL. The cards were highlighted with gold-foil lettering and logos. Each card number carried an 'SG' prefix.

COMPLETE SET (10) 5.00 12.00
STATED ODDS 1:8
SG1 Daunte Culpepper .40 1.00
SG2 Jamal Lewis .50 1.25
SG3 Peyton Manning 1.25 3.00
SG4 Edgerrin James .40 1.00
SG5 Randy Moss .40 1.00
SG6 Marshall Faulk .40 1.00
SG7 Mike Anderson .30 .75
SG8 Eddie George .50 1.25
SG9 Donovan McNabb .40 1.00
SG10 Cris Carter .50 1.25

2002 Topps Gallery

Released in September, 2002, this set contains 150 veterans and 50 rookies. The Hobby S.R.P. is $3.00/per pack. Each pack contains 5 cards. There were 24 packs per box, eight boxes per case.

COMPLETE SET (200) 25.00 60.00
COMP.SET w/o SP's (150) 15.00 40.00
UNPRICED PRESS PLATE/1 ODDS 1:617
1 Marshall Faulk .30 .75
2 Mark Brunell .30 .75
3 Jeff Garcia .25 .60
4 David Terrell .25 .60
5 Curtis Martin .30 .75
6 Terrell Davis .30 .75
7 Jake Plummer .25 .60
8 Eric Moulds .25 .60
9 Peyton Manning 1.00 2.50
10 Hines Ward .30 .75
11 Koren Robinson .25 .60
12 Eddie George .30 .75
13 Shane Matthews .25 .60
14 Trent Green .25 .60
15 Marcus Robinson .30 .75
16 Michael Vick .30 .75
17 Muhsin Muhammad .25 .60
18 Rocket Ismail .30 .75
19 Quincy Morgan .25 .60
20 Mike McMahon .25 .60
21 Randy Moss .30 .75
22 Willie Jackson .25 .60
23 Freddie Mitchell .25 .60
24 LaDainian Tomlinson .40 1.00
25 Warrick Dunn .25 .60
26 Zach Thomas .30 .75
27 Bill Schroeder .25 .60
28 Jon Kitna .25 .60
29 Rob Johnson .30 .75
30 Drew Bledsoe .30 .75
31 Ron Dayne .30 .75
32 Tim Brown .40 1.00
33 Michael Westbrook .25 .60
34 Terrell Owens .30 .75
35 Santana Moss .30 .75
36 Edgerrin James .30 .75
37 Ray Lewis .40 1.00
38 Chris Weinke .25 .60
39 Brian Griese .25 .60
40 Trent Dilfer .25 .60
41 Jay Fiedler .30 .75
42 Joe Horn .25 .60
43 Chad Johnson .25 .60
44 Plaxico Burress .25 .60
45 Trung Canidate .25 .60
46 Steve McNair .30 .75
47 Curtis Conway .30 .75
48 James Stewart .25 .60
49 James Jackson .25 .60
50 Tom Brady 2.00 5.00
51 Emmitt Smith .60 1.50
52 Michael Pittman .30 .75
53 Tony Gonzalez .30 .75
54 Daunte Culpepper .30 .75
55 Michael Strahan .30 .75
56 Keyshawn Johnson .30 .75
57 Marvin Harrison .30 .75
58 Brian Urlacher .40 1.00
59 Jeff Blake .30 .75
60 Chris Redman .25 .60
61 James McKnight .25 .60
62 Jerome Bettis .40 1.00
63 Shaun Alexander .25 .60
64 Rod Gardner .25 .60
65 Jimmy Smith .30 .75
66 Thomas Jones .25 .60
67 Peter Warrick .25 .60
68 Mike Anderson .25 .60
69 Ahman Green .30 .75
70 Amani Toomer .25 .60
71 Rich Gannon .30 .75
72 Vinny Testaverde .25 .60
73 Isaac Bruce .40 1.00
74 Derrick Mason .25 .60
75 John Abraham .30 .75
76 Shannon Sharpe .30 .75
77 Quincy Carter .25 .60
78 Todd Pinkston .25 .60
79 Drew Brees .75 2.00
80 Brad Johnson .30 .75
81 Garrison Hearst .25 .60
82 Anthony Thomas .30 .75
83 Brett Favre .75 2.00
84 Troy Brown .25 .60
85 Charlie Garner .30 .75
86 Kendrell Bell .25 .60
87 Darrell Jackson .30 .75
88 Ricky Williams .30 .75
89 Duce Staley .25 .60
90 Stephen Davis .25 .60
91 Dominic Rhodes .25 .60
92 Travis Henry .25 .60
93 David Boston .25 .60
94 Deuce McAllister .30 .75
95 Ike Hilliard .25 .60
96 Doug Flutie .30 .75
97 Torry Holt .30 .75
98 Keenan McCardell .30 .75
99 Rod Smith .30 .75
100 Donovan McNabb .30 .75
101 Corey Bradford .25 .60
102 Germane Crowell .25 .60
103 Michael Bennett .25 .60
104 Wayne Chrebet .25 .60
105 Mike Alstott .25 .60
106 Kevin Dyson .30 .75
107 Tim Couch .25 .60
108 Donald Hayes .25 .60
109 Maurice Smith .25 .60
110 Snoop Minnis .25 .60
111 Antowain Smith .30 .75
112 Kordell Stewart .25 .60
113 Kurt Warner .30 .75
114 Jerry Rice .75 2.00
115 Aaron Brooks .25 .60
116 Tiki Barber .30 .75
117 Marty Booker .25 .60
118 Qadry Ismail .25 .60
119 Peerless Price .25 .60
120 Marcus Pollard .25 .60
121 James Allen .25 .60
122 Junior Seau .30 .75
123 Fred Taylor .25 .60
124 Corey Dillon .25 .60
125 Lamar Smith .25 .60
126 Laveranues Coles .30 .75
127 James Thrash .30 .75
128 Kevan Barlow .25 .60
129 Matt Hasselbeck .25 .60
130 David Patten .25 .60
131 Antonio Freeman .40 1.00
132 Johnnie Morton .30 .75
133 Priest Holmes .25 .60
134 Cris Carter .40 1.00
135 Kevin Johnson .25 .60
136 Jim Miller .25 .60
137 Kerry Collins .25 .60
138 Joey Galloway .30 .75
139 Correll Buckhalter .25 .60
140 Chris Chambers .25 .60
141 Travis Taylor .25 .60
142 Ed McCaffrey .30 .75
143 J.J. Stokes .25 .60
144 Reggie Wayne .30 .75
145 Az-Zahir Hakim .25 .60
146 Tim Dwight .25 .60
147 Jevon Kearse .25 .60
148 Jamal Lewis .30 .75
149 Warren Sapp .30 .75
150 Jermaine Lewis .25 .60
151 William Green RC .50 1.25
152 Roy Williams RC .40 1.00
153 Kurt Kittner RC .40 1.00
154 Daniel Graham RC .50 1.25
155 Andre Davis RC .40 1.00
156 Donte Stallworth RC .60 1.50
157 Josh Reed RC .50 1.25
158 Rohan Davey RC .60 1.50
159 Wendell Bryant RC .40 1.00
160 Lito Sheppard RC .60 1.50
161 Najeh Davenport RC .40 1.00
162 Freddie Milons RC .40 1.00
163 Patrick Ramsey RC .50 1.25
164 Luke Staley RC .40 1.00
165 Maurice Morris RC .50 1.25
166 Dwight Freeney RC .75 2.00
167 Jeremy Shockey RC .60 1.50
168 Jabar Gaffney RC .40 1.00
169 DeShaun Foster RC .60 1.50
170 Chad Hutchinson RC .40 1.00
171 Tim Carter RC .50 1.25
172 Napoleon Harris RC .50 1.25
173 Kahlil Hill RC .40 1.00
174 Josh McCown RC .60 1.50
175 Ron Johnson RC .50 1.25
176 Marquise Walker RC .40 1.00
177 Joey Harrington RC .40 1.00
178 Travis Stephens RC .40 1.00
179 Julius Peppers RC 1.00 2.50
180 Ryan Sims RC .60 1.50
181 Albert Haynesworth RC .60 1.50
182 Phillip Buchanon RC .60 1.50
183 Jonathan Wells RC .50 1.25
184 Chester Taylor RC .60 1.50
185 Antonio Bryant RC .60 1.50
186 Adrian Peterson RC .50 1.25
187 Clinton Portis RC .60 1.50
188 Lamar Gordon RC .50 1.25
189 Reche Caldwell RC .50 1.25
190 Ashley Lelie RC .40 1.00
191 T.J. Duckett RC .40 1.00
192 Eric Crouch RC .60 1.50
193 David Garrard RC .50 1.25
194 Quentin Jammer RC .60 1.50
195 Ladell Betts RC .60 1.50
196 Antwaan Randle El RC .50 1.25
197 Cliff Russell RC .40 1.00
198 Javon Walker RC .60 1.50
199 John Henderson RC .50 1.25
200 David Carr RC .40 1.00

2002 Topps Gallery Rookie Variations

*VARIATIONS: 1X TO 2.5X BASIC CARDS
STATED ODDS 1:12 HOB/RET

2002 Topps Gallery Autographs

serted at a rate of 1:3281 for Group A, and 1:155 for Group B, these cards feature authentic autographs from some of todays top NFL stars. There was also an Artists Proofs version produced with each card hand serial numbered of 100 and inserted at a rate of 1:550.

GROUP A STATED ODDS 1:3281H, 1:3283R
GROUP B STATED ODDS 1:155 HOB/RET
*ART.PROOF/100: .6X TO 1.5X BASIC AU
ART.PROOF/100 ODDS 1:550 H, 1:551 R
AP PRINT RUN 100 SER.#'d SETS
GAB Aaron Brooks B 6.00 15.00
GAT Anthony Thomas B 8.00 20.00
GCC Chris Chambers B 6.00 15.00
GDS Duce Staley B 6.00 15.00
GHW Hines Ward B 30.00 60.00
GJA John Abraham B 8.00 20.00
GKB Kendrell Bell B 6.00 15.00
GMB Marty Booker B 6.00 15.00
GTB Tom Brady A 150.00 300.00

2002 Topps Gallery Heritage

serted at a rate of 1:12, this set features artists renderings of some of the NFL's most famous Rookie Cards.

STATED ODDS 1:12
NAMATH AU STATED ODDS 1:18701
GHBF Brett Favre 2.00 5.00
GHCD Corey Dillon .60 1.50
GHDC Daunte Culpepper .75 2.00
GHDM Dan Marino 2.50 6.00
GHDMC Donovan McNabb .75 2.00
GHEJ Edgerrin James .75 2.00
GHES Emmitt Smith 1.50 4.00
GHJL Jamal Lewis .75 2.00
GHJM Joe Montana 4.00 10.00
GHJN Joe Namath 2.00 5.00
GHJR Jerry Rice 2.00 5.00
GHKW Kurt Warner .75 2.00
GHMJ Marshall Faulk .75 2.00
GHMV Michael Vick .75 2.00
GHPM Peyton Manning 2.50 6.00
GHRM Randy Moss .75 2.00
GHTB Terry Bradshaw 1.50 4.00
GHTBR Tom Brady 5.00 12.00
GHAJN Joe Namath AU/25* 60.00 120.00

2002 Topps Gallery Heritage Relics

is set is a parallel of the Topps Gallery Heritage set, and features a swatch of game used memorabilia.

STATED ODDS 1:198 HOB/RET
GHRBF Brett Favre 8.00 20.00
GHRCD Corey Dillon 2.50 6.00
GHRDM Dan Marino 8.00 20.00
GHREJ Edgerrin James 3.00 8.00
GHRES Emmitt Smith 6.00 15.00
GHRJM Joe Montana 12.00 30.00
GHRJN Joe Namath 6.00 15.00
GHRJR Jerry Rice 8.00 20.00
GHRKW Kurt Warner 3.00 8.00
GHRMF Marshall Faulk 3.00 8.00

2002 Topps Gallery Originals Relics

serted at a rate of 1:66 for Group A, and 1:82 for Group B, these cards feature swatches of game used memorabilia of some of the toughest players in the NFL.

GROUP A ODDS 1:66 HOB/RET
GROUP B ODDS 1:82 HOB, 1:83 RET
GOAL Ashley Lelie B 2.50 6.00
GOBU Brian Urlacher A 4.00 10.00
GOCC Cris Carter A 4.00 10.00
GOCCH Chris Chambers A 2.50 6.00
GODB Drew Brees A 8.00 20.00
GODC David Carr B 2.50 6.00
GOEG Eddie George A 3.00 8.00
GOFT Fred Taylor A 2.50 6.00
GOJG Jeff Garcia A 2.50 6.00
GOJS Jimmy Smith A 3.00 8.00
GOKJ Keyshawn Johnson A 3.00 8.00
GOLT LaDainian Tomlinson A 4.00 10.00
GORD Rohan Davey B 4.00 10.00
GORJ Ron Johnson B 3.00 8.00
GOSD Stephen Davis A 2.50 6.00
GOSM Steve McNair A 3.00 8.00
GOTB Tim Brown A 4.00 10.00
GOTO Terrell Owens A 3.00 8.00
GOTS Travis Stephens B 2.50 6.00
GOWS Warren Sapp A 3.00 8.00

1996 Topps Gilt Edge Promos

1 Brett Favre 2.50 6.00
55 Steve Young 1.25 3.00

1996 Topps Gilt Edge

The 1996 Topps Gilt Edge set was issued in one series. This 90-card standard-size set was released in April 1996 and features the 84 members of the 1996 Pro Bowl roster, plus five players who had Pro Bowl-caliber seasons and one checklist card. Each card features Topps' new "gilt-edge" technology, placing gold foil edging around every card. The cards were issued in nine-card packs with a suggested retail price of $3.50 which included seven regular cards, a platinum card as well as a definitive edge card. Each case consisted of six boxes with 20 packs in each box. There are no Rookie Cards in this set.

COMPLETE SET (90) 6.00 15.00
1 Brett Favre 1.00 2.50
2 Kevin Glover .02 .10
3 Nate Newton .02 .10
4 Randall McDaniel .05 .15
5 William Roaf .02 .10
6 Lomas Brown .02 .10
7 Jay Novacek .02 .10
8 Emmitt Smith .75 2.00
9 Barry Sanders .75 2.00
10 Jerry Rice .50 1.25
11 Herman Moore .08 .25
12 Larry Centers .08 .25
13 Chester McGlockton .02 .10
14 Dan Saleaumua .02 .10
15 Bruce Smith .08 .25
16 Neil Smith .08 .25
17 Junior Seau .20 .50
18 Bryce Paup .02 .10
19 Greg Lloyd .08 .25
20 Terry McDaniel .02 .10
21 Dale Carter .02 .10
22 Carnell Lake .02 .10
23 Steve Atwater .02 .10
24 Elbert Shelley .02 .10
25 Brian Mitchell .02 .10
26 Jeff Feagles .02 .10
27 Morten Andersen .02 .10
28 Dan Marino 1.00 2.50
29 Dermontti Dawson .08 .20
30 Steve Wisniewski .02 .10
31 Bruce Matthews .02 .10
32 Bruce Armstrong .02 .10
33 Richmond Webb .02 .10
34 Ben Coates .08 .25
35 Marshall Faulk .25 .60
36 Chris Warren .08 .25
37 Carl Pickens .08 .25
38 Tim Brown .20 .50
39 Kimble Anders .08 .25
40 John Randle .08 .25
41 Eric Swann .02 .10
42 Reggie White .20 .50
43 Charles Haley .08 .25
44 Ken Norton .02 .10
45 Lee Woodall .02 .10
46 Ken Harvey .02 .10
47 Aeneas Williams .02 .10
48 Eric Davis .02 .10
49 Darren Woodson .08 .25
50 Merton Hanks .02 .10
51 Steve Tasker .02 .10
52 Glyn Milburn .02 .10
53 Jason Elam .08 .25
54 Darren Bennett .02 .10
55 Steve Young .40 1.00
56 Bart Oates .02 .10
57 Larry Allen .02 .10
58 Mark Tuinei .02 .10
59 Mark Chmura .08 .25
60 Michael Irvin .20 .50
61 Ricky Watters .08 .25
62 Cortez Kennedy .02 .10
63 Leslie O'Neal .02 .10
64 Bryan Cox .02 .10
65 Derrick Thomas .20 .50
66 Darryll Lewis .02 .10
67 Blaine Bishop .02 .10
68 Dana Stubblefield .08 .25
69 William Fuller .02 .10
70 Jessie Tuggle .02 .10
71 William Thomas .02 .10
72 Eric Allen .02 .10
73 Tim McDonald .02 .10
74 Jim Harbaugh .08 .25
75 Mark Stepnoski .02 .10
76 Keith Sims .02 .10
77 Gary Zimmerman .02 .10
78 Shannon Sharpe .08 .25
79 Anthony Miller .08 .25
80 Curtis Martin .40 1.00
81 Troy Aikman .50 1.25
82 Cris Carter .20 .50
83 Jeff Blake .20 .50
84 Yancey Thigpen .08 .25
85 Isaac Bruce .20 .50
86 Sam Mills .02 .10
87 Terrell Davis .40 1.00
88 Larry Brown .02 .10
89 Joey Galloway .20 .50
90 Checklist .02 .10

1996 Topps Gilt Edge Platinum

COMPLETE SET (90) 20.00 50.00
*PLATINUM: 1X TO 2.5X BASIC CARDS
ONE PLATINUM PER PACK

1996 Topps Gilt Edge Definitive Edge

Definitive Edge cards were randomly inserted in Gilt Edge packs at the approximate rate of 1:4 packs. This 15-card set features top players with a different theme for each card. There were five card designs with each used to cover three different themes.

COMPLETE SET (15) 10.00 25.00
STATED ODDS 1:4
1 Bruce Smith .30 .75
2 Brett Favre 3.00 8.00
3 Marcus Allen .60 1.50
4 Junior Seau .60 1.50
5 Deion Sanders .60 1.50
6 Jerry Rice 1.50 4.00
7 Steve Young 1.25 3.00
8 Drew Bledsoe 1.25 3.00
9 Michael Irvin .60 1.50
10 Reggie White .60 1.50
11 Dan Marino 3.00 8.00
12 John Alt .10 .30
13 Barry Sanders 2.50 6.00
14 Orlando Thomas .10 .30
15 Kordell Stewart .60 1.50

1998 Topps Gold Label Class 1

The 1998 Topps Gold Label set was printed on a prismatic 35 pt. Spectra-reflective rainbow stock and are gold foiled-stamped with the player's name and the Gold Label logo. In the foreground of each card is found a photo of a league standout with the background featuring quarterbacks passing and defensive players tackling. The backs carry career statistics and an insightful player commentary. Two parallel background variations for this set were also produced with the quarterbacks running (Class 2) and handing off the ball (Class 3) and defensive players running (Class 2) and pictured set before the snap (Class 3).

COMP.GOLD CLASS 1 (100) 30.00 60.00
1 John Elway .75 2.00
2 Rob Moore .30 .75
3 Jamal Anderson .40 1.00
4 Pat Johnson RC .50 1.25
5 Troy Aikman .60 1.50
6 Antowain Smith .40 1.00
7 Wesley Walls .40 1.00
8 Curtis Enis RC .50 1.25
9 Jimmy Smith .40 1.00
10 Terrell Davis .40 1.00
11 Marshall Faulk .40 1.00
12 Germane Crowell RC .40 1.00
13 Marcus Nash RC .40 1.00
14 Deion Sanders .40 1.00
15 Dorsey Levens .40 1.00
16 Corey Dillon .30 .75
17 Fred Taylor RC .75 2.00
18 Derrick Thomas .50 1.25
19 Kevin Dyson RC .50 1.25
20 Peyton Manning RC 8.00 20.00
21 Warren Sapp .40 1.00
22 Robert Holcombe RC .40 1.00
23 Joey Galloway .40 1.00
24 Garrison Hearst .30 .75
25 Brett Favre 1.00 2.50
26 Aeneas Williams .30 .75
27 Danny Kanell .30 .75
28 Robert Smith .30 .75
29 Brad Johnson .40 1.00

30 Dan Marino 1.00 2.50
31 Elvis Grbac .40 1.00
32 Terry Allen .40 1.00
33 Frank Sanders .30 .75
34 Peter Boulware .30 .75
35 Tim Brown .50 1.25
36 Keyshawn Johnson .40 1.00
37 Rae Carruth .30 .75
38 Michael Irvin .50 1.25
39 Brian Griese RC .75 2.00
40 Kordell Stewart .30 .75
41 Johnnie Morton .40 1.00
42 Robert Brooks .40 1.00
43 Keenan McCardell .40 1.00
44 Ben Coates .40 1.00
45 Jerry Rice 1.25 3.00
46 Tony Simmons RC .50 1.25
47 Irving Fryar .40 1.00
48 Jerome Pathon RC .50 1.25
49 Steve McNair .40 1.00
50 Warrick Dunn .30 .75
51 Skip Hicks RC .50 1.25
52 Andre Wadsworth RC .60 1.50
53 Chris Chandler .40 1.00
54 Curtis Conway .40 1.00
55 Eddie George .40 1.00
56 Jeff Blake .40 1.00
57 Greg Ellis RC .50 1.25
58 Scott Mitchell .40 1.00
59 Antonio Freeman .50 1.25
60 Drew Bledsoe .40 1.00
61 Mark Brunell .40 1.00
62 Andre Rison .40 1.00
63 Cris Carter .50 1.25
64 Jake Reed .40 1.00
65 Napoleon Kaufman .30 .75
66 Terry Glenn .40 1.00
67 Jason Sehorn .40 1.00
68 Rickey Dudley .30 .75
69 Junior Seau .40 1.00
70 Jerome Bettis .50 1.25
71 Curtis Martin .40 1.00
72 Warren Moon .50 1.25
73 Isaac Bruce .50 1.25
74 Mike Alstott .30 .75
75 Steve Young .60 1.50
76 Jacquez Green RC .50 1.25
77 Gus Frerotte .30 .75
78 Michael Jackson .30 .75
79 Carl Pickens .40 1.00
80 Bruce Smith .40 1.00
81 Shannon Sharpe .40 1.00
82 Herman Moore .40 1.00
83 Reggie White .50 1.25
84 Marvin Harrison .40 1.00
85 Jake Plummer .30 .75
86 Karim Abdul-Jabbar .30 .75
87 John Randle .50 1.25
88 Robert Edwards RC .50 1.25
89 Jeff George .40 1.00
90 Emmitt Smith .75 2.00
91 Terrell Owens .40 1.00
92 Trent Dilfer .40 1.00
93 Darrell Green .50 1.25
94 Andre Reed .50 1.25
95 Ryan Leaf RC .50 1.25
96 Rod Smith WR .40 1.00
97 O.J. McDuffie .40 1.00
98 John Avery RC .50 1.25
99 Charles Way .30 .75
100 Barry Sanders .75 2.00

1998 Topps Gold Label Class 1 Black

MPLETE SET (100) 200.00 400.00
*VETS: 2X TO 5X GOLD CLASS 1
*ROOKIES: 1.5X TO 4X GOLD CLASS 1
STATED ODDS 1:8

1998 Topps Gold Label Class 1 Red

ETS: 8X TO 20X GOLD CLASS 1
*ROOKIES: 6X TO 15X GOLD CLASS 1
RED/100 STATED ODDS 1:94
20 Peyton Manning 100.00 200.00

1998 Topps Gold Label Class 2

COMP.CLASS 2 GOLD (100) 75.00 150.00
*VETS: .6X TO 1.5X GOLD CLASS 1
*ROOKIES: .6X TO 1.2X GOLD CLASS 1
GOLD CLASS 2 STATED ODDS 1:2

1998 Topps Gold Label Class 2 Black

MPLETE SET (100) 300.00 600.00
*VETS: 3X TO 8X GOLD CLASS 1
*ROOKIES: 2.5X TO 6X GOLD CLASS 1
STATED ODDS 1:16

1998 Topps Gold Label Class 2 Red

*VETS/50: 15X TO 40X GOLD CLASS 1
*ROOKIES/50: 12X TO 30X GOLD CLASS 1
STATED ODDS 1:187
STATED PRINT RUN 50 SER.#'d SETS
20 Peyton Manning 150.00 300.00

1998 Topps Gold Label Class 3

COMP.CLASS 3 GOLD (100) 125.00 250.00
*VETS: 1X TO 2.5X GOLD CLASS 1
*ROOKIES: .8X TO 2X GOLD CLASS 1
GOLD CLASS 3 STATED ODDS 1:4

1998 Topps Gold Label Class 3 Black

ETS: 4X TO 10X GOLD CLASS 1
*ROOKIES: 3X TO 8X GOLD CLASS 1
STATED ODDS 1:32
20 Peyton Manning 50.00 120.00

1998 Topps Gold Label Class 3 Red

*VETS/25: 25X TO 60X GOLD CLASS 1
*ROOKIES/25: 20X TO 50X GOLD CLASS 1
STATED ODDS 1:375
STATED PRINT RUN 25 SER.#'d SETS
20 Peyton Manning 300.00 500.00

1999 Topps Gold Label Class 1

This 100 card standard-size set was issued in five card packs. A large number of parallels were issued and randomly inserted. Key Rookie Cards included Donovan McNabb, Edgerrin James, and Ricky Williams.

COMPLETE SET (100) 25.00 60.00
1 Terrell Davis .30 .75
2 Jake Plummer .25 .60
3 Mike Cloud RC .30 .75
4 D'Wayne Bates RC .30 .75
5 Jamal Anderson .30 .75
6 Cecil Collins RC .30 .75
7 Keyshawn Johnson .30 .75
8 Jerome Bettis .40 1.00
9 Ricky Watters .30 .75
10 Brett Favre .75 2.00
11 Joe Germaine RC .40 1.00
12 Eddie George .30 .75
13 Jevon Kearse RC .40 1.00
14 Skip Hicks .25 .60
15 James Johnson RC .30 .75
16 Terry Glenn .30 .75
17 Troy Edwards RC .30 .75
18 Karsten Bailey RC .30 .75
19 Trent Dilfer .25 .60
20 Barry Sanders .60 1.50
21 Vinny Testaverde .25 .60
22 Ed McCaffrey .30 .75
23 Shannon Sharpe .30 .75
24 Robert Smith .25 .60
25 Emmitt Smith .60 1.50
26 Rob Moore .25 .60
27 J.J. Stokes .25 .60
28 Champ Bailey RC .60 1.50
29 Napoleon Kaufman .25 .60
30 Fred Taylor .25 .60
31 Corey Dillon .25 .60
32 Sedrick Irvin RC .30 .75
33 Chris McAlister RC .30 .75
34 Warrick Dunn .25 .60
35 Isaac Bruce .40 1.00
36 Peerless Price RC .30 .75
37 Dorsey Levens .30 .75
38 Wayne Chrebet .25 .60
39 Randall Cunningham .30 .75
40 Dan Marino .75 2.00
41 Chris Chandler .30 .75
42 Mark Brunell .30 .75
43 Kevin Johnson RC .40 1.00
44 Natrone Means .30 .75
45 Jerome Pathon .25 .60
46 Daunte Culpepper RC .50 1.25
47 Akili Smith RC .30 .75
48 Keenan McCardell .30 .75
49 Steve McNair .30 .75
50 Randy Moss .30 .75
51 Terance Mathis .25 .60
52 Eric Moulds .25 .60
53 Rocket Ismail .30 .75
54 Cade McNown RC .30 .75
55 Kordell Stewart .25 .60
56 Rob Konrad RC .30 .75
57 Andre Rison .30 .75
58 Curtis Conway .30 .75
59 Chris Claiborne RC .30 .75
60 Jerry Rice 1.00 2.50
61 Peyton Manning 1.25 3.00
62 Jimmy Smith .30 .75
63 Doug Flutie .40 1.00
64 Frank Sanders .25 .60
65 Antowain Smith .25 .60
66 Curtis Enis .25 .60
67 Charlie Batch .25 .60
68 Marvin Harrison .30 .75
69 Garrison Hearst .25 .60
70 Ricky Williams RC .50 1.25
71 Torry Holt RC .60 1.50
72 Mike Alstott .25 .60
73 Drew Bledsoe .30 .75
74 O.J. McDuffie .30 .75
75 Donovan McNabb RC 2.00 5.00
76 Curtis Martin .30 .75
77 Priest Holmes .25 .60
78 Antonio Freeman .30 .75
79 Herman Moore .30 .75
80 Tim Couch RC .40 1.00
81 Troy Aikman .50 1.25
82 David Boston RC .30 .75
83 Tim Brown .40 1.00
84 Kevin Faulk RC .30 .75
85 Cris Carter .40 1.00
86 Marshall Faulk .30 .75
87 Shaun King RC .30 .75
88 Terrell Owens .30 .75
89 Carl Pickens .30 .75
90 Steve Young .50 1.25
91 Rod Smith .30 .75
92 Michael Irvin .40 1.00
93 Ike Hilliard .25 .60
94 Jon Kitna .25 .60
95 Brock Huard RC .30 .75
96 Joey Galloway .30 .75
97 Amos Zereoue RC .30 .75
98 Duce Staley .25 .60
99 John Elway .60 1.50
100 Edgerrin James RC .50 1.25

1999 Topps Gold Label Class 1 One to One

OVERALL ONE TO ONE STATED ODDS 1:839
NOT PRICED DUE TO SCARCITY

1999 Topps Gold Label Class 1 Black

MPLETE SET (100) 100.00 200.00
*BLACK 1 VETS: 1.2X TO 3X CLASS 1
*BLACK 1 ROOKIES: 1X TO 2.5X CLS 1
BLACK CLASS 1 ODDS 1:8

1999 Topps Gold Label Class 1 Red

MPLETE SET (100) 500.00 1000.00
*RED 1 VETS: 6X TO 15X CLASS 1
*RED 1 ROOKIES: 5X TO 12X CLS 1
CLASS 1 RED/100 ODDS 1:79

1999 Topps Gold Label Class 2

COMPLETE SET (100) 75.00 150.00
*CLASS 2 VETS: .6X TO 1.5X CLASS 1
*CLASS 2 ROOKIES: .5X TO 1.2X CLS 1
CLASS 2 STATED ODDS 1:2

1999 Topps Gold Label Class 2 One to One

OVERALL ONE TO ONE STATED ODDS 1:839
NOT PRICED DUE TO SCARCITY

1999 Topps Gold Label Class 2 Black

*BLACK 2 VETS: 2X TO 5X CLASS 1
*BLACK 2 ROOKIES: 1.5X TO 4X CLS 1
BLACK CLASS 2 ODDS 1:16

1999 Topps Gold Label Class 2 Red

ED 2 VETS: 8X TO 20X CLASS 1
*RED 2 ROOKIES: 3X TO 15X CLS 1
CLASS 2 RED/50 ODDS 1:157
STATED PRINT RUN 50 SER.#'d SETS

1999 Topps Gold Label Class 3

COMPLETE SET (100) 125.00 250.00
*CLASS 3 VETS: 1X TO 2.5X CLASS 1
*CLASS 3 ROOKIES: .8X TO 2X CLS 1
CLASS 3 STATED ODDS 1:4

1999 Topps Gold Label Class 3 One to One

OVERALL ONE TO ONE STATED ODDS 1:839
NOT PRICED DUE TO SCARCITY

1999 Topps Gold Label Class 3 Black

*BLACK 3 VETS: 2.5X TO 6X CLASS 1
*BLACK 3 ROOKIES: 2X TO 5X CLS 1
BLACK CLASS 3 ODDS 1:32

1999 Topps Gold Label Class 3 Red

*RED 3 VETS: 12X TO 30X CLASS 1
*RED 3 ROOKIES: 10X TO 25X CLS 1
CLASS 3 RED/25 ODDS 1:314
STATED PRINT RUN 25 SER.#'d SETS

1999 Topps Gold Label Race to Gold

sued one every 12 packs, these cards feature leading players who are chasing all-time records. Two parallels of this set were also issued. A black version was issued one every 48 packs and a red version was issued one every 1968 packs.

COMP.GOLD SET (15) 20.00 50.00
GOLD LABEL STATED ODDS 1:12
*BLACK LABEL: .8X TO 2X GOLD LABEL
BLACK LABEL STATED ODDS 1:48
*R1-R5 RED LABELS: 15X TO 35X GOLDS
R1-R5 RED LABEL PRINT RUN 13 SER.#'d.SETS
R1-R5 RED LABEL STATED ODDS 1:11,867
*R6-R10 RED LABELS: 7X TO 20X GOLDS
R6-R10 RED LAB.PRINT RUN 34 SER.#'d SETS
R6-R10 RED LABEL STATED ODDS 1:4638
*R11-R15 RED LABELS: 3X TO 8X GOLDS
R11-R15 RED LAB.PRINT RUN 80 SER.#'d SETS
R11-R15 RED LABEL STATED ODDS 1:1968
R1 Brett Favre 5.00 12.00
R2 Peyton Manning 5.00 12.00
R3 Drew Bledsoe 2.00 5.00
R4 Randall Cunningham 1.50 4.00
R5 Jake Plummer 1.00 2.50
R6 Emmitt Smith 3.00 8.00
R7 Terrell Davis 1.50 4.00
R8 Barry Sanders 5.00 12.00
R9 Eddie George 1.50 4.00
R10 Curtis Martin 1.50 4.00
R11 Antonio Freeman 1.50 4.00
R12 Eric Moulds 1.50 4.00
R13 Joey Galloway 1.00 2.50
R14 Rod Smith 1.00 2.50
R15 Randy Moss 4.00 10.00

2000 Topps Gold Label Class 1

Released in late October, Gold Label Features a 100-card set divided up into 80 veteran cards and 20 rookie cards. Base card stock is thick foilboard with two photos of each player; one close up, and a smaller action shot in the corner. Each card has a divider through the middle running from the top left corner to the bottom right corner stating which class each card is in. Gold Label was packaged in 24-pack boxes with packs containing five cards and carried a suggested retail price of $5.00.

COMPLETE SET (100) 15.00 40.00
1 Eric Moulds .20 .50
2 Muhsin Muhammad .20 .50
3 Patrick Jeffers .20 .50
4 Joey Galloway .25 .60
5 Edgerrin James .25 .60
6 Germane Crowell .20 .50
7 Ed McCaffrey .25 .60
8 Dorsey Levens .25 .60
9 Marcus Robinson .25 .60
10 Tony Gonzalez .25 .60
11 Robert Smith
12 Rich Gannon .25 .60
13 Jerry Rice .75 2.00
14 Mike Alstott .20 .50
15 Brad Johnson .25 .60
16 Emmitt Smith .50 1.25
17 Marvin Harrison .25 .60
18 Duce Staley .20 .50
19 Terry Glenn .25 .60
20 Terrell Owens .25 .60
21 Antonio Freeman .25 .60
22 Curtis Enis .20 .50
23 Michael Westbrook .20 .50
24 Cris Carter .30 .75
25 Tim Brown .30 .75
26 Terrell Davis .25 .60
27 Fred Taylor .20 .50
28 Amani Toomer .20 .50
29 Donovan McNabb .25 .60
30 Charlie Garner .25 .60
31 Kurt Warner .50 1.25
32 Antowain Smith .25 .60
33 Torry Holt .25 .60
34 Jake Plummer .20 .50
35 Steve Beuerlein .25 .60
36 Rocket Ismail .25 .60
37 Brett Favre .60 1.50
38 Mark Brunell .25 .60
39 Qadry Ismail .20 .50
40 Carl Pickens .25 .60
41 James Stewart .20 .50
42 Drew Bledsoe .25 .60
43 Keenan McCardell .25 .60
44 Jerome Bettis .30 .75
45 Jon Kitna .20 .50
46 Warrick Dunn .20 .50
47 Jevon Kearse .20 .50
48 Jamal Anderson .25 .60
49 Shaun King .20 .50
50 Ricky Williams .25 .60
51 Elvis Grbac .20 .50
52 Corey Dillon .20 .50
53 Brian Griese .20 .50
54 Steve Young .40 1.00
55 Tyrone Wheatley .20 .50
56 Daunte Culpepper .25 .60
57 Troy Aikman .40 1.00
58 Peyton Manning .75 2.00
59 Stephen Davis .20 .50
60 Keyshawn Johnson .25 .60
61 Doug Flutie .25 .60
62 Yancey Thigpen .20 .50
63 Jeff Blake .25 .60
64 Tony Banks .20 .50
65 Tim Couch .25 .60
66 Charlie Batch .20 .50
67 Rob Johnson .25 .60
68 Cade McNown .20 .50
69 Steve McNair .25 .60
70 Eddie George .25 .60
71 Isaac Bruce .30 .75
72 Ricky Watters .25 .60
73 Kordell Stewart .20 .50
74 Wayne Chrebet .20 .50
75 Curtis Martin .25 .60
76 Jimmy Smith .25 .60
77 Randy Moss .25 .60
78 Akili Smith .20 .50
79 Marshall Faulk .25 .60
80 Kerry Collins .20 .50
81 Ron Dayne RC .40 1.00
82 Chad Pennington RC .30 .75
83 Sylvester Morris RC .25 .60
84 Thomas Jones RC .30 .75
85 Shaun Alexander RC .40 1.00
86 Chris Redman RC .25 .60
87 Courtney Brown RC .30 .75
88 Jerry Porter RC .40 1.00
89 Ron Dugans RC .25 .60
90 Jamal Lewis RC .40 1.00
91 Travis Prentice RC .25 .60
92 Travis Taylor RC .25 .60
93 R.Jay Soward RC .25 .60
94 Peter Warrick RC .25 .60
95 Trung Canidate RC .25 .60
96 Tee Martin RC .25 .60
97 Bubba Franks RC .25 .60
98 Plaxico Burress RC .30 .75
99 J.R. Redmond RC .25 .60
100 Dennis Northcutt RC .25 .60

2000 Topps Gold Label Class 2

COMPLETE SET (100) 15.00 40.00
*CLASS 2: SAME VALUE AS CLASS 1

2000 Topps Gold Label Class 3

COMPLETE SET (100) 15.00 40.00
*CLASS 3: SAME VALUE AS CLASS 1

2000 Topps Gold Label Premium Parallel

COMPLETE SET (100) 125.00 250.00
*1-80 PREMIUM VETS: 2.5X TO 6X CLASS 1
*81-100 PREMIUM ROOKIES: 2X TO 5X
PREMIUM PRINT RUN 1000 SER.#'d SETS

2000 Topps Gold Label After Burners

Randomly inserted in packs at the rate of one in 23, this 14-card set features top player set against a "fire" background with gold foil highlights.

COMPLETE SET (14) 20.00 40.00
STATED ODDS 1:23
UNPRICED 1/1 ISSUED
A1 Brett Favre 3.00 8.00
A2 Corey Dillon 1.00 2.50
A3 Drew Bledsoe 1.25 3.00
A4 Cris Carter 1.50 4.00
A5 Jimmy Smith 1.25 3.00
A6 Edgerrin James 1.25 3.00
A7 Fred Taylor 1.00 2.50
A8 Tim Brown 1.50 4.00
A9 Marshall Faulk 1.25 3.00
A10 Steve Beuerlein 1.25 3.00
A11 Antonio Freeman 1.25 3.00
A12 Peyton Manning 4.00 10.00
A13 Mike Alstott 1.00 2.50
A14 Mark Brunell 1.25 3.00

2000 Topps Gold Label Bullion

ndomly inserted in packs at the rate of one in 32, this 10-card set features three players from the same team on an all gold foil board insert card.

COMPLETE SET (10) 25.00 50.00
STATED ODDS 1:32
UNPRICED 1/1 ISSUED
B1 Culpepper / Moss / Cris Carter 1.25 3.00
B2 James / Manning / Harrison 3.00 8.00
B3 B.Jhnson / S.Davis / Westbrk 1.00 2.50
B4 Taylor / Brunell / J.Smith 1.00 2.50
B5 E.Smith / Aikman / Galloway 2.00 5.00
B6 A.Smith / Dillon / Warrick .75 2.00
B7 M.Faulk / Warner / Bruce 2.00 5.00
B8 McNair / E.George / Kearse 1.00 2.50
B9 Sapp / King / Key.Johnson 1.00 2.50
B10 Levens / Favre / Freeman 2.50 6.00

2000 Topps Gold Label Graceful Giants

ndomly inserted in packs at the rate of one in 16, this 20-card set features top NFL stars on a foil board insert card with gold foil highlights.

COMPLETE SET (20) 25.00 50.00
STATED ODDS 1:16
UNPRICED 1/1 ISSUED
G1 Eddie George 1.00 2.50
G2 Randy Moss 1.00 2.50
G3 Keyshawn Johnson 1.00 2.50
G4 Warrick Dunn .75 2.00
G5 Jevon Kearse .75 2.00
G6 Sylvester Morris .75 2.00
G7 Ron Dayne 1.25 3.00
G8 Wayne Chrebet .75 2.00
G9 Steve McNair 1.00 2.50
G10 Courtney Brown 1.00 2.50
G11 Jacquez Green .75 2.00
G12 Daunte Culpepper 1.00 2.50
G13 Tony Gonzalez 1.00 2.50
G14 Mike Alstott .75 2.00
G15 Plaxico Burress 1.00 2.50
G16 Drew Bledsoe 1.00 2.50
G17 Travis Prentice .75 2.00
G18 Jerome Bettis 1.25 3.00
G19 Ricky Williams 1.00 2.50
G20 Jamal Lewis 1.25 3.00

2000 Topps Gold Label Holiday Match-Ups Fall

Randomly inserted in packs at the rate one in six, this 14-card set pairs players and gives stats and the results of their last meeting. Each card is die cut and has a Thanksgiving theme. Two different versions of each basic insert were produced with one or the other player's team name printed at the bottom of the cardback. Additionally, a one-of-one parallel set was also issued.

COMPLETE SET (14) 20.00 40.00
STATED ODDS 1:6
T1A R.Moss/T.Aikman 1.25 3.00
T1B R.Moss/T.Aikman 1.25 3.00
T2A D.Bledsoe/G.Crowell .75 2.00
T2B D.Bledsoe/G.Crowell .75 2.00
T3A C.Chandler/T.Brown 1.00 2.50
T3B C.Chandler/T.Brown 1.00 2.50
T4A R.Johnson/M.Alstott .75 2.00
T4B R.Johnson/M.Alstott .75 2.00
T5A C.McNown/W.Chrebet .60 1.50
T5B C.McNown/W.Chrebet .60 1.50
T6A C.Brown/J.Lewis 1.00 2.50
T6B C.Brown/J.Lewis 1.00 2.50
T7A T.Davis/J.Kitna .75 2.00
T7B T.Davis/J.Kitna .75 2.00
T8A T.Gonzalez/J.Seau .75 2.00
T8B T.Gonzalez/J.Seau .75 2.00
T9A Z.Thomas/P.Manning 2.50 6.00
T9B Z.Thomas/P.Manning 2.50 6.00
T10A R.Williams/M.Faulk .75 2.00
T10B R.Williams/M.Faulk .75 2.00
T11A D.Staley/B.Johnson .75 2.00
T11B D.Staley/B.Johnson .75 2.00
T12A J.Bettis/C.Dillon 1.00 2.50
T12B J.Bettis/C.Dillon 1.00 2.50
T13A S.McNair/M.Brunell .75 2.00
T13B S.McNair/M.Brunell .75 2.00
T14A R.Dayne/T.Jones 1.00 2.50
T14B R.Dayne/T.Jones 1.00 2.50

2000 Topps Gold Label Holiday Match-Ups Winter

Randomly inserted in packs at the rate one in six, this 14-card set pairs players and gives stats and the results of their last meeting. Each card is die cut and has a Christmas theme. Two different versions of each basic insert were produced with one or the other player's team name printed at the bottom of the cardback. Additionally, a one-of-one parallel set was also issued.

COMPLETE SET (14) 15.00 30.00
STATED ODDS 1:6
C1A J.Smith/K.Collins .75 2.00
C2A C.Garner/E.McCaffrey .75 2.00
C3A Ant.Smith/Sh.Alexander 1.00 2.50
C4A J.Plummer/M.Westbrook .60 1.50
C5A S.Beuerlein/R.Gannon .75 2.00
C6A C.Enis/C.Batch .60 1.50
C7A Ak.Smith/D.McNabb .75 2.00
C8A Syl.Morris/J.Anderson .75 2.00
C9A O.McDuffie/T.Glenn .75 2.00
C10A C.Carter/E.James 1.00 2.50
C11A C.Martin/T.Taylor .75 2.00
C12A P.Burress/J.Graham .75 2.00
C13A K.Warner/J.Blake 1.50 4.00
C14A S.King/B.Favre 2.00 5.00

2000 Topps Gold Label Rookie Autographs

Randomly inserted in packs overall at the rate of one in 56, this 19-card set features autographs from to 2000 draft picks on a foil board card with gold glitter along the top and bottom of the card. A Courtney Brown mail redemption card was produced but he never signed for the set.

OVERALL STATED ODDS 1:56
CP Chad Pennington 6.00 15.00
CR Chris Redman 5.00 12.00
DF Bubba Franks 5.00 12.00
DN Dennis Northcutt 5.00 12.00
JL Jamal Lewis 8.00 20.00
JP Jerry Porter 8.00 20.00
JR J.R. Redmond 5.00 12.00
PB Plaxico Burress 6.00 15.00
PW Peter Warrick 5.00 12.00
RD Ron Dayne 8.00 20.00
RS R.Jay Soward 5.00 12.00
SA Shaun Alexander 8.00 20.00
SM Sylvester Morris 5.00 12.00
TC Trung Canidate 5.00 12.00
TJ Thomas Jones 6.00 15.00
TM Tee Martin 5.00 12.00
TP Travis Prentice 5.00 12.00
TT Travis Taylor 5.00 12.00
RDU Ron Dugans 5.00 12.00

2012 Topps Gypsy Queen Mini National Convention

4 Andrew Luck 6.00 15.00
5 Robert Griffin III 6.00 15.00
6 Ryan Tannehill 2.50 6.00
7 Trent Richardson 2.50 6.00
8 Michael Floyd 1.50 4.00
9 Justin Blackmon 1.50 4.00

2001 Topps Heritage

In the summer of 2001 Topps released its Heritage set. The 146-card set featured the look of the 1956 Topps set and it included 110 veterans and 36 short printed rookies. The rookies were numbered to 1956. The cards were distributed in 8-card packs in boxes containing 24 packs. The cases contained 8 boxes. The packs carried a $3.00 SRP.

COMPLETE SET (146) 125.00 250.00
COMP.SET w/o SP's (110) 10.00 25.00
1 Ray Lewis .40 1.00
2 Peter Warrick .25 .60
3 James Stewart .25 .60
4 Junior Seau .30 .75
5 Jeff George .30 .75
6 Amani Toomer .25 .60
7 Elvis Grbac .30 .75
8 David Boston .25 .60
9 Jimmy Smith .30 .75
10 Warrick Dunn .25 .60
11 Hines Ward .30 .75
12 Joe Horn .25 .60
13 Stephen Davis .25 .60
14 Tyrone Wheatley .30 .75
15 Brian Urlacher .50 1.25
16 Fred Taylor .25 .60
17 Jerry Rice .75 2.00
18 Keyshawn Johnson .30 .75
19 Jay Fiedler .30 .75
20 Jamal Anderson .30 .75
21 Emmitt Smith .60 1.50
22 Tiki Barber .30 .75
23 Daunte Culpepper .30 .75
24 Torry Holt .30 .75
25 Peyton Manning 1.00 2.50
26 Eddie George .40 1.00
27 Jamal Lewis .40 1.00
28 Ricky Williams .30 .75
29 Ahman Green .30 .75
30 Ed McCaffrey .30 .75
31 Curtis Martin .30 .75
32 Isaac Bruce .40 1.00
33 Doug Flutie .30 .75
34 Steve McNair .30 .75
35 Donovan McNabb .30 .75
36 Keenan McCardell .30 .75
37 Charlie Batch .25 .60
38 Cade McNown .30 .75
39 Terrell Owens .30 .75
40 Brad Johnson .30 .75
41 Robert Smith .25 .60
42 Muhsin Muhammad .25 .60
43 Kurt Warner .60 1.50
44 Lamar Smith .30 .75
45 Brian Griese .25 .60
46 Trent Dilfer .25 .60
47 Jeff Garcia .25 .60
48 Derrick Mason .25 .60
49 Drew Bledsoe .30 .75
50 Marshall Faulk .30 .75
51 Corey Dillon .25 .60
52 Tony Gonzalez .30 .75
53 Chad Lewis .25 .60
54 Shaun Alexander .25 .60
55 Edgerrin James .30 .75
56 Eric Moulds .25 .60
57 Aaron Brooks .25 .60
58 Zach Thomas .30 .75
59 Jerome Bettis .40 1.00
60 Shannon Sharpe .30 .75
61 Kerry Collins .25 .60
62 Ricky Watters .30 .75
63 Tim Couch .25 .60
64 Marvin Harrison .30 .75
65 Tim Brown .40 1.00
66 Mark Brunell .30 .75
67 Wayne Chrebet .25 .60
68 Terry Glenn .30 .75
69 Mike Anderson .25 .60
70 Randy Moss .30 .75
71 Freddie Jones .25 .60
72 Ike Hilliard .25 .60
73 Derrick Alexander .25 .60
74 Travis Prentice .25 .60
75 Brett Favre .75 2.00
76 Rod Smith .30 .75
77 Troy Aikman .50 1.25
78 Cris Carter .40 1.00
79 Rich Gannon .30 .75
80 Charlie Garner .30 .75
81 Michael Pittman .30 .75
82 Jeff Graham .25 .60
83 Albert Connell .25 .60
84 Bill Schroeder .30 .75
85 Jeff Blake .30 .75
86 Jon Kitna .25 .60
87 Qadry Ismail .25 .60
88 Joey Galloway .30 .75
89 Charles Johnson .25 .60
90 Troy Brown .25 .60
91 Johnnie Morton .30 .75
92 Chris Chandler .30 .75
93 Donald Hayes .25 .60
94 Shaun King .25 .60
95 Vinny Testaverde .25 .60
96 James Allen .25 .60
97 Jake Plummer .25 .60
98 Antonio Freeman .40 1.00
99 Sean Dawkins .25 .60
100 Ron Dayne .30 .75
101 Rob Johnson .30 .75
102 Kordell Stewart .25 .60
103 Akili Smith .25 .60
104 Shawn Jefferson .25 .60
105 Germane Crowell .25 .60
106 Kevin Johnson .25 .60
107 Steve Beuerlein .30 .75
108 Marcus Robinson .30 .75
109 Peerless Price .25 .60
110 Jerome Pathon .25 .60
111 Sage Rosenfels RC 2.00 5.00
112 Quincy Morgan RC 2.00 5.00
113 Chad Johnson RC 2.50 6.00
114 Josh Heupel RC 2.50 6.00
115 Anthony Thomas RC 2.50 6.00
116 Drew Brees RC 40.00 80.00
117 Kevan Barlow RC 2.00 5.00
118 Chris Chambers RC 1.50 4.00
119 Mike McMahon RC 2.00 5.00
120 Todd Heap RC 2.00 5.00
121 Leonard Davis RC 2.50 6.00
122 Richard Seymour RC 2.50 6.00
123 Robert Ferguson RC 2.50 6.00
124 Andre Carter RC 2.00 5.00
125 Jesse Palmer RC 2.00 5.00
126 Travis Minor RC 2.00 5.00
127 Rudi Johnson RC 2.50 6.00
128 Rod Gardner RC 2.00 5.00
129 Snoop Minnis RC 1.50 4.00
130 Koren Robinson RC 2.00 5.00
131 Chris Weinke RC 2.00 5.00
132 James Jackson RC 1.50 4.00
133 Michael Vick RC 4.00 10.00
134 Marques Tuiasosopo RC 2.00 5.00
135 Michael Bennett RC 2.00 5.00
136 LaDainian Tomlinson RC 8.00 20.00
137 Freddie Mitchell RC 1.50 4.00
138 Deuce McAllister RC 2.50 6.00
139 Quincy Carter RC 2.00 5.00
140 Santana Moss RC 2.50 6.00
141 David Terrell RC 2.00 5.00
142 Reggie Wayne RC 3.00 8.00
143 Justin Smith RC 3.00 8.00
144 Gerard Warren RC 2.00 5.00
145 Travis Henry RC 2.00 5.00
146 Dan Morgan RC 2.00 5.00
NNO Checklist CL .20 .50

2001 Topps Heritage Retrofractor

*VETS 1-110: 4X TO 10X BASIC CARDS
*ROOKIES 111-146: .6X TO 1.5X
STATED PRINT RUN 556 SER.#'d SETS

2001 Topps Heritage 1956 All-Stars

Randomly inserted in packs of 2001 Topps Heritage, these 3 cards featured some All-Stars from the 1956 season. The cards carried 'HA' for the card numbering prefix. These were randomly inserted at a rate of 1:12 hobby, and 1:23 retail.

COMPLETE SET (3) 2.50 6.00
STATED ODDS 1:12
HACB Chuck Bednarik .75 2.00
HALM Lenny Moore .75 2.00
HAYT Y.A. Tittle 1.25 3.00

2001 Topps Heritage Classic Renditions

Randomly inserted in packs of 2001 Topps Heritage, these cards featured some current stars in classic threads. The cards featured drawings of players in throwback uniforms from the 1956 season. The cards carried a 'CR' prefix for the card numbering. These were randomly inserted at a rate of 1:8 hobby, and 1:15 retail.

COMPLETE SET (10) 6.00 15.00
STATED ODDS 1:8
CR1 Donovan McNabb .50 1.25
CR2 Brett Favre 1.25 3.00
CR3 Edgerrin James .50 1.25
CR4 Peyton Manning 1.50 4.00
CR5 Marvin Harrison .50 1.25
CR6 Kurt Warner 1.00 2.50
CR7 Marshall Faulk .50 1.25
CR8 Brian Urlacher .75 2.00
CR9 Jeff Garcia .40 1.00
CR10 Terrell Owens .50 1.25
CRABF Brett Favre AU 125.00 250.00
CRABU Brian Urlacher AU/25 60.00 120.00
CRAEJ Edgerrin James AU 100.00 200.00

2001 Topps Heritage Gridiron Collection Jersey

Randomly inserted in packs of 2001 Topps Heritage, these 11 cards featured some current stars with jersey swatches. The cards featured photos of players in their jersey that was used for the swatch. The cards carried a 'GC' prefix for the card numbering. These were randomly inserted at a rate of 1:287 hobby, and 1:288 retail.

STATED ODDS 1:287
GC1 Daunte Culpepper 4.00 10.00
GC2 Eddie George 5.00 12.00
GC3 Edgerrin James 4.00 10.00
GC4 Tony Gonzalez 4.00 10.00
GC5 Marvin Harrison 4.00 10.00
GC6 Jimmy Smith 4.00 10.00
GC7 Sam Cowart 3.00 8.00
GC9 Rod Woodson 5.00 12.00
GC10 Mo Lewis 3.00 8.00
GC11 Charles Woodson 5.00 12.00
GC12 Derrick Brooks 3.00 8.00

2001 Topps Heritage New Age Performers

Randomly inserted in packs of 2001 Topps Heritage at a rate of 1:8 hobby and 1:15 retail. This 15-card set featured current NFL stars and carried a 'NA' prefix on the card numbering.

COMPLETE SET (15) 12.50 30.00
STATED ODDS 1:8
NA1 Marshall Faulk .75 2.00
NA2 Jerry Rice 2.00 5.00
NA3 Marvin Harrison .75 2.00
NA4 Peyton Manning 2.50 6.00
NA5 Torry Holt .75 2.00
NA6 Isaac Bruce 1.00 2.50
NA7 Eddie George 1.00 2.50
NA8 Daunte Culpepper .75 2.00
NA9 Edgerrin James .75 2.00
NA10 Randy Moss .75 2.00
NA11 Jeff Garcia .60 1.50
NA12 Mike Anderson .60 1.50
NA13 Terrell Owens .75 2.00
NA14 Rod Smith .75 2.00
NA15 Cris Carter 1.00 2.50

2001 Topps Heritage Real One Autographs

Randomly inserted in packs of 2001 Topps Heritage at a rate of 1:377 hobby and 1:378 retail. This set featured former and current stars with the 2001 Heritage design with the Certified Topps Autograph stamp.

STATED ODDS 1:377
*RED INK/56: 1X TO 2.5X BASIC AUTO
RED INK SER.#'d PRINT RUN 56 SETS
THROAB Aaron Brooks 6.00 15.00
THROBU Brian Urlacher 30.00 50.00
THROCB Chuck Bednarik 10.00 25.00
THRODC Daunte Culpepper 8.00 20.00
THROEH Elroy Hirsch 40.00 100.00
THROEJ Edgerrin James 8.00 20.00
THROEM Eric Moulds 6.00 15.00
THROJL Jamal Lewis 10.00 25.00
THROJS Jimmy Smith 8.00 20.00
THROLM Lenny Moore 25.00 50.00
THROMA Mike Anderson 6.00 15.00
THROMH Marvin Harrison 12.00 30.00
THROOM Ollie Matson 30.00 50.00
THRORB Roosevelt Brown 25.00 50.00
THRORG Roosevelt Grier 12.00 30.00
THRORW Ricky Williams 8.00 20.00
THROSD Stephen Davis 6.00 15.00
THROTO Terrell Owens 8.00 20.00
THROWC Wayne Chrebet 6.00 15.00
THROYT Y.A. Tittle 25.00 50.00
THROJSC Joe Schmidt 20.00 40.00

2001 Topps Heritage Souvenir Seating

Randomly inserted in packs of 2001 Topps Heritage at a rate of 1:263 for both hobby and retail packs, this set was skip numbered. Each card includes a swatch from a stadium seat used during the 1950's at NFL stadiums. Cards: #S1, S2, S9 were not released in packs at the time of this product's release, but S1 and S2 have since surfaced on the secondary market.

STATED ODDS 1:263
SS1 Charley Conerly SP 30.00 60.00
SS2 Frank Gifford SP 30.00 60.00
SS3 Bart Starr 10.00 25.00
SS4 Paul Hornung SP 30.00 60.00
SS5 Johnny Unitas 10.00 25.00
SS6 Raymond Berry 6.00 15.00
SS7 Lenny Moore 5.00 12.00
SS8 Jim Brown 10.00 25.00
SS10 Chuck Bednarik 6.00 15.00

2001 Topps Heritage Then and Now

Randomly inserted in packs of 2001 Topps Heritage, these 3 cards featured some stars from the 1956 season teammed up with stars from the 2001. The cards carried 'HA' for the card numbering prefix. These were randomly inserted at a rate of 1:12 hobby, and 1:23 retail.

COMPLETE SET (3) 3.00 8.00
STATED ODDS 1:8
TNBL C.Bednarik/R.Lewis 1.00 2.50
TNMJ L.Moore/E.James 1.25 3.00
TNTG Y.Tittle/J.Garcia 1.25 3.00

2002 Topps Heritage

This 194-card set contains 154 veterans and 40 rookies. The rookies were inserted at a rate of 1:2. In addition, there were also several veteran SP's whose odds are not known. Boxes contained 24 packs of 8 cards. SRP was $3.00.

COMPLETE SET (194) 75.00 150.00
COMP.SET w/o SP's (154) 20.00 50.00
ROOKIE STATED ODDS 1:2
1 Jerome Bettis .50 1.25
2 Jeff Blake SP .60 1.50
3 Rod Smith .40 1.00
4 Eric Moulds .30 .75
5 Michael Vick .40 1.00
6 Randy Moss .40 1.00
7 Todd Pinkston .30 .75
8 Trung Canidate SP .50 1.25
9 Steve McNair .40 1.00
10 J.J. Stokes SP .50 1.25
11 Ricky Williams .40 1.00
12 Germane Crowell SP .50 1.25
13 Muhsin Muhammad SP .50 1.25
14 Michael Pittman SP .60 1.50
15 James Jackson SP .50 1.25
16 Dominic Rhodes .30 .75
17 Jay Fiedler .40 1.00
18 Marcus Robinson .40 1.00
19 Qadry Ismail SP .50 1.25
20 Michael Strahan .40 1.00
21 Koren Robinson .30 .75
22 James Allen SP .50 1.25
23 Chad Pennington .30 .75
24 Fred Taylor .30 .75
25 Corey Dillon .30 .75
26 Thomas Jones SP .50 1.25
27 Anthony Thomas .40 1.00
28 Priest Holmes .30 .75
29 Troy Brown .30 .75
30 Jerry Rice 1.00 2.50
31 Correll Buckhalter .30 .75
32 Drew Brees 1.00 2.50
33 Isaac Bruce .50 1.25
34 Warrick Dunn SP .50 1.25
35 Chris Chambers .30 .75
36 Antonio Freeman .50 1.25
37 Joey Galloway SP .60 1.50
38 Rob Johnson SP .60 1.50
39 Reggie Wayne .40 1.00
40 Santana Moss .40 1.00
41 Plaxico Burress .30 .75
42 Frank Wycheck SP .50 1.25
43 Johnnie Morton .40 1.00
44 Chris Weinke .30 .75
45 Rocket Ismail SP .60 1.50
46 Daunte Culpepper .40 1.00
47 Deuce McAllister SP .60 1.50
48 Terrell Owens .40 1.00
49 Michael Westbrook .30 .75
50 Tom Brady 2.50 6.00
51 Mike Anderson .30 .75
52 Jake Plummer .30 .75
53 Travis Taylor SP .50 1.25
54 Marcus Pollard SP .50 1.25
55 Zach Thomas .40 1.00
56 Duce Staley .30 .75
57 Trent Dilfer .30 .75
58 Keyshawn Johnson .40 1.00
59 Amani Toomer SP .50 1.25
60 David Terrell .30 .75
61 Robert Ferguson SP .60 1.50
62 Jeff Garcia .30 .75
63 Eddie George .40 1.00
64 Marshall Faulk .40 1.00
65 Travis Henry .30 .75
66 Tim Couch .30 .75
67 Mike McMahon .30 .75
68 John Abraham SP .60 1.50
69 James Thrash .40 1.00
70 Shaun Alexander .30 .75
71 Ike Hilliard SP .50 1.25
72 Brian Griese .30 .75
73 Ray Lewis .50 1.25
74 Jon Kitna .30 .75
75 Az-Zahir Hakim SP .50 1.25
76 Oronde Gadsden SP .50 1.25
77 Joe Horn .30 .75
78 Tim Brown .50 1.25
79 Kendrell Bell .30 .75
80 LaDainian Tomlinson .50 1.25
81 Brad Johnson .40 1.00
82 Tony Gonzalez .40 1.00
83 Bill Schroeder .30 .75
84 Quincy Carter .30 .75
85 Donald Hayes SP .50 1.25
86 Peyton Manning 1.25 3.00
87 Drew Bledsoe .40 1.00
88 Darrell Jackson .40 1.00
89 Rod Gardner .30 .75
90 Derrick Mason .30 .75
91 Byron Chamberlain SP .50 1.25
92 James McKnight SP .50 1.25
93 Kevin Johnson .30 .75
94 Terry Glenn .40 1.00
95 Marty Booker SP .50 1.25
96 Terrell Davis .40 1.00
97 Vinny Testaverde .30 .75
98 Hines Ward .40 1.00
99 Chad Lewis SP .50 1.25
100 Kurt Warner .40 1.00
101 Michael Bennett .30 .75
102 Edgerrin James .40 1.00
103 Corey Bradford SP .50 1.25
104 Chad Johnson SP .50 1.25
105 Alex Van Pelt .30 .75
106 Antowain Smith .40 1.00
107 Rich Gannon .40 1.00
108 Kevan Barlow SP .50 1.25
109 Mike Alstott SP .50 1.25
110 Kerry Collins SP .50 1.25
111 Jimmy Smith .40 1.00
112 Jermaine Lewis SP .50 1.25
113 Quincy Morgan SP .50 1.25
114 Maurice Smith SP .50 1.25
115 Willie Jackson .30 .75
116 Doug Flutie .40 1.00
117 Matt Hasselbeck .30 .75
118 Amos Zereoue SP .50 1.25
119 Lamar Smith .30 .75
120 Snoop Minnis .30 .75
121 Troy Hambrick SP .50 1.25
122 Shannon Sharpe SP .60 1.50
123 Laveranues Coles .40 1.00
124 Freddie Mitchell .30 .75
125 Kevin Dyson SP .60 1.50

126 Torry Holt .40 1.00
127 James Stewart SP .50 1.25
128 Brian Urlacher .50 1.25
129 David Boston .30 .75
130 Ron Dayne .40 1.00
131 Garrison Hearst .30 .75
132 Stephen Davis .30 .75
133 Donovan McNabb .40 1.00
134 David Patten .30 .75
135 Travis Minor SP .50 1.25
136 Peerless Price SP .50 1.25
137 Chris Redman SP .50 1.25
138 Ahman Green .40 1.00
139 Mark Brunell .40 1.00
140 Charlie Garner .40 1.00
141 Curtis Conway .40 1.00
142 Wayne Chrebet .30 .75
143 Kordell Stewart .30 .75
144 Peter Warrick .30 .75
145 Emmitt Smith .75 2.00
146 Jim Miller SP .50 1.25
147 Trent Green .30 .75
148 Cris Carter .50 1.25
149 Aaron Brooks .30 .75
150 Curtis Martin .40 1.00
151 Tiki Barber SP .60 1.50
152 Marvin Harrison .40 1.00
153 Tyrone Wheatley SP .60 1.50
154 Brett Favre 1.00 2.50
155 David Carr RC .60 1.50
156 Quentin Jammer RC 1.00 2.50
157 Julius Peppers RC 1.50 4.00
158 Mike Williams RC .60 1.50
159 Antwaan Randle El RC .75 2.00
160 Joey Harrington RC .60 1.50
161 Ashley Lelie RC .60 1.50
162 Marquise Walker RC .60 1.50
163 Rohan Davey RC 1.00 2.50
164 Patrick Ramsey RC .75 2.00
165 T.J. Duckett RC .60 1.50
166 DeShaun Foster RC 1.00 2.50
167 Donte Stallworth RC 1.00 2.50
168 William Green RC .75 2.00
169 Ron Johnson RC .75 2.00
170 Maurice Morris RC .75 2.00
171 Travis Stephens RC .60 1.50
172 Eric Crouch RC 1.00 2.50
173 David Garrard RC .75 2.00
174 Daniel Graham RC .75 2.00
175 Roy Williams RC .60 1.50
176 Jeremy Shockey RC 1.00 2.50
177 Josh McCown RC 1.00 2.50
178 Josh Reed RC .75 2.00
179 Andre Davis RC .60 1.50
180 Antonio Bryant RC 1.00 2.50
181 Clinton Portis RC 1.00 2.50
182 Javon Walker RC 1.00 2.50
183 Jabar Gaffney RC .60 1.50
184 Ladell Betts RC 1.00 2.50
185 Tim Carter RC .75 2.00
186 Reche Caldwell RC .75 2.00
187 Cliff Russell RC .60 1.50
188 Brian Westbrook SP RC 2.00 5.00
189 Freddie Milons RC .60 1.50
190 Phillip Buchanon RC 1.00 2.50
191 Lamar Gordon RC .75 2.00
192 Luke Staley RC .60 1.50
193 Albert Haynesworth RC 1.00 2.50
194 Kurt Kittner RC .60 1.50

2002 Topps Heritage Retrofractors

*VETS: 3X TO 8X BASIC CARDS
*VETS: 2X TO 5X BASIC SP
RETRO/557 ODDS 1:13 HOB, 1:14 RET
STATED PRINT RUN 557 SER.#'d SETS

2002 Topps Heritage Black Backs

STATED ODDS 1:2
1 Jerome Bettis .75 2.00
6 Randy Moss .60 1.50
27 Anthony Thomas .60 1.50
28 Priest Holmes .50 1.25
48 Terrell Owens .60 1.50
50 Tom Brady 4.00 10.00
62 Jeff Garcia .50 1.25
64 Marshall Faulk .60 1.50
70 Shaun Alexander .50 1.25
86 Peyton Manning 2.00 5.00
100 Kurt Warner .60 1.50
102 Edgerrin James .60 1.50
129 David Boston .50 1.25
133 Donovan McNabb .60 1.50
138 Ahman Green .60 1.50
150 Curtis Martin .60 1.50
152 Marvin Harrison .60 1.50
154 Brett Favre 1.50 4.00
155 David Carr .75 2.00
160 Joey Harrington .75 2.00
161 Ashley Lelie .75 2.00
163 Rohan Davey 1.25 3.00
164 Patrick Ramsey 1.00 2.50
166 DeShaun Foster 1.25 3.00
175 Roy Williams .75 2.00
179 Andre Davis .75 2.00
180 Antonio Bryant 1.25 3.00
184 Ladell Betts 1.25 3.00

2002 Topps Heritage 1957 Reprints

Inserted in packs at a rate of 1:6, this 10-card set is a reprint of 10 of the most notable names from the 1957 Topps set.
COMPLETE SET (10) 8.00 20.00
STATED ODDS 1:6 HOB, 1:12 RET
RAD Art Donovan .60 1.50
RBS Bart Starr 2.00 5.00
RCB Chuck Bednarik 1.00 2.50
RGB George Blanda .75 2.00
RGM Gino Marchetti .75 2.00
RPH Paul Hornung 1.00 2.50
RPS Pat Summerall 1.00 2.50
RRB Raymond Berry .75 2.00
RTM Tommy McDonald .75 2.00
RYT Y.A. Tittle 1.00 2.50

2002 Topps Heritage Classic Renditions

Inserted in hobby packs at a rate of 1:6 and retail at 1:12, this 10-card insert offers computer generated renderings of today's players wearing their clubs' uniform from 1957.
COMPLETE SET (10) 8.00 20.00
STATED ODDS 1:6 HOB, 1:12 RET
CRAT Anthony Thomas .75 2.00
CRDB David Boston .60 1.50
CREJ Edgerrin James .75 2.00
CRKB Kendrell Bell .60 1.50
CRKS Kordell Stewart .60 1.50
CRKW Kurt Warner .75 2.00
CRMF Marshall Faulk .75 2.00
CRMS Michael Strahan .75 2.00
CRPM Peyton Manning 2.50 6.00
CRTH Torry Holt .75 2.00

2002 Topps Heritage Classic Renditions Autographs

Inserted into packs at a rate of 1:10,990, this insert includes three cards of players who signed just 25 of their Classic Renditions inserts.
STATED ODDS 1:10990 HOB, 1:11904 RET
STATED PRINT RUN 25 SER.#'d SETS
CRAAT Anthony Thomas 15.00 40.00
CRAKB Kendrell Bell 12.00 30.00
CRAKW Kurt Warner 75.00 150.00

2002 Topps Heritage Gridiron Collection Jerseys

Inserted into packs at a rate of 1:64, this 13-card set includes jersey relics from a total of 13 current and retired superstars. Each card is serial numbered to 999. There is also a parallel version serial #'d to 25, which was randomly inserted into packs at the rate of 1:2572 hobby and 1:2580 retail packs.
JERSEY/999 ODDS 1:64 HOB/RET
STATED PRINT RUN 999 SER.#'d SETS
*FOIL/25: 1X TO 2.5X BASIC JSY/999
FOIL/25 ODDS 1:2572 H, 1:2580 R
FOIL PRINT RUN 25 SER.#'d SETS
GCBF Bubba Franks 2.50 6.00
GCCM Curtis Martin 3.00 8.00
GCEG Eddie George 3.00 8.00
GCES Emmitt Smith 6.00 15.00
GCJA John Abraham 3.00 8.00
GCJK Jevon Kearse 2.50 6.00
GCJN Joe Namath 6.00 15.00
GCJT Jeremiah Trotter 2.50 6.00
GCKJ Keyshawn Johnson 3.00 8.00
GCOK Olin Kreutz 5.00 12.00
GCRB Ronde Barber 2.50 6.00
GCTC Tim Couch 2.50 6.00
GCTO Terrell Owens 3.00 8.00

2002 Topps Heritage Hall of Fame Autographs

Inserted into packs at a rate of 1:8337 hobby packs, and 1:8928 retail packs, this 4-card insert set offers autographs from the four enshrinees of the 2002 Hall of Fame Class.
STATED ODDS 1:8337 HOB, 1:8928 RET
HOFDC Dave Casper 60.00 120.00
HOFDH Dan Hampton 125.00 200.00
HOFJK Jim Kelly 125.00 250.00
HOFJS John Stallworth 90.00 150.00

2002 Topps Heritage New Age Performers

This 15-card insert was inserted into packs at a rate of 1:8. The set showcases current stars whose performances have overshadowed NFL pioneers of the past.
COMPLETE SET (15) 15.00 40.00
STATED ODDS 1:8 HOB, 1:15 RET
NAP1 Donovan McNabb 1.00 2.50
NAP2 Kurt Warner 1.00 2.50
NAP3 Brett Favre 2.50 6.00
NAP4 Peyton Manning 3.00 8.00
NAP5 Stephen Davis .75 2.00
NAP6 Terrell Owens 1.00 2.50
NAP7 Anthony Thomas 1.00 2.50
NAP8 Jeff Garcia .75 2.00
NAP9 Marshall Faulk 1.00 2.50
NAP10 Edgerrin James 1.00 2.50
NAP11 David Boston .75 2.00
NAP12 Tim Couch .75 2.00
NAP13 Chris Chambers .75 2.00
NAP14 Marvin Harrison 1.00 2.50
NAP15 Curtis Martin 1.00 2.50

2002 Topps Heritage Real One Autographs

Inserted into packs at a rate of 1:199, this 21-card set includes an All-Star selection of players from 1957 to 2002. These players have signed their cards in blue ink. There is also a red ink parallel version of this set which was serial #'d to 57 and inserted into packs at a rate of 1:699 hobby, and 1:700 retail.
STATED ODDS 1:199 HOB/RET
HRAD Art Donovan 10.00 25.00
HRAT Anthony Thomas 10.00 25.00
HRBS Bart Starr 150.00 300.00
HRCB Chuck Bednarik 15.00 40.00
HRDB David Boston 8.00 20.00
HRDR Dominic Rhodes 8.00 20.00
HRGB George Blanda 20.00 50.00
HRGH Garrison Hearst 8.00 20.00
HRGM Gino Marchetti 20.00 40.00
HRHW Hines Ward 30.00 60.00
HRJA John Abraham 10.00 25.00
HRKB Kendrell Bell 8.00 20.00
HRMB Marty Booker 8.00 20.00
HRPH Paul Hornung 30.00 60.00
HRPHO Priest Holmes 8.00 20.00
HRPS Pat Summerall 30.00 60.00
HRRB Raymond Berry 15.00 40.00
HRTB Tom Brady 250.00 400.00
HRTM Tommy McDonald 12.00 30.00
HRYT Y.A. Tittle 15.00 40.00
HRZT Zach Thomas 10.00 25.00

2002 Topps Heritage Real One Autographs Red Ink

*RED INK/57: .6X TO 1.5X BASIC AU
RED INK/57 ODDS 1:699 H, 1:700 R
HRBS Bart Starr 125.00 250.00
HRTB Tom Brady 200.00 350.00

2005 Topps Heritage

This 400-card set was released in November, 2005. The set was issued in the hobby through eight-card packs with an $3 SRP which came 24 packs to a box. This set included 35 variations, most of which featured rookies in the style of the 1958 Topps football set. If the variations did not involve the 58 design; they were instead pictures of the players in throwback jerseys. There were also a grouping of short prints from cards 301-365 outside of the variations.
COMPLETE SET (400) 75.00 150.00
COMP.SET w/o SPs (300) 15.00 40.00
58T SP PRINTED WITH 1958 TOPPS DESIGN
TBJ SP PRINTED W/THROWBACK JER.PHOTO
1 Curtis Martin .30 .75
2 Javon Walker .25 .60
3 Derrick Mason .25 .60
4 Julius Jones .25 .60
5 Marc Bulger .25 .60
6 Reggie Wayne .30 .75
7 Isaac Bruce .40 1.00
8 Ray Lewis .40 1.00
9 Drew Bledsoe .30 .75
10 Michael Vick .30 .75
11 Charles Rogers .25 .60
12 Lee Evans .30 .75
13 Jake Plummer .25 .60
14 Edgerrin James .30 .75
15 Hines Ward .30 .75
16 Peyton Manning 1.00 2.50
17 Andre Johnson .30 .75
18 Trent Green .25 .60
19 Brian Westbrook .25 .60
20 Kevin Jones .25 .60
21 Deuce McAllister .30 .75
22 Marvin Harrison .30 .75
23 Dwight Freeney .25 .60
24 Ahman Green .30 .75
25 Plaxico Burress .25 .60
26 Daunte Culpepper .30 .75
27 Corey Dillon .25 .60
28 Joe Horn .25 .60
29 Torry Holt .30 .75
30 Randy Moss .30 .75
31 Drew Brees .40 1.00
32 Jonathan Vilma .25 .60
33 Jerome Bettis .40 1.00
34 Byron Leftwich .25 .60
35 Marshall Faulk .30 .75
36 Brett Favre .75 2.00
37 Steve McNair .30 .75
38 Rudi Johnson .25 .60
39 Tiki Barber .30 .75
40 Muhsin Muhammad .25 .60
41 Tony Gonzalez .30 .75
42 Chad Pennington .25 .60
43 Shaun Alexander .25 .60
44 Jamal Lewis .30 .75
45 Antonio Gates .40 1.00
46 LaDainian Tomlinson .40 1.00
47 Matt Hasselbeck .25 .60
48 Jake Delhomme .25 .60
49 Chad Johnson .25 .60
50 Willis McGahee .25 .60
51 Jason Witten .30 .75
52 J.P. Losman .25 .60
53 Donovan McNabb .30 .75
54A Eric Shelton RC .60 1.50
54B Eric Shelton 58T SP .75 2.00
55A Alex Smith QB RC 2.50 6.00
55B Alex Smith QB TBJ SP 3.00 8.00
56A Kyle Orton RC .60 1.50
56B Kyle Orton 58T SP .75 2.00
57A Andrew Walter RC .60 1.50
57B Andrew Walter TBJ SP .75 2.00
58A Ryan Moats RC .60 1.50
58B Ryan Moats 58T SP .75 2.00
59A Ciatrick Fason RC .60 1.50
59B Ciatrick Fason 58T SP .75 2.00
60A Vincent Jackson RC 1.00 2.50
60B Vincent Jackson 58T SP 1.25 3.00
61A Heath Miller RC 1.25 3.00
61B Heath Miller 58T SP 1.50 4.00
62A Carlos Rogers RC 1.00 2.50
62B Carlos Rogers TBJ SP 1.25 3.00
63A Terrence Murphy RC .60 1.50
63B Terrence Murphy 58T SP .75 2.00
64A Mike Williams .75 2.00
64B Mike Williams 58T SP 1.00 2.50
65A Vernand Morency RC .60 1.50
65B Vernand Morency 58T SP .75 2.00
66A Maurice Clarett .60 1.50
66B Maurice Clarett 58T SP .75 2.00
67A Roscoe Parrish RC .60 1.50
67B Roscoe Parrish 58T SP .75 2.00
68A Courtney Roby RC .60 1.50
68B Courtney Roby 58T SP .75 2.00
69 Tom Brady 1.50 4.00
70A David Greene RC .60 1.50
70B David Greene 58T SP .75 2.00
71A Antrel Rolle RC 1.00 2.50
71B Antrel Rolle 58T SP 1.25 3.00
72A Mark Bradley RC .60 1.50
72B Mark Bradley 58T SP .75 2.00
73A Frank Gore RC 1.25 3.00
73B Frank Gore 58T SP 1.50 4.00
74A Cedric Benson RC .60 1.50
74B Cedric Benson 58T SP .75 2.00
75A Derrick Johnson 62T RC .75 2.00
75B Derrick Johnson 58T SP 1.00 2.50
76A Reggie Brown RC .60 1.50
76B Reggie Brown 58T SP .75 2.00
77A Ronnie Brown RC .75 2.00
77B Ronnie Brown TBJ SP 1.00 2.50
78A Jason Campbell RC .60 1.50
78B Jason Campbell TBJ SP .75 2.00
79A Charlie Frye RC .60 1.50
79B Charlie Frye 58T SP .75 2.00
80 Jamie Sharper .25 .60
81 Tony Romo 6.00 15.00
82 Rod Smith .30 .75
83 Chester Taylor .30 .75
84 Marcus Robinson .25 .60
85 Terence Newman .25 .60
86 Aaron Brooks .25 .60
87 Kerry Collins .25 .60
88 Brandon Lloyd .25 .60
89 Michael Pittman .25 .60
90 Sean Taylor .40 1.00
91 Michael Lewis .25 .60
92 Jeremy Shockey .25 .60
93 Zach Thomas .30 .75
94 David Carr .25 .60
95 Champ Bailey .30 .75
96 Julius Peppers .30 .75
97 Brandon Stokley .25 .60
98 Deion Branch .25 .60
99 Charles Woodson .40 1.00
100 Darrell Jackson .25 .60
101 Ronde Barber .25 .60
102 Patrick Ramsey .30 .75
103 Warrick Dunn .25 .60
104 Takeo Spikes .25 .60
105 Thomas Jones .25 .60
106 T.J. Houshmandzadeh .25 .60
107 Najeh Davenport .25 .60
108 Nate Burleson .25 .60
109 Kelly Campbell .25 .60
110 LaVar Arrington .25 .60
111 Joey Harrington .25 .60
112 DeAngelo Hall .25 .60
113 Derrick Blaylock .25 .60
114 Michael Clayton .25 .60
115 Adam Archuleta .25 .60
116 Jason Taylor .30 .75
117 Donald Driver .30 .75
118 Dan Morgan .25 .60
119 Michael Jenkins .25 .60
120 Drew Henson .25 .60
121 Jay Fiedler .25 .60
122 Ladell Betts .25 .60
123 Jonathan Ogden .30 .75
124 Domanick Davis .25 .60
125 Sebastian Janikowski .25 .60
126 Cedrick Wilson .25 .60
127 Marcus Trufant .25 .60
128 Santana Moss .30 .75
129 Tatum Bell .25 .60
130 Jonathan Wells .25 .60
131 Laveranues Coles .25 .60
132 Josh McCown .30 .75
133 Antonio Bryant .25 .60
134 John Lynch .30 .75
135 Roy Williams WR .25 .60
136 Adam Vinatieri .25 .60
137 Dominic Rhodes .25 .60
138 Tyrone Calico .25 .60
139 Keenan McCardell .30 .75
140 Antonio Pierce .25 .60
141 Chris Chambers .25 .60
142 Bubba Franks .25 .60
143 Mike Vanderjagt .25 .60
144 Ernest Wilford .25 .60
145 Bertrand Berry .25 .60
146 David Garrard .25 .60
147 DeShaun Foster .30 .75
148 Rashaun Woods .25 .60
149 Wes Welker .30 .75
150 Allen Rossum .25 .60
151 Mike Anderson .25 .60
152 Keyshawn Johnson .30 .75
153 Alge Crumpler .30 .75
154 Dunta Robinson .25 .60
155 Kyle Boller .25 .60
156 William Green .25 .60
157 Peter Warrick .25 .60
158 Doug Gabriel .25 .60
159 Ashley Lelie .25 .60
160 Ronald Curry .25 .60
161 Keary Colbert .25 .60
162 Shawn Bryson .25 .60
163 Tim Rattay .25 .60
164 Jabar Gaffney .25 .60
165 Doug Jolley .25 .60
166 Keith Brooking .25 .60
167 Brian Urlacher .40 1.00
168 Chris Gamble .25 .60
169 Kurt Warner .30 .75
170 Duce Staley .25 .60
171 Steve Smith .40 1.00
172 Anquan Boldin .25 .60
173 Fred Taylor .25 .60
174 Donnie Edwards .25 .60
175 Clarence Moore .25 .60
176 Corey Bradford .25 .60
177 Dante Hall .25 .60
178 Warren Sapp .30 .75
179 Todd Heap .25 .60
180 Mewelde Moore .25 .60
181 John Abraham .25 .60
182 Rex Grossman .25 .60
183 Stephen Davis .25 .60
184 Greg Jones .25 .60
185 Jeremiah Trotter .25 .60
186 Carson Palmer .30 .75
187 Simeon Rice .25 .60
188 A.J. Feeley .25 .60
189 Matt Schaub .30 .75
190 Jamaar Taylor .25 .60
191 Joey Galloway .30 .75
192 Quentin Griffin .25 .60
193 Amani Toomer .25 .60
194 Michael Strahan .30 .75
195 Travis Henry .25 .60
196 Billy Volek .25 .60
197 Robert Ferguson .25 .60
198 Reggie Williams .25 .60
199 Jeff Garcia .25 .60
200 Mark Brunell .30 .75
201 Derrick Brooks .25 .60
202 Tommy Maddox .25 .60
203 William Henderson .25 .60
204 Bryant Johnson .25 .60
205 Philip Rivers .40 1.00
206 James Farrior .25 .60
207 Terrence McGee .30 .75
208 Bernard Berrian .25 .60
209 Gus Frerotte .25 .60
210 Mike Alstott .25 .60
211 Luke McCown .25 .60
212 Michael Bennett .25 .60
213 Kenechi Udeze .25 .60
214 Chris Perry .25 .60
215 Robert Gallery .25 .60
216 Lito Sheppard .30 .75
217 Brian Finneran .25 .60
218 Brian Griese .25 .60
219 Kevin Curtis .30 .75
220 LaMont Jordan .30 .75
221 Jerry Porter .25 .60
222 Reuben Droughns .25 .60
223 Dallas Clark .25 .60
224 Kevan Barlow .25 .60
225 Ken Lucas .25 .60
226 Lee Suggs .25 .60
227 Marcus Pollard .25 .60
228 David Givens .25 .60
229 T.J. Duckett .25 .60
230 Chris Simms .25 .60
231 Maurice Morris .25 .60
232 Chris McAllister .25 .60
233 Justin Fargas .30 .75
234 Jimmy Smith .30 .75
235 Aaron Stecker .25 .60
236 Donte Stallworth .25 .60
237 Darren Sproles RC 1.00 2.50
238 Justin McCareins .25 .60
239 Adrian McPherson RC .60 1.50
240 Brian Dawkins .40 1.00
241 Travis Taylor .25 .60
242 Fabian Washington RC .60 1.50
243 Jerramy Stevens .30 .75
244 Anthony Davis RC .60 1.50
245 Alex Smith TE RC .60 1.50
246 Ricky Williams .30 .75
247 Marion Barber RC .60 1.50
248 Marcus Spears RC .60 1.50
249 Mike Nugent RC .75 2.00
250 Dat Nguyen .25 .60
251 Derek Anderson RC .75 2.00
252 Terrence Holt .25 .60
253 Dane Looker .25 .60
254 Randy McMichael .25 .60
255 Craig Bragg RC .60 1.50
256 James Kilian RC .60 1.50
257 Airese Currie RC .60 1.50
258 Noah Herron RC .60 1.50
259 Dan Cody RC .60 1.50
260 Willie Parker .30 .75
261 Travis Johnson RC .60 1.50
262 Dan Orlovsky RC .60 1.50
263 Chris Baker .25 .60
264 Luis Castillo RC .75 2.00
265 Travis Daniels RC .75 2.00
266 Justin Miller RC .60 1.50
267 J.R. Russell RC .60 1.50
268 Lance Mitchell RC .75 2.00
269 T.A. McLendon RC .60 1.50
270 Jerricho Cotchery .25 .60
271 Chad Owens RC .60 1.50
272 Tab Perry RC .60 1.50
273 Corey Webster RC .75 2.00
274 Fred Gibson RC .60 1.50
275 Brandon Jones RC .75 2.00
276 DeWayne Robertson .25 .60
277 Brock Berlin RC .60 1.50
278 Nehemiah Broughton RC .75 2.00
279 Shaun Cody RC .75 2.00
280 Anthony Wright .25 .60
281 Damien Nash RC .75 2.00
282 Ryan Fitzpatrick RC 1.00 2.50
283 Paris Warren RC .75 2.00
284 Justin Tuck RC .75 2.00
285 Cedric Houston RC 1.00 2.50
286 Odell Thurman RC 1.00 2.50
287 Kirk Morrison RC 1.00 2.50
288 Josh Davis RC .60 1.50
289 Craphonso Thorpe RC .60 1.50
290 Sam Aiken .25 .60
291 Stanley Wilson RC .75 2.00
292 Jonathan Babineaux RC .60 1.50
293 Darryl Blackstock RC .60 1.50
294 Roydell Williams RC .75 2.00
295 Channing Crowder RC .75 2.00
296 Deandra Cobb RC .60 1.50
297 Larry Brackins RC .60 1.50
298 Bryant McFadden RC .75 2.00
299 Kevin Burnett RC .75 2.00
300 Barrett Ruud RC .75 2.00
301 Terrell Owens SP 1.25 3.00
302 Ben Roethlisberger SP 2.50 6.00
303 Eric Moulds SP 1.00 2.50
304 Eli Manning SP 2.50 6.00
305 Ed Reed SP 1.25 3.00
306 Larry Fitzgerald SP 1.50 4.00
307 Clinton Portis SP 1.00 2.50
308 Priest Holmes SP 1.00 2.50
309 Drew Bennett SP 1.25 3.00
310 Steven Jackson SP 1.00 2.50
311 Roy Williams S SP 1.00 2.50
312 Marcel Shipp SP 1.00 2.50
313 Peerless Price SP 1.00 2.50
314 Troy Vincent SP 1.25 3.00
315 Justin Gage SP 1.00 2.50
316 Nick Goings SP 1.00 2.50
317 Dennis Northcutt SP 1.00 2.50
318 Quincy Morgan SP 1.00 2.50
319 Darius Watts SP 1.00 2.50
320 Jason Elam SP 1.00 2.50
321 Nick Barnett SP 1.00 2.50
322 Tony Hollings SP 1.00 2.50
323 Samie Parker SP 1.00 2.50
324 Kelly Campbell SP 1.00 2.50
325 Kelly Holcomb SP 1.00 2.50
326 Darren Sharper SP 1.00 2.50
327 Tedy Bruschi SP 1.25 3.00
328 Ernie Conwell SP 1.00 2.50
329 Shaun Ellis SP 1.00 2.50
330 Teyo Johnson SP 1.00 2.50
331 Chris Brown SP 1.00 2.50
332 Quentin Jammer SP 1.00 2.50
333 Fred Smoot SP 1.00 2.50
334 Eric Parker SP 1.00 2.50
335 Steve Heiden SP 1.00 2.50
336 Troy Polamalu SP 1.50 4.00
337 Todd Pinkston SP 1.00 2.50
338 L.J. Smith SP 1.25 3.00
339 London Fletcher SP 1.25 3.00
340 Devery Henderson SP 1.00 2.50
341A Troy Williamson SP RC .75 2.00
341B Troy Williamson TBJ SP 1.00 2.50
342A J.J. Arrington SP RC 1.00 2.50
342B J.J. Arrington 58T SP 1.25 3.00
343A Cadillac Williams SP SP .75 2.00
343B Cadillac Williams TBJ SP 1.00 2.50
344A Aaron Rodgers SP RC 12.50 25.00
344B Aaron Rodgers 58T SP 12.00 30.00
345A Matt Jones SP RC .75 2.00
345B Matt Jones 58T SP 1.00 2.50
346A Roddy White SP RC 1.25 3.00
346B Roddy White 58T SP 1.50 4.00
347A Braylon Edwards SP RC .75 2.00
347B Braylon Edwards TBJ SP 1.00 2.50
348A Adam Jones SP RC .75 2.00
348B Adam Jones TBJ SP 1.00 2.50
349A Mark Clayton SP RC .75 2.00
349B Mark Clayton TBJ SP 1.00 2.50
350A Stefan LeFors SP RC .75 2.00
350B Stefan LeFors 58T SP 1.00 2.50
351 Alvin Pearman SP RC .75 2.00
352 Erasmus James SP RC .75 2.00
353 David Pollack SP RC .75 2.00
354 Brandon Jacobs SP RC 1.00 2.50
355 Chris Henry SP RC 1.00 2.50
356 Thomas Davis SP RC .75 2.00
357 Rasheed Marshall SP RC 1.00 2.50
358 Matt Roth SP RC .75 2.00
359 DeMarcus Ware SP RC 2.50 6.00
360 Matt Cassel SP RC .75 2.00
361 Stanford Routt SP RC 1.00 2.50
362 Marlin Jackson SP RC .75 2.00
363 Der.Johnson 59T SP ERR 1.00 2.50
364 Jerome Mathis SP RC 1.25 3.00
365 Lionel Gates SP RC .75 2.00
CL1 Checklist Card 1 .05 .15
CL2 Checklist Card 2 .05 .15
CL3 Checklist Card 3 .05 .15
CL4 Checklist Card 4 .05 .15

2005 Topps Heritage Felt Back Flashback

FELT BACK/199 ODDS 1:367 HOB
1 Michael Vick 10.00 25.00
2 Peyton Manning 10.00 25.00
3 Terrell Owens 6.00 15.00
4 Marvin Harrison 6.00 15.00
5 Shaun Alexander 7.50 20.00
6 Randy Moss 6.00 15.00
7 Tom Brady 15.00 40.00
8 LaDainian Tomlinson 6.00 15.00
9 Brett Favre 15.00 40.00
10 Donovan McNabb 7.50 20.00
11 Alex Smith QB 20.00 50.00
12 Ronnie Brown 20.00 50.00
13 Braylon Edwards 12.00 30.00
14 Cadillac Williams 12.00 30.00
15 Troy Williamson 8.00 20.00

2005 Topps Heritage Flashback Relics

GROUP A GOAL POST ODDS 1:151 HOB
GROUP B SEAT ODDS 1:837 HOB
GROUP C SEAT ODDS 1:725 HOB
FAV Adam Vinatieri A 12.50 30.00
FBF Brett Favre A 12.50 30.00
FJB Jim Brown C 7.50 20.00
FJE John Elway A 10.00 25.00
FJP Jim Plunkett A 6.00 15.00
FJR Jerry Rice A 7.50 20.00
FRS Roger Staubach A 7.50 20.00
FTB Tom Brady A 15.00 40.00
FTBR Terry Bradshaw B 8.00 20.00
FWP William Perry A 10.00 25.00

2005 Topps Heritage Foil

*VETERANS: 1.5X TO 4X BASIC VETS 1-300
*VETERANS: .3X TO .8X BASIC VET 301-340
*ROOKIES: .4X TO 1X BASIC ROOKIES 1-300
*ROOKIES: .3X TO .8X BASIC ROOK.341-365
FOIL SP ROOKIES TOO SCARCE TO PRICE
OVERALL FOIL STATED ODDS 1:4
58T SP PRINTED WITH 1958 TOPPS DESIGN
TBJ SP PRINTED W/THROWBACK JER.PHOTO
THC27A Aaron Rodgers 15.00 40.00

2005 Topps Heritage Foil Rainbow

*VETERANS: 8X TO 20X BASIC VETS 1-300
*VETERANS: 1.5X TO 4X BASIC VETS 301-340
*ROOKIES: 2.5X TO 6X BASIC ROOKIES 1-300
*ROOKIES: 2X TO 5X BASIC ROOKIES 341-365
FOIL RAINBOW/50 STATED ODDS 1:217
THC27 Aaron Rodgers 125.00 200.00

2005 Topps Heritage Gridiron Collection Relics

GROUP A ODDS 1:48, 911 HOB
GROUP B ODDS 1:124 HOB
GROUP C ODDS 1:121 HOB
GCRAS Alex Smith QB B 7.50 20.00
GCRBE Braylon Edwards B 3.00 8.00
GCRBS Barry Sanders C 10.00 25.00
GCRCW Cadillac Williams B 3.00 8.00
GCRJC Jason Campbell B 3.00 8.00
GCRJE John Elway C 10.00 25.00
GCRJM Joe Montana C 12.50 30.00
GCRJN Joe Namath A
GCRMA Marcus Allen C 5.00 12.00
GCRMC Mark Clayton B 3.00 8.00
GCRMJ Matt Jones B 3.00 8.00
GCRRB Ronnie Brown B 4.00 10.00
GCRRL Ronnie Lott C 4.00 10.00
GCRSY Steve Young C 6.00 15.00
GCRTW Troy Williamson B 3.00 8.00

2005 Topps Heritage New Age Performers

COMPLETE SET (15) 20.00 40.00
STATED ODDS 1:15
NAP1 Peyton Manning 2.50 6.00
NAP2 LaDainian Tomlinson 1.00 2.50
NAP3 Ben Roethlisberger 1.50 4.00
NAP4 Daunte Culpepper .75 2.00
NAP5 Randy Moss .75 2.00
NAP6 Shaun Alexander .60 1.50
NAP7 Marvin Harrison .75 2.00
NAP8 Brett Favre 2.00 5.00
NAP9 Tom Brady 4.00 10.00
NAP10 Michael Vick .75 2.00
NAP11 Terrell Owens .75 2.00
NAP12 Alex Smith QB 2.50 6.00
NAP13 Ronnie Brown .75 2.00
NAP14 Braylon Edwards .60 1.50
NAP15 Cadillac Williams .60 1.50

2005 Topps Heritage Real One Autographs

GROUP A ODDS 1:48,911 H
GROUP B ODDS 1:5675 H
GROUP C ODDS 1:3708 H
GROUP D ODDS 1:2451 H
GROUP E ODDS 1:1097 H
GROUP F ODDS 1:925 H
GROUP G ODDS 1:910 H
GROUP H ODDS 1:2185 H
GROUP I ODDS 1:202 H
GROUP J ODDS 1:1088 H
GROUP K ODDS 1:362 H
GROUP L ODDS 1:272 H
ROAAJ Adam Jones K 5.00 12.00
ROAAR Aaron Rodgers F 200.00 400.00
ROAAS Alex Smith QB D 15.00 40.00
ROAAW Andrew Walter G 8.00 20.00
ROAASM Alex Smith TE L 6.00 15.00
ROABA B.J. Askew I 5.00 12.00
ROABE Braylon Edwards G 10.00 25.00
ROABF Brett Favre A 150.00 300.00
ROABJ Brandon Jones L 5.00 12.00
ROACB Craig Bragg I 5.00 12.00
ROACF Ciatrick Fason F 8.00 20.00
ROACO Chad Owens J 5.00 12.00
ROACR Courtney Roby I 5.00 12.00
ROACW Cadillac Williams B 15.00 40.00
ROADJ Deacon Jones F 15.00 30.00
ROADJ Derrick Johnson I 8.00 20.00
ROAEC Earl Campbell D 25.00 50.00
ROAFG Frank Gore E 20.00 50.00
ROAHM Heath Miller F 10.00 25.00
ROAJA Joe Andruzzi I 5.00 12.00
ROAJB Jim Brown C 60.00 120.00
ROAJE John Elway B 100.00 200.00
ROAJM Joe Montana C 100.00 200.00
ROAJN Joe Namath C 60.00 120.00
ROAJMA Jerome Mathis K 5.00 12.00
ROAJMU James Mungro I 6.00 15.00
ROALM Lenny Moore E 12.00 30.00
ROALT Lawrence Taylor E 30.00 60.00
ROAMC Mark Clayton E 8.00 20.00
ROAMJ Matt Jones G 8.00 20.00
ROARB Ronnie Brown H 25.00 50.00
ROARC Ronald Curry I 6.00 15.00
ROARG Randall Gay I 6.00 15.00
ROARL Ronnie Lott B 40.00 80.00
ROARP Roscoe Parrish I 8.00 20.00
ROARW Roddy White D 10.00 25.00
ROATB Tatum Bell B 8.00 20.00
ROATW Troy Williamson E 8.00 20.00

2005 Topps Heritage Team Pennants

ONE PER BOX
1 Arizona Cardinals 2.00 5.00
2 Chicago Bears 2.50 6.00
3 Cleveland Browns 2.00 5.00
4 Detroit Lions 2.00 5.00
5 Green Bay Packers 3.00 8.00
6 Indianapolis Colts 2.00 5.00
7 New York Giants 2.50 6.00
8 Philadelphia Eagles 2.00 5.00
9 Pittsburgh Steelers 3.00 8.00
10 San Francisco 49ers 2.50 6.00
11 St. Louis Rams 2.00 5.00
12 Washington Redskins 2.50 6.00

2005 Topps Heritage Then and Now

COMPLETE SET (10) 12.50 30.00
STATED ODDS 1:15
TN1 B.Westbrook/L.Moore .75 2.00
TN2 J.Montana/T.Brady 4.00 10.00
TN3 G.Sayers/L.Tomlinson 2.00 5.00
TN4 Roethlisberger/J.Namath 3.00 8.00
TN5 E.Campbell/E.James 1.25 3.00
TN6 J.Lewis/J.Brown 2.00 5.00
TN7 B.Dawkins/R.Lott 1.25 3.00
TN8 L.Taylor/R.Lewis 1.25 3.00
TN9 O.Newsome/T.Gonzalez 1.00 2.50
TN10 D.Jones/D.Freeney 1.00 2.50

2006 Topps Heritage

This 407-card set was released in November, 2006. The set was issued into the hobby in eight-card packs, with a $3 SRP, which came 24 packs to a box. Some cards numbered between 1-133 and all cards numbered 311-407 were issued in shorter quantity than the other players in this set.
COMPLETE SET (497) 75.00 150.00
COMP.SET w/o SP's (207) 15.00 40.00
SPs: 1-90/95/100/101/107/109/111/121
SPs: 123/125/127/129/131/133/311-407
1 LaVar Arrington SP .40 1.00
2 Justin McCareins SP .40 1.00
3 Simeon Rice SP .40 1.00
4 Dennis Northcutt SP .40 1.00
5 Jason Campbell SP .40 1.00
6 Ricardo Colclough SP .40 1.00
7 Marion Barber SP .50 1.25
8 Samie Parker SP .40 1.00
9 Nick Barnett SP .40 1.00
10 David Garrard SP .40 1.00
11 Roy Williams S SP .40 1.00
12 Adrian Peterson SP .50 1.25
13 Marcus Robinson SP .40 1.00
14 Andrew Walter SP .40 1.00
15 Cedric Houston SP .40 1.00
16 John Abraham SP .40 1.00
17 Alex Smith TE SP .40 1.00
18 Travis Henry SP .40 1.00
19 Craig Krenzel SP .30 .75
20 Brian Dawkins SP .60 1.50
21 Bryant Young SP .40 1.00
22 Al Wilson SP .40 1.00
23 Nick Goings SP .40 1.00
24 Shaun Ellis SP .40 1.00
25 Marty Booker SP .40 1.00
26 Daniel Graham SP .40 1.00
27 Jim Sorgi SP .40 1.00
28 Sebastian Janikowski SP .40 1.00
29 Allen Rossum SP .40 1.00
30 Jim Kleinsasser SP .40 1.00
31 Lee Evans SP .50 1.25
32 Alex Brown SP .40 1.00
33 Steve Hutchinson SP .50 1.25
34 Sam Madison SP .40 1.00
35 Aaron Rodgers SP 1.50 4.00
36 Justin Griffith SP .30 .75
37 Terrence McGee SP .40 1.00
38 Odell Thurman SP .40 1.00
39 Marcus Trufant SP .40 1.00
40 Courtney Roby SP .40 1.00
41 Isaac Bruce SP .60 1.50
42 Ben Watson SP .40 1.00
43 Brandon Stokley SP .40 1.00
44 Koren Robinson SP .40 1.00
45 Mark Clayton SP .40 1.00
46 Darren Sproles SP .60 1.50
47 Matt Leinart SP RC .75 2.00
48 Terrell Owens SP .50 1.25
49 Antonio Pierce SP .40 1.00
50 Mark Brunell SP .50 1.25
51 T.J. Houshmandzadeh SP .40 1.00
52 Chris Gamble SP .40 1.00
53 Jason Witten SP .50 1.25
54 Michael Huff SP RC 1.00 2.50
55 Joey Porter SP .40 1.00
56 Eli Manning SP .50 1.25
57 Ladell Betts SP .40 1.00
58 Kevin Curtis SP .50 1.25
59 Reggie Williams SP .50 1.25
60 Alge Crumpler SP .50 1.25
61 Joseph Addai SP RC .75 2.00
62 Todd Heap SP .40 1.00
63 Trent Green SP .40 1.00
64 Muhsin Muhammad SP .40 1.00
65 Drew Bledsoe SP .50 1.25
66 LenDale White SP RC .75 2.00
67 Kris Mangum SP .30 .75
68 Troy Vincent SP .40 1.00
69 DeMarcus Ware SP .50 1.25
70 Brian Westbrook SP .40 1.00
71 Brandon Lloyd SP .40 1.00
72 Corey Dillon SP .40 1.00
73 Ernie Conwell SP .40 1.00
74 Laveranues Coles SP .40 1.00
75 Santana Moss SP .50 1.25
76 Alvis Whitted SP .30 .75
77 Demorrio Williams SP .75 2.00
78 Matt Hasselbeck SP .40 1.00
79 Billy Volek SP .40 1.00
80 Sean Taylor SP .60 1.50
81 Plaxico Burress SP .40 1.00
82 Frank Gore SP .50 1.25
83 Chris McAlister SP .40 1.00
84 Donnie Edwards SP .40 1.00
85 Ed Reed SP .50 1.25
86 Tarvaris Jackson SP RC .75 2.00
87 T.J. Duckett SP .40 1.00
88 Rex Grossman SP .40 1.00
89 Ronnie Brown SP .50 1.25
90 James Farrior SP .40 1.00
91 Mike Alstott .25 .60
92 Eddie Kennison .25 .60
93 Charlie Frye .30 .75
94 Deion Branch .25 .60
95 Brandon Jacobs SP .50 1.25
96 Larry Fitzgerald .30 .75
97 Domanick Davis .25 .60
98 Terrence Holt .25 .60
99 Dan Morgan .25 .60
100 Shaun Alexander SP .50 1.25
101 Shawne Merriman SP .60 1.50
102 Roddy White .25 .60
103 Ashley Lelie .25 .60
104 Jevon Kearse .25 .60
105 Andre Johnson .30 .75
106 Matt Mauck .25 .60
107 Dwight Freeney SP .50 1.25
108 Robert Gallery .25 .60
109 Chad Jackson SP RC 1.00 2.50
110 Marques Tuiasosopo .25 .60
111 LaMont Jordan SP .60 1.50
112 Taylor Jacobs .25 .60
113 Byron Leftwich .25 .60
114 Fabian Washington .25 .60
115 Michael Jenkins .25 .60
116 Steven Jackson .25 .60
117 Ronald Curry .25 .60
118 J.P. Losman .30 .75
119 Patrick Crayton .25 .60
120 Javon Walker .30 .75
121 Daunte Culpepper SP .60 1.50
122 Marc Bulger .25 .60
123 Kevin Jones SP .50 1.25
124 Tom Brady 1.25 3.00
125 Jay Cutler SP RC 1.25 3.00
126 Tony Gonzalez .30 .75
127 Warrick Dunn SP .50 1.25
128 Michael Strahan .30 .75
129 Demetrius Williams SP RC 1.00 2.50
130 Charles Woodson .40 1.00
131 Tiki Barber SP .60 1.50
132 Hines Ward .30 .75
133 Brian Calhoun SP RC 1.00 2.50
134 Torry Holt .30 .75
135 Priest Holmes .25 .60
136 Philip Rivers .40 1.00
137 Joey Harrington .25 .60
138 Donte Stallworth .25 .60
139 Ken Lucas .25 .60
140 Chad Morton .25 .60
141 Osi Umenyiora .25 .60
142 Jamal Lewis .30 .75
143 Derek Hagan RC .75 2.00
144 Deshaun Foster .30 .75
145 Michael Lewis .25 .60
146 Anquan Boldin .25 .60
147 Derrick Brooks .25 .60
148 Michael Turner .25 .60
149 Zach Thomas .30 .75
150 Carson Palmer .30 .75
151 Ryan Moats .25 .60
152 William Henderson .25 .60
153 Marcus Spears .25 .60
154 Travis Minor .25 .60
155 Scottie Vines .25 .60
156 Maurice Stovall RC .60 1.50
157 Dante Hall .25 .60
158 Chris Simms .25 .60
159 Zack Crockett .25 .60
160 Thomas Jones .25 .60
161 Marcus Pollard .25 .60
162 Troy Polamalu .40 1.00
163 LeRon McCoy .25 .60
164 Najeh Davenport .25 .60
165 Keenan McCardell .30 .75
166 Chris Brown .25 .60
167 Derrick Johnson .25 .60
168 Chad Pennington .25 .60
169 Adam Jones .25 .60
170 Terry Glenn .30 .75
171 Antonio Bryant .25 .60
172 Jerramy Stevens .30 .75
173 Antrel Rolle .25 .60
174 Randy McMichael .25 .60
175 Orlando Pace .25 .60
176 Chris Perry .30 .75
177 Drew Bennett .30 .75
178 Cedric Benson .25 .60
179 Ernest Wilford .25 .60
180 Dunta Robinson .25 .60
181 Reggie Wayne .30 .75
182 Lito Sheppard .30 .75
183 Maurice Drew RC 1.00 2.50
184 Todd Bouman .25 .60
185 Marlin Jackson .25 .60
186 D.J. Williams .25 .60
187 DeAngelo Hall .25 .60
188 Bubba Franks .25 .60
189 Greg Jones .25 .60
190 Dominic Rhodes .25 .60
191 Dallas Clark .25 .60
192 Dre Bly .25 .60
193 Charlie Whitehurst .25 .60
194 Will Demps RC .40 1.00
195 Champ Bailey .30 .75
196 Sinorice Moss RC .60 1.50
197 Jonathan Ogden .30 .75
198 Mike Peterson .25 .60
199 D.D. Lewis RC .60 1.50
200 Vincent Jackson .25 .60
201 Stefan Lefors .25 .60
202 Willie Parker .30 .75
203 Antwaan Randle El .25 .60
204 Keary Colbert .25 .60
205 Tyrone Calico .25 .60
206 Mike Williams .25 .60
207 David Carr .25 .60
208 Braylon Edwards .25 .60
209 Michael Clayton .25 .60
210 Jerome Mathis .25 .60
211 Fred Taylor .25 .60
212 Jake Delhomme .25 .60

213 Roy Williams WR .25 .60
214 Curtis Martin .30 .75
215 Terrell Suggs .25 .60
216 Troy Williamson .25 .60
217 Marshall Faulk .30 .75
218 D'Brickashaw Ferguson RC .60 1.50
219 Kelly Holcomb .25 .60
220 Matt Jones .25 .60
221 Michael Vick .30 .75
222 Deuce McAllister .30 .75
223 Eric Moulds .25 .60
224 Ike Taylor .25 .60
225 D.J. Hackett .25 .60
226 Keyshawn Johnson .30 .75
227 Josh McCown .25 .60
228 Joe Horn .25 .60
229 Jonathan Vilma .25 .60
230 Warren Sapp .30 .75
231 Reggie Brown .25 .60
232 Clinton Portis .25 .60
233 Derrick Burgess .25 .60
234 Bob Sanders .30 .75
235 Lofa Tatupu .25 .60
236 Justin Fargas .30 .75
237 Kellen Clemens RC .60 1.50
238 Richard Seymour .25 .60
239 Jeff Garcia .25 .60
240 Shaun Cody .25 .60
241 Brad Johnson .30 .75
242 Edgerrin James .30 .75
243 Terence Newman .25 .60
244 Bernard Berrian .25 .60
245 Mike Anderson .25 .60
246 Ahman Green .30 .75
247 Erron Kinney .25 .60
248 David Pollack .25 .60
249 Kevin Faulk .25 .60
250 Laurence Maroney RC .60 1.50
251 Chad Johnson .25 .60
252 Antonio Gates .40 1.00
253 Drew Brees .40 1.00
254 Jake Plummer .25 .60
255 Mario Williams RC 1.00 2.50
256 Chester Taylor .30 .75
257 Shawn Bryson .25 .60
258 J.J. Arrington .25 .60
259 Robert Ferguson .25 .60
260 Reuben Droughns .30 .75
261 Tab Perry .25 .60
262 Troy Brown .25 .60
263 Luis Castillo .25 .60
264 Quincy Morgan .25 .60
265 Damon Huard .25 .60
266 Walter Jones .25 .60
267 Kyle Vanden Bosch .25 .60
268 Doug Gabriel .25 .60
269 Deltha O'Neal .25 .60
270 Randy Moss .30 .75
271 Omar Jacobs RC .60 1.50
272 Kevan Barlow .25 .60
273 John Lynch .25 .60
274 Chris Cooley .25 .60
275 Zach Hilton .25 .60
276 Peter Warrick .25 .60
277 London Fletcher .30 .75
278 Nate Burleson .25 .60
279 Larry Foote .25 .60
280 Justin Miller .25 .60
281 Darius Watts .25 .60
282 Aaron Brooks .25 .60
283 Joey Galloway .30 .75
284 Darrell Jackson .30 .75
285 Alex Smith QB .30 .75
286 Vonnie Holliday .25 .60
287 Nathan Vasher .25 .60
288 Tatum Bell .25 .60
289 Olin Kreutz .25 .60
290 Duce Staley .25 .60
291 Courtney Anderson .25 .60
292 Tory James .25 .60
293 Mike Vanderjagt .25 .60
294 Mark Bradley .25 .60
295 Kurt Warner .30 .75
296 Ray Lewis .40 1.00
297 Kassim Osgood .25 .60
298 Trent Dilfer .25 .60
299 Justin Gage .25 .60
300 DeAngelo Williams RC .75 2.00
301 Luke McCown .25 .60
302 Charles Rogers .30 .75
303 Marcedes Lewis RC .60 1.50
304 Samari Rolle .25 .60
305 Greg Lewis .25 .60
306 Peter Boulware .25 .60
307 Donald Driver .30 .75
308 Travis Taylor .25 .60
309 Quentin Jammer .25 .60
310 Carlos Rogers .25 .60
311 Peyton Manning SP 5.00 12.00
312 Reggie Bush SP RC 1.25 3.00
313 Vernon Davis SP RC 1.00 2.50
314 Brett Favre SP 4.00 10.00
315 Cadillac Williams SP 1.50 4.00
316 Donovan McNabb SP 1.50 4.00
317 Jason Avant SP RC .75 2.00
318 Ben Roethlisberger SP 2.50 6.00
319 Steve Smith SP 2.00 5.00
320 Vince Young SP RC .75 2.00
321 Willis McGahee SP 1.25 3.00
322 Jeremy Shockey SP 1.25 3.00
323 Rudi Johnson SP 1.25 3.00
324 Brian Urlacher SP 2.00 5.00
325 Rod Smith SP 1.50 4.00
326 Santonio Holmes SP RC 1.00 2.50
327 Larry Johnson SP 1.25 3.00
328 Julius Jones SP 1.25 3.00
329 Marvin Harrison SP 1.50 4.00
330 Chris Chambers SP 1.25 3.00
331 Takeo Spikes SP 1.25 3.00
332 Brian Griese SP 1.25 3.00
333 Steve McNair SP 1.50 4.00
334 Willie McGinest SP 1.25 3.00
335 Tedy Bruschi SP 1.50 4.00
336 Roydell Williams SP 1.25 3.00
337 Patrick Ramsey SP 1.50 4.00
338 Kyle Boller SP 1.25 3.00
339 Bethel Johnson SP 1.25 3.00
340 Jerry Porter SP 1.25 3.00
341 Shawntae Spencer SP 1.25 3.00
342 Drew Carter SP 1.25 3.00
343 Jason Elam SP 1.25 3.00
344 Michael Pittman SP 1.25 3.00
345 Edell Shepherd SP RC .75 2.00
346 Maurice Hicks SP 1.25 3.00
347 Ron Dayne SP 1.50 4.00
348 Josh Reed SP 1.25 3.00
349 Lorenzo Neal SP 1.25 3.00
350 LaDainian Tomlinson SP 2.00 5.00
351 David Tyree SP 1.25 3.00
352 Keith Brooking SP 1.25 3.00
353 Devery Henderson SP 1.25 3.00
354 Daylon McCutcheon SP 1.25 3.00
355 Derrick Mason SP 1.25 3.00
356 Fred Smoot SP 1.25 3.00
357 Ronde Barber SP 1.25 3.00
358 Dan Kreider SP 1.25 3.00
359 Shayne Graham SP 1.25 3.00
360 [illegible] 1.25 3.00
361 Shawn Springs SP 1.25 3.00
362 Amani Toomer SP 1.25 3.00
363 Eric Parker SP 1.25 3.00
364 Jason Taylor SP 1.50 4.00
365 Keith Bulluck SP 1.25 3.00
366 Sam Gado SP 1.25 3.00
367 Cedrick Wilson SP 1.25 3.00
368 Mewelde Moore SP 1.25 3.00
369 Travis Daniels SP 1.25 3.00
370 Arnaz Battle SP 1.25 3.00
371 Kyle Orton SP 1.25 3.00
372 Dane Looker SP 1.25 3.00
373 Kellen Winslow SP 1.25 3.00
374 Julius Peppers SP 1.50 4.00
375 Jeremiah Trotter SP 1.25 3.00
376 L.J. Smith SP 1.25 3.00
377 Gibril Wilson SP 1.25 3.00
378 Adam Archuleta SP 1.25 3.00
379 Darren Sharper SP 1.25 3.00
380 Joe Jurevicius SP 1.25 3.00
381 Patrick Pass SP 1.25 3.00
382 A.J. Feeley SP 1.25 3.00
383 Leroy Hill SP 1.25 3.00
384 Corey Webster SP 1.25 3.00
385 Heath Miller SP 1.25 3.00
386 Cato June SP 1.50 4.00
387 Brad Hoover SP 1.25 3.00
388 Michael Boulware SP 1.25 3.00
389 Matt Schaub SP 1.25 3.00
390 Kirk Morrison SP 1.25 3.00
391 Kevin Carter SP 1.25 3.00
392 David Givens SP 1.50 4.00
393 Alvin Pearman SP 1.25 3.00
394 Brian Finneran SP 1.25 3.00
395 Ike Hilliard SP 1.25 3.00
396 Angelo Crowell SP 1.25 3.00
397 Charlie Adams SP 1.25 3.00
398 Neil Rackers SP 1.25 3.00
399 Brandon Jones SP 1.25 3.00
400 B.J. Sams SP 1.25 3.00
401 Kyle Johnson SP 1.25 3.00
402 Adam Vinatieri SP 1.25 3.00
403 Bryant Johnson SP 1.25 3.00
404 Bryan Fletcher SP 1.25 3.00
405 Channing Crowder SP 1.25 3.00
406 Jerricho Cotchery SP 1.25 3.00
407 A.J. Hawk SP RC 1.00 2.50
CL1 Checklist Card 1 .05 .15
CL2 Checklist Card 2 .05 .15
CL3 Checklist Card 3 .05 .15

2006 Topps Heritage Black Backs

*BLACK BACKS: .4X TO 1X RED BACKS

2006 Topps Heritage Chrome

CHROME/1952 ODDS 1:6 HOB
*REF.VETS: .6X TO 1.5X BASIC CHROME
*REF.ROOKIES: .6X TO 1.5X BASIC CHROME
REFRACT/552 ODDS 1:27 HOB
*BLACK REF.VETS: 1.2X TO 3X
*BLACK REF.ROOKIE: 1.5X TO 4X
BLK REFRACT/52 ODDS 1:294 HOB
THC1 Jeremy Shockey 1.25 3.00
THC2 Maurice Stovall 1.25 3.00
THC3 Donte Stallworth 1.25 3.00
THC4 Zach Thomas 1.50 4.00
THC5 Daunte Culpepper 1.50 4.00
THC6 Carson Palmer 1.50 4.00
THC7 Vernon Davis 1.50 4.00
THC8 A.J. Hawk 1.50 4.00
THC9 Plaxico Burress 1.25 3.00
THC10 Jamal Lewis 1.50 4.00
THC11 Shaun Alexander 1.25 3.00
THC12 LaMont Jordan 1.50 4.00
THC13 Marc Bulger 1.25 3.00
THC14 Chris Simms 1.25 3.00
THC15 Muhsin Muhammad 1.25 3.00
THC16 Ahman Green 1.50 4.00
THC17 Drew Bledsoe 1.50 4.00
THC18 David Carr 1.25 3.00
THC19 LenDale White 1.25 3.00
THC20 Joey Galloway 1.50 4.00
THC21 Michael Vick 1.50 4.00
THC22 Ray Lewis 2.00 5.00
THC23 Deuce McAllister 1.50 4.00
THC24 Marcedes Lewis 1.25 3.00
THC25 Eric Moulds 1.25 3.00
THC26 Julius Jones 1.25 3.00
THC27 Rudi Johnson 1.25 3.00
THC28 Chester Taylor 1.50 4.00
THC29 Todd Heap 1.25 3.00
THC30 Dante Hall 1.25 3.00
THC31 Trent Green 1.25 3.00
THC32 Rod Smith 1.50 4.00
THC33 Javon Walker 1.50 4.00
THC34 Omar Jacobs 1.25 3.00
THC35 Kevin Jones 1.25 3.00
THC36 Derek Hagan 1.50 4.00
THC37 Jason Avant 1.25 3.00
THC38 Deshaun Foster 1.50 4.00
THC39 Chris Brown 1.25 3.00
THC40 Takeo Spikes 1.25 3.00
THC41 Alge Crumpler 1.50 4.00
THC42 Tarvaris Jackson 1.25 3.00
THC43 Joseph Addai 1.25 3.00
THC44 Ben Roethlisberger 2.50 6.00
THC45 Chad Johnson 1.25 3.00
THC46 Ronnie Brown 1.50 4.00
THC47 Brian Urlacher 2.00 5.00
THC48 Laurence Maroney 1.25 3.00
THC49 Maurice Drew 2.00 5.00
THC50 Shawne Merriman 1.50 4.00
THC51 Vince Young 1.25 3.00
THC52 Corey Dillon 1.25 3.00
THC53 Steve Smith 2.00 5.00
THC54 Matt Hasselbeck 1.25 3.00
THC55 Willis McGahee 1.25 3.00
THC56 D'Brickashaw Ferguson 1.25 3.00
THC57 Chad Jackson 1.25 3.00
THC58 Clinton Portis 1.25 3.00
THC59 Santana Moss 1.50 4.00
THC60 Larry Johnson 1.25 3.00
THC61 Cadillac Williams 1.50 4.00
THC62 Tom Brady 6.00 15.00
THC63 Peyton Manning 5.00 12.00
THC64 Jay Cutler 1.50 4.00
THC65 Reggie Bush 2.00 5.00
THC66 Eli Manning 1.50 4.00
THC67 Brett Favre 4.00 10.00
THC68 Tony Gonzalez 1.50 4.00
THC69 Matt Leinart 1.25 3.00
THC70 Warrick Dunn 1.25 3.00
THC71 Terrell Owens 1.50 4.00
THC72 Anquan Boldin 1.25 3.00
THC73 LaDainian Tomlinson 2.00 5.00
THC74 Michael Strahan 1.50 4.00
THC75 Donovan McNabb 1.50 4.00
THC76 Demetrius Williams 1.25 3.00
THC77 Michael Huff 1.50 4.00
THC78 Charles Woodson 2.00 5.00
THC79 Byron Leftwich 1.25 3.00
THC80 Tiki Barber 1.50 4.00
THC81 Curtis Martin 1.50 4.00
THC82 Hines Ward 1.50 4.00
THC83 DeAngelo Williams 1.50 4.00
THC84 Brian Calhoun 1.25 3.00
THC85 Randy Moss 1.50 4.00
THC86 Torry Holt 1.50 4.00
THC87 Steven Jackson 1.25 3.00
THC88 Priest Holmes 1.25 3.00
THC89 Larry Fitzgerald 1.50 4.00
THC90 Philip Rivers 2.00 5.00
THC91 Domanick Davis 1.25 3.00
THC92 Santonio Holmes 1.00 [illegible]
THC93 Charlie Whitehurst 1.25 3.00
THC94 Antonio Gates 2.00 5.00
THC95 Fred Taylor 1.25 3.00
THC96 Drew Brees 2.00 5.00
THC97 Jake Delhomme 1.25 3.00
THC98 Jake Plummer 1.25 3.00
THC99 Roy Williams WR 1.25 3.00
THC100 Mario Williams 2.00 5.00
THC101 Drew Bennett 1.50 4.00
THC102 Sinorice Moss 1.25 3.00
THC103 Reggie Wayne 1.50 4.00
THC104 Willie Parker 1.50 4.00
THC105 Marvin Harrison 1.50 4.00
THC106 Joe Horn 1.25 3.00
THC107 Jonathan Vilma 1.25 3.00
THC108 Chris Chambers 1.25 3.00
THC109 Kellen Clemens 1.25 3.00
THC110 Edgerrin James 1.50 4.00

2006 Topps Heritage Flashbacks

COMPLETE SET (6) 5.00 12.00
STATED ODDS 1:5 HOB
FL1 Frank Gifford .75 2.00
FL2 Chuck Bednarik .60 1.50
FL3 Y.A. Tittle 1.00 2.50
FL4 Art Donovan .60 1.50
FL5 Hugh McElhenny .75 2.00
FL6 Lou Creekmur .60 1.50

2006 Topps Heritage Flashbacks Autographs

AUTO/25 ODDS 1:17,600 HOB
FAAD Art Donovan
FACB Chuck Bednarik 25.00 60.00
FAYT Y.A. Tittle 30.00 80.00

2006 Topps Heritage Flashbacks Relics

GIFFORD ODDS 1:17,150 HOB
BEDNARIK ODDS 1:1680 HOB
FRCB Chuck Bednarik 5.00 12.00
FRFG Frank Gifford 20.00 50.00

2006 Topps Heritage Gridiron Collection Jersey

STATED ODDS 1:45 HOB
GCAH A.J. Hawk 2.50 6.00
GCBC Brian Calhoun 2.00 5.00
GCCW Charlie Whitehurst 2.00 5.00
GCDH Derek Hagan 2.50 6.00
GCJA Jason Avant 2.00 5.00
GCJK Joe Klopfenstein 2.00 5.00
GCLW LenDale White 2.00 5.00
GCMH Michael Huff 2.50 6.00
GCMS Maurice Stovall 2.00 5.00
GCMW Mario Williams 3.00 8.00
GCRB Reggie Bush 3.00 8.00
GCSH Santonio Holmes 2.50 6.00
GCSM Sinorice Moss 2.00 5.00
GCTJ Tarvaris Jackson 2.00 5.00
GCTW Travis Wilson 2.00 5.00
GCVY Vince Young 2.00 5.00

2006 Topps Heritage Gridiron Collection Jersey Autographs

AUTO/25 ODDS 1:5850 HOB
GCRAAH A.J. Hawk 40.00 80.00
GCRABC Brian Calhoun 15.00 40.00
GCRADH Derek Hagan 15.00 40.00
GCRAJK Joe Klopfenstein
GCRALW LenDale White 40.00 80.00
GCRAMS Maurice Stovall
GCRAMW Mario Williams 20.00 50.00
GCRARB Reggie Bush 40.00 100.00
GCRASH Santonio Holmes 20.00 50.00
GCRASM Sinorice Moss 15.00 40.00
GCRATJ Tarvaris Jackson 30.00 80.00
GCRAVY Vince Young 25.00 60.00

2006 Topps Heritage Gridiron Collection Jersey Duals

DUAL/52 ODDS 1:5500 HOB
BL R.Bush/M.Leinart 5.00 12.00
BW R.Bush/L.White 5.00 12.00
HM S.Moss/S.Holmes 4.00 10.00
HS S.Holmes/M.Stovall 4.00 10.00
HW A.Hawk/M.Williams 5.00 12.00
YL V.Young/M.Leinart 3.00 8.00

2006 Topps Heritage In the Cards Autographs

GROUP A ODDS 1:70,000 HOB
GROUP B ODDS 1:5725 HOB
GROUP C ODDS 1:17,500 HOB
GROUP D ODDS 1:1208 HOB
GROUP E ODDS 1:1600 HOB
GROUP F ODDS 1:420 HOB
GROUP G ODDS 1:1680 HOB
UNPRICED SPECIAL EDITION #'d TO 6
HCAAH A.J. Hawk G 10.00 25.00
HCABF Brett Favre B 75.00 150.00
HCACJ Chad Jackson G 6.00 15.00
HCADA DeAngelo Williams D 12.00 30.00
HCADF D'Brickashaw Ferguson E 6.00 15.00
HCADM Dan Marino B 100.00 200.00
HCAES Emmitt Smith A 150.00 250.00
HCAJA Joseph Addai G 6.00 15.00
HCAJC Jay Cutler E 12.00 30.00
HCAJE John Elway B 75.00 150.00
HCAJK Joe Klopfenstein F 6.00 15.00
HCAJN Jerious Norwood G 6.00 15.00
HCAJN Joe Namath C 60.00 100.00
HCALP Leonard Pope E 10.00 25.00
HCALT LaDainian Tomlinson B 25.00 60.00
HCALW Leon Washington G 6.00 15.00
HCAMK Mathias Kiwanuka G 10.00 25.00
HCAML Matt Leinart D 6.00 15.00
HCAMW Mario Williams G 10.00 25.00
HCAPM Peyton Manning D 60.00 100.00
HCARB Reggie Bush D 8.00 20.00
HCASH Santonio Holmes D 8.00 20.00
HCATB Terry Bradshaw B 50.00 100.00
HCAVD Vernon Davis G 8.00 20.00
HCAVY Vince Young D 6.00 15.00
HCACJO Chad Johnson B 8.00 20.00
HCALWH LenDale White D 6.00 15.00

2006 Topps Heritage New Age Performers

COMPLETE SET (15) 8.00 20.00
STATED ODDS 1:8 HOB
NAP1 Brett Favre 2.50 6.00
NAP2 Steve Smith 1.25 3.00
NAP3 Tiki Barber 1.00 2.50
NAP4 Chad Johnson .75 2.00
NAP5 Tom Brady 4.00 10.00
NAP6 Carson Palmer 1.00 2.50
NAP7 LaDainian Tomlinson 1.25 3.00
NAP8 Larry Johnson .75 2.00
NAP9 Matt Hasselbeck .75 2.00
NAP10 Shaun Alexander .75 2.00
NAP11 Peyton Manning 3.00 8.00
NAP12 Ben Roethlisberger 1.50 4.00
NAP13 Reggie Bush .50 1.25
NAP14 Matt Leinart .30 .75
NAP15 Vince Young .30 .75

2006 Topps Heritage Real One Autographs

AUTO/200 ODDS 1:1055 HOB
*SPECIAL EDIT/52: .6X TO 1.5X BASIC INSERTS
SPEC.EDIT.AU/52 ODDS 1:4120 HOB
ROAAD Art Donovan 20.00 50.00
ROACB Chuck Bednarik 25.00 50.00
ROACT Charley Trippi 25.00 50.00
ROAGM Gino Marchetti 25.00 50.00
ROAHM Hugh McElhenny 25.00 50.00
ROAYA Y.A. Tittle UER 25.00 50.00

2006 Topps Heritage Then and Now

COMPLETE SET (5) 5.00 12.00
STATED ODDS 1:8 HOB
TN1 R.Bush/F.Gifford 1.00 2.50
TN2 B.Urlacher/C.Bednarik 1.00 2.50
TN3 D.Brees/Y.Tittle 1.00 2.50
TN4 M.Vick/C.Trippi .75 2.00
TN5 W.Sapp/A.Donovan .75 2.00

2015 Topps Heritage

1 Tom Brady 1.00 2.50
2 Dante Fowler Jr. RC .75 2.00
3 Jameis Winston RC 1.25 3.00
4 Amari Cooper RC 1.50 4.00
5 Aaron Rodgers .75 2.00
6 Kevin Johnson RC .50 1.25
7 Adrian Peterson .40 1.00
8 Ameer Abdullah RC .75 2.00
9 T.J. Yeldon RC .50 1.25
10 Marcus Mariota RC 2.00 5.00
11 Titus Davis RC .60 1.50
12 Sammie Coates RC .60 1.50
13 Stefon Diggs RC 1.25 3.00
14 Terry Bradshaw .75 2.00
15 Andrew Luck .50 1.25
16 Eddie Lacy .25 .60
17 Kevin White RC .60 1.50
18 Odell Beckham Jr. .40 1.00
19 Tyler Kroft RC .60 1.50
20 Peyton Manning .75 2.00
21 Steve Young .75 2.00
22 Vince Mayle RC .60 1.50
23 Clive Walford RC .50 1.25
24 Rashad Greene RC .50 1.25
25 Leonard Williams RC .50 1.25
26 Vic Beasley RC .60 1.50
27 Matt Jones RC .50 1.25
28 Jeremy Langford RC .50 1.25
29 Emmitt Smith 1.00 2.50
30 Drew Brees .40 1.00
31 Shaq Thompson RC .60 1.50
32 Sean Mannion RC .50 1.25
33 Terrence Magee RC .75 2.00
34 Jamison Crowder RC .60 1.50
35 Cody Fajardo RC .60 1.50
36 Eric Kendricks RC .50 1.25
37 Tevin Coleman RC .60 1.50
38 Bo Jackson .75 2.00
39 David Johnson RC 1.25 3.00
40 Ben Koyack RC .75 2.00
41 Duke Johnson RC .75 2.00
42 Levi Norwood RC .50 1.25
43 Calvin Johnson .40 1.00
44 Brett Favre 1.25 3.00
45 Devante Davis RC .60 1.50
46 Shane Carden RC .50 1.25
47 Justin Hardy RC .50 1.25
48 Jay Ajayi RC .75 2.00
49 Roger Staubach .75 2.00
50 Trae Waynes RC .50 1.25
51 DeVante Parker RC .75 2.00
52 Tony Lippett RC .50 1.25
54 Mike Davis RC .50 1.25
55 Dres Anderson RC .50 1.25
56 Le'Veon Bell .30 .75
57 Devin Smith RC .50 1.25
58 Bryce Petty RC .50 1.25
59 Jaelen Strong RC .60 1.50
60 Austin Hill RC .50 1.25
61 Eli Manning .30 .75
62 Deion Sanders .50 1.25
63 Marcus Murphy RC .50 1.25
64 Matthew Stafford .30 .75
65 Rob Gronkowski .40 1.00
66 Lawrence Taylor .60 1.50
67 Maxx Williams RC .50 1.25
68 Jamaal Charles .30 .75
69 Josh Harper RC .50 1.25
70 John Elway 1.00 2.50
71 Barry Sanders 1.00 2.50
72 Malcolm Brown RC .60 1.50
73 Marshawn Lynch .30 .75
74 Chris Conley RC .50 1.25
75 Jesse James RC .60 1.50
76 Buck Allen RC .60 1.50
77 Breshad Perriman RC .50 1.25
78 Devin Funchess RC .75 2.00
79 Dan Marino 1.25 3.00
80 Jerry Rice 1.00 2.50
81 David Cobb RC .50 1.25
82 Brett Hundley RC .50 1.25
83 Landon Collins RC .60 1.50
84 Tre McBride RC .50 1.25
85 Bud Dupree RC .60 1.50
86 Melvin Gordon RC 1.25 3.00
87 Jordy Nelson .30 .75
88 Cameron Artis-Payne RC .50 1.25
89 Antonio Brown .40 1.00
90 Dominique Brown RC .50 1.25
91 Tyler Lockett RC .75 2.00
92 Gale Sayers .60 1.50
93 Todd Gurley RC 2.00 5.00
94 Josh Robinson RC .50 1.25
95 Deontay Greenberry RC .50 1.25
96 Nelson Agholor RC .60 1.50
97 Kenny Bell RC .75 2.00
98 Dorial Green-Beckham RC .50 1.25
99 Eric Dickerson .50 1.25
100 Russell Wilson .50 1.25
101 Phillip Dorsett RC .50 1.25

2015 Topps High Tek

1 Tom Brady A 3.00 8.00
2 Jerry Rice A 2.00 5.00
3 John Elway A 2.00 5.00
4 Eli Manning A 1.00 2.50
5 Odell Beckham Jr. A 1.25 3.00
6 Dan Marino A 2.50 6.00
7 Jameis Winston A RC 1.25 3.00
8 Marcus Mariota A RC 2.00 5.00
9 Eric Dickerson A 1.00 2.50
10 Matt Forte A .75 2.00
11 Deion Sanders A 1.00 2.50
12 Drew Brees A 1.25 3.00
13 Kurt Warner A 1.00 2.50
14 Jerome Bettis A 1.25 3.00
15 Warren Moon A 1.25 3.00
16 Barry Sanders A 2.00 5.00
17 Howie Long A 1.25 3.00
18 Tim Brown A 1.25 3.00
19 Jordan Matthews A 1.00 2.50
20 Peyton Manning A 2.50 6.00
21 Kelvin Benjamin A 1.00 2.50
22 Joique Bell A .75 2.00
23 Alshon Jeffery A 1.00 2.50
24 Andre Williams A .75 2.00
25 Aaron Rodgers A 2.50 6.00
26 Donte Moncrief A 1.00 2.50
27 John Riggins A 1.00 2.50
28 Ryan Tannehill A 1.00 2.50
29 Antonio Brown A 1.25 3.00
30 Len Dawson A 1.25 3.00
31 Mike Evans A 1.00 2.50
32 Dwight Clark A 1.00 2.50
33 Sammy Watkins A 1.00 2.50
34 Ronnie Lott A 1.00 2.50
35 Emmanuel Sanders A 1.00 2.50
36 Terrell Davis A 1.00 2.50
37 Marshall Faulk A 1.00 2.50
38 Devin Smith RC .50 1.25
39 Shane Ray RC .50 1.25
40 Matthew Stafford A 1.00 2.50
41 Eddie Lacy A .75 2.00
42 Curtis Martin A 1.00 2.50
43 Trae Waynes RC .50 1.25
44 Davante Adams A 1.00 2.50
45 Russell Wilson A 1.50 4.00
46 Shaq Thompson A RC .60 1.50
47 Tre Mason A 1.00 2.50
48 Arik Armstead A RC .50 1.25
49 Maxx Williams A RC .50 1.25
50 Emmitt Smith A 2.00 5.00
51 Derek Carr A 1.25 3.00
52 Landon Collins A RC .60 1.50
53 Jeremy Hill A .75 2.00
54 Randy Gregory A RC .50 1.25
55 Dante Fowler Jr. A RC .75 2.00
56 Tre McBride A RC .50 1.25
57 David Johnson A RC 1.25 3.00
58 Alvin Dupree A RC .60 1.50
59 Greg Olsen A 1.00 2.50
60 Danny Shelton A RC .50 1.25
61 Vic Beasley A RC .60 1.50
62 Roger Craig A 1.00 2.50
63 Jamaal Charles A 1.00 2.50
64 Steve Young A 1.50 4.00
65 Isaiah Crowell A .75 2.00
66 Terry Bradshaw A 1.50 4.00
67 Clive Walford A RC .50 1.25
68 Jamison Crowder A RC .60 1.50
69 Martavis Bryant A .75 2.00
70 Terrance West A .75 2.00
71 Alfred Morris A .75 2.00
72 Brett Favre A 2.50 6.00
73 Nelson Agholor B RC .60 1.50
74 Garrett Grayson B RC .50 1.25
75 Luke Kuechly B 1.00 2.50
76 Bryce Petty B RC .50 1.25
77 Jeremy Langford B RC .50 1.25
78 Cameron Artis-Payne B RC .50 1.25
79 Kevin White B RC .60 1.50
80 Jaelen Strong B RC .60 1.50
81 Phillip Dorsett B RC .50 1.25
82 Ameer Abdullah B RC .75 2.00
83 Amari Cooper B RC 1.50 4.00
84 Breshad Perriman B RC .50 1.25
85 T.J. Yeldon B RC .50 1.25
86 Devin Funchess B RC .75 2.00
87 Lawrence Taylor B 1.25 3.00
88 Dorial Green-Beckham B RC .50 1.25
89 Ty Montgomery B RC .50 1.25
90 Mike Davis B RC .50 1.25
91 Kenny Bell B RC .75 2.00
92 Tony Lippett B RC .50 1.25
93 Bob Lilly B 1.00 2.50
94 Tyler Lockett B RC .75 2.00
95 Melvin Gordon B RC 1.25 3.00
96 Sammie Coates B RC .60 1.50
97 Clay Matthews B 1.25 3.00
98 Tevin Coleman B RC .60 1.50
99 DeVante Parker B RC .75 2.00
100 David Cobb B RC .50 1.25
101 Marshawn Lynch B 1.00 2.50
102 Brandon Marshall B .75 2.00
103 Sean Mannion B RC .50 1.25
104 Rashad Greene B RC .50 1.25
105 Javorius Allen B RC .60 1.50
106 Duke Johnson B RC .75 2.00
107 Leonard Williams B RC .50 1.25
108 Todd Gurley B RC 2.00 5.00
109 Chris Conley B RC .50 1.25
110 Victor Cruz B 1.00 2.50
111 Jay Ajayi B RC .75 2.00
112 Brett Hundley B RC .50 1.25

2015 Topps High Tek Blade

*BLADE: 2X TO 5X BASIC GROUP A

2015 Topps High Tek Chain Link

*CHAIN: .75X TO 2X BASIC GROUP B

2015 Topps High Tek Circuit Board

*CIRCUIT: .5X TO 1.2X BASIC GROUP A

2015 Topps High Tek Clouds Diffractor

*CLDS DFFRCTR: 2X TO 5X BASIC

2015 Topps High Tek Confetti Diffractor

*CNFTTI DFFRCTR: 1.2X TO 3X BASIC

2015 Topps High Tek Cubes

*CUBES: .75X TO 2X BASIC GROUP A

2015 Topps High Tek Diamonds

*DIAMONDS: 1.2X TO 3X BASIC GROUP B

2015 Topps High Tek Dots

*DOTS: .4X TO 1X BASIC GROUP B

2015 Topps High Tek Gold Rainbow Diffractor

*GOLD RNBW: 1.5X TO 4X BASIC

2015 Topps High Tek Grid

*GRID: 1.2X TO 3X BASIC GROUP B

2015 Topps High Tek Low TEK Diffractors

LTDAB Antonio Brown 5.00 12.00
LTDAM Alfred Morris 3.00 8.00
LTDDM Dan Marino 10.00 25.00
LTDEL Eddie Lacy 3.00 8.00
LTDES Emmanuel Sanders 4.00 10.00
LTDJB Jerome Bettis 5.00 12.00
LTDJE John Elway 8.00 20.00
LTDJH Jeremy Hill 3.00 8.00
LTDJR Jerry Rice 8.00 20.00
LTDMS Matthew Stafford 4.00 10.00
LTDOB Odell Beckham Jr. 5.00 12.00
LTDRT Ryan Tannehill 4.00 10.00
LTDSW Sammy Watkins 4.00 10.00
LTDTB Tim Brown 5.00 12.00
LTDTD Terrell Davis 4.00 10.00

2015 Topps High Tek Pipes

*PIPES: .5X TO 1.2X BASIC GROUP B

2015 Topps High Tek Purple Rainbow Diffractor

*PRPLE RNBW: .5X TO 1.2X BASIC

2015 Topps High Tek Pyramids

*PYRAMIDS: 1X TO 2.5X BASIC GROUP A

2015 Topps High Tek Spiral

*SPIRAL: .4X TO 1X BASIC GROUP A

2015 Topps High Tek Stripes

*STRIPES: 1.2X TO 3X BASIC GROUP A

2015 Topps High Tek Autographs

2 Jerry Rice
3 John Elway
4 Eli Manning 20.00 50.00
6 Dan Marino
7 Jameis Winston 30.00 60.00
8 Marcus Mariota 40.00 100.00
9 Eric Dickerson
10 Matt Forte
11 Deion Sanders
12 Drew Brees
13 Kurt Warner
15 Warren Moon
16 Barry Sanders 50.00 100.00
17 Howie Long
18 Tim Brown
19 Jordan Matthews 3.00 8.00
20 Peyton Manning
21 Kelvin Benjamin 3.00 8.00
22 Joique Bell 2.50 6.00
23 Alshon Jeffery 3.00 8.00
24 Andre Williams 2.50 6.00
25 Aaron Rodgers
27 John Riggins
28 Ryan Tannehill
31 Mike Evans 3.00 8.00
33 Sammy Watkins
35 Emmanuel Sanders 3.00 8.00
36 Terrell Davis
37 Marshall Faulk
38 Devin Smith 2.50 6.00
39 Shane Ray 2.50 6.00
41 Eddie Lacy
42 Curtis Martin
43 Trae Waynes 2.50 6.00
45 Russell Wilson
46 Shaq Thompson 3.00 8.00
48 Arik Armstead 2.50 6.00
50 Emmitt Smith
51 Derek Carr 15.00 30.00
52 Landon Collins 3.00 8.00
53 Jeremy Hill 2.50 6.00
55 Dante Fowler Jr. 4.00 10.00
56 Tre McBride 2.50 6.00
57 David Johnson 10.00 25.00
59 Greg Olsen 8.00 20.00
60 Danny Shelton 2.50 6.00
61 Vic Beasley 3.00 8.00
62 Roger Craig 3.00 8.00
64 Steve Young
65 Isaiah Crowell 2.50 6.00
66 Terry Bradshaw
67 Clive Walford 2.50 6.00
69 Martavis Bryant 2.50 6.00
72 Brett Favre
73 Nelson Agholor 3.00 8.00
75 Luke Kuechly 10.00 25.00
76 Bryce Petty 2.50 6.00
77 Jeremy Langford 2.50 6.00
78 Cameron Artis-Payne 2.50 6.00
79 Kevin White 3.00 8.00
80 Jaelen Strong 3.00 8.00
82 Ameer Abdullah 4.00 10.00
83 Amari Cooper
84 Breshad Perriman 2.50 6.00
86 Devin Funchess 4.00 10.00
89 Ty Montgomery 2.50 6.00
90 Mike Davis 2.50 6.00
91 Kenny Bell 4.00 10.00
92 Tony Lippett 2.50 6.00
94 Tyler Lockett 4.00 10.00
95 Melvin Gordon 8.00 20.00
96 Sammie Coates 3.00 8.00
97 Clay Matthews
98 Tevin Coleman 3.00 8.00
99 DeVante Parker
100 David Cobb 2.50 6.00
103 Sean Mannion 2.50 6.00
104 Rashad Greene 2.50 6.00
106 Duke Johnson 4.00 10.00
107 Leonard Williams 2.50 6.00
108 Todd Gurley 30.00 60.00
109 Chris Conley 2.50 6.00
110 Victor Cruz 3.00 8.00
111 Jay Ajayi 4.00 10.00
112 Brett Hundley 2.50 6.00

2015 Topps High Tek Autographs Clouds Diffractor

*CLOUD/25: .8X TO 2X BASIC AU
4 Eli Manning 50.00 100.00
12 Drew Brees 40.00 80.00
25 Aaron Rodgers 250.00 350.00
41 Eddie Lacy 12.00 30.00
66 Terry Bradshaw 50.00 100.00

2015 Topps High Tek Autographs Gold Diffractor

*GOLD/50: .6X TO 1.5X BASIC AU
8 Marcus Mariota 50.00 125.00
11 Deion Sanders 30.00 60.00

2015 Topps High Tek Autographs Tidal Diffractor

*TIDAL/99: .5X TO 1.2X BASIC AU
8 Marcus Mariota 50.00 125.00
108 Todd Gurley 30.00 60.00

2015 Topps High Tek Bright Horizons

BHAC Amari Cooper 5.00 12.00
BHAL Andrew Luck 6.00 15.00
BHJW Jameis Winston 4.00 10.00
BHKB Kelvin Benjamin 4.00 10.00
BHKW Kevin White 2.00 5.00
BHME Mike Evans 4.00 10.00
BHMG Melvin Gordon 4.00 10.00
BHMM Marcus Mariota 6.00 15.00
BHOB Odell Beckham Jr. 5.00 12.00
BHTG Todd Gurley 6.00 15.00

2015 Topps High Tek Bright Horizons Autographs

BHAL Andrew Luck/22
BHJW Jameis Winston/30
BHKB Kelvin Benjamin/50 6.00 15.00
BHKW Kevin White/30
BHME Mike Evans/50 6.00 15.00
BHMG Melvin Gordon/30
BHMM Marcus Mariota/30 75.00 125.00
BHTG Todd Gurley/30 50.00 100.00

2015 Topps High Tek DramaTEK Performers

DTPBF Brett Favre 10.00 25.00
DTPBS Barry Sanders 8.00 20.00
DTPDB Drew Brees 5.00 12.00
DTPEL Eddie Lacy 3.00 8.00
DTPES Emmitt Smith 8.00 20.00
DTPJB Jerome Bettis 5.00 12.00
DTPKB Kelvin Benjamin 4.00 10.00
DTPKW Kurt Warner 4.00 10.00
DTPMS Matthew Stafford 4.00 10.00
DTPOB Odell Beckham Jr. 5.00 12.00
DTPRT Ryan Tannehill 4.00 10.00
DTPRW Russell Wilson 6.00 15.00
DTPSY Steve Young 6.00 15.00
DTPTB Tim Brown 5.00 12.00
DTPTBR Terry Bradshaw 6.00 15.00

2015 Topps High Tek DramaTEK Performers Autographs

DTPABF Brett Favre
DTPABS Barry Sanders
DTPADB Drew Brees
DTPAEL Eddie Lacy 10.00 25.00
DTPAKB Kelvin Benjamin 6.00 15.00
DTPAKW Kurt Warner
DTPART Ryan Tannehill 10.00 25.00
DTPASY Steve Young 40.00 80.00
DTPATB Tim Brown 8.00 20.00
DTPATBR Terry Bradshaw

2015 Topps High Tek Tidal Diffractor

*TDL DFFRCTR: 1.2X TO 3X BASIC

1956 Topps Hocus Focus

The 1956 Topps Hocus Focus set is very similar in size and design to the 1948 Topps Magic Photos set. It contains at least 96 small (approximately 7/8" by 1 5/8") individual cards featuring a variety of sports and non-sport subjects. They were printed with both a series card number (by subject matter) on the back as well as a card number reflecting the entire set. The fronts were developed, much like a photograph, from a blank appearance by using moisture and sunlight. Due to varying degrees of photographic sensitivity, the clarity of these cards ranges from fully developed to poorly developed. A premium album holding 126-cards was also issued leading to the theory that there are actually 126 different cards. A few High Series (#97-126) cards have been discovered and cataloged below although a full 126-card checklist is yet unknown. The cards do reference the set name "Hocus Focus" on the backs unlike the 1948 Magic Photos. Finally, a slightly smaller version (roughly 7/8" by 1 7/16") of some of the cards has also been found, but a full checklist is not known.

10 Southern Cal Football 12.50 25.00

2011 Topps Inception

EXCH EXPIRATION: 8/31/2014
1 Troy Polamalu 2.50 6.00
2 Darren McFadden 1.50 4.00
3 Hakeem Nicks 1.50 4.00
4 Ryan Mathews 2.00 5.00
5 Mark Sanchez 1.50 4.00
6 Mike Williams 2.00 5.00
7 James Harrison 2.00 5.00
8 Dwight Freeney 1.50 4.00
9 Mike Wallace 1.50 4.00
10 Peyton Manning 5.00 12.00
11 Charles Woodson 2.50 6.00
12 Marshawn Lynch 2.00 5.00
13 Marcedes Lewis 1.50 4.00
14 Sidney Rice 1.50 4.00
15 Jonathan Stewart 1.50 4.00
16 Jerod Mayo 1.50 4.00
17 Dwayne Bowe 2.00 5.00
18 Matt Cassel 1.50 4.00
19 Peyton Hillis 1.50 4.00
20 Tom Brady 6.00 15.00
21 Santonio Holmes 1.50 4.00
22 Reggie Wayne 2.00 5.00
23 Josh Freeman 2.00 5.00
24 Knowshon Moreno 1.50 4.00
25 Ed Reed 2.00 5.00
26 Ronnie Brown 2.00 5.00
27 Sam Bradford 1.50 4.00
28 Jay Cutler 1.50 4.00
29 Eli Manning 2.00 5.00
30 Adrian Peterson 2.50 6.00
31 Beanie Wells 1.50 4.00
32 Arian Foster 1.50 4.00
33 Brian Urlacher 2.50 6.00
34 Greg Jennings 1.50 4.00
35 Pierre Garcon 2.00 5.00
36 Colt McCoy 1.50 4.00
37 Fred Jackson 1.50 4.00
38 Tony Gonzalez 2.00 5.00
39 Chris Ivory 2.00 5.00
40 Michael Vick 2.00 5.00
41 Ray Rice 1.50 4.00
42 Miles Austin 1.50 4.00
43 Hines Ward 2.00 5.00
44 Matthew Stafford 2.00 5.00
45 Ahmad Bradshaw 1.50 4.00
46 Rob Gronkowski 2.50 6.00
47 Marques Colston 1.50 4.00
48 Andre Johnson 2.00 5.00
48 Matt Schaub 1.50 4.00
49 Calvin Johnson 2.50 6.00
50 Roddy White 1.50 4.00
51 Antonio Gates 1.50 4.00
52 Larry Fitzgerald 2.00 5.00
53 LeSean McCoy 2.50 6.00
54 Ndamukong Suh 2.00 5.00
55 LeGarrette Blount 2.00 5.00
56 Philip Rivers 2.50 6.00
57 Steve Johnson 1.50 4.00
58 Santana Moss 2.00 5.00
59 Jason Witten 2.00 5.00
60 Maurice Jones-Drew 1.50 4.00
61 Matt Forte 1.50 4.00
62 Wes Welker 2.00 5.00
63 Tim Tebow 2.50 6.00
64 Jermichael Finley 1.50 4.00
65 Jordan Shipley 1.50 4.00
66 Matt Ryan 2.00 5.00
67 BenJarvus Green-Ellis 1.50 4.00
68 Matt Hasselbeck 1.50 4.00
69 Tony Romo 2.00 5.00
70 Ray Lewis 2.50 6.00
71 Vernon Davis 1.50 4.00
72 Dez Bryant 2.50 6.00
73 Chris Cooley 1.50 4.00
74 Shonn Greene 1.50 4.00
75 Brandon Lloyd 1.50 4.00
76 Jared Allen 1.50 4.00
77 Joe Flacco 2.00 5.00
78 Clay Matthews 2.50 6.00
79 Rashard Mendenhall 1.50 4.00
81 Darrelle Revis 1.50 4.00
82 Chris Johnson 1.50 4.00
83 Ben Roethlisberger 2.50 6.00
84 Malcom Floyd 1.50 4.00
85 Michael Turner 1.50 4.00
86 DeSean Jackson 2.00 5.00
87 James Starks 1.50 4.00
88 Zach Miller 1.50 4.00
89 Kenny Britt 1.50 4.00
90 Drew Brees 2.50 6.00
91 Danny Woodhead 2.00 5.00
92 Steven Jackson 1.50 4.00
93 Frank Gore 2.00 5.00
94 Percy Harvin 1.50 4.00
95 Braylon Edwards 1.50 4.00
96 Jamaal Charles 2.00 5.00
97 Julius Peppers 2.00 5.00
98 Brandon Marshall 2.00 5.00
99 Patrick Willis 2.00 5.00
100 Aaron Rodgers 5.00 12.00
101 Leonard Hankerson AU/199 RC 4.00 10.00
102 Ryan Mallett AU/199 RC 4.00 10.00
103 Ryan Williams AU RC EXCH 12.00 30.00
104 Mikel Leshoure AU RC 4.00 10.00
106 Jon Baldwin AU/500 RC 3.00 8.00
107 Torrey Smith AU/200 RC 4.00 10.00
108 Delone Carter AU/900 RC 3.00 8.00
109 Kyle Rudolph AU/900 RC 3.00 8.00
112 Randall Cobb AU/200 RC 6.00 15.00
113 Von Miller AU/199 RC 10.00 25.00
114 Daniel Thomas AU/200 RC 4.00 10.00
115 Jerrel Jernigan AU/500 RC 3.00 8.00
116 Shane Vereen AU/500 RC 4.00 10.00
117 DeMarco Murray AU/800 RC 6.00 15.00
118 Greg Little AU/800 RC 6.00 15.00
121 Titus Young AU/500 RC 4.00 10.00
122 Stevan Ridley AU/600 RC 3.00 8.00
123 Jordan Todman AU/900 RC 3.00 8.00
124 Alex Green AU/900 RC 3.00 8.00
126 Colin Kaepernick AU/500 RC 5.00 12.00
127 Austin Pettis AU/900 RC 3.00 8.00
128 Kendall Hunter AU/600 RC 6.00 15.00
129 Vincent Brown AU/900 RC 3.00 8.00
131 Taiwan Jones AU/900 RC 3.00 8.00
132 Bilal Powell AU/900 RC 4.00 10.00
133 Marcell Dareus AU/500 RC 3.00 8.00
134 Jamie Harper AU/600 RC 3.00 8.00
137 Edmond Gates AU/600 RC 3.00 8.00

2011 Topps Inception Blue

*1-100 VETS/209: .5X TO 1.2X BASIC CARDS
*ROOK.AU/150: .5X TO 1.2X AU RC/500-900
*ROOK.AU/150: .4X TO 1X AU RC/199-200
EXCH EXPIRATION: 8/31/2014

2011 Topps Inception Gray
*1-100 VETS/106: .6X TO 1.5X BASIC CARDS
*ROOK.AU/99: .6X TO 1.5X AU RC/500-900
*ROOK.AU/99: .5X TO 1.2X AU RC/199-200
EXCH EXPIRATION: 8/31/2014

2011 Topps Inception Green
*1-100 VETS/75: .8X TO 2X BASIC CARDS
*ROOK.AU/50: .8X TO 2X AU RC/500-900
*ROOK.AU/50: .6X TO 1.5X AU RC/199-200
EXCH EXPIRATION: 8/31/2014
105 Julio Jones AU 30.00 80.00
135 Cam Newton AU 75.00 150.00

2011 Topps Inception Red
*1-100 VETS/25: 1.2X TO 3X BASIC CARDS
*ROOK.AU/25: 1X TO 2.5X AU RC/500-900
*ROOK.AU/25: .8X TO 2X AU RC/199-200
EXCH EXPIRATION: 8/31/2014
105 Julio Jones AU 75.00 150.00
110 Mark Ingram AU EXCH 12.00 30.00
111 Andy Dalton AU 25.00 60.00
120 Jake Locker AU 8.00 20.00
125 Blaine Gabbert AU 8.00 20.00
130 A.J. Green AU 40.00 100.00
135 Cam Newton AU 125.00 250.00

2011 Topps Inception Dual Autographs
STATED PRINT RUN 25 SER.#'d SETS
EXCH EXPIRATION: 8/31/2014
DABS Baldwin/T.Smith EXCH 12.00 30.00
DACJ R.Cobb/J.Jernigan 20.00 50.00
DADG A.Dalton/A.Green 60.00 125.00
DADP A.Dalton/C.Ponder 40.00 100.00
DAGJ A.Green/J.Jones 100.00 200.00
DAGL B.Gabbert/J.Locker 12.00 30.00
DAGN B.Gabbert/C.Newton 75.00 150.00
DAIJ M.Ingram/J.Jones 50.00 100.00
DAIL Ingram/Leshoure 20.00 50.00
DALM J.Locker/R.Mallett 12.00 30.00
DAMV R.Mallett/S.Vereen 15.00 40.00
DANI Newton/Ingram EXCH 50.00 100.00
DAPR Ponder/Rudolph 60.00 120.00
DAVR S.Vereen/S.Ridley 15.00 40.00
DAWL Williams/Leshoure 25.00 60.00

2011 Topps Inception Rookie Autographs Silver Ink
*SILVER INK/25: .4X TO 1X RED AU/25
STATED PRINT RUN 25 SER.#'d SETS
SSAD Andy Dalton 25.00 50.00
SSAG A.J. Green 90.00 150.00
SSBG Blaine Gabbert 8.00 20.00
SSCK Colin Kaepernick 12.00 30.00
SSCN Cam Newton 100.00 200.00
SSCP Christian Ponder 8.00 20.00
SSDM DeMarco Murray 15.00 40.00
SSJJ Julio Jones 100.00 175.00
SSJL Jake Locker 8.00 20.00
SSMI Mark Ingram 12.00 30.00
SSRC Randall Cobb 12.00 30.00
SSRM Ryan Mallett 8.00 20.00

2011 Topps Inception Rookie Dual Jumbo Relics
STATED PRINT RUN 15 SER.#'d SETS
DJRBB J.Baldwin/V.Brown 5.00 12.00
DJRBS J.Baldwin/T.Smith 5.00 12.00
DJRCG R.Cobb/A.Green 8.00 20.00
DJRCJ R.Cobb/J.Jernigan 8.00 20.00
DJRDB A.Dalton/V.Brown 10.00 25.00
DJRDK A.Dalton/C.Kaepernick 10.00 25.00
DJRDP A.Dalton/C.Ponder 10.00 25.00
DJRGD A.Green/A.Dalton 12.00 30.00
DJRGJ A.Green/J.Jones 15.00 40.00
DJRGL B.Gabbert/J.Locker 5.00 12.00
DJRGN B.Gabbert/C.Newton 25.00 60.00
DJRGT E.Gates/D.Thomas 5.00 12.00
DJRID M.Ingram/M.Dareus 8.00 20.00
DJRIJ M.Ingram/J.Jones 15.00 40.00
DJRIL M.Ingram/M.Leshoure 8.00 20.00
DJRJD J.Jones/M.Dareus 15.00 40.00
DJRJH J.Jernigan/L.Hankerson 5.00 12.00
DJRJP J.Jernigan/B.Powell 6.00 15.00
DJRKG C.Kaepernick/A.Green 8.00 20.00
DJRKH C.Kaepernick/K.Hunter 8.00 20.00
DJRKP C.Kaepernick/A.Pettis 8.00 20.00
DJRKW C.Kaepernick/R.Williams 8.00 20.00
DJRLG G.Little/A.Green 12.00 30.00
DJRLH J.Locker/J.Harper 5.00 12.00
DJRLJ J.Locker/T.Jones 5.00 12.00
DJRLM J.Locker/R.Mallett 5.00 12.00
DJRLY M.Leshoure/T.Young 5.00 12.00
DJRMD V.Miller/M.Dareus 8.00 20.00
DJRMH D.Murray/K.Hunter 10.00 25.00
DJRMJ V.Miller/T.Jones 8.00 20.00
DJRMR R.Mallett/S.Ridley 5.00 12.00
DJRMV R.Mallett/S.Vereen 6.00 15.00
DJRND C.Newton/A.Dalton 15.00 40.00
DJRNI C.Newton/M.Ingram 25.00 60.00
DJRNJ C.Newton/J.Jones 25.00 60.00
DJRNM C.Newton/R.Mallett 25.00 60.00
DJRPH C.Ponder/L.Hankerson 5.00 12.00
DJRPT B.Powell/D.Thomas 6.00 15.00
DJRRG K.Rudolph/A.Green 5.00 12.00
DJRRP K.Rudolph/C.Ponder 5.00 12.00
DJRSL T.Smith/G.Little 6.00 15.00
DJRTB J.Todman/V.Brown 5.00 12.00
DJRTC D.Thomas/D.Carter 5.00 12.00
DJRTJ J.Todman/T.Jones 5.00 12.00
DJRTM D.Thomas/V.Miller 8.00 20.00
DJRTP J.Todman/B.Powell 6.00 15.00
DJRVR S.Vereen/S.Ridley 6.00 15.00
DJRWH R.Williams/J.Harper 5.00 12.00
DJRWL R.Williams/M.Leshoure 5.00 12.00
DJRYP T.Young/A.Pettis 5.00 12.00

2011 Topps Inception Rookie Jumbo Patch Autographs Red
RED JSY AU STATED PRINT RUN 25
*BASE AU/399-599: .2X TO .5X RED JSY AU/25
*BASE AU/150: .25X TO .5X RED JSY AU/25
*GRAY/75: .25X TO .6X RED JSY AU/25
*GREEN/50: .3X TO .8X RED JSY AU/25
AJPAD Andy Dalton 25.00 60.00
AJPAG A.J. Green 40.00 100.00
AJPAGR Alex Green 10.00 25.00
AJPAP Austin Pettis 10.00 25.00
AJPBG Blaine Gabbert 10.00 25.00
AJPBP Bilal Powell 12.00 30.00
AJPCK Colin Kaepernick 15.00 40.00
AJPCN Cam Newton 60.00 150.00
AJPCP Christian Ponder 10.00 25.00
AJPDB Da'Quan Bowers 10.00 25.00
AJPDC Delone Carter 10.00 25.00
AJPDM DeMarco Murray 20.00 50.00
AJPDT Daniel Thomas 10.00 25.00
AJPEG Edmond Gates 10.00 25.00
AJPGL Greg Little 15.00 40.00
AJPJB Jon Baldwin 10.00 25.00
AJPJH Jamie Harper 10.00 25.00
AJPJJ Julio Jones 100.00 200.00
AJPJJE Jerrel Jernigan 10.00 25.00
AJPJL Jake Locker 10.00 25.00
AJPJT Jordan Todman 10.00 25.00
AJPKH Kendall Hunter 10.00 25.00
AJPKR Kyle Rudolph 10.00 25.00
AJPLH Leonard Hankerson 10.00 25.00
AJPMD Marcell Dareus 10.00 25.00
AJPMI Mark Ingram 15.00 40.00
AJPML Mikel Leshoure 10.00 25.00
AJPRC Randall Cobb 15.00 40.00
AJPRM Ryan Mallett 10.00 25.00
AJPRW Ryan Williams 30.00 80.00
AJPSR Stevan Ridley 10.00 25.00
AJPSV Shane Vereen 12.00 30.00
AJPTJ Taiwan Jones 10.00 25.00
AJPTS Torrey Smith 10.00 25.00
AJPTY Titus Young 10.00 25.00
AJPVB Vincent Brown 10.00 25.00
AJPVM Von Miller 25.00 60.00

2011 Topps Inception Rookie Quad Patches
STATED PRINT RUN 15 SER.#'d SETS
GJBY Grn/Jons/Bldwin/Yng 40.00 80.00
GJCH Grn/Jons/Cobb/Hnkrsn 30.00 80.00
GLMD Gabb/Lckr/Mallt/Dlton 20.00 50.00
ILWT Ingrm/Lshre/Willi/Tdmn 15.00 40.00
JCHS Jons/Cbb/Hnkrsn/Smth 40.00 80.00
LWTV Leshre/Will/Tdmn/Vrn 12.00 30.00
NDGM Nwtn/Dreus/Gbbrt/Mlr 50.00 125.00
NGLM Nwtn/Gbbrt/Lckr/Mall 30.00 80.00
NLGP Nwtn/Lckr/Gabb/Pndr 50.00 125.00
TVRP Thm/Vrn/Ridly/Pwell 12.00 30.00

2011 Topps Inception Rookie Relics Jumbo Swatch
STATED PRINT RUN 158 SER.#'d SETS
*JUMBO PATCH/15: 1X TO 2.5X JUM.JSY/158
*JUMBO GRAY/75: .5X TO 1.2X JUM.JSY/158
*JUMBO GREEN/25: .6X TO 1.5X JUM.JSY/158
*JUMBO RED/10: .8X TO 2X JUMBO JSY/158
*PATCH/158: .5X TO 1.2X JUMBO JSY/158
*PATCH GRAY/75: .6X TO 1.5X JUM.JSY/158
*PATCH GREEN/25: .8X TO 2X JUM.JSY/158
*PATCH RED/10: 1X TO 2.5X JUMBO JSY/158
JRAD Andy Dalton 4.00 10.00
JRAG A.J. Green 5.00 12.00
JRAGR Alex Green 2.00 5.00
JRAP Austin Pettis 2.00 5.00
JRBG Blaine Gabbert 2.00 5.00
JRBP Bilal Powell 2.50 6.00
JRCK Colin Kaepernick 3.00 8.00
JRCN Cam Newton 10.00 25.00
JRCP Christian Ponder 2.00 5.00
JRDC Delone Carter 2.00 5.00
JRDM DeMarco Murray 4.00 10.00
JRDT Daniel Thomas 2.00 5.00
JREG Edmond Gates 2.00 5.00
JRGL Greg Little 2.50 6.00
JRJB Jon Baldwin 2.00 5.00
JRJH Jamie Harper 2.00 5.00
JRJJ Julio Jones 6.00 15.00
JRJJE Jerrel Jernigan 2.00 5.00
JRJL Jake Locker 2.00 5.00
JRJT Jordan Todman 2.00 5.00
JRKH Kendall Hunter 2.00 5.00
JRKR Kyle Rudolph 2.00 5.00
JRLH Leonard Hankerson 2.00 5.00
JRMD Marcell Dareus 2.00 5.00
JRMI Mark Ingram 3.00 8.00
JRML Mikel Leshoure 2.00 5.00
JRRC Randall Cobb 3.00 8.00
JRRM Ryan Mallett 2.00 5.00
JRRW Ryan Williams 2.00 5.00
JRSR Stevan Ridley 2.00 5.00
JRSV Shane Vereen 2.50 6.00
JRTJ Taiwan Jones 2.00 5.00
JRTS Torrey Smith 2.00 5.00
JRTY Titus Young 2.00 5.00
JRVB Vincent Brown 2.00 5.00
JRVM Von Miller 3.00 8.00

2012 Topps Inception
*ROOKIE AU: .25X TO .6X BLUE AU/150
TWO AUTOS PER BOX OVERALL
EXCH EXPIRATION: 6/30/2015
1 Cam Newton 1.50 4.00
2 Joe Flacco 1.25 3.00
3 Darren Sproles 1.25 3.00
4 Miles Austin 1.00 2.50
5 Josh Freeman 1.25 3.00
6 Steve Smith 1.25 3.00
7 Steven Jackson 1.00 2.50
8 Shonn Greene 1.00 2.50
9 Wes Welker 1.25 3.00
10 Calvin Johnson 1.50 4.00
11 Mike Wallace 1.00 2.50
12 Marques Colston 1.00 2.50
13 DeMarco Murray 1.25 3.00
14 Patrick Willis 1.25 3.00
15 C.J. Spiller 1.00 2.50
16 Ray Lewis 1.50 4.00
17 Jimmy Graham 1.50 4.00
18 Von Miller 1.25 3.00
19 Jason Witten 1.25 3.00
20 Aaron Rodgers 2.50 6.00
21 Chris Johnson 1.00 2.50
22 Michael Turner 1.00 2.50
23 LaDainian Tomlinson 1.50 4.00
24 Titus Young 1.00 2.50
25 Philip Rivers 1.50 4.00
26 Greg Jennings 1.00 2.50
27 Christian Ponder 1.00 2.50
28 Ryan Mathews 1.25 3.00
29 Matt Flynn 1.00 2.50
30 Adrian Peterson 1.50 4.00
31 Stevan Ridley 1.00 2.50
32 Reggie Bush 1.00 2.50
33 LeGarrette Blount 1.25 3.00
34 Tony Romo 1.25 3.00
35 Mark Sanchez 1.00 2.50
36 Antonio Gates 1.25 3.00
37 Jordy Nelson 1.25 3.00
38 Willis McGahee 1.00 2.50
39 Jake Locker 1.50 4.00
40 Tom Brady 4.00 10.00
41 Ben Roethlisberger 1.50 4.00
42 Darren McFadden 1.00 2.50
43 Matt Schaub 1.00 2.50
44 Beanie Wells 1.00 2.50
45 Steve Johnson 1.25 3.00
46 Julius Peppers 1.25 3.00
47 Vernon Davis 1.00 2.50
48 Roy Helu 1.00 2.50
49 Sidney Rice 1.00 2.50
50 Drew Brees 1.50 4.00
51 Fred Davis 1.00 2.50
52 Carson Palmer 1.25 3.00
53 Michael Bush 1.00 2.50
54 Jamaal Charles 1.25 3.00
55 Jared Allen 1.00 2.50
56 Marshawn Lynch 1.25 3.00
57 Andre Johnson 1.25 3.00
58 Jermichael Finley 1.00 2.50
59 LeSean McCoy 1.50 4.00
60 Eli Manning 1.25 3.00
61 Rob Gronkowski 1.50 4.00
62 Maurice Jones-Drew 1.00 2.50
63 Matthew Stafford 1.25 3.00
64 Ray Rice 1.00 2.50
65 Matt Ryan 1.25 3.00
66 Dez Bryant 1.50 4.00
67 Larry Fitzgerald 1.25 3.00
68 Ahmad Bradshaw 1.00 2.50
69 Jay Cutler 1.00 2.50
70 Michael Vick 1.25 3.00
71 Frank Gore 1.25 3.00
72 DeAngelo Williams 1.00 2.50
73 Vincent Jackson 1.00 2.50
74 Ryan Fitzpatrick 1.00 2.50
75 Matt Forte 1.00 2.50
76 Julio Jones 1.50 4.00
77 Fred Jackson 1.25 3.00
78 Alex Smith 1.25 3.00
79 Sam Bradford 1.00 2.50
80 Arian Foster 1.25 3.00
81 Hakeem Nicks 1.00 2.50
82 Tony Gonzalez 1.25 3.00
83 Andy Dalton 1.25 3.00
84 A.J. Green 1.50 4.00
85 Percy Harvin 1.00 2.50
86 Ben Tate 1.00 2.50
87 Tim Tebow 1.50 4.00
88 Aaron Hernandez 1.25 3.00
89 Mario Manningham 1.00 2.50
90 Troy Polamalu 1.50 4.00
91 Roddy White 1.00 2.50
92 BenJarvus Green-Ellis 1.25 3.00
93 Victor Cruz 1.25 3.00
94 Brandon Marshall 1.25 3.00
95 Ndamukong Suh 1.25 3.00
96 Jeremy Maclin 1.00 2.50
97 Kevin Kolb 1.00 2.50
98 Dwayne Bowe 1.25 3.00
99 Antonio Brown 1.50 4.00
100 Peyton Manning 3.00 8.00
102 Nick Foles AU RC 6.00 15.00
106 Ryan Broyles AU RC 5.00 12.00
108 Lamar Miller AU RC 4.00 10.00
113 Alshon Jeffery AU RC EXCH 8.00 20.00
114 Mohamed Sanu AU RC 4.00 10.00
115 Rueben Randle AU RC 5.00 12.00
116 Nick Toon AU RC 2.50 6.00
117 Doug Martin AU RC 4.00 10.00
118 LaMichael James AU RC 10.00 25.00
119 Bernard Pierce AU RC EXCH 2.50 6.00
121 Brian Quick AU RC 2.50 6.00
122 Jarius Wright AU RC 3.00 8.00
123 DeVier Posey AU RC 3.00 8.00
124 Dwayne Allen AU RC 3.00 8.00
125 Coby Fleener AU RC 2.50 6.00
126 Isaiah Pead AU RC 2.50 6.00
127 Robert Turbin AU RC 2.50 6.00
131 T.J. Graham AU RC 3.00 8.00
132 Joe Adams AU RC 2.50 6.00
133 Ronnie Hillman AU RC 2.50 6.00
134 Michael Egnew AU RC 2.50 6.00
141 Chris Givens AU RC EXCH 2.50 6.00

2012 Topps Inception Blue
*1-100 VETS/252: .6X TO 1.5X BASIC CARDS
101 Ryan Tannehill AU 6.00 15.00
102 Nick Foles AU 10.00 25.00
103 Michael Floyd AU 4.00 10.00
104 Kendall Wright AU 4.00 10.00
105 Brandon Weeden AU 15.00 40.00
106 Ryan Broyles AU 4.00 10.00
107 David Wilson AU 4.00 10.00
108 Lamar Miller AU 6.00 15.00
109 A.J. Jenkins AU 4.00 10.00
110 Andrew Luck AU 50.00 100.00
111 Brock Osweiler AU 4.00 10.00
112 Russell Wilson AU 60.00 120.00
113 Alshon Jeffery AU 15.00 30.00
114 Mohamed Sanu AU 6.00 15.00
115 Rueben Randle AU 8.00 20.00
116 Nick Toon AU 4.00 10.00
117 Doug Martin AU 6.00 15.00
118 LaMichael James AU 15.00 40.00
119 Bernard Pierce AU EXCH 4.00 10.00
120 Robert Griffin III AU 12.00 30.00
121 Brian Quick AU 4.00 10.00
122 Jarius Wright AU 5.00 12.00
123 DeVier Posey AU 5.00 12.00
124 Dwayne Allen AU 5.00 12.00
125 Coby Fleener AU 4.00 10.00
126 Isaiah Pead AU 4.00 10.00
127 Robert Turbin AU 4.00 10.00
129 Stephen Hill AU 4.00 10.00
130 Trent Richardson AU 12.00 30.00
131 T.J. Graham AU 5.00 12.00
132 Joe Adams AU 4.00 10.00
133 Ronnie Hillman AU 4.00 10.00
134 Michael Egnew AU 4.00 10.00
135 Justin Blackmon AU 4.00 10.00
141 Chris Givens AU 4.00 10.00

2012 Topps Inception Gold
*1-100 VETS/252: .8X TO 2X BASIC CARDS
*ROOKIE AU/99: .4X TO 1X BLUE AU/150

2012 Topps Inception Green
*1-100 VETS/75: 1X TO 2.5X BASIC CARDS
*ROOKIE AU/50: .5X TO 1.2X BLUE AU/150
110 Andrew Luck AU 75.00 150.00
112 Russell Wilson AU 75.00 150.00

2012 Topps Inception Red
*1-100 VETS/50: 1.5X TO 4X BASIC CARDS
*ROOKIE AU/25: .8X TO 2X BLUE AU/150
110 Andrew Luck AU 125.00 250.00
112 Russell Wilson AU 125.00 250.00

2012 Topps Inception Rookie Autographs Silver Ink
*SILVER INK/25: .8X TO 2X BLUE AU/150
STATED PRINT RUN 25 SER.#'d SETS
EXCH EXPIRATION: 6/30/2015
SSAL Andrew Luck 150.00 300.00
SSRG Robert Griffin III 75.00 150.00
SSRW Russell Wilson 125.00 250.00

2012 Topps Inception Dual Autographs
STATED PRINT RUN 25 SER.#'d SETS
EXCH EXPIRATION: 6/30/2015
DABF J.Blackmon/M.Floyd 60.00 120.00
DABR Blackmon/Richardson 25.00 60.00
DAGW R.Griffin III/K.Wright 15.00 40.00
DAJP L.James/I.Pead 25.00 60.00
DAJS A.Jeffery/M.Sanu 25.00 60.00
DALG A.Luck/R.Griffin III 100.00 200.00
DAOF B.Osweiler/N.Foles 30.00 80.00
DATH N.Toon/S.Hill 12.00 30.00
DATW R.Tannehill/B.Weeden 20.00 50.00
DAWB Weeden/Blackmon EXCH 75.00 125.00
DAWM D.Wilson/L.Miller 20.00 50.00

2012 Topps Inception Rookie Dual Jumbo Relics
STATED PRINT RUN 15 SER.#'d SETS
DJRBF J.Blackmon/M.Floyd 4.00 10.00
DJRBJ R.Broyles/A.Jeffery 8.00 20.00
DJRBR J.Blackmon/T.Richardson 4.00 10.00
DJRFA C.Fleener/D.Allen 4.00 10.00
DJRFW M.Floyd/K.Wright 4.00 10.00
DJRGT R.Griffin III/R.Tannehill 6.00 15.00
DJRGW R.Griffin III/K.Wright 5.00 12.00
DJRHG S.Hill/T.J. Graham 4.00 10.00
DJRJJ A.J. Jenkins/L.James 4.00 10.00
DJRJP L.James/I.Pead 4.00 10.00
DJRJS A.Jeffery/M.Sanu 8.00 20.00
DJRLA A.Luck/D.Allen 30.00 60.00
DJRLF A.Luck/C.Fleener 30.00 60.00
DJRLG A.Luck/R.Griffin III 30.00 80.00
DJRME L.Miller/M.Egnew 6.00 15.00
DJRMW D.Martin/D.Wilson 6.00 15.00
DJROF B.Osweiler/N.Foles 10.00 25.00
DJROH B.Osweiler/R.Hillman 4.00 10.00
DJRQP B.Quick/I.Pead 4.00 10.00
DJRRH R.Randle/S.Hill 4.00 10.00
DJRRM T.Richardson/D.Martin 6.00 15.00
DJRRW T.Richardson/D.Wilson 4.00 10.00
DJRRWE T.Richardson/B.Weeden 4.00 10.00
DJRRWI R.Randle/D.Wilson 4.00 10.00
DJRTE R.Tannehill/M.Egnew 6.00 15.00
DJRTH N.Toon/S.Hill 4.00 10.00
DJRTM R.Tannehill/L.Miller 6.00 15.00
DJRTS R.Tannehill/B.Osweiler 6.00 15.00
DJRTW N.Toon/R.Wilson 30.00 80.00
DJRTWE R.Tannehill/B.Weeden 6.00 15.00
DJRWA J.Wright/J.Adams 4.00 10.00
DJRWB B.Weeden/J.Blackmon 4.00 10.00
DJRWBR J.Wright/R.Broyles 4.00 10.00
DJRWJ K.Wright/A.Jeffery 8.00 20.00
DJRWJE K.Wright/A.J. Jenkins 4.00 10.00
DJRWM D.Wilson/L.Miller 6.00 15.00
DJRWT R.Wilson/R.Turbin 30.00 80.00

2012 Topps Inception Rookie Jumbo Patch Autographs
TWO AUTOS PER BOX OVERALL
*GOLD AU/75: .5X TO 1.2X PATCH AU
AJPAJ Alshon Jeffery 12.00 30.00
AJPAJJ A.J. Jenkins 5.00 12.00
AJPBO Brock Osweiler 5.00 12.00
AJPBP Bernard Pierce EXCH 5.00 12.00
AJPBQ Brian Quick 5.00 12.00
AJPCF Coby Fleener 5.00 12.00
AJPCGI Chris Givens 5.00 12.00
AJPDA Dwayne Allen 6.00 15.00
AJPDM Doug Martin 8.00 20.00
AJPDP DeVier Posey 6.00 15.00
AJPIP Isaiah Pead 5.00 12.00
AJPJA Joe Adams 5.00 12.00
AJPJW Jarius Wright 6.00 15.00
AJPLJ LaMichael James 5.00 12.00
AJPLM Lamar Miller 8.00 20.00
AJPME Michael Egnew 5.00 12.00
AJPMS Mohamed Sanu 8.00 20.00
AJPNF Nick Foles 12.00 30.00
AJPNT Nick Toon 5.00 12.00
AJPRB Ryan Broyles 5.00 12.00
AJPRH Ronnie Hillman 5.00 12.00
AJPRR Rueben Randle 6.00 15.00
AJPRTU Robert Turbin 5.00 12.00
AJPRW Russell Wilson 40.00 80.00
AJPSH Stephen Hill 5.00 12.00
AJPTG T.J. Graham 6.00 15.00
AJPTYH T.Y. Hilton 10.00 25.00

2012 Topps Inception Rookie Jumbo Patch Autographs Green
*GREEN AU/50: .6X TO 1.5X PATCH AU
STATED PRINT RUN 50 SER.#'d SETS
AJPKW Kendall Wright 8.00 20.00
AJPMF Michael Floyd 10.00 25.00

2012 Topps Inception Rookie Jumbo Patch Autographs Red
*RED AU/25: .8X TO 2X PATCH AU
RED PATCH AU PRINT RUN 25
AJPAL Andrew Luck 150.00 300.00
AJPBW Brandon Weeden 15.00 40.00
AJPDW David Wilson 10.00 25.00
AJPJB Justin Blackmon 10.00 25.00
AJPKW Kendall Wright 10.00 25.00
AJPMF Michael Floyd 12.00 30.00
AJPRG Robert Griffin III 60.00 120.00
AJPRT Ryan Tannehill 15.00 40.00
AJPRW Russell Wilson 100.00 200.00
AJPTR Trent Richardson 50.00 120.00

2012 Topps Inception Rookie Patch Autographs Gold Ink
*GOLD INK/25: .4X TO 1X RED PATCH AU/25
STATED PRINT RUN 25 SER.#'d SETS
GAPAL Andrew Luck 150.00 300.00
GAPRG Robert Griffin III 60.00 120.00
GAPRW Russell Wilson 100.00 200.00
GAPTR Trent Richardson 40.00 100.00

2012 Topps Inception Rookie Quad Patches
STATED PRINT RUN 15 SER.#'d SETS
QPBFRW Blkmn/Flyd/Rchrd/Wlsn 5.00 12.00
QPBFWJ Blkmn/Flyd/Wrht/Jnkns 5.00 12.00
QPGWWB RG3/Wrht/Wdn/Blkmn 20.00 50.00
QPLGBR Lck/RG3/Blkmn/Rchrn 25.00 60.00
QPLGTW Lck/RG3/Tnnhll/Wdn 50.00 120.00
QPRMWP Rchrd/Mrtn/Wlsn/Pd
QPWRMM Wrght/Rndl/Millr/Mrtn 8.00 20.00

2012 Topps Inception Rookie Relics Patch
STATED PRINT RUN 210 SER.#'d SETS
*PATCH BLUE/75: .4X TO 1X PATCH/210
*PATCH GOLD/50: .4X TO 1X PATCH/210
*PATCH GREEN/25: .5X TO 1.2X PATCH/210
*PATCH RED/10: .8X TO 2X PATCH/210
*JUMBO/165-169: .3X TO .8X PTCH/210
*JUMBO BLUE/75: .4X TO 1X PATCH/210
*JUMBO GOLD/50: .4X TO 1X PATCH/210
*JUM.PTCH GRN/25: .8X TO 2X PATCH/210
*JUM.PTCH RED/10: 1X TO 2.5X PATCH/210
RPAJ Alshon Jeffery 5.00 12.00
RPAJJ A.J. Jenkins 2.50 6.00
RPAL Andrew Luck 25.00 60.00
RPBO Brock Osweiler 2.50 6.00
RPBP Bernard Pierce 2.50 6.00
RPBQ Brian Quick 2.50 6.00
RPBW Brandon Weeden 2.50 6.00
RPCF Coby Fleener 2.50 6.00
RPCGI Chris Givens 2.50 6.00
RPDA Dwayne Allen 2.50 6.00
RPDM Doug Martin 4.00 10.00
RPDP DeVier Posey 2.50 6.00
RPDW David Wilson 2.50 6.00
RPIP Isaiah Pead 2.50 6.00
RPJA Joe Adams 2.50 6.00
RPJB Justin Blackmon 2.50 6.00
RPJW Jarius Wright 2.50 6.00
RPKW Kendall Wright 2.50 6.00
RPLJ LaMichael James 2.50 6.00
RPLM Lamar Miller 4.00 10.00
RPME Michael Egnew 2.50 6.00
RPMF Michael Floyd 6.00 15.00
RPMS Mohamed Sanu 4.00 10.00
RPNF Nick Foles 6.00 15.00
RPNT Nick Toon 2.50 6.00
RPRB Ryan Broyles 2.50 6.00
RPRG Robert Griffin III 3.00 8.00
RPRH Ronnie Hillman 2.50 6.00
RPRR Rueben Randle 2.50 6.00
RPRT Ryan Tannehill 4.00 10.00
RPRTU Robert Turbin 2.50 6.00
RPRW Russell Wilson 20.00 50.00
RPSH Stephen Hill 2.50 6.00
RPTG T.J. Graham 2.50 6.00
RPTR Trent Richardson 2.50 6.00

2013 Topps Inception
1 Joe Flacco 1.25 3.00
2 Dez Bryant 1.50 4.00
3 Vick Ballard 1.00 2.50
4 Andy Dalton 1.25 3.00
5 David Wilson 1.00 2.50
6 Santonio Holmes 1.00 2.50
7 Pierre Garcon 1.25 3.00
8 Justin Blackmon 1.00 2.50
9 Jacquizz Rodgers 1.25 3.00
10 Andrew Luck 2.50 6.00
12 Brandon Marshall 1.25 3.00
13 Jordy Nelson 1.25 3.00
14 Michael Vick 1.25 3.00
15 Trent Richardson 1.00 2.50
16 Cecil Shorts 1.00 2.50
17 Troy Polamalu 1.50 4.00
18 Tony Romo 1.25 3.00
19 Sam Bradford 1.00 2.50
20 Calvin Johnson 1.50 4.00
21 Ray Rice 1.00 2.50
22 Jason Witten 1.25 3.00
23 Matt Schaub 1.00 2.50
24 Eli Manning 1.25 3.00
25 Russell Wilson 3.00 8.00
26 Christian Ponder 1.00 2.50
27 Larry Fitzgerald 1.25 3.00
28 Frank Gore 1.25 3.00
29 Aldon Smith 1.00 2.50
30 Drew Brees 1.50 4.00
31 Julio Jones 1.50 4.00
32 Dennis Pitta 1.00 2.50
33 Jermaine Gresham 1.25 3.00
34 Richard Sherman 1.50 4.00
35 Maurice Jones-Drew 1.00 2.50
36 Clay Matthews 1.50 4.00
37 Vincent Jackson 1.00 2.50
38 Torrey Smith 1.00 2.50
39 Von Miller 1.25 3.00
40 Colin Kaepernick 1.25 3.00
41 Kendall Wright 1.00 2.50
42 Hakeem Nicks 1.00 2.50
43 Cam Newton 1.50 4.00
44 Demaryius Thomas 1.25 3.00
45 Steven Jackson 1.00 2.50
46 Eric Decker 1.00 2.50
47 Alfred Morris 1.00 2.50
48 Josh Freeman 1.25 3.00
49 Wes Welker 1.25 3.00
50 Aaron Rodgers 2.50 6.00
51 Chris Johnson 1.00 2.50
52 Kyle Rudolph 1.00 2.50
53 Anquan Boldin 1.00 2.50
54 Dwayne Bowe 1.25 3.00
55 Philip Rivers 1.50 4.00
56 Sidney Rice 1.00 2.50
57 T.Y. Hilton 1.25 3.00
58 Carson Palmer 1.25 3.00
59 LeSean McCoy 1.50 4.00
60 Adrian Peterson 1.50 4.00
61 Reggie Bush 1.00 2.50
62 Jamaal Charles 1.25 3.00
63 Rob Gronkowski 1.50 4.00
64 Vernon Davis 1.00 2.50
65 Stevan Ridley 1.00 2.50
66 Brandon Weeden 1.00 2.50
67 Darren McFadden 1.25 3.00
68 Jimmy Graham 1.50 4.00
69 Arian Foster 1.25 3.00
70 Tom Brady 4.00 10.00
71 Ben Roethlisberger 1.50 4.00
72 Randall Cobb 1.25 3.00
73 Jake Locker 1.25 3.00
74 A.J. Green 1.50 4.00
75 J.J. Watt 1.25 3.00
76 Jay Cutler 1.00 2.50
77 Reggie Wayne 1.25 3.00
78 Marshawn Lynch 1.25 3.00
79 DeMarco Murray 1.25 3.00
80 Robert Griffin III 1.00 2.50
81 C.J. Spiller 1.00 2.50
82 Ed Reed 1.25 3.00
83 Antonio Brown 1.50 4.00
84 Antonio Gates 1.25 3.00
85 Victor Cruz 1.25 3.00
86 Darren Sproles 1.25 3.00
87 Mark Ingram 1.25 3.00
88 Matt Ryan 1.25 3.00
89 Doug Martin 1.25 3.00
90 Andre Johnson 1.00 2.50
91 Ryan Tannehill 1.25 3.00
92 Percy Harvin 1.00 2.50
93 Brandon Myers 1.25 3.00
94 Matt Forte 1.00 2.50
95 Luke Kuechly 1.25 3.00
96 BenJarvus Green-Ellis 1.25 3.00
97 Matthew Stafford 1.25 3.00
98 Roddy White 1.00 2.50
99 Michael Crabtree 1.00 2.50
100 Peyton Manning 3.00 8.00
101 EJ Manuel AU RC 3.00 8.00
102 Cordarrelle Patterson AU RC 3.00 8.00
103 Mike Glennon AU RC 3.00 8.00
104 Zach Ertz AU RC 6.00 15.00
105 DeAndre Hopkins AU RC 5.00 12.00
106 Tyler Eifert AU RC 3.00 8.00
107 Matt Barkley AU RC 3.00 8.00
108 Tyler Wilson AU RC 3.00 8.00
109 Robert Woods AU RC 5.00 12.00
110 Geno Smith AU RC 3.00 8.00
111 Quinton Patton AU RC 3.00 8.00
112 Ryan Nassib AU RC 6.00 15.00
113 Terrance Williams AU RC 3.00 8.00
114 Markus Wheaton AU RC 3.00 8.00
115 Aaron Dobson AU RC 3.00 8.00
116 Giovani Bernard AU RC 3.00 8.00
117 Keenan Allen AU RC 8.00 20.00
118 Justin Hunter AU RC 3.00 8.00
119 Joseph Randle AU RC 3.00 8.00
120 Eddie Lacy AU RC 3.00 8.00
121 Marcus Lattimore AU RC 8.00 20.00
122 Montee Ball AU RC 8.00 20.00
124 Andre Ellington AU RC 3.00 8.00
125 Stepfan Taylor AU RC 4.00 10.00
126 Jordan Reed AU RC 5.00 12.00
127 Landry Jones AU RC 3.00 8.00
128 Le'Veon Bell AU RC 8.00 20.00
129 Mike Gillislee AU RC 5.00 12.00
130 Tavon Austin AU RC 4.00 10.00
131 Kenny Stills AU RC 3.00 8.00
132 Denard Robinson AU RC 3.00 8.00
133 Marquise Goodwin AU RC 3.00 8.00
134 Vance McDonald AU RC 5.00 12.00
135 Gavin Escobar AU RC 3.00 8.00
136 Johnathan Franklin AU RC 3.00 8.00
137 Stedman Bailey AU RC 3.00 8.00
138 Knile Davis AU RC 5.00 12.00
139 Christine Michael AU RC 3.00 8.00
140 Manti Te'o AU RC 4.00 10.00
141 Dion Jordan AU RC 3.00 8.00

2013 Topps Inception Green
*1-100 VETS/199: .6X TO 1.5X BASIC CARDS
*101-141 ROOKIE/99: .5X TO 1.2X AU RC

2013 Topps Inception Purple
*1-100 VETS/95: .8X TO 2X BASIC CARDS
*101-141 ROOKIE/75: .6X TO 1.5X AU RC

2013 Topps Inception Red
*1-100 VETS/25: 2X TO 5X BASIC CARDS
*101-141 ROOKIE/25: 1X TO 2.5X AU RC

2013 Topps Inception Yellow
*1-100 VETS/75: 1X TO 2.5X BASIC CARDS
*101-141 ROOKIE/50: .6X TO 1.5X AU RC

2013 Topps Inception Dual Autographs
DRAAA K.Allen/T.Austin 20.00 50.00
DRABL G.Bernard/E.Lacy 10.00 25.00
DRAEE T.Eifert/Z.Ertz 20.00 50.00
DRAET A.Ellington/S.Taylor 10.00 25.00
DRAHP J.Hunter/C.Patterson 10.00 25.00
DRALB M.Lattimore/M.Ball 10.00 25.00
DRARB D.Robinson/M.Ball 10.00 25.00
DRASB G.Smith/M.Barkley 10.00 25.00
DRAWM T.Wilson/Manuel 10.00 25.00
DRAWP T.Williams/Q.Patton 10.00 25.00

2013 Topps Inception Elements Autographs Fog
*RAIN/25: .4X TO 1X FOG/25
*SNOW/25: .4X TO 1X FOG/25
*WIND/25: .4X TO 1X FOG/25
EAAD Aaron Dobson 6.00 15.00
EAAE Andre Ellington 6.00 15.00
EADRO Denard Robinson 6.00 15.00
EAEJM EJ Manuel 6.00 15.00
EAEL Eddie Lacy 6.00 15.00
EAGB Giovani Bernard 6.00 15.00
EAGS Geno Smith 6.00 15.00
EAJF Johnathan Franklin 6.00 15.00
EAJH Justin Hunter 6.00 15.00
EAKA Keenan Allen 12.00 30.00
EALJ Landry Jones 6.00 15.00
EAMB Montee Ball 6.00 15.00
EAMBA Matt Barkley 6.00 15.00
EAMG Mike Gillislee 10.00 25.00
EAMGL Mike Glennon 6.00 15.00
EAML Marcus Lattimore 12.00 30.00
EAMT Manti Te'o 8.00 20.00
EAQP Quinton Patton 12.00 30.00
EARN Ryan Nassib 12.00 30.00
EARW Robert Woods 10.00 25.00
EAST Stepfan Taylor 8.00 20.00
EATA Tavon Austin 8.00 20.00
EATE Tyler Eifert 6.00 15.00
EATW Terrance Williams 6.00 15.00
EATWI Tyler Wilson 6.00 15.00

2013 Topps Inception Rookie Autographs Gold Ink
*GOLD/25: .8X TO 2X SILVER AU/50
*GOLD/25: .5X TO 1.2X SILVER AU/25
SSEJM EJ Manuel 10.00 25.00
SSEL Eddie Lacy 10.00 25.00
SSGS Geno Smith 10.00 25.00
SSMBA Montee Ball 10.00 25.00
SSTA Tavon Austin 12.00 30.00

2013 Topps Inception Rookie Autographs Silver Ink
STATED PRINT RUN 25-75
SSAD Aaron Dobson/50 15.00 40.00
SSAE Andre Ellington/75 5.00 12.00
SSCM Christine Michael/50 5.00 12.00
SSCP Cordarrelle Patterson/50 5.00 12.00
SSDH DeAndre Hopkins/25 20.00 50.00
SSDJ Dion Jordan/50 5.00 12.00
SSDRO Denard Robinson/75 5.00 12.00
SSEJM EJ Manuel/25 8.00 20.00
SSEL Eddie Lacy/50 5.00 12.00
SSGB Giovani Bernard/50 5.00 12.00
SSGE Gavin Escobar/50 5.00 12.00
SSGS Geno Smith/25 8.00 20.00
SSJF Johnathan Franklin/50 5.00 12.00
SSJH Justin Hunter/50 5.00 12.00
SSJR Joseph Randle/50 5.00 12.00
SSJRE Jordan Reed/75 8.00 20.00
SSKA Keenan Allen/50 10.00 25.00
SSKD Knile Davis/50 5.00 12.00
SSKS Kenny Stills/50 5.00 12.00
SSLB Le'Veon Bell/50 30.00 60.00
SSLJ Landry Jones/50 5.00 12.00
SSMB Matt Barkley/25 8.00 20.00
SSMBA Montee Ball/50 5.00 12.00
SSMG Mike Glennon/50 5.00 12.00
SSMGI Mike Gillislee/75 8.00 20.00
SSMGO Marquise Goodwin/50 5.00 12.00
SSML Marcus Lattimore/75 5.00 12.00
SSMT Manti Te'o/50 6.00 15.00
SSMW Markus Wheaton/50 5.00 12.00
SSQP Quinton Patton/50 10.00 25.00
SSRN Ryan Nassib/50 10.00 25.00
SSRW Robert Woods/50 8.00 20.00
SSSB Stedman Bailey/50 5.00 12.00
SSST Stepfan Taylor/50 6.00 15.00
SSTA Tavon Austin/25 10.00 25.00
SSTE Tyler Eifert/50 5.00 12.00
SSTW Tyler Wilson/50 5.00 12.00
SSTWI Terrance Williams/50 5.00 12.00
SSVM Vance McDonald/50 8.00 20.00
SSZE Zach Ertz/50 10.00 25.00

2013 Topps Inception Rookie Jumbo Patch Autographs Green
STATED PRINT RUN 75 SER.#'d SETS
EXCH EXPIRATION: 7/31/2016
*BASE/345: .3X TO .8X GREEN/75
*BASE/150: .4X TO 1X GREEN/75
*BASE/88: .4X TO 1X GREEN/75
*PURPLE/50: .5X TO 1.2X GREEN/75
*YELLOW/25: .8X TO 2X GREEN/75
IAJPAD Aaron Dobson 5.00 12.00
IAJPAE Andre Ellington 5.00 12.00
IAJPCM Christine Michael 10.00 25.00
IAJPCP Cordarrelle Patterson 5.00 12.00
IAJPDH DeAndre Hopkins 15.00 40.00
IAJPDJ Dion Jordan 5.00 12.00
IAJPDRO Denard Robinson 5.00 12.00
IAJPEJM EJ Manuel 5.00 12.00
IAJPEL Eddie Lacy 5.00 12.00
IAJPGB Giovani Bernard 5.00 12.00
IAJPGE Gavin Escobar 8.00 20.00
IAJPGS Geno Smith 5.00 12.00
IAJPJF Johnathan Franklin 5.00 12.00
IAJPJH Justin Hunter EXCH 5.00 12.00
IAJPJR Joseph Randle 5.00 12.00
IAJPJRE Jordan Reed EXCH 10.00 25.00
IAJPKA Keenan Allen 10.00 25.00
IAJPKD Knile Davis 8.00 20.00
IAJPKS Kenny Stills 5.00 12.00
IAJPLB Le'Veon Bell 40.00 80.00
IAJPLJ Landry Jones 5.00 12.00
IAJPMB Matt Barkley 8.00 20.00
IAJPMBA Montee Ball 5.00 12.00
IAJPMG Mike Glennon 5.00 12.00
IAJPMGI Mike Gillislee 8.00 20.00
IAJPMGO Marquise Goodwin 5.00 12.00
IAJPML Marcus Lattimore 15.00 40.00
IAJPMT Manti Te'o 6.00 15.00
IAJPMW Markus Wheaton 5.00 12.00
IAJPQP Quinton Patton 10.00 25.00
IAJPRN Ryan Nassib 8.00 20.00
IAJPRW Robert Woods 8.00 20.00
IAJPSB Stedman Bailey 10.00 25.00
IAJPST Stepfan Taylor 6.00 15.00
IAJPTA Tavon Austin 6.00 15.00
IAJPTE Tyler Eifert 5.00 12.00
IAJPTW Tyler Wilson 5.00 12.00
IAJPTWI Terrance Williams 5.00 12.00
IAJPVM Vance McDonald EXCH 8.00 20.00
IAJPZE Zach Ertz 10.00 25.00

2013 Topps Inception Rookie Relics Patch
*JUMBO/86: .3X TO .8X PATCH/93
*JUMBO GREEN/75: .3X TO .8X PATCH/93
*JUMBO PURPLE/50: .4X TO 1X PATCH/93
*JUMBO RED/10: 1X TO 2.5X PATCH/93
*JUMBO YELLOW/25: .6X TO 1.5X PATCH/93
*PATCH GREEN/75: .4X TO 1X PATCH/93
*PATCH PURPLE/50: .5X TO 1.2X PATCH/93
*PATCH RED/10: 1X TO 2.5X PATCH/93
*PATCH YELLOW/25: .6X TO 1.5X PATCH/93
RPAD Aaron Dobson 2.00 5.00
RPAE Andre Ellington 2.00 5.00
RPCM Christine Michael 2.00 5.00
RPCP Cordarrelle Patterson 2.00 5.00
RPDH DeAndre Hopkins 5.00 12.00
RPDJ Dion Jordan 2.00 5.00
RPDRO Denard Robinson 2.00 5.00
RPEJM EJ Manuel 8.00 20.00
RPEL Eddie Lacy 2.00 5.00
RPGB Giovani Bernard 2.00 5.00
RPGE Gavin Escobar 2.00 5.00
RPGS Geno Smith 2.00 5.00
RPJF Johnathan Franklin 2.00 5.00
RPJH Justin Hunter 2.00 5.00
RPJR Joseph Randle 2.00 5.00
RPJRE Jordan Reed 3.00 8.00
RPKA Keenan Allen 4.00 10.00
RPKD Knile Davis 2.00 5.00
RPKS Kenny Stills 2.00 5.00
RPLB Le'Veon Bell 6.00 15.00
RPLJ Landry Jones 2.00 5.00
RPMB Matt Barkley 2.00 5.00
RPMBA Montee Ball 3.00 8.00
RPMG Mike Glennon 2.00 5.00
RPMGI Mike Gillislee 2.00 5.00
RPMGO Marquise Goodwin 2.00 5.00
RPML Marcus Lattimore 2.00 5.00
RPMT Manti Te'o 2.50 6.00
RPMW Markus Wheaton 2.00 5.00
RPQP Quinton Patton 2.00 5.00
RPRN Ryan Nassib 2.00 5.00
RPRW Robert Woods 3.00 8.00
RPSB Stedman Bailey 2.00 5.00
RPST Stepfan Taylor 2.00 5.00
RPTA Tavon Austin 2.50 6.00
RPTE Tyler Eifert 2.00 5.00
RPTW Tyler Wilson 2.00 5.00
RPTWI Terrance Williams 2.00 5.00
RPVM Vance McDonald 2.50 6.00
RPZE Zach Ertz 4.00 10.00

2014 Topps Inception
*ROOKIE AU: .2X TO .5X MAGENTA AU/50
1 A.J. Green 1.50 4.00
2 Aaron Rodgers SP 3.00 8.00
3 Keenan Allen 1.25 3.00
4 Joe Flacco 1.25 3.00
5 Mike Wallace 1.00 2.50
6 Denarius Moore 1.00 2.50
7 Zac Stacy 1.00 2.50
8 Patrick Willis 1.25 3.00
9 Cecil Shorts 1.00 2.50
10 Larry Fitzgerald SP 1.25 3.00
11 Pierre Garcon 1.25 3.00
12 Ndamukong Suh 1.25 3.00
13 Drew Brees 1.50 4.00
14 Jay Cutler 1.00 2.50
15 Giovani Bernard 1.00 2.50
16 Eli Manning 1.25 3.00
17 Kendall Wright 1.00 2.50
18 Brandon Marshall 1.00 2.50
19 Robert Mathis 1.00 2.50
20 Ray Rice 1.00 2.50
21 Andre Johnson 1.25 3.00
22 Carson Palmer 1.25 3.00
23 EJ Manuel 1.00 2.50
24 Luke Kuechly 1.25 3.00
25 Ryan Tannehill 1.25 3.00
26 Jamaal Charles 1.25 3.00
27 Julius Thomas 1.00 2.50
28 Peyton Manning SP 3.00 8.00
29 T.Y. Hilton 1.25 3.00
30 Antonio Gates 1.00 2.50
31 Peyton Manning 3.00 8.00
32 Tom Brady SP 4.00 10.00
33 Cordarrelle Patterson 1.00 2.50
34 Frank Gore SP 1.25 3.00
35 Nick Foles 1.25 3.00
36 Russell Wilson 2.50 6.00
37 Antonio Brown 1.50 4.00
38 Clay Matthews 1.50 4.00
39 Barkevious Mingo 1.00 2.50
40 Alex Smith 1.25 3.00
41 Jason Witten 1.25 3.00
42 Andrew Luck 2.00 5.00
43 Torrey Smith 1.00 2.50
44 Terrell Suggs 1.00 2.50
45 Marshawn Lynch 1.25 3.00
46 Shonn Greene 1.00 2.50
47 Percy Harvin 1.00 2.50
48 Philip Rivers 1.50 4.00
49 Andy Dalton 1.25 3.00
50 Reggie Wayne 1.25 3.00
51 Matt Ryan 1.25 3.00
52 Mike Glennon 1.25 3.00
53 DeSean Jackson 1.25 3.00
54 Jordan Cameron 1.00 2.50
55 Earl Thomas 1.25 3.00
56 Doug Martin 1.25 3.00
57 Dez Bryant 1.50 4.00
58 Kenny Stills 1.00 2.50
59 Matthew Stafford 1.25 3.00
60 Michael Crabtree 1.00 2.50
61 Paul Posluszny 1.00 2.50
62 Calvin Johnson SP 1.50 4.00
63 Jordy Nelson 1.25 3.00
64 J.J. Watt 1.50 4.00
65 Le'Veon Bell 1.25 3.00
66 Demaryius Thomas 1.25 3.00
67 Ben Roethlisberger 1.50 4.00
68 Victor Cruz 1.25 3.00
69 Wes Welker 1.25 3.00
70 Troy Polamalu SP 1.50 4.00
71 Jimmy Graham 1.50 4.00
72 C.J. Spiller 1.00 2.50
73 Steve Smith 1.25 3.00
74 Shane Vereen 1.25 3.00
75 Geno Smith 1.00 2.50
76 Anquan Boldin 1.00 2.50
77 Darrelle Revis 1.00 2.50
78 Cam Newton 1.50 4.00
79 Josh Gordon 1.00 2.50
80 Kiko Alonso 1.00 2.50
81 LeSean McCoy 1.50 4.00
82 Andre Ellington 1.00 2.50
83 Manti Te'o 1.25 3.00
84 Tavon Austin 1.00 2.50
85 Muhammad Wilkerson 1.00 2.50
86 Richard Sherman 1.50 4.00
87 Eddie Lacy 1.00 2.50
88 Ryan Mathews 1.25 3.00
89 Julio Jones 1.50 4.00
90 Julius Peppers SP 1.25 3.00
91 Alfred Morris 1.00 2.50
92 Zach Ertz 1.25 3.00
93 Tony Romo 1.25 3.00
94 Von Miller 1.25 3.00
95 Drew Brees SP 1.50 4.00
96 Danny Amendola 1.25 3.00
97 Vincent Jackson 1.00 2.50
98 Roddy White 1.00 2.50
99 Aldon Smith 1.00 2.50
100 Alec Ogletree 1.00 2.50
101 Colin Kaepernick 1.25 3.00
102 Pierre Thomas 1.00 2.50
103 Patrick Peterson 1.00 2.50
104 Tyrann Mathieu 1.25 3.00
105 Alshon Jeffery 1.25 3.00
106 Reggie Bush 1.00 2.50
107 DeAndre Hopkins 1.25 3.00
108 Robert Griffin III 1.00 2.50
109 Rob Gronkowski 1.50 4.00
110 Adrian Peterson SP 1.50 4.00

2014 Topps Inception Green
*1-109 VETS: .6X TO 1.5X BASIC CARDS
*ROOKIE AU/99: .25X TO .6X MAGENTA AU/50
EXCH EXPIRATION: 7/31/2017

2014 Topps Inception Magenta
*1-109 VETS/75: 1X TO 2.5X BASIC CARDS
1R Johnny Manziel AU 10.00 25.00
2R Teddy Bridgewater AU 10.00 25.00
3R Jadeveon Clowney AU 8.00 20.00
5R Derek Carr AU 40.00 100.00
6R Eric Ebron AU 8.00 20.00
7R Mike Evans AU 15.00 40.00
8R Allen Robinson AU 10.00 25.00
9R Carlos Hyde AU 8.00 20.00
10R Tre Mason AU 6.00 15.00
11R Paul Richardson AU 12.00 30.00
12R Bishop Sankey AU 6.00 15.00
13R Jarvis Landry AU 12.00 30.00
14R Marqise Lee AU 8.00 20.00
15R Jordan Matthews AU 10.00 25.00
18R Jimmy Garoppolo AU 50.00 100.00
19R Jace Amaro AU 6.00 15.00
20R Blake Bortles AU 8.00 20.00
21R Sammy Watkins AU 30.00 80.00
22R Kelvin Benjamin AU 15.00 40.00
23R Donte Moncrief AU 6.00 15.00

26R Ka'Deem Carey AU 6.00 15.00
27R Jeremy Hill AU 8.00 20.00
28R Austin Seferian-Jenkins AU 6.00 15.00
30R Davante Adams AU 10.00 25.00
31R Odell Beckham Jr. AU 15.00 40.00
32R De'Anthony Thomas AU 6.00 15.00
33R Andre Williams AU 6.00 15.00
34R Brandin Cooks AU 10.00 25.00
35R Khalil Mack AU 50.00 125.00
36R Aaron Murray AU 6.00 15.00
37R Terrance West AU 6.00 15.00
39R Logan Thomas AU 6.00 15.00
41R Tom Savage AU 6.00 15.00
42R Charles Sims AU 6.00 15.00
46R Tajh Boyd AU 6.00 15.00
49R A.J. McCarron AU 6.00 15.00
51R Dri Archer AU 6.00 15.00
52R Devonta Freeman AU 10.00 25.00
53R Cody Latimer AU 8.00 20.00
54R Michael Sam AU 6.00 15.00

2014 Topps Inception Orange

*1-109 VETS/40: 1.2X TO 3X BASIC CARDS

2014 Topps Inception Purple

*1-109 VETS/99: .8X TO 2X BASIC CARDS
*ROOK.AU/75: .3X TO .8X MAGENTA AU/50

2014 Topps Inception Red

*1-109 VETS/50: 1.2X TO 3X BASIC CARDS
*ROOKIE AU/25: .5X TO 1.2X MAGENTA AU/50

2014 Topps Inception QB Inception Autographs

STATED PRINT RUN 20 SER.#'d SETS
QBIAAU Aaron Murray 4.00 10.00
QBIABB Blake Bortles 5.00 12.00
QBIADC Derek Carr 20.00 50.00
QBIAJG Jimmy Garoppolo 90.00 150.00
QBIAJM Johnny Manziel 6.00 15.00
QBIALT Logan Thomas 4.00 10.00
QBIATR Teddy Bridgewater 6.00 15.00
QBIATS Tom Savage 4.00 10.00

2014 Topps Inception Quad Autographs

STATED PRINT RUN 25 SER.#'d SETS
EXCH EXPIRATION: 7/31/2017
QRAAFWS Fmn/Achr/Wlms/Sms 15.00 40.00
QRABBMC Brtls/Brdg/Crr/Mnzl EX
QRACMSB Sm/Mnzl/Brdg/Clwn EX 50.00 100.00
QRACMWB Clwn/Mnzl/Brtl/Wtkn EX 50.00 100.00
QRAGTSB Svge/Byd/Thms/Grpplo 50.00 100.00
QRAHSMH Hyde/Snky/Msn/Hll 20.00 50.00
QRAMAMR Adms/Rsn/Mthw/Mcrf 30.00 60.00
QRAMMMM Mtbg/McCn/Mnzl/Mry 40.00 80.00
QRAWEBC Evn/Cks/Bckhm/Wtkns 100.00 200.00
QRAWEEB Wtkn/Evn/Ebrn/Bnjm EX 75.00 150.00

2014 Topps Inception Rookie Jumbo Patch Autographs

IAJPAR Allen Robinson 8.00 20.00
IAJPAS Austin Seferian-Jenkins 5.00 12.00
IAJPAU Aaron Murray 5.00 12.00
IAJPAW Andre Williams 5.00 12.00
IAJPBS Bishop Sankey 5.00 12.00
IAJPCH Carlos Hyde 6.00 15.00
IAJPCL Cody Latimer 6.00 15.00
IAJPCS Charles Sims 5.00 12.00
IAJPDA Davante Adams 8.00 20.00
IAJPDH Dri Archer 5.00 12.00
IAJPDM Donte Moncrief 5.00 12.00
IAJPDR Devonta Freeman 8.00 20.00
IAJPDT De'Anthony Thomas 5.00 12.00
IAJPJA Jace Amaro 5.00 12.00
IAJPJI Jeremy Hill 6.00 15.00
IAJPJL Jarvis Landry 12.00 30.00
IAJPJT Jordan Matthews 8.00 20.00
IAJPKB Kelvin Benjamin 8.00 20.00
IAJPKC Ka'Deem Carey 5.00 12.00
IAJPKM Khalil Mack 20.00 50.00
IAJPLT Logan Thomas 5.00 12.00
IAJPMS Michael Sam 5.00 12.00
IAJPOB Odell Beckham Jr. 12.00 30.00
IAJPPR Paul Richardson 10.00 25.00
IAJPTO Tajh Boyd 5.00 12.00
IAJPTS Tom Savage 5.00 12.00
IAJPTW Terrance West 5.00 12.00

2014 Topps Inception Rookie Jumbo Patch Autographs Green

*GREEN/75: .5X TO 1.2X PATCH AU
IAJPEE Eric Ebron 8.00 20.00
IAJPME Mike Evans 15.00 40.00
IAJPSW Sammy Watkins 10.00 25.00

2014 Topps Inception Rookie Jumbo Patch Autographs Magenta

*MAGENTA/25: .8X TO 2X PATCH AU
IAJPBB Blake Bortles 12.00 30.00
IAJPDC Derek Carr 40.00 80.00
IAJPEE Eric Ebron 12.00 30.00
IAJPJC Jadeveon Clowney 12.00 30.00
IAJPJM Johnny Manziel 15.00 40.00
IAJPME Mike Evans 25.00 60.00
IAJPOB Odell Beckham Jr. 60.00 125.00
IAJPSW Sammy Watkins 15.00 40.00
IAJPTB Teddy Bridgewater 15.00 40.00

2014 Topps Inception Rookie Jumbo Patch Autographs Purple

*PURPLE/50: .6X TO 1.5X PATCH AU
IAJPDC Derek Carr 30.00 60.00
IAJPJC Jadeveon Clowney 10.00 25.00
IAJPTB Teddy Bridgewater 12.00 30.00

2014 Topps Inception Rookie Relics Jumbo Patch

*GREEN/75: .4X TO 1X JUMBO/215
*PURPLE/50: .5X TO 1.2X JUMBO/215
*MAGENTA/25: 1X TO 2.5X JUMBO/215
*RED/10: 1.2X TO 3X JUMBO/215
RJRAM A.J. McCarron 1.50 4.00
RJRAR Allen Robinson 2.50 6.00
RJRAS Austin Seferian-Jenkins 1.50 4.00
RJRAU Aaron Murray 1.50 4.00
RJRAW Andre Williams 1.50 4.00
RJRBB Blake Bortles 2.00 5.00
RJRBC Brandin Cooks 2.50 6.00
RJRBS Bishop Sankey 1.50 4.00
RJRCH Carlos Hyde 2.00 5.00
RJRCL Cody Latimer 2.00 5.00
RJRCS Charles Sims 1.50 4.00
RJRDA Davante Adams 2.50 6.00
RJRDC Derek Carr 10.00 25.00
RJRDM Donte Moncrief 1.50 4.00
RJRDT De'Anthony Thomas 1.50 4.00
RJREE Eric Ebron 2.00 5.00
RJRJA Johnny Manziel 2.50 6.00
RJRJC Jadeveon Clowney 2.00 5.00
RJRJG Jimmy Garoppolo 12.00 30.00
RJRJH Jeremy Hill 2.00 5.00
RJRJL Jarvis Landry 3.00 8.00
RJRJM Jordan Matthews 2.50 6.00
RJRJR Jace Amaro 1.50 4.00
RJRKB Kelvin Benjamin 2.50 6.00
RJRKC Ka'Deem Carey 1.50 4.00
RJRKM Khalil Mack 6.00 15.00
RJRLT Logan Thomas 1.50 4.00
RJRME Mike Evans 4.00 10.00
RJRML Marqise Lee 2.00 5.00
RJRMS Michael Sam 1.50 4.00
RJROB Odell Beckham Jr 4.00 10.00
RJRPR Paul Richardson 2.00 5.00
RJRSW Sammy Watkins 2.50 6.00
RJRTB Teddy Bridgewater 2.50 6.00
RJRTM Tre Mason 1.50 4.00
RJRTO Tajh Boyd 1.50 4.00
RJRTS Tom Savage 1.50 4.00
RJRTW Terrance West 1.50 4.00
RJRDAR Dri Archer 1.50 4.00
RJRDFE Devonta Freeman 2.50 6.00

2014 Topps Inception Rookie Relics Patch

*PATCH/122: .5X TO 1.2X JUMBO PATCH/215
*GREEN/75: .5X TO 1.2X JUMBO PATCH/215
*PURPLE/50: .6X TO 1.5X JUMBO PATCH/215
*MAGENTA/25: .8X TO 2X JUMBO PATCH/215
*RED/10: 1.2X TO 3X JUMBO/215

2014 Topps Inception Silver Signings

*GOLD/25: .5X TO 1.2X SILVER/50
ISSAM A.J. McCarron 8.00 20.00
ISSAR Allen Robinson 12.00 30.00
ISSAS Austin Seferian-Jenkins 8.00 20.00
ISSAU Aaron Murray 8.00 20.00
ISSAW Andre Williams 8.00 20.00
ISSBB Blake Bortles 10.00 25.00
ISSBC Brandin Cooks 12.00 30.00
ISSBS Bishop Sankey 8.00 20.00
ISSCH Carlos Hyde 10.00 25.00
ISSDA Davante Adams 12.00 30.00
ISSDC Derek Carr 50.00 125.00
ISSDM Donte Moncrief 8.00 20.00
ISSDT De'Anthony Thomas 8.00 20.00
ISSEE Eric Ebron 10.00 25.00
ISSJA Johnny Manziel 12.00 30.00
ISSJC Jadeveon Clowney 10.00 25.00
ISSJG Jimmy Garoppolo 40.00 80.00
ISSJH Jeremy Hill 10.00 25.00
ISSJL Jarvis Landry 15.00 40.00
ISSJM Jordan Matthews 12.00 30.00
ISSJR Jace Amaro 8.00 20.00
ISSKB Kelvin Benjamin 12.00 30.00
ISSKC Ka'Deem Carey 8.00 20.00
ISSLT Logan Thomas 12.00 30.00
ISSME Mike Evans 20.00 50.00
ISSML Marqise Lee 10.00 25.00
ISSOB Odell Beckham Jr. 50.00 100.00
ISSPR Paul Richardson 15.00 40.00
ISSSW Sammy Watkins 12.00 30.00
ISSTB Teddy Bridgewater 20.00 50.00
ISSTM Tre Mason 8.00 20.00
ISSTO Tajh Boyd 8.00 20.00
ISSTS Tom Savage 8.00 20.00
ISSTW Terrance West 8.00 20.00
ISSZM Zach Mettenberger 8.00 20.00

2015 Topps Inception

*ROOKIE AU: .2X TO .5X ORANGE AU/50
1 Peyton Manning 3.00 8.00
2 J.J. Watt 1.50 4.00
3 Sammy Watkins 1.25 3.00
4 Geno Smith 1.00 2.50
5 Rob Gronkowski 1.50 4.00
6 Keenan Allen 1.25 3.00
7 Jay Cutler 1.00 2.50
8 Ryan Tannehill 1.25 3.00
9 Kelvin Benjamin 1.25 3.00
10 Eric Decker 1.00 2.50
11 Julio Jones 1.50 4.00
12 Teddy Bridgewater 1.25 3.00
13 Alex Smith 1.25 3.00
14 Demaryius Thomas 1.25 3.00
15 Mike Evans 1.25 3.00
16 Ryan Mathews 1.25 3.00
17 Richard Sherman 1.50 4.00
18 Bishop Sankey 1.00 2.50
19 Vincent Jackson 1.00 2.50
20 Andy Dalton 1.25 3.00
21 Tavon Austin 1.00 2.50
22 Alfred Morris 1.00 2.50
23 Jordy Nelson 1.25 3.00
24 Patrick Willis 1.25 3.00
25 Tom Brady 4.00 10.00
26 Blake Bortles 1.00 2.50
27 Johnny Manziel 1.25 3.00
28 Rashad Jennings 1.00 2.50
29 Terrell Suggs 1.00 2.50
30 Reggie Bush 1.00 2.50
31 Tony Romo 1.25 3.00
32 Cam Newton 1.50 4.00
33 Antonio Brown 1.50 4.00
34 Julius Thomas 1.00 2.50
35 Jordan Matthews 1.25 3.00
36 Eli Manning 1.25 3.00
37 Kendall Wright 1.00 2.50
38 Le'Veon Bell 1.25 3.00
39 Jadeveon Clowney 1.00 2.50
40 DeMarco Murray 1.25 3.00
41 Ben Roethlisberger 1.50 4.00
42 Matthew Stafford 1.25 3.00
43 Anquan Boldin 1.00 2.50
44 Toby Gerhart 1.00 2.50
45 Calvin Johnson 1.50 4.00
46 Marshawn Lynch 1.25 3.00
47 A.J. Green 1.50 4.00
48 Matt Ryan 1.25 3.00
49 Giovani Bernard 1.00 2.50
50 Russell Wilson 2.00 5.00
51 Von Miller 1.25 3.00
52 Ndamukong Suh 1.25 3.00
53 Kyle Orton 1.00 2.50
54 Andre Ellington 1.00 2.50
55 Arian Foster 1.25 3.00
56 Clay Matthews 1.50 4.00
57 Drew Brees 1.50 4.00
58 Michael Floyd 1.00 2.50
59 Brandon Marshall 1.00 2.50
60 Percy Harvin 1.00 2.50
61 Jordan Cameron 1.00 2.50
62 Matt Forte 1.00 2.50
63 Carson Palmer 1.25 3.00
64 Cordarrelle Patterson 1.00 2.50
65 Pierre Garcon 1.25 3.00
66 Philip Rivers 1.50 4.00
67 Jimmy Graham 1.50 4.00
68 DeSean Jackson 1.25 3.00
69 Derek Carr 1.50 4.00
70 Torrey Smith 1.00 2.50
71 LeSean McCoy 1.50 4.00
72 Odell Beckham Jr. 1.50 4.00
73 Danny Amendola 1.25 3.00
74 Jerick McKinnon 1.00 2.50
75 Mike Glennon 1.25 3.00
76 Roddy White 1.00 2.50
77 Eddie Lacy 1.00 2.50
78 Dez Bryant 1.50 4.00
79 Antonio Gates 1.00 2.50
80 Jamaal Charles 1.25 3.00
81 Nick Foles 1.25 3.00
82 Luke Kuechly 1.25 3.00
83 Michael Crabtree 1.00 2.50
84 Patrick Peterson 1.00 2.50
85 Robert Griffin III 1.00 2.50
86 Darrelle Revis 1.00 2.50
87 Colin Kaepernick 1.25 3.00
88 Earl Thomas 1.25 3.00
89 Brandin Cooks 1.25 3.00
90 Allen Robinson 1.25 3.00
91 Mark Ingram 1.25 3.00
92 Muhammad Wilkerson 1.00 2.50
93 Andrew Luck 2.00 5.00
94 Wes Welker 1.25 3.00
95 Joe Flacco 1.25 3.00
96 Alshon Jeffery 1.25 3.00
97 Mike Wallace 1.00 2.50
98 Khalil Mack 1.50 4.00
99 T.Y. Hilton 1.25 3.00
100 Aaron Rodgers 3.00 8.00
RA4 Amari Cooper AU RC 25.00 50.00

2015 Topps Inception Blue

*1-100 VETS/25: 1.5X TO 4X BASIC CARDS
*ROOK.AU/25: .5X TO 1.2X ORANGE AU/50
RA1 Jameis Winston AU
RA2 Marcus Mariota AU 75.00 150.00

2015 Topps Inception Green

*GREEN/150: .6X TO 1.5X BASIC CARDS

2015 Topps Inception Magenta

*1-100 VETS/99: 1X TO 2.5X BASIC CARDS
*ROOK.AU/99: .3X TO .8X ORANGE AU/50

2015 Topps Inception Orange

*1-100 VETS/50: 1.2X TO 2X BASIC CARDS
RA1 Jameis Winston AU 75.00 125.00
RA2 Marcus Mariota AU 100.00 200.00
RA3 Kevin White AU 8.00 20.00
RA5 Todd Gurley AU 30.00 80.00
RA6 Brett Hundley AU
RA7 DeVante Parker AU 20.00 50.00
RA8 Dorial Green-Beckham AU
RA9 Melvin Gordon AU 15.00 40.00
RA10 Jaelen Strong AU 8.00 20.00
RA11 Breshad Perriman AU 6.00 15.00
RA12 Devin Funchess AU 10.00 25.00
RA13 Phillip Dorsett AU 6.00 15.00
RA14 Devin Smith AU 6.00 15.00
RA15 Sammie Coates AU 15.00 40.00
RA16 Ameer Abdullah AU 10.00 25.00
RA17 Nelson Agholor AU 8.00 20.00
RA18 Rashad Greene AU 6.00 15.00
RA19 Tyler Lockett AU 10.00 25.00
RA20 Bryce Petty AU 6.00 15.00
RA21 Tevin Coleman AU 8.00 20.00
RA22 Duke Johnson AU 10.00 25.00
RA23 Jay Ajayi AU 12.00 30.00
RA25 T.J. Yeldon AU 6.00 15.00
RA26 Jeremy Langford AU 6.00 15.00
RA27 David Johnson AU 20.00 50.00
RA28 Sean Mannion AU 6.00 15.00
RA29 Justin Hardy AU 10.00 25.00
RA30 Matt Jones AU 6.00 15.00
RA31 Ty Montgomery AU 6.00 15.00
RA32 Mike Davis AU 6.00 15.00
RA33 Stefon Diggs AU 15.00 40.00
RA34 Jamison Crowder AU 8.00 20.00
RA35 David Cobb AU 6.00 15.00
RA36 Leonard Williams AU 6.00 15.00
RA37 Chris Conley AU 6.00 15.00
RA38 Maxx Williams AU 6.00 15.00
RA39 Javorius Allen AU 8.00 20.00
RA40 Vince Mayle AU 8.00 20.00
RA41 Karlos Williams AU 6.00 15.00
RA43 Cameron Artis-Payne AU 6.00 15.00
RA44 Clive Walford AU 6.00 15.00

2015 Topps Inception Purple

*1-100 VETS/125: .6X TO 1.5X BASIC CARDS
*ROOK.AU/150: .25X TO .6X MAGENTA AU/99

2015 Topps Inception Red

*1-100 VETS/75: 1X TO 2.5X BASIC CARDS
*ROOK.AU/75: .3X TO .8X ORANGE AU/50

2015 Topps Inception Gold Signings

*GOLD/25: .5X TO 1.2X SILVER AU/50
SSAA Ameer Abdullah 15.00 40.00
SSMM Marcus Mariota 75.00 150.00

2015 Topps Inception Quad Autographs

QRACPWG Cpr/White/Prkr/GrnBckhm 90.00 150.00
QRACWCS White/Strng/Cts/Cpr 75.00 150.00
QRADACL Lngfrd/Cbb/Dvs/Alln 40.00 80.00
QRAGAFS Abdllh/Fnchss/Grdn/Smth 50.00 100.00
QRAJAAC Clmn/Ajyi/Abdllh/Jhnsn
QRAMWGG Wnstn/Grdn/Grly/Mrta 125.00 250.00
QRASPAL Lcktt/Aghlr/Prrmn/Strng 50.00 100.00

2015 Topps Inception Quarterback Inception Autographs

QBIABH Brett Hundley 4.00 10.00
QBIABP Bryce Petty 4.00 10.00
QBIAJW Jameis Winston 125.00 200.00
QBIAMM Marcus Mariota 75.00 150.00
QBIASM Sean Mannion 4.00 10.00

2015 Topps Inception Rookie Jumbo Patch Autographs Magenta

STATED PRINT RUN 50 SER.#'d SETS
*BASE SILVER: .2X TO .5X MAGENTA/50
*GREEN/125: .25X TO .6X MAGENTA/50
*PURPLE/75: .3X TO .8X MAGENTA/50
AJPAA Ameer Abdullah 10.00 25.00
AJPAC Amari Cooper 30.00 60.00
AJPBH Brett Hundley 6.00 15.00
AJPBP Bryce Petty 6.00 15.00
AJPBPE Breshad Perriman 6.00 15.00
AJPCC Chris Conley 6.00 15.00
AJPDC David Cobb 6.00 15.00
AJPDF Devin Funchess 10.00 25.00
AJPDG Dorial Green-Beckham 6.00 15.00
AJPDJ Duke Johnson 10.00 25.00
AJPDJO David Johnson 25.00 60.00
AJPDP DeVante Parker 10.00 25.00
AJPDS Devin Smith 6.00 15.00
AJPJA Jay Ajayi 10.00 25.00
AJPJAL Javorius Allen 8.00 20.00
AJPJC Jamison Crowder 8.00 20.00
AJPJHA Justin Hardy 6.00 15.00
AJPJL Jeremy Langford 20.00 50.00
AJPJS Jaelen Strong 8.00 20.00
AJPJW Jameis Winston 125.00 200.00
AJPKW Kevin White 8.00 20.00
AJPKWI Karlos Williams 6.00 15.00
AJPLW Leonard Williams 6.00 15.00
AJPMD Mike Davis 6.00 15.00
AJPMG Melvin Gordon 25.00 60.00
AJPMJ Matt Jones 15.00 40.00
AJPMM Marcus Mariota 75.00 150.00
AJPMW Maxx Williams 6.00 15.00
AJPNA Nelson Agholor 8.00 20.00
AJPPD Phillip Dorsett 6.00 15.00
AJPRG Rashad Greene 6.00 15.00
AJPSC Sammie Coates 8.00 20.00
AJPSD Stefon Diggs 15.00 40.00
AJPSM Sean Mannion 6.00 15.00
AJPTC Tevin Coleman 8.00 20.00
AJPTG Todd Gurley 30.00 60.00
AJPTLO Tyler Lockett 10.00 25.00
AJPTM Ty Montgomery 6.00 15.00
AJPTY T.J. Yeldon 6.00 15.00
AJPVM Vince Mayle 8.00 20.00

2015 Topps Inception Rookie Jumbo Patch Autographs Red

*RED/25: .6X TO 1.5X MAGENTA/50
AJPJW Jameis Winston 175.00 300.00
AJPMM Marcus Mariota 100.00 200.00

2015 Topps Inception Rookie Relics Jumbo Patch

2014 Topps Inception Rookie Relics Jumbo Patch
2014 Topps Inception Rookie Relics Jumbo Patch
2014 Topps Inception Rookie Relics Jumbo Patch
RJPCC Chris Conley 2.00 5.00
RJRAA Ameer Abdullah 3.00 8.00
RJRAC Amari Cooper 6.00 15.00
RJRBH Brett Hundley 2.00 5.00
RJRBP Bryce Petty 2.00 5.00
RJRBPE Breshad Perriman 2.00 5.00
RJRDC David Cobb 2.00 5.00
RJRDF Devin Funchess 3.00 8.00
RJRDG Dorial Green-Beckham 2.00 5.00
RJRDJ Duke Johnson 3.00 8.00
RJRDJO David Johnson 5.00 12.00
RJRDP DeVante Parker 3.00 8.00
RJRDS Devin Smith 2.00 5.00
RJRGG Garrett Grayson 2.00 5.00
RJRJA Jay Ajayi 3.00 8.00
RJRJAL Javorius Allen 2.50 6.00
RJRJC Jamison Crowder 2.50 6.00
RJRJHA Justin Hardy 2.00 5.00
RJRJL Jeremy Langford 2.00 5.00
RJRJS Jaelen Strong 2.50 6.00
RJRJW Jameis Winston 12.00 30.00
RJRKW Kevin White 2.50 6.00
RJRLW Leonard Williams 2.00 5.00
RJRMD Mike Davis 2.00 5.00
RJRMG Melvin Gordon 5.00 12.00
RJRMJ Matt Jones 2.00 5.00
RJRMM Marcus Mariota 10.00 25.00
RJRMW Maxx Williams 2.00 5.00
RJRNA Nelson Agholor 2.50 6.00
RJRPD Phillip Dorsett 2.00 5.00
RJRRG Rashad Greene 2.00 5.00
RJRSC Sammie Coates 2.50 6.00
RJRSD Stefon Diggs 5.00 12.00
RJRSM Sean Mannion 2.00 5.00
RJRTC Tevin Coleman 2.50 6.00
RJRTG Todd Gurley 8.00 20.00
RJRTL Tyler Lockett 3.00 8.00
RJRTM Ty Montgomery 2.00 5.00
RJRTY T.J. Yeldon 2.00 5.00
RJRVM Vince Mayle 2.50 6.00

2015 Topps Inception Rookie Relics Patch

*PATCH/125: .4X TO 1X JUMBO PATCH/140
*MAGENTA/75: .5X TO 1.2X JUMBO PATCH/140
*RED/50: .6X TO 1.5X JUMBO PATCH/140
*ORANGE/25: .8X TO 2X JUMBO PATCH/140

2015 Topps Inception Silver Signings

SSAA Ameer Abdullah 12.00 30.00
SSAC Amari Cooper 30.00 80.00
SSBH Brett Hundley 15.00 40.00
SSBP Bryce Petty 8.00 20.00
SSBPR Breshad Perriman 8.00 20.00
SSCC Chris Conley 8.00 20.00
SSDC David Cobb 8.00 20.00
SSDF Devin Funchess 12.00 30.00
SSDG Dorial Green-Beckham 8.00 20.00
SSDJ Duke Johnson 12.00 30.00
SSDJO David Johnson 20.00 50.00
SSDP DeVante Parker 12.00 30.00
SSDS Devin Smith 8.00 20.00
SSJA Jay Ajayi
SSJAL Javorius Allen 12.00 30.00
SSJC Jamison Crowder 10.00 25.00
SSJHA Justin Hardy 8.00 20.00
SSJL Jeremy Langford 8.00 20.00
SSJS Jaelen Strong
SSJW Jameis Winston 100.00 200.00
SSKW Kevin White 20.00 40.00
SSLW Leonard Williams 8.00 20.00
SSMD Mike Davis 8.00 20.00
SSMG Melvin Gordon 25.00 60.00
SSMJ Matt Jones 8.00 20.00
SSMM Marcus Mariota 75.00 150.00
SSMW Maxx Williams 8.00 20.00
SSNA Nelson Agholor 10.00 25.00
SSPD Phillip Dorsett 8.00 20.00
SSRG Rashad Greene 10.00 25.00
SSSC Sammie Coates
SSSD Stefon Diggs 20.00 50.00
SSSM Sean Mannion 8.00 20.00
SSTC Tevin Coleman 10.00 25.00
SSTG Todd Gurley 75.00 150.00
SSTL Tyler Lockett 12.00 30.00
SSTM Ty Montgomery 8.00 20.00
SSTY T.J. Yeldon 8.00 20.00
SSVM Vince Mayle 10.00 25.00

2008 Topps Kickoff

This set was released on September 3, 2008. The base set consists of 220 cards. Cards 1-165 feature veterans, and cards 166-220 are rookies.
COMPLETE SET (220) 20.00 40.00
UNPRICED PRINT PLATE 1/1 ODDS 1:340
1 Drew Brees .20 .50
2 Peyton Manning .50 1.25
3 Eli Manning .15 .40
4 Steven Jackson .12 .30
5 Brian Westbrook .12 .30
6 Fred Taylor .12 .30
7 Terrell Owens .15 .40
8 Reggie Wayne .15 .40
9 Steve Smith .15 .40
10 Chad Pennington .12 .30
11 Jay Cutler .12 .30
12 Joey Harrington .12 .30
13 Kyle Boller .12 .30
14 Brett Favre .40 1.00
15 Kurt Warner .15 .40
16 Jason Campbell .12 .30
17 Shaun Alexander .12 .30
18 Maurice Jones-Drew .12 .30
19 Thomas Jones .12 .30
20 Selvin Young .12 .30
21 Brandon Jacobs .12 .30
22 Edgerrin James .15 .40
23 Chester Taylor .12 .30
24 Greg Jennings .12 .30
25 Jerricho Cotchery .12 .30
26 Joey Galloway .15 .40
27 Lee Evans .15 .40
28 Roy Williams WR .12 .30
29 Brandon Marshall .15 .40
30 Bobby Engram .12 .30
31 Antonio Gates .15 .40
32 Kellen Winslow .12 .30
33 Jeremy Shockey .12 .30
34 Heath Miller .12 .30
35 Vernon Davis .12 .30
36 Patrick Kerney .12 .30
37 Jared Allen .12 .30
38 DeMarcus Ware .15 .40
39 Brian Urlacher .20 .50
40 Champ Bailey .15 .40
41 Kellen Clemens .12 .30
42 JaMarcus Russell .12 .30
43 Matt Leinart .12 .30
44 Julius Jones .12 .30
45 Jerious Norwood .12 .30
46 James Jones .12 .30
47 Chris Chambers .12 .30
48 Sidney Rice .12 .30
49 Donte Stallworth .12 .30
50 Isaac Bruce .20 .50
51 Albert Haynesworth .12 .30
52 Julius Peppers .15 .40
53 Jon Beason .12 .30
54 Asante Samuel .12 .30
55 Roy Williams S .12 .30
56 Carson Palmer .15 .40
57 Tony Romo .15 .40
58 Willie Parker .15 .40
59 Clinton Portis .12 .30
60 LaDainian Tomlinson .20 .50
61 Joseph Addai .12 .30
62 Willis McGahee .12 .30
63 Anquan Boldin .12 .30
64 Randy Moss .15 .40
65 Andre Johnson .15 .40
66 Chad Johnson .12 .30
67 Larry Fitzgerald .15 .40
68 Jon Kitna .12 .30
69 Matt Hasselbeck .12 .30
70 Matt Schaub .12 .30
71 Jeff Garcia .12 .30
72 Sage Rosenfels .12 .30
73 Philip Rivers .20 .50
74 Cleo Lemon .12 .30
75 Brian Griese .12 .30
76 Warrick Dunn .12 .30
77 LenDale White .12 .30
78 Ryan Grant .15 .40
79 DeAngelo Williams .12 .30
80 Earnest Graham .12 .30
81 Torry Holt .15 .40
82 Derrick Mason .12 .30
83 Dwayne Bowe .15 .40
84 Donald Driver .15 .40
85 Shaun McDonald .12 .30
86 Chris Cooley .12 .30
87 Tony Gonzalez .15 .40
88 Dallas Clark .12 .30
89 Tony Scheffler .12 .30
90 Alge Crumpler .12 .30
91 Osi Umenyiora .12 .30
92 Michael Strahan .15 .40
93 Patrick Willis .15 .40
94 Ray Lewis .20 .50
95 Bob Sanders .15 .40
96 Troy Smith .15 .40
97 Jake Delhomme .12 .30
98 John Beck .12 .30
99 Reggie Bush .12 .30
100 Larry Johnson .12 .30
101 Rudi Johnson .12 .30
102 Ahmad Bradshaw .12 .30
103 Hines Ward .15 .40
104 Calvin Johnson .20 .50
105 Jerry Porter .12 .30
106 Reggie Williams .15 .40
107 Ted Ginn Jr. .12 .30
108 Terence Newman .12 .30
109 Troy Polamalu .20 .50
110 Devin Hester .15 .40
111 Tom Brady .60 1.50
112 Ben Roethlisberger .20 .50
113 Vince Young .12 .30
114 Adrian Peterson .20 .50
115 Marion Barber .12 .30
116 Marshawn Lynch .15 .40
117 Frank Gore .15 .40
118 Plaxico Burress .12 .30
119 Braylon Edwards .12 .30
120 David Garrard .12 .30
121 Trent Edwards .12 .30
122 Donovan McNabb .15 .40
123 Derek Anderson .12 .30
124 Marc Bulger .12 .30
125 Damon Huard .12 .30
126 Tarvaris Jackson .12 .30
127 DeShaun Foster .12 .30
128 Ron Dayne .12 .30
129 Kenny Watson .12 .30
130 Laurence Maroney .15 .40
131 Jamal Lewis .15 .40
132 Justin Fargas .12 .30
133 T.J. Houshmandzadeh .12 .30
134 Kevin Curtis .12 .30
135 Santonio Holmes .12 .30
136 Wes Welker .15 .40
137 Roddy White .12 .30
138 Marques Colston .12 .30
139 Bernard Berrian .12 .30
140 Santana Moss .12 .30
141 Owen Daniels .12 .30
142 Jason Witten .15 .40
143 Donald Lee .15 .40
144 Desmond Clark .12 .30
145 Zach Miller .12 .30
146 Mario Williams .15 .40
147 Ernie Sims .12 .30
148 Shawne Merriman .12 .30
149 Antonio Cromartie .12 .30
150 Ed Reed .15 .40
151 Brodie Croyle .15 .40
152 Rex Grossman .12 .30
153 Alex Smith QB .15 .40
154 Ronnie Brown .12 .30
155 Michael Turner .12 .30
156 Anthony Gonzalez .12 .30
157 Laveranues Coles .12 .30
158 Vincent Jackson .12 .30
159 Greg Olsen .15 .40
160 Jason Taylor .15 .40
161 Lofa Tatupu .12 .30
162 Marcus Trufant .12 .30
163 DeAngelo Hall .12 .30
164 Ronde Barber .12 .30
165 John Lynch .15 .40
166 Matt Ryan RC .75 2.00
167 Brian Brohm RC .25 .60
168 Andre Woodson RC .25 .60
169 Chad Henne RC .30 .75
170 Joe Flacco RC .50 1.25
171 John David Booty RC .25 .60
172 Colt Brennan RC .30 .75
173 Dennis Dixon RC .25 .60
174 Erik Ainge RC .25 .60
175 Josh Johnson RC .25 .60
176 Kevin O'Connell RC .25 .60
177 Anthony Morelli RC .25 .60
178 Darren McFadden RC .25 .60
179 Rashard Mendenhall RC .25 .60
180 Jonathan Stewart RC .40 1.00
181 Felix Jones RC .25 .60
182 Jamaal Charles RC .40 1.00
183 Chris Johnson RC .30 .75
184 Ray Rice RC .25 .60
185 Mike Hart RC .25 .60
186 Kevin Smith RC .25 .60
187 Steve Slaton RC .25 .60
188 Matt Forte RC .40 1.00
189 Tashard Choice RC .25 .60
190 Justin Forsett RC .30 .75
191 Harry Douglas RC .30 .75
192 DeSean Jackson RC .50 1.25
193 Malcolm Kelly RC .25 .60
194 Limas Sweed RC .25 .60
195 Mario Manningham RC .25 .60
196 James Hardy RC .25 .60
197 Early Doucet RC .25 .60
198 Donnie Avery RC .30 .75
199 Dexter Jackson RC .40 1.00
200 Devin Thomas RC .25 .60
201 Jordy Nelson RC .75 2.00
202 Eddie Royal RC .25 .60
203 Earl Bennett RC .40 1.00
204 Jerome Simpson RC .30 .75
205 Andre Caldwell RC .25 .60
206 Keenan Burton RC .25 .60
207 Dustin Keller RC .30 .75
208 Fred Davis RC .25 .60
209 John Carlson RC .25 .60
210 Jake Long RC .40 1.00
211 D.Rodgers-Cromartie RC .30 .75
212 Glenn Dorsey RC .25 .60
213 Sedrick Ellis RC .25 .60
214 Chris Long RC .30 .75
215 Vernon Gholston RC .25 .60
216 Derrick Harvey RC .25 .60
217 Jerod Mayo RC .40 1.00
218 Keith Rivers RC .25 .60
219 Leodis McKelvin RC .30 .75
220 Aqib Talib RC .40 1.00
CL1 Checklist 1 .02 .10
CL2 Checklist 2 .02 .10

2008 Topps Kickoff Silver Holofoil

*VETS 1-165: 3X TO 8X BASIC CARDS
*ROOKIES 166-220: .8X TO 2X BASIC CARDS
STATED PRINT RUN 1349 SER.#'d SETS

2008 Topps Kickoff Autographs

GROUP A ODDS 1:25,762 H, 1:15,237 J
GROUP B ODDS 1:1491 H, 1:997 J
GROUP C ODDS 1:900 H, 1:600 J
GROUP D ODDS 1:1975 H, 1:1350 J
GROUP A AU TOO SCARCE TO PRICE
KAAA Anthony Alridge C 2.50 6.00
KAAG Anthony Gonzalez B 5.00 12.00
KAAM Anthony Madison D 10.00 25.00
KAAV Adam Vinatieri B 12.00 30.00
KADH David Harris B 5.00 12.00
KADM Darren McFadden A 40.00 100.00
KAMK Mathias Kiwanuka B 5.00 12.00
KAMR Matt Ryan A 75.00 150.00
KAPS Paul Smith C 2.50 6.00
KART Ryan Torain C 3.00 8.00

2008 Topps Kickoff Puzzle

STATED ODDS 1:3
1 Peyton Manning 2.50 6.00
2 Tom Brady 3.00 8.00
3 Eli Manning .75 2.00
4 Tony Romo .75 2.00
5 Ben Roethlisberger 1.00 2.50
6 Drew Brees 1.00 2.50
7 LaDainian Tomlinson 1.00 2.50
8 Adrian Peterson 1.00 2.50
9 Willie Parker .75 2.00
10 Frank Gore .75 2.00
11 Willis McGahee .60 1.50
12 Steven Jackson .60 1.50
13 Chad Johnson .60 1.50
14 Reggie Wayne .75 2.00
15 Terrell Owens .75 2.00
16 Randy Moss .75 2.00
17 Braylon Edwards .60 1.50
18 Steve Smith .75 2.00
19 Antonio Gates .75 2.00
20 Tony Gonzalez .75 2.00
21 Matt Ryan 1.25 3.00
22 Brian Brohm .40 1.00
23 Darren McFadden .40 1.00
24 Rashard Mendenhall .40 1.00
25 Jonathan Stewart .60 1.50
26 Chad Henne .50 1.25
27 Felix Jones .40 1.00
28 Ray Rice .40 1.00

2008 Topps Kickoff Stars of the Game

STATED ODDS 1:6 HOB, 1:2 JUM
SGAG Antonio Gates 1.00 2.50
SGAP Adrian Peterson 1.25 3.00
SGBB Brian Brohm .50 1.25
SGBE Braylon Edwards .75 2.00
SGBR Ben Roethlisberger 1.25 3.00
SGCJ Chad Johnson .75 2.00
SGDB Drew Brees 1.25 3.00
SGDM Darren McFadden .50 1.25
SGEM Eli Manning 1.00 2.50
SGFG Frank Gore 1.00 2.50
SGJS Jonathan Stewart .75 2.00
SGLT LaDainian Tomlinson 1.25 3.00
SGMR Matt Ryan 1.50 4.00
SGPM Peyton Manning 3.00 8.00
SGRM Rashard Mendenhall .50 1.25
SGRM Randy Moss 1.00 2.50
SGRW Reggie Wayne 1.00 2.50
SGSJ Steven Jackson .75 2.00
SGSS Steve Smith 1.00 2.50
SGTB Tom Brady 4.00 10.00
SGTG Tony Gonzalez 1.00 2.50
SGTO Terrell Owens 1.00 2.50
SGTR Tony Romo 1.00 2.50
SGWM Willis McGahee .75 2.00
SGWP Willie Parker 1.00 2.50

2008 Topps Kickoff Tattoos

STATED ODDS 1:36 HOB, 1:9 JUM
TT1 Buffalo Bills .30 .75
TT2 Miami Dolphins .40 1.00
TT3 New England Patriots .40 1.00
TT4 New York Jets .40 1.00
TT5 Baltimore Ravens .30 .75
TT6 Cincinnati Bengals .30 .75
TT7 Cleveland Browns .30 .75
TT8 Pittsburgh Steelers .50 1.25
TT9 Houston Texans .30 .75
TT10 Indianapolis Colts .40 1.00
TT11 Jacksonville Jaguars .30 .75
TT12 Tennessee Titans .30 .75
TT13 Denver Broncos .40 1.00
TT14 Kansas City Chiefs .30 .75
TT15 Oakland Raiders .50 1.25
TT16 San Diego Chargers .30 .75
TT17 Dallas Cowboys .50 1.25
TT18 New York Giants .40 1.00
TT19 Philadelphia Eagles .30 .75
TT20 Washington Redskins .40 1.00
TT21 Chicago Bears .40 1.00
TT22 Detroit Lions .30 .75
TT23 Green Bay Packers .50 1.25
TT24 Minnesota Vikings .30 .75
TT25 Atlanta Falcons .30 .75
TT26 Carolina Panthers .30 .75
TT27 New Orleans Saints .30 .75
TT28 Tampa Bay Buccaneers .30 .75
TT29 Arizona Cardinals .30 .75
TT30 San Francisco 49ers .40 1.00
TT31 Seattle Seahawks .30 .75
TT32 St. Louis Rams .30 .75

2009 Topps Kickoff

COMPLETE SET (165) 15.00 40.00
TWO ROOKIES PER PACK
1 Larry Fitzgerald .15 .40
2 Anquan Boldin .12 .30
3 Roddy White .12 .30
4 Terrell Owens .15 .40
5 Steve Smith .15 .40
6 Chad Ochocinco .12 .30
7 Laveranues Coles .12 .30
8 Braylon Edwards .12 .30
9 Brandon Marshall .15 .40
10 Eddie Royal .12 .30
11 Calvin Johnson .20 .50
12 Greg Jennings .12 .30
13 Andre Johnson .15 .40
14 Anthony Gonzalez .12 .30
15 Reggie Wayne .15 .40
16 Dwayne Bowe .15 .40
17 Randy Moss .15 .40
18 Marques Colston .12 .30
19 Steve Smith .15 .40
20 Jerricho Cotchery .12 .30
21 DeSean Jackson .15 .40
22 Hines Ward .15 .40
23 Santonio Holmes .12 .30
24 Chris Chambers .12 .30
25 T.J. Houshmandzadeh .12 .30
26 Donnie Avery .12 .30
27 Antonio Bryant .12 .30
28 Santana Moss .15 .40
29 Jason Witten .15 .40
30 Dallas Clark .12 .30
31 Tony Gonzalez .15 .40
32 Jeremy Shockey .12 .30
33 Heath Miller .12 .30
34 Antonio Gates .15 .40
35 Vernon Davis .12 .30
36 John Carlson .15 .40
37 Kellen Winslow Jr. .12 .30
38 Chris Cooley .12 .30
39 Ed Reed .15 .40
40 Troy Polamalu .20 .50
41 Michael Turner .12 .30
42 Willis McGahee .12 .30
43 Marshawn Lynch .15 .40
44 DeAngelo Williams .12 .30
45 Jonathan Stewart .12 .30
46 Matt Forte .12 .30
47 Jamal Lewis .15 .40
48 Marion Barber .15 .40
49 Kevin Smith .12 .30
50 Steve Slaton .12 .30
51 Joseph Addai .12 .30
52 Maurice Jones-Drew .12 .30
53 Larry Johnson .12 .30
54 Jamaal Charles .15 .40
55 Ronnie Brown .12 .30
56 Adrian Peterson .20 .50
57 Chester Taylor .12 .30
58 Wes Welker .15 .40
59 Reggie Bush .12 .30
60 Brandon Jacobs .12 .30
61 Leon Washington .12 .30
62 Thomas Jones .12 .30
63 Darren McFadden .20 .50
64 Justin Fargas .12 .30
65 Brian Westbrook .12 .30
66 Willie Parker .12 .30
67 LaDainian Tomlinson .20 .50
68 Darren Sproles .15 .40
69 Frank Gore .15 .40
70 Steven Jackson .12 .30
71 Warrick Dunn .12 .30
72 Earnest Graham .12 .30
73 Chris Johnson .12 .30
74 LenDale White .12 .30
75 Clinton Portis .12 .30
76 Kurt Warner .15 .40
77 Matt Ryan .15 .40
78 Joe Flacco .15 .40
79 Trent Edwards .12 .30
80 Kyle Orton .12 .30
81 Carson Palmer .15 .40
82 Brady Quinn .12 .30
83 Tony Romo .15 .40
84 Jay Cutler .12 .30
85 Aaron Rodgers .40 1.00
86 Matt Schaub .12 .30
87 Peyton Manning .50 1.25
88 David Garrard .12 .30
89 Matt Cassel .12 .30
90 Chad Pennington .12 .30
91 Tarvaris Jackson .15 .40
92 Tom Brady .60 1.50
93 Drew Brees .20 .50
94 Eli Manning .15 .40
95 JaMarcus Russell .12 .30
96 Donovan McNabb .15 .40
97 Ben Roethlisberger .20 .50
98 Philip Rivers .20 .50
99 Matt Hasselbeck .12 .30
100 Marc Bulger .12 .30
101 Jason Campbell .12 .30
102 Ray Lewis .20 .50
103 Brian Urlacher .20 .50
104 Ernie Sims .12 .30
105 Joey Porter .15 .40
106 Jerod Mayo .15 .40
107 James Harrison .20 .50
108 Patrick Willis .15 .40
109 Julius Peppers .15 .40
110 DeMarcus Ware .15 .40
111 Brian Orakpo RC .30 .75
112 Pat White RC .30 .75
113 Malcolm Jenkins RC .25 .60
114 Nate Davis RC .25 .60
115 Rhett Bomar RC .25 .60
116 Matthew Stafford RC 1.25 3.00
117 Stephen McGee RC .25 .60
118 Aaron Maybin RC .30 .75
119 Josh Freeman RC .25 .60
120 Mark Sanchez RC .25 .60
121 B.J. Raji RC .30 .75
122 Javon Ringer RC .25 .60
123 Chris Wells RC .25 .60
124 Donald Brown RC .25 .60
125 Gartrell Johnson RC .25 .60
126 Glen Coffee RC .25 .60
127 Andre Brown RC .30 .75
128 Aaron Curry RC .40 1.00
129 Cedric Peerman RC .25 .60
130 Knowshon Moreno RC .25 .60
131 Shonn Greene RC .25 .60
132 LeSean McCoy RC .60 1.50
133 Rashad Jennings RC .30 .75
134 Brian Cushing RC .25 .60
135 James Davis RC .25 .60
136 Hakeem Nicks RC .30 .75
137 Austin Collie RC .25 .60
138 Eugene Monroe RC .25 .60
139 Brandon Tate RC .30 .75
140 Clay Matthews RC 1.00 2.50
141 Chase Coffman RC .25 .60
142 Brooks Foster RC .25 .60
143 Kenny Britt RC .40 1.00
144 Patrick Turner RC .25 .60
145 Darrius Heyward-Bey RC .40 1.00
146 Rey Maualuga RC .40 1.00
147 Deon Butler RC .25 .60
148 Derrick Williams RC .25 .60
149 Percy Harvin RC .25 .60
150 Jarett Dillard RC .25 .60
151 Jeremy Maclin RC .30 .75
152 Juaquin Iglesias RC .25 .60
153 Jared Cook RC .30 .75
154 James Laurinaitis RC .25 .60
155 Brandon Pettigrew RC .25 .60
156 Andre Smith RC .25 .60
157 Brian Robiskie RC .25 .60
158 Mohamed Massaquoi RC .25 .60
159 Ramses Barden RC .25 .60
160 Michael Crabtree RC .40 1.00
161 Michael Oher RC .40 1.00
162 Patrick Chung RC .25 .60
163 Louis Murphy RC .25 .60
164 William Moore RC .25 .60
165 Victor Harris RC .30 .75

2009 Topps Kickoff Silver Holofoil

*VETS 1-110: 3X TO 8X BASIC CARDS
*ROOKIES 111-165: .8X TO 2X
STATED PRINT RUN 2009 SER.#'d SETS

2009 Topps Kickoff Komics

STATED ODDS 1:4
1 Matt Ryan 1.00 2.50
2 Joe Flacco 1.00 2.50

3 Steve Slaton .75 2.00
4 Matt Forte .75 2.00
5 Chris Johnson .75 2.00
6 Jerod Mayo 1.00 2.50
7 Eddie Royal .75 2.00
8 Jake Long .75 2.00
9 Ryan Clady .75 2.00
10 Adrian Peterson 1.25 3.00
11 Drew Brees 1.25 3.00
12 Kurt Warner 1.00 2.50
13 Larry Fitzgerald 1.00 2.50
14 Michael Turner .75 2.00
15 James Harrison 1.25 3.00
16 Ben Roethlisberger 1.25 3.00
17 Philip Rivers 1.25 3.00
18 Santonio Holmes .75 2.00
19 Matt Cassel .75 2.00
20 Antonio Gates 1.00 2.50
21 Peyton Manning 3.00 8.00
22 Terrell Owens 1.00 2.50
23 Ed Reed 1.00 2.50
24 LaDainian Tomlinson 1.25 3.00
25 DeMarcus Ware 1.00 2.50
26 DeAngelo Williams .75 2.00
27 Brett Favre 2.50 6.00
28 Matthew Stafford 4.00 10.00
29 Michael Crabtree 1.25 3.00
30 Jeremy Maclin 1.00 2.50

2009 Topps Kickoff Stars of the Game

STATED ODDS 1:4
1 Peyton Manning 3.00 8.00
2 Larry Fitzgerald 1.00 2.50
3 Steve Slaton .75 2.00
4 Chris Johnson .75 2.00
5 Adrian Peterson 1.25 3.00
6 Aaron Rodgers 2.50 6.00
7 Jay Cutler .75 2.00
8 Steve Smith 1.00 2.50
9 Maurice Jones-Drew .75 2.00
10 Andre Johnson 1.00 2.50
11 Philip Rivers 1.25 3.00
12 Michael Turner .75 2.00
13 Calvin Johnson 1.25 3.00
14 Tony Romo 1.00 2.50
15 Reggie Wayne 1.00 2.50
16 Matt Forte .75 2.00
17 DeAngelo Williams .75 2.00
18 Frank Gore 1.00 2.50
19 Matt Ryan 1.00 2.50
20 Brian Westbrook .75 2.00
21 Kurt Warner 1.00 2.50
22 Clinton Portis .75 2.00
23 Brandon Jacobs .75 2.00
24 Steven Jackson .75 2.00
25 Drew Brees 1.25 3.00

2012 Topps Kickoff

COMPLETE SET (50) 8.00 20.00
1 Andrew Luck 2.00 5.00
2 Bernard Pierce .20 .50
3 Michael Egnew .20 .50
4 Nick Foles .50 1.25
5 Cam Newton .20 .50
6 Doug Martin .30 .75
7 Melvin Ingram .20 .50
8 Trent Richardson .20 .50
9 Kendall Wright .20 .50
10 Jerry Rice .30 .75
11 Mark Sanchez .12 .30
12 Brock Osweiler .20 .50
13 Joe Adams .20 .50
14 Dwayne Allen .20 .50
15 Jarius Wright .20 .50
16 Lamar Miller .30 .75
17 Justin Blackmon .20 .50
18 A.J. Jenkins .20 .50
19 Ronnie Hillman .20 .50
20 Dan Marino .40 1.00
21 Nick Toon .20 .50
22 Mohamed Sanu .30 .75
23 Isaiah Pead .20 .50
24 Matt Kalil .20 .50
25 Jim Brown .25 .60
26 Dontari Poe .20 .50
27 Brandon Weeden .20 .50
28 David Wilson .20 .50
29 Brian Quick .20 .50
30 John Elway .30 .75
31 Luke Kuechly .50 1.25
32 Tony Romo .15 .40
33 Chris Givens .20 .50
34 Michael Floyd .20 .50
35 Coby Fleener .20 .50
36 A.J. Green .20 .50
37 T.J. Graham .20 .50
38 Russell Wilson 1.50 4.00
39 Mark Barron .20 .50
40 Emmitt Smith .30 .75
41 Robert Turbin .20 .50
42 Rueben Randle .20 .50
43 Ryan Tannehill .30 .75
44 Alshon Jeffery .40 1.00
45 Stephen Hill .20 .50
46 DeVier Posey .20 .50
47 Ryan Broyles .20 .50
48 LaMichael James .20 .50
49 Patrick Willis .15 .40
50 Robert Griffin III .25 .60

2012 Topps Kickoff Autographs

3 Michael Egnew/160 2.50 6.00
4 Nick Foles/45 10.00 25.00
6 Doug Martin/45 6.00 15.00
7 Melvin Ingram/160 2.50 6.00
9 Kendall Wright/25 5.00 12.00
12 Brock Osweiler/25 5.00 12.00
13 Joe Adams/165 2.50 6.00
14 Dwayne Allen/160 2.50 6.00
15 Jarius Wright/160 2.50 6.00
16 Lamar Miller/25 8.00 20.00
17 Justin Blackmon/15 15.00 40.00
18 A.J. Jenkins/25 20.00 40.00
19 Ronnie Hillman/100 2.50 6.00
21 Nick Toon/160 2.50 6.00
22 Mohamed Sanu/45 6.00 15.00
23 Isaiah Pead/25 5.00 12.00
24 Matt Kalil/165 2.50 6.00
26 Dontari Poe/165 2.50 6.00
27 Brandon Weeden/15 25.00 60.00
28 David Wilson/25 5.00 12.00
29 Brian Quick/85 3.00 8.00
31 Luke Kuechly/45 10.00 25.00
33 Chris Givens/160 2.50 6.00
34 Michael Floyd/15 25.00 50.00
35 Coby Fleener/160 2.50 6.00
37 T.J. Graham/160 2.50 6.00
38 Russell Wilson/25 40.00 80.00
39 Mark Barron/45 4.00 10.00
41 Robert Turbin/160 2.50 6.00
42 Rueben Randle/45 4.00 10.00
43 Ryan Tannehill/15 8.00 20.00
44 Alshon Jeffery/25 10.00 25.00
45 Stephen Hill/25 12.00 30.00
46 DeVier Posey/45 4.00 10.00
47 Ryan Broyles/160 8.00 20.00
48 LaMichael James/45 12.00 30.00

2013 Topps Kickoff

COMPLETE SET (50) 8.00 20.00
INSERTS IN KICKOFF PACKS
1 EJ Manuel .20 .50
2 Robert Woods .30 .75
3 Giovani Bernard .20 .50
4 Montee Ball .20 .50
5 Eddie Lacy .20 .50
6 DeAndre Hopkins .50 1.25
7 Denard Robinson .20 .50
8 Cordarrelle Patterson .20 .50
9 Kenny Stills .20 .50
10 Geno Smith .20 .50
11 Matt Barkley .20 .50
12 Le'Veon Bell .60 1.50
13 Marcus Lattimore .20 .50
14 Tavon Austin .25 .60
15 Justin Hunter .20 .50
16 Tyler Wilson .20 .50
17 Dion Jordan .20 .50
18 Tyler Eifert .20 .50
19 Manti Te'o .25 .60
20 Andre Ellington .20 .50
21 Stepfan Taylor .20 .50
22 Marquise Goodwin .20 .50
23 Joseph Randle .20 .50
24 Gavin Escobar .20 .50
25 Terrance Williams .20 .50
26 Johnathan Franklin .20 .50
27 Knile Davis .20 .50
28 Mike Gillislee .20 .50
29 Aaron Dobson .20 .50
30 Ryan Nassib .20 .50
31 Zach Ertz .40 1.00
32 Landry Jones .20 .50
33 Markus Wheaton .20 .50
34 Keenan Allen .40 1.00
35 Vance McDonald .25 .60
36 Quinton Patton .20 .50
37 Christine Michael .20 .50
38 Stedman Bailey .20 .50
39 Mike Glennon .20 .50
40 Jordan Reed .30 .75
41 Deion Sanders .15 .40
42 Eric Dickerson .15 .40
43 Barry Sanders .30 .75
44 Randall Cunningham .15 .40
45 LaDainian Tomlinson .15 .40
46 Marshall Faulk .15 .40
47 Andrew Luck .30 .75
48 Robert Griffin III .12 .30
49 LeSean McCoy .20 .50
50 Jason Pierre-Paul .12 .30

2013 Topps Kickoff Autographs

EXCH EXPIRATION: 7/31/2016
1 EJ Manuel/25 20.00 40.00
2 Robert Woods/79 5.00 12.00
3 Giovani Bernard/79 3.00 8.00
4 Montee Ball/79 3.00 8.00
5 Eddie Lacy/79 3.00 8.00
6 DeAndre Hopkins/79 8.00 20.00
7 Denard Robinson/79 EXCH 3.00 8.00
8 Cordarrelle Patterson/79 3.00 8.00
9 Kenny Stills/79 3.00 8.00
10 Geno Smith/25 5.00 12.00
11 Matt Barkley/25 5.00 12.00
12 Le'Veon Bell/79 12.00 30.00
13 Marcus Lattimore/79 3.00 8.00
14 Tavon Austin/25 6.00 15.00
15 Justin Hunter/79 3.00 8.00
16 Tyler Wilson/79 3.00 8.00
17 Dion Jordan/79 3.00 8.00
18 Tyler Eifert/79 3.00 8.00
19 Manti Te'o/79 12.00 30.00
20 Andre Ellington/79 3.00 8.00
21 Stepfan Taylor/79 3.00 8.00
22 Marquise Goodwin/79 3.00 8.00
23 Joseph Randle/79 3.00 8.00
24 Gavin Escobar/79 3.00 8.00
25 Terrance Williams/79 3.00 8.00
26 Johnathan Franklin/79 3.00 8.00
27 Knile Davis/79 3.00 8.00
28 Mike Gillislee/79 3.00 8.00
29 Aaron Dobson/79 3.00 8.00
30 Ryan Nassib/79 3.00 8.00
31 Zach Ertz/79 6.00 15.00
32 Landry Jones/79 3.00 8.00
33 Markus Wheaton/79 3.00 8.00
34 Keenan Allen/79 6.00 15.00
35 Vance McDonald/79 4.00 10.00
36 Quinton Patton/79 8.00 20.00
37 Christine Michael/79 3.00 8.00
38 Stedman Bailey/79 3.00 8.00
39 Mike Glennon/79 3.00 8.00
40 Jordan Reed/79 8.00 20.00
41 Deion Sanders/25 25.00 50.00
42 Eric Dickerson/25 15.00 40.00
43 Barry Sanders/25 50.00 100.00
44 Randall Cunningham/25 15.00 40.00
45 LaDainian Tomlinson/25 15.00 40.00
46 Marshall Faulk/25 15.00 40.00
47 Andrew Luck/25 50.00 100.00
48 Robert Griffin III/25 12.00 30.00
49 LeSean McCoy/25 12.00 30.00
50 Jason Pierre-Paul/25 EXCH 8.00 20.00

1996 Topps Laser

The 1996 Topps Laser set was issued in one series totalling 128 cards. The 4-card packs carried a suggested retail of $5.00 each. The cards are all etch foil stamped, die-cut and UV coated.

COMPLETE SET (128) 15.00 40.00
1 Marshall Faulk .40 1.00
2 Alonzo Spellman .07 .20
3 Frank Sanders .15 .40
4 Anthony Pleasant .07 .20
5 Scott Mitchell .15 .40
6 Robert Brooks .30 .75
7 Robert Jones .07 .20
8 Phillippi Sparks .07 .20
9 Rodney Peete .07 .20
10 Kordell Stewart .30 .75
11 Ken Norton .07 .20
12 Brian Mitchell .07 .20
13 Ben Coates .15 .40
14 Quinn Early .07 .20
15 Emmitt Smith 1.25 3.00
16 Steve Bono .07 .20
17 Anthony Miller .15 .40
18 Mel Gray .07 .20
19 Neil O'Donnell .15 .40
20 Tim Brown .30 .75
21 Terrell Fletcher .07 .20
22 John Randle .15 .40
23 Fred Barnett .07 .20
24 Craig Heyward .07 .20
25 Ki-Jana Carter .15 .40
26 Eric Allen .07 .20
27 Warren Sapp .07 .20
28 Terry Wooden .07 .20
29 Darion Conner .07 .20
30 Mark Brunell .50 1.25
31 Vinny Testaverde .15 .40
32 Chris Calloway .07 .20
33 Steve Walsh .07 .20
34 Ken Dilger .15 .40
35 Bryan Cox .07 .20
36 Rob Moore .15 .40
37 Henry Thomas .07 .20
38 Henry Ellard .07 .20
39 Mark Chmura .15 .40
40 Jerry Rice .75 2.00
41 Michael Irvin .30 .75
42 Willie McGinest .07 .20
43 Steve McNair .60 1.50
44 Tamarick Vanover .15 .40
45 Cris Carter .30 .75
46 Levon Kirkland .07 .20
47 Terry McDaniel .07 .20
48 Jessie Tuggle .07 .20
49 O.J. McDuffie .15 .40
50 Bruce Smith .15 .40
51 Tyrone Hughes .07 .20
52 Tony Martin .15 .40
53 Hardy Nickerson .07 .20
54 Garrison Hearst .15 .40
55 Sam Mills .07 .20
56 Mark Carrier DB .07 .20
57 Quentin Coryatt .07 .20
58 Neil Smith .15 .40
59 Michael Westbrook .30 .75
60 Greg Lloyd .15 .40
61 Jeff Hostetler .07 .20
62 Wayne Chrebet .40 1.00
63 Herschel Walker .15 .40
64 Pepper Johnson .07 .20
65 John Elway 1.50 4.00
66 Reggie White .30 .75
67 James O.Stewart .15 .40
68 Bernie Parmalee .07 .20
69 Robert Smith .15 .40
70 Drew Bledsoe .50 1.25
71 Marvcus Patton .07 .20
72 Stan Humphries .15 .40
73 Darnay Scott .15 .40
74 Jim Kelly .30 .75
75 Terance Mathis .07 .20
76 Erik Kramer .07 .20
77 Marcus Allen .30 .75
78 Ernie Mills .07 .20
79 Harvey Williams .07 .20
80 Brett Favre 1.50 4.00
81 Seth Joyner .07 .20
82 Tyrone Poole .07 .20
83 Troy Aikman .75 2.00
84 Warren Moon .15 .40
85 Isaac Bruce .30 .75
86 Errict Rhett .15 .40
87 Rick Mirer .15 .40
88 Anthony Smith .07 .20
89 Bert Emanuel .15 .40
90 Junior Seau .30 .75
91 Terry Allen .15 .40
92 Brent Jones .07 .20
93 Adrian Murrell .15 .40
94 Dave Brown .07 .20
95 Bryce Paup .07 .20
96 Jim Everett .07 .20
97 Brian Washington .07 .20
98 Jim Harbaugh .15 .40
99 Shannon Sharpe .15 .40
100 Dan Marino 1.50 4.00
101 Curtis Martin .60 1.50
102 Ricky Watters .15 .40
103 Yancey Thigpen .15 .40
104 Trent Dilfer .30 .75
105 Joey Galloway .30 .75
106 Edgar Bennett .15 .40
107 Willie Jackson .15 .40
108 Mark Collins .07 .20
109 Rashaan Salaam .15 .40
110 Eric Metcalf .07 .20
111 Terrell Davis .60 1.50
112 Darryll Lewis .07 .20
113 Ken Harvey .07 .20
114 Rob Fredrickson .07 .20
115 Rodney Hampton .15 .40
116 Chris Slade .07 .20
117 Jeff George .15 .40
118 Lamar Lathon .07 .20
119 Curtis Conway .30 .75
120 Barry Sanders 1.25 3.00
121 Eric Zeier .07 .20
122 Jeff Blake .30 .75
123 Derrick Thomas .30 .75
124 Tyrone Wheatley .15 .40
125 Steve Young .60 1.50
126 Napoleon Kaufman .30 .75
127 Dave Meggett .07 .20
128 Kerry Collins .30 .75
P77 Marcus Allen Prototype .30 .75
CL Checklist Card .05 .15

1996 Topps Laser Bright Spots

Randomly inserted in packs at a rate of one in every 24, this 16-standard-sized card set features players considered to be the "bright spots" on their team. The card fronts feature laser die-cutting technology on a gold foil board with the player photo in color and the player's name in a bronze foil. The back of the card has the player's name and statistics.

COMPLETE SET (16) 25.00 60.00
STATED ODDS 1:24
1 Curtis Martin 3.00 8.00
2 Tom Carter .40 1.00
3 Dave Brown .40 1.00
4 Wayne Chrebet 2.00 5.00
5 Rashaan Salaam .75 2.00
6 Mark Brunell 2.50 6.00
7 Elvis Grbac .75 2.00
8 Errict Rhett .75 2.00
9 Isaac Bruce 1.50 4.00
10 Kerry Collins 1.50 4.00
11 Mario Bates .40 1.00
12 Joey Galloway 1.50 4.00
13 Napoleon Kaufman 1.50 4.00
14 Tamarick Vanover .75 2.00
15 Marshall Faulk 2.00 5.00
16 Terrell Davis 3.00 8.00

1996 Topps Laser Draft Picks

Randomly inserted in packs at a rate of one in 12, this 16-card standard-sized set contains rookies from the Class of 1996. The cards feature laser cutting and a holographic strip down the side of the card in which "96 Draft Picks" is laser cut into. The cards also feature a color player photo on the front, with the name at the bottom of the card. The backs feature a ghosted reverse of the front of the card, with the players name and college statistics listed.

COMPLETE SET (16) 15.00 40.00
STATED ODDS 1:12
1 Keyshawn Johnson 2.50 6.00
2 Lawrence Phillips 1.25 3.00
3 Bobby Hoying 1.50 4.00
4 Marco Battaglia .75 2.00
5 Kevin Hardy .75 2.00
6 Jerome Woods .75 2.00
7 Ray Mickens .75 2.00
8 John Mobley .75 2.00
9 Marvin Harrison 5.00 12.00
10 Walt Harris .75 2.00
11 Duane Clemons .75 2.00
12 Regan Upshaw .75 2.00
13 Brian Dawkins 3.00 8.00
14 Bobby Engram 1.25 3.00
15 Eddie Kennison 1.50 4.00
16 Jeff Lewis 1.25 3.00

1996 Topps Laser Stadium Stars

Randomly inserted in packs at a rate of one in 48, this 16-card standard-sized set when unfolded, is actually the size of two cards, as the laser sculpted holographic foil outside shows a team logo for the player on the inside of the card. The interior photo is a full bleed color photo with foil enhancements, while the back of the card has a color snapshot of the player and statistics comparing 1995 with career bests..

COMPLETE SET (16) 75.00 200.00
STATED ODDS 1:48
1 Barry Sanders 12.50 30.00
2 Jim Harbaugh 1.50 4.00
3 Tim Brown 3.00 8.00
4 Jim Everett .75 2.00
5 Brett Favre 15.00 40.00
6 Junior Seau 3.00 8.00
7 Greg Lloyd 1.50 4.00
8 Cris Carter 3.00 8.00
9 Emmitt Smith 12.50 30.00
10 Dan Marino 15.00 40.00
11 Jeff Blake 3.00 8.00
12 Darrell Green 1.50 4.00
13 John Elway 15.00 40.00
14 Marcus Allen 3.00 8.00
15 Steve Young 6.00 15.00
16 Drew Bledsoe 5.00 12.00

2011 Topps Legends

COMPLETE SET (165) 20.00 40.00
1 Joe Namath .30 .75
2 Junior Seau .20 .50
3 Vincent Brown RC .30 .75
4 Ray Rice .15 .40
5 Matt Ryan .20 .50
6 Roddy White .15 .40
7 Miles Austin .15 .40
8 Delone Carter RC .30 .75
9 Howie Long .25 .60
10 Roger Staubach .30 .75
11 Brian Urlacher .25 .60
12 Darrelle Revis .15 .40
13 Santana Moss .20 .50
14 Mikel Leshoure RC .30 .75
15 Jon Baldwin RC .30 .75
16 Niles Paul RC .30 .75
17 Felix Jones .15 .40
18 Matt Schaub .15 .40
19 Kurt Warner .20 .50
20 Marcus Allen .25 .60
21 Shane Vereen RC .40 1.00
22 Cecil Shorts RC .30 .75
23 Phil Simms .20 .50
24 Antonio Gates .15 .40
25 Jerrel Jernigan RC .30 .75
26 Champ Bailey .20 .50
27 Mark Sanchez .15 .40
28 Blaine Gabbert RC .30 .75
29 Jeremy Kerley RC .50 1.25
30 John Elway .40 1.00
31 Stevan Ridley RC .30 .75
32 Ndamukong Suh .20 .50
33 Drew Brees .25 .60
34 Ronald Johnson RC .30 .75
35 Virgil Green RC .30 .75
36 Hakeem Nicks .15 .40
37 Richard Dent .15 .40
38 Torrey Smith RC .30 .75
39 Tony Romo .20 .50
40 Franco Harris .25 .60
41 Christian Ponder RC .30 .75
42 Andy Dalton RC .60 1.50
43 Matt Cassel .15 .40
44 Dwayne Bowe .20 .50
45 Mark Ingram RC .50 1.25
46 Bilal Powell RC .40 1.00
47 Jamaal Charles .20 .50
48 Greg Little RC .40 1.00
49 Luke Stocker RC .30 .75
50 Joe Montana .60 1.50
51 Len Dawson .25 .60
52 Andre Johnson .20 .50
53 Reggie Wayne .20 .50
54 Charles Woodson .25 .60
55 Eli Manning .20 .50
56 Marcell Dareus RC .30 .75
57 Maurice Jones-Drew .15 .40
58 Wes Welker .20 .50
59 Sam Bradford .15 .40
60 Terry Bradshaw .30 .75
61 Leonard Hankerson RC .30 .75
62 Anquan Boldin .15 .40
63 Ryan Mallett RC .30 .75
64 Ryan Williams RC .30 .75
65 Troy Polamalu .25 .60
66 Kendall Hunter RC .30 .75
67 Julio Jones RC 1.00 2.50
68 LeGarrette Blount .20 .50
69 Julius Peppers .20 .50
70 Eric Dickerson .20 .50
71 Ahmad Bradshaw .15 .40
72 Ronnie Lott .20 .50
73 Da'Quan Bowers RC .30 .75
74 Edmond Gates RC .30 .75
75 Cam Newton RC 3.00 8.00
76 Fred Jackson .15 .40
77 Aldon Smith RC .30 .75
78 LaDainian Tomlinson .25 .60
79 Tandon Doss RC .30 .75
80 Jim Brown .30 .75
81 Jamie Harper RC .30 .75
82 A.J. Green RC .75 2.00
83 Michael Vick .20 .50
84 Chad Ochocinco .15 .40
85 Hines Ward .20 .50
86 Randall Cobb RC .50 1.25
87 Tim Tebow .25 .60
88 Chris Johnson .15 .40
89 Ed Reed .20 .50
90 Troy Aikman .30 .75
91 Nick Fairley RC .30 .75
92 Prince Amukamara RC .30 .75
93 Patrick Peterson RC .60 1.50
94 DeSean Jackson .20 .50
95 DeMarco Murray RC .60 1.50
96 Michael Turner .15 .40
97 Titus Young RC .30 .75
98 Daniel Thomas RC .30 .75
99 Kellen Winslow .15 .40
100 Dan Marino .50 1.25
101 Steve Young .30 .75
102 Matt Forte .15 .40
103 LeSean McCoy .25 .60
104 Dion Lewis RC .40 1.00
105 Mike Williams .20 .50
106 Thomas Jones .15 .40
107 Jacquizz Rodgers RC .30 .75
108 Aaron Rodgers .40 1.00
109 Mike Wallace .15 .40
110 Emmitt Smith .40 1.00
111 Arian Foster .15 .40
112 Josh Freeman .20 .50
113 Dwight Freeney .15 .40
114 Joe Flacco .20 .50
115 Tom Brady .60 1.50
116 Vernon Davis .15 .40
117 Kyle Rudolph RC .30 .75
118 Art Monk .25 .60
119 J.J. Watt RC 1.50 4.00
120 Bart Starr .40 1.00
121 Peyton Hillis .15 .40
122 Tony Gonzalez .20 .50
123 Jermichael Finley .15 .40
124 Marques Colston .15 .40
125 Jonathan Stewart .15 .40
126 Jim Plunkett .20 .50
127 Ray Lewis .25 .60
128 Steve Smith .20 .50
129 Austin Pettis RC .30 .75
130 Earl Campbell .25 .60
131 Calvin Johnson .25 .60
132 Steven Jackson .15 .40
133 Ben Roethlisberger .25 .60
134 Marshawn Lynch .20 .50
135 Ricky Stanzi RC .30 .75
136 Darren McFadden .15 .40
137 Jordan Todman RC .30 .75
138 Philip Rivers .25 .60
139 Adrian Peterson .25 .60
140 Tony Dorsett .25 .60
141 Jerome Bettis .25 .60
142 Larry Fitzgerald .20 .50
143 Steve Johnson .15 .40
144 Alex Green RC .30 .75
145 Tim Brown .25 .60
146 Frank Gore .20 .50
147 Percy Harvin .15 .40
148 Matt Hasselbeck .15 .40
149 Peyton Manning .50 1.25
150 Jerry Rice .40 1.00
151 Brandon Lloyd .15 .40
152 Von Miller RC .50 1.25
153 Santonio Holmes .15 .40
154 Brandon Marshall .20 .50
155 David Garrard .15 .40
156 Rashard Mendenhall .15 .40
157 Taiwan Jones RC .30 .75
158 Jimmy Smith RC .30 .75
159 Rob Housler RC .30 .75
160 Gale Sayers .25 .60
161 Jake Locker RC .30 .75
162 Colin Kaepernick RC .50 1.25
163 Patrick Willis .20 .50
164 Greg Salas RC .30 .75
165 Y.A. Tittle .25 .60

2011 Topps Legends Blue

*BLUE: .8X TO 2X BASIC CARDS
ONE PER PACK

2011 Topps Legends Bronze

*BRONZE/299: 2.5X TO 6X BASIC CARDS
BRONZE/299 ODDS 1:16 H, 1:22 R

2011 Topps Legends Gold

*GOLD/99: 4X TO 10X BASIC CARDS
GOLD/99 ODDS 1:49H, 1:65R

2011 Topps Legends Green

*GREEN/150: 3X TO 8X BASIC CARDS
GREEN/150 ODDS 1:32H, 1:44R

2011 Topps Legends Orange

*ORANGE/50: 6X TO 15X BASIC CARDS
ORANGE/50 ODDS 1:97H, 1;127R

2011 Topps Legends Purple

*PURPLE/10: 12X TO 30X BASIC CARDS
PURPLE PRINT RUN 10 SER.#'d SETS

2011 Topps Legends Red

*RED/75: 5X TO 12X BASIC CARDS
RED/75 ODDS 1:65H, 1:86R

2011 Topps Legends Aspiring Legacies

STATED ODDS 1:5 HOB/RET
ALAD Andy Dalton .60 1.50
ALAJG A.J. Green .75 2.00
ALAG Alex Green .30 .75
ALAP Austin Pettis .30 .75
ALBG Blaine Gabbert .30 .75
ALBP Bilal Powell .40 1.00
ALCK Colin Kaepernick .50 1.25
ALCN Cam Newton 1.50 4.00
ALCP Christian Ponder .30 .75
ALDC Delone Carter .30 .75
ALDM DeMarco Murray .60 1.50
ALDT Daniel Thomas .30 .75
ALEG Edmond Gates .30 .75
ALGL Greg Little .40 1.00
ALJB Jon Baldwin .30 .75
ALJH Jamie Harper .30 .75
ALJJ Julio Jones 1.00 2.50
ALJJE Jerrel Jernigan .30 .75
ALJL Jake Locker .30 .75
ALJT Jordan Todman .30 .75
ALKH Kendall Hunter .30 .75
ALKR Kyle Rudolph .30 .75
ALLH Leonard Hankerson .30 .75
ALMD Marcell Dareus .30 .75
ALMI Mark Ingram .50 1.25
ALML Mikel Leshoure .30 .75
ALRC Randall Cobb .50 1.25
ALRM Ryan Mallett .30 .75
ALRW Ryan Williams .30 .75
ALSR Stevan Ridley .30 .75
ALSV Shane Vereen .40 1.00
ALTJ Taiwan Jones .30 .75
ALTS Torrey Smith .30 .75
ALTY Titus Young .30 .75
ALVB Vincent Brown .30 .75
ALVM Von Miller .50 1.25

2011 Topps Legends Aspiring Legacies Jerseys

STATED ODDS 1:110 RET
*GOLD/50: .6X TO 1.5X BASIC JSY
*GREEN/150: .5X TO 1.2X BASIC JSY
*JUMBO/99: .6X TO 1.5X BASIC JSY
*RED/99: .5X TO 1.2X BASIC JSY
ALRAD Andy Dalton 2.50 6.00
ALRAG Alex Green 1.25 3.00
ALRAJG A.J. Green 3.00 8.00
ALRAP Austin Pettis 1.25 3.00
ALRBG Blaine Gabbert 1.25 3.00
ALRBP Bilal Powell 2.00 5.00
ALRCK Colin Kaepernick 2.00 5.00
ALRCN Cam Newton 6.00 15.00
ALRCP Christian Ponder 1.25 3.00
ALRDC Delone Carter 1.25 3.00
ALRDM DeMarco Murray 2.50 6.00
ALRDT Daniel Thomas 1.25 3.00
ALREG Edmond Gates 1.25 3.00
ALRGL Greg Little 2.00 5.00
ALRJB Jon Baldwin 1.25 3.00
ALRJH Jamie Harper 1.25 3.00
ALRJJ Julio Jones 4.00 10.00
ALRJJE Jerrel Jernigan 1.25 3.00
ALRJL Jake Locker 1.25 3.00
ALRJT Jordan Todman 1.25 3.00
ALRKH Kendall Hunter 1.25 3.00
ALRKR Kyle Rudolph 1.25 3.00
ALRLH Leonard Hankerson 1.25 3.00
ALRMD Marcell Dareus 1.25 3.00
ALRMI Mark Ingram 2.00 5.00
ALRML Mikel Leshoure 1.25 3.00
ALRRC Randall Cobb 2.00 5.00
ALRRM Ryan Mallett 1.25 3.00
ALRRW Ryan Williams 1.50 4.00
ALRSR Stevan Ridley 1.25 3.00
ALRSV Shane Vereen 1.50 4.00
ALRTJ Taiwan Jones 1.25 3.00
ALRTS Torrey Smith 1.25 3.00
ALRTY Titus Young 1.25 3.00
ALRVB Vincent Brown 1.25 3.00
ALRVM Von Miller 2.00 5.00

2011 Topps Legends Autographed Relics

JSY AU/25 ODDS 1:1065H, 1:3200R
EXCH EXPIRATION: 9/30/2014
AM Art Monk 50.00 100.00
EC Earl Campbell 25.00 50.00
ED Eric Dickerson 30.00 60.00
FH Franco Harris 30.00 60.00
GS Gale Sayers 30.00 60.00
HL Howie Long 30.00 60.00
JS Junior Seau 40.00 80.00
KS Ken Stabler 40.00 80.00
KW Kurt Warner 30.00 60.00
RL Ronnie Lott 25.00 50.00
SY Steve Young 40.00 80.00
TB Tim Brown 30.00 60.00
TBR Terry Bradshaw 50.00 100.00
TD Tony Dorsett 25.00 50.00
TT Thurman Thomas 20.00 40.00

2011 Topps Legends Autographs

STATED ODDS 1:1605 HOB, 1:4750 RET
EXCH EXPIRATION: 9/30/2014
LAAM Art Monk 40.00 80.00
LACH Chuck Howley
LAEC Earl Campbell 20.00 40.00
LAED Eric Dickerson 40.00 80.00
LAFB Fred Biletnikoff
LAFH Franco Harris 30.00 60.00
LAGS Gale Sayers 25.00 50.00
LAHL Howie Long 20.00 40.00
LAJB Jerome Bettis 40.00 80.00
LAJP Jim Plunkett
LAJS Junior Seau 25.00 50.00
LAKS Ken Stabler
LAKW Kurt Warner EXCH 25.00 50.00
LALB Larry Brown
LALD Len Dawson 25.00 50.00
LAMA Marcus Allen
LAOA Ottis Anderson EXCH 25.00 50.00
LAPS Phil Simms 15.00 30.00
LARD Richard Dent
LARL Ronnie Lott 15.00 30.00
LASY Steve Young 30.00 60.00
LATB Tim Brown 25.00 50.00
LATD Tony Dorsett
LATT Thurman Thomas
LAYT Y.A. Tittle 15.00 30.00

2011 Topps Legends Canton Hopefuls Autographs

STATED ODDS 1:2000H, 1:6000R
EXCH EXPIRATION: 9/30/2014
CHAAG Antonio Gates 8.00 20.00
CHAAJ Andre Johnson 15.00 30.00
CHAAP Adrian Peterson 40.00 80.00
CHACB Champ Bailey
CHADM Darren McFadden
CHAHN Hakeem Nicks
CHAHW Hines Ward 30.00 60.00
CHAJC Jamaal Charles
CHAKW Kellen Winslow 15.00 30.00
CHAMJ Maurice Jones-Drew
CHAMT Michael Turner 15.00 30.00
CHAPM Peyton Manning 60.00 120.00
CHAPW Patrick Willis 20.00 40.00
CHARL Ray Lewis
CHARW Reggie Wayne 15.00 30.00
CHASH Santonio Holmes
CHASJ Steven Jackson 15.00 30.00
CHASM Santana Moss
CHATJ Thomas Jones
CHATR Tony Romo 30.00 60.00

2011 Topps Legends Canton Hopefuls Autographed Relics

JSY AU/25 ODDS 1:1602H, 1:4750R
EXCH EXPIRATION: 9/30/2014
AG Antonio Gates 20.00 40.00
AJ Andre Johnson 20.00 40.00
DM Darren McFadden
HW Hines Ward 50.00 100.00
JC Jamaal Charles 12.00 30.00
MT Michael Turner 12.00 30.00
PM Peyton Manning 75.00 150.00
PW Patrick Willis 15.00 40.00
RL Ray Lewis 60.00 120.00
RW Reggie Wayne 20.00 40.00
TJ Thomas Jones 12.00 30.00

2011 Topps Legends Combo

STATED ODDS 1:10 HOB/RET
LCAC J.Addai/D.Carter .60 1.50
LCAM M.Allen/D.McFadden 1.50 4.00
LCBM T.Brady/R.Mallet 2.50 6.00
LCCG R.Cobb/A.Green .60 1.50
LCCJ E.Campbell/C.Johnson 1.00 2.50
LCGD A.Green/A.Dalton 1.00 2.50
LCGG D.Garrard/B.Gabbert .40 1.00
LCGJ A.Green/J.Jones 1.25 3.00
LCGN B.Gabbert/C.Newton 2.50 6.00
LCGT E.Gates/D.Thomas .40 1.00
LCID M.Ingram/M.Dareus .60 1.50
LCIJ M.Ingram/J.Jones 1.25 3.00
LCJP J.Jernigan/B.Powell .50 1.25
LCJY C.Johnson/T.Young .60 1.50
LCKH C.Kaepernick/K.Hunter .60 1.50
LCLH J.Locker/J.Harper .40 1.00
LCLY M.Leshoure/T.Young .40 1.00
LCMR J.Montana/J.Rice 2.50 6.00
LCPP A.Peterson/C.Ponder 1.50 5.00
LCRF A.Rodgers/B.Favre 2.50 6.00
LCRP K.Rudolph/C.Ponder .40 1.00
LCTB J.Todman/V.Brown .40 1.00
LCVR S.Vereen/S.Ridley .50 1.25
LCWB K.Warner/S.Bradford .75 2.00
LCYP T.Young/A.Pettis .40 1.00

2011 Topps Legends Combo Relics

STATED PRINT RUN 25 SER.#'d SETS
AC J.Addai/D.Carter 4.00 10.00
AM M.Allen/D.McFadden 8.00 20.00
BM T.Brady/R.Mallet 15.00 40.00
CG R.Cobb/A.Green 4.00 10.00
CJ E.Campbell/C.Johnson 10.00 25.00
GD A.Green/A.Dalton 6.00 15.00
GG D.Garrard/B.Gabbert 2.50 6.00
GJ A.Green/J.Jones 12.00 30.00
GN B.Gabbert/C.Newton 12.00 30.00
GT E.Gates/D.Thomas 2.50 6.00
ID M.Ingram/M.Dareus 4.00 10.00
IJ M.Ingram/J.Jones 8.00 20.00
JP J.Jernigan/B.Powell 3.00 8.00
JY C.Johnson/T.Young 6.00 15.00
KH C.Kaepernick/K.Hunter 4.00 10.00
LH J.Locker/J.Harper 2.50 6.00
LY M.Leshoure/T.Young 2.50 6.00
MR J.Montana/J.Rice 25.00 60.00
PP A.Peterson/C.Ponder 6.00 15.00
RF A.Rodgers/B.Favre 40.00 80.00
RP K.Rudolph/C.Ponder 2.50 6.00
TB J.Todman/V.Brown 4.00 10.00
VR S.Vereen/S.Ridley 3.00 8.00
WB K.Warner/S.Bradford 30.00 60.00
YP T.Young/A.Pettis 2.50 6.00

2011 Topps Legends Dual Autographs

DUAL AU/25 ODDS 1:1885H, 1:3400R
EXCH EXPRATION: 9/30/2014
AM M.Allen/McFadden 50.00 100.00
BT V.Brown/J.Todman 12.00 30.00
CG R.Cobb/A.Green 12.00 30.00
CH E.Campbell/J.Harper
JC T.Jones/D.Carter
JH T.Jones/K.Hunter 15.00 40.00
MM A.Monk/S.Moss 40.00 80.00
PR B.Powell/S.Ridley 15.00 40.00
TG D.Thomas/E.Gates 12.00 30.00
WB Warner/Bradford 30.00 60.00
YK S.Young/Kaepernick 160.00 300.00

2011 Topps Legends Future Legends Autographs

STATED ODDS 1:1275H, 1:4000R
EXCH EXPIRATION: 9/30/2014
FLAAD Andy Dalton 15.00 40.00
FLAAJG A.J. Green 25.00 50.00
FLAAG Alex Green EXCH 5.00 12.00
FLAAP Austin Pettis
FLABG Blaine Gabbert 5.00 12.00
FLABP Bilal Powell
FLACK Colin Kaepernick 8.00 20.00
FLACN Cam Newton 75.00 150.00
FLACP Christian Ponder 10.00 25.00
FLADC Delone Carter
FLADM DeMarco Murray 10.00 25.00
FLADT Daniel Thomas
FLAEG Edmond Gates
FLAGL Greg Little 6.00 15.00
FLAJB Jon Baldwin
FLAJH Jamie Harper 5.00 12.00
FLAJJE Jerrel Jernigan
FLAJJ Julio Jones
FLAJL Jake Locker 5.00 12.00
FLAJT Jordan Todman
FLAKH Kendall Hunter
FLAKR Kyle Rudolph 5.00 12.00
FLALH Leonard Hankerson
FLAMD Marcell Dareus
FLAMI Mark Ingram
FLAML Mikel Leshoure
FLARC Randall Cobb 8.00 20.00
FLARM Ryan Mallett 5.00 12.00
FLARW Ryan Williams
FLASR Stevan Ridley 5.00 12.00
FLASV Shane Vereen 6.00 15.00
FLATJ Taiwan Jones
FLATS Torrey Smith 5.00 12.00
FLATY Titus Young
FLAVB Vincent Brown 5.00 12.00
FLAVM Von Miller 12.00 30.00

2011 Topps Legends Future Legends Autographed Relics

JSY AU/25 ODDS 1:600H, 1:3650R
EXCH EXPIRATION: 9/30/2014
AG Alex Green 8.00 20.00
AJG A.J. Green 30.00 80.00
AP Austin Pettis 8.00 20.00
BG Blaine Gabbert 8.00 20.00
BP Bilal Powell
CN Cam Newton 75.00 150.00
DC Delone Carter
DM DeMarco Murray 15.00 40.00
DT Daniel Thomas 8.00 20.00
EG Edmond Gates
GL Greg Little 10.00 25.00
JH Jamie Harper
JJ Julio Jones 50.00 100.00
JJE Jerrel Jernigan
JL Jake Locker 8.00 20.00
JT Jordan Todman
KH Kendall Hunter 8.00 20.00
KR Kyle Rudolph EXCH 8.00 20.00
LH Leonard Hankerson
MD Marcell Dareus
ML Mikel Leshoure
RC Randall Cobb 12.00 30.00
SR Stevan Ridley 8.00 20.00
SV Shane Vereen 10.00 25.00
TJ Taiwan Jones
TS Torrey Smith 8.00 20.00
TY Titus Young
VB Vincent Brown
VM Von Miller 20.00 50.00

2011 Topps Legends Gridiron Legacies

STATED ODDS 1:4 HOB/RET
GLAM Art Monk .60 1.50
GLBF Brett Favre 1.25 3.00
GLCC Chris Cooley .40 1.00
GLCJ Chris Johnson .40 1.00
GLDB Drew Brees .60 1.50
GLDM Dan Marino 1.25 3.00
GLES Emmitt Smith 1.00 2.50
GLJE John Elway 1.00 2.50
GLJM Joe Montana 1.50 4.00
GLJN Joe Namath .75 2.00
GLJR Jerry Rice 1.00 2.50
GLKS Ken Stabler .60 1.50
GLLF Larry Fitzgerald .50 1.25
GLLT LaDainian Tomlinson .60 1.50
GLMA Marcus Allen .60 1.50
GLMF Matt Forte .40 1.00
GLMR Matt Ryan .50 1.25
GLMV Michael Vick .50 1.25
GLRS Roger Staubach .75 2.00
GLTA Troy Aikman .75 2.00
GLTB Terry Bradshaw .75 2.00
GLTBR Tim Brown .60 1.50
GLTG Tony Gonzalez .50 1.25
GLTOB Tom Brady 1.50 4.00
GLWW Wes Welker .50 1.25

2011 Topps Legends Gridiron Legacies Relics

STATED PRINT RUN 150 SER.#'d SETS
*OVERSIZE/15: 1X TO 2.5X BASIC JSY/150
GLRAM Art Monk 6.00 15.00
GLRBF Brett Favre 10.00 25.00
GLRCC Chris Cooley 4.00 10.00
GLRDB Drew Brees 4.00 10.00
GLRDM Dan Marino 10.00 25.00
GLRES Emmitt Smith 8.00 20.00
GLRJE John Elway 8.00 20.00
GLRJM Joe Montana 12.00 30.00
GLRKS Ken Stabler 6.00 15.00
GLRLF Larry Fitzgerald 3.00 8.00
GLRLT LaDainian Tomlinson 4.00 10.00
GLRMA Marcus Allen 5.00 12.00
GLRMF Matt Forte 2.50 6.00
GLRMR Matt Ryan 3.00 8.00
GLRMV Michael Vick 3.00 8.00
GLRRS Roger Staubach 6.00 15.00
GLRTA Troy Aikman 6.00 15.00
GLRTB Tim Brown 5.00 12.00
GLRTG Tony Gonzalez 3.00 8.00
GLRWW Wes Welker 3.00 8.00

2011 Topps Legends Reprint Autographs

RANDOM INSERTS IN HOBBY PACKS
EXCH EXPIRATION: 9/30/2014
36 Art Donovan 12.00 30.00
60 Lenny Moore 12.00 30.00
81 Fred Morrison 12.00 30.00
86 Y.A. Tittle 30.00 60.00
105 Mike McCormack 12.00 30.00

2011 Topps Legends Rookie Autographs

*BASE AUTO: .3X TO .8X BRONZE/99
GROUP A ODDS 1:253 H, 1:1307 R
GROUP B ODDS 1:79 H, 1:363 R
GROUP C ODDS 1:44 H, 1:238 R
RACN Cam Newton A 75.00 150.00

2011 Topps Legends Rookie Autographs Bronze

STATED PRINT RUN 99 SER.#'d SETS
RAAC Anthony Castonzo 3.00 8.00
RAAS Aldon Smith 3.00 8.00
RADB Da'Quan Bowers 3.00 8.00
RADE Darren Evans 4.00 10.00
RADH Dwayne Harris 3.00 8.00
RADL Derrick Locke 4.00 10.00
RADLE Dion Lewis 4.00 10.00
RADS Da'Rel Scott 3.00 8.00
RADT Daniel Thomas 3.00 8.00

RADW D.J. Williams	3.00	8.00
RAGL Greg Little	4.00	10.00
RAGS Greg Salas	3.00	8.00
RAJB Jon Baldwin	3.00	8.00
RAJH Jamie Harper	6.00	15.00
RAJHO Justin Houston	4.00	10.00
RAJJE Jerrel Jernigan	3.00	8.00
RAJK Jeremy Kerley	6.00	15.00
RAJR Jacquizz Rodgers	3.00	8.00
RAJW J.J. Watt	60.00	100.00
RALH Leonard Hankerson	3.00	8.00
RALS Luke Stocker	3.00	8.00
RAMH Mark Herzlich	3.00	8.00
RAMM Mike McNeill	6.00	15.00
RAMP Mike Pouncey	5.00	12.00
RANF Nick Fairley	3.00	8.00
RARH Robert Housler	3.00	8.00
RARJ Ronald Johnson	3.00	8.00
RARMO Rahim Moore	3.00	8.00
RARS Ricky Stanzi	3.00	8.00
RARW Ryan Williams	8.00	20.00
RASR Stevan Ridley	3.00	8.00
RASV Shane Vereen	4.00	10.00
RATS Torrey Smith	3.00	8.00
RATT Terrence Toliver	4.00	10.00
RATTA Tyrod Taylor	6.00	15.00
RAVG Virgil Green	3.00	8.00
RAVM Von Miller	8.00	20.00

2011 Topps Legends Rookie Autographs Red

*RED/50: .5X TO 1.2X BRONZE/99
RED PRINT RUN 50 SER.#'d SETS

RAAD Andy Dalton	12.00	30.00
RAAG Alex Green	10.00	25.00
RAAJG A.J. Green	40.00	80.00
RABG Blaine Gabbert	4.00	10.00
RACK Colin Kaepernick	6.00	15.00
RACP Christian Ponder	10.00	25.00
RAJJ Julio Jones	30.00	60.00
RAMI Mark Ingram	6.00	15.00
RARC Randall Cobb	6.00	15.00
RARM Ryan Mallett	4.00	10.00
RATS Torrey Smith	4.00	10.00

2011 Topps Legends Stamp of Approval Relics

STATED ODDS 1:580 H, 1:650 R

AP Austin Pettis	3.00	8.00
CH Chad Henne	6.00	15.00
CN Cam Newton	25.00	50.00
DB Dwayne Bowe	6.00	15.00
DC Delone Carter	3.00	8.00
EC Earl Campbell	15.00	30.00
EG Edmond Gates	3.00	8.00
JA Joseph Addai	5.00	12.00
JF Joe Flacco	6.00	15.00
JH Jamie Harper	3.00	8.00
JK Johnny Knox	5.00	12.00
JM Jeremy Maclin	5.00	12.00
JN Jordy Nelson	6.00	15.00
JT Jordan Todman	3.00	8.00
KH Kendall Hunter	3.00	8.00
LL LaRon Landry	5.00	12.00
MC Matt Cassel	5.00	12.00
TB Tim Brown	8.00	20.00
TJ Taiwan Jones	3.00	8.00
VB Vincent Brown	3.00	8.00

2011 Topps Legends Triple Autographs

STATED PRINT RUN 15 SER.#'d SETS

TAHBM F.Hris/Bettis/Mndnhl	100.00	175.00
TAHMM Hnkrsn/Monk/S.Moss	60.00	120.00
TAJAM T.Jnes/M.Aln/McFdn	60.00	120.00
TALYF Leshre/Young/Fairley	15.00	40.00
TAMVR Mallett/Vreen/Ridley	30.00	60.00

2008 Topps Letterman

This set was released on November 28, 2008. The base set consists of 100 cards. Cards 1-50 feature veterans serial numbered of 949, and cards 51-100 are rookies serial numbered of 419.

VETERAN PRINT RUN 949 SER.#'d SETS
ROOKIE PRINT RUN 419 SER.#'d SETS

1 Drew Brees	1.00	2.50
2 Tom Brady	3.00	8.00
3 Peyton Manning	2.50	6.00
4 Carson Palmer	.75	2.00
5 Ben Roethlisberger	1.00	2.50
6 Eli Manning	.75	2.00
7 Tony Romo	.75	2.00
8 Vince Young	.60	1.50
9 Matt Hasselbeck	.60	1.50
10 Derek Anderson	.60	1.50
11 Jay Cutler	.60	1.50
12 Philip Rivers	1.00	2.50
13 Steven Jackson	.60	1.50
14 Willie Parker	.75	2.00
15 Clinton Portis	.60	1.50
16 Adrian Peterson	1.00	2.50
17 LaDainian Tomlinson	1.00	2.50
18 Marion Barber	.60	1.50
19 Brian Westbrook	.60	1.50
20 Fred Taylor	.60	1.50
21 Marshawn Lynch	.75	2.00
22 Joseph Addai	.60	1.50
23 Willis McGahee	.60	1.50
24 Frank Gore	.75	2.00
25 Larry Johnson	.60	1.50
26 Brandon Jacobs	.60	1.50
27 Ryan Grant	.75	2.00
28 Chester Taylor	.60	1.50
29 Laurence Maroney	.75	2.00
30 Thomas Jones	.60	1.50
31 Chad Johnson	.60	1.50
32 Reggie Wayne	.75	2.00
33 Anquan Boldin	.60	1.50
34 Randy Moss	.75	2.00
35 Plaxico Burress	.60	1.50
36 Terrell Owens	.75	2.00
37 Andre Johnson	.75	2.00
38 Larry Fitzgerald	.75	2.00
39 Braylon Edwards	.60	1.50
40 Steve Smith	.75	2.00
41 T.J. Houshmandzadeh	.60	1.50
42 Torry Holt	.75	2.00
43 Brandon Marshall	.75	2.00
44 Wes Welker	.75	2.00
45 Dwayne Bowe	.75	2.00
46 Terry Bradshaw	1.50	4.00
47 Brett Favre	6.00	15.00
48 John Elway	2.00	5.00
49 Lawrence Taylor	1.25	3.00
50 Joe Namath	1.50	4.00
51 Matt Ryan RC	3.00	8.00
52 Brian Brohm RC	1.00	2.50
53 Chad Henne RC	1.25	3.00
54 Joe Flacco RC	2.00	5.00
55 Andre Woodson RC	1.00	2.50
56 John David Booty RC	1.00	2.50
57 Josh Johnson RC	1.00	2.50
58 Colt Brennan RC	1.25	3.00
59 Dennis Dixon RC	1.00	2.50
60 Erik Ainge RC	1.00	2.50
61 Kevin O'Connell RC	1.00	2.50
62 Darren McFadden RC	1.00	2.50
63 Rashard Mendenhall RC	1.00	2.50
64 Jonathan Stewart RC	1.50	4.00
65 Felix Jones RC	1.00	2.50
66 Jamaal Charles RC	1.50	4.00
67 Ray Rice RC	1.00	2.50
68 Chris Johnson RC	1.25	3.00
69 Mike Hart RC	1.00	2.50
70 Matt Forte RC	1.50	4.00
71 Kevin Smith RC	1.00	2.50
72 Steve Slaton RC	1.00	2.50
73 Malcolm Kelly RC	1.00	2.50
74 Limas Sweed RC	1.00	2.50
75 DeSean Jackson RC	2.00	5.00
76 James Hardy RC	1.00	2.50
77 Mario Manningham RC	1.00	2.50
78 Devin Thomas RC	1.00	2.50
79 Early Doucet RC	1.00	2.50
80 Andre Caldwell RC	1.00	2.50
81 Jordy Nelson RC	3.00	8.00
82 Eddie Royal RC	1.00	2.50
83 Earl Bennett RC	1.50	4.00
84 Donnie Avery RC	1.25	3.00
85 Dexter Jackson RC	1.50	4.00
86 Jerome Simpson RC	1.25	3.00
87 Harry Douglas RC	1.25	3.00
88 Keenan Burton RC	1.00	2.50
89 Marcus Smith RC	1.25	3.00
90 Dustin Keller RC	1.25	3.00
91 John Carlson RC	1.00	2.50
92 Jake Long RC	1.50	4.00
93 Chris Long RC	1.25	3.00
94 Vernon Gholston RC	1.00	2.50
95 Glenn Dorsey RC	1.00	2.50
96 Sedrick Ellis RC	1.00	2.50
97 Keith Rivers RC	1.00	2.50
98 Leodis McKelvin RC	1.25	3.00
99 D.Rodgers-Cromartie RC	1.25	3.00
100 Aqib Talib RC	1.50	4.00

2008 Topps Letterman Refractors

*VETS 1-45: 1.5X TO 4X BASIC CARDS
*LEGENDS 46-50: 1.2X TO 3X BASIC CARDS
*ROOKIES 51-100: .8X TO 2X BASIC CARDS
STATED PRINT RUN 99 SER.#'d SETS

47 Brett Favre	8.00	20.00

2008 Topps Letterman Xfractors

*VETS 1-45: 3X TO 8X BASIC CARDS
*LEGENDS 46-50: 2X TO 5X BASIC CARDS
*ROOKIES 51-100: 1.2X TO 3X BASIC CARDS
STATED PRINT RUN 25 SER.#'d SETS

47 Brett Favre	12.00	30.00

2008 Topps Letterman Authentic Relics Quad Autographs

BASE AUTO PRINT RUN 25-75
*REFRACTOR/15: .5X TO 1.2X BASE AU/75
REFRACTOR PRINT RUN 5-15
UNPRICED XFRACTOR AU PRINT RUN 3-5
UNPRICED SPRFRCTR AU PRINT RUN 1

AQRAC Andre Caldwell/75	6.00	15.00
AQRAG Anthony Gonzalez/25	10.00	25.00
AQRBE Braylon Edwards/25	10.00	25.00
AQRBM Brandon Marshall/25	12.00	30.00
AQRDA Donnie Avery/75	8.00	20.00
AQRDB Dwayne Bowe/25	12.00	30.00
AQRDH David Harris/75	8.00	20.00
AQREB Earl Bennett/75	10.00	25.00
AQRER Eddie Royal/75	6.00	15.00
AQRGD Glenn Dorsey/75 EXCH	6.00	15.00
AQRHD Harry Douglas/75	8.00	20.00
AQRJB John David Booty/75	6.00	15.00
AQRJC Jamaal Charles/75	10.00	25.00
AQRJL Jake Long/75	10.00	25.00
AQRJS Jerome Simpson/75	8.00	20.00
AQRMB Marion Barber/25	10.00	25.00
AQRMC Marques Colston/25	10.00	25.00
AQRMF Matt Forte/75	15.00	40.00
AQRML Marshawn Lynch/25	12.00	30.00
AQRRR Ray Rice/75	6.00	15.00
AQRSJ Steven Jackson/25	10.00	25.00
AQRSS Steve Slaton/75	6.00	15.00
AQRWW Wes Welker/25	30.00	60.00

2008 Topps Letterman Authentic Relics Quad Patch

UNPRICED QUAD PRINT RUN 10
UNPRICED REFRACTOR PRINT RUN 5
UNPRICED XFRACTOR PRINT RUN 3
UNPRICED SUPERFRACT PRINT RUN 1

2008 Topps Letterman Booklet Autographs

BASE AUTO PRINT RUN 15-46
UNPRICED REFRCTR PRINT RUN 10
UNPRICED XFRACTOR PRINT RUN 3
UNPRICED SUPERFRCTR PRINT RUN 1

ALBBE Braylon Edwards/46	20.00	50.00
ALBCB Colt Brennan/46	15.00	40.00
ALBCH Chad Henne/46	15.00	40.00
ALBDB Dwayne Bowe/46	25.00	60.00
ALBDD Dennis Dixon/46	25.00	60.00
ALBES Emmitt Smith/15	150.00	300.00
ALBFB Brett Favre/15	150.00	300.00
ALBFJ Felix Jones/46	12.00	30.00
ALBJA Joseph Addai/46	20.00	50.00
ALBJE John Elway/15	150.00	300.00
ALBJF Joe Flacco/46	40.00	80.00
ALBJH James Hardy/46	20.00	50.00
ALBJL Jake Long/46	20.00	50.00
ALBJM Joe Montana/15	200.00	400.00
ALBJN Joe Namath/15	125.00	200.00
ALBLS Limas Sweed/46	12.00	30.00
ALBLT Lawrence Taylor/15	60.00	120.00
ALBMB Marion Barber/46	30.00	80.00
ALBMF Matt Forte/46	20.00	50.00
ALBMR Matt Ryan/15	150.00	300.00
ALBPM Peyton Manning/15	150.00	250.00
ALBRR Ray Rice/15	15.00	40.00
ALBSJ Steven Jackson/46	25.00	60.00
ALBTBR Tom Brady/15	175.00	300.00

2008 Topps Letterman Patches

SER.#'d TO 9, TOTAL PRINT RUNS 36-126
*REFRACT/6: .5X TO 1.2X BASIC INSERT/9
REF.#'d TO 6, TOTAL PRINT RUNS 24-84
*XFRACT/3: .6X TO 1.5X BASIC INSERT/9
XFR.#'d TO 3, TOTAL PRINT RUNS 12-42
UNPRICED SUPR 1/1 TTL PRINT RUNS 4-14

LPAB Anquan Boldin/54*	6.00	15.00
LPAC Andre Caldwell/72*	4.00	10.00
LPAT Aqib Talib/45*	6.00	15.00
LPAW Andre Woodson/63*	4.00	10.00
LPBB Brian Brohm/45*	4.00	10.00
LPBR Ben Roethlisberger/126*	10.00	25.00
LPBS Barry Sanders/63*	20.00	50.00
LPBW Brian Westbrook/81*	6.00	15.00
LPCB Colt Brennan/63*	5.00	12.00
LPCL Chris Long/36*	5.00	12.00
LPCP Carson Palmer/54*	8.00	20.00
LPCW Chauncey Washington/90*	5.00	12.00
LPDA Donnie Avery/45*	5.00	12.00
LPDJ DeSean Jackson/63*	8.00	20.00
LPDM Dan Marino/54*	40.00	100.00
LPDT Devin Thomas/54*	4.00	10.00
LPES Emmitt Smith/45*	20.00	50.00
LPFG Frank Gore/36*	8.00	20.00
LPFJ Felix Jones/45*	4.00	10.00
LPFT Fred Taylor/54*	6.00	15.00
LPJC Jay Cutler/54*	6.00	15.00
LPJE John Elway/45*	30.00	80.00
LPJF Joe Flacco/54*	8.00	20.00
LPJH Jacob Hester/54*	4.00	10.00
LPJH James Hardy/45*	4.00	10.00
LPJJ Josh Johnson/63*	4.00	10.00
LPJM Joe Montana/63*	40.00	100.00
LPJN Joe Namath/54*	15.00	40.00
LPJN Jordy Nelson/54*	12.00	30.00
LPJR Jerry Rice/36*	30.00	80.00
LPJS Jonathan Stewart/63*	6.00	15.00
LPKW Kyle Wright/54*	4.00	10.00
LPLF Larry Fitzgerald/90*	8.00	20.00
LPLH Lavelle Hawkins/63*	5.00	12.00
LPLP Adrian Peterson/90*	10.00	25.00
LPLT Lawrence Taylor/54*	12.00	30.00
LPMF Matt Forte/45*	6.00	15.00
LPMH Marcus Henry/45*	4.00	10.00
LPMH Mike Hart/36*	4.00	10.00
LPMK Malcolm Kelly/45*	4.00	10.00
LPMR Matt Ryan/36*	12.00	30.00
LPRM Rashard Mendenhall/90*	4.00	10.00
LPRM Randy Moss/36*	8.00	20.00
LPSS Steve Slaton/54*	4.00	10.00
LPTA Troy Aikman/54*	15.00	40.00
LPTD Tony Dorsett/63*	15.00	40.00
LPTR Tony Romo/36*	8.00	20.00

2008 Topps Letterman Patches Autograph

SER.#'d TO 5-35; TOTAL PRINT RUNS 25-350
*REFRACTOR/4-9: .5X TO 1.2X BASIC AU/5-35
*XFRACTOR/3-15: .6X TO 1.5X BASIC AU/5-35

APAA Anthony Alridge/245*	6.00	15.00
APAC Andre Caldwell/280*	6.00	15.00
APAP Adrian Peterson/40*	75.00	150.00
APAT Aqib Talib/175*	10.00	25.00
APAW Andre Woodson/140*	6.00	15.00
APBB Brian Brohm/25*	8.00	20.00
APBS Barry Sanders/35*	75.00	150.00
APCB Colt Brennan/35*	10.00	25.00
APCW Chauncey Washington/350*	8.00	20.00
APDA Derek Anderson/40*	8.00	20.00
APDD Dennis Dixon/100*	6.00	15.00
APDM Dan Marino/30*	100.00	200.00
APDM Darren McFadden/40*	8.00	20.00
APDR Darius Reynaud/245*	6.00	15.00
APDT Devin Thomas/120*	6.00	15.00
APES Emmitt Smith/25*	125.00	250.00
APFJ Felix Jones/100*	6.00	15.00
APJA Joseph Addai/25*	8.00	20.00
APJE John Elway/25*	75.00	150.00
APJF Joe Flacco/120*	25.00	50.00
APJH Jacob Hester/120*	6.00	15.00
APJJ Josh Johnson/245*	6.00	15.00
APJM Joe Montana/35*	125.00	250.00
APJN Jordy Nelson/120*	25.00	50.00
APJR Jerry Rice/20*	100.00	200.00
APJS Jonathan Stewart/35*	12.00	30.00
APLH Lavelle Hawkins/245*	8.00	20.00
APLT Lawrence Taylor/30*	30.00	60.00
APMH Marcus Henry/175*	6.00	15.00
APMH Mike Hart/80*	6.00	15.00
APMR Matt Ryan/20*	100.00	200.00
APPA Allen Patrick/245*	6.00	15.00
APRM Rashard Mendenhall/200*	6.00	15.00
APSS Steve Slaton/120*	6.00	15.00

2008 Topps Letterman Patches Autograph Jersey Number

JERSEY # AU PRINT RUN 7-75
*REFRACT/25: .5X TO 1.2X BASIC AU/75

ANPAA Jake Long/75	10.00	25.00
ANPAB Ahmad Bradshaw/75	12.00	30.00
ANPAW Andre Woodson/75	6.00	15.00
ANPCH Chad Henne/75	8.00	20.00
ANPCJ Chris Johnson/75	8.00	20.00
ANPDD Dennis Dixon/75	6.00	15.00
ANPDK Dustin Keller/75	8.00	20.00
ANPDM Ray Rice/75	6.00	15.00
ANPDS Dantrell Savage/75	8.00	20.00
ANPFJ Felix Jones/75	6.00	15.00
ANPHD Harry Douglas/75	8.00	20.00
ANPJH Jacob Hester/75	6.00	15.00
ANPJJ Josh Johnson/75	6.00	15.00
ANPJM Jerod Mayo/75	10.00	25.00
ANPKB Chris Long/75	8.00	20.00
ANPLL Kevin O'Connell/75	6.00	15.00
ANPMS Keith Rivers/75	6.00	15.00
ANPRM Rashard Mendenhall/75	6.00	15.00
ANPRT Ryan Torain/75	8.00	20.00
ANPXO Xavier Omon/75	6.00	15.00

2008 Topps Letterman Patches Autograph RC Logo

RAPAA Adrian Arrington/79	6.00	15.00
RAPAC Andre Caldwell/79	6.00	15.00
RAPAP Allen Patrick/79	6.00	15.00
RAPBB Brian Brohm/19	10.00	25.00
RAPCH Chad Henne/19	12.00	30.00
RAPCJ Chris Johnson/79	8.00	20.00
RAPDA Donnie Avery/79	8.00	20.00
RAPDJ DeSean Jackson/79	12.00	30.00
RAPDM Darren McFadden/19	10.00	25.00
RAPDM Jake Long/79	10.00	25.00
RAPDR Darius Reynaud/79	6.00	15.00
RAPED Early Doucet/79	6.00	15.00
RAPFJ Felix Jones/19	10.00	25.00
RAPJB John David Booty/79	6.00	15.00
RAPJC Jamaal Charles/79	10.00	25.00
RAPJF Joe Flacco/19	30.00	80.00
RAPJH James Hardy/79	6.00	15.00
RAPJS Jonathan Stewart/19	15.00	40.00
RAPKO Kevin O'Connell/79	6.00	15.00
RAPKS Kevin Smith/79	6.00	15.00
RAPLH Lavelle Hawkins/79	8.00	20.00
RAPLS Limas Sweed/19	10.00	25.00
RAPMH Mike Hart/79	6.00	15.00
RAPMK Malcolm Kelly/79	6.00	15.00
RAPMR Matt Ryan/19	60.00	150.00
RAPOS Owen Schmitt/79	6.00	15.00
RAPPS Paul Smith/79	6.00	15.00
RAPRM Rashard Mendenhall/19	10.00	25.00
RAPRR Ray Rice/19	10.00	25.00
RAPSE Sedrick Ellis/79	6.00	15.00
RAPSS Steve Slaton/79	6.00	15.00

2008 Topps Letterman Patches Autograph Team Logo

TEAM LOGO AU PRINT RUN 7-75
*REFRACTOR/25: .5X TO 1.2X BASIC AU/75
REFRACTORS PRINT RUN 5-25
UNPRICED XFRACTOR PRINT RUN 3-10
UNPRICED SUPERFRACT PRINT RUN 1
SERIAL #'d UNDER 25 NOT PRICED

ATPBB Brian Brohm/75	6.00	15.00
ATPCJ Chris Johnson/75	8.00	20.00
ATPDA Donnie Avery/75	8.00	20.00
ATPDH David Harris/75	8.00	20.00
ATPDJ DeSean Jackson/75	12.00	30.00
ATPDJ Dexter Jackson/75	10.00	25.00
ATPDT Devin Thomas/75	6.00	15.00
ATPER Eddie Royal/75	6.00	15.00
ATPFJ Felix Jones/75	6.00	15.00
ATPGD Glenn Dorsey/75	6.00	15.00
ATPJH James Hardy/75	6.00	15.00
ATPJL Jake Long/75	10.00	25.00
ATPJN Jordy Nelson/75	25.00	50.00
ATPJS Jerome Simpson/75	8.00	20.00
ATPKS Kevin Smith/75	6.00	15.00
ATPMF Matt Forte/75	30.00	60.00
ATPRM Rashard Mendenhall/75	6.00	15.00
ATPRR Ray Rice/75	6.00	15.00
ATPSS Steve Slaton/75	6.00	15.00

2008 Topps Letterman Patches Jersey Number

STATED PRINT RUN 25 SER.#'d SETS
UNPRICED REFRACTOR PRINT RUN 5
UNPRICED XFRACTOR PRINT RUN 3
UNPRICED SUPERFRACTOR PRINT RUN 1

JNPAB Ahmad Bradshaw	8.00	20.00
JNPAP Adrian Peterson	8.00	20.00
JNPBB Brian Brohm	3.00	8.00
JNPBR Ben Roethlisberger	8.00	20.00
JNPBS Barry Sanders	12.00	30.00
JNPCB Colt Brennan	4.00	10.00
JNPCH Chad Henne	4.00	10.00
JNPCL Chris Long	4.00	10.00
JNPDA Derek Anderson	5.00	12.00
JNPDB Drew Brees	8.00	20.00
JNPDJ DeSean Jackson	6.00	15.00
JNPDK Dustin Keller	4.00	10.00
JNPDM Dan Marino	20.00	50.00
JNPDMC Darren McFadden	3.00	8.00
JNPEM Eli Manning	6.00	15.00
JNPES Emmitt Smith	15.00	40.00
JNPFJ Felix Jones	3.00	8.00
JNPHD Harry Douglas	4.00	10.00
JNPJA Joseph Addai	5.00	12.00
JNPJC Jamaal Charles	5.00	12.00
JNPJE John Elway	15.00	40.00
JNPJF Joe Flacco	6.00	15.00
JNPJH James Hardy	3.00	8.00
JNPJHE Jacob Hester	3.00	8.00
JNPJJ Josh Johnson	3.00	8.00
JNPJM Joe Montana	30.00	80.00
JNPJMA Jerod Mayo	5.00	12.00
JNPJS Jonathan Stewart	5.00	12.00
JNPKO Kevin O'Connell	3.00	8.00
JNPLF Larry Fitzgerald	6.00	15.00
JNPLT LaDainian Tomlinson	8.00	20.00
JNPMD Maurice Jones-Drew	5.00	12.00
JNPMF Matt Forte	5.00	12.00
JNPMH Matt Hasselbeck	5.00	12.00
JNPMR Matt Ryan	10.00	25.00
JNPPM Peyton Manning	20.00	50.00
JNPPR Philip Rivers	8.00	20.00
JNPRM Randy Moss	6.00	15.00
JNPRME Rashard Mendenhall	3.00	8.00
JNPRR Ray Rice	3.00	8.00
JNPRW Reggie Wayne	6.00	15.00
JNPSS Steve Slaton	3.00	8.00
JNPSY Selvin Young	5.00	12.00
JNPTB Tom Brady	25.00	60.00
JNPTO Terrell Owens	6.00	15.00

2008 Topps Letterman Patches Team Logos

STATED PRINT RUN 25 SER.#'d SETS
UNPRICED REFRACTOR PRINT RUN 5
UNPRICED XFRACTOR PRINT RUN 3
UNPRICED SUPERFRACTOR PRINT RUN 1

TLPAP Adrian Peterson	8.00	20.00
TLPBB Brian Brohm	3.00	8.00
TLPBE Braylon Edwards	5.00	12.00
TLPBJ Brandon Jacobs	5.00	12.00
TLPBS Barry Sanders	15.00	40.00
TLPBU Brian Urlacher	8.00	20.00
TLPCJ Chris Johnson	4.00	10.00
TLPCPO Clinton Portis	5.00	12.00
TLPDA Donnie Avery	4.00	10.00
TLPDJ Dexter Jackson	5.00	12.00
TLPDJA DeSean Jackson	6.00	15.00
TLPDM Darren McFadden	3.00	8.00
TLPDT Devin Thomas	3.00	8.00
TLPED Early Doucet	3.00	8.00
TLPER Eddie Royal	3.00	8.00
TLPFG Frank Gore	6.00	15.00
TLPFJ Felix Jones	3.00	8.00
TLPGD Glenn Dorsey	3.00	8.00
TLPJE John Elway	15.00	40.00
TLPJF Joe Flacco	6.00	15.00
TLPJH James Hardy	3.00	8.00
TLPJL Jake Long	5.00	12.00
TLPJN Joe Namath	12.00	30.00
TLPJNE Jordy Nelson	10.00	25.00
TLPJR JaMarcus Russell	5.00	12.00
TLPJS Jonathan Stewart	5.00	12.00
TLPJSI Jerome Simpson	4.00	10.00
TLPLT LaDainian Tomlinson	8.00	20.00
TLPMF Matt Forte	5.00	12.00
TLPMH Matt Hasselbeck	5.00	12.00
TLPML Marshawn Lynch	6.00	15.00
TLPMR Matt Ryan	10.00	25.00
TLPPM Peyton Manning	20.00	50.00
TLPRB Reggie Bush	5.00	12.00
TLPRG Ryan Grant	6.00	15.00
TLPRM Rashard Mendenhall	3.00	8.00
TLPRR Ray Rice	3.00	8.00
TLPSJ Steven Jackson	5.00	12.00
TLPSS Steve Smith	6.00	15.00
TLPSSL Steve Slaton	3.00	8.00
TLPTB Tom Brady	25.00	60.00
TLPTR Tony Romo	6.00	15.00
TLPVY Vince Young	5.00	12.00
TLPWM Willis McGahee	5.00	12.00
TLPWP Willie Parker	6.00	15.00

2014 Topps Magnetz

*SILVER: .6X TO 1.5X BASIC MAGENTZ
*GOLD: 1X TO 2.5X BASIC MAGENTZ

1A Keenan Allen	.40	1.00
1B Keenan Allen SP	1.25	3.00
2A Kiko Alonso	.30	.75
2B Kiko Alonso SP	1.00	2.50
3 Danny Amendola	.40	1.00
4 Champ Bailey	.40	1.00
5 Montee Ball	.30	.75
6 Joique Bell	.30	.75
7 Le'Veon Bell	.40	1.00
8 Giovani Bernard	.30	.75
9 Anquan Boldin	.30	.75
10 Blake Bortles	.40	1.00
11 NaVorro Bowman	.40	1.00
12 Sam Bradford	.30	.75
13A Tom Brady	1.25	3.00
13B Tom Brady SP	4.00	10.00
14A Drew Brees	.50	1.25
14B Drew Brees SP	1.50	4.00
15 Antonio Brown	.50	1.25
16A Dez Bryant	.50	1.25
16B Dez Bryant SP	1.50	4.00
17 Reggie Bush	.30	.75
18A Jamaal Charles	.40	1.00
18B Jamaal Charles SP	1.25	3.00
19 Jadeveon Clowney	.40	1.00
20 Randall Cobb	.40	1.00
21 Michael Crabtree	.30	.75
22A Victor Cruz	.40	1.00
22B Victor Cruz SP	1.25	3.00
23 Jay Cutler	.30	.75
24 Andy Dalton	.40	1.00
25 Vernon Davis	.30	.75
26 Andre Ellington	.30	.75
27A Larry Fitzgerald	.40	1.00
27B Larry Fitzgerald SP	1.25	3.00
28 Joe Flacco	.40	1.00
29 Michael Floyd	.30	.75
30 Nick Foles	.40	1.00
31 Matt Forte	.30	.75
32 Pierre Garcon	.40	1.00
33A Josh Gordon	.30	.75
33B Josh Gordon SP	1.00	2.50
34 Frank Gore	.40	1.00
35 Jimmy Graham	.50	1.25
36A A.J. Green	.50	1.25
36B A.J. Green SP	1.50	4.00
37A Robert Griffin III	.30	.75
37B Robert Griffin III SP	1.00	2.50
38 Rob Gronkowski	.50	1.25
39 T.Y. Hilton	.40	1.00
40 Justin Houston	.30	.75
41 DeSean Jackson	.40	1.00
42 Fred Jackson	.40	1.00
43 Vincent Jackson	.30	.75
44 Alshon Jeffery	.40	1.00
45 Andre Johnson	.40	1.00
46A Calvin Johnson	.50	1.25
46B Calvin Johnson SP	1.50	4.00
47 Chris Johnson	.30	.75
48A Julio Jones	.50	1.25
48B Julio Jones SP	1.50	4.00
49 Maurice Jones-Drew	.30	.75
50A Colin Kaepernick	.40	1.00
50B Colin Kaepernick SP	1.25	3.00
51 Luke Kuechly	.40	1.00
52 Eddie Lacy	.30	.75
53A Andrew Luck	.60	1.50
53B Andrew Luck SP	2.00	5.00
54 Marshawn Lynch	.40	1.00
55 Eli Manning	.40	1.00
56A Peyton Manning	2.00	5.00
56B Peyton Manning SP	6.00	15.00
57 EJ Manuel	.30	.75
58 Johnny Manziel	.50	1.25
59A Brandon Marshall	.30	.75
59B Brandon Marshall SP	1.00	2.50
60A Doug Martin	.40	1.00
60B Doug Martin SP	1.25	3.00
61 Ryan Mathews	.40	1.00
62A LeSean McCoy	.50	1.25
62B LeSean McCoy SP	1.50	4.00
63 Von Miller	.40	1.00
64 Knowshon Moreno	.30	.75
65 Alfred Morris	.30	.75
66 DeMarco Murray	.40	1.00
67 Jordy Nelson	.40	1.00
68A Cam Newton	.50	1.25
68B Cam Newton SP	1.50	4.00
69 Cordarrelle Patterson	.30	.75
70 Julius Peppers	.40	1.00
71A Adrian Peterson	.50	1.25
71B Adrian Peterson SP	1.50	4.00
72 Patrick Peterson	.30	.75
73 Jason Pierre-Paul	.30	.75
74A Troy Polamalu	.50	1.25
74B Troy Polamalu SP	1.50	4.00
75 Ray Rice	.30	.75
76 Trent Richardson	.30	.75
77 Philip Rivers	.50	1.25
78A Aaron Rodgers	1.00	2.50
78B Aaron Rodgers SP	3.00	8.00
79 Ben Roethlisberger	.50	1.25
80 Tony Romo	.40	1.00
81 Matt Ryan	.40	1.00
82 Richard Sherman	.50	1.25
83 Cecil Shorts	.30	.75
84 Alex Smith	.40	1.00
85 Geno Smith	.30	.75
86 Torrey Smith	.30	.75
87 C.J. Spiller	.30	.75
88 Zac Stacy	.30	.75
89 Matthew Stafford	.40	1.00
90 Rod Streater	.30	.75
91 Ndamukong Suh	.40	1.00
92 Ryan Tannehill	.40	1.00
93 Demaryius Thomas	.40	1.00
94 Pierre Thomas	.30	.75
95 Shane Vereen	.40	1.00
96 Bobby Wagner	.30	.75
97 Mike Wallace	.30	.75
98A J.J. Watt	.50	1.25
98B J.J. Watt SP	1.50	4.00
99 Wes Welker	.40	1.00
100 Roddy White	.30	.75
101A Russell Wilson	.75	2.00
101B Russell Wilson SP	2.50	6.00
102 Danny Woodhead	.40	1.00
103 Kendall Wright	.30	.75

1948 Topps Magic Photos

The 1948 Topps Magic Photos set contains 252 small (approximately 7/8" by 1 7/16") individual cards featuring sport and non-sport subjects. They were issued in 19 lettered series with cards numbered within each series. The fronts were developed, much like a photograph, from a "blank" appearance by using moisture and sunlight. Due to varying degrees of photographic sensitivity, the clarity of these cards ranges from fully developed to poorly developed. This set contains Topps' first baseball cards. A premium album holding 126-cards was also issued. The set is sometimes confused with Topps' 1956 Hocus-Focus set, although the cards in this set are slightly smaller than those in the Hocus-Focus set. The checklist below is presented by series. Poorly developed cards are considered in lesser condition and hence have lesser value. The catalog designation for this set is R714-27. Each type of card subject has a letter prefix as follows: Boxing Champions (A), All-American Basketball (B), All-American Football (C), Wrestling Champions (D), Track and Field Champions (E), Stars of Stage and Screen (F), American Dogs (G), General Sports (H), Movie Stars (J), Baseball Hall of Fame (K), Aviation Pioneers (L), Famous Landmarks (M), American Inventors (N), American Military Leaders (O), American Explorers (P), Basketball Thrills (Q), Football Thrills (R), Figures of the Wild West (S), and General Sports (T).

COMPLETE SET (252)	3000.00	5000.00
C1 Barney Poole	12.50	25.00
C2 Pete Elliott	7.50	15.00
C3 Doak Walker	25.00	50.00
C4 Bill Swiacki	10.00	20.00
C5 Bill Fischer	7.50	15.00
C6 Johnny Lujack	25.00	50.00
C7 Chuck Bednarik	25.00	50.00
C8 Joe Steffy	7.50	15.00
C9 George Connor	15.00	30.00
C10 Steve Suhey	10.00	20.00
C11 Bob Chappuis	10.00	20.00
C12 Bill Swiacki	7.50	15.00
Columbia 23		
Navy 14		
C13 Army-Notre Dame	12.50	25.00
R1 Wally Triplett	5.00	10.00
R2 Gil Stevenson	5.00	10.00
R3 Northwestern	5.00	10.00
R4 Yale vs. Columbia	5.00	10.00
R5 Cornell	5.00	10.00
NNO Sid Luckman Ad Poster	175.00	300.00

2009 Topps Magic

COMPLETE SET (250)	60.00	120.00
COMP.SET w/o SP's (200)	15.00	40.00
SP STATED ODDS 1:3		
1 Domenik Hixon	.20	.50
2 Brodie Croyle SP	1.50	4.00
3 LaDainian Tomlinson	.30	.75
4 Glen Coffee RC	.40	1.00
5 Cullen Harper RC	.40	1.00
6 DeMeco Ryans SP	2.00	5.00
7 Roddy White	.20	.50
8 Dexter Jackson	.20	.50
9 Derek Hagan	.20	.50
10 Zach Miller	.20	.50
11 Ryan Torain	.20	.50
12 Andrew Walter	.20	.50
13 Tarvaris Jackson	.25	.60
14 Felix Jones	.20	.50
15 Darren McFadden	.30	.75
16 Jason Campbell	.20	.50
17 Peyton Manning	.75	2.00
18 Kenny Irons SP	1.50	4.00
19 Bo Jackson	.60	1.50
20 Gartrell Johnson RC	.40	1.00
21 Ben Obomanu SP	2.00	5.00
22 Jerod Mayo	.25	.60
23 Courtney Taylor	.20	.50
24 Cadillac Williams	.25	.60
25 Nate Davis RC	.40	1.00
26 Robert Meachem SP	1.50	4.00
27 Isaiah Stanback SP	1.50	4.00
28 Earl Campbell	.50	1.25
29 Mathias Kiwanuka	.20	.50
30 Rashad Jennings RC	.50	1.25
31 Matt Ryan	.25	.60
32 Jamaal Charles	.25	.60
33 Marcus Griffin	.20	.50
34 John Beck SP	1.50	4.00
35 Justin Forsett SP	2.00	5.00
36 Lavelle Hawkins SP	1.50	4.00
37 DeSean Jackson	.25	.60
38 Marshawn Lynch	.25	.60
39 Brandon Marshall	.25	.60
40 Chase Coffman RC	.40	1.00
41 Kevin Smith	.20	.50
42 Aaron Ross	.20	.50
43 Gaines Adams	.20	.50
44 Tye Hill SP	1.50	4.00
45 Winston Justice	.20	.50
46 Chris Simms SP	1.50	4.00
47 Chris Brown SP	1.50	4.00
48 Limas Sweed	.25	.60
49 David Anderson	.20	.50
50 Donald Brown RC	.40	1.00
51 Joe Flacco	.25	.60
52 Dave Thomas SP	1.50	4.00
53 Dallas Baker	.20	.50
54 Andre Caldwell	.20	.50
55 Derrick Harvey SP	1.50	4.00
56 David Clowney	.20	.50
57 Percy Harvin RC	.40	1.00
58 Fred Taylor SP	1.50	4.00
59 DeShawn Wynn	.20	.50
60 Lorenzo Booker SP	1.50	4.00
61 Roy Williams WR	.20	.50
62 Chris Davis	.20	.50
63 Sebastian Janikowski SP	1.50	4.00
64 Greg Jones	.20	.50
65 James Laurinaitis RC	.40	1.00
66 Ernie Sims SP	1.50	4.00
67 Lawrence Timmons	.20	.50
68 Leon Washington	.20	.50
69 Kamerion Wimbley	.20	.50
70 Bernard Berrian	.20	.50
71 Selvin Young	.20	.50
72 Vince Young	.20	.50
73 Paul Williams	.20	.50
74 Reggie Brown	.20	.50
75 Sean Jones SP	1.50	4.00
76 Knowshon Moreno RC	.40	1.00
77 Matthew Stafford RC	2.00	5.00
78 Mohamed Massaquoi RC	.40	1.00
79 Leonard Pope SP	1.50	4.00
80 D.J. Shockley	.20	.50
81 Tashard Choice	.20	.50
82 P.J. Daniels SP	1.50	4.00
83 Colt Brennan	.25	.60
84 John Parker Wilson RC	.40	1.00
85 Donnie Avery	.20	.50
86 Kevin Kolb SP	1.50	4.00
87 Graham Harrell RC	.40	1.00
88 Rashard Mendenhall	.20	.50
89 Laurent Robinson	.20	.50
90 James Hardy	.25	.60
91 Antwaan Randle El	.20	.50
92 Scott Chandler	.20	.50
93 Chad Greenway	.20	.50
94 Ramses Barden RC	.40	1.00
95 Shonn Greene RC	.40	1.00
96 Aqib Talib	.20	.50
97 Michael Crabtree RC	.60	1.50
98 Yamon Figurs SP	1.50	4.00
99 Josh Freeman RC	.40	1.00
100 Jordy Nelson	.25	.60
101 Zach Thomas	.25	.60
102 Antonio Gates	.25	.60
103 Keenan Burton	.20	.50
104 Matt Forte	.20	.50
105 Terry Bradshaw SP	3.00	8.00
106 Ryan Moats	.20	.50
107 John David Booty	.25	.60
108 Brian Brohm	.20	.50
109 Michael Bush	.20	.50
110 Amobi Okoye	.20	.50
111 Kolby Smith SP	1.50	4.00
112 Joseph Addai	.20	.50
113 Dwayne Bowe	.25	.60
114 Michael Clayton	.20	.50
115 Craig Buster Davis	.20	.50
116 Early Doucet	.25	.60
117 Reggie Bush	.20	.50
118 Matt Flynn	.20	.50
119 Fred Davis	.20	.50
120 Kory Sheets RC	.50	1.25
121 Jacob Hester	.20	.50
122 LaRon Landry	.20	.50
123 Justin Fargas	.20	.50
124 Dwayne Jarrett	.20	.50
125 Ahmad Bradshaw SP	1.50	4.00
126 Randy Moss	.25	.60
127 Chad Pennington	.20	.50
128 Darrius Heyward-Bey RC	.60	1.50
129 Matt Leinart	.20	.50
130 Shawne Merriman SP	1.50	4.00
131 DeAngelo Williams SP	1.50	4.00
132 Frank Gore	.25	.60
133 Devin Hester	.25	.60
134 Ray Lewis	.30	.75
135 Willis McGahee	.20	.50
136 Greg Olsen SP	2.00	5.00
137 Roscoe Parrish	.20	.50
138 Antrel Rolle SP	1.50	4.00
139 Reggie Wayne	.25	.60
140 Kellen Winslow	.20	.50
141 Adrian Arrington	.20	.50
142 B.J. Askew	.20	.50
143 Jason Avant	.20	.50
144 Mark Sanchez RC	.40	1.00
145 Tom Brady	.75	2.00
146 Steve Breaston	.25	.60
147 Braylon Edwards	.20	.50
148 Leon Hall	.20	.50
149 Steve Smith USC	.25	.60
150 Mike Hart	.25	.60
151 Chad Henne	.25	.60
152 Drew Henson	.20	.50
153 Steve Hutchinson	.25	.60
154 Marlin Jackson SP	1.50	4.00
155 Ty Law	.30	.75
156 Mario Manningham	.20	.50
157 LaMarr Woodley	.20	.50
158 Javon Ringer RC	.40	1.00
159 LenDale White	.20	.50
160 Drew Stanton	.30	.75
161 Devin Thomas	.20	.50
162 Laurence Maroney	.25	.60
163 Alex Smith QB	.30	.75
164 Eli Manning	.40	1.00
165 Deuce McAllister SP	2.00	5.00
166 Patrick Willis	.25	.60
167 Jerious Norwood	.20	.50
168 Jordan Palmer	.20	.50
169 Chase Daniel RC	.50	1.25
170 Jeremy Maclin RC	.50	1.25
171 Jay Cutler	.20	.50
172 Brad Smith SP	1.50	4.00
173 Thomas Jones	.20	.50
174 Brandon Jackson SP	2.00	5.00
175 Nate Burleson	.20	.50
176 Alvin Pearman SP	1.50	4.00
177 Marcus Smith	.20	.50
178 Matt Schaub SP	1.50	4.00
179 DeAngelo Hall	.20	.50
180 Ronald Curry SP	1.50	4.00
181 Hakeem Nicks RC	.50	1.25
182 Kevin Jones	.20	.50
183 Willie Parker	.20	.50
184 Andre Brown RC	.50	1.25
185 DaJuan Morgan SP	1.50	4.00
186 Philip Rivers	.30	.75
187 Mario Williams	.25	.60
188 Vincent Jackson	.20	.50
189 Garrett Wolfe	.20	.50
190 Xavier Omon	.20	.50
191 John Carlson	.25	.60
192 Anthony Fasano	.20	.50
193 Julius Jones SP	1.50	4.00
194 Brady Quinn	.20	.50
195 Maurice Stovall SP	1.50	4.00
196 Bobby Carpenter	.20	.50
197 Chris Wells RC	.40	1.00
198 Joey Galloway	.25	.60
199 Vernon Gholston SP	1.50	4.00
200 Ted Ginn	.20	.50
201 Anthony Gonzalez	.20	.50
202 Eddie Royal	.20	.50
203 Michael Jenkins	.20	.50
204 Jason Hill	.20	.50
205 Troy Smith	.25	.60
206 Marc Bulger SP	1.50	4.00
207 Mark Bradley SP	1.50	4.00
208 Owen Schmitt SP	1.50	4.00
209 Juaquin Iglesias RC	.40	1.00
210 Malcolm Kelly	.20	.50
211 Allen Patrick SP	1.50	4.00
212 Adrian Peterson	.75	2.00
213 Tatum Bell	.20	.50
214 Brandon Pettigrew RC	.40	1.00
215 Kellen Clemens	.20	.50
216 Dennis Dixon	.20	.50
217 Jonathan Stewart	.20	.50
218 Demetrius Williams	.20	.50
219 Derek Anderson	.20	.50
220 Steven Jackson	.20	.50
221 Chad Johnson	.20	.50
222 Reggie Williams SP	1.50	4.00
223 Dan Connor	.20	.50
224 Derrick Williams SP RC	1.25	3.00
225 Larry Johnson	.20	.50
226 Pat White RC	.50	1.25
227 Paul Posluszny	.20	.50
228 Tony Dorsett	.50	1.25
229 LeSean McCoy RC	1.00	2.50
230 Dan Marino	1.25	3.00
231 Drew Brees	.30	.75
232 Dustin Keller	.20	.50
233 Kyle Orton SP	1.50	4.00
234 Steve Slaton	.20	.50
235 Kenny Britt RC	.60	1.50
236 Brian Leonard SP	1.50	4.00
237 Ray Rice	.20	.50
238 Kevin O'Connell	.20	.50
239 Lee Evans SP	2.00	5.00
240 James Jones	.20	.50
241 Eric Dickerson	.40	1.00
242 Jared Cook RC	.50	1.25
243 P.J. Hill RC	.40	1.00
244 Andre Hall	.20	.50
245 Rhett Bomar RC	.40	1.00
246 Trent Edwards	.20	.50
247 John Elway	1.00	2.50
248 Jim Brown	.60	1.50
249 Dwight Freeney	.20	.50
250 Joe Thomas	.25	.60
TMJR Jackie Robinson	8.00	20.00

2009 Topps Magic Mini

*VETS: 1.2X TO 3X BASIC CARDS
*VET SPs: .5X TO 1.2X BASIC CARDS
*RETIRED: 1.2X TO 3X BASIC CARDS
*RETIRED SPs: .5X TO 1.2X BASIC CARDS
*ROOKIES: .6X TO 1.5X BASIC CARDS
*ROOKIE SPs: .5X TO 1.2X BASIC CARDS
ONE MINI PER PACK OVERALL
MINI SP ODDS 1:12

2009 Topps Magic Mini Black

*VETS: 2.5X TO 6X BASIC CARDS
*VET SPs: .6X TO 1.5X BASIC CARDS
*RETIRED: 2.5X TO 6X BASIC CARDS
*RETIRED SPs: .6X TO 1.5X BASIC CARDS
*ROOKIES: 1X TO 2.5X BASIC CARDS
*ROOKIE SPs: .6X TO 1.5X BASIC CARDS
BLACK MINI ODDS 1:8
BLACK MINI SP ODDS 1:24

2009 Topps Magic 1948 Magic

STATED ODDS 1:6

M1 Vince Young	.75	2.00
M2 McCollum vs. Board of Educ.	.75	2.00
M3 Adrian Peterson	1.25	3.00
M4 Percy Harvin	.40	1.00
M5 Terry Bradshaw	1.50	4.00
M6 Marshall Plan	.75	2.00
M7 Tony Dorsett	1.25	3.00
M8 Knowshon Moreno	.40	1.00
M9 Bo Jackson	1.50	4.00
M10 World Heath Organization	.75	2.00
M11 Michael Crabtree	.60	1.50
M12 Berlin Blockage	.75	2.00
M13 Earl Campbell	1.25	3.00

Card	Low	High
M14 LeSean McCoy	1.00	2.50
M15 John Elway	2.00	5.00
M16 Israel Dec. Of Independ.	.75	2.00
M17 Jim Brown	1.50	4.00
M18 Harry Truman	.75	2.00
M19 Dan Marino	2.50	6.00
M20 Jeremy Maclin	.50	1.25
M21 Chris Johnson	.75	2.00
M22 Harry Truman	.75	2.00
M23 Steve Slaton	.75	2.00
M24 Arthur Miller Author	.75	2.00
M25 Reggie Bush	.75	2.00
M26 Matthew Stafford	2.00	5.00
M27 Mark Sanchez	.40	1.00
M28 LP Record	.75	2.00
M29 Eric Dickerson	1.00	2.50
M30 Maria Telkes	.75	2.00

2009 Topps Magic 1948 Magic Autographs

STATED ODDS 1:1480

Card	Low	High
AP Adrian Peterson	100.00	175.00
BJ Bo Jackson	75.00	125.00
DM Dan Marino	100.00	200.00
EC Earl Campbell	40.00	80.00
ED Eric Dickerson	50.00	100.00
JB Jim Brown	50.00	100.00
JE John Elway	75.00	150.00
MC Michael Crabtree	25.00	60.00
TB Terry Bradshaw	50.00	100.00
TD Tony Dorsett	30.00	60.00

2009 Topps Magic All Americans

STATED ODDS 1:8

Card	Low	High
AA1 John Elway	2.50	6.00
AA2 Knowshon Moreno	.60	1.50
AA3 Bo Jackson	2.00	5.00
AA4 LaDainian Tomlinson	1.50	4.00
AA5 Kevin Smith	1.00	2.50
AA6 Earl Campbell	1.50	4.00
AA7 Jeremy Maclin	.75	2.00
AA8 DeAngelo Williams	1.00	2.50
AA9 Shonn Greene	.60	1.50
AA10 Matt Ryan	1.25	3.00
AA11 Dan Marino	3.00	8.00
AA12 Peyton Manning	3.00	8.00
AA13 Donald Brown	.60	1.50
AA14 Eric Dickerson	1.25	3.00
AA15 Vince Young	1.00	2.50
AA16 Gale Sayers	1.50	4.00
AA17 Michael Crabtree	1.00	2.50
AA18 Jim Brown	2.00	5.00
AA19 Larry Fitzgerald	1.25	3.00
AA20 Adrian Peterson	1.50	4.00
AA21 Terry Bradshaw	2.00	5.00
AA22 Javon Ringer	1.00	2.50
AA23 Tony Dorsett	1.50	4.00
AA24 Darren McFadden	1.50	4.00
AA25 Reggie Bush	1.00	2.50

2009 Topps Magic Alumni

STATED ODDS 1:12

Card	Low	High
AB J.Addai/D.Bowe	1.00	2.50
BE T.Brady/B.Edwards	5.00	12.00
CH M.Crabtree/G.Harrell	.60	1.50
CV E.Campbell/V.Young	1.00	2.50
DS D.Dixon/J.Stewart	1.00	2.50
GM F.Gore/W.McGahee	1.25	3.00
JJ C.Johnson/S.Jackson	1.00	2.50
JL De.Jackson/Lynch	1.25	3.00
MC J.Maclin/C.Coffman	.50	1.25
MD D.Marino/T.Dorsett	3.00	8.00
PM Pennington/R.Moss	1.25	3.00
SM M.Stafford/K.Moreno	2.00	5.00
SW S.Slaton/P.White	1.00	2.50
WW R.Wayne/K.Winslow	1.25	3.00

2009 Topps Magic Alumni Autographs Dual

DUAL AUTO/25 ODDS 1:1025

Card	Low	High
AB J.Addai/D.Bowe	20.00	50.00
BE T.Brady/B.Edwards	150.00	250.00
CH M.Crabtree/G.Harrell	25.00	60.00
CV E.Campbell/V.Young	75.00	150.00
DS D.Dixon/J.Stewart	30.00	60.00
GM F.Gore/W.McGahee	30.00	60.00
JJ C.Johnson/S.Jackson	30.00	60.00
JL De.Jackson/Lynch	20.00	50.00
MC J.Maclin/C.Coffman	30.00	60.00
MD D.Marino/T.Dorsett	150.00	250.00
PM Pennington/R.Moss	75.00	150.00
SM M.Stafford/K.Moreno	75.00	150.00
SW S.Slaton/P.White	25.00	60.00
WW R.Wayne/K.Winslow	30.00	60.00

2009 Topps Magic Alumni Autographs Triple

TRIPLE AUTO/25 ODDS 1:1480

Card	Low	High
BBO M.Bush/Brohm/Okoye		
BSW R.Bush/Sanchez/L.White	100.00	200.00
CDM Coffman/Daniel/Maclin	40.00	80.00
DMM Dorsett/Marino/McCoy	175.00	300.00
GSG Ginn/T.Smith/Gonzalez	40.00	100.00
JWL Jenkins/Wells/Laurin	40.00	100.00
LBE Law/Brady/Edwards	175.00	300.00
MMW McAllister/Eli/Willis	100.00	200.00
MSM Moreno/Stafford/Massaq	100.00	200.00
WLW Wayne/R.Lewis/Winslow	75.00	150.00

2009 Topps Magic Autographs

GROUP 1A/25* ODDS 1:438
GROUP 1B/50* ODDS 1:650
GROUP 1C/250* ODDS 1:76
GROUP 1D ODDS 1:389
GROUP 1E ODDS 1:179
GROUP 1F ODDS 1:148
GROUP 2A/20* ODDS 1:35,000
GROUP 2B/25* ODDS 1:870
GROUP 2C/100* ODDS 1:91
GROUP 2D/150* ODDS 1:43
GROUP 2E ODDS 1:185
GROUP 2F ODDS 1:168
GROUP 2G ODDS 1:158
GROUP 2H ODDS 1:31

Card	Low	High
1 Domenik Hixon/100*	8.00	20.00
2 Brodie Croyle/150*	8.00	20.00
3 LaDainian Tomlinson/25*	100.00	200.00
4 Glen Coffee/150*	6.00	15.00
5 Cullen Harper/150*	6.00	15.00
6 DeMeco Ryans/150*	10.00	25.00
7 Roddy White/100*	8.00	20.00
8 Dexter Jackson 2H	4.00	10.00
9 Derek Hagan/150*	8.00	20.00
10 Zach Miller/25*	75.00	150.00
11 Ryan Torain 2E	4.00	10.00
12 Andrew Walter/100*	8.00	20.00
13 Tarvaris Jackson 2H	5.00	12.00
14 Felix Jones/250*	12.00	30.00
15 Darren McFadden/25*	60.00	120.00
16 Jason Campbell/25*	50.00	100.00
17 Peyton Manning/25*	175.00	300.00
18 Kenny Irons/20*	75.00	150.00
19 Bo Jackson/25*	125.00	200.00
20 Gartrell Johnson/150*	6.00	15.00
21 Ben Obomanu/100*	10.00	25.00
22 Jerod Mayo/150*	10.00	25.00
23 Courtney Taylor 2H	4.00	10.00
24 Cadillac Williams/25*	50.00	100.00
25 Nate Davis/250*	5.00	12.00
26 Robert Meachem/25*	60.00	120.00
27 Isaiah Stanback/100*	8.00	20.00
28 Earl Campbell/25*	75.00	150.00
29 Mathias Kiwanuka 2F	4.00	10.00
30 Rashad Jennings/150*	8.00	20.00
31 Matt Ryan/25*	125.00	250.00
32 Jamaal Charles/150*	10.00	25.00
33 Marcus Griffin 2H	4.00	10.00
34 John Beck/150*	8.00	20.00
35 Justin Forsett 2F	5.00	12.00
36 Lavelle Hawkins/150*	8.00	20.00
37 DeSean Jackson 1E	6.00	15.00
38 Marshawn Lynch/50*	25.00	50.00
39 Brandon Marshall/150*	10.00	25.00
40 Chase Coffman/150*	6.00	15.00
41 Kevin Smith 1G	6.00	15.00
42 Aaron Ross/150*	8.00	20.00
43 Gaines Adams/100*	8.00	20.00
44 Tye Hill/100*	8.00	20.00
45 Winston Justice/100*	8.00	20.00
46 Chris Simms/100*	8.00	20.00
47 Chris Brown/150*	8.00	20.00
48 Limas Sweed/100*	10.00	25.00
49 David Anderson/100*	8.00	20.00
50 Donald Brown/250*	12.00	30.00
51 Joe Flacco 1D	12.00	30.00
52 Dave Thomas/100*	8.00	20.00
53 Dallas Baker/100*	8.00	20.00
54 Andre Caldwell 2H	4.00	10.00
55 Derrick Harvey/150*	8.00	20.00
56 David Clowney 2E	4.00	10.00
57 Percy Harvin/250*	12.00	30.00
58 Fred Taylor/25*	50.00	100.00
59 DeShawn Wynn 2E	4.00	10.00
60 Lorenzo Booker/150*	8.00	20.00
61 Roy Williams WR 1E	6.00	15.00
62 Chris Davis 2F	4.00	10.00
63 Sebastian Janikowski/100*	12.00	30.00
64 Greg Jones/100*	8.00	20.00
65 James Laurinaitis/150*	6.00	15.00
66 Ernie Sims/150*	8.00	20.00
67 Lawrence Timmons/150*	8.00	20.00
68 Leon Washington 2G	4.00	10.00
69 Kamerion Wimbley/150*	8.00	20.00
70 Bernard Berrian/100*	8.00	20.00
71 Selvin Young/25*	60.00	120.00
72 Vince Young/25*	60.00	120.00
73 Paul Williams/150*	8.00	20.00
74 Reggie Brown/150*	8.00	20.00
75 Sean Jones/100*	8.00	20.00
76 Knowshon Moreno/50*	25.00	60.00
77 Matthew Stafford/50*	60.00	125.00
78 Mohamed Massaquoi/150*	6.00	15.00
79 Leonard Pope 2H	4.00	10.00
80 D.J. Shockley/100*	8.00	20.00
81 Tashard Choice/150*	8.00	20.00
82 P.J. Daniels 2H	4.00	10.00
83 Colt Brennan/100*	10.00	25.00
84 John Parker Wilson 2H	4.00	10.00
85 Donnie Avery/150*	8.00	20.00
86 Kevin Kolb/100*	10.00	25.00
87 Graham Harrell/150*	15.00	40.00
88 Rashard Mendenhall/250*	8.00	20.00
89 Laurent Robinson/150*	8.00	20.00
90 James Hardy/150*	10.00	25.00
91 Antwaan Randle El/100*	8.00	20.00
92 Scott Chandler 2H	4.00	10.00
93 Chad Greenway/100*	8.00	20.00
94 Ramses Barden/150*	6.00	15.00
95 Shonn Greene/150*	12.00	30.00
96 Aqib Talib 2G	4.00	10.00
97 Michael Crabtree/25*	30.00	80.00
98 Yamon Figurs 2E	4.00	10.00
99 Josh Freeman/50*	15.00	40.00
100 Jordy Nelson/150*	10.00	25.00
101 Zach Thomas/25*	60.00	120.00
102 Antonio Gates/50*	20.00	40.00
103 Keenan Burton 2G	4.00	10.00
104 Matt Forte 1G	10.00	25.00
105 Terry Bradshaw/25*	100.00	200.00
106 Ryan Moats/100*	8.00	20.00
107 John David Booty/100*	10.00	25.00
108 Brian Brohm/100*	8.00	20.00
109 Michael Bush/150*	8.00	20.00
110 Amobi Okoye/150*	8.00	20.00
111 Kolby Smith/50*	25.00	50.00
112 Joseph Addai/250*	6.00	15.00
113 Dwayne Bowe/250*	8.00	20.00
114 Michael Clayton/25*	40.00	80.00
115 Craig Buster Davis 2H	4.00	10.00
116 Early Doucet/150*	10.00	25.00
117 Reggie Bush/25*	75.00	150.00
118 Matt Flynn/150*	15.00	40.00
119 Fred Davis 2F	4.00	10.00
120 Kory Sheets/150*	8.00	20.00
121 Jacob Hester/150*	8.00	20.00
122 LaRon Landry/150*	8.00	20.00
123 Justin Fargas/100*	8.00	20.00
124 Dwayne Jarrett/100*	8.00	20.00
125 Ahmad Bradshaw/100*	12.00	30.00
126 Randy Moss/25*	100.00	200.00
127 Chad Pennington/25*	60.00	120.00
128 Darrius Heyward-Bey/50*	20.00	50.00
129 Matt Leinart/250*	20.00	40.00
130 Shawne Merriman/25*	50.00	100.00
131 DeAngelo Williams/50*	12.00	30.00
132 Frank Gore/250*	8.00	20.00
133 Devin Hester/150*	10.00	25.00
134 Ray Lewis/25*	125.00	200.00
135 Willis McGahee/25*	50.00	100.00
136 Greg Olsen/150*	10.00	25.00
137 Roscoe Parrish/100*	8.00	20.00
138 Antrel Rolle/100*	8.00	20.00
139 Reggie Wayne/25*	50.00	100.00
140 Kellen Winslow/25*	60.00	150.00
141 Adrian Arrington 2H	4.00	10.00
142 B.J. Askew/100*	8.00	20.00
143 Jason Avant/150*	8.00	20.00
144 Mark Sanchez/25*	75.00	150.00
145 Tom Brady/25*	150.00	250.00
146 Steve Breaston 2G	5.00	12.00
147 Braylon Edwards/25*	75.00	150.00
148 Leon Hall/100*	8.00	20.00
149 Steve Smith/100*	12.00	30.00
150 Mike Hart/150*	12.00	30.00
151 Chad Henne/150*	10.00	25.00
152 Drew Henson/100*	10.00	25.00
153 Steve Hutchinson/25*	125.00	250.00
154 Marlin Jackson/150*	8.00	20.00
155 Ty Law/100*	15.00	40.00
156 Mario Manningham/150*	8.00	20.00
157 LaMarr Woodley/150*	8.00	20.00
158 Javon Ringer/150*	6.00	15.00
159 LenDale White/100*	12.00	30.00
160 Drew Stanton/100*	12.00	30.00
161 Devin Thomas/150*	8.00	20.00
162 Laurence Maroney/25*	50.00	100.00
163 Alex Smith QB/150*	12.00	30.00
164 Eli Manning/25*	90.00	150.00
165 Deuce McAllister/25*	50.00	100.00
166 Patrick Willis 1D	8.00	20.00
167 Jerious Norwood/25*	50.00	100.00
168 Jordan Palmer/100*	8.00	20.00
169 Chase Daniel/150*	8.00	20.00
170 Jeremy Maclin/250*	6.00	15.00
171 Jay Cutler/50*	30.00	60.00
172 Brad Smith/100*	8.00	20.00
173 Thomas Jones/25*	60.00	120.00
174 Brandon Jackson/150*	10.00	25.00
175 Nate Burleson/150*	8.00	20.00
176 Alvin Pearman/100*	8.00	20.00
177 Marcus Smith 2E	4.00	10.00
178 Matt Schaub/100*	50.00	120.00
179 DeAngelo Hall/25*	40.00	80.00
180 Ronald Curry/100*	8.00	20.00
181 Hakeem Nicks/250*	6.00	15.00
182 Kevin Jones/25*	40.00	80.00
183 Willie Parker/25*	50.00	100.00
184 Andre Brown/150*	8.00	20.00
185 DaJuan Morgan 2G	4.00	10.00
186 Philip Rivers/50*	40.00	80.00
187 Mario Williams/100*	10.00	25.00
188 Vincent Jackson/25*	50.00	100.00
189 Garrett Wolfe/150*	8.00	20.00
190 Xavier Omon 2H	4.00	10.00
191 John Carlson 2H	5.00	12.00
192 Anthony Fasano/150*	8.00	20.00
193 Julius Jones/100*	12.00	30.00
194 Brady Quinn/25*	60.00	120.00
195 Maurice Stovall/100*	8.00	20.00
196 Bobby Carpenter/150*	8.00	20.00
197 Chris Wells/250*	20.00	40.00
198 Joey Galloway/100*	10.00	25.00
199 Vernon Gholston/150*	8.00	20.00
200 Ted Ginn/50*	25.00	50.00
201 Anthony Gonzalez/150*	8.00	20.00
202 Eddie Royal 1F	6.00	15.00
203 Michael Jenkins/150*	8.00	20.00
204 Jason Hill 2E	4.00	10.00
205 Troy Smith/100*	20.00	40.00
206 Marc Bulger/100*	10.00	25.00
207 Mark Bradley/100*	8.00	20.00
208 Owen Schmitt 2H	4.00	10.00
209 Juaquin Iglesias/150*	6.00	15.00
210 Malcolm Kelly/150*	8.00	20.00
211 Allen Patrick 2H	4.00	10.00
212 Adrian Peterson/25*	175.00	300.00
213 Tatum Bell/100*	8.00	20.00
214 Brandon Pettigrew/250*	5.00	12.00
215 Kellen Clemens/100*	8.00	20.00
216 Dennis Dixon/100*	15.00	30.00
217 Jonathan Stewart/250*	6.00	15.00
218 Demetrius Williams/150*	8.00	20.00
219 Derek Anderson/50*	20.00	40.00
220 Steven Jackson/25*	40.00	100.00
221 Chad Johnson/25*	60.00	120.00
222 Reggie Williams 2F	4.00	10.00
223 Dan Connor/150*	8.00	20.00
224 Derrick Williams/150*	6.00	15.00
225 Larry Johnson/25*	30.00	80.00
226 Pat White/250*	6.00	15.00
227 Paul Posluszny 2H	6.00	15.00
228 Tony Dorsett/25*	40.00	100.00
229 LeSean McCoy/250*	15.00	40.00
230 Dan Marino/25*	150.00	250.00
231 Drew Brees/25*	175.00	300.00
232 Dustin Keller/150*	8.00	20.00
233 Kyle Orton/100*	20.00	40.00
234 Steve Slaton 1F	10.00	25.00
235 Kenny Britt/250*	8.00	20.00
236 Brian Leonard/150*	8.00	20.00
237 Ray Rice/250*	6.00	15.00
238 Kevin O'Connell/150*	8.00	20.00
239 Lee Evans/100*	10.00	25.00
240 James Jones 2H	4.00	10.00
241 Eric Dickerson/25*	75.00	150.00
242 Jared Cook/150*	8.00	20.00
243 P.J. Hill/150*	6.00	15.00
244 Andre Hall/150*	8.00	20.00
245 Rhett Bomar/150*	6.00	15.00
246 Trent Edwards/150*	12.00	30.00
247 John Elway/25*	125.00	200.00
248 Jim Brown/25*	75.00	150.00
249 Dwight Freeney/100*	20.00	40.00
250 Joe Thomas/25*	60.00	120.00

2009 Topps Magic Thrills

STATED ODDS 1:10

Card	Low	High
MT1 2007 Fiesta Bowl	.75	2.00
MT2 Vince Young	.75	2.00
MT3 2003 Fiesta Bowl	.75	2.00
MT4 Vince Young	.75	2.00
MT5 Steve Slaton	.75	2.00
MT6 Tom Brady	4.00	10.00
MT7 Michael Robinson	.75	2.00
MT8 Marcus Spears	.75	2.00
MT9 Jason Campbell	.75	2.00
MT10 Eric Dickersom	1.00	2.50
MT11 Pat White	.50	1.25
MT12 Mark Sanchez	.40	1.00
MT13 Jeremy Maclin	.50	1.25
MT14 Chris Johnson	.75	2.00
MT15 2006 Insight Bowl	.75	2.00
MT16 Percy Harvin	.40	1.00
MT17 2008 Orange Bowl	.75	2.00
MT18 Kenny Britt	.60	1.50
MT19 Mike Hart	1.25	3.00
MT20 Quan Cosby	.75	2.00

2010 Topps Magic

Card	Low	High
COMPLETE SET (248)	25.00	60.00
COMP.SET w/o SP's (200)	15.00	30.00
SP STATED ODDS 1:3 HOB		
1 Jared Allen SP	1.50	4.00
2 Earl Thomas RC	1.00	2.50
3 Ricky Williams	.20	.50
4 Fred Jackson	.20	.50
5 Charles Scott SP RC	1.25	3.00
6 Matt Ryan	.20	.50
7 Chad Ochocinco	.15	.40
8 LeSean McCoy	.25	.60
9 Brent Celek	.15	.40
10 Myron Rolle RC	.40	1.00
11 Emmitt Smith	.60	1.50
12 Joe Namath SP	3.00	8.00
13 Knowshon Moreno	.15	.40
14 Hines Ward	.20	.50
15 Dwayne Bowe	.20	.50
16 Ndamukong Suh SP RC	3.00	8.00
17 Eric Berry RC	.60	1.50
18 Paul Hornung	.40	1.00
19 John Elway	.60	1.50
20 Marcus Easley RC	.40	1.00
21 Frank Gore SP	2.00	5.00
22 John Abraham	.15	.40
23 Chester Taylor	.15	.40
24 James Starks SP RC	1.50	4.00
25 Tim Tebow RC	2.00	5.00
26 Rob Gronkowski RC	1.25	3.00
27 Jerry Hughes SP RC	1.25	3.00
28 Kevin Smith	.15	.40
29 Todd Heap	.15	.40
30 Dezmon Briscoe SP RC	1.25	3.00
31 Braylon Edwards	.15	.40
32 Dan Marino	.75	2.00
33 Michael Bush	.15	.40
34 Brian Westbrook	.15	.40
35 Alex Smith QB SP	2.00	5.00
36 Kellen Clemens	.15	.40
37 James Hardy	.15	.40
38 Chad Henne	.20	.50
39 Bobby Carpenter SP	1.50	4.00
40 Ramses Barden	.20	.50
41 Marques Colston	.15	.40
42 Darren McFadden SP	1.50	4.00
43 Brooks Foster	.15	.40
44 Drew Brees	.25	.60
45 Jordan Shipley SP RC	1.25	3.00
46 James Casey	.15	.40
47 DeMarcus Ware	.20	.50
48 Reggie Wayne	.20	.50
49 Andre Johnson SP	2.00	5.00
50 Tony Romo	.20	.50
51 Jermaine Gresham RC	.40	1.00
52 Mike Williams RC	.40	1.00
53 Thomas Jones SP	1.50	4.00
54 Tony Gonzalez SP	2.00	5.00
55 David Anderson SP	1.50	4.00
56 Aaron Hernandez SP RC	1.25	3.00
57 Ed Wang RC	.60	1.50
58 David Harris SP	1.50	4.00
59 Juaquin Iglesias SP	1.50	4.00
60 Bob Sanders SP	2.00	5.00
61 Brian Orakpo	.15	.40
62 Jahvid Best RC	.40	1.00
63 Ed Reed	.20	.50
64 Gale Sayers SP	2.50	6.00
65 Sean Lee SP RC	2.50	6.00
66 Brandon LaFell RC	.60	1.50
67 Gerald McCoy RC	.40	1.00
68 Roddy White SP	1.50	4.00
69 Joey Galloway SP	2.00	5.00
70 Jonathan Crompton SP RC	1.25	3.00
71 Peyton Manning	.60	1.50
72 Deion Branch	.15	.40
73 Keith Rivers	.15	.40
74 William Moore	.15	.40
75 Jimmy Clausen RC	.40	1.00
76 Aaron Curry SP	2.00	5.00
77 Jared Odrick RC	.50	1.25
78 Sidney Rice SP	1.50	4.00
79 Santana Moss	.20	.50
80 Jimmy Graham SP RC	3.00	8.00
81 Rolando McClain RC	.40	1.00
82 Quan Cosby SP	1.50	4.00
83 Justin Gage	.15	.40
84 Andre Roberts SP RC	1.50	4.00
85 Rey Maualuga SP	1.50	4.00
86 LaDainian Tomlinson SP	2.50	6.00
87 Bernard Berrian	.15	.40
88 Chris Ogbonnaya	.15	.40
89 Dustin Keller SP	1.50	4.00
90 Mardy Gilyard RC	.40	1.00
91 Jacoby Ford RC	.40	1.00
92 Kevin Kolb	.15	.40
93 Antonio Gates	.20	.50
94 Joe McKnight RC	.40	1.00
95 Eli Manning	.20	.50
96 Ryan Mathews RC	.40	1.00
97 Armanti Edwards RC	.50	1.25
98 Arrelious Benn RC	.40	1.00
99 Cadillac Williams	.15	.40
100 Mark Sanchez	.15	.40
101 Joe Flacco	.20	.50
102 Philip Rivers	.25	.60
103 Tom Brady SP	3.00	8.00
104 Brandon Jacobs	.15	.40
105 Clinton Portis SP	1.50	4.00
106 Jason Witten	.20	.50
107 Willie Parker	.15	.40
108 Champ Bailey	.20	.50
109 Shonn Greene	.15	.40
110 Damian Williams RC	.40	1.00
111 Greg Jennings	.15	.40
112 Troy Polamalu	.25	.60
113 Jordy Nelson	.20	.50
114 Emmanuel Sanders RC	.60	1.50
115 Felix Jones	.15	.40
116 Carson Palmer	.20	.50
117 Derrick Morgan RC	.40	1.00
118 D.J. Williams	.15	.40
119 Steve Young SP	3.00	8.00
120 Percy Harvin SP	1.50	4.00
121 Dan LeFevour RC	.40	1.00
122 Richard Seymour	.15	.40
123 Mike Sims-Walker	.15	.40
124 Dexter McCluster RC	.50	1.25
125 Donovan McNabb	.20	.50
126 Patrick Willis	.20	.50
127 Brian Cushing	.15	.40
128 Marion Barber	.20	.50
129 Ben Tate RC	.40	1.00
130 Ahmad Bradshaw SP	1.50	4.00
131 Brian Urlacher SP	2.50	6.00
132 Steven Jackson	.15	.40
133 Chris Wells	.15	.40
134 James Jones	.15	.40
135 Robert Meachem	.15	.40
136 Brandon Gibson SP	1.50	4.00
137 Vernon Davis SP	1.50	4.00
138 Taylor Price SP RC	1.25	3.00
139 Montario Hardesty RC	.40	1.00
140 David Reed SP RC	1.25	3.00
141 Eddie Royal	.15	.40
142 Anthony Gonzalez	.15	.40
143 Riley Cooper RC	.40	1.00
144 Jacoby Jones	.15	.40
145 Marc Bulger SP	1.50	4.00
146 Sean Canfield RC	.40	1.00
147 Matt Cassel	.15	.40
148 Colt McCoy SP RC	3.00	8.00
149 Justin Forsett	.20	.50
150 Ronnie Lott	.30	.75
151 Mathias Kiwanuka	.15	.40
152 Joe Webb SP RC	1.25	3.00
153 Jerome Harrison	.15	.40
154 Tony Dorsett	.40	1.00
155 Brandon Marshall SP	2.00	5.00
156 Elvis Dumervil	.15	.40
157 Y.A. Tittle	.40	1.00
158 Greg Olsen	.20	.50
159 Josh Freeman	.20	.50
160 Darren Sproles	.20	.50
161 Chris Johnson	.15	.40
162 Hakeem Nicks	.15	.40
163 Matt Leinart	.15	.40
164 Bryan Bulaga RC	.40	1.00
165 Marcus Allen	.40	1.00
166 Johnny Knox	.15	.40
167 Jarett Dillard	.15	.40
168 Amobi Okoye	.15	.40
169 Dwight Freeney	.15	.40
170 Brett Favre	1.00	2.50
171 Ray Rice	.15	.40
172 Malcolm Kelly	.15	.40
173 Vincent Jackson	.15	.40
174 Adrian Peterson	.25	.60
175 Kellen Winslow Jr.	.15	.40
176 Darrius Heyward-Bey	.20	.50
177 John Carlson	.15	.40
178 Carlton Mitchell RC	.40	1.00
179 Marshawn Lynch	.20	.50
180 Santonio Holmes	.15	.40
181 Matt Forte	.15	.40
182 Fred Davis	.15	.40
183 Trent Edwards	.15	.40
184 Brian Brohm	.15	.40
185 Jonathan Dwyer RC	.40	1.00
186 Dez Bryant RC	1.00	2.50
187 Joseph Addai	.15	.40
188 Nate Burleson	.15	.40
189 Troy Aikman	.50	1.25
190 Maurice Jones-Drew	.15	.40
191 Zac Robinson RC	.50	1.25
192 DeAngelo Williams	.15	.40
193 Roger Staubach	.50	1.25
194 Wes Welker SP	2.00	5.00
195 Steve Smith	.20	.50
196 Vince Young	.15	.40
197 Tony Pike RC	.40	1.00
198 C.J. Spiller RC	.40	1.00
199 Demaryius Thomas RC	1.00	2.60
200 Rashard Mendenhall	.15	.40
201 Ray Lewis	.25	.60
202 Anthony Dixon RC	.40	1.00
203 Nnamdi Asomugha	.15	.40
204 Chad Greenway	.15	.40
205 Jim Brown	.50	1.25
206 Mike Kafka RC	.50	1.25
207 Michael Jenkins	.15	.40
208 Eric Decker RC	.50	1.25
209 Steve Slaton	.15	.40
210 Toby Gerhart RC	.40	1.00
211 Rashad Jennings	.15	.40
212 Malcolm Jenkins	.15	.40
213 Franco Harris	.40	1.00
214 Matthew Stafford	.20	.50
215 Paul Posluszny	.15	.40
216 Jerod Mayo	.20	.50
217 Fred Biletnikoff	.40	1.00
218 Aaron Rodgers	.50	1.25
219 Jake Long	.15	.40
220 Jamaal Charles	.20	.50
221 Willis McGahee	.15	.40
222 Tashard Choice	.15	.40
223 Larry Fitzgerald	.20	.50
224 Ben Roethlisberger	.25	.60
225 LaRon Landry	.15	.40
226 Early Doucet	.15	.40
227 Sammy Morris	.15	.40
228 Randy Moss	.20	.50
229 Chris Cooley	.15	.40
230 Cedric Benson	.15	.40
231 Mario Williams	.20	.50
232 Calvin Johnson	.25	.60
233 Cedric Peerman	.15	.40
234 Kyle Orton	.15	.40
235 Darrelle Revis	.15	.40
236 Golden Tate RC	.50	1.25
237 Reggie Bush	.15	.40
238 Jeremy Maclin	.15	.40
239 Derek Anderson	.15	.40
240 Devin Thomas	.15	.40
241 Sam Bradford RC	3.00	8.00
242 T.J. Houshmandzadeh	.15	.40
243 DeSean Jackson	.20	.50
244 Mohamed Massaquoi	.20	.50
245 Dennis Dixon	.15	.40
246 John Skelton RC	.50	1.25
247 Jonathan Stewart	.15	.40
248 James Davis	.15	.40

2010 Topps Magic Mini

*VETS: 1.2X TO 3X BASIC CARDS
*VET SP: .5X TO 1.2X BASIC SP
*ROOKIES: .5X TO 1.2X BASIC CARDS
*ROOKIE SP: .5X TO 1.2X BASIC SP RC
OVERALL MINI ODDS 1:1 HOB
MINI SP STATED ODDS 1:12 HOB

2010 Topps Magic Mini Black

*VETS: 2.5X TO 6X BASIC CARDS
*VET SP: .6X TO 1.5X BASIC SP
*ROOKIES: 1X TO 2.5X BASIC CARDS
*ROOKIE SP: .5X TO 1.5X BASIC RC SP
MINI BLACK STATED ODDS 1:8 HOB
MINI BLACK SP ODDS 1:24 HOB

2010 Topps Magic Mini Pigskin 50

*VETS/50: 4X TO 10X BASIC CARDS
*VETS/50: .6X TO 1.5X BASIC SP
*ROOKIE/50: 1.5X TO 4X BASIC RC
*ROOKIE/50: .6X TO 1.5X BASIC RC SP
MINI PIGSKIN/50 ODDS 1:37 HOB

2010 Topps Magic Autographs

TIER 1 GROUP A/15* ODDS 1:882 HOB
TIER 1 GROUP B/50* ODDS 1:333 HOB
TIER 1 GROUP C/100* ODDS 1:201 HOB
TIER 1 GROUP D ODDS 1:100 HOB
TIER 1 GROUP E ODDS 1:73 HOB
TIER 2 GROUP A/15* ODDS 1:1525 HOB
TIER 2 GROUP B/50* ODDS 1:615 HOB
TIER 2 GROUP C/100* ODDS 1:423 HOB
TIER 2 GROUP D ODDS 1:70 HOB
TIER 2 GROUP E ODDS 1:201 HOB
TIER 2 GROUP F ODDS 1:84 HOB
TIER 2 GROUP G ODDS 1:21 HOB
EXCH EXPIRATION: 12/31/2013

Card	Low	High
2 Earl Thomas 1C/100*	10.00	25.00
5 Charles Scott 2A/15*	30.00	60.00
6 Matt Ryan 1A/15*	75.00	135.00
7 Chad Ochocinco 1B/50*	30.00	60.00
8 LeSean McCoy 1C/100*	20.00	40.00
10 Myron Rolle 2D	6.00	15.00
11 Emmitt Smith 1A/15*	125.00	200.00
12 Joe Namath 1A/15*	100.00	175.00
15 Dwayne Bowe 1B/50*	20.00	40.00
16 Ndamukong Suh 1D	12.00	30.00
17 Eric Berry 1E	10.00	25.00
18 Paul Hornung 1C/100*	25.00	50.00
19 John Elway 1A/15*	100.00	200.00
20 Marcus Easley 2D	5.00	12.00
21 Frank Gore 1B/50*	30.00	60.00
23 Chester Taylor 2C/100*	8.00	20.00
24 James Starks 2D	5.00	12.00
25 Tim Tebow 1A/15*	125.00	250.00
26 Rob Gronkowski 2C/100*	25.00	50.00
27 Jerry Hughes 2D	6.00	15.00
30 Dezmon Briscoe 2A/15*	30.00	60.00
31 Braylon Edwards 1C/100*	10.00	25.00
32 Dan Marino 1A/15*	175.00	300.00
34 Brian Westbrook 1B/50*	10.00	25.00
36 Kellen Clemens 2F	6.00	15.00
37 James Hardy 2G	4.00	10.00
38 Chad Henne 2D	10.00	25.00
39 Bobby Carpenter 2G	4.00	10.00
40 Ramses Barden 2E	5.00	12.00
42 Darren McFadden 1A/15*	60.00	120.00
43 Brooks Foster 2G	5.00	12.00
44 Drew Brees 1D	40.00	80.00
45 Jordan Shipley 1E	4.00	10.00
46 James Casey 2A/15*	40.00	80.00
48 Reggie Wayne 1C/100*	15.00	40.00
50 Tony Romo 1A/15*	60.00	120.00
55 David Anderson 2F	5.00	12.00
56 Aaron Hernandez 2D	10.00	25.00
57 Ed Wang 2A/15*	50.00	100.00
58 David Harris 2F	4.00	10.00
59 Juaquin Iglesias 2G	5.00	12.00
62 Jahvid Best 1E	15.00	40.00
63 Ed Reed 1C/100*	30.00	60.00
64 Gale Sayers 1B/50*	50.00	100.00
65 Sean Lee 2C/100*	8.00	20.00
66 Brandon LaFell 2B/50*	10.00	25.00
67 Gerald McCoy 2B/50*	10.00	25.00
68 Roddy White 1D	10.00	25.00
69 Joey Galloway 2F	6.00	15.00
70 Jonathan Crompton 2F	5.00	12.00
71 Peyton Manning 1A/15*	100.00	200.00
72 Deion Branch 2E	8.00	20.00
73 Keith Rivers 2G	4.00	10.00
74 William Moore 2F	5.00	12.00
75 Jimmy Clausen 1A/15*	40.00	80.00
76 Aaron Curry 2E	8.00	20.00
77 Jared Odrick 2D	8.00	20.00
78 Sidney Rice 1B/50*	20.00	40.00
80 Jimmy Graham 2C/100*	20.00	50.00
82 Quan Cosby 2G	5.00	12.00
84 Andre Roberts 2D	5.00	12.00
85 Rey Maualuga 2B/50*	10.00	25.00
86 LaDainian Tomlinson 1B/50*	30.00	60.00
87 Bernard Berrian 2E	6.00	15.00
88 Chris Ogbonnaya 2A/15*	30.00	60.00
89 Dustin Keller 2A/15*	40.00	80.00
90 Mardy Gilyard 2D	6.00	15.00
01 Jacoby Ford 2D	8.00	20.00
92 Kevin Kolb 2A/15*	40.00	80.00
93 Antonio Gates 1B/50*	25.00	50.00
95 Eli Manning 1A/15*	75.00	150.00
96 Ryan Mathews 1D	8.00	20.00
97 Armanti Edwards 2D	6.00	15.00
98 Arrelious Benn 1E	6.00	15.00
101 Joe Flacco 1D	12.00	30.00
107 Willie Parker 2A/15*	75.00	150.00
109 Shonn Greene 1C/100*	12.00	30.00
110 Damian Williams 2B/50*	20.00	40.00
111 Greg Jennings 1C/100*	6.00	15.00
113 Jordy Nelson 2G	10.00	25.00
114 Emmanuel Sanders 2D	6.00	15.00
115 Felix Jones 1B/50*	12.00	30.00
117 Derrick Morgan 2B/50*	10.00	25.00
119 Steve Young 1B/50*	40.00	80.00
121 Dan LeFevour 2A/15*	40.00	80.00
123 Mike Sims-Walker 2C	6.00	15.00
124 Dexter McCluster 2B/50*	30.00	60.00
126 Patrick Willis 1B/50*	12.00	30.00
127 Brian Cushing 1E	6.00	15.00
129 Ben Tate 2A/15*	50.00	100.00
130 Ahmad Bradshaw 1B/50*	12.00	30.00
133 Chris Wells 1C/100*	10.00	25.00
134 James Jones 2G	5.00	12.00
136 Brandon Gibson 2A/15*	40.00	80.00
138 Taylor Price 2C/100*	6.00	15.00
139 Montario Hardesty 2A/15*	40.00	80.00
140 David Reed 2C/100*	6.00	15.00
142 Anthony Gonzalez 2B/50*	12.00	30.00
143 Riley Cooper 2D	6.00	15.00
144 Jacoby Jones 2E	6.00	15.00
145 Marc Bulger 2D	6.00	15.00
146 Sean Canfield 2D	5.00	12.00
148 Colt McCoy 1C/100*	20.00	50.00
149 Justin Forsett 2B/50*	8.00	20.00
150 Ronnie Lott 1D	15.00	40.00
151 Mathias Kiwanuka 2F	5.00	12.00
152 Joe Webb 2D	4.00	10.00
153 Jerome Harrison 2E	6.00	15.00
154 Tony Dorsett 1B/50*	40.00	80.00
155 Brandon Marshall 1A/15*	50.00	100.00
157 Y.A. Tittle 1B/50*	20.00	50.00
159 Josh Freeman 2A/15*	75.00	150.00
162 Hakeem Nicks 1D	8.00	20.00
163 Matt Leinart 2A/15*		
164 Bryan Bulaga 2B/50*	12.00	30.00
165 Marcus Allen 1B/50*	25.00	60.00
167 Jarett Dillard 2D	5.00	12.00
168 Amobi Okoye 2G	4.00	10.00
170 Brett Favre 1A/15*	150.00	300.00
171 Ray Rice 1A/15*	50.00	100.00
172 Malcolm Kelly 2G	4.00	10.00
174 Adrian Peterson 1A/15*	100.00	200.00
175 Kellen Winslow Jr. 1E	8.00	20.00
177 John Carlson 2B/50*	25.00	50.00
178 Carlton Mitchell 2D	5.00	12.00
179 Marshawn Lynch 2F	20.00	40.00
182 Fred Davis 2G	6.00	15.00
183 Trent Edwards 2A/15*		
184 Brian Brohm 2G	6.00	15.00
185 Jonathan Dwyer 2D	6.00	15.00
188 Nate Burleson 2A/15*	30.00	60.00
189 Troy Aikman 1A/15*	75.00	150.00
191 Zac Robinson 2D	5.00	12.00
192 DeAngelo Williams 1A/15*	40.00	80.00
193 Roger Staubach 1A/15*	60.00	120.00
196 Vince Young 1A/15*	25.00	60.00
197 Tony Pike 2B/50*	12.00	30.00
198 C.J. Spiller 1E	8.00	20.00
199 Demaryius Thomas 1E	10.00	25.00
201 Ray Lewis 1C/100*	50.00	100.00
202 Anthony Dixon 2D	8.00	20.00
205 Jim Brown 1A/15*	100.00	175.00
206 Mike Kafka 2A/15*	40.00	80.00
207 Michael Jenkins 2C	6.00	15.00
208 Eric Decker 2D	5.00	12.00
209 Steve Slaton 2B/50*	8.00	20.00
210 Toby Gerhart 2C/100*	20.00	40.00
211 Rashad Jennings 2G	5.00	12.00
212 Malcolm Jenkins 2G	5.00	12.00
213 Franco Harris 1C/100*	25.00	60.00
214 Matthew Stafford 1B/50*	20.00	50.00
215 Paul Posluszny 2B/50*	10.00	25.00
216 Jerod Mayo 1E	6.00	15.00
217 Fred Biletnikoff 1D	20.00	40.00
219 Jake Long 2F	6.00	15.00
220 Jamaal Charles 1D	12.00	30.00
221 Willis McGahee 1D	8.00	20.00
222 Tashard Choice 2B/50*	10.00	25.00
225 LaRon Landry 2F	6.00	15.00
226 Early Doucet 2G	5.00	12.00
227 Sammy Morris 2G	6.00	15.00
231 Mario Williams 1D	5.00	12.00
233 Cedric Peerman 2G	4.00	10.00
236 Golden Tate 1E	5.00	12.00
237 Reggie Bush 1A/15*	50.00	100.00
238 Jeremy Maclin 1C/100*	12.00	30.00
239 Derek Anderson 2G	6.00	15.00
240 Devin Thomas 2G	4.00	10.00
241 Sam Bradford 1B/50*	40.00	100.00
243 DeSean Jackson 1C/100*	12.00	30.00
244 Mohamed Massaquoi 2D	5.00	12.00
245 Dennis Dixon 2G	5.00	12.00
246 John Skelton 2A/15*	60.00	100.00
247 Jonathan Stewart 1D	8.00	20.00
248 James Davis 2D	5.00	12.00

2010 Topps Magic Autographs Dual

DUAL AU/25 ODDS 1:775 HOB
EXCH EXPIRATION: 12/31/2013

Card	Low	High
DAAJ Aikman/Jones-Drew	60.00	120.00
DABA F.Biletnikoff/M.Allen	40.00	80.00
DABB D.Brees/R.Bush	60.00	120.00
DABH J.Brown/M.Hardesty	40.00	100.00
DAJD F.Jones/Dorsett	25.00	60.00
DALW R.Lott/P.Willis	75.00	150.00
DAMAN P.Manning/E.Manning	125.00	225.00
DAMH Mendenhall/F.Harris	50.00	100.00
DAMM Marino/Marshall	100.00	175.00
DANS J.Namath/M.Sanchez	75.00	150.00
DARS T.Romo/R.Staubach	60.00	120.00
DASH G.Sayers/P.Hornung	50.00	100.00
DASP E.Smith/Peterson	125.00	250.00
DATE T.Tebow/J.Elway	150.00	300.00
DATG L.Tomlinson/S.Greene	50.00	100.00

2010 Topps Magic Autographs Triple

TRIPLE AU/25 ODDS 1:1150 HOB
EXCH EXPIRATION: 12/31/2013

Card	Low	High
TABME Brdfrd/P.Mann/Elway	200.00	350.00
TABMS Brees/Eli/Staubach	200.00	400.00
TADBA Dorsett/Bush/M.Alln	60.00	120.00
TAFPR Favre/Ptersn/S.Rice	150.00	250.00
TALGW Lwis/Gore/Wayne	90.00	150.00
TASSF Staff/Sanch/Flaco	60.00	120.00
TASTH E.Smth/Tebow/Hrvn	100.00	200.00
TASTS Spiller/Tmlnsn/Sayrs	50.00	120.00
TATEB Tate/Edwrds/Biltnkff	40.00	80.00
TATYA Tittle/S.Yng/Aikmn	100.00	200.00

2010 Topps Magic Historical Stamp of Approval

HISTORICAL STAMP/25 ODDS 1:358 HOB

Card	Low	High
HSAE Amelia Earhart	30.00	80.00
HSAES Albert Einstein	30.00	80.00
HSAGB Alexander Graham Bell	25.00	60.00
HSAH Alexander Hamilton	25.00	60.00
HSAJ Andrew Jackson	25.00	60.00
HSAL Abraham Lincoln	40.00	80.00
HSBC Buffalo Bill Cody	20.00	50.00
HSBF Benjamin Franklin	50.00	100.00
HSCP Casimir Pulaski	20.00	50.00
HSDMC Douglas MacArthur	25.00	60.00
HSEAP Edgar Allen Poe	25.00	60.00
HSEB Elizabeth Blackwell	20.00	50.00
HSER Eleanor Roosevelt	20.00	50.00
HSFAB Frederic Bartholdi	20.00	50.00
HSFD Frederick Douglas	20.00	50.00
HSFDR Franklin D. Roosevelt	25.00	60.00
HSFSF F. Scott Fitzgerald	20.00	50.00
HSFSK Francis Scott Key	25.00	60.00
HSGC Grover Cleveland	25.00	60.00
HSGE Geronimo	25.00	60.00
HSGP General Patton	25.00	60.00
HSGW George Washington	30.00	80.00
HSGWC George Washington Carver	25.00	60.00
HSHDT Henry David Thoreau	20.00	50.00
HSHK Helen Keller	20.00	50.00
HSJA Johnny Appleseed	20.00	50.00
HSJB James Buchanan	25.00	60.00
HSJFK John F. Kennedy	60.00	120.00
HSJH John Hanson	25.00	60.00
HSJJA John James Audubon	25.00	60.00
HSJM John Muir	20.00	50.00
HSJMO James Monroe	20.00	50.00
HSJPJ John Paul Jones	20.00	50.00
HSJQA John Quincy Adams	30.00	80.00
HSLC Lewis and Clark	20.00	50.00
HSLE Leif Erikson	20.00	50.00
HSMEW Mary Edwards Walker	20.00	50.00
HSMLK Martin Luther King	25.00	60.00
HSMMB Mary McLeod Bethune	20.00	50.00
HSNC Nicolaus Copernicus	20.00	50.00
HSNH Nathan Hale	20.00	50.00
HSOWW Orville and Wilbur Wright	20.00	50.00
HSPB Pearl Buck	20.00	50.00
HSPDL Ponce de Leon	20.00	50.00
HSRG Robert Goddard	15.00	40.00
HSRK Robert Kennedy	50.00	100.00
HSSB Simon Bolivar	20.00	50.00
HSSH Sam Houston	25.00	60.00
HSTE Thomas Edison	25.00	60.00
HSTJ Thomas Jefferson	25.00	60.00

2010 Topps Magic History's Best

Card	Low	High
COMPLETE SET (10)	8.00	20.00
STATED ODDS 1:12 HOBBY		
HB1 Emmitt Smith	1.50	4.00
HB2 Tom Brady	2.50	6.00
HB3 Ray Lewis	1.00	2.50
HB4 Brett Favre	2.00	5.00
HB5 Dan Marino	2.00	5.00
HB6 Peyton Manning	2.50	6.00
HB7 John Elway	1.50	4.00
HB8 Steve Young	1.25	3.00
HB9 Paul Hornung	1.00	2.50
HB10 LaDainian Tomlinson	1.00	2.50

2010 Topps Magic Magical Moments

Card	Low	High
COMPLETE SET (20)	8.00	20.00
STATED ODDS 1:4 HOBBY		
MM1 Andre Johnson	.60	1.50
MM2 Terrell Owens	.60	1.50
MM3 Wes Welker	.60	1.50
MM4 Brett Favre	1.50	4.00
MM5 Tony Romo	.60	1.50
MM6 Brandon Marshall	.60	1.50
MM7 Adrian Wilson	.50	1.25
MM8 Jamaal Charles	.60	1.50
MM9 LaDainian Tomlinson	.75	2.00
MM10 Peyton Manning	2.00	5.00
MM11 Matt Schaub	.50	1.25
MM12 Tom Brady	2.00	5.00
MM13 Fred Jackson	.60	1.50
MM14 Knowshon Moreno	.50	1.25
MM15 Elvis Dumervil	.50	1.25
MM16 Drew Brees	.75	2.00
MM17 Patrick Willis	.60	1.50
MM18 Shonn Greene	.50	1.25
MM19 Randy Moss	.60	1.50
MM20 Chris Johnson	.50	1.25

2010 Topps Magic Relics

RELIC/25 ODDS 1:153 HOBBY

Card	Low	High
1 Jared Allen	4.00	10.00
3 Ricky Williams	5.00	12.00
4 Fred Jackson	8.00	20.00
9 Brent Celek	4.00	10.00
13 Knowshon Moreno	4.00	10.00
14 Hines Ward	6.00	12.00
22 John Abraham	4.00	10.00
28 Kevin Smith	4.00	10.00
29 Todd Heap	4.00	10.00
33 Michael Bush	4.00	10.00
35 Alex Smith QB	5.00	12.00
41 Marques Colston	4.00	10.00
47 DeMarcus Ware	6.00	15.00
49 Andre Johnson	5.00	12.00
51 Jermaine Gresham	2.50	6.00
52 Mike Williams	2.50	6.00
53 Thomas Jones	4.00	10.00
54 Tony Gonzalez	5.00	12.00
60 Bob Sanders	6.00	15.00
61 Brian Orakpo	4.00	10.00
79 Santana Moss	5.00	12.00
81 Rolando McClain	2.50	6.00
83 Justin Gage	4.00	10.00
94 Joe McKnight	2.50	6.00
99 Cadillac Williams	4.00	10.00
100 Mark Sanchez	4.00	10.00
102 Philip Rivers	6.00	15.00
103 Tom Brady	12.00	30.00
104 Brandon Jacobs	4.00	10.00
105 Clinton Portis	4.00	10.00
106 Jason Witten	5.00	12.00
108 Champ Bailey	6.00	12.00
112 Troy Polamalu	6.00	15.00
116 Carson Palmer	5.00	12.00
118 D.J. Williams	4.00	10.00
120 Percy Harvin	4.00	10.00
122 Richard Seymour	4.00	10.00
125 Donovan McNabb	5.00	12.00
128 Marion Barber	5.00	12.00
131 Brian Urlacher	6.00	15.00
132 Steven Jackson	4.00	10.00
135 Robert Meachem	4.00	10.00
137 Vernon Davis	4.00	10.00
141 Eddie Royal	4.00	10.00
147 Matt Cassel	4.00	10.00
156 Elvis Dumervil	5.00	12.00
158 Greg Olsen	5.00	12.00
160 Darren Sproles	5.00	12.00
161 Chris Johnson	4.00	10.00
166 Johnny Knox	4.00	10.00
169 Dwight Freeney	4.00	10.00
173 Vincent Jackson	4.00	10.00
176 Darrius Heyward-Bey	5.00	12.00
180 Santonio Holmes	4.00	10.00
181 Matt Forte	4.00	10.00
186 Dez Bryant	10.00	25.00
187 Joseph Addai	4.00	10.00
190 Maurice Jones-Drew	4.00	10.00
194 Wes Welker	12.50	25.00
195 Steve Smith	5.00	12.00
200 Rashard Mendenhall	4.00	10.00
203 Nnamdi Asomugha	4.00	10.00
204 Chad Greenway	15.00	30.00
218 Aaron Rodgers	25.00	50.00
223 Larry Fitzgerald	5.00	12.00
224 Ben Roethlisberger	8.00	20.00
228 Randy Moss	5.00	12.00
229 Chris Cooley	6.00	12.00
230 Cedric Benson	4.00	10.00
232 Calvin Johnson	6.00	15.00
234 Kyle Orton	4.00	10.00
235 Darrelle Revis	4.00	10.00
242 T.J. Houshmandzadeh	4.00	10.00

2010 Topps Magic Rookie Stars

Card	Low	High
COMPLETE SET (20)	12.00	30.00
STATED ODDS 1:6 HOBBY		
RS1 Arrelious Benn	.50	1.25
RS2 Toby Gerhart	.50	1.25
RS3 Tim Tebow	1.50	4.00
RS4 C.J. Spiller	.50	1.25
RS5 Joe McKnight	.50	1.25
RS6 Jermaine Gresham	.50	1.25
RS7 Jahvid Best	.50	1.25
RS8 Golden Tate	.60	1.50
RS9 Ndamukong Suh	1.00	2.50
RS10 Montario Hardesty	.50	1.25
RS11 Ryan Mathews	.50	1.25
RS12 Demaryius Thomas	1.25	3.00
RS13 Rolando McClain	.50	1.25
RS14 Colt McCoy	.60	1.50
RS15 Jimmy Clausen	.50	1.25
RS16 Sam Bradford	.60	1.50
RS17 Rob Gronkowski	1.50	4.00
RS18 Dez Bryant	1.25	3.00
RS19 Dexter McCluster	.60	1.50
RS20 Eric Berry	.75	2.00

2011 Topps Magic Rookies

Card	Low	High
1A A.J. Green blue	1.50	4.00
1B A.J. Green orng SP	6.00	15.00
2 Aldon Smith	.60	1.50
3 Niles Paul	.60	1.50
4 Jon Baldwin	.60	1.50
5 Justin Houston	.75	2.00
6 Akeem Ayers	.60	1.50
7 Brandon Browner	.60	1.50
8 Dion Lewis	.75	2.00
9 DeMarco Murray	1.25	3.00
10A Mark Ingram prpl	1.00	2.50
10B Mark Ingram red SP	4.00	10.00
11 Ryan Kerrigan	.75	2.00
12 Lance Kendricks	.60	1.50
13 Marcell Dareus	.60	1.50
14 Stephen Paea	.60	1.50
15 Mike Pouncey	1.00	2.50
16 Terrence Toliver	.75	2.00
17 Terrelle Pryor	1.00	2.50
18 Muhammad Wilkerson	.60	1.50
19 Brooks Reed	.75	2.00
20A Jake Locker prpl	.60	1.50
20B Jake Locker blu SP	2.50	6.00
21 Vincent Brown	.60	1.50
22 Jacquizz Rodgers	.60	1.50
23 Ras-I Dowling	.60	1.50
24 Rahim Moore	.60	1.50
25 Patrick Peterson	1.25	3.00
26 Jeremy Kerley	1.00	2.50
27 Terrell McClain	.75	2.00
28 Dane Sanzenbacher	.60	1.50
29 Cecil Shorts	.60	1.50
30A Daniel Thomas prpl	.60	1.50
30B Daniel Thomas grn SP	2.50	6.00
31 Cameron Jordan	.75	2.00
32 Casey Matthews	.60	1.50
33 Virgil Green	.60	1.50
34 Owen Marecic	.60	1.50
35 Austin Pettis	.60	1.50
36 Darvin Adams	.60	1.50
37 Prince Amukamara	.60	1.50
38 Corey Liuget	.60	1.50
39 Luke Stocker	.60	1.50
40 Ryan Mallett	.60	1.50
41 Cameron Heyward	.75	2.00
42 Robert Quinn	.60	1.50
43 Aaron Williams	.60	1.50
44 Roy Helu	.60	1.50
45 Rob Housler	.60	1.50
46A Von Miller blue	1.00	2.50
46B Von Miller orng SP	4.00	10.00
47 Jamie Harper	.60	1.50
48 Mark Herzlich	.60	1.50
49 Edmond Gates	.60	1.50
50A Julio Jones prpl	2.00	5.00
50B Julio Jones red SP	8.00	20.00
51 Alex Green	.60	1.50
52 Jordan Todman	.60	1.50
53 J.J. Watt	4.00	10.00
54 Jimmy Smith	.60	1.50
55 Leonard Hankerson	.60	1.50
56 Greg Salas	.60	1.50
57 Nick Fairley	.60	1.50
58 Ryan Williams	.60	1.50
59 Tandon Doss	.60	1.50
60 Randall Cobb	1.00	2.50
61 Bilal Powell	.75	2.00
62 Denarius Moore	.60	1.50
63 Kyle Rudolph	.60	1.50
64 Dwayne Harris	.60	1.50
65 Jabaal Sheard	.60	1.50
66 Kendall Hunter	.60	1.50
67 Ronald Johnson	.60	1.50
68 Greg Jones	.75	2.00
69 K.J. Wright	1.00	2.50
70A Christian Ponder prpl	.60	1.50
70B Christian Ponder red SP	6.00	15.00
71 Greg McElroy	1.00	2.50
72 Tyrod Taylor	1.25	3.00
73 Da'Quan Bowers	.60	1.50
74 Colin Kaepernick	1.00	2.50
75 John Clay	1.00	2.50
76 Adrian Clayborn	.60	1.50
77 Mike McNeill	1.00	2.50
78 Kris Durham	.60	1.50
79 Titus Young	.60	1.50
80A Blaine Gabbert prpl	.60	1.50
80B Blaine Gabbert blu SP	2.50	6.00
81 Dontay Moch	.60	1.50
82 D.J. Williams	.60	1.50
83 Delone Carter	.60	1.50
84 Taiwan Jones	.60	1.50
85 Stevan Ridley	.60	1.50
86 Darren Evans	.75	2.00
87 Jerrel Jernigan	.60	1.50
88 Sione Fua	.60	1.50
89 Derrick Locke	.75	2.00
90A Andy Dalton prpl	1.25	3.00
90B Andy Dalton orng SP	5.00	12.00
91 Greg Little	.75	2.00
92 Phil Taylor	.60	1.50
93 Da'Rel Scott	.60	1.50
94 Shane Vereen	.75	2.00
95 Ricky Stanzi	.60	1.50
96 Brian Rolle	1.00	2.50
97 Doug Baldwin	3.00	8.00
98 Mikel Leshoure	.60	1.50
99 Torrey Smith	.60	1.50
100A Cam Newton prpl	3.00	8.00
100B Cam Newton blu SP	12.00	30.00

2011 Topps Magic Rookies Autographs

Card	Low	High
ONE AUTOGRAPH PER BOX		
1 A.J. Green SP	25.00	60.00
2 Aldon Smith	10.00	25.00
3 Niles Paul	6.00	15.00
4 Jon Baldwin	6.00	15.00
5 Justin Houston	4.00	10.00
6 Akeem Ayers	3.00	8.00
8 Dion Lewis	6.00	15.00
10 Mark Ingram SP	20.00	50.00
11 Ryan Kerrigan	8.00	20.00
12 Lance Kendricks	3.00	8.00
13 Marcell Dareus	6.00	15.00
14 Stephen Paea	6.00	15.00
15 Mike Pouncey	5.00	12.00
16 Terrence Toliver	4.00	10.00
20 Jake Locker SP	30.00	60.00
21 Vincent Brown	3.00	8.00
22 Jacquizz Rodgers	6.00	15.00
24 Rahim Moore	3.00	8.00
26 Jeremy Kerley	5.00	12.00
29 Cecil Shorts	3.00	8.00
30 Daniel Thomas	3.00	8.00
31 Cameron Jordan	4.00	10.00
33 Virgil Green	3.00	8.00
35 Austin Pettis	3.00	8.00
36 Darvin Adams	3.00	8.00
37 Prince Amukamara	6.00	15.00
39 Luke Stocker	3.00	8.00
40 Ryan Mallett SP	8.00	20.00
43 Aaron Williams	3.00	8.00
45 Rob Housler	3.00	8.00
46 Von Miller SP	25.00	60.00
47 Jamie Harper	6.00	15.00
48 Mark Herzlich	3.00	8.00
49 Edmond Gates	3.00	8.00
51 Alex Green		
52 Jordan Todman	4.00	10.00
53 J.J. Watt SP	50.00	80.00
55 Leonard Hankerson	3.00	8.00
56 Greg Salas	3.00	8.00
57 Nick Fairley	3.00	8.00
58 Ryan Williams	8.00	20.00
59 Tandon Doss	3.00	8.00
60 Randall Cobb SP	5.00	12.00
61 Bilal Powell	4.00	10.00
64 Dwayne Harris	3.00	8.00
66 Kendall Hunter	6.00	15.00
67 Ronald Johnson	3.00	8.00
70 Christian Ponder SP	25.00	60.00
71 Greg McElroy	5.00	12.00
72 Tyrod Taylor	6.00	15.00
73 Da'Quan Bowers	8.00	20.00
74 Colin Kaepernick	5.00	12.00
75 John Clay	15.00	30.00
76 Adrian Clayborn	3.00	8.00
77 Mike McNeill	5.00	12.00
79 Titus Young	15.00	30.00
80 Blaine Gabbert SP	3.00	8.00
82 D.J. Williams	3.00	8.00
83 Delone Carter	3.00	8.00
84 Taiwan Jones	8.00	20.00
86 Darren Evans	4.00	10.00
87 Jerrel Jernigan	3.00	8.00
89 Derrick Locke	4.00	10.00
93 Da'Rel Scott	3.00	8.00
94 Shane Vereen	4.00	10.00
95 Ricky Stanzi	8.00	20.00
98 Mikel Leshoure	3.00	8.00
100 Cam Newton SP	250.00	350.00

2011 Topps Magic Rookies Cut Autographs Black

Card	Low	High
1 A.J. Green	50.00	120.00
9 DeMarco Murray	12.00	30.00
10 Mark Ingram	40.00	80.00
50 Julio Jones	75.00	150.00
79 Titus Young	50.00	100.00
83 Delone Carter	30.00	60.00
91 Greg Little	30.00	60.00
100 Cam Newton	150.00	300.00

2012 Topps Magic

Card	Low	High
COMPLETE SET (275)	40.00	80.00
COMP.SET w/o SP's (220)	15.00	40.00
SP STATED ODDS 1:3 HOB		
1 Andrew Luck RC	2.50	6.00
2 Willis McGahee	.15	.40
3 Morris Claiborne RC	.25	.60
4 Jason Pierre-Paul	.15	.40
5 Joe Adams RC	.25	.60
6 Matt Cassel	.15	.40
7 Melvin Ingram RC	.25	.60
8 Darren McFadden	.15	.40
9 Clay Matthews	.25	.60
10 Wes Welker	.20	.50
11 Jermaine Kearse RC	.40	1.00
12 Patrick Willis	.20	.50
13 DeMarco Murray	.20	.50
14 James Laurinaitis	.15	.40
15 Bobby Rainey RC	.25	.60
16 Jahvid Best	.15	.40
17 Mario Williams	.15	.40
18 Jeff Fuller RC	.25	.60
19 Dwight Jones RC	.25	.60
20 Calvin Johnson	.25	.60
21 Champ Bailey	.20	.50
22 Kirk Cousins RC	1.00	2.50
23 Quinton Coples RC	.25	.60
24 Sam Bradford	.15	.40
25 Tommy Streeter RC	.25	.60
26 Rueben Randle RC	.25	.60
27 Mike Thomas	.20	.50
28 Matt Moore	.15	.40
29 Ben Tate	.15	.40
30 LeSean McCoy	.25	.60
31 A.J. Green	.25	.60
32 Alshon Jeffery RC	.50	1.25
33 Devon Still RC	.30	.75
34 Dustin Keller	.15	.40
35 Mark Sanchez	.15	.40
36 Dont'a Hightower RC	.40	1.00
37 Sidney Rice	.15	.40
38 T.J. Graham RC	.25	.60
39 Travis Benjamin RC	.25	.60
40 Steven Jackson	.15	.40
41 Mike Williams	.20	.50
42 Denarius Moore	.15	.40
43 Jabar Gaffney	.15	.40
44 Michael Floyd RC	.25	.60
45 Ronnie Hillman RC	.25	.60
46 Emmitt Smith	.60	1.50
47 James Starks	.15	.40
48 David DeCastro RC	.25	.60
49 Brian Urlacher	.25	.60
50 Larry Fitzgerald	.20	.50
51 Ahmad Bradshaw	.15	.40
52 Michael Egnew RC	.25	.60
53 Ryan Lindley RC	.25	.60
54 Stephen Hill RC	.25	.60
55 Jeremy Kerley	.15	.40
56 Daryl Richardson RC	.40	1.00
57 Cyrus Gray RC	.25	.60
58 Brock Osweiler RC	.25	.60
59 Tim Tebow	.25	.60
60 Ray Rice	.15	.40
61 Brandon Weeden RC	.25	.60
62 A.J. Hawk	.15	.40
63 Matt Schaub	.15	.40
64 Jermichael Finley	.15	.40
65 Frank Gore	.20	.50
66 Brandon Flowers	.15	.40
67 Vernon Davis	.15	.40
68 Steve Breaston	.15	.40
69 DeVier Posey RC	.25	.60
70 Eli Manning	.20	.50
71 Jason Babin	.15	.40
72 Joe Montana	.75	2.00
73 Chris Rainey RC	.25	.60
74 Anquan Boldin	.15	.40
75 Case Keenum RC	.50	1.25
76 Jared Allen	.15	.40
77 Hakeem Nicks	.15	.40
78 Doug Martin RC	.40	1.00
79 Davone Bess	.15	.40
80 Adrian Peterson	.25	.60
81 Philip Rivers	.25	.60
82 Lamar Miller RC	.40	1.00
83 Ray Lewis	.25	.60
84 Miles Austin	.15	.40
85 Darrelle Revis	.15	.40
86 Mark Ingram	.20	.50
87 Robert Turbin RC	.25	.60
88 Ed Reed	.20	.50
89 A.J. Jenkins RC	.25	.60
90 Marshawn Lynch	.20	.50
91 Beanie Wells	.15	.40
92 Chris Polk RC	.25	.60
93 Darren Sproles	.20	.50
94 Fred Jackson	.20	.50
95 Kevin Kolb	.15	.40
96 Matt Kalil RC	.25	.60
97 Nick Foles RC	.60	1.50
98 Roy Helu	.15	.40
99 Tony Romo	.20	.50
100 Robert Griffin III RC	.30	.75
101 Dre Kirkpatrick RC	.25	.60
102 DeAngelo Williams	.15	.40
103 James Casey	.15	.40
104 Jerry Rice	.60	1.50
105 Steve Smith	.20	.50
106 Von Miller	.20	.50
107 Santonio Holmes	.15	.40
108 Marvin Jones RC	.25	.60
109 Ryan Mathews	.20	.50
110 Greg Jennings	.15	.40
111 Juron Criner RC	.25	.60
112 Jeremy Maclin	.15	.40
113 Jamaal Charles	.20	.50
114 Dwayne Allen RC	.25	.60
115 Kendall Wright RC	.25	.60
116 Reggie Wayne	.20	.50
117 Michael Vick	.20	.50
118 Luke Kuechly RC	.60	1.50
119 Jacory Harris RC	.30	.75
120 Drew Brees	.25	.60
121 Rashard Mendenhall	.15	.40
122 Vincent Jackson	.15	.40
123 Bernard Pierce RC	.25	.60
124 Chandler Jones RC	.25	.60
125 Antonio Brown	.25	.60
126 Jason Witten	.20	.50
127 Torrey Smith	.15	.40
128 Josh Gordon RC	.60	1.50
129 Matt Ryan	.20	.50
130 Chris Johnson	.15	.40
131 Laurent Robinson	.15	.40
132 Andre Johnson	.20	.50
133 Mohamed Sanu RC	.40	1.00
134 Brandon Pettigrew	.15	.40
135 Brian Quick RC	.25	.60
136 Jake Locker	.25	.60
137 Ndamukong Suh	.20	.50
138 Percy Harvin	.15	.40
139 Demaryius Thomas	.25	.60
140 Victor Cruz	.20	.50
141 Bart Scott	.15	.40
142 Matt Forte	.15	.40
143 Tony Gonzalez	.20	.50
144 Greg Childs RC	.25	.60
145 Dez Bryant	.25	.60
146 Chad Greenway	.20	.50
147 Aaron Hernandez	.20	.50
148 Jim Kelly	.40	1.00
149 Jarius Wright RC	.25	.60
150 Arian Foster	.20	.50
151 Kellen Moore RC	.30	.75
152 Vick Ballard RC	.30	.75
153 LaMichael James RC	.25	.60
154 Jimmy Graham	.25	.60
155 Chandler Harnish RC	.25	.60
156 Darrius Heyward-Bey	.15	.40
157 Reggie Bush	.15	.40
158 Jacoby Ford	.15	.40
159 Nick Fairley	.15	.40
160 Rob Gronkowski	.25	.60
161 Christian Ponder	.15	.40
162 Golden Tate	.15	.40
163 Barry Sanders	.60	1.50
164 Nick Toon RC	.25	.60
165 Trent Richardson RC	.25	.60
166 Ryan Tannehill RC	.40	1.00
167 LeGarrette Blount	.20	.50
168 Knowshon Moreno	.15	.40
169 David Wilson RC	.25	.60
170 Julio Jones	.25	.60
171 BenJarvus Green-Ellis	.20	.50
172 Alex Smith	.20	.50
173 Devin Hester	.20	.50
174 Dwayne Bowe	.20	.50
175 Jay Cutler	.15	.40
176 Malcom Floyd	.15	.40
177 Mike Wallace	.15	.40
178 Pierre Garcon	.20	.50
179 Steve Johnson	.20	.50
180 Justin Blackmon RC	.25	.60
181 Russell Wilson RC	2.00	5.00
182 Cedric Benson	.15	.40
183 Chris Givens RC	.25	.60
184 Antonio Gates	.20	.50
185 Andy Dalton	.20	.50
186 Greg Olsen	.20	.50
187 Jordy Nelson	.20	.50
188 Ryan Broyles RC	.25	.60
189 Ben Roethlisberger	.25	.60
190 Maurice Jones-Drew	.15	.40
191 DeMarcus Ware	.25	.60
192 Coby Fleener RC	.25	.60
193 Justin Tuck	.15	.40
194 Isaiah Pead RC	.25	.60
195 Marvin McNutt RC	.25	.60
196 Michael Turner	.15	.40
197 Mark Barron RC	.25	.60
198 Julius Peppers	.20	.50
199 Andre Roberts	.20	.50
200 Aaron Rodgers	.40	1.00
201 Titus Young	.15	.40
202 Jacquizz Rodgers	.20	.50
203 Jerel Worthy RC	.25	.60
204 Marques Colston	.15	.40
205 Peyton Hillis	.15	.40
206 Michael Bush	.15	.40
207 Blaine Gabbert	.15	.40
208 Carson Palmer	.20	.50
209 Eric Decker	.15	.40
210 Matthew Stafford	.20	.50
211 Dontari Poe RC	.25	.60
212 Janoris Jenkins RC	.30	.75
213 Roddy White	.15	.40
214 Dexter McCluster	.15	.40
215 T.Y. Hilton RC	.50	1.25
216 Shonn Greene	.15	.40
217 Jim Brown	.50	1.25
218 Brandon Lloyd	.15	.40
219 C.J. Spiller	.15	.40
220 Cam Newton	.25	.60
221 Adrian Clayborn	.75	2.00
222 Colt McCoy	1.00	2.50
223 James Jones	1.00	2.50
224 Jonathan Stewart	.75	2.00
225 Lance Moore	.75	2.00
226 Devery Henderson	.75	2.00
227 Alfred Morris RC	.50	1.25
228 Owen Daniels	.75	2.00
229 Sean Lee	1.25	3.00
230 Peyton Manning	2.50	6.00
231 Fred Davis	.75	2.00
232 Colin Kaepernick	1.00	2.50
233 Joe Haden	.75	2.00
234 Michael Crabtree	.75	2.00
235 Heath Miller	.75	2.00
236 Randy Moss	1.00	2.50
237 Haloti Ngata	.75	2.00
238 DeMeco Ryans	.75	2.00
239 Brandon LaFell	.75	2.00
240 DeSean Jackson	1.00	2.50
241 Josh Freeman	1.00	2.50
242 Mario Manningham	.75	2.00
243 Patrick Peterson	.75	2.00
244 Brett Favre	2.50	6.00
245 Nate Burleson	.75	2.00
246 Ryan Fitzpatrick	.75	2.00
247 Ryan Mallett	1.00	2.50
248 Montario Hardesty	.75	2.00
249 Zach Miller	.75	2.00
250 Tom Brady	3.00	8.00
251 Joe Flacco	1.00	2.50
252 J.J. Watt	1.25	3.00
253 Prince Amukamara	.75	2.00
254 Stevan Ridley	.75	2.00
255 Dennis Pitta	.75	2.00
256 Brandon Jacobs	.75	2.00
257 Steve Young	1.50	4.00
258 Kenny Britt	.75	2.00
259 Isaac Redman	1.25	3.00
260 Troy Polamalu	1.25	3.00
261 Jon Baldwin	.75	2.00
262 Bobby Wagner RC	.75	2.00
263 B.J. Raji	.75	2.00
264 Matt Flynn	.75	2.00
265 Jermaine Gresham	.75	2.00
266 Randall Cobb	1.00	2.50
267 Toby Gerhart	.75	2.00
268 Lance Kendricks	.75	2.00
269 Jonathan Vilma	.75	2.00
270 Brandon Marshall	1.00	2.50
271 Charles Woodson	1.25	3.00
272 Nate Washington	.75	2.00
273 Josh Cribbs	.75	2.00
274 Damian Williams	.75	2.00
275 Santana Moss	1.00	2.50

2012 Topps Magic Mini

*1-220 VETS: .8X TO 2X BASIC CARDS
*1-220 ROOKIES: .5X TO 1.2X BASIC RC
*221-275 VET SP: .4X TO 1X BASIC SP
*221-275 ROOKIE SP: .5X TO 1.2X SP RC
ONE MINI PER PACK OVERALL

2012 Topps Magic Mini Black Border

Card	Low	High
*1-220 VETS: 2.5X TO 6X BASIC CARDS		
*1-220 ROOKIES: 1.5X TO 4X BASIC RC		
*221-275 VET SP: .8X TO 2X BASIC SP		
*221-275 ROOKIE SP: 1X TO 2.5X SP RC		
STATED ODDS 1:24 HOB		
1 Andrew Luck	10.00	25.00

2012 Topps Magic Mini Blue Border

*1-220 VETS: 1.2X TO 3X BASIC CARDS
*1-220 ROOKIES: .8X TO 2X BASIC RC
*221-275 VET SP: .6X TO 1.5X BASIC SP
*221-275 ROOKIE SP: .8X TO 2X SP RC
ONE PER RETAIL BOX

2012 Topps Magic Mini Pigskin 50

Card	Low	High
*1-220 VET/50: 4X TO 10X BASIC CARDS		
*1-220 ROOKIE/50: 2.5X TO 6X BASIC RC		
*221-275 VETS/50: .8X TO 2X BASIC SP		
*221-275 ROOKIE/50: 1.2X TO 3X SP RC		
PIGSKIN/50 ODDS 1:65 HOB		
1 Andrew Luck	25.00	50.00

2012 Topps Magic 1948 Magic

Card	Low	High
COMPLETE SET (20)	15.00	40.00
STATED ODDS 1:12 HOB		
1 A.J. Jenkins	.40	1.00
2 Andrew Luck	4.00	10.00
3 Brandon Weeden	.40	1.00
4 Coby Fleener	.40	1.00
5 Doug Martin	.60	1.50
6 Justin Blackmon	.40	1.00
7 Michael Floyd	.40	1.00
8 Robert Griffin III	.50	1.25
9 Ryan Tannehill	.60	1.50
10 Trent Richardson	.40	1.00
11 Aaron Rodgers	1.25	3.00
12 Darren McFadden	.50	1.25
13 LeSean McCoy	.75	2.00
14 Michael Vick	.60	1.50
15 Mike Wallace	.50	1.25
16 Torrey Smith	.50	1.25
17 Victor Cruz	.60	1.50
18 Von Miller	.60	1.50
19 Jerry Rice	1.50	4.00
20 Troy Aikman	1.25	3.00

2012 Topps Magic Autographs

Card	Low	High
STATED ODDS 1:9 HOB		
EXCH EXPIRATION: 12/31/2015		
1 Andrew Luck SP	300.00	500.00
5 Joe Adams SP	5.00	12.00
7 Melvin Ingram EXCH	2.00	5.00
8 Darren McFadden SP	20.00	40.00
11 Jermaine Kearse	5.00	12.00
12 Patrick Willis	30.00	60.00
15 Bobby Rainey	2.00	5.00
18 Jeff Fuller	2.00	5.00
19 Dwight Jones	2.00	5.00
22 Kirk Cousins SP	12.00	30.00
23 Quinton Coples	2.00	5.00
26 Rueben Randle	5.00	12.00
27 Mike Thomas SP	5.00	12.00
28 Matt Moore SP	8.00	20.00
29 Ben Tate	4.00	10.00
31 A.J. Green	15.00	30.00
32 Alshon Jeffery SP	15.00	30.00
33 Devon Still	2.50	6.00
36 Dont'a Hightower	3.00	8.00
37 Sidney Rice SP		
38 T.J. Graham SP	3.00	8.00
39 Travis Benjamin	2.00	5.00
42 Denarius Moore SP	6.00	15.00
43 Jabar Gaffney SP	8.00	20.00
44 Michael Floyd SP EXCH	20.00	50.00
45 Ronnie Hillman EXCH	2.00	5.00
48 David DeCastro	2.00	5.00
51 Ahmad Bradshaw SP	10.00	25.00
52 Michael Egnew SP	3.00	8.00
53 Ryan Lindley	2.00	5.00
54 Stephen Hill	2.00	5.00
55 Jeremy Kerley	4.00	10.00
56 Daryl Richardson	8.00	20.00
57 Cyrus Gray	2.00	5.00
58 Brock Osweiler	2.00	5.00
61 Brandon Weeden SP	15.00	40.00
63 Matt Schaub SP		
64 Jermichael Finley SP	6.00	15.00
65 Frank Gore SP	8.00	20.00
66 Brandon Flowers	4.00	10.00
67 Vernon Davis SP	25.00	50.00
68 Steve Breaston SP	4.00	10.00
69 DeVier Posey SP	3.00	8.00
70 Chris Rainey	2.00	5.00
75 Case Keenum	6.00	15.00
77 Hakeem Nicks SP	10.00	25.00
78 Doug Martin	3.00	8.00
79 Davone Bess	4.00	10.00
82 Lamar Miller SP	20.00	40.00
85 Darrelle Revis SP	30.00	60.00
86 Mark Ingram	5.00	12.00
87 Robert Turbin	2.00	5.00
89 A.J. Jenkins SP	12.50	25.00
90 Marshawn Lynch SP	20.00	40.00
91 Beanie Wells	10.00	25.00
92 Chris Polk SP EXCH	3.00	8.00
93 Darren Sproles SP EXCH	15.00	30.00
94 Fred Jackson SP EXCH	20.00	40.00
95 Kevin Kolb		
96 Matt Kalil	2.00	5.00
97 Nick Foles	25.00	50.00
98 Roy Helu SP	5.00	12.00
100 Robert Griffin III SP	30.00	60.00
101 Dre Kirkpatrick EXCH	2.00	5.00
103 James Casey	4.00	10.00
105 Steve Smith SP	10.00	25.00
106 Von Miller SP	20.00	40.00
107 Santonio Holmes SP	6.00	15.00
108 Marvin Jones	2.00	5.00
109 Ryan Mathews SP	6.00	15.00
110 Greg Jennings SP	15.00	40.00
111 Juron Criner	2.00	5.00
112 Jeremy Maclin SP		
114 Dwayne Allen SP	8.00	20.00
115 Kendall Wright SP	3.00	8.00
116 Reggie Wayne	6.00	15.00
118 Luke Kuechly	15.00	30.00
121 Rashard Mendenhall		
122 Vincent Jackson SP	8.00	20.00
124 Chandler Jones	2.00	5.00
125 Antonio Brown SP	8.00	20.00
127 Torrey Smith SP	8.00	20.00
128 Josh Gordon	5.00	12.00
129 Matt Ryan SP	40.00	80.00
131 Laurent Robinson SP	5.00	12.00
132 Andre Johnson SP	20.00	40.00
133 Mohamed Sanu	3.00	8.00
135 Brian Quick SP	3.00	8.00
136 Jake Locker	6.00	15.00
137 Ndamukong Suh SP	12.50	25.00
138 Percy Harvin SP	15.00	30.00
139 Demaryius Thomas	8.00	20.00
140 Victor Cruz SP	20.00	40.00
142 Matt Forte SP EXCH	20.00	40.00
144 Greg Childs	2.00	5.00
147 Aaron Hernandez	5.00	12.00
149 Jarius Wright	2.00	5.00
150 Arian Foster	5.00	12.00
151 Kellen Moore SP EXCH	4.00	10.00
152 Vick Ballard	2.50	6.00
153 LaMichael James SP	20.00	50.00
154 Jimmy Graham	8.00	20.00
155 Chandler Harnish	2.00	5.00
158 Jacoby Ford	4.00	10.00
159 Nick Fairley	4.00	10.00
161 Christian Ponder SP	4.00	10.00
162 Golden Tate	4.00	10.00
164 Nick Toon	3.00	8.00
165 Trent Richardson SP	40.00	80.00
166 Ryan Tannehill SP	3.00	8.00
167 LeGarrette Blount SP	5.00	12.00
169 David Wilson SP EXCH	3.00	8.00
174 Dwayne Bowe SP	12.50	25.00
176 Malcom Floyd	4.00	10.00
177 Mike Wallace	4.00	10.00
178 Pierre Garcon SP	15.00	30.00
180 Justin Blackmon SP EXCH		
181 Russell Wilson SP	250.00	400.00
182 Cedric Benson	4.00	10.00
188 Ryan Broyles	2.00	5.00
190 Maurice Jones-Drew SP	10.00	25.00
191 DeMarcus Ware SP	20.00	40.00
192 Coby Fleener	2.00	5.00
194 Isaiah Pead	3.00	8.00
195 Marvin McNutt	2.00	5.00
196 Michael Turner SP	15.00	30.00
197 Mark Barron	2.00	5.00
199 Andre Roberts	5.00	12.00
202 Jacquizz Rodgers	5.00	12.00
203 Jerel Worthy	2.00	5.00
204 Marques Colston SP	15.00	30.00
205 Peyton Hillis SP	6.00	15.00
206 Michael Bush	4.00	10.00
207 Blaine Gabbert	4.00	10.00
209 Eric Decker	4.00	10.00
211 Dontari Poe	2.00	5.00
212 Janoris Jenkins	2.50	6.00
213 Roddy White SP		
214 Dexter McCluster	4.00	10.00
215 T.Y. Hilton	4.00	10.00
216 Shonn Greene SP	4.00	10.00
221 Adrian Clayborn	4.00	10.00
222 Colt McCoy	5.00	12.00
227 Alfred Morris	2.00	5.00
229 Sean Lee	6.00	15.00
232 Colin Kaepernick	12.00	30.00
239 Brandon LaFell	4.00	10.00
247 Ryan Mallett	5.00	12.00
248 Montario Hardesty	4.00	10.00
249 Zach Miller	4.00	10.00
252 J.J. Watt	30.00	60.00
253 Prince Amukamara SP	4.00	10.00
261 Jon Baldwin	4.00	10.00
262 Bobby Wagner	3.00	8.00
265 Jermaine Gresham	4.00	10.00
267 Toby Gerhart	4.00	10.00
268 Lance Kendricks	4.00	10.00
269 Jonathan Vilma	4.00	10.00

2012 Topps Magic Charismatic Combos

Card	Low	High
COMPLETE SET (10)	5.00	12.00
STATED ODDS 1:12 HOB		
CCBW T.Brady/W.Welker	2.00	5.00
CCCM J.Cutler/B.Marshall	.60	1.50
CCMC E.Manning/V.Cruz	.60	1.50
CCNS C.Newton/S.Smith	.75	2.00
CCRJ A.Rodgers/G.Jennings	1.25	3.00
CCRW M.Ryan/R.White	.60	1.50
CCSJ M.Stafford/C.Johnson	.75	2.00
CCVJ M.Vick/D.Jackson	.60	1.50
CCMSJ M.Schaub/A.Johnson	.60	1.50
CCRWA B.Roethlisberger/M.Wallace	.75	2.00

2012 Topps Magic Dual Autographs

Card	Low	High
DUAL AU/25 ODDS 1:2410 HOB		
DAAF D.Allen/C.Fleener	10.00	25.00
DABA V.Ballard/D.Allen		
DABF Blackmon/Floyd EXCH	10.00	25.00
DAFJ M.Forte/A.Jeffery	20.00	50.00
DAHG R.Hillman/C.Gray	10.00	25.00
DAHH S.Hill/S.Holmes	10.00	25.00
DAHJ A.Hernandez/C.Jones	12.00	30.00
DAKH L.Kuechly/D.Hightower	25.00	60.00
DALG A.Luck/R.Griffin III	250.00	400.00
DAMM L.Miller/D.Martin	15.00	40.00
DAPS D.Poe/N.Suh	12.00	30.00
DAQA B.Quick/J.Adams	10.00	25.00
DARW R.Randle/D.Wilson	10.00	25.00
DARWE T.Richardson/B.Weeden	10.00	25.00
DAWT R.Wilson/R.Turbin	100.00	175.00

2012 Topps Magic Historical Coins

Card	Low	High
HISTORY COIN/25 ODDS 1:722 HOB		
HCAA Academy Awards	15.00	40.00
HCAE Amelia Earhart	15.00	40.00
HCAP Alcatraz	15.00	40.00
HCBR Babe Ruth	25.00	50.00
HCCC Charlie Chaplin	15.00	40.00
HCCG U.S. Coast Guard	15.00	40.00
HCCL Charles Lindbergh	15.00	40.00
HCFR Federal Reserve	15.00	40.00
HCGC Grand Central Terminal	15.00	40.00
HCGG The Great Gatsby	15.00	40.00
HCGT Gene Tunney	15.00	40.00
HCHD Hoover Dam	15.00	40.00
HCHG Harlem Globetrotters	15.00	40.00
HCHH Herbert Hoover	15.00	40.00
HCJD Joe DiMaggio	15.00	40.00
HCKK King Kong	15.00	40.00
HCLM Lincoln Memorial	15.00	40.00
HCLT Looney Toons Debut	15.00	40.00
HCMA Miss America Pageant	15.00	40.00
HCMM Mickey Mouse Debut	15.00	40.00
HCMO Monopoly	15.00	40.00
HCMR Mount Rushmore	15.00	40.00
HCMT Macy's Thanksgiving Parade	15.00	40.00
HCMW Minimum Wage	15.00	40.00
HCPC Panama Canal	15.00	40.00
HCPH Purple Heart	15.00	40.00
HCPP Pulitzer Prize	15.00	40.00
HCRB Baseball Radio Broadcast	15.00	40.00
HCSS Stop Sign	15.00	40.00
HCTM Time Magazine	15.00	40.00
HCTV Treaty of Versailles	15.00	40.00
HCWB Warner Bros.	15.00	40.00
HCWO Winter Olympics	15.00	40.00
HCWW Woodrow Wilson	15.00	40.00
HCYS Yankee Stadium Opens	15.00	40.00
HC18A 18th Amendment	15.00	40.00
HC19A 19th Amendment	15.00	40.00
HCESB Empire State Bldg.	15.00	40.00
HCFDR Franklin D. Roosevelt	15.00	40.00
HCFNG Baseball Night Game	15.00	40.00
HCGGB Golden Great Bridge	15.00	40.00
HCHGO Hank Gowdy	15.00	40.00
HCLMA LIFE Magazine	15.00	40.00
HCNPS National Parks	15.00	40.00
HCPOP Popeye	15.00	40.00
HCR66 Route 66	15.00	40.00
HCSEA Seabiscuit	15.00	40.00
HCSET Sporting Event Televised	15.00	40.00

2012 Topps Magic Magical Moments

Card	Low	High
COMPLETE SET (20)	5.00	12.00
STATED ODDS 1:6 HOB		
MMAB Antonio Brown	.50	1.25
MMAR Aaron Rodgers	.75	2.00
MMCN Cam Newton	.50	1.25
MMDB Drew Brees	.50	1.25
MMDM DeMarco Murray	.40	1.00
MMDS Darren Sproles	.40	1.00
MMEM Eli Manning	.40	1.00
MMJA Jared Allen	.30	.75
MMLM LeSean McCoy	.50	1.25
MMMF Matt Flynn	.30	.75
MMMJD Maurice Jones-Drew	.30	.75
MMML Marshawn Lynch	.40	1.00
MMMS Matthew Stafford	.40	1.00
MMPP Patrick Peterson	.30	.75
MMRG Rob Gronkowski	.50	1.25
MMSS Steve Smith	.40	1.00
MMTB Tom Brady	1.25	3.00
MMTS Torrey Smith	.30	.75
MMTT Tim Tebow	.50	1.25
MMVD Vernon Davis	.30	.75

2012 Topps Magic Relics

Card	Low	High
RELIC/25 ODDS 1:242 HOB		
6 Matt Cassel	5.00	12.00
9 Clay Matthews	8.00	20.00
10 Wes Welker	6.00	15.00
13 DeMarco Murray	6.00	15.00
14 James Laurinaitis	5.00	12.00
16 Jahvid Best	5.00	12.00
17 Mario Williams	5.00	12.00
21 Champ Bailey	6.00	15.00
24 Sam Bradford	5.00	12.00
30 LeSean McCoy	8.00	20.00
34 Dustin Keller	5.00	12.00
35 Mark Sanchez	5.00	12.00
40 Steven Jackson	5.00	12.00
41 Mike Williams	6.00	15.00
47 James Starks	5.00	12.00
49 Brian Urlacher	8.00	20.00
50 Larry Fitzgerald	6.00	15.00
55 Jordan Shipley	5.00	12.00
59 Tim Tebow	8.00	20.00
60 Ray Rice	5.00	12.00
62 A.J. Hawk	5.00	12.00
66 Rey Maualuga	5.00	12.00
70 Eli Manning	6.00	15.00
71 Jason Babin	5.00	12.00
74 Anquan Boldin	5.00	12.00
76 Jared Allen	5.00	12.00
79 Shane Vereen	5.00	12.00
80 Adrian Peterson	8.00	20.00
81 Philip Rivers	8.00	20.00
83 Ray Lewis	10.00	25.00
84 Miles Austin	5.00	12.00
85 Darrelle Revis	5.00	12.00
86 Mark Ingram	6.00	15.00
99 Tony Romo	6.00	15.00
102 DeAngelo Williams	5.00	12.00
103 Brian Orakpo	6.00	15.00
113 Jamaal Charles	6.00	15.00
116 Reggie Wayne	6.00	15.00
120 Drew Brees	8.00	20.00
123 Bernard Pierce	5.00	12.00
130 Chris Johnson	5.00	12.00
134 Brandon Pettigrew	5.00	12.00
136 Jake Locker	6.00	15.00
139 Demaryius Thomas	8.00	20.00
141 Bart Scott	5.00	12.00
143 Tony Gonzalez	6.00	15.00
145 Dez Bryant	8.00	20.00
146 Chad Greenway	6.00	15.00
150 Arian Foster	6.00	15.00
154 Jimmy Graham	8.00	20.00
156 Darrius Heyward-Bey	5.00	12.00
157 Reggie Bush	5.00	12.00
159 Earl Thomas	6.00	15.00
160 Rob Gronkowski	8.00	20.00
162 John Skelton	5.00	12.00
168 Knowshon Moreno	5.00	12.00
170 Julio Jones	8.00	20.00
173 Devin Hester	6.00	15.00
175 Jay Cutler	5.00	12.00
179 Steve Johnson	5.00	12.00
184 Antonio Gates	6.00	15.00
185 Andy Dalton	6.00	15.00
187 Jordy Nelson	6.00	15.00
189 Ben Roethlisberger	8.00	20.00
192 Coby Fleener	5.00	12.00
193 Justin Tuck	5.00	12.00
198 Julius Peppers	6.00	15.00
201 Titus Young	5.00	12.00
202 Jacquizz Rodgers	6.00	15.00
207 Blaine Gabbert	5.00	12.00
208 Carson Palmer	6.00	15.00
214 Richard Seymour	5.00	12.00
219 C.J. Spiller	5.00	12.00
220 Cam Newton	8.00	20.00

2012 Topps Magic Rookie Enchantment

Card	Low	High
COMPLETE SET (20)	12.00	30.00
STATED ODDS 1:5 HOB		
REAJ A.J. Jenkins	.40	1.00
REAL Andrew Luck	4.00	10.00
REBO Brock Osweiler	.40	1.00
REBW Brandon Weeden	.40	1.00
RECF Coby Fleener	.40	1.00
REDM Doug Martin	.60	1.50
REDW David Wilson	.40	1.00
REJB Justin Blackmon	.40	1.00
REKW Kendall Wright	.40	1.00
RELJ LaMichael James	.40	1.00
RELK Luke Kuechly	1.00	2.50
REMB Mark Barron	.40	1.00
REMC Morris Claiborne	.40	1.00
REMF Michael Floyd	.40	1.00
REMS Mohamed Sanu	.60	1.50
RERG Robert Griffin III	.50	1.25
RERT Ryan Tannehill	.60	1.50
RERTU Robert Turbin	.40	1.00
RESH Stephen Hill	.40	1.00
RETR Trent Richardson	.40	1.00

2012 Topps Magic Supernatural Stars

Card	Low	High
COMPLETE SET (40)	8.00	20.00
STATED ODDS 1:4 HOB		
SSAB Ahmad Bradshaw	.30	.75
SSAD Andy Dalton	.40	1.00
SSAF Arian Foster	.40	1.00
SSAG A.J. Green	.50	1.25
SSAJ Andre Johnson	.40	1.00
SSAP Adrian Peterson	.50	1.25
SSAS Alex Smith	.40	1.00
SSBM Brandon Marshall	.40	1.00
SSBR Ben Roethlisberger	.50	1.25
SSCJ Calvin Johnson	.50	1.25
SSDJ DeSean Jackson	.40	1.00
SSGJ Greg Jennings	.30	.75
SSHN Hakeem Nicks	.30	.75
SSJF Jermichael Finley	.30	.75
SSJG Jimmy Graham	.50	1.25
SSJJ Julio Jones	.50	1.25
SSJN Jordy Nelson	.40	1.00
SSJW Jason Witten	.40	1.00
SSLF Larry Fitzgerald	.40	1.00
SSMR Matt Ryan	.40	1.00
SSMS Matt Schaub	.30	.75
SSMT Michael Turner	.30	.75
SSMW Mike Wallace	.30	.75
SSPM Peyton Manning	1.00	2.50
SSPR Philip Rivers	.50	1.25
SSPW Patrick Willis	.40	1.00
SSRB Reggie Bush	.30	.75
SSRF Ryan Fitzpatrick	.30	.75
SSRR Ray Rice	.30	.75
SSSJ Steven Jackson	.30	.75
SSTG Tony Gonzalez	.40	1.00
SSTP Troy Polamalu	.50	1.25
SSTR Tony Romo	.40	1.00
SSVC Victor Cruz	.40	1.00
SSVM Von Miller	.40	1.00
SSWW Wes Welker	.40	1.00
SSCJO Chris Johnson	.30	.75
SSJFL Joe Flacco	.40	1.00
SSJPP Jason Pierre-Paul	.30	.75
SSMSA Mark Sanchez	.30	.75

2012 Topps Magic Triple Autographs

Card	Low	High
TRIPLE AU/25 ODDS 1:3600 HOB		
TABQJ Blckmn/Quick/Jffry EX	25.00	60.00
TAGHR Gaffney/Harvin/Rainey		
TAHPG Hiltn/Posey/Grhm	25.00	50.00
TAHRG Hillman/Rainey/Gray	25.00	50.00
TALGB Luck/RG3/Blckmn EX	250.00	400.00
TAMKH Millr/Kchly/Hghtwr	40.00	80.00
TAMMT Mrtn/Mllr/Trbin EXCH	25.00	60.00
TAPCB Poe/Kirkpatrick/Barron	15.00	40.00
TAWFL Wells/Floyd/Lindley EX	25.00	50.00
TAWGS Wallace/Gordon/Sanu		

2013 Topps Magic

Card	Low	High
COMP.SET w/o SP's (220)	12.00	30.00
1 Adrian Peterson	.25	.60
2 Vincent Jackson	.15	.40
3 Brian Hartline	.15	.40
4 Andy Dalton	.20	.50
5 Eli Manning	.20	.50
6 Haloti Ngata	.15	.40
7 Lonnie Pryor RC	.25	.60
8 Nico Johnson RC	.30	.75
9 Reggie Bush	.15	.40
10 Kayvon Webster RC	.30	.75
11 Dee Milliner RC	.25	.60
12 Aaron Mellette RC	.25	.60
13 Eric Fisher RC	.25	.60
14 Tyrann Mathieu RC	.40	1.00
15 Ray Graham RC	.25	.60
16 Miguel Maysonet RC	.25	.60
17 Markus Wheaton RC	.25	.60
18 Tyler Eifert RC	.25	.60
19 Onterio McCalebb RC	.30	.75
20 Stevan Ridley	.15	.40
21 Brett Favre	.50	1.25
22 Ace Sanders RC	.25	.60
23 Manti Te'o RC	.30	.75
24 Michael Crabtree	.15	.40
25 Andre Reed	.20	.50
26 Jimmy Graham	.25	.60
27 Alfred Morris	.15	.40
28 Daryl Richardson	.15	.40
29 DeAndre Hopkins RC	.60	1.50
30 Deion Sanders	.20	.50
31 Johnathan Cyprien RC	.25	.60
32 Dwayne Bowe	.20	.50
33 Cordarrelle Patterson RC	.25	.60
34 Kerwynn Williams RC	.25	.60
35 Corey Fuller RC	.25	.60
36 Le'Veon Bell RC	.75	2.00
37 Jarvis Jones RC	.25	.60
38 NaVorro Bowman	.20	.50
39 Jeremy Maclin	.15	.40
40 Roddy White	.15	.40
41 Alex Smith	.20	.50
42 Christine Michael RC	.25	.60
43 Denard Robinson RC	.25	.60
44 Giovani Bernard RC	.25	.60
45 Alshon Jeffery	.20	.50
46 DeMarco Murray	.20	.50
47 Steve Smith	.20	.50
48 Eric Reid RC	.30	.75
49 Mikel Leshoure	.15	.40
50 Peyton Manning	.50	1.25
51 Stevie Brown	.15	.40
52 Lance Moore	.15	.40
53 Marcel Reece	.15	.40
54 Dion Sims RC	.25	.60
55 Barry Sanders	.40	1.00
56 Matt Ryan	.20	.50
57 Golden Tate	.15	.40
58 Andre Roberts	.15	.40
59 Danario Alexander	.15	.40
60 Ryan Tannehill	.20	.50
61 Brandon Myers	.20	.50
62 John Jenkins RC	.25	.60
63 Matt Forte	.15	.40
64 Shane Vereen	.20	.50
65 Quinton Patton RC	.25	.60
66 Thurman Thomas	.20	.50
67 Eric Dickerson	.20	.50
68 Aaron Dobson RC	.25	.60
69 Bobby Wagner	.15	.40
70 Curtis Martin	.20	.50
71 Heath Miller	.15	.40
72 John Simon RC	.40	1.00
73 Tyler Bray RC	.25	.60
74 EJ Manuel RC	.25	.60
75 Kenny Stills RC	.25	.60
76 Josh Boyce RC	.25	.60
77 Antonio Gates	.20	.50
78 Bo Jackson	.30	.75
79 John Elway	.40	1.00
80 Joe Flacco	.20	.50

81 Marquise Goodwin RC .25 .60
82 Terrell Davis .20 .50
83 Randall Cunningham .20 .50
84 Mike Williams .20 .50
85 Vance McDonald RC .30 .75
86 Vick Ballard .15 .40
87 Montee Ball RC .25 .60
88 Steve Largent .25 .60
89 Brian Orakpo .20 .50
90 Zach Ertz RC .50 1.25
91 Jawan Jamison RC .25 .60
92 Barkevious Mingo RC .25 .60
93 Terrance Williams RC .25 .60
94 Patrick Peterson .15 .40
95 Luke Joeckel RC .25 .60
96 Datone Jones RC .25 .60
97 Marshall Faulk .20 .50
98 Khaseem Greene RC .25 .60
99 Trent Richardson .15 .40
100 Steve Young .30 .75
101 Tyler Wilson RC .25 .60
102 Earl Thomas .20 .50
103 Lamar Miller .15 .40
104 Bjoern Werner RC .25 .60
105 Cobi Hamilton RC .25 .60
106 Doug Martin .20 .50
107 Hakeem Nicks .15 .40
108 Conner Vernon RC .25 .60
109 Chris Gragg RC .25 .60
110 Landry Jones RC .25 .60
111 Jason Witten .20 .50
112 Joseph Randle RC .25 .60
113 Torrey Smith .15 .40
114 Rex Burkhead RC .30 .75
115 John Wetzel RC .30 .75
116 Andre Ellington RC .25 .60
117 D.J. Harper RC .30 .75
118 Chris Thompson RC .25 .60
119 Danny Amendola .20 .50
120 Johnathan Hankins RC .25 .60
121 David Wilson .15 .40
122 Stedman Bailey RC .25 .60
123 Jamaal Charles .20 .50
124 Robert Woods RC .40 1.00
125 Drew Brees .25 .60
126 Rob Gronkowski .25 .60
127 Jordan Reed RC .40 1.00
128 A.J. Green .25 .60
129 Dennis Johnson RC .25 .60
130 Barrett Jones RC .25 .60
131 Sam Montgomery RC .25 .60
132 Anquan Boldin .15 .40
133 Tavarres King RC .25 .60
134 Michael Vick .20 .50
135 C.J. Spiller .15 .40
136 Kenbrell Thompkins RC .40 1.00
137 Matt Barkley RC .25 .60
138 Tavon Austin RC .30 .75
139 Darren McFadden .20 .50
140 Jermaine Gresham .20 .50
141 LeSean McCoy .25 .60
142 Zac Dysert RC .25 .60
143 Josh Freeman .20 .50
144 Stepfan Taylor RC .25 .60
145 Chris Johnson .15 .40
146 Bacarri Rambo RC .30 .75
147 Ray Rice .15 .40
148 Gavin Escobar RC .25 .60
149 Ryan Nassib RC .25 .60
150 Geno Smith RC .25 .60
151 D.J. Hayden RC .25 .60
152 Mike Gillislee RC .25 .60
153 Zach Line RC .25 .60
154 Ryan Swope RC .25 .60
155 Justin Hunter RC .25 .60
156 Rodney Smith RC .25 .60
157 Dan Buckner RC .25 .60
158 Dan Marino .60 1.50
159 Reggie Wayne .20 .50
160 Marcus Allen .25 .60
161 Knile Davis RC .25 .60
162 Alex Okafor RC .25 .60
163 Dion Jordan RC .25 .60
164 Philip Lutzenkirchen RC .40 1.00
165 Joique Bell .20 .50
166 Shawn Williams RC .25 .60
167 Jeremy Kerley .15 .40
168 Frank Gore .20 .50
169 Blidi Wreh-Wilson RC .30 .75
170 Kenny Vaccaro RC .25 .60
171 Kenjon Barner RC .25 .60
172 Sheldon Richardson RC .25 .60
173 Randall Cobb .20 .50
174 Matthew Stafford .20 .50
175 Jermichael Finley .15 .40
176 Mike Glennon RC .25 .60
177 Ezekiel Ansah RC .25 .60
178 Kendall Wright .15 .40
179 Chance Warmack RC .25 .60
180 Maurice Jones-Drew .15 .40
181 Michael Williams RC .30 .75
182 Keenan Allen RC .50 1.25
183 Xavier Rhodes RC .25 .60
184 Chase Thomas RC .25 .60
185 Josh Gordon .15 .40
186 Cecil Shorts .15 .40
187 Marcus Lattimore RC .25 .60
188 Desmond Trufant RC .25 .60
189 James Laurinaitis .20 .50
190 Marshawn Lynch .20 .50
191 Sharrif Floyd RC .25 .60
192 Da'Rick Rogers .25 .60
193 Howie Long .25 .60
194 Alec Ogletree RC .25 .60
195 Pierre Garcon .20 .50
196 Matt Scott RC .25 .60
197 Jesse Williams RC .40 1.00
198 Marcus Davis RC .25 .60
199 Theo Riddick RC .25 .60
200 Robert Griffin III .15 .40
201 Jacquizz Rodgers .20 .50
202 Chris Harper RC .25 .60
203 Jamar Taylor RC .25 .60
204 Jason Pierre-Paul .15 .40
205 Robert Lester RC .25 .60
206 Joe Montana 1.00 2.50
207 Jordy Nelson .20 .50
208 Jonathan Dwyer .15 .40
209 Sidney Rice .15 .40
210 Brent Celek .15 .40
211 Eddie Lacy RC .25 .60
212 Lawrence Taylor .25 .60
213 Chris Givens .15 .40
214 BenJarvus Green-Ellis .20 .50
215 Jordan Poyer RC .25 .60
216 Brandon Jenkins RC .30 .75
217 Steve Johnson .20 .50
218 Warren Moon .25 .60
219 Johnathan Franklin RC .25 .60
220 Andrew Luck .40 1.00
221 Aaron Rodgers 1.50 4.00
222 Bruce Smith .75 2.00
223 J.J. Watt .75 2.00
224 Emmanuel Sanders .75 2.00
225 Kurt Warner .75 2.00
226 Jerome Bettis 1.00 2.50
227 Mohamed Sanu .60 1.50
228 Eric Decker .60 1.50
229 James Jones .60 1.50
230 Jim Kelly 1.00 2.50
231 Denarius Moore .60 1.50
232 Mark Ingram .75 2.00
233 Bernard Pierce .60 1.50
234 Zac Stacy RC .60 1.50
235 Jay Cutler .60 1.50
236 Ben Tate .60 1.50
237 Nick Mangold .60 1.50
238 Santonio Holmes .60 1.50
239 Larry Fitzgerald .75 2.00
240 Charles Tillman .75 2.00
241 Antonio Brown 1.00 2.50
242 Darren Sproles .75 2.00
243 Russell Wilson 2.00 5.00
244 Nate Washington .60 1.50
245 Eric Berry .75 2.00
246 Justin Blackmon .60 1.50
247 Philip Rivers 1.00 2.50
248 Dez Bryant 1.00 2.50
249 Jared Cook .60 1.50
250 Tom Brady 2.50 6.00
251 Ryan Mathews .75 2.00
252 Victor Cruz .75 2.00
253 Ben Roethlisberger 1.00 2.50
254 Rueben Randle .60 1.50
255 Kenny Britt .60 1.50
256 DeAngelo Williams .60 1.50
257 Ronnie Hillman .60 1.50
258 Tony Gonzalez .75 2.00
259 Ahmad Bradshaw .60 1.50
260 Jordan Cameron .60 1.50
261 T.Y. Hilton .75 2.00
262 Rod Woodson .75 2.00
263 Brandon Pettigrew .60 1.50
264 Ed Reed .75 2.00
265 Steven Jackson .60 1.50
266 Michael Floyd .60 1.50
267 Brandon LaFell .60 1.50
268 Sam Bradford .60 1.50
269 Julius Peppers .75 2.00
270 Wes Welker .75 2.00
271 Fred Jackson .75 2.00
272 Demaryius Thomas .75 2.00
273 Roger Craig .75 2.00
274 Coby Fleener .60 1.50
275 Joe Greene 1.00 2.50
276 Ndamukong Suh .75 2.00
277 DeMarcus Ware 1.00 2.50
278 Aldon Smith .60 1.50
279 Joe Staley .60 1.50
280 Marcedes Lewis .60 1.50
281 Pierre Thomas .75 2.00
282 Geno Atkins .60 1.50
283 Marlon Brown RC 1.00 2.50
284 Greg Olsen .75 2.00
285 Vernon Davis .60 1.50
286 Stephen Hill .60 1.50
287 Sean Lee .75 2.00
288 Marques Colston .60 1.50
289 Julio Jones 1.00 2.50
290 Patrick Willis .75 2.00
291 Matt Schaub .60 1.50
292 Brandon Marshall .75 2.00
293 Kyle Rudolph .60 1.50
294 DeSean Jackson .75 2.00
295 Richard Sherman 1.00 2.50
296 Eddie Royal .60 1.50
297 Margus Hunt RC .60 1.50
298 Mike Wallace .60 1.50
299 Troy Aikman 1.25 3.00
300 LaDainian Tomlinson .75 2.00
301 Colin Kaepernick .75 2.00
302 Arian Foster .75 2.00
303 Miles Austin .60 1.50
304 Cam Newton 1.00 2.50
305 Jared Allen .60 1.50
306 Greg Jennings .60 1.50
307 Percy Harvin .60 1.50
308 Brandon Weeden .60 1.50
309 Kevin Minter RC .60 1.50
310 Owen Daniels .60 1.50
311 Luke Kuechly .75 2.00
312 Fred Davis .60 1.50
313 Bilal Powell .60 1.50
314 Clay Matthews 1.00 2.50
315 Andre Johnson .60 1.50
316 Von Miller .75 2.00
317 Joe Thomas .60 1.50
318 Dwayne Allen .60 1.50
319 Darrius Heyward-Bey .60 1.50
320 Rashard Mendenhall .60 1.50
321 Carson Palmer .75 2.00
322 Julian Edelman 1.00 2.50
323 Santana Moss .75 2.00
324 Martellus Bennett .60 1.50
325 Troy Polamalu 1.00 2.50
326 Terrelle Pryor .75 2.00
327 Travis Kelce RC 1.50 4.00
328 Malcom Floyd .60 1.50
329 Tony Romo .75 2.00
330 Calvin Johnson 1.00 2.50

2013 Topps Magic Mini

*1-220 VETS: .8X TO 2X BASIC CARDS
*1-220 ROOKIES: .5X TO 1.2X BASIC RC
*221-330 SP: .5X TO 1.2X BASIC SP
ONE MINI PER PACK OVERALL

2013 Topps Magic Mini Green Border

*1-220 VETS: 1X TO 2.5X BASIC CARDS
*1-220 ROOKIES: .6X TO 1.5X BASIC RC
*221-330 SP: .5X TO 1.2X BASIC SP

2013 Topps Magic Mini Orange Border

*1-220 VETS: .8X TO 2X BASIC CARDS
*1-220 ROOKIES: .5X TO 1.2X BASIC RC
*221-330 SP: .5X TO 1.2X BASIC SP

2013 Topps Magic Mini Red Border

*1-220 VETS/50: 5X TO 12X BASIC CARDS
*1-220 ROOKIE/50: 3X TO 8X BASIC RC
*221-330 SP/50: 1.2X TO 3X BASIC SP

2013 Topps Magic 1948 Magic

COMPLETE SET (25) 25.00 60.00
1 Deion Sanders .75 2.00
2 Lawrence Taylor 1.00 2.50
3 Barry Sanders 1.50 4.00
4 Bo Jackson 1.25 3.00
5 Dan Marino 2.00 5.00
6 Adrian Peterson .75 2.00
7 Drew Brees .75 2.00
8 Tom Brady 2.00 5.00
9 Calvin Johnson .75 2.00
10 Arian Foster .60 1.50
11 Jamaal Charles .60 1.50
12 Peyton Manning 1.50 4.00
13 Colin Kaepernick .60 1.50
14 Jimmy Graham .75 2.00
15 Marshawn Lynch .60 1.50
16 EJ Manuel .40 1.00
17 Geno Smith .40 1.00
18 Cordarrelle Patterson .40 1.00
19 DeAndre Hopkins 1.00 2.50
20 Tavon Austin .50 1.25
21 Manti Te'o .50 1.25
22 Eddie Lacy .40 1.00
23 Giovani Bernard .40 1.00
24 Justin Hunter .40 1.00
25 Montee Ball .40 1.00

2013 Topps Magic Aerial Attack

AAAD Andy Dalton .60 1.50
AAAL Andrew Luck 1.25 3.00
AAAR Aaron Rodgers 1.25 3.00
AAAS Alex Smith .60 1.50
AABR Ben Roethlisberger .75 2.00
AABW Brandon Weeden .50 1.25
AACK Colin Kaepernick .60 1.50
AACN Cam Newton .75 2.00
AACP Carson Palmer .60 1.50
AADB Drew Brees .75 2.00
AAEM Eli Manning .60 1.50
AAJC Jay Cutler .50 1.25
AAJF Joe Flacco .60 1.50
AAMR Matt Ryan .60 1.50
AAMS Matthew Stafford .60 1.50
AAMSC Matt Schaub .50 1.25
AAMV Michael Vick .60 1.50
AAPM Peyton Manning 1.50 4.00
AAPR Philip Rivers .75 2.00
AARG Robert Griffin III .50 1.25
AART Ryan Tannehill .60 1.50
AARW Russell Wilson 1.50 4.00
AASB Sam Bradford .50 1.25
AATB Tom Brady 2.00 5.00
AATR Tony Romo .60 1.50

2013 Topps Magic Autographs

THREE PER HOBBY BOX, ONE PER RETAIL
1 Adrian Peterson SP
2 Vincent Jackson 5.00 12.00
3 Brian Hartline 5.00 12.00
5 Eli Manning SP
6 Haloti Ngata 5.00 12.00
7 Lonnie Pryor 2.00 5.00
8 Nico Johnson 3.00 8.00
10 Kayvon Webster 2.50 6.00
11 Dee Milliner 2.00 5.00
13 Eric Fisher SP
14 Tyrann Mathieu 3.00 8.00
15 Ray Graham 2.00 5.00
16 Miguel Maysonet 2.50 6.00
18 Tyler Eifert SP 4.00 10.00
19 Onterio McCalebb 2.50 6.00
20 Stevan Ridley 5.00 12.00
22 Ace Sanders 2.00 5.00
23 Manti Te'o SP
27 Alfred Morris 5.00 12.00
29 DeAndre Hopkins SP 8.00 20.00
30 Deion Sanders SP
32 Dwayne Bowe SP 10.00 25.00
33 Cordarrelle Patterson SP 4.00 10.00
35 Corey Fuller 2.00 5.00
36 Le'Veon Bell SP 25.00 50.00
38 Navorro Bowman 8.00 20.00
39 Jeremy Maclin SP
41 Alex Smith SP
42 Christine Michael SP
44 Giovani Bernard SP
47 Steve Smith SP
48 Eric Reid 5.00 12.00
49 Mikel Leshoure 5.00 12.00
50 Peyton Manning SP
51 Stevie Brown SP 4.00 10.00
53 Marcel Reece 2.00 5.00
54 Dion Sims 2.00 5.00
55 Barry Sanders SP 125.00 200.00
56 Matt Ryan SP
59 Danario Alexander 2.00 5.00
61 Brandon Myers 2.50 6.00
62 John Jenkins 2.50 6.00
63 Matt Forte SP
66 Thurman Thomas SP
68 Aaron Dobson 5.00 12.00
70 Curtis Martin SP
71 Heath Miller SP 8.00 20.00
72 John Simon 3.00 8.00
73 Tyler Bray 2.00 5.00
74 EJ Manuel SP 20.00 40.00
75 Kenny Stills 2.00 5.00
76 Josh Boyce 2.00 5.00
77 Antonio Gates SP
78 Bo Jackson SP
80 Joe Flacco SP 25.00 50.00
81 Marquise Goodwin 2.00 5.00
84 Mike Williams SP
07 Montee Ball SP 4.00 10.00
88 Steve Largent SP
89 Brian Orakpo SP 8.00 20.00
90 Zach Ertz 4.00 10.00
92 Barkevious Mingo 2.00 5.00
93 Terrance Williams SP 4.00 10.00
94 Patrick Peterson 8.00 20.00
95 Luke Joeckel 2.00 5.00
96 Datone Jones 2.00 5.00
97 Marshall Faulk SP 50.00 100.00
98 Khaseem Greene 2.00 5.00
101 Tyler Wilson SP
102 Earl Thomas 8.00 20.00
104 Bjoern Werner 2.00 5.00
105 Cobi Hamilton 2.00 5.00
109 Chris Gragg 2.00 5.00
110 Landry Jones 5.00 12.00
111 Jason Witten SP
112 Joseph Randle 2.00 5.00
115 John Wetzel 2.50 6.00
117 D.J. Harper 2.50 6.00
118 Chris Thompson 2.00 5.00
119 Danny Amendola 6.00 15.00
120 Johnathan Hankins 2.00 5.00
122 Stedman Bailey 2.00 5.00
124 Robert Woods SP
125 Drew Brees SP 50.00 100.00
127 Jordan Reed 3.00 8.00
128 A.J. Green SP 12.00 30.00
130 Barrett Jones 2.00 5.00
131 Sam Montgomery 2.00 5.00
132 Anquan Boldin SP
138 Tavon Austin SP
139 Darren McFadden SP
140 Jermaine Gresham SP
141 LeSean McCoy SP 15.00 40.00
142 Zac Dysert 2.00 5.00
143 Josh Freeman SP
144 Stepfan Taylor SP 15.00 40.00
145 Chris Johnson SP
147 Ray Rice SP
148 Gavin Escobar 2.00 5.00
149 Ryan Nassib SP 4.00 10.00
150 Geno Smith SP 4.00 10.00
151 D.J. Hayden 2.00 5.00
154 Ryan Swope 2.00 5.00
155 Justin Hunter SP 4.00 10.00
156 Rodney Smith 2.00 5.00
157 Dan Buckner 2.00 5.00
159 Reggie Wayne SP
162 Alex Okafor 2.00 5.00
163 Dion Jordan SP
164 Philip Lutzenkirchen 3.00 8.00
165 Joique Bell SP 8.00 20.00
166 Shawn Williams 2.00 5.00
167 Jeremy Kerley 5.00 12.00
168 Frank Gore SP
169 Blidi Wreh-Wilson 2.50 6.00
171 Kenjon Barner 2.00 5.00
173 Randall Cobb SP
174 Matthew Stafford SP 30.00 60.00
176 Mike Glennon SP
177 Ezekiel Ansah SP 6.00 15.00
179 Chance Warmack 2.00 5.00
180 Maurice Jones-Drew SP
182 Keenan Allen 10.00 25.00
183 Xavier Rhodes 4.00 10.00
184 Chase Thomas 2.50 6.00
188 Desmond Trufant SP 4.00 10.00
190 Marshawn Lynch SP 30.00 60.00
191 Sharrif Floyd 2.00 5.00
192 Da'Rick Rogers 2.00 5.00
193 Howie Long SP 25.00 50.00
194 Alec Ogletree 2.00 5.00
195 Pierre Garcon SP 10.00 25.00
196 Matt Scott 2.00 5.00
197 Jesse Williams 3.00 8.00
198 Marcus Davis 2.00 5.00
200 Robert Griffin III SP
201 Jacquizz Rodgers 6.00 15.00
203 Jamar Taylor 2.00 5.00
205 Robert Lester 2.50 6.00
207 Jordy Nelson SP 15.00 30.00
208 Jonathan Dwyer SP 6.00 15.00
210 Brent Celek SP
211 Eddie Lacy SP 40.00 100.00
212 Lawrence Taylor SP
214 BenJarvus Green-Ellis 6.00 15.00
215 Jordan Poyer 2.00 5.00
216 Brandon Jenkins 2.50 6.00
217 Steve Johnson 6.00 15.00
218 Warren Moon SP 30.00 60.00
220 Andrew Luck SP

2013 Topps Magic Dual Autographs

EXCH EXPIRATION: 12/31/2016
MDAAH D.Hopkins/T.Austin 15.00 40.00
MDABB M.Ball/L.Bell 20.00 50.00
MDABE M.Barkley/Z.Ertz 12.00 30.00
MDABS S.Bailey/K.Stills 6.00 15.00
MDADW R.Woods/A.Dobson 10.00 25.00
MDAJG D.Jordan/M.Gillislee 6.00 15.00
MDALF J.Franklin/E.Lacy 6.00 15.00
MDAML Michael/Lattimore EXCH 6.00 15.00
MDAMM B.Mingo/T.Mathieu 10.00 25.00
MDAMS G.Smith/E.Manuel 6.00 15.00
MDARM A.Morris/T.Richardson 12.00 30.00
MDASJ B.Jackson/B.Sanders 150.00 250.00
MDATJ J.Jones/M.Te'o 8.00 20.00
MDAWE G.Escobar/J.Witten 15.00 40.00
MDAWG M.Goodwin/R.Woods 10.00 25.00

2013 Topps Magic Ground and Pound

GAPAF Arian Foster .60 1.50
GAPAM Alfred Morris .50 1.25
GAPAP Adrian Peterson .75 2.00
GAPBGE BenJarvus Green-Ellis .60 1.50
GAPBP Bilal Powell .50 1.25
GAPCJ Chris Johnson .50 1.25
GAPCS C.J. Spiller .50 1.25
GAPDM Doug Martin .60 1.50
GAPDMC Darren McFadden .60 1.50
GAPDMU DeMarco Murray .60 1.50
GAPDR Daryl Richardson .50 1.25
GAPDS Darren Sproles .60 1.50
GAPDW David Wilson .50 1.25
GAPDWL DeAngelo Williams .50 1.25
GAPFG Frank Gore .60 1.50
GAPJC Jamaal Charles .60 1.50
GAPLM LeSean McCoy .75 2.00
GAPMF Matt Forte .50 1.25
GAPMJD Maurice Jones-Drew .50 1.25
GAPML Marshawn Lynch .60 1.50
GAPRB Reggie Bush .50 1.25
GAPRR Ray Rice .50 1.25
GAPSJ Steven Jackson .50 1.25
GAPSR Stevan Ridley .50 1.25
GAPTR Trent Richardson .50 1.25

2013 Topps Magic Rookie Enchantment

READ Aaron Dobson .40 1.00
REAO Alec Ogletree .40 1.00
RECM Christine Michael .40 1.00
RECP Cordarrelle Patterson .40 1.00
REDH DeAndre Hopkins 1.00 2.50
REDJ Dion Jordan .40 1.00
REDM Dee Milliner .40 1.00
REDR Denard Robinson .40 1.00
REDT Desmond Trufant .40 1.00
REEA Ezekiel Ansah .40 1.00
REEL Eddie Lacy .40 1.00
REEM EJ Manuel .40 1.00
REER Eric Reid .50 1.25
REGB Giovani Bernard .40 1.00
REGS Geno Smith .40 1.00
REJH Justin Hunter .40 1.00
REJJ Jarvis Jones .40 1.00
REKD Knile Davis .40 1.00
REKT Kenbrell Thompkins .60 1.50
RELB Le'Veon Bell 1.25 3.00
RELJ Luke Joeckel .40 1.00
REMB Matt Barkley .40 1.00
REMBA Montee Ball .40 1.00
REMG Marquise Goodwin .40 1.00
REMGL Mike Glennon .40 1.00
REMT Manti Te'o .50 1.25
REMW Markus Wheaton .40 1.00
RERW Robert Woods .60 1.50
REST Stepfan Taylor .40 1.00
RETA Tavon Austin .50 1.25
RETE Tyler Eifert .40 1.00
RETW Terrance Williams .40 1.00
REZE Zach Ertz .75 2.00

2013 Topps Magic Rookie Relics

MRRAD Aaron Dobson 2.50 6.00
MRRAE Andre Ellington 2.50 6.00
MRRCM Christine Michael 2.50 6.00
MRRCP Cordarrelle Patterson 2.50 6.00
MRRDH DeAndre Hopkins 6.00 15.00
MRRDJ Dion Jordan 2.50 6.00
MRRDR Denard Robinson 2.50 6.00
MRREL Eddie Lacy 2.50 6.00
MRREM EJ Manuel
MRRGS Geno Smith 2.50 6.00
MRRJF Johnathan Franklin 2.50 6.00
MRRJH Justin Hunter 2.50 6.00
MRRJR Jordan Reed 4.00 10.00
MRRKA Keenan Allen 5.00 12.00
MRRKD Knile Davis 2.50 6.00
MRRKS Kenny Stills 2.50 6.00
MRRMB Montee Ball 2.50 6.00
MRRMBA Matt Barkley 2.50 6.00
MRRMG Mike Glennon 2.50 6.00
MRRMT Manti Te'o 3.00 8.00
MRRRN Ryan Nassib 2.50 6.00
MRRSB Stedman Bailey 2.50 6.00
MRRTA Tavon Austin 3.00 8.00
MRRTE Tyler Eifert 2.50 6.00
MRRTW Tyler Wilson 2.50 6.00

2008 Topps Mayo

This set was released on January 28, 2009. The base set consists of 330 cards. Rookies and short prints are scattered throughout the set. This product was released with 8 cards per pack and 24 packs per hobby box.

COMPLETE SET (330) 60.00 120.00
COMP.SET w/o SP's (275) 20.00 40.00
UNPRICED PRINT PLATE PRINT RUN 1
1 Drew Brees .30 .75
2 Kyle Orton SP 1.00 2.50
3 LenDale White SP 1.00 2.50
4 Shaun McDonald .20 .50
5 Bobby Wade .20 .50
6 Javon Walker .25 .60
7 Owen Daniels .20 .50
8 Justin Tuck SP 1.00 2.50
9 Amobi Okoye .20 .50
10 Rich Eisen .20 .50
11 Fred Taylor SP 1.00 2.50
12 Ryan Torain SP RC 1.00 2.50
13 Steve Slaton RC .60 1.50
14 Jake Long SP RC 1.25 3.00
15 Peyton Manning .75 2.00
16 Jon Kitna .20 .50
17 Ryan Grant .25 .60
18 Brandon Stokley .20 .50
19 Troy Williamson SP 1.00 2.50
20 Reggie Brown .20 .50
21 Zach Miller .20 .50
22 Aaron Kampman SP 1.25 3.00
23 Albert Haynesworth .20 .50
24 Matt Cassel .20 .50
25 Selvin Young SP 1.00 2.50
26 Will Franklin SP RC 1.00 2.50
27 Matt Forte RC 1.00 2.50
28 Glenn Dorsey RC .60 1.50
29 Marc Bulger .20 .50
30 Jeff Garcia .20 .50
31 DeAngelo Williams .20 .50
32 Roydell Williams .20 .50
33 Sidney Rice .20 .50
34 James Jones SP 1.00 2.50
35 L.J. Smith .20 .50
36 Aaron Schobel .20 .50
37 Tommie Harris .20 .50
38 Tyler Thigpen .25 .60
39 LaDainian Tomlinson SP 1.50 4.00
40 Marcus Smith SP RC 1.00 2.50
41 Tashard Choice RC .60 1.50
42 Chris Long RC .75 2.00
43 Matt Moore SP 1.00 2.50
44 Chris Redman .20 .50
45 Laurence Maroney .25 .60
46 Larry Fitzgerald .25 .60
47 Donte Stallworth .20 .50
48 Marty Booker .20 .50
49 Greg Olsen .25 .60
50 Terrell Suggs .20 .50
51 Kevin Williams .20 .50
52 Derrick Ward .20 .50
53 Steven Jackson SP 1.00 2.50
54 Adrian Arrington SP RC .75 2.00
55 Tim Hightower RC .75 2.00
56 Chauncey Washington RC .75 2.00
57 Joe Thomas .25 .60
58 Matt Leinart SP 1.00 2.50
59 Jamal Lewis .25 .60
60 Braylon Edwards .20 .50
61 Steve Smith USC .25 .60
62 Mark Bradley .20 .50
63 Leonard Pope .20 .50
64 Dwight Freeney .20 .50
65 Adam Carriker .20 .50
66 Devery Henderson .20 .50
67 Willis McGahee SP 1.00 2.50
68 Fred Davis SP RC .75 2.00
69 Harry Douglas RC .75 2.00
70 Anthony Alridge SP RC .75 2.00
71 Rex Grossman .20 .50
72 Kellen Clemens .20 .50
73 Justin Fargas .20 .50
74 Steve Smith .25 .60
75 Hines Ward .25 .60
76 Muhsin Muhammad .20 .50
77 Randy McMichael .20 .50
78 Tamba Hali .20 .50
79 Archie Manning .25 .60
80 Orville Wright .20 .50
81 Michael Turner SP 1.00 2.50
82 Paul Smith RC .60 1.50
83 DeSean Jackson RC 1.25 3.00
84 Josh McCown .20 .50
05 John Deck .20 .50
86 LaMont Jordan SP 1.25 3.00
87 Greg Jennings .20 .50
88 Deion Branch .20 .50
89 David Patten .20 .50
90 Bob Sanders .25 .60
91 Luis Castillo .20 .50
92 Troy Aikman .40 1.00
93 Le'Ron McClain .30 .75
94 Todd Heap SP 1.00 2.50
95 Kyle Wright RC .60 1.50
96 Malcolm Kelly RC .60 1.50
97 Vince Young .20 .50
98 Troy Smith .25 .60
99 Reggie Bush .20 .50
100 Jerricho Cotchery .20 .50
101 Jerry Porter .20 .50
102 Ike Hilliard .20 .50
103 Ed Reed .25 .60
104 John Abraham .20 .50
105 Sterling Sharpe .25 .60
106 Brodie Croyle .25 .60
107 Jeremy Shockey SP 1.00 2.50
108 Andre Woodson RC .60 1.50
109 Limas Sweed RC .60 1.50
110 Jay Cutler .20 .50
111 Adrian Peterson .30 .75
112 Larry Johnson .20 .50
113 Joey Galloway .25 .60
114 Reggie Williams .25 .60
115 Justin McCareins .20 .50
116 Roy Williams S .20 .50
117 Julius Peppers .25 .60
118 Terry Bradshaw .40 1.00
119 James Harrison RC 3.00 8.00
120 Heath Miller SP 1.00 2.50
121 Chad Henne RC .75 2.00
122 Mario Manningham RC .60 1.50
123 J.P. Losman .20 .50
124 Willie Parker .25 .60
125 Rudi Johnson .20 .50
126 Lee Evans .25 .60
127 Marvin Harrison .25 .60
128 Isaac Bruce .30 .75
129 Kerry Rhodes .20 .50
130 Brian Urlacher SP 1.50 4.00
131 John Elway .50 1.25
132 LaMarr Woodley .25 .60
133 Calvin Johnson SP 1.50 4.00
134 Joe Flacco RC 1.25 3.00
135 James Hardy SP RC .75 2.00
136 Jason Campbell .20 .50
137 DeShaun Foster .20 .50
138 Ahmad Bradshaw .20 .50
139 Roy Williams WR .20 .50
140 Amani Toomer .20 .50
141 Bryant Johnson .20 .50
142 Troy Polamalu .30 .75
143 DeMarcus Ware .25 .60
144 Dan Marino .60 1.50
145 Grover Cleveland .20 .50
146 Plaxico Burress SP 1.00 2.50
147 Colt Brennan RC .75 2.00
148 Early Doucet RC .60 1.50
149 Matt Hasselbeck .20 .50
150 Jerious Norwood .20 .50
151 Leon Washington .20 .50
152 Arnaz Battle .20 .50
153 Ted Ginn Jr. .20 .50
154 Drew Bennett .20 .50
155 Brian Dawkins .30 .75
156 Patrick Willis .25 .60
157 Sonny Jurgensen .25 .60
158 Susan B. Anthony .20 .50
159 Terrell Owens SP 1.25 3.00
160 Dennis Dixon RC .60 1.50
161 Donnie Avery RC .75 2.00
162 Matt Schaub .20 .50
163 Kerry Collins .25 .60
164 Ronnie Brown .20 .50
165 Bobby Engram .20 .50
166 Laveranues Coles .20 .50
167 Antonio Gates .25 .60
168 LaRon Landry .25 .60
169 Ray Lewis .30 .75
170 Joe Namath .40 1.00
171 William Cody .20 .50
172 Andre Johnson SP 1.25 3.00
173 Erik Ainge RC .60 1.50
174 Dexter Jackson RC 1.00 2.50
175 Philip Rivers .30 .75
176 Marion Barber .20 .50
177 Chris Perry .20 .50
178 Torry Holt .25 .60
179 Anthony Gonzalez .20 .50
180 Kellen Winslow .20 .50
181 Adrian Wilson .20 .50
182 Shawne Merriman .20 .50
183 Lawrence Taylor .30 .75
184 William Rockefeller .20 .50
185 Brandon Marshall SP 1.25 3.00
186 Josh Johnson RC .60 1.50
187 Devin Thomas RC .60 1.50
188 Chad Pennington .20 .50
189 Brian Westbrook .20 .50
190 Ahman Green .25 .60
191 Derrick Mason .20 .50
192 Ernest Wilford .20 .50
193 Tony Scheffler .20 .50
194 Champ Bailey .25 .60
195 DeMeco Ryans .25 .60
196 Gale Sayers .30 .75
197 Gus Frerotte .20 .50
198 Dwayne Bowe SP 1.25 3.00
199 Kevin O'Connell RC .60 1.50
200 Jordy Nelson RC 2.00 5.00
201 Trent Edwards .20 .50
202 Kolby Smith .20 .50
203 Brian Leonard .20 .50
204 Mike Furrey .25 .60
205 Jabar Gaffney .20 .50
206 Donald Lee .25 .60
207 Antonio Cromartie .20 .50
208 Joey Porter .20 .50
209 Norman Rockwell .20 .50
210 Tom Brady SP 5.00 12.00
211 Nate Burleson SP 1.00 2.50
212 Funkmaster Flex SP 1.00 2.50
213 Keenan Burton RC .60 1.50
214 Donovan McNabb .25 .60
215 Marshawn Lynch .25 .60
216 Earnest Graham .20 .50
217 Donald Driver .25 .60
218 Mark Clayton .20 .50
219 Vernon Davis .20 .50
220 Asante Samuel .20 .50
221 Mike Vrabel .20 .50
222 King Edward VIII .20 .50
223 Warren Haynes SP 1.00 2.50
224 Antwaan Randle El SP 1.00 2.50
225 Darren McFadden RC .60 1.50
226 Earl Bennett RC 1.00 2.50
227 Derek Anderson .20 .50
228 Joseph Addai .20 .50
229 Julius Jones .20 .50
230 T.J. Houshmandzadeh .20 .50
231 Kevin Walter .25 .60
232 Chris Cooley .20 .50
233 Leon Hall .20 .50
234 D.J. Williams .20 .50
235 Guglielmo Marconi .20 .50
236 David Garrard SP 1.00 2.50
237 Vincent Jackson SP 1.00 2.50
238 Jonathan Stewart RC 1.00 2.50
239 Jerome Simpson RC .75 2.00
240 Kyle Boller .20 .50
241 Warrick Dunn .20 .50
242 Ricky Williams .25 .60
243 Kevin Curtis .20 .50
244 Justin Gage .20 .50
245 Tony Gonzalez .25 .60
246 DeAngelo Hall .20 .50
247 Antonio Pierce .20 .50
248 Claude Monet .20 .50
249 Carson Palmer SP 1.25 3.00
250 Laurent Robinson SP 1.00 2.50
251 Felix Jones RC .60 1.50
252 Andre Caldwell RC .60 1.50
253 JaMarcus Russell .20 .50
254 Frank Gore .25 .60
255 Dominic Rhodes .20 .50
256 Santonio Holmes .20 .50
257 J.T. O'Sullivan .20 .50
258 Dallas Clark .20 .50
259 Terence Newman .20 .50
260 Ernie Sims .20 .50
261 Paul Gauguin .20 .50
262 Ben Roethlisberger SP 1.50 4.00
263 Chris Chambers SP 1.00 2.50
264 John David Booty RC .60 1.50
265 Eddie Royal RC .60 1.50
266 Brady Quinn .20 .50
267 Maurice Jones-Drew .20 .50
268 Deuce McAllister .25 .60
269 Wes Welker .25 .60
270 Darrell Jackson .20 .50
271 Jason Witten .25 .60
272 Nate Clements .20 .50
273 A.J. Hawk .20 .50
274 Dr. John Harvey Kellogg .20 .50
275 Eli Manning SP 1.25 3.00
276 Matt Ryan SP RC 2.50 6.00
277 Jamaal Charles RC 1.00 2.50
278 Lavelle Hawkins RC .75 2.00
279 Jake Delhomme .20 .50
280 Thomas Jones .20 .50
281 Chad Johnson .20 .50
282 Roddy White .20 .50
283 Devard Darling .20 .50
284 Alge Crumpler .20 .50
285 Jared Allen .20 .50
286 Jonathan Vilma .20 .50
287 Milton Hershey .20 .50
288 Tony Romo SP 1.25 3.00
289 Brian Brohm SP RC .75 2.00
290 Chris Johnson RC .75 2.00
291 Vernon Gholston RC .60 1.50
292 Alex Smith QB .25 .60
293 Brandon Jacobs .20 .50
294 Reggie Wayne .25 .60
295 Marques Colston .20 .50
296 Ronald Curry .20 .50
297 Ben Watson .20 .50
298 Mario Williams .25 .60
299 Derrick Brooks .20 .50
300 Thomas Edison .20 .50
301 Brett Favre SP 3.00 8.00
302 Anthony Morelli SP RC .75 2.00
303 Ray Rice RC .60 1.50
304 Dustin Keller RC .75 2.00
305 Aaron Rodgers .60 1.50
306 Edgerrin James .25 .60
307 Anquan Boldin .20 .50
308 Bernard Berrian .20 .50
309 Dennis Northcutt .20 .50
310 Marcedes Lewis .20 .50
311 Jason Taylor .25 .60
312 Lofa Tatupu .20 .50
313 Arthur Conan Doyle .20 .50
314 Kurt Warner SP 1.25 3.00
315 Rashard Mendenhall SP RC .75 2.00
316 Mike Hart SP RC .75 2.00
317 Owen Schmitt RC .60 1.50
318 Tarvaris Jackson .20 .50
319 Chester Taylor .20 .50
320 Randy Moss .25 .60
321 Santana Moss .20 .50
322 Patrick Crayton .25 .60
323 Chris Baker .20 .50
324 Osi Umenyiora .20 .50
325 Shaun Rogers .20 .50
326 Rudyard Kipling .20 .50
327 Clinton Portis SP 1.00 2.50
328 Xavier Omon SP RC .75 2.00
329 Kevin Smith RC .60 1.50
330 Jacob Hester RC .60 1.50

2008 Topps Mayo Mini 1894 Sepia Backs

UNPRICED SEPIA BACK PRINT RUN 5
STATED ODDS 1:250 HOB

2008 Topps Mayo Mini Harvard Red Backs

*VETS: 8X TO 20X BASIC CARDS
*VET SPs: 1.5X TO 4X BASIC CARDS
*ROOKIES: 1.5X TO 4X BASIC CARDS
*ROOKIE SPs: 2X TO 5X BASIC CARDS
HARVARD RED BACK/25 ODDS 1:50 HOB

2008 Topps Mayo Mini Black Backs

*VETS: 1.5X TO 4X BASIC CARDS
*VET SPs: .5X TO 1.2X BASIC CARDS
*ROOKIES: .4X TO 1X BASIC CARDS
*ROOKIE SPs: .4X TO 1X BASIC CARDS
OVERALL MINI ODDS 1:1 HOBBY
SP MINI STATED ODDS 1:12 HOBBY

2008 Topps Mayo Mini Princeton Orange Backs

*VETS: 4X TO 10X BASIC CARDS
*VET SPs: .8X TO 2X BASIC CARDS
*ROOKIES: .8X TO 2X BASIC CARDS
*ROOKIE SPs: .6X TO 1.5X BASIC CARDS
PRINCETON ORANGE BACK ODDS 1:24 HOB

2008 Topps Mayo Mini Yale Blue Backs

*VETS: 3X TO 8X BASIC CARDS
*VET SPs: .6X TO 1.5X BASIC CARDS
*ROOKIES: .6X TO 1.5X BASIC CARDS
*ROOKIE SPs: .5X TO 1.2X BASIC CARDS
YALE BLUE BACK ODDS 1:13 HOB

2008 Topps Mayo Americana Autographs

GROUP A/190* ODDS 1:1000 HOB
GROUP B ODDS 1:1600 HOB
UNPRICED RED INK/10 ODDS 1:12,500 HOB
AAFF Funkmaster Flex/190* 15.00 40.00
AARE Rich Eisen/190* 15.00 40.00
AAWH Warren Haynes B 15.00 40.00

2008 Topps Mayo Americana Relics

GROUP A/50* ODDS 1:400 HOB
GROUP B ODDS 1:600 HOB
ARAF Al Franken A 12.00 30.00
ARCP Colin Powell A 12.00 30.00
ARCV Cornelius Vanderbilt A 12.00 30.00
ARER Eleanor Roosevelt A 12.00 30.00
ARFF Funkmaster Flex B 4.00 10.00
ARFL Fiorello LaGuardia A 12.00 30.00
ARGG George Gershwin A 12.00 30.00
ARHF Hamilton Fish A 12.00 30.00
ARHM Herman Melville A 12.00 30.00
ARHS Henry Stimson A 12.00 30.00
ARJJ John Jay A 12.00 30.00
ARJS Jonas Salk A 12.00 30.00
ARNR Norman Rockwell A 12.00 30.00
ARRE Rich Eisen Tie A 8.00 20.00
ARRG Rudy Giuliani A 12.00 30.00
ARRL Robert Livingston A 12.00 30.00
ARTR Theodore Roosevelt A 12.00 30.00
ARWH Warren Haynes B 12.00 30.00

2008 Topps Mayo Autographs

GROUP A/40* ODDS 1:1950 HOB
GROUP B/65* ODDS 1:3000 HOB
GROUP C/90* ODDS 1:4300 HOB
GROUP D/140* ODDS 1:920 HOB
GROUP E/190* ODDS 1:1000 HOB
GROUP F ODDS 1:193 HOB
GROUP G ODDS 1:1350 HOB
GROUP H ODDS 1:188 HOB
GROUP I ODDS 1:250 HOB
UNPRICED RED INK/10 ODDS 1:1420 HOB
EXCH EXPIRATION: 12/31/2011
AAH Ali Highsmith F 5.00 12.00
AAM Archie Manning/40* 20.00 40.00
AAW Andre Woodson F 4.00 10.00
ABF Brandon Flowers H 5.00 12.00
ACB Colt Brennan/65* 8.00 20.00
ACJ Chad Johnson/190* 8.00 20.00
ADA Donnie Avery H 5.00 12.00
ADBR Drew Brees/90* 30.00 60.00
ADJ DeSean Jackson H 8.00 20.00
ADMC Darren McFadden/65* 20.00 50.00
AEM Eli Manning/40* 50.00 100.00
AER Eddie Royal F 4.00 10.00
AFD Fred Davis/190* 4.00 10.00
AJC John Carlson I 4.00 10.00
AJE John Elway/40* 75.00 150.00
AJJ James Jones F 6.00 15.00
AJMO Josh Morgan I 4.00 10.00
AMC Marques Colston F 8.00 20.00
AMF Matt Forte H 15.00 40.00
AMK Malcolm Kelly F 4.00 10.00
AMR Matt Ryan/140* 50.00 100.00
APM Peyton Manning/40* 60.00 120.00
ASJ Sonny Jurgensen/140*
ASS Sterling Sharpe/140* 12.00 30.00
ATD Tony Dorsett/40* 30.00 60.00
AWF Will Franklin F 5.00 12.00
AWW Wes Welker G 25.00 50.00

2008 Topps Mayo Century Series Relics

GROUP A/50* ODDS 1:1200 HOB
GROUP B/100* ODDS 1:650 HOB
CSRAO Annie Oakley Stamp/100* 15.00 50.00
CSRFD Frederick Douglass Stamp/100* 15.00 40.00
CSRFS Ben Franklin Stamp/50* 20.00 50.00
CSRGC G.Cleveland Hankerchief A 20.00 50.00
CSRGS Ulysses S. Grant Stamp/50* 20.00 50.00
CSRLD Statue of Liberty Dime/50* 35.00 60.00
CSRSA Susan B. Anthony Stamp/100* 15.00 40.00
CSRTE Thomas Edison Stamp/100* 15.00 40.00
CSRUSM U.S.S. Maine Deck/100* 40.00 80.00
CSRWC William Cody Stamp/100* 15.00 40.00
CSRWS Daniel Webster Stamp/50* 20.00 50.00

2008 Topps Mayo Cut Signatures

UNPRICED CUT SIG/1 ODDS 1:35,328 HOB

2008 Topps Mayo Famous Ships

COMPLETE SET (19) 15.00 40.00
STATED ODDS 1:12 HOB
S1 Victoria 1.25 3.00
S2 Nina 1.25 3.00
S3 Pinta 1.25 3.00
S4 Santa Maria 1.25 3.00
S5 RMS Titanic 2.00 5.00
S6 Cutty Sark 1.25 3.00
S7 Queen Mary 2 1.25 3.00
S8 USS Arizona 1.25 3.00
S9 USS Monitor 1.25 3.00
S10 HMS Victory 1.25 3.00
S11 Appomattox 1.25 3.00
S12 Andrea Gail 1.25 3.00
S13 SS Andrea Doria 1.25 3.00

S14 RMS Carpathia 1.25 3.00
S15 RV Calypso 1.25 3.00
S16 Nimrod 1.25 3.00
S17 HMS Beagle 1.25 3.00
S18 HMS Bounty 1.25 3.00
S19 Golden Hind 1.25 3.00

2008 Topps Mayo Horses

STATED ODDS 1:48 HOB
H1 Appaloosa Horse 2.50 6.00
H2 Shetland Pony 2.50 6.00
H3 Tennessee Walking Horse 2.50 6.00
H4 Mustang 2.50 6.00
H5 Belgian Draft Horse 2.50 6.00
H6 American Miniature Horse 2.50 6.00
H7 Clydesdale 2.50 6.00
H8 Missouri Fox Trotter 2.50 6.00
H9 Morgan Horse 2.50 6.00
H10 American Paint Horse 2.50 6.00
H11 Chincoteague Pony 2.50 6.00
H12 Arabian Horse 2.50 6.00
H13 Canadian Horse 2.50 6.00
H14 Zebra 2.50 6.00
H15 Unicorn 2.50 6.00

2008 Topps Mayo Relics

GROUP A ODDS 1:38 HOB
GROUP B ODDS 1:32 HOB
RAB Anquan Boldin 2.50 6.00
RAG Antonio Gates 3.00 8.00
RAP Adrian Peterson 4.00 10.00
RBB Brian Brohm 2.00 5.00
RCH Chad Henne 2.50 6.00
RCJ Chad Johnson 2.50 6.00
RCJO Chris Johnson 2.50 6.00
RCP Carson Palmer 3.00 8.00
RCPO Clinton Portis 2.50 6.00
RDA Donnie Avery 2.50 6.00
RDG David Garrard 2.50 6.00
RDM Darren McFadden 6.00 15.00
RDW DeAngelo Williams 2.50 6.00
REM Eli Manning 5.00 12.00
RFG Frank Gore 4.00 10.00
RFJ Felix Jones 2.50 6.00
RGD Glenn Dorsey 2.00 5.00
RJB John David Booty 2.00 5.00
RJF Joe Flacco 10.00 25.00
RJG Jeff Garcia 2.50 6.00
RJH James Hardy 2.00 5.00
RJL Jake Long 3.00 8.00
RJS Jonathan Stewart 6.00 15.00
RLF Larry Fitzgerald 6.00 15.00
RLT LaDainian Tomlinson 6.00 15.00
RLW LenDale White 2.50 6.00
RMB Marion Barber 5.00 12.00
RMF Matt Forte 6.00 15.00
RMH Matt Hasselbeck 2.50 6.00
RMK Malcolm Kelly 2.00 5.00
RML Marshawn Lynch 3.00 8.00
RMR Matt Ryan 10.00 25.00
RPM Peyton Manning 8.00 20.00
RRG Ryan Grant 3.00 8.00
RRM Randy Moss 3.00 8.00
RRME Rashard Mendenhall 2.00 5.00
RRR Ray Rice 2.00 5.00
RRW Reggie Wayne 4.00 10.00
RSS Steve Slaton 2.00 5.00
RTG Tony Gonzalez 4.00 10.00
RTJ Thomas Jones 2.50 6.00
RWW Wes Welker 3.00 8.00

2008 Topps Mayo Super Bowl Match-ups

COMPLETE SET (33) 6.00 15.00
OVERALL ODDS 1:1 HOBBY
SB32A Denver Broncos .30 .75
SB32B Super Bowl XXXII .30 .75
SB32C Green Bay Packers .30 .75
SB33A Denver Broncos .30 .75
SB33B Super Bowl XXXIII .30 .75
SB33C Atlanta Falcons .30 .75
SB34A St. Louis Rams .30 .75
SB34B Super Bowl XXXIV .30 .75
SB34C Tennessee Titans .30 .75
SB35A Baltimore Ravens .30 .75
SB35B Super Bowl XXXV .30 .75
SB35C New York Giants .30 .75
SB36A New England Patriots .30 .75
SB36B Super Bowl XXXVI .30 .75
SB36C St. Louis Rams .30 .75
SB37A Tampa Bay Buccaneers .30 .75
SB37B Super Bowl XXXVII .30 .75
SB37C Oakland Raiders .30 .75
SB38A New England Patriots .30 .75
SB38B Super Bowl XXXVIII .30 .75
SB38C Carolina Panthers .30 .75
SB39A New England Patriots .30 .75
SB39B Super Bowl XXXIX .30 .75
SB39C Philadelphia Eagles .30 .75
SB40A Pittsburgh Steelers .30 .75
SB40B Super Bowl XL .30 .75
SB40C Seattle Seahawks .30 .75
SB41A Indianapolis Colts .30 .75
SB41B Super Bowl XLI .30 .75
SB41C Chicago Bears .30 .75
SB42A New York Giants .30 .75
SB42B Super Bowl XLII .30 .75
SB42C New England Patriots .30 .75

2009 Topps Mayo

COMPLETE SET (330) 40.00 80.00
COMP.SET w/o SP's (275) 15.00 40.00
276-330 SP ODDS 1:2 HOB
1 Benjamin Harrison Pres. .20 .50
2 Aaron Curry RC .60 1.50
3 Aaron Kampman .25 .60
4 Aaron Maybin RC .50 1.25
5 Aaron Rodgers .60 1.50
6 Adrian Peterson .30 .75
7 Adrian Wilson .20 .50
8 Ahmad Bradshaw .20 .50
9 Al Harris .20 .50
10 Albert Haynesworth .20 .50
11 Alex Smith QB .30 .75
12 Andre Brown RC .50 1.25
13 Andre Caldwell .20 .50
14 Andre Johnson .25 .60
15 Anquan Boldin .20 .50
16 Anthony Gonzalez .20 .50
17 Antoine Winfield .20 .50
18 Antonio Gates .25 .60
19 Antonio Pierce .20 .50
20 Antwaan Randle El .20 .50
21 Asante Samuel .20 .50
22 Austin Collie RC .40 1.00
23 B.J. Raji RC .50 1.25
24 Barry Sanders .60 1.50
25 Ben Roethlisberger .30 .75
26 Bernard Berrian .20 .50
27 Bo Scaife .20 .50
28 Bobby Engram .20 .50
29 Bobby Wade .20 .50
30 Bradie James .20 .50
31 Brady Quinn .20 .50
32 Brandon Marshall .25 .60
33 Brandon Pettigrew RC .40 1.00
34 Brandon Tate RC .50 1.25
35 Brian Cushing RC .40 1.00
36 Brian Dawkins .20 .50
37 Brian Hartline RC .60 1.50
38 Brian Orakpo RC .50 1.25
39 Brian Robiskie RC .40 1.00
40 Brian Urlacher .30 .75
41 Brian Westbrook .20 .50
42 Brooks Foster RC .40 1.00
43 Buffalo Bill .20 .50
44 Carson Palmer .25 .60
45 Cedric Benson .20 .50
46 Chad Ochocinco .20 .50
47 Champ Bailey .25 .60
48 Charles Woodson .30 .75
49 Chester Taylor .20 .50
50 Chris Chambers .20 .50
51 Chris Cooley .20 .50
52 Chris Johnson .20 .50
53 Chris Wells RC .40 1.00
54 Clay Matthews RC 1.50 4.00
55 Clinton Portis .20 .50
56 Grover Cleveland Pres. .20 .50
57 D'Qwell Jackson .20 .50
58 Dallas Clark .20 .50
59 Dan Marino .75 2.00
60 Darrelle Revis .20 .50
61 Darren McFadden .30 .75
62 Darrius Heyward-Bey RC .60 1.50
63 Daunte Culpepper .25 .60
64 DeAngelo Hall .20 .50
65 DeAngelo Williams .20 .50
66 Deion Branch .20 .50
67 DeMarcus Ware .25 .60
68 Derek Anderson .20 .50
69 Derrick Mason .20 .50
70 Derrick Ward .20 .50
71 Derrick Williams RC .40 1.00
72 DeSean Jackson .25 .60
73 Devery Henderson .20 .50
74 Devin Hester .25 .60
75 Domenik Hixon .20 .50
76 Donald Brown RC .40 1.00
77 Donald Driver .25 .60
78 Donnie Avery .20 .50
79 Donovan McNabb .25 .60
80 Drew Brees .30 .75
81 Dustin Keller .20 .50
82 Dwayne Bowe .25 .60
83 Dwight Freeney .20 .50
84 Orville Wright inventor .20 .50
85 Ed Reed .25 .60
86 Eddie Royal .20 .50
87 Eli Manning .25 .60
88 Ernie Sims .20 .50
89 Evander Hood RC .60 1.50
90 Annie Oakley .20 .50
91 Felix Jones .20 .50
92 Frank Gore .25 .60
93 Fred Jackson .25 .60
94 Fred Taylor .20 .50
95 Nikola Tesla engineer .20 .50
96 Gaines Adams .20 .50
97 Glen Coffee RC .40 1.00
98 Greg Camarillo .25 .60
99 Greg Jennings .20 .50
100 Greg Olsen .25 .60
101 William McKinley Pres. .20 .50
102 Heath Miller .20 .50
103 Hines Ward .25 .60
104 George Westinghouse entrepren. .20 .50
105 Isaac Bruce .30 .75
106 Theodore Roosevelt Pres. .20 .50
107 Jake Delhomme .20 .50
108 Jamaal Charles .25 .60
109 Jamal Lewis .25 .60
110 JaMarcus Russell .20 .50
111 James Farrior .20 .50
112 James Harrison .30 .75
113 Jared Allen .20 .50
114 Jared Cook RC .50 1.25
115 Jason Witten .25 .60
116 Jay Cutler .20 .50
117 Jeremy Maclin RC .50 1.25
118 Jeremy Shockey .20 .50
119 Jerious Norwood .20 .50
120 Jerod Mayo .25 .60
121 Jerricho Cotchery .20 .50
122 Jerry Rice .75 2.00
123 Jim Brown .50 1.25
124 Joe Flacco .25 .60
125 Joe Montana 1.25 3.00
126 Joey Galloway .25 .60
127 Joey Porter .25 .60
128 John Abraham .20 .50
129 John Carlson .25 .60
130 John Elway .60 1.50
131 Johnny Knox RC .50 1.25
132 Jon Beason .20 .50
133 Jonathan Stewart .20 .50
134 Jonathan Vilma .20 .50
135 Joseph Addai .20 .50
136 Josh Freeman RC .40 1.00
137 Josh Reed .20 .50
138 Juaquin Iglesias RC .40 1.00
139 Julian Peterson .20 .50
140 Julius Peppers .25 .60
141 Justin Fargas .20 .50
142 Justin Gage .20 .50
143 Justin Tuck .20 .50
144 Clara Barton nurse .20 .50
145 Kellen Winslow Jr. .20 .50
146 Kenny Britt RC .60 1.50
147 Kenny McKinley RC .40 1.00
148 Kerry Collins .20 .50
149 Kevin Faulk .20 .50
150 Kevin Smith .20 .50
151 Kevin Walter .25 .60
152 Kevin Williams .20 .50
153 Knowshon Moreno RC .40 1.00
154 Kris Jenkins .20 .50
155 Kurt Warner .25 .60
156 Kyle Orton .20 .50
157 LaDainian Tomlinson .30 .75
158 LaMarr Woodley .20 .50
159 Lance Briggs .25 .60
160 Lance Moore .20 .50
161 Larry English RC .50 1.25
162 Larry Fitzgerald .25 .60
163 Larry Johnson .20 .50
164 Laurence Maroney .25 .60
165 Laveranues Coles .20 .50
166 Le'Ron McClain .25 .60
167 Lee Evans .25 .60
168 LenDale White .20 .50
169 Leon Washington .20 .50
170 LeSean McCoy RC 1.00 2.50
171 London Fletcher .25 .60
172 Thomas Edison inventor .20 .50
173 Malcolm Jenkins RC .40 1.00
174 Marc Bulger .20 .50
175 Mario Williams .25 .60
176 Marion Barber .25 .60
177 Mark Clayton .20 .50
178 Mark Sanchez RC .40 1.00
179 Marques Colston .20 .50
180 Marshawn Lynch .25 .60
181 Mathias Kiwanuka .20 .50
182 Matt Cassel .20 .50
183 Matt Forte .20 .50
184 Matt Hasselbeck .20 .50
185 Matt Ryan .25 .60
186 Matt Schaub .20 .50
187 Matthew Stafford RC 2.00 5.00
188 Maurice Jones-Drew .20 .50
189 Mewelde Moore .20 .50
190 Michael Bush .20 .50
191 Michael Crabtree RC .60 1.50
192 Michael Jenkins .20 .50
193 Michael Turner .20 .50
194 Mike Goodson RC .50 1.25
195 Mike Thomas RC .40 1.00
196 Mike Wallace RC .60 1.50
197 Mohamed Massaquoi RC .40 1.00
198 Muhsin Muhammad .20 .50
199 Andrew Mellon banker .20 .50
200 Nate Davis RC .40 1.00
201 Nate Washington .20 .50
202 Nnamdi Asomugha .20 .50
203 Fred Grandy Congress .20 .50
204 Owen Daniels .20 .50
205 Barack Obama .30 .75
206 Pat White RC .50 1.25
207 Patrick Turner RC .40 1.00
208 Patrick Willis .25 .60
209 Percy Harvin RC .40 1.00
210 Peria Jerry RC .40 1.00
211 Peyton Manning .75 2.00
212 Philip Rivers .30 .75
213 Pierre Thomas .20 .50
214 Jay Ratliff .30 .75
215 Robert Jarvik inventor .20 .50
216 Ramses Barden RC .40 1.00
217 Randy Moss .25 .60
218 Rashard Mendenhall .20 .50
219 Ray Lewis .30 .75
220 Ray Rice .20 .50
221 Reggie Bush .20 .50
222 Reggie Wayne .25 .60
223 Rhett Bomar RC .40 1.00
224 Richard Seymour .20 .50
225 Ricky Williams .25 .60
226 Robert Ayers RC .40 1.00
227 Roddy White .20 .50
228 Ronde Barber .20 .50
229 Ronnie Brown .20 .50
230 Roscoe Parrish .20 .50
231 Roy Williams WR .20 .50
232 Ryan Grant .25 .60
233 Pawnee Bill .20 .50
234 Sage Rosenfels .20 .50
235 Santana Moss .25 .60
236 Shaun Hill .20 .50
237 Shaun Rogers .20 .50
238 Shonn Greene RC .40 1.00
239 Stephen McGee RC .40 1.00
240 Steve Slaton .20 .50
241 Steve Smith .25 .60
242 Steve Smith USC .25 .60
243 Steven Jackson .20 .50
244 Richmond Hobson Admiral .20 .50
245 T.J. Houshmandzadeh .20 .50
246 Tarvaris Jackson .25 .60
247 Tashard Choice .20 .50
248 Ted Ginn Jr. .20 .50
249 Terence Newman .20 .50
250 Terrell Owens .25 .60
251 Terrell Suggs .20 .50
252 Terry Bradshaw .50 1.25
253 Thomas Jones .20 .50
254 Tim Hightower .20 .50
255 Tom Brady 1.00 2.50
256 Tony Dorsett .40 1.00
257 Tony Gonzalez .25 .60
258 Tony Romo .25 .60
259 Torry Holt .25 .60
260 Edgerrin James .25 .60
261 Travis Beckum RC .40 1.00
262 Troy Aikman .50 1.25
263 Troy Polamalu .30 .75
264 Tyson Jackson RC .40 1.00
265 Paddy Doyle athlete .20 .50
266 John D. Rockefeller tycoon .20 .50
267 Vince Young .20 .50
268 Vincent Jackson .20 .50
269 Vontae Davis RC .40 1.00
270 Kevin Young track .20 .50
271 Wes Welker .25 .60
272 Willie Parker .20 .50
273 Willis McGahee .20 .50
274 Booker T. Washington .20 .50
275 Zach Miller .20 .50
276 Anthony Fasano .75 2.00
277 Antonio Bryant .75 2.00
278 Mike Powell track .75 2.00
279 Barrett Ruud .75 2.00
280 Brandon Jacobs .75 2.00
281 Braylon Edwards .75 2.00
282 Calvin Johnson 1.25 3.00
283 Chad Pennington .75 2.00
284 Chase Coffman RC .75 2.00
285 Chris Hope .75 2.00
286 Cortland Finnegan .75 2.00
287 Brett Favre 5.00 12.00
288 Darren Howard .75 2.00
289 Darren Sproles 1.00 2.50
290 David Garrard .75 2.00
291 Deon Butler RC .75 2.00
292 Dominic Rhodes .75 2.00
293 Earnest Graham .75 2.00
294 Gartrell Johnson RC .75 2.00
295 Gibril Wilson .75 2.00
296 Hakeem Nicks RC 1.00 2.50
297 J.T. O'Sullivan .75 2.00
298 James Casey RC 1.00 2.50
299 Jarett Dillard RC .75 2.00
300 Jason Campbell .75 2.00
301 Jason Smith RC .75 2.00
302 Michael Vick 1.00 2.50
303 Jeff Garcia .75 2.00
304 Joe Namath 1.50 4.00
305 Jon Kitna .75 2.00
306 Josh Cribbs .75 2.00
307 Julius Jones .75 2.00
308 Kenny Phillips .75 2.00
309 Kirk Morrison .75 2.00
310 Maurice Greene track .75 2.00
311 Louis Murphy RC .75 2.00
312 Manuel Johnson RC .75 2.00
313 Matt Leinart .75 2.00
314 Maurice Morris .75 2.00
315 Michael Griffin .75 2.00
316 Nick Collins .75 2.00
317 Pat Williams .75 2.00
318 Robert Mathis .75 2.00
319 Ryan Fitzpatrick .75 2.00
320 Sammy Morris .75 2.00
321 Santonio Holmes .75 2.00
322 Seneca Wallace .75 2.00
323 Ted Kennedy 1.00 2.50
324 Shawn Nelson RC .75 2.00
325 Steve Breaston 1.00 2.50
326 Tony Scheffler .75 2.00
327 Trent Cole .75 2.00
328 Trent Edwards .75 2.00
329 Tyler Thigpen .75 2.00
330 Jackie Joyner-Kersee track .75 2.00

2009 Topps Mayo Mini

*VETS 1-275: 1.5X TO 4X BASIC CARDS
*ROOKIES 1-275: .5X TO 1.2X BASIC CARDS
*VETS 276-330: .5X TO 1.2X BASIC CARDS
*ROOKIES 276-330: .4X TO 1X BASIC CARDS
276-330 STATED ODDS 1:12 HOB
331-360 SP INSERTED INSIDE RIP CARDS
287 Brett Favre 6.00 15.00
331 Adrian Peterson SP 8.00 20.00
332 Andre Johnson SP 6.00 15.00
333 Ben Roethlisberger SP 8.00 20.00
334 Brandon Marshall SP 6.00 15.00
335 Brian Westbrook SP 5.00 12.00
336 Calvin Johnson SP 8.00 20.00
337 Chris Wells SP 3.00 8.00
338 Clinton Portis SP 5.00 12.00
339 Donovan McNabb SP 6.00 15.00
340 Drew Brees SP 8.00 20.00
341 Eli Manning SP 6.00 15.00
342 Jay Cutler SP 5.00 12.00
343 Jeremy Maclin SP 4.00 10.00
344 Josh Freeman SP 3.00 8.00
345 Knowshon Moreno SP 3.00 8.00
346 LaDainian Tomlinson SP 8.00 20.00
347 Larry Fitzgerald SP 6.00 15.00
348 Mark Sanchez SP 3.00 8.00
349 Matt Ryan SP 6.00 15.00
350 Matthew Stafford SP 15.00 40.00
351 Michael Crabtree SP 5.00 12.00
352 Michael Turner SP 5.00 12.00
353 Peyton Manning SP 20.00 50.00
354 Philip Rivers SP 8.00 20.00
355 Reggie Wayne SP 6.00 15.00
356 Steve Smith SP 6.00 15.00
357 Steven Jackson SP 5.00 12.00
358 Terrell Owens SP 6.00 15.00
359 Tom Brady SP 25.00 60.00
360 Tony Romo SP 6.00 15.00

2009 Topps Mayo Mini Blue Back

*VETS 1-275: 4X TO 10X BASIC CARDS
*ROOKIES 1-275: 1X TO 2.5X BASIC CARDS
*VETS 276-330: .8X TO 2X BASIC CARDS
*ROOKIES 276-330: .6X TO 1.5X BASIC CARDS
BLUE BACK ODDS 1:24 HOB
287 Brett Favre 10.00 25.00

2009 Topps Mayo Mini Gold

*VETS 1-275: 4X TO 10X BASIC CARDS
*ROOKIES 1-275: 1X TO 2.5X BASIC CARDS
*VETS 276-330: .8X TO 2X BASIC CARDS
*ROOKIES 276-330: .6X TO 1.5X BASIC CARDS
GOLD STATED ODDS 1:21 HOB
287 Brett Favre 10.00 25.00

2009 Topps Mayo Mini Red Back

*VETS 1-275: 10 TO 25X BASIC CARDS
*ROOKIES 1-275: 2X TO 5X BASIC CARDS
*VETS 276-330: 2X TO 5X BASIC CARDS
*ROOKIES 276-330: 1X TO 2.5X BASIC CARDS
RED BACK/25 ODDS 1:82 HOB
287 Brett Favre 30.00 60.00

2009 Topps Mayo Silver

*VETS 1-275: 1.5X TO 4X BASIC CARDS
*ROOKIES 1-275: .5X TO 1.2X BASIC CARDS
*VETS 276-330: .5X TO 1.2X BASIC CARDS
*ROOKIES 276-330: .4X TO 1X BASIC CARDS
ONE SILVER PER PACK
287 Brett Favre 6.00 15.00

2009 Topps Mayo Americana Relics

GROUP A ODDS 1:33,000 HOB
GROUP B ODDS 1:1540 HOB
GROUP D ODDS 1:2100 HOB
MRAO Annie Oakley Brick B 25.00 50.00
MRBB Buffalo Bill Nickel A 30.00 60.00
MRBW Booker T. Washington Brick B 25.00 50.00
MRCE Columbian Exposition Handkerchief B 25.00 50.00
MRGC Grover Cleveland Floor B 30.00 60.00
MRHR Adm. H.G. Rickover Wood B 30.00 60.00
MRNT Nikola Tesla Brick B 25.00 50.00
MRRR Soldier Table B 30.00 60.00
MRTE Thomas Edison Brick B 25.00 50.00
MRTK Ted Kennedy Floor B 40.00 80.00
MRTR Theodore Roosevelt Floor B 40.00 80.00
MRWD William R. Day Tree A 30.00 60.00
MRWH Benjamin Harrsion Floor B 30.00 60.00
MRWM William McKinley Floor B 30.00 60.00
MRWN Wendell Neville Pants B 30.00 60.00
MRBB2 Buffalo Bill Brick B 25.00 50.00
MRRR2 Soldier Blanket B 30.00 60.00
MRRR3 Soldier Knapsack B 30.00 80.00
MRTK2 Ted Kennedy Banner D 20.00 50.00

2009 Topps Mayo Autographs

GROUP A ODDS 1:529 HOB
GROUP B ODDS 1:1330 HOB
GROUP C ODDS 1:160 HOB
GROUP D ODDS 1:90 HOB
GROUP E ODDS 1:96 HOB
GROUP F ODDS 1:86 HOB
UNPRICED RED INK INSERTED IN RIP CARDS
MAAC Austin Collie F 2.50 6.00
MAAP Adrian Peterson A 125.00 200.00
MABP Brandon Pettigrew E 2.50 6.00
MABR Brian Robiskie D 6.00 15.00
MACJ Chris Johnson A 40.00 80.00
MACL Chris Long A 8.00 20.00
MACWE Chris Wells C 12.00 30.00
MADA Donnie Avery C 6.00 15.00
MADB Donald Brown A 20.00 40.00
MADBR Drew Brees A 60.00 120.00
MADH Darrius Heyward-Bey A 12.00 30.00
MADJ DeSean Jackson C 8.00 20.00
MADW1 DeAngelo Williams A 12.00 30.00
MADW2 Derrick Williams E 2.50 6.00
MAGC Glen Coffee E 2.50 6.00
MAGJ1 Greg Jennings C 10.00 25.00
MAGJ2 Gartrell Johnson F 2.50 6.00
MAHN Hakeem Nicks D 3.00 8.00
MAJCU Jay Cutler A 40.00 80.00
MAJF1 Joe Flacco B 15.00 40.00
MAJF2 Josh Freeman A 12.00 30.00
MAJJK Jackie Joyner-Kersee Track C 8.00 20.00
MAJL James Laurinaitis E 6.00 15.00
MAJLO Jake Long F 5.00 12.00
MAJM Jeremy Maclin B 10.00 25.00
MAJS Jonathan Stewart A 12.00 30.00
MAKB Kenny Britt D 4.00 10.00
MAKM Knowshon Moreno A 15.00 40.00
MAKY Kevin Young Track C 5.00 12.00
MALF Larry Fitzgerald A 30.00 60.00
MALM LeSean McCoy D 12.00 30.00
MAMC Michael Crabtree A 30.00 80.00
MAMG Maurice Greene Track C 6.00 15.00
MAMM Mohamed Massaquoi C 6.00 15.00
MAMP Mike Powell Track C 6.00 15.00
MAMR Matt Ryan A 30.00 60.00
MAMS Matthew Stafford A 60.00 120.00
MAMSA Mark Sanchez A 50.00 100.00
MAMT Michael Turner A 12.00 30.00
MAMW Mario Williams A 8.00 20.00
MAPD Paddy Doyle Rec.Holder C 5.00 12.00
MAPH Percy Harvin D 6.00 15.00
MAPM Peyton Manning A 125.00 200.00
MAPR Philip Rivers A 25.00 50.00
MAPW1 Pat White D 3.00 8.00
MAPW2 Patrick Willis A 12.00 30.00
MARB Randy Barnes Track C
MARB2 Russell Byars Rec.Holder C 4.00 10.00
MARJ Robert Jarvik Inventor C 10.00 25.00
MARM Rey Maualuga F 4.00 10.00
MARW Roddy White D 6.00 15.00
MASGR Shonn Greene D 8.00 20.00

2009 Topps Mayo Cabinet Cards

ONE CABINET CARD PER HOBBY BOX
MCC1 Drew Brees 3.00 8.00
MCC2 Philip Rivers 3.00 8.00
MCC3 Peyton Manning 8.00 20.00
MCC4 Tom Brady 10.00 25.00
MCC5 Tony Romo 2.50 6.00
MCC6 Eli Manning 2.50 6.00
MCC7 Ben Roethlisberger 3.00 8.00
MCC8 Matt Ryan 2.50 6.00
MCC9 Adrian Peterson 3.00 8.00
MCC10 Clinton Portis 2.00 5.00
MCC11 LaDainian Tomlinson 3.00 8.00
MCC12 Steven Jackson 2.00 5.00
MCC13 Andre Johnson 2.50 6.00
MCC14 Larry Fitzgerald 2.50 6.00
MCC15 Knowshon Moreno .60 1.50
MCC16 Steve Smith 2.50 6.00
MCC17 Calvin Johnson 3.00 8.00
MCC18 Reggie Wayne 2.50 6.00
MCC19 Matthew Stafford 3.00 8.00
MCC20 Mark Sanchez .60 1.50

2009 Topps Mayo Cabinet Relics

STATED ODDS 1:73 HOBBY BOXES
MCR1 Drew Brees 20.00 40.00
MCR2 Aaron Rodgers 20.00 40.00
MCR3 Philip Rivers 12.00 30.00
MCR4 Peyton Manning 30.00 80.00
MCR5 Donovan McNabb 10.00 25.00
MCR6 Tony Romo 10.00 25.00
MCR7 Matt Ryan 10.00 25.00
MCR8 Ben Roethlisberger 12.00 30.00
MCR9 Adrian Peterson 12.00 30.00
MCR10 DeAngelo Williams 8.00 20.00
MCR11 Clinton Portis
MCR12 Thomas Jones
MCR13 Andre Johnson 10.00 25.00
MCR14 Larry Fitzgerald
MCR15 Steve Smith 10.00 25.00
MCR16 Calvin Johnson
MCR17 Matthew Stafford
MCR18 Mark Sanchez 3.00 8.00
MCR19 Knowshon Moreno 3.00 8.00
MCR20 Chris Wells 3.00 8.00

2009 Topps Mayo Celebrated Citizens

COMPLETE SET (15) 8.00 20.00
STATED ODDS 1:12
CC1 Samuel Adams 1.25 3.00
CC2 William Penn 1.25 3.00
CC3 Barack Obama 2.00 5.00
CC4 Andrew Hallidie 1.25 3.00
CC5 Henry Ford 1.25 3.00
CC6 Andrew Carnegie 1.25 3.00
CC7 Franklin D. Roosevelt 1.25 3.00
CC8 Stephen F. Austin 1.25 3.00
CC9 Janet Reno 1.25 3.00
CC10 John D. Rockeleller 1.25 3.00
CC11 Edgar Allan Poe 1.25 3.00
CC12 Henry Hudson 1.25 3.00
CC13 George Washington 1.25 3.00
CC14 David Crockett 1.25 3.00
CC15 William Tecumseh Sherman 1.25 3.00

2009 Topps Mayo Namesakes

COMPLETE SET (13) 15.00 40.00
STATED ODDS 1:48 HOB
NFL1 Bills 1.50 4.00
NFL2 Dolphins 1.50 4.00
NFL3 Eagles 1.50 4.00
NFL4 Falcons 1.50 4.00
NFL5 Colts 1.50 4.00
NFL6 Jaguars 1.50 4.00
NFL7 Lions 1.50 4.00
NFL8 Ravens 1.50 4.00
NFL9 Seahawks 1.50 4.00
NFL10 Bengals 1.50 4.00
NFL11 Jets 1.50 4.00
NFL12 Patriots 1.50 4.00
NFL13 Titans 1.50 4.00

2009 Topps Mayo Relics

GROUP A ODDS 1:239 HOB
GROUP B ODDS 1:85 HOB
GROUP C ODDS 1:38 HOB
MRAB Andre Brown C 2.00 5.00
MRABO Anquan Boldin A 3.00 8.00
MRAC Aaron Curry C 2.50 6.00
MRAG Antonio Gates A 4.00 10.00
MRAR Aaron Rodgers B 8.00 20.00
MRBM Brandon Marshall B 4.00 10.00
MRBP Brandon Pettigrew C 1.50 4.00
MRBR Brian Robiskie C 1.50 4.00
MRBRO Ben Roethlisberger B 5.00 12.00
MRBW Brian Westbrook B 3.00 8.00
MRCJ Calvin Johnson A 5.00 12.00
MRCW Chris Wells C 5.00 12.00
MRDA Donnie Avery B 3.00 8.00
MRDB Dwayne Bowe B 4.00 10.00
MRDB2 Donald Brown C 4.00 10.00
MRDBU Deon Butler C 1.50 4.00
MRDH Darrius Heyward-Bey C 2.50 6.00
MRDM Donovan McNabb B 4.00 10.00
MRDW DeAngelo Williams A 3.00 8.00
MRDW2 Derrick Williams C 1.50 4.00
MRER Eddie Royal B 3.00 8.00
MRGC Glen Coffee C 1.50 4.00
MRHN Hakeem Nicks C 2.00 5.00
MRJF Josh Freeman C 1.50 4.00
MRJI Juaquin Iglesias C 1.50 4.00
MRJM Jeremy Maclin C 4.00 10.00
MRJR Javon Ringer C 1.50 4.00
MRJS Jason Smith C 2.50 6.00
MRKB Kenny Britt C 2.50 6.00
MRKM Knowshon Moreno C 1.50 4.00
MRLF Larry Fitzgerald A 4.00 10.00
MRLM LeSean McCoy C 4.00 10.00
MRMC Marques Colston B 3.00 8.00
MRMC2 Michael Crabtree C 2.50 6.00
MRMF Matt Forte B 3.00 8.00
MRMJ Maurice Jones-Drew B 3.00 8.00
MRMM Mohamed Massaquoi C 1.50 4.00
MRMS Mark Sanchez C 6.00 15.00
MRMS2 Matthew Stafford C 6.00 15.00
MRMT Mike Thomas C 1.50 4.00
MRMW Mike Wallace C 2.50 6.00
MRND Nate Davis C 1.50 4.00
MRPH Percy Harvin C 4.00 10.00
MRPR Philip Rivers A 5.00 12.00
MRPT Patrick Turner C 2.50 6.00
MRPW Pat White C 2.00 5.00
MRRB Ramses Barden C 1.50 4.00
MRRB2 Ronnie Brown B 3.00 8.00
MRRBO Rhett Bomar C 2.50 6.00
MRRG Ryan Grant B 4.00 10.00
MRRRI Ray Rice B 3.00 8.00
MRSG Shonn Greene C 1.50 4.00
MRSJ Steven Jackson A 3.00 8.00
MRSM Stephen McGee C 1.50 4.00
MRSM2 Santana Moss B 4.00 10.00
MRSS1 Steve Smith B 4.00 10.00
MRSS2 Steve Smith USC B 4.00 10.00
MRTJ Tyson Jackson C 1.50 4.00
MRTJO Thomas Jones A 3.00 8.00

2009 Topps Mayo Rip Cards Ripped

PRICED WITH CLEANLY RIPPED BACKS
RC1 Drew Brees 3.00 8.00
RC2 Jay Cutler 2.00 5.00
RC3 Philip Rivers 3.00 8.00
RC4 Peyton Manning 8.00 20.00
RC5 Tom Brady 10.00 25.00
RC6 Donovan McNabb [illegible]
RC7 Tony Romo 2.50 6.00
RC8 Eli Manning 2.50 6.00
RC9 Ben Roethlisberger 3.00 8.00
RC10 Matt Ryan 2.50 6.00
RC11 Adrian Peterson 3.00 8.00
RC12 Clinton Portis 2.00 5.00
RC13 LaDainian Tomlinson 3.00 8.00
RC14 Steven Jackson 2.00 5.00
RC15 Brian Westbrook 2.00 5.00
RC16 Michael Turner 2.00 5.00
RC17 Andre Johnson 2.50 6.00
RC18 Larry Fitzgerald 2.50 6.00
RC19 Steve Smith 2.50 6.00
RC20 Calvin Johnson 3.00 8.00
RC21 Brandon Marshall 2.50 6.00
RC22 Reggie Wayne 2.50 6.00
RC23 Terrell Owens 2.50 6.00
RC24 Matthew Stafford 3.00 8.00
RC25 Mark Sanchez .60 1.50
RC26 Josh Freeman .60 1.50
RC27 Knowshon Moreno .60 1.50
RC28 Chris Wells .60 1.50
RC29 Michael Crabtree 1.00 2.50
RC30 Jeremy Maclin .75 2.00

2009 Topps Mayo Rip Cards Unripped

STATED ODDS 1:192 HOB
RC1 Drew Brees 25.00 60.00
RC2 Jay Cutler 15.00 40.00
RC3 Philip Rivers 25.00 60.00
RC4 Peyton Manning 40.00 80.00
RC5 Tom Brady 40.00 80.00
RC6 Donovan McNabb 20.00 50.00
RC7 Tony Romo 40.00 80.00
RC8 Eli Manning 20.00 50.00
RC9 Ben Roethlisberger 40.00 80.00
RC10 Matt Ryan 20.00 50.00
RC11 Adrian Peterson 40.00 80.00
RC12 Clinton Portis 15.00 40.00
RC13 LaDainian Tomlinson 25.00 60.00
RC14 Steven Jackson 15.00 40.00
RC15 Brian Westbrook 15.00 40.00
RC16 Michael Turner 15.00 40.00
RC17 Andre Johnson 15.00 40.00
RC18 Larry Fitzgerald 20.00 50.00
RC19 Steve Smith 20.00 50.00
RC20 Calvin Johnson 25.00 60.00
RC21 Brandon Marshall 20.00 50.00
RC22 Reggie Wayne 20.00 50.00
RC23 Terrell Owens 20.00 50.00
RC24 Matthew Stafford 25.00 60.00
RC25 Mark Sanchez 40.00 80.00
RC26 Josh Freeman 6.00 15.00
RC27 Knowshon Moreno 6.00 15.00
RC28 Chris Wells 6.00 15.00
RC29 Michael Crabtree 10.00 25.00
RC30 Jeremy Maclin 8.00 20.00

2009 Topps Mayo Stamp Relics

STATED ODDS 1:985
S1 1492 Landing of Columbus 15.00 40.00
S2 1901 East Express 15.00 40.00
S3 1898 Farming in the West 15.00 40.00
S4 Documentary Series of 1898 15.00 40.00
S5 1492 Columbus in Sight of Land 15.00 40.00

2009 Topps Mayo United States Governors

STATED ODDS 1:12 HOB
USG1 Bob Riley 1.00 2.50
USG2 Sean Parnell 1.00 2.50
USG3 Jan Brewer 1.00 2.50
USG4 Michael Dale Beebe 1.00 2.50
USG5 Arnold Schwarzenegger 1.00 2.50
USG6 Bill Ritter Jr. 1.00 2.50
USG7 M. Jodi Rell 1.00 2.50
USG8 Jack Markell 1.00 2.50
USG9 Charles Joseph Crist Jr. 1.00 2.50
USG10 Sonny Perdue 1.00 2.50
USG11 Linda Lingle 1.00 2.50
USG12 Butch Otter 1.00 2.50
USG13 Pat Quinn 1.00 2.50
USG14 Mitch Daniels 1.00 2.50
USG15 Chet Culver 1.00 2.50
USG16 Mark Parkinson 1.00 2.50
USG17 Steven L. Beshear 1.00 2.50
USG18 Bobby Jindal 1.00 2.50
USG19 John Elias Baldacci 1.00 2.50
USG20 Martin Joseph O'Malley 1.00 2.50
USG21 Deval Laurdine Patrick 1.00 2.50
USG22 Jennifer M. Granholm 1.00 2.50
USG23 Timothy Pawlenty 1.00 2.50
USG24 Haley Barbour 1.00 2.50
USG25 Jay Nixon 1.00 2.50
USG26 Brian Schweitzer 1.00 2.50
USG27 Dave Heineman 1.00 2.50
USG28 Jim Gibbons 1.00 2.50
USG29 John Lynch 1.00 2.50
USG30 Jon Stevens Corzine 1.00 2.50
USG31 Bill Richardson 1.00 2.50
USG32 David A. Paterson 1.00 2.50
USG33 Beverly Perdue 1.00 2.50
USG34 John Hoeven 1.00 2.50
USG35 Ted Strickland 1.00 2.50
USG36 Brad Henry 1.00 2.50
USG37 Ted Kulongoski 1.00 2.50
USG38 Edward G. Rendell 1.00 2.50
USG39 Donald L. Carcieri 1.00 2.50
USG40 Mark Sanford, Jr. 1.00 2.50
USG41 M. Michael Rounds 1.00 2.50
USG42 Phil Bredesen 1.00 2.50
USG43 Rick Perry 1.00 2.50
USG44 Gary Herbert 1.00 2.50
USG45 James H. Douglas 1.00 2.50
USG46 Tim Kaine 1.00 2.50
USG47 Christine Gregoire 1.00 2.50
USG48 Joe Manchin III 1.00 2.50
USG49 Jim Doyle 1.00 2.50
USG50 Dave Freudenthal 1.00 2.50

2009 Topps Mayo World's Fair Attractions

COMPLETE SET (14) 8.00 20.00
STATED ODDS 1:12 HOB
WF1 Ferris Wheel .75 2.00
WF2 1893 Chicago World's Fair .75 2.00
WF3 Court of Honor and the Grand Basin .75 2.00
WF4 Buffalo Bill .75 2.00
WF5 The White City .75 2.00
WF6 Thomas Edison .75 2.00
WF7 Idaho Building .75 2.00
WF8 John Bull Locomotive .75 2.00
WF9 Nikola Tesla .75 2.00
WF10 Viking .75 2.00
WF11 Eadweard Muybridge .75 2.00
WF12 Hamburger .75 2.00
WF13 Scott Joplin .75 2.00
WF14 Frederick Law Olmstead .75 2.00

2015 Topps Mega Box

*REFRACTOR: 1.2X TO 3X BASIC CARDS
1 Jameis Winston .50 1.25
2 Marcus Mariota .75 2.00
3 Melvin Gordon .50 1.25
4 Todd Gurley .75 2.00
5 Kevin White .25 .60
6 Amari Cooper .60 1.50

2013 Topps Mini

*VETS: .5X TO 1.2X BASIC CARDS
*ROOKIES: .4X TO 1X BASIC RC

2013 Topps Mini Gold

*VETS/58: 6X TO 15X BASIC MINI
*ROOKIES/58: 5X TO 12X BASIC MINI

2013 Topps Mini 1959 Mini

*MINI 1959: .4X TO 1X TOPPS 1959 MINI
STATED ODDS 1:6 MINI PACKS

2013 Topps Mini Autographs

AUTO/35-265 ODDS 1:40 MINI PACKS
MAAO Alex Okafor/265 3.00 8.00
MABJ Bo Jackson/35 50.00 100.00
MABM Barkevious Mingo/265 3.00 8.00
MACH Chris Harper/265 3.00 8.00
MACJ Chris Johnson/35
MACP Cordarrelle Patterson/50 5.00 12.00
MADH DeAndre Hopkins/35 12.00 30.00
MADJ Datone Jones/265 3.00 8.00
MADR Denard Robinson/265 3.00 8.00
MAEA Ezekiel Ansah/99 4.00 10.00
MAED Eric Dickerson/35 6.00 15.00
MAEF Eric Fisher
MAEJM EJ Manuel/35 5.00 12.00
MAEL Eddie Lacy/99 4.00 10.00
MAGB Giovani Bernard/99 4.00 10.00
MAGS Geno Smith/35 6.00 15.00
MAJN Jordy Nelson/35 10.00 25.00
MAJPP Jason Pierre-Paul
MAJW Jason Witten/35 20.00 40.00
MAKB Kenjon Barner/265 3.00 8.00
MAKV Kenny Vaccaro/265 3.00 8.00
MALT Lawrence Taylor/35 20.00 40.00
MAMB Montee Ball/99 4.00 10.00
MAME Matt Elam/265 3.00 8.00
MAMT Manti Te'o
MARW Robert Woods/99 6.00 15.00
MATA Tavon Austin/35 6.00 15.00
MATB Tyler Bray/99 4.00 10.00
MATE Tyler Eifert/265 3.00 8.00
MATM Tyrann Mathieu/265 5.00 12.00

2013 Topps Mini Relics

RELIC/25-57 ODDS 1:60 MINI PACKS
MRAD Aaron Dobson/57 2.50 6.00
MRAE Andre Ellington/57 2.50 6.00
MRAL Andrew Luck
MRCM Christine Michael/57 2.50 6.00
MRCP Cordarrelle Patterson/57 2.50 6.00
MRCW Cameron Wake/25 8.00 20.00
MRDH DeAndre Hopkins/57 6.00 15.00
MRDJ Dion Jordan/57 2.50 6.00
MRDR Denard Robinson/57 2.50 6.00
MREJM EJ Manuel/57 2.50 6.00
MREL Eddie Lacy/57 2.50 6.00
MRGB Giovani Bernard/57 2.50 6.00
MRGE Gavin Escobar/57 2.50 6.00
MRGS Geno Smith/57 2.50 6.00
MRJF Johnathan Franklin/57 2.50 6.00
MRJH Justin Hunter/57
MRJR Joseph Randle/57 2.50 6.00
MRJRE Jordan Reed/57 4.00 10.00
MRKA Keenan Allen/57 5.00 12.00
MRKD Knile Davis/57 2.50 6.00
MRKS Kenny Stills/57 2.50 6.00
MRLB Le'Veon Bell/57 8.00 20.00
MRLJ Landry Jones/57 2.50 6.00
MRMB Matt Barkley/57 2.50 6.00
MRMBA Montee Ball/57 2.50 6.00
MRMG Mike Glennon/57 2.50 6.00
MRMGI Mike Gillislee/57 2.50 6.00
MRMGO Marquise Goodwin/57 2.50 6.00
MRML Marcus Lattimore/57 2.50 6.00
MRMT Manti Te'o/57 3.00 8.00
MRMV Michael Vick
MRMW Markus Wheaton/57 2.50 6.00
MRQP Quinton Patton/57 2.50 6.00
MRRG3 Robert Griffin III
MRRN Ryan Nassib/57 2.50 6.00
MRRT Ryan Tannehill/25 5.00 12.00
MRRW Robert Woods/57 4.00 10.00
MRRWH Roddy White
MRRWI Russell Wilson/25 12.00 30.00
MRSB Stedman Bailey/57 2.50 6.00
MRST Stepfan Taylor/57 2.50 6.00
MRTA Tavon Austin/57 3.00 8.00
MRTB Tom Brady
MRTE Tyler Eifert/57 2.50 6.00
MRTR Tony Romo
MRTRI Trent Richardson/25 4.00 10.00
MRTW Tyler Wilson/57 2.50 6.00
MRTWI Terrance Williams/57 2.50 6.00
MRWM Vance McDonald/57 3.00 8.00
MRZE Zach Ertz/57 5.00 12.00

2013 Topps Museum Collection

COMPLETE SET (100) 40.00 80.00
1 Maurice Jones-Drew .40 1.00
2 Jamaal Charles .50 1.25
3 Andre Reed .50 1.25
4 Patrick Willis .50 1.25
5 Aaron Rodgers 1.00 2.50
6 Terrell Davis .50 1.25
7 Kenny Stills RC .40 1.00
8 Le'Veon Bell RC 1.25 3.00
9 Cameron Wake .40 1.00
10 Larry Fitzgerald .50 1.25
11 Stedman Bailey RC .40 1.00
12 LeSean McCoy .60 1.50
13 Justin Hunter RC .40 1.00
14 Deion Sanders .50 1.25
15 Johnathan Franklin RC .40 1.00
16 Vance McDonald RC .50 1.25
17 Andre Johnson .40 1.00
18 Robert Woods RC .60 1.50
19 Manti Te'o RC .50 1.25
20 Quinton Patton RC .40 1.00
21 DeMarcus Ware .60 1.50
22 Geno Smith RC .40 1.00
23 Colin Kaepernick .50 1.25
24 Montee Ball RC .40 1.00
25 Steve Largent .60 1.50
26 Ronnie Lott .50 1.25
27 Brandon Marshall .50 1.25
28 Cam Newton .60 1.50
29 Marshawn Lynch .50 1.25
30 Jason Pierre-Paul .40 1.00
31 Darrelle Revis .40 1.00
32 Ray Rice .40 1.00
33 Matthew Stafford .50 1.25
34 Troy Aikman .75 2.00
35 Philip Rivers .60 1.50
36 Matt Barkley RC .40 1.00
37 Matt Ryan .50 1.25
38 Eric Dickerson .50 1.25
39 Peyton Manning 2.50 6.00
40 Dion Jordan RC .40 1.00
41 Calvin Johnson .60 1.50
42 Mike Glennon RC .40 1.00
43 Ryan Tannehill .50 1.25
44 A.J. Green .60 1.50
45 Christine Michael RC .40 1.00
46 Bo Jackson .75 2.00
47 Brett Favre 1.25 3.00

48 Markus Wheaton RC .40 1.00
49 J.J. Watt .50 1.25
50 Giovani Bernard RC .40 1.00
51 Ben Roethlisberger .60 1.50
52 Eli Manning .50 1.25
53 Arian Foster .50 1.25
54 Barry Sanders 1.00 2.50
55 Jared Allen .40 1.00
56 Joe Montana 1.50 4.00
57 Knile Davis RC .40 1.00
58 Kurt Warner .50 1.25
59 Keenan Allen RC .75 2.00
60 Terrance Williams RC .40 1.00
61 Aaron Dobson RC .40 1.00
62 Luke Kuechly .50 1.25
63 Troy Polamalu .60 1.50
64 Drew Brees .60 1.50
65 Clay Matthews .60 1.50
66 Chris Johnson .40 1.00
67 Tom Brady 1.50 4.00
68 Aldon Smith .40 1.00
69 Reggie Wayne .50 1.25
70 DeAndre Hopkins RC 1.00 2.50
71 Robert Griffin III .40 1.00
72 Tony Romo .50 1.25
73 Adrian Peterson .60 1.50
74 Marcus Allen .60 1.50
75 Zach Ertz RC .75 2.00
76 Russell Wilson 1.25 3.00
77 Tyler Eifert RC .40 1.00
78 Marcus Lattimore RC .40 1.00
79 Denard Robinson RC .40 1.00
80 Stepfan Taylor RC .40 1.00
81 Eddie Lacy RC .40 1.00
82 Marshall Faulk .50 1.25
83 Wes Welker .50 1.25
84 Cordarrelle Patterson RC .40 1.00
85 Ryan Nassib RC .40 1.00
86 Jordan Reed RC .60 1.50
87 EJ Manuel RC .40 1.00
88 Tyler Wilson RC .40 1.00
89 Trent Richardson .40 1.00
90 Julio Jones .60 1.50
91 Joseph Randle RC .40 1.00
92 Von Miller .50 1.25
93 Doug Martin .50 1.25
94 Tavon Austin RC .50 1.25
95 Andrew Luck 1.00 2.50
96 Alfred Morris .40 1.00
97 C.J. Spiller .40 1.00
98 John Elway 1.00 2.50
99 Joe Flacco .50 1.25
100 Sam Bradford .40 1.00

2013 Topps Museum Collection Copper

*VETS: .6X TO 1.5X BASIC CARDS
*ROOKIES: .6X TO 1.5X BASIC RC

2013 Topps Museum Collection Ruby

*VETS/50: 2X TO 5X BASIC CARDS
*ROOKIES/50: 1.5X TO 4X BASIC RC

2013 Topps Museum Collection Sapphire

*VETS/99: 1.2X TO 3X BASIC CARDS
*ROOKIES/99: 1.2X TO 3X BASIC RC

2013 Topps Museum Collection Canvas Collection

CC1 Joe Montana 3.00 8.00
CC2 Troy Aikman 1.50 4.00
CC3 Eric Dickerson 1.00 2.50
CC4 Marshall Faulk 1.00 2.50
CC5 Marcus Allen 1.25 3.00
CC6 Bo Jackson 1.50 4.00
CC7 Steve Largent 1.25 3.00
CC8 Brett Favre 2.50 6.00
CC9 Barry Sanders 2.00 5.00
CC10 John Elway 2.00 5.00
CC11 Deion Sanders 1.00 2.50
CC12 Geno Smith .50 1.25
CC13 EJ Manuel .50 1.25
CC14 Tavon Austin .60 1.50
CC15 Peyton Manning 5.00 12.00
CC16 Andrew Luck 2.00 5.00
CC17 Robert Griffin III .75 2.00
CC18 Russell Wilson 2.50 6.00
CC19 Adrian Peterson 1.25 3.00
CC20 Calvin Johnson 1.25 3.00
CC21 Tom Brady 3.00 8.00
CC22 Colin Kaepernick 1.00 2.50
CC23 Drew Brees 1.25 3.00
CC24 Aaron Rodgers 2.00 5.00
CC25 Andre Johnson .75 2.00

2013 Topps Museum Collection Framed Museum Collection Autographs Silver

FRAMED SILVER/20 ODDS 1:58
MCFAAB Anquan Boldin 40.00 80.00
MCFAAD Aaron Dobson 10.00 25.00
MCFAAR Andre Reed 40.00 80.00
MCFABJ Bo Jackson 100.00 175.00
MCFACP Cordarrelle Patterson 10.00 25.00
MCFADH DeAndre Hopkins 40.00 80.00
MCFADJ Dion Jordan 10.00 25.00
MCFADR Denard Robinson 10.00 25.00
MCFAED Eric Dickerson EXCH 25.00 60.00
MCFAEJM EJ Manuel 25.00 60.00
MCFAEL Eddie Lacy 75.00 150.00
MCFAGB Giovani Bernard 10.00 25.00
MCFAGS Geno Smith 10.00 25.00
MCFAJH Justin Hunter 25.00 50.00
MCFAJM Joe Montana 175.00 300.00
MCFAJPP Jason Pierre-Paul 20.00 50.00
MCFAKW Kurt Warner 60.00 120.00
MCFALB Le'Veon Bell 40.00 80.00
MCFAMA Marcus Allen 50.00 100.00
MCFAMB Matt Barkley 10.00 25.00
MCFAMBA Montee Ball 10.00 25.00
MCFAMF Marshall Faulk 40.00 80.00
MCFAMG Mike Glennon 10.00 25.00
MCFAML Marcus Lattimore 40.00 80.00
MCFAMS Matthew Stafford 40.00 80.00
MCFAMT Manti Te'o 12.00 30.00
MCFAPM Peyton Manning 175.00 300.00
MCFARB Reggie Bush 40.00 80.00
MCFARL Ronnie Lott 40.00 80.00
MCFARW Robert Woods 40.00 80.00
MCFASL Steve Largent 40.00 80.00
MCFATA Troy Aikman 75.00 150.00
MCFATAU Tavon Austin 12.00 30.00
MCFATD Terrell Davis 25.00 60.00
MCFATE Tyler Eifert 10.00 25.00

2013 Topps Museum Collection Jumbo Patch Autographs

JUMBO PATCH AUTO/20 ODDS 1:101
*COPPER/15: .4X TO 1X JSY AU/20
*GOLD/10: .5X TO 1.2X JSY AU/20
MJPAAD Aaron Dobson 8.00 20.00
MJPACP Cordarrelle Patterson 8.00 20.00
MJPADH DeAndre Hopkins 20.00 50.00
MJPAEJM EJ Manuel 20.00 50.00
MJPAEL Eddie Lacy 100.00 175.00
MJPAGB Giovani Bernard 20.00 50.00
MJPAGS Geno Smith 8.00 20.00
MJPAJH Justin Hunter 8.00 20.00
MJPALB Le'Veon Bell 40.00 80.00
MJPAMB Matt Barkley 8.00 20.00
MJPAMBA Montee Ball 8.00 20.00
MJPAMG Mike Glennon 8.00 20.00
MJPAMT Manti Te'o 10.00 25.00
MJPAMW Markus Wheaton 8.00 20.00
MJPARN Ryan Nassib 15.00 40.00
MJPARW Robert Woods 12.00 30.00
MJPAST Stepfan Taylor 8.00 20.00
MJPATA Tavon Austin 10.00 25.00
MJPATE Tyler Eifert 8.00 20.00
MJPATW Terrance Williams 8.00 20.00

2013 Topps Museum Collection Jumbo Relics

JUMBO RELIC/75 ODDS 1:12
*COPPER/50: .5X TO 1.2X JUMBO JSY/75
*GOLD/25: .8X TO 2X JUMBO JSY/75
MJRAD Aaron Dobson 2.00 5.00
MJRAJG A.J. Green 5.00 12.00
MJRAL Andrew Luck 6.00 15.00
MJRCB Champ Bailey 3.00 8.00
MJRCK Colin Kaepernick 8.00 20.00
MJRCN Cam Newton 5.00 12.00
MJRCP Cordarrelle Patterson 2.00 5.00
MJRDH DeAndre Hopkins 4.00 10.00
MJRDJ Dion Jordan 2.00 5.00
MJRDM Doug Martin 3.00 8.00
MJRDMU DeMarco Murray 5.00 12.00
MJRDR Denard Robinson 2.00 5.00
MJRED Eric Decker 2.50 6.00
MJREJM EJ Manuel 4.00 10.00
MJREL Eddie Lacy 2.00 5.00
MJRFG Frank Gore 3.00 8.00
MJRGB Giovani Bernard 2.00 5.00
MJRGS Geno Smith 2.00 5.00
MJRJF Johnathan Franklin 2.00 5.00
MJRJH Justin Hunter 2.00 5.00
MJRJJ Julio Jones 4.00 10.00
MJRKA Keenan Allen 5.00 12.00
MJRLB Le'Veon Bell 5.00 12.00
MJRLM Lamar Miller 2.50 6.00
MJRMB Montee Ball 2.00 5.00
MJRMBA Matt Barkley 4.00 10.00
MJRMG Mike Glennon 2.00 5.00
MJRML Marcus Lattimore 4.00 10.00
MJRMT Manti Te'o 2.50 6.00
MJRMW Markus Wheaton 2.00 5.00
MJRNF Nick Foles 3.00 8.00
MJRRC Randall Cobb 3.00 8.00
MJRRG3 Robert Griffin III 2.50 6.00
MJRRT Ryan Tannehill 3.00 8.00
MJRRW Robert Woods 3.00 8.00
MJRRWI Russell Wilson 8.00 20.00
MJRSB Sam Bradford 2.50 6.00
MJRSR Stevan Ridley 2.50 6.00
MJRST Stepfan Taylor 2.00 5.00
MJRTA Tavon Austin 2.50 6.00
MJRTE Tyler Eifert 2.00 5.00
MJRTR Trent Richardson 2.50 6.00
MJRTRO Tony Romo 3.00 8.00
MJRTS Torrey Smith 2.50 6.00
MJRTW Terrance Williams 2.00 5.00
MJRVM Von Miller 3.00 8.00

2013 Topps Museum Collection Pro Bowl Jumbo Relics

PRO BOWL/75 ODDS 1:27
*COPPER/50: .5X TO 1.2X BASIC JSY/75
*GOLD/25: 1.2X TO 3X BASIC JSY/75
MPBJRAF Arian Foster 3.00 8.00
MPBJRAJG A.J. Green 4.00 10.00
MPBJRCG Chad Greenway 5.00 12.00
MPBJRCT Charles Tillman 4.00 10.00
MPBJRDB Drew Brees 4.00 10.00
MPBJRDT Demaryius Thomas 3.00 8.00
MPBJREB Eric Berry 3.00 8.00
MPBJREM Eli Manning 3.00 8.00
MPBJRET Earl Thomas 4.00 10.00
MPBJRGA Geno Atkins 2.50 6.00
MPBJRJA Jared Allen 2.50 6.00
MPBJRJB Jairus Byrd 2.50 6.00
MPBJRJG Jermaine Gresham 3.00 8.00
MPBJRJP Julius Peppers 4.00 10.00
MPBJRJPP Jason Pierre-Paul 2.50 6.00
MPBJRJW Jason Witten 3.00 8.00
MPBJRLW Leon Washington 2.50 6.00
MPBJRML Marshawn Lynch 3.00 8.00
MPBJRRW Reggie Wayne 3.00 8.00
MPBJRTD Thomas DeCoud 2.50 6.00
MPBJRTH Tamba Hali 2.50 6.00
MPBJRVJ Vincent Jackson 2.50 6.00

2013 Topps Museum Collection Pro Bowl Quad Relics

QUAD PRO BOWL/25 ODDS 1:81
*GOLD/10: .5X TO 1.2X BASIC QUAD/25
MPBQRAF Arian Foster 8.00 20.00
MPBQRAJG A.J. Green 10.00 25.00
MPBQRCG Chad Greenway 12.00 30.00
MPBQRCT Charles Tillman 15.00 40.00
MPBQRDB Drew Brees 12.00 30.00
MPBQRDT Demaryius Thomas 8.00 20.00
MPBQREB Eric Berry 8.00 20.00
MPBQREM Eli Manning 12.00 30.00
MPBQRET Earl Thomas 12.00 30.00
MPBQRGA Geno Atkins 6.00 15.00
MPBQRJA Jared Allen 6.00 15.00
MPBQRJB Jairus Byrd 6.00 15.00
MPBQRJG Jermaine Gresham 8.00 20.00
MPBQRJP Julius Peppers 12.00 30.00
MPBQRJPP Jason Pierre-Paul 6.00 15.00
MPBQRJW Jason Witten 8.00 20.00
MPBQRML Marshawn Lynch 8.00 20.00
MPBQRRW Reggie Wayne 8.00 20.00
MPBQRTH Tamba Hali 8.00 20.00
MPBQRVJ Vincent Jackson 6.00 15.00

2013 Topps Museum Collection Pro Bowl Signature Swatches Dual Relic Autographs

DUAL RELIC AU/30-55 ODDS 1:81
*COPPER/25: .5X TO 1.2X JSY AU/30-55
*GOLD/10: .6X TO 1.5X JSY AU/30-55
PBSSAJG A.J. Green 15.00 40.00
PBSSDB Drew Brees 75.00 135.00
PBSSDT Demaryius Thomas 12.00 30.00
PBSSEM Eli Manning 40.00 80.00
PBSSJG Jermaine Gresham 8.00 20.00
PBSSJPP Jason Pierre-Paul 8.00 20.00
PBSSJW Jason Witten 25.00 50.00
PBSSML Marshawn Lynch 30.00 60.00
PBSSRW Reggie Wayne 12.00 30.00
PBSSVJ Vincent Jackson 8.00 20.00

2013 Topps Museum Collection Quad Player Relics

QUAD RELIC/75 ODDS 1:22
*COPPER/50: .5X TO 1.2X QUAD JSY/75
*GOLD/25: .8X TO 2X QUAD JSY/75
MQRAHEE Efrt/Hpkn/Ertz/Astn 6.00 15.00
MQRAHPH Hpkn/Pttr/Hntr/Astn 6.00 15.00
MQRAPJG Alln/Ptrs/Gill/Jrdn 8.00 20.00
MQRBABG Brdf/Gvns/Astn/Bly 6.00 15.00
MQRBBBL Lcy/Ball/Brn/Bell 2.50 6.00
MQRCBBD Chrls/Ball/Dkr/Bwe 5.00 12.00
MQREEEM Efrt/Escr/McD/Ertz 5.00 12.00
MQRETAB Elngt/Astn/Tylr/Bly 5.00 12.00
MQRFJME Jcksn/Fls/Mcln/Ertz 5.00 12.00
MQRGBTW Brky/Glnn/Tnn/Wlsn 8.00 20.00
MQRGJBR J-D/Rbn/Blcm/Gbt 2.50 6.00
MQRGMTM Mlr/RG3/Tnh/Mrrs 3.00 8.00
MQRGRDB Byc/Dbsn/Rdly/Grnk 4.00 10.00
MQRJGAH Grn/Astn/Jns/Hpkns 6.00 15.00
MQRJRFH Fstr/Hpkns/Rbn/J-D 6.00 15.00
MQRKDLP Kprn/Ltmre/Ptn/Dvs 3.00 8.00
MQRLGWK Kprn/Wlsn/RG3/Lck 20.00 50.00
MQRLJWH Jhns/Hntr/Wrgt/Lkr 3.00 8.00
MQRMBWE Escb/Will/Brynt/Mry 8.00 20.00
MQRMSGB Smth/Brkly/Mnl/Glnn 2.50 6.00
MQRMSLG Mnl/Smth/Lck/RG3 6.00 15.00
MQRRLMB Lcy/Ball/Rch/Mrtn 3.00 8.00
MQRSWDG Dbsn/Gill/Smth/Wds 4.00 10.00
MQRTFBB Frnkn/Bell/Ball/Tylr 6.00 15.00
MQRTHWJ Wke/Jrdn/Hrtl/Tnn 3.00 8.00

2013 Topps Museum Collection Rookie Quad Relics

QUAD RELIC/75 STATED ODDS 1:15
*COPPER/50: .5X TO 1.2X JUMBO JSY/75
*GOLD/25: .8X TO 2X JUMBO JSY/75
MRQRAD Aaron Dobson 2.50 6.00
MRQRAE Andre Ellington 2.50 6.00
MRQRCM Christine Michael 2.50 6.00
MRQRCP Cordarrelle Patterson 2.50 6.00
MRQRDH DeAndre Hopkins 5.00 12.00
MRQRDJ Dion Jordan 2.50 6.00
MRQRDR Denard Robinson 2.50 6.00
MRQREJM EJ Manuel 2.50 6.00
MRQREL Eddie Lacy 2.50 6.00
MRQRGB Giovani Bernard 2.50 6.00
MRQRGE Gavin Escobar 2.50 6.00
MRQRGS Geno Smith 2.50 6.00
MRQRJF Johnathan Franklin 2.50 6.00
MRQRJH Justin Hunter 2.50 6.00
MRQRJR Joseph Randle 2.50 6.00
MRQRJRE Jordan Reed 4.00 10.00
MRQRKA Keenan Allen 6.00 15.00
MRQRKD Knile Davis 2.50 6.00
MRQRKS Kenny Stills 2.50 6.00
MRQRLB Le'Veon Bell 5.00 12.00
MRQRLJ Landry Jones 2.50 6.00
MRQRMB Matt Barkley 2.50 6.00
MRQRMBA Montee Ball 2.50 6.00
MRQRMG Mike Glennon 2.50 6.00
MRQRMGI Mike Gillislee 2.50 6.00
MRQRMGO Marquise Goodwin 2.50 6.00
MRQRML Marcus Lattimore 2.50 6.00
MRQRMT Manti Te'o 3.00 8.00
MRQRMW Markus Wheaton 2.50 6.00
MRQRQP Quinton Patton 2.50 6.00
MRQRRN Ryan Nassib 2.50 6.00
MRQRRW Robert Woods 4.00 10.00
MRQRSB Stedman Bailey 2.50 6.00
MRQRST Stepfan Taylor 2.50 6.00
MRQRTA Tavon Austin 3.00 8.00
MRQRTE Tyler Eifert 2.50 6.00
MRQRTW Tyler Wilson 2.50 6.00
MRQRTWI Terrance Williams 2.50 6.00
MRQRVM Vance McDonald 3.00 8.00
MRQRZE Zach Ertz 5.00 12.00

2013 Topps Museum Collection Signature Series Autographs

SIG SERIES/55-130 ODDS 1:10
EXCH EXPIRATION: 1/31/2017
*COPPER VETS/50: .4X TO 1X AU/55
*COPPER ROOK/50: .5X TO 1.2X AU/130
*COPPER ROOK/50: .4X TO 1X AU/55
*GOLD VETS/25: .5X TO 1.2X AU/55
*GOLD ROOKIE/25: .8X TO 2X AU/130
*GOLD ROOKIE/25: .6X TO 1.5X AU/55
SSAAB Anquan Boldin/55 15.00 40.00
SSAAD Aaron Dobson/55 3.00 8.00
SSAAE Andre Ellington/130 6.00 15.00
SSABJ Bo Jackson/55 40.00 80.00
SSACM Christine Michael/55 3.00 8.00
SSACP Cordarrelle Patterson/55 3.00 8.00
SSADA Danny Amendola/55 8.00 20.00
SSADH DeAndre Hopkins/55 8.00 20.00
SSADJ Dion Jordan/55 3.00 8.00
SSADR Denard Robinson/130 2.50 6.00
SSAEJM EJ Manuel/55 3.00 8.00
SSAEL Eddie Lacy/55 3.00 8.00
SSAGB Giovani Bernard/55 3.00 8.00
SSAGS Geno Smith/55 3.00 8.00
SSAGT Golden Tate/55 6.00 15.00
SSAJF Johnathan Franklin/130 2.50 6.00
SSAJH Justin Hunter/55 3.00 8.00
SSAJM Joe Montana/55 75.00 150.00
SSAJN Jordy Nelson/55 10.00 25.00
SSAJPP Jason Pierre-Paul/55 6.00 15.00
SSAJR Joseph Randle/130 2.50 6.00
SSAJRE Jordan Reed/130 4.00 10.00
SSAKA Keenan Allen/130 5.00 12.00
SSAKS Kenny Stills/130 2.50 6.00
SSAKW Kurt Warner/55 30.00 60.00
SSALB Le'Veon Bell/55 30.00 60.00
SSAMA Marcus Allen/55 20.00 40.00
SSAMBA Montee Ball/130 2.50 6.00
SSAMF Matt Forte/55 10.00 25.00
SSAMG Mike Glennon/55 3.00 8.00
SSAMGO Marquise Goodwin/55 3.00 8.00
SSAML Marcus Lattimore/130 2.50 6.00
SSAMLY Marshawn Lynch/55 40.00 80.00
SSAMS Matthew Stafford 20.00 40.00
SSAMT Manti Te'o/55 4.00 10.00
SSAMW Markus Wheaton/130 2.50 6.00
SSAMWI Mike Williams/55 EXCH 8.00 20.00
SSANB NaVorro Bowman/55 EXCH 10.00 25.00
SSAPM Peyton Manning/55 150.00 250.00
SSARB Reggie Bush/55 20.00 40.00
SSARL Ronnie Lott/55 20.00 40.00
SSARN Ryan Nassib/55 6.00 15.00
SSARW Robert Woods/55 5.00 12.00
SSASB Stedman Bailey/130 2.50 6.00
SSASL Steve Largent/55 20.00 40.00
SSAST Stepfan Taylor/130 2.50 6.00
SSASV Shane Vereen/55 8.00 20.00
SSATA Tavon Austin/55 4.00 10.00
SSATAI Troy Aikman/55 40.00 80.00
SSATD Terrell Davis/55 25.00 50.00
SSATE Tyler Eifert/130 2.50 6.00
SSATW Tyler Wilson/55 3.00 8.00
SSATWI Terrance Williams/130 2.50 6.00
SSAVM Vance McDonald/130 3.00 8.00
SSAZE Zach Ertz/130 5.00 12.00

2013 Topps Museum Collection Signature Series Dual Autographs

DUAL AUTO/25 STATED ODDS 1:62
DSSAAD D.Amendola/A.Dobson 25.00 50.00
DSSAAH T.Austin/D.Hopkins 20.00 50.00
DSSADJ T.Davis/B.Jackson 60.00 120.00
DSSALB M.Ball/E.Lacy 8.00 20.00
DSSAML R.Lott/J.Montana 150.00 250.00
DSSAMT D.Thomas/P.Manning 150.00 250.00
DSSAPH J.Hunter/C.Patterson 8.00 20.00
DSSASB G.Smith/M.Barkley 8.00 20.00
DSSATA K.Allen/M.Teâ€™o 30.00 60.00
DSSAWF M.Faulk/K.Warner 90.00 150.00

2013 Topps Museum Collection Signature Swatches Dual Relic Autographs

STATED PRINT RUN 55-95 ODDS 1:18
EXCH EXPIRATION: 1/31/2017
*COPPER VET/50: .5X TO 1.2X BASIC AU/80-95
*COPPER VET/50: .4X TO 1X BASIC AU/55
*COP.ROOK/50: .5X TO 1.2X BASIC AU/80-95
*COP.ROOK/50: .4X TO 1X BASIC AU/55
*GOLD VET/25: .6X TO 1.5X BASIC AU/80-95
*GOLD VET/25: .5X TO 1.2X BASIC AU/55
*GOLD ROOK/25: .6X TO 1.5X BASIC AU/80-95
*GOLD ROOK/25: .5X TO 1.2X BASIC AU/55
SSDRAAD Aaron Dobson/80 4.00 10.00
SSDRAAL Andrew Luck/55 50.00 100.00
SSDRAAM Alfred Morris/80 5.00 12.00
SSDRABO Brian Orakpo/95 6.00 15.00
SSDRACJS C.J. Spiller/80 5.00 12.00
SSDRACP C.Patterson/80 4.00 10.00
SSDRADA DeAndre Hopkins/55 12.00 30.00
SSDRADB Dwayne Bowe
SSDRADM Doug Martin/80 10.00 25.00
SSDRAEJM EJ Manuel/55 5.00 12.00
SSDRAEL Eddie Lacy/80 4.00 10.00
SSDRAGN Giovani Bernard/80 4.00 10.00
SSDRAGS Geno Smith/55 5.00 12.00
SSDRAJH Justin Hunter/80 4.00 10.00
SSDRAKA Keenan Allen/95 10.00 25.00
SSDRALB Le'Veon Bell/80 20.00 50.00
SSDRALM LeSean McCoy EXCH 20.00 40.00
SSDRALMI Lamar Miller/80 5.00 12.00
SSDRAMB Matt Barkley/55 5.00 12.00
SSDRAMBA Montee Ball/80 4.00 10.00
SSDRAMG Mike Glennon/95 4.00 10.00
SSDRAMT Manti Te'o/80 5.00 12.00
SSDRARC Randall Cobb/80 15.00 30.00
SSDRARCU Randall Cunningham
SSDRARW Robert Woods/80 6.00 15.00
SSDRASR Sidney Rice/55 6.00 15.00
SSDRASV Shane Vereen/80 6.00 15.00
SSDRATA Tavon Austin/55 6.00 15.00
SSDRATE Tyler Eifert/80 4.00 10.00
SSDRAZE Zach Ertz/95 8.00 20.00

2013 Topps Museum Collection Signature Swatches Triple Relic Autographs

*TRIP.ROOK/69-99: .4X TO 1X DUAL/80-95
TRIPLE AU/69-99 ODDS 1:22
*COPPER/50: .5X TO 1.2X BASIC TRIP/69
*GOLD/25: .6X TO 1.5X BASIC TRIP/69
SSTRACS Cecil Shorts/69 5.00 12.00
SSTRADM Darren McFadden/69 8.00 20.00
SSTRAHN Haloti Ngata/99 5.00 12.00
SSTRAJC Jamaal Charles/69 15.00 30.00
SSTRAMV Michael Vick/69 15.00 30.00
SSTRAMW Mike Williams/69 EXCH 6.00 15.00
SSTRARC Randall Cunningham/69 12.00 30.00

2014 Topps Museum Collection

COMPLETE SET (100) 30.00 60.00
1 Steve Young .75 2.00
2 Dan Marino 1.25 3.00
3 Barry Sanders 1.00 2.50
4 Emmitt Smith 1.00 2.50
5 Deion Sanders .50 1.25
6 Bo Jackson .75 2.00
7 Terry Bradshaw .75 2.00
8 Marshall Faulk .50 1.25
9 Troy Aikman .75 2.00
10 Brett Favre 1.25 3.00
11 Victor Cruz .50 1.25
12 Joe Namath .75 2.00
13 Eric Dickerson .50 1.25
14 Lawrence Taylor .60 1.50
15 Blake Bortles RC .50 1.25
16 Marcus Allen .60 1.50
17 Eric Ebron RC .50 1.25
18 Ronnie Lott .50 1.25
19 Logan Thomas RC .40 1.00
20 Jadeveon Clowney RC .50 1.25
21 Charles Sims RC .40 1.00
22 A.J. McCarron RC .40 1.00
23 Aaron Murray RC .40 1.00
24 Cody Latimer RC .50 1.25
25 Mike Evans RC 1.00 2.50
26 Devonta Freeman RC .60 1.50
27 David Fales RC .40 1.00
28 Jerick McKinnon RC .50 1.25
29 Tom Savage RC .40 1.00
30 Johnny Manziel RC .60 1.50
31 James White RC .75 2.00
32 Zach Mettenberger RC .40 1.00
33 Jeremy Hill RC .50 1.25
34 Martavis Bryant RC .50 1.25
35 Paul Richardson RC .50 1.25
36 Donte Moncrief RC .40 1.00
37 Khalil Mack RC 1.50 4.00
38 De'Anthony Thomas RC .40 1.00
39 Bishop Sankey RC .40 1.00
40 Carlos Hyde RC .50 1.25
41 Davante Adams RC .60 1.50
42 Jordan Matthews RC .60 1.50
43 Tre Mason RC .40 1.00
44 Jimmy Garoppolo RC 3.00 8.00
45 Brandin Cooks RC .60 1.50
46 Austin Seferian-Jenkins RC .40 1.00
47 Ka'Deem Carey RC .40 1.00
48 Odell Beckham Jr. RC 1.00 2.50
49 Kelvin Benjamin RC .60 1.50
50 Teddy Bridgewater RC .60 1.50
51 Marqise Lee RC .50 1.25
52 Sammy Watkins RC .60 1.50
53 Derek Carr RC 2.50 6.00
54 Terrance West RC .40 1.00
55 Richard Sherman .60 1.50
56 Andre Williams .40 1.00
57 J.J. Watt .60 1.50
58 Clay Matthews .60 1.50
59 Patrick Willis .50 1.25
60 Aaron Rodgers 1.25 3.00
61 Andrew Luck .75 2.00
62 Cam Newton .60 1.50
63 Colin Kaepernick .50 1.25
64 Drew Brees .60 1.50
65 Peyton Manning 1.25 3.00
66 Matt Ryan .50 1.25
67 Matthew Stafford .50 1.25
68 Nick Foles .50 1.25
69 Eli Manning .50 1.25
70 Russell Wilson 1.00 2.50
71 Robert Griffin III .40 1.00
72 Philip Rivers .60 1.50
73 Tom Brady 1.50 4.00
74 Tony Romo .50 1.25
75 Gale Sayers .60 1.50
76 Arian Foster .50 1.25
77 DeMarco Murray .50 1.25
78 Eddie Lacy .40 1.00
79 Giovani Bernard .40 1.00
80 Jamaal Charles .50 1.25
81 Le'Veon Bell .50 1.25
82 LeSean McCoy .60 1.50
83 Marshawn Lynch .50 1.25
84 Matt Forte .40 1.00
85 Jimmy Graham .60 1.50
86 Troy Polamalu .60 1.50
87 Reggie Bush .40 1.00
88 Rob Gronkowski .60 1.50
89 A.J. Green .60 1.50
90 Calvin Johnson .60 1.50
91 Andre Johnson .50 1.25
92 Brandon Marshall .40 1.00
93 Alshon Jeffery .50 1.25
94 Percy Harvin .40 1.00
95 Julio Jones .60 1.50
96 Demaryius Thomas .50 1.25
97 Frank Gore .50 1.25
98 Jordy Nelson .50 1.25
99 Larry Fitzgerald .50 1.25
100 Dez Bryant .60 1.50

2014 Topps Museum Collection Copper

*VETS: .6X TO 1.5X BASIC CARDS
*ROOKIES: .6X TO 1.5X BASIC RC

2014 Topps Museum Collection Ruby

*VETS/50: 2X TO 5X BASIC CARDS
*ROOKIES/50: 1.5X TO 4X BASIC RC
48 Odell Beckham Jr. 25.00 50.00

2014 Topps Museum Collection Sapphire

*VETS/99: 1.2X TO 3X BASIC CARDS
*ROOKIES/99: 1.2X TO 3X BASIC RC

2014 Topps Museum Collection Canvas Collection

CCAL Andrew Luck 1.50 4.00
CCAR Aaron Rodgers 2.50 6.00
CCBF Brett Favre 2.50 6.00
CCBJ Bo Jackson 1.50 4.00
CCCJ Calvin Johnson 1.25 3.00
CCCK Colin Kaepernick 1.00 2.50
CCCN Cam Newton 1.25 3.00
CCDB Drew Brees 1.25 3.00
CCDM Dan Marino 2.50 6.00
CCES Emmitt Smith 2.00 5.00
CCJE John Elway 2.00 5.00
CCJN Joe Namath 1.50 4.00
CCML Marshawn Lynch 1.00 2.50
CCPM Peyton Manning 2.50 6.00
CCRW Russell Wilson 2.00 5.00
CCSY Steve Young 1.50 4.00
CCTA Troy Aikman 1.50 4.00
CCTB Tom Brady 3.00 8.00
CCBSA Barry Sanders 2.00 5.00
CCTBRA Terry Bradshaw 1.50 4.00

2014 Topps Museum Collection Framed Museum Collection Autographs Silver

FAAL Andrew Luck 300.00 500.00
FAAR Aaron Rodgers 300.00 500.00
FABB Blake Bortles 15.00 40.00
FABC Brandin Cooks 20.00 50.00
FABF Brett Favre 150.00 300.00
FABJ Bo Jackson 150.00 250.00
FABM Brandon Marshall 12.00 30.00
FABS Bishop Sankey 12.00 30.00
FABSA Barry Sanders 200.00 300.00
FACH Carlos Hyde 15.00 40.00
FADB Drew Brees
FADM Dan Marino 100.00 200.00
FADS Deion Sanders 75.00 150.00
FAEL Eddie Lacy 12.00 30.00
FAES Emmitt Smith
FAJB Jerome Bettis 40.00 80.00
FAJC Jadeveon Clowney 15.00 40.00
FAJE John Elway 100.00 200.00
FAJH Jeremy Hill 15.00 40.00
FAJM Johnny Manziel EXCH 20.00 50.00
FAJMA Jordan Matthews 20.00 50.00
FAJN Joe Namath 75.00 150.00
FAKB Kelvin Benjamin 60.00 120.00
FALT Lawrence Taylor
FAME Mike Evans 30.00 80.00
FAML Marshawn Lynch EXCH 30.00 60.00
FAMS Matthew Stafford EXCH 30.00 60.00
FAMSI Mike Singletary 20.00 50.00
FAOB Odell Beckham Jr. 150.00 250.00
FAPM Peyton Manning 150.00 300.00
FASW Sammy Watkins 20.00 50.00
FASY Steve Young 60.00 120.00
FATB Teddy Bridgewater 50.00 100.00
FATBR Tom Brady 400.00 600.00
FATP Troy Polamalu 100.00 200.00

2014 Topps Museum Collection Jumbo Patch Autographs

JPAAM A.J. McCarron 5.00 12.00
JPABB Blake Bortles 6.00 15.00
JPABC Brandin Cooks 8.00 20.00
JPABS Bishop Sankey 5.00 12.00
JPACH Carlos Hyde 6.00 15.00
JPACL Cody Latimer 6.00 15.00
JPADC Derek Carr
JPAJC Jadeveon Clowney 6.00 15.00
JPAJG Jimmy Garoppolo 100.00 200.00
JPAJH Jeremy Hill 6.00 15.00
JPAJM Jordan Matthews 8.00 20.00
JPAKB Kelvin Benjamin 8.00 20.00
JPAME Mike Evans 12.00 30.00
JPAOB Odell Beckham Jr. 125.00 200.00
JPASW Sammy Watkins 0.00 20.00
JPATB Teddy Bridgewater 10.00 25.00
JPATM Tre Mason 5.00 12.00
JPATW Terrance West 5.00 12.00
JPAJMA Johnny Manziel 8.00 20.00
JPAJMC Jerick McKinnon 6.00 15.00

2014 Topps Museum Collection Jumbo Relics

*COPPER/50: .6X TO 1.5X JUMBO JSY/115
*GOLD/25: 1X TO 2.5X JUMBO JSY/115
MJRAL Andrew Luck 4.00 10.00
MJRAM A.J. McCarron 1.50 4.00
MJRAR Allen Robinson 2.50 6.00
MJRAS Austin Seferian-Jenkins 1.50 4.00
MJRAW Andre Williams 1.50 4.00
MJRBB Blake Bortles 2.00 5.00
MJRBC Brandin Cooks 2.50 6.00
MJRBS Bishop Sankey 1.50 4.00
MJRCH Carlos Hyde 2.00 5.00
MJRCL Cody Latimer 2.00 5.00
MJRCS Charles Sims 1.50 4.00
MJRDA Davante Adams 2.50 6.00
MJRDC Derek Carr 10.00 25.00
MJRDF Devonta Freeman 2.50 6.00
MJRDM Donte Moncrief 1.50 4.00
MJRDT De'Anthony Thomas 1.50 4.00
MJREE Eric Ebron 2.00 5.00
MJRJA Jace Amaro 1.50 4.00
MJRJC Jadeveon Clowney 2.00 5.00
MJRJG Jimmy Garoppolo 12.00 30.00
MJRJH Jeremy Hill 2.00 5.00
MJRJL Jarvis Landry 3.00 8.00
MJRJM Jordan Matthews 2.50 6.00
MJRKB Kelvin Benjamin 2.50 6.00
MJRKC Ka'Deem Carey 1.50 4.00
MJRKM Khalil Mack 6.00 15.00
MJRLB Le'Veon Bell 2.00 5.00
MJRLT Logan Thomas 1.50 4.00
MJRMB Montee Ball 2.00 5.00
MJRME Mike Evans 4.00 10.00
MJRML Marqise Lee 2.00 5.00
MJRNF Nick Foles 2.50 6.00
MJROB Odell Beckham Jr. 4.00 10.00
MJRPR Paul Richardson 2.00 5.00
MJRRG Robert Griffin III 2.00 5.00
MJRRT Ryan Tannehill 2.50 6.00
MJRRW Russell Wilson 5.00 12.00
MJRSW Sammy Watkins 2.50 6.00
MJRTR Teddy Bridgewater 2.50 6.00
MJRTM Tre Mason 1.50 4.00
MJRTS Tom Savage 1.50 4.00
MJRTW Terrance West 1.50 4.00
MJRAMU Aaron Murray 1.50 4.00
MJRDAR Dri Archer 1.50 4.00
MJRJMA Johnny Manziel 2.50 6.00

2014 Topps Museum Collection Pro Bowl Jumbo Relics

*COPPER/50: .5X TO 1.2X BASIC JSY/90-150
*COPPER/50: .4X TO 1X BASIC JSY/50-75
*GOLD/25: 1.2X TO 3X BASIC JSY/90-150
*GOLD/25: 1X TO 2.5X BASIC JSY/50-75
PBJRAC Antonio Cromartie/150 2.50 6.00
PBJRAJ Alshon Jeffery/75 4.00 10.00
PBJRAM Alfred Morris/100 5.00 12.00
PBJRAR Antrel Rolle/110 2.50 6.00
PBJRBA Branden Albert/150 2.50 6.00
PBJRBG Ben Grubbs/150 8.00 20.00
PBJRBM Brandon Marshall/50 3.00 8.00
PBJRCJ Cameron Jordan/125 2.50 6.00
PBJRDJ DeSean Jackson/100 3.00 8.00
PBJRDM DeMarco Murray/140 3.00 8.00
PBJREB Eric Berry/50 4.00 10.00
PBJRJC Jordan Cameron/50 3.00 8.00
PBJRJCH Jamaal Charles/50 5.00 12.00
PBJRJG Josh Gordon/50 3.00 8.00
PBJRJH Joe Haden/100 2.50 6.00
PBJRJHO Justin Houston/150 2.50 6.00
PBJRJW Jason Witten/50 4.00 10.00
PBJRKL Kyle Long
PBJRLK Luke Kuechly/150 10.00 25.00
PBJRMP Mike Pouncey/150 5.00 12.00
PBJRMW Mario Williams/50 3.00 8.00
PBJRMY Marshal Yanda/150 2.50 6.00
PBJRRM Robert Mathis/50 3.00 8.00
PBJRRQ Robert Quinn/90 3.00 8.00
PBJRTG Tony Gonzalez/150 2.50 6.00
PBJRTH Tamba Hali/150 2.50 6.00
PBJRTW Trent Williams/150 2.50 6.00

2014 Topps Museum Collection Pro Bowl Quad Relics

PRQRAJ Alshon Jeffery 8.00 20.00
PRQRAM Alfred Morris 6.00 15.00
PRQRAR Antrel Rolle 6.00 15.00
PRQRBF Brandon Flowers 6.00 15.00
PRQRBM Brandon Marshall 6.00 15.00
PRQRCJ Cameron Jordan 6.00 15.00
PRQRDJ DeSean Jackson 8.00 20.00
PRQRDM DeMarco Murray 8.00 20.00
PRQREB Eric Berry 8.00 20.00
PRQRJC Jordan Cameron 6.00 15.00
PRQRJCH Jamaal Charles 8.00 20.00
PRQRJG Josh Gordon 6.00 15.00
PRQRJH Joe Haden 6.00 15.00
PRQRJW Jason Witten 8.00 20.00
PRQRKL Kyle Long 6.00 15.00
PRQRLK Luke Kuechly 8.00 20.00
PRQRRM Robert Mathis 6.00 15.00
PRQRRQ Robert Quinn 8.00 20.00
PRQRTG Tony Gonzalez 6.00 15.00
PRQRTH Tamba Hali 6.00 15.00

2014 Topps Museum Collection Pro Bowl Signatures Swatches Dual Relic Autographs

PBDRAAJ Alshon Jeffery/120 12.00 30.00
PBDRAAM Alfred Morris/120 12.00 30.00
PBDRABM Brandon Marshall EXCH 25.00 50.00
PBDRAEB Eric Berry/120 12.00 30.00
PBDRAJC Jordan Cameron/120 6.00 15.00
PBDRAJCH Jamaal Charles/75 12.00 30.00
PBDRAJG Josh Gordon/100 6.00 15.00
PBDRAJW Jason Witten/80 25.00 50.00
PBDRAMR Marcel Reece/120 8.00 20.00
PBDRARM Robert Mathis/120 6.00 15.00

2014 Topps Museum Collection Quad Player Relics

*COPPER/50: .5X TO 1.2X QUAD JSY/99
FPQRBCGC Brs/Cks/Grhm/Clstn 4.00 10.00
FPQRBRMB Brdy/Mng/Brs/Rdgrs 20.00 50.00
FPQRBWBM Whtn/Brwn/Bll/Mllr 10.00 25.00
FPQRCFSH Fstr/Hkns/Svge/Clny 3.00 8.00
FPQRCJMF Mrshll/Ctlr/Jffry/Frte 3.00 8.00
FPQREWBM Mtws/Bhm/Evns/Wtns 6.00 15.00
FPQRFMMM Fles/Mcln/McCy/Mtws 4.00 10.00
FPQRGWKD Gre/Kprnck/Wlls/Dvs 8.00 20.00
FPQRLBGM Mnzl/Brtls/Griffin/Lck 10.00 25.00
FPQRLGBB Brgwtr/Brtls/Grffn/Lck 10.00 25.00
FPQRMBBC Crr/Brdgwtr/Mnzl/Brtls 10.00 25.00
FPQRMBGT Tnhll/Mnzl/Brgwtr/Grfn 10.00 25.00
FPQRMBTL Thms/Ltmr/Bll/Mnng 15.00 40.00
FPQRMBWT Mnzl/Tnnhll/Wlsn/Brtls 10.00 25.00
FPQRMHGB McCrrn/Brnrd/Grn/Hll 4.00 10.00
FPQRMHSF Hyde/Msn/Snky/Frmn 4.00 10.00
FPQRMRBW Bhm/Rdle/Wlms/Mng 6.00 15.00
FPQRNKWG Grfn/Wlsn/Nwtn/Kpck 10.00 25.00
FPQRRBMW Brnt/Mry/Rmo/Wtn 8.00 20.00
FPQRRLCM Lcy/Cbb/Mtws/Rgrs 30.00 60.00
FPQRRWJF Frmn/Whte/Ryn/Jnes 8.00 20.00
FPQRSHMH Hll/Msn/Snky/Hyde 3.00 8.00
FPQRWEBC Cks/Evns/Wkns/Bmn 10.00 25.00
FPQRWLMR Mchl/Lnch/Wlsn/Rdsn 15.00 30.00
FPQRWMCM Clwny/Mllr/Wlls/Mtthws

2014 Topps Museum Collection Quad Player Relics Gold

*GOLD/25: .8X TO 2X QUAD JSY/25
FPQRLBGM Mnzl/Brtls/Griffin/Lck 40.00 80.00

2014 Topps Museum Collection Rookie Quad Relios

*COPPER/50: .6X TO 1.5X JUMBO JSY/150
*GOLD/25: 1X TO 2.5X JUMBO JSY/150
RQRAM A.J. McCarron 2.00 5.00
RQRAMU Aaron Murray 2.00 5.00
RQRAR Allen Robinson 3.00 8.00
RQRAS Austin Seferian-Jenkins 2.00 5.00
RQRAW Andre Williams 2.00 5.00
RQRBB Blake Bortles 2.50 6.00
RQRBC Brandin Cooks 3.00 8.00
RQRBS Bishop Sankey 2.00 5.00
RQRCH Carlos Hyde 2.50 6.00
RQRCL Cody Latimer 2.50 6.00
RQRCS Charles Sims 2.00 5.00
RQRDA Davante Adams 3.00 8.00
RQRDC Derek Carr 8.00 20.00
RQRDF Devonta Freeman 3.00 8.00
RQRDM Donte Moncrief 2.00 5.00
RQRDT De'Anthony Thomas 2.00 5.00
RQREE Eric Ebron 2.50 6.00
RQRJC Jadeveon Clowney 2.50 6.00
RQRJG Jimmy Garoppolo 15.00 40.00
RQRJH Jeremy Hill 2.50 6.00
RQRJL Jarvis Landry 4.00 10.00
RQRJM Jordan Matthews 3.00 8.00
RQRJMA Johnny Manziel 3.00 8.00
RQRKB Kelvin Benjamin 3.00 8.00
RQRKC Ka'Deem Carey 2.00 5.00
RQRLT Logan Thomas 2.00 5.00
RQRME Mike Evans 5.00 12.00
RQRML Marqise Lee 2.50 6.00
RQROB Odell Beckham Jr. 5.00 12.00
RQRPR Paul Richardson 2.50 6.00
RQRSW Sammy Watkins 6.00 15.00
RQRTB Teddy Bridgewater 3.00 8.00
RQRTM Tre Mason 2.00 5.00
RQRTS Tom Savage 2.00 5.00
RQRTW Terrance West 2.00 5.00

2014 Topps Museum Collection Signature Series Autographs

SSAAE Andre Ellington/300 3.00 8.00
SSAAM Aaron Murray/350 3.00 8.00
SSAAMC A.J. McCarron/75 5.00 12.00
SSAAMO Alfred Morris/150 8.00 20.00
SSAAS Austin Seferian-Jenkins/150 4.00 10.00
SSAAW Andre Williams/350 3.00 8.00
SSABB Blake Bortles
SSABC Brandin Cooks/150 6.00 15.00
SSABJ Bo Jackson
SSABS Bishop Sankey/350 3.00 8.00
SSACL Cody Latimer EXCH
SSACM Clay Matthews
SSACP Cordarrelle Patterson/150 4.00 10.00
SSACS Charles Sims/150 4.00 10.00
SSADA Davante Adams/350 10.00 25.00
SSADC Derek Carr
SSADMA Doug Martin/75 6.00 15.00
SSAEE Eric Ebron/90 8.00 20.00
SSAEL Eddie Lacy/150 4.00 10.00
SSAFG Frank Gore
SSAGB Giovani Bernard/300 3.00 8.00
SSAJB Jerome Bettis
SSAJBR John Brown/350 5.00 12.00
SSAJC Jadeveon Clowney
SSAJCH Jamaal Charles/150
SSAJG Jimmy Garoppolo/75 75.00 150.00
SSAJGO Josh Gordon/75 5.00 12.00
SSAJH Jeremy Hill/150 5.00 12.00
SSAJM Johnny Manziel
SSAJMA Jordan Matthews/150 6.00 15.00
SSAJMK Jerick McKinnon/350 5.00 12.00
SSAJN Jordy Nelson
SSAJR John Riggins
SSAJT Julius Thomas/350 3.00 8.00
SSAJW James White/350 0.00 15.00
SSAKB Kelvin Benjamin/150 6.00 15.00
SSAKC Ka'Deem Carey/350 3.00 8.00
SSALM LeSean McCoy EXCH
SSAMA Marcus Allen/55
SSAMB Montee Ball/350 3.00 8.00
SSAMBR Martavis Bryant/350 4.00 10.00
SSAME Mike Evans
SSAMF Michael Floyd/75 5.00 12.00
SSAMFO Matt Forte/300 6.00 15.00
SSAMSI Mike Singletary/75 12.00 30.00
SSAPG Pierre Garcon/150 6.00 15.00
SSARC Roger Craig
SSARG Rob Gronkowski EXCH
SSARL Ronnie Lott/55
SSASW Sammy Watkins
SSATB Teddy Bridgewater
SSATS Tom Savage/75 6.00 15.00
SSATW Terrance West/350 3.00 8.00
SSAZS Zac Stacy/300 3.00 8.00

2014 Topps Museum Collection Signature Series Autographs Copper

*COPPER ROOK/50: .6X TO 1.5X BASIC AU/300-350
*COPPER ROOK/50: .5X TO 1.2X BASIC AU/150
*COPPER ROOK/50: .4X TO 1X BASIC AU/55-95
*COPPER VET/50: .75X TO 2X BASIC AU/300-350
*COPPER VET/50: .6X TO 1.5X BASIC AU/150
*COPPER VET/50: .5X TO 1.2X BASIC AU/55-95
SSAJM Johnny Manziel 8.00 20.00
SSAJN Jordy Nelson 25.00 50.00
SSASW Sammy Watkins 8.00 20.00

2014 Topps Museum Collection Signature Series Autographs Gold

*GOLD ROOK/25: .75X TO 8X BASIC AU/300-350
*GOLD ROOK/25: .6X TO 1.5X BASIC AU/150
*GOLD ROOK/25: .5X TO 1.2X BASIC AU/55-95
*GOLD VET/25: 1X TO 2.5X BASIC AU/300-350
*GOLD VET/25: .75X TO 2X BASIC AU/150
*GOLD VET/25: .6X TO 1.5X BASIC AU/55-95
SSAFG Frank Gore 25.00 50.00
SSAJB Jerome Bettis 60.00 120.00
SSAJC Jadeveon Clowney 8.00 20.00
SSAJN Jordy Nelson 30.00 60.00
SSAJR John Riggins 30.00 60.00
SSARC Roger Craig 12.00 30.00
SSARG Rob Gronkowski EXCH 40.00 80.00
SSASW Sammy Watkins 10.00 25.00

2014 Topps Museum Collection Signatures Swatches Dual Relic Autographs

SSDRAAE Andre Ellington/200 3.00 8.00
SSDRAAJ Alshon Jeffery/75 5.00 12.00
SSDRAAM A.J. McCarron EXCH 10.00 25.00
SSDRAAMU Aaron Murray/200 3.00 8.00
SSDRAAS Austin Seferian-Jenkins/75 4.00 10.00
SSDRAAW Andre Williams/200 3.00 8.00
SSDRABC Brandin Cooks/100 6.00 15.00
SSDRABS Bishop Sankey/200 3.00 8.00
SSDRACL Cody Latimer/200 4.00 10.00
SSDRACM Clay Matthews/75 30.00 60.00
SSDRACP Cordarrelle Patterson/75 4.00 10.00
SSDRACS Charles Sims/200 3.00 8.00
SSDRADA Davante Adams/200 5.00 12.00
SSDRADF Devonta Freeman/200 5.00 12.00
SSDRADM Doug Martin/75 5.00 12.00
SSDRAEL Eddie Lacy/75 15.00 30.00
SSDRAFG Frank Gore/75 12.00 30.00
SSDRAJC Jamaal Charles/75 10.00 25.00
SSDRAJG Jimmy Garoppolo/100 60.00 100.00
SSDRAJH Jeremy Hill EXCH 5.00 12.00
SSDRAJMC Jerick McKinnon/200 4.00 10.00
SSDRAKC Ka'Deem Carey/200 3.00 8.00
SSDRALT Logan Thomas/200 3.00 8.00
SSDRAMB Montee Ball/75 4.00 10.00
SSDRAMBR Martavis Bryant/200 4.00 10.00
SSDRAMF Matt Forte/75 8.00 20.00
SSDRANF Nick Foles/75 8.00 20.00
SSDRARG Rob Gronkowski 30.00 60.00
SSDRATW Terrance West/200 3.00 8.00
SSDRAZM Zach Mettenberger/200 3.00 8.00

2014 Topps Museum Collection Signatures Swatches Dual Relic Autographs Copper

*COPPER/50: .8X TO 2X DUAL JSY AU/200
*COPPER/50: .6X TO 1.5X DUAL JSY AU/75-100
SSDRAJG Jimmy Garoppolo 75.00 150.00
SSDRAMBR Martavis Bryant 8.00 20.00

2014 Topps Museum Collection Signatures Swatches Dual Relic Autographs Gold

*GOLD/25: 1X TO 2.5X DUAL JSY AU/200
*GOLD/25: .8X TO 2X DUAL JSY AU/75-100
SSDRAJG Jimmy Garoppolo 75.00 150.00
SSDRAMBR Martavis Bryant 10.00 25.00
SSDRARG Rob Gronkowski 40.00 80.00

2014 Topps Museum Collection Signatures Swatches Triple Relic Autographs

SSTRAAMU Aaron Murray/200 3.00 8.00
SSTRAAW Andre Williams/200 3.00 8.00
SSTRABB Blake Bortles
SSTRABC Brandin Cooks/100 6.00 15.00
SSTRABS Bishop Sankey/200 3.00 8.00
SSTRACL Cody Latimer/200 4.00 10.00
SSTRACSI Charles Sims/200 3.00 8.00
SSTRADC Derek Carr
SSTRADF Devonta Freeman/200 12.00 30.00
SSTRAEE Eric Ebron
SSTRAGB Giovani Bernard/200 5.00 12.00
SSTRAJC Jadeveon Clowney
SSTRAJG Jimmy Garoppolo/100 75.00 125.00
SSTRAJH Jeremy Hill EXCH 5.00 12.00
SSTRAJM Jordan Matthews/100 6.00 15.00
SSTRAJMA Johnny Manziel
SSTRAKB Kelvin Benjamin/200 5.00 12.00
SSTRALB Le'Veon Bell EXCH 12.00 30.00
SSTRALM LeSean McCoy EXCH
SSTRAME Mike Evans
SSTRAML Marqise Lee/100 5.00 12.00
SSTRAOB Odell Beckham Jr./100 40.00 80.00
SSTRASW Sammy Watkins
SSTRATB Teddy Bridgewater
SSTRATW Terrance West/200 3.00 8.00

2014 Topps Museum Collection Signatures Swatches Triple Relic Autographs Copper

*COPPER/50: .6X TO 1.5X TRIPLE JSY AU/200
*COPPER/50: .5X TO 1.2X TRIPLE JSY AU/100
SSTRAJG Jimmy Garoppolo 75.00 150.00

2014 Topps Museum Collection Signatures Swatches Triple Relic Autographs Gold

*GOLD/25: .8X TO 2X TRIPLE JSY AU/200
*GOLD/25: .6X TO 1.5X TRIPLE JSY AU/100
SSTRADC Derek Carr 40.00 80.00
SSTRAJG Jimmy Garoppolo 100.00 200.00

2015 Topps Museum Collection

1 Tom Brady 1.50 4.00
2 Bo Jackson .75 2.00
3 Adrian Peterson .60 1.50
4 Jamaal Charles .50 1.25
5 Marshawn Lynch .50 1.25
6 Eddie Lacy .40 1.00
7 Le'Veon Bell .50 1.25
8 Arian Foster .50 1.25
9 Antonio Brown .60 1.50
10 Rob Gronkowski .60 1.50
11 Jeremy Hill .40 1.00
12 DeMarco Murray .50 1.25

13 C.J. Anderson .50 1.25
14 Matt Forte .40 1.00
15 Demaryius Thomas .50 1.25
16 Ben Roethlisberger .60 1.50
17 Julio Jones .60 1.50
18 Russell Wilson .75 2.00
19 Aaron Rodgers 1.25 3.00
20 Peyton Manning 1.25 3.00
21 Jordy Nelson .50 1.25
22 Randall Cobb .50 1.25
23 Matthew Stafford .50 1.25
24 Eli Manning .50 1.25
25 Andrew Luck .75 2.00
26 LeSean McCoy .60 1.50
27 Sammy Watkins .50 1.25
28 Cam Newton .60 1.50
29 Calvin Johnson .60 1.50
30 Odell Beckham Jr. .60 1.50
31 Matt Ryan .50 1.25
32 Alshon Jeffery .50 1.25
33 Mike Evans .50 1.25
34 Kelvin Benjamin .50 1.25
35 Drew Brees .60 1.50
36 Ryan Tannehill .50 1.25
37 Philip Rivers .60 1.50
38 Tony Romo .50 1.25
39 Joe Flacco .50 1.25
40 Dez Bryant .60 1.50
41 Amari Cooper RC 1.00 2.50
42 Ameer Abdullah RC .50 1.25
43 Breshad Perriman RC .30 .75
44 Devin Funchess RC .50 1.25
45 Jameis Winston RC .75 2.00
46 Kevin White RC .40 1.00
47 Leonard Williams RC .30 .75
48 Nelson Agholor RC .40 1.00
49 Melvin Gordon RC .75 2.00
50 Marcus Mariota RC 1.25 3.00
51 Phillip Dorsett RC .30 .75
52 Tevin Coleman RC .40 1.00
53 Dorial Green-Beckham RC .30 .75
54 Todd Gurley RC 1.25 3.00
55 David Johnson RC .75 2.00
56 Duke Johnson RC .50 1.25
57 Matt Jones RC .30 .75
58 Tyler Lockett RC .50 1.25
59 DeVante Parker RC .50 1.25
60 Devin Smith RC .30 .75
61 Jaelen Strong RC .40 1.00
62 Maxx Williams RC .30 .75
63 T.J. Yeldon RC .30 .75
64 Deion Sanders .50 1.25
65 Emmitt Smith 1.00 2.50
66 Emmanuel Sanders .50 1.25
67 Golden Tate .40 1.00
68 Jerome Bettis .60 1.50
69 Jerry Rice 1.00 2.50
70 John Elway 1.00 2.50
71 Jordan Matthews .50 1.25
72 Lawrence Taylor .60 1.50
73 Marshall Faulk .50 1.25
74 Kurt Warner .50 1.25
75 LaDainian Tomlinson .50 1.25
76 Steve Young .75 2.00
77 Terrell Davis .50 1.25
78 Tim Brown .60 1.50
79 Terry Bradshaw .75 2.00
80 Brett Favre 1.25 3.00
81 Victor Cruz .50 1.25
82 Teddy Bridgewater .50 1.25
83 Barry Sanders 1.00 2.50
84 Eddie George .50 1.25
85 Dan Marino 1.25 3.00
86 A.J. Green .60 1.50
87 Justin Forsett .50 1.25
88 Jimmy Graham .60 1.50
89 DeAndre Hopkins .50 1.25
90 Blake Bortles .40 1.00
91 Ty Montgomery .40 1.00
92 Brandon Marshall .40 1.00
93 Greg Olsen .50 1.25
94 Luke Kuechly .50 1.25
95 J.J. Watt .60 1.50
96 Justin Houston .40 1.00
97 Darrelle Revis .40 1.00
98 Richard Sherman .60 1.50
99 Joe Haden .40 1.00
100 Patrick Peterson .40 1.00

2015 Topps Museum Collection 60th Anniversary Amethyst

*VETS/60: 2X TO 5X BASIC CARDS
*ROOKIES/60: 1.5X TO 4X BASIC RC

2015 Topps Museum Collection Copper

*VETS: .6X TO 1.5X BASIC CARDS
*ROOKIES: .6X TO 1.5X BASIC RC

2015 Topps Museum Collection Sapphire

*VETS/99: 1.2X TO 3X BASIC CARDS
*ROOKIES/99: 1.2X TO 3X BASIC RC
STATED ODDS 1:5 HOBBY

2015 Topps Museum Collection Canvas Collection

STATED ODDS 1:4 HOBBY
CCAA Ameer Abdullah .75 2.00
CCAC Amari Cooper 1.50 4.00
CCBR Ben Roethlisberger 1.25 3.00
CCDB Dez Bryant 1.25 3.00
CCDJ Duke Johnson 1.25 3.00
CCDP DeVante Parker 1.25 3.00
CCDT Demaryius Thomas 1.00 2.50
CCEG Eddie George 1.00 2.50
CCEL Eddie Lacy .75 2.00
CCEM Eli Manning 1.00 2.50
CCGS Gale Sayers 1.25 3.00
CCJB Jerome Bettis 1.25 3.00
CCJG Jimmy Graham 1.25 3.00
CCJJ Julio Jones 1.25 3.00
CCJR Jerry Rice 2.00 5.00
CCJW Jameis Winston 1.25 3.00
CCKW Kevin White .60 1.50
CCLB Le'Veon Bell 1.00 2.50
CCLT LaDainian Tomlinson 1.00 2.50
CCLT Lawrence Taylor 1.25 3.00
CCME Mike Evans 1.00 2.50
CCMG Melvin Gordon 1.25 3.00
CCMM Marcus Mariota 2.00 5.00
CCMR Matt Ryan 1.00 2.50
CCMS Mike Singletary 1.25 3.00
CCOB Odell Beckham Jr. 1.25 3.00
CCPR Philip Rivers 1.25 3.00
CCRG Rob Gronkowski 1.25 3.00
CCSW Sammy Watkins 1.00 2.50
CCTB Tim Brown 1.25 3.00
CCTBR Teddy Bridgewater 1.00 2.50
CCTG Todd Gurley 2.00 5.00
CCTL Tyler Lockett .75 2.00
CCTR Tony Romo 1.00 2.50
CCTY T.J. Yeldon .50 1.25

2015 Topps Museum Collection Jumbo Relics

*COPPER VET/50: .6X TO 1.5X BASIC JSY/99-135
*COPPER VET/50: .5X TO 1.2X BASIC JSY/175-249
*COPPER ROOK/50: .8X TO 2X BASIC JSY/175-249
*COPPER ROOK/50: 1X TO 2.5X BASIC JSY/99-135
*GOLD VET/25: .8X TO 2X BASIC JSY/175-249
*GOLD VET/25: .6X TO 1.5X BASIC JSY/99-135
*GOLD ROOK/25: 1X TO 2.5X BASIC JSY/175-249
*GOLD ROOK/25: .8X TO 2X BASIC JSY/99-135
MJRAA Ameer Abdullah/199 2.00 5.00
MJRAC Amari Cooper/249 4.00 10.00
MJRAJ Alshon Jeffery/99 2.50 6.00
MJRAL Andrew Luck/249 3.00 8.00
MJRBJ Bo Jackson/199 3.00 8.00
MJRBS Barry Sanders/199 4.00 10.00
MJRCN Cam Newton/249 2.50 6.00
MJRDG Dorial Green-Beckham/99 1.50 4.00
MJRDP DeVante Parker/99 2.50 6.00
MJRDT Demaryius Thomas/199 2.00 5.00
MJREL Eddie Lacy/199 1.50 4.00
MJRET Earl Thomas/175 2.00 5.00
MJRGG Garrett Grayson/99 1.50 4.00
MJRHW Hines Ward/99 2.50 6.00
MJRJC Jadeveon Clowney/99 2.00 5.00
MJRJE John Elway/199 4.00 10.00
MJRJH Jeremy Hill/125 2.00 5.00
MJRJJ Julio Jones/99 3.00 8.00
MJRJM Johnny Manziel/99 2.50 6.00
MJRJN Jordy Nelson/99 2.50 6.00
MJRJW Jameis Winston/249 5.00 12.00
MJRKB Kelvin Benjamin/99 2.50 6.00
MJRKW Kevin White/99 2.00 5.00
MJRLB Le'Veon Bell/249 2.00 5.00
MJRME Mike Evans/99 2.50 6.00
MJRMG Melvin Gordon/249 3.00 8.00
MJRMM Marcus Mariota/249 5.00 12.00
MJRMS Matthew Stafford/199 2.00 5.00
MJROB Odell Beckham Jr./249 2.50 6.00
MJRPD Phillip Dorsett/99 1.50 4.00
MJRRG Robert Griffin III/99 2.00 5.00
MJRRGR Rob Gronkowski/249 2.50 6.00
MJRRS Richard Sherman/199 2.50 6.00
MJRRW Russell Wilson/249 3.00 8.00
MJRSD Stefon Diggs/199 3.00 8.00
MJRSW Sammy Watkins/99 2.50 6.00
MJRTB Teddy Bridgewater/99 2.50 6.00
MJRTBR Tim Brown/99 3.00 8.00
MJRTBRA Tom Brady/125 8.00 20.00
MJRTC Tevin Coleman/99 2.00 5.00
MJRTG Todd Gurley/249 5.00 12.00
MJRTH T.Y. Hilton/99 2.50 6.00
MJRTY T.J. Yeldon/199 1.50 4.00
MJRVM Von Miller/135 2.50 6.00

2015 Topps Museum Collection Quad Player Relics

*COPPER/50: .5X TO 1.2X BASIC JSY/99
*GOLD/25: .6X TO 1.5X BASIC JSY/99
QRADST Andrsn/Sndrs/Dvs/Thms 3.00 8.00
QRBBBW Bll/Brwn/Btts/Wrd 20.00 40.00
QRBICC Brs/Cks/Ingrm/Clstn 4.00 10.00
QRCFJW Whte/Frte/Jffry/Ctlr 6.00 15.00
QRCJJJ Jhnsn/Clmn/Jhnsn/Jns 6.00 15.00
QRCWPA Cpr/Whte/Prkr/Aghlr 8.00 20.00
QRDHBG Hll/Grn/Brnrd/Dltn 4.00 10.00
QRFAPW Alln/Prrmn/Wllms/Flcco 3.00 8.00
QRFLSC Cnly/Lcktt/Fnchss/Strng 4.00 10.00
QRGGCW Cpr/Grdn/Whte/Grly 10.00 25.00
QRGGYA Grdn/Abdllh/Yldn/Grly 10.00 25.00
QRGPMH Mnn/Ptty/Hndly/Grysn 2.50 6.00
QRLHHD Hltn/Drstt/Lck/Hrrsn 5.00 12.00
QRMSCG GrnBckhm/Cbb/Snky/Mrta 8.00 20.00
QRNOFB Nwtn/Olsn/Bnjmn/Fnchss 6.00 15.00
QRPDSG GrnBckhm/Prrmn/Smth/Drstt 2.50 6.00
QRRCWJ Whte/Ryn/Clmn/Jns 4.00 10.00
QRRNCA Adms/Cbb/Nlsn/Rdgrs 15.00 30.00
QRRTGG Gts/Grdn/Rvrs/Tmlnsn 8.00 20.00
QRTMPL Tnnhll/Mllr/Lndry/Prkr 4.00 10.00
QRWLST Lnch/Thms/Shrmn/Wlsn 20.00 40.00
QRWMBB Wnstn/Mrta/Brdgwtr/Brtls 8.00 20.00
QRWMCW Cpr/Whte/Wnstn/Mrta 8.00 20.00
QRWMEJ Mrtn/Evns/Wnstn/Jcksn 8.00 20.00
QRWMGG Wnstn/Grly/Mrta/Grdn 8.00 20.00

2015 Topps Museum Collection Rookie Quad Relics

*COPPER/50: .5X TO 1.2X BASIC JSY/99
*GOLD/25: .6X TO 1.5X BASIC JSY
RQRAA Ameer Abdullah 3.00 8.00
RQRAC Amari Cooper 8.00 20.00
RQRBH Brett Hundley 2.00 5.00
RQRBP Breshad Perriman 2.00 5.00
RQRBPE Bryce Petty 2.00 5.00
RQRCC Chris Conley 2.00 5.00
RQRDG Dorial Green-Beckham 2.00 5.00
RQRDJ Duke Johnson 3.00 8.00
RQRDJO David Johnson 5.00 12.00
RQRDP DeVante Parker 3.00 8.00
RQRDS Devin Smith 2.00 5.00
RQRGG Garrett Grayson 2.00 5.00
RQRJA Jay Ajayi 3.00 8.00
RQRJAL Javorius Allen 2.50 6.00
RQRJC Jamison Crowder 2.50 6.00
RQRJL Jeremy Langford 2.00 5.00
RQRJS Jaelen Strong 2.50 6.00
RQRJW Jameis Winston 8.00 20.00
RQRKW Kevin White 2.50 6.00
RQRKW Karlos Williams 2.00 5.00
RQRLW Leonard Williams 2.00 5.00
RQRMG Melvin Gordon 5.00 12.00
RQRMJ Matt Jones 2.00 5.00
RQRMM Marcus Mariota 8.00 20.00
RQRMW Maxx Williams 2.00 5.00
RQRNA Nelson Agholor 2.50 6.00
RQRPD Phillip Dorsett 2.00 5.00
RQRRG Rashad Greene 2.00 5.00
RQRSC Sammie Coates 2.50 6.00
RQRSD Stefon Diggs 5.00 12.00
RQRSM Sean Mannion 2.00 5.00
RQRTC Tevin Coleman 2.50 6.00
RQRTG Todd Gurley 8.00 20.00
RQRTL Tyler Lockett 3.00 8.00
RQRTM Ty Montgomery 2.00 5.00
RQRTY T.J. Yeldon 2.00 5.00

2015 Topps Museum Collection Signature Series Autographs

SSAAA Ameer Abdullah/100 6.00 15.00
SSAAC Amari Cooper
SSAAG A.J. Green
SSAAJ Alshon Jeffery
SSABP Breshad Perriman/100 4.00 10.00
SSABPE Bryce Petty/100 4.00 10.00
SSABS Barry Sanders
SSACC Chris Conley/300 3.00 8.00
SSADC David Cobb/300 3.00 8.00
SSADFJ Dante Fowler Jr./150 6.00 15.00
SSADG Dorial Green-Beckham/100 4.00 10.00
SSADJ Duke Johnson/100 6.00 15.00
SSADJO David Johnson/300 12.00 30.00
SSADP DeVante Parker EXCH
SSADSM Devin Smith/100 4.00 10.00
SSAES Emmanuel Sanders/245 4.00 10.00
SSAJA Jay Ajayi/100 6.00 15.00
SSAJCR Jamison Crowder/300 4.00 10.00
SSAJH Jeremy Hill 4.00 10.00
SSAJL Jeremy Langford/300 3.00 8.00
SSAJM Jordan Matthews/150 5.00 12.00
SSAJR John Riggins/125 10.00 25.00
SSAJW Jameis Winston/300 8.00 20.00
SSAKWH Kevin White/350 4.00 10.00
SSALD Len Dawson EXCH
SSALW Leonard Williams EXCH 4.00 10.00
SSAMD Mike Ditka EXCH
SSAMM Marcus Mariota/300 40.00 80.00
SSAMW Maxx Williams/300 3.00 8.00
SSAPS Phil Simms/125 10.00 25.00
SSARL Ronnie Lott EXCH
SSASD Stefon Diggs/300 8.00 20.00
SSASM Sean Mannion/145 4.00 10.00
SSATC Tevin Coleman/300 4.00 10.00
SSATM Ty Montgomery/300 3.00 8.00
SSATY T.J. Yeldon/100 4.00 10.00

2015 Topps Museum Collection Signature Series Autographs Copper

*COPPER/50: .5X TO 1.2X BASIC AU/100-150
*COPPER/50: .6X TO 1.5X BASIC AU/245-350

2015 Topps Museum Collection Signatures Swatches Dual Relic Autographs

SSDRAC Amari Cooper
SSDRAL Andrew Luck
SSDRDG Dorial Green-Beckham
SSDRDJ Duke Johnson/100 6.00 15.00
SSDRDS Devin Smith/300 3.00 8.00
SSDREG Eddie George
SSDREL Eddie Lacy
SSDRES Emmitt Smith
SSDRESA Emmanuel Sanders
SSDRGO Greg Olsen
SSDRJH Jeremy Hill/300 3.00 8.00
SSDRJM Jordan Matthews/300 4.00 10.00
SSDRJR Jerry Rice
SSDRJW Jameis Winston
SSDRKB Kelvin Benjamin/150 10.00 25.00
SSDRKW Kevin White/300 4.00 10.00
SSDRLW Leonard Williams/255 3.00 8.00
SSDRMG Melvin Gordon
SSDRMM Marcus Mariota
SSDRMW Maxx Williams/300 3.00 8.00
SSDRRW Russell Wilson
SSDRTC Tevin Coleman/300 4.00 10.00
SSDRTG Todd Gurley/300 25.00 60.00
SSDRTL Tyler Lockett/300 5.00 12.00
SSDRTY T.J. Yeldon/300 3.00 8.00

2015 Topps Museum Collection Signatures Swatches Dual Relic Autographs Copper

*COPPER/50: .6X TO 1.5X BASIC JSY AU/255-300
*COPPER/50: .5X TO 1.2X BASIC JSY AU/100-150
SSDRAC Amari Cooper 40.00 80.00
SSDRJW Jameis Winston 50.00 100.00
SSDRMM Marcus Mariota 50.00 100.00

2015 Topps Museum Collection Signatures Swatches Dual Relic Autographs Gold

*GOLD/25: .8X TO 2X BASIC JSY AU/255-300
*GOLD/25: .6X TO 1.5X BASIC JSY AU/100-150

2015 Topps Museum Collection Signatures Swatches Triple Relic Autographs Copper

*COPPER/50: .6X TO 1.5X BASIC JSY AU/200-400
*COPPER/50: .5X TO 1.2X BASIC JSY AU/100-150
SSTRJW Jameis Winston 50.00 100.00
SSTRMM Marcus Mariota 40.00 100.00

2015 Topps Museum Collection Signatures Swatches Triple Relic Autographs Gold

*GOLD/25: .8X TO 2X BASIC JSY AU/200-400
*GOLD/25: .6X TO 1.5X BASIC JSY AU/100-150
SSTRJR Jerry Rice 100.00 200.00
SSTRJW Jameis Winston 125.00 200.00
SSTRMF Marshall Faulk 25.00 50.00
SSTRMR Matt Ryan 25.00 50.00

2009 Topps National Chicle

COMP.SET w/o SP's (173) 40.00 80.00
SP STATED ODDS 1:6
BASE CARDS #59, 99, 191 NOT ISSUED
1 Maurice Jones-Drew .20 .50
2 Nnamdi Asomugha .20 .50
3 Asante Samuel .20 .50
4 Vontae Davis RC .50 1.25
5 Brandon Jacobs .20 .50
6 Malcolm Jenkins RC .50 1.25
7 Mario Williams .25 .60
8 Julius Peppers .25 .60
9 Aaron Maybin RC .60 1.50
10 Matt Forte .20 .50
11 Tyson Jackson RC .50 1.25
12 Justin Tuck .20 .50
13 Jared Allen .20 .50
14 Brian Orakpo RC .60 1.50
15 Reggie Bush .20 .50
16 DeMarcus Ware .25 .60
17 Kris Jenkins .20 .50
18 B.J. Raji RC .60 1.50
19 Lance Briggs .25 .60
20 Drew Brees .30 .75
21 Jon Beason .20 .50
22 Johnny Knox SP RC 2.00 5.00
23 Aaron Curry RC .75 2.00
24 James Harrison SP 3.00 8.00
25 Anquan Boldin .20 .50
26 Clay Matthews SP RC 6.00 15.00
27 Brian Cushing RC .50 1.25
28 Joey Porter .25 .60
29 Patrick Willis .25 .60
30 Adrian Peterson .30 .75
31 Jason Smith RC .50 1.25
32 Nate Davis RC .50 1.25
33 Josh Freeman SP RC 1.50 4.00
34 Matt Cassel .20 .50
35 Ronnie Brown .20 .50
36 Dan Marino 1.00 2.50
37 Matthew Stafford RC 2.50 6.00
38 Matt Hasselbeck .20 .50
39 Brady Quinn .20 .50
40 LaDainian Tomlinson .30 .75
41 John Elway SP 5.00 12.00
42 JaMarcus Russell .20 .50
43 Joe Namath .60 1.50
44 Terry Bradshaw .60 1.50
45 Ryan Grant .25 .60
46 Joe Montana 1.50 4.00
47 Dan Marino SP 6.00 15.00
48 Troy Aikman .60 1.50
49 Stephen McGee RC .50 1.25
50 Steven Jackson .20 .50
51 Trent Edwards .20 .50
52 Mark Sanchez RC .50 1.25
53 David Garrard .20 .50
54 Chad Pennington SP 2.00 5.00
55 Kurt Warner .25 .60
56 Vince Young .20 .50
57 Jason Campbell .20 .50
58 Shonn Greene RC .50 1.25
60 DeAngelo Williams .20 .50
61 Tim Hightower .20 .50
62 Michael Turner .20 .50
63 Larry Johnson .20 .50
64 Jamal Lewis .25 .60
65 Donovan McNabb .25 .60
66 Cedric Peerman SP 2.00 5.00
67 Willis McGahee .20 .50
68 Mike Goodson .25 .60
69 Donald Brown SP RC 1.50 4.00
70 Patrick Turner RC .50 1.25
71 LenDale White .20 .50
72 Jerious Norwood SP 2.00 5.00
73 Barry Sanders SP 5.00 12.00
74 Felix Jones SP 2.00 5.00
75 Jay Cutler .20 .50
76 Rashard Mendenhall .20 .50
77 Ray Rice .20 .50
78 Darren Sproles .25 .60
79 Jim Brown .60 1.50
80 Larry Fitzgerald .25 .60
81 Tony Dorsett .50 1.25
82 Fred Taylor .20 .50
83 Andre Brown RC .60 1.50
84 Chris Wells RC .50 1.25
85 Matt Schaub .20 .50
86 Marshawn Lynch .25 .60
87 Jamaal Charles .25 .60
88 Chester Taylor .20 .50
89 Pierre Thomas .20 .50
90 Andre Johnson .25 .60
91 LeSean McCoy RC 1.25 3.00
92 Willie Parker .20 .50
93 Julius Jones .20 .50
94 Troy Polamalu .30 .75
95 Eli Manning .25 .60
96 Ed Reed SP 3.00 8.00
97 Brian Dawkins .20 .50
98 Tony Gonzalez .25 .60
100 Michael Vick .25 .60
101 Antonio Gates .25 .60
102 Greg Olsen .25 .60
103 Tony Scheffler .20 .50
104 Chris Cooley .20 .50
105 Ben Roethlisberger .30 .75
106 Dustin Keller SP 2.00 5.00
107 Shawn Nelson RC .50 1.25
108 Travis Beckum RC .50 1.25
109 Dallas Clark .20 .50
110 Chris Johnson .20 .50
111 John Carlson .25 .60
112 Chase Coffman RC .50 1.25
113 James Casey RC .60 1.50
114 Kellen Winslow Jr. .20 .50
115 Joe Flacco .25 .60
116 Jared Cook SP RC 2.00 5.00
117 Michael Jenkins .20 .50
118 Mike Thomas RC .50 1.25
119 Ted Ginn .20 .50
120 Reggie Wayne .25 .60
121 Percy Harvin RC .50 1.25
122 Hakeem Nicks RC .60 1.50
123 Mike Wallace RC .75 2.00
124 T.J. Houshmandzadeh .20 .50
125 Marques Colston .20 .50
126 Deion Branch .20 .50
127 Derrick Mason .20 .50
128 Brian Westbrook .20 .50
129 Roscoe Parrish .20 .50
130 Philip Rivers .30 .75
131 Brian Robiskie RC .50 1.25
132 Ramses Barden RC .50 1.25
133 Darrius Heyward-Bey RC .75 2.00
134 Jeremy Maclin SP RC 2.50 6.00
135 Kevin Smith .20 .50
136 Devery Henderson SP 2.00 5.00
137 Steve Smith USC .25 .60
138 Donnie Avery .20 .50
139 Santonio Holmes .20 .50
140 Matt Ryan .25 .60
141 Clinton Portis .20 .50
142 Manuel Johnson RC .50 1.25
143 Austin Collie RC .50 1.25
144 Jarett Dillard RC .50 1.25
145 Terrell Owens .25 .60
146 Braylon Edwards .20 .50
147 Chris Chambers .20 .50
148 Brian Hartline RC .75 2.00
149 Louis Murphy RC .50 1.25
150 Frank Gore .25 .60
151 Michael Crabtree RC .75 2.00
152 Jerry Rice 1.00 2.50
153 Torry Holt SP 2.50 6.00
154 Justin Gage .20 .50
155 Dwayne Bowe .25 .60
156 Juaquin Iglesias RC .50 1.25
157 Mohamed Massaquoi RC .50 1.25
158 Kevin Walter .25 .60
159 Isaac Bruce .30 .75
160 Tony Romo .25 .60
161 Donald Driver .25 .60
162 Mark Clayton .20 .50
163 Laveranues Coles .20 .50
164 Roy Williams WR .20 .50
165 Wes Welker .25 .60
166 Bobby Engram .20 .50
167 Joey Galloway .25 .60
168 Brooks Foster SP RC 1.50 4.00
169 Brandon Tate RC .60 1.50
170 Calvin Johnson .30 .75
171 Jerricho Cotchery .20 .50
172 DeSean Jackson .25 .60
173 Hines Ward .25 .60
174 Deon Butler RC .50 1.25
175 Roddy White .20 .50
176 Santana Moss .25 .60
177 Lee Evans SP 2.50 6.00
178 Andre Caldwell .20 .50
179 Brandon Marshall .25 .60
180 Aaron Rodgers .60 1.50
181 Derrick Williams SP RC 1.50 4.00
182 Devin Hester .25 .60
183 Anthony Gonzalez .20 .50
184 Bernard Berrian SP 2.00 5.00
185 Vincent Jackson .20 .50
186 Antonio Bryant .20 .50
187 Kenny Britt RC .75 2.00
188 Thomas Jones .20 .50
189 D'Qwell Jackson .20 .50
190 Peyton Manning SP 8.00 20.00
192 Knowshon Moreno RC .50 1.25
193 Marion Barber .25 .60
194 Chad Ochocinco SP 2.00 5.00
195 Jason Witten .25 .60
196 Greg Jennings .20 .50
197 Joseph Addai .20 .50
198 Steve Smith .25 .60
199 Tom Brady 1.00 2.50
200 Randy Moss .25 .60

2009 Topps National Chicle Mini

*VETS: 1.2X TO 3X BASIC CARDS
*VETS: .1X TO .3X BASIC SP
*RETIRED: 1X TO 2.5X BASIC CARDS
*RETIRED: .1X TO .3X BASIC SP
*ROOKIES: .5X TO 1.2X BASIC RC
*ROOKIES: .15X TO .4X BASIC SP RC
ONE MINI PER HOBBY PACK

2009 Topps National Chicle Mini Bazooka Back

*VETS: 2.5X TO 6X BASIC CARDS
*VETS: .25X TO .6X BASIC SP
*RETIRED: 2X TO 5X BASIC CARDS
*RETIRED: .3X TO .8X BASIC SP
*ROOKIES: .8X TO 2X BASIC RC
*ROOKIES: .25X TO .6X BASIC SP RC
STATED ODDS 1:12

2009 Topps National Chicle Mini Chicle Back

*VETS: 2X TO 5X BASIC CARDS
*VETS: .2X TO .5X BASIC SP
*RETIRED: 1.4X TO 4X BASIC CARDS
*RETIRED: .25X TO .6X BASIC SP
*ROOKIES: .6X TO 1.5X BASIC RC
*ROOKIES: .2X TO .5X BASIC SP RC
STATED ODDS 1:6

2009 Topps National Chicle Mini Topps Back

*VETS: 8X TO 20X BASIC CARDS
*VETS: .8X TO 2X BASIC SP
*RETIRED: 6X TO 15X BASIC CARDS
*RETIRED: 1X TO 2.5X BASIC SP
*ROOKIES: 2.5X TO 6X BASIC RC
*ROOKIES: .8X TO 2X BASIC SP RC
TOPPS/UMBRELLA BACK/25 ODDS 1:92 HOB

2009 Topps National Chicle Autographs

GROUP A ODDS 1:437 HOB
GROUP B ODDS 1:142 HOB
GROUP C ODDS 1:60 HOB
GROUP D ODDS 1:56 HOB
GROUP E ODDS 1:25 HOB
MCAMG Mike Goodson D 4.00 10.00
NCAAB Andre Brown E 4.00 10.00
NCAAC Aaron Curry C 5.00 12.00
NCAACB Drew Brees A 40.00 80.00
NCAACO Austin Collie E 8.00 20.00
NCAAP Adrian Peterson A 100.00 200.00
NCABB Bernard Berrian B 8.00 20.00
NCABF Brett Favre A 200.00 300.00
NCABH Brian Hartline D 5.00 12.00
NCABM Brandon Marshall B 8.00 20.00
NCABO Brian Orakpo D 4.00 10.00
NCABS Barry Sanders A 100.00 200.00
NCABT Brandon Tate C 6.00 15.00
NCACC Chase Coffman E 3.00 8.00
NCACW Chris Wells B 12.00 30.00
NCADBR Donald Brown A 12.00 30.00
NCADHB Darrius Heyward-Bey A
NCADJ DeSean Jackson B 10.00 25.00
NCADM Darren McFadden A
NCADMA Dan Marino A 75.00 150.00
NCADW Derrick Williams B 3.00 8.00
NCAGJ Greg Jennings B 10.00 25.00
NCAHN Hakeem Nicks C 4.00 10.00
NCAJA Joseph Addai A 10.00 25.00
NCAJB Jim Brown A 60.00 100.00
NCAJC1 Jamaal Charles C 8.00 20.00
NCAJC2 Jared Cook E 4.00 10.00
NCAJC3 Jay Cutler A 60.00 100.00
NCAJD Jarett Dillard E 4.00 10.00
NCAJE John Elway A 100.00 175.00
NCAJF Josh Freeman A 12.00 30.00
NCAJF Joe Flacco B 20.00 40.00
NCAJI Juaquin Iglesias D 3.00 8.00
NCAJM1 Jeremy Maclin A 12.00 30.00
NCAJM2 Joe Montana A 100.00 200.00
NCAJN Joe Namath A 75.00 150.00
NCAJR Jerry Rice A 125.00 200.00
NCAJS Jason Smith C 3.00 8.00
NCAKM Knowshon Moreno A 15.00 40.00
NCALJ Larry Johnson A 10.00 25.00
NCALM LeSean McCoy B 15.00 40.00
NCAMC Michael Crabtree A 20.00 50.00
NCAMJ Michael Jenkins E 4.00 10.00
NCAMS Matthew Stafford A 50.00 120.00
NCAMSA Mark Sanchez A 30.00 80.00
NCAMW Mike Wallace A 5.00 12.00
NCAND Nate Davis D 3.00 8.00
NCAPH Percy Harvin C 8.00 20.00
NCAPT Patrick Turner E 3.00 8.00
NCAPW Pat White B 4.00 10.00
NCARB Ramses Barden E 3.00 8.00
NCARR Ray Rice C 15.00 30.00
NCARW Reggie Wayne A 8.00 20.00
NCASG Shonn Greene C 10.00 25.00
NCASM Stephen McGee B 3.00 8.00
NCATA Troy Aikman A 60.00 120.00
NCATB1 Travis Beckum D 3.00 8.00
NCATB2 Terry Bradshaw A 60.00 100.00
NCATD Tony Dorsett A 30.00 60.00
NCATJ Tyson Jackson C 3.00 8.00
NCAWW Wes Welker C 12.00 30.00

2009 Topps National Chicle Cabinet

ONE CABINET PER HOBBY BOX
*ARTIST SIGN/50: 2X TO 5X BASIC CABINET
NCCC1 Peyton Manning 8.00 20.00
NCCC2 Andre Johnson 2.50 6.00
NCCC3 Clinton Portis 2.00 5.00
NCCC4 Jim Brown 4.00 10.00
NCCC5 Barry Sanders 5.00 12.00
NCCC6 Joe Namath 4.00 10.00
NCCC7 Tony Dorsett 3.00 8.00
NCCC8 Chris Wells 1.00 2.50
NCCC9 Donald Brown 1.00 2.50
NCCC10 Knowshon Moreno 1.00 2.50
NCCC11 Chris Johnson 2.00 5.00
NCCC12 Santonio Holmes 2.00 5.00
NCCC13 DeSean Jackson 2.50 6.00
NCCC14 Chad Ochocinco 2.00 5.00
NCCC15 Felix Jones 2.00 5.00
NCCC16 Matthew Stafford 5.00 12.00
NCCC17 Greg Jennings 2.00 5.00
NCCC18 Eli Manning 2.50 6.00
NCCC19 Terry Bradshaw 4.00 10.00
NCCC20 Aaron Rodgers 6.00 15.00
NCCC21 Michael Turner 2.00 5.00
NCCC22 Brian Westbrook 2.00 5.00
NCCC23 Joe Flacco 2.50 6.00
NCCC24 Tom Brady 10.00 25.00
NCCC25 Jay Cutler 2.00 5.00

2009 Topps National Chicle Dual Autographs

DUAL AUTO/20-25 ODDS 1:1690 HOB
CB M.Cassel/D.Bowe 25.00 50.00
FP B.Favre/Peterson 200.00 400.00
MM J.Maclin/L.McCoy 30.00 80.00
MS M.Stafford/M.Crabtree 30.00 80.00
MW P.Manning/R.Wayne 90.00 150.00
MWE K.Moreno/C.Wells 15.00 40.00
PH A.Peterson/P.Harvin 100.00 200.00
SC M.Sanchez/M.Cassel 40.00 100.00
SM M.Stafford/K.Moreno 40.00 80.00
SS M.Stafford/M.Sanchez 60.00 150.00

2009 Topps National Chicle Dual Relics

DUAL RELIC/25 ODDS 1:1150 HOB
BC D.Brees/M.Colston 15.00 30.00
BW R.Brown/P.White
FB L.Fitzgerald/A.Boldin 10.00 25.00
ME D.Marino/J.Elway 40.00 80.00
MN E.Manning/H.Nicks 10.00 25.00
MP S.Moss/C.Portis 8.00 20.00
MW P.Manning/R.Wayne 20.00 40.00
PH A.Peterson/P.Harvin 15.00 40.00
RB T.Romo/M.Barber 15.00 40.00
RG P.Rivers/A.Gates 10.00 25.00
RJ A.Rodgers/G.Jennings 15.00 40.00
SG M.Sanchez/S.Greene 15.00 40.00
SJ M.Stafford/C.Johnson 12.00 30.00
SW S.Smith/D.Williams 8.00 20.00
WM B.Westbrook/L.McCoy 8.00 20.00

2009 Topps National Chicle Era Icons

COMPLETE SET (14) 5.00 12.00
STATED ODDS 1:3 HOB
EI1 Amelia Earhart .50 1.25
EI2 Pennsylvania Railroad .50 1.25
EI3 Caroline Mikkelson .50 1.25
EI4 Sir Watson-Watt .50 1.25
EI5 Boulder Dam .50 1.25
EI6 Omaha .50 1.25
EI7 Franklin D. Roosevelt .50 1.25
EI8 Fort Knox .50 1.25
EI9 Danno O'Mahoney .50 1.25
EI10 Helen Jacobs .50 1.25
EI11 Roller Derby .50 1.25
EI12 Sir Malcolm Campbell .50 1.25
EI13 Porgy and Bess .50 1.25
EI14 China Clipper .50 1.25

2009 Topps National Chicle Era Icons Relics

Authentic Shirt Relic

ICON RELIC ODDS 1:139 HOB
AE Amelia Earhart Stamp 10.00 25.00
BD Boulder Dam Stamp 8.00 20.00
CL Charles Lindbergh Stamp 8.00 20.00
YS Yankee Stadium Stamp 12.00 30.00
FDR2 Franklin D. Roosevelt Stamp 8.00 20.00
FDR Franklin D. Roosevelt A Shirt 20.00 40.00

2009 Topps National Chicle Greatest Thrills

COMPLETE SET (10) 10.00 25.00
STATED ODDS 1:12 HOB
GT1 Santonio Holmes 1.00 2.50
GT2 David Tyree .75 2.00
GT3 Eli Manning 1.00 2.50
GT4 Kurt Warner 1.00 2.50
GT5 Terry Bradshaw 2.00 5.00
GT6 James Harrison 1.50 4.00
GT7 Tom Brady 4.00 10.00
GT8 John Elway 2.00 5.00
GT9 Willie Parker 1.00 2.50
GT10 Adam Vinatieri .75 2.00

2009 Topps National Chicle Greats of the Gridiron

STATED ODDS 1:24 HOB
GG1 Troy Aikman 2.50 6.00
GG2 Jerry Rice 4.00 10.00
GG3 Joe Montana 6.00 15.00
GG4 Joe Namath 2.50 6.00
GG5 Barry Sanders 3.00 8.00
GG6 Terry Bradshaw 2.50 6.00
GG7 John Elway 3.00 8.00
GG8 Brett Favre 4.00 10.00
GG9 Jim Brown 2.50 6.00
GG10 Tony Dorsett 2.00 5.00

2009 Topps National Chicle Relics

GROUP A ODDS 1:1285 HOB
GROUP B ODDS 1:25 HOB
NCRAB Andre Brown B 1.50 4.00
NCRAC Aaron Curry B 2.00 5.00
NCRAR Aaron Rodgers B 8.00 20.00
NCRBM Brandon Marshall B 3.00 8.00
NCRBP Brandon Pettigrew B 1.25 3.00
NCRBR Brian Robiskie B 1.25 3.00
NCRBS Barry Sanders A 12.00 30.00
NCRCW Chris Wells B 1.25 3.00
NCRDA Donnie Avery B 2.50 6.00
NCRDB1 Drew Brees B 4.00 10.00
NCRDB2 Deon Butler B 1.25 3.00
NCRDBR Donald Brown B 1.25 3.00
NCRDC Dallas Clark B 2.50 6.00
NCRDEW DeAngelo Williams B 2.50 6.00
NCRDHB Darrius Heyward-Bey B 2.00 5.00
NCRDM1 Dan Marino A 15.00 40.00
NCRDM2 Donovan McNabb B 3.00 8.00
NCRDMC Darren McFadden B 4.00 10.00
NCRDW Derrick Williams B 1.25 3.00
NCRFJ Felix Jones B 2.50 6.00
NCRHN Hakeem Nicks B 1.50 4.00
NCRJE John Elway A 12.00 30.00
NCRJF Josh Freeman B 1.25 3.00
NCRJI Juaquin Iglesias B 2.50 6.00
NCRJM Jeremy Maclin B 1.50 4.00
NCRJMO Joe Montana A 25.00 60.00
NCRJR Jerry Rice B 8.00 20.00
NCRJS Jason Smith B 2.00 5.00
NCRKB Kenny Britt B 2.00 5.00
NCRKM Knowshon Moreno B 1.25 3.00
NCRLE Lee Evans B 3.00 8.00
NCRLM LeSean McCoy B 3.00 8.00
NCRMC Michael Crabtree B 2.00 5.00
NCRMF Matt Forte B 2.50 6.00
NCRMJD Maurice Jones-Drew B 2.50 6.00
NCRMM Mohamed Massaquoi B 1.25 3.00
NCRMS Matthew Stafford B 6.00 15.00
NCRMSA Mark Sanchez B 1.25 3.00
NCRMT Mike Thomas B 1.25 3.00
NCRMW Mike Wallace B 2.00 5.00
NCRND Nate Davis B 1.25 3.00
NCRPH Percy Harvin B 1.25 3.00
NCRPT Patrick Turner B 2.00 5.00
NCRPW Pat White B 1.50 4.00
NCRRB Ramses Barden B 1.25 3.00
NCRRM Randy Moss B 5.00 12.00
NCRRR Ray Rice B 2.50 6.00
NCRSG Shonn Greene B 1.25 3.00
NCRSM Stephen McGee B 2.50 6.00
NCRSMO Santana Moss B 3.00 8.00
NCRTA Troy Aikman A 10.00 25.00
NCRTB Tom Brady B 12.00 30.00
NCRTBR Terry Bradshaw A 10.00 25.00
NCRTJ Tyson Jackson B 1.25 3.00

2009 Topps National Chicle Stars of the Gridiron

COMPLETE SET (10) 8.00 20.00
STATED ODDS 1:6 HOB
SG1 Tom Brady 3.00 8.00
SG2 Andre Johnson .75 2.00
SG3 Adrian Peterson 1.00 2.50
SG4 LaDainian Tomlinson 1.00 2.50
SG5 Brian Westbrook .60 1.50
SG6 Randy Moss .75 2.00
SG7 Clinton Portis .60 1.50
SG8 Steven Jackson .60 1.50
SG9 Larry Fitzgerald .75 2.00
SG10 Peyton Manning 2.50 6.00

2009 Topps National Chicle Youngsters of the Gridiron

COMPLETE SET (20) 20.00 50.00
STATED ODDS 1:4 HOB
YG1 Mark Sanchez .50 1.25
YG2 Chris Johnson .60 1.50
YG3 Pat White .60 1.50
YG4 Steve Slaton .60 1.50
YG5 Matthew Stafford 2.50 6.00
YG6 Eddie Royal .60 1.50
YG7 LeSean McCoy 1.25 3.00
YG8 Hakeem Nicks .60 1.50
YG9 Kevin Smith .60 1.50
YG10 Knowshon Moreno .50 1.25
YG11 Matt Forte .60 1.50
YG12 Jeremy Maclin .60 1.50
YG13 Darren McFadden 1.00 2.50
YG14 Percy Harvin .50 1.25
YG15 Donald Brown .50 1.25
YG16 Matt Ryan .75 2.00
YG17 Jonathan Stewart .60 1.50
YG18 Chris Wells .50 1.25
YG19 Joe Flacco .75 2.00
YG20 Michael Crabtree .75 2.00

2013 Topps National Convention 1952 Bowman

COMPLETE SET (8) 15.00 40.00
5 Geno Smith
6 Eddie Lacy
7 Tavon Austin
8 EJ Manuel

2015 Topps National Convention Allen and Ginter Die Cut

AGX71 Amari Cooper
AGX72 T.J. Yeldon
AGX73 Alshon Jeffery
AGX74 Emmitt Smith
AGX75 Dorial Green-Beckham
AGX76 Zach Mettenberger
AGX77 Gale Sayers
AGX78 Tom Brady
AGX79 Peyton Manning
AGX80 Aaron Rodgers
AGX81 Russell Wilson
AGX82 Andrew Luck
AGX83 J.J. Watt
AGX84 Luke Kuechly
AGX85 Drew Brees
AGX86 Tony Romo
AGX87 Odell Beckham Jr
AGX88 Dez Bryant
AGX89 Calvin Johnson
AGX90 Jameis Winston
AGX91 Terrance West
AGX92 Matt Forte
AGX93 Eddie Lacy
AGX94 Robbie Gould
AGX95 Marcus Mariota

2015 Topps National Convention Allen and Ginter Die Cut Autographs

ISSUED ON '15 NATIONAL CONVENTION
PRINT RUNS B/WN 8-80 COPIES PER
NO PRICING ON QTY 10 OR LESS
AGXAAC Amari Cooper
AGXAAJ Alshon Jeffery
AGXADG Dorial Green-Beckham/15
AGXADJ Duke Johnson
AGXAES Emmitt Smith
AGXAGS Gale Sayers
AGXAJG Jimmy Garoppolo
AGXAJW Jameis Winston/5
AGXAML Marshawn Lynch
AGXAMM Marcus Mariota/5
AGXAMW Maxx Williams
AGXAPD Phillip Dorsett
AGXATL Tyler Lockett
AGXATW Terrance West/40 8.00 20.00
AGXATY T.J. Yeldon/46

2006 Topps Paradigm

This 98-card set was released in April, 2007. The first 40 cards in this set feature a mix of active and retired greats while cards numbered 41-98 feature 2006 NFL rookies. Cards numbered 1-40 were issued to a stated print run of 169 serial numbered sets. The rookies are broken down into the following subsets; Cards with jersey swatches (41-59) issued to a stated print run of 249 serial numbered sets which were inserted at a stated rate of one in two; carrds with autographs (60-76) issued to a stated print run of 199 serial numbered sets which were inserted at a stated rate of one in three; and cards with both player-worn jersey swatches and autographs were issued to a stated print run of 99 serial numbered set which were inserted at a stated rate of one in eight. Cards numbered 61, 63, 66, 78 and 98 were never produced for this set.

1-40 PRINT RUN 169 SER.#'d SETS
JSY RC/249 STATED ODDS 1:2
JSY RC PRINT RUN 249 SER.#'d SETS
AU/199 RC STATED ODDS 1:3
AU/149 RC STATED ODDS 1:4
AUTO RC PRINT RUN 149-199
JSY AU/99 RC STATED ODDS 1:8
JSY AU RC PRINT RUN 99 SER.#'d SETS
1 Joe Namath 6.00 15.00
2 Dan Marino 15.00 40.00
3 Joe Montana 15.00 40.00
4 Terry Bradshaw 6.00 15.00
5 John Elway 8.00 20.00
6 Bart Starr 8.00 20.00
7 Barry Sanders 8.00 20.00
8 Emmitt Smith 8.00 20.00
9 Eric Dickerson 4.00 10.00
10 Earl Campbell 5.00 12.00
11 Jim Brown 6.00 15.00
12 Gale Sayers 5.00 12.00
13 Tony Dorsett 5.00 12.00
14 Jerry Rice 10.00 25.00
15 Brett Favre 10.00 25.00
16 Peyton Manning 12.00 30.00
17 Tom Brady 15.00 40.00
18 Michael Vick 4.00 10.00
19 Carson Palmer 4.00 10.00
20 Shaun Alexander 3.00 8.00
21 LaDainian Tomlinson 5.00 12.00
22 Larry Johnson 3.00 8.00
23 Frank Gore 4.00 10.00
24 Steve Smith 5.00 12.00
25 Chad Johnson 3.00 8.00
26 Johnny Unitas 8.00 20.00
27 Steve McNair 4.00 10.00
28 Donovan McNabb 4.00 10.00
29 Ben Roethlisberger 6.00 15.00
30 Tiki Barber 4.00 10.00
31 Corey Dillon 3.00 8.00
32 Edgerrin James 4.00 10.00
33 Clinton Portis 3.00 8.00
34 Tony Gonzalez 4.00 10.00
35 Jeremy Shockey 3.00 8.00
36 Marvin Harrison 4.00 10.00
37 Terrell Owens 4.00 10.00
38 Randy Moss 4.00 10.00
39 Torry Holt 4.00 10.00
40 Hines Ward 4.00 10.00
41 Kamerion Wimbley JSY RC 5.00 12.00
42 DeMeco Ryans JSY RC 5.00 12.00
43 Mathias Kiwanuka JSY RC 6.00 15.00
44 Ingle Martin JSY RC 5.00 12.00
45 Jerome Harrison JSY RC 4.00 10.00
46 Derek Hagan JSY RC 5.00 12.00
47 Joe Klopfenstein JSY RC 4.00 10.00
48 Willie Reid JSY RC 5.00 12.00
49 Devin Hester JSY RC 8.00 20.00
50 Tarvaris Jackson JSY RC 4.00 10.00
51 D.J. Shockley JSY RC 5.00 12.00
52 Brian Calhoun JSY RC 4.00 10.00
53 Anthony Fasano JSY RC 4.00 10.00
54 Hank Baskett JSY RC 4.00 10.00
55 Maurice Stovall JSY RC 4.00 10.00
56 Brad Smith JSY RC 5.00 12.00
57 Brandon Williams JSY RC 4.00 10.00
58 Travis Wilson JSY RC 4.00 10.00

59 Jason Avant JSY RC 4.00 10.00
60 Tye Hill AU/199 RC 5.00 12.00
62 Adam Jennings AU/199 RC 6.00 15.00
64 Cedric Humes AU/199 RC 5.00 12.00
65 P.J. Daniels AU/199 RC 5.00 12.00
67 David Thomas AU/199 RC 5.00 12.00
68 Dominique Byrd AU/199 RC 5.00 12.00
69 Quinton Ganther AU/199 RC 5.00 12.00
70 Ashton Youboty AU/199 RC 5.00 12.00
71 Bobby Carpenter AU/199 RC 5.00 12.00
72 Kellen Clemens AU/199 RC 5.00 12.00
73 Charlie Whitehurst AU/199 RC 5.00 12.00
74 Reggie McNeal AU/199 RC 5.00 12.00
75 Demetrius Williams AU/199 RC 5.00 12.00
76 Skyler Green AU/199 RC 5.00 12.00
77 Michael Huff AU/149 RC 8.00 20.00
79 Brodie Croyle AU/149 RC 6.00 15.00
80 Bruce Gradkowski AU/149 RC 8.00 20.00
81 Wali Lundy AU/149 RC 6.00 15.00
82 Jerious Norwood AU/149 RC 6.00 15.00
83 Mike Bell AU/99 RC 6.00 15.00
84 Marcedes Lewis AU/149 RC 6.00 15.00
85 Leonard Pope AU/149 RC 10.00 25.00
86 Chad Jackson AU/149 RC 6.00 15.00
87 Leon Washington AU/149 RC 6.00 15.00
88 Michael Robinson AU/149 RC 6.00 15.00
89 Mario Williams AU/149 RC 15.00 30.00
90 Joseph Addai AU/149 RC 6.00 15.00
91 Marques Colston AU/149 RC 10.00 25.00
92 Sinorice Moss AU/149 RC 6.00 15.00
93 Greg Jennings AU/149 RC 10.00 25.00
94 Matt Leinart JSY AU/99 RC 8.00 20.00
95 Vince Young JSY AU/99 RC 8.00 20.00
96 Sinorice Moss JSY AU/99 8.00 20.00
97 Reggie Bush JSY AU/99 RC 12.00 30.00
99 DeA.Williams JSY AU/99 RC 10.00 25.00
100 L.White JSY AU/99 RC 8.00 20.00
101 S.Holmes JSY AU/99 RC 10.00 25.00
102 Vernon Davis JSY AU/99 RC 10.00 25.00
103 A.J. Hawk JSY AU/99 RC 10.00 25.00

2006 Topps Paradigm Gold

*VETS 1-40: .8X TO 2X BASIC CARDS
VETS/25 STATED ODDS 1:8
VETERANS PRINT RUN 25 SER.#'d SETS
*JSY ROOK/25 #41-59: .5X TO 1.2X
ROOKIE JSY/25 ODDS 1:17
*AUTO ROOK/50: .5X TO 1.2X BASE AU/199
AUTO ROOKIE/50 ODDS 1:10-1:12
ROOKIE AUTO PRINT RUN 50

2006 Topps Paradigm Autographed NFL Logos

UNPRICED VETERAN 1/1 ODDS 1:825
UNPRICED ROOKIE 1/1 ODDS 1:298

2006 Topps Paradigm Autographed NFL Logos Dual

UNPRICED VETERAN 1/1 ODDS 1:1856
UNPRICED ROOKIE 1/1 ODDS 1:745

2006 Topps Paradigm Autographs

AUTO/149 STATED ODDS 1:11
*GOLD/50: .6X TO 1.2X BASIC AUTO/149
GOLD/50 STATED ODDS 1:31
TPABS Barry Sanders 60.00 120.00
TPAJB Jim Brown 50.00 100.00
TPAJM Joe Montana 60.00 120.00
TPAJN Joe Namath 50.00 100.00

2006 Topps Paradigm Career Highs Triple Jersey Autographs

PASSING/RUSHING YARDS ODDS 1:5
RECEIVING YARDS ODDS 1:6
TOUCHDOWNS STATED ODDS 1:9
STATED PRINT RUN 99 UNLESS NOTED
*GOLD/25: .5X TO 1.2X BASIC INSERTS
GOLD PASSING YARDS/25 ODDS 1:19
GOLD RUSHING YARDS/25 ODDS 1:20
GOLD RECEIVING YARDS/25 ODDS 1:23
PBF Brett Favre 100.00 200.00
PBG Bruce Gradkowski 10.00 25.00
PDM Dan Marino/56 75.00 150.00
PEM Eli Manning 40.00 100.00
PJC Jay Cutler 10.00 25.00
PJE John Elway 75.00 150.00
PJK Jim Kelly 30.00 60.00
PJM Joe Montana 75.00 150.00
PJN Joe Namath 60.00 120.00
PML Matt Leinart 8.00 20.00
PMV Michael Vick 20.00 50.00
PPM Peyton Manning 75.00 150.00
PTA Troy Aikman 40.00 100.00
PTB Terry Bradshaw 75.00 150.00
PTBR Tom Brady 150.00 250.00
PTR Tony Romo 40.00 100.00
PVY Vince Young 8.00 20.00
RBG Paul Hornung 25.00 50.00
RBS Barry Sanders 75.00 150.00
RDW DeAngelo Williams 10.00 25.00
REAG Antonio Gates 15.00 40.00
REC Earl Campbell 25.00 50.00
RECJ Chad Johnson 10.00 25.00
RED Eric Dickerson 25.00 50.00
REFB Fred Biletnikoff 25.00 50.00
REGJ Greg Jennings 12.00 30.00
REHB Hank Baskett 8.00 20.00
REJR Jerry Rice 75.00 150.00
RELJ Larry Johnson 10.00 25.00
RELT LaDainian Tomlinson/61 25.00 50.00
REMC Marques Colston 12.00 30.00
REMH Marvin Harrison 25.00 50.00
RERB Reggie Bush 12.00 30.00
RES Emmitt Smith 75.00 150.00
RESS Steve Smith/93 20.00 50.00
RETIB Tim Brown 25.00 50.00
RFG Frank Gore 12.00 30.00
RJN Jerious Norwood 8.00 20.00
RLJ Larry Johnson 10.00 25.00
RLT LaDainian Tomlinson/62 25.00 50.00
RMF Marshall Faulk 25.00 50.00
RMJD Maurice Drew 12.00 30.00
RRB Reggie Bush 12.00 30.00
RSA Shaun Alexander 10.00 25.00
TDBS Barry Sanders 75.00 150.00
TDDM Dan Marino
TDES Emmitt Smith/23 125.00 250.00
TDJR Jerry Rice 75.00 150.00
TDLJ Larry Johnson 10.00 25.00
TDMF Marshall Faulk 25.00 50.00
TDPM Peyton Manning 75.00 150.00
TDSA Shaun Alexander 10.00 25.00
TDTB Terry Bradshaw 75.00 150.00

2006 Topps Paradigm Dual Autograph Dual Patches

UNPRICED DUAL/10 ODDS 1:168
STATED PRINT RUN 10 SER.#'d SETS

2006 Topps Paradigm Dual Jersey Numbers Autographs

DUAL JSY AUTO/25 STATED ODDS 1:21
STATED PRINT RUN 25 SER.#'d SETS
JNABF Brett Favre 125.00 250.00
JNABS Barry Sanders 100.00 200.00
JNADM Dan Marino
JNAES Emmitt Smith
JNAJE John Elway 60.00 120.00
JNAJM Joe Montana 100.00 200.00
JNAJN Joe Namath 60.00 120.00
JNALM Laurence Maroney
JNAML Matt Leinart 30.00 80.00
JNAPM Peyton Manning 100.00 200.00
JNARB Reggie Bush 20.00 50.00
JNASA Shaun Alexander 40.00 80.00
JNATB Terry Bradshaw 75.00 150.00
JNATBR Tom Brady 150.00 250.00
JNAVY Vince Young 75.00 150.00

2006 Topps Paradigm Dual Jerseys

SILVER/99 STATED ODDS 1:4
SILVER PRINT RUN 99 SER.#'d SETS
*GOLD/25: .5X TO 1.2X BASIC DUAL JSY/99
GOLD/25 STATED ODDS 1:16
GOLD PRINT RUN 25 SER.#'d SETS
TPBSA Barry Sanders 6.00 15.00
TPCJ Chad Johnson 2.50 6.00
TPCP Carson Palmer 3.00 8.00
TPDM Dan Marino 8.00 20.00
TPES Emmitt Smith 6.00 15.00
TPFG Frank Gore 3.00 8.00
TPJE John Elway 6.00 15.00
TPJM Joe Montana 12.00 30.00
TPJN Joe Namath 5.00 12.00
TPJR Jerry Rice 8.00 20.00
TPJS Jeremy Shockey 2.50 6.00
TPJU Johnny Unitas 20.00 50.00
TPLJ Larry Johnson 2.50 6.00
TPLT LaDainian Tomlinson 4.00 10.00
TPMH Marvin Harrison 3.00 8.00
TPMV Michael Vick 3.00 8.00
TPPM Peyton Manning 10.00 25.00
TPSM Steve McNair 3.00 8.00
TPSS Steve Smith 4.00 10.00
TPTBR Tom Brady 12.00 30.00

2006 Topps Paradigm Namesake Relics Autographs

UNPRICED SILVER STATED ODDS 1:47
SILVER STATED PRINT RUN 2-4
UNPRICED GOLD 1/1 ODDS 1:115
GOLD STATED PRINT RUN 1

2006 Topps Paradigm Patch Frame Autographs

UNPRICED FRAMED AUTO/5 ODDS 1:190
STATED PRINT RUN 5 SER.#'d SETS

2006 Topps Paradigm Rookie Dual Jersey Autographs

SILVER/149 STATED ODDS 1:9
SILVER/249/250 STATED ODDS 1:6
SILVER/299 STATED ODDS 1:3
*GOLD/50: .6X TO 1.2X BASIC INSERTS
GOLD/50 STATED ODDS 1:16-1:28
GOLD PRINT RUN 50 SER.#'d SETS
AF Anthony Fasano/299 5.00 12.00
BG Bruce Gradkowski/249 6.00 15.00
BS Brad Smith/299 6.00 15.00
BW Brandon Williams/299 5.00 12.00
CJ Chad Jackson/249 5.00 12.00
CW Charlie Whitehurst/299 5.00 12.00
DH Devin Hester/299 10.00 25.00
DW Demetrius Williams/299 5.00 12.00
GJ Greg Jennings/149 8.00 20.00
HB Hank Baskett/250 5.00 12.00
JA Jason Avant/299 5.00 12.00
JN Jerious Norwood/249 5.00 12.00
MB Mike Bell/249 5.00 12.00
MC Marques Colston/149 8.00 20.00
ML Marcedes Lewis/249 5.00 12.00
MS Maurice Stovall/299 5.00 12.00
MW Mario Williams/149 8.00 20.00
SM Sinorice Moss/149 5.00 12.00
TJ Tarvaris Jackson/299 5.00 12.00
WL Wali Lundy/249 5.00 12.00
AD Joseph Addai/149 5.00 12.00
CA Brian Calhoun/299 5.00 12.00
MJD Maurice Drew/149 8.00 20.00

2007 Topps Performance

ROOKIE PRINT RUN 359 SER.#'d SETS
1 Drew Brees .75 2.00
2 Peyton Manning 2.00 5.00
3 Marc Bulger .50 1.25
4 Jon Kitna .50 1.25
5 Carson Palmer .60 1.50
6 Brett Favre 1.50 4.00
7 Tom Brady 2.50 6.00
8 Ben Roethlisberger .75 2.00
9 Philip Rivers .75 2.00
10 Chad Pennington .50 1.25
11 Eli Manning .60 1.50
12 Vince Young .50 1.25
13 Steve McNair .60 1.50
14 Tony Romo 1.00 2.50
15 Kurt Warner .60 1.50
16 Kyle Boller .50 1.25
17 Donovan McNabb .60 1.50
18 J.P. Losman .50 1.25
19 Matt Hasselbeck .50 1.25
20 Joey Harrington .60 1.50
21 Damon Huard .60 1.50
22 David Garrard .50 1.25
23 Trent Green .50 1.25
24 Jeff Garcia .50 1.25
25 Jason Campbell .50 1.25
26 Jay Cutler .50 1.25
27 Derek Anderson .50 1.25
28 Brian Griese .50 1.25
29 Matt Schaub .50 1.25
30 Daunte Culpepper .60 1.50
31 Joseph Addai .50 1.25
32 Maurice Jones-Drew .50 1.25
33 Steven Jackson .50 1.25
34 Brandon Jacobs .50 1.25
35 Willie Parker .60 1.50
36 LaDainian Tomlinson .75 2.00
37 Thomas Jones .50 1.25
38 Derrick Ward .60 1.50
39 Cedric Benson .50 1.25
40 Willis McGahee .50 1.25
41 Chester Taylor .50 1.25
42 Marion Barber .75 2.00
43 Frank Gore .60 1.50
44 DeShaun Foster .60 1.50
45 Brian Westbrook .50 1.25
46 Edgerrin James .60 1.50
47 Shaun Alexander .50 1.25
48 Warrick Dunn .50 1.25
49 LenDale White .60 1.50
50 Justin Fargas .50 1.25
51 Larry Johnson .50 1.25
52 Ronnie Brown .50 1.25
53 Fred Taylor .50 1.25
54 Clinton Portis .50 1.25
55 Travis Henry .60 1.50
56 Jamal Lewis .60 1.50
57 LaMont Jordan .60 1.50
58 Earnest Graham .60 1.50
59 Kenny Watson .60 1.50
60 Reggie Bush .50 1.25
61 Reggie Wayne .60 1.50
62 Torry Holt .60 1.50
63 Roy Williams WR .50 1.25
64 Chad Johnson .50 1.25
65 T.J. Houshmandzadeh .50 1.25
66 Randy Moss .60 1.50
67 Antwaan Randle El .50 1.25
68 Jerricho Cotchery .50 1.25
69 Plaxico Burress .50 1.25
70 Bernard Berrian .50 1.25
71 Derrick Mason .50 1.25
72 Terrell Owens .60 1.50
73 Steve Smith .60 1.50
74 Kevin Curtis .50 1.25
75 Shaun McDonald .50 1.25
76 Larry Fitzgerald .60 1.50
77 Santonio Holmes .50 1.25
78 Roddy White .50 1.25
79 Chris Chambers .50 1.25
80 Joey Galloway .60 1.50
81 Brandon Marshall .60 1.50
82 Braylon Edwards .50 1.25
83 Wes Welker .60 1.50
84 Donald Driver .60 1.50
85 Lee Evans .60 1.50
86 Greg Jennings .50 1.25
87 Kevin Walter .60 1.50
88 Ike Hilliard .50 1.25
89 Bobby Engram .50 1.25
90 Marques Colston .50 1.25
91 Antonio Gates .75 2.00
92 Kellen Winslow .50 1.25
93 Jason Witten .60 1.50
94 Dallas Clark .60 1.50
95 Tony Gonzalez .60 1.50
96 Jason Taylor .60 1.50
97 Ray Lewis .75 2.00
98 Shawne Merriman .50 1.25
99 Brian Urlacher .75 2.00
100 Champ Bailey .60 1.50
101 Trent Edwards RC 1.25 3.00
102 Kevin Kolb RC 1.50 4.00
103 JaMarcus Russell RC 1.25 3.00
104 Brady Quinn RC 1.25 3.00
105 John Beck RC 1.25 3.00
106 Drew Stanton RC 1.25 3.00
107 Troy Smith RC 1.25 3.00
108 Chris Leak RC 1.25 3.00
109 Adrian Peterson RC 4.00 10.00
110 Marshawn Lynch RC 2.50 6.00
111 Brandon Jackson RC 1.25 3.00
112 DeShawn Wynn RC 1.25 3.00
113 Tony Hunt RC 1.25 3.00
114 Dwayne Bowe RC 1.25 3.00
115 James Jones RC 1.25 3.00
116 Calvin Johnson RC 4.00 10.00
117 Sidney Rice RC 1.50 4.00
118 Laurent Robinson RC 2.00 5.00
119 Jacoby Jones RC 1.25 3.00
120 Greg Olsen RC 2.00 5.00
121 Steve Smith USC RC 1.25 3.00
122 Chris Davis RC 1.25 3.00
123 Ted Ginn Jr. RC 1.50 4.00
124 Dwayne Jarrett RC 1.50 4.00
125 Robert Meachem RC 1.50 4.00
126 Chris Henry RB RC 1.25 3.00
127 David Harris RC 1.25 3.00
128 Michael Bush RC 1.25 3.00
129 Yamon Figurs RC 1.25 3.00
130 Gaines Adams RC 1.50 4.00
131 Amobi Okoye RC 1.50 4.00
132 Patrick Willis RC 2.00 5.00
133 Paul Posluszny RC 1.25 3.00
134 LaMarr Woodley RC 2.50 6.00
135 LaRon Landry RC 2.00 5.00
136 Selvin Young RC 1.25 3.00
137 Brian Leonard RC 1.25 3.00
138 Scott Chandler RC 2.00 5.00
139 Anthony Gonzalez RC 1.25 3.00
140 Courtney Taylor RC 1.25 3.00
141 Mike Walker RC 2.00 5.00
142 Thomas Clayton RC 1.50 4.00
143 Ryne Robinson RC 1.50 4.00
144 Johnnie Lee Higgins RC 1.25 3.00
145 Lorenzo Booker RC 1.50 4.00
146 Craig Buster Davis RC 1.25 3.00
147 Antonio Pittman RC 1.25 3.00
148 Kolby Smith RC 1.25 3.00
149 Joe Thomas RC 2.00 5.00
150 Garrett Wolfe RC 1.25 3.00

2007 Topps Performance Bronze

*VETS/99: 1.5X TO 4X BASIC CARDS
*ROOKIES/199: .5X TO 1.2X BASIC CARDS
BRONZE STATED ODDS 1:2
1-100 BRONZE PRINT RUN 99 SER.#'d SETS
101-150 BRONZE PRINT RUN 199 SER.#'d SETS

2007 Topps Performance Gold

1-100 VETERAN/10 ODDS 1:20
101-150 ROOKIE/10 ODDS 1:39
UNPRICED GOLD PRINT RUN 10

2007 Topps Performance Silver

*VETS/50: 2.5X TO 6X BASIC CARDS
*ROOKIES/50: 1X TO 2.5X BASIC CARDS
1-100 VETERAN/50 ODDS 1:4
101-150 ROOKIE/50 ODDS 1:8
SILVER PRINT RUN 50 SER.#'d SETS

2007 Topps Performance Breakout Autographs

GROUP A ODDS 1:66
GROUP B ODDS 1:28
GROUP C ODDS 1:20
GROUP D ODDS 1:70
GROUP E ODDS 1:65
GROUP F ODDS 1:25
GROUP G ODDS 1:30
GROUP H ODDS 1:9
*BRONZE/50: .4X TO 1X BASE GROUP A-B
*BRONZE/50: .5X TO 1.2X BASE GROUP C-H
BRONZE/50 ODDS 1:16
*SILVER/25: .5X TO 1.2X BASE GROUP A-B
*SILVER/25: .6X TO 1.5X BASE GROUP C-H
SILVER/25 ODDS 1:33
UNPRICED GOLD/5 ODDS 1:155
BAAO Amobi Okoye C 3.00 8.00
BABJ Brandon Jackson E 2.50 6.00
BACW Cadillac Williams A 8.00 20.00
BADH David Harris B 3.00 8.00
BADS Drew Stanton B 3.00 8.00
BADW DeShawn Wynn H 2.50 6.00
BADWI DeAngelo Williams A 6.00 15.00
BAGJ Greg Jennings D 5.00 12.00
BAGO Greg Olsen C 4.00 10.00
BAJB John Beck C 2.50 6.00
BAJJO James Jones H 2.50 6.00
BAKK Kevin Kolb B 4.00 10.00
BALR Laurent Robinson F 4.00 10.00
BAMD Maurice Jones-Drew G 5.00 12.00
BAML Marshawn Lynch B 6.00 15.00
BAPW Patrick Willis C 10.00 25.00
BARW Roy Williams WR A 6.00 15.00
BASH Santonio Holmes A 6.00 15.00
BASJ Steven Jackson A 6.00 15.00
BASS Steve Smith USC F 2.50 6.00
BATE Trent Edwards C 2.50 6.00
BATG Ted Ginn Jr. B 8.00 20.00
BATH Tony Hunt B 3.00 8.00
BATR Tony Romo A 30.00 80.00
BAYF Yamon Figurs B 3.00 8.00

2007 Topps Performance Breakout Relics

BREAKOUT RELIC/50 ODDS 1:16
*BRONZE/25: .6X TO 1.5X BASIC JSY/50
BRONZE RELIC/25 ODDS 1:33
UNPRICED SILVER/10 ODDS 1:86
UNPRICED GOLD/5 ODDS 1:154
BADH David Harris 2.00 5.00
BRAO Amobi Okoye 2.50 6.00
BRBJ Brandon Jackson 2.00 5.00
BRCW Cadillac Williams 4.00 10.00
BRDS Drew Stanton 2.00 5.00
BRDW DeShawn Wynn 2.00 5.00
BRDWI DeAngelo Williams 3.00 8.00
BRGJ Greg Jennings 3.00 8.00
BRGO Greg Olsen 3.00 8.00
BRJB John Beck 2.00 5.00
BRJJO James Jones 2.00 5.00
BRKK Kevin Kolb 2.50 6.00
BRLR Laurent Robinson 3.00 8.00
BRMD Maurice Jones-Drew 3.00 8.00
BRML Marshawn Lynch 4.00 10.00
BRPW Patrick Willis 3.00 8.00
BRRW Roy Williams WR 3.00 8.00
BRSH Santonio Holmes 3.00 8.00
BRSJ Steven Jackson 3.00 8.00
BRSS Steve Smith USC 2.00 5.00
BRTE Trent Edwards 2.00 5.00
BRTG Ted Ginn Jr. 2.50 6.00
BRTH Tony Hunt 2.00 5.00
BRTR Tony Romo 15.00 40.00
BRYF Yamon Figurs 2.00 5.00

2007 Topps Performance Hall of Fame Autographed Relics

HOF RELIC AU/20 ODDS 1:102
UNPRICED DUAL RELIC AU/10 ODDS 1:194
UNPRICED QUAD RELIC AU/10 ODDS 1:387
HFARDM Dan Marino 100.00 200.00
HFARED Eric Dickerson 25.00 60.00
HFARFH Franco Harris 25.00 60.00
HFARJE John Elway 75.00 150.00
HFARJK Jim Kelly 60.00 120.00
HFARJM Joe Montana 100.00 200.00
HFARMA Marcus Allen 25.00 60.00
HFARSY Steve Young 50.00 100.00
HFARTA Troy Aikman 60.00 120.00
HFARTD Tony Dorsett 40.00 80.00

2007 Topps Performance Hall of Fame Autographed Relics Dual

UNPRICED DUAL RELIC AU/10 ODDS 1:194

2007 Topps Performance Hall of Fame Autographed Relics Quad

UNPRICED QUAD RELIC AU/10 ODDS 1:387

2007 Topps Performance Hall of Fame Autographs

HOF AUTO/20 ODDS 1:68
UNPRICED AUTO CUT/1 ODDS 1:1935
HFABS Barry Sanders 60.00 120.00
HFADM Dan Marino 100.00 200.00
HFAED Eric Dickerson 40.00 80.00
HFAFH Franco Harris 40.00 80.00
HFAGS Gale Sayers 50.00 100.00
HFAJB Jim Brown 60.00 120.00
HFAJE John Elway 75.00 150.00
HFAJM Joe Montana 75.00 150.00
HFAJN Joe Namath 60.00 120.00
HFAMA Marcus Allen 40.00 80.00
HFAPH Paul Hornung 30.00 60.00
HFARS Roger Staubach 60.00 120.00
HFATA Troy Aikman 60.00 120.00
HFATB Terry Bradshaw 60.00 120.00
HFATD Tony Dorsett 40.00 80.00

2007 Topps Performance Hall of Fame Autographs Dual

UNPRICED DUAL AU/10 ODDS 1:215

2007 Topps Performance Hall of Fame Cuts

UNPRICED AUTO CUT/1 ODDS 1:1935

2007 Topps Performance Rookie Autographed NFL Logos

UNPRICED NFL LOGO/1 ODDS 1:968

2007 Topps Performance Rookie Autographed NFL Logos Dual

UNPRICED NFL LOGO DUAL/1 ODDS 1:1935

2007 Topps Performance Rookie Autographed Relics

GROUP A ODDS 1:450
GROUP B ODDS 1:7
GROUP C ODDS 1:14
GROUP D/E ODDS 1:6
GROUP F ODDS 1:13
GROUP G ODDS 1:5
*BRONZE/50: .5X TO 1.2X AU JSY GRP B-H
*BRONZE/25: .6X TO 1.5X AU JSY GRP B
*BRONZE/15: .5X TO 1.2X AU JSY GRP A
BRONZE GRP A/15 ODDS 1:691
BRONZE GROUP B/50 ODDS 1:101
BRONZE GROUP C/50 ODDS 1:17
*SILVER/25: .6X TO 1.5X AU JSY GRP B-H
UNPRICED SLVR GRP A/15 ODDS 1:1076
UNPRICED SLVR GRP B/15 ODDS 1:173
SILVER GRP C/25 ODDS 1:34
UNPRICED GOLD/5 ODDS 1:114
UNPRICED PRINT PLATE/1 ODDS 1:138
UNPRICED NFL LOGO/1 ODDS 1:968
UNPRICED NFL LOGO DUAL/1 ODDS 1:1935
101 Trent Edwards D 4.00 10.00
102 Kevin Kolb B 5.00 12.00
103 JaMarcus Russell A 8.00 20.00
104 Brady Quinn B 4.00 10.00
105 John Beck D 4.00 10.00
106 Drew Stanton B 4.00 10.00
107 Troy Smith B 4.00 10.00
108 Chris Leak C 4.00 10.00
109 Adrian Peterson A 125.00 250.00
110 Marshawn Lynch B 8.00 20.00
111 Brandon Jackson B 4.00 10.00
112 DeShawn Wynn F 4.00 10.00
113 Tony Hunt B 4.00 10.00
114 Dwayne Bowe B 4.00 10.00
115 James Jones G 4.00 10.00
117 Sidney Rice B 6.00 15.00
118 Laurent Robinson D 6.00 15.00
119 Jacoby Jones B 4.00 10.00
120 Greg Olsen B 6.00 15.00
121 Steve Smith USC C 4.00 10.00
122 Chris Davis E 4.00 10.00
123 Ted Ginn Jr. B 5.00 12.00
124 Dwayne Jarrett B 5.00 12.00
125 Robert Meachem B 5.00 12.00
126 Chris Henry E 4.00 10.00
127 David Harris G 4.00 10.00
128 Michael Bush B 4.00 10.00
129 Yamon Figurs E 4.00 10.00
130 Gaines Adams B 5.00 12.00
131 Amobi Okoye D 5.00 12.00
132 Patrick Willis C 6.00 15.00
133 Paul Posluszny C 4.00 10.00
134 LaMarr Woodley D 8.00 20.00
135 LaRon Landry B 6.00 15.00

2007 Topps Performance Rookie Autographs

GROUP A ODDS 1:370
GROUP B ODDS 1:40
GROUP C ODDS 1:10
GROUP D ODDS 1:12
GROUP E ODDS 1:5
GROUP F/G ODDS 1:3
GROUP H ODDS 1:6
A.PETERSON OVERALL ODDS 1:78
101 Trent Edwards D 3.00 8.00
102 Kevin Kolb C 4.00 10.00
103 JaMarcus Russell A 20.00 50.00
104 Brady Quinn C 3.00 8.00
105 John Beck E 3.00 8.00
106 Drew Stanton D 3.00 8.00
107 Troy Smith B 4.00 10.00
108 Chris Leak C 3.00 8.00
109A Adrian Peterson/169 60.00 120.00
109B Adrian Peterson ROY/169 60.00 120.00
110 Marshawn Lynch C 20.00 50.00
111 Brandon Jackson C 3.00 8.00
112 DeShawn Wynn E 3.00 8.00
113 Tony Hunt B 4.00 10.00
114 Dwayne Bowe C 3.00 8.00
115 James Jones H 3.00 8.00
116 Calvin Johnson A 50.00 100.00
117 Sidney Rice B 5.00 12.00
118 Laurent Robinson F 5.00 12.00
119 Jacoby Jones E 3.00 8.00
120 Greg Olsen C 5.00 12.00
121 Steve Smith USC G 3.00 8.00
122 Chris Davis F 3.00 8.00
123 Ted Ginn Jr. B 5.00 12.00
124 Dwayne Jarrett C 4.00 10.00
125 Robert Meachem B 5.00 12.00
126 Chris Henry F 3.00 8.00
127 David Harris F 3.00 8.00
128 Michael Bush D 3.00 8.00
129 Yamon Figurs F 3.00 8.00
130 Gaines Adams D 4.00 10.00
131 Amobi Okoye E 4.00 10.00
132 Patrick Willis E 5.00 12.00
133 Paul Posluszny G 3.00 8.00
134 LaMarr Woodley E 6.00 15.00
135 LaRon Landry G 5.00 12.00

2007 Topps Performance Rookie Autographs Bronze

*BRONZE/50: .5X TO 1.2X BASIC AUTO
*BRONZE/25: .5X TO 1.2X BASE GRP A-B
*BRONZE/25: .6X TO 1.5X BASE GRP C-H
GROUP A/15 ODDS 1:692
GROUP B/25 ODDS 1:100
GROUP C/50 ODDS 1:17
A.PETERSON BRONZE OVERALL ODDS 1:197
BRONZE PRINT RUN 15-99
109A Adrian Peterson/99 60.00 120.00
109B Adrian Peterson ROY/99 60.00 120.00
110 Marshawn Lynch/50 30.00 60.00

2007 Topps Performance Rookie Autographs Gold

UNPRICED GOLD/5 ODDS 1:114
A.PETERSON GOLD OVERALL ODDS 1:807
GOLD STATED PRINT RUN 5-25
109A Adrian Peterson/25 125.00 250.00
109B Adrian Peterson ROY/25 125.00 250.00

2007 Topps Performance Rookie Autographs Red

A.PETERSON OVERALL RED ODDS 1:109
109A Adrian Peterson/135 60.00 120.00
109B Adrian Peterson ROY/135 60.00 120.00

2007 Topps Performance Rookie Autographs Silver

*SILVER/25: .6X TO 1.5X BASE GRP C-H
GROUP A/10 ODDS 1:1076
GROUP B/15 ODDS 1:173
GROUP C/25 ODDS 1:34
A.PETERSON SILVER OVERALL ODDS 1:262
SILVER PRINT RUN 10-75
104 Brady Quinn/25 5.00 12.00
109A Adrian Peterson/75 60.00 120.00
109B Adrian Peterson ROY/75 60.00 120.00
110 Marshawn Lynch/25 40.00 80.00

2007 Topps Performance Rookie Relics

ROOKIE RELIC/30 ODDS 1:20
*BRONZE/25: .4X TO 1X BASIC JSY/30
BRONZE/25 ODDS 1:23
UNPRICED SILVER/10 ODDS 1:62
UNPRICED GOLD/5 ODDS 1:110
101 Trent Edwards 2.00 5.00
102 Kevin Kolb 2.50 6.00
103 JaMarcus Russell 2.00 5.00
104 Brady Quinn 2.00 5.00
105 John Beck 2.00 5.00
106 Drew Stanton 2.00 5.00
107 Troy Smith 2.00 5.00
108 Chris Leak 2.00 5.00
109 Adrian Peterson 6.00 15.00
110 Marshawn Lynch 4.00 10.00
111 Brandon Jackson 2.00 5.00
112 DeShawn Wynn 2.00 5.00
113 Tony Hunt 2.00 5.00
114 Dwayne Bowe 2.00 5.00
115 James Jones 2.00 5.00
116 Calvin Johnson 6.00 15.00
117 Sidney Rice 2.50 6.00
118 Laurent Robinson 3.00 8.00
119 Jacoby Jones 2.00 5.00
120 Greg Olsen 3.00 8.00
121 Steve Smith USC 2.00 5.00
122 Chris Davis 2.00 5.00
123 Ted Ginn Jr. 2.50 6.00
124 Dwayne Jarrett 2.50 6.00
125 Robert Meachem 2.50 6.00
126 Chris Henry RB 2.00 5.00
127 David Harris 2.00 5.00
128 Michael Bush 2.00 5.00
129 Yamon Figurs 2.00 5.00
130 Gaines Adams 2.50 6.00
131 Amobi Okoye 2.50 6.00
132 Patrick Willis 3.00 8.00
133 Paul Posluszny 2.00 5.00
134 LaMarr Woodley 4.00 10.00
135 LaRon Landry 3.00 8.00

2007 Topps Performance Skill Sets Quarterbacks Triple Relics

SKILL SET QB/60 ODDS 1:22
*BRONZE/50: .4X TO 1X BASE JSY/60
BRONZE/50 ODDS 1:27
*SILVER/25: .5X TO 1.2X BASE JSY/60
SILVER/25 ODDS 1:54
UNPRICED RED/5 ODDS 1:258
UNPRICED GOLD/1 ODDS 1:1290
SSQBF Brett Favre 15.00 40.00
SSQBQ Brady Quinn 2.50 6.00
SSQBR Ben Roethlisberger 8.00 20.00
SSQDS Drew Stanton 2.50 6.00
SSQEM Eli Manning 6.00 15.00
SSQJB John Beck 2.50 6.00
SSQJE John Elway 15.00 40.00
SSQJR JaMarcus Russell 2.50 6.00
SSQKK Kevin Kolb 3.00 8.00
SSQML Matt Leinart 5.00 12.00
SSQTA Troy Aikman 12.00 30.00
SSQTE Trent Edwards 2.50 6.00
SSQTP Tom Brady 25.00 60.00
SSQTR Tony Romo 10.00 25.00
SSQTS Troy Smith 2.50 6.00

2007 Topps Performance Skill Sets Receivers Triple Relics

SKILL SET REC/60 ODDS 1:22
*BRONZE/50: .4X TO 1X BASE JSY/60
BRONZE/50 ODDS 1:27
*SILVER/25: .5X TO 1.2X BASE JSY/60
SILVER/25 ODDS 1:54
UNPRICED RED/5 ODDS 1:258
UNPRICED GOLD/1 ODDS 1:1290
SSWAG Anthony Gonzalez 2.50 6.00
SSWCJ Calvin Johnson 8.00 20.00
SSWDB Dwayne Bowe 2.50 6.00
SSWDJ Dwayne Jarrett 3.00 8.00
SSWJH Jason Hill 2.50 6.00
SSWJR Jerry Rice 20.00 50.00
SSWLF Larry Fitzgerald 6.00 15.00
SSWPW Paul Williams 2.50 6.00
SSWRM Randy Moss 6.00 15.00
SSWRM Robert Meachem 3.00 8.00
SSWSR Sidney Rice 3.00 8.00
SSWSS Steve Smith USC 2.50 6.00
SSWTB Tim Brown 10.00 25.00
SSWTG Ted Ginn Jr. 3.00 8.00
SSWYF Yamon Figurs 2.50 6.00

2007 Topps Performance Skill Sets Running Backs Triple Relics

SKILL SET RB/60 ODDS 1:22
*BRONZE/50: .4X TO 1X BASE JSY/60
BRONZE/50 ODDS 1:27
*SILVER/25: .5X TO 1.2X BASE JSY/60
SILVER/25 ODDS 1:54
UNPRICED RED/5 ODDS 1:258
UNPRICED GOLD/1 ODDS 1:1290
SSRAP Adrian Peterson 8.00 20.00
SSRBJ Brandon Jackson 2.50 6.00
SSRBL Brian Leonard 2.50 6.00
SSRDW DeAngelo Williams 5.00 *12.00
SSRES Emmitt Smith 15.00 40.00
SSRGW Garrett Wolfe 2.50 6.00
SSRJA Joseph Addai 5.00 12.00
SSRKI Kenny Irons 2.50 6.00
SSRLB Lorenzo Booker 3.00 8.00
SSRLM Laurence Maroney 6.00 15.00
SSRMB Michael Bush 2.50 6.00
SSRML Marshawn Lynch 5.00 12.00
SSRPH Paul Hornung 10.00 25.00
SSRSA Shaun Alexander 5.00 12.00
SSRAPI Antonio Pittman 2.50 6.00

2007 Topps Performance Triple Relic Signatures

UNPRICED TRIPLE RELIC/5 ODDS 1:387

2007 Topps Performance Triple Signatures

UNPRICED TRIPLE AU/5 ODDS 1:387
UNPRICED TRIP.RELIC AU/5 ODDS 1:387

2009 Topps Platinum

COMPLETE SET (165) 25.00 50.00
TWO ROOKIES PER HOBBY PACK
1 Drew Brees .25 .60
2 Kurt Warner .20 .50
3 Jay Cutler .15 .40
4 Aaron Rodgers .50 1.25
5 Philip Rivers .25 .60
6 Peyton Manning .60 1.50
7 Donovan McNabb .20 .50
8 Matt Cassel .15 .40
9 David Garrard .15 .40
10 Brett Favre 4.00 10.00
11 Tony Romo .20 .50
12 Matt Ryan .20 .50
13 Ben Roethlisberger .25 .60
14 Eli Manning .20 .50
15 Matt Schaub .15 .40
16 Joe Flacco .20 .50
17 Carson Palmer .20 .50
18 Tom Brady .75 2.00
19 Adrian Peterson .25 .60
20 Michael Turner .15 .40
21 DeAngelo Williams .15 .40
22 Clinton Portis .15 .40
23 Thomas Jones .15 .40
24 Steve Slaton .15 .40
25 Matt Forte .15 .40
26 Chris Johnson .15 .40
27 Ryan Grant .20 .50
28 LaDainian Tomlinson .25 .60
29 Brandon Jacobs .15 .40
30 Steven Jackson .15 .40
31 Marshawn Lynch .20 .50
32 Frank Gore .20 .50
33 Kevin Smith .15 .40
34 Brian Westbrook .15 .40
35 Ronnie Brown .15 .40
36 Marion Barber .20 .50
37 Jonathan Stewart .15 .40
38 Maurice Jones-Drew .15 .40
39 Willie Parker .15 .40
40 Darren McFadden .25 .60
41 Reggie Bush .15 .40
42 Joseph Addai .15 .40
43 LenDale White .15 .40
44 Felix Jones .15 .40
45 Ray Rice .15 .40
46 Fred Jackson .20 .50
47 Leon Washington .15 .40
48 Andre Johnson .20 .50
49 Larry Fitzgerald .20 .50
50 Steve Smith .20 .50
51 Roddy White .15 .40
52 Calvin Johnson .25 .60
53 Greg Jennings .15 .40
54 Brandon Marshall .20 .50
55 Antonio Bryant .15 .40
56 Wes Welker .20 .50
57 Reggie Wayne .20 .50
58 Marques Colston .15 .40
59 Terrell Owens .20 .50
60 Santana Moss .20 .50
61 Hines Ward .20 .50
62 Anquan Boldin .15 .40
63 Dwayne Bowe .20 .50
64 Roy Williams WR .15 .40
65 Donald Driver .20 .50
66 Randy Moss .20 .50
67 Eddie Royal .15 .40
68 DeSean Jackson .20 .50
69 T.J. Houshmandzadeh .15 .40
70 Jerricho Cotchery .15 .40
71 Santonio Holmes .15 .40
72 Chad Ochocinco .15 .40
73 Vincent Jackson .15 .40
74 Lee Evans .20 .50
75 Devin Hester .20 .50
76 Anthony Gonzalez .15 .40
77 Tony Gonzalez .20 .50
78 Jason Witten .20 .50
79 Dallas Clark .15 .40
80 Antonio Gates .20 .50
81 Chris Cooley .15 .40
82 Zach Miller .15 .40
83 Greg Olsen .20 .50
84 John Carlson .20 .50
85 Willis McGahee .15 .40
86 Fred Taylor .15 .40
87 John Abraham .15 .40
88 Jared Allen .15 .40
89 Julius Peppers .20 .50
90 Mario Williams .20 .50
91 Dwight Freeney .15 .40
92 DeMarcus Ware .20 .50
93 Joey Porter .20 .50
94 James Harrison .25 .60
95 LaMarr Woodley .15 .40
96 Patrick Willis .20 .50
97 Brian Urlacher .25 .60
98 Terrell Suggs .15 .40
99 Jerod Mayo .20 .50
100 Ray Lewis .25 .60
101 Charles Woodson .25 .60
102 Darrelle Revis .15 .40
103 Antoine Winfield .15 .40
104 Asante Samuel .15 .40
105 Chris Johnson CB .15 .40
106 Nnamdi Asomugha .15 .40
107 Champ Bailey .20 .50
108 Ed Reed .20 .50
109 Troy Polamalu .25 .60
110 Adrian Wilson .15 .40
111 Andre Brown RC .75 2.00
112 Aaron Curry RC 1.00 2.50
113 Brandon Pettigrew RC .60 1.50
114 Brian Robiskie RC .60 1.50
115 Chris Wells RC .60 1.50
116 Deon Butler RC .60 1.50
117 Donald Brown RC .60 1.50
118 Darrius Heyward-Bey RC 1.00 2.50
119 Derrick Williams RC .60 1.50
120 Glen Coffee RC .60 1.50
121 Hakeem Nicks RC .75 2.00
122 Josh Freeman RC .60 1.50
123 Juaquin Iglesias RC .60 1.60
124 Jeremy Maclin RC .75 2.00
125 Matthew Stafford RC 3.00 8.00
126 Javon Ringer RC .60 1.50
127 Jason Smith RC .60 1.50
128 Kenny Britt RC 1.00 2.50
129 Knowshon Moreno RC .60 1.50
130 LeSean McCoy RC 1.50 4.00
131 Michael Crabtree RC 1.00 2.50
132 Mohamed Massaquoi RC .60 1.50
133 Mark Sanchez RC .60 1.50
134 Mike Thomas RC .60 1.50
135 Mike Wallace RC 1.00 2.50
136 Nate Davis RC .60 1.50
137 Percy Harvin RC .60 1.50
138 Patrick Turner RC .60 1.50
139 Pat White RC .75 2.00
140 Ramses Barden RC .60 1.50
141 Rhett Bomar RC .60 1.50
142 Shonn Greene RC .60 1.50
143 Stephen McGee RC .60 1.50
144 Tyson Jackson RC .60 1.50
145 Chase Coffman RC .60 1.50
146 Tom Brandstater RC .75 2.00
147 Brian Orakpo RC .75 2.00
148 Malcolm Jenkins RC .60 1.50
149 Brian Cushing RC .60 1.50
150 Brian Hartline RC 1.00 2.50
151 Mike Goodson RC .75 2.00
152 Shawn Nelson RC .60 1.50
153 Austin Collie RC .60 1.50
154 Louis Murphy RC .60 1.50
155 Johnny Knox RC .75 2.00
156 Rashad Jennings RC .75 2.00
157 Jarett Dillard RC .60 1.50
158 Quan Cosby RC .60 1.50
159 Julian Edelman RC 3.00 8.00
160 James Laurinaitis RC .60 1.50
161 Gartrell Johnson RC .60 1.50
162 Brandon Gibson RC .75 2.00
163 James Davis RC .60 1.50
164 Rey Maualuga RC 1.00 2.50
165 Sammie Stroughter RC .60 1.50

2009 Topps Platinum Rookie Blue Refractors

*ROOKIES: 1.2X TO 3X BASIC CARDS
BLUE REFRACTOR/99 ODDS 1:76 HOB

2009 Topps Platinum Rookie Platinum Refractors 1549

*ROOKIES: .6X TO 1.5X BASIC CARDS
PLATINUM REF/1549 ODDS 1:5 HOB

2009 Topps Platinum Rookie Platinum Refractors 99

*ROOKIES: 1.2X TO 3X BASIC CARDS
PLATINUM REF/99 ODDS 1:40 HOB

2009 Topps Platinum Rookie Red Refractors

*ROOKIES: 3X TO 8X BASIC CARDS
RED REFRACTOR/25 ODDS 1:300 HOB
125 Matthew Stafford 60.00 120.00
133 Mark Sanchez 30.00 80.00

2009 Topps Platinum Rookie Refractors

*ROOKIES: .8X TO 2X BASIC CARDS
REFRACTOR/999 ODDS 1:8 HOB

2009 Topps Platinum Rookie White Refractors

*ROOKIES: 1X TO 2.5X BASIC CARDS
WHITE REFRACT/499 ODDS 1:15 HOB

2009 Topps Platinum Autographed Patches

STATED PRINT RUN 8-550
ARPAB Andre Brown/200 5.00 12.00
ARPAC Aaron Curry/450 6.00 15.00
ARPAP Adrian Peterson/90 90.00 150.00
ARPBM Brandon Marshall/150 10.00 25.00
ARPBP Brandon Pettigrew/150 8.00 20.00
ARPBR Brian Robiskie/300 4.00 10.00
ARPBW Chris Wells/450 12.00 30.00
ARPDB Deon Butler/150 4.00 10.00
ARPDBO Dwayne Bowe/150 8.00 20.00
ARPDBR Donald Brown/150 4.00 10.00
ARPDHB Darrius Heyward-Bey/110 6.00 15.00
ARPDM Dan Marino/110 75.00 135.00
ARPDW Derrick Williams/150 4.00 10.00
ARPGC Glen Coffee/150 4.00 10.00
ARPHN Hakeem Nicks/200 5.00 12.00
ARPJA Joseph Addai/110 12.00 30.00
ARPJF Josh Freeman/150 4.00 10.00
ARPJI Juaquin Iglesias/350 4.00 10.00
ARPJM Jeremy Maclin/150 5.00 12.00
ARPJR Javon Ringer/150 4.00 10.00
ARPJS Jason Smith/550 4.00 10.00
ARPKB Kenny Britt/200 6.00 15.00
ARPKM Knowshon Moreno/25 8.00 20.00
ARPLE Lee Evans/150 8.00 20.00
ARPLM LeSean McCoy/350 30.00 80.00
ARPMC Michael Crabtree/40 20.00 50.00
ARPMS Matt Stafford/8
ARPMSA Mark Sanchez/110 20.00 50.00
ARPMT Mike Thomas/150 4.00 10.00
ARPMW Mike Wallace/150 6.00 15.00
ARPPH Percy Harvin/300 8.00 20.00
ARPPT Patrick Turner/450 6.00 15.00
ARPPW Pat White/110 5.00 12.00
ARPRM Rashard Mendenhall/350 12.00 30.00
ARPRR Ray Rice/350 12.00 30.00
ARPSG Shonn Greene/150 4.00 10.00
ARPSS Steve Smith/350 10.00 25.00
ARPSSL Steve Slaton/150 6.00 15.00
ARPTJ Tyson Jackson/550 4.00 10.00

2009 Topps Platinum Autographed Patches Black Refractors

BLACK REF/25 ODDS 1:240 HOB
*RED REF/10: .5X TO 1.2X BLK REF/25
ARPAB Andre Brown 8.00 20.00
ARPAC Aaron Curry 10.00 25.00
ARPAP Adrian Peterson
ARPBM Brandon Marshall 12.00 30.00
ARPBP Brandon Pettigrew 6.00 15.00
ARPBR Brian Robiskie 6.00 15.00
ARPBW Chris Wells 6.00 15.00
ARPDB Deon Butler 6.00 15.00
ARPDBO Dwayne Bowe 12.00 30.00
ARPDBR Donald Brown 6.00 15.00
ARPDHB Darrius Heyward-Bey 10.00 25.00
ARPDM Dan Marino 100.00 200.00
ARPDW Derrick Williams 6.00 15.00
ARPGC Glen Coffee 6.00 15.00
ARPHN Hakeem Nicks 8.00 20.00
ARPJA Joseph Addai 10.00 25.00
ARPJF Josh Freeman 6.00 15.00
ARPJI Juaquin Iglesias 6.00 15.00
ARPJM Jeremy Maclin 8.00 20.00
ARPJR Javon Ringer 6.00 15.00
ARPJS Jason Smith 6.00 15.00
ARPKB Kenny Britt 10.00 25.00
ARPKM Knowshon Moreno 6.00 15.00
ARPLE Lee Evans 12.00 30.00
ARPLM LeSean McCoy 40.00 100.00
ARPMC Michael Crabtree 40.00 100.00
ARPMSA Mark Sanchez 40.00 100.00
ARPMT Mike Thomas 6.00 15.00
ARPMW Mike Wallace 10.00 25.00
ARPPH Percy Harvin 12.00 30.00
ARPPT Patrick Turner 6.00 15.00
ARPPW Pat White 8.00 20.00
ARPRM Rashard Mendenhall 10.00 25.00
ARPRR Ray Rice 20.00 50.00

ARPSG Shonn Greene 6.00 15.00
ARPSS Steve Smith 12.00 30.00
ARPSSL Steve Slaton 10.00 25.00
ARPTJ Tyson Jackson 6.00 15.00

2009 Topps Platinum Rookie Autographs

AUTO PRINT RUN 90-1550
111 Andre Brown/850 4.00 10.00
112 Aaron Curry/350 6.00 15.00
113 Brandon Pettigrew/100 4.00 10.00
114 Brian Robiskie/150 4.00 10.00
115 Chris Wells/50 6.00 15.00
116 Deon Butler/100 4.00 10.00
117 Donald Brown/90 5.00 12.00
118 Darrius Heyward-Bey/150 6.00 15.00
119 Derrick Williams/350 4.00 10.00
120 Glen Coffee/550 3.00 8.00
121 Hakeem Nicks/450 5.00 12.00
122 Josh Freeman/150 4.00 10.00
123 Juaquin Iglesias/550 3.00 8.00
124 Jeremy Maclin/150 5.00 12.00
126 Javon Ringer/1500 3.00 8.00
127 Jason Smith/650 3.00 8.00
128 Kenny Britt/150 6.00 15.00
130 LeSean McCoy/350 12.00 30.00
131 Michael Crabtree/50 20.00 50.00
133 Mark Sanchez/50 50.00 120.00
134 Mike Thomas/100 4.00 10.00
135 Mike Wallace/100 6.00 15.00
136 Nate Davis/650 3.00 8.00
137 Percy Harvin/850 3.00 8.00
138 Patrick Turner/450 4.00 10.00
139 Pat White/100 5.00 12.00
140 Ramses Barden/850 3.00 8.00
141 Rhett Bomar/850 3.00 8.00
142 Shonn Greene/550 3.00 8.00
143 Stephen McGee/450 4.00 10.00
144 Tyson Jackson/100 4.00 10.00
146 Tom Brandstater/450 5.00 12.00
148 Malcolm Jenkins/850 3.00 8.00
149 Brian Cushing/1550 6.00 15.00
152 Shawn Nelson/550 3.00 8.00
153 Austin Collie/450 4.00 10.00
155 Johnny Knox/1550 4.00 10.00
156 Rashad Jennings/1050 4.00 10.00
157 Jarett Dillard/1050 3.00 8.00
158 Quan Cosby/850 3.00 8.00
160 James Laurinaitis/850 3.00 8.00
162 Brandon Gibson/1050 4.00 10.00
163 James Davis/1050 3.00 8.00
164 Rey Maualuga/850 5.00 12.00

2009 Topps Platinum Rookie Autographs Black Refractors

BLACK REF AU/25 ODDS 1:270 HOB
*RED REF/10: .5X TO 1.2X BLACK REF/25
RED REFRACT/10 ODDS 1:535 HOB
111 Andre Brown 8.00 20.00
112 Aaron Curry 10.00 25.00
113 Brandon Pettigrew 6.00 15.00
114 Brian Robiskie 6.00 15.00
115 Chris Wells 6.00 15.00
116 Deon Butler 6.00 15.00
117 Donald Brown 6.00 15.00
118 Darrius Heyward-Bey 10.00 25.00
119 Derrick Williams 6.00 15.00
120 Glen Coffee 6.00 15.00
121 Hakeem Nicks 8.00 20.00
122 Josh Freeman 6.00 15.00
123 Juaquin Iglesias 6.00 15.00
124 Jeremy Maclin 8.00 20.00
126 Javon Ringer 6.00 15.00
127 Jason Smith 6.00 15.00
128 Kenny Britt 10.00 25.00
130 LeSean McCoy 20.00 50.00
131 Michael Crabtree 30.00 80.00
133 Mark Sanchez 75.00 200.00
134 Mike Thomas 6.00 15.00
135 Mike Wallace 10.00 25.00
136 Nate Davis 6.00 15.00
137 Percy Harvin 6.00 15.00
138 Patrick Turner 6.00 15.00
139 Pat White 8.00 20.00
140 Ramses Barden 6.00 15.00
141 Rhett Bomar 6.00 15.00
142 Shonn Greene 6.00 15.00
143 Stephen McGee 6.00 15.00
144 Tyson Jackson 6.00 15.00
146 Tom Brandstater 8.00 20.00
148 Malcolm Jenkins 6.00 15.00
149 Brian Cushing 12.00 30.00
152 Shawn Nelson 6.00 15.00
153 Austin Collie 6.00 15.00
155 Johnny Knox 8.00 20.00
156 Rashad Jennings 8.00 20.00
157 Jarett Dillard 6.00 15.00
158 Quan Cosby 6.00 15.00
160 James Laurinaitis 6.00 15.00
162 Brandon Gibson 8.00 20.00
163 James Davis 6.00 15.00
164 Rey Maualuga 10.00 25.00

2010 Topps Platinum Rookie Blue Refractors

*ROOKIES: 1.5X TO 4X BASIC CARDS
BLUE REF/99 ODDS 1:175 HOB

2010 Topps Platinum Rookie Platinum Black Refractors

*ROOKIES: 3X TO 8X BASIC CARDS
BLACK REFRACTOR/25 ODDS 1:765 HOB

2010 Topps Platinum Rookie Platinum Refractors

*ROOKIES: .6X TO 1.5X BASIC CARDS
PLATINUM REFRACTOR ODDS 1:6 HOB

2010 Topps Platinum Rookie Red Refractors

*ROOKIES: 3X TO 8X BASIC CARDS
RED REFRACTOR/25 ODDS 1:740 HOB

2010 Topps Platinum Rookie Refractors

*ROOKIES: .8X TO 2X BASIC CARDS
REFRACTOR/999 ODDS 1:116

2010 Topps Platinum Rookie White Refractors

*ROOKIES: 1X TO 2.5X BASIC CARDS
WHITE REFRACTOR/499 ODDS 1:34 HOB

2010 Topps Platinum Autographed Patch Duals

DUAL AU PATCH/25 ODDS 1:3340 HOB
BMC E.Berry/D.McCluster 25.00 00.00
BT J.Best/B.Tate 25.00 60.00
ET J.Elway/T.Tebow 150.00 300.00
HM M.Hardesty/J.McKnight 20.00 50.00
JR F.Jones/R.Rice 20.00 50.00
MC D.McCluster/J.Charles 25.00 60.00
PG A.Peterson/T.Gerhart 125.00 200.00
SM C.Spiller/R.Mathews 50.00 120.00
TB D.Thomas/D.Bryant 75.00 125.00
WM P.Willis/R.McClain 25.00 60.00

2010 Topps Platinum Autographed Patches

VETERAN PRINT RUN 120-300
ROOKIE PRINT RUN 200-800
EXCH EXPIRATION: 8/31/2013
*BLACK REF/99: .5X TO 1.2X VET/120-300
*BLACK REF/99: .8X TO 2X ROOKIE/500-800
*BLACK REF/99: .5X TO 1.2X ROOKIE/200-300
AB Arrelious Benn/800 5.00 12.00
AE Armanti Edwards/800 6.00 15.00
AG Anthony Gonzalez/140 8.00 20.00
AR Andre Roberts/800 6.00 15.00
BJ Brandon Jacobs/160 8.00 20.00
BL Brandon LaFell/500 8.00 20.00
BT Ben Tate/800 6.00 15.00
CH Chad Henne/120 10.00 25.00
CJS C.J. Spiller/200 8.00 20.00
CM Colt McCoy/200 6.00 15.00
CW Cadillac Williams/160 8.00 20.00
DB Dez Bryant/300 25.00 50.00
DBO Dwayne Bowe/160 10.00 25.00
DJ DeSean Jackson/180 8.00 20.00
DM Dexter McCluster/800 6.00 15.00
DM Darren McFadden/130 8.00 20.00
DT Demaryius Thomas/200 25.00 60.00
DW Damian Williams/500 5.00 12.00
EB Eric Berry/500 8.00 20.00
ED Eric Decker/800 6.00 15.00
ES Emmanuel Sanders/500 8.00 20.00
GM Gerald McCoy/500 5.00 12.00
GT Golden Tate/500 6.00 15.00
JA Joseph Addai/160 8.00 20.00
JB Jahvid Best/200 8.00 20.00
JC Jimmy Clausen/200 8.00 20.00
JD Jonathan Dwyer/500 5.00 12.00
JFR Josh Freeman/140 8.00 20.00
JG Jermaine Gresham/800 5.00 12.00
JM Joe McKnight EXCH 6.00 20.00
JMA Jerod Mayo/120 10.00 25.00
JS Jordan Shipley/500 5.00 12.00
KK Kevin Kolb/200 8.00 20.00
MC Marques Colston/200 8.00 20.00
ME Marcus Easley/800 5.00 12.00
MG Mardy Gilyard/800 5.00 12.00
MH Montario Hardesty/500 5.00 12.00
MK Mike Kafka/800 6.00 15.00
ML Marshawn Lynch/140 10.00 25.00
MW Mike Williams/800 5.00 12.00
MWI Mario Williams/120 10.00 25.00
NS Ndamukong Suh/500 12.00 30.00
PW Patrick Willis/300 12.00 30.00
RG Rob Gronkowski/800 50.00 100.00
RM Rolando McClain/500 5.00 12.00
RMA Ryan Mathews/200 8.00 20.00
SB Sam Bradford/200 20.00 50.00
TG Toby Gerhart/500 15.00 40.00
TP Taylor Price/800 5.00 12.00
TT Tim Tebow/300 20.00 50.00

2010 Topps Platinum Rookie Autographs

STATED PRINT RUN 400-1225
EXCH EXPIRATION: 8/31/2013
*BLACK REF/99: .8X TO 2X AUTO/900-1225
*BLACK REF/99: .6X TO 1.5X AUTO/400
*BLUE REF/599: .5X TO 1.2X AUTO/900-1225
6 Derrick Morgan/1099 3.00 8.00
7 Jordan Shipley/999 3.00 8.00
8 James Starks/1099 4.00 10.00
11 Tony Pike/1225 3.00 8.00
16 Montario Hardesty/999 3.00 8.00
21 Sean Canfield/1099 3.00 8.00
23 Mike Williams/900 3.00 8.00
28 Toby Gerhart/999 3.00 8.00
29 Anthony Dixon/900 3.00 8.00
34 Andre Roberts/900 4.00 10.00
35 Zac Robinson/1099 4.00 10.00
36 Ryan Mathews/400 4.00 10.00
41 Armanti Edwards/900 4.00 10.00
51 Dan LeFevour/1225 3.00 8.00
54 Charles Scott/1099 3.00 8.00
59 Earl Thomas/1099 10.00 25.00
61 Carlton Mitchell/1099 3.00 8.00
64 Arrelious Benn/400 4.00 10.00
65 Dezmon Briscoe/1099 3.00 8.00
69 Aaron Hernandez/1099 6.00 15.00
72 Jonathan Dwyer/400 4.00 10.00
73 Jermaine Gresham/999 3.00 8.00
75 Emmanuel Sanders/900 5.00 12.00
78 Golden Tate/400 5.00 12.00
83 Brandon LaFell/900 5.00 12.00
87 Dexter McCluster/400 5.00 12.00
91 Eric Berry/400 10.00 25.00
95 David Reed/900 3.00 8.00
98 Rolando McClain/900 3.00 8.00
101 Demaryius Thomas/400 10.00 25.00
102 Joe Webb/1099 3.00 8.00
103 Jimmy Graham/999 10.00 25.00
107 Ndamukong Suh/400 15.00 40.00
109 Damian Williams/1099 3.00 8.00
112 Taylor Price/900 3.00 8.00
116 Riley Cooper/1099 3.00 8.00
122 Rob Gronkowski/999 40.00 80.00
125 Marcus Easley/900 3.00 8.00
126 Jonathan Crompton/999 3.00 8.00
128 Gerald McCoy/400 4.00 10.00
132 Mike Kafka/999 4.00 10.00
135 Mardy Gilyard/999 3.00 8.00
138 John Skelton/999 4.00 10.00
142 Jacoby Ford/1099 3.00 8.00
144 Joe McKnight/999 3.00 8.00
146 Ben Tate/400 4.00 10.00
147 Anthony McCoy/1099 3.00 8.00
151 Eric Decker/900 4.00 10.00
152 Dez Bryant/400 40.00 80.00
157 Jahvid Best/400 4.00 10.00

2010 Topps Platinum Rookie Autographs Dual

STATED PRINT RUN 25 SER.#'d SETS
EXCH EXPIRATION: 8/31/2013
BB S.Bradford/D.Bryant 75.00 150.00
BC S.Bradford/J.Clausen 30.00 60.00
BM J.Best/D.McCluster 15.00 40.00
CT J.Clausen/G.Tate 30.00 80.00
GM Gerhart/McKnight EXCH 25.00 50.00
MS R.Mathews/C.Spiller 30.00 80.00
TC T.Tebow/J.Clausen 75.00 150.00
TH B.Tate/M.Hardesty 20.00 40.00
BMC S.Bradford/C.McCoy 30.00 60.00
BW A.Benn/M.Williams 20.00 50.00

2011 Topps Platinum

1 Cam Newton RC 2.50 6.00
2 Bilal Powell RC .60 1.50
3 Troy Polamalu .25 .60
4 Reggie Wayne .20 .50
6 Marques Colston .15 .40
7 Julio Jones RC 1.50 4.00
8 Jamie Harper RC .50 1.25
9 Matthew Stafford .20 .50
10 Adrian Peterson .25 .60
11 Randall Cobb RC .75 2.00
12 Ryan Kerrigan RC .60 1.50
13 A.J. Green RC 1.25 3.00
14 Shane Vereen RC .60 1.50
15 Stevan Ridley RC .50 1.25
16 Jeremy Kerley RC .75 2.00
17 Miles Austin .15 .40
18 Matt Schaub .15 .40
19 Jon Baldwin RC .50 1.25
20 Ray Rice .15 .40
21 Alex Green RC .50 1.25
22 Michael Turner .15 .40
23 Mike Williams .20 .50
24 Beanie Wells .15 .40
25 Ryan Mathews .20 .50
26 Kellen Winslow .15 .40
27 Von Miller RC .75 2.00
28 Tandon Doss RC .50 1.25
29 Roddy White .15 .40
30 Chris Johnson .15 .40
31 Percy Harvin .15 .40
32 DeAngelo Williams .15 .40
33 Dallas Clark .15 .40
35 Jonathan Stewart .15 .40
36 Knowshon Moreno .15 .40
38 Nick Fairley RC .50 1.25
39 Lance Kendricks RC .50 1.25
40 Andre Johnson .20 .50
41 Ray Lewis .25 .60
42 Jahvid Best .15 .40
44 Daniel Thomas RC .50 1.25
45 Brandon Marshall .20 .50
46 Dez Bryant .25 .60
47 Sidney Rice .15 .40
48 Shonn Greene .15 .40
49 LaDainian Tomlinson .25 .60
50 Blaine Gabbert RC .50 1.25
51 Jimmy Smith RC .50 1.25
53 Steven Jackson .15 .40
54 Cedric Benson .15 .40
55 Brian Urlacher .25 .60
56 Tony Romo .20 .50
58 D.J. Williams RC .50 1.25
59 Colin Kaepernick RC .75 2.00
60 Arian Foster .15 .40
61 Chris Cooley .15 .40
62 Edmond Gates RC .50 1.25
63 Santana Moss .20 .50
64 Marcell Dareus RC .50 1.25
65 Frank Gore .20 .50
66 Aldon Smith RC .50 1.25
67 Champ Bailey .20 .50
68 Jay Cutler .15 .40
69 Santonio Holmes .15 .40
70 Tom Brady .60 1.50
71 Greg Jennings .15 .40
72 Pierre Thomas .15 .40
73 Prince Amukamara RC .50 1.25
74 Ben Roethlisberger .25 .60
75 Matt Ryan .20 .50
76 Antonio Gates .15 .40
77 Thomas Jones .15 .40
78 Jordan Todman RC .50 1.25
79 Felix Jones .15 .40
80 Michael Vick .20 .50
81 Philip Rivers .25 .60
82 Darren McFadden .15 .40
83 Sam Bradford .15 .40
84 Josh Freeman .20 .50
85 Brandon Pettigrew .15 .40
86 J.J. Watt RC 2.50 6.00
88 Joseph Addai .15 .40
89 Joe Flacco .20 .50
90 Larry Fitzgerald .20 .50
91 Delone Carter RC .50 1.25
92 Calvin Johnson .25 .60
93 Jeremy Maclin .15 .40
94 Mikel Leshoure RC .50 1.25
95 Kenny Britt .15 .40
96 Austin Pettis RC .50 1.25
97 Kyle Rudolph RC .50 1.25
98 Mike Wallace .15 .40
99 Cameron Jordan RC .60 1.50
100 Peyton Manning .50 1.25
101 Vincent Brown RC .50 1.25
102 Braylon Edwards .15 .40
103 Jermichael Finley .15 .40
104 Hakeem Nicks .15 .40
105 Jerrel Jernigan RC .50 1.25
106 Ryan Williams RC .50 1.25
107 Da'Quan Bowers RC .50 1.25
108 Vincent Jackson .15 .40
109 Christian Ponder RC .50 1.25
110 Jamaal Charles .20 .50
111 Taiwan Jones RC .50 1.25
112 Marshawn Lynch .20 .50
113 LeSean McCoy .25 .60
114 DeMarco Murray RC 1.00 2.50
115 Cecil Shorts RC .50 1.25
116 Titus Young RC .50 1.25
117 Patrick Willis .20 .50
118 Brandon Lloyd .15 .40
119 Torrey Smith RC .50 1.25
120 Mark Ingram RC .75 2.00
121 Dwayne Bowe .20 .50
123 Matt Forte .15 .40
125 Jake Locker RC .50 1.25
126 Zach Miller .15 .40
127 Rashard Mendenhall .15 .40
129 Eli Manning .20 .50
130 Drew Brees .25 .60
131 Fred Jackson .15 .40
132 Andy Dalton RC 1.00 2.50
133 Jason Witten .20 .50
134 Ricky Stanzi RC .50 1.25
135 Steve Johnson .15 .40
136 Ryan Mallett RC .50 1.25
137 Leonard Hankerson RC .50 1.25
138 Ahmad Bradshaw .15 .40
139 Kendall Hunter RC .50 1.25
140 Maurice Jones-Drew .15 .40
142 Wes Welker .20 .50
143 Michael Crabtree .15 .40
144 DeSean Jackson .20 .50
145 Peyton Hillis .15 .40
146 Matt Cassel .15 .40
147 Vernon Davis .15 .40
148 Greg Little RC .60 1.50
150 Aaron Rodgers .40 1.00

2011 Topps Platinum Blue Refractors

*BLUE REF/299: 1.2X TO 3X BASIC INSERTS
BLUE REF/299 ODDS 1:49 HOB

2011 Topps Platinum Gold

*VETS: 1X TO 2.5X BASIC CARDS
ONE VETERAN PER HOBBY PACK
*ROOKIES: 3X TO 8X BASIC CARDS
ROOKIE/50 ODDS 1:293 HOB
86 J.J. Watt/50 40.00 80.00

2011 Topps Platinum Green

*VETS: 2X TO 5X BASIC CARDS
VETERAN STATED ODDS 1:10 HOB
*ROOKIES: 1X TO 2.5X BASIC CARDS
ROOKIE/499 ODDS 1:29 HOB

2011 Topps Platinum Red

*VETS: 3X TO 8X BASIC CARDS
VETERAN STATED ODDS 1:20 HOB
*ROOKIES/25: 4X TO 10X BASIC CARDS
ROOKIE/25 ODDS 1:586 HOB
1 Cam Newton/25 60.00 120.00
86 J.J. Watt/25 40.00 100.00

2011 Topps Platinum Purple Refractors

*PURPLE REF/99: 2X TO 5X BASIC RC
PURPLE REF/99 ODDS 1:48 HOB

2011 Topps Platinum Xfractors

*ROOKIES: .8X TO 2X BASIC RC
STATED ODDS 1:4 HOB

2011 Topps Platinum Die Cuts

STATED ODDS 1:20 HOB
PDCAD Andy Dalton 2.00 5.00
PDCAF Arian Foster 1.50 4.00
PDCAG A.J. Green 2.50 6.00
PDCAJ Andre Johnson 2.00 5.00
PDCAP Adrian Peterson 2.50 6.00
PDCAR Aaron Rodgers 4.00 10.00
PDCBG Blaine Gabbert 1.00 2.50
PDCCJ Chris Johnson 1.50 4.00
PDCCJO Calvin Johnson 2.50 6.00
PDCCN Cam Newton 5.00 12.00
PDCJB Jon Baldwin 1.00 2.50
PDCJJ Julio Jones 3.00 8.00
PDCJL Jake Locker 1.00 2.50
PDCKR Kyle Rudolph 1.00 2.50
PDCLF Larry Fitzgerald 2.00 5.00
PDCMD Marcell Dareus 1.00 2.50
PDCML Mikel Leshoure 1.00 2.50
PDCMV Michael Vick 2.00 5.00
PDCPA Prince Amukamara 1.00 2.50
PDCPP Patrick Peterson 2.00 5.00
PDCRM Ryan Mallett 1.00 2.50
PDCRW Ryan Williams 1.00 2.50
PDCTB Tom Brady 6.00 15.00
PDCTP Troy Polamalu 2.50 6.00
PDCTS Torrey Smith 1.00 2.50

2011 Topps Platinum Patch Autographs

STATED PRINT RUN 30 SER.#'d SETS
*GOLD REF/10: .5X TO 1.2X PATCH AU/30
*PURPLE REF/25: .4X TO 1X PATCH AU/30
EXCH EXPIRATION: 8/31/2014
AVPAG Antonio Gates 15.00 40.00
AVPCB Champ Bailey 25.00 50.00
AVPDM Darren McFadden 25.00 50.00
AVPDR Darrelle Revis 12.00 30.00
AVPGJ Greg Jennings 12.00 30.00
AVPJM Jerod Mayo EXCH 12.00 30.00
AVPJMA Jeremy Maclin 12.00 30.00
AVPJW Jason Witten 25.00 50.00
AVPLM LeSean McCoy 20.00 50.00
AVPMJD Maurice Jones-Drew 12.00 30.00
AVPPM Peyton Manning
AVPPW Patrick Willis 15.00 40.00
AVPRL Ray Lewis 75.00 150.00
AVPSJ Steven Jackson
AVPSR Sidney Rice 12.00 30.00

2011 Topps Platinum Rookie Autographs

STATED PRINT RUN 250-2175
*GREEN REF/150: .6X TO 1.5X AU/1450-2175
*GREEN REF/150: .5X TO 1.2X AU/808-1050
*GREEN REF/150: .4X TO 1X AU/250
EXCH EXPIRATION: 8/31/2014
2 Bilal Powell/250 5.00 12.00
5 Darvin Adams/1725 2.50 6.00
8 Jamie Harper/250 4.00 10.00
12 Ryan Kerrigan/1450 5.00 12.00
15 Stevan Ridley/250 4.00 10.00
16 Jeremy Kerley/2175 4.00 10.00
21 Alex Green/250 4.00 10.00
28 Tandon Doss/1725 2.50 6.00
34 Derrick Locke/1000 4.00 10.00
37 Justin Houston/1450 3.00 8.00
39 Lance Kendricks/808 3.00 8.00
43 Niles Paul/1450 2.50 6.00
44 Daniel Thomas/250 4.00 10.00
51 Jimmy Smith/1450 2.50 6.00
52 Da'Rel Scott/1050 3.00 8.00
57 Virgil Green/1000 3.00 8.00
58 D.J. Williams/1000 3.00 8.00
62 Edmond Gates/1000 3.00 8.00
66 Aldon Smith/808 3.00 8.00
73 Prince Amukamara/2175 2.50 6.00
78 Jordan Todman/250 4.00 10.00
86 J.J. Watt/1550 30.00 60.00
87 Rob Housler/1050 3.00 8.00
91 Delone Carter/250 4.00 10.00
96 Austin Pettis/1000 3.00 8.00
97 Kyle Rudolph/250 4.00 10.00
99 Cameron Jordan/1550 3.00 8.00
101 Vincent Brown/1000 3.00 8.00
105 Jerrel Jernigan/250 4.00 10.00
107 Da'Quan Bowers/250 4.00 10.00
111 Taiwan Jones/2175 2.50 6.00
114 DeMarco Murray/250 25.00 60.00
115 Cecil Shorts/1000 3.00 8.00
122 John Clay/1550 4.00 10.00
124 Rahim Moore/1000 3.00 8.00
128 Dwayne Harris/1725 2.50 6.00
139 Kendall Hunter/1000 3.00 8.00
141 Terrence Toliver/1000 4.00 10.00
149 Darren Evans/1000 4.00 10.00

2011 Topps Platinum Rookie Autographs Blue Refractors

*BLUE REF/99: .8X TO 2X AU/1450-2175
*BLUE REF/99: .6X TO 1.5X AU/808-1050
*BLUE REF/99: .5X TO 1.2X AU/250
86 J.J. Watt 60.00 125.00

2011 Topps Platinum Rookie Autographs Dual

STATED PRINT RUN 25 SER.#'d SETS
AP P.Amukamara/N.Paul 25.00 50.00
BL J.Baldwin/D.Lewis
CG R.Cobb/A.Green 15.00 40.00
DM M.Dareus/V.Miller 25.00 50.00
DP A.Dalton/C.Ponder 15.00 40.00
FB N.Fairley/D.Bowers 8.00 20.00
GT E.Gates/D.Thomas
HT K.Hunter/Todman EXCH 10.00 25.00
JD J.Jones/M.Dareus 40.00 80.00
JG J.Jernigan/E.Gates 15.00 40.00
KG C.Kaepernick/V.Green 20.00 50.00
LW M.Leshoure/R.Williams 20.00 50.00
MA V.Miller/P.Amukamara 20.00 50.00
MK R.Mallett/C.Kaepernick 20.00 50.00
MT D.Murray/D.Thomas 30.00 80.00
NF C.Newton/N.Fairley 40.00 100.00
SH T.Smith/L.Hankerson 10.00 25.00
SS T.Smith/D.Scott 10.00 25.00
VR S.Vereen/J.Rodgers
YP T.Young/A.Pettis 12.00 30.00

2011 Topps Platinum Rookie Jumbo Patch

STATED PRINT RUN 36 SER.#'d SETS
PRPAD Andy Dalton 8.00 20.00
PRPAG Alex Green 4.00 10.00
PRPAJG A.J. Green 15.00 40.00
PRPAP Austin Pettis 4.00 10.00
PRPBG Blaine Gabbert 4.00 10.00
PRPBP Bilal Powell 5.00 12.00
PRPCK Colin Kaepernick 6.00 15.00
PRPCN Cam Newton 20.00 50.00
PRPCP Christian Ponder 4.00 10.00
PRPDC Delone Carter 4.00 10.00
PRPDM DeMarco Murray 8.00 20.00
PRPDT Daniel Thomas 4.00 10.00
PRPEG Edmond Gates 4.00 10.00
PRPGL Greg Little 5.00 12.00
PRPJB Jon Baldwin 4.00 10.00
PRPJH Jamie Harper 4.00 10.00
PRPJJ Julio Jones 15.00 40.00
PRPJJE Jerrel Jernigan 4.00 10.00
PRPJL Jake Locker 15.00 40.00
PRPJT Jordan Todman 4.00 10.00
PRPKH Kendall Hunter 4.00 10.00
PRPKR Kyle Rudolph 4.00 10.00
PRPLH Leonard Hankerson 4.00 10.00
PRPMD Marcell Dareus 4.00 10.00
PRPMI Mark Ingram 6.00 15.00
PRPML Mikel Leshoure 4.00 10.00
PRPRC Randall Cobb 6.00 15.00
PRPRM Ryan Mallett 4.00 10.00
PRPRW Ryan Williams 4.00 10.00
PRPSR Stevan Ridley 4.00 10.00
PRPSV Shane Vereen 5.00 12.00
PRPTJ Taiwan Jones 4.00 10.00
PRPTS Torrey Smith 4.00 10.00
PRPTY Titus Young 4.00 10.00
PRPVB Vincent Brown 4.00 10.00
PRPVM Von Miller 6.00 15.00

2011 Topps Platinum Rookie Patch Autographs

STATED PRINT RUN 150-475
2 Bilal Powell/356 5.00 12.00
8 Jamie Harper/475 4.00 10.00
11 Randall Cobb/150 8.00 20.00
15 Stevan Ridley/199 5.00 12.00
16 Shane Vereen/199 6.00 15.00
21 Alex Green/475 4.00 10.00
27 Von Miller/150 12.00 30.00
28 Tandon Doss/356 4.00 10.00
37 Greg Salas/356 4.00 10.00
43 Niles Paul/356 4.00 10.00
44 Daniel Thomas/199 5.00 12.00
51 Dion Lewis/356 5.00 12.00
62 Edmond Gates/475 4.00 10.00
64 Marcell Dareus/150 5.00 12.00
73 Prince Amukamara/475 4.00 10.00
78 Jordan Todman/475 4.00 10.00
86 Torrey Smith/150 5.00 12.00
91 Delone Carter/475 4.00 10.00
94 Mikel Leshoure/150 5.00 12.00
96 Austin Pettis/475 4.00 10.00
97 Kyle Rudolph/150 5.00 12.00
101 Vincent Brown/475 4.00 10.00
105 Jerrel Jernigan/199 5.00 12.00
111 Taiwan Jones/475 8.00 20.00
114 DeMarco Murray/199 10.00 25.00
115 Cecil Shorts/356 4.00 10.00
116 Titus Young/150 5.00 12.00
137 Leonard Hankerson/150 5.00 12.00
139 Kendall Hunter/475 4.00 10.00
148 Greg Little/150 6.00 15.00

2011 Topps Platinum Rookie Patch Autographs Blue Refractors

*BLUE AU/75: .6X TO 1.5X BASIC AU/356-475
*BLUE AU/75: .5X TO 1.2X BASIC AU/150-199
1 Cam Newton 100.00 200.00
106 Ryan Williams 30.00 60.00

2011 Topps Platinum Rookie Patch Autographs Green Refractors

*GREEN AU/125: .5X TO 1.2X BASIC AU/356-475
*GREEN AU/125: .4X TO 1X BASIC AU/150-199
1 Cam Newton 125.00 250.00

2011 Topps Platinum Rookie Patch Autographs Purple Refractors

*PURPLE AU/25: 1.2X TO 3X BASIC AU/356-475
*PURPLE AU/25: 1X TO 2.5X BASIC AU/150-199
1 Cam Newton 250.00 400.00
11 Randall Cobb 20.00 50.00
50 Blaine Gabbert 12.00 30.00
59 Colin Kaepernick 20.00 50.00
106 Ryan Williams 40.00 80.00
120 Mark Ingram 20.00 50.00
132 Andy Dalton 25.00 60.00
136 Ryan Mallett 12.00 30.00

2011 Topps Platinum Rookie Patch Autographs Dual

STATED PRINT RUN 25 SER.#'d SETS
AP P.Amukamara/N.Paul 25.00 60.00
BL J.Baldwin/D.Lewis 20.00 50.00
CG R.Cobb/A.Green 12.00 30.00
DM M.Dareus/V.Miller 25.00 60.00
DP A.Dalton/C.Ponder 25.00 60.00
FB N.Fairley/D.Bowers 8.00 20.00
GJ A.Green/J.Jones 75.00 150.00
GT E.Gates/D.Thomas 25.00 60.00
HT K.Hunter/J.Todman
JD J.Jones/M.Dareus 50.00 100.00
JH J.Jernigan/Hankerson 15.00 40.00
KH Kaepernick/K.Hunter 20.00 50.00
LW M.Leshoure/R.Williams 15.00 40.00
MK R.Mallett/Kaepernick 20.00 50.00
MT D.Murray/D.Thomas 20.00 50.00
NF C.Newton/N.Fairley 40.00 100.00
PT B.Powell/D.Thomas 20.00 50.00
VR S.Vereen/J.Rodgers 12.00 30.00
YL T.Young/Leshoure EXCH 25.00 60.00
YP T.Young/Pettis EXCH 25.00 60.00

2012 Topps Platinum

COMPLETE SET (150) 25.00 60.00
COMP.SET w/o RC's (100) 10.00 25.00
1 Calvin Johnson .25 .60
2 Brandon Marshall .20 .50
3 Matt Schaub .15 .40
4 Aaron Hernandez .20 .50
5 Antonio Gates .20 .50
6 Jason Witten .20 .50
7 Ryan Mathews .20 .50
8 Miles Austin .15 .40
9 Vernon Davis .15 .40
10 Cam Newton .25 .60
11 Michael Vick .20 .50
12 Julio Jones .25 .60
13 Chris Johnson .15 .40
14 Darren McFadden .15 .40
15 Tim Tebow .25 .60
16 Jamaal Charles .20 .50
17 Ben Roethlisberger .25 .60
18 Michael Turner .15 .40
19 Jermichael Finley .15 .40
20 Aaron Rodgers .40 1.00
21 Steven Jackson .15 .40
22 Tony Gonzalez .20 .50
23 Jared Allen .15 .40
24 Troy Polamalu .25 .60
25 Frank Gore .20 .50
26 Ndamukong Suh .20 .50
27 Carson Palmer .20 .50
28 Patrick Willis .20 .50
29 Adrian Peterson .25 .60
30 Matthew Stafford .20 .50
31 Brian Urlacher .25 .60
32 Marques Colston .15 .40
33 Clay Matthews .25 .60
34 DeMarcus Ware .25 .60
35 Kyle Rudolph .15 .40
36 DeMarco Murray .20 .50
37 Fred Jackson .20 .50
38 Jonathan Stewart .15 .40
39 Percy Harvin .15 .40
40 Eli Manning .20 .50
41 Ahmad Bradshaw .15 .40
42 Andy Dalton .20 .50
43 Mark Ingram .20 .50
44 Darren Sproles .20 .50
45 Jay Cutler .15 .40
46 Roy Helu .15 .40
47 Josh Freeman .20 .50
48 Shonn Greene .15 .40
49 Reggie Bush .15 .40
50 Tom Brady .60 1.50
51 Dwayne Bowe .20 .50
52 Beanie Wells .15 .40
53 Joe Flacco .20 .50
54 Mike Tolbert .15 .40
55 Ryan Fitzpatrick .15 .40
56 Vincent Jackson .15 .40
57 Tony Romo .20 .50
58 Philip Rivers .25 .60
59 Michael Bush .15 .40
60 Peyton Manning .50 1.25
61 Felix Jones .15 .40
62 LeGarrette Blount .20 .50
63 Sam Bradford .15 .40
64 Mark Sanchez .15 .40
65 Alex Smith .20 .50
66 Willis McGahee .15 .40
67 Kendall Hunter .20 .50
68 LaDainian Tomlinson .25 .60
69 Brandon Lloyd .15 .40
70 Arian Foster .20 .50
71 Wes Welker .20 .50
72 DeSean Jackson .20 .50
73 Dez Bryant .25 .60
74 Michael Crabtree .15 .40
75 Christian Ponder .15 .40
76 Roddy White .15 .40
77 Matt Flynn .15 .40
78 Hakeem Nicks .15 .40
79 Jake Locker .25 .60
80 Ray Rice .15 .40
81 Kevin Kolb .15 .40
82 Matt Ryan .20 .50
83 LeSean McCoy .25 .60
84 Steve Smith .20 .50
85 Denarius Moore .15 .40
86 Maurice Jones-Drew .15 .40
87 Greg Jennings .15 .40
88 Larry Fitzgerald .20 .50
89 Santonio Holmes .15 .40
90 Andre Johnson .20 .50
91 Jordy Nelson .20 .50
92 Rob Gronkowski .25 .60
93 Jimmy Graham .25 .60
94 Victor Cruz .20 .50
95 Marshawn Lynch .20 .50
96 Mike Wallace .15 .40
97 A.J. Green .25 .60
98 Eric Decker .15 .40
99 Matt Forte .15 .40
100 Drew Brees .25 .60
101 Brock Osweiler RC .50 1.25
102 Brandon Weeden RC .50 1.25
103 Nick Foles RC 1.25 3.00
104 Kirk Cousins RC 2.00 5.00
105 Ryan Lindley RC .50 1.25
106 David Wilson RC .50 1.25
107 Lamar Miller RC .75 2.00
108 Doug Martin RC .75 2.00
109 Isaiah Pead RC .50 1.25
110 Ryan Tannehill RC .75 2.00
111 A.J. Jenkins RC .50 1.25
112 LaMichael James RC .50 1.25
113 Bernard Pierce RC .50 1.25
114 Chris Rainey RC .50 1.25
115 Ronnie Hillman RC .50 1.25
116 Cyrus Gray RC .50 1.25
117 Michael Floyd RC .50 1.25
118 Kendall Wright RC .50 1.25
119 Alshon Jeffery RC 1.00 2.50
120 Robert Griffin III RC 3.00 8.00
121 Mohamed Sanu RC .75 2.00
122 Rueben Randle RC .50 1.25
123 Nick Toon RC .50 1.25
124 Stephen Hill RC .50 1.25
125 Brian Quick RC .50 1.25
126 Joe Adams RC .50 1.25
127 Chris Givens RC .50 1.25
128 Juron Criner RC .50 1.25
129 Dwayne Allen RC .50 1.25
130 Trent Richardson RC .50 1.25
131 Coby Fleener RC .50 1.25
132 Morris Claiborne RC .50 1.25
133 Melvin Ingram RC .50 1.25
134 DeVier Posey RC .50 1.25
135 Jarius Wright RC .50 1.25
136 Janoris Jenkins RC .60 1.50
137 Luke Kuechly RC 1.25 3.00
138 Russell Wilson RC 8.00 20.00
139 Dre Kirkpatrick RC .50 1.25
140 Justin Blackmon RC .50 1.25
141 T.J. Graham RC .50 1.25
142 Marvin McNutt RC .50 1.25
143 Mark Barron RC .50 1.25
144 Robert Turbin RC .50 1.25
145 Michael Egnew RC .50 1.25
146 Ryan Broyles RC .50 1.25
147 T.Y. Hilton RC 1.00 2.50
148 Matt Kalil RC .50 1.25
149 Tommy Streeter RC .50 1.25
150 Andrew Luck RC 6.00 15.00

2012 Topps Platinum Black Refractors

*ROOKIES: .8X TO 2X BASIC RC
BLACK REF. ODDS 1:20 HOBBY

2012 Topps Platinum Blue Refractors

*ROOKIES/99: 1.5X TO 4X BASIC RC
BLUE REF/99 ODDS 1:278 HOB

2012 Topps Platinum Gold Refractors

*ROOKIES/50: 3X TO 8X BASIC RC
STATED PRINT RUN 50 SER.#'d SETS
120 Robert Griffin III 25.00 60.00
138 Russell Wilson 60.00 125.00
150 Andrew Luck 60.00 120.00

2012 Topps Platinum Orange Refractors

*ROOKIES: .5X TO 1.2X BASIC RC
THREE PER RETAIL VALUE PACK

2012 Topps Platinum Purple Refractors

*ROOKIES/75: 2.5X TO 6X BASIC RC
STATED PRINT RUN 75 SER.#'d SETS

2012 Topps Platinum Red

COMPLETE SET (100) 20.00 50.00
*VETERANS: 1X TO 2.5X BASIC CARDS

2012 Topps Platinum Red Refractors

*ROOKIES/25: 4X TO 10X BASIC RC
STATED PRINT RUN 25 SER.#'d SETS
120 Robert Griffin III 30.00 80.00
138 Russell Wilson 75.00 150.00
150 Andrew Luck 125.00 250.00

2012 Topps Platinum Xfractors

*ROOKIES: .6X TO 1.5X BASIC RC
STATED ODDS 1:4 HOBBY

2012 Topps Platinum Patch Autographs Refractors

REFRACTOR/99 ODDS 1:620 HOB
*PURPLE REF/25: .6X TO 1.5X BASIC INSERTS
AVPBG Blaine Gabbert/99 12.00 30.00
AVPCM Colt McCoy/99 10.00 25.00
AVPCP Christian Ponder/99 8.00 20.00
AVPDB Dez Bryant/99 15.00 40.00
AVPDM Darren McFadden/99 12.00 30.00
AVPDS Darren Sproles
AVPFJ Fred Jackson/99 25.00 50.00
AVPJM Jeremy Maclin/99 8.00 20.00
AVPMI Mark Ingram/99 10.00 25.00
AVPMS Mark Sanchez/99 8.00 20.00
AVPRH Roy Helu EXCH 8.00 20.00
AVPTS Torrey Smith/99 8.00 20.00

2012 Topps Platinum Rookie Autographs Blue Refractors

BLUE REF/99 ODDS 1:329 HOB
*BLACK REF/150: .3X TO .8X BLUE REF/99
*REFRACTOR AU: .25X TO .6X BLUE REF/99
105 Ryan Lindley 4.00 10.00
113 Bernard Pierce 4.00 10.00
114 Chris Rainey 4.00 10.00
115 Ronnie Hillman 4.00 10.00
116 Cyrus Gray 4.00 10.00
123 Nick Toon 4.00 10.00
126 Joe Adams 4.00 10.00
127 Chris Givens 4.00 10.00
128 Juron Criner 4.00 10.00
129 Dwayne Allen 4.00 10.00
131 Coby Fleener 4.00 10.00
133 Melvin Ingram 4.00 10.00
134 DeVier Posey 4.00 10.00
135 Jarius Wright 4.00 10.00
136 Janoris Jenkins 5.00 12.00
137 Luke Kuechly 15.00 40.00
139 Dre Kirkpatrick 4.00 10.00
141 Chandler Harnish 4.00 10.00
142 Marvin McNutt 4.00 10.00
143 Mark Barron 4.00 10.00
144 Robert Turbin 4.00 10.00
145 Devon Still 5.00 12.00
146 Ryan Broyles 8.00 20.00
147 T.Y. Hilton 8.00 20.00
148 Matt Kalil 4.00 10.00
152 Bo Levi Mitchell 4.00 10.00
153 Kellen Moore 5.00 12.00
154 T.J. Graham 6.00 15.00
155 Michael Egnew 4.00 10.00
156 Case Keenum 25.00 60.00
157 Jeff Fuller 4.00 10.00
158 Bobby Rainey 4.00 10.00
159 Jermaine Kearse 8.00 20.00
160 David DeCastro 4.00 10.00
161 Jacory Harris 5.00 12.00
162 Dwight Jones 4.00 10.00
163 Dontari Poe 4.00 10.00
164 Jerel Worthy 10.00 25.00
165 Greg Childs 4.00 10.00
166 Travis Benjamin 4.00 10.00

2012 Topps Platinum Rookie Autographs Purple Refractors

*PURPLE REF/25: .8X TO 2X BLUE REF/99
PURPLE REF/25 ODDS 1:1100 HOB
103 Nick Foles 20.00 50.00
108 Doug Martin 20.00 50.00
121 Mohamed Sanu 12.00 30.00
125 Brian Quick 8.00 20.00
151 Chris Polk 8.00 20.00

2012 Topps Platinum Rookie Autographs Dual

DUAL AUTO/25 ODDS 1:2530 HOB
DABF Blackmon/M.Floyd 8.00 20.00
DABR Blackmon/Richardson 20.00 50.00
DAFW M.Floyd/K.Wright 8.00 20.00
DAGW RG3/K.Wright 40.00 100.00
DAJJ L.James/A.Jenkins 25.00 50.00
DAJP L.James/I.Pead 25.00 50.00
DAJS A.Jeffery/M.Sanu 15.00 40.00
DALF A.Luck/C.Fleener 75.00 150.00
DALG A.Luck/RG3 350.00 500.00
DAOF B.Osweiler/N.Foles 15.00 40.00
DAOH B.Osweiler/R.Hillman 15.00 40.00
DARH Randle/S.Hill EXCH 15.00 40.00
DARW Richardson/Weeden 20.00 50.00
DATM Tannehill/L.Miller 12.00 30.00
DATW Tannehill/Weeden 12.00 30.00
DAWB Weeden/Blackmon 20.00 50.00
DAWM D.Wilson/L.Miller 15.00 40.00
DAWR D.Wilson/R.Randle 25.00 50.00
DAWT R.Wilson/R.Turbin 100.00 175.00
DARWI Richardson/D.Wilson 20.00 50.00

2012 Topps Platinum Rookie Die Cut

STATED ODDS 1:20 HOBBY
PDCAJ Alshon Jeffery 1.50 4.00
PDCAL Andrew Luck 12.00 30.00
PDCBO Brock Osweiler .75 2.00
PDCBP Bernard Pierce .75 2.00
PDCBQ Brian Quick .75 2.00
PDCBW Brandon Weeden .75 2.00
PDCCF Coby Fleener .75 2.00
PDCDM Doug Martin 1.25 3.00
PDCDW David Wilson .75 2.00
PDCIP Isaiah Pead .75 2.00
PDCJA Joe Adams .75 2.00
PDCJB Justin Blackmon .75 2.00
PDCKW Kendall Wright .75 2.00
PDCLJ LaMichael James .75 2.00
PDCLM Lamar Miller 1.25 3.00
PDCMF Michael Floyd .75 2.00
PDCMS Mohamed Sanu 1.25 3.00
PDCNF Nick Foles 2.00 5.00
PDCNT Nick Toon .75 2.00
PDCRG Robert Griffin III 6.00 15.00
PDCRH Ronnie Hillman .75 2.00
PDCRR Rueben Randle .75 2.00
PDCRT Ryan Tannehill 1.25 3.00
PDCSH Stephen Hill .75 2.00
PDCTR Trent Richardson .75 2.00

2012 Topps Platinum Rookie Jersey

*PATCH/71: 1X TO 2.5X BASIC JSY
PRRAL Andrew Luck 15.00 40.00
PRRBO Brock Osweiler 1.50 4.00
PRRBP Bernard Pierce 1.50 4.00
PRRBQ Brian Quick 1.50 4.00
PRRBW Brandon Weeden 1.50 4.00
PRRCF Coby Fleener 1.50 4.00
PRRDA Dwayne Allen 1.50 4.00
PRRDM Doug Martin 2.50 6.00
PRRDP DeVier Posey 1.50 4.00
PRRDW David Wilson 1.50 4.00
PRRIP Isaiah Pead 1.50 4.00
PRRJA Joe Adams 1.50 4.00
PRRJB Justin Blackmon 1.50 4.00
PRRJW Jarius Wright 1.50 4.00
PRRKW Kendall Wright 1.50 4.00
PRRLJ LaMichael James 1.50 4.00
PRRLM Lamar Miller 2.50 6.00
PRRME Michael Egnew 1.50 4.00
PRRMF Michael Floyd 1.50 4.00
PRRMS Mohamed Sanu 2.50 6.00
PRRNF Nick Foles 4.00 10.00
PRRNT Nick Toon 1.50 4.00
PRRRB Ryan Broyles 1.50 4.00
PRRRG Robert Griffin III 2.00 5.00
PRRRH Ronnie Hillman 1.50 4.00
PRRRR Rueben Randle 1.50 4.00
PRRRT Ryan Tannehill 2.50 6.00
PRRRW Russell Wilson 15.00 40.00
PRRSH Stephen Hill 1.50 4.00
PRRTG T.J. Graham 1.50 4.00
PRRTH T.Y. Hilton 3.00 8.00
PRRTR Trent Richardson 1.50 4.00
PRRAJJ A.J. Jenkins 1.50 4.00
PRRCGI Chris Givens 1.50 4.00
PRRRTU Robert Turbin 1.50 4.00

2012 Topps Platinum Rookie Patch Autographs Blue Refractors

*BLUE REF/25: .8X TO 2X GREEN REF/99
110 Ryan Tannehill 20.00 50.00
120 Robert Griffin III 75.00 150.00
130 Trent Richardson 40.00 100.00
138 Russell Wilson 200.00 350.00
150 Andrew Luck 350.00 500.00

2012 Topps Platinum Rookie Patch Autographs Green Refractors

GREEN REF/99 ODDS 1:178 HOBBY
*BLACK REF/125: .4X TO 1X GREEN REF/99
*REF/1001-1058: .3X TO .8X GREEN REF/99
*REF/250: .4X TO 1X GREEN REF/99
EXCH EXPIRATION: 8/31/2015
101 Brock Osweiler 6.00 15.00
102 Brandon Weeden 6.00 15.00
103 Nick Foles 30.00 80.00

106 David Wilson 6.00 15.00
107 Lamar Miller 10.00 25.00
108 Doug Martin 8.00 20.00
109 Isaiah Pead 6.00 15.00
110 Ryan Tannehill 10.00 25.00
111 A.J. Jenkins 6.00 15.00
112 LaMichael James 6.00 15.00
113 Bernard Pierce 12.00 30.00
114 Chris Rainey 6.00 15.00
115 Ronnie Hillman 6.00 15.00
116 Cyrus Gray 6.00 15.00
117 Michael Floyd 6.00 15.00
118 Kendall Wright 6.00 15.00
119 Alshon Jeffery 12.00 30.00
121 Mohamed Sanu 10.00 25.00
122 Rueben Randle 6.00 15.00
123 Nick Toon 6.00 15.00
124 Stephen Hill 6.00 15.00
125 Brian Quick 6.00 15.00
126 Joe Adams 6.00 15.00
127 Chris Givens 6.00 15.00
128 Juron Criner 6.00 15.00
129 Dwayne Allen 8.00 20.00
131 Coby Fleener 8.00 20.00
134 DeVier Posey 6.00 15.00
135 Jarius Wright 8.00 20.00
138 Russell Wilson 90.00 150.00
140 Justin Blackmon 6.00 15.00
144 Robert Turbin 6.00 15.00
146 Ryan Broyles 6.00 15.00
147 T.Y. Hilton 15.00 40.00
154 T.J. Graham 6.00 15.00
155 Michael Egnew 6.00 15.00
165 Greg Childs 6.00 15.00

2012 Topps Platinum Rookie Patch Autographs Dual

DUAL PATCH AU/25 ODDS 1:1192 HOB
DADPBF J.Blackmon/M.Floyd 8.00 20.00
DADPBR Blackmon/Richardson 25.00 60.00
DADPFW M.Floyd/K.Wright 8.00 20.00
DADPGW R.Griffin III/K.Wright 50.00 100.00
DADPJJ L.James/A.Jenkins 30.00 60.00
DADPJP L.James/I.Pead 30.00 60.00
DADPJS A.Jeffery/M.Sanu 20.00 50.00
DADPLF A.Luck/C.Fleener 75.00 150.00
DADPLG A.Luck/R.Griffin III 250.00 500.00
DADPOF B.Osweiler/N.Foles 12.00 30.00
DADPOH B.Osweiler/R.Hillman 12.00 30.00
DADPRH R.Randle/S.Hill 20.00 50.00
DADPRW Richardson/Weeden 40.00 100.00
DADPTH N.Toon/S.Hill 15.00 40.00
DADPTM R.Tannehill/L.Miller
DADPTW Tannehill/B.Weeden
DADPWB Weeden/Blackmon 25.00 60.00
DADPWR D.Wilson/R.Randle 30.00 60.00
DADPWT R.Wilson/R.Turbin 100.00 175.00
DADPRWI Richardson/D.Wilson 40.00 100.00

2013 Topps Platinum

COMPLETE SET (150) 20.00 50.00
COMP.SET w/o RC's (100) 8.00 20.00
ROOKIE STATED ODDS 1:2
1 Joe Flacco .20 .50
2 Jeremy Kerley .15 .40
3 Demaryius Thomas .20 .50
4 Tony Romo .20 .50
5 Brandon Pettigrew .15 .40
6 Ben Roethlisberger .25 .60
7 Philip Rivers .25 .60
8 Randall Cobb .20 .50
9 David Wilson .15 .40
10 Jake Locker .20 .50
11 Ray Rice .15 .40
12 Robert Griffin III .15 .40
13 DeAngelo Williams .15 .40
14 Brandon Weeden .15 .40
15 Alfred Morris .15 .40
16 DeSean Jackson .20 .50
17 Von Miller .20 .50
18 Reggie Bush .15 .40
19 Aaron Rodgers .40 1.00
20 C.J. Spiller .15 .40
21 Ryan Mathews .20 .50
22 Stevan Ridley .15 .40
23 Hakeem Nicks .15 .40
24 Michael Crabtree .15 .40
25 Percy Harvin .15 .40
26 Andre Johnson .15 .40
27 Wes Welker .20 .50
28 A.J. Green .25 .60
29 Vernon Davis .15 .40
30 Roddy White .15 .40
31 Russell Wilson .50 1.25
32 Christian Ponder .15 .40
33 Brandon Marshall .20 .50
34 Arian Foster .20 .50
35 Julius Peppers .20 .50
36 Kendall Wright .15 .40
37 Dwayne Bowe .20 .50
38 Jay Cutler .15 .40
39 Danny Amendola .20 .50
40 Andy Dalton .20 .50
41 Steven Jackson .15 .40
42 Drew Brees .25 .60
43 Justin Blackmon .15 .40
44 Santonio Holmes .15 .40
45 DeMarcus Ware .25 .60
46 Colin Kaepernick .20 .50
47 Ryan Tannehill .20 .50
48 Matthew Stafford .20 .50
49 Fred Davis .15 .40
50 Doug Martin .20 .50
51 Mike Wallace .15 .40
52 Darren McFadden .20 .50
53 Greg Jennings .15 .40
54 Troy Polamalu .25 .60
55 Torrey Smith .15 .40
56 Maurice Jones-Drew .15 .40
57 Jason Witten .20 .50
58 Sam Bradford .15 .40
59 Anquan Boldin .15 .40
60 Brian Orakpo .20 .50
61 Steve Smith .20 .50
62 Cam Newton .25 .60
63 Dez Bryant .25 .60
64 Kyle Rudolph .15 .40
65 Trent Richardson .15 .40
66 Reggie Wayne .20 .50
67 Antonio Gates .20 .50
68 Clay Matthews .25 .60
69 Peyton Manning .50 1.25
70 Miles Austin .15 .40
71 Michael Vick .20 .50
72 Frank Gore .20 .50
73 Rob Gronkowski .25 .60
74 Tom Brady .60 1.50
75 Josh Freeman .20 .50
76 Julio Jones .25 .60
77 Calvin Johnson .25 .60
78 Darrelle Revis .15 .40
79 Matt Schaub .15 .40
80 BenJarvus Green-Ellis .20 .50
81 Jimmy Graham .25 .60
82 LeSean McCoy .25 .60
83 Matt Forte .15 .40
84 DeMarco Murray .20 .50
85 Owen Daniels .15 .40
86 Chris Johnson .15 .40
87 Larry Fitzgerald .20 .50
88 Vincent Jackson .15 .40
89 Eli Manning .20 .50
90 Eric Decker .15 .40
91 Carson Palmer .20 .50
92 Victor Cruz .20 .50
93 J.J. Watt .20 .50
94 Jamaal Charles .20 .50
95 Andrew Luck .40 1.00
96 Ed Reed .20 .50
97 Adrian Peterson .25 .60
98 Matt Ryan .20 .50
99 Marshawn Lynch .20 .50
100 Darren Sproles .20 .50
101 Kenny Vaccaro RC .30 .75
102 Conner Vernon RC .30 .75
103 Dee Milliner RC .30 .75
104 EJ Manuel RC .30 .75
105 Arthur Brown RC .30 .75
106 Zach Line RC .30 .75
107 Tyrone Goard RC .30 .75
108 Matt Barkley RC .30 .75
109 Theo Riddick RC .30 .75
110 Andre Ellington RC .30 .75
111 Ryan Nassib RC .30 .75
112 Denard Robinson RC .30 .75
113 Quinton Patton RC .30 .75
114 Mike Glennon RC .30 .75
115 Giovani Bernard RC .30 .75
116 Justin Hunter RC .30 .75
117 Joseph Randle RC .30 .75
118 Dion Jordan RC .30 .75
119 Da'Rick Rogers RC .50 1.25
120 Manti Te'o RC .40 1.00
121 Montee Ball RC .30 .75
122 DeAndre Hopkins RC .75 2.00
123 Tavon Austin RC .40 1.00
124 Mike Gillislee RC .50 1.25
125 Stedman Bailey RC .30 .75
126 Zac Dysert RC .30 .75
127 Geno Smith RC .30 .75
128 Robert Woods RC .50 1.25
129 Ezekiel Ansah RC .30 .75
130 Stepfan Taylor RC .30 .75
131 Landry Jones RC .30 .75
132 Tyler Bray RC .30 .75
133 Desmond Trufant RC .30 .75
134 Tyler Wilson RC .30 .75
135 Rex Burkhead RC .40 1.00
136 Markus Wheaton RC .30 .75
137 Tyler Eifert RC .30 .75
138 Aaron Dobson RC .30 .75
139 Zeke Motta RC .40 1.00
140 Aaron Mellette RC .30 .75
141 Terrance Williams RC .30 .75
142 Zach Ertz RC .60 1.50
143 Cordarrelle Patterson RC .30 .75
144 Keenan Allen RC .60 1.50
145 Bjoern Werner RC .30 .75
146 Marcus Lattimore RC .30 .75
147 Johnathan Hankins RC .30 .75
148 Kenjon Barner RC .30 .75
149 Alec Ogletree RC .30 .75
150 Eddie Lacy RC .30 .75

2013 Topps Platinum Black Refractors

*101-150 ROOKIES: .8X TO 2X BASIC RC
STATED ODDS 1:20 HOBBY

2013 Topps Platinum Gold Refractors

*101-150 ROOKIES/50: 2.5X TO 6X BASIC RC
GOLD REF/50 ODDS 1:520 HOBBY

2013 Topps Platinum Orange Refractors

*101-150 ROOKIES: .6X TO 1.5X BASIC RC

2013 Topps Platinum Prism Refractors

*101-140 ROOKIES/99: 1.5X TO 4X BASIC RC
PRISM REF/99 ODDS 1:262 HOBBY
ALSO KNOWN AS FROST REFRACTORS

2013 Topps Platinum Purple Refractors

*101-150 ROOKIES/75: 2X TO 5X BASIC RC
PURPLE REF/75 ODDS 1:340 HOBBY

2013 Topps Platinum Red Refractors

*101-150 ROOKIES/25: 4X TO 10X BASIC RC
RED REFRACTOR ODDS 1:1034 HOBBY

2013 Topps Platinum Sapphire

*VETS: 1X TO 2.5X BASIC CARDS

2013 Topps Platinum Xfractors

*101-150 ROOKIES: .6X TO 1.5X BASIC RC
STATED ODDS 1:4 HOBBY

2013 Topps Platinum Camo Die Cut

CAMO STATED ODDS 1:240 HOBBY
*PINK DIE CUT: .4X TO 1X CAMO DC
ABMDCAF Arian Foster 2.00 5.00
ABMDCAL Andrew Luck 4.00 10.00
ABMDCAM Alfred Morris 1.50 4.00
ABMDCBG BenJarvus Green-Ellis 2.00 5.00
ABMDCBH Brian Hartline 1.50 4.00
ABMDCDB Drew Brees 3.00 8.00
ABMDCDH DeAndre Hopkins 2.00 5.00
ABMDCDR Denard Robinson .75 2.00
ABMDCED Eric Decker 1.50 4.00
ABMDCEL Eddie Lacy .75 2.00
ABMDCGS Geno Smith .75 2.00
ABMDCJG Jimmy Graham 2.50 6.00
ABMDCJP Jason Pierre-Paul 1.50 4.00
ABMDCLJ Landry Jones .75 2.00
ABMDCLM Lamar Miller 1.50 4.00
ABMDCMB Montee Ball .75 2.00
ABMDCMC Michael Crabtree 1.50 4.00
ABMDCML Marcus Lattimore .75 2.00
ABMDCMLY Marshawn Lynch 2.00 5.00
ABMDCMT Manti Te'o 1.00 2.50
ABMDCNB NaVorro Bowman 2.00 5.00
ABMDCRG Robert Griffin III 1.50 4.00
ABMDCSJ Steve Johnson 2.00 5.00
ABMDCTA Tavon Austin 1.00 2.50
ABMDCTE Tyler Eifert .75 2.00

2013 Topps Platinum Patch Autographs Refractors

PATCH AU/25-125 ODDS 1:459 HOB
EXCH EXPIRATION: 8/31/2016
*PRISM/15: .5X TO 1.2X PATCH AU/99-125
*PRISM/15: .4X TO 1X PATCH AU/25
*PURPLE/25: .5X TO 1.2X PATCH AU/99-125
*PURPLE/25: .4X TO 1X PATCH AU/25
AVPAL Andrew Luck/25 50.00 100.00
AVPAR Andre Roberts EXCH 5.00 12.00
AVPBG BenJarvus Green-Ellis/99 6.00 15.00
AVPBO Brian Orakpo/99 6.00 15.00
AVPDB Dwayne Bowe/99 6.00 15.00
AVPDM Doug Martin/99 10.00 25.00
AVPET Earl Thomas/125 12.00 30.00
AVPGT Golden Tate EXCH 5.00 12.00
AVPJC Jamaal Charles 10.00 25.00
AVPJG Jimmy Graham/99 12.00 30.00
AVPJL James Laurinaitis/99 8.00 20.00
AVPML Mikel Leshoure/99 5.00 12.00
AVPRT Ryan Tannehill/99 15.00 40.00
AVPSJ Steve Johnson/99 10.00 25.00
AVPVB Vick Ballard/125 5.00 12.00

2013 Topps Platinum Rookie Autographs Gold Refractors

*GOLD REF/15: .6X TO 1.5X PRISM AU/50
AEL Eddie Lacy 8.00 20.00
AEM EJ Manuel 20.00 50.00
AGS Geno Smith 8.00 20.00
AMBA Matt Barkley EXCH 8.00 20.00
AMGL Mike Glennon 8.00 20.00
ATA Tavon Austin 10.00 25.00

2013 Topps Platinum Rookie Autographs Prism Refractors

PRISM REF AU/50 ODDS 1:382 HOB
*BASE REFRACT: .2X TO .5X PRISM AU/50
*BLACK REF/150: .25X TO .6X PRISM AU/50
*BLUE REF/99: .3X TO .8X PRISM AU/50
AAB Arthur Brown 5.00 12.00
AAD Aaron Dobson 5.00 12.00
AAE Andre Ellington 5.00 12.00
ABR Bacarri Rambo 6.00 15.00
ABW Bjoern Werner 5.00 12.00
ACH Cobi Hamilton 5.00 12.00
ACHA Chris Harper 5.00 12.00
ACK Collin Klein 6.00 15.00
ACP Cordarrelle Patterson 5.00 12.00
ADH DeAndre Hopkins 12.00 30.00
ADJ Dion Jordan 5.00 12.00
ADM Dee Milliner EXCH 5.00 12.00
ADMO Damontre Moore 5.00 12.00
ADR Denard Robinson 5.00 12.00
ADRO Da'Rick Rogers 5.00 12.00
ADT Desmond Trufant 5.00 12.00
AEA Ezekiel Ansah EXCH 5.00 12.00
AEL Eddie Lacy 5.00 12.00
AGB Giovani Bernard 5.00 12.00
AJC Johnathan Cyprien 5.00 12.00
AJF Johnathan Franklin 5.00 12.00
AJFA Joseph Fauria 5.00 12.00
AJH Johnathan Hankins 5.00 12.00
AJHU Justin Hunter 5.00 12.00
AJJ Jawan Jamison 5.00 12.00
AJJO Jarvis Jones 10.00 25.00
AJR Joseph Randle 5.00 12.00
AJRE Jordan Reed 12.00 30.00
AKA Keenan Allen 15.00 40.00
AKB Kenjon Barner 5.00 12.00
AKD Knile Davis 5.00 12.00
AKS Kenny Stills 5.00 12.00
AKW Kerwynn Williams 5.00 12.00
ALJ Landry Jones 5.00 12.00
ALJO Luke Joeckel 5.00 12.00
AMB Montee Ball 5.00 12.00
AMG Mike Gillislee 5.00 12.00
AML Marcus Lattimore 5.00 12.00
AMS Matt Scott 5.00 12.00
AMT Manti Te'o 6.00 15.00
AMW Markus Wheaton 5.00 12.00
AQP Quinton Patton 5.00 12.00
ARB Rex Burkhead 12.00 30.00
ARG Ray Graham 5.00 12.00
ARN Ryan Nassib 5.00 12.00
ARW Robert Woods 8.00 20.00
ASB Stedman Bailey 5.00 12.00
AST Stepfan Taylor 5.00 12.00
ATB Tyler Bray 5.00 12.00
ATE Tyler Eifert 5.00 12.00
ATG Tyrone Goard 5.00 12.00
ATK Tavarres King 5.00 12.00
ATR Theo Riddick 5.00 12.00
ATW Terrance Williams 5.00 12.00
ATWI Tyler Wilson 5.00 12.00
AWD Will Davis 5.00 12.00
AZD Zac Dysert 5.00 12.00
AZE Zach Ertz 10.00 25.00
AZL Zach Line 5.00 12.00
AZM Zeke Motta 6.00 15.00

2013 Topps Platinum Rookie Autographs Purple Refractors

*PURPLE REF/25: .6X TO 1.5X PRISM AU/50
AEL Eddie Lacy 8.00 20.00
AEM EJ Manuel 8.00 20.00
AMBA Matt Barkley EXCH 8.00 20.00
AMGL Mike Glennon 8.00 20.00
ATA Tavon Austin 10.00 25.00

2013 Topps Platinum Rookie Autographs Dual

DUAL AUTO/25 ODDS 1:3150 HOB
DAAJ E.Ansah/D.Jordan 10.00 25.00
DAEE T.Eifert/Z.Ertz 20.00 50.00
DAGA M.Goodwin/T.Austin 12.00 30.00
DAGR M.Gillislee/J.Reed 15.00 40.00
DAJS L.Jones/K.Stills 10.00 25.00
DAJT J.Jones/M.Te'o 40.00 80.00
DALL E.Lacy/M.Lattimore 10.00 25.00
DAMT D.Milliner/D.Trufant
DANG R.Nassib/M.Glennon 10.00 25.00
DAPH C.Patterson/J.Hunter 10.00 25.00
DAPR Q.Patton/D.Rogers 20.00 50.00
DARM J.Randle/C.Michael 10.00 25.00
DASB G.Smith/M.Barkley 10.00 25.00
DAWA R.Woods/T.Austin 15.00 40.00
DAWB M.Wheaton/S/Bailey 10.00 25.00

2013 Topps Platinum Rookie Jersey

RANDOM INSERTS IN RETAIL BOXES
*PATCH/59: .8X TO 2X BASIC JSY
PRRAD Aaron Dobson 1.50 4.00
PRRAE Andre Ellington 1.50 4.00
PRRCM Christine Michael 1.50 4.00
PRRCP Cordarrelle Patterson 1.50 4.00
PRRDH DeAndre Hopkins 4.00 10.00
PRRDR Denard Robinson 1.50 4.00
PRREL Eddie Lacy 1.50 4.00
PRREM EJ Manuel 1.50 4.00
PRRGB Giovani Bernard 1.50 4.00
PRRGS Geno Smith 1.50 4.00
PRRJF Johnathan Franklin 1.50 4.00
PRRJH Justin Hunter 1.50 4.00
PRRJR Joseph Randle 1.50 4.00
PRRKA Keenan Allen 3.00 8.00
PRRKD Knile Davis 1.50 4.00
PRRKS Kenny Stills 1.50 4.00
PRRLJ Landry Jones 1.50 4.00
PRRMB Matt Barkley 1.50 4.00
PRRMBA Montee Ball 1.50 4.00
PRRMG Mike Glennon 1.50 4.00
PRRMGI Mike Gillislee 1.50 4.00
PRRML Marcus Lattimore 1.50 4.00
PRRMT Manti Te'o 2.00 5.00
PRRMW Markus Wheaton 1.50 4.00
PRRQP Quinton Patton 1.50 4.00
PRRRN Ryan Nassib 1.50 4.00
PRRRW Robert Woods 2.50 6.00
PRRSB Stedman Bailey 1.50 4.00
PRRST Stepfan Taylor 1.50 4.00
PRRTA Tavon Austin 2.00 5.00
PRRTB Tyler Bray 1.50 4.00
PRRTE Tyler Eifert 1.50 4.00
PRRTW Tyler Wilson 1.50 4.00
PRRTWI Terrance Williams 1.50 4.00
PRRZE Zach Ertz 3.00 8.00

2013 Topps Platinum Rookie Patch Autographs Blue Refractors

*BLUE/25: .6X TO 1.5X GREEN AU/99
BLUE REF AU/25 ODDS 1:684 HOB
ARPEM EJ Manuel 8.00 20.00
ARPGS Geno Smith 8.00 20.00
ARPMB Matt Barkley 8.00 20.00

2013 Topps Platinum Rookie Patch Autographs Green Refractors

GREEN REF AU/99 ODDS 1:189 HOB
*BLACK REF/125: .3X TO .8X GREEN AU/99
*BASE REF/872-1000: .2X TO .5X GRN AU/99
*BASE REF/250-484: .25X TO .6X GRN AU/99
EXCH EXPIRATION: 8/31/2016
ARPAD Aaron Dobson 5.00 12.00
ARPAE Andre Ellington 15.00 40.00
ARPCM Christine Michael 20.00 50.00
ARPCP Cordarrelle Patterson 5.00 12.00
ARPDH DeAndre Hopkins 15.00 40.00
ARPDJ Dion Jordan 5.00 12.00
ARPDRO Denard Robinson EXCH 5.00 12.00
ARPEL Eddie Lacy 5.00 12.00
ARPGB Giovani Bernard 5.00 12.00
ARPGE Gavin Escobar 5.00 12.00
ARPJF Johnathan Franklin 5.00 12.00
ARPJH Justin Hunter 10.00 25.00
ARPJR Joseph Randle 5.00 12.00
ARPJRE Jordan Reed 8.00 20.00
ARPKA Keenan Allen 20.00 50.00
ARPKD Knile Davis 5.00 12.00
ARPKS Kenny Stills 15.00 40.00
ARPLB Le'Veon Bell 25.00 60.00
ARPLJ Landry Jones 5.00 12.00
ARPMBA Montee Ball 5.00 12.00
ARPMG Mike Glennon 5.00 12.00
ARPMGI Mike Gillislee 5.00 12.00
ARPMGO Marquise Goodwin 5.00 12.00
ARPML Marcus Lattimore 15.00 40.00
ARPMT Manti Te'o 6.00 15.00
ARPMW Markus Wheaton 5.00 12.00
ARPQP Quinton Patton 12.00 30.00
ARPRN Ryan Nassib 5.00 12.00
ARPRW Robert Woods 8.00 20.00
ARPSB Stedman Bailey 5.00 12.00
ARPST Stepfan Taylor 5.00 12.00
ARPTA Tavon Austin 6.00 15.00
ARPTE Tyler Eifert 5.00 12.00
ARPTK Tavarres King 5.00 12.00
ARPTW Tyler Wilson 5.00 12.00
ARPTWI Terrance Williams 5.00 12.00
ARPZE Zach Ertz 12.00 30.00

2013 Topps Platinum Rookie Patch Autographs Prism Refractors

*PRISM/50: .5X TO 1.2X GREEN AU/99
PRISM REF AU/50 ODDS 1:342 HOB
ARPEM EJ Manuel 6.00 15.00

2013 Topps Platinum Rookie Patch Autographs Dual

DUAL PATCH AU/25 ODDS 1:1628 HOB
DADPAB T.Austin/G.Bernard 15.00 40.00
DADPAH T.Austin/D.Hopkins 40.00 80.00
DADPBB M.Barkley/L.Bell
DADPBE M.Barkley/Z.Ertz 25.00 60.00
DADPBL G.Bernard/E.Lacy 12.00 30.00
DADPBN M.Barkley/R.Nassib 12.00 30.00
DADPBW L.Bell/M.Wheaton 40.00 100.00
DADPEE Z.Ertz/T.Eifert 30.00 80.00
DADPGD Goodwin/A.Dobson 30.00 80.00
DADPGW M.Glennon/T.Wilson 12.00 30.00
DADPHP J.Hunter/C.Patterson 12.00 30.00
DADPMW E.Manuel/R.Woods 40.00 80.00
DADPRS Robinson/K.Stills EXCH 12.00 30.00
DADPSN G.Smith/R.Nassib 12.00 30.00
DADPTA M.Te'o/K.Allen 30.00 60.00
DADPWW Wheaton/R.Woods

2014 Topps Platinum

COMPLETE SET (150) 25.00 50.00
COMP.SET w/o RC's (100) 8.00 20.00
ONE ROOKIE PER HOBBY PACK OVERALL
1 Eddie Lacy .15 .40
2 Eli Manning .20 .50
3 Alshon Jeffery .20 .50
4 Ryan Mathews .20 .50
5 Jordy Nelson .20 .50
6 Jamaal Charles .20 .50
7 Richard Sherman .25 .60
8 Keenan Allen .20 .50
9 Cecil Shorts .15 .40
10 J.J. Watt .25 .60
11 Giovani Bernard .15 .40
12 Andy Dalton .20 .50
13 Pierre Garcon .20 .50
14 Troy Polamalu .25 .60
15 Cordarrelle Patterson .15 .40
16 Jay Cutler .15 .40
17 Russell Wilson .40 1.00
18 Drew Brees .25 .60
19 Matt Ryan .20 .50
20 Rob Gronkowski .25 .60
21 Peyton Manning .50 1.25
22 Randall Cobb .20 .50
23 Matt Forte .15 .40
24 Alfred Morris .15 .40
25 Larry Fitzgerald .20 .50
26 EJ Manuel .15 .40
27 Patrick Willis .20 .50
28 Calvin Johnson .25 .60
29 T.Y. Hilton .20 .50
30 Victor Cruz .20 .50
31 Denarius Moore .15 .40
32 Adrian Peterson .25 .60
33 Kendall Wright .15 .40
34 Brandon Marshall .15 .40
35 Ryan Tannehill .20 .50
36 Bernard Pierce .15 .40
37 A.J. Green .25 .60
38 Earl Thomas .20 .50
39 Antonio Brown .25 .60
40 Pierre Thomas .15 .40
41 Julian Edelman .25 .60
42 DeSean Jackson .20 .50
43 Aaron Rodgers .50 1.25
44 Colin Kaepernick .20 .50
45 Percy Harvin .15 .40
46 Clay Matthews .25 .60
47 Joe Flacco .20 .50
48 Michael Crabtree .15 .40
49 DeAndre Hopkins .20 .50
50 Luke Kuechly .20 .50
51 Matthew Stafford .20 .50
52 Julius Thomas .15 .40
53 Jimmy Graham .25 .60
54 LeSean McCoy .25 .60
55 Julio Jones .25 .60
56 Jordan Cameron .15 .40
57 Ndamukong Suh .20 .50
58 Vincent Jackson .15 .40
59 Josh Gordon .15 .40
60 Brian Hartline .15 .40
61 Dez Bryant .25 .60
62 Marshawn Lynch .20 .50
63 Wes Welker .20 .50
64 Ace Sanders .15 .40
65 Philip Rivers .25 .60
66 Robert Griffin III .15 .40
67 Andrew Luck .30 .75
68 Roddy White .15 .40
69 Patrick Peterson .15 .40
70 Frank Gore .20 .50
71 DeMarco Murray .20 .50
72 Robert Mathis .15 .40
73 Robert Quinn .20 .50
74 Nick Foles .20 .50
75 Geno Smith .15 .40
76 Cam Newton .25 .60
77 Tom Brady .60 1.50
78 Sheldon Richardson .15 .40
79 Kiko Alonso .15 .40
80 Tony Romo .20 .50
81 Von Miller .20 .50
82 Alex Smith .20 .50
83 Mike Wallace .15 .40
84 Reggie Wayne .20 .50
85 Eric Berry .20 .50
86 Zach Ertz .20 .50
87 Darrelle Revis .15 .40
88 Torrey Smith .15 .40
89 Sean Lee .20 .50
90 Le'Veon Bell .20 .50
91 Mike Glennon .20 .50
92 Reggie Bush .15 .40
93 Tavon Austin .15 .40
94 Andre Johnson .20 .50
95 NaVorro Bowman .20 .50
96 Terrell Suggs .15 .40
97 C.J. Spiller .15 .40
98 Montee Ball .15 .40
99 Demaryius Thomas .20 .50
100 Arian Foster .20 .50
101 Jeremy Hill RC .40 1.00
102 Derek Carr RC 2.00 5.00
103 Cody Latimer RC .40 1.00
104 Dri Archer RC .30 .75
105 Jace Amaro RC .30 .75
106 Kelvin Benjamin RC .50 1.25
107 Davante Adams RC .50 1.25
108 Teddy Bridgewater RC .50 1.25
109 Shaquelle Evans RC .30 .75
110 Andre Williams RC .30 .75
111 De'Anthony Thomas RC .30 .75
112 Aaron Donald RC .75 2.00
113 Marqise Lee RC .40 1.00
114 C.J. Fiedorowicz RC .30 .75
115 Aaron Murray RC .30 .75
116 Blake Bortles RC .40 1.00
117 Odell Beckham Jr. RC 3.00 8.00
118 Jarvis Landry RC .60 1.50
119 Sammy Watkins RC .50 1.25
120 Charles Sims RC .30 .75
121 Tre Mason RC .30 .75
122 Jalen Saunders RC .30 .75
123 John Brown RC .50 1.25
124 A.J. McCarron RC .30 .75
125 Tajh Boyd RC .30 .75
126 Johnny Manziel RC .50 1.25
127 Carlos Hyde RC .40 1.00
128 Terrance West RC .30 .75
129 Tom Savage RC .30 .75
130 Devonta Freeman RC .50 1.25
131 Jadeveon Clowney RC .40 1.00
132 Bishop Sankey RC .30 .75
133 Khalil Mack RC 1.25 3.00
134 Devin Street RC .30 .75
135 Darqueze Dennard RC .40 1.00
136 Jordan Matthews RC .50 1.25
137 Ha Ha Clinton-Dix RC .40 1.00
138 Brandin Cooks RC .50 1.25
139 Kevin Norwood RC .30 .75
140 Eric Ebron RC .40 1.00
141 Paul Richardson RC .40 1.00
142 Ka'Deem Carey RC .30 .75
143 Jimmy Garoppolo RC 2.50 6.00
144 Austin Seferian-Jenkins RC .30 .75
145 Michael Sam RC .30 .75
146 Logan Thomas RC .30 .75
147 Donte Moncrief RC .30 .75
148 Allen Robinson RC .50 1.25
149 Lache Seastrunk RC .30 .75
150 Mike Evans RC .75 2.00

2014 Topps Platinum Black Refractors

*BLACK REF: .8X TO 2X BASIC RC
STATED ODDS 1:20

2014 Topps Platinum Blue Wave Refractors

*BLUE WAVE: 1X TO 2.5X BASIC CARDS
ONE PER HOBBY PACK

2014 Topps Platinum Camo Refractors

*CAMO REF/10: 6X TO 15X BASIC RC

2014 Topps Platinum Gold Refractors

*GOLD REF/50: 2.5X TO 6X BASIC RC

2014 Topps Platinum Orange Refractors

*101-50 ORANGE: .5X TO 1.2X BASIC RC

2014 Topps Platinum Pink Refractors

*PINK REF/10: 6X TO 15X BASIC RC

2014 Topps Platinum Pulsar Refractors

*PULSAR/99: 1.5X TO 4X BASIC RC

2014 Topps Platinum Purple Refractors

*PURPLE REF/75: 2X TO 5X BASIC RC

2014 Topps Platinum Red Refractors

*RED REF/25: 4X TO 10X BASIC RC

2014 Topps Platinum Xfractors

*XFRACTOR: .5X TO 1.2X BASIC RC
STATED ODDS 1:4

2014 Topps Platinum Autographs Black Refractors

*BLACK RED/150: .5X TO 1.2X BASIC REF
57 Derek Carr 15.00 40.00
58 Jimmy Garoppolo 50.00 100.00

2014 Topps Platinum Autographs Blue Refractors

*BLUE REF/99: .6X TO 1.5X BASIC REF
15 A.J. McCarron 3.00 8.00
42 Odell Beckham Jr. 100.00
52 Mike Evans 10.00 25.00
58 Jimmy Garoppolo 60.00 125.00

2014 Topps Platinum Autographs Gold Refractors

*GOLD REF/15: 1.2X TO 3X BASIC REF
14 Teddy Bridgewater 50.00 100.00
30 Blake Bortles 8.00 20.00
42 Odell Beckham Jr. 100.00 200.00
55 Sammy Watkins 10.00 25.00
58 Jimmy Garoppolo 125.00 250.00

2014 Topps Platinum Autographs Pulsar Refractors

*PULSAR REF/50: .8X TO 2X BASIC REF
14 Teddy Bridgewater 25.00 50.00
15 A.J. McCarron 4.00 10.00
30 Blake Bortles 5.00 12.00
42 Odell Beckham Jr. 75.00 150.00
52 Mike Evans 12.00 30.00
55 Sammy Watkins 6.00 15.00
58 Jimmy Garoppolo 75.00 150.00

2014 Topps Platinum Autographs Purple Refractors

*PURPLE REF/25: 1X TO 2.5X BASIC REF
14 Teddy Bridgewater
30 Blake Bortles 6.00 15.00
42 Odell Beckham Jr.
52 Mike Evans 15.00 40.00
58 Jimmy Garoppolo 100.00 200.00

2014 Topps Platinum Autographs Refractors

STATED ODDS 1:14
EXCH EXPIRATION: 10/31/2017
1 Davante Adams 6.00 15.00
2 Darqueze Dennard 2.50 6.00
4 Zach Mettenberger 2.00 5.00
6 Terrance West 2.00 5.00
7 David Fales 2.00 5.00
8 Devonta Freeman 8.00 20.00
9 Jadeveon Clowney 2.50 6.00
10 Ka'Deem Carey 2.00 5.00
12 Jordan Matthews 3.00 8.00
13 Ha Ha Clinton-Dix 2.50 6.00
14 Teddy Bridgewater 10.00 25.00
16 Eric Ebron
17 Tajh Boyd 2.00 5.00
18 Devin Street 2.00 5.00
19 Brandon Coleman 2.00 5.00
20 Josh Huff 2.50 6.00
21 James White 4.00 10.00
22 Taylor Lewan 2.00 5.00
23 Bradley Roby 2.00 5.00
24 Cody Latimer
25 Bishop Sankey 2.00 5.00
26 Tom Savage 2.00 5.00
27 Deone Bucannon 2.00 5.00
28 Rob Blanchflower 2.00 5.00
29 Jeremy Hill 2.50 6.00
30 Blake Bortles 2.50 6.00
31 Jason Verrett 2.00 5.00
33 Will Clarke 2.00 5.00
36 Brandin Cooks 3.00 8.00
37 Isaiah Burse 2.00 5.00
38 Logan Thomas 2.00 5.00
39 Kelvin Benjamin 3.00 8.00
40 Connor Shaw 2.00 5.00
42 Odell Beckham Jr. 40.00 80.00
43 Jerick McKinnon 2.50 6.00
44 Tre Mason 2.00 5.00
45 DaQuan Jones 2.50 6.00
46 Andre Williams 2.00 5.00
47 Marqise Lee
49 Jace Amaro 2.00 5.00
50 Donte Moncrief 2.00 5.00
51 Dri Archer 2.00 5.00
52 Mike Evans 8.00 20.00
54 Allen Robinson
55 Sammy Watkins 3.00 8.00
56 Antonio Richardson 3.00 8.00
57 Derek Carr 30.00 80.00
58 Jimmy Garoppolo 12.50 25.00
60 Ryan Shazier 3.00 8.00
61 Austin Seferian-Jenkins 2.00 5.00
62 Cyril Richardson 2.00 5.00
64 Johnny Manziel 10.00 25.00
65 Aaron Murray 2.00 5.00
66 Greg Robinson 2.00 5.00
67 C.J. Fiedorowicz 2.00 5.00
68 Stephen Morris 2.00 5.00
69 Troy Niklas 2.00 5.00
70 John Brown 3.00 8.00
72 Lache Seastrunk 2.00 5.00
73 Shaq Evans 2.00 5.00
74 Aaron Donald 8.00 20.00
76 Kevin Norwood 2.00 5.00
77 Jared Abbrederis 2.00 5.00
79 Jordan Lynch 2.50 6.00
80 Robert Herron 2.00 5.00

2014 Topps Platinum Camo Die Cut

*PINK DIE CUT: .4X TO 1X CAMO DC
BSDCAG A.J. Green 2.50 6.00
BSDCAJ Alshon Jeffery 2.00 5.00
BSDCAL Andrew Luck 3.00 8.00
BSDCAM Alfred Morris 1.50 4.00
BSDCAR Aaron Rodgers 5.00 12.00
BSDCBB Blake Bortles 1.00 2.50
BSDCDB Drew Brees 2.50 6.00
BSDCDC Derek Carr 5.00 12.00
BSDCEE Eric Ebron 2.00 5.00
BSDCJC Jadeveon Clowney 1.00 2.50
BSDCJCA Jordan Cameron 1.50 4.00
BSDCJE Julian Edelman 2.50 6.00
BSDCJM Johnny Manziel 1.25 3.00
BSDCJT Julius Thomas 1.50 4.00
BSDCJW J.J. Watt 2.50 6.00
BSDCKB Kelvin Benjamin 1.25 3.00
BSDCLM LeSean McCoy 2.50 6.00
BSDCME Mike Evans 2.00 5.00
BSDCML Marshawn Lynch 2.00 5.00
BSDCOB Odell Beckham Jr. 2.00 5.00
BSDCRG Rob Gronkowski 2.50 6.00
BSDCRW Russell Wilson 4.00 10.00
BSDCSW Sammy Watkins 1.25 3.00
BSDCTB Teddy Bridgewater 1.25 3.00
BSDCVC Victor Cruz 2.00 5.00

2014 Topps Platinum Patch Autographs Refractors

AVPBH Brian Hartline/172 6.00 15.00
AVPJR Jordan Reed/172 6.00 15.00
AVPMF Matt Forte/172 6.00 15.00
AVPML Marshawn Lynch/30 30.00 80.00
AVPRM Ryan Mathews/172 8.00 20.00
AVPSV Shane Vereen
AVPVC Victor Cruz

2014 Topps Platinum Rookie Autographs Dual

STATED PRINT RUN 25 SER.#'d SETS
DABW A.Williams/O.Beckham 90.00 150.00
DAES C.Sims/M.Evans 12.00 30.00
DAHM A.McCarron/J.Hill

2014 Topps Platinum Rookie Die Cut

STATED ODDS 1:20
PDCAM Aaron Murray .50 1.25
PDCAMC A.J. McCarron .50 1.25
PDCAR Allen Robinson .75 2.00
PDCBB Blake Bortles .60 1.50
PDCBS Bishop Sankey .50 1.25
PDCCH Carlos Hyde .60 1.50
PDCCL Cody Latimer .60 1.50
PDCDA Davante Adams .75 2.00
PDCDC Derek Carr 3.00 8.00
PDCDF Devonta Freeman .75 2.00
PDCEE Eric Ebron .60 1.50
PDCJC Jadeveon Clowney .60 1.50
PDCJG Jimmy Garoppolo 4.00 10.00
PDCJM Johnny Manziel .75 2.00
PDCJMA Jordan Matthews .75 2.00
PDCKB Kelvin Benjamin .75 2.00
PDCKM Khalil Mack 2.00 5.00
PDCME Mike Evans 1.25 3.00
PDCML Marqise Lee .60 1.50
PDCMS Michael Sam .50 1.25
PDCOB Odell Beckham Jr. 1.25 3.00
PDCSW Sammy Watkins .75 2.00
PDCTB Teddy Bridgewater .75 2.00
PDCTM Tre Mason .50 1.25
PDCTS Tom Savage .50 1.25

2014 Topps Platinum Rookie Jersey

*PATCH/68: .8X TO 2X BASIC JSY
PRRAM Aaron Murray 1.50 4.00
PRRAMC A.J. McCarron 1.50 4.00
PRRAR Allen Robinson 2.50 6.00
PRRAS Austin Seferian-Jenkins 1.50 4.00
PRRAW Andre Williams 1.50 4.00
PRRBB Blake Bortles 2.00 5.00
PRRBC Brandin Cooks 2.50 6.00
PRRBS Bishop Sankey 1.50 4.00
PRRCH Carlos Hyde 2.00 5.00
PRRCL Cody Latimer 2.00 5.00
PRRDA Davante Adams 2.50 6.00
PRRDAR Dri Archer 1.50 4.00
PRRDC Derek Carr 10.00 25.00
PRRDF Devonta Freeman 2.50 6.00
PRRDM Donte Moncrief 1.50 4.00
PRRDT De'Anthony Thomas 1.50 4.00
PRREE Eric Ebron 2.00 5.00
PRRJA Jace Amaro 1.50 4.00
PRRJC Jadeveon Clowney 2.00 5.00
PRRJG Jimmy Garoppolo 12.00 30.00
PRRJH Jeremy Hill 2.00 5.00
PRRJL Jarvis Landry 3.00 8.00
PRRJM Johnny Manziel 2.50 6.00
PRRJMA Jordan Matthews 2.50 6.00
PRRKB Kelvin Benjamin 2.50 6.00
PRRKC Ka'Deem Carey 1.50 4.00
PRRKM Khalil Mack 6.00 15.00
PRRME Mike Evans 4.00 10.00
PRRML Marqise Lee 2.00 5.00
PRROB Odell Beckham Jr. 10.00 25.00
PRRPR Paul Richardson 2.00 5.00
PRRSW Sammy Watkins 2.50 6.00
PRRTB Teddy Bridgewater 2.50 6.00
PRRTM Tre Mason 1.50 4.00
PRRTS Tom Savage 1.50 4.00

2014 Topps Platinum Rookie Patch Autographs Blue Refractors

*BLUE REF/25: .8X TO 2X PATCH AU REF
ARPBB Blake Bortles 40.00 80.00
ARPDC Derek Carr 40.00 100.00
ARPJM Johnny Manziel
ARPJM2 Johnny Manziel
ARPME Mike Evans
ARPOB Odell Beckham Jr. 60.00 125.00
ARPSW Sammy Watkins
ARPTB Teddy Bridgewater 25.00 50.00

2014 Topps Platinum Rookie Patch Autographs Refractors

STATED ODDS 1:35
*BLACK REF/125: .5X TO 1.2X REF.JSY AU
*GREEN REF/99: .5X TO 1.2X PATCH AU REF
*PULSAR REF/50: .6X TO 1.5X PATCH AU REF
ARPAD Aaron Donald 8.00 20.00
ARPAM Aaron Murray 3.00 8.00
ARPAMC A.J. McCarron 3.00 8.00
ARPAR Allen Robinson 5.00 12.00
ARPAS Austin Seferian-Jenkins 3.00 8.00
ARPAW Andre Williams 3.00 8.00
ARPBB Blake Bortles 4.00 10.00
ARPBC Brandin Cooks 5.00 12.00
ARPBS Bishop Sankey 3.00 8.00
ARPCH Carlos Hyde 4.00 10.00
ARPCL Cody Latimer 4.00 10.00
ARPCS Charles Sims 8.00 20.00
ARPDA Davante Adams 5.00 12.00
ARPDAR Dri Archer 3.00 8.00
ARPDC Derek Carr 20.00 50.00
ARPDF Devonta Freeman 12.00 30.00
ARPDM Donte Moncrief 3.00 8.00
ARPEE Eric Ebron 4.00 10.00
ARPJA Jace Amaro 3.00 8.00
ARPJC Jadeveon Clowney 4.00 10.00
ARPJG Jimmy Garoppolo 50.00 100.00
ARPJH Jeremy Hill 4.00 10.00
ARPJL Jarvis Landry 12.00 30.00
ARPJM Johnny Manziel 5.00 12.00
ARPJM2 Johnny Manziel 5.00 12.00
ARPJMA Jordan Matthews 5.00 12.00
ARPJMC Jerick McKinnon 4.00 10.00
ARPJW James White 6.00 15.00
ARPKB Kelvin Benjamin 5.00 12.00
ARPKC Ka'Deem Carey 3.00 8.00
ARPLT Logan Thomas 3.00 8.00
ARPME Mike Evans 12.00 30.00
ARPML Marqise Lee 4.00 10.00
ARPOB Odell Beckham Jr. 30.00 60.00
ARPPR Paul Richardson 6.00 15.00
ARPSW Sammy Watkins 5.00 12.00
ARPTB Teddy Bridgewater 15.00 40.00
ARPTBO Tajh Boyd 3.00 8.00
ARPTM Tre Mason 8.00 20.00
ARPTS Tom Savage 6.00 15.00
ARPTW Terrance West 3.00 8.00

2014 Topps Platinum Rookie Patch Autographs Dual

DADPBB Bortles/Bridgewater/25 25.00 50.00

2015 Topps Platinum

1 Odell Beckham Jr. .25 .60
2 Cam Newton .25 .60
3 Aaron Rodgers .50 1.25
4 Robert Mathis .15 .40
5 Tom Brady .60 1.50
6 Randall Cobb .20 .50
7 Colin Kaepernick .20 .50
8 Dwayne Allen .15 .40
9 Robert Quinn .20 .50
10 Tony Romo .20 .50
11 Greg Hardy .15 .40
12 Patrick Peterson .15 .40
13 Karlos Dansby .15 .40
14 DeAndre Hopkins .20 .50
15 Drew Brees .25 .60
16 Teddy Bridgewater .20 .50
17 J.J. Watt .25 .60
18 Peyton Manning .50 1.25
19 Matt Forte .15 .40
20 Andrew Luck .30 .75
21 C.J. Anderson .20 .50
22 Matt Ryan .20 .50
23 Alshon Jeffery .20 .50
24 Jordy Nelson .20 .50
25 Philip Rivers .25 .60
26 Darren McFadden .15 .40
27 Joique Bell .15 .40
28 Jason Pierre-Paul .15 .40
29 Terrell Suggs .15 .40
30 Golden Tate .15 .40
31 Darrelle Revis .15 .40
32 Jared Allen .15 .40
33 Dez Bryant .25 .60
34 Rob Gronkowski .25 .60
35 Eli Manning .20 .50
36 Matthew Stafford .20 .50
37 Mark Ingram .20 .50
38 A.J. Green .25 .60
39 Chandler Jones .15 .40
40 Giovani Bernard .15 .40
41 Jamaal Charles .20 .50
42 T.Y. Hilton .20 .50
43 Martellus Bennett .15 .40
44 Vernon Davis .15 .40
45 Richard Sherman .25 .60
46 Antonio Gates .15 .40
47 Jeremy Hill .15 .40
48 Ryan Tannehill .20 .50
49 Calvin Johnson .25 .60
50 Russell Wilson .30 .75
51 LeSean McCoy .25 .60
52 Jason Witten .20 .50
53 Emmanuel Sanders .20 .50
54 Greg Olsen .20 .50
55 Ben Roethlisberger .25 .60
56 Jordan Matthews .20 .50
57 Antonio Brown .25 .60
58 Jimmy Graham .25 .60
59 Justin Forsett .20 .50
60 Alfred Morris .15 .40
61 Clay Matthews .25 .60
62 Arian Foster .20 .50
63 DeSean Jackson .20 .50
64 DeMarcus Ware .20 .50
65 Jordan Reed .15 .40
66 C.J. Mosley .25 .60
67 Lamar Miller .15 .40
68 Frank Gore .20 .50
69 Marcell Dareus .15 .40
70 Le'Veon Bell .20 .50
71 Ndamukong Suh .20 .50
72 Latavius Murray .15 .40
73 Mike Evans .20 .50
74 Von Miller .20 .50
75 Tim Jennings .15 .40
76 Joe Flacco .20 .50
77 DeMarco Murray .20 .50
78 Cameron Wake .15 .40
79 Luke Kuechly .20 .50
80 Mario Williams .15 .40

81 Lavonte David .15 .40
82 Gerald McCoy .15 .40
83 Jay Cutler .15 .40
84 Travis Kelce .25 .60
85 Julius Thomas .15 .40
86 Demaryius Thomas .20 .50
87 Kelvin Benjamin .20 .50
88 Jonathan Stewart .15 .40
89 Julian Edelman .25 .60
90 Robert Griffin III .15 .40
91 Marshawn Lynch .20 .50
92 Zach Ertz .20 .50
93 Sam Bradford .15 .40
94 DeAndre Levy .15 .40
95 Sammy Watkins .20 .50
96 Julio Jones .25 .60
97 Eddie Lacy .15 .40
98 Joe Haden .15 .40
99 Brandon Marshall .15 .40
100 Jordan Cameron .15 .40
101 Jameis Winston RC .75 2.00
102 Phillip Dorsett RC .30 .75
103 Todd Gurley RC 1.25 3.00
104 Jamison Crowder RC .40 1.00
105 Melvin Gordon RC .75 2.00
106 Mike Davis RC .30 .75
107 Kenny Bell RC .50 1.25
108 Devin Smith RC .30 .75
109 Rashad Greene RC .30 .75
110 Brett Hundley RC .30 .75
111 Matt Jones RC .30 .75
112 Tyler Kroft RC .40 1.00
113 Jay Ajayi RC .50 1.25
114 Amari Cooper RC 1.00 2.50
115 David Cobb RC .30 .75
116 Vince Mayle RC .40 1.00
117 Clive Walford RC .30 .75
118 Breshad Perriman RC .30 .75
119 Ty Montgomery RC .30 .75
120 DeVante Parker RC .50 1.25
121 T.J. Yeldon RC .30 .75
122 Dorial Green-Beckham RC .30 .75
123 Duke Johnson RC .50 1.25
124 Andrus Peat RC .30 .75
125 Marcus Mariota RC 1.25 3.00
126 Jaelen Strong RC .40 1.00
127 Jeremy Langford RC .30 .75
128 Chris Conley RC .30 .75
129 Karlos Williams RC .30 .75
130 David Johnson RC .75 2.00
131 Sammie Coates RC .40 1.00
132 Garrett Grayson RC .30 .75
133 Javorius Allen RC .40 1.00
134 Tevin Coleman RC .40 1.00
135 Brandon Scherff RC .50 1.25
136 Ameer Abdullah RC .50 1.25
137 Tyler Lockett RC .50 1.25
138 Kevin White RC .40 1.00
139 Vic Beasley RC .40 1.00
140 Maxx Williams RC .30 .75
141 Stefon Diggs RC .75 2.00
142 Justin Hardy RC .30 .75
143 Trae Waynes RC .30 .75
144 Nelson Agholor RC .40 1.00
146 Bryce Petty RC .30 .75
147 Sean Mannion RC .30 .75
148 Alvin Dupree RC .40 1.00
149 Cameron Artis-Payne RC .30 .75
150 Leonard Williams RC .30 .75

2015 Topps Platinum Black Refractors
*BLACK REF/50: 2.5X TO 6X BASIC RC

2015 Topps Platinum Gold
*GOLD: 1X TO 2.5X BASIC CARDS

2015 Topps Platinum Orange Refractors
*ORANGE: .6X TO 1.5X BASIC RC
INSERTED IN HANGER PACKS

2015 Topps Platinum Pulsar Refractors
*PULSAR/99: 1.5X TO 4X BASIC RC

2015 Topps Platinum Purple Refractors
*PURPLE REF/75: 2X TO 5X BASIC RC

2015 Topps Platinum Red Refractors
*RED REF/25: 4X TO 10X BASIC RC

2015 Topps Platinum Sapphire Refractors
*SAPPHIRE REF: .8X TO 2X BASIC RC

2015 Topps Platinum Xfractors
*XFRACTOR: .5X TO 1.2X BASIC RC

2015 Topps Platinum Autographs Refractors
ARAA Ameer Abdullah 3.00 8.00
ARAAR Arik Armstead 2.00 5.00
ARAC Amari Cooper
ARACA Alex Carter 2.00 5.00
ARAD Alvin Dupree 2.50 6.00
ARAG Antwan Goodley 2.00 5.00
ARAH Austin Hill 2.00 5.00
ARAP Andrus Peat 2.00 5.00
ARBJ Byron Jones 3.00 8.00
ARBK Ben Koyack 3.00 8.00
ARBM Benardrick McKinney 2.00 5.00
ARBP Breshad Perriman 2.00 5.00
ARBPE Bryce Petty 2.00 5.00
ARBS Brandon Scherff 3.00 8.00
ARCA Cameron Artis-Payne 2.00 5.00
ARCW Clive Walford 2.00 5.00
ARDA Dres Anderson 2.00 5.00
ARDC David Cobb 2.00 5.00
ARDD Devante Davis 2.50 6.00
ARDF Devin Funchess
ARDFJ Dante Fowler Jr. 3.00 8.00
ARDG Deontay Greenberry 2.00 5.00
ARDH Danielle Hunter 2.50 6.00
ARDJ Duke Johnson 3.00 8.00
ARDP Denzel Perryman 2.00 5.00
ARDS Devin Smith 2.00 5.00
ARDSN Danny Shelton 2.00 5.00
AREH Eli Harold 2.00 5.00
AREK Eric Kendricks 2.00 5.00
ARJAJ Jay Ajayi 3.00 8.00
ARJC Jamison Crowder 2.50 6.00
ARJH Jeff Heuerman 2.50 6.00
ARJHA Justin Hardy 2.00 5.00
ARJHR Josh Harper 2.00 5.00
ARJL Jeremy Langford
ARJR Josh Robinson 2.00 5.00
ARJS Jaelen Strong 2.50 6.00
ARJW Jameis Winston
ARKB Kenny Bell 3.00 8.00
ARKJ Kevin Johnson 2.00 5.00
ARKW Kevin White
ARKWI Karlos Williams 2.00 5.00
ARLC Landon Collins 2.50 6.00
ARLCO La'el Collins 2.50 6.00
ARLM Lorenzo Mauldin 2.00 5.00
ARLW Leonard Williams 2.00 5.00
ARMB Malcom Brown 2.00 5.00
ARMD Mike Davis 2.00 5.00
ARMG Melvin Gordon 10.00 25.00
ARMJ Matt Jones
ARMM Marcus Mariota EXCH
ARMP Marcus Peters 8.00 20.00
ARNA Nelson Agholor 2.50 6.00
AROO Owamagbe Odighizuwa 2.50 6.00
ARPD Phillip Dorsett
ARPDA Paul Dawson 2.50 6.00
ARPW P.J. Williams 2.50 6.00
ARRG Rashad Greene 2.00 5.00
ARSR Shane Ray 2.00 5.00
ARST Shaq Thompson 2.50 6.00
ARTC Tevin Coleman 2.50 6.00
ARTD Titus Davis 2.50 6.00
ARTF Trey Flowers 3.00 8.00
ARTG Todd Gurley 50.00 100.00
ARTK Tyler Kroft 2.50 6.00
ARTL Tyler Lockett
ARTLI Tony Lippett 2.00 5.00
ARTM Ty Montgomery
ARTMB Tre McBride 2.00 5.00
ARTY T.J. Yeldon 2.00 5.00

2015 Topps Platinum Autographs Gold Refractors
*GOLD/99: .6X TO 1.5X BASIC AU
ARTG Todd Gurley 40.00 80.00

2015 Topps Platinum Autographs Pulsar Refractors
*PULSAR/50: .75X TO 2X BASIC AU
ARJW Jameis Winston 75.00 125.00

2015 Topps Platinum Autographs Purple Refractors
*PURPLE/25: 1X TO 2.5X BASIC AU

2015 Topps Platinum Camo Die Cut
*PINK DIE CUT: .4X TO 1X CAMO DC
BSDRAA Ameer Abdullah 1.25 3.00
BSDRAB Antonio Brown 2.50 6.00
BSDRAC Amari Cooper 2.50 6.00
BSDRAG A.J. Green 2.50 6.00
BSDRAL Andrew Luck 3.00 8.00
BSDRAR Aaron Rodgers 5.00 12.00
BSDRBH Brett Hundley .75 2.00
BSDRBP Breshad Perriman .75 2.00
BSDRCA C.J. Anderson 2.00 5.00
BSDRCJ Calvin Johnson 2.50 6.00
BSDRDB Dez Bryant 2.50 6.00
BSDRDBR Drew Brees 2.50 6.00
BSDRDG Dorial Green-Beckham .75 2.00
BSDRDJ Duke Johnson 1.25 3.00
BSDRDM DeMarco Murray 2.00 5.00
BSDRDP DeVante Parker 1.25 3.00
BSDREL Eddie Lacy 1.50 4.00
BSDREM Eli Manning 2.00 5.00
BSDRGG Garrett Grayson .75 2.00
BSDRJA Jay Ajayi 1.25 3.00
BSDRJC Jamaal Charles 2.00 5.00
BSDRJG Jimmy Graham 2.50 6.00
BSDRJH Jeremy Hill 1.50 4.00
BSDRJN Jordy Nelson 2.00 5.00
BSDRJS Jaelen Strong 1.00 2.50
BSDRJW Jameis Winston 2.00 5.00
BSDRKB Kelvin Benjamin 2.00 5.00
BSDRKW Kevin White 1.00 2.50
BSDRLB Le'Veon Bell 2.00 5.00
BSDRME Mike Evans 2.00 5.00
BSDRMF Matt Forte 1.50 4.00
BSDRMG Melvin Gordon 2.00 5.00
BSDRML Marshawn Lynch 2.00 5.00
BSDRMM Marcus Mariota 3.00 8.00
BSDROB Odell Beckham Jr. 2.50 6.00
BSDRPD Phillip Dorsett .75 2.00
BSDRPM Peyton Manning 5.00 12.00
BSDRRG Rob Gronkowski 2.50 6.00
BSDRRW Russell Wilson 3.00 8.00
BSDRSC Sammie Coates 1.00 2.50
BSDRTB Tom Brady 6.00 15.00
BSDRTC Tevin Coleman 1.00 2.50
BSDRTG Todd Gurley 3.00 8.00
BSDRTY T.J. Yeldon .75 2.00

2015 Topps Platinum Platinum Players Die Cut
PDCAA Ameer Abdullah .75 2.00
PDCAC Amari Cooper 1.50 4.00
PDCAG A.J. Green 1.50 4.00
PDCAL Andrew Luck 2.00 5.00
PDCAR Aaron Rodgers 3.00 8.00
PDCDB Drew Brees 1.50 4.00
PDCEL Eddie Lacy 1.00 2.50
PDCEM Eli Manning 1.25 3.00
PDCJG Jimmy Graham 1.50 4.00
PDCJH Jeremy Hill 1.00 2.50
PDCJW Jameis Winston 1.25 3.00
PDCKB Kelvin Benjamin 1.25 3.00
PDCKW Kevin White .60 1.50
PDCLB Le'Veon Bell 1.25 3.00
PDCME Mike Evans 1.25 3.00
PDCMG Melvin Gordon 1.25 3.00
PDCML Marshawn Lynch 1.25 3.00
PDCMM Marcus Mariota 2.00 5.00
PDCOB Odell Beckham Jr. 1.50 4.00
PDCPM Peyton Manning 3.00 8.00
PDCRG Rob Gronkowski 1.50 4.00
PDCRW Russell Wilson 2.00 5.00
PDCTB Tom Brady 4.00 10.00
PDCTG Todd Gurley 2.00 5.00
PDCTY T.J. Yeldon .50 1.25

2015 Topps Platinum Rookie Jersey
PRRAA Ameer Abdullah 2.50 6.00
PRRAC Amari Cooper 6.00 15.00
PRRBH Brett Hundley 4.00 10.00
PRRBP Breshad Perriman 1.50 4.00
PRRBPE Bryce Petty 1.50 4.00
PRRCC Chris Conley 1.50 4.00
PRRDC David Cobb 1.50 4.00
PRRDG Dorial Green-Beckham 1.50 4.00
PRRDJ Duke Johnson 2.50 6.00
PRRDJO David Johnson 4.00 10.00
PRRDP DeVante Parker 2.50 6.00
PRRDS Devin Smith 1.50 4.00
PRRGG Garrett Grayson 1.50 4.00
PRRJA Jay Ajayi 2.50 6.00
PRRJAL Javorius Allen 2.00 5.00
PRRJC Jamison Crowder 2.00 5.00
PRRJHD Justin Hardy 1.50 4.00
PRRJL Jeremy Langford 1.50 4.00
PRRJS Jaelen Strong 2.00 5.00
PRRJW Jameis Winston 6.00 15.00
PRRKW Karlos Williams 1.50 4.00
PRRKW Kevin White 4.00 10.00
PRRLW Leonard Williams 1.50 4.00
PRRMD Mike Davis 1.50 4.00
PRRMG Melvin Gordon 5.00 12.00
PRRMJ Matt Jones 1.50 4.00
PRRMM Marcus Mariota 6.00 15.00
PRRMW Maxx Williams 1.50 4.00
PRRNA Nelson Agholor 2.00 5.00
PRRPD Phillip Dorsett 1.50 4.00
PRRRG Rashad Greene 1.50 4.00
PRRSC Sammie Coates 2.00 5.00
PRRSD Stefon Diggs 4.00 10.00
PRRSM Sean Mannion 1.50 4.00
PRRTC Tevin Coleman 2.00 5.00
PRRTG Todd Gurley 8.00 20.00
PRRTL Tyler Lockett 2.50 6.00
PRRTM Ty Montgomery 1.50 4.00
PRRTY T.J. Yeldon 1.50 4.00

2015 Topps Platinum Rookie Patch Autographs
ARPAA Ameer Abdullah
ARPAC Amari Cooper
ARPBP Breshad Perriman 3.00 8.00
ARPCC Chris Conley 3.00 8.00
ARPCW Clive Walford 3.00 8.00
ARPDC David Cobb 3.00 8.00
ARPDJ Duke Johnson 5.00 12.00
ARPDP DeVante Parker
ARPDS Devin Smith 3.00 8.00
ARPJA Jay Ajayi 5.00 12.00
ARPJC Jamison Crowder 4.00 10.00
ARPJH Jeff Heuerman 4.00 10.00
ARPJJ Jesse James 4.00 10.00
ARPJL Jeremy Langford 3.00 8.00
ARPJS Jaelen Strong 4.00 10.00
ARPJW Jameis Winston 75.00 150.00
ARPKB Kenny Bell 5.00 12.00
ARPKW Kevin White
ARPLW Leonard Williams 3.00 8.00
ARPMD Mike Davis 3.00 8.00
ARPMG Melvin Gordon
ARPMJ Matt Jones
ARPMM Marcus Mariota
ARPMW Maxx Williams 3.00 8.00
ARPNA Nelson Agholor 4.00 10.00
ARPRG Rashad Greene 3.00 8.00
ARPSC Sammie Coates 4.00 10.00
ARPSD Stefon Diggs 8.00 20.00
ARPTC Tevin Coleman 4.00 10.00
ARPTG Todd Gurley
ARPTL Tyler Lockett 5.00 12.00
ARPTM Ty Montgomery 3.00 8.00
ARPTY T.J. Yeldon
ARPVM Vince Mayle 4.00 10.00
ARPBPY Bryce Petty 3.00 8.00
ARPDGB Dorial Green-Beckham
ARPJAL Javorius Allen 4.00 10.00
ARPJHD Justin Hardy 3.00 8.00
ARPKWM Karlos Williams 3.00 8.00
ARPTMB Tre McBride 3.00 8.00

2015 Topps Platinum Rookie Patch Autographs Refractors
ARPAA Ameer Abdullah
ARPAC Amari Cooper
ARPBP Breshad Perriman 3.00 8.00
ARPCC Chris Conley 3.00 8.00
ARPCW Clive Walford 3.00 8.00
ARPDC David Cobb 3.00 8.00
ARPDJ Duke Johnson 5.00 12.00
ARPDP DeVante Parker
ARPDS Devin Smith 3.00 8.00
ARPJA Jay Ajayi
ARPJC Jamison Crowder 4.00 10.00
ARPJH Jeff Heuerman 4.00 10.00
ARPJJ Jesse James 4.00 10.00
ARPJL Jeremy Langford 3.00 8.00
ARPJS Jaelen Strong 4.00 10.00
ARPJW Jameis Winston
ARPKB Kenny Bell 5.00 12.00
ARPKW Kevin White
ARPLW Leonard Williams 3.00 8.00
ARPMD Mike Davis 3.00 8.00
ARPMG Melvin Gordon
ARPMJ Matt Jones
ARPMM Marcus Mariota
ARPMW Maxx Williams 3.00 8.00
ARPNA Nelson Agholor
ARPRG Rashad Greene 3.00 8.00
ARPSC Sammie Coates 4.00 10.00
ARPSD Stefon Diggs 8.00 20.00
ARPTC Tevin Coleman 4.00 10.00
ARPTG Todd Gurley
ARPTL Tyler Lockett 5.00 12.00
ARPTM Ty Montgomery 3.00 8.00
ARPTY T.J. Yeldon
ARPVM Vince Mayle 4.00 10.00
ARPBPY Bryce Petty 3.00 8.00
ARPDGB Dorial Green-Beckham 12.00 30.00
ARPJAL Javorius Allen 4.00 10.00
ARPJHD Justin Hardy 3.00 8.00
ARPKWM Karlos Williams 3.00 8.00
ARPTMB Tre McBride 3.00 8.00

2015 Topps Platinum Rookie Patch Autographs Black Refractors
*BLACK/125: .5X TO 1.2X BASIC JSY AU

2015 Topps Platinum Rookie Patch Autographs Green Refractors
*GREEN/99: .6X TO 1.5X BASIC JSY AU

2015 Topps Platinum Rookie Patch Autographs Sapphire Refractors
*SAPPHIRE/25: 1X TO 2.5X BASIC INSERTS
ARPJW Jameis Winston 125.00 200.00

2015 Topps Platinum Rookie Patch Autographs Dual
DADPAP J.Allen/B.Perriman 10.00 25.00
DADPAY T.Yeldon/A.Abdullah 12.00 30.00
DADPCA C.Artis-Payne/S.Coates 10.00 25.00
DADPCH T.Coleman/J.Hardy 10.00 25.00
DADPCP D.Parker/A.Cooper 50.00 100.00
DADPCW A.Cooper/K.White 50.00 100.00
DADPCY A.Cooper/T.Yeldon 50.00 100.00
DADPGC D.Cobb/D.Green-Beckham 8.00 20.00
DADPGG M.Gordon/T.Gurley 40.00 80.00
DADPGY R.Greene/T.Yeldon 8.00 20.00
DADPJC M.Jones/J.Crowder 10.00 25.00
DADPJM V.Mayle/D.Johnson 12.00 30.00
DADPPA D.Parker/J.Ajayi 12.00 30.00
DADPPS B.Petty/D.Smith 8.00 20.00
DADPWM M.Mariota/J.Winston 100.00 200.00

2011 Topps Precision
ONE AUTO PER PACK OVERALL
EXCH EXPIRATION: 1/31/2015
1 Adrian Peterson 1.50 4.00
2 Sidney Rice 1.00 2.50
3 Sam Bradford 1.00 2.50
4 Patrick Willis 1.25 3.00
5 Roger Staubach 2.00 5.00
6 Jim Brown 2.00 5.00
7 Maurice Jones-Drew 1.00 2.50
8 Frank Gore 1.25 3.00
9 Marques Colston 1.00 2.50
10 Larry Fitzgerald 1.25 3.00
11 DeAngelo Williams 1.00 2.50
12 Greg Jennings 1.00 2.50
13 Tony Dorsett 1.50 4.00
14 DeMarcus Ware 1.25 3.00
15 DeSean Jackson 1.25 3.00
16 Mike Wallace 1.00 2.50
17 Calvin Johnson 1.50 4.00
18 Reggie Bush 1.00 2.50
19 Dwayne Bowe 1.25 3.00
20 Roddy White 1.00 2.50
21 Peyton Hillis 1.00 2.50
22 Shonn Greene 1.00 2.50
23 Earl Campbell 1.50 4.00
24 Jason Witten 1.25 3.00
25 Knowshon Moreno 1.00 2.50
26 Rashard Mendenhall 1.00 2.50
27 Vincent Jackson 1.00 2.50
28 Ben Roethlisberger 1.50 4.00
29 Phil Simms 1.25 3.00
30 Chris Johnson 1.00 2.50
31 Brandon Lloyd 1.00 2.50
32 Charles Woodson 1.50 4.00
33 Ndamukong Suh 1.25 3.00
34 Tony Romo 1.25 3.00
35 Philip Rivers 1.50 4.00
36 Vernon Davis 1.00 2.50
37 Miles Austin 1.00 2.50
38 Dez Bryant 1.50 4.00
39 Jimmy Graham 1.50 4.00
40 Andre Johnson 1.25 3.00
41 Chad Ochocinco 1.00 2.50
42 Percy Harvin 1.00 2.50
43 Terry Bradshaw 2.00 5.00
44 Brandon Marshall 1.25 3.00
45 Joe Flacco 1.25 3.00
46 Peyton Manning 3.00 8.00
47 Mike Williams 1.25 3.00
48 Cedric Benson 1.00 2.50
49 Josh Freeman 1.25 3.00
50 Aaron Rodgers 3.00 8.00
51 Mario Manningham 1.00 2.50
52 Pierre Thomas 1.00 2.50
53 Kenny Britt 1.00 2.50
54 Santonio Holmes 1.00 2.50
55 Clay Matthews 1.50 4.00
56 Felix Jones 1.00 2.50
57 LeSean McCoy 1.50 4.00
58 Thurman Thomas 1.25 3.00
59 Ray Lewis 1.50 4.00
60 Jamaal Charles 1.25 3.00
61 Joe Namath 2.00 5.00
62 Dallas Clark 1.00 2.50
63 Ahmad Bradshaw 1.00 2.50
64 Ryan Mathews 1.25 3.00
65 Eli Manning 1.25 3.00
66 Matt Schaub 1.00 2.50
67 Darren McFadden 1.00 2.50
68 Ray Rice 1.00 2.50
69 Gale Sayers 1.50 4.00
70 Arian Foster 1.00 2.50
71 Matt Forte 1.00 2.50
72 Steve Smith 1.25 3.00
73 Hakeem Nicks 1.00 2.50
74 Franco Harris 1.50 4.00
75 Steven Jackson 1.00 2.50
76 Matthew Stafford 1.25 3.00
77 Steve Johnson 1.00 2.50
78 Antonio Gates 1.00 2.50
79 Anquan Boldin 1.00 2.50
80 Tom Brady 4.00 10.00
81 Len Dawson 1.50 4.00
82 Marshawn Lynch 1.25 3.00
83 Austin Collie 1.00 2.50
84 Kurt Warner 1.25 3.00
85 Beanie Wells 1.00 2.50
86 Owen Daniels 1.00 2.50
87 Michael Turner 1.00 2.50
88 Eric Dickerson 1.25 3.00
89 LeGarrette Blount 1.25 3.00
90 Drew Brees 1.50 4.00
91 Tim Hightower 1.00 2.50
92 Marcus Allen 1.50 4.00
93 Santana Moss 1.25 3.00
94 Jermichael Finley 1.00 2.50
95 Reggie Wayne 1.25 3.00
96 Jahvid Best 1.00 2.50
97 Joseph Addai 1.00 2.50
98 Matt Ryan 1.25 3.00
99 Jeremy Maclin 1.00 2.50
100 Michael Vick 1.25 3.00
105 Colin Kaepernick AU RC 6.00 15.00
106 Ryan Mallett AU RC 4.00 10.00
107 Jonathan Baldwin AU RC 4.00 10.00
108 Ryan Williams AU RC 4.00 10.00
109 Mikel Leshoure AU RC 4.00 10.00
111 Marcell Dareus AU RC 4.00 10.00
112 Von Miller AU RC 10.00 25.00
113 Randall Cobb AU RC 6.00 15.00
114 Leonard Hankerson AU RC 4.00 10.00
115 Greg Little AU RC 5.00 12.00
116 Torrey Smith AU RC 4.00 10.00
117 Alex Green AU RC 8.00 20.00
118 Jerrel Jernigan AU RC 4.00 10.00
119 DeMarco Murray AU RC 8.00 20.00
121 Shane Vereen AU RC 5.00 12.00
122 Stevan Ridley AU RC 4.00 10.00
123 Delone Carter AU RC 4.00 10.00
124 Jamie Harper AU RC 5.00 12.00
125 Taiwan Jones AU RC 5.00 12.00
126 Bilal Powell AU RC 5.00 12.00
127 Jordan Todman AU RC 4.00 10.00
128 Edmond Gates AU RC 4.00 10.00
129 Kendall Hunter AU RC 8.00 20.00
131 Vincent Brown AU RC 5.00 12.00
132 Roy Helu AU RC 6.00 15.00
133 Terrelle Pryor AU SP RC 6.00 15.00
134 Titus Young AU RC 4.00 10.00
135 Kyle Rudolph AU RC 4.00 10.00
136 Austin Pettis AU RC 4.00 10.00
137 Daniel Thomas AU RC 4.00 10.00

2011 Topps Precision Autographs Gold
*GOLD VETS/50: .5X TO 1.2X RED AU/99
GOLD VETERANS PRINT RUN 50
UNPRICED GOLD LEGEND PRINT RUN 10
PCVADB Drew Brees/50 40.00 80.00

2011 Topps Precision Autographs Green
*GREEN VETS/25: .6X TO 1.5X RED AU/99
GREEN PRINT RUN 25 SER.#'d SETS
PCVADB Drew Brees 40.00 100.00

2011 Topps Precision Autographs Red
VETERAN STATED PRINT RUN 99
LEGEND STATED PRINT RUN 25
*BASE VETS: .3X TO .8X RED AU/99
*BASE LEGENDS: .3X TO .8X RED AU/99
PCRAAM Art Monk/25 20.00 50.00
PCRAEC Earl Campbell/25 20.00 50.00
PCRAED Eric Dickerson/25 20.00 50.00
PCRAFB Fred Biletnikoff/25 20.00 50.00
PCRAFH Franco Harris/25 20.00 50.00
PCRAGS Gale Sayers/25 25.00 60.00
PCRAJB Jerome Bettis/25 40.00 100.00
PCRAJBR Jim Brown/25 40.00 80.00
PCRAJN Joe Namath/25 50.00 100.00
PCRAKS Ken Stabler/25 20.00 50.00
PCRAKW Kurt Warner/25
PCRALD Len Dawson/25 15.00 40.00
PCRAMA Marcus Allen/25 20.00 50.00
PCRAPS Phil Simms/25 15.00 40.00
PCRARL Ronnie Lott/25 20.00 50.00
PCRARS Roger Staubach/25 50.00 100.00
PCRATB Terry Bradshaw/25 50.00 100.00
PCRATBR Tim Brown/25 20.00 50.00
PCRATD Tony Dorsett/25 30.00 60.00
PCRATT Thurman Thomas/25 15.00 40.00
PCRAYT Y.A. Tittle/25 15.00 40.00
PCVAAB Ahmad Bradshaw/99 6.00 15.00
PCVAABE Arrelious Benn/99 4.00 10.00
PCVAAR Antrel Rolle/99 4.00 10.00
PCVAAW Adrian Wilson/99 4.00 10.00
PCVABL Brandon Lloyd/99 4.00 10.00
PCVACS C.J. Spiller/99 4.00 10.00
PCVADBE Davone Bess/99 4.00 10.00
PCVADH DeAngelo Hall/99 4.00 10.00
PCVADM Derrick Mason/99 4.00 10.00
PCVAEB Eric Berry/99 6.00 15.00
PCVAGO Greg Olsen/99 5.00 12.00
PCVAJF Jacoby Ford/99 5.00 12.00
PCVAJG Jermaine Gresham/99 4.00 10.00
PCVAJGR Jimmy Graham/99 6.00 15.00
PCVAJM Jerod Mayo/99 5.00 12.00
PCVAJP Jason Pierre-Paul/99 10.00 25.00
PCVALB LeGarrette Blount/99 5.00 12.00
PCVAML Marshawn Lynch/99 15.00 40.00
PCVAMW Mike Wallace/99 4.00 10.00
PCVANW Nate Washington/99 5.00 12.00
PCVARM Robert Mathis/99 6.00 15.00
PCVARW Roddy White/99 6.00 15.00
PCVASB Steve Breaston/99 4.00 10.00
PCVASJ Steve Johnson/99 6.00 15.00
PCVATH Todd Heap/99 4.00 10.00
PCVATJ Thomas Jones/99 6.00 15.00
PCVATP Taylor Price/99 4.00 10.00
PCVATW T.J. Ward/99 6.00 15.00
PCVAVD Vernon Davis/99 8.00 20.00

2011 Topps Precision Autographs Dual
STATED PRINT RUN 25 SER.#'d SETS
PCDABS J.Baldwin/T.Smith 8.00 20.00
PCDACG R.Cobb/A.Green 12.00 30.00
PCDADG A.Dalton/A.J. Green 40.00 80.00
PCDADM M.Dareus/V.Miller EXCH 20.00 50.00
PCDAFJ J.Ford/T.Jones 10.00 25.00
PCDAGJ A.J. Green/J.Jones 60.00 120.00
PCDAGL B.Gabbert/J.Locker 8.00 20.00
PCDAIL M.Ingram/M.Leshoure 12.00 30.00
PCDAKH C.Kaepernick/K.Hunter 12.00 30.00
PCDAKW K.Kolb/R.Williams 8.00 20.00
PCDALH G.Little/L.Hankerson 10.00 25.00
PCDALY M.Leshoure/T.Young 8.00 20.00
PCDAMR R.Mallett/S.Ridley 8.00 20.00
PCDAMT B.Marshall/D.Thomas 15.00 40.00
PCDAMV R.Mallett/S.Vereen 10.00 25.00
PCDANG C.Newton/A.J. Green 75.00 150.00
PCDANI C.Newton/M.Ingram 50.00 100.00
PCDANJ C.Newton/J.Jones 75.00 150.00
PCDAPR C.Ponder/K.Rudolph 25.00 60.00
PCDASY M.Stafford/T.Young 20.00 50.00
PCDATB J.Todman/V.Brown 12.00 30.00
PCDATG D.Thomas/E.Gates 8.00 20.00
PCDAVR S.Vereen/S.Ridley 10.00 25.00
PCDALHA J.Locker/J.Harper 8.00 20.00
PCDANGA C.Newton/B.Gabbert 75.00 150.00

2011 Topps Precision Autographs Triple
STATED PRINT RUN 15 SER.#'d SETS
BCI Brees/Colston/Ingram 150.00 250.00
CJC Cassel/T.Jones/Charles 15.00 40.00
FMB Fairley/V.Miller/Bowers 10.00 25.00
GSL A.J. Green/T.Smith/Little 50.00 100.00
JCG Jennings/Cobb/A.Green
KWW Kolb/Wells/Williams 30.00 60.00
LYF Leshoure/Young/Fairley 10.00 25.00
MHL C.McCoy/Hillis/Little 25.00 50.00
MVR Mallett/Vereen/Ridley 20.00 50.00
RBM Romo/D.Bryant/D.Murray 75.00 150.00
RML Ridley/Murray/D.Lewis 25.00 50.00
RPC Ridley/Powell/Carter 20.00 50.00
RWJ M.Ryan/R.White/J.Jones 60.00 120.00
TMR D.Thomas/Murray/Ridley 25.00 50.00
YHL T.Young/Hankerson/Little 15.00 40.00

2011 Topps Precision Rookie Autographs Gold Ink
*GOLD INK/50: .6X TO 1.5X BASIC AU
GOLD INK STATED PRINT RUN 50
EXCH EXPIRATION: 1/31/2015
101 Jake Locker 8.00 20.00
102 Blaine Gabbert 8.00 20.00
104 Andy Dalton 15.00 40.00
120 A.J. Green 40.00 100.00
138 Cam Newton 100.00 200.00

2011 Topps Precision Rookie Autographs Red Ink
*RED INK/75: .5X TO 1.2X BASIC AU
RED INK STATED PRINT RUN 75
103 Christian Ponder 6.00 15.00
104 Andy Dalton 15.00 40.00
110 Mark Ingram 30.00 60.00

2011 Topps Precision Rookie Autographs White Ink
*WHITE INK/25: .8X TO 2X BASIC AU
WHITE INK STATED PRINT RUN 25
101 Jake Locker 10.00 25.00
102 Blaine Gabbert 10.00 25.00
103 Christian Ponder 10.00 25.00
110 Mark Ingram 40.00 100.00

2011 Topps Precision Rookie Jumbo Relic Autographs Green
GREEN PRINT RUN 25 SER.#'d SETS
*BASE JSY AU: .25X TO .6X GREEN JSY AU/25
*GOLD/30: .3X TO .8X GREEN JSY AU/25
*RED/50: .3X TO .8X GREEN JSY AU/25
EXCH EXPIRATION: 1/31/2015
RAJRAD Andy Dalton 20.00 40.00
RAJRAG A.J. Green 50.00 100.00
RAJRAGR Alex Green 8.00 20.00
RAJRAP Austin Pettis 8.00 20.00
RAJRBG Blaine Gabbert 8.00 20.00
RAJRBP Bilal Powell 10.00 25.00
RAJRCK Colin Kaepernick 12.00 30.00
RAJRCN Cam Newton 100.00 200.00
RAJRCP Christian Ponder 8.00 20.00
RAJRDC Delone Carter 8.00 20.00
RAJRDM DeMarco Murray 15.00 40.00
RAJRDT Daniel Thomas 8.00 20.00
RAJREG Edmond Gates 8.00 20.00
RAJRGL Greg Little 10.00 25.00
RAJRJB Jonathan Baldwin 8.00 20.00
RAJRJH Jamie Harper 10.00 25.00
RAJRJE Jerrel Jernigan 8.00 20.00
RAJRJL Jake Locker 8.00 20.00
RAJRJT Jordan Todman 8.00 20.00
RAJRKH Kendall Hunter 8.00 20.00
RAJRKR Kyle Rudolph 8.00 20.00
RAJRLH Leonard Hankerson 8.00 20.00
RAJRMD Marcell Dareus 8.00 20.00
RAJRMI Mark Ingram 25.00 60.00
RAJRML Mikel Leshoure 8.00 20.00
RAJRRC Randall Cobb 12.00 30.00
RAJRRM Ryan Mallett 8.00 20.00
RAJRRW Ryan Williams 8.00 20.00
RAJRSR Stevan Ridley 8.00 20.00
RAJRSV Shane Vereen 10.00 25.00
RAJRTJ Taiwan Jones 8.00 20.00
RAJRTS Torrey Smith 8.00 20.00
RAJRTY Titus Young 8.00 20.00
RAJRVB Vincent Brown 8.00 20.00
RAJRVM Von Miller 20.00 50.00

2011 Topps Precision Veteran Patch Relic Autographs
STATED PRINT RUN 15 SER.#'d SETS
VAPAB Ahmad Bradshaw 10.00 25.00
VAPAG Antonio Gates 10.00 25.00
VAPBL Brandon Lloyd 10.00 25.00
VAPDM Darren McFadden 15.00 40.00
VAPHW Hines Ward 50.00 100.00
VAPJC Jamaal Charles 12.00 30.00
VAPLM LeSean McCoy 15.00 40.00
VAPMS Mark Sanchez 12.00 30.00
VAPSJ Steve Johnson
VAPVD Vernon Davis 15.00 40.00

2010 Topps Prime
COMPLETE SET (150) 40.00 80.00
COMP.SET w/o RC's (100) 15.00 30.00
ROOKIE/999 STATED ODDS 1:4 HOB
HOBBY CARDS PRINTED ON THICK STOCK
1 Tim Tebow RC 2.00 5.00
2 Trent Williams RC .75 2.00
3 Miles Austin .20 .50
4 Matt Forte .20 .50
5 Armanti Edwards RC .75 2.00
6 Mike Wallace .20 .50
7 Donovan McNabb .25 .60
8 Jay Cutler .20 .50
9 Derrick Morgan RC .60 1.50
10 Jimmy Clausen RC .60 1.50
11 Knowshon Moreno .20 .50
12 Arrelious Benn RC .60 1.50
13 James Laurinaitis .25 .60
14 Kellen Winslow .20 .50
15 Reggie Bush .20 .50
16 Jacoby Ford RC .60 1.50
17 Carlton Mitchell RC .60 1.50
18 Beanie Wells .20 .50
19 Troy Polamalu .30 .75
20 Colt McCoy RC .75 2.00
21 Kevin Kolb .20 .50
22 Eric Berry RC 1.00 2.50
23 Joe Webb RC .60 1.50
24 Jared Allen .20 .50
25 Ed Wang RC 1.00 2.50
26 Randy Moss .25 .60
27 Santana Moss .25 .60
28 Rolando McClain RC .60 1.50
29 Felix Jones .20 .50
30 Ryan Mathews RC .60 1.50
31 Darrelle Revis .20 .50
32 Damian Williams RC .60 1.50
33 Shonn Greene .20 .50
34 Marion Barber .25 .60
35 LeSean McCoy .30 .75
36 Matt Ryan .25 .60
37 Brent Celek .20 .50
38 Rashard Mendenhall .20 .50
39 Clinton Portis .20 .50
40 C.J. Spiller RC .60 1.50
41 Joe Flacco .25 .60
42 Rob Gronkowski RC 2.00 5.00
43 Ronnie Brown .20 .50
44 Ryan Grant .25 .60
45 Fred Jackson .25 .60
46 Andre Roberts RC .75 2.00
47 Josh Freeman .25 .60
48 Mike Kafka RC .75 2.00
49 Gerald McCoy RC .60 1.50
50 Dez Bryant RC 1.50 4.00
51 Vincent Jackson .20 .50
52 DeAngelo Williams .20 .50
53 Dexter McCluster RC .75 2.00
54 Jonathan Dwyer RC .60 1.50
55 Earl Thomas RC 1.50 4.00
56 Sean Lee RC 1.25 3.00
57 Montario Hardesty RC .60 1.50
58 Cedric Benson .20 .50
59 Chad Ochocinco .20 .50
60 Demaryius Thomas RC 1.50 4.00
61 Jerry Hughes RC .60 1.50
62 Mario Williams .25 .60
63 Dwight Freeney .20 .50
64 Brandon LaFell RC 1.00 2.50
65 Emmanuel Sanders RC 1.00 2.50
66 Riley Cooper RC .60 1.50
67 Jamaal Charles .25 .60
68 David Reed RC .60 1.50
69 Mardy Gilyard RC .60 1.50
70 Jahvid Best RC .60 1.50
71 Devin Hester .25 .60
72 Jared Odrick RC .75 2.00
73 Nnamdi Asomugha .20 .50
74 Michael Turner .20 .50
75 Eric Decker RC .75 2.00
76 Ray Rice .20 .50
77 Robert Meachem .20 .50
78 Steve Smith .25 .60
79 Cadillac Williams .20 .50
80 Ndamukong Suh RC 1.25 3.00
81 John Skelton RC .75 2.00
82 Sean Canfield RC .60 1.50
83 Jonathan Stewart .20 .50
84 DeMeco Ryans .20 .50
85 Brian Dawkins .20 .50
86 Brandon Marshall .25 .60
87 Santonio Holmes .20 .50
88 Brett Favre .60 1.50
89 Jason Witten .25 .60
90 Ben Tate RC .60 1.50
91 Dallas Clark .20 .50
92 Jordan Shipley RC .60 1.50
93 Steven Jackson .20 .50
94 Marcus Easley RC .60 1.50
95 Joe McKnight RC .60 1.50
96 Mike Williams RC .60 1.50
97 Sidney Rice .20 .50
98 Jermaine Gresham RC .60 1.50
99 Greg Jennings .20 .50
100 Sam Bradford RC .75 2.00
101 Pierre Thomas .20 .50
102 Roddy White .20 .50
103 Reggie Wayne .25 .60
104 Brandon Jacobs .20 .50
105 Patrick Willis .25 .60
106 Hakeem Nicks .20 .50
107 Pierre Garcon .25 .60
108 Frank Gore .25 .60
109 Carson Palmer .25 .60
110 Peyton Manning .75 2.00
111 Antonio Gates .25 .60
112 Bryan Bulaga RC .60 1.50
113 Mark Sanchez .20 .50
114 Dwayne Bowe .25 .60
115 DeMarcus Ware .25 .60
116 Steve Smith USC .20 .50
117 LaDainian Tomlinson .30 .75
118 Chad Henne .25 .60
119 Calvin Johnson .30 .75
120 Adrian Peterson .30 .75
121 Tony Gonzalez .25 .60
122 Michael Crabtree .20 .50
123 Jon Beason .20 .50
124 Vernon Davis .20 .50
125 Philip Rivers .30 .75
126 DeSean Jackson .25 .60
127 Aaron Rodgers .60 1.50
128 Larry Fitzgerald .25 .60
129 Percy Harvin .20 .50
130 Tom Brady .75 2.00
131 Taylor Price RC .60 1.50
132 Hines Ward .25 .60
133 Eli Manning .25 .60
134 Wes Welker .25 .60
135 Kenny Britt .20 .50
136 Andre Johnson .25 .60
137 Tony Romo .25 .60
138 Jeremy Maclin .20 .50
139 Toby Gerhart RC .60 1.50
140 Chris Johnson .20 .50
141 Matthew Stafford .25 .60
142 Mike Sims-Walker .20 .50
143 Golden Tate RC .75 2.00
144 Joseph Addai .20 .50
145 Matt Schaub .20 .50
146 Marques Colston .20 .50
147 Thomas Jones .20 .50
148 Maurice Jones-Drew .20 .50
149 Anquan Boldin .20 .50
150 Drew Brees .30 .75

2010 Topps Prime Black
*ROOKIES: 1.5X TO 4X BASIC CARDS
BLACK/25 ODDS 1:133 HOBBY

2010 Topps Prime Blue
*VETS/50: 4X TO 10X BASIC CARDS
VETS/50 STATED ODDS 1:34 HOB
*ROOKIES/199: .8X TO 2X BASIC CARDS
ROOKIE/199 STATED ODDS 1:17 HOB

2010 Topps Prime Gold
*VETS/199: 2.5X TO 6X BASIC CARDS
VET/199 STATED ODDS 1:9 HOB
*ROOKIES/699: .5X TO 1.2X BASIC CARDS
ROOKIE/699 STATED ODDS 1:5 HOB

2010 Topps Prime Red
*ROOKIES: 1X TO 2.5X BASIC CARDS
RED/75 STATED ODDS 1:45 HOB

2010 Topps Prime Retail
*RETAIL VETS: .3X TO .8X HOBBY
*RETAIL ROOKIES: .2X TO .5X HOBBY
RETAIL CARDS PRINTED ON THIN STOCK

2010 Topps Prime Retail Bronze
*VETS: 1.5X TO 4X BASIC HOBBY
*ROOKIES: .4X TO 1X BASIC HOBBY
RETAIL BRONZE PRINT RUN 1379

2010 Topps Prime 2nd Quarter
*GOLD/25: .6X TO 1.5X BASIC INSERTS
2Q1 T.Tebow/S.Bradford 5.00 12.00
2Q2 P.Manning/J.Addai 4.00 10.00
2Q3 J.McKnight/A.McCoy .60 1.50
2Q4 R.McClain/J.Ford .60 1.50
2Q5 T.Romo/D.Bryant 1.50 4.00
2Q6 J.Clausen/G.Tate .75 2.00
2Q7 E.Berry/M.Hardesty 1.00 2.50
2Q8 J.Best/N.Suh 1.25 3.00
2Q9 D.McCluster/E.Berry .75 2.00
2Q10 B.Sanders/E.Berry 1.00 2.50
2Q11 M.Kafka/R.Cooper .75 2.00
2Q12 J.Dwyer/E.Sanders 1.00 2.50
2Q13 S.Bradford/M.Gilyard .75 2.00
2Q14 A.Benn/M.Williams .60 1.50
2Q15 R.Gronkowski/T.Price 2.00 5.00
2Q16 N.Suh/G.McCoy 1.25 3.00
2Q17 D.Bryant/D.Thomas 1.50 4.00
2Q18 D.McCluster/A.Benn .75 2.00
2Q19 C.Spiller/M.Easley .60 1.50
2Q20 C.Spiller/R.Mathews .60 1.50
2Q21 R.McClain/R.Seymour .60 1.50
2Q22 C.McCoy/M.Hardesty .75 2.00
2Q23 T.Tebow/D.Thomas 1.50 4.00
2Q24 T.Tebow/E.Decker 2.00 5.00
2Q25 D.Thomas/E.Decker 1.50 4.00
2Q26 J.Gresham/J.Shipley .60 1.50
2Q27 B.LaFell/A.Edwards 1.00 2.50
2Q28 J.Gresham/R.Gronkowski 2.00 5.00
2Q29 A.Smith/P.Willis 1.25 3.00
2Q30 J.Clausen/B.LaFell 1.00 2.50

2010 Topps Prime 2nd Quarter Relics
DUAL JSY/275-355 ODDS 1:20 HOB
*GOLD/25: .6X TO 1.5X BASIC JSY/275
BG S.Bradford/M.Gilyard/355 2.00 5.00
BH E.Berry/M.Hardesty/355 2.50 6.00
BS J.Best/N.Suh/355 3.00 8.00
BT D.Bryant/D.Thomas/355 4.00 10.00
BW A.Benn/M.Williams/355 1.50 4.00
CL J.Clausen/B.LaFell/355 2.50 6.00
CT J.Clausen/G.Tate/355 2.00 5.00
DS J.Dwyer/E.Sanders/355 2.50 6.00
GG J.Gresham/R.Gronkowski/355 5.00 12.00
GP R.Gronkowski/T.Price/355 5.00 12.00
GS J.Gresham/J.Shipley/355 1.50 4.00
KC M.Kafka/R.Cooper/275 2.00 5.00
LE B.LaFell/A.Edwards/355 2.50 6.00
MA P.Manning/J.Addai/275 10.00 25.00
MB D.McCluster/E.Berry/355 2.00 5.00
MCB D.McCluster/A.Benn/355 2.00 5.00
MF R.McClain/J.Ford/275 1.50 4.00
MH C.McCoy/M.Hardesty/355 2.00 5.00
MM J.McKnight/A.McCoy/275 1.50 4.00
MS R.McClain/R.Seymour/275 1.50 4.00
RB T.Romo/D.Bryant/275 4.00 10.00
SB B.Sanders/E.Berry/275 2.50 6.00
SE C.Spiller/M.Easley/355 1.50 4.00
SM N.Suh/G.McCoy/355 3.00 8.00
SM C.Spiller/R.Mathews/355 1.50 4.00
SW A.Smith/P.Willis/275 3.00 8.00
TB T.Tebow/S.Bradford/355 5.00 12.00
TD T.Tebow/E.Decker/355 6.00 15.00
THD D.Thomas/E.Decker/355 4.00 10.00
TT T.Tebow/D.Thomas/355 4.00 10.00

2010 Topps Prime 3rd Quarter
*GOLD/25: .6X TO 1.5X BASIC INSERTS
3Q1 Tebow/Thomas/Decker 2.00 5.00
3Q2 Tebow/Cooper/Hernandez 2.00 5.00
3Q3 Bradford/McCoy/Gresham .75 2.00
3Q4 Peterson/Johnson/Drew 1.50 4.00
3Q5 Clausen/Edwards/LaFell 1.00 2.50
3Q6 McCoy/Hardesty/Mitchell .75 2.00
3Q7 Benn/McCoy/Williams .60 1.50
3Q8 McCoy/Shipley/Thomas 1.50 4.00
3Q9 Young/Gage/Williams 1.00 2.50
3Q10 Best/Gerhart/McKnight .60 1.50
3Q11 Thomas/Dwyer/Morgan 1.50 4.00
3Q12 Bradford/Tebow/Clausen 5.00 12.00
3Q13 Spiller/Mathews/Best .60 1.50
3Q14 Gerhart/Tate/Hardesty .60 1.50
3Q15 Bryant/Thomas/Benn 1.50 4.00
3Q16 Tate/Williams/LaFell 1.00 2.50
3Q17 Benson/Gresham/Shipley .60 1.50
3Q18 Gilyard/Williams/Price .60 1.50
3Q19 Suh/McCoy/Berry 1.25 3.00
3Q20 Best/Gerhart/Williams .60 1.50
3Q21 Spiller/McKnight/Price .60 1.50
3Q22 Gresham/Dwyer/Hardesty .60 1.50
3Q23 Thomas/Mathews/McClain 1.50 4.00
3Q24 Bradford/Thomas/Spiller 1.50 4.00
3Q25 Tebow/Bryant/Mathews 2.00 5.00
3Q26 Clausen/McCluster/Best .75 2.00
3Q27 McCoy/Benn/Gerhart .75 2.00
3Q28 Edwards/Tomlinson/McKnight 1.50 4.00
3Q29 Brady/Gronkowski/Price 4.00 10.00
3Q30 Tate/Thomas/McCoy .75 2.00

2010 Topps Prime 3rd Quarter Relics
TRIPLE JSY/199-275 ODDS 1:27 HOB
*GOLD/25: .6X TO 1.5X BASIC TRIPLE
BGM Best/Gerhart/McKnght/275 2.00 5.00
BGP Brady/Grnkwski/Price/199 12.00 30.00
BGS Bensn/Greshm/Shiply/199 2.00 5.00
BGW Best/Gerhart/Williams/275 2.00 5.00
BMG Bradfrd/McCy/Grshm/275 2.50 6.00
BMW Benn/G.McCy/Willims/275 2.00 5.00
BTB Bryant/Thomas/Benn/275 6.00 15.00
BTC Bradfrd/Tebw/Clausn/275 6.00 15.00
BTS Bradfrd/Thoms/Spiller/275 5.00 12.00
CEL Clausn/Edwrds/LaFell/199 5.00 12.00
CMB Clausen/McClstr/Best/275 2.50 6.00
ETM Edwrds/Tmlnsn/McKnt/199 5.00 12.00
GDH Greshm/Dwyr/Hardsty/275 2.00 5.00
GTH Gerhart/Tate/Hardesty/275 2.00 5.00
GWP Gilyard/Williams/Price/275 2.00 5.00
MBG McCy/Benn/Gerhart/275 6.00 15.00
MHM C.McCy/Hrdsty/Mitchll/199 2.50 6.00
MST McCy/Shiply/Thoms/199 6.00 15.00
PJJ Ptrsn/Johnsn/Jns-Drw/199 5.00 12.00
SMB Spiller/Mathews/Best/275 2.00 5.00
SMCB Suh/McCoy/Berry/275 4.00 10.00
SMP Spiller/McKnight/Price/275 2.00 5.00
TBM Tebow/Bryant/Mathews/275 8.00 20.00
TCH Tebow/Cooper/Hern/199 8.00 20.00
TDM Thomas/Dwyer/Morgan/199 5.00 12.00
TMM Thms/Mathws/McCln/275 6.00 15.00
TTD Tbw/Thms/Dckr/275 8.00 20.00
TTM Tate/Thomas/McCoy/199 2.50 6.00
TWL Tate/Williams/LaFell/275 3.00 8.00
YGW Young/Gage/Williams/199 3.00 8.00

2010 Topps Prime 4th Quarter
*GOLD/25: .6X TO 1.5X BASIC INSERTS
4Q1 Spllr/Bst/Mthws/Tte .60 1.50
4Q2 Gerhrt/McKnt/Hrdsty/Dixn .60 1.50
4Q3 Tbw/Clsen/Brdfrd/McCy 2.00 5.00
4Q4 Brynt/McClstr/Thms/Bnn 1.50 4.00
4Q5 Tate/LaFl/Will/Sandrs 1.00 2.50
4Q6 Plmr/Shply/Brdy/Prce 4.00 10.00
4Q7 Gilyard/Easley/Will/Ford .60 1.50

Card	Low	High
4Q8 Grshm/Hern/Grnk/Grhm	2.00	5.00
4Q9 Suh/Brry/McCy/Thms	1.50	4.00
4Q10 Edwrds/Tmlin/Dwyr/Sndrs	1.50	4.00
4Q11 Spllr/Dwyr/Thms/Grhm	1.50	4.00
4Q12 Brdfrd/Brynt/McCy/Shply	1.50	4.00
4Q13 Ptrsn/Grhrt/Sltn/Tte	1.50	4.00
4Q14 Clausn/Tate/McCy/Shiply	.75	2.00
4Q15 Bst/Grnk/Grhrt/Will	2.00	5.00
4Q16 McClstr/Dixon/Berry/McCln	.75	2.00
4Q17 McClstr/LaFll/Hrdsty/Tate	1.00	2.50
4Q18 Spillr/Will/McKn/Prce	.75	2.00
4Q19 Suh/Bst/McCy/Bnn	1.25	3.00
4Q20 LaFll/Edwrds/Grshm/Shiply	1.00	2.50
4Q21 Barber/Jones/Moss/Portis	1.25	3.00
4Q22 McCtr/Thms/Mths/McCn	1.50	4.00
4Q23 Tbw/Spllr/Brynt/Grshm	2.00	5.00
4Q24 Brdfrd/Spllr/Suh/McCy	1.25	3.00
4Q25 Brdfrd/Spllr/Tbw/Mthws	2.00	5.00
4Q26 Brdfrd/Brynt/Tbw/Thms	2.00	5.00
4Q27 Brynt/Splr/Thms/Mthws	1.50	4.00
4Q28 Mnng/Brdy/Rmo/Brdfrd	2.50	6.00
4Q29 Brdfrd/Glyrd/Tbw/Dckr	2.00	5.00
4Q30 Best/Gerhart/Hrdsty/Dwyer	.60	1.50

2010 Topps Prime 4th Quarter Relics

QUAD JSY/124-175 ODDS 1:43 HOB
*GOLD/25: .6X TO 1.5X BASIC QUAD

Card	Low	High
BBMS Brad/Bryn/McC/Shp/175	6.00	15.00
BBTT Brad/Bryn/Tbw/Thms/175	8.00	20.00
BGGW Bst/Grnk/Grhrt/Wll/175	8.00	20.00
BGHD Bst/Grhrt/Hrsy/Dwyr/175	2.50	6.00
BGTD Brd/Glyrd/Tbw/Dck/175	8.00	20.00
BJMP Brbr/Jns/Mss/Prts/124	5.00	12.00
BMTB Byn/MCs/Ths/Bnn/175	8.00	20.00
BSSM Brd/Spll/Suh/McC/175	5.00	12.00
BSTM Brdf/Spll/Tbw/Mts/175	8.00	20.00
CTMS Clsn/Tte/MCy/Shp/175	3.00	8.00
DSTM Bryn/Spll/Thms/Mthw/175	8.00	20.00
ETDS Edd/Tmln/Dwyr/Sndr/124	4.00	10.00
GEWF Glyrd/Esly/Will/Frd/124	2.50	6.00
GHGG Grsm/Hrn/Grnk/Grhm/124	8.00	20.00
GMHD Grht/McKn/Hrdst/Dixn/175	2.50	6.00
LEGS LFll/Edrd/Grsh/Shply/175	5.00	12.00
MBRB Mnng/Brdy/Rmo/Brfd/124	10.00	25.00
MDBM McCst/Dixn/Brry/McCn/124	3.00	8.00
MLHT McClst/LFll/Hrdsty/Tte/175	4.00	10.00
MTMM McClt/Thm/Mthw/McCl/175	6.00	15.00
PGST Ptrsn/Grhrt/Sltn/Tte/124	6.00	15.00
PSBP Plmr/Shply/Brdy/Prce/124	6.00	15.00
SBMB Suh/Bst/McCy/Bnn/175	5.00	12.00
SBMT Spillr/Bst/Mthws/Tte/175	2.50	6.00
SBMTH Suh/Brry/McCy/Thms/124	8.00	20.00
SDTG Spllr/Dwyr/Thms/Grhm/124	6.00	15.00
SWMP Splr/Will/McKnt/Prce/124	6.00	15.00
TCBM Tbw/Clsn/Brad/McC/175	8.00	20.00
TLWS Tte/LaFll/Will/Sndrs/175	4.00	10.00
TSBG Tbw/Splr/Brynt/Grshm/175	10.00	25.00

2010 Topps Prime Autographed Relics Level 1

*LEVEL 1/20: .8X TO 2X LEVEL 4
*LEVEL 1/10: 1X TO 2.5X LEVEL 4
LEVEL 1 PRINT RUN 10-20

Card	Low	High
PL1CM Colt McCoy/20	15.00	40.00
PL1DB Dez Bryant/10		
PL1SB Sam Bradford/20	40.00	80.00
PL1TT Tim Tebow/20	75.00	200.00

2010 Topps Prime Autographed Relics Level 4

STATED PRINT RUN 30 SER.#'d SETS
*LEVEL 3/25: .6X TO 1.5X LEVEL 4
*LEVEL 2/15: .8X TO 2X LEVEL 4
EXCH EXPIRATION: 11/30/2013

Card	Low	High
PL4AB Arrelious Benn	6.00	15.00
PL4AE Armanti Edwards	8.00	20.00
PL4AR Andre Roberts	8.00	20.00
PL4BL Brandon LaFell	10.00	25.00
PL4BT Ben Tate	6.00	15.00
PL4CM Colt McCoy	8.00	20.00
PL4CS C.J. Spiller	6.00	15.00
PL4DB Dez Bryant	40.00	80.00
PL4DM Dexter McCluster	8.00	20.00
PL4DT Demaryius Thomas	15.00	40.00
PL4DW Damian Williams	6.00	15.00
PL4EB Eric Berry	10.00	25.00
PL4ED Eric Decker	8.00	20.00
PL4ES Emmanuel Sanders	10.00	25.00
PL4GT Golden Tate	12.00	30.00
PL4JB Jahvid Best	6.00	15.00
PL4JC Jimmy Clausen	6.00	15.00
PL4JD Jonathan Dwyer	6.00	15.00
PL4JG Jermaine Gresham	6.00	15.00
PL4JS Jordan Shipley	6.00	15.00
PL4ME Marcus Easley	6.00	15.00
PL4MG Mardy Gilyard	6.00	15.00
PL4MH Montario Hardesty	6.00	15.00
PL4MK Mike Kafka	8.00	20.00
PL4MW Mike Williams	6.00	15.00
PL4NS Ndamukong Suh	20.00	50.00
PL4RG Rob Gronkowski	60.00	120.00
PL4RM Ryan Mathews	6.00	15.00
PL4SB Sam Bradford	20.00	50.00
PL4TG Toby Gerhart	6.00	15.00
PL4TP Taylor Price	6.00	15.00
PL4TT Tim Tebow	50.00	120.00

2010 Topps Prime Autographed Relics Level 5

STATED PRINT RUN 75-499
EXCH EXPIRATION: 11/30/2013

Card	Low	High
PL5AB Arrelious Benn/499	3.00	8.00
PL5AD Anthony Dixon/299	5.00	12.00
PL5AE Armanti Edwards/499	4.00	10.00
PL5AG Antonio Gates/150	12.00	30.00
PL5AH Aaron Hernandez/299	5.00	12.00
PL5AM Anthony McCoy/299	5.00	12.00
PL5AP Adrian Peterson/75	60.00	120.00
PL5AR Andre Roberts/499	4.00	10.00
PL5BL Brandon LaFell/499	5.00	12.00
PL5BT Ben Tate/499	3.00	8.00
PL5CH Chad Henne/75	12.00	30.00
PL5CM Colt McCoy/150	8.00	20.00
PL5CS C.J. Spiller/399	4.00	10.00
PL5CT Chester Taylor/150	10.00	25.00
PL5DL Dan LeFevour/299	5.00	12.00
PL5DM Darren McFadden/150	15.00	40.00
PL5DMC Dexter McCluster/499	4.00	10.00
PL5DMO Derrick Morgan/299	5.00	12.00
PL5DT Demaryius Thomas/399	10.00	25.00
PL5DW Damian Williams/499	3.00	8.00
PL5ED Eric Decker/499	4.00	10.00
PL5ES Emmanuel Sanders/499	5.00	12.00
PL5FJ Felix Jones/150	15.00	40.00
PL5GRA Jimmy Graham/299	10.00	25.00
PL5GT Golden Tate/499	6.00	15.00
PL5JB Jahvid Best/399	4.00	10.00
PL5JC Jimmy Clausen/150	6.00	15.00
PL5JD Jonathan Dwyer/499	3.00	8.00
PL5JF Jacoby Ford/299	5.00	12.00
PL5JG Jermaine Gresham/499	3.00	8.00
PL5JS Jordan Shipley/499	3.00	8.00
PL5KK Kevin Kolb/150	10.00	25.00
PL5KM Knowshon Moreno/150	10.00	25.00
PL5MC Marques Colston/150	10.00	25.00
PL5ME Marcus Easley/399	4.00	10.00
PL5MG Mardy Gilyard/499	3.00	8.00
PL5MH Montario Hardesty/499	3.00	8.00
PL5MJD Maurice Jones-Drew/150	10.00	25.00
PL5MK Mike Kafka/499	4.00	10.00
PL5NS Ndamukong Suh/299	12.00	30.00
PL5PM Peyton Manning/150	60.00	120.00
PL5RC Riley Cooper/299	5.00	12.00
PL5RG Rob Gronkowski/499	40.00	80.00
PL5RM Ryan Mathews/399	4.00	10.00
PL5SB Sam Bradford/150	20.00	50.00
PL5SR Sidney Rice/150	10.00	25.00
PL5SS Steve Slaton/75	10.00	25.00
PL5TG Toby Gerhart/499	3.00	8.00
PL5TP Taylor Price/150	6.00	15.00
PL5TR Tony Romo/150	30.00	60.00

2010 Topps Prime Rookie

*GOLD/25: .8X TO 2X BASIC INSERTS

Card	Low	High
PR1 Sam Bradford	.60	1.50
PR2 Ndamukong Suh	1.00	2.50
PR3 Eric Berry	.75	2.00
PR4 C.J. Spiller	.50	1.25
PR5 Ryan Mathews	.50	1.25
PR6 Jermaine Gresham	.50	1.25
PR7 Demaryius Thomas	1.25	3.00
PR8 Dez Bryant	1.25	3.00
PR9 Tim Tebow	1.50	4.00
PR10 Jahvid Best	.50	1.25
PR11 Dexter McCluster	.60	1.50
PR12 Arrelious Benn	.50	1.25
PR13 Rob Gronkowski	1.50	4.00
PR14 Jimmy Clausen	.50	1.25
PR15 Toby Gerhart	.50	1.25
PR16 Ben Tate	.50	1.25
PR17 Montario Hardesty	.50	1.25
PR18 Golden Tate	.60	1.50
PR19 Damian Williams	.50	1.25
PR20 Brandon LaFell	.75	2.00
PR21 Jordan Shipley	.50	1.25
PR22 Colt McCoy	.60	1.50
PR23 Eric Decker	.60	1.50
PR24 Joe McKnight	.50	1.25
PR25 Jonathan Dwyer	.50	1.25
PR26 Emmanuel Sanders	.75	2.00
PR27 Mike Williams	.50	1.25
PR28 Mardy Gilyard	.50	1.25
PR29 Taylor Price	.50	1.25
PR30 Rolando McClain	.50	1.25
PR31 Gerald McCoy	.50	1.25
PR32 Marcus Easley	.50	1.25
PR33 Andre Roberts	.60	1.50
PR34 Mike Kafka	.60	1.50
PR35 Armanti Edwards	.60	1.50

2010 Topps Prime Rookie Autographs

STATED PRINT RUN 149-599
EXCH EXPIRATION: 11/30/2013

Card	Low	High
PARAB Arrelious Benn/399	3.00	8.00
PARADX Anthony Dixon/599	2.50	6.00
PARAE Armanti Edwards/599	3.00	8.00
PARAM Anthony McCoy/599	2.50	6.00
PARAR Andre Roberts/149	5.00	12.00
PARBB Bryan Bulaga/599	2.50	6.00
PARBL Brandon LaFell/149	6.00	15.00
PARBT Ben Tate/299	3.00	8.00
PARCM Carlton Mitchell/599	2.50	6.00
PARCMC Colt McCoy/149	5.00	12.00
PARCS C.J. Spiller/299	3.00	8.00
PARCSC Charles Scott/149	4.00	10.00
PARDL Dan LeFevour/399	3.00	8.00
PARDMC Dexter McCluster/399	4.00	10.00
PARDR David Reed/149	4.00	10.00
PARDT Demaryius Thomas/149	10.00	25.00
PARDW Damian Williams/299	3.00	8.00
PARED Eric Decker/299	4.00	10.00
PARES Emmanuel Sanders/599	10.00	25.00
PARET Earl Thomas/399	10.00	25.00
PARGRA Jimmy Graham/149	8.00	20.00
PARGT Golden Tate/399	4.00	10.00
PARJB Jahvid Best/299	3.00	8.00
PARJC Jimmy Clausen/149	4.00	10.00
PARJCR Jonathan Crompton/599	2.50	6.00
PARJD Jonathan Dwyer/299	3.00	8.00
PARJF Jacoby Ford/599	2.50	6.00
PARJG Jermaine Gresham/399	3.00	8.00
PARJH Jerry Hughes/599	2.50	6.00
PARJO Jared Odrick/599	6.00	15.00
PARJS John Skelton/599	3.00	8.00
PARJSH Jordan Shipley/599	2.50	6.00
PARJST James Starks/599	3.00	8.00
PARJW Joe Webb/149	4.00	10.00
PARME Marcus Easley/599	2.50	6.00
PARMG Mardy Gilyard/599	2.50	6.00
PARMH Montario Hardesty/149	4.00	10.00
PARMK Mike Kafka/149	5.00	12.00
PARNS Ndamukong Suh/149	15.00	40.00
PARRC Riley Cooper/599	5.00	12.00
PARRG Rob Gronkowski/299	25.00	50.00
PARRM Ryan Mathews/299	3.00	8.00
PARSB Sam Bradford/149	15.00	40.00
PARSC Sean Canfield/599	2.50	6.00
PARSL Sean Lee/149	8.00	20.00
PARTG Toby Gerhart/149	4.00	10.00
PARTP Tony Pike/149	4.00	10.00
PARTPR Taylor Price/599	2.50	6.00
PARTT Tim Tebow/149	30.00	80.00
PARTW Trent Williams/599	3.00	8.00

2010 Topps Prime Rookie Autographs Gold

*GOLD/25: 1X TO 2.5X BASIC AU/599
*GOLD/25: .8X TO 2X BASIC AU/299-399
*GOLD/25: .6X TO 1.5X BASIC AU/149
GOLD/25 STATED ODDS 1:196 HOB

Card	Low	High
PARCMC Colt McCoy	8.00	20.00
PARTT Tim Tebow	40.00	100.00

2010 Topps Prime Rookie Relics

ROOKIE RELIC/420 ODDS 1:14 HOB
*GOLD/25: .6X TO 1.5X BASIC JSY/420

Card	Low	High
PRRAB Arrelious Benn	1.25	3.00
PRRAE Armanti Edwards	1.50	4.00
PRRAR Andre Roberts	1.50	4.00
PRRBL Brandon LaFell	2.00	5.00
PRRBT Ben Tate	1.25	3.00
PRRCM Colt McCoy	1.50	4.00
PRRCS C.J. Spiller	1.25	3.00
PRRDB Dez Bryant	5.00	12.00
PRRDM Dexter McCluster	1.50	4.00
PRRDT Demaryius Thomas	3.00	8.00
PRRDW Damian Williams	1.25	3.00
PRREB Eric Berry	2.00	5.00
PRRED Eric Decker	1.50	4.00
PRRES Emmanuel Sanders	2.00	5.00
PRRGM Gerald McCoy	1.25	3.00
PRRGT Golden Tate	1.50	4.00
PRRJB Jahvid Best	2.50	6.00
PRRJC Jimmy Clausen	1.25	3.00
PRRJD Jonathan Dwyer	1.25	3.00
PRRJG Jermaine Gresham	1.25	3.00
PRRJM Joe McKnight	1.25	3.00
PRRJS Jordan Shipley	1.25	3.00
PRRME Marcus Easley	1.25	3.00
PRRMG Mardy Gilyard	1.25	3.00
PRRMH Montario Hardesty	1.25	3.00
PRRMK Mike Kafka	1.50	4.00
PRRMW Mike Williams	1.25	3.00
PRRNS Ndamukong Suh	2.50	6.00
PRRRG Rob Gronkowski	4.00	10.00
PRRRM Ryan Mathews	1.25	3.00
PRRRM Rolando McClain	1.25	3.00
PRRSB Sam Bradford	1.50	4.00
PRRTG Toby Gerhart	1.25	3.00
PRRTP Taylor Price	1.25	3.00
PRRTT Tim Tebow	4.00	10.00

2011 Topps Prime

Card	Low	High
COMPLETE SET (150)	30.00	80.00
COMP.SET w/o RC's (100)	12.00	30.00

ROOKIE/930 STATED ODDS 1:4 HOB

Card	Low	High
1 Aaron Rodgers	.50	1.25
2 Jamie Harper RC	.60	1.50
3 Bilal Powell RC	.75	2.00
4 Brandon Lloyd	.20	.50
5 Sam Bradford	.20	.50
6 Antonio Gates	.20	.50
7 Mark Ingram RC	1.00	2.50
8 Shonn Greene	.20	.50
9 DeMarco Murray RC	1.25	3.00
10 Andre Johnson	.25	.60
11 Rashard Mendenhall	.20	.50
12 Rob Housler RC	.60	1.50
13 Jonathan Stewart	.20	.50
14 Delone Carter RC	.60	1.50
15 Prince Amukamara RC	.60	1.50
16 Michael Turner	.20	.50
17 LaDainian Tomlinson	.30	.75
18 Dwayne Harris RC	.60	1.50
19 Philip Rivers	.30	.75
20 Adrian Peterson	.30	.75
21 Nick Fairley RC	.60	1.50
22 Percy Harvin	.20	.50
23 Titus Young RC	.60	1.50
24 D.J. Williams RC	.60	1.50
25 Lee Evans	.25	.60
26 Jeremy Maclin	.20	.50
27 Jordan Todman RC	.60	1.50
28 Calvin Johnson	.30	.75
29 Jacquizz Rodgers RC	.60	1.50
30 Arian Foster	.20	.50
31 A.J. Green RC	1.50	4.00
32 Josh Freeman	.25	.60
33 Ryan Mathews	.25	.60
34 Austin Pettis RC	.60	1.50
35 Jared Allen	.20	.50
36 Anquan Boldin	.20	.50
37 Kyle Rudolph RC	.60	1.50
38 LeGarrette Blount	.25	.60
39 Cedric Benson	.20	.50
40 Chris Johnson	.20	.50
41 Steven Jackson	.20	.50
42 Troy Polamalu	.30	.75
43 Mike Williams	.25	.60
44 Ryan Mallett RC	.60	1.50
45 Torrey Smith RC	.60	1.50
46 Tony Gonzalez	.25	.60
47 Colin Kaepernick RC	1.00	2.50
48 Brandon Jacobs	.20	.50
49 Eli Manning	.25	.60
50 Cam Newton RC	3.00	8.00
51 Rahim Moore RC	.60	1.50
52 Julio Jones RC	2.00	5.00
53 Da'Rel Scott RC	.60	1.50
54 Greg Salas RC	.60	1.50
55 Randall Cobb RC	1.00	2.50
56 Marcell Dareus RC	.60	1.50
57 Alex Green RC	.60	1.50
58 Matt Forte	.20	.50
59 Mike Williams	.25	.60
60 Clay Matthews	.30	.75
61 Christian Ponder RC	.60	1.50
62 Greg Jennings	.20	.50
63 Shane Vereen RC	.75	2.00
64 Ray Rice	.20	.50
65 Marshawn Lynch	.25	.60
66 Peyton Hillis	.20	.50
67 Ben Roethlisberger	.30	.75
68 Jon Baldwin RC	.60	1.50
69 Joe Flacco	.25	.60
70 Drew Brees	.30	.75
71 Jamaal Charles	.25	.60
72 Pierre Garcon	.25	.60
73 Stephen Tulloch	.20	.50
74 Dion Lewis RC	.75	2.00
75 Michael Crabtree	.20	.50
76 Hakeem Nicks	.20	.50
77 Beanie Wells	.20	.50
78 Von Miller RC	1.00	2.50
79 Miles Austin	.20	.50
80 Larry Fitzgerald	.25	.60
81 Jahvid Best	.20	.50
82 Jake Locker RC	.60	1.50
83 Blaine Gabbert RC	.60	1.50
84 Chad Ochocinco	.20	.50
85 DeSean Jackson	.25	.60
86 Dwayne Bowe	.25	.60
87 Ricky Stanzi RC	.60	1.50
88 James Starks	.20	.50
89 Jimmy Graham	.30	.75
90 Mark Sanchez	.20	.50
91 Leonard Hankerson RC	.60	1.50
92 Knowshon Moreno	.20	.50
93 Taiwan Jones RC	.60	1.50
94 Ed Reed	.25	.60
95 Dez Bryant	.30	.75
96 Kendall Hunter RC	.60	1.50
97 Vincent Jackson	.20	.50
98 Kenny Britt	.20	.50
99 Jerod Mayo	.20	.50
100 Peyton Manning	.60	1.50
101 Darren McFadden	.20	.50
102 C.J. Spiller	.20	.50
103 Santana Moss	.25	.60
104 Ray Lewis	.30	.75
105 Matt Schaub	.20	.50
106 Marcedes Lewis	.20	.50
107 Marques Colston	.20	.50
108 Ryan Williams RC	.60	1.50
109 Steve Johnson	.20	.50
110 Matt Ryan	.25	.60
111 Roddy White	.20	.50
112 Austin Collie	.20	.50
113 Andy Dalton RC	1.25	3.00
114 Stevan Ridley RC	.60	1.50
115 Jason Witten	.25	.60
116 Matt Cassel	.20	.50
117 Daniel Thomas RC	.60	1.50
118 Luke Stocker RC	.60	1.50
119 Virgil Green RC	.60	1.50
120 Maurice Jones-Drew	.20	.50
121 Santonio Holmes	.20	.50
122 Brandon Marshall	.25	.60
123 Felix Jones	.20	.50
124 LeSean McCoy	.30	.75
125 Mike Wallace	.20	.50
126 Patrick Willis	.25	.60
127 Jeremy Kerley RC	1.00	2.50
128 Reggie Wayne	.25	.60
129 DeMarcus Ware	.25	.60
130 Michael Vick	.25	.60
131 Dallas Clark	.20	.50
132 Brian Urlacher	.30	.75
133 Sidney Rice	.20	.50
134 Steve Smith	.25	.60
135 Wes Welker	.25	.60
136 Frank Gore	.25	.60
137 Jerrel Jernigan RC	.60	1.50
138 Davone Bess	.20	.50
139 Malcom Floyd	.20	.50
140 Tony Romo	.25	.60
141 Braylon Edwards	.20	.50
142 Ahmad Bradshaw	.20	.50
143 Vincent Brown RC	.60	1.50
144 Vernon Davis	.20	.50
145 Edmond Gates RC	.60	1.50
146 Mikel Leshoure RC	.60	1.50
147 Jay Cutler	.20	.50
148 Greg Little RC	.75	2.00
149 Hines Ward	.25	.60
150 Tom Brady	.75	2.00

2011 Topps Prime Aqua

*AQUA VETS: .8X TO 2X BASIC CARDS
RANDOM INSERTS IN HOBBY PACKS

2011 Topps Prime Blue

*BLUE/599: .5X TO 1.2X BASIC ROOKIES
BLUE/599 STATED ODDS 1:6

2011 Topps Prime Gold

*GOLD/699: .5X TO 1.2X BASIC ROOKIES
GOLD/699 STATED ODDS 1:5

2011 Topps Prime Green

*GREEN/99: 1X TO 2.5X BASIC ROOKIES
GREEN/99 STATED ODDS 1:33

2011 Topps Prime Powder Blue

*BLUE VETS/75: 3X TO 8X BASIC CARDS
POWDER BLUE/75 ODDS 1:22

2011 Topps Prime Purple

*PURPLE/399: .6X TO 1.5X BASIC ROOKIES
PURPLE/399 STATED ODDS 1:9

2011 Topps Prime Rainbow

*RAINBOW/25: 1.5X TO 4X BASIC ROOKIES
RAINBOW/25 STATED ODDS 1:130

Card	Low	High
50 Cam Newton	40.00	80.00

2011 Topps Prime Red

*RED/499: .5X TO 1.2X BASIC ROOKIES
RED/499 STATED ODDS 1:7

2011 Topps Prime Retail

*VETS: .3X TO .8X BASIC CARDS
*ROOKIES: .2X TO .5X BASIC CARDS

2011 Topps Prime Retail Bronze

*VETS: 1.2X TO 3X BASIC HOBBY
*ROOKIES: .4X TO 1X BASIC HOBBY
RANDOM INSERTS IN RETAIL PACKS

2011 Topps Prime Autographed Relics Level 3

*LEV.THREE/25: 1X TO 2.5X LEV.SIX/515
*LEV.THREE/25: .8X TO 2X LEV.SIX/199
*LEV.THREE/25: .5X TO 1.2X LEV.SIX/50
LEVEL THREE PRINT RUN 25

2011 Topps Prime Autographed Relics Level 4

LEVEL FOUR STATED PRINT RUN 15
*LEVEL TWO/15: .5X TO 1.2X LEV.FOUR/15
*LEVEL THREE/25: .4X TO 1X LEV.FOUR/15

Card	Low	High
PIVAD Andy Dalton	50.00	100.00
PIVAG Alex Green	10.00	25.00
PIVAJG A.J. Green	75.00	150.00
PIVAP Austin Pettis	10.00	25.00
PIVBG Blaine Gabbert	10.00	25.00
PIVBP Bilal Powell	12.00	30.00
PIVCK Colin Kaepernick	15.00	40.00
PIVCN Cam Newton	150.00	300.00
PIVCP Christian Ponder	10.00	25.00
PIVDC Delone Carter	10.00	25.00
PIVDM DeMarco Murray	20.00	50.00
PIVDT Daniel Thomas	10.00	25.00
PIVEG Edmond Gates	10.00	25.00
PIVGL Greg Little	12.00	30.00
PIVJB Jon Baldwin	20.00	50.00
PIVJH Jamie Harper	10.00	25.00
PIVJJ Julio Jones	100.00	200.00
PIVJJE Jerrel Jernigan	10.00	25.00
PIVJL Jake Locker	10.00	25.00
PIVJT Jordan Todman	10.00	25.00
PIVKH Kendall Hunter	20.00	50.00
PIVKR Kyle Rudolph	10.00	25.00
PIVLH Leonard Hankerson	10.00	25.00
PIVMD Marcell Dareus	10.00	25.00
PIVMI Mark Ingram	15.00	40.00
PIVML Mikel Leshoure	10.00	25.00
PIVRC Randall Cobb	15.00	40.00
PIVRM Ryan Mallett	10.00	25.00
PIVRW Ryan Williams	25.00	60.00
PIVSR Stevan Ridley	10.00	25.00
PIVSV Shane Vereen	12.00	30.00
PIVTJ Taiwan Jones	25.00	60.00
PIVTS Torrey Smith	10.00	25.00
PIVTY Titus Young	10.00	25.00
PIVVB Vincent Brown	10.00	25.00
PIVVM Von Miller	25.00	60.00

2011 Topps Prime Autographed Relics Level 6

STATED PRINT RUN 50-515
EXCH EXPIRATION: 9/30/2014

Card	Low	High
PVIAD Andy Dalton/515	10.00	25.00
PVIAG Alex Green/515	4.00	10.00
PVIAGA Antonio Gates/50	10.00	25.00
PVIAJ Andre Johnson/50	30.00	60.00
PVIAJG A.J. Green/199	20.00	50.00
PVIAP Austin Pettis/50	8.00	20.00
PVIAR Antrel Rolle/100	8.00	20.00
PVIBG Blaine Gabbert/199	5.00	12.00
PVIBP Bilal Powell/199	6.00	15.00
PVICB Champ Bailey/100	12.00	30.00
PVICK Colin Kaepernick/199	8.00	20.00
PVICN Cam Newton/199	50.00	120.00
PVICP Christian Ponder/515	4.00	10.00
PVIDC Delone Carter/199	5.00	12.00
PVIDM DeMarco Murray/199	10.00	25.00
PVIDMC Darren McFadden/100	15.00	40.00
PVIDR Darrelle Revis/50	25.00	50.00
PVIDT Daniel Thomas/515	4.00	10.00
PVIEG Edmond Gates/515	4.00	10.00
PVIGJ Greg Jennings/100	8.00	20.00
PVIGL Greg Little/515	5.00	12.00
PVIHW Hines Ward/50	30.00	60.00
PVIJB Jon Baldwin/515	8.00	20.00
PVIJH Jamie Harper/515	4.00	10.00
PVIJJ Julio Jones/515	25.00	50.00
PVIJJE Jerrel Jernigan/515	4.00	10.00
PVIJL Jake Locker/199	5.00	12.00
PVIJT Jordan Todman/50	8.00	20.00
PVIJW Jason Witten/100	20.00	40.00
PVIKH Kendall Hunter/515	8.00	20.00
PVIKM Knowshon Moreno/50	10.00	25.00
PVIKR Kyle Rudolph/515	5.00	12.00
PVILH Leonard Hankerson/515	4.00	10.00
PVIMD Marcell Dareus/199	5.00	12.00
PVIMI Mark Ingram/199	8.00	20.00
PVIMJ Maurice Jones-Drew/50	10.00	25.00
PVIML Mikel Leshoure/50	10.00	25.00
PVIRC Randall Cobb/515	6.00	15.00
PVIRL Ray Lewis/100	40.00	80.00
PVIRM Ryan Mallett/515	4.00	10.00
PVIRW Ryan Williams/515	10.00	25.00
PVISG Shonn Greene/100	8.00	20.00
PVISR Sidney Rice/100	8.00	20.00
PVISRI Stevan Ridley/515	4.00	10.00
PVISV Shane Vereen/515	5.00	12.00
PVITJ Taiwan Jones/199	10.00	25.00
PVITS Torrey Smith/515	4.00	10.00
PVITY Titus Young	5.00	12.00
PVIVB Vincent Brown/515	4.00	10.00
PVIVM Von Miller/515	10.00	25.00

2011 Topps Prime Autographed Relics Level 6 Gold

*GOLD/25: .8X TO 2X LEVEL SIX/515
*GOLD/25: .6X TO 1.5X LEVEL SIX/199
*GOLD/25: .5X TO 1.2X LEVEL SIX/100
*GOLD/25: .4X TO 1X LEVEL SIX/50 VETS
*GOLD/25: .4X TO 1X LEVEL SIX/50 ROOK
GOLD STATED PRINT RUN 25

Card	Low	High
PVICN Cam Newton	75.00	150.00

2011 Topps Prime Dual

Card	Low	High
COMPLETE SET (20)	10.00	25.00

RANDOM INSERTS IN PACKS
*GOLD/50: .8X TO 2X BASIC INSERTS
*SILVER HOLO/25: 1X TO 2.5X BASIC INSERTS

Card	Low	High
AR J.Addai/S.Ridley	.50	1.25
BP M.Bush/B.Powell	.60	1.50
CG R.Cobb/A.Green	.75	2.00
GD A.Green/A.Dalton	1.25	3.00
GJ A.Green/J.Jones	1.50	4.00
ID M.Ingram/M.Dareus	.75	2.00
JD J.Jones/M.Dareus	1.50	4.00
JP J.Jernigan/B.Powell	.60	1.50
KH Kaepernick/K.Hunter	.75	2.00
LH J.Locker/J.Harper	.50	1.25
LY M.Leshoure/T.Young	.50	1.25
MB L.McCoy/J.Baldwin	.75	2.00
MH S.Moss/L.Hankerson	.60	1.50
MV R.Mallett/S.Vereen	.60	1.50
NL H.Nicks/G.Little	.60	1.50
PM A.Peterson/D.Murray	1.50	4.00
RP K.Rudolph/C.Ponder	.50	1.25
TB J.Todman/V.Brown	.50	1.25
VR S.Vereen/S.Ridley	.60	1.50
YP T.Young/A.Pettis	.50	1.25

2011 Topps Prime Dual Relics

STATED PRINT RUN 398 SER.#'d SETS
*GOLD/50: .6X TO 1.5X BASIC DUAL JSY
*SLVR HOLO/25: .8X TO 2X BASIC DUAL JSY

Card	Low	High
AR J.Addai/S.Ridley	1.50	4.00
BP M.Bush/B.Powell	2.50	6.00
CG R.Cobb/A.Green	2.50	6.00
GD A.Green/A.Dalton	4.00	10.00
GJ A.Green/J.Jones	6.00	15.00
ID M.Ingram/M.Dareus	2.50	6.00
JD J.Jones/M.Dareus	5.00	12.00
JP J.Jernigan/B.Powell	2.00	5.00
KH Kaepernick/K.Hunter	2.50	6.00
LH J.Locker/J.Harper	1.50	4.00
LY M.Leshoure/T.Young	1.50	4.00
MB L.McCoy/J.Baldwin	2.50	6.00
MH S.Moss/L.Hankerson	2.00	5.00
MV R.Mallett/S.Vereen	2.00	5.00
NL H.Nicks/G.Little	2.00	5.00
PM A.Peterson/D.Murray	5.00	12.00
RP K.Rudolph/C.Ponder	1.50	4.00
TB J.Todman/V.Brown	1.50	4.00
VR S.Vereen/S.Ridley	2.00	5.00
YP T.Young/A.Pettis	1.50	4.00

2011 Topps Prime Quad

RANDOM INSERTS IN PACKS
*GOLD/50: .8X TO 2X BASIC INSERTS
*SILVER HOLO/25: 1X TO 2.5X BASIC INSERTS

Card	Low	High
BWMV Brady/Welker/Mallett/Vern	2.50	6.00
GJCH Green/Jones/Cobb/Hnkrsn	2.00	5.00
GLMD Gabbert/Lockr/Malltt/Daltn	1.25	3.00
ILWT Ingrm/Leshre/Willms/Tdmn	1.00	2.50
JCHS Jones/Cobb/Hnkrsn/Smith	2.00	5.00
LWTV Leshre/Willms/Todmn/Vern	.75	2.00
NGGJ Newtn/Gabbrt/Green/Jnes	3.00	8.00
NLGP Newtn/Lockr/Gabbrt/Pondr	3.00	8.00
PDKM Pondr/Daltn/Kprnck/Malltt	1.25	3.00
PHPR Petersn/Harvn/Pondr/Rdlph	1.00	2.50

2011 Topps Prime Quad Relics

STATED PRINT RUN 350 SER.#'d SETS
*GOLD/50: .5X TO 1.2X BASIC QUAD
*SLVR HOLO/25: .6X TO 1.5X BASIC QUAD

Card	Low	High
BWMV Brdy/Wlkr/Mlltt/Vrn	12.00	30.00
GJCH Grn/Jns/Cbb/Hnkrsn	6.00	15.00
GLMD Gbbrt/Lckr/Mlltt/Dltn	4.00	10.00
ILWT Ingrm/Lshre/Wllms/Tdmn	3.00	8.00
JCHS Jns/Cbb/Hnkrsn/Smth	6.00	15.00
LWTV Lshre/Wllms/Tdmn/Vrn	5.00	12.00
NGGJ Nwtn/Gbbrt/Grn/Jns	12.00	30.00
NLGP Nwtn/Lckr/Gbbrt/Pndr	12.00	30.00
PDKM Pndr/Dltn/Kprnck/Mlltt	4.00	10.00
PHPR Ptrsn/Hrvn/Pndr/Rdlph	10.00	25.00

2011 Topps Prime Rookie

Card	Low	High
COMPLETE SET (35)	15.00	40.00

RANDOM INSERTS IN PACKS
*GOLD/50: .8X TO 2X BASIC INSERTS
*SILVER HOLO/25: 1X TO 2.5X BASIC INSERTS

Card	Low	High
PRAD Andy Dalton	1.00	2.50
PRAG Alex Green	.50	1.25
PRAJG A.J. Green	1.25	3.00
PRAP Austin Pettis	.50	1.25
PRBG Blaine Gabbert	.50	1.25
PRBP Bilal Powell	.60	1.50
PRCK Colin Kaepernick	.75	2.00
PRCN Cam Newton	2.50	6.00
PRCP Christian Ponder	.50	1.25
PRDC Delone Carter	.50	1.25
PRDM DeMarco Murray	1.00	2.50
PRDT Daniel Thomas	.50	1.25
PRGL Greg Little	.60	1.50
PRJB Jon Baldwin	.50	1.25
PRJH Jamie Harper	.50	1.25
PRJJ Julio Jones	1.50	4.00
PRJJE Jerrel Jernigan	.50	1.25
PRJL Jake Locker	.50	1.25
PRJT Jordan Todman	.50	1.25
PRKH Kendall Hunter	.50	1.25
PRKR Kyle Rudolph	.50	1.25
PRLH Leonard Hankerson	.50	1.25
PRMD Marcell Dareus	.50	1.25
PRMI Mark Ingram	.75	2.00
PRML Mikel Leshoure	.50	1.25
PRRC Randall Cobb	.75	2.00
PRRM Ryan Mallett	.50	1.25
PRRW Ryan Williams	.50	1.25
PRSR Stevan Ridley	.50	1.25
PRSV Shane Vereen	.60	1.50
PRTJ Taiwan Jones	.50	1.25
PRTS Torrey Smith	.50	1.25
PRTY Titus Young	.50	1.25
PRVB Vincent Brown	.50	1.25
PRVM Von Miller	.75	2.00

2011 Topps Prime Rookie Autographs

STATED PRINT RUN 99-450
EXCH EXPIRATION: 9/30/2014

Card	Low	High
2 Jamie Harper/250	4.00	10.00
3 Bilal Powell/99	6.00	15.00
7 Mark Ingram/99	8.00	20.00
9 DeMarco Murray/200	20.00	50.00
12 Rob Housler/450	3.00	8.00
14 Delone Carter/99	5.00	12.00
15 Prince Amukamara/450	3.00	8.00
18 Dwayne Harris/450	3.00	8.00
21 Nick Fairley/400	3.00	8.00
23 Titus Young	4.00	10.00
24 D.J. Williams/450	3.00	8.00
27 Jordan Todman		
29 Jacquizz Rodgers/450	3.00	8.00
31 A.J. Green/99	25.00	50.00
37 Kyle Rudolph/250	4.00	10.00
44 Ryan Mallett/99	5.00	12.00
45 Torrey Smith/270	4.00	10.00
47 Colin Kaepernick/99	8.00	20.00
50 Cam Newton/200	50.00	100.00
51 Rahim Moore/450	3.00	8.00
52 Julio Jones/99	20.00	50.00
53 Da'Rel Scott/450	3.00	8.00
54 Greg Salas/450	3.00	8.00
55 Randall Cobb/270	6.00	15.00
56 Marcell Dareus		
57 Alex Green/400	3.00	8.00
61 Christian Ponder/99	5.00	12.00
63 Shane Vereen/250	5.00	12.00
68 Jon Baldwin/99	5.00	12.00
74 Dion Lewis/450	4.00	10.00
78 Von Miller/99	12.00	30.00
82 Jake Locker/99	5.00	12.00
83 Blaine Gabbert/99	5.00	12.00
87 Ricky Stanzi/400	3.00	8.00
91 Leonard Hankerson/270	4.00	10.00
93 Taiwan Jones/99	5.00	12.00
96 Kendall Hunter/250	4.00	10.00
108 Ryan Williams/99	5.00	12.00
113 Andy Dalton/99	10.00	25.00
114 Stevan Ridley/250	4.00	10.00
117 Daniel Thomas/250	4.00	10.00
118 Luke Stocker/450	3.00	8.00
119 Virgil Green/450	3.00	8.00
127 Jeremy Kerley/450	5.00	12.00
137 Jerrel Jernigan/250	4.00	10.00
143 Vincent Brown		
145 Edmond Gates/250	4.00	10.00
146 Mikel Leshoure EXCH	4.00	10.00
148 Greg Little/270	5.00	12.00
151 Aldon Smith/400	3.00	8.00
152 J.J. Watt/450	30.00	60.00
153 Adrian Clayborn EXCH	4.00	10.00
154 Ryan Kerrigan/450	4.00	10.00
155 Aaron Williams/450	3.00	8.00

2011 Topps Prime Rookie Autographs Gold

*GOLD/50: .8X TO 2X BASIC AU/400-450
*GOLD/50: .6X TO 1.5X BASIC AU/200-270
*GOLD/50: .5X TO 1.2X BASIC AU/99
STATED PRINT RUN 50 SER.#'d SETS

2011 Topps Prime Rookie Autographs Silver Holofoil

*SLV HOLO/25: 1X TO 2.5X BASIC AU/400-450
*SLV HOLO/25: .8X TO 2X BASIC AU/200-270
*SLV HOLO/25: .6X TO 1.5X BASIC AU/99
STATED PRINT RUN 25 SER.#'d SETS

2011 Topps Prime Rookie Jumbo Relics

SILVER PRINT RUN 318 SER.#'d SETS
*GOLD/50: .6X TO 1.5X BASIC JSY/318
*SLVR HOLO/25: .8X TO 2X BASIC JSY/318

Card	Low	High
PRJAD Andy Dalton	3.00	8.00
PRJAG Alex Green	1.50	4.00
PRJAP Austin Pettis	1.50	4.00
PRJBG Blaine Gabbert	1.50	4.00
PRJBP Bilal Powell	2.00	5.00
PRJCK Colin Kaepernick	2.50	6.00
PRJCN Cam Newton	8.00	20.00
PRJCP Christian Ponder	1.50	4.00
PRJDC Delone Carter	1.50	4.00
PRJDM DeMarco Murray	6.00	15.00
PRJDT Daniel Thomas	1.50	4.00
PRJEG Edmond Gates	1.50	4.00
PRJGL Greg Little	2.00	5.00
PRJJB Jon Baldwin	1.50	4.00
PRJJH Jamie Harper	1.50	4.00
PRJJJ Julio Jones	6.00	15.00
PRJJE Jerrel Jernigan	1.50	4.00
PRJJL Jake Locker	1.50	4.00
PRJJT Jordan Todman	1.50	4.00
PRJKH Kendall Hunter	1.50	4.00
PRJKR Kyle Rudolph	1.50	4.00
PRJLH Leonard Hankerson	1.50	4.00
PRJMD Marcell Dareus	1.50	4.00
PRJMI Mark Ingram	2.50	6.00
PRJML Mikel Leshoure	1.50	4.00
PRJRC Randall Cobb	2.50	6.00
PRJRM Ryan Mallett	1.50	4.00
PRJRW Ryan Williams	1.50	4.00
PRJSR Stevan Ridley	1.50	4.00
PRJSV Shane Vereen	2.00	5.00
PRJTJ Taiwan Jones	1.50	4.00
PRJTS Torrey Smith	1.50	4.00
PRJTY Titus Young	1.50	4.00
PRJVB Vincent Brown	1.50	4.00
PRJVM Von Miller	2.50	6.00
PRJAJG A.J. Green	4.00	10.00

2011 Topps Prime Triple

RANDOM INSERTS IN PACKS
*GOLD/50: .8X TO 2X BASIC INSERTS
*SILVER HOLO/25: 1X TO 2.5X BASIC INSERTS

Card	Low	High
CJH Carter/Jones/Harper	.50	1.25
GJB Green/Jones/Baldwin	1.50	4.00
HCJ Hunter/Carter/Jones	.50	1.25
IWV Ingram/Williams/Vereen	.75	2.00
JBP Jernigan/Brown/Pettis	.50	1.25
JDI Jones/Dareus/Ingram	1.50	4.00
JLY Johnson/Leshre/Young	.75	2.00
LTM Leshre/Thomas/Murray	1.00	2.50
MRB P.Mann/Rodgers/Brady	2.50	6.00
MVR Mallett/Vereen/Ridley	.60	1.50
NLG Newton/Locker/Gabbert	2.50	6.00
NMD Newton/Miller/Dareus	2.50	6.00
PDK Ponder/Dalton/Kpernick	1.00	2.50
RBT Rivers/Brown/Todman	.75	2.00
YSL Young/Smith/Little	.60	1.50

2011 Topps Prime Triple Relics

STATED PRINT RUN 388
*GOLD/50: .6X TO 1.5X BASIC TRIPLE
*SLVR HOLO/25: .8X TO 2X BASIC TRIPLE

Card	Low	High
CJH Carter/Jones/Harper	3.00	8.00
GJB Green/Jones/Baldwin	6.00	15.00
HCJ Hunter/Carter/Jones	3.00	8.00
IWV Ingram/Williams/Vereen	2.50	6.00
JBP Jernigan/Brown/Pettis	3.00	8.00
JDI Jones/Dareus/Ingram	8.00	20.00
JLY Johnson/Leshre/Young	5.00	12.00
LTM Leshre/Thomas/Murray	3.00	8.00
MRB P.Mann/Rodgers/Brady	12.00	30.00
MVR Mallett/Vereen/Ridley	2.00	5.00
NLG Newton/Locker/Gabbert	10.00	25.00
NMD Newton/Miller/Dareus	10.00	25.00
PDK Ponder/Dalton/Kpernick	3.00	8.00
RBT Rivers/Brown/Todman	4.00	10.00
YSL Young/Smith/Little	4.00	10.00

2011 Topps Prime Veteran

Card	Low	High
COMPLETE SET (20)	8.00	20.00

RANDOM INSERTS IN PACKS
*GOLD/50: 1X TO 2.5X BASIC INSERTS
*SILVER HOLO/25: 1.2X TO 3X BASIC INSERTS

Card	Low	High
PVAP Adrian Peterson	1.00	2.50
PVBU Brian Urlacher	1.00	2.50
PVCJ Calvin Johnson	1.00	2.50
PVER Eddie Royal	.60	1.50
PVHN Hakeem Nicks	.60	1.50
PVJA Joseph Addai	.60	1.50
PVJW Jason Witten	.75	2.00
PVKM Knowshon Moreno	.60	1.50
PVLF Larry Fitzgerald	.75	2.00
PVLM LeSean McCoy	1.00	2.50
PVMB Michael Bush	.60	1.50
PVPH Percy Harvin	.60	1.50
PVPR Philip Rivers	1.00	2.50
PVRL Ray Lewis	1.00	2.50
PVSM Santana Moss	.75	2.00
PVTB Tom Brady	2.50	6.00
PVTG Tony Gonzalez	.75	2.00
PVTP Troy Polamalu	1.00	2.50
PVTR Tony Romo	.75	2.00
PVWW Wes Welker	.75	2.00

2011 Topps Prime Veteran Relics

STATED PRINT RUN 99 SER.#'d SETS
*GOLD/50: .5X TO 1.2X BASIC JSY
*SILVER HOLO/25: .8X TO 2X BASIC JSY

Card	Low	High
PVRAP Adrian Peterson	5.00	12.00
PVRBU Brian Urlacher	5.00	12.00
PVRCJ Calvin Johnson	5.00	12.00
PVRER Eddie Royal	3.00	8.00
PVRHN Hakeem Nicks	3.00	8.00
PVRJA Joseph Addai	3.00	8.00
PVRJW Jason Witten	4.00	10.00
PVRKM Knowshon Moreno	3.00	8.00
PVRLF Larry Fitzgerald	4.00	10.00
PVRLM LeSean McCoy	5.00	12.00
PVRMB Michael Bush	3.00	8.00
PVRPH Percy Harvin	3.00	8.00
PVRPR Philip Rivers	5.00	12.00
PVRRL Ray Lewis	5.00	12.00
PVRSM Santana Moss	4.00	10.00
PVRTB Tom Brady	12.00	30.00
PVRTG Tony Gonzalez	4.00	10.00
PVRTP Troy Polamalu	5.00	12.00
PVRTR Tony Romo	4.00	10.00
PVRWW Wes Welker	4.00	10.00

2012 Topps Prime

Card	Low	High
COMPLETE SET (150)	40.00	80.00
COMP.SET w/o RCs (100)	10.00	25.00

ONE ROOKIE PER HOBBY PACK

Card	Low	High
1 Andrew Luck RC	4.00	10.00
2 DeAngelo Williams	.20	.50
3 Jason Pierre-Paul	.20	.50
4 DeSean Jackson	.25	.60
5 Nick Foles RC	1.00	2.50
6 Nick Toon RC	.40	1.00
7 Randy Moss	.25	.60
8 Dez Bryant	.30	.75
9 T.J. Graham RC	.40	1.00
10 Cam Newton	.30	.75
11 A.J. Jenkins RC	.40	1.00
12 Jarius Wright RC	.40	1.00
13 LeGarrette Blount	.25	.60
14 Darren McFadden	.20	.50
15 Coby Fleener RC	.40	1.00
16 Jared Allen	.20	.50
17 Beanie Wells	.20	.50
18 Brock Osweiler RC	.40	1.00
19 Matt Ryan	.25	.60
20 Eli Manning	.25	.60
21 Joe Adams RC	.40	1.00
22 Tim Tebow	.30	.75
23 Jason Witten	.25	.60
24 Andre Johnson	.25	.60
25 Peyton Hillis	.20	.50
26 Kevin Kolb	.20	.50
27 Chris Rainey RC	.40	1.00
28 Rueben Randle RC	.40	1.00
29 Mark Barron RC	.40	1.00
30 Aaron Rodgers	.50	1.25
31 Ryan Mathews	.25	.60
32 Mike Wallace	.20	.50
33 Roy Helu	.20	.50
34 Mohamed Sanu RC	.60	1.50
35 Laurent Robinson	.20	.50
36 Steve Smith	.25	.60
37 Patrick Willis	.25	.60
38 Alshon Jeffery RC	.75	2.00
39 Christian Ponder	.20	.50
40 Trent Richardson RC	.40	1.00
41 Marques Colston	.20	.50
42 Wes Welker	.25	.60
43 Sam Bradford	.20	.50
44 Alex Smith	.25	.60
45 Darren Sproles	.25	.60
46 Kendall Wright RC	.40	1.00
47 Matt Forte	.20	.50
48 Ndamukong Suh	.25	.60
49 LaMichael James RC	.40	1.00
50 Tom Brady	.75	2.00
51 Juron Criner RC	.40	1.00
52 Julio Jones	.30	.75
53 Torrey Smith	.20	.50
54 Tony Gonzalez	.25	.60
55 Adrian Peterson	.30	.75
56 Hakeem Nicks	.20	.50
57 Roddy White	.20	.50
58 Vernon Davis	.20	.50
59 Chris Johnson	.20	.50
60 Maurice Jones-Drew	.20	.50
61 Von Miller	.25	.60
62 Philip Rivers	.30	.75
63 Reggie Bush	.20	.50
64 Ryan Fitzpatrick	.20	.50
65 Lamar Miller RC	.60	1.50
66 Ben Roethlisberger	.30	.75
67 Isaiah Pead RC	.40	1.00
68 Marshawn Lynch	.25	.60
69 Brian Quick RC	.40	1.00
70 Justin Blackmon RC	.40	1.00
71 Mario Williams	.20	.50
72 Antonio Brown	.30	.75
73 Shonn Greene	.20	.50
74 Michael Egnew RC	.40	1.00
75 Chris Givens RC	.40	1.00
76 Steve Johnson	.25	.60
77 Doug Martin RC	.60	1.50
78 Russell Wilson RC	3.00	8.00
79 Tony Romo	.25	.60
80 Arian Foster	.25	.60
81 Kirk Cousins RC	1.50	4.00
82 Dre Kirkpatrick RC	.40	1.00
83 Greg Jennings	.20	.50
84 Jeremy Maclin	.20	.50
85 Jay Cutler	.20	.50
86 Joe Flacco	.25	.60
87 Ryan Tannehill RC	.60	1.50
88 Jake Locker	.30	.75
89 Luke Kuechly RC	1.00	2.50
90 Calvin Johnson	.30	.75
91 Ronnie Hillman RC	.40	1.00
92 Matt Flynn	.20	.50
93 Aaron Hernandez	.25	.60
94 Ryan Lindley RC	.40	1.00
95 Jermichael Finley	.20	.50
96 Dwayne Allen RC	.40	1.00
97 Michael Vick	.25	.60
98 DeVier Posey RC	.40	1.00
99 Brandon Weeden RC	.40	1.00
100 Peyton Manning	.60	1.50
101 Victor Cruz	.25	.60
102 Anquan Boldin	.20	.50
103 Robert Turbin RC	.40	1.00
104 Josh Freeman	.25	.60
105 Fred Jackson	.25	.60
106 DeMarco Murray	.25	.60
107 Melvin Ingram RC	.40	1.00
108 Jamaal Charles	.25	.60
109 Dontari Poe RC	.40	1.00
110 Larry Fitzgerald	.25	.60
111 Dwayne Bowe	.25	.60
112 Mark Sanchez	.20	.50
113 Matthew Stafford	.25	.60
114 Mario Manningham	.20	.50
115 Greg Childs RC	.40	1.00
116 Steven Jackson	.20	.50
117 Cyrus Gray RC	.40	1.00
118 Percy Harvin	.20	.50
119 A.J. Green	.30	.75
120 Rob Gronkowski	.30	.75
121 Ahmad Bradshaw	.20	.50
122 Jordy Nelson	.25	.60
123 Antonio Gates	.25	.60
124 Brandon Marshall	.25	.60

125 Greg Little .20 .50
126 Andy Dalton .25 .60
127 Michael Turner .20 .50
128 Matt Schaub .20 .50
129 LeSean McCoy .30 .75
130 Drew Brees .30 .75
131 Tommy Streeter RC .40 1.00
132 Chandler Harnish RC .40 1.00
133 Willis McGahee .20 .50
134 Vincent Jackson .20 .50
135 T.Y. Hilton RC .75 2.00
136 Ryan Broyles RC .40 1.00
137 David Wilson RC .40 1.00
138 Carson Palmer .25 .60
139 Troy Polamalu .30 .75
140 Jimmy Graham .30 .75
141 Travis Benjamin RC .40 1.00
142 Michael Floyd RC .40 1.00
143 Miles Austin .20 .50
144 LaDainian Tomlinson .30 .75
145 Ray Lewis .30 .75
146 Frank Gore .25 .60
147 Stephen Hill RC .40 1.00
148 Bernard Pierce RC .40 1.00
149 Ray Rice .20 .50
150 Robert Griffin III RC .50 1.25

2012 Topps Prime Copper

*COPPER/350: .8X TO 2X BASIC RC
COPPER/350 ODDS 1:13 HOBBY

2012 Topps Prime Copper Rainbow

*ROOKIES/50: 1.5X TO 4X BASIC RC

2012 Topps Prime Gold

*VETS: 1X TO 2.5X BASIC CARDS
ONE PARALLEL PER HOBBY PACK OVERALL
*ROOKIES/250: 8X TO 2X BASIC RC
GOLD ROOKIE/250 ODDS 1:18 HOBBY

2012 Topps Prime Silver Rainbow

*ROOKIES: 1.2X TO 3X BASIC RC
STATED ODDS 1:45 HOBBY

2012 Topps Prime Retail

*RETAIL VETS: .3X TO .8X HOBBY
*RETAIL ROOKIES: .3X TO .8X HOBBY RC
RETAIL PRINTED ON THINNER STOCK

2012 Topps Prime Retail Blue

*VETS: .8X TO 2X BASIC CARDS
*ROOKIES: .4X TO 1X HOBBY RC
THREE PER RETAIL VALUE PACK

2012 Topps Prime Autographed Relics Level 2

*SILVER/15: 1.5X TO 4X LEVEL 5/700-780
*SILVER/15: 1.2X TO 3X LEVEL 5/250-300
PIIAL Andrew Luck 300.00 500.00
PIIRG Robert Griffin III 50.00 100.00
PIIRW Russell Wilson 200.00 350.00

2012 Topps Prime Autographed Relics Level 4

*SILVER/15: 1X TO 2.5X LEVEL 5/700-780
*SILVER/15: .8X TO 2X LEVEL 5/250-300
PIVAL Andrew Luck 175.00 300.00
PIVRG Robert Griffin III 40.00 80.00
PIVRW Russell Wilson 150.00 250.00

2012 Topps Prime Autographed Relics Level 5

EXCH EXPIRATION: 8/31/2015
PVAG A.J. Green/100 15.00 40.00
PVAJ A.J. Jenkins/250 4.00 10.00
PVAJE Alshon Jeffery/250 12.00 30.00
PVAL Andrew Luck/300 75.00 150.00
PVBG Blaine Gabbert/100 8.00 20.00
PVBO Brock Osweiler/250 4.00 10.00
PVBQ Brian Quick/250 4.00 10.00
PVBW Brandon Weeden/250 4.00 10.00
PVCF Coby Fleener/780 3.00 8.00
PVCG Chris Givens/780 3.00 8.00
PVCGR Cyrus Gray/700 3.00 8.00
PVCM Colt McCoy/100 10.00 25.00
PVCP Christian Ponder/100 8.00 20.00
PVCRA Chris Rainey/780 3.00 8.00
PVDA Dwayne Allen/780 EXCH 3.00 8.00
PVDB Dez Bryant/100 12.00 30.00
PVDM Doug Martin/780 5.00 12.00
PVDP DeVier Posey/780 3.00 8.00
PVGC Greg Childs/700 3.00 8.00
PVIP Isaiah Pead/250 4.00 10.00
PVJA Joe Adams/700 EXCH 3.00 8.00
PVJB Justin Blackmon/250 4.00 10.00
PVJC Juron Criner/700 3.00 8.00
PVJMA Jeremy Maclin/100 8.00 20.00
PVJW Jarius Wright/780 3.00 8.00
PVKW Kendall Wright/250 EXCH 4.00 10.00
PVLJ LaMichael James/250 4.00 10.00
PVLM Lamar Miller/250 6.00 15.00
PVME Michael Egnew/780 3.00 8.00
PVMF Michael Floyd/780 3.00 8.00
PVMI Mark Ingram/100 10.00 25.00
PVMS Mohamed Sanu/250 6.00 15.00
PVNF Nick Foles/250 25.00 50.00
PVNT Nick Toon/780 3.00 8.00
PVRB Ryan Broyles/780 3.00 8.00
PVRG Robert Griffin III/300 20.00 50.00
PVRH Ronnie Hillman/780 3.00 8.00
PVRR Rueben Randle/250 4.00 10.00
PVRT Ryan Tannehill/250 6.00 15.00
PVRTU Robert Turbin/780 3.00 8.00
PVRW Russell Wilson/250 75.00 150.00
PVSB Sam Bradford/100 20.00 50.00
PVSH Stephen Hill/250 4.00 10.00
PVTG T.J. Graham/780 3.00 8.00
PVTH T.Y. Hilton/700 6.00 15.00
PVTR Trent Richardson/250 12.00 30.00
PVTS Torrey Smith/100 EXCH 8.00 20.00
PVVM Von Miller/100 10.00 25.00

2012 Topps Prime Autographed Relics Level 5 Copper

*COPPER/50: .6X TO 1.5X LEVEL 5/700-780
*COPPER/50: .5X TO 1.2X LEVEL 5/250-300
PVAL Andrew Luck 100.00 200.00
PVRG Robert Griffin III 25.00 60.00
PVRW Russell Wilson 100.00 175.00

2012 Topps Prime Autographed Relics Level 5 Gold

*GOLD/25: .8X TO 2X LEVEL 5/700-780
*GOLD/25: .6X TO 1.5X LEVEL 5/250-300
PVAL Andrew Luck 125.00 250.00
PVRG Robert Griffin III 30.00 80.00
PVRW Russell Wilson 125.00 200.00

2012 Topps Prime Autographed Relics Level 5 Silver Rainbow

*SILVER/15: 1X TO 2.5X LEVEL 5/700-780
*SILVER/15: .8X TO 2X LEVEL 5/250-300
PVAL Andrew Luck 200.00 300.00
PVRG Robert Griffin III 40.00 100.00
PVRW Russell Wilson 150.00 250.00

2012 Topps Prime Dual Combo Relics

STATED PRINT RUN 405 SER.#'d SETS
*COPPER/25: .6X TO 1.5X DUAL COMBO/405
DCRBF J.Blackmon/M.Floyd 1.25 3.00
DCRBR J.Blackmon/T.Richardson 1.25 3.00
DCRFW M.Floyd/K.Wright 1.25 3.00
DCRGN R.Griffin III/C.Newton 2.00 5.00
DCRGW R.Griffin III/K.Wright 1.50 4.00
DCRJJ L.James/A.Jenkins 1.25 3.00
DCRJP L.James/I.Pead 1.25 3.00
DCRJS A.Jeffery/M.Sanu 2.50 6.00
DCRLF A.Luck/C.Fleener 6.00 15.00
DCRLG A.Luck/R.Griffin III 10.00 25.00
DCRLN A.Luck/C.Newton 12.00 30.00
DCROF B.Osweiler/N.Foles 3.00 8.00
DCROH B.Osweiler/R.Hillman 1.25 3.00
DCRRH R.Randle/S.Hill 3.00 8.00
DCRRW T.Richardson/B.Weeden 1.25 3.00
DCRTH N.Toon/S.Hill 3.00 8.00
DCRTM R.Tannehill/L.Miller 2.00 5.00
DCRTW R.Tannehill/B.Weeden 2.00 5.00
DCRWB B.Weeden/J.Blackmon 1.25 3.00
DCRWT R.Wilson/R.Turbin 8.00 20.00

2012 Topps Prime Dual Relics

*DUAL JSY/235-306: .4X TO 1X SINGLE JSY/266
STATED PRINT RUN 235-306
*COPPER/25: .6X TO 1.5X SINGLE JSY/266

2012 Topps Prime Primed Rookies

STATED ODDS 1:10 HOBBY
PRAJ A.J. Jenkins .75 2.00
PRAL Andrew Luck 8.00 20.00
PRBO Brock Osweiler .75 2.00
PRBP Bernard Pierce .75 2.00
PRBQ Brian Quick .75 2.00
PRBW Brandon Weeden .75 2.00
PRCF Coby Fleener .75 2.00
PRCG Chris Givens .75 2.00
PRCH Chandler Harnish .75 2.00
PRCR Chris Rainey .75 2.00
PRDA Dwayne Allen .75 2.00
PRDK Dre Kirkpatrick .75 2.00
PRDM Doug Martin 1.25 3.00
PRDP DeVier Posey .75 2.00
PRDW David Wilson .75 2.00
PRGC Greg Childs .75 2.00
PRIP Isaiah Pead .75 2.00
PRJA Joe Adams .75 2.00
PRJB Justin Blackmon .75 2.00
PRJW Jarius Wright .75 2.00
PRKC Kirk Cousins 3.00 8.00
PRKW Kendall Wright .75 2.00
PRLJ LaMichael James .75 2.00
PRLK Luke Kuechly 2.00 5.00
PRLM Lamar Miller 1.25 3.00
PRMB Mark Barron .75 2.00
PRME Michael Egnew .75 2.00
PRMF Michael Floyd .75 2.00
PRMI Melvin Ingram .75 2.00
PRMS Mohamed Sanu 1.25 3.00
PRNF Nick Foles 2.00 5.00
PRNT Nick Toon .75 2.00
PRRB Ryan Broyles .75 2.00
PRRG Robert Griffin III 1.00 2.50
PRRH Ronnie Hillman .75 2.00
PRRL Ryan Lindley .75 2.00
PRRR Rueben Randle .75 2.00
PRRT Ryan Tannehill 1.25 3.00
PRRW Russell Wilson 6.00 15.00
PRSH Stephen Hill .75 2.00
PRTB Travis Benjamin .75 2.00
PRTG T.J. Graham .75 2.00
PRTH T.Y. Hilton 1.50 4.00
PRTR Trent Richardson .75 2.00
PRTS Tommy Streeter .75 2.00
PRAJE Alshon Jeffery 1.50 4.00
PRCGR Cyrus Gray .75 2.00
PRDPO Dontari Poe .75 2.00
PRJCR Juron Criner .75 2.00
PRRTU Robert Turbin .75 2.00

2012 Topps Prime Primetimers

STATED ODDS 1:5 HOBBY
*SILVER RETAIL: .4X TO 1X HOBBY
PTAB Ahmad Bradshaw .60 1.50
PTAD Andy Dalton .75 2.00
PTAF Arian Foster .75 2.00
PTAG A.J. Green 1.00 2.50
PTAH Aaron Hernandez .75 2.00
PTAJ Andre Johnson .75 2.00
PTAP Adrian Peterson 1.00 2.50
PTAR Aaron Rodgers 1.50 4.00
PTAS Alex Smith .75 2.00
PTBM Brandon Marshall .75 2.00
PTBR Ben Roethlisberger 1.00 2.50
PTBW Beanie Wells .60 1.50
PTCB Cedric Benson .60 1.50
PTCJ Calvin Johnson 1.00 2.50
PTCN Cam Newton 1.00 2.50
PTCP Carson Palmer .75 2.00
PTCS C.J. Spiller .60 1.50
PTDB Drew Brees 1.00 2.50
PTDJ DeSean Jackson .75 2.00
PTDM Darren McFadden .60 1.50
PTDS Darren Sproles .75 2.00
PTDW DeAngelo Williams .60 1.50
PTEM Eli Manning .75 2.00
PTFD Fred Davis .60 1.50
PTFG Frank Gore .75 2.00
PTFJ Fred Jackson .75 2.00
PTGJ Greg Jennings .60 1.50
PTHN Hakeem Nicks .60 1.50
PTJA Jared Allen .60 1.50
PTJC Jay Cutler .60 1.50
PTJF Josh Freeman .75 2.00
PTJG Jimmy Graham 1.00 2.50
PTJJ Julio Jones 1.00 2.50
PTJL Jake Locker 1.00 2.50
PTJN Jordy Nelson .75 2.00
PTJP Julius Peppers .75 2.00
PTJW Jason Witten .75 2.00
PTKK Kevin Kolb .60 1.50
PTKM Knowshon Moreno .60 1.50
PTLB LeGarrette Blount .75 2.00
PTLF Larry Fitzgerald .75 2.00
PTLM LeSean McCoy 1.00 2.50
PTLT LaDainian Tomlinson 1.00 2.50
PTMA Miles Austin .60 1.50
PTMC Marques Colston .60 1.50
PTMF Matt Flynn .60 1.50
PTML Marshawn Lynch .75 2.00
PTMR Matt Ryan .75 2.00
PTMS Matthew Stafford .75 2.00
PTMT Michael Turner .60 1.50
PTMV Michael Vick .75 2.00
PTMW Mike Wallace .60 1.50
PTNS Ndamukong Suh .75 2.00
PTPH Peyton Hillis .60 1.50
PTPM Peyton Manning 2.00 5.00
PTPR Philip Rivers 1.00 2.50
PTPW Patrick Willis .75 2.00
PTRB Reggie Bush .60 1.50
PTRF Ryan Fitzpatrick .60 1.50
PTRG Rob Gronkowski 1.00 2.50
PTRH Roy Helu .60 1.50
PTRM Ryan Mathews .75 2.00
PTRR Ray Rice .60 1.50
PTRW Roddy White .60 1.50
PTSB Sam Bradford .60 1.50
PTSG Shonn Greene .60 1.50
PTSJ Steven Jackson .60 1.50
PTSR Stevan Ridley .60 1.50
PTSS Steve Smith .75 2.00
PTTB Tom Brady 2.50 6.00
PTTG Tony Gonzalez .75 2.00
PTTP Troy Polamalu 1.00 2.50
PTTR Tony Romo .75 2.00
PTTT Tim Tebow 1.00 2.50
PTVC Victor Cruz .75 2.00
PTVD Vernon Davis .60 1.50
PTVJ Vincent Jackson .60 1.50
PTVM Von Miller .75 2.00
PTWM Willis McGahee .60 1.50
PTWW Wes Welker .75 2.00
PTABO Anquan Boldin .60 1.50
PTAGA Antonio Gates .75 2.00
PTCJO Chris Johnson .60 1.50
PTCPO Christian Ponder .60 1.50
PTDBO Dwayne Bowe .75 2.00
PTDBR Dez Bryant 1.00 2.50
PTDMU DeMarco Murray .75 2.00
PTDTO Demaryius Thomas 1.00 2.50
PTJCH Jamaal Charles .75 2.00
PTJFI Jermichael Finley .60 1.50
PTJFL Joe Flacco .75 2.00
PTJPP Jason Pierre-Paul .60 1.50
PTMCR Michael Crabtree .60 1.50
PTMFO Matt Forte .60 1.50
PTMJD Maurice Jones-Drew .60 1.50
PTMSA Mark Sanchez .60 1.50
PTMSC Matt Schaub .60 1.50
PTMWI Mario Williams .60 1.50
PTPHA Percy Harvin .60 1.50
PTTGE Toby Gerhart .60 1.50

2012 Topps Prime Quad Combo Relics

STATED PRINT RUN 86-610
*COPPER/25: .6X TO 1.5X QUAD COMBO/610
QCRBFWJ Blkmn/Fld/Wrht/Jnkns 1.50 4.00
QCRBGTC Blkm/Grn/Thm/Crbt UER 6.00 15.00
QCRGWWB RG3/Wrt/Wdn/Blkmn 2.00 5.00
QCRLGRB Lck/RG3/Rcdsn/Blck 12.00 30.00
QCRLGTW Lck/RG3/Tnn/Wdn 15.00 40.00
QCRLNBS Lck/Nwtn/Brdf/Stf/86 15.00 40.00
QCRLOGT Lck/Oswlr/RG3/Tann 15.00 40.00
QCRRISM Rchrd/Ingm/Spl/Mrno 2.00 5.00
QCRWRMM Wrht/Rndl/Mlr/Mrtin 2.50 6.00

2012 Topps Prime Quad Relics

*QUAD JSY/146-155: .6X TO 1.5X SNGL JSY/266
QUAD RELIC/146-155 ODDS 1:58 HOB
*COPPER/25: .6X TO 1.5X SINGLE JSY/266

2012 Topps Prime Relics

STATED PRINT RUN 266 SER.#'d SETS
*COPPER/25: .6X TO 1.5X BASIC JSY/266
PRAJ A.J. Jenkins 1.50 4.00
PRAJE Alshon Jeffery 3.00 8.00
PRAL Andrew Luck 12.00 30.00
PRBO Brock Osweiler 1.50 4.00
PRBP Bernard Pierce 1.50 4.00
PRBQ Brian Quick 1.50 4.00
PRBW Brandon Weeden 1.50 4.00
PRCF Coby Fleener 1.50 4.00
PRCG Chris Givens 1.50 4.00
PRDA Dwayne Allen 1.50 4.00
PRDM Doug Martin 2.50 6.00
PRDP DeVier Posey 1.50 4.00
PRIP Isaiah Pead 1.50 4.00
PRJA Joe Adams 1.50 4.00
PRJB Justin Blackmon 1.50 4.00
PRJW Jarius Wright 1.50 4.00
PRKW Kendall Wright 1.50 4.00
PRLJ LaMichael James 1.50 4.00
PRLM Lamar Miller 2.50 6.00
PRME Michael Egnew 1.50 4.00
PRMF Michael Floyd 1.50 4.00
PRMS Mohamed Sanu 2.50 6.00
PRNF Nick Foles 4.00 10.00
PRNT Nick Toon 1.50 4.00
PRRB Ryan Broyles 1.50 4.00
PRRG Robert Griffin III 2.00 5.00
PRRH Ronnie Hillman 1.50 4.00
PRRR Rueben Randle 1.50 4.00
PRRT Ryan Tannehill 2.50 6.00
PRRTU Robert Turbin 1.50 4.00
PRRW Russell Wilson 8.00 20.00
PRSH Stephen Hill 1.50 4.00
PRTG T.J. Graham 1.50 4.00
PRTR Trent Richardson 1.50 4.00

2012 Topps Prime Rookie Autographs

ROOKIE AU/260-286 ODDS 1:22 HOB
EXCH EXPIRATION: 8/31/2015
1 Andrew Luck/260 60.00 125.00
5 Nick Foles/286 15.00 40.00
6 Nick Toon/286 2.50 6.00
9 T.J. Graham/286 2.50 6.00
11 A.J. Jenkins/286 2.50 6.00
12 Jarius Wright/286 2.50 6.00
15 Coby Fleener/286 2.50 6.00
18 Brock Osweiler/260 2.50 6.00
21 Joe Adams/286 2.50 6.00
27 Chris Rainey/286 2.50 6.00
28 Rueben Randle/286 2.50 6.00
29 Mark Barron/286 2.50 6.00
34 Mohamed Sanu/286 4.00 10.00
38 Alshon Jeffery/286 8.00 20.00
40 Trent Richardson/260 12.00 30.00
46 Kendall Wright/260 2.50 6.00
49 LaMichael James/260 2.50 6.00
51 Juron Criner/286 2.50 6.00
65 Lamar Miller/260 4.00 10.00
67 Isaiah Pead/260 2.50 6.00
69 Brian Quick/286 2.50 6.00
70 Justin Blackmon/260 2.50 6.00
74 Michael Egnew/286 2.50 6.00
75 Chris Givens/286 2.50 6.00
77 Doug Martin/260 4.00 10.00
78 Russell Wilson/286 60.00 125.00
81 Kirk Cousins/286 12.00 30.00
82 Dre Kirkpatrick/286 2.50 6.00
87 Ryan Tannehill/260 4.00 10.00
89 Luke Kuechly/286 8.00 20.00
91 Ronnie Hillman/260 2.50 6.00
94 Ryan Lindley/286 2.50 6.00
96 Dwayne Allen/286 2.50 6.00
98 DeVier Posey/286 2.50 6.00
99 Brandon Weeden/260 2.50 6.00
103 Robert Turbin/286 2.50 6.00
107 Melvin Ingram/286 2.50 6.00
109 Dontari Poe/286 2.50 6.00
115 Greg Childs/286 2.50 6.00
117 Cyrus Gray/286 2.50 6.00
132 Chandler Harnish/286 2.50 6.00
135 T.Y. Hilton/286 5.00 12.00
136 Ryan Broyles/286 2.50 6.00
137 David Wilson/260 2.50 6.00
141 Travis Benjamin/286 2.50 6.00
142 Michael Floyd/260 2.50 6.00
147 Stephen Hill/286 2.50 6.00
150 Robert Griffin III/260 20.00 50.00
151 Matt Kalil/286 2.50 6.00
152 Chris Polk/260 2.50 6.00

2012 Topps Prime Rookie Autographs Copper

*COPPER/99: .5X TO 1.2X BASIC AU
COPPER/99 ODDS 1:48 HOB

2012 Topps Prime Rookie Autographs Copper Rainbow

*COPPER RNBW/25: .8X TO 2X BASIC AU
COPPER RAINBOW/25 ODDS 1:190 HOB
1 Andrew Luck 100.00 200.00
78 Russell Wilson 100.00 175.00

2012 Topps Prime Rookie Autographs Gold

*GOLD/75: .6X TO 1.5X BASIC AU
GOLD/75 STATED ODDS 1:63 HOB
1 Andrew Luck 100.00 200.00
78 Russell Wilson 90.00 150.00

2012 Topps Prime Rookie Autographs Silver Rainbow

*SILVER RNBW/50: .6X TO 1.5X BASIC AU
SILVER RAINBOW/50 ODDS 1:95 HOB
1 Andrew Luck 100.00 200.00
78 Russell Wilson 90.00 150.00

2012 Topps Prime Triple Combo Relics

STATED PRINT RUN 559 SER.#'d SETS
*COPPER/25: .8X TO 2X TRIPLE COMBO/559
TCRBFW Blackmon/Floyd/Wright 1.25 3.00
TCRBGT Blackmon/Green/Thomas 2.00 5.00
TCRFWJ Floyd/Wright/Jeffery 2.50 6.00
TCRLFG Luck/Fleener/Gerhart 10.00 25.00
TCRLFH Luck/Fleener/Hilton 10.00 25.00
TCRLGT Luck/Griffin III/Tannehill 6.00 15.00
TCRLNB Luck/Newton/Bradford 12.00 30.00
TCROWF Osweiler/Weeden/Foles 3.00 8.00
TCRQGP Quick/Givens/Pead 3.00 8.00
TCRRHJ Randle/Hill/Jeffery 2.50 6.00
TCRRIS Richardson/Ingram/Spiller 1.50 4.00
TCRWHR Wright/Hill/Randle 3.00 8.00

2012 Topps Prime Triple Relics

*TRIPLE JSY/194: .5X TO 1.2X SINGLE JSY/266
STATED PRINT RUN 194 SER.#'d SETS
*COPPER/25: .8X TO 2X SINGLE JSY/266

2013 Topps Prime

COMP.SET w/o RC's (100) 10.00 25.00
ONE ROOKIE PER HOBBY PACK
1 Andrew Luck .50 1.25
2 Matt Ryan .25 .60
3 Russell Wilson .60 1.50
4 NaVorro Bowman .25 .60
5 Joe Flacco .25 .60
6 Patrick Peterson .20 .50
7 Colin Kaepernick .25 .60
8 Doug Martin .25 .60
9 Drew Brees .30 .75
10 Eli Manning .25 .60
11 Julio Jones .30 .75
12 Tom Brady .75 2.00
13 Steve Johnson .25 .60
14 Justin Blackmon .20 .50
15 Brandon Marshall .25 .60
16 Danny Amendola .25 .60
17 Mike Wallace .20 .50
18 Peyton Manning .60 1.50
19 Miles Austin .20 .50
20 Ed Reed .25 .60
21 Frank Gore .25 .60
22 David Wilson .20 .50
23 Arian Foster .25 .60
24 Marshawn Lynch .25 .60
25 Adrian Peterson .30 .75
26 Percy Harvin .20 .50
27 Ray Rice .20 .50
28 C.J. Spiller .20 .50
29 DeMarco Murray .25 .60
30 Dwayne Allen .20 .50
31 Reggie Bush .20 .50
32 Jacquizz Rodgers .25 .60
33 Trent Richardson .20 .50
34 Randall Cobb .25 .60
35 Tony Romo .25 .60
36 Steve Smith .25 .60
37 Eric Decker .20 .50
38 Jeremy Kerley .20 .50
39 Steven Jackson .20 .50
40 Andre Johnson .20 .50
41 Sidney Rice .20 .50
42 BenJarvus Green-Ellis .25 .60
43 Troy Polamalu .30 .75
44 Lamar Miller .20 .50
45 Andy Dalton .25 .60
46 Alfred Morris .20 .50
47 Aaron Rodgers .50 1.25
48 Jonathan Dwyer .20 .50
49 Ben Roethlisberger .30 .75
50 Robert Griffin .20 .50
51 Demaryius Thomas .25 .60
52 Clay Matthews .30 .75
53 Vick Ballard .20 .50
54 Bobby Wagner .20 .50
55 Greg Jennings .20 .50
56 Wes Welker .25 .60
57 Jason Witten .25 .60
58 T.Y. Hilton .25 .60
59 Richard Sherman .30 .75
60 Jamaal Charles .25 .60
61 Josh Freeman .25 .60
62 Antonio Gates .25 .60
63 Christian Ponder .20 .50
64 Janoris Jenkins .20 .50
65 LeSean McCoy .30 .75
66 Larry Fitzgerald .25 .60
67 Kendall Wright .20 .50
68 Brandon Weeden .20 .50
69 DeMarcus Ware .30 .75
70 Brandon Myers .25 .60
71 Chris Givens .20 .50
72 Michael Crabtree .20 .50
73 Cecil Shorts .20 .50
74 Jimmy Graham .30 .75
75 J.J. Watt .25 .60
76 Brandon Pettigrew .20 .50
77 Stevan Ridley .20 .50
78 Rob Gronkowski .30 .75
79 Cam Newton .30 .75
80 Victor Cruz .25 .60
81 Darren McFadden .25 .60
82 Torrey Smith .20 .50
83 Vincent Jackson .20 .50
84 Roddy White .20 .50
85 Vernon Davis .20 .50
86 Chris Johnson .20 .50
87 Reggie Wayne .25 .60
88 Hakeem Nicks .20 .50
89 Ryan Tannehill .25 .60
90 Jason Pierre-Paul .20 .50
91 Von Miller .25 .60
92 Kyle Rudolph .20 .50
93 Golden Tate .20 .50
94 Dez Bryant .30 .75
95 Nick Foles .25 .60
96 Darren Sproles .25 .60
97 Matt Forte .20 .50
98 Luke Kuechly .25 .60
99 A.J. Green .30 .75
100 Calvin Johnson .30 .75
101 Geno Smith RC .40 1.00
102 Jordan Reed RC .60 1.50
103 Stepfan Taylor RC .40 1.00
104 Dion Jordan RC .40 1.00
105 Cordarrelle Patterson RC .40 1.00
106 Markus Wheaton RC .40 1.00
107 Johnathan Franklin RC .40 1.00
108 Le'Veon Bell RC 1.25 3.00
109 Robert Woods RC .60 1.50
110 Ace Sanders RC .40 1.00
111 Landry Jones RC .40 1.00
112 Bjoern Werner RC .40 1.00
113 Keenan Allen RC .75 2.00
114 DeAndre Hopkins RC 1.00 2.50
115 Giovani Bernard RC .40 1.00
116 Marquise Goodwin RC .40 1.00
117 Marcus Lattimore RC .40 1.00
118 Manti Te'o RC .50 1.25
119 Andre Ellington RC .40 1.00
120 Tyrann Mathieu RC .60 1.50
121 Mike Glennon RC .40 1.00
122 Stedman Bailey RC .40 1.00
123 Tavarres King RC .40 1.00
124 Aaron Dobson RC .40 1.00
125 Tavon Austin RC .50 1.25
126 Barkevious Mingo RC .40 1.00
127 Joseph Randle RC .40 1.00
128 Quinton Patton RC .40 1.00
129 Vance McDonald RC .50 1.25
130 Eric Fisher RC .40 1.00
131 EJ Manuel RC .40 1.00
132 Luke Joeckel RC .40 1.00
133 Gavin Escobar RC .40 1.00
134 Christine Michael RC .40 1.00
135 Kenny Stills RC .40 1.00
136 Ryan Nassib RC .40 1.00
137 Knile Davis RC .40 1.00
138 Terrance Williams RC .40 1.00
139 Tyler Eifert RC .40 1.00
140 Mike Gillislee RC .40 1.00
141 Jarvis Jones RC .40 1.00
142 Tyler Wilson RC .40 1.00
143 Justin Hunter RC .40 1.00
144 Desmond Trufant RC .40 1.00
145 Montee Ball RC .40 1.00
146 Zach Ertz RC .75 2.00
147 Matt Barkley RC .40 1.00
148 Dee Milliner RC .40 1.00
149 Denard Robinson RC .40 1.00
150 Eddie Lacy RC .40 1.00

2013 Topps Prime Copper

*COPPER/350: .8X TO 2X BASIC RC

2013 Topps Prime Gold

*VETS: 1X TO 2.5X BASIC CARDS
*ROOKIES/250: .8X TO 2X BASIC RC

2013 Topps Prime Retail

*1-100 VETS: .3X TO .8X BASIC CARDS
*101-150 ROOKIES: .3X TO .8X BASIC RC

2013 Topps Prime Retail Blue

*VETS: .8X TO 2X BASIC CARDS
*ROOKIES: .4X TO 1X BASIC CARDS

2013 Topps Prime Silver Rainbow

*SLVR RAINBOW/50: 1.5X TO 4X BASIC RC

2013 Topps Prime Autographed Relics Level 2

*LEVEL TWO/15: 1.5X TO 4X SLV AU/449
*LEVEL TWO/15: 1.2X TO 3X SLV AU/200
PIIEL Eddie Lacy 10.00 25.00
PIIEM EJ Manuel 40.00 100.00
PIIGS Geno Smith 10.00 25.00

2013 Topps Prime Autographed Relics Level 3

*LEV.THREE/15: 1.5X TO 4X SLV AU/449
*LEV.THREE/15: 1.2X TO 3X SLV AU/200
PIIIEL Eddie Lacy 10.00 25.00
PIIIEM EJ Manuel 40.00 100.00
PIIIGS Geno Smith 10.00 25.00

2013 Topps Prime Autographed Relics Level 5 Silver

EXCH EXPIRATION: 10/31/2016
PVAD Aaron Dobson/449 2.50 6.00
PVAE Andre Ellington/449 2.50 6.00
PVAL Andrew Luck/150 40.00 80.00
PVAM Alfred Morris/150 8.00 20.00
PVBH Brian Hartline/200 5.00 12.00
PVCM Christine Michael/449 2.50 6.00
PVCP Cordarrelle Patterson/200 3.00 8.00
PVCS Cecil Shorts/200 5.00 12.00
PVDH DeAndre Hopkins/200 8.00 20.00
PVDJ Dion Jordan/449 2.50 6.00
PVDR Denard Robinson/449 2.50 6.00
PVDT Demaryius Thomas/200 EXCH 8.00 20.00
PVEL Eddie Lacy/449 2.50 6.00
PVEM EJ Manuel/200 15.00 40.00
PVGB Giovani Bernard/449 2.50 6.00
PVGE Gavin Escobar/449 2.50 6.00
PVGS Geno Smith/200 3.00 8.00
PVHN Haloti Ngata/200 6.00 15.00
PVJF Johnathan Franklin/449 2.50 6.00
PVJH Justin Hunter/449 EXCH 6.00 15.00
PVJR Joseph Randle/449 2.50 6.00
PVJRE Jordan Reed/449 6.00 15.00
PVKA Keenan Allen/449 5.00 12.00
PVKD Knile Davis/449 2.50 6.00
PVKS Kenny Stills/449 2.50 6.00
PVLB Le'Veon Bell/449 10.00 25.00
PVLJ Landry Jones/449 2.50 6.00
PVLM LeSean McCoy/150 8.00 20.00
PVMB Matt Barkley/200 3.00 8.00
PVMBA Montee Ball/449 2.50 6.00
PVMG Mike Glennon/200 3.00 8.00
PVMGI Mike Gillislee/449 2.50 6.00
PVMGO Marquise Goodwin/449 2.50 6.00
PVML Marcus Lattimore/449 2.50 6.00
PVMT Manti Te'o/200 4.00 10.00
PVMW Markus Wheaton/449 2.50 6.00
PVQP Quinton Patton/449 EXCH 2.50 6.00
PVRN Ryan Nassib/449 2.50 6.00
PVRW Robert Woods/449 4.00 10.00
PVSB Stedman Bailey/449 2.50 6.00
PVSJ Steve Johnson/200 8.00 20.00
PVSR Stevan Ridley/200 5.00 12.00
PVSS Steve Smith/200 15.00 30.00
PVST Stepfan Taylor/449 2.50 6.00
PVTA Tavon Austin/200 4.00 10.00
PVTE Tyler Eifert/449 2.50 6.00
PVTW Tyler Wilson/449 2.50 6.00
PVTWI Terrance Williams/449 2.50 6.00
PVVM Vance McDonald/449 3.00 8.00
PVZE Zach Ertz/449 5.00 12.00

2013 Topps Prime Autographed Relics Level 5 Copper

*COPP.VET/50: .5X TO 1.2X SLVR AU/150-200
*COPP.ROOK/50: .6X TO 1.5X SLVR AU/449
*COPP.ROOK/50: .5X TO 1.2X SLVR AU/200
PVAL Andrew Luck
PVEM EJ Manuel 20.00 50.00
PVGS Geno Smith 4.00 10.00

2013 Topps Prime Autographed Relics Level 5 Copper Rainbow

*COP.RAIN.VET/15: .8X TO 2X SLVR/150-200
*COP.RAIN.RK/15: 1X TO 2.5X SLVR AU/449
*COP.RAIN.RK/15: .8X TO 2X SLVR AU/200
PVAL Andrew Luck
PVEM EJ Manuel 40.00 100.00
PVGS Geno Smith 6.00 15.00

2013 Topps Prime Autographed Relics Level 5 Gold

*GOLD VET/25: .6X TO 1.5X SLVR AU/150-200
*GOLD ROOK/25: .8X TO 2X SLVR AU/449
*GOLD ROOK/25: .6X TO 1.5X SLVR AU/200
PVAL Andrew Luck
PVEM EJ Manuel 25.00 60.00
PVGS Geno Smith 5.00 12.00

2013 Topps Prime Autographs

ROOKIE AUTO ODDS 1:26 HOB
EXCH EXPIRATION: 10/31/2016
1 Andrew Luck/50 60.00 100.00
4 NaVorro Bowman/150 8.00 20.00
6 Patrick Peterson/150 10.00 25.00
13 Steve Johnson/150 5.00 12.00
16 Danny Amendola/150 8.00 20.00
21 Frank Gore/150 8.00 20.00
22 David Wilson/150 4.00 10.00
31 Reggie Bush 15.00 40.00
32 Jacquizz Rodgers/150 5.00 12.00
34 Randall Cobb/150 8.00 20.00
36 Steve Smith/150 8.00 20.00
38 Jeremy Kerley/150 4.00 10.00
41 Sidney Rice/150 5.00 12.00
42 BenJarvus Green-Ellis/150 5.00 12.00
48 Jonathan Dwyer/150 4.00 10.00
50 Robert Griffin 30.00 80.00
51 Demaryius Thomas EXCH 5.00 12.00
54 Bobby Wagner/150 4.00 10.00
61 Josh Freeman/150 5.00 12.00
70 Brandon Myers/150 5.00 12.00
73 Cecil Shorts/150 4.00 10.00
74 Jimmy Graham/150 10.00 25.00
77 Stevan Ridley/150 4.00 10.00
90 Jason Pierre-Paul/150 4.00 10.00
93 Golden Tate/150 4.00 10.00
101 Geno Smith/130 3.00 8.00
102 Jordan Reed/250 6.00 15.00
103 Stepfan Taylor/250 2.50 6.00
104 Dion Jordan/250 2.50 6.00
105 Cordarrelle Patterson/180 2.50 6.00
106 Markus Wheaton/250 2.50 6.00
107 Johnathan Franklin/250 2.50 6.00
108 Le'Veon Bell/250 12.00 30.00
109 Robert Woods/250 4.00 10.00
111 Landry Jones/250 2.50 6.00
112 Bjoern Werner/250 2.50 6.00
113 Keenan Allen/250 6.00 15.00
114 DeAndre Hopkins/180 6.00 15.00
115 Giovani Bernard/250 2.50 6.00
116 Marquise Goodwin/250 2.50 6.00
117 Marcus Lattimore/250 2.50 6.00
118 Manti Te'o/180 3.00 8.00
119 Andre Ellington EXCH 2.50 6.00
121 Mike Glennon/180 2.50 6.00
122 Stedman Bailey/250 2.50 6.00
124 Aaron Dobson/250 2.50 6.00
125 Tavon Austin/180 3.00 8.00
127 Joseph Randle EXCH 2.50 6.00
129 Vance McDonald/250 3.00 8.00
131 EJ Manuel/130 3.00 8.00
133 Gavin Escobar/250 2.50 6.00
134 Christine Michael/250 2.50 6.00
135 Kenny Stills/250 2.50 6.00
136 Ryan Nassib/250 2.50 6.00
137 Knile Davis/250 2.50 6.00
138 Terrance Williams/250 2.50 6.00
139 Tyler Eifert/250 2.50 6.00
140 Mike Gillislee/250 2.50 6.00
142 Tyler Wilson EXCH 2.50 6.00
143 Justin Hunter EXCH 2.50 6.00
145 Montee Ball/250 2.50 6.00
146 Zach Ertz/250 5.00 12.00
147 Matt Barkley/130 3.00 8.00
149 Denard Robinson/250 2.50 6.00
150 Eddie Lacy/250 2.50 6.00

2013 Topps Prime Autographs Copper

*VETS/25: .5X TO 1.2X BASIC AU/150
*ROOKIE/99: .5X TO 1.2X BASIC AU/180-250
*ROOKIE/99: .4X TO 1X BASIC AU/130
1 Andrew Luck 75.00 125.00

2013 Topps Prime Autographs Gold

*VETS/15: .6X TO 1.5X BASIC AU/150
*ROOKIE/75: .4X TO 1X BASIC AU/130
*ROOKIE/75: .5X TO 1.2X BASIC AU/180-250
1 Andrew Luck

2013 Topps Prime Autographs Silver Rainbow

*ROOKIE/25: .8X TO 2X BASIC AU/180-250
*ROOKIE/25: .6X TO 1.5X BASIC AU/130

2013 Topps Prime Dual Combo Relics

STATED PRINT RUN 330 SER.#'d SETS
*COPPER/25: .6X TO 1.5X BASIC DUAL/330
DCRBA J.Blackmon/T.Austin 2.00 5.00
DCRBB G.Bernard/L.Bell 5.00 12.00
DCRBW L.Bell/M.Wheaton 5.00 12.00
DCRDW A.Dobson/T.Williams 1.50 4.00
DCREB T.Eifert/G.Bernard 1.50 4.00
DCREE T.Eifert/Z.Ertz 3.00 8.00
DCRGS R.Griffin/G.Smith 1.50 4.00
DCRLF E.Lacy/J.Franklin 1.50 4.00
DCRLM A.Luck/E.Manuel 6.00 15.00
DCRLR M.Lattimore/D.Robinson 1.50 4.00
DCRMD D.McFadden/K.Davis 2.00 5.00
DCRMG D.Martin/M.Glennon 2.00 5.00
DCRMJ V.Miller/D.Jordan 2.00 5.00
DCRMR D.Murray/J.Randle 2.00 5.00
DCRMS E.Manuel/G.Smith 1.50 4.00
DCRPH C.Patterson/J.Hunter 1.50 4.00
DCRRL T.Richardson/E.Lacy 1.50 4.00
DCRTA M.Te'o/K.Allen 3.00 8.00
DCRTG R.Tannehill/M.Gillislee 2.00 5.00
DCRWB R.Woods/M.Barkley 2.50 6.00

2013 Topps Prime Prime Performance

STATED ODDS 1:10 HOB, 1:12 RET
PPAJ Alshon Jeffery .75 2.00
PPAL Andrew Luck 1.50 4.00
PPAM Alfred Morris .60 1.50
PPBP Bernard Pierce .60 1.50
PPBW Brandon Weeden .60 1.50
PPCG Chris Givens .60 1.50
PPDA Dwayne Allen .60 1.50
PPDM Doug Martin .75 2.00
PPDP DeVier Posey .60 1.50
PPDW David Wilson .60 1.50
PPJB Justin Blackmon .60 1.50
PPJG Josh Gordon .60 1.50
PPJJ Janoris Jenkins .60 1.50
PPKW Kendall Wright .60 1.50
PPLM Lamar Miller .60 1.50
PPMF Michael Floyd .60 1.50
PPMS Mohamed Sanu .60 1.50
PPNF Nick Foles .75 2.00
PPRG Robert Griffin .60 1.50
PPRH Ronnie Hillman .60 1.50
PPRT Ryan Tannehill .75 2.00
PPRW Russell Wilson 2.00 5.00
PPTH T.Y. Hilton .75 2.00
PPTR Trent Richardson .60 1.50
PPVB Vick Ballard .60 1.50

2013 Topps Prime Prime Performance Relics

PPAJ Alshon Jeffery 4.00 10.00
PPAL Andrew Luck 8.00 20.00
PPAM Alfred Morris 3.00 8.00
PPBP Bernard Pierce 3.00 8.00
PPBW Brandon Weeden 3.00 8.00
PPCG Chris Givens 3.00 8.00
PPDA Dwayne Allen 3.00 8.00
PPDM Doug Martin 4.00 10.00
PPDP DeVier Posey 3.00 8.00
PPDW David Wilson 3.00 8.00
PPJB Justin Blackmon 3.00 8.00
PPJG Josh Gordon 3.00 8.00
PPJJ Janoris Jenkins 3.00 8.00
PPKW Kendall Wright 3.00 8.00
PPLM Lamar Miller 3.00 8.00
PPMF Michael Floyd 3.00 8.00
PPMS Mohamed Sanu 3.00 8.00
PPNF Nick Foles 4.00 10.00
PPRG Robert Griffin 3.00 8.00
PPRH Ronnie Hillman 3.00 8.00
PPRT Ryan Tannehill 4.00 10.00
PPRW Russell Wilson 6.00 15.00
PPTH T.Y. Hilton 4.00 10.00
PPTR Trent Richardson 3.00 8.00
PPVB Vick Ballard 3.00 8.00

2013 Topps Prime Primed Rookies

STATED ODDS 1:10 HOB, 1:12 RET
PRCM Christine Michael .60 1.50
PRCP Cordarrelle Patterson .60 1.50
PRDH DeAndre Hopkins 1.50 4.00
PRDR Denard Robinson .60 1.50
PREL Eddie Lacy .60 1.50
PREM EJ Manuel .60 1.50
PRGB Giovani Bernard .60 1.50
PRGS Geno Smith .60 1.50
PRJF Johnathan Franklin .60 1.50
PRJH Justin Hunter .60 1.50
PRKA Keenan Allen 1.25 3.00
PRLB Le'Veon Bell 2.00 5.00
PRMB Matt Barkley .60 1.50
PRMBA Montee Ball .60 1.50
PRMG Marquise Goodwin .60 1.50
PRMGL Mike Glennon .60 1.50
PRML Marcus Lattimore .60 1.50
PRMT Manti Te'o .75 2.00
PRMW Markus Wheaton .60 1.50
PRRW Robert Woods 1.00 2.50
PRSB Stedman Bailey .60 1.50
PRTA Tavon Austin .75 2.00
PRTE Tyler Eifert .60 1.50
PRTW Terrance Williams .60 1.50
PRZE Zach Ertz 1.25 3.00

2013 Topps Prime Primetimers

PTAF Arian Foster .75 2.00
PTAG A.J. Green 1.00 2.50
PTAJ Andre Johnson .60 1.50
PTAL Andrew Luck 1.50 4.00
PTAM Alfred Morris .60 1.50
PTAP Adrian Peterson 1.00 2.50
PTAR Aaron Rodgers 1.50 4.00
PTBM Brandon Marshall .75 2.00
PTBR Ben Roethlisberger 1.00 2.50
PTBW Bobby Wagner .60 1.50
PTCJ Calvin Johnson 1.00 2.50
PTCK Colin Kaepernick .75 2.00
PTCM Clay Matthews 1.00 2.50
PTCN Cam Newton 1.00 2.50
PTCS C.J. Spiller .60 1.50
PTDB Dez Bryant 1.00 2.50
PTDBR Drew Brees 1.00 2.50
PTDM Doug Martin .75 2.00
PTDS Darren Sproles .75 2.00
PTDW David Wilson .60 1.50
PTEM Eli Manning .75 2.00
PTFG Frank Gore .75 2.00
PTHN Hakeem Nicks .60 1.50
PTJF Joe Flacco .75 2.00
PTJG Jimmy Graham 1.00 2.50
PTJJ Julio Jones 1.00 2.50
PTJJE Janoris Jenkins .60 1.50
PTJW Jason Witten .75 2.00
PTJWA J.J. Watt .75 2.00
PTLF Larry Fitzgerald .75 2.00
PTLK Luke Kuechly .75 2.00
PTLM LeSean McCoy 1.00 2.50
PTMC Michael Crabtree .60 1.50
PTML Marshawn Lynch .75 2.00
PTMR Matt Ryan .75 2.00
PTPM Peyton Manning 2.00 5.00
PTPP Patrick Peterson .60 1.50
PTRG Rob Gronkowski 1.00 2.50
PTRG3 Robert Griffin .60 1.50
PTRR Ray Rice .60 1.50
PTRS Richard Sherman 1.00 2.50
PTRW Reggie Wayne .75 2.00
PTRWI Roddy White .60 1.50
PTRWS Russell Wilson 2.00 5.00
PTTB Tom Brady 2.50 6.00
PTTR Trent Richardson .60 1.50
PTVC Victor Cruz .75 2.00
PTVD Vernon Davis .60 1.50
PTVJ Vincent Jackson .60 1.50
PTWW Wes Welker .75 2.00

2013 Topps Prime Quad Combo Relics

*COPPER/25: .6X TO 1.5X QUAD/373
QCRAHEE An/Hs/Et/Ez 3.00 8.00
QCRAHPH An/Hs/Pn/Hr 3.00 8.00
QCRAPJG An/Pn/Jn/Gs 1.25 3.00
QCRBBBL Bd/Bl/Bl/Ly 8.00 20.00
QCRBGAB By/Gs/An/Bd 1.50 4.00
QCREEEM Et/Ez/Er/Md 2.50 6.00
QCRGJBR Gt/Js/Bn/Rn 2.00 5.00
QCRMBWE My/Bt/Ws/Er 2.00 5.00
QCRMJWG Ml/Jn/Ws/Gn 2.00 5.00
QCRMSGB Ml/Sh/Gn/By 1.25 3.00

2013 Topps Prime Relics

*COPPER/25: .6X TO 1.5X RELIC/170
*DUAL RELIC/165: .4X TO 1X RELIC/170
*DUAL COPPER/99: .5X TO 1.2X RELIC/170
*DUAL COP.RAIN/25: .6X TO 1.5X RELIC/170
*DUAL GOLD/75: .5X TO 1.2X RELIC/170
*QUAD RELIC/99: .6X TO 1.5X RELIC/170
*QUAD COPPER/94: .6X TO 1.5X RELIC/170
*QUAD COP.RAIN/25: .8X TO 2X RELIC/170
*QUAD GOLD/75: .6X TO 1.5X RELIC/170
PRAD Aaron Dobson 1.25 3.00
PRAE Andre Ellington 1.25 3.00
PRCM Christine Michael 1.25 3.00
PRCP Cordarrelle Patterson 1.25 3.00
PRDH DeAndre Hopkins 3.00 8.00
PRDJ Dion Jordan 1.25 3.00
PRDR Denard Robinson 1.25 3.00
PREL Eddie Lacy 1.25 3.00
PREM EJ Manuel 1.25 3.00
PRGB Giovani Bernard 1.25 3.00
PRGE Gavin Escobar 1.25 3.00
PRGS Geno Smith 1.25 3.00
PRJF Johnathan Franklin 1.25 3.00
PRJH Justin Hunter 1.25 3.00
PRJR Joseph Randle 1.25 3.00
PRJRE Jordan Reed 2.00 5.00
PRKA Keenan Allen 2.50 6.00
PRKD Knile Davis 1.25 3.00
PRKS Kenny Stills 1.25 3.00
PRLB Le'Veon Bell 4.00 10.00
PRLJ Landry Jones 1.25 3.00
PRMB Matt Barkley 1.25 3.00
PRMBA Montee Ball 1.25 3.00
PRMG Mike Glennon 1.25 3.00
PRMGI Mike Gillislee 1.25 3.00
PRMGO Marquise Goodwin 1.25 3.00
PRML Marcus Lattimore 1.25 3.00
PRMT Manti Te'o 1.50 4.00
PRMW Markus Wheaton 1.25 3.00
PRQP Quinton Patton 1.25 3.00
PRRN Ryan Nassib 1.25 3.00
PRRW Robert Woods 2.00 5.00
PRSB Stedman Bailey 1.25 3.00
PRST Stepfan Taylor 1.25 3.00
PRTA Tavon Austin 1.50 4.00
PRTE Tyler Eifert 1.25 3.00
PRTW Tyler Wilson 1.25 3.00
PRTWI Terrance Williams 1.25 3.00
PRVM Vance McDonald 1.50 4.00
PRZE Zach Ertz 2.50 6.00

2014 Topps Prime

COMP.SET w/o SP's (150) 30.00 60.00
1A Peyton Manning wht .60 1.50
1B P.Manning SP blue 4.00 10.00
2 Patrick Peterson .20 .50
3A Andrew Luck wht .40 1.00
3B Andrew Luck SP blu 2.50 6.00
4A Torrey Smith wht .20 .50
4B Torrey Smith SP purp 1.25 3.00
5A Kendall Wright .20 .50
5B Kendall Wright SP 1.25 3.00
6 Keenan Allen .25 .60
7 DeMarco Murray .25 .60
8A Matthew Stafford wht .25 .60
8B Matthew Stafford SP blu 1.50 4.00
9 Mike Glennon .25 .60
10A Alshon Jeffery blu .25 .60
10B Alshon Jeffery SP wht 1.50 4.00
11A Cordarrelle Patterson catch .20 .50
11B Cordarrelle Patterson SP celeb 1.25 3.00
12A T.Y. Hilton .25 .60
12B T.Y. Hilton SP 1.50 4.00
13A Brandon Marshall .20 .50
13B Brandon Marshall SP 1.25 3.00
14A Colin Kaepernick run .25 .60
14B C.Kaepernick SP celeb 1.50 4.00
15 Arian Foster .25 .60
16 DeAndre Hopkins .25 .60
17 Joe Flacco .25 .60

Card	Low	High
18 Reggie Wayne	.25	.60
19 Montee Ball	.20	.50
20A Michael Crabtree red	.20	.50
20B Michael Crabtree SP wht	1.25	3.00
21 Eli Manning	.25	.60
22A Julio Jones	.30	.75
22B Julio Jones SP	2.00	5.00
23 EJ Manuel	.20	.50
24 Julius Thomas	.20	.50
25A Adrian Peterson wht	.30	.75
25B Adrian Peterson SP prpl	2.00	5.00
26A Larry Fitzgerald	.25	.60
26B Larry Fitzgerald SP	1.50	4.00
27 Patrick Willis	.25	.60
28A Demaryius Thomas	.25	.60
28B Demaryius Thomas SP	1.50	4.00
29A Jamaal Charles	.25	.60
29B Jamaal Charles SP	1.50	4.00
30A Darrelle Revis	.20	.50
30B Darrelle Revis SP	1.25	3.00
31 Randall Cobb	.25	.60
32A Eddie Lacy	.20	.50
32B Eddie Lacy SP	1.25	3.00
33 Nick Foles	.25	.60
34A Tony Romo	.25	.60
34B Tony Romo SP	1.50	4.00
35A Dez Bryant	.30	.75
35B Dez Bryant SP	2.00	5.00
36 Robert Quinn	.25	.60
37A J.J. Watt	.30	.75
37B J.J. Watt SP	2.00	5.00
38A Von Miller	.25	.60
38B Von Miller SP	1.50	4.00
39 Ray Rice	.20	.50
40 Earl Thomas	.25	.60
41 Jay Cutler	.20	.50
42 Andy Dalton	.25	.60
43 Robert Mathis	.20	.50
44 Marshawn Lynch	.25	.60
45 Denarius Moore	.20	.50
46A LeSean McCoy	.30	.75
46B LeSean McCoy SP	2.00	5.00
47A Ryan Tannehill	.25	.60
47B Ryan Tannehill SP	1.50	4.00
48A Pierre Garcon	.25	.60
48B Pierre Garcon SP	1.50	4.00
49 Eric Berry	.25	.60
50A Calvin Johnson	.30	.75
50B Calvin Johnson SP	2.00	5.00
51A Kiko Alonso	.20	.50
51B Kiko Alonso SP	1.25	3.00
52A Andre Johnson	.25	.60
52B Andre Johnson SP	1.50	4.00
53A DeSean Jackson	.25	.60
53B DeSean Jackson SP	1.50	4.00
54 Troy Polamalu	.30	.75
55 Sheldon Richardson	.20	.50
56 Matt Ryan	.25	.60
57 Ndamukong Suh	.25	.60
58A Cam Newton	.30	.75
58B Cam Newton SP	2.00	5.00
59A Tavon Austin	.20	.50
59B Tavon Austin SP	1.25	3.00
60A A.J. Green	.30	.75
60B A.J. Green SP	2.00	5.00
61A Matt Forte	.20	.50
61B Matt Forte SP	1.25	3.00
62 Alfred Morris	.20	.50
63 Philip Rivers	.30	.75
64A Aaron Rodgers	.60	1.50
64B Aaron Rodgers SP	4.00	10.00
65A Clay Matthews	.30	.75
65B Clay Matthews SP	2.00	5.00
66A Victor Cruz	.25	.60
66B Victor Cruz SP	1.50	4.00
67 Brian Hartline	.20	.50
68 Terrell Suggs	.20	.50
69 Jordan Cameron	.20	.50
70A Rob Gronkowski	.30	.75
70B Rob Gronkowski SP	2.00	5.00
71 Alex Smith	.25	.60
72 Le'Veon Bell	.25	.60
73A Luke Kuechly	.25	.60
73B Luke Kuechly SP	1.50	4.00
74 Zach Ertz	.25	.60
75 Russell Wilson	.50	1.25
76 Reggie Bush	.20	.50
77 Percy Harvin	.20	.50
78A Geno Smith	.20	.50
78B Geno Smith SP	1.25	3.00
79A Antonio Brown	.30	.75
79B Antonio Brown SP	2.00	5.00
80 Ryan Mathews	.25	.60
81A Tom Brady	.75	2.00
81B Tom Brady SP	5.00	12.00
82 Julian Edelman	.30	.75
83 Mike Wallace	.20	.50
84A Frank Gore	.25	.60
84B Frank Gore SP	1.50	4.00
85 Ace Sanders	.20	.50
86A NaVorro Bowman	.25	.60
86B NaVorro Bowman SP	1.50	4.00
87A Jimmy Graham	.30	.75
87B Jimmy Graham SP	2.00	5.00
88A Wes Welker	.25	.60
88B Wes Welker SP	1.50	4.00
89 Roddy White	.20	.50
90A Josh Gordon	.20	.50
90B Josh Gordon SP	1.25	3.00
91 Pierre Thomas	.20	.50
92A Giovani Bernard	.20	.50
92B Giovani Bernard SP	1.25	3.00
93A Richard Sherman	.30	.75
93B Richard Sherman SP	2.00	5.00
94A Robert Griffin III	.20	.50
94B Robert Griffin III SP	1.25	3.00
95 Jordy Nelson	.25	.60
96 Vincent Jackson	.20	.50
97 Cecil Shorts	.20	.50
98 Sean Lee	.25	.60
99 C.J. Spiller	.20	.50
100A Drew Brees	.30	.75
100B Drew Brees SP	2.00	5.00
101A Mike Evans RC	1.00	2.50
101B Mike Evans SP	2.50	6.00
102 David Fales RC	.40	1.00
103A Jace Amaro RC	.40	1.00
103B Jace Amaro SP	1.00	2.50
104A Kelvin Benjamin RC	.60	1.50
104B Kelvin Benjamin SP	1.50	4.00
105 Donte Moncrief RC	.40	1.00
106A Bishop Sankey RC	.40	1.00
106B Bishop Sankey SP	1.00	2.50
107A Allen Robinson RC	.60	1.50
107B Allen Robinson SP	1.50	4.00
108A Jordan Matthews RC	.60	1.50
108B Jordan Matthews SP	1.50	4.00
109 Jerick McKinnon RC	.50	1.25
110A Michael Sam RC	.40	1.00
110B Michael Sam SP	1.00	2.50
111A Logan Thomas RC	.40	1.00
111B Logan Thomas SP	1.00	2.50
112A A.J. McCarron RC	.40	1.00
112B A.J. McCarron SP	1.00	2.50
113A Josh Huff RC	.50	1.25
113B Josh Huff SP	1.25	3.00
114A Jeremy Hill RC	.50	1.25
114B Jeremy Hill SP	1.25	3.00
115A Marqise Lee RC	.50	1.25
115B Marqise Lee SP	1.25	3.00
116A Eric Ebron RC	.50	1.25
116B Eric Ebron SP	1.25	3.00
117A Charles Sims RC	.40	1.00
117B Charles Sims SP	1.00	2.50
118A Jimmy Garoppolo RC	3.00	8.00
118B Jimmy Garoppolo SP	8.00	20.00
119A Paul Richardson RC	.50	1.25
119B Paul Richardson SP	1.25	3.00
120A Austin Seferian-Jenkins RC	.40	1.00
120B Austin Seferian-Jenkins SP	1.00	2.50
121A Teddy Bridgewater RC	.60	1.50
121B Teddy Bridgewater SP	8.00	20.00
122A De'Anthony Thomas RC	.40	1.00
122B De'Anthony Thomas SP	1.00	2.50
123 Khalil Mack RC	1.50	4.00
124 Troy Niklas RC	.40	1.00
125A Derek Carr RC	2.50	6.00
125B Derek Carr SP	6.00	15.00
126A James White RC	.75	2.00
126B James White SP	2.00	5.00
127 Anthony Barr RC	.40	1.00
128 C.J. Mosley RC	.50	1.25
129A Tajh Boyd RC	.40	1.00
129B Tajh Boyd SP	1.00	2.50
130A Aaron Murray RC	.40	1.00
130B Aaron Murray SP	1.00	2.50
131A Carlos Hyde RC	.50	1.25
131B Carlos Hyde SP	1.25	3.00
132A Andre Williams RC	.40	1.00
132B Andre Williams SP	1.00	2.50
133 Tom Savage RC	.40	1.00
134A Blake Bortles RC	.50	1.25
134B Blake Bortles SP	1.25	3.00
135A Zach Mettenberger RC	.40	1.00
135B Zach Mettenberger SP	1.00	2.50
136A Davante Adams RC	.60	1.50
136B Davante Adams SP	1.50	4.00
137A Devonta Freeman RC	.60	1.50
137B Devonta Freeman SP	1.50	4.00
138A Tre Mason RC	.40	1.00
138B Tre Mason SP	1.00	2.50
139A Cody Latimer RC	.50	1.25
139B Cody Latimer SP	1.25	3.00
140A Jadeveon Clowney RC	.50	1.25
140B Jadeveon Clowney SP	1.25	3.00
141A Brandin Cooks RC	.60	1.50
141B Brandin Cooks SP	1.50	4.00
142 Ha Ha Clinton-Dix RC	.50	1.25
143A Dri Archer RC	.40	1.00
143B Dri Archer SP	1.00	2.50
144A Johnny Manziel RC pass	.60	1.50
144B J.Manziel SP pointing	2.00	5.00
145A Jarvis Landry RC	.75	2.00
145B Jarvis Landry SP	2.00	5.00
146A Sammy Watkins RC	.60	1.50
146B Sammy Watkins SP	1.50	4.00
147A Terrance West RC	.40	1.00
147B Terrance West SP	1.00	2.50
148 Martavis Bryant RC	.50	1.25
149A Ka'Deem Carey RC	.40	1.00
149B Ka'Deem Carey SP	1.00	2.50
150A Odell Beckham Jr. RC	1.00	2.50
150B Odell Beckham Jr. SP	2.50	6.00

2014 Topps Prime Autographed Relics Level 5

EXCH EXPIRATION: 9/30/2017

Card	Low	High
PVAJ Alshon Jeffery	10.00	25.00
PVAM A.J. McCarron	3.00	8.00
PVAR Allen Robinson	5.00	12.00
PVAS Austin Seferian-Jenkins	3.00	8.00
PVAU Aaron Murray	3.00	8.00
PVAW Andre Williams	8.00	20.00
PVBB Blake Bortles	4.00	10.00
PVBC Brandin Cooks	5.00	12.00
PVBS Bishop Sankey	3.00	8.00
PVCH Carlos Hyde EXCH	4.00	10.00
PVCL Cody Latimer	4.00	10.00
PVCS Charles Sims	3.00	8.00
PVCSP C.J. Spiller	6.00	15.00
PVDA Davante Adams	5.00	12.00
PVDC Derek Carr	40.00	80.00
PVDF Devonta Freeman	5.00	12.00
PVDM Donte Moncrief	3.00	8.00
PVDR Dri Archer	3.00	8.00
PVDT De'Anthony Thomas	3.00	8.00
PVEE Eric Ebron	4.00	10.00
PVEL Eddie Lacy	6.00	15.00
PVFG Frank Gore	10.00	25.00
PVGB Giovani Bernard	6.00	15.00
PVJA Johnny Manziel	5.00	12.00
PVJC Jadeveon Clowney	4.00	10.00
PVJG Jimmy Garoppolo	50.00	100.00
PVJH Jeremy Hill	4.00	10.00
PVJJ Julio Jones	30.00	60.00
PVJK Jerick McKinnon	4.00	10.00
PVJL Jarvis Landry	6.00	15.00
PVJM Jordan Matthews	5.00	12.00
PVJR Jace Amaro	3.00	8.00
PVKB Kelvin Benjamin	20.00	40.00
PVKC Ka'Deem Carey	3.00	8.00
PVKM Khalil Mack EXCH	25.00	50.00
PVLB Le'Veon Bell EXCH	8.00	20.00
PVLT Logan Thomas	8.00	20.00
PVME Mike Evans	8.00	20.00
PVML Marqise Lee	4.00	10.00
PVMLY Marshawn Lynch EXCH	25.00	50.00
PVMS Matthew Stafford	15.00	40.00
PVMSA Michael Sam EXCH	3.00	8.00
PVOB Odell Beckham Jr. EXCH	30.00	60.00
PVPR Paul Richardson	6.00	15.00
PVRG Rob Gronkowski	25.00	50.00
PVSW Sammy Watkins	5.00	12.00
PVTB Teddy Bridgewater	20.00	50.00
PVTM Tre Mason	3.00	8.00
PVTO Tajh Boyd	3.00	8.00
PVTS Tom Savage	3.00	8.00
PVTW Terrance West	8.00	20.00
PVZM Zach Mettenberger	3.00	8.00

2014 Topps Prime Autographed Relics Level 5 Copper

*ROOKIES/50: .6X TO 1.5X BASIC JSY AU

2014 Topps Prime Autographed Relics Level 5 Gold

*GOLD ROOK/25: .8X TO 2X BASIC JSY AU

2014 Topps Prime Autographs

EXCH EXPIRATION: 9/30/2017

Card	Low	High
101R Mike Evans	6.00	15.00
102R David Fales EXCH	2.50	6.00
104R Kelvin Benjamin	4.00	10.00
105R Donte Moncrief	2.50	6.00
106R Bishop Sankey	2.50	6.00
107R Allen Robinson	4.00	10.00
108R Jordan Matthews	4.00	10.00
109R Jerick McKinnon	3.00	8.00
110R Michael Sam	2.50	6.00
111R Logan Thomas	2.50	6.00
112R A.J. McCarron	2.50	6.00
113R Josh Huff	3.00	8.00
114R Jeremy Hill	3.00	8.00
115R Marqise Lee	3.00	8.00
116R Eric Ebron	3.00	8.00
117R Charles Sims	2.50	6.00
118R Jimmy Garoppolo	20.00	50.00
119R Paul Richardson	3.00	8.00
120R Austin Seferian-Jenkins	2.50	6.00
121R Teddy Bridgewater	10.00	25.00
123R Khalil Mack	10.00	25.00
124R Troy Niklas	2.50	6.00
125R Derek Carr	25.00	60.00
126R James White	5.00	12.00
127R Anthony Barr	2.50	6.00
129R Tajh Boyd	2.50	6.00
130R Aaron Murray	2.50	6.00
131R Carlos Hyde	3.00	8.00
132R Andre Williams	2.50	6.00
134R Blake Bortles		
135R Zach Mettenberger	2.50	6.00
137R Devonta Freeman	4.00	10.00
138R Tre Mason		
139R Cody Latimer	3.00	8.00
140R Jadeveon Clowney	3.00	8.00
141R Brandin Cooks	4.00	10.00
142R Ha Ha Clinton-Dix	3.00	8.00
143R Dri Archer	2.50	6.00
144R Johnny Manziel EXCH	4.00	10.00
145R Jarvis Landry	5.00	12.00
146R Sammy Watkins	4.00	10.00
147R Terrance West	2.50	6.00
148R Martavis Bryant	3.00	8.00
149R Ka'Deem Carey	2.50	6.00
150R Odell Beckham Jr. EXCH	40.00	80.00
8V Matthew Stafford		
10V Alshon Jeffery		
11V Cordarrelle Patterson		
12V T.Y. Hilton	6.00	15.00
24V Julius Thomas EXCH	8.00	20.00
32V Eddie Lacy	5.00	12.00
40V Earl Thomas	15.00	40.00
44V Marshawn Lynch	15.00	30.00
46V LeSean McCoy		
65V Clay Matthews		
69V Jordan Cameron	5.00	12.00
70V Rob Gronkowski		
82V Julian Edelman EXCH	15.00	40.00
92V Giovani Bernard	5.00	12.00
95V Jordy Nelson	12.00	30.00
101V Brett Favre SP	100.00	175.00
104V Zac Stacy EXCH	5.00	12.00
105V Jordan Reed	5.00	12.00
107V Keenan Allen	8.00	20.00
108V Montee Ball	5.00	12.00
109V Le'Veon Bell EXCH	15.00	40.00

2014 Topps Prime Autographs Copper

*ROOKIES/99: .5X TO 1.2X BASIC AU
*VETERANS/25: .6X TO 1.5X BASIC AU

Card	Low	High
118R Jimmy Garoppolo	25.00	60.00

2014 Topps Prime Autographs Copper Rainbow

*ROOKIES/50: .6X TO 1.5X BASIC AU

Card	Low	High
118R Jimmy Garoppolo	30.00	80.00
121R Teddy Bridgewater	25.00	60.00
134R Blake Bortles	5.00	12.00

2014 Topps Prime Autographs Gold

*VETERANS/15: .6X TO 1.5X BASIC AU
*ROOKIES/75: .5X TO 1.2X BASIC AU

Card	Low	High
118R Jimmy Garoppolo	30.00	60.00
121R Teddy Bridgewater	20.00	50.00
134R Blake Bortles	4.00	10.00

2014 Topps Prime Autographs Silver Rainbow

*SILVR ROOK/25: .8X TO 2X BASIC AU

Card	Low	High
121R Teddy Bridgewater	30.00	80.00
134R Blake Bortles	6.00	15.00

2014 Topps Prime Dual Combo Relics

*COPPER/25: .8X TO 2X BASIC DUAL/142

Card	Low	High
DCRBL B.Bortles/M.Lee	5.00	12.00
DCRBM T.Bridgewater/J.Manziel	2.50	6.00
DCRBN C.Newton/K.Benjamin	2.50	6.00
DCRBP C.Patterson/T.Bridgewater	2.50	6.00
DCRDW A.Williams/O.Beckham Jr.	4.00	10.00
DCRCS T.Savage/J.Clowney	2.00	5.00
DCRES M.Evans/C.Sims	4.00	10.00
DCRHB J.Hill/G.Bernard	2.00	5.00
DCRHM J.Hill/A.McCarron	2.00	5.00
DCRLB O.Beckham Jr./J.Landry	4.00	10.00
DCRMB J.Manziel/B.Bortles	5.00	12.00
DCRME J.Manziel/M.Evans	10.00	25.00
DCRMS T.Mason/B.Sankey	1.50	4.00
DCRMW S.Watkins/E.Manuel	2.50	6.00
DCRSH C.Hyde/B.Sankey	2.00	5.00
DCRTM D.Thomas/A.Murray	1.50	4.00
DCRWB S.Watkins/T.Boyd	2.50	6.00
DCRWE M.Evans/S.Watkins	4.00	10.00
DCRABE D.Archer/L.Bell	4.00	10.00
DCRBLA M.Ball/C.Latimer	2.00	5.00

2014 Topps Prime Prime Patches

*COPPER RAIN/25: .6X TO 1.5X RELIC
*DUAL/140: .4X TO 1X BASIC JSY
*DUAL COPPER/99: .5X TO 1.2X RELIC
*DUAL COP. RAIN/25: .6X TO 1.5X RELIC
*DUAL GOLD/75: .5X TO 1.2X RELIC
*QUAD/140: .4X TO 1X RELIC
*QUAD COPP/99: .5X TO 1.2X RELIC
*QUAD COP. RAIN/25: .8X TO 2X RELIC
*QUAD GOLD/75: .6X TO 1.5X RELIC

Card	Low	High
PPAM Aaron Murray	1.25	3.00
PPAR Allen Robinson	2.00	5.00
PPAS Austin Seferian-Jenkins	1.25	3.00
PPAW Andre Williams	1.25	3.00
PPBB Blake Bortles	1.50	4.00
PPBC Brandin Cooks	2.00	5.00
PPBS Bishop Sankey	1.25	3.00
PPCH Carlos Hyde	1.50	4.00
PPCL Cody Latimer	1.50	4.00
PPCS Charles Sims	1.25	3.00
PPDA Davante Adams	2.00	5.00
PPDC Derek Carr	4.00	10.00
PPDF Devonta Freeman	2.00	5.00
PPDM Donte Moncrief	1.25	3.00
PPDT De'Anthony Thomas	1.25	3.00
PPEE Eric Ebron	1.50	4.00
PPJA Jace Amaro	1.25	3.00
PPJC Jadeveon Clowney	1.50	4.00
PPJG Jimmy Garoppolo	10.00	25.00
PPJH Jeremy Hill	1.50	4.00
PPJL Jarvis Landry	2.50	6.00
PPJM Johnny Manziel	2.00	5.00
PPKB Kelvin Benjamin	2.00	5.00
PPKC Ka'Deem Carey	1.25	3.00
PPKM Khalil Mack	5.00	12.00
PPLT Logan Thomas	1.25	3.00
PPME Mike Evans	3.00	8.00
PPML Marqise Lee	1.50	4.00
PPMS Michael Sam	1.25	3.00
PPOB Odell Beckham Jr.	3.00	8.00
PPPR Paul Richardson	1.50	4.00
PPSW Sammy Watkins	2.00	5.00
PPTB Teddy Bridgewater	2.00	5.00
PPTM Tre Mason	1.25	3.00
PPTS Tom Savage	1.25	3.00
PPTW Terrance West	1.25	3.00
PPAMC A.J. McCarron	1.25	3.00
PPDAR Dri Archer	1.25	3.00
PPJMA Jordan Matthews	2.00	5.00
PPTBO Tajh Boyd	1.25	3.00

2014 Topps Prime Prime Performance

Card	Low	High
COMPLETE SET (25)	12.00	30.00
PPAD Aaron Dobson	.60	1.50
PPAE Andre Ellington	.60	1.50
PPAS Ace Sanders	.60	1.50
PPCP Cordarrelle Patterson	.60	1.50
PPDH DeAndre Hopkins	.75	2.00
PPDM Dee Milliner	.60	1.50
PPEA Ezekiel Ansah	.60	1.50
PPEL Eddie Lacy	.60	1.50
PPEM EJ Manuel	.60	1.50
PPGB Giovani Bernard	.60	1.50
PPGS Geno Smith	.60	1.50
PPJJ Jarvis Jones	.60	1.50
PPJR Jordan Reed	.60	1.50
PPKA Keenan Allen	.75	2.00
PPKS Kenny Stills	.60	1.50
PPLB Le'Veon Bell	.75	2.00
PPMB Montee Ball	.60	1.50
PPMG Marquise Goodwin	.60	1.50
PPML Mike Glennon	.75	2.00
PPMW Markus Wheaton	.60	1.50
PPRW Robert Woods	.75	2.00
PPTA Tavon Austin	.60	1.50
PPTE Tyler Eifert	.75	2.00
PPTW Terrance Williams	.60	1.50
PPZE Zach Ertz	.75	2.00

2014 Topps Prime Prime Performance Relics

Card	Low	High
PPRAD Aaron Dobson	3.00	8.00
PPRAE Andre Ellington	3.00	8.00
PPRAS Ace Sanders	3.00	8.00
PPRCP Cordarrelle Patterson	3.00	8.00
PPRDH DeAndre Hopkins	4.00	10.00
PPRDM Dee Milliner	3.00	8.00
PPREA Ezekiel Ansah	3.00	8.00
PPREL Eddie Lacy	3.00	8.00
PPREM EJ Manuel	3.00	8.00
PPRGB Giovani Bernard	3.00	8.00
PPRGS Geno Smith	3.00	8.00
PPRJJ Jarvis Jones	3.00	8.00
PPRJR Jordan Reed	3.00	8.00
PPRKA Keenan Allen	4.00	10.00
PPRKS Kenny Stills	3.00	8.00
PPRLB Le'Veon Bell	4.00	10.00
PPRMB Montee Ball	3.00	8.00
PPRMG Marquise Goodwin	3.00	8.00
PPRML Mike Glennon	4.00	10.00
PPRMW Markus Wheaton	3.00	8.00
PPRRW Robert Woods	4.00	10.00
PPRTA Tavon Austin	3.00	8.00
PPRTE Tyler Eifert	4.00	10.00
PPRTW Terrance Williams	3.00	8.00
PPRZE Zach Ertz	4.00	10.00

2014 Topps Prime Primed Rookies

Card	Low	High
PROAMC A.J. McCarron	.60	1.50
PROAW Andre Williams	.60	1.50
PROBB Blake Bortles	.75	2.00
PROBC Brandin Cooks	1.00	2.50
PROBS Bishop Sankey	.60	1.50
PROCH Carlos Hyde	.75	2.00
PRODC Derek Carr	4.00	10.00
PROEE Eric Ebron	.75	2.00
PROJC Jadeveon Clowney	.75	2.00
PROJG Jimmy Garoppolo	5.00	12.00
PROJH Jeremy Hill	.75	2.00
PROJM Johnny Manziel	1.00	2.50
PROJMA Jordan Matthews	1.00	2.50
PROKB Kelvin Benjamin	1.00	2.50
PROKM Khalil Mack	2.50	6.00
PROME Mike Evans	1.50	4.00
PROML Marqise Lee	.75	2.00
PROAM Michael Sam	.60	1.50
PROOB Odell Beckham Jr.	1.50	4.00
PROSW Sammy Watkins	1.00	2.50
PROTB Teddy Bridgewater	1.00	2.50
PROTM Tre Mason	.60	1.50
PROTS Tom Savage	.60	1.50
PROTW Terrance West	.60	1.50
PROZM Zach Mettenberger	.60	1.50

2014 Topps Prime Primetimers

Card	Low	High
COMPLETE SET (50)	15.00	30.00
PTAB Antonio Brown	1.00	2.50
PTAG A.J. Green	1.00	2.50
PTAJ Alshon Jeffery	.75	2.00
PTAL Andrew Luck	1.25	3.00
PTAM Alfred Morris	.60	1.50
PTAP Adrian Peterson	1.00	2.50
PTAR Aaron Rodgers	2.00	5.00
PTBM Brandon Marshall	.60	1.50
PTCJ Calvin Johnson	1.00	2.50
PTCK Colin Kaepernick	.75	2.00
PTCN Cam Newton	1.00	2.50
PTCP Cordarrelle Patterson	.60	1.50
PTCT Charles Tillman	.75	2.00
PTDB Drew Brees	1.00	2.50
PTDE Darrelle Revis	.60	1.50
PTDJ DeSean Jackson	.75	2.00
PTDR Dez Bryant	1.00	2.50
PTDT Demaryius Thomas	.75	2.00
PTEB Eric Berry	.75	2.00
PTEL Eddie Lacy	.60	1.50
PTET Earl Thomas	.75	2.00
PTFG Frank Gore	.75	2.00
PTJA Jason Witten	.75	2.00
PTJC Jamaal Charles	.75	2.00
PTJG Josh Gordon	.60	1.50
PTJJ Julio Jones	1.00	2.50
PTJR Jimmy Graham	1.00	2.50
PTJW J.J. Watt	1.00	2.50
PTKA Keenan Allen	.75	2.00
PTKL Kiko Alonso	.60	1.50
PTLF Larry Fitzgerald	.75	2.00
PTLK Luke Kuechly	.75	2.00
PTLM LeSean McCoy	1.00	2.50
PTMF Matt Forte	.60	1.50
PTML Marshawn Lynch	.75	2.00
PTNB NaVorro Bowman	.75	2.00
PTNS Ndamukong Suh	.75	2.00
PTPG Pierre Garcon	.75	2.00
PTPM Peyton Manning	2.00	5.00
PTPP Patrick Peterson	.60	1.50
PTRB Reggie Bush	.60	1.50
PTRG Robert Griffin III	.60	1.50
PTRI Russell Wilson	1.50	4.00
PTRM Robert Mathis	.60	1.50
PTRS Richard Sherman	1.00	2.50
PTRW Reggie Wayne	.75	2.00
PTTB Tom Brady	2.50	6.00
PTVC Victor Cruz	.75	2.00
PTVJ Vincent Jackson	.60	1.50
PTZS Zac Stacy	.60	1.50

2014 Topps Prime Quad Combo Relics

*QUAD COP. RAIN/25: .6X TO 1.5X QUAD/142

Card	Low	High
QCRAPWE Alln/Wtkns/Pttrsn/Evns	5.00	12.00
QCRBBLW Wlsn/Brgwtr/Lck/Brtls	12.00	30.00
QCRBMBC Brgwtr/Mnzl/Brtls/Crr	12.00	30.00
QCRGSES Glnn/Sms/Evns/SfJnkns	5.00	12.00
QCRGSMM Svg/Grp/McCr/Mrry	15.00	40.00
QCRLBSM Lcy/Bll/Msn/Snky	2.50	6.00
QCRLGMB RG3/Mnzl/Brtls/Lck	12.00	30.00
QCRMWSW Spllr/Wds/Mnl/Wtkns	3.00	8.00
QCRSHHM Msn/Snky/Hll/Hyde	2.50	6.00
QCRWEBB Evns/Wtkns/Bckh/Bnjmn	5.00	12.00

2002 Topps Pristine

Released in December 2002, this set features 50 veterans and 120 rookies. The rookie portion of the set, cards 51-170 were broken into three tiers: common (C), uncommon (U), and rare (R). The uncommon cards were serial #'d to 999, and the rares were serial #d to 499. Boxes contained 5 triple packs, containing a total of 8 cards. The first pack contained an uncirculated refractor, the second pack contained a memorabilia card, and the third pack contained veteran and rookie cards.

Card	Low	High
COMP.SET w/o SP's (50)	20.00	50.00
1 Peyton Manning	2.50	6.00
2 Darrell Jackson	.75	2.00
3 Donovan McNabb	.75	2.00
4 Rod Smith	.75	2.00
5 Daunte Culpepper	.75	2.00
6 Drew Brees	2.00	5.00
7 Stephen Davis	.60	1.50
8 Kurt Warner	.75	2.00
9 Eric Moulds	.60	1.50
10 Jake Plummer	.60	1.50
11 Chris Weinke	.60	1.50
12 Brian Griese	.60	1.50
13 Corey Bradford	.60	1.50
14 Trent Green	.60	1.50
15 Tom Brady	5.00	12.00
16 Jeff Garcia	.60	1.50
17 Tiki Barber	.75	2.00
18 Eddie George	.75	2.00
19 Jamal Lewis	.75	2.00
20 Troy Brown	.60	1.50
21 Priest Holmes	.60	1.50
22 Jimmy Smith	.75	2.00
23 Tim Brown	1.00	2.50
24 Plaxico Burress	.60	1.50
25 Aaron Brooks	.60	1.50
26 Marshall Faulk	.75	2.00
27 Steve McNair	.75	2.00
28 Curtis Martin	.75	2.00
29 Corey Dillon	.60	1.50
30 Tim Couch	.60	1.50
31 Michael Vick	.75	2.00
32 David Boston	.60	1.50
33 Kordell Stewart	.60	1.50
34 Jerome Bettis	1.00	2.50
35 Keyshawn Johnson	.75	2.00
36 Torry Holt	.75	2.00
37 Shaun Alexander	.60	1.50
38 Brett Favre	2.00	5.00
39 Marvin Harrison	.75	2.00
40 Randy Moss	.75	2.00
41 Jerry Rice	2.00	5.00
42 LaDainian Tomlinson	1.00	2.50
43 Terrell Owens	.75	2.00
44 Edgerrin James	.75	2.00
45 Anthony Thomas	.75	2.00
46 Drew Bledsoe	.75	2.00
47 Ahman Green	.75	2.00
48 Ricky Williams	.75	2.00
49 Tony Gonzalez	.75	2.00
50 Emmitt Smith	1.50	4.00
51 Joey Harrington C RC	.60	1.50
52 Joey Harrington U	.75	2.00
53 Joey Harrington R	1.00	2.50
54 Josh McCown C RC	1.00	2.50
55 Josh McCown U	1.25	3.00
56 Josh McCown R	1.50	4.00
57 Antwaan Randle El C RC	.75	2.00
58 Antwaan Randle El U	1.00	2.50
59 Antwaan Randle El R	1.25	3.00
60 Reche Caldwell C RC	.75	2.00
61 Reche Caldwell U	1.00	2.50
62 Reche Caldwell R	1.25	3.00
63 Jason McAddley C RC	.75	2.00
64 Jason McAddley U	1.00	2.50
65 Jason McAddley R	1.25	3.00
66 Ashley Lelie C RC	.60	1.50
67 Ashley Lelie U	.75	2.00
68 Ashley Lelie R	1.00	2.50
69 Travis Stephens C RC	.60	1.50
70 Travis Stephens U	.75	2.00
71 Travis Stephens R	1.00	2.50
72 Chad Hutchinson C RC	.60	1.50
73 Chad Hutchinson U	.75	2.00
74 Chad Hutchinson R	1.00	2.50
75 Quentin Jammer C RC	1.00	2.50
76 Quentin Jammer U	1.25	3.00
77 Quentin Jammer R	1.50	4.00
78 Tim Carter C RC	.75	2.00
79 Tim Carter U	1.00	2.50
80 Tim Carter R	1.25	3.00
81 Antonio Bryant C RC	1.00	2.50
82 Antonio Bryant U	1.25	3.00
83 Antonio Bryant R	1.50	4.00
84 Cliff Russell C RC	.60	1.50
85 Cliff Russell U	.75	2.00
86 Cliff Russell R	1.00	2.50
87 Rohan Davey C RC	1.00	2.50
88 Rohan Davey U	1.25	3.00
89 Rohan Davey R	1.50	4.00
90 Javon Walker C RC	1.00	2.50
91 Javon Walker U	1.25	3.00
92 Javon Walker R	1.50	4.00
93 T.J. Duckett C RC	.60	1.50
94 T.J. Duckett U	.75	2.00
95 T.J. Duckett R	1.00	2.50
96 Donte Stallworth C RC	1.00	2.50
97 Donte Stallworth U	1.25	3.00
98 Donte Stallworth R	1.50	4.00
99 Andre Davis C RC	.60	1.50
100 Andre Davis U	.75	2.00
101 Andre Davis R	1.00	2.50
102 Mike Williams C RC	.60	1.50
103 Mike Williams U	.75	2.00
104 Mike Williams R	1.00	2.50
105 Freddie Milons C RC	.60	1.50
106 Freddie Milons U	.75	2.00
107 Freddie Milons R	1.00	2.50
108 John Henderson C RC	.75	2.00
109 John Henderson U	1.00	2.50
110 John Henderson R	1.25	3.00
111 DeShaun Foster C RC	1.00	2.50
112 DeShaun Foster U	1.25	3.00
113 DeShaun Foster R	1.50	4.00
114 Josh Reed C RC	.75	2.00
115 Josh Reed U	1.00	2.50
116 Josh Reed R	1.25	3.00
117 Jabar Gaffney C RC	.60	1.50
118 Jabar Gaffney U	.75	2.00
119 Jabar Gaffney R	1.00	2.50
120 Clinton Portis C RC	1.00	2.50
121 Clinton Portis U	1.25	3.00
122 Clinton Portis R	1.50	4.00
123 Jeremy Shockey C RC	1.00	2.50
124 Jeremy Shockey U	1.50	4.00
125 Jeremy Shockey R	1.50	4.00
126 Dwight Freeney C RC	1.25	3.00
127 Dwight Freeney U	1.50	4.00
128 Dwight Freeney R	2.00	5.00
129 Brian Westbrook C RC	1.25	3.00
130 Brian Westbrook U	1.50	4.00
131 Brian Westbrook R	2.00	5.00
132 Randy Fasani C RC	.60	1.50
133 Randy Fasani U	.75	2.00
134 Randy Fasani R	1.00	2.50
135 Julius Peppers C RC	1.50	4.00
136 Julius Peppers U	2.00	5.00
137 Julius Peppers R	2.50	6.00
138 Patrick Ramsey C RC	.75	2.00
139 Patrick Ramsey U	1.00	2.50
140 Patrick Ramsey R	1.25	3.00
141 William Green C RC	.75	2.00
142 William Green U	1.00	2.50
143 William Green R	1.25	3.00
144 Daniel Graham C RC	.75	2.00
145 Daniel Graham U	1.00	2.50
146 Daniel Graham R	1.25	3.00
147 Ron Johnson C RC	.75	2.00
148 Ron Johnson U	1.00	2.50
149 Ron Johnson R	1.25	3.00
150 Maurice Morris C RC	.75	2.00
151 Maurice Morris U	1.00	2.50
152 Maurice Morris R	1.25	3.00
153 Eric Crouch C RC	1.00	2.50
154 Eric Crouch U	1.25	3.00
155 Eric Crouch R	1.50	4.00
156 Roy Williams C RC	.60	1.50
157 Roy Williams U	.75	2.00
158 Roy Williams R	1.00	2.50
159 Ladell Betts C RC	1.00	2.50
160 Ladell Betts U	1.25	3.00
161 Ladell Betts R	1.50	4.00
162 David Garrard C RC	.75	2.00
163 David Garrard U	1.00	2.50
164 David Garrard R	1.25	3.00
165 Marquise Walker C RC	.60	1.50
166 Marquise Walker U	.75	2.00
167 Marquise Walker R	1.00	2.50
168 David Carr C RC	.60	1.50
169 David Carr U	.75	2.00
170 David Carr R	1.00	2.50
ESA1 Emmitt Smith AU	175.00	300.00
ESJ1 Emmitt Smith JSY	12.00	30.00

2002 Topps Pristine Gold Refractors

*1-50 VETS: 3X TO 8X BASIC CARDS
*ROOKIE C 51-170: 2.5X TO 6X
*ROOKIE U 51-170: 2X TO 5X
*ROOKIE R 51-170: 1.5X TO 4X
ONE PER HOBBY BOX
STATED PRINT RUN 79 SER.#'d SETS

2002 Topps Pristine Refractors

*1-50 VET/349: 2X TO 5X BASIC CARDS
1-50 VET/349 ODDS 1:5
1-50 VET PRINT RUN 349
*51-170 ROOKIE C/999: 1X TO 2.5X
51-170 ROOKIE C PRINT RUN 999
*51-170 ROOKIE U/499: 1X TO 2.5X
51-170 ROOKIE U/499 ODDS 1:5
51-170 ROOKIE U PRINT RUN 499
*51-170 ROOKIE R/199: 1.2X TO 3X
51-170 ROOKIE R/199 ODDS 1:11
51-170 ROOKIE R PRINT RUN 199

2002 Topps Pristine All-Rookie Team Jerseys

This set features jersey swatches from top 2002 rookies. Group A stated odds were 1:30, Group B 1:50, and Group C 1:46.

GROUP A STATED ODDS 1:30
GROUP B STATED ODDS 1:50
GROUP C STATED ODDS 1:46

Card	Low	High
TRRAL Ashley Lelie A	2.50	6.00
TRRCP Clinton Portis A	4.00	10.00
TRRJG Jabar Gaffney A	2.50	6.00
TRRJP Julius Peppers B	6.00	15.00
TRRMW Mike Williams C	2.50	6.00

2002 Topps Pristine Autographs

This set features authentic player autographs. Stated odds were as follows: Group A 1:637, Group B 1:36, Group C 1:160, Group D 1:26, Group E 1:154, Group F 1:41, and Group G 1:64.

GROUP A STATED ODDS 1:637
GROUP B STATED ODDS 1:36
GROUP C STATED ODDS 1:160
GROUP D STATED ODDS 1:26
GROUP E STATED ODDS 1:154
GROUP F STATED ODDS 1:41
GROUP G STATED ODDS 1:64

Card	Low	High
PAD Andre Davis B	5.00	12.00
PAL Ashley Lelie D	5.00	12.00
PBF Brett Favre C	75.00	150.00
PBM Bryant McKinnie F	5.00	12.00
PCR Cliff Russell G	5.00	12.00
PDC David Carr B	5.00	12.00
PDF DeShaun Foster B	8.00	20.00
PDG David Garrard D	10.00	25.00
PJH Joey Harrington A	8.00	20.00
PJM Josh McCown D	8.00	20.00
PJR Josh Reed D	6.00	15.00
PJW Javon Walker B	8.00	20.00
PKC Kelly Campbell B	6.00	15.00
PKK Kurt Kittner B	5.00	12.00
PPR Patrick Ramsey B	6.00	15.00
PRD Rohan Davey F	8.00	20.00
PRJ Ron Johnson B	6.00	15.00
PTS Travis Stephens D	5.00	12.00
PWG William Green C	6.00	15.00
PDRC Reche Caldwell D	6.00	15.00
PTJD T.J. Duckett B	8.00	20.00

2002 Topps Pristine Driving Foroc Jerseys

This set features authentic jerseys of some of the NFL's top offensive producers. Group A stated odds were 1:126, Group B 1:110, Group C 1:31, Group D 1:18, Group E 1:25, and Group F 1:33.

GROUP A STATED ODDS 1:126
GROUP B STATED ODDS 1:110
GROUP C STATED ODDS 1:31
GROUP D STATED ODDS 1:18
GROUP E STATED ODDS 1:25
GROUP F STATED ODDS 1:33

Card	Low	High
DFAB Aaron Brooks D	2.50	6.00
DFAT Anthony Thomas D	3.00	8.00
DFBF Brett Favre B	8.00	20.00
DFCM Curtis Martin C	3.00	8.00
DFDF Doug Flutie E	3.00	8.00
DFKW Kurt Warner E	3.00	8.00
DFLT LaDainian Tomlinson D	4.00	10.00
DFMB Mark Brunell F	3.00	8.00
DFMF Marshall Faulk C	3.00	8.00
DFSD Stephen Davis A	2.50	6.00

2002 Topps Pristine Nickel Package Jerseys

This set features jersey swatches from some of the NFL's top defensive stars. Group A stated odds were 1:238, Group B 1:185, Group C 1:60, Group D 1:49, and Group E 1:35.

GROUP A STATED ODDS 1:238
GROUP B STATED ODDS 1:185
GROUP C STATED ODDS 1:60
GROUP D STATED ODDS 1:49
GROUP E STATED ODDS 1:35

Card	Low	High
NPJK Jevon Kearse B	2.50	6.00
NPJP Julius Peppers D	6.00	15.00
NPJS Justin Smith C	3.00	8.00
NPRW Roy Williams E	2.50	6.00
NPTV Troy Vincent A	3.00	8.00

2002 Topps Pristine Patches

Inserted at a rate of 1:49, this set features authentic patch swatches, with each card being serial #'d to 100.

PATCH/100 STATED ODDS 1:49
STATED PRINT RUN 100 SER.#'d SETS

Card	Low	High
PPAB Aaron Brooks	4.00	10.00
PPAT Anthony Thomas	5.00	12.00
PPBF Brett Favre	12.00	30.00
PPBG Brian Griese	4.00	10.00
PPCM Curtis Martin	5.00	12.00
PPDF Doug Flutie	5.00	12.00
PPDG Darrell Green	6.00	15.00
PPDS Duce Staley	4.00	10.00
PPEG Eddie George	5.00	12.00
PPES Emmitt Smith	10.00	25.00
PPJG Jeff Garcia	4.00	10.00
PPJR Jerry Rice	12.00	30.00
PPKJ Keyshawn Johnson	5.00	12.00
PPKW Kurt Warner	5.00	12.00
PPMB Mark Brunell	5.00	12.00
PPMF Marshall Faulk	5.00	12.00
PPTO Terrell Owens	5.00	12.00

2002 Topps Pristine Portions Jerseys

This set features cards with swatches of authentic game worn jerseys. Stated odds were as follows: Group A 1:74, Group B 1:63, Group C 1:29, Group D 1:55, Group E 1:46, Group F 1:46, and Group G 1:40.

GROUP A STATED ODDS 1:74
GROUP B STATED ODDS 1:63
GROUP C STATED ODDS 1:29
GROUP D STATED ODDS 1:55
GROUP E STATED ODDS 1:46
GROUP F STATED ODDS 1:46
GROUP G STATED ODDS 1:40

Card	Low	High
PPBRG Brian Griese B	2.50	6.00
PPRDB Drew Brees G	8.00	20.00
PPRDG Darrell Green F	4.00	10.00
PPREG Eddie George C	3.00	8.00
PPRES Emmitt Smith A	10.00	25.00
PPRJG Jeff Garcia E	2.50	6.00
PPRJR Jerry Rice F	8.00	20.00
PPRKJ Keyshawn Johnson D	3.00	8.00
PPRTO Terrell Owens D	3.00	8.00

2002 Topps Pristine Rookie Premiere Jerseys

This set features jersey swatches from many top 2002 rookies. Stated odds were as follows: Group A 1:97, Group B 1:72, Group C 1:63, Group D 1:55, Group E 1:49, Group F 1:15, Group G 1:21, Group H 1:20, Group I 1:18, Group J 1:18, and Group K 1:31.

GROUP A STATED ODDS 1:97
GROUP B STATED ODDS 1:72
GROUP C STATED ODDS 1:63
GROUP D STATED ODDS 1:55
GROUP E STATED ODDS 1:49
GROUP F STATED ODDS 1:15
GROUP G STATED ODDS 1:21
GROUP H STATED ODDS 1:20
GROUP I STATED ODDS 1:18
GROUP J STATED ODDS 1:18
GROUP K STATED ODDS 1:31

Card	Low	High
RPRAB Antonio Bryant I	4.00	10.00
RPRAD Andre Davis H	2.50	6.00
RPRCP Clinton Portis F	4.00	10.00
RPRDC Reche Caldwell E	3.00	8.00
RPRDF DeShaun Foster L	4.00	10.00
RPRDG David Garrard G	3.00	8.00
RPRDS Donte Stallworth I	4.00	10.00
RPREC Eric Crouch G	4.00	10.00
RPRGR Daniel Graham D	3.00	8.00
RPRJG Jabar Gaffney I	2.50	6.00
RPRJH Joey Harrington F	2.50	6.00
RPRJM Josh McCown H	4.00	10.00
RPRJR Josh Reed K	3.00	8.00
RPRJS Jeremy Shockey K	4.00	10.00
RPRJW Javon Walker J	4.00	10.00
RPRMW Marquise Walker A	2.50	6.00
RPRPR Patrick Ramsey B	3.00	8.00
RPRTC Tim Carter F	3.00	8.00
RPRTD T.J. Duckett C	2.50	6.00
RPRWG William Green J	3.00	8.00

2003 Topps Pristine

Released in November of 2003, this set features 50 veterans and 99 rookies. The rookie portion of this set, cards 51-149, is broken into three tiers: common, uncommon, and rare. Uncommon rookies were inserted at a rate of 1:2, and are serial numbered to 1499. Rare rookies were inserted at a rate of 1:5, and are serial numbered to 499. Boxes contained 5 triple packs, and each pack contained a total of 8 cards. The first pack contained an uncirculated refractor, the second pack contained a memorabilia card, and the third pack contained veteran and rookie cards. The pack SRP was $30.

Card	Low	High
COMP.SET w/o SP's (50)	15.00	40.00
U ROOKIE/1499 ODDS 1:2		
R ROOKIE/499 ODDS 1:5		
1 Brett Favre	1.50	4.00
2 Rich Gannon	.60	1.50
3 Randy Moss	.60	1.50
4 Travis Henry	.50	1.25
5 Troy Brown	.50	1.25
6 Darrell Jackson	.60	1.50
7 Steve McNair	.60	1.50
8 Plaxico Burress	.50	1.25
9 Jerry Rice	1.50	4.00
10 Donovan McNabb	.60	1.50
11 Marty Booker	.50	1.25
12 Joey Galloway	.60	1.50
13 Peerless Price	.50	1.25
14 Emmitt Smith	1.25	3.00
15 David Carr	.50	1.25
16 Priest Holmes	.50	1.25
17 LaDainian Tomlinson	.75	2.00
18 Hines Ward	.60	1.50
19 Tiki Barber	.60	1.50
20 Fred Taylor	.50	1.25
21 Marvin Harrison	.60	1.50
22 Marshall Faulk	.60	1.50
23 Terrell Owens	.60	1.50
24 Patrick Ramsey	.60	1.50
25 Michael Vick	.60	1.50
26 Tom Brady	3.00	8.00
27 Shaun Alexander	.50	1.25
28 Derrick Mason	.50	1.25
29 Keyshawn Johnson	.75	2.00
30 Ricky Williams	.60	1.50
31 Ahman Green	.60	1.50
32 Joey Harrington	.50	1.25
33 Corey Dillon	.50	1.25
34 Jamal Lewis	.60	1.50
35 Drew Bledsoe	.60	1.50
36 Tommy Maddox	.50	1.25
37 Kurt Warner	.60	1.50
38 Deuce McAllister	.60	1.50
39 Curtis Martin	.60	1.50
40 Chad Pennington	.50	1.25
41 Trent Green	.50	1.25
42 Edgerrin James	.60	1.50
43 Clinton Portis	.50	1.25
44 Eric Moulds	.50	1.25
45 Peyton Manning	2.00	5.00
46 Jeff Garcia	.50	1.25
47 Daunte Culpepper	.60	1.50
48 Tim Couch	.50	1.25
49 Drew Brees	.75	2.00
50 Aaron Brooks	.50	1.25
51 Anquan Boldin C RC	1.25	3.00
52 Anquan Boldin U	1.50	4.00
53 Anquan Boldin R	2.50	6.00
54 Andre Johnson C RC	2.00	5.00
55 Andre Johnson U	2.50	6.00
56 Andre Johnson R	4.00	10.00
57 Artose Pinner C RC	.75	2.00
58 Artose Pinner U	1.00	2.50
59 Artose Pinner R	1.50	4.00
60 Bryant Johnson C RC	1.25	3.00
61 Bryant Johnson U	1.50	4.00
62 Bryant Johnson R	2.50	6.00
63 Bethel Johnson C RC	.75	2.00
64 Bethel Johnson U	1.00	2.50
65 Bethel Johnson R	1.50	4.00
66 Byron Leftwich C RC	1.00	2.50
67 Byron Leftwich U	1.25	3.00
68 Byron Leftwich R	2.00	5.00
69 Brian St.Pierre C RC	.75	2.00

70 Brian St.Pierre U 1.00 2.50
71 Brian St.Pierre R 1.50 4.00
72 Chris Brown C RC .75 2.00
73 Chris Brown U 1.00 2.50
74 Chris Brown R 1.50 4.00
75 Carson Palmer C RC 1.50 4.00
76 Carson Palmer U 2.00 5.00
77 Carson Palmer R 3.00 8.00
78 Charles Rogers C RC 1.00 2.50
79 Charles Rogers U 1.25 3.00
80 Charles Rogers R 2.00 5.00
81 Chris Simms C RC .75 2.00
82 Chris Simms U 1.00 2.50
83 Chris Simms R 1.50 4.00
84 Dallas Clark C RC 1.25 3.00
85 Dallas Clark U 1.50 4.00
86 Dallas Clark R 2.50 6.00
87 Dave Ragone C RC .75 2.00
88 Dave Ragone U 1.00 2.50
89 Dave Ragone R 1.50 4.00
90 DeWayne Robertson C RC 1.00 2.50
91 DeWayne Robertson U 1.25 3.00
92 DeWayne Robertson R 2.00 5.00
93 Justin Fargas C RC 1.25 3.00
94 Justin Fargas U 1.50 4.00
95 Justin Fargas R 2.50 6.00
96 Kyle Boller C RC .75 2.00
97 Kyle Boller U 1.00 2.50
98 Kyle Boller R 1.50 4.00
99 Kevin Curtis C RC .75 2.00
100 Kevin Curtis U 1.00 2.50
101 Kevin Curtis R 1.50 4.00
102 Ken Dorsey C RC 1.00 2.50
103 Ken Dorsey U 1.25 3.00
104 Ken Dorsey R 2.00 5.00
105 Kelley Washington C RC .75 2.00
106 Kelley Washington U 1.00 2.50
107 Kelley Washington R 1.50 4.00
108 Kliff Kingsbury C RC 1.25 3.00
109 Kliff Kingsbury U 1.50 4.00
110 Kliff Kingsbury R 2.50 6.00
111 Larry Johnson C RC 1.00 2.50
112 Larry Johnson U 1.25 3.00
113 Larry Johnson R 2.00 5.00
114 Musa Smith C RC .75 2.00
115 Musa Smith U 1.00 2.50
116 Musa Smith R 1.50 4.00
117 Marcus Trufant C RC 1.00 2.50
118 Marcus Trufant U 1.25 3.00
119 Marcus Trufant R 2.00 5.00
120 Nate Burleson C RC 1.00 2.50
121 Nate Burleson U 1.25 3.00
122 Nate Burleson R 2.00 5.00
123 Onterrio Smith C RC .75 2.00
124 Onterrio Smith U 1.00 2.50
125 Onterrio Smith R 1.50 4.00
126 Rex Grossman C RC 1.00 2.50
127 Rex Grossman U 1.25 3.00
128 Rex Grossman R 2.00 5.00
129 Seneca Wallace C RC 1.00 2.50
130 Seneca Wallace U 1.25 3.00
131 Seneca Wallace R 2.00 5.00
132 Tyrone Calico C RC .75 2.00
133 Tyrone Calico U 1.00 2.50
134 Tyrone Calico R 1.50 4.00
135 Taylor Jacobs C RC .75 2.00
136 Taylor Jacobs U 1.00 2.50
137 Taylor Jacobs R 1.50 4.00
138 Teyo Johnson C RC 1.00 2.50
139 Teyo Johnson U 1.25 3.00
140 Teyo Johnson R 2.00 5.00
141 Terence Newman C RC 1.25 3.00
142 Terence Newman U 1.50 4.00
143 Terence Newman R 2.50 6.00
144 Terrell Suggs C RC 1.00 2.50
145 Terrell Suggs U 1.25 3.00
146 Terrell Suggs R 2.00 5.00
147 Willis McGahee C RC 1.00 2.50
148 Willis McGahee U 1.25 3.00
149 Willis McGahee R 2.00 5.00

2003 Topps Pristine Gold Refractors

*VETS 1-50: 2X TO 5X BASIC CARDS
1-50 VETERAN PRINT RUN 150
*C ROOKIES 51-149: 1.5X TO 4X
C ROOKIES PRINT RUN 75
*U ROOKIES 51-149: 1.5X TO 4X
U ROOKIES PRINT RUN 50
*R ROOKIES 51-149: 1.5X TO 4X
R ROOKIES PRINT RUN 25
ONE PER HOBBY BOX

2003 Topps Pristine Refractors

*1-50 VETS/99: 2.5X TO 6X BASIC CARDS
*51-149 C ROOKIES/1449: .8X TO 2X
*51-149 U ROOKIES/499: .8X TO 2X
*51-149 R ROOKIES/99: 1X TO 2.5X

2003 Topps Pristine All-Rookie Team Jerseys

Randomly inserted in packs, cards in this set feature green backgrounds and event worn jerseys from the Rookie Premiere Photo Shoot. Group odds are as follows: Group A: 1:88, Group B: 1:74, and Group C: 1:14. An uncirculated refractor parallel of this set exists, and was inserted at a rate of 1:345. The Refractors parallels are serial numbered to 25.

GROUP A STATED ODDS 1:88
GROUP B STATED ODDS 1:74
GROUP C STATED ODDS 1:14
*REFRACTOR/25: 1.5X TO 4X BASIC JSY
REFRACTOR/25 STATED ODDS 1:345
ARTAJ Andre Johnson C 6.00 15.00
ARTBJ Bryant Johnson A 4.00 10.00
ARTBL Byron Leftwich C 3.00 8.00
ARTCP Carson Palmer C 10.00 25.00
ARTCR Charles Rogers C 3.00 8.00
ARTKB Kyle Boller C 2.50 6.00
ARTLJ Larry Johnson A 3.00 8.00
ARTRG Rex Grossman A 3.00 8.00
ARTWM Willis McGahee B 8.00 20.00

2003 Topps Pristine All-Star Endorsements Jersey Autographs

This set features game worn jersey swatches and authentic player autographs on the card. The group odds are as follows: Group A: 1:138, Group B: 1:34, and Group C: 1:44. Please note that Bryant Young, Jonathon Ogden, and Marty Booker were issued as exchange cards in packs. The exchange expiration deadline was 10/31/2005.

GROUP A STATED ODDS 1:138
GROUP B STATED ODDS 1:34
GROUP C STATED ODDS 1:44
ASEDM Deuce McAllister A 10.00 25.00
ASELK Lincoln Kennedy B 8.00 20.00
ASEMB Marty Booker B 8.00 20.00
ASEOK Olin Kreutz C 12.00 30.00
ASETG Tony Gonzalez A 10.00 25.00
ASEWR Willie Roaf C 25.00 50.00

2003 Topps Pristine Autographs

This set features authentic player autographs signed directly on the card. The group odds are as follows: Group A: 1:3350, Group B: 1:455, Group C: 1:20, Group D: 1:110, Group E: 1:48, and Group F 1:31. Please note that a Gold parallel of this set exists with each serial numbered to 25.

GROUP A STATED ODDS 1:3350
GROUP B STATED ODDS 1:455
GROUP C STATED ODDS 1:20
GROUP D STATED ODDS 1:110
GROUP E STATED ODDS 1:48
GROUP F STATED ODDS 1:31
PEBJ Bryant Johnson C 8.00 20.00
PEBL Byron Leftwich C 6.00 15.00
PEBS Barry Sanders B 50.00 100.00
PECB Chris Brown C 5.00 12.00
PECS Chris Simms F 12.00 30.00
PEDM Dan Marino A 125.00 250.00
PEJF Justin Fargas E 8.00 20.00
PEJR Jerry Rice B 75.00 150.00
PEKB Kyle Boller E 5.00 12.00
PEKW Kelly Washington C 5.00 12.00
PELJ Larry Johnson C 6.00 15.00
PERG Rex Grossman C 6.00 15.00
PETC Tyrone Calico D 5.00 12.00
PETJ Taylor Jacobs C 5.00 12.00
PETJO Teyo Johnson F 6.00 15.00
PETS Terrell Suggs F 6.00 15.00

2003 Topps Pristine Autographs Gold

*GOLD/25: .8X TO 2X BASIC AUTO
GOLD PRINT RUN 25 SERIAL #'d SETS
PEBS Barry Sanders 100.00 200.00
PEDM Dan Marino 125.00 250.00
PEJR Jerry Rice 100.00 200.00

2003 Topps Pristine Gems Relics

This set features game worn jersey patches. The group odds are as follows: Group A: 1:248, Group B: 1:121, Group C: 1:57, and Group D: 1:51.

GROUP A STATED ODDS 1:248
GROUP B STATED ODDS 1:121
GROUP C STATED ODDS 1:57
GROUP D STATED ODDS 1:51
PGABU Brian Urlacher C 5.00 12.00
PGACP Clinton Portis C 3.00 8.00
PGADM Deuce McAllister D 4.00 10.00
PGADS Duce Staley C 3.00 8.00
PGAJK Jevon Kearse D 3.00 8.00
PGAJS Jeremy Shockey B 3.00 8.00
PGAJT Jason Taylor D 4.00 10.00
PGARW Ricky Williams C 4.00 10.00
PGAT Amani Toomer B 3.00 8.00
PGATH Anthony Thomas B 4.00 10.00
PGATO Terrell Owens C 4.00 10.00
PGAZT Zach Thomas C 4.00 10.00
PGCP Chad Pennington A 4.00 10.00
PGDC David Carr A 4.00 10.00
PGJH Joey Harrington A 4.00 10.00

2003 Topps Pristine Igniters Relics

This set features game worn jersey swatches. Players in Group A were inserted at a rate of 1:33, and players in Group B were inserted at a rate of 1:10. Please note that there is an uncirculated refractor parallel of this set that was inserted at a rate of 1:634. The Refractors are serial numbered to 25.

GROUP A STATED ODDS 1:33
GROUP B STATED ODDS 1:10
*REFRACTOR/25: 1X TO 2.5X BASIC JSY
REFRACTOR/25 ODDS 1:634
PICP Chad Pennington A 2.00 5.00
PIJH Joey Harrington B 2.00 5.00
PIJS Jeremy Shockey B 2.00 5.00
PIJT Jason Taylor B 2.50 6.00
PITO Terrell Owens A 2.50 6.00

2003 Topps Pristine Minis

Inserted at a rate of one per box, this set features miniature cards of established NFL superstars and promising rookies. A Jerry Rice authentic mini card autograph was inserted at a rate of 1:648.

STATED ODDS ONE PER BOX
RICE AU STATED ODDS 1:648
PM1 Michael Vick .75 2.00
PM2 Brett Favre 2.00 5.00
PM3 Marvin Harrison .75 2.00
PM4 Chad Pennington .60 1.50
PM5 Priest Holmes .60 1.50
PM6 LaDainian Tomlinson 1.00 2.50
PM7 Drew Bledsoe .75 2.00
PM8 Ricky Williams .75 2.00
PM9 Randy Moss .75 2.00
PM10 Donovan McNabb .75 2.00
PM11 Peyton Manning 2.50 6.00
PM12 Deuce McAllister .75 2.00
PM13 Steve McNair .75 2.00
PM14 Clinton Portis .60 1.50
PM15 Jerry Rice 2.00 5.00
PM16 Terrell Owens .75 2.00
PM17 Marshall Faulk .75 2.00
PM18 Rich Gannon .75 2.00
PM19 Tom Brady 4.00 10.00
PM20 Jamal Lewis .75 2.00
PM21 Carson Palmer 1.25 3.00
PM22 Andre Johnson 1.50 4.00
PM23 Willis McGahee .75 2.00
PM24 Bryant Johnson 1.00 2.50
PM25 Byron Leftwich .75 2.00
PM26 Justin Fargas 1.00 2.50
PM27 Anquan Boldin 1.00 2.50
PM28 Rex Grossman .75 2.00
PM29 Larry Johnson .75 2.00
PM30 Taylor Jacobs .60 1.50
PM31 Kyle Boller .60 1.50
PM32 Tyrone Calico .60 1.50
PM33 Bethel Johnson .60 1.50
PM34 Charles Rogers .75 2.00
PM35 Teyo Johnson .75 2.00
PM36 Musa Smith .60 1.50
PM37 Kelley Washington .60 1.50
PM38 Chris Brown .60 1.50
PM39 Dallas Clark 1.00 2.50
PM40 Chris Simms .60 1.50
NNO Jerry Rice AUTO 60.00 120.00

2003 Topps Pristine Performance

This set features game worn jersey swatches. Group odds are as follows: Group A: 1:37, Group B: 1:33, Group C: 1:4. Please note that there is an uncirculated refractor parallel of this set that was inserted at a rate of 1:311. Refractors are serial numbered to 25.

GROUP A STATED ODDS 1:37
GROUP B STATED ODDS 1:33
GROUP C STATED ODDS 1:4
*REFRACTOR/25: 2X TO 5X BASIC JSY
REFRACTOR/25 ODDS 1:311
PPAT Amani Toomer C 2.50 6.00
PPATH Anthony Thomas C 3.00 8.00
PPBU Brian Urlacher C 4.00 10.00
PPCP Clinton Portis C 2.50 6.00
PPDC David Carr A 2.50 6.00
PPDM Deuce McAllister C 3.00 8.00
PPDS Duce Staley C 2.50 6.00
PPJK Jevon Kearse C 2.50 6.00
PPRW Ricky Williams C 3.00 8.00
PPZT Zach Thomas B 3.00 8.00

2003 Topps Pristine Rookie Premiere Jerseys

Randomly inserted in packs, cards in this set feature blue backgrounds and event worn jerseys from the Rookie Premiere Photo Shoot. Group odds are as follows: Group A: 1:137, Group B: 1:46, Group C: 1:74, Group D: 1:27, Group E: 1:7, Group F: 1:36, and Group G: 1:6. An uncirculated refractor parallel of this set exists, and was inserted at a rate of 1:179. Refractors are serial numbered to 25.

GROUP A STATED ODDS 1:137
GROUP B STATED ODDS 1:46
GROUP C STATED ODDS 1:74
GROUP D STATED ODDS 1:27
GROUP E STATED ODDS 1:7
GROUP F STATED ODDS 1:36
GROUP G STATED ODDS 1:6
*REFRACTOR/25: 1.5X TO 4X BASIC JSY
REFRACTOR/25 STATED ODDS 1:179
REFRACTOR PRINT RUN 25 #'d SETS
RPRAJ Andre Johnson E 6.00 15.00
RPRAP Artose Pinner G 2.50 6.00
RPRBJ Bethel Johnson G 2.50 6.00
RPRBL Byron Leftwich E 3.00 8.00
RPRCR Charles Rogers E 3.00 8.00
RPRDC Dallas Clark A 4.00 10.00
RPRDR DeWayne Robertson E 3.00 8.00
RPRKB Kyle Boller G 2.50 6.00
RPRKC Kevin Curtis E 2.50 6.00
RPRKD Ken Dorsey E 3.00 8.00
RPRKK Kliff Kingsbury G 4.00 10.00
RPRKW Kelly Washington D 2.50 6.00
RPRLJ Larry Johnson D 3.00 8.00
RPRMS Musa Smith G 2.50 6.00
RPRMT Marcus Trufant C 3.00 8.00
RPRNB Nate Burleson G 3.00 8.00
RPRSW Seneca Wallace B 3.00 8.00
RPRTC Tyrone Calico B 2.50 6.00
RPRTN Terence Newman E 4.00 10.00
RPRTS Terrell Suggs F 3.00 8.00

2004 Topps Pristine

Topps Pristine was initially released in mid-November 2004. The base set consists of 149-cards including 33-rookies produced with three levels of base set cards (common - C, Rare - R, and Uncommon - U). Hobby boxes contained 5-packs of 8-cards and carried an S.R.P. of $30 per pack. Two parallel sets and a variety of inserts can be found seeded in packs highlighted by the Personal Endorsement Autograph inserts.

COMP.SET w/o SP's (50) 15.00 40.00
R/499 STATED ODDS 1:4
R STATED PRINT RUN 499 SER.#'d SETS
UNPRICED PRESS PLATES #'d OF 1
1 Michael Vick .60 1.50
2 Tony Gonzalez .60 1.50
3 Terrell Owens .60 1.50
4 Brett Favre 1.50 4.00
5 Jamal Lewis .60 1.50
6 Tim Rattay .50 1.25
7 Ricky Williams .60 1.50
8 Edgerrin James .60 1.50
9 Torry Holt .60 1.50
10 Randy Moss .60 1.50
11 Derrick Mason .50 1.25
12 Joe Horn .50 1.25
13 Marvin Harrison .60 1.50
14 Carson Palmer .60 1.50
15 Anquan Boldin .50 1.25
16 Quincy Carter .50 1.25
17 Byron Leftwich .50 1.25
18 Eric Moulds .50 1.25
19 Marc Bulger .50 1.25
20 Ahman Green .60 1.50
21 Jeff Garcia .50 1.25
22 Laveranues Coles .50 1.25
23 Hines Ward .60 1.50
24 Santana Moss .60 1.50
25 LaDainian Tomlinson .75 2.00
26 Domanick Davis .50 1.25
27 Stephen Davis .50 1.25
28 Tiki Barber .60 1.50
29 Chris Chambers .50 1.25
30 Priest Holmes .50 1.25
31 Chad Pennington .50 1.25
32 Shaun Alexander .50 1.25
33 Brad Johnson .60 1.50
34 Marshall Faulk .60 1.50
35 Peyton Manning 2.00 5.00
36 Jake Plummer .50 1.25
37 Clinton Portis .50 1.25
38 Matt Hasselbeck .50 1.25
39 Amani Toomer .50 1.25
40 Steve McNair .60 1.50
41 Daunte Culpepper .60 1.50
42 Fred Taylor .50 1.25
43 Joey Harrington .50 1.25
44 Jake Delhomme .50 1.25
45 Deuce McAllister .60 1.50
46 Chad Johnson .50 1.25
47 Travis Henry .50 1.25
48 Corey Dillon .50 1.25
49 Tom Brady 3.00 8.00
50 Donovan McNabb .60 1.50
51 Ben Roethlisberger C RC 6.00 15.00
52 Ben Roethlisberger U 8.00 20.00
53 Ben Roethlisberger R 10.00 25.00
54 Ben Troupe C RC .75 2.00
55 Ben Troupe U 1.00 2.50
56 Ben Troupe R 1.25 3.00
57 Ben Watson C RC 1.00 2.50
58 Ben Watson U 1.25 3.00
59 Ben Watson R 1.50 4.00
60 Bernard Berrian C RC .75 2.00
61 Bernard Berrian U 1.00 2.50
62 Bernard Berrian R 1.25 3.00
63 Cedric Cobbs C RC .75 2.00
64 Cedric Cobbs U 1.00 2.50
65 Cedric Cobbs R 1.25 3.00
66 Chris Perry C RC .75 2.00
67 Chris Perry U 1.00 2.50
68 Chris Perry R 1.25 3.00
69 Darius Watts C RC .75 2.00
70 Darius Watts U 1.00 2.50
71 Darius Watts R 1.25 3.00
72 DeAngelo Hall C RC 1.25 3.00
73 DeAngelo Hall U 1.50 4.00
74 DeAngelo Hall R 2.00 5.00
75 Derrick Hamilton C RC .75 2.00
76 Derrick Hamilton U 1.00 2.50
77 Derrick Hamilton R 1.25 3.00
78 Devard Darling C RC .75 2.00
79 Devard Darling U 1.00 2.50
80 Devard Darling R 1.25 3.00
81 Devery Henderson C RC .75 2.00
82 Devery Henderson U 1.00 2.50
83 Devery Henderson R 1.25 3.00
84 Dunta Robinson C RC .75 2.00
85 Dunta Robinson U 1.00 2.50
86 Dunta Robinson R 1.25 3.00
87 Eli Manning C RC 6.00 15.00
88 Eli Manning U 8.00 20.00
89 Eli Manning R 10.00 25.00
90 Greg Jones C RC .75 2.00
91 Greg Jones U 1.00 2.50
92 Greg Jones R 1.25 3.00
93 J.P. Losman C RC .75 2.00
94 J.P. Losman U 1.00 2.50
95 J.P. Losman R 1.25 3.00
96 Julius Jones C RC .75 2.00
97 Julius Jones U 1.00 2.50
98 Julius Jones R 1.25 3.00
99 Keary Colbert C RC .75 2.00
100 Keary Colbert U 1.00 2.50
101 Keary Colbert R 1.25 3.00
102 Kellen Winslow C RC .75 2.00
103 Kellen Winslow U 1.00 2.50
104 Kellen Winslow R 1.25 3.00
105 Kevin Jones C RC 1.00 2.50
106 Kevin Jones U 1.00 2.50
107 Kevin Jones R 1.50 4.00
108 Larry Fitzgerald C RC 3.00 8.00
109 Larry Fitzgerald U 4.00 10.00
110 Larry Fitzgerald R 5.00 12.00
111 Lee Evans C RC 1.25 3.00
112 Lee Evans U 1.50 4.00
113 Lee Evans R 2.00 5.00
114 Luke McCown C RC .75 2.00
115 Luke McCown U 1.00 2.50
116 Luke McCown R 1.25 3.00
117 Matt Schaub C RC .75 2.00
118 Matt Schaub U 1.00 2.50
119 Matt Schaub R 1.25 3.00
120 Mewelde Moore C RC 1.00 2.50
121 Mewelde Moore U 1.25 3.00
122 Mewelde Moore R 1.50 4.00
123 Michael Clayton C RC 1.00 2.50
124 Michael Clayton U 1.25 3.00
125 Michael Clayton R 1.50 4.00
126 Michael Jenkins C RC .75 2.00
127 Michael Jenkins U 1.00 2.50
128 Michael Jenkins R 1.25 3.00
129 Philip Rivers C RC 2.50 6.00
130 Philip Rivers U 3.00 8.00
131 Philip Rivers R 4.00 10.00
132 Rashaun Woods C RC .75 2.00
133 Rashaun Woods U 1.00 2.50
134 Rashaun Woods R 1.25 3.00
135 Reggie Williams C RC .75 2.00
136 Reggie Williams U 1.00 2.50
137 Reggie Williams R 1.25 3.00
138 Robert Gallery C RC 1.00 2.50
139 Robert Gallery U 1.25 3.00
140 Robert Gallery R 1.50 4.00
141 Roy Williams C RC .75 2.00
142 Roy Williams U 1.00 2.50
143 Roy Williams R 1.25 3.00
144 Steven Jackson C RC 1.25 3.00
145 Steven Jackson U 1.50 4.00
146 Steven Jackson R 2.00 5.00
147 Tatum Bell C RC .75 2.00
148 Tatum Bell U 1.00 2.50
149 Tatum Bell R 1.25 3.00

2004 Topps Pristine Gold Refractors

*VETS 1-50: 1.5X TO 4X BASIC CARDS
*C ROOKIES 51-149: 2X TO 5X BASE CARD
1-50/C ROOKIES/99: ONE PER HOBBY BOX
*U ROOKIES 51-149: 3X TO 8X BASE CARD
U ROOKIES PRINT RUN 25 SER.#'d SETS
UNPRICED R ROOKIES PRINT RUN 10

2004 Topps Pristine Refractors

*VETSS 1-50: 1.5X TO 4X BASIC CARDS
1-50 VETERAN/99 ODDS 1:13
*C ROOKIES 51-149: .8X TO 2X BASE CARD
51-149 C ROOKIE PRINT RUN 1099
*U ROOKIES 51-149: .8X TO 2X BASE CARD
51-149 U ROOKIES/499 ODDS 1:4
*R ROOKIES 51-149: 1.2X TO 3X BASE CARD
51-149 R ROOKIE/99 ODDS 1:19
ONE REFRACTOR PER HOBBY PACK

2004 Topps Pristine All-Pro Endorsement Jersey Autographs

GROUP A STATED ODDS 1:308
GROUP 8 STATED ODDS 1:202
GROUP C STATED ODDS 1:175
GROUP D STATED ODDS 1:86
APEAC Alge Crumpler D 10.00 25.00
APEDF Dwight Freeney B 15.00 40.00
APEDH Dante Hall C 10.00 25.00
APEPM Peyton Manning A 75.00 135.00
APESE Shaun Ellis A 10.00 25.00

2004 Topps Pristine Clutch Performers Jersey

GROUP A STATED ODDS 1:20
GROUP B STATED ODDS 1:19
GROUP C STATED ODDS 1:31
*REFRACTOR/25: 1.5X TO 4X BASIC JSY
REFRACTOR/25 STATED ODDS 1:510
CPAB Aaron Brooks A 2.50 6.00
CPDB Deion Branch B 2.50 6.00
CPDH Dante Hall A 2.50 6.00
CPJH Joey Harrington C 2.50 6.00
CPTL Ty Law B 4.00 10.00

2004 Topps Pristine Fantasy Favorites Jersey

GROUP A STATED ODDS 1:121
GROUP B STATED ODDS 1:77
GROUP C STATED ODDS 1:67
GROUP D STATED ODDS 1:48
GROUP E STATED ODDS 1:42
GROUP F STATED ODDS 1:37
GROUP G STATED ODDS 1:18
GROUP H STATED ODDS 1:33
GROUP I STATED ODDS 1:28
*REFRACTOR/25: 2X TO 5X BASIC JSY
REFRACTOR/25 STATED ODDS 1:254
FFCM Curtis Martin C 2.50 6.00
FFDM Donovan McNabb I 2.50 6.00
FFJW Javon Walker D 2.00 5.00
FFMF Marshall Faulk H 2.50 6.00
FFMV Michael Vick A 6.00 15.00
FFPB Plaxico Burress B 2.00 5.00
FFPM Peyton Manning G 8.00 20.00
FFRJ Rudi Johnson G 2.00 5.00
FFRM Randy Moss F 2.50 6.00
FFSM Santana Moss E 2.50 6.00

2004 Topps Pristine Minis

STATED ODDS 1:6
VICK AUTO STATED ODDS 1:472
PM1 Michael Vick 1.50 4.00
PM2 Randy Moss 1.50 4.00
PM3 Marshall Faulk 1.50 4.00
PM4 Deuce McAllister 1.50 4.00
PM5 Peyton Manning 5.00 12.00
PM6 Donovan McNabb 1.50 4.00
PM7 Jamal Lewis 1.50 4.00
PM8 Tom Brady 8.00 20.00
PM9 Torry Holt 1.50 4.00
PM10 Priest Holmes 1.25 3.00
PM11 Clinton Portis 1.25 3.00
PM12 Terrell Owens 1.50 4.00
PM13 Anquan Boldin 1.25 3.00
PM14 Ahman Green 1.50 4.00
PM15 Brett Favre 4.00 10.00
PM16 Chris Perry 1.25 3.00
PM17 Greg Jones 1.25 3.00
PM18 Derrick Hamilton 1.25 3.00
PM19 Keary Colbert 1.25 3.00
PM20 Reggie Williams 1.25 3.00
PM21 Philip Rivers 3.00 8.00
PM22 Steven Jackson 1.50 4.00
PM23 Luke McCown 1.25 3.00
PM24 Kevin Jones 1.25 3.00
PM25 Darius Watts 1.25 3.00
PM26 Eli Manning 8.00 20.00
PM27 Michael Jenkins 1.25 3.00
PM28 Lee Evans 2.00 5.00
PM29 Julius Jones 1.00 2.50
PM30 Matt Schaub 1.00 2.50
PM31 Roy Williams WR 1.00 2.50
PM32 Tatum Bell 1.25 3.00
PM33 Rashaun Woods 1.25 3.00
PM34 Michael Clayton 1.50 4.00
PM35 Devery Henderson 1.25 3.00
PM36 Larry Fitzgerald 4.00 10.00
PM37 J.P. Losman 1.25 3.00
PM38 Kellen Winslow 1.25 3.00
PM39 Ben Roethlisberger 8.00 20.00
PMAMV Michael Vick AU 30.00 60.00

2004 Topps Pristine Minis Jersey

JERSEY STATED ODDS 1:312
PMRBR Ben Roethlisberger 100.00 200.00
PMRDM Donovan McNabb 25.00 60.00
PMREM Eli Manning 75.00 150.00
PMRMF Marshall Faulk 20.00 50.00
PMRMV Michael Vick 60.00 120.00
PMRPM Peyton Manning 75.00 150.00
PMRRM Randy Moss 50.00 100.00
PMRRW Roy Williams WR 20.00 50.00
PMRSJ Steven Jackson 6.00 15.00

2004 Topps Pristine Personal Endorsement Autographs

GROUP A STATED ODDS 1:029
GROUP B STATED ODDS 1:734
GROUP C STATED ODDS 1:480
GROUP D STATED ODDS 1:412
GROUP E STATED ODDS 1:97
GROUP F STATED ODDS 1:167
GROUP G STATED ODDS 1:24
GROUP H STATED ODDS 1:8
PEBB Bernard Berrian F 5.00 12.00
PECPE Chris Perry D 5.00 12.00
PEDF Dwight Freeney G 6.00 15.00
PEDHA Derrick Hamilton H 5.00 12.00
PEDHE Devery Henderson H 5.00 12.00
PEDRH Drew Henson E 5.00 12.00
PEEM Eli Manning E 40.00 100.00
PEGJ Greg Jones G 5.00 12.00
PEJC Jerricho Cotchery H 6.00 15.00
PEJPL J.P. Losman G 5.00 12.00
PEJV Jonathan Vilma G 6.00 15.00
PEKJ Kevin Jones G 6.00 15.00
PEMJ Michael Jenkins H 5.00 12.00
PEMV Michael Vick C 25.00 50.00
PEPKS P.K. Sam H 5.00 12.00
PEPM Peyton Manning B 75.00 150.00
PEPR Philip Rivers E 25.00 50.00
PERW Roy Williams WR A 5.00 12.00
PESE Shaun Ellis H 5.00 12.00
PETB Tatum Bell H 5.00 12.00

2004 Topps Pristine Personal Endorsement Autographs Gold

*GOLD/25: 1X TO 2.5X BASIC AUTO
GOLD/25 STATED ODDS 1:127 HOB
PEEM Eli Manning 150.00 300.00
PEPM Peyton Manning 175.00 300.00

2004 Topps Pristine Pristine Gems Jersey

GROUP A STATED ODDS 1:624
GROUP B STATED ODDS 1:87
GROUP C STATED ODDS 1:102
PGAB Aaron Brooks C 2.50 6.00
PGDM Donovan McNabb C 3.00 8.00
PGJPL J.P. Losman B 2.50 6.00
PGKJ Kevin Jones B 3.00 8.00
PGLF Larry Fitzgerald B 8.00 20.00
PGMF Marshall Faulk C 3.00 8.00
PGMV Michael Vick A 3.00 8.00
PGPM Peyton Manning B 10.00 25.00
PGRJ Rudi Johnson B 2.50 6.00
PGRM Randy Moss B 3.00 8.00
PGRW Roy Williams WR B 2.00 5.00
PGSM Santana Moss A 3.00 8.00

2004 Topps Pristine Real Deal Jersey

GROUP A STATED ODDS 1:1263
GROUP B STATED ODDS 1:154
*REFRACTOR/25: 1.5X TO 4X BASIC DUAL
REFRACTOR/25 ODDS 1:510
RDEL E.Manning/J.Losman B 12.00 30.00
RDFW Fitzgerald/Ro.Will. B 6.00 15.00
RDMR E.Mann/Roethlis. B 15.00 40.00
RDPJ C.Perry/K.Jones B 5.00 12.00
RDRC P.Rivers/M.Clayton A 5.00 12.00

2004 Topps Pristine Rookie Revolution Jersey

OUP A STATED ODDS 1:123
GROUP B STATED ODDS 1:30
GROUP C STATED ODDS 1:16
GROUP D STATED ODDS 1:23
GROUP E STATED ODDS 1:41
GROUP F STATED ODDS 1:19
GROUP G STATED ODDS 1:18
GROUP H STATED ODDS 1:6
GROUP I STATED ODDS 1:30
GROUP J STATED ODDS 1:10
*REFRACTOR/25: 1.5X TO 4X BASIC JSY
REFRACTOR/25 ODDS 1:111
RRBB Bernard Berrian E 2.00 5.00
RRBR Ben Roethlisberger A 15.00 40.00
RRBW Ben Watson G 2.50 6.00
RRCC Cedric Cobbs E 2.00 5.00
RRCP Chris Perry H 2.00 5.00
RRDD Devard Darling G 2.00 5.00
RRDHA Derrick Hamilton D 2.00 5.00
RRDHE Devery Henderson G 2.00 5.00
RRDR Dunta Robinson E 2.00 5.00
RRDW Darius Watts F 2.00 5.00
RREM Eli Manning B 20.00 40.00
RRGJ Greg Jones F 2.00 5.00
RRJJ Julius Jones I 2.00 5.00
RRJPL J.P. Losman G 2.00 5.00
RRKC Keary Colbert I 2.00 5.00
RRKJ Kevin Jones D 2.50 6.00
RRLF Larry Fitzgerald G 6.00 15.00
RRMC Michael Clayton C 2.50 6.00
RRMM Mewelde Moore I 2.50 6.00
RRMS Matt Schaub B 2.00 5.00
RRRG Robert Gallery C 2.50 6.00
RRRW Roy Williams WR C 2.00 5.00
RRRWO Rashaun Woods G 2.00 5.00

2005 Topps Pristine

This 172-card set was released in November, 2005. The set was issued in the hobby in seven-card packs with an $30 SRP Which came five packs to a box, Cards number 1-100 were the heaviest printed cards with cards numbered 101-166 had either a game-worn jersey relic (101-145) ; an autograph (146-167) or both a game-worn jersey relic and an autograph (168-172).

COMP.SET w/o SP's (100) 25.00 60.00
OVERALL JSY U STATED ODDS 1:6
JSY U PRINT RUN 900 UNLESS NOTED
AU R/100 STATED ODDS 1:37
JSY AU S/25 STATED ODDS 1:675
UNPRICED PRINT.PLATES PRINT RUN 1 SET
1 Tiki Barber C .75 2.00
2 LaDainian Tomlinson C 1.00 2.50
3 Drew Bennett C .75 2.00
4 Jake Delhomme C .60 1.50
5 Deuce McAllister C .75 2.00
6 Jerome Bettis C 1.00 2.50
7 Javon Walker C .60 1.50
8 Marshall Faulk C .75 2.00
9 Trent Green C .60 1.50
10 Travis Henry C .60 1.50
11 Eli Manning C 1.50 4.00
12 Donovan McNabb C .75 2.00
13 Priest Holmes C .60 1.50
14 Brandon Stokley C .60 1.50
15 Curtis Martin C .75 2.00
16 Muhsin Muhammad C .60 1.50
17 Corey Dillon C .60 1.50
18 Fred Taylor C .60 1.50
19 Michael Vick C .75 2.00
20 Michael Jenkins C .60 1.50
21 Chris Brown C .60 1.50
22 Willis McGahee C .60 1.50
23 Drew Bledsoe C .75 2.00
24 Michael Clayton C .60 1.50
25 Kerry Collins C .60 1.50
26 Jason Witten C .75 2.00
27 Clinton Portis C .60 1.50
28 Marc Bulger C .60 1.50
29 Julius Jones C .60 1.50
30 Chad Pennington C .60 1.50
31 Kevin Jones C .60 1.50
32 Domanick Davis C .60 1.50
33 Reggie Wayne C .75 2.00
34 Jimmy Smith C .75 2.00
35 Byron Leftwich C .60 1.50
36 Randy Moss C .75 2.00
37 Isaac Bruce C 1.00 2.50
38 LaMont Jordan C .75 2.00
39 Edgerrin James C .75 2.00
40 Aaron Brooks C .60 1.50
41 Steven Jackson C .60 1.50
42 Cedric Benson C RC 1.00 2.50
43 Brian Westbrook C .60 1.50
44 Andrew Walter C RC 1.00 2.50
45 Andre Johnson C .75 2.00
46 David Greene C RC 1.00 2.50
47 David Carr C .60 1.50
48 Marion Barber C RC 1.00 2.50
49 Warrick Dunn C .60 1.50
50 Terrence Murphy C RC 1.00 2.50
51 Dante Hall C .60 1.50
52 Willie Parker C .75 2.00
53 Laveranues Coles C .60 1.50
54 DeMarcus Ware C RC 3.00 8.00
55 Santana Moss C .75 2.00
56 Alvin Pearman C RC 1.00 2.50
57 Keary Colbert C .60 1.50
58 Carlos Rogers C RC 1.50 4.00
59 Jeremy Shockey C .60 1.50
60 Craig Bragg C RC 1.00 2.50
61 Daunte Culpepper C .75 2.00
62 Charlie Frye C RC 1.00 2.50
63 DeShaun Foster C .75 2.00
64 Chad Owens C RC 1.00 2.50
65 Dunta Robinson C .60 1.50
66 Mike Nugent C RC 1.25 3.00
67 Jonathan Vilma C .60 1.50
68 Erasmus James C RC 1.00 2.50
69 Randy McMichael C .60 1.50
70 Stefan LeFors C RC 1.00 2.50
71 Ben Roethlisberger C 1.50 4.00
72 Tab Perry C RC 1.00 2.50
73 Joey Harrington C .60 1.50
74 Adrian McPherson C RC 1.00 2.50
75 Roy Williams WR C .60 1.50
76 Vincent Jackson C RC 1.50 4.00
77 Lee Suggs C .60 1.50
78 Ryan Moats C RC 1.00 2.50
79 Plaxico Burress C .60 1.50
80 Chris Henry C RC 1.25 3.00
81 Larry Fitzgerald C 1.00 2.50
82 Travis Johnson C RC 1.00 2.50
83 Terrell Owens C .75 2.00
84 Fabian Washington C RC 1.00 2.50
85 Stephen Davis C .60 1.50
86 Odell Thurman C RC 1.50 4.00
87 Tatum Bell C .60 1.50
88 Roddy White C RC 1.50 4.00
89 J.P. Losman C .60 1.50
90 J.J. Arrington C RC 1.25 3.00
91 Thomas Jones C .60 1.50
92 Eric Shelton C RC 1.00 2.50
93 Charles Rogers C .60 1.50
94 Matt Jones C RC 1.00 2.50
95 Chris Chambers C .60 1.50
96 Jerome Mathis C RC 1.50 4.00
97 Darrell Jackson C .60 1.50
98 Justin Miller C RC 1.00 2.50
99 Donte Stallworth C .60 1.50
100 Brandon Jacobs C RC 1.25 3.00
101 Alex Smith QB JSY U RC 8.00 20.00
102 Mark Clayton JSY U RC 2.00 5.00
103 Antrel Rolle JSY U RC 3.00 8.00
104 Kyle Orton JSY/500 U RC 2.00 5.00
105 Roscoe Parrish JSY U RC 2.00 5.00
106 Vernand Morency JSY U RC 2.00 5.00
107 Maurice Clarett JSY U 2.00 5.00
108 Mark Bradley JSY U RC 2.00 5.00
109 Reg.Brown JSY/500 U RC 2.00 5.00
110 Ronnie Brown JSY U RC 2.50 6.00
111 B.Edwards JSY/500 U RC 2.00 5.00
112 T.Williamson JSY/500 U RC 2.00 5.00
113 Cadillac Williams JSY U RC 2.00 5.00
114 Ricky Williams JSY/500 U 3.00 8.00
115 Jake Plummer JSY/500 U 2.50 6.00
116 Brian Urlacher JSY U 4.00 10.00
117 Joe Horn JSY/500 U 2.50 6.00
118 Anquan Boldin JSY/500 U 2.50 6.00
119 Carson Palmer JSY U 3.00 8.00
120 Rudi Johnson JSY/500 U 2.50 6.00
121 Matt Hasselbeck JSY/500 U 2.50 6.00
123 Steve McNair JSY/500 U 3.00 8.00
124 Shaun Alexander JSY U 2.50 6.00
125 Julius Peppers JSY/500 U 3.00 8.00
126 Dwight Freeney JSY/500 U 2.50 6.00
127 Patrick Kerney JSY U 2.50 6.00
128 Drew Brees JSY U 4.00 10.00
129 Tony Gonzalez JSY/500 U 3.00 8.00
130 Alge Crumpler JSY/500 U 3.00 8.00
131 Chad Johnson JSY/500 U 2.50 6.00
132 M.Muhammad JSY/500 U 2.50 6.00
133 Zach Thomas JSY/500 U 3.00 8.00
134 Marvin Harrison JSY U 3.00 8.00
135 LaVar Arrington JSY U 2.50 6.00
136 Eric Moulds JSY U 2.50 6.00
137 Michael Strahan JSY U 3.00 8.00
138 Jamal Lewis JSY/500 U 3.00 8.00
139 Ray Lewis JSY U 4.00 10.00
140 Hines Ward JSY/500 U 3.00 8.00
141 Peyton Manning JSY/500 U 10.00 25.00
142 Tom Brady JSY/500 U 15.00 40.00
143 Ahman Green JSY/500 U 3.00 8.00
144 Trent Green JSY/500 U 2.50 6.00
145 Brett Favre JSY/500 U 8.00 20.00
146 Aaron Rodgers AU R RC 250.00 400.00
147 Adam Jones AU R RC 5.00 12.00
148 Alex Smith QB AU R 20.00 50.00
149 Antrel Rolle AU R 8.00 20.00
150 Braylon Edwards AU R 5.00 12.00
151 Ciatrick Fason AU R RC 5.00 12.00
152 Courtney Roby AU R RC 5.00 12.00
153 Craphonso Thorpe AU R RC 5.00 12.00
154 Dan Cody AU R RC 5.00 12.00
155 Dan Orlovsky AU R RC 5.00 12.00
156 Darren Sproles AU R RC 20.00 40.00
157 David Pollack AU R RC 5.00 12.00
158 Derrick Johnson AU R RC 6.00 15.00
159 Frank Gore AU R RC 10.00 25.00
160 Heath Miller AU R RC 10.00 25.00
161 Jason Campbell AU R RC 5.00 12.00
162 Kyle Orton AU R 20.00 40.00
163 Mike Williams AU R 6.00 15.00
164 Ronnie Brown AU R 6.00 15.00
165 Troy Williamson AU R 5.00 12.00
166 Vernand Morency AU R 5.00 12.00
167 Deion Branch AU R 5.00 12.00
168 Brett Favre JSY AU S 150.00 300.00
169 Joe Montana JSY AU S 175.00 300.00
170 Barry Sanders JSY AU S 125.00 250.00
171 Tom Brady JSY AU S 175.00 300.00
172 Dan Marino JSY AU S 125.00 250.00

2005 Topps Pristine Die Cuts

*VETERANS 1-100: 1.2X TO 3X BASIC CARDS
*ROOKIES 1-100: .8X TO 2X BASIC CARDS
1-100 C/115 STATED ODDS 1:2
*VET.JSYs 114-145: .6X TO 1.5X BASIC CARDS
*ROOKIE JSY 101-113: .6X TO 1.5X
101-145 U JSY/45 STATED ODDS 1:18
*ROOKIE AUs 146-167: .6X TO 1.5X
146-167 R AU/20 STATED ODDS 1:193
UNPRICED S JSY AU/5 ODDS 1:3837
146 Aaron Rodgers AU R 400.00 600.00

2005 Topps Pristine In The Name Letter Patches

STATED ODDS 1:1145
UNPRICED PER LETTER PRINT RUN 1

2005 Topps Pristine Personal Endorsements Autographs

1500 STATED ODDS 1:3
U/250 STATED ODDS 1:36
R/50 STATED ODDS 1:276
S/25 STATED ODDS 1:1705
UNPRICED UNCIRC.PRINT RUN 3 SETS
UNPRICED DUAL/5 STATED ODDS 1:1023
AJ Adam Jones/250 U 6.00 15.00
AR Antrel Rolle/250 U 6.00 15.00
AW Andrew Walter/250 U 6.00 15.00
CB Craig Bragg/1500 C 4.00 10.00
CC Channing Crowder/1500 C 5.00 12.00
CH Chris Henry/250 U 6.00 15.00
CL Chase Lyman/1500 C 4.00 10.00
CW Cadillac Williams/250 U 30.00 80.00
DA Derek Anderson/1500 C 5.00 12.00
DB Deion Branch/50 R 20.00 40.00
DC Deandra Cobb/1500 C 4.00 10.00
DJ Derrick Johnson/1500 C 5.00 12.00
DN Damien Nash/1500 C 5.00 12.00
DR Dante Ridgeway/1500 C 4.00 10.00
EC Earl Campbell/50 R 25.00 50.00
HM Heath Miller/250 U 10.00 25.00
JC Jason Campbell/250 U 15.00 30.00
JM Joe Montana/25 S 100.00 200.00
JN Joe Namath/25 S 100.00 200.00
JR J.R. Russell/1500 C 4.00 10.00
KH Kay-Jay Harris/1500 C 4.00 10.00
LT Lawrence Taylor/50 R 40.00 80.00
MB Marion Barber/1500 C 4.00 10.00
MC Matt Cassel/1500 C 4.00 10.00
MC Mark Clayton/250 U 8.00 20.00
MH Marvin Harrison/50 R 20.00 40.00
MW Mike Williams/50 R 8.00 20.00
NB Nate Burleson/250 U 6.00 15.00
NH Noah Herron/1500 C 4.00 10.00
RF Ryan Fitzpatrick/1500 C 6.00 15.00
RM Rasheed Marshall/1500 C 5.00 12.00
RP Roscoe Parrish/1500 C 4.00 10.00
RW Roydell Williams/1500 C 5.00 12.00
SL Stefan LeFors/1500 C 4.00 10.00
TM Terrence Murphy/1500 C 4.00 10.00
DJO Deacon Jones/50 R 15.00 40.00

2005 Topps Pristine Personal Pieces Common

GROUP A ODDS 1:14
GROUP B ODDS 1:16
GROUP C/750 ODDS 1:3
UNPRICED UNCIRC/3 ODDS 1:533
AC Alge Crumpler/750 4.00 10.00
AG Antonio Gates/500 4.00 10.00
AR Antrel Rolle/1000 4.00 10.00
AS Alex Smith QB/1000 8.00 20.00
BE Braylon Edwards/500 5.00 12.00
BL Byron Leftwich/1000 4.00 10.00
BU Brian Urlacher/1000 4.00 10.00
CJ Chad Johnson/500 5.00 12.00
CP Carson Palmer/1000 5.00 12.00
CW Cadillac Williams/1000 4.00 10.00
DB Drew Brees/750 4.00 10.00
DF Dwight Freeney/1000 4.00 10.00
DM Deuce McAllister/500 4.00 10.00
EM Eric Moulds/1000 3.00 8.00
FT Fred Taylor/1000 3.00 8.00
JH Joe Horn/750 4.00 10.00
JL J.P. Losman/1000 4.00 10.00
JP Jake Plummer/750 4.00 10.00
JT Jason Taylor/1000 3.00 8.00
JV Jonathan Vilma/1000 4.00 10.00
KO Kyle Orton/1000 4.00 10.00
LA LaVar Arrington/1000 4.00 10.00
LE Lee Evans/1000 3.00 8.00
LT LaDainian Tomlinson/500 5.00 12.00
MB Mark Bradley/1000 3.00 8.00
MC Mark Clayton/1000 3.00 8.00
MH Matt Hasselbeck/500 5.00 12.00
MM Muhsin Muhammad/750 3.00 8.00
MS Michael Strahan/1000 3.00 8.00
PK Patrick Kerney/1000 3.00 8.00
RB Ronnie Brown/1000 6.00 15.00
RJ Rudi Johnson/500 4.00 10.00
RP Roscoe Parrish/1000 4.00 10.00
RW Ricky Williams/500 4.00 10.00
SA Shaun Alexander/1000 5.00 12.00
SM Steve McNair/500 4.00 10.00
TG Tony Gonzalez/750 4.00 10.00
TS Takeo Spikes/1000 3.00 8.00
TW Troy Williamson/1000 3.00 8.00
VM Vernand Morency/1000 3.00 8.00
WM Willis McGahee/1000 3.00 8.00
ZT Zach Thomas/500 5.00 12.00
DMA Derrick Mason/1000 3.00 8.00
JPE Julius Peppers/1000 4.00 10.00
MBU Marc Bulger/1000 3.00 8.00
MCL Maurice Clarett/750 3.00 8.00
MHA Marvin Harrison/1000 4.00 10.00
RBR Reggie Brown/1000 3.00 8.00
TGR Trent Green/500 4.00 10.00

2005 Topps Pristine Personal Pieces Rare

RARE/75 STATED ODDS 1:120
UNPRICED UNCIRC/3 ODDS 1:1163
PPRAS Alex Smith QB 15.00 40.00
PPRBE Braylon Edwards 10.00 25.00
PPRCW Cadillac Williams 10.00 25.00
PPRLT LaDainian Tomlinson 10.00 25.00
PPRMHA Marvin Harrison 8.00 20.00
PPRPM Peyton Manning 10.00 25.00
PPRRB Ronnie Brown 12.50 30.00
PPRSA Shaun Alexander 10.00 25.00
PPRTW Troy Williamson 6.00 15.00

2005 Topps Pristine Personal Pieces Scarce

UNPRICED SCARCE/10 ODDS 1:2257
UNPRICED UNCIRC/3 ODDS 1:6396

2005 Topps Pristine Personal Pieces Uncommon

COMMON/200 STATED ODDS 1:18
UNPRICED UNCIRC/3 ODDS 1:1163
PPUAG Antonio Gates 5.00 12.00
PPUAR Antrel Rolle 5.00 12.00
PPUAS Alex Smith QB 10.00 25.00
PPUCJ Chad Johnson 6.00 15.00
PPUCP Carson Palmer 8.00 20.00
PPUCW Cadillac Williams 6.00 15.00
PPUDB Drew Brees 5.00 12.00
PPUDM Deuce McAllister 5.00 12.00
PPULT LaDainian Tomlinson 6.00 15.00
PPUMC Mark Clayton 4.00 10.00
PPUMCL Maurice Clarett 4.00 10.00
PPUMHA Marvin Harrison 5.00 12.00
PPUPM Peyton Manning 7.50 20.00
PPURB Ronnie Brown 8.00 20.00
PPURJ Rudi Johnson 5.00 12.00
PPURW Ricky Williams 5.00 12.00
PPURBR Reggie Brown 4.00 10.00
PPUSA Shaun Alexander 8.00 20.00
PPUSM Steve McNair 5.00 12.00
PPUTG Tony Gonzalez 5.00 12.00
PPUTW Troy Williamson 4.00 10.00
PPUTGR Trent Green 5.00 12.00
PPUZT Zach Thomas 6.00 15.00

2005 Topps Pristine Pro Bowl Leather

PRO BOWL LEATHER/50 ODDS 1:164
PBLDC Daunte Culpepper 6.00 15.00
PBLDM Donovan McNabb 6.00 15.00
PBLJB Jerome Bettis 12.00 30.00
PBLLT LaDainian Tomlinson 8.00 20.00
PBLMH Marvin Harrison 6.00 15.00
PBLMV Michael Vick
PBLPM Peyton Manning 12.50 30.00
PBLTB Tom Brady 15.00 40.00
PBLTG Tony Gonzalez
PBLTBA Tiki Barber 6.00 15.00

2005 Topps Pristine Pro Bowl Paydirt

O BOWL PAYDIRT/25 ODDS 1:419
PBPAG Antonio Gates 10.00 25.00
PBPBW Brian Westbrook 10.00 25.00

PBPHW Hines Ward 10.00 25.00
PBPLT LaDainian Tomlinson
PBPMH Marvin Harrison 10.00 25.00
PBPMV Michael Vick 12.50 30.00
PBPPM Peyton Manning 15.00 40.00
PBPTH Torry Holt 10.00 25.00

2005 Topps Pristine Selective Swatch

UNPRICED SELECT.SWATCH/1 ODDS 1:4263

2005 Topps Pristine Uncirculated

ETERANS 1-100: 1.2X TO 3X BASIC CARDS
*ROOKIES 1-100: .8X TO 2X BASIC CARDS
1-100 C PRINT RUN 750 SER.#'d SETS
*VET.JSYs 114-145: .6X TO 1.5X BASIC CARDS
*ROOKIE JSY 101-113: .6X TO 1.5X
101-145 U JSY PRINT RUN 100 SER.#'d SETS
*ROOKIE AU 146-167: .6X TO 1.5X BASIC AUTO
146-167 R AU PRINT RUN 20 SER.#'d SETS
UNPRICED S JSY AU PRINT RUN 5 SETS
ONE UNCIRCULATED CARD PER BOX
146 Aaron Rodgers AU R 500.00 800.00

2005 Topps Pristine 50th Anniversary Patches

50TH ANNIV.PATCH/150 ODDS 1:27
PRAJ Adam Jones 3.00 8.00
PRARO Antrel Rolle 3.00 8.00
PRAS Alex Smith QB 10.00 25.00
PRAW Andrew Walter 3.00 8.00
PRBE Braylon Edwards 6.00 15.00
PRCF Charlie Frye 3.00 8.00
PRCR Carlos Rogers 3.00 8.00
PRCW Cadillac Williams 6.00 15.00
PRJC Jason Campbell 5.00 12.00
PRJJA J.J. Arrington 3.00 8.00
PRKO Kyle Orton 4.00 10.00
PRMB Mark Bradley 3.00 8.00
PRMC Maurice Clarett 3.00 8.00
PRMCL Mark Clayton 3.00 8.00
PRMJ Matt Jones 4.00 10.00
PRRB Ronnie Brown 10.00 25.00
PRRBR Reggie Brown 3.00 8.00
PRRW Roddy White 4.00 10.00
PRTM Terrence Murphy 3.00 8.00
PRTW Troy Williamson 3.00 8.00

2001 Topps Reserve

Realesed in November 2001, this 150 card set was issued in six box cases which included 10 packs of cards per box. A dealer ordering this product also received one autographed mini-helmet on top of each box as a premium for ordering the product. The base cards 1-100 feature veterans, while the rookie cards were short printed (serial numbered of 999) and inserted at a 1:5 ratio for hobby packs and 1:9 for retail.

COMP.SET w/o SP's (100) 30.00 60.00
ROOKIE/999 ODDS 1:5 HOB, 1:9 RET
1 Jeff Garcia .30 .75
2 Joe Horn .30 .75
3 Jeff George .40 1.00
4 Ed McCaffrey .40 1.00
5 Keenan McCardell .40 1.00
6 Jerome Bettis .50 1.25
7 Jake Plummer .30 .75
8 Doug Flutie .40 1.00
9 Wayne Chrebet .30 .75
10 Brett Favre 1.00 2.50
11 Emmitt Smith .75 2.00
12 Derrick Mason .30 .75
13 Lamar Smith .40 1.00
14 Brian Urlacher .60 1.50
15 Kurt Warner .75 2.00
16 Jerry Rice 1.00 2.50
17 Tony Gonzalez .40 1.00
18 Jeff Blake .40 1.00
19 Warrick Dunn .30 .75
20 Vinny Testaverde .30 .75
21 Peyton Manning 1.25 3.00
22 Drew Bledsoe .40 1.00
23 Tim Dwight .40 1.00
24 Brad Johnson .40 1.00
25 Peter Warrick .30 .75
26 Steve McNair .40 1.00
27 James Thrash .40 1.00
28 Kordell Stewart .30 .75
29 Randy Moss .40 1.00
30 Brian Griese .30 .75
31 Curtis Martin .40 1.00
32 Ike Hilliard .30 .75
33 Torry Holt .40 1.00
34 James Allen .30 .75
35 Jay Fiedler .40 1.00
36 Junior Seau .40 1.00
37 Troy Brown .30 .75
38 Ricky Williams .40 1.00
39 Charlie Garner .40 1.00
40 Eddie George .50 1.25
41 Stephen Davis .30 .75
42 Tim Couch .30 .75
43 Jimmy Smith .40 1.00
44 Trent Green .30 .75
45 Rod Smith .40 1.00
46 Isaac Bruce .50 1.25
47 Oronde Gadsden .30 .75
48 Keyshawn Johnson .40 1.00
49 Jeff Graham .30 .75
50 Mark Brunell .40 1.00
51 Cade McNown .40 1.00
52 Terry Glenn .40 1.00
53 Derrick Alexander .30 .75
54 Ron Dayne .40 1.00
55 Shaun Alexander .30 .75
56 Chris Chandler .40 1.00
57 Rob Johnson .40 1.00
58 Germane Crowell .30 .75
59 Cris Carter .50 1.25
60 Ahman Green .40 1.00
61 Marshall Faulk .40 1.00
62 Darrell Jackson .40 1.00
63 Duce Staley .30 .75
64 Kevin Johnson .30 .75
65 Muhsin Muhammad .30 .75
66 Elvis Grbac .40 1.00
67 Fred Taylor .30 .75
68 Marcus Robinson .40 1.00
69 Edgerrin James .40 1.00
70 Kerry Collins .30 .75
71 Daunte Culpepper .40 1.00
72 Matt Hasselbeck .30 .75
73 Akili Smith .30 .75
74 Aaron Brooks .30 .75
75 Tim Biakabutuka .30 .75
76 Ray Lewis .50 1.25
77 David Boston .30 .75
78 Donovan Mcnabb .40 1.00
79 Marvin Harrison .40 1.00
80 Rich Gannon .40 1.00
81 Tony Richardson .30 .75
82 Peerless Price .30 .75
83 Jamal Anderson .40 1.00
84 Mike Anderson .30 .75
85 Terrell Owens .40 1.00
86 Antonio Freeman .50 1.25
87 Charlie Batch .30 .75
88 Jamal Lewis .50 1.25
89 Jon Kitna .30 .75
90 Joey Galloway .40 1.00
91 Tyrone Wheatley .40 1.00
92 Jeff Lewis .30 .75
93 Eric Moulds .30 .75
94 Shawn Jefferson .30 .75
95 Tiki Barber .40 1.00
96 Tim Brown .50 1.25
97 Corey Dillon .30 .75
98 Tony Banks .30 .75
99 James Stewart .30 .75
100 Amani Toomer .30 .75
101 Freddie Mitchell RC 1.25 3.00
102 James Jackson RC 1.25 3.00
103 Michael Bennett RC 1.50 4.00
104 LaDainian Tomlinson RC 6.00 15.00
105 Gerard Warren RC 1.50 4.00
106 Dan Morgan RC 1.50 4.00
107 Alge Crumpler RC 2.00 5.00
108 Mike McMahon RC 1.50 4.00
109 Justin Smith RC 2.50 6.00
110 Chris Weinke RC 1.50 4.00
111 Rudi Johnson RC 2.00 5.00
112 Rod Gardner RC 1.50 4.00
113 Koren Robinson RC 1.50 4.00
114 Andre Carter RC 1.50 4.00
115 Kevan Barlow RC 1.50 4.00
116 Jesse Palmer RC 1.50 4.00
117 Anthony Thomas RC 2.00 5.00
118 Michael Vick RC 3.00 8.00
119 Sage Rosenfels RC 1.50 4.00
120 Chad Johnson RC 2.00 5.00
121 Robert Ferguson RC 2.00 5.00
122 Quincy Carter RC 1.50 4.00
123 Travis Minor RC 1.50 4.00
124 Travis Henry RC 1.50 4.00
125 Reggie Wayne RC 2.50 6.00
126 David Terrell RC 1.50 4.00
127 Josh Heupel RC 2.00 5.00
128 Deuce McAllister RC 2.00 5.00
129 Todd Heap RC 1.50 4.00
130 Drew Brees RC 50.00 100.00
131 Snoop Minnis RC 1.25 3.00
132 Marques Tuiasosopo RC 1.50 4.00
133 Santana Moss RC 2.00 5.00
134 Quincy Morgan RC 1.50 4.00
135 Chris Chambers RC 1.25 3.00
136 Richard Seymour RC 2.00 5.00
137 LaMont Jordan RC 2.00 5.00
138 Eddie Berlin RC 1.25 3.00
139 Correll Buckhalter RC 1.25 3.00
140 Justin McCareins RC 1.50 4.00
141 Vinny Sutherland RC 1.25 3.00
142 Chris Taylor RC 1.25 3.00
143 Scotty Anderson RC 1.25 3.00
144 Nate Clements RC 1.50 4.00
145 Darnerien McCants RC 1.50 4.00
146 Dan Alexander RC 1.50 4.00
147 A.J. Feeley RC 1.50 4.00
148 Chris Barnes RC 1.25 3.00
149 Dee Brown RC 1.25 3.00
150 Milton Wynn RC 1.25 3.00
NNO Checklist Card .02 .10

2001 Topps Reserve Autographs

serted at a rate of 1:9 hobby and 1:37 retail packs, these 32-cards feature a mix of signed cards by veterans and rookies. A few players did not sign cards in time to appear in packs, they were issued as exchange cards with an expiration date of November 1, 2003.

OVERALL STATED ODDS 1:9 HOB, 1:37 RET
TRAB Aaron Brooks 4.00 10.00
TRCC Chris Chambers 4.00 10.00
TRCJ Chad Johnson 6.00 15.00
TRCW Chris Weinke 5.00 12.00
TRDB Drew Brees 200.00 400.00
TRDC Daunte Culpepper 5.00 12.00
TRDM Derrick Mason 4.00 10.00
TRDMO Dan Morgan 5.00 12.00
TRDT David Terrell 5.00 12.00
TREM Eric Moulds 4.00 10.00
TRJB Josh Booty 5.00 12.00
TRJH Joe Horn 4.00 10.00
TRJJ James Jackson 4.00 10.00
TRJL Jamal Lewis 6.00 15.00
TRJP Jesse Palmer 5.00 12.00
TRJS Jimmy Smith 5.00 12.00
TRJT James Thrash 5.00 12.00
TRKB Kevan Barlow 5.00 12.00
TRKR Koren Robinson 5.00 12.00
TRLS Lamar Smith 5.00 12.00
TRLT LaDainian Tomlinson 50.00 120.00
TRMA Mike Anderson 4.00 10.00
TRMB Michael Bennett 5.00 12.00
TRMV Michael Vick 25.00 60.00
TRQM Quincy Morgan 5.00 12.00
TRRG Rod Gardner 5.00 12.00
TRRWA Reggie Wayne 25.00 50.00
TRSM Santana Moss 10.00 25.00
TRSMO Sammy Morris 4.00 10.00
TRTH Travis Henry 5.00 12.00
TRWJ Willie Jackson 4.00 10.00

2001 Topps Reserve Jerseys

Issued at a rate of 1:39 hobby and 1:107 retail for regular jerseys and 1:33 hobby and 1:97 retail for Pro Bowl jerseys, this 10-card set features swatches from player worn or game worn jerseys from NFL players.

REGULAR JERSEY ODDS 1:39H, 1:107R
PRO BOWL JERSEY ODDS 1:33H, 1:97R
TRRBB Blaine Bishop PB 2.50 6.00
TRRDB Derrick Brooks PB 2.50 6.00
TRRFW Frank Wycheck PB 2.50 6.00
TRRMA Mike Alstott 2.50 6.00
TRRMB Mark Brunell 3.00 8.00
TRRML Mo Lewis PB 2.50 6.00
TRRSM Sam Madison PB 2.50 6.00
TRRSR Samari Rolle PB 2.50 6.00
TRRSS Shannon Sharpe 3.00 8.00
TRRTH Torry Holt 3.00 8.00

2001 Topps Reserve Mini Helmet Autographs

Issued as a hobby box topper, these 20 mini-helmets featured signatures by a variety of 2001 NFL rookies. Each helmet includes the Topps Hologram of authenticity. Redemption cards for signed helmets were randomly seeded in retail packs at the rate of 1:108.

ONE PER HOBBY BOX
RETAIL REDEMPTION CARD ODDS 1:108
1 Dan Alexander 10.00 25.00
2 Kevan Barlow 10.00 25.00
4 Drew Brees 40.00 80.00
5 Rod Gardner 10.00 25.00
6 Travis Henry 10.00 25.00
7 Josh Heupel 12.00 30.00
8 James Jackson 8.00 20.00
9 Peyton Manning 40.00 80.00
10 Justin McCareins 10.00 25.00
11 Travis Minor 10.00 25.00
12 Dan Morgan 10.00 25.00
13 Santana Moss 20.00 50.00
14 Bobby Newcombe 10.00 25.00
15 Jesse Palmer 10.00 25.00
16 Ken-Yon Rambo 8.00 20.00
17 Koren Robinson 10.00 25.00
18 Vinny Sutherland 8.00 20.00
19 Michael Vick 20.00 50.00
20 Chris Weinke 10.00 25.00

2001 Topps Reserve Rookie Premier Jerseys

Issued at a rate of 1:23 hobby and 1:66 retail, these seven cards feature jersey swatches from some leading 2001 NFL rookies.

COMPLETE SET (8) 30.00 60.00
STATED ODDS 1:23 HOB, 1:66 RET
TRRDM Dan Morgan 4.00 10.00
TRRJJ James Jackson 3.00 8.00
TRRMM Snoop Minnis 3.00 8.00
TRRMT Marques Tuiasosopo 4.00 10.00
TRRQM Quincy Morgan 4.00 10.00
TRRRJ Rudi Johnson 5.00 12.00
TRRTM Travis Minor 4.00 10.00
TRRMCC Mike McMahon

2002 Topps Reserve

This 150 card set consists of 100 veterans and 50 rookies. The rookies were randomly inserted packs, and were serial #'d to 999. Boxes contained 10 packs of 5 cards and one mini-helmet. The box SRP was $75.

COMP.SET w/o SP's (100) 15.00 40.00
ROOKIE PRINT RUN 999 SER.#'d SETS
1 Michael Vick .40 1.00
2 Chris Chambers .30 .75
3 Laveranues Coles .40 1.00
4 Koren Robinson .30 .75
5 Rod Gardner .30 .75
6 James Thrash .40 1.00
7 Michael Bennett .30 .75
8 Rocket Ismail .40 1.00
9 Peter Warrick .30 .75
10 Drew Bledsoe .40 1.00
11 Marcus Robinson .40 1.00
12 Tiki Barber .40 1.00
13 LaDainian Tomlinson .50 1.25
14 Eddie George .40 1.00
15 Mike McMahon .30 .75
16 Joe Horn .30 .75
17 Tom Brady 2.50 6.00
18 Edgerrin James .40 1.00
19 Mike Anderson .30 .75
20 Lamar Smith .30 .75
21 Chris Redman .30 .75
22 David Boston .30 .75
23 Ike Hilliard .30 .75
24 Jeff Garcia .30 .75
25 Michael Pittman .40 1.00
26 Torry Holt .40 1.00
27 Priest Holmes .30 .75
28 Germane Crowell .30 .75
29 David Terrell .30 .75
30 Tim Couch .30 .75
31 Terry Glenn .40 1.00
32 Qadry Ismail .30 .75
33 Aaron Brooks .30 .75
34 Donovan McNabb .40 1.00
35 Jerome Bettis .50 1.25
36 Stephen Davis .30 .75
37 Trent Green .30 .75
38 Chris Weinke .30 .75
39 Derrick Alexander .30 .75
40 Ahman Green .40 1.00
41 Antowain Smith .40 1.00
42 Garrison Hearst .30 .75
43 Keyshawn Johnson .40 1.00
44 Plaxico Burress .30 .75
45 Marvin Harrison .40 1.00
46 Ray Lewis .50 1.25
47 Jake Plummer .30 .75
48 Daunte Culpepper .40 1.00
49 Troy Brown .30 .75
50 Emmitt Smith .75 2.00
51 Jerry Rice 1.00 2.50
52 Duce Staley .30 .75
53 Kurt Warner .40 1.00
54 Derrick Mason .30 .75
55 Brad Johnson .40 1.00
56 Fred Taylor .30 .75
57 Jimmy Smith .40 1.00
58 Sylvester Morris .30 .75
59 Quincy Morgan .30 .75
60 Jamal Lewis .40 1.00
61 Warrick Dunn .30 .75
62 Rod Smith .40 1.00
63 Deuce McAllister .40 1.00
64 Hines Ward .40 1.00
65 Steve McNair .40 1.00
66 Ricky Williams .40 1.00
67 Anthony Thomas .40 1.00
68 Eric Moulds .30 .75
69 Travis Taylor .30 .75
70 Tim Brown .50 1.25
71 Kordell Stewart .30 .75
72 Shaun Alexander .30 .75
73 Peyton Manning 1.25 3.00
74 Marty Booker .30 .75
75 Brett Favre 1.00 2.50
76 Santana Moss .40 1.00
77 James Allen .30 .75
78 Tony Gonzalez .40 1.00
79 Mark Brunell .40 1.00
80 Randy Moss .40 1.00
81 Jay Fiedler .40 1.00
82 Muhsin Muhammad .30 .75
83 Travis Henry .30 .75
84 Amani Toomer .30 .75
85 Freddie Mitchell .30 .75
86 Terrell Owens .40 1.00
87 Drew Brees 1.00 2.50
88 Darrell Jackson .40 1.00
89 Curtis Martin .40 1.00
90 Snoop Minnis .30 .75
91 Quincy Carter .30 .75
92 Corey Dillon .30 .75
93 Rich Gannon .40 1.00
94 Vinny Testaverde .30 .75
95 Jim Miller .30 .75
96 Kevin Johnson .30 .75
97 Brian Griese .30 .75
98 Kerry Collins .30 .75
99 Brian Urlacher .50 1.25
100 Marshall Faulk .40 1.00
101 David Carr RC 1.25 3.00
102 Donte Stallworth RC 2.00 5.00
103 Marquise Walker RC 1.25 3.00
104 Eric Crouch RC 2.00 5.00
105 Jake Schifino RC 1.25 3.00
106 Rohan Davey RC 2.00 5.00
107 David Garrard RC 1.50 4.00
108 Julius Peppers RC 3.00 8.00
109 DeShaun Foster RC 2.00 5.00
110 Roy Williams RC 1.25 3.00
111 Javon Walker RC 2.00 5.00
112 Matt Schobel RC 1.50 4.00
113 Clinton Portis RC 2.00 5.00
114 Albert Haynesworth RC 2.00 5.00
115 Jeremy Shockey RC 2.00 5.00
116 Antwaan Randle El RC 1.50 4.00
117 Maurice Morris RC 1.50 4.00
118 Andre Davis RC 1.25 3.00
119 Chad Hutchinson RC 1.25 3.00
120 Lito Sheppard RC 2.00 5.00
121 Daniel Graham RC 1.50 4.00
122 Jabar Gaffney RC 1.25 3.00
123 Josh McCown RC 2.00 5.00
124 Randy Fasani RC 1.25 3.00
125 Patrick Ramsey RC 1.50 4.00
126 Tim Carter RC 1.50 4.00
127 Ladell Betts RC 2.00 5.00
128 Jonathan Wells RC 1.50 4.00
129 Jason McAddley RC 1.50 4.00
130 Kurt Kittner RC 1.25 3.00
131 Josh Reed RC 1.50 4.00
132 T.J. Duckett RC 1.25 3.00
133 John Henderson RC 1.50 4.00
134 Travis Stephens RC 1.25 3.00
135 William Green RC 1.50 4.00
136 Freddie Milons RC 1.25 3.00
137 Ashley Lelie RC 1.25 3.00
138 Brian Westbrook RC 2.50 6.00
139 Antonio Bryant RC 2.00 5.00
140 Cliff Russell RC 1.25 3.00
141 Reche Caldwell RC 1.50 4.00
142 Aaron Lockett RC 1.25 3.00
143 Mike Williams RC 1.25 3.00
144 Ron Johnson RC 1.50 4.00
145 Herb Haygood RC 1.25 3.00
146 Dwight Freeney RC 2.50 6.00
147 Josh Scobey RC 1.50 4.00
148 Luke Staley RC 1.25 3.00
149 Jerramy Stevens RC 2.00 5.00
150 Joey Harrington RC 1.25 3.00
NNO Joe Namath AUTO

2002 Topps Reserve Autographs

is set features authentic autographs on a crisp, clean card design. Stated odds for this set were as follows: Group A 1:134, Group B 1:67, Group C 1:14, Group D 1:17, Group E 1:13, Group F 1:6, Group G 1:17, Group H 1:14, Group I 1:12, and Group J 1:8.

GROUP A STATED ODDS 1:134
GROUP B STATED ODDS 1:67
GROUP C STATED ODDS 1:14
GROUP D STATED ODDS 1:17
GROUP E STATED ODDS 1:13
GROUP F STATED ODDS 1:6
GROUP G STATED ODDS 1:17
GROUP H STATED ODDS 1:14
GROUP I STATED ODDS 1:12
GROUP J STATED ODDS 1:8
RAAT Anthony Thomas F 5.00 12.00
RABF Brett Favre B 75.00 150.00
RABS Bill Schroeder H 4.00 10.00
RABU Brian Urlacher C 20.00 40.00
RACC Chris Chambers G 4.00 10.00
RADM Derrick Mason J 4.00 10.00
RADT David Terrell C 4.00 10.00
RAJG Jeff Garcia C 6.00 12.00
RAJR Jerry Rice A 60.00 125.00
RALJ LaMont Jordan E 6.00 12.00
RALS Lamar Smith D 4.00 10.00
RALT LaDainian Tomlinson I 20.00 50.00
RAMR Marcus Robinson D
RARD Richard Dent E 10.00 25.00
RASM Sammy Morris F 4.00 10.00
RATS Tai Streets F 4.00 10.00
RAWJ Willie Jackson F 4.00 10.00

2002 Topps Reserve Jerseys

This set features cards with authentic jersey swatches. The stated odds for these cards were as follows: Group A 1:64, Group B 1:52, Group C 1:16, Group D 1:46, Group E 1:35, and Group F 1:26.

GROUP A STATED ODDS 1:64
GROUP B STATED ODDS 1:52
GROUP C STATED ODDS 1:16
GROUP D STATED ODDS 1:46
GROUP E STATED ODDS 1:35
GROUP F STATED ODDS 1:26
RRCD Corey Dillon C 2.50 6.00
RRCG Charlie Garner B 3.00 8.00
RRDB Drew Brees C 8.00 20.00
RRDC Daunte Culpepper D 3.00 8.00
RRDM Dan Marino F DP 8.00 20.00
RRDS Duce Staley E DP 2.50 6.00
RREG Eddie George A 3.00 8.00
RREJ Edgerrin James D 3.00 8.00
RREM Eric Moulds A 2.50 6.00
RRFT Fred Taylor C 2.50 6.00
RRJN Joe Namath C 6.00 15.00
RRJS Jimmy Smith C 3.00 8.00
RRKJ Keyshawn Johnson C 3.00 8.00
RRMA Mike Alstott F 2.50 6.00
RRMB Mark Brunell A 3.00 8.00
RRPM Peyton Manning C 10.00 25.00
RRRG Rich Gannon B 3.00 8.00
RRSC Sam Cowart B 2.50 6.00
RRSM Steve McNair C 3.00 8.00
RRTG Tony Gonzalez D 3.00 8.00
RRTM Travis Minor C 2.50 6.00
RRTO Terrell Owens C 3.00 8.00

2002 Topps Reserve Mini Helmet Autographs

serted one per box, this set is composed of signed mini-helmets from many of the NFL best past and present players. Each helmet was serial #'d to various quantities as listed below. Most helmets with a print run of 25 or fewer are not priced due to market scarcity.

STATED ODDS ONE PER BOX
SERIAL #'d/25 OR LESS NOT PRICED
3 Mike Anderson/250 20.00 40.00
5 Kevan Barlow/80 30.00 60.00
8 Deion Branch/500 20.00 40.00
9 Drew Brees/65 40.00 80.00
12 Antonio Bryant/800 20.00 40.00
13 Tim Carter/1000 12.50 25.00
14 Dave Casper/500 15.00 30.00
15 Mark Clayton/570 20.00 40.00
16 Laveranues Coles/229 15.00 30.00
18 Roger Craig/66 25.00 50.00
20 Andre Davis/900 15.00 30.00
21 Eric Dickerson/41 50.00 100.00
22 Rod Gardner/70 25.00 50.00
24 Roosevelt Grier/480 15.00 30.00
26 Rodney Hampton/480 15.00 30.00
27 Lester Hayes/35 20.00 50.00
29 Travis Henry/160 25.00 50.00
31 Darrell Jackson/214 15.00 30.00
36 Deacon Jones/551 20.00 40.00
42 Don Maynard/55 25.00 50.00
43 Justin McCareins/55 15.00 30.00
44 Tommy McDonald/543 12.50 25.00
47 Travis Minor/144 15.00 30.00
48 Joe Montana/30 150.00 250.00
49 Dan Morgan/55 20.00 40.00
50 Santana Moss/48 30.00 60.00
52 Christian Okoye/189 15.00 30.00
53 Jesse Palmer/154 12.50 25.00
54 Drew Pearson/451 15.00 30.00
59 Gale Sayers/260 35.00 60.00
63 Otis Sistrunk/500 12.50 25.00
64 Steve Smith/500 20.00 40.00
69 Chris Weinke/178 15.00 30.00

2011 Topps Rising Rookies

COMPLETE SET (200) 15.00 40.00
FIVE ROOKIES PER PACK ON AVERAGE
1 Aaron Rodgers .40 1.00
2 Calvin Johnson .25 .60
3 Philip Rivers .25 .60
4 Frank Gore .20 .50
5 Patrick Willis .20 .50
6 Colt McCoy .15 .40
7 Maurice Jones-Drew .15 .40
8 Miles Austin .15 .40
9 Andre Johnson .20 .50
10 Chris Johnson .15 .40
11 Jason Witten .20 .50
12 DeAngelo Williams .15 .40
13 Ray Rice .15 .40
14 Steven Jackson .15 .40
15 Jay Cutler .15 .40
16 Tony Romo .20 .50
17 Vernon Davis .15 .40
18 Anquan Boldin .15 .40
19 Brandon Lloyd .15 .40
20 Peyton Manning .50 1.25
21 LeGarrette Blount .20 .50
22 Steve Smith USC .15 .40
23 Brian Urlacher .25 .60
24 David Garrard .15 .40
25 Arian Foster .15 .40
26 Knowshon Moreno .15 .40
27 Mark Sanchez .15 .40
28 Tim Tebow .25 .60
29 LaDainian Tomlinson .25 .60
30 Adrian Peterson .25 .60
31 Reggie Wayne .20 .50
32 Matt Cassel .15 .40
33 Percy Harvin .15 .40
34 DeMarcus Ware .20 .50
35 Jared Allen .15 .40
36 Brandon Marshall .20 .50
37 Darrelle Revis .15 .40
38 Joe Flacco .20 .50
39 Mike Williams .20 .50
40 Tom Brady .60 1.50
41 Dallas Clark .15 .40
42 Darren McFadden .15 .40
43 Jeremy Maclin .15 .40
44 Dez Bryant .25 .60
45 Hakeem Nicks .15 .40
46 Peyton Hillis .15 .40
47 Ray Lewis .25 .60
48 Justin Tuck .15 .40
49 Marques Colston .15 .40
50 Michael Vick .20 .50
51 Ben Roethlisberger .25 .60
52 Rob Gronkowski .25 .60
53 Matt Forte .15 .40
54 Braylon Edwards .15 .40
55 BenJarvus Green-Ellis .15 .40
56 Matt Schaub .15 .40
57 Wes Welker .20 .50
58 Charles Woodson .25 .60
59 Matthew Stafford .20 .50
60 Matt Ryan .20 .50
61 Austin Collie .15 .40
62 Danny Woodhead .20 .50
63 Eli Manning .20 .50
64 Greg Jennings .15 .40
65 Ed Reed .20 .50
66 Ryan Mathews .20 .50
67 Hines Ward .20 .50
68 Jonathan Stewart .15 .40
69 Jermichael Finley .15 .40
70 Roddy White .15 .40
71 Jerod Mayo .15 .40
72 Marshawn Lynch .20 .50
73 Santana Moss .20 .50
74 DeSean Jackson .20 .50
75 Kenny Britt .15 .40
76 Clay Matthews .25 .60
77 Sam Bradford .15 .40
78 Santonio Holmes .15 .40
79 Michael Turner .15 .40
80 Larry Fitzgerald .20 .50
81 Antonio Gates .15 .40
82 Jamaal Charles .20 .50
83 Ryan Torain .15 .40
84 Ndamukong Suh .20 .50
85 Ahmad Bradshaw .15 .40
86 Malcom Floyd .15 .40
87 Julius Peppers .20 .50
88 Rashard Mendenhall .15 .40
89 Marcedes Lewis .15 .40
90 Drew Brees .25 .60
91 LeSean McCoy .25 .60
92 Dwight Freeney .15 .40
93 Tony Gonzalez .20 .50
94 James Harrison .20 .50
95 Dwayne Bowe .20 .50
96 Mike Wallace .15 .40
97 Steve Johnson .15 .40
98 Josh Freeman .20 .50
99 Deion Branch .15 .40
100 Troy Polamalu .25 .60
101 Patrick Peterson RC .60 1.50
102 Aldon Smith RC .30 .75
103 Daniel Thomas RC .30 .75
104 Ryan Mallett RC .30 .75
105 Greg Little RC .40 1.00
106 Mike Pouncey RC .50 1.25
107 Greg Salas RC .30 .75
108 Delone Carter RC .30 .75
109 Julio Jones RC 1.00 2.50
110 Da'Quan Bowers RC .30 .75
111 Torrey Smith RC .30 .75
112 Kyle Rudolph RC .30 .75
113 Kendall Hunter RC .30 .75
114 Prince Amukamara RC .30 .75
115 Jon Baldwin RC .30 .75
116 Aldrick Robinson RC .40 1.00
117 T.J. Yates RC .30 .75
118 Stephen Paea RC .30 .75
119 Aaron Williams RC .30 .75
120 Jake Locker RC .30 .75
121 Robert Quinn RC .30 .75
122 Adrian Clayborn RC .30 .75
123 Marcell Dareus RC .30 .75
124 Akeem Ayers RC .30 .75
125 Christian Ponder RC .30 .75
126 Andy Dalton RC .60 1.50
127 Ricky Stanzi RC .30 .75
128 Colin Kaepernick RC .50 1.25
129 Randall Cobb RC .50 1.25
130 Cam Newton RC 1.50 4.00
131 Shane Vereen RC .40 1.00
132 DeMarco Murray RC .60 1.50
133 Stevan Ridley RC .30 .75
134 Christian Ballard RC .30 .75
135 Dion Lewis RC .40 1.00
136 Luke Stocker RC .30 .75
137 Lance Kendricks RC .30 .75
138 D.J. Williams RC .30 .75
139 Jerrel Jernigan RC .30 .75
140 Mark Ingram RC .50 1.25
141 Tandon Doss RC .30 .75
142 Titus Young RC .30 .75
143 Austin Pettis RC .30 .75
144 Ryan Kerrigan RC .40 1.00
145 Cameron Jordan RC .40 1.00
146 J.J. Watt RC 1.50 4.00
147 Dontay Moch RC .30 .75
148 Marvin Austin RC .30 .75
149 Vincent Brown RC .30 .75
150 A.J. Green RC .75 2.00
151 Brandon Harris RC .30 .75
152 Curtis Brown RC .30 .75
153 Brooks Reed RC .40 1.00
154 Jabaal Sheard RC .30 .75
155 Leonard Hankerson RC .30 .75
156 Dwayne Harris RC .30 .75
157 Roy Helu RC .30 .75
158 Cameron Heyward RC .40 1.00
159 Justin Houston RC .40 1.00
160 Blaine Gabbert RC .30 .75
161 Ronald Johnson RC .30 .75
162 Taiwan Jones RC .30 .75
163 Bruce Carter RC .30 .75
164 Greg McElroy RC .50 1.25
165 Colin McCarthy RC .40 1.00
166 Rahim Moore RC .30 .75
167 Niles Paul RC .30 .75
168 Bilal Powell RC .40 1.00
169 Jacquizz Rodgers RC .30 .75
170 Mikel Leshoure RC .30 .75
171 Cecil Shorts RC .30 .75
172 Tyrod Taylor RC .60 1.50
173 Jordan Todman RC .30 .75
174 Brandon Burton RC .40 1.00
175 Martez Wilson RC .30 .75
176 Anthony Allen RC .30 .75
177 Allen Bailey RC .30 .75
178 Quan Sturdivant RC .40 1.00
179 Jordan Cameron RC .40 1.00
180 Ryan Williams RC .30 .75
181 Nathan Enderle RC .30 .75
182 Ras-I Dowling RC .30 .75
183 Edmond Gates RC .30 .75
184 Jamie Harper RC .30 .75
185 Robert Housler RC .30 .75
186 Jeremy Kerley RC .50 1.25
187 Denarius Moore RC .30 .75
188 Anthony Castonzo RC .30 .75
189 Casey Matthews RC .30 .75
190 Nick Fairley RC .30 .75
191 Evan Royster RC .30 .75
192 Quinton Carter RC .30 .75
193 Jimmy Smith RC .30 .75
194 Virgil Green RC .30 .75
195 Ryan Whalen RC .30 .75
196 Da'Rel Scott RC .30 .75
197 Alex Green RC .30 .75
198 Phil Taylor RC .30 .75
199 Muhammad Wilkerson RC .30 .75
200 Von Miller RC .50 1.25

2011 Topps Rising Rookies Black

UNPRICED BLACK/1 ODDS 1:2856 HOB

2011 Topps Rising Rookies Blue

*BLUE/1339: .8X TO 2X BASIC CARDS
BLUE/1399 STATED ODDS 1:6 HOB

2011 Topps Rising Rookies Gold

OLD: .5X TO 1.2X BASIC CARDS
GOLD STATED ODDS 1:1 HOB

2011 Topps Rising Rookies Green

*GREEN/25: 4X TO 10X BASIC CARDS
GREEN/25 STATED ODDS 1:322 HOB

2011 Topps Rising Rookies Orange

*ORANGE: 1.2X TO 3X BASIC CARDS
ORANGE STATED PRINT RUN 1:65 HOB

2011 Topps Rising Rookies Red

*RED/99: 2X TO 5X BASIC CARDS
RED/99 STATED ODDS 1:81 HOB

2011 Topps Rising Rookies Combine Competition

RANDOM INSERTS IN PACKS
CCBL J.Baldwin/G.Little .50 1.25
CCCJ R.Cobb/J.Jernigan .60 1.50
CCGJ A.Green/J.Jones 1.25 3.00
CCHY L.Hankerson/T.Young .40 1.00
CCIL M.Ingram/M.Leshoure .60 1.50
CCLP J.Locker/C.Ponder .40 1.00
CCMW V.Miller/M.Wilson .60 1.50
CCNG C.Newton/B.Gabbert 2.00 5.00
CCPA P.Peterson/Amukamara .75 2.00
CCSG T.Smith/E.Gates .40 1.00
CCVC S.Vereen/D.Carter .50 1.25
CCWG D.Williams/V.Green .40 1.00
CCWT R.Williams/J.Todman .40 1.00

2011 Topps Rising Rookies Draft Selection

RANDOM INSERTS IN PACKS
DSAB Ahmad Bradshaw .60 1.50
DSAR Aaron Rodgers 1.50 4.00
DSBJ Brandon Jacobs .60 1.50
DSBL Brandon Lloyd .60 1.50
DSBR Ben Roethlisberger 1.00 2.50
DSBU Brian Urlacher 1.00 2.50
DSCB Champ Bailey .75 2.00
DSCC Chris Cooley .60 1.50
DSCJ Calvin Johnson 1.00 2.50
DSDF D'Brickashaw Ferguson .60 1.50
DSDG David Garrard .60 1.50
DSDH Devery Henderson .60 1.50
DSDK Dustin Keller .75 2.00
DSDM Derrick Mason .60 1.50
DSER Ed Reed .75 2.00
DSFJ Felix Jones .60 1.50
DSGO Greg Olsen .75 2.00
DSJA Jared Allen .60 1.50
DSJC Jerricho Cotchery .60 1.50
DSJK Johnny Knox .60 1.50
DSJL James Laurinaitis .60 1.50
DSJP Julius Peppers .75 2.00
DSKB Kenny Britt .60 1.50
DSKO Kyle Orton .60 1.50
DSLM LaMarr Woodley .60 1.50
DSLT Lawrence Timmons .60 1.50
DSMB Michael Bush .60 1.50
DSMC Michael Crabtree .60 1.50
DSMH Matt Hasselbeck .60 1.50
DSMT Michael Turner .60 1.50
DSMW Mario Williams .60 1.50
DSNA Nnamdi Asomugha .60 1.50
DSPH Percy Harvin .60 1.50
DSPM Peyton Manning 2.00 5.00
DSPP Paul Posluszny .60 1.50
DSPR Philip Rivers 1.00 2.50
DSPW Patrick Willis .75 2.00
DSRM Robert Meachem .60 1.50
DSRS Richard Seymour .60 1.50
DSSB Steve Breaston .60 1.50
DSTG Tony Gonzalez .75 2.00
DSTH Todd Heap .60 1.50
DSABO Anquan Boldin .60 1.50
DSAJH A.J. Hawk .60 1.50
DSCBE Cedric Benson .60 1.50
DSCHJ Chris Johnson .60 1.50
DSDHT Devin Hester .75 2.00
DSDMC Darren McFadden .60 1.50
DSJAV Jason Avant .60 1.50
DSJCU Jay Cutler .60 1.50

2011 Topps Rising Rookies Draft Selection Jerseys

RANDOM INSERTS IN PACKS
DSSAB Ahmad Bradshaw 2.50 6.00
DSSAR Aaron Rodgers 10.00 25.00
DSSBJ Brandon Jacobs 2.50 6.00
DSSBL Brandon Lloyd 2.50 6.00
DSSBR Ben Roethlisberger 4.00 10.00
DSSBU Brian Urlacher 4.00 10.00
DSSCB Champ Bailey 3.00 8.00
DSSCC Chris Cooley 2.50 6.00
DSSCJ Calvin Johnson 4.00 10.00
DSSDF D'Brickashaw Ferguson 2.50 6.00
DSSDG David Garrard 2.50 6.00
DSSDH Devery Henderson 2.50 6.00
DSSDK Dustin Keller 3.00 8.00
DSSDM Derrick Mason 2.50 6.00
DSSER Ed Reed 3.00 8.00
DSSFJ Felix Jones 2.50 6.00
DSSGO Greg Olsen 3.00 8.00
DSSJA Jared Allen 2.50 6.00
DSSJC Jerricho Cotchery 2.50 6.00
DSSJK Johnny Knox 2.50 6.00
DSSJL James Laurinaitis 2.50 6.00
DSSJP Julius Peppers 3.00 8.00
DSSKB Kenny Britt 2.50 6.00
DSSKO Kyle Orton 2.50 6.00
DSSLM LaMarr Woodley 4.00 10.00
DSSLT Lawrence Timmons 4.00 10.00
DSSMB Michael Bush 2.50 6.00
DSSMC Michael Crabtree 2.50 6.00
DSSMH Matt Hasselbeck 2.50 6.00
DSSMT Michael Turner 2.50 6.00
DSSMW Mario Williams 2.50 6.00
DSSNA Nnamdi Asomugha 2.50 6.00
DSSPH Percy Harvin 2.50 6.00
DSSPM Peyton Manning 10.00 25.00
DSSPP Paul Posluszny 2.50 6.00
DSSPR Philip Rivers 4.00 10.00
DSSPW Patrick Willis 3.00 8.00
DSSRM Robert Meachem 2.50 6.00
DSSRS Richard Seymour 2.50 6.00
DSSSB Steve Breaston 2.50 6.00
DSSTG Tony Gonzalez 3.00 8.00
DSSTH Todd Heap 2.50 6.00
DSSABO Anquan Boldin 2.50 6.00
DSSAJH A.J. Hawk 2.50 6.00
DSSCBE Cedric Benson 2.50 6.00
DSSCHJ Chris Johnson 2.50 6.00
DSSDHT Devin Hester 3.00 8.00
DSSDMC Darren McFadden 2.50 6.00
DSSJAV Jason Avant 2.50 6.00
DSSJCU Jay Cutler 2.50 6.00

2011 Topps Rising Rookies Dual Autographs

STATED PRINT RUN 25 SER.#'d SETS
UNPRICED GOLD AU PRINT RUN 5
EXCH EXPIRATION: 5/31/2014
DAAS Amukamara/N.Suh 30.00 60.00
DABF D.Bowers/N.Fairley 15.00 40.00
DABS J.Baldwin/T.Smith 20.00 50.00
DAGB B.Gabbert/S.Bradford 30.00 80.00
DAGJ Green/J.Jones EXCH 60.00 120.00
DAGN B.Gabbert/C.Newton 75.00 150.00
DAIL Ingram/Leshoure 12.00 30.00
DAIM M.Ingram/R.Mathews
DALM Leshoure/Menden EXCH 20.00 50.00
DAMP D.Murray/A.Peterson 100.00 175.00
DANF C.Newton/N.Fairley 75.00 150.00
DANT C.Newton/T.Tebow 100.00 200.00
DARG Rudolph/Gresham EXCH 15.00 40.00
DASH T.Smith/L.Hankerson 20.00 50.00
DAGBR A.Green/D.Bryant 40.00 80.00

2011 Topps Rising Rookies Freshman Impressions Autograph Jerseys

ATED PRINT RUN 25 SER.#'d SETS
UNPRICED JUMBO AU PRINT RUN 5
UNPRICED JUMBO PATCH AU PRINT RUN 1
UNPRICED PATCH AU PRINT RUN 10
FIARAB Arrelious Benn 6.00 15.00
FIARAE Armanti Edwards 6.00 15.00
FIARAH Aaron Hernandez 10.00 25.00
FIARAR Andre Roberts 8.00 20.00
FIARBL Brandon LaFell 6.00 15.00
FIARBT Ben Tate 10.00 25.00
FIARCJS C.J. Spiller 6.00 15.00
FIARCM Colt McCoy 15.00 40.00
FIARDB Dez Bryant 25.00 50.00
FIARDM Dexter McCluster 10.00 25.00
FIARDT Demaryius Thomas
FIARDW Damian Williams
FIAREB Eric Berry 10.00 25.00
FIARED Eric Decker 6.00 15.00
FIARES Emmanuel Sanders 10.00 25.00
FIARET Earl Thomas 8.00 20.00
FIARGM Gerald McCoy 6.00 15.00
FIARGT Golden Tate 6.00 15.00
FIARJB Jahvid Best 6.00 15.00
FIARJC Jimmy Clausen 10.00 25.00
FIARJG Jermaine Gresham
FIARJGR Jimmy Graham 25.00 50.00
FIARJM Joe McKnight 10.00 25.00
FIARJS Jordan Shipley
FIARME Marcus Easley
FIARMH Montario Hardesty 8.00 20.00
FIARMK Mike Kafka 6.00 15.00
FIARMW Mike Williams 12.00 30.00
FIARNS Ndamukong Suh 25.00 50.00
FIARRG Rob Gronkowski 25.00 50.00
FIARRM Ryan Mathews 15.00 40.00
FIARSB Sam Bradford 30.00 80.00
FIARTG Toby Gerhart 10.00 25.00
FIARTP Taylor Price 6.00 15.00
FIARTT Tim Tebow 75.00 135.00

2011 Topps Rising Rookies Freshman Impressions Autographs

NDOM INSERTS IN PACKS
FIAAB Arrelious Benn 4.00 10.00
FIAAE Armanti Edwards 4.00 10.00
FIAAH Aaron Hernandez 6.00 15.00
FIAAR Andre Roberts 5.00 12.00
FIABL Brandon LaFell 4.00 10.00
FIABT Ben Tate 4.00 10.00
FIACJS C.J. Spiller 4.00 10.00
FIACM Colt McCoy 15.00 40.00
FIADB Dez Bryant 20.00 40.00
FIADM Dexter McCluster 6.00 15.00
FIADT Demaryius Thomas 10.00 20.00
FIADW Damian Williams 4.00 10.00
FIAEB Eric Berry 6.00 15.00
FIAED Eric Decker 6.00 12.00
FIAES Emmanuel Sanders 5.00 12.00
FIAGM Gerald McCoy 4.00 10.00
FIAGT Golden Tate 4.00 10.00
FIAJB Jahvid Best 4.00 10.00
FIAJC Jimmy Clausen 8.00 20.00
FIAJF Jacoby Ford 5.00 12.00
FIAJG Jermaine Gresham 4.00 10.00
FIAJGR Jimmy Graham 8.00 20.00
FIAJM Joe McKnight 6.00 15.00
FIAJS Jordan Shipley 6.00 15.00
FIAME Marcus Easley 4.00 10.00
FIAMH Montario Hardesty 5.00 12.00
FIAMK Mike Kafka 5.00 12.00
FIAMW Mike Williams 8.00 20.00
FIANS Ndamukong Suh 12.00 30.00
FIARG Rob Gronkowski 15.00 30.00
FIARM Ryan Mathews
FIASB Sam Bradford 20.00 50.00
FIATG Toby Gerhart 5.00 12.00
FIATP Taylor Price 4.00 10.00
FIATT Tim Tebow 30.00 80.00

2011 Topps Rising Rookies Freshman Impressions Jerseys

NDOM INSERTS IN PACKS
*JUMBO/10: .8X TO 2X BASIC JSY
UNPRICED JUMBO PATCH PRINT RUN 1
FIRAB Arrelious Benn 3.00 8.00
FIRAE Armanti Edwards 3.00 8.00
FIRAR Andre Roberts 4.00 10.00
FIRBL Brandon LaFell 3.00 8.00
FIRBT Ben Tate 3.00 8.00
FIRCJS C.J. Spiller 3.00 8.00
FIRCM Colt McCoy 3.00 8.00
FIRDB Dez Bryant 5.00 12.00
FIRDM Dexter McCluster 3.00 8.00
FIRDT Demaryius Thomas 5.00 12.00
FIRDW Damian Williams 3.00 8.00
FIREB Eric Berry 4.00 10.00
FIRED Eric Decker 3.00 8.00
FIRES Emmanuel Sanders 5.00 12.00
FIRET Earl Thomas 5.00 12.00
FIRGM Gerald McCoy 3.00 8.00
FIRGT Golden Tate 3.00 8.00
FIRJB Jahvid Best 3.00 8.00
FIRJC Jimmy Clausen 3.00 8.00
FIRJG Jermaine Gresham 3.00 8.00
FIRJGR Jimmy Graham 5.00 12.00
FIRJM Joe McKnight 4.00 10.00
FIRJS Jordan Shipley 3.00 8.00
FIRME Marcus Easley 3.00 8.00
FIRMG Mardy Gilyard 3.00 8.00
FIRMH Montario Hardesty 4.00 10.00
FIRMK Mike Kafka 3.00 8.00
FIRMW Mike Williams 4.00 10.00
FIRNS Ndamukong Suh 4.00 10.00

FIRRG Rob Gronkowski 5.00 12.00
FIRRM Ryan Mathews 4.00 10.00
FIRSB Sam Bradford 3.00 8.00
FIRTG Toby Gerhart 4.00 10.00
FIRTP Taylor Price 3.00 8.00
FIRTT Tim Tebow 8.00 20.00

2011 Topps Rising Rookies Freshman Impressions Jerseys Patch

*PATCH/25: .8X TO 2X BASIC JSY
STATED PRINT RUN 25 SER.#'d SETS
FIRSB Sam Bradford 25.00 60.00
FIRTT Tim Tebow 25.00 60.00

2011 Topps Rising Rookies NFL Draft

RANDOM INSERTS IN PACKS
DRAD Andy Dalton .75 2.00
DRAJG A.J. Green 1.00 2.50
DRAP Austin Pettis .40 1.00
DRBG Blaine Gabbert .40 1.00
DRCK Colin Kaepernick .60 1.50
DRCN Cam Newton 2.00 5.00
DRCP Christian Ponder .40 1.00
DRCS Cecil Shorts .40 1.00
DRDB Da'Quan Bowers .40 1.00
DRDL Dion Lewis .50 1.25
DRDM DeMarco Murray .75 2.00
DRDT Daniel Thomas .40 1.00
DRGL Greg Little .50 1.25
DRGS Greg Salas .40 1.00
DRJB Jon Baldwin .40 1.00
DRJJ Julio Jones 1.25 3.00
DRJJE Jerrel Jernigan .40 1.00
DRJL Jake Locker .40 1.00
DRJR Jacquizz Rodgers .40 1.00
DRJT Jordan Todman .40 1.00
DRKH Kendall Hunter .40 1.00
DRKR Kyle Rudolph .40 1.00
DRLH Leonard Hankerson .40 1.00
DRLK Lance Kendricks .40 1.00
DRLS Luke Stocker .40 1.00
DRMI Mark Ingram .60 1.50
DRML Mikel Leshoure .40 1.00
DRNF Nick Fairley .40 1.00
DRNP Niles Paul .40 1.00
DRPA Prince Amukamara .40 1.00
DRPP Patrick Peterson .75 2.00
DRRC Randall Cobb .60 1.50
DRRM Ryan Mallett .40 1.00
DRRW Ryan Williams .40 1.00
DRSR Stevan Ridley .40 1.00
DRSV Shane Vereen .50 1.25
DRTD Tandon Doss .40 1.00
DRTS Torrey Smith .40 1.00
DRTY Titus Young .40 1.00
DRVM Von Miller .60 1.50

2011 Topps Rising Rookies NFL Draft Autographs

ATED PRINT RUN 10-260
*NFL SHIELD AU: .4X TO 1X DRAFT AU
UNPRICED RED INK PRINT RUN 5
EXCH EXPIRATION: 5/31/2014
DRAAD Andy Dalton/50 12.00 30.00
DRAAJG A.J. Green/25 25.00 60.00
DRAAP Austin Pettis/260 6.00 15.00
DRABG Blaine Gabbert EXCH 12.00 30.00
DRACK Colin Kaepernick/100 6.00 15.00
DRACN Cam Newton/10
DRACP Christian Ponder/50 10.00 25.00
DRACS Cecil Shorts/260 3.00 8.00
DRADB Da'Quan Bowers
DRADC Delone Carter EXCH 4.00 10.00
DRADL Dion Lewis/260 4.00 10.00
DRADM DeMarco Murray/100 6.00 15.00
DRADT Daniel Thomas/260 3.00 8.00
DRAGL Greg Little/100 5.00 12.00
DRAGS Greg Salas/260 3.00 8.00
DRAJB Jon Baldwin/50 5.00 12.00
DRAJJ Julio Jones/25 25.00 50.00
DRAJJE Jerrel Jernigan/100 4.00 10.00
DRAJL Jake Locker/25 6.00 15.00
DRAJR Jacquizz Rodgers/260 3.00 8.00
DRAJT Jordan Todman/260 3.00 8.00
DRAKH Kendall Hunter/260 3.00 8.00
DRAKR Kyle Rudolph/100 4.00 10.00
DRALH Leonard Hankerson/100 8.00 20.00
DRALK Lance Kendricks/260 3.00 8.00
DRALS Luke Stocker/100 4.00 10.00
DRAMI Mark Ingram/10
DRAML Mikel Leshoure/50 10.00 25.00
DRANF Nick Fairley
DRANP Niles Paul/260 3.00 8.00
DRAPA Prince Amukamara/100 4.00 10.00
DRARC Randall Cobb/100 6.00 15.00
DRARM Ryan Mallett/25 12.00 30.00
DRARW Ryan Williams/50 20.00 40.00
DRASR Stevan Ridley/260 3.00 8.00
DRASV Shane Vereen/260 4.00 10.00
DRATD Tandon Doss/260 3.00 8.00
DRATS Torrey Smith/50 5.00 12.00
DRATY Titus Young/100 4.00 10.00
DRAVM Von Miller/50 12.00 30.00

2011 Topps Rising Rookies NFL Draft Patch Autographs

ATED PRINT RUN 10-170
*NFL SHLD PATCH: .4X TO 1X DRFT PCH AU
UNPRICED RED INK PRINT RUN 5
EXCH EXPIRATION: 5/31/2014
RAPAD Andy Dalton/40 15.00 40.00
RAPAJG A.J. Green/25 30.00 80.00
RAPAP Austin Pettis/170 8.00 20.00
RAPBG Blaine Gabbert/10
RAPCK Colin Kaepernick/65 10.00 25.00
RAPCN Cam Newton/10
RAPCP Christian Ponder/25 40.00 80.00
RAPCS Cecil Shorts/170 4.00 10.00
RAPDB Da'Quan Bowers/40 6.00 15.00
RAPDC Delone Carter EXCH 5.00 12.00
RAPDL Dion Lewis/170 5.00 12.00
RAPDM DeMarco Murray
RAPDT Daniel Thomas/115 4.00 10.00
RAPGL Greg Little/65 8.00 20.00
RAPGS Greg Salas/170 4.00 10.00
RAPJB Jon Baldwin/40 6.00 15.00
RAPJJ Julio Jones/25 25.00 60.00
RAPJJE Jerrel Jernigan/65 6.00 15.00
RAPJL Jake Locker/25
RAPJR Jacquizz Rodgers/170 4.00 10.00
RAPJT Jordan Todman/115 5.00 12.00
RAPKH Kendall Hunter/170 4.00 10.00
RAPKR Kyle Rudolph/65 6.00 15.00
RAPLH Leonard Hankerson 6.00 15.00
RAPLK Lance Kendricks/170 4.00 10.00
RAPLS Luke Stocker/115 5.00 12.00
RAPML Mikel Leshoure/25 12.00 30.00
RAPNF Nick Fairley/40 6.00 15.00
RAPNP Niles Paul/170 4.00 10.00
RAPPA Prince Amukamara/40 6.00 15.00
RAPRC Randall Cobb/40 10.00 25.00
RAPRM Ryan Mallett/25 8.00 20.00
RAPRW Ryan Williams
RAPSR Stevan Ridley/170 4.00 10.00
RAPSV Shane Vereen/115 6.00 15.00
RAPTD Tandon Doss/115 5.00 12.00
RAPTS Torrey Smith/40 6.00 15.00
RAPTY Titus Young/40 6.00 15.00
RAPVM Von Miller/40 15.00 40.00

2011 Topps Rising Rookies Playmaker

RANDOM INSERTS IN PACKS
PAG Antonio Gates .60 1.50
PAP Adrian Peterson 1.00 2.50
PBE Braylon Edwards .60 1.50
PCG Chad Greenway .75 2.00
PCP Clinton Portis .60 1.50
PDB Dwayne Bowe .75 2.00
PDBR Drew Brees 1.00 2.50
PDH David Harris .60 1.50
PDJ DeSean Jackson .75 2.00
PDR Darrelle Revis .60 1.50
PER Eddie Royal .60 1.50
PFJ Fred Jackson .60 1.50
PGJ Greg Jennings .60 1.50
PHN Hakeem Nicks .60 1.50
PJA Joseph Addai .60 1.50
PJC Jamaal Charles .75 2.00
PJF Joe Flacco .75 2.00
PJN Jordy Nelson .75 2.00
PJW Jason Witten .75 2.00
PLL LaRon Landry .60 1.50
PLM LeSean McCoy 1.00 2.50
PMF Matt Forte .60 1.50
PMJD Maurice Jones-Drew .60 1.50
PMS Matthew Stafford .75 2.00
PRL Ray Lewis 1.00 2.50
PRM Rashard Mendenhall .60 1.50
PRW Reggie Wayne .75 2.00
PRWH Roddy White .60 1.50
PSH Santonio Holmes .60 1.50
PSJ Steven Jackson .60 1.50

2011 Topps Rising Rookies Playmaker Autograph Jerseys

STATED PRINT RUN 25 SER.#'d SETS
UNPRICED JUMBO PRINT RUN 5
UNPRICED JUMBO PATCH PRINT RUN 1
UNPRICED PATCH PRINT RUN 10
PARAG Antonio Gates 8.00 20.00
PARAP Adrian Peterson 60.00 120.00
PARBE Braylon Edwards 8.00 20.00
PARCG Chad Greenway 20.00 40.00
PARCP Clinton Portis 8.00 20.00
PARDB Dwayne Bowe 10.00 25.00
PARDBR Drew Brees 30.00 60.00
PARDH David Harris
PARDJ DeSean Jackson 12.00 30.00
PARDR Darrelle Revis 12.00 30.00
PARER Eddie Royal 8.00 20.00
PARFJ Fred Jackson 40.00 80.00
PARGJ Greg Jennings 8.00 20.00
PARHN Hakeem Nicks 8.00 20.00
PARJA Joseph Addai 8.00 20.00
PARJC Jamaal Charles 12.00 30.00
PARJF Joe Flacco 15.00 40.00
PARJN Jordy Nelson 10.00 25.00
PARJW Jason Witten
PARLL LaRon Landry
PARLM LeSean McCoy 12.00 30.00
PARMF Matt Forte 8.00 20.00
PARMJD Maurice Jones-Drew 8.00 20.00
PARMS Matthew Stafford 40.00 80.00
PARRL Ray Lewis 50.00 100.00
PARRM Rashard Mendenhall 8.00 20.00
PARRW Reggie Wayne 12.00 30.00
PARRWH Roddy White 12.00 30.00
PARSH Santonio Holmes 8.00 20.00
PARSJ Steven Jackson 8.00 20.00

2011 Topps Rising Rookies Playmaker Autographs

STATED PRINT RUN 20 SER.#'d SETS
PAAG Antonio Gates 10.00 25.00
PAAP Adrian Peterson 40.00 100.00
PABE Braylon Edwards 6.00 15.00
PACG Chad Greenway 15.00 30.00
PACP Clinton Portis 6.00 15.00
PADB Dwayne Bowe 8.00 20.00
PADBR Drew Brees 30.00 60.00
PADH David Harris 6.00 15.00
PADJ DeSean Jackson 10.00 25.00
PADR Darrelle Revis 6.00 15.00
PAER Eddie Royal
PAFJ Fred Jackson 40.00 80.00
PAGJ Greg Jennings 6.00 15.00
PAHN Hakeem Nicks 10.00 25.00
PAJA Joseph Addai 6.00 15.00
PAJC Jamaal Charles
PAJF Joe Flacco 15.00 30.00
PAJN Jordy Nelson 10.00 25.00
PAJW Jason Witten 15.00 30.00
PALL LaRon Landry 6.00 15.00
PALM LeSean McCoy 10.00 25.00
PAMF Matt Forte 6.00 15.00
PAMJD Maurice Jones-Drew 6.00 15.00
PAMS Matthew Stafford 25.00 50.00
PARL Ray Lewis 30.00 60.00
PARM Rashard Mendenhall 6.00 15.00
PARW Reggie Wayne 8.00 20.00
PARWH Roddy White 6.00 15.00
PASH Santonio Holmes 6.00 15.00
PASJ Steven Jackson 6.00 15.00

2011 Topps Rising Rookies Playmaker Jerseys

NDOM INSERTS IN PACKS
*PATCH/25: .8X TO 2X BASIC JSY
*JUMBO/10: 1X TO 2.5X BASIC JSY
UNPRICED JUMBO PATCH PRINT RUN 1
PSAG Antonio Gates 2.50 6.00
PSAP Adrian Peterson 4.00 10.00
PSBE Braylon Edwards 2.50 6.00
PSCG Chad Greenway 3.00 8.00
PSCP Clinton Portis 2.50 6.00
PSDB Dwayne Bowe 3.00 8.00
PSDBR Drew Brees 4.00 10.00
PSDH David Harris 2.50 6.00
PSDJ DeSean Jackson 3.00 8.00
PSDR Darrelle Revis 2.50 6.00
PSER Eddie Royal 2.50 6.00
PSFJ Fred Jackson 5.00 12.00
PSGJ Greg Jennings 2.50 6.00
PSHN Hakeem Nicks 2.50 6.00
PSJA Joseph Addai 2.50 6.00
PSJC Jamaal Charles 3.00 8.00
PSJF Joe Flacco 3.00 8.00
PSJN Jordy Nelson 3.00 8.00
PSJW Jason Witten 3.00 8.00
PSLL LaRon Landry 2.50 6.00
PSLM LeSean McCoy 4.00 10.00
PSMF Matt Forte 2.50 6.00
PSMJD Maurice Jones-Drew 2.50 6.00
PSMS Matthew Stafford 3.00 8.00
PSRL Ray Lewis 4.00 10.00
PSRM Rashard Mendenhall 2.50 6.00
PSRW Reggie Wayne 3.00 8.00
PSRWH Roddy White 2.50 6.00
PSSH Santonio Holmes 2.50 6.00
PSSJ Steven Jackson 2.50 6.00

2011 Topps Rising Rookies Rookie Autographs

RANDOM INSERTS IN PACKS
*RED INK/15: .6X TO 1.5X BASIC AU
EXCH EXPIRATION: 5/31/2014
102 Aldon Smith 3.00 8.00
103 Daniel Thomas 3.00 8.00
104 Ryan Mallett 3.00 8.00
105 Greg Little 4.00 10.00
106 Mike Pouncey 10.00 25.00
107 Greg Salas 3.00 8.00
108 Delone Carter 3.00 8.00
109 Julio Jones EXCH 20.00 50.00
110 Da'Quan Bowers 3.00 8.00
111 Torrey Smith 3.00 8.00
112 Kyle Rudolph EXCH 3.00 8.00
113 Kendall Hunter 3.00 8.00
114 Prince Amukamara 3.00 8.00
115 Jon Baldwin 3.00 8.00
118 Stephen Paea 3.00 8.00
119 Aaron Williams 3.00 8.00
120 Jake Locker 3.00 8.00
123 Marcell Dareus 3.00 8.00
125 Christian Ponder EXCH 3.00 8.00
126 Andy Dalton 20.00 50.00
127 Ricky Stanzi 3.00 8.00
128 Colin Kaepernick 5.00 12.00
129 Randall Cobb 5.00 12.00
130 Cam Newton 60.00 120.00
131 Shane Vereen 4.00 10.00
132 DeMarco Murray 6.00 15.00
133 Stevan Ridley 3.00 8.00
135 Dion Lewis 4.00 10.00
136 Luke Stocker 3.00 8.00
137 Lance Kendricks 3.00 8.00
139 Jerrel Jernigan 3.00 8.00
140 Mark Ingram 5.00 12.00
141 Tandon Doss 3.00 8.00
142 Titus Young 3.00 8.00
143 Austin Pettis 6.00 15.00
146 J.J. Watt 40.00 80.00
149 Vincent Brown 3.00 8.00
150 A.J. Green 25.00 50.00
155 Leonard Hankerson 3.00 8.00
159 Justin Houston 4.00 10.00
160 Blaine Gabbert
161 Ronald Johnson 3.00 8.00
162 Taiwan Jones 3.00 8.00
166 Rahim Moore 3.00 8.00
167 Niles Paul 3.00 8.00
168 Bilal Powell 4.00 10.00
169 Jacquizz Rodgers 3.00 8.00
170 Mikel Leshoure 3.00 8.00
171 Cecil Shorts 3.00 8.00
172 Tyrod Taylor 6.00 15.00
173 Jordan Todman 3.00 8.00
180 Ryan Williams 25.00 50.00
183 Edmond Gates 3.00 8.00
184 Jamie Harper 3.00 8.00
186 Jeremy Kerley 5.00 12.00
188 Anthony Castonzo 3.00 8.00
190 Nick Fairley 3.00 8.00
193 Jimmy Smith 6.00 15.00
194 Virgil Green 6.00 15.00
196 Da'Rel Scott 6.00 15.00
197 Alex Green 3.00 8.00
200 Von Miller 8.00 20.00

2011 Topps Rising Rookies Rookie Team Patches

rds from this set were randomly seeded in special retail boxes and each features a manufactured patch of an NFL team logo. Note that many cards were issued with the incorrect team patch on them since this set was intended to reflect a "mock draft." The swatches were easy to remove and reapply creating numerous, possibly countless, possible variations so no variations are listed below. We list just the original team swatch.

STATED PRINT RUN 1074 SER.#'d SETS.
RTPAA Jake Locker 2.00 5.00
RTPAS Aldon Smith 2.00 5.00
RTPAW Corey Liuget 2.00 5.00
RTPBG Blaine Gabbert 2.00 5.00
RTPCJ Cameron Heyward 2.50 6.00
RTPAC Adrian Clayborn 2.00 5.00
RTPCN Cam Newton 10.00 25.00
RTPCP Christian Ponder 2.00 5.00
RTPDB Da'Quan Bowers 2.00 5.00
RTPGC Gabe Carimi 2.50 6.00
RTPJH Jon Baldwin 2.50 6.00
RTPJJ Julio Jones 6.00 15.00
RTPJS Jimmy Smith 2.00 5.00
RTPMD Marcell Dareus 2.00 5.00
RTPMI Mark Ingram 3.00 8.00
RTPMP Mike Pouncey 3.00 8.00
RTPMW Muhammad Wilkerson 2.00 5.00
RTPNF Nick Fairley 2.00 5.00
RTPNS Nate Solder 2.00 5.00
RTPPA Prince Amukamara 2.00 5.00
RTPPP Patrick Peterson 4.00 10.00
RTPPT Phil Taylor 2.00 5.00
RTPRC Christian Ballard 2.00 5.00
RTPRK Ryan Kerrigan 2.50 6.00
RTPML Mikel Leshoure 2.00 5.00
RTPRQ Robert Quinn 2.00 5.00
RTPTS Torrey Smith 2.00 5.00
RTPVM Von Miller 3.00 8.00
RTPACA Anthony Castonzo 2.00 5.00
RTPAJG A.J. Green 5.00 12.00
RTPJJW J.J. Watt 10.00 25.00
RTPTSM Tyron Smith 2.50 6.00

2011 Topps Rising Rookies Triple Autographs

ATED PRINT RUN 25 SER.#'d SETS
UNPRICED GOLD PRINT RUN 5
EXCH EXPIRATION: 5/31/2014
TABDF Bowrs/Dreus/Frly 20.00 50.00
TABMS Bowers/Miller/Smith
TAGJS Green/Jones/Smith 60.00 120.00
TAHCB Hankersn/Cobb/Baldwin 20.00 50.00
TAIJD Ingrm/Jnes/Dareus EX 60.00 120.00
TAILW Ingram/Leshre/Will 50.00 100.00
TAMSI Moreno/Spiller/Ingram 40.00 80.00
TANGL Nwtn/Gbbrt/Lcker 175.00 300.00
TASBG Stfrd/Brdfrd/Gbbrt 30.00 80.00
TASHL Smith/Hankerson/Little 25.00 60.00

2008 Topps Rookie Progression

This set was released on May 21, 2008. The base set consists of 220 cards, which have some rookie cards scattered among the veterans and legends. Each pack contained at least one rookie card.

COMPLETE SET (220) 30.00 60.00
1 Drew Brees .40 1.00
2 Jon Kitna .25 .60
3 Tom Brady 1.25 3.00
4 Chad Pennington .25 .60
5 Steve McNair .30 .75
6 Josh McCown .25 .60
7 Matt Hasselbeck .25 .60
8 David Garrard .25 .60
9 Jay Cutler .25 .60
10 Matt Schaub .25 .60
11 Daunte Culpepper .30 .75
12 Kellen Clemens .25 .60
13 John Beck .25 .60
14 Trent Edwards .25 .60
15 Steven Jackson .25 .60
16 Willie Parker .30 .75
17 Derrick Ward .25 .60
18 Julius Jones .25 .60
19 DeShaun Foster .25 .60
20 Shaun Alexander .25 .60
21 Reggie Bush .25 .60
22 Clinton Portis .25 .60
23 Ron Dayne .25 .60
24 Maurice Jones-Drew .25 .60
25 Warrick Dunn .25 .60
26 Adrian Peterson .40 1.00
27 Brian Leonard .25 .60
28 Greg Jennings .25 .60
29 Torry Holt .30 .75
30 T.J. Houshmandzadeh .25 .60
31 Jerricho Cotchery .25 .60
32 Derrick Mason .25 .60
33 Kevin Curtis .25 .60
34 Kevin Walter .30 .75
35 Joey Galloway .30 .75
36 Anquan Boldin .25 .60
37 Santonio Holmes .25 .60
38 Lee Evans .30 .75
39 Dwayne Bowe .30 .75
40 Laurent Robinson .25 .60
41 Antonio Gates .30 .75
42 Chris Cooley .25 .60
43 Owen Daniels .25 .60
44 Patrick Kerney .25 .60
45 Gaines Adams .25 .60
46 Jon Beason .25 .60
47 Antonio Cromartie .25 .60
48 Bob Sanders .30 .75
49 Reggie Nelson .25 .60
50 John Elway .75 2.00
51 Allen Patrick RC .50 1.25
52 Steve Young .60 1.50
53 Bruce Davis RC .60 1.50
54 Cliff Avril RC .75 2.00
55 Chevis Jackson RC .50 1.25
56 Peyton Manning 1.00 2.50
57 Carson Palmer .30 .75
58 Ben Roethlisberger .40 1.00
59 Eli Manning .30 .75
60 Tony Romo .30 .75
61 Donovan McNabb .30 .75
62 Joey Harrington .25 .60
63 Jeff Garcia .25 .60
64 Derek Anderson .25 .60
65 Rex Grossman .25 .60
66 Kyle Boller .25 .60
67 Sage Rosenfels .25 .60
68 JaMarcus Russell .25 .60
69 Jerious Norwood .25 .60
70 Thomas Jones .25 .60
71 LaDainian Tomlinson .40 1.00
72 Cedric Benson .25 .60
73 Marion Barber .25 .60
74 Brian Westbrook .25 .60
75 LenDale White .25 .60
76 Ronnie Brown .25 .60
77 Travis Henry .25 .60
78 Kenny Watson .25 .60
79 Fred Taylor .25 .60
80 Ryan Grant .30 .75
81 Marshawn Lynch .30 .75
82 Selvin Young .25 .60
83 Wes Welker .30 .75
84 Roy Williams WR .25 .60
85 Randy Moss .30 .75
86 Plaxico Burress .25 .60
87 Terrell Owens .30 .75
88 Andre Johnson .30 .75
89 Roddy White .25 .60
90 Brandon Marshall .30 .75
91 Donald Driver .30 .75
92 Hines Ward .30 .75
93 Ike Hilliard .25 .60
94 James Jones .25 .60
95 Calvin Johnson .40 1.00
96 Kellen Winslow .25 .60
97 Tony Gonzalez .30 .75
98 Osi Umenyiora .25 .60
99 Mario Williams .30 .75
100 D.J. Williams .25 .60
101 Ernie Sims .25 .60
102 Marcus Trufant .25 .60
103 Sean Taylor .40 1.00
104 Troy Aikman .60 1.50
105 Dan Marino 1.00 2.50
106 Dantrell Savage RC .60 1.50
107 DJ Hall RC .50 1.25
108 Eddie Royal RC .50 1.25
109 Harry Douglas RC .60 1.50
110 Marcus Griffin RC .50 1.25
111 Marc Bulger .25 .60
112 Peyton Hillis RC .75 2.00
113 Philip Rivers .40 1.00
114 Vince Young .25 .60
115 Kurt Warner .30 .75
116 Cleo Lemon .25 .60
117 Damon Huard .25 .60
118 Jason Campbell .25 .60
119 Brian Griese .25 .60
120 Tarvaris Jackson .25 .60
121 J.P. Losman .25 .60
122 Troy Smith .30 .75
123 Brady Quinn .25 .60
124 Joseph Addai .25 .60
125 Laurence Maroney .30 .75
126 Brandon Jacobs .25 .60
127 Willis McGahee .25 .60
128 Frank Gore .30 .75
129 Edgerrin James .30 .75
130 Kevin Jones .25 .60
131 DeAngelo Williams .25 .60
132 Jamal Lewis .30 .75
133 Chester Taylor .25 .60
134 Earnest Graham .25 .60
135 Justin Fargas .25 .60
136 Kolby Smith .25 .60
137 Marques Colston .25 .60
138 Reggie Wayne .30 .75
139 Chad Johnson .25 .60
140 Amani Toomer .25 .60
141 Bernard Berrian .25 .60
142 Steve Smith .30 .75
143 Larry Fitzgerald .30 .75
144 Chris Chambers .25 .60
145 Braylon Edwards .25 .60
146 David Patten .25 .60
147 Bobby Engram .25 .60
148 Shaun McDonald .25 .60
149 Anthony Gonzalez .25 .60
150 Sidney Rice .25 .60
151 Jason Witten .30 .75
152 Greg Olsen .30 .75
153 Jared Allen .25 .60
154 DeMarcus Ware .30 .75
155 Nick Barnett .25 .60
156 Patrick Willis .30 .75
157 Ed Reed .30 .75
158 Asante Samuel .25 .60
159 Rafael Little RC .60 1.50
160 Joe Montana 1.50 4.00
161 Lawrence Jackson RC .50 1.25
162 Chauncey Washington RC .60 1.50
163 Keenan Burton RC .50 1.25
164 John Carlson RC .50 1.25
165 Dorien Bryant RC .60 1.50
166 Adarius Bowman RC .60 1.50
167 Ali Highsmith RC .50 1.25
168 Andre Woodson RC .50 1.25
169 Darren McFadden RC .50 1.25
170 Brian Brohm RC .50 1.25
171 Brandon Flowers RC .60 1.50
172 Matt Ryan RC 1.50 4.00
173 Calais Campbell RC .60 1.50
174 Quentin Groves RC .60 1.50
175 Curtis Lofton RC .60 1.50
176 Justin Forsett RC .60 1.50
177 Lavelle Hawkins RC .60 1.50
178 DeSean Jackson RC 1.00 2.50
179 Dan Connor RC .50 1.25
180 Dennis Dixon RC .50 1.25
181 Derrick Harvey RC .50 1.25
182 Erik Ainge RC .50 1.25
183 Earl Bennett RC .75 2.00
184 Early Doucet RC .50 1.25
185 Erin Henderson RC .60 1.50
186 Felix Jones RC .50 1.25
187 James Hardy RC .50 1.25
188 Jonathan Stewart RC .75 2.00
189 Kenny Phillips RC .50 1.25
190 Keith Rivers RC .50 1.25
191 Kevin Smith RC .50 1.25
192 Mike Jenkins RC .50 1.25
193 Malcom Kelly RC .50 1.25
194 Mike Hart RC .50 1.25
195 Chad Henne RC .60 1.50
196 Jake Long RC .75 2.00
197 Mario Manningham RC .50 1.25
198 Rashard Mendenhall RC .50 1.25
199 Reggie Smith RC .50 1.25
200 Ray Rice RC .50 1.25
201 Steve Slaton RC .50 1.25
202 Tracy Porter RC .60 1.50
203 Jerod Mayo RC .75 2.00
204 John David Booty RC .50 1.25
205 Fred Davis RC .50 1.25
206 Sedrick Ellis RC .50 1.25
207 Chris Johnson RC .60 1.50
208 Andre Caldwell RC .50 1.25
209 Tashard Choice RC .50 1.25
210 Glenn Dorsey RC .50 1.25
211 Vernon Gholston RC .50 1.25
212 Chris Long RC .60 1.50
213 Xavier Adibi RC .50 1.25
214 Donnie Avery RC .60 1.50
215 Colt Brennan RC .60 1.50
216 Kentwan Balmer RC .50 1.25
217 Jamaal Charles RC .75 2.00
218 Limas Sweed RC .50 1.25
219 Matt Forte RC .75 2.00
220 Owen Schmitt RC .50 1.25

2008 Topps Rookie Progression Bronze

ETS: 1.5X TO 4X BASIC CARDS
*ROOKIES: .6X TO 1.5X BASIC CARDS
BRONZE/389 STATED ODDS 1:8S

2008 Topps Rookie Progression Gold

*VETS: 2.5X TO 6X BASIC CARDS
*ROOKIES: 1X TO 2.5X BASIC CARDS
GOLD/199 STATED ODDS 1:15

2008 Topps Rookie Progression Platinum

*VETS: 3X TO 8X BASIC CARDS
*ROOKIES: 1.2X TO 3X BASIC CARDS
PLATINUM/99 STATED ODDS 1:29

2008 Topps Rookie Progression Silver

*VETS: 2X TO 5X BASIC CARDS
*ROOKIES: .8X TO 2X BASIC CARDS
SILVER/299 STATED ODDS 1:10

2008 Topps Rookie Progression Game Worn Jerseys

GROUP A ODDS 1:2300
GROUP B ODDS 1:3117
GROUP C ODDS 1:1400
GROUP D ODDS 1:4950
GROUP E ODDS 1:263
GROUP F ODDS 1:623
GROUP G ODDS 1:207
GROUP H ODDS 1:339
AB Adarius Bowman A 4.00 10.00
AC Andre Caldwell A 3.00 8.00
AH Ali Highsmith A 3.00 8.00
AP Adrian Peterson E 4.00 10.00
AW Andre Woodson A 3.00 8.00
BD Bruce Davis H 2.50 6.00
BU Brian Urlacher E 4.00 10.00
BW Brian Westbrook E 2.50 6.00
CB Colt Brennan B 3.00 8.00
CH Chad Henne B 3.00 8.00
CW Chauncey Washington D 2.50 6.00
DA Donnie Avery A 4.00 10.00
DB Dorien Bryant B 3.00 8.00
DBO Dwayne Bowe E 3.00 8.00
DC Dan Connor A 3.00 8.00
DD Donald Driver E 3.00 8.00
DH DJ Hall C 2.00 5.00
DJ Dexter Jackson G 3.00 8.00
DM Donovan McNabb E 3.00 8.00
DR Dominique Rodgers-Cromartie C 2.50 6.00
DS Dantrell Savage C 2.50 6.00
DST Donte Stallworth E 2.50 6.00
EA Erik Ainge B 2.50 6.00
ER Eddie Royal A 3.00 8.00
FT Fred Taylor E 2.50 6.00
HD Harry Douglas A 4.00 10.00
JA Joseph Addai E 2.50 6.00
JB John David Booty B 2.50 6.00
JF Justin Forsett A 4.00 10.00
JF Joe Flacco C 4.00 10.00
JG Joey Galloway E 3.00 8.00
JH Jacob Hester A 3.00 8.00
JN Jordy Nelson G 6.00 15.00
KR Keith Rivers A 3.00 8.00
LH Lavelle Hawkins A 4.00 10.00
LJ Lawrence Jackson G 2.00 5.00
LM Leodis McKelvin F 2.50 6.00
LT LaDainian Tomlinson E 4.00 10.00
MF Matt Forte A 5.00 12.00
MG Marcus Griffin C 2.00 5.00
ML Marshawn Lynch E 3.00 8.00
MS Marcus Smith H 2.50 6.00
PH Peyton Hillis G 3.00 8.00
RL Rafael Little E 2.50 6.00
SE Sedrick Ellis F 2.00 5.00
SM Shawne Merriman E 2.50 6.00
TC Tashard Choice A 3.00 8.00
TO Terrell Owens E 3.00 8.00
VY Vince Young E 2.50 6.00
YB Yvenson Bernard C 3.00 8.00

2008 Topps Rookie Progression Game Worn Jerseys Bronze

ONZE/189 GRP A ODDS 1:284
BRONZE/249 GRP B ODDS 1:84
*GOLD/99: .5X TO 1.2X BRONZE JSYs
GOLD/99 ODDS 1:154
*PLATINUM/29: .8X TO 2X BRONZE JSYs
PLATINUM/29 ODDS 1:650
*SILVER/179: .4X TO 1X BRONZE JSYs
SILVER/179 ODDS 1:84
AB Adarius Bowman/189 2.50 6.00
AC Andre Caldwell/189 2.00 5.00
AH Ali Highsmith/249 2.50 6.00
AP Adrian Peterson/249 4.00 10.00
AW Andre Woodson/189 4.00 10.00
BD Bruce Davis/249 2.50 6.00
BU Brian Urlacher/249 4.00 10.00
BW Brian Westbrook/249 2.50 8.00
CB Colt Brennan/189 2.50 6.00
CH Chad Henne/189 2.50 6.00
CW Chauncey Washington/249 2.50 6.00
DA Donnie Avery/189 2.50 6.00
DB Dorien Bryant/189 2.50 6.00
DBO Dwayne Bowe/249 3.00 8.00
DC Dan Connor/189 2.00 5.00
DD Donald Driver/249 3.00 8.00
DH DJ Hall/249 2.00 5.00
DJ Dexter Jackson/249 3.00 8.00
DM Donovan McNabb/249 3.00 8.00
DR Dominique Rodgers-Cromartie/249 2.50 6.00
DS Dantrell Savage/249 2.50 6.00
DST Donte Stallworth/249 2.50 6.00
EA Erik Ainge/189 5.00 12.00
ER Eddie Royal/189 2.00 5.00
FT Fred Taylor/249 2.50 6.00
HD Harry Douglas/189 2.50 6.00
JA Joseph Addai/249 2.50 6.00
JB John David Booty/189 2.00 5.00
JF Joe Flacco/249 4.00 10.00
JFO Justin Forsett/189 2.50 6.00
JG Joey Galloway/249 3.00 8.00
JH Jacob Hester/189 2.00 5.00
JN Jordy Nelson/249 6.00 15.00
KR Keith Rivers/189 2.00 5.00
LH Lavelle Hawkins/189 2.50 6.00
LJ Lawrence Jackson/249 3.00 8.00
LM Leodis McKelvin/249 2.50 6.00
LT LaDainian Tomlinson/249 4.00 10.00
MF Matt Forte/189 3.00 8.00
MG Marcus Griffin/249 2.00 5.00
ML Marshawn Lynch/249 3.00 8.00
MS Marcus Smith/249 2.50 6.00
PH Peyton Hillis/249 3.00 8.00
RL Rafael Little/249 2.50 6.00
SE Sedrick Ellis/249 2.00 5.00
SM Shawne Merriman/249 2.50 6.00
TC Tashard Choice/189 2.00 5.00
TO Terrell Owens/249 3.00 8.00
VY Vince Young/249 2.50 6.00
YB Yvenson Bernard/249 3.00 8.00

2008 Topps Rookie Progression Game Worn Jerseys Dual

GROUP A ODDS 1:4650
GROUP B ODDS 1:861
*BRONZE/99: .3X TO .8X BASIC DUAL
BRONZE/99 ODDS 1:306
*SILVER/50: .4X TO 1X BASIC DUAL
SILVER/50 ODDS 1:620
*GOLD/25: .5X TO 1.2X BASIC DUAL
GOLD/25 ODDS 1:1300
UNPRICED PLATINUM/10 ODDS 1:2950
PDRAB D.Avery/D.Bryant A 4.00 10.00
PDRAF E.Aingle/J.Flacco A 6.00 15.00
PDRAH J.Addai/J.Hester B 3.00 8.00
PDRBH J.Booty/C.Henne B 4.00 10.00
PDRCF T.Choice/J.Forsett A 4.00 10.00
PDRCH A.Caldwell/D.Hall B 3.00 8.00
PDRCR D.Connor/K.Rivers A 3.00 8.00
PDRDG T.DeCoud/M.Griffin B 3.00 8.00
PDREJ S.Ellis/L.Jackson B 3.00 8.00
PDRHB L.Hawkins/A.Bowman A 4.00 10.00
PDRJH C.Jackson/A.Highsmith B 3.00 8.00
PDRLF M.Lynch/J.Forsett B 4.00 10.00
PDRMR L.McKelvin/D.Rodgers B 4.00 10.00
PDRMW D.McNabb/B.Westbrook B 4.00 10.00
PDRPT A.Peterson/L.Tomlinson B 15.00 40.00
PDRPW T.Porter/D.Wolfe B 4.00 10.00
PDRRD E.Royal/H.Douglas B 4.00 10.00
PDRSB D.Savage/Y.Bernard B 5.00 12.00
PDRTC F.Taylor/A.Caldwell B 3.00 8.00
PDRTT T.Thomas/D.Tribble B 3.00 8.00
PDRUC B.Urlacher/D.Connor B 5.00 12.00
PDRUM B.Urlacher/S.Merriman B 5.00 12.00
PDRWB A.Woodson/C.Brennan A 4.00 10.00
PDRWF C.Washington/M.Forte A 5.00 12.00
PDRYP V.Young/A.Peterson B 15.00 40.00

2008 Topps Rookie Progression Game Worn Jerseys Triple

BASE TRIPLE ODDS 1:1035
*BRONZE/99: .3X TO .8X BASIC TRIPLE
BRONZE/99 ODDS 1:512
*SILVER/50: .4X TO 1X BASIC TRIPLE
SILVER/50 ODDS 1:1035
*GOLD/25: .5X TO 1.2X BASIC TRIPLE
GOLD/25 ODDS 1:2150
UNPRICED PLATINUM/10 ODDS 1:5050
BAF Brennan/Ainge/Flacco 6.00 15.00
BAH Bryant/Avery/Hall 4.00 10.00
BHW Booty/Henne/Woodson 4.00 10.00
CFF Choice/Forsett/Forte 5.00 12.00
CRH Connor/Rivers/Highsmith 3.00 8.00
DWM Davis/Wheeler/Moffitt 4.00 10.00
HCB Hawkins/Caldwell/Bowman 4.00 10.00
HHJ Hester/Highsmith/Jackson 3.00 8.00
JER Jackson/Ellis/Rivers 3.00 8.00
JTT Jackson/Tribble/Thomas 3.00 8.00
LRA Laws/Robertson/Avril 5.00 12.00
NRD Nelson/Royal/Douglas 4.00 10.00
OBD Owens/Bowe/Driver 6.00 15.00
RMP Cromartie/McKelvin/Porter 4.00 10.00
WHH Washington/Hester/Hillis 3.00 8.00

2008 Topps Rookie Progression Game Worn Jerseys Quad

BASE QUAD ODDS 1:3225
*BRONZE/50: .3X TO .8X BASIC QUAD
BRONZE/50 ODDS 1:1558
*SILVER/25: .4X TO 1X BASIC QUAD
SILVER/25 ODDS 1:3250
UNPRICED GOLD/10 ODDS 1:7550
UNPRICED PLATINUM/1 ODDS 1:90,000
1 Choice/Forte/Ptrsn/Lynch 20.00 50.00
2 Henne/Wdson/Yng/McN 5.00 12.00
3 Forsett/Hawk/Sav/Bwmn 5.00 12.00
4 Flacco/Ainge/Brenn/Booty 8.00 20.00
5 Gallo/Stallw/Smith/Jcksn 6.00 15.00
6 Caldwell/Avery/Bryant/Hall 5.00 12.00
7 Merr/Urlach/Connor/Rivers 6.00 15.00
8 Taylr/Wstbrk/Addai/Tomlin 6.00 15.00
9 Griffin/Castil/DeCoud/Wlfe 4.00 10.00
10 Booty/Wash/Wdson/Little 4.00 10.00

2008 Topps Rookie Progression Legends

RONZE/389: .5X TO 1.2X BASIC INSERTS
L/R/V BRONZE/389 ODDS 1:16
*SILVER/299: .6X TO 1.5X BASIC INSERTS
L/R/V SILVER/299 ODDS 1:21
*GOLD/199: .8X TO 2X BASIC INSERTS
L/R/V GOLD/199 ODDS 1:32
*PLATINUM/50: 1X TO 2.5X BASIC INSERTS
L/R/V PLATINUM/50 ODDS 1:125
PLAG Antonio Gates .60 1.50
PLBE Braylon Edwards .50 1.25
PLBR Ben Roethlisberger .75 2.00
PLBW Brian Westrbook .50 1.25
PLCP Carson Palmer .60 1.50
PLDB Drew Brees .75 2.00
PLDM Dan Marino 1.50 4.00
PLFT Fred Taylor .50 1.25
PLJE John Elway 1.25 3.00
PLJL Jamal Lewis .60 1.50
PLJM Joe Montana 2.50 6.00
PLLF Larry Fitzgerald .60 1.50
PLLT LaDainian Tomlinson .75 2.00
PLPM Peyton Manning 2.00 5.00
PLRM Randy Moss .60 1.50
PLSJ Steven Jackson .50 1.25
PLSY Steve Young 1.00 2.50
PLTA Troy Aikman 1.00 2.50
PLTB Tom Brady 2.50 6.00
PLTO Terrell Owens .60 1.50

2008 Topps Rookie Progression Legends Game Worn Jerseys Bronze

BRONZE/99 ODDS 1:1525
*SILVER/79: .4X TO 1X BRONZE JSY
SILVER/79 ODDS 1:1942
*GOLD/50: .5X TO 1.2X BRONZE JSY
GOLD/50 ODDS 1:3117
UNPRICED L/V/R PLAT.AU/20 ODDS 1:554
PLDM Dan Marino 12.00 30.00
PLJE John Elway 10.00 25.00
PLJM Joe Montana 20.00 50.00
PLSY Steve Young 6.00 15.00
PLTA Troy Aikman 8.00 20.00

2008 Topps Rookie Progression Rookie Autographs Blue

BLUE GROUP A/79 ODDS 1:290
BLUE GROUP B/299 ODDS 1:1505
BLUE GROUP C/499 ODDS 1:895
BLUE GROUP D/999 ODDS 1:149
*RED VERSION: SAME PRICE
166 Adarius Bowman/999 3.00 8.00
168 Andre Woodson/79 4.00 10.00
169 Darren McFadden/79 4.00 10.00
170 Brian Brohm/79 4.00 10.00
172 Matt Ryan/79 30.00 80.00
178 DeSean Jackson/79 8.00 20.00
180 Dennis Dixon/79 4.00 10.00
184 Early Doucet/79 4.00 10.00
186 Felix Jones/79 4.00 10.00
188 Jonathan Stewart/79 6.00 15.00
189 Kenny Phillips/499 2.50 6.00
193 Malcolm Kelly/79 4.00 10.00
194 Mike Hart/79 4.00 10.00
195 Chad Henne/79 5.00 12.00
196 Jake Long/299 5.00 12.00
197 Mario Manningham/79 8.00 20.00
198 Rashard Mendenhall/79 4.00 10.00
200 Ray Rice/79 4.00 10.00
201 Steve Slaton/79 4.00 10.00
204 John David Booty/79 4.00 10.00
205 Fred Davis/999 2.50 6.00
207 Chris Johnson/999 3.00 8.00
215 Colt Brennan/79 5.00 12.00
218 Limas Sweed/79 4.00 10.00

2008 Topps Rookie Progression Rookie Autographs Blue Bronze

BRONZE/35 ODDS 1:271
*SILVER/20: .6X TO 1.5X BRONZE AU/35
SILVER/20 ODDS 1:497
UNPRICED GOLD/10 ODDS 1:892
UNPRICED PLATINUM/1 ODDS 1:9000
RED VERSION SAME PRICE
166 Adarius Bowman 6.00 15.00
168 Andre Woodson 5.00 12.00
169 Darren McFadden 5.00 12.00
170 Brian Brohm 5.00 12.00
172 Matt Ryan 30.00 80.00
178 DeSean Jackson 10.00 25.00
180 Dennis Dixon 5.00 12.00
184 Early Doucet 5.00 12.00
186 Felix Jones 5.00 12.00
188 Jonathan Stewart 8.00 20.00
189 Kenny Phillips 5.00 12.00
193 Malcolm Kelly 5.00 12.00
194 Mike Hart 5.00 12.00
195 Chad Henne 6.00 15.00
196 Jake Long 8.00 20.00
197 Mario Manningham 10.00 25.00
198 Rashard Mendenhall 5.00 12.00
200 Ray Rice 5.00 12.00
201 Steve Slaton 5.00 12.00
204 John David Booty 5.00 12.00
205 Fred Davis 5.00 12.00
207 Chris Johnson 6.00 15.00
210 Glenn Dorsey
215 Colt Brennan 6.00 15.00
218 Limas Sweed 5.00 12.00

2008 Topps Rookie Progression Rookies

RONZE/389: .5X TO 1.2X BASIC INSERTS
L/R/V BRONZE/389 ODDS 1:16
*SILVER/299: .6X TO 1.5X BASIC INSERTS
L/R/V SILVER/299 ODDS 1:21
*GOLD/199: .8X TO 2X BASIC INSERTS
L/R/V GOLD/199 ODDS 1:32
*PLATINUM/50: 1X TO 2.5X BASIC INSERTS
L/R/V PLATINUM/50 ODDS 1:125
PRAB Adarius Bowman .60 1.50
PRAC Andre Caldwell .50 1.25
PRAH Ali Highsmith .50 1.25
PRAW Andre Woodson .50 1.25
PRBB Brian Brohm .50 1.25
PRBM Ben Moffitt .50 1.25
PRCB Colt Brennan .60 1.50
PRCG Charles Godfrey .50 1.25
PRCH Chad Henne .60 1.50
PRCJ Chris Johnson .60 1.50
PRCW Chauncey Washington .60 1.50
PRDA Donnie Avery .60 1.50
PRDB Dorien Bryant .60 1.50
PRDC Dan Connor .50 1.25
PRDH DJ Hall .50 1.25
PRDR Darrell Robertson .50 1.25
PRDRC Dominique Rodgers-Cromartie .60 1.50
PRDS Dantrell Savage .60 1.50
PREA Erik Ainge .50 1.25
PRED Early Doucet .50 1.25
PRER Eddie Royal .50 1.25
PRFD Fred Davis .50 1.25
PRHD Harry Douglas .60 1.50
PRJB John David Booty .50 1.25
PRJF Joe Flacco 1.00 2.50
PRJFO Justin Forsett .60 1.50
PRJH Jacob Hester .50 1.25
PRJN Jordy Nelson 1.50 4.00
PRKB Keenan Burton .50 1.25
PRKD Kellen Davis .50 1.25
PRKR Keith Rivers .50 1.25
PRLH Lavelle Hawkins .60 1.50
PRLJ Lawrence Jackson .50 1.25
PRLM Leodis McKelvin .60 1.50
PRLS Limas Sweed .50 1.25
PRMF Matt Forte .75 2.00
PRMG Marcus Griffin .50 1.25
PRMJ Mike Jenkins .50 1.25
PRMR Matt Ryan 1.50 4.00
PRMRU Martin Rucker .50 1.25
PRMS Marcus Smith .60 1.50
PRPH Peyton Hillis .75 2.00
PRQG Quentin Groves .60 1.50
PRRL Rafael Little .60 1.50
PRSE Sedrick Ellis .50 1.25
PRTC Tashard Choice .50 1.25
PRTD Thomas DeCoud .50 1.25
PRTP Tracy Porter .60 1.50
PRTZ Tom Zbikowski .60 1.50
PRYB Yvenson Bernard .75 2.00

2008 Topps Rookie Progression Rookies Game Worn Jerseys Bronze

ONZE PRINT RUN 299 SER.#'d SETS
*SILVER/199: .5X TO 1.2X BRONZE JSY
SILVER PRINT RUN 199 SER.#'d SETS
*GOLD/99: .6X TO 1.5X BRONZE JSY
GOLD PRINT RUN 99 SER.#'d SETS
UNPRICED L/V/R PLAT.AU/20 ODDS 1:554
PRAB Adarius Bowman 2.50 6.00
PRAC Andre Caldwell 2.00 5.00
PRAH Ali Highsmith 2.00 5.00
PRAW Andre Woodson 2.00 5.00
PRCB Colt Brennan 2.50 6.00
PRCH Chad Henne 2.50 6.00
PRCJ Chris Johnson 2.50 6.00
PRCW Chauncey Washington 2.50 6.00
PRDA Donnie Avery 2.50 6.00
PRDB Dorien Bryant 2.50 6.00
PRDC Dan Connor 2.00 5.00
PRDH DJ Hall 2.00 5.00

PRDS Dantrell Savage 2.50 6.00
PREA Erik Ainge 2.00 5.00
PRED Early Doucet 2.00 5.00
PRER Eddie Royal 2.00 5.00
PRFD Fred Davis 2.00 5.00
PRHD Harry Douglas 2.50 6.00
PRJB John David Booty 2.00 5.00
PRJF Joe Flacco 4.00 10.00
PRJFO Justin Forsett 2.50 6.00
PRJH Jacob Hester 2.00 5.00
PRKB Keenan Burton 2.00 5.00
PRKR Keith Rivers 2.00 5.00
PRLH Lavelle Hawkins 2.50 6.00
PRLS Limas Sweed 2.00 5.00
PRMF Matt Forte 3.00 8.00
PRRL Rafael Little 2.50 6.00
PRTC Tashard Choice 2.00 5.00
PRYB Yvenson Bernard 3.00 8.00

2008 Topps Rookie Progression Signatures

GROUP A ODDS 1:1664
GROUP B ODDS 1:381
GROUP C ODDS 1:602
GROUP D ODDS 1:179
GROUP E ODDS 1:150
GROUP F ODDS 1:449
GROUP G ODDS 1:299
GROUP H ODDS 1:112
GROUP I ODDS 1:45
GROUP J ODDS 1:149
AB Adarius Bowman I 3.00 8.00
AW Andre Woodson B 3.00 8.00
BB Brian Brohm A 8.00 20.00
BJ Brandon Jacobs A 6.00 15.00
BW Brian Westbrook A 12.00 30.00
CB Colt Brennan A 10.00 25.00
CH Chad Henne A
CJ Chris Johnson J 3.00 8.00
CL Chris Long D 3.00 8.00
DA Derek Anderson A 8.00 20.00
DC Dan Connor E 2.50 6.00
DD Dennis Dixon B 8.00 20.00
DF De'Cody Fagg H 3.00 8.00
DH DJ Hall I 2.50 6.00
DJ DeSean Jackson B 6.00 15.00
DM Darren McFadden A 5.00 12.00
EA Erik Ainge E 2.50 6.00
EB Earl Bennett I 4.00 10.00
ED Early Doucett C 2.50 6.00
ES Ernie Sims E 3.00 8.00
FD Fred Davis H 2.50 6.00
FJ Felix Jones A 5.00 12.00
GD Glenn Dorsey D EXCH
GJ Greg Jennings B 3.00 8.00
JB John David Booty B 3.00 8.00
JF Joe Flacco B 6.00 15.00
JH James Hardy D 2.50 6.00
JL Jake Long F 4.00 10.00
JS Jonathan Stewart A 25.00 50.00
KR Keith Rivers D 2.50 6.00
KS Kevin Smith G 2.50 6.00
LS Limas Sweed B 3.00 8.00
LT LaDainian Tomlinson A 25.00 50.00
MB Marion Barber A 15.00 40.00
MH Mike Hart B 3.00 8.00
MK Malcolm Kelly C 2.50 6.00
ML Marshawn Lynch A 10.00 25.00
MM Mario Manningham D 2.50 6.00
MR Matt Ryan A 50.00 100.00
PM Peyton Manning A
PW Patrick Willis B 6.00 15.00
RG Ryan Grant B EXCH
RM Rashard Mendenhall A 5.00 12.00
RR Ray Rice E 2.50 6.00
RW Roddy White B 3.00 8.00
SS Steve Slaton B 3.00 8.00
TC Tashard Choice I 2.50 6.00
WW Wes Welker C 15.00 30.00

2008 Topps Rookie Progression Signatures Bronze

BRONZE/35 ODDS 1:282
*SILVER/20: .6X TO 1.5X BRONZE AU/35
AB Adarius Bowman 6.00 15.00
AW Andre Woodson 5.00 12.00
BB Brian Brohm 5.00 12.00
BJ Brandon Jacobs 8.00 20.00
BW Brian Westbrook 8.00 20.00
CB Colt Brennan 6.00 15.00
CH Chad Henne 6.00 15.00
CJ Chris Johnson 6.00 15.00
CL Chris Long 6.00 15.00
DA Derek Anderson 8.00 20.00
DC Dan Connor 5.00 12.00
DD Dennis Dixon 5.00 12.00
DF De'Cody Fagg 6.00 15.00
DH DJ Hall 5.00 12.00
DJ DeSean Jackson 10.00 25.00
DM Darren McFadden 5.00 12.00
EA Erik Ainge 5.00 12.00
EB Earl Bennett 8.00 20.00
ED Early Doucett 5.00 12.00
ES Ernie Sims 8.00 20.00
FD Fred Davis 5.00 12.00
FJ Felix Jones 5.00 12.00
GD Glenn Dorsey EXCH
GJ Greg Jennings 8.00 20.00
JB John David Booty 5.00 12.00
JF Joe Flacco 10.00 25.00
JH James Hardy 5.00 12.00
JL Jake Long 8.00 20.00
JS Jonathan Stewart 8.00 20.00
KR Keith Rivers 5.00 12.00
KS Kevin Smith 5.00 12.00
LS Limas Sweed 5.00 12.00
LT LaDainian Tomlinson 30.00 60.00
MB Marion Barber
MH Mike Hart 5.00 12.00
MK Malcolm Kelly 5.00 12.00
ML Marshawn Lynch 15.00 40.00
MM Mario Manningham 5.00 12.00
MR Matt Ryan 40.00 100.00
PM Peyton Manning 60.00 100.00
PW Patrick Willis 10.00 25.00
RG Ryan Grant EXCH
RM Rashard Mendenhall 5.00 12.00
RR Ray Rice 5.00 12.00
RW Roddy White 8.00 20.00
SS Steve Slaton 5.00 12.00
TC Tashard Choice 5.00 12.00
WW Wes Welker 25.00 50.00

2008 Topps Rookie Progression Signatures Dual

DUAL AUTO/20 ODDS 1:1663
GJ R.Grant/G.Jennings 8.00 20.00
HJ L.Hawkins/D.Jackson 25.00 50.00
HM M.Hall/M.Manningham 20.00 30.00
JB B.Jacobs/M.Barber 25.00 60.00
LF M.Lynch/J.Forsett 25.00 50.00
MA P.Manning/E.Ainge 75.00 150.00
MJ D.McFadden/F.Jones 8.00 20.00
RB M.Ryan/B.Brohm 100.00 200.00
RS R.Rice/S.Slaton 8.00 20.00
SB D.Savage/A.Bowman 20.00 40.00
SK L.Sweed/M.Kelly 20.00 50.00
SM J.Stewart/R.Mendenhall 12.00 30.00
TM L.Tomlinson/D.McFadden 12.00 30.00
WB A.Woodson/C.Brennan 12.00 30.00
WJ B.Westbrook/C.Johnson 10.00 25.00

2008 Topps Rookie Progression Signatures Triple

UNPRICED TRIPLE AU/10 ODDS 1:5030

2008 Topps Rookie Progression Veterans

RONZE/389: .5X TO 1.2X BASIC INSERTS
L/R/V BRONZE/389 ODDS 1:16
*SILVER/299: .6X TO 1.5X BASIC INSERTS
L/R/V SILVER/299 ODDS 1:21
*GOLD/199: .8X TO 2X BASIC INSERTS
L/R/V GOLD/199 ODDS 1:32
*PLATINUM/50: 1X TO 2.5X BASIC INSERTS
L/R/V PLATINUM/50 ODDS 1:125
PVAG Antonio Gates .75 2.00
PVAP Adrian Peterson 1.00 2.50
PVBE Braylon Edwards .60 1.50
PVBJ Brandon Jacobs .60 1.50
PVBM Brandon Marshall .75 2.00
PVBR Ben Roethlisberger 1.00 2.50
PVBW Brian Westrbook .60 1.50
PVCP Carson Palmer .75 2.00
PVCPO Clinton Portis .60 1.50
PVDA Derek Anderson .60 1.50
PVDB Drew Brees 1.00 2.50
PVDH Devin Hester .75 2.00
PVFT Fred Taylor .60 1.50
PVJA Joseph Addai .60 1.50
PVJL Jamal Lewis .75 2.00
PVKW Kellen Winslow .60 1.50
PVLF Larry Fitzgerald .75 2.00
PVLT LaDainian Tomlinson 1.00 2.50
PVPM Peyton Manning 2.50 6.00
PVRM Randy Moss .75 2.00
PVRW Reggie Wayne .75 2.00
PVSH Santonio Holmes .60 1.50
PVSJ Steven Jackson .60 1.50
PVTB Tom Brady 3.00 8.00
PVTH T.J. Houshmandzadeh .60 1.50
PVTO Terrell Owens .75 2.00
PVTR Tony Romo .75 2.00
PVVY Vince Young .60 1.50
PVWP Willie Parker .75 2.00

2008 Topps Rookie Progression Veterans Game Worn Jerseys Bronze

BRONZE PRINT RUN 299 SER.#'d SETS
*SILVER/199: .5X TO 1.2X BRONZE JSYs
SILVER PRINT RUN 199 SER.#'d SETS
*GOLD/99: .6X TO 1.5X BRONZE JSYs
GOLD PRINT RUN 99 SER.#'d SETS
UNPRICED L/V/R PLAT.AU/20 ODDS 1:554
PVAG Antonio Gates 3.00 8.00
PVBE Braylon Edwards 2.50 6.00
PVBJ Brandon Jacobs 2.50 6.00
PVBM Brandon Marshall 3.00 8.00
PVDA Derek Anderson 2.50 6.00
PVDB Drew Brees 4.00 10.00
PVDH Devin Hester 5.00 12.00
PVJA Joseph Addai 2.50 6.00
PVKW Kellen Winslow 2.50 6.00
PVLT LaDainian Tomlinson 4.00 10.00
PVPM Peyton Manning 10.00 25.00
PVRM Randy Moss 3.00 8.00
PVRW Reggie Wayne 3.00 8.00
PVSH Santonio Holmes 2.50 6.00
PVSJ Steven Jackson 2.50 6.00
PVTH T.J. Houshmandzadeh 2.50 6.00
PVTR Tony Romo 3.00 8.00
PVVY Vince Young 2.50 6.00
PVWP Willie Parker 3.00 8.00

2008 Topps Rookie Progression Veterans Game Worn Jerseys Platinum Autographs

TERAN PLAT.AU/20 ODDS 1:554
PVAG Antonio Gates 15.00 40.00
PVBE Braylon Edwards 12.00 30.00
PVBJ Brandon Jacobs 12.00 30.00
PVBM Brandon Marshall 15.00 40.00
PVDA Derek Anderson 12.00 30.00
PVDB Drew Brees 40.00 80.00
PVDH Devin Hester 15.00 40.00
PVJA Joseph Addai 12.00 30.00
PVKW Kellen Winslow 12.00 30.00
PVLT LaDainian Tomlinson 30.00 60.00
PVPM Peyton Manning 75.00 150.00
PVRM Randy Moss 40.00 80.00
PVRW Reggie Wayne 15.00 40.00
PVSH Santonio Holmes 12.00 30.00
PVSJ Steven Jackson 12.00 30.00
PVTH T.J. Houshmandzadeh 12.00 30.00
PVTR Tony Romo 50.00 100.00
PVVY Vince Young 12.00 30.00
PVWP Willie Parker 15.00 40.00

1998 Topps Season Opener

MPLETE SET (165) 30.00 80.00
*STARS: .4X TO 1X BASE TOPPS
SEASON OPENER RETAIL ONLY PRODUCT
1 Peyton Manning RC 8.00 20.00
2 Jerome Pathon RC 1.00 2.50
3 Duane Starks RC .50 1.25
4 Brian Simmons RC .75 2.00
5 Keith Brooking RC 1.00 2.50
6 Robert Edwards RC .75 2.00
7 Curtis Enis RC .50 1.25
8 John Avery RC .75 2.00
9 Fred Taylor RC 1.50 4.00
10 Germane Crowell RC .75 2.00
11 Hines Ward RC 4.00 10.00
12 Marcus Nash RC .50 1.25
13 Jacquez Green RC .75 2.00
14 Joe Jurevicius RC 1.00 2.50
15 Greg Ellis RC .50 1.25
16 Brian Griese RC 1.50 4.00
17 Tavian Banks RC .75 2.00
18 Robert Holcombe RC .75 2.00
19 Skip Hicks RC .75 2.00
20 Ahman Green RC 2.00 5.00
21 Takeo Spikes RC 1.00 2.50
22 Randy Moss RC 5.00 12.00
23 Andre Wadsworth RC .75 2.00
24 Jason Peter RC .50 1.25
25 Grant Wistrom RC .75 2.00
26 Charles Woodson RC 2.00 5.00
27 Kevin Dyson RC 1.00 2.50
28 Pat Johnson RC .75 2.00
29 Tim Dwight RC 1.00 2.50
30 Ryan Leaf RC 1.00 2.50

1999 Topps Season Opener

leased as a retail product, this 165-card set incorporates the 1999 Topps card-stock but is enhanced with a foil "Season Opener" stamp.

COMPLETE SET (165) 20.00 40.00
1 Jerry Rice .50 1.25
2 Emmitt Smith .30 .75
3 Curtis Martin .15 .40
4 Ed McCaffrey .15 .40
5 Oronde Gadsden .12 .30
6 Byron Bam Morris .12 .30
7 Michael Irvin .20 .50
8 Shannon Sharpe .15 .40
9 Levon Kirkland .12 .30
10 Fred Taylor .12 .30
11 Andre Reed .20 .50
12 Chad Brown .12 .30
13 Skip Hicks .12 .30
14 Tim Dwight .15 .40
15 Michael Sinclair .12 .30
16 Carl Pickens .15 .40
17 Derrick Alexander WR .12 .30
18 Kevin Greene .20 .50
19 Duce Staley .12 .30
20 Dan Marino .40 1.00
21 Frank Sanders .12 .30
22 Ricky Proehl .12 .30
23 Frank Wycheck .15 .40
24 Andre Rison .15 .40
25 Natrone Means .15 .40
26 Steve McNair .15 .40
27 Vonnie Holliday .12 .30
28 Charles Woodson .20 .50
29 Rob Moore .12 .30
30 John Elway .30 .75
31 Derrick Thomas .20 .50
32 Jake Plummer .12 .30
33 Mike Alstott .12 .30
34 Keenan McCardell .15 .40
35 Mark Chmura .12 .30
36 Keyshawn Johnson .15 .40
37 Priest Holmes .12 .30
38 Antonio Freeman .15 .40
39 Ty Law .20 .50
40 Jamal Anderson .15 .40
41 Courtney Hawkins .12 .30
42 James Jett .12 .30
43 Aaron Glenn .12 .30
44 Jimmy Smith .15 .40
45 Michael McCrary .12 .30
46 Junior Seau .15 .40
47 Bill Romanowski .15 .40
48 Mark Brunell .15 .40
49 Yancey Thigpen .12 .30
50 Steve Young .25 .60
51 Cris Carter .20 .50
52 Vinny Testaverde .12 .30
53 Zach Thomas .15 .40
54 Kordell Stewart .12 .30
55 Tim Biakabutuka .15 .40
56 J.J. Stokes .12 .30
57 Jon Kitna .12 .30
58 Jacquez Green .12 .30
59 Marvin Harrison .15 .40
60 Barry Sanders .30 .75
61 Darrell Green .20 .50
62 Terance Mathis .12 .30
63 Ricky Watters .15 .40
64 Chris Chandler .15 .40
65 Cameron Cleeland .12 .30
66 Rod Smith .15 .40
67 Freddie Jones .12 .30
68 Adrian Murrell .12 .30
69 Terrell Owens .15 .40
70 Troy Aikman .25 .60
71 John Mobley .12 .30
72 Corey Dillon .12 .30
73 Rickey Dudley .12 .30
74 Randall Cunningham .15 .40
75 Muhsin Muhammad .12 .30
76 Stephen Boyd .12 .30
77 Tony Gonzalez .15 .40
78 Deion Sanders .15 .40
79 Ben Coates .15 .40
80 Brett Favre .40 1.00
81 Shawn Springs .12 .30
82 Dorsey Levens .15 .40
83 Ray Buchanan .12 .30
84 Charlie Batch .12 .30
85 John Randle .20 .50
86 Eddie George .15 .40
87 Ray Lewis .20 .50
88 Johnnie Morton .15 .40
89 Kevin Hardy .12 .30
90 O.J. McDuffie .15 .40
91 Herman Moore .15 .40
92 Tim Brown .20 .50
93 Bert Emanuel .15 .40
94 Elvis Grbac .12 .30
95 Peter Boulware .12 .30
96 Curtis Conway .15 .40
97 Doug Flutie .20 .50
98 Jake Reed .15 .40
99 Ike Hilliard .12 .30
100 Randy Moss .15 .40
101 Warren Sapp .15 .40
102 Bruce Smith .15 .40
103 Joey Galloway .15 .40
104 Napoleon Kaufman .12 .30
105 Warrick Dunn .12 .30
106 Wayne Chrebet .12 .30
107 Robert Brooks .15 .40
108 Antowain Smith .12 .30
109 Trent Dilfer .12 .30
110 Peyton Manning .60 1.50
111 Isaac Bruce .20 .50
112 John Lynch .15 .40
113 Terry Glenn .15 .40
114 Garrison Hearst .12 .30
115 Jerome Bettis .20 .50
116 Darnay Scott .12 .30
117 Lamar Thomas .12 .30
118 Chris Spielman .15 .40
119 Robert Smith .12 .30
120 Drew Bledsoe .15 .40
121 Reidel Anthony .12 .30
122 Wesley Walls .15 .40
123 Eric Moulds .12 .30
124 Terrell Davis .15 .40
125 Dale Carter .12 .30
126 Charles Johnson .12 .30
127 Steve Atwater .15 .40
128 Jim Harbaugh .15 .40
129 Tony Martin .15 .40
130 Kerry Collins .12 .30
131 Trent Green .12 .30
132 Marshall Faulk .15 .40
133 Rocket Ismail .15 .40
134 Warren Moon .20 .50
135 Jerris McPhail .12 .30
136 Damon Gibson .12 .30
137 Jim Pyne .12 .30
138 Antonio Langham .12 .30
139 Freddie Solomon .12 .30
140 Randy Moss SH .15 .40
141 John Elway SH .30 .75
142 Doug Flutie SH .20 .50
143 Emmitt Smith SH .30 .75
144 Terrell Davis SH .15 .40
145 Troy Edwards RC .40 1.00
146 Torry Holt RC .75 2.00
147 Tim Couch RC .50 1.25
148 Sedrick Irvin RC .40 1.00
149 Ricky Williams RC .60 1.50
150 Peerless Price RC .40 1.00
151 Mike Cloud RC .40 1.00
152 Kevin Faulk RC .40 1.00
153 Kevin Johnson RC .50 1.25
154 James Johnson RC .40 1.00
155 Edgerrin James RC .60 1.50
156 D'Wayne Bates RC .40 1.00
157 Donovan McNabb RC 2.50 6.00
158 David Boston RC .40 1.00
159 Daunte Culpepper RC .60 1.50
160 Champ Bailey RC .75 2.00
161 Cecil Collins RC .40 1.00
162 Cade McNown RC .40 1.00
163 Brock Huard RC .40 1.00
164 Akili Smith RC .40 1.00
165 Checklist Card .10 .30

1999 Topps Season Opener Autographs

Randomly inserted in packs at a rate of 1 in 7126 packs, these were hand signed cards of the number one picks within there respective drafts the two players who signed cards were number one draft picks Peyton Manning and Tim Couch.

STATED ODDS 1:7126
A1 Tim Couch 30.00 80.00
A2 Peyton Manning 60.00 150.00

1999 Topps Season Opener Football Fever

ese contest cards were inserted one per pack in 1999 Topps Season Opener. Each card featured a player and a game date. If that player passed for 300-yards, rushed for 100-yards, or caught passes for 100-yards during that date's game then the card was a winner. Winning entries were to be sent to Topps for a chance at various prizes including a trip to the 2000 Pro Bowl game. There were 7-winning cards as noted below.

COMPLETE SET (55) 10.00 20.00
ONE PER PACK
F1A Brett Favre 9/26 W .75 2.00
F1B Brett Favre 10/17 .40 1.00
F1C Brett Favre 11/07 .40 1.00
F1D Brett Favre 11/29 .40 1.00
F2A Jake Plummer 9/27 .07 .20
F2B Jake Plummer 10/03 .07 .20
F2C Jake Plummer 10/31 .07 .20
F2D Jake Plummer 12/05 .07 .20
F3A Drew Bledsoe 9/19 .15 .40
F3B Drew Bledsoe 10/03 W .30 .75
F3C Drew Bledsoe 10/24 .15 .40
F3D Drew Bledsoe 12/05 .15 .40
F4A Peyton Manning 9/12 .30 .75
F4B Peyton Manning 10/17 .30 .75
F4C Peyton Manning 10/24 .30 .75
F4D Peyton Manning 12/12 .30 .75
F5A Tim Couch 10/10 .08 .25
F5B Tim Couch 11/21 .08 .25
F5C Tim Couch 11/28 .08 .25
F5D Tim Couch 12/05 .08 .25
F6A Terrell Davis 9/13 .10 .30
F6B Terrell Davis 10/03 .10 .30
F6C Terrell Davis 10/31 .10 .30
F6D Terrell Davis 12/19 .10 .30
F7A Jamal Anderson 9/12 .10 .30
F7B Jamal Anderson 10/17 .10 .30
F7C Jamal Anderson 10/25 .10 .30
F7D Jamal Anderson 12/05 .10 .30
F8A Curtis Martin 9/12 .10 .30
F8B Curtis Martin 10/17 W .25 .60
F8C Curtis Martin 10/24 W .25 .60
F8D Curtis Martin 11/21 .10 .30
F9A Fred Taylor 9/26 .08 .25
F9B Fred Taylor 10/17 .08 .25
F9C Fred Taylor 10/31 W .20 .50
F9D Fred Taylor 12/12 .08 .25
F10A Ricky Williams 10/3 .20 .50
F10B Ricky Williams 10/10 .20 .50
F10C Ricky Williams 10/31 W .40 1.00
F10D Ricky Williams 12/12 .20 .50
F11A Antonio Freeman 9/26 .10 .30
F11B Antonio Freeman 11/29 .10 .30
F11C Antonio Freeman 12/12 .10 .30
F12A Jerry Rice 9/19 .25 .60
F12B Jerry Rice 10/24 .25 .60
F12C Jerry Rice 11/29 .25 .60
F13A Jimmy Smith 10/17 .07 .20
F13B Jimmy Smith 10/31 .07 .20
F13C Jimmy Smith 12/13 .07 .20
F14A Randy Moss 10/24 .30 .75
F14B Randy Moss 11/08 .30 .75
F14C Randy Moss 12/20 W .60 1.50
F15A Torry Holt 10/03 .20 .50
F15B Torry Holt 10/24 .20 .50
F15C Torry Holt 12/05 .20 .50

2000 Topps Season Opener

Released as a retail product, Topps Season Opener utilizes the same card stock as the regular Topps Set but replaced the blue border with a burgandy one and each card has a silver foil Season Opener stamp. Topps Season Opener was packaged in 24-pack boxes with each pack containing seven cards plus one Football Fever card.

COMPLETE SET (220) 15.00 40.00
1 Tyrone Wheatley .10 .25
2 Carl Pickens .12 .30
3 Zach Thomas .12 .30
4 Jacquez Green .10 .25
5 Sean Dawkins .10 .25
6 Brad Johnson .12 .30
7 Jerry Rice .40 1.00
8 Doug Flutie .12 .30
9 Cade McNown .10 .25
10 Rod Smith .12 .30
11 Kevin Hardy .10 .25
12 Marvin Harrison .12 .30
13 David Boston .10 .25
14 Priest Holmes .10 .25
15 Keith Poole .10 .25
16 Troy Edwards .10 .25
17 Robert Smith .10 .25
18 Kevin Lockett .10 .25
19 Johnnie Morton .12 .30
20 Terrell Davis .12 .30
21 Corey Bradford .10 .25
22 Keyshawn Johnson .12 .30
23 Tony Banks .10 .25
24 Matthew Hatchette .10 .25
25 Troy Aikman .20 .50
26 Natrone Means .12 .30
27 Peerless Price .12 .30
28 Bruce Smith .12 .30
29 Tim Couch .12 .30
30 Terrell Owens .12 .30
31 O.J. McDuffie .12 .30
32 Troy Brown .10 .25
33 Corey Dillon .10 .25
34 Cam Cleeland .10 .25
35 Brian Griese .10 .25
36 Shawn Springs .10 .25
37 Marcus Robinson .12 .30
38 Jermaine Lewis .10 .25
39 Olandis Gary .12 .30
40 Tony Gonzalez .12 .30
41 Frank Wycheck .12 .30
42 Jon Kitna .10 .25
43 Muhsin Muhammad .10 .25
44 Jerome Bettis .15 .40
45 Darrin Chiaverini .10 .25
46 Steve McNair .12 .30
47 Charlie Batch .10 .25
48 Steve Beuerlein .12 .30
49 Dorsey Levens .12 .30
50 Jim Harbaugh .12 .30
51 Jonathan Linton .10 .25
52 Napoleon Kaufman .12 .30
53 Curtis Enis .10 .25
54 Darnay Scott .12 .30
55 Tim Dwight .12 .30
56 Mikhael Ricks .10 .25
57 Kevin Dyson .12 .30
58 Antonio Freeman .12 .30
59 E.G. Green .10 .25
60 Jake Plummer .10 .25
61 Bill Schroeder .12 .30
62 Shaun King .10 .25
63 Michael Basnight .10 .25
64 Vinny Testaverde .10 .25
65 Rob Johnson .12 .30
66 Jeff Blake .12 .30
67 Marshall Faulk .12 .30
68 Keenan McCardell .12 .30
69 Michael Westbrook .10 .25
70 Yancey Thigpen .10 .25
71 Akili Smith .10 .25
72 Charles Woodson .15 .40
73 Qadry Ismail .10 .25
74 Pat Johnson .10 .25
75 Rocket Ismail .12 .30
76 Terrence Wilkins .10 .25
77 Herman Moore .10 .25
78 Jevon Kearse .10 .25
79 Oronde Gadsden .12 .30
80 Errict Rhett .12 .30
81 Ed McCaffrey .12 .30
82 Mike Alstott .10 .25
83 Stephen Alexander .10 .25
84 Mark Brunell .12 .30
85 Jeff George .12 .30
86 Stephen Davis .10 .25
87 Germane Crowell .10 .25
88 Charlie Garner .12 .30
89 Kordell Stewart .10 .25
90 Tim Biakabutuka .12 .30
91 Jim Miller .10 .25
92 Eddie George .12 .30
93 Joe Montgomery .10 .25
94 Wayne Chrebet .10 .25
95 Freddie Jones .10 .25
96 Ricky Proehl .10 .25
97 Warren Sapp .12 .30
98 Derrick Mayes .10 .25
99 Daunte Culpepper .12 .30
100 Torry Holt .12 .30
101 Isaac Bruce .15 .40
102 Kevin Johnson .10 .25
103 Antowain Smith .12 .30
104 Rob Moore .10 .25
105 Joey Galloway .12 .30
106 Rickey Dudley .10 .25
107 Terry Glenn .12 .30
108 Ike Hilliard .10 .25
109 Jeff Graham .10 .25
110 J.J. Stokes .12 .30
111 Steve Young .20 .50
112 Albert Connell .10 .25
113 Tony Brackens .10 .25
114 James Johnson .10 .25
115 Tim Brown .15 .40
116 Terance Mathis .10 .25
117 Peyton Manning .40 1.00
118 Kerry Collins .10 .25
119 Duce Staley .10 .25
120 Torrance Small .10 .25
121 Curtis Martin .12 .30
122 Damon Huard .10 .25
123 Derrick Alexander .10 .25
124 Jimmy Smith .12 .30
125 Cris Carter .15 .40
126 Jamal Anderson .12 .30
127 Eric Moulds .10 .25
128 Drew Bledsoe .12 .30
129 Ricky Williams .12 .30
130 Andre Hastings .10 .25
131 Amani Toomer .10 .25
132 Rich Gannon .12 .30
133 Richard Huntley .10 .25
134 Donovan McNabb .12 .30
135 Jermaine Fazande .10 .25
136 Randy Moss .12 .30
137 Champ Bailey .12 .30
138 Elvis Grbac .10 .25
139 Warrick Dunn .10 .25
140 John Randle .15 .40
141 Edgerrin James .12 .30
142 Tony Martin .12 .30
143 Chris Chandler .12 .30
144 Stephen Boyd .10 .25
145 Az-Zahir Hakim .10 .25
146 Tony Simmons .10 .25
147 Pete Mitchell .10 .25
148 Junior Seau .12 .30
149 Ricky Watters .12 .30
150 Michael Pittman .10 .25
151 Fred Taylor .10 .25
152 Charles Johnson .10 .25
153 Jason Tucker .10 .25
154 Brett Favre .30 .75
155 Patrick Jeffers .10 .25
156 Curtis Conway .12 .30
157 Frank Sanders .10 .25
158 James Stewart .10 .25
159 Emmitt Smith .25 .60
160 Jessie Armstead .10 .25
161 Wesley Walls .10 .25
162 Kent Graham .10 .25
163 Kurt Warner .25 .60
164 Shawn Jefferson .10 .25
165 Jammi German .10 .25
166 Jay Riemersma .10 .25
167 Fred Lane .10 .25
168 Jamir Miller .10 .25
169 David LaFleur .10 .25
170 David Sloan .10 .25
171 Jerome Pathon .10 .25
172 Sam Madison .10 .25
173 Tiki Barber .12 .30
174 Yatil Green .10 .25
175 Checklist .08 .25
176 Kurt Warner HL .20 .50
177 Brett Favre HL .25 .60
178 Marshall Faulk HL .10 .25
179 Jevon Kearse HL .07 .20
180 Edgerrin James CL .10 .25
181 Troy Aikman CS .15 .40
182 Terrell Davis CS .10 .25
183 Steve Beuerlein CS .10 .25
184 Tim Brown CS .12 .30
185 Randy Moss CS .10 .25
186 Drew Bledsoe CS .10 .25
187 Curtis Martin CS .10 .25
188 Shannon Sharpe CS .10 .25
189 Brett Favre CS .25 .60
190 Brad Johnson CS .10 .25
191 Tony Gonzalez CS .10 .25
192 Jon Kitna CS .07 .20
193 Peyton Manning CS .30 .75
194 Mark Brunell CS .10 .25
195 Cade McNown CS .08 .25
196 Jim Harbaugh CS .10 .25
197 Shaun King CS .08 .25
198 Kurt Warner CS .20 .50
199 Eddie George CS .10 .25
200 Ricky Williams CS .10 .25
201 Curtis Keaton RC .25 .60
202 Tee Martin RC .25 .60
203 Thomas Jones RC .30 .75
204 Giovanni Carmazzi RC .25 .60
205 Courtney Brown RC .30 .75
206 Shaun Alexander RC .40 1.00
207 Travis Taylor RC .25 .60
208 Dennis Northcutt RC .25 .60
209 Trung Canidate RC .25 .60
210 Jamal Lewis RC .40 1.00
211 R.Jay Soward RC .25 .60
212 Sylvester Morris RC .25 .60
213 Ron Dugans RC .25 .60
214 Chris Redman RC .25 .60
215 Plaxico Burress RC .30 .75
216 Peter Warrick RC .25 .60
217 Travis Prentice RC .25 .60
218 Ron Dayne RC .40 1.00
219 J.R. Redmond RC .25 .60
220 Chad Pennington RC .30 .75

2000 Topps Season Opener Autographs

ndomly inserted in packs at the overall rate of one in 2319, this 4-card set features authentic player signatures. Each card is stamped with a foil "Topps Certified Autograph" stamp.

AUTO/100-300 OVERALL ODDS 1:2296
A1 Kurt Warner/100 30.00 60.00
A2 Marvin Harrison/300 15.00 30.00
A3 Stephen Davis/300 10.00 25.00
A4 Joe Montana/200 60.00 120.00

2000 Topps Season Opener Football Fever

ndomly inserted in packs at the rate of one in one, this 15-card set features players with a specified goal to reach for each date listed on the card. Group A, F1A-F5C, features quarterbacks who must eclipse the 300 yard mark for passing. Group B1, F6A-F10D, features running backs who must rush for more than 100 yards. Group C, F11A-F15D, features receivers who must beat the 100 yard mark. Four different card variations were issued for each player featuring a unique date. Winning cards could be mailed into Topps for entry into their prize drawing. The cards are not numbered, so they have been issued numbers in accordance to the checklist.

COMPLETE SET (55) 6.00 15.00
F1A Brett Favre .30 .75
F1B Brett Favre .30 .75
F1C Brett Favre .30 .75
F1D Brett Favre .30 .75
F2A Kurt Warner .25 .60
F2B Kurt Warner .25 .60
F2C Kurt Warner .25 .60
F2D Kurt Warner .25 .60
F3A Brad Johnson .12 .30
F3B Brad Johnson .12 .30
F3C Brad Johnson .12 .30
F3D Brad Johnson .12 .30
F4A Peyton Manning .40 1.00
F4B Peyton Manning .40 1.00
F4C Peyton Manning .40 1.00
F4D Peyton Manning .40 1.00
F5A Drew Bledsoe .12 .30
F5B Drew Bledsoe .12 .30
F5C Drew Bledsoe .12 .30
F5D Drew Bledsoe .12 .30
F6A Terrell Davis .12 .30
F6B Terrell Davis .12 .30
F6C Terrell Davis .12 .30
F6D Terrell Davis .12 .30
F7A Edgerrin James .12 .30
F7B Edgerrin James .12 .30
F7C Edgerrin James .12 .30
F7D Edgerrin James .12 .30
F8A Stephen Davis .10 .25
F8B Stephen Davis .10 .25
F8C Stephen Davis .10 .25
F8D Stephen Davis .10 .25
F9A Fred Taylor .10 .25
F9B Fred Taylor .10 .25
F9C Fred Taylor .10 .25
F9D Fred Taylor .10 .25
F10A Jamal Lewis .10 .25
F10B Jamal Lewis .10 .25
F10C Jamal Lewis .10 .25
F10D Jamal Lewis .10 .25
F11A Marvin Harrison .12 .30
F11B Marvin Harrison .12 .30
F11C Marvin Harrison .12 .30
F11D Marvin Harrison .12 .30
F12A Isaac Bruce .15 .40
F12B Isaac Bruce .15 .40
F12C Isaac Bruce .15 .40
F12D Isaac Bruce .15 .40
F13A Jimmy Smith .12 .30
F13B Jimmy Smith .12 .30
F13C Jimmy Smith .12 .30
F13D Jimmy Smith .12 .30
F14A Randy Moss .12 .30
F14B Randy Moss .12 .30
F14C Randy Moss .12 .30
F14D Randy Moss .12 .30
F15A Peter Warrick .10 .25
F15B Peter Warrick .10 .25
F15C Peter Warrick .10 .25
F15D Peter Warrick .10 .25

2004 Topps Signature

pps Signature was initially released in late-December 2004. The base set consists of 96-cards including 20-rookies serial numbered to 499 and 21-signed rookie cards serial numbered between 299 and 1499. Hobby boxes contained 4-packs of 5-cards and carried an S.R.P. of $50 per pack with one autographed card per pack. Two parallel sets and a variety of autographed inserts can be found seeded in packs highlighted by the Canton Cuts 1/1 autographs.

COMP.SET w/o SP's (55) 15.00 40.00
56-75 ROOKIE/499 STATED ODDS 1:3
ROOKIE AU/299 GROUP A ODDS 1:15
ROOKIE AU/999 GROUP B ODDS 1:11
ROOKIE AU/1099 GROUP C ODDS 1:4
ROOKIE AU/1499 GROUP D ODDS 1:3
1 Tom Brady 3.00 8.00
2 Chad Johnson .50 1.25
3 Amani Toomer .50 1.25
4 Shaun Alexander .50 1.25
5 Terrell Owens .60 1.50
6 Jake Delhomme .50 1.25
7 Eric Moulds .50 1.25
8 Fred Taylor .50 1.25
9 Mark Brunell .60 1.50
10 Priest Holmes .50 1.25
11 Marvin Harrison .60 1.50
12 Jeff Garcia .50 1.25
13 Brad Johnson .60 1.50
14 Laveranues Coles .50 1.25
15 LaDainian Tomlinson .75 2.00
16 Anquan Boldin .50 1.25
17 Curtis Martin .60 1.50
18 Joe Horn .50 1.25
19 Domanick Davis .50 1.25
20 Jamal Lewis .60 1.50
21 Steve Smith .75 2.00
22 Aaron Brooks .50 1.25
23 Hines Ward .60 1.50
24 Marc Bulger .50 1.25
25 Randy Moss .60 1.50
26 Jerry Rice 1.50 4.00
27 Tiki Barber .60 1.50
28 Jake Plummer .50 1.25
29 Travis Henry .50 1.25
30 Michael Vick .60 1.50
31 Matt Hasselbeck .50 1.25
32 Santana Moss .60 1.50
33 Corey Dillon .50 1.25
34 Byron Leftwich .50 1.25
35 Clinton Portis .50 1.25
36 Derrick Mason .50 1.25
37 Tim Rattay .50 1.25
38 Chris Chambers .50 1.25
39 Joey Harrington .50 1.25
40 Deuce McAllister .60 1.50
41 Tony Gonzalez .60 1.50
42 Kurt Warner .60 1.50
43 Carson Palmer .60 1.50
44 Marshall Faulk .60 1.50
45 Peyton Manning 2.00 5.00
46 Ahman Green .60 1.50
47 Torry Holt .60 1.50
48 Chad Pennington .50 1.25
49 Trent Green .50 1.25
50 Brett Favre 1.50 4.00
51 Stephen Davis .50 1.25
52 Steve McNair .60 1.50
53 Daunte Culpepper .60 1.50
54 Edgerrin James .60 1.50
55 Donovan McNabb .60 1.50
56 Sean Taylor RC 8.00 20.00
57 Darius Watts RC 1.25 3.00
58 Ben Troupe RC 1.25 3.00
59 Josh Harris RC 1.25 3.00
60 Jeff Smoker RC 1.50 4.00
61 Mewelde Moore RC 1.50 4.00
62 Reggie Williams RC 1.25 3.00
63 Ben Watson RC 1.50 4.00
64 Rashaun Woods RC 1.25 3.00
65 Kellen Winslow RC 1.25 3.00
66 Robert Gallery RC 1.50 4.00
67 Steven Jackson RC 2.00 5.00
68 Craig Krenzel RC 1.25 3.00
69 DeAngelo Hall RC 2.00 5.00
70 Devard Darling RC 1.25 3.00
71 Julius Jones RC 1.25 3.00
72 Derrick Hamilton RC 1.25 3.00
73 Devery Henderson RC 1.25 3.00
74 Dunta Robinson RC 1.25 3.00
75 Larry Fitzgerald RC 5.00 12.00
76 Chris Perry AU/999 RC 5.00 12.00
77 J.P. Losman AU/1099 RC 5.00 12.00
78 Lee Evans AU/1099 RC 8.00 20.00
79 Cedric Cobbs AU/1499 RC 5.00 12.00
80 Philip Rivers AU/299 RC 50.00 100.00
81 Greg Jones AU/1499 RC 5.00 12.00
82 Michael Clayton AU/1099 RC 6.00 15.00
83 Jonathan Vilma AU/1499 RC 6.00 15.00
84 Jerricho Cotchery AU/1499 RC 6.00 15.00
85 Roy Williams AU/299 RC 8.00 20.00
86 Keary Colbert AU/1499 RC 5.00 12.00
87 Luke McCown AU/1499 RC 5.00 12.00
88 Bernard Berrian AU/1499 RC 5.00 12.00
89 Michael Jenkins AU/1499 RC 5.00 12.00
90 Eli Manning AU/299 RC 60.00 150.00
91 Matt Schaub AU/1499 RC 5.00 12.00
92 Tatum Bell AU/1099 RC 5.00 12.00
93 Roethlisberger AU/299 RC 150.00 300.00
94 Kevin Jones AU/1099 RC 6.00 15.00
95 Cody Pickett AU/999 RC 5.00 12.00
96 Drew Henson AU/299 RC 6.00 15.00

2004 Topps Signature Blue

-55 VETS/50: 2.5X TO 6X BASE CARDS
*56-75 ROOKIES/50: .6X TO 1.5X BASE RC
1-75 BLUE/50 STATED ODDS 1:6
*ROOKIE AU: .6X TO 1.5X BASE AU
ROOKIE AU/50 ODDS 1:39
*RK.JSY AU: .8X TO 2X JSY AU/999-1499
*RK.JSY AU: .5X TO 1.2X JSY AU/299
ROOKIE JSY AU/50 ODDS 1:43
90 Eli Manning JSY AU 150.00 300.00
93 Roethlisberger JSY AU 175.00 350.00

2004 Topps Signature Gold

75 GOLD STATED ODDS 1:286
ROOKIE AU STATED ODDS 1:1847
ROOKIE JSY AU STATED ODDS 1:2032
UNPRICED GOLD PRINT RUN 1 SET

2004 Topps Signature Autographs Green

GROUP A STATED ODDS 1:72
GROUP B STATED ODDS 1:12
*BLUE/50: .5X TO 1.2X GRP A AU
*BLUE/50: .6X TO 1.5X GRP B AU
BLUE/50 STATED ODDS 1:62
UNPRICED GOLD/1 ODDS 1:2903
ACB Chris Brown A 8.00 20.00
ADD Domanick Davis B 6.00 15.00
AJE John Elway A 100.00 200.00
AJM Justin McCareins B 6.00 15.00
AKB Kevan Barlow B 6.00 15.00
AMV Michael Vick A 20.00 50.00
ASS Steve Smith B 10.00 25.00

2004 Topps Signature Buy Back Autographs

STATED ODDS 1:813
JE1 John Elway 87T 75.00 150.00
JE2 John Elway 88T 75.00 150.00

1997 Topps Stars

e 1997 Topps Stars hobby only set was issued in one series of 125-cards and was distributed in seven-card packs with a suggested retail price of $3. The set features color photos of 100 current NFL stars and 25 1997 NFL draft picks printed on heavy 20 point card stock with diffraction and matte gold foil stamping. The backs carry player and statistical information.

COMPLETE SET (125) 10.00 25.00
1 Brett Favre 1.00 2.50
2 Michael Jackson .15 .40
3 Simeon Rice .15 .40
4 Thurman Thomas .25 .60
5 Karim Abdul-Jabbar .25 .60
6 Marvin Harrison .25 .60
7 John Elway 1.00 2.50
8 Carl Pickens .15 .40
9 Rod Woodson .15 .40
10 Kerry Collins .25 .60
11 Cortez Kennedy .08 .25
12 William Fuller .08 .25
13 Michael Irvin .25 .60
14 Tyrone Braxton .08 .25
15 Steve Young .30 .75
16 Keith Lyle .08 .25
17 Blaine Bishop .08 .25
18 Jeff Hostetler .08 .25
19 Levon Kirkland .08 .25
20 Barry Sanders .75 2.00
21 Deion Sanders .25 .60
22 Jamal Anderson .25 .60
23 Eric Davis .08 .25
24 Hardy Nickerson .08 .25
25 LeRoy Butler .08 .25
26 Mark Brunell .30 .75
27 Aeneas Williams .08 .25
28 Curtis Martin .30 .75
29 Wayne Chrebet .25 .60
30 Jerry Rice .50 1.25
31 Jake Reed .15 .40
32 Wayne Martin .08 .25
33 Derrick Alexander WR .15 .40
34 Isaac Bruce .25 .60
35 Terrell Davis .30 .75
36 Jerome Bettis .25 .60
37 Keenan McCardell .15 .40
38 Derrick Thomas .25 .60
39 Jason Sehorn .15 .40
40 Keyshawn Johnson .25 .60
41 Jeff Blake .15 .40
42 Terry Allen .25 .60
43 Ben Coates .15 .40
44 William Thomas .08 .25
45 Bryce Paup .08 .25
46 Bryant Young .08 .25
47 Eric Swann .08 .25
48 Tim Brown .25 .60
49 Tony Martin .15 .40
50 Eddie George .25 .60
51 Sam Mills .08 .25
52 Terry McDaniel .08 .25
53 Darren Woodson .08 .25
54 Ashley Ambrose .08 .25
55 Drew Bledsoe .30 .75
56 Larry Centers .15 .40
57 Ty Detmer .15 .40

58 Merton Hanks .08 .25
59 Charles Johnson .15 .40
60 Dan Marino 1.00 2.50
61 Joey Galloway .15 .40
62 Junior Seau .25 .60
63 Brett Perriman .08 .25
64 Wesley Walls .15 .40
65 Chad Brown .08 .25
66 Henry Ellard .08 .25
67 Keith Jackson .08 .25
68 John Randle .15 .40
69 Chester McGlockton .08 .25
70 Emmitt Smith .75 2.00
71 Vinny Testaverde .15 .40
72 Steve Atwater .08 .25
73 Irving Fryar .15 .40
74 Gus Frerotte .08 .25
75 Terry Glenn .25 .60
76 Anthony Johnson .08 .25
77 Jimmy Smith .15 .40
78 Terrell Buckley .08 .25
79 Kimble Anders .15 .40
80 Cris Carter .25 .60
81 Dave Meggett .08 .25
82 Shannon Sharpe .15 .40
83 Adrian Murrell .15 .40
84 Herman Moore .15 .40
85 Bruce Smith .15 .40
86 Lamar Lathon .08 .25
87 Ken Harvey .08 .25
88 Curtis Conway .15 .40
89 Alfred Williams .08 .25
90 Troy Aikman .50 1.25
91 Carnell Lake .08 .25
92 Michael Sinclair .08 .25
93 Ricky Watters .15 .40
94 Kevin Greene .15 .40
95 Reggie White .25 .60
96 Tyrone Hughes .08 .25
97 Dale Carter .08 .25
98 Rob Moore .15 .40
99 Tony Tolbert .08 .25
100 Willie McGinest .08 .25
101 Orlando Pace RC .40 1.00
102 Yatil Green RC .20 .50
103 Antowain Smith RC 1.50 4.00
104 David LaFleur RC .08 .25
105 Jake Plummer RC 2.50 6.00
106 Will Blackwell RC .20 .50
107 Dwayne Rudd RC .40 1.00
108 Corey Dillon RC 2.50 6.00
109 Pat Barnes RC .40 1.00
110 Peter Boulware RC .40 1.00
111 Tony Gonzalez RC 2.50 6.00
112 Renaldo Wynn RC .08 .25
113 Darrell Russell RC .08 .25
114 Bryant Westbrook RC .08 .25
115 James Farrior RC .40 1.00
116 Joey Kent RC .20 .50
117 Rae Carruth RC .08 .25
118 Jim Druckenmiller RC .20 .50
119 Byron Hanspard RC .15 .40
120 Ike Hilliard RC .75 2.00
121 Kevin Lockett RC .20 .50
122 Tom Knight RC .08 .25
123 Shawn Springs RC .20 .50
124 Troy Davis RC .20 .50
125 Darnell Autry RC .20 .50
NNO Checklist Card .08 .25
PP36 Jerome Bettis Promo .60 1.50

1997 Topps Stars Foil

MPLETE SET (125) 400.00 800.00
*STARS: 10X TO 25X BASIC CARDS
*RCs: 3X TO 8X HI
STATED ODDS 1:18

1997 Topps Stars Future Pro Bowlers

Randomly inserted in hobby packs only at a rate of one in 12, this 15-card set features color photos of players expected to make the trip to Hawaii to the Pro Bowl. Each card was printed on rainbow foilboard stock and laser die cut.

COMPLETE SET (15) 15.00 40.00
STATED ODDS 1:12 HOBBY
FPB1 Ike Hilliard 1.50 4.00
FPB2 Tom Knight .75 2.00
FPB3 David LaFleur .75 2.00
FPB4 Byron Hanspard 1.25 3.00
FPB5 Kevin Lockett 1.25 3.00
FPB6 Rae Carruth .75 2.00
FPB7 Jim Druckenmiller 1.25 3.00
FPB8 Darnell Autry 1.25 3.00
FPB9 Joey Kent 1.50 4.00
FPB10 Peter Boulware 1.25 3.00
FPB11 Orlando Pace 1.50 4.00
FPB12 Troy Davis 1.25 3.00
FPB13 Antowain Smith 4.00 8.00
FPB14 Bryant Westbrook .75 2.00
FPB15 Yatil Green 1.25 3.00

1997 Topps Stars Rookie Reprints

Randomly inserted in hobby packs at a rate of one in 64, this 10-card set features reprints of the Topps Rookie Cards of former gridiron greats who are in the Pro Football Hall of Fame. Each of the players also signed a number of the cards which were randomly inserted at the rate of 1:128.

COMPLETE SET (10) 30.00 60.00
STATED ODDS 1:64
AUTOGRAPH STATED ODDS 1:128
1 George Blanda 2.50 6.00
2 Dick Butkus 4.00 10.00
3 Len Dawson UER 2.50 6.00
4 Jack Ham 2.00 5.00
5 Sam Huff 2.00 5.00
6 Deacon Jones 2.50 6.00
7 Ray Nitschke 2.50 6.00
8 Gale Sayers 4.00 10.00
9 Randy White 2.00 5.00
10 Kellen Winslow 2.00 5.00

1997 Topps Stars Rookie Reprints Autographs

Randomly inserted in hobby packs only at a rate of one in 128, this 10-card set is parallel to the regular Hall of Fame Rookie Reprints set. The difference is found in the authentic autograph of the player and the Topps Certified Autograph Stamp printed on the cards.

STATED ODDS 1:128 HOBBY
1 George Blanda 40.00 80.00
2 Dick Butkus 50.00 80.00
3 Len Dawson 15.00 40.00
4 Jack Ham 30.00 60.00
5 Sam Huff 30.00 60.00
6 Deacon Jones 15.00 40.00
7 Ray Nitschke 125.00 200.00
8 Gale Sayers 40.00 80.00
9 Randy White 25.00 50.00
10 Kellen Winslow 20.00 40.00

1997 Topps Stars Pro Bowl Memories

ndomly inserted in hobby packs at a rate of one in 24, this 10-card set features color photos of ten perennial Pro Bowl players printed on die-cut diffraction foilboard stock.

COMPLETE SET (10) 25.00 60.00
STATED ODDS 1:24
PBM1 Barry Sanders 6.00 15.00
PBM2 Jeff Blake 1.25 3.00
PBM3 Ken Harvey .75 2.00
PBM4 Brett Favre 8.00 20.00
PBM5 Jerry Rice 4.00 10.00
PBM6 John Elway 8.00 20.00
PBM7 Marshall Faulk 2.00 5.00
PBM8 Steve Young 2.50 6.00
PBM9 Mark Brunell 2.50 6.00
PBM10 Troy Aikman 4.00 10.00

1997 Topps Stars Pro Bowl Stars

Randomly inserted in hobby packs at a rate of one in 24, this 30-card set features color photos of players who were named to the 1997 Pro Bowl and are printed on embossed uniluster card stock.

COMPLETE SET (30) 40.00 100.00
STATED ODDS 1:24
PB1 Brett Favre 8.00 20.00
PB2 Mark Brunell 3.00 8.00
PB3 Kerry Collins 2.50 6.00
PB4 Drew Bledsoe 3.00 8.00
PB5 Barry Sanders 8.00 20.00
PB6 Terrell Davis 3.00 8.00
PB7 Terry Allen 2.50 6.00
PB8 Jerome Bettis 2.50 6.00
PB9 Ricky Watters 1.50 4.00
PB10 Curtis Martin 3.00 8.00
PB11 Emmitt Smith 8.00 20.00
PB12 Kimble Anders 1.50 4.00
PB13 Jerry Rice 5.00 12.00
PB14 Carl Pickens 1.50 4.00
PB15 Herman Moore 1.50 4.00
PB16 Tony Martin 1.50 4.00
PB17 Isaac Bruce 2.50 6.00
PB18 Tim Brown 2.50 6.00
PB19 Wesley Walls 1.50 4.00
PB20 Shannon Sharpe 1.50 4.00
PB21 Dana Stubblefield 1.00 2.50
PB22 Reggie White 2.50 6.00
PB23 Bruce Smith 1.50 4.00
PB24 Bryant Young 1.00 2.50
PB25 Junior Seau 2.50 6.00
PB26 Kevin Greene 1.50 4.00
PB27 Derrick Thomas 2.50 6.00
PB28 Chad Brown 1.00 2.50
PB29 Deion Sanders 2.50 6.00
PB30 Rod Woodson 1.50 4.00

1998 Topps Stars Promos

COMPLETE SET (6) 2.50 6.00
PP1 Terrell Davis .40 1.00
PP2 Herman Moore .30 .75
PP3 Brett Favre 1.25 3.00
PP4 Eddie George .30 .75
PP5 Jerome Bettis .40 1.00
PP6 Barry Sanders .75 2.00

1998 Topps Stars

e 1998 Topps Stars set was issued in one series totalling 150 standard size cards. The six-card packs retail for $3.00 each. The 20 pt. stock cards are borderless with a matte gold-foil stamping and UV coating. The set is sequentially numbered within one of five groups: Red Star (1 of 8799), Bronze Star (1 of 8799), Silver Star (1 of 3999), Gold Star (1 of 1999) and Gold Star Rainbow (1 of 99). Red Star and Bronze Star are considered regular cards. The player selection and categories are also based upon the five-star system which includes: Arm Strength, Accuracy, Mobility, Consistency and Leadership. A complete checklist card of the 1998 Topps Stars set was seeded in packs at the rate of 1:5.

COMP.RED SET (150) 30.00 80.00
1 John Elway 2.00 5.00
2 Duane Starks RC .40 1.00
3 Bruce Smith .30 .75
4 Jeff Blake .30 .75
5 Carl Pickens .30 .75
6 Shannon Sharpe .30 .75
7 Jerome Pathon RC 1.00 2.50
8 Jimmy Smith .30 .75
9 Elvis Grbac .30 .75
10 Mark Brunell .50 1.25
11 Karim Abdul-Jabbar .50 1.25
12 Terry Glenn .50 1.25
13 Larry Centers .20 .50
14 Jeff George .30 .75
15 Terry Allen .50 1.25
16 Charles Johnson .20 .50
17 Chris Spielman .20 .50
18 Ahman Green RC 2.50 6.00
19 Kevin Dyson RC 1.00 2.50
20 Dan Marino 2.00 5.00
21 Andre Wadsworth RC .60 1.50
22 Chris Chandler .30 .75
23 Kerry Collins .30 .75
24 Erik Kramer .20 .50
25 Warrick Dunn .50 1.25
26 Michael Irvin .50 1.25
27 Herman Moore .30 .75
28 Dorsey Levens .50 1.25
29 Cris Carter .50 1.25
30 Drew Bledsoe .75 2.00
31 Kevin Greene .30 .75
32 Charles Way .20 .50
33 Bobby Hoying .30 .75
34 Tony Banks .30 .75
35 Steve Young .60 1.50
36 Trent Dilfer .50 1.25
37 Warren Sapp .30 .75
38 Skip Hicks RC .60 1.50
39 Michael Jackson .20 .50
40 Curtis Martin .50 1.25
41 Thurman Thomas .50 1.25
42 Corey Dillon .50 1.25
43 Brian Griese RC 2.00 5.00
44 Marshall Faulk .60 1.50
45 Isaac Bruce .50 1.25
46 Fred Taylor RC 1.50 4.00
47 Andre Rison .30 .75
48 O.J. McDuffie .30 .75
49 John Avery RC .60 1.50
50 Terrell Davis .50 1.25
51 Robert Edwards RC .60 1.50
52 Keyshawn Johnson .50 1.25
53 Rickey Dudley .20 .50
54 Hines Ward RC 5.00 10.00
55 Irving Fryar .30 .75
56 Freddie Jones .20 .50
57 Michael Sinclair .20 .50
58 Darnay Scott .30 .75
59 Tim Dwight RC 1.00 2.50
60 Tim Brown .50 1.25
61 Ray Lewis .50 1.25
62 Curtis Enis RC .40 1.00
63 Emmitt Smith 1.50 4.00
64 Scott Mitchell .30 .75
65 Antonio Freeman .50 1.25
66 Randy Moss RC 4.00 10.00
67 Peyton Manning RC 8.00 20.00
68 Danny Kanell .30 .75
69 Charlie Garner .30 .75
70 Mike Alstott .50 1.25
71 Grant Wistrom RC .60 1.50
72 Jacquez Green RC .60 1.50
73 Gus Frerotte .20 .50
74 Peter Boulware .20 .50
75 Jerry Rice 1.00 2.50
76 Antowain Smith .50 1.25
77 Brian Simmons RC .60 1.50
78 Rod Smith .30 .75
79 Marvin Harrison .50 1.25
80 Ryan Leaf RC 1.00 2.50
81 Keenan McCardell .30 .75
82 Derrick Thomas .50 1.25
83 Zach Thomas .50 1.25
84 Ben Coates .30 .75
85 Rob Moore .30 .75
86 Wayne Chrebet .50 1.25
87 Napoleon Kaufman .50 1.25
88 Levon Kirkland .20 .50
89 Junior Seau .50 1.25
90 Eddie George .50 1.25
91 Warren Moon .50 1.25
92 Anthony Simmons RC .60 1.50
93 Steve McNair .50 1.25
94 Frank Sanders .30 .75
95 Joey Galloway .30 .75
96 Jamal Anderson .50 1.25
97 Rae Carruth .20 .50
98 Curtis Conway .30 .75
99 Greg Ellis RC .40 1.00
100 Kordell Stewart .50 1.25
101 Germane Crowell RC .60 1.50
102 Mark Chmura .30 .75
103 Robert Smith .50 1.25
104 Andre Hastings .20 .50
105 Reggie White .50 1.25
106 Jessie Armstead .20 .50
107 Kevin Hardy .20 .50
108 Robert Holcombe RC .60 1.50
109 Garrison Hearst .50 1.25
110 Jerome Bettis .50 1.25
111 Reidel Anthony .30 .75
112 Michael Westbrook .30 .75
113 Pat Johnson RC .60 1.50
114 Andre Reed .30 .75
115 Charles Woodson RC 2.50 6.00
116 Takeo Spikes RC 1.00 2.50
117 Marcus Nash RC .40 1.00
118 Tavian Banks RC .30 .75
119 Tony Gonzalez .50 1.25
120 Jake Plummer .50 1.25
121 Tony Simmons RC .60 1.50
122 Aaron Glenn .20 .50
123 Ricky Watters .30 .75
124 Kimble Anders .30 .75
125 Barry Sanders 1.50 4.00
126 Terance Mathis .30 .75
127 Wesley Walls .30 .75
128 Bobby Engram .30 .75
129 Johnnie Morton .30 .75
130 Brett Favre 2.00 5.00
131 Brad Johnson .50 1.25
132 John Randle .30 .75
133 Chris Sanders .20 .50
134 Joe Jurevicius RC 1.00 2.50
135 Deion Sanders .50 1.25
136 Terrell Owens .50 1.25
137 Darrell Green .30 .75
138 Jermaine Lewis .30 .75
139 James Stewart .30 .75
140 Troy Aikman 1.00 2.50
141 Hardy Nickerson .20 .50
142 Blaine Bishop .20 .50
143 Keith Brooking RC 1.00 2.50
144 Jason Peter RC .40 1.00
145 Jake Reed .30 .75
146 Jason Sehorn .30 .75
147 Robert Brooks .30 .75
148 J.J. Stokes .30 .75
149 Michael Strahan .30 .75
150 Glenn Foley .30 .75
NNO Checklist Card .20 .50

1998 Topps Stars Bronze

COMPLETE SET (150) 30.00 80.00
*BRONZE CARDS: SAME PRICE AS RED
STATED PRINT RUN 8799 SER.#'d SETS

1998 Topps Stars Gold

COMP.GOLD SET (150) 125.00 250.00
*GOLD VETS: 1.2X TO 3X BASIC CARDS
*GOLD ROOKIES: .8X TO 2X BASIC CARDS
GOLD/1999 ODDS 1:2

1998 Topps Stars Gold Rainbow

OLD RBW.VETS: 8X TO 20X BASIC CARDS
*GOLD RBW.ROOKIES: 2.5X TO 6X
GOLD RAINBOW/99 ODDS 1:41

1998 Topps Stars Silver

COMP.SILVER SET (150) 50.00 120.00
*SILVER/3999: .6X TO 1.5X BASIC CARDS
SILVER PRINT RUN 3999 SER.#'d SETS

1998 Topps Stars Galaxy

Randomly inserted in packs at the rate of one in 611, this 10-card set features color photos of top stars printed on a galaxy background with bronze foil stamping. Only 100 serial-numbered sets were produced. Three parallel versions of this set were also produced with different foil stamping: Silver (inserted 1:814 packs and sequentially numbered to 75), Gold (inserted 1:1222 packs and sequentially numbered to 50), and Gold Rainbow (inserted 1:12,215 packs and sequentially numbered to only five).

BRONZE/100 STATED ODDS 1:611
*SILVER/75: .5X TO 1.2X BRONZE/100
SILVER/75 STATED ODDS 1:814
*GOLD/50: .6X TO 1.5X BRONZE/100
GOLD/50 STATED ODDS 1:1222
UNPRICED GOLD RBW/5 ODDS 1:12,215
G1 Brett Favre 30.00 80.00
G2 Barry Sanders 25.00 60.00
G3 Jerry Rice 15.00 40.00
G4 Herman Moore 5.00 12.00
G5 Tim Brown 8.00 20.00
G6 Steve Young 10.00 25.00
G7 Cris Carter 8.00 20.00
G8 John Elway 30.00 80.00
G9 Mark Brunell 6.00 15.00
G10 Terrell Davis 8.00 20.00

1998 Topps Stars Luminaries

Randomly inserted in packs at the rate of one in 407, this 15-card set features color images of the top three players from each of the "five-tool" categories (Arm Strength, Accuracy, Mobility, Consistency, and Leadership) printed on a bronze foil background. Only 100 serial-numbered sets were printed. Three parallel versions of this set were also produced with different foil stamping: Silver (inserted 1:543 packs and sequentially numbered to 75), Gold (inserted 1:814 packs and sequentially numbered to 50), and Gold Rainbow (inserted 1:8144 packs and sequentially numbered to only five).

BRONZE/100 STATED ODDS 1:407
*SILVER/75: .4X TO 1X BRONZE/100
SILVER/75 STATED ODDS 1:543
*GOLD/50: .5X TO 1.2X BRONZE/100
GOLD/50 STATED ODDS 1:814
UNPRICED GOLD RBW/5 ODDS 1:8144
L1 Brett Favre 40.00 100.00
L2 Steve Young 12.50 30.00
L3 John Elway 40.00 100.00
L4 Barry Sanders 30.00 80.00
L5 Terrell Davis 10.00 25.00
L6 Eddie George 10.00 25.00
L7 Herman Moore 2.50 6.00
L8 Tim Brown 10.00 25.00
L9 Jerry Rice 20.00 50.00
L10 Junior Seau 10.00 25.00
L11 Bruce Smith 10.00 25.00
L12 John Randle 6.00 15.00
L13 Peyton Manning 75.00 150.00
L14 Ryan Leaf 6.00 15.00
L15 Curtis Enis 2.50 6.00

1998 Topps Stars Rookie Reprints

Randomly inserted in packs at a rate of one in 24, this eight-card set features reprints of the original Topps Rookie cards of eight NFL Hall of Famers.

COMPLETE SET (8) 12.50 25.00
STATED ODDS 1:24
1 Walter Payton 6.00 15.00
2 Don Maynard 1.50 4.00
3 Charlie Joiner 1.25 3.00
4 Fred Biletnikoff 1.50 4.00
5 Paul Hornung 1.50 4.00
6 Gale Sayers 2.50 6.00
7 John Hannah .75 2.00
8 Paul Warfield 1.50 4.00

1998 Topps Stars Rookie Reprints Autographs

Randomly inserted in packs at a rate of one in 153, this eight-card set features reprints of the Topps Rookie cards of eight NFL Hall of Famers signed and carrying the Topps Certified Autograph Issue stamp for authenticity. The set is sequentially numbered to 500.

STATED ODDS 1:153
1 Walter Payton 300.00 600.00
2 Don Maynard 15.00 30.00
3 Charlie Joiner 15.00 30.00
4 Fred Biletnikoff 30.00 60.00
5 Paul Hornung 35.00 60.00
6 Gale Sayers 35.00 60.00
7 John Hannah 15.00 30.00
8 Paul Warfield 15.00 30.00

1998 Topps Stars Supernovas

Randomly inserted into packs at the rate of one in 611, this 10-card set features color action images of players who have proven that they either possess all of the five tools or excel dramatically in one and printed on a large bronze foil star background. Only 100 serial-numbered sets were produced. Three parallel versions of this set were also produced with different foil stamping: Silver (inserted 1:814 packs and sequentially numbered to 75), Gold (inserted 1:1222 packs and sequentially numbered to 50), and Gold Rainbow (inserted 1:12,215 packs and sequentially numbered to only five).

BRONZE/100 STATED ODDS 1:611
*SILVER/75: .5X TO 1.2X BRONZE/100
SILVER/75 STATED ODDS 1:814
*GOLD/50: .6X TO 1.5X BRONZE/100
GOLD/50 STATED ODDS 1:1222
UNPRICED GOLD RBW/5 ODDS 1:12,215
S1 Ryan Leaf 4.00 10.00
S2 Curtis Enis 2.50 6.00
S3 Kevin Dyson 4.00 10.00
S4 Randy Moss 30.00 80.00
S5 Peyton Manning 75.00 150.00
S6 Duane Starks 2.50 6.00
S7 Grant Wistrom 2.50 6.00
S8 Charles Woodson 10.00 25.00
S9 Fred Taylor 8.00 20.00
S10 Andre Wadsworth 4.00 10.00

1999 Topps Stars Promos

Sent out for promotional purposes, this 6-card set previewed the base card product for the 1999 Topps Stars release.

COMPLETE SET (6) 2.50 6.00
PP1 Chris Chandler .40 1.00
PP2 Charlie Batch .40 1.00
PP3 Jake Plummer .50 1.25
PP4 Terrell Davis .75 2.00
PP5 Keyshawn Johnson .50 1.25
PP6 Warrick Dunn .50 1.25

1999 Topps Stars

Released as a 140-card set, the 1999 Topps Stars set was printed on thick 24 point card stock with foil stamping and a flood-gloss finish. Four different versions, destinguished by the number of foil stars on the card front, of the base set were released ranging from one star to four stars, and parallels for each set level were released also. Topps stars was packaged in 24-pack boxes containing 6-card packs and carried a suggested retail price of $3.00.

COMPLETE SET (140) 20.00 50.00
1 Champ Bailey RC .50 1.25
2 Akili Smith RC .25 .60
3 Randy Moss .25 .60
4 Cade McNown RC .25 .60
5 Torry Holt RC .50 1.25
6 Troy Edwards RC .25 .60
7 David Boston RC .25 .60
8 Edgerrin James RC .40 1.00
9 Daunte Culpepper RC .40 1.00
10 Tim Couch RC .30 .75
11 Ricky Williams RC .40 1.00
12 Fred Taylor .20 .50
13 Barry Sanders .50 1.25
14 Emmitt Smith .50 1.25
15 Jerry Rice .75 2.00
16 Jake Plummer .20 .50
17 Terrell Owens .25 .60
18 Eric Moulds .20 .50
19 Dan Marino .60 1.50
20 Steve McNair .25 .60
21 Donovan McNabb RC 2.00 5.00
22 Curtis Martin .25 .60
23 Peyton Manning 1.00 2.50
24 Garrison Hearst .20 .50
25 Eddie George .25 .60
26 Antonio Freeman .25 .60
27 Doug Flutie .30 .75
28 Kevin Faulk RC .25 .60
29 Brett Favre .60 1.50
30 Randall Cunningham .25 .60
31 Mark Brunell .25 .60
32 Keyshawn Johnson .25 .60
33 Terrell Davis .25 .60
34 Drew Bledsoe .25 .60
35 Jerome Bettis .30 .75
36 Charlie Batch .20 .50
37 Steve Young .40 1.00
38 Jamal Anderson .25 .60
39 Troy Aikman .40 1.00
40 John Elway .50 1.25
41 Amos Zereoue RC .25 .60
42 J.J. Stokes .20 .50
43 Antowain Smith .20 .50
44 Jimmy Smith .25 .60
45 Shaun King RC .25 .60
46 Jevon Kearse RC .30 .75
47 Sedrick Irvin RC .25 .60
48 Rod Smith .25 .60
49 Kevin Johnson RC .30 .75
50 Joey Galloway .25 .60
51 Mike Cloud RC .25 .60
52 D'Wayne Bates RC .25 .60
53 Peerless Price RC .25 .60
54 Herman Moore .25 .60
55 Rob Konrad RC .25 .60
56 James Johnson RC .25 .60
57 Cecil Collins RC .25 .60
58 Wayne Chrebet .20 .50
59 Cris Carter .30 .75
60 Tim Brown .30 .75
61 Frank Wycheck .25 .60
62 Charles Woodson .30 .75
63 Antoine Winfield RC .25 .60
64 Ryan Leaf .25 .60
65 Ricky Watters .25 .60
66 Yancey Thigpen .20 .50
67 Michael Westbrook .20 .50
68 Vinny Testaverde .20 .50
69 Kordell Stewart .20 .50
70 Duce Staley .20 .50
71 Shannon Sharpe .25 .60
72 Junior Seau .25 .60
73 Bruce Smith .25 .60
74 Frank Sanders .20 .50
75 Lawrence Phillips .25 .60
76 Robert Smith .20 .50
77 Andre Reed .30 .75
78 Darnay Scott .20 .50
79 Adrian Murrell .20 .50
80 Ricky Proehl .20 .50
81 Zach Thomas .25 .60
82 Deion Sanders .25 .60
83 Andre Rison .25 .60
84 Jake Reed .25 .60
85 Carl Pickens .25 .60
86 John Randle .30 .75
87 Jerome Pathon .20 .50
88 Brock Huard RC .25 .60
89 Elvis Grbac .20 .50
90 Curtis Enis .20 .50
91 Rickey Dudley .20 .50
92 Amani Toomer .20 .50
93 Robert Brooks .25 .60
94 Derrick Alexander .20 .50
95 Reidel Anthony .20 .50
96 Mark Chmura .20 .50
97 Trent Dilfer .20 .50
98 Ebenezer Ekuban RC .25 .60
99 Tony Banks .25 .60
100 Terry Glenn .25 .60
101 Andre Hastings .20 .50
102 Ike Hilliard .20 .50
103 Michael Irvin .30 .75
104 Napoleon Kaufman .20 .50
105 Dorsey Levens .25 .60
106 Ed McCaffrey .25 .60
107 Natrone Means .25 .60
108 Skip Hicks .20 .50
109 James Jett .20 .50
110 Priest Holmes .20 .50
111 Tim Dwight .25 .60
112 Curtis Conway .25 .60
113 Jeff Blake .25 .60
114 Karim Abdul-Jabbar .20 .50
115 Karsten Bailey RC .25 .60
116 Chris Chandler .25 .60
117 Germane Crowell .20 .50
118 Warrick Dunn .20 .50
119 Bert Emanuel .25 .60
120 Jermaine Fazande RC .25 .60
121 Joe Germaine RC .30 .75
122 Tony Gonzalez .25 .60
123 Jacquez Green .20 .50
124 Marvin Harrison .25 .60
125 Corey Dillon .20 .50
126 Ben Coates .25 .60
127 Chris Claiborne RC .25 .60
128 Isaac Bruce .30 .75
129 Mike Alstott .20 .50
130 Andy Katzenmoyer RC .30 .75
131 Jon Kitna .20 .50
132 Keenan McCardell .25 .60
133 Johnnie Morton .25 .60
134 O.J. McDuffie .25 .60
135 Chris McAlister .20 .50
136 Terance Mathis .20 .50
137 Thurman Thomas .25 .60
138 Jermaine Lewis .20 .50
139 Rob Moore .20 .50
140 Brad Johnson .25 .60

1999 Topps Stars Parallel

COMPLETE SET (140) 250.00 500.00
*STARS: 3X TO 8X HI COL.
*RCs: 1.2X TO 3X
STATED ODDS 1:15
CARDS SERIAL NUMBERED TO 299

1999 Topps Stars Two Star

COMPLETE SET (60) 15.00 40.00
*TWO STARS: SAME PRICE AS 1 STAR
ONE OR TWO CARDS PER PACK

1999 Topps Stars Two Star Parallel

COMPLETE SET (60) 250.00 500.00
*STARS: 4X TO 10X HI COL.
*ROOKIES: 1.5X TO 4X
STATED ODDS 1:42
CARDS SERIAL NUMBERED TO 249

1999 Topps Stars Three Star

COMPLETE SET (40) 12.50 30.00
*THREE STARS: SAME PRICE AS 1 STAR
ONE PER PACK

1999 Topps Stars Three Star Parallel

COMPLETE SET (40) 250.00 500.00
*STARS: 5X TO 12X HI COL.
*ROOKIES: 2X TO 5X
STATED ODDS 1:79
CARDS SERIAL NUMBERED TO 199

1999 Topps Stars Four Star

COMPLETE SET (10) 10.00 25.00
*FOUR STARS: SAME PRICE AS 1 STAR
STATED ODDS 1:4

1999 Topps Stars Four Star Parallel

COMPLETE SET (10) 75.00 150.00
*STARS: 5X TO 12X
*ROOKIES: 2.5X TO 6X
STATED ODDS 1:634
CARDS SERIAL NUMBERED TO 99

1999 Topps Stars Autographs

Randomly inserted in packs at one in 419, this 6-card set features three 1999's top rookies and three veteran standouts on cards containing each respective players autograph. Three versions of this set were released, the base card contains a blue background, red background cards were seeded at one in 629 packs, and gold background cards were seeded at one in 2528 packs. Card backs carry an "A" prefix.

BLUE BACKGROUND STATED ODDS 1:419
GOLD BACKGROUND STATED ODDS 1:2528
RED BACKGROUND STATED ODDS 1:629
A1 Tim Couch B 10.00 25.00
A2 Torry Holt B 12.00 30.00
A3 David Boston B 8.00 30.00
A4 Fred Taylor R 12.00 30.00
A5 Marshall Faulk R 20.00 50.00
A6 Randy Moss G 30.00 80.00

1999 Topps Stars New Dawn

ndomly inserted in packs at the rate of one in 31, this 20-card set features top rookies on cards with topps' super-premium select metallization treatment and foil stamping. Card backs carry an "N" prefix.

COMPLETE SET (20) 50.00 100.00
STATED ODDS 1:31
STATED PRINT RUN 1000 SER.#'d SETS
N1 Tim Couch 1.25 3.00
N2 Kevin Faulk 1.25 3.00
N3 Troy Edwards 1.00 2.50
N4 Champ Bailey 1.50 4.00
N5 Peerless Price 1.25 3.00
N6 Kevin Johnson 1.25 3.00
N7 Edgerrin James 5.00 12.00
N8 Daunte Culpepper 5.00 12.00
N9 Torry Holt 3.00 8.00
N10 Donovan McNabb 6.00 15.00
N11 Shaun King 1.00 2.50
N12 Mike Cloud 1.00 2.50
N13 Cade McNown 1.00 2.50
N14 David Boston 1.25 3.00
N15 James Johnson 1.00 2.50
N16 Karsten Bailey 1.00 2.50
N17 Sedrick Irvin .60 1.50
N18 Akili Smith 1.00 2.50
N19 D'Wayne Bates 1.00 2.50
N20 Ricky Williams 2.50 6.00

1999 Topps Stars Rookie Relics

Randomly inserted in packs at one in 209, this set was available in two versions. Torry Holt jersey cards were available from packs, while Kurt Warner and Donovan McNabb cards were redemptions for the piece of memorabilia that appeared on the redemption card.

COMPLETE SET (3) 40.00 100.00
STATED ODDS 1:209
RR1 Kurt Warner 12.00 30.00
RR2 Torry Holt 12.00 30.00
RR3 Donovan McNabb 12.00 30.00

1999 Topps Stars Rookie Reprints

Randomly inserted in packs at one in 16, this set features reprints of Roger Staubach and Terry Bradshaw rookie cards on white card stock with a glossy finish.

COMPLETE SET (2) 4.00 10.00
STATED ODDS 1:16
1 Roger Staubach 2.00 5.00
2 Terry Bradshaw 2.00 5.00

1999 Topps Stars Rookie Reprints Autographs

Randomly inserted in packs at the rate of one in 629, this set parallels the base Rookie Reprints set in an autographed version. Card fronts contain a Topps stamp of authenticity, and card backs carry an "RA" prefix.

STATED ODDS 1:629
RA1 Roger Staubach 60.00 120.00
RA2 Terry Bradshaw 60.00 120.00

1999 Topps Stars Stars of the Game

Randomly inserted in packs at the rate of one in 31, this 10-card set features NFL veterans that have proven their greatness over the span of their careers. Each card is sequentially numbered to 1999. Card backs carry an "S" prefix.

COMPLETE SET (10) 40.00 80.00
STATED ODDS 1:31
STATED PRINT RUN 1999 SER.#'d SETS
S1 Jamal Anderson 1.50 4.00
S2 Dan Marino 5.00 12.00
S3 Barry Sanders 5.00 12.00
S4 Brett Favre 5.00 12.00
S5 Emmitt Smith 3.00 8.00
S6 Fred Taylor 1.50 4.00
S7 Kurt Warner 7.50 20.00
S8 Randy Moss 4.00 10.00
S9 Peyton Manning 6.00 15.00
S10 Terrell Davis 1.50 4.00

1999 Topps Stars Zone of Their Own

Randomly inserted in packs at the rate of one in 31, this 10-card set features both rookies and veterans in a set that is sequentially numbered to 1999. Card backs carry a "Z" prefix.

COMPLETE SET (10) 20.00 50.00
STATED ODDS 1:31
STATED PRINT RUN 1999 SER.#'d SETS
Z1 Randy Moss 4.00 10.00
Z2 Eddie George 1.50 4.00
Z3 Tim Brown 1.50 4.00
Z4 Curtis Martin 1.50 4.00
Z5 Brett Favre 5.00 12.00
Z6 Barry Sanders 5.00 12.00
Z7 Warrick Dunn 1.50 4.00
Z8 Terrell Davis 1.50 4.00
Z9 Ricky Williams 2.00 5.00
Z10 Doug Flutie 1.50 4.00

2000 Topps Stars Promos

Sent out for promotional purposes, this 6-card set previewed the base card product for the 2000 Topps Stars release.

COMPLETE SET (6) 2.50 6.00
PP1 Keyshawn Johnson .50 1.25
PP2 Dorsey Levens .50 1.25
PP3 Rich Gannon .50 1.25
PP4 Michael Westbrook .40 1.00
PP5 Mike Alstott .40 1.00
PP6 Edgerrin James .50 1.25

2000 Topps Stars

sued as a 175-card base set, Topps Stars is comprised of 120 regular issue player cards, five Retired Stars, 20 Heroes of Hawaii, five Hawaiian Future, and 25 Rookie cards. Base cards are borderless and feature player action shots and silver foil highlights. Topps Stars was packaged in 24-pack boxes with packs containing six cards and carried a suggested retail price of $3.00.

COMPLETE SET (175) 15.00 40.00
1 Keyshawn Johnson .25 .60
2 Marcus Robinson .25 .60
3 Antonio Freeman .25 .60
4 Jake Plummer .20 .50
5 Zach Thomas .25 .60
6 Kordell Stewart .20 .50
7 Mike Alstott .20 .50
8 Fred Taylor .20 .50
9 J.J. Stokes .25 .60
10 Emmitt Smith .50 1.25
11 Derrick Mayes .20 .50
12 Stephen Davis .20 .50
13 Jamal Anderson .25 .60
14 Antowain Smith .25 .60
15 Steve Beuerlein .25 .60
16 Olandis Gary .25 .60
17 Rickey Dudley .20 .50
18 Sean Dawkins .20 .50
19 Mark Brunell .25 .60
20 Brett Favre .60 1.50
21 Jim Harbaugh .25 .60
22 Darnay Scott .25 .60
23 Herman Moore .20 .50
24 Drew Bledsoe .25 .60
25 Priest Holmes .20 .50
26 Albert Connell .20 .50
27 Ike Hilliard .20 .50
28 Charlie Garner .25 .60
29 Jimmy Smith .25 .60
30 Randy Moss .25 .60
31 Peerless Price .25 .60
32 Terrell Davis .25 .60
33 Troy Edwards .20 .50
34 Kevin Dyson .25 .60
35 O.J. McDuffie .25 .60
36 Troy Aikman .40 1.00
37 Frank Sanders .20 .50
38 Bobby Engram .20 .50
39 Tyrone Wheatley .20 .50
40 Ricky Williams .25 .60
41 Warrick Dunn .20 .50
42 Elvis Grbac .20 .50
43 Dorsey Levens .25 .60
44 Curtis Conway .25 .60
45 Johnnie Morton .25 .60
46 Ed McCaffrey .25 .60
47 Kevin Johnson .20 .50
48 Muhsin Muhammad .20 .50
49 Terance Mathis .20 .50
50 Eddie George .25 .60
51 Daunte Culpepper .25 .60
52 Jeff Graham .20 .50
53 Jon Kitna .20 .50
54 Marvin Harrison .25 .60
55 Steve McNair .25 .60
56 Jeff Blake .25 .60
57 Carl Pickens .25 .60
58 Germane Crowell .20 .50
59 Rob Moore .20 .50
60 Marshall Faulk .25 .60
61 Jerome Bettis .30 .75
62 Michael Westbrook .20 .50
63 Keenan McCardell .25 .60
64 Shannon Sharpe .25 .60
65 Rod Smith .25 .60
66 Curtis Enis .20 .50
67 Vinny Testaverde .20 .50
68 Freddie Jones .20 .50
69 Jevon Kearse .20 .50
70 Jerry Rice .75 2.00
71 Champ Bailey .25 .60
72 Peyton Manning .75 2.00
73 Rich Gannon .25 .60
74 Cris Carter .30 .75
75 Doug Flutie .25 .60
76 Corey Dillon .20 .50
77 Tony Gonzalez .25 .60
78 Shaun King .20 .50
79 Terrell Owens .25 .60
80 Dan Marino .60 1.50
81 Curtis Martin .25 .60
82 Patrick Jeffers .20 .50
83 Brian Griese .20 .50
84 Akili Smith .20 .50
85 Charlie Batch .20 .50
86 Tim Dwight .25 .60
87 Robert Smith .20 .50
88 Duce Staley .20 .50
89 Jacquez Green .20 .50
90 Steve Young .40 1.00
91 Tony Martin .25 .60
92 Az-Zahir Hakim .20 .50
93 Tim Brown .30 .75
94 Donovan McNabb .25 .60
95 Chris Chandler .25 .60
96 Tim Couch .25 .60
97 Tim Biakabutuka .25 .60
98 Terry Glenn .25 .60
99 Wayne Chrebet .20 .50
100 Kurt Warner .50 1.25
101 Qadry Ismail .20 .50
102 Torry Holt .25 .60
103 Ray Lucas .20 .50
104 James Johnson .20 .50
105 Errict Rhett .25 .60
106 James Stewart .20 .50
107 Tony Banks .20 .50
108 Amani Toomer .20 .50
109 Isaac Bruce .30 .75
110 Brad Johnson .25 .60
111 Kerry Collins .20 .50
112 Eric Moulds .20 .50
113 Rocket Ismail .25 .60
114 Keith Poole .20 .50
115 Rob Johnson .25 .60
116 Deion Sanders .25 .60
117 Ricky Watters .25 .60
118 Cade McNown .20 .50
119 Joey Galloway .25 .60
120 Edgerrin James .25 .60
121 Franco Harris .30 .75
122 Steve Largent .30 .75
123 Joe Montana 1.00 2.50
124 Deacon Jones .25 .60
125 Ronnie Lott .30 .75
126 Mark Brunell HH .20 .50
127 Rich Gannon HH .20 .50
128 Tony Gonzalez HH .20 .50
129 Randy Moss HH .20 .50
130 Kurt Warner HH .40 1.00
131 Marvin Harrison HH .20 .50
132 Jimmy Smith HH .20 .50
133 Edgerrin James HH .20 .50
134 Corey Dillon HH .15 .40
135 Peyton Manning HH .60 1.50
136 Brad Johnson HH .20 .50
137 Steve Beuerlein HH .20 .50
138 Emmitt Smith HH .40 1.00
139 Marshall Faulk HH .20 .50
140 Mike Alstott HH .15 .40
141 Deacon Jones HH .20 .50
142 Joe Montana HH .75 2.00
143 Franco Harris HH .25 .60
144 Steve Largent HH .25 .60
145 Ronnie Lott HH .25 .60
146 Chad Pennington HF .20 .50
147 Peter Warrick HF .15 .40
148 Plaxico Burress HF .20 .50
149 Thomas Jones HF .20 .50
150 Jamal Lewis HF .25 .60
151 Travis Taylor RC .20 .50
152 Shaun Alexander RC .30 .75
153 Dez White RC .20 .50
154 Thomas Jones RC .25 .60
155 Curtis Keaton RC .20 .50
156 Courtney Brown RC .25 .60
157 Danny Farmer RC .20 .50
158 Trung Canidate RC .20 .50
159 R.Jay Soward RC .20 .50
160 Jamal Lewis RC .30 .75
161 Todd Pinkston RC .20 .50
162 Reuben Droughns RC .20 .50
163 Ron Dugans RC .20 .50
164 Ron Dayne RC .30 .75
165 Laveranues Coles RC .25 .60
166 Sylvester Morris RC .20 .50
167 Peter Warrick RC .20 .50
168 Dennis Northcutt RC .20 .50
169 Tee Martin RC .20 .50
170 Brian Urlacher RC 1.00 2.50
171 Chris Redman RC .20 .50
172 Chad Pennington RC .25 .60
173 J.R. Redmond RC .20 .50
174 Travis Prentice RC .20 .50
175 Plaxico Burress RC .25 .60

2000 Topps Stars Green

*VETS 1-125: 3X TO 8X BASIC CARDS
1-125 VETERAN PRINT RUN 299
*VETS 126-150: 10X TO 25X
*ROOKIES 126-150: 10X TO 25X
*ROOKIES 151-175: 8X TO 20X
126-175 STATED PRINT RUN 99

2000 Topps Stars Pro Bowl Jerseys

Randomly inserted in packs at the rate of one in 85, this 65-card set features player action photos coupled with a swatch of a game worn Pro Bowl jersey cut out in the shape of the Pro Bowl logo.

STATED ODDS 1:85
KMC Kevin Mawae 6.00 15.00
MBP Mitch Berger 8.00 20.00
TTP Tom Tupa 6.00 15.00
AZTI Zach Thomas 8.00 20.00
BDFS Brian Dawkins 10.00 25.00
BJQB Brad Johnson 8.00 20.00
BMOG Bruce Matthews 6.00 15.00
CBOLB Chad Brown 6.00 15.00
CCWR Cris Carter 10.00 25.00
CDRB Corey Dillon 6.00 15.00
CKILB Cortez Kennedy 8.00 20.00
CLFS Carnell Lake 6.00 15.00
CWCB Charles Woodson 10.00 25.00
DBOLB Derrick Brooks 6.00 15.00
DCOLB Dexter Coakley 6.00 15.00
DRILM Darrell Russell 6.00 15.00
DSST Detron Smith 6.00 15.00
DSTE David Sloan 6.00 15.00
EGRB Eddie George 8.00 20.00
EJRB Edgerrin James 8.00 20.00
ESRB Emmitt Smith 15.00 40.00
FWTE Frank Wycheck 8.00 20.00
GMKR Glyn Milburn 6.00 15.00
HNILB Hardy Nickerson 6.00 15.00
IBWR Isaac Bruce 10.00 25.00
JKDE Jevon Kearse 6.00 15.00
JSWR Jimmy Smith 8.00 20.00
KCDE Kevin Carter 6.00 15.00
KHOLB Kevin Hardy 6.00 15.00
KJWR Keyshawn Johnson 8.00 20.00

KWQB Kurt Warner 15.00 40.00
LEILM Luther Elliss 6.00 15.00
LMSS Lawyer Milloy 6.00 15.00
LSFS Lance Schulters 6.00 15.00
LSOT Leon Searcy 6.00 15.00
MAFB Mike Alstott 6.00 15.00
MBQB Mark Brunell 8.00 20.00
MFRB Marshall Faulk 8.00 20.00
MHWR Marvin Harrison 8.00 20.00
MMDE Michael McCrary 6.00 15.00
MMWR Muhsin Muhammad 6.00 15.00
MSDE Michael Strahan 8.00 20.00
OMPK Olindo Mare 6.00 15.00
OPOT Orlando Pace 6.00 15.00
PBOL Peter Boulware 6.00 15.00
RGQB Rich Gannon 8.00 20.00
RMOG Randall McDaniel 8.00 20.00
RMWR Randy Moss 8.00 20.00
RPDE Robert Porcher 6.00 15.00
RWFS Rod Woodson 10.00 25.00
SBIL Stephen Boyd 6.00 15.00
SBQB Steve Beuerlein 8.00 20.00
SDRB Stephen Davis 6.00 15.00
SGFB Sam Gash 6.00 15.00
SLOT Leon Searcy 6.00 15.00
SMCB Sam Madison 6.00 15.00
TBDE Tony Brackens 6.00 15.00
TGTE Tony Gonzalez 8.00 20.00
TJOG Tre Johnson 6.00 15.00
TLCB Todd Lyght 6.00 15.00
TMKR Tremain Mack 6.00 15.00
TPILM Trevor Pryce 6.00 15.00
WROT William Roaf 6.00 15.00
WSIL Warren Sapp 8.00 20.00
WWTE Wesley Walls 6.00 15.00

2000 Topps Stars Autographs

ndomly inserted in packs at the rate of one in 411, this 11-card set features authentic player autographs coupled with a foil "Topps Certified Autograph" stamp. Some were issued via mail redemption cards that carried an expiration date of 2/28/2001. A Franco Harris mail redemption card was produced but he never signed for the set.

STATED ODDS 1:411
CC Cris Carter 15.00 40.00
CR Chris Redman 10.00 25.00
DG Darrell Green 30.00 60.00
DJ Deacon Jones 15.00 40.00
EJ Edgerrin James 12.00 30.00
JM Joe Montana 50.00 120.00
KC Kevin Carter 10.00 25.00
KW Kurt Warner 20.00 50.00
RD Ron Dayne 15.00 40.00
RL Ronnie Lott 12.00 30.00
SL Steve Largent 15.00 40.00

2000 Topps Stars Pro Bowl Powerhouse

ndomly inserted in packs at the rate of one in 12, this 15-card set features players that have performed well in the Pro Bowl and are ready for a repeat performance.

COMPLETE SET (15) 7.50 20.00
STATED ODDS 1:12
PB1 Kurt Warner 1.00 2.50
PB2 Warren Sapp .50 1.25
PB3 Marvin Harrison .50 1.25
PB4 Kevin Carter .40 1.00
PB5 Jimmy Smith .50 1.25
PB6 Stephen Davis .40 1.00
PB7 Edgerrin James .50 1.25
PB8 Tony Gonzalez .50 1.25
PB9 Sam Madison .40 1.00
PB10 Mike Alstott .40 1.00
PB11 Marshall Faulk .50 1.25
PB12 Jevon Kearse .40 1.00
PB13 Kevin Hardy .40 1.00
PB14 Peyton Manning 1.50 4.00
PB15 Randy Moss .50 1.25

2000 Topps Stars Progression

ndomly inserted in packs at the rate of one in 15, this 5-card set highlights an NFL timeline and traces the lineage of players from the past to players of today.

COMPLETE SET (5) 4.00 10.00
STATED ODDS 1:15
P1 Montana 2.50 6.00
Favre
Pennington
P2 D.Jones .60 1.50
Kearse
C.Brown
P3 Lott .75 2.00
Lynch
Grant
P4 Largent .75 2.00
R.Moss
Warrick
P5 Harris .60 1.50
E.James
T.Jones

2000 Topps Stars Walk of Fame

ndomly seeded in packs at the rate of one in eight, this 15-card set spotlights top players of today and compares their stats to a star from the past.

COMPLETE SET (15) 7.50 20.00
STATED ODDS 1:8
W1 Randy Moss .40 1.00
W2 Kurt Warner .75 2.00
W3 Jimmy Smith .40 1.00
W4 Cris Carter .50 1.25
W5 Brett Favre 1.00 2.50
W6 Ricky Williams .40 1.00
W7 Marvin Harrison .40 1.00
W8 Fred Taylor .30 .75
W9 Eddie George .40 1.00
W10 Edgerrin James .40 1.00
W11 Jevon Kearse .30 .75
W12 Emmitt Smith .75 2.00
W13 Marshall Faulk .40 1.00
W14 Terrell Davis .40 1.00
W15 Peyton Manning 1.25 3.00

2012 Topps Strata

COMPLETE SET (150) 15.00 40.00
1 Robert Griffin III RC .30 .75
2 Joe Adams RC .25 .60
3 DeMarco Murray .25 .60
4 Beanie Wells .20 .50
5 Morris Claiborne RC .25 .60
6 Ryan Tannehill RC .40 1.00
7 Steve Johnson .25 .60
8 LaMichael James RC .25 .60
9 Quinton Coples RC .25 .60
10 Calvin Johnson .30 .75
11 Jason Witten .25 .60
12 Mario Williams .20 .50
13 A.J. Jenkins RC .25 .60
14 Vernon Davis .20 .50
15 Josh Freeman .25 .60
16 Fletcher Cox RC .40 1.00
17 Hakeem Nicks .20 .50
18 Doug Martin RC .40 1.00
19 Darrelle Revis .20 .50
20 Maurice Jones-Drew .20 .50
21 Brian Quick RC .25 .60
22 Jordy Nelson .25 .60
23 Tony Romo .25 .60
24 Bruce Irvin RC .30 .75
25 Rob Gronkowski .30 .75
26 Fred Jackson .25 .60
27 Jeremy Maclin .20 .50
28 Ryan Broyles RC .25 .60
29 Russell Wilson RC 2.00 5.00
30 Andre Johnson .25 .60
31 Mario Manningham .20 .50
32 Antonio Gates .25 .60
33 Michael Floyd RC .25 .60
34 Jake Locker .30 .75
35 Ronnie Hillman RC .25 .60
36 Kevin Kolb .20 .50
37 Andy Dalton .25 .60
38 Dwayne Bowe .25 .60
39 Mark Sanchez .20 .50
40 Adrian Peterson .30 .75
41 Frank Gore .25 .60
42 Antonio Brown .30 .75
43 LeGarrette Blount .25 .60
44 Matt Ryan .25 .60
45 DeMarcus Ware .30 .75
46 Patrick Willis .25 .60
47 Miles Austin .20 .50
48 Ryan Mathews .25 .60
49 Lamar Miller RC .40 1.00
50 Aaron Rodgers .50 1.25
51 Nick Toon RC .25 .60
52 Willis McGahee .20 .50
53 Dont'a Hightower RC .40 1.00
54 Aaron Hernandez .25 .60
55 Steve Smith .25 .60
56 Michael Crabtree .20 .50
57 Roddy White .20 .50
58 Jay Cutler .20 .50
59 Matt Schaub .20 .50
60 Peyton Manning .60 1.50
61 Luke Kuechly RC .60 1.50
62 Shea McClellin RC .30 .75
63 Philip Rivers .30 .75
64 Randy Moss .25 .60
65 Harrison Smith RC .25 .60
66 Greg Jennings .20 .50
67 T.J. Graham RC .25 .60
68 Whitney Mercilus RC .25 .60
69 Joe Flacco .25 .60
70 Larry Fitzgerald .25 .60
71 Matt Flynn .20 .50
72 Marshawn Lynch .25 .60
73 Brandon Weeden RC .25 .60
74 Jermichael Finley .20 .50
75 Trent Richardson RC .25 .60
76 Michael Vick .25 .60
77 Chandler Jones RC .25 .60
78 Rueben Randle RC .25 .60
79 Chris Johnson .20 .50
80 Cam Newton .30 .75
81 Mohamed Sanu RC .40 1.00
82 Matthew Stafford .25 .60
83 Dez Bryant .30 .75
84 Mike Wallace .20 .50
85 Kendall Wright RC .25 .60
86 Alex Smith .25 .60
87 Darren McFadden .20 .50
88 Jimmy Graham .30 .75
89 Roy Helu .20 .50
90 Victor Cruz .25 .60
91 Arian Foster .25 .60
92 Darren Sproles .25 .60
93 Stephen Hill RC .25 .60
94 Bernard Pierce RC .25 .60
95 C.J. Spiller .20 .50
96 Mark Barron RC .25 .60
97 Stevan Ridley .20 .50
98 Robert Turbin RC .25 .60
99 Sidney Rice .20 .50
100 Tom Brady .75 2.00
101 Peyton Hillis .20 .50
102 Michael Turner .20 .50
103 Carson Palmer .25 .60
104 Reggie Wayne .25 .60
105 Steven Jackson .20 .50
106 Ben Roethlisberger .30 .75
107 Chris Givens RC .25 .60
108 Coby Fleener RC .25 .60
109 Wes Welker .25 .60
110 Ray Rice .20 .50
111 Troy Polamalu .30 .75
112 Isaiah Pead RC .25 .60
113 Jarius Wright RC .25 .60
114 A.J. Green .30 .75
115 Reggie Bush .20 .50
116 Dwayne Allen RC .25 .60
117 Melvin Ingram RC .25 .60
118 Matt Forte .20 .50
119 Ryan Fitzpatrick .20 .50
120 Drew Brees .30 .75
121 Julio Jones .30 .75
122 David Wilson RC .25 .60
123 Tim Tebow .30 .75
124 Nick Foles RC .60 1.50
125 Justin Blackmon RC .25 .60
126 Clay Matthews .30 .75
127 Alshon Jeffery RC .50 1.25
128 Michael Egnew RC .25 .60
129 Brock Osweiler RC .25 .60
130 Eli Manning .25 .60
131 Anquan Boldin .20 .50
132 Dre Kirkpatrick RC .25 .60
133 Percy Harvin .20 .50
134 Courtney Upshaw RC .30 .75
135 Sam Bradford .20 .50
136 Jared Allen .20 .50
137 Michael Brockers RC .25 .60
138 Vincent Jackson .20 .50
139 Brandon Marshall .25 .60
140 LeSean McCoy .30 .75
141 Ndamukong Suh .25 .60
142 Shonn Greene .20 .50
143 Tony Gonzalez .25 .60
144 Marques Colston .20 .50
145 Ahmad Bradshaw .20 .50
146 DeVier Posey RC .25 .60
147 Laurent Robinson .20 .50
148 DeSean Jackson .25 .60
149 Christian Ponder .20 .50
150 Andrew Luck RC 2.50 6.00

2012 Topps Strata Blue

*ROOKIES/50: 2.5X TO 6X HOBBY RC

2012 Topps Strata Bronze

*ROOKIES/150: 1.2X TO 3X HOBBY RC

2012 Topps Strata Gold

*ROOKIES/99: 2X TO 5X HOBBY RC

2012 Topps Strata Green

*ROOKIES/10: 8X TO 20X HOBBY RC

2012 Topps Strata Retail

COMPLETE SET (150) 15.00 40.00
*RETAIL: .3X TO .8X HOBBY

2012 Topps Strata Clear Cut Rookie Relic Autographs Blue Patch

*BASE JSY AU: .25X TO .6X BLUE/75
*BRONZE/150: .25X TO .6X BLUE/75
*GOLD/99: .3X TO .8X BLUE/75
*GREEN/55: .5X TO 1.2X BLUE/75
CCARAJ A.J. Jenkins 6.00 15.00
CCARAJE Alshon Jeffery 12.00 30.00
CCARAL Andrew Luck 75.00 150.00
CCARBO Brock Osweiler 6.00 15.00
CCARBP Bernard Pierce EXCH 12.00 30.00
CCARBQ Brian Quick 6.00 15.00
CCARBW Brandon Weeden 6.00 15.00
CCARCF Coby Fleener 6.00 15.00
CCARCG Chris Givens 6.00 15.00
CCARDA Dwayne Allen 6.00 15.00
CCARDM Doug Martin 10.00 25.00
CCARDP DeVier Posey 6.00 15.00
CCARDPO DeVier Posey 6.00 15.00
CCARDW David Wilson 6.00 15.00
CCARGC Greg Childs 6.00 15.00
CCARIP Isaiah Pead 6.00 15.00
CCARJA Joe Adams 6.00 15.00
CCARJB Justin Blackmon 6.00 15.00
CCARJC Juron Criner 6.00 15.00
CCARJW Jarius Wright 6.00 15.00
CCARKW Kendall Wright 6.00 15.00
CCARLJ LaMichael James 6.00 15.00
CCARLM Lamar Miller 10.00 25.00
CCARME Michael Egnew 6.00 15.00
CCARMF Michael Floyd 6.00 15.00
CCARMS Mohamed Sanu 10.00 25.00
CCARNF Nick Foles 15.00 40.00
CCARNT Nick Toon 6.00 15.00
CCARNTO Nick Toon 6.00 15.00
CCARRB Ryan Broyles 6.00 15.00
CCARRBR Ryan Broyles 6.00 15.00
CCARRG Robert Griffin III 30.00 80.00
CCARRH Ronnie Hillman 6.00 15.00
CCARROT Robert Turbin 6.00 15.00
CCARRR Rueben Randle 6.00 15.00
CCARRT Ryan Tannehill 10.00 25.00
CCARRTU Robert Turbin 6.00 15.00
CCARRW Russell Wilson 150.00 300.00
CCARSH Stephen Hill 6.00 15.00
CCARTG T.J. Graham 6.00 15.00
CCARTH T.Y. Hilton 12.00 30.00
CCARTJG T.J. Graham 6.00 15.00
CCARTR Trent Richardson 25.00 60.00

2012 Topps Strata Clear Cut Rookie Relic Autographs Red Patch

*RED/30: .6X TO 1.5X BLUE/75
CCARAL Andrew Luck 150.00 250.00
CCARDM Doug Martin 15.00 40.00
CCARRW Russell Wilson 200.00 400.00
CCARTR Trent Richardson 25.00 60.00

2012 Topps Strata Rookie Autographs

*BRONZE/150: .4X TO 1X BASIC AUTO
EXCH EXPIRATION: 11/30/2015
RAAJ Alshon Jeffery
RABP Bernard Pierce
RABQ Brian Quick
RABR Bobby Rainey 2.50 6.00
RACF Coby Fleener 2.50 6.00
RACG Cyrus Gray 2.50 6.00
RACGI Chris Givens EXCH 2.50 6.00
RACH Chandler Harnish 2.50 6.00
RACK Case Keenum 20.00 50.00
RACP Chris Polk
RACR Chris Rainey EXCH 2.50 6.00
RADA Dwayne Allen 2.50 6.00
RADD David DeCastro 2.50 6.00
RADJ Dwight Jones 2.50 6.00
RADK Dre Kirkpatrick EXCH 2.50 6.00
RADM Doug Martin
RADP DeVier Posey 2.50 6.00
RADPO Dontari Poe 2.50 6.00
RADS Devon Still 3.00 8.00
RAGC Greg Childs 2.50 6.00
RAIP Isaiah Pead
RAJA Joe Adams 2.50 6.00
RAJC Juron Criner 2.50 6.00
RAJF Jeff Fuller 2.50 6.00
RAJH Jacory Harris 3.00 8.00
RAJJ Janoris Jenkins 3.00 8.00
RAJK Jermaine Kearse 6.00 15.00
RAJW Jarius Wright 2.50 6.00
RAJWO Jerel Worthy 2.50 6.00
RAKC Kirk Cousins 10.00 25.00
RAKM Kellen Moore 3.00 8.00
RALJ LaMichael James 2.50 6.00
HALK Luke Kuechly 8.00 20.00
RAMB Mark Barron EXCH 2.50 6.00
RAME Michael Egnew 2.50 6.00
RAMI Melvin Ingram 2.50 6.00
RAMK Matt Kalil 2.50 6.00
RAMM Marvin McNutt 2.50 6.00
RAMS Mohamed Sanu
RANF Nick Foles 20.00 40.00
RANT Nick Toon 2.50 6.00
RARB Ryan Broyles 2.50 6.00
RARH Ronnie Hillman 2.50 6.00
RARL Ryan Lindley 2.50 6.00
RARR Rueben Randle
RART Robert Turbin 2.50 6.00
RATB Travis Benjamin 2.50 6.00
RATJG T.J. Graham 2.50 6.00
RATYH T.Y. Hilton 5.00 12.00

2012 Topps Strata Rookie Autographs Blue

*BLUE/75: .6X TO 1.5X BASIC AU
RADM Doug Martin 6.00 15.00
RAKC Kirk Cousins 15.00 40.00
RALJ LaMichael James 4.00 10.00
RANF Nick Foles 25.00 60.00

2012 Topps Strata Rookie Autographs Gold

RAJK Jermaine Kearse 10.00 25.00
RALJ LaMichael James 3.00 8.00
RANF Nick Foles 20.00 50.00

2012 Topps Strata Rookie Autographs Green

*GREEN/50: .8X TO 2X BASIC AU
RADM Doug Martin 8.00 20.00
RAKC Kirk Cousins 20.00 50.00
RALJ LaMichael James 5.00 12.00
RANF Nick Foles 30.00 80.00

2012 Topps Strata Rookie Autographs Red

*RED/25: 1X TO 2.5X BASIC AU
RADM Doug Martin 10.00 25.00
RALJ LaMichael James 6.00 15.00
RANF Nick Foles 40.00 100.00

2012 Topps Strata Rookie Die Cut

STATED ODDS 1:18 HOB, 1:24 RET
RDCAJ Alshon Jeffery 2.00 5.00
RDCAJJ A.J. Jenkins 1.00 2.50
RDCAL Andrew Luck 10.00 25.00
RDCBO Brock Osweiler 1.00 2.50
RDCBP Bernard Pierce 1.00 2.50
RDCBQ Brian Quick 1.00 2.50
RDCBW Brandon Weeden 1.00 2.50
RDCCF Coby Fleener 1.00 2.50
RDCCG Chris Givens 1.00 2.50
RDCDA Dwayne Allen 1.00 2.50
RDCDM Doug Martin 1.50 4.00
RDCDP DeVier Posey 1.00 2.50
RDCDW David Wilson 1.00 2.50
RDCIP Isaiah Pead 1.00 2.50
RDCJA Joe Adams 1.00 2.50
RDCJB Justin Blackmon 1.00 2.50
RDCJW Jarius Wright 1.00 2.50
RDCKW Kendall Wright 1.00 2.50
RDCLJ LaMichael James 1.00 2.50
RDCLM Lamar Miller 1.50 4.00
RDCME Michael Egnew 1.00 2.50
RDCMF Michael Floyd 1.00 2.50
RDCMS Mohamed Sanu 1.50 4.00
RDCNF Nick Foles 2.50 6.00
RDCNT Nick Toon 1.00 2.50
RDCRB Ryan Broyles 1.00 2.50
RDCRG Robert Griffin III 6.00 15.00
RDCRH Ronnie Hillman 1.00 2.50
RDCRR Rueben Randle 1.00 2.50
RDCRT Ryan Tannehill 1.50 4.00
RDCRTU Robert Turbin 1.00 2.50
RDCRW Russell Wilson 8.00 20.00
RDCSH Stephen Hill 1.00 2.50
RDCTG T.J. Graham 1.00 2.50
RDCTR Trent Richardson 1.00 2.50

2012 Topps Strata Rookie Jersey Autographs

EXCH EXPIRATION: 11/30/2015
SSRAJ Alshon Jeffery 20.00 50.00
SSRAJJ A.J. Jenkins 10.00 25.00
SSRAL Andrew Luck 125.00 250.00
SSRBO Brock Osweiler EXCH 10.00 25.00
SSRBP Bernard Pierce 10.00 25.00
SSRBQ Brian Quick 10.00 25.00
SSRBW Brandon Weeden 10.00 25.00
SSRCF Coby Fleener 10.00 25.00
SSRCG Chris Givens 10.00 25.00
SSRDA Dwayne Allen 10.00 25.00
SSRDM Doug Martin 15.00 40.00
SSRDP DeVier Posey 10.00 25.00
SSRDW David Wilson 10.00 25.00
SSRGC Greg Childs 10.00 25.00
SSRIP Isaiah Pead 10.00 25.00
SSRJA Joe Adams 10.00 25.00
SSRJB Justin Blackmon 10.00 25.00
SSRJC Juron Criner 10.00 25.00
SSRJW Jarius Wright 10.00 25.00
SSRKW Kendall Wright 10.00 25.00
SSRLJ LaMichael James 10.00 25.00
SSRLM Lamar Miller 15.00 40.00
SSRME Michael Egnew 10.00 25.00
SSRMF Michael Floyd 10.00 25.00
SSRMS Mohamed Sanu 15.00 40.00
SSRNF Nick Foles 25.00 60.00
SSRNT Nick Toon 10.00 25.00
SSRRB Ryan Broyles 10.00 25.00
SSRRG Robert Griffin III 60.00 120.00
SSRRH Ronnie Hillman 10.00 25.00
SSRRR Rueben Randle 10.00 25.00
SSRRT Ryan Tannehill 15.00 40.00
SSRRTU Robert Turbin 25.00 50.00
SSRRW Russell Wilson 175.00 300.00
SSRSH Stephen Hill 10.00 25.00
SSRTG T.J. Graham 10.00 25.00
SSRTH T.Y. Hilton 20.00 50.00
SSRTR Trent Richardson EXCH 50.00 100.00

2012 Topps Strata Rookie Jersey Autographs Patch

*PATCH/15: .6X TO 1.5X JSY AU/40
SSRAL Andrew Luck 400.00 800.00
SSRRG Robert Griffin III 100.00 200.00
SSRRW Russell Wilson 350.00 500.00

2012 Topps Strata Rookie Jerseys

*PATCH/80: .6X TO 1.5X BASIC JSY/296
*BRONZE/150: .5X TO 1.2X BASIC JSY/296
*GOLD/99: .5X TO 1.2X BASIC JSY/296
*GREEN PATCH/65: .6X TO 1.5X BASIC JSY/296
*RED PATCH/41: .8X TO 2X BASIC JSY/296
RRAJ Alshon Jeffery 3.00 8.00
RRAJJ A.J. Jenkins 1.50 4.00
RRAL Andrew Luck 12.00 30.00
RRBO Brock Osweiler 1.50 4.00
RRBP Bernard Pierce 1.50 4.00
RRBQ Brian Quick 1.50 4.00
RRBW Brandon Weeden 1.50 4.00
RRCF Coby Fleener 1.50 4.00
RRCG Chris Givens 1.50 4.00
RRDA Dwayne Allen 1.50 4.00
RRDM Doug Martin 2.50 6.00
RRDP DeVier Posey 1.50 4.00
RRGC Greg Childs 1.50 4.00
RRIP Isaiah Pead 1.50 4.00
RRJA Joe Adams 1.50 4.00
RRJB Justin Blackmon 1.50 4.00
RRJC Juron Criner 1.50 4.00
RRJW Jarius Wright 1.50 4.00
RRKW Kendall Wright 1.50 4.00
RRLJ LaMichael James 1.50 4.00
RRLM Lamar Miller 2.50 6.00
RRME Michael Egnew 1.50 4.00
RRMF Michael Floyd 1.50 4.00
RRMS Mohamed Sanu 2.50 6.00
RRNF Nick Foles 4.00 10.00
RRNT Nick Toon 1.50 4.00
RRRB Ryan Broyles 1.50 4.00
RRRG Robert Griffin III 2.00 5.00
RRRH Ronnie Hillman 1.50 4.00
RRRR Rueben Randle 1.50 4.00
RRRT Ryan Tannehill 2.50 6.00
RRRTU Robert Turbin 1.50 4.00
RRRW Russell Wilson 8.00 20.00
RRSH Stephen Hill 1.50 4.00
RRTG T.J. Graham 1.50 4.00
RRTH T.Y. Hilton 3.00 8.00
RRTR Trent Richardson 1.50 4.00

2013 Topps Strata

COMPLETE SET (150) 15.00 40.00
1 Percy Harvin .20 .50
2 Reggie Bush .20 .50
3 Ryan Nassib RC .25 .60
4 Landry Jones RC .25 .60
5 Calvin Johnson .30 .75
6 Danny Amendola .25 .60
7 Ben Roethlisberger .30 .75
8 Jake Locker .25 .60
9 Stedman Bailey RC .25 .60
10 Adrian Peterson .30 .75
11 Kenjon Barner RC .25 .60
12 Matt Barkley RC .25 .60
13 Vance McDonald RC .30 .75
14 Wes Welker .25 .60
15 Robert Woods RC .40 1.00
16 Antonio Cromartie .20 .50
17 Giovani Bernard RC .25 .60
18 Luke Kuechly .25 .60
19 Rob Gronkowski .30 .75
20 Steve Johnson .25 .60
21 Justin Blackmon .20 .50
22 Charles Tillman .25 .60
23 C.J. Spiller .20 .50
24 Knile Davis RC .25 .60
25 Jay Cutler .20 .50
26 Patrick Willis .25 .60
27 BenJarvus Green-Ellis .25 .60
28 Vincent Jackson .20 .50
29 Antonio Brown .30 .75
30 Aaron Rodgers .50 1.25
31 Dee Milliner RC .25 .60
32 Quinton Patton RC .25 .60
33 Alex Smith .25 .60
34 Eli Manning .25 .60
35 LeSean McCoy .30 .75
36 Dion Jordan RC .25 .60
37 Cecil Shorts .20 .50
38 Tyler Eifert RC .25 .60
39 Darren Sproles .25 .60
40 Roddy White .20 .50
41 Andre Johnson .20 .50
42 Reggie Wayne .25 .60
43 Jamaal Charles .25 .60
44 Larry Fitzgerald .25 .60
45 Michael Vick .25 .60
46 Jarvis Jones RC .25 .60
47 Aldon Smith .20 .50
48 Doug Martin .25 .60
49 Anquan Boldin .20 .50
50 Stepfan Taylor RC .25 .60
51 Keenan Allen RC .50 1.25
52 Mike Glennon RC .25 .60
53 Christian Ponder .20 .50
54 Eric Reid RC .30 .75
55 Josh Boyce RC .25 .60
56 Alfred Morris .20 .50
57 Mike Wallace .20 .50
58 Joe Flacco .25 .60
59 Santonio Holmes .20 .50
60 Markus Wheaton RC .25 .60
61 Eric Decker .20 .50
62 Jared Allen .20 .50
63 Torrey Smith .20 .50
64 Ed Reed .25 .60
65 Manti Te'o RC .30 .75
66 Matt Ryan .25 .60
67 Jimmy Graham .30 .75
68 Tavarres King RC .25 .60
69 Brandon Weeden .20 .50
70 Troy Polamalu .30 .75
71 Dwayne Bowe .25 .60
72 Matt Forte .20 .50
73 Gavin Escobar RC .25 .60
74 Patrick Peterson .20 .50
75 Darren McFadden .25 .60
76 Hakeem Nicks .20 .50
77 Frank Gore .25 .60
78 Earl Thomas .25 .60
79 James Laurinaitis .25 .60
80 Von Miller .25 .60
81 Denarius Moore .20 .50
82 Andrew Luck .50 1.25
83 EJ Manuel RC .25 .60
84 Steven Jackson .20 .50
85 Russell Wilson .60 1.50
86 Christine Michael RC .25 .60
87 Tony Romo .25 .60
88 Sam Bradford .20 .50
89 Andre Ellington RC .25 .60
90 Montee Ball RC .25 .60
91 Victor Cruz .25 .60
92 Aaron Dobson RC .25 .60
93 Marshawn Lynch .25 .60
94 DeAndre Hopkins RC .60 1.50
95 Tom Brady .75 2.00
96 A.J. Green .30 .75
97 Tyler Wilson RC .25 .60
98 Stevan Ridley .20 .50
99 Colin Kaepernick .25 .60
100 Mike Gillislee RC .25 .60
101 Richard Sherman .30 .75
102 Vernon Davis .20 .50
103 Clay Matthews .30 .75
104 Pierre Garcon .25 .60
105 Matt Schaub .20 .50
106 Terrance Williams RC .25 .60
107 Trent Richardson .20 .50
108 Matthew Stafford .25 .60
109 Chris Johnson .20 .50
110 Kenny Stills RC .25 .60
111 D.J. Hayden RC .25 .60
112 Ezekiel Ansah RC .25 .60
113 Peyton Manning .60 1.50
114 Cam Newton .30 .75
115 DeMarco Murray .25 .60
116 Johnathan Franklin RC .25 .60
117 Geno Smith RC .25 .60
118 David Wilson .20 .50
119 Antonio Gates .25 .60
120 J.J. Watt .25 .60
121 Carson Palmer .25 .60
122 Maurice Jones-Drew .20 .50
123 Josh Freeman .25 .60
124 Denard Robinson RC .25 .60
125 Eddie Lacy RC .25 .60
126 Brandon Marshall .25 .60
127 Arian Foster .25 .60
128 Barkevious Mingo RC .25 .60
129 Cordarrelle Patterson RC .25 .60
130 Dez Bryant .30 .75
131 Cobi Hamilton RC .25 .60
132 Andy Dalton .25 .60
133 Steve Smith .25 .60
134 Drew Brees .30 .75
135 Philip Rivers .30 .75
136 Justin Hunter RC .25 .60
137 Zach Ertz RC .50 1.25
138 Ray Rice .20 .50
139 Marquise Goodwin RC .25 .60
140 Demaryius Thomas .25 .60
141 Jason Witten .25 .60
142 Robert Griffin III .20 .50
143 Le'Veon Bell RC .75 2.00
144 Ryan Tannehill .25 .60
145 Marcus Lattimore RC .25 .60
146 Julio Jones .30 .75
147 Jordan Reed RC .40 1.00
148 Randall Cobb .25 .60
149 Tavon Austin RC .30 .75
150 Joseph Randle RC .25 .60

2013 Topps Strata Blue

*ROOKIES/50: 2.5X TO 6X BASIC RC

2013 Topps Strata Bronze

*ROOKIES/150: 1.2X TO 3X BASIC RC

2013 Topps Strata Green

*ROOKIES/10: 6X TO 15X BASIC RC

2013 Topps Strata Gold

*ROOKIES/99: 1.5X TO 4X BASIC CARDS

2013 Topps Strata Orange

*VETS: 1.2X TO 3X BASIC CARDS
*ROOKIES: 1X TO 2.5X BASIC RC

2013 Topps Strata Retail

*ROOKIES: .3X TO .8X BASIC RC

2013 Topps Strata Retail Black Onyx

*VETS: 1.2X TO 3X BASIC CARDS
*ROOKIES: 1X TO 2.5X BASIC RC

2013 Topps Strata Autographs

3 Ryan Nassib SP 4.00 10.00
4 Landry Jones SP 4.00 10.00
9 Stedman Bailey 2.00 5.00
11 Kenjon Barner 2.00 5.00
12 Matt Barkley SP 2.00 5.00
13 Vance McDonald 2.50 6.00
17 Giovani Bernard SP 2.00 5.00
32 Quinton Patton 2.00 5.00
38 Tyler Eifert 2.00 5.00
46 Ryan Swope SP 2.00 5.00
52 Mike Glennon SP 2.00 5.00
54 Chris Harper 2.00 5.00
60 Markus Wheaton 2.00 5.00
65 Manti Te'o SP 2.50 6.00
68 Tavarres King SP 2.00 5.00
73 Gavin Escobar 2.00 5.00
83 EJ Manuel SP 2.00 5.00
90 Montee Ball 2.00 5.00
92 Aaron Dobson SP 2.00 5.00
94 DeAndre Hopkins SP 5.00 12.00
100 Mike Gillislee 2.00 5.00
110 Kenny Stills 2.00 5.00
116 Johnathan Franklin 2.00 5.00
117 Geno Smith SP 2.00 5.00
125 Eddie Lacy SP 2.00 5.00
129 Cordarrelle Patterson SP 2.00 5.00
136 Justin Hunter SP 2.00 5.00
137 Zach Ertz 4.00 10.00
143 Le'Veon Bell SP 10.00 25.00
145 Marcus Lattimore 8.00 20.00
147 Jordan Reed 3.00 8.00
149 Tavon Austin SP 2.50 6.00
151 D.J. Hayden 2.00 5.00
152 Jarvis Jones 5.00 12.00
153 Alec Ogletree 2.00 5.00
154 Da'Rick Rogers 2.00 5.00
155 Tyrann Mathieu 3.00 8.00
156 Alex Okafor 2.00 5.00
157 Michael Williams 2.50 6.00
170 Dion Sims 2.00 5.00

2013 Topps Strata Autographs Bronze

*BRONZE ROOK/150: .5X TO 1.2X BASIC AU
159 Danny Amendola 6.00 15.00
160 Lance Moore 5.00 12.00
161 Brent Celek 5.00 12.00
162 Andre Roberts 5.00 12.00
163 Jonathan Dwyer 5.00 12.00
165 Marcel Reece 5.00 12.00

2013 Topps Strata Autographs Green

*GRN VET/50: .6X TO 1.5X BRONZE AU/150
*GRN ROOK/50: .8X TO 2X BASIC AU
34 Eli Manning 30.00 60.00

2013 Topps Strata Autographs Gold

*GLD VET/99: .5X TO 1.2X BRONZE AU/150
*GOLD ROOK/99: .6X TO 1.5X BASIC AU

2013 Topps Strata Autographs Red

*RED VET/25: .8X TO 2X BRONZE AU/150
*RED ROOK/25: 1X TO 2.5X BASIC AU
34 Eli Manning 40.00 80.00

2013 Topps Strata Autographs Blue

*BLU VET/75: .5X TO 1.2X BRONZE AU/150
*BLU ROOK/75: .6X TO 1.5X BASIC AU

2013 Topps Strata Clear Cut Rookie Relic Autographs

*BLUE/50: .6X TO 1.5X BASIC JSY AU
*BRONZE/150: .5X TO 1.2X BASIC JSY AU
*GOLD/75: .6X TO 1.5X BASIC JSY AU
*GREEN/25: 1X TO 2.5X BASIC JSY AU
EXCH EXPIRATION: 11/30/2016
CCARAD Aaron Dobson 3.00 8.00
CCARAE Andre Ellington 3.00 8.00
CCARCM Christine Michael 3.00 8.00
CCARCP Cordarrelle Patterson 3.00 8.00
CCARDH DeAndre Hopkins 8.00 20.00
CCARDJ Dion Jordan 3.00 8.00
CCARDR Denard Robinson EXCH 3.00 8.00
CCAREJM EJ Manuel 3.00 8.00
CCAREL Eddie Lacy 3.00 8.00
CCARGB Giovani Bernard 3.00 8.00
CCARGE Gavin Escobar 3.00 8.00
CCARGS Geno Smith 3.00 8.00
CCARJF Johnathan Franklin 3.00 8.00
CCARJH Justin Hunter 3.00 8.00
CCARJR Joseph Randle 3.00 8.00
CCARJRE Jordan Reed 5.00 12.00
CCARKA Keenan Allen 6.00 15.00
CCARKD Knile Davis 3.00 8.00
CCARKS Kenny Stills 3.00 8.00
CCARLB Le'Veon Bell 15.00 40.00
CCARLJ Landry Jones 3.00 8.00
CCARMB Matt Barkley 3.00 8.00
CCARMBA Montee Ball 3.00 8.00
CCARMG Mike Glennon 3.00 8.00
CCARMGI Mike Gillislee 3.00 8.00
CCARMGO Marquise Goodwin 3.00 8.00
CCARML Marcus Lattimore 3.00 8.00
CCARMT Manti Te'o 4.00 10.00
CCARMW Markus Wheaton 3.00 8.00
CCARQP Quinton Patton 3.00 8.00
CCARRN Ryan Nassib 3.00 8.00
CCARRW Robert Woods 5.00 12.00
CCARSB Stedman Bailey 6.00 15.00
CCARST Stepfan Taylor 3.00 8.00
CCARTA Tavon Austin 4.00 10.00
CCARTE Tyler Eifert 3.00 8.00
CCARTW Tyler Wilson 3.00 8.00
CCARTWI Terrance Williams 3.00 8.00
CCARVM Vance McDonald 4.00 10.00
CCARZE Zach Ertz 6.00 15.00

2013 Topps Strata Clear Cut Rookie Relic Autographs Red Patch

*RED/15: 1.2X TO 3X BASIC JSY AU
CCAREL Eddie Lacy 10.00 25.00

2013 Topps Strata Shadowbox Jersey Autographs

*RED PATCH/15: .6X TO 1.5X JSY AU/35
SSRAD Aaron Dobson 8.00 20.00
SSRAE Andre Ellington 5.00 12.00
SSRAJG A.J. Green EXCH
SSRCJS C.J. Spiller EXCH
SSRCM Christine Michael 12.00 30.00
SSRCP Cordarrelle Patterson 5.00 12.00
SSRDH DeAndre Hopkins 15.00 40.00
SSRDJ Dion Jordan 5.00 12.00
SSRDR Denard Robinson 5.00 12.00
SSREJM EJ Manuel 5.00 12.00
SSREL Eddie Lacy 5.00 12.00
SSREM Eli Manning EXCH
SSRGB Giovani Bernard 5.00 12.00
SSRGE Gavin Escobar 5.00 12.00
SSRGS Geno Smith 5.00 12.00
SSRJF Johnathan Franklin 5.00 12.00
SSRJH Justin Hunter
SSRJR Joseph Randle 5.00 12.00
SSRJRE Jordan Reed 12.00 30.00
SSRKA Keenan Allen
SSRKD Knile Davis 5.00 12.00
SSRKS Kenny Stills 5.00 12.00
SSRLB Le'Veon Bell 15.00 40.00
SSRLJ Landry Jones 5.00 12.00
SSRMB Matt Barkley 5.00 12.00
SSRMBA Montee Ball 5.00 12.00
SSRMG Mike Glennon 5.00 12.00
SSRMGI Mike Gillislee 5.00 12.00
SSRMGO Marquise Goodwin 5.00 12.00
SSRML Marcus Lattimore 15.00 40.00
SSRMT Manti Te'o 6.00 15.00
SSRMW Markus Wheaton 5.00 12.00
SSRQP Quinton Patton 5.00 12.00
SSRRN Ryan Nassib 10.00 25.00
SSRRR Ray Rice EXCH
SSRRW Robert Woods 15.00 40.00
SSRRWA Reggie Wayne EXCH
SSRSB Stedman Bailey
SSRSC Santa Claus 75.00 135.00
SSRST Stepfan Taylor 5.00 12.00
SSRTA Tavon Austin 6.00 15.00
SSRTE Tyler Eifert 5.00 12.00
SSRTW Tyler Wilson 5.00 12.00
SSRTWI Terrance Williams 5.00 12.00
SSRVM Vance McDonald 6.00 15.00
SSRZE Zach Ertz 10.00 25.00

2013 Topps Strata Jerseys

*BLUE PATCH/70: .5X TO 1.2X JSY/213
*BRONZE/150: .4X TO 1X JSY/213
*GOLD PATCH/90: .5X TO 1.2X JSY/213
*GREEN PATCH/35: .8X TO 2X JSY/213
*RED PATCH/10: 1.2X TO 3X JSY/213
SRAD Aaron Dobson 1.25 3.00
SRADA Andy Dalton 2.50 6.00
SRAE Andre Ellington 1.25 3.00
SRAM Alfred Morris 2.00 5.00
SRCM Christine Michael 1.25 3.00
SRCP Cordarrelle Patterson 1.25 3.00
SRDB Dez Bryant 3.00 8.00
SRDH DeAndre Hopkins 3.00 8.00
SRDJ Dion Jordan 1.25 3.00
SRDR Denard Robinson 1.25 3.00
SREJM EJ Manuel 1.25 3.00
SREL Eddie Lacy 1.25 3.00
SRFJ Fred Jackson 2.50 6.00
SRGB Giovani Bernard 1.25 3.00
SRGE Gavin Escobar 1.25 3.00
SRGS Geno Smith 1.25 3.00
SRJF Johnathan Franklin 1.25 3.00
SRJH Justin Hunter 1.25 3.00
SRJJ Julio Jones 3.00 8.00
SRJR Joseph Randle 1.25 3.00
SRJRE Jordan Reed 2.00 5.00
SRKA Keenan Allen 2.50 6.00
SRKD Knile Davis 1.25 3.00
SRKS Kenny Stills 1.25 3.00
SRLB Le'Veon Bell 4.00 10.00
SRLF Larry Fitzgerald 2.50 6.00
SRLJ Landry Jones 1.25 3.00
SRMB Matt Barkley 1.25 3.00
SRMBA Montee Ball 1.25 3.00
SRMG Mike Glennon 1.25 3.00
SRMGI Mike Gillislee 1.25 3.00
SRMGO Marquise Goodwin 1.25 3.00
SRML Marcus Lattimore 1.25 3.00
SRMT Manti Te'o 1.50 4.00
SRMW Markus Wheaton 1.25 3.00
SRNS Ndamukong Suh 2.50 6.00
SRQP Quinton Patton 1.25 3.00
SRRN Ryan Nassib 1.25 3.00
SRRT Ryan Tannehill 2.50 6.00
SRRW Robert Woods 2.00 5.00
SRSB Stedman Bailey 1.25 3.00
SRSBR Sam Bradford 2.00 5.00
SRST Stepfan Taylor 1.25 3.00
SRTA Tavon Austin 1.50 4.00
SRTE Tyler Eifert 1.25 3.00
SRTR Tony Romo 2.50 6.00
SRTW Tyler Wilson 1.25 3.00
SRTWI Terrance Williams 1.25 3.00
SRVM Vance McDonald 1.50 4.00
SRZE Zach Ertz 2.50 6.00

2013 Topps Strata Rookie Die Cut

RDCAD Aaron Dobson .60 1.50
RDCAO Alec Ogletree .60 1.50
RDCAOK Alex Okafor .60 1.50
RDCBM Barkevious Mingo .60 1.50
RDCCH Chris Harper .60 1.50
RDCCP Cordarrelle Patterson .60 1.50
RDCDH DeAndre Hopkins 1.50 4.00
RDCDJ Dion Jordan .60 1.50
RDCDJH D.J. Hayden .60 1.50
RDCDR Da'Rick Rogers .60 1.50
RDCDRO Denard Robinson .60 1.50
RDCDS Dion Sims .60 1.50
RDCDT Desmond Trufant .60 1.50
RDCEJM EJ Manuel .60 1.50
RDCEL Eddie Lacy .60 1.50
RDCGB Giovani Bernard .60 1.50
RDCGE Gavin Escobar .60 1.50
RDCGS Geno Smith .60 1.50
RDCJF Johnathan Franklin .60 1.50
RDCJH Justin Hunter .60 1.50
RDCJJ Jarvis Jones .60 1.50
RDCJJA Jawan Jamison .60 1.50
RDCJR Jordan Reed 1.00 2.50
RDCKB Kenjon Barner .60 1.50
RDCKS Kenny Stills .60 1.50
RDCLB Le'Veon Bell 2.00 5.00
RDCLJ Landry Jones .60 1.50
RDCLJO Luke Joeckel .60 1.50
RDCMB Matt Barkley .60 1.50
RDCMBA Montee Ball .60 1.50
RDCMG Mike Glennon .60 1.50
RDCMGI Mike Gillislee .60 1.50
RDCML Marcus Lattimore .60 1.50
RDCMT Manti Te'o .75 2.00
RDCMW Markus Wheaton .60 1.50
RDCMWI Michael Williams .75 2.00
RDCQP Quinton Patton .60 1.50
RDCRB Rex Burkhead .75 2.00
RDCRG Ray Graham .60 1.50
RDCRN Ryan Nassib .60 1.50
RDCRS Ryan Swope .60 1.50
RDCSB Stedman Bailey .60 1.50
RDCTA Tavon Austin .75 2.00
RDCTB Tyler Bray .60 1.50
RDCTE Tyler Eifert .60 1.50
RDCTK Tavarres King .60 1.50
RDCTM Tyrann Mathieu 1.00 2.50
RDCVM Vance McDonald .75 2.00
RDCZD Zac Dysert .60 1.50
RDCZE Zach Ertz 1.25 3.00

2013 Topps Strata Shadow Box

SSRAD Aaron Dobson 6.00 15.00
SSRAE Andre Ellington 5.00 12.00
SSRAJG A.J. Green
SSRCJS C.J. Spiller 6.00 15.00
SSRCM Christine Michael 4.00 10.00
SSRCP Cordarrelle Patterson
SSRDH DeAndre Hopkins 6.00 15.00
SSRDJ Dion Jordan
SSRDR Denard Robinson 4.00 10.00
SSREJM EJ Manuel
SSREL Eddie Lacy 4.00 10.00
SSREM Eli Manning 12.00 30.00
SSRGB Giovani Bernard
SSRGE Gavin Escobar 4.00 10.00
SSRGS Geno Smith 4.00 10.00
SSRJF Johnathan Franklin 4.00 10.00
SSRJH Justin Hunter
SSRJR Joseph Randle 4.00 10.00
SSRJRE Jordan Reed 6.00 15.00
SSRKA Keenan Allen 8.00 20.00
SSRKD Knile Davis 4.00 10.00
SSRKS Kenny Stills
SSRLB Le'Veon Bell 8.00 20.00
SSRLJ Landry Jones
SSRMB Matt Barkley
SSRMBA Montee Ball 4.00 10.00
SSRMG Mike Glennon 4.00 10.00
SSRMGI Mike Gillislee
SSRMGO Marquise Goodwin 4.00 10.00
SSRML Marcus Lattimore 6.00 15.00
SSRMT Manti Te'o 5.00 12.00
SSRMW Markus Wheaton 4.00 10.00
SSRQP Quinton Patton 4.00 10.00
SSRRN Ryan Nassib 8.00 20.00
SSRRR Ray Rice 6.00 15.00
SSRRW Robert Woods 6.00 15.00
SSRRWA Reggie Wayne 8.00 20.00
SSRSB Stedman Bailey 4.00 10.00
SSRST Stepfan Taylor 4.00 10.00
SSRTA Tavon Austin 5.00 12.00
SSRTE Tyler Eifert 5.00 12.00
SSRTW Tyler Wilson
SSRTWI Terrance Williams 4.00 10.00
SSRVM Vance McDonald 6.00 15.00
SSRZE Zach Ertz 5.00 12.00

2014 Topps Strata

ROOKIE SP STATED ODDS 1:96 HOBBY
1 Calvin Johnson .30 .75
2 Ryan Tannehill .25 .60
3 Robert Griffin III .20 .50
4 Frank Gore .25 .60
5 Larry Fitzgerald .25 .60
6 Jordan Cameron .20 .50
7 Eddie Lacy .20 .50
8 Russell Wilson .50 1.25
9 Arian Foster .25 .60
10 Ndamukong Suh .25 .60
11 Cam Newton .30 .75
12 Marshawn Lynch .25 .60
13 Trent Richardson .20 .50
14 Dez Bryant .30 .75
15 Percy Harvin .20 .50
16 Shane Vereen .25 .60
17 DeMarco Murray .25 .60
18 Mike Wallace .20 .50
19 Andre Ellington .20 .50
20 Vincent Jackson .20 .50
21 Carson Palmer .25 .60
22 Jake Locker .25 .60
23 Colin Kaepernick .25 .60

24 Alshon Jeffery .25 .60
25 EJ Manuel .20 .50
26 Randall Cobb .25 .60
27 Michael Floyd .20 .50
28 T.Y. Hilton .25 .60
29 Julius Thomas .20 .50
30 Michael Crabtree .20 .50
31 Cordarrelle Patterson .20 .50
32 Darrelle Revis .20 .50
33 Andrew Luck .40 1.00
34 Wes Welker .25 .60
35 Stevan Ridley .20 .50
36 Rob Gronkowski .30 .75
37 Pierre Garcon .25 .60
38 Le'Veon Bell .25 .60
39 Aaron Rodgers .60 1.50
40 Rashad Jennings .20 .50
41 Toby Gerhart .20 .50
42 Maurice Jones-Drew .20 .50
43 Reggie Wayne .25 .60
44 Doug Martin .25 .60
45 Joique Bell .20 .50
46 Zac Stacy .20 .50
47 Jason Pierre-Paul .20 .50
48 Von Miller .25 .60
49 Demaryius Thomas .25 .60
50 LeSean McCoy .30 .75
51 C.J. Spiller .20 .50
52 Patrick Willis .25 .60
53 Sam Bradford .20 .50
54 Steven Jackson .20 .50
55 Matt Forte .20 .50
56 Jay Cutler .20 .50
57 Jamaal Charles .25 .60
58 Earl Thomas .25 .60
59 Geno Smith .20 .50
60 Matthew Stafford .25 .60
61 Nick Foles .25 .60
62 Vernon Davis .20 .50
63 Bernard Pierce .20 .50
64 Clay Matthews .30 .75
65 Brandon Marshall .20 .50
66 Joe Flacco .25 .60
67 Philip Rivers .30 .75
68 A.J. Green .30 .75
69 DeSean Jackson .25 .60
70 Antonio Brown .30 .75
71 J.J. Watt .30 .75
72 Matt Ryan .25 .60
73 Knowshon Moreno .20 .50
74 Tom Brady .75 2.00
75 Alfred Morris .20 .50
76 Luke Kuechly .25 .60
77 Richard Sherman .30 .75
78 Jordan Reed .20 .50
79 Ben Tate .20 .50
80 Julio Jones .30 .75
81 Brian Hoyer .20 .50
82 Montee Ball .20 .50
83 Drew Brees .30 .75
84 Marques Colston .20 .50
85 Eli Manning .25 .60
86 Peyton Manning .60 1.50
87 Jordy Nelson .25 .60
88 Jason Witten .25 .60
89 Andre Johnson .25 .60
90 Ryan Mathews .25 .60
91 Victor Cruz .25 .60
92 Josh Gordon .20 .50
93 Reggie Bush .20 .50
94 Chris Johnson .20 .50
95 Jimmy Graham .30 .75
96 Ben Roethlisberger .30 .75
97 Troy Polamalu .30 .75
98 Giovani Bernard .20 .50
99 Tony Romo .25 .60
100 Keenan Allen .25 .60
101 Cassius Marsh RC .30 .75
102 Martavis Bryant RC .30 .75
103A Terrance West RC .25 .60
103B Terrance West SP .60 1.50
104 Austin Seferian-Jenkins RC .25 .60
105A Odell Beckham Jr. RC .60 1.50
105B Odell Beckham Jr. SP 6.00 15.00
106 Xavier Grimble RC .30 .75
107 Michael Sam RC .25 .60
108 Deone Bucannon RC .25 .60
109 Marion Grice RC .25 .60
110A Jadeveon Clowney RC .30 .75
110B Jadeveon Clowney SP .75 2.00
111 Charles Sims RC .25 .60
112 Cody Hoffman RC .25 .60
113 Ka'Deem Carey RC .25 .60
114A Carlos Hyde RC .30 .75
114B Carlos Hyde SP .75 2.00
115 Greg Robinson RC .25 .60
116 Stephon Tuitt RC .40 1.00
117A Kelvin Benjamin RC .40 1.00
117B Kelvin Benjamin SP 1.00 2.50
118A Cody Latimer RC .30 .75
118B Cody Latimer SP .75 2.00
119 Zach Mettenberger RC .25 .60
120 Kyle Van Noy RC .30 .75
121 Bruce Ellington RC .25 .60
122A Brandin Cooks RC .40 1.00
122B Brandin Cooks SP 1.00 2.50
123A Jordan Matthews RC .40 1.00
123B Jordan Matthews SP 1.00 2.50
124A Derek Carr RC 1.50 4.00
124B Derek Carr SP 4.00 10.00
125 Timmy Jernigan RC .25 .60
126 Darqueze Dennard RC .30 .75
127 Henry Josey RC .25 .60
128 Troy Niklas RC .25 .60
129 Zack Martin RC .30 .75
130 Josh Huff RC .30 .75
131 Devin Street RC .25 .60
132 Paul Richardson RC .30 .75
133 Davante Adams RC .40 1.00
134 Richard Rodgers RC .40 1.00
135 Jarvis Landry RC .50 1.25
136 Garrett Gilbert RC .25 .60
137 Jeff Mathews RC .30 .75
138 Isaiah Crowell RC .30 .75
139 C.J. Fiedorowicz RC .25 .60
140 Anthony Barr RC .25 .60
141A Jimmy Garoppolo RC 2.00 5.00
141B Jimmy Garoppolo SP 5.00 12.00
142 Kony Ealy RC .30 .75
143A A.J. McCarron RC .25 .60
143B A.J. McCarron SP .60 1.50
144 Ra'Shede Hageman RC .25 .60
145 David Fales RC .25 .60
146 Stephen Morris RC .25 .60
147 Trey Millard RC .30 .75
148A Blake Bortles RC .30 .75
148B Blake Bortles SP .75 2.00
149 Jace Amaro RC .25 .60
150 C.J. Mosley RC .30 .75
151 Ryan Grant RC .25 .60
152A Sammy Watkins RC .40 1.00
152B Sammy Watkins SP 1.00 2.50
153 Dri Archer RC .25 .60
154 Calvin Pryor RC .25 .60
155 Jake Matthews RC .25 .60
156 Ha Ha Clinton-Dix RC .30 .75
157 Robert Herron RC .25 .60
158 Marqise Lee RC .30 .75
159 Connor Shaw RC .25 .60
160 Kevin Norwood RC .25 .60
161 Trent Murphy RC .25 .60
162 Brandon Coleman RC .25 .60
163 Cyrus Kouandjio RC .30 .75
164 Jerick McKinnon RC .30 .75
165 John Brown RC .40 1.00
166A Eric Ebron RC .30 .75
166B Eric Ebron SP .75 2.00
167 Jeremy Hill RC .30 .75
168 Arthur Lynch RC .25 .60
169 Jeff Janis RC .25 .60
170 Michael Campanaro RC .25 .60
171 Taylor Lewan RC .25 .60
172 Scott Crichton RC .25 .60
173A Tre Mason RC .25 .60
173B Tre Mason SP .60 1.50
174 Tajh Boyd RC .25 .60
175 Ryan Shazier RC .40 1.00
176A Bishop Sankey RC .25 .60
176B Bishop Sankey SP .60 1.50
177 Aaron Murray RC .25 .60
178 Jason Verrett RC .25 .60
179 Donte Moncrief RC .25 .60
180 James White RC .50 1.25
181 Storm Johnson RC .25 .60
182A Tom Savage RC .25 .60
182B Tom Savage SP .60 1.50
183 Justin Gilbert RC .25 .60
184 Louis Nix RC .25 .60
185A Teddy Bridgewater RC .40 1.00
185B Teddy Bridgewater SP 6.00 15.00
186 De'Anthony Thomas RC .25 .60
187A Mike Evans RC .60 1.50
187B Mike Evans SP 1.50 4.00
188 Devonta Freeman RC .40 1.00
189 Lorenzo Taliaferro RC .25 .60
190 Aaron Donald RC .60 1.50
191 Lache Seastrunk RC .25 .60
192 Andre Williams RC .25 .60
193 Logan Thomas RC .25 .60
194 Pierre Desir RC .25 .60
195 Jalen Saunders RC .25 .60
196 Khalil Mack RC 1.00 2.50
197 Allen Robinson RC .40 1.00
198 Mike Davis RC .25 .60
199 Bradley Roby RC .25 .60
200A Johnny Manziel RC .40 1.00
200B Johnny Manziel SP 1.00 2.50

2014 Topps Strata Black

*1-100 VETS: 1X TO 2.5X BASIC CARDS
*101-200 ROOKIES: .8X TO 2X BASIC RC
INSERTS IN RETAIL BLASTER BOXES

2014 Topps Strata Bronze

*ROOKIES/150: 1.2X TO 3X BASIC RC

2014 Topps Strata Gold

*VETS: 1.2X TO 3X BASIC CARDS
*ROOKIES: .75X TO 2X BASIC CARDS

2014 Topps Strata Retail

*RETAIL: .3X TO .8X HOBBY

2014 Topps Strata Retail Purple

*1-100 VETS: .8X TO 2X BASIC CARDS
*101-200 ROOKIES: .6X TO 1.5X BASIC RC
THREE PER RETAIL JUMBO PACK

2014 Topps Strata Sapphire

*ROOKIES/50: 2.5X TO 6X BASIC RC

2014 Topps Strata Topaz

*ROOKIES/99: 1.5X TO 4X BASIC CARDS

2014 Topps Strata Autographs

STATED ODDS 1:56 HOBBY
*BRONZE/150: .5X TO 1.2X BASIC AU
*TOPAZ/99: .6X TO 1.5X BASIC AU
*SAPPHIRE/75: .6X TO 1.5X BASIC AU
*EMERALD/50: .75X TO 2X BASIC AU
*RUBY/25: 1X TO 2.5X BASIC AU
6 Jordan Cameron 3.00 8.00
7 Eddie Lacy 3.00 8.00
24 Alshon Jeffery 6.00 15.00
28 T.Y. Hilton
29 Julius Thomas 3.00 8.00
61 Nick Foles
82 Montee Ball 3.00 8.00
98 Giovani Bernard
100 Keenan Allen 4.00 10.00
101 David Fales 2.00 5.00
102 Troy Niklas 2.00 5.00
103 Xavier Grimble 2.50 6.00
106 Cody Hoffman 2.00 5.00
109 Terrance West 2.00 5.00
110 Kony Ealy 2.50 6.00
113 Trey Millard 2.50 6.00
115 Andre Williams 2.00 5.00
119 Ka'Deem Carey 2.00 5.00
120 C.J. Fiedorowicz 2.00 5.00
123 Tajh Boyd 2.00 5.00
126 Deone Bucannon 2.00 5.00
127 Jason Verrett 2.00 5.00
128 Brandon Coleman 2.00 5.00
135 Garrett Gilbert 2.00 5.00
136 Jared Abbrederis 2.00 5.00
137 Jace Amaro 2.00 5.00
139 Josh Huff 2.50 6.00
144 Isaiah Crowell 2.50 6.00
145 Bishop Sankey 2.00 5.00
150 Robert Herron 2.00 5.00
153 Lache Seastrunk 2.00 5.00
154 Lorenzo Taliaferro 2.00 5.00
162 Jeremy Hill 2.50 6.00
164 Ryan Shazier 3.00 8.00
168 Anthony Barr 2.00 5.00
170 Logan Thomas 2.00 5.00
172 Arthur Lynch 2.00 5.00
175 Henry Josey 2.00 5.00
177 James White 4.00 10.00
179 Ha Ha Clinton-Dix 2.50 6.00
181 Scott Crichton 2.00 5.00
185 Darqueze Dennard 2.50 6.00
187 Marqise Lee 2.50 6.00
188 Kyle Van Noy 2.50 6.00
189 Stephon Tuitt 3.00 8.00
190 Zach Mettenberger 2.00 5.00
193 Marion Grice 2.00 5.00
194 Martavis Bryant 2.50 6.00
199 Mike Davis 2.00 5.00
200 Stephen Morris 2.00 5.00

2014 Topps Strata Clear Cut Rookie Relic Autographs

*JSY AU: .25X TO .6X SAPPHIRE/75
CCARJM Johnny Manziel EXCH 4.00 10.00

2014 Topps Strata Clear Cut Rookie Relic Autographs Emerald

*EMERALD/50: .5X TO 1.2X SAPPHIRE/75
CCARTB Teddy Bridgewater 15.00 40.00

2014 Topps Strata Clear Cut Rookie Relic Autographs Ruby

*RUBY/25: .6X TO 1.5X SAPPHIRE/75

2014 Topps Strata Clear Cut Rookie Relic Autographs Sapphire

*BRONZE/150: .3X TO .8X SAPPHIRE/75
*TOPAZ/90: .4X TO 1X SAPPHIRE/75
CCARAM A.J. McCarron 4.00 10.00
CCARAMU Aaron Murray 4.00 10.00
CCARAR Allen Robinson 6.00 15.00
CCARAS Austin Seferian-Jenkins 4.00 10.00
CCARAW Andre Williams 6.00 15.00
CCARBB Blake Bortles 5.00 12.00
CCARBC Brandin Cooks 6.00 15.00
CCARBE Bruce Ellington 4.00 10.00
CCARBS Bishop Sankey 4.00 10.00
CCARCL Cody Latimer 5.00 12.00
CCARCS Charles Sims 4.00 10.00
CCARDA Davante Adams 10.00 25.00
CCARDAR Dri Archer EXCH 4.00 10.00
CCARDC Derek Carr 30.00 60.00
CCARDF Devonta Freeman 12.00 30.00
CCARDFA David Fales 4.00 10.00
CCARDM Donte Moncrief 4.00 10.00
CCAREE Eric Ebron 5.00 12.00
CCARJA Jace Amaro 4.00 10.00
CCARJC Jadeveon Clowney EXCH 5.00 12.00
CCARJG Jimmy Garoppolo 75.00 150.00
CCARJH Jeremy Hill 5.00 12.00
CCARJHU Josh Huff 5.00 12.00
CCARJL Jarvis Landry 15.00 40.00
CCARJM Jerick McKinnon 5.00 12.00
CCARJMA Jordan Matthews 6.00 15.00
CCARKB Kelvin Benjamin 6.00 15.00
CCARKC Ka'Deem Carey 4.00 10.00
CCARLT Logan Thomas 4.00 10.00
CCARMB Martavis Bryant 5.00 12.00
CCARME Mike Evans 12.00 30.00
CCARML Marqise Lee 5.00 12.00
CCARPR Paul Richardson 8.00 20.00
CCARSW Sammy Watkins 25.00 60.00
CCARTB Teddy Bridgewater 12.00 30.00
CCARTBO Tajh Boyd 4.00 10.00
CCARTM Tre Mason 4.00 10.00
CCARTS Tom Savage 4.00 10.00
CCARTW Terrance West 4.00 10.00
CCARZM Zach Mettenberger 4.00 10.00

2014 Topps Strata Die Cut Autographs

ASDCBS Bishop Sankey
ASDCLM LeSean McCoy 15.00 40.00
ASDCMB Montee Ball 10.00 25.00
ASDCME Mike Evans
ASDCML Marshawn Lynch
ASDCNF Nick Foles
ASDCRG Rob Gronkowski EXCH 40.00 80.00
ASDCSW Sammy Watkins
ASDCTB Teddy Bridgewater

2014 Topps Strata Die Cuts

STATED ODDS 1:12 HOBBY
SDCAF Arian Foster 1.00 2.50
SDCAG A.J. Green 1.25 3.00
SDCAL Andrew Luck 1.50 4.00
SDCAM Alfred Morris .75 2.00
SDCAR Aaron Rodgers 2.50 6.00
SDCBB Blake Bortles .75 2.00
SDCBM Brandon Marshall .75 2.00
SDCBS Bishop Sankey .60 1.50
SDCCH Carlos Hyde .75 2.00
SDCCJ Calvin Johnson 1.25 3.00
SDCCK Colin Kaepernick 1.00 2.50
SDCCM Clay Matthews 1.25 3.00
SDCCN Cam Newton 1.25 3.00
SDCDB Dez Bryant 1.25 3.00
SDCDC Derek Carr 4.00 10.00
SDCDJ DeSean Jackson 1.00 2.50
SDCDM DeMarco Murray 1.00 2.50
SDCDT Demaryius Thomas 1.00 2.50
SDCFG Frank Gore 1.00 2.50
SDCJC Jamaal Charles 1.00 2.50
SDCJG Jimmy Graham 1.25 3.00
SDCJJ Julio Jones 1.25 3.00
SDCJM Johnny Manziel 1.00 2.50
SDCJN Jordy Nelson 1.00 2.50
SDCJW J.J. Watt 1.25 3.00
SDCLB Le'Veon Bell 1.00 2.50
SDCLM LeSean McCoy 1.25 3.00
SDCMB Montee Ball .75 2.00
SDCME Mike Evans 1.50 4.00
SDCMF Matt Forte .75 2.00
SDCML Marshawn Lynch 1.00 2.50
SDCMR Matt Ryan 1.00 2.50
SDCMS Matthew Stafford 1.00 2.50
SDCNF Nick Foles 1.00 2.50
SDCOB Odell Beckham Jr. 1.50 4.00
SDCPH Percy Harvin .75 2.00
SDCPM Peyton Manning 2.50 6.00
SDCRG Robert Griffin III .75 2.00
SDCRS Richard Sherman 1.25 3.00
SDCRT Ryan Tannehill 1.00 2.50
SDCRW Russell Wilson 2.00 5.00
SDCSW Sammy Watkins 1.00 2.50
SDCTB Tom Brady 3.00 8.00
SDCTM Tre Mason .60 1.50
SDCTR Tony Romo 1.00 2.50
SDCDBR Drew Brees 1.25 3.00
SDCDMA Doug Martin 1.00 2.50
SDCJCL Jadeveon Clowney .75 2.00
SDCRGR Rob Gronkowski 1.25 3.00
SDCTBR Teddy Bridgewater 1.00 2.50

2014 Topps Strata Jerseys

*BRONZE/150: .5X TO 1.2X JSY
*TOPAZ PATCH/90: .6X TO 1.5X JSY
*SAPPHIRE PATCH/75: .6X TO 1.5X JSY
SRAG A.J. Green 3.00 8.00
SRAL Andrew Luck 4.00 10.00
SRAM A.J. McCarron 1.00 2.50
SRAR Allen Robinson 1.50 4.00
SRAS Austin Seferian-Jenkins 1.00 2.50
SRAW Andre Williams 1.00 2.50
SRBB Blake Bortles 1.25 3.00
SRBC Brandin Cooks 1.50 4.00
SRBS Bishop Sankey 1.00 2.50
SRCH Carlos Hyde 1.25 3.00
SRCL Cody Latimer 1.25 3.00
SRCN Cam Newton 3.00 8.00
SRCS Charles Sims 1.00 2.50
SRDA Davante Adams 3.00 8.00
SRDC Derek Carr 6.00 15.00
SRDF Devonta Freeman 1.50 4.00
SRDM Donte Moncrief 1.00 2.50
SRDT De'Anthony Thomas 1.00 2.50
SREE Eric Ebron 1.25 3.00
SREL Eddie Lacy 2.00 5.00
SREM Eli Manning 2.50 6.00
SRFG Frank Gore 2.50 6.00
SRJA Jace Amaro 1.00 2.50
SRJC Jadeveon Clowney 1.25 3.00
SRJG Jimmy Garoppolo 4.00 10.00
SRJH Jeremy Hill 1.25 3.00
SRJL Jarvis Landry 2.00 5.00
SRJM Johnny Manziel 1.50 4.00
SRJW James White 2.00 5.00
SRKB Kelvin Benjamin 1.50 4.00
SRKC Ka'Deem Carey 1.00 2.50
SRKM Khalil Mack 4.00 10.00
SRLM LeSean McCoy 3.00 8.00
SRLT Logan Thomas 1.00 2.50
SRMB Montee Ball 2.00 5.00
SRME Mike Evans 2.50 6.00
SRML Marqise Lee 1.25 3.00
SROB Odell Beckham Jr. 6.00 15.00
SRPR Paul Richardson 1.25 3.00
SRRG Robert Griffin III 2.00 5.00
SRRW Russell Wilson 5.00 12.00
SRSW Sammy Watkins 1.50 4.00
SRTB Teddy Bridgewater 1.50 4.00
SRTM Tre Mason 1.00 2.50
SRTS Tom Savage 1.00 2.50
SRTW Terrance West 1.00 2.50
SRAMU Aaron Murray 1.00 2.50
SRDAR Dri Archer 1.00 2.50
SRJMA Jordan Matthews 1.50 4.00
SRMBR Martavis Bryant 1.25 3.00

2014 Topps Strata Jerseys Emerald Patch

*EMERALD PATCH/50: .8X TO 2X JSY
SROB Odell Beckham Jr. 5.00 12.00

2014 Topps Strata Jerseys Ruby Patch

*RUBY PATCH/25: 1X TO 2.5X JSY
SROB Odell Beckham Jr. 6.00 15.00

2014 Topps Strata Quarterback Die Cut Autographs

OVERAL DIE CUT AU ODDS 1:4820 HOBBY
AQDCAM Aaron Murray 8.00 20.00
AQDCBB Blake Bortles 10.00 25.00
AQDCDC Derek Carr
AQDCDF David Fales
AQDCJG Jimmy Garoppolo
AQDCJM Johnny Manziel
AQDCMS Matthew Stafford
AQDCNF Nick Foles
AQDCTS Tom Savage
AQDCZM Zach Mettenberger

2014 Topps Strata Quarterback Die Cuts

STATED ODDS 1:8 HOBBY
QDCAD Andy Dalton .75 2.00
QDCAL Andrew Luck 1.25 3.00
QDCAM A.J. McCarron .50 1.25
QDCAR Aaron Rodgers 2.00 5.00
QDCAS Alex Smith .75 2.00
QDCBB Blake Bortles .60 1.50
QDCCK Colin Kaepernick .75 2.00
QDCCN Cam Newton 1.00 2.50
QDCDB Drew Brees 1.00 2.50
QDCDC Derek Carr 3.00 8.00
QDCDF David Fales .50 1.25
QDCEM EJ Manuel .60 1.50
QDCGS Geno Smith .60 1.50
QDCJC Jay Cutler .60 1.50
QDCJG Jimmy Garoppolo 4.00 10.00
QDCJL Jake Locker .75 2.00
QDCJM Johnny Manziel .75 2.00
QDCLT Logan Thomas .50 1.25
QDCMR Matt Ryan .75 2.00
QDCMS Matthew Stafford .75 2.00
QDCNF Nick Foles .75 2.00
QDCPM Peyton Manning 2.00 5.00
QDCPR Philip Rivers 1.00 2.50
QDCRG Robert Griffin III .60 1.50
QDCRT Ryan Tannehill .75 2.00
QDCRW Russell Wilson 1.50 4.00
QDCSB Sam Bradford .60 1.50
QDCTB Teddy Bridgewater .75 2.00
QDCTR Tony Romo .75 2.00
QDCTS Tom Savage .50 1.25
QDCZM Zach Mettenberger .50 1.25
QDCAMU Aaron Murray .50 1.25
QDCEMA Eli Manning .75 2.00
QDCTBO Tajh Boyd .50 1.25
QDCTBR Tom Brady 2.50 6.00

2014 Topps Strata Relic Autographs

SSRAM A.J. McCarron 5.00 12.00
SSRAMO Alfred Morris
SSRAMU Aaron Murray 5.00 12.00
SSRAR Allen Robinson 8.00 20.00
SSRAS Austin Seferian-Jenkins
SSRAW Andre Williams 5.00 12.00
SSRBB Blake Bortles 6.00 15.00
SSRBS Bishop Sankey 5.00 12.00
SSRCH Carlos Hyde 6.00 15.00
SSRCL Cody Latimer 6.00 15.00
SSRCS Charles Sims 5.00 12.00
SSRDA Davante Adams 8.00 20.00
SSRDAR Dri Archer 5.00 12.00
SSRDC Derek Carr 40.00 80.00
SSRDF Devonta Freeman 8.00 20.00
SSRDFA David Fales 5.00 12.00
SSRDM Donte Moncrief 5.00 12.00
SSRDMA Doug Martin
SSREE Eric Ebron 6.00 15.00
SSREL Eddie Lacy
SSRJA Jace Amaro 5.00 12.00
SSRJC Jadeveon Clowney 6.00 15.00
SSRJG Jimmy Garoppolo 50.00 100.00
SSRJH Jeremy Hill 6.00 15.00
SSRJHU Josh Huff 6.00 15.00
SSRJL Jarvis Landry 10.00 25.00
SSRJM Johnny Manziel EXCH 8.00 20.00
SSRJMA Jordan Matthews 8.00 20.00
SSRKB Kelvin Benjamin 30.00 80.00
SSRKC Ka'Deem Carey 5.00 12.00
SSRLM LeSean McCoy
SSRLT Logan Thomas
SSRME Mike Evans 25.00 60.00
SSRML Marqise Lee 6.00 15.00
SSRMS Michael Sam 5.00 12.00
SSRPR Paul Richardson 12.00 30.00
SSRRW Russell Wilson
SSRSW Sammy Watkins 30.00 80.00
SSRTB Teddy Bridgewater 30.00 80.00
SSRTBO Tajh Boyd 5.00 12.00
SSRTM Tre Mason 5.00 12.00
SSRTS Tom Savage 5.00 12.00
SSRTW Terrance West 8.00 15.00
SSRZM Zach Mettenberger 5.00 12.00

2014 Topps Strata Shadowbox Autographs

SSAAM Alfred Morris 10.00 25.00
SSAAMC A.J. McCarron 5.00 12.00
SSAAMU Aaron Murray 5.00 12.00
SSAAR Allen Robinson 8.00 20.00
SSAAS Austin Seferian-Jenkins 5.00 12.00
SSAAW Andre Williams 5.00 12.00
SSABC Brandin Cooks 8.00 20.00
SSABS Bishop Sankey 5.00 12.00
SSACH Carlos Hyde 6.00 15.00
SSACL Cody Latimer 6.00 15.00
SSACS Charles Sims 5.00 12.00
SSADA DaVante Adams 8.00 20.00
SSADAR Dri Archer
SSADC Derek Carr 30.00 80.00
SSADF David Fales
SSADFR DeVonta Freeman 8.00 20.00
SSADM Doug Martin
SSADMO Donte Moncrief 5.00 12.00
SSAEE Eric Ebron 6.00 15.00
SSAEL Eddie Lacy 10.00 25.00
SSAJC Jamaal Charles
SSAJCL Jadeveon Clowney
SSAJG Jimmy Garoppolo 50.00 100.00
SSAJH Josh Huff 6.00 15.00
SSAJHI Jeremy Hill 6.00 15.00
SSAJL Jarvis Landry 10.00 25.00
SSAJM Jordan Matthews 8.00 20.00
SSAJMA Johnny Manziel EXCH 8.00 20.00
SSAJW James White 10.00 25.00
SSAKB Kelvin Benjamin 8.00 20.00
SSAKC Ka'Deem Carey 5.00 12.00
SSALM LeSean McCoy
SSALT Logan Thomas 5.00 12.00
SSAME Mike Evans 12.00 30.00
SSAML Marqise Lee 6.00 15.00
SSAOB Odell Beckham Jr. 40.00 80.00
SSAPR Paul Richardson
SSASW Sammy Watkins 8.00 20.00
SSATB Teddy Bridgewater 15.00 40.00
SSATM Tre Mason 5.00 12.00
SSATS Tom Savage 5.00 12.00
SSATW Terrance West 8.00 20.00
SSAZM Zach Mettenberger 5.00 12.00

2015 Topps Strata Autographs

*ROOK/600-800: .2X TO .5X BLACK AU/50
*ROOK/150: .25X TO .6X BLACK AU/50
*VETS/600-800: .2X TO .5X BLACK AU/50
SAAA Ameer Abdullah/150 4.00 10.00
SAAC Amari Cooper
SAAL Andrew Luck
SABH Brett Hundley/800 2.00 5.00
SABP Breshad Perriman
SABPE Bryce Petty/600 2.00 5.00
SACA C.J. Anderson/150 3.00 8.00
SADFJ Dante Fowler Jr./800 3.00 8.00
SADG Dorial Green-Beckham
SADJ Duke Johnson/600 3.00 8.00
SADJO David Johnson/800 8.00 20.00
SADM Donte Moncrief/800 2.50 6.00
SADS Devin Smith
SAES Emmanuel Sanders/800 4.00 10.00
SAJA Jay Ajayi/600 3.00 8.00
SAJAL Javorius Allen EXCH
SAJC Jamaal Charles
SAJM Jordan Matthews
SAJW Jameis Winston
SAKW Kevin White/150 3.00 8.00
SALC Landon Collins/800 2.50 6.00
SAMB Martavis Bryant/800 3.00 8.00
SAMG Melvin Gordon
SAMM Marcus Mariota
SAPD Phillip Dorsett
SARC Roger Craig
SARGR Rashad Greene/800 2.00 5.00
SASC Sammie Coates/800 2.50 6.00
SAST Shaq Thompson/800 2.50 6.00
SATC Tevin Coleman/800 2.50 6.00
SATD Titus Davis/800 2.50 6.00
SATG Todd Gurley/99 20.00 50.00
SATK Travis Kelce
SATL Tyler Lockett/800 3.00 8.00
SATLI Tony Lippett/800 3.00 8.00
SATM Tre McBride/800 2.00 5.00
SATMO Ty Montgomery/600 2.00 5.00
SATW Trae Waynes/800 2.00 5.00
SATY T.J. Yeldon/150 2.50 6.00
SAVB Vic Beasley/800 2.50 6.00

2015 Topps Strata Autographs Blue

SATG Todd Gurley 20.00 50.00

2015 Topps Strata Autographs Gold

*GOLD/25: .5X TO 1.2X BLACK AU/50

2015 Topps Strata Autographs Green

*GREEN/75: .3X TO .8X BLACK AU/50
SAAC Amari Cooper 25.00 50.00
SAJW Jameis Winston 40.00 80.00
SAMM Marcus Mariota 40.00 80.00
SATG Todd Gurley 25.00 50.00

2015 Topps Strata Clear Cut Rookie Relic Autographs

CCAPAA Ameer Abdullah 5.00 12.00
CCAPAC Amari Cooper 20.00 50.00
CCAPBH Brett Hundley 3.00 8.00
CCAPBP Breshad Perriman 3.00 8.00
CCAPBPE Bryce Petty 3.00 8.00
CCAPCA Cameron Artis-Payne 3.00 8.00
CCAPCC Chris Conley EXCH 3.00 8.00
CCAPDC David Cobb 3.00 8.00
CCAPDF Devin Funchess
CCAPDG Dorial Green-Beckham 3.00 8.00
CCAPDJ Duke Johnson 5.00 12.00
CCAPDJO David Johnson 8.00 20.00
CCAPDP DeVante Parker 5.00 12.00
CCAPDS Devin Smith 3.00 8.00
CCAPJA Jay Ajayi 5.00 12.00
CCAPJC Jamison Crowder 4.00 10.00
CCAPJHA Justin Hardy 3.00 8.00
CCAPJL Jeremy Langford 3.00 8.00
CCAPJS Jaelen Strong 4.00 10.00
CCAPJW Jameis Winston
CCAPKW Kevin White
CCAPKWI Karlos Williams 3.00 8.00
CCAPLW Leonard Williams 3.00 8.00
CCAPMD Mike Davis 3.00 8.00
CCAPMG Melvin Gordon
CCAPMJ Matt Jones 3.00 8.00
CCAPMM Marcus Mariota
CCAPMW Maxx Williams 3.00 8.00
CCAPNA Nelson Agholor 4.00 10.00
CCAPPD Phillip Dorsett 3.00 8.00
CCAPRG Rashad Greene 3.00 8.00
CCAPSC Sammie Coates 4.00 10.00
CCAPSM Sean Mannion 3.00 8.00
CCAPTC Tevin Coleman 4.00 10.00
CCAPTG Todd Gurley
CCAPTL Tyler Lockett 5.00 12.00
CCAPTMO Ty Montgomery 3.00 8.00
CCAPTY T.J. Yeldon 3.00 8.00
CCAPVM Vince Mayle 4.00 10.00

2015 Topps Strata Clear Cut Rookie Relic Autographs Black

*BLACK/50: .6X TO 1.5X BASIC JSY AU
CCAPTG Todd Gurley 40.00 100.00

2015 Topps Strata Clear Cut Rookie Relic Autographs Blue

*BLUE/99: .5X TO 1.2X BASIC JSY AU

2015 Topps Strata Clear Cut Rookie Relic Autographs Gold

*GOLD/25: .8X TO 2X BASIC JSY AU

2015 Topps Strata Clear Cut Rookie Relic Autographs Green

*GREEN/75: .5X TO 1.2X BASIC JSY AU
CCAPMM Marcus Mariota 50.00 100.00
CCAPTG Todd Gurley 30.00 80.00

2015 Topps Strata Signatures

SSAA Ameer Abdullah 5.00 12.00
SSAC Amari Cooper
SSBJ Bo Jackson
SSBP Breshad Perriman 3.00 8.00
SSBPE Bryce Petty 3.00 8.00
SSCC Chris Conley 3.00 8.00
SSDC David Cobb 3.00 8.00
SSDG Dorial Green-Beckham 3.00 8.00
SSDJ Duke Johnson 5.00 12.00
SSDJO David Johnson 15.00 40.00
SSDP DeVante Parker 5.00 12.00
SSDS Devin Smith 3.00 8.00
SSEL Eddie Lacy 3.00 8.00
SSJA Jay Ajayi 5.00 12.00
SSJAL Javorius Allen 4.00 10.00
SSJC Jamaal Charles 4.00 10.00
SSJH Jeremy Hill 3.00 8.00
SSJL Jeremy Langford 3.00 8.00
SSJW Jameis Winston/31 75.00 100.00
SSKB Kelvin Benjamin 4.00 10.00
SSKW Kevin White 4.00 10.00
SSKWI Karlos Williams 3.00 8.00
SSLW Leonard Williams 3.00 8.00
SSMD Mike Davis 3.00 8.00
SSME Mike Evans 4.00 10.00
SSMG Melvin Gordon 8.00 20.00
SSMM Marcus Mariota
SSMS Matthew Stafford
SSMW Maxx Williams 3.00 8.00
SSPD Phillip Dorsett 3.00 8.00
SSRGR Rashad Greene 3.00 8.00
SSRS Roger Staubach
SSSC Sammie Coates 4.00 10.00
SSSW Sammy Watkins 4.00 10.00
SSTC Tevin Coleman 4.00 10.00
SSTG Todd Gurley
SSTL Tyler Lockett 5.00 12.00
SSTM Ty Montgomery 3.00 8.00
SSTY T.J. Yeldon 3.00 8.00
SSVM Vince Mayle 4.00 10.00

1981 Topps Red Border Stickers

This set of 28 red-bordered stickers was distributed as a separate issue (inside a football capsule) unlike the "Coming Soon" subsets, which were inserted in with the regular football card wax packs. The stickers were actually sold in vending machines for 25 cents a sticker. They are the same size as the regular Topps stickers (1 15/16" by 2 9/16") and tougher to find than the other "Coming Soon" sticker subsets distributed in later years. The numbering in this set is completely different from the sticker numbering in the 1981 Topps 262-sticker set. There was one sticker issued for each team.

COMPLETE SET (28) 20.00 40.00
1 Steve Bartkowski .50 1.25
2 Bert Jones .50 1.25
3 Joe Cribbs .50 1.25
4 Walter Payton 6.00 15.00
5 Ross Browner .40 1.00
6 Brian Sipe .50 1.25
7 Tony Dorsett 2.00 5.00
8 Randy Gradishar .50 1.25
9 Billy Sims .60 1.50
10 James Lofton .60 1.50
11 Mike Barber .40 1.00
12 Art Still .40 1.00
13 Jack Youngblood .50 1.25
14 David Woodley .40 1.00
15 Ahmad Rashad .60 1.50
16 Russ Francis .40 1.00
17 Archie Manning .60 1.50
18 Dave Jennings .40 1.00
19 Richard Todd .40 1.00
20 Lester Hayes .50 1.25
21 Ron Jaworski .50 1.25
22 Franco Harris 1.25 3.00
23 Ottis Anderson .60 1.50
24 John Jefferson .50 1.25
25 Freddie Solomon .40 1.00
26 Steve Largent 1.25 3.00
27 Lee Roy Selmon .60 1.50
28 Art Monk 1.50 4.00

1981 Topps Stickers

ke the 1981 baseball stickers, the 1981 Topps football stickers were also printed in Italy, each sticker measuring 1 15/16" by 2 9/16". The 262-card (sticker) set contains 22 All-Pro foil cards (numbers 121-142). The foil cards are somewhat more difficult to obtain, and a premium price is placed upon them. The card numbers begin with players from the AFC East teams and continue through the AFC Central and West divisions with teams within each division listed alphabetically. Card number 151 begins the NFC East teams, and a similar progression through the NFC divisions completes the remaining cards of the set. The backs contain a 1981 copyright date. On the inside back cover of the sticker album the company offered (via direct mail-order) any ten different stickers (but no more than two foil) of your choice for 1.00; this is one reason why the values of the most popular players in these sticker sets are somewhat depressed compared to traditional card set prices. The front cover of the sticker album features a Buffalo Bills player. The following players are shown in their Rookie Card year or earlier: Dwight Clark, Jacob Green (two years early), Dan Hampton, Art Monk, Anthony Munoz (one year early), and Kellen Winslow.

COMPLETE SET (262) 10.00 25.00
1 Brian Sipe LL .04 .10
2 Dan Fouts LL .12 .30
3 John Jefferson LL .04 .10
4 Bruce Harper LL .04 .10
5 J.T. Smith LL .04 .10
6 Luke Prestridge LL .04 .10
7 Lester Hayes LL .04 .10
8 Gary Johnson LL .04 .10
9 Bert Jones .08 .20
10 Fred Cook .04 .10
11 Roger Carr .04 .10
12 Greg Landry .04 .10
13 Raymond Butler .04 .10
14 Bruce Laird .04 .10
15 Ed Simonini .04 .10
16 Curtis Dickey .04 .10
17 Joe Cribbs .04 .10
18 Joe Ferguson .04 .10
19 Ben Williams .04 .10
20 Jerry Butler .04 .10
21 Roland Hooks .04 .10
22 Fred Smerlas .04 .10
23 Frank Lewis .04 .10
24 Mark Brammer .04 .10
25 David Woodley .04 .10
26 Nat Moore .04 .10
27 Uwe Von Schamann .04 .10
28 Vern Den Herder .04 .10
29 Tony Nathan .04 .10
30 Duriel Harris .04 .10
31 Don McNeal .04 .10
32 Delvin Williams .04 .10
33 Stanley Morgan .04 .10
34 John Hannah .08 .20
35 Horace Ivory .04 .10
36 Steve Nelson .04 .10
37 Steve Grogan .08 .20
38 Vagas Ferguson .04 .10
39 John Smith .04 .10
40 Mike Haynes .04 .10
41 Mark Gastineau .04 .10
42 Wesley Walker .04 .10
43 Joe Klecko .04 .10
44 Chris Ward .04 .10
45 Johnny Lam Jones .04 .10
46 Marvin Powell .04 .10
47 Richard Todd .04 .10
48 Greg Buttle .04 .10
49 Eddie Edwards .04 .10
50 Dan Ross .04 .10
51 Ken Anderson .12 .30
52 Ross Browner .04 .10
53 Don Bass .04 .10
54 Jim LeClair .04 .10
55 Pete Johnson .04 .10
56 Anthony Munoz .40 1.00
57 Brian Sipe .04 .10
58 Mike Pruitt .04 .10
59 Greg Pruitt .04 .10
60 Thom Darden .04 .10
61 Ozzie Newsome .12 .30
62 Dave Logan .04 .10
63 Lyle Alzado .08 .20
64 Reggie Rucker .04 .10
65 Robert Brazile .04 .10
66 Mike Barber .04 .10
67 Carl Roaches .04 .10
68 Ken Stabler .10 1.00
69 Gregg Bingham .04 .10
70 Mike Renfro .04 .10
71 Leon Gray .04 .10
72 Rob Carpenter .04 .10
73 Franco Harris .15 .40
74 Jack Lambert .12 .30
75 Jim Smith .04 .10
76 Mike Webster .08 .20
77 Sidney Thornton .04 .10
78 Joe Greene .12 .30
79 John Stallworth .08 .20
80 Tyrone McGriff .04 .10
81 Randy Gradishar .04 .10
82 Haven Moses .04 .10
83 Riley Odoms .04 .10
84 Matt Robinson .04 .10
85 Craig Morton .04 .10
86 Rulon Jones .04 .10
87 Rick Upchurch .04 .10
88 Jim Jensen .04 .10
89 Art Still .04 .10
90 J.T. Smith .04 .10
91 Steve Fuller .04 .10
92 Gary Barbaro .04 .10
93 Ted McKnight .04 .10
94 Bob Grupp .04 .10
95 Henry Marshall .04 .10
96 Mike Williams .04 .10
97 Jim Plunkett .08 .20
98 Lester Hayes .04 .10
99 Cliff Branch .08 .20
100 John Matuszak .04 .10
101 Matt Millen .04 .10
102 Kenny King .04 .10
103 Ray Guy .04 .10
104 Ted Hendricks .08 .20
105 John Jefferson .08 .20
106 Fred Dean .08 .20
107 Dan Fouts .15 .40
108 Charlie Joiner .12 .30
109 Kellen Winslow .60 1.50
110 Gary Johnson .04 .10
111 Mike Thomas .04 .10
112 Louie Kelcher .04 .10
113 Jim Zorn .04 .10
114 Terry Beeson .04 .10
115 Jacob Green .08 .20
116 Steve Largent .30 .75
117 Dan Doornink .04 .10
118 Manu Tuiasosopo .04 .10
119 John Sawyer .04 .10
120 Jim Jodat .04 .10
121 Walter Payton FOIL 1.50 4.00
122 Brian Sipe FOIL .12 .30
123 Joe Cribbs FOIL .12 .30
124 James Lofton FOIL .20 .50
125 John Jefferson FOIL .12 .30
126 Leon Gray FOIL .08 .20
127 Joe DeLamielleure FOIL .12 .30
128 Mike Webster FOIL .12 .30
129 John Hannah FOIL .12 .30
130 Mike Kenn FOIL .08 .20
131 Kellen Winslow FOIL .60 1.50
132 Lee Roy Selmon FOIL .20 .50
133 Randy White FOIL .20 .50
134 Gary Johnson FOIL .08 .20
135 Art Still FOIL .08 .20
136 Robert Brazile FOIL .08 .20
137 Nolan Cromwell FOIL .08 .20
138 Ted Hendricks FOIL .12 .30
139 Lester Hayes FOIL .12 .30
140 Randy Gradishar FOIL .12 .30
141 Lemar Parrish FOIL .08 .20
142 Donnie Shell FOIL .12 .30
143 Ron Jaworski LL .04 .10
144 Archie Manning LL .04 .10
145 Walter Payton LL .40 1.00
146 Billy Sims LL .08 .20
147 James Lofton LL .08 .20
148 Dave Jennings LL .04 .10
149 Nolan Cromwell LL .04 .10
150 Al(Bubba) Baker LL .04 .10
151 Tony Dorsett .50 1.25
152 Harvey Martin .04 .10
153 Danny White .08 .20
154 Pat Donovan .04 .10
155 Drew Pearson .08 .20
156 Robert Newhouse .04 .10
157 Randy White .12 .30
158 Butch Johnson .04 .10
159 Dave Jennings .04 .10
160 Brad Van Pelt .04 .10
161 Phil Simms .20 .50
162 Mike Friede .04 .10
163 Billy Taylor .04 .10
164 Gary Jeter .04 .10
165 George Martin .04 .10
166 Earnest Gray .04 .10
167 Ron Jaworski .08 .20
168 Bill Bergey .04 .10
169 Wilbert Montgomery .04 .10
170 Charlie Smith WR .04 .10
171 Jerry Robinson .04 .10
172 Herman Edwards .04 .10
173 Harold Carmichael .08 .20
174 Claude Humphrey .04 .10
175 Ottis Anderson .10 .25
176 Jim Hart .04 .10
177 Pat Tilley .04 .10
178 Rush Brown .04 .10
179 Tom Brahaney .04 .10
180 Dan Dierdorf .10 .25
181 Wayne Morris .04 .10
182 Doug Marsh .04 .10
183 Art Monk .60 1.50
184 Clarence Harmon .04 .10
185 Lemar Parrish .04 .10
186 Joe Theismann .15 .40
187 Joe Lavender .04 .10
188 Wilbur Jackson .04 .10
189 Dave Butz .04 .10
190 Coy Bacon .04 .10
191 Walter Payton 1.25 3.00
192 Alan Page .08 .20
193 Vince Evans .08 .20
194 Roland Harper .04 .10
195 Dan Hampton .25 .60
196 Gary Fencik .04 .10
197 Mike Hartenstine .04 .10
198 Robin Earl .04 .10
199 Billy Sims .10 .25
200 Leonard Thompson .04 .10
201 Jeff Komlo .04 .10
202 Al(Bubba) Baker .04 .10
203 Eddie Murray .04 .10
204 Dexter Bussey .04 .10
205 Tom Ginn .04 .10
206 Freddie Scott .04 .10
207 James Lofton .15 .40
208 Mike Butler .04 .10
209 Lynn Dickey .04 .10
210 Gerry Ellis .04 .10
211 Eddie Lee Ivery .04 .10
212 Ezra Johnson .04 .10
213 Paul Coffman .04 .10
214 Aundra Thompson .04 .10
215 Ahmad Rashad .08 .20
216 Tommy Kramer .04 .10
217 Matt Blair .04 .10
218 Sammie White .04 .10
219 Ted Brown .04 .10
220 Joe Senser .04 .10
221 Rickey Young .04 .10
222 Randy Holloway .04 .10
223 Lee Roy Selmon .12 .30
224 Doug Williams .04 .10
225 Ricky Bell .04 .10

226 David Lewis .04 .10
227 Gordon Jones .04 .10
228 Dewey Selmon .04 .10
229 Jimmie Giles .04 .10
230 Mike Washington .04 .10
231 William Andrews .04 .10
232 Jeff Van Note .04 .10
233 Steve Bartkowski .04 .10
234 Junior Miller .04 .10
235 Lynn Cain .04 .10
236 Joel Williams .04 .10
237 Alfred Jenkins .04 .10
238 Kenny Johnson .04 .10
239 Jack Youngblood .08 .20
240 Elvis Peacock .04 .10
241 Cullen Bryant .04 .10
242 Dennis Harrah .04 .10
243 Billy Waddy .04 .10
244 Nolan Cromwell .04 .10
245 Doug France .04 .10
246 Johnnie Johnson .04 .10
247 Archie Manning .08 .20
248 Tony Galbreath .04 .10
249 Wes Chandler .04 .10
250 Stan Brock .04 .10
251 Ike Harris .04 .10
252 Russell Erxleben .04 .10
253 Jimmy Rogers .04 .10
254 Tom Myers .04 .10
255 Dwight Clark .30 .75
256 Earl Cooper .04 .10
257 Steve DeBerg .08 .20
258 Randy Cross .04 .10
259 Freddie Solomon .04 .10
260 Jim Miller P .04 .10
261 Charle Young .04 .10
262 Bobby Leopold .04 .10
NNO Sticker Album .75 2.00

1982 Topps Coming Soon Stickers

This 16-sticker set advertises "Coming Soon" on the sticker backs. All stickers in this small set were gold bordered foil stickers; these "Coming Soon" stickers were inserted in the regular issue 1982 Topps football card wax packs. They are the same size as the regular Topps stickers with the same sticker numbers as well; hence the set is skip-numbered.

COMPLETE SET (16) 2.00 5.00
5 MVP Super Bowl XVI .75 2.00
6 NFC Championship .08 .20
9 Super Bowl XVI .60 1.50
71 Tommy Kramer .08 .20
73 George Rogers .12 .30
75 Tom Skladany .08 .20
139 Nolan Cromwell AP .08 .20
143 Jack Lambert AP .20 .50
144 Lawrence Taylor AP .40 1.00
150 Billy Sims AP .15 .40
154 Ken Anderson AP .20 .50
159 John Hannah AP .15 .40
160 Anthony Munoz AP .40 1.00
220 Ken Anderson .20 .50
221 Dan Fouts .20 .50
222 Frank Lewis .08 .20

1982 Topps Stickers

The 1982 Topps football sticker set contains 288 stickers and is similar in format to the 1981 sticker set. The stickers measure 1 15/16" by 2 9/16". This year's stickers have yellow borders compared to the white borders of the previous year. Stickers numbered 1-10, 70-77, 139-160, and 220-227 are foils. Stickers numbered 1 and 2 combine to portray the San Francisco 49ers, Super Bowl XVI Champions. Sticker numbers 3 and 4 combine to form the Super Bowl XVI theme art trophy. Stickers are numbered essentially in team order, with the teams themselves ordered alphabetically by team name within conference. Those stickers that are asterisked in the checklist below are those that were also included in the "Coming Soon" sticker set inserted in early 1982 football wax packs. The backs contain a 1982 copyright date. On the inside back cover of the sticker album the company offered (via direct mail-order) any ten different stickers (but no more than two foil) of your choice for 1.00; this is one reason why the values of the most popular players in these sticker sets are somewhat depressed compared to traditional card set prices. The front cover of the sticker album features Joe Montana. The following players are shown in their Rookie Card year: James Brooks, Cris Collinsworth, Ronnie Lott, Anthony Munoz, Lawrence Taylor, and Everson Walls.

COMPLETE SET (288) 10.00 25.00
1 Super Bowl XVI .40 1.00
Champs, San Francisco
49ers Team (L) FOIL
2 Super Bowl XVI .30 .75
Champs, San Francisco
49ers Team (R) FOIL
3 Super Bowl XVI .08 .20
Theme Art
trophy (top) FOIL
4 Super Bowl XVI .08 .20
Theme Art
trophy (bottom) FOIL
5 MVP Joe Montana 2.00 5.00
Super Bowl XVI * FOIL
6 1981 NFC Champions .04 .10
49'ers FOIL *
7 1981 AFC Champions .08 .20
(Ken Anderson
handing off) FOIL
8 Super Bowl XVI .10 .25
(Ken Anderson
dropping back) FOIL
9 Super Bowl XVI 1.50 4.00
(Joe Montana
handing off) * FOIL
10 Super Bowl XVI .20 .50
(line blocking) FOIL
11 Steve Bartkowski .04 .10
12 William Andrews .04 .10
13 Lynn Cain .04 .10
14 Wallace Francis .04 .10
15 Alfred Jackson .04 .10
16 Alfred Jenkins .04 .10
17 Mike Kenn .04 .10
18 Junior Miller .04 .10
19 Vince Evans .04 .10
20 Walter Payton 1.25 3.00
21 Dave Williams RB .04 .10
22 Brian Baschnagel .04 .10
23 Rickey Watts .04 .10
24 Ken Margerum .04 .10
25 Revie Sorey .04 .10
26 Gary Fencik .04 .10
27 Matt Suhey .04 .10
28 Danny White .08 .20
29 Tony Dorsett .15 .40
30 Drew Pearson .08 .20
31 Rafael Septien .04 .10
32 Pat Donovan .04 .10
33 Herb Scott .04 .10
34 Ed Too Tall Jones .08 .20
35 Randy White .10 .25
36 Tony Hill .04 .10
37 Eric Hipple .04 .10
38 Billy Sims .08 .20
39 Dexter Bussey .04 .10
40 Freddie Scott .04 .10
41 David Hill .04 .10
42 Eddie Murray .04 .10
43 Tom Skladany .04 .10
44 Doug English .04 .10
45 Al(Bubba) Baker .04 .10
46 Lynn Dickey .04 .10
47 Gerry Ellis .04 .10
48 Harlan Huckleby .04 .10
49 James Lofton .15 .40
50 John Jefferson .04 .10
51 Paul Coffman .04 .10
52 Jan Stenerud .04 .10
53 Rich Wingo .04 .10
54 Wendell Tyler .04 .10
55 Preston Dennard .04 .10
56 Billy Waddy .04 .10
57 Frank Corral .04 .10
58 Jack Youngblood .04 .10
59 Pat Thomas .04 .10
60 Rod Perry .04 .10
61 Nolan Cromwell .04 .10
62 Tommy Kramer .04 .10
63 Rickey Young .04 .10
64 Ted Brown .04 .10
65 Ahmad Rashad .10 .25
66 Sammie White .04 .10
67 Joe Senser .04 .10
68 Ron Yary .04 .10
69 Matt Blair .04 .10
70 Joe Montana FOIL 2.50 6.00
71 Tommy Kramer * FOIL .06 .15
72 Alfred Jenkins FOIL .06 .15
73 George Rogers * FOIL .06 .15
74 Wendell Tyler FOIL .06 .15
75 Tom Skladany * FOIL .06 .15
76 Everson Walls FOIL .10 .25
77 Curtis Greer FOIL .06 .15
78 Archie Manning .08 .20
79 Dave Waymer .04 .10
80 George Rogers .08 .20
81 Jack Holmes .04 .10
82 Toussaint Tyler .04 .10
83 Wayne Wilson .04 .10
84 Russell Erxleben .04 .10
85 Elois Grooms .04 .10
86 Phil Simms .08 .20
87 Scott Brunner .04 .10
88 Rob Carpenter .04 .10
89 Johnny Perkins .04 .10
90 Dave Jennings .04 .10
91 Harry Carson .04 .10
92 Lawrence Taylor .60 1.50
93 Beasley Reece .04 .10
94 Mark Haynes .04 .10
95 Ron Jaworski .04 .10
96 Wilbert Montgomery .04 .10
97 Hubie Oliver .04 .10
98 Harold Carmichael .04 .10
99 Jerry Robinson .04 .10
100 Stan Walters .04 .10
101 Charlie Johnson NT .04 .10
102 Roynell Young .04 .10
103 Tony Franklin .04 .10
104 Neil Lomax .08 .20
105 Jim Hart .04 .10
106 Ottis Anderson .08 .20
107 Stump Mitchell .04 .10
108 Pat Tilley .04 .10
109 Rush Brown .04 .10
110 E.J. Junior .04 .10
111 Ken Greene .04 .10
112 Mel Gray .04 .10
113 Joe Montana 2.00 5.00
114 Ricky Patton .04 .10
115 Earl Cooper .04 .10
116 Dwight Clark .10 .25
117 Freddie Solomon .04 .10
118 Randy Cross .04 .10
119 Fred Dean .08 .20
120 Ronnie Lott .40 1.00
121 Dwight Hicks .04 .10
122 Doug Williams .04 .10
123 Jerry Eckwood .04 .10
124 James Owens .04 .10
125 Kevin House .04 .10
126 Jimmie Giles .04 .10
127 Charley Hannah .04 .10
128 Lee Roy Selmon .10 .25
129 Hugh Green .04 .10
130 Joe Theismann .12 .30
131 Joe Washington .04 .10
132 John Riggins .10 .25
133 Art Monk .20 .50
134 Ricky Thompson .04 .10
135 Don Warren .04 .10
136 Perry Brooks .04 .10
137 Mike Nelms .04 .10
138 Mark Moseley .04 .10
139 Nolan Cromwell * AP FOIL .06 .15
140 Dwight Hicks AP FOIL .06 .15
141 Ronnie Lott AP FOIL .60 1.50
142 Harry Carson AP FOIL .10 .25
143 Jack Lambert * AP FOIL .15 .40
144 Lawrence Taylor * AP FOIL .75 2.00
145 Mel Blount AP FOIL .12 .30
146 Joe Klecko AP FOIL .06 .15
147 Randy White AP FOIL .15 .40
148 Doug English AP FOIL .06 .15
149 Fred Dean AP FOIL .08 .20
150 Billy Sims * AP FOIL .12 .30
151 Tony Dorsett AP FOIL .50 1.25
152 James Lofton AP FOIL .25 .60
153 Alfred Jenkins AP FOIL .10 .25
154 Ken Anderson * AP FOIL .15 .40
155 Kellen Winslow AP FOIL .25 .60
156 Marvin Powell AP FOIL .06 .15
157 Randy Cross AP FOIL .06 .15
158 Mike Webster AP FOIL .10 .25
159 John Hannah * AP FOIL .12 .30
160 Anthony Munoz * AP FOIL .40 1.00
161 Curtis Dickey .04 .10
162 Randy McMillan .04 .10
163 Roger Carr .04 .10
164 Raymond Butler .04 .10
165 Reese McCall .04 .10
166 Ed Simonini .04 .10
167 Herb Orvis .04 .10
168 Nesby Glasgow .04 .10
169 Joe Ferguson .04 .10
170 Joe Cribbs .04 .10
171 Jerry Butler .04 .10
172 Frank Lewis .04 .10
173 Mark Brammer .04 .10
174 Fred Smerlas .04 .10
175 Jim Haslett .04 .10
176 Charles Romes .04 .10
177 Bill Simpson .04 .10
178 Ken Anderson .10 .25
179 Charles Alexander .04 .10
180 Pete Johnson .04 .10
181 Isaac Curtis .04 .10
182 Cris Collinsworth .20 .50
183 Pat McInally .04 .10
184 Anthony Munoz .20 .50
185 Louis Breeden .04 .10
186 Jim Breech .04 .10
187 Brian Sipe .08 .20
188 Charles White .04 .10
189 Mike Pruitt .04 .10
190 Reggie Rucker .04 .10
191 Dave Logan .04 .10
192 Ozzie Newsome .10 .25
193 Dick Ambrose .04 .10
194 Joe DeLamielleure .04 .10
195 Ricky Feacher .04 .10
196 Craig Morton .04 .10
197 Dave Preston .04 .10
198 Rick Parros .04 .10
199 Rick Upchurch .04 .10
200 Steve Watson .04 .10
201 Riley Odoms .04 .10
202 Randy Gradishar .04 .10
203 Steve Foley .04 .10
204 Ken Stabler .15 .40
205 Gifford Nielsen .04 .10
206 Tim Wilson .04 .10
207 Ken Burrough .04 .10
208 Mike Renfro .04 .10
209 Greg Stemrick .04 .10
210 Robert Brazile .04 .10
211 Gregg Bingham .04 .10
212 Steve Fuller .04 .10
213 Bill Kenney .04 .10
214 Joe Delaney .04 .10
215 Henry Marshall .04 .10
216 Nick Lowery .04 .10
217 Art Still .04 .10
218 Gary Green .04 .10
219 Gary Barbaro .04 .10
220 Ken Anderson * FOIL .15 .40
221 Dan Fouts * FOIL .20 .50
222 Frank Lewis * FOIL .06 .15
222 Steve Watson FOIL .06 .15
223 James Brooks FOIL .25 .60
224 Chuck Muncie FOIL .06 .15
225 Pat McInally FOIL .06 .15
226 John Harris FOIL .06 .15
227 Joe Klecko FOIL .06 .15
228 David Woodley .04 .10
229 Tony Nathan .04 .10
230 Andra Franklin .04 .10
231 Nat Moore .04 .10
232 Duriel Harris .04 .10
233 Uwe Von Schamann .04 .10
234 Bob Baumhower .04 .10
235 Glenn Blackwood .04 .10
236 Tommy Vigorito .04 .10
237 Steve Grogan .04 .10
238 Matt Cavanaugh .04 .10
239 Tony Collins .04 .10
240 Vagas Ferguson .04 .10
241 John Smith .04 .10
242 Stanley Morgan .04 .10
243 John Hannah .04 .10
244 Steve Nelson .04 .10
245 Don Hasselbeck .04 .10
246 Richard Todd .04 .10
247 Bruce Harper .04 .10
248 Wesley Walker .04 .10
249 Jerome Barkum .04 .10
250 Marvin Powell .04 .10
251 Mark Gastineau .04 .10
252 Joe Klecko .04 .10
253 Darrol Ray .04 .10
254 Marty Lyons .04 .10
255 Marc Wilson .04 .10
256 Kenny King .04 .10
257 Mark Van Eeghen .04 .10
258 Cliff Branch .04 .10
259 Bob Chandler .04 .10
260 Ray Guy .04 .10
261 Ted Hendricks .08 .20
262 Lester Hayes .04 .10
263 Terry Bradshaw .40 1.00
264 Franco Harris .15 .40
265 John Stallworth .08 .20
266 Jim Smith .04 .10
267 Mike Webster .04 .10
268 Jack Lambert .10 .25
269 Mel Blount .08 .20
270 Donnie Shell .04 .10
271 Bennie Cunningham .04 .10
272 Dan Fouts .12 .30
273 Chuck Muncie .04 .10
274 James Brooks .12 .30
275 Charlie Joiner .08 .20
276 Wes Chandler .04 .10
277 Kellen Winslow .15 .40
278 Doug Wilkerson .04 .10
279 Gary Johnson .04 .10
280 Rolf Benirschke .04 .10
281 Jim Zorn .04 .10
282 Theotis Brown .04 .10
283 Dan Doornink .04 .10
284 Steve Largent .40 1.00
285 Sam McCullum .04 .10
286 Efren Herrera .04 .10
287 Manu Tuiasosopo .04 .10
288 John Harris .04 .10
288 Sticker Album 1.25 3.00

1983 Topps Stickers

The 1983 Topps football sticker set (330) is similar to the previous years in that it contains stickers, foil stickers, and an accompanying album to house one's sticker collection. The foil stickers are noted in the checklist below by "FOIL"; foils are numbers 1-4, 73-80, 143-152, and 264-271. On the inside back cover of the sticker album the company offered (via direct mail-order) any ten different stickers (but no more than two foil) of your choice for 1.00; this is one reason why the values of the most popular players in these sticker sets are somewhat depressed compared to traditional card set prices. The following players are shown in their Rookie Card year: Marcus Allen, Jim McMahon, and Mike Singletary.

COMPLETE SET (330) 10.00 25.00
1 Franco Harris .30 .75
(Left half) FOIL
2 Franco Harris .15 .40
(Right half) FOIL
3 Walter Payton FOIL 1.50 4.00
4 Walter Payton FOIL 1.50 4.00
5 John Riggins .12 .30
6 Tony Dorsett .20 .50
7 Mark Van Eeghen .04 .10
8 Chuck Muncie .04 .10
9 Wilbert Montgomery .04 .10
10 Greg Pruitt .04 .10
11 Sam Cunningham .04 .10
12 Ottis Anderson .08 .20
13 Mike Pruitt .04 .10
14 Dexter Bussey .04 .10
15 Mike Pagel .04 .10
16 Curtis Dickey .04 .10
17 Randy McMillan .04 .10
18 Raymond Butler .04 .10
19 Nesby Glasgow .04 .10
20 Zachary Dixon .04 .10
21 Matt Bouza .04 .10
22 Johnie Cooks .04 .10
23 Curtis Brown .04 .10
24 Joe Cribbs .04 .10
25 Roosevelt Leaks .04 .10
26 Jerry Butler .04 .10
27 Frank Lewis .04 .10
28 Fred Smerlas .04 .10
29 Ben Williams .04 .10
30 Joe Ferguson .04 .10
31 Isaac Curtis .04 .10
32 Cris Collinsworth .08 .20
33 Anthony Munoz .08 .20
34 Max Montoya .04 .10
35 Ross Browner .04 .10
36 Reggie Williams .04 .10
37 Ken Riley .04 .10
38 Pete Johnson .04 .10
39 Ken Anderson .10 .25
40 Charles White .04 .10
41 Dave Logan .04 .10
42 Doug Dieken .04 .10
43 Ozzie Newsome .08 .20
44 Tom Cousineau .04 .10
45 Bob Golic .04 .10
46 Brian Sipe .04 .10
47 Paul McDonald .04 .10
48 Mike Pruitt .04 .10
49 Luke Prestridge .04 .10
50 Randy Gradishar .04 .10
51 Rulon Jones .04 .10
52 Rick Parros .04 .10
53 Steve DeBerg .04 .10
54 Tom Jackson .04 .10
55 Rick Upchurch .04 .10
56 Steve Watson .04 .10
57 Robert Brazile .04 .10
58 Willie Tullis .04 .10
59 Archie Manning .08 .20
60 Gifford Nielsen .04 .10
61 Harold Bailey .04 .10
62 Carl Roaches .04 .10
63 Gregg Bingham .04 .10
64 Daryl Hunt .04 .10
65 Gary Green .04 .10
66 Gary Barbaro .04 .10
67 Bill Kenney .04 .10
68 Joe Delaney .04 .10
69 Henry Marshall .04 .10
70 Nick Lowery .04 .10
71 Jeff Gossett .04 .10
72 Art Still .04 .10
73 Ken Anderson FOIL .10 .25
74 Dan Fouts FOIL .15 .40
75 Wes Chandler FOIL .10 .25
76 James Brooks FOIL .10 .25
77 Rick Upchurch FOIL .04 .10
78 Luke Prestridge FOIL .04 .10
79 Jesse Baker FOIL .04 .10
80 Freeman McNeil FOIL .10 .25
81 Ray Guy .04 .10
82 Jim Plunkett .08 .20
83 Lester Hayes .04 .10
84 Kenny King .04 .10
85 Cliff Branch .08 .20
86 Todd Christensen .04 .10
87 Lyle Alzado .08 .20
88 Ted Hendricks .08 .20
89 Rod Martin .04 .10
90 David Woodley .04 .10
91 Ed Newman .04 .10
92 Earnie Rhone .04 .10
93 Don McNeal .04 .10
94 Glenn Blackwood .04 .10
95 Andra Franklin .04 .10
96 Nat Moore .04 .10
97 Lyle Blackwood .04 .10
98 A.J. Duhe .04 .10
99 Tony Collins .04 .10
100 Stanley Morgan .04 .10
101 Pete Brock .04 .10
102 Steve Nelson .04 .10
103 Steve Grogan .04 .10
104 Mark Van Eeghen .04 .10
105 Don Hasselbeck .04 .10
106 John Hannah .08 .20
107 Mike Haynes .04 .10
108 Wesley Walker .04 .10
109 Marvin Powell .04 .10
110 Joe Klecko .04 .10
111 Bobby Jackson .04 .10
112 Richard Todd .04 .10
113 Lance Mehl .04 .10
114 Johnny Lam Jones .04 .10
115 Mark Gastineau .04 .10
116 Freeman McNeil .04 .10
117 Franco Harris .15 .40
118 Mike Webster .08 .20
119 Mel Blount .08 .20
120 Donnie Shell .04 .10
121 Terry Bradshaw .40 1.00
122 John Stallworth .08 .20
123 Jack Lambert .10 .25
124 Dwayne Woodruff .04 .10
125 Bennie Cunningham .04 .10
126 Charlie Joiner .08 .20
127 Kellen Winslow .12 .30
128 Rolf Benirschke .04 .10
129 Louie Kelcher .04 .10
130 Chuck Muncie .04 .10
131 Wes Chandler .04 .10
132 Gary Johnson .04 .10
133 James Brooks .08 .20
134 Dan Fouts .15 .40
135 Jacob Green .04 .10
136 Michael Jackson .04 .10
137 Jim Zorn .04 .10
138 Sherman Smith .04 .10
139 Keith Simpson .04 .10
140 Steve Largent .40 1.00
141 John Harris .04 .10
142 Jeff West .04 .10
143 Ken Anderson .10 .25
(top) FOIL
144 Ken Anderson .10 .25
(bottom) FOIL
145 Tony Dorsett .30 .75
(top) FOIL
146 Tony Dorsett .30 .75
(bottom) FOIL
147 Dan Fouts .15 .40
(top) FOIL
148 Dan Fouts .15 .40
(bottom) FOIL
149 Joe Montana 2.00 5.00
(top) FOIL
150 Joe Montana 2.00 5.00
(bottom) FOIL
151 Mark Moseley .04 .10
(top) FOIL
152 Mark Moseley .04 .10
(bottom) FOIL
153 Richard Todd .04 .10
154 Butch Johnson .04 .10
155 Gary Hogeboom UER .04 .10
(Bill on back)
156 A.J. Duhe .04 .10
157 Kurt Sohn .04 .10
158 Drew Pearson .08 .20
159 John Riggins .10 .25
160 Pat Donovan .04 .10
161 John Hannah .08 .20
162 Jeff Van Note .04 .10
163 Randy Cross .04 .10
164 Marvin Powell .04 .10
165 Kellen Winslow .10 .25
166 Dwight Clark .08 .20
167 Wes Chandler .04 .10
168 Tony Dorsett .15 .40
169 Freeman McNeil .04 .10
170 Ken Anderson .08 .20
171 Mark Moseley .04 .10
172 Mark Gastineau .04 .10
173 Gary Johnson .04 .10
174 Randy White .10 .25
175 Ed Too Tall Jones .08 .20
176 Hugh Green .04 .10
177 Harry Carson .04 .10
178 Lawrence Taylor .15 .40
179 Lester Hayes .04 .10
180 Mark Haynes .04 .10
181 Dave Jennings .04 .10
182 Nolan Cromwell .04 .10
183 Tony Peters .04 .10
184 Jimmy Cefalo .04 .10
185 A.J. Duhe .04 .10
186 John Riggins .10 .25
187 Charlie Brown .04 .10
188 Mike Nelms .04 .10
189 Mark Murphy .04 .10
190 Fulton Walker .04 .10
191 Marcus Allen 1.25 3.00
192 Chip Banks .04 .10
193 Charlie Brown .04 .10
194 Bob Crable .04 .10
195 Vernon Dean .04 .10
196 Jim McMahon .40 1.00
197 Tootie Robbins .04 .10
198 Luis Sharpe .04 .10
199 Rohn Stark .04 .10
200 Lester Williams .04 .10
201 Leo Wisniewski .04 .10
202 Butch Woolfolk .04 .10
203 Mike Kenn .04 .10
204 R.C. Thielemann .04 .10
205 Buddy Curry .04 .10
206 Steve Bartkowski .04 .10
207 Alfred Jackson .04 .10
208 Don Smith .04 .10
209 Alfred Jenkins .04 .10
210 Fulton Kuykendall .04 .10
211 William Andrews .04 .10
212 Gary Fencik .04 .10
213 Walter Payton 1.25 3.00
214 Mike Singletary .40 1.00
215 Otis Wilson .04 .10
216 Matt Suhey .04 .10
217 Dan Hampton .10 .25
218 Emery Moorehead .04 .10
219 Mike Hartenstine .04 .10
220 Danny White .08 .20
221 Drew Pearson .08 .20
222 Rafael Septien .04 .10
223 Ed Too Tall Jones .08 .20
224 Everson Walls .04 .10
225 Randy White .10 .25
226 Harvey Martin .04 .10
227 Tony Hill .04 .10
228 Tony Dorsett .15 .40
229 Billy Sims .08 .20
230 Leonard Thompson .04 .10
231 Eddie Murray .04 .10
232 Doug English .04 .10
233 Ken Fantetti .04 .10
234 Tom Skladany .04 .10
235 Freddie Scott .04 .10
236 Eric Hipple .04 .10
237 David Hill .04 .10
238 John Jefferson .04 .10
239 Paul Coffman .04 .10
240 Ezra Johnson .04 .10
241 Mike Douglass .04 .10
242 Mark Lee .04 .10
243 John Anderson .04 .10
244 Jan Stenerud .08 .20
245 Lynn Dickey .04 .10
246 James Lofton .12 .30
247 Vince Ferragamo .04 .10
248 Preston Dennard .04 .10
249 Jack Youngblood .08 .20
250 Mike Guman .04 .10
251 LeRoy Irvin .04 .10
252 Mike Lansford .04 .10
253 Kent Hill .04 .10
254 Nolan Cromwell .04 .10
255 Doug Martin .04 .10
256 Greg Coleman .04 .10
257 Ted Brown .04 .10
258 Mark Mullaney .04 .10
259 Joe Senser .04 .10
260 Randy Holloway .04 .10
261 Matt Blair .04 .10
262 Sammie White .04 .10
263 Tommy Kramer .04 .10
264 Joe Theismann FOIL .15 .40
265 Joe Montana FOIL 2.50 6.00
266 Dwight Clark FOIL .10 .25
267 Mike Nelms FOIL .04 .10
268 Carl Birdsong FOIL .04 .10
269 Everson Walls FOIL .04 .10
270 Doug Martin FOIL .04 .10
271 Tony Dorsett FOIL .50 1.25
272 Russell Erxleben .04 .10
273 Stan Brock .04 .10
274 Jeff Groth .04 .10
275 Bruce Clark .04 .10
276 Ken Stabler .15 .40
277 George Rogers .04 .10
278 Derland Moore .04 .10
279 Wayne Wilson .04 .10
280 Lawrence Taylor .15 .40
281 Harry Carson .04 .10
282 Brian Kelley .04 .10
283 Brad Van Pelt .04 .10
284 Earnest Gray .04 .10
285 Dave Jennings .04 .10
286 Rob Carpenter .04 .10
287 Scott Brunner .04 .10
288 Ron Jaworski .04 .10
289 Jerry Robinson .04 .10
290 Frank LeMaster .04 .10
291 Wilbert Montgomery .04 .10
292 Tony Franklin .04 .10
293 Harold Carmichael .08 .20
294 John Spagnola .04 .10
295 Herman Edwards .04 .10
296 Ottis Anderson .04 .10
297 Carl Birdsong .04 .10
298 Doug Marsh .04 .10
299 Neil Lomax .04 .10
300 Rush Brown .04 .10
301 Pat Tilley .04 .10
302 Wayne Morris .04 .10
303 Dan Dierdorf .08 .20
304 Roy Green .08 .20
305 Joe Montana 1.50 4.00
306 Randy Cross .04 .10
307 Freddie Solomon .04 .10
308 Jack Reynolds .04 .10
309 Ronnie Lott .15 .40
310 Renaldo Nehemiah .04 .10
311 Russ Francis .04 .10
312 Dwight Clark .08 .20
313 Doug Williams .04 .10
314 Bill Capece .04 .10
315 Mike Washington .04 .10
316 Hugh Green .04 .10
317 Kevin House .04 .10
318 Lee Roy Selmon .10 .25
319 Neal Colzie .04 .10
320 Jimmie Giles .04 .10
321 Cedric Brown .04 .10
322 Tony Peters .04 .10
323 Neal Olkewicz .04 .10
324 Dexter Manley .04 .10
325 Joe Theismann .12 .30
326 Rich Milot .04 .10
327 Mark Moseley .04 .10
328 Art Monk .15 .40
329 Mike Nelms .04 .10
330 John Riggins .10 .25
NNO Sticker Album .75 2.00

1983 Topps Sticker Boxes

The 1983 Topps Sticker Box set contains 12 boxes each containing two large cards (24 cards total) on the side of the box itself and 35 stickers inside. Cards, when cut, measure approximately 2 1/2" by 3 1/2". These blank-backed cards are unnumbered but each box is numbered on a white box tab. The player on top is offense and the lower player is defense. Number 10 was not issued. Prices below reflect the value of the uncut boxes not including the stickers inside the box.

COMPLETE SET (12) 50.00 100.00
1 Pat Donovan 3.00 8.00
M.Gastineau
2 Wes Chandler 3.00 8.00
Nolan Cromwell
3 Marvin Powell 4.00 10.00
Too Tall Jones
4 Ken Anderson 4.00 10.00
Tony Peters
5 Freeman McNeil 6.00 15.00
L.Taylor
6 Mark Moseley 3.00 8.00
Dave Jennings
7 Dwight Clark 4.00 10.00
Mike Haynes
8 Jeff Van Note 3.00 8.00
Harry Carson
9 Tony Dorsett 8.00 20.00
Hugh Green
11 Randy Cross 3.00 8.00
Gary Johnson
12 Kellen Winslow 4.00 10.00
Lester Hayes
13 John Hannah 6.00 15.00
Randy White

1984 Topps Stickers

The 1984 Topps Football sticker set is similar to the previous years in that it contains stickers, foil stickers, and an accompanying album to house one's collection. Many of these stickers were printed two players per card. In the checklist below the dual player stickers are listed according to the player with the lowest sticker number. The foil stickers are noted by "FOIL" in the checklist below. On the inside back cover of the sticker album the company offered (via direct mail-order) any 10 different stickers of your choice for 1.00; this is one reason why the values of the most popular players in these sticker sets are somewhat depressed compared to traditional card set prices. The sticker album features Charlie Joiner on the front cover and Dan Fouts on the back cover. The following players are shown in their Rookie Card year: Deron Cherry, Roger Craig, Eric Dickerson, Mark Duper, John Elway, Chris Hinton, Howie Long, Dan Marino, and Jackie Slater.

COMPLETE SET (186) 15.00 35.00
1 Super Bowl XVIII FOIL .12 .30
Plunkett
Allen UL
2 Super Bowl XVIII FOIL .08 .20
Plunkett
Allen UR
3 Super Bowl XVIII FOIL .08 .20
Plunkett
Allen LL
4 Super Bowl XVIII FOIL .08 .20
Plunkett
Allen LR
5 Marcus Allen FOIL .50 1.25
(Super Bowl MVP)
6 Walter Payton 1.25 3.00
7 Mike Richardson .04 .10
157 Pete Johnson
8 Jim McMahon .04 .10
158 Reggie Williams
9 Mike Hartenstine .04 .10
159 Isaac Curtis
10 Mike Singletary .08 .20
11 Willie Gault .04 .10
12 Terry Schmidt .04 .10
162 Charles Alexander
13 Emery Moorehead .04 .10
163 Ray Horton
14 Leslie Frazier .04 .10
164 Steve Kreider
15 Jack Thompson .04 .10
165 Ben Williams
16 Booker Reese .04 .10
166 Frank Lewis
17 James Wilder .04 .10
167 Roosevelt Leaks
18 Lee Roy Selmon .08 .20
19 Hugh Green .04 .10
20 Gerald Carter .04 .10
170 Joe Danelo
21 Steve Wilson .04 .10
171 Chris Keating
22 Michael Morton .04 .10
172 Jerry Butler
23 Kevin House .04 .10
24 Ottis Anderson .04 .10
25 Lionel Washington .04 .10
175 Barney Chavous
26 Pat Tilley .04 .10
176 Zach Thomas WR
27 Curtis Greer .04 .10
177 Luke Prestridge
28 Roy Green .04 .10
29 Carl Birdsong .04 .10
30 Neil Lomax .04 .10
180 Steve Foley
31 Lee Nelson .04 .10
181 Sammy Winder
32 Stump Mitchell .04 .10
182 Rick Upchurch
33 Tony Hill .04 .10
183 Bobby Jones
34 Everson Walls .04 .10
184 Matt Bahr
35 Danny White .04 .10
185 Doug Dieken
36 Tony Dorsett .20 .50
37 Ed Too Tall Jones .08 .20
38 Rafael Septien .04 .10
188 Tom Cousineau
39 Doug Cosbie .04 .10
189 Paul McDonald
40 Drew Pearson .08 .20
190 Clay Matthews
41 Randy White .08 .20
42 Ron Jaworski .04 .10
43 Anthony Griggs .04 .10
193 Chuck Muncie
44 Hubie Oliver .04 .10
194 Linden King
45 Wilbert Montgomery .08 .20
195 Charlie Joiner
46 Dennis Harrison .04 .10
47 Mike Quick .04 .10
48 Jerry Robinson .04 .10
198 James Brooks
49 Michael Williams/199 Mike Green LB .04 .10
50 Herman Edwards .04 .10
200 Rolf Benirschke
51 Steve Bartkowski .04 .10
201 Henry Marshall
52 Mick Luckhurst .04 .10
202 Nick Lowery
53 Mike Pitts .04 .10
203 Jerry Blanton
54 William Andrews .04 .10
55 R.C. Thielemann .04 .10
56 Buddy Curry .04 .10
206 Billy Jackson
57 Billy Johnson .04 .10
207 Art Still
58 Ralph Giacomarro .04 .10
208 Theotis Brown
59 Mike Kenn .04 .10
60 Joe Montana 1.50 4.00
61 Fred Dean .06 .15
211 Nesby Glasgow
62 Dwight Clark .04 .10
212 Mike Pagel
63 Wendell Tyler .04 .10
213 Ray Donaldson
64 Dwight Hicks .04 .10
65 Ronnie Lott .12 .30
66 Roger Craig .12 .30
216 Rohn Stark
67 Fred Solomon .04 .10
217 Randy McMillan
68 Ray Wersching .04 .10
218 Vernon Maxwell
69 Brad Van Pelt .04 .10
219 A.J. Duhe
70 Butch Woolfolk .04 .10
220 Andra Franklin
71 Terry Kinard .04 .10
221 Ed Newman
72 Lawrence Taylor .15 .40
73 Ali Haji-Sheikh .04 .10
74 Mark Haynes .04 .10
224 Bob Baumhower
75 Rob Carpenter .04 .10
225 Reggie Roby
76 Earnest Gray .04 .10
226 Dwight Stephenson
77 Harry Carson .04 .10
78 Billy Sims .08 .20
79 Eddie Murray .04 .10
229 Freeman McNeil
80 William Gay .04 .10
230 Bruce Harper
81 Leonard Thompson .04 .10
231 Wesley Walker
82 Doug English .04 .10
83 Eric Hipple .04 .10
84 Ken Fantetti .04 .10
234 Johnny Lam Jones
85 Bruce McNorton .04 .10
235 Lance Mehl
86 James Jones .04 .10
236 Pat Ryan
87 Lynn Dickey .04 .10
237 Florian Kempf
88 Ezra Johnson .04 .10
238 Carl Roaches
89 Jan Stenerud .04 .10
239 Gregg Bingham
90 James Lofton .08 .20
91 Larry McCarren .04 .10
92 John Jefferson .04 .10
242 Doug France
93 Mike Douglass .04 .10
243 Chris Dressel
94 Gerry Ellis .04 .10
244 Willie Tullis
95 Paul Coffman .04 .10
96 Eric Dickerson .30 .75
97 Jackie Slater .08 .20
247 Brian Holloway
98 Carl Ekern .04 .10
248 Stanley Morgan
99 Vince Ferragamo .04 .10
249 Rick Sanford
100 Kent Hill .04 .10
101 Nolan Cromwell .04 .10
102 Jack Youngblood .08 .20
252 Andre Tippett
103 John Misko .04 .10
253 Steve Grogan
104 Mike Barber .04 .10
254 Clayton Weishuhn
105 Jeff Bostic .08 .20
255 Jim Plunkett
106 Mark Murphy .04 .10
256 Rod Martin
107 Joe Jacoby .04 .10
257 Lester Hayes
108 John Riggins .08 .20
109 Joe Theismann .08 .20
110 Russ Grimm .08 .20
260 Ted Hendricks
111 Neal Olkewicz .04 .10
261 Greg Pruitt
112 Charlie Brown WR .25 .60
262 Howie Long
113 Dave Butz .04 .10
114 George Rogers .04 .10
115 Jim Kovach .04 .10
265 Jacob Green
116 Dave Wilson .04 .10
266 Bruce Scholtz
117 Johnnie Poe .20 .50
267 Steve Largent
118 Russell Erxleben .04 .10
119 Rickey Jackson .30 .75
120 Jeff Groth .04 .10
270 Dave Brown DB
121 Richard Todd .04 .10
271 Zachary Dixon
122 Wayne Wilson .04 .10
272 Norm Johnson
123 Steve Dils .15 .40
273 Terry Bradshaw
124 Benny Ricardo .04 .10
274 Keith Willis
125 John Turner .04 .10
275 Gary Anderson K
126 Ted Brown .04 .10
127 Greg Coleman .04 .10
128 Darrin Nelson .04 .10
278 Calvin Sweeney
129 Scott Studwell .04 .10
279 Rick Woods
130 Tommy Kramer .04 .10
280 Bennie Cunningham
131 Doug Martin .04 .10
132 Nolan Cromwell 2.50 6.00
144 Dan Marino
All-Pro FOIL
133 Carl Birdsong .04 .10
145 Ali Haji-Sheikh
All-Pro FOIL
134 Deron Cherry .08 .20
146 Eric Dickerson
All-Pro FOIL
135 Ronnie Lott .12 .30
147 Curt Warner
All-Pro FOIL
136 Lester Hayes .08 .20
148 James Lofton
All-Pro FOIL
137 Lawrence Taylor .15 .40
149 Todd Christensen
All-Pro FOIL
138 Jack Lambert .08 .20
150 Cris Collinsworth
All-Pro FOIL
139 Chip Banks .04 .10
151 Mike Kenn
All-Pro FOIL
140 Lee Roy Selmon .08 .20
152 Russ Grimm
All-Pro FOIL
141 Fred Smerlas .04 .10
153 Jeff Bostic
All-Pro FOIL
142 Doug English .08 .20
154 John Hannah
All-Pro FOIL
143 Doug Betters .08 .20
155 Anthony Munoz

All-Pro FOIL
156 Ken Anderson .08 .20
160 Anthony Munoz .08 .20
161 Cris Collinsworth .04 .10
168 Joe Ferguson .04 .10
169 Fred Smerlas .04 .10
173 Eugene Marve .04 .10
174 Louis Wright .04 .10
178 Steve Watson .04 .10
179 John Elway 2.50 6.00
186 Mike Pruitt .04 .10
187 Chip Banks .04 .10
191 Ozzie Newsome .08 .20
192 Dan Fouts .12 .30
196 Wes Chandler .04 .10
197 Kellen Winslow .08 .20
204 Bill Kenney .04 .10
205 Carlos Carson .04 .10
209 Deron Cherry .08 .20
210 Curtis Dickey .04 .10
214 Raul Allegre .04 .10
215 Chris Hinton .04 .10
222 Dan Marino 2.50 6.00
223 Doug Betters .04 .10
227 Mark Duper .15 .40
228 Mark Gastineau .04 .10
232 Marvin Powell .04 .10
233 Joe Klecko .04 .10
240 Tim Smith .04 .10
241 Jesse Baker .04 .10
245 Robert Brazile .04 .10
246 Tony Collins .04 .10
250 John Hannah .08 .20
251 Rich Camarillo .04 .10
258 Marcus Allen .30 .75
259 Todd Christensen .04 .10
263 Vann McElroy .04 .10
264 Curt Warner .08 .20
268 Kenny Easley .04 .10
269 Dave Krieg .08 .20
276 Franco Harris .08 .20
277 Mike Webster .04 .10
281 Jack Lambert .08 .20
282 Curt Warner .08 .20
283 Todd Christensen
FOIL
NNO Sticker Album .75 2.00
(Charlie Joiner
and Dan Fouts)

1985 Topps Coming Soon Stickers

This set of 30 white-bordered stickers are usually referred to as the "Coming Soon" stickers as they were inserted in the regular issue 1985 Topps football card wax packs and prominently mention "Coming Soon" on the sticker backs. They are the same size as the regular Topps stickers (approximately 2 1/8" by 3") and were not very difficult to find. Unlike many of the sticker cards in the regular set, this subset only contains one player per sticker. This is a skip-numbered set due to the fact that these stickers have the same numbers as the regular sticker issue.

COMPLETE SET (30) 3.00 8.00
6 Ken Anderson .08 .20
15 Greg Bell .04 .10
24 John Elway 1.00 2.50
33 Ozzie Newsome .08 .20
42 Charlie Joiner .08 .20
51 Bill Kenney .06 .15
60 Randy McMillan .04 .10
69 Dan Marino 1.00 2.50
77 Mark Clayton .08 .20
78 Mark Gastineau .06 .15
87 Warren Moon .40 1.00
96 Tony Eason .04 .10
105 Marcus Allen .25 .60
114 Steve Largent .20 .50
123 John Stallworth .06 .15
156 Walter Payton .50 1.25
165 James Wilder .04 .10
174 Neil Lomax .06 .15
183 Tony Dorsett .15 .40
192 Mike Quick .04 .10
201 William Andrews .06 .15
210 Joe Montana 1.00 2.50
214 Dwight Clark .08 .20
219 Lawrence Taylor .12 .30
228 Billy Sims .06 .15
237 James Lofton .12 .30
246 Eric Dickerson .12 .30
255 John Riggins .10 .25
268 George Rogers .06 .15
284 Tommy Kramer .06 .15

1985 Topps Stickers

The 1985 Topps Football sticker set is similar to the previous years in that it contains stickers and an accompanying album to house one's sticker collection. However, there are no foil stickers in this set. Some of the stickers are half the size of others; those paired stickers sharing a card with another player are indicated parenthetically by the other player's sticker number in the checklist below. On the inside back cover of the sticker album the company offered (via direct mail-order) any ten different stickers of your choice for 1.00; this is one reason why the values of the most popular players in these sticker sets are somewhat depressed compared to traditional card set prices. The front cover of the sticker album features Dan Marino, Joe Montana, Walter Payton, Eric Dickerson, Art Monk, and Charlie Joiner; the back cover shows a team photo of the San Francisco 49ers. The stickers are checklisted below according to special subsets and teams. The following players are shown in their Rookie Card year or earlier: Mark Clayton, Richard Dent, Henry Ellard, Boomer Esiason (one year early), Craig James, Louis Lipps, Warren Moon, Ken O'Brien, and Darryl Talley.

COMPLETE SET (173) 20.00 40.00
1 Super Bowl XIX 1.50 4.00
Joe Montana LH
2 Super Bowl XIX .75 2.00
Joe Montana RH
3 Super Bowl XIX .04 .10
Roger Craig LH
4 Super Bowl XIX .04 .10
Roger Craig RH
5 Super Bowl XIX .04 .10
Wendell Tyler
6 Ken Anderson .08 .20
7 M.L. Harris .08 .20
157 Dan Hampton
8 Eddie Edwards .04 .10
158 Wille Gault
9 Louis Breeden .04 .10
160 Matt Suhoy
10 Larry Kinnebrew .04 .10
11 Isaac Curtis .04 .10
161 Mike Singletary
12 James Brooks .04 .10
162 Gary Fencik
13 Jim Breech .08 .20
163 Jim McMahon
14 Boomer Esiason .20 .50
164 Bob Thomas
15 Greg Bell .04 .10
16 Fred Smerlas .04 .10
166 Steve DeBerg
17 Joe Ferguson .04 .10
167 Mark Cotney
18 Ken Johnson DE .04 .10
168 Adger Armstrong
19 Darryl Talley .08 .20
169 Gerald Carter
20 Preston Dennard .04 .10
170 David Logan
21 Charles Romes .04 .10
171 Hugh Green
22 Jim Haslett .08 .20
172 Lee Roy Selmon
23 Byron Franklin .04 .10
24 John Elway 2.00 5.00
25 Rulon Jones .04 .10
175 Otis Armstrong
26 Butch Johnson .04 .10
176 Al Bubba Baker
27 Rich Karlis .04 .10
177 E.J. Junior
28 Sammy Winder .04 .10
29 Tom Jackson .04 .10
179 Pat Tilley
30 Mike Harden .04 .10
180 Stump Mitchell
31 Steve Watson .04 .10
181 Lionel Washington
32 Steve Foley .04 .10
182 Curtis Greer
33 Ozzie Newsome .08 .20
34 Al Gross .04 .10
184 Gary Hogeboom
35 Paul McDonald .04 .10
185 Jim Jeffcoat
36 Matt Bahr .04 .10
186 Danny White
37 Charles White .04 .10
187 Michael Downs
38 Don Rogers .04 .10
188 Doug Cosbie
39 Mike Pruitt .04 .10
189 Tony Hill
40 Reggie Camp .04 .10
190 Rafael Septien
41 Boyce Green .04 .10
42 Charlie Joiner .04 .10
43 Dan Fouts .08 .20
193 Ray Ellis
44 Keith Ferguson .04 .10
194 John Spagnola
45 Pete Holohan .04 .10
195 Dennis Harrison
46 Earnest Jackson .04 .10
47 Wes Chandler .04 .10
197 Greg Brown
48 Gill Byrd .08 .20
198 Ron Jaworski
49 Kellen Winslow .08 .20
199 Paul McFadden
50 Billy Ray Smith .04 .10
200 Wes Hopkins
51 Bill Kenney .04 .10
52 Herman Heard .04 .10
202 Mike Pitts
53 Art Still .04 .10
203 Steve Bartkowski
54 Nick Lowery .04 .10
204 Gerald Riggs
55 Deron Cherry .04 .10
205 Alfred Jackson
56 Henry Marshall .04 .10
206 Don Smith DE
57 Mike Bell .04 .10
207 Mike Kenn
58 Todd Blackledge .04 .10
208 Kenny Johnson
59 Carlos Carson .04 .10
60 Randy McMillan .04 .10
61 Donnell Thompson .04 .10
211 Wendell Tyler
62 Raymond Butler .04 .10
212 Keena Turner
63 Ray Donaldson .04 .10
213 Ray Wersching
64 Art Schlichter .04 .10
65 Rohn Stark .04 .10
215 Dwaine Board
66 Johnie Cooks .08 .20
216 Roger Craig
67 Mike Pagel .08 .20
217 Ronnie Lott
68 Eugene Daniel .04 .10
218 Freddie Solomon
69 Dan Marino 2.00 5.00
70 Pete Johnson .04 .10
220 Zeke Moyatt
71 Tony Nathan .04 .10
221 Harry Carson
72 Glenn Blackwood .04 .10
222 Rob Carpenter RB
73 Woody Bennett .04 .10
223 Bobby Johnson WR
74 Dwight Stephenson .04 .10
224 Joe Morris
75 Mark Duper .04 .10
225 Mark Haynes
76 Doug Betters .04 .10
226 Lionel Manuel
77 Mark Clayton .12 .30
78 Mark Gastineau .04 .10
79 Johnny Lam Jones .04 .10
229 Leonard Thompson
80 Mickey Shuler .04 .10
230 James Jones FB
81 Tony Paige .08 .20
231 Eddie Murray
82 Freeman McNeil .04 .10
83 Russell Carter .04 .10
233 Gary Danielson
84 Wesley Walker .04 .10
234 Curtis Green
85 Bruce Harper .04 .10
235 Bobby Watkins
86 Ken O'Brien .08 .20
236 Doug English
87 Warren Moon .30 .75
88 Jesse Baker .04 .10
238 Eddie Lee Ivery
89 Carl Roaches .04 .10
239 Mike Douglass
90 Carter Hartwig .04 .10
240 Gerry Ellis
91 Larry Moriarty .04 .10
241 Tim Lewis
92 Robert Brazile .04 .10
242 Paul Coffman
93 Oliver Luck .04 .10
243 Tom Flynn
94 Willie Tullis .04 .10
244 Ezra Johnson
95 Tim Smith .04 .10
96 Tony Eason .04 .10
97 Stanley Morgan .04 .10
247 Jack Youngblood
98 Mosi Tatupu .04 .10
248 Doug Smith C
99 Raymond Clayborn .04 .10
249 Jeff Kemp
100 Andre Tippett .04 .10
101 Craig James .08 .20
251 Mike Lansford
102 Derrick Ramsey .04 .10
252 Henry Ellard
103 Tony Collins .04 .10
253 LeRoy Irvin
104 Tony Franklin .04 .10
254 Ron Brown
105 Marcus Allen .20 .50
106 Chris Bahr .04 .10
256 Dexter Manley
107 Marc Wilson .04 .10
257 Darrell Green
108 Howie Long .08 .20
258 Joe Theismann
109 Bill Pickel .04 .10
259 Mark Malone
110 Mike Haynes .04 .10
260 Clint Didier
111 Malcolm Barnwell .04 .10
261 Vernon Dean
112 Rod Martin .04 .10
262 Calvin Muhammad
113 Todd Christensen .04 .10
114 Steve Largent .20 .50
115 Curt Warner .04 .10
265 Hoby Brenner
116 Kenny Easley .04 .10
266 Dave Wilson
117 Jacob Green .04 .10
267 Hokie Gajan
118 Daryl Turner .04 .10
119 Norm Johnson .06 .15
269 Rickey Jackson
120 Dave Krieg .08 .20
270 Brian Hansen
121 Eric Lane .04 .10
271 Dave Waymer
122 Jeff Bryant .04 .10
272 Richard Todd
123 John Stallworth .04 .10
124 Donnie Shell .04 .10
274 Ted Brown
125 Gary Anderson .04 .10
275 Leo Lewis
126 Mark Malone .04 .10
276 Scott Studstill
127 Sam Washington .04 .10
277 Alfred Anderson
128 Frank Pollard .04 .10
278 Rufus Bess
129 Mike Merriweather .04 .10
279 Darrin Nelson
130 Walter Abercrombie .04 .10
280 Greg Coleman
131 Louis Lipps .04 .10
132 Mark Clayton .08 .20
144 Todd Bell
133 Randy Cross .04 .10
145 Richard Dent
134 Eric Dickerson .12 .30
146 Kenny Easley
135 John Hannah .04 .10
147 Mark Gastineau
136 Mike Kenn .08 .20
148 Dan Hampton
137 Dan Marino 1.50 4.00
149 Mark Haynes
138 Art Monk .08 .20
150 Mike Haynes
139 Anthony Munoz .04 .10
151 E.J. Junior
140 Ozzie Newsome .04 .10
152 Rod Martin
141 Walter Payton 1.25 3.00
153 Steve Nelson
142 Jan Stenerud .04 .10
154 Reggie Roby
143 Dwight Stephenson .08 .20
155 Lawrence Taylor
156 Walter Payton 1.50 4.00
160 Richard Dent .20 .50
165 James Wilder .04 .10
173 Kevin House .04 .10
174 Neil Lomax .04 .10
178 Roy Green .04 .10
183 Tony Dorsett .20 .50
191 Randy White .08 .20
192 Mike Quick .04 .10
196 Wilbert Montgomery .04 .10
201 William Andrews .04 .10
209 Stacey Bailey .04 .10
210 Joe Montana 2.00 5.00
214 Dwight Clark .04 .10
219 Lawrence Taylor .12 .30
227 Phil Simms .08 .20
228 Billy Sims .04 .10
232 William Gay .04 .10
237 James Lofton .08 .20
245 Lynn Dickey .04 .10
246 Eric Dickerson .12 .30
250 Kent Hill .04 .10
255 John Riggins .08 .20
263 Art Monk .08 .20
264 Bruce Clark .04 .10
268 George Rogers .04 .10
273 Jan Stenerud .04 .10
281 Tommy Kramer .04 .10
282 Joe Montana 2.50 6.00
283 Dan Marino
284 Brian Hansen .04 .10
285 Jim Arnold
NNO Sticker Album .75 2.00

1986 Topps Stickers

The 1986 Topps Football sticker set is similar to the previous years in that it contains stickers, foil stickers, and an accompanying album to house one's sticker collection. The stickers measure approximately 2 1/8" by 3". The sticker design shows an inverted L-shaped border in an accent color. The stickers are numbered on the front and on the back. The sticker backs are printed in brown ink on white stock. Sticker pairs are identified below by parenthetically listing the other member of the pair. On the inside back cover of the sticker album the company offered (via direct mail-order) any ten different stickers of your choice for 1.00; this is one reason why the values of the most popular players in these sticker sets are somewhat depressed compared to traditional card set prices. The front cover of the sticker album features Walter Payton and several other Chicago Bears players; the back cover shows a team photo of the Chicago Bears. The stickers are checklisted below according to special subsets and teams. The following players are shown in their Rookie Card year: Anthony Carter, Gary Clark, Bernie Kosar, Andre Reed, Bruce Smith, Al Toon, Reggie White, and Steve Young.

COMPLETE SET (173) 12.50 25.00
1 Walter Payton LH .50 1.25
2 Walter Payton RH .40 1.00
3 Richard Dent LH .04 .10
4 Richard Dent RH .04 .10
5 Richard Dent FOIL .08 .20
Super Bowl MVP
6 Walter Payton 1.25 3.00
7 William Perry .04 .10
8 Jim McMahon .04 .10
158 Cris Collinsworth
9 Richard Dent .04 .10
159 Eddie Edwards
10 Jim Covert .04 .10
160 James Griffin
11 Dan Hampton .04 .10
161 Jim Breech
12 Mike Singletary .04 .10
162 Eddie Brown WR
13 Jay Hilgenberg .04 .10
163 Ross Browner
14 Otis Wilson .04 .10
164 James Brooks
15 Jimmie Giles .04 .10
16 Kevin House .04 .10
166 Jerry Butler
17 Jeremiah Castille .04 .10
167 Don Wilson
18 James Wilder .04 .10
19 Donald Igwebuike .04 .10
169 Jim Haslett
20 David Logan .04 .10
170 Bruce Mathison
21 Jeff Davis .30 .75
171 Bruce Smith
22 Frank Garcia .04 .10
172 Joe Cribbs
23 Steve Young .75 2.00
173 Charles Romes
24 Stump Mitchell .04 .10
25 E.J. Junior .04 .10
26 J.T. Smith 1.00 2.50
176 John Elway
27 Pat Tilley .04 .10
177 Sammy Winder
28 Neil Lomax .04 .10
178 Louis Wright
29 Leonard Smith .04 .10
179 Steve Watson
30 Ottis Anderson .04 .10
180 Dennis Smith
31 Curtis Greer .04 .10
181 Mike Harden
32 Roy Green .04 .10
182 Vance Johnson
33 Tony Dorsett .15 .40
34 Tony Hill .04 .10
184 Chip Banks
35 Doug Cosbie .04 .10
185 Bob Golic
36 Everson Walls .04 .10
37 Randy White .08 .20
187 Ozzie Newsome
38 Rafael Septien .12 .30
188 Bernie Kosar
39 Mike Renfro .04 .10
189 Don Rogers
40 Danny White .04 .10
190 Al Gross
41 Ed Too Tall Jones .04 .10
191 Clarence Weathers
42 Earnest Jackson .04 .10
43 Mike Quick .04 .10
44 Wes Hopkins .04 .10
194 Wes Chandler
45 Reggie White .40 1.00
195 Kellen Winslow
46 Greg Brown .04 .10
196 Gary Anderson RB
47 Paul McFadden .04 .10
197 Charlie Joiner
48 John Spagnola .04 .10
198 Ralf Mojsiejenko
49 Ron Jaworski .04 .10
199 Bob Thomas
50 Herman Hunter .04 .10
200 Tim Spencer
51 Gerald Riggs .04 .10
52 Mike Pitts .04 .10
202 Bill Maas
53 Buddy Curry .04 .10
203 Herman Heard
54 Billy Johnson .04 .10
55 Rick Donnelly .04 .10
205 Nick Lowery
56 Rick Bryan .04 .10
206 Bill Kenney
57 Bobby Butler .04 .10
207 Albert Lewis
58 Mick Luckhurst/208 Art Still .04 .10
59 Mike Kenn .04 .10
209 Stephone Paige
60 Roger Craig .08 .20
61 Joe Montana 1.50 4.00
62 Michael Carter .04 .10
212 Albert Bentley
63 Eric Wright .04 .10
213 Eugene Daniel
64 Dwight Clark .04 .10
214 Pat Beach
65 Ronnie Lott .04 .10
215 Cliff Odom
66 Carlton Williamson .04 .10
216 Duane Bickett
67 Wendell Tyler .04 .10
217 George Wonsley
68 Dwaine Board .04 .10
218 Randy McMillan
69 Joe Morris .04 .10
70 Leonard Marshall .04 .10
220 Dwight Stephenson
71 Lionel Manue .04 .10
221 Roy Foster
72 Harry Carson .04 .10
73 Phil Simms .04 .10
223 Mark Duper
74 Sean Landeta .04 .10
224 Fuad Reveiz
75 Lawrence Taylor .08 .20
225 Reggie Roby
76 Elvis Patterson .04 .10
226 Tony Nathan
77 George Adams .04 .10
227 Ron Davenport
78 James Jones FB .04 .10
79 Leonard Thompson .04 .10
80 William Graham .04 .10
230 Mark Gastineau
81 Mark Nichols .04 .10
231 Ken O'Brien
82 William Gay .04 .10
232 Lance Mehl
83 Jimmy Williams .04 .10
233 Al Toon
84 Billy Sims .04 .10
234 Mickey Shuler
85 Bobby Watkins .04 .10
235 Pat Leahy
86 Eddie Murray .04 .10
236 Wesley Walker
87 James Lofton .08 .20
88 Jessie Clark .12 .30
238 Warren Moon
89 Tim Lewis .04 .10
239 Mike Rozier
90 Eddie Lee Ivery .04 .10
91 Phillip Epps .04 .10
241Tim Smith
92 Ezra Johnson .04 .10
242 Butch Woolfolk
93 Mike Douglass .04 .10
243 Willie Drewrey
94 Paul Coffman .04 .10
244 Keith Bostic
95 Randy Scott .04 .10
245 Jesse Baker
96 Eric Dickerson .08 .20
97 Dale Hatcher .04 .10
98 Ron Brown .04 .10
248 Tony Eason
99 LeRoy Irvin .04 .10
249 Andre Tippett
100 Kent Hill .04 .10
250 Tony Collins
101 Dennis Harrah .04 .10
251 Brian Holloway
102 Jackie Slater .04 .10
252 Irving Fryar
103 Mike Wilcher .04 .10
253 Raymond Clayborn
104 Doug Smith .04 .10
254 Steve Nelson
105 Art Monk .08 .20
106 Joe Jacoby .04 .10
256 Mike Haynes
107 Russ Grimm .04 .10
257 Todd Christensen
108 George Rogers .04 .10
109 Dexter Manley .04 .10
259 Lester Hayes
110 Jay Schroeder .04 .10
260 Rod Martin
111 Gary Clark .15 .40
261 Dokie Williams
112 Curtis Jordan .04 .10
262 Chris Bahr
113 Charles Mann .04 .10
263 Bill Pickel
114 Morten Andersen .04 .10
115 Rickey Jackson .04 .10
116 Glen Redd .04 .10
266 Fredd Young
117 Bobby Hebert .08 .20
267 Dave Krieg
118 Hoby Brenner .04 .10
268 Daryl Turner
119 Brian Hansen .04 .10
269 John Harris
120 Dave Waymer .04 .10
270 Randy Edwards
121 Bruce Clark .04 .10
271 Kenny Easley
122 Wayne Wilson .04 .10
272 Jacob Green
123 Joey Browner .08 .20
124 Darrin Nelson .04 .10
274 Mike Webster
125 Keith Millard .04 .10
275 Walter Abercrombie
126 Anthony Carter .12 .30
127 Buster Rhymes .04 .10
277 Frank Pollard
128 Steve Jordan .08 .20
278 Mike Merriweather
129 Greg Coleman .04 .10
279 Mark Malone
130 Ted Brown .04 .10
280 Donnie Shell
131 John Turner .08 .20
281 John Stallworth
132 Harry Carson .15 .40
144 Marcus Allen AP FOIL
133 Deron Cherry .04 .10
145 Gary Anderson K AP FOIL
134 Richard Dent .08 .20
146 Doug Cosbie AP FOIL
135 Mike Haynes .08 .20
147 Jim Covert AP FOIL
136 Wes Hopkins .08 .20
148 John Hannah AP FOIL
137 Joe Klecko .04 .10
149 Jay Hilgenberg AP FOIL
138 Leonard Marshall .04 .10
150 Kent Hill AP FOIL
139 Karl Mecklenburg .04 .10
151 Brian Holloway AP FOIL
140 Rohn Stark .20 .50
152 Steve Largent AP FOIL
141 Lawrence Taylor 1.00 2.50
153 Dan Marino AP FOIL
142 Andre Tippett .08 .20
154 Art Monk AP FOIL
143 Everson Walls .75 2.00
155 Walter Payton AP FOIL
156 Anthony Munoz .08 .20
157 Boomer Esiason .12 .30
165 Greg Bell .04 .10
168 Andre Reed .30 .75
174 Karl Mecklenburg .04 .10
175 Rulon Jones .04 .10
183 Kevin Mack .04 .10
186 Earnest Byner .08 .20
192 Lionel James .04 .10
193 Dan Fouts .12 .30
201 Deron Cherry .04 .10
204 Carlos Carson .04 .10
210 Rohn Stark .04 .10
211 Chris Hinton .04 .10
219 Dan Marino 1.50 4.00
222 Mark Clayton .08 .20
228 Freeman McNeil .04 .10
229 Joe Klecko .04 .10
237 Drew Hill .04 .10
240 Mike Munchak .04 .10
246 Craig James .08 .20
247 John Hannah .08 .20
255 Marcus Allen .15 .40
258 Howie Long .08 .20
264 Curt Warner .04 .10
265 Steve Largent .20 .50
273 Gary Anderson K .04 .10
276 Louis Lipps .04 .10
282 Marcus Allen .20 .50
284 Kevin Butler FOIL
283 Ken O'Brien .08 .20
285 Roger Craig FOIL
NNO Sticker Album .75 2.00

1987 Topps Stickers

The 1987 Topps Football sticker set is similar to the previous years in that it contains stickers, foil stickers, and an accompanying album to house one's sticker collection. The stickers are approximately 2 1/8" by 3" and are in full-color with a white border with little footballs in each corner. The stickers are numbered on the front in the lower left hand border. Several feature two players per sticker card; they are designated in the checklist below along with the card number of the paired player. The sticker backs are printed in red on white stock. On the inside back cover of the sticker album the company offered (via direct mail-order) any ten different stickers of your choice for 1.00; this is one reason why the values of the most popular players in these sticker sets are somewhat depressed compared to traditional card set prices. The front cover of the sticker album shows New York Giants art. The following players are shown in their Rookie Card year: Keith Byars, Randall Cunningham, Kenneth Davis, Jim Everett, Doug Flutie, Ernest Givins, Jim Kelly, Leslie O'Neal and Herschel Walker.

COMPLETE SET (173) 10.00 20.00
1 Phil Simms .08 .20
Super Bowl MVP
2 Super Bowl XXI .04 .10
Phil Simms UL
3 Super Bowl XXI .04 .10
Phil Simms UR
4 Super Bowl XXI .04 .10
Phil Simms LL
5 Super Bowl XXI .04 .10
Phil Simms LR
6 Mike Singletary .08 .20
7 Jim Covert .08 .20
156 Boomer Esiason
8 Willie Gault .08 .20
157 Anthony Munoz
9 Jim McMahon .08 .20
158 Tim McGee
10 Doug Flutie .40 1.00
159 Max Montoya
11 Richard Dent .04 .10
160 Jim Breach
12 Kevin Butler .04 .10
161 Tim Krumrie
13 Wilber Marshall .04 .10
162 Eddie Brown WR
14 Walter Payton .75 2.00
15 Calvin Magee .04 .10
16 David Logan .04 .10
165 Charles Romes
17 Jeff Davis .04 .10
166 Robb Riddick
18 Gerald Carter .04 .10
167 Eugene Marve
19 James Wilder .04 .10
20 Chris Washington .04 .10
168 Chris Burkett
21 Phil Freeman .10 .25
169 Bruce Smith
22 Frank Garcia .04 .10
170 Greg Bell
23 Donald Igwebuike .04 .10
171 Pete Metzelaars
24 Al(Bubba) Baker .04 .10
175 Mike Harden
25 Vai Sikahema .04 .10
176 Gerald Willhite
26 Leonard Smith .04 .10
177 Rulon Jones
27 Ron Wolfley .04 .10
178 Rick Hunley
28 J.T. Smith .04 .10
29 Roy Green .04 .10
179 Mark Jackson
30 Cedric Mack .04 .10
180 Rich Karlis
31 Neil Lomax .04 .10
181 Sammy Winder
32 Stump Mitchell .04 .10
33 Herschel Walker .15 .40
34 Danny White .04 .10
184 Kevin Mack
35 Michael Downs .04 .10
185 Bob Golic
36 Randy White .08 .20
186 Ozzie Newsome
37 Eugene Lockhart .04 .10
188 Gerald McNeil
38 Mike Sherrard .08 .20
189 Hanford Dixon
39 Jim Jeffcoat .04 .10
190 Cody Risien
40 Tony Hill .04 .10
191 Chris Rockins
41 Tony Dorsett .12 .30
42 Keith Byars .04 .10
192 Gill Byrd
43 Andre Waters .08 .20
193 Kellen Winslow
44 Kenny Jackson .04 .10
194 Billy Ray Smith
45 John Teltschik .04 .10
195 Wes Chandler
46 Roynell Young .08 .20
196 Leslie O'Neal
47 Randall Cunningham .20 .50
197 Ralf Mojsiejenko
48 Mike Reichenbach .04 .10
198 Lee Williams
49 Reggie White .20 .50
50 Mike Quick .04 .10
51 Bill Fralic .04 .10
201 Stephone Paige
52 Sylvester Stamps .04 .10
202 Irv Eatman
53 Bret Clark .04 .10
203 Bill Kenney
54 William Andrews .04 .10
204 Dino Hackett
55 Buddy Curry .04 .10
205 Carlos Carson
56 David Archer .04 .10
206 Art Still
57 Rick Bryan .04 .10
207 Lloyd Burruss
58 Gerald Riggs .04 .10
59 Charlie Brown .04 .10
60 Joe Montana 1.00 2.50
61 Jerry Rice .75 2.00
62 Carlton Williamson .04 .10
212 Cliff Odom
63 Roger Craig .08 .20
213 Randy McMillan
64 Ronnie Lott .08 .20
214 Chris Hinton
65 Dwight Clark .04 .10
215 Matt Bouza
66 Jeff Stover .04 .10
216 Ray Donaldson
67 Charles Haley .08 .20
217 Bill Brooks
68 Ray Wersching .04 .10
218 Jack Trudeau
69 Lawrence Taylor .12 .30
70 Joe Morris .04 .10
71 Carl Banks .04 .10
221 Dwight Stephenson
72 Mark Bavaro .04 .10
222 Mark Clayton
73 Harry Carson .04 .10
223 Roy Foster
74 Phil Simms .08 .20
224 John Offerdahl
75 Jim Burt .04 .10
225 Lorenzo Hampton
76 Brad Benson .04 .10
226 Reggie Roby
77 Leonard Marshall .04 .10
227 Tony Nathan
78 Jeff Chadwick .04 .10
79 Devon Mitchell .04 .10
228 Johnny Hector
80 Chuck Long .04 .10
229 Wesley Walker
81 Demetrious Johnson .04 .10
230 Mark Gastineau
82 Herman Hunter .04 .10
231 Ken O'Brien
83 Keith Ferguson .04 .10
232 Dave Jennings
84 Garry James .04 .10
233 Mickey Shuler
85 Leonard Thompson .04 .10
234 Joe Klecko
86 James Jones FB .04 .10
87 Kenneth Davis .08 .20
88 Brian Noble .08 .20
237 Warren Moon
89 Al Del Greco .04 .10
238 Dean Steinkubler
90 Mark Lee .04 .10
239 Mike Rozier
91 Randy Wright .04 .10
92 Tim Harris .08 .20
240 Ray Childress
93 Phillip Epps .04 .10
241 Tony Zendejas
94 Walter Stanley .04 .10
242 John Grimsley
95 Eddie Lee Ivery .04 .10
243 Jesse Baker
96 Doug Smith .08 .20
247 Steve Grogan
97 Jerry Gray .04 .10
248 Garin Veris
98 Dennis Harrah .04 .10
249 Stanley Morgan
99 Jim Everett .08 .20
250 Fred Marion
100 Jackie Slater .04 .10
251 Raymond Clayborn
101 Vince Newsome .04 .10
252 Mosi Tatupu
102 LeRoy Irvin .04 .10
253 Tony Eason
103 Henry Ellard .04 .10
104 Eric Dickerson .12 .30
105 George Rogers .08 .20
256 Howie Long
106 Darrell Green .08 .20
257 Marcus Allen
107 Art Monk .08 .20
258 Vann McElroy
108 Neal Olkewicz .08 .20
260 Mike Haynes
109 Russ Grimm .04 .10
261 Sean Jones
110 Dexter Manley .08 .20
262 Jim Plunkett
111 Kelvin Bryant .04 .10
263 Chris Bahr
112 Jay Schroeder .04 .10
113 Gary Clark .08 .20
114 Rickey Jackson .04 .10
115 Eric Martin .04 .10
264 Dave Krieg
116 Dave Waymer .04 .10
265 Jacob Green
117 Morten Andersen .04 .10
266 Norm Johnson
118 Bruce Clark .04 .10
267 Fredd Young
119 Hoby Brenner .04 .10
269 Dave Brown DB
120 Brian Hansen .04 .10
270 Kenny Easley
121 Dave Wilson .04 .10
271 Bobby Joe Edmonds
122 Rueben Mayes .04 .10
123 Tommy Kramer .04 .10
124 Joey Browner .04 .10
274 Mark Malone
125 Anthony Carter .08 .20
275 Bryan Hinkle
126 Keith Millard .04 .10
276 Earnest Jackson
127 Steve Jordan .04 .10
128 Chuck Nelson .04 .10
277 Keith Willis
129 Issiac Holt .04 .10
278 Walter Abercrombie
130 Darrin Nelson .04 .10
279 Donnie Shell
131 Gary Zimmerman .20 .50
280 John Stallworth
132 Mark Bavaro .04 .10
146 Darrell Green AP FOIL
133 Jim Covert .12 .30
147 Ronnie Lott AP FOIL
134 Eric Dickerson .08 .20
148 Bill Maas AP FOIL
135 Bill Fralic .04 .10
149 Dexter Manley AP FOIL
136 Tony Franklin .04 .10
150 Karl Mecklenburg AP FOIL
137 Dennis Harrah .12 .30
151 Mike Singletary AP FOIL
138 Dan Marino .75 2.00
152 Rohn Stark AP FOIL
139 Joe Morris .12 .30
153 Lawrence Taylor AP FOIL
140 Jerry Rice .60 1.50
154 Andre Tippett AP FOIL
141 Cody Risien .15 .40
155 Reggie White AP FOIL
142 Dwight Stephenson .08 .20
282 Eric Dickerson AP FOIL
143 Al Toon .75 2.00
283 Dan Marino AP FOIL
144 Deron Cherry .04 .10
284 Tony Franklin AP FOIL
145 Hanford Dixon .04 .10
285 Todd Christensen AP FOIL
163 James Brooks .04 .10
164 Cris Collinsworth .04 .10
172 Jim Kelly .40 1.00
173 Andre Reed .15 .40
174 John Elway .75 2.00
182 Karl Mecklenburg .04 .10
183 Bernie Kosar .08 .20
187 Brian Brennan .04 .10
199 Gary Anderson RB .04 .10
200 Dan Fouts .12 .30
208 Deron Cherry .04 .10
209 Bill Maas .04 .10
210 Gary Hogeboom .04 .10
211 Rohn Stark .04 .10
219 Mark Duper .04 .10
220 Dan Marino .75 2.00
235 Freeman McNeil .04 .10
236 Al Toon .04 .10
244 Ernest Givins .08 .20
245 Drew Hill .04 .10
246 Tony Franklin .04 .10
254 Andre Tippett .04 .10
255 Todd Christensen .04 .10
259 Dokie Williams .04 .10
268 Steve Largent .20 .50
272 Curt Warner .04 .10
273 Mike Merriweather .04 .10
281 Louis Lipps .04 .10
NNO Sticker Album .75 2.00

1988 Topps Stickers

The 1988 Topps Football sticker set is very similar to the previous years in that it contains stickers, foil stickers, and an accompanying album to house one's sticker collection. The stickers measure approximately 2 1/8" by 3" and have a distinctive red border with an inner frame of small yellow footballs. The stickers are numbered on the front. The sticker backs are actually part of a different set. The foil sticker subset contains pairs of All-Pros (AP) and are so indicated in the checklist below. Stickers 2-5 are actually a large four-part action photo of Super Bowl XXII action with Doug Williams handing off to Timmy Smith. On the inside back cover of the sticker album the company offered (via direct mail-order) any ten different stickers of your choice for 1.00; this is one reason why the values of the most popular players in these sticker sets are somewhat depressed compared to traditional card set prices. The front cover of the sticker album features an action photo of the Washington Redskins; the back cover depicts Doug Williams artwork. The following players are shown in their Rookie Card year: Neal Anderson, Cornelius Bennett, Brian Bosworth, Ronnie Harmon, Bo Jackson, Clyde Simmons, Webster Slaughter, Pat Swilling, Vinny Testaverde, and Wade Wilson.

COMPLETE SET (173) 4.00 10.00
1 Super Bowl XXII MVP .04 .10
Doug Williams

2 Super Bowl XXII .04 .10
Redskins vs. Broncos
Doug Williams UL
3 Super Bowl XXII .04 .10
Redskins vs. Broncos
Doug Williams UR
4 Super Bowl XXII .04 .10
Redskins vs. Broncos
Doug Williams LL
5 Super Bowl XXII .04 .10
Redskins vs. Broncos
Doug Williams LR
6 Neal Anderson .04 .10
234 Alex Gordon
7 Willie Gault .04 .10
224 Paul Lankford
8 Dennis Gentry .04 .10
219 Dwight Stephenson
9 Dave Duerson .04 .10
197 Lee Williams
10 Steve McMichael .04 .10
266 Norm Johnson
11 Dennis McKinnon .04 .10
230 Freeman McNeil
12 Mike Singletary .04 .10
209 Paul Palmer
13 Jim McMahon .04 .10
14 Richard Dent .04 .10
15 Vinny Testaverde .20 .50
167 Ronnie Harmon
16 Gerald Carter .04 .10
187 Brian Brennan
17 Jeff Smith .04 .10
185 Earnest Byner
18 Chris Washington .04 .10
212 Bill Brooks
19 Bobby Futrell .04 .10
231 Johnny Hector
20 Calvin Magee .04 .10
182 Mike Harden
21 Ron Holmes .04 .10
169 Chris Burkett
22 Ervin Randle .04 .10
23 James Wilder .04 .10
24 Neil Lomax .04 .10
25 Robert Awalt .04 .10
161 Tim Krumrie
26 Leonard Smith .04 .10
177 Karl Mecklenburg
27 Stump Mitchell .04 .10
178 Mark Haynes
28 Vai Sikahema .04 .10
280 Harry Newsome
29 Freddie Joe Nunn .04 .10
222 John Bosa
30 Earl Ferrell .04 .10
223 Jackie Shipp
31 Roy Green .04 .10
157 Stanford Jennings
32 J.T. Smith .04 .10
33 Michael Downs .04 .10
34 Herschel Walker .08 .20
35 Roger Ruzek .04 .10
269 Dave Krieg
36 Ed Too Tall Jones .04 .10
245 Sean Jones
37 Everson Walls .04 .10
252 Ronnie Lippett
38 Bill Bates .04 .10
213 Dean Biasucci
39 Doug Cosbie .04 .10
179 Rulon Jones
40 Eugene Lockhart .04 .10
186 Webster Slaughter
41 Danny White .04 .10
205 Dino Hackett
42 Randall Cunningham .20 .50
43 Reggie White .20 .50
44 Anthony Toney .08 .20
256 James Lofton
45 Mike Quick .04 .10
248 Stephen Starring
46 John Spagnola .04 .10
235 Harry Hamilton
47 Clyde Simmons .04 .10
275 Dwight Stone
48 Andre Waters .04 .10
261 Greg Townsend
49 Keith Byars .04 .10
265 Jacob Green
50 Jerome Brown .08 .20
240 Warren Moon
51 John Rade .04 .10
52 Rick Donnelly .04 .10
53 Scott Campbell .04 .10
160 Boomer Esiason
54 Floyd Dixon .04 .10
246 Stanley Morgan
55 Gerald Riggs .04 .10
236 Mickey Shuler
56 Bill Fralic .04 .10
267 Brian Bosworth
57 Mike Gann .04 .10
165 Andre Reed
58 Tony Casillas .04 .10
168 Shane Conlan
59 Rick Bryan .04 .10
257 Vance Mueller
60 Jerry Rice .50 1.25
61 Ronnie Lott .08 .20
62 Ray Wersching .04 .10
220 John Offerdahl
63 Charles Haley .04 .10
281 Dwayne Woodruff
64 Joe Montana .75 2.00
190 Clay Matthews
65 Joe Cribbs .04 .10
221 Troy Stradford
66 Mike Wilson .04 .10
203 Christian Okoye
67 Roger Craig .04 .10
251 Rich Camarillo
68 Michael Walter .04 .10
162 Anthony Munoz
69 Mark Bavaro .04 .10
70 Carl Banks .04 .10
71 George Adams .04 .10
274 Frank Pollard
72 Phil Simms .04 .10
216 Mike Prior
73 Lawrence Taylor .08 .20
181 Vance Johnson
74 Joe Morris .04 .10
198 Curtis Adams
75 Lionel Manuel .04 .10
204 Deron Cherry
76 Sean Landeta .04 .10
210 Jack Trudeau
77 Harry Carson .04 .10
159 Scott Fulhage
78 Chuck Long .12 .30
166 Cornelius Bennett
79 James Jones .04 .10
259 Todd Christensen
80 Garry James .04 .10
158 Eddie Brown WR
81 Gary Lee .04 .10
176 Sammy Winder
82 Jim Arnold .04 .10
260 Vann McElroy
83 Dennis Gibson .04 .10
232 Pat Leahy
84 Mike Cofer .04 .10
242 Alonzo Highsmith
85 Pete Mandley .04 .10
86 James Griffin .04 .10
87 Randy Wright .04 .10
206 Mike Bell
88 Phillip Epps .04 .10
191 Kevin Mack
89 Brian Noble .04 .10
249 Steve Grogan
90 Johnny Holland .04 .10
258 Jerry Robinson
91 Dave Brown .04 .10
156 Larry Kinnebrew
92 Brent Fullwood .04 .10
207 Stephone Paige
93 Kenneth Davis .04 .10
194 Gary Anderson RB
94 Tim Harris .04 .10
95 Walter Stanley .04 .10
96 Charles White .04 .10
97 Jackie Slater .04 .10
98 Jim Everett .12 .30
271 Steve Largent
99 Mike Lansford .04 .10
200 Ralf Mojsiejenko
100 Henry Ellard .04 .10
199 Vencie Glenn
101 Dale Hatcher .04 .10
170 Mark Kelso
102 Jim Collins .04 .10
268 Bobby Joe Edmonds
103 Jerry Gray .04 .10
214 Cliff Odom
104 LeRoy Irvin .04 .10
276 Mike Merriweather
105 Darrell Green .04 .10
106 Doug Williams .04 .10
107 Gary Clark .04 .10
247 Garin Veris
108 Charles Mann .04 .10
171 Robb Riddick
109 Art Monk .08 .20
270 Kenny Easley
110 Barry Wilburn .04 .10
196 Elvis Patterson
111 Alvin Walton .04 .10
188 Carl Hairston
112 Dexter Manley .04 .10
233 Ken O'Brien
113 Kelvin Bryant .04 .10
180 Ricky Nattiel
114 Morten Andersen .04 .10
115 Rueben Mayes .04 .10
244 Keith Bostic
116 Brian Hansen .04 .10
279 Gary Anderson K
117 Dalton Hilliard .04 .10
241 Drew Hill
118 Rickey Jackson .04 .10
195 Chip Banks
119 Eric Martin .04 .10
189 Mike Johnson LB
120 Mel Gray .04 .10
278 Delton Hall
121 Bobby Hebert .04 .10
215 Barry Krauss
122 Pat Swilling .08 .20
123 Anthony Carter .04 .10
124 Wade Wilson .04 .10
225 Mark Duper
125 Darrin Nelson .04 .10
250 Irving Fryar
126 D.J. Dozier .04 .10
239 Ernest Givins
127 Chris Doleman .08 .20
128 Henry Thomas .04 .10
255 Howie Long
129 Jesse Solomon .04 .10
211 Albert Bentley
130 Neal Guggemos .04 .10
243 Mike Munchak
131 Joey Browner .04 .10
208 Bill Kenney
132 Carl Banks .04 .10
152 Jackie Slater AP FOIL
133 Joey Browner .04 .10
145 Mark Bavaro AP FOIL
134 Hanford Dixon .60 1.50
147 John Elway AP FOIL
135 Rick Donnelly .04 .10
149 Mike Munchak AP FOIL
136 Kenny Easley .04 .10
155 Charles White AP FOIL
137 Darrell Green .40 1.00
151 Jerry Rice AP FOIL
138 Bill Maas .04 .10
148 Bill Fralic AP FOIL
139 Mike Singletary .12 .30
153 J.T. Smith AP FOIL
140 Bruce Smith .12 .30
154 Dwight Stephenson AP FOIL
141 Andre Tippett .08 .20
146 Eric Dickerson AP FOIL
142 Reggie White .15 .40
150 Anthony Munoz AP FOIL
143 Fredd Young .04 .10
144 Morten Andersen AP FOIL
163 Jim Breech .04 .10
164 Reggie Williams .04 .10
172 Bruce Smith .08 .20
173 Jim Kelly .20 .50
174 Jim Ryan .04 .10
175 John Elway .75 2.00
183 Frank Minnifield .04 .10
184 Bernie Kosar .04 .10
192 Kellen Winslow .04 .10
193 Billy Ray Smith .04 .10
201 Carlos Carson .04 .10
202 Bill Maas .04 .10
217 Eric Dickerson .08 .20
218 Duane Bickett .04 .10
226 Dan Marino .75 2.00
227 Mark Clayton .04 .10
228 Bob Crable .04 .10
229 Al Toon .04 .10
237 Mike Rozier .04 .10
238 Al Smith .04 .10
253 Andre Tippett .04 .10
254 Fred Marion .04 .10
262 Bo Jackson .30 .75
263 Marcus Allen .15 .40
264 Curt Warner .04 .10
272 Fredd Young .04 .10
273 David Little .04 .10
277 Earnest Jackson .04 .10
282 J.T. Smith .04 .10
283 Charles White
284 Reggie White .08 .20
285 Morten Andersen
NNO Sticker Album .75 2.00

1988 Topps Sticker Backs

These cards are actually the backs of the Topps stickers and can be found with a variety of "front" sticker combinations. The cards are numbered in fine print in the statistical section of the card. The 67 cards in the set are generally a selection of popular players with all of them being quarterbacks, running backs, or receivers. The cards measure approximately 2 1/8" by 3". The cards are checklisted below alphabetically according to teams. We've priced these card "backs" below at a level that would include a lower priced sticker attached to the front. Combinations of star player fronts and backs may carry premiums.

COMPLETE SET (67) 2.00 5.00
1 Doug Williams .04 .10
2 Gary Clark .04 .10
3 John Elway .50 1.25
4 Sammy Winder .04 .10
5 Vance Johnson .04 .10
6 Joe Montana .50 1.25
7 Roger Craig .04 .10
8 Jerry Rice .30 .75
9 Rueben Mayes .04 .10
10 Eric Martin .04 .10
11 Neal Anderson .04 .10
12 Willie Gault .04 .10
13 Bernie Kosar .04 .10
14 Kevin Mack .04 .10
15 Webster Slaughter .08 .20
16 Warren Moon .12 .30
17 Mike Rozier .04 .10
18 Drew Hill .04 .10
19 Eric Dickerson .08 .20
20 Bill Brooks .04 .10
21 Curt Warner .04 .10
22 Steve Largent .12 .30
23 Darrin Nelson .04 .10
24 Anthony Carter .04 .10
25 Earnest Jackson .04 .10
26 Weegie Thompson .04 .10
27 Stephen Starring .04 .10
28 Stanley Morgan .04 .10
29 Dan Marino .50 1.25
30 Troy Stradford .04 .10
31 Mark Clayton .04 .10
32 Curtis Adams .04 .10
33 Kellen Winslow .08 .20
34 Jim Kelly .15 .40
35 Ronnie Harmon .04 .10
36 Chris Burkett .04 .10
37 Randall Cunningham .12 .30
38 Anthony Toney .04 .10
39 Mike Quick .04 .10
40 Neil Lomax .04 .10
41 Stump Mitchell .04 .10
42 J.T. Smith .04 .10
43 Herschel Walker .08 .20
44 Herschel Walker .08 .20
45 Joe Morris .04 .10
46 Mark Bavaro .04 .10
47 Charles White .04 .10
48 Henry Ellard .08 .20
49 Ken O'Brien .04 .10
50 Freeman McNeil .04 .10
51 Al Toon .04 .10
52 Kenneth Davis .04 .10
53 Walter Stanley .04 .10
54 Marcus Allen .12 .30
55 James Lofton .08 .20
56 Boomer Esiason .08 .20
57 Larry Kinnebrew .04 .10
58 Eddie Brown .04 .10
59 James Wilder .04 .10
60 Gerald Carter .04 .10
61 Christian Okoye .04 .10
62 Carlos Carson .04 .10
63 James Jones FB .04 .10
64 Pete Mandley .04 .10
65 Gerald Riggs .04 .10
66 Floyd Dixon .04 .10
67 Checklist Card .04 .10

2010 Topps Supreme

STATED PRINT RUN 209 SER.#'d SETS
1 Drew Brees 2.00 5.00
2 Armanti Edwards RC 1.50 4.00
3 Jahvid Best RC 1.25 3.00
4 Colt McCoy RC 1.50 4.00
5 C.J. Spiller RC 1.25 3.00
6 Ben Tate RC 1.25 3.00
7 Hakeem Nicks 1.25 3.00
8 LeSean McCoy 2.00 5.00
9 Troy Polamalu 2.00 5.00
10 Larry Fitzgerald 1.50 4.00
11 Emmitt Smith 3.00 8.00
12 Aaron Rodgers 4.00 10.00
13 Antonio Gates 1.50 4.00
14 Toby Gerhart RC 1.25 3.00
15 Roddy White 1.25 3.00
16 Mark Sanchez 1.25 3.00
17 Kenny Britt 1.25 3.00
18 Kareem Jackson RC 1.25 3.00
19 Major Wright RC 1.25 3.00
20 Ray Lewis 2.00 5.00
21 Jared Allen 1.25 3.00
22 LaDainian Tomlinson 2.00 5.00
23 Matt Schaub 1.25 3.00
24 Donovan McNabb 1.50 4.00
25 Dez Bryant RC 3.00 8.00
26 Tyson Alualu RC 1.25 3.00
27 Darren McFadden 1.25 3.00
28 Jermaine Gresham RC 1.25 3.00
29 Joe Namath 2.50 6.00
30 Peyton Manning 5.00 12.00
31 Damian Williams RC 1.25 3.00
32 Jordan Shipley RC 1.25 3.00
33 Dexter McCluster RC 1.50 4.00
34 Dwight Freeney 1.25 3.00
35 Michael Turner 1.25 3.00
36 Marques Colston 1.25 3.00
37 Golden Tate RC 1.50 4.00
38 Jimmy Clausen RC 1.25 3.00
39 Mardy Gilyard RC 1.25 3.00
40 Eric Dickerson 1.50 4.00
41 Ray Rice 1.25 3.00
42 Art Monk 2.00 5.00
43 Rolando McClain RC 1.25 3.00
44 Emmanuel Sanders RC 2.00 5.00
45 Tony Romo 1.50 4.00
46 Rob Gronkowski RC 4.00 10.00
47 Joe Flacco 1.50 4.00
48 Gerald McCoy RC 1.25 3.00
49 Marcus Allen 2.00 5.00
50 Dan Marino 4.00 10.00
51 Wes Welker 1.50 4.00
52 Sean Weatherspoon RC 1.25 3.00
53 Shonn Greene 1.25 3.00
54 Andre Roberts RC 1.50 4.00
55 Philip Rivers 2.00 5.00
56 Tim Brown 2.00 5.00
57 Anquan Boldin 1.25 3.00
58 Ryan Torain 1.25 3.00
59 Franco Harris 2.00 5.00
60 Vernon Davis 1.25 3.00
61 Brett Favre 4.00 10.00
62 Josh Freeman 1.50 4.00
63 Rashard Mendenhall 1.25 3.00
64 Ryan Mathews RC 1.25 3.00
65 Taylor Price RC 1.25 3.00
66 Patrick Willis 1.50 4.00
67 Brandon Marshall 1.50 4.00
68 Arian Foster 1.50 4.00
69 Brandon LaFell RC 2.00 5.00
70 Demaryius Thomas RC 3.00 8.00
71 Tom Brady 5.00 12.00
72 Mike Kafka RC 1.50 4.00
73 DeAngelo Williams 1.25 3.00
74 Jonathan Dwyer RC 1.25 3.00
75 Tim Tebow RC 10.00 25.00
76 Jamaal Charles 1.50 4.00
77 Jason Pierre-Paul RC 2.00 5.00
78 Eric Decker RC 1.50 4.00
79 Eli Manning 1.50 4.00
80 Cris Carter 2.00 5.00
81 Joe Montana 6.00 15.00
82 Andre Johnson 1.50 4.00
83 Darrelle Revis 1.25 3.00
84 Marcus Easley RC 1.25 3.00
85 Joe McKnight RC 1.25 3.00
86 Mario Williams 1.50 4.00
87 Mike Williams RC 1.25 3.00
88 Eric Berry RC 2.00 5.00
89 Montario Hardesty RC 1.25 3.00
90 Sam Bradford RC 1.50 4.00
91 Randy Moss 2.50 6.00
92 Reggie Wayne 1.50 4.00
93 Maurice Jones-Drew 1.25 3.00
94 Arrelious Benn RC 1.25 3.00
95 Ndamukong Suh RC 2.50 6.00
96 Howie Long 2.00 5.00
97 Justin Tuck 1.25 3.00
98 Adrian Peterson 2.00 5.00
99 Jay Cutler 1.25 3.00
100 Chris Johnson 1.25 3.00

2010 Topps Supreme Black

*VETS/25: 1.2X TO 3X BASIC CARDS
*ROOKIES/25: .8X TO 2X BASIC CARDS
STATED PRINT RUN 25 SER.#'d SETS

2010 Topps Supreme Blue

*VETS/62: .8X TO 2X BASIC CARDS
*ROOKIES/62: .5X TO 1.2X BASIC CARDS
BLUE STATED PRINT RUN 62

2010 Topps Supreme Autographed Dual Relics

STATED PRINT RUN 10-50
*TRIPLE AU/50: .4X TO 1X DUAL JSY AU/50
TRIPLE JSY AU PRINT RUN 10-50
SADRBF Brett Favre 150.00 250.00
SADRCM Colt McCoy/50 8.00 20.00
SADRCS C.J. Spiller/25 8.00 20.00
SADRDB Drew Brees/15 40.00 80.00
SADRDR Darrelle Revis/15 25.00 50.00
SADRDT Demaryius Thomas/25 20.00 50.00
SADRED Eric Dickerson/15 25.00 50.00
SADREM Eli Manning/50 50.00 100.00
SADRJB Jahvid Best/25 8.00 20.00
SADRJC Jimmy Clausen/50 6.00 15.00
SADRJF Joe Flacco/15 30.00 60.00
SADRJM Joe Montana/25 100.00 175.00
SADRJN Joe Namath/25 60.00 120.00
SADRNS Ndamukong Suh/25 40.00 80.00
SADRPM Peyton Manning/50 100.00 200.00
SADRRM Ryan Mathews/25 8.00 20.00
SADRSB Sam Bradford/50 20.00 40.00
SADRSH Santonio Holmes/15 15.00 40.00
SADRTR Tony Romo/15 40.00 80.00
SADRTT Tim Tebow/50 50.00 120.00

2010 Topps Supreme Autographs

STATED PRINT RUN 10-75
EXCH EXPIRATION: 1/31/2014
SAAG Antonio Gates/25 12.00 30.00
SABM Brandon Marshall/25 12.00 30.00
SADJ DeSean Jackson/25 10.00 25.00
SAEM Eli Manning/55 40.00 80.00
SAFG Frank Gore/25 12.00 30.00
SAJE John Elway/55 60.00 120.00
SAJM Joe Montana/55 60.00 120.00
SAJN Joe Namath/55 40.00 80.00
SAMS Matthew Stafford/25 30.00 60.00
SAPM Peyton Manning/55 60.00 120.00
SARL Ray Lewis/25 40.00 80.00
SATR Tony Romo/55 30.00 60.00
SARCM Colt McCoy/50 6.00 15.00
SARCS C.J. Spiller/50 5.00 12.00
SARDM Dexter McCluster/15 10.00 25.00
SARDT Demaryius Thomas/50 12.00 30.00
SAREB Eric Berry/15 20.00 60.00
SARGM Gerald McCoy/15 8.00 20.00
SARJB Jahvid Best/50 5.00 12.00
SARJC Jimmy Clausen/50 5.00 12.00
SARJG Jermaine Gresham/15 8.00 20.00
SARJS Jordan Shipley/15 8.00 20.00
SARNS Ndamukong Suh/50 30.00 60.00
SARRM Ryan Mathews/50 5.00 12.00
SARSB Sam Bradford/50 30.00 60.00
SARTT Tim Tebow/75 50.00 120.00

2010 Topps Supreme Dual Autographs

STATED PRINT RUN 10-50
MM P.Manning/Eli/50 100.00 200.00
TM Tmlinsn/Mathws/50 40.00 100.00

2010 Topps Supreme Rookie Quad Relics

STATED PRINT RUN 15 SER.#'d SETS
EACH HAS 2 CARDS OF EQUAL VALUE
*TRIPLE/15: .4X TO 1X QUAD/15
SRQRAB Arrelious Benn 5.00 12.00
SRQRBL Brandon LaFell 8.00 20.00
SRQRCM Colt McCoy 6.00 15.00
SRQRCS C.J. Spiller 5.00 12.00
SRQRDB Dez Bryant 20.00 50.00
SRQRDM Dexter McCluster 6.00 15.00
SRQRDT Demaryius Thomas 12.00 30.00
SRQREB Eric Berry 8.00 20.00
SRQRGM Gerald McCoy 5.00 12.00
SRQRGT Golden Tate 6.00 15.00
SRQRJD Jonathan Dwyer 5.00 12.00
SRQRJG Jermaine Gresham 5.00 12.00
SRQRJM Joe McKnight 5.00 12.00
SRQRJS Jordan Shipley 5.00 12.00
SRQRMK Mike Kafka 6.00 15.00
SRQRMW Mike Williams 5.00 12.00
SRQRNS Ndamukong Suh 10.00 25.00
SRQRRG Rob Gronkowski 15.00 40.00
SRQRRM Ryan Mathews 5.00 12.00
SRQRABE Arrelious Benn 5.00 12.00
SRQRBLA Brandon LaFell 8.00 20.00
SRQRCMC Colt McCoy 6.00 15.00
SRQRCSP C.J. Spiller 5.00 12.00
SRQRDBR Dez Bryant 20.00 50.00
SRQRDMC Dexter McCluster 6.00 15.00
SRQRDTH Demaryius Thomas 12.00 30.00
SRQREBE Eric Berry 8.00 20.00
SRQRGMC Gerald McCoy 5.00 12.00
SRQRGTA Golden Tate 6.00 15.00
SRQRJDW Jonathan Dwyer 5.00 12.00
SRQRJGR Jermaine Gresham 5.00 12.00
SRQRJMC Joe McKnight 5.00 12.00
SRQRJSH Jordan Shipley 5.00 12.00
SRQRMKA Mike Kafka 6.00 15.00
SRQRMWI Mike Williams 5.00 12.00
SRQRNSU Ndamukong Suh 10.00 25.00
SRQRRGR Rob Gronkowski 15.00 40.00
SRQRRMA Ryan Mathews 5.00 12.00
SRQRRMC Rolando McClain 5.00 12.00
SRQRRMCL Rolando McClain 5.00 12.00

2010 Topps Supreme Rookie Relic Quad Combos

STATED PRINT RUN 15 SER.#'d SETS
BBMS Brdfrd/Brynt/C.McC/Shp 6.00 15.00
BGGW Best/Grhrt/Gron/Will 8.00 20.00
BGTT Brdfrd/Glyrd/Tbw/Thm 8.00 20.00
BGWL Best/Gerhrt/Will/LaFll 4.00 10.00
BMBR Brdfrd/G.McC/Bryn/Rbn 6.00 15.00
BRBK Brdfrd/Rbrts/Brynt/Kfka 6.00 15.00
BSMM Brynt/Spllr/McCl/Mthws 12.00 30.00
BSTM Brdfrd/Spllr/Tbw/Mthws 8.00 20.00
BSWM Best/Suh/Willm/G.McCy 5.00 12.00
BTMT Brynt/Thms/McClstr/Tte 12.00 30.00
BTSG Brdfrd/Thms/Splr/Grshm 6.00 15.00
BWLS Benn/Williams/LaFell/Sanders 6.00 15.00
CMBG Clsn/McClstr/Best/Grhm 6.00 15.00
CMMT Clsn/McCy/McCls/Tte 10.00 25.00
CTMS Clsn/G.Tte/C.McCy/Shply 10.00 25.00
GEWS Gilyard/Easley/Williams/Shipley 6.00 15.00
GPGS Gronkowski/Price/Gresham/Shipley 6.00 15.00
GSDS Gresham/Shipley/Dwyer/Sanders 6.00 15.00
GSLE Gresham/Shipley/LaFell/Edwards 6.00 15.00
GTHM Grhrt/B.Tte/Hrdsty/McKn 2.50 6.00
HSTW Hardsty/Sndrs/B.Tte/Will 4.00 10.00
KCDS Kafka/Coopr/Dwyr/Sndrs 6.00 15.00
MBFM McClstr/Berry/Frd/McCln 8.00 20.00
MHDS McCy/Hrdsty/Dwyr/Sndrs 4.00 10.00
MHGS McCy/Hrdsty/Grshm/Shply 3.00 8.00
MTMM McClt/Thms/Mtws/McCl 6.00 15.00
MTMT McCy/Tte/McC/Tte 10.00 25.00
SEGP Spllr/Esly/Grnkki/Prce 8.00 20.00
SEMH Spillr/Esly/McCy/Hrdsty 3.00 8.00
SMBT Spilr/Mthws/Bst/Tte 2.50 6.00
STDG Spillr/Thoms/Dwyer/Grhm 6.00 15.00
TBBM Tbw/Brynt/Brdfrd/McClstr 8.00 20.00
TBCM Tebw/Brdfrd/Clsn/C.McCy 8.00 20.00
TBMG Thms/Brry/McKn/Gronk 8.00 20.00
TBSM Thms/Brynt/Spllr/Mthws 6.00 15.00
TBTB Tebw/Brdfrd/Thms/Brynt 8.00 20.00
TDBG Tebw/Dckr/Brdfrd/Gilyrd 8.00 20.00
TDFS Thmas/Dwyr/Ford/Spillr 6.00 15.00
TDMB Thoms/Dckr/McCls/Brry 8.00 20.00
TDWB Thoms/Dckr/Will/Benn 8.00 20.00
THCT Tebw/Hern/Clsen/Tte 15.00 40.00
THDG B.Tte/Hrdst/Dwyr/Grhrt 2.50 6.00
TMLT Tebw/McCls/LaFll/Tte 15.00 40.00
TTCL Tebw/Thom/Clsn/LaFll 15.00 40.00
TWTW G.Tte/Will/B.Tte/D.Will 8.00 20.00
WBGP Will/Benn/Gronk/Price 6.00 15.00
WBLE Will/Benn/LaFll/Edwrds 6.00 15.00
WGEM Will/Gilyrd/Easly/Mtchl 6.00 15.00
SMBTH Suh/G.McCy/Berry/Thms 8.00 20.00
TBMGR Tebw/Brynt/Mthws/Grnk 15.00 40.00

2011 Topps Supreme

STATED PRINT RUN 429 SER.#'d SETS
1 Joe Namath 2.50 6.00
2 Vincent Brown RC 1.25 3.00
3 Jon Baldwin RC 1.25 3.00
4 Mark Sanchez 1.25 3.00
5 Sam Bradford 1.25 3.00
6 Mikel Leshoure RC 1.25 3.00
7 LeSean McCoy 2.00 5.00
8 Matt Ryan 1.50 4.00
9 Mark Ingram RC 2.00 5.00
10 Terry Bradshaw 2.50 6.00
11 Howie Long 2.00 5.00
12 Knowshon Moreno 1.25 3.00
13 Taiwan Jones RC 1.25 3.00
14 Peyton Hillis 1.25 3.00
15 Dwayne Bowe 1.50 4.00
16 Franco Harris 2.00 5.00
17 Leonard Hankerson RC 1.25 3.00
18 Marcell Dareus RC 1.25 3.00
19 Eric Berry 1.50 4.00
20 Emmitt Smith 3.00 8.00
21 Mike Wallace 1.25 3.00
22 Arian Foster 1.25 3.00
23 Philip Rivers 2.00 5.00
24 Shane Vereen RC 1.50 4.00
25 Andy Dalton RC 2.50 6.00
26 Bart Starr 3.00 8.00
27 Dez Bryant 2.00 5.00
28 DeSean Jackson 1.50 4.00
29 Ronnie Lott 1.50 4.00
30 Tom Brady 5.00 12.00
31 Phil Simms 1.50 4.00
32 Charles Woodson 2.00 5.00
33 A.J. Green RC 3.00 8.00
34 Matt Schaub 1.25 3.00
35 Randall Cobb RC 2.00 5.00
36 Marques Colston 1.25 3.00
37 Andre Johnson 1.50 4.00
38 Bilal Powell RC 1.50 4.00
39 Jeremy Maclin 1.25 3.00
40 Adrian Peterson 2.00 5.00
41 Reggie Wayne 1.50 4.00
42 DeMarco Murray RC 2.50 6.00
43 Kendall Hunter RC 1.25 3.00
44 Maurice Jones-Drew 1.25 3.00
45 Jamie Harper RC 1.25 3.00
46 Daniel Thomas RC 1.25 3.00
47 Patrick Willis 1.50 4.00
48 Kyle Rudolph RC 1.25 3.00
49 Drew Brees 2.00 5.00
50 Dan Marino 4.00 10.00
51 Frank Gore 1.50 4.00
52 Greg Little RC 1.50 4.00
53 Larry Fitzgerald 1.50 4.00
54 Alex Green RC 1.25 3.00
55 Ben Roethlisberger 2.00 5.00
56 Von Miller RC 2.00 5.00
57 Jordan Todman RC 1.25 3.00
58 Edmond Gates RC 1.25 3.00
59 Jared Allen 1.25 3.00
60 Peyton Manning 4.00 10.00
61 Austin Pettis RC 1.25 3.00
62 Tony Dorsett 2.00 5.00
63 Torrey Smith RC 1.25 3.00
64 Ray Rice 1.25 3.00
65 Ryan Mallett RC 1.25 3.00
66 Titus Young RC 1.25 3.00
67 Tony Romo 1.50 4.00
68 Delone Carter RC 1.25 3.00
69 Miles Austin 1.25 3.00
70 Aaron Rodgers 3.00 8.00
71 Julio Jones RC 4.00 10.00
72 Ahmad Bradshaw 1.25 3.00
73 Colin Kaepernick RC 2.00 5.00
74 Jerrel Jernigan RC 1.25 3.00
75 Ray Lewis 2.00 5.00
76 Roddy White 1.25 3.00
77 Hakeem Nicks 1.25 3.00
78 Darren McFadden 1.25 3.00
79 Kevin Kolb 1.25 3.00
80 Jerry Rice 3.00 8.00
81 Rashard Mendenhall 1.25 3.00
82 Jake Locker RC 1.25 3.00
83 Chris Johnson 1.25 3.00
84 Christian Ponder RC 1.25 3.00
85 DeAngelo Williams 1.25 3.00
86 Roger Staubach 2.50 6.00
87 Ryan Williams RC 1.25 3.00
88 Ndamukong Suh 1.50 4.00
89 Eli Manning 1.50 4.00
90 Michael Vick 1.50 4.00
91 Jamaal Charles 1.50 4.00
92 Cam Newton RC 6.00 15.00
93 Steven Jackson 1.25 3.00
94 Stevan Ridley RC 1.25 3.00
95 Blaine Gabbert RC 1.25 3.00
96 Greg Jennings 1.25 3.00
97 Michael Turner 1.25 3.00
98 Calvin Johnson 2.00 5.00
99 Mike Williams 1.50 4.00
100 Joe Montana 5.00 12.00

2011 Topps Supreme Green

*VETS/15: 1.5X TO 4X BASIC CARDS
*RETIRED/15: 1.5X TO 4X BASIC CARDS
*ROOKIES/15: 1.2X TO 3X BASIC CARDS

2011 Topps Supreme Purple

*VETS/75: .8X TO 2X BASIC CARDS
*RETIRED/75: .8X TO 2X BASIC CARDS
*ROOKIES/75: .6X TO 1.5X BASIC CARDS

2011 Topps Supreme Red

*VETS/99: .8X TO 2X BASIC CARDS
*RETIRED/99: .8X TO 2X BASIC CARDS
*ROOKIES/99: .6X TO 1.5X BASIC CARDS

2011 Topps Supreme Sepia

*VETS/30: 1X TO 2.5X BASIC CARDS
*RETIRED/30: 1X TO 2.5X BASIC CARDS
*ROOKIES/30: .8X TO 2X BASIC CARDS

2011 Topps Supreme Autographed Dual Relics

*DUAL VETS/15: .5X TO 1.2X AU RELIC/50
*DUAL ROOKIE/15: .6X TO 1.5X AU RELIC/50
STATED PRINT RUN 15 SER.#'d SETS
UNPRICED DUAL JUMBO AU PRINT RUN 15
UNPRICED DUAL PATCH AU PRINT RUN 10
SADRCN Cam Newton 200.00 300.00
SADRDM DeMarco Murray 25.00 60.00
SADRJJ Julio Jones 50.00 100.00

2011 Topps Supreme Autographed Relics

STATED PRINT RUN 50 SER.#'d SETS
UNPRICED JUMBO AU PRINT RUN 10
UNPRICED QUAD AU PRINT RUN 10
UNPRICED SIX AU PRINT RUN 10
EXCH EXPIRATION: 12/31/2014
SARAD Andy Dalton 15.00 40.00
SARAJG A.J. Green 40.00 80.00
SARAP Austin Pettis 8.00 20.00
SARBG Blaine Gabbert 8.00 20.00
SARCK Colin Kaepernick 12.00 30.00
SARCN Cam Newton 60.00 125.00
SARCP Christian Ponder 15.00 40.00
SARDB Drew Brees 50.00 100.00
SARDM DeMarco Murray 15.00 40.00
SARDT Daniel Thomas 8.00 20.00
SARGL Greg Little 10.00 25.00
SARJB Jon Baldwin 8.00 20.00
SARJJE Jerrel Jernigan 8.00 20.00
SARJL Jake Locker 8.00 20.00
SARJM Joe Montana 75.00 150.00
SARJR Jerry Rice 90.00 150.00
SARKH Kendall Hunter 15.00 40.00
SARKR Kyle Rudolph 10.00 25.00
SARLH Leonard Hankerson 8.00 20.00
SARMD Marcell Dareus 8.00 20.00
SARMF Matt Forte 10.00 25.00
SARMI Mark Ingram 12.00 30.00
SARML Mikel Leshoure 8.00 20.00
SARMR Matt Ryan 25.00 50.00
SARMT Michael Turner 10.00 25.00
SARMV Michael Vick 15.00 40.00
SARRC Randall Cobb 12.00 30.00
SARRL Ray Lewis 60.00 120.00
SARRM Ryan Mallett 8.00 20.00
SARRW Ryan Williams 8.00 20.00
SARSJ Steve Johnson 10.00 25.00
SARSR Stevan Ridley 8.00 20.00
SARSV Shane Vereen 10.00 25.00
SARTR Tony Romo 30.00 80.00
SARTS Torrey Smith 8.00 20.00
SARTY Titus Young 8.00 20.00
SARVM Von Miller 20.00 50.00

2011 Topps Supreme Autographed Relics Red

*RED VETS/20: .5X TO 1.2X AU RELIC/50
*RED ROOKIES/20: .6X TO 1.5X AU RELIC/50
AUTO RED PRINT RUN 20 SER.#'d SETS
EXCH EXPIRATION: 12/31/2014
SARCN Cam Newton 75.00 150.00
SARDM DeMarco Murray EXCH 25.00 60.00

2011 Topps Supreme Autographs

BLUE STATED PRINT RUN 27
UNPRICED GREEN PRINT RUN 10
*RED/20: .4X TO 1X BLUE AU/7
EXCH EXPIRATION: 12/31/2014
SAAF Arian Foster 12.00 30.00
SAAJ Andre Johnson 15.00 40.00
SAAP Adrian Peterson 50.00 100.00
SABS Bart Starr 60.00 120.00
SADB Drew Brees 40.00 80.00
SADJ DeSean Jackson 12.00 30.00
SADM Dan Marino 75.00 150.00
SAGJ Greg Jennings 12.00 30.00
SAHL Howie Long 20.00 50.00
SAJM Joe Montana 75.00 150.00
SAJMA Jeremy Maclin 12.00 30.00
SAJN Joe Namath 50.00 100.00
SAJR Jerry Rice 90.00 150.00
SAMA Miles Austin EXCH 12.00 30.00
SAMC Marques Colston 12.00 30.00
SAMV Michael Vick 30.00 60.00
SAMW Mike Wallace 12.00 30.00
SAPH Peyton Hillis 12.00 30.00
SAPM Peyton Manning 50.00 100.00
SAPS Phil Simms 15.00 40.00
SARR Ray Rice 12.00 30.00
SARW Roddy White 12.00 30.00
SASB Sam Bradford 15.00 40.00
SATB Terry Bradshaw 50.00 100.00
SATR Tony Romo 30.00 60.00
SATT Tim Tebow 30.00 80.00

2011 Topps Supreme Dual Autographs

STATED PRINT RUN 25 SER.#'d SETS
UNPRICED JSY AU PRINT RUN 5
UNPRICED PATCH AU PRINT RUN 1
SDABB D.Bowe/J.Baldwin 12.00 30.00
SDABS J.Baldwin/T.Smith 10.00 25.00
SDACG R.Cobb/A.Green 15.00 40.00
SDACJ M.Cassel/T.Jones 12.00 30.00
SDADB A.Dalton/V.Brown 20.00 50.00
SDADK A.Dalton/Kaepernick 20.00 50.00
SDADP A.Dalton/C.Ponder 25.00 60.00
SDADS T.Dorsett/E.Smith 125.00 250.00
SDAGD A.Green/A.Dalton 75.00 150.00
SDAGL B.Gabbert/J.Locker 10.00 25.00
SDAGN B.Gabbert/C.Newton 100.00 200.00
SDAID M.Ingram/M.Dareus 15.00 40.00
SDAIL M.Ingram/M.Leshoure 15.00 40.00
SDAJB V.Jackson/V.Brown 10.00 25.00
SDAJH J.Jernigan/L.Hankerson 10.00 25.00
SDAJP J.Jernigan/B.Powell 12.00 30.00
SDAKG C.Kaepernick/A.Green 15.00 40.00
SDAKH C.Kaepernick/K.Hunter 15.00 40.00
SDALG G.Little/A.Green 40.00 80.00
SDALH J.Locker/J.Harper 10.00 25.00
SDALM J.Locker/R.Mallett 10.00 25.00
SDALY M.Leshoure/T.Young 10.00 25.00
SDAMH S.Moss/L.Hankerson 12.00 30.00
SDAMR J.Montana/J.Rice 200.00 300.00
SDAMV R.Mallett/S.Vereen 12.00 30.00
SDANM C.Newton/R.Mallett 40.00 80.00
SDANS J.Namath/M.Sanchez 60.00 120.00
SDAPH C.Ponder/Hankerson 20.00 50.00
SDAPJ Peterson/Jones-Drew 60.00 120.00
SDARG K.Rudolph/A.Green 10.00 25.00
SDARP K.Rudolph/C.Ponder 10.00 25.00
SDASL T.Smith/G.Little 12.00 30.00
SDATB J.Todman/V.Brown 10.00 25.00
SDATC D.Thomas/D.Carter 10.00 25.00
SDATJ J.Todman/T.Jones 10.00 25.00
SDATM D.Thomas/V.Miller 25.00 60.00
SDATP J.Todman/B.Powell 12.00 30.00
SDAVR S.Vereen/S.Ridley 12.00 30.00
SDAWH R.Williams/J.Harper 15.00 40.00
SDAWL R.Williams/Leshoure 15.00 40.00
SDAYP T.Young/A.Pettis 10.00 25.00
SDACJE R.Cobb/J.Jernigan 15.00 40.00
SDAMHU D.Murray/K.Hunter 20.00 50.00
SDAMRI R.Mallett/S.Ridley 10.00 25.00
SDAMRO Manning/Rodgers EX 250.00 400.00

2011 Topps Supreme Eight Piece Relics

STATED PRINT RUN 20 SER.#'d SETS
UNPRICED PLATINUM PRINT RUN 1
1 Running Backs 25.00 60.00
2 Quarterbacks 40.00 80.00
3 Rookie WR and RB 25.00 50.00
4 Rookie WR and QB 15.00 40.00
5 Rookie WR and QB 12.00 30.00
6 Rookie WR and QB 20.00 50.00
7 Rookie WR and QB 15.00 40.00
8 Rookie WR and QB 12.00 30.00
9 Rookie QB and RB 15.00 40.00
10 Rookie QB and RB 30.00 80.00
11 Rookie QB and RB 20.00 50.00
12 Rookie WR and RB 12.00 30.00
13 Rookie QB and RB 15.00 40.00

2011 Topps Supreme Rookie Autographs

STATED PRINT RUN 55-175
EXCH EXPIRATION: 12/31/2014
SRAAD Andy Dalton/55 15.00 40.00
SRAAG Alex Green/55 6.00 15.00
SRAAJG A.J. Green/90 20.00 40.00
SRAAP Austin Pettis/55 6.00 15.00
SRABG Blaine Gabbert/90 5.00 12.00
SRABP Bilal Powell/55 8.00 20.00
SRACK Colin Kaepernick/90 8.00 20.00
SRACN Cam Newton/175 60.00 120.00
SRACP Christian Ponder/90 5.00 12.00
SRADC Delone Carter 6.00 15.00
SRADM DeMarco Murray/55 12.00 30.00
SRADT Daniel Thomas/55 6.00 15.00
SRAEG Edmond Gates/55 6.00 15.00
SRAGL Greg Little/55 8.00 20.00
SRAJB Jon Baldwin/90 5.00 12.00
SRAJH Jamie Harper/55 6.00 15.00
SRAJJE Jerrel Jernigan/55 6.00 15.00
SRAJL Jake Locker/175 5.00 12.00
SRAJT Jordan Todman/55 6.00 15.00
SRAKH Kendall Hunter/55 12.00 30.00
SRALH Leonard Hankerson/55 8.00 20.00
SRALK Lance Kendricks/55 8.00 20.00
SRAMD Marcell Dareus/90 5.00 12.00
SRAMI Mark Ingram/175 8.00 20.00
SRAML Mikel Leshoure/90 5.00 12.00
SRARC Randall Cobb/55 10.00 25.00
SRARH Roy Helu/90 5.00 12.00
SRARM Ryan Mallett/90 5.00 12.00
SRARW Ryan Williams/90 5.00 12.00
SRASR Stevan Ridley/55 12.00 30.00
SRASV Shane Vereen/55 8.00 20.00
SRATJ Taiwan Jones/55 6.00 15.00
SRATP Terrelle Pryor/90 8.00 20.00
SRATS Torrey Smith/55 6.00 15.00
SRATY Titus Young/90 5.00 12.00
SRAVB Vincent Brown/55 8.00 20.00
SRAVM Von Miller 15.00 40.00

2011 Topps Supreme Rookie Autographs Green

*GREEN/15: .8X TO 2X BASIC AU/90-175
*GREEN/15: .6X TO 1.5X BASIC AU/55
GREEN PRINT RUN 15 SER.#'d SETS

2011 Topps Supreme Rookie Autographs Purple

*PURPLE/25: .6X TO 1.5X BASIC AU/90-175
*PURPLE/25: .5X TO 1.2X BASIC AU/55
PURPLE STATED PRINT RUN 25
SRAAD Andy Dalton 50.00 100.00

2011 Topps Supreme Rookie Autographs Red

*RED/50: .5X TO 1.2X BASIC AU/90-175
*RED/50: .4X TO 1X BASIC AU/55
RED PRINT RUN 50 SER.#'d SETS

2011 Topps Supreme Rookie Quad Relics

STATED PRINT RUN 25-30
MOST HAVE TWO CARDS OF EQUAL VALUE
SRQRAD1 Andy Dalton/25 6.00 15.00
SRQRAD2 Andy Dalton/30 6.00 15.00
SRQRAJG1 A.J. Green/30 8.00 20.00
SRQRAJG2 A.J. Green
SRQRBG1 Blaine Gabbert/25 3.00 8.00
SRQRBG2 Blaine Gabbert/30 3.00 8.00
SRQRCK1 Colin Kaepernick/25 5.00 12.00
SRQRCK2 Colin Kaepernick/30 5.00 12.00
SRQRCN1 Cam Newton/30 15.00 40.00
SRQRCN2 Cam Newton/30 15.00 40.00
SRQRCP1 Christian Ponder/25 3.00 8.00
SRQRCP2 Christian Ponder/30 3.00 8.00
SRQRGL1 Greg Little/25 4.00 10.00
SRQRGL2 Greg Little/30 4.00 10.00
SRQRJB1 Jon Baldwin/30 3.00 8.00
SRQRJB2 Jon Baldwin/25 3.00 8.00
SRQRJJ1 Julio Jones/30 10.00 25.00
SRQRJJ2 Julio Jones/25 10.00 25.00
SRQRJL1 Jake Locker/25 3.00 8.00
SRQRJL2 Jake Locker 3.00 8.00
SRQRLH1 Leonard Hankerson/25 3.00 8.00
SRQRLH2 Leonard Hankerson
SRQRMD1 Marcell Dareus/30 3.00 8.00
SRQRMD2 Marcell Dareus
SRQRMI1 Mark Ingram/30 5.00 12.00
SRQRMI2 Mark Ingram/25 5.00 12.00
SRQRML1 Mikel Leshoure/30 3.00 8.00
SRQRML2 Mikel Leshoure/25 3.00 8.00
SRQRRC1 Randall Cobb/30 5.00 12.00
SRQRRC2 Randall Cobb/25 5.00 12.00
SRQRRM1 Ryan Mallett/30 3.00 8.00
SRQRRM2 Ryan Mallett/25 3.00 8.00
SRQRRW1 Ryan Williams/30 3.00 8.00
SRQRRW2 Ryan Williams/25 3.00 8.00
SRQRTS1 Torrey Smith/30 3.00 8.00
SRQRTS2 Torrey Smith/25 3.00 8.00
SRQRTY1 Titus Young/30 3.00 8.00
SRQRTY2 Titus Young/25 3.00 8.00
SRQRVM1 Von Miller/30 5.00 12.00
SRQRVM2 Von Miller/25 5.00 12.00

2011 Topps Supreme Rookie Relic Die Cuts

STATED PRINT RUN 55 SER.#'d SETS
SRDCAD Andy Dalton 5.00 12.00
SRDCAG Alex Green 2.50 6.00
SRDCAP Austin Pettis 2.50 6.00
SRDCBG Blaine Gabbert 2.50 6.00
SRDCBP Bilal Powell 3.00 8.00
SRDCCK Colin Kaepernick 4.00 10.00
SRDCCN Cam Newton 12.00 30.00
SRDCCP Christian Ponder 2.50 6.00
SRDCDC Delone Carter 2.50 6.00
SRDCDM DeMarco Murray 5.00 12.00
SRDCDT Daniel Thomas 2.50 6.00
SRDCGL Greg Little 3.00 8.00
SRDCJB Jon Baldwin 2.50 6.00
SRDCJH Jamie Harper 2.50 6.00
SRDCJJ Julio Jones 8.00 20.00
SRDCJL Jake Locker 2.50 6.00
SRDCJT Jordan Todman 2.50 6.00
SRDCKH Kendall Hunter 2.50 6.00
SRDCKR Kyle Rudolph 2.50 6.00
SRDCLH Leonard Hankerson 2.50 6.00
SRDCMD Marcell Dareus 2.50 6.00

SRDCMI Mark Ingram 4.00 10.00
SRDCML Mikel Leshoure 2.50 6.00
SRDCRC Randall Cobb 4.00 10.00
SRDCRM Ryan Mallett 2.50 6.00
SRDCRW Ryan Williams 2.50 6.00
SRDCSR Stevan Ridley 2.50 6.00
SRDCSV Shane Vereen 3.00 8.00
SRDCTS Torrey Smith 2.50 6.00
SRDCTY Titus Young 2.50 6.00
SRDCVB Vincent Brown 2.50 6.00
SRDCVM Von Miller 4.00 10.00
SRDCAJG A.J. Green 6.00 15.00
SRDCJJE Jerrel Jernigan 2.50 6.00

2011 Topps Supreme Rookie Relic Quad Combos

STATED PRINT RUN 25 SER.#'d SETS
BCGR Baldwin/Cobb/Green/Ridley 4.00 10.00
BSCL Baldwin/Smith/Cobb/Little 4.00 10.00
CLBG Cobb/Little/Brown/Gates 4.00 10.00
CYPB Cobb/Young/Pettis/Brown 4.00 10.00
GBJY Grn/Bldwn/Jrngn/Yng 6.00 15.00
GDPK Gabb/Dltn/Pndr/Kprnck 5.00 12.00
GJIT Grn/Jones/Ingr/Thmas 10.00 25.00
GJLP Green/Jern/Little/Pettis 6.00 15.00
GJYG Green/Jons/Yng/Gates 10.00 25.00
GLDK Gabb/Lckr/Dltn/Kprnick 5.00 12.00
GLMK Gabb/Lckr/Mallt/Kprnck 4.00 10.00
GLMP Gabb/Lckr/Mallt/Pnder 2.50 6.00
GLND Gabb/Lckr/Nwtn/Dlton 12.00 30.00
GLNK Gabb/Lckr/Nwtn/Kprnk 12.00 30.00
GLNM Gabb/Lckr/Nwtn/Mallt 12.00 30.00
GLNP Gabb/Lckr/Nwtn/Pndr 12.00 30.00
GLPK Gabb/Lckr/Pndr/Kprnk 4.00 10.00
GNMD Gabb/Nwtn/Mllt/Dltn 12.00 30.00
GNMK Gabb/Nwtn/Mllt/Kprk 12.00 30.00
GSCB Grn/Smith/Cbb/Brwn 6.00 15.00
ITRG Ingrm/Tdmn/Rdly/Grn 4.00 10.00
ITTH Ingrm/Thm/Tdmn/Hntr 4.00 10.00
ITVH Ingrm/Thms/Vern/Hntr 4.00 10.00
JBLY Jones/Baldwin/Little/Young 8.00 20.00
JCJH Jones/Cobb/Jernigan/Hankerson 8.00 20.00
JSHP Jones/Smith/Hankerson/Pettis 8.00 20.00
JSLH Jones/Smith/Little/Hankerson 8.00 20.00
LMDK Lock/Mall/Dltn/Kprnk 5.00 12.00
LMDP Lock/Mall/Dltn/Pondr 5.00 12.00
LNDK Lock/Nwtn/Dltn/Kprk 12.00 30.00
LNMP Lock/Nwtn/Mall/Pndr 12.00 30.00
LSVH Little/Smith/Vereen/Harper 3.00 8.00
MDPK Mall/Dltn/Pndr/Kprnk 5.00 12.00
MHCP Mrry/Hntr/Crte/Pwell 5.00 12.00
MTHR Mrry/Tdmn/Hntr/Rdly 5.00 12.00
NDPK Nwtn/Dltn/Pndr/Kprk 12.00 30.00
PGDL Pndr/Gbrt/Dltn/Lckr 5.00 12.00
SLYH Smith/Little/Young/Hankerson 3.00 8.00
SYBG Smith/Young/Brown/Gates 2.50 6.00
TMHG Thms/Mrry/Hntr/Grn 5.00 12.00
WMHR Will/Mrry/Hrpe/Rdly 5.00 12.00
WTVC Williams/Thomas/Vereen/Carter 3.00 8.00
WTVR Williams/Thomas/Vereen/Ridley 3.00 8.00

2011 Topps Supreme Six Piece Relics

STATED PRINT RUN 25 SER.#'d SETS
1 Thm/Mur/Tdm/Pow/Rid/Grn 12.00 30.00
2 Bwe/Jhn/Jhn/Bld/Hrp/Yng 10.00 25.00
3 Grn/Smt/Lit/Yng/Hnk/Pts 15.00 40.00
4 McF/Ptr/Bwe/Mlt/Mur/Rid 12.00 30.00
5 Grn/Cb/Jrn/Lit/Yng/Pet 12.00 30.00
6 Gab/Loc/Nwt/Dlt/Pnd/Kpr 20.00 50.00
7 Gab/Loc/Nwt/Mal/Pnd/Kpr 20.00 50.00
8 Nwt/Gab/Loc/Grn/Jns/Ing 25.00 60.00
9 Loc/Nwt/Mal/Dlt/Pnd/Kpr 20.00 50.00
10 Gab/Loc/Nwt/Mal/Dlt/Pnd 25.00 60.00
11 Gab/Loc/Mal/Dlt/Pnd/Kpr 20.00 50.00
12 Ing/Thm/Tdm/Hrp/Hnt/Pwl 15.00 40.00
13 Thm/Tdm/Hnt/Pwl/Rid/Grn 12.00 30.00

2011 Topps Supreme Veteran Quad Relics

STATED PRINT RUN 20 SER.#'d SETS
EACH HAS TWO CARDS OF EQUAL VALUE
SVQRAG1 Antonio Gates 5.00 12.00
SVQRAG2 Antonio Gates 5.00 12.00
SVQRCJ1 Chris Johnson 5.00 12.00
SVQRCJ2 Chris Johnson 5.00 12.00
SVQRDB1 Dwayne Bowe 6.00 15.00
SVQRDB2 Dwayne Bowe 6.00 15.00
SVQRDM1 Darren McFadden 5.00 12.00
SVQRDM2 Darren McFadden 5.00 12.00
SVQRDR1 Darrelle Revis 5.00 12.00
SVQRDR2 Darrelle Revis 5.00 12.00
SVQRJC1 Jamaal Charles 6.00 15.00
SVQRJC2 Jamaal Charles 6.00 15.00
SVQRMS1 Mark Sanchez 5.00 12.00
SVQRMS2 Mark Sanchez 5.00 12.00
SVQRMV1 Michael Vick 6.00 15.00
SVQRMV2 Michael Vick 6.00 15.00
SVQRTB1 Tom Brady 15.00 40.00
SVQRTB2 Tom Brady 15.00 40.00
SVQRTR1 Tony Romo 6.00 15.00
SVQRTR2 Tony Romo 6.00 15.00

2012 Topps Supreme

1 Andrew Luck RC 30.00 60.00
2 Maurice Jones-Drew 1.00 2.50
3 Marques Colston 1.00 2.50
4 Warren Moon 1.50 4.00
5 Eli Manning 1.25 3.00
6 Philip Rivers 1.50 4.00
7 Adrian Peterson 1.50 4.00
8 Brandon Weeden RC 1.00 2.50
9 A.J. Green 1.50 4.00
10 Emmitt Smith 3.00 8.00
11 Wes Welker 1.25 3.00
12 Coby Fleener RC 1.00 2.50
13 Joe Montana 4.00 10.00
14 Michael Turner 1.00 2.50
15 Alfred Morris RC 1.00 2.50
16 Dwayne Allen RC 1.00 2.50
17 David Wilson RC 1.00 2.50
18 Vernon Davis 1.00 2.50
19 Brock Osweiler RC 1.00 2.50
20 Aaron Rodgers 3.00 8.00
21 Patrick Willis 1.25 3.00
22 Peyton Manning 6.00 15.00
23 Russell Wilson RC 20.00 40.00
24 Troy Polamalu 1.50 4.00
25 Rob Gronkowski 1.50 4.00
26 Michael Vick 1.25 3.00
27 Andre Johnson 1.25 3.00
28 Von Miller 1.25 3.00
29 LeSean McCoy 1.50 4.00
30 Arian Foster 1.25 3.00
31 DeVier Posey RC 1.00 2.50
32 Mohamed Sanu RC 1.50 4.00
33 Troy Aikman 2.00 5.00
34 Michael Floyd RC 1.00 2.50
35 Jimmy Graham 1.50 4.00
36 Victor Cruz 1.25 3.00
37 Steve Smith 1.25 3.00
38 Stephen Hill RC 1.00 2.50
39 DeMarco Murray 1.25 3.00
40 John Elway 2.50 6.00
41 Jerry Rice 3.00 8.00
42 Ronnie Hillman RC 1.00 2.50
43 Jermichael Finley 1.00 2.50
44 Steven Jackson 1.00 2.50
45 Drew Brees 1.50 4.00
46 Isaiah Pead RC 1.00 2.50
47 Dan Marino 3.00 8.00
48 Jim Brown 2.00 5.00
49 Nick Toon RC 1.00 2.50
50 Justin Blackmon RC 1.00 2.50
51 Mike Wallace 1.00 2.50
52 Rueben Randle RC 1.00 2.50
53 Hakeem Nicks 1.00 2.50
54 Greg Jennings 1.00 2.50
55 Ndamukong Suh 1.25 3.00
56 Matt Ryan 1.25 3.00
57 Matt Forte 1.00 2.50
58 Larry Fitzgerald 1.25 3.00
59 Nick Foles RC 2.50 6.00
60 Tom Brady 4.00 10.00
61 Mark Barron RC 1.00 2.50
62 Tony Romo 1.25 3.00
63 Ryan Mathews 1.25 3.00
64 Ryan Broyles RC 1.00 2.50
65 Luke Kuechly RC 2.50 6.00
66 Michael Egnew RC 1.00 2.50
67 Matthew Stafford 1.25 3.00
68 Kendall Wright RC 1.00 2.50
69 Joe Flacco 1.25 3.00
70 Calvin Johnson 1.50 4.00
71 Ryan Tannehill RC 1.50 4.00
72 Julio Jones 1.50 4.00
73 Darren McFadden 1.00 2.50
74 Frank Gore 1.25 3.00
75 Cam Newton 1.50 4.00
76 Brandon Marshall 1.25 3.00
77 Marshawn Lynch 1.25 3.00
78 T.J. Graham RC 1.00 2.50
79 Steve Young 2.00 5.00
80 Trent Richardson RC 1.00 2.50
81 Jared Allen 1.00 2.50
82 Lamar Miller RC 1.50 4.00
83 Andy Dalton 1.25 3.00
84 Robert Turbin RC 1.00 2.50
85 Ahmad Bradshaw 1.00 2.50
86 Alshon Jeffery RC 2.00 5.00
87 Chris Johnson 1.00 2.50
88 Jarius Wright RC 1.00 2.50
89 LaMichael James RC 1.00 2.50
90 Ray Rice 1.00 2.50
91 Doug Martin RC 1.50 4.00
92 Jordy Nelson 1.25 3.00
93 Jamaal Charles 1.25 3.00
94 Roddy White 1.00 2.50
95 Brian Quick RC 1.00 2.50
96 Joe Namath 2.50 6.00
97 A.J. Jenkins RC 1.00 2.50
98 Darren Sproles 1.25 3.00
99 Morris Claiborne RC 1.00 2.50
100 Robert Griffin III RC 5.00 12.00

2012 Topps Supreme Blue

*VETS/96: .5X TO 1.2X BASIC CARDS
*ROOKIES/96: .5X TO 1.2X BASIC CARDS

2012 Topps Supreme Green

*VETS/15: 1.2X TO 3X BASIC CARDS
*ROOKIES/15: 1.2X TO 3X BASIC CARDS
1 Andrew Luck 100.00 200.00

2012 Topps Supreme Purple

*VETS/75: .6X TO 1.5X BASIC CARDS
*ROOKIES/75: .6X TO 1.5X BASIC CARDS

2012 Topps Supreme Sepia

*VETS/40: .8X TO 2X BASIC CARDS
*ROOKIES/40: .8X TO 2X BASIC CARDS

2012 Topps Supreme Autographed Dual Relics

EXCH EXPIRATION: 2/28/2016
SADRAF Arian Foster
SADRAJ A.J. Jenkins EXCH 8.00 20.00
SADRAJE Alshon Jeffery 15.00 40.00
SADRAL Andrew Luck 175.00 300.00
SADRBG Blaine Gabbert 12.00 30.00
SADRBO Brock Osweiler 8.00 20.00
SADRBQ Brian Quick 8.00 20.00
SADRBW Brandon Weeden 8.00 20.00
SADRCF Coby Fleener
SADRDA Dwayne Allen
SADRDM Doug Martin 12.00 30.00
SADRDP DeVier Posey 8.00 20.00
SADRDW David Wilson 8.00 20.00
SADRIP Isaiah Pead 8.00 20.00
SADRJB Justin Blackmon 8.00 20.00
SADRJG Josh Gordon 20.00 50.00
SADRJGR Jimmy Graham
SADRJM Joe Montana
SADRJMA Jeremy Maclin 12.00 30.00
SADRJR Jerry Rice
SADRKW Kendall Wright 8.00 20.00
SADRLJ LaMichael James EXCH 8.00 20.00
SADRLM Lamar Miller 12.00 30.00
SADRLMC LeSean McCoy
SADRMF Michael Floyd 8.00 20.00
SADRMFO Matt Forte
SADRNF Nick Foles 50.00 125.00
SADRNT Nick Toon 8.00 20.00
SADRPH Percy Harvin
SADRRB Ryan Broyles 8.00 20.00
SADRRG Robert Griffin III 100.00 200.00
SADRRH Ronnie Hillman 8.00 20.00
SADRRM Ryan Mathews 15.00 40.00
SADRRR Rueben Randle 8.00 20.00
SADRRT Ryan Tannehill 12.00 30.00
SADRRTU Robert Turbin 8.00 20.00
SADRRW Russell Wilson 150.00 250.00
SADRSH Stephen Hill 8.00 20.00
SADRTR Trent Richardson 30.00 80.00
SADRVM Von Miller

2012 Topps Supreme Autographed Relics

EXCH EXPIRATION: 2/28/2016
*BLUE/25: .5X TO 1.2X JSY AU/51
SARAJ A.J. Jenkins 5.00 12.00
SARAJE Alshon Jeffery 10.00 25.00
SARAL Andrew Luck 90.00 150.00
SARBO Brock Osweiler 5.00 12.00
SARBQ Brian Quick 5.00 12.00
SARBW Brandon Weeden 5.00 12.00
SARCF Coby Fleener 5.00 12.00
SARDA Dwayne Allen 5.00 12.00
SARDM Doug Martin 8.00 20.00
SARDP DeVier Posey 5.00 12.00
SARDW David Wilson 5.00 12.00
SARFJ Fred Jackson 12.00 30.00
SARIP Isaiah Pead 5.00 12.00
SARJB Justin Blackmon 5.00 12.00
SARJG Josh Gordon 12.00 30.00
SARJGR Jimmy Graham 12.00 30.00
SARJM Joe Montana 75.00 125.00
SARJMA Jeremy Maclin 8.00 20.00
SARJN Joe Namath 50.00 100.00
SARJW Jarius Wright 5.00 12.00
SARKW Kendall Wright 5.00 12.00
SARLJ LaMichael James 5.00 12.00
SARLM Lamar Miller 8.00 20.00
SARMF Michael Floyd 5.00 12.00
SARMFO Matt Forte 8.00 20.00
SARMJD Maurice Jones-Drew 8.00 20.00
SARNF Nick Foles 30.00 80.00
SARNT Nick Toon 5.00 12.00
SARRB Ryan Broyles 5.00 12.00
SARRG Rob Gronkowski 20.00 40.00
SARRG3 Robert Griffin III 60.00 120.00
SARRH Ronnie Hillman 5.00 12.00
SARRR Rueben Randle 5.00 12.00
SARRT Ryan Tannehill 8.00 20.00
SARRTU Robert Turbin 5.00 12.00
SARRW Russell Wilson 100.00 175.00
SARSH Stephen Hill 5.00 12.00
SARTR Trent Richardson 5.00 12.00
SARTS Torrey Smith EXCH 8.00 20.00
SARWM Willis McGahee 8.00 20.00

2012 Topps Supreme Autographs

*BLUE/25: .5X TO 1.2X BASIC AU/46
EXCH EXPIRATION: 2/28/2016
SAAF Arian Foster 10.00 25.00
SAAG A.J. Green 12.00 30.00
SADB Drew Brees 40.00 80.00
SAFG Frank Gore EXCH 10.00 25.00
SAGJ Greg Jennings EXCH 8.00 20.00
SAJM Joe Montana 60.00 120.00
SAJN Joe Namath 40.00 80.00
SAJP Jim Plunkett 10.00 25.00
SAJR Jerry Rice
SALD Len Dawson 12.00 30.00
SAMS Matthew Stafford 25.00 50.00
SAMW Mike Wallace 8.00 20.00
SAPS Phil Simms 10.00 25.00
SARG Rob Gronkowski EXCH 25.00 50.00
SARS Roger Staubach 30.00 60.00
SASS Steve Smith 12.00 30.00
SAVC Victor Cruz 15.00 40.00
SAVJ Vincent Jackson 8.00 20.00
SAWM Warren Moon 15.00 40.00
SAYT Y.A. Tittle 12.00 30.00

2012 Topps Supreme Dual Autographs

ABC A.Bradshaw/V.Cruz 30.00 60.00
SDABF J.Blackmon/M.Floyd 20.00 50.00
SDABQ J.Blackmon/B.Quick 15.00 40.00
SDABR D.Brees/M.Ryan 60.00 120.00
SDABS J.Brown/E.Smith 150.00 250.00
SDABW J.Blackmon/K.Wright 20.00 50.00
SDADH Davis/Hernandez 15.00 40.00
SDAFA C.Fleener/D.Allen 12.00 30.00
SDAFL A.Foster/M.Lynch 40.00 100.00
SDAFR B.Favre/A.Rodgers 250.00 400.00
SDAGB R.Griffin III/J.Blackmon 75.00 150.00
SDAGH Gronk/Hernandez EXCH 50.00 100.00
SDAGR R.Griffin III/Richardson 60.00 120.00
SDAGW R.Griffin III/K.Wright 75.00 150.00
SDAHJ S.Hill/A.Jeffery 12.00 30.00
SDAHN Holmes/H.Nicks EXCH 15.00 40.00
SDAIR M.Ingram/Richardson 30.00 80.00
SDAJS A.Jeffery/M.Sanu 15.00 40.00
SDAKF J.Kelly/D.Fouts 50.00 100.00
SDALB A.Luck/J.Blackmon 75.00 150.00
SDALF A.Luck/C.Fleener 75.00 150.00
SDALG A.Luck/R.Griffin III 150.00 300.00
SDALR A.Luck/T.Richardson 75.00 150.00
SDAMF D.McFadden/M.Forte 15.00 40.00
SDAMW D.Martin/D.Wilson 20.00 50.00
SDANC H.Nicks/V.Cruz EXCH 30.00 80.00
SDAOH B.Osweiler/R.Hillman
SDAPH A.Peterson/P.Harvin 60.00 120.00
SDAQP B.Quick/I.Pead 15.00 40.00
SDARB Richardson/Blackmon 20.00 50.00
SDARG T.Romo/R.Griffin III 125.00 200.00
SDARW R.Randle/D.Wilson 30.00 60.00
SDASG M.Sanchez/S.Greene 15.00 40.00
SDATH N.Toon/S.Hill 12.00 30.00
SDATM R.Tannehill/L.Miller 40.00 80.00
SDATO R.Tannehill/B.Osweiler 20.00 50.00
SDAVM M.Vick/J.Maclin 20.00 50.00
SDAWB B.Weeden/J.Blackmon 20.00 50.00
SDAWD P.Willis/V.Davis EXCH 30.00 60.00
SDAWJ K.Wright/A.Jeffery 15.00 40.00
SDAWM M.Wallace/J.Maclin 15.00 40.00
SDAWR B.Weeden/Richardson 40.00 100.00
SDAWT R.Wilson/N.Toon 75.00 150.00
SDAFJD M.Jones-Drew/A.Foster 25.00 60.00
SDAGBL B.Gabbert/J.Blackmon 20.00 40.00
SDAGJD B.Gabbert/Jones-Drew 15.00 30.00
SDAPHA Ponder/P.Harvin EXCH 30.00 60.00
SDARWI T.Richardson/D.Wilson 25.00 60.00
SDASGR Stafford/A.Green EXCH 25.00 60.00
SDASPP N.Suh/J.Pierre-Paul 20.00 50.00
SDAWTU R.Wilson/R.Turbin 100.00 175.00

2012 Topps Supreme Eight Piece Relics

SEPR1 Luck/RGIII/Key Rookies 1 25.00 60.00
SEPR2 Luck/RGIII/Key Rookies 2 25.00 60.00
SEPR3 Luck/RGIII/Key Rookies 1 25.00 60.00
SEPR4 Rookie WRs and RBs 15.00 40.00
SEPR5 Gnts/Rams/Shwk/Clts 30.00 60.00
SEPR6 Defensive and TE Vets
SEPR7 QB Vets and Rookies 25.00 60.00
SEPR8 Rookie WRs 15.00 40.00
SEPR9 Rookie RBs 20.00 50.00
SEPR10 WR Vets and Rookies 20.00 50.00
SEPR11 9ers/Clts/Shwk/Rams 30.00 60.00
SEPR13 Bears and Panthers 25.00 50.00
SEPR14 Veteran RBs and QBs 15.00 40.00
SEPR15 Charg/Brwns/Skins/Jags
SEPR16 Bears/Jets/Rams/Cards 20.00 40.00

2012 Topps Supreme Rookie Autographs

SRAAJE Alshon Jeffery 15.00 30.00
SRAAL Andrew Luck 75.00 150.00
SRABO Brock Osweiler 4.00 10.00
SRABQ Brian Quick 4.00 10.00
SRABW Brandon Weeden 4.00 10.00
SRACF Coby Fleener 4.00 10.00
SRACJ Chandler Jones 4.00 10.00
SRADA Dwayne Allen 4.00 10.00
SRADM Doug Martin 6.00 15.00
SRADP DeVier Posey 4.00 10.00
SRADW David Wilson 4.00 10.00
SRAIP Isaiah Pead 4.00 10.00
SRAJB Justin Blackmon 4.00 10.00
SRAJC Juron Criner 4.00 10.00
SRAJG Josh Gordon 10.00 25.00
SRAJJ Janoris Jenkins 5.00 12.00
SRAJW Jarius Wright 4.00 10.00
SRAKW Kendall Wright 4.00 10.00
SRALM Lamar Miller 8.00 20.00
SRAME Michael Egnew 4.00 10.00
SRAMF Michael Floyd 4.00 10.00
SRAMS Mohamed Sanu 6.00 15.00
SRANF Nick Foles 12.00 30.00
SRANT Nick Toon 4.00 10.00
SRARB Ryan Broyles 4.00 10.00
SRARG3 Robert Griffin III 25.00 60.00
SRARH Ronnie Hillman 4.00 10.00
SRARR Rueben Randle 4.00 10.00
SRART Ryan Tannehill 6.00 15.00
SRARTU Robert Turbin 4.00 10.00
SRARW Russell Wilson 75.00 150.00
SRASH Stephen Hill 4.00 10.00
SRATG T.J. Graham 4.00 10.00
SRATH T.Y. Hilton 8.00 20.00
SRATR Trent Richardson 10.00 25.00

2012 Topps Supreme Rookie Autographs Blue

*BLUE/50: .5X TO 1.2X BASIC AU/85
SRAAL Andrew Luck 100.00 200.00
SRARW Russell Wilson 100.00 200.00

2012 Topps Supreme Rookie Autographs Green

*GREEN/15: .8X TO 2X BASIC AU/85
SRAAL Andrew Luck 150.00 300.00
SRARW Russell Wilson 150.00 300.00
SRATR Trent Richardson 20.00 50.00

2012 Topps Supreme Rookie Autographs Purple

*PURPLE/25: .6X TO 1.5X BASIC AU/85
SRAAL Andrew Luck 125.00 250.00
SRARW Russell Wilson 125.00 250.00

2012 Topps Supreme Rookie Quad Relics

SRQRAJ A.J. Jenkins 3.00 8.00
SRQRAJE Alshon Jeffery 6.00 15.00
SRQRAL Andrew Luck 25.00 60.00
SRQRAM Alfred Morris 3.00 8.00
SRQRBO Brock Osweiler 3.00 8.00
SRQRBQ Brian Quick 5.00 12.00
SRQRBW Brandon Weeden 3.00 8.00
SRQRCF Coby Fleener 3.00 8.00
SRQRDA Dwayne Allen 3.00 8.00
SRQRDK Dre Kirkpatrick 3.00 8.00
SRQRDM Doug Martin 5.00 12.00
SRQRDP DeVier Posey 5.00 12.00
SRQRDW David Wilson 3.00 8.00
SRQRIP Isaiah Pead 5.00 12.00
SRQRJA Joe Adams 5.00 12.00
SRQRJB Justin Blackmon 3.00 8.00
SRQRJC Juron Criner 5.00 12.00
SRQRJG Josh Gordon 8.00 20.00
SRQRJJ Janoris Jenkins 4.00 10.00
SRQRJW Jarius Wright 3.00 8.00
SRQRKW Kendall Wright 3.00 8.00
SRQRLJ LaMichael James 3.00 8.00
SRQRLM Lamar Miller 5.00 12.00
SRQRME Michael Egnew 5.00 12.00
SRQRMF Michael Floyd 3.00 8.00
SRQRMS Mohamed Sanu 5.00 12.00
SRQRNF Nick Foles 8.00 20.00
SRQRNT Nick Toon 5.00 12.00
SRQRRB Ryan Broyles 3.00 8.00
SRQRRG3 Robert Griffin III 25.00 60.00
SRQRRH Ronnie Hillman 3.00 8.00
SRQRRR Rueben Randle 3.00 8.00
SRQRRT Ryan Tannehill 5.00 12.00
SRQRRTU Robert Turbin 3.00 8.00
SRQRRW Russell Wilson 20.00 50.00
SRQRSH Stephen Hill 3.00 8.00
SRQRTG T.J. Graham 5.00 12.00
SRQRTH T.Y. Hilton 6.00 15.00
SRQRTR Trent Richardson 3.00 8.00
SRQRVB Vick Ballard 4.00 10.00

2012 Topps Supreme Rookie Relic Die Cuts

SRDCAJ A.J. Jenkins 3.00 8.00
SRDCAJE Alshon Jeffery 6.00 15.00
SRDCAL Andrew Luck 25.00 60.00
SRDCAM Alfred Morris 3.00 8.00
SRDCBO Brock Osweiler 3.00 8.00
SRDCBQ Brian Quick 3.00 8.00
SRDCBW Brandon Weeden 3.00 8.00
SRDCCF Coby Fleener 3.00 8.00
SRDCDA Dwayne Allen 3.00 8.00
SRDCDK Dre Kirkpatrick 3.00 8.00
SRDCDM Doug Martin 5.00 12.00
SRDCDP DeVier Posey 3.00 8.00
SRDCDW David Wilson 3.00 8.00
SRDCIP Isaiah Pead 3.00 8.00
SRDCJB Justin Blackmon 3.00 8.00
SRDCJG Josh Gordon 8.00 20.00
SRDCKW Kendall Wright 3.00 8.00
SRDCLJ LaMichael James 3.00 8.00
SRDCLM Lamar Miller 5.00 12.00
SRDCMB Mark Barron 3.00 8.00
SRDCME Michael Egnew 3.00 8.00
SRDCMF Michael Floyd 3.00 8.00
SRDCMS Mohamed Sanu 5.00 12.00
SRDCNF Nick Foles 8.00 20.00
SRDCRB Ryan Broyles 3.00 8.00
SRDCRG3 Robert Griffin III 12.00 30.00
SRDCRH Ronnie Hillman 3.00 8.00
SRDCRR Rueben Randle 3.00 8.00
SRDCRT Ryan Tannehill 5.00 12.00
SRDCRTU Robert Turbin 3.00 8.00
SRDCRW Russell Wilson 20.00 50.00
SRDCSH Stephen Hill 3.00 8.00
SRDCTG T.J. Graham 3.00 8.00
SRDCTH T.Y. Hilton 6.00 15.00
SRDCTR Trent Richardson 3.00 8.00

2012 Topps Supreme Rookie Relic Quad Combos

BFWM Blckmn/Flyd/Wdn/Mrtin 4.00 10.00
BPCW Bryles/Psey/Criner/Wrght 6.00 15.00
CHJJ Coples/Hill/Jenkins/James 2.50 6.00
CPHG Coples/Poe/Hill/Gray 6.00 15.00
FAMR Flner/Alln/Mrris/Rchrdsn 4.00 10.00
FJJW Flyd/Jenkns/Jeffry/Wright 5.00 12.00
FLJJ Flyd/Lndly/Jnkins/James 2.50 6.00
FLOH Foles/Lndly/Oswler/Hrnsh 6.00 15.00
FLSK Floyd/Lndly/Sanu/Kirkpt 6.00 15.00
FLWR Floyd/Lindly/Wilsn/Rndle 2.50 6.00
FRCH Foles/Rndle/Crinr/Hillmn 6.00 15.00
GMWR RG3/Morris/Wilson/Rndle 3.00 8.00
GTAE Grahm/Toon/Allen/Egnw 6.00 15.00
GWRK RG3/Wrght/Rchrds/Kirkpt 12.00 30.00
HGSH Hill/Graham/Sanu/Hilton 5.00 12.00
JJFA Jnkins/Jmes/Flner/Allen 2.50 6.00
KJFA Krkpt/Jnkns/Flner/Allen 6.00 15.00
LFGG Luck/Fler/RG3/Gordn 25.00 60.00
LGBF Luck/RG3/Blckmn/Floyd 25.00 60.00
LGTW Luck/RG3/Tnnhill/Wden 15.00 40.00
LHAB Luck/Hilton/Allen/Ballrd 25.00 60.00
LTBM Luck/Tnnhil/Ballrd/Miller 15.00 40.00
MEJH Millr/Egnw/Jnes/Hghtwr 4.00 10.00
MKTA Martin/Kchly/Toon/Adms 6.00 15.00
MTHB Morris/Turbn/Hillmn/Bllrd 3.00 8.00
MTQT Martin/Toon/Qck/Turbn 4.00 10.00
OHFM Oswlr/Hillmn/Fles/McNtt 6.00 15.00
PHCW Posey/Hilton/Crinr/Wrght 5.00 12.00
QGPR Qck/Pead/Gvns/Rchrds 4.00 10.00
QHJR Quick/Hill/Jeffery/Rndle 5.00 12.00
QPWT Quick/Pead/Wgnr/Turbn 4.00 10.00
RBWP Rchrds/Blckm/Wrght/Pce 2.50 6.00
RWBG Rchrd/Wden/Bnjmn/Grdn 6.00 15.00
RWTW Rchrd/Wlsn/Tnnhll/Wlsn 15.00 40.00
SGBA Sanu/Grhm/Bnjmn/Adms 6.00 15.00
TJHC Turbin/Jnkns/Hllmn/Crinr 2.50 6.00
TJPR Turbn/Jmes/Prce/Rainy 2.50 6.00
TWFO Tnnhill/Wilsn/Fols/Oswlr 15.00 40.00
WARB Wriht/Adms/Rchrds/Bllrd 4.00 10.00
WGMB Wriht/Grdn/Millr/Bnjmin 6.00 15.00
WHOF Wrght/Hltn/Oswlr/Foles 6.00 15.00
WJKH Wriht/Jefry/Krkptrk/Hltn 5.00 12.00
WMRF Wilsn/Mrris/Rndle/Fles 6.00 15.00
WROH Wdn/Rchrds/Oswlr/Hllmn 2.50 6.00
WTTE Wilsn/Trbin/Tnnhill/Egnw 15.00 40.00

2012 Topps Supreme Six Piece Relics

SSPR2 Rch/Mrt/Pd/Wls/Mlr/Hl 5.00 12.00
SSPR3 Wright/Blackmon
Quick/Floyd/Hill/Jeffery 6.00 15.00
SSPR4 Wd/Rch/Wls/Trb/Lk/Bl 25.00 60.00
SSPR5 Wilson/Randle
Jenkins/James/Osweiler/Hillman 3.00 8.00
SSPR6 Lk/Fln/Hlt/Tn/EgMl 25.00 50.00
SSPR7 Lkr/Jh/Wrg/Snc/Grn/Hl 10.00 25.00
SSPR9 Brd/Qk/Pd/Lk/Hlt/Fln 25.00 60.00
SSPR10 Qk/Hl/Jf/Bry/Rnd/Snu
SSPR11 Bs/Mlr/Mrn/Hlm/Chr/Gry
SSPR12 Gonzalez/Graham
Hernandez/Fleener/Allen/Egnew 10.00 25.00
SSPR13 Hst/Jfr/Lkr/Wr/Jn-D/Blkm
SSPR14 Weeden/Osweiler
Foles/Blackmon/Quick/Jenkins 8.00 20.00
SSPR15 Trn/Frt/Grn/Mrt/Hlm/Trb
SSPR16 Spl/Grh/Snc/Hl/Grk/Tn 5.00 12.00
SSPR17 Sproles/Ingram
Bradshaw/Randle/Green/Sanu 10.00 25.00
SSPR18 Fst/McF/Gn/Jns/Wt/Gts
SSPR19 Witten/Murray
Gates/Mathews/Gonzalez/Turner 8.00 20.00
SSPR20 Fly/Wrg/Mrt/Wl/Jnk/Jms 5.00 12.00
SSPR21 Jffs/Hll/Plc/Bry/Ps/Snu

2012 Topps Supreme Veteran Quad Relics

SVQRAF Arian Foster 8.00 20.00
SVQRAF2 Arian Foster 8.00 20.00
SVQRAP Adrian Peterson
SVQRBU Brian Urlacher 10.00 25.00
SVQRCN Cam Newton 10.00 25.00
SVQRCN2 Cam Newton 10.00 25.00
SVQRDM DeMarco Murray 8.00 20.00
SVQRDR Darrelle Revis 6.00 15.00
SVQRDT Demaryius Thomas 10.00 25.00
SVQRDW DeAngelo Williams 6.00 15.00
SVQREM Eli Manning
SVQRGJ Greg Jennings 6.00 15.00
SVQRHN Hakeem Nicks 6.00 15.00
SVQRJJ Julio Jones 10.00 25.00
SVQRJP Julius Peppers 8.00 20.00
SVQRJW Jason Witten 8.00 20.00
SVQRJW2 Jason Witten 8.00 20.00
SVQRMR Matt Ryan 8.00 20.00
SVQRMS Mark Sanchez 6.00 15.00
SVQRMT Michael Turner 6.00 15.00
SVQRMT2 Michael Turner 6.00 15.00
SVQRMW Mike Wallace 6.00 15.00
SVQRMWI Mike Williams 8.00 20.00
SVQRPR Philip Rivers 10.00 25.00
SVQRPW Patrick Willis 8.00 20.00
SVQRRG Rob Gronkowski 10.00 25.00
SVQRRL Ray Lewis 15.00 40.00
SVQRSR Stevan Ridley 6.00 15.00
SVQRTR Tony Romo 8.00 20.00
SVQRTR2 Tony Romo 8.00 20.00

2013 Topps Supreme

ATED PRINT RUN 170 SER.#'d SETS
1 Peyton Manning 4.00 10.00
2 Drew Brees 2.00 5.00
4 Robert Griffin III 1.25 3.00
5 Tyler Eifert RC 1.00 2.50
6 Ray Rice 1.25 3.00
7 Lawrence Taylor 2.00 5.00
8 Julius Thomas 1.25 3.00
9 Matthew Stafford 1.50 4.00
10 Robert Woods RC 1.50 4.00
11 Victor Cruz 1.50 4.00
12 Tony Romo 1.50 4.00
13 T.Y. Hilton 1.50 4.00
14 Montee Ball RC 1.25 3.00
15 Aaron Rodgers 3.00 8.00
16 Tyrann Mathieu RC 1.50 4.00
17 Marlon Brown RC 1.50 4.00
18 DeSean Jackson 1.50 4.00
19 Matt Ryan 1.50 4.00
20 Colin Kaepernick 1.50 4.00
21 Andre Johnson 1.25 3.00
22 Philip Rivers 2.00 5.00
23 DeAndre Hopkins RC 2.50 6.00
24 DeMarco Murray 1.50 4.00
25 Geno Smith RC 1.00 2.50
26 Zach Ertz RC 2.00 5.00
27 Marcus Allen 2.00 5.00
28 Jordy Nelson 1.50 4.00
29 Matt Forte 1.25 3.00
30 Brett Favre 4.00 10.00
31 Russell Wilson 4.00 10.00
32 Eddie Lacy RC 1.00 2.50
33 Dez Bryant 2.00 5.00
34 Dion Jordan RC 1.00 2.50
35 Calvin Johnson 2.00 5.00
36 Marshawn Lynch 1.50 4.00
37 Matt Barkley RC 1.00 2.50
38 Keenan Allen RC 2.00 5.00
39 Le'Veon Bell RC 3.00 8.00
40 Terrance Williams RC 1.00 2.50
41 Eric Decker 1.25 3.00
42 Zac Stacy RC 1.00 2.50
43 Kurt Warner 1.50 4.00
44 Andre Brown 1.50 4.00
45 Brandon Marshall 1.50 4.00
46 Joe Flacco 1.50 4.00
47 LaDainian Tomlinson 1.50 4.00
48 Manti Te'o RC 1.25 3.00
49 Jay Cutler 1.25 3.00
50 Andrew Luck 3.00 8.00
51 Cordarrelle Patterson RC 1.00 2.50
52 Julio Jones 2.00 5.00
53 Kenny Stills RC 1.00 2.50
54 Eli Manning 1.50 4.00
55 Darren McFadden 1.50 4.00
56 Barry Sanders 3.00 8.00
57 Justin Houston 1.25 3.00
58 Tony Gonzalez 1.50 4.00
59 Kiko Alonso RC 1.25 3.00
60 Luke Kuechly 1.50 4.00
61 Richard Sherman 2.00 5.00
62 Tom Brady 5.00 12.00
63 Alfred Morris 1.25 3.00
64 Andre Reed 1.50 4.00
65 Curtis Martin 1.50 4.00
66 Jimmy Graham 2.00 5.00
67 Patrick Peterson 1.25 3.00
68 Andre Ellington RC 1.00 2.50
69 Giovani Bernard RC 1.00 2.50
70 Denard Robinson RC 1.00 2.50
71 Rob Gronkowski 2.00 5.00
72 Jamaal Charles 1.50 4.00
73 Frank Gore 1.50 4.00
74 Jason Witten 1.50 4.00
75 Tavon Austin RC 1.25 3.00
76 Eric Reid RC 1.25 3.00
77 Eric Dickerson 1.50 4.00
78 LeSean McCoy 2.00 5.00
79 Bo Jackson 2.50 6.00
80 Jarvis Jones RC 1.00 2.50
81 C.J. Spiller 1.25 3.00
82 J.J. Watt 1.50 4.00
83 Torrey Smith 1.25 3.00
84 A.J. Green 2.00 5.00
85 Larry Fitzgerald 1.50 4.00
86 Stevan Ridley 1.25 3.00
87 Reggie Bush 1.25 3.00
88 Jordan Cameron 1.25 3.00
89 Mike Glennon RC 1.00 2.50
90 Ezekiel Ansah RC 1.00 2.50
91 Kenbrell Thompkins RC 1.50 4.00
92 Vernon Davis 1.25 3.00
93 Demaryius Thomas 1.50 4.00
94 Arian Foster 1.50 4.00
95 Cam Newton 2.00 5.00
96 Antonio Gates 1.50 4.00
97 Antonio Brown 2.00 5.00
98 EJ Manuel RC 1.00 2.50
99 Doug Martin 1.50 4.00
100 Adrian Peterson 2.00 5.00

2013 Topps Supreme Blue

ETS/112: .5X TO 1.2X BASIC CARDS
*ROOKIES/112: .5X TO 1.2X BASIC CARDS

2013 Topps Supreme Green

*VETS/50: .8X TO 2X BASIC CARDS
*ROOKIES/50: .8X TO 2X BASIC RC

2013 Topps Supreme Purple

*VETS/99: .5X TO 1.2X BASIC CARDS
*ROOKIES/99: .5X TO 1.2X BASIC CARDS

2013 Topps Supreme Sepia

*VETS/75: .6X TO 1.5X BASIC CARDS
*ROOKIES/75: .6X TO 1.5X BASIC CARDS

2013 Topps Supreme Autographed Quad Relics

*QUAD AU/15: .5X TO 1.2X JSY AU/30
SAQRJM Joe Montana 125.00 200.00
SAQRPM Peyton Manning 150.00 250.00

2013 Topps Supreme Autographed Relics

EXCH EXPIRATION: 2/28/2017
SARAD Aaron Dobson 4.00 10.00
SARAG Antonio Gates 10.00 25.00
SARCM Christine Michael 4.00 10.00
SARCP Cordarrelle Patterson 4.00 10.00
SARDH DeAndre Hopkins 10.00 25.00
SARDJ Dion Jordan 4.00 10.00
SARDM Dan Marino 75.00 150.00
SARDMC Darren McFadden 10.00 25.00
SAREL Eddie Lacy EXCH 4.00 10.00
SAREM EJ Manuel 15.00 40.00
SAREMA Eli Manning 40.00 80.00
SARFG Frank Gore 10.00 25.00
SARGB Giovani Bernard 4.00 10.00
SARGS Geno Smith 4.00 10.00
SARJC Jamaal Charles 10.00 25.00
SARJF Joe Flacco 12.00 30.00
SARJFR Johnathan Franklin 4.00 10.00
SARJH Justin Hunter 4.00 10.00
SARJM Jeremy Maclin 8.00 20.00
SARJR Jordan Reed EXCH 6.00 15.00
SARKS Kenny Stills 4.00 10.00
SARLB Le'Veon Bell 15.00 40.00
SARMB Matt Barkley 4.00 10.00
SARMBA Montee Ball 4.00 10.00
SARMF Matt Forte 8.00 20.00
SARMG Mike Glennon 4.00 10.00
SARMGI Mike Gillislee 4.00 10.00
SARMR Matt Ryan 12.00 30.00
SARMT Manti Te'o 5.00 12.00
SARMW Mike Williams 10.00 25.00
SARPM Peyton Manning 125.00 200.00
SARRC Randall Cobb 10.00 25.00
SARRW Robert Woods 6.00 15.00
SARSB Stedman Bailey 4.00 10.00
SARSR Stevan Ridley 8.00 20.00
SARST Stepfan Taylor 4.00 10.00
SARTA Tavon Austin 5.00 12.00
SARTE Tyler Eifert 4.00 10.00
SARZE Zach Ertz 8.00 20.00

2013 Topps Supreme Autographs

*BLUE/20: .5X TO 1.2X BASIC AU/31
EXCH EXPIRATION: 2/28/2017
SAAB Anquan Boldin EXCH 8.00 20.00
SAAG A.J. Green 12.00 30.00
SAAL Andrew Luck 50.00 100.00
SAAR Andre Reed 12.00 30.00
SAAS Alex Smith 10.00 25.00
SABF Brett Favre 60.00 120.00
SABJ Bo Jackson 40.00 80.00
SABS Barry Sanders 75.00 150.00
SABSM Bruce Smith 15.00 40.00
SACM Curtis Martin 15.00 40.00
SACS C.J. Spiller 8.00 20.00
SAED Eric Dickerson 15.00 40.00
SAES Emmitt Smith 100.00 175.00
SAHL Howie Long 15.00 40.00
SAHM Heath Miller 8.00 20.00
SAJB Jerome Bettis 50.00 100.00
SAJC Jamaal Charles 12.00 30.00
SAJF Josh Freeman 10.00 25.00
SAJK Jim Kelly 25.00 50.00
SAJN Jordy Nelson 10.00 25.00
SAJPP Jason Pierre-Paul 8.00 20.00
SAJW Jason Witten 20.00 40.00
SAKW Kurt Warner 25.00 50.00
SALT LaDainian Tomlinson 12.00 30.00
SALTA Lawrence Taylor 30.00 60.00
SAMA Marcus Allen 15.00 40.00
SAMC Michael Crabtree 8.00 20.00
SAMF Matt Forte 8.00 20.00
SAMR Matt Ryan 10.00 25.00
SAMS Matthew Stafford 12.00 30.00
SARC Roger Craig 12.00 30.00
SARW Rod Woodson 25.00 50.00
SASR Stevan Ridley 8.00 20.00
SATT Thurman Thomas 12.00 30.00
SAWM Warren Moon 15.00 40.00

2013 Topps Supreme Dual Autographs

SDAABU R.Bush/M.Allen 15.00 40.00
SDAAD D.Amendola/A.Dobson 10.00 25.00
SDABB G.Bernard/M.Ball 8.00 20.00
SDABBE J.Bettis/L.Bell 75.00 135.00
SDABE Z.Ertz/M.Barkley 12.00 30.00
SDABEI T.Eifert/G.Bernard 8.00 20.00
SDABEL G.Bernard/E.Lacy 8.00 20.00
SDABG Green-Ellis/G.Bernard 10.00 25.00
SDABL L.Bell/E.Lacy 25.00 60.00
SDABLA E.Lacy/M.Ball 8.00 20.00
SDADB M.Ball/T.Davis 25.00 60.00
SDAEM P.Manning/J.Elway 200.00 300.00
SDAFL M.Forte/E.Lacy 8.00 20.00
SDAGG J.Graham/Gronkowski 40.00 80.00
SDAGW M.Glennon/T.Wilson 8.00 20.00
SDAJH J.Hunter/C.Johnson 25.00 50.00
SDAJS V.Jackson/S.Smith 12.00 30.00
SDAKT T.Thomas/J.Kelly 40.00 80.00
SDALE J.Elway/A.Luck 200.00 350.00
SDALL S.Largent/M.Lynch 60.00 120.00
SDALS B.Smith/H.Long 40.00 80.00
SDAMB M.Barkley/E.Manuel
SDAMS G.Smith/E.Manuel 8.00 20.00
SDAMSM D.Milliner/G.Smith 8.00 20.00
SDAMW R.Woods/E.Manuel 12.00 30.00
SDANC R.Cobb/J.Nelson 30.00 60.00
SDAPH C.Patterson/D.Hopkins 25.00 50.00
SDAPHU J.Hunter/C.Patterson 8.00 20.00
SDAPPT L.Taylor/J.Pierre-Paul 30.00 60.00
SDARSA M.Ryan/D.Sanders 75.00 135.00
SDARW A.Reed/R.Woods 12.00 30.00
SDASA T.Austin/G.Smith 10.00 25.00
SDASB M.Stafford/R.Bush 60.00 120.00
SDASM C.Martin/G.Smith
SDATA M.Te'o/K.Allen 25.00 50.00
SDAVC M.Vick/R.Cunningham 30.00 60.00
SDAWB J.Bettis/R.Woodson 100.00 175.00
SDAWD A.Dobson/R.Woods 12.00 30.00
SDAWF K.Warner/M.Faulk 90.00 150.00
SDAWS R.Woodson/D.Sanders 75.00 125.00

2013 Topps Supreme Dual Autographs Patch

SDAPBL E.Lacy/L.Bell 30.00 80.00
SDAPDB M.Ball/T.Davis 30.00 80.00
SDAPFA M.Faulk/T.Austin 30.00 80.00
SDAPFR R.Rice/J.Flacco 40.00 80.00
SDAPGB Glennon/M.Barkley 10.00 25.00
SDAPGM R.Griffin III/A.Morris 10.00 25.00
SDAPJH C.Johnson/J.Hunter 20.00 50.00
SDAPLM A.Luck/E.Manuel 125.00 200.00
SDAPMB M.Ball/D.Martin
SDAPMC J.Charles/McFadden 25.00 60.00
SDAPMG Manuel/M.Goodwin 15.00 40.00
SDAPMS E.Manuel/G.Smith 10.00 25.00
SDAPMT D.Marino/R.Tannehill 100.00 200.00
SDAPMY J.Montana/S.Young
SDAPOT M.Te'o/B.Orakpo 15.00 40.00
SDAPPH Patterson/D.Hopkins
SDAPRT G.Tate/S.Rice 20.00 50.00
SDAPSH D.Hopkins/C.Spiller 20.00 50.00
SDAPTG Tomlinson/A.Gates 75.00 125.00
SDAPWF K.Warner/M.Faulk 90.00 150.00

2013 Topps Supreme Rookie Autographs

EXCH EXPIRATION: 2/28/2017
*BLUE/40: .5X TO 1.2X BASIC AU/75
*PURPLE/25: .6X TO 1.5X BASIC AU/75
SRAAD Aaron Dobson 3.00 8.00
SRAAS Ace Sanders 3.00 8.00
SRACM Christine Michael 3.00 8.00
SRACP Cordarrelle Patterson 3.00 8.00
SRADH DeAndre Hopkins 8.00 20.00
SRADJ Dion Jordan 3.00 8.00
SRAEF Eric Fisher 3.00 8.00
SRAEL Eddie Lacy EXCH 3.00 8.00
SRAEM EJ Manuel 3.00 8.00
SRAGB Giovani Bernard 3.00 8.00
SRAGS Geno Smith 3.00 8.00
SRAJB Josh Boyce 3.00 8.00
SRAKB Kenjon Barner 3.00 8.00
SRAKT Kenbrell Thompkins 5.00 12.00
SRALB Le'Veon Bell 15.00 40.00
SRAMB Montee Ball 3.00 8.00
SRAMG Mike Glennon 3.00 8.00
SRAMT Manti Te'o 4.00 10.00
SRARW Robert Woods 5.00 12.00
SRAST Stepfan Taylor 3.00 8.00
SRATA Tavon Austin 4.00 10.00
SRATE Tyler Eifert 3.00 8.00
SRATM Tyrann Mathieu 5.00 12.00
SRATW Terrance Williams 3.00 8.00
SRAZE Zach Ertz 6.00 15.00

2013 Topps Supreme Rookie Quad Relics

*BLUE/15: .5X TO 1.2X BASIC JSY/25
SRQRAD Aaron Dobson 2.50 6.00
SRQRCM Christine Michael 2.50 6.00
SRQRCP Cordarrelle Patterson 2.50 6.00
SRQRDH DeAndre Hopkins 6.00 15.00
SRQRDR Denard Robinson 2.50 6.00
SRQREL Eddie Lacy 2.50 6.00
SRQREM EJ Manuel 2.50 6.00
SRQRGB Giovani Bernard 2.50 6.00
SRQRGS Geno Smith 2.50 6.00
SRQRJH Justin Hunter 5.00 12.00
SRQRKA Keenan Allen 5.00 12.00
SRQRLB Le'Veon Bell 8.00 20.00
SRQRMB Montee Ball 2.50 6.00
SRQRMG Mike Glennon 2.50 6.00
SRQRMT Manti Te'o 3.00 8.00
SRQRRW Robert Woods 4.00 10.00
SRQRTA Tavon Austin 3.00 8.00
SRQRTE Tyler Eifert 2.50 6.00
SRQRVM Vance McDonald 3.00 8.00
SRQRMBA Matt Barkley 2.50 6.00

2013 Topps Supreme Rookie Relic Die Cuts

*PURPLE/25: .6X TO 1.5X BASIC JSY
SRDCAD Aaron Dobson 2.00 5.00
SRDCAE Andre Ellington 2.00 5.00
SRDCCM Christine Michael 2.00 5.00
SRDCCP Cordarrelle Patterson 2.00 5.00
SRDCDH DeAndre Hopkins 5.00 12.00
SRDCDJ Dion Jordan 2.00 5.00
SRDCDR Denard Robinson 2.00 5.00
SRDCEL Eddie Lacy 2.00 5.00
SRDCEM EJ Manuel 3.00 8.00
SRDCGB Giovani Bernard 2.00 5.00
SRDCGS Geno Smith 2.00 5.00
SRDCJF Johnathan Franklin 2.00 5.00
SRDCJH Justin Hunter 2.00 5.00
SRDCJR Jordan Reed 3.00 8.00
SRDCKA Keenan Allen 4.00 10.00
SRDCKD Knile Davis 2.00 5.00
SRDCKS Kenny Stills 2.00 5.00
SRDCLB Le'Veon Bell 6.00 15.00
SRDCMB Montee Ball 2.00 5.00
SRDCMBA Matt Barkley 3.00 8.00
SRDCMG Mike Glennon 2.00 5.00
SRDCMGO Marquise Goodwin 2.00 5.00
SRDCML Marcus Lattimore 2.00 5.00
SRDCMT Manti Te'o 2.50 6.00
SRDCMW Markus Wheaton 2.00 5.00
SRDCRN Ryan Nassib 2.00 5.00
SRDCRW Robert Woods 3.00 8.00
SRDCSB Stedman Bailey 2.00 5.00
SRDCST Stepfan Taylor 2.00 5.00
SRDCTA Tavon Austin 2.50 6.00
SRDCTE Tyler Eifert 2.00 5.00
SRDCTW Terrance Williams 2.00 5.00
SRDCTWI Tyler Wilson 2.00 5.00
SRDCVM Vance McDonald 2.50 6.00
SRDCZE Zach Ertz 4.00 10.00

2013 Topps Supreme Veteran Quad Relics

SVQRAB Antonio Brown 8.00 20.00
SVQRAF Arian Foster 5.00 12.00
SVQRAG A.J. Green 6.00 15.00
SVQRAL Andrew Luck 10.00 25.00
SVQRCJ Chris Johnson 4.00 10.00
SVQRCK Colin Kaepernick 6.00 15.00
SVQRCN Cam Newton 6.00 15.00
SVQRDB Drew Brees 6.00 15.00
SVQRDEZ Dez Bryant 6.00 15.00
SVQRDM Doug Martin 5.00 12.00
SVQRED Eric Decker 4.00 10.00
SVQRJC Jay Cutler 4.00 10.00
SVQRJCH Jamaal Charles 5.00 12.00
SVQRJG Jimmy Graham 6.00 15.00
SVQRJJ Julio Jones 6.00 15.00
SVQRLF Larry Fitzgerald 5.00 12.00
SVQRMC Marques Colston 4.00 10.00
SVQRMF Matt Forte 4.00 10.00
SVQRPM Peyton Manning 40.00 80.00
SVQRRC Randall Cobb 5.00 12.00
SVQRRG Robert Griffin III 4.00 10.00
SVQRRGR Rob Gronkowski 6.00 15.00
SVQRRW Russell Wilson 12.00 30.00
SVQRVD Vernon Davis 4.00 10.00
SVQRVM Von Miller 5.00 12.00

2014 Topps Supreme

STATED PRINT RUN 162 SER.#'d SETS
1 Russell Wilson 3.00 8.00
2 Alshon Jeffery 1.50 4.00
3 Bishop Sankey RC 1.00 2.50
4 Andrew Luck 2.50 6.00
5 Jarvis Landry RC 2.00 5.00
6 Tre Mason RC 1.00 2.50
7 LeSean McCoy 2.00 5.00
8 John Brown RC 1.50 4.00
9 Sammy Watkins RC 1.50 4.00
10 Eli Manning 1.50 4.00
11 Matt Ryan 1.50 4.00
12 Jordan Cameron 1.25 3.00
13 Carlos Hyde RC 1.25 3.00
14 Joe Flacco 1.50 4.00
15 Paul Richardson RC 1.25 3.00
16 Montee Ball 1.25 3.00
17 Antonio Brown 2.00 5.00
18 Reggie Bush 1.25 3.00
19 Ben Roethlisberger 2.00 5.00
20 Larry Fitzgerald 1.50 4.00
21 Brett Favre 4.00 10.00
22 Dan Marino 4.00 10.00
23 Jadeveon Clowney RC 1.25 3.00
24 Nick Foles 1.50 4.00
25 Jerome Bettis 2.00 5.00
26 Terrance West RC 1.00 2.50
27 Julius Thomas 1.25 3.00
28 Blake Bortles RC 1.25 3.00
29 Tony Romo 1.50 4.00
30 Cam Newton 2.00 5.00
31 Philip Rivers 2.00 5.00
32 Robert Griffin III 1.25 3.00
33 Demaryius Thomas 1.50 4.00
34 Troy Polamalu 2.00 5.00
35 A.J. Green 2.00 5.00
36 Marshawn Lynch 1.50 4.00
37 Matthew Stafford 1.50 4.00
38 Dez Bryant 2.00 5.00
39 Brandin Cooks RC 1.50 4.00
40 Terry Bradshaw 2.50 6.00
41 Alfred Morris 1.25 3.00
42 Bo Jackson 3.00 8.00
43 Roddy White 1.25 3.00
44 Steve Young 2.50 6.00
45 Brandon Marshall 1.25 3.00

46 Luke Kuechly 1.50 4.00
47 Aaron Murray RC 1.00 2.50
48 Marshall Faulk 1.50 4.00
49 Kelvin Benjamin RC 1.50 4.00
50 Peyton Manning 4.00 10.00
51 Le'Veon Bell 1.50 4.00
52 J.J. Watt 2.00 5.00
53 Earl Thomas 1.50 4.00
54 Mike Evans RC 2.50 6.00
55 Rob Gronkowski 2.00 5.00
56 Jerick McKinnon RC 1.25 3.00
57 Teddy Bridgewater RC 1.50 4.00
58 Marqise Lee RC 1.25 3.00
59 Julio Jones 2.00 5.00
60 Jamaal Charles 1.50 4.00
61 Jordy Nelson 1.50 4.00
62 Richard Sherman 2.00 5.00
63 Troy Aikman 2.50 6.00
64 Percy Harvin 1.25 3.00
65 Michael Crabtree 1.25 3.00
66 Clay Matthews 2.00 5.00
67 Colin Kaepernick 1.50 4.00
68 Derek Carr RC 6.00 15.00
69 Wes Welker 1.50 4.00
70 Ryan Mathews 1.50 4.00
71 Barry Sanders 3.00 8.00
72 Drew Brees 2.00 5.00
73 C.J. Spiller 1.25 3.00
74 Reggie Wayne 1.50 4.00
75 Arian Foster 1.50 4.00
76 Pierre Garcon 1.50 4.00
77 DeAndre Hopkins 1.50 4.00
78 Matt Forte 1.25 3.00
79 DeSean Jackson 1.50 4.00
80 Ryan Tannehill 1.50 4.00
81 Tom Brady 5.00 12.00
82 Eddie Lacy 1.25 3.00
83 Aaron Rodgers 4.00 10.00
84 DeMarco Murray 1.50 4.00
85 Deion Sanders 1.50 4.00
86 Emmitt Smith 3.00 8.00
87 Jeremy Hill RC 1.25 3.00
88 Johnny Manziel RC 1.50 4.00
89 Jordan Matthews 2.00 5.00
90 Keenan Allen 1.50 4.00
91 A.J. McCarron RC 1.00 2.50
92 Victor Cruz 1.50 4.00
93 Eric Ebron RC 1.25 3.00
94 Cordarrelle Patterson 1.25 3.00
95 Giovani Bernard 1.25 3.00
96 Davante Adams RC 1.50 4.00
97 Odell Beckham Jr. RC 2.50 6.00
98 Jimmy Graham 2.00 5.00
99 Calvin Johnson 2.00 5.00
100 Joe Namath 2.50 6.00

2014 Topps Supreme Blue

*BLUE/144: .4X TO 1X BASIC CARDS/162

2014 Topps Supreme Green

*GREEN/25: .8X TO 2X BASIC CARDS/162

2014 Topps Supreme Purple

*PURPLE/99: .5X TO 1.2X BASIC CARDS/162

2014 Topps Supreme Sepia

*SEPIA/50: .6X TO 1.5X BASIC CARDS/162

2014 Topps Supreme Autographed Quad Relics

EXCH EXPIRATON: 2/28/2018
SAQRAG A.J. Green 20.00 50.00
SAQRAJ Alshon Jeffery
SAQRAM Aaron Murray 8.00 20.00
SAQRAMC A.J. McCarron EXCH 8.00 20.00
SAQRAR Allen Robinson 12.00 30.00
SAQRAS Austin Seferian-Jenkins 8.00 20.00
SAQRAW Andre Williams 8.00 20.00
SAQRBB Blake Bortles 10.00 25.00
SAQRBC Brandin Cooks 12.00 30.00
SAQRBS Bishop Sankey 8.00 20.00
SAQRCH Carlos Hyde EXCH 10.00 25.00
SAQRCL Cody Latimer 10.00 25.00
SAQRCS Charles Sims 8.00 20.00
SAQRDA Davante Adams 12.00 30.00
SAQRDAR Dri Archer 8.00 20.00
SAQRDC Derek Carr 40.00 100.00
SAQRDF Devonta Freeman 30.00 60.00
SAQRDM Donte Moncrief 8.00 20.00
SAQREE Eric Ebron 12.00 30.00
SAQRGB Giovani Bernard 12.00 30.00
SAQRJC Jadeveon Clowney 10.00 25.00
SAQRJG Jimmy Garoppolo 50.00 100.00
SAQRJH Jeremy Hill
SAQRJJ Julio Jones EXCH 20.00 50.00
SAQRJL Jarvis Landry
SAQRJM Johnny Manziel 12.00 30.00
SAQRJMA Jordan Matthews 12.00 30.00
SAQRJMC Jerick McKinnon 10.00 25.00
SAQRKB Kelvin Benjamin 12.00 30.00
SAQRKC Ka'Deem Carey 10.00 25.00
SAQRLB Le'Veon Bell EXCH 15.00 40.00
SAQRLM LeSean McCoy EXCH 20.00 50.00
SAQRME Mike Evans 40.00 80.00
SAQRML Marqise Lee 10.00 25.00
SAQROB Odell Beckham Jr. 60.00 125.00
SAQRPR Paul Richardson 10.00 25.00
SAQRSW Sammy Watkins 12.00 30.00
SAQRTBR Teddy Bridgewater 40.00 80.00
SAQRTS Tom Savage 8.00 20.00
SAQRTW Terrance West 8.00 20.00

2014 Topps Supreme Autographed Relics

SAPAM Aaron Murray/75 4.00 10.00
SAPAS Austin Seferian-Jenkins/75 4.00 10.00
SAPBB Blake Bortles 8.00 20.00
SAPBC Brandin Cooks/50 8.00 20.00
SAPBS Bishop Sankey/75 4.00 10.00
SAPCM Clay Matthews/25 40.00 80.00
SAPDA Davante Adams/75 6.00 15.00
SAPDC Derek Carr/30 50.00 100.00
SAPEE Eric Ebron/30 8.00 20.00
SAPES Emmitt Smith/25 100.00 175.00
SAPFG Frank Gore/30 12.00 30.00
SAPJC Jadeveon Clowney/30 8.00 20.00
SAPJG Jimmy Garoppolo/50 60.00 125.00
SAPJGO Josh Gordon/75 8.00 20.00
SAPJH Jeremy Hill EXCH 5.00 12.00
SAPJM Johnny Manziel/25
SAPJMA Jordan Matthews/50 8.00 20.00
SAPJMC Jerick McKinnon/75 5.00 12.00
SAPJN Joe Namath/25 60.00 100.00
SAPKB Kelvin Benjamin/75 6.00 15.00
SAPKC Ka'Deem Carey/65 6.00 15.00
SAPME Mike Evans/30 15.00 40.00
SAPML Marqise Lee/75 5.00 12.00
SAPOB Odell Beckham Jr./30 40.00 100.00
SAPRG Rob Gronkowski/75 EXCH 12.00 30.00
SAPSW Sammy Watkins/30 10.00 25.00
SAPTBR Teddy Bridgewater
SAPTBRA Tom Brady/25 350.00 600.00
SAPTS Tom Savage/75 4.00 10.00
SAPTW Terrance West

2014 Topps Supreme Autographed Relics Blue Patch

*BLUE/25: .8X TO 2X JSY AU/75
*BLUE/25: .6X TO 1.5X JSY AU/50-65
*BLUE/25: .5X TO 1.2X JSY AU/30
SAPCM Clay Matthews 50.00 100.00
SAPES Emmitt Smith 100.00 200.00
SAPJN Joe Namath 75.00 120.00
SAPOB Odell Beckham Jr.
SAPTBRA Tom Brady 500.00 700.00

2014 Topps Supreme Autographs

SAAB Antonio Brown/50 10.00 25.00
SAAE Andre Ellington/75 5.00 12.00
SAAGA Antonio Gates/30 8.00 20.00
SAAJ Alshon Jeffery/50 8.00 20.00
SAAM Alfred Morris/50 6.00 15.00
SABJ Bo Jackson
SADM Dan Marino
SADS Deion Sanders
SAFG Frank Gore/50 8.00 20.00
SAGB Giovani Bernard/50 6.00 15.00
SAJB Jerome Bettis/30 40.00 100.00
SAJCH Jamaal Charles/50 10.00 25.00
SAJE John Elway
SAJN Jordy Nelson EXCH 20.00 50.00
SAJT Julius Thomas/65 5.00 12.00
SAMA Marcus Allen EXCH 20.00 50.00
SAMFO Matt Forte/50 6.00 15.00
SAMSI Mike Singletary/50 10.00 25.00
SAPG Pierre Garcon/50 6.00 15.00
SARB Reggie Bush/50 6.00 15.00
SARC Roger Craig/50 8.00 20.00
SARG Rob Gronkowski EXCH 20.00 40.00
SARL Ronnie Lott/50 15.00 40.00
SARWA Reggie Wayne/30 10.00 25.00
SARWO Rod Woodson/50 20.00 40.00
SASL Steve Largent/30 20.00 40.00
SATB Tom Brady
SATP Troy Polamalu/50 80.00
SATT Thurman Thomas/30 10.00 25.00
SAVJ Vincent Jackson/30 8.00 20.00

2014 Topps Supreme Autographs Blue

*BLUE/20: .8X TO 2X BASIC AU/65-75
*BLUE/20: .6X TO 1.5X BASIC AU/50
*BLUE/20: .5X TO 1.2X BASIC AU/30
SABJ Bo Jackson 50.00 100.00
SADM Dan Marino 90.00 150.00
SADS Deion Sanders 40.00 80.00
SAJE John Elway 60.00 120.00
SATB Tom Brady 200.00 350.00

2014 Topps Supreme Dual Autographs

SDABCO O.Beckham/B.Cooks 40.00 100.00
SDABE M.Evans/K.Benjamin 40.00 80.00
SDABEB E.Ebron/R.Bush 10.00 25.00
SDABM J.Manziel/Bridgewater 15.00 40.00
SDABW A.Williams/O.Beckham 40.00 100.00
SDACH J.Clowney/D.Hopkins 25.00 50.00
SDACS T.Savage/J.Clowney 30.00 60.00
SDACT J.Clowney/L.Taylor
SDACW B.Cooks/S.Watkins 12.00 30.00
SDAEG E.Ebron/R.Gronkowski
SDAES C.Sims/M.Evans 20.00 50.00
SDAFR A.Rodgers/B.Favre
SDAGB G.Bernard/A.Green 30.00 60.00
SDAGS J.Garoppolo/T.Savage 50.00 100.00
SDAHL J.Landry/J.Hill EXCH 40.00 80.00
SDAHM A.McCarron/J.Hill
SDALB Beckham/J.Landry EXCH 40.00 100.00
SDALR A.Robinson/M.Lee
SDALW R.Wilson/A.Luck 150.00 250.00
SDAMB J.Manziel/B.Bortles 50.00 100.00
SDAME M.Evans/J.Manziel 40.00 80.00
SDAMF B.Favre/J.Manziel 100.00 200.00
SDAMFO N.Foles/L.McCoy
SDAMH C.Hyde/T.Mason 10.00 25.00
SDAMJ B.Marshall/Jeffery EXCH 25.00 50.00
SDAMM P.Manning/E.Manning 150.00 250.00
SDAMMC A.Murray/A.McCarron 8.00 20.00
SDASH B.Sankey/J.Hill 10.00 25.00
SDASS B.Sanders/E.Smith 125.00 250.00
SDASST B.Sanders/Stafford EXCH 125.00 200.00
SDAST M.Smith/E.Thomas EXCH 30.00 60.00
SDAWE M.Evans/S.Watkins 20.00 50.00
SDAWF T.West/D.Freeman 12.00 30.00
SDAWL M.Lynch/R.Wilson 125.00 200.00

2014 Topps Supreme Dual Autographs Patch

SDAPBCA D.Carr/T.Bridgewater 50.00 100.00
SDAPBCO O.Beckham/B.Cooks 100.00 200.00
SDAPBCR O.Beckham/V.Cruz 150.00 125.00
SDAPBE K.Benjamin/M.Evans 50.00 100.00
SDAPBL B.Bortles/M.Lee 75.00 150.00
SDAPBM T.Bridgewater/J.Manziel 20.00 50.00
SDAPBMA P.Manning/T.Brady 500.00 900.00
SDAPBMC J.McKinnon/T.Brdgwtr 20.00 50.00
SDAPBW A.Williams/O.Beckham 60.00 125.00
SDAPBWA O.Beckham/S.Watkins 60.00 125.00
SDAPCS J.Clowney/T.Savage 25.00 50.00
SDAPES A.SfrnJnkns/M.Evans 40.00 80.00
SDAPJF A.Jeffery/M.Forte 30.00 60.00
SDAPJW R.White/J.Jones 50.00 100.00
SDAPMB B.Bortles/J.Manziel 100.00 200.00
SDAPMBE O.Beckham/E.Manning 300.00 500.00
SDAPSS B.Sanders/E.Smith 250.00 400.00
SDAPWB K.Benjamin/S.Watkins 15.00 40.00
SDAPWE M.Evans/S.Watkins
SDAPWM J.Manziel/S.Watkins 100.00 200.00

2014 Topps Supreme Rookie Autographs

SRAAM Aaron Murray/75 3.00 8.00
SRAAR Allen Robinson/100 4.00 10.00
SRAAW Andre Williams/100 2.50 6.00
SRABB Blake Bortles
SRABC Brandin Cooks/50 5.00 12.00
SRABS Bishop Sankey/100 2.50 6.00
SRACS Charles Sims/100 2.50 6.00
SRADAR Dri Archer/99 2.50 6.00
SRADC Derek Carr/50 30.00 80.00
SRADF Devonta Freeman/125 4.00 10.00
SRAJC Jadeveon Clowney
SRAJG Jimmy Garoppolo/50 40.00 80.00
SRAJH Jeremy Hill/100 3.00 8.00
SRAJMA Jordan Matthews/100 4.00 10.00
SRAKB Kelvin Benjamin/50 5.00 12.00
SRAKC Ka'Deem Carey/100 2.50 6.00
SRALT Lorenzo Taliaferro/125 2.50 6.00
SRAME Mike Evans/50 10.00 25.00
SRAOB Odell Beckham Jr./50 40.00 80.00
SRATBR Teddy Bridgewater
SRATM Tre Mason/50 3.00 8.00
SRATS Tom Savage/50 3.00 8.00
SRATW Terrance West/99 2.50 6.00
SRAZM Zach Mettenberger/115 2.50 6.00

2014 Topps Supreme Rookie Autographs Blue

*BLUE/50: .5X TO 1.2X BASIC AU/99-115
*BLUE/50: .4X TO 1X BASIC AU/50-75
SRABB Blake Bortles 4.00 10.00
SRAJC Jadeveon Clowney 4.00 10.00
SRAJM Johnny Manziel 15.00 40.00
SRAOB Odell Beckham Jr. 40.00 80.00
SRATBR Teddy Bridgewater 15.00 40.00

2014 Topps Supreme Rookie Autographs Purple

*PURPLE/25: .8X TO 2X BASIC AU/99-115
*PURPLE/25: .6X TO 1.5X BASIC AU/50-75
SRABB Blake Bortles 6.00 15.00
SRADC Derek Carr 40.00 100.00
SRAOB Odell Beckham Jr. 50.00 100.00

2014 Topps Supreme Rookie Quad Relics

*BLUE/15: .5X TO 1.2X QUAD JSY/36
EACH PLAYER HAS 2 CARDS OF EQUAL VALUE
SRQPAM Aaron Murray 2.50 6.00
SRQPAMC A.J. McCarron 2.50 6.00
SRQPAMCC A.J. McCarron 2.50 6.00
SRQPAMU Aaron Murray 2.50 6.00
SRQPAR Allen Robinson 4.00 10.00
SRQPARO Allen Robinson 4.00 10.00
SRQPBB Blake Bortles 3.00 8.00
SRQPBC Brandin Cooks 4.00 10.00
SRQPBCO Brandin Cooks 4.00 10.00
SRQPBS Bishop Sankey 2.50 6.00
SRQPBSA Bishop Sankey 2.50 6.00
SRQPCH Carlos Hyde 3.00 8.00
SRQPCHY Carlos Hyde 3.00 8.00
SRQPDC Derek Carr 8.00 20.00
SRQPDCA Derek Carr 8.00 20.00
SRQPDF Devonta Freeman 4.00 10.00
SRQPDFR Devonta Freeman 4.00 10.00
SRQPEE Eric Ebron 3.00 8.00
SRQPEEB Eric Ebron 3.00 8.00
SRQPJC Jadeveon Clowney 3.00 8.00
SRQPJCL Jadeveon Clowney 3.00 8.00
SRQPJG Jimmy Garoppolo 20.00 50.00
SRQPJGA Jimmy Garoppolo 20.00 50.00
SRQPJM Johnny Manziel 4.00 10.00
SRQPJMA Johnny Manziel 4.00 10.00
SRQPKB Kelvin Benjamin 8.00 20.00
SRQPKBE Kelvin Benjamin 8.00 20.00
SRQPME Mike Evans 6.00 15.00
SRQPMEV Mike Evans 6.00 15.00
SRQPOB Odell Beckham Jr. 30.00 60.00
SRQPOBE Odell Beckham Jr. 30.00 60.00
SRQPSW Sammy Watkins 10.00 25.00
SRQPSWA Sammy Watkins 10.00 25.00
SRQPTB Teddy Bridgewater 4.00 10.00
SRQPTBR Teddy Bridgewater 4.00 10.00
SRQPTM Tre Mason 2.50 6.00
SRQPTMA Tre Mason 2.50 6.00
SRQPTS Tom Savage 2.50 6.00
SRQPTSA Tom Savage 2.50 6.00

2014 Topps Supreme Rookie Relic Die Cuts

SRDRAD Aaron Donald 6.00 15.00
SRDRAM Aaron Murray 2.50 6.00
SRDRAMU A.J. McCarron 2.50 6.00
SRDRAR Allen Robinson 4.00 10.00
SRDRAS Austin Seferian-Jenkins 2.50 6.00
SRDRBB Blake Bortles 3.00 8.00
SRDRBC Brandin Cooks 4.00 10.00
SRDRBS Bishop Sankey 2.50 6.00
SRDRCH Carlos Hyde 3.00 8.00
SRDRCL Cody Latimer 3.00 8.00
SRDRCS Charles Sims 2.50 6.00
SRDRDA Davante Adams 4.00 10.00
SRDRDC Derek Carr 15.00 40.00
SRDRDF Devonta Freeman 4.00 10.00
SRDRDT De'Anthony Thomas 2.50 6.00
SRDREE Eric Ebron 3.00 8.00
SRDRJC Jadeveon Clowney 3.00 8.00
SRDRJG Jimmy Garoppolo 20.00 50.00
SRDRJH Jeremy Hill 3.00 8.00
SRDRJL Jarvis Landry 5.00 12.00
SRDRJM Jerick McKinnon 3.00 8.00
SRDRJMA Johnny Manziel 4.00 10.00
SRDRJMAT Jordan Matthews 4.00 10.00
SRDRKB Kelvin Benjamin 4.00 10.00
SRDRKC Ka'Deem Carey 2.50 6.00
SRDRKM Khalil Mack 10.00 25.00
SRDRME Mike Evans 6.00 15.00
SRDRML Marqise Lee 3.00 8.00
SRDROB Odell Beckham Jr. 6.00 15.00
SRDRPR Paul Richardson 3.00 8.00
SRDRSW Sammy Watkins 4.00 10.00
SRDRTBR Teddy Bridgewater 4.00 10.00
SRDRTM Tre Mason 2.50 6.00
SRDRTS Tom Savage 2.50 6.00
SRDRTW Terrance West 2.50 6.00

2014 Topps Supreme Rookie Relic Quad Combos

STATED PRINT RUN 20 SER.#'d SETS
*BLUE/15: .4X TO 1X QUAD JSY/20
SRQCAMRB Bck/Rchrd/Mthws/Arch 15.00 40.00
SRQCBCGS Crr/Grplo/Brgwtr/Svge 20.00 50.00
SRQCBCMM Brgwtr/McCrn/Crr/Mrry
SRQCBMBC Mnzl/Crr/Brgwtr/Brtls 15.00 40.00
SRQCCLBB Bjmn/Bchm/Cks/Lee 15.00 40.00
SRQCCLMR Rrdsn/Lee/Mthws/Cks 5.00 12.00
SRQCFHHC Frmn/Hll/Hyde/Cry 4.00 10.00
SRQCGSBT Grpplo/Crr/Svge/Thms
SRQCGSMM Mry/Svge/Grplo/McCrn 20.00 50.00
SRQCLCMM Mncrf/Cks/Lee/Mtthws
SRQCMMBT Thms/McCrn/Mrry/Crr 8.00 20.00
SRQCMRBB Mthw/Rchrd/Bjmn/Bck 15.00 40.00
SRQCSHHM Snky/Hll/Msn/Hyde 3.00 8.00
SRQCSMWF Frmn/Wst/Msn/Snky 4.00 10.00
SRQCSWFW Wllms/Frmn/Sms/Wst 4.00 10.00
SRQCSWSM Snky/Msn/Wst/Sims 2.50 6.00
SRQCWEBB Wtkns/Evns/Bck/Bjmn 15.00 40.00
SRQCWECL Wtkns/Lee/Cks/Evns 6.00 15.00
SRQCWEMR Evns/Wkns/Mthw/Rchrd 6.00 15.00
SRQCWFHH Hll/Hyde/Wst/Frmn 4.00 10.00

2014 Topps Supreme Veterans Quad Relics

SVQRAF Arian Foster 6.00 15.00
SVQRAG Antonio Gates 5.00 12.00
SVQRAJ Alshon Jeffery 6.00 15.00
SVQRAL Andrew Luck 10.00 25.00
SVQRAR Aaron Rodgers 25.00 50.00
SVQRARO Antrel Rolle 5.00 12.00
SVQRCN Cam Newton 8.00 20.00
SVQRCS C.J. Spiller 5.00 12.00
SVQRDB Drew Brees 8.00 20.00
SVQRDT Demaryius Thomas 6.00 15.00
SVQREB Eric Berry 6.00 15.00
SVQREM Eli Manning 6.00 15.00
SVQRFG Frank Gore 6.00 15.00
SVQRJJ Julio Jones 8.00 20.00
SVQRMF Matt Forte 5.00 12.00
SVQRPM Peyton Manning
SVQRRC Randall Cobb 10.00 25.00
SVQRRG Robert Griffin III 5.00 12.00
SVQRRGR Rob Gronkowski 8.00 20.00
SVQRRT Ryan Tannehill 6.00 15.00
SVQRRW Roddy White 5.00 12.00
SVQRTH T.Y. Hilton 6.00 15.00
SVQRTP Troy Polamalu 20.00 40.00
SVQRTR Tony Romo 6.00 15.00
SVQRVD Vernon Davis 5.00 12.00

2015 Topps Supreme

*COPPER/194: .5X TO 1.2X BASIC CARDS
*VIOLET/99: .6X TO 1.5X BASIC CARDS
*GOLD/50: .8X TO 2X BASIC CARDS
*GREEN/25: 1X TO 2.5X BASIC CARDS
1 Tom Brady 5.00 12.00
2 Calvin Johnson 2.00 5.00
3 Marshawn Lynch 1.50 4.00
4 Aaron Rodgers 4.00 10.00
5 J.J. Watt 2.00 5.00
6 Andrew Luck 2.50 6.00
7 Jamaal Charles 1.50 4.00
8 Le'Veon Bell 1.50 4.00
9 Richard Sherman 2.00 5.00
10 Rob Gronkowski 2.00 5.00
11 Peyton Manning 4.00 10.00
12 Drew Brees 2.00 5.00
13 Antonio Brown 2.00 5.00
14 Demaryius Thomas 1.50 4.00
15 Russell Wilson 2.50 6.00
16 Dez Bryant 2.00 5.00
17 Julio Jones 2.00 5.00
18 Odell Beckham Jr. 2.00 5.00
19 Eddie Lacy 1.25 3.00
20 Cam Newton 2.00 5.00
21 Jordy Nelson 1.50 4.00
22 DeMarco Murray 1.50 4.00
23 Adrian Peterson 2.00 5.00
24 Jimmy Graham 2.00 5.00
25 Ben Roethlisberger 2.00 6.00
26 A.J. Green 2.00 5.00
27 LeSean McCoy 2.00 5.00
28 Arian Foster 1.50 4.00
29 Matthew Stafford 1.50 4.00
30 Alshon Jeffery 1.50 4.00
31 Matt Forte 1.25 3.00
32 Tony Romo 1.50 4.00
33 Clay Matthews 2.00 5.00
34 Mike Evans 1.50 4.00
35 Kelvin Benjamin 1.50 4.00
36 Sammy Watkins 1.50 4.00
37 Matt Ryan 1.50 4.00
38 Eli Manning 1.50 4.00
39 Colin Kaepernick 1.50 4.00
40 Brett Favre 4.00 10.00
41 John Elway 3.00 8.00
42 Ryan Tannehill 1.50 4.00
43 Emmitt Smith 3.00 8.00
44 Steve Young 2.50 6.00
45 Dan Marino 4.00 10.00
46 Bo Jackson 2.50 6.00
47 Marshall Faulk 1.50 4.00
48 Barry Sanders 3.00 8.00
49 Terrell Davis 1.50 4.00
50 Deion Sanders 1.50 4.00
51 Eric Dickerson 1.50 4.00
52 Lawrence Taylor 2.00 5.00
53 Ronnie Lott 1.50 4.00
54 Troy Polamalu 2.00 5.00
55 Joe Greene 2.00 5.00
56 Tim Brown 2.00 5.00
57 Paul Hornung 2.00 5.00
58 Jerry Rice 3.00 8.00
59 Kurt Warner 1.50 4.00
60 Phil Simms 1.50 4.00
61 Roger Staubach 2.50 6.00
62 Marcus Allen 2.00 5.00
63 Warren Moon 2.00 5.00
64 Tony Dorsett 2.00 5.00
65 Terry Bradshaw 2.50 6.00
66 Mike Ditka 2.00 5.00
67 DeVante Parker RC 1.50 4.00
68 Devin Funchess RC 1.50 4.00
69 Amari Cooper RC 3.00 8.00
70 Marcus Mariota RC 4.00 10.00
71 Kevin White RC 1.25 3.00
72 Melvin Gordon RC 2.50 6.00
73 Dorial Green-Beckham RC 1.00 2.50
74 Brett Hundley RC 1.00 2.50
75 Jameis Winston RC 2.50 6.00
76 Tevin Coleman RC 1.25 3.00
77 Maxx Williams RC 1.00 2.50
78 Ameer Abdullah RC 1.50 4.00
79 Ty Montgomery RC 1.00 2.50
80 Todd Gurley RC 4.00 10.00
81 Nelson Agholor RC 1.25 3.00
82 T.J. Yeldon RC 1.00 2.50
83 Mike Davis RC 1.00 2.50
84 Tyler Lockett RC 1.50 4.00
85 Bryce Petty RC 1.00 2.50
86 Matt Jones RC 1.00 2.50
87 Phillip Dorsett RC 1.00 2.50
88 Jay Ajayi RC 1.50 4.00
89 Breshad Perriman RC 1.00 2.50
90 Garrett Grayson RC 1.00 2.50
91 Sean Mannion RC 1.00 2.50
92 Chris Conley RC 1.00 2.50
93 Gale Sayers 2.00 5.00
94 Earl Campbell 2.00 5.00
95 Franco Harris 2.00 5.00
96 Hines Ward 1.50 4.00
97 Jarryd Hayne 2.00 5.00
98 C.J. Anderson 1.50 4.00
99 Frank Gore 1.50 4.00
100 Randall Cobb 1.50 4.00

2015 Topps Supreme Autograph Patches

SAPAA Ameer Abdullah/45 6.00 15.00
SAPAC Amari Cooper/45 40.00 80.00
SAPBPR Breshad Perriman
SAPBPT Bryce Petty
SAPCA C.J. Anderson/45 10.00 25.00
SAPDF Devin Funchess/45 6.00 15.00
SAPDH DeAndre Hopkins/45 10.00 25.00
SAPDJ Duke Johnson/45 6.00 15.00
SAPDP DeVante Parker/45 6.00 15.00
SAPEL Eddie Lacy/45 15.00 30.00
SAPES Emmanuel Sanders/45 10.00 25.00
SAPGO Greg Olsen/45 15.00 30.00
SAPJH Jeremy Hill/45 8.00 20.00
SAPJM Jordan Matthews/45 10.00 25.00
SAPJN Jordy Nelson/45 25.00 50.00
SAPJS Jaelen Strong/50 5.00 12.00
SAPJW Jameis Winston/30 90.00 150.00
SAPKB Kelvin Benjamin/45 10.00 25.00
SAPKW Kevin White/45 5.00 12.00
SAPMD Mike Davis/45 4.00 10.00
SAPMG Melvin Gordon/45 10.00 25.00
SAPMJ Matt Jones/50 4.00 10.00
SAPMM Marcus Mariota/30 60.00 125.00
SAPNA Nelson Agholor/45 5.00 12.00
SAPPD Phillip Dorsett/45 4.00 10.00
SAPTG Todd Gurley/45 30.00 60.00
SAPTH T.Y. Hilton/55 10.00 25.00
SAPTL Tyler Lockett/55 6.00 15.00
SAPTM Ty Montgomery/45 4.00 10.00
SAPTY T.J. Yeldon/45 4.00 10.00

2015 Topps Supreme Autographs

SAAGR A.J. Green
SAAJG A.J. Green
SAAL Andrew Luck/35 60.00 120.00
SAAR Aaron Rodgers
SABF Brett Favre
SACA C.J. Anderson/35 8.00 20.00
SADCA Derek Carr/50 20.00 40.00
SADCL Dwight Clark/35 8.00 20.00
SADH DeAndre Hopkins/35 8.00 20.00
SADM DeMarco Murray
SAEL Eddie Lacy/50 6.00 15.00
SAESA Emmanuel Sanders/35 8.00 20.00
SAESM Emmitt Smith
SAGS Gale Sayers/35 20.00 40.00
SAHW Hines Ward/50 30.00 60.00
SAJH Jeremy Hill/35 6.00 15.00
SAJM Jordan Matthews/35 8.00 20.00
SAJN Jordy Nelson/50 12.00 30.00
SAKB Kelvin Benjamin/35 8.00 20.00
SALK Luke Kuechly/35 25.00 50.00
SAME Mike Evans/35 8.00 20.00
SAMF Matt Forte/35 6.00 15.00
SAMR Matt Ryan
SAMSI Mike Singletary/35 10.00 25.00
SAMST Matthew Stafford
SAPH Paul Hornung/35 10.00 25.00
SAPS Phil Simms
SARG Rob Gronkowski
SART Ryan Tannehill/45 8.00 20.00
SASW Sammy Watkins
SATBI Teddy Bridgewater
SATBR Tim Brown/50 12.00 30.00
SATDA Terrell Davis/35 20.00 40.00
SATDO Tony Dorsett/47 20.00 40.00
SATH T.Y. Hilton/55 8.00 20.00

2015 Topps Supreme Autographs Gold

*GOLD AU/20-25: .5X TO 1.2X BASIC AU/35-55
SAAL Andrew Luck/25 75.00 150.00
SABF Brett Favre/25 90.00 150.00

2015 Topps Supreme Dual Autographs

SDAAM N.Agholor/J.Matthews 6.00 15.00
SDAAS E.Sanders/C.Anderson 8.00 20.00
SDABC T.Brown/A.Cooper 40.00 80.00
SDABF K.Benjamin/D.Funchess 8.00 20.00
SDABG J.Greene/T.Bradshaw
SDABH F.Harris/T.Bradshaw
SDABS R.Staubach/T.Bradshaw 150.00 250.00
SDACC A.Cooper/D.Carr 30.00 60.00
SDACI M.Ingram/B.Cooks 6.00 15.00
SDAEM P.Manning/J.Elway
SDAFA D.Funchess/C.Artis-Payne 8.00 20.00
SDAFJ M.Forte/A.Jeffery 20.00 40.00
SDAHD P.Dorsett/T.Hilton 6.00 15.00
SDAJW K.White/A.Jeffery 12.00 30.00
SDAKO L.Kuechly/G.Olsen 30.00 60.00
SDALG F.Gore/A.Luck 50.00 100.00
SDALN J.Nelson/E.Lacy 25.00 50.00
SDAML P.Manning/A.Luck
SDAMM P.Manning/E.Manning
SDAMN C.Matthews/J.Nelson 25.00 60.00
SDAMR A.Rodgers/P.Manning
SDANC J.Nelson/R.Cobb 25.00 50.00
SDAPL J.Landry/D.Parker
SDAPW B.Perriman/M.Williams 5.00 12.00
SDARS J.Rice/B.Sanders
SDASD T.Dorsett/R.Staubach
SDASF M.Forte/G.Sayers 20.00 40.00
SDASM P.Simms/E.Manning
SDAST L.Taylor/P.Simms 50.00 100.00
SDATL J.Landry/R.Tannehill
SDATP D.Parker/R.Tannehill
SDATS B.Sanders/L.Tomlinson
SDAWE M.Evans/J.Winston 40.00 80.00
SDAWM J.Winston/M.Mariota 100.00 200.00
SDAWS R.Sherman/R.Wilson
SDAYR S.Young/J.Rice
SDAGHI A.Green/J.Hill 10.00 25.00
SDAMMA J.Matthews/D.Murray 6.00 15.00
SDASSA M.Singletary/G.Sayers
SDASSM E.Smith/B.Sanders

2015 Topps Supreme Quad Relics

SQPAB Antonio Brown 8.00 20.00
SQPAG A.J. Green 8.00 20.00
SQPAJ Alshon Jeffery 6.00 15.00
SQPAL Andrew Luck 10.00 25.00
SQPAR Aaron Rodgers 15.00 40.00
SQPCN Cam Newton 8.00 20.00
SQPDBE Drew Brees 8.00 20.00
SQPDBY Dez Bryant 8.00 20.00
SQPDM DeMarco Murray 6.00 15.00
SQPDT Demaryius Thomas 6.00 15.00
SQPEL Eddie Lacy 5.00 12.00
SQPEM Eli Manning 6.00 15.00
SQPJJ Julio Jones 8.00 20.00
SQPLB Le'Veon Bell 6.00 15.00
SQPME Mike Evans 6.00 15.00
SQPMS Matthew Stafford/25 6.00 15.00
SQPOB Odell Beckham Jr. 8.00 20.00
SQPRC Randall Cobb 6.00 15.00
SQPRGO Rob Gronkowski 8.00 20.00
SQPRS Richard Sherman 8.00 20.00
SQPRW Russell Wilson 10.00 25.00
SQPTH T.Y. Hilton 6.00 15.00
SQPTR Tony Romo 6.00 15.00

2015 Topps Supreme Rookie Autographs Gold

*ROOK AU/75: .3X TO .8X BASIC AU/50
SRAAA Ameer Abdullah 6.00 15.00
SRAAC Amari Cooper 40.00 80.00
SRABH Brett Hundley 4.00 10.00
SRABP Bryce Petty 4.00 10.00
SRABPE Breshad Perriman 4.00 10.00
SRACA Cameron Artis-Payne 4.00 10.00
SRACC Chris Conley 4.00 10.00
SRACW Clive Walford 4.00 10.00
SRADC David Cobb 4.00 10.00
SRADF Devin Funchess 6.00 15.00
SRADGB Dorial Green-Beckham 4.00 10.00
SRADJ David Johnson 12.00 30.00
SRADJU Duke Johnson 6.00 15.00
SRADS Devin Smith 4.00 10.00
SRAJC Jamison Crowder 5.00 12.00
SRAJJ Jesse James 5.00 12.00
SRAJS Jaelen Strong 5.00 12.00
SRAJW Jameis Winston 10.00 25.00
SRAKW Karlos Williams 4.00 10.00
SRAKWH Kevin White 5.00 12.00
SRAMD Mike Davis 4.00 10.00
SRAMG Melvin Gordon 10.00 25.00
SRAMM Marcus Mariota 50.00 100.00
SRAMW Maxx Williams 4.00 10.00
SRANA Nelson Agholor 5.00 12.00
SRASD Stefon Diggs 10.00 25.00
SRASM Sean Mannion 4.00 10.00
SRATG Todd Gurley 40.00 100.00
SRATLO Tyler Lockett 6.00 15.00
SRATMO Ty Montgomery 4.00 10.00
SRATY T.J. Yeldon 4.00 10.00

2015 Topps Supreme Rookie Autographs Green

*GREEN/25: .6X TO 1.5X GOLD AU/50
SRAAC Amari Cooper 40.00 100.00

2015 Topps Supreme Rookie Quad Patches

*GOLD/25: .5X TO 1.2X BASIC JSY/50
SRQPAAB Ameer Abdullah 4.00 10.00
SRQPACO Amari Cooper 10.00 25.00
SRQPACP Amari Cooper 10.00 25.00
SRQPAMA Ameer Abdullah 4.00 10.00
SRQPBHD Brett Hundley 2.50 6.00
SRQPBHU Brett Hundley 2.50 6.00
SRQPBPR Breshad Perriman 2.50 6.00
SRQPBPT Bryce Petty 2.50 6.00
SRQPDFN Devin Funchess 4.00 10.00
SRQPDFU Devin Funchess 4.00 10.00
SRQPDGB Dorial Green-Beckham 2.50 6.00
SRQPDPA DeVante Parker 4.00 10.00
SRQPDPR DeVante Parker 4.00 10.00
SRQPDRG Dorial Green-Beckham 2.50 6.00
SRQPGGA Garrett Grayson 2.50 6.00
SRQPGGR Garrett Grayson 2.50 6.00
SRQPJAJ Jay Ajayi 4.00 10.00
SRQPJSR Jaelen Strong 3.00 8.00
SRQPJST Jaelen Strong 3.00 8.00
SRQPJWI Jameis Winston 10.00 25.00
SRQPJWN Jameis Winston 10.00 25.00
SRQPKWH Kevin White 3.00 8.00
SRQPKWI Kevin White 3.00 8.00
SRQPMGO Melvin Gordon 6.00 15.00
SRQPMGR Melvin Gordon 6.00 15.00
SRQPMJ Matt Jones 2.50 6.00
SRQPMM Marcus Mariota 10.00 25.00
SRQPMMA Marcus Mariota 10.00 25.00
SRQPNAG Nelson Agholor 3.00 8.00
SRQPNAH Nelson Agholor 3.00 8.00
SRQPPDO Phillip Dorsett 2.50 6.00
SRQPPDR Phillip Dorsett 2.50 6.00
SRQPSM Sean Mannion 2.50 6.00
SRQPTCL Tevin Coleman 3.00 8.00
SRQPTCO Tevin Coleman 3.00 8.00
SRQPTGR Todd Gurley 12.00 30.00
SRQPTGU Todd Gurley 12.00 30.00
SRQPTJY T.J. Yeldon 2.50 6.00
SRQPTL Tyler Lockett 4.00 10.00
SRQPTYE T.J. Yeldon 2.50 6.00

2015 Topps Supreme Rookie Quad Patches Combo

SRQCCGDL Cpr/Dvs/Grdn/Lcktt 8.00 20.00
SRQCCPGA Aghlr/GrnBckhm/Cpr/Prkr 8.00 20.00
SRQCCPGP Prkr/Cpr/GrnBckhm/Prrmn 8.00 20.00
SRQCCPYA Abdllh/Cpr/Yldn/Prkr 8.00 20.00
SRQCCWGG Cpr/White/Grly/Grdn 10.00 25.00
SRQCCWPA Cpr/White/Prkr/Aghlr 8.00 20.00
SRQCDWAM Mntgmry/White/Abdllh/Dggs 5.00 12.00
SRQCFWBR Wllms/Bsly/Ry/Fwlr 3.00 8.00
SRQCGAYC Clmn/Grdn/Abdllh/Yldn 5.00 12.00
SRQCGAYJ Abdllh/Jns/Yldn/Grdn 5.00 12.00
SRQCGDYS Drstt/Yldn/Strng/GrnBckhm 2.50 6.00
SRQCGGYA Yldn/Grdn/Grly/Abdllh 10.00 25.00
SRQCGMPH Hndly/Ptty/Mnn/Grysn 2.00 5.00
SRQCHMWL Mntgmry/Lngfrd/White/Hndly 2.50 6.00
SRQCMGCP Prkr/Grdn/Cpr/Mrta 10.00 25.00
SRQCPAYG Yldn/Grne/Prkr/Ajyi 3.00 8.00
SRQCWGCW Wnstn/Whte/Cpr/Grly 10.00 25.00
SRQCWMCG Mrta/Wnstn/Grly/Cpr 10.00 25.00
SRQCWMGG Wnstn/Grly/Mrta/Grdn 10.00 25.00
SRQCWMGM Mrta/Grysn/Mnn/Wnstn 10.00 25.00

2015 Topps Take It to the House

1 Marcus Mariota 1.00 2.50
2 Jaelen Strong .30 .75
3 Sammie Coates .30 .75
4 Jeremy Langford .25 .60
5 Melvin Gordon .60 1.50
6 Tevin Coleman .30 .75
7 Brett Hundley .25 .60
8 DeVante Parker .40 1.00
9 Dorial Green-Beckham .25 .60
10 Jameis Winston .60 1.50
11 Breshad Perriman .25 .60
12 Devin Funchess .40 1.00
13 Phillip Dorsett .25 .60
14 Devin Smith .25 .60
15 Amari Cooper .75 2.00
16 Ameer Abdullah .40 1.00
17 Nelson Agholor .30 .75
18 Rashad Greene .25 .60
19 Tyler Lockett .40 1.00
20 Todd Gurley 1.00 2.50
21 Duke Johnson .40 1.00
22 Jay Ajayi .40 1.00
23 Bryce Petty .25 .60
24 Maxx Williams .25 .60
25 Kevin White .30 .75
26 David Johnson .60 1.50
27 Ty Montgomery .25 .60
28 T.J. Yeldon .25 .60
29 Mike Davis .25 .60
30 Aaron Rodgers .50 1.25
31 Sean Mannion .25 .60
32 Javorius Allen .30 .75
33 Karlos Williams .25 .60
34 Tony Lippett .25 .60
35 Marshawn Lynch .20 .50
36 Vince Mayle .30 .75
37 David Cobb .25 .60
38 Kenny Bell .40 1.00
39 Chris Conley .25 .60
40 Leonard Williams .25 .60
41 Tre McBride .25 .60
42 Justin Hardy .25 .60
43 Jamison Crowder .30 .75
44 Clive Walford .25 .60
45 Andrew Luck .30 .75
46 Nick O'Leary .25 .60
47 Matt Jones .25 .60
48 Austin Hill .25 .60
49 Deontay Greenberry .25 .60
50 Russell Wilson .30 .75
51 Randy Gregory .25 .60
52 Dante Fowler Jr. .40 1.00
53 Shane Ray .25 .60
54 Alvin Dupree .30 .75
55 Tom Brady .60 1.50
56 Vic Beasley .30 .75
57 Eddie Lacy .15 .40
58 DeMarco Murray .20 .50
59 Stefon Diggs .60 1.50
60 Le'Veon Bell .20 .50
61 Levi Norwood .25 .60
62 Cameron Artis-Payne .25 .60
63 Jeff Heuerman .30 .75
64 Jesse James .30 .75
65 Drew Brees .25 .60
66 Trae Waynes .25 .60
67 LeSean McCoy .25 .60
68 Calvin Johnson .25 .60
69 Adrian Peterson .25 .60
70 Odell Beckham Jr. .25 .60
71 Antonio Brown .25 .60
72 Rob Gronkowski .25 .60
73 Jimmy Graham .25 .60
74 A.J. Green .25 .60
75 Peyton Manning .50 1.25
76 Eli Manning .20 .50
77 Jordy Nelson .20 .50
78 Matthew Stafford .20 .50
79 Richard Sherman .25 .60
80 J.J. Watt .25 .60
81 John Elway .40 1.00
82 Brett Favre .50 1.25
83 Emmitt Smith .40 1.00
84 Steve Young .30 .75
85 Dan Marino .50 1.25
86 Barry Sanders .40 1.00
87 Malcolm Brown .20 .50
88 Bo Jackson .30 .75
89 Deion Sanders .20 .50
90 Roger Staubach .30 .75
91 Gale Sayers .25 .60
92 Eric Dickerson .20 .50
93 Kaelin Clay .15 .40
94 Josh Robinson .15 .40
95 Jerry Rice .40 1.00
96 Terry Bradshaw .30 .75
97 Dominique Brown .15 .40
98 Josh Harper .15 .40
99 Ben Koyack .25 .60
100 Jamaal Charles .20 .50

2015 Topps Take It to the House Autographs

1 Marcus Mariota
3 Sammie Coates 4.00 10.00
4 Jeremy Langford 3.00 8.00
5 Melvin Gordon
6 Tevin Coleman 4.00 10.00
7 Brett Hundley 3.00 8.00
8 DeVante Parker 5.00 12.00
9 Dorial Green-Beckham 3.00 8.00
10 Jameis Winston
11 Breshad Perriman 3.00 8.00
12 Devin Funchess 5.00 12.00
14 Devin Smith 3.00 8.00
15 Amari Cooper
16 Ameer Abdullah 5.00 12.00
17 Nelson Agholor 4.00 10.00
18 Rashad Greene 3.00 8.00
19 Tyler Lockett 5.00 12.00
20 Todd Gurley 40.00 80.00
21 Duke Johnson 5.00 12.00
22 Jay Ajayi 5.00 12.00
25 Kevin White 4.00 10.00
27 Ty Montgomery 3.00 8.00
28 T.J. Yeldon 3.00 8.00
29 Mike Davis 3.00 8.00
33 Karlos Williams 3.00 8.00
34 Tony Lippett 3.00 8.00
36 Vince Mayle 4.00 10.00
37 David Cobb 3.00 8.00
38 Kenny Bell 5.00 12.00
39 Chris Conley 3.00 8.00
42 Justin Hardy 3.00 8.00
43 Jamison Crowder 4.00 10.00
44 Clive Walford 3.00 8.00
45 Andrew Luck
49 Deontay Greenberry 3.00 8.00
50 Russell Wilson
52 Dante Fowler Jr. 5.00 12.00
57 Eddie Lacy 15.00 40.00
58 DeMarco Murray 4.00 10.00
61 Levi Norwood 3.00 8.00
62 Cameron Artis-Payne 3.00 8.00
75 Peyton Manning
76 Eli Manning 4.00 10.00
82 Brett Favre 60.00 120.00
85 Dan Marino
86 Barry Sanders
91 Gale Sayers 15.00 40.00
97 Dominique Brown 3.00 8.00
98 Josh Harper 3.00 8.00
99 Ben Koyack 5.00 12.00

2003 Topps Total

Released in August of 2003, this 550-card set includes 440 veterans and 110 rookies. Boxes contained 36 packs of 10 cards. Pack SRP was $1.
COMPLETE SET (550) 40.00 80.00
1 Rich Gannon .20 .50
2 Travis Henry .15 .40
3 Brian Finneran .15 .40
4 Ed Hartwell .15 .40
5 Az-Zahir Hakim .15 .40
6 Rodney Peete .15 .40
7 David Terrell .15 .40
8 Matt Schobel .20 .50
9 Andre Davis .15 .40
10 Dexter Coakley .20 .50
11 Rod Smith .20 .50
12 Damerien McCants .15 .40
13 Robert Ferguson .15 .40
14 Kailee Wong .15 .40
15 James Mungro .15 .40
16 Fred Taylor .15 .40
17 Tony Gonzalez .20 .50
18 Randall Godfrey .15 .40
19 Robert Thomas .15 .40
20 Rohan Davey .15 .40
21 Terrell Owens .20 .50
22 Ron Dayne .20 .50
23 Charlie Batch .15 .40
24 Brian Westbrook .15 .40
25 Plaxico Burress .15 .40
26 Reche Caldwell .15 .40
27 Fred Beasley .15 .40
28 Anthony Simmons .15 .40
29 Rod Woodson .20 .50
30 Derrick Brooks .15 .40
31 Shaun Ellis .15 .40
32 Ladell Betts .15 .40
33 Russell Davis .15 .40
34 Warrick Dunn .15 .40
35 Jeremy Shockey .15 .40
36 Alex Van Pelt .15 .40
37 Todd Douman .15 .40
38 Kelly Campbell .15 .40
39 Justin Smith .20 .50
40 Jamel White .15 .40
41 La'Roi Glover .15 .40
42 Ian Gold .15 .40
43 Robert Porcher .15 .40
44 Jermaine Lewis .15 .40
45 Marvin Harrison .20 .50
46 Darren Sharper .15 .40
47 Jamie Sharper .15 .40
48 Tony Richardson .15 .40
49 Moe Williams .15 .40
50 Ricky Williams .20 .50
51 Ty Law .25 .60
52 Donte Stallworth .15 .40
53 Shannon Sharpe .20 .50
54 Santana Moss .20 .50
55 Charlie Garner .20 .50
56 Brian Dawkins .25 .60
57 Dan Campbell .15 .40
58 William Green .15 .40
59 Ron Dugans .15 .40
60 Darrell Jackson .20 .50
61 Marc Bulger .15 .40
62 Joe Jurevicius .20 .50
63 Erron Kinney .15 .40
64 Champ Bailey .20 .50
65 Peerless Price .15 .40
66 Gary Baxter .15 .40
67 Chris Redman .15 .40
68 London Fletcher .20 .50
69 Dee Brown .15 .40
70 Anthony Thomas .20 .50
71 Jake Delhomme .15 .40
72 Dorsey Levens .20 .50
73 Roy Williams .15 .40
74 Ashley Lelie .15 .40
75 Joey Harrington .15 .40
76 William Henderson .15 .40
77 Corey Bradford .15 .40
78 Reggie Wayne .20 .50
79 Kyle Brady .15 .40
80 Trent Green .15 .40
81 Bill Romanowski .20 .50
82 Chike Okeafor RC .30 .75
83 David Patten .15 .40
84 Terrelle Smith .15 .40
85 Kerry Collins .15 .40
86 Derrick Mason .15 .40
87 Trung Canidate .15 .40
88 A.J. Feeley .15 .40
89 Jason Gildon .20 .50
90 Doug Flutie .20 .50
91 Tai Streets .15 .40
92 Keith Newman .15 .40
93 Adam Archuleta .15 .40
94 Simeon Rice .15 .40
95 Eddie George .20 .50
96 Frank Sanders .15 .40
97 Freddie Jones .15 .40
98 Charles Johnson .15 .40
99 Keith Traylor .20 .50
100 Drew Bledsoe .20 .50
101 Muhsin Muhammad .15 .40
102 Marques Anderson .15 .40
103 Donald Hayes .15 .40
104 Quincy Morgan .15 .40
105 Chad Hutchinson .15 .40
106 Mike Anderson .15 .40
107 Randy McMichael .15 .40
108 Vonnie Holliday .15 .40
109 Marcus Coleman .15 .40
110 Edgerrin James .20 .50
111 Michael Lewis .15 .40
112 Wayne Chrebet .15 .40
113 Antwaan Randle El .15 .40
114 Byron Chamberlain .15 .40
115 Jeff Garcia .15 .40
116 Kim Herring .15 .40
117 Kenny Holmes .15 .40
118 John Lynch .20 .50

119 Doug Jolley .15 .40
120 Duce Staley .15 .40
121 Kordell Stewart .15 .40
122 Stephen Alexander .15 .40
123 Andre Carter .15 .40
124 Bobby Engram .15 .40
125 Marshall Faulk .20 .50
126 Peter Simon RC .15 .40
127 Alge Crumpler .20 .50
128 Kenny Watson .15 .40
129 Duane Starks .15 .40
130 Jeff Blake .20 .50
131 Todd Heap .15 .40
132 Bobby Shaw .15 .40
133 Ricky Proehl .20 .50
134 John Abraham .20 .50
135 T.J. Houshmandzadeh .15 .40
136 Brian Urlacher .25 .60
137 Darren Woodson .20 .50
138 Steve Beuerlein .20 .50
139 Cory Schlesinger .15 .40
140 Ahman Green .20 .50
141 Jabar Gaffney .15 .40
142 Eddie Drummond .15 .40
143 Stacey Mack .15 .40
144 Johnnie Morton .20 .50
145 Chris Chambers .15 .40
146 Jim Kleinsasser .15 .40
147 Tebucky Jones .15 .40
148 Marcus Pollard .15 .40
149 Tony Brackens .15 .40
150 Chad Pennington .15 .40
151 Kevin Faulk .15 .40
152 Michael Lewis .15 .40
153 Mark Bruener .15 .40
154 Tim Dwight .15 .40
155 Jerry Rice .50 1.25
156 Trent Dilfer .15 .40
157 Jon Ritchie .15 .40
158 Michael Pittman .15 .40
159 Lamar Gordon .15 .40
160 Rod Gardner .15 .40
161 Ken Dilger .15 .40
162 Doug Johnson .15 .40
163 Peter Boulware .20 .50
164 Jevon Kearse .15 .40
165 Julius Peppers .25 .60
166 Chris Chandler .20 .50
167 Lorenzo Neal .15 .40
168 Kevin Johnson .15 .40
169 Kevin Hardy .15 .40
170 KaRon Coleman .15 .40
171 James Stewart .15 .40
172 Tony Fisher .15 .40
173 Billy Miller .15 .40
174 Phillip Crosby .15 .40
175 Priest Holmes .15 .40
176 Elvis Joseph .15 .40
177 Bryan Gilmore .15 .40
178 D'Wayne Bates .15 .40
179 Quincy Carter .15 .40
180 Joe Horn .15 .40
181 Anthony Henry .15 .40
182 Anthony Becht .15 .40
183 Mike Peterson .15 .40
184 James Thrash .15 .40
185 Jerome Bettis .25 .60
186 Marcellus Wiley .15 .40
187 Tim Rattay .15 .40
188 Maurice Morris .15 .40
189 Jason Taylor .20 .50
190 Keyshawn Johnson .25 .60
191 John Simon .15 .40
192 Fred Smoot .15 .40
193 Wendell Bryant .15 .40
194 Brandon Stokley .15 .40
195 Kurt Warner .20 .50
196 Steve Smith .25 .60
197 Dez White .15 .40
198 Jim Miller .15 .40
199 Robert Griffith .15 .40
200 Michael Vick .20 .50
201 Antonio Bryant .15 .40
202 Laveranues Coles .15 .40
203 Kalimba Edwards .15 .40
204 Bubba Franks .20 .50
205 David Carr .15 .40
206 Dwight Freeney .15 .40
207 Eric Johnson .20 .50
208 Reggie Tongue .15 .40
209 Cam Cleeland .15 .40
210 Michael Bennett .15 .40
211 Antowain Smith .20 .50
212 Warren Sapp .20 .50
213 Ike Hilliard .15 .40
214 Olandis Gary .15 .40
215 Tim Brown .25 .60
216 Kevin Dyson .15 .40
217 Eddie Kennison .15 .40
218 Junior Seau .20 .50
219 Donnie Edwards .15 .40
220 Shaun Alexander .15 .40
221 Terrence Wilkins .15 .40
222 Garrison Hearst .15 .40
223 Keith Bulluck .15 .40
224 Zeron Flemister .15 .40
225 Jake Plummer .15 .40
226 Chad Johnson .15 .40
227 Travis Taylor .15 .40
228 Josh Reed .15 .40
229 James Farrior .15 .40
230 Marty Booker .15 .40
231 Todd Pinkston .15 .40
232 Dennis Northcutt .15 .40
233 Troy Hambrick .15 .40
234 Roland Williams .15 .40
235 Bill Schroeder .15 .40
236 Javon Walker .20 .50
237 Kevin Swayne .15 .40
238 Dominic Rhodes .15 .40
239 David Garrard .15 .40
240 Mike Maslowski RC .15 .40
241 Travis Minor .15 .40
242 Terry Glenn .20 .50
243 Deion Branch .15 .40
244 Adrian Peterson .15 .40
245 Tiki Barber .20 .50
246 Ray Lewis .25 .60
247 Marques Tuiasosopo .15 .40
248 Chad Lewis .20 .50
249 Takeo Spikes .15 .40
250 LaDainian Tomlinson .25 .60
251 Stephen Davis .15 .40
252 Koren Robinson .20 .50
253 Daylon McCutcheon .15 .40
254 Rob Johnson .20 .50
255 Donovan McNabb .20 .50
256 Derrius Thompson .15 .40
257 Marcel Shipp .15 .40
258 Keith Brooking .20 .50
259 Chris McAlister .20 .50
260 Eric Moulds .15 .40
261 Amos Zereoue .15 .40
262 Drew Brees .25 .60
263 Jon Kitna .15 .40
264 Brad Johnson .20 .50
265 Emmitt Smith .40 1.00
266 Trevor Pryce .20 .50
267 Mike McMahon .15 .40
268 Patrick Ramsey .20 .50
269 Jonathan Wells .15 .40
270 Mark Brunell .20 .50
271 Marc Boerigter .15 .40
272 Rob Konrad .15 .40
273 Derrick Alexander .15 .40
274 Joey Galloway .20 .50
275 Peyton Manning .60 1.50
276 Najeh Davenport .15 .40
277 Jesse Palmer .15 .40
278 LaMont Jordan .20 .50
279 Ernie Conwell .15 .40
280 Hines Ward .20 .50
281 Freddie Mitchell .20 .50
282 Curtis Conway .15 .40
283 Cedrick Wilson .20 .50
284 Troy Brown .15 .40
285 Torry Holt .20 .50
286 Mike Alstott .20 .50
287 Frank Wycheck .15 .40
288 Jeremiah Trotter .20 .50
289 Tyrone Wheatley .20 .50
290 David Boston .15 .40
291 Jay Fiedler .15 .40
292 Troy Walters .15 .40
293 Warrick Holdman .15 .40
294 Peter Warrick .15 .40
295 Tim Couch .15 .40
296 Aaron Glenn .15 .40
297 Deuce McAllister .20 .50
298 Michael Strahan .20 .50
299 Tom Brady 1.00 2.50
300 Brett Favre .50 1.25
301 Isaac Bruce .25 .60
302 Jimmy Smith .20 .50
303 Dante Hall .15 .40
304 James McKnight .15 .40
305 Daunte Culpepper .20 .50
306 Lawyer Milloy .15 .40
307 Jerome Pathon .15 .40
308 Steve McNair .20 .50
309 Vinny Testaverde .20 .50
310 Tommy Maddox .15 .40
311 Amani Toomer .15 .40
312 Aaron Brooks .15 .40
313 Gus Frerotte .15 .40
314 Kevan Barlow .15 .40
315 Matt Hasselbeck .15 .40
316 Clinton Portis .20 .50
317 Keenan McCardell .20 .50
318 Zach Thomas .20 .50
319 Curtis Martin .20 .50
320 Jamal Lewis .20 .50
321 T.J. Duckett .15 .40
322 Jerry Porter .15 .40
323 Randy Moss .20 .50
324 Rosevelt Colvin .15 .40
325 Corey Dillon .15 .40
326 Kelly Holcomb .15 .40
327 Josh McCown .20 .50
328 Ed McCaffrey .20 .50
329 Mikhael Ricks .15 .40
330 Donald Driver .20 .50
331 Darling/Thompson/McKinnon .15 .40
332 Hall/Carpenter/Buchanon .15 .40
333 Thomas/Weaver/Gregg RC .15 .40
334 Winfield/Wire/Clements .20 .50
335 Morgan/Fields/Witherspoon .20 .50
336 Brown/Robinson RC/Daniels .15 .40
337 Powell RC/Thornton/Williams RC .15 .40
338 Taylor RC/Little/Bentley .15 .40
339 Ekuban/Ellis/Myers .25 .60
340 Gard/Dalton RC/Berry RC .30 .75
341 Green/Curry RC/Holmes .15 .40
342 Hunt RC/KGB/Walker RC .15 .40
343 Walker/Deloach RC/Payne .15 .40
344 Bratzke/Washington/Morris .15 .40
345 Henderson/Coleman/Stroud .20 .50
346 Hicks/Browning RC/Sims .15 .40
347 A.Ogunleye RC/Chester RC .75 2.00
348 Robbins/Mixon/Johnstone .20 .50
349 Phifer/Johnson/Bruschi .20 .50
350 Grant/Chase RC/Howard .20 .50
351 Short/Jones RC/Barrow .25 .60
352 Jones/Lewis/Cowart .15 .40
353 Barton/Parrella/Harris .20 .50
354 Whiting/Simon/Walker .20 .50
355 Smith/Hamp/von Oel .40 1.00
356 Williams RC/Fisk/Johnson .15 .40
357 Smith/Ulbrich/Peterson .15 .40
358 Cochran RC/Eaton/Randle .20 .50
359 Lewis/Wistrom/Little .15 .40
360 Rudd/Spires/Quarles RC .15 .40
361 Haynesworth/Carter/Smith .25 .60
362 Smith/Armstead/Upshaw .20 .50
363 Ad.Wilson/Dex.Jackson RC .15 .40
364 F.Wakefield/K.Vanden .15 .40
365 K.Kasper/J.McAddley .15 .40
366 B.Smith/P.Kerney .15 .40
367 M.Jenkins/T.Taylor .15 .40
368 C.Draft/M.Stewart .15 .40
369 J.Hunter/R.Johnson .15 .40
370 C.Fuller/E.Reed .15 .40
371 A.Schobel/J.Posey RC .20 .50
372 P.Williams/S.Adams .20 .50
373 D.Grant/M.Minter .15 .40
374 B.Buckner/K.Jenkins .15 .40
375 R.Howard RC/T.Cousin RC .15 .40
376 M.Brown/M.Green .15 .40
377 J.Azumah/R.W.McQuarters .15 .40
378 B.Simmons/S.Foley .15 .40
379 A.Hawkins/J.Burris .15 .40
380 Jo.Armour RC/M.Manuel .15 .40
381 G.Warren/D.Roye .15 .40
382 C.Brown/K.Lang .15 .40
383 D.Ross/M.Edwards .15 .40
384 A.Singleton RC/D.Nguyen .20 .50
385 A.Wilson/J.Mobley .15 .40
386 D.O'Neal/K.Kennedy .15 .40
387 L.Elliss/S.Rogers .15 .40
388 C.Cash/D.Bly .15 .40
389 B.Walker/C.Harris .15 .40
390 H.Navies RC/N.Diggs .15 .40
391 A.Harris/M.McKenzie .20 .50
392 C.Clemons/J.Foreman .15 .40
393 E.Brown/M.Stevens .15 .40
394 B.Scioli/L.Tripplett .15 .40
395 D.Macklin/W.Harris .15 .40
396 A.Ayodele/H.Douglas .15 .40
397 F.Bryant/J.Craft RC .15 .40
398 D.Darius/M.McCree .15 .40
399 S.Fujita/S.Barber .15 .40
400 E.Warfield RC/W.Bartee .20 .50
401 G.Wesley/J.Woods .15 .40
402 P.Surtain/S.Madison .15 .40
403 B.Marion/S.Knight .15 .40
404 G.Biekert/H.Crockett .15 .40
405 C.Claiborne/C.Hovan .15 .40
406 C.Chavous/K.Irvin .15 .40
407 C.Fauria/D.Graham .15 .40
408 O.Smith/R.Harrison .20 .50
409 A.Pleasant/R.Seymour .15 .40
410 D.Smith/S.Hodge .15 .40
411 A.Ambrose/D.Carter .15 .40
412 M.Mitchell/D.Rodgers .15 .40
413 W.Allen/W.Peterson .20 .50
414 C.Griffin/K.Hamilton .15 .40
415 O.Stoutmire/S.Williams .15 .40
416 A.Beasley/D.Abraham .20 .50
417 J.McGraw/S.Garnes .15 .40
418 C.Woodson/T.Duchenon .25 .60
419 T.Bryant/T.Armstrong .15 .40
420 B.Taylor/T.Vincent .20 .50
421 C.Emmons/N.Wayne .15 .40
422 B.Alexander/C.Hope .15 .40
423 J.Porter/K.Bell .25 .60
424 C.Scott/D.Washington .15 .40
425 B.Leber/R.McNeil .15 .40
426 Q.Jammer/T.Cody .15 .40
427 A.Plummer/J.Webster .15 .40
428 T.Parrish/Z.Bronson .15 .40
429 I.Mili/J.Stevens .20 .50
430 K.Lucas/S.Springs .15 .40
431 C.Brown/O.Huff .15 .40
432 J.Duncan/T.Polley .15 .40
433 A.Williams/T.Fisher .20 .50
434 B.Kelly/R.Barber .15 .40
435 A.Stecker/K.Williams .15 .40
436 D.Bennett/J.McCareins .20 .50
437 L.Schulters/T.Williams .15 .40
438 A.Dyson/S.Rolle .20 .50
439 I.Ohalete/M.Bowen .15 .40
440 B.Noble/D.Wilkinson .20 .50
441 Charles Rogers RC .40 1.00
442 Jimmy Kennedy RC .40 1.00
443 Kelley Washington RC .30 .75
444 Trent Smith RC .40 1.00
445 Rashean Mathis RC .30 .75
446 Brian St.Pierre RC .30 .75
447 Bethel Johnson RC .30 .75
448 Alonzo Jackson RC .30 .75
449 Arnaz Battle RC .50 1.25
450 Carson Palmer RC .60 1.50
451 Michael Haynes RC .30 .75
452 LaBrandon Toefield RC .30 .75
453 Earnest Graham RC .50 1.25
454 Walter Young RC .30 .75
455 Terry Pierce RC .30 .75
456 Talman Gardner RC .30 .75
457 J.T. Wall RC .30 .75
458 DeWayne Robertson RC .40 1.00
459 Bradie James RC .50 1.25
460 Andre Johnson RC .75 2.00
461 Bobby Wade RC .40 1.00
462 Chris Davis RC .40 1.00
463 Kliff Kingsbury RC .50 1.25
464 Osi Umenyiora RC .60 1.50
465 Domanick Davis RC .40 1.00
466 Sam Aiken RC .40 1.00
467 Ty Warren RC .40 1.00
468 Terence Newman RC .60 1.50
469 Zuriel Smith RC .30 .75
470 Willis McGahee RC .40 1.00
471 David Kircus RC .40 1.00
472 Billy McMullen RC .30 .75
473 Antwoine Sanders RC .30 .75
474 Adrian Madise RC .30 .75
475 Byron Leftwich RC .40 1.00
476 Justin Gage RC .40 1.00
477 Jason Witten RC 1.25 3.00
478 Lee Suggs RC .30 .75
479 Kareem Kelly RC .30 .75
480 Rex Grossman RC .40 1.00
481 Nate Burleson RC .40 1.00
482 Chris Brown RC .30 .75
483 Julian Battle RC .40 1.00
484 Carl Ford RC .30 .75
485 Angelo Crowell RC .40 1.00
486 Bennie Joppru RC .30 .75
487 Aaron Walker RC .40 1.00
488 Brandon Green RC .30 .75
489 L.J. Smith RC .50 1.25
490 Ken Dorsey RC .40 1.00
491 Eugene Wilson RC .50 1.25
492 Chaun Thompson RC .30 .75
493 Kevin Curtis RC .50 1.25
494 Marcus Trufant RC .40 1.00
495 Andrew Williams RC .30 .75
496 Visanthe Shiancoe RC .50 1.25
497 Terrence Edwards RC .30 .75
498 Rien Long RC .30 .75
499 Nick Barnett RC .50 1.25
500 Larry Johnson RC .40 1.00
501 Ken Hamlin RC .50 1.25
502 Johnathan Sullivan RC .30 .75
503 Jeremi Johnson RC .30 .75
504 William Joseph RC .30 .75
505 Boss Bailey RC .40 1.00
506 Anquan Boldin RC .50 1.25
507 Dave Ragone RC .30 .75
508 DeJuan Groce RC .30 .75
509 Rashad Moore RC .30 .75
510 Mike Doss RC .40 1.00
511 Kenny Peterson RC .40 1.00
512 Justin Griffith RC .40 1.00
513 Jordan Gross RC .30 .75
514 Terrence Holt RC .30 .75
515 Seneca Wallace RC .40 1.00
516 Ovie Mughelli RC .30 .75
517 Jerome McDougle RC .30 .75
518 Kevin Williams RC .50 1.25
519 Musa Smith RC .30 .75
520 Teyo Johnson RC .40 1.00
521 Victor Hobson RC .30 .75
522 Cory Redding RC .40 1.00
523 Cecil Sapp RC .30 .75
524 Brandon Lloyd RC .50 1.25
525 Chris Simms RC .30 .75
526 Artose Pinner RC .30 .75
527 DeWayne White RC .30 .75
528 Doug Gabriel RC .40 1.00
529 Calvin Pace RC .30 .75
530 Onterrio Smith RC .30 .75
531 Terrell Suggs RC .40 1.00
532 Ronald Bellamy RC .40 1.00
533 Jimmy Wilkerson RC .40 1.00
534 Travis Anglin RC .30 .75
535 Tyrone Calico RC .30 .75
536 Keenan Howry RC .30 .75
537 Gibran Hamdan RC .30 .75
538 Bryant Johnson RC .50 1.25
539 Brad Banks RC .40 1.00
540 Justin Fargas RC .50 1.25
541 B.J. Askew RC .40 1.00
542 J.R. Tolver RC .40 1.00
543 Tully Banta-Cain RC .50 1.25
544 Shaun McDonald RC .40 1.00
545 Taylor Jacobs RC .30 .75
546 Ricky Manning RC .40 1.00
547 Dallas Clark RC .50 1.25
548 Juston Wood RC .30 .75
549 Andre Woolfolk RC .30 .75
550 Kyle Boller RC .30 .75
CL1 Checklist Card 1 .02 .10
CL2 Checklist Card 2 .02 .10
CL3 Checklist Card 3 .02 .10
CL4 Checklist Card 4 .02 .10

2003 Topps Total Silver

*VETS 1-440: 1X TO 2.5X BASIC CARDS
*ROOKIES 441-550: .8X TO 2X
ONE SILVER PER PACK

2003 Topps Total Award Winners

COMPLETE SET (20) 7.50 20.00
STATED ODDS 1:6
AW1 Rich Gannon .50 1.25
AW2 Derrick Brooks .40 1.00
AW3 Clinton Portis .40 1.00
AW4 Julius Peppers .60 1.50
AW5 Priest Holmes .40 1.00
AW6 Kerry Collins .40 1.00
AW7 Tom Brady 2.50 6.00
AW8 Brett Favre 1.25 3.00
AW9 Chad Pennington .40 1.00
AW10 Ricky Williams .50 1.25
AW11 Deuce Mcallister .50 1.25
AW12 Shaun Alexander .40 1.00
AW13 Marvin Harrison .50 1.25
AW14 Randy Moss .50 1.25
AW15 Terrell Owens .50 1.25
AW16 Hines Ward .50 1.25
AW17 Jason Taylor .50 1.25
AW18 Brian Urlacher .60 1.50
AW19 Rod Woodson .50 1.25
AW20 Brian Kelly .40 1.00

2003 Topps Total Signatures

This set features authentic player autographs from seven NFL superstars. Groups A and B were inserted 1:2046 packs. Group C was inserted 1:387 packs. Group D was inserted 1:268 packs. The overall stated odds were 1:185.

GROUP A, B STATED ODDS 1:2046
GROUP C STATED ODDS 1:387
GROUP D STATED ODDS 1:268
OVERALL STATED ODDS 1:185
TSCJ Chad Johnson C 6.00 15.00
TSDN Dennis Northcutt B 6.00 15.00
TSJJ Joe Jurevicius A 8.00 20.00
TSJT Jason Taylor A 20.00 40.00
TSLB Ladell Betts D 6.00 15.00
TSMB Marc Boerigter D 6.00 15.00
TSTB Todd Bouman D 6.00 15.00

2003 Topps Total Team Checklists

Randomly inserted into packs, this set features player images on the front, and a team checklist on the back.

COMPLETE SET (32) 10.00 25.00
TC1 Emmitt Smith .60 1.50
TC2 Michael Vick .30 .75
TC3 Ray Lewis .40 1.00
TC4 Drew Bledsoe .30 .75
TC5 Stephen Davis .25 .60
TC6 Brian Urlacher .40 1.00
TC7 Corey Dillon .25 .60
TC8 Tim Couch .25 .60
TC9 Chad Hutchinson .40 1.00
TC10 Clinton Portis .25 .60
TC11 Joey Harrington .25 .60
TC12 Brett Favre .75 2.00
TC13 David Carr .25 .60
TC14 Peyton Manning 1.00 2.50
TC15 Jimmy Smith .30 .75
TC16 Priest Holmes .25 .60
TC17 Ricky Williams .30 .75
TC18 Randy Moss .30 .75
TC19 Tom Brady 1.50 4.00
TC20 Deuce Mcallister .30 .75
TC21 Jeremy Shockey .25 .60
TC22 Chad Pennington .25 .60
TC23 Rich Gannon .30 .75
TC24 Donovan Mcnabb .30 .75
TC25 Hines Ward .30 .75
TC26 LaDainian Tomlinson .40 1.00
TC27 Terrell Owens .30 .75
TC28 Shaun Alexander .25 .60
TC29 Marshall Faulk .30 .75
TC30 Warren Sapp .30 .75
TC31 Steve Mcnair .30 .75
TC32 Patrick Ramsey .30 .75

2003 Topps Total Total Production

COMPLETE SET (10) 5.00 12.00
STATED ODDDS 1:12
TP1 Tom Brady 2.50 6.00
TP2 Peyton Manning 1.50 4.00
TP3 Brett Favre 1.25 3.00
TP4 Priest Holmes .40 1.00
TP5 Shaun Alexander .40 1.00
TP6 Ricky Williams .50 1.25
TP7 Clinton Portis .40 1.00
TP8 Terrell Owens .50 1.25
TP9 Hines Ward .50 1.25
TP10 Marvin Harrison .50 1.25

2003 Topps Total Total Topps

COMPLETE SET (20) 10.00 25.00
STATED ODDS 1:6
TT1 Rich Gannon .50 1.25
TT2 Peyton Manning 1.50 4.00
TT3 Brett Favre 1.25 3.00
TT4 Steve McNair .50 1.25
TT5 Chad Pennington .40 1.00
TT6 Michael Vick .50 1.25
TT7 Ricky Williams .40 1.00
TT8 Priest Holmes .40 1.00
TT9 LaDainian Tomlinson .60 1.50
TT10 Clinton Portis .40 1.00
TT11 Travis Henry .40 1.00
TT12 Deuce McAllister .50 1.25
TT13 Marvin Harrison .50 1.25
TT14 Jerry Rice 1.25 3.00
TT15 Randy Moss .50 1.25
TT16 Hines Ward .50 1.25
TT17 Terrell Owens .50 1.25
TT18 Derrick Brooks .40 1.00
TT19 Brian Urlacher .60 1.50
TT20 Jason Taylor .50 1.25

2004 Topps Total

Topps Total was initially released in mid-August 2004. The base set consists of 440-cards including 110-rookies making it the largest base set of the year. Hobby boxes contained 36-packs of 10-cards and carried an S.R.P. of $1 per pack. Two parallel sets and a variety of inserts can be found seeded in packs.

COMPLETE SET (440) 40.00 80.00
1 Donovan McNabb .25 .60
2 Zach Thomas .25 .60
3 Randy Moss .25 .60
4 Kerry Collins .20 .50
5 Hines Ward .25 .60
6 Tyrone Calico .25 .60
7 Patrick Ramsey .25 .60
8 Jeff Garcia .20 .50
9 Aveion Cason .20 .50
10 Stephen Davis .20 .50
11 Marcel Shipp .20 .50
12 T.J. Duckett .20 .50
13 Chris McAlister .20 .50
14 Peter Warrick .20 .50
15 Ahman Green .25 .60
16 Deion Branch .20 .50
17 David Boston .20 .50
18 Wayne Chrebet .20 .50
19 Michael Strahan .25 .60
20 Arnaz Battle .25 .60
21 Darrell Jackson .25 .60
22 Chris Chandler .25 .60
23 Charlie Garner .25 .60
24 James Thrash .20 .50
25 LaDainian Tomlinson .30 .75
26 Jerry Porter .20 .50
27 Jerome Pathon .20 .50
28 Jerome Bettis .30 .75
29 Eddie George .25 .60
30 Jamal Lewis .25 .60
31 Ricky Proehl .25 .60
32 Josh Reed .20 .50
33 David Terrell .20 .50
34 Antonio Bryant .25 .60
35 Domanick Davis .20 .50
36 Artose Pinner .20 .50
37 Jed Weaver .20 .50
38 Johnnie Morton .25 .60
39 Troy Edwards .20 .50
40 Marvin Harrison .25 .60
41 Chris Hovan .20 .50
42 Boo Williams .20 .50
43 Ike Hilliard .20 .50
44 Sam Cowart .20 .50
45 Shaun Alexander .20 .50
46 Freddie Mitchell .20 .50
47 Garrison Hearst .20 .50
48 Joe Jurevicius .20 .50
49 Freddie Jones .20 .50
50 Michael Vick .25 .60
51 Mike Rucker .20 .50
52 Carson Palmer .25 .60
53 Az-Zahir Hakim .20 .50
54 Billy Miller .20 .50
55 Chad Pennington .20 .50
56 Charles Woodson .30 .75
57 Andre Carter .20 .50
58 Maurice Morris .25 .60
59 Leonard Little .20 .50
60 Travis Henry .20 .50
61 Thomas Jones .20 .50
62 Dennis Northcutt .20 .50
63 Quentin Griffin .20 .50
64 Joey Harrington .20 .50
65 Edgerrin James .25 .60
66 Cortez Hankton .20 .50
67 Jason Taylor .25 .60
68 Eddie Kennison .25 .60
69 Ty Law .30 .75
70 Aaron Brooks .25 .60
71 Antonio Gates .30 .75
72 Antwaan Randle El .25 .60
73 Kevan Barlow .20 .50
74 Chris Brown .20 .50
75 Clinton Portis .25 .60
76 Rod Gardner .20 .50
77 Isaac Bruce .30 .75
78 Mike Alstott .30 .75
79 Brian Westbrook .25 .60
80 Amani Toomer .20 .50
81 Justin Fargas .25 .60
82 Michael Bennett .25 .60
83 Dante Hall .20 .50
84 Marcus Pollard .20 .50
85 Fred Taylor .20 .50
86 Tai Streets .20 .50
87 Robert Ferguson .20 .50
88 Roy Williams S .25 .60
89 Lee Suggs .25 .60
90 Chad Johnson .25 .60
91 DeShaun Foster .25 .60
92 Alge Crumpler .25 .60
93 Travis Taylor .20 .50
94 London Fletcher .25 .60
95 Priest Holmes .25 .60
96 A.J. Feeley .20 .50
97 Kevin Faulk .20 .50
98 Shaun Ellis .20 .50
99 Tim Dwight .20 .50
100 Peyton Manning .75 2.00
101 Dane Looker .20 .50
102 Mark Brunell .25 .60
103 Bryant Johnson .20 .50
104 Kelley Washington .20 .50
105 Rex Grossman .25 .60
106 William Green .20 .50
107 Keyshawn Johnson .25 .60
108 Trevor Pryce .20 .50
109 Donald Driver .25 .60
110 David Carr .20 .50
111 Marcus Robinson .20 .50
112 Justin McCareins .20 .50
113 Tim Brown .30 .75
114 James Farrior .20 .50
115 Deuce McAllister .25 .60
116 Simeon Rice .20 .50
117 Koren Robinson .25 .60
118 Kassim Osgood .20 .50
119 Tim Rattay .20 .50
120 Laveranues Coles .25 .60
121 Brian Finneran .20 .50
122 Todd Heap .20 .50
123 Bobby Shaw .20 .50
124 Anthony Thomas .25 .60
125 Brett Favre .60 1.50
126 Dwight Freeney .20 .50
127 Randy McMichael .20 .50
128 David Givens .20 .50
129 Rich Gannon .20 .50
130 Tiki Barber .25 .60
131 Terrell Owens .25 .60
132 Drew Bennett .20 .50
133 Shawn Bryson .20 .50
134 Jabar Gaffney .20 .50
135 Jake Delhomme .25 .60
136 Warrick Dunn .20 .50
137 Brandon Lloyd .20 .50
138 Brad Johnson .20 .50
139 Jon Kitna .20 .50
140 Marshall Faulk .25 .60
141 Javon Walker .20 .50
142 Nate Burleson .20 .50
143 Jimmy Smith .25 .60
144 Adewale Ogunleye .20 .50
145 Trent Green .20 .50
146 Richard Seymour .20 .50
147 Donte' Stallworth .20 .50
148 Curtis Martin .25 .60
149 Todd Pinkston .20 .50
150 Steve McNair .25 .60
151 Josh McCown .25 .60
152 Ray Lewis .30 .75
153 Muhsin Muhammad .20 .50
154 Quincy Morgan .20 .50
155 Jake Plummer .20 .50
156 Jason Witten .20 .50
157 Dallas Clark .20 .50
158 Onterrio Smith .20 .50
159 Jeremy Shockey .25 .60
160 Ricky Williams .25 .60
161 Jevon Kearse .20 .50
162 Plaxico Burress .20 .50
163 Drew Brees .30 .75
164 Bobby Engram .20 .50
165 Torry Holt .25 .60
166 Ladell Betts .20 .50
167 Kelly Holcomb .20 .50
168 Vinny Testaverde .20 .50
169 Marty Booker .20 .50
170 Rudi Johnson .20 .50
171 Andra Davis .20 .50
172 Kurt Warner .25 .60
173 Troy Brown .20 .50
174 Jerry Rice .60 1.50
175 Daunte Culpepper .25 .60
176 Darren Sharper .20 .50
177 Charles Rogers .20 .50
178 Ashley Lelie .20 .50
179 Correll Buckhalter .20 .50
180 Anquan Boldin .25 .60
181 Terrell Suggs .25 .60
182 Reggie Wayne .25 .60
183 Duce Staley .20 .50
184 Donnie Edwards .20 .50
185 Joe Horn .20 .50
186 LaVar Arrington .20 .50
187 Keenan McCardell .20 .50
188 Cedrick Wilson .20 .50
189 Bubba Franks .20 .50
190 Santana Moss .25 .60
191 Peerless Price .20 .50
192 Kyle Boller .20 .50
193 Julius Peppers .25 .60
194 Drew Bledsoe .25 .60
195 Marc Bulger .20 .50
196 Brian Urlacher .30 .75
197 Andre' Davis .20 .50
198 Terry Glenn .20 .50
199 Champ Bailey .20 .50
200 Tom Brady 1.25 3.00
201 Chris Chambers .20 .50
202 Tommy Maddox .20 .50
203 Derrick Brooks .25 .60
204 Corey Dillon .20 .50
205 Matt Hasselbeck .20 .50
206 Keith Brooking .20 .50
207 Steve Smith .30 .75
208 Tony Gonzalez .25 .60
209 Joey Galloway .25 .60
210 Derrick Mason .20 .50
211 Quincy Carter .20 .50
212 Rod Smith .25 .60
213 Andre Johnson .25 .60
214 Rod Woodson .25 .60
215 Byron Leftwich .20 .50
216 Kevin Dyson .20 .50
217 Keith Bulluck .20 .50
218 Eric Moulds .20 .50
219 Jamie Sharper .20 .50
220 Takeo Spikes .20 .50
221 C.Pace/F.Wakefield .20 .50
222 B.Smith/P.Kerney .25 .60
223 E.Reed/G.Baxter .25 .60
224 A.Schobel/J.Posey .20 .50
225 K.Jenkins/B.Buckner .25 .60
226 J.Smith/D.Clemons .25 .60
227 M.Haynes/B.Robinson .20 .50
228 C.Brown/G.Warren .25 .60
229 T.Newman/D.Woodson .25 .60
230 R.Johnson/M.Fatafehi .20 .50
231 R.Porcher/J.Hall RC .30 .75
232 K.Gbaja-Biamila/C.Hunt .20 .50
233 A.Glenn/M.Coleman .25 .60
234 N.Harper RC/J.Jefferson .25 .60
235 H.Douglas/T.Brackens .20 .50
236 V.Holliday/E.Hicks .20 .50
237 S.Knight/A.Freeman .20 .50
238 S.Martin/N.Rogers .20 .50
239 R.Colvin/W.McGinest .25 .60
240 O.Stoutmire/S.Williams .20 .50
241 E.Barton/V.Hobson .20 .50
242 W.Sapp/T.Washington .25 .60
243 C.Simon/D.Walker .25 .60
244 T.Polamalu/M.Logan 1.00 2.50
245 J.Williams/A.Dingle RC .20 .50
246 B.Young/B.Whiting .25 .60
247 K.Hamlin/D.Robinson RC .20 .50
248 D.Lewis/R.Pickett .20 .50
249 A.McFarland/G.Spires .20 .50
250 A.Haynesworth/R.Long .20 .50
251 I.Ohalete/M.Bowen .20 .50
252 B.Berry/K.King .25 .60
253 E.Johnson/E.Jasper .20 .50
254 C.Tillman/J.Azumah .25 .60
255 M.Wiley/L.Glover .25 .60
256 S.Rogers/D.Wilkinson .25 .60
257 G.Walker/R.Smith .20 .50
258 M.Doss/I.Bashir .25 .60
259 M.Stroud/J.Henderson .20 .50
260 R.Sims/J.Browning .25 .60
261 J.Seau/M.Greenwood .30 .75
262 K.Williams/K.Mixon .20 .50
263 T.Warren/K.Traylor .20 .50
264 W.Allen/W.Peterson .20 .50
265 D.Barrett/R.Tongue .20 .50
266 P.Buchanon/D.Gibson .25 .60
267 L.Sheppard/S.Brown .20 .50
268 B.Taylor/M.Trufant .25 .60
269 M.Washington/M.Barrow .20 .50
270 C.Draft/M.Stewart .20 .50
271 M.Brown/M.Green .20 .50
272 E.Brown/M.McCree .20 .50
273 P.Surtain/S.Madison .20 .50
274 B.Dawkins/M.Lewis .20 .50
275 S.Springs/F.Smoot .20 .50
276 McKinnon/Fisher/Thompson .20 .50
277 Webster/McBride RC/Scott RC .30 .75
278 Boulware/Hartwell/Thomas .20 .50
279 Vincent/Milloy/Clements .25 .60
280 Witherspoon/Morgan/Fields .25 .60
281 Simmons/Hardy/Webster .25 .60
282 Odom RC/Brown/Briggs 1.00 2.50
283 Holdman/Thompson/Lang .20 .50
284 Nguyen/Coakley/Singleton .20 .50
285 Wilson/Spragan RC/Holland .20 .50
286 Holmes/J.Davis RC/Bailey .20 .50
287 Barnett/Diggs/Navies .20 .50
288 Foreman/Peek/Wong .20 .50
289 Brock RC/Reagor/Tripplett .25 .60
290 Ayodele/Favors/Peterson .20 .50
291 Barber/Maslowsk/Fujita .20 .50
292 Claiborne/Henderson/Nattiel .25 .60
293 Bruschi/Phifer/Vrabel .30 .75
294 Grant/Howard/Sullivan .20 .50
295 Robbins/Joseph/Umenyiora .20 .50
296 Abra/Rober/Fergus.RC .50 1.25
297 Harris/Rudd/Brayton .25 .60
298 Simoneau/Wayne/Jones .20 .50
299 Porter/Bell/Haggans RC .40 1.00
300 Jammer/Davis/Florence .20 .50
301 Peterson/Ulbrich/Smith .25 .60
302 Simmons/Huff/Brown .20 .50
303 Tinoisamoa/Polley/Thomas .20 .50
304 Quarles/Wyms/Nece .20 .50
305 Carter/Hall/Simon .20 .50
306 Griffin/Daniels/Wynn .20 .50
307 Jackson/Wilson/Macklin .20 .50
308 Gregg/Douglas/Weaver .20 .50
309 Williams/Denney/Adams .25 .60
310 Hawkins/Minter/Manning .20 .50
311 James/Herring/Beckett .20 .50
312 Griffith/Little/Henry .20 .50
313 Lynch/Ferg.RC/Hern.RC .25 .60
314 Bly/Marion/Bryant .20 .50
315 Harris/Roman/McKenzie .25 .60
316 Thorn/Morris/Brackett RC .30 .75
317 Mathis/Darius/Bolden RC .20 .50
318 Warfield/Wesley/Woods .20 .50
319 Winfield/Russell RC/Chavous .25 .60
320 Harrison/Wilson/Poole .20 .50
321 Rodgers/Ruff/Hodge .20 .50
322 Green/Greisen/Emmons .20 .50
323 Von Oelhoffen/Smith/Hampton .20 .50
324 Godfrey/Foley/Leber .20 .50
325 Plummer/Parrish/Rumph .20 .50
326 Okeafor/Wistrom/Moore .25 .60
327 Archuleta/Williams/Butler .20 .50
328 Barber/Smith/Phillips .20 .50
329 Dyson/Schulters/Williams .20 .50
330 Thomas/Bellamy/Jones .20 .50
331 Philip Rivers RC 1.25 3.00
332 Dwan Edwards RC .40 1.00
333 Ben Watson RC .50 1.25
334 Karlos Dansby RC .50 1.25
335 Cedric Cobbs RC .40 1.00
336 Chris Perry RC .40 1.00
337 Darius Watts RC .40 1.00
338 Ricardo Colclough RC .40 1.00
339 Derrick Hamilton RC .40 1.00
340 Devard Darling RC .40 1.00
341 Daryl Smith RC .40 1.00
342 Luke McCown RC .40 1.00
343 Dunta Robinson RC .40 1.00
344 Keith Smith RC .40 1.00
345 Ben Hartsock RC .40 1.00
346 J.P. Losman RC .40 1.00
347 Chris Cooley RC .50 1.25
348 Keary Colbert RC .40 1.00
349 Tommie Harris RC .50 1.25
350 Eli Manning RC 3.00 8.00
351 Kevin Jones RC .50 1.25
352 Lee Evans RC .60 1.50
353 D.J. Williams RC .60 1.50
354 Ben Troupe RC .40 1.00
355 Mewelde Moore RC .50 1.25
356 Michael Clayton RC .50 1.25
357 Michael Jenkins RC .40 1.00
358 Adimchinobe Echemandu RC .50 1.25
359 Rashaun Woods RC .40 1.00
360 Bernard Berrian RC .40 1.00
361 Carlos Francis RC .40 1.00
362 Roy Williams RC .40 1.00
363 Sean Taylor RC 2.50 6.00
364 Steven Jackson RC .60 1.50
365 Tatum Bell RC .40 1.00
366 Jonathan Vilma RC .50 1.25
367 Derrick Strait RC .40 1.00
368 Andy Hall RC .40 1.00
369 Jason Babin RC .60 1.50
370 Will Smith RC .50 1.25
371 Kenechi Udeze RC .50 1.25
372 Vince Wilfork RC .60 1.50
373 Ahmad Carroll RC .40 1.00
374 Marquise Hill RC .40 1.00
375 Ben Roethlisberger RC 3.00 8.00
376 Chris Gamble RC .40 1.00
377 Junior Siavii RC .40 1.00
378 Teddy Lehman RC .40 1.00
379 Antwan Odom RC .40 1.00
380 DeAngelo Hall RC .60 1.50
381 Nathan Vasher RC .60 1.50
382 B.J. Symons RC .40 1.00
383 Reggie Williams RC .40 1.00
384 Michael Boulware RC .60 1.50
385 Matt Schaub RC .40 1.00
386 Sean Jones RC .40 1.00
387 Courtney Watson RC .40 1.00
388 Nathaniel Adibi RC .40 1.00
389 Devery Henderson RC .40 1.00
390 Greg Jones RC .40 1.00
391 Joey Thomas RC .40 1.00
392 Drew Carter RC .50 1.25
393 Julius Jones RC .40 1.00
394 Keyaron Fox RC .50 1.25
395 Darrion Scott RC .50 1.25
396 Rich Gardner RC .50 1.25
397 Jeff Smoker RC .50 1.25
398 Will Poole RC .60 1.50
399 Samie Parker RC .40 1.00
400 Larry Fitzgerald RC 1.50 4.00
401 Jerricho Cotchery RC .50 1.25
402 Ernest Wilford RC .50 1.25
403 Johnnie Morant RC .40 1.00
404 Craig Krenzel RC .40 1.00
405 Michael Turner RC .40 1.00
406 D.J. Hackett RC .40 1.00
407 P.K. Sam RC .40 1.00
408 Triandos Luke RC .40 1.00
409 Josh Harris RC .40 1.00
410 Drew Henson RC .40 1.00
411 John Navarre RC .40 1.00
412 Cody Pickett RC .40 1.00
413 Clarence Moore RC .40 1.00
414 Michael Gaines RC .40 1.00
415 Derek Abney RC .40 1.00
416 Dontarrious Thomas RC .50 1.25
417 Reggie Torbor RC .40 1.00
418 Ryan Krause RC .40 1.00
419 Travis LaBoy RC .50 1.25
420 Kellen Winslow RC .40 1.00
421 Keiwan Ratliff RC .40 1.00
422 Gilbert Gardner RC .40 1.00
423 Jamaar Taylor RC .40 1.00
424 Matt Ware RC .60 1.50
425 Stuart Schweigert RC .50 1.25
426 Marcus Tubbs RC .40 1.00
427 Brandon Chillar RC .50 1.25
428 Shawntae Spencer RC .40 1.00
429 Marquis Cooper RC .40 1.00
430 Derrick Ward RC .60 1.50
431 Tim Euhus RC .40 1.00
432 Patrick Crayton RC .60 1.50
433 Caleb Miller RC .40 1.00
434 Donnell Washington RC .50 1.25
435 Thomas Tapeh RC .50 1.25
436 Randy Starks RC .40 1.00
437 Sloan Thomas RC .50 1.25
438 Maurice Mann RC .40 1.00
439 Jim Sorgi RC .50 1.25
440 Nate Lawrie RC .40 1.00

2004 Topps Total First Edition

COMPLETE SET (440) 60.00 150.00
*FRST EDIT.VETS: 1X TO 2.5X BASIC CARDS
*FE ROOKIES: .8X TO 2X BASIC CARDS

2004 Topps Total Silver

MPLETE SET (440) 100.00 200.00
*SILVER VETS: 1.2X TO 3X BASIC CARDS
*SLVR ROOK: 1X TO 2.5X BASIC CARDS
ONE PER PACK

2004 Topps Total Award Winners

COMPLETE SET (20) 10.00 25.00
STATED ODDS 1:9 HOB/RET
AW1 Jamal Lewis .60 1.50
AW2 Ahman Green .60 1.50
AW3 Priest Holmes .50 1.25
AW4 Torry Holt .60 1.50
AW5 Randy Moss .60 1.50
AW6 Chris Chambers .50 1.25
AW7 LaDainian Tomlinson .75 2.00
AW8 Peyton Manning 2.00 5.00
AW9 Marc Bulger .50 1.25
AW10 Brett Favre 1.50 4.00
AW11 Steve McNair .60 1.50
AW12 Daunte Culpepper .60 1.50
AW13 Michael Strahan .60 1.50
AW14 Adewale Ogunleye .60 1.50
AW15 Jamie Sharper .50 1.25
AW16 Micheal Barrow .50 1.25
AW17 Mike Vanderjagt .50 1.25
AW18 Anquan Boldin .50 1.25
AW19 Terrell Suggs .50 1.25
AW20 Tom Brady 4.00 10.00

2004 Topps Total Signatures

GROUP A ODDS 1:33,480 H, 1:17,383 R
GROUP B ODDS 1:11,160 H, 1:6773 R
GROUP C ODDS 1:427 HOB, 1:3369 RET
GROUP D ODDS 1:4058 HOB, 1:2173 RET
GROUP E ODDS 1:2829 HOB, 1:1644 RET
OVERALL AUTO ODDS 1:327 HOB, 1:605 RET
TSBS Brandon Stokley D 8.00 20.00
TSCC Cedric Cobbs C 8.00 20.00
TSCP Chad Pennington A 10.00 25.00
TSDD Domanick Davis B 8.00 20.00
TSKC Keary Colbert C 8.00 20.00
TSMCL Michael Clayton E 10.00 25.00
TSNB Nate Burleson C 10.00 25.00

2004 Topps Total Team Checklists

MPLETE SET (32) 15.00 40.00
TTC1 Anquan Boldin .30 .75
TTC2 Michael Vick .40 1.00
TTC3 Jamal Lewis .40 1.00
TTC4 Travis Henry .30 .75
TTC5 Jake Delhomme .30 .75
TTC6 Brian Urlacher .50 1.25
TTC7 Chad Johnson .30 .75
TTC8 Jeff Garcia .30 .75
TTC9 Keyshawn Johnson .40 1.00
TTC10 Jake Plummer .30 .75
TTC11 Joey Harrington .30 .75
TTC12 Brett Favre 1.00 2.50
TTC13 Domanick Davis .30 .75
TTC14 Peyton Manning 1.25 3.00
TTC15 Byron Leftwich .30 .75
TTC16 Priest Holmes .30 .75
TTC17 Ricky Williams .40 1.00
TTC18 Randy Moss .40 1.00
TTC19 Tom Brady 2.00 5.00

TTC20 Deuce McAllister .40 1.00
TTC21 Amani Toomer .30 .75
TTC22 Chad Pennington .30 .75
TTC23 Jerry Rice 1.00 2.50
TTC24 Donovan McNabb .40 1.00
TTC25 Hines Ward .40 1.00
TTC26 LaDainian Tomlinson .50 1.25
TTC27 Kevan Barlow .30 .75
TTC28 Matt Hasselbeck .30 .75
TTC29 Torry Holt .40 1.00
TTC30 Keenan McCardell .30 .75
TTC31 Steve McNair .40 1.00
TTC32 Clinton Portis .30 .75

2004 Topps Total Total Production

COMPLETE SET (10) 6.00 15.00
STATED ODDS 1:18 HOB/RET
TP1 Brett Favre 2.00 5.00
TP2 Peyton Manning 2.50 6.00
TP3 Priest Holmes .60 1.50
TP4 Jon Kitna .60 1.50
TP5 Matt Hasselbeck .60 1.50
TP6 Daunte Culpepper .75 2.00
TP7 Ahman Green .75 2.00
TP8 LaDainian Tomlinson 1.00 2.50
TP9 Randy Moss .75 2.00
TP10 Shaun Alexander .60 1.50

2004 Topps Total Total Topps

COMPLETE SET (20) 10.00 25.00
STATED ODDS 1:9 HOB/RET
TT1 Peyton Manning 2.50 6.00
TT2 Steve McNair .75 2.00
TT3 Torry Holt .75 2.00
TT4 Brett Favre 2.00 5.00
TT5 Jamal Lewis .75 2.00
TT6 Deuce McAllister .75 2.00
TT7 Randy Moss .75 2.00
TT8 Marvin Harrison .75 2.00
TT9 Ahman Green .75 2.00
TT10 Tom Brady 4.00 10.00
TT11 Shaun Alexander .60 1.50
TT12 LaDainian Tomlinson 1.00 2.50
TT13 Daunte Culpepper .75 2.00
TT14 Hines Ward .75 2.00
TT15 Anquan Boldin .60 1.50
TT16 Priest Holmes .60 1.50
TT17 Derrick Mason .60 1.50
TT18 Donovan McNabb .75 2.00
TT19 Clinton Portis .60 1.50
TT20 Terrell Owens .75 2.00

2005 Topps Total

This 550-card set was released in August, 2005. The hobby version of this product was issued in 10-card packs with an 99 cent SPR which came 36 packs to a box. An 110-card rookie subset (441-550) is included in this set. An interesting aspect of this set is the inclusion of many multi-player cards, which expands thc number of players in this set by a sigificant amoun t.

COMPLETE SET (550) 30.00 80.00
COMP.PACKERS TIN (20) 10.00 20.00
COMP.STEELERS TIN (20) 10.00 20.00
1 Michael Vick .25 .60
2 O.Kreutz/Q.Mitchell RC .25 .60
3 Re.Williams/Garrard/T.Edwards .20 .50
4 Terence Newman .20 .50
5 D.Jolley/C.Baker .20 .50
6 D.Clark/S.Will.RC/B.Hamilton .20 .50
7 Terrell Owens .25 .60
8 I.Ohalete/A.Wilson .20 .50
9 G.Walker/Payne/Rob.Smith .20 .50
10 Quentin Jammer .20 .50
11 Ke.Smith/D.Bly .20 .50
12 C.Taylor/Ogden/B.Sams .25 .60
13 Torry Holt .25 .60
14 W.Henderson/N.Davenport .20 .50
15 J.Siavii/Hicks/J.Allen .20 .50
16 Keith Bulluck .20 .50
17 K.Irvin/C.Chavous .20 .50
18 F.Jackson/A.Bryant/A.Davis .20 .50
19 Michael Pittman .20 .50
20 Vanderjagt/H.Smith RC .20 .50
21 J.Winborn/Ulbrich/D.Smith .20 .50
22 Reggie Wayne .25 .60
23 S.Lechler/Janikowski .20 .50
24 K.Mathis RC/J.Webster/B.Scott .20 .50
25 Daunte Culpepper .25 .60
26 W.Peterson/W.Allen .20 .50
27 T.Walter/F.Adams/L.Allen .30 .75
28 Tauscher/M.Flanagan/Clifton RC .20 .50
29 Jerome Bettis .30 .75
30 M.Brown/R.McQuarters .20 .50
31 Andre Johnson .25 .60
32 Toefield/G.Jones/Fuamatu-Ma'Afala .20 .50
33 G.Lewis/B.McMullen .25 .60
34 Kyle Boller .20 .50
35 Kacyvenski/T.White RC/Bates .20 .50
36 Chris Brown .20 .50
37 J.Phillips/B.Kelly .20 .50
38 Saturday RC/Diem RC/Ta.Glenn 4.00 10.00
39 Clinton Portis .20 .50
40 M.Scifres/N.Kaeding .20 .50
41 Ke.Williams/Udeze/Johnstone .20 .50
42 Tony Parrish .20 .50
43 D.Armstrong/J.Gaffney .20 .50
44 F.Bryant/C.Cash/Te.Holt .20 .50
45 Kerry Collins .20 .50
46 M.Strong/M.Morris .20 .50
47 Robertson/J.Abraham/S.Ellis .20 .50
48 Darrell Jackson .20 .50
49 P.Price/A.Rossum .20 .50
50 A.Henry/N.Jones RC/Frazier RC .20 .50
51 Steven Jackson .20 .50
52 R.Sims/J.Browning .20 .50
53 Robbins/Umenyiora/W.Joseph .30 .75
54 Billy Volek .20 .50
55 A.Ayodele/Da.Smith .20 .50
56 I.Scott RC/Odom/T.Johnson .20 .50
57 Onterrio Smith .20 .50
58 M.Stover/D.Zastudil RC .20 .50
59 Hunt/Gbaja-Biamila/Kampman RC .20 .50
60 Dante Hall .20 .50
61 J.Peterson/B.Young .20 .50
62 Hardwick RC/Olivea RC/Oben .20 .50
63 Chad Pennington .20 .50
64 D.Clark/A.Moorehead .20 .50
65 B.Taylor/K.Richard RC .20 .50
66 K.Walker/J.Wade RC .20 .50
67 Jeremy Shockey .20 .50
68 Daylon McCutcheon .20 .50
69 Coakley/Claiborne/Tinoisamoa .20 .50
70 Roy Williams WR .20 .50
71 L.Schulters/Ta.Williams .20 .50
72 S.Brown/Hood RC/Wynn .30 .75
73 Sean Taylor .30 .75
74 L.Little/B.Chillar .20 .50
75 Boiman/R.Starks/Clauss RC .20 .50
76 Lee Suggs .20 .50
77 P.Crayton/T.Glenn .20 .50
78 Dansby/Darling/G.Hayes .20 .50
79 Nick Barnett .20 .50
80 R.Coleman/A.Lake RC .20 .50
81 Berrian/J.Gage/D.Clark .20 .50
82 Dominic Rhodes .20 .50
83 C.Moore/R.Hymes .20 .50
84 Fraley RC/Runyan/T.Thomas .20 .50
85 Philip Rivers .30 .75
86 A.Harris/A.Carroll .20 .50
87 B.Sanders/Doss/J.Jefferson .50 1.25
88 Cesaire RC/Ja.Will/Dingle .20 .50
89 Eric Moulds .20 .50
90 P.Zellner RC/R.Davis .20 .50
91 K.Wong/Babin/A.Peek .20 .50
92 Tony Richardson .20 .50
93 G.Wesley/J.Woods .20 .50
94 Fabini/Goodwin RC/K.Mawae .20 .50
95 Tatum Bell .20 .50
96 K.Lewis RC/C.Emmons .20 .50
97 J.Galloway/W.Heller .25 .60
98 Tom Brady 1.25 3.00
99 R.Babers/B.Walker .20 .50
100 Mickens/McGraw/Buckley .20 .50
101 Zach Thomas .25 .60
102 Co.Brown RC/A.Weaver .20 .50
103 A.Will/J.Butler/K.Garrett .25 .60
104 Troy Polamalu .30 .75
105 W.Sapp/T.Washington .25 .60
106 T.Johnson/Crockett/Morant .20 .50
107 Chris McAlister .20 .50
108 C.Stanley RC/K.Brown .20 .50
109 Drew Henson .20 .50
110 James Hall .20 .50
111 S.Player/N.Rackers .20 .50
112 D.Watts/A.Lelie .20 .50
113 J.David/N.Harper .20 .50
114 R.Curry/D.Gabriel .20 .50
115 R.Colclough/W.Williams .25 .60
116 C.Tillman/J.Azumah .25 .60
117 M.Kemoeatu RC/Ad.Thomas .30 .75
118 M.Roman/J.Thomas .20 .50
119 D.Henderson/M.Lewis .20 .50
120 M.Furrey/Manumaleuna .30 .75
121 R.Mahe/C.Buckhalter .20 .50
122 E.Kinney/T.Fleming .20 .50
123 W.Dunn/T.Duckett .20 .50
124 T.Euhus/M.Campbell .20 .50
125 P.Hunter/A.Glenn .20 .50
126 R.Tongue/D.Barrett .20 .50
127 S.Morris/L.Gordon .20 .50
128 R.Clark RC/S.Springs .60 1.50
129 J.Miller/A.Vinatieri .20 .50
130 E.Warfield/W.Bartee .20 .50
131 Me.Moore/M.Bennett .20 .50
132 N.Goings/B.Hoover .20 .50
133 Q.Harris/D.Macklin .20 .50
134 E.Drummond/R.Swinton .20 .50
135 J.Fargas/A.Whitted .25 .60
136 N.Clements/T.McGee RC .25 .60
137 T.Hollings/J.Wells .20 .50
138 D.Cooper RC/K.Thomas RC .20 .50
139 P.Dawson/D.Frost RC .20 .50
140 J.McCown/J.Navarre .25 .60
141 G.Ellis/K.Coleman .20 .50
142 G.Wilson/B.Alexander .20 .50
143 A.Woolfolk/L.Thompson .20 .50
144 E.Conwell/B.Williams .20 .50
145 D.Akers/Di.Johnson RC .20 .50
146 Hillenmeyer RC/L.Briggs .50 1.25
147 R.Mathis RC/G.Brackett .50 1.25
148 J.Rice/R.Alexander .60 1.50
149 E.Coleman/D.Strait .20 .50
150 J.Hartwig RC/B.Troupe .20 .50
151 S.Davis/D.Florence .20 .50
152 P.Buchanon/M.Coleman .20 .50
153 S.Heiden/A.Shea .20 .50
154 T.Spikes/L.Fletcher .25 .60
155 T.Laboy/A.Odom .20 .50
156 A.Toomer/M.Cloud .20 .50
157 L.Tynes RC/C.Horn .25 .60
158 N.Diggs/P.Lenon RC .20 .50
159 R.Long/A.Haynesworth .20 .50
160 B.Askew/J.Sowell .20 .50
161 John Carney/Mitch Berger .20 .50
162 K.Campbell/J.Wiggins .20 .50
163 Jerramy Stevens .25 .60
164 Willis McGahee .20 .50
165 Ed Reed .25 .60
166 Muhsin Muhammad .20 .50
167 Donovin Darius .20 .50
168 E.J. Henderson .20 .50
169 Tony Banks .20 .50
170 Fred Taylor .20 .50
171 Jeremiah Trotter .20 .50
172 Adam Archuleta .20 .50
173 Marcus Trufant .20 .50
174 Steve McNair .25 .60
175 Ben Roethlisberger .50 1.25
176 Derrick Blaylock .20 .50
177 Michael Strahan .25 .60
178 Robert Gallery .20 .50
179 Drew Brees .30 .75
180 David Kircus .20 .50
181 Robert Ferguson .20 .50
182 Jim Sorgi .20 .50
183 Alge Crumpler .25 .60
184 DeShaun Foster .25 .60
185 Reuben Droughns .20 .50
186 Charles Grant .20 .50
187 Jason Taylor .25 .60
188 James Thrash .25 .60
189 LaDainian Tomlinson .30 .75
190 Tim Rattay .20 .50
191 Jeff Garcia .20 .50
192 Jerricho Cotchery .20 .50
193 Chris Simms .20 .50
194 Jevon Kearse .20 .50
195 Kyle Brady .20 .50
196 Trent Green .20 .50
197 Antoine Winfield .25 .60
198 Deion Branch .20 .50
199 Rudi Johnson .20 .50
200 Lee Evans .25 .60
201 Stephen Davis .20 .50
202 Darnell Dockett .20 .50
203 Kurt Warner .25 .60
204 Quincy Morgan .20 .50
205 Daimon Shelton .20 .50
206 Champ Bailey .25 .60
207 Jamal Lewis .25 .60
208 Brett Favre .60 1.50
209 Charles Woodson .30 .75
210 Koren Robinson .20 .50
211 Chris Chambers .20 .50
212 Dave Ragone .20 .50
213 Travis Minor .20 .50
214 Simeon Rice .20 .50
215 Tommy Maddox .20 .50
216 Aaron Stecker .20 .50
217 Dwight Freeney .20 .50
218 Thomas Jones .20 .50
219 Patrick Ramsey .25 .60
220 Travis Taylor .20 .50
221 Chris Weinke .20 .50
222 Marc Bulger .20 .50
223 James Farrior .20 .50
224 Billy Miller .20 .50
225 Mike Peterson .20 .50
226 Eddie Kennison .20 .50
227 Aaron Brooks .20 .50
228 Plaxico Burress .20 .50
229 Jerry Porter .20 .50
230 Joey Harrington .20 .50
231 Bubba Franks .20 .50
232 Michael Jenkins .20 .50
233 Larry Fitzgerald .30 .75
234 Troy Vincent .25 .60
235 Chad Johnson .20 .50
236 Roy Williams S .20 .50
237 Corey Dillon .20 .50
238 Donovan McNabb .25 .60
239 Marcus Robinson .20 .50
240 Derrick Brooks .20 .50
241 David Bowens RC .20 .50
242 Renaldo Wynn .20 .50
243 Kevan Barlow .20 .50
244 Antonio Gates .30 .75
245 Duce Staley .20 .50
246 Ernest Wilford .20 .50
247 Kevin Jones .20 .50
248 Julius Peppers .25 .60
249 Terrell Suggs .20 .50
250 Bertrand Berry .20 .50
251 Brian Simmons .20 .50
252 Jake Plummer .20 .50
253 Brian Urlacher .30 .75
254 Justin McCareins .20 .50
255 L.J. Smith .25 .60
256 Matt Hasselbeck .20 .50
257 Rashaun Woods .20 .50
258 Rodney Harrison .20 .50
259 Brandon Stokley .20 .50
260 Tony Gonzalez .25 .60
261 J.P. Losman .20 .50
262 DeAngelo Hall .20 .50
263 Jake Delhomme .20 .50
264 Shaun Rogers .20 .50
265 Donald Driver .25 .60
266 Will Smith .20 .50
267 Brian Westbrook .20 .50
268 A.J. Feeley .20 .50
269 Marshall Faulk .25 .60
270 Marques Tuiasosopo .20 .50
271 Curtis Martin .25 .60
272 Jason Witten .25 .60
273 Kellen Winslow .20 .50
274 Corey Bradford .20 .50
275 Samari Rolle .20 .50
276 Anquan Boldin .20 .50
277 Adrian Peterson .20 .50
278 Javon Walker .20 .50
279 Fred Smoot .20 .50
280 Mike Alstott .20 .50
281 Randy McMichael .20 .50
282 Jay Fiedler .20 .50
283 Jamie Sharper .20 .50
284 Eli Manning .50 1.25
285 Todd Pinkston .20 .50
286 La'Roi Glover .20 .50
287 Chris Perry .20 .50
288 David Carr .20 .50
289 Bryant Johnson .20 .50
290 Ray Lewis .30 .75
291 Tommie Harris .20 .50
292 Joe Horn .20 .50
293 Rod Smith .25 .60
294 Michael Clayton .20 .50
295 Tyrone Calico .20 .50
296 Santana Moss .25 .60
297 Hines Ward .25 .60
298 Jonathan Vilma .20 .50
299 Randy Moss .25 .60
300 Donte Stallworth .20 .50
301 Isaac Bruce .30 .75
302 Brian Griese .20 .50
303 Dennis Northcutt .20 .50
304 Michael Green .20 .50
305 Marvin Harrison .25 .60
306 Jimmy Smith .25 .60
307 Patrick Kerney .20 .50
308 Todd Heap .20 .50
309 Dan Morgan .20 .50
310 Charles Rogers .20 .50
311 Dunta Robinson .20 .50
312 Deuce McAllister .25 .60
313 Ronde Barber .20 .50
314 Brandon Lloyd .20 .50
315 Tiki Barber .25 .60
316 LaMont Jordan .25 .60
317 Lito Sheppard .25 .60
318 Laveranues Coles .20 .50
319 Drew Bennett .25 .60
320 Julius Jones .20 .50
321 Ahman Green .25 .60
322 Domanick Davis .20 .50
323 Byron Leftwich .20 .50
324 Nate Burleson .20 .50
325 David Givens .20 .50
326 Trent Dilfer .20 .50
327 T.J. Houshmandzadeh .20 .50
328 Keith Brooking .20 .50
329 Derrick Mason .20 .50
330 Ken Lucas .20 .50
331 Rex Grossman .20 .50
332 Edgerrin James .25 .60
333 Priest Holmes .20 .50
334 Donnie Edwards .20 .50
335 Pierson Prioleau RC .20 .50
336 Shaun Alexander .20 .50
337 D.J. Williams .20 .50
338 Peyton Manning .75 2.00
339 Carson Palmer .25 .60
340 Keyshawn Johnson .25 .60
341 Tory James .20 .50
342 Drew Bledsoe .25 .60
343 Chris Gamble .20 .50
344 Mi.Lewis/B.Dawkins .30 .75
345 Forney/McClure RC/Weiner RC .20 .50
346 R.Smart/Kasay/J.Kyle .20 .50
347 J.Ferguson/Reeves/Nguyen .20 .50
348 Crocker/Lehan RC/M.Jameson .20 .50
349 Tyree/Ja.Taylor/T.Carter .20 .50
350 H.Thomas/D.Jones/Simoneau .20 .50
351 Royal/McCants/T.Jacobs .20 .50
352 Welker/D.Thompson/Gilmore .25 .60
353 D.Lewis/Pickett/Ty.Jackson .20 .50
354 F.Brown/F.Thomas/J.Bellamy .20 .50
355 Asomugha/M.Anderson/Schweigert .25 .60
356 M.Stroud/J.Hender/Favors .20 .50
357 W.Shields/Roaf/B.Waters RC .20 .50
358 Hamilton/Nalen/Lepsis .20 .50
359 J.Smith/Geathers/D.Clemons .25 .60
360 Wire/R.Baker/L.Milloy .20 .50
361 Ayanbadejo/J.Scobey/Hambrick .20 .50
362 St.Smith/Proehl/Colbert .30 .75
363 N.Harris/D.Thomas/Offord .20 .50
364 L.Neal/M.Turner/Pinnock .30 .75
365 Faneca/M.Smith RC/Hartings .50 1.25
366 E.Moore/Pope/Ayanbadejo RC .25 .60
367 A.Plummer/Jo.Hanson RC/Spencer .20 .50
368 L.Betts/Brunell/C.Morton .25 .60
369 Pace/Timmerman/McCollum .20 .50
370 B.Thomas/Barton/Hobson .20 .50
371 S.Barber/K.Fox/K.Mitchell .20 .50
372 K.Edwards/Wilkinson/Redding .20 .50
373 Co.Jackson RC/Lang/McKinley .20 .50
374 Bannan/R.Edwards/S.Adams .20 .50
375 M.Schaub/D.White/Finneran .25 .60
376 Short/A.Wallace RC/K.Jenkins .20 .50
377 Leach/Carswell/Putzier .20 .50
378 Vrabel/T.Johnson/Bruschi .30 .75
379 Kiel/Je.Wilson RC/Fletcher .20 .50
380 Engelber/To.Brown RC/A.Adams .20 .50
381 Quarles/Gooch/D.White .20 .50
382 Madison/W.Poole/R.Howard .20 .50
383 Schneck RC/Gardocki/J.Reed .20 .50
384 J.Mitchell RC/Gross/Brzezinski RC .20 .50
385 Greisen/B.Green/A.Pierce .20 .50
386 C.Simon/D.Walker/McDougle .20 .50
387 D.Graham/Fauria/B.Watson .25 .60
388 E.Johnson/R.John/M.Coleman .20 .50
389 June/D.Thornton/Hutchins .25 .60
390 Teague/R.Tucker/M.Will.T .20 .50
391 M.Haynes/A.Brown/Ogunleye .20 .50
392 Ulmer RC/Br.Smith/De.Williams .20 .50
393 K.Faulk/Pass/Be.Johnson .20 .50
394 Tobeck RC/W.Jones/S.Hutchin .25 .60
395 V.Holliday/Y.Bell RC/K.Carter .20 .50
396 L.Foote/J.Porter/Al.Jackson .20 .50
397 Looker/K.Curtis/S.McDonald .25 .60
398 L.Marshall RC/C.Griffin/D.Evans .25 .60
399 D.Klecko/Izzo/R.Colvin .20 .50
400 M.Holland/Bentley/Gandy .20 .50
401 Petitgout/McKenzie RC/J.Whittle RC .20 .50
402 Sykes RC/Fatafehi/A.Wilson .20 .50
403 Meester RC/Ma.Will/Manuwai RC .20 .50
404 M.Schobel/K.Washing/Warrick .20 .50
405 M.Minter/R.Manning/C.Branch .20 .50
406 Jo.Reed/Jo.Smith/Aiken .20 .50
407 Birk/Liwienski/McKinnie .20 .50
408 Godfrey/Foley/Leber .20 .50
409 McFarland/Wyms/G.Spires .20 .50
410 E.Perry/Do.Lee/Booker .20 .50
411 Von Oelhoffen/Hoke RC/Aa.Smith .25 .60
412 B.Mitchell/Wistrom/Ra.Moore .20 .50
413 J.Green/Wilfork/T.Warren .25 .60
414 Middlebrooks/Lynch/N.Ferguson .25 .60
415 Reagor/R.Brock/Jo.Williams .20 .50
416 J.Dunn/S.Parker/La.Johnson .20 .50
417 La.Johnson/M.Wilkins RC/C.Miller .20 .50
418 Buckner/Moorehead/M.Rucker .20 .50
419 Denney/Kelsay/A.Schobel .20 .50
420 Singleton/B.James/K.O'Neil RC .20 .50
421 C.Thompson/Boyer/An.Davis .20 .50
422 D.Grant/Richardson RC/R.Mathis .20 .50
423 Schlesinger/Bryson/Pinner .20 .50
424 S.Johnson RC/R.Davis/Ru.Jones .20 .50
425 Phifer/Banta-Cain/McGinest .25 .60
426 McCardell/Osgood/E.Parker .25 .60
427 C.Woodard/Bernard/A.Cochran .20 .50
428 A.Battle/A.Walker/E.Johnson .20 .50
429 Salave'a RC/M.Wash/L.Arrington .20 .50
430 L.Mays/C.Wilson/Randle El .20 .50
431 D.Starks/E.Wilson/R.Gay .20 .50
432 Q.Griffin/M.Anderson/C.Sapp .20 .50
433 J.Thornton/L.Moore RC/Powell .20 .50
434 M.Gaines/Hankton/Seidman .20 .50
435 M.Haggan RC/Posey/A.Crowell .20 .50
436 O'Neal/M.Williams/K.Ratliff .20 .50
437 M.Light RC/Koppen RC/S.Neal RC .20 .50
438 C.Watson/D.Rodgers/J.Allen .20 .50
439 M.Boulware/Hamlin/Bierria RC .20 .50
440 T.Rogers RC/Unck RC/Roye .20 .50
441 Frank Gore RC .75 2.00
442 Mike Patterson RC .40 1.00
443 DeMarcus Ware RC 1.25 3.00
444 Chris Henry RC .50 1.25
445 Thomas Davis RC .40 1.00
446 Justin Miller RC .40 1.00
447 Shaun Cody RC .50 1.25
448 Alex Barron RC .40 1.00
449 Brock Berlin RC .40 1.00
450 Travis Johnson RC .40 1.00
451 Jerome Mathis RC .60 1.50
452 Lance Mitchell RC .50 1.25
453 Marlin Jackson RC .40 1.00
454 Charlie Frye RC .40 1.00
455 Luis Castillo RC .50 1.25
456 Fred Gibson RC .40 1.00
457 Dustin Fox RC .50 1.25
458 Ryan Fitzpatrick RC .60 1.50
459 Dan Orlovsky RC .40 1.00
460 Justin Tuck RC .50 1.25
461 Corey Webster RC .50 1.25
462 Travis Daniels RC .50 1.25
463 J.J. Arrington RC .50 1.25
464 David Greene RC .40 1.00
465 Alvin Pearman RC .40 1.00
466 Manuel White RC .50 1.25
467 Paris Warren RC .50 1.25
468 Patrick Estes RC .40 1.00
469 Cedric Houston RC .60 1.50
470 David Pollack RC .40 1.00
471 Craig Bragg RC .40 1.00
472 Vincent Jackson RC .60 1.50
473 Adam Jones RC .40 1.00
474 Matt Jones RC .40 1.00
475 Stefan LeFors RC .40 1.00
476 Heath Miller RC .75 2.00
477 Ryan Moats RC .50 1.25
478 Vernand Morency RC .50 1.25
479 Terrence Murphy RC .40 1.00
480 Kyle Orton RC .40 1.00
481 Roscoe Parrish RC .40 1.00
482 Courtney Roby RC .40 1.00
483 Aaron Rodgers RC 6.00 12.00
484 Carlos Rogers RC .60 1.50
485 Antrel Rolle RC .60 1.50
486 Eric Shelton RC .40 1.00
487 Alex Smith QB RC 1.50 4.00
488 Andrew Walter RC .40 1.00
489 Roddy White RC .60 1.50
490 Cadillac Williams RC .40 1.00
491 Mike Williams .50 1.25
492 Troy Williamson RC .40 1.00
493 Kirk Morrison RC .60 1.50
494 Tab Perry RC .40 1.00
495 Chad Owens RC .40 1.00
496 Lofa Tatupu RC .50 1.25
497 Craphonso Thorpe RC .40 1.00
498 Ryan Riddle RC .40 1.00
499 Marcus Maxwell RC .40 1.00
500 Barrett Ruud RC .50 1.25
501 Stanley Wilson RC .50 1.25
502 Mike Nugent RC .50 1.25
503 Eric King RC .40 1.00
504 Darryl Blackstock RC .40 1.00
505 Attiyah Ellison RC .40 1.00
506 Donte Nicholson RC .40 1.00
507 Airese Currie RC .40 1.00
508 Larry Brackins RC .40 1.00
509 Joel Dreessen RC .50 1.25
510 Cedric Benson RC .40 1.00
511 Mark Bradley RC .40 1.00
512 Reggie Brown RC .40 1.00
513 Ronnie Brown RC .50 1.25
514 Jason Campbell RC .40 1.00
515 Maurice Clarett .50 1.25
516 Mark Clayton RC .40 1.00
517 Braylon Edwards RC .40 1.00
518 Ciatrick Fason RC .40 1.00
519 Dan Cody RC .40 1.00
520 Taylor Stubblefield RC .40 1.00
521 J.R. Russell RC .40 1.00
522 Rian Wallace RC .50 1.25
523 Anthony Davis RC .40 1.00
524 Derek Anderson RC .50 1.25
525 Boomer Grigsby RC .60 1.50
526 Rasheed Marshall RC .50 1.25
527 Adrian McPherson RC .40 1.00
528 Noah Herron RC .40 1.00
529 Bryant McFadden RC .50 1.25
530 Lionel Gates RC .40 1.00
531 Matt Roth RC .40 1.00
532 Derrick Johnson RC .50 1.25
533 Stanford Routt RC .50 1.25
534 Brandon Jacobs RC .50 1.25
535 Kevin Burnett RC .50 1.25
536 Ryan Claridge RC .40 1.00
537 James Kilian RC .40 1.00
538 Oshiomogho Atogwe RC .50 1.25
539 Fabian Washington RC .40 1.00
540 Marion Barber RC .40 1.00
541 Anttaj Hawthorne RC .40 1.00
542 Zach Tuiasosopo RC .40 1.00
543 Ellis Hobbs RC .60 1.50
544 Alex Smith TE RC .40 1.00
545 Erasmus James RC .40 1.00
546 Channing Crowder RC .50 1.25
547 Kelvin Hayden RC .50 1.25
548 Darren Sproles RC .60 1.50
549 Marcus Spears RC .40 1.00
550 Dante Ridgeway RC .40 1.00
CL1 Checklist 1 .02 .10
CL2 Checklist 2 .02 .10
CL3 Checklist 3 .02 .10
CL4 Checklist 4 .02 .10
BR1 Ben Roethlisberger Jumbo 3.00 6.00
VL1 Vince Lombardi Jumbo 3.00 6.00

2005 Topps Total First Edition

COMPLETE SET (55) 125.00 250.00
*STARS: 1X TO 2.5X BASIC CARDS
*ROOKIES: .8X TO 2X BASIC CARDS

2005 Topps Total Silver

COMPLETE SET (550) 60.00 150.00
*STARS: 1.2X TO 3X BASIC CARDS
*ROOKIES: .8X TO 2X BASIC CARDS
ONE SILVER PER PACK

2005 Topps Total Award Winners

COMPLETE SET (20) 12.50 25.00
STATED ODDS 1:12 HOB/RET
AW1 Curtis Martin .75 2.00
AW2 Shaun Alexander .60 1.50
AW3 Daunte Culpepper .75 2.00
AW4 Trent Green .60 1.50
AW5 Muhsin Muhammad .60 1.50
AW6 Chad Johnson .60 1.50
AW7 LaDainian Tomlinson 1.00 2.50
AW8 Marvin Harrison .75 2.00
AW9 Dwight Freeney .60 1.50
AW10 Adam Vinatieri .60 1.50
AW11 Dante Hall .60 1.50
AW12 Joe Horn .60 1.50
AW13 Tony Gonzalez .75 2.00
AW14 Donovan McNabb .75 2.00
AW15 Corey Dillon .60 1.50
AW16 Peyton Manning 2.50 6.00
AW17 Ed Reed .75 2.00
AW18 Ben Roethlisberger 1.50 4.00
AW19 Jonathan Vilma .60 1.50
AW20 Deion Branch .60 1.50

2005 Topps Total Rookie Jerseys

STATED ODDS 1:8 SPECIAL RETAIL
1 Alex Smith QB 7.50 20.00
2 Mark Clayton 2.50 6.00
3 Antrel Rolle 4.00 10.00
4 Kyle Orton 2.50 6.00
5 Roscoe Parrish 2.50 6.00
6 Vernand Morency 2.50 6.00
7 Maurice Clarett 2.50 6.00
8 Mark Bradley 2.50 6.00
9 Reggie Brown 2.50 6.00

2005 Topps Total Signatures

OUP A ODDS 1:18,092 H, 1:3860 R
GROUP B ODDS 1:234 H, 1:1924 R
GROUP C ODDS 1:1528 H, 1:1522 R
TSAG Antonio Gates A 10.00 25.00
TSDB Drew Bennett A 20.00 40.00
TSJS Junior Siavii C 5.00 12.00
TSLW LeVar Woods B 5.00 12.00
TSMH Marquise Hill B 5.00 12.00
TSTS Trent Smith B 5.00 12.00

2005 Topps Total Team Checklists

COMPLETE SET (32) 12.50 30.00
TC1 Larry Fitzgerald .50 1.25
TC2 Michael Vick .40 1.00
TC3 Jamal Lewis .40 1.00
TC4 Willis McGahee .30 .75
TC5 Jake Delhomme .30 .75
TC6 Muhsin Muhammad .30 .75
TC7 Rudi Johnson .30 .75
TC8 Reuben Droughns .30 .75
TC9 Drew Bledsoe .40 1.00
TC10 Jake Plummer .30 .75
TC11 Kevin Jones .30 .75
TC12 Brett Favre 1.00 2.50
TC13 Domanick Davis .30 .75
TC14 Peyton Manning 1.25 3.00
TC15 Byron Leftwich .30 .75
TC16 Trent Green .30 .75
TC17 Chris Chambers .30 .75
TC18 Daunte Culpepper .40 1.00
TC19 Tom Brady 2.00 5.00
TC20 Joe Horn .30 .75
TC21 Tiki Barber .40 1.00
TC22 Curtis Martin .40 1.00
TC23 Randy Moss .40 1.00
TC24 Donovan McNabb .40 1.00
TC25 Ben Roethlisberger .75 2.00
TC26 LaDainian Tomlinson .50 1.25
TC27 Brandon Lloyd .30 .75
TC28 Shaun Alexander .30 .75
TC29 Torry Holt .40 1.00
TC30 Michael Clayton .30 .75
TC31 Drew Bennett .40 1.00
TC32 Clinton Portis .30 .75

2005 Topps Total Total Production

COMPLETE SET (10) 10.00 20.00
STATED ODDS 1:18 HOB/RET
TP1 Peyton Manning 2.50 6.00
TP2 Daunte Culpepper .75 2.00
TP3 LaDainian Tomlinson 1.00 2.50
TP4 Muhsin Muhammad .60 1.50
TP5 Shaun Alexander .60 1.50
TP6 Marvin Harrison .75 2.00
TP7 Priest Holmes .60 1.50
TP8 Donovan McNabb .75 2.00
TP9 Terrell Owens .75 2.00
TP10 Brett Favre 2.00 5.00

2005 Topps Total Total Topps

MPLETE SET (20) 15.00 30.00
STATED ODDS 1:6 HOB/RET
TT1 Tom Brady 4.00 10.00
TT2 LaDainian Tomlinson 1.00 2.50
TT3 Terrell Owens .75 2.00
TT4 Priest Holmes .60 1.50
TT5 Daunte Culpepper .75 2.00
TT6 Curtis Martin .75 2.00
TT7 Joe Horn .60 1.50
TT8 Trent Green .60 1.50
TT9 Edgerrin James .75 2.00
TT10 Randy Moss .75 2.00
TT11 Michael Vick .75 2.00
TT12 Tony Gonzalez .75 2.00
TT13 Marvin Harrison .75 2.00
TT14 Corey Dillon .60 1.50
TT15 Rudi Johnson .60 1.50
TT16 Peyton Manning 2.50 6.00
TT17 Muhsin Muhammad .60 1.50
TT18 Shaun Alexander .60 1.50
TT19 Brett Favre 2.00 5.00
TT20 Donovan McNabb .75 2.00

2006 Topps Total

This 550-card set was released in August, 2006. The set was issued into the hobby in 30-card packs with an $3 SRP which came 24 packs to a box. The first 440 cards in this set feature a mix of single and multi-player veteran cards, while cards numbered 441-550 feature 2006 rookies.

COMPLETE SET (550) 25.00 60.00
1 C.Webster/S.Madison .20 .50
2 Randy Moss .25 .60
3 Garcia/Parry/Detmer .20 .50
4 Matt Jones .20 .50
5 C.Brown/G.Earl .20 .50
6 Anderson/Steinbach/Braham .20 .50
7 DeAngelo Hall .20 .50
8 J.P. Losman .25 .60
9 Kevin Jones .20 .50
10 K.Dorsey/F.Gore .25 .60
11 Nichol/Pearson RC/Allen .20 .50
12 Brandon Lloyd .20 .50
13 Jeremiah Trotter .20 .50
14 Stone/Grove/Sims .20 .50
15 Drew Brees .30 .75
16 Jason Taylor .25 .60
17 Tony Gonzalez .25 .60
18 Brandon Stokley .20 .50
19 Jake Plummer .20 .50
20 Braylon Edwards .20 .50
21 Berrian/Maynard/Gould RC .20 .50
22 B.Sams/M.Stover .20 .50
23 Darling/Huff/Dansby .20 .50
24 Julius Peppers .25 .60
25 Ferguson/Spears/Ellis .20 .50
26 D.Lee/D.Martin .20 .50
27 B.Johnson/B.Johnson .25 .60
28 Bethel Johnson .20 .50
29 Ellis/Robertson/Thomas .20 .50
30 Willie Parker .25 .60
31 E.Shepherd/I.Hilliard .20 .50
32 Troupe/Scaife/Mauck .20 .50
33 Marc Bulger .20 .50
34 M.Trufant/M.Boulware .20 .50
35 Hardwick/Oben/Olivea .20 .50
36 Ray Lewis .30 .75
37 S.Lefors/C.Weinke .20 .50
38 Kaesviharn/Pollack/Ohalete .20 .50
39 G.Jones/A.Pearman .20 .50
40 Allen/Hicks/Sims .20 .50
41 Tiki Barber .25 .60
42 N.Asomugha/F.Washington .30 .75
43 Lewis/Adams/Emanuel .30 .75
44 Rodney Harrison .20 .50
45 H.Smith/A.Vinatieri .20 .50
46 Orlovsky/Kitna/Bryson .20 .50
47 Bubba Franks .20 .50
48 A.Wilson/I.Gold .20 .50
49 Davis/Thompson/McGinest .20 .50
50 Nathan Vasher .20 .50
51 J.Greer/T.Vincent .20 .50
52 Rossum/Ptrsn/Koenen RC .20 .50
53 DeMarcus Ware .25 .60
54 L.Diamond RC/Booker .20 .50
55 McKinnie/Birk/Hutchinson .25 .60
56 Cole/Kearse/Patterson .20 .50
57 Tubbs/Wistrom/Fisher .20 .50
58 Curtis Martin .25 .60
59 D.Macklin/A.Rolle .20 .50
60 Lejeune/Howard/Bell .20 .50
61 Reggie Brown .20 .50
62 M.McKenzie/F.Thomas .20 .50
63 Fletcher/Hartsock/Sorgi .20 .50
64 Larry Fitzgerald .25 .60
65 E.Moulds/V.Morency .20 .50
66 Williams/Barnes/Naeole .20 .50
67 Trent Green .20 .50
68 D.Sproles/M.Turner .30 .75
69 Chillar/Glover/Tinoisamoa .25 .60
70 Chris Gamble .20 .50
71 A.Jones/M.Waddell .20 .50
72 Marshall/Washington/Daniels .20 .50
73 Hines Ward .25 .60
74 S.Knight/P.Surtain .20 .50
75 McKinney/Wade/Wiegert .20 .50
76 Rod Smith .25 .60
77 D.Henson/T.Romo 2.00 5.00
78 Franklin RC/Gregg/Pryce .20 .50
79 David Garrard .20 .50
80 D.Smith/M.Peterson .20 .50
81 Bowens/Traylor/Roth .20 .50
82 Simeon Rice .20 .50
83 M.Douglas/B.Young .20 .50
84 Thornton/Reynolds RC/Sirmon .20 .50
85 T.J. Houshmandzadeh .20 .50
86 L.Betts/J.Campbell .20 .50
87 Smith/Hartings/Faneca .20 .50
88 Antonio Pierce .20 .50
89 C.Kluwe/R.Longwell .20 .50
90 Thomas/Manning/Poppinga .20 .50
91 Willis McGahee .20 .50
92 K.Smith/T.Holt .20 .50
93 Wilson/Samuel/Hobbs .25 .60
94 Pace/Timmerman/Barron .20 .50
95 Fred Taylor .20 .50
96 M.Doss/B.Sanders .25 .60
97 Joe/Briggs/Ayanbadejo .25 .60
98 Daunte Culpepper .25 .60
99 C.Perry/T.Perry .25 .60
100 Whitted/Janikowski/Lechler .20 .50
101 Julius Jones .20 .50
102 C.Lavalais/R.Coleman .20 .50
103 Rucker/Ciurciu RC/Wallace .20 .50
104 Rex Grossman .20 .50
105 Dunta Robinson .20 .50
106 Bockwoldt/Craft/Gleason .20 .50
107 Chad Pennington .20 .50
108 Heath Miller .20 .50
109 D.Hackett/N.Burleson .20 .50
110 Drew Bennett .25 .60
111 Williams/Godfrey/Castillo .20 .50
112 Doug Gabriel .20 .50
113 A.Toomer/B.Jacobs .20 .50
114 Travis Taylor .20 .50
115 Troy Fleming .20 .50
116 Todd Heap .20 .50
117 Reese/Williams/Boley .20 .50
118 Odell Thurman .20 .50
119 D.Watts/J.Walker .25 .60
120 Scobee/Hanson RC/Toefield .20 .50
121 Donovan McNabb .25 .60
122 A.Smith TE/A.Becht .20 .50
123 Adam Archuleta .20 .50
124 J.J. Arrington .20 .50
125 Johnson/Simmons/Miller .20 .50
126 Andruzzi/Bentley/Tucker .20 .50
127 Aaron Rodgers .75 2.00
128 Brown/Gardner/Hobson .20 .50
129 Antonio Bryant .20 .50
130 Isaac Bruce .30 .75
131 Quarles/Nece/Ruud .20 .50
132 Williams/Elam/Sauerbrun .20 .50
133 B.Hoover/N.Goings .20 .50
134 Ward/Carter/Rolle .20 .50
135 Dante Hall .20 .50
136 Tom Brady 1.00 2.50
137 R.Moats/C.Buckhalter .20 .50
138 Arnaz Battle .20 .50
139 Bernard/Hill/Lewis RC .20 .50
140 Kampman/Gbaja-Biamila/Jenkins .25 .60
141 Fowler RC/James/Burnett .20 .50
142 Warrick Dunn .20 .50
143 Eli Manning .25 .60
144 Clark/Brayton/Morrison .20 .50
145 Zach Thomas .25 .60
146 Anderson/Babin/Greenwood .20 .50
147 Ron Dayne .25 .60
148 D.Zastudil/P.Dawson .20 .50
149 Williams/Mosley/Johnson .20 .50
150 Donte Stallworth .20 .50
151 Shawne Merriman .25 .60
152 Thompson/Hentrich/Bironas .20 .50
153 Clinton Portis .20 .50
154 R.Curry/J.Morant .20 .50
155 Dwight Freeney .20 .50
156 B.Russell/D.McCutcheon .20 .50
157 Brown/Green/Tillman .25 .60
158 Takeo Spikes .20 .50
159 Kurt Warner .25 .60
160 Jonathan Vilma .20 .50
161 James Farrior .20 .50
162 D.Florence/Q.Jammer .20 .50
163 Kevan Barlow .20 .50
164 Haggans/Hampton/Smith .20 .50
165 Walter Jones .20 .50
166 Mayberry/Jacox RC/Holland .20 .50
167 Byron Leftwich .20 .50
168 Mike Williams WR .20 .50
169 Jason Witten .25 .60
170 Dennis Northcutt .20 .50
171 Baker/Clements/Wire .20 .50
172 Ronnie Cruz .20 .50
173 E.Henderson/E.James .20 .50
174 LaMont Jordan .25 .60
175 Tyrone Calico .20 .50
176 Nalen/Foster/Hamilton .20 .50
177 Sam Gado .20 .50
178 Randy McMichael .20 .50
179 Brown/Sheppard/Ware .25 .60
180 L.Little/A.Hargrove .20 .50
181 Cadillac Williams .25 .60
182 Feely/Morton/Tyree .20 .50
183 Dallas Clark .20 .50
184 Faggins/Sanders/Coleman .20 .50
185 V.Holliday/K.Carter .20 .50
186 Smith/Ulbrich/Winborn .20 .50
187 S.Player/N.Rackers .20 .50
188 Steve Smith .30 .75
189 Cassel/Graham/Watson .20 .50
190 J.Porter/L.Foote .20 .50
191 Jamal Lewis .25 .60
192 Michael Jenkins .20 .50
193 Michael Strahan .25 .60
194 Kyle Vanden Bosch .20 .50
195 Shields/Roaf/Waters .20 .50
196 Terry Glenn .25 .60
197 Griffith/Green/Wilson .20 .50
198 Philip Rivers .30 .75
199 Tuck/Joseph/Robbins .20 .50
200 LaDainian Tomlinson .30 .75
201 J.David/N.Harper .20 .50
202 Hall/Bailey/Rogers .20 .50
203 Donald Driver .25 .60
204 Reuben Droughns .25 .60
205 Wahle/Gross/Wharton .20 .50
206 Jonathan Ogden .25 .60
207 J.Bullocks/D.Smith .20 .50
208 Nugent/Miller/Graham RC .20 .50
209 Matt Hasselbeck .20 .50
210 Derrick Brooks .20 .50
211 Foxworth/Lynch/Ferguson .20 .50
212 Stewart/Unck/Fisk .20 .50
213 M.Will.T/Anderson RC/Villarrial .20 .50
214 Saturday/Glenn/Diem .20 .50
215 Larry Johnson .20 .50
216 Marcus Robinson .20 .50
217 Aaron Brooks .20 .50
218 Smith/Bartrum/Spach .20 .50
219 Steven Jackson .20 .50
220 Roy Williams WR .20 .50
221 L.Polite/P.Crayton .20 .50
222 Carson Palmer .25 .60
223 Brown/Kreutz/Tait .20 .50
224 Charles Woodson .30 .75
225 J.Payton/T.Henry .20 .50
226 K.Rhodes/E.Coleman .20 .50
227 Ronnie Brown .25 .60
228 David Carr .20 .50
229 Terence Newman .25 .60
230 Grigsby/Bell/Mitchell .20 .50
231 M.Vrabel/R.Colvin .25 .60
232 Heitmann/Smiley/Harris .20 .50
233 Joey Galloway .25 .60
234 Keith Bulluck .20 .50
235 Hall/Frost/Brown .20 .50
236 Dockett/Smith/Okeafor .20 .50
237 Mike Anderson .20 .50
238 Kellen Winslow .20 .50
239 Tatum Bell .20 .50
240 A.Pinner/C.Schlesinger .20 .50
241 Roman/Underwood/Collins .25 .60
242 Reggie Wayne .25 .60
243 Reggie Williams .25 .60
244 Pope/Spragan/Crowder .20 .50
245 Courtney Watson .20 .50
246 G.Lewis/B.McMullen .20 .50
247 Troy Polamalu .30 .75
248 Smoker/Faulk/Looker .20 .50
249 Keyshawn Johnson .25 .60
250 J.Babineaux/C.Davis .20 .50
251 Marcel Shipp .20 .50
252 Brian Urlacher .30 .75
253 Haynesworth/LaBoy/Starks .20 .50
254 Derrick Burgess .20 .50
255 Harris/Thomas/Leber .20 .50
256 Henderson/Stroud/Hayward .20 .50
257 Travis Minor .20 .50
258 Rivera/Petitti/Johnson .20 .50
259 D.J. Williams .20 .50
260 Terrell Owens .25 .60
261 C.Wilson/D.Kreider .20 .50
262 Antonio Gates .30 .75
263 Ronde Barber .20 .50
264 Bryant Johnson .20 .50
265 Brett Favre .60 1.50
266 C.Stanley/K.Brown .20 .50
267 McKenzie/Petitgout/O'Hara .40 1.00
268 Chris Cooley .20 .50
269 Steve McNair .25 .60
270 Smith/Thornton/Geathers .20 .50
271 McClure/Forney/Lehr RC .20 .50
272 B.Sapp RC/Bartee/Wesley .20 .50
273 Jeremy Shockey .25 .60
274 Chad Johnson .25 .60
275 Vincent RC/Flynn RC/Mulitalo .20 .50
276 Deuce McAllister .25 .60
277 Sapp/Kelly/Hamilton .25 .60
278 B.Manumaleuna/R.Fitzpatrick .30 .75
279 Spires/White/Wyms .20 .50
280 Josh McCown .20 .50
281 Derrick Johnson LB .20 .50
282 T.Bryant/C.Grant .20 .50
283 C.Houston/D.Blaylock .20 .50
284 David Givens .25 .60
285 Lindell/McGee/Moorman .20 .50
286 Charlie Frye .25 .60
287 Ahman Green .25 .60
288 Darren Sharper .20 .50
289 Justin McCareins .20 .50
290 Lofa Tatupu .20 .50
291 Brock/Reagor/Thomas .20 .50
292 Muhsin Muhammad .20 .50
293 Derrick Mason .20 .50
294 Jones/Mare/Welker .25 .60
295 Stecker/Henderson/Conwell .20 .50
296 Mawae/Roos/Olson .20 .50
297 M.Bradley/A.Peterson .20 .50
298 John Abraham .20 .50
299 Dockery/Rabach/Samuels .20 .50
300 Peyton Manning .75 2.00
301 Alge Crumpler .25 .60
302 Mathis/Richardson/Grant .20 .50
303 Tedy Bruschi .25 .60
304 Snee/Diehl RC/Rymer RC .40 1.00

305 J.Stevens/P.Warrick .25 .60
306 Trent Dilfer .20 .50
307 Marion Barber .25 .60
308 Robert Ferguson .20 .50
309 Chester Taylor .25 .60
310 Jerry Porter .20 .50
311 Buenning/Walker/Wade .20 .50
312 DeShaun Foster .25 .60
313 R.Parrish/K.Holcomb .20 .50
314 Chris Brown .20 .50
315 Woody/Backus/Raiola .20 .50
316 Andre Johnson .25 .60
317 S.Graham/K.Larson .20 .50
318 Mangum/Gaines/Shelton .20 .50
319 Ben Roethlisberger .40 1.00
320 T.Devoe/C.Adams .20 .50
321 Jake Delhomme .20 .50
322 Chris Chambers .20 .50
323 Chris Simms .20 .50
324 Ed Reed .25 .60
325 Charles Rogers .25 .60
326 Eddie Kennison .20 .50
327 Seymour/Warren/Wilfork .25 .60
328 Lorenzo Neal .20 .50
329 Taylor Jacobs .20 .50
330 K.Mathis/L.Milloy .20 .50
331 Glenn/Henry/Reeves .20 .50
332 B.Dawkins/M.Lewis .30 .75
333 Edgerrin James .25 .60
334 Lee Evans .25 .60
335 Pat Williams .20 .50
336 Arrington/Torbor/Moore .20 .50
337 Roy Williams S .20 .50
338 Joe Horn .20 .50
339 Keenan McCardell .25 .60
340 Lee RC/Nedney/Hicks .20 .50
341 Mark Brunell .25 .60
342 Jimmy Smith .25 .60
343 Deltha O'Neal .20 .50
344 Chris McAlister .20 .50
345 T.Williamson/J.Kleinsasser .20 .50
346 N.Herron/A.Thurman .20 .50
347 A.Brown/A.Ogunleye .20 .50
348 Michael Vick .25 .60
349 Laveranues Coles .20 .50
350 Alex Smith QB .25 .60
351 Billy Volek .20 .50
352 Cato June .25 .60
353 J.Jurevicius/F.Jackson .20 .50
354 Keary Colbert .20 .50
355 Griffith/Schaub/White .20 .50
356 Smith/Payne/Walker .20 .50
357 Samie Parker .20 .50
358 Plaxico Burress .20 .50
359 R.Bartell/O.Atogwe .20 .50
360 C.Roby/R.Williams .20 .50
361 Springs/Harris/Prioleau .20 .50
362 A.Crowell/L.Fletcher .25 .60
363 Nick Barnett .20 .50
364 Antoine Winfield .20 .50
365 Will Smith .20 .50
366 J.Cotchery/B.Askew .20 .50
367 Brian Westbrook .20 .50
368 Jerome Mathis .20 .50
369 C.Moore/D.Darling .20 .50
370 Eric Parker .20 .50
371 Bly/Wilson/Kennedy .20 .50
372 Champ Bailey .25 .60
373 Cedric Benson .20 .50
374 Gray RC/Tobeck/Locklear .20 .50
375 L.Tynes/D.Colquitt .20 .50
376 Dan Morgan .20 .50
377 Posey/Schobel/Kelsay .20 .50
378 Ekuban/Brown/Myers .20 .50
379 Reed/Colclough/Gardocki .20 .50
380 M.Pollard/S.Vines .20 .50
381 McQuarters/Butler/Deloatch .20 .50
382 Fred Smoot .20 .50
383 Walter/Anderson/Crockett .20 .50
384 Dominic Rhodes .20 .50
385 T.Thompson/M.Vanderjagt .25 .60
386 Sullivan/Melton/Bryant .20 .50
387 M.Scifres/N.Kaeding .20 .50
388 Erron Kinney .20 .50
389 Bergen/Edwards/McCoy .20 .50
390 B.Jones/K.Brady .20 .50
391 McKinley/Pool/Baxter .20 .50
392 Jackson/Giordano/Hayden .20 .50
393 Keith Brooking .20 .50
394 Josh Reed .20 .50
395 Thomas Jones .20 .50
396 D.Johnson CB/S.Spencer .20 .50
397 Woolfolk/Clauss/Gardner .20 .50
398 Kyle Boller .20 .50
399 P.Pass/K.Faulk .20 .50
400 Routt/Schweigert/Riddle .20 .50
401 Donnie Edwards .20 .50
402 Michael Clayton .20 .50
403 Kasay/Kyle/Robertson .20 .50
404 A.Carroll/A.Harris .25 .60
405 Priest Holmes .20 .50
406 Jabar Gaffney .20 .50
407 Mewelde Moore .20 .50
408 Torry Holt .25 .60
409 Mark Clayton .20 .50
410 Shaun Alexander .20 .50
411 T.Tillman/T.Daniels .20 .50
412 Deion Branch .20 .50
413 Fraley/Andrews/Darilek RC .20 .50
414 Anquan Boldin .20 .50
415 T.James/K.Ratliff .20 .50
416 Ernest Wilford .20 .50
417 Moore/Jones/Kendall .20 .50
418 Brian Griese .20 .50
419 B.Kelly/J.Phillips .20 .50
420 Patrick Ramsey .25 .60
421 Corey Dillon .20 .50
422 Santana Moss .25 .60
423 Thomas/Edwards/Boulware .20 .50
424 Ashley Lelie .20 .50
425 G.Wilson/W.Demps .30 .75
426 Darrell Jackson .25 .60
427 Williams/Udeze/Scott .20 .50
428 K.Lucas/M.Minter .20 .50
429 Lee Suggs .20 .50
430 Kaczur/Mruczkowski/Gorin .20 .50
431 Robert Gallery .20 .50
432 Osgood/Feeley/Jackson .20 .50
433 Domanick Davis .20 .50
434 Osi Umenyiora .20 .50
435 Drew Bledsoe .25 .60
436 J.Gage/E.Berlin .20 .50
437 Rudi Johnson .20 .50
438 J.Fargas/M.Tuiasosopo .25 .60
439 Antwaan Randle El .20 .50
440 Marvin Harrison .25 .60
441 Brandon Marshall RC .75 2.00
442 Wali Lundy RC .40 1.00
443 Bruce Gradkowski RC .50 1.25
444 Leonard Pope RC .60 1.50
445 Omar Jacobs RC .40 1.00
446 Travis Wilson RC .40 1.00
447 Derek Hagan RC .50 1.25
448 Devin Hester RC .75 2.00
449 Willie Reid RC .50 1.25
450 A.J. Hawk RC .50 1.25
451 DeAngelo Williams RC .50 1.25
452 Ashton Youboty RC .40 1.00
453 Abdul Hodge RC .40 1.00
454 Leon Washington RC .40 1.00
455 D'Qwell Jackson RC .40 1.00
456 Johnathan Joseph RC .50 1.25
457 Antonio Cromartie RC .50 1.25
458 Michael Robinson RC .40 1.00
459 Tye Hill RC .40 1.00
460 Mathias Kiwanuka RC .60 1.50
461 Vince Young RC .40 1.00
462 DeMeco Ryans RC .50 1.25
463 Brodrick Bunkley RC .50 1.25
464 Jay Cutler RC .50 1.25
465 Brad Smith RC .50 1.25
466 Elvis Dumervil RC .60 1.50
467 Cory Rodgers RC .40 1.00
468 Davin Joseph RC .50 1.25
469 Rocky McIntosh RC .40 1.00
470 Jason Avant RC .40 1.00
471 Anthony Schlegel RC .50 1.25
472 Kamerion Wimbley RC .50 1.25
473 Joseph Addai RC .40 1.00
474 Ernie Sims RC .40 1.00
475 Jimmy Williams RC .40 1.00
476 LenDale White RC .40 1.00
477 Brandon Williams RC .40 1.00
478 Ko Simpson RC .50 1.25
479 Jerious Norwood RC .40 1.00
480 P.J. Daniels RC .40 1.00
481 Mario Williams RC .60 1.50
482 Santonio Holmes RC .50 1.25
483 Joe Klopfenstein RC .40 1.00
484 Matt Leinart RC .40 1.00
485 Danieal Manning RC .60 1.50
486 Andre Hall RC .50 1.25
487 Chad Greenway RC .60 1.50
488 Chad Jackson RC .40 1.00
489 Skyler Green RC .40 1.00
490 Donte Whitner RC .50 1.25
491 Bobby Carpenter RC .40 1.00
492 Jovon Bouknight RC .50 1.25
493 Vernon Davis RC .50 1.25
494 Kevin McMahan RC .50 1.25
495 D.J. Shockley RC .50 1.25
496 A.J. Nicholson RC .40 1.00
497 Brian Calhoun RC .40 1.00
498 Tim Day RC .50 1.25
499 Devin Aromashodu RC .40 1.00
500 Charlie Whitehurst RC .40 1.00
501 Sinorice Moss RC .40 1.00
502 Maurice Stovall RC .40 1.00
503 Laurence Maroney RC .40 1.00
504 James Anderson RC .40 1.00
505 Darnell Bing RC .50 1.25
506 Jerome Harrison RC .40 1.00
507 Daniel Bullocks RC .40 1.00
508 Will Blackmon RC .40 1.00
509 Marcedes Lewis RC .40 1.00
510 Lawrence Vickers RC .50 1.25
511 Marques Hagans RC .40 1.00
512 Jeremy Bloom RC .40 1.00
513 Dominique Byrd RC .40 1.00
514 Tarvaris Jackson RC .40 1.00
515 Dusty Dvoracek RC .60 1.50
516 Brodie Croyle RC .40 1.00
517 Demetrius Williams RC .40 1.00
518 Jason Allen RC .50 1.25
519 Mike Hass RC .40 1.00
520 Nick Mangold RC .50 1.25
521 Brett Basanez RC .60 1.50
522 Ben Obomanu RC .50 1.25
523 Tamba Hali RC .60 1.50
524 Gabe Watson RC .40 1.00
525 Kelly Jennings RC .50 1.25
526 Reggie Bush RC .60 1.50
527 Bernard Pollard RC .50 1.25
528 Reggie McNeal RC .40 1.00
529 Jonathan Orr RC .50 1.25
530 Haloti Ngata RC .50 1.25
531 David Thomas RC .40 1.00
532 Ingle Martin RC .50 1.25
533 Anthony Fasano RC .40 1.00
534 Winston Justice RC .50 1.25
535 Manny Lawson RC .50 1.25
536 Kellen Clemens RC .40 1.00
537 Adam Jennings RC .50 1.25
538 Thomas Howard RC .40 1.00
539 Cedric Humes RC .40 1.00
540 Garrett Mills RC .50 1.25
541 Jeff Webb RC .50 1.25
542 Michael Huff RC .50 1.25
543 Gerris Wilkinson RC UER .40 1.00
544 Maurice Drew RC .60 1.50
545 John McCargo RC .40 1.00
546 Todd Watkins RC .40 1.00
547 Marcus Vick RC .40 1.00
548 Greg Jennings RC .60 1.50
549 P.J. Pope RC .60 1.50
550 D'Brickashaw Ferguson RC .40 1.00
CL1 Checklist Card 1 .05 .15
CL2 Checklist Card 2 .05 .15
CL3 Checklist Card 3 .05 .15
CL4 Checklist Card 4 .05 .15
CL5 Checklist Card 5 .05 .15
CL6 Checklist Card 6 .05 .15

2006 Topps Total Black

*VETS 1-440: 3X TO 8X BASIC CARDS
*ROOKIES 441-550: 1.5X TO 4X BASIC CARDS
BLACK/50 STATED ODDS 1:11

2006 Topps Total Blue

*VETS 1-440: .8X TO 2X BASIC CARDS
*ROOKIES 441-550: .5X TO 1.2X
STATED ODDS 1.5:1

2006 Topps Total Gold

ETS 1-440: 2.5X TO 6X BASIC CARDS
*ROOKIES 441-550: 1.2X TO 3X BASIC CARDS
STATED ODDS 1:10 HOB, 1:12 RET

2006 Topps Total Red

*VETERANS 1-440: 1X TO 2.5X BASIC CARDS
*ROOKIES 441-550: .6X TO 1.5X
STATED ODDS 1:1 HOB, 1:4 RET

2006 Topps Total Silver

*VETERANS 1-440: 1.5X TO 4X BASIC CARDS
*ROOKIES 441-550: .8X TO 2X BASIC CARDS
STATED ODDS 1:4 HOB, 1:6 RET

2006 Topps Total Award Winners

COMPLETE SET (20) 10.00 25.00
STATED ODDS 1:8 HOB/RET
AW1 Carson Palmer .60 1.50
AW2 Tom Brady 2.50 6.00
AW3 Brett Favre 1.50 4.00
AW4 Larry Johnson .50 1.25
AW5 Ben Roethlisberger 1.00 2.50
AW6 Chad Johnson .50 1.25
AW7 Derrick Burgess .50 1.25
AW8 Cadillac Williams .60 1.50
AW9 Shaun Alexander .50 1.25
AW10 Tedy Bruschi .60 1.50
AW11 Marvin Harrison .60 1.50
AW12 Brian Urlacher .75 2.00
AW13 Steve Smith .75 2.00
AW14 Matt Hasselbeck .50 1.25
AW15 Jonathan Vilma .50 1.25
AW16 Shawne Merriman .60 1.50
AW17 Peyton Manning 2.00 5.00
AW18 Larry Fitzgerald .60 1.50
AW19 Shaun Alexander .50 1.25
AW20 Hines Ward .60 1.50

2006 Topps Total Rookie Jerseys

D3 1:8 TARGET RETAIL PACKS
32TE A.J. Hawk 2.50 6.00
33TE Brandon Marshall 4.00 10.00
34TE Brandon Williams 2.00 5.00
35TE Brian Calhoun 2.00 5.00
36TE Chad Jackson 2.00 5.00
37TE Charlie Whitehurst 2.00 5.00
38TE DeAngelo Williams 2.50 6.00
39TE Demetrius Williams 2.00 5.00
40TE Derek Hagan 2.50 6.00
41TE Jason Avant 2.00 5.00
42TE Jerious Norwood 2.00 5.00
43TE Joe Klopfenstein 2.00 5.00
44TE Kellen Clemens 2.00 5.00
45TE Laurence Maroney 2.00 5.00
46TE LenDale White 2.00 5.00
47TE Leon Washington 2.00 5.00
48TE Marcedes Lewis 2.00 5.00
49TE Mario Williams 3.00 8.00
50TE Matt Leinart 2.00 5.00
51TE Maurice Drew 3.00 8.00
52TE Maurice Stovall 2.00 5.00
53TE Michael Huff 2.50 6.00
54TE Michael Robinson 2.00 5.00
55TE Omar Jacobs 2.00 5.00
56TE Reggie Bush 3.00 8.00
57TE Santonio Holmes 2.50 6.00
58TE Sinorice Moss 2.00 5.00
59TE Tarvaris Jackson 2.00 5.00
60TE Travis Wilson 2.00 5.00
61TE Vernon Davis 2.50 6.00
62TE Vince Young 2.00 5.00

2006 Topps Total Signatures

GROUP A ODDS 1:5100 H, 1:7400 R
GROUP B ODDS 1:1310 H, 1:2550
GROUP C ODDS 1:385 H, 1:1000 R
TSBS Brad Smith 6.00 15.00
TSCT Chester Taylor 15.00 40.00
TSDH Devin Hester 12.00 30.00
TSJA Jason Avant 8.00 20.00
TSMD Maurice Drew 20.00 40.00
TSMH Michael Huff 10.00 25.00
TSSM Shawne Merriman 12.00 30.00
TSSS Steve Smith 30.00 60.00
TSTP Troy Polamalu

2006 Topps Total Sports Illustrated For Kids

MPLETE SET (25) 8.00 20.00
STATED ODDS 1:1
1 Shaun Alexander .30 .75
2 Larry Johnson .30 .75
3 LaDainian Tomlinson .50 1.25
4 Clinton Portis .30 .75
5 Tiki Barber .40 1.00
6 Edgerrin James .40 1.00
7 Rudi Johnson .30 .75
8 Cadillac Williams .40 1.00
9 Peyton Manning 1.25 3.00
10 Ronnie Brown .40 1.00
11 Steven Jackson .30 .75
12 Tony Gonzalez .40 1.00
13 LaMont Jordan .40 1.00
14 Terrell Owens .40 1.00
15 Steve Smith .50 1.25
16 Chad Johnson .30 .75
17 Torry Holt .40 1.00
18 Marvin Harrison .40 1.00
19 Larry Fitzgerald .40 1.00
20 Randy Moss .40 1.00
21 Antonio Gates .50 1.25
22 Reggie Bush .50 1.25
23 Tom Brady 1.50 4.00
24 Jeremy Shockey .30 .75
25 Donovan McNabb .40 1.00

2006 Topps Total Team Checklists

ATED ODDS 1:4
1 Edgerrin James .25 .60
2 Michael Vick .25 .60
3 Steve McNair .25 .60
4 Willis McGahee .20 .50
5 Steve Smith .30 .75
6 Brian Urlacher .30 .75
7 Carson Palmer .25 .60
8 Charlie Frye .25 .60
9 Terrell Owens .25 .60
10 Jake Plummer .20 .50
11 Roy Williams WR .20 .50
12 Brett Favre .60 1.50
13 Mario Williams .40 1.00
14 Peyton Manning .75 2.00
15 Byron Leftwich .20 .50
16 Larry Johnson .20 .50
17 Daunte Culpepper .25 .60
18 Chester Taylor .25 .60
19 Tom Brady 1.00 2.50
20 Reggie Bush .40 1.00
21 Tiki Barber .25 .60
22 Curtis Martin .25 .60
23 Randy Moss .25 .60
24 Donovan McNabb .25 .60
25 Ben Roethlisberger .40 1.00
26 LaDainian Tomlinson .30 .75
27 Vernon Davis .30 .75
28 Shaun Alexander .20 .50
29 Marc Bulger .20 .50
30 Cadillac Williams .25 .60
31 Vince Young .25 .60
32 Clinton Portis .20 .50

2006 Topps Total Total Production

COMPLETE SET (10) 6.00 15.00
STATED ODDS 1:16 HOB/RET
TP1 Shaun Alexander .50 1.25
TP2 Larry Johnson .50 1.25
TP3 Carson Palmer .60 1.50
TP4 Peyton Manning 2.00 5.00
TP5 Tom Brady 2.50 6.00
TP6 Drew Brees .75 2.00
TP7 LaDainian Tomlinson .75 2.00
TP8 Chris Chambers .50 1.25
TP9 Marvin Harrison .60 1.50
TP10 Steve Smith .75 2.00

2006 Topps Total Total Topps

MPLETE SET (20) 10.00 25.00
STATED ODDS 1:8 HOB/RET
TT1 Peyton Manning 2.00 5.00
TT2 Ben Roethlisberger 1.00 2.50
TT3 Steve Smith .75 2.00
TT4 Carson Palmer .60 1.50
TT5 Larry Johnson .50 1.25
TT6 Tiki Barber .60 1.50
TT7 Chad Johnson .50 1.25
TT8 LaDainian Tomlinson .75 2.00
TT9 Michael Vick .60 1.50
TT10 Edgerrin James .60 1.50
TT11 Cadillac Williams .60 1.50
TT12 Tom Brady 2.50 6.00
TT13 Antonio Gates .75 2.00
TT14 Hines Ward .60 1.50
TT15 Trent Green .50 1.25
TT16 Rudi Johnson .50 1.25
TT17 Donovan Mcnabb .60 1.50
TT18 Shaun Alexander .50 1.25
TT19 Marvin Harrison .60 1.50
TT20 Brett Favre 1.50 4.00

2007 Topps Total

This 550-card set was released in August, 2007. The set was issued into the hobby in 10-card packs, with a 99 cent SRP, which came 36 packs to a box. Cards numbered 1-440 feature veteran players in a mix of single and multi-player cards while cards numbered 441-550 feature 2007 NFL rookies.

COMPLETE SET (550) 25.00 60.00
UNPRICED PRINT PLATES SER.#'d TO 1
1 Cadillac Williams .25 .60
2 Marcel Shipp .20 .50
Troy Walters
3 Kerry Collins .20 .50
Brandon Jones
4 J.J. Arrington .25 .60
5 Albert Haynesworth .20 .50
6 DeAngelo Hall .20 .50
7 Kyle Vanden Bosch .20 .50
Travis LaBoy
Andre Woolfolk
8 Kyle Boller .20 .50
Justin Green
Demetrius Williams
9 Anquan Boldin .20 .50
10 Anthony Thomas .20 .50
11 Orlando Huff .20 .50
Leonard Pope
Darnell Dockett
12 Mike Rucker .20 .50
Kris Jenkins
13 Musa Smith .20 .50
Mike Anderson
14 DeShaun Foster .25 .60
15 Mark Clayton .20 .50
16 Mike Minter
Ken Lucas
Richard Marshall
17 Ed Reed .25 .60
18 Devin Hester .25 .60
19 Brian Moorman .20 .50
Craig Nall
Rian Lindell
20 Jamal Lewis .25 .60
21 Chris Gamble .20 .50
22 Kenny Wright .20 .50
Leigh Bodden
Tim Carter
23 Tommie Harris .20 .50
Tank Johnson
24 Ryan Tucker .20 .50
Kevin Shaffer RC
Hank Fraley
25 Brad Maynard .20 .50
Robbie Gould
Adrian Peterson Bears
26 Terence Newman .20 .50
Anthony Henry
27 T.J. Houshmandzadeh .20 .50
28 Travis Henry .25 .60
29 Julius Jones .20 .50
30 Kyle Johnson .20 .50
Nick Ferguson
Dre Bly
31 Leonard Davis .20 .50
Marco Rivera
Andre Gurode
32 Aaron Kampman .25 .60
Kabeer Gbaja-Biamila
33 Demetrin Veal RC .20 .50
Gerard Warren
34 Brett Favre .60 1.50
35 Mike Bell .25 .60
36 Ron Dayne .25 .60
37 Jon Kitna .20 .50
38 Kris Brown .20 .50
Dexter Wynn
Samkon Gado
39 Daniel Bullocks .20 .50
Fernando Bryant
Kenoy Kennedy
40 Peyton Manning .75 2.00
41 Matt Schaub .20 .50
42 Matt Jones .25 .60
43 Jim Sorgi .20 .50
Ben Utecht
44 Dennis Northcutt .20 .50
Josh Scobee
Alvin Pearman
45 Dallas Clark .25 .60
46 Kris Wilson .20 .50
Michael Bennett
47 Jeff Saturday .20 .50
Tarik Glenn
Ryan Diem
48 Daunte Culpepper .25 .60
49 Damon Huard .25 .60
50 Bryant McKinnie .25 .60
Matt Birk
Steve Hutchinson
51 Ty Law .30 .75
52 Rosevelt Colvin .25 .60
Mike Vrabel
53 Brian Waters .20 .50
Casey Wiegmann RC
Will Shields
54 Chad Jackson .20 .50
55 Bobby Wade .20 .50
Tony Richardson
56 Tedy Bruschi .25 .60
57 Antoine Winfield .20 .50
58 Jammal Brown .20 .50
Jeff Faine
Jon Stinchcomb
59 Matt Light .20 .50
Logan Mankins
Dan Koppen
60 Michael Strahan .25 .60
61 Marques Colston .20 .50
62 Johnnie Morant .20 .50
Ronald Curry
63 Will Demps .20 .50
Gibril Wilson
64 Warren Sapp .25 .60
65 William Joseph .20 .50
Fred Robbins
Barry Cofield
66 Chris Carr .20 .50
Sebastian Janikowski
Shane Lechler
67 Cedric Houston .20 .50
68 Nate Washington .20 .50
69 Jonathan Vilma .20 .50
70 Willie Parker .25 .60
71 Sheldon Brown .20 .50
Lito Sheppard
72 Najeh Davenport .20 .50
Charlie Batch
Dan Kreider
73 Jevon Kearse .20 .50
74 Luis Castillo .20 .50
Jamal Williams
75 Darren Howard .20 .50
Jerome McDougle
Trent Cole
76 Vernon Davis .20 .50
77 Antonio Gates .30 .75
78 Chris Gray .20 .50
Chris Spencer
Walter Jones
79 Terrence Kiel .20 .50
Drayton Florence
Marlon McCree
80 V. Adeyanju/L.Glover .20 .50
81 Ashley Lelie .25 .60
82 Torry Holt .25 .60
83 Maurice Morris .20 .50
Mack Strong
84 Jermaine Phillips .20 .50
Will Allen
Shelton Quarles
85 Shaun Alexander .20 .50
86 Vince Young .20 .50
87 Orlando Pace .20 .50
Alex Barron
Andy McCollum
88 Brandon Lloyd .20 .50
89 Joey Galloway .25 .60
90 Neil Rackers .20 .50
Scott Player
91 Peter Sirmon .20 .50
David Thornton
92 Bryant Johnson .20 .50
93 Bo Scaife .20 .50
Cortland Finnegan
Reynaldo Hill
94 John Abraham .20 .50
95 Jason Campbell .20 .50
96 Kelly Gregg .25 .60
Bart Scott
Haloti Ngata
97 Adrian Wilson .20 .50
98 Drew Carter .20 .50
Keary Colbert
99 Michael Jenkins .20 .50
D.J. Shockley
Roddy White
100 Jake Delhomme .20 .50
101 Terrell Suggs .20 .50
Trevor Pryce
102 Thomas Davis .20 .50
James Anderson
Dan Morgan
103 Todd Heap .20 .50
104 Bernard Berrian .20 .50
105 Peerless Price .20 .50
106 Chris Henry .20 .50
107 Daimon Shelton .20 .50
Robert Royal
Ryan Neufeld
108 Kellen Winslow .20 .50
109 Rex Grossman .20 .50
110 Kamerion Wimbley .20 .50
D'Qwell Jackson
Andra Davis
111 Levi Jones .20 .50
Willie Anderson
112 Bradie James .20 .50
Akin Ayodele
113 Deltha O'Neal .20 .50
114 Javon Walker .25 .60
115 Jeremi Johnson .20 .50
Doug Johnson
Reggie Kelly
116 Quincy Morgan .20 .50
Jason Elam
Paul Ernster
117 Roy Williams S .20 .50
118 Donald Driver .25 .60
119 Miles Austin .50 1.25
Mat McBriar
Sam Hurd
120 Dunta Robinson .20 .50
Dexter McCleon
121 Devale Ellis RC .20 .50
Shaun McDonald
122 Wali Lundy .20 .50
123 Tatum Bell .20 .50
124 Owen Daniels .20 .50
Mark Bruener
Jeb Putzier
125 Marquand Manuel .20 .50
Nick Collins
Al Harris
126 Morlon Greenwood .20 .50
Shawn Barber
Shantee Orr
127 Ahman Green .25 .60
128 Marvin Harrison .25 .60
129 Josh Thomas .20 .50
Corey Simon
Raheem Brock
130 Chris Naeole .20 .50
Brad Meester
Maurice Williams
131 Marcus Stroud .20 .50
John Henderson
132 Kendrell Bell .20 .50
Derrick Johnson
133 Byron Leftwich .20 .50
134 Trent Green .20 .50
135 Samie Parker .20 .50
136 Mewelde Moore .20 .50
137 Chris Chambers .20 .50
138 Chris Kluwe .20 .50
Artose Pinner
Ryan Longwell
139 Travis Daniels .20 .50
Michael Lehan
Keith Adams
140 Richard Seymour .20 .50
141 Jim Kleinsasser .20 .50
Brooks Bollinger
142 Fred Thomas .20 .50
Mike McKenzie
143 Darren Sharper .20 .50
144 Will Smith .20 .50
145 Ellis Hobbs .20 .50
Asante Samuel
Chad Scott
146 Simns/Shanle RC/Fujita .20 .50
147 Devery Henderson .20 .50
148 Jeremy Shockey .20 .50
149 Antonio Pierce .20 .50
Reggie Torbor
150 Zack Crockett .20 .50
Justin Fargas
151 Jerricho Cotchery .20 .50
152 Dominic Rhodes .20 .50
153 D'Brickashaw Ferguson .20 .50
Nick Mangold
Pete Kendall
154 Nnamdi Asomugha .20 .50
Fabian Washington
Stuart Schweigert
155 Andrew Walter .20 .50
156 Cedrick Wilson .20 .50
157 Dirk Johnson .20 .50
David Akers
Reno Mahe
158 Troy Polamalu .30 .75
159 Casey Hampton .20 .50
Aaron Smith
160 Alan Faneca .20 .50
Max Starks
Marvel Smith
161 Shawne Merriman .20 .50
162 Shaun Phillips .20 .50
Randall Godfrey
163 Jonas Jennings .30 .75
Larry Allen
Kwame Harris
164 Nate Clements .20 .50
165 Marcus Pollard .20 .50
Seneca Wallace
166 Marcus Trufant .20 .50
Jordan Babineaux RC
Kelly Jennings
167 Nate Burleson .20 .50
168 Isaac Bruce .30 .75
169 Deion Branch .20 .50
170 Alex Smith TE .20 .50
Anthony Becht
171 Brandon Chillar .20 .50
Pisa Tinoisamoa
Will Witherspoon
172 Mark Jones .20 .50
Matt Bryant
Josh Bidwell
173 Michael Clayton .20 .50
174 LenDale White .25 .60
175 Lamont Thompson .20 .50
Chris Hope
176 Chris Cooley .20 .50
177 Santana Moss .25 .60
178 Chike Okeafor .20 .50
Bertrand Berry
179 Chris Samuels .20 .50
Jon Jansen
Randy Thomas
180 Matt Leinart .20 .50
181 Michael Vick .25 .60
182 Antrel Rolle .20 .50
Roderick Hood
Terrence Holt
183 Michael Koenen .20 .50
Morten Andersen
Allen Rossum
184 Joe Horn .20 .50
185 Chris McAlister .20 .50
Samari Rolle
186 Steve McNair .25 .60
187 Roscoe Parrish .20 .50
188 Sam Koch .25 .60
Jonathan Ogden
Matt Stover
189 J.P. Losman .20 .50
190 J.Kasay/J.Baker RC .20 .50
191 Kiwaukee Thomas .20 .50
Ko Simpson
Donte Whitner
192 Steve Smith .25 .60
193 Cedric Benson .20 .50
194 Rashied Davis .20 .50
195 Bryan Robinson .25 .60
Justin Smith
196 Mark Bradley .20 .50
Brian Griese
Desmond Clark
197 Dexter Jackson .20 .50
Keiwan Ratliff
Johnathan Joseph
198 Carson Palmer .25 .60
199 Joe Jurevicius .20 .50
200 Willie McGinest .20 .50
201 Terry Glenn .25 .60
202 Joshua Cribbs .30 .75
Phil Dawson
Dave Zastudil
203 DeMarcus Ware .25 .60
Greg Ellis
Marcus Spears
204 Bobby Carpenter .20 .50
Aaron Glenn
205 Cory Redding .20 .50
Shaun Rogers
206 Champ Bailey .25 .60
207 T.J. Duckett .20 .50
208 Damien Woody .20 .50
Dominic Raiola
Jeff Backus
209 Kevin Jones .20 .50
210 Greg Jennings .20 .50
211 Cullen Jenkins .20 .50
Corey Williams
Ryan Pickett
212 Anthony Weaver .20 .50
Jason Babin
213 Andre Johnson .25 .60
214 Kevin Walter .25 .60
Jameel Cook
Derrick Lewis
215 Hunter Smith .20 .50
Terrence Wilkins
Adam Vinatieri
216 Bob Sanders .25 .60
217 Greg Jones .20 .50
David Garrard
218 Reggie Wayne .25 .60
219 Fred Taylor .20 .50
220 Eddie Kennison .20 .50
221 Marty Booker .20 .50
222 Jeff Webb .20 .50
Rod Gardner
Dustin Colquitt
223 Ronnie Brown .20 .50
224 Channing Crowder .20 .50
Joey Porter
225 Jason Allen .20 .50
Renaldo Hill
Yeremiah Bell
226 Tarvaris Jackson .20 .50
227 Kevin Williams .20 .50
Pat Williams
228 Kenechi Udeze .20 .50
Darrion Scott
Dwight Smith
229 Tom Brady 1.00 2.50
230 Roman Harper .20 .50
Josh Bullocks
231 James Sanders .30 .75
Rodney Harrison
Stephen Gostkowski
232 Terrance Copper .25 .60
233 Brandon Jacobs .20 .50
234 Drew Brees .30 .75
235 Bryan Thomas .20 .50
Shaun Ellis
236 Amani Toomer .20 .50
237 Justin Miller .20 .50
238 Jared Lorenzen .25 .60
David Tyree
Sinorice Moss
239 Brad Smith .20 .50
Chris Baker
240 Derrick Burgess .20 .50
Tyler Brayton
241 Jerry Porter .25 .60
242 Michael Huff .25 .60
243 Jeremiah Trotter .20 .50
244 Kirk Morrison .20 .50
Sam Williams
Thomas Howard
245 Shawn Andrews .20 .50
William Thomas
Jon Runyan
246 Santonio Holmes .20 .50
247 Jerame Tuman .20 .50
Heath Miller
248 Eric Parker .20 .50
249 Quentin Jammer .20 .50
250 Marcus McNeill .20 .50
Nick Hardwick
Mike Goff RC
251 Mark Roman .20 .50
Jeff Ulbrich
Shawntae Spencer
252 Walt Harris .20 .50
Michael Lewis
253 LeRoy Hill .20 .50
Lofa Tatupu
254 Bryant Young .20 .50
255 Darrell Jackson .20 .50
256 Deon Grant .20 .50
Brian Russell
Michael Boulware
257 Drew Bennett .20 .50
258 Steven Jackson .20 .50
259 Dane Looker .20 .50
Gus Frerotte
Corey Chavous
260 Ike Hilliard .20 .50
Michael Pittman
261 Simeon Rice .20 .50
262 Roydell Williams .20 .50
263 Mark Brunell .25 .60
James Thrash
264 Ben Troupe .20 .50
Kevin Mawae
Erron Kinney
265 Clinton Portis .20 .50
266 Larry Fitzgerald .25 .60
267 Carlos Rogers .20 .50
Fred Smoot
Shawn Springs
268 Gerald Hayes .20 .50
Calvin Pace
Karlos Dansby
269 Warrick Dunn .20 .50
270 Keith Brooking .20 .50
Brian Finneran
271 Kynan Forney .20 .50
Wayne Gandy
Todd McClure
272 Jerious Norwood .20 .50
273 Josh Reed .20 .50
Shaud Williams
274 Willis McGahee .20 .50
275 Terrence McGee .20 .50
276 Ronnie Prude .20 .50
Jarret Johnson
Dawan Landry
277 Lee Evans .25 .60
278 Keyshawn Johnson .25 .60
279 Jordan Gross .20 .50
Mike Wahle
Will Montgomery
280 Alex Brown .20 .50
Adewale Ogunleye
281 Muhsin Muhammad .20 .50
282 Olin Kreutz .20 .50
John Tait
Fred Miller
283 Glenn Holt RC .25 .60
Kyle Larson
Shayne Graham
284 Chris Perry .20 .50
285 Derek Anderson .20 .50
Ken Dorsey
286 Chad Johnson .20 .50
287 Charlie Frye .25 .60
288 Orpheus Roye .20 .50
Ted Washington
Robaire Smith
289 Jason Witten .25 .60
290 Tony Romo .40 1.00
291 D.J. Williams .20 .50
Ian Gold
Al Wilson
292 Ebenezer Ekuban .20 .50
Kenard Lang
293 Paris Lenon .20 .50
Boss Bailey
294 Rod Smith .25 .60
295 Mike Furrey .25 .60
296 Nick Harris .20 .50
Jason Hanson
Eddie Drummond
297 Robert Ferguson .20 .50
298 Charles Woodson .30 .75
299 Chad Clifton .20 .50
Mark Tauscher
Rob Davis
300 Travis Johnson .20 .50
C.C. Brown
Glenn Earl
301 Mario Williams .25 .60
302 Anthony McFarland .20 .50
Robert Mathis
303 George Wrighster .20 .50
Marcedes Lewis
304 Joseph Addai .20 .50
305 Maurice Jones-Drew .20 .50
306 Ernest Wilford .20 .50
307 Donovin Darius .20 .50
Nick Greisen
Mike Peterson
308 Larry Johnson .20 .50
309 Derek Hagan .20 .50
310 Ron Edwards .20 .50
James Reed
Jimmy Wilkerson
311 Zach Thomas .25 .60
312 Vonnie Holliday .20 .50
Keith Traylor
313 Jason Rader .20 .50
L.J. Shelton
Cleo Lemon
314 Chester Taylor .20 .50
315 Jabar Gaffney .20 .50
Reche Caldwell
316 E.J. Henderson .20 .50
Dontarrious Thomas
Ben Leber
317 Donte Stallworth .25 .60
318 Jamie Martin .20 .50
Mike Karney
319 Hollis Thomas .20 .50
Brian Young
Charles Grant
320 Reuben Droughns .25 .60
321 Eli Manning .25 .60
322 Corey Webster .20 .50
R.W. McQuarters
Sam Madison
323 Erik Coleman .20 .50
Kerry Rhodes
324 Chad Pennington .20 .50
325 DeWayne Robertson .20 .50
Kimo Von Oelhoffen
Andre Dyson
326 Courtney Anderson .20 .50
Robert Gallery
Randal Williams
327 Randy Moss .25 .60
328 Brodrick Bunkley .20 .50
Mike Patterson
329 Correll Buckhalter .20 .50
330 Donovan McNabb .25 .60
331 Chris Gardocki .20 .50
Jeff Reed
332 Vincent Jackson .20 .50
333 Ben Roethlisberger .30 .75
334 Philip Rivers .30 .75
335 Larry Foote .20 .50
Clark Haggans
James Farrior
336 Billy Volek .20 .50
Brandon Manumaleuna
Nate Kaeding

337 Alex Smith QB .25 .60
338 Marques Douglas .20 .50
Manny Lawson
339 Maurice Hicks .20 .50
Joe Nedney
Andy Lee
340 D.J. Hackett .20 .50
341 Julian Peterson .20 .50
342 Patrick Kerney .20 .50
Bryce Fisher
Rocky Bernard
343 Randy McMichael .20 .50
Joe Klopfenstein
344 Leonard Little .20 .50
345 Jeff Garcia .20 .50
346 Cato June .20 .50
Derrick Brooks
347 Mike Alstott .20 .50
348 Keith Bulluck .20 .50
349 Kevin Carter .20 .50
Greg Spires
Chris Hovan
350 Courtney Roby .20 .50
Craig Hentrich
Rob Bironas
351 London Fletcher .25 .60
Marcus Washington
352 Edgerrin James .25 .60
353 Antwaan Randle El .20 .50
354 Kurt Warner .25 .60
Gabe Watson
Sean Morey
355 Renaldo Wynn .20 .50
Phillip Daniels
Andre Carter
356 Roy Williams WR .20 .50
357 Alge Crumpler .25 .60
358 Brian Dawkins .30 .75
359 Chris Crocker .20 .50
Lawyer Milloy
Jimmy Williams
360 Reggie Bush .20 .50
361 Chris Kelsay .20 .50
Angelo Crowell
362 Sean Taylor .30 .75
363 Aaron Schobel .20 .50
364 Rock Cartwright .20 .50
Ladell Betts
Mike Sellers
365 DeAngelo Williams .20 .50
366 Grady Jackson .20 .50
Rod Coleman
367 David Carr .20 .50
Brad Hoover
Michael Gaines
368 Derrick Mason .20 .50
369 Brian Urlacher .30 .75
370 Ray Lewis .30 .75
371 Robert Geathers .20 .50
Madieu Williams
Landon Johnson
372 Langston Walker .20 .50
Jason Peters
Derrick Dockery
373 Jason Wright .20 .50
Jerome Harrison
374 Julius Peppers .25 .60
375 Braylon Edwards .20 .50
376 Lance Briggs .25 .60
Mark Anderson
377 Jay Cutler .20 .50
378 Nathan Vasher .25 .60
Charles Tillman
Ricky Manning Jr
379 Brandon Marshall .25 .60
Daniel Graham
Patrick Ramsey
380 Rudi Johnson .20 .50
381 Ernie Sims .20 .50
382 Marion Barber .25 .60
383 Bubba Franks .75 2.00
Aaron Rodgers
384 Terrell Owens .25 .60
385 Vernand Morency .25 .60
386 Brad Johnson .25 .60
Anthony Fasano
Patrick Crayton
387 Nick Barnett .20 .50
Will Blackmon
Abdul Hodge
388 John Engelberger .20 .50
Elvis Dumervil
389 DeMeco Ryans .25 .60
390 John Lynch .25 .60
391 Rashean Mathis .20 .50
392 Shawn Bryson .20 .50
Brian Calhoun
Dan Campbell
393 Brian Williams .20 .50
Paul Spicer
Reggie Hayward
394 A.J. Hawk .20 .50
395 Tamba Hali .20 .50
Jared Allen
396 Gary Brackett .20 .50
Rob Morris
397 Jason Taylor .25 .60
398 Dwight Freeney .20 .50
399 Donnie Spragan .20 .50
Matt Roth
Travares Tillman
400 Marlin Jackson .20 .50
Matt Giordano
Antoine Bethea
401 Ty Warren .20 .50
Vince Wilfork
402 Reggie Williams .25 .60
403 Wes Welker .25 .60
404 Tony Gonzalez .25 .60
405 Laurence Maroney .25 .60
406 Patrick Surtain .20 .50
Greg Wesley
Sammy Knight
407 Steve Weatherford RC .20 .50
Michael Lewis
John Carney
408 Will Allen .20 .50
Andre Goodman
409 Plaxico Burress .20 .50
410 Troy Williamson .20 .50
411 Victor Hobson .20 .50
Eric Barton
412 Ben Watson .25 .60
Matt Cassel
Kevin Faulk
413 Justin McCareins .20 .50
Mike Nugent
Ben Graham
414 Deuce McAllister .25 .60
415 LaMont Jordan .25 .60
416 Osi Umenyiora .20 .50
Mathias Kiwanuka
417 Reggie Brown .20 .50
418 Shaun O'Hara .25 .60
Kareem McKenzie
Chris Snee
419 Hines Ward .25 .60
420 Leon Washington .20 .50
421 Ike Taylor .20 .50
Deshea Townsend
Bryant McFadden
422 Laveranues Coles .20 .50
423 Lorenzo Neal .20 .50
Michael Turner
424 Dhani Jones .20 .50
Takeo Spikes
425 Frank Gore .25 .60
426 Brian Westbrook .20 .50
427 Michael Robinson .25 .60
Moran Norris
Trent Dilfer
428 Kevin Curtis .25 .60
Hank Baskett
Greg Lewis
429 Fakhir Brown .20 .50
Tye Hill
430 LaDainian Tomlinson .30 .75
431 Marc Bulger .20 .50
432 Matt Wilhelm .20 .50
Igor Olshansky
Antonio Cromartie
433 Chris Simms .20 .50
434 Derek Smith LB .20 .50
Tully Banta-Cain
435 Ronde Barber .20 .50
Brian Kelly
Phillip Buchanon
436 Arnaz Battle .20 .50
437 David Givens .20 .50
438 Matt Hasselbeck .20 .50
439 Cornelius Griffin .20 .50
Rocky McIntosh
440 Dominique Byrd .20 .50
Jeff Wilkins
Aaron Walker
441 JaMarcus Russell RC .40 1.00
442 Brady Quinn RC .40 1.00
443 Drew Stanton RC .40 1.00
444 Troy Smith RC .40 1.00
445 Kevin Kolb RC .50 1.25
446 Trent Edwards RC .40 1.00
447 John Beck RC .40 1.00
448 Jordan Palmer RC .50 1.25
449 Chris Leak RC .40 1.00
450 Isiah Stanback RC .40 1.00
451 Tyler Palko RC .60 1.50
452 Jared Zabransky RC .40 1.00
453 Jeff Rowe RC .40 1.00
454 Zac Taylor RC .50 1.25
455 Lester Ricard RC .50 1.25
456 Adrian Peterson RC 1.25 3.00
457 Marshawn Lynch RC .75 2.00
458 Brandon Jackson RC .40 1.00
459 Michael Bush RC .40 1.00
460 Kenny Irons RC .40 1.00
461 Antonio Pittman RC .40 1.00
462 Tony Hunt RC .40 1.00
463 Darius Walker RC .40 1.00
464 Dwayne Wright RC .40 1.00
465 Lorenzo Booker RC .50 1.25
466 Kenneth Darby RC .40 1.00
467 Chris Henry RC .40 1.00
468 Selvin Young RC .40 1.00
469 Brian Leonard RC .40 1.00
470 Ahmad Bradshaw RC .60 1.50
471 Gary Russell RC .50 1.25
472 Kolby Smith RC .40 1.00
473 Thomas Clayton RC .50 1.25
474 Garrett Wolfe RC .40 1.00
475 Calvin Johnson RC 1.25 3.00
476 Ted Ginn Jr. RC .50 1.25
477 Dwayne Jarrett RC .50 1.25
478 Dwayne Bowe RC .40 1.00
479 Sidney Rice RC .50 1.25
480 Robert Meachem RC .50 1.25
481 Anthony Gonzalez RC .40 1.00
482 Craig Buster Davis RC .40 1.00
483 Aundrae Allison RC .40 1.00
484 Chansi Stuckey RC .50 1.25
485 David Clowney RC .40 1.00
486 Steve Smith RC .40 1.00
487 Courtney Taylor RC .40 1.00
488 Paul Williams RC .40 1.00
489 Johnnie Lee Higgins RC .40 1.00
490 Rhema McKnight RC .40 1.00
491 Jason Hill RC .40 1.00
492 Dallas Baker RC .40 1.00
493 Greg Olsen RC .60 1.50
494 Yamon Figurs RC .40 1.00
495 Scott Chandler RC .60 1.50
496 Matt Spaeth RC .60 1.50
497 Ben Patrick RC .50 1.25
498 Clark Harris RC .50 1.25
499 Martrez Milner RC .40 1.00
500 Joe Newton RC .40 1.00
501 Alan Branch RC .40 1.00
502 Amobi Okoye RC .50 1.25
503 DeMarcus Tank Tyler RC .40 1.00
504 Justin Harrell RC .40 1.00
505 Brandon Mebane RC .50 1.25
506 Gaines Adams RC .50 1.25
507 Jamaal Anderson RC .50 1.25
508 Adam Carriker RC .40 1.00
509 Jarvis Moss RC .40 1.00
510 Charles Johnson RC .40 1.00
511 Anthony Spencer RC .50 1.25
512 Quentin Moses RC .40 1.00
513 LaMarr Woodley RC .75 2.00
514 Victor Abiamiri RC .40 1.00
515 Ray McDonald RC .50 1.25
516 Tim Crowder RC .50 1.25
517 Patrick Willis RC .60 1.50
518 Brandon Siler RC .40 1.00
519 David Harris RC .40 1.00
520 Buster Davis RC .50 1.25
521 Lawrence Timmons RC .60 1.50
522 Paul Posluszny RC .40 1.00
523 Jon Beason RC .40 1.00
524 Rufus Alexander RC .40 1.00
525 Earl Everett RC .40 1.00
526 Stewart Bradley RC .40 1.00
527 Prescott Burgess RC .40 1.00
528 Leon Hall RC .40 1.00
529 Darrelle Revis RC .50 1.25
530 Aaron Ross RC .40 1.00
531 Daymeion Hughes RC .40 1.00
532 Marcus McCauley RC .40 1.00
533 Chris Houston RC .40 1.00
534 Tanard Jackson RC .40 1.00
535 Jonathan Wade RC .40 1.00
536 Josh Wilson RC .50 1.25
537 Eric Wright RC .40 1.00
538 A.J. Davis RC .40 1.00
539 David Irons RC .40 1.00
540 LaRon Landry RC .60 1.50
541 Reggie Nelson RC .40 1.00
542 Michael Griffin RC .40 1.00
543 Brandon Meriweather RC .50 1.25
544 Eric Weddle RC .50 1.25
545 Aaron Rouse RC .40 1.00
546 Josh Gattis RC .40 1.00
547 Joe Thomas RC .60 1.50
548 Levi Brown RC .40 1.00
549 Tony Ugoh RC .40 1.00
550 Ryan Kalil RC .40 1.00

2007 Topps Total 1st Edition Copper

*1ST EDIT.VETS: 1.2X TO 3X BASIC CARDS
*1ST EDIT.ROOKIE: .5X TO 1.5X BASIC CARDS
1ST EDITION ODDS 1:2

2007 Topps Total Black

*BLACK VETS: 4X TO 10X BASIC CARDS
*BLACK ROOKIES: 2X TO 5X BASIC CARDS
BLACK/50 STATED ODDS 1:10

2007 Topps Total Blue

*BLUE VETS: 1.2X TO 3X BASIC CARDS
*BLUE ROOKIES: .6X TO 1.5X BASIC CARDS
BLUE STATED ODDS 1:2

2007 Topps Total Gold

*GOLD VETS: 3X TO 8X BASIC CARDS
*GOLD ROOKIES: 1.5X TO 4X BASIC CARDS
GOLD STATED ODDS 1:12

2007 Topps Total Red

*RED VETS: 1.5X TO 4X BASIC CARDS
*RED ROOKIES: .8X TO 2X BASIC CARDS
STATED ODDS 1:4

2007 Topps Total Silver

*SILVER VETS: 2X TO 5X BASIC CARDS
*SILVER ROOKIES: 1X TO 2.5X BASIC CARDS
STATED ODDS 1:6

2007 Topps Total Award Winners

STATED ODDS 1:8
AW1 Peyton Manning 2.00 5.00
AW2 Drew Brees .75 2.00
AW3 LaDainian Tomlinson .75 2.00
AW4 LaDainian Tomlinson .75 2.00
AW5 Chad Johnson .50 1.25
AW6 Terrell Owens .60 1.50
AW7 Shawne Merriman .50 1.25
AW8 Vince Young .50 1.25
AW9 DeMeco Ryans .60 1.50
AW10 Chad Pennington .50 1.25
AW11 Jason Taylor .60 1.50
AW12 LaDainian Tomlinson .75 2.00
AW13 Champ Bailey .60 1.50
AW14 Zach Thomas .60 1.50
AW15 Peyton Manning 2.00 5.00
AW16 Jon Kitna .50 1.25
AW17 Peyton Manning 2.00 5.00
AW18 Andre Johnson .60 1.50
AW19 Hank Baskett .60 1.50
AW20 Chester Taylor .50 1.25

2007 Topps Total Signatures

GROUP A ODDS 1:10,750
GROUP B ODDS 1:2175
GROUP C ODDS 1:400
UNPRICED PRINT PLATES SER.#'d TO 1
DW Darius Walker C 6.00 15.00
FG Frank Gore A 40.00 80.00
GJ Greg Jennings B 8.00 20.00
JC Jerricho Cotchery A 10.00 25.00
JH Jason Hill B 8.00 20.00
KJ Kevin Jones B 6.00 15.00
MC Marques Colston A
MJ Maurice Jones-Drew A 10.00 25.00
SJ Steven Jackson A
SS Steve Smith USC B 10.00 25.00
SY Selvin Young C 10.00 25.00
TJ Thomas Jones A
TP Tyler Palko C 6.00 15.00
DWI DeAngelo Williams A

2007 Topps Total Team Checklists

TC1 Matt Leinart .30 .75
TC2 Michael Vick .40 1.00
TC3 Ray Lewis .50 1.25
TC4 Lee Evans .40 1.00
TC5 Steve Smith WR .40 1.00
TC6 Brian Urlacher .50 1.25
TC7 Chad Johnson .30 .75
TC8 Braylon Edwards .30 .75
TC9 Tony Romo .60 1.50
TC10 Jay Cutler .30 .75
TC11 Roy Williams WR .30 .75
TC12 Brett Favre 1.00 2.50
TC13 Andre Johnson .40 1.00
TC14 Peyton Manning 1.25 3.00
TC15 Fred Taylor .30 .75
TC16 Larry Johnson .30 .75
TC17 Ronnie Brown .30 .75
TC18 Chester Taylor .30 .75
TC19 Tom Brady 1.50 4.00
TC20 Reggie Bush .30 .75
TC21 Eli Manning .40 1.00
TC22 Chad Pennington .30 .75
TC23 JaMarcus Russell .30 .75
TC24 Donovan McNabb .40 1.00
TC25 Willie Parker .40 1.00
TC26 LaDainian Tomlinson .50 1.25
TC27 Frank Gore .40 1.00
TC28 Shaun Alexander .30 .75
TC29 Torry Holt .40 1.00
TC30 Cadillac Williams .40 1.00
TC31 Vince Young .30 .75
TC32 Clinton Portis .30 .75

2007 Topps Total Total Production

STATED ODDS 1:16
TP1 LaDainian Tomlinson .75 2.00
TP2 Peyton Manning 2.00 5.00
TP3 Carson Palmer .60 1.50
TP4 Drew Brees .75 2.00
TP5 Marc Bulger .50 1.25
TP6 Tom Brady 2.50 6.00
TP7 Eli Manning .60 1.50
TP8 Rex Grossman .50 1.25
TP9 Philip Rivers .75 2.00
TP10 Jon Kitna .50 1.25

2007 Topps Total Total Topps

STATED ODDS 1:8
TT1 Peyton Manning 2.00 5.00
TT2 Tom Brady 2.50 6.00
TT3 Carson Palmer .60 1.50
TT4 LaDainian Tomlinson .75 2.00
TT5 Shaun Alexander .50 1.25
TT6 Larry Johnson .50 1.25
TT7 Chad Johnson .50 1.25
TT8 Marvin Harrison .60 1.50
TT9 Steve Smith .60 1.50
TT10 Drew Brees .75 2.00
TT11 Donovan McNabb .60 1.50
TT12 Steven Jackson .50 1.25
TT13 Frank Gore .60 1.50
TT14 Torry Holt .60 1.50
TT15 Terrell Owens .60 1.50
TT16 Brett Favre 1.50 4.00
TT17 Willie Parker .60 1.50
TT18 Philip Rivers .75 2.00
TT19 Rudi Johnson .50 1.25
TT20 Roy Williams WR .50 1.25

2014 Topps Translucent

ISSUED VIA TOPPS.COM IN TWO CARD PACKS
1 Davante Adams
2 Dri Archer 6.00 15.00
3 Odell Beckham Jr.
4 Kelvin Benjamin
5 Blake Bortles 8.00 20.00
6 Teddy Bridgewater
7 Martavis Bryant 8.00 20.00
8 Ka'Deem Carey 6.00 15.00
9 Derek Carr 60.00 120.00
10 Jadeveon Clowney 8.00 20.00
11 Brandin Cooks 10.00 25.00
12 Aaron Donald 15.00 40.00
13 Eric Ebron 8.00 20.00
14 Mike Evans 50.00 100.00
15 David Fales 6.00 15.00
16 C.J. Fiedorowicz 6.00 15.00
17 Devonta Freeman 10.00 25.00
18 Jimmy Garoppolo 30.00 80.00
19 Jeremy Hill 8.00 20.00
20 Carlos Hyde
21 Jarvis Landry
22 Cody Latimer 8.00 20.00
23 Johnny Manziel
24 Tre Mason
25 Jordan Matthews 10.00 25.00
26 A.J. McCarron 6.00 15.00
27 Jerick McKinnon 8.00 20.00
28 Zach Mettenberger 6.00 15.00
29 Aaron Murray 6.00 15.00
30 Kevin Norwood 6.00 15.00
31 Paul Richardson 8.00 20.00
32 Allen Robinson 10.00 25.00
33 Bishop Sankey 6.00 15.00
34 Tom Savage 6.00 15.00
35 Lache Seastrunk 6.00 15.00
36 Austin Seferian-Jenkins 6.00 15.00
37 Charles Sims 6.00 15.00
38 Lorenzo Taliaferro 6.00 15.00
39 Logan Thomas 6.00 15.00
40 Sammy Watkins
41 Terrance West 6.00 15.00
42 James White 12.00 30.00
43 Andre Williams 6.00 15.00

2010 Topps Tribute

1 Drew Brees 1.50 4.00
2 Ray Lewis 1.50 4.00
3 Devin McCourty RC 1.00 2.50
4 Tony Romo 1.25 3.00
5 Percy Harvin 1.00 2.50
6 Joe Namath 2.00 5.00
7 Ahmad Bradshaw 1.00 2.50
8 John Conner RC .75 2.00
9 Sean Weatherspoon RC .75 2.00
10 Chris Johnson 1.00 2.50
11 Arian Foster 1.25 3.00
12 Kyle Wilson RC .75 2.00
13 Arrelious Benn RC .75 2.00
14 Anquan Boldin 1.00 2.50
15 LaDainian Tomlinson 1.50 4.00
16 Kareem Jackson RC .75 2.00
17 LeGarrette Blount RC 1.50 4.00
18 Rashard Mendenhall 1.00 2.50
19 Chris Ivory RC 2.00 5.00
20 Sam Bradford RC 4.00 10.00
21 Anthony Dixon RC .75 2.00
22 Dan Marino 3.00 8.00
23 Rob Gronkowski RC 2.50 6.00
24 Mark Sanchez 1.00 2.50
25 Eric Dickerson 1.25 3.00
26 Chad Ochocinco 1.00 2.50
27 Eli Manning 1.25 3.00
28 Jason Pierre-Paul RC 1.25 3.00
29 Miles Austin 1.00 2.50
30 Frank Gore 1.25 3.00
31 Jimmy Clausen RC .75 2.00
32 Patrick Robinson RC 1.00 2.50
33 DeSean Jackson 1.25 3.00
34 Derrick Morgan RC .75 2.00
35 Troy Polamalu 1.50 4.00
36 Franco Harris 1.50 4.00
37 Jerry Hughes RC .75 2.00
38 Aaron Hernandez RC .75 2.00
39 Emmitt Smith 2.50 6.00
40 Adrian Peterson 1.50 4.00
41 Tyson Alualu RC .75 2.00
42 Michael Turner 1.00 2.50
43 T.J. Ward RC 1.25 3.00
44 Jordan Shipley RC .75 2.00
45 Michael Vick 1.25 3.00
46 Jahvid Best RC .75 2.00
47 Larry Fitzgerald 1.25 3.00
48 Austin Collie 1.00 2.50
49 Darrelle Revis 1.00 2.50
50 Tim Tebow RC 6.00 15.00
51 Reggie Wayne 1.25 3.00
52 Donovan McNabb 1.25 3.00
53 Joe Haden RC 1.25 3.00
54 Gale Sayers 1.50 4.00
55 Rolando McClain RC .75 2.00
56 Patrick Willis 1.25 3.00
57 John Elway 2.50 6.00
58 Jermaine Gresham RC .75 2.00
59 Eric Berry RC 1.25 3.00
60 Peyton Manning 4.00 10.00
61 Brandon Marshall 1.25 3.00
62 Ndamukong Suh RC 1.50 4.00
63 Joe Montana 5.00 12.00
64 Colt McCoy RC 1.00 2.50
65 LeSean McCoy 1.50 4.00
66 Kyle Orton 1.00 2.50
67 Steve Young 2.00 5.00
68 Hakeem Nicks 1.00 2.50
69 Steven Jackson 1.00 2.50
70 Maurice Jones-Drew 1.00 2.50
71 Troy Aikman 2.00 5.00
72 Tony Dorsett 1.50 4.00
73 Mike Williams RC .75 2.00
74 Ryan Mathews RC .75 2.00
75 Wes Welker 1.25 3.00
76 Thurman Thomas 1.25 3.00
77 Nate Allen RC 1.25 3.00
78 Max Hall RC 1.25 3.00
79 Dallas Clark 1.00 2.50
80 Dez Bryant RC 2.00 5.00
81 Brett Favre 3.00 8.00
82 Roger Staubach 2.00 5.00
83 Toby Gerhart RC .75 2.00
84 Ray Rice 1.00 2.50
85 Calvin Johnson 1.50 4.00
86 Demaryius Thomas RC 2.00 5.00
87 Joe Flacco 1.25 3.00
88 C.J. Spiller RC .75 2.00
89 Philip Rivers 1.50 4.00
90 Tom Brady 4.00 10.00
91 Golden Tate RC 1.00 2.50
92 Dexter McCluster RC 1.00 2.50
93 Matt Ryan 1.25 3.00
94 Earl Campbell 1.50 4.00
95 Gerald McCoy RC .75 2.00
96 Matt Schaub 1.00 2.50
97 Earl Thomas RC 2.00 5.00
98 Andre Johnson 1.25 3.00
99 Terrell Owens 1.25 3.00
100 Aaron Rodgers 2.00 5.00

2010 Topps Tribute Black

*VETS: .8X TO 2X BASIC CARDS
*ROOKIES: .8X TO 2X BASIC CARDS
BLACK PRINT RUN 75 SER.#'d SETS

2010 Topps Tribute Blue

*VETS: .8X TO 2X BASIC CARDS
*ROOKIES: .8X TO 2X BASIC CARDS
BLUE PRINT RUN 89 SER.#'d SETS

2010 Topps Tribute Gold

*VETS: 2X TO 5X BASIC CARDS
*ROOKIES: 2.5X TO 6X BASIC CARDS
GOLD PRINT RUN 20 SER.#'d SETS
20 Sam Bradford 20.00 50.00
30 Tim Tebow 30.00 80.00

2010 Topps Tribute Green

*VETS: 1X TO 2.5X BASIC CARDS
*ROOKIES: 1X TO 2.5X BASIC CARDS
GREEN PRINT RUN 50 SER.#'d SETS

2010 Topps Tribute Autographed Dual Relics

DUAL JSY AUTO PRINT RUN 20-99
*BLACK/30: .5X TO 1.2X BASIC INSERT/55-99
*BLACK/30: .4X TO 1X BASIC INSERT/20
*BLUE/50: .4X TO 1X BASIC INSERT/55-99
EXCH EXPIRATION: 1/31/2014
ADRAB Arrelious Benn/55 5.00 12.00
ADRABE Arrelious Benn/55 5.00 12.00
ADRAD Anthony Dixon/99 5.00 12.00
ADRAH Aaron Hernandez/99 5.00 12.00
ADRBL Brandon LaFell/60 8.00 20.00
ADRBLA Brandon LaFell/99 8.00 20.00
ADRBT Ben Tate/55 5.00 12.00
ADRBTA Ben Tate/55 5.00 12.00
ADRCM Colt McCoy/20 8.00 20.00
ADRCMI Carlton Mitchell/99 5.00 12.00
ADRCP Clinton Portis/20 15.00 40.00
ADRCS C.J. Spiller/20 6.00 15.00
ADRCSP C.J. Spiller/20 6.00 15.00
ADRDB Drew Brees/20 40.00 80.00
ADRDM Dexter McCluster/60 6.00 15.00
ADRDMC Dexter McCluster/55 6.00 15.00
ADRDT Demaryius Thomas/20 25.00 50.00
ADRDTH Demaryius Thomas/20 25.00 50.00
ADRDW Damian Williams/55 5.00 12.00
ADRDWI Damian Williams/55 5.00 12.00
ADREB Eric Berry/55 8.00 20.00
ADREM Eli Manning/20 50.00 100.00
ADRFH Franco Harris/20 30.00 60.00
ADRGTA Golden Tate/55 6.00 15.00
ADRJB Jahvid Best/20 6.00 15.00
ADRJBE Jahvid Best/20 6.00 15.00
ADRJC Jimmy Clausen/20 6.00 15.00
ADRJD Jonathan Dwyer/99 5.00 12.00
ADRJDW Jonathan Dwyer/99 5.00 12.00
ADRJF Joe Flacco/55 20.00 40.00
ADRJG Jermaine Gresham/55 5.00 12.00
ADRJGR Jermaine Gresham/55 5.00 12.00
ADRJK Johnny Knox/60 8.00 20.00
ADRJN Joe Namath/20 50.00 100.00
ADRJS Jordan Shipley/99 5.00 12.00
ADRJSH Jordan Shipley/99 5.00 12.00
ADRJST James Starks/99 6.00 15.00
ADRKS Ken Stabler/20 30.00 60.00
ADRLT LaDainian Tomlinson/20 20.00 50.00
ADRMF Matt Forte/20 10.00 25.00
ADRMG Mardy Gilyard EXCH 5.00 12.00
ADRMH Montario Hardesty/55 5.00 12.00
ADRMHA Montario Hardesty/55 5.00 12.00
ADRMK Mike Kafka/55 6.00 15.00
ADRMKA Mike Kafka/55 6.00 15.00
ADRNS Ndamukong Suh/20 30.00 80.00
ADRNSU Ndamukong Suh/20 30.00 80.00
ADRPM Peyton Manning/20 100.00 200.00
ADRRC Riley Cooper/99 5.00 12.00
ADRRG Rob Gronkowski/99 25.00 60.00
ADRRM Ryan Mathews/20 6.00 15.00
ADRRMA Ryan Mathews/20 6.00 15.00
ADRSB Sam Bradford/20 20.00 50.00
ADRSC Sean Canfield/60 5.00 12.00
ADRSY Steve Young/20 50.00 100.00
ADRTG Toby Gerhart/55 5.00 12.00
ADRTGE Toby Gerhart/55 5.00 12.00
ADRTP Taylor Price/99 5.00 12.00
ADRTPR Taylor Price/99 5.00 12.00
ADRTT Tim Tebow/20 40.00 100.00
ADRTTH Thurman Thomas/20 15.00 40.00

2010 Topps Tribute Autographed Dual Relics Gold

*GOLD/15: .5X TO 1.2X BASIC INSERT/55-99
*GOLD/15: .4X TO 1X BASIC INSERT/20
GOLD PRINT RUN 15 SER.#'d SETS
ADRBF Brett Favre 100.00 200.00
ADRER Ed Reed 40.00 80.00
ADRES Emmitt Smith 100.00 200.00
ADRKK Kevin Kolb 20.00 40.00
ADRRL Ray Lewis 50.00 100.00

2010 Topps Tribute Autographed Quad Relics

*QUAD JSY AU: .4X TO 1X DUAL JSY AU
QUAD JSY AUTO PRINT RUN 20-99
*BLACK/30: .5X TO 1.2X BASIC INSERT/55-99
*BLUE/50: .4X TO 1X BASIC INSERT/55-99
*GOLD/15: .5X TO 1.2X BASIC INSERT/55-99
*GOLD/15: .4X TO 1X BASIC INSERT/20
EXCH EXPIRATION: 1/31/2014
AQRDR Darrelle Revis/20 20.00 40.00
AQRGMC Gerald McCoy/55 5.00 12.00

2010 Topps Tribute Autographed Triple Relics

*TRIPLE JSY AU: .4X TO 1X DUAL JSY AU
TIPLE JSY AUTO PRINT RUN 20-99
*BLACK/30: .5X TO 1.2X BASIC TRIPLE/55-99
*BLACK/30: .4X TO 1X BASIC TRIPLE/20
*BLUE/50: .4X TO 1X BASIC TRIPLE/55-99
*GOLD/15: .5X TO 1.2X BASIC TRIPLE/55-99
*GOLD/15: .4X TO 1X BASIC TRIPLE/20
EXCH EXPIRATION: 1/31/2014
ATRDR Darrelle Revis/20 20.00 40.00
ATRDRE David Reed/99 5.00 12.00
ATREC Earl Campbell/20 30.00 60.00
ATRED Eric Decker/99 6.00 15.00
ATREDK Eric Decker/99 6.00 15.00
ATRJSK John Skelton/99 6.00 15.00

2010 Topps Tribute Dual Autographs

STATED PRINT RUN 20 SER.#'d SETS
DABS J.Best/C.Spiller 15.00 40.00
DABT S.Bradford/T.Tebow 100.00 200.00
DADB E.Dickerson/S.Bradford 50.00 100.00
DAET J.Elway/T.Tebow 150.00 300.00
DAGD F.Gore/A.Dixon 25.00 60.00
DAHG Hernandez/R.Gronkowski 50.00 100.00
DAMM P.Manning/E.Manning 100.00 200.00
DAMS D.McCluster/C.Spiller 15.00 40.00
DATM D.Thomas/D.McCluster 20.00 50.00

2010 Topps Tribute Dual Player Relics

STATED PRINT RUN 15 SER.#'d SETS
DCRBM T.Brady/R.Moss
DCRBR D.Brees/A.Rodgers 20.00 50.00
DCRBT D.Bryant/D.Thomas 12.00 30.00
DCRET J.Elway/T.Tebow 40.00 80.00
DCRFP B.Favre/A.Peterson 30.00 60.00
DCRGD F.Gore/A.Dixon
DCRBSP J.Best/C.Spiller 10.00 25.00

2010 Topps Tribute Relic Dual Swatch

STATED PRINT RUN 45 SER.#'d SETS
*BLACK/15: .5X TO 1.2X BASIC DUAL JSY/45
*BLUE/30: .4X TO 1X BASIC DUAL JSY/45
*QUAD JSY/45: .4X TO 1X BASIC DUAL JSY/45
*QUAD BLACK/15: .5X TO 1.2X DUAL JSY/45
*QUAD BLUE/30: .4X TO 1X DUAL JSY/45
DRAB Arrelious Benn 2.50 6.00
DRAR Aaron Rodgers 12.00 30.00
DRBC Brent Celek 5.00 12.00
DRBL Brandon LaFell 4.00 10.00
DRBR Ben Roethlisberger 8.00 20.00
DRBT Ben Tate 2.50 6.00
DRCC Chris Cooley 5.00 12.00
DRCM Colt McCoy 3.00 8.00
DRCS C.J. Spiller 2.50 6.00
DRCSP C.J. Spiller 2.50 6.00
DRDB Dez Bryant 6.00 15.00
DRDBR Dez Bryant 6.00 15.00
DRDM Dexter McCluster 3.00 8.00
DRDMC Dexter McCluster 3.00 8.00
DRDT Demaryius Thomas 6.00 15.00
DRDTH Demaryius Thomas 6.00 15.00
DRDW Damian Williams 2.50 6.00
DREB Eric Berry 4.00 10.00
DREM Eli Manning 6.00 15.00
DRGT Golden Tate 3.00 8.00
DRJB Jahvid Best 2.50 6.00
DRJBE Jahvid Best 2.50 6.00
DRJC Jimmy Clausen 2.50 6.00
DRJCL Jimmy Clausen 2.50 6.00
DRJD Jonathan Dwyer 2.50 6.00
DRJG Jermaine Gresham 2.50 6.00
DRJGR Jermaine Gresham 2.50 6.00
DRJS Jordan Shipley 2.50 6.00
DRMC Matt Cassel 5.00 12.00
DRMH Montario Hardesty 2.50 6.00
DRMJD Maurice Jones-Drew 5.00 12.00
DRRG Rob Gronkowski 8.00 20.00
DRRM Ryan Mathews 2.50 6.00
DRRMA Ryan Mathews 2.50 6.00
DRRMO Randy Moss 6.00 15.00
DRSB Sam Bradford 3.00 8.00
DRSBR Sam Bradford 3.00 8.00
DRSM Santana Moss 6.00 15.00
DRTG Toby Gerhart 2.50 6.00
DRTT Tim Tebow 8.00 20.00
DRTTE Tim Tebow 8.00 20.00

2010 Topps Tribute Relic Triple Swatch

*TRIPLE JSY/45: .4X TO 1X DUAL JSY/45
STATED PRINT RUN 45 SER.#'d SETS
*BLACK/15: .5X TO 1.2X BASIC DUAL JSY/45
*BLUE/30: .4X TO 1X BASIC DUAL JSY/45
TRKK Kevin Kolb 5.00 12.00

2006 Topps Triple Threads

This 149-card set was released in January, 2007. This set was issued into the hobby in six-card packs, with an $100 SRP, which came 2 packs to a box. Cards numbered 1-100 feature veterans while cards numbered 102-150 are 2006 with both player-worn jersey swatches and signatures. The veteran cards were issued to a stated print run of 1199 serial numbered sets while cards numbered 102-150 were issued to a stated print run of 99 serial numbered sets. Interesting, card number 101, which was intended to be Vince Young, was never released.

COMP.SET w/o RC's (100) 75.00 150.00
1-100 PRINT RUN 1199 SER.#'d SETS
JSY AU/99 ROOKIE ODDS 1:8
1 Shaun Alexander 1.00 2.50
2 Carson Palmer 1.25 3.00
3 Randy Moss 1.25 3.00
4 Dan Marino 4.00 10.00
5 Terrell Owens 1.25 3.00
6 Trent Green 1.00 2.50
7 Brian Westbrook 1.00 2.50
8 Terry Bradshaw 2.50 6.00
9 Steven Jackson 1.00 2.50
10 Emmitt Smith 3.00 8.00
11 Ben Roethlisberger 2.00 5.00
12 Daunte Culpepper 1.25 3.00
13 Edgerrin James 1.25 3.00
14 Santana Moss 1.25 3.00
15 Larry Johnson 1.00 2.50
16 Johnny Unitas 3.00 8.00
17 Eric Moulds 1.00 2.50
18 LaDainian Tomlinson 1.50 4.00
19 Donovan McNabb 1.25 3.00
20 Fred Taylor 1.00 2.50
21 Hines Ward 1.25 3.00
22 Eli Manning 1.25 3.00
23 Tatum Bell 1.00 2.50
24 Donald Driver 1.25 3.00
25 Drew Bledsoe 1.25 3.00
26 Clinton Portis 1.00 2.50
27 Tony Gonzalez 1.25 3.00
28 Plaxico Burress 1.00 2.50
29 Shawne Merriman 1.25 3.00
30 Cadillac Williams 1.25 3.00
31 Larry Fitzgerald 1.25 3.00
32 Jake Plummer 1.00 2.50
33 Willis McGahee 1.00 2.50
34 Joe Namath 2.50 6.00
35 Ahman Green 1.25 3.00
36 Marvin Harrison 1.25 3.00
37 Ronnie Brown 1.25 3.00
38 Joe Montana 6.00 15.00
39 Deuce McAllister 1.25 3.00
40 Philip Rivers 1.50 4.00
41 Marion Barber 1.25 3.00
42 Chris Chambers 1.00 2.50
43 Jason Witten 1.25 3.00
44 Brett Favre 3.00 8.00
45 Anquan Boldin 1.00 2.50
46 Tiki Barber 1.25 3.00
47 Byron Leftwich 1.00 2.50
48 Steve Smith 1.50 4.00
49 Willie Parker 1.25 3.00
50 Darrell Jackson 1.25 3.00
51 David Carr 1.00 2.50
52 Chris Brown 1.00 2.50
53 Aaron Brooks 1.00 2.50
54 Donte Stallworth 1.00 2.50
55 Michael Vick 1.25 3.00
56 Curtis Martin 1.25 3.00
57 T.J. Houshmandzadeh 1.00 2.50
58 Steve McNair 1.25 3.00
59 Reggie Wayne 1.25 3.00
60 DeShaun Foster 1.25 3.00
61 Chad Johnson 1.00 2.50
62 Domanick Davis 1.00 2.50
63 Braylon Edwards 1.00 2.50
64 Drew Brees 1.50 4.00
65 Kevin Jones 1.00 2.50
66 Alge Crumpler 1.25 3.00
67 Lee Evans 1.25 3.00
68 Matt Hasselbeck 1.00 2.50
69 Jamal Lewis 1.25 3.00
70 Aaron Rodgers 4.00 10.00
71 Joey Galloway 1.25 3.00
72 LaMont Jordan 1.25 3.00
73 Mark Brunell 1.25 3.00
74 Torry Holt 1.25 3.00
75 Chester Taylor 1.25 3.00
76 Jake Delhomme 1.00 2.50
77 Doak Walker 2.00 5.00
78 Corey Dillon 1.00 2.50
79 Antonio Gates 1.50 4.00
80 Marc Bulger 1.00 2.50
81 Walter Payton 4.00 10.00
82 Mark Clayton 1.00 2.50
83 Brian Urlacher 1.50 4.00
84 Julius Jones 1.00 2.50
85 Tom Brady 5.00 12.00
86 Joe Horn 1.00 2.50
87 John Elway 3.00 8.00
88 Reggie Brown 1.00 2.50
89 Warrick Dunn 1.00 2.50
90 Charlie Frye 1.25 3.00
91 Isaac Bruce 1.50 4.00
92 Jim Thorpe 2.50 6.00
93 Drew Bennett 1.25 3.00
94 Brad Johnson 1.25 3.00
95 Chad Pennington 1.00 2.50
96 Andre Johnson 1.25 3.00
97 Todd Heap 1.00 2.50
98 Rudi Johnson 1.00 2.50
99 Jeremy Shockey 1.00 2.50
100 Peyton Manning 4.00 10.00
102 A.J. Hawk JSY AU RC 10.00 25.00
103 Reggie Bush JSY AU RC 12.00 30.00
104 Matt Leinart JSY AU RC 8.00 20.00
105 Mario Williams JSY AU RC 12.00 30.00
106 S.Holmes JSY AU RC 10.00 25.00
107 DeA.Williams JSY AU RC 10.00 25.00
108 Jay Cutler JSY AU RC 10.00 25.00
109 J.Norwood JSY AU RC 8.00 20.00
110 Chad Jackson JSY AU RC 8.00 20.00
111 T.Jackson JSY AU RC 8.00 20.00
112 Brian Calhoun JSY AU RC 8.00 20.00
113 L.Maroney JSY AU RC 8.00 20.00
114 Maurice Stovall JSY AU RC 8.00 20.00
115 Travis Wilson JSY AU RC 8.00 20.00
116 Omar Jacobs JSY AU RC 8.00 20.00
117 Michael Huff JSY AU RC 10.00 25.00
118 Br.Williams JSY AU RC 8.00 20.00
119 Kellen Clemens JSY AU RC 8.00 20.00
120 Jason Avant JSY AU RC 8.00 20.00
121 M.Robinson JSY AU RC 8.00 20.00
122 M.Lewis JSY AU RC 8.00 20.00
123 B.Marshall JSY AU RC 15.00 40.00
124 Vernon Davis JSY AU RC 10.00 25.00
125 Dem.Williams JSY AU RC 8.00 20.00
126 C.Whitehurst JSY AU RC 8.00 20.00
127 Sinorice Moss JSY AU RC 8.00 20.00
128 Maurice Drew JSY AU RC 20.00 50.00
129 Derek Hagan JSY AU RC 10.00 25.00
130 L.Washington JSY AU RC 8.00 20.00
131 Joseph Addai JSY AU RC 8.00 20.00
132 Joe Klopfenstein JSY AU RC 8.00 20.00
133 LenDale White JSY AU RC 8.00 20.00
134 Anthony Fasano JSY AU RC 8.00 20.00
135 Mike Bell JSY AU RC 8.00 20.00
136 Will Blackmon JSY AU RC 8.00 20.00
137 B.Gradkowski JSY AU RC 10.00 25.00
138 Marques Hagans JSY AU RC 8.00 20.00
139 Jerome Harrison JSY AU RC 8.00 20.00
140 Devin Hester JSY AU RC 15.00 40.00
141 Greg Jennings JSY AU RC 12.00 30.00
142 M.Kiwanuka JSY AU RC 12.00 30.00
143 Ingle Martin JSY AU RC 10.00 25.00
144 Willie Reid JSY AU RC 10.00 25.00
145 Cory Rodgers JSY AU RC 8.00 20.00
146 Brad Smith JSY AU RC 10.00 25.00
147 Hank Baskett JSY AU RC 8.00 20.00
148 Kamerion Wimbley JSY AU RC 10.00 25.00
149 DeMeco Ryans JSY AU RC 10.00 25.00
150 David Anderson JSY AU RC 10.00 25.00

2006 Topps Triple Threads Emerald

*VETS 1-100: .6X TO 1.5X BASIC CARDS
*RETIRED: .6X TO 1.5X BASIC CARDS
1-100 #'d OF 199 STATED ODDS 1:2
*ROOKIE JSY AU: .5X TO 1.2X BASIC CARDS
ROOKIE JSY AU/50 ODDS 1:16
101 Vince Young JSY AU 20.00 50.00

2006 Topps Triple Threads Gold

*VETS 1-100: .8X TO 2X BASIC CARDS
*RETIRED: .8X TO 2X BASIC CARDS
1-100 #'d OF 99 STATED ODDS 1:2
*ROOKIE JSY AU: .8X TO 2X BASIC CARDS
ROOKIE JSY AU/25 STATED ODDS 1:32
101 Vince Young JSY AU 30.00 60.00

2006 Topps Triple Threads Platinum

VETERANS STATED ODDS 1:399
ROOKIES STATED ODDS 1:798
UNPRICED PLATINUM PRINT RUN 1

2006 Topps Triple Threads Sapphire

*VETS 1-100: 2X TO 5X BASIC CARDS
*RETIRED: 2X TO 5X BASIC CARDS
1-100 #'d OF 25 STATED ODDS 1:16
VETERANS PRINT RUN 25 SER.#'d SETS
UNPRICED ROOKIE JSY AU/10 ODDS 1:79
ROOKIES PRINT RUN 10 SER.#'d SETS

2006 Topps Triple Threads Sepia

*VETS 1-100: .5X TO 1.2X BASIC CARDS
*RETIRED 1-100: .5X TO 1.2X BASIC CARDS
1-100 PRINT RUN 499 SER.#'d SETS
*ROOKIE JSY AU: .5X TO 1.2X BASIC CARDS
ROOKIE JSY AU/75 ODDS 1:11
ROOKIES PRINT RUN 75 SER.#'d SETS
101 Vince Young JSY AU 20.00 40.00

2006 Topps Triple Threads Autographed Relic Combos Red

D/36 STATED ODDS 1:94
RED PRINT RUN 36 SER.#'d SETS
*SEPIA/27: .5X TO 1.2X RED/36
SEPIA/27 STATED ODDS 1:127
SEPIA PRINT RUN 27 SER.#'d SETS
*EMERALD/18: .5X TO 1.2X RED/36
EMERALD/18 STATED ODDS 1:182
EMERALD PRINT RUN 18 SER.#'d SETS
UNPRICED GOLD/9 ODDS 1:368
GOLD PRINT RUN 9 SER.#'d SETS
UNPRICED SAPPHIRE/3 ODDS 1:1136
SAPPHIRE PRINT RUN 3 SER.#'d SETS
UNPRICED PLATINUM 1/1 ODDS 1:3126
UNPRICED PRINT.PLATE 1/1 ODDS 1:1137
1 Leinart/Bush/White 20.00 50.00
2 Klopfen/Lewis/Davis 15.00 40.00
3 Moss/Holmes/Hagan 15.00 40.00
4 Calhoun/Maroney/Addai 12.00 30.00
5 Williams/Bush/Young 20.00 50.00
6 P.Man/Hrrisn/Addai 75.00 200.00
7 Namath/Peyton/Eli 125.00 250.00
8 Favre/Elway/Marino 300.00 500.00
9 Tomlin/Rivers/Merriman 50.00 120.00
10 Jacobs/Jackson/Clemens 12.00 30.00
11 V.Davis/Whthrst/Washin 15.00 40.00
12 Young/Huff/Simms 15.00 40.00

2006 Topps Triple Threads Autographed Relic Red

RED/18 STATED ODDS 1:15
RED PRINT RUN 18 SER.#'d SETS
*GOLD/9: .6X TO 1.2X RED/18
GOLD/9 STATED ODDS 1:28
GOLD PRINT RUN 9 SER.#'d SETS
UNPRICED SAPPHIRE/3 ODDS 1:83
SAPPHIRE PRINT RUN 3 SER.#'d SETS
UNPRICED PLATINUM/1 ODDS 1:248
UNPRICED PRINT PLATE/1 ODDS 1:62
EACH PLAYER HAS 3 CARDS PRICED EQUALLY
1 Peyton Manning 125.00 225.00
4 LaDainian Tomlinson 25.00 60.00
7 Michael Vick 40.00 80.00
10 Emmitt Smith 125.00 250.00
13 Matt Leinart 20.00 50.00
16 Reggie Bush 20.00 50.00
19 Vince Young 30.00 80.00
22 Chad Johnson 20.00 40.00
25 A.J. Hawk 30.00 80.00
28 Eli Manning 60.00 120.00
31 Steve Smith 20.00 40.00
34 LenDale White 20.00 40.00
37 Santonio Holmes 30.00 60.00
40 Mario Williams 20.00 40.00
43 Vernon Davis 20.00 50.00
46 Sinorice Moss 15.00 30.00
49 Joe Namath 75.00 150.00
52 Chad Jackson 15.00 30.00
55 DeAngelo Williams 25.00 60.00
58 Laurence Maroney 15.00 40.00
61 Brett Favre 125.00 250.00
64 Joe Montana 100.00 200.00
67 Dan Marino 125.00 250.00
70 John Elway 100.00 200.00
73 Jim Kelly 50.00 100.00
76 Eric Dickerson 40.00 100.00
79 Shawne Merriman 20.00 40.00
82 Rudi Johnson 20.00 40.00
85 Marc Bulger 20.00 40.00
88 Chris Brown 12.50 25.00
91 Tatum Bell 15.00 30.00
94 Brian Calhoun 15.00 30.00

97 Maurice Drew 30.00 80.00
100 Derek Hagan 15.00 30.00
103 Michael Huff 15.00 30.00
106 Tarvaris Jackson 15.00 30.00
109 Joseph Addai 20.00 40.00
112 Jay Cutler 15.00 40.00
115 Maurice Stovall 12.00 30.00
118 Demetrius Williams 15.00 30.00
121 Kellen Clemens 20.00 40.00
124 Omar Jacobs 15.00 30.00
127 Brandon Marshall 20.00 50.00
130 Michael Robinson 15.00 30.00
133 Brandon Williams 20.00 40.00
136 Jerious Norwood 20.00 40.00
139 Travis Wilson 20.00 40.00
142 Jason Avant 15.00 30.00
145 Marcedes Lewis 15.00 30.00
148 Mike Bell 15.00 30.00
151 Joe Klopfenstein 12.50 25.00
154 Charlie Whitehurst 20.00 40.00
157 Larry Johnson 20.00 40.00
160 Philip Rivers 40.00 80.00

2006 Topps Triple Threads Relic Combos Red

RED/36 STATED ODDS 1:15
*SEPIA/27: .4X TO 1X RED/36
SEPIA/27 STATED ODDS 1:19
*EMERALD/18: .5X TO 1.2X RED/36
EMERALD/18 STATED ODDS 1:28
1 M.Allen/B.Sanders/E.Smith 15.00 40.00
2 Unitas/Elway/Namath 40.00 100.00
3 E.Smith/Alxndr/B.Sanders 15.00 40.00
4 Alxndr/Holmes/Faulk 8.00 20.00
5 Dickerson/J.Lewis/B.Sand 15.00 40.00
6 Strahan/Freeney/J.Taylor 8.00 20.00
7 Reed/O'Neal/Law 10.00 25.00
8 Favre/Elway/Marino 30.00 80.00
9 James/R.Moss/Portis 8.00 20.00
10 Montana/Marino/Taylor 30.00 80.00
11 Warner/P.Manning/McNair 25.00 60.00
12 Vilma/Urlacher/Thomas 10.00 25.00
13 J.Lewis/Dillon/Payton 20.00 50.00
14 Allen/B.Sanders/Payton 25.00 60.00
15 E.Smith/Rice/M.Allen 20.00 50.00
16 Leinart/Bush/White 8.00 20.00
17 E.Manning/Barber/Strahan 8.00 20.00
18 Montana/Stovall/J.Jones 30.00 80.00
19 Bush/DeA.Will/Maroney 8.00 20.00
20 Roeth/Ward/Holmes 25.00 60.00
21 Palmer/M.Allen/Mi.Will 10.00 25.00
22 Leinart/Cutler/Young 6.00 15.00
23 Brady/Jackson/Maroney 30.00 80.00
24 Klopfen/M.Lewis/V.Davis 6.00 15.00
25 McNabb/Re.Brown/Avant 8.00 20.00
26 Martin/Marino/Fitzgerald 20.00 50.00
27 Favre/Montana/Marino 30.00 80.00
28 Boldin/Roeth/C.Williams 12.00 30.00
29 Payton/Faulk/M.Allen 20.00 50.00
30 Tomlinson/Rivers/Gates 10.00 25.00
31 McNabb/Freeney/M.Harsn 8.00 20.00
32 Bledsoe/Witten/J.Jones 8.00 20.00
33 James/Shockey/Portis 8.00 20.00
34 Young/Benson/Simms 6.00 15.00
35 Jacobs/T.Jackson/Clemens 6.00 15.00
36 E.Smith/C.Jackson/F.Taylor 15.00 40.00
37 Johnson/Gonzalez/Green 8.00 20.00
38 Roeth/R.Moss/Pennington 12.00 30.00
39 Palmer/Ch.Jhnsn/R.Jhnsn 8.00 20.00
40 P.Manning/Alxndr/S.Smith 25.00 60.00
41 Drew/M.Lewis/M.Jones 8.00 20.00
42 Si.Moss/Holmes/Hagan 8.00 20.00
43 Brady/L.Jhnsn/C.Jhnsn 30.00 80.00
44 Favre/Alxndr/S.Smith 20.00 50.00
45 Si.Moss/Sa.Moss/Gore 8.00 20.00
46 Calhoun/Maroney/Addai 6.00 15.00
47 Suggs/Peppers/Vilma 8.00 20.00
48 Holt/S.Jackson/Bulger 8.00 20.00
49 Bush/Horn/Stallworth 8.00 20.00
50 Strahan/L.Taylor/Umenyiora 10.00 25.00
51 Ma.Will/Bush/Young 8.00 20.00
52 L.Taylor/Peppers/Dunn 10.00 25.00
53 Favre/Green/Hawk 20.00 50.00
54 Delhomme/Foster/S.Smith 10.00 25.00
55 V.Davis/Whitehurst/Washin 6.00 15.00
56 Heap/R.Lewis/J.Lewis 10.00 25.00
57 Pennington/Martin/Clemens 8.00 20.00
58 Dunn/Washington/Boldin 6.00 15.00
59 Fitzgerald/Rolle/Boldin 8.00 20.00
60 Warner/Brady/Ward 30.00 80.00
61 Alxndr/Holmes/E.Smith 15.00 40.00
62 P.Mann/M.Hrrisn/Freeney 25.00 60.00
63 Losman/Evans/McGahee 8.00 20.00
64 C.Williams/Simms/Stovall 8.00 20.00
65 Plummer/Cutler/T.Bell 6.00 15.00
66 L.Jhnsn/Robnsn/Arrington 6.00 15.00
67 Vick/Crumpler/R.White 8.00 20.00
68 Wilson/Marshall/Dem.Will 12.00 30.00
69 Namath/P.Mann/E.Mann 25.00 60.00
70 Addai/D.Davis/Mi.Clayton 6.00 15.00
71 Marino/Rice/E.Smith 30.00 80.00
72 Ma.Will/A.Jhnsn/Carr 10.00 25.00
73 K.Jones/Mi.Will/R.Will 6.00 15.00
74 T.Jackson/Wlmsn/Moore 6.00 15.00
75 Edwards/Frye/Wilson 8.00 20.00
76 Alxndr/Hassel/Trufant 6.00 15.00
77 Young/A.Jones/L.White 6.00 15.00
78 R.Moss/Huff/Walter 8.00 20.00
79 Ro.Brwn/Hagan/Chambers 8.00 20.00
80 Vilma/R.Lewis/Reed 10.00 25.00

2006 Topps Triple Threads Relic Red

D/36 STATED ODDS 1:9
RED PRINT RUN 36 SER.#'d SETS
*SEPIA/27: .4X TO 1X RED/36
SEPIA/27 STATED ODDS 1:12
SEPIA PRINT RUN 27 SER.#'d SETS
*EMERALD/18: .5X TO 1.2X RED/36
EMERALD/18 ODDS 1:17
EMERALD PRINT RUN 18 SER.#'d SETS
*GOLD/9: .6X TO 1.5X RED/36
GOLD/9 STATED ODDS 1:33
GOLD PRINT RUN 9 SER.#'d SETS
UNPRICED SAPPHIRE/3 ODDS 1:98
SAPPHIRE PRINT RUN 3 SER.#'d SETS
UNPRICED PLATINUM 1/1 ODDS 1:293
EACH PLAYER HAS 3 CARDS PRICED EQUALLY
TTR1 Peyton Manning 25.00 60.00
TTR4 LaDainian Tomlinson 10.00 25.00
TTR7 Michael Vick 8.00 20.00
TTR10 Emmitt Smith 25.00 60.00
TTR13 Matt Leinart 5.00 12.00
TTR16 Randy Moss 8.00 20.00
TTR19 Cadillac Williams 8.00 20.00
TTR22 Tom Brady 30.00 80.00
TTR25 Lawrence Taylor 15.00 40.00
TTR28 Reggie Bush 8.00 20.00
TTR31 Carson Palmer 8.00 20.00
TTR34 Hines Ward 8.00 20.00
TTR37 Ronnie Brown 8.00 20.00
TTR40 Vince Young 5.00 12.00
TTR43 Chad Johnson 6.00 15.00
TTR46 A.J. Hawk 6.00 15.00
TTR49 Johnny Unitas 20.00 50.00
TTR52 Eli Manning 8.00 20.00
TTR55 Steve Smith 10.00 25.00
TTR58 Shaun Alexander 6.00 15.00
TTR61 LenDale White 5.00 12.00
TTR64 Donovan McNabb 8.00 20.00
TTR67 Santonio Holmes 6.00 15.00
TTR70 Mario Williams 8.00 20.00
TTR73 Vernon Davis 6.00 15.00
TTR76 Jeremy Shockey 6.00 15.00
TTR79 Marvin Harrison 8.00 20.00
TTR82 Ben Roethlisberger 12.00 30.00
TTR85 Tiki Barber 8.00 20.00
TTR88 Sinorice Moss 5.00 12.00
TTR91 Joe Namath 20.00 50.00
TTR94 Jerry Rice 30.00 80.00
TTR97 Curtis Martin 8.00 20.00
TTR100 Chad Jackson 5.00 12.00
TTR103 Clinton Portis 6.00 15.00
TTR106 DeAngelo Williams 6.00 15.00
TTR109 Barry Sanders 25.00 60.00
TTR112 Edgerrin James 8.00 20.00
TTR115 Laurence Maroney 5.00 12.00
TTR118 Brett Favre 20.00 50.00
TTR121 Walter Payton 30.00 80.00
TTR124 Joe Montana 25.00 60.00
TTR127 Larry Johnson 6.00 15.00
TTR130 Dan Marino 30.00 80.00
TTR133 John Elway 25.00 60.00

2007 Topps Triple Threads

is 149-card set was released in January, 2008. The set was issued into the hobby in six-card packs with an $100 SRP which came two packs to a box. Cards numbered 1-80 feature veterans and cards numbered 81-100 feature retired greats. All cards numbered 1-100 were issued to a stated print run of 1449 serial numbered sets. Cards numbered 101-149 are 2007 NFL rookies with both player-worn swatches and a signature. All cards numbered 101-149 were issued to a stated print run of 99 serial numbered sets.
1-100 PRINT RUN 1449 SER.#'d SETS
JSY AU ROOKIE PRINT RUN 99
1 Peyton Manning 4.00 10.00
2 Carson Palmer 1.25 3.00
3 Tom Brady 5.00 12.00
4 Drew Brees 1.50 4.00
5 Marc Bulger 1.00 2.50
6 Donovan McNabb 1.25 3.00
7 Eli Manning 1.25 3.00
8 Jay Cutler 1.00 2.50
9 Vince Young 1.00 2.50
10 Brett Favre 3.00 8.00
11 Matt Hasselbeck 1.00 2.50
12 Tony Romo 2.00 5.00
13 Philip Rivers 1.50 4.00
14 Matt Leinart 1.00 2.50
15 Ben Roethlisberger 1.50 4.00
16 Chad Pennington 1.00 2.50
17 Alex Smith QB 1.25 3.00
18 Matt Schaub 1.00 2.50
19 Steve McNair 1.25 3.00
20 Rex Grossman 1.00 2.50
21 Jason Campbell 1.00 2.50
22 Trent Green 1.00 2.50
23 J.P. Losman 1.00 2.50
24 Byron Leftwich 1.00 2.50
25 Jake Delhomme 1.00 2.50
26 LaDainian Tomlinson 1.50 4.00
27 Steven Jackson 1.00 2.50
28 Shaun Alexander 1.00 2.50
29 Larry Johnson 1.00 2.50
30 Brian Westbrook 1.00 2.50
31 Joseph Addai 1.00 2.50
32 Reggie Bush 1.00 2.50
33 Frank Gore 1.25 3.00
34 Willie Parker 1.25 3.00
35 Laurence Maroney 1.25 3.00
36 Maurice Jones-Drew 1.00 2.50
37 Travis Henry 1.25 3.00
38 Clinton Portis 1.00 2.50
39 Ronnie Brown 1.00 2.50
40 Thomas Jones 1.00 2.50
41 Willis McGahee 1.00 2.50
42 Edgerrin James 1.25 3.00
43 Brandon Jacobs 1.00 2.50
44 Ahman Green 1.25 3.00
45 Cedric Benson 1.00 2.50
46 Cadillac Williams 1.25 3.00
47 Warrick Dunn 1.00 2.50
48 Jamal Lewis 1.25 3.00
49 Julius Jones 1.00 2.50
50 DeAngelo Williams 1.00 2.50
51 Fred Taylor 1.00 2.50
52 Chester Taylor 1.00 2.50
53 DeShaun Foster 1.25 3.00
54 Chad Johnson 1.00 2.50
55 Marvin Harrison 1.25 3.00
56 Torry Holt 1.25 3.00
57 Terrell Owens 1.25 3.00
58 Reggie Wayne 1.25 3.00
59 Steve Smith 1.25 3.00
60 Roy Williams WR 1.00 2.50
61 Randy Moss 1.25 3.00
62 Andre Johnson 1.25 3.00
63 Larry Fitzgerald 1.25 3.00
64 Anquan Boldin 1.00 2.50
65 Javon Walker 1.25 3.00
66 Laveranues Coles 1.00 2.50
67 Hines Ward 1.25 3.00
68 Lee Evans 1.25 3.00
69 Marques Colston 1.00 2.50
70 Braylon Edwards 1.00 2.50
71 Santana Moss 1.25 3.00
72 Jerricho Cotchery 1.00 2.50
73 Greg Jennings 1.00 2.50
74 Antonio Gates 1.50 4.00
75 Tony Gonzalez 1.25 3.00
76 Jeremy Shockey 1.00 2.50
77 Alge Crumpler 1.25 3.00
78 Champ Bailey 1.25 3.00
79 Shawne Merriman 1.00 2.50
80 Jason Taylor 1.25 3.00
81 Troy Aikman 2.00 5.00
82 Terry Bradshaw 2.00 5.00
83 Jim Brown 2.00 5.00
84 Earl Campbell 1.50 4.00
85 Len Dawson 1.50 4.00
86 Eric Dickerson 1.25 3.00
87 Tony Dorsett 1.50 4.00
88 John Elway 2.50 6.00
89 Marshall Faulk 1.25 3.00
90 Franco Harris 1.50 4.00
91 Dan Marino 3.00 8.00
92 Joe Montana 5.00 12.00
93 Joe Namath 2.00 5.00
94 Walter Payton 3.00 8.00
95 Jerry Rice 3.00 8.00
96 Barry Sanders 2.50 6.00
97 Gale Sayers 1.50 4.00
98 Bart Starr 2.50 6.00
99 Roger Staubach 2.00 5.00
100 Steve Young 2.00 5.00
101 Gaines Adams JSY AU RC 8.00 20.00
102 David Harris JSY AU RC 6.00 15.00
103 Paul Poluszny JSY AU RC 6.00 15.00
104 L.Timmons JSY AU RC 10.00 25.00
105 Patrick Willis JSY AU RC 15.00 40.00
106 John Beck JSY AU RC 6.00 15.00
107 Trent Edwards JSY AU RC 6.00 15.00
108 Kevin Kolb JSY AU RC 8.00 20.00
109 Chris Leak JSY AU RC 6.00 15.00
110 Jordan Palmer JSY AU RC 8.00 20.00
111 Brady Quinn JSY AU RC 6.00 15.00
112 J.Russell JSY AU RC 6.00 15.00
113 Troy Smith JSY AU RC 6.00 15.00
114 Isaiah Stanback JSY AU RC 6.00 15.00
115 Drew Stanton JSY AU RC 6.00 15.00
116 Lorenzo Booker JSY AU RC 8.00 20.00
117 Michael Bush JSY AU RC 6.00 15.00
118 Chris Henry RB JSY AU RC 6.00 15.00
119 Tony Hunt JSY AU RC 6.00 15.00
120 B.Jackson JSY AU RC 6.00 15.00
121 Brian Leonard JSY AU RC 6.00 15.00
122 M.Lynch JSY AU RC 20.00 50.00
123 A.Peterson JSY AU RC 100.00 200.00
124 Antonio Pittman JSY AU RC 6.00 15.00
125 Garrett Wolfe JSY AU RC 6.00 15.00
126 LaRon Landry JSY AU RC 10.00 25.00
127 Greg Olsen JSY AU RC 10.00 25.00
128 A.Allison JSY AU RC 6.00 15.00
129 D.Bowe JSY AU RC 6.00 15.00
130 Steve Breaston JSY AU RC 6.00 15.00
131 C.Davis JSY AU RC 6.00 15.00
132 Chris Davis JSY AU RC 6.00 15.00
133 Yamon Figurs JSY AU RC 6.00 15.00
134 Joel Filani JSY AU RC 6.00 15.00
135 Ted Ginn JSY AU RC 8.00 20.00
136 A.Gonzalez JSY AU RC 6.00 15.00
137 Roy Hall JSY AU RC 10.00 25.00
138 Jason Hill JSY AU RC 6.00 15.00
139 Dwayne Jarrett JSY AU RC 8.00 20.00
140 Calvin Johnson JSY AU RC 75.00 150.00
141 Jacoby Jones JSY AU RC 6.00 15.00
142 J.Lee Higgins JSY AU RC 6.00 15.00
143 R.Meachem JSY AU RC 8.00 20.00
144 Sidney Rice JSY AU RC 8.00 20.00
145 Ryne Robinson JSY AU RC 8.00 20.00
146 Steve Smith JSY AU RC 6.00 15.00
147 Chansi Stuckey JSY AU RC 8.00 20.00
148 Paul Williams JSY AU RC 6.00 15.00
149 Joe Thomas JSY AU RC 10.00 25.00

2007 Topps Triple Threads Emerald

*VETS/199 1-100: .6X TO 1.5X BASIC CARDS
*RETIRED/199 1-100: .6X TO 1.5X BASIC CARDS
*ROOKIES/69 101-150: .4X TO 1X
EMERALD 1-100 PRINT RUN 199
EMERALD 101-150 PRINT RUN 69
123 Adrian Peterson JSY AU 100.00 200.00
140 Calvin Johnson JSY AU 75.00 150.00

2007 Topps Triple Threads Gold

*VETS/99 1-100: .8X TO 2X BASIC CARDS
*RETIRED/99 1-100: .8X TO 2X BASIC CARDS
*ROOKIES/25 101-150: .5X TO 1.2X
GOLD 1-100 PRINT RUN 99
GOLD 101-150 PRINT RUN 25
123 Adrian Peterson JSY AU 125.00 250.00
140 Calvin Johnson JSY AU 175.00 300.00

2007 Topps Triple Threads Platinum

UNPRICED PLATINUM PRINT RUN 1

2007 Topps Triple Threads Rookie Autographed Relic Prime

*ROOKIES/25: .6X TO 1.5X BASIC CARDS
STATED PRINT RUN 25 SER.#'d SETS
UNPRICED PRIME BLACK PRINT RUN 1
UNPRICED PRINT PLATE PRINT RUN 1
123 Adrian Peterson JSY AU 250.00 500.00
140 Calvin Johnson JSY AU 75.00 150.00

2007 Topps Triple Threads Rookie Autographed Relic Prime Red

*ROOKIES/10: 1X TO 2.5X BASIC CARDS
PRIME RED PRINT RUN 10
123 Adrian Peterson JSY AU 400.00 750.00

2007 Topps Triple Threads Sapphire

ETS/25 1-100: 2X TO 5X BASIC CARDS
*RETIRED/25 1-100: 2X TO 5X BASIC CARDS
*ROOKIES/10 101-150: .75X TO 1.5X
SAPPHIRE 1-100 PRINT RUN 25
SAPPHIRE 101-150 PRINT RUN 10
123 Adrian Peterson JSY AU 250.00 500.00
140 Calvin Johnson JSY AU 200.00 350.00

2007 Topps Triple Threads Sepia

*VETS/639 1-80: .5X TO 1.2X BASIC CARDS
*RETIRED/639 81-100: .5X TO 1.2X BASE CARD
*ROOKIES/89 101-150: .4X TO 1X
SEPIA 1-100 PRINT RUN 639
SEPIA 101-149 PRINT RUN 89

2007 Topps Triple Threads Autographed Relic Red

RED PRINT RUN 18 SER.#'d SETS
*GOLD/9: .5X TO 1.2X RED/18
GOLD STATED PRINT RUN 9
UNPRICED SAPPHIRE PRINT RUN 3
UNPRICED PLATINUM PRINT RUN 1
UNPRICED PRINT PLATES PRINT RUN 1
EACH PLAYER HAS 3 CARDS PRICED EQUALLY
1 John Beck 8.00 20.00
4 Lorenzo Booker 10.00 25.00
7 Dwayne Bowe 8.00 20.00
10 Michael Bush 8.00 20.00
13 Trent Edwards 8.00 20.00
16 JaMarcus Russell 8.00 20.00
19 Ted Ginn Jr. 10.00 25.00
22 Anthony Gonzalez 8.00 20.00
25 Chris Henry RB 8.00 20.00
28 Jason Hill 8.00 20.00
31 Tony Hunt 8.00 20.00
34 Brandon Jackson 8.00 20.00
37 Dwayne Jarrett 10.00 25.00
40 Kevin Kolb 10.00 25.00
43 Brian Leonard 8.00 20.00
46 Marshawn Lynch 15.00 40.00
49 Robert Meachem 10.00 25.00
52 Greg Olsen 12.00 30.00
55 Antonio Pittman 8.00 20.00
58 Brady Quinn 15.00 40.00
61 Steve Smith USC 8.00 20.00
64 Drew Stanton 8.00 20.00
67 Calvin Johnson 60.00 120.00
70 Adrian Peterson 150.00 300.00
73 Paul Williams 8.00 20.00
76 Terry Bradshaw 75.00 150.00
79 Jim Brown 50.00 120.00
82 Eric Dickerson 50.00 100.00
85 Tony Dorsett 40.00 100.00
88 Dan Marino 125.00 250.00
91 Joe Montana 100.00 200.00
94 Jerry Rice 100.00 175.00
97 Barry Sanders 100.00 200.00
100 Paul Hornung 30.00 80.00
103 Joe Namath 60.00 120.00
106 Shaun Alexander 15.00 40.00
109 Tom Brady 250.00 400.00
112 Drew Brees 40.00 80.00
115 Reggie Bush 15.00 40.00
118 Marques Colston 15.00 40.00
121 Brett Favre 150.00 250.00
124 Maurice Jones-Drew 15.00 40.00
127 Joey Galloway 20.00 50.00
130 Antonio Gates 25.00 60.00
133 Tony Gonzalez 20.00 50.00
136 Frank Gore 20.00 50.00
139 Marvin Harrison 20.00 50.00
142 Steven Jackson 15.00 40.00
145 Chad Johnson 15.00 40.00
148 Larry Johnson 15.00 40.00
151 Julius Jones 15.00 40.00
154 Matt Leinart 15.00 40.00
157 Peyton Manning 100.00 175.00
160 Eli Manning 50.00 100.00
163 Shawne Merriman 15.00 40.00
166 Willie Parker 20.00 50.00
169 Tony Romo 30.00 80.00
172 Reggie Wayne 20.00 50.00
175 LaDainian Tomlinson 50.00 100.00
178 Vince Young 15.00 40.00

2007 Topps Triple Threads Autographed Relic Combos Red

RED PRINT RUN 36 SER.#'d SETS
*SEPIA/27: .6X TO 1.2X RED/36
SEPIA PRINT RUN 27 SER.#'d SETS
*EMERALD/18: .75X TO 1.5X RED/36
EMERALD PRINT RUN 18 SER.#'d SETS
UNPRICED GOLD PRINT RUN 9
UNPRICED SAPPHIRE PRINT RUN 3
UNPRICED PLATINUM PRINT RUN 1
UNPRICED PRINT PLATES PRINT RUN 1
1 Allen/Leinart/Bush 40.00 100.00
2 Ginn/T.Smith/Gonzalez 20.00 50.00
3 P.Man/Brady/Elway 250.00 450.00
4 Young/Montana/Rice 250.00 400.00
5 P.Mann/Yng/Montana 250.00 400.00
6 Peppers/Gonz/Gates 50.00 100.00
7 Eli/Quinn/Young 50.00 120.00
8 Kolb/Stanton/Beck 25.00 60.00
9 Bowe/Meach/Jarrett 20.00 50.00
10 Bush/Henry/Jackson 20.00 50.00
11 Beck/Booker/Ginn 15.00 40.00
12 Horng/Brdshw/Namath 100.00 175.00
13 Sanders/Brown/Dorsett 125.00 250.00

2007 Topps Triple Threads Dual Crest Rookie Autographed Relic Combos

UNPRICED DUAL AUTO PRINT RUN 1

2007 Topps Triple Threads HOF Autographed Relic Red

RED PRINT RUN 18 SER.#'d SETS
*GOLD/9: .5X TO 1.2X RED/18
GOLD STATED PRINT RUN 9
UNPRICED SAPPHIRE PRINT RUN 3
UNPRICED PLATINUM PRINT RUN 1
UNPRICED PRINT PLATES PRINT RUN 1
TTH1 Marcus Allen 40.00 80.00
TTH2 Jim Brown 60.00 120.00
TTH3 Tony Dorsett 50.00 100.00
TTH4 Joe Namath 60.00 120.00
TTH5 Barry Sanders 100.00 175.00
TTH6 Terry Bradshaw 75.00 150.00
TTH7 Eric Dickerson 50.00 100.00
TTH8 Paul Hornung 30.00 80.00
TTH9 Joe Montana 125.00 200.00
TTH10 Dan Marino 150.00 250.00

2007 Topps Triple Threads Relic Red

RED PRINT RUN 36 SER.#'d SETS
*SEPIA/27: .4X TO 1X RED/36
SEPIA PRINT RUN 27 SER.#'d SETS
*EMERALD/18: .5X TO 1.2X RED/36
EMERALD PRINT RUN 18 SER.#'d SETS
*GOLD/9: .6X TO 1.5X RED/36
GOLD STATED PRINT RUN 9
UNPRICED SAPPHIRE PRINT RUN 3
UNPRICED PLATINUM PRINT RUN 1
*PRIME RED/18: .6X TO 1.5X RED/36
PRIME RED PRINT RUN 18
*PRIME GOLD/9: .8X TO 2X RED/36
PRIME GOLD PRINT RUN 9
UNPRICED PRIME PLAT.PRINT RUN 1
UNPRICED PRIME SAPPHIRE PRINT RUN 3
PLAYERS HAVE THREE CARDS OF EQUAL VALUE
TTR1 JaMarcus Russell 2.50 6.00
TTR4 Brady Quinn 2.50 6.00
TTR7 Adrian Peterson 8.00 20.00
TTR10 Marshawn Lynch 5.00 12.00
TTR13 Calvin Johnson 8.00 20.00
TTR16 Ted Ginn Jr. 3.00 8.00
TTR19 Dwayne Bowe 2.50 6.00
TTR22 Robert Meachem 3.00 8.00
TTR25 Drew Stanton 2.50 6.00
TTR28 Dwayne Jarrett 3.00 8.00
TTR31 John Elway 25.00 60.00
TTR34 Dan Marino 30.00 80.00
TTR37 Joe Montana 25.00 60.00
TTR40 Joe Namath 20.00 50.00
TTR43 Jim Brown 20.00 50.00
TTR46 Barry Sanders 25.00 60.00
TTR49 Eric Dickerson 12.00 30.00
TTR52 Tony Dorsett 15.00 40.00
TTR55 Terry Bradshaw 20.00 50.00
TTR58 Roger Staubach 20.00 50.00
TTR61 Peyton Manning 20.00 50.00
TTR64 Drew Brees 10.00 25.00
TTR67 Carson Palmer 8.00 20.00
TTR70 Brett Favre 20.00 50.00
TTR73 Vince Young 6.00 15.00
TTR76 Tom Brady 30.00 80.00
TTR79 Philip Rivers 10.00 25.00
TTR82 Matt Leinart 6.00 15.00
TTR85 LaDainian Tomlinson 10.00 25.00
TTR88 Larry Johnson 6.00 15.00
TTR91 Steven Jackson 6.00 15.00
TTR94 Frank Gore 8.00 20.00
TTR97 Reggie Bush 6.00 15.00
TTR100 Willie Parker 8.00 20.00
TTR103 Rudi Johnson 6.00 15.00
TTR106 Shaun Alexander 6.00 15.00
TTR109 Laurence Maroney 8.00 20.00
TTR112 Chad Johnson 6.00 15.00
TTR115 Marvin Harrison 8.00 20.00
TTR118 Roy Williams WR 6.00 15.00
TTR121 Reggie Wayne 8.00 20.00
TTR124 Torry Holt 8.00 20.00
TTR127 Terrell Owens 8.00 20.00
TTR130 Andre Johnson 8.00 20.00
TTR133 Steve Smith 8.00 20.00

2007 Topps Triple Threads Relic Combos Red

RED PRINT RUN 36 SER.#'d SETS
*SEPIA/27: .5X TO 1.2X RED/36
SEPIA PRINT RUN 27 SER.#'d SETS
*EMERALD/18: .6X TO 1.5X RED/36
EMERALD PRINT RUN 18 SER.#'d SETS
UNPRICED GOLD PRINT RUN 9
UNPRICED SAPPHIRE PRINT RUN 3
UNPRICED PLATINUM PRINT RUN 1
1 Brees/Colston/Bush 12.00 30.00
2 Brady/Maroney/Moss 40.00 100.00
3 P.Mann/Harrison/Wayne 20.00 50.00
4 Rivers/Tomlin/Gates 12.00 30.00
5 Johnson/Johnson/Palmer 10.00 25.00
6 Romo/Owens/Jones 20.00 50.00
7 Bulger/Holt/Jackson 10.00 25.00
8 Eli/Burress/Shockey 15.00 40.00
9 Roeth/Parker/Ward 12.00 30.00
10 Cutler/Henry/Walker 10.00 25.00
11 Marino/Favre/Elway 50.00 100.00
12 Brees/P.Mann/Bulger 20.00 50.00
13 E.Smith/Payton/Sndrs 50.00 100.00
14 Tomlin/Johnson/Gore 12.00 30.00
15 Jhnsn/Hrrisn/Will.WR 10.00 25.00
16 Smith/Allen/Payton 25.00 60.00
17 Eli/McAllister/Willis 8.00 20.00
18 Boldin/Coles/Walker 10.00 25.00
19 Hall/Law/Woodson 12.00 30.00
20 Russell/Bowe/Davis 5.00 12.00
21 Quinn/Walker/McKnight 5.00 12.00
22 Elway/Marino/Brady 50.00 100.00
23 Jackson/Johnson/Housh 8.00 20.00
24 Leinart/Bush/Palmer 10.00 25.00
25 Olsen/Winslow/Shock 12.00 30.00
26 Gore/McGahee/James 10.00 25.00
27 Williams/Brown/Irons 10.00 25.00
28 Rivers/Holt/Cotchery 12.00 30.00
29 Merriman/Davis/Jordan 10.00 25.00
30 Meach/Price/Stallworth 10.00 25.00
31 Ginn/Galloway/Glenn 6.00 15.00
32 Ginn/Smith/Gonzalez 6.00 15.00
33 Freeney/McNabb/Harrison 10.00 25.00
34 Crumpler/Parker/Peppers 10.00 25.00
35 Peppers/Gonzalez/Gates 12.00 30.00
36 Petrsn/Will.S/Clayton 25.00 60.00
37 Moss/A.Jhnsn/Wayne 10.00 25.00
38 Sanders/Allen/Bush 20.00 50.00
39 Colston/Housh/Driver 10.00 25.00
40 Russll/Ca.Jhnsn/Thomas 20.00 50.00
41 Young/Leinart/Cutler 8.00 20.00
42 Bush/Maroney/Addai 10.00 25.00
43 Ca.Jhnsn/Ginn/Bowe 15.00 40.00
44 Stanton/Beck/Kolb 6.00 15.00
45 Eli/Rivers/Roeth 6.00 15.00
46 Penn/Leftwich/Moss 10.00 25.00
47 Roeth/Cad.Will/Young 12.00 30.00
48 Portis/James/Vilma 10.00 25.00
49 Lewis/Jones/Alexander 10.00 25.00
50 Jones/Lewis/McGahee 10.00 25.00
51 P.Mann/Brady/Elway 50.00 100.00
52 Young/Montana/Rice 50.00 100.00
53 Leinart/Bush/Jarrett 10.00 25.00
54 Aikman/Elway/Marino 20.00 50.00
55 Jones/Randle El/Smith 10.00 25.00
56 Battle/Boldin/Ward 10.00 25.00
57 P.Mann/Montana/Yng 40.00 80.00
58 Roeth/Losman/Leinart 12.00 30.00
59 Palmer/Brees/Romo 20.00 50.00
60 Tomlinson/Gore/J.Jones 12.00 30.00
61 James/Bnson/Ru.Jhnsn 10.00 25.00
62 Parker/Jackson/Maroney 10.00 25.00
63 Taylor/Peterson/Dunn 25.00 60.00
64 Brown/Allen/Harris 20.00 50.00
65 Chambers/Walker/Gallo 10.00 25.00
66 Edwards/Burress/Rivers 12.00 30.00
67 Johnson/Holt/Owens 15.00 40.00
68 Will.WR/Fitz/Smith QB 10.00 25.00
69 Gates/Jennings/Johnson 12.00 30.00
70 McGahee/Brown/Hester 10.00 25.00
71 Allen/Davis/Bush 12.00 30.00
72 Johnson/Johnson/Johnson 10.00 25.00
73 Bradshaw/Harris/Ward 40.00 80.00
74 Leinart/Boldin/Fitzgerald 10.00 25.00
75 Tomlin/Sanders/Martin 20.00 50.00
76 Eli/Romo/McNabb 15.00 40.00
77 Roeth/Palmer/Quinn 20.00 50.00
78 Rivers/Russell/Cutler 15.00 40.00
79 P.Mann/Palmer/Russell 20.00 50.00
80 A.Johnson/Fitz/Edwrds 10.00 25.00
81 Namath/Bradshaw/Brady 40.00 80.00
82 Hornung/Montana/Quinn 20.00 50.00
83 Sanders/Dorsett/Brown 25.00 60.00
84 Brown/Namath/Bradshaw 30.00 60.00
85 Elway/Marino/Montana 50.00 100.00

2007 Topps Triple Threads Relic Double Combos Red

RED STATED PRINT RUN 36
*SEPIA/27: .4X TO 1X RED/36
SEPIA STATED PRINT RUN 27
*EMERALD/18: .5X TO 1.2X RED/36
EMERALD STATED PRINT RUN 18
UNPRICED GOLD PRINT RUN 9
UNPRICED SAPPHIRE PRINT RUN 3
UNPRICED PLATINUM PRINT RUN 1
1 Peyton Manning 6X Jsy 30.00 80.00
2 HOF RBs 30.00 80.00
3 #12 QBs 60.00 120.00
4 SB MVPs 100.00 200.00
5 #1 PICK 50.00 100.00
6 HOF QBs 75.00 150.00
7 PAC TEN 12.00 30.00
8 BIG TEN 40.00 100.00
9 SEC RBs 20.00 50.00
10 Jim Brown 6X Jsy 20.00 50.00
11 AFC QBs 40.00 100.00
12 NFC QBs 40.00 100.00
13 07 QBs 15.00 40.00
14 Johnny Unitas 6X Jsy 30.00 80.00
15 Terry Bradshaw 6X Jsy 25.00 60.00
16 07 WRs 20.00 40.00
17 NEW QBs 15.00 40.00
18 COWBOY 75.00 150.00
19 STEELERS 75.00 150.00
20 SF 49ers 50.00 100.00

2008 Topps Triple Threads

This set was released on January 23, 2009. The base set consists of 134 cards. Cards 1-100 feature veterans, and cards 101-134 are autographed jersey rookies serial numbered of 89. This product was released with 6 cards per pack and 2 packs per hobby box.
1-100 PRINT RUN 779 SER.#'d SETS
101-134 JSY AU RC/89 ODDS 1:10
1 Drew Brees 1.50 4.00
2 Tom Brady 5.00 12.00
3 Peyton Manning 4.00 10.00
4 Carson Palmer 1.25 3.00
5 Ben Roethlisberger 1.50 4.00
6 Eli Manning 1.25 3.00
7 Tony Romo 1.25 3.00
8 Vince Young 1.00 2.50
9 Jon Kitna 1.00 2.50
10 Matt Hasselbeck 1.00 2.50
11 Derek Anderson 1.00 2.50
12 Jay Cutler 1.00 2.50
13 Donovan McNabb 1.25 3.00
14 Philip Rivers 1.50 4.00
15 Jason Campbell 1.00 2.50
16 David Garrard 1.00 2.50
17 Jeff Garcia 1.00 2.50
18 Marc Bulger 1.00 2.50
19 Matt Schaub 1.00 2.50
20 Tarvaris Jackson 1.00 2.50
21 Matt Leinart 1.00 2.50
22 Trent Edwards 1.00 2.50
23 JaMarcus Russell 1.00 2.50
24 Brodie Croyle 1.25 3.00
25 Aaron Rodgers 3.00 8.00
26 Steven Jackson 1.00 2.50
27 Willie Parker 1.25 3.00
28 Clinton Portis 1.00 2.50
29 Adrian Peterson 1.50 4.00
30 LaDainian Tomlinson 1.50 4.00
31 Marion Barber 1.00 2.50
32 Brian Westbrook 1.00 2.50
33 Fred Taylor 1.00 2.50
34 Marshawn Lynch 1.25 3.00
35 Joseph Addai 1.00 2.50
36 Willis McGahee 1.00 2.50
37 Frank Gore 1.25 3.00
38 Jamal Lewis 1.25 3.00
39 Edgerrin James 1.25 3.00
40 Thomas Jones 1.00 2.50
41 LenDale White 1.00 2.50
42 Justin Fargas 1.00 2.50
43 Brandon Jacobs 1.00 2.50
44 Ryan Grant 1.25 3.00
45 Larry Johnson 1.00 2.50
46 Laurence Maroney 1.25 3.00
47 Maurice Jones-Drew 1.00 2.50
48 Ronnie Brown 1.00 2.50
49 Reggie Bush 1.00 2.50
50 DeAngelo Williams 1.00 2.50
51 Chad Johnson 1.00 2.50
52 Reggie Wayne 1.25 3.00
53 Anquan Boldin 1.00 2.50
54 Randy Moss 1.25 3.00
55 Plaxico Burress 1.00 2.50
56 Terrell Owens 1.25 3.00
57 Andre Johnson 1.25 3.00
58 Larry Fitzgerald 1.25 3.00
59 Braylon Edwards 1.00 2.50
60 Steve Smith 1.25 3.00
61 Brandon Marshall 1.25 3.00
62 Roddy White 1.00 2.50
63 Marques Colston 1.00 2.50
64 Torry Holt 1.25 3.00
65 Wes Welker 1.25 3.00
66 Bobby Engram 1.00 2.50
67 T.J. Houshmandzadeh 1.00 2.50
68 Jerricho Cotchery 1.00 2.50
69 Kevin Curtis 1.00 2.50
70 Derrick Mason 1.00 2.50
71 Donald Driver 1.25 3.00
72 Joey Galloway 1.25 3.00
73 Dwayne Bowe 1.25 3.00
74 Chris Chambers 1.00 2.50
75 Santonio Holmes 1.00 2.50
76 Tony Gonzalez 1.25 3.00
77 Jason Witten 1.25 3.00
78 Kellen Winslow 1.00 2.50
79 Antonio Gates 1.25 3.00
80 Chris Cooley 1.00 2.50
81 Vernon Davis 1.00 2.50
82 Dallas Clark 1.00 2.50
83 Jason Taylor 1.25 3.00
84 Shawne Merriman 1.00 2.50
85 Champ Bailey 1.25 3.00
86 Patrick Willis 1.25 3.00
87 Ray Lewis 1.50 4.00
88 DeMarcus Ware 1.25 3.00
89 Bob Sanders 1.25 3.00
90 Devin Hester 1.25 3.00
91 Brett Favre 3.00 8.00
92 John Elway 2.50 6.00
93 Joe Montana 5.00 12.00
94 Barry Sanders 2.50 6.00
95 Walter Payton 3.00 8.00
96 Joe Namath 2.00 5.00
97 Paul Hornung 1.50 4.00
98 Troy Aikman 2.00 5.00
99 Lawrence Taylor 1.50 4.00
100 Emmitt Smith 2.50 6.00
101 Matt Ryan JSY AU RC 40.00 80.00
102 D.McFadden JSY AU RC 5.00 12.00
103 J.Stewart JSY AU RC 8.00 20.00
104 Joe Flacco JSY AU RC 20.00 50.00
105 Felix Jones JSY AU RC 5.00 12.00
106 R.Mendenhall JSY AU RC 5.00 12.00
107 Brian Brohm JSY AU RC 5.00 12.00
108 Chris Johnson JSY AU RC 6.00 15.00
109 Donnie Avery JSY AU RC 6.00 15.00
110 Devin Thomas JSY AU RC 5.00 12.00
111 Chad Henne JSY AU RC 6.00 15.00
112 Ray Rice JSY AU RC 5.00 12.00
113 DeSean Jackson JSY AU RC 10.00 25.00
114 Malcolm Kelly JSY AU RC 5.00 12.00
115 Limas Sweed JSY AU RC 5.00 12.00
116 Kevin Smith JSY AU RC 5.00 12.00
117 Jamaal Charles JSY AU RC 8.00 20.00
118 Steve Slaton JSY AU RC 5.00 12.00
119 Jordy Nelson JSY AU RC 15.00 40.00
120 James Hardy JSY AU RC 5.00 12.00
121 Jake Long JSY AU RC 8.00 20.00
122 Glenn Dorsey JSY AU RC 5.00 12.00
123 Eddie Royal JSY AU RC 5.00 12.00
124 Matt Forte JSY AU RC 20.00 40.00
125 Jerome Simpson JSY AU RC 6.00 15.00
126 Dexter Jackson JSY AU RC 8.00 20.00
127 Earl Bennett JSY AU RC 8.00 20.00
128 Early Doucet JSY AU RC 5.00 12.00
129 Harry Douglas JSY AU RC 6.00 15.00
130 Kevin O'Connell JSY AU RC 5.00 12.00
131 M.Manningham JSY AU RC 10.00 25.00
132 Andre Caldwell JSY AU RC 5.00 12.00
133 Dustin Keller JSY AU RC 6.00 15.00
134 John David Booty JSY AU RC 5.00 12.00

2008 Topps Triple Threads Emerald

*VETS 1-100: .6X TO 1.5X BASIC CARDS
1-100 VETERAN/149 ODDS 1:2
*ROOKIES 101-134: .5X TO 1.2X BASIC CARDS
1-100 ROOKIE JSY AU/50 ODDS 1:16

2008 Topps Triple Threads Gold

*VETS 1-100: .8X TO 2X BASIC CARDS
1-100 VETERAN/99 ODDS 1:3
*ROOKIES 101-134: .8X TO 2X BASIC CARDS
101-134 ROOKIE JSY AU/25 ODDS 1:32
101 Matt Ryan JSY AU 75.00 150.00
104 Joe Flacco JSY AU 40.00 100.00
108 Chris Johnson JSY AU 10.00 25.00

2008 Topps Triple Threads Platinum

UNPRICED PLATINUM VET.ODDS 1:262
UNPRICED PLAT JSY AU ODDS 1:752

2008 Topps Triple Threads Rookie Autographed Relic Prime

*PRIME.25: .8X TO 2X BASE JSY AU/89
PRIME SILVER/25 ODDS 1:32
UNPRICED PRIME BLACK/1 ODDS 1:752
UNPRICED PRINT PLATE PRINT RUN 1
101 Matt Ryan 100.00 200.00
104 Joe Flacco 50.00 100.00

2008 Topps Triple Threads Rookie Autographed Relic Prime Red

*RED/10: 1X TO 2.5X BASIC JSY AU/89
RED JSY AU PRINT RUN 10
101 Matt Ryan 250.00 500.00
104 Joe Flacco 100.00 200.00
105 Felix Jones 12.00 30.00
108 Chris Johnson 15.00 40.00
111 Chad Henne 15.00 40.00
112 Ray Rice 12.00 30.00

2008 Topps Triple Threads Sapphire

*VETS 1-100: 1.2X TO 3X BASIC CARDS
1-100 VETERAN/25 ODDS 1:11
*ROOKIES 101-134: .8X TO 2X BASIC CARDS
101-134 ROOKIE JSY AU/10 ODDS 1:76
101 Matt Ryan JSY AU 150.00 300.00
104 Joe Flacco JSY AU 60.00 125.00
108 Chris Johnson JSY AU 12.00 30.00
112 Ray Rice JSY AU 10.00 25.00

2008 Topps Triple Threads Sepia

*VETS 1-100: .5X TO 1.2X BASIC CARDS
1-100 VETERAN/249 ODDS 1:2
*ROOKIES 101-134: .4X TO 1X BASIC CARDS
101-134 ROOKIE JSY AU/75 ODDS 1:11

2008 Topps Triple Threads Autographed Relic Triple Red

RED STATED PRINT RUN 6-36
*SEPIA/15: .5X TO 1.2X RED/36
SEPIA STATED PRINT RUN 5-15
UNPRICED EMERALD PRINT RUN 4
UNPRICED GOLD PRINT RUN 3
UNPRICED SAPPHIRE PRINT RUN 2
UNPRICED PLATINUM PRINT RUN 1
UNPRICED PRINT PLATE PRINT RUN 1
4 Jones/Johnson/Rice/36 20.00 50.00
5 Forte/Smith/Slaton/36 50.00 100.00
6 Royal/Jackson/Hardy/36 30.00 80.00
11 Flacco/Jcksn/Smpsn/36 25.00 60.00
12 Forte/Johnson/Smith/36 20.00 50.00

2008 Topps Triple Threads Relic Red

RED/17 STATED ODDS 1:12
*SEPIA/12: .4X TO 1X RED/17
SEPIA/12 STATED ODDS 1:16
*EMERALD/9: .4X TO 1X RED/17
EMERALD/9 STATED ODDS 1:22
*GOLD/6: .5X TO 1.2X RED/17
GOLD/6 STATED ODDS 1:32
UNPRICED SAPPHIRE/3 ODDS 1:64
UNPRICED PLATINUM/1 ODDS 1:194
UNPRICED PRIME RED/9 ODDS 1:64
UNPRICED PRIME GOLD/6 ODDS 1:96
UNPRICED PRIME SAPPHIRE/3 ODDS 1:194
UNPRICED PRIME PLATINUM/1 ODDS 1:564
PLAYERS HAVE THREE CARDS OF EQUAL VALUE
TTR1 Matt Ryan 15.00 40.00
TTR4 Darren McFadden 5.00 12.00
TTR7 Jonathan Stewart 8.00 20.00
TTR10 Joe Flacco 10.00 25.00
TTR13 Felix Jones 5.00 12.00
TTR16 Rashard Mendenhall 5.00 12.00
TTR19 Brian Brohm 5.00 12.00
TTR22 Chad Henne 6.00 15.00
TTR25 Devin Thomas 5.00 12.00
TTR28 Limas Sweed 5.00 12.00
TTR31 Brett Favre 25.00 60.00
TTR34 John Elway 25.00 60.00
TTR37 Joe Montana 50.00 120.00
TTR40 Barry Sanders 25.00 60.00
TTR43 Walter Payton 30.00 80.00
TTR46 Joe Namath 20.00 50.00
TTR49 Matt Leinart 8.00 20.00
TTR52 Troy Aikman 20.00 50.00
TTR55 Lawrence Taylor 15.00 40.00
TTR58 Emmitt Smith 25.00 60.00
TTR61 Eli Manning 10.00 25.00
TTR64 Peyton Manning 30.00 80.00
TTR67 Ben Roethlisberger 25.00 60.00
TTR70 Tom Brady 40.00 100.00
TTR73 Tony Romo 10.00 25.00
TTR76 Drew Brees 12.00 30.00
TTR79 Philip Rivers 12.00 30.00
TTR82 Jay Cutler 8.00 20.00
TTR85 Vince Young 8.00 20.00
TTR88 LaDainian Tomlinson 12.00 30.00
TTR91 Adrian Peterson 30.00 80.00
TTR94 Marshawn Lynch 10.00 25.00
TTR97 Steven Jackson 8.00 20.00
TTR100 Willie Parker 10.00 25.00
TTR103 Willis McGahee 8.00 20.00
TTR106 Frank Gore 10.00 25.00
TTR109 Joseph Addai 8.00 20.00
TTR112 Terrell Owens 10.00 25.00
TTR115 Randy Moss 10.00 25.00
TTR118 Chad Johnson 8.00 20.00
TTR121 Reggie Wayne 10.00 25.00
TTR124 Andre Johnson 10.00 25.00
TTR127 Larry Fitzgerald 10.00 25.00
TTR130 Braylon Edwards 8.00 20.00
TTR133 Plaxico Burress 8.00 20.00

2008 Topps Triple Threads Relic Combos Red

RED/22 STATED ODDS 1:16
*SEPIA/15: .5X TO 1.2X RED/22
SEPIA/15 STATED ODDS 1:22
UNPRICED EMERALD/9 ODDS 1:36
UNPRICED GOLD/6 ODDS 1:54
UNPRICED SAPPHIRE/3 ODDS 1:107
UNPRICED PLATINUM/1 ODDS 1:322
TTRC1 Brady/Moss/Maroney 20.00 50.00
TTRC2 Romo/Barber/Owens 8.00 20.00
TTRC3 Manning/Jacobs/Burress 12.00 30.00
TTRC4 Brees/Bush/Colston 10.00 25.00
TTRC5 Leinart/Fitzgerald/Boldin 8.00 20.00
TTRC6 Bulger/Jackson/Holt 8.00 20.00
TTRC7 Roeth/Parker/Ward 20.00 50.00
TTRC8 Palmer/Johnson/Housh 8.00 20.00
TTRC9 Anderson/Edwards/Wins 6.00 15.00
TTRC10 Manning/Addai/Wayne 25.00 60.00
TTRC11 Rivers/Tomlinson/Gates 10.00 25.00
TTRC12 Favre/Marino/Elway 40.00 80.00
TTRC13 Brady/Brees/Romo 30.00 80.00
TTRC14 Smith/Payton/Sanders 40.00 80.00
TTRC15 Tomlin/Petersn/Wstbrk 10.00 25.00
TTRC16 Rice/Brown/Bruce 15.00 40.00
TTRC17 Wayne/Moss/Johnson 8.00 20.00
TTRC18 Brady/Romo/Roeth 30.00 80.00
TTRC19 Smith/Allen/Tomlinson 25.00 60.00
TTRC20 Tomlin/Ptrson/Addai 10.00 25.00
TTRC21 Moss/Edwards/Owens 8.00 20.00
TTRC22 Henne/Mannham/Lng 5.00 12.00
TTRC23 Russell/Addai/Bowe 8.00 20.00
TTRC24 Long/Long/Ryan 15.00 40.00
TTRC25 K.Smith/Mrshll/Smuel 4.00 10.00
TTRC26 Ryan/Henne/Brohm 15.00 40.00
TTRC27 Flacco/O'Conn/Booty 6.00 15.00
TTRC28 McFad/Stwrt/Menden 5.00 12.00
TTRC29 Jones/Johnson/Rice 4.00 10.00
TTRC30 Forte/Smith/Slaton 5.00 12.00
TTRC31 Kelly/Thomas/Sweed 6.00 15.00
TTRC32 Jackson/Mnnham/Doucet 6.00 15.00
TTRC33 Hardy/Avery/Nelson 10.00 25.00
TTRC34 Palmer/Leinart/Booty 8.00 20.00
TTRC35 Owens/Moss/Harrison 8.00 20.00
TTRC36 Rodgers/Lynch/Jackson 10.00 25.00
TTRC37 Romo/Westbrk/Owens 15.00 40.00
TTRC38 Edwards/Toomer/Manningham 6.00 15.00
TTRC39 Roeth/Young/Ptersn 10.00 25.00
TTRC40 Urlacher/Merriman/Willis 10.00 25.00
TTRC41 Burress/Mason/Thomas 6.00 15.00
TTRC42 Moss/D.Thms/M.Klly 6.00 15.00
TTRC43 Young/Will.WR/Sweed 6.00 15.00
TTRC44 Tomlinson/Taylor/Dunn 10.00 25.00
TTRC45 Grant/J.Jns/Walker 8.00 20.00
TTRC46 Williams/Adams/Long 6.00 15.00
TTRC47 Bush/Petersn/McFad 10.00 25.00
TTRC48 Petersn/Kelly/Will.S 10.00 25.00
TTRC49 Bowe/Davis/Doucet 6.00 15.00
TTRC50 Brady/Henne/Griese 15.00 40.00
TTRC51 D.Andrsn/Jcksn/Jhnsn 6.00 15.00
TTRC52 Burress/Tmer/Mnninghm 6.00 15.00
TTRC53 Peterson/Lewis/Payton 40.00 80.00
TTRC54 Ward/Holmes/Sweed 6.00 15.00
TTRC55 Brady/Tomlin/P.Mann 30.00 80.00
TTRC56 Roeth/Taylor/Gates 15.00 40.00
TTRC57 Ryan/Kelly/Charles 15.00 40.00
TTRC58 Petersn/Stewart/Jones 10.00 25.00
TTRC59 McGah/Brown/Lynch 8.00 20.00
TTRC60 Roeth/Leinart/Henne 8.00 20.00
TTRC61 White/Fargas/Grant 8.00 20.00
TTRC62 Owens/Moss/Holt 8.00 20.00
TTRC63 Marino/Dorsett/Fitzg 40.00 80.00
TTRC64 Fitzg/Will.WR/D.Thms 8.00 20.00
TTRC65 Petersn/Owens/Tomlin 10.00 25.00
TTRC66 Rice/Owens/Moss 15.00 40.00
TTRC67 Romo/Parker/Gates 8.00 20.00
TTRC68 Bush/White/Fargas 6.00 15.00
TTRC69 Anderson/Grant/Welker 8.00 20.00
TTRC70 McFad/McGah/McAllis 4.00 10.00
TTRC71 Brohm/Rice/Slaton 3.00 8.00
TTRC72 Flacco/D.Jcksn/Smpsn 6.00 15.00
TTRC73 Bush/Tomlin/McFad 5.00 12.00
TTRC74 Petersn/Willis/Thomas 10.00 25.00
TTRC75 Forte/Johnson/Smith 5.00 12.00
TTRC76 S.Jcksn/Lynch/Stwart 5.00 12.00
TTRC77 Portis/McGah/James 8.00 20.00
TTRC78 Burress/Wayne/Ward 8.00 20.00
TTRC79 Peterson/Lynch/Bowe 10.00 25.00
TTRC80 Brady/Elway/Montana 40.00 80.00

2009 Topps Triple Threads

1-100 VETERAN PRINT RUN 799
101-134 ROOKIE JSY AU PRINT RUN 35-70
1 Drew Brees 1.50 4.00
2 Kurt Warner 1.25 3.00
3 Jay Cutler 1.00 2.50
4 Aaron Rodgers 3.00 8.00
5 Philip Rivers 1.50 4.00
6 Peyton Manning 4.00 10.00
7 Donovan McNabb 1.25 3.00
8 Matt Cassel 1.00 2.50

9 Chad Pennington 1.00 2.50
10 David Garrard 1.00 2.50
11 Brett Favre 6.00 15.00
12 Tony Romo 1.25 3.00
13 Matt Ryan 1.25 3.00
14 Ben Roethlisberger 1.50 4.00
15 Jake Delhomme 1.00 2.50
16 Jason Campbell 1.00 2.50
17 Eli Manning 1.25 3.00
18 Matt Schaub 1.00 2.50
19 Kyle Orton 1.00 2.50
20 Joe Flacco 1.25 3.00
21 Marc Bulger 1.00 2.50
22 JaMarcus Russell 1.00 2.50
23 Trent Edwards 1.00 2.50
24 Kerry Collins 1.00 2.50
25 Matt Hasselbeck 1.00 2.50
26 Brady Quinn 1.00 2.50
27 Carson Palmer 1.25 3.00
28 Tom Brady 5.00 12.00
29 Adrian Peterson 1.50 4.00
30 Michael Turner 1.00 2.50
31 DeAngelo Williams 1.00 2.50
32 Clinton Portis 1.00 2.50
33 Thomas Jones 1.00 2.50
34 Steve Slaton 1.00 2.50
35 Matt Forte 1.00 2.50
36 Chris Johnson 1.00 2.50
37 Ryan Grant 1.25 3.00
38 LaDainian Tomlinson 1.50 4.00
39 Brandon Jacobs 1.00 2.50
40 Steven Jackson 1.00 2.50
41 Marshawn Lynch 1.25 3.00
42 Frank Gore 1.25 3.00
43 Derrick Ward 1.00 2.50
44 Jamal Lewis 1.25 3.00
45 Kevin Smith 1.00 2.50
46 Brian Westbrook 1.00 2.50
47 Ronnie Brown 1.00 2.50
48 Marion Barber 1.25 3.00
49 Larry Johnson 1.00 2.50
50 Cedric Benson 1.00 2.50
51 Jonathan Stewart 1.00 2.50
52 Maurice Jones-Drew 1.00 2.50
53 Willie Parker 1.00 2.50
54 Darren McFadden 1.50 4.00
55 Reggie Bush 1.00 2.50
56 Joseph Addai 1.00 2.50
57 Andre Johnson 1.25 3.00
58 Larry Fitzgerald 1.25 3.00
59 Steve Smith 1.25 3.00
60 Roddy White 1.00 2.50
61 Calvin Johnson 1.50 4.00
62 Greg Jennings 1.00 2.50
63 Brandon Marshall 1.25 3.00
64 Antonio Bryant 1.00 2.50
65 Wes Welker 1.25 3.00
66 Reggie Wayne 1.25 3.00
67 Marques Colston 1.00 2.50
68 Terrell Owens 1.25 3.00
69 Santana Moss 1.25 3.00
70 Hines Ward 1.25 3.00
71 Anquan Boldin 1.00 2.50
72 Dwayne Bowe 1.25 3.00
73 Roy Williams WR 1.00 2.50
74 Donald Driver 1.25 3.00
75 Randy Moss 1.25 3.00
76 Eddie Royal 1.00 2.50
77 Bernard Berrian 1.00 2.50
78 DeSean Jackson 1.25 3.00
79 T.J. Houshmandzadeh 1.00 2.50
80 Braylon Edwards 1.00 2.50
81 Jerricho Cotchery 1.00 2.50
82 Santonio Holmes 1.00 2.50
83 Torry Holt 1.25 3.00
84 Chad Ochocinco 1.00 2.50
85 Tony Gonzalez 1.25 3.00
86 Jason Witten 1.25 3.00
87 Dallas Clark 1.00 2.50
88 DeMarcus Ware 1.25 3.00
89 Ed Reed 1.25 3.00
90 Patrick Willis 1.25 3.00
91 Terry Bradshaw 2.00 5.00
92 Earl Campbell 1.50 4.00
93 Bo Jackson 2.00 5.00
94 Joe Montana 5.00 12.00
95 Dan Marino 3.00 8.00
96 Jim Brown 2.00 5.00
97 Tony Dorsett 1.50 4.00
98 Joe Namath 2.00 5.00
99 Jerry Rice 3.00 8.00
100 John Elway 2.50 6.00
101 Andre Brown JSY AU/70 RC 8.00 20.00
102 Aaron Curry JSY AU/70 RC 10.00 25.00
103 B.Pettigrew JSY AU/70 RC 6.00 15.00
104 B.Robiskie JSY AU/70 RC 6.00 15.00
105 Chris Wells JSY AU/35 RC 8.00 20.00
106 Deon Butler JSY AU/70 RC 6.00 15.00
107 D.Brown JSY AU/35 RC 8.00 20.00
108 D.Heyward-Bey JSY AU/35 RC 12.00 30.00
109 D.Williams JSY AU/70 RC 6.00 15.00
110 Glen Coffee JSY AU/70 RC 6.00 15.00
111 H.Nicks JSY AU/70 RC 8.00 20.00
112 J.Freeman JSY AU/35 RC 8.00 20.00
113 J.Iglesias JSY AU/70 RC 6.00 15.00
114 Jeremy Maclin JSY AU/35 RC 10.00 25.00
115 M.Stafford JSY AU/35 RC 50.00 100.00
116 J.Ringer JSY AU/70 RC 6.00 15.00
117 Jason Smith JSY AU/70 RC 6.00 15.00
118 Kenny Britt JSY AU/70 RC 10.00 25.00
119 K.Moreno JSY AU/35 RC 8.00 20.00
120 L.McCoy JSY AU/70 RC 15.00 40.00
121 M.Crabtree JSY AU/35 RC 12.00 30.00
122 M.Massaquoi JSY AU/70 RC 6.00 15.00
123 M.Sanchez JSY AU/35 RC 8.00 20.00
124 Mike Thomas JSY AU/70 RC 6.00 15.00
125 M.Wallace JSY AU/70 RC 10.00 25.00
126 Nate Davis JSY AU/70 RC 6.00 15.00
127 Percy Harvin JSY AU/70 RC 6.00 15.00
128 P.Turner JSY AU/70 RC 6.00 15.00
129 Pat White JSY AU/70 RC 8.00 20.00
130 R.Barden JSY AU/70 RC 6.00 15.00
131 Rhett Bomar JSY AU/70 RC 6.00 15.00
132 S.Greene JSY AU/70 RC 6.00 15.00
133 S.McGee JSY AU/70 RC 6.00 15.00
134 T.Jackson JSY AU/70 RC 6.00 15.00

2009 Topps Triple Threads Emerald

*VETS 1-100: .6X TO 1.5X BASIC CARDS
1-100 VETERAN PRINT RUN 149
*ROOKIE: .6X TO 1.5X BASIC JSY AU/70
*ROOKIE: .5X TO 1.2X BASIC JSY AU/35
101-134 ROOKIE JSY AU PRINT RUN 50

2009 Topps Triple Threads Gold

*VETS 1-100: .8X TO 2X BASIC CARDS
1-100 VETERAN PRINT RUN 99
*ROOKIE: .6X TO 1.5X BASIC JSY AU/70
*ROOKIE: .5X TO 1.2X BASIC JSY AU/35
101-134 ROOKIE JSY AU PRINT RUN 15

2009 Topps Triple Threads Sapphire

*VETS 1-100: 1.5X TO 4X BASIC CARDS
1-100 VETERAN PRINT RUN 25
*ROOKIE: .8X TO 2X BASIC JSY AU/70
*ROOKIE: .6X TO 1.5X BASIC JSY AU/35
101-134 ROOKIE JSY AU PRINT RUN 10

2009 Topps Triple Threads Sepia

*VETS 1-100: .5X TO 1.2X BASIC CARDS
1-100 VETERAN PRINT RUN 249
*ROOKIE: .5X TO 1.2X BASIC JSY AU/70
*ROOKIE: .4X TO 1X BASIC JSY AU/35
101-134 ROOKIE JSY AU PRINT RUN 30

2009 Topps Triple Threads Rookie Autographed Relic Prime Sepia

*ROOKIE/30: .6X TO 1.5X BASIC JSY AU/70
*ROOKIE/20: .6X TO 1.5X BASIC JSY AU/35
PRIME SEPIA PRINT RUN 20-30

2009 Topps Triple Threads Rookie Autographed Relic Prime Sapphire

*ROOKIE/15: .8X TO 2X BASIC JSY AU/70
*ROOKIE/15: .6X TO 1.5X BASIC JSY AU/35
PRIME SAPPHIRE PRINT RUN 15

2009 Topps Triple Threads Autographed Relic Combos Red

D STATED PRINT RUN 25
*SEPIA/12: .5X TO 1.2X RED/36
*SEPIA/12: .4X TO 1X RED/15
1 Sayrs/Brown/Sandrs/15 100.00 200.00
2 Stffrd/Sanchz/Frman/15 50.00 120.00
3 Moreno/Wells/Brown/36 15.00 40.00
4 Crabtr/Hywrd/Maclin/15 20.00 50.00
5 Aikmn/P.Mnn/Stffrd/15 100.00 200.00
6 Brdy/Mntna/Brdshw/15 250.00 400.00
7 Tmlinsn/Ptrsn/Bsh/15 100.00 200.00
8 Marino/Drstt/McCy/15 100.00 250.00
9 Brees/Haslbck/Romo/36 60.00 120.00
10 Wells/Brwn/McCy/36 40.00 80.00
11 Harvin/Nicks/Britt/36 30.00 80.00
12 Hywrd-By/Curry/Nicks/36 20.00 50.00

2009 Topps Triple Threads Autographed Relics Red

RED STATED PRINT RUN 15-25
*GOLD/10: .6X TO 1.5X RED/25
*GOLD/10: .5X TO 1.2X RED/15
EACH HAS THREE CARDS OF EQUAL VALUE
TTRA1 Drew Brees/15 60.00 120.00
TTRA4 Matt Ryan/15 40.00 80.00
TTRA7 Eli Manning/15 40.00 80.00
TTRA10 Frank Gore/25 15.00 40.00
TTRA13 Matthew Stafford/15 40.00 100.00
TTRA16 Joe Flacco/25 25.00 50.00
TTRA19 Mark Sanchez/15 8.00 20.00
TTRA22 Brady Quinn/15 15.00 40.00
TTRA28 Pat White/25 8.00 20.00
TTRA31 Eric Dickerson/15 30.00 60.00
TTRA34 Peyton Manning/15 100.00 175.00
TTRA37 Josh Freeman/15 8.00 20.00
TTRA40 Bo Jackson/15 50.00 100.00
TTRA49 Knowshon Moreno/15 8.00 20.00
TTRA52 Darren McFadden/15 25.00 50.00
TTRA61 Chris Wells/25 6.00 15.00
TTRA67 Donald Brown/25 6.00 15.00
TTRA70 LeSean McCoy/25 25.00 60.00
TTRA73 Percy Harvin/25 6.00 15.00
TTRA76 Jeremy Maclin/25 8.00 20.00
TTRA79 Darrius Heyward-Bey/25 10.00 25.00
TTRA82 Shonn Greene/25 6.00 15.00
TTRA85 Hakeem Nicks/25 8.00 20.00
TTRA88 Kenny Britt/25 10.00 25.00
TTRA91 Michael Crabtree/15 12.00 30.00
TTRA94 Dan Marino/15 100.00 200.00
TTRA106 Terry Bradshaw/15 50.00 100.00

2009 Topps Triple Threads Relic Red

D STATED PRINT RUN 25
*EMERALD/9: .5X TO 1.2X RED/25
*PURPLE/20: .4X TO 1X RED/25
*SEPIA/18: .4X TO 1X RED/25
*PRIME/15: .6X TO 1.5X RED/25
EACH HAS THREE CARDS OF EQUAL VALUE
TTR1 Matthew Stafford 10.00 25.00
TTR2 Matthew Stafford 10.00 25.00
TTR3 Matthew Stafford 10.00 25.00
TTR4 Mark Sanchez 2.50 6.00
TTR5 Mark Sanchez 2.50 6.00
TTR6 Mark Sanchez 2.50 6.00
TTR7 Josh Freeman 2.50 6.00
TTR8 Josh Freeman 2.50 6.00
TTR9 Josh Freeman 2.50 6.00
TTR10 Knowshon Moreno 2.50 6.00
TTR11 Knowshon Moreno 2.50 6.00
TTR12 Knowshon Moreno 2.50 6.00
TTR13 Donald Brown 2.50 6.00
TTR14 Donald Brown 2.50 6.00
TTR15 Donald Brown 2.50 6.00
TTR16 Chris Wells 8.00 20.00
TTR17 Chris Wells 8.00 20.00
TTR18 Chris Wells 8.00 20.00
TTR19 Darrius Heyward-Bey 4.00 10.00
TTR20 Darrius Heyward-Bey 4.00 10.00
TTR21 Darrius Heyward-Bey 4.00 10.00
TTR22 Michael Crabtree 4.00 10.00
TTR23 Michael Crabtree 4.00 10.00
TTR24 Michael Crabtree 4.00 10.00
TTR25 Jeremy Maclin 3.00 8.00
TTR26 Jeremy Maclin 4.00 10.00
TTR27 Jeremy Maclin 3.00 8.00
TTR28 Percy Harvin 2.50 6.00
TTR29 Percy Harvin 2.50 6.00
TTR30 Percy Harvin 2.50 6.00
TTR31 Drew Brees 10.00 25.00
TTR32 Drew Brees 10.00 25.00
TTR33 Drew Brees 10.00 25.00
TTR34 Peyton Manning 25.00 60.00
TTR35 Peyton Manning 25.00 60.00
TTR36 Peyton Manning 25.00 60.00
TTR37 Tom Brady 20.00 50.00
TTR38 Tom Brady 20.00 50.00
TTR39 Tom Brady 20.00 50.00
TTR40 Philip Rivers 10.00 25.00
TTR41 Philip Rivers 10.00 25.00
TTR42 Philip Rivers 10.00 25.00
TTR43 Ben Roethlisberger 10.00 25.00
TTR44 Ben Roethlisberger 10.00 25.00
TTR45 Ben Roethlisberger 10.00 25.00
TTR46 Adrian Peterson 10.00 25.00
TTR47 Adrian Peterson 10.00 25.00
TTR48 Adrian Peterson 10.00 25.00
TTR49 LaDainian Tomlinson 10.00 25.00
TTR50 LaDainian Tomlinson 10.00 25.00
TTR51 LaDainian Tomlinson 10.00 25.00
TTR52 Clinton Portis 6.00 15.00
TTR53 Clinton Portis 6.00 15.00
TTR54 Clinton Portis 6.00 15.00
TTR55 Matt Forte 6.00 15.00
TTR56 Matt Forte 6.00 15.00
TTR57 Matt Forte 6.00 15.00
TTR58 Frank Gore 10.00 25.00
TTR59 Frank Gore 10.00 25.00
TTR60 Frank Gore 10.00 25.00
TTR61 Andre Johnson 8.00 20.00
TTR62 Andre Johnson 8.00 20.00
TTR63 Andre Johnson 8.00 20.00
TTR64 Larry Fitzgerald 8.00 20.00
TTR65 Larry Fitzgerald 8.00 20.00
TTR66 Larry Fitzgerald 8.00 20.00
TTR67 Steve Smith 8.00 20.00
TTR68 Steve Smith 8.00 20.00
TTR69 Steve Smith 8.00 20.00
TTR70 DeAngelo Williams 6.00 15.00
TTR71 DeAngelo Williams 6.00 15.00
TTR72 DeAngelo Williams 6.00 15.00
TTR73 Randy Moss 8.00 20.00
TTR74 Randy Moss 8.00 20.00
TTR75 Randy Moss 8.00 20.00
TTR76 Terry Bradshaw 12.00 30.00
TTR77 Terry Bradshaw 12.00 30.00
TTR78 Terry Bradshaw 12.00 30.00
TTR79 Earl Campbell 10.00 25.00
TTR80 Earl Campbell 10.00 25.00
TTR81 Earl Campbell 10.00 25.00
TTR82 Bo Jackson 12.00 30.00
TTR83 Bo Jackson 12.00 30.00
TTR84 Bo Jackson 12.00 30.00
TTR85 Dan Marino 25.00 60.00
TTR86 Dan Marino 25.00 60.00
TTR87 Dan Marino 25.00 60.00
TTR88 John Elway 20.00 50.00
TTR89 John Elway 20.00 50.00
TTR90 John Elway 20.00 50.00

2009 Topps Triple Threads Relic Combos Red

RED STATED PRINT RUN 25
*SEPIA/15: .5X TO 1.2X RED/25
1 Manning/Addai/Wayne 25.00 60.00
2 Romo/Barber/Williams 15.00 40.00
3 Fitzgerald/Boldin/Breaston 8.00 20.00
4 Bowe/Dorsey/Jackson 8.00 20.00
5 Brady/Moss/Welker 30.00 80.00
6 Bradshaw/Ward/Holmes 15.00 40.00
7 Brees/Bush/Colston 10.00 25.00
8 Aikman/Manning/Stafford 15.00 40.00
9 Brown/Dickerson/Dorsett 15.00 40.00
10 White/Brown/Ginn 4.00 10.00
11 Montana/Rice/TO 40.00 100.00
12 Sanchez/Jones/Cotchery 12.00 30.00
13 Delhomme/Williams/Smith 8.00 20.00
14 Moreno/Brown/Britt 10.00 25.00
15 Jones-Drw/Rice/Wstbrk 6.00 15.00
16 Elway/Roeth/Brady 40.00 100.00
17 Dickerson/Faulk/Jackson 12.00 30.00
18 Favre/Marino/Manning 30.00 80.00
19 Roethr/Ryan/Flacco 10.00 25.00
20 Stewart/Forte/Slaton 6.00 15.00
21 Gore/Jackson/Tomlinson 10.00 25.00
22 Rodgers/Grant/Jennings 20.00 50.00
23 Johnson/Fitz/S.Smith 8.00 20.00
24 Stafford/Sanders/Jhnsn 12.00 30.00
25 Williams/Jacobs/White 6.00 15.00
26 Stafford/Sanchez/Frman 12.00 30.00
27 White/McGee/Davis 4.00 10.00
28 Moreno/Brown/Wells 10.00 25.00
29 McCoy/Greene/Coffee 8.00 20.00
30 Hywrd-By/Crabtree/Maclin 5.00 12.00
31 Harvin/Nicks/Britt 5.00 12.00
32 Stafford/Pettigrew/Williams 12.00 30.00
33 Davis/Coffee/Crabtree 5.00 12.00
34 Nicks/Barden/Brown 4.00 10.00
35 Stafford/Moreno/Mssquoi 10.00 25.00
36 Palmer/Leinart/Sanchez 12.00 30.00
37 Moss/Johnson/Hywrd-By 5.00 12.00
38 Ochocinco/Jennings/Gates 8.00 20.00
39 Brown/Allen/Long 12.00 30.00
40 McNabb/McCoy/Maclin 8.00 20.00
41 Russell/McFadd/Hywrd-By 5.00 12.00
42 Lewis/Merriman/Curry 10.00 25.00
43 Namath/Manning/Sanchez 6.00 15.00
44 Payton/Brown/Smith 20.00 50.00
45 Peterson/Portis/Dickerson 10.00 25.00
46 Parker/Peppers/Nicks 4.00 10.00
47 McGahee/Lewis/Reed 10.00 25.00
48 Manning/Rivers/Roeth 10.00 25.00
49 Rodgers/Lynch/Jackson 20.00 50.00
50 Avery/Hester/Royal 8.00 20.00
51 Stewart/Mendenhall/Jones 6.00 15.00
52 Tomlinson/Taylor/Timmons 10.00 25.00
53 Elway/Namath/Favre 25.00 60.00
54 Urlacher/Willis/Lewis 10.00 25.00
55 Rice/White/Taylor 25.00 60.00
56 Urlacher/Hawk/Curry 8.00 20.00
57 Johnson/Williams/Butler 6.00 15.00
58 Ware/Peppers/Williams 8.00 20.00
59 Rice/Ward/Holmes 25.00 60.00
60 Marino/Fitzgerald/McCoy 25.00 60.00

2009 Topps Triple Threads Relic Double Combos Red

STATED PRINT RUN 20
*SEPIA/15: .4X TO 1X RED/20
1 By/Mn/Fr/Mo/Ey/Mt 100.00 200.00
2 Sl/Sz/Fn/Wt/Me/Ds 30.00 80.00
3 Mo/Bn/Ws/My/Gn/Ce 20.00 50.00
4 Hd/Cr/Mn/Hv/Nk/Bt 15.00 40.00
5 Mq/Rk/Bn/Wl/Tr/Wl 15.00 40.00
6 Bn/Rr/Br/Is/Ts/Pr 15.00 40.00
7 Rs/Sh/Dw/Wl/Js/Be 25.00 60.00
8 Rs/Mn/By/Rh/Pm/Sh 40.00 100.00
9 Bs/Rm/Rn/Eli/Rs/Sd 30.00 80.00
10 Tn/Js/Sn/Jn/Lh/Dw 25.00 60.00
11 Pn/Wl/Ps/Fe/Gt/Js 30.00 80.00
12 Sh/Tn/An/Pn/Bn/Fk
13 Mn/Re/Mn/Wn/By/Ms

2009 Topps Triple Threads Relic XXIV Red

RED PRINT RUN 15
*SEPIA/9: .4X TO 1X RED/15
TFR1 Matthew Stafford 40.00 100.00
TFR2 Mark Sanchez 5.00 12.00
TFR3 Jerry Rice 75.00 150.00
TFR4 Earl Campbell 40.00 80.00
TFR5 Bo Jackson 50.00 100.00
TFR6 Dan Marino 75.00 150.00
TFR7 Knowshon Moreno 20.00 50.00
TFR8 Chris Wells 25.00 60.00
TFR9 Michael Crabtree 20.00 50.00
TFR10 Jeremy Maclin 15.00 40.00
TFR11 Tom Brady 75.00 150.00
TFR13 Peyton Manning 75.00 150.00
TFR14 Andre Johnson 30.00 60.00
TFR15 Aaron Rodgers 60.00 150.00

2010 Topps Triple Threads

101A-135B ROOKIE JSY AU PRINT RUN 99
A FEATURE RC DIE CUT/B TEAM DIE CUT
A/B JSY AU ROOKIES OF EQUAL VALE
EXCH EXPIRATION: 10/31/2013
1 Peyton Manning 2.50 6.00
2 Ray Rice .60 1.50
3 Marques Colston .60 1.50
4 LeSean McCoy 1.00 2.50
5 Aaron Rodgers 2.00 5.00
6 Anquan Boldin .60 1.50
7 Antonio Gates .75 2.00
8 Steve Smith USC .60 1.50
9 Jonathan Stewart .60 1.50
10 Drew Brees 1.00 2.50
11 Hakeem Nicks .60 1.50
12 Steven Jackson .60 1.50
13 Pierre Garcon .75 2.00
14 Matt Ryan .75 2.00
15 Pierre Thomas .60 1.50
16 Shonn Greene .60 1.50
17 Matt Schaub .60 1.50
18 Cedric Benson .60 1.50
19 Mark Sanchez .60 1.50
20 Adrian Peterson 1.00 2.50
21 Kyle Orton .60 1.50
22 Jerome Harrison .60 1.50
23 Kevin Kolb .60 1.50
24 Randy Moss .75 2.00
25 Vince Young .60 1.50
26 Miles Austin .60 1.50
27 Chad Henne .75 2.00
28 Chris Johnson .60 1.50
29 Carson Palmer .75 2.00
30 Chad Ochocinco .60 1.50
31 DeAngelo Williams .60 1.50
32 Thomas Jones .60 1.50
33 Donald Driver .75 2.00
34 Matt Forte .60 1.50
35 Philip Rivers 1.00 2.50
36 Ryan Grant .75 2.00
37 Joe Flacco .75 2.00
38 Brandon Jacobs .60 1.50
39 LaDainian Tomlinson 1.00 2.50
40 Brett Favre 4.00 8.00
41 Frank Gore .75 2.00
42 Dwayne Bowe .75 2.00
43 Beanie Wells .60 1.50
44 Ben Roethlisberger 1.00 2.50
45 Felix Jones .60 1.50
46 Percy Harvin .60 1.50
47 Knowshon Moreno .60 1.50
48 Sidney Rice .60 1.50
49 Ronnie Brown .60 1.50
50 Eli Manning .75 2.00
51 Joseph Addai .60 1.50
52 Tony Romo .75 2.00
53 Larry Fitzgerald .75 2.00
54 Jared Allen .60 1.50
55 Rashard Mendenhall .60 1.50
56 Reggie Wayne .75 2.00
57 Darren McFadden .60 1.50
58 Lee Evans .75 2.00
59 Reggie Bush .60 1.50
60 Troy Polamalu 1.00 2.50
61 Andre Johnson .75 2.00
62 Dallas Clark .60 1.50
63 Greg Jennings .60 1.50
64 Donovan McNabb .75 2.00
65 Steve Smith .75 2.00
66 Fred Jackson .75 2.00
67 Calvin Johnson 1.00 2.50
68 Patrick Willis .75 2.00
69 Brandon Marshall .75 2.00
70 Tom Brady 2.50 6.00
71 Vincent Jackson .60 1.50
72 Clinton Portis .60 1.50
73 Wes Welker .75 2.00
74 Jamaal Charles .75 2.00
75 Jay Cutler .60 1.50
76 Mike Sims-Walker .60 1.50
77 Hines Ward .75 2.00
78 David Garrard .60 1.50
79 Eddie Royal .60 1.50
80 Maurice Jones-Drew .60 1.50
81 DeSean Jackson .75 2.00
82 Matthew Stafford .75 2.00
83 Michael Turner .60 1.50
84 Santonio Holmes .60 1.50
85 Roddy White .60 1.50
86 Tony Gonzalez .75 2.00
87 DeMarcus Ware .75 2.00
88 Jason Witten .75 2.00
89 Santana Moss .75 2.00
90 Darrelle Revis .60 1.50
91 Troy Aikman 1.50 4.00
92 Marcus Allen 1.25 3.00
93 Ronnie Lott 1.00 2.50
94 Dan Marino 2.50 6.00
95 Emmitt Smith 2.00 5.00
96 Thurman Thomas 1.00 2.50
97 Eric Dickerson 1.00 2.50
98 Gale Sayers 1.25 3.00
99 Jim Brown 1.50 4.00
100 John Elway 2.00 5.00
101A Sam Bradford JSY AU RC 20.00 50.00
101B Sam Bradford JSY AU RC 20.00 50.00
102A N.Suh JSY AU RC 12.00 30.00
102B N.Suh JSY AU RC 12.00 30.00
103B Charles Scott JSY AU RC 6.00 15.00
104A C.J. Spiller JSY AU RC 6.00 15.00
104B C.J. Spiller JSY AU RC 6.00 15.00
105A Ryan Mathews JSY AU RC 6.00 15.00
105B Ryan Mathews JSY AU RC 6.00 15.00
106A Anthony McCoy JSY AU RC 6.00 15.00
106B Anthony McCoy JSY AU RC 6.00 15.00
107A D.Thomas JSY AU RC 15.00 40.00
107B D.Thomas JSY AU RC 15.00 40.00
108B Dez Bryant JSY AU RC 40.00 80.00
109A Tim Tebow JSY AU RC 15.00 40.00
110A Jahvid Best JSY AU RC 6.00 15.00
110B Jahvid Best JSY AU RC 6.00 15.00
111A D.McCluster JSY AU RC 8.00 20.00
111B D.McCluster JSY AU RC 8.00 20.00
112A Arrelious Benn JSY AU RC 6.00 15.00
112B R.Gronkowski JSY AU RC 6.00 15.00
113A R.Gronkowski JSY AU RC 30.00 60.00
113B Rob Gronkowski JSY AU RC 30.00 60.00
114A Jimmy Clausen JSY AU RC 6.00 15.00
114B Jimmy Clausen JSY AU RC 6.00 15.00
115A Toby Gerhart JSY AU RC 8.00 20.00
115B Toby Gerhart JSY AU RC 8.00 20.00
116A Ben Tate JSY AU RC 6.00 15.00
116B Ben Tate JSY AU RC 6.00 15.00
117A M.Hardesty JSY AU RC 6.00 15.00
117B M.Hardesty JSY AU RC 6.00 15.00
118A Golden Tate JSY AU RC 8.00 20.00
118B Golden Tate JSY AU RC 8.00 20.00
119A Damian Williams JSY AU RC 6.00 15.00
119B Damian Williams JSY AU RC 6.00 15.00
120A Brandon LaFell JSY AU RC 10.00 25.00
120B Brandon LaFell JSY AU RC 10.00 25.00
121A Jordan Shipley JSY AU RC 6.00 15.00
121B Jordan Shipley JSY AU RC 6.00 15.00
122A Colt McCoy JSY AU RC 6.00 15.00
122B Colt McCoy JSY AU RC 6.00 15.00
123A Eric Decker JSY AU RC 8.00 20.00
123B Eric Decker JSY AU RC 8.00 20.00
124A Derrick Morgan JSY AU RC 6.00 15.00
124B Derrick Morgan JSY AU RC 6.00 15.00
125A Jonathan Dwyer JSY AU RC 6.00 15.00
125B Jonathan Dwyer JSY AU RC 6.00 15.00
126A E.Sanders JSY AU RC 12.00 30.00
126B E.Sanders JSY AU RC 12.00 30.00
127A M.Williams JSY AU RC 6.00 15.00
127B M.Williams JSY AU RC 6.00 15.00
128A Mardy Gilyard JSY AU RC 6.00 15.00
128B Mardy Gilyard JSY AU RC 6.00 15.00
129A Gerald McCoy JSY AU RC 10.00 25.00
129B Gerald McCoy JSY AU RC 10.00 25.00
130A Marcus Easley JSY AU RC 6.00 15.00
130B Marcus Easley JSY AU RC 6.00 15.00
131A Andre Roberts JSY AU RC 6.00 15.00
131B Andre Roberts JSY AU RC 6.00 15.00
132A Mike Kafka JSY AU RC 8.00 20.00
132B Mike Kafka JSY AU RC 8.00 20.00
133A A.Edwards JSY AU RC 8.00 20.00
133B A.Edwards JSY AU RC 8.00 20.00
134A Earl Thomas JSY AU RC 15.00 40.00
135A Sean Canfield JSY AU RC 6.00 15.00

2010 Topps Triple Threads Emerald

*VETS 1-90: .6X TO 1.5X BASIC CARDS
*RETIRED 91-100: .6X TO 1.5X BASIC CARDS
1-100 STATED PRINT RUN 299
*ROOKIE JSY AU: .5X TO 1.2X BASIC CARDS
101-135 ROOKIE JSY AU PRINT RUN 50
101A Sam Bradford JSY AU 40.00 100.00
101B Sam Bradford JSY AU 40.00 100.00
109A Tim Tebow JSY AU 25.00 60.00

2010 Topps Triple Threads Gold

*VETS 1-90: 1X TO 2.5X BASIC CARDS
*RETIRED 91-100: 1X TO 2.5X BASIC CARDS
1-100 STATED PRINT RUN 99
*ROOKIE JSY AU: .6X TO 1.5X BASIC CARDS
101-135 ROOKIE JSY AU PRINT RUN 25
101A Sam Bradford JSY AU 50.00 120.00
101B Sam Bradford JSY AU 50.00 120.00
108B Dez Bryant JSY AU 50.00 100.00
109A Tim Tebow JSY AU 30.00 80.00
109B Tim Tebow JSY AU 30.00 80.00

2010 Topps Triple Threads Ruby

*VETS 1-90: 2X TO 5X BASIC CARDS
*RETIRED 91-100: 2X TO 5X BASIC CARDS
1-100 STATED PRINT RUN 25
101-135 UNPRICED JSY AU PRINT RUN 10

2010 Topps Triple Threads Autographed Relic Combos

STATED PRINT RUN 27 SER.#'d SETS
*EMERALD/18: .5X TO 1.2X BASIC INSERTS
EXCH EXPIRATION: 10/13/2012
1 Montana/Young/Lott 100.00 200.00
2 Bradford/McCoy/Clausen 25.00 60.00
3 Spiller/Mathews/Best 10.00 25.00
4 Thomas/McCluster/Benn 20.00 50.00
5 R.Lewis/Willis/Mayo 30.00 80.00
6 Bradford/McCoy/Shipley 30.00 80.00
7 Manning/Addai/Wayne 75.00 150.00
8 Jones-Drew/Mathews/Best 10.00 25.00
9 Tate/Hardesty/McCluster 15.00 40.00
10 Clausen/Williams/LaFell 15.00 40.00
11 McCoy/Benn/Will 25.00 60.00
12 Frman/Will/Benn 15.00 40.00
13 Benn/Decker/Kafka 25.00 50.00
14 Spiller/Thomas/Dwyer 25.00 60.00
15 D.Williams/Gerhart/Best 20.00 50.00
16 Roberts/G.Tate/Gilyard 15.00 40.00
17 Gore/Jns-Drw/Jcksn 25.00 50.00
18 Mathews/Thoms/McClslr 25.00 80.00
19 Brees/Bush/Colston 50.00 100.00
20 Will/Easley/Gilyard EXCH 20.00 50.00
21 Bradford/Thomas/Spiller 25.00 60.00

2010 Topps Triple Threads Autographed Relic Duals

JSY AU PRINT RUN 18
TTARP1 P.Manning/R.Wayne
TTARP2 T.Aikman/T.Romo 100.00 200.00
TTARP3 E.Smith/T.Dorsett
TTARP4 M.Hardesty/B.Tate 15.00 40.00
TTARP5 P.Manning/E.Manning 150.00 250.00
TTARP6 R.Mendenhall/F.Harris 40.00 80.00

2010 Topps Triple Threads Autographed Relics

STATED PRINT RUN 18 SER.#'d SETS
*GOLD/9: .5X TO 1.2X BASIC AU/18
EXCH EXPIRATION: 10/31/2013
EACH HAS 2-3 CARDS OF EQUAL VALUE
TTRA1 Peyton Manning 100.00 200.00
TTRA2 Peyton Manning 100.00 200.00
TTRA3 Peyton Manning 100.00 200.00
TTRA4 Mark Sanchez 40.00 80.00
TTRA5 Mark Sanchez 40.00 80.00
TTRA6 Mark Sanchez 20.00 50.00
TTRA7 Sam Bradford 75.00 200.00
TTRA8 Sam Bradford 75.00 200.00
TTRA9 Sam Bradford 75.00 200.00
TTRA10 John Elway 75.00 150.00
TTRA11 John Elway 75.00 150.00
TTRA12 John Elway 75.00 150.00
TTRA13 Knowshon Moreno 20.00 40.00
TTRA14 Knowshon Moreno 20.00 40.00
TTRA15 Knowshon Moreno 20.00 40.00
TTRA16 Sidney Rice 15.00 40.00
TTRA17 Sidney Rice 15.00 40.00
TTRA18 Sidney Rice 15.00 40.00
TTRA19 Adrian Peterson 75.00 150.00
TTRA20 Adrian Peterson 75.00 150.00
TTRA21 Adrian Peterson 75.00 150.00
TTRA22 Earl Campbell 30.00 60.00
TTRA23 Earl Campbell 30.00 60.00
TTRA24 Earl Campbell 30.00 60.00
TTRA25 Matt Ryan 30.00 60.00
TTRA26 Matt Ryan 30.00 60.00
TTRA27 Matt Ryan 30.00 60.00
TTRA28 Marques Colston 20.00 40.00
TTRA29 Marques Colston 20.00 40.00
TTRA30 Franco Harris 30.00 60.00
TTRA31 Dan Marino 100.00 200.00
TTRA32 Dan Marino 100.00 200.00
TTRA33 Dan Marino 100.00 200.00
TTRA34 Eli Manning 50.00 100.00
TTRA35 Eli Manning 50.00 100.00
TTRA36 Eli Manning 50.00 100.00
TTRA37 Jimmy Clausen 15.00 40.00
TTRA38 Jimmy Clausen 15.00 40.00
TTRA39 Jimmy Clausen 15.00 40.00
TTRA40 Ryan Mathews 10.00 25.00
TTRA41 Ryan Mathews 10.00 25.00
TTRA42 Ryan Mathews 10.00 25.00
TTRA43 Ben Tate 10.00 25.00
TTRA44 Ben Tate 10.00 25.00
TTRA45 Ben Tate 10.00 25.00
TTRA46 C.J. Spiller 10.00 25.00
TTRA47 C.J. Spiller 10.00 25.00
TTRA48 C.J. Spiller 10.00 25.00
TTRA49 Kevin Kolb 10.00 25.00
TTRA50 Kevin Kolb 10.00 25.00
TTRA51 Kevin Kolb 10.00 25.00
TTRA52 Emmitt Smith 100.00 200.00
TTRA53 Emmitt Smith 100.00 200.00
TTRA54 Emmitt Smith 100.00 200.00
TTRA55 Joe Flacco 30.00 60.00
TTRA56 Joe Flacco 30.00 60.00
TTRA57 Joe Flacco 30.00 60.00
TTRA58 Marcus Allen 25.00 50.00
TTRA59 Marcus Allen 25.00 50.00
TTRA60 Marcus Allen 25.00 50.00
TTRA61 Montario Hardesty 8.00 20.00
TTRA62 Montario Hardesty 8.00 20.00
TTRA63 Montario Hardesty 8.00 20.00
TTRA64 Jahvid Best 15.00 40.00
TTRA65 Jahvid Best 15.00 40.00
TTRA66 Jahvid Best 15.00 40.00
TTRA67 Jonathan Dwyer 15.00 40.00
TTRA68 Jonathan Dwyer 15.00 40.00
TTRA69 Jonathan Dwyer 15.00 40.00
TTRA70 Dexter McCluster 15.00 40.00
TTRA71 Dexter McCluster 15.00 40.00
TTRA72 Dexter McCluster 15.00 40.00
TTRA73 LaDainian Tomlinson 30.00 60.00
TTRA74 LaDainian Tomlinson 30.00 60.00
TTRA75 LaDainian Tomlinson 30.00 60.00
TTRA76 Percy Harvin 20.00 40.00
TTRA77 Percy Harvin 20.00 40.00
TTRA78 Percy Harvin 20.00 40.00
TTRA79 Demaryius Thomas 25.00 50.00
TTRA80 Demaryius Thomas 25.00 50.00
TTRA81 Demaryius Thomas 25.00 50.00
TTRA82 Rashard Mendenhall 12.00 30.00
TTRA83 Rashard Mendenhall 12.00 30.00
TTRA84 Rashard Mendenhall 12.00 30.00
TTRA85 Frank Gore 20.00 40.00
TTRA86 Frank Gore 20.00 40.00
TTRA87 Frank Gore 20.00 40.00
TTRA88 Tim Tebow 75.00 150.00
TTRA89 Thurman Thomas 30.00 60.00
TTRA90 Matthew Stafford 30.00 60.00
TTRA91 Brett Favre 125.00 250.00
TTRA92 Brett Favre 125.00 250.00
TTRA93 Brett Favre 125.00 250.00
TTRA94 Eric Dickerson 25.00 50.00
TTRA95 Eric Dickerson 25.00 50.00
TTRA96 Eric Dickerson 25.00 50.00
TTRA97 Drew Brees 50.00 100.00
TTRA98 Drew Brees 50.00 100.00
TTRA99 Drew Brees 50.00 100.00
TTRA100 Colt McCoy 30.00 80.00
TTRA101 Colt McCoy 30.00 80.00
TTRA102 Colt McCoy 20.00 50.00
TTRA103 DeAngelo Williams 20.00 40.00
TTRA104 DeAngelo Williams 20.00 40.00
TTRA105 DeAngelo Williams 20.00 40.00
TTRA106 Matthew Stafford 30.00 60.00
TTRA107 Matthew Stafford 30.00 60.00

2010 Topps Triple Threads Relic

STATED PRINT RUN 36 SER.#'d SETS
*EMERALD/18: .5X TO 1.2X BASIC JSY/36
*GOLD/9: .6X TO 1.5X BASIC JSY/36
*SEPIA/27: .4X TO 1X BASIC JSY/36
EACH HAS THREE CARDS OF EQUAL VALUE
TTR1 Tony Romo 6.00 15.00
TTR2 Tony Romo 6.00 15.00
TTR3 Tony Romo 6.00 15.00
TTR4 Sam Bradford 4.00 10.00
TTR5 Sam Bradford 4.00 10.00
TTR6 Sam Bradford 4.00 10.00
TTR7 Jimmy Clausen 3.00 8.00
TTR8 Jimmy Clausen 3.00 8.00
TTR9 Jimmy Clausen 3.00 8.00
TTR10 Tim Tebow 10.00 25.00
TTR11 Tim Tebow 10.00 25.00
TTR12 Tim Tebow 10.00 25.00
TTR13 C.J. Spiller 3.00 8.00
TTR14 C.J. Spiller 3.00 8.00
TTR15 C.J. Spiller 3.00 8.00
TTR16 Ryan Mathews 3.00 8.00
TTR17 Ryan Mathews 3.00 8.00
TTR18 Ryan Mathews 3.00 8.00
TTR19 Jahvid Best 3.00 8.00
TTR20 Jahvid Best 3.00 8.00
TTR21 Jahvid Best 3.00 8.00
TTR22 Demaryius Thomas 8.00 20.00
TTR23 Demaryius Thomas 8.00 20.00
TTR24 Demaryius Thomas 8.00 20.00
TTR25 Dez Bryant 8.00 20.00
TTR26 Dez Bryant 8.00 20.00
TTR27 Dez Bryant 8.00 20.00
TTR28 Golden Tate 4.00 10.00
TTR29 Golden Tate 4.00 10.00
TTR30 Golden Tate 4.00 10.00
TTR31 Dexter McCluster 8.00 20.00
TTR32 Dexter McCluster 8.00 20.00
TTR33 Dexter McCluster 8.00 20.00
TTR34 Ben Tate 3.00 8.00
TTR35 Ben Tate 3.00 8.00
TTR36 Ben Tate 3.00 8.00
TTR37 Colt McCoy 4.00 10.00
TTR38 Colt McCoy 4.00 10.00
TTR39 Colt McCoy 4.00 10.00
TTR40 Jonathan Dwyer 3.00 8.00
TTR41 Jonathan Dwyer 3.00 8.00
TTR42 Jonathan Dwyer 3.00 8.00
TTR43 Toby Gerhart 3.00 8.00
TTR44 Toby Gerhart 3.00 8.00
TTR45 Toby Gerhart 3.00 8.00
TTR46 Montario Hardesty 3.00 8.00
TTR47 Montario Hardesty 3.00 8.00
TTR48 Montario Hardesty 3.00 8.00
TTR49 Joe McKnight 3.00 8.00
TTR50 Joe McKnight 3.00 8.00
TTR51 Joe McKnight 3.00 8.00
TTR52 Mike Williams 3.00 8.00
TTR53 Mike Williams 3.00 8.00
TTR54 Mike Williams 3.00 8.00
TTR55 Eric Decker 6.00 15.00
TTR56 Eric Decker 6.00 15.00
TTR57 Eric Decker 6.00 15.00
TTR58 Arrelious Benn 3.00 8.00
TTR59 Arrelious Benn 3.00 8.00
TTR60 Arrelious Benn 3.00 8.00
TTR61 Steven Jackson 5.00 12.00
TTR62 Steven Jackson 5.00 12.00
TTR63 Steven Jackson 5.00 12.00
TTR64 Brandon Jacobs 8.00 20.00
TTR65 Brandon Jacobs 8.00 20.00
TTR66 Brandon Jacobs 8.00 20.00
TTR67 Tom Brady 15.00 40.00
TTR68 Tom Brady 15.00 40.00
TTR69 Tom Brady 15.00 40.00
TTR70 Peyton Manning 15.00 40.00
TTR71 Peyton Manning 15.00 40.00
TTR72 Peyton Manning 15.00 40.00
TTR73 Maurice Jones-Drew 5.00 12.00
TTR74 Maurice Jones-Drew 5.00 12.00
TTR75 Maurice Jones-Drew 5.00 12.00
TTR76 Larry Fitzgerald 6.00 15.00
TTR77 Larry Fitzgerald 6.00 15.00
TTR78 Larry Fitzgerald 6.00 15.00
TTR79 Eric Dickerson 10.00 25.00
TTR80 Eric Dickerson 10.00 25.00
TTR81 Eric Dickerson 10.00 25.00
TTR82 Tony Dorsett 12.00 30.00
TTR83 Tony Dorsett 12.00 30.00
TTR84 Tony Dorsett 12.00 30.00
TTR85 Marcus Allen 12.00 30.00
TTR86 Marcus Allen 12.00 30.00
TTR87 Marcus Allen 12.00 30.00
TTR88 Dan Marino 25.00 60.00
TTR89 Dan Marino 25.00 60.00
TTR90 Dan Marino 25.00 60.00
TTR91 Dwayne Bowe 6.00 15.00
TTR92 Dwayne Bowe 6.00 15.00
TTR93 Dwayne Bowe 6.00 15.00
TTR94 Andre Johnson 6.00 15.00
TTR95 Andre Johnson 6.00 15.00
TTR96 Andre Johnson 6.00 15.00
TTR97 Chris Johnson 5.00 12.00
TTR98 Chris Johnson 5.00 12.00
TTR99 Chris Johnson 5.00 12.00
TTR100 Mike Kafka 4.00 10.00
TTR101 Mike Kafka 4.00 10.00
TTR102 Mike Kafka 4.00 10.00
TTR103 Ray Lewis 12.00 30.00
TTR104 Ray Lewis 12.00 30.00
TTR105 Ray Lewis 12.00 30.00
TTR106 Jeremy Maclin 5.00 12.00
TTR107 Jeremy Maclin 5.00 12.00
TTR108 Jeremy Maclin 5.00 12.00
TTR109 Knowshon Moreno 5.00 12.00
TTR110 Knowshon Moreno 5.00 12.00
TTR111 Knowshon Moreno 5.00 12.00
TTR112 Rashard Mendenhall 5.00 12.00
TTR113 Rashard Mendenhall 5.00 12.00
TTR114 Rashard Mendenhall 5.00 12.00
TTR115 Joe Montana 40.00 100.00
TTR116 Joe Montana 40.00 100.00
TTR117 Joe Montana 40.00 100.00
TTR118 Santana Moss 6.00 15.00
TTR119 Santana Moss 6.00 15.00
TTR120 Santana Moss 6.00 15.00
TTR121 Willis McGahee 5.00 12.00
TTR122 Willis McGahee 5.00 12.00
TTR123 Willis McGahee 5.00 12.00
TTR124 Adrian Peterson 15.00 40.00
TTR125 Adrian Peterson 15.00 40.00
TTR126 Adrian Peterson 15.00 40.00
TTR127 Troy Polamalu 8.00 20.00
TTR128 Troy Polamalu 8.00 20.00
TTR129 Troy Polamalu 8.00 20.00
TTR130 Ed Reed 10.00 25.00
TTR131 Ed Reed 10.00 25.00
TTR132 Ed Reed 10.00 25.00
TTR133 Philip Rivers 8.00 20.00
TTR134 Philip Rivers 8.00 20.00
TTR135 Philip Rivers 8.00 20.00
TTR136 Steve Smith 6.00 15.00
TTR137 Steve Smith 6.00 15.00
TTR138 Steve Smith 6.00 15.00
TTR139 Roddy White 5.00 12.00
TTR140 Roddy White 5.00 12.00
TTR141 Roddy White 5.00 12.00
TTR142 Thurman Thomas 10.00 25.00
TTR143 Thurman Thomas 10.00 25.00
TTR144 Thurman Thomas 10.00 25.00
TTR145 Matthew Stafford 6.00 15.00
TTR146 Matthew Stafford 6.00 15.00
TTR147 Matthew Stafford 6.00 15.00
TTR148 Earl Campbell 12.00 30.00
TTR149 Earl Campbell 12.00 30.00
TTR150 Earl Campbell 12.00 30.00
TTR151 Troy Aikman 12.00 30.00
TTR152 Troy Aikman 12.00 30.00
TTR153 Troy Aikman 12.00 30.00
TTR154 Roger Staubach 15.00 40.00
TTR155 Roger Staubach 15.00 40.00
TTR156 Roger Staubach 15.00 40.00
TTR157 Eric Berry 5.00 12.00
TTR158 Eric Berry 5.00 12.00
TTR159 Eric Berry 5.00 12.00

2010 Topps Triple Threads Relic Combos

STATED PRINT RUN 36 SER.#'d SETS
*EMERALD/18: .5X TO 1.2X BASIC JSY/36
*SEPIA/27: .4X TO 1X BASIC JSY/36
TTRC1 Johnson/Fitzgerald/Moss 6.00 15.00
TTRC2 Johnsn/Petrsn/Jnes-Drw 8.00 20.00
TTRC3 Sanchez/Stafford/Flacco 6.00 15.00
TTRC4 Mannng/Wyne/Dickrsn 15.00 40.00
TTRC5 Romo/Jones/Witten 6.00 15.00
TTRC6 Manning/Romo/Kolb 6.00 15.00
TTRC7 Gore/Jones-Drew/S.Jcksn 6.00 15.00
TTRC8 Royal/Thomas/Decker 8.00 20.00
TTRC9 Stafford/Bradford/Clausen 4.00 10.00
TTRC10 Staubach/Dorsett/Smith 20.00 50.00
TTRC11 Ryan/White/Gonzalez 6.00 15.00
TTRC12 Dumervil/Allen/Suh 6.00 15.00
TTRC13 Montana/Marino/Elway 25.00 60.00
TTRC14 Montana/Brady/Clausen 20.00 50.00
TTRC15 Lott/Polamalu/Reed 8.00 20.00
TTRC16 Palmer/Shipley/Gresham 4.00 10.00
TTRC17 Leinart/Fitzgerald/Roberts 6.00 15.00
TTRC18 Sanchz/Tomlnsn/McKnght 8.00 20.00
TTRC19 Cassel/Bowe/McCluster 4.00 10.00
TTRC20 Ware/Freeney/Williams 6.00 15.00
TTRC21 Henne/Marshall/Williams 6.00 15.00
TTRC22 Stafford/Johnson/Best 10.00 25.00
TTRC23 Brady/Welker/Maroney 20.00 50.00
TTRC24 Moss/Portis/Thomas 6.00 15.00
TTRC25 Roeth/Mndnhall/Dwyer 8.00 20.00
TTRC26 Forte/Hester/Bennett 6.00 15.00
TTRC27 Willis/McClain/Mayo 4.00 10.00
TTRC28 Young/Johnson/Williams 5.00 12.00
TTRC29 Roeth/Ward/Sanders 8.00 20.00
TTRC30 Tebow/Thomas/Decker 10.00 25.00
TTRC31 Mathews/Best/Gerhart 3.00 8.00
TTRC32 McCoy/Benn/Williams 3.00 8.00
TTRC33 Grnkwski/Price/Hernndz 10.00 25.00
TTRC34 Tebow/Hernandez/Dixon 10.00 25.00
TTRC35 Asomugha/Revis/Bailey 6.00 15.00
TTRC36 Palmer/Flacco/McCoy 4.00 10.00
TTRC37 Rivers/Tebow/Cassel 10.00 25.00
TTRC38 McCluster/Hardesty/LaFell 5.00 12.00
TTRC39 Clausen/LaFell/Edwards 5.00 12.00
TTRC40 Spiller/Mathews/Best 3.00 8.00
TTRC41 Johnson/Slaton/Tate 6.00 15.00
TTRC42 Roberts/Edwards/Price 4.00 10.00
TTRC43 Hester/Olsen/Forte 10.00 25.00
TTRC44 Colston/White/Smith 6.00 15.00
TTRC45 Spiller/Thomas/Dwyer 8.00 20.00
TTRC46 Bradford/McCoy/Bryant 15.00 40.00
TTRC47 Benn/Decker/Kafka 4.00 10.00
TTRC48 Williams/Easley/Gilyard 3.00 8.00
TTRC49 Williams/McKnight/Best 3.00 8.00
TTRC50 Bradford/Clausen/McCoy 4.00 10.00
TTRC51 Williams/LaFell/Sanders 5.00 12.00
TTRC52 Best/Gerhart/Williams 3.00 8.00
TTRC53 Tate/Hardesty/Dixon 3.00 8.00
TTRC54 Brdfrd/McCy/Grshm 4.00 10.00
TTRC55 Tate/Hardesty/McCluster 4.00 10.00
TTRC56 Grshm/Thms/Brynt 8.00 20.00
TTRC57 Brdfrd/Tbw/Clsn 10.00 25.00
TTRC58 Suh/McCoy/Berry 6.00 15.00
TTRC59 Gerhart/Tate/Hardesty 3.00 8.00
TTRC60 Brynt/Thms/McClstr 8.00 20.00

2010 Topps Triple Threads Relic Double Combos

STATED PRINT RUN 36 SER.#'d SETS
*EMERALD/18: .5X TO 1.2X BASIC JSY/36
*SEPIA/27: .4X TO 1X BASIC JSY/36
1 Ptrsn/Fitz/Mnn/Splr/Brdfrd 20.00 50.00
2 Stbch/Akmn/Rm/Drstt/Jns 50.00 100.00
3 Mrno/Mntn/Elwy/Nmth/Aik 60.00 120.00
4 Splr/Mthws/Bst/Grhrt/Hrd 25.00 60.00
5 Brdfd/Tbw/Clsn/Spllr/Bst 15.00 40.00
6 Tbw/McClstr/Hrd/Tte/Dxn 40.00 80.00
7 Brd/Bryn/McCy/McCy/Suh 20.00 50.00
8 Will/Glyrd/Esly/Thms/Frd 8.00 25.00
9 Splr/Thms/Dwyr/Tte/Hrd 15.00 40.00
10 Mnn/Brdy/Rvrs/Fvr/Ryn 60.00 120.00
11 R.Staubach/T.Dorsett 30.00 80.00
12 B.Favre/A.Rodgers 40.00 100.00
13 R.Lewis/E.Reed 25.00 50.00
14 M.Allen/R.Bush 20.00 40.00
15 D.Marino/L.Fitzgerald 50.00 100.00

2010 Topps Triple Threads Relic XXIV

STATED PRINT RUN 18 SER.#'d SETS
*GOLD/9: .6X TO 1.5X BASIC JSY/18
TFR1 Brett Favre 50.00 120.00
TFR2 Sam Bradford 5.00 12.00
TFR3 Peyton Manning 25.00 60.00
TFR4 DeMarcus Ware 8.00 20.00
TFR5 Dan Marino 25.00 60.00
TFR6 C.J. Spiller 4.00 10.00
TFR7 Chris Johnson 6.00 15.00
TFR8 Hines Ward 12.00 30.00
TFR9 Demaryius Thomas 10.00 25.00
TFR10 Marcus Allen 12.00 30.00
TFR11 Dez Bryant 10.00 25.00
TFR12 LaDainian Tomlinson 15.00 40.00
TFR13 Jimmy Clausen 4.00 10.00
TFR14 Clinton Portis 6.00 15.00
TFR15 Thurman Thomas 10.00 25.00
TFR16 Ryan Mathews 4.00 10.00
TFR17 Tim Tebow 12.00 30.00
TFR18 Steve Young 15.00 40.00

2010 Topps Triple Threads Rookie and Rising Star Autographed Relic Dual

STATED PRINT RUN 50 SER.#'d SETS
*GOLD/25: .5X TO 1.2X BASIC AU/50
1 S.Bradford/D.Bryant 50.00 100.00
2 P.Harvin/D.McCluster
3 C.Spiller/J.Dwyer 20.00 50.00
4 R.Mathews/J.Best 20.00 50.00
5 T.Aikman/S.Bradford 60.00 120.00
6 M.Sanchez/J.Clausen 20.00 50.00

2010 Topps Triple Threads Sepia

*VETS 1-90: .5X TO 1.2X BASIC CARDS
*RETIRED 91-100: .5X TO 1.2X BASIC CARDS
1-100 STATED PRINT RUN 499
*ROOKIE JSY AU: .4X TO 1X BASIC CARDS
101-135 ROOKIE JSY AU PRINT RUN 70

2011 Topps Triple Threads

100 VETERAN PRINT RUN 999
101-136 ROOKIE JSY AU PRINT RUN 99
EXCH EXPIRATION: 11/30/2014
1 Tom Brady 3.00 8.00

2 LeGarrette Blount 1.00 2.50
3 Jamaal Charles 1.00 2.50
4 Brian Urlacher 1.25 3.00
5 Matt Schaub .75 2.00
6 Ed Reed 1.00 2.50
7 Marshawn Lynch 1.00 2.50
8 Jay Cutler .75 2.00
9 Jahvid Best .75 2.00
10 Drew Brees 1.25 3.00
11 Frank Gore 1.00 2.50
12 Mike Williams 1.00 2.50
13 Hakeem Nicks .75 2.00
14 Steven Jackson .75 2.00
15 Rob Gronkowski 1.25 3.00
16 Roddy White .75 2.00
17 Mark Sanchez .75 2.00
18 Maurice Jones-Drew .75 2.00
19 LeSean McCoy 1.25 3.00
20 LaDainian Tomlinson 1.25 3.00
21 Michael Turner .75 2.00
22 Nnamdi Asomugha .75 2.00
23 Chad Ochocinco .75 2.00
24 Sam Bradford .75 2.00
25 Calvin Johnson 1.25 3.00
26 Tim Tebow 1.25 3.00
27 Fred Jackson .75 2.00
28 Jerome Bettis 1.25 3.00
29 Dwayne Bowe 1.00 2.50
30 Adrian Peterson 1.25 3.00
31 Brandon Lloyd .75 2.00
32 Junior Seau 1.00 2.50
33 Sidney Rice .75 2.00
34 Gale Sayers 1.25 3.00
35 Matt Hasselbeck .75 2.00
36 Ryan Mathews 1.00 2.50
37 Josh Freeman 1.00 2.50
38 Greg Jennings .75 2.00
39 Jonathan Stewart .75 2.00
40 Larry Fitzgerald 1.00 2.50
41 Brandon Marshall 1.00 2.50
42 Clay Matthews 1.25 3.00
43 Matt Forte .75 2.00
44 Jerod Mayo .75 2.00
45 Dan Marino 2.50 6.00
46 David Garrard .75 2.00
47 Wes Welker 1.00 2.50
48 Jerry Rice 2.00 5.00
49 Chris Johnson .75 2.00
50 Aaron Rodgers 2.00 5.00
51 Dez Bryant 1.25 3.00
52 DeSean Jackson 1.00 2.50
53 Anquan Boldin .75 2.00
54 John Elway 2.00 5.00
55 Brett Favre 2.50 6.00
56 Arian Foster .75 2.00
57 Jeremy Maclin .75 2.00
58 Percy Harvin .75 2.00
59 Tony Romo 1.00 2.50
60 Tony Gonzalez 1.00 2.50
61 Joe Flacco 1.00 2.50
62 Terry Bradshaw 1.50 4.00
63 Antonio Gates .75 2.00
64 Matt Ryan 1.00 2.50
65 Steve Johnson .75 2.00
66 Santana Moss 1.00 2.50
67 Jordy Nelson 1.00 2.50
68 Andre Johnson 1.00 2.50
69 Knowshon Moreno .75 2.00
70 Philip Rivers 1.25 3.00
71 Steve Smith 1.00 2.50
72 Vernon Davis .75 2.00
73 DeMarcus Ware 1.00 2.50
74 Austin Collie .75 2.00
75 Matthew Stafford 1.00 2.50
76 Marcedes Lewis .75 2.00
77 Joe Montana 3.00 8.00
78 Marques Colston .75 2.00
79 Reggie Wayne 1.00 2.50
80 Troy Polamalu 1.25 3.00
81 Peyton Hillis .75 2.00
82 Mike Wallace .75 2.00
83 Shonn Greene .75 2.00
84 Darren McFadden .75 2.00
85 Eli Manning 1.00 2.50
86 Pierre Thomas .75 2.00
87 Matt Cassel .75 2.00
88 Rashard Mendenhall .75 2.00
89 Miles Austin .75 2.00
90 Michael Vick 1.00 2.50
91 BenJarvus Green-Ellis .75 2.00
92 Ahmad Bradshaw .75 2.00
93 Ndamukong Suh 1.00 2.50
94 Santonio Holmes .75 2.00
95 Justin Tuck .75 2.00
96 Ben Roethlisberger 1.25 3.00
97 Joseph Addai .75 2.00
98 Ray Rice .75 2.00
99 Joe Namath 1.50 4.00
100 Peyton Manning 2.50 6.00
103A Vincent Brown JSY AU RC 5.00 12.00
103C Vincent Brown MFL JSY AU RC 5.00 12.00
103B Vincent Brown SD JSY AU RC 5.00 12.00
104A Daniel Thomas JSY AU RC 5.00 12.00
104B Daniel Thomas NFL JSY AU RC 5.00 12.00
104C Daniel Thomas MIA JSY AU RC 5.00 12.00
105A Kyle Rudolph JSY AU RC 5.00 12.00
105B Kyle Rudolph NFL JSY AU RC 5.00 12.00
105C Kyle Rudolph MIN JSY AU RC 5.00 12.00
106A Bilal Powell JSY AU RC 6.00 15.00
106B Bilal Powell NFL JSY AU RC 6.00 15.00
106C Bilal Powell NYJ JSY AU RC 6.00 15.00
107A Jordan Todman JSY AU RC 5.00 12.00
107B Jordan Todman NFL JSY AU RC 5.00 12.00
107C Jordan Todman SD JSY AU RC 5.00 12.00
109A Shane Vereen JSY AU RC 6.00 15.00
109B Shane Vereen NFL JSY AU RC 6.00 15.00
109C Shane Vereen NE JSY AU RC 6.00 15.00
110 Cam Newton JSY AU RC 60.00 120.00
112A Kendall Hunter JSY AU RC 12.00 30.00
112B Kendall Hunter NFL JSY AU RC 12.00 30.00
112C Kendall Hunter SF JSY AU RC 12.00 30.00
115A Jerrel Jernigan JSY AU RC 5.00 12.00
115B Jerrel Jernigan NFL JSY AU RC 5.00 12.00
115C Jerrel Jernigan NYG JSY AU RC 5.00 12.00
119A Alex Green JSY AU RC 5.00 12.00
119B Alex Green NFL JSY AU RC 5.00 12.00
119C Alex Green GB JSY AU RC 5.00 12.00
125A Edmond Gates JSY AU RC 5.00 12.00
125B Edmond Gates NFL JSY AU RC 5.00 12.00
125C Edmond Gates MIA JSY AU RC 5.00 12.00
126A Austin Pettis JSY AU RC 5.00 12.00
126B Austin Pettis NFL JSY AU RC 5.00 12.00
126C Austin Pettis STL JSY AU RC 5.00 12.00
127A Jamie Harper JSY AU RC 5.00 12.00
127B Jamie Harper NFL JSY AU RC 5.00 12.00
127C Jamie Harper TEN JSY AU RC 5.00 12.00
129A Stevan Ridley JSY AU RC 5.00 12.00
129B Stevan Ridley NFL JSY AU RC 5.00 12.00
129C Stevan Ridley NE JSY AU RC 5.00 12.00
132A Delone Carter JSY AU RC 5.00 12.00
132B Delone Carter NFL JSY AU RC 5.00 12.00
132C Delone Carter IND JSY AU RC 5.00 12.00
134A D.Murray JSY AU RC 10.00 25.00
134B DeMarco Murray NFL JSY AU RC 10.00 25.00
134C DeMarco Murray DAL JSY AU RC 10.00 25.00
135A Taiwan Jones JSY AU RC 5.00 12.00
135B Taiwan Jones NFL JSY AU RC 5.00 12.00
135C Taiwan Jones OAK JSY AU RC 6.00 12.00

2011 Topps Triple Threads Emerald

ETS/250: .6X TO 1.5X BASIC CARDS
*ROOKIE JSY AU/50: .5X TO 1.2X BASIC AU
101A Torrey Smith JSY AU 12.00 30.00
113A Leonard Hankerson JSY AU 6.00 15.00
116A Greg Little JSY AU 8.00 20.00
121A Randall Cobb JSY AU 10.00 25.00

2011 Topps Triple Threads Gold

*VETS/99: 1X TO 2.5X BASIC CARDS
*ROOKIE JSY AU/25: .8X TO 2X BASIC AU

2011 Topps Triple Threads Ruby

*VETS/25: 2X TO 5X BASIC CARDS
1-100 VETERAN PRINT RUN 25
UNPRICED ROOKIE JSY AU PRINT RUN 10

2011 Topps Triple Threads Sepia

ETS/300: .5X TO 1.2X BASIC CARDS
*ROOKIE AU/70: .4X TO 1X BASIC JSY AU

2011 Topps Triple Threads Autographed Relic Combos

STATED PRINT RUN 27 SER.#'d SETS
*EMERALD/18: .5X TO 1.2X COMBO AU/27
RC1 Vick/Jackson/Maclin 40.00 80.00
RC3 Moreno/Tebow/Miller 40.00 100.00
RC4 Cobb/Leshoure/Rudolph 30.00 60.00
RC5 Newton/Miller/Dareus 50.00 120.00
RC6 Newton/Locker/Gabbert 60.00 120.00
RC8 Ingram/Williams/Vereen 15.00 40.00
RC9 Ponder/Dalton/Kaeper 50.00 100.00
RC10 Mallett/Vereen/Ridley 12.00 30.00
RC11 Jernigan/Brown/Pettis 10.00 25.00
RC13 Young/Smith/Little 12.00 30.00
RC14 Leshre/Thms/Mury 20.00 50.00
RC15 Kaeper/Young/Pettis 50.00 100.00
RC16 Hankrsn/Jernign/Mury 20.00 50.00
RC17 Brees/Colstn/Ingram 90.00 150.00
RC19 Hunter/Carter/Jones 10.00 25.00
RC21 A.Green/Smith/Little 25.00 60.00

2011 Topps Triple Threads Autographed Relic Duals

STATED PRINT RUN 18 SER.#'d SETS
EXCH EXPIRATION: 11/30/2014
TTARP1 M.Vick/D.Jackson 60.00 120.00
TTARP2 A.Peterson/D.Murray 125.00 200.00
TTARP3 J.Elway/T.Tebow 150.00 300.00
TTARP4 D.Brees/P.Manning 175.00 300.00
TTARP5 Favre/Rodgers 400.00 600.00
TTARP6 R.Staubach/T.Romo 75.00 150.00

2011 Topps Triple Threads Autographed Relics

STATED PRINT RUN 18 SER.#'d SETS
*SEPIA/9: .5X TO 1.2X BASIC AU/18
TTAR1 Vincent Brown 8.00 20.00
TTAR2 Vincent Brown 8.00 20.00
TTAR3 Knowshon Moreno 12.00 30.00
TTAR4 Knowshon Moreno 12.00 30.00
TTAR5 Jerrel Jernigan 8.00 20.00
TTAR6 Jerrel Jernigan 8.00 20.00
TTAR10 Phil Simms 15.00 40.00
TTAR11 A.J. Green 50.00 100.00
TTAR12 A.J. Green 50.00 100.00
TTAR13 Hines Ward 50.00 100.00
TTAR14 Hines Ward 50.00 100.00
TTAR15 Drew Brees 75.00 150.00
TTAR16 Drew Brees 75.00 150.00
TTAR17 Daniel Thomas 8.00 20.00
TTAR18 Daniel Thomas 8.00 20.00
TTAR19 Santana Moss 15.00 40.00
TTAR20 Santana Moss 15.00 40.00
TTAR21 Darrelle Revis
TTAR22 Darrelle Revis
TTAR23 Matt Cassel 12.00 30.00
TTAR24 Matt Cassel 12.00 30.00
TTAR25 Christian Ponder 8.00 20.00
TTAR26 Christian Ponder 8.00 20.00
TTAR27 Kendall Hunter 8.00 20.00
TTAR28 Kendall Hunter 8.00 20.00
TTAR29 Earl Campbell 40.00 80.00
TTAR30 Earl Campbell 40.00 80.00
TTAR31 Julio Jones 40.00 80.00
TTAR32 Julio Jones 40.00 80.00
TTAR33 Andy Dalton 30.00 80.00
TTAR34 Andy Dalton 30.00 80.00
TTAR35 Jamaal Charles 15.00 40.00
TTAR36 Jamaal Charles 15.00 40.00
TTAR37 Colin Kaepernick 40.00 80.00
TTAR38 Colin Kaepernick 40.00 80.00
TTAR39 Ryan Mallett 8.00 20.00
TTAR40 Ryan Mallett 8.00 20.00
TTAR41 Zach Miller 12.00 30.00
TTAR42 Zach Miller 10.00 25.00
TTAR43 Joe Flacco 30.00 60.00
TTAR44 Joe Flacco 30.00 60.00
TTAR45 Jon Baldwin 8.00 20.00
TTAR46 Jon Baldwin 8.00 20.00
TTAR47 Ryan Williams 8.00 20.00
TTAR48 Ryan Williams 8.00 20.00
TTAR49 DeSean Jackson 15.00 40.00
TTAR50 DeSean Jackson 15.00 40.00
TTAR51 Mikel Leshoure 8.00 20.00
TTAR52 Mikel Leshoure 8.00 20.00
TTAR53 Alex Green 8.00 20.00
TTAR54 Alex Green 8.00 20.00
TTAR55 DeMarco Murray 15.00 40.00
TTAR56 DeMarco Murray 15.00 40.00
TTAR57 Greg Little 10.00 25.00
TTAR58 Greg Little 10.00 25.00
TTAR59 Kyle Rudolph 8.00 20.00
TTAR60 Kyle Rudolph 8.00 20.00
TTAR61 Leonard Hankerson 8.00 20.00
TTAR62 Leonard Hankerson 8.00 20.00
TTAR63 Marcell Dareus 8.00 20.00
TTAR64 Marcell Dareus 8.00 20.00
TTAR65 Randall Cobb 12.00 30.00
TTAR66 Randall Cobb 12.00 30.00
TTAR67 Titus Young 8.00 20.00
TTAR68 Titus Young 8.00 20.00
TTAR69 Torrey Smith 8.00 20.00
TTAR70 Torrey Smith 8.00 20.00
TTAR71 Von Miller 20.00 50.00

2011 Topps Triple Threads Autographed Unity Relics

ATED PRINT RUN 90 SER.#'d SETS
*EMERALD/50: .5X TO 1.2X BASIC AU/90
*GOLD/25: .6X TO 1.5X BASIC AU/90
*SEPIA/75: .4X TO 1X BASIC AU/90
TTUAR1 Steve Breaston 5.00 12.00
TTUAR2 Steve Breaston 5.00 12.00
TTUAR3 Steve Breaston 5.00 12.00
TTUAR4 Ryan Williams 4.00 10.00
TTUAR5 Ryan Williams 4.00 10.00
TTUAR6 Ryan Williams 4.00 10.00
TTUAR7 Chris Cooley 6.00 15.00
TTUAR8 DeAngelo Hall 6.00 15.00
TTUAR9 Leonard Hankerson 4.00 10.00
TTUAR10 Jon Baldwin 4.00 10.00
TTUAR11 Jon Baldwin 4.00 10.00
TTUAR12 Jon Baldwin 4.00 10.00
TTUAR13 Titus Young 4.00 10.00
TTUAR14 Brandon Pettigrew 6.00 15.00
TTUAR15 Mikel Leshoure 4.00 10.00
TTUAR16 Jamie Harper 4.00 10.00
TTUAR17 Earl Campbell 20.00 40.00
TTUAR18 Jake Locker 4.00 10.00
TTUAR19 Dwayne Bowe 8.00 20.00
TTUAR20 Matt Cassel 6.00 15.00
TTUAR21 Jon Baldwin 4.00 10.00
TTUAR22 Kyle Rudolph 4.00 10.00
TTUAR23 Kyle Rudolph 4.00 10.00
TTUAR24 Kyle Rudolph 4.00 10.00
TTUAR25 Marques Colston 6.00 15.00
TTUAR26 Marques Colston 6.00 15.00
TTUAR27 Marques Colston 6.00 15.00
TTUAR28 Shonn Greene 6.00 15.00
TTUAR29 Dustin Keller 5.00 12.00
TTUAR30 Bilal Powell 5.00 12.00
TTUAR31 Bilal Powell 5.00 12.00
TTUAR32 Shonn Greene 6.00 15.00
TTUAR33 Dustin Keller 5.00 12.00
TTUAR34 Dustin Keller 5.00 12.00
TTUAR35 Bilal Powell 5.00 12.00
TTUAR36 Shonn Greene 6.00 15.00
TTUAR37 Tony Dorsett 20.00 50.00
TTUAR38 Tony Dorsett 20.00 50.00
TTUAR39 Tony Dorsett 20.00 50.00
TTUAR40 Jordan Todman 4.00 10.00
TTUAR41 Antonio Gates 6.00 15.00
TTUAR42 Vincent Brown 4.00 10.00
TTUAR43 Vernon Davis 6.00 15.00
TTUAR44 Patrick Willis 12.00 30.00
TTUAR45 Colin Kaepernick 25.00 60.00
TTUAR46 Colin Kaepernick 25.00 60.00
TTUAR47 Vernon Davis 6.00 15.00
TTUAR48 Patrick Willis 12.00 30.00
TTUAR49 Patrick Willis 12.00 30.00
TTUAR50 Colin Kaepernick 25.00 60.00
TTUAR51 Vernon Davis 6.00 15.00
TTUAR52 DeAngelo Hall 6.00 15.00
TTUAR53 Leonard Hankerson 4.00 10.00
TTUAR54 Chris Cooley 6.00 15.00
TTUAR55 Stevan Ridley 4.00 10.00
TTUAR56 Ryan Mallett 4.00 10.00
TTUAR57 Shane Vereen 5.00 12.00
TTUAR58 Shane Vereen 5.00 12.00
TTUAR59 Stevan Ridley 4.00 10.00
TTUAR60 Ryan Mallett 4.00 10.00
TTUAR61 Ryan Mallett 4.00 10.00
TTUAR62 Shane Vereen 5.00 12.00
TTUAR63 Stevan Ridley 4.00 10.00
TTUAR64 A.J. Green 25.00 50.00
TTUAR65 A.J. Green 25.00 50.00
TTUAR66 A.J. Green 25.00 50.00

2011 Topps Triple Threads Relic

STATED PRINT RUN 36 SER.#'d SETS
*EMERALD/18: .5X TO 1.2X BASIC JSY/36
*GOLD/9: .6X TO 1.5X BASIC JSY/36
*SEPIA/27: .4X TO 1X BASIC JSY/36
MOST HAVE THREE CARDS OF EQUAL VALUE
TTR1 Cam Newton 15.00 40.00
TTR2 Cam Newton 15.00 40.00
TTR3 Cam Newton 15.00 40.00
TTR4 Jake Locker 4.00 10.00
TTR5 Jake Locker 4.00 10.00
TTR6 Jake Locker 4.00 10.00
TTR7 Mark Ingram 12.00 30.00
TTR8 Mark Ingram 12.00 30.00
TTR9 Mark Ingram 12.00 30.00
TTR10 Blaine Gabbert 4.00 10.00
TTR11 Blaine Gabbert 4.00 10.00
TTR12 Blaine Gabbert 4.00 10.00
TTR13 A.J. Green 10.00 25.00
TTR14 A.J. Green 10.00 25.00
TTR15 A.J. Green 10.00 25.00
TTR16 Christian Ponder 4.00 10.00
TTR17 Christian Ponder 4.00 10.00
TTR18 Christian Ponder 4.00 10.00
TTR19 Julio Jones 12.00 30.00
TTR20 Julio Jones 12.00 30.00
TTR21 Julio Jones 12.00 30.00
TTR22 Andy Dalton 8.00 20.00
TTR23 Andy Dalton 8.00 20.00
TTR24 Andy Dalton 8.00 20.00
TTR25 Colin Kaepernick 6.00 15.00
TTR26 Colin Kaepernick 6.00 15.00
TTR27 Colin Kaepernick 6.00 15.00
TTR28 Ryan Mallett 4.00 10.00
TTR29 Ryan Mallett 4.00 10.00
TTR30 Ryan Mallett 4.00 10.00
TTR31 Jon Baldwin 4.00 10.00
TTR32 Jon Baldwin 4.00 10.00
TTR33 Jon Baldwin 4.00 10.00
TTR34 Ryan Williams 4.00 10.00
TTR35 Ryan Williams 4.00 10.00
TTR36 Ryan Williams 4.00 10.00
TTR37 Mikel Leshoure 4.00 10.00
TTR38 Mikel Leshoure 4.00 10.00
TTR39 Mikel Leshoure 4.00 10.00
TTR40 Titus Young 4.00 10.00
TTR41 Titus Young 4.00 10.00
TTR42 Titus Young 4.00 10.00
TTR43 Marcell Dareus 4.00 10.00
TTR44 Marcell Dareus 4.00 10.00
TTR45 Marcell Dareus 4.00 10.00
TTR46 DeMarco Murray 8.00 20.00
TTR47 DeMarco Murray 8.00 20.00
TTR48 DeMarco Murray 8.00 20.00
TTR49 Greg Little 5.00 12.00
TTR50 Greg Little 5.00 12.00
TTR51 Greg Little 5.00 12.00
TTR52 Leonard Hankerson 4.00 10.00
TTR53 Leonard Hankerson 4.00 10.00
TTR54 Leonard Hankerson 4.00 10.00
TTR55 Randall Cobb 6.00 15.00
TTR56 Randall Cobb 6.00 15.00
TTR57 Randall Cobb 6.00 15.00
TTR58 Torrey Smith 4.00 10.00
TTR59 Torrey Smith 4.00 10.00
TTR60 Torrey Smith 4.00 10.00
TTR61 Kyle Rudolph 4.00 10.00
TTR62 Kyle Rudolph 4.00 10.00
TTR63 Kyle Rudolph 4.00 10.00
TTR64 Daniel Thomas 4.00 10.00
TTR65 Daniel Thomas 4.00 10.00
TTR66 Daniel Thomas 4.00 10.00
TTR67 Nnamdi Asomugha 5.00 12.00
TTR68 Nnamdi Asomugha 5.00 12.00
TTR69 Nnamdi Asomugha 5.00 12.00
TTR70 Marion Barber 5.00 12.00
TTR71 Marion Barber 5.00 12.00
TTR72 Marion Barber 5.00 12.00
TTR73 Tom Brady 20.00 50.00
TTR74 Tom Brady 20.00 50.00
TTR75 Tom Brady 20.00 50.00
TTR76 Jay Cutler 5.00 12.00
TTR77 Jay Cutler 5.00 12.00
TTR78 Jay Cutler 5.00 12.00
TTR79 Larry Fitzgerald 6.00 15.00
TTR80 Larry Fitzgerald 6.00 15.00
TTR81 Larry Fitzgerald 6.00 15.00
TTR82 Matt Forte 5.00 12.00
TTR83 Matt Forte 5.00 12.00
TTR84 Matt Forte 5.00 12.00
TTR85 Alex Green 4.00 10.00
TTR86 Alex Green 4.00 10.00
TTR87 Alex Green 4.00 10.00
TTR88 Tony Gonzalez 6.00 15.00
TTR89 Tony Gonzalez 6.00 15.00
TTR90 Tony Gonzalez 6.00 15.00
TTR91 Frank Gore 6.00 15.00
TTR92 Frank Gore 6.00 15.00
TTR93 Frank Gore 6.00 15.00
TTR94 LaDainian Tomlinson 8.00 20.00
TTR95 LaDainian Tomlinson 8.00 20.00
TTR96 Terry Bradshaw 15.00 40.00
TTR97 Devin Hester 8.00 20.00
TTR98 Devin Hester 8.00 20.00
TTR99 Devin Hester 8.00 20.00
TTR100 Brian Urlacher 8.00 20.00
TTR101 Brian Urlacher 8.00 20.00
TTR102 Brian Urlacher 8.00 20.00
TTR103 Chris Johnson 5.00 12.00
TTR104 Chris Johnson 5.00 12.00
TTR105 Chris Johnson 5.00 12.00
TTR106 Felix Jones 5.00 12.00
TTR107 Felix Jones 5.00 12.00
TTR108 Felix Jones 5.00 12.00
TTR109 Jim Plunkett 10.00 25.00
TTR110 Jim Plunkett 10.00 25.00
TTR111 Jim Plunkett 10.00 25.00
TTR112 Troy Polamalu 8.00 20.00
TTR113 Troy Polamalu 8.00 20.00
TTR114 Troy Polamalu 8.00 20.00
TTR115 Ed Reed 8.00 20.00
TTR116 Ed Reed 8.00 20.00
TTR117 Ed Reed 8.00 20.00

2011 Topps Triple Threads Relic Combos

STATED PRINT RUN 36 SER.#'d SETS
*EMERALD/18: .5X TO 1.2X COMBO/36
*SEPIA/27: .4X TO 1X COMBO/36
TTRC1 Namath/Montana/Elway 40.00 80.00
TTRC2 Ryan/Stafford/Sanchez 10.00 25.00
TTRC3 Nelson/Royal/Jackson 6.00 15.00
TTRC4 Murray/Hunter/Thomas 6.00 15.00
TTRC5 T.Jnes/McFadd/M.Bush 5.00 12.00
TTRC6 Pslzny/Willis/Harris 6.00 15.00
TTRC7 Willms/R.Bush/V.Yng 5.00 12.00
TTRC8 Willms/Jns-Drw/Addai 5.00 12.00
TTRC9 McFadd/CJ/Charles 6.00 15.00
TTRC10 Willis/Lewis/Urlacher 12.00 30.00
TTRC11 Caldwell/Harvin/Murphy 5.00 12.00
TTRC12 Smith/Little/Hankerson 4.00 10.00
TTRC13 Newton/A.Green/Jones 15.00 40.00
TTRC14 Elway/Tebow/Orton 15.00 40.00
TTRC15 Brady/Manning/Marino 30.00 60.00
TTRC16 Rice/Smith/Tomlinson 15.00 40.00
TTRC17 Smith/Tomlinson/Allen 15.00 40.00
TTRC18 Young/Rivers/Romo 12.00 30.00
TTRC19 Manning/Brady/Young 20.00 50.00
TTRC20 Favre/Marino/Elway 30.00 80.00
TTRC21 Roeth/Ryan/Flacco 10.00 25.00
TTRC22 Rice/Thomas/Smith 15.00 40.00
TTRC23 Smith/Harris/Thomas 15.00 40.00
TTRC24 Montana/Favre/Marino 30.00 80.00
TTRC25 Newton/Miller/Dareus 15.00 40.00
TTRC26 Newton/Locker/Gabbert 15.00 40.00
TTRC27 A.Green/J.Jons/Baldwin 10.00 25.00
TTRC28 Ingram/Williams/Vereen 5.00 12.00
TTRC29 Hunter/Carter/T.Jnes 3.00 8.00
TTRC30 Ponder/Dalton/Kaeper 6.00 15.00
TTRC31 Mallett/Vereen/Ridley 4.00 10.00
TTRC32 Jernigan/Brown/Pettis 3.00 8.00
TTRC33 J.Jnes/Dareus/Ingram 10.00 25.00
TTRC34 T.Yng/Smith/Little 4.00 10.00
TTRC35 Leshre/Thomas/Murray 6.00 15.00
TTRC36 Carter/T.Jnes/Harper 6.00 15.00
TTRC37 KaeperT.Young/Pettis 5.00 12.00
TTRC38 Powell/Vereen/Thomas 4.00 10.00
TTRC39 A.Green/Smith/Little 8.00 20.00
TTRC40 Hnkrsn/Jernign/Murray 6.00 15.00

2011 Topps Triple Threads Relic Double Combos

STATED PRINT RUN 36 SER.#'d SETS
*EMERALD/18: .5X TO 1.2X DOUBLE COMBO/36
*SEPIA/27: .4X TO 1X DOUBLE COMBO/36
TTRDC1 Michael Vick 12.00 30.00
TTRDC2 Dan Marino 25.00 60.00
TTRDC3 Brett Favre 30.00 80.00
TTRDC4 Brian Urlacher 15.00 40.00
TTRDC5 Louis Murphy 10.00 25.00
TTRDC6 Wes Welker 12.00 30.00
TTRDC7 Devin Hester 15.00 40.00
TTRDC8 Jay Cutler 10.00 25.00
TTRDC9 Tim Tebow 15.00 40.00
TTRDC10 Tony Romo 12.00 30.00
TTRDC11 Maurice Jones-Drew 10.00 25.00
TTRDC12 Cal.Johnsn/T.Young 12.00 30.00
TTRDC13 CJ/J.Harper 8.00 20.00
TTRDC14 D.Sproles/D.Thomas 10.00 25.00
TTRDC15 Jason Campbell 10.00 25.00

2011 Topps Triple Threads Rookies and Rising Stars Autographed Relics

STATED PRINT RUN 50 SER.#'d SETS
*SEPIA/25: .5X TO 1.2X DUAL AU/50
1 R.White/J.Jones 40.00 80.00
2 D.Jackson/S.Vereen 12.00 30.00
3 J.Maclin/B.Gabbert 20.00 50.00
4 L.McCoy/J.Baldwin 15.00 40.00
5 Pettigrew/K.Rudolph 10.00 25.00
6 S.Greene/B.Powell 15.00 40.00

2011 Topps Triple Threads Super Bowl Legends Relics

STATED PRINT RUN 18 SER.#'d SETS
TTSBL1 Jerry Rice 20.00 50.00
TTSBL2 Joe Namath 15.00 40.00
TTSBL3 Roger Staubach 15.00 40.00
TTSBL4 Tom Brady 15.00 40.00
TTSBL5 Aaron Rodgers 50.00 100.00
TTSBL6 Kurt Warner 15.00 40.00
TTSBL7 Drew Brees 12.00 30.00
TTSBL8 Joe Montana 30.00 80.00
TTSBL9 Marcus Allen 12.00 30.00
TTSBL10 Peyton Manning 15.00 40.00
TTSBL11 Phil Simms 10.00 25.00
TTSBL12 Troy Aikman 15.00 40.00
TTSBL13 Emmitt Smith 20.00 50.00
TTSBL14 Steve Young 15.00 40.00
TTSBL15 John Elway 20.00 50.00

2011 Topps Triple Threads Unity Relics

STATED PRINT RUN 36 SER.#'d SETS
*EMERALD/18: .5X TO 1.2X BASIC JSY/36
*GOLD/9: .6X TO 1.5X BASIC JSY/36
*SEPIA/27: .4X TO 1X BASIC JSY/36
MOST HAVE THREE CARDS OF EQUAL VALUE
TTUSR1 Dan Marino 15.00 40.00
TTUSR2 Dan Marino 15.00 40.00
TTUSR3 Dan Marino 15.00 40.00
TTUSR4 Cam Newton 15.00 40.00
TTUSR5 Cam Newton 15.00 40.00
TTUSR6 Cam Newton 15.00 40.00
TTUSR7 Phil Simms 5.00 12.00
TTUSR8 Phil Simms 5.00 12.00
TTUSR9 Phil Simms 5.00 12.00
TTUSR10 Brett Favre 12.00 30.00
TTUSR11 Brett Favre 12.00 30.00
TTUSR12 Brett Favre 12.00 30.00
TTUSR13 Mark Sanchez 3.00 8.00
TTUSR14 Mark Sanchez 3.00 8.00
TTUSR15 Mark Sanchez 3.00 8.00
TTUSR16 Jason Witten 5.00 12.00
TTUSR17 Jason Witten 5.00 12.00
TTUSR18 Jason Witten 5.00 12.00
TTUSR19 Jason Avant 3.00 8.00
TTUSR20 Jason Avant 3.00 8.00
TTUSR21 Jason Avant 3.00 8.00
TTUSR22 Jordy Nelson 6.00 15.00
TTUSR23 Jordy Nelson 6.00 15.00
TTUSR24 Jordy Nelson 6.00 15.00
TTUSR25 Tom Brady 12.00 30.00
TTUSR26 Tom Brady 12.00 30.00
TTUSR27 Tom Brady 12.00 30.00
TTUSR28 Austin Pettis 2.50 6.00
TTUSR29 Austin Pettis 2.50 6.00
TTUSR30 Austin Pettis 2.50 6.00
TTUSR31 Steven Jackson 3.00 8.00
TTUSR32 Steven Jackson 3.00 8.00
TTUSR33 Steven Jackson 3.00 8.00
TTUSR34 Taiwan Jones 2.50 6.00
TTUSR35 Taiwan Jones 2.50 6.00
TTUSR36 Taiwan Jones 2.50 6.00
TTUSR37 Bilal Powell 3.00 8.00
TTUSR38 Bilal Powell 3.00 8.00
TTUSR39 Bilal Powell 3.00 8.00
TTUSR40 Delone Carter 2.50 6.00
TTUSR41 Delone Carter 2.50 6.00
TTUSR42 Delone Carter 2.50 6.00
TTUSR43 Jordan Todman 2.50 6.00
TTUSR44 Jordan Todman 2.50 6.00
TTUSR45 Jordan Todman 2.50 6.00
TTUSR46 Jason Campbell 3.00 8.00
TTUSR47 Ken Stabler 6.00 15.00
TTUSR48 Jim Plunkett 6.00 15.00
TTUSR49 Jim Plunkett 6.00 15.00
TTUSR50 Jason Campbell 3.00 8.00
TTUSR51 Ken Stabler 6.00 15.00
TTUSR52 Ken Stabler 6.00 15.00
TTUSR53 Jim Plunkett 6.00 15.00
TTUSR54 Jason Campbell 3.00 8.00
TTUSR55 Fred Biletnikoff 8.00 20.00
TTUSR56 Louis Murphy 3.00 8.00
TTUSR57 Darrius Heyward-Bey 3.00 8.00
TTUSR58 Darrius Heyward-Bey 3.00 8.00
TTUSR59 Fred Biletnikoff 8.00 20.00
TTUSR60 Louis Murphy 3.00 8.00
TTUSR61 Louis Murphy 3.00 8.00
TTUSR62 Darrius Heyward-Bey 3.00 8.00
TTUSR63 Fred Biletnikoff 8.00 20.00
TTUSR64 Champ Bailey 4.00 10.00
TTUSR65 Eddie Royal 3.00 8.00
TTUSR66 Von Miller 4.00 10.00
TTUSR67 Von Miller 4.00 10.00
TTUSR68 Champ Bailey 4.00 10.00
TTUSR69 Eddie Royal 3.00 8.00
TTUSR70 Eddie Royal 3.00 8.00
TTUSR71 Von Miller 4.00 10.00
TTUSR72 Champ Bailey 4.00 10.00
TTUSR73 Richard Seymour 3.00 8.00
TTUSR74 Howie Long 8.00 20.00
TTUSR75 Rolando McClain 3.00 8.00
TTUSR76 Rolando McClain 3.00 8.00
TTUSR77 Richard Seymour 3.00 8.00
TTUSR78 Howie Long 8.00 20.00
TTUSR79 Howie Long 8.00 20.00
TTUSR80 Rolando McClain 3.00 8.00
TTUSR81 Richard Seymour 3.00 8.00
TTUSR82 Andre Caldwell 3.00 8.00
TTUSR83 Andy Dalton 5.00 12.00
TTUSR84 A.J. Green 6.00 15.00
TTUSR85 A.J. Green 6.00 15.00
TTUSR86 Andre Caldwell 3.00 8.00
TTUSR87 Andy Dalton 5.00 12.00
TTUSR88 Andy Dalton 5.00 12.00
TTUSR89 A.J. Green 6.00 15.00
TTUSR90 Andre Caldwell 3.00 8.00
TTUSR91 DeMarco Murray 5.00 12.00
TTUSR92 DeMarco Murray 5.00 12.00
TTUSR93 DeMarco Murray 5.00 12.00
TTUSR94 Ryan Williams 2.50 6.00
TTUSR95 Ryan Williams 2.50 6.00
TTUSR96 Ryan Williams 2.50 6.00
TTUSR97 Jon Baldwin 2.50 6.00
TTUSR98 Jon Baldwin 2.50 6.00
TTUSR99 Jon Baldwin 2.50 6.00
TTUSR100 Marcell Dareus 2.50 6.00
TTUSR101 Marcell Dareus 2.50 6.00
TTUSR102 Marcell Dareus 2.50 6.00
TTUSR103 Jerrel Jernigan 2.50 6.00
TTUSR104 Jerrel Jernigan 2.50 6.00
TTUSR105 Jerrel Jernigan 2.50 6.00
TTUSR106 Mario Williams 3.00 8.00
TTUSR107 Mario Williams 3.00 8.00
TTUSR108 Mario Williams 3.00 8.00
TTUSR109 Art Monk 10.00 25.00
TTUSR110 Santana Moss 4.00 10.00
TTUSR111 Leonard Hankerson 2.50 6.00
TTUSR112 Leonard Hankerson 2.50 6.00
TTUSR113 Art Monk 10.00 25.00
TTUSR114 Santana Moss 4.00 10.00
TTUSR115 Santana Moss 4.00 10.00
TTUSR116 Leonard Hankerson 2.50 6.00
TTUSR117 Art Monk 10.00 25.00
TTUSR118 Torrey Smith 2.50 6.00
TTUSR119 Torrey Smith 2.50 6.00
TTUSR120 Torrey Smith 2.50 6.00
TTUSR121 Titus Young 2.50 6.00
TTUSR122 Titus Young 2.50 6.00
TTUSR123 Titus Young 2.50 6.00
TTUSR124 Greg Little 3.00 8.00
TTUSR125 Greg Little 3.00 8.00
TTUSR126 Greg Little 3.00 8.00
TTUSR127 Edmond Gates 2.50 6.00
TTUSR128 Edmond Gates 2.50 6.00
TTUSR129 Edmond Gates 2.50 6.00
TTUSR130 Daniel Thomas 2.50 6.00
TTUSR131 Daniel Thomas 2.50 6.00
TTUSR132 Daniel Thomas 2.50 6.00
TTUSR133 Dustin Keller 4.00 10.00
TTUSR134 Dustin Keller 4.00 10.00
TTUSR135 Dustin Keller 4.00 10.00
TTUSR136 Stevan Ridley 2.50 6.00
TTUSR137 Ryan Mallett 2.50 6.00
TTUSR138 Shane Vereen 3.00 8.00
TTUSR139 Shane Vereen 3.00 8.00
TTUSR140 Stevan Ridley 2.50 6.00
TTUSR141 Ryan Mallett 2.50 6.00
TTUSR142 Ryan Mallett 2.50 6.00
TTUSR143 Shane Vereen 3.00 8.00
TTUSR144 Stevan Ridley 2.50 6.00
TTUSR145 Joe Montana 20.00 50.00
TTUSR146 Colin Kaepernick 4.00 10.00
TTUSR147 Kendall Hunter 2.50 6.00
TTUSR148 Kendall Hunter 2.50 6.00
TTUSR149 Joe Montana 20.00 50.00
TTUSR150 Colin Kaepernick 4.00 10.00
TTUSR151 Colin Kaepernick 4.00 10.00
TTUSR152 Kendall Hunter 2.50 6.00
TTUSR153 Joe Montana 15.00 40.00
TTUSR154 Jared Allen 5.00 12.00
TTUSR155 Christian Ponder 2.50 6.00
TTUSR156 Kyle Rudolph 2.50 6.00
TTUSR157 Kyle Rudolph 2.50 6.00
TTUSR158 Jared Allen 5.00 12.00
TTUSR159 Christian Ponder 2.50 6.00
TTUSR160 Christian Ponder 2.50 6.00
TTUSR161 Kyle Rudolph 2.50 6.00
TTUSR162 Jared Allen 5.00 12.00
TTUSR163 Devery Henderson 3.00 8.00
TTUSR164 Robert Meachem 3.00 8.00
TTUSR165 Mark Ingram 4.00 10.00
TTUSR166 Mark Ingram 4.00 10.00
TTUSR167 Devery Henderson 3.00 8.00
TTUSR168 Robert Meachem 3.00 8.00
TTUSR169 Robert Meachem 3.00 8.00
TTUSR170 Mark Ingram 4.00 10.00
TTUSR171 Devery Henderson 3.00 8.00
TTUSR172 Blaine Gabbert 2.50 6.00
TTUSR173 Blaine Gabbert 2.50 6.00
TTUSR174 Blaine Gabbert 2.50 6.00
TTUSR175 Randall Cobb 4.00 10.00
TTUSR176 Alex Green 2.50 6.00
TTUSR177 A.J. Hawk 3.00 8.00

2012 Topps Triple Threads

COMP.SET w/o RC's (100) 60.00 120.00
1-100 VETERAN PRINT RUN 989
101-135 ROOKIE JSY AU PRINT RUN 99
EXCH EXPIRATION: 11/30/2015
SOME ROOKIES HAVE TWO OR THREE VARIATIONS OF EQUAL VALUE
1 Eli Manning 1.00 2.50
2 DeMarcus Ware 1.25 3.00
3 Ben Roethlisberger 1.25 3.00
4 Carson Palmer 1.00 2.50
5 Isaac Redman 1.25 3.00
6 Brett Favre 2.50 6.00
7 Victor Cruz 1.00 2.50
8 Josh Freeman 1.00 2.50
9 Sidney Rice .75 2.00
10 Drew Brees 1.25 3.00
11 Matt Hasselbeck .75 2.00
12 Joe Flacco 1.00 2.50
13 Fred Jackson 1.00 2.50
14 Steve Smith 1.00 2.50
15 Jason Pierre-Paul .75 2.00
16 John Elway 2.00 5.00
17 Ryan Mathews 1.00 2.50
18 Darren McFadden .75 2.00
19 Santonio Holmes .75 2.00
20 Calvin Johnson 1.25 3.00
21 Steve Young 1.50 4.00
22 Emmitt Smith 2.00 5.00
23 Joe Namath 2.00 5.00
24 Julio Jones 1.25 3.00
25 Arian Foster 1.00 2.50
26 Sam Bradford .75 2.00
27 Michael Vick 1.00 2.50
28 Alex Smith 1.00 2.50
29 Jay Cutler .75 2.00
30 Ray Rice .75 2.00
31 Darren Sproles 1.00 2.50
32 Dwayne Bowe 1.00 2.50
33 Michael Turner .75 2.00
34 Ryan Fitzpatrick .75 2.00
35 Malcom Floyd .75 2.00
36 Tony Gonzalez 1.00 2.50
37 Roddy White .75 2.00
38 Jeremy Maclin .75 2.00
39 Percy Harvin .75 2.00
40 Maurice Jones-Drew .75 2.00
41 Marques Colston .75 2.00
42 Darrelle Revis .75 2.00
43 Troy Polamalu 1.25 3.00
44 Mike Wallace .75 2.00
45 Philip Rivers 1.25 3.00
46 Wes Welker 1.00 2.50
47 Kurt Warner 1.00 2.50
48 Miles Austin .75 2.00
49 Dan Marino 2.50 6.00
50 Aaron Rodgers 2.00 5.00
51 Demaryius Thomas 1.25 3.00
52 Rob Gronkowski 1.25 3.00
53 Matt Ryan 1.00 2.50
54 Tony Romo 1.00 2.50
55 Patrick Willis 1.00 2.50
56 Christian Ponder .75 2.00
57 Beanie Wells .75 2.00
58 Shonn Greene .75 2.00
59 Reggie Wayne 1.00 2.50
60 LeSean McCoy 1.25 3.00
61 Jared Allen .75 2.00
62 DeMarco Murray 1.00 2.50
63 Joe Montana 3.00 8.00
64 Mark Sanchez .75 2.00
65 Steven Jackson .75 2.00
66 Matt Schaub .75 2.00
67 DeAngelo Williams .75 2.00
68 Hakeem Nicks .75 2.00
69 Roy Helu .75 2.00
70 Tom Brady 3.00 8.00
71 Chris Johnson .75 2.00
72 Larry Fitzgerald 1.00 2.50
73 Frank Gore 1.00 2.50
74 A.J. Green 1.25 3.00
75 Matthew Stafford 1.00 2.50
76 Aaron Hernandez 1.00 2.50
77 DeSean Jackson 1.00 2.50
78 Jonathan Stewart .75 2.00
79 Reggie Bush .75 2.00
80 Andre Johnson 1.00 2.50
81 Vernon Davis .75 2.00
82 Ahmad Bradshaw .75 2.00
83 Marshawn Lynch 1.00 2.50
84 Steve Johnson 1.00 2.50
85 Dez Bryant 1.25 3.00
86 Jimmy Graham 1.25 3.00
87 Jermichael Finley .75 2.00
88 Greg Jennings .75 2.00
89 LeGarrette Blount 1.00 2.50
90 Cam Newton 1.25 3.00
91 Jordy Nelson 1.00 2.50
92 Jake Locker 1.25 3.00
93 Jerry Rice 2.00 5.00
94 Matt Forte .75 2.00
95 Antonio Gates 1.00 2.50
96 Andy Dalton 1.00 2.50
97 Kenny Britt .75 2.00
98 Willis McGahee .75 2.00
99 Adrian Peterson 1.25 3.00
100 Peyton Manning 2.50 6.00
103 B.Weeden 3QB JSY AU RC 5.00 12.00
104A Nick Foles 9QB JSY AU RC 30.00 60.00
104B Nick Foles PHI JSY AU RC 30.00 60.00
105 David Wilson 34RB JSY AU RC 5.00 12.00
106 Lamar Miller 44RB JSY AU RC 8.00 20.00
107A D.Martin 22RB JSY AU RC 8.00 20.00
107B Doug Martin TB JSY AU RC 8.00 20.00
108A Isaiah Pead 24RB JSY AU RC 5.00 12.00
108B Isaiah Pead STL JSY AU RC 5.00 12.00
109A L.James 23RB JSY AU RC 5.00 12.00
109B LaMichael James SF JSY AU RC 5.00 12.00
111A T.Y. Hilton 13WR JSY AU RC 10.00 25.00
111B T.Y. Hilton IND JSY AU RC 10.00 25.00
112A Ronnie Hillman 34RB JSY AU RC 5.00 12.00
112B Ronnie Hillman DEN JSY AU RC 5.00 12.00
112C Ronnie Hillman RH JSY AU RC 5.00 12.00
114 M.Floyd 15WR JSY AU RC 5.00 12.00
115A Michael Egnew 84TE JSY AU RC 5.00 12.00
115B Michael Egnew MIA JSY AU RC 5.00 12.00
115C Michael Egnew ME JSY AU RC 5.00 12.00
116A Jarius Wright 17WR JSY AU RC 5.00 12.00
116C Jarius Wright JW JSY AU RC 5.00 12.00
117A Mohamed Sanu 12WR JSY AU RC 8.00 20.00
117B Mohamed Sanu CIN JSY AU RC 8.00 20.00
117C Mohamed Sanu MS JSY AU RC 8.00 20.00
118A Rueben Randle 82WR JSY AU RC 5.00 12.00
118B Rueben Randle NYG JSY AU RC 5.00 12.00
119A Nick Toon 88WR JSY AU RC 5.00 12.00
119C Nick Toon NT JSY AU RC 5.00 12.00
121 Stephen Hill 84WR JSY AU RC 5.00 12.00
122A Brian Quick 83WR JSY AU RC 5.00 12.00
122B Brian Quick STL JSY AU RC 5.00 12.00
123A Joe Adams 15WR JSY AU RC 5.00 12.00
123B Joe Adams CAR JSY AU RC 5.00 12.00
123C Joe Adams JA JSY AU RC 5.00 12.00
124A Dwayne Allen 83TE JSY AU RC 5.00 12.00
124B Dwayne Allen IND JSY AU RC 5.00 12.00
125A Coby Fleener 80TE JSY AU RC 5.00 12.00
125B Coby Fleener IND JSY AU RC 5.00 12.00
126 Juron Criner OAK JSY AU RC 5.00 12.00
127A R.Turbin 22RB JSY AU RC EX 6.00 15.00
128A A.J. Jenkins 17WR JSY AU RC 5.00 12.00
128B A.J. Jenkins SF JSY AU RC 5.00 12.00
129A DeVier Posey 11WR JSY AU RC 5.00 12.00
129B DeVier Posey HOU JSY AU RC 5.00 12.00
129C DeVier Posey DP JSY AU RC 5.00 12.00
131A R.Wilson 3QB JSY AU RC 90.00 150.00
131B Russell Wilson SEA JSY AU RC 90.00 150.00
132A Ryan Broyles 84WR JSY AU RC 5.00 12.00
132B Ryan Broyles DET JSY AU RC 5.00 12.00
133A T.J. Graham 11WR JSY AU RC 5.00 12.00
133B T.J. Graham BUF JSY AU RC 5.00 12.00
134 K.Wright 13WR JSY AU RC EX 5.00 12.00
135 A.Jeffery 17WR JSY AU RC 10.00 25.00

2012 Topps Triple Threads Emerald

*1-100 VETS/170: .6X TO 1.5X BASIC CARDS
*101-135 JSY AU/50: .5X TO 1.2X BASIC JSY AU
SOME HAVE MULTIPLE CARDS OF EQUAL VALUE
101 R.Tannehill 17QB JSY AU 10.00 25.00
102A B.Osweiler 6QB JSY AU 6.00 15.00
113 J.Blackmon 14WR JSY AU 6.00 15.00

2012 Topps Triple Threads Gold

*1-100 VETS/99: 1X TO 2.5X BASIC CARDS
*101-135 JSY AU/25: .8X TO 2X BASIC JSY AU
SOME HAVE MULTIPLE CARDS OF EQUAL VALUE
101 R.Tannehill 17QB JSY AU 15.00 40.00
102A B.Osweiler 6QB JSY AU 10.00 25.00
107A Doug Martin 22RB JSY AU 15.00 40.00
110 Andrew Luck 12QB JSY AU 200.00 400.00
113A J.Blackmon 14WR JSY AU 10.00 25.00
120 R.Griffin III 10QB JSY AU 60.00 120.00
131A Russell Wilson 3QB JSY AU 125.00 200.00
131B Russell Wilson SEA JSY AU 125.00 200.00

2012 Topps Triple Threads Onyx

*1-100 VETS/50: 1.2X TO 3X BASIC CARDS

2012 Topps Triple Threads Sapphire

*1-100 VETS/25: 2X TO 5X BASIC CARDS
1-100 VETERAN STATED PRINT RUN 25
101-135 UNPRICED JSY AU PRINT RUN 10

2012 Topps Triple Threads Sepia

*1-100 VETS/310: .5X TO 1.2X BASIC CARDS
*101-135 JSY AU/70: .4X TO 1X JSY AU/99
SOME HAVE MULTIPLE CARDS OF EQUAL VALUE
101 Ryan Tannehill JSY AU 8.00 20.00
102 Brock Osweiler JSY AU 5.00 12.00
110 Andrew Luck JSY AU 150.00 300.00
113 Justin Blackmon JSY AU 5.00 12.00
120 Robert Griffin III JSY AU 60.00 120.00
130 Trent Richardson JSY AU 20.00 50.00
131 Russell Wilson JSY AU 75.00 150.00

2012 Topps Triple Threads Autographed Relic Combos

*EMERALD/18: .5X TO 1.2X COMBO AU/27
EXCH EXPIRATION: 11/30/2015
TTARC1 Luck/Richardson/RG3 100.00 200.00
TTARC2 Tannehill/Egnew/Miller 50.00 120.00
TTARC3 Floyd/Blackmon/Wright 20.00 50.00
TTARC4 Martin/Wilson/Richrdsn 40.00 100.00
TTARC5 Jcksn/Grhm/Jhnsn EXCH 30.00 60.00
TTARC6 Tannhill/Griffin/Luck 100.00 200.00
TTARC7 Fleener/Allen/Luck EX 150.00 250.00
TTARC8 Randle/Jeffery/Hill 20.00 50.00
TTARC9 Rice/Young/Montana 250.00 400.00
TTARC10 Randle/Cruz/Nicks EX 40.00 80.00
TTARC11 Vick/Maclin/McCoy EX 30.00 60.00
TTARC12 Foles/Wilson/Osweiler 50.00 100.00
TTARC13 Blckmn/Gabbert/Jns-Drw 15.00 40.00
TTARC14 Jenkins/Quick/Floyd 30.00 60.00
TTARC15 Broyles/Jeffery/Wright 15.00 40.00

2012 Topps Triple Threads Autographed Relic Double Combos

*GOLD/18: .6X TO 1.2X DBL COMBO/27
TTARDC1 Hall of Fame QBs EXCH 500.00 800.00
TTARDC2 Luck/RG3/Rook. 100.00 200.00
TTARDC3 Rookie WRs and RBs 50.00 100.00
TTARDC4 Luck/RG3/Mrtin/Rooks 200.00 400.00
TTARDC5 Star Runng Backs 40.00 80.00
TTARDC6 Receivr and RBs EXCH 25.00 60.00
TTARDC7 Star Receivers 50.00 100.00
TTARDC8 Tight Ends 40.00 80.00
TTARDC9 Rookie Receivers 50.00 100.00
TTARDC12 Luck/RG3/RookQB 100.00 200.00

2012 Topps Triple Threads Autographed Relic Pairs

STATED PRINT RUN 18 SER.#'d SETS
EXCH EXPIRATION: 11/30/2015
TTARP1 A.Luck/R.Griffin III 250.00 500.00
TTARP2 R.Griffin III/K.Wright 75.00 150.00
TTARP3 Weeden/Richardson 20.00 50.00
TTARP4 Blackmon/Richardson 40.00 100.00
TTARP5 M.Sanchez/S.Greene 15.00 40.00
TTARP6 Ryan/M.Schaub 30.00 80.00
TTARP7 L.Miller/W.McGahee 25.00 50.00
TTARP8 D.Wilson/R.Randle 30.00 60.00
TTARP9 C.Fleener/A.Luck 75.00 150.00

2012 Topps Triple Threads Autographed Relics

EXCH EXPIRATION: 11/30/2015
TTAR1 A.J. Jenkins
TTAR2 A.J. Green 40.00 80.00
TTAR3 Alshon Jeffery
TTAR4 Andrew Luck 200.00 350.00
TTAR5 Andrew Luck 200.00 350.00
TTAR6 Arian Foster 10.00 25.00
TTAR7 Brandon Weeden 8.00 20.00
TTAR8 Brian Quick 8.00 20.00
TTAR9 Michael Vick 30.00 60.00
TTAR10 Cedric Benson 8.00 20.00
TTAR11 Coby Fleener 8.00 20.00
TTAR12 Lamar Miller 12.00 30.00
TTAR13 David Wilson
TTAR14 Doug Martin 12.00 30.00
TTAR15 Brandon Lloyd 8.00 20.00
TTAR16 Mohamed Sanu 12.00 30.00
TTAR17 Jahvid Best
TTAR18 Jahvid Best
TTAR19 Jeremy Maclin 8.00 20.00
TTAR20 Jerry Rice 125.00 200.00
TTAR21 Jerry Rice
TTAR22 Jimmy Graham 40.00 80.00
TTAR23 Nick Toon 8.00 20.00
TTAR24 Ronnie Hillman 8.00 20.00
TTAR25 Justin Blackmon 8.00 20.00
TTAR26 Kendall Wright 8.00 20.00
TTAR27 Russell Wilson 125.00 200.00
TTAR28 LaMichael James 8.00 20.00
TTAR29 Michael Turner
TTAR30 Michael Floyd 8.00 20.00
TTAR31 Mike Wallace 12.00 30.00
TTAR32 Mark Ingram 8.00 20.00
TTAR33 Mark Ingram 8.00 20.00
TTAR34 Blaine Gabbert
TTAR35 Blaine Gabbert
TTAR36 Robert Griffin III 60.00 120.00
TTAR37 Robert Griffin III
TTAR38 Robert Turbin EXCH 8.00 20.00
TTAR39 Ryan Tannehill 40.00 80.00
TTAR40 Ryan Mathews 10.00 25.00
TTAR41 Ryan Mathews 10.00 25.00
TTAR42 Torrey Smith 12.00 30.00
TTAR43 Stephen Hill 8.00 20.00
TTAR44 Steve Johnson
TTAR45 Trent Richardson 30.00 80.00
TTAR46 Rueben Randle 8.00 20.00
TTAR47 Von Miller 15.00 40.00

2012 Topps Triple Threads Quarterback Immortal Relics

*GOLD/18: .5X TO 1.2X BASIC JSY/36
TTQI1 Steve Young 12.00 30.00
TTQI2 John Elway 12.00 30.00
TTQI3 Joe Montana 20.00 50.00
TTQI4 Joe Namath 15.00 40.00
TTQI5 Tony Romo 6.00 15.00

TTQI6 Andrew Luck 25.00 60.00
TTQI7 Robert Griffin III 3.00 8.00
TTQI8 Brett Favre 20.00 50.00
TTQI9 Dan Marino 15.00 40.00
TTQI10 Mark Sanchez 5.00 12.00
TTQI11 Cam Newton 10.00 25.00
TTQI12 Michael Vick 6.00 15.00
TTQI13 Eli Manning 6.00 15.00
TTQI14 Matt Ryan 6.00 15.00
TTQI15 Jay Cutler 5.00 12.00

2012 Topps Triple Threads Relic

*GOLD/9: .6X TO 1.5X BASIC JSY/36
*GOLD ROOK/9: .5X TO 1.2X BASIC JSY/36
*EMERALD/18: .5X TO 1.2X BASIC JSY/36
*SEPIA/27: .4X TO 1X BASIC JSY/36
MOST HAVE MULTIPLE CARDS OF EQUAL VALUE
TTR1 Andrew Luck 25.00 60.00
TTR2 Andrew Luck 25.00 60.00
TTR3 Andrew Luck 25.00 60.00
TTR4 Robert Griffin III 3.00 8.00
TTR5 Robert Griffin III 3.00 8.00
TTR6 Robert Griffin III 3.00 8.00
TTR7 Ryan Tannehill 4.00 10.00
TTR8 Ryan Tannehill 4.00 10.00
TTR9 Ryan Tannehill 4.00 10.00
TTR10 Brock Osweiler 2.50 6.00
TTR11 Brock Osweiler 2.50 6.00
TTR12 Brock Osweiler 2.50 6.00
TTR13 Brandon Weeden 2.50 6.00
TTR14 Brandon Weeden 2.50 6.00
TTR15 Brandon Weeden 2.50 6.00
TTR16 Trent Richardson 2.50 6.00
TTR17 Trent Richardson 2.50 6.00
TTR18 Trent Richardson 2.50 6.00
TTR19 David Wilson 2.50 6.00
TTR20 David Wilson 2.50 6.00
TTR21 Doug Martin 4.00 10.00
TTR22 Doug Martin 4.00 10.00
TTR23 Doug Martin 4.00 10.00
TTR24 LaMichael James 2.50 6.00
TTR25 LaMichael James 2.50 6.00
TTR26 LaMichael James 2.50 6.00
TTR27 Justin Blackmon 2.50 6.00
TTR28 Justin Blackmon 2.50 6.00
TTR29 Justin Blackmon 2.50 6.00
TTR30 Michael Floyd 2.50 6.00
TTR31 Michael Floyd 2.50 6.00
TTR32 Michael Floyd 2.50 6.00
TTR33 Rueben Randle 2.50 6.00
TTR34 Rueben Randle 2.50 6.00
TTR35 Rueben Randle 2.50 6.00
TTR36 Stephen Hill 2.50 6.00
TTR37 Stephen Hill 2.50 6.00
TTR38 Stephen Hill 2.50 6.00
TTR39 Brian Quick 2.50 6.00
TTR40 Brian Quick 2.50 6.00
TTR41 Brian Quick 2.50 6.00
TTR42 Dwayne Allen 2.50 6.00
TTR43 Dwayne Allen 2.50 6.00
TTR44 Dwayne Allen 2.50 6.00
TTR45 Coby Fleener 2.50 6.00
TTR46 Coby Fleener 2.50 6.00
TTR47 Coby Fleener 2.50 6.00
TTR48 Russell Wilson 20.00 50.00
TTR49 Russell Wilson 20.00 50.00
TTR50 Russell Wilson 20.00 50.00
TTR51 Joe Montana
TTR52 Joe Montana
TTR53 Aaron Rodgers
TTR54 Kendall Wright 2.50 6.00
TTR55 Kendall Wright 2.50 6.00
TTR56 Kendall Wright 2.50 6.00
TTR57 Alshon Jeffery 5.00 12.00
TTR58 Alshon Jeffery 5.00 12.00
TTR59 Alshon Jeffery 5.00 12.00
TTR60 Cam Newton 8.00 20.00
TTR61 Cam Newton 8.00 20.00
TTR62 Jamaal Charles 6.00 15.00
TTR63 Jamaal Charles 6.00 15.00
TTR64 Julio Jones 8.00 20.00
TTR65 Julio Jones 8.00 20.00
TTR66 Julio Jones 8.00 20.00
TTR67 A.J. Green 8.00 20.00
TTR68 A.J. Green 8.00 20.00
TTR69 A.J. Green 8.00 20.00
TTR70 Julius Peppers 6.00 15.00
TTR71 Julius Peppers 6.00 15.00
TTR72 Julius Peppers 6.00 15.00
TTR73 Santana Moss 6.00 15.00
TTR74 Santana Moss 6.00 15.00
TTR75 Santana Moss 6.00 15.00
TTR76 Aaron Hernandez 6.00 15.00
TTR77 Aaron Hernandez 6.00 15.00
TTR78 Aaron Hernandez 6.00 15.00
TTR79 Larry Fitzgerald 6.00 15.00
TTR80 Larry Fitzgerald 6.00 15.00
TTR81 Marques Colston 5.00 12.00
TTR82 Marques Colston 5.00 12.00
TTR83 Marques Colston 5.00 12.00
TTR84 Bernard Pierce 2.50 6.00
TTR85 Mark Ingram 6.00 15.00
TTR86 Jerry Rice 12.00 30.00
TTR87 Jerry Rice 12.00 30.00
TTR88 Arian Foster 6.00 15.00
TTR89 Arian Foster 6.00 15.00
TTR90 Arian Foster 6.00 15.00
TTR91 Maurice Jones-Drew 5.00 12.00
TTR92 Maurice Jones-Drew 5.00 12.00
TTR93 Maurice Jones-Drew 5.00 12.00
TTR94 Mark Sanchez 5.00 12.00
TTR95 Mark Sanchez 5.00 12.00
TTR96 Darrelle Revis 5.00 12.00
TTR97 Darrelle Revis 5.00 12.00
TTR98 Jeremy Maclin 5.00 12.00
TTR99 Jeremy Maclin 5.00 12.00
TTR100 Ray Lewis 10.00 25.00
TTR101 Ray Lewis 10.00 25.00
TTR102 Ray Lewis 10.00 25.00
TTR103 Miles Austin 5.00 12.00
TTR104 Miles Austin 5.00 12.00
TTR105 Michael Turner 5.00 12.00
TTR106 Michael Turner 5.00 12.00
TTR107 Vernon Davis 5.00 12.00
TTR108 Vernon Davis 5.00 12.00
TTR109 Vernon Davis 5.00 12.00
TTR110 Darren McFadden 5.00 12.00
TTR111 Darren McFadden 5.00 12.00
TTR112 Michael Vick 6.00 15.00
TTR113 Michael Vick 6.00 15.00
TTR114 Patrick Willis 6.00 15.00
TTR115 Patrick Willis 6.00 15.00
TTR116 Champ Bailey 6.00 15.00
TTR117 Champ Bailey 6.00 15.00
TTR118 Champ Bailey 6.00 15.00
TTR119 Antonio Gates 6.00 15.00
TTR120 Antonio Gates 6.00 15.00
TTR121 Antonio Gates 6.00 15.00
TTR122 Tony Romo 6.00 15.00
TTR123 Tony Romo 6.00 15.00

2012 Topps Triple Threads Relic Combos

*EMERALD/18: .5X TO 1.2X BASIC COMBO/36
*SEPIA/27: .4X TO 1X BASIC COMBO/36
TTRC1 Tannehill/Griffin III/Luck 30.00 80.00
TTRC2 Wilson/Martin/Richrdsn 5.00 12.00
TTRC3 Wright/Floyd/Blackmon 3.00 8.00
TTRC4 Allen/Fleener/Luck 30.00 60.00
TTRC5 Weedn/Richrdsn/McCy 12.00 30.00
TTRC6 Hillman/Osweiler/Miller 4.00 10.00
TTRC7 Toon/Colston/Brees 15.00 40.00
TTRC8 Randle/Wilson/Manning 10.00 25.00
TTRC9 Jenkins/James/Smith 10.00 25.00
TTRC10 Griffin III/Martin/Floyd 5.00 12.00
TTRC11 Jenkins/Quick/Wright 8.00 20.00
TTRC12 Blackmn/Luck/Richrdsn 25.00 60.00
TTRC13 Pierce/Flacco/Lewis 12.00 30.00
TTRC14 Griffin III/Martin/Floyd 5.00 12.00
TTRC15 Wilson/Miller/Hill 5.00 12.00
TTRC16 Austin/Romo/Murray 6.00 15.00
TTRC17 Bailey/Green/Moreno 8.00 20.00
TTRC18 McCoy/Charles/Shipley 6.00 15.00
TTRC19 Rice/Jones-Drew/Turner 8.00 20.00
TTRC20 Peterson/Forte/Jackson 10.00 25.00
TTRC21 Randle/Jeffery/Adams 6.00 15.00
TTRC22 Nicks/Tuck/Bradshaw 15.00 40.00
TTRC23 Rivers/Schaub/Brady 20.00 50.00
TTRC24 Ryan/Brees/Newton 10.00 25.00
TTRC25 Tannehill/Marino/Bush 20.00 50.00
TTRC26 Hillman/Miller/Pierce 8.00 20.00
TTRC27 Young/Rice/Owens 15.00 40.00
TTRC28 Lewis/Boldin/Smith 12.00 30.00
TTRC29 Jackson/Spiller/Johnson 10.00 25.00
TTRC30 Moreno/Mthws/McFad 8.00 20.00
TTRC31 Jeffery/Hill/Quick 6.00 15.00
TTRC32 Rchrdsn/Jnes/McFad 5.00 12.00
TTRC33 Wlkr/Jhnsn/Cruz EXCH 25.00 50.00
TTRC34 Brady/Marino/Brees 20.00 50.00
TTRC35 Hilton/Toon/Sanu 10.00 25.00
TTRC36 Cutler/Peppers/Urlacher 12.00 30.00
TTRC37 Manning/Rodgers/Brees 20.00 40.00
TTRC38 Berry/Cassel/Bowe 8.00 20.00
TTRC39 Johnson/Foster/Jones-D 10.00 25.00
TTRC40 Newton/Dareus/Ingram 10.00 25.00
TTRC41 Wilson/Weeden/Foles 25.00 60.00
TTRC42 Cruz/Fitzg/Wallce EXCH 25.00 50.00
TTRC43 Pead/James/Turbin 3.00 8.00
TTRC44 Vick/Hall/Wilson 4.00 10.00
TTRC45 Hernan/Harvin/Rainey 6.00 15.00

2012 Topps Triple Threads Rookie Jumbo Relics

*EMERALD/50: .5X TO 1.2X BASIC JSY/99
*GOLD/25: .6X TO 1.5X BASIC JSY/99
*SAPPHIRE/10: .8X TO 2X BASIC JSY/99
*SEPIA/75: .4X TO 1X BASIC JSY/99
MOST HAVE TWO CARDS OF EQUAL VALUE
TTRJR1 A.J. Jenkins 2.00 5.00
TTRJR2 Alshon Jeffery 4.00 10.00
TTRJR3 Andrew Luck 15.00 40.00
TTRJR4 Andrew Luck 15.00 40.00
TTRJR5 Bernard Pierce 2.00 5.00
TTRJR6 Bernard Pierce 2.00 5.00
TTRJR7 Brandon Weeden 2.00 5.00
TTRJR8 Brandon Weeden 2.00 5.00
TTRJR9 Brian Quick 2.00 5.00
TTRJR10 Brian Quick 2.00 5.00
TTRJR11 Brock Osweiler 2.00 5.00
TTRJR12 Brock Osweiler 2.00 5.00
TTRJR13 Coby Fleener 2.00 5.00
TTRJR14 David Wilson 2.00 5.00
TTRJR15 David Wilson 2.00 5.00
TTRJR16 DeVier Posey 2.00 5.00
TTRJR17 Doug Martin 3.00 8.00
TTRJR18 Doug Martin 3.00 8.00
TTRJR19 Dwayne Allen 2.00 5.00
TTRJR20 Isaiah Pead 2.00 5.00
TTRJR21 Isaiah Pead 2.00 5.00
TTRJR22 Jarius Wright 2.00 5.00
TTRJR23 Joe Adams 2.00 5.00
TTRJR24 Justin Blackmon 2.00 5.00
TTRJR25 Justin Blackmon 2.00 5.00
TTRJR26 Kendall Wright 2.00 5.00
TTRJR27 Kendall Wright 2.00 5.00
TTRJR28 Lamar Miller 3.00 8.00
TTRJR29 Lamar Miller 3.00 8.00
TTRJR30 LaMichael James 2.00 5.00
TTRJR31 Michael Floyd 2.00 5.00
TTRJR32 Michael Floyd 2.00 5.00
TTRJR33 Michael Egnew 2.00 5.00
TTRJR34 Michael Egnew 2.00 5.00
TTRJR35 Mohamed Sanu 3.00 8.00
TTRJR36 Nick Toon 2.00 5.00
TTRJR37 T.Y. Hilton 4.00 10.00
TTRJR38 Nick Foles 5.00 12.00
TTRJR39 Nick Foles 5.00 12.00
TTRJR40 Robert Griffin III 2.50 6.00
TTRJR41 Robert Griffin III 2.50 6.00
TTRJR42 Robert Turbin 2.00 5.00
TTRJR43 Robert Turbin 2.00 5.00
TTRJR44 Ronnie Hillman 2.00 5.00
TTRJR45 Rueben Randle 2.00 5.00
TTRJR46 Russell Wilson 10.00 25.00
TTRJR47 Russell Wilson 10.00 25.00
TTRJR48 Ryan Tannehill 3.00 8.00
TTRJR49 Ryan Tannehill 3.00 8.00
TTRJR50 Ryan Broyles 2.00 5.00
TTRJR51 Stephen Hill 2.00 5.00
TTRJR52 T.J. Graham 2.00 5.00
TTRJR53 T.Y. Hilton 4.00 10.00
TTRJR54 Trent Richardson 2.00 5.00
TTRJR55 Trent Richardson 2.00 5.00
TTRJR56 Stephen Hill 2.00 5.00
TTRJR57 Alshon Jeffery 4.00 10.00
TTRJR58 Joe Adams 2.00 5.00
TTRJR59 Dwayne Allen 2.00 5.00
TTRJR60 Rueben Randle 2.00 5.00
TTRJR61 LaMichael James 2.00 5.00
TTRJR62 Ronnie Hillman 2.00 5.00
TTRJR63 Jarius Wright 2.00 5.00
TTRJR64 Mohamed Sanu 3.00 8.00

2012 Topps Triple Threads Rookie Quarterback Booklets

A.LUCK/RG3/10 600.00 1000.00

2012 Topps Triple Threads Rookies Autographed Relics Sepia

SEPIA STATED PRINT RUN 75
*EMERALD/50: .5X TO 1.2X SEPIA/75
*BASE RED/99: .4X TO 1X SEPIA/75
SOME HAVE TWO CARDS OF EQUAL VALUE
TTRAR1 Joe Adams 4.00 10.00
TTRAR2 Joe Adams 4.00 10.00
TTRAR3 Dwayne Allen 4.00 10.00
TTRAR4 Dwayne Allen 4.00 10.00
TTRAR5 Justin Blackmon 4.00 10.00
TTRAR6 Ryan Broyles 4.00 10.00
TTRAR7 Ryan Broyles 4.00 10.00
TTRAR8 Cyrus Gray 4.00 10.00
TTRAR9 Michael Egnew 4.00 10.00
TTRAR10 Michael Egnew 4.00 10.00
TTRAR11 Coby Fleener 4.00 10.00
TTRAR12 Coby Fleener 4.00 10.00
TTRAR13 Michael Floyd 4.00 10.00
TTRAR14 Nick Foles 20.00 50.00
TTRAR15 Nick Foles 20.00 50.00
TTRAR16 T.J. Graham 4.00 10.00
TTRAR17 T.J. Graham 4.00 10.00
TTRAR18 Robert Griffin III 25.00 60.00
TTRAR19 Stephen Hill 4.00 10.00
TTRAR20 Ronnie Hillman 4.00 10.00
TTRAR21 Ronnie Hillman 4.00 10.00
TTRAR22 T.Y. Hilton 8.00 20.00
TTRAR23 T.Y. Hilton 8.00 20.00
TTRAR24 LaMichael James 4.00 10.00
TTRAR25 Alshon Jeffery 8.00 20.00
TTRAR26 A.J. Jenkins 4.00 10.00
TTRAR27 Andrew Luck 125.00 250.00
TTRAR28 Doug Martin 6.00 15.00
TTRAR29 Doug Martin 6.00 15.00
TTRAR30 Lamar Miller 6.00 15.00
TTRAR31 Lamar Miller 6.00 15.00
TTRAR32 Brock Osweiler 4.00 10.00
TTRAR33 Isaiah Pead 4.00 10.00
TTRAR34 Isaiah Pead 4.00 10.00
TTRAR35 Brian Quick 4.00 10.00
TTRAR36 Rueben Randle 4.00 10.00
TTRAR37 DeVier Posey 4.00 10.00
TTRAR38 DeVier Posey 4.00 10.00
TTRAR39 Brian Quick 4.00 10.00
TTRAR40 Brian Quick 4.00 10.00
TTRAR41 Rueben Randle 4.00 10.00
TTRAR42 Trent Richardson 15.00 40.00
TTRAR43 Mohamed Sanu 6.00 15.00
TTRAR44 Ryan Tannehill 6.00 15.00
TTRAR45 Nick Toon 4.00 10.00
TTRAR46 Nick Toon 4.00 10.00
TTRAR47 Robert Turbin 4.00 10.00
TTRAR48 Robert Turbin 4.00 10.00
TTRAR49 Brandon Weeden 4.00 10.00
TTRAR50 Russell Wilson 100.00 175.00
TTRAR51 Russell Wilson 100.00 175.00
TTRAR52 David Wilson 4.00 10.00
TTRAR53 Kendall Wright 4.00 10.00
TTRAR54 Jarius Wright 4.00 10.00
TTRAR55 Jarius Wright 4.00 10.00
TTRAR56 Mohamed Sanu 6.00 15.00
TTRAR57 David Wilson 4.00 10.00
TTRAR58 Cyrus Gray 4.00 10.00
TTRAR59 Kendall Wright 4.00 10.00
TTRAR61 Stephen Hill 4.00 10.00
TTRAR62 LaMichael James 4.00 10.00
TTRAR63 Alshon Jeffery 15.00 40.00
TTRAR64 A.J. Jenkins 4.00 10.00
TTRAR65 Doug Martin 6.00 15.00
TTRAR66 Lamar Miller 6.00 15.00
TTRAR67 Brock Osweiler 4.00 10.00
TTRAR68 Isaiah Pead 4.00 10.00

2012 Topps Triple Threads Rookies Autographed Relics Gold

*BASE GOLD/25: .8X TO 2X SEPIA/75
SOME HAVE TWO CARDS OF EQUAL VALUE
TTRAR27 Andrew Luck 200.00 400.00
TTRAR50 Russell Wilson 175.00 300.00

2013 Topps Triple Threads

ROOKIE PRINT RUN 99 SER.#'d SETS
EXCH EXPIRATION: 11/30/2016
1 Marshawn Lynch 1.00 2.50
2 Clay Matthews 1.25 3.00
3 Stevan Ridley .75 2.00
4 Joe Montana 4.00 10.00
5 Von Miller 1.00 2.50
6 Darren McFadden 1.00 2.50
7 Aaron Rodgers 2.00 5.00
8 Ryan Tannehill 1.00 2.50
9 Earl Thomas 1.00 2.50
10 Roddy White .75 2.00
11 J.J. Watt 1.00 2.50
12 LaDainian Tomlinson 1.00 2.50
13 Robert Griffin III .75 2.00
14 Alex Smith 1.00 2.50
15 Antonio Brown 1.25 3.00
16 Andy Dalton 1.00 2.50
17 Ben Roethlisberger 1.25 3.00
18 Colin Kaepernick 1.00 2.50
19 Randall Cobb 1.00 2.50
20 Victor Cruz 1.00 2.50
21 Steven Jackson .75 2.00
22 Brandon Marshall 1.00 2.50
23 Santonio Holmes .75 2.00
24 Calvin Johnson 1.25 3.00
25 A.J. Green 1.25 3.00
26 Alfred Morris .75 2.00
27 Matt Forte .75 2.00
28 Tony Romo 1.00 2.50
29 Jared Allen .75 2.00
30 Jake Locker 1.00 2.50
31 Russell Wilson 2.50 6.00
32 Dwayne Bowe 1.00 2.50
33 Andrew Luck 2.00 5.00
34 Carson Palmer 1.00 2.50
35 Jairus Byrd .75 2.00
36 Eric Dickerson 1.00 2.50
37 Arian Foster 1.00 2.50
38 Percy Harvin .75 2.00
39 Brandon Weeden .75 2.00
40 Matt Schaub .75 2.00
41 Jason Witten 1.00 2.50
42 Luke Kuechly 1.00 2.50
43 Tom Brady 3.00 8.00
44 John Elway 2.00 5.00
45 Jerry Rice 2.00 5.00
46 Antonio Gates 1.00 2.50
47 Dan Marino 2.50 6.00
48 Demaryius Thomas 1.00 2.50
49 Vincent Jackson .75 2.00
50 Ray Rice .75 2.00
51 Trent Richardson .75 2.00
52 Marshall Faulk 1.00 2.50
53 Julio Jones 1.25 3.00
54 LeSean McCoy 1.25 3.00
55 Justin Blackmon .75 2.00
56 Jay Cutler .75 2.00
57 Dez Bryant 1.25 3.00
58 Wes Welker 1.00 2.50
59 Cam Newton 1.25 3.00
60 DeMarco Murray 1.00 2.50
61 Maurice Jones-Drew .75 2.00
62 Eli Manning 1.00 2.50
63 Aldon Smith .75 2.00
64 Philip Rivers 1.25 3.00
65 Larry Fitzgerald 1.00 2.50
66 Eric Decker .75 2.00
67 Adrian Peterson 1.25 3.00
68 Steve Young 1.50 4.00
69 Lawrence Taylor 1.25 3.00
70 Joe Flacco 1.00 2.50
71 Michael Vick 1.00 2.50
72 David Wilson .75 2.00
73 Vernon Davis .75 2.00
74 Sam Bradford .75 2.00
75 Emmitt Smith 2.00 5.00
76 Troy Polamalu 1.25 3.00
77 Hakeem Nicks .75 2.00
78 Matthew Stafford 1.00 2.50
79 Barry Sanders 2.00 5.00
80 James Laurinaitis 1.00 2.50
81 Matt Ryan 1.00 2.50
82 Rob Gronkowski 1.25 3.00
83 Reggie Wayne 1.00 2.50
84 Richard Sherman 1.25 3.00
85 Jimmy Graham 1.25 3.00
86 Christian Ponder .75 2.00
87 Patrick Peterson .75 2.00
88 Drew Brees 1.25 3.00
89 C.J. Spiller .75 2.00
90 Darren Sproles 1.00 2.50
91 Andre Johnson .75 2.00
92 Chris Johnson .75 2.00
93 Doug Martin 1.00 2.50
94 Mike Wallace .75 2.00
95 Jamaal Charles 1.00 2.50
96 Frank Gore 1.00 2.50
97 Josh Freeman 1.00 2.50
98 Peyton Manning 2.50 6.00
99 Patrick Willis 1.00 2.50
100 Deion Sanders 1.00 2.50
101 Keenan Allen JSY AU RC 10.00 25.00
102 Tavon Austin JSY AU RC 6.00 15.00
103 Stedman Bailey JSY AU RC 5.00 12.00
104 Montee Ball JSY AU RC 5.00 12.00
105 Matt Barkley JSY AU RC 5.00 12.00
106 Le'Veon Bell JSY AU RC 25.00 50.00
107 Giovani Bernard JSY AU RC 5.00 12.00
108 Knile Davis JSY AU RC 5.00 12.00
109 Aaron Dobson JSY AU RC 5.00 12.00
110 Tyler Eifert JSY AU RC 5.00 12.00
111 Andre Ellington JSY AU RC 5.00 12.00
112 Zach Ertz JSY AU RC 10.00 25.00
113 Gavin Escobar JSY AU RC 5.00 12.00
114 J.Franklin JSY AU RC 5.00 12.00
115 Mike Gillislee JSY AU RC EXCH 5.00 12.00
116 Mike Glennon JSY AU RC 15.00 40.00
117 M.Goodwin JSY AU RC 5.00 12.00
118 D.Hopkins JSY AU RC EXCH 12.00 30.00
119 Justin Hunter JSY AU RC 5.00 12.00
120 Landry Jones JSY AU RC 5.00 12.00
121 Dion Jordan JSY AU RC 5.00 12.00
122 Eddie Lacy JSY AU RC 5.00 12.00
123 Marcus Lattimore JSY AU RC 5.00 12.00
124 EJ Manuel JSY AU RC 5.00 12.00
125 V.McDonald JSY AU RC 6.00 15.00
126 Christine Michael JSY AU RC 5.00 12.00
127 Ryan Nassib JSY AU RC 5.00 12.00
128 C.Patterson JSY AU RC 5.00 12.00
129 Quinton Patton JSY AU RC 5.00 12.00
130 Joseph Randle JSY AU RC 5.00 12.00
131 Jordan Reed JSY AU RC 8.00 20.00
132 D.Robinson JSY AU RC 5.00 12.00
133 Geno Smith JSY AU RC 5.00 12.00
134 Kenny Stills JSY AU RC EXCH 5.00 12.00
135 Stepfan Taylor JSY AU RC 5.00 12.00
136 Manti Te'o JSY AU RC 6.00 15.00
137 Markus Wheaton JSY AU RC 5.00 12.00
138 T.Williams JSY AU RC 5.00 12.00
139 Tyler Wilson JSY AU RC 5.00 12.00
140 Robert Woods JSY AU RC 8.00 20.00
141 Tyler Bray JSY AU RC 5.00 12.00
145 Josh Boyce JSY AU RC 5.00 12.00
149 Ray Graham JSY AU RC 5.00 12.00
151 Keenan Allen JSY AU RC 12.00 30.00
152 Montee Ball JSY AU RC 5.00 12.00
153 Andre Ellington JSY AU RC 5.00 12.00
159 Kenny Stills JSY AU RC EXCH 5.00 12.00

2013 Topps Triple Threads Emerald

*1-100 VETS/170: .6X TO 1.5X BASIC CARDS
*101-159 ROOKIE/50: .5X TO 1.2X JSY AU/99
117 Marquise Goodwin JSY AU 6.00 15.00
157 Jordan Reed JSY AU 10.00 25.00

2013 Topps Triple Threads Gold

*1-100 VETS/99: 1X TO 2.5X BASIC CARDS
*101-159 ROOKIE/25: .6X TO 1.5X JSY AU/99

2013 Topps Triple Threads Purple

*1-100 VETS/320: .5X TO 1.2X BASIC CARDS
*101-159 ROOKIE/70: .4X TO 1X JSY AU/99

2013 Topps Triple Threads Ruby

*1-100 VETS/50: 1.2X TO 3X BASIC CARDS
*101-159 ROOKIE/15: .8X TO 2X JSY AU/99

2013 Topps Triple Threads Sapphire

*1-100 VETS/25: 1.5X TO 4X BASIC CARDS
*101-159 ROOKIE/10: 1X TO 2.5X JSY AU/99

2013 Topps Triple Threads Autographed Relic Trios

EXCH EXPIRATION: 11/30/2016
*EMERALD/18: .5X TO 1.2X COMBO AU/27
TTARTBBB Bll/Bll/Brnrd 40.00 100.00
TTARTCLF Lcy/Frnkln/Cbb 40.00 80.00
TTARTDFP Ptrsn/Dckrsn/Flk 75.00 150.00
TTARTGBE Grn/Efrt/Brnrd 40.00 80.00
TTARTGWW RG3/Wrght/Wlliams 40.00 80.00
TTARTJBR Blckmn/JnsDrw/Rbnsn 12.00 30.00
TTARTLGW Wilson/RG3/Luck 175.00 300.00
TTARTMAH Hpkns/Astn/Mnl EX 30.00 80.00
TTARTMML Lcy/Mrtn/Mrrs EX 50.00 100.00
TTARTMYR Rce/Mntna/Yng EX 250.00 400.00
TTARTSAB Bly/Astn/Smth 15.00 40.00
TTARTSHE Elgtn/Hpkns/Splr EX 40.00 80.00
TTARTTDB Dckr/Thms/Bll 50.00 100.00
TTARTVFB Fls/Vck/Brkly 50.00 120.00
TTARTWRM Wlsn/Rce/Mchl 50.00 100.00

2013 Topps Triple Threads Autographed Relic Double Trios

*GOLD/18: .5X TO 1.2X DOUBLE COMBO/27
AHPHWD Hr/Dn/Pn/Hs/An/Ws 30.00 80.00
BBBLMD Ml/Ds/Ly/Bl/Bd/Bl 60.00 120.00
GWGEEE Wn/Et/Ez/Gs/Er/Gi 40.00 80.00
JJFHRH Rn/Hr/Fr/Hs/Jw/Jn 40.00 80.00
LGTMSB By/Gn/Tl/Ml/Lk/Sh 150.00 300.00
LGTWMS Tl/Gn/Wn/Ml/Sh/Lk 150.00 300.00
MMESSD Ss/Sh/Ey/Mo/Ma/Dn 500.00 750.00
MSGBNW Wn/By/Gn/Sh/Ml/Nb 12.00 30.00
V3MMCE Ck/Ez/Mn/Vk/By/My 60.00 150.00
WRDBFR Dn/Wn/Fo/Rn/Re/Bd 50.00 100.00

2013 Topps Triple Threads Autographed Relics

TTARAD Aaron Dobson
TTARAJG A.J. Green 30.00 80.00
TTARAL Andrew Luck 100.00 200.00
TTARBH Brian Hartline 10.00 25.00
TTARBO Brian Orakpo
TTARCJS C.J. Spiller 15.00 40.00
TTARCP Cordarrelle Patterson 8.00 20.00
TTARDB Dwayne Bowe 15.00 40.00
TTARDH DeAndre Hopkins 20.00 50.00
TTARDJ Dion Jordan
TTARDM Dan Marino 100.00 200.00
TTARDR Denard Robinson 15.00 40.00
TTARDS Deion Sanders
TTARED Eric Dickerson 50.00 100.00
TTAREJM EJ Manuel 40.00 80.00
TTAREL Eddie Lacy 60.00 120.00
TTAREM Eli Manning 40.00 80.00
TTARGB Giovani Bernard
TTARGS Geno Smith 8.00 20.00
TTARJF Joe Flacco 30.00 60.00
TTARJH Justin Hunter 15.00 40.00
TTARJL James Laurinaitis EXCH 15.00 40.00
TTARJR Jerry Rice 100.00 200.00
TTARKA Keenan Allen 40.00 80.00
TTARKD Knile Davis
TTARKS Kenny Stills
TTARLB Le'Veon Bell 40.00 80.00
TTARMB Matt Barkley 8.00 20.00
TTARMBA Montee Ball 8.00 20.00
TTARMC Michael Crabtree
TTARMG Marquise Goodwin 8.00 20.00
TTARML Marcus Lattimore 8.00 20.00
TTARMT Manti Te'o 10.00 25.00
TTARMV Michael Vick 20.00 50.00
TTAROP Quinton Patton 15.00 40.00
TTARRC Randall Cobb 12.00 30.00
TTARRG Robert Griffin III 40.00 80.00
TTARRT Ryan Tannehill 30.00 60.00
TTARRW Robert Woods
TTARSB Stedman Bailey
TTARSV Shane Vereen EXCH 12.00 30.00
TTARSY Steve Young 30.00 60.00
TTARTA Tavon Austin 10.00 25.00
TTARTE Tyler Eifert 8.00 20.00
TTARTW Terrance Williams 8.00 20.00

2013 Topps Triple Threads Autographed Relic Pairs

TTARPBE M.Barkley/Z.Ertz 30.00 60.00
TTARPBL M.Ball/E.Lacy
TTARPGB A.Green/G.Bernard
TTARPGW A.Gates/J.Witten
TTARPLG A.Luck/R.Griffin
TTARPLW A.Luck/R.Wayne
TTARPMS E.Manuel/G.Smith
TTARPMT E.Manning/L.Taylor
TTARPPP A.Peterson/C.Patterson 125.00 200.00
TTARPTA M.Te'o/K.Allen

2013 Topps Triple Threads Relics

*EMERALD/18: .5X TO 1.2X BASIC JSY/36
*GOLD/9: .6X TO 1.5X BASIC JSY/36
*PURPLE/27: .4X TO 1X BASIC JSY/36
MOST HAVE 2-3 CARDS OF EQUAL VALUE
TTRAD Aaron Dobson 2.50 6.00
TTRAD2 Aaron Dobson 6.00 15.00
TTRAD3 Aaron Dobson 2.50 6.00
TTRAE Andre Ellington 2.50 6.00
TTRAE2 Andre Ellington 2.50 6.00
TTRAE3 Andre Ellington 6.00 15.00
TTRAL Andrew Luck 12.00 30.00
TTRAL2 Andrew Luck 12.00 30.00
TTRAM Alfred Morris 5.00 12.00
TTRCK Colin Kaepernick 6.00 15.00
TTRCK2 Colin Kaepernick 6.00 15.00
TTRCM Christine Michael 2.50 6.00
TTRCM2 Christine Michael 2.50 6.00
TTRCM3 Christine Michael 2.50 6.00
TTRCN Cam Newton 10.00 25.00
TTRCN2 Cam Newton 10.00 25.00
TTRCP Cordarrelle Patterson 2.50 6.00
TTRCP2 Cordarrelle Patterson 2.50 6.00
TTRCP3 Cordarrelle Patterson 2.50 6.00
TTRDB Dez Bryant 8.00 20.00
TTRDE DeMarco Murray 6.00 15.00
TTRDE2 DeMarco Murray 6.00 15.00
TTRDE3 DeMarco Murray 6.00 15.00
TTRDH DeAndre Hopkins 6.00 15.00
TTRDH2 DeAndre Hopkins 6.00 15.00
TTRDH3 DeAndre Hopkins 6.00 15.00
TTRDJ Dion Jordan 2.50 6.00
TTRDJ2 Dion Jordan 2.50 6.00
TTRDJ3 Dion Jordan 2.50 6.00
TTRDM Doug Martin 8.00 20.00
TTRDR Denard Robinson 2.50 6.00
TTRDR2 Denard Robinson 2.50 6.00
TTRDR3 Denard Robinson 2.50 6.00
TTRED Eric Decker 8.00 20.00
TTRED2 Eric Decker 8.00 20.00
TTREL Eddie Lacy 2.50 6.00
TTREL2 Eddie Lacy 2.50 6.00
TTREL3 Eddie Lacy 2.50 6.00
TTREM EJ Manuel 2.50 6.00
TTREM2 EJ Manuel 2.50 6.00
TTRGB Giovani Bernard 2.50 6.00
TTRGB2 Giovani Bernard 2.50 6.00
TTRGB3 Giovani Bernard 2.50 6.00
TTRGE Gavin Escobar 2.50 6.00
TTRGE2 Gavin Escobar 2.50 6.00
TTRGE3 Gavin Escobar 2.50 6.00
TTRGS Geno Smith 2.50 6.00
TTRGS2 Geno Smith 2.50 6.00
TTRGS3 Geno Smith 2.50 6.00
TTRJA Jared Allen 5.00 12.00
TTRJA2 Jared Allen 10.00 25.00
TTRJC Jay Cutler 8.00 20.00
TTRJF Johnathan Franklin 2.50 6.00
TTRJF2 Johnathan Franklin 2.50 6.00
TTRJF3 Johnathan Franklin 2.50 6.00
TTRJH Justin Hunter 2.50 6.00
TTRJH2 Justin Hunter 2.50 6.00
TTRJH3 Justin Hunter 2.50 6.00
TTRJJ Julio Jones 8.00 20.00
TTRJO Jordan Reed 4.00 10.00
TTRJO2 Jordan Reed 4.00 10.00
TTRJO3 Jordan Reed 4.00 10.00
TTRJP Julius Peppers 8.00 20.00
TTRJR Joseph Randle 2.50 6.00
TTRJR2 Joseph Randle 2.50 6.00
TTRKA Keenan Allen 5.00 12.00
TTRKA2 Keenan Allen 5.00 12.00
TTRKA3 Keenan Allen 5.00 12.00
TTRKD Knile Davis 2.50 6.00
TTRKD2 Knile Davis 2.50 6.00
TTRKD3 Knile Davis 2.50 6.00
TTRKS Kenny Stills 2.50 6.00
TTRKS2 Kenny Stills 2.50 6.00
TTRKS3 Kenny Stills 2.50 6.00
TTRLB Le'Veon Bell 8.00 20.00
TTRLB2 Le'Veon Bell 8.00 20.00
TTRLB3 Le'Veon Bell 10.00 25.00
TTRLF Larry Fitzgerald 6.00 15.00
TTRLJ Landry Jones 2.50 6.00
TTRLJ2 Landry Jones 2.50 6.00
TTRLJ3 Landry Jones 2.50 6.00
TTRMA Matt Barkley 5.00 15.00
TTRMA2 Matt Barkley 5.00 12.00
TTRMA3 Matt Barkley 5.00 12.00
TTRMB Montee Ball 2.50 6.00
TTRMB2 Montee Ball 2.50 6.00
TTRMB3 Montee Ball 2.50 6.00
TTRMG Mike Glennon 2.50 6.00
TTRMG2 Mike Glennon 2.50 6.00
TTRMG3 Mike Glennon 2.50 6.00
TTRMI Miles Austin 5.00 12.00
TTRMK Mike Gillislee 2.50 6.00
TTRMK2 Mike Gillislee 2.50 6.00
TTRMK3 Mike Gillislee 2.50 6.00
TTRMS Matt Schaub 5.00 12.00
TTRMT Manti Te'o 3.00 8.00
TTRMT2 Manti Te'o 3.00 8.00
TTRMT3 Manti Te'o 3.00 8.00
TTRMW Markus Wheaton 2.50 6.00
TTRMW2 Markus Wheaton 2.50 6.00
TTRMW3 Markus Wheaton 2.50 6.00
TTRRG Robert Griffin III 5.00 12.00
TTRRG2 Robert Griffin III 5.00 12.00
TTRRN Ryan Nassib 2.50 6.00
TTRRN2 Ryan Nassib 2.50 6.00
TTRRN3 Ryan Nassib 2.50 6.00
TTRRO Roddy White 5.00 12.00
TTRRT Ryan Tannehill 6.00 15.00
TTRRT2 Ryan Tannehill 6.00 15.00
TTRRU Russell Wilson 15.00 40.00
TTRRU2 Russell Wilson 15.00 40.00
TTRRW Robert Woods 4.00 10.00
TTRRW2 Robert Woods 4.00 10.00
TTRSB Sam Bradford 5.00 12.00
TTRST Stepfan Taylor 2.50 6.00
TTRST2 Stepfan Taylor 2.50 6.00
TTRST3 Stepfan Taylor 2.50 6.00
TTRTA Tavon Austin 6.00 15.00
TTRTA2 Tavon Austin 6.00 15.00
TTRTA3 Tavon Austin 6.00 15.00
TTRTE Tyler Eifert 2.50 6.00
TTRTE2 Tyler Eifert 2.50 6.00
TTRTE3 Tyler Eifert 2.50 6.00
TTRTR Trent Richardson 5.00 12.00
TTRTR2 Trent Richardson 5.00 12.00
TTRTR3 Trent Richardson 5.00 12.00
TTRTS Torrey Smith 5.00 12.00
TTRTS2 Torrey Smith 5.00 12.00
TTRTS3 Torrey Smith 8.00 20.00
TTRTW Terrance Williams 2.50 6.00
TTRTW2 Terrance Williams 2.50 6.00
TTRTW3 Terrance Williams 2.50 6.00
TTRTY Tyler Wilson 2.50 6.00
TTRTY2 Tyler Wilson 2.50 6.00
TTRTY3 Tyler Wilson 2.50 6.00
TTRVM Von Miller 6.00 15.00
TTRZE Zach Ertz 5.00 12.00
TTRZE2 Zach Ertz 5.00 12.00
TTRZE3 Zach Ertz 5.00 12.00

2013 Topps Triple Threads Relics Trios

*EMERALD/18: .5X TO 1.2X COMBO/36
*PURPLE/27: .4X TO 1X COMBO/36
TTRTBAB Bly/Astn/Brdfrd 4.00 10.00
TTRTBGR Brdy/Rdly/Grnkwski 20.00 50.00
TTRTCFP Frte/Pprs/Ctlr 8.00 20.00
TTRTCWJ Clstn/Jcksn/Whte 5.00 12.00
TTRTDGB Brnrd/Dltn/Grn 8.00 20.00
TTRTEEE Efrt/Escbr/Ertz 6.00 15.00
TTRTFGJ Ftzgrld/Grn/Jns 8.00 20.00
TTRTFMR Mnnng/Flcco/Rdgrs 12.00 30.00
TTRTFRS Flcco/Rce/Smith 6.00 15.00
TTRTGGW Grhm/Gts/Wttn 8.00 20.00
TTRTGKN Grffn/Kprnck/Nwtn 8.00 20.00
TTRTGWG Wttn/Grnkwski/Gts 8.00 20.00
TTRTGWW Wllms/Grffn/Wrght 8.00 20.00
TTRTHDW Whtn/Hntr/Dbsn 5.00 12.00
TTRTHPH Hntr/Pttrsn/Hpkns 8.00 20.00
TTRTJJF JnDrw/Fstr/Jhnsn 6.00 15.00
TTRTJPW Wrght/Jhnsn/Pttrsn 8.00 20.00
TTRTKGD Gre/Dvs/Kprnck 6.00 15.00
TTRTKWB Kprnck/Brdfrd/Wlsn 10.00 25.00
TTRTLGT Tnnhll/Lck/Grffn 12.00 30.00
TTRTLGW Wlsn/Grffn/Lck 15.00 40.00
TTRTMCM McFddn/Mthws/Chrls 6.00 15.00
TTRTMJS Jhnsn/Spllr/Mnul 4.00 10.00
TTRTMLN Mnul/Lck/Nwtn 8.00 20.00
TTRTMMM Mrry/Mrrs/McCy 8.00 20.00
TTRTMSG Mnul/Glnnn/Smth 3.00 8.00
TTRTRMB Brynt/Rmo/Mrry 8.00 20.00
TTRTRMG Gts/Rvrs/Mthws 8.00 20.00
TTRTRMM Rchrdsn/Mrtn/Mrrs 6.00 15.00
TTRTRWJ Jns/Ryn/Whte 8.00 20.00
TTRTSAB Astn/Bly/Smth 4.00 10.00
TTRTSHE Hpkns/Ellngtn/Spllr 8.00 20.00
TTRTSMT Mnl/Tnnhll/Smth 4.00 10.00
TTRTTEM Ellngtn/Mchl/Tylr 3.00 8.00
TTRTVFB Brkly/Fls/Vck 4.00 10.00
TTRTVMJ Jcksn/Vck/McCy 8.00 20.00

2013 Topps Triple Threads Rookie Autograph Relics

*EMERALD/50: .5X TO 1.2X BASIC INSERTS
*GOLD/25: .6X TO 1.5X BASIC INSERTS
*PURPLE/70: .4X TO 1X BASIC INSERTS
*SAPPHIRE/10: 1X TO 2.5X BASIC INSERTS
SOME HAVE TWO CARDS OF EQUAL VALUE
TTRARAD Aaron Dobson 4.00 10.00
TTRARAD2 Aaron Dobson 4.00 10.00
TTRARAE Andre Ellington 4.00 10.00
TTRARAE2 Andre Ellington 4.00 10.00
TTRARCM Christine Michael 12.00 30.00
TTRARCM2 Christine Michael 12.00 30.00
TTRARCP Cordarrelle Patterson 4.00 10.00
TTRARCP2 Cordarrelle Patterson 4.00 10.00
TTRARDH DeAndre Hopkins 10.00 25.00
TTRARDH2 DeAndre Hopkins 10.00 25.00
TTRARDJ Dion Jordan 4.00 10.00
TTRARDR Denard Robinson 4.00 10.00
TTRARDR2 Denard Robinson 4.00 10.00
TTRAREL Eddie Lacy 4.00 10.00
TTRAREL2 Eddie Lacy 4.00 10.00
TTRAREM EJ Manuel 4.00 10.00
TTRARGB Giovani Bernard 4.00 10.00
TTRARGB2 Giovani Bernard 12.00 30.00
TTRARGE Gavin Escobar 4.00 10.00
TTRARGE2 Gavin Escobar 4.00 10.00
TTRARGS Geno Smith 4.00 10.00
TTRARJF Johnathan Franklin 4.00 10.00
TTRARJF2 Johnathan Franklin 4.00 10.00
TTRARJH Justin Hunter 4.00 10.00
TTRARJH2 Justin Hunter 4.00 10.00
TTRARJR Jordan Reed 6.00 15.00
TTRARJR2 Jordan Reed 6.00 15.00
TTRARJRA Joseph Randle 4.00 10.00
TTRARKA Keenan Allen 6.00 15.00
TTRARKA2 Keenan Allen 6.00 15.00
TTRARKD Knile Davis 4.00 10.00
TTRARKS Kenny Stills 4.00 10.00
TTRARKS2 Kenny Stills 4.00 10.00
TTRARLB Le'Veon Bell 12.00 30.00
TTRARLB2 Le'Veon Bell 20.00 50.00
TTRARLJ Landry Jones 4.00 10.00
TTRARMB Montee Ball 4.00 10.00
TTRARMB2 Montee Ball 4.00 10.00
TTRARMBA Matt Barkley 4.00 10.00
TTRARMG Mike Gillislee 4.00 10.00
TTRARMGL Mike Glennon 4.00 10.00
TTRARMGO Marquise Goodwin 4.00 10.00
TTRARML Marcus Lattimore 4.00 10.00
TTRARMT Manti Te'o 5.00 12.00
TTRARMT2 Manti Te'o 5.00 12.00
TTRARMW Markus Wheaton 4.00 10.00
TTRARQP Quinton Patton 4.00 10.00
TTRARRN Ryan Nassib 4.00 10.00
TTRARRN2 Ryan Nassib 4.00 10.00
TTRARRW Robert Woods 6.00 15.00
TTRARSB Stedman Bailey 4.00 10.00
TTRARST Stepfan Taylor 4.00 10.00
TTRARST2 Stepfan Taylor 4.00 10.00
TTRARTA Tavon Austin 5.00 12.00
TTRARTA2 Tavon Austin 5.00 12.00
TTRARTE Tyler Eifert 4.00 10.00
TTRARTE2 Tyler Eifert 4.00 10.00
TTRARTW Terrance Williams 4.00 10.00
TTRARVM Vance McDonald 5.00 12.00
TTRARZE Zach Ertz 8.00 20.00
TTRARZE2 Zach Ertz 8.00 20.00

2013 Topps Triple Threads Rookie Jumbo Relics

*EMERALD/50: .5X TO 1.2X BASIC JSY/99
*GOLD/25: .6X TO 1.5X BASIC JSY/99
*PURPLE/75: .4X TO 1X BASIC JSY/99
*SAPPHIRE/10: 1X TO 2.5X BASIC JSY/99
SOME HAVE TWO CARDS OF EQUAL VALUE
TTRJRAD Aaron Dobson 1.50 4.00
TTRJRAD2 Aaron Dobson 1.50 4.00
TTRJRAE Andre Ellington 1.50 4.00
TTRJRCM Christine Michael 1.50 4.00
TTRJRCM2 Christine Michael 1.50 4.00
TTRJRCP Cordarrelle Patterson 1.50 4.00
TTRJRCP2 Cordarrelle Patterson 1.50 4.00
TTRJRDH DeAndre Hopkins 4.00 10.00
TTRJRDH2 DeAndre Hopkins 4.00 10.00
TTRJRDJ Dion Jordan 1.50 4.00
TTRJRDJ2 Dion Jordan 1.50 4.00
TTRJRDR Denard Robinson 1.50 4.00
TTRJRDR2 Denard Robinson 1.50 4.00
TTRJREL Eddie Lacy 1.50 4.00
TTRJREL2 Eddie Lacy 1.50 4.00
TTRJREM EJ Manuel 1.50 4.00
TTRJRGB Giovani Bernard 1.50 4.00
TTRJRGB2 Giovani Bernard 1.50 4.00
TTRJRGE Gavin Escobar 1.50 4.00
TTRJRGS Geno Smith 1.50 4.00
TTRJRGS2 Geno Smith 1.50 4.00
TTRJRJF Johnathan Franklin 1.50 4.00
TTRJRJF2 Johnathan Franklin 1.50 4.00
TTRJRJH Justin Hunter 1.50 4.00
TTRJRJH2 Justin Hunter 1.50 4.00
TTRJRJO Jordan Reed 2.50 6.00
TTRJRJO2 Jordan Reed 2.50 6.00
TTRJRJR Joseph Randle 1.50 4.00
TTRJRKA Keenan Allen 3.00 8.00
TTRJRKA2 Keenan Allen 3.00 8.00
TTRJRKD Knile Davis 1.50 4.00
TTRJRKD2 Knile Davis 1.50 4.00
TTRJRKS Kenny Stills 1.50 4.00
TTRJRKS2 Kenny Stills 1.50 4.00
TTRJRLB Le'Veon Bell 5.00 12.00
TTRJRLJ Landry Jones 1.50 4.00
TTRJRMA Matt Barkley 1.50 4.00
TTRJRMA2 Matt Barkley 1.50 4.00
TTRJRMB Montee Ball 2.00 5.00
TTRJRMB2 Montee Ball 1.50 4.00
TTRJRMG Mike Glennon 1.50 4.00
TTRJRMG2 Mike Glennon 1.50 4.00
TTRJRMGO Marquise Goodwin 1.50 4.00
TTRJRMI Mike Gillislee 1.50 4.00
TTRJRML Marcus Lattimore 1.50 4.00
TTRJRMT Manti Te'o 2.00 5.00
TTRJRMT2 Manti Te'o 2.00 5.00
TTRJRMW Markus Wheaton 1.50 4.00
TTRJRQP Quinton Patton 1.50 4.00
TTRJRRG Ray Graham 1.50 4.00
TTRJRRN Ryan Nassib 1.50 4.00
TTRJRRN2 Ryan Nassib 1.50 4.00
TTRJRRW Robert Woods 2.50 6.00
TTRJRSB Stedman Bailey 1.50 4.00
TTRJRST Stepfan Taylor 1.50 4.00
TTRJRTA Tavon Austin 2.00 5.00
TTRJRTA2 Tavon Austin 2.00 5.00
TTRJRTE Tyler Eifert 1.50 4.00
TTRJRTE2 Tyler Eifert 1.50 4.00
TTRJRTW Terrance Williams 1.50 4.00
TTRJRTY Tyler Wilson 1.50 4.00
TTRJRTY2 Tyler Wilson 1.50 4.00
TTRJRVM Vance McDonald 2.00 5.00
TTRJRZE Zach Ertz 3.00 8.00
TTRJRZE2 Zach Ertz 3.00 8.00

2013 Topps Triple Threads Transparencies Autographs

TTTAD Aaron Dobson 6.00 15.00
TTTAE Andre Ellington 6.00 15.00
TTTCM Christine Michael 12.00 30.00
TTTCP Cordarrelle Patterson 6.00 15.00
TTTDH DeAndre Hopkins 15.00 40.00
TTTDJ Dion Jordan 6.00 15.00
TTTDR Denard Robinson 6.00 15.00
TTTEJM EJ Manuel 6.00 15.00
TTTEL Eddie Lacy 50.00 100.00
TTTGB Giovani Bernard 6.00 15.00
TTTGE Gavin Escobar 6.00 15.00
TTTGS Geno Smith 6.00 15.00
TTTJF Johnathan Franklin 6.00 15.00
TTTJH Justin Hunter 12.00 30.00
TTTJR Joseph Randle 6.00 15.00
TTTJRE Jordan Reed 15.00 40.00
TTTKA Keenan Allen 25.00 60.00
TTTKD Knile Davis 6.00 15.00
TTTKS Kenny Stills 15.00 40.00
TTTLB Le'Veon Bell 30.00 60.00
TTTLJ Landry Jones 6.00 15.00
TTTMB Matt Barkley 6.00 15.00
TTTMBA Montee Ball 6.00 15.00
TTTMG Mike Glennon 6.00 15.00
TTTMGI Mike Gillislee 6.00 15.00
TTTMGO Marquise Goodwin 6.00 15.00
TTTML Marcus Lattimore 25.00 50.00
TTTMT Manti Te'o 8.00 20.00
TTTMW Markus Wheaton 6.00 15.00
TTTQP Quinton Patton 6.00 15.00
TTTRN Ryan Nassib 12.00 30.00
TTTRW Robert Woods 10.00 25.00
TTTSB Stedman Bailey 6.00 15.00
TTTST Stepfan Taylor 6.00 15.00
TTTTA Tavon Austin 8.00 20.00
TTTTE Tyler Eifert 6.00 15.00
TTTTW Tyler Wilson 6.00 15.00
TTTTWI Terrance Williams 6.00 15.00
TTTVM Vance McDonald 8.00 20.00
TTTZE Zach Ertz 12.00 30.00

2014 Topps Triple Threads

1 Colin Kaepernick 1.00 2.50
2 Eric Berry 1.00 2.50
3 Cordarrelle Patterson .75 2.00
4 NaVorro Bowman 1.00 2.50
5 Reggie Wayne 1.00 2.50
6 J.J. Watt 1.25 3.00
7 Randall Cobb 1.00 2.50
8 Vincent Jackson .75 2.00
9 Marshawn Lynch 1.00 2.50
10 Brandon Marshall .75 2.00
11 Von Miller 1.00 2.50
12 Jamaal Charles 1.00 2.50
13 Brian Hartline .75 2.00
14 Matt Forte .75 2.00
15 Luke Kuechly 1.00 2.50
16 Jordy Nelson 1.00 2.50
17 Rod Streater .75 2.00
18 Bernard Pierce .75 2.00
19 C.J. Spiller .75 2.00
20 Reggie Bush .75 2.00
21 Patrick Peterson .75 2.00
22 DeAndre Hopkins 1.00 2.50
23 Arian Foster 1.00 2.50
24 Tavon Austin .75 2.00
25 Tony Romo 1.00 2.50
26 Peyton Manning 2.50 6.00
27 Richard Sherman 1.25 3.00
28 Denarius Moore .75 2.00
29 Alfred Morris .75 2.00
30 Jimmy Graham 1.25 3.00
31 DeMarco Murray 1.00 2.50
32 Robert Griffin III .75 2.00
33 T.Y. Hilton 1.00 2.50
34 Jay Cutler .75 2.00
35 Pierre Thomas .75 2.00
36 Tom Brady 3.00 8.00
37 Le'Veon Bell 1.00 2.50
38 Demaryius Thomas 1.00 2.50
39 Larry Fitzgerald 1.00 2.50
40 DeSean Jackson 1.00 2.50
41 Andre Johnson 1.00 2.50
42 Andy Dalton 1.00 2.50
43 Eddie Lacy .75 2.00
44 Kiko Alonso .75 2.00
45 Torrey Smith .75 2.00
46 Jordan Cameron .75 2.00
47 Philip Rivers 1.25 3.00
48 Terrell Suggs .75 2.00
49 Antonio Brown 1.25 3.00
50 Percy Harvin .75 2.00
51 Matt Ryan 1.00 2.50
52 Alshon Jeffery 1.00 2.50
53 Aaron Rodgers 2.50 6.00
54 Calvin Johnson 1.25 3.00
55 Julio Jones 1.25 3.00
56 Michael Crabtree .75 2.00
57 Cam Newton 1.25 3.00
58 Rob Gronkowski 1.25 3.00
59 A.J. Green 1.25 3.00
60 Roddy White .75 2.00
61 Robert Quinn 1.00 2.50
62 Andrew Luck 1.50 4.00
63 Keenan Allen 1.00 2.50
64 Clay Matthews 1.25 3.00
65 Wes Welker 1.00 2.50
66 Nick Foles 1.00 2.50
67 Julius Thomas .75 2.00
68 Mike Glennon 1.00 2.50
69 Earl Thomas 1.00 2.50
70 Matthew Stafford 1.00 2.50
71 Dez Bryant 1.25 3.00
72 Ryan Tannehill 1.00 2.50
73 Eli Manning 1.00 2.50
74 Pierre Garcon 1.00 2.50
75 Sean Lee 1.00 2.50
76 Alex Smith 1.00 2.50
77 EJ Manuel .75 2.00
78 Darrelle Revis .75 2.00
79 Ace Sanders .75 2.00
80 LeSean McCoy 1.25 3.00
81 Patrick Willis 1.00 2.50
82 Giovani Bernard .75 2.00
83 Drew Brees 1.25 3.00
84 Ndamukong Suh 1.00 2.50
85 Julian Edelman 1.25 3.00
86 Sheldon Richardson .75 2.00
87 Troy Polamalu 1.25 3.00
88 Montee Ball .75 2.00
89 Geno Smith .75 2.00
90 Frank Gore 1.00 2.50
91 Mike Wallace .75 2.00
92 Ryan Mathews 1.00 2.50
93 Russell Wilson 2.00 5.00
94 Kendall Wright .75 2.00

95 Josh Gordon .75 2.00
96 Robert Mathis .75 2.00
97 Cecil Shorts .75 2.00
98 Victor Cruz 1.00 2.50
99 Joe Flacco 1.00 2.50
100 Zach Ertz 1.00 2.50
101 Davante Adams JSY AU RC 6.00 15.00
102 Davante Adams JSY AU RC 6.00 15.00
103 Jace Amaro JSY AU RC 4.00 10.00
104 Jace Amaro JSY AU RC 4.00 10.00
105 Dri Archer JSY AU RC 4.00 10.00
106 Dri Archer JSY AU RC 4.00 10.00
107 Odell Beckham Jr. JSY AU RC 40.00 80.00
108 Kelvin Benjamin JSY AU RC 6.00 15.00
110 Tajh Boyd JSY AU RC 4.00 10.00
111 Tajh Boyd JSY AU RC 4.00 10.00
112 Teddy Bridgewater JSY AU RC 30.00 60.00
113 Ka'Deem Carey JSY AU RC 4.00 10.00
114 Ka'Deem Carey JSY AU RC 4.00 10.00
115 Derek Carr JSY AU RC 30.00 60.00
116 Jadeveon Clowney JSY AU RC 5.00 12.00
117 Brandin Cooks JSY AU RC 10.00 25.00
118 Eric Ebron JSY AU RC 5.00 12.00
119 Mike Evans JSY AU RC 20.00 50.00
120 Devonta Freeman JSY AU RC EXCH 6.00 15.00
121 Devonta Freeman JSY AU RC EXCH 6.00 15.00
122 Jimmy Garoppolo JSY AU RC 30.00 60.00
123 Jeremy Hill JSY AU RC 5.00 12.00
124 Jeremy Hill JSY AU RC 5.00 12.00
125 Carlos Hyde JSY AU RC EXCH 5.00 12.00
126 Carlos Hyde JSY AU RC EXCH 5.00 12.00
127 Jarvis Landry JSY AU RC 8.00 20.00
128 Jarvis Landry JSY AU RC 8.00 20.00
129 Cody Latimer JSY AU RC 5.00 12.00
130 Cody Latimer JSY AU RC 5.00 12.00
131 Marqise Lee JSY AU RC 5.00 12.00
132 Marqise Lee JSY AU RC 5.00 12.00
133 Khalil Mack JSY AU RC EXCH 15.00 40.00
134 Khalil Mack JSY AU RC EXCH 15.00 40.00
135 Johnny Manziel JSY AU RC 15.00 40.00
137 Jordan Matthews JSY AU RC 6.00 15.00
138 Jordan Matthews JSY AU RC 6.00 15.00
139 A.J. McCarron JSY AU RC 4.00 10.00
140 Donte Moncrief JSY AU RC 4.00 10.00
141 Donte Moncrief JSY AU RC 4.00 10.00
142 Aaron Murray JSY AU RC 4.00 10.00
143 Aaron Murray JSY AU RC 4.00 10.00
144 Paul Richardson JSY AU RC 8.00 20.00
145 Allen Robinson JSY AU RC 6.00 15.00
146 Allen Robinson JSY AU RC 6.00 15.00
147 Michael Sam JSY AU RC 4.00 10.00
148 Michael Sam JSY AU RC 4.00 10.00
149 Bishop Sankey JSY AU RC 4.00 10.00
150 Bishop Sankey JSY AU RC 4.00 10.00
151 Austin Seferian-Jenkins JSY AU RC 4.00 10.00
152 Austin Seferian-Jenkins JSY AU RC 4.00 10.00
153 Charles Sims JSY AU RC 4.00 10.00
155 Sammy Watkins JSY AU RC 6.00 15.00
156 Terrance West JSY AU RC 4.00 10.00

2014 Topps Triple Threads Emerald

*1-100 VETS/199: .6X TO 1.5X BASIC CARDS
*101-159 ROOKIE/50: .5X TO 1.2X JSY AU/99
122 Jimmy Garoppolo JSY AU 60.00 125.00

2014 Topps Triple Threads Gold

*1-100 VETS/99: 1X TO 2.5X BASIC CARDS
*101-159 ROOKIE/25: .6X TO 1.5X JSY AU/99
107 Odell Beckham Jr. JSY AU 60.00 125.00
122 Jimmy Garoppolo JSY AU 100.00 200.00

2014 Topps Triple Threads Purple

*1-100 VETS/399: .5X TO 1.2X BASIC CARDS
*101-159 ROOKIE/70: .4X TO 1X JSY AU/99
122 Jimmy Garoppolo JSY AU 40.00 80.00

2014 Topps Triple Threads Ruby

*1-100 VETS/50: 1.2X TO 3X BASIC CARDS
*101-159 ROOKIE/15: .8X TO 2X JSY AU/99

2014 Topps Triple Threads Sapphire

*1-100 VETS/25: 1.5X TO 4X BASIC CARDS

2014 Topps Triple Threads Autographed Relic Double Trios

TTARDC3 Ens/Wkns/Brwtr/Brls/Ern/Mnzl 100.00 200.00
TTARDC4 Mthws/Mncf Adms/Ltmr/Rbsn/Rrdsn 75.00 150.00
TTARDC6 Brgwtr/Brtls/Crr/Grplo/Mnzl/Svge 100.00 200.00
TTARDC7 Lee/Bjmn/Cks/Bkhm/Wkns/Evns 200.00 300.00
TTARDC8 Hde/Hll/Msn/Snky/Sms/Wst
TTARDC13 Brtls/McCrn/Lee/Mnzl/Wst/Hll 100.00 200.00
TTARDC14 Jfry/Frmn/Cry/Jns/Wllms/Crz 50.00 100.00
TTARDC15 Bsh/Frte/Frmn/Cry/Whte/Ebrn 50.00 100.00

2014 Topps Triple Threads Autographed Relic Pairs Gold

*GOLD/18: .5X TO 1.2X COMBO AU/27
TTARP4 S.Watkins/M.Evans 75.00 150.00
TTARP8 B.Bortles/M.Lee 15.00 40.00

2014 Topps Triple Threads Autographed Relic Trios

EXCH EXPIRATION: 11/30/2017
TTART1 Manziel/Bortles/Bridgewater 20.00 50.00
TTART2 Evans/Ebron/Watkins 60.00 120.00
TTART3 Mason/Hill/Hyde 15.00 40.00
TTART4 Evans/Benjamin/Watkins 75.00 150.00
TTART5 Carey/Forte/Jeffery 15.00 40.00
TTART6 Savage/Garoppolo/Carr 50.00 100.00
TTART7 Ebron/Bush/Stafford 15.00 40.00
TTART11 Charles/Morris/McCoy 25.00 60.00
TTART13 Robinson/Bortles/Lee 20.00 50.00
TTART14 Cruz/Jeffery/Jones 25.00 60.00
TTART17 Adams/Latimer/Robinson 20.00 50.00
TTART18 Richardson/Moncrief/Matthews 40.00 80.00
TTART20 Sims/Hill/West 15.00 40.00
TTART21 Lee/Cooks/Benjamin 40.00 100.00
TTART22 Garoppolo/Murray/McCarron 30.00 80.00

2014 Topps Triple Threads Autographed Relic Trios Emerald

*EMERALD/18: .5X TO 1.2X COMBO AU/36
TTART1 Manziel/Bortles/Bridgewater 25.00 60.00

2014 Topps Triple Threads Autographed Relics

TTARAG Antonio Gates 10.00 25.00
TTARAJ Alshon Jeffery 15.00 40.00
TTARAL Andrew Luck 150.00 250.00
TTARBB Blake Bortles 10.00 25.00
TTARBH Brian Hartline 10.00 25.00
TTARBM Brandon Marshall 60.00 120.00
TTARCS C.J. Spiller 12.00 30.00
TTARDM Dan Marino 150.00 250.00
TTAREL Eddie Lacy 10.00 25.00
TTAREM Eli Manning 75.00 150.00
TTARES Emmitt Smith 100.00 200.00
TTARFG Frank Gore
TTARJC Jamaal Charles
TTARJG Josh Gordon 10.00 25.00
TTARJM Johnny Manziel 12.00 30.00
TTARJW Jason Witten 40.00 80.00
TTARKB Kelvin Benjamin 12.00 30.00
TTARLB Le'Veon Bell
TTARME Mike Evans 20.00 50.00
TTARMF Matt Forte 25.00 50.00
TTARMJ Marvin Jones 10.00 25.00
TTARMS Matthew Stafford 40.00 80.00
TTARPT Pierre Thomas 10.00 25.00
TTARRB Reggie Bush 15.00 40.00
TTARRC Randall Cobb 12.00 30.00
TTARRG Rob Gronkowski
TTARRW Roddy White 10.00 25.00
TTARSJ Stevie Johnson 12.00 30.00
TTARSR Stevan Ridley 10.00 25.00
TTARSW Sammy Watkins
TTARTA Tavon Austin 10.00 25.00
TTARTB Teddy Bridgewater
TTARTM Tre Mason 15.00 40.00
TTARTR Tony Romo 50.00 100.00
TTARAGR A.J. Green
TTARGSA Gale Sayers 40.00 80.00
TTARJCL Jadeveon Clowney 10.00 25.00
TTARMWH Markus Wheaton 10.00 25.00
TTARRWI Russell Wilson
TTARRWO Robert Woods 12.00 30.00

2014 Topps Triple Threads Hand Stamped Autographs

TTHSAW Andre Williams EXCH 75.00 150.00
TTHSBB Blake Bortles EXCH 40.00 80.00
TTHSCH Carlos Hyde EXCH 30.00 60.00
TTHSEE Eric Ebron EXCH 60.00 120.00
TTHSJC Jadeveon Clowney EXCH 40.00 100.00
TTHSJG Jimmy Garoppolo EXCH
TTHSJM Jordan Matthews EXCH 75.00 150.00
TTHSME Mike Evans EXCH 90.00 150.00
TTHSOB Odell Beckham Jr. EXCH 300.00 500.00
TTHSTB Teddy Bridgewater EXCH 75.00 150.00

2014 Topps Triple Threads Relics

MOST HAVE MULTIPLE CARDS OF EQUAL VALUE
TTR1 Nick Fairley 5.00 12.00
TTR4 Dez Bryant 8.00 20.00
TTR7 Reggie Bush 5.00 12.00
TTR10 Jamaal Charles 6.00 15.00
TTR19 Marques Colston 5.00 12.00
TTR22 Victor Cruz 6.00 15.00
TTR25 Jay Cutler 5.00 12.00
TTR28 D'Brickashaw Ferguson 5.00 12.00
TTR31 Larry Fitzgerald 6.00 15.00
TTR40 Matt Forte 5.00 12.00
TTR49 Antonio Gates 5.00 12.00
TTR52 Tony Gonzalez 5.00 12.00
TTR55 Josh Gordon 5.00 12.00
TTR58 Mario Williams 5.00 12.00
TTR61 Brian Hartline 5.00 12.00
TTR64 DeSean Jackson 6.00 15.00
TTR70 Alshon Jeffery 8.00 20.00
TTR73 Julio Jones 8.00 20.00
TTR76 Marvin Jones 5.00 12.00
TTR79 Nick Mangold 5.00 12.00
TTR82 Eli Manning 10.00 25.00
TTR85 Knowshon Moreno 5.00 12.00
TTR97 Tony Romo 10.00 25.00
TTR100 Matt Ryan 6.00 15.00
TTR103 Cecil Shorts 5.00 12.00
TTR106 Emmitt Smith 20.00 40.00
TTR109 C.J. Spiller 5.00 12.00
TTR118 Matthew Stafford 6.00 15.00
TTR130 Roddy White 5.00 12.00
TTR142 Adrian Clayborn 5.00 12.00
TTR145 DeMarcus Ware 6.00 15.00
TTR148 Peyton Manning 40.00 80.00
TTR149 Aaron Rodgers 20.00 40.00
TTR150 Joe Namath 20.00 40.00
TTR151 Gale Sayers 10.00 25.00
TTR152 Dan Marino 25.00 50.00
TTR153 Marshall Faulk 6.00 15.00
TTR155 Tom Brady 20.00 40.00
TTR156 Eric Dickerson 12.00 30.00
TTR157 Drew Brees 8.00 20.00
TTR159 Steve Young 10.00 25.00
TTR160 Deion Sanders 10.00 25.00
TTR162 Marshawn Lynch 25.00 50.00
TTR163 LeSean McCoy 12.00 30.00
TTR164 Russell Wilson 15.00 40.00
TTR165 Pierre Thomas 5.00 12.00
TTR171 Osi Umenyiora 5.00 12.00
TTR174 Markus Wheaton 5.00 12.00
TTR180 Brian Hartline 5.00 12.00
TTR183 Fred Jackson 6.00 15.00
TTR186 Stevie Johnson 6.00 15.00

2014 Topps Triple Threads Relics Trios

*EMERALD/18: .5X TO 1.2X BASIC INSERT/36
*PURPLE/27: .5X TO 1.2X BASIC INSERT/36
TTRT1 Bridgewater/Manziel/Bortles 4.00 10.00
TTRT2 Evans/Watkins/Ebron 6.00 15.00
TTRT3 Mason/Hill/Hyde 3.00 8.00
TTRT4 Benjamin/Evans/Watkins 6.00 15.00
TTRT5 Carey/Forte/Jeffery 6.00 15.00
TTRT6 Savage/Carr/Garoppolo 20.00 50.00
TTRT7 Ebron/Bush/Stafford 3.00 8.00
TTRT11 Morris/Charles/McCoy 8.00 20.00
TTRT13 Bortles/Robinson/Lee 4.00 10.00
TTRT14 Cruz/Jeffery/Jones 8.00 20.00
TTRT15 Wallace/Fitzgerald/White 6.00 15.00
TTRT16 Thomas/Mason/Sankey 2.50 6.00
TTRT17 Latimer/Adams/Robinson 4.00 10.00
TTRT18 Matthews/Richardson/Moncrief 4.00 10.00
TTRT19 Wilson/Manning/Rodgers 25.00 50.00
TTRT20 Sims/Hill/West 3.00 8.00
TTRT21 Lee/Benjamin/Cooks 4.00 10.00
TTRT22 McCarron/Garoppolo/Murray 20.00 50.00
TTRT23 Boyd/Thomas/Savage 2.50 6.00
TTRT25 Jones/Freeman/White 8.00 20.00
TTRT26 Cruz/Williams/Beckham 6.00 15.00
TTRT27 Evans/Beckham/Cooks 6.00 15.00
TTRT28 Adams/Latimer/Cooks 4.00 10.00
TTRT29 Robinson/Matthews/Cooks 4.00 10.00
TTRT30 Richardson/Cooks/Moncrief 4.00 10.00
TTRT31 Robinson/Matthews/Richardson 4.00 10.00
TTRT32 Latimer/Beckham/Richardson 6.00 15.00
TTRT33 Landry/Wallace/Hartline 5.00 12.00
TTRT34 Smith/Romo/Bryant 6.00 15.00
TTRT35 Lee/Robinson/Shorts 4.00 10.00
TTRT36 Jeffery/Cutler/Forte 6.00 15.00
TTRT37 Cooks/Colston/Graham 4.00 10.00
TTRT38 Beckham/Manning/Cruz 6.00 15.00
TTRT39 Davis/Hyde/Gore 3.00 8.00
TTRT40 Jones/Ryan/White 8.00 20.00
TTRT41 Garoppolo/Thomas/Boyd 20.00 50.00
TTRT42 Thomas/Williams/Freeman 4.00 10.00
TTRT43 Williams/West/Thomas 2.50 6.00
TTRT44 Hill/Sankey/Thomas 3.00 8.00
TTRT46 Murray/Charles/Thomas 3.00 8.00
TTRT48 Bell/Archer/Wheaton 6.00 15.00
TTRT49 Cooks/Benjamin/Evans 6.00 15.00

2014 Topps Triple Threads Rookie Autograph Relics Gold

*GOLD/25: .6X TO 1.5X BASIC AU/99
TTRAR1 Teddy Bridgewater
TTRAR2 Blake Bortles 6.00 15.00
TTRAR3 Jadeveon Clowney 6.00 15.00
TTRAR37 Jimmy Garoppolo 60.00 150.00
TTRAR51 Odell Beckham Jr. 60.00 150.00

2014 Topps Triple Threads Rookie Jumbo Relics

*EMERALD/50: .5X TO 1.2X BASIC JSY/99
*GOLD/25: .6X TO 1.5X BASIC JSY/99
*PURPLE/75: .4X TO 1X BASIC JSY/99
*SAPPHIRE/10: 1X TO 2.5X BASIC JSY/99
SOME HAVE TWO CARDS OF EQUAL VALUE
TTRJR1 Davante Adams 2.50 6.00
TTRJR2 Jace Amaro 1.50 4.00
TTRJR3 Jace Amaro 1.50 4.00
TTRJR4 Odell Beckham Jr. 4.00 10.00
TTRJR5 Odell Beckham Jr. 4.00 10.00
TTRJR6 Kelvin Benjamin 2.50 6.00
TTRJR7 Kelvin Benjamin 2.50 6.00
TTRJR8 Blake Bortles 2.00 5.00
TTRJR9 Blake Bortles 2.00 5.00
TTRJR10 Tajh Boyd 1.50 4.00
TTRJR11 Tajh Boyd 1.50 4.00
TTRJR12 Teddy Bridgewater 6.00 15.00
TTRJR13 Teddy Bridgewater 6.00 15.00
TTRJR14 Cody Latimer 2.00 5.00
TTRJR15 Ka'Deem Carey 1.50 4.00
TTRJR16 Ka'Deem Carey
TTRJR17 Derek Carr 10.00 25.00
TTRJR18 Derek Carr 10.00 25.00
TTRJR19 Jadeveon Clowney 2.00 5.00
TTRJR20 Jadeveon Clowney 2.00 5.00
TTRJR21 Brandin Cooks 2.50 6.00
TTRJR22 Brandin Cooks 2.50 6.00
TTRJR23 Eric Ebron 2.00 5.00
TTRJR24 Eric Ebron 2.00 5.00
TTRJR25 Mike Evans 4.00 10.00
TTRJR26 Mike Evans 4.00 10.00
TTRJR27 Devonta Freeman 2.50 6.00
TTRJR28 Devonta Freeman 2.50 6.00
TTRJR29 Jimmy Garoppolo 4.00 10.00
TTRJR30 Jimmy Garoppolo 4.00 10.00
TTRJR31 Jeremy Hill 2.00 5.00
TTRJR32 Jeremy Hill 2.00 5.00
TTRJR33 Carlos Hyde 2.00 5.00
TTRJR34 Carlos Hyde 2.00 5.00
TTRJR35 Jarvis Landry 3.00 8.00
TTRJR36 Marqise Lee 2.00 5.00
TTRJR37 Marqise Lee 2.00 5.00
TTRJR38 Terrance West 1.50 4.00
TTRJR39 Terrance West 1.50 4.00
TTRJR40 Johnny Manziel 2.50 6.00
TTRJR41 Johnny Manziel 2.50 6.00
TTRJR42 Tre Mason 1.50 4.00
TTRJR43 Tre Mason 1.50 4.00
TTRJR44 Jordan Matthews 2.50 6.00
TTRJR45 A.J. McCarron 1.50 4.00
TTRJR46 A.J. McCarron 1.50 4.00
TTRJR47 Michael Sam 1.50 4.00
TTRJR48 Michael Sam 1.50 4.00
TTRJR49 Donte Moncrief 1.50 4.00
TTRJR50 Aaron Murray 1.50 4.00
TTRJR51 Aaron Murray 1.50 4.00
TTRJR52 Allen Robinson 2.50 6.00
TTRJR53 Allen Robinson 2.50 6.00
TTRJR54 Bishop Sankey 1.50 4.00
TTRJR55 Bishop Sankey 1.50 4.00
TTRJR56 Austin Seferian-Jenkins 1.50 4.00
TTRJR57 Austin Seferian-Jenkins 1.50 4.00
TTRJR58 Khalil Mack 6.00 15.00
TTRJR59 Khalil Mack 6.00 15.00
TTRJR60 Logan Thomas 1.50 4.00
TTRJR61 Logan Thomas 1.50 4.00
TTRJR62 Sammy Watkins 2.50 6.00
TTRJR63 Sammy Watkins 2.50 6.00
TTRJR64 Andre Williams 1.50 4.00
TTRJR65 Andre Williams 1.50 4.00
TTRJR66 Jordan Matthews 2.50 6.00
TTRJR67 Jarvis Landry 3.00 8.00
TTRJR68 Cody Latimer 2.00 5.00
TTRJR69 Charles Sims 1.50 4.00
TTRJR70 Charles Sims 1.50 4.00
TTRJR71 Dri Archer 1.50 4.00
TTRJR72 Dri Archer 1.50 4.00
TTRJR73 Davante Adams 2.50 6.00
TTRJR74 Donte Moncrief 1.50 4.00

2014 Topps Triple Threads Transparencies Autographs

*EMERALD/30: .5X TO 1.2X BASIC AU/65
TTTAM A.J. McCarron
TTTAMU Aaron Murray 5.00 12.00
TTTAR Allen Robinson 8.00 20.00
TTTASJ Austin Seferian-Jenkins 5.00 12.00
TTTAW Andre Williams
TTTBB Blake Bortles 6.00 15.00
TTTBC Brandin Cooks 8.00 20.00
TTTBS Bishop Sankey 5.00 12.00
TTTCF C.J. Fiedorowicz 5.00 12.00
TTTCS Charles Sims 5.00 12.00
TTTCSH Connor Shaw 5.00 12.00
TTTDA Davante Adams 8.00 20.00
TTTDC Derek Carr 25.00 50.00
TTTDM Donte Moncrief 5.00 12.00
TTTEE Eric Ebron 6.00 15.00
TTTJA Jace Amaro 5.00 12.00
TTTJC Jadeveon Clowney 6.00 15.00
TTTJG Jimmy Garoppolo 40.00 80.00
TTTJHI Jeremy Hill 6.00 15.00
TTTJL Jarvis Landry
TTTJLY Jordan Lynch 6.00 15.00
TTTJM Johnny Manziel
TTTJMA Jordan Matthews 8.00 20.00
TTTJW James White 10.00 25.00
TTTKB Kelvin Benjamin
TTTKC Ka'Deem Carey 5.00 12.00
TTTLS Lache Seastrunk 5.00 12.00
TTTLT Logan Thomas 5.00 12.00
TTTMB Martavis Bryant 6.00 15.00
TTTME Mike Evans 12.00 30.00
TTTML Marqise Lee 6.00 15.00
TTTOB Odell Beckham Jr.
TTTSM Stephen Morris 5.00 12.00
TTTSW Sammy Watkins 8.00 20.00
TTTTB Teddy Bridgewater 40.00 80.00
TTTTBO Tajh Boyd
TTTTM Tre Mason
TTTTS Tom Savage 5.00 12.00
TTTTW Terrance West 5.00 12.00
TTTZM Zach Mettenberger 5.00 12.00

2015 Topps Triple Threads

SOME PLAYERS HAVE MULT. CARDS OF EQUAL VALUE
EXCH EXPIRATION: 10/31/17
1 Calvin Johnson 1.25 3.00
2 Marshawn Lynch 1.00 2.50
3 Aaron Rodgers 2.50 6.00
4 J.J. Watt 1.25 3.00
5 Tom Brady 3.00 8.00
6 Andrew Luck 1.50 4.00
7 Jamaal Charles 1.00 2.50
8 Le'Veon Bell 1.00 2.50
9 Richard Sherman 1.25 3.00
10 Rob Gronkowski 1.25 3.00
11 Peyton Manning 2.50 6.00
12 Drew Brees 1.25 3.00
13 Antonio Brown 1.25 3.00
14 Demaryius Thomas 1.00 2.50
15 Russell Wilson 1.50 4.00
16 Dez Bryant 1.25 3.00
17 Julio Jones 1.25 3.00
18 Odell Beckham Jr. 1.25 3.00
19 Eddie Lacy .75 2.00
20 Ndamukong Suh 1.00 2.50
21 Jordy Nelson 1.00 2.50
22 Cam Newton 1.25 3.00
23 DeMarco Murray 1.00 2.50
24 Adrian Peterson 1.25 3.00
25 Jimmy Graham 1.25 3.00
26 Luke Kuechly 1.00 2.50
27 LeSean McCoy 1.25 3.00
28 A.J. Green 1.25 3.00
29 Earl Thomas 1.00 2.50
30 Ben Roethlisberger 1.25 3.00
31 Terrell Suggs .75 2.00
32 Matt Forte .75 2.00
33 Randall Cobb 1.00 2.50
34 Philip Rivers 1.25 3.00
35 Kam Chancellor 1.25 3.00
36 Arian Foster 1.00 2.50
37 Matthew Stafford 1.00 2.50
38 Alshon Jeffery 1.00 2.50
39 Jeremy Hill .75 2.00
40 T.Y. Hilton 1.00 2.50
41 Tony Romo 1.00 2.50
42 Clay Matthews 1.25 3.00
43 Mike Evans 1.00 2.50
44 Kelvin Benjamin 1.00 2.50
45 C.J. Anderson 1.00 2.50
46 Brandon Marshall .75 2.00
47 Sammy Watkins 1.00 2.50
48 [illegible] 1.00 2.50
49 DeSean Jackson 1.00 2.50
50 Frank Gore 1.00 2.50
51 Joe Flacco 1.00 2.50
52 Eli Manning 1.00 2.50
53 Colin Kaepernick 1.00 2.50
54 Alfred Morris .75 2.00
55 Larry Fitzgerald 1.00 2.50
56 Ryan Tannehill 1.00 2.50
57 Antonio Gates .75 2.00
58 Golden Tate .75 2.00
59 Jeremy Maclin .75 2.00
60 John Elway 2.00 5.00
61 Brett Favre 2.50 6.00
62 Emmitt Smith 2.00 5.00
63 Steve Young 1.50 4.00
64 Dan Marino 2.50 6.00
65 Bo Jackson 1.50 4.00
66 Marshall Faulk 1.00 2.50
67 Barry Sanders 2.00 5.00
68 Terrell Davis 1.00 2.50
69 Earl Campbell 1.25 3.00
70 Deion Sanders 1.00 2.50
71 Eric Dickerson 1.00 2.50
72 Lawrence Taylor 1.25 3.00
73 Ronnie Lott 1.00 2.50
74 Gale Sayers 1.25 3.00
75 Mike Singletary 1.25 3.00
76 Troy Polamalu 1.25 3.00
77 Joe Greene 1.25 3.00
78 Tim Brown 1.25 3.00
79 Paul Hornung 1.25 3.00
80 Jerry Rice 2.00 5.00
81 Kurt Warner 1.00 2.50
82 Phil Simms 1.00 2.50
83 Roger Staubach 1.50 4.00
84 Jim Kelly 1.25 3.00
85 Marcus Allen 1.25 3.00
86 Warren Moon 1.25 3.00
87 Steve Largent 1.25 3.00
88 Len Dawson 1.25 3.00
89 Robert Griffin III .75 2.00
90 Blake Bortles .75 2.00
91 Curtis Martin 1.00 2.50
92 Tony Dorsett 1.25 3.00
93 Terry Bradshaw 1.50 4.00
94 Darrelle Revis .75 2.00
95 Johnny Manziel 1.00 2.50
96 Teddy Bridgewater 1.00 2.50
97 Howie Long 1.25 3.00
98 Sam Bradford .75 2.00
99 Nick Foles 1.00 2.50
100 LaDainian Tomlinson 1.00 2.50
101 Jameis Winston JSY AU RC
102 Marcus Mariota JSY AU RC
103 Amari Cooper JSY AU RC 30.00 60.00
104 Kevin White JSY AU RC 5.00 12.00
105 Melvin Gordon JSY AU RC 10.00 25.00
106 Todd Gurley JSY AU RC 40.00 80.00
107 DeVante Parker JSY AU RC 6.00 15.00
108 Nelson Agholor JSY AU RC 6.00 15.00
109 Jaelen Strong JSY AU RC 5.00 12.00
110 Marcus Mariota JSY AU RC
111 Brett Hundley JSY AU RC
112 Devin Funchess JSY AU RC 6.00 15.00
113 Phillip Dorsett JSY AU RC 4.00 10.00
114 Dorial Green-Beckham JSY AU RC 4.00 10.00
115 Ameer Abdullah JSY AU RC 6.00 15.00
116 Devin Smith JSY AU RC 4.00 10.00
117 T.J. Yeldon JSY AU RC 4.00 10.00
118 T.J. Yeldon JSY AU RC 4.00 10.00
119 Duke Johnson JSY AU RC 6.00 15.00
120 Jay Ajayi JSY AU RC 6.00 15.00
121 Sean Mannion JSY AU RC 4.00 10.00
122 Ty Montgomery JSY AU RC 4.00 10.00
123 Chris Conley JSY AU RC 4.00 10.00
124 David Johnson JSY AU RC 10.00 25.00
125 Jeremy Langford JSY AU RC 4.00 10.00
126 Tevin Coleman JSY AU RC 5.00 12.00
129 Sammie Coates JSY AU RC 5.00 12.00
131 Maxx Williams JSY AU RC 4.00 10.00
132 Maxx Williams JSY AU RC 4.00 10.00
133 Mike Davis JSY AU RC 4.00 10.00
134 Mike Davis JSY AU RC 4.00 10.00
135 Tyler Lockett JSY AU RC 6.00 15.00
136 Tyler Lockett JSY AU RC 6.00 15.00
137 Stefon Diggs JSY AU RC 10.00 25.00
138 Rashad Greene JSY AU RC 4.00 10.00
139 Bryce Petty JSY AU RC 4.00 10.00
140 Bryce Petty JSY AU RC 4.00 10.00
142 Justin Hardy JSY AU RC 4.00 10.00
143 Justin Hardy JSY AU RC 4.00 10.00
144 David Cobb JSY AU RC 4.00 10.00
145 David Cobb JSY AU RC 4.00 10.00
146 Nelson Agholor JSY AU RC 6.00 15.00
147 Ameer Abdullah JSY AU RC 6.00 15.00
148 Jameis Winston JSY AU RC
149 Breshad Perriman JSY AU RC 4.00 10.00
150 Amari Cooper JSY AU RC 30.00 60.00
151 Kevin White JSY AU RC 5.00 12.00
152 Melvin Gordon JSY AU RC 10.00 25.00
153 Todd Gurley JSY AU RC 40.00 80.00
154 Jameis Winston JSY AU RC
155 Marcus Mariota JSY AU RC
161 Jamison Crowder JSY AU RC 5.00 12.00
167 Jeremy Langford JSY AU RC 4.00 10.00
171 Jay Ajayi JSY AU RC 6.00 15.00
172 T.J. Yeldon JSY AU RC 4.00 10.00

2015 Topps Triple Threads Emerald

*1-100 VETS/199: .6X TO 1.5X BASIC CARDS
*101-159 ROOKIE/50: .5X TO 1.2X JSY AU/99
101 Jameis Winston JSY AU 60.00 120.00
102 Marcus Mariota JSY AU 75.00 150.00
106 Todd Gurley JSY AU 60.00 120.00

2015 Topps Triple Threads Gold

*1-100 VETS/99: 1X TO 2.5X BASIC CARDS
*101-155 ROOKIE/25: .6X TO 1.5X JSY AU/99
102 Marcus Mariota JSY AU 100.00 200.00

2015 Topps Triple Threads Purple

*1-100 VETS/232: .5X TO 1.2X BASIC CARDS
*101-155 ROOKIE/70: .4X TO 1X JSY AU/99
101 Jameis Winston JSY AU 50.00 100.00
102 Marcus Mariota JSY AU 50.00 125.00
106 Todd Gurley JSY AU 40.00 80.00

2015 Topps Triple Threads Ruby

*1-100 VETS/50: 1.2X TO 3X BASIC CARDS
*101-155 ROOKIE/15: .8X TO 2X JSY AU/99
101 Jameis Winston JSY AU 75.00 150.00

2015 Topps Triple Threads Sapphire

*1-100 VETS/25: 1.5X TO 4X BASIC CARDS

2015 Topps Triple Threads Autographed Relic Pairs

TTARP2 T.Brown/A.Cooper 75.00 150.00
TTARP5 A.Cooper/D.Carr 60.00 125.00
TTARP7 M.Mariota/J.Winston 150.00 300.00
TTARP8 T.Gurley/M.Gordon 75.00 150.00
TTARP9 J.Nelson/E.Lacy 50.00 100.00
TTARP10 L.Tomlinson/M.Gordon
TTARP11 G.Sayers/M.Singletary 15.00 40.00
TTARP12 B.Sanders/M.Stafford
TTARP14 C.Matthews/J.Nelson 40.00 80.00
TTARP16 K.White/A.Jeffery 12.00 30.00
TTARP18 M.Evans/J.Winston
TTARP20 N.Agholor/J.Matthews 12.00 30.00
TTARP21 D.Parker/J.Ajayi
TTARP22 J.Rice/B.Sanders
TTARP24 R.Wilson/A.Luck 125.00 250.00
TTARP25 K.Benjamin/D.Funchess 15.00 40.00
TTARP26 T.Yeldon/B.Bortles

2015 Topps Triple Threads Autographed Relics

TTARAG A.J. Green 15.00 40.00
TTARAL Andrew Luck
TTARBS Barry Sanders 100.00 200.00
TTARDC Derek Carr 30.00 60.00
TTARDM Dan Marino 75.00 150.00
TTARDMU DeMarco Murray
TTAREL Eddie Lacy 25.00 50.00
TTARJE John Elway 75.00 150.00
TTARJH Jeremy Hill 10.00 25.00
TTARJL Jarvis Landry 12.00 30.00
TTARJN Jordy Nelson
TTARJR Jerry Rice
TTARKB Kelvin Benjamin
TTARMA Marcus Allen
TTARME Mike Evans 12.00 30.00
TTARMS Matthew Stafford 25.00 50.00
TTARRC Randall Cobb
TTARRW Russell Wilson 60.00 120.00
TTARTB Tim Brown
TTARTBR Terry Bradshaw 75.00 150.00

2015 Topps Triple Threads Gridiron Legends Autographs

GLABF Brett Favre 100.00 200.00
GLACM Curtis Martin 12.00 30.00
GLADC Dwight Clark 12.00 30.00
GLAGS Gale Sayers 15.00 40.00
GLAJG Joe Greene 15.00 40.00
GLAKW Kurt Warner 25.00 50.00
GLALD Len Dawson 15.00 40.00
GLALT Lawrence Taylor 30.00 60.00
GLAMS Mike Singletary 12.00 30.00
GLAPH Paul Hornung 15.00 40.00
GLAPS Phil Simms 12.00 30.00
GLARC Roger Craig 12.00 30.00
GLARL Ronnie Lott 12.00 30.00
GLASL Steve Largent
GLATB Tim Brown
GLATDO Tony Dorsett 30.00 60.00

2015 Topps Triple Threads Relics

*PURPLE/27: .4X TO 1X BASIC JSY/36
*EMERALD/18: .5X TO 1.2X BASIC JSY/36
*GOLD/9: .6X TO 1.5X BASIC JSY/36
MOST HAVE MULTIPLE CARDS OF EQUAL VALUE
TTRAA1 Ameer Abdullah 3.00 8.00
TTRAA2 Ameer Abdullah 3.00 8.00
TTRAA3 Ameer Abdullah 3.00 8.00
TTRAC1 Amari Cooper 6.00 15.00
TTRAC2 Amari Cooper 6.00 15.00
TTRAC3 Amari Cooper 6.00 15.00
TTRAG1 Antonio Gates 5.00 12.00
TTRAG2 Antonio Gates 5.00 12.00
TTRAG3 Antonio Gates 5.00 12.00
TTRAG1 A.J. Green 8.00 20.00
TTRAG2 A.J. Green 8.00 20.00
TTRAG3 A.J. Green 8.00 20.00
TTRAJ1 Alshon Jeffery 6.00 15.00
TTRAJ2 Alshon Jeffery 6.00 15.00
TTRAJ3 Alshon Jeffery 6.00 15.00
TTRAL1 Andrew Luck 10.00 25.00
TTRAL2 Andrew Luck 10.00 25.00
TTRAL3 Andrew Luck 10.00 25.00
TTRBB1 Blake Bortles 5.00 12.00
TTRBB2 Blake Bortles 5.00 12.00
TTRBB3 Blake Bortles 5.00 12.00
TTRCA1 C.J. Anderson 6.00 15.00
TTRCA2 C.J. Anderson 6.00 15.00
TTRCA3 C.J. Anderson 6.00 15.00
TTRCN1 Cam Newton 8.00 20.00
TTRCN2 Cam Newton 8.00 20.00
TTRCN3 Cam Newton 8.00 20.00
TTRDC1 Derek Carr 8.00 20.00
TTRDC2 Derek Carr 8.00 20.00
TTRDC3 Derek Carr 8.00 20.00
TTRDH1 DeAndre Hopkins 6.00 15.00
TTRDH2 DeAndre Hopkins 6.00 15.00
TTRDH3 DeAndre Hopkins 6.00 15.00
TTRDM1 DeMarco Murray 6.00 15.00
TTRDM2 DeMarco Murray 6.00 15.00
TTRDM3 DeMarco Murray 6.00 15.00
TTRDP1 DeVante Parker 3.00 8.00
TTRDP2 DeVante Parker 3.00 8.00
TTRDP3 DeVante Parker 3.00 8.00
TTRDRE1 Darrelle Revis 5.00 12.00
TTRDRE2 Darrelle Revis 5.00 12.00
TTRDRE3 Darrelle Revis 5.00 12.00
TTRDT1 Demaryius Thomas 6.00 15.00
TTRDT2 Demaryius Thomas 6.00 15.00
TTRDT3 Demaryius Thomas 6.00 15.00
TTREL1 Eddie Lacy 5.00 12.00
TTREL2 Eddie Lacy 5.00 12.00
TTREL3 Eddie Lacy 5.00 12.00
TTRES1 Emmanuel Sanders 6.00 15.00
TTRES2 Emmanuel Sanders 6.00 15.00
TTRES3 Emmanuel Sanders 6.00 15.00
TTRET1 Earl Thomas 6.00 15.00
TTRET2 Earl Thomas 6.00 15.00
TTRET3 Earl Thomas 6.00 15.00
TTRJC1 Jamaal Charles 6.00 15.00
TTRJC2 Jamaal Charles 6.00 15.00
TTRJC3 Jamaal Charles 6.00 15.00
TTRJJ1 Julio Jones 8.00 20.00
TTRJJ2 Julio Jones 8.00 20.00
TTRJJ3 Julio Jones 8.00 20.00
TTRJL1 Jarvis Landry 6.00 15.00
TTRJL2 Jarvis Landry 6.00 15.00
TTRJL3 Jarvis Landry 6.00 15.00
TTRJMA1 Jordan Matthews 6.00 15.00
TTRJMA2 Jordan Matthews 6.00 15.00
TTRJMA3 Jordan Matthews 6.00 15.00
TTRJN1 Jordy Nelson 6.00 15.00
TTRJN2 Jordy Nelson 6.00 15.00
TTRJN3 Jordy Nelson 6.00 15.00
TTRJW1 Jameis Winston 5.00 12.00
TTRJW2 Jameis Winston 5.00 12.00
TTRJW3 Jameis Winston 5.00 12.00
TTRKB1 Kelvin Benjamin 6.00 15.00
TTRKB2 Kelvin Benjamin 6.00 15.00
TTRKB3 Kelvin Benjamin 4.00 10.00
TTRKW1 Kevin White 2.50 6.00
TTRKW2 Kevin White 2.50 6.00
TTRKW3 Kevin White 2.50 6.00
TTRLB1 Le'Veon Bell 6.00 15.00
TTRLB2 Le'Veon Bell 6.00 15.00
TTRLB3 Le'Veon Bell 6.00 15.00
TTRME1 Mike Evans 6.00 15.00
TTRME2 Mike Evans 6.00 15.00
TTRME3 Mike Evans 6.00 15.00
TTRMG1 Melvin Gordon 5.00 12.00
TTRMG2 Melvin Gordon 5.00 12.00
TTRMG3 Melvin Gordon 5.00 12.00
TTRMM1 Marcus Mariota 8.00 20.00
TTRMM2 Marcus Mariota 8.00 20.00
TTRMM3 Marcus Mariota 8.00 20.00
TTRMR1 Matt Ryan 6.00 15.00
TTRMR2 Matt Ryan 6.00 15.00
TTRMR3 Matt Ryan 6.00 15.00
TTRMS1 Matthew Stafford 6.00 15.00
TTRMS2 Matthew Stafford 6.00 15.00
TTRMS3 Matthew Stafford 6.00 15.00
TTRNA1 Nelson Agholor 2.50 6.00
TTRNA2 Nelson Agholor 2.50 6.00
TTRNA3 Nelson Agholor 2.50 6.00
TTROB1 Odell Beckham Jr. 8.00 20.00
TTROB2 Odell Beckham Jr. 8.00 20.00
TTROB3 Odell Beckham Jr. 8.00 20.00
TTRPR1 Philip Rivers 8.00 20.00
TTRPR2 Philip Rivers 8.00 20.00
TTRPR3 Philip Rivers 8.00 20.00
TTRRC1 Randall Cobb 6.00 15.00
TTRRC2 Randall Cobb 6.00 15.00
TTRRC3 Randall Cobb 6.00 15.00
TTRRG1 Robert Griffin III 5.00 12.00
TTRRG2 Robert Griffin III 5.00 12.00
TTRRG3 Robert Griffin III 5.00 12.00
TTRRS1 Richard Sherman 8.00 20.00
TTRRS2 Richard Sherman 8.00 20.00
TTRRS3 Richard Sherman 8.00 20.00
TTRRT1 Ryan Tannehill 6.00 15.00
TTRRT2 Ryan Tannehill 6.00 15.00
TTRRT3 Ryan Tannehill 6.00 15.00
TTRRW1 Russell Wilson 10.00 25.00
TTRRW2 Russell Wilson 10.00 25.00
TTRRW3 Russell Wilson 10.00 25.00
TTRSW1 Sammy Watkins 6.00 15.00
TTRSW2 Sammy Watkins 6.00 15.00
TTRSW3 Sammy Watkins 6.00 15.00
TTRTB1 Teddy Bridgewater 6.00 15.00
TTRTB2 Teddy Bridgewater 6.00 15.00
TTRTB3 Teddy Bridgewater 6.00 15.00
TTRTG1 Todd Gurley 8.00 20.00
TTRTG2 Todd Gurley 8.00 20.00
TTRTG3 Todd Gurley 8.00 20.00
TTRTH1 T.Y. Hilton 6.00 15.00
TTRTH2 T.Y. Hilton 6.00 15.00
TTRTH3 T.Y. Hilton 6.00 15.00

2015 Topps Triple Threads Relics Trios

*PURPLE/27: .4X TO 1X BASIC JSY/36
*EMERALD/18: .5X TO 1.2X BASIC JSY/36
TTRAJB Alln/Jcksn/Brwn 15.00 40.00
TTRAMM Mtthws/Aghlr/Mrry 3.00 8.00
TTRBNF Nwtn/Bnjmn/Fnchss 4.00 10.00
TTRBRW Witten/Bryant/Romo 8.00 20.00
TTRCCK Klce/Cnly/Chrls 4.00 10.00
TTRCCM Cpr/Mck/Crr 8.00 20.00
TTRCNA Adms/Cbb/Nlsn 6.00 15.00
TTRCWP Cpr/Whte/Prkr 8.00 20.00
TTRDFG Grly/Dckrsn/Flk 12.00 30.00
TTRFWJ Frte/Whte/Jffry 3.00 8.00
TTRGGY Grdn/Grly/Yldn 12.00 30.00
TTRHBG Grn/Hll/Brnrd 8.00 20.00
TTRHLD Drstt/Hltn/Lck 5.00 12.00
TTRJRC Clmn/Ryn/Jns 4.00 10.00
TTRJWE Wnstn/Evns/Jcksn 12.00 30.00
TTRKNB Bnjmn/Kchly/Nwtn 12.00 30.00
TTRLTP Lndry/Prkr/Tnnhll 4.00 10.00
TTRMBC Crz/Mnng/Bckhm 10.00 25.00
TTRMLN Nlsn/Mtthws/Lcy 8.00 20.00
TTRMTA Mnng/Andrsn/Thms 12.00 30.00
TTRRBB Bll/Rthlsbrgr/Brwn 12.00 30.00
TTRRLN Lcy/Rdgrs/Nlsn 20.00 50.00
TTRSSJ Sndrs/Jhnsn/Stffrd 20.00 50.00
TTRTAS Andrsn/Sndrs/Thms 6.00 15.00
TTRTRG Grdn/Rvrs/Gts 6.00 15.00
TTRTSL Shrmn/Lnch/Thms 8.00 20.00
TTRWLS Lnch/Shrmn/Wlsn 10.00 25.00
TTRWMH Mrta/Hndly/Wnstn 10.00 25.00
TTRWWN Nwtn/Wnstn/Wlsn 6.00 15.00
TTRYBR Yldn/Rbnsn/Brtls 6.00 15.00

2015 Topps Triple Threads Rookie Autograph Relics

TTRARAA Ameer Abdullah 5.00 12.00
TTRARAAB Ameer Abdullah 5.00 12.00
TTRARAC Amari Cooper 20.00 50.00
TTRARBH Brett Hundley 3.00 8.00
TTRARBP Breshad Perriman 3.00 8.00
TTRARBPE Bryce Petty 3.00 8.00
TTRARBPET Bryce Petty 3.00 8.00
TTRARCA Cameron Artis-Payne 3.00 8.00
TTRARCAP Cameron Artis-Payne 3.00 8.00
TTRARCC Chris Conley 3.00 8.00
TTRARCCO Chris Conley 3.00 8.00
TTRARCW Clive Walford 3.00 8.00
TTRARDC David Cobb 3.00 8.00
TTRARDF Devin Funchess 5.00 12.00
TTRARDG Dorial Green-Beckham 3.00 8.00
TTRARDJ Duke Johnson 5.00 12.00
TTRARDJO David Johnson 8.00 20.00
TTRARDP DeVante Parker 5.00 12.00
TTRARDS Devin Smith 3.00 8.00
TTRARDSM Devin Smith 3.00 8.00
TTRARDUJO Duke Johnson 5.00 12.00
TTRARJA Jay Ajayi 5.00 12.00
TTRARJAJ Jay Ajayi 5.00 12.00
TTRARJC Jamison Crowder 4.00 10.00
TTRARJH Justin Hardy 3.00 8.00
TTRARJHA Justin Hardy 3.00 8.00
TTRARJJ Jesse James 4.00 10.00
TTRARJJA Jesse James 4.00 10.00
TTRARJL Jeremy Langford 3.00 8.00
TTRARJLA Jeremy Langford 3.00 8.00
TTRARJR Josh Robinson 3.00 8.00
TTRARJS Jaelen Strong 4.00 10.00
TTRARJW Jameis Winston
TTRARKB Kenny Bell 5.00 12.00
TTRARKW Kevin White 4.00 10.00
TTRARMD Mike Davis 3.00 8.00
TTRARMDA Mike Davis 3.00 8.00
TTRARMG Melvin Gordon 8.00 20.00
TTRARMM Marcus Mariota
TTRARMW Maxx Williams 3.00 8.00
TTRARNA Nelson Agholor 4.00 10.00
TTRARNAG Nelson Agholor 4.00 10.00
TTRARRG Rashad Greene 3.00 8.00
TTRARRGR Rashad Greene 3.00 8.00
TTRARSM Sean Mannion 3.00 8.00
TTRARSMA Sean Mannion 3.00 8.00
TTRARTCO Tevin Coleman 4.00 10.00
TTRARTG Todd Gurley 25.00 50.00
TTRARTL Tyler Lockett 5.00 12.00
TTRARTLO Tyler Lockett 5.00 12.00
TTRARTM Ty Montgomery 3.00 8.00
TTRARTMC Tre McBride 3.00 8.00
TTRARTMO Ty Montgomery 3.00 8.00
TTRARTW Trae Waynes 3.00 8.00
TTRARTY T.J. Yeldon 3.00 8.00
TTRARTYE T.J. Yeldon 3.00 8.00
TTRARVB Vic Beasley 4.00 10.00
TTRARVM Vince Mayle 4.00 10.00

2015 Topps Triple Threads Rookie Autograph Relics Emerald

*EMERALD/50: .5X TO 1.2X BASIC JSY AU/99
TTRARMM Marcus Mariota 50.00 100.00

2015 Topps Triple Threads Rookie Autograph Relics Purple

STATED PRINT RUN 75 SER.#'d SETS

2015 Topps Triple Threads Rookie Jumbo Relics

*PURPLE/75: .4X TO 1.2X BASIC JSY/99
*EMERALD/50: .5X TO 1.2X BASIC JSY/50
*GOLD/25: .6X TO 1.5X BASIC JSY/99
SOME PLAYERS HAVE MULT. CARDS OF EQUAL VALUE
TTRJRAA Ameer Abdullah 2.50 6.00
TTRJRAAB Ameer Abdullah 2.50 6.00
TTRJRAC Amari Cooper 5.00 12.00
TTRJRACO Amari Cooper 5.00 12.00
TTRJRACOO Amari Cooper 5.00 12.00
TTRJRBH Brett Hundley 1.50 4.00
TTRJRBHU Brett Hundley 1.50 4.00
TTRJRBP Breshad Perriman 1.50 4.00
TTRJRBPE Bryce Petty 1.50 4.00
TTRJRBPET Bryce Petty 1.50 4.00
TTRJRCA Cameron Artis-Payne 1.50 4.00
TTRJRCCO Chris Conley 1.50 4.00
TTRJRDCO David Cobb 1.50 4.00
TTRJRDF Devin Funchess 2.50 6.00
TTRJRDG Dorial Green-Beckham 1.50 4.00
TTRJRDGB Dorial Green-Beckham 1.50 4.00
TTRJRDJ Duke Johnson 2.50 6.00
TTRJRDJO David Johnson 4.00 10.00
TTRJRDP DeVante Parker 2.50 6.00
TTRJRDPA DeVante Parker 2.50 6.00
TTRJRDS Devin Smith 1.50 4.00
TTRJRDU Duke Johnson 2.50 6.00
TTRJRGG Garrett Grayson 1.50 4.00
TTRJRJA Jay Ajayi 2.50 6.00
TTRJRJAJ Jay Ajayi 2.50 6.00
TTRJRJAL Javorius Allen 2.00 5.00
TTRJRJL Jeremy Langford 1.50 4.00
TTRJRJS Jaelen Strong 2.00 5.00
TTRJRJW Jameis Winston 8.00 20.00
TTRJRJWI Jameis Winston 8.00 20.00
TTRJRJWIN Jameis Winston 8.00 20.00
TTRJRKW Kevin White 2.00 5.00
TTRJRKWH Kevin White 2.00 5.00
TTRJRKWI Karlos Williams 1.50 4.00
TTRJRLW Leonard Williams 1.50 4.00
TTRJRMDA Mike Davis 1.50 4.00
TTRJRMG Melvin Gordon 4.00 10.00
TTRJRMGO Melvin Gordon 4.00 10.00
TTRJRMGOR Melvin Gordon 4.00 10.00
TTRJRMJ Matt Jones 1.50 4.00
TTRJRMM Marcus Mariota 6.00 15.00
TTRJRMMA Marcus Mariota 6.00 15.00
TTRJRMMAR Marcus Mariota 6.00 15.00
TTRJRMW Maxx Williams 1.50 4.00
TTRJRNA Nelson Agholor 2.00 5.00
TTRJRPD Phillip Dorsett 1.50 4.00
TTRJRRG Rashad Greene 1.50 4.00
TTRJRSC Sammie Coates 2.00 5.00
TTRJRSDI Stefon Diggs 4.00 10.00
TTRJRSM Sean Mannion 1.50 4.00
TTRJRTC Tevin Coleman 2.00 5.00
TTRJRTCO Tevin Coleman 2.00 5.00
TTRJRTG Todd Gurley 8.00 20.00
TTRJRTGU Todd Gurley 8.00 20.00
TTRJRTGUR Todd Gurley 8.00 20.00
TTRJRTJY T.J. Yeldon 1.50 4.00
TTRJRTLO Tyler Lockett 5.00 12.00
TTRJRTM Ty Montgomery 1.50 4.00
TTRJRTYE T.J. Yeldon 1.50 4.00

2015 Topps Triple Threads Transparencies Autographs

TTTAA Ameer Abdullah 8.00 20.00
TTTAC Amari Cooper
TTTBH Brett Hundley
TTTBP Bryce Petty 5.00 12.00
TTTBPE Breshad Perriman 5.00 12.00
TTTCC Chris Conley 5.00 12.00
TTTDC David Cobb 5.00 12.00
TTTDF Devin Funchess 8.00 20.00
TTTDJ David Johnson 12.00 30.00
TTTDP DeVante Parker 8.00 20.00
TTTDS Devin Smith 5.00 12.00
TTTJW Jameis Winston
TTTKW Kevin White 6.00 15.00
TTTKWI Karlos Williams
TTTMG Melvin Gordon 12.00 30.00
TTTMM Marcus Mariota 50.00 100.00
TTTNA Nelson Agholor
TTTPD Phillip Dorsett 5.00 12.00
TTTSC Sammie Coates 6.00 15.00
TTTTC Tevin Coleman
TTTTG Todd Gurley 25.00 60.00
TTTTL Tyler Lockett 20.00 50.00
TTTTM Ty Montgomery
TTTTY T.J. Yeldon

2005 Topps Turkey Red

This 299-card set was released in January, 2006. The set was issued in the hobby in eight-card packs with an $4 SRP which came 24 packs to a box. Cards numbered 181-230 form a rookie subset.

COMPLETE SET (299) 125.00 250.00
COMP.SET w/o SP's (249) 25.00 60.00
SP STATED ODDS 1:4
1A Eli Manning .60 1.50
1B Eli Manning Ad Back 3.00 8.00
2 Clinton Portis .25 .60
3 Charles Woodson .40 1.00
4A Ray Lewis .40 1.00
4B Ray Lewis Ad Back 2.00 5.00
5 Michael Clayton .25 .60
6 Eric Moulds .25 .60
7 Derrick Blaylock .25 .60
8 Carson Palmer .30 .75
9 Zach Thomas .30 .75
10 Dallas Clark .25 .60
11 DeAngelo Hall .25 .60
12 Terrell Owens .30 .75
13 Brian Griese .25 .60
14 Dunta Robinson .25 .60
15 Kevan Barlow .25 .60
16 Jake Plummer .25 .60
17 James Farrior .25 .60
18A Peyton Manning 1.00 2.50
18B Peyton Manning Ad Back 5.00 12.00
19 Michael Bennett .25 .60
20 Brian Urlacher .40 1.00
21 Dante Hall .25 .60
22 Deion Branch .25 .60
23 Billy Volek .25 .60
24 Donald Driver .30 .75
25 LaDainian Tomlinson CL .30 .75
26 Donte Stallworth CL .20 .50
27 Joey Galloway .30 .75
28 Joey Harrington .25 .60
29 T.J. Houshmandzadeh .25 .60
30 LaDainian Tomlinson .40 1.00
31 Darius Watts .25 .60
32 Chris Gamble .25 .60
33 Javon Walker .25 .60
34 Kevin Curtis .30 .75
35 Steven Jackson .25 .60
36 J.P. Losman .25 .60
37A Champ Bailey .30 .75
37B Champ Bailey Ad Back 1.50 4.00
38 Tiki Barber .30 .75
39 LaVar Arrington .25 .60
40 Byron Leftwich .25 .60
41 Edgerrin James .30 .75
42 DeShaun Foster .30 .75
43 Darrell Jackson .25 .60
44 Julius Peppers .30 .75
45 David Carr .25 .60
46 Drew Bennett .30 .75
47 Antonio Gates .40 1.00
48A Deuce McAllister .30 .75
48B Deuce McAllister Ad Back 1.50 4.00
49 Patrick Ramsey .30 .75
50 Antonio Bryant .25 .60
51 Quentin Jammer .25 .60
52 Chris Drown .25 .60
53 Eddie Kennison .25 .60
54 Steve McNair .30 .75
55 Corey Bradford .25 .60
56 Chris Perry .25 .60
57 Curtis Martin .30 .75

58 Mewelde Moore .25 .60
59 Travis Taylor .25 .60
60 Chad Pennington .25 .60
61 Chad Johnson .25 .60
62 Kyle Boller .25 .60
63 Tyrone Calico .25 .60
64 Michael Pittman .25 .60
65 Kerry Collins .25 .60
66 Keary Colbert .25 .60
67 LaMont Jordan CL .25 .60
68 Robert Gallery .25 .60
69 Derrick Mason .25 .60
70 Brian Dawkins .40 1.00
71 Chris Simms .25 .60
72 Marc Bulger .25 .60
73 Stephen Davis .25 .60
74 Kurt Warner .30 .75
75 Todd Heap .25 .60
76 Domanick Davis CL .20 .50
77 Shaun Alexander .25 .60
78 Jerry Porter .25 .60
79 Chester Taylor .30 .75
80A Michael Vick .30 .75
80B Michael Vick Ad Back 1.50 4.00
81 Justin McCareins .25 .60
82 Fred Taylor .25 .60
83 Laveranues Coles .25 .60
84 Steve Smith .40 1.00
85 Sean Taylor .40 1.00
86 Marvin Harrison .30 .75
87 Ashley Lelie .25 .60
88 Willis McGahee .25 .60
89 Terence Newman .25 .60
90 Joe Horn .25 .60
91 Lee Suggs .25 .60
92 Keyshawn Johnson .30 .75
93 Desmond Clark .25 .60
94 T.J. Duckett .25 .60
95 Reggie Wayne .30 .75
96 Donte Stallworth .25 .60
97 Clarence Moore .25 .60
98 Jason Witten .30 .75
99 Jake Delhomme .25 .60
100 Julius Jones .25 .60
101 Ben Troupe .25 .60
102 Hines Ward .30 .75
103 Domanick Davis .25 .60
104 B.J. Sams .25 .60
105 Marcus Robinson .25 .60
106 Devery Henderson .25 .60
107 Matt Hasselbeck .25 .60
108 Antonio Pierce .25 .60
109 Santana Moss .30 .75
110 Adam Vinatieri .25 .60
111 Michael Strahan .30 .75
112 Greg Jones .25 .60
113 Drew Brees .40 1.00
114 Marcus Robinson .25 .60
115 Michael Jenkins .25 .60
116 Randy McMichael .25 .60
117 Jonathan Vilma .25 .60
118 Greg Lewis .30 .75
119 Ernest Wilford .25 .60
120 Warrick Dunn .25 .60
121 Shaun Alexander CL .20 .50
122 Donnie Edwards .25 .60
123 Antwaan Randle El .25 .60
124 Rod Smith .30 .75
125 Ed Reed .30 .75
126 Muhsin Muhammad .25 .60
127 L.J. Smith .30 .75
120 Chris Chambers .25 .60
129 Matt Schaub .30 .75
130 Andre Johnson .30 .75
131 Thomas Jones .25 .60
132 Robert Ferguson .25 .60
133 Jeremy Shockey .25 .60
134 William Green .25 .60
135A Ben Roethlisberger .60 1.50
135B Ben Roethlisberger Ad Back 3.00 8.00
136A Donovan McNabb .30 .75
136B Donovan McNabb Ad Back 1.50 4.00
137 Duce Staley .25 .60
138 Larry Fitzgerald .40 1.00
139 Charles Rogers .25 .60
140 Mark Brunell .30 .75
141 Kevin Jones .25 .60
142 LaMont Jordan .30 .75
143 Aaron Brooks .25 .60
144 Brian Westbrook .25 .60
145 Larry Johnson .25 .60
146 Tommy Maddox .25 .60
147 Corey Dillon .25 .60
148 William Henderson .25 .60
149 Tony Hollings .25 .60
150 Lee Evans .30 .75
151 Kelly Holcomb .25 .60
152 Reuben Droughns .25 .60
153 Keenan McCardell .30 .75
154 Ricky Williams .30 .75
155 Rashaun Woods .25 .60
156 D.J. Williams .25 .60
157 Tom Brady 1.50 4.00
158 Eric Parker .25 .60
159 Mike Anderson .25 .60
160 Roy Williams WR .25 .60
161 Mike Vanderjagt .25 .60
162 Ronald Curry .25 .60
163 Priest Holmes .25 .60
164 Bernard Berrian .25 .60
165 Brian Finneran .25 .60
166 Tony Gonzalez .30 .75
167 Chris McAlister .25 .60
168 Gus Frerotte .25 .60
169 Bryant Johnson .25 .60
170 Jay Fiedler .25 .60
171 Bubba Franks .25 .60
172 Tony Romo 5.00 10.00
173 Jamal Lewis .30 .75
174 Torry Holt .30 .75
175 Ladell Betts .25 .60
176 Bertrand Berry .25 .60
177 Josh McCown .30 .75
178 Jonathan Wells .25 .60
179 Plaxico Burress .25 .60
180 Rudi Johnson .25 .60
181 Cedric Benson RC .50 1.25
182 Carlos Rogers RC .75 2.00
183 Terrence Murphy RC .50 1.25
184 Frank Gore RC 1.00 2.50
185 Vincent Jackson RC .75 2.00
186 Ciatrick Fason RC .50 1.25
187 Alex Smith QB RC 2.00 5.00
188 Mike Williams .60 1.50
189 Kyle Orton RC .50 1.25
190A Ronnie Brown grn RC .60 1.50
190B Ronnie Brown white 4.00 10.00
191 Charlie Frye RC .50 1.25
192 Mark Bradley RC .50 1.25
193 Antrel Rolle RC .75 2.00
194 Roscoe Parrish RC .50 1.25
195 Ryan Moats RC .50 1.25
196 Andrew Walter RC .50 1.25
197 Troy Williamson RC .50 1.25
198 Cadillac Williams RC .50 1.25
199 Adam Jones RC .50 1.25
200 Braylon Edwards RC .50 1.25
201 Vernand Morency RC .50 1.25
202 Ryan Fitzpatrick RC .75 2.00
203 Heath Miller RC 1.00 2.50
204 Eric Shelton RC .50 1.25
205 Jason Campbell RC .40 1.00
206 David Pollack RC .50 1.25
207 Stefan LeFors RC .50 1.25
208 DeMarcus Ware RC 1.50 4.00
209 J.J. Arrington RC .60 1.50
210 Marion Barber RC .50 1.25
211 Samkon Gado RC .75 2.00
212 Roddy White RC .75 2.00
213 Brandon Jacobs RC .60 1.50
214 Mark Clayton RC .50 1.25
215 Alex Smith TE RC .50 1.25
216 Darren Sproles RC .75 2.00
217 Fabian Washington RC .50 1.25
218 Brandon Jones RC .60 1.50
219 Derrick Johnson RC .60 1.50
220 Dan Orlovsky RC .50 1.25
221 Aaron Rodgers RC 10.00 20.00
222 Cedric Houston RC .75 2.00
223 Reggie Brown RC .50 1.25
224 Scottie Vines RC .75 2.00
225 Willie Parker .30 .75
226 Matt Jones RC .50 1.25
227 Odell Thurman RC .75 2.00
228 Alvin Pearman RC .50 1.25
229 Chris Henry RC .60 1.50
230 Courtney Roby RC .50 1.25
231 Isaac Bruce .40 1.00
232 Warrick Dunn CL .20 .50
233 Willis McGahee CL .20 .50
234 Marcus Pollard .25 .60
235 Jason Taylor .30 .75
236 Joe Namath 2.50 6.00
237 Joe Montana 5.00 12.00
238 Barry Sanders 2.50 6.00
239 Jim Brown 2.00 5.00
240 Terry Bradshaw 2.00 5.00
241 Ahman Green .30 .75
242 Tiki Barber CL .25 .60
243 Julius Jones CL .20 .50
244 Daunte Culpepper .30 .75
245 Edgerrin James CL .25 .60
246 Trent Green 2.00 5.00
247 Dwight Freeney 2.00 5.00
248A Brett Favre 5.00 12.00
248B Brett Favre Ad Back 6.00 15.00
249 Marshall Faulk 2.50 6.00
250 Jerome Bettis 3.00 8.00
251 Nate Burleson 2.00 5.00
252 Brandon Lloyd 2.00 5.00
253 Randy Moss 2.50 6.00
254 Drew Bledsoe 2.50 6.00
255 Brandon Stokley 2.00 5.00
256 Takeo Spikes 2.00 5.00
257 Philip Rivers 3.00 8.00
258 Lito Sheppard 2.50 6.00
259 Jimmy Smith 2.50 6.00
260 Tatum Bell 2.00 5.00
261 Allen Rossum 2.00 5.00
262 Amani Toomer 2.00 5.00
263 Jabar Gaffney 2.00 5.00
264 Jonathan Ogden 2.50 6.00
265 John Abraham 2.00 5.00
266 Aaron Stecker 2.00 5.00
267 Jason Elam 2.00 5.00
268 Najeh Davenport 2.00 5.00
269 Alge Crumpler 2.50 6.00
270 Roy Williams S 2.00 5.00
271 Trent Dilfer 2.00 5.00
272 Anquan Boldin 2.00 5.00
273 Artose Pinner 2.00 5.00
274 David Garrard 2.00 5.00
275 Terry Glenn 2.00 5.00
276 Adam Archuleta 2.00 5.00
277 Jeremiah Trotter 2.00 5.00
278 Travis Henry 2.00 5.00
279 Rex Grossman 2.00 5.00
280 Maurice Morris 2.00 5.00
281 Mike Alstott 2.00 5.00
282 Justin Gage 2.00 5.00
283 Dennis Northcutt 2.00 5.00
284 David Givens 2.00 5.00
285 Dominic Rhodes 2.00 5.00
286 Gerald Ford 2.00 5.00
287 Ronald Reagan 2.00 5.00
288 John F. Kennedy 2.00 5.00
289 Ulysses S. Grant 2.00 5.00
CL1 Jumbo Checklist 1 .40 1.00
CL2 Jumbo Checklist 2 .40 1.00

2005 Topps Turkey Red Black

*VETERANS 1-245: 4X TO 10X BASIC CARDS
*VETS 1-245: .8X TO 2X BASIC AD BACKS
*ROOKIES: 1.2X TO 3X BASIC CARDS
*RETIRED 236-240: 1X TO 2.5X BASIC CARDS
*VETERANS 246-285: .5X TO 1.2X
*PRESIDENTS 286-289: .6X TO 1.5X
BLACK STATED ODDS 1:20 HOB/RET
190B Ronnie Brown Ad Back 6.00 15.00
248A Brett Favre
248B Brett Favre Ad Back 10.00 25.00

2005 Topps Turkey Red Gold

*VETERANS 1-245: 8X TO 20X BASIC CARDS
*VETS 1-245: 1.5X TO 4X BASIC AD BACKS
*ROOKIES: 2.5X TO 6X BASIC CARDS
*RETIRED 236-240: 2X TO 5X BASIC CARDS
*VETERANS 246-285: 1X TO 2.5X
*PRESIDENTS 286-289: 1.2X TO 3X
GOLD/50 ODDS 1:41 HOB, 1:42 RET
190B Ronnie Brown Ad Back 20.00 50.00
248A Brett Favre 20.00 50.00
248B Brett Favre Ad Back 20.00 50.00

2005 Topps Turkey Red Red

*VETERANS 1-245: 1.2X TO 3X BASIC CARDS
*VETS 1-245: .3X TO .8X BASIC AD BACKS
*ROOKIES: .6X TO 1.5X BASIC CARDS
*RETIRED 236-240: .4X TO 1X BASIC CARDS
*VETERANS 246-285: .15X TO .4X
*PRESIDENTS 286-289: .4X TO 1X
OVERALL PARALLEL ODDS 1:1
190B Ronnie Brown Ad Back 2.50 6.00
248A Brett Favre 2.50 6.00
248B Brett Favre Ad Back 3.00 8.00

2005 Topps Turkey Red White

*VETERANS 1-245: 1.5X TO 4X BASIC CARDS
*VETS 1-245: .4X TO 1X BASIC AD BACKS
*ROOKIES: .8X TO 2X BASIC CARDS
*RETIRED 236-240: .5X TO 1.2X BASIC CARDS
*VETERANS 246-285: .2X TO .5X
*PRESIDENTS 286-289: .5X TO 1.2X
STATED ODDS 1:4 HOB/RET

2005 Topps Turkey Red Autographs Gray

GROUP A ODDS 1:1514 H, 1:8042 R
GROUP B ODDS 1:1020 H, 1:4530 R
GROUP C ODDS 1:237 H, 1:1292 R
GROUP D ODDS 1:342 H, 1:2096 R
GROUP E ODDS 1:458 H, 1:2432 R
GROUP F ODDS 1:79 H, 1:1565 R
TRAAR Aaron Rodgers B 175.00 300.00
TRABB Bernard Berrian C 6.00 15.00
TRABE Braylon Edwards C 12.00 30.00
TRACB Craig Bragg C 6.00 15.00
TRACP Chad Pennington A 20.00 40.00
TRADJ Deacon Jones C 12.00 30.00
TRADS Darren Sproles D 12.00 30.00
TRADBO David Bowens F 4.00 10.00
TRAEC Earl Campbell A 20.00 50.00
TRAEH Ed Hartwell F 4.00 10.00
TRAEW Ernest Wilford E 4.00 10.00
TRAJB Jim Brown A 60.00 100.00
TRAJC Jason Campbell C 15.00 40.00
TRAJN Joe Namath A 60.00 100.00
TRAKO Kyle Orton 10.00 25.00
TRAMC Mark Clayton A 20.00 40.00
TRAMJ Matt Jones B 12.00 30.00
TRAMS Mark Simoneau F 5.00 12.00
TRAPM Peyton Manning A 75.00 135.00
TRARB Ronnie Brown A 60.00 100.00
TRARC Ronald Curry 6.00 15.00
TRARM Ryan Moats B 10.00 25.00
TRASL Stefan LeFors C 6.00 15.00
TRASM Santana Moss C 10.00 25.00
TRATB Terry Bradshaw A 60.00 100.00
TRATBR Tom Brady A 100.00 200.00

2005 Topps Turkey Red Autographs Red

RED/199 GROUP A ODDS 1:144 H, 1:765 R
RED/50 GROUP B ODDS 1: 353 H, 1:2165 R
*BLACK/50: .6X TO 1.5X REDS
BLACK/10 NOT PRICED DUE TO SCARCITY
BLACK GROUP A ODDS 1:566H, 1:3417R
BLACK GROUP B ODDS 1:2236H, 1:8089R
*GOLD/25: .8X TO 2X REDS
GOLD/5 NOT PRICED DUE TO SCARCITY
GOLD/25 GROUP A ODDS 1:1278H, 1:5430R
GOLD/5 GROUP B ODDS 1:7029H, 1:12,010R
*WHITE/25: .5X TO 1.2X REDS
*WHITE/99: .5X TO 1.2X REDS
WHITE/99 GROUP A ODDS 1:266H, 1:2120R
WHITE/25 GROUP B ODDS 1: 775H, 1:3570R
WOOD 1/1 ODDS 1:24,600H,1:24,628 R
TRAAR Aaron Rodgers/50 B 300.00 450.00
TRABB Bernard Berrian/199 A 6.00 15.00
TRABE Braylon Edwards/50 B 15.00 40.00
TRACB Craig Bragg/199 A 6.00 15.00
TRACP Chad Pennington/50 B 12.50 30.00
TRADJ Deacon Jones/50 B 15.00 40.00
TRADS Darren Sproles/199 12.00 30.00
TRADBO David Bowens/199 A 5.00 12.00
TRAEC Earl Campbell/50 B 30.00 50.00
TRAEH Ed Hartwell/199 A 5.00 12.00
TRAEW Ernest Wilford/199 A 6.00 15.00
TRAJB Jim Brown/50 B 60.00 100.00
TRAJC Jason Campbell/50 B 25.00 50.00
TRAJN Joe Namath/50 B 60.00 100.00
TRAKO Kyle Orton/50 B 12.50 30.00
TRAMC Mark Clayton/199 A 10.00 25.00
TRAMJ Matt Jones/50 B 15.00 40.00
TRAMS Mark Simoneau/199 A 5.00 12.00
TRAPM Peyton Manning/50 B 75.00 150.00
TRARB Ronnie Brown/50 B 40.00 80.00
TRARC Ronald Curry/199 A 5.00 12.00
TRARM Ryan Moats/199 A 8.00 20.00
TRASL Stefan LeFors/50 B 10.00 25.00
TRASM Santana Moss/50 B 12.50 30.00
TRATB Terry Bradshaw/50 B 60.00 100.00
TRATBR Tom Brady/50 B 150.00 250.00

2005 Topps Turkey Red B-18 Blankets Yellow

STATED ODDS 1:2 BOXES
*WHITE BACKGROUND: .4X TO 1X YELLOW
BF Brett Favre 10.00 25.00
CW Cadillac Williams 4.00 10.00
LT LaDainian Tomlinson 4.00 10.00
MV Michael Vick 6.00 15.00
PM Peyton Manning 8.00 20.00
RB Ronnie Brown 5.00 12.00
RM Randy Moss 4.00 10.00
TB Tom Brady 8.00 20.00

2005 Topps Turkey Red Cabinet

STATED ODDS 1:BOX
TRAL Abraham Lincoln 6.00 15.00
TRBC Bill Clinton 12.50 30.00
TRBF Brett Favre 15.00 40.00
TRBR Ben Roethlisberger 12.00 30.00
TRCP Carson Palmer 6.00 15.00
TRCW Cadillac Williams 5.00 12.00
TREM Eli Manning 12.00 30.00
TRJA John Adams 6.00 15.00
TRJJ Jack Johnson 6.00 15.00
TRLT LaDainian Tomlinson 8.00 20.00
TRMV Michael Vick 6.00 15.00
TRPM Peyton Manning 20.00 50.00
TRRB Ronnie Brown 6.00 15.00
TRRM Randy Moss 6.00 15.00
TRSA Shaun Alexander 5.00 12.00
TRTB Tom Brady 30.00 80.00

2005 Topps Turkey Red Cabinet Autographed Relics

OVERALL CABINET ODDS 1:2 BOXES
TRARBR Ben Roethlisberger/50 125.00 250.00
TRARCW Cadillac Williams/75 30.00 80.00
TRARDM Dan Marino/25 200.00 350.00
TRARJA J.J. Arrington/175 15.00 40.00
TRARJE John Elway/25 175.00 300.00
TRARJM Joe Montana/25 175.00 300.00
TRARKO Kyle Orton/100 25.00 50.00
TRARLT Lawrence Taylor/50 60.00 120.00
TRARMB Mark Bradley/175 10.00 25.00
TRARMC Mark Clayton/100 15.00 40.00
TRARMJ Matt Jones/100 25.00 60.00
TRARPM Peyton Manning/25 175.00 300.00
TRARRB Ronnie Brown/50 60.00 120.00
TRARTB Tom Brady/25 200.00 350.00
TRARTW Troy Williamson/75 20.00 50.00

2005 Topps Turkey Red Cut Signatures

UNPRICED CUT AU/1 ODDS 1:21,866 HOB

2005 Topps Turkey Red Relics Gray

STATED ODDS 1:67 HOB, 1:75 RET
*BLACK/99: .8X TO 2X BASIC CARDS
BLACK/99 ODDS 1:220 HOB, 1:278 RET
*GOLD/25: 1.2X TO 3X BASIC CARDS
GOLD/25 ODDS 1:1009 H, 1:1059 R
*RED/299: .5X TO 1.2X BASIC CARDS
RED/299 ODDS 1:84 HOB/RET
*WHITE/199: .6X TO 1.5X BASIC CARDS
WHITE/199 ODDS 1:86 HOB, 1:265 RET
UNPRICED WOOD/1 ODDS 1:25,689H,1:26,270R
TRRAJ Andre Johnson 4.00 10.00
TRRBR Ben Roethlisberger 12.50 30.00
TRRCB Chris Brown 4.00 10.00
TRRCC Chris Chambers 4.00 10.00
TRRCD Corey Dillon 4.00 10.00
TRRCJ Chad Johnson 5.00 12.00
TRRDB Drew Brees 5.00 12.00
TRRDC Daunte Culpepper 5.00 12.00
TRRDD Domanick Davis 4.00 10.00
TRRDM Deuce McAllister 4.00 10.00
TRRDCA David Carr 4.00 10.00
TRRHW Hines Ward 6.00 15.00
TRRIB Isaac Bruce 4.00 10.00
TRRJA John Abraham 4.00 10.00
TRRJL J.P. Losman 4.00 10.00
TRRJS Jeremy Shockey 5.00 12.00
TRRPH Priest Holmes 5.00 12.00
TRRRW Roy Williams S 5.00 12.00
TRRSA Shaun Alexander 6.00 15.00
TRRSD Stephen Davis 4.00 10.00
TRRTB Tom Brady 8.00 20.00
TRRTG Tony Gonzalez 4.00 10.00
TRRTH Torry Holt 5.00 12.00
TRRTS Terrell Suggs 4.00 10.00
TRRWD Warrick Dunn 4.00 10.00

2006 Topps Turkey Red

This 328-card set was released in November, 2006. The set was issued into the hobby eight-card packs, with a $4 SRP, which came 24 packs to a box. Cards numbered 1-180 and 231-315 are veterans while cards numbered 181-230 feature 2006 rookies. Some of the cards in this set were produced to shorter quantities than the other cards in the set are those cards are notated in our checklist with an SP.

COMPLETE SET (328) 100.00 200.00
COMP.SET w/o SP's (274) 20.00 50.00
UNPRICED PRINT PLATES #'d TO 1
UNPRICED SUEDE PRINT RUN 1
1 LaVar Arrington .20 .50
2 Heath Miller .20 .50
3 Antwaan Randle El .20 .50
4 Derrick Mason .20 .50
5 Deshaun Foster .25 .60
6 Andre Johnson .25 .60
7 Jonathan Vilma .20 .50
8 Trent Dilfer .20 .50
9 Tatum Bell .20 .50
10 Bubba Franks .20 .50
11 T.J. Houshmandzadeh .20 .50
12 Adam Vinatieri .20 .50
13 Quentin Jammer .20 .50
14 Jim Kleinsasser .20 .50
15 Priest Holmes .20 .50
16 Courtney Roby .20 .50
17 Chris Simms .20 .50
18 Terry Glenn .25 .60
19 Jonathan Ogden .25 .60
20 Andrew Walter .20 .50
21 Lito Sheppard .25 .60
22 Kevan Barlow .20 .50
23 Santana Moss .25 .60
24 Kelly Holcomb .20 .50
25 Thomas Jones .20 .50
26 Dennis Northcutt .20 .50
27 Najeh Davenport .20 .50
28 Edgerrin James .25 .60
29 Kevin Curtis .25 .60
30 Brian Griese .20 .50
31 Jason Taylor .25 .60
32 T.J. Duckett .20 .50
33 Antonio Bryant .20 .50
34 Donald Driver .25 .60
35 Brian Westbrook .20 .50
36 Lofa Tatupu .20 .50
37 Ben Troupe .20 .50
38 Chris Cooley .20 .50
39 Josh McCown .20 .50
40 Chris Perry .25 .60
41 Joe Horn .20 .50
42 Kyle Boller .20 .50
43 Keyshawn Johnson .25 .60
44 Frank Gore .25 .60
45 Terence Newman .20 .50
46 Devery Henderson .20 .50
47 Michael Strahan .25 .60
48 Ladell Betts .20 .50
49 Patrick Ramsey .25 .60
50 Anquan Boldin .20 .50
51 Nathan Vasher .20 .50
52 Dominic Rhodes .20 .50
53 Travis Minor .20 .50
54 Torry Holt .25 .60
55 Sam Gado .20 .50
56 Fred Taylor .20 .50
57 Braylon Edwards .20 .50
58 Tyrone Calico .20 .50
59 Derrick Burgess .20 .50
60 Chester Taylor .25 .60
61 Julius Peppers .25 .60
62 L.J. Smith .20 .50
63 Keenan McCardell .25 .60
64 Lee Evans .25 .60
65 Champ Bailey .25 .60
66 Alex Smith QB .25 .60
67 Tedy Bruschi .25 .60
68 Roddy White .20 .50
69 Marty Booker .20 .50
70 Fred Smoot .20 .50
71 A.J. Feeley .20 .50
72 Kellen Winslow .20 .50
73 Curtis Martin .25 .60
74 Ronald Curry .20 .50
75 Sam Madison .20 .50
76 Keary Colbert .20 .50
77 Marcus Pollard .20 .50
78 James Farrior .20 .50
79 Travis Henry .20 .50
80 Samari Rolle .20 .50
81 Rodney Harrison .20 .50
82 Matt Schaub .20 .50
83 Philip Rivers .30 .75
84 DeMarcus Ware .25 .60
85 Reggie Wayne .25 .60
86 Derrick Johnson .20 .50
87 Travis Taylor .20 .50
88 Antonio Pierce .20 .50
89 Jamal Lewis .25 .60
90 Aaron Brooks .20 .50
91 Michael Pittman .20 .50
92 Jerricho Cotchery .20 .50
93 Shayne Graham .20 .50
94 Dante Hall .20 .50
95 Warrick Dunn .20 .50
96 Mewelde Moore .20 .50
97 Brandon Lloyd .20 .50
98 Chris Gamble .20 .50
99 Odell Thurman .20 .50
100 Osi Umenyiora .20 .50
101 Jerry Porter .20 .50
102 Brandon Stokley .20 .50
103 Clinton Portis .20 .50
104 Quentin Jammer .20 .50
105 Reuben Droughns .25 .60
106 Jason Campbell .20 .50
107 LaBrandon Toefield .20 .50
108 Nate Burleson .20 .50
109 Antrel Rolle .20 .50
110A Steve McNair PS .25 .60
110B Steve McNair YS .25 .60
111A Chad Johnson PBB .20 .50
111B Chad Johnson No PBB .20 .50
112 Steven Jackson .20 .50
113 Ron Dayne .25 .60
114 Deion Branch .20 .50
115 Ed Reed .25 .60
116 Ty Law .30 .75
117 Drew Bledsoe .25 .60
118 Chris McAlister .20 .50
119 Plaxico Burress .20 .50
120 Aaron Rodgers .75 2.00
121 Tony Gonzalez .25 .60
122 David Givens .25 .60
123 Michael Vick .25 .60
124 Antonio Gates .30 .75
125 Darrell Jackson .25 .60
126 Adam Jones .20 .50
127 LaDainian Tomlinson CL .25 .60
128 Chad Pennington .20 .50
129 Kevin Faulk .20 .50
130 Isaac Bruce .30 .75
131 Tom Brady CL .75 2.00
132 Deuce McAllister .25 .60
133 Laveranues Coles .20 .50
134 Donnie Edwards .20 .50
135 Brian Urlacher CL .25 .60
136 Dallas Clark .20 .50
137 Drew Bennett .25 .60
138 Domanick Davis .20 .50
139 Cadillac Williams CL .20 .50
140 David Garrard .20 .50
141 Shaun Alexander CL .15 .40
142 Troy Williamson .20 .50
143 Steve Smith CL .25 .60
144 Jake Plummer .20 .50
145 Carson Palmer CL .20 .50
146 DeAngelo Hall .20 .50
147 Michael Vick CL .20 .50
148 Kyle Vanden Bosch .20 .50
149 Larry Johnson CL .15 .40
150 LaDainian Tomlinson .30 .75
151 Dunta Robinson .20 .50
152 Muhsin Muhammad .20 .50
153 Steven Jackson CL .15 .40
154 David Pollack .20 .50
155 Mark Brunell .25 .60
156 Donovan McNabb .25 .60
157 Jeremy Shockey .20 .50
158 Corey Dillon .20 .50
159 Mark Clayton .20 .50
160 Vincent Jackson .20 .50
161 Kurt Warner .25 .60
162 Marcus Robinson .20 .50
163 Takeo Spikes .20 .50
164 Vernand Morency .20 .50
165 J.P. Losman .25 .60
166 Matt Jones .20 .50
167 Rod Smith .25 .60
168 Steve Smith .30 .75
169 Michael Vick .25 .60
170 Mike Vanderjagt .20 .50
171 Amani Toomer .20 .50
172 Deltha O'Neal .20 .50
173 Michael Jenkins .20 .50
174 David Carr .20 .50
175 Chris Brown .20 .50
176 Kevin Jones .20 .50
177 Roy Williams S .20 .50
178 Marvin Harrison .25 .60
179 Drew Brees .30 .75
180 John Abraham .20 .50
181 Joseph Addai RC SP 1.25 3.00
182 Sinorice Moss RC SP 1.25 3.00
183A Vince Young PS RC .50 1.25
183B Vince Young OS SP 1.25 3.00
184 Vernon Davis RC SP 1.50 4.00
185 Brandon Williams RC SP 1.25 3.00
186 Derek Hagan RC SP 1.50 4.00
187 Brian Calhoun RC SP 1.25 3.00
188 Mario Williams RC SP 2.00 5.00
189 DeAngelo Williams RC SP 1.50 4.00
190 Jay Cutler RC SP 1.50 4.00
191 A.J. Hawk RC SP 1.50 4.00
192 Reggie Bush RC .75 2.00
193 Laurence Maroney RC SP 1.25 3.00
194 D'Brickashaw Ferguson RC SP 1.25 3.00
195 Jason Avant RC SP 1.25 3.00
196 Brodie Croyle RC SP 1.25 3.00
197 Michael Huff RC SP 1.50 4.00
198 LenDale White RC SP 1.25 3.00
199 Marcedes Lewis RC SP 1.25 3.00
200 Travis Wilson RC SP 1.25 3.00
201 Haloti Ngata RC SP 1.50 4.00
202 Greg Jennings RC SP 2.00 5.00
203 Leon Washington RC SP 1.25 3.00
204 Tamba Hali RC SP 2.00 5.00
205 Santonio Holmes RC SP 1.50 4.00
206 Jerome Harrison RC SP 1.25 3.00
207 Tarvaris Jackson RC SP 1.25 3.00
208 Mathias Kiwanuka RC SP 2.00 5.00
209 Omar Jacobs RC SP 1.25 3.00
210 Alan Zemaitis RC SP 1.25 3.00
211 Demetrius Williams RC SP 1.25 3.00
212 Bobby Carpenter RC SP 1.25 3.00
213 Tye Hill RC SP 1.25 3.00
214 Chad Jackson RC SP 1.25 3.00
215 Joe Klopfenstein RC SP 1.25 3.00
216 Kamerion Wimbley RC SP 1.50 4.00
217 Michael Robinson RC SP 1.25 3.00
218 David Thomas RC SP 1.25 3.00
219 Charlie Whitehurst RC SP 1.25 3.00
220 Jerious Norwood RC SP 1.25 3.00
221 Druce Gradkowski RC SP 1.50 4.00
222 Kellen Clemens RC SP 1.25 3.00
223 Thomas Howard RC SP 1.25 3.00
224 Anthony Fasano RC SP 1.25 3.00
225 Maurice Drew RC SP 2.00 5.00
226 Antonio Cromartie RC SP 1.50 4.00
227 Mike Bell RC SP 1.25 3.00
228 D'Qwell Jackson RC SP 1.25 3.00
229A Matt Leinart TIB RC .50 1.25
229B Matt Leinart SIB SP 1.25 3.00
230 Maurice Stovall RC SP 1.25 3.00
231A Carson Palmer WJ .25 .60
231B Carson Palmer BJ .25 .60
232 Courtney Anderson .20 .50
233 D.J. Williams .20 .50
234 Chris Chambers .20 .50
235 Zach Thomas .25 .60
236 Reggie Brown .20 .50
237 Cadillac Williams .25 .60
238 Randy McMichael .20 .50
239 Brian Urlacher .30 .75
240 Cedric Houston .20 .50
241 Marc Bulger .20 .50
242 Mike Anderson .20 .50
243 Allen Rossum .20 .50
244 William Henderson .20 .50
245 Eddie Kennison .20 .50
246 Adam Archuleta .20 .50
247 Ryan Moats .20 .50
248 D.J. Hackett .20 .50
249 Marion Barber .25 .60
250 Mike Alstott .20 .50
251 Shawne Merriman .25 .60
252 Byron Leftwich .20 .50
253 Dan Morgan .20 .50
254 Ronnie Brown .25 .60
255 Mark Bradley .20 .50
256 Mike Williams .20 .50
257 Ronde Barber .20 .50
258 Bernard Berrian .20 .50
259 Gibril Wilson .20 .50
260 Scottie Vines .20 .50
261 Rex Grossman .20 .50
262 Daniel Graham .20 .50
263 Ernest Wilford .20 .50
264 Javon Walker .25 .60
265 Corey Webster .20 .50
266 Jon Kitna .20 .50
267 Arnaz Battle .20 .50
268 Robert Ferguson SP 1.50 4.00
269 Cedric Benson .20 .50
270 Michael Clayton .20 .50
271 Brandon Jacobs .20 .50
272 Jason Witten SP 2.00 5.00
273A Randy Moss BS .25 .60
273B Randy Moss PS .25 .60
274 Daunte Culpepper SP 2.00 5.00
275 Ronnie Brown .25 .60
276 Dwight Freeney .20 .50
277 LaMont Jordan .25 .60
278 Jeremiah Trotter .20 .50
279A Hines Ward PO sky .25 .60
279B Hines Ward BY sky .25 .60
280A Tom Brady PBB 1.00 2.50
280B Tom Brady No PBB 1.00 2.50
281 Charles Woodson .30 .75
282A Shaun Alexander GJ .20 .50
282B Shaun Alexander WJ .20 .50
283 Eric Moulds .20 .50
284A Ben Roethlisberger BS .40 1.00
284B Ben Roethlisberger PS .40 1.00
285 Matt Hasselbeck .20 .50
286 Willis McGahee .20 .50
287 Carlos Rogers .20 .50
288 Brett Favre .60 1.50
289 Larry Fitzgerald .25 .60
290 Billy Volek .20 .50
291 Julius Jones .20 .50
292 Trent Green .20 .50
293 Ashley Lelie .20 .50
294 Eli Manning .25 .60
295 Alge Crumpler .25 .60
296 Rudi Johnson .20 .50
297 Troy Polamalu .30 .75
298 Roy Williams WR .20 .50
299 Willie Parker .25 .60
300 Jake Delhomme .20 .50
301 Champ Bailey .25 .60
302 Ahman Green .25 .60
303 Robert Gallery .20 .50
304 Todd Heap .20 .50
305 Joey Harrington .20 .50
306 Terrell Owens .25 .60
307 Joey Galloway .25 .60
308A Larry Johnson OS .20 .50
308A Larry Johnson PS .20 .50
309 Brian Dawkins .30 .75
310 Ray Lewis .30 .75
311A Tiki Barber OS .25 .60
311B Tiki Barber BS SP 2.00 5.00
312 Donte Stallworth .20 .50
313 Eric Parker .20 .50
314 Charlie Frye .25 .60
315A Peyton Manning BYS .75 2.00
315B Peyton Manning OS SP 15.00 40.00

2006 Topps Turkey Red Black

*VETERANS: 3X TO 8X BASIC CARDS
*VETERAN SPs: .5X TO 1.2X BASIC CARDS
*ROOKIES: 1X TO 2.5X BASIC CARDS
*ROOKIE SPs: .4X TO 1X BASIC CARDS
BLACK STATED ODDS 1:24

2006 Topps Turkey Red Gold

*VETERANS: 6X TO 15X BASIC CARDS
*VETERAN SPs: 1X TO 2.5X BASIC CARDS
*ROOKIES: 2.5X TO 6X BASIC CARDS
*ROOKIE SPs: 1X TO 2.5X BASIC CARDS
GOLD/50 STATED ODDS 1:78

2006 Topps Turkey Red Red

*VETERANS: 1.2X TO 3X BASIC CARDS
*VETERAN SPs: .2X TO .5X BASIC CARDS
*ROOKIES: .5X TO 1.2X BASIC CARDS
*ROOKIE SPs: .2X TO .5X BASIC CARDS
OVERALL PARALLEL ODDS 1:1

2006 Topps Turkey Red Suede

UNPRICED SUEDE PRINT RUN 1

2006 Topps Turkey Red White

*VETERANS: 1.5X TO 4X BASIC CARDS
*VETERAN SPs: .25X TO .6X BASIC CARDS
*ROOKIES: .6X TO 1.5X BASIC CARDS
*ROOKIE SPs: .25X TO .6X BASIC CARDS
STATED ODDS 1:4

2006 Topps Turkey Red Cabinet

UNPRICED SUEDE PRINT RUN 1
AH A.J. Hawk 1.50 4.00
BF Brett Favre 8.00 20.00
BR Ben Roethlisberger 5.00 12.00
CJ Chad Johnson 2.50 6.00
CJA Chad Jackson 1.25 3.00
CP Carson Palmer 3.00 8.00
CW Cadillac Williams 3.00 8.00
DC Daunte Culpepper 3.00 8.00
DW DeAngelo Williams 1.50 4.00
EJ Edgerrin James 3.00 8.00
HW Hines Ward 3.00 8.00
JA Joseph Addai 1.25 3.00
JC Jay Cutler 1.50 4.00
LJ Larry Johnson 2.50 6.00
LM Laurence Maroney 1.25 3.00
LT LaDainian Tomlinson 4.00 10.00
LW LenDale White 1.25 3.00
MH Marvin Harrison 3.00 8.00
ML Matt Leinart 1.25 3.00
MW Mario Williams 2.00 5.00
PM Peyton Manning 10.00 25.00
RB Ronnie Brown 3.00 8.00
RBU Reggie Bush 2.00 5.00
RM Randy Moss 3.00 8.00
SA Shaun Alexander 2.50 6.00
SH Santonio Holmes 1.50 4.00
SM Sinorice Moss 1.25 3.00
TB Tiki Barber 3.00 8.00
TBR Tom Brady 12.00 30.00
TO Terrell Owens 3.00 8.00
VD Vernon Davis 1.50 4.00
VY Vince Young 1.25 3.00

2006 Topps Turkey Red Cabinet Autographed Relics

STATED PRINT RUN 75-500
CJ Chad Jackson/500 10.00 25.00
CW Charlie Whitehurst/500 10.00 25.00
ES Emmitt Smith/75 125.00 250.00
JM Joe Montana/75 75.00 150.00
LM Laurence Maroney/300 12.00 30.00
LT LaDainian Tomlinson/75 90.00 150.00
MD Maurice Drew/500 12.00 30.00
ML Matt Leinart/150 15.00 40.00
PM Peyton Manning/75 100.00 200.00
RB Reggie Bush/75 15.00 40.00
SH Santonio Holmes/150 15.00 40.00
TB Tatum Bell/225 15.00 30.00
VD Vernon Davis/225 15.00 40.00
VY Vince Young/150 15.00 40.00

2006 Topps Turkey Red Cabinet Autographed Relics Duals

STATED PRINT RUN 25 SER.#'d SETS
UNPRICED SUEDE PRINT RUN 1
BS R.Bush/E.Smith 100.00 200.00
ML P.Manning/M.Leinart 150.00 300.00
MM J.Montana/P.Manning 300.00 450.00
TB L.Tomlinson/R.Bush 100.00 200.00
YL V.Young/M.Leinart 40.00 100.00

2006 Topps Turkey Red Autographs Red

GROUP B/199 ODDS 1:308
GROUP A/50 ODDS 1:720
*WHITE/25-99: .5X TO 1.2X RED/50-199
*BLACK/50: .6X TO 1.5X RED/199
*GOLD/25: .8X TO 2X RED/199
*GRAY GRP E-G: .4X TO 1X RED/199
*GRAY GRP B-C: .5X TO 1.2X RED/199
*GRAY GRP B-C: .4X TO 1X RED/50
*GRAY GRP A: .5X TO 1.2X RED/50
AH A.J. Hawk/50 10.00 25.00
BF Brett Favre/50 90.00 150.00
BM Brandon Marshall/199 8.00 20.00
BW Brandon Williams/199 5.00 12.00
CG Chad Greenway/199 8.00 20.00
CJ Chad Jackson/199 5.00 12.00
DW DeAngelo Williams/50 12.00 30.00
DWI Demetrius Williams/199 5.00 12.00
ES Emmitt Smith/50 75.00 150.00
JA Joseph Addai/50 8.00 20.00
JC Jay Cutler/50 10.00 25.00
JE John Elway/50 75.00 150.00
JM Joe Montana/50 90.00 150.00
LM Laurence Maroney/199 5.00 12.00
LW LenDale White/199 5.00 12.00
MD Maurice Drew/50 12.00 30.00
MK Mathias Kiwanuka/50 12.00 30.00
ML Matt Leinart/50 8.00 20.00
MLE Marcedes Lewis/199 5.00 12.00
MW Mario Williams/199 8.00 20.00
PM Peyton Manning/50 60.00 120.00
RB Reggie Bush/50 20.00 50.00
SH Santonio Holmes/199 6.00 15.00
SM Sinorice Moss/199 5.00 12.00
TW Travis Wilson/199 5.00 12.00
VY Vince Young/50 15.00 40.00
WR Willie Reid/199 6.00 15.00

2006 Topps Turkey Red Relics Gray

*BLACK/99: .8X TO 2X GRAY RELIC
BLACK/99 STATED ODDS 1:524
*GOLD/25: 1.2X TO 3X GRAY RELIC
GOLD/25 STATED ODDS 1:2144
*RED/399: .5X TO 1.2X GRAY RELIC
RED/399 STATED ODDS 1:83
UNPRICED SUEDE PRINT RUN 1
*WHITE/199: .6X TO 1.5X GRAY RELIC
WHITE/199 STATED ODDS 1:260
AB Anquan Boldin 2.00 5.00
AH A.J. Hawk 2.50 6.00
BU Brian Urlacher 3.00 8.00
CC Chris Chambers 2.00 5.00
DD Domanick Davis 2.00 5.00
EM Eric Moulds 2.00 5.00
FG Frank Gore 2.50 6.00
JV Jonathan Vilma 2.00 5.00
LA LaVar Arrington 2.00 5.00
MB Marc Bulger 2.00 5.00
MC Michael Clayton 2.00 5.00
MF Marshall Faulk 2.50 6.00
MH Marvin Harrison 2.50 6.00
MJ Matt Jones 2.00 5.00
ML Matt Leinart 2.00 5.00
RB Reggie Bush 3.00 8.00
RL Ray Lewis 3.00 8.00
SD Stephen Davis 2.00 5.00
SH Santonio Holmes 2.50 6.00
SJ Steven Jackson 2.00 5.00
TB Tatum Bell 2.00 5.00
TBR Tom Brady 10.00 25.00
TG Trent Green 2.00 5.00
VD Vernon Davis 2.50 6.00
VY Vince Young 2.00 5.00

2006 Topps Turkey Red B-18 Blankets White

*YELLOW: .4X TO 1X WHITE
BR Ben Roethlisberger 4.00 10.00
CP Carson Palmer 2.50 6.00
LT LaDainian Tomlinson 3.00 8.00
ML Matt Leinart .75 2.00
PM Peyton Manning 8.00 20.00
RB Reggie Bush 1.25 3.00
SA Shaun Alexander 2.00 5.00
TB Tiki Barber 2.50 6.00
TB Tom Brady 10.00 25.00
VY Vince Young .75 2.00

2012 Topps Turkey Red

*MINI: .5X TO 1.2X BASIC CARDS
1A A.Luck set to pass 10.00 25.00
1B A.Luck SP passing 30.00 60.00
2 Joe Adams .50 1.25
3 T.Y. Hilton 1.00 2.50
4 Melvin Ingram .50 1.25
5 David DeCastro .50 1.25
6 Case Keenum 1.00 2.50
7 Zach Brown .50 1.25
8 Mohamed Sanu .75 2.00
9 Nick Perry .60 1.50
10A D.Wilson yellow sky .50 1.25
10B D.Wilson SP red sky 1.25 3.00
11 Nick Foles 1.25 3.00
12 Brandon Bolden .50 1.25
13 LaVon Brazill .75 2.00
14 Nick Toon .50 1.25
15 Quinton Coples .50 1.25
16 Brock Osweiler .50 1.25
17 Stephon Gilmore .60 1.50
18 Chris Polk .50 1.25
19 Jarius Wright .50 1.25
20 Morris Claiborne .50 1.25
21 Lamar Miller .75 2.00
22 Ronnie Hillman .50 1.25
23 Courtney Upshaw .60 1.50
24 Dan Herron .50 1.25
25 Brian Quick .50 1.25
26 LaMichael James .50 1.25
27 Robert Turbin .50 1.25
28 Dwight Bentley .60 1.50
29 Mychal Kendricks .75 2.00
30A B.Weeden dropback 1.25 3.00
30B B.Weeden SP pass 3.00 8.00
31 Cyrus Gray .50 1.25
32 Chandler Jones .50 1.25
33 Dwayne Allen .50 1.25
34 Alfred Morris .50 1.25
35 Travis Benjamin .50 1.25
36 Kendall Reyes .50 1.25
37 Marvin McNutt .50 1.25
38 Juron Criner .50 1.25
39 Jerel Worthy .50 1.25
40A Michael Floyd left .50 1.25
40B M.Floyd SP right 1.25 3.00
41 Chandler Harnish .50 1.25
42 Michael Egnew .50 1.25
43 Harrison Smith .50 1.25
44 Whitney Mercilus .50 1.25
45 Jared Crick .50 1.25
46 Dre Kirkpatrick .50 1.25
47 Jeff Fuller .50 1.25
48 Shea McClellin .60 1.50
49 Brandon Taylor .50 1.25
50A Trent Richardson run .50 1.25
50B T.Richardson SP catch 1.25 3.00
51 Ryan Lindley .50 1.25
52 Matt Kalil .50 1.25
53 Jermaine Kearse .75 2.00
54 T.J. Graham .50 1.25
55 Stephen Hill .50 1.25
56 Bobby Wagner .75 2.00
57 Dwight Jones .50 1.25
58 Vinny Curry .60 1.50
59 Coby Fleener .50 1.25
60A Ryan Tannehill right .75 2.00
60B R.Tannehill SP fwd 1.50 4.00
61 Michael Brockers .50 1.25
62 A.J. Jenkins .50 1.25
63 Kirk Cousins 2.00 5.00
64 Ryan Broyles .50 1.25
65 DeVier Posey .50 1.25
66 Marvin Jones .50 1.25
67 Andre Branch .50 1.25
68 Lavonte David .75 2.00
69 Rishard Matthews .50 1.25
70A Justin Blackmon run .50 1.25
70B J.Blackmon SP cut 1.25 3.00
71 Alshon Jeffery 1.25 3.00
72 Josh Gordon 1.25 3.00
73 Isaiah Pead .50 1.25
74 Bruce Irvin .60 1.50
75 Luke Kuechly 1.25 3.00
76 Kellen Moore .60 1.50
77 Fletcher Cox .75 2.00
78 Chris Rainey .50 1.25
79 Bernard Pierce .50 1.25
80A Doug Martin run .75 2.00
80B Doug Martin SP catch 2.00 5.00
81 Dont'a Hightower .75 2.00
82 Vick Ballard .60 1.50

83 Dontari Poe .50 1.25
84 Trumaine Johnson .50 1.25
85A Kendall Wright catch .50 1.25
85B Kendall Wright SP run 1.25 3.00
86 Orson Charles .50 1.25
87 Devon Still .60 1.50
88 Derek Wolfe .60 1.50
89 Rueben Randle .50 1.25
90 Mark Barron .50 1.25
91 Janoris Jenkins .60 1.50
92 Greg Childs .50 1.25
93 Keshawn Martin .60 1.50
94 Devon Wylie .50 1.25
95 Tavon Wilson .60 1.50
96 Jeff Demps .60 1.50
97 Bobby Rainey .50 1.25
98 Chris Givens .50 1.25
99 Russell Wilson 8.00 20.00
100A Robert Griffin III GB 3.00 8.00
100B Robert Griffin III SP YB 8.00 20.00

2012 Topps Turkey Red Autographs

ONE AUTOGRAPH PER BOX
STATED PRINT RUN 5-500
3 T.Y. Hilton/50 6.00 15.00
4 Melvin Ingram/50 3.00 8.00
5 David DeCastro/169 2.50 6.00
6 Case Keenum/169 12.00 30.00
14 Nick Toon/50 3.00 8.00
15 Quinton Coples/50 3.00 8.00
22 Ronnie Hillman/50 3.00 8.00
31 Cyrus Gray/50 3.00 8.00
33 Dwayne Allen/50 3.00 8.00
34 Alfred Morris/50 3.00 8.00
35 Travis Benjamin/169 2.50 6.00
37 Marvin McNutt/500 2.00 5.00
38 Juron Criner/50 3.00 8.00
41 Chandler Harnish/50 3.00 8.00
42 Michael Egnew/50 3.00 8.00
47 Jeff Fuller/169 2.50 6.00
51 Ryan Lindley/50 3.00 8.00
54 T.J. Graham/50 3.00 8.00
59 Coby Fleener/50 3.00 8.00
64 Ryan Broyles/50 3.00 8.00
65 DeVier Posey/50 3.00 8.00
66 Marvin Jones/500 2.00 5.00
75 Luke Kuechly/50 10.00 25.00
78 Chris Rainey/50 3.00 8.00
82 Vick Ballard/299 3.00 8.00
83 Dontari Poe/169 2.50 6.00
87 Devon Still/169 3.00 8.00
90 Mark Barron/444 2.00 5.00
91 Janoris Jenkins/500 2.50 6.00
103 Jarius Wright/50 3.00 8.00
107 Dre Kirkpatrick/50 3.00 8.00
108 Jermaine Kearse/154 6.00 15.00

2013 Topps Turkey Red

*MINI: .5X TO 1.2X BASIC CARDS
1A Eddie Lacy run 3.00 8.00
1B Eddie Lacy SP catch 8.00 20.00
2 Onterio McCalebb .60 1.50
3 Tyler Wilson .50 1.25
4A EJ Manuel scrmbl .50 1.25
4B EJ Manuel SP pass 1.25 3.00
5A C.Patterson right .50 1.25
5B C.Patterson SP left 1.25 3.00
6 Tyler Bray .50 1.25
7 Joseph Randle .50 1.25
8 Sheldon Richardson .50 1.25
9 Knile Davis .50 1.25
10 Ezekiel Ansah .50 1.25
11 Marcus Lattimore .50 1.25
12 Vance McDonald .60 1.50
13 Robert Lester .50 1.25
14 Chris Gragg .50 1.25
15 Bjoern Werner .50 1.25
16 Chase Thomas .50 1.25
17 Jamar Taylor .50 1.25
18A Montee Ball run .50 1.25
18B M.Ball SP catch 1.25 3.00
19 Mike Glennon .50 1.25
20 Chance Warmack .50 1.25
21 Alex Okafor .50 1.25
22 Corey Fuller .50 1.25
23 Jesse Williams .75 2.00
24 Landry Jones .50 1.25
25 Miguel Maysonet .50 1.25
26 Jordan Poyer .50 1.25
27 Giovani Bernard .50 1.25
28 Tyler Eifert .50 1.25
29 Dion Sims .50 1.25
30 Khaseem Greene .50 1.25
31 Christine Michael .50 1.25
32 Rodney Smith .50 1.25
33 Rex Burkhead .60 1.50
34 Chris Thompson .50 1.25
35 Eric Fisher .50 1.25
36 Brandon Jenkins .60 1.50
37 Justin Hunter .50 1.25
38 Aaron Mellette .50 1.25
39 Johnathan Cyprien .50 1.25
40A Manti Te'o cutting .60 1.50
40B Manti Te'o SP frwrd 1.50 4.00
41A Tavon Austin run .60 1.50
41B Tavon Austin SP catch 1.50 4.00
42 Keenan Allen 1.00 2.50
43 Dan Buckner .50 1.25
44 Nico Johnson .60 1.50
45 Blidi Wreh-Wilson .60 1.50
46 Kayvon Webster .60 1.50
47A Matt Barkley scrmbl .50 1.25
47B Matt Barkley SP pass 1.25 3.00
48 Ryan Swope .50 1.25
49 Stepfan Taylor .50 1.25
50 Barrett Jones .50 1.25
51 D.J. Harper .60 1.50
52 Jordan Reed .75 2.00
53 John Wetzel .60 1.50
54 Zac Dysert .50 1.25
55 Terrance Williams .50 1.25
56 Markus Wheaton .50 1.25
57 Johnathan Franklin .50 1.25
58 Xavier Rhodes .50 1.25
59 John Simon .75 2.00
60 Kenny Stills .50 1.25
61 Kenbrell Thompkins .75 2.00
62 Zach Ertz 1.00 2.50
63 Gavin Escobar .50 1.25
64 Shawn Williams .50 1.25
65 Kenjon Barner .50 1.25
66 Stedman Bailey .50 1.25
67 Le'Veon Bell 1.50 4.00
68 Dee Milliner .50 1.25
69 Robert Woods .75 2.00
70 Matt Scott .50 1.25
71 Dennis Johnson .50 1.25
72 Sam Montgomery .50 1.25
73 Sharrif Floyd .50 1.25
74 Barkevious Mingo .50 1.25
75 Mike Gillislee .50 1.25
76 Tavarres King .50 1.25
77 T.J. McDonald .50 1.25
78 Datone Jones .50 1.25
79 Ryan Nassib .50 1.25
80 Quinton Patton .50 1.25
81 Tyrone Goard .50 1.25
82 Luke Joeckel .50 1.25
83 Conner Vernon .50 1.25
84 Denard Robinson .50 1.25
85 Dion Jordan .50 1.25
86 Philip Lutzenkirchen .75 2.00
87 Johnathan Hankins .50 1.25
88 Marcus Davis .50 1.25
89 Aaron Dobson .50 1.25
90 Theo Riddick .50 1.25
91A Geno Smith scrmbl .50 1.25
91B G.Smith SP drop back 1.25 3.00
92 Da'Rick Rogers .50 1.25
93 Marquise Goodwin .50 1.25
94 John Jenkins .50 1.25
95A Tyrann Mathieu white .75 2.00
95B Tyrann Mathieu SP red 2.00 5.00
96 Ray Graham .50 1.25
97A DeAndre Hopkins run 1.25 3.00
97B D.Hopkins SP catch 3.00 8.00
98 Arthur Brown .50 1.25
99 Andre Ellington .50 1.25
100 Desmond Trufant .50 1.25

2013 Topps Turkey Red Autographs

E PER BOX
1 Eddie Lacy
2 Onterio McCalebb 3.00 8.00
4 EJ Manuel
5 Cordarrelle Patterson
7 Joseph Randle 2.50 6.00
9 Knile Davis 2.50 6.00
11 Marcus Lattimore 8.00 20.00
13 Robert Lester 4.00 10.00
14 Chris Gragg 2.50 6.00
15 Bjoern Werner 2.50 6.00
16 Chase Thomas 3.00 8.00
17 Jamar Taylor 2.50 6.00
18 Montee Ball 2.50 6.00
20 Chance Warmack 2.50 6.00
21 Alex Okafor 2.50 6.00
22 Corey Fuller 2.50 6.00
23 Jesse Williams 4.00 10.00
24 Landry Jones 2.50 6.00
25 Miguel Maysonet 3.00 8.00
26 Jordan Poyer 2.50 6.00
27 Giovani Bernard 2.50 6.00
28 Tyler Eifert
29 Dion Sims 2.50 6.00
30 Khaseem Greene 5.00 12.00
31 Christine Michael 2.50 6.00
32 Rodney Smith 2.50 6.00
34 Chris Thompson 2.50 6.00
36 Brandon Jenkins 4.00 10.00
37 Justin Hunter 2.50 6.00
38 Aaron Mellette 4.00 10.00
39 Johnathan Cyprien 2.50 6.00
40 Manti Te'o
41 Tavon Austin 3.00 8.00
42 Keenan Allen 5.00 12.00
43 Dan Buckner 2.50 6.00
44 Nico Johnson 4.00 10.00
45 Blidi Wreh-Wilson 3.00 8.00
46 Kayvon Webster 4.00 10.00
47 Matt Barkley 2.50 6.00
48 Ryan Swope 2.50 6.00
49 Stepfan Taylor 2.50 6.00
50 Barrett Jones 4.00 10.00
51 D.J. Harper 3.00 8.00
52 Jordan Reed 6.00 15.00
56 Markus Wheaton 2.50 6.00
59 John Simon 4.00 10.00
60 Kenny Stills 2.50 6.00
61 Kenbrell Thompkins 4.00 10.00
62 Zach Ertz 5.00 12.00
63 Gavin Escobar 2.50 6.00
66 Stedman Bailey 2.50 6.00
67 Le'Veon Bell
68 Dee Milliner 2.50 6.00
70 Matt Scott 2.50 6.00
72 Sam Montgomery 2.50 6.00
73 Sharrif Floyd 6.00 15.00
74 Barkevious Mingo 2.50 6.00
75 Mike Gillislee 2.50 6.00
77 T.J. McDonald 2.50 6.00
78 Datone Jones 2.50 6.00
85 Dion Jordan 2.50 6.00
87 Johnathan Hankins 2.50 6.00
88 Marcus Davis 2.50 6.00
89 Aaron Dobson
91 Geno Smith
92 Da'Rick Rogers 2.50 6.00
94 John Jenkins 3.00 8.00
96 Ray Graham 3.00 8.00
97 DeAndre Hopkins
100 Desmond Trufant 2.50 6.00

2014 Topps Turkey Red

1A Johnny Manziel .75 2.00
1B Johnny Manziel SP
2 Jarvis Landry 1.00 2.50
3 Will Sutton .60 1.50
4 Michael Sam .50 1.25
5 Ryan Shazier .75 2.00
6A Derek Carr 3.00 8.00
6B Derek Carr SP
7 Timmy Jernigan .50 1.25
8 Michael Campanaro .50 1.25
9 Brandin Cooks .75 2.00
10 Arthur Lynch .50 1.25
11 Devonta Freeman .75 2.00
12 Tom Savage .50 1.25
13 Stephen Morris .50 1.25
14 Darqueze Dennard .60 1.50
15 Jared Abbrederis .50 1.25
16 Dominique Easley .50 1.25
17 Jason Verrett .50 1.25
18 Troy Niklas .50 1.25
19 C.J. Mosley .60 1.50
20 Zach Mettenberger .50 1.25
21 Andre Williams .50 1.25
22 John Brown .75 2.00
23 Jordan Matthews .75 2.00
24 Trey Millard .60 1.50
25 Richard Rodgers .75 2.00
26 Jimmy Garoppolo 4.00 10.00
27 Trent Murphy .50 1.25
28 Jeff Janis .50 1.25
29 James White 1.00 2.50
30 Khalil Mack 2.00 5.00
31 Charles Sims .50 1.25
32 Anthony Barr .50 1.25
33 Jeremy Hill .60 1.50
34 De'Anthony Thomas .50 1.25
35A Tre Mason .50 1.25
35B Tre Mason SP
36 Kelvin Benjamin .75 2.00
37A Bishop Sankey .50 1.25
37B Bishop Sankey SP
38 Lache Seastrunk .50 1.25
39 Paul Richardson .60 1.50
40 Henry Josey .50 1.25
41 C.J. Fiedorowicz .50 1.25
42 Connor Shaw .50 1.25
43 Cody Latimer .60 1.50
44 Calvin Pryor .50 1.25
45 Jake Matthews .50 1.25
46 Donte Moncrief .50 1.25
47A Jadeveon Clowney .60 1.50
47B Jadeveon Clowney SP 1.25 3.00
48 Aaron Murray .50 1.25
49 Ra'Shede Hageman .50 1.25
50A Blake Bortles .60 1.50
50B Blake Bortles SP 1.25 3.00
51 Kyle Van Noy .60 1.50
52 Damien Williams .50 1.25
53 Jordan Lynch .60 1.50
54 Isaiah Crowell .60 1.50
55 Allen Robinson .75 2.00
56 Davante Adams .75 2.00
57A Eric Ebron .60 1.50
57B Eric Ebron SP 1.25 3.00
58 Bradley Roby .50 1.25
59 Ka'Deem Carey .50 1.25
60 Odell Beckham Jr. 1.25 3.00
61 Tajh Boyd .50 1.25
62 Rajion Neal .50 1.25
63 Bruce Ellington .50 1.25
64 Jerick McKinnon .60 1.50
65 A.J. McCarron .50 1.25
66 Stephon Tuitt .75 2.00
67 Dri Archer .50 1.25
68 Josh Huff .60 1.50
69 Greg Robinson .50 1.25
70 Aaron Donald 1.25 3.00
71 Martavis Bryant .60 1.50
72 Kevin Norwood .50 1.25
73 Marqise Lee .60 1.50
74 Ryan Grant .50 1.25
75 Cassius Marsh .60 1.50
76 Deone Bucannon .50 1.25
77 Carlos Hyde .60 1.50
78 Zack Martin .60 1.50
79 Kony Ealy .60 1.50
80 Jalen Saunders .50 1.25
81 Devin Street .50 1.25
82 Marion Grice .50 1.25
83A Sammy Watkins .75 2.00
83B Sammy Watkins SP
84 Colt Lyerla .75 2.00
85A Mike Evans 1.25 3.00
85B Mike Evans SP
86 Ha Ha Clinton-Dix .60 1.50
87 Scott Crichton .50 1.25
88 Garrett Gilbert .50 1.25
89 Logan Thomas .50 1.25
90 Jace Amaro .50 1.25
91 Austin Seferian-Jenkins .50 1.25
92 Shaquelle Evans .50 1.25
93 David Fales .50 1.25
94 Terrance West .50 1.25
95 Ahmad Dixon .50 1.25
96 Xavier Grimble .60 1.50
97 Brandon Coleman .50 1.25
98 Robert Herron .50 1.25
99 Taylor Lewan .50 1.25
100A Teddy Bridgewater .75 2.00
100B Teddy Bridgewater SP

2014 Topps Turkey Red Mini

*MINI: .8X TO 2X BASIC CARDS
ONE PER PACK

2014 Topps Turkey Red Autographs

ONE PER BOX
1 Johnny Manziel 6.00 15.00
2 Jarvis Landry
3 Will Sutton 5.00 12.00
6 Derek Carr 25.00 60.00
8 Michael Campanaro 4.00 10.00
9 Brandin Cooks 6.00 15.00
10 Arthur Lynch 4.00 10.00
11 Devonta Freeman 6.00 15.00
12 Tom Savage
13 Stephen Morris 4.00 10.00
14 Darqueze Dennard 5.00 12.00
15 Jared Abbrederis 4.00 10.00
16 Dominique Easley 4.00 10.00
18 Troy Niklas 4.00 10.00
19 C.J. Mosley 5.00 12.00
20 Zach Mettenberger 4.00 10.00
21 Andre Williams 4.00 10.00
22 John Brown 6.00 15.00
23 Jordan Matthews 6.00 25.00
24 Trey Millard 5.00 12.00
26 Jimmy Garoppolo 30.00 80.00
28 Jeff Janis 4.00 10.00
29 James White 8.00 20.00
31 Charles Sims 4.00 10.00
32 Anthony Barr 4.00 10.00
33 Jeremy Hill 5.00 12.00
36 Kelvin Benjamin 6.00 15.00
37 Bishop Sankey
38 Lache Seastrunk 4.00 10.00
40 Henry Josey 4.00 10.00
41 C.J. Fiedorowicz 4.00 10.00
42 Connor Shaw 4.00 10.00
43 Cody Latimer 5.00 12.00
44 Calvin Pryor 4.00 10.00
45 Jake Matthews 4.00 10.00
47 Jadeveon Clowney 5.00 12.00
48 Aaron Murray 4.00 10.00
50 Blake Bortles
51 Kyle Van Noy 5.00 12.00
52 Damien Williams 4.00 10.00
53 Jordan Lynch 5.00 12.00
54 Isaiah Crowell 5.00 12.00
55 Allen Robinson 6.00 15.00
56 Davante Adams 8.00 20.00
57 Eric Ebron 5.00 12.00
58 Bradley Roby 4.00 10.00
59 Ka'Deem Carey 4.00 10.00
61 Tajh Boyd 4.00 10.00
62 Rajion Neal 4.00 10.00
63 Bruce Ellington 4.00 10.00
64 Jerick McKinnon 5.00 12.00
65 A.J. McCarron
66 Stephon Tuitt 6.00 15.00
67 Dri Archer 4.00 10.00
69 Greg Robinson 4.00 10.00
70 Aaron Donald 10.00 25.00
71 Martavis Bryant 5.00 12.00
72 Kevin Norwood 4.00 10.00
75 Cassius Marsh 5.00 12.00
76 Deone Bucannon 4.00 10.00
79 Kony Ealy 5.00 12.00
81 Devin Street 4.00 10.00
82 Marion Grice 4.00 10.00
83 Sammy Watkins 6.00 15.00
85 Mike Evans 10.00 25.00
86 Ha Ha Clinton-Dix 5.00 12.00
88 Garrett Gilbert 4.00 10.00
89 Logan Thomas 4.00 10.00
90 Jace Amaro 4.00 10.00
91 Austin Seferian-Jenkins 4.00 10.00
93 David Fales 4.00 10.00
94 Terrance West 4.00 10.00
95 Ahmad Dixon 4.00 10.00
96 Xavier Grimble 5.00 12.00
97 Brandon Coleman 4.00 10.00
98 Robert Herron 4.00 10.00
99 Taylor Lewan 4.00 10.00
100 Teddy Bridgewater

2007 Topps TX Exclusive

is 225-card set was released in August, 2007. The set was issued into the hobby in five-card packs, with a $20 SRP, which came 12 packs to a box. Cards numbered 1-100 feature veterans, while cards 101-200 feature 2007 NFL Rookie Cards issued to stated print runs between 399 and 1049 cards and the set concludes with cards 201-225 which feature retired greats and were issued to a stated print run of 1099 serial numbered cards and were inserted into packs at a stated rate of one in six.

COMP.SET w/o SP's (100) 10.00 25.00
101-200 ROOKIE PRINT RUN 399-1049
201-225 RETIRED/1099 ODDS 1:6
1 Peyton Manning 1.25 3.00
2 Carson Palmer .40 1.00
3 Tom Brady 1.50 4.00
4 Drew Brees .50 1.25
5 Rex Grossman .30 .75
6 Donovan McNabb .40 1.00
7 Eli Manning .40 1.00
8 Philip Rivers .50 1.25
9 Brett Favre 1.00 2.50
10 Marc Bulger .30 .75
11 Michael Vick .40 1.00
12 Tony Romo .60 1.50
13 Matt Hasselbeck .30 .75
14 Jake Delhomme .30 .75
15 Ben Roethlisberger .50 1.25
16 Alex Smith QB .40 1.00
17 Chad Pennington .30 .75
18 Steve McNair .40 1.00
19 Trent Green .30 .75
20 David Carr .30 .75
21 Vince Young .30 .75
22 Jay Cutler .30 .75
23 Matt Leinart .30 .75
24 Jason Campbell .30 .75
25 Bruce Gradkowski .30 .75
26 Larry Johnson .30 .75
27 Frank Gore .40 1.00
28 LaDainian Tomlinson .50 1.25
29 Cedric Benson .30 .75
30 Chester Taylor .30 .75
31 Thomas Jones .30 .75
32 Steven Jackson .30 .75
33 Willie Parker .40 1.00
34 Rudi Johnson .30 .75
35 Fred Taylor .30 .75
36 Warrick Dunn .30 .75
37 Julius Jones .30 .75
38 Brian Westbrook .30 .75
39 Ronnie Brown .30 .75
40 Travis Henry .40 1.00
41 Jamal Lewis .40 1.00
42 Cadillac Williams .40 1.00
43 Edgerrin James .40 1.00
44 Ahman Green .40 1.00
45 Deuce McAllister .40 1.00
46 Deshaun Foster .40 1.00
47 Tatum Bell .30 .75
48 Willis McGahee .30 .75
49 Kevin Jones .30 .75
50 Corey Dillon .30 .75
51 Clinton Portis .30 .75
52 Shaun Alexander .30 .75
53 Laurence Maroney .40 1.00
54 Maurice Jones-Drew .30 .75
55 Jerious Norwood .30 .75
56 Mike Bell .40 1.00
57 Leon Washington .30 .75
58 Chad Johnson .30 .75
59 Roy Williams WR .30 .75
60 Andre Johnson .40 1.00
61 Reggie Wayne .40 1.00
62 Steve Smith .40 1.00
63 Donald Driver .40 1.00
64 Anquan Boldin .30 .75
65 Lee Evans .40 1.00
66 Eric Moulds .30 .75
67 Javon Walker .40 1.00
68 Terrell Owens .40 1.00
69 Laveranues Coles .30 .75
70 Marvin Harrison .40 1.00
71 Darrell Jackson .30 .75
72 Torry Holt .40 1.00
73 Hines Ward .40 1.00
74 Joey Galloway .40 1.00
75 T.J. Houshmandzadeh .30 .75
76 Plaxico Burress .30 .75
77 Jerricho Cotchery .30 .75
78 Joe Horn .30 .75
79 Mike Furrey .40 1.00
80 Braylon Edwards .30 .75
81 Mark Bradley .30 .75
82 Larry Fitzgerald .40 1.00
83 Terry Glenn .40 1.00
84 Michael Clayton .30 .75
85 Muhsin Muhammad .30 .75
86 Randy Moss .40 1.00
87 Chris Chambers .30 .75
88 Santana Moss .40 1.00
89 Keyshawn Johnson .40 1.00
90 Santonio Holmes .30 .75
91 Marques Colston .30 .75
92 Greg Jennings .30 .75
93 Vernon Davis .30 .75
94 Chris Cooley .30 .75
95 Alge Crumpler .40 1.00
96 Tony Gonzalez .40 1.00
97 Ben Watson .30 .75
98 Todd Heap .30 .75
99 Antonio Gates .50 1.25
100 Jeremy Shockey .30 .75
101 Brady Quinn/399 RC 1.50 4.00
102 Joe Thomas/1049 RC 1.50 4.00
103 Calvin Johnson/399 RC 5.00 12.00
104 Adrian Peterson/399 RC 5.00 12.00
105 JaMarcus Russell/399 RC 1.50 4.00
106 Marshawn Lynch/399 RC 3.00 8.00
107 Alan Branch/1049 RC 1.00 2.50
108 Levi Brown/799 RC 1.00 2.50
109 Gaines Adams/599 RC 1.50 4.00
110 Trent Edwards/1049 RC 1.00 2.50
111 Dwayne Jarrett/1049 RC 1.25 3.00
112 Leon Hall/1049 RC 1.00 2.50
113 Kenneth Darby/599 RC 1.25 3.00
114 John Beck/599 RC 1.25 3.00
115 Marcus McCauley/1049 RC 1.00 2.50
116 Ted Ginn Jr./399 RC 2.00 5.00
117 Kenny Irons/1049 RC 1.00 2.50
118 LaRon Landry/599 RC 2.00 5.00
119 Reggie Nelson/1049 RC 1.00 2.50
120 Quentin Moses/1049 RC 1.00 2.50
121 Ray McDonald/1049 RC 1.25 3.00
122 Drew Stanton/599 RC 1.25 3.00
123 Garrett Wolfe/1049 RC 1.00 2.50
124 Greg Olsen/799 RC 1.50 4.00
125 Troy Smith/599 RC 1.25 3.00
126 Chris Henry/1049 RC 1.00 2.50
127 Patrick Willis/1049 RC 1.50 4.00
128 Chris Leak/799 RC 1.00 2.50
129 Paul Posluszny/799 RC 1.00 2.50
130 Steve Breaston/599 RC 1.25 3.00
131 Brandon Meriweather/799 RC 1.25 3.00
132 Thomas Clayton/1049 RC 1.25 3.00
133 Rhema McKnight/1049 RC 1.00 2.50
134 Anthony Spencer/1049 RC 1.25 3.00
135 Amobi Okoye/799 RC 1.25 3.00
136 Daymeion Hughes/1049 RC 1.00 2.50
137 Michael Bush/1049 RC 1.00 2.50
138 H.B. Blades/1049 RC 1.00 2.50
139 Michael Griffin/799 RC 1.00 2.50
140 Justin Harrell/1049 RC 1.00 2.50
141 Victor Abiamiri/1049 RC 1.00 2.50
142 Aundrae Allison/799 RC 1.00 2.50
143 Jared Zabransky/799 RC 1.00 2.50
144 Martrez Milner/799 RC 1.00 2.50
145 Adam Carriker/799 RC 1.00 2.50
146 Paul Williams/599 RC 1.25 3.00
147 Tanard Jackson/1049 RC 1.00 2.50
148 Marcus Thomas/1049 RC 1.25 3.00
149 Selvin Young/1049 RC 1.00 2.50
150 Jamaal Anderson/799 RC 1.25 3.00
151 David Harris/1049 RC 1.00 2.50
152 Vincent Marshall/1049 RC 1.25 3.00
153 Buster Davis/1049 RC 1.25 3.00
154 Jon Beason/799 RC 1.00 2.50
155 Tim Crowder/1049 RC 1.25 3.00
156 Brian Leonard/1049 RC 1.00 2.50
157 LaMarr Woodley/1049 RC 2.00 5.00
158 DeMarcus Tank Tyler/1049 RC 1.00 2.50
159 John Wendling/1049 RC 1.25 3.00
160 Aaron Ross/1049 RC 1.00 2.50
161 Earl Everett/1049 RC 1.00 2.50
162 Tony Hunt/599 RC 1.25 3.00
163 Craig Buster Davis/1049 RC 1.00 2.50
164 Rufus Alexander/1049 RC 1.00 2.50
165 Aaron Rouse/799 RC 1.00 2.50
166 Lorenzo Booker/599 RC 1.50 4.00
167 Kevin Kolb/1049 RC 1.25 3.00
168 David Irons/799 RC 1.00 2.50
169 Sidney Rice/599 RC 1.50 4.00
170 Johnnie Lee Higgins/799 RC 1.00 2.50
171 Tyler Palko/1049 RC 1.50 4.00
172 Robert Meachem/1049 RC 1.25 3.00
173 Prescott Burgess/1049 RC 1.00 2.50
174 Jordan Palmer/799 RC 1.25 3.00
175 Darius Walker/799 RC 1.00 2.50
176 Drew Tate/799 RC 1.25 3.00
177 Chris Davis/1049 RC 1.00 2.50
178 Michael Johnson/1049 RC 1.25 3.00
179 Matt Spaeth/1049 RC 1.50 4.00
180 Yamon Figurs/1049 RC 1.00 2.50
181 Joel Filani/1049 RC 1.00 2.50
182 Jason Hill/599 RC 1.25 3.00
183 Anthony Gonzalez/1049 RC 1.00 2.50
184 Chansi Stuckey/1049 RC 1.25 3.00
185 Antonio Pittman/799 RC 1.00 2.50
186 Dallas Baker/1049 RC 1.00 2.50
187 Sabby Piscitelli/1049 RC 1.00 2.50
188 Brandon Jackson/1049 RC 1.00 2.50
189 Darrelle Revis/1049 RC 1.25 3.00
190 David Clowney/1049 RC 1.00 2.50
191 Courtney Taylor/1049 RC 1.00 2.50
192 Eric Weddle/1049 RC 1.25 3.00
193 Lawrence Timmons/799 RC 1.50 4.00
194 Scott Chandler/1049 RC 1.50 4.00
195 Dwayne Bowe/399 RC 1.50 4.00
196 Kolby Smith/1049 RC 1.00 2.50
197 Jarvis Moss/1049 RC 1.00 2.50
198 Isaiah Stanback/1049 RC 1.00 2.50
199 Steve Smith USC/599 RC 1.25 3.00
200 Joe Newton/1049 RC 1.00 2.50
201 Troy Aikman 2.50 6.00
202 Terry Bradshaw 2.50 6.00
203 John Elway 3.00 8.00
204 Roger Staubach 2.50 6.00
205 Steve Young 2.50 6.00
206 Jim Plunkett 1.50 4.00
207 Dan Marino 4.00 10.00
208 Jim Kelly 2.00 5.00
209 Joe Namath 2.50 6.00
210 Joe Montana 6.00 15.00
211 Earl Campbell 2.00 5.00
212 Paul Hornung 2.00 5.00
213 Eric Dickerson 1.50 4.00
214 Emmitt Smith 3.00 8.00
215 Jim Brown 2.50 6.00
216 Marshall Faulk 1.50 4.00
217 Barry Sanders 3.00 8.00
218 Thurman Thomas 1.50 4.00
219 Marcus Allen 2.00 5.00
220 Tony Dorsett 2.00 5.00
221 Fred Biletnikoff 2.00 5.00
222 Tim Brown 2.00 5.00
223 Jerry Rice 4.00 10.00
224 Lawrence Taylor 2.00 5.00
225 Rod Woodson 1.50 4.00

2007 Topps TX Exclusive Bronze

*VETS 1-100: 2.5X TO 6X BASIC CARDS
*ROOKIES: .6X TO 1.5X BASIC RC/1049
*ROOKIES: .6X TO 1.5X BASIC RC/799
*ROOKIES: .5X TO 1.2X BASIC RC/599
*ROOKIES: .4X TO 1X BASIC RC/399
*RETIRED 201-225: .4X TO 1X BASIC CARDS
BRONZE/149 STATED ODDS 1:5 HOB

2007 Topps TX Exclusive Gold

*VETS 1-100: 10X TO 25X BASIC CARDS
*ROOKIES: 3X TO 8X BASIC RC/1049
*ROOKIES: 3X TO 8X BASIC RC/799
*ROOKIES: 2.5X TO 6X BASIC RC/599
*ROOKIES: 2X TO 5X BASIC RC/399
*RETIRED 201-225: 2.5X TO 6X
GOLD/10 STATED ODDS 1:74 HOB

2007 Topps TX Exclusive Silver

*VETS 1-100: 4X TO 10X BASIC CARDS
*ROOKIES: 1.2X TO 3X BASIC RC/1049
*ROOKIES: 1.2X TO 3X BASIC RC/799
*ROOKIES: 1X TO 2.5X BASIC RC/599
*ROOKIES: .8X TO 2X BASIC RC/399
*RETIRED 201-225: 1X TO 2.5X
SILVER/49 STATED ODDS 1:15 HOB

2007 Topps TX Exclusive Franchise Winning Ticket

WIN.TICKET/299 ODDS 1:9
*BRONZE/99: .5X TO 1.2X BASIC INSERTS
BRONZE PRINT RUN 99 SER.#'d SETS
*SILVER/49: .6X TO 1.5X BASIC INSERTS
SILVER/49 ODDS 1:113
*GOLD/25: 1X TO 2.5X BASIC INSERTS
GOLD/25 ODDS 1:221
AG Antonio Gates 2.00 5.00
AJ Andre Johnson 1.50 4.00
CJ Chad Johnson 1.25 3.00
CP Carson Palmer 1.50 4.00
DB Drew Brees 2.00 5.00
FG Frank Gore 1.50 4.00
GJ Greg Jennings 1.25 3.00
JA Joseph Addai 1.25 3.00
JC Jay Cutler 1.25 3.00
JS Jeremy Shockey 1.25 3.00
JW Javon Walker 1.50 4.00
LF Larry Fitzgerald 1.50 4.00
LJ Larry Johnson 1.25 3.00
LM Laurence Maroney 1.50 4.00
LT LaDainian Tomlinson 2.00 5.00
MC Marques Colston 1.25 3.00
MH Marvin Harrison 1.50 4.00
MJD Maurice Jones-Drew 1.25 3.00
ML Matt Leinart 1.25 3.00
PM Peyton Manning 5.00 12.00
PR Philip Rivers 2.00 5.00
RB Reggie Bush 1.25 3.00
RW Roy Williams WR 1.25 3.00
SA Shaun Alexander 1.25 3.00
SS Steve Smith 1.50 4.00
TG Tony Gonzalez 1.50 4.00
TM Tom Brady 6.00 15.00
TR Tony Romo 2.50 6.00
VY Vince Young 1.25 3.00
WM Willis McGahee 1.25 3.00

2007 Topps TX Exclusive Franchise Winning Ticket Dual

DUAL/149 STATED ODDS 1:74
*BRONZE/49: .5X TO 1.2X BASIC INSERTS
BRONZE PRINT RUN 49 SER.#'d SETS
*SILVER/25: .6X TO 1.5X BASIC INSERTS
SILVER/25 STATED ODDS 1:442
*GOLD/10: 1.5X TO 4X BASIC INSERTS
GOLD/10 STATED ODDS 1:1100
BM T.Brady/L.Maroney 10.00 25.00
CB R.Bush/D.Brees 3.00 8.00
CW J.Cutler/J.Walker 2.50 6.00
DS J.Delhomme/S.Smith 2.50 6.00
GS F.Gore/A.Smith QB 2.50 6.00
HA Hasselbeck/Alexander 2.00 5.00
JG L.Johson/T.Gonzalez 2.50 6.00
LF M.Leinart/L.Fitzgerald 2.50 6.00
MH P.Manning/Harrison 8.00 20.00
MS E.Manning/Shockey 2.50 6.00
PJ C.Palmer/Ch.Johnson 2.50 6.00
RJ T.Romo/J.Jones 4.00 10.00
TR Tomlinson/P.Rivers 3.00 8.00
VD M.Vick/W.Dunn 2.50 6.00
YW V.Young/L.White 2.50 6.00

2007 Topps TX Exclusive Franchise Winning Ticket Jersey

BASE JSY/199 ODDS 1:28
*PATCH/15: 1.2X TO 3X BASIC JSY/199
PATCH/15 ODDS 1:395
AG Antonio Gates 4.00 10.00
AJ Andre Johnson 3.00 8.00
CJ Chad Johnson 2.50 6.00
CP Carson Palmer 3.00 8.00
DB Drew Brees 4.00 10.00
FG Frank Gore 3.00 8.00
GJ Greg Jennings 2.50 6.00
JA Joseph Addai 2.50 6.00
JC Jay Cutler 2.50 6.00
JS Jeremy Shockey 2.50 6.00
JW Javon Walker 3.00 8.00
LF Larry Fitzgerald 3.00 8.00
LJ Larry Johnson 2.50 6.00
LM Laurence Maroney 3.00 8.00
LT LaDainian Tomlinson 4.00 10.00
MC Marques Colston 2.50 6.00
MH Marvin Harrison 3.00 8.00
MJD Maurice Jones-Drew 2.50 6.00
ML Matt Leinart 2.50 6.00
PM Peyton Manning 10.00 25.00
PR Philip Rivers 4.00 10.00
RB Reggie Bush 2.50 6.00
RW Roy Williams WR 2.50 6.00
SA Shaun Alexander 2.50 6.00
SS Steve Smith 3.00 8.00
TB Tom Brady 12.00 30.00
TG Tony Gonzalez 3.00 8.00
TR Tony Romo 5.00 12.00
VY Vince Young 2.50 6.00
WM Willis McGahee 2.50 6.00

2007 Topps TX Exclusive Franchise Winning Ticket Jersey Autographs

STATED PRINT RUN 10 SER.#'d SETS
UNPRICED PATCH AU PRINT RUN 5
AG Antonio Gates 15.00 40.00
CJ Chad Johnson 20.00 50.00
DB Drew Brees 60.00 120.00
FG Frank Gore 25.00 60.00
GJ Greg Jennings 15.00 40.00
JA Joseph Addai 25.00 60.00
LJ Larry Johnson 25.00 60.00
LM Laurence Maroney 25.00 60.00
LT LaDainian Tomlinson 60.00 120.00
MC Marques Colston 25.00 60.00
MH Marvin Harrison 40.00 80.00
MJD Maurice Jones-Drew 20.00 50.00
ML Matt Leinart 30.00 80.00
PM Peyton Manning 125.00 250.00
RW Roy Williams WR 20.00 50.00
SA Shaun Alexander 25.00 60.00
SS Steve Smith 20.00 50.00
TB Tom Brady 150.00 300.00
TG Tony Gonzalez 15.00 40.00
TR Tony Romo 125.00 250.00
VY Vince Young 40.00 100.00
WM Willis McGahee 15.00 40.00

2007 Topps TX Exclusive Franchise Winning Ticket Dual Jersey

DUAL JSY/49 ODDS 1:230
PATCH/5 ODDS 1:2209
BB R.Bush/D.Brees 12.50 30.00
BM T.Brady/Maroney 12.50 30.00
CW J.Cutler/J.Walker 10.00 25.00
DS J.Delhomme/S.Smith 6.00 15.00
GS F.Gore/A.Smith QB 8.00 20.00
HA Hasselbeck/Alexander 6.00 15.00
JG L.Johnson/T.Gonzalez 6.00 15.00
LF M.Leinart/L.Fitzgerald 10.00 25.00
MH P.Manning/Harrison 12.00 30.00
MS E.Manning/Shockey 8.00 20.00
PJ C.Palmer/Ch.Johnson 6.00 15.00
RJ T.Romo/J.Jones 20.00 50.00
TR L.Tomlinson/P.Rivers 10.00 25.00
VD M.Vick/W.Dunn 6.00 15.00
YW V.Young/L.White 10.00 25.00

2007 Topps TX Exclusive Post Season Ticket

BASE/499 STATED ODDS 1:20
*BRONZE/99: .6X TO 1.5X BASIC INSERTS
BRONZE/99 ODDS 1:99
*SILVER/49: .8X TO 2X BASIC INSERTS
SILVER/49 ODDS 1:199
*GOLD/10: 2X TO 5X BASIC INSERTS
GOLD/10 ODDS 1:972
BF Brett Favre 3.00 8.00
BU Brian Urlacher 1.50 4.00
DJ Darrell Jackson 1.00 2.50
FT Fred Taylor 1.00 2.50
JD Jake Delhomme 1.00 2.50
LT LaDainian Tomlinson 1.50 4.00
MH Marvin Harrison 1.25 3.00
MHA Matt Hasselbeck 1.00 2.50
PM Peyton Manning 4.00 10.00
RS Rod Smith 1.25 3.00
SA Shaun Alexander 1.00 2.50
SM Steve McNair 1.25 3.00
SS Steve Smith 1.25 3.00
TB Tom Brady 5.00 12.00
TBR Troy Brown 1.00 2.50
TG Tony Gonzalez 1.25 3.00
TH Torry Holt 1.25 3.00

2007 Topps TX Exclusive Post Season Ticket Jersey

JSY/199 ODDS 1:50
*PATCH/25: 1X TO 2.5X BASIC JSY/199
PATCH/25 ODDS 1:406
BF Brett Favre 8.00 20.00
BU Brian Urlacher 4.00 10.00
DJ Darrell Jackson 2.50 6.00
FT Fred Taylor 2.50 6.00
JD Jake Delhomme 2.50 6.00
LT LaDainian Tomlinson 4.00 10.00
MH Marvin Harrison 3.00 8.00
MH Matt Hasselbeck 2.50 6.00
PM Peyton Manning 10.00 25.00
RS Rod Smith 3.00 8.00
SA Shaun Alexander 2.50 6.00
SM Steve McNair 3.00 8.00
SS Steve Smith 3.00 8.00
TB Troy Brown 2.50 6.00
TB Tom Brady 12.00 30.00
TG Tony Gonzalez 3.00 8.00
TH Torry Holt 3.00 8.00

2007 Topps TX Exclusive Post Season Ticket Jersey Autographs

STATED PRINT RUN 15 SER.#'d SETS
UNPRICED PATCH PRINT RUN 5
BF Brett Favre 175.00 300.00
FT Fred Taylor 20.00 40.00
JD Jake Delhomme 30.00 60.00
LT LaDainian Tomlinson 40.00 100.00
MH Matt Hasselbeck 30.00 60.00
MH Marvin Harrison 40.00 80.00
PM Peyton Manning 125.00 250.00
SS Steve Smith 20.00 40.00
TB Tom Brady 150.00 300.00
TG Tony Gonzalez 20.00 40.00

2007 Topps TX Exclusive Pro Bowl Ticket Stub Autographs

PRO BOWL AUTO/25 ODDS 1:691
UNPRICED GOLD SER.#'d TO 1
AG Antonio Gates 30.00 60.00
BDR Drew Brees 50.00 100.00
CJ Chad Johnson 40.00 80.00
LJ Larry Johnson 50.00 100.00
LT LaDainian Tomlinson 75.00 150.00
MH Marvin Harrison 40.00 80.00
PM Peyton Manning 150.00 300.00
SM Shawne Merriman 50.00 100.00
SS Steve Smith 30.00 60.00
TG Tony Gonzalez 30.00 60.00

2007 Topps TX Exclusive Rookie Autographs

GROUP A ODDS 1:1691
GROUP B ODDS 1:837
GROUP C ODDS 1:222
GROUP D ODDS 1:70
GROUP E ODDS 1:166
GROUP F ODDS 1:42
GROUP G ODDS 1:18
GROUP H ODDS 1:17
AA Aundrae Allison G 3.00 8.00
AG Anthony Gonzalez E 3.00 8.00
AO Amobi Okoye G 4.00 10.00
AP Adrian Peterson A 150.00 300.00
API Antonio Pittman G 3.00 8.00
BQ Brady Quinn B 6.00 15.00
CJ Calvin Johnson A 60.00 120.00
CL Chris Leak G 3.00 8.00
DB Dwayne Bowe D 10.00 25.00
DJ Dwayne Jarrett C 4.00 10.00
DS Drew Stanton D 3.00 8.00
DW Darius Walker H 3.00 8.00
GO Greg Olsen D 5.00 12.00
GW Garrett Wolfe F 3.00 8.00
IS Isaiah Stanback H 3.00 8.00
JH Jason Hill F 3.00 8.00
JR JaMarcus Russell B 5.00 12.00
LG Luke Getsy H 5.00 12.00
LH Leon Hall F 3.00 8.00
LL LaRon Landry G 5.00 12.00
MB Michael Bush D 3.00 8.00
ML Marshawn Lynch C 12.00 30.00
RM Robert Meachem G 4.00 10.00
SR Sidney Rice D 4.00 10.00
SS Steve Smith USC H 3.00 8.00
SY Selvin Young F 3.00 8.00
TG Ted Ginn Jr. C 4.00 10.00
TH Tony Hunt E 3.00 8.00
TP Tyler Palko H 5.00 12.00
TS Troy Smith D 3.00 8.00

2007 Topps TX Exclusive Season Ticket

BASE/399 STATED ODDS 1:22
*BRONZE/99: .6X TO 1.5X BASIC INSERTS
BRONZE/99 ODDS 1:88
*SILVER/49: .8X TO 2X BASIC INSERTS
SILVER/49 ODDS 1:199
*GOLD/10: 2X TO 5X BASIC INSERTS
GOLD/10 ODDS 1:972
BD Brian Dawkins 1.50 4.00
BF Brett Favre 3.00 8.00
BU Brian Urlacher 1.50 4.00
CJ Chad Johnson 1.00 2.50
CP Chad Pennington 1.00 2.50
DB Derrick Brooks 1.00 2.50
DD Donald Driver 1.25 3.00
DM Deuce McAllister 1.25 3.00
FT Fred Taylor 1.00 2.50
JH Joe Horn 1.00 2.50
LT LaDainian Tomlinson 1.50 4.00
MH Marvin Harrison 1.25 3.00
MHA Matt Hasselbeck 1.00 2.50
PM Peyton Manning 4.00 10.00
RL Ray Lewis 1.50 4.00
SA Shaun Alexander 1.00 2.50
TG Tony Gonzalez 1.25 3.00
TH Torry Holt 1.25 3.00
ZT Zach Thomas 1.25 3.00

2007 Topps TX Exclusive Season Ticket Jersey

JSY/199 ODDS 1:44
*PATCH/25: 1X TO 2.5X BASIC JSY/199
PATCH/25 ODDS 1:363
BD Brian Dawkins 4.00 10.00
BF Brett Favre 8.00 20.00
BU Brian Urlacher 4.00 10.00
CJ Chad Johnson 2.50 6.00
CP Chad Pennington 2.50 6.00
DB Derrick Brooks 2.50 6.00
DD Donald Driver 3.00 8.00
DM Deuce McAllister 3.00 8.00
FT Fred Taylor 2.50 6.00
JH Joe Horn 2.50 6.00
LT LaDainian Tomlinson 4.00 10.00
MH Matt Hasselbeck 2.50 6.00
MH Marvin Harrison 3.00 8.00
PM Peyton Manning 10.00 25.00
RL Ray Lewis 4.00 10.00
SA Shaun Alexander 2.50 6.00
TG Tony Gonzalez 3.00 8.00
TH Torry Holt 3.00 8.00
ZT Zach Thomas 3.00 8.00

2007 Topps TX Exclusive Season Ticket Jersey Autographs

STATED PRINT RUN 10 SER.#'d SETS
UNPRICED PATCH PRINT RUN 5
CJ Chad Johnson 25.00 50.00
CP Chad Pennington 25.00 50.00
DB Derrick Brooks 25.00 50.00
DM Deuce McAllister 25.00 50.00
FT Fred Taylor 30.00 60.00
JH Joe Horn 15.00 40.00
LT LaDainian Tomlinson 75.00 150.00
MH Matt Hasselbeck 30.00 60.00
PM Peyton Manning 125.00 250.00
RL Ray Lewis 60.00 120.00
SA Shaun Alexander 30.00 60.00
TG Tony Gonzalez 15.00 40.00
ZT Zach Thomas 40.00 80.00

2007 Topps TX Exclusive Super Bowl Ticket Stub

STATED ODDS 1:6
ARE Antwaan Randle El 6.00 15.00
AV Adam Vinatieri 6.00 15.00
BR Ben Roethlisberger 10.00 25.00
BU Brian Urlacher 8.00 20.00
DF Dwight Freeney 5.00 12.00
DH Devin Hester 6.00 15.00
DJ Darrell Jackson 5.00 12.00
HM Heath Miller 5.00 12.00
JA Joseph Addai 8.00 20.00
LT Lota Tatupu 5.00 12.00
MH Marvin Harrison 6.00 15.00
MH Matt Hasselbeck 5.00 12.00
MM Muhsin Muhammad 5.00 12.00
PM Peyton Manning 12.50 30.00
RW Reggie Wayne 5.00 12.00
SA Shaun Alexander 6.00 15.00

TJ Thomas Jones 5.00 12.00
TP Troy Polamalu 8.00 20.00
WP Willie Parker 6.00 15.00

2007 Topps TX Exclusive Super Bowl Ticket Stub Autographs

GROUP A ODDS 1:483
GROUP B ODDS 1:167
GROUP C ODDS 1:371
GROUP D ODDS 1:222
GROUP E ODDS 1:42
GROUP F ODDS 1:93
GROUP G ODDS 1:34
GROUP H ODDS 1:28
GROUP I ODDS 1:21
ARE Antwaan Randle El E 10.00 25.00
AS Asante Samuel D 15.00 40.00
BD Brian Dawkins E 15.00 40.00
CW Cedrick Wilson I 8.00 20.00
DB Deion Branch B 12.00 30.00
DB Derrick Brooks B 40.00 80.00
DJ2 Dexter Jackson B 12.00 30.00
DJ3 Dhani Jones E 6.00 15.00
DM Dan Morgan G 6.00 15.00
GW Grant Wistrom H 6.00 15.00
HM Heath Miller I 15.00 40.00
JA Joseph Addai C 15.00 40.00
JD Jake Delhomme B 12.00 30.00
JF James Farrior I 10.00 25.00
JJ Joe Jurevicius B 12.00 30.00
JR Jerry Rice A 125.00 200.00
JS Jerramy Stevens H 5.00 12.00
JT Jeremiah Trotter E 8.00 20.00
KF Kevin Faulk G 8.00 20.00
KJ Kris Jenkins F 8.00 20.00
LJS L.J. Smith G 6.00 15.00
LT Lofa Tatupu G 8.00 20.00
MA Mike Alstott B 40.00 80.00
MB Michael Boulware H 5.00 12.00
MH1 Marvin Harrison A 25.00 60.00
MH2 Matt Hasselbeck B 15.00 40.00
MM1 Muhsin Muhammad XXXVIII C 8.00 20.00
MM2 Muhsin Muhammad XLI D 8.00 20.00
MS Mack Strong H 6.00 15.00
PM Peyton Manning A 150.00 300.00
RC Rosevelt Colvin G 8.00 20.00
RH Rodney Harrison E 15.00 40.00
RW Reggie Wayne C 30.00 60.00
SA Shaun Alexander A 30.00 60.00
SJ Sebastian Janikowski B 20.00 40.00
SS Steve Smith B 30.00 60.00
TB Tim Brown A 30.00 80.00
TBR Tom Brady A 300.00 500.00
TJ Thomas Jones E 12.00 30.00
TL Ty Law E 8.00 20.00
VW Vince Wilfork E 8.00 20.00
WJ Walter Jones I 12.00 30.00
WP Willie Parker D 30.00 60.00

2007 Topps TX Exclusive Ticket 2 Stardom

BASE/499 STATED ODDS 1:16
*BRONZE/99: .6X TO 1.5X BASIC INSERTS
BRONZE/99 ODDS 1:76
*SILVER/49: .8X TO 2X BASIC INSERTS
SILVER/49 ODDS 1:154
*GOLD/10: 2X TO 5X BASIC INSERTS
GOLD/10 ODDS 1:751
AS Alex Smith QB 1.25 3.00
BJ Brandon Jacobs 1.00 2.50
BR Ben Roethlisberger 1.50 4.00
CW Cadillac Williams 1.25 3.00
DH DeAngelo Hall 1.00 2.50
DW DeAngelo Williams 1.00 2.50
FG Frank Gore 1.25 3.00
GJ Greg Jennings 1.00 2.50
JA Joseph Addai 1.00 2.50
JCO Jerricho Cotchery 1.00 2.50
JCU Jay Cutler 1.00 2.50
KJ Kevin Jones 1.00 2.50
LF Larry Fitzgerald 1.25 3.00
LM Laurence Maroney 1.25 3.00
MC Marques Colston 1.00 2.50
ML Matt Leinart 1.00 2.50
PR Philip Rivers 1.50 4.00
RB Reggie Bush 1.00 2.50
RW Roy Williams WR 1.00 2.50
SJ Steven Jackson 1.00 2.50
SM Shawne Merriman 1.00 2.50
VY Vince Young 1.00 2.50

2007 Topps TX Exclusive Ticket 2 Stardom Jersey

ATED PRINT RUN 199 SER.#'d SETS
*PATCH/49: .8X TO 2X BASIC JSY/199
PATCH PRINT RUN 49 SER.#'d SETS
AS Alex Smith QB 3.00 8.00
BJ Brandon Jacobs 2.50 6.00
BR Ben Roethlisberger 4.00 10.00
CW Cadillac Williams 3.00 8.00
DH DeAngelo Hall 2.50 6.00
DW DeAngelo Williams 2.50 6.00
FG Frank Gore 3.00 8.00
GJ Greg Jennings 2.50 6.00
JA Joseph Addai 2.50 6.00
JC Jay Cutler 2.50 6.00
JC Jerricho Cotchery 2.50 6.00
KJ Kevin Jones 2.50 6.00
LF Larry Fitzgerald 3.00 8.00
LM Laurence Maroney 3.00 8.00
MC Marques Colston 2.50 6.00
ML Matt Leinart 2.50 6.00
PR Philip Rivers 4.00 10.00
RB Reggie Bush 2.50 6.00
RW Roy Williams WR 2.50 6.00
SJ Steven Jackson 2.50 6.00
SM Shawne Merriman 2.50 6.00
VY Vince Young 2.50 6.00

2007 Topps TX Exclusive Ticket 2 Stardom Jersey Autographs

STATED PRINT RUN 25 SER.#'d SETS
UNPRICED PATCH PRINT RUN 5
AS Alex Smith QB 15.00 40.00
CW Cadillac Williams 15.00 40.00
DH DeAngelo Hall 12.00 30.00
DW DeAngelo Williams 12.00 30.00
FG Frank Gore 15.00 40.00
GJ Greg Jennings 12.00 30.00
JA Joseph Addai 12.00 30.00
JC Jerricho Cotchery 12.00 30.00
KJ Kevin Jones 12.00 30.00
LM Laurence Maroney 15.00 40.00
MC Marques Colston 15.00 40.00
ML Matt Leinart 12.00 30.00
RB Reggie Bush 12.00 30.00
RW Roy Williams WR 12.00 30.00
SJ Steven Jackson 12.00 30.00
SM Shawne Merriman 12.00 30.00
VY Vince Young 12.00 30.00

2007 Topps TX Exclusive Ticket to Hawaii

SE/499 STATED ODDS 1:14
*BRONZE/99: .6X TO 1.5X BASIC INSERTS
BRONZE/99 ODDS 1:70
*SILVER/49: .8X TO 2X BASIC INSERTS
SILVER/49 ODDS 1:141
*GOLD/10: 2X TO 5X BASIC INSERTS
GOLD/10 ODDS 1:698
AC Alge Crumpler 1.25 3.00
AJ Andre Johnson 1.25 3.00
CJ Chad Johnson 1.00 2.50
CP Carson Palmer 1.25 3.00
DB Drew Brees 1.50 4.00
DD Donald Driver 1.25 3.00
DH Devin Hester 1.25 3.00
DHA DeAngelo Hall 1.00 2.50
ER Ed Reed 1.25 3.00
FG Frank Gore 1.25 3.00
JP Julius Peppers 1.25 3.00
JPE Julian Peterson 1.00 2.50
JT Jason Taylor 1.25 3.00
LJ Larry Johnson 1.00 2.50
LT LaDainian Tomlinson 1.50 4.00
PM Peyton Manning 4.00 10.00
RW Reggie Wayne 1.25 3.00
SH Steve Hutchinson 1.25 3.00
SJ Steven Jackson 1.00 2.50
SM Shawne Merriman 1.00 2.50
SS Steve Smith 1.25 3.00
TG Tarik Glenn 1.00 2.50
TR Tony Romo 2.00 5.00
VY Vince Young 1.00 2.50

2007 Topps TX Exclusive Ticket to Hawaii Jersey

STATED PRINT RUN 249 SER.#'d SETS
*PATCH/49: .8X TO 2X BASIC JSY/199
PATCH PRINT RUN 49 SER.#'d SETS
AC Alge Crumpler 3.00 8.00
AJ Andre Johnson 3.00 8.00
CJ Chad Johnson 2.50 6.00
CP Carson Palmer 3.00 8.00
DB Drew Brees 4.00 10.00
DD Donald Driver 3.00 8.00
DH Devin Hester 6.00 15.00
DHA DeAngelo Hall 2.50 6.00
ER Ed Reed 3.00 8.00
FG Frank Gore 3.00 8.00
JP Julius Peppers 3.00 8.00
JPE Julian Peterson 4.00 10.00
JT Jason Taylor 3.00 8.00
LJ Larry Johnson 2.50 6.00
LT LaDainian Tomlinson 4.00 10.00
PM Peyton Manning 10.00 25.00
RW Reggie Wayne 3.00 8.00
SH Steve Hutchinson 3.00 8.00
SJ Steven Jackson 2.50 6.00
SM Shawne Merriman 2.50 6.00
SS Steve Smith 3.00 8.00
TG Tarik Glenn 3.00 8.00
TR Tony Romo 12.50 30.00
VY Vince Young 2.50 6.00

2007 Topps TX Exclusive Ticket to Hawaii Jersey Autographs

STATED PRINT RUN 25 SER.#'d SETS
UNPRICED PATCH PRINT RUN 5
CJ Chad Johnson 20.00 40.00
DB Drew Brees 40.00 80.00
DHA DeAngelo Hall 12.00 30.00
FG Frank Gore 25.00 50.00
JP Julius Peppers
LJ Larry Johnson 15.00 40.00
LT LaDainian Tomlinson 60.00 120.00
PM Peyton Manning 150.00 250.00
RW Reggie Wayne 30.00 60.00
SH Steve Hutchinson 20.00 40.00
SJ Steven Jackson 25.00 50.00
SM Shawne Merriman 25.00 50.00
SS Steve Smith
TG Tarik Glenn 20.00 40.00
TR Tony Romo 100.00 175.00
VY Vince Young 50.00 120.00

2009 Topps Unique

COMPLETE SET (200) 50.00 100.00
COMP.SET w/o SP's (150) 15.00 30.00
SHORT PRINT/1829 ODDS 1:2
1 Drew Brees/1829 1.25 3.00
2 Julius Jones .20 .50
3 Ray Lewis .30 .75
4 Devin Hester .25 .60
5 Jamal Lewis .25 .60
6 Darren Sharper .20 .50
7 Brian Urlacher .30 .75
8 Darren Sproles .25 .60
9 Greg Olsen .25 .60
10 Ted Ginn .20 .50
11 Tony Gonzalez/1829 1.00 2.50
12 Fred Jackson .25 .60
13 Owen Daniels .20 .50
14 Patrick Willis .25 .60
15 DeMarcus Ware .25 .60
16 Earl Bennett/1829 1.00 2.50
17 Chris Cooley .20 .50
18 Nate Burleson .20 .50
19 Laurent Robinson .20 .50
20 Matt Forte .20 .50
21 Willis McGahee/1829 .75 2.00
22 Muhsin Muhammad .20 .50
23 Antonio Cromartie/1829 .75 2.00
24 Patrick Crayton .20 .50
25 Steve Breaston .25 .60
26 Steve Smith USC .25 .60
27 Chris Chambers .20 .50
28 Zach Miller .20 .50
29 Fred Taylor .20 .50
30 Adrian Peterson .30 .75
31 Kellen Winslow/1829 .75 2.00
32 Vernon Davis .20 .50
33 Visanthe Shiancoe .25 .60
34 Jerious Norwood .20 .50
35 Dustin Keller/1829 .75 2.00
36 Donnie Avery/1829 .75 2.00
37 Michael Vick .25 .60
38 Josh Morgan .20 .50
39 Rashard Mendenhall/1829 .75 2.00
40 Steven Jackson/1829 .75 2.00
41 Ahmad Bradshaw .20 .50
42 Michael Bush .20 .50
43 Jeremy Shockey/1829 .75 2.00
44 Jairus Byrd RC .75 2.00
45 Darrelle Revis .20 .50
46 Dallas Clark/1829 .75 2.00
47 Chester Taylor/1829 .75 2.00
48 Chaz Schilens .20 .50
49 Ricky Williams .25 .60
50 Tom Brady 1.00 2.50
51 Mark Clayton/1829 .75 2.00
52 John Carlson/1829 1.00 2.50
53 Asante Samuel .20 .50
54 Peyton Manning .75 2.00
55 Aaron Rodgers .60 1.50
56 Philip Rivers/1829 1.25 3.00
57 Kurt Warner .25 .60
58 Donovan McNabb .25 .60
59 Matt Ryan .25 .60
60 DeAngelo Williams .20 .50
61 Tony Romo .25 .60
62 Carson Palmer .25 .60
63 Matt Schaub .20 .50
64 Matt Hasselbeck/1829 .75 2.00
65 Brett Favre 1.25 3.00
66 David Garrard .20 .50
67 Chad Pennington .20 .50
68 Ben Roethlisberger/1829 1.25 3.00
69 Kyle Orton .20 .50
70 Michael Turner .20 .50
71 Joe Flacco .25 .60
72 Trent Edwards/1829 .75 2.00
73 Eli Manning .25 .60
74 Matt Cassel .20 .50
75 Jake Delhomme .20 .50
76 Kerry Collins/1829 .75 2.00
77 JaMarcus Russell .20 .50
78 Brady Quinn .20 .50
79 Marc Bulger .20 .50
80 Larry Fitzgerald .25 .60
81 Domenik Hixon .20 .50
82 Isaac Bruce .30 .75
83 LaDainian Tomlinson .30 .75
84 Tim Hightower .20 .50
85 Jay Cutler/1829 .75 2.00
86 Jason Campbell .20 .50
87 Maurice Jones-Drew/1829 .75 2.00
88 Roddy White .20 .50
89 Brandon Jacobs/1829 .75 2.00
90 Andre Johnson/1829 1.00 2.50
91 T.J. Houshmandzadeh/1829 .75 2.00
92 Santonio Holmes .20 .50
93 Cedric Benson/1829 .75 2.00
94 Calvin Johnson .30 .75
95 Steve Slaton .20 .50
96 Greg Jennings/1829 .75 2.00
97 Marion Barber .25 .60
98 Steve Smith .25 .60
99 Clinton Portis .20 .50
100 Brian Westbrook .20 .50
101 Reggie Bush .20 .50
102 Anquan Boldin .20 .50
103 Pierre Thomas .20 .50
104 Ronnie Brown/1829 .75 2.00
105 Ryan Grant .25 .60
106 Marques Colston .20 .50
107 Kevin Smith .20 .50
108 Wes Welker/1829 1.00 2.50
109 Dwayne Bowe .25 .60
110 Chris Johnson .20 .50
111 Vincent Jackson .20 .50
112 Thomas Jones/1829 .75 2.00
113 Jason Witten .25 .60
114 Eddie Royal .20 .50
115 Ed Reed .25 .60
116 Chad Ochocinco/1829 .75 2.00
117 Joseph Addai .20 .50
118 Terrell Owens .25 .60
119 Anthony Gonzalez .20 .50
120 Randy Moss .25 .60
121 DeSean Jackson .25 .60
122 Braylon Edwards .20 .50
123 LenDale White .20 .50
124 Darren McFadden/1829 1.25 3.00
125 Derrick Mason .20 .50
126 Laveranues Coles .20 .50
127 Antonio Gates .25 .60
128 Felix Jones/1829 .75 2.00
129 Antonio Bryant .20 .50
130 Reggie Wayne/1829 1.00 2.50
131 Donald Driver .25 .60
132 Hines Ward/1829 1.00 2.50
133 Leon Washington .20 .50
134 Brandon Marshall .25 .60
135 Troy Polamalu .30 .75
136 Roy Williams WR/1829 .75 2.00
137 Jerricho Cotchery .20 .50
138 Ray Rice .20 .50
139 Kevin Walter .25 .60
140 Frank Gore .25 .60
141 Lee Evans .25 .60
142 Bernard Berrian .20 .50
143 Derrick Ward/1829 .75 2.00
144 Marshawn Lynch/1829 1.00 2.50
145 Jonathan Stewart .20 .50
146 Larry Johnson .20 .50
147 Willie Parker .20 .50
148 Santana Moss .25 .60
149 Torry Holt .25 .60
150 Matthew Stafford RC 2.50 6.00
151 Aaron Curry RC .75 2.00
152 Rashad Jennings RC .60 1.50
153 Brian Robiskie/1829 RC .60 1.50
154 Deon Butler RC .50 1.25
155 Chris Wells RC .50 1.25
156 Aaron Maybin/1829 RC .75 2.00
157 Darrius Heyward-Bey/1829 RC 1.00 2.50
158 Derrick Williams RC .50 1.25
159 Glen Coffee RC .50 1.25
160 Hakeem Nicks RC .60 1.50
161 Josh Freeman/1829 RC .60 1.50
162 Juaquin Iglesias RC .50 1.25
163 Mike Goodson RC .60 1.50
164 Andre Brown RC .60 1.50
165 Percy Harvin RC .50 1.25
166 Jason Smith RC .50 1.25
167 Kenny Britt RC .75 2.00
168 Rhett Bomar RC .50 1.25
169 Nate Davis RC .50 1.25
170 Knowshon Moreno RC .50 1.25
171 Mohamed Massaquoi RC .50 1.25
172 Bernard Scott RC .75 2.00
173 Mike Thomas/1829 RC .60 1.50
174 Mike Wallace RC .75 2.00
175 LeSean McCoy/1829 RC 1.50 4.00
176 Javon Ringer/1829 RC .60 1.50
177 Patrick Turner/1829 RC .60 1.50
178 Pat White RC .60 1.50
179 Ramses Barden RC .50 1.25
180 Michael Crabtree RC .75 2.00
181 Shonn Greene/1829 RC .60 1.50
182 Stephen McGee RC .50 1.25
183 Tyson Jackson RC .50 1.25
184 B.J. Raji RC .60 1.50
185 Donald Brown RC .50 1.25
186 Brian Orakpo RC .60 1.50
187 Malcolm Jenkins RC .50 1.25
188 Brian Cushing RC .50 1.25
189 Brian Hartline/1829 RC 1.00 2.50
190 Jeremy Maclin RC .60 1.50
191 Louis Murphy RC .50 1.25
192 Austin Collie RC .50 1.25
193 Gartrell Johnson/1829 RC .60 1.50
194 Jared Cook RC .60 1.50
195 Brandon Pettigrew RC .50 1.25
196 Shawn Nelson RC .50 1.25
197 Sammie Stroughter/1829 RC .60 1.50
198 Chase Coffman RC .50 1.25
199 James Davis RC .50 1.25
200 Mark Sanchez RC .50 1.25

2009 Topps Unique Bronze

*VETS: 2.5X TO 6X BASIC CARDS
*VETS: .6X TO 1.5X BASIC SP
*ROOKIES: .8X TO 2X BASIC CARDS
*ROOKIES: .6X TO 1.5X BASIC SP RC
BRONZE/99 ODDS 1:10

2009 Topps Unique Gold

*VETS: 4X TO 10X BASIC CARDS
*VETS: 1X TO 2.5X BASIC SP
*ROOKIES: 1.2X TO 3X BASIC CARDS
*ROOKIES: 1X TO 2.5X BASIC SP RC
GOLD/25 ODDS 1:37

2009 Topps Unique Red

*VETS: 2X TO 5X BASIC CARDS
*VETS: .5X TO 1.2X BASIC SP
*ROOKIES: .5X TO 1.2X BASIC CARDS
*ROOKIES: .4X TO 1X BASIC SP RC
RED/799 ODDS 1:2

2009 Topps Unique Alone At The Top

COMPLETE SET (10) 8.00 20.00
STATED ODDS 1:12
*BRONZE/99: 1X TO 2.5X BASIC INSERTS
*GOLD/25: 1.2X TO 3X BASIC INSERTS
AT1 Adrian Peterson 1.00 2.50
AT2 Drew Brees 1.00 2.50
AT3 Andre Johnson .75 2.00
AT4 DeAngelo Williams .60 1.50
AT5 Philip Rivers 1.00 2.50
AT6 Larry Fitzgerald .75 2.00
AT7 D'Qwell Jackson .60 1.50
AT8 DeMarcus Ware .75 2.00
AT9 Ed Reed .75 2.00
AT10 Drew Brees 1.00 2.50

2009 Topps Unique Dynamic Dual Autographs

AL AUTO/25 ODDS 1:729
BB T.Brady/D.Brees 150.00 300.00
BM D.Bowe/B.Marshall 20.00 40.00
BN K.Britt/H.Nicks 20.00 40.00
CH Crabtree/Heyward-Bey 20.00 50.00
MW R.Moss/R.Wayne 30.00 80.00
OE C.Ochocinco/B.Edwards 20.00 40.00
PH A.Peterson/P.Harvin 75.00 150.00
PT A.Peterson/Tomlinson 75.00 150.00
RW M.Ryan/R.White 40.00 80.00
WM C.Wells/K.Moreno 20.00 50.00

2009 Topps Unique Dynamic Dual Jerseys

DUAL JERSEY/79 ODDS 1:93
JA J.Addai/D.Brown 2.50 6.00
BB D.Brees/R.Bush 6.00 15.00
BM T.Brady/R.Moss 10.00 25.00
NB R.Barden/H.Nicks 3.00 8.00
BF L.Fitzgerald/A.Boldin 4.00 10.00
GG F.Gore/G.Coffee 2.50 6.00
HF D.Hester/M.Forte 4.00 10.00
BJ F.Jones/M.Barber 6.00 15.00
JS A.Johnson/S.Slaton 4.00 10.00
MJ E.Manning/B.Jacobs 6.00 15.00
MM L.McCoy/J.Maclin 6.00 15.00
MS S.Moss/C.Portis 4.00 10.00
MW D.McNabb/B.Westbrook 4.00 10.00
PH Peterson/P.Harvin 2.50 6.00
RB J.Ringer/K.Britt 4.00 10.00
RG P.Rivers/A.Gates 5.00 12.00
RJ A.Rodgers/G.Jennings 8.00 20.00
RMA B.Robiskie/M.Massaquoi 2.50 6.00
SK M.Sanchez/D.Keller 10.00 25.00
SP M.Stafford/B.Pettigrew 8.00 20.00
WS D.Williams/S.Smith 4.00 10.00
MR B.Marshall/E.Royal 4.00 10.00
RM K.Moreno/E.Royal 2.50 6.00
RW T.Romo/J.Witten 4.00 10.00
RWH M.Ryan/R.White 4.00 10.00

2009 Topps Unique Game Breakers Autographs

STATED PRINT RUN 25-1000
BB Bernard Berrian/150 5.00 12.00
BF Brett Favre/25 175.00 300.00
BQ Brady Quinn/25 15.00 40.00
DB Drew Brees/50 40.00 80.00
EM Eli Manning/50 40.00 80.00
FG Frank Gore/100 6.00 15.00
GC Glen Coffee/250 3.00 8.00
HN Hakeem Nicks/100 4.00 10.00
JA Joseph Addai/100 5.00 12.00
JC Jamaal Charles/500 6.00 15.00
JD James Davis/1000 2.50 6.00
JF1 Joe Flacco/200 10.00 25.00
JF2 Josh Freeman/100 3.00 8.00
JK Johnny Knox/750 3.00 8.00
JM Jeremy Maclin/100 10.00 25.00
JS Jonathan Stewart/100 8.00 20.00
LE Lee Evans/100 5.00 12.00
LM LeSean McCoy/400 8.00 20.00
MC Matt Cassel/100 8.00 20.00
MR Matt Ryan/50 25.00 50.00
PH Percy Harvin/200 10.00 25.00
PM Peyton Manning/25 75.00 150.00
PW Pat White/400 4.00 10.00
RJ Rashad Jennings/500 3.00 8.00
RR Ray Rice/400 10.00 25.00
SS Steve Smith USC/500 5.00 12.00
TE Trent Edwards/250 5.00 12.00
WW Wes Welker/50 15.00 40.00

2009 Topps Unique Game Breakers Jersey

GAME BREAKER JERSEY/199 ODDS 1:37
AJ Andre Johnson 3.00 8.00
AP Adrian Peterson 4.00 10.00
BJ Brandon Jacobs 2.50 6.00
BM Brandon Marshall 3.00 8.00
BR Ben Roethlisberger 4.00 10.00
BW Brian Westbrook 2.50 6.00
CP Clinton Portis 2.50 8.00
DW DeAngelo Williams 2.50 6.00
EM Eli Manning 3.00 8.00
FG Frank Gore 3.00 8.00
GJ Greg Jennings 2.50 6.00
JA Joseph Addai 2.50 6.00
JS Jonathan Stewart 2.50 6.00
LF Larry Fitzgerald 3.00 8.00
MB Marion Barber 3.00 8.00
MF Matt Forte 2.50 6.00
MJD Maurice Jones-Drew 2.50 6.00
PM Peyton Manning 10.00 25.00
PR Philip Rivers 4.00 10.00
RB Reggie Bush 2.50 6.00
RM Randy Moss 3.00 8.00
RW Reggie Wayne 3.00 8.00
SH Santonio Holmes 2.50 6.00
SS Steve Slaton 2.50 6.00
TR Tony Romo 3.00 8.00

2009 Topps Unique Game Breakers Jersey Autographs

ME BREAKER JSY AU/25 ODDS 1:729
BJ Brandon Jacobs 8.00 20.00
BW Brian Westbrook
DW DeAngelo Williams 8.00 20.00
FG Frank Gore
JC Jay Cutler 8.00 20.00
JF Joe Flacco 20.00 40.00
JS Jonathan Stewart 8.00 20.00
MB Marion Barber
MR Matt Ryan 25.00 50.00
MS Mark Sanchez
SS Steve Slaton 8.00 20.00

2009 Topps Unique Jumbo Relic Patch

JUMBO PATCH/10-20 ODDS 1:289
SERIAL #'d UNDER 20 NOT PRICED
AJ Andre Johnson/20 12.00 30.00
AV Adam Vinatieri/20 20.00 50.00
BF Brett Favre/20 75.00 150.00
BR B.J. Raji/20 12.00 30.00
BU Brian Urlacher/20 20.00 50.00
DW Derrick Williams/20 10.00 25.00
EH Evander Hood/20 15.00 40.00
JPW John Parker Wilson/20 10.00 25.00
JS1 Jeremy Shockey/20 12.00 30.00
KC Kevin Curtis/20 12.00 30.00
KS Kevin Smith/20 12.00 30.00
MO Michael Oher/20 15.00 40.00
MT Mike Thomas/20 10.00 25.00
MTH Mike Thomas/20 10.00 25.00
PT Patrick Turner/20 10.00 25.00
QC Quan Cosby/20 12.00 30.00
SN Shawn Nelson/20 12.00 30.00
SS2 Steve Smith/20 15.00 40.00
TG Tony Gonzalez/20 15.00 40.00
TH1 Todd Heap/20 12.00 30.00
TH2 Torry Holt/20 15.00 40.00
TP Troy Polamalu/20 20.00 50.00

2009 Topps Unique Prime Time Patches

STATED PRINT RUN 25-99
PTP1 Joseph Addai/50 4.00 10.00
PTP2 Donnie Avery/50 4.00 10.00
PTP3 Donnie Avery/40 4.00 10.00
PTP4 Marion Barber/99 5.00 12.00
PTP5 Anquan Boldin/50 4.00 10.00
PTP6 Anquan Boldin/40 4.00 10.00
PTP7 Dwayne Bowe/50 5.00 12.00
PTP8 Dwayne Bowe/40 5.00 12.00
PTP9 Terry Bradshaw/50 8.00 20.00
PTP10 Tom Brady/99 15.00 40.00
PTP11 Tom Brady/40 20.00 50.00
PTP12 Drew Brees/75 6.00 15.00
PTP13 Kenny Britt/50 3.00 8.00
PTP14 Kenny Britt/40 3.00 8.00
PTP16 Ronnie Brown/50 4.00 10.00
PTP17 Ronnie Brown/40 4.00 10.00
PTP18 Reggie Bush/50 4.00 10.00
PTP19 Reggie Bush/40 4.00 10.00
PTP20 Brian Westbrook/50 4.00 10.00
PTP21 Brian Westbrook/40 4.00 10.00
PTP22 Dallas Clark/50 4.00 10.00
PTP23 Dallas Clark/40 4.00 10.00
PTP25 Laveranues Coles/75 4.00 10.00
PTP26 Marques Colston/50 4.00 10.00
PTP27 Chris Cooley/75 4.00 10.00
PTP28 Jerricho Cotchery/50 4.00 10.00
PTP29 Jerricho Cotchery/40 4.00 10.00
PTP33 Brian Dawkins/50 6.00 15.00
PTP34 Brian Dawkins/40 6.00 15.00
PTP35 Donald Driver/75 5.00 12.00
PTP36 Braylon Edwards/50 4.00 10.00
PTP37 Trent Edwards/50 4.00 10.00
PTP38 Trent Edwards/40 4.00 10.00
PTP39 John Elway/50 10.00 25.00
PTP40 Lee Evans/50 5.00 12.00
PTP41 Lee Evans/40 5.00 12.00
PTP42 Brett Favre/25 20.00 50.00
PTP43 Larry Fitzgerald/50 5.00 12.00
PTP44 Joe Flacco/50 5.00 12.00
PTP46 Antonio Gates/50 5.00 12.00
PTP47 Antonio Gates/40 5.00 12.00
PTP48 Ted Ginn/50 4.00 10.00
PTP49 Ted Ginn/40 4.00 10.00
PTP50 Anthony Gonzalez/50 4.00 10.00
PTP51 Anthony Gonzalez/50 4.00 10.00
PTP52 Tony Gonzalez/50 5.00 12.00
PTP53 Tony Gonzalez/40 5.00 12.00
PTP54 Frank Gore/99 5.00 12.00
PTP55 Frank Gore/40 5.00 12.00
PTP56 Marvin Harrison/50 5.00 12.00
PTP57 Marvin Harrison/40 5.00 12.00
PTP59 Matt Hasselbeck/50 4.00 10.00
PTP60 Matt Hasselbeck/40 4.00 10.00
PTP61 Devin Hester/75 5.00 12.00
PTP62 Santonio Holmes/50 4.00 10.00
PTP63 T.J. Houshmandzadeh/50 4.00 10.00
PTP64 T.J. Houshmandzadeh/40 4.00 10.00
PTP65 DeSean Jackson/50 5.00 12.00
PTP66 Steven Jackson/99 4.00 10.00
PTP67 Steven Jackson/40 4.00 10.00
PTP68 Vincent Jackson/75 4.00 10.00
PTP69 Edgerrin James/50 5.00 12.00
PTP70 Edgerrin James/40 5.00 12.00
PTP71 Greg Jennings/75 4.00 10.00
PTP72 Andre Johnson/50 5.00 12.00
PTP73 Andre Johnson/40 5.00 12.00
PTP74 Calvin Johnson/50 6.00 15.00
PTP75 Calvin Johnson/40 6.00 15.00
PTP76 Chad Ochocinco/50 4.00 10.00
PTP77 Chad Ochocinco/40 4.00 10.00
PTP78 Felix Jones/50 4.00 10.00
PTP79 Felix Jones/40 4.00 10.00
PTP80 Maurice Jones-Drew/50 4.00 10.00
PTP81 Maurice Jones-Drew/40 4.00 10.00
PTP82 Jamal Lewis/50 5.00 12.00
PTP83 Ray Lewis/50 6.00 15.00
PTP84 Ray Lewis/40 6.00 15.00
PTP85 Marshawn Lynch/50 5.00 12.00
PTP86 Marshawn Lynch/40 5.00 12.00
PTP89 Peyton Manning/50 15.00 40.00
PTP90 Dan Marino/50 15.00 40.00
PTP91 DeAngelo Williams/50 4.00 10.00
PTP92 DeAngelo Williams/40 4.00 10.00
PTP94 Darren McFadden/75 6.00 15.00
PTP95 Willis McGahee/50 4.00 10.00
PTP96 Willis McGahee/40 4.00 10.00
PTP97 Donovan McNabb/50 5.00 12.00
PTP98 Donovan McNabb/40 5.00 12.00
PTP99 Rashard Mendenhall/50 4.00 10.00
PTP100 Rashard Mendenhall/40 4.00 10.00
PTP101 Joe Montana/25 25.00 60.00
PTP103 Randy Moss/50 5.00 12.00
PTP104 Randy Moss/40 5.00 12.00
PTP105 Santana Moss/75 5.00 12.00
PTP106 Hakeem Nicks/50 5.00 12.00
PTP107 Greg Olsen/75 5.00 12.00
PTP108 Terrell Owens/50 5.00 12.00
PTP109 Terrell Owens/40 5.00 12.00
PTP110 Terrell Owens/50 5.00 12.00
PTP111 Terrell Owens/40 5.00 12.00
PTP112 Carson Palmer/50 5.00 12.00
PTP113 Carson Palmer/40 5.00 12.00
PTP114 Willie Parker/50 4.00 10.00
PTP115 Willie Parker/40 4.00 10.00
PTP116 Adrian Peterson/50 10.00 25.00
PTP117 Adrian Peterson/40 10.00 25.00
PTP118 Clinton Portis/50 4.00 10.00
PTP119 Clinton Portis/40 4.00 10.00
PTP120 Brady Quinn/50 4.00 10.00
PTP121 Brady Quinn/40 4.00 10.00
PTP122 Ed Reed/50 5.00 12.00
PTP123 Ed Reed/40 5.00 12.00
PTP125 Ray Rice/50 4.00 10.00
PTP126 Ray Rice/50 4.00 10.00
PTP127 Aaron Rodgers/75 10.00 25.00
PTP128 Ben Roethlisberger/50 6.00 15.00
PTP129 Eddie Royal/50 4.00 10.00
PTP130 Eddie Royal/40 4.00 10.00
PTP131 JaMarcus Russell/50 4.00 10.00
PTP132 JaMarcus Russell/40 4.00 10.00
PTP133 Matt Ryan/50 5.00 12.00
PTP135 Jeremy Shockey/50 4.00 10.00
PTP136 Jeremy Shockey/40 4.00 10.00
PTP137 Steve Slaton/50 4.00 10.00
PTP139 Steve Smith/50 5.00 12.00
PTP140 Steve Smith/40 5.00 12.00
PTP141 Matthew Stafford/50 10.00 25.00
PTP142 Jonathan Stewart/50 4.00 10.00
PTP143 Fred Taylor/50 4.00 10.00
PTP144 Fred Taylor/40 4.00 10.00
PTP145 LaDainian Tomlinson/50 6.00 15.00
PTP146 LaDainian Tomlinson/40 6.00 15.00
PTP147 Brian Urlacher/50 6.00 15.00
PTP148 Brian Urlacher/40 6.00 15.00
PTP149 Michael Vick/50 5.00 12.00
PTP150 Michael Vick/40 5.00 12.00
PTP151 Hines Ward/50 8.00 20.00
PTP152 Hines Ward/40 8.00 20.00
PTP153 Kurt Warner/75 5.00 12.00
PTP154 Reggie Wayne/50 5.00 12.00

2009 Topps Unique Triple Threat Jersey

TRIPLE JERSEY/25 ODDS 1:260
BBB Bomar/A.Brown/Barden 6.00 15.00
BBC Brees/Bush/Colston 8.00 20.00
BMW Brady/Moss/Welker 25.00 60.00
CHM Crabtree/Harvin/Maclin 5.00 12.00
CPM Campbell/Portis/Moss 6.00 15.00
DCC Davis/Coffee/Crabtree 5.00 12.00
ELE Edwards/Lynch/Evans 6.00 15.00
FRM Flacco/Rice/McGahee 6.00 15.00
GJT Garrard/Jones-Drew/Thomas 5.00 12.00
JMM Jackson/Maclin/McCoy 8.00 20.00
JWR Johnson/White/Ringer 5.00 12.00
MBW Moreno/Brown/Wells 10.00 25.00
MJN Eli/Jacobs/Nicks 4.00 10.00
MRM Moreno/Royal/Marshall 10.00 25.00
MWB Manning/Wayne/Brown 12.00 30.00
MWJ McNabb/Westbrook/Jackson 6.00 15.00
QEM Quinn/Edwards/Massaquoi 5.00 12.00
RBJ Romo/Barber/Jones 6.00 15.00
RGJ Rodgers/Grant/Jennings 12.00 30.00
RMH Russell/McFad/Hywrd-By 5.00 12.00
RMW Roeth/Mndnhll/Wllace 5.00 12.00
RTG Rivers/Tomlinson/Gates 8.00 20.00
SGK Sanchez/Greene/Keller 10.00 25.00
SPW Stafford/Pettigrew/Williams 10.00 25.00
SSF Stafford/Sanchez/Freeman 15.00 40.00
BGW P.White/R.Brown/Ginn 4.00 10.00
WFB Warner/Fitzgerald/Boldin 6.00 15.00
WSS Williams/S.Smith/Stewart 6.00 15.00

2009 Topps Unique Unique Unis

COMPLETE SET (20) 12.00 30.00
STATED ODDS 1:6
*BRONZE/99: 1X TO 2.5X BASIC INSERTS
*GOLD/25: 1.2X TO 3X BASIC INSERTS
UU1 Donovan McNabb .75 2.00
UU2 Brett Favre 4.00 10.00
UU3 Frank Gore .75 2.00
UU4 Tom Brady 3.00 8.00
UU5 Brian Westbrook .60 1.50
UU6 Tony Romo .75 2.00
UU7 Josh Freeman .60 1.50
UU8 LaDainian Tomlinson 1.00 2.50
UU9 Mark Sanchez .40 1.00
UU10 Terrell Owens .75 2.00
UU11 Philip Rivers 1.00 2.50
UU12 Ronnie Brown .60 1.50
UU13 Chris Johnson .60 1.50
UU14 Matt Forte .60 1.50
UU15 Adrian Peterson 1.00 2.50
UU16 Kyle Orton .60 1.50
UU17 Zach Miller .60 1.50
UU18 Steven Jackson .60 1.50
UU19 Dwayne Bowe .75 2.00
UU20 Ben Roethlisberger 1.00 2.50

2009 Topps Unique Unparalleled Performances

STATED ODDS 1:6
*BRONZE/99: 1X TO 2.5X BASIC INSERTS
*GOLD/25: 1.2X TO 3X BASIC INSERTS
UP1 Drew Brees 1.00 2.50
UP2 Andre Johnson .75 2.00
UP3 Michael Turner .60 1.50
UP4 Matt Forte .60 1.50
UP5 Tom Brady 3.00 8.00
UP6 Steven Jackson .60 1.50
UP7 Philip Rivers 1.00 2.50
UP8 Terrell Owens .75 2.00
UP9 Steve Smith .75 2.00
UP10 Adrian Peterson 1.00 2.50
UP11 Larry Fitzgerald .75 2.00
UP12 Frank Gore .75 2.00
UP13 Reggie Wayne .75 2.00
UP14 Brian Westbrook .60 1.50
UP15 Peyton Manning 2.50 6.00
UP16 DeAngelo Williams .60 1.50
UP17 Randy Moss .75 2.00
UP18 Maurice Jones-Drew .60 1.50
UP19 Clinton Portis .60 1.50
UP20 LaDainian Tomlinson 1.00 2.50

2010 Topps Unrivaled

COMP.SET w/o RC's (100) 8.00 20.00
151-200 ROOKIE/999 ODDS 1:8 HOB
1 Steven Jackson .20 .50
2 Joseph Addai .20 .50
3 Matthew Stafford .25 .60
4 Randy Moss .25 .60
5 Brandon Marshall .25 .60
6 Ray Lewis .30 .75
7 Nnamdi Asomugha .20 .50
8 Vincent Jackson .20 .50
9 Beanie Wells .20 .50
10 Ryan Grant .25 .60
11 Pierre Garcon .25 .60
12 Jonathan Vilma .20 .50
13 Shonn Greene .20 .50
14 Tony Romo .25 .60
15 Jon Beason .20 .50
16 Marques Colston .20 .50
17 Vince Young .20 .50
18 Vernon Davis .20 .50
19 Mike Wallace .20 .50
20 Patrick Willis .25 .60
21 Eli Manning .25 .60
22 DeAngelo Williams .20 .50
23 Mike Sims-Walker .20 .50
24 Troy Polamalu .30 .75
25 Jamaal Charles .25 .60
26 Knowshon Moreno .20 .50
27 LeSean McCoy .30 .75
28 Cedric Benson .20 .50
29 Dallas Clark .20 .50
30 Pierre Thomas .20 .50
31 DeSean Jackson .25 .60
32 Jonathan Stewart .20 .50
33 Lee Evans .25 .60
34 Darren McFadden .20 .50
35 Jay Cutler .20 .50
36 Philip Rivers .30 .75
37 Roddy White .20 .50
38 Calvin Johnson .30 .75
39 Ronnie Brown .20 .50
40 Chris Cooley .20 .50
41 Percy Harvin .20 .50
42 Carson Palmer .25 .60
43 Drew Brees .30 .75
44 Clinton Portis .20 .50
45 Reggie Wayne .25 .60
46 Hines Ward .25 .60
47 Mark Sanchez .20 .50
48 Brian Urlacher .30 .75
49 Jerome Harrison .20 .50
50 Kevin Kolb .20 .50
51 Tony Gonzalez .25 .60
52 Steve Smith .20 .50
53 T.J. Houshmandzadeh .20 .50
54 Justin Forsett .25 .60
55 Jeremy Maclin .20 .50
56 Ricky Williams .25 .60
57 Chad Henne .25 .60
58 Steve Smith .25 .60
59 Steve Slaton .20 .50
60 Brent Celek .20 .50
61 Asante Samuel .20 .50
62 Hakeem Nicks .20 .50
63 Matt Schaub .20 .50
64 Miles Austin .20 .50
65 Michael Crabtree .20 .50
66 Maurice Jones-Drew .20 .50
67 Rashard Mendenhall .20 .50
68 Joe Flacco .25 .60
69 Sidney Rice .20 .50
70 Donovan McNabb .25 .60
71 Aaron Rodgers .60 1.50
72 Fred Jackson .25 .60
73 Felix Jones .20 .50
74 Brett Favre .60 1.50
75 Chris Johnson .20 .50
76 Matt Ryan .25 .60
77 Adrian Peterson .30 .75
78 Andre Johnson .25 .60
79 Antonio Gates .25 .60
80 Tom Brady .75 2.00
81 Frank Gore .25 .60
82 Kellen Winslow .20 .50
83 Matt Forte .20 .50
84 Anquan Boldin .20 .50
85 Chad Ochocinco .20 .50
86 Greg Jennings .20 .50
87 Reggie Bush .20 .50
88 Jared Allen .20 .50
89 Santana Moss .25 .60
90 Braylon Edwards .20 .50
91 Brandon Jacobs .20 .50
92 Darrelle Revis .20 .50
93 Dwayne Bowe .25 .60
94 Peyton Manning .75 2.00
95 Thomas Jones .20 .50
96 James Laurinaitis .25 .60
97 Michael Turner .20 .50
98 Ray Rice .20 .50
99 Donald Brown .20 .50
100 Larry Fitzgerald .25 .60
101 Anthony McCoy RC 1.00 2.50
102 Anthony Dixon RC 1.00 2.50
103 Ryan Mathews RC 1.00 2.50
104 Mike Kafka RC 1.25 3.00
105 Brandon Ghee RC 1.00 2.50
106 Ndamukong Suh RC 2.00 5.00
107 C.J. Spiller RC 1.00 2.50
108 Montario Hardesty RC 1.00 2.50
109 Dan Williams RC 1.00 2.50
110 Eric Decker RC 1.25 3.00
111 Brandon LaFell RC 1.50 4.00
112 Rob Gronkowski RC 3.00 8.00
113 Aaron Hernandez RC 1.00 2.50
114 Jacoby Ford RC 1.00 2.50
115 Mike Williams RC 1.00 2.50
116 Demaryius Thomas RC 2.50 6.00
117 Tony Pike RC 1.00 2.50
118 Jimmy Clausen RC 1.00 2.50
119 John Skelton RC 1.25 3.00
120 Jonathan Crompton RC 1.00 2.50
121 Andre Roberts RC 1.25 3.00
122 Bryan Bulaga RC 1.00 2.50
123 Jimmy Graham RC 2.50 6.00
124 Jahvid Best RC 1.00 2.50
125 Taylor Price RC 1.00 2.50
126 Colt McCoy RC 1.25 3.00
127 Armanti Edwards RC 1.25 3.00
128 Carlton Mitchell RC 1.00 2.50
129 Dez Bryant RC 2.50 6.00
130 Damian Williams RC 1.00 2.50
131 Jonathan Dwyer RC 1.00 2.50
132 Jordan Shipley RC 1.00 2.50
133 Arrelious Benn RC 1.00 2.50
134 Charles Scott RC 1.00 2.50
135 Toby Gerhart RC 1.00 2.50
136 Tim Tebow RC 3.00 8.00
137 Ben Tate RC 1.00 2.50
138 Dexter McCluster RC 1.25 3.00
139 Sean Lee RC 2.00 5.00
140 Dan LeFevour RC 1.00 2.50
141 Jerry Hughes RC 1.00 2.50
142 Gerald McCoy RC 1.00 2.50
143 Sam Bradford RC 1.25 3.00
144 Riley Cooper RC 1.00 2.50
145 James Starks RC 1.25 3.00
146 Emmanuel Sanders RC 1.50 4.00
147 Marcus Easley RC 1.00 2.50
148 Mardy Gilyard RC 1.00 2.50
149 Trent Williams RC 1.25 3.00
150 Golden Tate RC 1.25 3.00

2010 Topps Unrivaled Black

*VETS 1-100: 4X TO 10X BASIC CARDS
*ROOKIES 101-150: .6X TO 1.5X BASIC CARDS
BLACK/99 STATED ODDS 1:37 HOB

2010 Topps Unrivaled Gold 499

*VETS: 2X TO 5X BASIC CARDS
*ROOKIES: .4X TO 1X BASIC CARDS
GOLD/499 STATED ODDS 1:8 HOB

2010 Topps Unrivaled Gold 759

*VETS: 1.5X TO 4X BASIC CARDS
VETS GOLD/759 ODDS 1:6 HOB

2010 Topps Unrivaled Red

*VETS 1-100: 8X TO 20X BASIC CARDS
*ROOKIES 101-150: 1.5X TO 4X BASIC CARDS
RED/25 STATED ODDS 1:140 HOB

2010 Topps Unrivaled Silver

*VETS: 2.5X TO 6X BASIC CARDS
*ROOKIES: .5X TO 1.2X BASIC CARDS
SILVER PRINT RUN 299 SER.#'d SETS

2010 Topps Unrivaled Autographed Patch

GROUP A ODDS 1:1052 HOB
GROUP B ODDS 1:334 HOB
GROUP C ODDS 1:153 HOB
GROUP D ODDS 1:183 HOB
GROUP E ODDS 1:65 HOB
*VET JUMBO/15: .8X TO 2X AU/149
*VET JUMBO/15: .6X TO 1.5X AU/50-100
*ROOKIE JUMBO/15: .8X TO 2X AU/149-349
*ROOKIE JUMBO/15: .5X TO 1.2X AU/50-100
*ROOKIE JUMBO/15: .5X TO 1X AU/30
EXCH EXPIRATION: 10/31/2013
UAPAB Arrelious Benn/349 5.00 12.00
UAPAD Anthony Dixon/249 5.00 12.00
UAPAE Armanti Edwards/349 6.00 15.00
UAPAH Aaron Hernandez/149 8.00 20.00
UAPAP Adrian Peterson/149 40.00 100.00
UAPAR Andre Roberts/349 6.00 15.00
UAPBB Bernard Berrian/149 6.00 15.00
UAPBE Braylon Edwards/149 6.00 15.00
UAPBL Brandon LaFell/349 8.00 20.00
UAPBT Ben Tate/249 5.00 12.00
UAPCMC Colt McCoy/50 10.00 25.00
UAPCO Chad Ochocinco/100 8.00 20.00
UAPCS C.J. Spiller/100 6.00 15.00
UAPCSC Charles Scott/249 5.00 12.00
UAPCT Chester Taylor/149 6.00 15.00
UAPDB Dez Bryant/30 60.00 120.00
UAPDBO Dwayne Bowe/149 8.00 20.00
UAPDMC Dexter McCluster/349 6.00 15.00
UAPDT Demaryius Thomas/100 12.00 30.00
UAPDW DeAngelo Williams/100 8.00 20.00
UAPDWI Damian Williams/349 5.00 12.00
UAPED Eric Decker/349 6.00 15.00
UAPES Emmanuel Sanders/349 8.00 20.00
UAPFG Frank Gore/50 12.00 30.00
UAPFJ Felix Jones/50 10.00 25.00
UAPGM Gerald McCoy/149 5.00 12.00
UAPGT Golden Tate/349 8.00 20.00
UAPJB Jahvid Best/100 6.00 15.00
UAPJC Jimmy Clausen/50 8.00 20.00
UAPJD Jonathan Dwyer/249 5.00 12.00
UAPJF Jacoby Ford/349 5.00 12.00
UAPJG1 Jermaine Gresham/249 5.00 12.00
UAPJG2 Jermaine Gresham/221 5.00 12.00
UAPJGR Jimmy Graham/349 10.00 25.00
UAPJM Jeremy Maclin/149 6.00 15.00
UAPJN Jordy Nelson/149 8.00 20.00
UAPJS James Starks/249 6.00 15.00
UAPJSH Jordan Shipley/349 5.00 12.00

UAPKM Knowshon Moreno/100 8.00 20.00
UAPLL LaRon Landry/149 6.00 15.00
UAPLT LaDainian Tomlinson/50 25.00 60.00
UAPMC Matt Cassel/149 6.00 15.00
UAPME Marcus Easley/349 5.00 12.00
UAPMG Mardy Gilyard/349 5.00 12.00
UAPMH Montario Hardesty/249 5.00 12.00
UAPMK Mike Kafka/349 6.00 15.00
UAPMR Matt Ryan/149 25.00 60.00
UAPMW Mike Williams/249 5.00 12.00
UAPNS Ndamukong Suh/100 20.00 50.00
UAPPH Percy Harvin/100 6.00 15.00
UAPPP Paul Posluszny/149 6.00 15.00
UAPRG Rob Gronkowski/149 25.00 60.00
UAPRM Ryan Mathews/100 6.00 15.00
UAPRMA Rey Maualuga/149 6.00 15.00
UAPSB Sam Bradford/50 30.00 60.00
UAPSJ Steven Jackson/100 8.00 20.00
UAPSR Sidney Rice/100 8.00 20.00
UAPTG Toby Gerhart/349 5.00 12.00
UAPTT Tim Tebow/30 60.00 120.00
UAPWM Willis McGahee/149 6.00 15.00

2010 Topps Unrivaled Autographed Patch Black

*VETS: .6X TO 1.5X BASIC AU/149
*VETS: .5X TO 1.2X BASIC AU/100
*VETS: .4X TO 1X BASIC AU/50
*ROOKIES: .6X TO 1.5X BASIC AU/149-349
*ROOKIES: .5X TO 1.2X BASIC AU/100
*ROOKIES: .4X TO 1X BASIC AU/30-50
AU PATCH BLACK/50 ODDS 1:157 HOB
UAPAP Adrian Peterson 40.00 100.00
UAPCMC Colt McCoy 25.00 60.00
UAPSB Sam Bradford 30.00 60.00

2010 Topps Unrivaled Greats

GREATS/499 ODDS 1:39 HOB
UGDM Dan Marino 3.00 8.00
UGED Eric Dickerson 1.25 3.00
UGES Emmitt Smith 2.50 6.00
UGET Earl Campbell 1.50 4.00
UGGS Gale Sayers 1.50 4.00
UGJE John Elway 2.50 6.00
UGJM Joe Montana 5.00 12.00
UGJN Joe Namath 2.00 5.00
UGMA Marcus Allen 1.50 4.00
UGRL Ronnie Lott 1.25 3.00
UGRS Roger Staubach 2.00 5.00
UGSY Steve Young 2.00 5.00
UGTA Troy Aikman 2.00 5.00
UGTD Tony Dorsett 1.50 4.00
UGTT Thurman Thomas 1.25 3.00

2010 Topps Unrivaled Greats Jerseys

GREATS JSY/199 ODDS 1:422 HOB
UGRDM Dan Marino 12.00 30.00
UGREC Earl Campbell 6.00 15.00
UGRED Eric Dickerson 5.00 12.00
UGRES Emmitt Smith 10.00 25.00
UGRGS Gale Sayers 6.00 15.00
UGRJE John Elway 10.00 25.00
UGRJM Joe Montana 20.00 50.00
UGRJN Joe Namath 8.00 20.00
UGRMA Marcus Allen 6.00 15.00
UGRRL Ronnie Lott 5.00 12.00
UGRRS Roger Staubach 8.00 20.00
UGRSY Steve Young 8.00 20.00
UGRTA Troy Aikman 8.00 20.00
UGRTD Tony Dorsett 6.00 15.00
UGRTT Thurman Thomas 5.00 12.00

2010 Topps Unrivaled Rookie Autographs

GROUP A ODDS 1:10,175 HOB
GROUP B ODDS 1:321 HOB
GROUP C ODDS 1:36 HOB
GROUP D ODDS 1:53 HOB
GROUP E ODDS 1:58 HOB
EXCH EXPIRATION: 10/31/2013
101 Anthony McCoy/780 2.50 6.00
102 Anthony Dixon/680 2.50 6.00
103 Ryan Mathews/125 3.00 8.00
104 Mike Kafka/480 3.00 8.00
105 Brandon Ghee/780 2.50 6.00
106 Ndamukong Suh/125 15.00 40.00
107 C.J. Spiller/125 3.00 8.00
108 Montario Hardesty/480 2.50 6.00
109 Dan Williams/780 2.50 6.00
110 Eric Decker/480 3.00 8.00
111 Brandon LaFell/680 4.00 10.00
112 Rob Gronkowski/480 30.00 60.00
113 Aaron Hernandez/480 8.00 20.00
114 Jacoby Ford/680 2.50 6.00
115 Mike Williams/480 2.50 6.00
116 Demaryius Thomas/125 8.00 20.00
117 Tony Pike/480 2.50 6.00
118 Jimmy Clausen/125 3.00 8.00
119 John Skelton/480 3.00 8.00
120 Jonathan Crompton/480 2.50 6.00
121 Andre Roberts/680 3.00 8.00
122 Bryan Bulaga/780 2.50 6.00
123 Jimmy Graham/480 12.00 30.00
124 Jahvid Best/125 3.00 8.00
125 Taylor Price/680 2.50 6.00
126 Colt McCoy/125 4.00 10.00
127 Armanti Edwards/480 3.00 8.00
128 Carlton Mitchell/780 2.50 6.00
129 Dez Bryant/20 30.00 60.00
130 Damian Williams/680 2.50 6.00
131 Jonathan Dwyer/480 2.50 6.00
132 Jordan Shipley/480 2.50 6.00
133 Arrelious Benn/480 2.50 6.00
134 Charles Scott/780 2.50 6.00
135 Toby Gerhart/480 2.50 6.00
136 Tim Tebow/20 60.00 150.00
137 Ben Tate/480 2.50 6.00
138 Dexter McCluster/680 3.00 8.00
139 Sean Lee/480 5.00 12.00
140 Dan LeFevour/480 2.50 6.00
141 Jerry Hughes/480 2.50 6.00
142 Gerald McCoy/125 3.00 8.00
143 Sam Bradford/125 25.00 60.00
144 Riley Cooper/480 2.50 6.00
145 James Starks/780 3.00 8.00
146 Emmanuel Sanders/680 4.00 10.00
147 Marcus Easley/680 2.50 6.00
148 Mardy Gilyard/680 2.50 6.00
149 Trent Williams/780 3.00 8.00
150 Golden Tate/480 5.00 12.00

2010 Topps Unrivaled Rookie Autographs Black

*BLACK AU: .5X TO 1.2X BASIC AU/480-780
*BLACK AU: .4X TO 1X BASIC AU/125
BLACK AU/99 ODDS 1:78 HOB
129 Dez Bryant/48 20.00 50.00
143 Sam Bradford 25.00 60.00

2010 Topps Unrivaled Rookie Autographs Dual

DUAL AUTO/25 ODDS 1:1040 HOB
BM1 S.Bradford/C.McCoy 30.00 60.00
BM2 J.Best/D.McCluster 12.00 30.00
BW A.Benn/M.Williams 10.00 25.00
CL J.Clausen/B.LaFell 15.00 40.00
CT J.Clausen/G.Tate 12.00 30.00
DB D.McCluster/C.Spiller 12.00 30.00
DG J.Dwyer/T.Gerhart 15.00 40.00
MB R.Mathews/J.Best 10.00 25.00
MG R.Mathews/T.Gerhart 10.00 25.00
MH C.McCoy/M.Hardesty 25.00 60.00
SC S.Bradford/J.Clausen 30.00 60.00
SM C.Spiller/R.Mathews 10.00 25.00
TH B.Tate/M.Hardesty 10.00 25.00
BBR S.Bradford/C.Spiller 12.00 30.00
SMC N.Suh/G.McCoy 25.00 60.00

2010 Topps Unrivaled Rookies

ROOKIE/199 ODDS 1:105 HOB
URAB Arrelious Benn 1.25 3.00
URCM Colt McCoy 1.50 4.00
URCS C.J. Spiller 1.25 3.00
URDB Dez Bryant 3.00 8.00
URDT Demaryius Thomas 3.00 8.00
URDW Damian Williams 1.25 3.00
UREB Eric Berry 2.00 5.00
URGM Gerald McCoy 1.25 3.00
URGT Golden Tate 1.50 4.00
URJB Jahvid Best 1.25 3.00
URJC Jimmy Clausen 1.25 3.00
URJD Jonathan Dwyer 1.25 3.00
URJG Jermaine Gresham 1.25 3.00
URJM Joe McKnight 1.25 3.00
URJS Jordan Shipley 1.25 3.00
URMG Mardy Gilyard 1.25 3.00
URMH Montario Hardesty 1.25 3.00
URMW Mike Williams 1.25 3.00
URNS Ndamukong Suh 2.50 6.00
URRG Rob Gronkowski 4.00 10.00
URRM Rolando McClain 1.25 3.00
URSB Sam Bradford 1.50 4.00
URTT Tim Tebow 4.00 10.00
URDMC Dexter McCluster 1.50 4.00
URRMA Ryan Mathews 1.25 3.00

2010 Topps Unrivaled Rookies Jerseys

ROOKIE JSY/99 ODDS 1:507 HOB
URRAB Arrelious Benn 2.50 6.00
URRCM Colt McCoy 3.00 8.00
URRCS C.J. Spiller 2.50 6.00
URRDB Dez Bryant 6.00 15.00
URRDT Demaryius Thomas 6.00 15.00
URRDW Damian Williams 2.50 6.00
URREB Eric Berry 4.00 10.00
URRGM Gerald McCoy 2.50 6.00
URRGT Golden Tate 3.00 8.00
URRJB Jahvid Best 2.50 6.00
URRJC Jimmy Clausen 2.50 6.00
URRJD Jonathan Dwyer 2.50 6.00
URRJG Jermaine Gresham 2.50 6.00
URRJM Joe McKnight 2.50 6.00
URRJS Jordan Shipley 2.50 6.00
URRMG Mardy Gilyard 2.50 6.00
URRMH Montario Hardesty 2.50 6.00
URRMW Mike Williams 2.50 6.00
URRNS Ndamukong Suh 5.00 12.00
URRRG Rob Gronkowski 8.00 20.00
URRRM Rolando McClain 2.50 6.00
URRSB Sam Bradford 3.00 8.00
URRTT Tim Tebow 8.00 20.00
URRDMC Dexter McCluster 3.00 8.00
URRRMA Ryan Mathews 2.50 6.00

2010 Topps Unrivaled Trio

TRIO/299 ODDS 1:174 HOB
ABM Allen/Bush/McKnight 2.50 6.00
DPB Dickerson/Portis/Best 2.50 6.00
DTM Dorsett/Tomlinson/Mathews 3.00 8.00
EBT Elway/Brady/Tebow 5.00 12.00
HFG Hornung/Forte/Gerhart 2.50 6.00
MMB Montana/P.Mann/Bradford 5.00 12.00
MRC Marino/Romo/Clausen 4.00 10.00
SGM Sayers/Gore/Mathews 3.00 8.00
SPS E.Smth/Petersn/Spiller 4.00 10.00
SRB Staubach/Ryan/Bradford 4.00 10.00

2010 Topps Unrivaled Trio Jerseys

TRIO JSY STATED ODDS 1:1300 HOB
ABM Allen/Bush/McKnight 6.00 15.00
DPB Dickerson/Portis/Best 5.00 12.00
DTM Dorsett/Tomlinson/Mathews
EBT Elway/Brady/Tebow 25.00 50.00
HFG Hornung/Forte/Gerhart 6.00 15.00
MMB Montana/P.Mann/Bradford 25.00 50.00
MRC Marino/Romo/Clausen 20.00 40.00
SGM Sayers/Gore/Mathews 12.00 30.00
SPS E.Smth/Petersn/Spiller 10.00 25.00
SRB Staubach/Ryan/Bradford 6.00 15.00

2010 Topps Unrivaled Veterans

VETERANS/999 ODDS 1:21 HOB
UVAG Antonio Gates 1.25 3.00
UVAP Adrian Peterson 1.50 4.00
UVBD Brian Dawkins 1.00 2.50
UVBE Braylon Edwards 1.00 2.50
UVCP Clinton Portis 1.00 2.50
UVCP Carson Palmer 1.25 3.00
UVDH Devin Hester 1.25 3.00
UVDM DeMarcus Ware 1.25 3.00
UVED Elvis Dumervil 1.00 2.50
UVFJ Fred Jackson 1.25 3.00
UVHW Hines Ward 1.25 3.00
UVJA Jared Allen 1.00 2.50
UVLT LaDainian Tomlinson 1.50 4.00
UVMF Matt Forte 1.00 2.50
UVMR Matt Ryan 1.25 3.00
UVNA Nnamdi Asomugha 1.00 2.50
UVRM Robert Meachem 1.00 2.50
UVSH Santonio Holmes 1.00 2.50
UVSR Sidney Rice 1.00 2.50
UVTH T.J. Houshmandzadeh 1.00 2.50
UVTJ Thomas Jones 1.00 2.50
UVVJ Vincent Jackson 1.00 2.50
UVVY Vince Young 1.00 2.50
UVWW Wes Welker 1.25 3.00
UVC.J. Calvin Johnson 1.50 4.00

2010 Topps Unrivaled Veterans Jerseys

VETERANS JSY/199 ODDS 1:140 HOB
UVRAG Antonio Gates 3.00 8.00
UVRAP Adrian Peterson 4.00 10.00
UVRBD Brian Dawkins 2.50 6.00
UVRBE Braylon Edwards 2.50 6.00
UVRCP Carson Palmer 3.00 8.00
UVRCP Clinton Portis 2.50 6.00
UVRDH Devin Hester 3.00 8.00
UVRDW DeMarcus Ware 3.00 8.00
UVRED Elvis Dumervil 2.50 6.00
UVRFJ Fred Jackson 5.00 12.00
UVRHW Hines Ward 4.00 10.00
UVRJA Jared Allen 2.50 6.00
UVRLT LaDainian Tomlinson 5.00 12.00
UVRMF Matt Forte 2.50 6.00
UVRMR Matt Ryan 3.00 8.00
UVRNA Nnamdi Asomugha 2.50 6.00
UVRRM Robert Meachem 2.50 6.00
UVRSH Santonio Holmes 2.50 6.00
UVRSR Sidney Rice 2.50 6.00
UVRTJ Thomas Jones 2.50 6.00
UVRVJ Vincent Jackson 2.50 6.00
UVRVY Vince Young 2.50 6.00
UVRWW Wes Welker 3.00 8.00
UVRTJH T.J. Houshmandzadeh 2.50 6.00
UVRC.J. Calvin Johnson 4.00 10.00

2009 Topps Update

MP.SET w/o VAR (330) 20.00 50.00
COMMON CARD (1-330) .12 .30
COMMON SP VAR (1-330) 5.00 12.00
SP VAR ODDS 1:32 HOBBY
COMMON RC (1-330) 4.00 1.00
PRINTING PLATE ODDS 1:615 HOBBY
PLATE PRINT RUN 1 SET PER COLOR
BLACK-CYAN-MAGENTA-YELLOW ISSUED
NO PLATE PRICING DUE TO SCARCITY
UH320 Mark Schlereth/Daniel Schlereth .12 .30

2009 Topps Update Black

ATED ODDS 1:44 HOBBY
STATED PRINT RUN 58 SER.#'d SETS
UH320 Mark Schlereth/Daniel Schlereth 4.00 10.00

2009 Topps Update Gold Border

*GOLD VET: 2.5X TO 6X BASIC
*GOLD RC: .75X TO 2X BASIC RC
STATED ODDS 1:3 HOBBY
STATED PRINT RUN 2009 SER.#'d SETS

2012 Topps Valor

ATED PRINT RUN 170 SER.#'d SETS
1 Ray Lewis 2.50 6.00
2 Brian Urlacher 2.50 6.00
3 BenJarvus Green-Ellis 2.00 5.00
4 Fred Jackson 2.00 5.00
5 LeSean McCoy 2.50 6.00
6 Coby Fleener RC 1.25 3.00
7 Darrelle Revis 1.50 4.00
8 Wes Welker 2.00 5.00
9 Tony Romo 2.00 5.00
10 Andrew Luck RC 50.00 100.00
11 Von Miller 2.00 5.00
12 A.J. Green 2.50 6.00
13 Jimmy Graham 2.50 6.00
14 Tony Gonzalez 2.00 5.00
15 Jason Pierre-Paul 1.50 4.00
16 Luke Kuechly RC 3.00 8.00
17 Peyton Manning 8.00 20.00
18 Chris Johnson 1.50 4.00
19 Josh Gordon RC 3.00 8.00
20 Tom Brady 6.00 15.00
21 Brandon Marshall 2.00 5.00
22 Mohamed Sanu RC 2.00 5.00
23 DeMarcus Ware 2.50 6.00
24 Vernon Davis 1.50 4.00
25 Trent Richardson RC 1.25 3.00
26 Ben Roethlisberger 6.00 15.00
27 Mario Williams 1.50 4.00
28 Antonio Gates 2.00 5.00
29 James Laurinaitis 1.50 4.00
30 Calvin Johnson 2.50 6.00
31 Clay Matthews 2.50 6.00
32 Anquan Boldin 1.50 4.00
33 Stephen Hill RC 1.25 3.00
34 Marshawn Lynch 2.00 5.00
35 Russell Wilson RC 30.00 60.00
36 Ed Reed 2.00 5.00
37 Jamaal Charles 2.00 5.00
38 Michael Vick 2.00 5.00
39 Darren McFadden 1.50 4.00
40 Aaron Rodgers 6.00 15.00
41 Ndamukong Suh 2.00 5.00
42 Mark Sanchez 1.50 4.00
43 Adrian Peterson 2.50 6.00
44 Isaiah Pead RC 1.25 3.00
45 Ray Rice 1.50 4.00
46 Brock Osweiler RC 1.25 3.00
47 Lamar Miller RC 2.00 5.00
48 Larry Fitzgerald 2.00 5.00
49 Courtney Upshaw RC 1.50 4.00
50 Jim Brown 3.00 8.00
51 Quinton Coples RC 1.25 3.00
52 Matthew Stafford 2.00 5.00
53 Dan Fouts 2.00 5.00
54 Andy Dalton 2.00 5.00
55 Ryan Tannehill RC 2.00 5.00
56 Chandler Jones RC 1.25 3.00
57 Brandon Weeden RC 1.25 3.00
58 Philip Rivers 2.50 6.00
59 Andre Johnson 2.00 5.00
60 Robert Griffin III RC 1.50 4.00
61 Michael Floyd RC 1.25 3.00
62 Alshon Jeffery RC 2.50 6.00
63 Steven Jackson 1.50 4.00
64 LaMichael James RC 1.25 3.00
65 Julio Jones 2.50 6.00
66 Michael Turner 1.50 4.00
67 A.J. Jenkins RC 1.25 3.00
68 Ryan Broyles RC 1.25 3.00
69 Alfred Morris RC 1.25 3.00
70 Eli Manning 2.00 5.00
71 Victor Cruz 2.00 5.00
72 Rob Gronkowski 2.50 6.00
73 Jim Kelly 2.50 6.00
74 Brian Orakpo 2.00 5.00
75 Justin Blackmon RC 1.25 3.00
76 Rueben Randle RC 1.25 3.00
77 Dwayne Allen RC 1.25 3.00
78 Michael Egnew RC 1.25 3.00
79 David Wilson RC 1.25 3.00
80 Drew Brees 2.50 6.00
81 Jim Plunkett 2.00 5.00
82 Vincent Jackson 1.50 4.00
83 Earl Thomas 2.00 5.00
84 Brian Quick RC 1.25 3.00
85 Patrick Willis 2.00 5.00
86 Kurt Warner 2.00 5.00
87 Arian Foster 2.00 5.00
88 Kendall Wright RC 1.25 3.00
89 Frank Gore 2.00 5.00
90 Cam Newton 2.50 6.00
91 Jared Allen 1.50 4.00
92 Doug Martin RC 2.00 5.00
93 DeMarco Murray 2.00 5.00
94 Melvin Ingram RC 1.25 3.00
95 Matt Forte 1.50 4.00
96 Nick Foles RC 3.00 8.00
97 Mark Barron RC 1.25 3.00
98 Tim Tebow 2.50 6.00
99 Robert Turbin RC 1.25 3.00
100 Troy Polamalu 2.50 6.00

2012 Topps Valor Glory

*VETS/50: .8X TO 2X BASIC CARD/170
*ROOKIES/50: .6X TO 1.5X BASIC RC/170
10 Andrew Luck 60.00 150.00

2012 Topps Valor Autographs

*BASE AU/146-170: .3X TO .8X COURAGE/70
*BASE AU/75: .4X TO 1X COURAGE/70
VAAL Andrew Luck/75 60.00 125.00
VARG Robert Griffin III/75 5.00 12.00
VARH Ronnie Hillman/170 3.00 8.00

2012 Topps Valor Autographs Courage

*HONOR/50: .4X TO 1X COURAGE AU/70
VAAJ Alshon Jeffery 8.00 20.00
VAAJJ A.J. Jenkins 4.00 10.00
VAAL Andrew Luck 60.00 125.00
VABO Brock Osweiler 4.00 10.00
VABQ Brian Quick 4.00 10.00
VABW Brandon Weeden 4.00 10.00
VACF Coby Fleener 4.00 10.00
VACG Chris Givens 4.00 10.00
VACJ Chandler Jones 4.00 10.00
VADA Dwayne Allen 4.00 10.00
VADM Doug Martin 6.00 15.00
VADP DeVier Posey 4.00 10.00
VADW David Wilson 4.00 10.00
VAIP Isaiah Pead 4.00 10.00
VAJB Justin Blackmon 4.00 10.00
VAJC Juron Criner 4.00 10.00
VAJG Josh Gordon 10.00 25.00
VAJW Jarius Wright 4.00 10.00
VAKW Kendall Wright 4.00 10.00
VALJ LaMichael James 4.00 10.00
VALK Luke Kuechly 15.00 40.00
VALM Lamar Miller 6.00 15.00
VAME Michael Egnew 4.00 10.00
VAMF Michael Floyd 4.00 10.00
VAMJ Marvin Jones 4.00 10.00
VAMS Mohamed Sanu 6.00 15.00
VANF Nick Foles 25.00 60.00
VANT Nick Toon 4.00 10.00
VAQC Quinton Coples 4.00 10.00
VARB Ryan Broyles 4.00 10.00
VARR Rueben Randle 4.00 10.00
VART Ryan Tannehill 6.00 15.00
VARTU Robert Turbin 4.00 10.00
VASH Stephen Hill 4.00 10.00
VATB Travis Benjamin 4.00 10.00
VATJG T.J. Graham 4.00 10.00
VATR Trent Richardson 4.00 10.00
LATYH T.Y. Hilton 8.00 20.00
VAVB Vick Ballard 6.00 15.00

2012 Topps Valor Autographs Glory

*GLORY/25: .5X TO 1.2X COURAGE AU/70
VAAL Andrew Luck 75.00 150.00

2012 Topps Valor Centurion Autographs Strength

EXCH EXPIRATION: 2/28/2016
*BASE AU/304-500: .25X TO .6X STRENGTH/50
*BASE AU/92-250: .3X TO .8X STRENGTH/50
*DISCIPLINE/25: .5X TO 1.2X STRENGTH/50
*SPEED/70: .4X TO 1X STRENGTH/50
CAAB Ahmad Bradshaw 6.00 15.00
CAAF Arian Foster 20.00 40.00
CAAH Aaron Hernandez 8.00 20.00
CAAR Andre Roberts 6.00 15.00
CABT Ben Tate 6.00 15.00
CACB Cedric Benson 6.00 15.00
CADF Dan Fouts 15.00 40.00
CADM Denarius Moore 8.00 20.00
CAED Eric Decker 6.00 15.00
CAFG Frank Gore 8.00 20.00
CAGJ Greg Jennings 10.00 25.00
CAJB Jim Brown 40.00 80.00
CAJGR Jermaine Gresham 6.00 15.00
CAJIG Jimmy Graham 10.00 25.00
CAJJW J.J. Watt 40.00 100.00
CAJK Jim Kelly 20.00 50.00
CAJM Jeremy Maclin 6.00 15.00
CAJP Jim Plunkett EXCH 10.00 25.00
CAJPP Jason Pierre-Paul 6.00 15.00
CAJV Jonathan Vilma 6.00 15.00
CAKW Kurt Warner 25.00 50.00
CAMC Marques Colston 6.00 15.00
CAMF Malcom Floyd 6.00 15.00
CAMI Mark Ingram 8.00 20.00
CAMR Matt Ryan 30.00 60.00
CAMV Michael Vick 12.00 30.00
CAMW Mike Wallace 6.00 15.00
CANS Ndamukong Suh 10.00 25.00
CAPG Pierre Garcon 8.00 20.00
CAPH Percy Harvin EXCH 10.00 25.00
CAPW Patrick Willis EXCH 15.00 30.00
CASG Shonn Greene 6.00 15.00
CASH Santonio Holmes 6.00 15.00
CASL Sean Lee 15.00 30.00
CASR Sidney Rice EXCH 6.00 15.00
CASS Steve Smith 12.00 30.00
CATR Tony Romo 30.00 60.00
CATS Torrey Smith 6.00 15.00
CAVC Victor Cruz 12.00 30.00
CAVD Vernon Davis EXCH 6.00 15.00
CAVM Von Miller EXCH 8.00 20.00

2012 Topps Valor Field Armor Patches

*DISCIPLINE/25: .6X TO 1.5X BASIC PATCH/150
*SPEED/70: .5X TO 1.2X BASIC PATCH/150
*STRENGTH/50: .5X TO 1.2X BASIC PATCH/150
FAPAJ Alshon Jeffery 4.00 10.00
FAPAJJ A.J. Jenkins 2.00 5.00
FAPAL Andrew Luck 20.00 50.00
FAPBO Brock Osweiler 2.00 5.00
FAPBP Bernard Pierce 2.00 5.00
FAPBQ Brian Quick 2.00 5.00
FAPBW Brandon Weeden 2.00 5.00
FAPCF Coby Fleener 2.00 5.00
FAPCG Chris Givens 2.00 5.00
FAPCJ Chandler Jones 2.00 5.00
FAPDA Dwayne Allen 2.00 5.00
FAPDK Dre Kirkpatrick 2.00 5.00
FAPDM Doug Martin 3.00 8.00
FAPDP DeVier Posey 2.00 5.00
FAPDW David Wilson 2.00 5.00
FAPIP Isaiah Pead 2.00 5.00
FAPJB Justin Blackmon 2.00 5.00
FAPJG Josh Gordon 5.00 12.00
FAPJW Jarius Wright 4.00 10.00
FAPKW Kendall Wright 2.00 5.00
FAPLJ LaMichael James 2.00 5.00
FAPLM Lamar Miller 3.00 8.00
FAPMB Mark Barron 2.00 5.00
FAPME Michael Egnew 2.00 5.00
FAPMF Michael Floyd 2.00 5.00
FAPMS Mohamed Sanu 3.00 8.00
FAPNF Nick Foles 5.00 12.00
FAPNT Nick Toon 2.00 5.00
FAPRB Ryan Broyles 2.00 5.00
FAPRG Robert Griffin III 2.50 6.00
FAPRH Ronnie Hillman 2.00 5.00
FAPRR Rueben Randle 2.00 5.00
FAPRT Ryan Tannehill 3.00 8.00
FAPRTU Robert Turbin 2.00 5.00
FAPRW Russell Wilson 15.00 40.00
FAPSH Stephen Hill 2.00 5.00
FAPTJG T.J. Graham 2.00 5.00
FAPTR Trent Richardson 2.00 5.00
FAPTYH T.Y. Hilton 4.00 10.00
FAPVB Vick Ballard 5.00 12.00

2012 Topps Valor Legionary Autographs

*BASE AU/146-170: .3X TO .8X SPEED/70
*BASE AU/75-100: .4X TO 1X SPEED/70
EXCH EXPIRATION: 2/28/2016
LAAL Andrew Luck/75 60.00 125.00
LARG Robert Griffin III/75 5.00 12.00
LARH Ronnie Hillman/170 3.00 8.00

2012 Topps Valor Legionary Autographs Discipline

*DISCIPLINE/25: .5X TO 1.2X SPEED/70
LAAL Andrew Luck 75.00 150.00
LART Ryan Tannehill 8.00 20.00
LATR Trent Richardson 5.00 12.00

2012 Topps Valor Legionary Autographs Speed

*STRENGTH/50: .4X TO 1X SPEED/70
EXCH EXPIRATION: 2/28/2016
LAAJ Alshon Jeffery 8.00 20.00
LAAJJ A.J. Jenkins 4.00 10.00
LAAL Andrew Luck 60.00 125.00
LABO Brock Osweiler 4.00 10.00
LABQ Brian Quick 4.00 10.00
LABW Brandon Weeden 4.00 10.00
LACF Coby Fleener 4.00 10.00
LACG Chris Givens 4.00 10.00
LACJ Chandler Jones 4.00 10.00
LACR Chris Rainey 4.00 10.00
LADA Dwayne Allen 4.00 10.00
LADM Doug Martin 6.00 15.00
LADP DeVier Posey 4.00 10.00
LADW David Wilson 4.00 10.00
LAIP Isaiah Pead 4.00 10.00
LAJB Justin Blackmon 4.00 10.00
LAJC Juron Criner 4.00 10.00
LAJG Josh Gordon 10.00 25.00
LAJW Jarius Wright 4.00 10.00
LAKW Kendall Wright 4.00 10.00
LALJ LaMichael James 4.00 10.00
LALM Lamar Miller 6.00 15.00
LAME Michael Egnew 4.00 10.00
LAMF Michael Floyd 4.00 10.00
LAMJ Marvin Jones 4.00 10.00
LAMM Marvin McNutt 4.00 10.00
LAMS Mohamed Sanu 6.00 15.00
LANF Nick Foles 25.00 60.00
LANT Nick Toon 4.00 10.00
LAQC Quinton Coples 4.00 10.00
LARB Ryan Broyles 4.00 10.00
LARR Rueben Randle 4.00 10.00
LART Ryan Tannehill 6.00 15.00
LARTU Robert Turbin 4.00 10.00
LASH Stephen Hill 4.00 10.00
LATB Travis Benjamin 4.00 10.00
LATJG T.J. Graham 4.00 10.00
LATYH T.Y. Hilton 8.00 20.00
LAVB Vick Ballard 6.00 15.00

2012 Topps Valor Shield of Honor Patch Autographs

SOHAJ Alshon Jeffery 15.00 40.00
SOHAJJ A.J. Jenkins 8.00 20.00
SOHAL Andrew Luck 100.00 200.00
SOHBO Brock Osweiler 8.00 20.00
SOHBQ Brian Quick 8.00 20.00
SOHBW Brandon Weeden 8.00 20.00
SOHCF Coby Fleener 8.00 20.00
SOHDA Dwayne Allen 8.00 20.00
SOHDH Dont'a Hightower 12.00 30.00
SOHDK Dre Kirkpatrick 8.00 20.00
SOHDM Doug Martin 12.00 30.00
SOHDP DeVier Posey 8.00 20.00
SOHDW David Wilson 8.00 20.00
SOHIP Isaiah Pead 8.00 20.00
SOHJA Joe Adams 8.00 20.00
SOHJB Justin Blackmon 8.00 20.00
SOHJC Juron Criner 8.00 20.00
SOHJG Josh Gordon 20.00 50.00
SOHJW Jarius Wright 8.00 20.00
SOHKW Kendall Wright
SOHLJ LaMichael James 8.00 20.00
SOHLK Luke Kuechly 30.00 60.00
SOHLM Lamar Miller 12.00 30.00
SOHME Michael Egnew 8.00 20.00
SOHMF Michael Floyd 8.00 20.00
SOHMS Mohamed Sanu 12.00 30.00
SOHNF Nick Foles 50.00 125.00
SOHNT Nick Toon 12.00 30.00
SOHRB Ryan Broyles 8.00 20.00
SOHRH Ronnie Hillman 8.00 20.00
SOHRR Rueben Randle 8.00 20.00
SOHRT Ryan Tannehill 12.00 30.00
SOHRTU Robert Turbin 15.00 40.00
SOHRW Russell Wilson 125.00 250.00
SOHSH Stephen Hill 8.00 20.00
SOHTJG T.J. Graham 8.00 20.00
SOHTR Trent Richardson 30.00 80.00
SOHTYH T.Y. Hilton 15.00 40.00
SOHVB Vick Ballard 10.00 25.00

2014 Topps Valor

COMPLETE SET (200) 20.00 40.00
1 Jadeveon Clowney RC .40 1.00
2 Joe Namath .50 1.25
3 Darqueze Dennard RC .40 1.00
4 J.J. Watt .40 1.00
5 Pierre Thomas .25 .60
6 Dri Archer RC .30 .75
7 Andrew Luck .50 1.25
8 Eli Manning .30 .75
9 Montee Ball .25 .60
10 Andre Williams RC .30 .75
11 Joe Flacco .30 .75
12 Derek Carr RC 2.00 5.00
13 Patrick Peterson .25 .60
14 Tajh Boyd RC .30 .75
15 Percy Harvin .25 .60
16 Ray Rice .25 .60
17 Marshall Faulk .30 .75
18 Andre Johnson .30 .75
19 Gale Sayers .40 1.00
20 Michael Crabtree .25 .60
21 Matt Ryan .30 .75
22 Donte Moncrief RC .30 .75
23 Earl Thomas .30 .75
24 Alfred Morris .25 .60
25 Calvin Johnson .40 1.00
26 Odell Beckham Jr. RC .75 2.00
27 Eric Berry .30 .75
28 Cecil Shorts .25 .60
29 Blake Bortles RC .40 1.00
30 Clay Matthews .40 1.00
31 Logan Thomas RC .30 .75
32 Deion Sanders .30 .75
33 David Fales RC .30 .75
34 Paul Richardson RC .40 1.00
35 Shane Vereen .30 .75
36 Carlos Hyde RC .40 1.00
37 Jason Pierre-Paul .25 .60
38 Josh Gordon .25 .60
39 Jarvis Landry RC .60 1.50
40 Terrell Suggs .25 .60
41 Von Miller .30 .75
42 Brandin Cooks RC .50 1.25
43 Luke Kuechly .30 .75
44 Tom Savage RC .30 .75
45 Austin Seferian-Jenkins RC .30 .75
46 Matthew Stafford .30 .75
47 Ryan Mathews .30 .75
48 Khalil Mack RC 1.25 3.00
49 Steve Smith .30 .75
50 Johnny Manziel RC .50 1.25
51 Devonta Freeman RC .50 1.25
52 Richard Sherman .40 1.00
53 Zac Stacy .25 .60
54 Jordan Matthews RC .50 1.25
55 Mike Wallace .25 .60
56 Robert Griffin III .25 .60
57 Matt Forte .25 .60
58 Torrey Smith .25 .60
59 Troy Polamalu .40 1.00
60 Jamaal Charles .30 .75
61 Davante Adams RC .50 1.25
62 Victor Cruz .30 .75
63 Connor Shaw RC .30 .75
64 Jason Witten .30 .75
65 Martavis Bryant RC .40 1.00
66 Kyle Fuller RC .30 .75
67 Marshawn Lynch .30 .75
68 Jimmy Garoppolo RC 2.50 6.00
69 Cordarrelle Patterson .25 .60
70 Darrelle Revis .25 .60
71 Taylor Lewan RC .30 .75
72 Isaiah Crowell RC .40 1.00
73 Philip Rivers .40 1.00
74 Bradley Roby RC .30 .75
75 Andy Dalton .30 .75
76 Devin Street RC .30 .75
77 DeSean Jackson .30 .75
78 Aaron Rodgers .75 2.00
79 De'Anthony Thomas RC .30 .75
80 Tom Brady 1.00 2.50
81 Julio Jones .40 1.00
82 Joe Montana 1.00 2.50
83 Keenan Allen .30 .75
84 Steve Young .50 1.25
85 Jordy Nelson .30 .75
86 Jerick McKinnon RC .40 1.00
87 Cody Latimer RC .40 1.00
88 Knowshon Moreno .25 .60
89 Bo Jackson .50 1.25
90 Marqise Lee RC .40 1.00
91 Terry Bradshaw .50 1.25
92 Bruce Ellington RC .30 .75
93 Vernon Davis .25 .60
94 Ndamukong Suh .30 .75
95 Zach Ertz .30 .75
96 Michael Sam RC .30 .75
97 C.J. Mosley RC .40 1.00
98 Ha Ha Clinton-Dix RC .40 1.00
99 Arian Foster .30 .75
100 Adrian Peterson .40 1.00
101 Patrick Willis .30 .75
102 Robert Quinn .30 .75
103 Stephen Morris RC .30 .75
104 NaVorro Bowman .30 .75
105 Jay Cutler .25 .60
106 DeMarco Murray .30 .75
107 Robert Herron RC .30 .75
108 Rob Gronkowski .40 1.00
109 C.J. Spiller .25 .60
110 Frank Gore .30 .75
111 Marcus Allen .40 1.00
112 Storm Johnson RC .30 .75
113 Jeremy Hill RC .40 1.00
114 James White RC .60 1.50
115 Terrance West RC .30 .75
116 Jake Matthews RC .30 .75
117 Ryan Tannehill .30 .75
118 Le'Veon Bell .30 .75
119 Larry Fitzgerald .30 .75
120 Roddy White .25 .60
121 Charles Sims RC .30 .75
122 Ka'Deem Carey RC .30 .75
123 Giovani Bernard .25 .60
124 Ben Roethlisberger .40 1.00
125 Troy Aikman .50 1.25
126 John Riggins .30 .75
127 Calvin Pryor RC .30 .75
128 Wes Welker .30 .75
129 Randall Cobb .30 .75
130 Dee Ford RC .30 .75
131 Michael Vick .30 .75
132 Alex Smith .30 .75
133 Ryan Shazier RC .50 1.25
134 Sam Bradford .25 .60
135 Antonio Brown .40 1.00
136 Tavon Austin .25 .60
137 Eric Decker .25 .60
138 Julian Edelman .40 1.00
139 Emmitt Smith .60 1.50
140 Golden Tate .30 .75
141 Aaron Murray RC .30 .75
142 Greg Robinson RC .30 .75
143 Geno Atkins .25 .60
144 Julius Thomas .25 .60
145 Eric Ebron RC .40 1.00
146 Jimmy Graham .40 1.00
147 Jordan Reed .25 .60
148 Jared Abbrederis RC .30 .75
149 LeSean McCoy .40 1.00
150 Sammy Watkins RC .50 1.25
151 Barry Sanders .60 1.50
152 A.J. McCarron RC .30 .75
153 Demaryius Thomas .30 .75
154 Kam Chancellor .40 1.00
155 T.Y. Hilton .30 .75
156 Colin Kaepernick .30 .75
157 Michael Floyd .25 .60
158 Brett Favre .75 2.00
159 Reggie Bush .25 .60
160 Mike Evans RC .75 2.00
161 Geno Smith .25 .60
162 Stevan Ridley .25 .60
163 EJ Manuel .25 .60
164 Marques Colston .25 .60
165 Reggie Wayne .30 .75
166 Drew Brees .40 1.00
167 Tre Mason RC .30 .75
168 Troy Niklas RC .30 .75
169 Jace Amaro RC .30 .75
170 Allen Robinson RC .50 1.25
171 Cameron Wake .25 .60
172 Alshon Jeffery .30 .75
173 Dez Bryant .40 1.00
174 Anthony Barr RC .30 .75
175 Eddie Lacy .25 .60
176 Josh Huff RC .40 1.00
177 Nick Foles .30 .75
178 Jordan Cameron .25 .60
179 Tony Romo .30 .75
180 Zach Mettenberger RC .30 .75
181 Bishop Sankey RC .30 .75
182 Pierre Garcon .30 .75
183 Teddy Bridgewater RC .50 1.25
184 Russell Wilson .60 1.50
185 Kelvin Benjamin RC .50 1.25
186 Cam Newton .40 1.00
187 Robert Mathis .25 .60
188 Jake Locker .30 .75
189 Dan Marino .75 2.00
190 Trent Richardson .25 .60
191 Kendall Wright .25 .60
192 Aaron Donald RC .75 2.00
193 John Elway .60 1.50
194 Vincent Jackson .25 .60
195 Sheldon Richardson .25 .60
196 A.J. Green .40 1.00
197 DeAndre Hopkins .30 .75
198 Kiko Alonso .25 .60
199 Brandon Marshall .25 .60
200 Peyton Manning 1.25 3.00

2014 Topps Valor Courage

*VETS/399: 1.5X TO 4X BASIC CARDS
*ROOKIES/399: 1X TO 2.5X BASIC RC

2014 Topps Valor Discipline

*VETS/299: 1.5X TO 4X BASIC CARDS
*ROOKIES/299: 1X TO 2.5X BASIC RC

2014 Topps Valor Glory

*VETS/199: 2X TO 5X BASIC CARDS
*ROOKIES/199: 1.2X TO 3X BASIC RC

2014 Topps Valor Speed

*VETS: 1X TO 2.5X BASIC CARDS
*ROOKIES: .6X TO 1.5X BASIC RC

2014 Topps Valor Strength

*VETS/499: 1.2X TO 3X BASIC CARDS
*ROOKIES/499: .8X TO 2X BASIC RC

2014 Topps Valor Valor

*VETS/99: 2.5X TO 6X BASIC CARDS
*ROOKIES/99: 1.5X TO 4X BASIC RC

2014 Topps Valor Retail

COMPLETE SET (200) 12.00 30.00
*RETAIL VETS: .3X TO .8X HOBBY
*RETAIL ROOKIES: .3X TO .8X HOBBY RC

2014 Topps Valor Retail Courage

*VETS/399: 1.5X TO 4X BASIC HOBBY
*ROOKIES/399: 1X TO 2.5X HOBBY RC

2014 Topps Valor Retail Discipline

*VETS/299: 1.5X TO 4X BASIC HOBBY
*ROOKIES/299: 1X TO 2.5X HOBBY RC

2014 Topps Valor Retail Glory

*VETS/199: 2X TO 5X BASIC HOBBY
*ROOKIES/199: 1.2X TO 3X HOBBY RC

2014 Topps Valor Retail Speed

*VETS: 1X TO 2.5X BASIC HOBBY
*ROOKIES: .6X TO 1.5X HOBBY RC

2014 Topps Valor Retail Strength

*VETS/499: 1.2X TO 3X BASIC HOBBY
*ROOKIES/499: .8X TO 2X HOBBY RC

2014 Topps Valor Retail Valor

*VETS/99: 2.5X TO 6X BASIC HOBBY
*ROOKIES/99: 1.5X TO 4X HOBBY RC

2014 Topps Valor Autographs

*BASE AU: .3X TO .8X COURAGE/50
VABB Blake Bortles 3.00 8.00
VAJM Johnny Manziel 4.00 10.00
VATB Teddy Bridgewater 20.00 50.00

2014 Topps Valor Autographs Courage

*SPEED/99: .3X TO .8X COURAGE/50
*STRENGTH/75: .4X TO 1X COURAGE/50
VAAB Anthony Barr 3.00 8.00
VAAM Aaron Murray 3.00 8.00
VAAMC A.J. McCarron 8.00 20.00
VAAR Allen Robinson 5.00 12.00
VAASJ Austin Seferian-Jenkins 3.00 8.00
VAAW Andre Williams 3.00 8.00
VABC Brandin Cooks 5.00 12.00
VABE Bruce Ellington 3.00 8.00
VABG Brandon Coleman 3.00 8.00
VABS Bishop Sankey 3.00 8.00
VACL Cody Latimer 4.00 10.00
VACM Clay Mathews 20.00 40.00
VACS Charles Sims 3.00 8.00
VADA Davante Adams 5.00 12.00
VADAR Dri Archer 3.00 8.00
VADC Derek Carr 20.00 50.00
VADF David Fales 3.00 8.00
VADFR Devonta Freeman 5.00 12.00
VADM Donte Moncrief 3.00 8.00
VADS Devin Street 3.00 8.00
VAEE Eric Ebron 4.00 10.00
VAGG Garrett Gilbert 3.00 8.00
VAJAB Jared Abbrederis 3.00 8.00
VAJC Jadeveon Clowney 4.00 10.00
VAJG Jimmy Garoppolo 30.00 60.00
VAJH Jeremy Hill 4.00 10.00
VAJL Jarvis Landry 6.00 15.00
VAJM Johnny Manziel
VAJMA Jordan Matthews 5.00 12.00
VAJW James White 6.00 15.00
VAKB Kelvin Benjamin 15.00 30.00
VAKC Ka'Deem Carey 3.00 8.00
VALM LeSean McCoy 12.00 30.00
VAMB Martavis Bryant 4.00 10.00
VAME Mike Evans 8.00 20.00
VAMG Marion Grice 3.00 8.00
VAML Marqise Lee 4.00 10.00
VAMLY Marshawn Lynch 15.00 30.00
VAMS Michael Sam 3.00 8.00
VAOB Odell Beckham Jr. EXCH 40.00 80.00
VARG Rob Gronkowski EXCH 20.00 40.00
VARH Robert Herron 3.00 8.00
VASW Sammy Watkins 5.00 12.00
VATB Teddy Bridgewater
VATBO Tajh Boyd 3.00 8.00
VATN Troy Niklas 3.00 8.00
VATS Tom Savage 3.00 8.00
VATW Terrance West 3.00 8.00
VAZM Zach Mettenberger 3.00 8.00

2014 Topps Valor Autographs Discipline

*DISCIPLINE/25: .5X TO 1.2X COURAGE/50
VACM Clay Matthews 25.00 50.00
VAJG Jimmy Garoppolo 50.00 100.00
VALM LeSean McCoy 15.00 40.00
VAOB Odell Beckham Jr. 40.00 100.00
VARG Rob Gronkowski 25.00 50.00
VARW Russell Wilson 40.00 80.00
VAMLY Marshawn Lynch 20.00 40.00

2014 Topps Valor Jumbo Relics

ONE PER HOBBY BOX OVERALL
*COURAGE/50: .6X TO 1.5X BASIC JSY
*DISCIPLINE/25: .8X TO 2X BASIC JSY
*SPEED/99: .5X TO 1.2X BASIC JSY
*STRENGTH/75: .5X TO 1.2X BASIC JSY
VJRAL Andrew Luck 5.00 12.00
VJRAM Aaron Murray 1.50 4.00
VJRAMC A.J. McCarron 1.50 4.00
VJRASJ Austin Seferian-Jenkins 1.50 4.00
VJRAW Andre Williams 1.50 4.00
VJRBB Blake Bortles 2.00 5.00
VJRBC Brandin Cooks 2.50 6.00
VJRBS Bishop Sankey 1.50 4.00
VJRCH Carlos Hyde 2.00 5.00
VJRCL Cody Latimer 2.00 5.00
VJRCN Cam Newton 4.00 10.00
VJRCS Charles Sims 1.50 4.00
VJRDA Dri Archer 1.50 4.00
VJRDC Derek Carr 5.00 12.00
VJRDF Devonta Freeman 2.50 6.00
VJRDM Donte Moncrief 1.50 4.00
VJRDMA Doug Martin 3.00 8.00
VJRDT De'Anthony Thomas 1.50 4.00
VJREE Eric Ebron 2.00 5.00
VJREL Eddie Lacy 2.50 6.00
VJRJC Jadeveon Clowney 2.00 5.00
VJRJG Jimmy Garoppolo 12.00 30.00
VJRJH Jeremy Hill 2.00 5.00
VJRJL Jarvis Landry 3.00 8.00
VJRJM Johnny Manziel 2.50 6.00
VJRJMA Jordan Matthews 2.50 6.00
VJRKB Kelvin Benjamin 2.50 6.00
VJRKC Ka'Deem Carey 1.50 4.00
VJRLB Le'Veon Bell 3.00 8.00
VJRLT Logan Thomas 1.50 4.00
VJRMB Montee Ball 2.50 6.00
VJRME Mike Evans 4.00 10.00
VJRML Marqise Lee 2.00 5.00
VJRMS Michael Sam 1.50 4.00
VJRNF Nick Foles 3.00 8.00
VJROB Odell Beckham Jr. 4.00 10.00
VJRRG Robert Griffin III 2.50 6.00
VJRRW Russell Wilson 6.00 15.00
VJRSW Sammy Watkins 2.50 6.00
VJRTB Tajh Boyd 1.50 4.00
VJRTBR Teddy Bridgewater 2.50 6.00
VJRTM Tre Mason 1.50 4.00
VJRTS Tom Savage 1.50 4.00
VJRTW Terrance West 1.50 4.00
VJRZM Zach Mettenberger 1.50 4.00

2014 Topps Valor Patches

*PATCH: .4X TO 1X JUMBO RELIC
*COURAGE/50: .6X TO 1.5X BASIC PATCH
*DISCIPLINE/25: .8X TO 2X BASIC PATCH
*SPEED/99: .5X TO 1.2X BASIC PATCH
*STRENGTH/75: .5X TO 1.2X BASIC PATCH

2014 Topps Valor Rookie Relics

*COURAGE/50: .6X TO 1.5X BASIC JSY
*DISCIPLINE/25: .8X TO 2X BASIC JSY
*SPEED/99: .5X TO 1.2X BASIC JSY
*STRENGTH/75: .5X TO 1.2X BASIC JSY
VRRAM Aaron Murray 1.25 3.00
VRRAMC A.J. McCarron 1.25 3.00
VRRAR Allen Robinson 2.00 5.00
VRRASJ Austin Seferian-Jenkins 1.25 3.00
VRRAW Andre Williams 1.25 3.00
VRRBB Blake Bortles 1.50 4.00
VRRBC Brandin Cooks 2.00 5.00
VRRBS Bishop Sankey 1.25 3.00
VRRCH Carlos Hyde 1.50 4.00
VRRCL Cody Latimer 1.50 4.00
VRRCS Charles Sims 1.25 3.00
VRRDA Davante Adams 2.00 5.00
VRRDAR Dri Archer 1.25 3.00
VRRDC Derek Carr 4.00 10.00
VRRDF Devonta Freeman 2.00 5.00
VRRDM Donte Moncrief 1.25 3.00
VRRDT De'Anthony Thomas 1.25 3.00
VRREE Eric Ebron 1.50 4.00
VRRJA Jace Amaro 1.25 3.00
VRRJC Jadeveon Clowney 1.50 4.00
VRRJG Jimmy Garoppolo 10.00 25.00
VRRJH Jeremy Hill 1.50 4.00
VRRJL Jarvis Landry 2.50 6.00
VRRJM Johnny Manziel 2.00 5.00
VRRJMA Jordan Matthews 2.00 5.00
VRRKB Kelvin Benjamin 2.00 5.00
VRRKC Ka'Deem Carey 1.25 3.00
VRRKM Khalil Mack 5.00 12.00

VRRLT Logan Thomas 1.25 3.00
VRRMB Martavis Bryant 1.50 4.00
VRRME Mike Evans 3.00 8.00
VRRML Marqise Lee 1.50 4.00
VRRMS Michael Sam 1.25 3.00
VRROB Odell Beckham Jr. 3.00 8.00
VRRPR Paul Richardson 1.50 4.00
VRRSW Sammy Watkins 2.00 5.00
VRRTB Tajh Boyd 1.25 3.00
VRRTBR Teddy Bridgewater 2.00 5.00
VRRTM Tre Mason 1.25 3.00
VRRTS Tom Savage 1.25 3.00
VRRTW Terrance West 1.25 3.00
VRRZM Zach Mettenberger 1.25 3.00

2014 Topps Valor Shield of Honor Patch Autographs

*HONOR PATCH AU: .3X TO .8X COURAGE/50

2014 Topps Valor Shield of Honor Patch Autographs Courage

*SPEED/99: .3X TO .8X COURAGE/50
*STRENGTH/75: .4X TO 1X COURAGE/50
SOHAM Aaron Murray 4.00 10.00
SOHAMC A.J. McCarron 10.00 25.00
SOHAR Allen Robinson 6.00 15.00
SOHASJ Austin Seferian-Jenkins 4.00 10.00
SOHAW Andre Williams 4.00 10.00
SOHBB Blake Bortles EXCH 5.00 12.00
SOHBC Brandin Cooks 6.00 15.00
SOHBS Bishop Sankey 4.00 10.00
SOHCH Carlos Hyde 5.00 12.00
SOHCL Cody Latimer 5.00 12.00
SOHCS Charles Sims 4.00 10.00
SOHDA Dri Archer 4.00 10.00
SOHDAD Davante Adams 6.00 15.00
SOHDC Derek Carr 20.00 40.00
SOHDF Devonta Freeman 6.00 15.00
SOHDM Donte Moncrief 4.00 10.00
SOHDT De'Anthony Thomas 4.00 10.00
SOHEE Eric Ebron 5.00 12.00
SOHJC Jimmy Garoppolo 50.00 100.00
SOHJCL Jadeveon Clowney 5.00 12.00
SOHJHI Jeremy Hill 5.00 12.00
SOHJL Jarvis Landry 10.00 25.00
SOHJM Jordan Matthews 6.00 15.00
SOHJMA Johnny Manziel 6.00 15.00
SOHKB Kelvin Benjamin 6.00 15.00
SOHKC Ka'Deem Carey 4.00 10.00
SOHKM Khalil Mack 30.00 80.00
SOHLT Logan Thomas 4.00 10.00
SOHMB Martavis Bryant
SOHME Mike Evans 12.00 30.00
SOHML Marqise Lee 5.00 12.00
SOHMLY Marshawn Lynch
SOHMS Michael Sam 4.00 10.00
SOHOB Odell Beckham Jr. 50.00 100.00
SOHRG Rob Gronkowski EXCH
SOHSW Sammy Watkins 6.00 15.00
SOHTB Tajh Boyd 4.00 10.00
SOHTBR Teddy Bridgewater 15.00 40.00
SOHTM Tre Mason EXCH 4.00 10.00
SOHTS Tom Savage 4.00 10.00
SOHTW Terrance West 4.00 10.00
SOHZM Zach Mettenberger 4.00 10.00

2014 Topps Valor Shield of Honor Patch Autographs Discipline

*DISCIPLINE/25: .5X TO 1.2X COURAGE/50
SOHAP Adrian Peterson
SOHBSA Barry Sanders 100.00 175.00
SOHDB Drew Brees 40.00 80.00
SOHJC Jimmy Garoppolo 60.00 125.00

2015 Topps Valor

1 Ben Roethlisberger .40 1.00
2 Garrett Grayson RC .30 .75
3 Russell Wilson .50 1.25
4 Melvin Gordon RC .75 2.00
5 Tom Brady 1.00 2.50
6 Tony Romo .30 .75
7 Mario Williams .25 .60
8 Alvin Dupree RC .40 1.00
9 Ryan Kerrigan .25 .60
10 Peyton Manning .75 2.00
11 Geno Atkins .25 .60
12 Aaron Rodgers .75 2.00
13 Sheldon Richardson .25 .60
14 Shane Ray .25 .60
15 Patrick Peterson .25 .60
16 Ryan Tannehill .30 .75
17 DeMarcus Ware .30 .75
18 Colin Kaepernick .30 .75
19 Vontae Davis .25 .60
20 Andrew Luck .50 1.25
21 Benardrick McKinney RC .30 .75
22 Clay Matthews .40 1.00
23 Von Miller .30 .75
24 Cam Newton .40 1.00
25 Richard Sherman .40 1.00
26 J.J. Watt .40 1.00
27 Danny Shelton RC .30 .75
28 Derek Carr .40 1.00
29 Andrus Peat RC .30 .75
30 Dan Marino .75 2.00
31 Dominique Rodgers-Cromartie .25 .60
32 Cameron Wake .25 .60
33 Lawrence Taylor .40 1.00
34 Cameron Artis-Payne RC .30 .75
35 Eric Kendricks RC .30 .75
36 Alex Smith .30 .75
37 Kevin Johnson RC .30 .75
38 Paul Dawson RC .40 1.00
39 Brett Hundley RC .30 .75
40 Eli Manning .30 .75
41 Duke Johnson RC .50 1.25
42 Eddie Goldman RC .30 .75
43 Vic Beasley RC .40 1.00
44 Steve Young .50 1.25
45 Desmond Trufant .25 .60
46 Jason Pierre-Paul .25 .60
47 Ameer Abdullah RC .50 1.25
48 Javorius Allen RC .40 1.00
49 Jameis Winston RC .75 2.00
50 Arik Armstead RC .30 .75
51 Matt Ryan .30 .75
52 Bryce Petty RC .30 .75
53 Nick Foles .30 .75
54 Byron Maxwell .25 .60
55 Brent Grimes RC .30 .75
56 Marcus Mariota RC 1.25 3.00
57 Denzel Perryman RC .30 .75
58 Terrell Suggs .25 .60
59 Drew Brees .40 1.00
60 Randy Gregory RC .30 .75
61 Dante Fowler Jr. RC .50 1.25
62 Joe Flacco .30 .75
63 Justin Houston RC .30 .75
64 Ndamukong Suh .30 .75
65 Aaron Donald .40 1.00
66 Luke Kuechly .30 .75
67 Shaq Thompson RC .40 1.00
68 Sean Mannion RC .30 .75
69 Len Dawson .40 1.00
70 Terry Bradshaw .50 1.25
71 Roger Staubach .50 1.25
72 Teddy Bridgewater .30 .75
73 Philip Rivers .40 1.00
74 Johnny Manziel .30 .75
75 David Cobb RC .30 .75
76 Darrelle Revis .25 .60
77 Bob Lilly .30 .75
78 Deion Sanders .30 .75
79 David Johnson RC .75 2.00
80 Jay Ajayi RC .50 1.25
81 Owamagbe Odighizuwa RC .40 1.00
82 Blake Bortles .25 .60
83 Andy Dalton .30 .75
84 Prince Amukamara .25 .60
85 John Elway .60 1.50
86 Robert Griffin III .25 .60
87 Lawrence Timmons .25 .60
88 Robert Quinn .30 .75
89 Phil Simms .30 .75
90 Matthew Stafford .30 .75
91 Brandon Scherff RC .50 1.25
92 Joe Haden .25 .60
93 La'el Collins RC .40 1.00
94 Julius Peppers .30 .75
95 Leonard Williams RC .30 .75
96 C.J. Mosley RC .50 1.25
97 Trae Waynes RC .30 .75
98 Gerald McCoy .25 .60
99 Khalil Mack .40 1.00
100 Jadeveon Clowney .25 .60
101 Jeremy Langford RC .30 .75
102 Sammie Coates RC .40 1.00
103 Josh Robinson RC .30 .75
104 Malcolm Brown RC .40 1.00
105 Victor Cruz .30 .75
106 DeAndre Hopkins .30 .75
107 LeSean McCoy .40 1.00
108 Lamar Miller .25 .60
109 Dorial Green-Beckham RC .30 .75
110 Jeff Heuerman RC .40 1.00
111 Ronnie Lott .30 .75
112 Demaryius Thomas .30 .75
113 Earl Thomas .30 .75
114 Paul Hornung .40 1.00
115 C.J. Anderson .30 .75
116 Dez Bryant .40 1.00
117 Le'Veon Bell .30 .75
118 Steve Smith .30 .75
119 Jamaal Charles .30 .75
120 Torry Holt .30 .75
121 DeVante Parker RC .50 1.25
122 Jaelen Strong RC .40 1.00
123 Breshad Perriman RC .30 .75
124 Brandon Marshall .25 .60
125 Rashad Greene RC .30 .75
126 T.J. Yeldon RC .30 .75
127 Rashad Jennings .25 .60
128 Mike Evans .30 .75
129 Phillip Dorsett RC .30 .75
130 Jordan Matthews .30 .75
131 John Riggins .30 .75
132 DeMarco Murray .30 .75
133 Charles Woodson .40 1.00
134 Tyler Lockett RC .50 1.25
135 Terrell Davis .30 .75
136 Muhammad Wilkerson .25 .60
137 Alfred Morris .25 .60
138 Jimmy Graham .40 1.00
139 Davante Adams .30 .75
140 Kelvin Benjamin .30 .75
141 Tre McBride RC .30 .75
142 Andre Ellington .25 .60
143 Greg Olsen .30 .75
144 Calvin Johnson .40 1.00
145 Jeremy Hill .25 .60
146 Barry Sanders .60 1.50
147 Maxx Williams RC .30 .75
148 Chris Conley RC .30 .75
149 Alshon Jeffery .30 .75
150 Emmitt Smith .60 1.50
151 Jeremy Maclin .25 .60
152 Emmanuel Sanders .30 .75
153 Vincent Jackson .25 .60
154 Joique Bell .25 .60
155 Gale Sayers .40 1.00
156 Antonio Brown .40 1.00
157 Travis Kelce .40 1.00
158 Amari Cooper RC 1.00 2.50
159 Martavis Bryant .25 .60
160 Marshall Faulk .30 .75
161 Matt Forte .25 .60
162 A.J. Green .40 1.00
163 Arian Foster .30 .75
164 Denard Robinson .25 .60
165 Eric Berry .30 .75
166 Dwight Clark .30 .75
167 Kevin White RC .40 1.00
168 Jerry Rice .60 1.50
169 Sammy Watkins .30 .75
170 Randall Cobb .30 .75
171 Golden Tate .25 .60
172 Jordy Nelson .30 .75
173 DeSean Jackson .30 .75
174 Tre Mason .30 .75
175 Odell Beckham Jr. .40 1.00
176 Tevin Coleman RC .40 1.00
177 Julio Jones .40 1.00
178 Andre Williams .25 .60
179 Terrence Magee RC .50 1.25
180 Clive Walford RC .30 .75
181 Todd Gurley RC 1.25 3.00
182 T.Y. Hilton .30 .75
183 Tony Lippett RC .30 .75
184 Jerome Bettis .40 1.00
185 Karlos Williams RC .30 .75
186 Julian Edelman .40 1.00
187 Kenny Bell RC .50 1.25
188 Marshawn Lynch .30 .75
189 Tim Brown .40 1.00
190 Bo Jackson .50 1.25
191 Nelson Agholor RC .40 1.00
192 Giovani Bernard .25 .60
193 Eddie Lacy .25 .60
194 Mark Ingram .30 .75
195 Jonathan Stewart .25 .60
196 Devin Smith RC .30 .75
197 Stefon Diggs RC .75 2.00
198 Kam Chancellor .40 1.00
199 Devin Funchess RC .50 1.25
200 Rob Gronkowski .40 1.00

2015 Topps Valor Courage

*VETS/299: 1.5X TO 4X BASIC CARDS
*ROOKIES/299: 1X TO 2.5X BASIC RC

2015 Topps Valor Discipline

*VETS/199: 2X TO 5X BASIC CARDS
*ROOKIES/199: 1.2X TO 3X BASIC RC

2015 Topps Valor Glory

*VETS/99: 2.5X TO 6X BASIC CARDS
*ROOKIES/99: 1.5X TO 4X BASIC RC

2015 Topps Valor Honor

*VETS: 1X TO 2.5X HOBBY CARDS
*ROOKIES: .6X TO 1.5X HOBBY RC

2015 Topps Valor Speed

*VETS: 1X TO 2.5X BASIC CARDS

2015 Topps Valor Strength

*VETS: 1.2X TO 3X BASIC CARDS
*ROOKIES: .8X TO 2X BASIC RC

2015 Topps Valor Autographs Courage

3 Russell Wilson
4 Melvin Gordon
8 Alvin Dupree 4.00 10.00
14 Shane Ray 3.00 8.00
34 Cameron Artis-Payne 3.00 8.00
35 Eric Kendricks 3.00 8.00
37 Kevin Johnson 3.00 8.00
38 Paul Dawson 4.00 10.00
39 Brett Hundley
41 Duke Johnson
47 Ameer Abdullah 5.00 12.00
49 Jameis Winston 60.00 120.00
56 Marcus Mariota 50.00 100.00
59 Drew Brees
61 Dante Fowler Jr. 5.00 12.00
67 Shaq Thompson 4.00 10.00
79 David Johnson 12.00 30.00
80 Jay Ajayi 5.00 12.00
97 Trae Waynes 3.00 8.00
101 Jeremy Langford 3.00 8.00
102 Sammie Coates 6.00 15.00
103 Josh Robinson 3.00 8.00
104 Malcolm Brown 4.00 10.00
108 Lamar Miller 6.00 15.00
109 Dorial Green-Beckham 3.00 8.00
110 Jeff Heuerman 4.00 10.00
115 C.J. Anderson 8.00 20.00
121 DeVante Parker
122 Jaelen Strong 4.00 10.00
123 Breshad Perriman 3.00 8.00
125 Rashad Greene 3.00 8.00
126 T.J. Yeldon 3.00 8.00
128 Mike Evans
129 Phillip Dorsett 3.00 8.00
130 Jordan Matthews 6.00 15.00
134 Tyler Lockett 10.00 25.00
140 Kelvin Benjamin 8.00 20.00
141 Tre McBride 3.00 8.00
145 Jeremy Hill 6.00 15.00
147 Maxx Williams 3.00 8.00
148 Chris Conley 3.00 8.00
152 Emmanuel Sanders 15.00 30.00
154 Joique Bell 6.00 15.00
157 Travis Kelce 10.00 25.00
158 Amari Cooper 25.00 50.00
167 Kevin White 4.00 10.00
175 Odell Beckham Jr.
176 Tevin Coleman 4.00 10.00
180 Clive Walford 3.00 8.00
181 Todd Gurley 20.00 50.00
183 Tony Lippett 3.00 8.00
189 Tim Brown
191 Nelson Agholor 4.00 10.00
196 Devin Smith 3.00 8.00
199 Devin Funchess 5.00 12.00

2015 Topps Valor Autographs

*BASE AU/800: .2X TO .5X COURAGE AU/50
*BASE AU/176-512: .25X TO .6X COURAGE AU/50
*BASE AU/100: .3X TO .8X COURAGE AU/50
104 Malcolm Brown/800 2.00 5.00

2015 Topps Valor Autographs Discipline

*DISCIPLINE/25: .5X TO 1.2X COURAGE AU/50

2015 Topps Valor Autographs Speed

*SPEED/99: .3X TO .8X COURAGE AU/50

2015 Topps Valor Autographs Strength

*STRENGTH/75: .3X TO .8X COURAGE AU/50

2015 Topps Valor Battle Cry

STATED ODDS 1:10 HOBBY
BCAB Antonio Brown 1.00 2.50
BCBC Brian Cushing .60 1.50
BCCK Colin Kaepernick .75 2.00
BCCM Clay Matthews 1.00 2.50
BCCN Cam Newton 1.00 2.50
BCDR Darrelle Revis .60 1.50
BCGO Greg Olsen .75 2.00
BCJW J.J. Watt 1.00 2.50
BCLM LeSean McCoy 1.00 2.50
BCOB Odell Beckham Jr. 1.00 2.50
BCPR Philip Rivers 1.00 2.50
BCRG Rob Gronkowski 1.00 2.50
BCRS Richard Sherman 1.00 2.50
BCTS Terrell Suggs .60 1.50
BCJWI Jason Witten .75 2.00

2015 Topps Valor Gridiron Warriors

STATED ODDS 1:4 HOBBY
GWAJ Alshon Jeffery .60 1.50
GWAL Andrew Luck 1.00 2.50
GWBJ Bo Jackson 1.00 2.50
GWBL Bob Lilly .60 1.50
GWDB Drew Brees .75 2.00
GWDC Dwight Clark .60 1.50
GWEL Eddie Lacy .50 1.25
GWEM Eli Manning .60 1.50
GWGO Greg Olsen .60 1.50
GWHL Howie Long .75 2.00
GWJB Jerome Bettis .75 2.00
GWJC Jamaal Charles .60 1.50
GWJE John Elway 1.25 3.00
GWJR Jerry Rice 1.25 3.00
GWLK Luke Kuechly .60 1.50
GWLT Lawrence Taylor .75 2.00
GWME Mike Evans .60 1.50
GWMF Matt Forte .50 1.25
GWOB Odell Beckham Jr. .75 2.00
GWPM Peyton Manning 1.50 4.00
GWPS Phil Simms .60 1.50
GWRS Roger Staubach 1.00 2.50
GWRT Ryan Tannehill .60 1.50
GWTB Tim Brown .75 2.00
GWTD Terrell Davis .60 1.50

2015 Topps Valor Gridiron Warriors Autographs

GWABJ Bo Jackson 30.00 60.00
GWADC Dwight Clark 8.00 20.00
GWAEL Eddie Lacy 6.00 15.00
GWAEM Eli Manning 25.00 50.00
GWAGO Greg Olsen 8.00 20.00
GWAJB Jerome Bettis 30.00 60.00
GWAJE John Elway 50.00 100.00
GWALK Luke Kuechly 15.00 40.00
GWALT Lawrence Taylor 25.00 50.00
GWAME Mike Evans 8.00 20.00
GWAMF Matt Forte 6.00 15.00
GWAOB Odell Beckham Jr. 30.00 60.00
GWAPM Peyton Manning 100.00 200.00
GWARS Roger Staubach 30.00 80.00
GWATD Terrell Davis 8.00 20.00

2015 Topps Valor Jumbo Relics

*SPEED/99: .5X TO 1.2X BASIC JSY/300
*STRENGTH/75: .5X TO 1.2X BASIC JSY/300
*COURAGE/50: .6X TO 1.5X BASIC JSY/300
*DISCIPLINE/25: .8X TO 2X BASIC JSY/300
VJRAA Ameer Abdullah 2.00 5.00
VJRAC Amari Cooper 4.00 10.00
VJRBH Brett Hundley 1.25 3.00
VJRBP Breshad Perriman 1.25 3.00
VJRBPE Bryce Petty 1.25 3.00
VJRCA Cameron Artis-Payne 1.25 3.00
VJRCC Chris Conley 1.25 3.00
VJRDAJ David Johnson 3.00 8.00
VJRDC David Cobb 1.25 3.00
VJRDF Devin Funchess 2.00 5.00
VJRDG Dorial Green-Beckham 1.25 3.00
VJRDP DeVante Parker 2.00 5.00
VJRDS Devin Smith 1.25 3.00
VJRDUJ Duke Johnson 2.00 5.00
VJRGG Garrett Grayson 1.25 3.00
VJRJA Jay Ajayi 2.00 5.00
VJRJAL Javorius Allen 1.50 4.00
VJRJC Jadeveon Clowney 2.00 5.00
VJRJH Jeremy Hill 2.00 5.00
VJRJL Jeremy Langford 1.25 3.00
VJRJM Johnny Manziel 2.50 6.00
VJRJS Jaelen Strong 1.50 4.00
VJRJW Jameis Winston 6.00 15.00
VJRKB Kenny Bell 2.00 5.00
VJRKBE Kelvin Benjamin 2.50 6.00
VJRKW Kevin White 1.50 4.00
VJRKWI Karlos Williams 1.25 3.00
VJRMD Mike Davis 1.25 3.00
VJRME Mike Evans 2.50 6.00
VJRMG Melvin Gordon 3.00 8.00
VJRMM Marcus Mariota 5.00 12.00
VJRMW Maxx Williams 1.25 3.00
VJRNA Nelson Agholor 1.50 4.00
VJROB Odell Beckham Jr. 3.00 8.00
VJRPD Phillip Dorsett 1.25 3.00
VJRRG Rashad Greene 1.25 3.00
VJRSC Sammie Coates 1.50 4.00
VJRSD Stefon Diggs 3.00 8.00
VJRSM Sean Mannion 1.25 3.00
VJRTC Tevin Coleman 1.50 4.00
VJRTG Todd Gurley 5.00 12.00
VJRTL Tyler Lockett 2.00 5.00
VJRTM Tre McBride 1.25 3.00
VJRTY T.J. Yeldon 1.25 3.00
VJRTYM Ty Montgomery 1.25 3.00

2015 Topps Valor Patches

*SPEED/99: .5X TO 1.2X BASIC JSY/289
*STRENGTH/75: .5X TO 1.2X BASIC JSY/289
*COURAGE/50: .6X TO 1.5X BASIC JSY/289
*DISCIPLINE/25: .8X TO 2X BASIC JSY/289
VPAA Ameer Abdullah 2.00 5.00
VPAC Amari Cooper 4.00 10.00
VPBB Blake Bortles 2.00 5.00
VPBH Brett Hundley 1.25 3.00
VPBP Breshad Perriman 1.25 3.00
VPBPE Bryce Petty 1.25 3.00
VPCA Cameron Artis-Payne 1.25 3.00
VPCC Chris Conley 1.25 3.00
VPDAJ David Johnson 3.00 8.00
VPDC Derek Carr 3.00 8.00
VPDCO David Cobb 1.25 3.00
VPDF Devin Funchess 2.00 5.00
VPDG Dorial Green-Beckham 1.25 3.00
VPDP DeVante Parker 2.00 5.00
VPDS Devin Smith 1.25 3.00
VPDUJ Duke Johnson 2.00 5.00
VPGG Garrett Grayson 1.25 3.00
VPJA Jay Ajayi 2.00 5.00
VPJAL Javorius Allen 1.50 4.00
VPJC Jadeveon Clowney 2.00 5.00
VPJL Jeremy Langford 1.25 3.00
VPJS Jaelen Strong 1.50 4.00
VPJW Jameis Winston 6.00 15.00
VPKB Kenny Bell 2.00 5.00
VPKW Kevin White 1.50 4.00
VPKWI Karlos Williams 1.25 3.00
VPMD Mike Davis 1.25 3.00
VPMG Melvin Gordon 5.00 12.00
VPMM Marcus Mariota 5.00 12.00
VPMW Maxx Williams 1.25 3.00
VPNA Nelson Agholor 1.50 4.00
VPOB Odell Beckham Jr. 3.00 8.00
VPPD Phillip Dorsett 1.25 3.00
VPRG Rashad Greene 1.25 3.00
VPSC Sammie Coates 1.50 4.00
VPSD Stefon Diggs 3.00 8.00
VPSM Sean Mannion 1.25 3.00
VPSW Sammy Watkins 2.50 6.00
VPTB Teddy Bridgewater 2.50 6.00
VPTC Tevin Coleman 1.50 4.00
VPTG Todd Gurley 4.00 10.00
VPTL Tyler Lockett 2.00 5.00
VPTM Tre McBride 1.25 3.00
VPTY T.J. Yeldon 1.25 3.00
VPTYM Ty Montgomery 1.25 3.00

2015 Topps Valor Rookie Relics

*SPEED/99: .5X TO 1.2X BASIC JSY
*STRENGTH/75: .5X TO 1.2X BASIC JSY
*COURAGE/50: .6X TO 1.5X BASIC JSY
*DISCIPLINE: .8X TO 2X BASIC JSY
VRRAA Ameer Abdullah 2.00 5.00
VRRAC Amari Cooper 4.00 10.00
VRRBH Brett Hundley 1.25 3.00
VRRBP Breshad Perriman 1.25 3.00
VRRBPE Bryce Petty 1.25 3.00
VRRCC Chris Conley 1.25 3.00
VRRDAJ David Johnson 3.00 8.00
VRRDCO David Cobb 1.25 3.00
VRRDF Devin Funchess 2.00 5.00
VRRDG Dorial Green-Beckham 1.25 3.00
VRRDP DeVante Parker 2.00 5.00
VRRDS Devin Smith 1.25 3.00
VRRDUJ Duke Johnson 2.00 5.00
VRRGG Garrett Grayson 1.25 3.00
VRRJA Jay Ajayi 2.00 5.00
VRRJAL Javorius Allen 1.50 4.00
VRRJC Jamison Crowder 1.50 4.00
VRRJL Jeremy Langford 1.25 3.00
VRRJS Jaelen Strong 1.50 4.00
VRRJW Jameis Winston 6.00 15.00
VRRKB Kenny Bell 2.00 5.00
VRRKW Kevin White 1.50 4.00
VRRKWI Karlos Williams 1.25 3.00
VRRLW Leonard Williams 1.25 3.00
VRRMD Mike Davis 1.25 3.00
VRRMG Melvin Gordon 3.00 8.00
VRRMM Marcus Mariota 5.00 12.00
VRRMW Maxx Williams 1.25 3.00
VRRNA Nelson Agholor 1.50 4.00
VRRPD Phillip Dorsett 1.25 3.00
VRRRG Rashad Greene 1.25 3.00
VRRSC Sammie Coates 1.50 4.00
VRRSD Stefon Diggs 3.00 8.00
VRRSM Sean Mannion 1.25 3.00
VRRTC Tevin Coleman 1.50 4.00
VRRTG Todd Gurley 4.00 10.00
VRRTL Tyler Lockett 2.00 5.00
VRRTY T.J. Yeldon 1.25 3.00
VRRTYM Ty Montgomery 1.25 3.00
VRRVMA Vince Mayle 1.50 4.00

2015 Topps Valor Shield of Honor Patch Autographs

*BASIC JSY AU/100: .3X TO .8X COURAGE/50
*BASIC JSY AU/227-525: .25X TO .6X COURAGE/50
*BASIC JSY AU/800: .2X TO .5X COURAGE/50
SHAMM Marcus Mariota 40.00 80.00

2015 Topps Valor Shield of Honor Patch Autographs Courage

SHAAA Ameer Abdullah 6.00 15.00
SHAAC Amari Cooper 40.00 80.00
SHABH Brett Hundley 4.00 10.00
SHABP Breshad Perriman
SHABPE Bryce Petty 4.00 10.00
SHACA Cameron Artis-Payne 4.00 10.00
SHACC Chris Conley 4.00 10.00
SHACW Clive Walford 4.00 10.00
SHADA Davante Adams
SHADAJ David Johnson 12.00 30.00
SHADF Devin Funchess 6.00 15.00
SHADG Dorial Green-Beckham
SHADP DeVante Parker 6.00 15.00
SHADS Devin Smith
SHADUJ Duke Johnson 6.00 15.00
SHAJA Jay Ajayi 6.00 15.00
SHAJAL Javorius Allen 5.00 12.00
SHAJC Jamison Crowder 5.00 12.00
SHAJH Justin Hardy 4.00 10.00
SHAJL Jeremy Langford 4.00 10.00
SHAJS Jaelen Strong 5.00 12.00
SHAJW Jameis Winston
SHAKB Kelvin Benjamin 10.00 25.00
SHAKW Kevin White 5.00 12.00
SHAKWI Karlos Williams 4.00 10.00
SHAMB Martavis Bryant 8.00 20.00
SHAMD Mike Davis 4.00 10.00
SHAME Mike Evans
SHAMG Melvin Gordon 10.00 25.00
SHAMJ Matt Jones 4.00 10.00
SHAMM Marcus Mariota 50.00 100.00
SHAMW Maxx Williams 4.00 10.00
SHANA Nelson Agholor
SHAOB Odell Beckham Jr. 30.00 60.00
SHAPD Phillip Dorsett 4.00 10.00
SHARG Rashad Greene 4.00 10.00
SHASC Sammie Coates 10.00 25.00
SHASM Sean Mannion 4.00 10.00
SHASW Sammy Watkins 10.00 25.00
SHATC Tevin Coleman 5.00 12.00
SHATG Todd Gurley 25.00 60.00
SHATL Tyler Lockett 6.00 15.00
SHATM Ty Montgomery 4.00 10.00
SHATMB Tre McBride 4.00 10.00
SHATY T.J. Yeldon 4.00 10.00
SHAVM Vince Mayle 5.00 12.00

2015 Topps Valor Shield of Honor Patch Autographs Discipline

*DISCIPLINE/25: .5X TO 1.2X COURAGE/50
SHAMM Marcus Mariota 60.00 150.00

2015 Topps Valor Shield of Honor Patch Autographs Speed

*SPEED/99: .3X TO .8X COURAGE/50
SHAMM Marcus Mariota 50.00 125.00

2015 Topps Valor Shield of Honor Patch Autographs Strength

*STRENGTH/75: .3X TO .8X COURAGE/50
SHAMM Marcus Mariota 50.00 125.00

2015 Topps Valor Valor

*VETS/50: 3X TO 8X BASIC CARDS
*ROOKIES/50: 2X TO 5X BASIC RC

2001 Topps XFL Promos

Distributed to hobby dealers and at various wrestling events, these cards were produced to promote the release of the 2001 Topps XFL footbal card product.
COMPLETE SET (8) 2.00 4.00
P1 Scott Milanovich .30 .75
P2 James Bostic .20 .50
P3 Rashaan Salaam .40 1.00
P4 Jeff Brohm .30 .75
P5 Chuck Clements .20 .50
P6 Pat Barnes .30 .75
P7 Charles Puleri .20 .50
P8 John Avery .40 1.00

2001 Topps XFL

Topps issued the first set featuring players from the XFL in April 2001. This would prove to be the only year the XFL existed. The cards were released in 8-card packs. The set was broken down into: 79-player cards, 4-team vs. team (LB) cards, 16-Girls on Fire cheerleader cards and 1-checklist. Many players in the set had previous NFL cards.
COMPLETE SET (100) 12.50 25.00
1 Mike Pawlawski .50 1.25
2 Todd Doxzon .10 .30
3 James Bostic .30 .75
4 Jim Druckenmiller .20 .50
5 Mario Bailey .10 .30
6 Mike Cawley .20 .50
7 Dino Philyaw .10 .30
8 Aaron Bailey .20 .50
9 Juan Johnson .20 .50
10 Kaipo McGuire .10 .30
11 Toya Jones .10 .30
12 Todd Floyd .10 .30
13 Jamie Baisley .10 .30
14 Brian Shay .20 .50
15 Eric England .10 .30
16 Curtis Alexander .10 .30
17 Tim Lester .30 .75
18 Dialleo Burks .10 .30
19 Charles Puleri .30 .75
20 Zechariah Lord .10 .30
21 Chrys Chukwuma .10 .30
22 Rickey Brady .20 .50
23 Rashaan Salaam .60 1.50
24 Jermaine Copeland .20 .50
25 Butler By'not'e .10 .30
26 Tommy Maddox 1.25 3.00
27 Mike Furrey 1.25 3.00
28 Ed Smith .10 .30
29 Pat Barnes .40 1.00
30 James Hundon .20 .50
31 John Avery .40 1.00
32 James Willis .10 .30
33 Larry Ryans .10 .30
34 Vaughn Dunbar .10 .30
35 John Williams .10 .30
36 Casey Weldon .40 1.00
37 Roell Preston .20 .50
38 Jeff Brohm .40 1.00
39 Rashaan Shehee .20 .50
40 Kevin Swayne .20 .50
41 Ben Snell .10 .30
42 James Williams UER .10 .30
43 Corte McGuffey .20 .50
44 Charles Jordan .20 .50
45 Frank Leatherwood .10 .30
46 Dwayne Sabb .10 .30
47 Shannon Culver .10 .30
48 Brent Moss .20 .50
49 Zola Davis .10 .30
50 Ryan Clement .30 .75
51 Tyji Armstrong .10 .30
52 Paul Failla .10 .30
53 Michael Blair .20 .50
54 Corey Ivy .30 .75
55 Daryl Hobbs .20 .50
56 Paul Lacoste .10 .30
57 Damon Gourdine .10 .30
58 Wendell Davis .10 .30
59 Joe Cummings .10 .30
60 Stephen Fisher .10 .30
61 Stepfret Williams .30 .75
62 Brandon Sanders .10 .30
63 Michael Black .20 .50
64 Scott Milanovich .40 1.00
65 Brian Roche .10 .30
66 Darnell McDonald .20 .50
67 Marcus Hinton .10 .30
68 Quincy Jackson .10 .30
69 Roosevelt Potts .20 .50
70 Rod Smart .75 2.00
71 Keith Elias .10 .30
72 Latario Rachal .10 .30
73 Mike Sutton .10 .30
74 Kirby DarDar .20 .50
75 Derrick Clark .20 .50
76 Antonio Edwards .10 .30
77 Marcus Crandell .20 .50
78 Jerry Crafts .10 .30
79 Brian Roberson .20 .50
80 Las Vegas vs New York LB .10 .30
81 Orlando vs Chicago LB .10 .30
82 San Francisco vs Los Angeles LB .10 .30
83 Memphis vs Birmingham LB .10 .30
84 Kat GF .10 .30
85 Rose GF .10 .30
86 Dana GF .10 .30
87 Lisa Michelle GF .10 .30
88 Kiushin GF .10 .30
89 Youn GF .10 .30
90 Sunni GF .10 .30
91 Cicely GF .10 .30
92 Tanisha GF .10 .30
93 Krissy GF .10 .30
94 TK GF .10 .30
95 Jensi GF .10 .30
96 Jenny GF .10 .30
97 Karla GF .10 .30
98 Jenny GF .10 .30
99 Susanne GF .10 .30
100 Checklist .10 .30

2001 Topps XFL Endzone Autographs

Randomly inserted at a rate of one in 28 packs. This set features authentic player autographs on a horizontal card.
1 Tommy Maddox 8.00 20.00
2 Tim Lester 6.00 15.00
3 Rickey Brady 6.00 15.00
4 Wally Richardson 6.00 15.00
5 Michael Black 6.00 15.00
6 Jermaine Copeland 6.00 15.00
7 LeShon Johnson 6.00 15.00
8 Chrys Chukwuma 6.00 15.00
9 Mike Archie 6.00 15.00
10 Rashaan Shehee 6.00 15.00
11 Roell Preston 6.00 15.00
12 Mike Furrey 6.00 15.00
13 Keith Elias 6.00 15.00
14 Ken Oxendine 6.00 15.00
15 Paul Failla 6.00 15.00
16 Dino Philyaw 6.00 15.00
17 Todd Doxzon 6.00 15.00
18 Chris Brantley 6.00 15.00

2001 Topps XFL Gridiron Gear

ndomly inserted at a rate of one in 190 packs. This set features authentic player memorabilia including game used footballs and jerseys. The footballs appear tougher to pull than the jerseys.
1F John Avery FB 5.00 12.00
1J John Avery JSY 4.00 10.00
2F Rashaan Salaam FB 5.00 12.00
2J Rashaan Salaam JSY 4.00 10.00
3F Jeff Brohm FB 5.00 12.00
3J Jeff Brohm JSY 4.00 10.00
4F James Bostic FB 5.00 12.00
4J James Bostic JSY 4.00 10.00
5F Pat Barnes FB 5.00 12.00
5J Pat Barnes JSY 4.00 10.00
6F Scott Milanovich FB 5.00 12.00
6J Scott Milanovich JSY 4.00 10.00
7F Charles Puleri FB 5.00 12.00
7J Charles Puleri JSY 4.00 10.00
8F Chuck Clements FB 5.00 12.00
8J Chuck Clements JSY 4.00 10.00

2001 Topps XFL Loaded Cannon

Randomly inserted at a rate of one in 8 packs. This set features full color photographs on a silver foil background of top quarterbacks.
COMPLETE SET (8) 10.00 25.00
1 Tommy Maddox 2.00 5.00
2 Casey Weldon 2.00 5.00
3 Marcus Crandell 2.00 5.00
4 Jeff Brohm 2.00 5.00
5 Ryan Clement 2.00 5.00
6 Mike Pawlawski 2.00 5.00
7 Charles Puleri 2.00 5.00
8 Tim Lester 2.00 5.00

2001 Topps XFL Logo Stickers

Randomly inserted at a rate of one in 2 packs. This set features various XFL logos in a sticker format.
COMPLETE SET (10) 1.50 4.00
1 Los Angeles Xtreme .20 .50
2 Birmingham Thunderbolts .20 .50
3 Memphis Maniax .20 .50
4 Orlando Rage .20 .50
5 Las Vegas Outlaws .20 .50
6 San Francisco Demons .20 .50
7 New York Hitmen .20 .50
8 Chicago Enforcers .20 .50
9 XFL Logo .20 .50
10 XFL Football .20 .50

2004 Toronto Sun Superstar Quarterbacks Stickers

This set of stickers was sponsored by the Toronto Sun and Mac's Stores and released in Canada. The stickers were issued on numbered blankbacked sheets of seven or eight stickers per sheet. When seperated, each sticker measures roughly 1 1/2" by 2 /18" and each includes its own sticker number on the front. An album was issued to house the set with one page devoted to each of the 12-quarterbacks in the set. Each player has six-different stickers featuring different photos. We've cataloged them below as full sheets instead of cut out stickers.
COMPLETE SET (10) 10.00 20.00
1 Sheet 1 1.25 3.00
2 Sheet 2 .75 2.00
3 Sheet 3 1.00 2.50
4 Sheet 4 .75 2.00
5 Sheet 5 1.25 3.00
6 Sheet 6 1.00 2.50
7 Sheet 7 1.25 3.00
8 Sheet 8 .75 2.00
9 Sheet 9 1.25 3.00
10 Sheet 10 1.25 3.00
NNO Album 2.00 5.00

2011 Totally Certified

COMP.SET w/o RC's (100) 10.00 25.00
151-200 ROOKIE AU PRINT RUN 299
201-236 ROOKIE JSY AU PRINT RUN 99-499
EXCH EXPIRATION: 9/14/2013
1 Fred Jackson .30 .75
2 Ryan Fitzpatrick .30 .75
3 Steve Johnson .30 .75
4 BenJarvus Green-Ellis .30 .75
5 Tom Brady 1.25 3.00
6 Wes Welker .40 1.00
7 Mark Sanchez .30 .75
8 Santonio Holmes .30 .75
9 Shonn Greene .30 .75
10 Brandon Marshall .40 1.00
11 Brian Hartline .40 1.00
12 Reggie Bush .30 .75
13 Ben Roethlisberger .50 1.25
14 Mike Wallace .30 .75
15 Rashard Mendenhall .30 .75
16 Troy Polamalu .50 1.25
17 Cedric Benson .30 .75
18 Jermaine Gresham .30 .75
19 Jerome Simpson .30 .75
20 Anquan Boldin .30 .75
21 Joe Flacco .40 1.00
22 Ray Lewis .50 1.25
23 Ray Rice .30 .75
24 Colt McCoy .30 .75
25 Josh Cribbs .30 .75
26 Peyton Hillis .30 .75
27 Andre Johnson .40 1.00
28 Arian Foster .30 .75
29 Matt Schaub .30 .75
30 Chris Johnson .30 .75
31 Kenny Britt .30 .75
32 Matt Hasselbeck .30 .75
33 Maurice Jones-Drew .30 .75
34 Mike Thomas .40 1.00
35 Paul Posluszny .30 .75
36 Dallas Clark .30 .75
37 Joseph Addai .30 .75
38 Peyton Manning 1.00 2.50
39 Reggie Wayne .40 1.00
40 Dwayne Bowe .40 1.00
41 Jamaal Charles .40 1.00
42 Matt Cassel .30 .75
43 Philip Rivers .50 1.25
44 Ryan Mathews .40 1.00
45 Vincent Jackson .30 .75
46 Carson Palmer .40 1.00
47 Darren McFadden .30 .75
48 Darrius Heyward-Bey .30 .75
49 Eric Decker .30 .75
50 Tim Tebow .50 1.25
51 Willis McGahee .30 .75
52 Ahmad Bradshaw .30 .75
53 Eli Manning .40 1.00
54 Hakeem Nicks .30 .75
55 DeSean Jackson .40 1.00
56 LeSean McCoy .50 1.25
57 Michael Vick .40 1.00
58 DeMarcus Ware .40 1.00
59 Dez Bryant .50 1.25
60 Tony Romo .40 1.00
61 Fred Davis .30 .75
62 London Fletcher .40 1.00
63 Ryan Torain .30 .75
64 Aaron Rodgers .75 2.00
65 Greg Jennings .30 .75
66 James Starks .30 .75
67 Calvin Johnson .50 1.25
68 Jahvid Best .30 .75
69 Matthew Stafford .40 1.00
70 Brian Urlacher .50 1.25
71 Jay Cutler .30 .75
72 Matt Forte .30 .75
73 Adrian Peterson .50 1.25
74 Jared Allen .30 .75
75 Percy Harvin .30 .75
76 Drew Brees .50 1.25
77 Jimmy Graham .50 1.25
78 Marques Colston .30 .75
79 Josh Freeman .40 1.00
80 LeGarrette Blount .40 1.00
81 Mike Williams .40 1.00
82 Matt Ryan .40 1.00
83 Michael Turner .30 .75
84 Roddy White .30 .75
85 DeAngelo Williams .30 .75
86 Greg Olsen .40 1.00
87 Jonathan Stewart .30 .75
88 Steve Smith WR .40 1.00
89 Alex Smith QB .40 1.00
90 Frank Gore .40 1.00
91 Vernon Davis .30 .75
92 Leon Washington .30 .75
93 Marshawn Lynch .40 1.00
94 Sidney Rice .30 .75
95 Brandon Lloyd .30 .75
96 Sam Bradford .30 .75
97 Steven Jackson .30 .75
98 Beanie Wells .30 .75
99 Kevin Kolb .30 .75
100 Larry Fitzgerald .40 1.00
151 A.Williams AU/299 RC 3.00 8.00
152 A.Clayborn AU/299 RC 3.00 8.00
153 A.Ayers AU/299 RC EXCH 3.00 8.00
154 A.Smith AU/299 RC EXCH
155 A.Bradford AU/299 RC 3.00 8.00
156 B.Harris AU/299 RC 3.00 8.00
157 C.Heyward AU/299 RC 4.00 10.00
158 C.Jordan AU/299 RC 4.00 10.00
159 C.Shorts AU/299 RC 3.00 8.00
160 C.Liuget AU/299 RC 3.00 8.00
161 D.Williams AU/299 RC 3.00 8.00
162 D.Bowers AU/299 RC 3.00 8.00
163 D.Scott AU/299 RC 3.00 8.00
164 D.Moore AU/299 RC 8.00 20.00
165 D.Lewis AU/299 RC 4.00 10.00
166 G.Jones AU/299 RC 4.00 10.00
167 G.Salas AU/299 RC 3.00 8.00
168 J.J. Watt AU/299 RC 30.00 60.00
169 J.Rodgers AU/299 RC 3.00 8.00
170 J.Kerley AU/299 RC 5.00 12.00
171 J.Smith AU/299 RC 3.00 8.00
172 J.White AU/299 RC 3.00 8.00
173 J.Thomas AU/299 RC 4.00 10.00
174 J.Houston AU/299 RC 4.00 10.00
175 K.Durham AU/299 RC 3.00 8.00
176 L.Kendricks AU/299 RC 3.00 8.00
177 L.Stocker AU/299 RC 3.00 8.00
178 N.Enderle AU/299 RC 3.00 8.00
179 Niles Paul AU/299 RC 3.00 8.00
180 Phil Taylor AU/299 RC 3.00 8.00
181 P.Amukamara AU/299 RC 3.00 8.00
182 R.Moore AU/299 RC 3.00 8.00
183 Ricky Stanzi AU/299 RC 3.00 8.00
184 R.Helu AU/299 RC EXCH 3.00 8.00
185 Ryan Kerrigan AU/299 RC 4.00 10.00
186 T.J. Yates AU/299 RC 3.00 8.00
187 Tandon Doss AU/299 RC 3.00 8.00
188 Terrelle Pryor AU/299 RC 5.00 12.00
189 Tyrod Taylor AU/299 RC 6.00 15.00
190 Joe Lefeged AU/299 RC 4.00 10.00
191 J.Williams AU/299 RC EXCH 5.00 12.00
192 K.J. Wright AU/299 RC 5.00 12.00
193 Mason Foster AU/299 RC 3.00 8.00
194 Casey Matthews AU/299 RC 3.00 8.00
195 Anthony Allen AU/299 RC 3.00 8.00
196 Armond Smith AU/299 RC 4.00 10.00
197 D.Sanzenbacher AU/299 RC 3.00 8.00
198 Doug Baldwin AU/299 RC 8.00 20.00
199 LaQuan Williams AU/299 RC 4.00 10.00
200 Mark Herzlich AU/299 RC 3.00 8.00
201 A.J. Green JSY AU/299 RC 20.00 40.00
202 Alex Green JSY AU/499 RC 4.00 10.00
203 Andy Dalton JSY AU/399 RC 8.00 20.00
204 A.Pettis JSY AU/499 RC 4.00 10.00
205 B.Powell JSY AU/99 RC 8.00 20.00
206 B.Gabbert JSY AU/299 RC 5.00 12.00
207 Cam Newton JSY AU/299 RC 60.00 120.00
208 C.Ponder JSY AU/299 RC 5.00 12.00
209 Clyde Gates JSY AU/499 RC 4.00 10.00
210 C.Kaepernick JSY AU/399 RC 6.00 15.00
211 D.Thomas JSY AU/499 RC 4.00 10.00
212 Delone Carter JSY AU/499 RC 4.00 10.00
213 D.Murray JSY AU/99 RC 30.00 80.00
214 G.Little JSY AU/499 RC 5.00 12.00
215 Jake Locker JSY AU/299 RC 5.00 12.00
216 J.Harper JSY AU/499 RC 4.00 10.00
217 J.Jernigan JSY AU/499 RC 4.00 10.00
218 J.Baldwin JSY AU/499 RC 4.00 10.00
219 J.Todman JSY AU/499 RC 4.00 10.00
220 J.Jones JSY AU/399 RC EXCH 20.00 40.00
221 K.Hunter JSY AU/499 RC 8.00 20.00
222 Kyle Rudolph JSY AU/499 RC 4.00 10.00
223 L.Hankerson JSY AU/499 RC 4.00 10.00
224 M.Dareus JSY AU/499 RC 4.00 10.00
225 Mark Ingram JSY AU/299 RC 8.00 20.00
226 Leshoure JSY AU/399 RC EXCH 4.00 10.00
227 Randall Cobb JSY AU/99 RC 10.00 25.00
228 Ryan Mallett JSY AU/299 RC 5.00 12.00
229 R.Williams JSY AU/399 RC 4.00 10.00
230 S.Vereen JSY AU/499 RC EXCH 5.00 12.00
231 Stevan Ridley JSY AU/499 RC 4.00 10.00
232 Taiwan Jones JSY AU/499 RC 4.00 10.00
233 Titus Young JSY AU/499 RC 4.00 10.00
234 Torrey Smith JSY AU/499 RC 4.00 10.00
235 V.Brown JSY AU/499 RC 4.00 10.00
236 Von Miller JSY AU/499 RC 15.00 30.00

2011 Totally Certified Blue

*1-100 VETS/50: 3X TO 8X BASIC CARDS
STATED PRINT RUN 50 SER.#'d SETS

2011 Totally Certified Blue Materials

STATED PRINT RUN 12-249
1 Fred Jackson/25 4.00 10.00
2 Ryan Fitzpatrick/249 2.50 6.00
3 Steve Johnson/199 2.50 6.00
4 BenJarvus Green-Ellis/99 5.00 12.00
5 Tom Brady/249 10.00 25.00
6 Wes Welker/99 4.00 10.00
7 Mark Sanchez/249 2.50 6.00
9 Shonn Greene/249 2.50 6.00
10 Brandon Marshall/249 3.00 8.00
11 Brian Hartline/249 3.00 8.00
14 Mike Wallace/249 2.50 6.00
17 Cedric Benson/249 2.50 6.00
18 Jermaine Gresham/249 2.50 6.00

20 Anquan Boldin/249 2.50 6.00
21 Joe Flacco/249 3.00 8.00
22 Ray Lewis/249 4.00 10.00
23 Ray Rice/249 2.50 6.00
24 Colt McCoy/249 2.50 6.00
25 Josh Cribbs/249 2.50 6.00
26 Peyton Hillis/99 3.00 8.00
27 Andre Johnson/99 4.00 10.00
28 Arian Foster/49 5.00 12.00
29 Matt Schaub/249 2.50 6.00
30 Chris Johnson/199 2.50 6.00
31 Kenny Britt/249 2.50 6.00
32 Matt Hasselbeck/249 2.50 6.00
33 Maurice Jones-Drew/249 2.50 6.00
34 Mike Thomas/249 3.00 8.00
36 Dallas Clark/249 2.50 6.00
37 Joseph Addai/249 2.50 6.00
38 Peyton Manning/49 10.00 25.00
39 Reggie Wayne/99 4.00 10.00
40 Dwayne Bowe/249 3.00 8.00
41 Jamaal Charles/249 3.00 8.00
42 Matt Cassel/249 2.50 6.00
43 Philip Rivers/249 4.00 10.00
44 Ryan Mathews/199 3.00 8.00
45 Vincent Jackson/249 2.50 6.00
47 Darren McFadden/249 2.50 6.00
50 Tim Tebow/249 4.00 10.00
52 Ahmad Bradshaw/249 2.50 6.00
53 Eli Manning/249 3.00 8.00
54 Hakeem Nicks/249 2.50 6.00
55 DeSean Jackson/12 6.00 15.00
56 LeSean McCoy/80 5.00 12.00
57 Michael Vick/99 4.00 10.00
58 DeMarcus Ware/249 4.00 10.00
59 Dez Bryant/99 5.00 12.00
60 Tony Romo/249 3.00 8.00
62 London Fletcher/249 3.00 8.00
63 Ryan Torain/249 2.50 6.00
64 Aaron Rodgers/99 10.00 25.00
67 Calvin Johnson/99 5.00 12.00
68 Jahvid Best/199 2.50 6.00
69 Matthew Stafford/99 4.00 10.00
70 Brian Urlacher/249 4.00 10.00
71 Jay Cutler/249 2.50 6.00
72 Matt Forte/249 2.50 6.00
73 Adrian Peterson/49 5.00 12.00
74 Jared Allen/249 4.00 10.00
75 Percy Harvin/199 2.50 6.00
76 Drew Brees/249 4.00 10.00
78 Marques Colston/249 2.50 6.00
82 Matt Ryan/249 3.00 8.00
83 Michael Turner/249 2.50 6.00
84 Roddy White/99 3.00 8.00
85 DeAngelo Williams/199 2.50 6.00
90 Frank Gore/249 3.00 8.00
91 Vernon Davis/199 2.50 6.00
96 Sam Bradford/249 2.50 6.00
97 Steven Jackson/249 2.50 6.00
98 Beanie Wells/99 3.00 8.00
100 Larry Fitzgerald/249 3.00 8.00

2011 Totally Certified Gold

*1-100 VETS/25: 5X TO 12X BASIC CARDS
*151-200 ROOK.AU25: .8X TO 2X AU RC/299
*RK.JSY AU/20-25: 1.2X TO 3X JSY AU/399-499
*ROOK.JSY AU/20-25: 1X TO 2.5X JSY AU/299
*ROOK.JSY AU/20-25: .8X TO 2X JSY AU/99
GOLD STATED PRINT RUN 12-25
201 A.J. Green JSY AU/25 60.00 120.00
203 Andy Dalton JSY AU/25 25.00 60.00
207 Cam Newton JSY AU/25 150.00 300.00
215 Jake Locker JSY AU/25 12.00 30.00

2011 Totally Certified Gold Materials Prime

GOLD STATED PRINT RUN 1-49
2 Ryan Fitzpatrick/49 5.00 12.00
4 BenJarvus Green-Ellis/49 8.00 20.00
6 Wes Welker/49 6.00 15.00
7 Mark Sanchez/49 5.00 12.00
8 Santonio Holmes/49 5.00 12.00
9 Shonn Greene/49 5.00 12.00
10 Brandon Marshall/49 6.00 15.00
11 Brian Hartline/49 6.00 15.00
17 Cedric Benson/49 5.00 12.00
20 Anquan Boldin/49 5.00 12.00
21 Joe Flacco/49 6.00 15.00
22 Ray Lewis/49 8.00 20.00
23 Ray Rice/49 5.00 12.00
25 Josh Cribbs/49 5.00 12.00
30 Chris Johnson/49 5.00 12.00
32 Matt Hasselbeck/49 5.00 12.00
33 Maurice Jones-Drew/49 5.00 12.00
34 Mike Thomas/49 6.00 15.00
37 Joseph Addai/25 6.00 15.00
40 Dwayne Bowe/49 6.00 15.00
41 Jamaal Charles/49 6.00 15.00
42 Matt Cassel/49 5.00 12.00
43 Philip Rivers/49 8.00 20.00
44 Ryan Mathews/49 6.00 15.00
45 Vincent Jackson/49 5.00 12.00
47 Darren McFadden/49 5.00 12.00
50 Tim Tebow/49 8.00 20.00
52 Ahmad Bradshaw/49 5.00 12.00
53 Eli Manning/49 6.00 15.00
54 Hakeem Nicks/49 5.00 12.00
55 DeSean Jackson/49 6.00 15.00
58 DeMarcus Ware/49 8.00 20.00
59 Dez Bryant/49 8.00 20.00
60 Tony Romo/49 6.00 15.00
62 London Fletcher/49 6.00 15.00
63 Ryan Torain/25 6.00 15.00
67 Calvin Johnson/49 8.00 20.00
70 Brian Urlacher/49 8.00 20.00
71 Jay Cutler/25 6.00 15.00
72 Matt Forte/49 5.00 12.00
76 Drew Brees/49 8.00 20.00
78 Marques Colston/49 5.00 12.00
83 Michael Turner/49 5.00 12.00
84 Roddy White/49 5.00 12.00
90 Frank Gore/49 6.00 15.00
97 Steven Jackson/49 5.00 12.00
100 Larry Fitzgerald/49 6.00 15.00

2011 Totally Certified Gold Signatures

STATED PRINT RUN 8-15
1 Aaron Rodgers/15 150.00 250.00
4 Charles Woodson/15 150.00 250.00
5 Drew Brees/15 50.00 100.00
6 Larry Fitzgerald/15 30.00 60.00
7 Mark Sanchez/15 15.00 40.00
8 Matthew Stafford/15 30.00 60.00
10 Peyton Manning/15 75.00 150.00
11 Ray Rice/15 30.00 60.00
12 Tim Tebow/15 50.00 120.00
14 Troy Polamalu/15 40.00 80.00
15 Antonio Gates/15 8.00 20.00
16 Matt Forte/15 8.00 20.00
17 Ben Roethlisberger/15
18 Brandon Lloyd/15 8.00 20.00
19 Clay Matthews/15 30.00 60.00
20 Roddy White/15 8.00 20.00
21 Dwayne Bowe/15 8.00 20.00
22 Greg Jennings/15 8.00 20.00
23 Hakeem Nicks/15 8.00 20.00
24 LeSean McCoy/15 12.00 30.00
25 Jahvid Best/15 8.00 20.00
26 Jerod Mayo/15 8.00 20.00
27 Marques Colston/15 8.00 20.00
28 Matt Schaub/15 8.00 20.00
29 Mike Tolbert/15 8.00 20.00
30 Mike Wallace/15 8.00 20.00
31 Nnamdi Asomugha/15 12.00 30.00
[illegible]

33 Pierre Thomas/15 12.00 30.00
34 Ryan Mathews/15 10.00 25.00
35 Shonn Greene/15 8.00 20.00
36 Vernon Davis/15 12.00 30.00
37 Tony Romo/15 40.00 80.00
38 Brian Hartline/15 10.00 25.00
39 C.J. Spiller/15 8.00 20.00
40 Chad Greenway/15 12.00 30.00
41 Chris Cooley/15 8.00 20.00
43 DeAngelo Williams/15 8.00 20.00
44 DeSean Jackson/15 10.00 25.00
45 Donald Driver/15 20.00 50.00
46 Eli Manning/15 60.00 120.00
47 Fred Davis/15 6.00 15.00
48 Greg Olsen/15 10.00 25.00
49 Jared Allen/15 20.00 40.00
50 Joe Flacco/15
101 Archie Manning AU/15 20.00 50.00
102 Ace Parker AU/15 15.00 40.00
103 Doug Williams AU/15 15.00 40.00
104 Floyd Little AU/15 12.00 30.00
105 Frank Gifford AU/15 15.00 40.00
106 Fred Williamson AU/15 12.00 30.00
107 Gary Collins AU/15 12.00 30.00
108 Henry Ellard AU/15 12.00 30.00
109 Jim Taylor AU/15 15.00 40.00
110 John Taylor AU/15 15.00 40.00
111 Lydell Mitchell AU/15 12.00 30.00
112 Mel Renfro AU/15 12.00 30.00
113 Ottis Anderson AU/15 12.00 30.00
114 Rosey Grier AU/15 15.00 40.00
115 Russ Grimm AU/15 12.00 30.00
116 Willie Davis AU/15 12.00 30.00
117 Alan Page AU/15 12.00 30.00
119 Bart Starr AU/15 90.00 150.00
120 Bob Lilly AU/15 15.00 40.00
121 Bobby Bell AU/15 12.00 30.00
122 Charley Taylor AU/15 12.00 30.00
123 Charlie Joiner AU/15 12.00 30.00
124 Chuck Bednarik AU/15 12.00 30.00
125 Dave Casper AU/15 12.00 30.00
126 Deion Sanders AU/15 40.00 80.00
127 Earl Campbell AU/15 20.00 50.00
128 Forrest Gregg AU/15 12.00 30.00
130 Hugh McElhenny AU/15 15.00 40.00
131 Jack Lambert AU/15 40.00 80.00
132 Jack Youngblood AU/15 12.00 30.00
133 James Lofton AU/15 12.00 30.00
134 Jan Stenerud AU/15 15.00 40.00
135 Jim Otto AU/15 12.00 30.00
136 Joe Greene AU/15 40.00 80.00
138 Barry Sanders AU/15 60.00 120.00
140 Cris Carter AU/15 20.00 50.00
141 Dan Marino AU/15 125.00 200.00
145 Jim Kelly AU/15 20.00 50.00
146 Joe Montana AU/15 90.00 150.00
147 Joe Namath AU/15 60.00 120.00
148 John Elway AU/15 60.00 120.00

2011 Totally Certified Freshman Fabric Signatures Red

*RED/200-300: .5X TO 1.2X JSY AU/399-499
*RED/175-300: .4X TO 1X JSY AU/299
RED STATED PRINT RUN 175-300
207 Cam Newton JSY AU/175 50.00 100.00
210 Colin Kaepernick JSY AU/300 8.00 20.00

2011 Totally Certified Future Materials

STATED PRINT RUN 499 SER.#'d SETS
*PRIME/17-49: .8X TO 2X BASIC JSY/499
1 Randall Cobb 2.50 6.00
2 Blaine Gabbert 1.50 4.00
3 Ryan Mallett 1.50 4.00
4 Julio Jones 5.00 12.00
5 A.J. Green 4.00 10.00
6 Colin Kaepernick 2.50 6.00
7 Austin Pettis 1.50 4.00
8 Marcell Dareus 1.50 4.00
9 Titus Young 1.50 4.00
10 Von Miller 2.50 6.00
11 Mark Ingram 2.50 6.00
12 Christian Ponder 1.50 4.00
13 DeMarco Murray 3.00 8.00
14 Jake Locker 1.50 4.00
15 Mikel Leshoure 1.50 4.00
16 Jonathan Baldwin 1.50 4.00
17 Ryan Williams 1.50 4.00
18 Delone Carter 1.50 4.00
19 Alex Green 3.00 8.00
20 Kyle Rudolph 1.50 4.00
21 Stevan Ridley 1.50 4.00
22 Vincent Brown 1.50 4.00
23 Clyde Gates 1.50 4.00
24 Daniel Thomas 1.50 4.00
25 Andy Dalton 3.00 8.00
26 Kendall Hunter 1.50 4.00
27 Jamie Harper 1.50 4.00
28 Greg Little 2.00 5.00
29 Leonard Hankerson 1.50 4.00
30 Shane Vereen 2.00 5.00
31 Jerrel Jernigan 1.50 4.00
32 Bilal Powell 2.00 5.00
33 Cam Newton 8.00 20.00
34 Jordan Todman 1.50 4.00
35 Torrey Smith 1.50 4.00
36 Taiwan Jones 1.50 4.00

2011 Totally Certified Heritage Collection Jerseys

STATED PRINT RUN 50-249
*PRIME/30-49: .6X TO 1.5X BASIC JSY/199-249
*PRIME/15-25: .8X TO 2X BASIC JSY/199-249
*PRIME/49: .6X TO 1.5X BASIC JSY/100
*PRIME/45: .5X TO 1.2X BASIC JSY/50
1 Alan Page/249 3.00 8.00
2 Y.A. Tittle/249 5.00 12.00
3 Bo Jackson/249 8.00 20.00
4 Bob Hayes/199 5.00 12.00
5 Boomer Esiason/249 4.00 10.00
6 Buck Buchanan/249 3.00 8.00
7 Chuck Howley/249 5.00 12.00
8 Cris Carter/249 5.00 12.00
9 Curtis Martin/249 4.00 10.00
10 Dan Marino/249 10.00 25.00
11 Deion Sanders/249 6.00 15.00
12 Doak Walker/249 6.00 15.00
13 Don Maynard/249 4.00 10.00
14 Don Meredith/249 8.00 20.00
15 Doug Flutie/249 4.00 10.00
16 Ed Too Tall Jones/249 3.00 8.00
17 Eddie George/249 4.00 10.00
18 Eric Dickerson/249 4.00 10.00
19 Ernie Davis/50 15.00 40.00
20 Fran Tarkenton/249 5.00 12.00
21 Franco Harris/249 5.00 12.00
22 Gale Sayers/249 5.00 12.00
23 George Blanda/249 4.00 10.00
24 Irving Fryar/249 3.00 8.00
25 Jay Novacek/249 4.00 10.00
26 Jerome Bettis/249 8.00 20.00
27 Jerry Rice/249 8.00 20.00
28 Jerry Rice/249 8.00 20.00
29 Jim Brown/249 6.00 15.00
30 Jim McMahon/249 4.00 10.00
31 Jim Otto/249 4.00 10.00
32 Jim Parker/249 3.00 8.00
33 Jim Plunkett/249 4.00 10.00
34 Jim Thorpe/100 60.00 100.00
35 Joe Greene/249 5.00 12.00
36 Joe Montana/200 12.00 30.00
37 Joe Montana/249 12.00 30.00
38 Joe Namath/240 8.00 20.00
39 Joe Perry/100 5.00 12.00
[illegible] 6.00 15.00

41 John Hadl/249 3.00 8.00
42 Keith Jackson/249 3.00 8.00
43 Ken Stabler/249 5.00 12.00
44 Keyshawn Johnson/249 4.00 10.00
45 Larry Csonka/249 4.00 10.00
46 Len Dawson/249 5.00 12.00
47 Marshall Faulk/249 4.00 10.00
48 Mike Ditka/249 6.00 15.00
49 Mike Singletary/249 5.00 12.00
50 Warren Sapp/215 4.00 10.00
51 Paul Warfield/249 4.00 10.00
52 Phil Simms/249 4.00 10.00
53 Randall Cunningham/249 5.00 12.00
54 Richard Dent/249 3.00 8.00
55 Rickey Jackson/199 3.00 8.00
56 Rod Woodson/249 5.00 12.00
57 Roger Staubach/249 6.00 15.00
58 Ronnie Lott/249 4.00 10.00
59 Shannon Sharpe/249 5.00 12.00
60 Steve Young/249 6.00 15.00
61 Tony Dorsett/249 5.00 12.00
62 Troy Aikman/249 6.00 15.00
63 Walter Payton/249 15.00 30.00
64 Warren Moon/249 5.00 12.00

2011 Totally Certified HRX Video Cards

STATED PRINT RUN 40 SER.#'d SETS
UNPRICED AUTO PRINT RUN 10
EXCH EXPIRATION: 9/14/2013
1 Andy Dalton 25.00 60.00
2 Cam Newton 125.00 250.00
3 Mark Ingram 50.00 100.00
4 Tim Tebow 150.00 300.00

2011 Totally Certified Piece of the Game

STATED PRINT RUN 7-199
*PRIME/38-49: .8X TO 2X BASIC JSY/125-199
*PRIME/15-25: 1X TO 2.5X BASIC JSY/125-199
1 Matt Ryan/199 3.00 8.00
2 Roddy White/7
3 Anquan Boldin/199 2.50 6.00
4 Joe Flacco/199 3.00 8.00
5 Ray Lewis/199 4.00 10.00
6 Ray Rice/199 2.50 6.00
7 C.J. Spiller/199 2.50 6.00
8 Ryan Fitzpatrick/199 2.50 6.00
9 Brian Urlacher/199 4.00 10.00
10 Devin Hester/199 3.00 8.00
11 Johnny Knox/199 2.50 6.00
12 Felix Jones/199 2.50 6.00
13 Eddie Royal/199 2.50 6.00
14 Knowshon Moreno/199 2.50 6.00
15 Tim Tebow/199 4.00 10.00
16 Matthew Stafford/148 3.00 8.00
17 Clay Matthews/199 5.00 12.00
18 Matt Schaub/199 2.50 6.00
19 Dwight Freeney/125 2.50 6.00
20 Pierre Garcon/145 3.00 8.00
21 Reggie Wayne/177 3.00 8.00
22 Maurice Jones-Drew/172 2.50 6.00
23 Dexter McCluster/190 2.50 6.00
24 Matt Cassel/149 2.50 6.00
25 Tamba Hali/149 2.50 6.00
26 Anthony Fasano/149 2.50 6.00
27 Brian Hartline/149 3.00 8.00
28 Chad Greenway/149 3.00 8.00
29 Devery Henderson/149 2.50 6.00
30 Marques Colston/149 2.50 6.00
31 Pierre Thomas /149 2.50 6.00
32 Ahmad Bradshaw/149 2.50 6.00
33 Brandon Jacobs/149 2.50 6.00
34 Eli Manning/149 3.00 8.00
35 Hakeem Nicks/149 2.50 6.00
36 Darrelle Revis/149 2.50 6.00
37 LaDainian Tomlinson/149 4.00 10.00
38 Mark Sanchez/149 2.50 6.00
39 Darren McFadden/149 2.50 6.00
40 Jacoby Ford/149 3.00 8.00
41 Antonio Gates/149 2.50 6.00
42 Malcom Floyd/149 2.50 6.00
43 Vincent Jackson/149 2.50 6.00
44 Frank Gore/149 3.00 8.00
45 Patrick Willis/149 3.00 8.00
46 Steven Jackson/149 2.50 6.00
47 Earnest Graham/149 2.50 6.00
48 Kellen Winslow Jr./195 2.50 6.00
49 Chris Johnson/149 2.50 6.00
50 Cortland Finnegan/149 2.50 6.00
51 Marc Mariani/149 3.00 8.00
52 Brian Orakpo/149 4.00 10.00
53 Chris Cooley/149 2.50 6.00
54 Santana Moss/149 3.00 8.00
55 Beanie Wells/149 2.50 6.00
56 Larry Fitzgerald/149 3.00 8.00
57 Tony Gonzalez/149 3.00 8.00
58 Jay Cutler/149 2.50 6.00
59 Julius Peppers/149 3.00 8.00
60 Cedric Benson/149 2.50 6.00
61 Jordan Shipley/149 2.50 6.00
62 Josh Cribbs/149 2.50 6.00
63 Miles Austin/149 2.50 6.00
64 Owen Daniels/149 2.50 6.00
65 Dallas Clark/149 2.50 6.00
66 Joseph Addai/149 2.50 6.00
67 Mike Thomas/149 3.00 8.00
68 Tom Brady/149 10.00 25.00
69 Sebastian Janikowski/149 6.00 15.00
70 Brent Celek/149 2.50 6.00
71 Sam Bradford/149 2.50 6.00
72 Kenny Britt/149 2.50 6.00
73 Michael Turner/149 2.50 6.00
74 Ed Reed/149 3.00 8.00
75 Haloti Ngata/149 2.50 6.00

2011 Totally Certified Stitches in Time

STATED PRINT RUN 35-200
*PRIME/25: .6X TO 1.5X QUAD/115-200
*PRIME/25: .5X TO 1.2X QUAD/35
1 Smith/Pytn/Sndrs/Mrtin/35 30.00 60.00
2 Bettis/Tmlin/Dckrsn/Drstt/200 10.00 25.00
3 Fvre/Mrno/P.Mann/Elwy/100 40.00 80.00
4 Rice/Owens/Moss/Carter/199 12.00 30.00
5 Turnr/Btks/Single/Urlch/70 20.00 40.00
6 Craig/Gore/Jones/Davis/125 8.00 20.00
7 Mere/Staub/Aikmn/Rmo/150 30.00 60.00
8 Kelly/Thoms/Reed/Smith/75 15.00 40.00
9 Elwy/Dvis/McCaf/Shrpe/150 15.00 40.00
10 Starr/Grgg/Jrdn/Hrnung/150 15.00 40.00
11 Plunk/Stablr/Brwn/Hndr/150 12.00 30.00
12 White/Smith/Strah/Ware/115 10.00 25.00
13 Wdsn/Sndrs/Reed/Asom/150 12.00 30.00
14 Eli/Roeth/Brees/Rdgers/90 20.00 40.00
15 Brdshw/Stall/Grne/Hrris/145 20.00 40.00
16 Ptrsn/Formn/Cartr/Hrvin/150 12.00 30.00
17 Jones-D/Rice/Trnr/Gore/150 10.00 25.00
18 Johnsn/Welkr/Jhnsn/Fitz/150 10.00 25.00
19 Gonzalez/Witten/Gates/Davis/150 6.00 15.00
20 Ward/Stafford/Moreno/Green/150 8.00 20.00
21 Lewis/Reed/Gore/Hester/150 10.00 25.00
22 Brady/Henne/Harris/Manningham/150 8.00 20.00
23 Eli/McClus/Willis/Grn-Ellis/35 12.00 30.00
24 McCoy/Shipley/Benson/Charles/150 6.00 15.00
25 Cassel/Lott/Matthews/Sanchez/150 8.00 20.00

2011 Totally Certified Team Panini Material Autographs

STATED PRINT RUN 25-30
1 Anquan Boldin/30 10.00 25.00
2 Arian Foster/25 25.00 50.00
3 BenJarvus Green-Ellis/30 20.00 50.00
4 Colt McCoy/25 10.00 25.00
5 Darren McFadden/30 10.00 25.00
6 Dez Bryant/30 15.00 40.00
7 Jamaal Charles/25 15.00 40.00
8 Jay Cutler/25 10.00 25.00
10 LaDainian Tomlinson/30 40.00 80.00
11 Percy Harvin/30 10.00 25.00
12 Philip Rivers/25 25.00 50.00
13 Sam Bradford/25 15.00 40.00
14 Santonio Holmes/30 10.00 25.00

2012 Totally Certified

MP.SET w/o RC's (100) 10.00 25.00
101-200 ROOKIE AU PRINT RUN 99-299
201-235 ROOK.JSY AU PRINT RUN 49-199
EXCH EXPIRATION: 9/20/2014
1 Tom Brady 1.25 3.00
2 Wes Welker .40 1.00
3 Rob Gronkowski .50 1.25
4 Ray Rice .30 .75
5 Torrey Smith .30 .75
6 Andy Dalton .40 1.00
7 A.J. Green .50 1.25
8 Greg Little .30 .75
9 Josh Cribbs .30 .75
10 Ben Roethlisberger .50 1.25
11 Antonio Brown .50 1.25
12 Arian Foster .40 1.00
13 Matt Schaub .30 .75
14 Reggie Wayne .40 1.00
15 Robert Mathis .30 .75
16 Marcedes Lewis .30 .75
17 Maurice Jones-Drew .30 .75
18 Chris Johnson .30 .75
19 Kenny Britt .30 .75
20 Fred Jackson .40 1.00
21 Steve Johnson .40 1.00
22 Reggie Bush .30 .75
23 Brian Hartline .40 1.00
24 Shonn Greene .30 .75
25 Santonio Holmes .30 .75
26 Peyton Manning 1.25 3.00
27 Willis McGahee .30 .75
28 Jamaal Charles .40 1.00
29 Dwayne Bowe .40 1.00
30 Darren McFadden .30 .75
31 Darrius Heyward-Bey .30 .75
32 Philip Rivers .50 1.25
33 Antonio Gates .40 1.00
34 Ryan Mathews .40 1.00
35 Jay Cutler .30 .75
36 Brandon Marshall .40 1.00
37 Matt Forte .30 .75
38 Matthew Stafford .40 1.00
39 Calvin Johnson .50 1.25
40 Aaron Rodgers .75 2.00
41 Jordy Nelson .40 1.00
42 Greg Jennings .30 .75
43 Christian Ponder .30 .75
44 Adrian Peterson .50 1.25
45 Percy Harvin .30 .75
46 Julio Jones .50 1.25
47 Roddy White .30 .75
48 Michael Turner .30 .75
49 Cam Newton .50 1.25
50 Steve Smith .40 1.00
51 Drew Brees .50 1.25
52 Marques Colston .30 .75
53 Josh Freeman .40 1.00
54 Vincent Jackson .30 .75
55 Tony Romo .40 1.00
56 Dez Bryant .50 1.25
57 Victor Cruz .40 1.00
58 Hakeem Nicks .30 .75
59 Eli Manning .40 1.00
60 LeSean McCoy .50 1.25
61 Michael Vick .40 1.00
62 Fred Davis .30 .75
63 Pierre Garcon .40 1.00
64 Larry Fitzgerald .40 1.00
65 Patrick Peterson .30 .75
66 Alex Smith .40 1.00
67 Patrick Willis .40 1.00
68 Marshawn Lynch .40 1.00
69 Sidney Rice .30 .75
70 Sam Bradford .30 .75
71 Steven Jackson .30 .75
72 Doug Flutie .40 1.00
73 Drew Bledsoe .40 1.00
74 Fran Tarkenton .50 1.25
75 Jerome Bettis .50 1.25
76 Jake Plummer .30 .75
77 Jim Plunkett .40 1.00
78 Kellen Winslow .30 .75
79 Rod Smith .30 .75
80 Rod Woodson .40 1.00
81 Sterling Sharpe .40 1.00
82 Steve Largent .50 1.25
83 Tim Brown .50 1.25
84 Warren Sapp .40 1.00
85 Thurman Thomas .40 1.00
86 Ronnie Lott .40 1.00
87 Bernie Kosar .40 1.00
88 Bo Jackson .60 1.50
89 Bob Griese .50 1.25
90 Boomer Esiason .40 1.00
91 Charlie Joiner .30 .75
92 Cris Collinsworth .40 1.00
93 Cris Carter .50 1.25
94 Dave Casper .30 .75
95 Dick Butkus .60 1.50
96 Ed McCaffrey .30 .75
97 Eric Dickerson .40 1.00
98 Fred Taylor .30 .75
99 Gale Sayers .50 1.25
100 Jim McMahon .40 1.00
101 Alfred Morris AU/290 RC 2.50 6.00
102 Andre Branch AU/290 RC 2.50 6.00
103 Greg Zuerlein AU/290 RC 4.00 10.00
104 B.J. Cunningham AU/290 RC 2.50 6.00
105 Bobby Rainey AU/290 RC 2.50 6.00
106 Bobby Wagner AU/290 RC 4.00 10.00
107 B.Bolden AU/290 RC 2.50 6.00
108 Bruce Irvin AU/290 RC 3.00 8.00
109 Bryce Brown AU/290 RC 2.50 6.00
110 Blair Walsh AU/290 RC 10.00 25.00
111 Chandler Harnish AU/290 RC 2.50 6.00
112 C.Jones AU/290 RC 2.50 6.00
113 Chris Polk AU/290 RC 2.50 6.00
114 Chris Rainey AU/290 RC 2.50 6.00
115 Damaris Johnson AU/290 RC 2.50 6.00
116 C.Upshaw AU/290 RC 3.00 8.00
117 Cyrus Gray AU/290 RC 2.50 6.00
118 D.Richardson AU/290 RC 8.00 20.00
119 Deonte Thompson AU/290 RC 3.00 8.00
120 David DeCastro AU/290 RC 2.50 6.00
121 Evan Rodriguez AU/290 RC 3.00 8.00
122 Deangelo Peterson AU/290 RC 2.50 6.00
123 Devon Still AU/290 RC 3.00 8.00
124 Devon Wylie AU/290 RC 2.50 6.00
125 D.Hightower AU/290 RC EX 4.00 10.00
126 Dontari Poe AU/290 RC 2.50 6.00
127 Dre Kirkpatrick AU/290 RC 2.50 6.00
128 Jeff Demps AU/290 RC 3.00 8.00
129 Josh Cooper AU/290 RC 3.00 8.00
130 Fletcher Cox AU/290 RC 4.00 10.00
131 George Iloka AU/290 RC 2.50 6.00
132 Jorvorskie Lane AU/290 RC 3.00 8.00
133 Rod Streater AU/290 RC 4.00 10.00
134 Harrison Smith AU/290 RC 5.00 12.00
135 Janoris Jenkins AU/290 RC 3.00 8.00
136 Jared Crick AU/290 RC 2.50 6.00
137 Josh Gordon AU/290 RC [illegible]
138 Jonathan Martin AU/290 RC 2.50 6.00
139 Juron Criner AU/290 RC 2.50 6.00
140 Kellen Moore AU/290 RC 3.00 8.00
141 Keshawn Martin AU/290 RC 3.00 8.00
142 Kevin Zeitler AU/290 RC 2.50 6.00
143 Kirk Cousins AU/99 RC 15.00 40.00
144 Ladarius Green AU/290 RC 2.50 6.00
145 Josh Norman AU/290 RC 3.00 8.00
146 Lavonte David AU/290 RC 4.00 10.00
147 Luke Kuechly AU/290 RC 10.00 20.00
148 Justin Tucker AU/290 RC 8.00 20.00
149 Mark Barron AU/290 RC 2.50 6.00
150 Kris Adams AU/290 RC 4.00 10.00
151 Marvin Jones AU/290 RC 2.50 6.00
152 Lance Dunbar AU/290 RC 5.00 12.00
153 Matt Kalil AU/290 RC 2.50 6.00
154 Melvin Ingram AU/290 RC 2.50 6.00
155 Michael Brockers AU/290 RC 2.50 6.00
156 Michael Smith AU/290 RC 3.00 8.00
157 Morris Claiborne AU/99 RC 3.00 8.00
158 Mychal Kendricks AU/290 RC 4.00 10.00
159 Nick Perry AU/290 RC 3.00 8.00
160 Orson Charles AU/290 RC 2.50 6.00
161 Quinton Coples AU/290 RC 2.50 6.00
162 Riley Reiff AU/290 RC 2.50 6.00
163 Rishard Matthews AU/290 RC 2.50 6.00
164 Ronnell Lewis AU/290 RC 2.50 6.00
165 Ryan Lindley AU/290 RC 2.50 6.00
166 S.McClellin AU/290 RC 3.00 8.00
167 Stephon Gilmore AU/290 RC 3.00 8.00
168 T.Y. Hilton AU/290 RC 5.00 12.00
169 Miles Burris AU/290 RC 4.00 10.00
170 Terrance Ganaway AU/290 RC 3.00 8.00
171 Nigel Bradham AU/290 RC 3.00 8.00
172 Tommy Streeter AU/290 RC 2.50 6.00
173 Travis Benjamin AU/290 RC 2.50 6.00
174 Vick Ballard AU/290 RC 3.00 8.00
175 Vinny Curry AU/290 RC 3.00 8.00
176 Vontaze Burfict AU/290 RC 3.00 8.00
177 Whitney Mercilus AU/290 RC 2.50 6.00
178 Zach Brown AU/290 RC 2.50 6.00
179 Derek Wolfe AU/290 RC EXCH 3.00 8.00
180 Tavon Wilson AU/290 RC 3.00 8.00
181 Kendall Reyes AU/290 RC 2.50 6.00
182 Jerel Worthy AU/290 RC EXCH 2.50 6.00
183 C.Hayward AU/290 RC 2.50 6.00
184 Trumaine Johnson AU/290 RC 2.50 6.00
185 Josh Robinson AU/290 RC 4.00 10.00
186 Olivier Vernon AU/290 RC 4.00 10.00
187 Brandon Taylor AU/290 RC 2.50 6.00
188 Demario Davis AU/290 RC 2.50 6.00
189 Brandon Hardin AU/290 RC 3.00 8.00
190 Jamell Fleming AU/290 RC 2.50 6.00
191 Tyrone Crawford AU/290 RC 2.50 6.00
192 Mike Martin AU/290 RC 3.00 8.00
193 Bill Bentley AU/290 RC 3.00 8.00
194 Sean Spence AU/290 RC 3.00 8.00
195 Omar Bolden AU/290 RC 3.00 8.00
196 Coty Sensabaugh AU/290 RC 3.00 8.00
197 Adrien Robinson AU/290 RC 2.50 6.00
198 Rhett Ellison AU/290 RC 3.00 8.00
199 Najee Goode AU/290 RC 2.50 6.00
200 James Hanna AU/290 RC 2.50 6.00
201 A.Luck JSY AU/199 RC 60.00 125.00
202 A.J. Jenkins JSY AU/199 RC 4.00 10.00
203 A.Jeffery JSY AU/199 RC 8.00 20.00
204 B.Pierce JSY AU/199 RC 8.00 20.00
205 B.Weeden JSY AU/199 RC 4.00 10.00
206 Brian Quick JSY AU/199 RC 4.00 10.00
207 B.Osweiler JSY AU/199 RC 4.00 10.00
208 Chris Givens JSY AU/199 RC 4.00 10.00
209 Coby Fleener JSY AU/199 RC 4.00 10.00
210 D.Wilson JSY AU/199 RC 4.00 10.00
211 DeVier Posey JSY AU/199 RC EXCH 4.00 10.00
212 D.Martin JSY AU/199 RC 6.00 15.00
213 Dwayne Allen JSY AU/199 RC 4.00 10.00
214 Isaiah Pead JSY AU/199 RC 4.00 10.00
215 Jarius Wright JSY AU/199 RC 4.00 10.00
216 Joe Adams JSY AU/199 RC 4.00 10.00
217 J.Blackmon JSY AU/99 RC 5.00 12.00
218 K.Wright JSY AU/199 RC 4.00 10.00
219 Lamar Miller JSY AU/199 RC 6.00 15.00
220 L.James JSY AU/199 RC 4.00 10.00
221 Michael Egnew JSY AU/199 RC 4.00 10.00
222 M.Floyd JSY AU/199 RC 4.00 10.00
223 Mohamed Sanu JSY AU/199 RC 6.00 15.00
224 Nick Foles JSY AU/199 RC 20.00 50.00
225 Nick Toon JSY AU/49 RC 6.00 15.00
226 R.Griffin III JSY AU/199 RC 5.00 12.00
227 Robert Turbin JSY AU/199 RC 4.00 10.00
228 Ronnie Hillman JSY AU/199 RC 4.00 10.00
229 R.Randle JSY AU/99 RC 5.00 12.00
230 R.Wilson JSY AU/199 RC EX 50.00 100.00
231 Ryan Broyles JSY AU/199 RC 4.00 10.00
232 R.Tannehill JSY AU/199 RC 6.00 15.00
233 Stephen Hill JSY AU/199 RC 4.00 10.00
234 T.J. Graham JSY AU/199 RC 4.00 10.00
235 T.Richardson JSY AU/199 RC 4.00 10.00

2012 Totally Certified Blue

*1-100 VETS/199: 1.5X TO 4X BASIC CARDS
*101-200 ROOK.AU/99: .5X TO 1.2X AU RC/290
*101-200 ROOK.AU/49: .5X TO 1.2X AU RC/99
*201-235 JSY AU/59-99: .5X TO 1.2X JSY AU/199
*201-235 JSY AU/49: .5X TO 1.2X JSY AU/99
201 Andrew Luck JSY AU/99 60.00 150.00
230 Russell Wilson JSY AU/26 75.00 150.00

2012 Totally Certified Gold

-100 VETS/25: 5X TO 12X BASIC CARDS
*101-200 ROOK.AU/25: .8X TO 2X AU RC/290
*101-200 ROOK.AU/25: .6X TO 1.5X AU RC/99
*201-235 JSY AU/24-25: .8X TO 2X JSY AU/199
*201-235 JSY AU/25: .5X TO 1.2X JSY AU/49
201 Andrew Luck JSY AU 200.00 300.00
230 Russell Wilson JSY AU/25 150.00 250.00

2012 Totally Certified Gold Materials Prime

*GOLD/49: .8X TO 2X BASIC JSY/299
*GOLD/49: .5X TO 1.2X BASIC JSY/49
*GOLD/15-25: 1X TO 2.5X BASIC JSY/149-299
*GOLD/25: .8X TO 2X BASIC JSY/99
*GOLD/25: .6X TO 1.5X BASIC JSY/49
40 Adrian Peterson/25 20.00 50.00
42 Tom Brady/15 30.00 60.00

2012 Totally Certified Red Materials

*BLUE/99: .5X TO 1.2X BASIC JSY/299
*BLUE/49: .6X TO 1.5X BASIC JSY/149-199
*BLUE/49: .5X TO 1.2X BASIC JSY/99
*BLUE/25: .8X TO 2X BASIC JSY/199
1 Beanie Wells/299 2.00 5.00
2 Larry Fitzgerald/299 2.50 6.00
3 Matt Ryan/299 2.50 6.00
4 Michael Turner/299 2.00 5.00
5 Roddy White/299 2.00 5.00
6 Joe Flacco/299 2.50 6.00
7 Ray Rice/299 2.00 5.00
8 Ray Lewis/299 3.00 8.00
9 Ed Reed/299 2.50 6.00
10 Ryan Fitzpatrick/299 2.00 5.00
11 Steve Johnson/299 2.50 6.00
12 Steve Smith/299 2.50 6.00
14 DeAngelo Williams/299 2.00 5.00
15 Jonathan Stewart/299 2.00 5.00
16 Jay Cutler/299 2.00 5.00
17 Matt Forte/299 2.00 5.00
18 Devin Hester/299 2.50 6.00
19 Andy Dalton/299 2.50 6.00
20 A.J. Green/299 3.00 8.00
21 Jermaine Gresham/299 2.00 5.00
22 Tony Romo/299 2.50 6.00
23 Jason Witten/299 2.50 6.00
24 [illegible] 2.00 5.00
25 Miles Austin/299 2.00 5.00
26 Von Miller/199 2.50 6.00
27 Demaryius Thomas/299 3.00 8.00
28 Knowshon Moreno/299 2.00 5.00
29 Anquan Boldin/299 2.00 5.00
30 Eric Decker/299 2.00 5.00
31 Donald Driver/49 5.00 12.00
32 Andre Johnson/99 3.00 8.00
33 Arian Foster/299 2.50 6.00
35 Marcedes Lewis/299 2.00 5.00
36 Maurice Jones-Drew/99 2.50 6.00
37 Matt Cassel/299 2.00 5.00
38 Jamaal Charles/299 2.50 6.00
39 Dwayne Bowe/299 2.50 6.00
40 Adrian Peterson/299 3.00 8.00
41 Percy Harvin/299 2.00 5.00
42 Tom Brady/299 8.00 20.00
43 Wes Welker/299 2.50 6.00
44 Drew Brees/299 3.00 8.00
45 Marques Colston/299 2.00 5.00
47 Eli Manning/299 2.50 6.00
48 Hakeem Nicks/299 2.00 5.00
49 Shonn Greene/299 2.00 5.00
50 Reggie Bush/299 2.00 5.00
51 Mark Sanchez/299 2.00 5.00
52 Darren McFadden/299 2.00 5.00
53 Carson Palmer/299 2.50 6.00
54 DeSean Jackson/299 2.50 6.00
55 Jeremy Maclin/299 2.00 5.00
56 Jimmy Graham/299 3.00 8.00
58 Troy Polamalu/299 3.00 8.00
59 Daniel Thomas/299 2.00 5.00
60 Philip Rivers/299 3.00 8.00
61 Antonio Gates/299 2.50 6.00
62 Ryan Mathews/299 2.50 6.00
63 Darrius Heyward-Bey/299 2.00 5.00
64 Torrey Smith/299 2.00 5.00
65 Vernon Davis/299 2.00 5.00
66 Steven Jackson/299 2.00 5.00
68 Sam Bradford/299 2.00 5.00
70 Chris Johnson/49 3.00 8.00
71 Brian Orakpo/299 2.50 6.00
72 London Fletcher/299 3.00 8.00
73 Santana Moss/299 2.50 6.00
75 Felix Jones/299 2.00 5.00
76 Christian Ponder/299 2.00 5.00
77 Darren Sproles/49 4.00 10.00
78 Michael Vick/299 2.50 6.00
79 Mike Wallace/299 2.00 5.00
80 Sean Lee/299 3.00 8.00
81 Kevin Walter/149 2.00 5.00
82 Brian Urlacher/299 3.00 8.00
83 Tony Gonzalez/299 2.50 6.00
84 Dustin Keller/299 2.00 5.00
87 Ahmad Bradshaw/199 2.00 5.00
89 Tony Moeaki/299 2.00 5.00
90 Michael Crabtree/299 2.00 5.00
91 C.J. Spiller/299 2.00 5.00
92 Sidney Rice/299 2.00 5.00
93 Kenny Britt/299 2.00 5.00
94 Davone Bess/299 2.00 5.00
95 Fred Jackson/299 2.50 6.00
96 Elvis Dumervil/299 2.00 5.00
97 Jared Allen/299 2.00 5.00
98 Lance Briggs/49 4.00 10.00
99 Jay Ratliff/299 2.50 6.00
100 Willis McGahee/299 2.00 5.00

2012 Totally Certified Blue Signatures

8 Greg Little/49 5.00 12.00
9 Josh Cribbs/25
19 Kenny Britt/49 8.00 20.00
41 Jordy Nelson/15
62 Fred Davis/25 6.00 15.00
77 Jim Plunkett/25 10.00 25.00
78 Kellen Winslow/25 8.00 20.00
91 Charlie Joiner/49 8.00 20.00

2012 Totally Certified Gold Signatures

11 Antonio Brown/25 10.00 25.00
14 Reggie Wayne/15 8.00 20.00
15 Robert Mathis/25 8.00 20.00
17 Maurice Jones-Drew/25 6.00 15.00
19 Kenny Britt/25 6.00 15.00
25 Santonio Holmes/25 6.00 15.00
43 Christian Ponder/25 6.00 15.00
53 Josh Freeman/25 8.00 20.00
65 Patrick Peterson/25 6.00 15.00
84 Warren Sapp/25
91 Charlie Joiner/25 8.00 20.00
94 Dave Casper/25 8.00 20.00

2012 Totally Certified Down and Dirty Materials

*PRIME/49: .8X TO 2X BASIC JSY/154-299
*PRIME/49: .5X TO 1.2X BASIC JSY/44
*PRIME/17: 1X TO 2.5X BASIC JSY/299
1 Doug Martin/299 2.50 6.00
2 A.J. Jenkins/299 1.50 4.00
3 Alshon Jeffery/299 3.00 8.00
4 Andrew Luck/299 12.00 30.00
5 Bernard Pierce/299 1.50 4.00
6 Brandon Weeden/299 1.50 4.00
7 Brian Quick/299 1.50 4.00
8 Brock Osweiler/299 1.50 4.00
9 Chris Givens/299 1.50 4.00
11 David Wilson/299 1.50 4.00
12 DeVier Posey/299 1.50 4.00
13 Dwayne Allen/299 1.50 4.00
14 Isaiah Pead/299 1.50 4.00
15 Jarius Wright/299 1.50 4.00
16 Joe Adams/299 1.50 4.00
17 Justin Blackmon/186 1.50 4.00
18 Kendall Wright/299 1.50 4.00
19 Lamar Miller/299 2.50 6.00
20 LaMichael James/299 1.50 4.00
21 Michael Egnew/299 1.50 4.00
22 Michael Floyd/299 1.50 4.00
23 Mohamed Sanu/44 4.00 10.00
24 Nick Foles/299 4.00 10.00
26 Robert Griffin III/299 2.00 5.00
27 Robert Turbin/299 1.50 4.00
28 Ronnie Hillman/299 1.50 4.00
30 Russell Wilson/299 10.00 25.00
31 Ryan Broyles/154 1.50 4.00
32 Ryan Tannehill/299 2.50 6.00
33 Stephen Hill/262 1.50 4.00
34 T.J. Graham/299 1.50 4.00
35 Trent Richardson/299 1.50 4.00

2012 Totally Certified Future Signature Materials

1 Robert Griffin III/175 4.00 10.00
2 A.J. Jenkins/175 3.00 8.00
3 Alshon Jeffery/175 6.00 15.00
4 Andrew Luck/175 60.00 125.00
5 Bernard Pierce/175 6.00 15.00
6 Brandon Weeden/175 3.00 8.00
7 Brian Quick/175 3.00 8.00
8 Brock Osweiler/175 3.00 8.00
9 Chris Givens/175 3.00 8.00
10 Coby Fleener/167 3.00 8.00
11 David Wilson/175 3.00 8.00
12 DeVier Posey/175 3.00 8.00
13 Doug Martin/175 5.00 12.00
14 Dwayne Allen/175 3.00 8.00
15 Isaiah Pead/175 3.00 8.00
16 Jarius Wright/175 3.00 8.00
17 Joe Adams/175 3.00 8.00
18 Justin Blackmon/175 3.00 8.00
19 Kendall Wright/175 3.00 8.00
20 Lamar Miller/175 5.00 12.00
21 LaMichael James/175 3.00 8.00
22 Michael Egnew/175 3.00 8.00
23 Michael Floyd/175 3.00 8.00
24 Mohamed Sanu/175 5.00 12.00
25 Nick Foles/175 12.00 30.00
27 Robert Turbin/175 3.00 8.00
28 Ronnie Hillman/175 3.00 8.00
29 Rueben Randle/100 3.00 8.00
30 Russell Wilson/175 60.00 125.00
31 Ryan Broyles/175 3.00 8.00
32 Ryan Tannehill/175 5.00 12.00
33 Stephen Hill/175 3.00 8.00
34 T.J. Graham/175 3.00 8.00
35 Trent Richardson/175 12.00 30.00

2012 Totally Certified Future Signature Materials Prime

*PRIME/49: .8X TO 2X BASIC AU/175
*PRIME/18-21: 1X TO 2.5X BASIC AU/175
4 Andrew Luck/49 100.00 200.00
30 Russell Wilson/49 100.00 175.00

2012 Totally Certified HRX Video Cards

EXCH EXPIRATION: 9/20/2014
1 Trent Richardson 40.00 100.00
2 Andrew Luck 150.00 250.00
3 Justin Blackmon 25.00 60.00
4 Robert Griffin III 15.00 40.00
5 Ryan Tannehill 15.00 40.00

2012 Totally Certified Stitches in Time

1 Jim Kelly/199 5.00 12.00
2 Dez Bryant/25 6.00 15.00
3 Philip Rivers/199 4.00 10.00
4 Von Miller/25 5.00 12.00
6 Joe Flacco/149 3.00 8.00
7 Reggie Bush/49 3.00 8.00
8 A.J. Green/49 5.00 12.00
9 Matt Forte/99 2.50 6.00
10 Larry Fitzgerald/199 4.00 10.00
11 Wes Welker/199 5.00 12.00
12 Frank Gore/25 5.00 12.00
13 Jimmy Graham/49 5.00 12.00
14 Jonathan Stewart/25 4.00 10.00
15 Darrius Heyward-Bey/99 2.50 6.00
16 Matt Ryan/199 3.00 8.00
17 Adrian Peterson/199 4.00 10.00
18 Darren Sproles/49 4.00 10.00
19 Kevin Walter/99 2.50 6.00
20 Andy Dalton/99 3.00 8.00
21 Randall Cunningham/49 5.00 12.00
22 Jake Plummer/99 3.00 8.00
23 Walter Payton/99 15.00 40.00
24 Barry Sanders/99 8.00 20.00
25 Joe Namath/199 6.00 15.00
26 D.Keller/F.Davis/99 3.00 8.00
27 A.Johnson/D.Thomas/99 5.00 12.00
28 M.Lewis/V.Davis/99 3.00 8.00
29 Ponder/S.Bradford/199 3.00 8.00
30 M.Colston/M.Wallace/3
31 C.Portis/S.Moss/99 4.00 10.00
32 D.Brees/T.Brady/199 10.00 25.00
33 D.Jackson/M.Vick/99 4.00 10.00
34 McFadden/F.Jones/199 3.00 8.00
35 D.Driver/E.Decker/49 8.00 20.00
36 D.Bowe/J.Charles/199 4.00 10.00
37 D.Hester/J.Cutler/199 4.00 10.00
38 Bradshaw/Jackson/99 3.00 8.00
39 Taylor/Jones-Drew/184 3.00 8.00
40 C.Carter/P.Harvin/49 8.00 20.00
41 E.George/R.Lewis/49 8.00 20.00
42 K.Andrsn/Newsome/30
43 C.Dillon/C.Martin/7
44 Esiason/Collinsworth/99 5.00 12.00
45 J.Elway/T.Davis/199 10.00 25.00
46 Nicks/White/Johnson/34 6.00 15.00
48 Eli/Ryan/Fitzpatrick/49 6.00 15.00
49 Gates/Miller/Gonzalez/25 8.00 20.00
50 Reed/Lewis/Suggs/99 8.00 20.00
51 Esiason/Young/Moon/35 8.00 20.00
52 Keller/Sanchz/Greene/199 4.00 10.00
53 Baily/Wdson/Finngn/27 10.00 25.00
54 Williams/Stewart/Smith/24 8.00 20.00
55 Turner/Rice/Mathews/99 5.00 12.00
56 Warner/Faulk/Holt/89 6.00 15.00
57 Montana/Cassel/Holmes/93 12.00 30.00
58 Urlacher/Butkus/Briggs/20 15.00 40.00
61 Witt/Nvck/Romo/Akmn/199 15.00 40.00
63 Reed/Blount/Suggs/Pola/99 10.00 25.00
64 Celk/Orkpo/Austin/T.Brbr/15
65 Garcia/Rice/Crab/Lott/199 12.00 30.00

2012 Totally Certified Stitches in Time Prime

2 Dez Bryant/49 6.00 15.00
4 Von Miller/25 8.00 20.00
8 A.J. Green/25 8.00 20.00
9 Matt Forte/25 5.00 12.00
10 Larry Fitzgerald/20 8.00 20.00
11 Wes Welker/49 5.00 12.00
13 Jimmy Graham/25 8.00 20.00
16 Matt Ryan/20 6.00 15.00
17 Adrian Peterson/25 8.00 20.00
19 Kevin Walter/49 4.00 10.00
20 Andy Dalton/49 5.00 12.00
22 Jake Plummer/49 5.00 12.00
23 Walter Payton/25 20.00 50.00
24 Barry Sanders/25 15.00 40.00
25 Joe Namath/49 10.00 25.00
26 D.Keller/F.Davis/25 6.00 15.00
28 M.Lewis/V.Davis/30 6.00 15.00
29 C.Ponder/S.Bradford/49 5.00 12.00
31 C.Portis/S.Moss/49 6.00 15.00
32 D.Brees/T.Brady/49 20.00 50.00
33 D.Jackson/M.Vick/25 8.00 20.00
34 D.McFadden/F.Jones/49 5.00 12.00
37 D.Hester/J.Cutler/49 6.00 15.00
39 F.Taylor/M.Jones-Drew/49 5.00 12.00
41 E.George/R.Lewis/49 8.00 20.00
42 K.Anderson/O.Newsome/25 10.00 25.00
43 C.Dillon/C.Martin/49 8.00 20.00
44 B.Esiason/C.Collinsworth/49 8.00 20.00
45 J.Elway/T.Davis/15 20.00 50.00
47 Boldin/Henderson/Cribbs/15 8.00 20.00
48 Manning/Ryan/Fitzpatrick/15 10.00 25.00
50 Reed/Lewis/Suggs/49 25.00 50.00
54 Williams/Stewart/Smith/22 10.00 25.00
56 Warner/Faulk/Holt/34 12.00 30.00
57 Montana/Cassel/Holmes/25 25.00 60.00
59 Smith/Bettis/Allen/18 25.00 60.00
63 Reed/Blount/Suggs/Pola/25 20.00 50.00
65 Garcia/Rice/Crabtree/Lott/49 30.00 60.00

2012 Totally Certified Team Panini Material Autographs

*PRIME/25: .8X TO 2X BASIC AU/50
*PRIME/25: .6X TO 1.5X BASIC AU/25
2 Darren McFadden/25 8.00 20.00
4 Eric Decker/25 8.00 20.00
5 Hakeem Nicks/25 8.00 20.00
7 Jeremy Maclin/50 6.00 15.00
8 Marcedes Lewis/50 6.00 15.00
9 Marques Colston/25 8.00 20.00
10 Matt Forte/25 8.00 20.00
11 Michael Turner/15 8.00 20.00
12 Ray Rice/25 8.00 20.00
15 Shonn Greene/25 8.00 20.00
16 Steve Smith/50 8.00 20.00
17 Von Miller/25 10.00 25.00
18 Andy Dalton/25 10.00 25.00
19 Arian Foster/25 20.00 40.00
21 Ryan Mathews/25 10.00 25.00
22 C.J. Spiller/50 10.00 25.00
23 Kenny Britt/50 6.00 15.00
25 Brian Orakpo/50 8.00 20.00
27 Beanie Wells/25 8.00 20.00
28 Sam Bradford/25 20.00 40.00
29 Fred Davis/50 6.00 15.00

2013 Totally Certified

151-210 ROOKIE AU PRINT RUN 325-499
EXCH EXPIRATION: 5/27/2015
211-250 ROOKIE ODDS 1:1 OVERALL

1 Larry Fitzgerald .40 1.00
2 Matt Ryan .40 1.00
3 Julio Jones .50 1.25
4 Joe Flacco .40 1.00
5 Ray Rice .30 .75
6 C.J. Spiller .30 .75
7 Cam Newton .50 1.25
8 Jay Cutler .30 .75
9 Brandon Marshall .40 1.00
10 Andy Dalton .40 1.00
11 A.J. Green .50 1.25
12 Josh Gordon .30 .75
13 Tony Romo .40 1.00
14 Dez Bryant .50 1.25
15 Peyton Manning 1.00 2.50
16 Wes Welker .40 1.00
17 Matthew Stafford .40 1.00
18 Calvin Johnson .50 1.25
19 Aaron Rodgers .75 2.00
20 Jordy Nelson .40 1.00
21 Matt Schaub .30 .75
22 Arian Foster .40 1.00
23 Andrew Luck .75 2.00
24 Trent Richardson .30 .75
25 Maurice Jones-Drew .30 .75
26 Jamaal Charles .40 1.00
27 Ryan Tannehill .40 1.00
28 Mike Wallace .30 .75
29 Christian Ponder .30 .75
30 Adrian Peterson .50 1.25
31 Tom Brady 1.25 3.00
32 Danny Amendola .40 1.00
33 Drew Brees .50 1.25
34 Eli Manning .40 1.00
35 Mark Sanchez .30 .75
36 Darren McFadden .40 1.00
37 Michael Vick .40 1.00
38 LeSean McCoy .50 1.25
39 Ben Roethlisberger .50 1.25
40 Philip Rivers .50 1.25
41 Ryan Mathews .40 1.00
42 Colin Kaepernick .40 1.00
43 Anquan Boldin .30 .75
44 Russell Wilson 1.00 2.50
45 Percy Harvin .30 .75
46 Sam Bradford .30 .75
47 Doug Martin .40 1.00
48 Chris Johnson .30 .75
49 Robert Griffin III .30 .75
50 Alfred Morris .30 .75
51 Andre Johnson TH .50 1.25
52 Robert Griffin III TH .50 1.25
53 Dez Bryant TH .75 2.00
54 Matthew Stafford TH .60 1.50
55 Brandon Marshall TH .60 1.50
56 Joe Flacco TH .60 1.50
57 Tom Brady TH 2.00 5.00
58 Miles Austin TH .50 1.25
59 Aaron Rodgers TH 1.25 3.00
60 Donald Driver TH .60 1.50
61 Chris Johnson TH .50 1.25
62 DeMarcus Ware TH .75 2.00
63 Jason Witten TH .60 1.50
64 Roddy White TH .50 1.25
65 Calvin Johnson TH .75 2.00
66 Brett Favre TH 1.50 4.00
67 Tony Romo TH .60 1.50
68 Champ Bailey TH .60 1.50
69 Michael Vick TH .60 1.50
70 Peyton Manning TH 1.50 4.00
71 Marvin Harrison TH .60 1.50
72 Cris Carter TH .75 2.00
73 Barry Sanders TH 1.25 3.00
74 Eddie George TH .60 1.50
75 Emmitt Smith TH 1.25 3.00
76 Deion Sanders TH .60 1.50
77 Troy Aikman TH 1.00 2.50
78 Michael Irvin TH .75 2.00
79 Warren Moon TH .75 2.00
80 Danny White TH .60 1.50
81 Randy White TH .60 1.50
82 Tony Dorsett TH .75 2.00
83 Walter Payton TH 1.50 4.00
84 Earl Campbell TH .75 2.00
85 Bob Griese TH .75 2.00
86 Larry Csonka TH .75 2.00
87 John Riggins TH .60 1.50
88 Roger Staubach TH 1.00 2.50
89 Alan Page TH .50 1.25
90 Len Dawson TH .75 2.00
91 Fred Biletnikoff TH .75 2.00
92 Lance Alworth TH .60 1.50
93 Bart Starr TH 1.25 3.00
94 Jim Taylor TH .60 1.50
95 Don Maynard TH .60 1.50
96 Paul Hornung TH .75 2.00
97 Bulldog Turner TH .60 1.50
98 Ace Parker TH .50 1.25
99 Dutch Clark TH .60 1.50
100 Red Grange TH 1.00 2.50
151 Aaron Mellette AU/499 RC 2.00 5.00
152 Ace Sanders AU/499 RC 2.00 5.00
154 Alex Okafor AU/499 RC 2.00 5.00
155 Arthur Brown AU/499 RC 2.00 5.00
157 Bjoern Werner AU/499 RC 2.00 5.00
158 B.Wreh-Wilson AU/399 RC 2.50 6.00
159 C.Warmack AU/325 RC 2.00 5.00
160 Alan Bonner AU/499 RC 2.00 5.00
161 B.Sorensen AU/499 RC 2.00 5.00
162 Brice Butler AU/499 RC 2.00 5.00
163 C.Thompson AU/499 RC 2.00 5.00
164 K.Thompkins AU/499 RC 3.00 8.00
165 Corey Fuller AU/349 RC 2.00 5.00
166 C.Carradine AU/499 RC 2.00 5.00
167 D.Hopkins AU/399 RC 2.00 5.00
168 D.J. Hayden AU/499 RC 3.00 8.00
169 D.Moore AU/499 RC 2.00 5.00
170 D.Rogers AU/499 RC 2.00 5.00
171 Darius Slay AU/399 RC 2.00 5.00
172 Datone Jones AU/499 RC 2.00 5.00
173 Jon Bostic AU/499 RC 4.00 10.00
175 Justin Brown AU/499 RC 3.00 8.00
176 D.Trufant AU/499 RC 2.00 5.00
177 Dion Sims AU/499 RC 2.00 5.00
178 L.Murray AU/499 RC 8.00 20.00
179 Eric Reid AU/499 RC 5.00 12.00
180 E.Ansah AU/499 RC 2.00 5.00
182 Luke Willson AU/499 RC 3.00 8.00
183 J.Cyprien AU/499 RC 2.00 5.00
184 J.Banks AU/499 RC 2.00 5.00
186 Josh Boyce AU/499 RC 2.00 5.00
187 Kenjon Barner AU/499 RC 2.00 5.00
188 K.Vaccaro AU/499 RC 2.00 5.00
189 Kevin Minter AU/499 RC 2.00 5.00
190 Mychal Rivera AU/499 RC 2.00 5.00
191 Cierre Wood AU/499 RC EXCH 2.00 5.00
192 Margus Hunt AU/499 RC 2.00 5.00
193 M.Wilson AU/499 RC 3.00 8.00
194 Matt Elam AU/499 RC 2.00 5.00
195 Ray Graham AU/499 RC 2.00 5.00
196 Robert Alford AU/499 RC 2.00 5.00
197 R.Shepard AU/499 RC 2.00 5.00
199 Rex Burkhead AU/499 RC 6.00 15.00
200 Rodney Smith AU/499 RC 2.00 5.00
201 Jeff Tuel AU/499 RC 2.00 5.00
202 Earl Wolff AU/499 RC 3.00 8.00
203 S.Montgomery AU/499 RC 2.00 5.00
204 Tavarres King AU/499 RC 2.00 5.00
205 Theo Riddick AU/499 RC 2.00 5.00
206 Travis Kelce AU/499 RC 12.00 30.00
207 Tyler Bray AU/499 RC 2.00 5.00
208 T.Mathieu AU/499 RC 6.00 15.00
209 X.Rhodes AU/499 RC 2.00 5.00
210 Zac Dysert AU/499 RC 2.00 5.00
211 Aaron Dobson RC .50 1.25
212 Andre Ellington RC .50 1.25
213 Christine Michael RC .50 1.25
214 Cordarrelle Patterson RC .50 1.25
215 DeAndre Hopkins RC 1.25 3.00
216 Denard Robinson RC .50 1.25
217 Dion Jordan RC .50 1.25
218 Eddie Lacy RC .50 1.25
219 EJ Manuel RC .50 1.25
220 Gavin Escobar RC .50 1.25
221 Geno Smith RC .50 1.25
222 Giovani Bernard RC .50 1.25
223 Johnathan Franklin RC .50 1.25
224 Jordan Reed RC .75 2.00
225 Joseph Randle RC .50 1.25
226 Justin Hunter RC .50 1.25
227 Keenan Allen RC 1.00 2.50
228 Kenny Stills RC .50 1.25
229 Knile Davis RC .50 1.25
230 Landry Jones RC .50 1.25
231 Le'Veon Bell RC 1.50 4.00
232 Manti Te'o RC .60 1.50
233 Marcus Lattimore RC .50 1.25
234 Markus Wheaton RC .50 1.25
235 Marquise Goodwin RC .50 1.25
236 Matt Barkley RC .50 1.25
237 Mike Gillislee RC .50 1.25
238 Mike Glennon RC .50 1.25
239 Montee Ball RC .50 1.25
240 Quinton Patton RC .50 1.25
241 Robert Woods RC .75 2.00
242 Ryan Nassib RC .50 1.25
243 Stedman Bailey RC .50 1.25
244 Stepfan Taylor RC .50 1.25
245 Tavon Austin RC .60 1.50
246 Terrance Williams RC .50 1.25
247 Tyler Eifert RC .50 1.25
248 Tyler Wilson RC .50 1.25
249 Vance McDonald RC .60 1.50
250 Zach Ertz RC 1.00 2.50

2013 Totally Certified Blue

*1-50 VETS/99: 2X TO 5X BASIC CARDS
*51-100 TH/99: 1.2X TO 3X BASIC TH
*211-250 ROOK/99: 1X TO 2.5X BASIC RC
*151-210 RK.AU/25: .8X TO 2X AU/325-499

2013 Totally Certified Gold

*1-50 VETS/25: 3X TO 8X BASIC CARDS
*51-100 TH/25: 2X TO 5X BASIC TH
*211-250 ROOK/25: 1.5X TO 4X BASIC RC

2013 Totally Certified Red

*1-50 VETS: 1.2X TO 3X BASIC CARDS
*51-100 TH: .8X TO 2X BASIC TH
*211-250 ROOKIE: .6X TO 1.5X BASIC RC
*151-210 RK.AU/99: .5X TO 1.2X AU/325-499

2013 Totally Certified Red Materials

*BLUE/49-99: .5X TO 1.2X RED/149-299
*BLUE/49: .4X TO 1X RED/99
*BLUE/25: .5X TO 1.2X RED/49-99
*GOLD/25: .8X TO 2X RED/149-299
*GOLD/25: .6X TO 1.5X RED/49-99
1 Reggie Wayne/99 3.00 8.00
2 Matt Ryan/299 2.50 6.00
3 Bernard Pierce/299 2.00 5.00
4 Brian Cushing/299 2.00 5.00
5 Colin Kaepernick/49 3.00 8.00
6 C.J. Spiller/199 2.00 5.00
7 Roddy White/199 2.00 5.00
8 Kam Chancellor/99 5.00 12.00
9 Sidney Rice/49 2.50 6.00
10 DeMarcus Ware/199 3.00 8.00
11 Larry Fitzgerald/299 2.50 6.00
12 Arian Foster/99 3.00 8.00
13 Jason Witten/299 2.50 6.00
14 Chad Greenway/299 2.50 6.00
15 Chris Johnson/199 2.00 5.00
16 Julio Jones/99 4.00 10.00
17 Cam Newton/299 3.00 8.00
18 DeSean Jackson/299 2.50 6.00
19 Jonathan Stewart/49 2.50 6.00
20 Robert Turbin/49 2.50 6.00
21 Philip Rivers/299 3.00 8.00
22 Jeremy Maclin/299 2.00 5.00
23 Golden Tate/99 2.50 6.00
25 LeSean McCoy/199 3.00 8.00
26 Marques Colston/199 2.00 5.00
27 DeMarco Murray/299 2.50 6.00
28 A.J. Green/299 3.00 8.00
29 Dez Bryant/49 4.00 10.00
30 Darren McFadden/299 2.50 6.00
31 DeAngelo Williams/299 2.00 5.00
32 Maurice Jones-Drew/199 2.00 5.00
33 Jay Cutler/299 2.00 5.00
34 Nate Washington/299 2.00 5.00
35 James Laurinaitis/299 2.50 6.00
36 Matt Forte/299 2.00 5.00
37 Marcedes Lewis/99 2.50 6.00
38 Hakeem Nicks/49 2.50 6.00
39 Andy Dalton/199 2.50 6.00
40 Mario Manningham/299 2.00 5.00
41 Mike Williams/99 3.00 8.00
42 Dwayne Bowe/299 2.50 6.00
43 Jimmy Graham/199 3.00 8.00
44 Janoris Jenkins/99 2.50 6.00
45 Dre Kirkpatrick/299 2.00 5.00
46 Steve Johnson/299 2.50 6.00
47 Champ Bailey/299 2.50 6.00
48 Joe Flacco/299 2.50 6.00
49 Christian Ponder/199 2.00 5.00
50 Demaryius Thomas/149 2.50 6.00
51 Jake Locker/299 2.50 6.00
52 Jacob Tamme/149 2.00 5.00
53 Greg Olsen/99 3.00 8.00
54 Justin Blackmon/99 2.50 6.00
55 Matt Schaub/199 2.00 5.00
56 Dexter McCluster/299 2.50 6.00
57 Kendall Wright/299 2.00 5.00
58 Alfred Morris/199 2.00 5.00
59 Derrick Johnson/299 2.00 5.00
60 D'Qwell Jackson/299 2.00 5.00
61 Eric Berry/299 2.50 6.00
62 Fred Jackson/199 2.50 6.00
63 Greg Little/299 2.00 5.00
64 Fred Davis/299 2.00 5.00
65 Jamaal Charles/299 2.50 6.00
66 Jermaine Gresham/299 2.50 6.00
67 Joe Haden/299 2.00 5.00
68 Jacoby Jones/299 2.00 5.00
69 Lance Briggs/299 2.50 6.00
70 Leonard Hankerson/299 2.00 5.00
71 Brock Osweiler/299 2.50 6.00
72 Michael Vick/299 2.50 6.00
73 Ray Rice/299 2.00 5.00
74 Robert Meachem/299 2.00 5.00
75 Ronnie Hillman/299 2.00 5.00
76 Ryan Kerrigan/299 2.00 5.00
77 Ryan Tannehill/199 2.50 6.00
78 Sam Bradford/299 2.00 5.00
79 Ryan Mathews/299 2.50 6.00
80 Tamba Hali/199 2.00 5.00
81 Terrell Suggs/299 2.00 5.00
82 BenJarvus Green-Ellis/99 3.00 8.00
83 Tony Romo/299 2.50 6.00
84 Josh Morgan/299 2.00 5.00
85 Rahim Moore/299 2.00 5.00
86 Blaine Gabbert/299 2.00 5.00
87 Donald Brown/299 2.00 5.00
88 DeAngelo Hall/299 2.00 5.00
89 Darren Sproles/49 3.00 8.00
90 Brandon Weeden/299 2.00 5.00
91 Robert Griffin III/299 2.00 5.00
92 Eli Manning/299 2.50 6.00
93 Eric Decker/199 2.00 5.00
94 London Fletcher/299 2.50 6.00
95 Malcom Floyd/299 2.00 5.00
96 Haloti Ngata /299 2.00 5.00
97 DeMeco Ryans/299 2.00 5.00
98 Pierre Garcon/199 2.50 6.00
99 Antonio Gates/299 2.50 6.00
100 Brian Hartline/299 2.00 5.00

2013 Totally Certified Gold Signatures

*GOLD ROOKIE/25: .8X TO 2X RED/299

2013 Totally Certified Red Signatures

51 Herman Moore TH/99 6.00 15.00
73 Eddie George TH/99 15.00 40.00
75 Deion Sanders TH/49 20.00 40.00
77 Michael Irvin TH/49 15.00 30.00
80 Danny White TH/99 8.00 20.00
86 Larry Csonka TH/99 15.00 30.00
90 Len Dawson TH/25 12.00 30.00
96 Paul Hornung TH/25
97 Donald Driver TH/99 15.00 40.00
103 Michael Floyd/99 5.00 12.00
104 Andrew Hawkins/99
107 Brian Quick/99 5.00 12.00
109 Cecil Shorts/99 5.00 12.00
110 Clay Matthews/49 20.00 40.00
111 Colin Kaepernick/7
114 David Wilson/99 5.00 12.00
119 Justin Houston/49
121 Jeremy Kerley/99
126 Lamar Miller/99 5.00 12.00
129 Julian Edelman/25 50.00 100.00
135 Charles Clay/99 6.00 15.00
136 Nate Washington/99
137 Nick Foles/99 12.00 30.00
140 Rashard Mendenhall/49
143 Jordan Cameron/99
145 Ryan Tannehill/49 15.00 40.00
147 Sean Lee/99 8.00 20.00
149 Richard Sherman/99 40.00 100.00
211 Aaron Dobson FF/299 2.50 6.00
212 Andre Ellington FF/299 2.50 6.00
213 Christine Michael FF/299 2.50 6.00
214 Cordarrelle Patterson FF/299 2.50 6.00
215 DeAndre Hopkins FF/299 6.00 15.00
216 Denard Robinson FF/299 2.50 6.00
217 Dion Jordan FF/299 2.50 6.00
218 Eddie Lacy FF/299 2.50 6.00
219 EJ Manuel FF/299 2.50 6.00
220 Gavin Escobar FF/299 2.50 6.00
221 Geno Smith FF/299 2.50 6.00
222 Giovani Bernard FF/299 2.50 6.00
223 Johnathan Franklin FF/299 2.50 6.00
224 Jordan Reed FF/299 4.00 10.00
225 Joseph Randle FF/299 2.50 6.00
226 Justin Hunter FF/299 5.00 12.00
227 Keenan Allen FF/299 5.00 12.00
228 Kenny Stills FF/299 2.50 6.00
229 Knile Davis FF/299 2.50 6.00
230 Landry Jones FF/299 2.50 6.00
231 Le'Veon Bell FF/299 8.00 20.00
232 Manti Te'o FF/299 3.00 8.00
233 Marcus Lattimore FF/299 2.50 6.00
234 Markus Wheaton FF/299 2.50 6.00
235 Marquise Goodwin FF/299 2.50 6.00
236 Matt Barkley FF/299 2.50 6.00
237 Mike Gillislee FF/299 2.50 6.00
238 Mike Glennon FF/299 2.50 6.00
239 Montee Ball FF/299 2.50 6.00
240 Quinton Patton FF/299 2.50 6.00
241 Robert Woods FF/299 4.00 10.00
242 Ryan Nassib FF/299 2.50 6.00
243 Stedman Bailey FF/299 2.50 6.00
244 Stepfan Taylor FF/299 2.50 6.00
245 Tavon Austin FF/299 3.00 8.00
246 Terrance Williams FF/299 2.50 6.00
247 Tyler Eifert FF/299 2.50 6.00
248 Tyler Wilson FF/299 2.50 6.00
249 Vance McDonald FF/299 3.00 8.00
250 Zach Ertz FF/299 5.00 12.00

2013 Totally Certified Future Signature Materials

*PRIME/49: .6X TO 1.5X JSY AU/149
1 Aaron Dobson 2.50 6.00
2 Andre Ellington 2.50 6.00
3 Christine Michael 2.50 6.00
4 Cordarrelle Patterson 2.50 6.00
5 DeAndre Hopkins 6.00 15.00
6 Denard Robinson 2.50 6.00
7 Dion Jordan 2.50 6.00
8 Eddie Lacy 2.50 6.00
9 EJ Manuel 2.50 6.00
10 Gavin Escobar 2.50 6.00
11 Geno Smith 2.50 6.00
12 Giovani Bernard 2.50 6.00
13 Johnathan Franklin 2.50 6.00
14 Jordan Reed 4.00 10.00
15 Joseph Randle 2.50 6.00
16 Justin Hunter 2.50 6.00
17 Keenan Allen 5.00 12.00
18 Kenny Stills 2.50 6.00
19 Knile Davis 2.50 6.00
20 Landry Jones 2.50 6.00
21 Le'Veon Bell 8.00 20.00
22 Manti Te'o 3.00 8.00
23 Marcus Lattimore 2.50 6.00
24 Markus Wheaton 2.50 6.00
25 Marquise Goodwin 2.50 6.00
26 Matt Barkley 2.50 6.00
27 Mike Gillislee 2.50 6.00
28 Mike Glennon 2.50 6.00
29 Montee Ball 2.50 6.00
30 Quinton Patton 2.50 6.00
31 Robert Woods 4.00 10.00
32 Ryan Nassib 2.50 6.00
33 Stedman Bailey 2.50 6.00
34 Stepfan Taylor 2.50 6.00
35 Tavon Austin 3.00 8.00
36 Terrance Williams 2.50 6.00
37 Tyler Eifert 2.50 6.00
38 Tyler Wilson 2.50 6.00
39 Vance McDonald 3.00 8.00
40 Zach Ertz 5.00 12.00

2013 Totally Certified Rookie Roll Call Materials

*PRIME/25: .8X TO 2X BASIC JSY/299
1 Aaron Dobson 1.25 3.00
2 Andre Ellington 1.25 3.00
3 Christine Michael 1.25 3.00
4 Cordarrelle Patterson 1.25 3.00
5 DeAndre Hopkins 3.00 8.00
6 Denard Robinson 1.25 3.00
7 Dion Jordan 1.25 3.00
8 Eddie Lacy 1.25 3.00
9 EJ Manuel 1.25 3.00
10 Gavin Escobar 1.25 3.00
11 Geno Smith 1.25 3.00
12 Giovani Bernard 1.25 3.00
13 Johnathan Franklin 1.25 3.00
14 Jordan Reed 2.00 5.00
15 Joseph Randle 1.25 3.00
16 Justin Hunter 1.25 3.00
17 Keenan Allen 2.50 6.00
18 Kenny Stills 1.25 3.00
19 Knile Davis 1.25 3.00
20 Landry Jones 1.25 3.00
21 Le'Veon Bell 4.00 10.00
22 Manti Te'o 1.50 4.00
23 Marcus Lattimore 1.25 3.00
24 Markus Wheaton 1.25 3.00
25 Marquise Goodwin 1.25 3.00
26 Matt Barkley 1.25 3.00
27 Mike Gillislee 1.25 3.00
28 Mike Glennon 1.25 3.00
29 Montee Ball 1.25 3.00
30 Quinton Patton 1.25 3.00
31 Robert Woods 2.00 5.00
32 Ryan Nassib 1.25 3.00
33 Stedman Bailey 1.25 3.00
34 Stepfan Taylor 1.25 3.00
35 Tavon Austin 1.50 4.00
36 Terrance Williams 1.25 3.00
37 Tyler Eifert 1.25 3.00
38 Tyler Wilson 1.25 3.00
39 Vance McDonald 1.50 4.00
40 Zach Ertz 2.50 6.00

2013 Totally Certified Stitches in Time

*1-25 PRIME/25: 1X TO 2.5X BASIC JSY/299
*1-25 PRIME/25: .6X TO 1.5X BASIC JSY/49-99
*26-45 PRIME/25: .8X TO 2X DUAL JSY/299
*26-45 PRIME/25: .6X TO 1.5X DUAL JSY/99-199
*26-45 PRIME/25: .5X TO 1.2X DUAL JSY/49
*27-55 PRM/20-25: .6X TO 1.5X TRPL/199-299
1 Arian Foster/99 4.00 10.00
2 BenJarvus Green-Ellis/49 4.00 10.00
3 Brent Celek/99 3.00 8.00
4 Christian Ponder/99 3.00 8.00
5 C.J. Spiller/99 3.00 8.00
6 Darren McFadden/299 2.50 6.00
7 DeMarco Murray/299 2.50 6.00
8 DeSean Jackson/299 2.50 6.00
9 Hakeem Nicks/49 3.00 8.00
10 Dwayne Bowe/299 2.50 6.00
11 Torrey Smith/299 2.00 5.00
12 Malcom Floyd/299 2.00 5.00
13 Matt Schaub/299 2.00 5.00
14 Peyton Manning/49 15.00 40.00
15 Ray Rice/299 2.00 5.00
16 Robert Griffin III/299 2.00 5.00
17 Sam Bradford/299 2.00 5.00
18 Santonio Holmes/299 2.00 5.00
19 Steve Johnson/299 2.50 6.00
20 Tamba Hali/299 2.00 5.00
21 Bill Romanowski/299 2.50 6.00
22 Dan Marino/299 8.00 20.00
23 Marshall Faulk/299 3.00 8.00
24 Shaun Alexander/299 2.50 6.00
25 Ted Hendricks/299 2.50 6.00
26 A.Morris/Peterson/299 5.00 12.00
27 A.Dalton/A.Green/299 5.00 12.00
28 K.Chancellor/B.Irvin/149 6.00 15.00
29 Claiborne/Kirkpatrick/49 5.00 12.00
30 Gresham/Gonzalez/299 4.00 10.00
31 Laurinaitis/J.Jenkins/149 5.00 12.00
32 D.Ware/T.Suggs/299 5.00 12.00
33 D.Thomas/E.Decker/299 4.00 10.00
34 D.Martin/R.Hillman/299 4.00 10.00
35 S.Rice/G.Tate/49 5.00 12.00
36 Tannehill/B.Hartline/299 4.00 10.00
37 J.Cutler/B.Marshall/49 6.00 15.00
38 J.Witten/J.Graham/299 5.00 12.00
39 M.Vick/J.Maclin/99 5.00 12.00
40 M.Ryan/R.White/299 4.00 10.00
41 M.Alstott/W.Dunn/199 4.00 10.00
42 J.Rice/J.Montana/299 25.00 60.00
43 Greenway/J.Allen/299 5.00 12.00
44 W.Payton/Campbell/199 15.00 40.00
45 T.Aikman/T.Romo/299 8.00 20.00
46 Kprnck/Dvs/Gre/99 12.00 30.00
47 Wyne/Hrrsn/Clrk/199 4.00 10.00
48 Blckmn/Wdn/Brynt/99 6.00 15.00
49 Clstn/Jns/Jcksn/25 8.00 20.00
50 Grcn/Grffn/Dvs/49 5.00 12.00
51 Mthws/Rvrs/Gts/299 5.00 12.00
52 Flcco/Mnnng/Brs/299 6.00 15.00
53 Nwtn/Mnnng/Stffrd/199 10.00 25.00
54 Cnnnghm/Essn/Plmmr/299 5.00 12.00
55 Tmlnsn/Lws/Btts/299 6.00 15.00
56 Bail/Wood/Edw/Deion/199 8.00 20.00
57 Yng/Elwy/Mam/Mont/299 30.00 80.00
58 Chrls/John/Morr/Orkp/199 4.00 10.00
59 Fitz/Bwe/Aust/Smith/25
60 Tylr/Jns-D/Smt/Murr/49 15.00 40.00

2013 Totally Certified Team Panini Material Autographs

*PRIME AU/25: .5X TO 1.2X JSY AU/49-99
EXCH EXPIRATION: 5/27/2015
1 Adrian Peterson/25 EXCH
2 Drew Brees/25 60.00 120.00
3 Ryan Tannehill/25
5 Darren McFadden/25
6 Demaryius Thomas/25 EXCH 15.00 40.00
7 Jimmy Graham/25 EXCH 20.00 50.00
10 Jamaal Charles/25
11 Cam Newton/25
12 Steve Johnson/25
13 Andy Dalton/49 15.00 40.00
14 Sam Bradford/25 12.00 30.00
15 Golden Tate/49
16 Alfred Morris/25 EXCH 12.00 30.00
17 Kenny Britt/99 10.00 25.00
18 Antonio Gates/25 12.00 30.00
19 Lamar Miller/49
20 Dez Bryant/25 25.00 50.00

2014 Totally Certified

ONE ROOKIE PER HOBBY PACK
1 Andre Ellington .30 .75
2 Carson Palmer .40 1.00
3 Larry Fitzgerald .40 1.00
4 Julio Jones .50 1.25
5 Matt Ryan .40 1.00
6 Roddy White .30 .75
7 Joe Flacco .40 1.00
8 Terrell Suggs .30 .75
9 Steve Smith .40 1.00
10 C.J. Spiller .30 .75
11 EJ Manuel .30 .75
12 Robert Woods .40 1.00
13 Cam Newton .50 1.25
14 DeAngelo Williams .30 .75
15 Jerricho Cotchery .30 .75
16 Brandon Marshall .30 .75
17 Jay Cutler .30 .75
18 Matt Forte .30 .75
19 A.J. Green .50 1.25
20 Andy Dalton .40 1.00
21 Giovani Bernard .30 .75
22 Ben Tate .30 .75
23 Josh Gordon .30 .75
24 Brian Hoyer .30 .75
25 DeMarco Murray .40 1.00
26 Dez Bryant .50 1.25
27 Tony Romo .40 1.00
28 Demaryius Thomas .40 1.00
29 Peyton Manning 1.00 2.50
30 Wes Welker .40 1.00
31 Calvin Johnson .50 1.25
32 Matthew Stafford .40 1.00
33 Reggie Bush .30 .75
34 Aaron Rodgers 1.00 2.50
35 Eddie Lacy .30 .75
36 Randall Cobb .40 1.00
37 Andre Johnson .40 1.00
38 Arian Foster .40 1.00
39 Ryan Fitzpatrick .30 .75
40 Andrew Luck .60 1.50
41 Reggie Wayne .40 1.00
42 Trent Richardson .30 .75
43 Cecil Shorts .30 .75
44 Chad Henne .30 .75
45 Toby Gerhart .30 .75
46 Alex Smith .40 1.00
47 Dwayne Bowe .40 1.00
48 Jamaal Charles .40 1.00
49 Brian Hartline .30 .75
50 Lamar Miller .30 .75
51 Ryan Tannehill .40 1.00
52 Adrian Peterson .50 1.25
53 Cordarrelle Patterson .30 .75
54 Matt Cassel .30 .75
55 Rob Gronkowski .50 1.25
56 Stevan Ridley .30 .75
57 Tom Brady 1.25 3.00
58 Drew Brees .50 1.25
59 Jimmy Graham .50 1.25
60 Marques Colston .30 .75
61 Eli Manning .40 1.00
62 Rashad Jennings .30 .75
63 Victor Cruz .40 1.00
64 Eric Decker .30 .75
65 Geno Smith .30 .75
66 Chris Johnson .30 .75
67 Darren McFadden .30 .75
68 Matt Schaub .30 .75
69 James Jones .30 .75
70 Jeremy Maclin .30 .75
71 LeSean McCoy .50 1.25
72 Nick Foles .40 1.00
73 Antonio Brown .50 1.25
74 Ben Roethlisberger .50 1.25
75 Le'Veon Bell .40 1.00
76 Antonio Gates .30 .75
77 Philip Rivers .50 1.25
78 Ryan Mathews .40 1.00
79 Colin Kaepernick .40 1.00
80 Frank Gore .40 1.00
81 Michael Crabtree .30 .75
82 Marshawn Lynch .40 1.00
83 Richard Sherman .50 1.25
84 Russell Wilson .75 2.00
85 Sam Bradford .30 .75
86 Tavon Austin .30 .75
87 Zac Stacy .30 .75
88 Doug Martin .40 1.00
89 Josh McCown .30 .75
90 Vincent Jackson .30 .75
91 Jake Locker .40 1.00
92 Kendall Wright .30 .75
93 Nate Washington .30 .75
94 Alfred Morris .30 .75
95 Pierre Garcon .40 1.00
96 Robert Griffin III .30 .75
97 Barry Sanders 1.00 2.50
98 Joe Montana 2.00 5.00
99 Dan Marino 1.25 3.00
100 Emmitt Smith 1.00 2.50
101 Deone Bucannon RC .50 1.25
102 John Brown RC .75 2.00
103 Troy Niklas RC .50 1.25
104 Jake Matthews RC .50 1.25
105 Ra'Shede Hageman RC .50 1.25
106 C.J. Mosley RC .60 1.50
107 Michael Campanaro RC .50 1.25
108 Timmy Jernigan RC .50 1.25
109 Kony Ealy RC .60 1.50
110 Tyler Gaffney RC .50 1.25
111 David Fales RC .50 1.25
112 Kyle Fuller RC .50 1.25
113 Darqueze Dennard RC .60 1.50
114 James Wilder Jr. RC .60 1.50
115 Connor Shaw RC .50 1.25
116 Isaiah Crowell RC .60 1.50
117 Devin Street RC .50 1.25
118 L'Damian Washington RC .60 1.50
119 Zack Martin RC .60 1.50
120 Bradley Roby RC .50 1.25
121 Kyle Van Noy RC .60 1.50
122 Ha Ha Clinton-Dix RC .60 1.50
123 Jared Abbrederis RC .50 1.25
124 Jeff Janis RC .50 1.25
125 Rajion Neal RC .50 1.25
126 C.J. Fiedorowicz RC .50 1.25
127 Louis Nix III RC .50 1.25
128 Dee Ford RC .50 1.25
129 Allen Hurns RC .60 1.50
130 Anthony Barr RC .50 1.25
131 Jerick McKinnon RC .60 1.50
132 Scott Crichton RC .50 1.25
133 Dominique Easley RC .50 1.25
134 James White RC 1.00 2.50
135 Brandon Coleman RC .50 1.25
136 Calvin Pryor RC .50 1.25
137 Shaq Evans RC .50 1.25
138 Mike Davis RC .50 1.25
139 Ed Reynolds RC .50 1.25
140 Josh Huff RC .60 1.50
141 Marcus Smith RC .50 1.25
142 Martavis Bryant RC .60 1.50
143 Ryan Shazier RC .75 2.00
144 Jason Verrett RC .50 1.25
145 Marion Grice RC .50 1.25
146 Tevin Reese RC .50 1.25
147 Bruce Ellington RC .50 1.25
148 Chris Borland RC .50 1.25
149 Jimmie Ward RC .60 1.50
150 Kevin Norwood RC .50 1.25
151 Aaron Donald RC 1.25 3.00
152 Greg Robinson RC .50 1.25
153 Lamarcus Joyner RC .60 1.50
154 Michael Sam RC .50 1.25
155 Robert Herron RC .50 1.25
156 Antonio Andrews RC .50 1.25
157 Zach Mettenberger RC .50 1.25
158 Cody Hoffman RC .50 1.25
159 Lache Seastrunk RC .50 1.25
160 Trent Murphy RC .50 1.25
161 Logan Thomas RC .50 1.25
162 Devonta Freeman RC .75 2.00
163 Sammy Watkins RC .75 2.00
164 Kelvin Benjamin RC .75 2.00
165 Ka'Deem Carey RC .50 1.25
166 A.J. McCarron RC .50 1.25
167 Jeremy Hill RC .60 1.50
168 Johnny Manziel RC .75 2.00
169 Terrance West RC .50 1.25
170 Cody Latimer RC .60 1.50
171 Eric Ebron RC .60 1.50
172 Davante Adams RC .75 2.00
173 Jadeveon Clowney RC .60 1.50
174 Tom Savage RC .50 1.25
175 Donte Moncrief RC .50 1.25
176 Allen Robinson RC .75 2.00
177 Blake Bortles RC .60 1.50
178 Marqise Lee RC .60 1.50
179 Aaron Murray RC .50 1.25
180 De'Anthony Thomas RC .50 1.25
181 Jarvis Landry RC 1.00 2.50
182 Teddy Bridgewater RC .75 2.00
183 Asa Watson RC .50 1.25
184 Jimmy Garoppolo RC 4.00 10.00
185 Brandin Cooks RC .75 2.00
186 Andre Williams RC .50 1.25
187 Odell Beckham Jr. RC 1.00 2.50
188 Jace Amaro RC .50 1.25
189 Tajh Boyd RC .50 1.25
190 Derek Carr RC 3.00 8.00
191 Khalil Mack RC 2.00 5.00
192 Jordan Matthews RC .75 2.00
193 Dri Archer RC .50 1.25
194 Carlos Hyde RC .60 1.50
195 Paul Richardson RC .60 1.50
196 Tre Mason RC .50 1.25
197 Austin Seferian-Jenkins RC .50 1.25
198 Charles Sims RC .50 1.25
199 Mike Evans RC 1.25 3.00
200 Bishop Sankey RC .50 1.25

2014 Totally Certified Mirror Platinum Blue

*1-100 VETS/10: 6X TO 15X BASIC CARDS
*101-200 ROOKIES/10: 2X TO 5X BASIC RC

2014 Totally Certified Mirror Platinum Red

*1-100 VETS/25: 3X TO 8X BASIC CARDS
*101-200 ROOKIES/25: 1.2X TO 3X BASIC RC

2014 Totally Certified Platinum Blue

*1-100 VETS/50: 2.5X TO 6X BASIC CARDS
*101-200 ROOKIES/50: 1X TO 2.5X BASIC RC

2014 Totally Certified Platinum Gold

*1-100 VETS/25: 3X TO 8X BASIC CARDS
*101-200 ROOKIES/25: 1.2X TO 3X BASIC RC

2014 Totally Certified Platinum Red

*1-100 VETS/100: 2X TO 5X BASIC CARDS
*101-200 ROOKIES/100: .8X TO 2X BASIC RC

2014 Totally Certified Certified Fabrics

ONE AU OR JSY PER HOBBY PACK
*BLUE/50: .6X TO 1.5X BASIC JSY
*BLUE/25: .8X TO 2X BASIC JSY
*GOLD/25: 1X TO 2.5X BASIC JSY
*RED/100: .5X TO 1.2X BASIC JSY
*RED/50: .6X TO 1.5X BASIC JSY
*RED/25: .8X TO 2X BASIC JSY
CFAB Antonio Brown 3.00 8.00
CFAD Andy Dalton 2.50 6.00
CFAG A.J. Green 3.00 8.00
CFAM Alfred Morris 2.00 5.00
CFAP Adrian Peterson 3.00 8.00
CFBH Brian Hartline 2.00 5.00
CFBO Brian Orakpo 2.00 5.00
CFCN Cam Newton 3.00 8.00
CFCP Cordarrelle Patterson 2.00 5.00
CFCS Cecil Shorts 2.00 5.00
CFCSP C.J. Spiller 2.00 5.00
CFDAT Daniel Thomas 2.00 5.00
CFDB Dwayne Bowe 2.50 6.00
CFDBR Dez Bryant 3.00 8.00
CFDE Dannell Ellerbe 2.00 5.00
CFDET Demaryius Thomas 2.50 6.00
CFDM Doug Martin 2.50 6.00
CFDMC Darren McFadden 2.00 5.00
CFDMU DeMarco Murray 2.50 6.00
CFDW Danny Woodhead 2.50 6.00
CFED Eric Decker 2.00 5.00
CFGB Giovani Bernard 2.00 5.00
CFHM Heath Miller 2.00 5.00
CFJC Jordan Cameron 2.00 5.00
CFJCH Jamaal Charles 2.50 6.00
CFJCU Jay Cutler 2.00 5.00
CFJF Joe Flacco 2.50 6.00
CFJG Jimmy Graham 3.00 8.00
CFJH Justin Houston 2.00 5.00
CFJHU Justin Hunter 2.00 5.00
CFJK Jeremy Kerley 2.00 5.00
CFLF Larry Fitzgerald 2.50 6.00
CFLM LeSean McCoy 3.00 8.00
CFMB Matt Barkley 2.00 5.00
CFMBA Montee Ball 2.00 5.00
CFMC Michael Crabtree 2.00 5.00
CFMF Matt Forte 2.00 5.00
CFML Marshawn Lynch 2.50 6.00
CFMR Matt Ryan 2.50 6.00
CFMS Matthew Stafford 2.50 6.00
CFMT Manti Te'o 2.50 6.00
CFNW Nate Washington 2.00 5.00
CFPR Philip Rivers 3.00 8.00
CFPT Pierre Thomas 2.00 5.00
CFRM Robert Mathis 2.00 5.00
CFRR Rueben Randle 2.00 5.00
CFRT Ryan Tannehill 2.50 6.00
CFRW Robert Woods 2.50 6.00
CFSC Scott Chandler 2.00 5.00
CFSG Shonn Greene 2.00 5.00
CFSS Steve Smith 2.50 6.00
CFTA Tavon Austin 2.00 5.00
CFTB Tom Brady 8.00 20.00
CFTH Tamba Hali 2.00 5.00
CFTR Trent Richardson 2.00 5.00
CFTRO Tony Romo 2.50 6.00
CFTS Terrell Suggs 2.00 5.00
CFVD Vernon Davis 2.00 5.00
CFVJ Vincent Jackson 2.00 5.00
CFZM Zach Miller 2.00 5.00

2014 Totally Certified Clear Cloth

*BLUE/50: .5X TO 1.2X BASIC JSY/100
*GOLD/25: .6X TO 1.5X BASIC JSY/100
CCAG Antonio Gates 3.00 8.00
CCAGR A.J. Green 5.00 12.00
CCAL Andrew Luck 6.00 15.00
CCAP Adrian Peterson 5.00 12.00
CCAS Alex Smith 4.00 10.00
CCBP Bilal Powell 3.00 8.00
CCCK Colin Kaepernick 4.00 10.00
CCCN Cam Newton 5.00 12.00
CCDB Drew Brees 5.00 12.00
CCDM Darren McFadden 3.00 8.00
CCFJ Fred Jackson 4.00 10.00
CCJC Jamaal Charles 4.00 10.00
CCJF Joe Flacco 4.00 10.00
CCLF Larry Fitzgerald 4.00 10.00
CCMF Matt Forte 3.00 8.00
CCMR Matt Ryan 4.00 10.00
CCMW Mike Wallace 3.00 8.00
CCNF Nick Foles 4.00 10.00
CCNW Nate Washington 3.00 8.00
CCPG Pierre Garcon 4.00 10.00
CCPM Peyton Manning 10.00 25.00
CCRS Richard Sherman 8.00 20.00
CCSB Sam Bradford 3.00 8.00
CCTR Tony Romo 4.00 10.00
CCVJ Vincent Jackson 3.00 8.00

2014 Totally Certified Epix Play Memorabilia Red

*BLUE/50: .6X TO 1.5X RED JSY
*GOLD/25: 1X TO 2.5X RED JSY
EPAP Adrian Peterson 3.00 8.00
EPBS Barry Sanders 8.00 20.00
EPCK Colin Kaepernick 2.50 6.00
EPDB Drew Brees 3.00 8.00
EPDM Dan Marino 10.00 25.00
EPEM Eli Manning 2.50 6.00
EPJE John Elway 8.00 20.00
EPJM Johnny Manziel 2.00 5.00
EPJMO Joe Montana 12.00 30.00
EPJN Joe Namath 6.00 15.00
EPMF Marshall Faulk 4.00 10.00
EPPM Peyton Manning 6.00 15.00
EPRW Russell Wilson 5.00 12.00
EPTB Tom Brady 8.00 20.00
EPTD Terrell Davis 2.00 5.00

2014 Totally Certified Rookie Autograph Jerseys

*MIRR.RED/25: .6X TO 1.5X BASIC AU
*PLAT.GOLD/25: .8X TO 2X BASIC AU
*PLAT.RED/50-100: .5X TO 1.2X BASIC AU
161 Logan Thomas 3.00 8.00
162 Devonta Freeman 5.00 12.00
163 Sammy Watkins 15.00 40.00
164 Kelvin Benjamin 5.00 12.00
165 Ka'Deem Carey 3.00 8.00
166 A.J. McCarron 3.00 8.00
167 Jeremy Hill 4.00 10.00
168 Johnny Manziel 5.00 12.00
169 Terrance West 3.00 8.00
170 Cody Latimer 4.00 10.00
171 Eric Ebron 4.00 10.00
172 Davante Adams 5.00 12.00
173 Jadeveon Clowney 4.00 10.00
174 Tom Savage 3.00 8.00
175 Donte Moncrief 3.00 8.00
176 Allen Robinson
177 Blake Bortles 4.00 10.00
178 Marqise Lee 4.00 10.00
179 Aaron Murray 3.00 8.00
181 Jarvis Landry 6.00 15.00
182 Teddy Bridgewater 5.00 12.00
183 Asa Watson 3.00 8.00
184 Jimmy Garoppolo 25.00 50.00
185 Brandin Cooks 5.00 12.00
186 Andre Williams 3.00 8.00
188 Jace Amaro 3.00 8.00
189 Tajh Boyd 3.00 8.00
190 Derek Carr 30.00 60.00
192 Jordan Matthews 5.00 12.00
196 Tre Mason 3.00 8.00
197 Austin Seferian-Jenkins 3.00 8.00
198 Charles Sims 3.00 8.00
199 Mike Evans 8.00 20.00
200 Bishop Sankey 3.00 8.00

2014 Totally Certified Rookie Autograph Jerseys Prime Platinum Blue

*PLAT.BLUE/50: .5X TO 1.2X BASIC AU
*PLAT.BLUE/25: .6X TO 1.5X BASIC AU
184 Jimmy Garoppolo/25 30.00 80.00
187 Odell Beckham Jr./25 50.00 100.00

2014 Totally Certified Rookie Clear Cloth

*BLUE/50: .5X TO 1.2X BASIC JSY/100
*GOLD/25: .6X TO 1.5X BASIC JSY/100
RCCAM A.J. McCarron 2.00 5.00
RCCBB Blake Bortles 2.50 6.00
RCCBC Brandin Cooks 3.00 8.00
RCCBS Bishop Sankey 2.00 5.00
RCCCL Cody Latimer 2.50 6.00
RCCDA Davante Adams 3.00 8.00
RCCDAR Dri Archer 2.00 5.00
RCCDC Derek Carr 6.00 15.00
RCCDM Donte Moncrief 2.00 5.00
RCCDT De'Anthony Thomas 2.00 5.00
RCCEE Eric Ebron 2.50 6.00
RCCJC Jadeveon Clowney 2.50 6.00
RCCJH Jeremy Hill 2.50 6.00
RCCJL Jarvis Landry 4.00 10.00
RCCJM Johnny Manziel 3.00 8.00
RCCJMA Jordan Matthews 3.00 8.00
RCCKB Kelvin Benjamin 3.00 8.00
RCCKC Ka'Deem Carey 2.00 5.00
RCCME Mike Evans 5.00 12.00
RCCML Marqise Lee 2.50 6.00
RCCOB Odell Beckham Jr. 8.00 20.00
RCCPR Paul Richardson 2.50 6.00
RCCSW Sammy Watkins 3.00 8.00
RCCTB Teddy Bridgewater 3.00 8.00
RCCTM Tre Mason 2.00 5.00

2014 Totally Certified Rookie Penmanship Red

RPAB Anthony Barr 3.00 8.00
RPAM A.J. McCarron
RPAMU Aaron Murray 3.00 8.00
RPAW Andre Williams 3.00 8.00
RPBB Blake Bortles 4.00 10.00
RPBC Brandin Cooks 5.00 12.00
RPBS Bishop Sankey 3.00 8.00
RPCH Cody Hoffman 3.00 8.00
RPCL Cody Latimer 4.00 10.00
RPCM C.J. Mosley 4.00 10.00
RPCS Charles Sims 3.00 8.00
RPDA Davante Adams 5.00 12.00
RPDC Derek Carr 20.00 50.00
RPDF David Fales 3.00 8.00
RPDM Donte Moncrief 3.00 8.00
RPDS Devin Street 3.00 8.00
RPEE Eric Ebron 4.00 10.00
RPJC Jadeveon Clowney 4.00 10.00
RPJG Jimmy Garoppolo
RPJH Jeremy Hill 4.00 10.00
RPJM Johnny Manziel 5.00 12.00
RPJMA Jordan Matthews 5.00 12.00
RPKB Kelvin Benjamin 5.00 12.00
RPKC Ka'Deem Carey 3.00 8.00
RPKM Khalil Mack
RPKN Kevin Norwood 3.00 8.00
RPLT Logan Thomas
RPLW L'Damian Washington
RPME Mike Evans
RPMG Marion Grice 3.00 8.00
RPPR Paul Richardson
RPSW Sammy Watkins 5.00 12.00
RPTB Teddy Bridgewater 5.00 12.00
RPTG Tyler Gaffney 3.00 8.00
RPTM Tre Mason 3.00 8.00
RPTR Tevin Reese 3.00 8.00
RPTS Tom Savage
RPTW Terrance West 3.00 8.00

2014 Totally Certified Rookie Penmanship Blue

RPAB Anthony Barr/25 5.00 12.00
RPAMU Aaron Murray/25 5.00 12.00
RPAR Allen Robinson/25 8.00 20.00
RPAW Andre Williams/25
RPBC Brandin Cooks/25 8.00 20.00
RPBE Bruce Ellington/25 5.00 12.00
RPBS Bishop Sankey/25 5.00 12.00
RPCH Cody Hoffman/25 5.00 12.00
RPCHY Carlos Hyde/25 6.00 15.00
RPCL Cody Latimer/25 6.00 15.00
RPCM C.J. Mosley/25 6.00 15.00
RPCP Calvin Pryor/25 5.00 12.00
RPCS Charles Sims/25 5.00 12.00
RPDA Davante Adams/25
RPDAR Dri Archer/25 5.00 12.00
RPDF David Fales/25 5.00 12.00
RPDM Donte Moncrief/25 5.00 12.00
RPDS Devin Street/25 5.00 12.00
RPDT De'Anthony Thomas/25
RPDV Devonta Freeman/25 8.00 20.00
RPEE Eric Ebron/25
RPJH Jeremy Hill/25 6.00 15.00
RPJHU Josh Huff/25 6.00 15.00
RPJL Jarvis Landry/25
RPJMA Jordan Matthews/25 8.00 20.00
RPKB Kelvin Benjamin/25 8.00 20.00
RPKC Ka'Deem Carey/25 5.00 12.00
RPKM Khalil Mack/25 20.00 50.00
RPKN Kevin Norwood/25 5.00 12.00
RPLT Logan Thomas/25 5.00 12.00
RPLW L'Damian Washington/25 6.00 15.00
RPMB Martavis Bryant/25
RPMG Marion Grice/25 5.00 12.00
RPOB Odell Beckham Jr./25 50.00 100.00
RPPR Paul Richardson/25 10.00 25.00
RPTG Tyler Gaffney/25 5.00 12.00
RPTM Tre Mason/25
RPTR Tevin Reese/25 5.00 12.00
RPTS Tom Savage/25 5.00 12.00
RPTW Terrance West/25 5.00 12.00

2014 Totally Certified Rookie Roll Call Jerseys

*BLUE/50: .6X TO 1.5X BASIC JSY
*GOLD/25: .8X TO 2X BASIC JSY
*RED/100: .5X TO 1.2X BASIC JSY
RCCAM A.J. McCarron 1.25 3.00
RCCAMU Aaron Murray 1.25 3.00
RCCAR Allen Robinson 2.00 5.00
RCCAS Austin Seferian-Jenkins 1.25 3.00

RCCAW Asa Watson 1.25 3.00
RCCAWI Andre Williams 1.25 3.00
RCCBB Blake Bortles 1.50 4.00
RCCBC Brandin Cooks 2.00 5.00
RCCBS Bishop Sankey 1.25 3.00
RCCCH Carlos Hyde 1.50 4.00
RCCCL Cody Latimer 1.50 4.00
RCCCS Charles Sims 1.25 3.00
RCCDA Davante Adams 2.00 5.00
RCCDAR Dri Archer 1.25 3.00
RCCDC Derek Carr 4.00 10.00
RCCDF Devonta Freeman 2.50 6.00
RCCDM Donte Moncrief 1.25 3.00
RCCDT De'Anthony Thomas 1.25 3.00
RCCEE Eric Ebron 1.50 4.00
RCCJA Jace Amaro 1.25 3.00
RCCJC Jadeveon Clowney 1.50 4.00
RCCJG Jimmy Garoppolo 10.00 25.00
RCCJH Jeremy Hill 1.50 4.00
RCCJL Jarvis Landry 2.50 6.00
RCCJM Johnny Manziel 2.00 5.00
RCCJMA Jordan Matthews 2.00 5.00
RCCKB Kelvin Benjamin 2.00 5.00
RCCKC Ka'Deem Carey 1.25 3.00
RCCKM Khalil Mack 5.00 12.00
RCCLT Logan Thomas 1.25 3.00
RCCME Mike Evans 3.00 8.00
RCCML Marqise Lee 1.50 4.00
RCCOB Odell Beckham Jr. 6.00 15.00
RCCPR Paul Richardson 1.50 4.00
RCCSW Sammy Watkins 2.00 5.00
RCCTB Tajh Boyd 1.25 3.00
RCCTBR Teddy Bridgewater 2.00 5.00
RCCTM Tre Mason 1.25 3.00
RCCTS Tom Savage 1.25 3.00
RCCTW Terrance West 1.25 3.00

2014 Totally Certified Rookie Signatures Mirror Red

*MIRROR RED/25: .5X TO 1.2X RED AU/50
142 Martavis Bryant 6.00 15.00

2014 Totally Certified Rookie Signatures Platinum Blue

*PLAT.BLUE/25: .5X TO 1.2X RED AU/50
142 Martavis Bryant 6.00 15.00

2014 Totally Certified Rookie Signatures Platinum Red

*BASIC AU: .25X TO .6X RED AU/50
101 Deone Bucannon 4.00 10.00
102 John Brown 6.00 15.00
103 Troy Niklas 4.00 10.00
104 Jake Matthews 4.00 10.00
105 Ra'Shede Hageman 4.00 10.00
106 C.J. Mosley 5.00 12.00
107 Michael Campanaro 4.00 10.00
108 Timmy Jernigan 4.00 10.00
109 Kony Ealy 5.00 12.00
110 Tyler Gaffney 4.00 10.00
111 David Fales 4.00 10.00
112 Kyle Fuller 4.00 10.00
113 Darqueze Dennard 5.00 12.00
114 James Wilder Jr. 5.00 12.00
115 Connor Shaw 4.00 10.00
116 Isaiah Crowell 5.00 12.00
117 Devin Street 4.00 10.00
118 L'Damian Washington 5.00 12.00
119 Zack Martin 8.00 20.00
121 Kyle Van Noy 5.00 12.00
122 Ha Ha Clinton-Dix 5.00 12.00
123 Jared Abbrederis 8.00 20.00
124 Jeff Janis 4.00 10.00
125 Rajion Neal 4.00 10.00
126 C.J. Fiedorowicz 4.00 10.00
127 Louis Nix III 4.00 10.00
128 Dee Ford 4.00 10.00
129 Allen Hurns 5.00 12.00
130 Anthony Barr 4.00 10.00
131 Jerick McKinnon 5.00 12.00
132 Scott Crichton 4.00 10.00
133 Dominique Easley 4.00 10.00
135 Brandon Coleman 4.00 10.00
136 Calvin Pryor 4.00 10.00
137 Shaq Evans 4.00 10.00
138 Mike Davis 4.00 10.00
139 Ed Reynolds 4.00 10.00
140 Josh Huff 5.00 12.00
141 Marcus Smith 4.00 10.00
143 Ryan Shazier 6.00 15.00
144 Jason Verrett 4.00 10.00
145 Marion Grice 4.00 10.00
146 Tevin Reese 4.00 10.00
148 Chris Borland 4.00 10.00
149 Jimmie Ward 5.00 12.00
150 Kevin Norwood 4.00 10.00
151 Aaron Donald 15.00 40.00
152 Greg Robinson 4.00 10.00
153 Lamarcus Joyner 5.00 12.00
154 Michael Sam 8.00 20.00
155 Robert Herron 4.00 10.00
156 Antonio Andrews 4.00 10.00
158 Cody Hoffman 4.00 10.00
159 Lache Seastrunk 4.00 10.00
160 Trent Murphy 4.00 10.00

2014 Totally Certified Stitches in Time

STBUF J.Kelly/S.Watkins 3.00 8.00
STCHI K.Carey/M.Singletary 5.00 12.00
STCIN A.McCarron/B.Esiason 4.00 10.00
STCOW D.Murray/T.Dorsett 6.00 15.00
STDAL T.Romo/T.Aikman 8.00 20.00
STDEN C.Latimer/T.Davis 4.00 10.00
STDET B.Sanders/E.Ebron 8.00 20.00
STGB B.Favre/D.Adams 10.00 25.00
STIND D.Moncrief/M.Harrison 3.00 8.00
STJAC B.Bortles/F.Taylor 2.50 6.00
STKC A.Murray/L.Dawson 10.00 25.00
STMIA D.Marino/J.Landry
STMIN F.Tarkenton/T.Bridgewater 3.00 8.00
STNE J.Garoppolo/T.Brady 25.00 60.00
STNYG A.Toomer/O.Beckham Jr. 5.00 12.00
STNYJ G.Smith/J.Namath 12.00 30.00
STOAK D.Carr/J.Plunkett 12.00 30.00
STPIT D.Archer/J.Bettis 5.00 12.00
STRAI H.Long/K.Mack 12.00 30.00
STSEA P.Richardson/S.Largent 5.00 12.00
STSF C.Hyde/J.Rice 8.00 20.00
STSTL M.Faulk/T.Mason 4.00 10.00
STTB M.Evans/W.Dunn 5.00 12.00
STTEN B.Sankey/E.George 4.00 10.00

2014 Totally Certified Stitches in Time Trios

ST3CB Wdsn/Sndrs/Shrmn 15.00 40.00
ST3DC Brynt/Smth/Stbch 20.00 50.00
ST3DE Lng/Clwny/Alln
ST3KC Mrry/Smth/Mntna
ST3MD Grse/Mrno/Tnnhll
ST3MV Crtr/Trkntn/Brdgwtr
ST3PS Archr/Btts/Bll 12.00 30.00
ST3QB Mrno/Mnzl/Brdy 20.00 50.00
ST3TT Snky/Cmpbll/Grge 12.00 30.00
ST3WR Jhnsn/Rce/Wtkns 12.00 30.00

2000 Totino's Pizza

These cards were actually part of a contest in which one had to accumulate more than one player to qualify for various prizes. The Eddie George card was good for the Grand Prize of which only 5 were made. The cards were printed on the inside of Totino's Pizza boxes are were to be cut off of the box by the collector. Each card features a small black and white photo with a brief write-up on the player. There are two versions of each card: white stock cards measure roughly 3 1/2" by 3 1/2" when cut from the product package and the brown stock cards measure roughly [illegible] cut. The contest expired 2/29/2000.

COMPLETE SET (4) 1.20 3.00
1 Mike Alstott .40 1.00
2 Eddie George WIN
3 Marshall Faulk .50 1.25
4 John Randle .40 1.00
5 Charles Woodson .20 .50

1977 Touchdown Club

This 50-card set was initially targeted toward football autograph collectors as the set featured only living (at the time) ex-football players many of whom were or are now in the Pro Football Hall of Fame in Canton, Ohio. The set was originally sold for $5.95 along with a printed address list for the players in the set. The cards are black and white (typically showing the player in his prime) and are numbered on the back. The cards measure approximately 2 1/4" by 3 1/4". Card backs list career honors the player received.

COMPLETE SET (50) 60.00 120.00
1 Red Grange 4.00 8.00
2 George Halas 4.00 8.00
3 Benny Friedman UER 1.00 2.50
4 Cliff Battles 1.25 3.00
5 Mike Michalske 1.25 3.00
6 George McAfee 1.50 3.00
7 Beattie Feathers 1.25 3.00
8 Ernie Caddel 1.00 2.50
9 George Musso 1.25 3.00
10 Sid Luckman 2.50 5.00
11 Cecil Isbell 1.25 3.00
12 Bronko Nagurski 4.00 8.00
13 Hunk Anderson 1.00 2.50
14 Dick Farman 1.00 2.50
15 Aldo Forte 1.00 2.50
16 Ki Aldrich 1.00 2.50
17 Jim Lee Howell 1.00 2.50
18 Ray Flaherty 1.25 3.00
19 Hampton Pool 1.00 2.50
20 Alex Wojciechowicz 1.25 3.00
21 Bill Osmanski 1.00 2.50
22 Hank Soar 1.00 2.50
23 Dutch Clark 1.50 3.00
24 Joe Muha 1.00 2.50
25 Don Hutson 2.00 4.00
26 Jim Poole 1.00 2.50
27 Charley Malone 1.00 2.50
28 Charley Trippi 1.50 3.00
29 Andy Farkas 1.00 2.50
30 Clarke Hinkle 1.25 3.00
31 Gary Famiglietti 1.00 2.50
32 Bulldog Turner 1.50 3.00
33 Sammy Baugh 4.00 8.00
34 Pat Harder 1.00 2.50
35 Tuffy Leemans 1.00 2.50
36 Ken Strong 1.50 3.00
37 Barney Poole 1.00 2.50
38 Frank(Bruiser) Kinard 1.25 3.00
39 Buford Ray 1.00 2.50
40 Clarence(Ace) Parker 1.25 3.00
41 Buddy Parker 1.00 2.50
42 Mel Hein 1.25 3.00
43 Ed Danowski 1.00 2.50
44 Bill Dudley 1.50 3.00
45 Paul Stenn 1.00 2.50
46 George Connor 1.25 3.00
47 George Sauer Sr. 1.00 2.50
48 Armand Niccolai 1.00 2.50
49 Tony Canadeo 1.25 3.00
50 Bill Willis 1.50 4.00

1989 Touchdown UK

This contest card set was produced by NFL Properties UK, sponsored by Touchdown magazine, and distributed through Team and Small Shredded Wheats packages in Great Britain. Each card is unnumbered and features a color photo of NFL action without specific identification of players. Small silver scratch-off boxes also appear on the cardfront with contest rules covering the cardback. We've included known players that appear on each card below.

COMPLETE SET (30) 300.00 500.00
1 Duel for the Ball 6.00 15.00
Rams vs. Chargers
2 Safety Blitz Pressures QB 6.00 15.00
Todd Blackledge
3 Powerful Kick-off 6.00 15.00
Scott Norwood
4 Kick-off Starts the Game 6.00 15.00
Gary Anderson K
5 Dennis Gentry 6.00 15.00
Joey Browner
6 Field Goal Attempt Sails 8.00 20.00
Packers vs. 49ers
7 Atlanta's QB Finds Receiver 8.00 20.00
Chris Miller
8 Afred Anderson 8.00 20.00
Bill Bate
9 End Zone Ballet for a TD 6.00 15.00
Jonathan Hayes vs. Bears
10 Bengals' QB Throws a Pass 10.00 25.00
Boomer Esiason
11 Breaking up a Reception 6.00 15.00
Gill Byrd
Ron Heller TE
12 Mark Clayton 6.00 15.00
Dwayne Woodruff
13 Cincinnati's QB Let's One Fly 10.00 25.00
Boomer Esiason
14 Eddie Brown WR vs Steelers 6.00 15.00
15 Fighting for a Fumble 6.00 15.00
Delton Hall
16 Warren Moon 12.00 30.00
Reggie Williams
17 Juggling the Ball 8.00 20.00
Gary Anderson RB vs. Cowboys
18 Reaching High for Completion 6.00 15.00
Chris Burkett
19 Saints QB fires a Bomb 8.00 20.00
Bobby Hebert
20 James Pruitt 6.00 15.00
Ray Horton
21 Ball Pops Loose 8.00 20.00
Dino Hackett
Neal Anderson
22 Kevin Butler 8.00 20.00
Steve McMichael
23 Ball Flies Loose After Punt 6.00 15.00
Bill Renner vs. Giant
24 Phil Simms 12.00 30.00
Jumbo Elliott
Jesse Penn
25 Marc Wilson 8.00 20.00
Leslie O'Neal
26 Steelers Defense Causes a Fumble#(John Swain 6.00
15.00
27 Mark Malone 6.00 15.00
Markus Koch
Craig Wolfley
28 Long Pass From Broncos QB 40.00 80.00
29 Punt From the End Zone 6.00 15.00
30 Bears Pass 8.00 20.00
[illegible]

2005 Tri-Cities Fever NFL

COMPLETE SET (26) 7.50 15.00
1 Jeremy Bohannon .30 .75
2 Antar Brame .30 .75
3 Ron Childs .30 .75
4 Jason Cobb .30 .75
5 Jarvis Dunn .30 .75
6 Zach Fife .30 .75
7 Thomas Ford .30 .75
8 Nick Hannah .30 .75
9 Michael Hodges Jr. .30 .75
10 Josh Jelinek .30 .75
11 Josh Jelmberg .30 .75
12 Rhodri Kirwan .30 .75
13 Nick Lano .30 .75
14 Karl Kuhau-leftee .30 .75
15 Scott Lunde .30 .75
16 Ray Marshall .30 .75
17 Brian Meier .30 .75
18 Paris Moore .30 .75
19 Mike Rigell .30 .75
20 Michael Che Romero .30 .75
21 Brandon Schillinger .30 .75
22 Lucien Scott .30 .75
23 Tyler Thomas .30 .75
24 Mac Tuiaea .30 .75
25 Cheerleaders Card .30 .75
26 Cover Card .30 .75

2010 TRISTAR Obak

COMMON CARD (1-109) .20 .50
COMMON VAR (1-109) .40 1.00
COMMON SP (110-120) 1.50 4.00
THREE SPs PER BOX
73 Andy Farkas .20 .50
101 Howard Cassady .20 .50
104 Kyle Rote Sr. .20 .50
105 Charlie Ward .30 .75

2010 TRISTAR Obak Black

*BLACK: 2.5X TO 6X BASIC
*BLACK VAR: 1.2X TO 3X BASIC VAR
*BLACK SP: .5X TO 1.2X BASIC SP
OVERALL PARALLEL ODDS 1:10
STATED PRINT RUN 50 SER.#'d SETS

2010 TRISTAR Obak Mini T212

STATED ODDS ONE PER PACK
35 Charlie Ward .30 .75

2010 TRISTAR Obak Mini T212 Black

*BLACK: 1X TO 2.5X BASIC
*BLACK VAR: .6X TO 1.5X BASIC VAR
STATED ODDS 1:20
STATED PRINT RUN 50 SER.#'d SETS

2010 TRISTAR Obak Autographs

ERALL AUTO ODDS 1:5
STATED PRINT RUN 125 SER.#'d SETS
A81 Charlie Ward 4.00 10.00

2010 TRISTAR Obak Autographs Black

*BLACK: .5X TO 1.2X BROWN
OVERALL AUTO ODDS 1:5
STATED PRINT RUN 50 SER.#'d SETS
A58 Toby Gerhart 8.00 20.00

2010 TRISTAR Obak Autographs Brown

*BROWN: .5X TO 1.2X BASIC
OVERALL AUTO ODDS 1:5
STATED PRINT RUN 75 SER.#'d SETS
A54 Howard Cassady 8.00 20.00

2010 TRISTAR Obak National Convention VIP

COMPLETE SET (12)
N6 Andy Farkas 1.50 4.00

2011 TRISTAR Obak National Convention VIP

NP4 Roger Staubach
NP5 Terry Bradshaw
NP6 Gale Sayers
NP9 Stan Musial/Bob Kalsu 2.50 6.00

2011 TRISTAR Pursuit Obak Preview

TWO OBAK CARDS PER BOX
ANNC'D PRINT RUN OF 311 SETS
P6A Billy Johnson .60 1.50
P6B Billy Johnson .60 1.50
Square Around Number
P7 William Heffelfinger .60 1.50

2011 TRISTAR Obak

COMP.SET w/o SP's (110)
1 Sammy Baugh .30 .75
2 Dutch Clark .25 .60
3 Red Grange .40 1.00
4 Mel Hein .20 .50
5 Fats Henry .20 .50
6 Cal Hubbard .20 .50
7 Don Hutson .25 .60
8 Curly Lambeau .30 .75
9 Tim Mara .20 .50
10 George Preston Marshall .20 .50
11 Johnny Blood McNally .20 .50
12 Bronko Nagurski .30 .75
13 Ernie Nevers .25 .60
14 Bart Starr .50 1.25
15 Johnny Unitas .50 1.25
16 Paul Hornung .30 .75
17 Terry Bradshaw .40 1.00
18 Earl Campbell .30 .75
19 Morten Andersen .20 .50
20 Roger Staubach .40 1.00
21 Gale Sayers .30 .75
22 Gino Cappelletti .20 .50
23 Jim Otto .20 .50
24 Jim Parker .20 .50
25 Norm Van Brocklin .25 .60
26 Vince Lombardi .50 1.25
27 John Heisman .20 .50
28 Paul Bear Bryant .30 .75
29 Doak Walker .30 .75
30 Douglas MacArthur .20 .50
31 Joe Carr .20 .50
32 Bert Bell .20 .50
33 Robert Maxwell .20 .50
34 John Outland .20 .50
35 Henry Rutgers .20 .50
36 King Camp Gillette .20 .50
37 Darrell Royal .20 .50
38 Angelo Bertelli .20 .50
39 Bo Jackson .50 1.25
40 John Cappelletti .20 .50
41 John David Crow .20 .50
42 Howard Cassady .20 .50
43 Billy Sims .25 .60
44 Johnny Lattner .30 .75
45 Steve Owens .20 .50
46 Frank Sinkwich .20 .50
47 Mike Rozier .30 .75
48 Larry Kelley .20 .50
49 Andre Ware .25 .60
50 Charlie Ward .20 .50
51 Tom Dempsey .20 .50
52 Benny Friedman .20 .50
53 Paul Robeson .20 .50
54 Corbett Davis .20 .50
55 Sam Francis .20 .50
56 Tommy Nobis .20 .50
57 Lem Barney .20 .50
58 Dennis Byrd .20 .50
59 Bobby Douglass .20 .50
60 Kurt Warner .25 .60
61 Quentin Coryatt .20 .50
62 Poe Brothers .20 .50
63 Ray Childress .20 .50
64 Lydell Mitchell .20 .50
65 Chuck Hughes .20 .50
66 Johanna Spyri .20 .50
67 Caspar Whitney .20 .50
68 John Moses Brunswick .20 .50
69 Bob Lilly .25 .60
70 Elroy Hirsch .25 .60
71 Dante Hall .20 .50
72 Christian Okoye .20 .50
73 Ickey Woods .20 .50
74 Harry Beecher .20 .50
75 Roger Craig .25 .60
76 Beattie Feathers .20 .50
77 Joe Foss .20 .50
78 Ray Guy .20 .50
79 Graham McNamee .20 .50
80 Joe Perry .25 .60
81 Emlen Tunnell .20 .50
82 Emory Bellard .20 .50
83 Walter Camp .20 .50
84 Eddie Cochems .20 .50
85 William Webb Ellis .20 .50
86 Ray Flaherty .20 .50
87 Charles Follis .20 .50
88 Ralph Hay .20 .50
89 Pudge Heffelfinger .20 .50
90 Fritz Pollard .20 .50
91 Cadet Joseph Reeves .20 .50
92 John Tate Riddell .20 .50
93 Bradbury Robinson .20 .50
94 AmosAlonzo Stagg .20 .50
95 A.E. Staley .20 .50
96 George Taliaferro .20 .50
97 Fielding Yost .20 .50
98 Lyndon B. Johnson .20 .50
99 Dwight Eisenhower .20 .50
100 Gerald Ford .25 .60
101 John Kennedy .30 .75
102 Richard Nixon .20 .50
103 Ronald Reagan .30 .75
104 Rocky Bleier .25 .60
105 Maurice Footsie Britt .20 .50
106 Jack Chevigney .20 .50
107 Bob Kalsu .20 .50
108 Yale Lary .20 .50
109 Eddie LeBaron .20 .50
110 Jack Lummus .25 .60
111 Charlie Ward SP 1.25 3.00
112 Rocky Bleier SP 1.50 4.00
113 Maurice Footsie Britt SP 1.25 3.00
114 Al Blozis SP 1.25 3.00
115 Jack Chevigney SP 1.25 3.00
116 Bob Kalsu SP 1.25 3.00
117 Eddie LeBaron SP 1.25 3.00
118 Jack Lummus SP 1.50 4.00
119 Johnny Poe SP 1.25 3.00
120 Fritz Pollard SP 1.25 3.00

2011 TRISTAR Obak Gold

*111-120 GOLD/50: .6X TO 1.5X BASIC SP

2011 TRISTAR Obak Green

*1-110 GREEN/25: 3X TO 8X BASIC CARDS
*111-120 GREEN/25: .8X TO 2X BASIC CARDS

2011 TRISTAR Obak Orange

*1-110 ORANGE/10: 5X TO 12X BASIC CARDS
*111-120 ORANGE/10: 1.2X TO 3X BASIC SP

2011 TRISTAR Obak Orange 75

*111-120 ORANGE/75: .5X TO 1.2X BASIC SP

2011 TRISTAR Obak Autographs

*BASE AU/100: .3X TO .8X BROWN/50
STATED PRINT RUN 100 SER.#'d SETS
A1 Morten Andersen 5.00 12.00
A5 Dennis Byrd 5.00 12.00
A7 Gino Cappelletti 5.00 12.00
A8 John Cappelletti 5.00 12.00
A12 Eric Crouch 6.00 15.00
A14 Tom Dempsey 5.00 12.00
A15 Bobby Douglass 5.00 12.00
A17 Ray Guy 6.00 15.00
A18 Dante Hall 5.00 12.00
A19 Paul Hornung 8.00 20.00
A22 Johnny Lattner 6.00 15.00
A23 Eddie LeBaron 6.00 15.00
A26 Lydell Mitchell 5.00 12.00
A29 Christian Okoye 5.00 12.00
A30 Jim Otto 5.00 12.00
A34 Mike Rozier 5.00 12.00
A36 Billy Sims 6.00 15.00
A39 Charlie Ward 6.00 15.00

2011 TRISTAR Obak Autographs Brown

STATED PRINT RUN 50 SER.#'d SETS
A1 Morten Andersen 6.00 15.00
A2 Lem Barney 6.00 15.00
A3 Rocky Bleier 10.00 25.00
A5 Dennis Byrd 6.00 15.00
A7 Gino Cappelletti 6.00 15.00
A8 John Cappelletti 6.00 15.00
A9 Ray Childress 6.00 15.00
A10 Quentin Coryatt 6.00 15.00
A11 Roger Craig 8.00 20.00
A12 Eric Crouch 8.00 20.00
A14 Tom Dempsey 6.00 15.00
A15 Bobby Douglass 6.00 15.00
A16 Toby Gerhart 8.00 20.00
A17 Ray Guy 8.00 20.00
A18 Dante Hall 6.00 15.00
A19 Paul Hornung 10.00 25.00
A21 Yale Lary 6.00 15.00
A22 Johnny Lattner 8.00 20.00
A23 Eddie LeBaron 8.00 20.00
A25 Bob Lilly 8.00 20.00
A26 Lydell Mitchell 6.00 15.00
A27 Ozzie Newsome 8.00 20.00
A28 Tommy Nobis 6.00 15.00
A29 Christian Okoye 6.00 15.00
A30 Jim Otto 6.00 15.00
A31 Steve Owens 6.00 15.00
A32 Mel Renfro 6.00 15.00
A34 Mike Rozier 6.00 15.00
A36 Billy Sims 8.00 20.00
A38 George Taliaferro 6.00 15.00
A39 Charlie Ward 6.00 15.00
A40 Andre Ware 8.00 20.00
A41 Ickey Woods 6.00 15.00

2011 TRISTAR Obak Autographs Green

*GREEN AU/25: .5X TO 1.2X BROWN/50
STATED PRINT RUN 25 SER.#'d SETS
A13 John David Crow 8.00 20.00
A35 Gale Sayers 15.00 40.00

2011 TRISTAR Obak Autographs Orange

*ORANGE AU/75: .3X TO .8X BROWN/50
STATED PRINT RUN 75 SER.#'d SETS

2011 TRISTAR Obak Cut Signatures Blue

BLUE PRINT RUN 50 SER.#'d SETS
*BRONZE/75: .4X TO 1X BLUE/50
24 Bob Gain 6.00 15.00
34 Brad Johnson 6.00 15.00
37 Lee Roy Jordan 6.00 15.00
59 Philip Rivers 12.00 30.00
62 Junior Seau 25.00 50.00
64 Don Shula 15.00 30.00
69 Jim Stillwagon 6.00 15.00
72 Pat Summerall 10.00 25.00
75 Vinny Testaverde 6.00 15.00
79 Charley Trippi 6.00 15.00
84 Charles White 6.00 15.00

2011 TRISTAR Obak Cut Signatures Green

GREEN AUTO PRINT RUN 25
4 Terry Baker 12.00 30.00
6 Sammy Baugh 40.00 80.00
7 Joe Bellino 8.00 20.00
13 David Carr 8.00 20.00
18 Richard Dent 12.00 30.00
34 Brad Johnson 8.00 20.00
37 Lee Roy Jordan 8.00 20.00
48 Warren McVea 8.00 20.00
50 Craig Morton 8.00 20.00
51 Jay Novacek 10.00 25.00
55 William Perry 8.00 20.00
59 Philip Rivers 15.00 40.00
60 George Rogers 10.00 25.00
62 Junior Seau 30.00 60.00
63 Jerry Sherk 8.00 20.00
64 Don Shula 15.00 40.00
69 Jim Stillwagon 8.00 20.00
72 Pat Summerall 10.00 25.00
78 Y.A. Tittle 12.00 30.00
79 Charley Trippi 8.00 20.00
84 Charles White 8.00 20.00
89 Danny Wuerffel 8.00 20.00

1983 Tudor Figurines

Produced by Tudor Games, these figurines were produced for each NFL team's quarterback. Although the statues are not specifically identified, they were designed to represent that team's 1983 quarterback. The pieces were rather crudely done with each appearing to be exact in design save for the team uniform. They are listed below by the product code number on the package (also in team alphabetical order) and are priced as opened statues. Complete sealed packages are valued at double the prices below.

COMPLETE SET (28) 220.00 550.00
2001 Jim McMahon 8.00 20.00
2002 Ken Anderson 8.00 20.00
2003 Joe Ferguson 6.00 15.00
2004 John Elway 40.00 100.00
2005 Brian Sipe 6.00 15.00
2006 Doug Williams 6.00 15.00
2007 Jim Hart 6.00 15.00
2008 Dan Fouts 10.00 25.00
2009 Steve Fuller 6.00 15.00
2010 Bert Jones 8.00 20.00
2011 Danny White 8.00 20.00
2012 David Woodley 6.00 15.00
2013 Ron Jaworski 6.00 15.00
2014 Steve Bartkowski 8.00 20.00
2015 Joe Montana 50.00 125.00
2016 Phil Simms 8.00 20.00
2017 Richard Todd 6.00 15.00
2018 Eric Hipple 6.00 15.00
2019 Archie Manning 15.00 40.00
2020 Lynn Dickey 6.00 15.00
2021 Steve Grogan 8.00 20.00
2022 Jim Plunkett 8.00 20.00
2023 Vince Ferragamo 6.00 15.00
2024 Joe Theismann 15.00 40.00
2025 Ken Stabler 12.00 30.00
2026 Jim Zorn 6.00 15.00
2027 Terry Bradshaw 20.00 50.00
2028 Tommy Kramer 6.00 15.00

2011 TRISTAR Obak T212 Mini

ONE MINI PER PACK
*BROWN/75: 1.5X TO 4X BASIC INSERTS
*GREEN/25: 2.5X TO 6X BASIC INSERTS
1 Sammy Baugh .50 1.25
2 Bronko Nagurski .50 1.25
3 Earl Campbell .50 1.25
4 Terry Bradshaw .60 1.50
5 Bart Starr .75 2.00
6 Johnny Unitas .75 2.00
7 Bob Lilly .40 1.00
8 Vince Lombardi .75 2.00
9 John Heisman .30 .75
10 Bo Jackson .60 1.50
11 John Cappelletti .30 .75
12 Benny Friedman .30 .75
13 Gale Sayers .50 1.25
14 Walter Camp .30 .75
15 Kurt Warner .40 1.00
16 Poe Brothers .30 .75
17 Harry Beecher .30 .75
18 Paul Bear Bryant .50 1.25
19 Charles Follis .30 .75
20 Pudge Heffelfinger .30 .75
21 Fritz Pollard .30 .75
22 Gerald Ford .40 1.00
23 John Kennedy .50 1.25
24 Rocky Bleier .40 1.00

2011 TRISTAR Obak T4 Cabinets

ONE T4 CABINET PER HOBBY BOX
*BROWN/50: .5X TO 1.2X BASIC INSERTS
*GREEN/25: .6X TO 1.5X BASIC INSERTS
T4F1 G.Ford/F.Yost 1.50 4.00
T4F2 C.Follis/E.Tunnell 1.50 4.00
T4F3 R.Bleier/T.Bradshaw 2.00 5.00
T4F4 E.LeBaron/A.A.Stagg 1.50 4.00
T4F5 P.Hornung/B.Starr 4.00 10.00
T4F6 D.Royal/E.Campbell 2.50 6.00
T4F7 J.Cappelletti/J.Heisman 1.50 4.00
T4F8 T.Gerhart/W.Camp 2.00 5.00
T4F9 Staubach/Bradshaw 3.00 8.00
T4F10 C.Ward/R.Maxwell 1.50 4.00
T4F11 P.Hornung/B.Bell 2.50 6.00
T4F12 G.Sayers/R.Grange 3.00 8.00
T4F13 Y.Lary/J.D.Crow 1.50 4.00
T4F14 J.Lattner/J.Chevigne 1.50 4.00
T4F15 B.Lilly/S.Baugh 2.50 6.00

1989 TV-4 NFL Quarterbacks

The 1989 TV-4 NFL Quarterbacks set features 20 cards measuring approximately 2 7/16" by 3 1/8". The fronts are borderless and show attractive color action and portrait drawings of each quarterback. The drawings were performed by artist J.C. Ford. The vertically oriented backs list career highlights. The TV-4 refers to a London (England) television station, which distributed the cards. The cards were distributed in England and were intended to promote the National Football League, which had begun playing pre-season games there.

COMPLETE SET (20) 20.00 40.00
1 Dutch Clark .50 1.25
2 Sammy Baugh .60 1.50
3 Bob Waterfield .50 1.25
4 Sid Luckman .60 1.50
5 Otto Graham .60 1.50
6 Bobby Layne .60 1.50
7 Norm Van Brocklin .50 1.25
8 George Blanda .50 1.25
9 Y.A. Tittle .50 1.25
10 Johnny Unitas 1.50 4.00
11 Bart Starr 1.50 4.00
12 Sonny Jurgensen .50 1.25
13 Joe Namath 1.50 4.00
14 Fran Tarkenton .60 1.50
15 Roger Staubach 1.25 3.00
16 Terry Bradshaw 1.25 3.00
17 Dan Fouts .50 1.25
18 Joe Montana 4.00 10.00
19 John Elway 3.00 8.00
20 Dan Marino 3.00 8.00

1997 UD3

The 1997 Upper Deck UD3 set was issued in one series totalling 90 cards. The set contains the topical subsets: Prime Choice Rookie (1-30), Eye of a Champion (31-60), and Pigskin Heroes (61-90). Each of the three subsets were printed using different insert quality printing technologies. Prime Choice Rookies display color action player photos using Light F/X technology. Eye of a Champion utilizes CEL Chrome technology. Pigskin Heroes features color player action photos and player images using Electric embossed technology and printed on a pigskin-look background.

COMPLETE SET (90) 20.00 50.00
1 Orlando Pace RC .50 1.25
2 Walter Jones RC .75 2.00
3 Tony Gonzalez RC 1.50 4.00
4 David LaFleur RC .20 .50
5 Jim Druckenmiller RC .30 .75
6 Jake Plummer RC 1.50 4.00
7 Pat Barnes RC .30 .75
8 Ike Hilliard RC .60 1.50
9 Reidel Anthony RC .50 1.25
10 Rae Carruth RC .20 .50
11 Yatil Green RC .30 .75
12 Joey Kent RC .50 1.25
13 Will Blackwell RC .30 .75
14 Kevin Lockett RC .30 .75
15 Warrick Dunn RC 1.25 3.00
16 Antowain Smith RC 1.25 3.00
17 Troy Davis RC .30 .75
18 Byron Hanspard RC .30 .75
19 Corey Dillon RC 1.50 4.00
20 Darnell Autry RC .30 .75
21 Peter Boulware RC .50 1.25
22 Darrell Russell RC .20 .50
23 Kenny Holmes RC .50 1.25
24 Reinard Wilson RC .30 .75
25 Renaldo Wynn RC .20 .50
26 Dwayne Rudd RC .50 1.25
27 James Farrior RC .50 1.25
28 Shawn Springs RC .30 .75
29 Bryant Westbrook RC .20 .50
30 Tom Knight RC .20 .50
31 Barry Sanders EC 1.50 4.00
32 Brett Favre EC 2.00 5.00
33 Brian Mitchell EC .20 .50
34 Curtis Martin EC .60 1.50
35 Dan Marino EC 2.00 5.00
36 Deion Sanders EC .50 1.25
37 Drew Bledsoe EC .60 1.50
38 Eddie George EC .50 1.25
39 Edgar Bennett EC .20 .50
40 Emmitt Smith EC 1.50 4.00
41 Isaac Bruce EC .50 1.25
42 Jerome Bettis EC .50 1.25
43 Jerry Rice EC 1.00 2.50
44 John Elway EC 2.00 5.00
45 Junior Seau EC .50 1.25
46 Karim Abdul-Jabbar EC .50 1.25
47 Kerry Collins EC .50 1.25
48 Marshall Faulk EC .60 1.50
49 Marvin Harrison EC .50 1.25
50 Michael Irvin EC .50 1.25
51 Natrone Means EC .30 .75
52 Reggie White EC .50 1.25
53 Ricky Watters EC .30 .75
54 Stan Humphries EC .30 .75
55 Steve Young EC .60 1.50
56 Terry Glenn EC .50 1.25
57 Thurman Thomas EC .50 1.25
58 Tony Martin EC .30 .75
59 Troy Aikman EC 1.00 2.50
60 Vinny Testaverde EC .30 .75
61 Anthony Johnson PH .20 .50
62 Bobby Engram EC .30 .75
63 Carl Pickens PH .30 .75
64 Cris Carter PH .30 .75
65 Derrick Witherspoon PH .20 .50
66 Eddie Kennison PH .30 .75
67 Eric Swann PH .20 .50
68 Gus Frerotte PH .30 .75
69 Herman Moore PH .30 .75
70 Irving Fryar PH .30 .75
71 Jamal Anderson PH .50 1.25
72 Jeff Blake PH .50 1.25
73 Jim Harbaugh PH .30 .75
74 Joey Galloway PH .30 .75
75 Keenan McCardell PH .30 .75
76 Kevin Greene PH .30 .75
77 Keyshawn Johnson PH .50 1.25
78 Kordell Stewart PH .50 1.25
79 Marcus Allen PH .50 1.25
80 Mario Bates PH .20 .50
81 Mark Brunell PH .60 1.50
82 Michael Jackson PH .30 .75
83 Mike Alstott PH .50 1.25
84 Scott Mitchell PH .30 .75
85 Shannon Sharpe PH .30 .75
86 Steve McNair PH .60 1.50
87 Terrell Davis PH .60 1.50
88 Tim Brown PH .50 1.25
89 Ty Detmer PH .30 .75
90 Tyrone Wheatley PH .30 .75

1997 UD3 Generation Excitement

Randomly inserted in packs at the rate of one in 11, this 15-card set features two color action images of the same player printed on a die cut Light F/X card.

COMPLETE SET (15) 50.00 120.00
STATED ODDS 1:11
GE1 Jerry Rice 5.00 12.00
GE2 Carl Pickens 1.50 4.00
GE3 Curtis Conway 1.50 4.00
GE4 John Elway 10.00 25.00
GE5 Ike Hilliard 2.50 6.00
GE6 Marvin Harrison 2.50 6.00
GE7 Emmitt Smith 8.00 20.00
GE8 Barry Sanders 8.00 20.00
GE9 Deion Sanders 2.50 6.00
GE10 Rae Carruth .75 2.00
GE11 Curtis Martin 3.00 8.00
GE12 Terry Glenn 2.50 6.00
GE13 Napoleon Kaufman 2.50 6.00
GE14 Kordell Stewart 2.50 6.00
GE15 Jake Plummer 3.00 8.00

1997 UD3 Marquee Attraction

Randomly inserted in packs at the rate of one in 144, this 15-card set features color action photos of top players printed on die-cut cards using Cel Chrome technology.

COMPLETE SET (15) 100.00 250.00
STATED ODDS 1:144
MA1 Steve Young 8.00 20.00
MA2 Troy Aikman 12.50 30.00
MA3 Keyshawn Johnson 6.00 15.00
MA4 Marcus Allen 6.00 15.00
MA5 Dan Marino 25.00 60.00
MA6 Mark Brunell 6.00 15.00
MA7 Eddie George 6.00 15.00
MA8 Brett Favre 15.00 40.00
MA9 Drew Bledsoe 8.00 20.00
MA10 Eddie Kennison 4.00 10.00
MA11 Terrell Davis 8.00 20.00
MA12 Warrick Dunn 6.00 15.00
MA13 Yatil Green 2.00 5.00
MA14 Troy Davis 2.00 5.00
MA15 Shawn Springs 2.00 5.00

1997 UD3 Signature Performers

Randomly inserted in packs at the rate of one in 1500, this four-card set features color action photos of top players in black-and-gold borders printed on a die-cut card and autographed in the white space below the picture.

COMPLETE SET (4) 100.00 200.00
STATED ODDS 1:1500
PF1 Curtis Martin 30.00 60.00
PF2 Troy Aikman 60.00 120.00
PF3 Marcus Allen 25.00 60.00
PF4 Eddie George 15.00 40.00

1998 UD3

The 1998 UD Cubed set contains 270 standard size cards. The 3-card packs retail for $3.99 each. The set contains the subsets: Future Shock-Embossed (1-30; 1:6), Next Wave-Embossed (31-60; 1:4), Upper Realm-Embossed (61-90; 1:125), Future Shock-Light F/X (91-120; 1:12), Next Wave-Light F/X (121-150; 1:1.5), Upper Realm-Light F/X (151-180; 1:6), Future Shock-Rainbow (181-210; 1:1.33), Next Wave-Rainbow (211-240; 1:12), and Upper Realm-Rainbow (241-270; 1:24).

1 Peyton Manning FE 15.00 30.00
2 Ryan Leaf FE 2.00 5.00
3 Andre Wadsworth FE 1.25 3.00
4 Charles Woodson FE 2.00 5.00
5 Curtis Enis FE .75 2.00
6 Grant Wistrom FE 1.25 3.00
7 Greg Ellis FE .75 2.00
8 Fred Taylor FE 2.00 5.00
9 Duane Starks FE .75 2.00
10 Keith Brooking FE 2.00 5.00
11 Takeo Spikes FE 2.00 5.00
12 Jason Peter FE .75 2.00
13 Anthony Simmons FE 1.25 3.00
14 Kevin Dyson FE 2.00 5.00
15 Brian Simmons FE 1.25 3.00
16 Robert Edwards FE 1.25 3.00
17 Randy Moss FE 8.00 20.00
18 John Avery FE 1.25 3.00
19 Marcus Nash FE .75 2.00
20 Jerome Pathon FE 2.00 5.00
21 Jacquez Green FE 1.25 3.00
22 Robert Holcombe FE 1.25 3.00
23 Pat Johnson FE 1.25 3.00
24 Germane Crowell FE 1.25 3.00
25 Joe Jurevicius FE 2.00 5.00
26 Skip Hicks FE 1.25 3.00
27 Ahman Green FE 3.00 8.00
28 Brian Griese FE 2.50 6.00
29 Hines Ward FE 5.00 12.00
30 Tavian Banks FE 1.25 3.00
31 Warrick Dunn NE 1.50 4.00
32 Jake Plummer NE 1.50 4.00
33 Derrick Mayes NE 1.00 2.50
34 Napoleon Kaufman NE 1.50 4.00
35 Jamal Anderson NE 1.50 4.00
36 Marvin Harrison NE 1.50 4.00
37 Jermaine Lewis NE 1.00 2.50
38 Corey Dillon NE 1.50 4.00
39 Keyshawn Johnson NE 1.50 4.00
40 Mike Alstott NE 1.50 4.00
41 Bobby Hoying NE 1.00 2.50
42 Keenan McCardell NE 1.00 2.50
43 Will Blackwell NE .60 1.50
44 Peter Boulware NE .60 1.50
45 Tony Banks NE 1.00 2.50
46 Rod Smith WR NE 1.00 2.50
47 Tony Gonzalez NE 1.50 4.00
48 Antowain Smith NE 1.00 2.50
49 Rae Carruth NE .60 1.50
50 J.J. Stokes NE 1.00 2.50
51 Brad Johnson NE 1.50 4.00
52 Shawn Springs NE .60 1.50
53 Elvis Grbac NE .60 1.50
54 Jimmy Smith NE 1.00 2.50
55 Terry Glenn NE 1.50 4.00
56 Tiki Barber NE 1.50 4.00
57 Gus Frerotte NE .60 1.50
58 Danny Wuerffel NE 1.00 2.50
59 Fred Lane NE .60 1.50
60 Todd Collins NE .60 1.50
61 Barry Sanders UE 2.50 6.00
62 Troy Aikman UE 1.50 4.00
63 Dan Marino UE 3.00 8.00
64 Drew Bledsoe UE 1.25 3.00
65 Dorsey Levens UE .75 2.00
66 Jerome Bettis UE .75 2.00
67 John Elway UE 3.00 8.00
68 Steve Young UE 1.00 2.50
69 Terrell Davis UE .75 2.00
70 Kordell Stewart UE .50 1.25
71 Jeff George UE .50 1.25
72 Emmitt Smith UE 2.50 6.00
73 Irving Fryar UE .50 1.25
74 Brett Favre UE 3.00 8.00
75 Eddie George UE .75 2.00
76 Terry Allen UE .75 2.00
77 Warren Moon UE .75 2.00
78 Mark Brunell UE .75 2.00
79 Robert Smith UE .75 2.00
80 Jerry Rice UE 1.50 4.00
81 Tim Brown UE .75 2.00
82 Carl Pickens UE .50 1.25
83 Joey Galloway UE .50 1.25
84 Herman Moore UE .50 1.25
85 Adrian Murrell UE .50 1.25
86 Thurman Thomas UE .75 2.00
87 Robert Brooks UE .50 1.25
88 Michael Irvin UE .75 2.00
89 Andre Rison UE .50 1.25
90 Marshall Faulk UE 1.00 2.50
91 Peyton Manning FF 20.00 50.00
92 Ryan Leaf FF 3.00 8.00
93 Andre Wadsworth FF 2.00 5.00
94 Charles Woodson FF 3.00 8.00
95 Curtis Enis FF 1.25 3.00
96 Grant Wistrom FF 2.00 5.00
97 Greg Ellis FF 1.25 3.00
98 Fred Taylor FF 3.00 8.00
99 Duane Starks FF 1.25 3.00
100 Keith Brooking FF 3.00 8.00
101 Takeo Spikes FF 3.00 8.00
102 Jason Peter FF 1.25 3.00
103 Anthony Simmons FF 2.00 5.00
104 Kevin Dyson FF 3.00 8.00
105 Brian Simmons FF 2.00 5.00
106 Robert Edwards FF 2.00 5.00
107 Randy Moss FF 8.00 20.00
108 John Avery FF 2.00 5.00
109 Marcus Nash FF 1.25 3.00
110 Jerome Pathon FF 3.00 8.00
111 Jacquez Green FF 2.00 5.00
112 Robert Holcombe FF 2.00 5.00
113 Pat Johnson FF 2.00 5.00
114 Germane Crowell FF 2.00 5.00
115 Joe Jurevicius FF 3.00 8.00
116 Skip Hicks FF 2.00 5.00
117 Ahman Green FF 5.00 12.00
118 Brian Griese FF 4.00 10.00
119 Hines Ward FF 7.50 20.00
120 Tavian Banks FF 2.00 5.00
121 Warrick Dunn NF .75 2.00
122 Jake Plummer NF .75 2.00
123 Derrick Mayes NF .50 1.25
124 Napoleon Kaufman NF .75 2.00
125 Jamal Anderson NF .75 2.00
126 Marvin Harrison NF .75 2.00
127 Jermaine Lewis NF .50 1.25
128 Corey Dillon NF .75 2.00
129 Keyshawn Johnson NF .75 2.00
130 Mike Alstott NF .75 2.00
131 Bobby Hoying NF .50 1.25
132 Keenan McCardell NF .50 1.25
133 Will Blackwell NF .30 .75
134 Peter Boulware NF .30 .75
135 Tony Banks NF .50 1.25

136 Rod Smith NF .50 1.25
137 Tony Gonzalez NF .75 2.00
138 Antowain Smith NF .50 1.25
139 Rae Carruth NF .30 .75
140 J.J. Stokes NF .50 1.25
141 Brad Johnson NF .75 2.00
142 Shawn Springs NF .30 .75
143 Elvis Grbac NF .30 .75
144 Jimmy Smith NF .50 1.25
145 Terry Glenn NF .75 2.00
146 Tiki Barber NF .75 2.00
147 Gus Frerotte NF .30 .75
148 Danny Wuerffel NF .50 1.25
149 Fred Lane NF .30 .75
150 Todd Collins NF .30 .75
151 Barry Sanders UF 6.00 15.00
152 Troy Aikman UF 4.00 10.00
153 Dan Marino UF 7.50 20.00
154 Drew Bledsoe UF 3.00 8.00
155 Dorsey Levens UF 2.00 5.00
156 Jerome Bettis UF 2.00 5.00
157 John Elway UF 7.50 20.00
158 Steve Young UF 2.50 6.00
159 Terrell Davis UF 2.00 5.00
160 Kordell Stewart UF 1.25 3.00
161 Jeff George UF 1.25 3.00
162 Emmitt Smith UF 6.00 15.00
163 Irving Fryar UF 1.25 3.00
164 Brett Favre UF 7.50 20.00
165 Eddie George UF 2.00 5.00
166 Terry Allen UF 2.00 5.00
167 Warren Moon UF 2.00 5.00
168 Mark Brunell UF 2.00 5.00
169 Robert Smith UF 2.00 5.00
170 Jerry Rice UF 4.00 10.00
171 Tim Brown UF 2.00 5.00
172 Carl Pickens UF 1.25 3.00
173 Joey Galloway UF 1.25 3.00
174 Herman Moore UF 1.25 3.00
175 Adrian Murrell UF 1.25 3.00
176 Thurman Thomas UF 2.00 5.00
177 Robert Brooks UF 1.25 3.00
178 Michael Irvin UF 2.00 5.00
179 Andre Rison UF 1.25 3.00
180 Marshall Faulk UF 2.50 6.00
181 Peyton Manning FR RC 8.00 20.00
182 Ryan Leaf FR RC 1.00 2.50
183 Andre Wadsworth FR RC .60 1.50
184 Charles Woodson FR RC 1.00 2.50
185 Curtis Enis FR RC .40 1.00
186 Grant Wistrom FR RC .60 1.50
187 Greg Ellis FR RC .40 1.00
188 Fred Taylor FR RC 1.25 3.00
189 Duane Starks FR RC .40 1.00
190 Keith Brooking FR RC 1.00 2.50
191 Takeo Spikes FR RC 1.00 2.50
192 Jason Peter FR RC .40 1.00
193 Anthony Simmons FR RC .60 1.50
194 Kevin Dyson FR RC 1.00 2.50
195 Brian Simmons FR RC .60 1.50
196 Robert Edwards FR RC .60 1.50
197 Randy Moss FR RC 6.00 15.00
198 John Avery FR RC .60 1.50
199 Marcus Nash FR RC .40 1.00
200 Jerome Pathon FR RC 1.00 2.50
201 Jacquez Green FR RC .60 1.50
202 Robert Holcombe FR RC .60 1.50
203 Pat Johnson FR RC .60 1.50
204 Germane Crowell FR RC .60 1.50
205 Joe Jurevicius FR RC 1.00 2.50
206 Skip Hicks FR RC .60 1.50
207 Ahman Green FR RC 2.00 5.00
208 Brian Griese FR RC 1.50 4.00
209 Hines Ward FR RC 4.00 8.00
210 Tavian Banks FR RC .60 1.50
211 Warrick Dunn NR 3.00 8.00
212 Jake Plummer NR 3.00 8.00
213 Derrick Mayes NR 2.00 5.00
214 Napoleon Kaufman NR 3.00 8.00
215 Jamal Anderson NR 3.00 8.00
216 Marvin Harrison NR 3.00 8.00
217 Jermaine Lewis NR 2.00 5.00
218 Corey Dillon NR 3.00 8.00
219 Keyshawn Johnson NR 3.00 8.00
220 Mike Alstott NR 3.00 8.00
221 Bobby Hoying NR 2.00 5.00
222 Keenan McCardell NR 2.00 5.00
223 Will Blackwell NR 1.25 3.00
224 Peter Boulware NR 1.25 3.00
225 Tony Banks NR 2.00 5.00
226 Rod Smith NR 2.00 5.00
227 Tony Gonzalez NR 3.00 8.00
228 Antowain Smith NR 1.25 3.00
229 Rae Carruth NR 1.25 3.00
230 J.J. Stokes NR 2.00 5.00
231 Brad Johnson NR 3.00 8.00
232 Shawn Springs NR 1.25 3.00
233 Elvis Grbac NR 1.25 3.00
234 Jimmy Smith NR 2.00 5.00
235 Terry Glenn NR 3.00 8.00
236 Tiki Barber NR 2.00 5.00
237 Gus Frerotte NR 1.25 3.00
238 Danny Wuerffel NR 2.00 5.00
239 Fred Lane NR 1.25 3.00
240 Todd Collins NR 1.25 3.00
241 Barry Sanders UR 12.50 30.00
242 Troy Aikman UR 7.50 20.00
243 Dan Marino UR 15.00 40.00
244 Drew Bledsoe UR 6.00 15.00
245 Dorsey Levens UR 4.00 10.00
246 Jerome Bettis UR 4.00 10.00
247 John Elway UR 15.00 40.00
248 Steve Young UR 5.00 12.00
249 Terrell Davis UR 4.00 10.00
250 Kordell Stewart UR 2.50 6.00
251 Jeff George UR 2.50 6.00
252 Emmitt Smith UR 12.50 30.00
253 Irving Fryar UR 2.50 6.00
254 Brett Favre UR 15.00 40.00
255 Eddie George UR 4.00 10.00
256 Terry Allen UR 4.00 10.00
257 Warren Moon UR 4.00 10.00
258 Mark Brunell UR 4.00 10.00
259 Robert Smith UR 4.00 10.00
260 Jerry Rice UR 7.50 20.00
261 Tim Brown UR 4.00 10.00
262 Carl Pickens UR 2.50 6.00
263 Joey Galloway UR 2.50 6.00
264 Herman Moore UR 2.50 6.00
265 Adrian Murrell UR 2.50 6.00
266 Thurman Thomas UR 4.00 10.00
267 Robert Brooks UR 2.50 6.00
268 Michael Irvin UR 4.00 10.00
269 Andre Rison UR 2.50 6.00
270 Marshall Faulk UR 5.00 12.00
P243 Dan Marino UR Promo 1.25 3.00
(no card number on back)

1998 UD3 Die Cuts

COMP.EMB.DIE CUT (90) 200.00 400.00
*EMB.DIE CUT 1-30: SAME PRICE
*EMB.DIE CUT 31-60: .5X TO 1.2X HI COL.
*EMB.DIE CUT 61-90: 1.2X TO 3X HI COL.
EMBOSSED PRINT RUN 2000 SERIAL #'d SETS
*FX DIE CUT 91-120: .5X TO 1.2X HI COL.
*FX DIE CUT 121-150: 2X TO 5X HI COL.
*FX DIE CUT 151-180: .5X TO 1.2X HI COL.
FX STATED PRINT RUN 1000 SETS
*RAINBOW DIE CUT 181-210: 6X TO 15X HI
*RAINBOW DIE CUT 211-240: 2X TO 5X HI
*RAINBOW DIE CUT 241-270: 1.5X TO 4X
RAINBOW PRINT RUN 100 SETS

2002 UD Authentics

Released in mid-September 2002, this set contains 90 veterans, 50 rookies, and 8 flashback cards. The Missing Rookies flashback cards are serial #'d to either 1989 or 1990. Boxes contained 18 packs of 5 cards. SRP was $6.99 per pack.

COMP.SET w/o SP's (90) 10.00 25.00
1 Jake Plummer .25 .60
2 David Boston .25 .60
3 Thomas Jones .25 .60
4 Michael Vick .30 .75
5 Warrick Dunn .25 .60
6 Jamal Lewis .30 .75
7 Chris Redman .25 .60
8 Travis Taylor .25 .60
9 Drew Bledsoe .30 .75
10 Eric Moulds .25 .60
11 Travis Henry .25 .60
12 Chris Weinke .25 .60
13 Muhsin Muhammad .25 .60
14 Anthony Thomas .30 .75
15 Jim Miller .25 .60
16 Marty Booker .25 .60
17 Corey Dillon .25 .60
18 Jon Kitna .25 .60
19 Peter Warrick .25 .60
20 Tim Couch .25 .60
21 Emmitt Smith .60 1.50
22 Joey Galloway .30 .75
23 Quincy Carter .25 .60
24 Brian Griese .25 .60
25 Terrell Davis .30 .75
26 Shannon Sharpe .30 .75
27 Germane Crowell .25 .60
28 James Stewart .25 .60
29 Az-Zahir Hakim .25 .60
30 Brett Favre .75 2.00
31 Ahman Green .30 .75
32 Terry Glenn .30 .75
33 Jermaine Lewis .25 .60
34 James Allen .25 .60
35 Corey Bradford .25 .60
36 Edgerrin James .30 .75
37 Marvin Harrison .30 .75
38 Peyton Manning 1.00 2.50
39 Jimmy Smith .30 .75
40 Mark Brunell .30 .75
41 Trent Green .25 .60
42 Johnnie Morton .30 .75
43 Priest Holmes .25 .60
44 Ricky Williams .30 .75
45 Chris Chambers .25 .60
46 Jay Fiedler .30 .75
47 Daunte Culpepper .30 .75
48 Randy Moss .30 .75
49 Michael Bennett .25 .60
50 Troy Brown .25 .60
51 Antowain Smith .30 .75
52 Tom Brady 2.00 5.00
53 Aaron Brooks .25 .60
54 Deuce McAllister .30 .75
55 Joe Horn .25 .60
56 Amani Toomer .25 .60
57 Kerry Collins .25 .60
58 Ron Dayne .30 .75
59 Chad Pennington .25 .60
60 Curtis Martin .30 .75
61 Vinny Testaverde .25 .60
62 Jerry Rice .75 2.00
63 Rich Gannon .30 .75
64 Tim Brown .40 1.00
65 Donovan McNabb .30 .75
66 Duce Staley .25 .60
67 James Thrash .30 .75
68 Plaxico Burress .25 .60
69 Jerome Bettis .40 1.00
70 Kordell Stewart .25 .60
71 Doug Flutie .30 .75
72 Drew Brees .75 2.00
73 LaDainian Tomlinson .40 1.00
74 Garrison Hearst .25 .60
75 Jeff Garcia .25 .60
76 Terrell Owens .30 .75
77 Ricky Watters .30 .75
78 Shaun Alexander .25 .60
79 Trent Dilfer .25 .60
80 Isaac Bruce .40 1.00
81 Kurt Warner .30 .75
82 Marshall Faulk .30 .75
83 Keyshawn Johnson .30 .75
84 Michael Pittman .30 .75
85 Brad Johnson .30 .75
86 Eddie George .30 .75
87 Jevon Kearse .25 .60
88 Steve McNair .30 .75
89 Shane Matthews .25 .60
90 Stephen Davis .25 .60
91 Josh McCown RC 2.00 5.00
92 Kurt Kittner RC 1.25 3.00
93 T.J. Duckett RC 1.25 3.00
94 Wes Pate RC 1.25 3.00
95 Chester Taylor RC 2.00 5.00
96 Ron Johnson RC 1.50 4.00
97 Lamont Brightful RC 1.25 3.00
98 Josh Reed RC 1.50 4.00
99 Randy Fasani RC 1.25 3.00
100 DeShaun Foster RC 2.00 5.00
101 Julius Peppers RC 3.00 8.00
102 William Green RC 1.50 4.00
103 Andre Davis RC 1.25 3.00
104 Chad Hutchinson RC 1.25 3.00
105 Antonio Bryant RC 2.00 5.00
106 Roy Williams RC 1.25 3.00
107 Clinton Portis RC 2.00 5.00
108 Herb Haygood RC 1.25 3.00
109 Ashley Lelie RC 1.25 3.00
110 Joey Harrington RC 1.25 3.00
111 Luke Staley RC 1.25 3.00
112 Javon Walker RC 2.00 5.00
113 David Carr RC 1.25 3.00
114 Jonathan Wells RC 1.50 4.00
115 Jabar Gaffney RC 1.25 3.00
116 Brian Allen RC 1.25 3.00
117 David Garrard RC 1.50 4.00
118 Leonard Henry RC 1.25 3.00
119 Rohan Davey RC 2.00 5.00
120 Deion Branch RC 2.00 5.00
121 J.T. O'Sullivan RC 1.50 4.00
122 Donte Stallworth RC 2.00 5.00
123 Tim Carter RC 1.50 4.00
124 Daryl Jones RC 1.25 3.00
125 Ronald Curry RC 1.25 3.00
126 Napoleon Harris RC 1.50 4.00
127 Brian Westbrook RC 2.50 6.00
128 Antwaan Randle El RC 1.50 4.00
129 Reche Caldwell RC 1.50 4.00
130 Quentin Jammer RC 2.00 5.00
131 Brandon Doman RC 1.25 3.00
132 Maurice Morris RC 1.50 4.00
133 Eric Crouch RC 2.00 5.00
134 Lamar Gordon RC 1.50 4.00
135 Travis Stephens RC 1.25 3.00
136 Marquise Walker RC 1.25 3.00
137 Jake Schifino RC 1.25 3.00
138 Patrick Ramsey RC 1.50 4.00
139 Ladell Betts RC 2.00 5.00
140 Cliff Russell RC 1.25 3.00
141 Chris Chandler MR/1989 1.25 3.00
142 Tim Brown MR/1989 1.50 4.00
143 Wesley Walls MR/1989 1.25 3.00
144 Rod Woodson MR/1989 1.50 4.00
145 Rich Gannon MR/1990 1.25 3.00
146 Emmitt Smith MR/1990 2.50 6.00
147 Junior Seau MR/1990 1.25 3.00
148 Shannon Sharpe MR/1990 1.25 3.00

2002 UD Authentics Gold 25

*1-90 VETS: 8X TO 20X BASIC CARDS
*91-140 ROOKIES: 1X TO 2.5X BASIC CARDS
*141-149 FLASHBACK: 2X TO 5X
STATED PRINT RUN 25 SER.#'d SETS

2002 UD Authentics All-Star Authentics

Inserted at a rate of 1:18, this set features a swatch of game used memorabilia. There is also a gold parallel available that is serial #'d to 25.

STATED ODDS 1:18
*GOLD/25: 1.2X TO 3X BASIC JSY
GOLD PRINT RUN 25 SER.#'d SETS
AABL Drew Bledsoe 3.00 8.00
AABO David Boston 2.50 6.00
AACB Courtney Brown 2.50 6.00
AACM Curtis Martin 3.00 8.00
AACS Corey Simon 2.50 6.00
AADF Doug Flutie 3.00 8.00
AADW Darren Woodson 3.00 8.00
AAEJ Edgerrin James 3.00 8.00
AAEM Eric Moulds 2.50 6.00
AAJP Jake Plummer 2.50 6.00
AAJS Junior Seau 3.00 8.00
AAPH Priest Holmes 2.50 6.00
AAPP Peerless Price 2.50 6.00
AARG Rod Gardner 2.50 6.00
AASD Stephen Davis 2.50 6.00
AASM Steve McNair 3.00 8.00
AATC Tim Couch 2.50 6.00
AATJ Thomas Jones 2.50 6.00
AATW Terrence Wilkins 2.50 6.00

2002 UD Authentics American Authentics Level 1

Inserted at a rate of 1:216, this set features authentic autographs on a card design resembling the American Flag. A few cards were issued in smaller quantity as notated next to the player's name in our checklist.

STATED ODDS 1:216
UNPRICED LEVEL 1 GOLD SER.#'d OF 15
*LEVEL 2: .8X TO 2X LEVEL 1
LEVEL 2 PRINT RUN 25 SER.#'d SETS
UNPRICED LEVEL 2 GOLD SER.#'d OF 5
ST1AT Anthony Thomas 7.50 20.00
ST1DC Daunte Culpepper/56* 20.00 40.00
ST1LT LaDainian Tomlinson SP 20.00 50.00
ST1PM Peyton Manning 50.00 100.00
ST1TG Tony Gonzalez/56* 20.00 40.00

2002 UD Authentics Glory Bound Jerseys

Inserted at a rate of 1:18, this set features a swatch of event used memorabilia from some of the NFL's top 2002 rookies.

STATED ODDDS 1:18
*GOLD/25: 1.2X TO 3X BASIC JSY
GOLD PRINT RUN 25 SER.#'d SETS
GBJAB Antonio Bryant 3.00 8.00
GBJAL Ashley Lelie 2.00 5.00
GBJCP Clinton Portis 3.00 8.00
GBJDC David Carr 2.00 5.00
GBJDF DeShaun Foster 3.00 8.00
GBJDG David Garrard 2.50 6.00
GBJDS Donte Stallworth 3.00 8.00
GBJJG Jabar Gaffney 2.00 5.00
GBJJH Joey Harrington 2.00 5.00
GBJJM Josh McCown 3.00 8.00
GBJJP Julius Peppers 5.00 12.00
GBJJR Josh Reed 2.50 6.00
GBJJW Javon Walker 3.00 8.00
GBJLB Ladell Betts 3.00 8.00
GBJMM Maurice Morris 2.50 6.00
GBJMW Marquise Walker 2.00 5.00
GBJPR Patrick Ramsey 2.50 6.00
GBJRD Rohan Davey 3.00 8.00
GBJRJ Ron Johnson 2.50 6.00
GBJRW Roy Williams 2.00 5.00
GBJTD T.J. Duckett 2.00 5.00
GBJTS Travis Stephens 2.00 5.00
GBJWG William Green 2.50 6.00

2002 UD Authentics Rumble Backs

Inserted at a rate of 1:18, this set showcases many of the NFL's premier running backs.

COMPLETE SET (20) 20.00 50.00
STATED ODDS 1:18
RB1 Emmitt Smith 2.00 5.00
RB2 Marshall Faulk 1.00 2.50
RB3 Edgerrin James 1.00 2.50
RB4 Terrell Davis 1.00 2.50
RB5 Anthony Thomas 1.00 2.50
RB6 LaDainian Tomlinson 1.25 3.00
RB7 Curtis Martin 1.00 2.50
RB8 Jerome Bettis 1.25 3.00
RB9 Ricky Watters 1.00 2.50
RB10 Ricky Williams 1.00 2.50
RB11 Eddie George 1.00 2.50
RB12 Jamal Lewis 1.00 2.50
RB13 Corey Dillon .75 2.00
RB14 Warrick Dunn .75 2.00
RB15 Ahman Green 1.00 2.50
RB16 Priest Holmes .75 2.00
RB17 Duce Staley .75 2.00
RB18 Michael Bennett .75 2.00
RB19 Deuce McAllister 1.00 2.50
RB20 Ron Dayne 1.00 2.50

2009 UD Black

1-90 VETERAN PRINT RUN 250
91-131 ROOKIE AU PRINT RUN 199-399
1 Greg Jennings 5.00 12.00
2 Darrell Green 6.00 15.00
3 Larry Fitzgerald 6.00 15.00
4 Kurt Warner 6.00 15.00
5 Matt Ryan 6.00 15.00
6 Michael Turner 5.00 12.00
7 Bubba Smith 5.00 12.00
8 Ray Lewis 8.00 20.00
9 Thurman Thomas 6.00 15.00
10 Ed Reed 6.00 15.00
11 Jim Kelly 8.00 20.00
12 Jerry Kramer 6.00 15.00
13 Jonathan Stewart 5.00 12.00
14 Deacon Jones 6.00 15.00
15 Billy Sims 6.00 15.00
16 Anthony Munoz 6.00 15.00
17 Ken Anderson 6.00 15.00
18 Mike Ditka 8.00 20.00
19 Gale Sayers 8.00 20.00
20 Matt Forte 5.00 12.00
21 Jack Youngblood 5.00 12.00
22 Marshawn Lynch 6.00 15.00
23 Jerricho Cotchery 5.00 12.00
24 Roger Staubach 12.00 30.00
25 Emmitt Smith 12.00 30.00
26 Bob Lilly 6.00 15.00
27 Daryl Johnston 6.00 15.00
28 Randy White 8.00 20.00
29 Troy Aikman 10.00 25.00
30 Tony Romo 10.00 25.00
31 Merlin Olsen 5.00 12.00
32 Paul Hornung 8.00 20.00
33 Felix Jones 5.00 12.00
34 DeMarcus Ware 6.00 15.00
35 Brandon Marshall 6.00 15.00
36 Lem Barney 5.00 12.00
37 John Elway 15.00 40.00
38 Calvin Johnson 8.00 20.00
39 Barry Sanders 10.00 25.00
40 Kevin Smith 5.00 12.00
41 Aaron Rodgers 15.00 40.00
42 Andre Johnson 6.00 15.00
43 Steve Slaton 5.00 12.00
44 Peyton Manning 15.00 40.00
45 Earl Campbell 8.00 20.00
46 Reggie Wayne 6.00 15.00
47 Maurice Jones-Drew 5.00 12.00
48 Dwayne Bowe 6.00 15.00
49 Bob Griese 6.00 15.00
50 Joey Porter 6.00 15.00
51 Ron Yary 5.00 12.00
52 Adrian Peterson 8.00 20.00
53 Alan Page 5.00 12.00
54 Tom Brady 25.00 60.00
55 Matt Cassel 5.00 12.00
56 Drew Brees 8.00 20.00
57 Brandon Jacobs 5.00 12.00
58 Marques Colston 5.00 12.00
59 Lawrence Taylor 8.00 20.00
60 Eli Manning 6.00 15.00
61 Don Maynard 6.00 15.00
62 Brett Favre 15.00 40.00
63 Jason Campbell 5.00 12.00
64 Fred Biletnikoff 8.00 20.00
65 Kellen Winslow Sr. 6.00 15.00
66 Darren McFadden 8.00 20.00
67 Brian Dawkins 5.00 12.00
68 Brian Westbrook 5.00 12.00
69 Chuck Bednarik 6.00 15.00
70 L.C. Greenwood 5.00 12.00
71 Ronnie Brown 5.00 12.00
72 Ben Roethlisberger 12.00 30.00
73 Terry Bradshaw 10.00 25.00
74 Harry Carson 5.00 12.00
75 Franco Harris 8.00 20.00
76 Rocky Bleier 6.00 15.00
77 Jack Ham 6.00 15.00
78 Ronnie Lott 6.00 15.00
79 LaDainian Tomlinson 8.00 20.00
80 Antonio Gates 6.00 15.00
81 Steve Young 10.00 25.00
82 Jerry Rice 15.00 40.00
83 Roger Craig 6.00 15.00
84 Frank Gore 6.00 15.00
85 Tom Rathman 5.00 12.00
86 Jim Zorn 5.00 12.00
87 Derrick Brooks 5.00 12.00
88 Chris Johnson 5.00 12.00
89 Joe Theismann 8.00 20.00
90 Clinton Portis 5.00 12.00
91 Andre Smith AU/399 RC 5.00 12.00
92 Nate Davis AU/399 RC 5.00 12.00
93 Jason Smith AU/399 RC 5.00 12.00
94 B.J. Raji AU/399 RC 10.00 25.00
95 James Davis AU/399 RC 5.00 12.00
96 Donald Brown AU/199 RC 12.00 30.00
97 Mike Wallace AU/399 RC 8.00 20.00
98 Percy Harvin AU/399 RC 12.00 30.00
99 Glen Coffee AU/399 RC 5.00 12.00
100 M.Stafford AU/199 RC 40.00 100.00
101 K.Moreno AU/199 RC 6.00 15.00
102 M.Massaquoi AU/399 RC 5.00 12.00
103 Vontae Davis AU/399 RC 5.00 12.00
104 Shonn Greene AU/399 RC 5.00 12.00
105 Josh Freeman AU/199 RC 6.00 15.00
106 Mike Goodson AU/399 RC 6.00 15.00
107 Brandon Tate AU/399 RC 6.00 15.00
108 D.Heyward-Bey AU/399 RC 8.00 20.00
109 Javon Ringer AU/399 RC 5.00 12.00
110 Derrick Williams AU/399 RC 5.00 12.00
111 Clay Matthews AU/399 RC 30.00 60.00
112 Jeremy Maclin AU/199 RC 8.00 20.00
113 Patrick Turner AU/399 RC 5.00 12.00
114 Hakeem Nicks AU/399 RC 6.00 15.00
115 Chris Wells AU/199 RC 15.00 40.00
116 J.Laurinaitis AU/399 RC 5.00 12.00
117 Malcolm Jenkins AU/399 RC 5.00 12.00
118 B.Pettigrew AU/399 RC 5.00 12.00
119 Juaquin Iglesias AU/399 RC 5.00 12.00
120 LeSean McCoy AU/199 RC 15.00 40.00
122 Ramses Barden AU/399 RC 5.00 12.00
123 Brian Orakpo AU/399 RC 6.00 15.00
124 M.Crabtree AU/199 RC 10.00 25.00
125 Brian Cushing AU/399 RC 5.00 12.00
126 Mark Sanchez AU/399 RC 15.00 40.00
127 Rey Maualuga AU/399 RC 8.00 20.00
128 S.McGee AU/399 RC 5.00 12.00
129 Eugene Monroe AU/399 RC 5.00 12.00
130 Alphonso Smith AU/399 RC 5.00 12.00
131 Aaron Curry AU/399 RC 8.00 20.00
132 Pat White AU/399 RC 6.00 15.00

2009 UD Black Autographs

STATED PRINT RUN 10-75
SERIAL #'d UNDER 25 NOT PRICED
1 Greg Jennings/75 15.00 40.00
2 Darrell Green/25 30.00 60.00
7 Bubba Smith/75 15.00 40.00
8 Ray Lewis/25 60.00 120.00
9 Thurman Thomas/25 20.00 50.00
11 Jim Kelly/25 50.00 100.00
12 Jerry Kramer/75 15.00 40.00
13 Jonathan Stewart/25 12.00 30.00
14 Deacon Jones/75 15.00 40.00
15 Billy Sims/75 15.00 40.00
16 Anthony Munoz/25 20.00 50.00
17 Ken Anderson/75 12.00 30.00
19 Gale Sayers/25 30.00 60.00
20 Matt Forte/35 12.00 30.00
21 Jack Youngblood/75 12.00 30.00
22 Marshawn Lynch/25 12.00 30.00
26 Bob Lilly/50 15.00 40.00
27 Daryl Johnston/75 15.00 40.00
28 Randy White/25 20.00 50.00
31 Merlin Olsen/25 15.00 40.00
32 Paul Hornung/75 15.00 40.00
34 DeMarcus Ware/50 15.00 40.00
35 Brandon Marshall/25 15.00 40.00
36 Lem Barney/75 12.00 30.00
40 Kevin Smith/75 10.00 25.00
43 Steve Slaton/50 10.00 25.00
44 Peyton Manning/25 100.00 175.00
45 Earl Campbell/50 20.00 50.00
46 Reggie Wayne/25 20.00 50.00
47 Maurice Jones-Drew/50 15.00 40.00
48 Dwayne Bowe/35 15.00 40.00
49 Bob Griese/25 25.00 60.00
50 Joey Porter/75 12.00 30.00
51 Ron Yary/75 12.00 30.00
53 Alan Page/50 12.00 30.00
57 Brandon Jacobs/25 12.00 30.00
58 Marques Colston/75 15.00 40.00
59 Lawrence Taylor/25 30.00 60.00
60 Eli Manning/25 50.00 100.00
61 Don Maynard/50 12.00 30.00
63 Jason Campbell/25 12.00 30.00
64 Fred Biletnikoff/35 25.00 60.00
65 Kellen Winslow Sr./50 12.00 30.00
68 Brian Westbrook/25 12.00 30.00
70 L.C. Greenwood/75 20.00 50.00
71 Ronnie Brown/25 12.00 30.00
74 Harry Carson/75 12.00 30.00
76 Rocky Bleier/75 20.00 50.00
77 Jack Ham/25 30.00 80.00
78 Ronnie Lott/50 15.00 40.00
83 Roger Craig/75 15.00 40.00
85 Tom Rathman/75 15.00 40.00
86 Jim Zorn/75 12.00 30.00
87 Derrick Brooks/50 15.00 40.00
88 Chris Johnson/50 25.00 50.00
89 Joe Theismann/25 20.00 50.00
90 Clinton Portis/25 12.00 30.00

2009 UD Black Biography Plaque Autographs

STATED PRINT RUN 5-50
SERIAL #'d UNDER 25 NOT PRICED
BPSBL Bob Lilly/50 15.00 40.00
BPSDJ Deacon Jones/50 15.00 40.00
BPSGJ Greg Jennings/50 20.00 50.00
BPSGS Gale Sayers/25 30.00 60.00
BPSJA Jared Allen/50 30.00 60.00
BPSJK Jim Kelly/25 50.00 100.00
BPSJT Joe Theismann/25 20.00 50.00
BPSJY Jack Youngblood/50 12.00 30.00
BPSKA Ken Anderson/50 12.00 30.00
BPSKW Kurt Warner/25 40.00 80.00
BPSLA Steve Largent/25 25.00 60.00
BPSLT Lawrence Taylor/25 25.00 60.00
BPSMC Marques Colston/50 20.00 50.00
BPSMR Matt Ryan/25 40.00 80.00
BPSMT Michael Turner/25 12.00 30.00
BPSPA Alan Page/50 12.00 30.00
BPSPM Peyton Manning/25 100.00 200.00
BPSRB Rocky Bleier/25 25.00 60.00
BPSRW Randy White/50 15.00 40.00
BPSSL Steve Slaton/25 12.00 30.00

2009 UD Black Cut Autographs

CUT AUTO PRINT RUN 1-172
SERIAL #'d UNDER 15 NOT PRICED
BCAW Arnie Weinmeister/18 40.00 80.00
BCBA Red Badgro/28 30.00 60.00
BCBB Bert Bell/32 30.00 60.00
BCBN Bronko Nagurski/17 150.00 225.00
BCCC Charley Conerly/172 25.00 50.00
BCCH Clarke Hinkle/15 100.00 200.00
BCDL Dick Lane/25 40.00 80.00
BCEH Elroy Hirsch/85 20.00 50.00
BCES Ernie Stautner/24 20.00 50.00
BCFG Frank Gatski/43 20.00 50.00
BCGC George Connor/81 20.00 50.00
BCGM George McAfee/88 20.00 50.00
BCGU Gene Upshaw/35 30.00 60.00
BCJP Jim Parker/24 30.00 60.00
BCLA Dante Lavelli/85 20.00 50.00
BCLC Lou Creekmur/34 20.00 50.00
BCLG Lou Groza/22 30.00 60.00
BCLN Leo Nomellini/21 30.00 60.00
BCMU George Musso/37 20.00 50.00
BCOG Otto Graham/20 40.00 80.00
BCRF Ray Flaherty/15 40.00 80.00
BCRN Ray Nitschke/18 75.00 150.00
BCSB Sammy Baugh/53 40.00 80.00
BCTC Tony Canadeo/34 20.00 50.00
BCTF Tom Fears/21 30.00 60.00
BCTL Tom Landry/26 125.00 250.00
BCWE Weeb Ewbank/42 20.00 50.00

2009 UD Black Dual Autographs

STATED PRINT RUN 5-35
BG S.Greene/D.Brown/25 15.00 40.00
BM D.Brees/A.Manning/25 75.00 150.00
CJ B.Jacobs/E.Campbell/35 20.00 50.00
CS C.Johnson/Slaton/35 30.00 60.00
FD J.Freeman/Davis/25 15.00 40.00
HB Heyward-By/Britt/35 15.00 40.00
HC M.Crabtree/G.Harrell/25 20.00 50.00
JD J.Ringer/D.Moore/35 15.00 40.00
JL Laurinaitis/M.Jenkins/35 15.00 40.00
JO D.Jones/M.Olsen/35 30.00 60.00
JW D.Ware/E.Jones/35 40.00 80.00
LH C.Howley/B.Lilly/35 30.00 60.00
MC Coffman/J.Maclin/35 15.00 40.00
MS Sanchez/Maualuga/25 25.00 60.00
MW K.Moreno/C.Wells/25 20.00 50.00
NF B.Foster/Nicks/35 20.00 50.00
PC Pettigrew/J.Cook/35 10.00 25.00
PK A.Karras/A.Page/25 25.00 50.00
PW Portis/Westbrook/25 15.00 40.00
SF M.Forte/J.Stewart/35 25.00 50.00
SM Morono/Stafford/25 50.00 120.00
SS Stafford/Sanchez/25 40.00 100.00
WR C.Wells/B.Robiskie/25 25.00 50.00

2009 UD Black Dual Player Autographs on Jersey

DUAL JSY AU PRINT RUN 15-25
SERIAL #'d UNDER 25 NOT PRICED
DPCS E.Campbell/Slaton/25 50.00 100.00
DPEL L.Evans/M.Lynch/25 20.00 40.00

2009 UD Black Film Slides Autographs

ATED PRINT RUN 9-75
FSAP Adrian Peterson/28 100.00 200.00
FSBL Rocky Bleier/50 30.00 60.00
FSBS Barry Sanders/20 75.00 135.00
FSCP Clinton Portis/26 12.00 30.00
FSES Emmitt Smith/22 100.00 175.00
FSFB Fred Biletnikoff/50 20.00 50.00
FSFH Franco Harris/32 25.00 60.00
FSJT Joe Theismann/50 15.00 40.00
FSLB Lem Barney/75 12.00 30.00
FSLT Lawrence Taylor/15 30.00 80.00
FSMF Matt Forte/22 12.00 30.00
FSMR Matt Ryan/25 40.00 80.00
FSMT Michael Turner/25 12.00 30.00
FSPM Peyton Manning/18 75.00 135.00
FSRB Ronnie Brown/23 12.00 30.00
FSRY Ron Yary/75 12.00 30.00
FSSL Steve Largent/25 25.00 60.00
FSTO LaDainian Tomlinson/21 30.00 60.00

2009 UD Black Lustrous Materials Patch Autographs

STATED PRINT RUN 5-30
SERIAL #'d UNDER 25 NOT PRICED
LPAB Anquan Boldin/30 20.00 50.00
LPBJ Brandon Jacobs/50 12.00 30.00
LPBM Brandon Marshall/50 15.00 40.00
LPBW Brian Westbrook/50 15.00 40.00
LPCP Clinton Portis/50 10.00 25.00
LPDB Dwayne Bowe/50 15.00 40.00
LPDM Donovan McNabb/15 25.00 60.00
LPFG Frank Gore/30 20.00 50.00
LPGJ Greg Jennings/50 20.00 50.00
LPJO Chris Johnson/50 15.00 40.00
LPJT Joe Theismann/50 20.00 50.00
LPKS Kevin Smith/50 12.00 30.00
LPKW Kurt Warner/30 50.00 100.00
LPMC Marques Colston/50 20.00 50.00
LPMF Matt Forte/50 15.00 40.00
LPMJ Maurice Jones-Drew/50 15.00 40.00
LPMR Matt Ryan/30 40.00 80.00
LPMS Mike Singletary/50 30.00 60.00
LPPM Peyton Manning/50 100.00 175.00
LPTR Tony Romo/30 50.00 100.00

2009 UD Black Quad Autographs

STATED PRINT RUN 20
ROOKQB Frm/Snch/Stf/Dvs/20 75.00 200.00
ROOKRB Mrn/Wls/McC/Brwn 50.00 120.00
ROOKWR Nks/Crbt/Mcln/Hrv/20 20.00 50.00

2009 UD Black Quad Jersey Autographs

STATED PRINT RUN 5-75
UNPRICED 1/1 PATCHES EXIST
SERIAL #'d UNDER 25 NOT PRICED
1PQAH A.J. Hawk/75 12.00 30.00
1PQBJ Bo Jackson/34 50.00 100.00
1PQBY Billy Sims/75 10.00 25.00
1PQCP Clinton Portis/25 20.00 50.00
1PQFG Frank Gore/50 15.00 40.00
1PQJO Chris Johnson/75 20.00 50.00
1PQJS Jonathan Stewart/75 12.00 30.00
1PQKA Ken Anderson/25 20.00 50.00
1PQKW Kellen Winslow Sr./75 12.00 30.00
1PQML Marshawn Lynch/25 12.00 30.00
1PQMR Matt Ryan/25 40.00 80.00
1PQPS Phil Simms/75 15.00 40.00
1PQRB Ronnie Brown/25 15.00 40.00
1PQRC Roger Craig/75 15.00 40.00
1PQSS Steve Slaton/50 10.00 25.00
1PQTA Troy Aikman/25 50.00 100.00
1PQTR Tony Romo/25 40.00 80.00

2009 UD Black Quad Jersey Autographs Patch

QUAD PATCH AUTO PRINT RUN 5-50
SERIAL #'d UNDER 25 NOT PRICED
1PQAH A.J. Hawk/50 12.00 30.00
1PQBY Billy Sims/50 15.00 40.00
1PQDB Derrick Brooks/50 25.00 60.00
1PQFG Frank Gore/25 15.00 40.00
1PQGJ Greg Jennings/25 20.00 50.00
1PQJH Jack Ham/25 20.00 50.00
1PQJO Chris Johnson/50 15.00 40.00
1PQJS Jonathan Stewart/50 15.00 40.00
1PQKA Ken Anderson/25 15.00 40.00
1PQKW Kellen Winslow Sr./25 20.00 50.00
1PQMF Matt Forte/50 30.00 60.00
1PQML Marshawn Lynch/50 15.00 40.00
1PQMR Matt Ryan/25 50.00 100.00
1PQPS Phil Simms/35 20.00 50.00
1PQRB Ronnie Brown/26 20.00 50.00
1PQRC Roger Craig/50 15.00 40.00
1PQSS Steve Slaton/25 15.00 40.00
1PQTR Tony Romo/25 40.00 80.00

2009 UD Black Triple Autographs

TRIPLE AUTO PRINT RUN 5-25
HGW Hill/Willis/Gore/25 40.00 80.00
PHI McNb/Wstbrk/Jcksn/15 50.00 100.00
RAM Olsen/Gabriel/Jones/25 40.00 80.00
RBS Grne/Ringr/Moore/25 25.00 60.00
RUN Wells/McCoy/Moreno/15 40.00 100.00
NFCE Wstbrk/Prts/Jcbs/25 25.00 60.00
PASS Sanchez/Harrell/Staff/15 75.00 150.00
CATCH Crbtr/Mcln/Hrvn/15 25.00 60.00
GENES A.Mann/Peyton/Eli/15 250.00 400.00

2011 UD Black Lustrous Rookie Materials Signatures

1-7 STATED PRINT RUN 35
8-35 STATED PRINT RUN 75
INSERTS IN 2011 EXQUISITE COLL
EXCH EXPIRATION: 7/31/2014
1 Jake Locker/35 10.00 25.00
2 Mark Ingram/35 15.00 40.00
3 A.J. Green/35 40.00 100.00
4 Cam Newton/35 100.00 200.00
5 Blaine Gabbert/35 10.00 25.00
6 Julio Jones/35 40.00 100.00
7 Christian Ponder/35 10.00 25.00
8 Ryan Williams/75 25.00 50.00
9 Randall Cobb/75 12.00 30.00
10 Greg Salas/75 8.00 20.00
11 Jerrel Jernigan/75 8.00 20.00
12 Leonard Hankerson/75 8.00 20.00
13 Kendall Hunter/75 8.00 20.00
14 Niles Paul/75 10.00 25.00
15 Dion Lewis/75 10.00 25.00
16 DeMarco Murray/75 EXCH 15.00 40.00
17 Tandon Doss/75 8.00 20.00
18 Ronald Johnson/75 8.00 20.00
19 Greg Little/75 10.00 25.00
20 Titus Young/75 8.00 20.00
21 Vincent Brown/75 8.00 20.00
22 Mikel Leshoure/75 8.00 20.00
23 Jacquizz Rodgers/75 8.00 20.00
24 Jonathan Baldwin/75 15.00 40.00
25 Roy Helu/75 8.00 20.00
26 Shane Vereen/75 10.00 25.00
27 Torrey Smith/75 8.00 20.00
28 Austin Pettis/75 8.00 20.00
29 Ryan Mallett/75 8.00 20.00
30 Kyle Rudolph/75 8.00 20.00
31 Daniel Thomas/75 8.00 20.00
32 Andy Dalton/75 15.00 40.00
33 Colin Kaepernick/75 12.00 30.00
34 Delone Carter/75 8.00 20.00
35 Dwayne Harris/75 8.00 20.00

2011 UD Black Signatures

SERTS IN 2011 EXQUISITE COLL
BAC Anthony Carter/60 10.00 25.00
BAD Andy Dalton/60 20.00 50.00
BAG Archie Griffin/45 25.00 50.00
BAP Adrian Peterson/45 40.00 80.00
BAR Aaron Rodgers/60 100.00 200.00
BAW Andre Ware/60 12.00 30.00
BBB Brian Bosworth/60 15.00 40.00
BBG Blaine Gabbert/60 10.00 25.00
BBS Barry Sanders/45 50.00 120.00
BCC Cris Carter/60 15.00 40.00
BCK Colin Kaepernick/60 15.00 40.00
BCN Cam Newton/60 60.00 120.00
BCP Christian Ponder/45 10.00 25.00
BCW Charles White/60 10.00 25.00
BDB Drew Brees/45 40.00 80.00
BDF Doug Flutie/45 15.00 40.00
BDL Daryle Lamonica/60 10.00 25.00
BDM Dan Marino/45 90.00 175.00
BEG Eddie George/45 50.00 120.00
BEM Eric Metcalf/60 10.00 25.00
BGS Gale Sayers/45 25.00 50.00
BHW Herschel Walker/45 25.00 50.00
BJB Jonathan Baldwin/60 10.00 25.00
BJE John Elway/45 75.00 150.00
BJJ Julio Jones/45 40.00 100.00
BJL Jake Locker/60 10.00 25.00
BJO Johnny Rodgers/60 10.00 25.00
BJP Jim Plunkett/60 12.00 30.00
BJR Jerry Rice/45 60.00 120.00
BMI Mark Ingram/60 15.00 40.00
BON Ozzie Newsome/45 12.00 30.00
BRG Roman Gabriel/60 10.00 25.00
BRW Ryan Williams/60 10.00 25.00
BSO Steve Owens/60 10.00 25.00
BTA Troy Aikman/45 30.00 60.00
BTB Tim Brown/45 25.00 50.00
BTD Tony Dorsett/45 25.00 50.00
BTT Thurman Thomas/45 12.00 30.00
BTY Titus Young/60 10.00 25.00
BVM Von Miller/60 25.00 60.00
BWM Warren Moon/45 15.00 40.00

2012 UD Black Lustrous Legends Materials Signatures

BLL1 John Elway 60.00 120.00
BLL2 Dan Marino 90.00 150.00
BLL3 Drew Bledsoe 40.00 80.00
BLL4 Vinny Testaverde 15.00 40.00
BLL5 Bo Jackson
BLL7 Bart Starr 60.00 120.00
BLL9 Earl Campbell
BLL12 Daryle Lamonica 15.00 40.00

2012 UD Black Lustrous Rookie Materials Signatures

BRL1 Brandon Weeden 8.00 20.00
BRL2 Doug Martin 12.00 30.00
BRL3 Justin Blackmon 8.00 20.00
BRL4 Michael Floyd 8.00 20.00
BRL5 Robert Griffin III 10.00 25.00
BRL6 Ryan Tannehill 12.00 30.00
BRL7 Trent Richardson 20.00 50.00
BRL8 Kendall Wright 5.00 12.00
BRL9 Brock Osweiler 5.00 12.00
BRL10 Nick Foles 12.00 30.00
BRL11 A.J. Jenkins 5.00 12.00
BRL12 Case Keenum 10.00 25.00
BRL13 Kellen Moore 6.00 15.00
BRL14 Russell Wilson 100.00 200.00
BRL15 Kirk Cousins 20.00 50.00
BRL16 Isaiah Pead 5.00 12.00
BRL17 LaMichael James 5.00 12.00
BRL19 Coby Fleener 5.00 12.00
BRL20 Brian Quick 5.00 12.00
BRL21 Stephen Hill 5.00 12.00
BRL22 Alshon Jeffery 10.00 25.00
BRL23 Ryan Broyles 5.00 12.00
BRL24 Rueben Randle 5.00 12.00
BRL25 DeVier Posey 5.00 12.00
BRL26 Mohamed Sanu 8.00 20.00
BRL27 Travis Benjamin 5.00 12.00
BRL28 Jarius Wright 5.00 12.00
BRL29 Nick Toon 5.00 12.00
BRL30 Juron Criner 5.00 12.00

2012 UD Black Signatures

BAC Anthony Carter/65 8.00 20.00
UDBAJ Alshon Jeffery/65 12.00 30.00
UDBAR Aaron Rodgers/35 125.00 200.00
UDBAW Andre Ware/65 8.00 20.00
UDBBJ Bo Jackson/65 50.00 100.00
UDBBS Barry Sanders/35 75.00 150.00
UDBBW Brandon Weeden/65 8.00 20.00
UDBCW Charlie Ward/99 15.00 40.00
UDBDF Doug Flutie/65 10.00 25.00
UDBDM Doug Martin/65 12.00 30.00
UDBGB Gary Beban/65 8.00 20.00
UDBGR George Rogers/65 10.00 25.00
UDBHW Herschel Walker/65 15.00 40.00
UDBJB Justin Blackmon/65 8.00 20.00
UDBJE John Elway/35 60.00 120.00
UDBJL Johnny Lattner/65 8.00 20.00
UDBJN Joe Namath/35 50.00 100.00
UDBJP Jake Plummer/65 8.00 20.00
UDBJR Jerry Rice/35 60.00 120.00
UDBJW Jason White/65 8.00 20.00
UDBKM Ken MacAfee/99 6.00 15.00
UDBLJ LaMichael James/65 8.00 20.00
UDBMD Dan Marino/35 75.00 150.00
UDBMF Michael Floyd/65 12.00 30.00
UDBMR Mike Rozier/99 10.00 25.00
UDBMS Mohamed Sanu/65 10.00 25.00
UDBNT Nick Toon/99 8.00 20.00
UDBPH Paul Hornung/65 12.00 30.00
UDBRB Ryan Broyles/65 8.00 20.00
UDBRG Robert Griffin III/65 10.00 25.00
UDBRJ Johnny Rodgers/99 8.00 20.00
UDBRW Russell Wilson/65 75.00 150.00
UDBST Bart Starr/65 50.00 100.00
UDBSY Steve Young/35 40.00 80.00
UDBTA Troy Aikman/35 40.00 80.00
UDBTF Tommie Frazier/99 8.00 20.00
UDBTR Trent Richardson/65 8.00 20.00
UDBTT Tim Tebow/65 30.00 60.00
UDBVT Vinny Testaverde/65 12.00 30.00
UDBWJ Joe Washington/65 10.00 25.00

2013 UD Black Rookie Lustrous Jersey

INSERTED IN 2013 EXQUISITE COLLECTION
EXCH EXPIRATION: 5/20/2016
BRL1 Geno Smith/25 6.00 15.00
BRL2 Matt Barkley/25 6.00 15.00
BRL3 EJ Manuel/25 6.00 15.00
BRL4 Giovani Bernard/25 6.00 15.00
BRL5 Tavon Austin/25 8.00 20.00
BRL6 DeAndre Hopkins/25
BRL7 Manti Te'o/25 25.00 50.00
BRL8 Mike Glennon/75 5.00 12.00
BRL9 Ryan Nassib/75 5.00 12.00
BRL10 Zac Dysert/75 5.00 12.00
BRL11 Tyler Eifert/75 5.00 12.00
BRL12 C.Patterson/75 EXCH
BRL13 Justin Hunter/75 10.00 25.00
BRL14 Le'Veon Bell/75 25.00 50.00
BRL15 Robert Woods/75 EXCH 8.00 20.00
BRL16 Zach Ertz/75 10.00 25.00
BRL17 Aaron Dobson/75 5.00 12.00
BRL18 Marcus Lattimore/75 5.00 12.00
BRL19 Johnathan Franklin/75 5.00 12.00
BRL20 Landry Jones/75 EXCH
BRL21 Terrance Williams/75 5.00 12.00
BRL22 Keenan Allen/75 EXCH 10.00 25.00
BRL23 Denard Robinson/75 5.00 12.00
BRL24 Stedman Bailey/75 10.00 25.00
BRL25 Markus Wheaton/75 5.00 12.00
BRL26 Eddie Lacy/75 5.00 12.00
BRL27 Mike Gillislee/75 5.00 12.00
BRL28 Joseph Randle/75 5.00 12.00
BRL29 Kenny Stills/75 10.00 25.00
BRL30 Montee Ball/75 5.00 12.00

2014 UD Black Lustrous Legends Jersey Signatures

BLLEC Earl Campbell
BLLEG Eddie George
BLLHW Hines Ward 60.00 125.00
BLLJB Jerome Bettis
BLLJE John Elway
BLLMA Marcus Allen
BLLMS Matthew Stafford 75.00 150.00
BLLSY Steve Young
BLLTB Tim Brown
BLLTD Terrell Davis 10.00 25.00

2014 UD Black Rookie Lustrous Jersey Signatures

BRL1 Johnny Manziel/25
BRL2 Sammy Watkins/25
BRL3 Teddy Bridgewater/25
BRL4 Mike Evans/25 30.00 80.00
BRL5 Blake Bortles/25
BRL6 Brandin Cooks/25 20.00 50.00
BRL7 Derek Carr/25
BRL8 Aaron Murray/75 8.00 20.00
BRL9 Marqise Lee/75 10.00 25.00
BRL10 Carlos Hyde/75 EXCH 10.00 25.00
BRL11 Eric Ebron/75 10.00 25.00
BRL12 Tom Savage/75 8.00 20.00
BRL13 Jarvis Landry/75 15.00 40.00
BRL14 Bishop Sankey/75
BRL15 Paul Richardson/75 10.00 25.00
BRL16 Jimmy Garoppolo/75 60.00 150.00
BRL17 Bruce Ellington/75 8.00 20.00
BRL18 Jeremy Hill/75 10.00 25.00
BRL19 Josh Huff/75 10.00 25.00
BRL20 Logan Thomas/75 EXCH 8.00 20.00
BRL21 Kelvin Benjamin/75 EXCH 12.00 30.00
BRL22 Ka'Deem Carey/75 8.00 20.00
BRL23 Terrance West/75 8.00 20.00
BRL24 Michael Sam/75 8.00 20.00
BRL25 Allen Robinson/75 12.00 30.00
BRL26 De'Anthony Thomas/75 EXCH 8.00 20.00
BRL27 Lache Seastrunk/75 8.00 20.00
BRL28 Zach Mettenberger/75
BRL29 Davante Adams/75 12.00 30.00
BRL30 Charles Sims/75 8.00 20.00

2014 UD Black Signatures

UDBAG Ahman Green/60 10.00 25.00
UDBBC Brandin Cooks/30 15.00 40.00
UDBBI Bishop Sankey/60 12.00 30.00
UDBBK Bernie Kosar/30
UDBBW Brian Westbrook/30 10.00 25.00
UDBCC Chris Cooley/60 8.00 20.00

UDBDC Derek Carr/30 60.00 150.00
UDBDS Donnie Shell/60 8.00 20.00
UDBDT De'Anthony Thomas/60 8.00 20.00
UDBEE Eric Ebron/60 10.00 25.00
UDBGJ Jimmy Garoppolo/60 60.00 150.00
UDBJG Jeff Garcia/60 8.00 20.00
UDBJH Jeremy Hill/60 10.00 25.00
UDBKA Ken Anderson/60 10.00 25.00
UDBKB Kelvin Benjamin/30 15.00 40.00
UDBME Mike Evans/30 20.00 50.00
UDBML Marqise Lee/30 EXCH 12.00 30.00
UDBOB Odell Beckham Jr./30 100.00 200.00
UDBPW Peter Warrick/60 8.00 20.00
UDBRB Ronde Barber/60 8.00 20.00
UDBSS Steve Slaton/60 8.00 20.00
UDBSW Sammy Watkins/30 15.00 40.00
UDBTD Terrell Davis/30 6.00 15.00
UDBTS Tom Savage/60 8.00 20.00
UDBTW Terrance West/60 8.00 20.00
UDBZM Zach Mettenberger/60

1998 UD Choice Previews

The 1998 Upper Deck UD Choice Previews set was issued in one series totalling 55 cards. The cards were intended to give collectors a sneak preview of the "new" set that replaced Collector's Choice. The cards were packaged 6-cards per pack with 24-packs per box and no inserts.

COMPLETE SET (55) 4.00 10.00
2 Rob Moore .15 .40
4 Larry Centers .08 .25
7 Jamal Anderson .25 .60
12 Byron Hanspard .08 .25
15 Jermaine Lewis .15 .40
20 Eric Moulds .25 .60
22 Bruce Smith .15 .40
26 Rae Carruth .08 .25
28 Winslow Oliver .08 .25
32 Erik Kramer .08 .25
35 Curtis Conway .15 .40
39 Jeff Blake .15 .40
40 Carl Pickens .15 .40
49 Deion Sanders .25 .60
53 Ed McCaffrey .15 .40
55 John Mobley .08 .25
58 Scott Mitchell .15 .40
62 Bryant Westbrook .08 .25
67 Reggie White .25 .60
70 LeRoy Butler .08 .25
72 Marshall Faulk .30 .75
76 Quentin Coryatt .08 .25
77 Keenan McCardell .15 .40
80 Jimmy Smith .15 .40
84 Andre Rison .15 .40
86 Tony Gonzalez .25 .60
92 Yatil Green .08 .25
96 Brad Johnson .25 .60
98 Jake Reed .15 .40
103 Troy Davis .08 .25
104 Andre Hastings .08 .25
110 Terry Glenn .25 .60
111 Ben Coates .15 .40
115 Danny Kanell .15 .40
119 Tiki Barber .25 .60
122 Glenn Foley .15 .40
124 Kyle Brady .08 .25
129 Jeff George .15 .40
131 Darrell Russell .08 .25
136 Irving Fryar .15 .40
137 Mike Mamula .08 .25
143 Levon Kirkland .08 .25
147 Greg Lloyd .08 .25
150 Orlando Pace .08 .25
151 Isaac Bruce .25 .60
155 Natrone Means .15 .40
157 Tony Martin .15 .40
161 Merton Hanks .08 .25
165 J.J. Stokes .15 .40
168 Chad Brown .08 .25
173 Trent Dilfer .25 .60
175 Warren Sapp .15 .40
180 Steve McNair .25 .60
186 Gus Frerotte .08 .25
191 Cris Dishman .08 .25

1998 UD Choice

The 1998 UD Choice set consists of 438 standard size cards. The set is divided into Series One with 255 cards and Series Two with 183 cards. The 12-card packs retail for a suggested price of $1.29 each. The set contains the subsets: Rookie Class (193-222), DYOC Winners (223-252), and Domination Next (256-285). The Domination Next subset was randomly inserted in packs at a rate of 1:4. An SE parallel version was also produced and sequentially numbered to 2,000. The card fronts feature color action game photos within a white border. The Upper Deck logo is found in the bottom right corner with the featured player's name, number, and team in the opposite corner.

COMPLETE SET (438) 25.00 60.00
COMP.SERIES 1 (255) 12.50 30.00
COMP.SERIES 2 (183) 12.50 30.00
COMP.FACT.SER.1 (275) 20.00 40.00
1 Jake Plummer .20 .50
2 Rob Moore .10 .30
3 Simeon Rice .10 .30
4 Larry Centers .07 .20
5 Aeneas Williams .07 .20
6 Chris Gedney .07 .20
7 Jamal Anderson .20 .50
8 Michael Booker .07 .20
9 Ronnie Bradford RC .07 .20
10 Cornelius Bennett .07 .20
11 Terance Mathis .10 .30
12 Byron Hanspard .07 .20
13 Peter Boulware .07 .20
14 Jonathan Ogden .07 .20
15 Jermaine Lewis .10 .30
16 Tony Siragusa .07 .20
17 Brian Kinchen .07 .20
18 Michael Jackson .07 .20
19 Doug Flutie .20 .50
20 Eric Moulds .20 .50
21 Antowain Smith .20 .50
22 Bruce Smith .10 .30
23 Jay Riemersma .07 .20
24 Ruben Brown .07 .20
25 Fred Lane .07 .20
26 Rae Carruth .07 .20
27 Wesley Walls .10 .30
28 Winslow Oliver .07 .20
29 Tyrone Poole .07 .20
30 Lamar Lathon .07 .20
31 Anthony Johnson .07 .20
32 Erik Kramer .07 .20
33 Darnell Autry .07 .20
34 Bobby Engram .10 .30
35 Curtis Conway .10 .30
36 Jeff Jaeger .07 .20
37 Chris Penn .07 .20
38 Corey Dillon .20 .50
39 Jeff Blake .10 .30
40 Carl Pickens .10 .30
41 Ki-Jana Carter .07 .20
42 Reinard Wilson .07 .20
43 Tremain Mack .07 .20
44 Troy Aikman .40 1.00
45 Larry Allen .07 .20
46 Darren Woodson .07 .20
47 Anthony Miller .07 .20
48 Erik Williams .07 .20
49 Deion Sanders .20 .50
50 Richie Cunningham .07 .20
51 John Elway .75 2.00
52 Steve Atwater .07 .20
53 Ed McCaffrey .10 .30
54 Maa Tanuvasa .07 .20
55 John Mobley .07 .20
56 Bill Romanowski .07 .20
57 Shannon Sharpe .10 .30
58 Scott Mitchell .10 .30
59 Jason Hanson .07 .20
60 Herman Moore .10 .30
61 Luther Elliss .07 .20
62 Bryant Westbrook .07 .20
63 Kevin Abrams RC .10 .30
64 Brett Favre .75 2.00
65 Gilbert Brown .07 .20
66 Antonio Freeman .20 .50
67 Reggie White .20 .50
68 Mark Chmura .10 .30
69 Seth Joyner .07 .20
70 LeRoy Butler .07 .20
71 Marvin Harrison .20 .50
72 Marshall Faulk .25 .60
73 Ken Dilger .07 .20
74 Steve Morrison .07 .20
75 Zack Crockett .07 .20
76 Quentin Coryatt .07 .20
77 Keenan McCardell .10 .30
78 Mark Brunell .20 .50
79 Renaldo Wynn .07 .20
80 Jimmy Smith .10 .30
81 James O. Stewart .10 .30
82 Kevin Hardy .07 .20
83 Marcus Allen .20 .50
84 Andre Rison .10 .30
85 Pete Stoyanovich .07 .20
86 Tony Gonzalez .20 .50
87 Derrick Thomas .20 .50
88 Rich Gannon .20 .50
89 Elvis Grbac .10 .30
90 Dan Marino .75 2.00
91 Lawrence Phillips .07 .20
92 Yatil Green .07 .20
93 Zach Thomas .20 .50
94 Olindo Mare RC .07 .20
95 Charles Jordan .07 .20
96 Brad Johnson .20 .50
97 Cris Carter .20 .50
98 Jake Reed .10 .30
99 Ed McDaniel .07 .20
100 Dwayne Rudd .07 .20
101 Leroy Hoard .07 .20
102 Danny Wuerffel .10 .30
103 Troy Davis .07 .20
104 Andre Hastings .07 .20
105 Nicky Savoie .07 .20
106 Willie Roaf .07 .20
107 Ray Zellars .07 .20
108 Tedy Bruschi .40 1.00
109 Drew Bledsoe .30 .75
110 Terry Glenn .20 .50
111 Ben Coates .10 .30
112 Willie Clay .07 .20
113 Chris Slade .07 .20
114 Larry Whigham .07 .20
115 Danny Kanell .10 .30
116 Jessie Armstead .07 .20
117 Phillippi Sparks .07 .20
118 Michael Strahan .10 .30
119 Tiki Barber .20 .50
120 Charles Way .07 .20
121 Chris Calloway .07 .20
122 Glenn Foley .10 .30
123 Wayne Chrebet .20 .50
124 Kyle Brady .07 .20
125 Keyshawn Johnson .20 .50
126 Aaron Glenn .07 .20
127 James Farrior .07 .20
128 Victor Green .07 .20
129 Jeff George .10 .30
130 Rickey Dudley .07 .20
131 Darrell Russell .07 .20
132 Tim Brown .20 .50
133 James Trapp .07 .20
134 Napoleon Kaufman .20 .50
135 Bobby Hoying .10 .30
136 Irving Fryar .10 .30
137 Mike Mamula .07 .20
138 Troy Vincent .07 .20
139 Bobby Taylor .07 .20
140 Chris Boniol .07 .20
141 Jerome Bettis .20 .50
142 Charles Johnson .07 .20
143 Levon Kirkland .07 .20
144 Carnell Lake .07 .20
145 Will Blackwell .07 .20
146 Tim Lester .07 .20
147 Greg Lloyd .07 .20
148 Tony Banks .10 .30
149 Ryan McNeil .07 .20
150 Orlando Pace .07 .20
151 Isaac Bruce .20 .50
152 Eddie Kennison .10 .30
153 Leslie O'Neal .07 .20
154 Darren Bennett .07 .20
155 Natrone Means .10 .30
156 Junior Seau .20 .50
157 Tony Martin .10 .30
158 Rodney Harrison .10 .30
159 Freddie Jones .07 .20
160 Terrell Owens .20 .50
161 Merton Hanks .07 .20
162 Chris Doleman .07 .20
163 Steve Young .25 .60
164 Chuck Levy .07 .20
165 J.J. Stokes .10 .30
166 Ken Norton .07 .20
167 Bennie Blades .07 .20
168 Chad Brown .07 .20
169 Warren Moon .20 .50
170 Cortez Kennedy .07 .20
171 Darryl Williams .07 .20
172 Michael Sinclair .07 .20
173 Trent Dilfer .20 .50
174 Mike Alstott .20 .50
175 Warren Sapp .10 .30
176 Reidel Anthony .10 .30
177 Derrick Brooks .20 .50
178 Horace Copeland .07 .20
179 Hardy Nickerson .07 .20
180 Steve McNair .20 .50
181 Anthony Dorsett .07 .20
182 Chris Sanders .07 .20
183 Derrick Mason .10 .30
184 Eddie George .20 .50
185 Blaine Bishop .07 .20
186 Gus Frerotte .07 .20
187 Terry Allen .20 .50
188 Darrell Green .10 .30
189 Ken Harvey .07 .20
190 Matt Turk .07 .20
191 Cris Dishman [illegible]
192 Keith Thibodeaux RC .07 .20
193 Peyton Manning RC 5.00 12.00
194 Ryan Leaf RC .40 1.00
195 Charles Woodson RC .50 1.25
196 Andre Wadsworth RC .25 .60
197 Keith Brooking RC .40 1.00
198 Jason Peter RC .15 .40
199 Curtis Enis RC .15 .40
200 Randy Moss RC 3.00 8.00
201 Tra Thomas RC .15 .40
202 Robert Edwards RC .25 .60
203 Kevin Dyson RC .40 1.00
204 Fred Taylor RC .60 1.50
205 Corey Chavous RC .40 1.00
206 Grant Wistrom RC .25 .60
207 Vonnie Holliday RC .25 .60
208 Brian Simmons RC .25 .60
209 Jeremy Staat RC .15 .40
210 Alonzo Mayes RC .15 .40
211 Anthony Simmons RC .25 .60
212 Sam Cowart RC .25 .60
213 Flozell Adams RC .15 .40
214 Terry Fair RC .25 .60
215 Germane Crowell RC .25 .60
216 Robert Holcombe RC .25 .60
217 Jacquez Green RC .25 .60
218 Skip Hicks RC .25 .60
219 Takeo Spikes RC .40 1.00
220 Az-Zahir Hakim RC .40 1.00
221 Ahman Green RC 1.25 3.00
222 Chris Fuamatu-Ma'afala RC .25 .60
223 Darnell Autry DYOC .07 .20
224 John Randle DYOC .10 .30
225 Scott Mitchell DYOC .07 .20
226 Troy Aikman DYOC .20 .50
227 Terrell Davis DYOC .20 .50
228 Kordell Stewart DYOC .20 .50
229 Warrick Dunn DYOC .20 .50
230 Craig Newsome DYOC .07 .20
231 Brett Favre DYOC .25 .60
232 Kordell Stewart DYOC .20 .50
233 Barry Sanders DYOC .25 .60
234 Dan Marino DYOC .25 .60
235 Dan Marino DYOC .25 .60
236 Tamarick Vanover DYOC .07 .20
237 Warrick Dunn DYOC .20 .50
238 Andre Rison DYOC .07 .20
239 Dan Marino DYOC .25 .60
240 Reggie White DYOC .20 .50
241 Tim Brown DYOC .20 .50
242 Joe Montana DYOC .25 .60
243 Robert Brooks DYOC .10 .30
244 Danny Kanell DYOC .07 .20
245 Emmitt Smith DYOC .25 .60
246 Barry Sanders DYOC .25 .60
247 Brett Favre DYOC .30 .75
248 Brett Favre DYOC .30 .75
249 Jerome Bettis DYOC .07 .20
250 Kordell Stewart DYOC .20 .50
251 Terrell Davis DYOC .20 .50
252 Drew Bledsoe DYOC .20 .50
253 Troy Aikman CL .20 .50
254 Dan Marino CL .30 .75
255 Warrick Dunn CL .20 .50
256 Peyton Manning DN 7.50 15.00
257 Ryan Leaf DN .75 2.00
258 Andre Wadsworth DN .60 1.50
259 Charles Woodson DN .75 2.00
260 Curtis Enis DN .40 1.00
261 Grant Wistrom DN .60 1.50
262 Greg Ellis DN RC .40 1.00
263 Fred Taylor DN .75 2.00
264 Duane Starks DN RC .40 1.00
265 Keith Brooking DN .75 2.00
266 Takeo Spikes DN .75 2.00
267 Anthony Simmons DN .60 1.50
268 Kevin Dyson DN .75 2.00
269 Robert Edwards DN .60 1.50
270 Randy Moss DN 4.00 10.00
271 John Avery DN RC .60 1.50
272 Marcus Nash DN RC .40 1.00
273 Jerome Pathon DN RC .75 2.00
274 Jacquez Green DN .60 1.50
275 Robert Holcombe DN .60 1.50
276 Pat Johnson DN RC .60 1.50
277 Germane Crowell DN .60 1.50
278 Tony Simmons DN RC .60 1.50
279 Joe Jurevicius DN RC .75 2.00
280 Skip Hicks DN .40 1.00
281 Sam Cowart DN .60 1.50
282 Rashaan Shehee DN RC .60 1.50
283 Brian Griese DN RC 1.50 4.00
284 Tim Dwight DN RC .75 2.00
285 Ahman Green DN 1.50 4.00
286 Adrian Murrell .10 .30
287 Corey Chavous .20 .50
288 Eric Swann .07 .20
289 Frank Sanders .10 .30
290 Eric Metcalf .07 .20
291 Jammi German RC .15 .40
292 Eugene Robinson .07 .20
293 Chris Chandler .10 .30
294 Tony Martin .10 .30
295 Jessie Tuggle .07 .20
296 Errict Rhett .10 .30
297 Jim Harbaugh .10 .30
298 Eric Green .10 .30
299 Ray Lewis .20 .50
300 Jamie Sharper .07 .20
301 Fred Coleman RC .15 .40
302 Rob Johnson .10 .30
303 Quinn Early .07 .20
304 Thurman Thomas .20 .50
305 Andre Reed .10 .30
306 Sean Gilbert .07 .20
307 Kerry Collins .10 .30
308 Jason Peter .07 .20
309 Michael Bates .07 .20
310 William Floyd .10 .30
311 Alonzo Mayes RC .15 .40
312 Tony Parrish RC .40 1.00
313 Walt Harris .07 .20
314 Edgar Bennett .07 .20
315 Jeff Jaeger .07 .20
316 Brian Simmons .10 .30
317 David Dunn .07 .20
318 Ashley Ambrose .07 .20
319 Darnay Scott .10 .30
320 Neil O'Donnell .10 .30
321 Flozell Adams .10 .30
322 Stepfret Williams .07 .20
323 Emmitt Smith .60 1.50
324 Michael Irvin .20 .50
325 Chris Warren .10 .30
326 Eric Brown RC .15 .40
327 Rod Smith WR .10 .30
328 Terrell Davis .20 .50
329 Neil Smith .10 .30
330 Darrien Gordon .07 .20
331 Curtis Alexander RC .15 .40
332 Barry Sanders .60 1.50
333 David Sloan .07 .20
334 Johnnie Morton .10 .30
335 Robert Porcher .07 .20
336 Tommy Vardell .07 .20
337 Vonnie Holliday .10 .30
338 Dorsey Levens .20 .60
339 Derrick Mayes .10 .30
340 Robert Brooks .10 .30
341 Raymont Harris .07 .20
342 E.G. Green RC .25 .60
343 Torrance Small .07 .20
344 [illegible] .07 .20
345 Aaron Bailey .07 .20
346 Jeff Burris .07 .20
347 Donovin Darius RC .25 .60
348 Tavian Banks RC .10 .30
349 Aaron Beasley .07 .20
350 Tony Brackens .07 .20
351 Bryce Paup .07 .20
352 Chester McGlockton .07 .20
353 Leslie O'Neal .07 .20
354 Derrick Alexander WR .10 .30
355 Kimble Anders .10 .30
356 Tamarick Vanover .07 .20
357 Brock Marion .07 .20
358 Larry Shannon RC .15 .40
359 Karim Abdul-Jabbar .20 .50
360 Troy Drayton .07 .20
361 O.J. McDuffie .10 .30
362 John Randle .10 .30
363 David Palmer .07 .20
364 Robert Smith .20 .50
365 Kailee Wong RC .15 .40
366 Duane Clemons .07 .20
367 Kyle Turley RC .40 1.00
368 Sean Dawkins .07 .20
369 Lamar Smith .10 .30
370 Cameron Cleeland RC .15 .40
371 Keith Poole .07 .20
372 Tebucky Jones RC .15 .40
373 Willie McGinest .07 .20
374 Ty Law .10 .30
375 Lawyer Milloy .10 .30
376 Tony Carter .07 .20
377 Shaun Williams RC .25 .60
378 Brian Alford RC .15 .40
379 Tyrone Wheatley .10 .30
380 Jason Sehorn .10 .30
381 David Patten RC .40 1.00
382 Scott Frost RC .15 .40
383 Mo Lewis .07 .20
384 Kevin Williams DB RC .15 .40
385 Curtis Martin .20 .50
386 Vinny Testaverde .10 .30
387 Mo Collins RC .15 .40
388 James Jett .10 .30
389 Eric Allen .07 .20
390 Jon Ritchie RC .25 .60
391 Harvey Williams .07 .20
392 Tra Thomas .07 .20
393 Rodney Peete .07 .20
394 Hugh Douglas UER .07 .20
395 Charlie Garner .10 .30
396 Karl Hankton RC .25 .60
397 Kordell Stewart .20 .50
398 George Jones .07 .20
399 Earl Holmes .07 .20
400 Hines Ward RC 2.50 5.00
401 Jason Gildon .07 .20
402 Ricky Proehl .07 .20
403 Az-Zahir Hakim .07 .20
404 Amp Lee .07 .20
405 Eric Hill LB .07 .20
406 Leonard Little RC .40 1.00
407 Charlie Jones .07 .20
408 Craig Whelihan RC .07 .20
409 Terrell Fletcher .07 .20
410 Kenny Bynum RC .15 .40
411 Mikhael Ricks RC .25 .60
412 R.W. McQuarters RC .25 .60
413 Jerry Rice .40 1.00
414 Garrison Hearst .20 .50
415 Ty Detmer .10 .30
416 Gabe Wilkins .07 .20
417 Michael Black RC .40 1.00
418 James McKnight .20 .50
419 Darrin Smith .07 .20
420 Joey Galloway .10 .30
421 Ricky Watters .10 .30
422 Warrick Dunn .20 .50
423 Brian Kelly RC .25 .60
424 Bert Emanuel .10 .30
425 John Lynch .10 .30
426 Regan Upshaw .07 .20
427 Yancey Thigpen .07 .20
428 Kenny Holmes .07 .20
429 Frank Wycheck .07 .20
430 Samari Rolle RC .15 .40
431 Brian Mitchell .07 .20
432 Stephen Alexander RC .25 .60
433 Jamie Asher .07 .20
434 Michael Westbrook .10 .30
435 Dana Stubblefield .07 .20
436 Dan Wilkinson .07 .20
437 Dan Marino CL .25 .60
438 Jerry Rice CL .20 .50
DY2 Troy Aikman DYOC .50 1.25

1998 UD Choice Choice Reserve

COMP.CHOICE RES. (255) 400.00 800.00
*VETS: 3X TO 8X BASIC CARDS
*ROOKIES: 1.2X TO 3X BASIC CARDS
CHOICE RESERVE STATED ODDS 1:6

1998 UD Choice Domination Next SE

*DOM NEXT SE: 1.5X TO 3X BASE CARD HI

1998 UD Choice Prime Choice Reserve

*STARS: 20X TO 50X BASE CARD HI
*ROOKIES: 8X TO 20X BASE CARD HI
PRIME CHOICE RES. PRINT RUN 100 SETS
193 Peyton Manning 175.00 300.00
256 Peyton Manning DN 175.00 300.00

1998 UD Choice Jumbos

These cards were issued in special retail boxes and are an enlarged version of basic issue cards.

1998 UD Choice Mini Bobbing Head

Randomly inserted in packs at a rate of one in 4, this 30-card insert set features 30 players that fold into stand-up figures with a removable bobbing head.

COMPLETE SET (30) 12.50 25.00
STATED ODDS 1:4
M1 Jake Plummer .50 1.25
M2 Jamal Anderson .50 1.25
M3 Michael Jackson .20 .50
M4 Bruce Smith .30 .75
M5 Rae Carruth .20 .50
M6 Curtis Conway .30 .75
M7 Jeff Blake .30 .75
M8 Troy Aikman 1.00 2.50
M9 Michael Irvin .50 1.25
M10 Terrell Davis .50 1.25
M11 Barry Sanders 1.50 4.00
M12 Herman Moore .30 .75
M13 Reggie White .50 1.25
M14 Dorsey Levens .50 1.25
M15 Marvin Harrison .50 1.25
M16 Keenan McCardell .30 .75
M17 Andre Rison .30 .75
M18 Dan Marino 2.00 5.00
M19 Curtis Martin .50 1.25
M20 Keyshawn Johnson .50 1.25
M21 Tim Brown .50 1.25
M22 Kordell Stewart .50 1.25
M23 Greg Lloyd .20 .50
M24 Junior Seau .50 1.25
M25 Jerry Rice 1.00 2.50
M26 Merton Hanks .20 .50
M27 Joey Galloway .30 .75
M28 Warrick Dunn .50 1.25
M29 Warren Sapp .30 .75
M30 Darrell Green .30 .75

1998 UD Choice Starquest

Randomly inserted one in every pack, this 30-card set is the first of a four-tier insert set. The card front features a color action photo on a blue mod design background. Green, red, and gold foil parallel versions were also produced with insertion rates of 1:7 packs for Green and 1:23 for Red. Only 100 Gold sets were printed.

COMPLETE BLUE SET (30) 7.50 15.00
BLUE STATED ODDS 1:1H, 20 PER FACT.SET
*GREENS: 1.2X TO 3X BASIC INSERTS
GREEN STATED ODDS 1:7
*REDS: 2.5X TO 6X BASIC INSERTS
RED STATED ODDS 1:23
*GOLD/100: 20X TO 50X BASIC INSERTS
GOLD STATED PRINT RUN 100 SETS
1 Warren Moon .25 .60
2 Jerry Rice .50 1.25
3 Jeff George .15 .40
4 Brett Favre 1.00 2.50
5 Junior Seau .25 .60
6 Cris Carter .15 .40
7 John Elway 1.00 2.50
8 Troy Aikman .50 1.25
9 Steve Young .30 .75
10 Kordell Stewart .25 .60
11 Drew Bledsoe .40 1.00
12 Dorsey Levens .25 .60
13 Dan Marino 1.00 2.50
14 Joey Galloway .15 .40
15 Antonio Freeman .25 .60
16 Jake Plummer .25 .60
17 Corey Dillon .25 .60
18 Mark Brunell .25 .60
19 Andre Rison .15 .40
20 Barry Sanders .75 2.00
21 Deion Sanders .25 .60
22 Emmitt Smith .75 2.00
23 Antowain Smith .25 .60
24 Herman Moore .15 .40
25 Napoleon Kaufman .25 .60
26 Jerome Bettis .25 .60
27 Eddie George .25 .60
28 Warrick Dunn .25 .60
29 Adrian Murrell .15 .40
30 Terrell Davis .25 .60

1998 UD Choice Starquest/Rookquest Blue

e 1998 UD Choice Starquest/Rookquest Blue set consists of 30 cards with blue foil stamping. The cards are randomly inserted in every pack of 1998 UD Choice cards. The "double-fronts" feature the traditional Starquest tiers exhibiting two players. One side features a veteran and the other side showcases a rookie. The player's name is found in the upper right corner with the Upper Deck logo in the opposite corner. Green, red, and gold foil parallel versions were also produced with insertion rates of 1:7 packs for Green and 1:23 for Red. Only 100 Gold sets were printed.

COMPLETE SET (30) 15.00 30.00
BLUE STATED ODDS ONE PER PACK
*GREENS: 1.5X TO 3X HI COL.
GREEN STATED ODDS 1:7
*REDS: 3.5X TO 7X HI COL.
RED STATED ODDS 1:23
*GOLDS: 20X TO 40X HI COL.
GOLD STATED PRINT RUN 100 SETS
SR1 J.Elway / P.Manning 3.00 8.00
SR2 D.Bledsoe / R.Leaf .50 1.25
SR3 B.Sanders / Ta.Banks .75 2.00
SR4 B.Favre / V.Holliday 1.00 2.50
SR5 J.Seau / T.Spikes .30 .75
SR6 D.Sanders / C.Woodson .40 1.00
SR7 J.Rice / R.Moss 2.50 6.00
SR8 R.White / A.Wadsworth .20 .50
SR9 E.Smith / F.Taylor .60 1.50
SR10 M.Irvin / K.Dyson .30 .75
SR11 T.Aikman / S.Williams .50 1.25
SR12 J.Bettis / C.Enis .30 .75
SR13 D.Marino / B.Griese 1.25 3.00
SR14 S.Young / R.W.McQuarters .40 1.00
SR15 D.Stubblefield / G.Ellis .08 .25
SR16 J.Plummer / P.Johnson .30 .75
SR17 C.Dillon / R.Shehee .30 .75
SR18 M.Brunell / J.Pathon .30 .75
SR19 A.Rison / J.Green .20 .50
SR20 M.Alstott / J.Ritchie .20 .50
SR21 D.Levens / A.Green .75 2.00
SR22 K.Stewart / H.Ward 1.25 3.00
SR23 A.Smith / S.Hicks .20 .50
SR24 H.Moore / G.Crowell .20 .50
SR25 K.Greene / J.Peter .20 .50
SR26 K.Johnson / M.Nash .20 .50
SR27 E.George / R.Holcombe .30 .75
SR28 W.Dunn / J.Avery .08 .25
SR29 T.Vanover / T.Dwight .30 .75
SR30 T.Davis / R.Edwards .30 .75

2004 UD Diamond All-Star

UD Diamond All-Star was initially released in mid-July 2004 as a retail-only product. The base set consists of 120-cards including 30-short printed rookies. Retail boxes contained 24-packs of 6-cards and carried an S.R.P. of $2.99 per pack. Two parallel sets and a variety of inserts can be found seeded in packs highlighted by the Stars of 2004 Autographs inserts.

COMP.SET w/o SP's (90) 7.50 20.00
ROOKIE STATED ODDS 1:6
1 Michael Vick .15 .40
2 Julius Peppers .15 .40
3 Roy Williams S .12 .30
4 Ahman Green .15 .40
5 Trent Green .12 .30
6 Tom Brady .75 2.00
7 Rich Gannon .15 .40
8 Drew Brees .20 .50
9 Brad Johnson .15 .40
10 Todd Heap .12 .30
11 Chad Johnson .12 .30
12 Ashley Lelie .12 .30
13 Marvin Harrison .15 .40
14 Daunte Culpepper .15 .40
15 Amani Toomer .12 .30
16 Terrell Owens .15 .40
17 Shaun Alexander .12 .30
18 Mark Brunell .15 .40
19 Drew Bledsoe .15 .40
20 Rudi Johnson .12 .30
21 Charles Rogers .12 .30
22 Edgerrin James .15 .40
23 Randy Moss .15 .40
24 Tiki Barber .15 .40
25 Hines Ward .15 .40
26 Koren Robinson .12 .30
27 Laveranues Coles .12 .30
28 Travis Henry .12 .30
29 Carson Palmer .15 .40
30 Joey Harrington .12 .30
31 Byron Leftwich .12 .30
32 Moe Williams .12 .30
33 Chad Pennington .12 .30
34 Duce Staley .12 .30
35 Marshall Faulk .15 .40
36 Clinton Portis .12 .30
37 Marcel Shipp .12 .30
38 Eric Moulds .12 .30
39 Andre Davis .12 .30
40 Brett Favre .40 1.00
41 Fred Taylor .12 .30
42 Ty Law .20 .50
43 Santana Moss .15 .40
44 Tommy Maddox .12 .30
45 Torry Holt .15 .40
46 Peerless Price .12 .30
47 Stephen Davis .12 .30
48 Quincy Carter .12 .30
49 David Carr .12 .30
50 Dante Hall .12 .30
51 Deuce McAllister .15 .40
52 Jerry Rice .40 1.00
53 Tim Rattay .12 .30
54 Derrick Brooks .12 .30
55 Warrick Dunn .12 .30
56 Anthony Thomas .15 .40
57 Keyshawn Johnson .15 .40
58 Domanick Davis .12 .30
59 Ricky Williams .15 .40
60 Aaron Brooks .12 .30
61 Tim Brown .20 .50
62 Brandon Lloyd .15 .40
63 Steve McNair .15 .40
64 Kyle Boller .12 .30
65 Brian Urlacher .20 .50
66 Jake Plummer .12 .30
67 Peyton Manning .50 1.25
68 Chris Chambers .12 .30
69 Jeremy Shockey .12 .30
70 Brian Westbrook .12 .30
71 Matt Hasselbeck .12 .30
72 Derrick Mason .12 .30
73 Anquan Boldin .12 .30
74 Jake Delhomme .12 .30
75 Jeff Garcia .12 .30
76 Donald Driver .15 .40
77 Priest Holmes .12 .30
78 Corey Dillon .12 .30
79 Curtis Martin .15 .40
80 LaDainian Tomlinson .20 .50
81 Marc Bulger .12 .30
82 Jamal Lewis .15 .40
83 Marty Booker .12 .30
84 Quentin Griffin .12 .30
85 Andre Johnson .15 .40
86 Junior Seau .20 .50
87 Joe Horn .12 .30
88 Donovan McNabb .15 .40
89 Kevan Barlow .12 .30
90 Eddie George .15 .40
91 Eli Manning RC 5.00 12.00
92 Larry Fitzgerald RC 2.50 6.00
93 Ben Roethlisberger RC 5.00 12.00
94 Roy Williams RC .60 1.50
95 Derrick Hamilton RC .60 1.50
96 Kellen Winslow RC .60 1.50
97 Bernard Berrian RC .60 1.50
98 Steven Jackson RC 1.00 2.50
99 DeAngelo Hall RC 1.00 2.50
100 Kevin Jones RC .75 2.00
101 Reggie Williams RC .60 1.50
102 Michael Clayton RC .75 2.00
103 Rashaun Woods RC .60 1.50
104 Devery Henderson RC .60 1.50
105 Ben Troupe RC .60 1.50
106 Cedric Cobbs RC .60 1.50
107 Lee Evans RC 1.00 2.50
108 Luke McCown RC .60 1.50
109 Chris Perry RC .60 1.50
110 J.P. Losman RC .60 1.50
111 Philip Rivers RC 2.00 5.00
112 Michael Jenkins RC .60 1.50
113 Greg Jones RC .60 1.50
114 Darius Watts RC .60 1.50
115 Tatum Bell RC .60 1.50
116 Ben Watson RC .75 2.00
117 Drew Henson RC .60 1.50
118 Keary Colbert RC .60 1.50
119 Matt Schaub RC .60 1.50
120 Julius Jones RC .60 1.50

2004 UD Diamond All-Star Gold Honors

OLD VETS: 10X TO 25X BASIC CARDS
*GOLD ROOKIES: 2.5X TO 6X
STATED PRINT RUN 50 SER.#'d SETS

2004 UD Diamond All-Star Silver Honors

MPLETE SET (12) 50.00 120.00
*SILVER VETS: 2X TO 5X BASIC CARDS
*SILVER ROOKIES: .6X TO 1.5X
OVERALL GOLD/SILVER ODDS 1:6

2004 UD Diamond All-Star Dean's List Jersey

ERALL INSERT ODDS 1:24
DLAG Ahman Green 3.00 8.00
DLBF Brett Favre 8.00 20.00
DLBU Brian Urlacher 4.00 10.00
DLCP Clinton Portis SP 3.00 8.00
DLDC Daunte Culpepper 3.00 8.00
DLDM Donovan McNabb 3.00 8.00
DLLT LaDainian Tomlinson 4.00 10.00
DLMH Marvin Harrison 3.00 8.00
DLMV Michael Vick SP 4.00 10.00
DLPH Priest Holmes 2.50 6.00
DLPM Peyton Manning 10.00 25.00
DLRM Randy Moss 3.00 8.00
DLRW Ricky Williams 3.00 8.00
DLSM Steve McNair 3.00 8.00
DLTB Tom Brady 15.00 40.00
DLTH Torry Holt 3.00 8.00

2004 UD Diamond All-Star Future Gems Jersey

ERALL INSERT ODDS 1:24
FGAB Anquan Boldin SP 2.50 6.00
FGAJ Andre Johnson SP 3.00 8.00
FGBJ Bethel Johnson 2.50 6.00
FGBL Byron Leftwich 2.50 6.00
FGCB Chris Brown 2.50 6.00
FGCP Carson Palmer 3.00 8.00
FGCR Charles Rogers SP 2.50 6.00
FGDC Dallas Clark 2.50 6.00
FGDD Domanick Davis SP 2.50 6.00
FGJF Justin Fargas 3.00 8.00
FGKB Kyle Boller 2.50 6.00
FGKW Kelley Washington 2.50 6.00
FGLJ Larry Johnson 2.50 6.00
FGLS Lee Suggs 3.00 8.00
FGOS Onterrio Smith 2.50 6.00
FGRG Rex Grossman 2.50 6.00
FGTC Tyrone Calico 3.00 8.00
FGTN Terence Newman 3.00 8.00
FGTS Terrell Suggs 2.50 6.00
FGWM Willis McGahee 2.50 6.00

2004 UD Diamond All-Star Premium Stars

OVERALL INSERT ODDS 1:24
PS1 Michael Vick 1.00 2.50
PS2 Brett Favre 2.50 6.00
PS3 Peyton Manning 3.00 8.00
PS4 Randy Moss 1.00 2.50
PS5 Clinton Portis .75 2.00
PS6 Donovan McNabb 1.00 2.50
PS7 LaDainian Tomlinson 1.25 3.00
PS8 Jerry Rice 2.50 6.00
PS9 Ricky Williams 1.00 2.50
PS10 Chad Pennington .75 2.00
PS11 Priest Holmes .75 2.00
PS12 Tom Brady 5.00 12.00
PS13 Deuce McAllister 1.00 2.50
PS14 Michael Strahan 1.00 2.50
PS15 Steve McNair 1.00 2.50

2004 UD Diamond All-Star Promo

ONE PER PACK
AS1 Eli Manning 3.00 8.00
AS2 Larry Fitzgerald 1.50 4.00
AS3 Ben Roethlisberger 3.00 8.00
AS4 Philip Rivers 1.25 3.00
AS5 Roy Williams WR .40 1.00
AS6 Steven Jackson .60 1.50
AS7 Kellen Winslow Jr. .40 1.00
AS8 Reggie Williams .40 1.00
AS9 Sean Taylor 2.50 6.00
AS10 Chris Gamble .40 1.00
AS11 DeAngelo Hall .60 1.50
AS12 Kevin Jones .50 1.25
AS13 Teddy Lehman .40 1.00
AS14 Michael Clayton .50 1.25
AS15 Rashaun Woods .40 1.00
AS16 Karlos Dansby .50 1.25
AS17 Ben Troupe .40 1.00
AS18 Kenechi Udeze .50 1.25
AS19 Lee Evans .60 1.50
AS20 Jonathan Vilma .50 1.25
AS21 J.P. Losman .40 1.00
AS22 Michael Jenkins .40 1.00
AS23 Greg Jones .40 1.00
AS24 Carlos Francis .40 1.00
AS25 Devery Henderson .40 1.00
AS26 Michael Turner .40 1.00
AS27 Chris Perry .40 1.00
AS28 Keary Colbert .40 1.00
AS29 Matt Schaub .40 1.00
AS30 Cody Pickett .40 1.00
AS31 Julius Jones .40 1.00
AS32 Tommie Harris .50 1.25
AS33 Will Smith .50 1.25
AS34 Vince Wilfork .60 1.50
AS35 D.J. Williams .60 1.50
AS36 Joey Thomas .40 1.00
AS37 Antwan Odom .40 1.00
AS38 Dunta Robinson .40 1.00
AS39 Craig Krenzel .40 1.00
AS40 Cedric Cobbs .40 1.00
AS41 Tatum Bell .40 1.00
AS42 B.J. Symons .40 1.00
AS43 P.K. Sam .40 1.00
AS44 Jerricho Cotchery .50 1.25
AS45 John Navarre .40 1.00
AS46 Josh Harris .40 1.00
AS47 Will Poole .60 1.50
AS48 Matt Ware .60 1.50
AS49 Samie Parker .40 1.00
AS50 Drew Henson .40 1.00
AS51 Michael Boulware .60 1.50
AS52 Jared Lorenzen .50 1.25
AS53 Derrick Strait .40 1.00
AS54 Ben Watson .50 1.25
AS55 Ernest Wilford .50 1.25
AS56 Darius Watts .40 1.00
AS57 Devard Darling .40 1.00
AS58 Bob Sanders .75 2.00
AS59 Stuart Schweigert .50 1.25
AS60 Robert Gallery .50 1.25
AS61 Mewelde Moore .50 1.25
AS62 Johnnie Morant .40 1.00
AS63 Bernard Berrian .40 1.00
AS64 Kris Wilson .50 1.25
AS65 Ben Hartsock .40 1.00
AS66 Jeff Smoker .50 1.25
AS67 Luke McCown .40 1.00
AS68 Derrick Hamilton .40 1.00
AS69 Wild Card .60 1.50

2004 UD Diamond All-Star Stars of 2004 Autographs

STATED PRINT RUN 100 SER.#'d SETS
BL Brandon Lloyd 4.00 10.00
CC Chris Chambers 4.00 10.00
DD Domanick Davis 4.00 10.00
TG Tony Gonzalez 15.00 40.00
CJ Chad Johnson 5.00 12.00

2004 UD Diamond Pro Sigs

UD Diamond Pro Sigs was initially released in early October 2004. The base set consists of 140-cards including 50-short printed rookie cards. Hobby boxes contained 24-packs of 6-cards and carried an S.R.P. of $2.99 per pack. One partial parallel set and a variety of inserts can be found seeded in packs highlighted by the multi-tiered Signature Collection inserts.

COMP.SET w/o SP's (90) 7.50 20.00
91-140 ROOKIE STATED ODDS 1:6
1 Marcel Shipp .15 .40
2 Anquan Boldin .15 .40
3 Michael Vick .20 .50
4 Peerless Price .15 .40
5 Warrick Dunn .15 .40
6 Todd Heap .15 .40
7 Kyle Boller .15 .40
8 Jamal Lewis .20 .50
9 Drew Bledsoe .20 .50
10 Travis Henry .15 .40
11 Eric Moulds .15 .40
12 Julius Peppers .20 .50
13 Stephen Davis .15 .40
14 Jake Delhomme .15 .40
15 Anthony Thomas .20 .50
16 Brian Urlacher .25 .60
17 Marty Booker .15 .40
18 Chad Johnson .15 .40
19 Rudi Johnson .15 .40
20 Carson Palmer .20 .50
21 Andre Davis .15 .40
22 Jeff Garcia .15 .40
23 Eddie George .20 .50
24 Vinny Testaverde .15 .40
25 Keyshawn Johnson .20 .50
26 Ashley Lelie .15 .40
27 Jake Plummer .15 .40
28 Quentin Griffin .15 .40
29 Charles Rogers .15 .40

30 Joey Harrington .15 .40
31 Ahman Green .20 .50
32 Brett Favre .50 1.25
33 Donald Driver .20 .50
34 David Carr .15 .40
35 Domanick Davis .15 .40
36 Andre Johnson .20 .50
37 Marvin Harrison .20 .50
38 Edgerrin James .20 .50
39 Peyton Manning .60 1.50
40 Byron Leftwich .15 .40
41 Fred Taylor .15 .40
42 Trent Green .15 .40
43 Dante Hall .15 .40
44 Priest Holmes .15 .40
45 Ricky Williams .20 .50
46 Chris Chambers .15 .40
47 Junior Seau .25 .60
48 Daunte Culpepper .20 .50
49 Randy Moss .20 .50
50 Moe Williams .15 .40
51 Tom Brady 1.00 2.50
52 Deion Branch .15 .40
53 Corey Dillon .15 .40
54 Deuce McAllister .20 .50
55 Aaron Brooks .15 .40
56 Joe Horn .15 .40
57 Michael Strahan .20 .50
58 Tiki Barber .20 .50
59 Jeremy Shockey .15 .40
60 Chad Pennington .15 .40
61 Santana Moss .20 .50
62 Curtis Martin .20 .50
63 Rich Gannon .20 .50
64 Jerry Rice .50 1.25
65 Jerry Porter .15 .40
66 Terrell Owens .20 .50
67 Brian Westbrook .15 .40
68 Donovan McNabb .20 .50
69 Hines Ward .20 .50
70 Duce Staley .15 .40
71 Tommy Maddox .15 .40
72 Drew Brees .25 .60
73 LaDainian Tomlinson .25 .60
74 Tim Rattay .15 .40
75 Brandon Lloyd .20 .50
76 Kevan Barlow .15 .40
77 Shaun Alexander .15 .40
78 Koren Robinson .15 .40
79 Matt Hasselbeck .15 .40
80 Marshall Faulk .20 .50
81 Torry Holt .20 .50
82 Marc Bulger .15 .40
83 Brad Johnson .20 .50
84 Derrick Brooks .15 .40
85 Steve McNair .20 .50
86 Derrick Mason .15 .40
87 Chris Brown .15 .40
88 Mark Brunell .20 .50
89 Laveranues Coles .15 .40
90 Clinton Portis .15 .40
91 Eli Manning RC 6.00 15.00
92 Larry Fitzgerald RC 3.00 8.00
93 Ben Roethlisberger RC 6.00 15.00
94 Roy Williams RC .75 2.00
95 Sean Taylor RC 5.00 12.00
96 Kellen Winslow RC .75 2.00
97 Chris Gamble RC .75 2.00
98 Steven Jackson RC 1.25 3.00
99 DeAngelo Hall RC 1.25 3.00
100 Kevin Jones RC 1.00 2.50
101 Reggie Williams RC .75 2.00
102 Michael Clayton RC 1.00 2.50
103 Rashaun Woods RC .75 2.00
104 D.J. Williams RC 1.25 3.00
105 Ben Troupe RC .75 2.00
106 Mewelde Moore RC 1.00 2.50
107 Lee Evans RC 1.25 3.00
108 Jonathan Vilma RC 1.00 2.50
109 Chris Perry RC .75 2.00
110 J.P. Losman RC .75 2.00
111 Philip Rivers RC 2.50 6.00
112 Michael Jenkins RC .75 2.00
113 Greg Jones RC .75 2.00
114 John Navarre RC .75 2.00
115 Jerricho Cotchery RC 1.00 2.50
116 Michael Turner RC .75 2.00
117 Drew Henson RC .75 2.00
118 Keary Colbert RC .75 2.00
119 Matt Schaub RC .75 2.00
120 Cody Pickett RC .75 2.00
121 Luke McCown RC .75 2.00
122 P.K. Sam RC .75 2.00
123 Ernest Wilford RC 1.00 2.50
124 Will Smith RC 1.00 2.50
125 Bernard Berrian RC .75 2.00
126 Robert Gallery RC 1.00 2.50
127 Ben Watson RC 1.00 2.50
128 Devery Henderson RC .75 2.00
129 Jeff Smoker RC 1.00 2.50
130 Josh Harris RC .75 2.00
131 Julius Jones RC .75 2.00
132 Dunta Robinson RC .75 2.00
133 Tatum Bell RC .75 2.00
134 Cedric Cobbs RC .75 2.00
135 Devard Darling RC .75 2.00
136 Johnnie Morant RC .75 2.00
137 Derrick Hamilton RC .75 2.00
138 Darius Watts RC .75 2.00
139 Tommie Harris RC 1.00 2.50
140 B.J. Symons RC .75 2.00

2004 UD Diamond Pro Sigs Rookie Gold

OOKIES: .8X TO 2X BASIC CARDS
STATED PRINT RUN 349 SER.#'d SETS

2004 UD Diamond Pro Sigs Signature Collection

ATED ODDS 1:24
UNPRICED PLATINUM PRINT RUN 10
SCAR Antwaan Randle El 5.00 12.00
SCBB Bernard Berrian 5.00 12.00
SCBC Brandon Chillar 6.00 15.00
SCBF Brett Favre SP 75.00 150.00
SCBH Ben Hartsock SP 5.00 12.00
SCBJ B.J. Symons 5.00 12.00
SCBL Brandon Lloyd 6.00 15.00
SCBR Ben Roethlisberger SP 100.00 200.00
SCBT Ben Troupe 5.00 12.00
SCBW Ben Watson 6.00 15.00
SCCB Chris Brown SP 5.00 12.00
SCCC Cedric Cobbs 5.00 12.00
SCCF Clarence Farmer 5.00 12.00
SCCJ Chad Johnson SP 5.00 12.00
SCCL Casey Clausen 6.00 15.00
SCCP Cody Pickett 5.00 12.00
SCDA Dante Hall SP
SCDD Devard Darling 5.00 12.00
SCDE Derrick Mason SP 5.00 12.00
SCDH DeAngelo Hall 8.00 20.00
SCDV Devery Henderson SP
SCDW Darius Watts SP 5.00 12.00
SCEM Eli Manning 100.00 200.00
SCEW Ernest Wilford 6.00 15.00
SCGJ Greg Jones 5.00 12.00
SCHE Todd Heap SP 5.00 12.00
SCJC Jerricho Cotchery 6.00 15.00
SCJE Jesse Palmer SP 5.00 12.00
SCJG Joey Galloway SP 6.00 15.00
SCJM Johnnie Morant 5.00 12.00
SCJN John Navarre 5.00 12.00
SCJP J.P. Losman 5.00 12.00
SCJS Jeff Smoker 6.00 15.00
SCJV Jonathan Vilma 6.00 16.00
SCKC Keary Colbert 5.00 12.00
SCKJ Kevin Jones 6.00 15.00
SCKU Kenechi Udeze 6.00 15.00
SCLE Lee Evans SP 8.00 20.00
SCLM Luke McCown 5.00 12.00
SCMC Michael Clayton 6.00 15.00
SCMJ Michael Jenkins 5.00 12.00
SCMS Matt Schaub 12.00 30.00
SCPE Chris Perry 5.00 12.00
SCPM Peyton Manning SP 40.00 80.00
SCQW Quincy Wilson 5.00 12.00
SCRA Rashaun Woods 5.00 12.00
SCRE Reggie Williams 5.00 12.00
SCRG Robert Gallery 6.00 15.00
SCRJ Rudi Johnson SP 5.00 12.00
SCRW Roy Williams WR SP 5.00 12.00
SCSJ Steven Jackson 8.00 20.00
SCSP Samie Parker 5.00 12.00
SCTH Tommie Harris 6.00 15.00
SCTR Travis Henry 5.00 12.00
SCVW Vince Wilfork 8.00 20.00
SCWM Willis McGahee SP 5.00 12.00
SCWS Will Smith 6.00 15.00
SCZT Zach Thomas SP 10.00 25.00

2004 UD Diamond Pro Sigs Signature Collection Gold

*GOLD/25: 1X TO 2.5X BASIC AU
STATED PRINT RUN 25 SER.#'d SETS
SCBF Brett Favre 125.00 250.00
SCBR Ben Roethlisberger 125.00 250.00
SCEM Eli Manning 150.00 250.00
SCPM Peyton Manning 75.00 150.00

2001 UD Game Gear

This 110 card set was issued in early fall, 2001. The set is broken down into a 90 card veteran base set and a 20 card rookie subset. The Rookie Card were numbered from 90 through 110 and had different print runs. Cards numbered 91 through 100 had a print run of 1000 sets while cards numbered 101 through 110 had a print run of 500 sets.

COMP.SET w/o SP's (90) 12.00 30.00
1 Jake Plummer .25 .60
2 David Boston .25 .60
3 Jamal Anderson .30 .75
4 Shawn Jefferson .25 .60
5 Jamal Lewis .40 1.00
6 Elvis Grbac .30 .75
7 Ray Lewis .40 1.00
8 Rob Johnson .30 .75
9 Shawn Bryson .25 .60
10 Muhsin Muhammad .25 .60
11 Jeff Lewis .25 .60
12 Marcus Robinson .30 .75
13 James Allen .25 .60
14 Brian Urlacher .50 1.25
15 Cade McNown .30 .75
16 Peter Warrick .25 .60
17 Akili Smith .25 .60
18 Corey Dillon .25 .60
19 Tim Couch .25 .60
20 Kevin Johnson .25 .60
21 Emmitt Smith .60 1.50
22 Rocket Ismail .30 .75
23 Joey Galloway .30 .75
24 Terrell Davis .30 .75
25 Brian Griese .25 .60
26 Ed McCaffrey .30 .75
27 Mike Anderson .25 .60
28 Charlie Batch .25 .60
29 Germane Crowell .25 .60
30 James Stewart .25 .60
31 Brett Favre .75 2.00
32 Dorsey Levens .30 .75
33 Ahman Green .30 .75
34 Peyton Manning 1.00 2.50
35 Edgerrin James .30 .75
36 Marvin Harrison .30 .75
37 Mark Brunell .30 .75
38 Jimmy Smith .30 .75
39 Fred Taylor .25 .60
40 Tony Gonzalez .30 .75
41 Derrick Alexander .25 .60
42 Trent Green .25 .60
43 Lamar Smith .30 .75
44 Oronde Gadsden .25 .60
45 Zach Thomas .30 .75
46 Randy Moss .30 .75
47 Daunte Culpepper .30 .75
48 Doug Chapman .25 .60
49 Cris Carter .40 1.00
50 Drew Bledsoe .30 .75
51 Terry Glenn .30 .75
52 Troy Brown .25 .60
53 Ricky Williams .30 .75
54 Jeff Blake .30 .75
55 Aaron Brooks .25 .60
56 Joe Horn .25 .60
57 Kerry Collins .25 .60
58 Ron Dayne .30 .75
59 Amani Toomer .25 .60
60 Tiki Barber .30 .75
61 Vinny Testaverde .25 .60
62 Curtis Martin .30 .75
63 Wayne Chrebet .25 .60
64 Rich Gannon .30 .75
65 Jerry Rice .75 2.00
66 Tim Brown .40 1.00
67 Duce Staley .25 .60
68 Donovan McNabb .30 .75
69 Jerome Bettis .40 1.00
70 Kordell Stewart .25 .60
71 Marshall Faulk .30 .75
72 Kurt Warner .60 1.50
73 Torry Holt .30 .75
74 Isaac Bruce .40 1.00
75 Doug Flutie .30 .75
76 Junior Seau .30 .75
77 Jeff Garcia .25 .60
78 Terrell Owens .30 .75
79 Matt Hasselbeck .25 .60
80 Shaun Alexander .25 .60
81 Ricky Watters .30 .75
82 Keyshawn Johnson .30 .75
83 Brad Johnson .30 .75
84 Warrick Dunn .25 .60
85 Mike Alstott .25 .60
86 Eddie George .40 1.00
87 Steve McNair .30 .75
88 Jeff George .30 .75
89 Michael Westbrook .25 .60
90 Stephen Davis .25 .60
91 Mike McMahon RC 1.25 3.00
92 James Jackson RC 1.00 2.50
93 Quincy Morgan RC 1.25 3.00
94 Travis Minor RC 1.25 3.00
95 Chris Chambers RC 1.00 2.50
96 Jesse Palmer RC 1.25 3.00
97 Santana Moss RC 1.50 4.00
98 Marques Tuiasosopo RC 1.25 3.00
99 Freddie Mitchell RC 1.00 2.50
100 Kevan Barlow RC 1.25 3.00
101 Michael Vick RC 3.00 8.00
102 Chris Weinke RC 1.50 4.00
103 Reggie Wayne RC 2.50 6.00
104 Robert Ferguson RC 2.00 5.00
105 Michael Bennett RC 1.50 4.00
106 Deuce McAllister RC 2.00 5.00
107 Drew Brees RC 40.00 80.00
108 LaDainian Tomlinson RC 6.00 15.00
109 Koren Robinson RC 1.50 4.00
110 Rod Gardner RC 1.50 4.00
EJ Edgerrin James SAMPLE .00 1.50

2001 UD Game Gear Rookie Jerseys

-100 PRINT RUN 1000
101-110 PRINT RUN 500
91 Mike McMahon 3.00 8.00
92 James Jackson 2.50 6.00
93 Quincy Morgan 3.00 8.00
94 Travis Minor 3.00 8.00
95 Chris Chambers 2.50 6.00
96 Jesse Palmer 3.00 8.00
97 Santana Moss 4.00 10.00
98 Marques Tuiasosopo 3.00 8.00
99 Freddie Mitchell 2.50 6.00
100 Kevan Barlow 3.00 8.00
101 Michael Vick 6.00 15.00
102 Chris Weinke 3.00 8.00
103 Reggie Wayne 5.00 12.00
104 Robert Ferguson 4.00 10.00
105 Michael Bennett 3.00 8.00
106 Deuce McAllister 4.00 10.00
107 Drew Brees 20.00 50.00
108 LaDainian Tomlinson 15.00 40.00
109 Koren Robinson 3.00 8.00
110 Rod Gardner 3.00 8.00

2001 UD Game Gear Autographs

sued at a rate of one in 18, these cards featured the player's signature in a trapped autograph format. A few cards were signed in significantly lesser quantity and those cards along with their announced print runs are notated in our checklist. The Terrell Davis cards apparently was not issued in packs but surfaced at a later date.

STATED ODDS 1:18
ATGS Anthony Thomas 8.00 20.00
AZGS Az-Zahir Hakim 5.00 12.00
CCGS Chris Chambers 5.00 12.00
CJGS Chad Johnson 8.00 20.00
CWGS Chris Weinke SP/390* 6.00 15.00
DBGS Drew Brees 200.00 400.00
DMGS Dan Morgan 6.00 15.00
DTGS David Terrell 6.00 15.00
DUGS Deuce McAllister 8.00 20.00
GAGS Rich Gannon SP/360* 8.00 20.00
GWGS Gerard Warren 6.00 15.00
JBGS Jim Brown SP/295* 30.00 80.00
JGGS Jeff Garcia 5.00 12.00
JLGS Jamal Lewis SP/295* 8.00 20.00
JNGS Joe Namath SP/295* 50.00 100.00
JRGS John Riggins SP/395* 20.00 50.00
KRGS Koren Robinson 6.00 15.00
KYGS Ken-Yon Rambo 5.00 12.00
LTGS LaDainian Tomlinson 20.00 50.00
MBGS Michael Bennett 6.00 15.00
MVGS Michael Vick SP/195* 20.00 50.00
PMGS Peyton Manning 50.00 100.00
RDGS Ron Dayne 6.00 15.00
RGGS Rod Gardner SP/150* 8.00 20.00
RMGS Randy Moss SP/95* 50.00 100.00
RWGS Reggie Wayne 10.00 25.00
SMGS Santana Moss 6.00 15.00
TDGS Terrell Davis 10.00 25.00
TGGS Tony Gonzalez 10.00 25.00

2001 UD Game Gear Helmets

Issued at a rate of one in 108, these 29 cards feature a piece of a player's helmet on the card.

STATED ODDS 1:108
ASH Akili Smith 5.00 12.00
ATH Amani Toomer 5.00 12.00
CDH Corey Dillon 5.00 12.00
CWH Chris Weinke 6.00 15.00
DMH Deuce McAllister 8.00 20.00
DTH David Terrell 6.00 15.00
ESH Emmitt Smith 12.00 30.00
FTH Fred Taylor 5.00 12.00
IBH Isaac Bruce 8.00 20.00
JRH Jerry Rice 15.00 40.00
JSH Jason Sehorn 6.00 15.00
KBH Kevan Barlow 6.00 15.00
KMH Keenan McCardell 6.00 15.00
KRH Koren Robinson 6.00 15.00
KWH Kurt Warner 12.00 30.00
LTH LaDainian Tomlinson 12.00 30.00
MFH Marshall Faulk 6.00 15.00
MVH Michael Vick 6.00 15.00
PWH Peter Warrick 5.00 12.00
RGH Rod Gardner 6.00 15.00
RWH Reggie Wayne 5.00 12.00
SMH Santana Moss 8.00 20.00
TAH Troy Aikman 10.00 25.00
TBH Tiki Barber 6.00 15.00
TJH Thomas Jones 5.00 12.00
DBOH David Boston 5.00 12.00
DBRH Drew Brees 15.00 40.00
MBEH Michael Bennett 6.00 15.00
MBRH Mark Brunell 6.00 15.00

2001 UD Game Gear Jerseys

Issued at a rate of one in 18, these 18 cards feature a jersey swatch along with the player photo on the card.

STATED ODDS 1:18
AHJ Az-Zahir Hakim 3.00 8.00
BFJ Brett Favre 10.00 25.00
DBJ Drew Bledsoe 4.00 10.00
EGJ Eddie George 5.00 12.00
ESJ Emmitt Smith 8.00 20.00
JRJ Jerry Rice 10.00 25.00
MBJ Mark Brunell 4.00 10.00
MFJ Marshall Faulk 4.00 10.00
PMJ Peyton Manning 12.00 30.00
RDJ Ron Dayne 4.00 10.00
RGJ Rich Gannon 4.00 10.00
RWJ Ricky Williams 4.00 10.00
SMJ Steve McNair 4.00 10.00
TAJ Troy Aikman 6.00 15.00
TCJ Tim Couch 3.00 8.00
TGJ Terry Glenn 4.00 10.00
WCJ Wayne Chrebet 3.00 8.00
WDJ Warrick Dunn 3.00 8.00

2001 UD Game Gear Uniforms

Inserted in packs at a rate of one in 18, these 15 cards feature a game-used uniform swatch on it.

STATED ODDS 1:18
CBU Courtney Brown 3.00 8.00
CCU Cris Carter 5.00 12.00
DCU Daunte Culpepper 4.00 10.00
DMU Dan Marino 10.00 25.00
FMU Freddie Mitchell 3.00 8.00
JAU Jessie Armstead 3.00 8.00
JBU Jim Brown 10.00 25.00
JLU Jamal Lewis 5.00 12.00
JPU Jim Plunkett 4.00 10.00
KCU Kerry Collins 3.00 8.00
RDU Ron Dayne 4.00 10.00
RLU Ray Lewis 5.00 12.00
RMU Randy Moss 4.00 10.00
THU Torry Holt 4.00 10.00
WPU Walter Payton 12.00 30.00

2000 UD Graded

Released in mid January 2001, this 160-card set features 90 base cards sequentially numbered to 1500, 45 rookie cards, numbers 91-135, sequentially numbered to 1325, the first 855 of which were graded and inserted at the rate of one in two packs, and 25 autographed rookie cards, numbers 136-165, where card numbers 136-155 are sequentially numbered to 500 and card numbers 156-165 are sequentially numbered to 250. Of the autographed rookie cards, a total of 1217 cards were not graded, and graded versions were inserted at the rate of one in six packs. Card numbers 138, 139, 147, 148, and 163 were not issued. Cards are white along the top and the bottom with grey stripes, vertical on base cards and horizontal on rookie subsets, silver foil highlights and color player photographs. Serial numbers are placed on all of the card fronts. Graded versions of this set were encased with a blue SGC label so as not to be confused with cards graded after the initial packout. Upper Deck Graded series was packaged in 6-pack boxes with packs containing three ungraded and one graded card and carried a suggested retail price of $49.99.

COMP.SET w/o RC's (90) 50.00 100.00
91-135 ROOKIE PRINT RUN 1325
136-155 ROOKIE AU PRINT RUN 500
156-165 ROOKIE AU PRINT RUN 250
1 Jake Plummer .75 2.00
2 David Boston .75 2.00
3 Jamal Anderson 1.00 2.50
4 Shawn Jefferson .75 2.00
5 Qadry Ismail .75 2.00
6 Tony Banks .75 2.00
7 Priest Holmes .75 2.00
8 Rob Johnson 1.00 2.50
9 Eric Moulds .75 2.00
10 Steve Beuerlein 1.00 2.50
11 Muhsin Muhammad .75 2.00
12 Donald Hayes .75 2.00
13 Tim Biakabutuka 1.00 2.50
14 Cade McNown .75 2.00
15 Marcus Robinson 1.00 2.50
16 James Allen .75 2.00
17 Akili Smith .75 2.00
18 Corey Dillon .75 2.00
19 Tim Couch 1.00 2.50
20 Kevin Johnson .75 2.00
21 Troy Aikman 1.50 4.00
22 Emmitt Smith 2.00 5.00
23 Rocket Ismail 1.00 2.50
24 Terrell Davis 1.00 2.50
25 Rod Smith 1.00 2.50
26 Brian Griese .75 2.00
27 Charlie Batch .75 2.00
28 James Stewart .75 2.00
29 Germane Crowell .75 2.00
30 Brett Favre 2.50 6.00
31 Antonio Freeman 1.00 2.50
32 Dorsey Levens 1.00 2.50
33 Peyton Manning 3.00 8.00
34 Edgerrin James 1.00 2.50
35 Marvin Harrison 1.00 2.50
36 Mark Brunell 1.00 2.50
37 Jimmy Smith 1.00 2.50
38 Fred Taylor .75 2.00
39 Elvis Grbac .75 2.00
40 Tony Gonzalez 1.00 2.50
41 Lamar Smith .75 2.00
42 Jay Fiedler 1.00 2.50
43 Randy Moss 1.00 2.50
44 Daunte Culpepper 1.00 2.50
45 Robert Smith .75 2.00
46 Cris Carter 1.25 3.00
47 Drew Bledsoe 1.00 2.50
48 Kevin Faulk .75 2.00
49 Terry Glenn 1.00 2.50
50 Ricky Williams 1.00 2.50
51 Jeff Blake 1.00 2.50
52 Joe Horn 1.00 2.50
53 Kerry Collins .75 2.00
54 Amani Toomer .75 2.00
55 Tiki Barber 1.00 2.50
56 Wayne Chrebet .75 2.00
57 Curtis Martin 1.00 2.50
58 Vinny Testaverde .75 2.00
59 Tyrone Wheatley .75 2.00
60 Tim Brown 1.25 3.00
61 Rich Gannon 1.00 2.50
62 Duce Staley .75 2.00
63 Charles Johnson .75 2.00
64 Donovan McNabb 1.00 2.50
65 Bobby Shaw RC .75 2.00
66 Kordell Stewart .75 2.00
67 Jerome Bettis 1.25 3.00
68 Marshall Faulk 1.00 2.50
69 Isaac Bruce 1.25 3.00
70 Torry Holt 1.00 2.50
71 Kurt Warner 2.00 5.00
72 Neil Smith .75 2.00
73 Ryan Leaf 1.00 2.50
74 Curtis Conway 1.00 2.50
75 Jeff Garcia .75 2.00
76 Charlie Garner 1.00 2.50
77 Jerry Rice 3.00 8.00
78 Ricky Watters 1.00 2.50
79 Brock Huard .75 2.00
80 Jon Kitna .75 2.00
81 Keyshawn Johnson 1.00 2.50
82 Jacquez Green .75 2.00
83 Mike Alstott .75 2.00
84 Shaun King .75 2.00
85 Eddie George 1.00 2.50
86 Kevin Dyson 1.00 2.50
87 Steve McNair 1.00 2.50
88 Brad Johnson 1.00 2.50
89 Stephen Davis .75 2.00
90 Jeff George 1.00 2.50
91 Ron Dixon RC 2.00 5.00
92 Avion Black RC 2.00 5.00
93 Hank Poteat RC 2.00 5.00
94 Doug Chapman RC 2.00 5.00
95 Drew Haddad RC 2.00 5.00
96 Rondell Mealey RC 2.00 5.00
97 Spergon Wynn RC 2.00 5.00
98 Keith Bulluck RC 2.50 6.00
99 John Abraham RC 3.00 8.00
100 Rob Morris RC 2.50 6.00
101 Jerry Porter RC 3.00 8.00
102 Laveranues Coles RC 2.50 6.00
103 Jarious Jackson RC 2.50 6.00
104 Tom Brady RC 250.00 400.00
105 Jonas Lewis RC 2.00 5.00
106 Todd Husak RC 2.00 5.00
107 Shyrone Stith RC 2.00 5.00
108 Sammy Morris RC 2.00 5.00
109 Corey Simon RC 2.50 6.00
110 Chad Morton RC 2.50 6.00
111 Brian Urlacher RC 10.00 25.00
112 Anthony Becht RC 2.00 5.00
113 Chris Cole RC 2.50 6.00
114 Anthony Lucas RC 2.00 5.00
115 Charles Lee RC 2.00 5.00
116 JaJuan Dawson RC 2.00 5.00
117 Darrell Jackson RC 2.00 5.00
118 Gari Scott RC 2.00 5.00
119 Windrell Hayes RC 2.00 5.00
120 Paul Smith RC 2.00 5.00
121 Mareno Philyaw RC 2.00 5.00
122 Trevor Gaylor RC 2.00 5.00
123 Muneer Moore RC 2.00 5.00
124 Michael Wiley RC 2.00 5.00
125 Ronney Jenkins RC 2.00 5.00
126 Frank Moreau RC 2.00 5.00
127 Dante Hall RC 2.00 5.00
128 Darren Howard RC 2.00 5.00
129 Todd Pinkston RC 2.00 5.00
130 Mike Anderson RC 2.00 5.00
131 Doug Johnson RC 2.00 5.00
132 Shaun Ellis RC 2.50 6.00
133 James Williams RC 2.00 5.00
134 Ron Dugans RC 2.00 5.00
135 Frank Murphy RC 2.00 5.00
136 Dez White AU RC 6.00 15.00
137 Danny Farmer AU RC 6.00 15.00
140 Reuben Droughns AU RC 6.00 15.00
141 Jamal Lewis AU RC 10.00 25.00
142 J.R. Redmond AU RC 6.00 15.00
143 Tee Martin AU RC 6.00 15.00
144 Giovanni Carmazzi AU RC 6.00 15.00
145 Tim Rattay AU RC 8.00 20.00
146 Trung Canidate AU RC 6.00 15.00
149 Chris Coleman AU RC 6.00 15.00
150 Corey Moore AU RC 6.00 15.00
151 Troy Walters AU RC 6.00 15.00
152 Joe Hamilton AU RC 6.00 15.00
153 Kwame Cavil AU RC 6.00 15.00
154 Dennis Northcutt AU RC 6.00 15.00
155 Travis Taylor AU RC 6.00 15.00
156 Curtis Keaton AU RC 8.00 20.00
157 Shaun Alexander AU RC 12.00 30.00
158 Chad Pennington AU RC 10.00 25.00
159 Sylvester Morris AU RC 8.00 20.00
160 Plaxico Burress AU RC 10.00 25.00
161 Ron Dayne AU RC 12.00 30.00
162 Courtney Brown AU RC 10.00 25.00
164 Peter Warrick AU RC 8.00 20.00
165 Chris Redman AU RC 8.00 20.00

2000 UD Graded Jerseys

Randomly inserted in packs, this 21-card set contains cards with swatches of game jerseys in the lower right hand corner. Jersey swatches are overlayed so it appears that three square swatches are present on the card front. The cards resemble the base version and are highlighted with silver foil. A total of 2127 ungraded cards were issued in this 21-card set.

GBF Brett Favre 15.00 40.00
GCC Cris Carter 8.00 20.00
GDB Drew Bledsoe 6.00 15.00
GDM Dan Marino 20.00 50.00
GEJ Edgerrin James SP 8.00 20.00
GES Emmitt Smith SP 15.00 40.00
GIB Isaac Bruce SP 10.00 25.00
GJR Jerry Rice 20.00 50.00
GKJ Keyshawn Johnson 6.00 15.00
GKW Kurt Warner SP 15.00 40.00
GMB Mark Brunell SP 8.00 20.00
GPM Peyton Manning 15.00 40.00
GPW Peter Warrick 5.00 12.00
GRD Ron Dayne 8.00 20.00
GRJ Rob Johnson 6.00 15.00
GRM Randy Moss 6.00 15.00
GSK Shaun King 5.00 12.00
GSM Steve McNair SP 8.00 20.00
GTA Troy Aikman 12.50 30.00
GTH Torry Holt 6.00 15.00
GTJ Thomas Jones 6.00 15.00

2001 UD Graded

This 135 card set was issued in five card packs with a SRP of $49.99 per pack with six packs per box. The first 45 cards in the set feature leading NFL players while the other 90 cards are split with two different versions of 2001 NFL rookies. Each of these players have an action and a portrait shot. The rookies also have three different tiers of print runs: Cards numbered 46 to 55 have a print run of 500 serial numbered sets, cards numbered 56 to 65 have a print run of 750 serial numbered sets and cards numbered 66 through 90 have a print run of 900 serial numbered sets.

COMP.SET w/o SP's (45) 25.00 60.00
56-65: TWO VERSIONS SER.#'d TO 750 EACH
1 Jake Plummer .50 1.25
2 Jamal Anderson .60 1.50
3 Jamal Lewis .75 2.00
4 Rob Johnson .60 1.50
5 Muhsin Muhammad .50 1.25
6 Marcus Robinson .60 1.50
7 Peter Warrick .50 1.25
8 Corey Dillon .50 1.25
9 Tim Couch .50 1.25
10 Emmitt Smith 1.25 3.00
11 Terrell Davis .60 1.50
12 Brian Griese .50 1.25
13 Charlie Batch .50 1.25
14 Brett Favre 1.50 4.00
15 Peyton Manning 2.00 5.00
16 Edgerrin James .60 1.50
17 Mark Brunell .60 1.50
18 Fred Taylor .50 1.25
19 Tony Gonzalez .60 1.50
20 Trent Green .50 1.25
21 Lamar Smith .60 1.50
22 Randy Moss .60 1.50
23 Daunte Culpepper .60 1.50
24 Drew Bledsoe .60 1.50
25 Ricky Williams .60 1.50
26 Kerry Collins .50 1.25
27 Ron Dayne .60 1.50
28 Vinny Testaverde .50 1.25
29 Curtis Martin .60 1.50
30 Rich Gannon .60 1.50
31 Charlie Garner .60 1.50
32 Duce Staley .50 1.25
33 Donovan McNabb .60 1.50
34 Jerome Bettis .75 2.00
35 Marshall Faulk .60 1.50
36 Kurt Warner 1.25 3.00
37 Doug Flutie .60 1.50
38 Jeff Garcia .50 1.25
39 Terrell Owens .60 1.50
40 Matt Hasselbeck .50 1.25
41 Keyshawn Johnson .60 1.50
42 Mike Alstott .50 1.25
43 Eddie George .75 2.00
44 Steve McNair .60 1.50
45 Stephen Davis .50 1.25
46 Michael Bennett Action RC 2.50 6.00
46P Michael Bennett Portrait RC 2.50 6.00
47 Drew Brees Action RC 25.00 50.00
47P Drew Brees Portrait RC 25.00 50.00
48 Chad Johnson Action RC 3.00 8.00
48P Chad Johnson Portrait RC 3.00 8.00
49 Deuce McAllister Action RC 3.00 8.00
49P Deuce McAllister Portrait RC 3.00 8.00
50 Santana Moss Action RC 3.00 8.00
50P Santana Moss Portrait RC 3.00 8.00
51 Koren Robinson Action RC 2.50 6.00
51P Koren Robinson Portrait RC 2.50 6.00
52 David Terrell Action RC 2.50 6.00
52P David Terrell Portrait RC 2.50 6.00
53 LaDain Tomlinson Act RC 10.00 25.00
53P LaDain Tomlinson Port RC 10.00 25.00
54 Michael Vick Action RC 5.00 12.00
54P Michael Vick Portrait RC 5.00 12.00
55 Chris Weinke Action RC 2.50 6.00
55P Chris Weinke Portrait RC 2.50 6.00
56 Reggie Wayne Action RC 3.00 8.00
56P Reggie Wayne Portrait RC 3.00 8.00
57 Anthony Thomas Action RC 2.50 6.00
57P Anthony Thomas Portrait RC 2.50 6.00
58 Sage Rosenfels Action RC 2.00 5.00
58P Sage Rosenfels Portrait RC 2.00 5.00
59 Rod Gardner Action RC 2.00 5.00
59P Rod Gardner Portrait RC 2.00 5.00
60 Quincy Morgan Action RC 2.00 5.00
60P Quincy Morgan Portrait RC 2.00 5.00
61 Freddie Mitchell Action RC 1.50 4.00
61P Freddie Mitchell Portrait RC 1.50 4.00
62 Gerard Warren Action RC 2.00 5.00
62P Gerard Warren Portrait RC 2.00 5.00
63 James Jackson Action RC 1.50 4.00
63P James Jackson Portrait RC 1.50 4.00
64 Travis Henry Action RC 2.00 5.00
64P Travis Henry Portrait RC 2.00 5.00
65 Chris Chambers Action RC 1.50 4.00
65P Chris Chambers Portrait RC 1.50 4.00
66 Vinny Sutherland Action RC 1.50 4.00
66P Vinny Sutherland Portrait RC 1.50 4.00
67 Todd Heap Action RC 2.00 5.00
67P Todd Heap Portrait RC 2.00 5.00
68 Dan Morgan Action RC 2.00 5.00
68P Dan Morgan Portrait RC 2.00 5.00
69 Rudi Johnson Action RC 2.50 6.00
69P Rudi Johnson Portrait RC 2.50 6.00
70 Quincy Carter Action RC 2.00 5.00
70P Quincy Carter Portrait RC 2.00 5.00
71 Kevin Kasper Action RC 1.50 4.00
71P Kevin Kasper Portrait RC 1.50 4.00
72 Scotty Anderson Action RC 1.50 4.00
72P Scotty Anderson Portrait RC 1.50 4.00
73 Mike McMahon Action RC 2.00 5.00
73P Mike McMahon Portrait RC 2.00 5.00
74 Robert Ferguson Action RC 2.50 6.00
74P Robert Ferguson Portrait RC 2.50 6.00
75 Snoop Minnis Action RC 1.50 4.00
75P Snoop Minnis Portrait RC 1.50 4.00
76 Josh Heupel Action RC 2.50 6.00
76P Josh Heupel Portrait RC 2.50 6.00
77 Travis Minor Action RC 2.00 5.00
77P Travis Minor Portrait RC 2.00 5.00
78 Justin Smith Action RC 3.00 8.00
78P Justin Smith Portrait RC 3.00 8.00
79 Jesse Palmer Action RC 2.00 5.00
79P Jesse Palmer Portrait RC 2.00 5.00
80 Marques Tuiasosopo Act RC 2.00 5.00
80P Marques Tuiasosopo Port RC 2.00 5.00
81 A.J. Feeley Action RC 2.00 5.00
81P A.J. Feeley Portrait RC 2.00 5.00
82 Correll Buckhalter Act RC 1.50 4.00
82P Correll Buckhalter Portrait RC 1.50 4.00
83 Kevan Barlow Action RC 2.00 5.00
83P Kevan Barlow Portrait RC 2.00 5.00
84 Alex Bannister Action RC 1.50 4.00
84P Alex Bannister Portrait RC 1.50 4.00
85 Josh Booty Action RC 2.00 5.00
85P Josh Booty Portrait RC 2.00 5.00
86 Eddie Berlin Action RC 1.50 4.00
86P Eddie Berlin Portrait RC 1.50 4.00
87 Andre Carter Action RC 2.00 5.00
87P Andre Carter Portrait RC 2.00 5.00
88 LaMont Jordan Action RC 2.50 6.00
88P LaMont Jordan Portrait RC 2.50 6.00
89 Ken-Yon Rambo Action RC 1.50 4.00
89P Ken-Yon Rambo Portrait RC 1.50 4.00
90 Alge Crumpler Action RC 2.50 6.00
90P Alge Crumpler Portrait RC 2.50 6.00

2001 UD Graded Rookie Autographs

Randomly inserted in packs, these cards are a quasi-parallel of the Rookie cards in the 2001 UD Graded series. Only cards numbered from 46 through 65 were issued in this fashion. Cards numbered 46 through 55 have a print run of 500 serial numbered sets, while cards numbered 56-65 have a print run of 750 serial numbered sets.

46-55 PRINT RUN 500
56-65 PRINT RUN 750
46 Michael Bennett/500 8.00 20.00
47 Drew Brees/500 400.00 800.00
48 Chad Johnson/500 10.00 25.00
49 Deuce McAllister/500 10.00 25.00
50 Santana Moss/500 10.00 25.00
51 Koren Robinson/500 8.00 20.00
52 David Terrell/500 8.00 20.00
53 LaDainian Tomlinson/500 25.00 60.00
54 Michael Vick/500 25.00 60.00
55 Chris Weinke/500 8.00 20.00
56 Reggie Wayne/750 30.00 60.00
57 Anthony Thomas/750 10.00 25.00
58 Sage Rosenfels/750 8.00 20.00
59 Rod Gardner/750 8.00 20.00
60 Quincy Morgan/750 8.00 20.00
61 Freddie Mitchell/750 6.00 15.00
62 Gerard Warren/750 8.00 20.00
63 James Jackson/750 6.00 15.00
64 Travis Henry/750 8.00 20.00
65 Chris Chambers/750 6.00 15.00

2001 UD Graded Rookie Jerseys

milar to the UD Graded Rookie Autograph insert set, these cards are a partial parallel to the regular UD Graded set. Cards numbered 46 to 65 were issued for this set and picture the player along with a game-used jersey swatch with blue foil highlights. The cards were serial numbered to either 500 or 750 on the front. While most Drew Brees cards feature the correct second number (500) of the serial number, a few have been found to have 100 incorrectly printed as the second number of the serial numbering string.

STATED PRINT RUN 500-750
46 Michael Bennett/500 5.00 12.00
47 Drew Brees/500 25.00 60.00
48 Chad Johnson/500 6.00 15.00
49 Deuce McAllister/500 6.00 15.00
50 Santana Moss/500 6.00 15.00
51 Koren Robinson/500 5.00 12.00
52 David Terrell/500 5.00 12.00
53 LaDainian Tomlinson/500 20.00 50.00
54 Michael Vick/500 10.00 25.00
55 Chris Weinke/500 5.00 12.00
56 Reggie Wayne/750 8.00 20.00
57 Anthony Thomas/750 6.00 15.00
58 Sage Rosenfels/750 5.00 12.00
59 Rod Gardner/750 5.00 12.00
60 Quincy Morgan/750 5.00 12.00
61 Freddie Mitchell/750 4.00 10.00
62 Gerard Warren/750 5.00 12.00
63 James Jackson/750 4.00 10.00
64 Travis Henry/750 5.00 12.00
65 Chris Chambers/750 4.00 10.00

2001 UD Graded Jerseys

Issued at a rate of one every two packs, this 21 card set feature leading players along a game-worn jersey piece of these players on the card.

STATED ODDS 1:2
*BLUE/125: .5X TO 1.2X BASIC JSYs
BF Brett Favre 10.00 25.00
CB Charlie Batch 3.00 8.00
CC Cris Carter 5.00 12.00
CH Chris Chandler 4.00 10.00
DB David Boston 3.00 8.00
DC Daunte Culpepper 4.00 10.00
JL Jamal Lewis 5.00 12.00
JR Jerry Rice 10.00 25.00
JS Jimmy Smith 4.00 10.00
KJ Keyshawn Johnson 4.00 10.00
KM Keenan McCardell 4.00 10.00
KW Kurt Warner 8.00 20.00
MB Mark Brunell 4.00 10.00
MF Marshall Faulk 4.00 10.00
PM Peyton Manning 12.00 30.00
PW Peter Warrick 3.00 8.00
RD Ron Dayne 4.00 10.00
RM Randy Moss 4.00 10.00
SS Shannon Sharpe 4.00 10.00
TB Tiki Barber 4.00 10.00

2002 UD Graded

This 200 card set consists of 90 veterans and 110 rookies. Cards 91-150 were serial #'d to 700, cards 151-180 were numbered to 550 and autographed, and cards 181-200 were numbered to 250 and autographed. Please note that some cards were only available as redemptions with an expiration date of 9/30/2005. Pack SRP was $49.99. Each pack contained one PSA graded rookie and 4 regular cards.

COMP.SET w/o SP's (90) 20.00 50.00
151-180 ROOKIE AUTO PRINT RUN 550
1 David Boston .30 .75
2 Frank Sanders .30 .75
3 Jake Plummer .30 .75
4 Shawn Jefferson .30 .75
5 Michael Vick .40 1.00
6 Warrick Dunn .30 .75
7 Chris Redman .30 .75
8 Ray Lewis .50 1.25
9 Travis Taylor .30 .75
10 Drew Bledsoe .40 1.00
11 Eric Moulds .30 .75
12 Travis Henry .30 .75
13 Chris Weinke .30 .75
14 Muhsin Muhammad .30 .75
15 Anthony Thomas .40 1.00
16 Brian Urlacher .50 1.25
17 Jim Miller .30 .75
18 Corey Dillon .30 .75
19 Jon Kitna .30 .75
20 Peter Warrick .30 .75
21 James Jackson .30 .75
22 Kevin Johnson .30 .75
23 Tim Couch .30 .75
24 Emmitt Smith .75 2.00
25 Joey Galloway .40 1.00
26 Quincy Carter .30 .75
27 Brian Griese .30 .75
28 Shannon Sharpe .40 1.00
29 Terrell Davis .40 1.00
30 Az-Zahir Hakim .30 .75
31 Germane Crowell .30 .75
32 Mike McMahon .30 .75
33 Ahman Green .40 1.00
34 Brett Favre 1.00 2.50
35 Terry Glenn .40 1.00
36 Jermaine Lewis .30 .75
37 James Allen .30 .75
38 Edgerrin James .40 1.00
39 Marvin Harrison .40 1.00
40 Peyton Manning 1.25 3.00
41 Fred Taylor .30 .75
42 Jimmy Smith .40 1.00
43 Mark Brunell .40 1.00
44 Priest Holmes .30 .75
45 Trent Green .30 .75
46 Chris Chambers .30 .75
47 Jay Fiedler .40 1.00
48 Ricky Williams .40 1.00
49 Daunte Culpepper .40 1.00
50 Michael Bennett .30 .75
51 Randy Moss .40 1.00
52 Antowain Smith .40 1.00
53 Tom Brady 2.50 6.00
54 Troy Brown .30 .75
55 Aaron Brooks .30 .75
56 Deuce McAllister .40 1.00
57 Joe Horn .30 .75
58 Kerry Collins .30 .75
59 Ron Dayne .40 1.00
60 Chad Pennington .30 .75
61 Curtis Martin .40 1.00
62 Vinny Testaverde .30 .75
63 Jerry Rice 1.00 2.50
64 Rich Gannon .40 1.00
65 Tim Brown .50 1.25
66 Donovan McNabb .40 1.00
67 Duce Staley .30 .75
68 Freddie Mitchell .30 .75
69 Hines Ward .40 1.00
70 Jerome Bettis .50 1.25
71 Kordell Stewart .30 .75
72 Doug Flutie .40 1.00
73 Drew Brees 1.00 2.50
74 LaDainian Tomlinson .50 1.25
75 Garrison Hearst .30 .75
76 Jeff Garcia .30 .75
77 Terrell Owens .40 1.00
78 Koren Robinson .30 .75
79 Shaun Alexander .30 .75
80 Trent Dilfer .30 .75
81 Isaac Bruce .50 1.25
82 Kurt Warner .40 1.00
83 Marshall Faulk .40 1.00
84 Brad Johnson .40 1.00
85 Keyshawn Johnson .40 1.00
86 Rob Johnson .40 1.00
87 Eddie George .40 1.00
88 Steve McNair .40 1.00
89 Rod Gardner .30 .75
90 Stephen Davis .30 .75
91 Daniel Graham A RC 1.50 4.00
92 Josh McCown A RC 2.00 5.00
93 Josh Scobey A RC 1.50 4.00
94 T.J. Duckett A RC 1.25 3.00
95 Ronald Curry A RC 1.25 3.00
96 Kalimba Edwards A RC 1.50 4.00
97 Chester Taylor A RC 2.00 5.00
98 Randy Fasani A RC 1.25 3.00
99 Adrian Peterson A RC 1.50 4.00
100 Chad Hutchinson A RC 1.25 3.00
101 Javon Walker A RC 2.00 5.00
102 Jonathan Wells A RC 1.50 4.00
103 David Garrard A RC 1.50 4.00
104 Leonard Henry A RC 1.25 3.00
105 Dusty Bonner A RC 1.25 3.00
106 Donte Stallworth A RC 2.00 5.00
107 J.T. O'Sullivan A RC 1.50 4.00
108 Mike Williams A RC 1.25 3.00
109 Tim Carter A RC 1.50 4.00
110 Larry Ned A RC 1.25 3.00
111 Brian Westbrook A RC 2.50 6.00
112 Freddie Milons A RC 1.25 3.00
113 Ed Reed A RC 8.00 20.00
114 Antwaan Randle El A RC 1.50 4.00
115 Julius Peppers A RC 3.00 8.00
116 Quentin Jammer A RC 2.00 5.00
117 John Henderson A RC 1.50 4.00
118 Travis Stephens A RC 1.25 3.00
119 Ladell Betts A RC 2.00 5.00
120 Cliff Russell A RC 1.25 3.00
121 Daniel Graham P RC 1.50 4.00
122 Josh McCown P RC 2.00 5.00
123 Josh Scobey P RC 1.50 4.00
124 T.J. Duckett P RC 1.25 3.00
125 Ronald Curry P RC 1.25 3.00
126 Kalimba Edwards P RC 1.50 4.00
127 Chester Taylor P RC 2.00 5.00
128 Randy Fasani P RC 1.25 3.00
129 Adrian Peterson P RC 1.50 4.00
130 Chad Hutchinson P RC 1.25 3.00
131 Javon Walker P RC 2.00 5.00
132 Jonathan Wells P RC 1.50 4.00
133 David Garrard P RC 1.50 4.00
134 Leonard Henry P RC 1.25 3.00
135 Dusty Bonner P RC 1.25 3.00
136 Donte Stallworth P RC 2.00 5.00
137 J.T. O'Sullivan P RC 1.50 4.00
138 Mike Williams P RC 1.25 3.00
139 Tim Carter P RC 1.50 4.00
140 Larry Ned P RC 1.25 3.00
141 Brian Westbrook P RC 2.50 6.00
142 Freddie Milons P RC 1.25 3.00
143 Ed Reed P RC 8.00 20.00
144 Antwaan Randle El P RC 1.50 4.00
145 Julius Peppers P RC 3.00 8.00
146 Quentin Jammer P RC 2.00 5.00
147 John Henderson P RC 1.50 4.00
148 Travis Stephens P RC 1.25 3.00
149 Ladell Betts P RC 2.00 5.00
150 Cliff Russell P RC 1.25 3.00
151 Ron Johnson A AU RC 6.00 15.00
152 Josh Reed A AU RC 6.00 15.00
153 DeShaun Foster A AU RC 8.00 20.00
154 Andre Davis A AU RC 5.00 12.00
155 Antonio Bryant A AU RC 8.00 20.00
156 Roy Williams A AU RC 5.00 12.00
157 Woody Dantzler A AU RC 6.00 15.00
158 Luke Staley A AU RC 5.00 12.00
159 Jabar Gaffney A AU RC 5.00 12.00
160 Rohan Davey A AU RC 8.00 20.00
161 Brandon Doman A AU RC 5.00 12.00
162 Napoleon Harris A AU RC 6.00 15.00
163 Reche Caldwell A AU RC 6.00 15.00
164 Kelly Campbell A AU RC 6.00 15.00
165 Eric Crouch A AU RC 8.00 20.00
166 Ron Johnson P AU RC 6.00 15.00
167 Josh Reed P AU RC 6.00 15.00

168 DeShaun Foster P AU RC 8.00 20.00
169 Andre Davis P AU RC 5.00 12.00
170 Antonio Bryant P AU RC 8.00 20.00
171 Roy Williams P AU RC 5.00 12.00
172 Woody Dantzler P AU RC 6.00 15.00
173 Luke Staley P AU RC 5.00 12.00
174 Jabar Gaffney P AU RC 5.00 12.00
175 Rohan Davey P AU RC 8.00 20.00
176 Brandon Doman P AU RC 5.00 12.00
177 Napoleon Harris P AU RC 6.00 15.00
178 Reche Caldwell P AU RC 6.00 15.00
179 Kelly Campbell P AU RC 6.00 15.00
180 Eric Crouch P AU RC 8.00 20.00
181 Kurt Kittner A AU RC 6.00 15.00
182 Jeremy Shockey A AU RC 10.00 25.00
183 William Green A AU RC 8.00 20.00
184 Clinton Portis A AU RC 10.00 25.00
185 Ashley Lelie A AU RC 6.00 15.00
186 Joey Harrington A AU RC 6.00 15.00
187 David Carr A AU RC 6.00 15.00
188 Maurice Morris A AU RC 8.00 20.00
189 Marquise Walker A AU RC 6.00 15.00
190 Patrick Ramsey A AU RC 8.00 20.00
191 Kurt Kittner P AU RC 6.00 15.00
192 Jeremy Shockey P AU RC 10.00 25.00
193 William Green P AU RC 8.00 20.00
194 Clinton Portis P AU RC 10.00 25.00
195 Ashley Lelie P AU RC 6.00 15.00
196 Joey Harrington P AU RC 6.00 15.00
197 David Carr P AU RC 6.00 15.00
198 Maurice Morris P AU RC 8.00 20.00
199 Marquise Walker P AU RC 6.00 15.00
200 Patrick Ramsey P AU RC 8.00 20.00

2002 UD Graded Gold

*1-90 VETS: 5X TO 12X BASIC CARDS
*91-150 ROOKIES: 1X TO 2.5X
*151-180 ROOKIES: .8X TO 2X
*181-200 ROOKIES: .6X TO 1.5X
GOLD PRINT RUN 75 SER.#'d SETS

2002 UD Graded Dual Game Jerseys

This set features two swatches of game used jersey from many of the NFL's best players. Each card was serial numbered of 100.
STATED PRINT RUN 100 SER.#'d SETS
BP100 D.Bledsoe/P.Price 6.00 15.00
BS100 M.Brunell/J.Smith 6.00 15.00
BT100 D.Brees/L.Tomlinson 15.00 40.00
CM100 D.Culpepper/R.Moss 6.00 15.00
FC100 J.Fiedler/C.Chambers 6.00 15.00
FS100 J.Seau/D.Flutie 6.00 15.00
GR100 R.Gannon/J.Rice 15.00 40.00
JC100 T.Couch/Kev.Johnson 5.00 12.00
JP100 M.Pittman/Key.Johnson 6.00 15.00
MJ100 P.Manning/E.James 20.00 50.00
MT100 C.Martin/V.Testaverde 6.00 15.00
PB100 J.Plummer/D.Boston 5.00 12.00
SB100 K.Stewart/K.Bell 5.00 12.00
SS100 C.Simon/D.Staley 5.00 12.00
TB100 A.Thomas/M.Booker 6.00 15.00
WF100 B.Favre/K.Warner 15.00 40.00
WH100 K.Warner/T.Holt 6.00 15.00

2002 UD Graded Jerseys

Randomly inserted into packs, these cards feature swatches of game used jersey and are serial numbered to varying quantities.
STATED PRINT RUN 50-200
UNPRICED GOLD PRINT RUN 10-15
G1AN Mike Anderson/200 2.50 6.00
G1BA Brad Johnson/200 3.00 8.00
G1BL Drew Bledsoe/200 3.00 8.00
G1BO David Boston/200 2.50 6.00
G1BR Drew Brees/200 8.00 20.00
G1BU Brian Urlacher/200 4.00 10.00
G1CM Curtis Martin/200 3.00 8.00
G1CP Chad Pennington/200 2.50 6.00
G1CW Chris Weinke/200 2.50 6.00
G1DB Drew Bledsoe/200 3.00 8.00
G1DF Doug Flutie/200 3.00 8.00
G1EG Eddie George/200 3.00 8.00
G1EJ Edgerrin James/200 3.00 8.00
G1JJ J.J. Stokes/200 2.50 6.00
G1JS Junior Seau/200 3.00 8.00
G1KJ Keyshawn Johnson/200 3.00 8.00
G1KW Kurt Warner/200 3.00 8.00
G1LT LaDainian Tomlinson/200 4.00 10.00
G1MA Mike Alstott/200 2.50 6.00
G1MB Mark Brunell/200 3.00 8.00
G1MF Marshall Faulk/200 3.00 8.00
G1MN Peyton Manning/200 10.00 25.00
G1MO Johnnie Morton/200 3.00 8.00
G1MS Michael Strahan/200 3.00 8.00
G1PH Priest Holmes/200 2.50 6.00
G1PM Peyton Manning/200 10.00 25.00
G1RA Ron Dayne/200 3.00 8.00
G1RD Ron Dayne/200 3.00 8.00
G1RG Rod Gardner/200 2.50 6.00
G1RG Rich Gannon/200 3.00 8.00
G1RM Randy Moss/200 3.00 8.00
G1SD Stephen Davis/200 2.50 6.00
G1SE Junior Seau/200 3.00 8.00
G1SM Steve McNair/200 3.00 8.00
G1TC Tim Couch/200 2.50 6.00
G1TD Terrell Davis/200 3.00 8.00
G1TG Trent Green/200 2.50 6.00
G1TJ Thomas Jones/200 2.50 6.00
G1TO Terrell Owens/200 3.00 8.00
G1TT Travis Taylor/200 2.50 6.00
G1VT Vinny Testaverde/200 2.50 6.00
G1WE Chris Weinke/200 2.50 6.00
G2DB Drew Bledsoe/100 4.00 10.00
G2EJ Edgerrin James/100 4.00 10.00
G2JP Jake Plummer/100 3.00 8.00
G2JR Jerry Rice/100 10.00 25.00
G2KW Kurt Warner/100 4.00 10.00
G2RM Randy Moss/100 4.00 10.00
G2SD Stephen Davis/100 3.00 8.00
G2SM Steve McNair/100 4.00 10.00
G2TC Tim Couch/100 3.00 8.00
G2TO Terrell Owens/100 4.00 10.00
G3BO David Boston/50 4.00 10.00
G3CA David Carr/50 4.00 10.00
G3CB Champ Bailey/50 5.00 12.00
G3CM Curtis Martin/50 5.00 12.00
G3CO Courtney Brown/50 4.00 10.00
G3DS Duce Staley/50 4.00 10.00
G3EG Eddie George/50 5.00 12.00
G3EJ Edgerrin James/50 5.00 12.00
G3IB Isaac Bruce/50 6.00 15.00
G3KS Kordell Stewart/50 4.00 10.00
G3KW Kurt Warner/50 5.00 12.00
G3MB Mark Brunell/50 5.00 12.00
G3MH Marvin Harrison/50 5.00 12.00
G3PM Peyton Manning/50 15.00 40.00
G3RD Ron Dayne/50 5.00 12.00
G3RG Rich Gannon/50 5.00 12.00
G3RM Randy Moss/50 5.00 12.00
G3SM Steve McNair/50 5.00 12.00
G3TB Tim Brown/50 6.00 15.00
G3TC Tim Couch/50 4.00 10.00
G3TD Terrell Davis/50 5.00 12.00
G3TO Terrell Owens/50 5.00 12.00
G4AT Anthony Thomas/75 4.00 10.00
G4BF Brett Favre/75 10.00 25.00
G4BO David Boston/75 3.00 8.00
G4BR Drew Brees/75 10.00 25.00
G4CM Curtis Martin/75 4.00 10.00
G4DB Drew Bledsoe/75 4.00 10.00
G4DC Daunte Culpepper/75 4.00 10.00
G4DF Doug Flutie/75 4.00 10.00
G4DM Dan Marino/75 10.00 25.00
G4DS Duce Staley/75 3.00 8.00
G4EJ Edgerrin James/75 4.00 10.00
G4EM Eric Moulds/75 3.00 8.00
G4FO DeShaun Foster/75 5.00 12.00
G4IB Isaac Bruce/75 5.00 12.00
G4JE John Elway/75 8.00 20.00
G4JH Joey Harrington/75 3.00 8.00
G4JP Jake Plummer/75 3.00 8.00
G4JR Jerry Rice/75 10.00 25.00
G4JS James Stewart/75 3.00 8.00
G4KS Kordell Stewart/75 3.00 8.00
G4KW Kurt Warner/75 4.00 10.00
G4MB Mark Brunell/75 4.00 10.00
G4MH Marvin Harrison/75 4.00 10.00
G4PM Peyton Manning/75 12.00 30.00
G4PR Patrick Ramsey/75 4.00 10.00
G4RG Rich Gannon/75 4.00 10.00
G4SD Stephen Davis/75 3.00 8.00
G4SM Steve McNair/75 4.00 10.00
G4TH Torry Holt/75 4.00 10.00
G4WS Warren Sapp/75 4.00 10.00
G5AT Anthony Thomas/75 4.00 10.00
G5BF Brett Favre/75 10.00 25.00
G5BO David Boston/75 3.00 8.00
G5BU Brian Urlacher/75 5.00 12.00
G5CA David Carr/75 3.00 8.00
G5CM Curtis Martin/75 4.00 10.00
G5CP Chad Pennington/75 3.00 8.00
G5DC Daunte Culpepper/75 4.00 10.00
G5DF Doug Flutie/75 4.00 10.00
G5EM Eric Moulds/75 3.00 8.00
G5JH Joey Harrington/75 3.00 8.00
G5JL Jamal Lewis/75 4.00 10.00
G5JP Jake Plummer/75 3.00 8.00
G5JR Jerry Rice/75 10.00 25.00
G5JS James Stewart/75 3.00 8.00
G5KJ Keyshawn Johnson/75 4.00 10.00
G5KW Kurt Warner/75 4.00 10.00
G5LT LaDainian Tomlinson/75 5.00 12.00
G5MB Mark Brunell/75 4.00 10.00
G5PM Peyton Manning/75 12.00 30.00
G5RL Ray Lewis/75 5.00 12.00
G5WD Warrick Dunn/75 3.00 8.00
G6AT Anthony Thomas/50 5.00 12.00
G6BF Brett Favre/50 12.00 30.00
G6BO David Boston/50 4.00 10.00
G6CG Charlie Garner/50 5.00 12.00
G6DC David Carr/50 4.00 10.00
G6DF Doug Flutie/50 5.00 12.00
G6JR Jerry Rice/50 12.00 30.00
G6KW Kurt Warner/50 5.00 12.00
G6LT LaDainian Tomlinson/50 6.00 15.00
G6TJ Thomas Jones/50 4.00 10.00

2002 UD Graded Rookie Jerseys

This set features cards with jersey swatches from many of the NFL's top 2002 rookies. Most cards were serial #'d to 350, with the exceptions being noted below numbered to 50. There was also a gold parallel serial #'d to 125 or 10.
STATED PRINT RUN 50-350
*GOLD/125: .5X TO 1.2X JSY/350
GOLD PRINT RUN 10-125
AB500 Antonio Bryant 4.00 10.00
AD500 Andre Davis 2.50 6.00
AL500 Ashley Lelie 2.50 6.00
CP500 Clinton Portis 4.00 10.00
CR500 Cliff Russell 2.50 6.00
DC500 David Carr 2.50 6.00
DF500 DeShaun Foster 4.00 10.00
DG500 Daniel Graham 3.00 8.00
DS500 Donte Stallworth 4.00 10.00
EC500 Eric Crouch 4.00 10.00
EL500 Antwaan Randle El 3.00 8.00
JG500 Jabar Gaffney 2.50 6.00
JH500 Joey Harrington/50 4.00 10.00
JM500 Josh McCown 4.00 10.00
JP500 Julius Peppers 6.00 15.00
JR500 Josh Reed 3.00 8.00
JS500 Jeremy Shockey 4.00 10.00
LB500 Ladell Betts 4.00 10.00
MM500 Maurice Morris 3.00 8.00
MW500 Marquise Walker 2.50 6.00
PR500 Patrick Ramsey 3.00 8.00
RC500 Reche Caldwell 3.00 8.00
RD500 Rohan Davey 4.00 10.00
RJ500 Ron Johnson 3.00 8.00
RW500 Roy Williams 2.50 6.00
TC500 Tim Carter 3.00 8.00
TJ500 T.J. Duckett 2.50 6.00
TS500 Travis Stephens 2.50 6.00
WA500 Javon Walker 4.00 10.00
WG500 William Green 3.00 8.00
RGDC David Carr/50 4.00 10.00
RGDS Donte Stallworth/50 6.00 15.00
RGJP Julius Peppers/50 10.00 25.00
RGWG William Green/50 5.00 12.00

2013 UD Infinite Industry Summit Exclusives

STATED PRINT RUN 150 SER. #'d SETS
EX3 Robert Griffin III 20.00 50.00

1999 UD Ionix

The 1999 Upper Deck Ionix set was issued in one series for a total of 90 cards and was distributed in four-card packs with a suggested retail price of $4.99. The fronts feature action color photos of 60 veterans and 30 rookies printed on thick, double-laminated metalized cards.. The Rookie subset cards have an insertion rate of 1:4 packs.
COMPLETE SET (90) 40.00 100.00
COMP.SET w/o SP's (60) 12.50 25.00
1 Jake Plummer .25 .60
2 Adrian Murrell .25 .60
3 Jamal Anderson .30 .75
4 Chris Chandler .30 .75
5 Priest Holmes .25 .60
6 Michael Jackson .25 .60
7 Antowain Smith .25 .60
8 Doug Flutie .40 1.00
9 Tim Biakabutuka .30 .75
10 Muhsin Muhammad .25 .60
11 Erik Kramer .30 .75
12 Curtis Enis .25 .60
13 Corey Dillon .25 .60
14 Ty Detmer .25 .60
15 Justin Armour .25 .60
16 Troy Aikman .50 1.25
17 Emmitt Smith .60 1.50
18 John Elway .60 1.50
19 Terrell Davis .30 .75
20 Barry Sanders .60 1.50
21 Charlie Batch .25 .60
22 Brett Favre .75 2.00
23 Dorsey Levens .30 .75
24 Marshall Faulk .30 .75
25 Peyton Manning 1.25 3.00
26 Mark Brunell .30 .75
27 Fred Taylor .25 .60
28 [illegible]
29 Andre Rison .30 .75
30 Dan Marino .75 2.00
31 Karim Abdul-Jabbar .25 .60
32 Randall Cunningham .30 .75
33 Randy Moss .30 .75
34 Drew Bledsoe .30 .75
35 Terry Glenn .30 .75
36 Danny Wuerffel .30 .75
37 Kent Graham .25 .60
38 Gary Brown .25 .60
39 Vinny Testaverde .25 .60
40 Keyshawn Johnson .30 .75
41 Napoleon Kaufman .25 .60
42 Tim Brown .40 1.00
43 Koy Detmer .25 .60
44 Duce Staley .25 .60
45 Kordell Stewart .25 .60
46 Jerome Bettis .40 1.00
47 Isaac Bruce .40 1.00
48 Robert Holcombe .25 .60
49 Jim Harbaugh .30 .75
50 Natrone Means .30 .75
51 Steve Young .50 1.25
52 Jerry Rice 1.00 2.50
53 Jon Kitna .25 .60
54 Joey Galloway .30 .75
55 Warrick Dunn .25 .60
56 Trent Dilfer .25 .60
57 Steve McNair .30 .75
58 Eddie George .30 .75
59 Skip Hicks .25 .60
60 Michael Westbrook .25 .60
61 Tim Couch RC .60 1.50
62 Ricky Williams RC .75 2.00
63 Daunte Culpepper RC .75 2.00
64 Akili Smith RC .50 1.25
65 Donovan McNabb RC 4.00 10.00
66 Michael Bishop RC .60 1.50
67 Brock Huard RC .50 1.25
68 Torry Holt RC 1.00 2.50
69 Cade McNown RC .50 1.25
70 Shaun King RC .50 1.25
71 Champ Bailey RC 1.00 2.50
72 Chris Claiborne RC .50 1.25
73 Jevon Kearse RC .60 1.50
74 D'Wayne Bates RC .50 1.25
75 David Boston RC .50 1.25
76 Edgerrin James RC .75 2.00
77 Sedrick Irvin RC .50 1.25
78 Dameane Douglas RC .50 1.25
79 Troy Edwards RC .50 1.25
80 Ebenezer Ekuban RC .50 1.25
81 Kevin Faulk RC .50 1.25
82 Joe Germaine RC .60 1.50
83 Kevin Johnson RC .60 1.50
84 Andy Katzenmoyer RC .60 1.50
85 Rob Konrad RC .50 1.25
86 Chris McAlister RC .50 1.25
87 Peerless Price RC .50 1.25
88 Tai Streets RC .60 1.50
89 Autry Denson RC .50 1.25
90 Amos Zereoue RC .50 1.25

1999 UD Ionix Reciprocal

MPLETE SET (90) 200.00 400.00
*RECIP.STARS 1-60: 1.2X TO 3X HI COL.
RECIP.1-60 STATED ODDS 1:6
*RECIPROCAL RCs 61-90: .6X TO 1.5X
RECIP.61-90 STATED ODDS 1:19

1999 UD Ionix Astronomix

Randomly inserted into packs at the rate of one in 23, this 25-card set highlights the great statistical achievements of 25 top NFL stars.
COMPLETE SET (25) 100.00 200.00
STATED ODDS 1:23
A1 Keyshawn Johnson 2.50 6.00
A2 Emmitt Smith 5.00 12.00
A3 Eddie George 2.50 6.00
A4 Fred Taylor 2.50 6.00
A5 Peyton Manning 8.00 20.00
A6 John Elway 8.00 20.00
A7 Brett Favre 8.00 20.00
A8 Terrell Davis 2.50 6.00
A9 Mark Brunell 2.50 6.00
A10 Dan Marino 8.00 20.00
A11 Randall Cunningham 2.50 6.00
A12 Steve McNair 2.50 6.00
A13 Jamal Anderson 2.50 6.00
A14 Barry Sanders 8.00 20.00
A15 Jake Plummer 1.50 4.00
A16 Drew Bledsoe 3.00 8.00
A17 Jerome Bettis 2.50 6.00
A18 Jerry Rice 5.00 12.00
A19 Warrick Dunn 2.50 6.00
A20 Steve Young 3.00 8.00
A21 Terrell Owens 2.50 6.00
A22 Ricky Williams 2.00 5.00
A23 Akili Smith .75 2.00
A24 Cade McNown .75 2.00
A25 David Boston 1.00 2.50

1999 UD Ionix Electric Forces

Randomly inserted in packs at the rate of one in six, this 20-card set features action color photos of some of the most collectible NFL stars printed on cards using graphic technology.
COMPLETE SET (20) 30.00 60.00
STATED ODDS 1:6
EF1 Ricky Williams .75 2.00
EF2 Tim Couch .40 1.00
EF3 Daunte Culpepper 1.50 4.00
EF4 Akili Smith .30 .75
EF5 Cade McNown .30 .75
EF6 Donovan McNabb 2.00 5.00
EF7 Brock Huard .40 1.00
EF8 Michael Bishop .40 1.00
EF9 Torry Holt 1.00 2.50
EF10 Peerless Price .40 1.00
EF11 Peyton Manning 2.50 6.00
EF12 Jake Plummer .50 1.25
EF13 John Elway 2.50 6.00
EF14 Mark Brunell .75 2.00
EF15 Steve Young 1.00 2.50
EF16 Jamal Anderson .75 2.00
EF17 Kordell Stewart .50 1.25
EF18 Eddie George .75 2.00
EF19 Fred Taylor .75 2.00
EF20 Brett Favre 2.50 6.00

1999 UD Ionix HoloGrFX

Randomly inserted into packs at the rate of one in 1,500, this 10-card set features color action photos of some of Football's most collectible players printed on cards that combine rainbow foil and Ionix technology.
COMPLETE SET (10) 150.00 400.00
STATED ODDS 1:1500
H1 Ricky Williams 15.00 30.00
H2 Tim Couch 15.00 30.00
H3 Cade McNown 10.00 25.00
H4 Peyton Manning 30.00 80.00
H5 Jake Plummer 10.00 25.00
H6 Randy Moss 25.00 60.00
H7 Barry Sanders 30.00 80.00
H8 Jamal Anderson 15.00 30.00
H9 Terrell Davis 15.00 30.00
H10 Brett Favre 30.00 80.00

1999 UD Ionix Power F/X

Randomly inserted into packs at the rate of one in 11, this set features color action photos of the most talented rookies and supreme veterans printed on cards using Ionix technology.
COMPLETE SET (9) 20.00 40.00
STATED ODDS 1:11
[illegible]
P2 Randy Moss 2.50 6.00
P3 Terrell Davis 1.00 2.50
P4 Steve Young 1.25 3.00
P5 Dan Marino 3.00 8.00
P6 Warrick Dunn 1.00 2.50
P7 Keyshawn Johnson 1.00 2.50
P8 Barry Sanders 3.00 8.00
P9 Tim Couch .60 1.50
P10 Ricky Williams 1.25 3.00

1999 UD Ionix UD Authentics

Randomly inserted into packs, this set features color action autographed cards of top rookies. Reportedly, 100 of each card was produced except for Ricky Williams who signed only 50 cards. Some cards were issued via mail redemptions that carried an expiration date of 7/15/2000. Unlike the other UD Authentics cards issued in packs in 1999, the Ionix inserts do not have the brand logo printed on the cards.
AS Akili Smith 25.00 50.00
BH Brock Huard 25.00 50.00
CM Cade McNown 25.00 50.00
DC Daunte Culpepper 40.00 80.00
DM Donovan McNabb 40.00 100.00
MB Michael Bishop 25.00 50.00
RW Ricky Williams 25.00 50.00
SK Shaun King 25.00 50.00
TC Tim Couch 25.00 50.00
TH Torry Holt 25.00 60.00

1999 UD Ionix Warp Zone

Randomly inserted into packs at the rate of one in 108, this 15-card set features color action player photos printed on cards with a special holographic foil enhancement.
COMPLETE SET (15) 50.00 120.00
STATED ODDS 1:108
W1 Ricky Williams 3.00 8.00
W2 Tim Couch 1.50 4.00
W3 Cade McNown 1.25 3.00
W4 Daunte Culpepper 6.00 15.00
W5 Akili Smith 1.25 3.00
W6 Brock Huard 1.50 4.00
W7 Donovan McNabb 8.00 20.00
W8 Jake Plummer 1.50 4.00
W9 Jamal Anderson 2.50 6.00
W10 John Elway 8.00 20.00
W11 Randy Moss 6.00 15.00
W12 Terrell Davis 2.50 6.00
W13 Troy Aikman 5.00 12.00
W14 Barry Sanders 8.00 20.00
W15 Fred Taylor 2.50 6.00

2000 UD Ionix

Released as a 120-card set and a retail only product, UD Ionix features 60 base veteran cards and 60 Futuristic Rookie cards sequentially numbered to 2000. Base Issue cards are all foil and have colored backgrounds to match the featured player's team colors. Ionix was packaged in 24-pack boxes with packs containing four cards and carried a suggested retail price of $3.99.
COMPLETE SET (120) 150.00 300.00
COMP.SET w/o RC's (60) 5.00 12.00
61-120 ROOKIE PRINT RUN 2000
1 Jake Plummer .12 .30
2 Jamal Anderson .15 .40
3 Qadry Ismail .12 .30
4 Rob Johnson .15 .40
5 Eric Moulds .12 .30
6 Muhsin Muhammad .12 .30
7 Patrick Jeffers .12 .30
8 Cade McNown .12 .30
9 Marcus Robinson .15 .40
10 Akili Smith .12 .30
11 Corey Dillon .12 .30
12 Tim Couch .15 .40
13 Kevin Johnson .12 .30
14 Troy Aikman .25 .60
15 Emmitt Smith .30 .75
16 Rocket Ismail .15 .40
17 Terrell Davis .15 .40
18 Olandis Gary .15 .40
19 Charlie Batch .12 .30
20 James Stewart .12 .30
21 Brett Favre .40 1.00
22 Antonio Freeman .15 .40
23 Peyton Manning .50 1.25
24 Edgerrin James .15 .40
25 Marvin Harrison .15 .40
26 Mark Brunell .15 .40
27 Fred Taylor .12 .30
28 Elvis Grbac .12 .30
29 Tony Gonzalez .15 .40
30 O.J. McDuffie .15 .40
31 Damon Huard .12 .30
32 Randy Moss .15 .40
33 Cris Carter .20 .50
34 Drew Bledsoe .15 .40
35 Terry Glenn .15 .40
36 Ricky Williams .15 .40
37 Kerry Collins .12 .30
38 Amani Toomer .12 .30
39 Keyshawn Johnson .15 .40
40 Vinny Testaverde .12 .30
41 Tim Brown .20 .50
42 Rich Gannon .15 .40
43 Duce Staley .12 .30
44 Donovan McNabb .15 .40
45 Troy Edwards .12 .30
46 Jerome Bettis .20 .50
47 Marshall Faulk .15 .40
48 Kurt Warner .30 .75
49 Junior Seau .15 .40
50 Jeff Graham .12 .30
51 Charlie Garner .15 .40
52 Jerry Rice .50 1.25
53 Ricky Watters .15 .40
54 Jon Kitna .12 .30
55 Mike Alstott .12 .30
56 Shaun King .12 .30
57 Eddie George .15 .40
58 Steve McNair .15 .40
59 Brad Johnson .15 .40
60 Stephen Davis .12 .30
61 Ahmed Plummer RC 1.25 3.00
62 Courtney Brown RC 1.50 4.00
63 Deltha O'Neal RC 1.25 3.00
64 Chad Morton RC 1.50 4.00
65 Corey Simon RC 1.50 4.00
66 Hank Poteat RC 1.25 3.00
67 Raynoch Thompson RC 1.25 3.00
68 Darren Howard RC 1.25 3.00
69 Rondell Mealey RC 1.25 3.00
70 Marcus Knight RC 1.25 3.00
71 Keith Bulluck RC UER 1.50 4.00
72 John Abraham RC 2.00 5.00
73 Rob Morris RC 1.50 4.00
74 Chris Redman RC 1.25 3.00
75 Joe Hamilton RC 1.25 3.00
76 Jarious Jackson RC 1.50 4.00
77 Tom Brady RC 250.00 500.00
78 Chad Pennington RC 1.50 4.00
79 Tee Martin RC 1.25 3.00
80 Giovanni Carmazzi RC 1.25 3.00
81 Tim Rattay RC 1.50 4.00
82 Marc Bulger RC 1.50 4.00
83 Todd Husak RC 1.25 3.00
84 Curtis Keaton RC 1.25 3.00
85 Ron Dayne RC 2.00 5.00
86 Shaun Alexander RC 2.00 5.00
87 Thomas Jones RC 1.50 4.00
88 Reuben Droughns RC 1.25 3.00
89 Jamal Lewis RC 2.00 5.00
90 J.R. Redmond RC 1.25 3.00
91 Travis Prentice RC 1.25 3.00
92 Shyrone Stith RC 1.25 3.00
93 Chris Hovan RC 1.50 4.00
94 Michael Wiley RC 1.25 3.00
95 Trung Canidate RC 1.25 3.00
96 Sebastian Janikowski RC 2.00 5.00
97 Brian Urlacher RC 6.00 15.00
98 Bubba Franks RC 1.25 3.00
99 Anthony Becht RC 1.25 3.00
100 Chris Cole RC 1.50 4.00
101 R.Jay Soward RC 1.25 3.00
102 Peter Warrick RC 1.25 3.00
103 Plaxico Burress RC 1.50 4.00
104 Sylvester Morris RC 1.25 3.00
105 Dez White RC 1.25 3.00
106 Travis Taylor RC 1.25 3.00
107 Trevor Gaylor RC 1.25 3.00
108 Anthony Lucas RC 1.25 3.00
109 Sherrod Gideon RC 1.25 3.00
110 Todd Pinkston RC 1.25 3.00
111 Dennis Northcutt RC 1.25 3.00
112 Jerry Porter RC 2.00 5.00
113 Ron Dugans RC 1.25 3.00
114 Laveranues Coles RC 1.50 4.00
115 Darrell Jackson RC 1.25 3.00
116 Danny Farmer RC 1.25 3.00
117 Gari Scott RC 1.25 3.00
118 JaJuan Dawson RC 1.25 3.00
119 Troy Walters RC 1.25 3.00
120 Quinton Spotwood RC 1.25 3.00

2000 UD Ionix High Voltage

Randomly inserted in packs at the rate of one in four, this 15-card set features color player action photos on an all holofoil card with gold borders.
COMPLETE SET (15) 4.00 10.00
STATED ODDS 1:4
HV1 Fred Taylor .30 .75
HV2 Michael Westbrook .30 .75
HV3 James Stewart .30 .75
HV4 Keyshawn Johnson .40 1.00
HV5 Marcus Robinson .40 1.00
HV6 Charlie Batch .30 .75
HV7 Marvin Harrison .40 1.00
HV8 Olandis Gary .40 1.00
HV9 Curtis Martin .40 1.00
HV10 Isaac Bruce .50 1.25
HV11 Jake Plummer .30 .75
HV12 Shaun King .30 .75
HV13 Jimmy Smith .40 1.00
HV14 Muhsin Muhammad .30 .75
HV15 Rocket Ismail .40 1.00

2000 UD Ionix Majestix

ndomly inserted in packs at the rate of one in 11, this 15-card set features a gold foil outline border framing color action photos on an all holofoil card stock.
COMPLETE SET (15) 10.00 25.00
STATED ODDS 1:11
M1 Steve Young 1.00 2.50
M2 Jerry Rice 2.00 5.00
M3 Troy Aikman 1.00 2.50
M4 Emmitt Smith 1.25 3.00
M5 Vinny Testaverde .50 1.25
M6 Cris Carter .75 2.00
M7 Brett Favre 1.50 4.00
M8 Eddie George .60 1.50
M9 Herman Moore .50 1.25
M10 Drew Bledsoe .60 1.50
M11 Tim Brown .75 2.00
M12 Steve Beuerlein .60 1.50
M13 Brad Johnson .60 1.50
M14 Mark Brunell .60 1.50
M15 Randy Moss .60 1.50

2000 UD Ionix Rookie Xtreme

Randomly inserted in packs at the rate of one in 11, this 15-card set showcased top picks from the 2000 NFL draft. Each card is printed on holographic foil and has gold foil highlights.
COMPLETE SET (15) 12.50 30.00
STATED ODDS 1:11
RX1 Trung Canidate .25 .60
RX2 Peter Warrick .25 .60
RX3 Plaxico Burress .30 .75
RX4 Jamal Lewis .40 1.00
RX5 Thomas Jones .30 .75
RX6 Chad Pennington .30 .75
RX7 Chris Redman .25 .60
RX8 Ron Dayne .40 1.00
RX9 Courtney Brown .30 .75
RX10 Corey Simon .30 .75
RX11 Shaun Alexander .40 1.00
RX12 Dez White .25 .60
RX13 J.R. Redmond .25 .60
RX14 Shyrone Stith .25 .60
RX15 Travis Taylor .25 .60

2000 UD Ionix Sunday Best

Randomly inserted in packs at the rate of one in 23, this 15-card set features marquee players that perform to their prime week after week. Full color action shots are set against a holofoil background.
COMPLETE SET (15) 10.00 25.00
STATED ODDS 1:23
SB1 Stephen Davis .60 1.50
SB2 Brian Griese .60 1.50
SB3 Corey Dillon .60 1.50
SB4 Muhsin Muhammad .60 1.50
SB5 Charlie Batch .60 1.50
SB6 Shaun King .60 1.50
SB7 Germane Crowell .60 1.50
SB8 Drew Bledsoe .75 2.00
SB9 Jake Plummer .60 1.50
SB10 Torry Holt .75 2.00
SB11 Marcus Robinson .75 2.00
SB12 Ricky Williams .75 2.00
SB13 Tim Couch .75 2.00
SB14 Kevin Johnson .60 1.50
SB15 Warrick Dunn .60 1.50

2000 UD Ionix Super Trio

Randomly inserted in packs at the rate of one in 23, this 15-card set features full color action photography set on a holofoil backdrop that is colored to match each respective player's team colors.
COMPLETE SET (15) 12.50 30.00
STATED ODDS 1:23
ST1 Peyton Manning 2.50 6.00
ST2 Edgerrin James .75 2.00
ST3 Marvin Harrison .75 2.00
ST4 Kurt Warner 1.50 4.00
ST5 Marshall Faulk .75 2.00
ST6 Isaac Bruce 1.00 2.50
ST7 Mark Brunell .75 2.00
ST8 Fred Taylor .60 1.50
ST9 Jimmy Smith .75 2.00
ST10 Troy Aikman 1.25 3.00
ST11 Emmitt Smith 1.50 4.00
ST12 Rocket Ismail .75 2.00
ST13 Brad Johnson .75 2.00
ST14 Stephen Davis .60 1.50
ST15 Michael Westbrook .60 1.50

2000 UD Ionix UD Authentics

Randomly seeded in packs, this 52-card set features authentic player autographs in a "whiteout" box in the lower right hand corner. The level one Blue autographs were serial numbered out of 300 and the Gold level 2 cards serial numbered of 100. The Green parallel issue of all 52-cards was serial numbered of 25-sets. Some autographs were issued through redemption cards with an expiration date of 2/28/2001.
BLUE STATED PRINT RUN 300
GOLD STATED PRINT RUN 100
*GREEN/25: 1X TO 2.5X BLUE AU/300
*GREEN/25: .6X TO 1.5X HI GOLD AU/100
GREEN STATED PRINT RUN 25
BG Brian Griese B 4.00 10.00
BJ Brad Johnson G 8.00 20.00
BU Brian Urlacher B 20.00 50.00
CA Champ Bailey B 5.00 12.00
CB Charlie Batch B 4.00 10.00
CC Cris Carter B 8.00 20.00
CN Chris Coleman B 4.00 10.00
CP Chad Pennington G 8.00 20.00
CR Chris Redman G 6.00 15.00
DA David Boston B 4.00 10.00
DF Danny Farmer B 4.00 10.00
DL Dorsey Levens G 8.00 20.00
DN Dennis Northcutt B 4.00 10.00
EJ Edgerrin James G 8.00 20.00
EM Eric Moulds G 6.00 15.00
FR Bubba Franks B 4.00 10.00
IB Isaac Bruce B 6.00 15.00
JH Joe Hamilton B 4.00 10.00
JL Jamal Lewis G 10.00 25.00
JP Jake Plummer G 6.00 15.00
KJ Keyshawn Johnson G 8.00 20.00
KW Kurt Warner G 20.00 50.00
MB Mark Brunell G 8.00 20.00
MC Cade McNown G 6.00 15.00
MF Marshall Faulk G 12.00 30.00
MH Marvin Harrison G 8.00 20.00
MW Michael Wiley B 4.00 10.00
OG Olandis Gary B 5.00 12.00
PM Peyton Manning G 50.00 100.00
PW Peter Warrick G 6.00 15.00
RD Ron Dayne G 10.00 25.00
RJ Rob Johnson B 5.00 12.00
RL Ray Lucas B 4.00 10.00
RM Randy Moss G 25.00 60.00
RS R.Jay Soward B 4.00 10.00
SA Shaun Alexander B 6.00 15.00
SG Sherrod Gideon B 4.00 10.00
SL Sylvester Morris G 6.00 15.00
TA Troy Aikman G 25.00 60.00
TB Tim Brown B 10.00 25.00
TC Tim Couch G 8.00 20.00
TD Terrell Davis G 8.00 20.00
TH Torry Holt G 8.00 20.00
TJ Thomas Jones G 8.00 20.00
TM Tee Martin B 4.00 10.00
TO Terrell Owens B 10.00 25.00
TP Travis Prentice B 4.00 10.00
TR Tim Rattay B 5.00 12.00
TW Troy Walters B 4.00 10.00
WC Wayne Chrebet B 4.00 10.00

2000 UD Ionix Warp Zone

Randomly inserted in packs at the rate of one in 239, this 15-card set features player action shots against a green background. Cards are all holofoil and have silver foil highlights.
COMPLETE SET (15) 60.00 150.00
STATED ODDS 1:239
WZ1 Marshall Faulk 3.00 8.00
WZ2 Kurt Warner 6.00 15.00
WZ3 Peyton Manning 10.00 25.00
WZ4 Edgerrin James 3.00 8.00
WZ5 Brett Favre 8.00 20.00
WZ6 Tim Couch 3.00 8.00
WZ7 Ricky Williams 3.00 8.00
WZ8 Mark Brunell 3.00 8.00
WZ9 Fred Taylor 2.50 6.00
WZ10 Terrell Davis 3.00 8.00
WZ11 Dan Marino 8.00 20.00
WZ12 Randy Moss 3.00 8.00
WZ13 Emmitt Smith 6.00 15.00
WZ14 Eddie George 3.00 8.00
WZ15 Steve McNair 3.00 8.00

2008 UD Masterpieces

This set was released on November 4, 2008. The base set consists of 105 cards. Cards 1-99 feature veterans with several rookie cards mixed in, and cards 101-110 are short-printed rookies.
COMPLETE SET (105) 75.00 135.00
COMP.SET w/o SP's (86) 15.00 40.00
91-99 TW ODDS 1:12 HOBBY
101-110 RC ODDS 1:6 HOBBY
1 Donnie Avery RC .60 1.50
2 Adrian Peterson .50 1.25
3 D.Tyree/E.Manning .40 1.00
4 Alan Ameche .30 .75
5 Barry Sanders .75 2.00
6 Bart Starr .75 2.00
7 Ben Roethlisberger .50 1.25
8 Brett Favre 1.00 2.50
9 Bob Sanders .40 1.00
10 Brett Favre 1.00 2.50
11 Brian Urlacher .50 1.25
12 Earl Bennett RC .75 2.00
13 Champ Bailey .40 1.00
14 Chuck Bednarik .40 1.00
15 Dan Marino 1.00 2.50
16 Brian Bosworth .50 1.25
17 Devin Thomas RC .50 1.25
18 Andre Caldwell RC .50 1.25
19 Desmond Howard .30 .75
20 Devin Hester .40 1.00
21 Dick Butkus .60 1.50
22 Harry Douglas RC .60 1.50
23 Don Shula .50 1.25
24 Donovan McNabb .40 1.00
25 Kevin O'Connell RC .50 1.25
26 Doug Flutie .40 1.00
27 Drew Pearson .40 1.00
28 Dwight Clark .40 1.00
29 Early Doucet RC .50 1.25
30 Ed Podolak .30 .75
31 Eli Manning .40 1.00
32 Joe Flacco RC 1.00 2.50
33 James Hardy RC .50 1.25
34 Franco Harris .50 1.25
35 Frank Reich .30 .75
36 Dexter Jackson RC .75 2.00
37 Gale Sayers .50 1.25
38 Chris Johnson RC .60 1.50
39 Herm Edwards .30 .75
40 Howard Cosell .40 1.00
41 Dustin Keller RC .60 1.50
42 Jamaal Charles RC .75 2.00
43 Jim Brown .60 1.50
44 Jim Thorpe .60 1.50
46 Joe Montana 1.50 4.00
47 Joe Namath .60 1.50
48 John David Booty RC .50 1.25
49 John Elway .75 2.00
50 Johnny Unitas .75 2.00
51 Jordy Nelson RC 1.50 4.00
52 Kellen Winslow Sr. .40 1.00
53 Eddie Royal RC .50 1.25
54 Kevin Dyson .30 .75
55 Kevin Dyson .30 .75
56 Kevin Smith RC .60 1.50
57 LaDainian Tomlinson .50 1.25
58 Limas Sweed RC .50 1.25
60 Malcolm Kelly RC .50 1.25
61 Mario Manningham RC .50 1.25
62 Marvin Harrison .40 1.00
63 Jerome Simpson RC .60 1.50
64 Matt Forte RC .75 2.00
66 Chris Long RC .60 1.50
67 Paul Hornung .50 1.25
68 Peyton Manning 1.25 3.00
69 Randy Moss .40 1.00
71 Ray Rice RC .30 .75
72 Red Grange .60 1.50
73 Lester Hayes .40 1.00
74 Sammy Baugh .50 1.25
75 [illegible]
76 Steve Slaton RC .50 1.25
77 Billy Sims .40 1.00
78 Jack Lambert .50 1.25
79 Scott Norwood .30 .75
80 Snow Plow Game .30 .75
81 Terrell Owens .40 1.00
82 Terry Bradshaw .60 1.50
83 Tom Brady 1.50 4.00
84 Tom Brady 1.50 4.00
85 Tony Romo .40 1.00
86 Vince Lombardi .75 2.00
87 Vince Young .30 .75
88 Walter Payton 1.00 2.50
89 Wes Welker .40 1.00
90 Y.A. Tittle .50 1.25
91 Peterson/Butkus TW 4.00 10.00
92 Unitas/P.Mann TW 5.00 12.00
93 Favre/Hornung TW 4.00 10.00
94 R.Moss/M.Blount TW 3.00 8.00
95 Horn/Mont/Theis/Quinn TW 5.00 12.00
96 B.Sanders/Swann TW 4.00 10.00
97 Hornung/Favre TW 4.00 10.00
98 Tarkenton/Peterson TW 4.00 10.00
99 E.ManningTittle TW 4.00 10.00
101 Rashard Mendenhall SP RC .75 2.00
102 Brian Brohm SP RC .75 2.00
103 Chad Henne SP RC 1.00 2.50
104 Jake Long SP RC 1.25 3.00
105 Felix Jones SP RC .75 2.00
106 Darren McFadden SP RC .75 2.00
107 DeSean Jackson SP RC 1.50 4.00
108 Glenn Dorsey SP RC .75 2.00
109 Jonathan Stewart SP RC 1.25 3.00
110 Matt Ryan SP RC 2.50 6.00

2008 UD Masterpieces Framed Black

*VETS: 1X TO 2.5X BASIC CARDS
*ROOKIES: .6X TO 1.5X BASIC CARDS

2008 UD Masterpieces Framed Blue 150

*VETS:1.2 X TO 3X BASIC CARDS
*ROOKIES: .8X TO 2X BASIC CARDS
STATED PRINT RUN 150 SER.#'d SETS

2008 UD Masterpieces Framed Burgundy

*VETS 1-90: 3X TO 8X BASIC CARDS
*ROOKIES 1-90: 2X TO 5X BASIC CARDS
*TIME WARP 91-99: .8X TO 2X BASIC CARDS
*ROOKIES 101-110: 1.5X TO 4X BASIC CARDS
STATED PRINT RUN 10-25 SER.#'d SETS

2008 UD Masterpieces Framed Brown 99

*VETS: 1.5X TO 4X BASIC CARDS
*ROOKIES: 1X TO 2.5X BASIC CARDS
STATED PRINT RUN 99 SER.#'d SETS

2008 UD Masterpieces Framed Green 50

*VETS 1-90: 2X TO 5X BASIC CARDS
*ROOKIES 1-90: 1.2X TO 3X BASIC CARDS
*TIME WARP 91-99: .5X TO 1.2X BASIC CARDS
*ROOKIES 101-110: .8X TO 2X BASIC CARDS
STATED PRINT RUN 50 SER.#'d SETS

2008 UD Masterpieces Framed Green 75

*VETS 1-90: 2X TO 5X BASIC CARDS
*ROOKIES 1-90: 1.2X TO 3X BASIC CARDS
*TIME WARP 91-99: .5X TO 1.2X BASIC CARDS
*ROOKIES 101-110: .8X TO 2X BASIC CARDS
STATED PRINT RUN 75 SER.#'d SETS

2008 UD Masterpieces Framed Light Blue 10

*VETS 1-90: 4X TO 10X BASIC CARDS
*ROOKIES 1-90: 2.5X TO 6X BASIC CARDS
*TIME WARP 91-99: .8X TO 2X BASIC CARDS
*ROOKIES 101-110: 1.5X TO 4X BASIC CARDS
STATED PRINT RUN 10 SERIAL #'D SETS

2008 UD Masterpieces Framed Blue 50

*VETS 1-90: 2X TO 5X BASIC CARDS
*ROOKIES 1-90: 1.2X TO 3X BASIC CARDS
*TIME WARP 91-99: .5X TO 1.2X BASIC CARDS
*ROOKIES 101-110: .8X TO 2X BASIC CARDS
STATED PRINT RUN 50 SER.#'d SETS

2008 UD Masterpieces Framed Red 199

*VETS: 1.2X TO 3X BASIC CARDS
*ROOKIES: .8X TO 2X BASIC CARDS
STATED PRINT RUN 199 SER.#'d SETS

2008 UD Masterpieces Framed Silver

*VETS/RET/50-89: 2X TO 5X BASIC CARDS
*VETS/RET/30-49: 2.5X TO 6X BASIC CARDS
*VETS/RET/15-29: 3X TO 8X BASIC CARDS
*ROOKIES/50-89: 1.2X TO 3X BASIC CARDS
*ROOKIES/30-49: 1.5X TO 4X BASIC CARDS
*ROOKIES/15-29: 2X TO 5X BASIC CARDS
STATED PRINT RUN 1-89

2008 UD Masterpieces Captured on Canvas Jerseys

*PATCH/50: .6X TO 1.5X BASIC INSERTS
PATCH PRINT RUN 50 SER.#'d SETS
OVERALL JERSEY ODDS 1:6 HOBBY
CC1 Tom Brady 12.00 30.00
CC2 Dexter Jackson 2.50 6.00
CC3 Anquan Boldin 2.50 6.00
CC4 Brian Brohm 1.50 4.00
CC5 Brian Westbrook 2.50 6.00
CC6 Calvin Johnson 4.00 10.00
CC7 Chad Henne 2.00 5.00
CC8 Chad Johnson 2.50 6.00
CC9 Chris Cooley 4.00 10.00
CC10 Chris Johnson 2.00 5.00
CC11 Brett Favre 8.00 20.00
CC12 Tony Romo 3.00 8.00
CC13 Dallas Clark 2.50 6.00
CC14 Darren McFadden 1.50 4.00
CC15 Devin Thomas 1.50 4.00
CC16 DeMarcus Ware 3.00 8.00
CC17 Harry Douglas 2.00 5.00
CC18 DeSean Jackson 3.00 8.00
CC19 Devin Hester 3.00 8.00
CC20 Kevin O'Connell 1.50 4.00
CC21 Braylon Edwards 2.50 6.00
CC22 Dwayne Bowe 3.00 8.00
CC23 Early Doucet 1.50 4.00
CC24 Ed Reed 3.00 8.00
CC25 Dustin Keller 2.00 5.00
CC26 Felix Jones 1.50 4.00
CC27 James Hardy 1.50 4.00
CC29 Roy Williams WR 2.50 6.00
CC30 Greg Olsen 3.00 8.00
CC31 Jamaal Charles 2.50 6.00
CC32 Jay Cutler 2.50 6.00
CC35 Joe Flacco 3.00 8.00
CC36 Glenn Dorsey 1.50 4.00
CC37 Joey Galloway 3.00 8.00
CC38 John David Booty 1.50 4.00
CC39 Jonathan Stewart 5.00 12.00
CC40 Jordy Nelson 5.00 12.00
CC41 LaDainian Tomlinson 4.00 10.00
CC42 [illegible]

CC43 JaMarcus Russell 2.50 6.00
CC44 Willis McGahee 2.50 6.00
CC45 Limas Sweed 1.50 4.00
CC46 Malcolm Kelly 1.50 4.00
CC47 Mario Manningham 1.50 4.00
CC48 Andre Caldwell 1.50 4.00
CC49 Matt Forte 2.50 6.00
CC50 Matt Leinart 2.50 6.00
CC51 Matt Ryan 5.00 12.00
CC52 Michael Clayton 2.50 6.00
CC53 Jake Long 2.50 6.00
CC54 Jerome Simpson 2.00 5.00
CC55 Rashard Mendenhall 1.50 4.00
CC56 Ray Rice 1.50 4.00
CC57 Ryan Grant 3.00 8.00
CC58 Steve Slaton 1.50 4.00
CC59 Steven Jackson 2.50 6.00
CC60 Reggie Bush 2.50 6.00

2008 UD Masterpieces Stroke Of Genius Autographs

SOG1 Adrian Arrington 3.00 8.00
SOG2 Andre Woodson 3.00 8.00
SOG3 Ben Roethlisberger SP
SOG4 Ben Watson 6.00 15.00
SOG5 Billy Sims 10.00 25.00
SOG6 Bo Jackson SP 100.00 200.00
SOG7 Marc Bulger 6.00 15.00
SOG8 Dallas Clark 6.00 15.00
SOG10 Brian Bosworth 12.00 30.00
SOG11 Brian Brohm SP 3.00 8.00
SOG12 Calais Campbell 4.00 10.00
SOG13 Jamal Lewis 8.00 20.00
SOG14 Chad Henne 4.00 10.00
SOG15 Chad Johnson SP 10.00 25.00
SOG16 Chris Johnson 4.00 10.00
SOG17 Chris Long 6.00 15.00
SOG18 Jamaal Charles 5.00 12.00
SOG19 Colt Brennan SP 4.00 10.00
SOG20 Dan Marino
SOG21 Trent Edwards 6.00 15.00
SOG22 Darren McFadden SP 15.00 40.00
SOG23 Daryl Johnston 15.00 30.00
SOG24 Devin Thomas 3.00 8.00
SOG25 DeMarcus Ware 10.00 25.00
SOG26 Dennis Dixon 3.00 8.00
SOG27 Derek Anderson 6.00 15.00
SOG28 DeSean Jackson 6.00 15.00
SOG29 Y.A. Tittle 20.00 40.00
SOG30 Dick Butkus SP 60.00 100.00
SOG31 Kevin O'Connell 3.00 8.00
SOG33 Eli Manning SP 50.00 100.00
SOG34 Erik Ainge 3.00 8.00
SOG35 Felix Jones 3.00 8.00
SOG37 Fred Davis 3.00 8.00
SOG38 Glenn Dorsey 3.00 8.00
SOG40 Jack Ham SP 25.00 50.00
SOG42 Jake Long 5.00 12.00
SOG43 Jason Campbell SP 15.00 30.00
SOG45 Jeff Garcia SP 15.00 30.00
SOG46 Jerry Kramer 10.00 25.00
SOG48 Joe Flacco 20.00 50.00
SOG50 Joe Namath SP 200.00 400.00
SOG51 John David Booty SP 3.00 8.00
SOG52 John Elway SP 125.00 200.00
SOG53 Jonathan Stewart SP 10.00 25.00
SOG54 Jordy Nelson 10.00 25.00
SOG55 Ken Stabler SP 20.00 40.00
SOG56 Kenny Phillips 3.00 8.00
SOG58 Kevin Smith 3.00 8.00
SOG59 Kurt Warner SP 40.00 80.00
SOG60 LaDainian Tomlinson SP 30.00 60.00
SOG63 Leodis McKelvin 4.00 10.00
SOG64 Lester Hayes SP 10.00 25.00
SOG65 Limas Sweed 3.00 8.00
SOG66 Malcolm Kelly 3.00 8.00
SOG67 Jerome Simpson 4.00 10.00
SOG68 Matt Flynn 3.00 8.00
SOG69 Matt Forte 12.00 30.00
SOG70 Matt Ryan SP 60.00 120.00
SOG71 Dexter Jackson 5.00 12.00
SOG73 Michael Huff 6.00 15.00
SOG74 Mike Hart 3.00 8.00
SOG75 Mike Jenkins 3.00 8.00
SOG76 Owen Schmitt 3.00 8.00
SOG77 Patrick Willis 8.00 20.00
SOG78 Paul Hornung SP 15.00 30.00
SOG79 Peyton Manning SP 60.00 120.00
SOG80 Rashard Mendenhall 3.00 8.00
SOG81 Ray Rice 3.00 8.00
SOG82 Roger Craig 10.00 25.00
SOG83 Roman Gabriel 30.00 60.00
SOG84 Cadillac Williams SP 8.00 20.00
SOG85 Steve Slaton 3.00 8.00
SOG86 Tashard Choice 3.00 8.00
SOG87 Tom Rathman 10.00 25.00
SOG88 Tony Romo SP

2005 UD Mini Jersey Collection

This 100-card set was released in December, 2005. This set was issued through Upper Deck's retail outlets and these cards were available in three-card packs with a $5.99 SRP which came 18 packs to a box. Cards numbered 1-70 feature veterans sequenced in team alphabetical order; while cards numbered 71-85 feature leading 2005 NFL rookies and the set concludes with a season review subset (cards 86-100).

COMPLETE SET (100) 20.00 50.00
1 Kurt Warner .30 .75
2 Anquan Boldin .25 .60
3 Michael Vick .30 .75
4 Warrick Dunn .25 .60
5 Kyle Boller .25 .60
6 Ray Lewis .40 1.00
7 Jake Delhomme .25 .60
8 DeShaun Foster .30 .75
9 Carson Palmer .30 .75
10 Chad Johnson .25 .60
11 Rudi Johnson .25 .60
12 Kellen Winslow .25 .60
13 Lee Suggs .25 .60
14 Julius Jones .25 .60
15 Drew Bledsoe .30 .75
16 Tatum Bell .25 .60
17 Jake Plummer .25 .60
18 Roy Williams WR .25 .60
19 Kevin Jones .25 .60
20 Brett Favre .75 2.00
21 Ahman Green .30 .75
22 David Carr .25 .60
23 Andre Johnson .30 .75
24 Peyton Manning 1.00 2.50
25 Edgerrin James .30 .75
26 Marvin Harrison .30 .75
27 Byron Leftwich .25 .60
28 Fred Taylor .25 .60
29 Priest Holmes .25 .60
30 Trent Green .25 .60
31 Tony Gonzalez .30 .75
32 A.J. Feeley .25 .60
33 Randy McMichael .25 .60
34 Daunte Culpepper .30 .75
35 Nate Burleson .25 .60
36 Tom Brady 1.50 4.00
37 Corey Dillon .25 .60
38 Aaron Brooks .25 .60
39 Joe Horn .25 .60
40 Deuce McAllister .30 .75
41 Eli Manning .60 1.50
42 Tiki Barber .30 .75
43 Jeremy Shockey .25 .60
44 Chad Pennington .25 .60
45 Curtis Martin .30 .75
46 Santana Moss .30 .75
47 Randy Moss .30 .75
48 Kerry Collins .25 .60
49 Donovan McNabb .30 .75
50 Terrell Owens .30 .75
51 Brian Westbrook .25 .60
52 Ben Roethlisberger .60 1.50
53 Jerome Bettis .40 1.00
54 Drew Brees .40 1.00
55 LaDainian Tomlinson .40 1.00
56 Kevan Barlow .25 .60
57 Tim Rattay .25 .60
58 Matt Hasselbeck .25 .60
59 Shaun Alexander .25 .60
60 Darrell Jackson .25 .60
61 Marc Bulger .25 .60
62 Steven Jackson .25 .60
63 Torry Holt .30 .75
64 Michael Pittman .25 .60
65 Brian Griese .25 .60
66 Michael Clayton .25 .60
67 Steve McNair .30 .75
68 Drew Bennett .30 .75
69 Clinton Portis .25 .60
70 Patrick Ramsey .30 .75
71 Alex Smith QB RC 2.00 5.00
72 Aaron Rodgers RC 10.00 20.00
73 Jason Campbell RC .50 1.25
74 Ronnie Brown RC .60 1.50
75 Cadillac Williams RC .50 1.25
76 Cedric Benson RC .50 1.25
77 J.J. Arrington RC .60 1.50
78 Braylon Edwards RC .50 1.25
79 Troy Williamson RC .50 1.25
80 Mike Williams .60 1.50
81 Matt Jones RC .50 1.25
82 Mark Clayton RC .50 1.25
83 Roddy White RC .75 2.00
84 Reggie Brown RC .50 1.25
85 Eric Shelton RC .50 1.25
86 Peyton Manning SR 1.00 2.50
87 Ben Roethlisberger SR .60 1.50
88 Julius Jones SR .25 .60
89 Michael Vick SR .30 .75
90 Tom Brady SR 1.50 4.00
91 Corey Dillon SR .25 .60
92 Terrell Owens SR .30 .75
93 Donovan McNabb SR .30 .75
94 Priest Holmes SR .25 .60
95 Kevin Jones SR .25 .60
96 Jerome Bettis SR .40 1.00
97 Torry Holt SR .30 .75
98 Clinton Portis SR .25 .60
99 Drew Brees SR .40 1.00
100 Tiki Barber SR .30 .75
NNO Checklist Card .05 .15

2005 UD Mini Jersey Collection Replica Jerseys Autographs

STATED ODDS 1:360
AW Andrew Walter 50.00 100.00
CF Charlie Frye 50.00 100.00
CR Carlos Rogers 50.00 100.00
DG David Greene 50.00 100.00
DO Dan Orlovsky 50.00 100.00
KO Kyle Orton 60.00 100.00
RW Roddy White 30.00 60.00
VM Vernand Morency 50.00 100.00

2005 UD Mini Jersey Collection Replica Jerseys White

ONE MINI JERSEY PER PACK
*DARK: 1X TO 2.5X WHITE JERSEYS
DARK STATED ODDS 1:18
BF Brett Favre 8.00 20.00
BL Byron Leftwich 2.50 6.00
BR Ben Roethlisberger 5.00 12.00
BU Brian Urlacher 2.50 6.00
CP1 Chad Pennington 2.50 6.00
CP2 Carson Palmer 3.00 8.00
DB Drew Bledsoe 2.50 6.00
DC Daunte Culpepper 2.50 6.00
DM Donovan McNabb 3.00 8.00
EM Eli Manning 4.00 10.00
JJ Julius Jones 3.00 8.00
KJ Kevin Jones 2.50 6.00
LT LaDainian Tomlinson 2.50 6.00
MH Marvin Harrison 2.50 6.00
MV Michael Vick 4.00 10.00
PM Peyton Manning 5.00 12.00
RM Randy Moss 2.50 6.00
TB1 Tom Brady 5.00 12.00
TB2 Tedy Bruschi 2.50 6.00
TO Terrell Owens 2.50 6.00

2003 UD Patch Collection

Released in October of 2003, this set consists of 162 cards, including 105 veterans and 57 rookies. Cards 1-90 are veterans. Rookies 91-120 were inserted at a rate of 1:4, rookies 121-132 were inserted at a rate of 1:20, and rookies 133-147 were inserted at a rate of 1:40. Cards 121-147 feature collectible patches on the card front. Cards 148-162 were inserted at a rate of 1:40 and also feature collectible patches on card front. A Peyton Manning sample card was produced to preview this set and that card can be located at the end of our checklist. Boxes contained 20 packs of 5 cards. SRP was $3.99.

COMP.SET w/o SP's (90) 7.50 20.00
1 Peyton Manning 1.00 2.50
2 Aaron Brooks .25 .60
3 Joey Harrington .25 .60
4 Brett Favre .75 2.00
5 Donovan McNabb .30 .75
6 Jeff Garcia .25 .60
7 Michael Vick .30 .75
8 David Carr .25 .60
9 Drew Brees .40 1.00
10 Chad Pennington .25 .60
11 Daunte Culpepper .30 .75
12 Tom Brady 1.50 4.00
13 Kurt Warner .30 .75
14 Brad Johnson .30 .75
15 Josh McCown .30 .75
16 Drew Bledsoe .30 .75
17 Rich Gannon .30 .75
18 Tim Couch .25 .60
19 Keyshawn Johnson .40 1.00
20 Travis Henry .25 .60
21 LaDainian Tomlinson .40 1.00
22 Emmitt Smith .60 1.50
23 Michael Bennett .25 .60
24 Mark Brunell .30 .75
25 Steve McNair .30 .75
26 Clinton Portis .25 .60
27 Eddie George .30 .75
28 Marshall Faulk .30 .75
29 Curtis Martin .30 .75
30 Ahman Green .30 .75
31 Priest Holmes .25 .60
32 Edgerrin James .30 .75
33 Deuce McAllister .30 .75
34 Ricky Williams .30 .75
35 Anthony Thomas .30 .75
36 Jerome Bettis .40 1.00
37 Shaun Alexander .25 .60
38 Jake Plummer .25 .60
39 Patrick Ramsey .30 .75
40 Laveranues Coles .25 .60
41 David Boston .25 .60
42 Jay Fiedler .25 .60
43 Garrison Hearst .25 .60
44 Corey Dillon .25 .60
45 Charlie Garner .30 .75
46 Fred Taylor .25 .60
47 Chad Hutchinson .25 .60
48 Quincy Carter .25 .60
49 Kevan Barlow .25 .60
50 Tommy Maddox .25 .60
51 Kordell Stewart .25 .60
52 Chris Redman .25 .60
53 Jamal Lewis .30 .75
54 Zach Thomas .30 .75
55 Junior Seau .30 .75
56 Chris Chambers .25 .60
57 Matt Hasselbeck .25 .60
58 Marc Bulger .25 .60
59 Isaac Bruce .40 1.00
60 Torry Holt .30 .75
61 Kelly Holcomb .25 .60
62 Plaxico Burress .25 .60
63 Ray Lewis .40 1.00
64 Brian Urlacher .40 1.00
65 Tim Brown .40 1.00
66 William Green .25 .60
67 Kevin Johnson .25 .60
68 Trent Green .25 .60
69 Santana Moss .30 .75
70 Tony Gonzalez .30 .75
71 Rod Smith .30 .75
72 Ashley Lelie .25 .60
73 Peerless Price .25 .60
74 Antonio Bryant .25 .60
75 Duce Staley .25 .60
76 Darrell Jackson .30 .75
77 Jeremy Shockey .25 .60
78 Kerry Collins .25 .60
79 Koren Robinson .30 .75
80 Jerry Rice .75 2.00
81 Terrell Owens .30 .75
82 Antwaan Randle El .25 .60
83 Donte Stallworth .25 .60
84 Randy Moss .30 .75
85 Chad Johnson .25 .60
86 Hines Ward .30 .75
87 Rod Gardner .25 .60
88 Marvin Harrison .30 .75
89 Eric Moulds .25 .60
90 Julius Peppers .40 1.00
91 Nate Hybl RC 1.00 2.50
92 Lon Sheriff RC .75 2.00
93 Gerald Hayes RC 1.00 2.50
94 B.J. Askew RC 1.00 2.50
95 Artose Pinner RC .75 2.00
96 Domanick Davis RC 1.00 2.50
97 LaBrandon Toefield RC .75 2.00
98 Lee Suggs RC .75 2.00
99 Cecil Sapp RC .75 2.00
100 Kelley Washington RC .75 2.00
101 Kevin Curtis RC .75 2.00
102 Zuriel Smith RC .75 2.00
103 Carl Ford RC .75 2.00
104 Travis Anglin RC .75 2.00
105 Terrence Edwards RC .75 2.00
106 Troy Polamalu RC 12.50 25.00
107 Nate Burleson RC 1.00 2.50
108 Cecil Moore RC .75 2.00
109 Kassim Osgood RC 1.25 3.00
110 Teyo Johnson RC 1.00 2.50
111 Jason Witten RC 3.00 8.00
112 Vishante Shiancoe RC 1.25 3.00
113 Kevin Ware RC .75 2.00
114 Mike Pinkard RC .75 2.00
115 Donald Lee RC 1.00 2.50
116 Justin Gage RC 1.00 2.50
117 Adrian Madise RC .75 2.00
118 Anthony Adams RC 1.00 2.50
119 Dan Curley RC .75 2.00
120 Dallas Clark RC 1.25 3.00
121 Kyle Boller RI RC 1.50 4.00
122 Chris Simms RI RC 1.50 4.00
123 Dave Ragone RI RC 1.50 4.00
124 Kliff Kingsbury RI RC 2.50 6.00
125 Brad Banks RI RC 2.00 5.00
126 Gibran Hamdan RI RC 1.50 4.00
127 Ken Dorsey RI RC 2.00 5.00
128 Seneca Wallace RI RC 2.00 5.00
129 Brian St.Pierre RI RC 1.50 4.00
130 Rex Grossman RI RC 2.00 5.00
131 Brooks Bollinger RI RC 2.00 5.00
132 Jason Gesser RI RC 2.00 5.00
133 Carson Palmer RI RC 4.00 10.00
134 Byron Leftwich RI RC 2.50 6.00
135 Charles Rogers RI RC 2.50 6.00
136 Andre Johnson RI RC 5.00 12.00
137 Willis McGahee RI RC 2.50 6.00
138 Larry Johnson RI RC 2.50 6.00
139 Musa Smith RI RC 2.00 5.00
140 Chris Brown RI RC 2.00 5.00
141 Onterrio Smith RI RC 2.00 5.00
142 Justin Fargas RI RC 3.00 8.00
143 Bryant Johnson RI RC 3.00 8.00
144 Taylor Jacobs RI RC 2.00 5.00
145 Bethel Johnson RI RC 2.00 5.00
146 Tyrone Calico RI RC 2.00 5.00
147 Anquan Boldin RI RC 3.00 8.00
148 Michael Vick AP 2.00 5.00
149 Brett Favre AP 5.00 12.00
150 Chad Pennington AP 1.50 4.00
151 Kurt Warner AP 2.00 5.00
152 David Carr AP 1.50 4.00
153 Donovan McNabb AP 2.00 5.00
154 LaDainian Tomlinson AP 2.50 6.00
155 Marshall Faulk AP 2.00 5.00
156 Emmitt Smith AP 4.00 10.00
157 Jerry Rice AP 5.00 12.00
158 Terrell Owens AP 2.00 5.00
159 Brian Urlacher AP 2.50 6.00
160 Randy Moss AP 2.00 5.00
161 Ricky Williams AP 2.00 5.00
162 Peyton Manning AP 6.00 15.00
P162 Peyton Manning AP SAMPLE 1.50 4.00

2003 UD Patch Collection Gold Patches

*ROOKIES 121-132: 1.5X TO 4X BASE
*ROOKIES 133-147: 1.2X TO 3X BASE
*AP VETS 148-162: 2X TO 5X BASE
STATED PRINT RUN 25 SER.#'d SETS

2003 UD Patch Collection Jumbo Patches

Inserted one per box, each card features a collectible patch swatch. A gold version numbered to 25 was also produced.

STATED ODDS ONE PER BOX
*GOLD/25: 1.2X TO 3X BASIC INSERTS
GOLD PRINT RUN 25 SER.#'d SETS
AJ Andre Johnson 3.00 8.00
BF Brett Favre 6.00 15.00
BL Byron Leftwich 1.50 4.00
BU Brian Urlacher 3.00 8.00
CP Chad Pennington 2.00 5.00
DB Drew Brees 3.00 8.00
DC David Carr 2.00 5.00
DM Donovan McNabb 2.50 6.00
ES Emmitt Smith 5.00 12.00
JH Joey Harrington 2.00 5.00
JR Jerry Rice 6.00 15.00
JS Jeremy Shockey 2.00 5.00
KB Kyle Boller 2.00 5.00
LJ Larry Johnson 1.50 4.00
LT LaDainian Tomlinson 3.00 8.00
MC Deuce McAllister 2.50 6.00
MF Marshall Faulk 2.50 6.00
MV Michael Vick 2.50 6.00
PM Peyton Manning 8.00 20.00
PO Clinton Portis 2.00 5.00
RM Randy Moss 2.50 6.00
RW Ricky Williams 2.50 6.00
SC Carson Palmer 2.50 6.00
TO Terrell Owens 2.50 6.00

2003 UD Patch Collection Jumbo Patches Autographs

Randomly inserted as box toppers, this set features authentic player autographs. Each card is serial numbered to 50.

PRINT RUN 50 SERIAL #'d SETS
PM Peyton Manning 60.00 100.00
TO Terrell Owens

2003 UD Patch Collection Signature Patches

Inserted at a rate of 1:410, this set features authentic player autographs. A Gold verson serial numbered to 25 was also produced.

STATED ODDS 1:410
*GOLD/25: .8X TO 2X BASIC AUTO
*GOLD/25: .6X TO 1.5X BASIC AU SP
GOLD PRINT RUN 25 SER.#'d SETS
SPAB Aaron Brooks 8.00 20.00
SPBL Byron Leftwich 10.00 25.00
SPCH Chad Pennington 8.00 20.00
SPCJ Chad Johnson 8.00 20.00
SPCP Carson Palmer SP 75.00 150.00
SPDB Drew Brees SP 30.00 60.00
SPJG Jeff Garcia 8.00 20.00
SPJJ James Jackson 8.00 20.00
SPKB Kevan Barlow 8.00 20.00
SPPM Peyton Manning 60.00 120.00
SPRG Rod Gardner 8.00 20.00
SPRJ Rudi Johnson 8.00 20.00
SPRW Reggie Wayne 15.00 40.00
SPTH Todd Heap 8.00 20.00
SPWM Willis McGahee SP 25.00 50.00

2003 UD Patch Collection All Upper Deck Patches

Inserted at a rate of 1:22, this set features collectible patches on the card front. There is a Gold parallel of this set that features collectible patches with gold highlights. The Gold patches are hand numbered to 25.

STATED ODDS 1:22
*GOLD/25: 1.5X TO 4X BASIC INSERTS
GOLD PRINT RUN 25 SER.#'d SETS
UD1 Edgerrin James 2.00 5.00
UD2 Aaron Brooks 1.50 4.00
UD3 Steve McNair 2.00 5.00
UD4 Tim Couch 1.50 4.00
UD5 Tom Brady 10.00 25.00
UD6 Joey Harrington 1.50 4.00
UD7 Jeremy Shockey 1.50 4.00
UD8 Daunte Culpepper 2.00 5.00
UD9 Jeff Garcia 1.50 4.00
UD10 David Boston 1.50 4.00
UD11 Deuce McAllister 2.00 5.00
UD12 Ahman Green 2.00 5.00
UD13 Tim Brown 2.50 6.00
UD14 Shaun Alexander 1.50 4.00
UD15 Laveranues Coles 1.50 4.00
UD16 Priest Holmes 1.50 4.00
UD17 Clinton Portis 1.50 4.00
UD18 Marvin Harrison 2.00 5.00
UD19 Drew Bledsoe 2.00 5.00
UD20 Corey Dillon 1.50 4.00
UD21 Drew Brees 2.50 6.00

2002 UD Piece of History

Released in late May 2002, this 162 card set features 100 veterans and 62 rookies. Most rookies were serial #'d to 2002, with some being serial #'d to 500, and others being serial #'d to 500 and also containing a jersey swatch. Cards were issued in 24 pack boxes with 5 cards per pack. SRP was $2.99 per pack.

COMP.SET w/o SP's (100) 10.00 25.00
1 David Boston .25 .60
2 Jake Plummer .25 .60
3 Chris Chandler .30 .75
4 Jamal Anderson .30 .75
5 Michael Vick .30 .75
6 Elvis Grbac .25 .60
7 Qadry Ismail .25 .60
8 Ray Lewis .40 1.00
9 Eric Moulds .25 .60
10 Rob Johnson .30 .75
11 Travis Henry .25 .60
12 Chris Weinke .25 .60
13 Donald Hayes .25 .60
14 Muhsin Muhammad .25 .60
15 Anthony Thomas .30 .75
16 Brian Urlacher .40 1.00
17 David Terrell .25 .60
18 Jim Miller .25 .60
19 Marty Booker .25 .60
20 Corey Dillon .25 .60
21 Jon Kitna .25 .60
22 Peter Warrick .25 .60
23 James Jackson .25 .60
24 Kevin Johnson .25 .60
25 Tim Couch .25 .60
26 Emmitt Smith .60 1.50
27 Quincy Carter .25 .60
28 Rocket Ismail .30 .75
29 Brian Griese .25 .60
30 Ed McCaffrey .30 .75
31 Rod Smith .30 .75
32 Terrell Davis .30 .75
33 Charlie Batch .25 .60
34 James Stewart .25 .60
35 Mike McMahon .25 .60
36 Ahman Green .30 .75
37 Antonio Freeman .40 1.00
38 Bill Schroeder .25 .60
39 Brett Favre .75 2.00
40 Dominic Rhodes .25 .60
41 Edgerrin James .30 .75
42 Marvin Harrison .30 .75
43 Peyton Manning 1.00 2.50
44 Jimmy Smith .30 .75
45 Mark Brunell .30 .75
46 Priest Holmes .25 .60
47 Tony Gonzalez .30 .75
48 Trent Green .25 .60
49 Chris Chambers .25 .60
50 Jay Fiedler .30 .75
51 Lamar Smith .25 .60
52 Uronde Gadsden .25 .60
53 Daunte Culpepper .30 .75
54 Michael Bennett .25 .60
55 Randy Moss .30 .75
56 Antowain Smith .30 .75
57 Drew Bledsoe .30 .75
58 Tom Brady 2.00 5.00
59 Troy Brown .25 .60
60 Aaron Brooks .25 .60
61 Joe Horn .25 .60
62 Michael Strahan .30 .75
63 Kerry Collins .25 .60
64 Ron Dayne .30 .75
65 Tiki Barber .30 .75
66 Curtis Martin .30 .75
67 Laveranues Coles .30 .75
68 Santana Moss .30 .75
69 Vinny Testaverde .25 .60
70 Jerry Rice .75 2.00
71 Rich Gannon .30 .75
72 Tim Brown .40 1.00
73 Donovan McNabb .30 .75
74 Duce Staley .25 .60
75 Freddie Mitchell .25 .60
76 James Thrash .30 .75
77 Jerome Bettis .40 1.00
78 Kendrell Bell .25 .60
79 Kordell Stewart .25 .60
80 Doug Flutie .30 .75
81 Junior Seau .30 .75
82 LaDainian Tomlinson .40 1.00
83 Garrison Hearst .25 .60
84 Jeff Garcia .25 .60
85 Terrell Owens .30 .75
86 Matt Hasselbeck .25 .60
87 Ricky Watters .30 .75
88 Shaun Alexander .25 .60
89 Isaac Bruce .40 1.00
90 Kurt Warner .30 .75
91 Marshall Faulk .30 .75
92 Torry Holt .30 .75
93 Brad Johnson .30 .75
94 Keyshawn Johnson .30 .75
95 Mike Alstott .25 .60
96 Warrick Dunn .25 .60
97 Eddie George .30 .75
98 Steve McNair .30 .75
99 Stephen Davis .25 .60
100 Tony Banks .25 .60
101 Antonio Bryant RC 2.00 5.00
102 Adrian Peterson RC 1.50 4.00
103 Brian Poli-Dixon RC 1.25 3.00
104 Kyle Johnson RC 1.25 3.00
105 Clinton Portis RC 2.00 5.00
106 David Carr/500 RC 2.50 6.00
107 Rocky Calmus RC 1.50 4.00
108 Eric Crouch RC 2.00 5.00
109 Jeremy Shockey RC 2.00 5.00
110 Jabar Gaffney RC 1.25 3.00
111 Damien Anderson RC 1.25 3.00
112 Josh Reed RC 1.50 4.00
113 Lamar Gordon RC 1.50 4.00
114 Julius Peppers/500 RC 6.00 15.00
115 Kelly Campbell RC 1.50 4.00
116 Leonard Henry RC 1.25 3.00
117 Chad Hutchinson/500 RC 2.50 6.00
118 Luke Staley RC 1.25 3.00
119 Josh Scobey RC 1.50 4.00
120 Marquise Walker RC 1.25 3.00
121 Roy Williams RC 1.25 3.00
122 Patrick Ramsey RC 1.50 4.00
123 Ashley Lelie/500 RC 2.50 6.00
124 Rohan Davey RC 2.00 5.00
125 Ron Johnson RC 1.50 4.00
126 T.J. Duckett RC 1.25 3.00
127 Cliff Russell RC 1.25 3.00
128 William Green/500 RC 3.00 8.00
129 Reche Caldwell RC 1.50 4.00
130 Donte Stallworth RC 2.00 5.00
131 Javon Walker RC 2.00 5.00
132 David Garrard RC 1.50 4.00
133 Quentin Jammer RC 2.00 5.00
134 Ladell Betts RC 2.00 5.00
135 Freddie Milons RC 1.25 3.00
136 Brian Westbrook RC 2.50 6.00
137 John Henderson RC 1.50 4.00
138 Kalimba Edwards RC 1.50 4.00
139 Daniel Graham RC 1.50 4.00
140 Josh McCown RC 2.00 5.00
141 Joey Harrington/500 JSY RC 3.00 8.00
142 Phillip Buchanon/500 JSY RC 5.00 12.00
143 Maurice Morris/1500 JSY RC 3.00 8.00
144 George Godsey/1500 JSY RC 2.50 6.00
145 J.T. O'Sullivan/1500 JSY RC 3.00 8.00
146 Kurt Kittner/500 JSY RC 3.00 8.00
147 DeShaun Foster/500 JSY RC 5.00 12.00
148 Ant Randle El/1500 JSY RC 3.00 8.00
149 Woody Dantzler/1500 JSY RC 3.00 8.00
150 Randy Fasani/1500 JSY RC 2.50 6.00
151 Kahlil Hill/1500 JSY RC 2.50 6.00
152 Atrews Bell/1500 JSY RC 2.50 6.00
153 Eric McCoo/1500 JSY RC 2.50 6.00
154 Ricky Williams/1500 JSY RC 3.00 8.00
155 Albert Haynesworth/500 RC 5.00 12.00
156 Lamont Thompson/1500 JSY RC 3.00 8.00
157 Andre Davis/1500 JSY RC 2.50 6.00
158 Travis Stephens/500 JSY RC 3.00 8.00
159 Delvon Flowers/1500 JSY RC 2.50 6.00
160 Robert Thomas/1500 JSY RC 2.50 6.00
161 Marq Anderson/1500 JSY RC 3.00 8.00
162 Keny Coleman/1500 JSY RC 2.50 6.00

2002 UD Piece of History Hitmakers

Inserted at a rate of 1:30, this six card set features past Butkus award winners.

COMPLETE SET (6) 4.00 10.00
STATED ODDS 1:30
HM1 Dan Morgan .60 1.50
HM2 Chris Claiborne .60 1.50
HM3 Marvin Jones .60 1.50
HM4 Andy Katzenmoyer .60 1.50
HM5 Rocky Calmus .75 2.00
HM6 Kevin Hardy .60 1.50

2002 UD Piece of History Hitmakers Jerseys

Inserted at a rate of 1:336, this 6 card set features past Butkus award winners along with a swatch of game used jersey.

STATED ODDDS 1:336
HMJBU Brian Urlacher SP 6.00 15.00
HMJCC Chris Claiborne 2.50 6.00
HMJDM Dan Morgan 2.50 6.00
HMJJS Junior Seau 3.00 8.00
HMJRH Rodney Harrison 2.50 6.00
HMJRL Ray Lewis SP 6.00 15.00

2002 UD Piece of History National Honors

Inserted at a rate of 1:9, this 11 card set honors Heisman Trophy winners currently playing in the NFL.

COMPLETE SET (11) 7.50 20.00
STATED ODDS 1:9
NH1 Doug Flutie 1.00 2.50
NH2 Chris Weinke .75 2.00
NH3 Desmond Howard 1.00 2.50
NH4 Ty Detmer .75 2.00
NH5 Eric Crouch 1.25 3.00
NH6 Ricky Williams 1.00 2.50
NH7 Ron Dayne 1.00 2.50
NH8 Vinny Testaverde .75 2.00
NH9 Charles Woodson 1.25 3.00
NH10 Tim Brown 1.25 3.00
NH11 Eddie George 1.00 2.50

2002 UD Piece of History National Honors Jerseys

Inserted at a rate of 1:168, this 11-card set features Heisman Trophy winners along with a swatch of game used jersey. Upper Deck provided print run totals on the two most difficult cards to find.

STATED ODDS 1:168
NHJCWE Chris Weinke 2.50 6.00
NHJCWO Charles Woodson/52* 10.00 25.00
NHJDF Doug Flutie 3.00 8.00
NHJDH Desmond Howard 3.00 8.00
NHJEG Eddie George 3.00 8.00
NHJMA Marcus Allen 10.00 25.00
NHJRD Ron Dayne SP 3.00 8.00
NHJRW Ricky Williams/52* 8.00 20.00
NHJTB Tim Brown 4.00 10.00
NHJVT Vinny Testaverde 2.50 6.00

2002 UD Piece of History Rookie Glory

Inserted at a rate of 1:7, this 13 card set features players who had outstanding rookie campaigns.

COMPLETE SET (13) 12.50 30.00
STATED ODDS 1:7
RG1 Brian Urlacher 1.25 3.00
RG2 Anthony Thomas 1.00 2.50
RG3 Emmitt Smith 2.00 5.00
RG4 Mike Anderson .75 2.00
RG5 Edgerrin James 1.00 2.50
RG6 Randy Moss 1.00 2.50
RG7 Curtis Martin 1.00 2.50
RG8 Charles Woodson 1.25 3.00
RG9 Hugh Douglas .75 2.00
RG10 Jerome Bettis 1.25 3.00
RG11 Kendrell Bell .75 2.00
RG12 Warrick Dunn .75 2.00
RG13 Jevon Kearse .75 2.00

2002 UD Piece of History Rookie Glory Jerseys

Inserted at a rate of 1:108, this 12 card set features players who had outstanding rookie campaigns, and also include a game worn jersey swatch.

STATED ODDS 1:108
RGJAT Anthony Thomas 3.00 8.00
RGJBU Brian Urlacher 4.00 10.00
RGJCM Curtis Martin 3.00 8.00
RGJCW Charles Woodson/52* 40.00 80.00
RGJDC Daunte Culpepper/92* 3.00 8.00
RGJEJ Edgerrin James SP 4.00 10.00
RGJHD Hugh Douglas 2.50 6.00
RGJJK Jevon Kearse SP 4.00 10.00
RGJLT LaDainian Tomlinson 4.00 10.00
RGJMB Michael Bennett 2.50 6.00
RGJPM Peyton Manning 10.00 25.00
RGJRM Randy Moss SP 5.00 12.00
RGJWD Warrick Dunn 2.50 6.00

2002 UD Piece of History Run to History

Inserted at a rate of 1:30, this 13 card set features some of the top rushers in the NFL today.

COMPLETE SET (6) 7.50 20.00
STATED ODDS 1:30
RH1 Luke Staley 1.00 2.50
RH2 Ricky Williams 1.25 3.00
RH3 Ron Dayne 1.25 3.00
RH4 LaDainian Tomlinson 1.50 4.00
RH5 Garrison Hearst 1.00 2.50
RH6 Eddie George 1.25 3.00

2002 UD Piece of History Run to History Jerseys

Inserted at a rate of 1:336, this 6 card set features some of the top rushers in the NFL today, along with a swatch of game used jersey.

STATED ODDS 1:336
RHJEG Eddie George 3.00 8.00
RHJEJ Edgerrin James 3.00 8.00
RHJJL Jamal Lewis 3.00 8.00
RHJLT LaDainian Tomlinson SP 4.00 10.00
RHJRD Ron Dayne 3.00 8.00
RHJRW Ricky Williams/82* 8.00 20.00

2002 UD Piece of History The Big Game

Inserted at a rate of 1:6, this 30 card set features players who step up in the big games.

COMPLETE SET (30) 30.00 80.00
STATED ODDS 1:6
BG1 Chris Chandler 1.00 2.50
BG2 Trent Dilfer .75 2.00
BG3 Darren Sharper .75 2.00
BG4 Jamal Lewis 1.00 2.50
BG5 Ray Lewis 1.25 3.00
BG6 Rod Woodson 1.25 3.00
BG7 Bruce Smith 1.00 2.50
BG8 Emmitt Smith 2.00 5.00
BG9 Larry Allen 1.25 3.00
BG10 Ed McCaffrey 1.00 2.50
BG11 Rod Smith 1.00 2.50
BG12 Terrell Davis 1.00 2.50
BG13 John Elway 2.00 5.00
BG14 Brett Favre 2.50 6.00
BG15 Antonio Freeman 1.25 3.00
BG16 Dorsey Levens 1.00 2.50
BG17 Drew Bledsoe 1.00 2.50
BG18 Tom Brady 6.00 15.00
BG19 Troy Brown .75 2.00
BG20 Michael Strahan 1.00 2.50
BG21 Jessie Armstead .75 2.00
BG22 Junior Seau 1.00 2.50
BG23 Jerry Rice 2.50 6.00
BG24 Ricky Watters 1.00 2.50
BG25 Kurt Warner 1.00 2.50
BG26 Marshall Faulk 1.00 2.50
BG27 London Fletcher 1.00 2.50
BG28 Isaac Bruce 1.25 3.00
BG29 Steve McNair 1.00 2.50
BG30 Darrell Green 1.25 3.00

2002 UD Piece of History The Big Game Jerseys

Inserted at a rate of 1:48, this 30 card set features players who step up in the big games. Each card also includes a game worn jersey swatch.

STATED ODDS 1:48
*PATCH/25: 1.2X TO 3X BASIC JSY
*PATCH/25: 1X TO 2.5X BASIC JSY SP
PATCH PRINT RUN 25 SER.#'d SETS
BGJBF Brett Favre 8.00 20.00
BGJBS Bruce Smith 3.00 8.00
BGJCC Chris Chandler SP 4.00 10.00
BGJCM Curtis Martin SP 4.00 10.00
BGJDB Drew Bledsoe 3.00 8.00
BGJDG Darrell Green 4.00 10.00
BGJDM Dan Marino 8.00 20.00
BGJIB Isaac Bruce SP 5.00 12.00
BGJJA Jessie Armstead 2.50 6.00
BGJJE John Elway SP 8.00 20.00
BGJJK Jim Kelly 4.00 10.00
BGJJL Jamal Lewis SP 4.00 10.00
BGJJR Jerry Rice 8.00 20.00
BGJJS Junior Seau 3.00 8.00
BGJKW Kurt Warner 3.00 8.00
BGJLA Larry Allen 4.00 10.00
BGJLF London Fletcher 3.00 8.00
BGJMF Marshall Faulk 3.00 8.00
BGJMS Michael Strahan 3.00 8.00
BGJOP Orlando Pace 2.50 6.00
BGJRD Ron Dayne 3.00 8.00
BGJRL Ray Lewis 4.00 10.00
BGJRW Rod Woodson 4.00 10.00
BGJSM Steve McNair SP 4.00 10.00
BGJSY Steve Young SP 6.00 15.00
BGJTD Trent Dilfer 2.50 6.00
BGJTT Travis Taylor 2.50 6.00

2005 UD Portraits

This 200-card set was released in October, 2005. The set was issued in eight-card hobby packs with an $125 SRP. Cards numbered 1-100 feature veterans in team alphabetical order while cards 101-200 feature 2005 rookies and those cards were issued to a stated print run of 425 serial numbered sets.

DRAFT PICK PRINT RUN 425 SER.#'d SETS
1 Larry Fitzgerald 1.25 3.00
2 Anquan Boldin .75 2.00
3 Josh McCown 1.00 2.50
4 Michael Vick 1.00 2.50
5 Alge Crumpler 1.00 2.50
6 Peerless Price .75 2.00
7 Ray Lewis 1.25 3.00
8 Jamal Lewis 1.00 2.50
9 Todd Heap .75 2.00
10 Derrick Mason .75 2.00
11 J.P. Losman .75 2.00
12 Willis McGahee .75 2.00
13 Eric Moulds .75 2.00
14 Jake Delhomme .75 2.00
15 DeShaun Foster 1.00 2.50
16 Steve Smith 1.25 3.00
17 Brian Urlacher 1.25 3.00
18 Rex Grossman .75 2.00
19 Muhsin Muhammad .75 2.00
20 Carson Palmer 1.00 2.50
21 Rudi Johnson .75 2.00
22 Chad Johnson .75 2.00
23 Julius Jones .75 2.00
24 Keyshawn Johnson 1.00 2.50
25 Drew Bledsoe 1.00 2.50
26 Tatum Bell .75 2.00
27 Jake Plummer .75 2.00
28 Ashley Lelie .75 2.00
29 Roy Williams WR .75 2.00
30 Kevin Jones .75 2.00
31 Joey Harrington .75 2.00
32 Brett Favre 2.50 6.00
33 Ahman Green 1.00 2.50
34 Javon Walker .75 2.00
35 David Carr .75 2.00
36 Andre Johnson 1.00 2.50
37 Domanick Davis .75 2.00
38 Peyton Manning 3.00 8.00
39 Reggie Wayne 1.00 2.50
40 Edgerrin James 1.00 2.50
41 Marvin Harrison 1.00 2.50
42 Byron Leftwich .75 2.00
43 Fred Taylor .75 2.00
44 Jimmy Smith 1.00 2.50
45 Priest Holmes .75 2.00
46 Larry Johnson .75 2.00
47 Trent Green .75 2.00
48 A.J. Feeley .75 2.00
49 Chris Chambers .75 2.00
50 Randy McMichael .75 2.00
51 Daunte Culpepper 1.00 2.50
52 Onterrio Smith .75 2.00
53 Nate Burleson .75 2.00
54 Tom Brady 5.00 12.00
55 Corey Dillon .75 2.00
56 Deion Branch .75 2.00
57 David Givens .75 2.00
58 Aaron Brooks .75 2.00
59 Deuce McAllister 1.00 2.50
60 Joe Horn .75 2.00
61 Eli Manning 2.00 5.00
62 Jeremy Shockey .75 2.00
63 Tiki Barber 1.00 2.50
64 Chad Pennington .75 2.00
65 Curtis Martin 1.00 2.50
66 Jonathan Vilma .75 2.00
67 Kerry Collins .75 2.00
68 Jerry Porter .75 2.00
69 Randy Moss 1.00 2.50
70 Donovan McNabb 1.00 2.50
71 Terrell Owens 1.00 2.50
72 Brian Dawkins 1.25 3.00
73 Brian Westbrook .75 2.00
74 Ben Roethlisberger 2.00 5.00
75 Jerome Bettis 1.25 3.00
76 Hines Ward 1.00 2.50
77 Duce Staley .75 2.00
78 Drew Brees 1.25 3.00
79 LaDainian Tomlinson 1.25 3.00
80 Antonio Gates 1.25 3.00
81 Eric Parker .75 2.00
82 Tim Rattay .75 2.00
83 Kevan Barlow .75 2.00
84 Eric Johnson .75 2.00
85 Shaun Alexander .75 2.00
86 Darrell Jackson .75 2.00
87 Matt Hasselbeck .75 2.00
88 Marc Bulger .75 2.00
89 Steven Jackson .75 2.00
90 Marshall Faulk 1.00 2.50
91 Torry Holt 1.00 2.50
92 Michael Pittman .75 2.00
93 Brian Griese .75 2.00
94 Michael Clayton .75 2.00
95 Steve McNair 1.00 2.50
96 Billy Volek .75 2.00
97 Chris Brown .75 2.00
98 Clinton Portis .75 2.00
99 Patrick Ramsey 1.00 2.50
100 Santana Moss 1.00 2.50
101 Aaron Rodgers RC 15.00 30.00
102 Alex Smith QB RC 5.00 12.00
103 Charlie Frye RC 1.25 3.00
104 Andrew Walter RC 1.25 3.00
105 Jason Campbell RC 1.25 3.00
106 Dan Orlovsky RC 1.25 3.00
107 Derek Anderson RC 1.50 4.00
108 Kyle Orton RC 1.25 3.00
109 David Greene RC 1.25 3.00
110 James Kilian RC 1.25 3.00
111 Matt Jones RC 1.25 3.00
112 Cedric Benson RC 1.25 3.00
113 Ronnie Brown RC 1.50 4.00
114 Cadillac Williams RC 1.25 3.00
115 Ciatrick Fason RC 1.25 3.00
116 Vernand Morency RC 1.25 3.00
117 Eric Shelton RC 1.25 3.00
118 Maurice Clarett 1.25 3.00
119 Marion Barber RC 1.25 3.00
120 Anthony Davis RC 1.25 3.00
121 J.J. Arrington RC 1.50 4.00
122 Ryan Moats RC 1.25 3.00
123 Frank Gore RC 2.50 6.00
124 Alvin Pearman RC 1.25 3.00
125 Darren Sproles RC 2.00 5.00
126 Cedric Houston RC 2.00 5.00
127 Braylon Edwards RC 1.25 3.00
128 Troy Williamson RC 1.25 3.00
129 Mark Clayton RC 1.25 3.00
130 Chris Henry RC 1.50 4.00
131 Roddy White RC 2.00 5.00
132 Fred Gibson RC 1.25 3.00
133 Craphonso Thorpe RC 1.25 3.00
134 Terrence Murphy RC 1.25 3.00
135 Roydell Williams RC 1.50 4.00
136 Roscoe Parrish RC 1.25 3.00
137 Reggie Brown RC 1.25 3.00
138 Craig Bragg RC 1.25 3.00
139 Larry Brackins RC 1.25 3.00
140 Rasheed Marshall RC 1.50 4.00
141 J.R. Russell RC 1.25 3.00
142 Vincent Jackson RC 2.00 5.00
143 Dante Ridgeway RC 1.25 3.00
144 Chad Owens RC 1.25 3.00
145 Airese Currie RC 1.25 3.00
146 Marcus Maxwell RC 1.25 3.00
147 Paris Warren RC 1.50 4.00
148 Tab Perry RC 1.25 3.00
149 Jerome Mathis RC 2.00 5.00
150 Courtney Roby RC 1.25 3.00
151 Heath Miller RC 2.50 6.00
152 Alex Smith TE RC 1.25 3.00
153 Kevin Everett RC 2.00 5.00
154 Travis Johnson RC 1.25 3.00
155 Mike Patterson RC 1.25 3.00
156 DeMarcus Ware RC 4.00 10.00
157 Erasmus James RC 1.25 3.00
158 Dan Cody RC 1.25 3.00
159 David Pollack RC 1.25 3.00
160 Shaun Cody RC 1.50 4.00
161 Matt Roth RC 1.25 3.00
162 Marcus Spears RC 1.25 3.00

163 Jonathan Babineaux RC 1.25 3.00
164 Justin Tuck RC 1.50 4.00
165 Channing Crowder RC 1.50 4.00
166 Odell Thurman RC 2.00 5.00
167 Barrett Ruud RC 1.50 4.00
168 Lance Mitchell RC 1.50 4.00
169 Derrick Johnson RC 1.50 4.00
170 Shawne Merriman RC 2.00 5.00
171 Kevin Burnett RC 1.50 4.00
172 Darryl Blackstock RC 1.25 3.00
173 Antrel Rolle RC 2.00 5.00
174 Adam Jones RC 1.50 4.00
175 Fabian Washington RC 1.25 3.00
176 Carlos Rogers RC 2.00 5.00
177 Corey Webster RC 1.50 4.00
178 Justin Miller RC 1.25 3.00
179 Eric Green RC 1.25 3.00
180 Marlin Jackson RC 1.25 3.00
181 Luis Castillo RC 1.50 4.00
182 Thomas Davis RC 1.25 3.00
183 Kirk Morrison RC 2.00 5.00
184 Vincent Fuller RC 1.50 4.00
185 Donte Nicholson RC 1.25 3.00
186 Brodney Pool RC 2.00 5.00
187 Mike Nugent RC 1.50 4.00
188 Timmy Chang RC 1.25 3.00
189 Matt Cassel RC 1.25 3.00
190 Adrian McPherson RC 1.25 3.00
191 Gino Guidugli RC 1.25 3.00
192 Stefan LeFors RC 1.25 3.00
193 Marcus Randall RC 1.50 4.00
194 Brandon Jacobs RC 1.50 4.00
195 Walter Reyes RC 1.25 3.00
196 Mark Bradley RC 1.25 3.00
197 Josh Bullocks RC 1.50 4.00
198 Chase Lyman RC 1.25 3.00
199 Harry Williams RC 1.50 4.00
200 Mike Williams 1.50 4.00

2005 UD Portraits Gold

*VETERANS: 1X TO 2.5X BASIC CARDS
*ROOKIES: .8X TO 2X BASIC CARDS
GOLD PRINT RUN 75 SER.#'d SETS

2005 UD Portraits Platinum

*VETERANS: 2.5X TO 6X BASIC CARDS
*ROOKIES: 1.5X TO 4X BASIC CARDS
PLATINUM PRINT RUN 30 SER.#'d SETS

2005 UD Portraits Memorable Materials

TWO MEMORABLE MATERIALS PER BOX
UNPRICED AUTOS PRINT RUN 15 SETS
MMAB Anquan Boldin 2.50 6.00
MMAG Ahman Green 3.00 8.00
MMAN Antrel Rolle 3.00 8.00
MMAO Antonio Gates 2.50 6.00
MMAR Aaron Rodgers 20.00 40.00
MMAS Alex Smith QB 6.00 15.00
MMAW Andrew Walter 2.50 6.00
MMBD Brian Dawkins 3.00 8.00
MMBE Braylon Edwards 3.00 8.00
MMBL Byron Leftwich 2.50 6.00
MMBR Ben Roethlisberger 7.50 20.00
MMCA Carlos Rogers 2.50 6.00
MMCF Charlie Frye 2.50 6.00
MMCI Ciatrick Fason 2.50 6.00
MMCP Carson Palmer 3.00 8.00
MMCR Chris Brown 2.50 6.00
MMCW Cadillac Williams 5.00 12.00
MMDM Donovan McNabb 4.00 10.00
MMDS Deion Sanders 3.00 8.00
MMJA J.J. Arrington 2.50 6.00
MMJC Jason Campbell 3.00 8.00
MMJJ Julius Jones 4.00 10.00
MMJL J.P. Losman 3.00 8.00
MMKO Kyle Orton 2.50 6.00
MMLJ LaMont Jordan 3.00 8.00
MMMA Mark Clayton 2.50 6.00
MMMB Marc Bulger 2.50 6.00
MMMC Michael Clayton 2.50 6.00
MMMM Muhsin Muhammad 2.50 6.00
MMMO Maurice Clarett 2.50 6.00
MMMV Michael Vick 5.00 12.00
MMMY Mark Bradley 3.00 8.00
MMPM Peyton Manning 5.00 12.00
MMRB Ronnie Brown 6.00 15.00
MMRE Reggie Brown 2.50 6.00
MMRM Ryan Moats 3.00 8.00
MMRO Roddy White 3.00 8.00
MMRP Roscoe Parrish 2.50 6.00
MMRW Reggie Wayne 2.50 6.00
MMTW Troy Williamson 2.50 6.00
MMVM Vernand Morency 2.50 6.00

2005 UD Portraits Memorable Materials Autographs

MMSAB Anquan Boldin 10.00 25.00
MMSAG Ahman Green 12.00 30.00
MMSAN Antrel Rolle 12.00 30.00
MMSAO Antonio Gates 15.00 40.00
MMSAR Aaron Rodgers 200.00 350.00
MMSAS Alex Smith QB 30.00 80.00
MMSAW Andrew Walter 8.00 20.00
MMSBD Brian Dawkins
MMSBE Braylon Edwards 8.00 20.00
MMSBL Byron Leftwich 10.00 25.00
MMSBR Ben Roethlisberger
MMSCA Carlos Rogers 12.00 30.00
MMSCF Charlie Frye 8.00 20.00
MMSCI Ciatrick Fason
MMSCP Carson Palmer 12.00 30.00
MMSCR Chris Brown 10.00 25.00
MMSCW Cadillac Williams 8.00 20.00
MMSDM Donovan McNabb 12.00 30.00
MMSDS Deion Sanders 40.00 80.00
MMSJA J.J. Arrington 10.00 25.00
MMSJC Jason Campbell 8.00 20.00
MMSJJ Julius Jones
MMSJL J.P. Losman 10.00 25.00
MMSKO Kyle Orton 8.00 20.00
MMSLJ LaMont Jordan 10.00 25.00
MMSMA Mark Clayton 8.00 20.00
MMSMB Marc Bulger 10.00 25.00
MMSMC Michael Clayton
MMSMM Muhsin Muhammad
MMSMO Maurice Clarett
MMSMV Michael Vick 40.00 80.00
MMSMY Mark Bradley 8.00 20.00
MMSPM Peyton Manning 60.00 120.00
MMSRB Ronnie Brown 10.00 25.00
MMSRE Reggie Brown
MMSRM Ryan Moats
MMSRO Roddy White
MMSRP Roscoe Parrish
MMSRW Reggie Wayne 12.00 30.00
MMSTW Troy Williamson 8.00 20.00
MMSVM Vernand Morency 8.00 20.00

2005 UD Portraits Rookie Signature Portait Duals 8x10

STATED PRINT RUN 45 SER.#'d SETS
DRP1 A.Smith QB/A.Rodgers 150.00 250.00
DRP2 C.Williams/Ro.Brown 15.00 40.00
DRP3 M.Clayton/B.Edwards 15.00 40.00
DRP4 Rod.White/Williamson 25.00 60.00
DRP5 C.Benson/V.Morency 15.00 40.00
DRP6 D.Greene/D.Pollack 15.00 40.00
DRP7 A.Rolle/Mar.Jackson 25.00 60.00
DRP8 C.Frye/A.Walter 15.00 40.00
DRP9 C.Fason/R.Moats 15.00 40.00
DRP10 A.Rodgers/J.Arrington 75.00 150.00
DRP11 F.Gore/R.Parrish 30.00 80.00
DRP12 J.Campbell/Ro.Brown 20.00 50.00
DRP13 R.Parrish/C.Thorpe 15.00 40.00
DRP14 [illegible] 15.00 40.00
DRP15 Er.James/A.Hawthorne 15.00 40.00
DRP16 B.Edwards/M.Williams 20.00 50.00
DRP17 M.Barber/F.Gore 10.00 25.00
DRP18 M.Williams/M.Clarett 20.00 50.00

2005 UD Portraits Scrapbook Materials

ONE PER BOX
SBAB Anquan Boldin 2.50 6.00
SBAG Ahman Green 3.00 8.00
SBAN Antrel Rolle 4.00 10.00
SBAR Aaron Rodgers SP 20.00 50.00
SBAS Alex Smith QB 5.00 12.00
SBAW Andrew Walter 2.50 6.00
SBBE Braylon Edwards 1.50 4.00
SBBF Brett Favre 8.00 20.00
SBBR Ben Roethlisberger 6.00 15.00
SBCA Carlos Rogers 4.00 10.00
SBCB Cedric Benson 2.50 6.00
SBCF Charlie Frye 2.50 6.00
SBCI Ciatrick Fason 2.50 6.00
SBCP Carson Palmer SP 4.00 10.00
SBCW Cadillac Williams 1.50 4.00
SBDB Drew Bennett 3.00 8.00
SBDM Donovan McNabb 3.00 8.00
SBDR Drew Bledsoe 3.00 8.00
SBEM Eli Manning 6.00 15.00
SBFG Frank Gore 3.00 8.00
SBHM Heath Miller 3.00 8.00
SBJA J.J. Arrington 3.00 8.00
SBJC Jason Campbell 1.50 4.00
SBJJ Julius Jones 2.50 6.00
SBJL J.P. Losman SP 3.00 8.00
SBKO Kyle Orton 1.50 4.00
SBLE Lee Evans 3.00 8.00
SBMA Mark Clayton 2.50 6.00
SBMB Mark Bradley 2.50 6.00
SBMC Michael Clayton 2.50 6.00
SBMO Maurice Clarett 3.00 8.00
SBMV Michael Vick 3.00 8.00
SBMW Mike Williams 3.00 8.00
SBPM Peyton Manning 10.00 25.00
SBRB Ronnie Brown 2.00 5.00
SBRE Reggie Wayne 3.00 8.00
SBRW Roy Williams WR 2.50 6.00
SBSJ Steven Jackson 2.50 6.00
SBTB Tiki Barber 3.00 8.00
SBTW Troy Williamson 2.50 6.00
SBVJ Vincent Jackson 2.50 6.00
SBVM Vernand Morency 3.00 8.00

2005 UD Portraits Scrapbook Moments

STATED PRINT RUN 425 SER.#'d SETS
1 Aaron Brooks .75 2.00
2 Anthony Davis .75 2.00
3 Antonio Gates 1.25 3.00
4 Ahman Green 1.00 2.50
5 Antrel Rolle 1.00 2.50
6 Anquan Boldin .75 2.00
7 Aaron Rodgers 8.00 20.00
8 Alex Smith QB 2.50 6.00
9 Andrew Walter .60 1.50
10 Braylon Edwards .60 1.50
11 Brett Favre 2.50 6.00
12 Ben Roethlisberger 2.00 5.00
13 Cedric Benson .60 1.50
14 Charlie Frye .60 1.50
15 Ciatrick Fason .75 2.00
16 Carson Palmer 1.00 2.50
17 Cadillac Williams .60 1.50
18 Drew Bennett 1.00 2.50
19 Carlos Rogers 1.00 2.50
20 Donovan McNabb 1.00 2.50
21 Drew Bledsoe 1.00 2.50
22 Eli Manning 2.00 5.00
23 Frank Gore 1.25 3.00
24 Heath Miller 1.25 3.00
25 J.J. Arrington .75 2.00
26 Joe Horn .75 2.00
27 Julius Jones .75 2.00
28 Jack Lambert 1.50 4.00
29 J.P. Losman .75 2.00
30 Jason Campbell .60 1.50
31 Jason White 1.00 2.50
32 Kyle Orton .60 1.50
33 Lee Evans 1.00 2.50
34 Mark Clayton .60 1.50
35 Marc Bulger .75 2.00
36 Michael Clayton .60 1.50
37 David Greene .75 2.00
38 Maurice Clarett .60 1.50
39 Michael Vick 1.00 2.50
40 Mark Bradley .75 2.00
41 Paul Hornung 1.50 4.00
42 Peyton Manning 3.00 8.00
43 Ronnie Brown .75 2.00
44 Reggie Wayne 1.00 2.50
45 Roy Williams WR .75 2.00
46 Steven Jackson .75 2.00
47 Tiki Barber 1.00 2.50
48 Troy Williamson .60 1.50
49 Vincent Jackson 1.00 2.50
50 Vernand Morency .60 1.50
UDPKG Roy Williams Promo .40 1.00

2005 UD Portraits Scrapbook Signatures

UNPRICED AUTO PRINT RUN 20 SETS
SSAB Aaron Brooks 10.00 25.00
SSAG Antonio Gates 15.00 40.00
SSAH Ahman Green 12.00 30.00
SSAQ Anquan Boldin 10.00 25.00
SSAR Aaron Rodgers 300.00 600.00
SSAS Alex Smith QB 75.00 150.00
SSAW Andrew Walter 10.00 25.00
SSBF Brett Favre 150.00 250.00
SSBR Ben Roethlisberger 75.00 125.00
SSCB Cedric Benson 10.00 25.00
SSCI Ciatrick Fason 10.00 25.00
SSCW Cadillac Williams 10.00 25.00
SSDG David Greene 10.00 25.00
SSDM Donovan McNabb 25.00 50.00
SSDR Drew Bledsoe 12.00 30.00
SSEM Eli Manning 40.00 80.00
SSFG Frank Gore 12.00 30.00
SSJA J.J. Arrington 12.00 30.00
SSJJ Julius Jones 6.00 15.00
SSJK Jack Lambert 30.00 60.00
SSJL J.P. Losman 10.00 25.00
SSKO Kyle Orton 10.00 25.00
SSLE Lee Evans 12.00 30.00
SSMB Marc Bulger 10.00 25.00
SSMC Michael Clayton 10.00 25.00
SSMU Maurice Clarett 10.00 25.00
SSMY Mark Bradley 10.00 25.00
SSPH Paul Hornung 20.00 40.00
SSPM Peyton Manning 75.00 125.00
SSRE Reggie Wayne 12.00 30.00
SSRW Roy Williams WR 10.00 25.00
SSTB Tiki Barber 12.00 30.00
SSTW Troy Williamson 10.00 25.00
SSVJ Vincent Jackson 15.00 40.00

2005 UD Portraits Signature Portraits 8x10

ONE 8X10 AUTO PER BOX
SP1 Ahman Green 15.00 40.00
SP2 Byron Leftwich SP 25.00 50.00
SP3 Michael Vick SP 25.00 60.00
SP4 Peyton Manning 75.00 150.00
SP5 Antonio Gates 15.00 40.00
SP6 Lee Evans 10.00 25.00
SP7 Bob Griese 20.00 50.00
SP8 Michael Clayton 12.50 30.00
SP9 Archie Manning 20.00 50.00
SP10 Jack Lambert 40.00 80.00
SP11 Ben Roethlisberger SP 100.00 175.00
SP12 Steven Jackson 15.00 40.00
SP13 Marc Bulger 12.50 30.00
SP14 Drew Bledsoe SP 25.00 60.00
SP15 Rudi Johnson 15.00 40.00
SP16 Julius Jones 15.00 40.00
SP17 Carson Palmer SP 20.00 50.00
SP18 Roy Williams WR 15.00 40.00
SP19 Fred Taylor 12.50 30.00
SP20 Eli Manning SP 75.00 125.00
SP21 Donovan McNabb SP 60.00 100.00
SP22 Brett Favre SP 125.00 250.00
SP23 J.P. Losman 15.00 40.00
SP24 Domanick Davis 10.00 25.00
SP25 Joe Horn 10.00 25.00
SP26 Tiki Barber 15.00 40.00
SP27 Steve Largent 30.00 60.00
SP28 Bernie Kosar 15.00 40.00
SP29 Paul Hornung 20.00 50.00
SP30 Charlie Joiner 15.00 40.00
SP31 George Blanda 30.00 60.00
SP32 Gale Sayers SP 50.00 100.00
SP33 Fran Tarkenton 20.00 50.00
SP34 Dan Marino SP 125.00 250.00
SP35 John Elway SP 125.00 250.00
SP36 Joe Montana SP 125.00 250.00
SP37 Jack Ham 15.00 40.00
SP38 Raymond Berry 15.00 40.00
SP39 Don Maynard 15.00 40.00
SP40 LaDainian Tomlinson 40.00 80.00
SP41 Len Dawson 20.00 50.00
SP42 Joe Theismann 15.00 40.00
SP43 Joe Greene 30.00 60.00
SP44 Marcus Allen 25.00 50.00
SP45 Mike Singletary SP 30.00 60.00
SP46 Deion Sanders 50.00 100.00
SP47 Troy Aikman 60.00 120.00
SP48 Kyle Orton 15.00 40.00
SP49 Charlie Frye 10.00 25.00
SP50 Andrew Walter 10.00 25.00
SP51 Dan Orlovsky 10.00 25.00
SP52 David Greene 10.00 25.00
SP53 Heath Miller 12.00 30.00
SP54 Vernand Morency 12.50 30.00
SP55 Mike Williams 10.00 25.00
SP56 Ciatrick Fason 10.00 25.00
SP57 J.J. Arrington 10.00 25.00
SP58 Braylon Edwards 20.00 50.00
SP59 Art Donovan 12.50 30.00
SP60 Mark Clayton 10.00 25.00
SP61 Ronnie Brown 30.00 60.00
SP62 Cadillac Williams 25.00 60.00
SP63 Cedric Benson 10.00 25.00
SP64 Alex Smith QB 25.00 60.00
SP65 Aaron Rodgers 125.00 250.00
SP66 Jason Campbell 15.00 40.00
SP67 Roddy White 15.00 40.00
SP68 Roscoe Parrish 10.00 25.00
SP69 Troy Williamson 10.00 25.00
SP70 Maurice Clarett 10.00 25.00
SP71 Antrel Rolle 10.00 25.00
SP72 Reggie Brown 10.00 25.00

2005 UD Portraits Signature Portraits Dual 8x10

DUAL PRINT RUN 45 SER.#'D SETS
UNPRICED TRIPLE SIGS #'d TO 10
UNPRICED QUAD SIGS #'d TO 5
DSP1 P.Manning/R.Wayne 90.00 150.00
DSP2 M.Vick/A.Crumpler 40.00 80.00
DSP3 B.Favre/A.Green 125.00 250.00
DSP4 L.Evans/J.Losman 20.00 50.00
DSP5 D.McAllister/J.Horn 20.00 50.00
DSP6 D.Bledsoe/J.Jones 25.00 60.00
DSP7 D.McNabb/B.Dawkins 90.00 150.00
DSP8 C.Palmer/Ch.Johnson 20.00 50.00
DSP9 M.Bulger/S.Jackson 25.00 60.00

2002-03 UD SuperStars

This 300 card set was released in March, 2003. This set was issued in five card packs with an $3 SRP. The packs were issued in 24 pack boxes which came 12 boxes to a case. The final 50 cards of the set featured two rookies from different sports.

COMPLETE SET (300) 30.00 80.00
10 Jake Plummer .20 .50
21 Michael Vick .40 1.00
38 Tom Brady .60 1.50
39 Antowain Smith .20 .50
40 Drew Bledsoe .40 1.00
52 Anthony Thomas .25 .60
60 Corey Dillon .25 .60
63 Tim Couch .15 .40
70 Brian Griese .25 .60
72 Dirk Nowitzki .50 1.25
73 Emmitt Smith .75 2.00
74 Quincy Carter .20 .50
90 Ricky Williams .25 .60
92 Ahman Green .30 .75
93 Brett Favre .75 2.00
105 Edgerrin James .40 1.00
106 Peyton Manning .60 1.50
107 Mark Brunell .25 .60
108 Jimmy Smith .15 .40
111 Priest Holmes .30 .75
125 Steve McNair .25 .60
126 Eddie George .25 .60
133 Daunte Culpepper .25 .60
134 Randy Moss .50 1.25
140 Aaron Brooks .25 .60
141 Deuce McAllister .40 1.00
163 Curtis Martin .30 .75
164 Chad Pennington .40 1.00
176 Jerry Rice .60 1.50
177 Rich Gannon .20 .50
189 Donovan McNabb .40 1.00
195 Jerome Bettis .30 .75
196 Kordell Stewart .15 .40
206 LaDainian Tomlinson .40 1.00
214 Jeff Garcia .25 .60
215 Terrell Owens .40 1.00
224 Shaun Alexander .15 .40
233 Kurt Warner .30 .75
234 Marshall Faulk .30 .75
248 Stephen Davis .15 .40
251 J.McCown .30 .75
J.Valverde
252 D.Devore .20 .50
W.Bryant
253 T.Duckett .40 1.00
I.Kovalchuk
256 F.Sanchez .75 2.00
R.Davey
257 J.Peppers .75 2.00
E.Cole
259 K.Kane .20 .50
R.Mason Jr.
260 E.Almonte .30 .75
A.Peterson
261 A.Davis 1.50 4.00
R.Nash
262 D.Wagner .60 1.50
W.Green
263 C.Esslinger 1.50 4.00
C.Portis
264 C.Hutchinson .50 1.25
C.Jacobsen
265 A.Lelie .75 2.00
R.Reyes
266 N.Hilario .40 1.00
N.Kulovich
267 J.Harrington 1.25 3.00
T.Prince
268 H.Zetterberg 1.50 4.00
K.Edwards
270 M.Dunleavy .40 1.00
P.Buchanon
271 B.Puffer .20 .50
J.Gaffney
272 B.Nachbar .20 .50
J.Wells
273 D.Carr 4.00 10.00
Y.Ming
274 J.Brito .20 .50
R.Sims
275 K.Ishii .30 .75
K.Rush
277 L.Martinez .20 .50
C.Nall
278 M.Haislip .60 1.50
J.Walker
279 K.Frederick .50 1.25
S.Hill
280 D.Stallworth .60 1.50
C.Borchardt
281 T.Yates 1.00 2.50
J.Shockey
282 J.Cerda .20 .50
T.Carter
286 A.Burnside .60 1.50
A.Randle El
287 B.Howard .20 .50
R.Caldwell
288 O.Perez .40 1.00
Q.Jammer
289 L.Ugueto .20 .50
J.Stevens
290 M.Morris .20 .50
M.Thornton
291 S.Taguchi .30 .75
L.Gordon
292 J.Simontacchi .20 .50
R.Thomas
293 F.Escalona .20 .50
M.Walker
294 B.Backe .30 .75
T.Stephens
296 P.Ramsey .60 1.50
J.Dixon

2002-03 UD SuperStars Gold

*GOLD 1-250: 2.5X TO 6X BASIC
*GOLD MATSUI: 6X TO 12X BASIC
*GOLD 251-300: 2X TO 5X BASIC

2002-03 UD SuperStars Benchmarks

Inserted at a stated rate of one in 20, these 10 cards feature two athletes from different sports with something in common. It could be being a legendary figure in the sport or playing in the same city.

B2 B.Bonds 2.50 6.00
J.Rice
B3 M.Faulk 1.00 2.50
T.Gwynn
B5 A.Iverson 1.00 2.50
D.McNabb
B6 N.Garciaparra 2.00 5.00
T.Brady
B7 K.Garnett 1.50 4.00
R.Moss
B8 S.Sosa 1.25 3.00
A.Thomas
B9 M.McGwire 2.50 6.00
K.Warner

2002-03 UD SuperStars City All-Stars Dual Jersey

Inserted at a stated rate of one in 32, these 43 cards featured two jersey swatches from star athletes from the same city. Some cards were issued in smaller quantities and we have notated that information with an SP in our database.

ABBD A.Brooks/B.Davis 6.00 15.00
ADDM A.Davis/D.Miles 5.00 12.00
ADPW A.Dunn/P.Warrick 4.00 10.00
BGJS B.Griese/J.Sakic 6.00 15.00
DBTH D.Brees/T.Hoffman 6.00 15.00
DCTO D.Culpepper/T.Hunter 8.00 20.00
ECRG E.Chavez/R.Gannon 6.00 15.00
EJJO E.James/J.O'Neal 5.00 12.00
JBJF J.Fiedler/J.Beckett 4.00 10.00
JGCB J.Gaffney/C.Biggio 6.00 15.00
JGJS J.Garcia/J.Snow 6.00 15.00
JLDS J.LeClair/D.Staley 6.00 15.00
JPLG J.Plummer/L.Gonzalez 4.00 10.00
LTRK L.Tomlinson/R.Klesko 6.00 15.00
MFJD M.Faulk/J.Drew 6.00 15.00
MVAJ M.Vick/A.Jones 10.00 25.00
PHMS P.Holmes/M.Sweeney 6.00 15.00
PLAM P.Lo Duca/A.Miller 6.00 15.00
RACP R.Alomar/C.Pennington 6.00 15.00
RDBW R.Dayne/B.Williams 6.00 15.00
SAEM S.Alexander/E.Martinez 6.00 15.00
SDJS S.Davis/J.Stackhouse SP 6.00 15.00
SMPG S.McNair/P.Gasol 10.00 25.00
THJD T.Holt/J.Drew 5.00 12.00
TORA T.Owens/R.Aurilia 6.00 15.00
WSMB W.Szczerbiak/M.Bennett 5.00 12.00

2002-03 UD SuperStars City All-Stars Triple Jersey

Randomly inserted in packs, these cards featured three game-used jersey swatches from all-stars from the same city. These cards were issued to a stated print run of 250 serial numbered sets.

CVT Chipper 12.00 30.00
Vick
Terry
IGS Ichiro 10.00 25.00
Payton
Alexander
JCK Griffey 10.00 25.00
Dillon
K.Martin
JDW Jacque 10.00 25.00
Culp
Szczerbiak
JDY Bagwell 15.00 40.00
Carr
Ming
JKA Kendall/Stewart/Kovalev 15.00 30.00
JMK Drew/Faulk/Tkachuk 10.00 25.00
JSB Harrington 25.00 50.00
Yzer
Wallace
MJA Prior 5.00 12.00
J.Will
A.Thomas
MJC Piazza 10.00 25.00
Kidd
C.Martin
MJJ Tejada 10.00 25.00
J.Rich
Rice
OTD Vizquel 10.00 25.00
Couch
D.Wag
PTP Pedro 10.00 25.00
Brady
Pierce

2002-03 UD SuperStars Keys to the City

Inserted at a stated rate of one in six. These 10 cards feature two star athletes from the same city.

COMPLETE SET (10) 10.00 25.00
K3 M.McGwire 1.50 4.00
K.Warner
K4 B.Urlacher 1.00 2.50
S.Sosa
K5 P.Martinez 1.00 2.50
T.Brady
K7 M.Piazza .75 2.00
C.Martin
K8 J.Bagwell 1.50 4.00
D.Carr
K9 S.Yzerman 1.25 3.00
J.Harrington
K10 A.Rodriguez 1.25 3.00
E.Smith

2002-03 UD SuperStars Legendary Leaders Dual Jersey

Inserted at a stated rate of one in 96, these 20 cards feature game-worn jersey pieces from two star athletes from the same city.

AIDM A.Iverson/D.McNabb 10.00 25.00
DCJB D.Carr/J.Bagwell 6.00 15.00
EJJO E.James/J.O'Neal 6.00 15.00
ESAR E.Smith/A.Rodriguez 15.00 40.00
JGKC J.Giambi/K.Collins 4.00 10.00
JKCP J.Kidd/C.Pennington 8.00 20.00
JRCD K.Griffey Jr./C.Dillon 6.00 15.00
JRJR J.Rice/J.Richardson 10.00 25.00
JSTG J.Seau/T.Gwynn 6.00 15.00
JWAT J.Williams/A.Thomas 6.00 15.00
KGRM K.Garnett/R.Moss 15.00 30.00
KWMM K.Warner/M.McGwire 20.00 50.00
PMTD P.Martinez/T.Brady 30.00 80.00
RMPM R.Miller/P.Manning 15.00 30.00
SSBU S.Sosa/B.Urlacher 8.00 20.00
SYJH S.Yzerman/J.Harrington 10.00 25.00
TCOV T.Couch/O.Vizquel 4.00 10.00

2002-03 UD SuperStars Legendary Leaders Triple Jersey

Randomly inserted in packs, these 18 cards feature game-used jersey swatches from three athletes. This set is significant by the usage of game-worn swatches of soccer great David Beckham. Each card was issued to a stated print run of 250 serial numbered sets.

ADJ Iverson 20.00 50.00
McNabb
Roenick
AEM A.Rod/Emmitt/Modano 20.00 50.00
CJS Ripken/Jagr/Davis 12.50 30.00
GMS Maddux 12.50 30.00
Vick
A-Rahim
JDM Giambi/Bledsoe/Messier 10.00 25.00
KJT Malone 10.00 25.00
Rice
Gwynn
LBP Walker/Griese/Roy 15.00 40.00
MCA Piazza/C.Penn/Yashin 10.00 25.00
MPS McGwire/Manning/Yzer 30.00 80.00
PPT Pedro 20.00 50.00
Pierce
Brady
RJM Clemens/Rice/Lemieux 30.00 60.00
SEB Sosa/Daze/Urlacher 10.00 25.00
SKM Sosa 15.00 40.00
Kobe
Faulk
TEM Gwynn/Emmitt/Lemieux 12.50 30.00

2002-03 UD SuperStars Magic Moments

Inserted at a stated rate of one in five, this 20 card set featured a mix of active and retired players along with history about key moments in their career.

COMPLETE SET (20) 10.00 25.00
MM11 Kurt Warner .50 1.25
MM12 Brett Favre 1.25 3.00
MM13 Tom Brady 1.00 2.50

2002-03 UD SuperStars Rookie Review

Inserted at a stated rate of one in 20, these 10 cards feature two athletes who made their American professional debut in the same year.

R2 I.Suzuki 2.00 5.00
M.Vick
R4 V.Carter 1.25 3.00
P.Manning
R5 E.Smith 2.00 5.00
S.Sosa
R6 M.Prior .75 2.00
D.Brees
R10 D.Jeter 1.50 4.00
J.Bettis

2002-03 UD SuperStars Spokesmen

Issued as a three-card pack topper, these 30 cards feature a mix of players who were also serving as spokesmen for Upper Deck.

*BLACK: 1.25X TO 3X BASIC SPOKESMEN
BLACK/GOLD INSERTS IN SPOKESMEN PACKS
BLACK PRINT RUN 250 SERIAL #'d SETS
*GOLD/25: 3X TO 8X BASIC INSERTS
GOLD PRINT RUN 25 SERIAL #'d SETS
UD11 Peyton Manning 1.25 3.00
UD26 Peyton Manning 1.25 3.00

2003 Ultimate Collection

Released in September of 2003, this set consists of 107 cards including 55 veterans and 52 rookies. Each veteran is serial numbered to 750. The non-autographed rookies are serial numbered to 750 or 250, and the autographed rookies are serial numbered to 250.

1 Peyton Manning 2.50 6.00
2 Aaron Brooks .60 1.50
3 Joey Harrington .60 1.50
4 Brett Favre 2.00 5.00
5 Donovan McNabb .75 2.00
6 Jeff Garcia .60 1.50
7 Michael Vick .75 2.00
8 David Carr .60 1.50
9 Drew Brees 1.00 2.50
10 Chad Pennington .60 1.50
11 Drew Bledsoe .75 2.00
12 Tom Brady 4.00 10.00
13 Kurt Warner .75 2.00
14 Brad Johnson .75 2.00
15 Jay Fiedler .60 1.50
16 Tim Couch .60 1.50
17 Trent Green .60 1.50
18 Daunte Culpepper .75 2.00
19 Keyshawn Johnson 1.00 2.50
20 Garrison Hearst .60 1.50
21 LaDainian Tomlinson 1.00 2.50
22 Emmitt Smith 1.50 4.00
23 Steve McNair .75 2.00
24 Chris Redman .60 1.50
25 Chad Hutchinson .60 1.50
26 Deuce McAllister .75 2.00
27 Eddie George .75 2.00
28 Marshall Faulk .75 2.00
29 Ahman Green .75 2.00
30 Julius Peppers 1.00 2.50
31 Priest Holmes .60 1.50
32 Edgerrin James .75 2.00
33 Jerry Rice 2.00 5.00
34 Ricky Williams .75 2.00
35 Anthony Thomas .75 2.00
36 Jerome Bettis 1.00 2.50
37 Shaun Alexander .60 1.50
38 Randy Moss .75 2.00
39 Jeremy Shockey .60 1.50
40 Patrick Ramsey .75 2.00
41 Clinton Portis .60 1.50
42 Terrell Owens .75 2.00
43 Corey Dillon .60 1.50
44 Mark Brunell .75 2.00
45 Rich Gannon .75 2.00
46 Curtis Martin .75 2.00
47 Josh McCown .75 2.00
48 Kerry Collins .60 1.50
49 Peerless Price .60 1.50
50 David Boston .60 1.50
51 Plaxico Burress .60 1.50
52 Marvin Harrison .75 2.00
53 Travis Henry .60 1.50
54 Brian Urlacher 1.00 2.50
55 Jake Plummer .60 1.50
56 Dave Ragone/750 RC 2.00 5.00
57 Brian St.Pierre AU/250 RC 8.00 20.00
58 Tony Romo/750 RC 20.00 40.00
59 Dallas Clark/750 RC 3.00 8.00
60 Kirk Farmer/750 RC 2.50 6.00
61 Juston Wood/750 RC 2.00 5.00
62 Justin Gage/750 RC 2.50 6.00
63 Sam Aiken/750 RC 2.50 6.00
64 LaBrandon Toefield/750 RC 2.00 5.00
65 L.J. Smith/750 RC 3.00 8.00
66 Domanick Davis/750 RC 2.50 6.00
67 Artose Pinner/750 RC 2.00 5.00
68 Dahrran Diedrick/750 RC 2.00 5.00
69 Lee Suggs/750 RC 2.00 5.00
70 Bethel Johnson/750 RC 2.00 5.00
71 Tyrone Calico/750 RC 2.00 5.00
72 Kevin Curtis/750 RC 2.00 5.00
73 Bobby Wade/750 RC 2.50 6.00
74 Brandon Lloyd/750 RC 3.00 8.00
75 Bryant Johnson/750 RC 3.00 8.00
76 J.R. Tolver/750 RC 2.50 6.00
77 Billy McMullen/750 RC 2.00 5.00
78 Nate Burleson/750 RC 2.50 6.00
79 Jason Johnson AU/250 RC 8.00 20.00
80 Talman Gardner/250 RC 5.00 12.00
81 Anquan Boldin/250 RC 8.00 20.00
82 Musa Smith/250 RC 5.00 12.00
83 Teyo Johnson/250 RC 6.00 15.00
84 Kyle Boller AU/250 RC 8.00 20.00
85 Carson Palmer AU/250 RC 40.00 100.00
86 Byron Leftwich AU/250 RC 10.00 25.00
87 Earnest Graham AU/250 RC 12.00 30.00
88 Chris Brown AU/250 RC 8.00 20.00
89 Chris Simms AU/250 RC 8.00 20.00
90 Kliff Kingsbury AU/250 RC 12.00 30.00
91 Jason Gesser/750 RC 2.50 6.00
92 Brad Banks AU/250 RC 10.00 25.00
93 Ken Dorsey AU/250 RC 10.00 25.00
94 Rex Grossman AU/250 RC 10.00 25.00
95 Willis McGahee AU/250 RC 12.00 30.00
96 Larry Johnson AU/250 RC 10.00 25.00
97 Quentin Griffin AU/250 RC 10.00 25.00
98 Onterrio Smith AU/250 RC 8.00 20.00
99 Justin Fargas AU/250 RC 12.00 30.00
100 Kareem Kelly AU/250 RC 8.00 20.00
101 Arnaz Battle AU/250 RC 12.00 30.00
102 Kel Washington AU/250 RC 8.00 20.00
103 Seneca Wallace AU/250 RC 10.00 25.00
104 Taylor Jacobs AU/250 RC 8.00 20.00
105 Andre Johnson/750 RC 5.00 12.00
106 Charles Rogers/250 RC 6.00 15.00
107 Terrell Suggs AU/250 RC 15.00 40.00

2003 Ultimate Collection Gold

*VETS 1-55: 1X TO 2.5X BASIC CARDS
1-55 VETERAN PRINT RUN 75
*ROOKIES/75: .8X TO 2X RC/750
*ROOKIES/25: .8X TO 2X RC/250
*ROOK.AU/25: .6X TO 1.5X AU/250
56-107 ROOKIE PRINT RUN 25-75
58 Tony Romo/75 75.00 125.00
85 Carson Palmer AU/25 125.00 250.00
94 Rex Grossman AU/25 15.00 40.00
95 Willis McGahee AU/25 50.00 120.00
96 Larry Johnson AU/25 50.00 120.00

2003 Ultimate Collection Buy Back Autographs

Randomly inserted into packs, this set features cards released in previous Upper Deck products that were bought back by the company for use in this product. Each card is autographed by the player and is embossed and serial numbered to various quantities. We've only listed below the card with sufficient market information for pricing. Please note that Terrell Owens was issued in packs as an exchange card.

STATED PRINT RUN 1-36
SER.#'d UNDER 25 NOT PRICED
1 S.Alexander 02SP/19 15.00 40.00
3 S.Alexander 02UDG/35 15.00 40.00
4 S.Alexander 02UDSS/36 15.00 40.00
13 A.Brooks 02UDG/20 15.00 40.00
15 A.Brooks 02UDSS/23 15.00 40.00
26 T.Couch 02SP/24 15.00 40.00
27 T.Couch 02UDA/19 15.00 40.00
28 T.Couch 02UDG/28 15.00 40.00
35 J.Garcia 01UDPPJsy/29 15.00 40.00
37 J.Garcia 02UDSS/24 15.00 40.00
38 R.Gardner 02SP/29 15.00 40.00
40 R.Gardner 02UDSS/24 15.00 40.00
43 P.Manning 01UDPPJsy/29 60.00 120.00
44 P.Manning 02SPLC/25 60.00 120.00
48 P.Manning 02UDSS/24 60.00 120.00
54 T.Owens 02UDG/20 25.00 50.00
58 A.Thomas 02UDG/34 15.00 40.00
60 A.Thomas 02UDSS/35 15.00 40.00
62 L.Tomlinson 02UDG/20 40.00 80.00

2003 Ultimate Collection Game Jerseys

Randomly inserted into packs, this set features authentic game worn jersey swatches. Each card is serial numbered to 250 or 99. A gold parallel set also exists, with each card serial numbered to 25. Six of the best players also were issued in an autographed parallel version with those being serial numbered to 25. A Gold Autograph version was also produced and serial numbered of 10.

STATED PRINT RUN 99-250
*GOLD/25: 1X TO 2.5X BASE JSY/250
*GOLD/25: .6X TO 1.5X BASE JSY/99
GOLD STATED PRINT RUN 25
UJAB Aaron Brooks/250 3.00 8.00
UJAG Ahman Green/250 4.00 10.00
UJBA Tom Brady/250 20.00 50.00
UJBF Brett Favre/250 10.00 25.00
UJBR Drew Brees/250 5.00 12.00
UJBS Barry Sanders/99 15.00 40.00
UJBU Brian Urlacher/250 5.00 12.00
UJCP1 Chad Pennington/250 3.00 8.00
UJCP2 Clinton Portis/250 3.00 8.00
UJDA Dan Marino/99 20.00 50.00
UJDB Drew Bledsoe/250 4.00 10.00
UJDC Daunte Culpepper/250 4.00 10.00
UJDM Donovan McNabb/250 4.00 10.00
UJEJ Edgerrin James/250 4.00 10.00
UJFT Fran Tarkenton/99 10.00 25.00
UJJE John Elway/99 12.00 30.00
UJJG Jeff Garcia/250 3.00 8.00
UJJK Jim Kelly/99 10.00 25.00
UJJM Joe Montana/99 40.00 80.00
UJJN Joe Namath/99 15.00 40.00
UJJR Jerry Rice/250 10.00 25.00
UJKJ Keyshawn Johnson/250 5.00 12.00
UJKW Kurt Warner/250 4.00 10.00
UJLT LaDainian Tomlinson/250 5.00 12.00
UJMA Marcus Allen/99 10.00 25.00
UJMC Deuce McAllister/250 4.00 10.00
UJMF Marshall Faulk/250 4.00 10.00
UJMV Michael Vick/250 4.00 10.00
UJPH Priest Holmes/250 3.00 8.00
UJPM Peyton Manning/250 12.00 30.00
UJRM Randy Moss/250 4.00 10.00
UJRW Ricky Williams/250 4.00 10.00
UJST Bart Starr/99 20.00 50.00
UJSY Steve Young/99 12.00 30.00
UJTA Troy Aikman/99 12.00 30.00
UJTC Tim Couch/250 3.00 8.00
UJTO Terrell Owens/250 4.00 10.00
UJWP Walter Payton/99 25.00 60.00

2003 Ultimate Collection Game Jersey Autographs

Randomly inserted into packs, this 6-card set features game worn jersey swatches and authentic player autographs. Each card is serial numbered to 25. A gold parallel version exists, with each card serial numbered to 10.

STATED PRINT RUN 25 SER.#'d SETS
GOLD/10 NOT PRICED DUE TO SCARCITY
UJSBS Bart Starr 125.00 250.00
UJSDM Dan Marino 125.00 250.00
UJSJM Joe Montana 125.00 250.00
UJSJN Joe Namath 100.00 175.00
UJSMV Michael Vick 60.00 100.00
UJSPM Peyton Manning 100.00 200.00

2003 Ultimate Collection Game Jersey Duals

Randomly inserted into packs, this set features two swatches of authentic game worn jersey. Each card is serial numbered to various quantities. A gold parallel also exists, with each card serial numbered to 25. Six of the best cards also were issued in an autographed parallel version with those being serial numbered to 25. A Gold Autograph version was also produced and serial numbered of 10.

STATED PRINT RUN 99-250
*GOLD/25: .8X TO 2X BASE DUAL/250
*GOLD/25: .5X TO 1.2X BASE DUAL/99-100
GOLD PRINT RUN 25 SER.#'d SETS
UDJAM T.Aikman/P.Manning/99 25.00 60.00
UDJBC A.Brooks/T.Couch/250 4.00 10.00
UDJCB D.Carr/T.Brady/250 25.00 60.00
UDJFM M.Faulk/C.Martin/250 5.00 12.00
UDJFR B.Favre/J.Rice/250 12.00 30.00
UDJHB J.Harrington/D.Brees/250 6.00 15.00
UDJHW P.Holmes/R.Williams/250 5.00 12.00
UDJKB J.Kelly/D.Bledsoe/250 10.00 25.00
UDJMC D.Marino/D.Carr/99 20.00 50.00
UDJMS D.McAllstr/B.Sndrs/100 15.00 40.00
UDJMV D.McNabb/M.Vick/250 5.00 12.00
UDJMG1 D.McNabb/J.Garcia/250 5.00 12.00
UDJMG2 J.Montana/J.Garcia/99 30.00 80.00
UDJNP Namath/Pennington/99 15.00 40.00
UDJPD C.Portis/T.Davis/250 5.00 12.00
UDJPF W.Payton/M.Faulk/99 30.00 80.00
UDJPM C.Pennington/R.Moss/250 5.00 12.00
UDJPT W.Payton/A.Thomas/250 12.00 30.00
UDJPW W.Payton/R.Williams/99 30.00 80.00
UDJRO J.Rice/T.Owens/250 12.00 30.00
UDJSF B.Starr/B.Favre/99 40.00 100.00
UDJST Sanders/Tomlinson/99 15.00 40.00
UDJTC F.Trkntn/D.Culpppr/99 10.00 25.00
UDJYV S.Young/M.Vick/99 12.00 30.00

2003 Ultimate Collection Game Jersey Duals Autographs

Randomly inserted into packs, this set features two authentic autographs. Each card is serial numbered to 25. A gold parallel version also exists, with each card serial numbered to 10.

STATED PRINT RUN 25 SER.#'d SETS
GOLD/10 NOT PRICED DUE TO SCARCITY
DJSEM J.Elway/D.McNabb 200.00 400.00
DJSMM D.Marino/P.Manning 300.00 500.00
DJSNP J.Namath/C.Pennington 125.00 250.00
DJSSF B.Starr/B.Favre 400.00 550.00
DJSVM M.Vick/D.McNabb 75.00 150.00
DJSYV S.Young/M.Vick 100.00 200.00

2003 Ultimate Collection Game Jersey Duals Patches

Randomly inserted into packs, this set features two jersey patch swatches. Each card is serial numbered to 25. A gold parallel also exists, with each card serial numbered to 10 or less.

STATED PRINT RUN 25 SER.#'d SETS
UNPRICED PATCH GOLD PRINT RUN 3-10
DGPAM T.Aikman/P.Manning 60.00 150.00
DGPBR M.Brunell/D.Ragone 20.00 50.00
DGPBW T.Bradshaw/K.Warner 30.00 80.00
DGPJM E.James/W.McGahee 12.00 30.00
DGPMC R.Moss/D.Culpepper 20.00 50.00
DGPMF D.Marino/J.Fiedler 50.00 125.00
DGPMG J.Montana/J.Garcia 80.00 200.00
DGPPT W.Payton/A.Thomas 50.00 125.00
DGPRM J.Rice/R.Moss 50.00 125.00
DGPRO J.Rice/T.Owens 50.00 125.00
DGPSF B.Starr/B.Favre 80.00 200.00
DGPVM M.Vick/D.McNabb 20.00 50.00

2003 Ultimate Collection Game Jersey Patches

Randomly inserted into packs, this set features game worn jersey patches. Each card is serial numbered to various quantities. A gold parallel also exists, with each card serial numbered to 25 or less.

STATED PRINT RUN 25-175
*GOLD/25: 1X TO 2.5X BASE PATCH/141-175
*GOLD/25: .8X TO 2X BASE PATCH/99
GOLD PRINT RUN 10-25
GJPAB Aaron Brooks/175 5.00 12.00
GJPAG Ahman Green/175 6.00 15.00
GJPBA Barry Sanders/25 50.00 120.00
GJPBF Brett Favre/99 20.00 50.00
GJPBS Bart Starr/25 40.00 100.00
GJPBU Brian Urlacher/175 8.00 20.00
GJPCA David Carr/175 5.00 12.00
GJPCP1 Chad Pennington/99 6.00 15.00
GJPCP2 Clinton Portis/175 5.00 12.00
GJPDC Daunte Culpepper/175 6.00 15.00
GJPDB1 Drew Bledsoe/175 6.00 15.00
GJPDB2 Drew Brees/99 10.00 25.00
GJPDM1 Dan Marino/25 60.00 150.00
GJPDM2 Deuce McAllister/175 6.00 15.00
GJPDM3 Donovan McNabb/99 8.00 20.00
GJPEG Eddie George/175 6.00 15.00
GJPEJ Edgerrin James/99 8.00 20.00
GJPES Emmitt Smith/175 12.00 30.00
GJPFT Fran Tarkenton/99 12.00 30.00
GJPJE John Elway/99 20.00 50.00
GJPJG Jeff Garcia/175 5.00 12.00
GJPJM Joe Montana/25 60.00 150.00
GJPJN Joe Namath/25 40.00 100.00
GJPJR Jerry Rice/175 15.00 40.00
GJPKJ Keyshawn Johnson/175 8.00 20.00
GJPKW Kurt Warner/99 8.00 20.00
GJPLT LaDainian Tomlinson/175 8.00 20.00
GJPMF Marshall Faulk/175 6.00 15.00
GJPMV Michael Vick/99 8.00 20.00
GJPPH Priest Holmes/175 5.00 12.00
GJPPM Peyton Manning/175 20.00 50.00
GJPRM Randy Moss/175 6.00 15.00
GJPRW Ricky Williams/99 8.00 20.00
GJPSY Steve Young/25 30.00 80.00
GJPTA Troy Aikman/99 15.00 40.00
GJPTC Tim Couch/175 5.00 12.00
GJPTO Terrell Owens/175 6.00 15.00
GJPTB1 Terry Bradshaw/25 30.00 80.00
GJPTB2 Tom Brady/175 30.00 80.00
GJPWP Walter Payton/25 60.00 150.00

2003 Ultimate Collection Ultimate Signatures

Randomly inserted into packs, this set features authentic player autographs. Please note that Brett Favre, Bart Starr, David Carr, Dan Marino, Fran Tarkenton, John Elway, Joe Montana, Joe Namath, Jerry Rice, Steve Young, Troy Aikman, and Terry Bradshaw are all serial numbered to 25. All others are not serial numbered. In addition, Randy Moss was issued in packs as an exchange card but never signed for the set. A gold parallel also exists, with each card serial numbered to 50 or 10.

*GOLD/50: .6X TO 1.5X BASE AUTO
GOLD STATED PRINT RUN 10-50
USAB Aaron Brooks 8.00 20.00
USBA Barry Sanders 90.00 150.00

USBB Brad Banks 8.00 20.00
USBF Brett Favre/25 175.00 300.00
USBL Byron Leftwich 8.00 20.00
USBS Bart Starr/25 100.00 200.00
USCH Chad Pennington 8.00 20.00
USCP Carson Palmer 75.00 125.00
USCS Chris Simms 12.00 30.00
USDB Drew Brees 30.00 60.00
USDC David Carr/25 10.00 25.00
USDE Deuce McAllister 10.00 25.00
USDM Dan Marino/25 125.00 250.00
USFT Fran Tarkenton/25 30.00 60.00
USJE John Elway/25 100.00 200.00
USJF Justin Fargas 10.00 25.00
USJK Jim Kelly 20.00 50.00
USJM Joe Montana/25 125.00 250.00
USJN Joe Namath/25 75.00 135.00
USJR Jerry Rice/25 100.00 200.00
USKK Kliff Kingsbury 10.00 25.00
USKS Ken Stabler 25.00 50.00
USLT LaDainian Tomlinson 20.00 50.00
USMA Marcus Allen 20.00 40.00
USPM Peyton Manning 75.00 125.00
USRG Rex Grossman 8.00 20.00
USSU Donovan McNabb 20.00 50.00
USSY Steve Young/25 90.00 150.00
USTA Troy Aikman/25 75.00 150.00
USTB Terry Bradshaw/25 75.00 150.00
USTC Tim Couch 8.00 20.00

2003 Ultimate Collection Ultimate Signatures Duals

Randomly inserted into packs, this set features two authentic autographs. Each card is serial numbered to 50 or 25. A gold parallel also exists, with each card serial numbered to 25 or 10.

DSBT Brees/Tomlinson/50 75.00 150.00
DSGM J.Garcia/J.Montana/25 100.00 200.00
DSGY J.Garcia/S.Young/25 75.00 150.00
DSMF D.Marino/J.Fiedler/25 125.00 250.00
DSMM P.Mann/A.Mann/50 100.00 200.00
DSMP P.Manning/Palmer/50 100.00 200.00
DSMY Montana/S.Young/25 200.00 400.00
DSNP Namath/Penning/25 75.00 150.00
DSPL Palmer/Leftwich/50 30.00 80.00
DSSF B.Starr/B.Favre/25 300.00 500.00
DSSS P.Simms/C.Simms/50 30.00 60.00

2003 Ultimate Collection Ultimate Signatures Duals Gold

SER.#'d TO 10 NOT PRICED
DSBT Brees/Tomlinson/25 60.00 150.00
DSMM P.Mann/A.Mann/25 125.00 200.00
DSMP P.Manning/Palmer/25 125.00 250.00
DSPL Palmer/Leftwich/25 50.00 120.00
DSSS P.Simms/C.Simms/25 40.00 100.00

2004 Ultimate Collection

Ultimate Collection was initially released in late December 2004 and remained one of the hottest products of the year. The base set consists of 135-cards including 64-veterans serial numbered to 750 as well as multi-level numbered rookie cards and autographed rookie cards. Hobby boxes contained 4-packs of 4-cards and carried an S.R.P. of $100 per pack. Three parallel sets and a variety of inserts can be found seeded in packs highlighted by a huge checklist of Buy Back Autographs and the Ultimate Signatures inserts.

1-65 VETERAN PRINT RUN 750
66-91/99A/133-135 PRINT RUN 750
92-98 ROOKIE PRINT RUN 250
99B-124/131-132 AU RC PRINT RUN 250
125-130 AU RC PRINT RUN 150 SER.#'d SETS
UNPRICED PLATINUM PRINT RUN 10
1 Emmitt Smith 2.50 6.00
2 Anquan Boldin 1.00 2.50
3 Michael Vick 1.25 3.00
4 Peerless Price 1.00 2.50
5 Kyle Boller 1.00 2.50
6 Jamal Lewis 1.25 3.00
7 Drew Bledsoe 1.25 3.00
8 Travis Henry 1.00 2.50
9 Stephen Davis 1.00 2.50
10 Jake Delhomme 1.00 2.50
11 Rex Grossman 1.00 2.50
12 Brian Urlacher 1.50 4.00
13 Carson Palmer 1.25 3.00
14 Chad Johnson 1.00 2.50
15 Jeff Garcia 1.00 2.50
16 Keyshawn Johnson 1.25 3.00
17 Roy Williams S 1.00 2.50
18 Jake Plummer 1.00 2.50
19 Joey Harrington 1.00 2.50
20 Charles Rogers 1.00 2.50
21 Ahman Green 1.25 3.00
22 Brett Favre 3.00 8.00
23 David Carr 1.00 2.50
24 Domanick Davis 1.00 2.50
25 Andre Johnson 1.25 3.00
26 Edgerrin James 1.25 3.00
27 Peyton Manning 4.00 10.00
28 Marvin Harrison 1.25 3.00
29 Byron Leftwich 1.00 2.50
30 Fred Taylor 1.00 2.50
31 Priest Holmes 1.00 2.50
32 Tony Gonzalez 1.25 3.00
33 Trent Green 1.00 2.50
34 Ricky Williams 1.25 3.00
35 Chris Chambers 1.00 2.50
36 Jay Fiedler 1.00 2.50
37 Randy Moss 1.25 3.00
38 Daunte Culpepper 1.25 3.00
39 Tom Brady 6.00 15.00
40 Corey Dillon 1.00 2.50
41 Deuce McAllister 1.25 3.00
42 Aaron Brooks 1.00 2.50
43 Tiki Barber 1.25 3.00
44 Jeremy Shockey 1.00 2.50
45 Chad Pennington 1.00 2.50
46 Curtis Martin 1.25 3.00
47 Santana Moss 1.25 3.00
48 Jerry Rice 3.00 8.00
49 Rich Gannon 1.25 3.00
50 Donovan McNabb 1.25 3.00
51 Terrell Owens 1.25 3.00
52 Hines Ward 1.25 3.00
53 Plaxico Burress 1.00 2.50
54 LaDainian Tomlinson 1.50 4.00
55 Tim Rattay 1.00 2.50
56 Matt Hasselbeck 1.00 2.50
57 Shaun Alexander 1.00 2.50
58 Marc Bulger 1.00 2.50
59 Marshall Faulk 1.25 3.00
60 Torry Holt 1.25 3.00
61 Brad Johnson 1.25 3.00
62 Steve McNair 1.25 3.00
63 Chris Brown 1.00 2.50
64 Mark Brunell 1.25 3.00
65 Clinton Portis 1.00 2.50
66 Michael Turner RC 2.00 5.00
67 Kris Wilson RC 2.50 6.00
68 Jeff Smoker RC 2.50 6.00
69 Adimchinobe Echemandu RC 2.50 6.00
71 Thomas Tapeh RC 2.50 6.00
72 Chris Cooley RC 2.50 6.00
73 Cody Pickett RC 2.00 5.00
74 P.K. Sam RC 2.00 5.00
75 Ben Hartsock RC 2.00 5.00
76 Tim Euhus RC 2.00 5.00
77 Jammal Lord RC 2.00 5.00
78 Ricardo Colclough RC 2.00 5.00
79 D.J. Hackett RC 2.00 5.00
80 Ahmad Carroll RC 2.00 5.00
81 Troy Fleming RC 2.00 5.00
82 John Navarre RC 2.00 5.00
83 Craig Krenzel RC 2.00 5.00
84 Johnnie Morant RC 2.00 5.00
85 D.J. Williams RC 3.00 8.00
86 Jarrett Payton RC 2.50 6.00
87 Quincy Wilson RC 2.00 5.00
88 B.J. Symons RC 2.00 5.00
89 Tommie Harris RC 2.50 6.00
90 Jonathan Vilma RC 2.50 6.00
91 Karlos Dansby RC 2.50 6.00
92 Jerricho Cotchery RC 3.00 8.00
93 Samie Parker RC 2.50 6.00
94 Carlos Francis RC 2.50 6.00
95 Jim Sorgi RC 3.00 8.00
96 Derrick Hamilton RC 2.50 6.00
97 Dunta Robinson RC 2.50 6.00
98 Chris Gamble RC 2.50 6.00
99A Josh Harris RC 2.00 5.00
99B Devery Henderson AU RC 6.00 15.00
100 Julius Jones AU RC 10.00 25.00
101 Cedric Cobbs AU RC 6.00 15.00
102 Greg Jones AU RC 6.00 15.00
103 Tatum Bell AU RC 6.00 15.00
104 Michael Jenkins AU RC 6.00 15.00
105 Devard Darling AU RC 6.00 15.00
106 Lee Evans AU RC 10.00 25.00
107 Keary Colbert AU RC 6.00 15.00
108 Bernard Berrian AU RC 6.00 15.00
109 Ben Watson AU RC 8.00 20.00
110 Matt Schaub AU RC 10.00 25.00
111 Darius Watts AU RC 6.00 15.00
112 Kevin Jones AU RC 8.00 20.00
113 Luke McCown AU RC 6.00 15.00
114 DeAngelo Hall AU RC 10.00 25.00
115 Rashaun Woods AU RC 6.00 15.00
116 Michael Clayton AU RC 8.00 20.00
117 Ben Troupe AU RC 6.00 15.00
118 B.J. Sams AU RC 6.00 15.00
119 Reggie Williams AU RC 6.00 15.00
120 Chris Perry AU RC 6.00 15.00
121 Roy Williams AU RC 6.00 15.00
122 Robert Gallery AU RC 8.00 20.00
123 J.P. Losman AU RC 6.00 15.00
124 Steven Jackson AU RC 15.00 40.00
125 Drew Henson AU RC 6.00 15.00
126 Kellen Winslow AU RC 10.00 25.00
127 B.Roethlisberger AU RC 150.00 300.00
128 Philip Rivers AU RC 30.00 80.00
129 Larry Fitzgerald AU RC 75.00 150.00
130 Eli Manning AU RC 125.00 250.00
131 Ernest Wilford AU RC 8.00 20.00
132 Mewelde Moore AU RC 8.00 20.00
133 Will Smith RC 2.50 6.00
134 Kenechi Udeze RC 2.50 6.00
135 Matt Mauck RC 2.00 5.00

2004 Ultimate Collection Gold

*VETS: .8X TO 2X BASIC CARDS
*ROOKIES/75: .8X TO 2X BASIC RC/750
1-91/99A/133-135 PRINT RUN 75 SETS
*ROOKIES/25: 1X TO 2.5X BASE RC/250
92-98 STATED PRINT RUN 25 SETS

2004 Ultimate Collection HoloGold

*VETS: 1.2X TO 3X BASE CARDS
*ROOKIES/30: 1.2X TO 3X BASIC RC/750
1-91/99A/133-135 PRINT RUN 30 SETS
UNPRICED 92-98 PRINT RUN 5 SETS

2004 Ultimate Collection Buy Back Autographs

SER.#'d UNDER 22 NOT PRICED
BBCC1 C.Chambers 01UDRT/25 12.00 30.00
BBCC2 C.Chambers 01UDORG/20 12.00 30.00
BBCJ1 C.Johnson 03SPA/26 15.00 40.00
BBCJ2 C.Johnson 03SPSIG/42 15.00 40.00
BBCJ3 C.Johnson 03SS/45 15.00 40.00
BBCJ4 C.Johnson 03UDGJ/33 15.00 40.00
BBDB1 D.Bledsoe 00UDGJ/21
BBDE3 D.McAllister 03SPA/26 15.00 40.00
BBDK D.Mason 03SPA/40 12.50 30.00
BBFT F.Tarkenton 03SPSIG/28 15.00 40.00
BBJO3 J.McCown 03SPA/27 12.50 30.00
BBJO4 J.McCown 03SPSIG/22 12.50 30.00
BBJO5 J.McCown 03UDSOS/24 12.50 30.00
BBKS2 K.Stabler 03SPSIG/26 25.00 60.00
BBRA R.White 01UDLTT/33 15.00 40.00
BBRW3 R.Will.S 03UDGJ/31 15.00 40.00
BBTH2 T.Henry 03SPA/36 10.00 25.00
BBTH4 T.Henry 03SPSIG/46 10.00 25.00
BBTH5 T.Henry 03SS/39 10.00 25.00
BBTO T.Heap 03SS/30 10.00 25.00
BBZT2 Z.Thomas 04SPxSS/50 12.50 30.00

2004 Ultimate Collection Game Jerseys

STATED PRINT RUN 175 SER.#'d SETS
*GOLD: 1X TO 2.5X BASIC JSY/175
GOLD PRINT RUN 25 SER.#'d SETS
UGJBF Brett Favre 8.00 20.00
UGJBL Byron Leftwich 2.50 6.00
UGJBS Barry Sanders 8.00 20.00
UGJCA Carson Palmer 3.00 8.00
UGJCL Clinton Portis 2.50 6.00
UGJCP Chad Pennington 2.50 6.00
UGJDA David Carr 2.50 6.00
UGJDC Daunte Culpepper 3.00 8.00
UGJDM Deuce McAllister 3.00 8.00
UGJDO Donovan McNabb 3.00 8.00
UGJED Eric Dickerson 5.00 12.00
UGJES Emmitt Smith 8.00 20.00
UGJFT Fran Tarkenton 5.00 12.00
UGJJE John Elway 8.00 20.00
UGJJM Joe Montana 15.00 40.00
UGJJN Joe Namath 8.00 20.00
UGJJR Jerry Rice 8.00 20.00
UGJJS Jeremy Shockey 2.50 6.00
UGJLS Lynn Swann 12.00 30.00
UGJLT LaDainian Tomlinson 4.00 10.00
UGJMA Dan Marino 10.00 25.00
UGJMF Marshall Faulk 3.00 8.00
UGJMH Marvin Harrison 3.00 8.00
UGJMV Michael Vick 3.00 8.00
UGJPH Priest Holmes 2.50 6.00
UGJPM Peyton Manning 10.00 25.00
UGJPS Phil Simms 4.00 10.00
UGJRM Randy Moss 3.00 8.00
UGJRS Roger Staubach 6.00 15.00
UGJRW Ricky Williams 3.00 8.00
UGJSM Steve McNair 3.00 8.00
UGJSY Steve Young 6.00 15.00
UGJTA Troy Aikman 6.00 15.00
UGJTB Tom Brady 15.00 40.00
UGJTE Terry Bradshaw 6.00 15.00
UGJTO Terrell Owens 3.00 8.00
UGJWP Walter Payton 20.00 50.00

2004 Ultimate Collection Game Jersey Autographs

STATED PRINT RUN 25 SER.#'d SETS
UGJSBF Brett Favre 175.00 300.00
UGJSCP Chad Pennington 15.00 40.00
UGJSDA Daunte Culpepper 20.00 50.00
UGJSDC David Carr 15.00 40.00
UGJSDM Deuce McAllister 20.00 50.00
UGJSDO Donovan McNabb 30.00 80.00
UGJSJE John Elway 125.00 250.00
UGJSJM Joe Montana 125.00 250.00
UGJSJN Joe Namath 100.00 175.00
UGJSJT Joe Theismann 25.00 60.00
UGJSLT LaDainian Tomlinson 25.00 60.00
UGJSMV Michael Vick 25.00 60.00
UGJSPM Peyton Manning 125.00 250.00
UGJSSM Steve McNair 20.00 50.00
UGJSTB Tom Brady 125.00 250.00

2004 Ultimate Collection Game Jersey Duals

STATED PRINT RUN 99 SER.#'d SETS
*GOLD/15: .8X TO 2X BASIC DUAL
GOLD STATED PRINT RUN 15
UNPRICED DUAL AU PRINT RUN 15 SETS
BP T.Brady/C.Pennington 30.00 80.00
CF D.Carr/B.Favre 15.00 40.00
CM D.Culpepper/S.McNair 6.00 15.00
EM J.Elway/J.Montana 25.00 60.00
EP E.Manning/P.Rivers 20.00 50.00
FM B.Favre/P.Manning 20.00 50.00
HJ P.Holmes/E.James 6.00 15.00
LP B.Leftwich/C.Palmer 6.00 15.00
LR L.Fitzgerald/R.Moss 10.00 25.00
MB J.Montana/T.Brady 30.00 80.00
MM D.Marino/J.Montana 25.00 60.00
MO R.Moss/T.Owens 6.00 15.00
MR R.Moss/J.Rice 15.00 40.00
NU J.Namath/J.Unitas 20.00 50.00
OM T.Owens/D.McNabb 6.00 15.00
PG C.Portis/A.Green 6.00 15.00
PM C.Pennington/P.Manning 20.00 50.00
PS W.Payton/G.Sayers 30.00 80.00
RO J.Rice/T.Owens 15.00 40.00
SA R.Staubach/T.Aikman 10.00 25.00
SF E.Smith/M.Faulk 12.00 30.00
SG J.Shockey/T.Gonzalez 6.00 15.00
SP B.Sanders/W.Payton 30.00 80.00
SW J.Shockey/K.Winslow Jr. 5.00 12.00
TL L.Taylor/R.Lott 8.00 20.00
TM L.Tomlinson/D.McAllister 8.00 20.00
UT B.Urlacher/Z.Thomas 8.00 20.00
VB M.Vick/T.Brady 15.00 40.00
VM M.Vick/M.Brunell 10.00 25.00
WH Ri.Williams/P.Holmes 6.00 15.00

2004 Ultimate Collection Game Jersey Dual Autographs

PRICED DUAL JSY AU PRINT RUN 15
UNPRICED DUAL PATCH AU PRINT RUN 5

2004 Ultimate Collection Game Jersey Dual Patches

STATED PRINT RUN 25 SER.#'d SETS
UNPRICED GOLD PRINT RUN 10
AE T.Aikman/J.Elway 25.00 60.00
BP T.Brady/C.Pennington 30.00 80.00
FV B.Favre/M.Vick 40.00 100.00
MC R.Moss/D.Culpepper 20.00 50.00
MM D.Marino/J.Montana 50.00 120.00
NU J.Namath/J.Unitas 50.00 100.00
PS P.Manning/S.McNair 30.00 80.00
SM B.Sanders/D.McAllister 30.00 80.00
VM M.Vick/D.McNabb 25.00 60.00
WT Ri.Williams/L.Tomlinson 20.00 50.00

2004 Ultimate Collection Game Jersey Logo Autographs

UNPRICED AU PRINT RUN 1 SET

2004 Ultimate Collection Game Jersey Patches

STATED PRINT RUN 150 SER.#'d SETS
*GOLD/25: .8X TO 2X BASIC PTCH/150
GOLD PRINT RUN 25 SER.#'d SETS
UNPRICED AUTO PRINT RUN 10 SETS
UPAG Ahman Green 6.00 15.00
UPBF Brett Favre 15.00 40.00
UPBL Byron Leftwich 5.00 12.00
UPBS Barry Sanders 15.00 40.00
UPBU Brian Urlacher 8.00 20.00
UPCA Carson Palmer 6.00 15.00
UPCC Cris Carter 8.00 20.00
UPCL Clinton Portis 5.00 12.00
UPCP Chad Pennington 5.00 12.00
UPDA David Carr 5.00 12.00
UPDB Drew Bledsoe 6.00 15.00
UPDC Daunte Culpepper 6.00 15.00
UPDE Deuce McAllister 6.00 15.00
UPDM Donovan McNabb 6.00 15.00
UPED Eric Dickerson 10.00 25.00
UPEJ Edgerrin James 6.00 15.00
UPES Emmitt Smith 12.00 30.00
UPFT Fran Tarkenton 10.00 25.00
UPGS Gale Sayers 10.00 25.00
UPJE John Elway 15.00 40.00
UPJM Joe Montana 20.00 50.00
UPJN Joe Namath 15.00 40.00
UPJR Jerry Rice 15.00 40.00
UPJS Jeremy Shockey 5.00 12.00
UPJU Johnny Unitas 20.00 50.00
UPLT LaDainian Tomlinson 8.00 20.00
UPMA Dan Marino 20.00 50.00
UPMB Mark Brunell 6.00 15.00
UPMF Marshall Faulk 6.00 15.00
UPMH Marvin Harrison 6.00 15.00
UPMV Michael Vick 6.00 15.00
UPPH Priest Holmes 5.00 12.00
UPPM Peyton Manning 20.00 50.00
UPRM Randy Moss 6.00 15.00
UPRS Roger Staubach 12.00 30.00
UPRW Ricky Williams 6.00 15.00
UPSM Steve McNair 6.00 15.00
UPTA Troy Aikman 12.00 30.00
UPTB Tom Brady 30.00 80.00
UPTO Terrell Owens 6.00 15.00
UPWP Walter Payton 30.00 80.00
UPZT Zach Thomas 6.00 15.00

2004 Ultimate Collection Game Jersey Patches Autographs

UNPRICED AU PRINT RUN 10 SER.#'d SETS

2004 Ultimate Collection Game Jersey Super Patches

SUPER PATCH PRINT RUN 15
USPBF Brett Favre 40.00 100.00
USPCP Chad Pennington 12.00 30.00
USPDE Deuce McAllister 15.00 40.00
USPDM Donovan McNabb 15.00 40.00
USPES Emmitt Smith 30.00 80.00
USPJR Jerry Rice 40.00 100.00
USPMV Michael Vick 15.00 40.00
USPPM Peyton Manning 50.00 120.00
USPRM Randy Moss 15.00 40.00
USPTB Tom Brady 80.00 200.00

2004 Ultimate Collection Rookie Jerseys

STATED PRINT RUN 199 SER.#'d SETS
*GOLD/25: .6X TO 1.5X BASIC JSY/199
GOLD PRINT RUN 25 SER.#'d SETS
UNPRICED AUTO PRINT RUN 1
URJBR Ben Roethlisberger 20.00 50.00
URJCC Cedric Cobbs 2.50 6.00
URJCP Chris Perry 2.50 6.00
URJDD Devard Darling 2.50 6.00
URJDE Devery Henderson 2.50 6.00
URJEM Eli Manning 15.00 40.00
URJGJ Greg Jones 2.50 6.00
URJJJ Julius Jones 2.50 6.00
URJJP J.P. Losman 2.50 6.00
URJKJ Kevin Jones 3.00 8.00
URJKW Kellen Winslow Jr. 2.50 6.00
URJLE Lee Evans 4.00 10.00
URJLF Larry Fitzgerald 10.00 25.00
URJMC Michael Clayton 3.00 8.00
URJMJ Michael Jenkins 2.50 6.00
URJPR Philip Rivers 12.00 30.00
URJRA Rashaun Woods 2.50 6.00
URJRO Roy Williams WR 2.50 6.00
URJRW Reggie Williams 2.50 6.00
URJSJ Steven Jackson 4.00 10.00
URJTB Tatum Bell 2.50 6.00

2004 Ultimate Collection Ultimate Signatures

UNPRICED QUAD AU PRINT RUN 5 SETS
USAG Ahman Green/100 10.00 25.00
USAR Andy Reid/100 10.00 25.00
USBF Brett Favre/25 175.00 300.00
USBL Byron Leftwich/275 6.00 15.00
USBP Bill Parcells/25 40.00 80.00
USBR Roethlisberger/100 125.00 250.00
USBS Barry Sanders/25 100.00 200.00
USCC Chris Chambers/275 6.00 15.00
USCJ Chad Johnson/275 6.00 15.00
USDB Drew Bledsoe/275 8.00 20.00
USEC Earl Campbell/275 20.00 40.00
USEM Eli Manning/100 100.00 200.00
USFT Fran Tarkenton/275 20.00 40.00
USHL Howie Long/100 25.00 50.00
USJE John Elway/25 100.00 200.00
USJF John Fox/100 8.00 20.00
USJG Jon Gruden/100 10.00 25.00
USJJ Jimmy Johnson/100 12.00 30.00
USJM Joe Montana/25 100.00 200.00
USJN Joe Namath/25 75.00 150.00
USJP J.P. Losman/275 6.00 15.00
USJT Joe Theismann/275 10.00 25.00
USKB Kyle Boller/275 6.00 15.00
USKJ Kevin Jones/275 8.00 20.00
USKW Kellen Winslow Jr./100 8.00 20.00
USLD Len Dawson/275 10.00 25.00
USMB Mark Brunell/275 10.00 25.00
USMV Michael Vick/25 20.00 50.00
USPH Paul Hornung/275 15.00 40.00
USPM Peyton Manning/25 100.00 200.00
USPR Philip Rivers/275 30.00 80.00
USRG Rex Grossman/275 10.00 25.00
USRW Roy Williams WR/275 6.00 15.00
USTA Troy Aikman/25 50.00 100.00
USTB Tom Brady/25 250.00 400.00
USTH Travis Henry/275 6.00 15.00
USTS Tony Siragusa/275 10.00 25.00
USWI Kellen Winslow Sr./100 12.00 30.00

2004 Ultimate Collection Ultimate Signatures Duals

AS Aikman/Staubach/50 90.00 150.00
CV Culpepper/Vick/25 50.00 100.00
EA Elway/Aikman/25 125.00 250.00
FM Favre/Manning/25 250.00 400.00
JG Johnson/Gruden/25 25.00 60.00
MF McNabb/Favre/25 175.00 300.00
MG McAllister/Green/50 25.00 50.00
MM P.Manning/Eli/50 250.00 400.00
MN Montana/Namath/25 250.00 400.00
MT D.McAll/Tomlinson/50 25.00 60.00
PF Pennington/Favre/50 100.00 200.00
PR Parcells/Reid/25 25.00 60.00
SP McNair/Manning/25 100.00 200.00
TB Theismann/Brunell/50 15.00 40.00
TG Tomlinson/Green/50 40.00 100.00
TS Tarkenton/Stabler/25 50.00 100.00
WW Winslow/Winslow/50 25.00 60.00

2004 Ultimate Collection Ultimate Signatures Quads

UNPRICED QUAD PRINT RUN 5

2005 Ultimate Collection

This 289-card set was released in January, 2006. The set was issued in the hobby in four-card packs with an $100 SRP which came four packs to a box. Cards numbered 1-100 feature veterans in alphabetical order by team while cards 101-269 feature rookies with cards numbered 200-249 all having autographs. All cards in this set are serial numbered, Cards numbered 1-100 and 270-289 were all issued to a stated print run of 550 serial numbered sets while cards numbered 101-200 and 250-269 were issued to a stated print run of 235 serial numbered sets. The signed rookies were issued to a stated print run of 225 serial numbered sets unless specifically notated in our checklist.

1-100/270-289 PRINT RUN 550 SER.#'d SETS
101-200/250-269 PRINT RUN 235 SETS
ROOKIE AUTO PRINT RUN 99-225
1 Larry Fitzgerald 1.50 4.00
2 Anquan Boldin 1.00 2.50
3 Kurt Warner 1.25 3.00
4 Michael Vick 1.25 3.00
5 Warrick Dunn 1.00 2.50
6 Alge Crumpler 1.25 3.00
7 Ray Lewis 1.50 4.00
8 Deion Sanders 1.25 3.00
9 Kyle Boller 1.00 2.50
10 Derrick Mason 1.00 2.50
11 J.P. Losman 1.00 2.50
12 Willis McGahee 1.00 2.50
13 Lee Evans 1.25 3.00
14 Eric Moulds 1.00 2.50
15 Jake Delhomme 1.00 2.50
16 Keary Colbert 1.00 2.50
17 DeShaun Foster 1.25 3.00
18 Brian Urlacher 1.50 4.00
19 Rex Grossman 1.00 2.50
20 Muhsin Muhammad 1.00 2.50
21 Carson Palmer 1.25 3.00
22 Rudi Johnson 1.00 2.50
23 Chad Johnson 1.00 2.50
24 Julius Jones 1.00 2.50
25 Keyshawn Johnson 1.25 3.00
26 Drew Bledsoe 1.25 3.00
27 Tatum Bell 1.00 2.50
28 Jake Plummer 1.00 2.50
29 Ashley Lelie 1.00 2.50
30 Roy Williams WR 1.00 2.50
31 Kevin Jones 1.00 2.50
32 Jeff Garcia 1.00 2.50
33 Brett Favre 3.00 8.00
34 Ahman Green 1.25 3.00
35 Javon Walker 1.00 2.50
36 David Carr 1.00 2.50
37 Andre Johnson 1.25 3.00
38 Domanick Davis 1.00 2.50
39 Peyton Manning 4.00 10.00
40 Reggie Wayne 1.25 3.00
41 Edgerrin James 1.25 3.00
42 Marvin Harrison 1.25 3.00
43 Byron Leftwich 1.00 2.50
44 Fred Taylor 1.00 2.50
45 Jimmy Smith 1.25 3.00
46 Priest Holmes 1.00 2.50
47 Larry Johnson 1.00 2.50
48 Trent Green 1.00 2.50
49 A.J. Feeley 1.00 2.50
50 Chris Chambers 1.00 2.50
51 Randy McMichael 1.00 2.50
52 Daunte Culpepper 1.25 3.00
53 Michael Bennett 1.00 2.50
54 Nate Burleson 1.00 2.50
55 Tom Brady 6.00 15.00
56 Corey Dillon 1.00 2.50
57 Deion Branch 1.00 2.50
58 David Givens 1.00 2.50
59 Aaron Brooks 1.00 2.50
60 Deuce McAllister 1.25 3.00
61 Joe Horn 1.00 2.50
62 Eli Manning 2.50 6.00
63 Jeremy Shockey 1.00 2.50
64 Tiki Barber 1.25 3.00
65 Chad Pennington 1.00 2.50
66 Curtis Martin 1.25 3.00
67 Laveranues Coles 1.00 2.50
68 Kerry Collins 1.00 2.50
69 LaMont Jordan 1.25 3.00
70 Randy Moss 1.25 3.00
71 Donovan McNabb 1.25 3.00
72 Terrell Owens 1.25 3.00
73 Brian Dawkins 1.50 4.00
74 Brian Westbrook 1.00 2.50
75 Ben Roethlisberger 2.50 6.00
76 Jerome Bettis 1.50 4.00
77 Hines Ward 1.25 3.00
78 Duce Staley 1.00 2.50
79 Drew Brees 1.50 4.00
80 LaDainian Tomlinson 1.50 4.00
81 Antonio Gates 1.50 4.00
82 Tim Rattay 1.00 2.50
83 Kevan Barlow 1.00 2.50
84 Eric Johnson 1.00 2.50
85 Shaun Alexander 1.00 2.50
86 Darrell Jackson 1.00 2.50
87 Matt Hasselbeck 1.00 2.50
88 Marc Bulger 1.00 2.50
89 Steven Jackson 1.00 2.50
90 Marshall Faulk 1.25 3.00
91 Torry Holt 1.25 3.00
92 Michael Pittman 1.00 2.50
93 Brian Griese 1.00 2.50
94 Michael Clayton 1.00 2.50
95 Steve McNair 1.25 3.00
96 Drew Bennett 1.25 3.00
97 Chris Brown 1.00 2.50
98 Clinton Portis 1.00 2.50
99 Patrick Ramsey 1.25 3.00
100 Santana Moss 1.25 3.00
101 James Kilian RC 2.50 6.00
102 Marlin Jackson RC 2.50 6.00
103 Corey Webster RC 3.00 8.00
104 Ryan Claridge RC 2.50 6.00
105 David Pollack RC 2.50 6.00
106 Deandra Cobb RC 2.50 6.00
107 Anttaj Hawthorne RC 2.50 6.00
108 Erasmus James RC 2.50 6.00
109 Dan Cody RC 2.50 6.00
110 Jerome Mathis RC 4.00 10.00
111 Barrett Ruud RC 3.00 8.00
112 Kevin Burnett RC 3.00 8.00
113 Jason White RC 4.00 10.00
114 Chase Lyman RC 2.50 6.00
115 Cedric Houston RC 4.00 10.00
116 Roydell Williams RC 3.00 8.00
117 Fred Gibson RC 2.50 6.00
118 Dustin Colquitt RC 3.00 8.00
119 Rasheed Marshall RC 3.00 8.00
120 Walter Reyes RC 2.50 6.00
121 Craig Bragg RC 2.50 6.00
122 Marcus Maxwell RC 2.50 6.00
123 LeRon McCoy RC 2.50 6.00
124 Harry Williams RC 3.00 8.00
125 Larry Brackins RC 2.50 6.00
126 J.R. Russell RC 2.50 6.00
127 Manuel White RC 3.00 8.00
128 Brandon Jones RC 3.00 8.00
129 Eric King RC 2.50 6.00
130 Travis Johnson RC 2.50 6.00
131 Mike Patterson RC 2.50 6.00
132 Marcus Spears RC 2.50 6.00
133 Darryl Blackstock RC 2.50 6.00
134 Michael Boley RC 4.00 10.00
135 Leroy Hill RC 4.00 10.00
136 Channing Crowder RC 3.00 8.00
137 Odell Thurman RC 4.00 10.00
138 Lance Mitchell RC 3.00 8.00
139 Jerome Collins RC 3.00 8.00
140 Stanford Routt RC 3.00 8.00
141 Justin Miller RC 2.50 6.00
142 Bryant McFadden RC 3.00 8.00
143 Eric Green RC 2.50 6.00
144 Fabian Washington RC 2.50 6.00
145 Antonio Perkins RC 3.00 8.00
146 Shaun Cody RC 3.00 8.00
147 Jonathan Babineaux RC 2.50 6.00
148 Ronald Bartell RC 3.00 8.00
149 Luis Castillo RC 3.00 8.00
150 Chris Carr RC 2.50 6.00
151 Justin Tuck RC 3.00 8.00
152 Brodney Pool RC 3.00 8.00
153 Matt Roth RC 2.50 6.00
154 DeMarcus Ware RC 8.00 20.00
155 Josh Bullocks RC 3.00 8.00
156 Vincent Fuller RC 3.00 8.00
157 Donte Nicholson RC 2.50 6.00
158 Rashied Davis RC 4.00 10.00
159 Nick Collins RC 4.00 10.00
160 Mike Nugent RC 3.00 8.00
161 Tyson Thompson RC 2.50 6.00
162 Darrent Williams RC 4.00 10.00
163 Kelvin Hayden RC 3.00 8.00
164 Oshiomogho Atogwe RC 3.00 8.00
165 Ryan Fitzpatrick RC 4.00 10.00
166 Stanley Wilson RC 3.00 8.00
167 Vonta Leach RC 3.00 8.00
168 Ellis Hobbs RC 4.00 10.00
169 Scott Starks RC 3.00 8.00
170 Lionel Gates RC 2.50 6.00
171 Alvin Pearman RC 2.50 6.00
172 Damien Nash RC 3.00 8.00
173 Noah Herron RC 2.50 6.00
174 Domonique Foxworth RC 3.00 8.00
175 Derrick Johnson CB RC 2.50 6.00
176 Lofa Tatupu RC 3.00 8.00
177 Daven Holly RC 2.50 6.00
178 Dante Ridgeway RC 2.50 6.00
179 Airese Currie RC 2.50 6.00
180 Adam Bergen RC 2.50 6.00
181 Kirk Morrison RC 4.00 10.00
182 Alfred Fincher RC 3.00 8.00
183 Jordan Beck RC 3.00 8.00
184 Sean Considine RC 2.50 6.00
185 Tab Perry RC 2.50 6.00
186 Travis Daniels RC 3.00 8.00
187 Paris Warren RC 3.00 8.00
188 Marviel Underwood RC 3.00 8.00
189 Jerome Carter RC 2.50 6.00
190 Kerry Rhodes RC 3.00 8.00
191 James Sanders RC 2.50 6.00
192 Stephen Spach RC 2.50 6.00
193 Bo Scaife RC 3.00 8.00
194 Andre Frazier RC 4.00 10.00
195 Alex Barron RC 2.50 6.00
196 Jammal Brown RC 4.00 10.00
197 Nehemiah Broughton RC 3.00 8.00
198 Elton Brown RC 2.50 6.00
199 David Baas RC 2.50 6.00
200 Joel Dreessen RC 3.00 8.00
201 Maurice Clarett AU/120 6.00 15.00
202 Craphonso Thorpe AU RC 5.00 12.00
203 Adam Jones AU RC 5.00 12.00
204 Mark Bradley AU RC 5.00 12.00
205 Vincent Jackson AU RC 8.00 20.00
206 Antrel Rolle AU RC 8.00 20.00
207 Heath Miller AU RC 10.00 25.00
208 Anthony Davis AU RC 5.00 12.00
209 Terrence Murphy AU RC 5.00 12.00
210 Chris Henry AU RC 6.00 15.00
211 Roscoe Parrish AU RC 5.00 12.00
212 Stefan LeFors AU RC 5.00 12.00
213 Derek Anderson AU RC 6.00 15.00
214 Darren Sproles AU RC 10.00 25.00
215 Adrian McPherson AU RC 5.00 12.00
216 Frank Gore AU RC 30.00 60.00
217 Marion Barber AU RC 5.00 12.00
218 Ryan Moats AU RC 5.00 12.00
219 Carlos Rogers AU RC 8.00 20.00
220 Vernand Morency AU RC 5.00 12.00
221 J.J. Arrington AU RC 6.00 15.00
222 Courtney Roby AU RC 5.00 12.00
223 Dan Orlovsky AU RC 5.00 12.00
224 Kyle Orton AU RC 15.00 40.00
225 David Greene AU RC 5.00 12.00
226 Roddy White AU/150 RC 10.00 25.00
227 Matt Jones AU/99 RC 6.00 15.00
228 Reggie Brown AU/150 RC 6.00 15.00
229 Mark Clayton AU/150 RC 6.00 15.00
230 Eric Shelton AU/150 RC 6.00 15.00
231 Ciatrick Fason AU/150 RC 6.00 15.00
232 Jason Campbell AU/150 RC 30.00 60.00
233 Charlie Frye AU/150 RC 6.00 15.00
234 Andrew Walter AU/150 RC 6.00 15.00
235 Troy Williamson AU/120 RC 6.00 15.00
236 Braylon Edwards AU/99 RC 20.00 50.00
237 Mike Williams AU/99 8.00 20.00
238 Cedric Benson AU/99 RC 6.00 15.00
239 Cadillac Williams AU/99 RC 6.00 15.00
240 Ronnie Brown AU/99 RC 8.00 20.00
241 Alex Smith QB AU/99 RC 40.00 100.00
242 Aaron Rodgers AU/99 RC 500.00 900.00
243 Matt Cassel AU RC 15.00 40.00
244 Brandon Jacobs AU RC 6.00 15.00
245 Alex Smith TE AU RC 5.00 12.00
246 Derrick Johnson AU RC 6.00 15.00
247 Chad Owens AU RC 5.00 12.00
248 Thomas Davis AU RC 5.00 12.00
249 Shawne Merriman AU RC 8.00 20.00
250 Gino Guidugli RC 2.50 6.00
251 Timmy Chang RC 2.50 6.00
252 Todd Mortensen RC 2.50 6.00
253 Bryan Randall RC 3.00 8.00
254 Brock Berlin RC 2.50 6.00
255 T.A. McLendon RC 2.50 6.00
256 Kay-Jay Harris RC 2.50 6.00
257 Bobby Purify RC 3.00 8.00
258 Steve Savoy RC 2.50 6.00
259 Keron Henry RC 2.50 6.00
260 Josh Davis RC 2.50 6.00
261 Chauncey Stovall RC 2.50 6.00
262 Efrem Hill RC 2.50 6.00
263 Sione Pouha RC 2.50 6.00
264 Jesse Lumsden RC 2.50 6.00
265 Vincent Burns RC 2.50 6.00
266 Brady Poppinga RC 4.00 10.00
267 Boomer Grigsby RC 4.00 10.00
268 Robert McCune RC 3.00 8.00
269 Fred Amey RC 2.50 6.00
270 T.J. Duckett 1.00 2.50
271 Jamal Lewis 1.25 3.00
272 Rod Gardner 1.00 2.50
273 Thomas Jones 1.00 2.50
274 Jason Witten 1.25 3.00
275 Roy Williams S 1.00 2.50
276 Mike Anderson 1.00 2.50
277 Joey Harrington 1.00 2.50
278 Charles Rogers 1.00 2.50
279 Donald Driver 1.25 3.00
280 Jabar Gaffney 1.00 2.50
281 Reggie Williams 1.00 2.50
282 Tony Gonzalez 1.25 3.00
283 Ricky Williams 1.25 3.00
284 Mewelde Moore 1.00 2.50
285 Plaxico Burress 1.00 2.50
286 Jerry Porter 1.00 2.50
287 Brandon Lloyd 1.00 2.50
288 Isaac Bruce 1.50 4.00
289 LaVar Arrington 1.00 2.50

2005 Ultimate Collection Gold Holofoil

*VETERANS: 1.2X TO 3X BASIC CARDS
*ROOKIES: .6X TO 1.5X BASIC CARDS
STATED PRINT RUN 40 SER.#'d SETS

2005 Ultimate Collection Game Jersey

STATED PRINT RUN 99 SER.#'d SETS
*GOLD: .5X TO 1.2X BASIC JERSEYS
GOLD PRINT RUN 50 SER.#'d SETS
*PLATINUM: .6X TO 1.5X BASIC JERSEYS
PLATINUM PRINT RUN 25 SER.#'d SETS
*PATCHES: .6X TO 1.5X BASIC JERSEYS
PATCH PRINT RUN 50 SER.#'d SETS
*GOLD PATCHES: .8X TO 2X BASIC JERSEYS
GOLD PATCH PRINT RUN 35 SER.#'d SETS
*PLAT.PATCHES: 1.2X TO 3X BASIC JERSEYS
PLATINUM PATCH PRINT RUN 20 SER.#'d SETS
UNPRICED PATCH AU PRINT RUN 15 SETS
GJAB Aaron Brooks 3.00 8.00
GJAG Ahman Green 4.00 10.00
GJAJ Andre Johnson 4.00 10.00
GJBE Tatum Bell 4.00 10.00
GJBF Brett Favre 12.50 30.00
GJBK Bernie Kosar 5.00 12.00
GJBL Byron Leftwich 4.00 10.00
GJBR Ben Roethlisberger 12.50 30.00
GJBS Barry Sanders 15.00 30.00
GJBU Brian Urlacher 4.00 10.00
GJBW Brian Westbrook 3.00 8.00
GJCD Corey Dillon 3.00 8.00
GJCH Chad Pennington 4.00 10.00
GJCL Clinton Portis 4.00 10.00
GJCM Curtis Martin 4.00 10.00
GJCP Carson Palmer 4.00 10.00
GJCU Daunte Culpepper 4.00 10.00
GJDA David Carr 3.00 8.00
GJDB Drew Bledsoe 4.00 10.00
GJDC Donovan McNabb 5.00 12.00
GJDD Domanick Davis 3.00 8.00
GJDE Deuce McAllister 3.00 8.00
GJDE Derrick Mason 3.00 8.00
GJDM Dan Marino 15.00 40.00
GJDR Drew Brees 3.00 8.00
GJDS Deion Sanders 6.00 15.00
GJEJ Edgerrin James 4.00 10.00
GJEM Eli Manning 10.00 25.00
GJFT Fred Taylor 3.00 8.00
GJJB Jerome Bettis 7.50 20.00
GJJE John Elway 12.50 30.00
GJJH Joey Harrington 4.00 10.00
GJJJ Julius Jones 5.00 12.00
GJJL Jamal Lewis 4.00 10.00
GJJM Joe Montana 20.00 40.00
GJJP J.P. Losman 3.00 8.00
GJJR Jerry Rice 7.50 20.00
GJJS Jeremy Shockey 4.00 10.00
GJJW Javon Walker 4.00 10.00
GJKJ Kevin Jones 4.00 10.00
GJKS Ken Stabler 6.00 15.00
GJLF Larry Fitzgerald 4.00 10.00
GJLT LaDainian Tomlinson 4.00 10.00
GJMA Marcus Allen 6.00 15.00
GJMB Marc Bulger 3.00 8.00
GJMF Marshall Faulk 4.00 10.00
GJMH Marvin Harrison 4.00 10.00
GJMS Mike Singletary 5.00 12.00
GJMV Michael Vick 6.00 15.00
GJON Ozzie Newsome 5.00 12.00
GJPH Priest Holmes 4.00 10.00
GJPM Peyton Manning 7.50 20.00
GJPR Philip Rivers 4.00 10.00
GJPS Phil Simms 6.00 15.00
GJRE Reggie Wayne 3.00 8.00
GJRI Ricky Williams 4.00 10.00
GJRL Ray Lewis 4.00 10.00
GJRM Randy Moss 4.00 10.00
GJRS Roger Staubach 7.50 20.00
GJRW Roy Williams WR 4.00 10.00
GJSA Shaun Alexander 5.00 12.00
GJSL Steve Largent 6.00 15.00
GJSM Steve McNair 4.00 10.00
GJSY Steve Young 7.50 20.00
GJTA Troy Aikman 7.50 20.00
GJTB Tom Brady 10.00 25.00
GJTD Tony Dorsett 5.00 12.00
GJTG Tony Gonzalez 3.00 8.00
GJTH Torry Holt 4.00 10.00
GJTO Terrell Owens 4.00 10.00
GJWD Warrick Dunn 3.00 8.00
GJWM Willis McGahee 3.00 8.00
GJWP Walter Payton 15.00 40.00

2005 Ultimate Collection Game Jersey Autographs

STATED PRINT RUN 25 SER.#'d SETS
*PATCH AU/15: .5X TO1.2X JSY AU/25
AGJAG Ahman Green 15.00 40.00
AGJAR Aaron Rodgers 400.00 700.00
AGJAS Alex Smith QB 75.00 150.00
AGJBE Braylon Edwards 20.00 50.00
AGJBF Brett Favre 100.00 200.00
AGJBJ Bo Jackson 50.00 100.00
AGJBL Byron Leftwich 15.00 40.00
AGJBR Ben Roethlisberger 75.00 150.00
AGJBS Barry Sanders 100.00 200.00
AGJCB Cedric Benson 25.00 60.00
AGJCP Carson Palmer 25.00 60.00
AGJCW Cadillac Williams 12.00 30.00
AGJDE Deuce McAllister 12.50 30.00
AGJDM Dan Marino 150.00 300.00
AGJDS Deion Sanders 40.00 80.00
AGJEJ Edgerrin James 20.00 50.00
AGJEM Eli Manning 90.00 150.00
AGJJE John Elway 100.00 200.00
AGJJL J.P. Losman 12.50 30.00
AGJJM Joe Montana 125.00 250.00
AGJLT LaDainian Tomlinson 30.00 80.00
AGJMB Marc Bulger 15.00 40.00
AGJMC Michael Clayton 12.50 30.00
AGJMS Mike Singletary 25.00 60.00
AGJMV Michael Vick 40.00 80.00
AGJMW Mike Williams 15.00 40.00
AGJPM Peyton Manning 100.00 200.00
AGJRB Ronnie Brown 20.00 50.00
AGJRO Roy Williams WR 12.50 30.00
AGJRP Roscoe Parrish 12.50 30.00
AGJRS Roger Staubach 50.00 100.00
AGJRW Reggie Wayne 20.00 50.00
AGJSJ Steven Jackson 20.00 50.00
AGJTA Troy Aikman 50.00 100.00
AGJTB Tiki Barber 25.00 60.00
AGJTD Tony Dorsett 25.00 60.00
AGJTG Trent Green 12.50 30.00
AGJWH Roddy White 12.00 30.00

2005 Ultimate Collection Game Jersey Duals

ATED PRINT RUN 50 SER.#'d SETS
*PATCH/25: .5X TO 1.2X BASIC DUAL JSY
*GOLD/15: .6X TO 1.5X BASIC DUAL JSY
DJBB C.Benson/R.Brown 6.00 15.00
DJBJ M.Bulger/S.Jackson 5.00 12.00
DJBS D.Bledsoe/R.Staubach 10.00 25.00
DJCB M.Clayton/R.Brown 5.00 12.00
DJCW J.Campbell/C.Williams 5.00 12.00
DJDM B.Dawkins/D.McNabb 8.00 20.00
DJEA Manning/Roethlisberger 20.00 50.00
DJEM J.Elway/J.Montana 25.00 60.00
DJEW B.Edwards/M.Williams 6.00 15.00
DJFG B.Favre/A.Green 15.00 40.00
DJJA J.Jones/T.Aikman 10.00 25.00
DJJB V.Jackson/M.Bradley 8.00 20.00
DJJD J.Jones/T.Dorsett 8.00 20.00
DJJM E.James/P.Manning 20.00 50.00
DJJP J.Elway/P.Manning 20.00 50.00
DJJR S.Jackson/R.Brown 6.00 15.00
DJLP B.Leftwich/C.Palmer 6.00 15.00
DJLR J.Losman/B.Roethlisberger 12.00 30.00
DJMA E.Manning/P.Manning 20.00 50.00
DJMB R.Moats/R.Brown 5.00 12.00
DJMG D.McAllister/A.Green 6.00 15.00
DJMM D.Marino/J.Montana 40.00 80.00
DJMR E.Manning/A.Rodgers 25.00 60.00
DJMV D.McNabb/M.Vick 6.00 15.00
DJMW M.Clayton/R.Williams WR 5.00 12.00
DJOC K.Orton/J.Campbell 5.00 12.00
DJPL R.Parrish/J.Losman 5.00 12.00
DJPM C.Palmer/E.Manning 12.00 30.00
DJPW R.Parrish/R.White 8.00 20.00
DJRA A.Rodgers/J.Arrington 20.00 50.00
DJRS A.Rodgers/A.Smith 20.00 50.00
DJSF E.Shelton/C.Fason 5.00 12.00
DJSM A.Smith/J.Montana 25.00 60.00
DJTM L.Tomlinson/D.McAllister 8.00 20.00
DJTR T.Williamson/R.White 8.00 20.00
DJWB C.Williams/B.Edwards 6.00 15.00
DJWE R.Williams/B.Edwards 5.00 12.00
DJWF A.Walter/C.Frye 5.00 12.00
DJWJ C.Williams/B.Jackson 10.00 25.00
DJWP R.Wayne/R.Parrish 6.00 15.00
DJWW M.Williams/T.Williamson 6.00 15.00

2005 Ultimate Collection Rookie Jerseys

STATED PRINT RUN 99 SER.#'d SETS
*GOLD/50: .5X TO 1.2X BASIC JSY/99
GOLD PRINT RUN 50 SER.#'d SETS
*PLATINUM/25: .6X TO 1.5X BASIC JSY/99
PLATINUM PRINT RUN 25 SER.#'d SETS
*PATCH/50: .6X TO 1.5X BASIC JSY/99
PATCH PRINT RUN 50 SER.#'d SETS
*GOLD PATCH/20: 1.2X TO 3X BASIC JSY/99
GOLD PATCH PRINT RUN 20 SER.#'d SETS
RJAR Aaron Rodgers 40.00 100.00
RJAS Alex Smith QB 10.00 25.00
RJAW Andrew Walter 2.50 6.00
RJBE Braylon Edwards 2.50 6.00
RJCB Cedric Benson 2.50 6.00
RJCF Charlie Frye 2.50 6.00
RJCI Ciatrick Fason 2.50 6.00
RJCW Cadillac Williams 2.50 6.00
RJES Eric Shelton 2.50 6.00
RJHM Heath Miller 5.00 12.00
RJJC Jason Campbell 2.50 6.00
RJJJ J.J. Arrington 3.00 8.00
RJMB Mark Bradley 2.50 6.00
RJMC Mark Clayton 2.50 6.00
RJMJ Matt Jones 2.50 6.00
RJMO Maurice Clarett 2.50 6.00
RJMW Mike Williams 3.00 8.00
RJRB Reggie Brown 2.50 6.00
RJRO Ronnie Brown 3.00 8.00
RJRP Roscoe Parrish 2.50 6.00
RJRW Roddy White 4.00 10.00
RJSL Stefan LeFors 2.50 6.00
RJTW Troy Williamson 2.50 6.00

RJVJ Vincent Jackson 4.00 10.00
RJVM Vernand Morency 2.50 6.00

2005 Ultimate Collection Ultimate Signatures

ERALL AUTO STATED ODDS 1:4
UNPRICED GOLD PRINT RUN 10 SER.#'d SETS
UNPRICED HOLOFOIL/5 ISSUED VIA MAIL
UNPRICED QUAD AU PRINT RUN 5 SETS
UNPRICED TRIPLE AU PRINT RUN 15 SETS
UNPRICED EIGHT AU PRINT RUN 1 SET
USAB Anquan Boldin/99 7.50 20.00
USAD Art Donovan/99 12.50 25.00
USAJ A.J. Feeley/99 6.00 15.00
USAM Adrian McPherson/99 6.00 15.00
USAN Antrel Rolle/99 7.50 20.00
USAR Aaron Rodgers/75 250.00 400.00
USAS Alex Smith QB/25 40.00 100.00
USAW Andrew Walter/99 12.50 30.00
USBE Braylon Edwards/75 12.00 30.00
USBJ Bo Jackson/75 40.00 80.00
USBK Bernie Kosar/99 12.50 30.00
USBS Barry Sanders/25 100.00 200.00
USCB Cedric Benson/75 12.50 30.00
USCF Charlie Frye/99 12.50 30.00
USCI Ciatrick Fason/99 6.00 15.00
USCL Maurice Clarett/75 6.00 15.00
USCP Carson Palmer/25 15.00 40.00
USCR Courtney Roby/99 6.00 15.00
USCW Cadillac Williams/75 20.00 50.00
USDD Domanick Davis/99 6.00 15.00
USDF Dan Fouts/25 25.00 60.00
USDJ Deacon Jones/99 12.50 30.00
USDM Dan Marino/25 125.00 250.00
USDO Don Maynard/99 6.00 15.00
USDS Deion Sanders/25 40.00 80.00
USEC Earl Campbell/75 20.00 40.00
USEJ Edgerrin James/25 20.00 50.00
USEM Eli Manning/25 90.00 150.00
USES Eric Shelton/99 6.00 15.00
USFH Franco Harris/75 40.00 80.00
USFR Fran Tarkenton/75 20.00 40.00
USGB George Blanda/75 25.00 50.00
USGS Gale Sayers/25 40.00 80.00
USJA J.J. Arrington/99 12.50 30.00
USJC Jason Campbell/99 12.00 30.00
USJH Joe Horn/99 6.00 15.00
USJJ Julius Jones/25 20.00 50.00
USJK Jim Kelly/25 40.00 80.00
USJL James Lofton/75 7.50 20.00
USJO Adam Jones/99 7.50 20.00
USJP Jim Plunkett/75 7.50 20.00
USJP J.P. Losman/99 7.50 20.00
USJT Joe Theismann/99 12.50 30.00
USKO Kyle Orton/99 15.00 40.00
USLA Larry Johnson/99 12.00 30.00
USLE Lee Evans/99 6.00 15.00
USLJ LaMont Jordan/99 6.00 15.00
USMA Marcus Allen/75 12.50 30.00
USMB Marc Bulger/75 6.00 15.00
USMC Mark Clayton/99 12.50 30.00
USMI Michael Clayton/99 7.50 20.00
USMS Mike Singletary/75 12.50 30.00
USMV Michael Vick/25 40.00 80.00
USMW Mike Williams/99 12.50 30.00
USNB Nate Burleson/99 6.00 15.00
USPM Peyton Manning/75 60.00 120.00
USRB Reggie Brown/99 12.50 30.00
USRD Andre Reed/99 7.50 20.00
USRE Reggie Wayne/99 15.00 30.00
USRO Ronnie Brown/99 30.00 80.00
USRP Roscoe Parrish/99 7.50 20.00
USRS Roger Staubach/25 60.00 100.00
USSJ Steven Jackson/75 12.50 30.00
USSL Steve Largent/75 12.50 30.00
USTA Troy Aikman/25 50.00 100.00
USTB Tiki Barber/99 10.00 25.00
USTD Tony Dorsett/25 20.00 50.00
USTG Trent Green/75 7.50 20.00
USTW Troy Williamson/99 12.50 30.00
USWH Roddy White/99 15.00 30.00

2005 Ultimate Collection Ultimate Signatures Duals

AL PRINT RUN 35 SER.#'d SETS
DSAB T.Aikman/D.Bledsoe 40.00 80.00
DSBJ M.Bulger/S.Jackson 25.00 50.00
DSBP G.Blanda/J.Plunkett 40.00 80.00
DSBS C.Benson/G.Sayers 40.00 80.00
DSBW C.Benson/R.Williams 30.00 60.00
DSCT J.Campbell/J.Theismann 30.00 60.00
DSEW B.Edwards/M.Williams 20.00 50.00
DSFH B.Favre/P.Hornung 150.00 250.00
DSGM A.Green/D.McAllister 20.00 40.00
DSJC S.Jackson/E.Campbell 25.00 50.00
DSJS J.Jones/B.Sanders 60.00 120.00
DSKL J.Kelly/J.Losman 30.00 60.00
DSLR S.Largent/A.Reed 30.00 60.00
DSMA P.Manning/T.Aikman 100.00 200.00
DSPC C.Palmer/C.Collinsworth 30.00 60.00
DSPJ J.Plunkett/B.Jackson 60.00 120.00
DSRM Roethlisberger/Marino 150.00 300.00
DSRS A.Rodgers/A.Smith 175.00 300.00
DSWB C.Williams/R.Brown 60.00 120.00
DSWC T.Williamson/M.Clayton 20.00 40.00

2006 Ultimate Collection

is 360-card set was released in November, 2006. The set was issued in the hobby in four-card packs, with an $100 SRP, which came four packs to a box. Cards numbered 1-200 feature veterans in alphabetical team order while cards 201-360 feature 2006 rookies. Within the rookie grouping: Cards numbered 201-260 were signed by the player to different serial numbered print runs, which information we have notated in our checklist. A few players did not return their signatures in time for pack out and the exchange deadline for those cards was November 15, 2009.
1-200 VET PRINT RUN 525
UNPRICED PRINT PLATE AUs #'d TO 1
1 Kurt Warner 1.50 4.00
2 Edgerrin James 1.50 4.00
3 Larry Fitzgerald 1.50 4.00
4 Anquan Boldin 1.25 3.00
5 Antrel Rolle 1.25 3.00
6 Karlos Dansby 1.25 3.00
7 Michael Vick 1.50 4.00
8 Warrick Dunn 1.25 3.00
9 DeAngelo Hall 1.25 3.00
10 Alge Crumpler 1.50 4.00
11 Roddy White 1.25 3.00
12 Michael Jenkins 1.25 3.00
13 Steve McNair 1.50 4.00
14 Jamal Lewis 1.50 4.00
15 Derrick Mason 1.25 3.00
16 Todd Heap 1.25 3.00
17 Mark Clayton 1.25 3.00
18 Ray Lewis 2.00 5.00
19 J.P. Losman 1.50 4.00
20 Willis McGahee 1.25 3.00
21 Lee Evans 1.50 4.00
22 Roscoe Parrish 1.25 3.00
23 Takeo Spikes 1.25 3.00
24 Nate Clements 1.25 3.00
25 Jake Delhomme 1.25 3.00
26 DeShaun Foster 1.50 4.00
27 Steve Smith 2.00 5.00
28 Keary Colbert 1.25 3.00
29 Julius Peppers 1.50 4.00
30 Chris Gamble 1.25 3.00
31 Rex Grossman 1.25 3.00
32 Thomas Jones 1.25 3.00
33 Cedric Benson 1.25 3.00
34 Muhsin Muhammad 1.25 3.00
35 Brian Urlacher 2.00 5.00
36 Nathan Vasher 1.25 3.00
37 Carson Palmer 1.50 4.00
38 Rudi Johnson 1.25 3.00
39 Chad Johnson 1.25 3.00
40 T.J. Houshmandzadeh 1.25 3.00
41 Odell Thurman 1.25 3.00
42 Deltha O'Neal 1.25 3.00
43 Charlie Frye 1.50 4.00
44 Reuben Droughns 1.50 4.00
45 Braylon Edwards 1.25 3.00
46 Joe Jurevicius 1.25 3.00
47 Kellen Winslow 1.25 3.00
48 Willie McGinest 1.25 3.00
49 Drew Bledsoe 1.50 4.00
50 Julius Jones 1.25 3.00
51 Terrell Owens 1.50 4.00
52 Terry Glenn 1.50 4.00
53 Jason Witten 1.50 4.00
54 DeMarcus Ware 1.50 4.00
55 Roy Williams S 1.25 3.00
56 Jake Plummer 1.25 3.00
57 Tatum Bell 1.25 3.00
58 Rod Smith 1.50 4.00
59 Javon Walker 1.50 4.00
60 Stephen Alexander 1.25 3.00
61 Champ Bailey 1.50 4.00
62 John Lynch 1.25 3.00
63 Jon Kitna 1.25 3.00
64 Kevin Jones 1.25 3.00
65 Roy Williams WR 1.25 3.00
66 Mike Williams 1.25 3.00
67 Marcus Pollard 1.25 3.00
68 Dre Bly 1.25 3.00
69 Brett Favre 4.00 10.00
70 Ahman Green 1.50 4.00
71 Donald Driver 1.50 4.00
72 Robert Ferguson 1.25 3.00
73 Charles Woodson 2.00 5.00
74 Kabeer Gbaja-Biamila 1.25 3.00
75 David Carr 1.25 3.00
76 Domanick Davis 1.25 3.00
77 Andre Johnson 1.50 4.00
78 Eric Moulds 1.25 3.00
79 Jeb Putzier 1.25 3.00
80 Dunta Robinson 1.25 3.00
81 Peyton Manning 5.00 12.00
82 Dominic Rhodes 1.25 3.00
83 Reggie Wayne 1.50 4.00
84 Marvin Harrison 1.50 4.00
85 Dallas Clark 1.25 3.00
86 Dwight Freeney 1.25 3.00
87 Bob Sanders 1.50 4.00
88 Byron Leftwich 1.25 3.00
89 Fred Taylor 1.25 3.00
90 Matt Jones 1.25 3.00
91 Ernest Wilford 1.25 3.00
92 Greg Jones 1.25 3.00
93 Mike Peterson 1.25 3.00
94 Trent Green 1.25 3.00
95 Larry Johnson 1.25 3.00
96 Samie Parker 1.25 3.00
97 Eddie Kennison 1.25 3.00
98 Tony Gonzalez 1.50 4.00
99 Patrick Surtain 1.25 3.00
100 Daunte Culpepper 1.50 4.00
101 Ronnie Brown 1.50 4.00
102 Chris Chambers 1.25 3.00
103 Marty Booker 1.25 3.00
104 Randy McMichael 1.25 3.00
105 Jason Taylor 1.50 4.00
106 Zach Thomas 1.50 4.00
107 Brad Johnson 1.50 4.00
108 Chester Taylor 1.50 4.00
109 Travis Taylor 1.25 3.00
110 Troy Williamson 1.25 3.00
111 Darren Sharper 1.25 3.00
112 Antoine Winfield 1.25 3.00
113 Tom Brady 6.00 15.00
114 Corey Dillon 1.25 3.00
115 Deion Branch 1.25 3.00
116 Ben Watson 1.25 3.00
117 Tedy Bruschi 1.50 4.00
118 Richard Seymour 1.25 3.00
119 Rodney Harrison 1.25 3.00
120 Drew Brees 2.00 5.00
121 Deuce McAllister 1.50 4.00
122 Joe Horn 1.25 3.00
123 Donte Stallworth 1.25 3.00
124 Will Smith 1.25 3.00
125 Fred Thomas 1.25 3.00
126 Eli Manning 1.50 4.00
127 Tiki Barber 1.50 4.00
128 Plaxico Burress 1.25 3.00
129 Jeremy Shockey 1.25 3.00
130 Osi Umenyiora 1.25 3.00
131 Michael Strahan 1.50 4.00
132 LaVar Arrington 1.25 3.00
133 Chad Pennington 1.25 3.00
134 Curtis Martin 1.50 4.00
135 Laveranues Coles 1.25 3.00
136 Justin McCareins 1.25 3.00
137 Jonathan Vilma 1.25 3.00
138 Shaun Ellis 1.25 3.00
139 Aaron Brooks 1.25 3.00
140 LaMont Jordan 1.50 4.00
141 Randy Moss 1.50 4.00
142 Doug Gabriel 1.25 3.00
143 Jerry Porter 1.25 3.00
144 Derrick Burgess 1.25 3.00
145 Donovan McNabb 1.50 4.00
146 Brian Westbrook 1.25 3.00
147 Reggie Brown 1.25 3.00
148 L.J. Smith 1.25 3.00
149 Jevon Kearse 1.25 3.00
150 Brian Dawkins 2.00 5.00
151 Ben Roethlisberger 2.50 6.00
152 Willie Parker 1.50 4.00
153 Hines Ward 1.50 4.00
154 Cedrick Wilson 1.25 3.00
155 Heath Miller 1.25 3.00
156 Joey Porter 1.25 3.00
157 Troy Polamalu 2.00 5.00
158 Philip Rivers 2.00 5.00
159 LaDainian Tomlinson 2.00 5.00
160 Keenan McCardell 1.50 4.00
161 Eric Parker 1.25 3.00
162 Antonio Gates 2.00 5.00
163 Shawne Merriman 1.50 4.00
164 Donnie Edwards 1.25 3.00
165 Alex Smith QB 1.50 4.00
166 Frank Gore 1.50 4.00
167 Antonio Bryant 1.25 3.00
168 Eric Johnson 1.25 3.00
169 Bryant Young 1.25 3.00
170 Shawntae Spencer 1.25 3.00
171 Matt Hasselbeck 1.25 3.00
172 Shaun Alexander 1.25 3.00
173 Darrell Jackson 1.50 4.00
174 Nate Burleson 1.25 3.00
175 Lofa Tatupu 1.25 3.00
176 Julian Peterson 1.25 3.00
177 Marc Bulger 1.25 3.00
178 Steven Jackson 1.25 3.00
179 Torry Holt 1.50 4.00
180 Kevin Curtis 1.50 4.00
181 Isaac Bruce 2.00 5.00
182 Leonard Little 1.25 3.00
183 Chris Simms 1.25 3.00
184 Cadillac Williams 1.50 4.00
185 Joey Galloway 1.50 4.00
186 Michael Clayton 1.25 3.00
187 Derrick Brooks 1.25 3.00
188 Ronde Barber 1.25 3.00
189 Billy Volek 1.25 3.00
190 Chris Brown 1.25 3.00
191 Drew Bennett 1.50 4.00
192 Travis Henry 1.25 3.00
193 Ben Troupe 1.25 3.00
194 Kyle Vanden Bosch 1.25 3.00
195 Sean Taylor 2.00 5.00
196 Mark Brunell 1.50 4.00
197 Clinton Portis 1.25 3.00
198 Santana Moss 1.50 4.00
199 Antwaan Randle El 1.25 3.00
200 Jason Campbell 1.25 3.00
201 Matt Leinart AU/99 RC 10.00 25.00
202 DeA.Williams AU/99 RC 25.00 50.00
203 Jay Cutler AU/99 RC 12.00 30.00
204 Joseph Addai AU/99 RC 10.00 25.00
205 L.Maroney AU/150 RC 6.00 15.00
206 Reggie Bush AU/99 RC 20.00 50.00
207 Santonio Holmes AU/99 RC 12.00 30.00
208 Vernon Davis AU/99 RC 12.00 30.00
209 Vince Young AU/99 RC 15.00 40.00
210 LenDale White AU/150 RC 6.00 15.00
211 Jerious Norwood AU/150 RC 6.00 15.00
212 Travis Wilson AU/150 RC 6.00 15.00
213 Brian Calhoun AU/150 RC 6.00 15.00
214 A.J. Hawk AU/99 RC 12.00 30.00
215 Greg Jennings AU/150 RC 10.00 25.00
216 Mario Williams AU/99 RC 15.00 40.00
217 Maurice Drew AU/150 RC 25.00 60.00
218 Marcedes Lewis AU/150 RC 6.00 15.00
219 Skyler Green AU/275 RC 5.00 12.00
220 Derek Hagan AU/150 RC 8.00 20.00
221 Tarvaris Jackson AU/150 RC 6.00 15.00
222 Chad Jackson AU/150 RC 6.00 15.00
223 Sinorice Moss AU/99 RC 10.00 25.00
224 Kellen Clemens AU/150 RC 6.00 15.00
225 Leon Washington AU/150 RC 6.00 15.00
226 Michael Huff AU/150 RC 8.00 20.00
227 Omar Jacobs AU/150 RC 6.00 15.00
228 Charlie Whitehurst AU/150 RC 6.00 15.00
229 Michael Robinson AU/150 RC 6.00 15.00
230 Brandon Williams AU/150 RC 6.00 15.00
231 Leonard Pope AU/275 RC 8.00 20.00
232 Greg Lee AU/275 RC 5.00 12.00
233 D.J. Shockley AU/275 RC 6.00 15.00
234 Dem.Williams AU/275 RC 5.00 12.00
235 Reggie McNeal AU/275 RC 5.00 12.00
236 Jerome Harrison AU/275 RC 5.00 12.00
237 Anthony Fasano AU/275 RC 5.00 12.00
238 B.Marshall AU/275 RC 10.00 25.00
239 Ernie Sims AU/275 RC 5.00 12.00
240 Cory Rodgers AU/275 RC 5.00 12.00
241 Will Blackmon AU/275 RC 5.00 12.00
242 DeMeco Ryans AU/275 RC 6.00 15.00
243 Owen Daniels AU/275 RC 8.00 20.00
244 Josh Betts AU/275 RC 6.00 15.00
245 Chad Greenway AU/275 RC 8.00 20.00
246 Mike Hass AU/275 RC 5.00 12.00
247 Mathias Kiwanuka AU/275 RC 8.00 20.00
248 D.Ferguson AU/275 RC 5.00 12.00
249 Brad Smith AU/275 RC 6.00 15.00
250 Thomas Howard AU/275 RC 5.00 12.00
251 Jason Avant AU/275 RC 5.00 12.00
252 Brodrick Bunkley AU/275 RC 6.00 15.00
253 Willie Reid AU/275 RC 6.00 15.00
254 Kelly Jennings AU/275 RC 6.00 15.00
255 Jimmy Williams AU/275 RC 5.00 12.00
256 Joe Klopfenstein AU/275 RC 5.00 12.00
257 Tye Hill AU/275 RC 5.00 12.00
258 Dominique Byrd AU/275 RC 5.00 12.00
259 Maurice Stovall AU/150 RC 6.00 15.00
260 Bruce Gradkowski AU/275 RC 6.00 15.00
261 Abdul Hodge RC 2.50 6.00
262 Adam Jennings RC 3.00 8.00
263 Ahmad Brooks RC 4.00 10.00
264 Andrew Whitworth RC 2.50 6.00
265 Anthony Schlegel RC 3.00 8.00
266 Anthony Smith RC 4.00 10.00
267 Antonio Cromartie RC 3.00 8.00
268 Ashton Youboty RC 2.50 6.00
269 Ben Obomanu RC 3.00 8.00
270 Bennie Brazell RC 3.00 8.00
271 Bernard Pollard RC 3.00 8.00
272 Bobby Carpenter RC 2.50 6.00
273 Brett Basanez RC 4.00 10.00
274 Brett Elliott RC 4.00 10.00
275 Brodie Croyle RC 2.50 6.00
276 Calvin Lowry RC 4.00 10.00
277 Cedric Griffin RC 3.00 8.00
278 Cedric Humes RC 2.50 6.00
279 Charles Davis RC 3.00 8.00
280 Charles Gordon RC 2.50 6.00
281 Chris Gocong RC 3.00 8.00
282 Claude Wroten RC 2.50 6.00
283 Clint Ingram RC 4.00 10.00
284 Cody Hodges RC 3.00 8.00
285 Corey Bramlet RC 3.00 8.00
286 Cory Ross RC 4.00 10.00
287 Damien Rhodes RC 3.00 8.00
288 Danieal Manning RC 4.00 10.00
289 Daniel Bullocks RC 2.50 6.00
290 Darnell Bing RC 3.00 8.00
291 Darrell Hackney RC 3.00 8.00
292 Darryl Tapp RC 3.00 8.00
293 Daryn Colledge RC 4.00 10.00
294 David Anderson RC 3.00 8.00
295 David Kirtman RC 3.00 8.00
296 David Pittman RC 3.00 8.00
297 David Thomas RC 2.50 6.00
298 Davin Joseph RC 3.00 8.00
299 Andre Hall RC 3.00 8.00
300 Delanie Walker RC 5.00 12.00
301 Demetrius Summers RC 2.50 6.00
302 Devin Aromashodu RC 2.50 6.00
303 Devin Hester RC 5.00 12.00
304 Donte Whitner RC 3.00 8.00
305 D'Qwell Jackson RC 2.50 6.00
306 Dusty Dvoracek RC 4.00 10.00
307 Elvis Dumervil RC 4.00 10.00
308 Eric Smith RC 3.00 8.00
309 Freddie Keiaho RC 3.00 8.00
310 Frostee Rucker RC 3.00 8.00
311 Garrett Mills RC 3.00 8.00
312 Gerris Wilkinson RC 2.50 6.00
313 Haloti Ngata RC 3.00 8.00
314 Ingle Martin RC 3.00 8.00
315 J.D. Runnels RC 3.00 8.00
316 James Anderson RC 2.50 6.00
317 Jason Allen RC 3.00 8.00
318 Jason Pociask RC 3.00 8.00
319 Hank Baskett RC 2.50 6.00
320 Jeff King RC 3.00 8.00
321 Jeff Webb RC 3.00 8.00
322 Jeremy Bloom RC 2.50 6.00
323 Jeremy Trueblood RC 3.00 8.00
324 Joel Klatt RC 3.00 8.00
325 John McCargo RC 2.50 6.00
326 Johnathan Joseph RC 3.00 8.00
327 Jon Alston RC 2.50 6.00
328 Jonathan Orr RC 3.00 8.00
329 Kamerion Wimbley RC 3.00 8.00
330 Kent Smith RC 4.00 10.00
331 Kevin McMahan RC 3.00 8.00
332 Ko Simpson RC 3.00 8.00
333 Lawrence Vickers RC 3.00 8.00
334 Manny Lawson RC 3.00 8.00
335 Marcus Demps RC 2.00 5.00
336 Marcus McNeill RC 2.50 6.00
337 Marcus Vick RC 2.50 6.00
338 Marques Colston RC 4.00 10.00
339 Marques Hagans RC 2.50 6.00
340 Matt Shelton RC 4.00 10.00
341 Nick Mangold RC 3.00 8.00
342 P.J. Daniels RC 2.50 6.00
343 P.J. Pope RC 4.00 10.00
344 Miles Austin RC 3.00 8.00
345 Quinn Sypniewski RC 3.00 8.00
346 Richard Marshall RC 2.50 6.00
347 Richie Ross RC 3.00 8.00
348 Rocky McIntosh RC 2.50 6.00
349 Roman Harper RC 3.00 8.00
350 Ryan Cook RC 3.00 8.00
351 Mike Bell RC 2.50 6.00
352 Deuce Lutui RC 3.00 8.00
353 Tamba Hali RC 4.00 10.00
354 Tim Massaquoi RC 3.00 8.00
355 Todd Watkins RC 2.50 6.00
356 Tony Scheffler RC 4.00 10.00
357 Drew Olson RC 2.50 6.00
358 Wali Lundy RC 2.50 6.00
359 Wendell Mathis RC 3.00 8.00
360 Winston Justice RC 3.00 8.00

2006 Ultimate Collection Gold

*VETS 1-200: 1X TO 2.5X BASIC CARDS
*ROOKIES 261-360: .6X TO 1.5X BASIC CARDS
STATED PRINT RUN 50 SER.#'d SETS
UNPRICED GOLD AU PRINT RUN 10

2006 Ultimate Collection Achievements Signatures

STATED PRINT RUN 25 SER.#'d SETS
BF Brett Favre 125.00 200.00
BR Ben Roethlisberger 60.00 120.00
CW Cadillac Williams 25.00 50.00
LJ Larry Johnson 25.00 60.00
LT LaDainian Tomlinson 75.00 135.00
PM Peyton Manning 90.00 150.00
SS Steve Smith 15.00 40.00
SY Steve Young 50.00 80.00
TB Tiki Barber 25.00 50.00

2006 Ultimate Collection Game Jersey Autographs

STATED PRINT RUN 30-35
UNPRICED AU COMBO PRINT RUN 1
UNPRICED LOGO PATCH PRINT RUN 1
UNPRICED AU PATCH PRINT RUN 15
ULTAC Alge Crumpler 12.00 30.00
ULTAD Tarvaris Jackson 10.00 25.00
ULTAG Antonio Gates 15.00 40.00
ULTAJ A.J. Hawk 12.00 30.00
ULTBC Brian Calhoun 10.00 25.00
ULTBF Brett Favre 125.00 200.00
ULTBL Byron Leftwich 10.00 25.00
ULTBM Brandon Marshall 20.00 50.00
ULTBR Ben Roethlisberger 60.00 120.00
ULTBU Reggie Bush 25.00 60.00
ULTBW Brandon Williams 10.00 25.00
ULTCA Cadillac Williams 12.00 30.00
ULTCF Charlie Frye 12.00 30.00
ULTCJ Chad Jackson 10.00 25.00
ULTCW Charlie Whitehurst 10.00 25.00
ULTDG David Givens 12.00 30.00
ULTDH Derek Hagan 12.00 30.00
ULTDW DeAngelo Williams 20.00 50.00
ULTEM Eli Manning 50.00 80.00
ULTFO DeShaun Foster 12.00 30.00
ULTJJ Julius Jones 10.00 25.00
ULTJK Joe Klopfenstein 10.00 25.00
ULTJN Jerious Norwood 10.00 25.00
ULTJO LaMont Jordan 12.00 30.00
ULTKC Kellen Clemens 10.00 25.00
ULTKJ Keyshawn Johnson 12.00 30.00
ULTLE Marcedes Lewis 10.00 25.00
ULTLJ Larry Johnson 10.00 25.00
ULTLM Laurence Maroney 10.00 25.00
ULTLT LaDainian Tomlinson 50.00 100.00
ULTLW LenDale White 10.00 25.00
ULTMB Marc Bulger 10.00 25.00
ULTMD Maurice Drew 15.00 40.00
ULTMH Michael Huff 12.00 30.00
ULTMI Mike Williams 10.00 25.00
ULTML Matt Leinart 10.00 25.00
ULTMR Michael Robinson 10.00 25.00
ULTMS Maurice Stovall 10.00 25.00
ULTMW Mario Williams 15.00 40.00
ULTNB Nate Burleson 10.00 25.00
ULTOJ Omar Jacobs 10.00 25.00
ULTPM Peyton Manning 90.00 150.00
ULTPR Philip Rivers 15.00 40.00
ULTRB Ronnie Brown 12.00 30.00
ULTRJ Rudi Johnson 10.00 25.00
ULTRW Reggie Wayne 12.00 30.00
ULTSH Santonio Holmes 12.00 30.00
ULTSM Sinorice Moss 10.00 25.00
ULTSS Steve Smith 15.00 40.00
ULTTA Lofa Tatupu 10.00 25.00
ULTTB Tiki Barber 12.00 30.00
ULTTH T.J. Houshmandzadeh/30 10.00 25.00
ULTTJ Thomas Jones 10.00 25.00
ULTVD Vernon Davis 12.00 30.00
ULTVY Vince Young 10.00 25.00
ULTWA Leon Washington 10.00 25.00
ULTWI Demetrius Williams 10.00 25.00

2006 Ultimate Collection Jerseys

STATED PRINT RUN 99 SER.#'d SETS
*PATCH SLVR/50 .6X TO 1.5X BASIC JSYs
PATCHES PRINT RUN 50 SER.#'d SETS
*PATCH GLD/30: .8X TO 2X BASIC JSYs
GOLD PATCH PRINT RUN 30
*SILVER/75: .4X TO 1X BASIC JSYs
SILVER PRINT RUN 75 SER.#'d SETS
*SPECTRUM/40: .6X TO 1.5X BASIC JSYs
SPECTRUM PRINT RUN 40 SER.#'d SETS
ULAB Anquan Boldin 3.00 8.00
ULAG Ahman Green 3.00 8.00
ULAS Alex Smith QB 4.00 10.00
ULBE Braylon Edwards 4.00 10.00
ULBF Brett Favre 8.00 20.00
ULBL Byron Leftwich 3.00 8.00
ULBR Ben Roethlisberger 6.00 15.00
ULBS Barry Sanders 10.00 25.00
ULBU Brian Urlacher 4.00 10.00
ULCJ Chad Johnson 3.00 8.00
ULCP Carson Palmer 4.00 10.00
ULCW Cadillac Williams 3.00 8.00
ULDB Drew Bledsoe 4.00 10.00
ULDC Daunte Culpepper 4.00 10.00
ULDD Domanick Davis 3.00 8.00
ULDF DeShaun Foster 3.00 8.00
ULDM Dan Marino 12.00 30.00
ULDO Donovan McNabb 4.00 10.00
ULDR Drew Brees 4.00 10.00
ULEJ Edgerrin James 4.00 10.00
ULEM Eli Manning 5.00 12.00
ULGA Antonio Gates 4.00 10.00
ULGR Trent Green 3.00 8.00
ULJD Jake Delhomme 3.00 8.00
ULJH Joe Horn 3.00 8.00
ULJJ Julius Jones 4.00 10.00
ULJK Jim Kelly 6.00 15.00
ULJL Jamal Lewis 3.00 8.00
ULJO LaMont Jordan 3.00 8.00
ULJP Jake Plummer 3.00 8.00
ULJS Jeremy Shockey 4.00 10.00
ULJT Jason Taylor 3.00 8.00
ULKS Ken Stabler 8.00 20.00
ULLF Larry Fitzgerald 4.00 10.00
ULLJ Larry Johnson 4.00 10.00
ULLT LaDainian Tomlinson 6.00 15.00
ULMC Deuce McAllister 3.00 8.00
ULMH Marvin Harrison 4.00 10.00
ULMV Michael Vick 4.00 10.00
ULPB Plaxico Burress 3.00 8.00
ULPH Priest Holmes 3.00 8.00
ULPM Peyton Manning 6.00 15.00
ULRB Ronnie Brown 4.00 10.00
ULRL Ray Lewis 4.00 10.00
ULRM Randy Moss 4.00 10.00
ULRS Rod Smith 3.00 8.00
ULRW Reggie Wayne 3.00 8.00
ULSA Shaun Alexander 4.00 10.00
ULSS Steve Smith 4.00 10.00
ULTB Tom Brady 6.00 15.00
ULTG Tony Gonzalez 3.00 8.00
ULTH Joe Theismann 6.00 15.00
ULTI Tiki Barber 4.00 10.00
ULTO Terrell Owens 4.00 10.00
ULTW Troy Williamson 3.00 8.00
ULWI Roy Williams WR 4.00 10.00
ULWM Willis McGahee 4.00 10.00
ULCB1 Champ Bailey 3.00 8.00
ULCB2 Cedric Benson 4.00 10.00

2006 Ultimate Collection Jerseys Dual

DUAL PRINT RUN 99 SER.#'d SETS
*PATCH/50: .5X TO 1.2X BASIC DUALS
PATCH PRINT RUN 50 SER.#'d SETS
UDBF Boldin/Fitzgerald 6.00 15.00
UDBH C.Bailey/M.Huff 6.00 15.00
UDBL R.Bush/M.Leinart 6.00 15.00
UDBM D.Brees/D.McAllister 8.00 20.00
UDBO D.Bledsoe/T.Owens 6.00 15.00
UDBR Brady/Roethlisberger 12.00 30.00
UDBW R.Brown/L.White 6.00 15.00
UDBY C.Benson/V.Young 8.00 20.00
UDCB D.Culpepper/R.Brown 6.00 15.00
UDCK Crumpler/Klopfenstein 6.00 15.00
UDCS C.Jackson/S.Holmes 6.00 15.00
UDDC J.Delhomme/K.Clemens 6.00 15.00
UDDL D.Williams/L.Maroney 10.00 25.00
UDEL E.James/L.Maroney 6.00 15.00
UDFD D.Foster/M.Drew 6.00 15.00
UDFM B.Favre/P.Manning 15.00 40.00
UDGD A.Gates/V.Davis 3.00 8.00
UDGG T.Gonzalez/A.Gates 6.00 15.00
UDHA Hasselbeck/Alexander 6.00 15.00
UDHH A.Hawk/S.Holmes 8.00 20.00
UDJH L.Johnson/P.Holmes 6.00 15.00
UDJM L.Jordan/W.McGahee 6.00 15.00
UDJS J.Jones/M.Stovall 6.00 15.00
UDJW R.Johnson/C.Williams 6.00 15.00
UDLD M.Lewis/M.Drew 6.00 15.00
UDLJ B.Leftwich/O.Jacobs 6.00 15.00
UDME D.Marino/J.Elway 20.00 50.00
UDMH R.Moss/M.Harrison 6.00 15.00
UDMM P.Manning/E.Manning 12.00 30.00
UDMY D.McNabb/V.Young 8.00 20.00
UDOJ T.Owens/C.Jackson 5.00 12.00
UDPB J.Plummer/T.Bell 5.00 12.00
UDPL C.Palmer/M.Leinart 8.00 20.00
UDSB B.Sanders/R.Bush 20.00 50.00
UDSJ S.Smith/C.Johnson 6.00 15.00
UDTD T.Barber/D.Williams 8.00 20.00
UDTH L.Tatupu/A.Hawk 6.00 15.00
UDTJ Tomlinson/L.Johnson 8.00 20.00
UDTW J.Taylor/M.Williams 5.00 12.00
UDVY M.Vick/V.Young 8.00 20.00
UDWM R.Wayne/S.Moss 4.00 10.00

2006 Ultimate Collection Jerseys Triple

TRIPLE PRINT RUN 50 SER.#'d SETS
*TRI PATCH/25: .5X TO 1.2X BASIC TRIPLES
TRIPLE PATCH PRINT RUN 25
AJJ Alex/James/Johnson 10.00 25.00
BBS Barber/Burress/Shockey 10.00 25.00
BMH Brees/McAllister/Horn 10.00 25.00
BMS Bledsoe/Manning/Smith QB 12.00 30.00
BWM Bush/Williams/Maroney 12.00 30.00
DFP Delh/Foster/Peppers 6.00 15.00
DLK Davis/Lewis/Klopfenstein 4.00 10.00
FBR Favre/Brady/Roeth 25.00 60.00
GHG Green/Holmes/Gonzalez 6.00 15.00
JHM Jackson/Holmes/Moss 10.00 25.00
JWB Johnson/Williams/Brown 8.00 20.00
LYC Leinart/Young/Clemens 15.00 40.00
MCL McNabb/Culp/Leftwich 8.00 20.00
PBS Plummer/Bell/Smith 6.00 15.00
RTG Rivers/Tomlinson/Gates 12.00 30.00
SJO Smith/Johnson/Owens 10.00 25.00
VPM Vick/Palmer/Manning 12.00 30.00
WHH Williams/Hawk/Huff 10.00 25.00

2006 Ultimate Collection Jerseys Quad

QUAD PRINT RUN 25 SER.#'d SETS
*QUAD PATCH/20: .5X TO 1.2 X
BMWW Bsh/Mron/DeA.W/Wht 15.00 40.00
HJMD Hlms/Jcksn/Moss/Dvis 10.00 25.00
MSOJ Mss/Smith/Owns/Chad 15.00 40.00
RMMB Roeth/P.Mnn/McNbb/Brdy 30.00 80.00
TAJJ Tmlnsn/Alex/LJ/James 20.00 50.00
YWCJ V.Yng/White/Clmns/Jcksn 25.00 60.00

2006 Ultimate Collection Rookie Jerseys

STATED PRINT RUN 99 SER.#'d SETS
*PATCH GLD/25: .8X TO 2X BASIC JSYs
PATCH GOLD PRINT RUN 25
*PATCH SLVR/50: .6X TO 1.5X BASIC JSYs
PATCH SILVER PRINT RUN 50
*SILVER/75: .4X TO 1X BASIC JSYs
SILVER PRINT RUN 75 SER.#'d SETS
*SPECTRUM/40: .6X TO 1.5X BASIC JSYs
SPECTRUM PRINT RUN 40 SER.#'d SETS
URAH A.J. Hawk 3.00 8.00
URBC Brian Calhoun 2.50 6.00
URBM Brandon Marshall 5.00 12.00
URBW Brandon Williams 2.50 6.00
URCJ Chad Jackson 2.50 6.00
URCW Charlie Whitehurst 2.50 6.00
URDH Derek Hagan 3.00 8.00
URDW DeAngelo Williams 3.00 8.00
URJA Jason Avant 2.50 6.00
URJK Joe Klopfenstein 2.50 6.00
URJN Jerious Norwood 2.50 6.00
URKC Kellen Clemens 2.50 6.00
URLE Matt Leinart 2.50 6.00
URLM Laurence Maroney 2.50 6.00
URLW LenDale White 2.50 6.00
URMD Maurice Drew 4.00 10.00
URMH Michael Huff 3.00 8.00
URML Marcedes Lewis 2.50 6.00
URMR Michael Robinson 2.50 6.00
URMS Maurice Stovall 2.50 6.00
URMW Mario Williams 4.00 10.00
UROJ Omar Jacobs 2.50 6.00
URRB Reggie Bush 4.00 10.00
URSH Santonio Holmes 3.00 8.00
URSM Sinorice Moss 2.50 6.00
URTJ Tarvaris Jackson 2.50 6.00
URTW Travis Wilson 2.50 6.00
URVD Vernon Davis 3.00 8.00
URVY Vince Young 2.50 6.00
URWA Leon Washington 2.50 6.00

2006 Ultimate Collection Stat Patches

ATED PRINT RUN 50 SER.#'d SETS
AB Anquan Boldin 6.00 15.00
AG Ahman Green 6.00 15.00
BA Tiki Barber 8.00 20.00
BF Brett Favre 15.00 40.00
BL Byron Leftwich 6.00 15.00
BR Ben Roethlisberger 12.00 30.00
BW Brian Westbrook 6.00 15.00
CB Champ Bailey 6.00 15.00
CC Chris Chambers 6.00 15.00
CD Corey Dillon 6.00 15.00
CJ Chad Johnson 6.00 15.00
CM Curtis Martin 8.00 20.00
CP Carson Palmer 8.00 20.00
DB Drew Bledsoe 8.00 20.00
DC Daunte Culpepper 8.00 20.00
DM Dan Marino 15.00 40.00
DO Donovan McNabb 8.00 20.00
DR Drew Brees 8.00 20.00
EJ Edgerrin James 8.00 20.00
EM Eli Manning 10.00 25.00
FT Fred Taylor 6.00 15.00
GA Antonio Gates 8.00 20.00
HA Matt Hasselbeck 6.00 15.00
JD Jake Delhomme 6.00 15.00
JS Jeremy Shockey 8.00 20.00
JW Javon Walker 6.00 15.00
LF Larry Fitzgerald 8.00 20.00
LJ Larry Johnson 8.00 20.00
LT LaDainian Tomlinson 8.00 20.00
MC Deuce McAllister 6.00 15.00
MH Marvin Harrison 8.00 20.00
MV Michael Vick 8.00 20.00
PB Plaxico Burress 6.00 15.00
PM Peyton Manning 12.00 30.00
PO Clinton Portis 8.00 20.00
RJ Rudi Johnson 6.00 15.00
RL Ray Lewis 8.00 20.00
RM Randy Moss 8.00 20.00
SS Steve Smith 8.00 20.00
TB Tom Brady 12.00 30.00
TG Trent Green 6.00 15.00
TH Torry Holt 6.00 15.00
TO Terrell Owens 8.00 20.00
PH1 Priest Holmes 27 6.00 15.00
PH2 Priest Holmes 86 6.00 15.00
RW1 Reggie Wayne 28 6.00 15.00
RW2 Reggie Wayne 83 6.00 15.00
SA1 Shaun Alexander 28 8.00 20.00
SA2 Shaun Alexander 89 8.00 20.00
TG1 Tony Gonzalez 56 6.00 15.00
TG2 Tony Gonzalez 78 6.00 15.00

2006 Ultimate Collection Super Jerseys

STATED PRINT RUN 50 SER.#'d SETS
UNPRICED PATCH PRINT RUN 10
SUPAG Antonio Gates 10.00 25.00
SUPAS Alex Smith QB 10.00 25.00
SUPBA Tiki Barber 10.00 25.00
SUPBF Brett Favre 20.00 50.00
SUPBR Ben Roethlisberger 15.00 40.00
SUPBU Reggie Bush 10.00 25.00
SUPCB Champ Bailey 8.00 20.00
SUPCJ Chad Johnson 8.00 20.00
SUPCP Carson Palmer 10.00 25.00
SUPCW Cadillac Williams 10.00 25.00
SUPDC Daunte Culpepper 10.00 25.00
SUPDF DeShaun Foster 8.00 20.00
SUPDM Donovan McNabb 10.00 25.00
SUPEJ Edgerrin James 10.00 25.00
SUPEM Eli Manning 12.00 30.00
SUPGR Trent Green 8.00 20.00
SUPJD Jake Delhomme 8.00 20.00
SUPJJ Julius Jones 10.00 25.00
SUPJO LaMont Jordan 8.00 20.00
SUPJP Jake Plummer 8.00 20.00
SUPJS Jeremy Shockey 10.00 25.00
SUPLJ Larry Johnson 10.00 25.00
SUPLT LaDainian Tomlinson 10.00 25.00
SUPMH Matt Hasselbeck 8.00 20.00
SUPML Matt Leinart 6.00 15.00
SUPMV Michael Vick 10.00 25.00
SUPPM Peyton Manning 15.00 40.00
SUPRB Ronnie Brown 10.00 25.00
SUPRM Randy Moss 10.00 25.00
SUPSA Shaun Alexander 10.00 25.00
SUPSS Steve Smith 10.00 25.00
SUPTB Tom Brady 15.00 40.00
SUPTG Tony Gonzalez 8.00 20.00
SUPTO Terrell Owens 10.00 25.00

2006 Ultimate Collection Ultimate Scripts

STATED PRINT RUN 35 SER.#'d SETS
USCAF Anthony Fasano 6.00 15.00
USCAG Antonio Gates 10.00 25.00
USCAH A.J. Hawk 12.00 30.00
USCAI Troy Aikman 50.00 100.00
USCAV Jason Avant 6.00 15.00
USCBB Brodrick Bunkley 8.00 20.00
USCBC Brian Calhoun 6.00 15.00
USCBE Braylon Edwards 6.00 15.00
USCBF Brett Favre 100.00 200.00
USCBG Bruce Gradkowski 8.00 20.00
USCBL Byron Leftwich 6.00 15.00
USCBM Brandon Marshall 15.00 40.00
USCBO Bob Griese 10.00 25.00
USCBR Ben Roethlisberger 60.00 100.00
USCBS Brad Smith 8.00 20.00
USCBU Reggie Bush 10.00 25.00
USCBW Brandon Williams 6.00 15.00
USCCG Chad Greenway 10.00 25.00
USCCJ Chad Jackson 6.00 15.00
USCCU Kevin Curtis 8.00 20.00
USCCW Charlie Whitehurst 6.00 15.00
USCDA Dan Fouts 12.00 30.00
USCDB Dominique Byrd 6.00 15.00
USCDE Demetrius Williams 6.00 15.00
USCDG David Givens 8.00 20.00
USCDH Derek Hagan 8.00 20.00
USCDM Dan Marino 100.00 200.00
USCDR Drew Bledsoe 8.00 20.00
USCDS D.J. Shockley 8.00 20.00
USCDW DeAngelo Williams 15.00 40.00
USCEM Eli Manning 50.00 80.00
USCES Ernie Sims 6.00 15.00
USCFO DeShaun Foster 8.00 20.00
USCGJ Greg Jennings 10.00 25.00
USCGL Greg Lee 6.00 15.00
USCHA Mike Hass 6.00 15.00
USCHI Tye Hill 6.00 15.00
USCHO T.J. Houshmandzadeh 6.00 15.00
USCJA Joseph Addai 6.00 15.00
USCJB Josh Betts 8.00 20.00
USCJC Jay Cutler 8.00 20.00
USCJE John Elway 75.00 150.00
USCJH Jerome Harrison 6.00 15.00
USCJJ Julius Jones 6.00 15.00
USCJK Joe Klopfenstein 6.00 15.00
USCJN Jerious Norwood 6.00 15.00
USCJO Keyshawn Johnson 8.00 20.00
USCJW Jimmy Williams 6.00 15.00
USCKC Kellen Clemens 6.00 15.00
USCKJ Kelly Jennings 8.00 20.00
USCLA LaMont Jordan 8.00 20.00
USCLE Matt Leinart 6.00 15.00
USCLJ Larry Johnson 6.00 15.00
USCLM Laurence Maroney 6.00 15.00
USCLO Lofa Tatupu 6.00 15.00
USCLP Leonard Pope 10.00 25.00
USCLT LaDainian Tomlinson 30.00 80.00
USCLW LenDale White 6.00 15.00
USCMA Derrick Mason 6.00 15.00
USCMD Maurice Drew 25.00 60.00
USCMH Michael Huff 8.00 20.00
USCMK Mathias Kiwanuka 10.00 25.00
USCML Marcedes Lewis 6.00 15.00
USCMM Muhsin Muhammad 6.00 15.00
USCMR Michael Robinson 6.00 15.00
USCMS Maurice Stovall 6.00 15.00
USCMV Michael Vick 20.00 50.00
USCMW Mario Williams 12.00 30.00
USCOD Owen Daniels 10.00 25.00
USCPH Paul Hornung 12.00 30.00
USCPM Peyton Manning 60.00 120.00
USCPR Philip Rivers 20.00 60.00
USCRB Ronnie Brown 8.00 20.00
USCRJ Rudi Johnson 6.00 15.00
USCRM Reggie McNeal 6.00 15.00
USCRO Cory Rodgers 6.00 15.00
USCRW Reggie Wayne 12.00 30.00
USCRY DeMeco Ryans 8.00 20.00
USCSH Santonio Holmes 8.00 20.00
USCSS Steve Smith EXCH 12.00 30.00
USCSY Steve Young 30.00 80.00
USCTA Tarvaris Jackson 6.00 15.00
USCTB Tiki Barber 12.00 30.00
USCTH Thomas Howard 6.00 15.00
USCTJ Thomas Jones 6.00 15.00
USCTW Travis Wilson 6.00 15.00
USCVD Vernon Davis 8.00 20.00
USCVY Vince Young 6.00 15.00
USCWA Leon Washington 6.00 15.00
USCWB Will Blackmon 6.00 15.00
USCWI Cadillac Williams 8.00 20.00
USCWR Willie Reid 8.00 20.00

2006 Ultimate Collection Ultimate Signatures

STATED PRINT RUN 25-99
UNPRICED PRINT PLATES SER.#'d TO 1
USAH A.J. Hawk/99 20.00 50.00
USBA Ronde Barber/99 10.00 25.00
USBC Brian Calhoun/99 8.00 20.00
USBE Braylon Edwards/99 10.00 25.00
USBF Brett Favre/25 125.00 225.00
USBL Drew Bledsoe/25 15.00 40.00
USBR Reggie Brown/99 8.00 20.00
USBU Reggie Bush/25 12.00 30.00
USCJ Chad Jackson/99 10.00 25.00
USCP Carson Palmer/25
USCS Chris Simms/99 8.00 20.00
USCU Kevin Curtis/99 6.00 15.00
USCW Cadillac Williams/25 15.00 40.00
USDB Drew Bennett/99 6.00 15.00
USDF D'Brickashaw Ferguson/99 6.00 15.00
USDG David Givens/99 6.00 15.00
USDM Deuce McAllister/75 8.00 20.00
USDW DeAngelo Williams/75 25.00 50.00
USEM Eli Manning/25 50.00 80.00
USFO DeShaun Foster/99 6.00 15.00
USGJ Greg Jennings/99 6.00 15.00
USHO T.J. Houshmandzadeh/99 8.00 20.00
USJA Joseph Addai/99 12.00 30.00
USJC Jay Cutler/25 15.00 40.00
USJO LaMont Jordan/75 6.00 15.00
USJW Jason Witten/99 20.00 40.00
USKC Kellen Clemens/99 10.00 25.00
USKO Kyle Orton/99 6.00 15.00
USLE Byron Leftwich/25 12.00 30.00
USLJ Larry Johnson/25 15.00 40.00
USLM Laurence Maroney/75 10.00 25.00
USLT LaDainian Tomlinson/25 40.00 80.00
USLW LenDale White/75 10.00 25.00
USMA Derrick Mason/99 6.00 15.00
USMB Marc Bulger/75 8.00 20.00
USMC Mark Clayton/75 8.00 20.00
USMD Maurice Drew/99 20.00 50.00
USMH Michael Huff/99 10.00 25.00
USML Matt Leinart/25 15.00 40.00
USMW Mario Williams/75 12.00 30.00
USNB Nate Burleson/99 6.00 15.00
USPM Peyton Manning/25 75.00 150.00
USRB Ronnie Brown/75 10.00 25.00
USRJ Rudi Johnson/99 10.00 25.00
USRO Ben Roethlisberger/25 60.00 120.00
USRW Reggie Wayne/99 12.00 30.00
USSH Santonio Holmes/75 20.00 40.00
USSM Sinorice Moss/99 10.00 25.00
USSS Steve Smith/75 10.00 25.00
USTA Lofa Tatupu/99 12.00 30.00
USTB Tiki Barber/25 20.00 50.00
USTH Thomas Jones/75 10.00 25.00
USTJ Tarvaris Jackson/99 10.00 25.00
USVD Vernon Davis/75 6.00 15.00
USVY Vince Young/25 60.00 120.00
USWH Charlie Whitehurst/99 10.00 25.00
USWI Mike Williams/99 6.00 15.00
USWP Willie Parker/99 10.00 25.00

2006 Ultimate Collection Ultimate Signatures Duals

ATED PRINT RUN 25 SER.#'d SETS
AS Aikman/Staubach 75.00 150.00
BB T.Barber/R.Barber 40.00 100.00
BG D.Bennett/D.Givens 15.00 40.00
BJ Benson/T.Jones 25.00 60.00
BM R.Bush/D.McAllister 2.00 50.00
BS R.Bush/G.Sayers 30.00 80.00
CM M.Clayton/D.Mason 30.00 60.00
EC J.Elway/J.Cutler 150.00 250.00
FW Foster/D.Williams 25.00 60.00
GD A.Gates/V.Davis 15.00 40.00
GJ T.Green/L.Johnson 25.00 60.00
HP F.Harris/W.Parker 50.00 100.00
HR S.Holmes/W.Reid 25.00 60.00
HS A.Hawk/E.Sims 30.00 80.00
JB L.Jordan/A.Brooks 15.00 40.00
JH R.Johnson/Houshmand 25.00 50.00
JM C.Jackson/L.Maroney 20.00 50.00
LD M.Lewis/M.Drew 30.00 80.00
LY M.Leinart/V.Young 20.00 50.00
MF Marino/Favre 175.00 350.00
MM P.Manning/E.Manning 150.00 250.00
OM K.Orton/M.Muhammad 15.00 40.00
SJ S.Smith/K.Johnson 20.00 50.00
ST B.Sanders/L.Tomlinson 125.00 250.00
TE T.Barber/E.Manning 75.00 125.00
WA R.Wayne/J.Addai 25.00 60.00
WB C.Williams/R.Brown 25.00 60.00
WF J.Witten/A.Fasano 40.00 80.00
WG Ma.Williams/Greenwood 25.00 60.00
YW V.Young/L.White 25.00 60.00

2006 Ultimate Collection Ultimate Signatures Triples

TRIPLE SIGNATURE PRINT RUN 20
ADS Aikman/Dawson/Stabler 75.00 150.00
BWB Brown/Williams/Benson 40.00 100.00
HSG Hawk/Sims/Greenway 40.00 100.00
JJP Johnson/Jordan/Parker 30.00 60.00
JTB Johnson/Tomlinson/Barber 40.00 80.00
LBW Leinart/Bush/White 20.00 50.00
SAB Staubach/Aikman/Bledsoe 75.00 150.00
WMA Williams/Maroney/Addai 40.00 80.00
YLC Young/Leinart/Cutler 30.00 60.00

2007 Ultimate Collection

This 160-card set was released in November, 2007. The set was issued into the hobby in four-card packs, with an $100 SRP, which came four packs to a box. Cards numbered 1-100 feature veterans issued to a stated print run of 400 serial numbered sets while cards number 101-160 were all signed by the player. Those Rookie Cards were broken down thusly: Cards numbered 101-110 were issued to a stated print run of 99 serial numbered sets, cards numbered 111-127 were issued to a stated print run of 150 serial numbered sets and cards numbered 128-160 were all issued to a stated print run of 250 serial numbered sets.
1-100 PRINT RUN 400 SER.#'d SETS

101-110 ROOKIE AU PRINT RUN 99
111-127 ROOKIE AU PRINT RUN 150
128-160 ROOKIE AU PRINT RUN 250
1 Matt Leinart 1.50 4.00
2 Edgerrin James 2.00 5.00
3 Larry Fitzgerald 2.00 5.00
4 Anquan Boldin 1.50 4.00
5 Marion Barber 2.00 5.00
6 Jerious Norwood 1.50 4.00
7 Alge Crumpler 2.00 5.00
8 Steve McNair 2.00 5.00
9 Willis McGahee 1.50 4.00
10 Mark Clayton 1.50 4.00
11 J.P. Losman 1.50 4.00
12 Anthony Thomas 1.50 4.00
13 Lee Evans 2.00 5.00
14 Jake Delhomme 1.50 4.00
15 DeAngelo Williams 1.50 4.00
16 Steve Smith 2.00 5.00
17 Rex Grossman 1.50 4.00
18 Cedric Benson 1.50 4.00
19 Brian Urlacher 2.50 6.00
20 Carson Palmer 2.00 5.00
21 Rudi Johnson 1.50 4.00
22 Chad Johnson 1.50 4.00
23 T.J. Houshmandzadeh 1.50 4.00
24 Charlie Frye 2.00 5.00
25 Kellen Winslow 1.50 4.00
26 Braylon Edwards 1.50 4.00
27 Tony Romo 3.00 8.00
28 Julius Jones 1.50 4.00
29 Terrell Owens 2.00 5.00
30 Jay Cutler 1.50 4.00
31 Travis Henry 2.00 5.00
32 Javon Walker 2.00 5.00
33 Jon Kitna 1.50 4.00
34 Roy Williams WR 1.50 4.00
35 Tatum Bell 1.50 4.00
36 Brett Favre 5.00 12.00
37 Donald Driver 2.00 5.00
38 Greg Jennings 1.50 4.00
39 Matt Schaub 1.50 4.00
40 Ahman Green 2.00 5.00
41 Andre Johnson 2.00 5.00
42 Peyton Manning 6.00 15.00
43 Joseph Addai 1.50 4.00
44 Marvin Harrison 2.00 5.00
45 Reggie Wayne 2.00 5.00
46 Byron Leftwich 1.50 4.00
47 Maurice Jones-Drew 1.50 4.00
48 Fred Taylor 1.50 4.00
49 Brodie Croyle 2.00 5.00
50 Larry Johnson 1.50 4.00
51 Tony Gonzalez 2.00 5.00
52 Trent Green 1.50 4.00
53 Ronnie Brown 1.50 4.00
54 Chris Chambers 1.50 4.00
55 Tarvaris Jackson 1.50 4.00
56 Chester Taylor 1.50 4.00
57 Troy Williamson 1.50 4.00
58 Tom Brady 8.00 20.00
59 Laurence Maroney 2.00 5.00
60 Randy Moss 2.00 5.00
61 Drew Brees 2.50 6.00
62 Reggie Bush 1.50 4.00
63 Deuce McAllister 2.00 5.00
64 Marques Colston 1.50 4.00
65 Eli Manning 2.00 5.00
66 Brandon Jacobs 1.50 4.00
67 Plaxico Burress 1.50 4.00
68 Chad Pennington 1.50 4.00
69 Thomas Jones 1.50 4.00
70 Laveranues Coles 1.50 4.00
71 LaMont Jordan 2.00 5.00
72 Dominic Rhodes 1.50 4.00
73 Ronald Curry 1.50 4.00
74 Donovan McNabb 2.00 5.00
75 Brian Westbrook 1.50 4.00
76 Reggie Brown 1.50 4.00
77 Ben Roethlisberger 2.50 6.00
78 Willie Parker 2.00 5.00
79 Hines Ward 2.00 5.00
80 Philip Rivers 2.50 6.00
81 LaDainian Tomlinson 2.50 6.00
82 Antonio Gates 2.50 6.00
83 Alex Smith QB 2.00 5.00
84 Frank Gore 2.00 5.00
85 Darrell Jackson 1.50 4.00
86 Matt Hasselbeck 1.50 4.00
87 Shaun Alexander 1.50 4.00
88 Deion Branch 1.50 4.00
89 Marc Bulger 1.50 4.00
90 Steven Jackson 1.50 4.00
91 Torry Holt 2.00 5.00
92 Jeff Garcia 1.50 4.00
93 Cadillac Williams 2.00 5.00
94 Joey Galloway 2.00 5.00
95 Vince Young 1.50 4.00
96 LenDale White 2.00 5.00
97 David Givens 1.50 4.00
98 Jason Campbell 1.50 4.00
99 Clinton Portis 1.50 4.00
100 Santana Moss 2.00 5.00
101 Adrian Peterson AU/99 RC 150.00 300.00
102 Brady Quinn AU/99 RC 10.00 25.00
103 Calvin Johnson AU/99 RC 100.00 175.00
104 Dwayne Bowe AU/99 RC 10.00 25.00
105 JaMarcus Russell AU/99 RC 10.00 25.00
106 Kevin Kolb AU/99 RC 12.00 30.00
107 Marshawn Lynch AU/99 RC 40.00 80.00
108 Robert Meachem AU/99 RC 12.00 30.00
109 Sidney Rice AU/99 RC 12.00 30.00
110 Ted Ginn AU/99 RC 12.00 30.00
111 Anthony Gonzalez AU/150 RC 6.00 15.00
112 Brian Leonard AU/150 RC 6.00 15.00
113 Chris Henry AU/150 RC 6.00 15.00
114 Chris Leak AU/150 RC 6.00 15.00
115 Drew Stanton AU/150 RC 6.00 15.00
116 Dwayne Jarrett AU/150 RC 8.00 20.00
117 Gaines Adams AU/150 RC 8.00 20.00
118 Greg Olsen AU/150 RC 10.00 25.00
119 Jason Hill AU/150 RC 6.00 15.00
120 Joe Thomas AU/150 RC 10.00 25.00
121 Kenny Irons AU/150 RC 6.00 15.00
122 LaRon Landry AU/150 RC 10.00 25.00
123 Leon Hall AU/150 RC 6.00 15.00
124 Lorenzo Booker AU/150 RC 8.00 20.00
125 Michael Bush AU/150 RC 6.00 15.00
126 Steve Smith AU/150 RC 6.00 15.00
127 Trent Edwards AU/150 RC 6.00 15.00
128 Amobi Okoye AU/250 RC 6.00 15.00
129 Antonio Pittman AU/250 RC 5.00 12.00
130 Aundrae Allison AU/250 RC 5.00 12.00
131 Brandon Jackson AU/250 RC 5.00 12.00
132 Brandon Meriweather AU/250 RC 6.00 15.00
133 Chansi Stuckey AU/250 RC 6.00 15.00
134 Craig Buster Davis AU/250 RC 5.00 12.00
135 Dallas Baker AU/250 RC 5.00 12.00
136 Darrelle Revis AU/250 RC 15.00 30.00
137 David Ball AU/250 RC 5.00 12.00
138 David Clowney AU/250 RC 5.00 12.00
139 Daymeion Hughes AU/250 RC 5.00 12.00
140 Dwayne Wright AU/250 RC 5.00 12.00
141 Eric Wright AU/250 RC 5.00 12.00
142 Garrett Wolfe AU/250 RC 5.00 12.00
143 John Beck AU/250 RC 5.00 12.00
144 Johnnie Lee Higgins AU/250 RC 5.00 12.00
145 Jordan Palmer AU/250 RC 6.00 15.00
146 Kenneth Darby AU/250 RC 5.00 12.00
147 Kolby Smith AU/250 RC 5.00 12.00
148 LaMarr Woodley AU/250 RC 15.00 30.00
149 Lawrence Timmons AU/250 RC 8.00 20.00
150 Legedu Naanee AU/250 RC 6.00 15.00
151 Matt Moore AU/250 RC 8.00 20.00
152 Paul Williams AU/250 RC 5.00 12.00
153 Quentin Moses AU/250 RC 5.00 12.00
154 Reggie Nelson AU/250 RC 5.00 12.00
155 Rhema McKnight AU/250 RC 5.00 12.00
156 Selvin Young AU/250 RC 5.00 12.00
157 Syvelle Newton AU/250 RC 6.00 15.00
158 Tony Hunt AU/250 RC 5.00 12.00
159 Tyler Palko AU/250 RC 8.00 20.00
160 Zach Miller AU/250 RC 5.00 12.00

2007 Ultimate Collection Achievement Patches

STATED PRINT RUN 99 SER.#'d SETS
UAPAG Anthony Gonzalez 2.50 6.00
UAPAP Adrian Peterson 8.00 20.00
UAPBF Brett Favre 12.00 30.00
UAPBO Dwayne Bowe 2.50 6.00
UAPBQ Brady Quinn 2.50 6.00
UAPCJ Chad Johnson 4.00 10.00
UAPCP Carson Palmer 5.00 12.00
UAPDB Drew Brees 6.00 15.00
UAPDJ Dwayne Jarrett 3.00 8.00
UAPDM Donovan McNabb 5.00 12.00
UAPEM Eli Manning 5.00 12.00
UAPGI Ted Ginn Jr. 3.00 8.00
UAPGR Trent Green 4.00 10.00
UAPHW Hines Ward 5.00 12.00
UAPJB John Beck 2.50 6.00
UAPJM Joe Montana 15.00 40.00
UAPJO Calvin Johnson 8.00 20.00
UAPJR JaMarcus Russell 2.50 6.00
UAPJT Jason Taylor 5.00 12.00
UAPKK Kevin Kolb 3.00 8.00
UAPLF Larry Fitzgerald 5.00 12.00
UAPLJ Larry Johnson 4.00 10.00
UAPLT LaDainian Tomlinson 6.00 15.00
UAPLY Marshawn Lynch 5.00 12.00
UAPMH Marvin Harrison 5.00 12.00
UAPML Matt Leinart 4.00 10.00
UAPPM Peyton Manning 15.00 40.00
UAPRB Reggie Bush 4.00 10.00
UAPRL Ray Lewis 6.00 15.00
UAPRM Robert Meachem 3.00 8.00
UAPRW Roy Williams WR 4.00 10.00
UAPSS Steve Smith 5.00 12.00
UAPSY Steve Young 12.00 30.00
UAPTB Tom Brady 15.00 40.00
UAPTG Tony Gonzalez 5.00 12.00
UAPTH Torry Holt 5.00 12.00
UAPTO Terrell Owens 5.00 12.00
UAPVY Vince Young 4.00 10.00
UAPWD Warrick Dunn 4.00 10.00

2007 Ultimate Collection Game Patches

STATED PRINT RUN 99 SER.#'d SETS
UGPAG Ahman Green 5.00 12.00
UGPAS Alex Smith QB 5.00 12.00
UGPBE Cedric Benson 4.00 10.00
UGPBF Brett Favre 15.00 40.00
UGPBF2 Brett Favre 15.00 40.00
UGPBL Byron Leftwich 4.00 10.00
UGPBR Ben Roethlisberger 6.00 15.00
UGPBW Brian Westbrook 4.00 10.00
UGPCB Champ Bailey 5.00 12.00
UGPCJ Chad Johnson 4.00 10.00
UGPCP Carson Palmer 5.00 12.00
UGPCW Cadillac Williams 5.00 12.00
UGPDB Drew Brees 6.00 15.00
UGPDD Donald Driver 5.00 12.00
UGPDM Donovan McNabb 5.00 12.00
UGPDW DeAngelo Williams 4.00 10.00
UGPEJ Edgerrin James 5.00 12.00
UGPEJ2 Edgerrin James 5.00 12.00
UGPES Emmitt Smith 12.00 30.00
UGPFG Frank Gore 5.00 12.00
UGPGA Antonio Gates 6.00 15.00
UGPHA Marvin Harrison 5.00 12.00
UGPHW Hines Ward 5.00 12.00
UGPJJ Julius Jones 4.00 10.00
UGPJT Jason Taylor 5.00 12.00
UGPLC Laveranues Coles 4.00 10.00
UGPLE Lee Evans 5.00 12.00
UGPLF Larry Fitzgerald 5.00 12.00
UGPLM Laurence Maroney 5.00 12.00
UGPLT LaDainian Tomlinson 6.00 15.00
UGPLT2 LaDainian Tomlinson 6.00 15.00
UGPMB Marc Bulger 4.00 10.00
UGPMH Matt Hasselbeck 4.00 10.00
UGPPM Peyton Manning 15.00 40.00
UGPPM2 Peyton Manning 15.00 40.00
UGPPO Clinton Portis 4.00 10.00
UGPPR Philip Rivers 6.00 15.00
UGPRB Reggie Bush 4.00 10.00
UGPRO Ronnie Brown 4.00 10.00
UGPRW Reggie Wayne 5.00 12.00
UGPSA Shaun Alexander 4.00 10.00
UGPSJ Steven Jackson 4.00 10.00
UGPSM Steve McNair 5.00 12.00
UGPTB Tom Brady 25.00 50.00
UGPTH T.J. Houshmandzadeh 4.00 10.00
UGPTR Tony Romo 8.00 20.00
UGPVY Vince Young 4.00 10.00
UGPWI Roy Williams WR 4.00 10.00
UGPWM Willis McGahee 4.00 10.00

2007 Ultimate Collection Materials Autographs

STATED PRINT RUN 1-25
UMAB Anquan Boldin 12.00 30.00
UMAD Joseph Addai
UMAS Alex Smith QB 25.00 50.00
UMBF Brett Favre 150.00 250.00
UMBJ Brandon Jacobs 12.00 30.00
UMBU Reggie Bush 20.00 50.00
UMCL Mark Clayton 10.00 25.00
UMCT Chester Taylor 10.00 25.00
UMDR Drew Bennett
UMEM Eli Manning 60.00 120.00
UMEM2 Eli Manning 60.00 120.00
UMFG Frank Gore 20.00 40.00
UMHO T.J. Houshmandzadeh 12.00 30.00
UMJT Joe Theismann 20.00 40.00
UMLE Lee Evans 10.00 25.00
UMLT LaDainian Tomlinson 40.00 80.00
UMMB Marc Bulger 10.00 25.00
UMML Matt Leinart 20.00 40.00
UMML2 Matt Leinart 20.00 40.00
UMMQ Marques Colston 10.00 25.00
UMTR Tony Romo
UMWP Willie Parker 20.00 40.00

2007 Ultimate Collection Materials Dual

STATED PRINT RUN 75 SER.#'d SETS
*PATCH/25: .8X TO 2X BASIC DUAL/75
PATCH PRINT RUN 25 SER.#'d SETS
1 P.Manning/T.Brady 30.00 80.00
2 R.Bush/D.McAllister 5.00 12.00
3 S.Merriman/P.Willis 3.00 8.00
4 L.Tomlinson/A.Peterson 20.00 50.00
5 T.Gonzalez/A.Gates 6.00 15.00
6 T.Romo/T.Owens 8.00 20.00
7 S.Smith/D.Williams 5.00 12.00
8 J.Jones/T.Jones 4.00 10.00
9 R.Brown/C.Williams 5.00 12.00
10 M.Jones-Drew/M.Lynch 8.00 20.00
11 T.Ginn Jr./C.Johnson 6.00 15.00
12 M.Harrison/A.Gonzalez 2.50 6.00
13 P.Manning/E.Manning 15.00 40.00
14 C.Pennington/T.Brady 20.00 50.00
15 B.Favre/P.Manning 25.00 60.00
17 B.Quinn/M.Leinart 2.00 5.00
18 V.Young/R.Bush 4.00 10.00
19 E.James/F.Gore 5.00 12.00
20 S.Jackson/S.Alexander 4.00 10.00
21 L.Washington/L.Coles 4.00 10.00
22 R.Bush/M.Leinart 4.00 10.00
23 T.Holt/S.Rice 2.50 6.00
24 M.Bush/J.Russell 2.00 5.00
25 M.Leinart/C.Palmer 5.00 12.00
26 D.Stanton/C.Johnson 6.00 15.00
27 R.Bush/R.Meachem 5.00 12.00
28 P.Rivers/B.Roethlisberger 6.00 15.00
29 H.Ward/C.Bailey 5.00 12.00
30 L.Maroney/L.Washington 5.00 12.00
31 A.Peterson/M.Lynch 15.00 40.00
32 S.Smith USC/D.Jarrett 2.50 6.00
33 W.Parker/W.McGahee 5.00 12.00
34 C.Johnson/T.Houshmandzadeh 4.00 10.00
35 C.Palmer/C.Johnson 5.00 12.00
36 P.Manning/M.Harrison 12.00 30.00
37 J.Russell/B.Quinn 2.00 5.00
38 W.McGahee/F.Gore 5.00 12.00
39 S.Alexander/M.Bush 2.00 5.00
40 A.Boldin/L.Fitzgerald 5.00 12.00

2007 Ultimate Collection Materials Quad

QUAD PRINT RUN 25 SER.#'d SETS
UNPRICED PATCH PRINT RUN 10
1 James/Gore/Jackson/Alex 12.00 30.00
2 Tomlin/Gore/Jcksn/Jhnsn 15.00 40.00
3 Bush/Lnart/Young/J-Drew 20.00 50.00
4 Hass/Alex/Roeth/Parker 15.00 40.00
5 Mann/Hrrisn/Wyne/Addai 30.00 80.00
6 Romo/Brees/Palmer/Addai 30.00 80.00
7 Will.WR/Meach/Fitz/Bowe 6.00 15.00
8 Beck/Ginn/Stanton/Jhnsn 15.00 40.00
9 Bush/Leinart/Palmer/Allen 15.00 40.00
10 Smith USC/Jarr/Smith/Pitt 6.00 15.00
11 Coles/Walk/Ward/Evans 12.00 30.00
12 Wayne/Boldin/Smith/Holt 12.00 30.00
13 Portis/Gore/McGa/James 12.00 30.00
14 Holt/Bruce/Fitz/Boldin 15.00 40.00
15 Will.WR/Driver/Bold/Smith 12.00 30.00
16 Hill/Willis/Bush/Higgins 8.00 20.00
18 Russell/Quinn/Kolb/Beck 6.00 15.00
19 Maron/White/Wash/J-Drew 12.00 30.00
20 Palmer/Leinart/Bush/White 12.00 30.00
21 Lynch/Peterson/Jcksn/Irns 40.00 100.00
22 Jhnsn/Wyne/Hrrisn/Evans 12.00 30.00
23 Stant/Kolb/Figrs/Smith USC 6.00 15.00
24 Brady/Mann/Roeth/Penn 40.00 100.00
25 Dunn/McAll/D.Will/Cadill 12.00 30.00
26 Russell/Petrson/Ginn/Olsen 30.00 80.00
27 Favre/Eli/Peyton/Brady 75.00 150.00
28 Russ/Quinn/Peyton/McNbb 20.00 50.00
29 Jhnsn/Ginn/Bowe/Meach 15.00 40.00
30 T.Smith/Gonz/Pittman/Ginn 10.00 25.00

2007 Ultimate Collection Materials Silver

SILVER RUN 125 SER.#'d SETS
*GOLD/99: .5X TO 1.2X SILVER/125
GOLD PRINT RUN 99 SER.#'d SETS
*PATCH/35: 1X TO 2.5X SILVER/125
PATCHES PRINT RUN 35 SER.#'d SETS
UMAB Anquan Boldin 2.50 6.00
UMAC Alge Crumpler 3.00 8.00
UMAG Antonio Gates 4.00 10.00
UMAH A.J. Hawk 2.50 6.00
UMAJ Andre Johnson 3.00 8.00
UMAS Alex Smith QB 3.00 8.00
UMBD Brian Dawkins 4.00 10.00
UMBF Brett Favre 8.00 20.00
UMBJ Brandon Jacobs 2.50 6.00
UMBL Byron Leftwich 2.50 6.00
UMBM Marc Bulger 2.50 6.00
UMBR Ben Roethlisberger 4.00 10.00
UMTE2 Tedy Bruschi 3.00 8.00
UMBU Brian Urlacher 4.00 10.00
UMBW Brian Westbrook 2.50 6.00
UMCA Jason Campbell 2.50 6.00
UMCB Cedric Benson 2.50 6.00
UMCJ Chad Johnson 2.50 6.00
UMCL Michael Clayton 2.50 6.00
UMCO Marques Colston 2.50 6.00
UMCP Carson Palmer 3.00 8.00
UMCT Chester Taylor 2.50 6.00
UMDB Drew Bennett 2.50 6.00
UMDD Donald Driver 3.00 8.00
UMDE Deion Branch 2.50 6.00
UMDM Donovan McNabb 3.00 8.00
UMDM2 Donovan McNabb 3.00 8.00
UMDR Drew Brees 4.00 10.00
UMDW DeAngelo Williams 2.50 6.00
UMEJ Edgerrin James 3.00 8.00
UMEM Eli Manning 3.00 8.00
UMER Ed Reed 3.00 8.00
UMFG Frank Gore 3.00 8.00
UMFT Fred Taylor 2.50 6.00
UMGL Terry Glenn 3.00 8.00
UMHA Matt Hasselbeck 2.50 6.00
UMMH Marvin Harrison 3.00 8.00
UMHO T.J. Houshmandzadeh 2.50 6.00
UMHW Hines Ward 3.00 8.00
UMIB Isaac Bruce 4.00 10.00
UMJA Joseph Addai 2.50 6.00
UMJC Jay Cutler 2.50 6.00
UMJG Joey Galloway 3.00 8.00
UMJH Joe Horn 2.50 6.00
UMJL Jamal Lewis 3.00 8.00
UMJM Joe Montana 10.00 25.00
UMJN Jerious Norwood 2.50 6.00
UMJP Julius Peppers 3.00 8.00
UMJS Jeremy Shockey 2.50 6.00
UMJS2 Jeremy Shockey 2.50 6.00
UMJT Joe Theismann 4.00 10.00
UMJW Javon Walker 3.00 8.00
UMKW Kellen Winslow 2.50 6.00
UMLC Laveranues Coles 2.50 6.00
UMLE Lee Evans 3.00 8.00
UMLF Larry Fitzgerald 3.00 8.00
UMLJ Larry Johnson 2.50 6.00
UMLM Laurence Maroney 3.00 8.00
UMLT LaDainian Tomlinson 4.00 10.00
UMLW LenDale White 3.00 8.00
UMEM2 Eli Manning 3.00 8.00
UMMB Marion Barber 3.00 8.00
UMMC Mark Clayton 2.50 6.00
UMME Shawne Merriman 2.50 6.00
UMMH2 Marvin Harrison 3.00 8.00
UMMJ Maurice Jones-Drew 2.50 6.00
UMML Matt Leinart 2.50 6.00
UMML2 Matt Leinart 2.50 6.00
UMWM Willis McGahee 2.50 6.00
UMPB Plaxico Burress 2.50 6.00
UMPE Chad Pennington 2.50 6.00
UMPM Peyton Manning 8.00 20.00
UMPM2 Peyton Manning 8.00 20.00
UMPO Clinton Portis 2.50 6.00
UMPR Philip Rivers 4.00 10.00
UMRB Reggie Bush 2.50 6.00
UMRG Rex Grossman 2.50 6.00
UMRO Ronnie Brown 2.50 6.00
UMRW Reggie Wayne 3.00 8.00
UMSA Shaun Alexander 2.50 6.00
UMSH Santonio Holmes 2.50 6.00
UMSJ Steven Jackson 2.50 6.00
UMME2 Shawne Merriman 2.50 6.00
UMSS Steve Smith 3.00 8.00
UMST Steve McNair 3.00 8.00
UMTB Tom Brady 12.00 30.00
UMTB2 Tom Brady 12.00 30.00
UMTE Tedy Bruschi 3.00 8.00
UMTG Trent Green 2.50 6.00
UMTH Todd Heap 2.50 6.00
UMTO Terrell Owens 3.00 8.00
UMTR Tony Romo 5.00 12.00
UMTW Troy Williamson 2.50 6.00
UMVY Vince Young 2.50 6.00
UMWA Leon Washington 2.50 6.00
UMWD Warrick Dunn 2.50 6.00
UMWI Roy Williams WR 2.50 6.00
UMWM2 Willis McGahee 2.50 6.00
UMWP Willie Parker 3.00 8.00

2007 Ultimate Collection Materials Triple

TRIPLE PRINT RUN 50 SER.#'d SETS
*PATCH/15: .8X TO 2X BASIC TRIPLE/50
PATCH STATED PRINT RUN 15
1 L.Jhnsn/S.Jcksn/Tomlin 10.00 25.00
2 Bulger/Holt/Bruce 10.00 25.00
3 Manning/Hrrisn/Wayne 25.00 60.00
4 Brady/Manning/Roeth 30.00 80.00
5 Ward/Parker/Roeth 10.00 25.00
6 Johnson/Ginn Jr./Bowe 10.00 25.00
7 Johnson/Housh/Palmer 8.00 20.00
8 Hunt/Bush/Wolfe 6.00 15.00
9 Peterson/Lynch/Irons 20.00 50.00
10 Adams/Thomas/Willis 5.00 12.00
11 Eli/Shockey/Burress 8.00 20.00
12 Russell/Quinn/Kolb 4.00 10.00
13 Gore/McGahee/James 8.00 20.00
14 Smith/Pittman/Gonzalez 6.00 15.00
15 Boldin/Fitzger/Leinart 8.00 20.00
16 Meach/Gonz/Johnson 12.00 30.00
17 Brees/Hassel/Favre 20.00 50.00
18 Romo/Manning/McNbb 20.00 50.00
19 Favre/Driver/Jennings 20.00 50.00
20 Stanton/Beck/Edwards 3.00 8.00
21 Russell/Quinn/Smith 6.00 15.00
22 Rice/Jarrett/Smith USC 4.00 10.00
23 Bush/Tomlinson/James 10.00 25.00
24 Benson/Urlach/Grssmn 10.00 25.00
25 Russell/Peterson/Jhnsn 25.00 60.00
26 Jones/Romo/Owens 20.00 50.00
27 Holt/Boldin/Owens 8.00 20.00
29 D.Will/J-Drew/Washing 6.00 15.00
30 Henry/Leonard/Jackson 6.00 15.00

2007 Ultimate Collection Rookie Materials Matchup

STATED PRINT RUN 99 SER.#'d SETS
AT G.Adams/J.Thomas 3.00 8.00
AW P.Willis/G.Adams 3.00 8.00
BK K.Kolb/J.Beck 2.50 6.00
EB T.Edwards/J.Beck 2.00 5.00
EL M.Lynch/T.Edwards 4.00 10.00
FW Y.Figurs/P.Williams 2.00 5.00
GB A.Gonzalez/D.Bowe 2.00 5.00
GG T.Ginn Jr./A.Gonzalez 2.50 6.00
GM R.Meachem/T.Ginn Jr. 2.50 6.00
HL C.Henry RB/M.Lynch 4.00 10.00
HW J.Higgins/P.Williams 2.00 5.00
IJ K.Irons/B.Jackson 2.00 5.00
JG C.Johnson/T.Ginn Jr. 6.00 15.00
JR S.Rice/D.Jarrett 2.50 6.00
JS C.Johnson/D.Stanton 6.00 15.00
KH T.Hunt/K.Kolb 2.50 6.00
LB B.Leonard/M.Bush 2.00 5.00
MH R.Meachem/J.Hill 2.50 6.00
PR A.Peterson/S.Rice 6.00 15.00
QR J.Russell/B.Quinn 2.00 5.00
QT B.Quinn/J.Thomas 3.00 8.00
RH S.Rice/J.Higgins 2.50 6.00
SE D.Stanton/T.Edwards 2.00 5.00
SH S.Smith USC/J.Hill 2.00 5.00
SJ D.Jarrett/S.Smith USC 2.50 6.00
SK K.Kolb/D.Stanton 2.50 6.00
SP A.Pittman/T.Smith 2.00 5.00
WA P.Willis/G.Adams 3.00 8.00
WH P.Willis/J.Hill 3.00 8.00
WO G.Olsen/G.Wolfe 3.00 8.00

2007 Ultimate Collection Rookie Materials Matchup Autographs

ATED PRINT RUN 5-25
FW P.Williams/Y.Figurs 20.00 50.00
GB A.Gonzalez/D.Bowe 50.00 100.00
GG T.Ginn Jr./A.Gonzalez 50.00 100.00
GM T.Ginn Jr./R.Meachem 25.00 60.00
HW J.Higgins/P.Williams 20.00 50.00
LB B.Leonard/M.Bush 25.00 60.00
MH R.Meachem/J.Hill 20.00 50.00
QT B.Quinn/J.Thomas 30.00 80.00
SK D.Stanton/K.Kolb 15.00 40.00

2007 Ultimate Collection Rookie Materials Silver

RONZE TRIPLE/25: 1X TO 2.5X BASIC SILVER
BRONZE TRIPLE SWATCH PRINT RUN 25
*GOLD/99: .5X TO 1.2X BASIC SILVER
GOLD PRINT RUN 50 SER.#'d SETS
*GREEN/50: .6X TO 1.5X BASIC SLVR
GREEN TRIPLE SWATCH PRINT RUN 50
*HOLOSILVER PATCH/50: .6X TO 1.5X BASIC SILVER
HOLOSILVER PATCH PRINT RUN 50 SER.#'d SETS
URMAG Anthony Gonzalez 1.50 4.00
URMAP Adrian Peterson 5.00 12.00
URMBJ Brandon Jackson 1.50 4.00
URMBL Brian Leonard 1.50 4.00
URMBQ Brady Quinn 1.50 4.00
URMCH Chris Henry RB 1.50 4.00
URMCJ Calvin Johnson 5.00 12.00
URMDB Dwayne Bowe 1.50 4.00
URMDJ Dwayne Jarrett 2.00 5.00
URMDS Drew Stanton 1.50 4.00
URMGA Gaines Adams 2.00 5.00
URMGO Greg Olsen 2.50 6.00
URMJB John Beck 1.50 4.00
URMJH Jason Hill 1.50 4.00
URMJR JaMarcus Russell 1.50 4.00
URMJT Joe Thomas 2.50 6.00
URMKI Kenny Irons 1.50 4.00
URMKK Kevin Kolb 2.00 5.00
URMMB Michael Bush 1.50 4.00
URMML Marshawn Lynch 3.00 8.00
URMPW Paul Williams 1.50 4.00
URMRM Robert Meachem 2.00 5.00
URMSR Sidney Rice 2.00 5.00
URMSS Steve Smith USC 1.50 4.00
URMTE Trent Edwards 1.50 4.00
URMTG Ted Ginn Jr. 2.00 5.00
URMTH Tony Hunt 1.50 4.00
URMTS Troy Smith 1.50 4.00
URMWI Patrick Willis 2.50 6.00
URMYF Yamon Figurs 1.50 4.00

2007 Ultimate Collection Rookie Rewind Super Patches

STATED PRINT RUN 99 SER.#'d SETS
AH A.J. Hawk 6.00 15.00
DW DeAngelo Williams 6.00 15.00
KC Kellen Clemens 6.00 15.00
LM Laurence Maroney 8.00 20.00
LW Leon Washington 6.00 15.00
MJ Maurice Jones-Drew 6.00 15.00
ML Matt Leinart 6.00 15.00
RB Reggie Bush 6.00 15.00
SH Santonio Holmes 6.00 15.00
VY Vince Young 6.00 15.00

2007 Ultimate Collection Rookie Signatures Gold

*GOLD/25: .6X TO 1.5X BASE RC/99
*GOLD/25: .6X TO 1.5X BASE RC/150
*GOLD/25: .8X TO 2X BASE RC/250
STATED PRINT RUN 25 SER.#'d SETS
UNPRICED NFL LOGO AU PRINT RUN 1
UNPRICED HOLOFOIL SER.#'d TO 10
101 Adrian Peterson 200.00 400.00
102 Brady Quinn 10.00 25.00
103 Calvin Johnson 100.00 200.00
106 Kevin Kolb 30.00 80.00
109 Sidney Rice 60.00 120.00

2007 Ultimate Collection Sunday Stars Signatures

*GOLD/50: .6X TO 1.5X BASIC AUTOS
GOLD PRINT RUN 50 SER.#'d SETS
SSAB Alan Branch 4.00 10.00
SSAG Anthony Gonzalez 4.00 10.00
SSAP Adrian Peterson SP 100.00 200.00
SSBB Bernard Berrian SP 5.00 12.00
SSCJ Chad Johnson SP 6.00 15.00
SSDB Dallas Baker 4.00 10.00
SSDJ Darrell Jackson 4.00 10.00
SSDS Drew Stanton 4.00 10.00
SSFG Frank Gore SP 6.00 15.00
SSGO Greg Olsen 6.00 15.00
SSJC Jerricho Cotchery 4.00 10.00
SSJF Joel Filani 4.00 10.00
SSLT L.Tomlinson Blue Ink 20.00 50.00
SSLTR L.Tomlinson Red Ink 40.00 80.00
SSMG Michael Griffin 4.00 10.00
SSML Marshawn Lynch SP 20.00 50.00
SSPH Paul Hornung SP 12.50 25.00
SSPP Paul Posluszny 6.00 15.00
SSSN Syvelle Newton 5.00 12.00
SSVJ Vincent Jackson 4.00 10.00
SSWP Willie Parker SP 8.00 20.00

2007 Ultimate Collection Ultimate Ink

ATED PRINT RUN 10-25
INKAB Alan Branch 6.00 15.00
INKAG Anthony Gonzalez 6.00 15.00
INKBL Brian Leonard 6.00 15.00
INKBS Barry Sanders 75.00 150.00
INKBU Reggie Bush 25.00 50.00
INKCJ Chad Johnson 6.00 15.00
INKCL Mark Clayton 6.00 15.00
INKCO Jerricho Cotchery 6.00 15.00
INKCT Chester Taylor 6.00 15.00
INKCW Cadillac Williams 8.00 20.00
INKDJ Dwayne Jarrett 8.00 20.00
INKDM Dan Marino 75.00 150.00
INKDP Drew Pearson 10.00 25.00
INKGJ Greg Jennings 6.00 15.00
INKGR Gary Russell 8.00 20.00
INKJA Joseph Addai 6.00 15.00
INKKD Kenneth Darby 6.00 15.00
INKKK Kevin Kolb 8.00 20.00
INKKS Kolby Smith 6.00 15.00
INKMB Marc Bulger 6.00 15.00
INKMC Marques Colston 6.00 15.00
INKMG Michael Griffin 6.00 15.00
INKML Marshawn Lynch 30.00 60.00
INKMS Matt Schaub 6.00 15.00
INKRC Roger Craig 10.00 25.00
INKSY Steve Young/10 90.00 150.00
INKTG Ted Ginn Jr. 8.00 20.00
INKTH T.J. Houshmandzadeh 6.00 15.00
INKTP Tyler Palko 10.00 25.00
INKVJ Vincent Jackson 6.00 15.00
INKWI Paul Williams 6.00 15.00
INKYO Selvin Young 6.00 15.00
INKZM Zach Miller 6.00 15.00

2007 Ultimate Collection Ultimate Inscriptions

ATED PRINT RUN 25 SER.#'d SETS
UIAA Aundrae Allison 6.00 15.00
UIAB Anquan Boldin 6.00 15.00
UIAG Anthony Gonzalez 6.00 15.00
UIBA David Ball 6.00 15.00
UIBE Drew Bennett 6.00 15.00
UIBJ Brandon Jacobs 6.00 15.00
UIBL Brian Leonard 6.00 15.00
UICJ Chad Johnson 6.00 15.00
UICS Chansi Stuckey 8.00 20.00
UIDB Dallas Baker 6.00 15.00
UIDJ Dwayne Jarrett 8.00 20.00
UIDP Drew Pearson 10.00 25.00
UIDT Drew Tate 8.00 20.00
UIFG Frank Gore 8.00 20.00
UIGJ Greg Jennings 6.00 15.00
UIGO Greg Olsen 10.00 25.00
UIGS Gale Sayers 40.00 80.00
UIIS Isaiah Stanback 6.00 15.00
UIJL John Lynch 25.00 50.00
UIJP Jordan Palmer 8.00 20.00
UIJR Jeff Rowe 6.00 15.00
UIJZ Jared Zabransky 6.00 15.00
UIKK Kevin Kolb 8.00 20.00
UIMC Mark Clayton 6.00 15.00
UIMG Michael Griffin 6.00 15.00
UIMM Marcus McCauley 6.00 15.00
UIMO Matt Moore 10.00 25.00
UIPH Paul Hornung 12.00 30.00
UIQM Quentin Moses 6.00 15.00
UIRB Reggie Bush 50.00 100.00
UIRC Roger Craig 10.00 25.00
UIRM Robert Meachem 8.00 20.00
UITG Ted Ginn Jr. 8.00 20.00
UIVJ Vincent Jackson 6.00 15.00
UIWI Paul Williams 6.00 15.00
UIWP Willie Parker 12.00 30.00
UIWY DeShawn Wynn 6.00 15.00
UIYF Yamon Figurs 6.00 15.00
UIZM Zach Miller 6.00 15.00

2007 Ultimate Collection Ultimate Signatures

*GOLD/50: .6X TO 1.5X BASIC AUTOS
GOLD PRINT RUN 5-50
USAB Alan Branch 4.00 10.00
USAG Anthony Gonzalez 4.00 10.00
USBJ Brandon Jacobs SP 20.00 40.00
USBL Brian Leonard 4.00 10.00
USBM Brandon Meriweather 5.00 12.00
USBO Anquan Boldin SP 6.00 15.00
USBQ Brady Quinn SP
USCS Chansi Stuckey 5.00 12.00
USCT Courtney Taylor 4.00 10.00
USDJ Dwayne Jarrett SP 5.00 12.00
USDS Drew Stanton 4.00 10.00
USEW Eric Wright 4.00 10.00
USGJ Greg Jennings 6.00 15.00
USGO Greg Olsen 6.00 15.00
USGR Gary Russell 5.00 12.00
USIS Isaiah Stanback 4.00 10.00
USJA Jamaal Anderson 5.00 12.00
USJF Joel Filani 4.00 10.00
USJH Johnnie Lee Higgins 4.00 10.00
USJR JaMarcus Russell SP 30.00 80.00
USJT Joe Thomas 6.00 15.00
USJZ Jared Zabransky 4.00 10.00
USKK Kevin Kolb SP 10.00 25.00
USLB Lorenzo Booker 5.00 12.00
USLH Leon Hall SP 4.00 10.00
USLL LaRon Landry SP 6.00 15.00
USLN Legedu Naanee 5.00 12.00
USLT Lawrence Timmons 6.00 15.00
USMB Michael Bush 4.00 10.00
USMC Rhema McKnight 4.00 10.00
USMG Michael Griffin 4.00 10.00
USQM Quentin Moses 4.00 10.00
USRM Robert Meachem SP 5.00 12.00
USRN Reggie Nelson 4.00 10.00
USTG Ted Ginn Jr. SP 5.00 12.00
USTM Tyrone Moss 4.00 10.00
USWI Paul Williams 4.00 10.00
USYF Yamon Figurs 4.00 10.00
USZM Zach Miller 4.00 10.00

2007 Ultimate Collection Ultimate Signatures Duals

STATED PRINT RUN 35 SER.#'d SETS
DSBS M.Bulger/M.Schaub 12.00 30.00
DSCG R.Craig/F.Gore 15.00 40.00
DSFW Y.Figurs/P.Williams 12.00 30.00
DSGG T.Ginn/A.Gonzalez 15.00 40.00
DSGH M.Griffin/L.Hall 12.00 30.00
DSHM J.Higgins/Z.Miller 12.00 30.00
DSJH C.Johnson/T.Housh 15.00 40.00
DSLN L.Landry/R.Nelson 12.00 30.00
DSLO B.Leonard/G.Olsen 15.00 40.00
DSPL A.Peterson/M.Lynch 125.00 250.00
DSPS J.Palmer/I.Stanback 12.00 30.00
DSSG A.Smith QB/F.Gore 30.00 60.00
DSSJ B.Sndrs/Ca.Jhnsn 100.00 200.00
DSSK D.Stanton/K.Kolb 12.00 30.00
DSTB Tomlinson/Bush 30.00 80.00

2007 Ultimate Collection Ultimate Signatures Triples

IPLE AU PRINT RUN 5-15
TSGBM Gnn/Bwe/Mchm 15.00 40.00
TSLBP Lndry/Blds/Plmr 20.00 50.00
TSMFM Mnnng/Fvre/Mntna 175.00 300.00
TSMLQ Mnnng/Lnrt/Qunn 75.00 150.00
TSMMN Mnnng/Mntna/Nmth
TSNWB Nlsn/Wynn/Bkr 12.00 30.00
TSRBA Rssll/Bwe/Addi
TSRJP Rssll/Jhnsn/Ptrsn 125.00 250.00
TSSBL Sndrs/Bsh/Lynch 100.00 175.00
TSSKP Stntn/Klb/Plmr 15.00 40.00
TSSTJ Smth/Tmlnsn/Jhnsn 100.00 175.00

2007 Ultimate Collection Write of Passage Signatures

*GOLD/50: .5X TO 1.2X BASIC AUTOS
GOLD PRINT RUN 5-50
WPAA Aundrae Allison 4.00 10.00
WPAG Anthony Gonzalez 4.00 10.00
WPBL Brian Leonard 4.00 10.00
WPCT Chester Taylor 4.00 10.00
WPCW Cadillac Williams SP 10.00 25.00
WPDJ Dwayne Jarrett 5.00 12.00
WPDS Drew Stanton 4.00 10.00
WPDW DeShawn Wynn 4.00 10.00
WPGJ Greg Jennings 4.00 10.00
WPJA Joseph Addai SP 20.00 40.00
WPKK Kevin Kolb 5.00 12.00
WPML Marshawn Lynch SP 15.00 40.00
WPMM Marcus McCauley 4.00 10.00
WPQM Quentin Moses 4.00 10.00
WPRB Reggie Brown 4.00 10.00
WPRM Robert Meachem 5.00 12.00
WPRO Jeff Rowe 4.00 10.00
WPSY Selvin Young 8.00 20.00
WPTG Ted Ginn SP 5.00 12.00
WPTH Tony Hunt 4.00 10.00
WPTM Tyrone Moss 4.00 10.00
WPWI Paul Williams 4.00 10.00

2008 Ultimate Collection

This set was released on February 17, 2009. The base set consists of 214 cards. Cards 1-130 feature veterans serial numbered of 275, and cards 131-200 are rookies serial numbered of 275. Cards 201-221 are autographed jersey rookie cards serial numbered of 99-375. This product was released with 4 cards per pack and 1 pack per hobby box.

1-130 STATED PRINT RUN 275
131-200 ROOKIE PRINT RUN 275
201-221 JSY AU RC PRINT RUN 99-375
1 Jake Delhomme 1.50 4.00
2 Trent Edwards 1.50 4.00
3 Marshawn Lynch 2.00 5.00
4 Jason Taylor 2.00 5.00
5 Chad Pennington 1.50 4.00
6 Ronnie Brown 1.50 4.00
7 Thomas Jones 1.50 4.00
8 Brett Favre 5.00 12.00
9 Jerricho Cotchery 1.50 4.00
10 Tom Brady 8.00 20.00
11 Randy Moss 2.00 5.00
12 Laurence Maroney 2.00 5.00
13 Ed Reed 2.00 5.00
14 Ray Lewis 2.50 6.00
15 Willis McGahee 1.50 4.00
16 Carson Palmer 2.00 5.00
17 Chad Johnson 1.50 4.00
18 T.J. Houshmandzadeh 1.50 4.00
19 Derek Anderson 1.50 4.00
20 Braylon Edwards 1.50 4.00
21 Kellen Winslow 1.50 4.00
22 Ben Roethlisberger 2.50 6.00
23 Troy Polamalu 2.50 6.00
24 Santonio Holmes 1.50 4.00
25 DeMeco Ryans 2.00 5.00
26 Andre Johnson 2.00 5.00
27 Matt Schaub 1.50 4.00
28 Peyton Manning 6.00 15.00
29 Reggie Wayne 2.00 5.00
30 Dallas Clark 1.50 4.00
31 David Garrard 1.50 4.00
32 Fred Taylor 1.50 4.00
33 Maurice Jones-Drew 1.50 4.00
34 Vince Young 1.50 4.00
35 Alge Crumpler 1.50 4.00
36 LenDale White 1.50 4.00
37 Jay Cutler 1.50 4.00
38 Marvin Harrison 2.00 5.00
39 Brandon Marshall 2.00 5.00
40 Brodie Croyle 2.00 5.00
41 Dwayne Bowe 2.00 5.00
42 Larry Johnson 1.50 4.00
43 JaMarcus Russell 1.50 4.00
44 Ronald Curry 1.50 4.00
45 Jeremy Shockey 1.50 4.00
46 LaDainian Tomlinson 2.50 6.00
47 Antonio Cromartie 1.50 4.00
48 Antonio Gates 2.00 5.00
49 Shawne Merriman 1.50 4.00
50 Tony Romo 2.00 5.00
51 Terrell Owens 2.00 5.00
52 Marion Barber 1.50 4.00
53 Zach Thomas 2.00 5.00
54 Eli Manning 2.00 5.00
55 Plaxico Burress 1.50 4.00
56 Brandon Jacobs 1.50 4.00
57 Antonio Pierce 1.50 4.00
58 Donovan McNabb 2.00 5.00
59 Asante Samuel 1.50 4.00
60 Brian Westbrook 1.50 4.00
61 Jason Campbell 1.50 4.00
62 Clinton Portis 1.50 4.00
63 Chris Cooley 1.50 4.00
64 Kyle Orton 1.50 4.00
65 Brian Urlacher 2.50 6.00
66 Lance Briggs 2.00 5.00
67 Ernie Sims 1.50 4.00
68 Roy Williams 1.50 4.00
69 Calvin Johnson 2.50 6.00
70 Greg Jennings 1.50 4.00
71 Ryan Grant 2.00 5.00
72 Aaron Rodgers 5.00 12.00
73 A.J. Hawk 1.50 4.00
74 Tarvaris Jackson 1.50 4.00
75 Adrian Peterson 2.50 6.00
76 Bernard Berrian 1.50 4.00
77 Michael Turner 1.50 4.00
78 Jerious Norwood 1.50 4.00
79 Kurt Warner 2.00 5.00
80 DeAngelo Williams 1.50 4.00
81 Steve Smith 2.00 5.00
82 Dwayne Jarrett 2.00 5.00
83 Drew Brees 2.50 6.00
84 Reggie Bush 1.50 4.00
85 Marques Colston 1.50 4.00
86 Jeff Garcia 1.50 4.00
87 Joey Galloway 2.00 5.00
88 Hines Ward 2.00 5.00
89 Matt Leinart 1.50 4.00
90 Larry Fitzgerald 2.00 5.00
91 Edgerrin James 2.00 5.00
92 Marc Bulger 1.50 4.00
93 Torry Holt 2.00 5.00
94 Steven Jackson 1.50 4.00
95 Ricky Williams 2.00 5.00
96 Frank Gore 2.00 5.00
97 Vernon Davis 1.50 4.00
98 Matt Hasselbeck 1.50 4.00
99 Julius Jones 1.50 4.00
100 Deion Branch 1.50 4.00
101 Barry Sanders 4.00 10.00
102 Billy Sims 2.00 5.00
103 Bo Jackson 3.00 8.00
104 Brian Bosworth 2.50 6.00
105 Dan Marino 5.00 12.00
106 Daryl Johnston 2.00 5.00
107 Dick Butkus 3.00 8.00
108 Rod Woodson 2.00 5.00
109 Fran Tarkenton 2.50 6.00
110 Franco Harris 2.50 6.00
111 Herschel Walker 2.50 6.00
112 Jack Lambert 2.50 6.00
113 Jerry Kramer 2.00 5.00
114 Jim Brown 3.00 8.00
115 Jim Kelly 2.50 6.00
116 Joe Greene 2.50 6.00
117 Joe Montana 8.00 20.00
118 Joe Namath 3.00 8.00
119 John Elway 4.00 10.00
120 Ken Stabler 2.50 6.00
121 Ken Anderson 2.00 5.00
122 Emmitt Smith 4.00 10.00
123 Mel Blount 2.00 5.00
124 Paul Hornung 2.50 6.00
125 Roger Craig 2.00 5.00
126 Roman Gabriel 1.50 4.00
127 Bruce Smith 2.00 5.00
128 Terry Bradshaw 3.00 8.00
129 Tom Rathman 2.00 5.00
130 Y.A. Tittle 2.50 6.00
131 Kregg Lumpkin RC 3.00 8.00
132 Antoine Cason RC 2.50 6.00
133 Aqib Talib RC 3.00 8.00
134 Mike Tolbert RC 3.00 8.00
135 Chris Johnson RC 2.50 6.00
136 Bruce Davis RC 2.50 6.00
137 Calais Campbell RC 2.50 6.00
138 Jordy Nelson RC 6.00 15.00
139 Chevis Jackson RC 2.00 5.00
140 Chris Ellis RC 2.00 5.00
141 Brad Cottam RC 2.00 5.00
142 Will Franklin RC 2.50 6.00
143 Early Doucet RC 2.00 5.00
144 DaJuan Morgan RC 2.50 6.00
145 Mike Hart RC 2.00 5.00
146 Davone Bess RC 2.50 6.00
147 Tom Santi RC 2.50 6.00
148 Dennis Dixon RC 2.00 5.00
149 D.Rodgers-Cromartie RC 2.50 6.00
150 Jerod Mayo RC 3.00 8.00
151 Dexter Jackson RC 3.00 8.00
152 Fred Davis RC 2.00 5.00
153 Dwight Lowery RC 2.50 6.00
154 Colt Brennan RC 2.50 6.00
155 Erik Ainge RC 2.00 5.00
156 Frank Okam RC 2.00 5.00
157 Glenn Dorsey RC 2.00 5.00
158 Gosder Cherilus RC 2.50 6.00
159 Harry Douglas RC 2.50 6.00
160 Eddie Royal RC 2.00 5.00
161 Jacob Hester RC 2.00 5.00
162 Jacob Tamme RC 2.50 6.00
163 Chauncey Washington RC 2.50 6.00
164 Jermichael Finley RC 2.00 5.00
165 John Carlson RC 2.00 5.00
166 Jerome Simpson RC 2.50 6.00
167 Spencer Larsen RC 2.00 5.00
168 Josh Johnson RC 2.00 5.00
169 Keenan Burton RC 2.00 5.00
170 Keith Rivers RC 2.00 5.00
171 Kellen Davis RC 2.00 5.00
172 Kenny Phillips RC 2.00 5.00
173 Kevin O'Connell RC 2.00 5.00
174 Mike Cox RC 2.50 6.00
175 Lavelle Hawkins RC 2.50 6.00
176 Lawrence Jackson RC 2.00 5.00
177 Leodis McKelvin RC 2.50 6.00
178 Mario Manningham RC 2.00 5.00
179 Matt Flynn RC 2.00 5.00
180 Mike Jenkins RC 2.00 5.00
181 Owen Schmitt RC 2.00 5.00
182 Steve Johnson RC 6.00 15.00
183 Charles Godfrey RC 2.00 5.00
184 Peyton Hillis RC 3.00 8.00
185 Phillip Merling RC 2.00 5.00
186 Quentin Groves RC 2.50 6.00
187 Ryan Clady RC 2.50 6.00
188 Andre Caldwell RC 2.00 5.00
189 Ryan Torain RC 2.50 6.00
190 Sam Baker RC 2.00 5.00
191 Tracy Porter RC 2.50 6.00
192 Sedrick Ellis RC 2.00 5.00
193 Shawn Crable RC 2.00 5.00
194 Tashard Choice RC 2.00 5.00
195 Terrell Thomas RC 2.00 5.00
196 Tom Zbikowski RC 2.50 6.00
197 Trevor Laws RC 2.00 5.00
198 Vernon Gholston RC 2.00 5.00
199 Xavier Adibi RC 2.00 5.00
200 Chris Long RC 2.50 6.00
201 D.McFadden JSY AU/99 RC 10.00 25.00
202 DeS.Jackson JSY AU/375 RC 12.00 30.00
203 Brian Brohm JSY AU/99 RC 10.00 25.00
204 Matt Ryan JSY AU/99 RC 100.00 200.00
205 J.Stewart JSY AU/99 RC 12.00 30.00
206 D.Avery JSY AU/375 RC 8.00 20.00
207 Chad Henne JSY AU/375 RC 8.00 20.00
208 Jake Long JSY AU/375 RC 10.00 25.00
209 Mendenhall JSY AU/99 RC 10.00 25.00
210 Felix Jones JSY AU/375 RC 6.00 15.00
211 Dustin Keller JSY AU/375 RC 8.00 20.00
212 J.Charles JSY AU/375 RC 12.00 30.00
215 Matt Forte JSY AU/375 RC 20.00 50.00
216 Kevin Smith JSY AU/375 RC 6.00 15.00
217 Ray Rice JSY AU/375 RC 6.00 15.00
218 Steve Slaton JSY AU/375 RC 6.00 15.00
219 Joe Flacco JSY AU/99 RC 40.00 80.00
220 D.Thomas JSY AU/375 RC 6.00 15.00
221 J.Booty JSY AU/375 RC 6.00 15.00

2008 Ultimate Collection 1997 Legends Autographs

179 Steve Young 75.00 150.00
180 Emmitt Smith SP 400.00 700.00
181 Barry Sanders 300.00 500.00
182 Brett Favre SP 800.00 1200.00
183 Rod Woodson 30.00 80.00
184 Jerry Rice SP 350.00 600.00
185 Jim Kelly 50.00 120.00
186 Troy Aikman 100.00 200.00
187 John Elway 300.00 500.00
189 Daryl Johnston SP 50.00 100.00
191 Marshall Faulk 30.00 80.00
193 Bo Jackson 50.00 100.00
194 Tom Rathman 30.00 80.00
195 Brian Bosworth 30.00 80.00

2008 Ultimate Collection Rookie Material Patch Autographs
ROOKIE PATCH PRINT RUN 10-15
202 DeSean Jackson/15 30.00 80.00
206 Donnie Avery/15 20.00 50.00
207 Chad Henne/15 20.00 50.00
208 Jake Long/15 25.00 60.00
209 Rashard Mendenhall/15 15.00 40.00
210 Felix Jones/15 15.00 40.00
211 Dustin Keller/15 20.00 50.00
212 Jamaal Charles/15 25.00 60.00
214 Malcolm Kelly/15 15.00 40.00
215 Matt Forte/15 25.00 60.00
216 Kevin Smith/15 15.00 40.00
217 Ray Rice/15 15.00 40.00
218 Steve Slaton/15 15.00 40.00
220 Devin Thomas/15 15.00 40.00
221 John David Booty/15 15.00 40.00

2008 Ultimate Collection Ultimate Signature Jerseys
STATED PRINT RUN 5-45
UAJ2 Jamal Lewis/30 10.00 25.00
UAJ5 Tony Romo/40 40.00 80.00
UAJ8 Eli Manning/35 40.00 80.00
UAJ9 Bob Sanders/40
UAJ10 Eli Manning/35 40.00 80.00
UAJ11 Chad Johnson/35 10.00 25.00
UAJ12 Clinton Portis/25 15.00 40.00
UAJ16 Joseph Addai/30 10.00 25.00
UAJ17 Eli Manning/15 50.00 100.00
UAJ18 Peyton Manning/15 75.00 150.00
UAJ19 Kurt Warner/35 50.00 100.00
UAJ20 Peyton Manning/35 60.00 120.00
UAJ23 Larry Johnson/35 15.00 40.00
UAJ24 Marshawn Lynch/35 15.00 40.00
UAJ25 Peyton Manning/15 75.00 150.00
UAJ26 Peyton Manning/15 100.00 200.00
UAJ27 Roy Williams WR/20 15.00 40.00
UAJ28 Tony Romo/40 40.00 80.00
UAJ29 Marion Barber/30 15.00 40.00
UAJ30 Eli Manning/15 50.00 100.00

2008 Ultimate Collection Ultimate Dual Autograph Jerseys
DUAL AUTO JSY PRINT RUN 5-45
SERIAL #'d UNDER 15 NOT PRICED
5 Ds.Jcksn/Kelly/30 20.00 50.00
6 J.Stewart/L.Johnson/15 25.00 60.00
7 A.Hawk/D.Ware/35 20.00 50.00
10 Lynch/Mendenhall/25 30.00 60.00
11 Stewart/Mendenhall/25 20.00 50.00
12 D.Bowe/R.Williams WR/25 20.00 50.00
13 Bo Jcksn/Mendenhall/25 60.00 120.00
16 D.Thomas/Sweed/45 EXCH 20.00 50.00
17 J.Cmpbll/Grrard/30 EXCH 20.00 50.00
18 Petersn/M.Kelly/15 100.00 200.00
19 F.Tarkenton/J.Booty/35 20.00 50.00
20 C.Henne/B.Griese/25
21 Forte/K.Smth/45 25.00 60.00

2008 Ultimate Collection Ultimate Foursomes Jerseys Gold
STATED PRINT RUN 25-50
*PRIME/15: .5X TO 1.2X BASIC FOUR/50
PRIME PRINT RUN 15 SER.#'d SETS
1 Toml/Ptersn/Parkr/Taylr 15.00 40.00
2 Brdy/P.Mnn/Rmo/Roeth 20.00 50.00
3 Toml/Ptrsn/James/Bush 15.00 40.00
4 Tmlin/Brees/Rivers/Bush 10.00 25.00
5 Hrrisn/Moss/TO/Ch.Jhnsn 8.00 20.00
6 Brady/Eli/Moss/Burress 30.00 80.00
7 Urlch/Hwk/Brschi/Mrrimn 10.00 25.00
8 Shcky/Eli/Watsn/Brady/25 30.00 80.00
9 Eli/P.Mann/Brdy/Rmo 30.00 80.00
10 McNbb/Wrnr/V.Yng/Brees 10.00 25.00
11 Moss/Smith/Wayne/Fitz 8.00 20.00
12 Plmr/Andrsn/Grrard/P.Mann 25.00 60.00
13 Andrsn/P.Mnn/Blgr/Plmr 25.00 60.00
14 Roeth/Ward/P.Mnn/Hrrisn 25.00 60.00
15 Romo/Barber/Owens/Ware 8.00 20.00
16 Gnzlz/Shcky/Gtes/Wtsn 8.00 20.00
17 LJ/Tmlinsn/Lwis/Portis 10.00 25.00
18 Brady/Palmr/Rivers/Cutler 30.00 80.00
20 Wstbrk/Toml/Ptersn/Jcksn 15.00 40.00
21 Grrard/Eli/Roeth/Rdgrs 15.00 40.00
22 McNb/Wstbrk/P.Mnn/Hrsn 25.00 60.00
23 Brady/Marny/Welkr/Moss 30.00 80.00
24 Leinart/Bush/V.Yng/Quinn 6.00 15.00
25 Eli/Roeth/McNbb/Warnr 10.00 25.00
26 LJ/Tomlin/Grant/Bush 10.00 25.00
27 Roeth/Prkr/Andrsn/Lwis 10.00 25.00
28 B.Sndrs/Wdsn/Baly/Reed 10.00 25.00
29 Brdy/Welkr/P.Mnn/Wyne 30.00 80.00

2008 Ultimate Collection Ultimate Foursomes Jerseys Patch Holofoil
*PATCH HOLO/20: .5X TO 1.2X JSY GOLD/50
STATED PRINT RUN 20 SER.#'d SETS
19 McNbb/Cmpbll/Yng/Rssll 10.00 25.00
30 LJ/Tomlin/Wstbrk/Jcksn 12.00 30.00

2008 Ultimate Collection Ultimate Futures Autograph Jerseys
STATED PRINT RUN 15-35
URAJ1 Devin Thomas/35 8.00 20.00
URAJ2 Brian Brohm/15 15.00 40.00
URAJ3 Chad Henne/35 10.00 25.00
URAJ4 Kevin Smith/35 8.00 20.00
URAJ6 DeSean Jackson/35 15.00 40.00
URAJ7 Felix Jones/35 8.00 20.00
URAJ8 Joe Flacco/35 15.00 40.00
URAJ9 John David Booty/35 8.00 20.00
URAJ10 Jonathan Stewart/15 20.00 50.00
URAJ13 Matt Ryan/15 50.00 100.00
URAJ14 Matt Forte/35 12.00 30.00

2008 Ultimate Collection Ultimate Futures Foursomes Jerseys Patch Holofoil
FUTURE FOUR PATCH PRINT RUN 25
*FUTURE FOUR JSY/50: .3X TO .8X PATCH/25
FUTURE FOUR JERSEY PRINT RUN 50
*FUT.FOUR PRIME/25: .4X TO 1X PATCH/25
FUTURE FOUR PRIME PRINT RUN 25
1 McFdd/Jnes/Stew/Mndnhll 6.00 15.00
2 Brohm/Henne/Flacco/Ryan 12.00 30.00
3 Rice/Slaton/Johnson/Smith 5.00 12.00
4 Royal/Kelly/Rice/Johnson 4.00 10.00
5 Brohm/Hnne/Dglas/Mnghm 5.00 12.00
6 Stewart/Forte/Rice/Charles 6.00 15.00
7 Henne/Flacco/Ryan/O'Con 12.00 30.00
8 Jacksn/Douct/Kelly/Mnghm 8.00 20.00
9 Brohm/Sweed/Nlsn/Mndhll 12.00 30.00
10 Dorsey/McFad/Doucet/Jnes 4.00 10.00
11 Forte/Slaton/Johnsn/Mndhll 6.00 15.00
12 Brohm/Hnne/Booty/O'Con 5.00 12.00
13 McFad/Stew/Forte/Johnsn 6.00 15.00
14 Stew/Forte/Johnsn/Mndhll 6.00 15.00
15 McFad/Jacksn/Keller/Ryan 12.00 30.00

2008 Ultimate Collection Ultimate Generations Foursomes Jerseys Gold
STATED PRINT RUN 50 SER.#'d SETS
*SILVER/25: .5X TO 1.2X GOLD QUAD/50
PRIME SILVER PRINT RUN 25
UNPRICED PATCH PRINT RUN 10-20
2 Brady/Hnne/Moss/J.Rce 30.00 80.00
4 Plmr/Andrsn/Roeth/Brdshw 15.00 40.00
5 Sandrs/Toml/McFdd/Craig 15.00 40.00
8 Ryan/McFdd/P.Mnn/Tmlin 15.00 40.00
9 Butkus/Ham/Merrimn/Willis 15.00 40.00
11 Deion/Reed/Plmlu/Blount 10.00 25.00
12 Flacco/Roeth/Syers/Forte 8.00 20.00
14 Tmlinsn/C.Jhnsn/Bo/Forte 8.00 20.00
15 P.Mann/Palmr/Eli/Booty 25.00 60.00
16 K.Smth/B.Sndrs/Emmitt/F.Jns 20.00 50.00
17 Parkr/Mndnhll/Paytn/Forte 25.00 60.00
19 Bush/Young/Booty/Chrles 10.00 25.00
20 Stabch/Aikm/Theis/Cmpbll 20.00 50.00
21 Payton/Sayrs/Forte/Hestr 25.00 60.00
22 Elwy/Ctlr/Roeth/Brdshw 20.00 50.00
24 Palmr/Booty/Sweed/R.Will 8.00 20.00
27 Trkntn/Andrsn/P.Mnn/Ryan
28 Emmtt/F.Jns/O.Andrsn/Jcbs 20.00 50.00
30 Butkus/Urlchr/Ham/Hawk 15.00 40.00
31 Deion/Reed/Pola/Blount 12.00 30.00
32 Favre/Eli/Rodgrs/P.Mann 25.00 60.00
33 Wnslw Jr./Gts/Gnzlz/Kellr 8.00 20.00
34 C.Jhnsn/Eli/Flcco/Sweed 8.00 20.00
37 Elway/Cutlr/Favre/Rodgrs 25.00 60.00
39 Boswrth/Hwk/Butks/Wre 15.00 40.00

2008 Ultimate Collection Ultimate Highlight Signatures
STATED PRINT RUN 5-35
UHA2 LaDainian Tomlinson/15 40.00 80.00
UHA8 Paul Hornung/35 20.00 50.00
UHA10 Bo Jackson/30 40.00 100.00
UHA15 Matt Ryan/15 50.00 100.00
UHA17 Chad Johnson/35 10.00 25.00
UHA18 Tony Romo/20 40.00 80.00
UHA20 Roger Craig/35 15.00 40.00

2008 Ultimate Collection Ultimate Imagery Signatures
STATED PRINT RUN 5-15
UIA1 LaDainian Tomlinson/15 40.00 100.00
UIA2 Dan Marino
UIA5 Peyton Manning/15 75.00 150.00
UIA6 Eli Manning/15 50.00 100.00
UIA10 Dick Butkus/20 30.00 60.00

2008 Ultimate Collection Ultimate Inscriptions
STATED PRINT RUN 10-45
UI1 Bo Jackson/15 40.00 100.00
UI2 Paul Hornung/35 20.00 50.00
UI3 Adrian Peterson/15 125.00 200.00
UI6 Daryl Johnston/35 25.00 50.00
UI9 Chad Johnson/25 12.00 30.00
UI11 Eli Manning/15 50.00 100.00
UI12 LaDainian Tomlinson/15 50.00 100.00
UI13 Steve Young/15 60.00 120.00
UI14 Don Maynard/45 10.00 25.00
UI16 Felix Jones/45 8.00 20.00
UI17 Peyton Manning/15 75.00 150.00
UI18 Marion Barber/25 20.00 50.00
UI19 Joe Greene/25 25.00 60.00
UI20 Brian Bosworth/35 EXCH 40.00 80.00

2008 Ultimate Collection Ultimate Inscriptions Dual
STATED PRINT RUN 5-25
1 B.Jcksn/Bosworth/25 50.00 100.00
3 P.Manning/T.Romo/15 150.00 300.00
6 E.Manning/P.Manning/15 250.00 400.00
8 R.Will WR/C.Johnson/15 15.00 40.00
9 J.Ham/J.Greene/15 60.00 120.00
10 F.Harris/Mendenhall/25 60.00 120.00
11 Sayers/Butkus/15 EXCH 60.00 120.00
14 M.Barber/M.Lynch/15 40.00 80.00
15 P.Hornung/Y.Tittle/15 EXCH

2008 Ultimate Collection Ultimate Legendary Signature Jerseys
STATED PRINT RUN 5-25
SERIAL #'d UNDER 15 NOT PRICED
ULAJ3 Bo Jackson/15 60.00 150.00
ULAJ4 Bo Jackson/15 60.00 150.00
ULAJ7 Dick Butkus/15 EXCH 40.00 100.00
ULAJ8 Brian Bosworth/15 40.00 80.00
ULAJ11 Fran Tarkenton/20 40.00 80.00
ULAJ12 Fran Tarkenton/20 40.00 80.00
ULAJ21 Joe Theismann/25 25.00 60.00
ULAJ22 Joe Theismann/25 25.00 60.00
ULAJ28 Ken Anderson/25 EXCH 12.00 30.00

2008 Ultimate Collection Ultimate Legendary Foursomes Jerseys Gold
STATED PRINT RUN 50 SER.#'d SETS
*PATCH/20: .5X TO 1.2X LEGEND.FOUR/50
PATCH PRINT RUN 10-20
*PRIME/15: .5X TO 1.2X LEGEND.FOUR/50
PRIME PRINT RUN 15 SER.#'d SETS
1 Craig/Jackson/Sanders/Smith 25.00 60.00
5 Smith/Sayers/Sanders/Sims 25.00 60.00
7 Butkus/Syrs/Payton/McMah 40.00 100.00
10 Kelly/McMah/Tarken/Elway

2008 Ultimate Collection Ultimate Legendary Signatures
STATED PRINT RUN 10-30
SERIAL #'d UNDER 15 NOT PRICED
USL3 Bart Starr/20 75.00 150.00
USL4 Y.A. Tittle/30
USL5 Franco Harris/15 40.00 80.00
USL6 Jerry Kramer/15 20.00 50.00
USL11 Paul Hornung/15 20.00 50.00
USL14 Bob Griese/15 30.00 60.00

2008 Ultimate Collection Ultimate Numbers Signatures
STATED PRINT RUN 4-85
SERIAL #'d UNDER 15 NOT PRICED
UNA1 Dick Butkus/51 40.00 80.00
UNA2 Darren McFadden/20
UNA3 LaDainian Tomlinson/21 40.00 80.00
UNA7 Barry Sanders/20 60.00 120.00
UNA8 Chad Johnson/85 10.00 25.00
UNA10 Wes Welker/83 20.00 40.00
UNA13 Peyton Manning/18 75.00 150.00
UNA14 Marshawn Lynch/23 15.00 40.00
UNA16 Roger Craig/33 15.00 40.00
UNA17 Brian Bosworth/55 20.00 50.00
UNA19 Gale Sayers/40 30.00 80.00

2008 Ultimate Collection Ultimate Patch Gold
PATCH PRINT RUN 40 SER.#'d SETS
AH A.J. Hawk 6.00 15.00
AR Aaron Rodgers 15.00 40.00
BC Brodie Croyle 15.00 40.00
BS Bob Sanders 15.00 40.00
CH Chad Henne 5.00 12.00
CJ Chad Johnson 6.00 15.00
CP Clinton Portis 6.00 15.00
CW Cadillac Williams 10.00 25.00
DA Derek Anderson 12.00 30.00
JA Joseph Addai 6.00 15.00
JR Jerry Rice 15.00 40.00
JS Jonathan Stewart 6.00 15.00
KS Kevin Smith 4.00 10.00
LJ Larry Johnson 6.00 15.00
LT LaDainian Tomlinson 10.00 25.00
MB Marion Barber 6.00 15.00
RM Rashard Mendenhall 4.00 10.00
RW Roy Williams WR 6.00 15.00

2008 Ultimate Collection Ultimate Patch Autographs
STATED PRINT RUN 5-25
SERIAL #'d UNDER 15 NOT PRICED
UPAD Joseph Addai/15 15.00 40.00
UPAH A.J. Hawk/20 15.00 40.00
UPAR Aaron Rodgers/20
UPBC Brodie Croyle/20 15.00 40.00
UPBS Bob Sanders/20
UPCH Chad Henne/15 20.00 50.00
UPCP Clinton Portis/15 15.00 40.00
UPDA Derek Anderson/15 12.00 30.00
UPDB Dick Butkus/15 50.00 100.00
UPEM Eli Manning/15 50.00 100.00
UPFJ Felix Jones/15 12.00 30.00
UPGS Gale Sayers/20 40.00 80.00
UPJF Joe Flacco/25 75.00 150.00
UPJO Chad Johnson/15 12.00 30.00
UPJS Jonathan Stewart/25 25.00 60.00
UPKS Kevin Smith/25 15.00 40.00
UPKW Kurt Warner/20 35.00 60.00
UPLJ Larry Johnson/15 15.00 40.00
UPMB Marion Barber/20 15.00 40.00
UPME Rashard Mendenhall/20 12.00 30.00
UPML Marshawn Lynch/20 20.00 50.00
UPMR Matt Ryan/15 60.00 120.00
UPPM Peyton Manning/15 75.00 150.00
UPRW Roy Williams WR/20 15.00 40.00
UPTR Tony Romo/15 50.00 100.00
UPWI Kellen Winslow Sr./15 15.00 40.00

2008 Ultimate Collection Ultimate Patch Prime Silver
PRIME PRINT RUN 15 SER.#'d SETS
UPAP Adrian Peterson 15.00 40.00
UPBF Brett Favre 30.00 80.00
UPBJ Bo Jackson 20.00 50.00
UPDB Dick Butkus 20.00 50.00
UPEM Eli Manning 12.00 30.00
UPES Emmitt Smith 25.00 60.00
UPGS Gale Sayers 15.00 40.00
UPJF Joe Flacco 10.00 25.00
UPJK Jim Kelly 15.00 40.00
UPJR Jerry Rice 30.00 80.00
UPKW Kurt Warner 12.00 30.00
UPLT LaDainian Tomlinson 15.00 40.00
UPMC Darren McFadden 5.00 12.00
UPMR Matt Ryan 15.00 40.00
UPPM Peyton Manning 40.00 100.00
UPRM Randy Moss 12.00 30.00
UPSA Barry Sanders 25.00 60.00
UPSY Steve Young 20.00 50.00
UPTB Tom Brady 50.00 120.00
UPTR Tony Romo 12.00 30.00
UPWI Kellen Winslow Sr. 12.00 30.00

2008 Ultimate Collection Ultimate Rookie Autographs Trios
ATED PRINT RUN 15-35
1 McFad/Stewart/Mndhll/15 50.00 100.00
2 Thomas/Hardy/Kelly/25 15.00 40.00
4 Booty/Ellis/Rvrs/25 12.00 30.00
5 Flacco/Ryan/Henne/15 100.00 200.00
6 Bty/Brhm/Wdsn/25 15.00 40.00
7 Jcksn/Douct/Kelly/25 25.00 60.00
9 Forte/Smith/Mendenhall/35 50.00 120.00
11 C.Jhn/K.Smth/Frte/25 40.00 100.00
12 Rice/Slaton/Charles/35 40.00 100.00
14 Kllr/Dvis/Crlsn/25 12.00 30.00
15 Stewart/Smith/Jones/25 30.00 80.00

2008 Ultimate Collection Ultimate Rookie Big Materials
STATED PRINT RUN 40 SER.#'d SETS
URBM3 Chad Henne 10.00 25.00
URBM4 Chris Johnson 10.00 25.00
URBM6 Darren McFadden 8.00 20.00
URBM7 DeSean Jackson 15.00 40.00
URBM8 Early Doucet 10.00 25.00
URBM9 Felix Jones 8.00 20.00
URBM12 Joe Flacco 15.00 40.00
URBM13 Jonathan Stewart 20.00 50.00
URBM14 Kevin Smith 8.00 20.00
URBM15 Malcolm Kelly 8.00 20.00
URBM17 Matt Forte 12.00 30.00
URBM18 Matt Ryan 15.00 40.00
URBM19 Rashard Mendenhall 8.00 20.00
URBM21 Steve Slaton 8.00 20.00

2008 Ultimate Collection Ultimate Seasons Jerseys Autographs
STATED PRINT RUN 5-20
UNPRICED PATCH PRINT RUN 5-10
SERIAL #'d UNDER 15 NOT PRICED
*PLAYERS W/MULTIPLE CARDS: SAME PRICE
USEA5 Joe Flacco/20 40.00 80.00
USEA6 Joe Flacco/20 40.00 80.00
USEA7 Joe Flacco/20 40.00 80.00
USEA13 Felix Jones/15 12.00 30.00
USEA14 Felix Jones/15 12.00 30.00
USEA15 Felix Jones/15 12.00 30.00
USEA16 Felix Jones/15 12.00 30.00
USEA23 Chad Johnson/15 10.00 25.00
USEA24 Chad Johnson/15 10.00 25.00
USEA33 Rashard Mendenhall/15 12.00 30.00
USEA34 Rashard Mendenhall/15 12.00 30.00
USEA41 Jack Ham/15 50.00 100.00
USEA42 Jack Ham/15 50.00 100.00
USEA43 Jack Ham/15 50.00 100.00
USEA44 Jack Ham/15 50.00 100.00
USEA45 Fran Tarkenton/15 40.00 80.00
USEA46 Fran Tarkenton/15 40.00 80.00
USEA47 Fran Tarkenton/15 40.00 80.00
USEA48 Fran Tarkenton/15 40.00 80.00
USEA49 Matt Forte/15 40.00 100.00
USEA50 Matt Forte/15 40.00 100.00
USEA53 Tony Romo/15 50.00 100.00
USEA54 Tony Romo/15 50.00 100.00
USEA55 Tony Romo/15 50.00 100.00
USEA57 Brian Brohm/15 12.00 30.00
USEA65 Paul Hornung/15 20.00 50.00
USEA66 Paul Hornung/15 20.00 50.00
USEA67 Paul Hornung/15 20.00 50.00
USEA68 Paul Hornung/15 20.00 50.00
USEA69 Clinton Portis/15 20.00 50.00
USEA70 Clinton Portis/15 20.00 50.00
USEA71 Clinton Portis/15 20.00 50.00
USEA72 Clinton Portis/15 20.00 50.00
USEA73 Kurt Warner/15 40.00 100.00
USEA74 Kurt Warner/15 40.00 100.00
USEA75 Kurt Warner/15 40.00 100.00
USEA76 Kurt Warner/15 40.00 100.00
USEA81 Eli Manning/15 50.00 100.00
USEA82 Eli Manning/15 50.00 100.00
USEA83 Eli Manning/15 50.00 100.00
USEA84 Eli Manning/15 50.00 100.00
USEA95 Paul Hornung/15 20.00 50.00
USEA96 Paul Hornung/15 20.00 50.00
USEA97 Dick Butkus/15 40.00 100.00
USEA98 Dick Butkus/15 40.00 100.00
USEA99 Dick Butkus/15 40.00 100.00
USEA100 Dick Butkus/15 40.00 100.00

2008 Ultimate Collection Ultimate Signature Plays
STATED PRINT RUN 5-20
SERIAL #'d UNDER 15 NOT PRICED
USP4 Bert Jones/15 15.00 40.00
USP5 Billy Sims/15 20.00 50.00
USP6 Bo Jackson/15 40.00 100.00
USP9 Brian Bosworth/15 40.00 80.00
USP14 Rashard Mendenhall/15 10.00 25.00
USP17 Felix Jones/20 10.00 25.00
USP19 Don Maynard/15 12.00 30.00
USP27 Marshawn Lynch/15 12.00 30.00
USP34 Gale Sayers/15 40.00 80.00
USP35 Y.A. Tittle/15 15.00 40.00

2008 Ultimate Collection Ultimate Signatures
STATED PRINT RUN 15-35
US1 Adrian Peterson/15 125.00 200.00
US2 Roy Williams WR/20 15.00 40.00
US3 Eli Manning/20 50.00 100.00
US4 LaDainian Tomlinson/15 50.00 100.00
US5 Peyton Manning/20 75.00 150.00
US6 Peyton Manning/20 75.00 150.00
US7 Adrian Peterson/15 125.00 200.00
US8 LaDainian Tomlinson/15 30.00 80.00
US10 Larry Johnson/25 15.00 40.00
US11 Clinton Portis/30 15.00 40.00
US12 Tony Romo/35 40.00 80.00
US13 Eli Manning/20 50.00 100.00
US14 Tony Romo/35 40.00 80.00
US15 Chad Johnson/25 8.00 20.00

2008 Ultimate Collection Ultimate Signatures Duals
STATED PRINT RUN 10-35
SERIAL #'d UNDER 15 NOT PRICED
2 C.Henne/B.Brohm/25 20.00 50.00
6 J.Flacco/C.Henne/25 40.00 80.00
7 D.Butkus/A.Hawk/25 50.00 100.00
8 B.Starr/B.Brohm/15 75.00 150.00
9 A.Manning/E.Manning/25 60.00 120.00
10 P.Manning/M.Ryan/15 175.00 300.00
11 J.Lewis/D.Anderson/25 20.00 50.00
12 P.Manning/E.Manning/15 150.00 250.00
13 T.Edwards/M.Lynch/15 25.00 60.00
16 J.Stewart/F.Jones/25 15.00 40.00
17 T.Aikman/T.Romo/15 125.00 200.00
18 J.Stewart/R.Mendenhall/25 15.00 40.00
19 B.Brohm/J.Nelson/25 40.00 80.00
20 D.Maynard/W.Welker/35 30.00 60.00

2008 Ultimate Collection Ultimate Signatures Triples
STATED PRINT RUN 5-35
SERIAL #'d UNDER 15 NOT PRICED
1 Henne/Flacco/Booty/25 40.00 80.00
2 Tark/Theis/Andsn/25 40.00 80.00
3 Ch.Jhn/Ds.Jck/Bw/35 25.00 60.00
5 Ttle/O.Andrsn/Eli/25 50.00 100.00
7 Shcky/Wins.Sr./Clark/25

2008 Ultimate Collection Ultimate Six Jerseys
COMMON CARD 20.00 50.00
STATED PRINT RUN 20 SER.#'d SETS
UNPRICED PATCH PRINT RUN 5
1 McF/Tmln/Ryn/Mnn/Klly/Jhns 25.00 60.00
2 Jhns/Jcks/Dcet/Ric/Bldn/Klly 20.00 50.00
5 Ric/Mss/Win/Win/P.Mnn/Eli 40.00 100.00
6 Hrn/Brh/Fvre/Stb/Aik/Rmo 30.00 80.00
8 Snds/Smt/Pyt/Frt/Smt/Jnes 60.00 150.00
9 Hrrs/Prkr/Mnd/Smt/Brbr/Jns 25.00 60.00
10 Brdy/O'Cn/Trk/Bty/Rdg/Brh 10.00 25.00
13 Pyt/Sms/Smt/Tml/Pet/McF 30.00 80.00
16 Yng/Rce/Brd/Ms/Cmp/Thm 50.00 120.00
18 Jhns/Cld/Wrd/Swd/Hlt/Avry 12.00 30.00
19 Kly/Edw/Fvr/Rdgr/Stbc/Aik 60.00 120.00
22 Wstbk/Jns/Hrs/Prkr/Crg/Gre 10.00 25.00
23 Mnn/Eli/Brd/Rth/Rdg/Brhm 40.00 100.00
24 Mnn/Flco/Plm/Ryn/Rth/Brh 20.00 50.00
25 Bsrt/Btk/Wlis/Hwk/Lmb/Sms 20.00 50.00
26 Stb/Aik/Rmo/Jns/Man/Flco 20.00 50.00
27 Aik/Rmo/Plmr/And/Mss/Rce 30.00 80.00
28 Syr/Frt/Sms/Snd/Lmbt/Hwk 25.00 60.00
29 Snd/Smt/Jck/McF/Pyt/Frt 50.00 120.00
31 Hrs/Mnd/Snd/Smt/Brbr/Jns 25.00 60.00
34 Btk/Hwk/Sng/Url/Blnt/Snds 20.00 50.00
35 Btk/Bsr/Lmbr/Mrm/Hwk/Wil 20.00 50.00
36 Mn/Brh/Tml/Frte/Mss/Swd 40.00 100.00
37 Smt/Jck/Mss/Swd/Hlt/Thm 20.00 50.00
38 Ptrs/McF/Prk/Mnd/Brbr/Jns 10.00 25.00
39 Brdy/Hne/Rdg/Brh/Eli/Ryn 30.00 80.00
42 Mnd/Brb/Frte/LJ/Jhn/Ptrn 30.00 80.00

2009 Ultimate Collection
1-150 VET/LEGEND PRINT RUN 375
151-200 ROOKIE PRINT RUN 375
201-220 ROOKIE AU PRINT RUN 99-399
EXCH EXPIRATION: 2/3/2012
1 Larry Fitzgerald 1.50 4.00
2 Anquan Boldin 1.25 3.00
3 Steve Breaston 1.50 4.00
4 Adrian Wilson 1.25 3.00
5 Kurt Warner 1.50 4.00
6 Michael Turner 1.25 3.00
7 Roddy White 1.25 3.00
8 Tony Gonzalez 1.50 4.00
9 Matt Ryan 1.50 4.00
10 Ray Rice 1.25 3.00
11 Ed Reed 1.50 4.00
12 Joe Flacco 1.50 4.00
13 Marshawn Lynch 1.50 4.00
14 Terrell Owens 1.50 4.00
15 Lee Evans 1.50 4.00
16 Trent Edwards 1.25 3.00
17 DeAngelo Williams 1.25 3.00
18 Jonathan Stewart 1.25 3.00
19 Steve Smith 1.50 4.00
20 Julius Peppers 1.50 4.00
21 Jake Delhomme 1.25 3.00
22 Matt Forte 1.25 3.00
23 Devin Hester 1.50 4.00
24 Jay Cutler 1.25 3.00
25 Chad Johnson 1.25 3.00
26 Carson Palmer 1.50 4.00
27 Jamal Lewis 1.50 4.00
28 Braylon Edwards 1.25 3.00
29 Brady Quinn 1.25 3.00
30 Marion Barber 1.50 4.00
31 Jason Witten 1.50 4.00
32 DeMarcus Ware 1.50 4.00
33 Tony Romo 1.50 4.00
34 Brandon Marshall 1.50 4.00
35 Eddie Royal 1.25 3.00
36 Tony Scheffler 1.25 3.00
37 Brian Dawkins 1.25 3.00
38 Kyle Orton 1.25 3.00
39 Kevin Smith 1.25 3.00
40 Calvin Johnson 2.00 5.00
41 Ryan Grant 1.50 4.00
42 Greg Jennings 1.25 3.00
43 Donald Driver 1.50 4.00
44 Charles Woodson 2.00 5.00
45 Aaron Rodgers 4.00 10.00
46 Steve Slaton 1.25 3.00
47 Andre Johnson 1.50 4.00
48 Matt Schaub 1.25 3.00
49 Reggie Wayne 1.50 4.00
50 Anthony Gonzalez 1.25 3.00
51 Peyton Manning 5.00 12.00
52 Bob Sanders 1.50 4.00
53 Maurice Jones-Drew 1.25 3.00
54 David Garrard 1.25 3.00
55 Dwayne Bowe 1.50 4.00
56 Matt Cassel 1.25 3.00
57 Ronnie Brown 1.25 3.00
58 Ted Ginn Jr. 1.25 3.00
59 Chad Pennington 1.25 3.00
60 Adrian Peterson 2.00 5.00
61 Bernard Berrian 1.25 3.00
62 Brett Favre 4.00 10.00
63 Wes Welker 1.50 4.00
64 Randy Moss 1.50 4.00
65 Tom Brady 6.00 15.00
66 Pierre Thomas 1.25 3.00
67 Marques Colston 1.25 3.00
68 Drew Brees 2.00 5.00
69 Brandon Jacobs 1.25 3.00
70 Eli Manning 1.50 4.00
71 Thomas Jones 1.25 3.00
72 Darren McFadden 2.00 5.00
73 JaMarcus Russell 1.25 3.00
74 Brian Westbrook 1.25 3.00
75 DeSean Jackson 1.50 4.00
76 Donovan McNabb 1.50 4.00
77 Willie Parker 1.25 3.00
78 Hines Ward 1.50 4.00
79 Santonio Holmes 1.25 3.00
80 James Harrison 2.00 5.00
81 Ben Roethlisberger 2.00 5.00
82 Troy Polamalu 2.00 5.00
83 LaDainian Tomlinson 2.00 5.00
84 Vincent Jackson 1.25 3.00
85 Philip Rivers 2.00 5.00
86 Frank Gore 1.50 4.00
87 Patrick Willis 1.50 4.00
88 Shaun Hill 1.25 3.00
89 T.J. Houshmandzadeh 1.25 3.00
90 Matt Hasselbeck 1.25 3.00
91 Steven Jackson 1.25 3.00
92 Donnie Avery 1.25 3.00
93 Marc Bulger 1.25 3.00
94 Derrick Ward 1.25 3.00
95 Antonio Bryant 1.25 3.00
96 Chris Johnson 1.25 3.00
97 Clinton Portis 1.25 3.00
98 Santana Moss 1.50 4.00
99 Chris Cooley 1.25 3.00
100 Jason Campbell 1.25 3.00
101 Barry Sanders 4.00 10.00
102 Emmitt Smith 4.00 10.00
103 Dan Marino 5.00 12.00
104 Fred Biletnikoff 2.50 6.00
105 Jerry Rice 5.00 12.00
106 Bo Jackson 3.00 8.00
107 Earl Campbell 2.50 6.00
108 Paul Hornung 2.50 6.00
109 Roger Staubach 3.00 8.00
110 Bob Griese 2.50 6.00
111 Bob Lilly 2.00 5.00
112 Billy Sims 2.00 5.00
113 Steve Young 3.00 8.00
114 Alex Karras 2.00 5.00
115 Deacon Jones 2.00 5.00
116 Ken Anderson 2.00 5.00
117 Steve Largent 2.50 6.00
118 Don Maynard 2.00 5.00
119 Troy Aikman 3.00 8.00
120 Alan Page 1.50 4.00
121 Lawrence Taylor 2.50 6.00
122 Harry Carson 1.50 4.00
123 Roger Craig 2.00 5.00
124 Darrell Green 2.00 5.00
125 Randall Cunningham 2.00 5.00
126 Lem Barney 1.50 4.00
127 Donnie Shell 1.50 4.00
128 Daryl Johnston 2.00 5.00
129 Terry Bradshaw 3.00 8.00
130 Franco Harris 2.50 6.00
131 Roman Gabriel 1.50 4.00
132 Rocky Bleier 2.00 5.00
133 Joe Theismann 2.50 6.00
134 Phil Simms 2.00 5.00
135 Jim Kelly 2.50 6.00
136 Kellen Winslow Sr. 2.00 5.00
137 L.C. Greenwood 1.50 4.00
138 Warren Moon 2.50 6.00
139 Tim Brown 2.50 6.00
140 Doug Flutie 2.00 5.00
141 Thurman Thomas 2.00 5.00
142 Gale Sayers 2.50 6.00
143 Fran Tarkenton 2.50 6.00
144 Chuck Howley 1.50 4.00
145 Randy White 2.50 6.00
146 Archie Manning 2.00 5.00
147 Bubba Smith 1.50 4.00
148 Rod Woodson 2.00 5.00
149 Cliff Harris 2.00 5.00
150 Drew Bledsoe 2.00 5.00
151 Aaron Maybin RC 2.00 5.00
152 Julian Edelman RC 15.00 30.00
153 Tom Brandstater RC 2.00 5.00
154 Brian Cushing RC 1.50 4.00
155 Rey Maualuga RC 2.50 6.00
156 Clay Matthews RC 6.00 15.00
157 Brian Orakpo RC 2.00 5.00
158 B.J. Raji RC 2.00 5.00
159 Johnny Knox RC 2.00 5.00
160 Eugene Monroe RC 1.50 4.00
161 Louis Murphy RC 1.50 4.00
162 Tyson Jackson RC 1.50 4.00
163 Stephen McGee RC 1.50 4.00
164 Darius Butler RC 2.00 5.00
165 Brandon Tate RC 2.00 5.00
166 Derrick Williams RC 1.50 4.00
167 Mike Wallace RC 2.50 6.00
168 Mike Thomas RC 1.50 4.00
169 Glen Coffee RC 1.50 4.00
170 Jason Smith RC 1.50 4.00
171 Andre Brown RC 2.00 5.00
172 Robert Ayers RC 1.50 4.00
173 Malcolm Jenkins RC 1.50 4.00
174 Patrick Turner RC 1.50 4.00
175 Travis Beckum RC 1.50 4.00
176 Chase Coffman RC 1.50 4.00
177 James Laurinaitis RC 1.50 4.00
178 Curtis Painter RC 1.50 4.00
179 Duke Robinson RC 1.50 4.00
180 Andre Smith RC 1.50 4.00
181 Larry English RC 2.00 5.00
182 Michael Johnson RC 1.50 4.00
183 Patrick Chung RC 1.50 4.00
184 Vontae Davis RC 1.50 4.00
185 Brooks Foster RC 1.50 4.00
186 Rashad Jennings RC 2.00 5.00
187 William Moore RC 1.50 4.00
188 Evander Hood RC 2.50 6.00
189 Peria Jerry RC 1.50 4.00
190 Michael Oher RC 2.50 6.00
191 Alex Mack RC 1.50 4.00
192 Louis Delmas RC 2.00 5.00
193 Alphonso Smith RC 1.50 4.00
194 Richard Quinn RC 2.00 5.00
195 Fili Moala RC 1.50 4.00
196 Deon Butler RC 1.50 4.00
197 Brian Hartline RC 2.50 6.00
198 Mike Goodson RC 2.00 5.00
199 Austin Collie RC 1.50 4.00
200 Javon Ringer RC 1.50 4.00
201 M.Stafford AU/99 RC 50.00 120.00
202 Mark Sanchez AU/99 RC 25.00 60.00
203 Chris Wells AU/99 RC 20.00 50.00
204 K.Moreno AU/99 RC 8.00 20.00
205 M.Crabtree AU/99 RC 12.00 30.00
206 D.Heyward-Bey AU/99 RC 12.00 30.00
207 Donald Brown AU/99 RC 8.00 20.00
208 Percy Harvin AU/399 RC 4.00 10.00
209 Jeremy Maclin AU/399 RC 5.00 12.00
210 Josh Freeman AU/99 RC 6.00 15.00
211 B.Pettigrew AU/399 RC 4.00 10.00
212 Aaron Curry AU/399 RC 6.00 15.00
213 Kenny Britt AU/399 RC 6.00 15.00
214 LeSean McCoy AU/199 RC 25.00 50.00
215 Pat White AU/399 RC 5.00 12.00
216 Shonn Greene AU/399 RC 4.00 10.00
217 Hakeem Nicks AU/399 RC 5.00 12.00
219 Juaquin Iglesias AU/399 RC 4.00 10.00
220 Nate Davis AU/399 RC 4.00 10.00

2009 Ultimate Collection Ultimate Rookie Signatures Blue
*BLUE INK/35: .6X TO 1.5X BASE AU RC/399
*BLUE INK/35: .4X TO 1X BASE AU RC/99-199
*BLUE INK/15: .5X TO 1.2X BASE AU RC/99
BLUE INK PRINT RUN 15-35

2009 Ultimate Collection 1997 Legends Autographs
EXCH EXPIRATION: 2/3/2012
196 Bruce Smith 125.00 250.00
197 Tim Brown 50.00 100.00
198 Dan Marino 600.00 1000.00
200 Darrell Green
201 Phil Simms 500.00 800.00
202 Lawrence Taylor EXCH 100.00 175.00
204 Harry Carson 20.00 50.00
205 Merlin Olsen 30.00 80.00
206 Earl Campbell 90.00 150.00
207 Randall Cunningham 20.00 50.00
208 Warren Moon 50.00 120.00
211 Doug Flutie 40.00 100.00
212 Drew Bledsoe 30.00 80.00
213 Herman Moore 20.00 50.00
214 Andre Reed 20.00 50.00
215 Mike Alstott 25.00 60.00
216 Christian Okoye 20.00 50.00

2009 Ultimate Collection Ultimate Dual Autograph Jerseys
DUAL JSY AU PRINT RUN 5-20
DSJBC L.Briggs/A.Curry/20 20.00 40.00
DSJBP Brooks/J.Porter/20 15.00 40.00
DSJFD N.Davis/J.Freeman/20 25.00 50.00

2009 Ultimate Collection Ultimate Enshrinement Signatures
ENSHRINEMENT AU PRINT RUN 10-25
EAP Alan Page/25 12.00 30.00
EDM Don Maynard/15 15.00 40.00
EEC Earl Campbell/15 20.00 50.00
EGS Gale Sayers/15 40.00 80.00
EHC Harry Carson/25 12.00 30.00
EKW Kellen Winslow Sr./15 20.00 50.00
ELB Lem Barney/25 12.00 30.00
EMS Mike Singletary/15 20.00 50.00
ESL Steve Largent/15 30.00 60.00

2009 Ultimate Collection Ultimate Enshrinements Dual Signatures
DUAL AU PRINT RUN 5-25
EDJO M.Olsen/D.Jones/15 60.00 100.00
EDLM S.Largent/Maynard/15 15.00 40.00
EDPJ A.Page/D.Jones/25 20.00 50.00
EDWB L.Barney/Woodson/15 50.00 100.00

2009 Ultimate Collection Ultimate Future Six Jerseys
STATED PRINT RUN 99 SER.#'d SETS
*GOLD/25: .5X TO 1.2X BASIC SIX JSY
*PATCH/25: .8X TO 2X BASIC SIX JSY
1 Cof/McC/Grn/Wll/Rng/Mrn 5.00 12.00
2 McG/Bmr/Stf/Snch/Frm/Dv 10.00 25.00
3 Crb/Hrv/Mcl/Hyw/Brd/Brt 3.00 8.00
4 Igl/Hyw/Mcl/Msg/Hrv/Crb 3.00 8.00
5 Cry/Snc/Hyw/Stf/Jck 3.00 8.00
6 Mrn/Brn/Wls/Grn/McC/Brn 5.00 12.00
7 Stf/Ptg/Hyw/Mrn/Jck/Smh 10.00 25.00
8 Bmr/Brn/Brd/Crb/Dv/Cof 2.50 6.00
9 Crb/Brn/Hrv/Wls/Hyw/Mrn 2.00 5.00
10 Wlm/Ptg/Stf/Crb/Cof/Dvs 8.00 20.00
11 Stf/Ptg/Wlm/Bmr/Brd/Brn 10.00 25.00
12 Brd/Wlm/Crb/Hrv/Msg/Rbk 2.00 5.00
13 Rbk/Mcl/Wlc/Hyw/Igl/Trn 8.00 20.00
14 Trn/Wht/Thm/Hyw/Crb/Rbk 2.00 5.00
15 Snc/Dvs/Frm/Stf/Bmr/Wht 10.00 25.00

2009 Ultimate Collection Ultimate Futures Autograph Jerseys
STATED PRINT RUN 20 SER.#'d SETS
FSJAC Aaron Curry 10.00 25.00
FSJBP Brandon Pettigrew 6.00 15.00
FSJBR Brian Robiskie 6.00 15.00
FSJCW Chris Wells 6.00 15.00
FSJDB Donald Brown 6.00 15.00
FSJDH Darrius Heyward-Bey 10.00 25.00
FSJHN Hakeem Nicks 8.00 20.00
FSJJF Josh Freeman 6.00 15.00
FSJJI Juaquin Iglesias 6.00 15.00
FSJKB Kenny Britt 10.00 25.00
FSJKM Knowshon Moreno 6.00 15.00
FSJLM LeSean McCoy 25.00 60.00
FSJMC Michael Crabtree 20.00 50.00
FSJMS Matthew Stafford 75.00 150.00
FSJND Nate Davis 6.00 15.00
FSJPH Percy Harvin 6.00 15.00
FSJPT Patrick Turner 6.00 15.00
FSJSA Mark Sanchez 30.00 80.00
FSJSG Shonn Greene 6.00 15.00
FSJSM Stephen McGee 6.00 15.00

2009 Ultimate Collection Ultimate Generations Signature
STATED PRINT RUN 5-25
HHLB Lrints/Hwk/Ham/Brks/25 30.00 60.00
LWCT Crry/LT/Lwis/Wllis/25
SJWJ Smth//Jns/Wllm/Jcksn/25

2009 Ultimate Collection Ultimate Generations Six Jerseys
STATED PRINT RUN 35-75
*GOLD/25: .5X TO 1.2X BASIC SIX JSY
*PATCH/15: .6X TO 1.5X BASIC SIX JSY
1 Fvr/Klly/Snch/Stff/Man/Brd 25.00 60.00
2 Ptrs/Smt/Hrr/Mrn/Hrn/Crg 20.00 50.00
3 Rd/Myn/Biltn/Crbt/Mss/Lrgt 15.00 40.00
4 Pge/Hyn/Smth/Jns/Wht/Jck 8.00 20.00
5 Cry/Btk/Ham/LT/Wls/Lwis 15.00 40.00
6 Brs/Eli/Trk/Mnn/Stb/Brds 25.00 60.00
7 Smt/Crg/Tml/Ptrs/Wtb/Snd 20.00 50.00
8 Prts/Wlls/Ptr/Brwn/Brb/Mrn 12.00 30.00
9 Mrn/Sm/Mc/Wl/Th/Snd/35 15.00 40.00
10 Hyw/Bldn/Hrv/Crbt/Mss/Jhn 20.00 50.00
11 Jhns/Brt/Mcln/Msg/Ftz/Jhns 10.00 25.00
12 Kly/Stff/Mnn/Sms/Stb/Brdy 15.00 40.00
13 Trn/Jhn/Crbt/Wyn/Rbk/Jhn 15.00 40.00
14 Sms/Eli/Bmr/McG/Rmo/Aik 12.00 30.00
15 Grs/Pnn/Mrn/Stb/Rmo/Aik 15.00 40.00
16 Picc/Smt/Jns/Brbr/Frt/Pyt 40.00 100.00
17 Fvr/Mrn/Snch/Ryn/Stf/Mnn 25.00 60.00
18 Crg/Yng/Rce/Crb/Cle/Dvs 20.00 50.00
19 Rd/Kly/Evns/Lyn/Thm/Edw 8.00 20.00
20 Rth/Hrrs/Wrd/Swn/Brd/Prk 12.00 30.00
21 Ptr/Snd/Jhn/Mrn/Hrn/Pyt 25.00 60.00
22 Ham/LT/Sng/Lws/Brk/Hwk 12.00 30.00
23 Frm/Snc/Eli/Wrn/Stf/Rvrs 15.00 40.00
25 Hrs/Wrd/Swn/Wlc/Mnd/Prk
26 Hyw/Blt/Ric/Swn/Crbt/Wlc
27 Smt/Brb/Jck/Mc/Snd/Smt/35 20.00 50.00
28 Snd/Sms/Pic/Smt/Frt/Pytn 25.00 60.00
30 Snc/McN/Frm/Rthl/Stf/Brdy 20.00 50.00
31 Rmo/Aik/Kly/Edw/McN/Cng 15.00 40.00
33 Snd/Jhn/Cmp/Smt/Frt/Pytn 25.00 60.00
34 Snd/Picc/Cmp/Smt/Syr/Hrn 30.00 80.00
35 Rd/Crtr/Myn/Blt/Rce/Lrg 12.00 30.00

2009 Ultimate Collection Ultimate Inscriptions
STATED PRINT RUN 20 SER.#'d SETS
EXCH EXPIRATION: 2/3/2012
IAC Aaron Curry 15.00 40.00
IAH Albert Haynesworth 10.00 25.00
IAP Alan Page 15.00 40.00
IBR Ben Roethlisberger 60.00 120.00
IBW Brian Westbrook 12.00 30.00
IDG Darrell Green
IDJ Deacon Jones 25.00 50.00
IEC Earl Campbell 40.00 80.00
IJK Jim Kelly 30.00 60.00
IKM Knowshon Moreno 8.00 20.00
ILB Lance Briggs 25.00 50.00
IMC Michael Crabtree 40.00 80.00
IMS Matthew Stafford 40.00 100.00
IPM Peyton Manning 125.00 250.00
IRC Randall Cunningham 25.00 50.00
IRL Ronnie Lott 40.00 80.00
ISA Mark Sanchez 25.00 60.00
ITB Tim Brown 15.00 40.00

2009 Ultimate Collection Ultimate Inscriptions Dual
DUAL AUTO PRINT RUN 5-35
HM J.Maclin/P.Harvin/35 25.00 60.00
LZ S.Largent/J.Zorn/35 40.00 80.00

2009 Ultimate Collection Ultimate Legendary Signatures
STATED PRINT RUN 10-45
LAK Alex Karras/35 EXCH 12.00 30.00
LAP Alan Page/40 10.00 25.00
LTB Tim Brown/35 15.00 40.00
LEC Earl Campbell/35 20.00 50.00
LJK Jim Kelly/20 30.00 60.00
LLB Lem Barney/50 10.00 25.00
LLT Lawrence Taylor/20
LPS Phil Simms/15 12.00 30.00
LRW Randy White/45 15.00 40.00
LWO Rod Woodson/35 EXCH 25.00 50.00

2009 Ultimate Collection Ultimate Legendary Six Jerseys
SIX JERSEY PRINT RUN 35-75
1 Mar/Ths/Elw/Stb/Brd/Mn/75 30.00 60.00
2 Snd/Cmp/Syr/Tml/Crg/Pyt/35 30.00 60.00
5 Mar/Trk/Elw/Stb/Brd/Aik/75 30.00 60.00
6 Mar/Kel/Ths/Elw/Sim/Cun/35 30.00 80.00
7 Snd/Elw/Hrn/Stb/Aik/Pyt/30 30.00 80.00
15 Lil/Smt/Rce/Crg/Yng/Aik/35 30.00 60.00
17 Hrs/Thm/Snd/Cmp/Smt/Cr/35 30.00 60.00
20 Yng/Crg/Smt/Aik/BrdHrs/35 30.00 60.00

2009 Ultimate Collection Ultimate Loyality Signatures
STATED PRINT RUN 10-45
LYAK Alex Karras/25 15.00 40.00
LYBG Bob Griese/20 25.00 60.00
LYDJ Daryl Johnston/35
LYFB Fred Biletnikoff/25 20.00 50.00
LYGS Gale Sayers/25 30.00 60.00
LYHC Harry Carson/35 12.00 30.00
LYJH Jack Ham/20 15.00 40.00
LYJK Jim Kelly/15 30.00 80.00
LYJT Joe Theismann/45 20.00 50.00
LYKR Jerry Kramer/35 15.00 40.00
LYKW Kellen Winslow Sr./45 12.00 30.00
LYLB Lem Barney/35 12.00 30.00
LYLG L.C. Greenwood/25 12.00 30.00
LYLT Lawrence Taylor/25
LYMS Mike Singletary/25 20.00 50.00
LYPH Paul Hornung/35 15.00 40.00
LYPM Peyton Manning/25 75.00 150.00
LYRB Rocky Bleier/45 15.00 40.00
LYRL Ray Lewis/25 50.00 100.00
LYRW Reggie Wayne/25 12.00 30.00
LYSL Steve Largent/25 20.00 50.00
LYWH Randy White/25 20.00 50.00

2009 Ultimate Collection Ultimate Patch
STATED PRINT RUN 10-50
U1 Adrian Peterson 8.00 20.00
U2 LaDainian Tomlinson 8.00 20.00
U3 Randy Moss 6.00 15.00
U4 Peyton Manning 20.00 50.00
U5 Eli Manning 6.00 15.00
U6 Tony Romo 6.00 15.00
U7 Ben Roethlisberger 8.00 20.00
U8 Matt Ryan 10.00 25.00
U9 Pat White 4.00 10.00
U10 A.J. Hawk 5.00 12.00
U11 Tom Brady 25.00 60.00
U12 Donovan McNabb 6.00 15.00
U13 Patrick Willis 8.00 20.00
U14 Ray Lewis 8.00 20.00
U15 Brett Favre 15.00 40.00
U18 Brandon Jacobs 5.00 12.00
U19 Calvin Johnson 8.00 20.00
U20 Reggie Bush 5.00 12.00
U21 Drew Brees 8.00 20.00
U22 Matthew Stafford 15.00 40.00
U23 Knowshon Moreno 3.00 8.00
U24 Mark Sanchez 3.00 8.00
U25 Josh Freeman 3.00 8.00
U26 Darrius Heyward-Bey 5.00 12.00
U27 Michael Crabtree 5.00 12.00
U28 Donald Brown 3.00 8.00
U29 Chris Wells 3.00 8.00
U30 Jeremy Maclin 4.00 10.00
U31 Percy Harvin 3.00 8.00
U32 LeSean McCoy 8.00 20.00
U33 Aaron Curry 5.00 12.00
U34 Shonn Greene 3.00 8.00
U35 Chris Johnson 5.00 12.00
U36 Matt Forte 5.00 12.00
U37 Jonathan Stewart 5.00 12.00
U39 Brian Robiskie 3.00 8.00
U40 Walter Payton 20.00 50.00
U41 Fred Biletnikoff 12.00 30.00

2009 Ultimate Collection Ultimate Patch Autographs
STATED PRINT RUN 5-25
U9 Pat White/20 40.00 80.00
U13 Patrick Willis/15 30.00 60.00
U30 Jeremy Maclin/15 30.00 80.00
U31 Percy Harvin/20 25.00 60.00
U32 LeSean McCoy/20 30.00 80.00
U33 Aaron Curry/20 20.00 50.00
U34 Shonn Greene/15 30.00 80.00
U36 Matt Forte/20 30.00 80.00

2009 Ultimate Collection Ultimate Rookie Autographs Trios
STATED PRINT RUN 3-45
EXCH EXPIRATION: 2/3/2012
BBN Nicks/Barden/Bomar/25 12.00 30.00
CCA Curry/Ayers/Cushing/45
HMB Harvin/Maclin/Britt/25 20.00 50.00
HMD McGee/Harrell/Davis/25 15.00 40.00
JDC Jenkins/Chung/Davis/45 10.00 25.00
LCE Curry/Laurin/English/15 12.00 30.00
MCM Matth/Cush/Maual/35 40.00 100.00
PBC Coffman/Pett/Beckm/45 10.00 25.00
RCH Hywrd/Rbisk/Crbtr/15 25.00 60.00
RMG McCoy/Greene/Ringer/25 25.00 60.00
SMH Moreno/Heyward/Staff/15 50.00 120.00
SSF Stafford/Sanchz/Frman/15 100.00 200.00
SWP Stafford/PettiWilliams/15 75.00 150.00
TTW Wallace/Thomas/Turner/25 6.00 15.00
WFD White/Freeman/Davis/25 20.00 50.00

2009 Ultimate Collection Ultimate Rookie Big Materials
STATED PRINT RUN 99 SER.#'d SETS
B1 Mark Sanchez 4.00 10.00
B2 Matthew Stafford 25.00 60.00
B3 Josh Freeman 4.00 10.00
B4 Chris Wells 4.00 10.00
B5 Knowshon Moreno 4.00 10.00
B6 Donald Brown 4.00 10.00
B7 Shonn Greene 4.00 10.00
B8 Darrius Heyward-Bey 6.00 15.00
B9 Michael Crabtree 6.00 15.00
B10 Percy Harvin 4.00 10.00

B11 Jeremy Maclin 5.00 12.00
B12 Brandon Pettigrew 4.00 10.00
B13 Hakeem Nicks 5.00 12.00
B14 Aaron Curry 6.00 15.00
B15 Kenny Britt 6.00 15.00
B16 LeSean McCoy 10.00 25.00
B17 Brian Robiskie 4.00 10.00
B18 Nate Davis 4.00 10.00
B19 Pat White 5.00 12.00
B20 Javon Ringer 4.00 10.00
B21 Ramses Barden 6.00 15.00

2009 Ultimate Collection Ultimate Signatures Duals

DUAL AUTO PRINT RUN 5-65
EXCH EXPIRATION: 2/3/2012
DBG B.Griese/D.Brees/15 50.00 100.00
DBL L.Briggs/R.Lewis/25 40.00 80.00
DBW P.White/R.Brown/35 15.00 40.00
DCB D.Bowe/M.Cassel/25 12.00 30.00
DCH Heyward/Crabtree/25 20.00 50.00
DGB D.Brown/S.Greene/35 8.00 20.00
DHA J.Allen/Hynswrth/45 30.00 50.00
DHM P.Harvin/Maclin/35 30.00 80.00
DHW Haynswrth/Wlliams/35 10.00 25.00
DJR C.Johnson/J.Ringer/45 25.00 50.00
DSB L.Briggs/Singletary/25 30.00 60.00
DLM S.Largent/D.Maynard/35 25.00 50.00
DMM E.Mnning/P.Mnning/15 200.00 350.00
DRS M.Ryan/M.Stafford/15 50.00 120.00
DTR M.Ryan/M.Turner/15 30.00 80.00
DWB Warner/Boldin/25 30.00 60.00
DWM C.Wells/K.Moreno/25 30.00 80.00

2009 Ultimate Collection Ultimate Signatures Quads

QUAD AUTO PRINT RUN 5-25
LBPW Prtr/Will/Lws/Brgs/15 100.00 200.00
LCCE Curry/Laur/Engl/Csh/25 30.00 80.00
PJOK Page/Karrs/Jnes/Olsn/25
SMCP Morno/Pett/Staff/Crbtr/15 50.00 120.00
SSFD Davs/Frmn/Snchz/Staff/15 40.00 100.00
WMMB Mrno/Brwn/McCy/Wlls/15 30.00 80.00

2009 Ultimate Collection Ultimate Signature Jerseys

STATED PRINT RUN 10-25
SJAB Anquan Boldin/15 12.00 30.00
SJAP Adrian Peterson/15 100.00 200.00
SJBJ Brandon Jacobs/25 12.00 30.00
SJBM Brandon Marshall/15 12.00 30.00
SJCJ Chris Johnson/15 40.00 80.00
SJDC Dallas Clark/25 15.00 40.00
SJDW DeMarcus Ware/25 15.00 40.00
SJFG Frank Gore/15 12.00 30.00
SJJA Jared Allen/25 40.00 80.00
SJKS Kevin Smith/15 12.00 30.00
SJKW Kurt Warner/15 50.00 100.00
SJLB Lance Briggs/15 25.00 50.00
SJLE Lee Evans/15 12.00 30.00
SJMF Matt Forte/25 15.00 40.00
SJMR Matt Ryan/15 50.00 100.00
SJPM Peyton Manning/15 100.00 175.00
SJPW Patrick Willis/15 25.00 50.00
SJRB Ronnie Brown/15 15.00 40.00
SJRL Ray Lewis/15 90.00 150.00
SJSS Steve Slaton/15 12.00 30.00

2009 Ultimate Collection Ultimate Six Jerseys

STATED PRINT RUN 50-99
*GOLD/25: .5X TO 1.2X BASIC SIX JSY
*PATCH/20: .6X TO 1.5X BASIC SIX JSY
1 Wrn/Eli/Mnn/Brs/McNb/Brdy 15.00 40.00
2 Jns/Tmln/Wtbk/Trn/Ptrs/Prt 15.00 40.00
3 Johnson/Fitzgerald
Wayne/Jennings/Moss/Johnson/99 10.00 25.00
4 Brdy/Rvr/Rmo/Rth/Mnn/Wrn 15.00 40.00
5 Url/Hyn/Aln/Tat/Lws/Will 15.00 40.00
6 Mn/Clk/Clst/Bsh/Brs/Wn/99 20.00 50.00
7 Rth/Hlms/Prk/Wrnr/Ftz/Bldn 12.00 30.00
8 Forte/McFadden/Smith
Slaton/Johnson/Jones/99 10.00 25.00
9 Brbr/Rmo/Brs/Bsh/Trnr/Ryn 12.00 30.00
10 Frt/Hstr/Url/Hwk/Jng/Rdg/99 15.00 40.00
11 Rm/Ctlr/Eli/Ryn/McN/Mn/99 12.00 30.00
12 Wbk/Ptr/Frt/Lch/Jhn/Stn/99 15.00 40.00
13 Brd/Ms/Wkr/Mn/Clk/Wyn/99 15.00 40.00
14 McF/Rs/Hyw/Rrs/Gts/Tml/99 10.00 25.00
15 Rmo/Brbr/Eli/Jcb/Wstb/McNb 12.00 30.00
16 Trnr/Ptr/Bsh/Frt/Sltn/Wllms 12.00 30.00
17 Johnson/Moss/Marshall
Bowe/Fitzgerald/Boldin 10.00 25.00
18 Addai/Parker/Jones-Drew
Brown/Johnson/Tomlinson/99 10.00 25.00
19 Gates/Witten/Miller/Clark
Shockey/Cooley 10.00 25.00
20 Cb/Es/Pr/Rs/Sb/Pn 12.00 30.00
21 Wtn/Brbr/Rmo/Ncks/Jcbs/Eli 6.00 15.00
22 Jacobs/Forte/Portis/Gore/Grant/Slaton 10.00 25.00
23 Johnson/Reed/Lewis/Wayne/Portis/Hester 10.00 25.00
24 Plm/Rth/Qnn/Flco/Pnn/Grrd 12.00 30.00
25 Brd/Flc/Ryn/Sch/Mnn/Std/99 20.00 50.00
26 Haynesworth/Curry/Ware
Mayo/Jackson/Williams 8.00 20.00
27 Jn/Ws/Bn/Ps/Tr/Bh 15.00 40.00
28 Ncks/Smt/Brdn/Jcbs/Bmr/Eli 4.00 10.00
29 Brd/Smt/Ncks/Msq/Rbsk/Edw 4.00 10.00
30 Mn/Add/Clk/Gts/Rrs/Tml/99 15.00 40.00

2012 Ultimate Collection

TWO PER UPPER DECK HOBBY BOX
1 Rueben Randle 1.25 3.00
2 Alfonzo Dennard 1.25 3.00
3 Alshon Jeffery 2.50 6.00
4 Brock Osweiler 1.25 3.00
5 B.J. Cunningham 1.25 3.00
6 Brandon Bolden 1.25 3.00
7 Brandon Thompson 1.50 4.00
8 Brandon Weeden 1.25 3.00
9 Brian Quick 1.25 3.00
10 Case Keenum 2.50 6.00
11 Chandler Harnish 1.25 3.00
12 Stephen Hill 1.25 3.00
13 Dwayne Allen 1.25 3.00
14 Courtney Upshaw 1.50 4.00
15 Cyrus Gray 1.25 3.00
16 Dan Herron 1.25 3.00
17 Davin Meggett 1.25 3.00
18 DeVier Posey 1.25 3.00
19 Doug Martin 2.00 5.00
20 Dwight Jones 1.25 3.00
21 Fozzy Whittaker 1.25 3.00
22 Gerell Robinson 1.25 3.00
23 Isaiah Pead 1.25 3.00
24 Dre Kirkpatrick 1.25 3.00
25 Jarius Wright 1.25 3.00
26 Jarrett Boykin 3.00 8.00
27 Bernard Pierce 1.25 3.00
28 Jeff Fuller 1.25 3.00
29 Jermaine Kearse 2.00 5.00
30 Joe Adams 1.25 3.00
31 Juron Criner 1.25 3.00
32 Justin Blackmon 1.25 3.00
33 Kellen Moore 1.50 4.00
34 Kendall Wright 1.25 3.00
35 Keshawn Martin 1.50 4.00
36 Kirk Cousins 5.00 12.00
37 LaMichael James 1.25 3.00
38 Chris Givens 1.25 3.00
39 Marc Tyler 1.25 3.00
40 Marquis Maze 1.25 3.00
41 Marvin McNutt 1.25 3.00
42 Ronnie Hillman 1.25 3.00
43 Melvin Ingram 1.25 3.00
44 Michael Egnew 1.25 3.00
45 Michael Floyd 1.25 3.00
46 Mohamed Sanu 2.00 5.00
47 Luke Kuechly 3.00 8.00
48 Nick Foles 3.00 8.00
49 Nick Toon 1.25 3.00
50 Quinton Coples 1.25 3.00
51 Rishard Matthews 1.25 3.00
52 Robert Griffin III 1.50 4.00
53 Russell Wilson 8.00 20.00
54 Ryan Broyles 1.25 3.00
55 Ryan Lindley 1.25 3.00
56 Ryan Tannehill 2.00 5.00
57 Tauren Poole 1.25 3.00
58 Tommy Streeter 1.25 3.00
59 Trent Richardson 1.25 3.00
60 T.J. Graham 1.25 3.00
61 Andrew Luck/525 15.00 40.00

2012 Ultimate Collection Rookie Autographs

EXCH EXPIRATION: 11/21/2015
2 Brandon Weeden 25.00 60.00
3 Robert Griffin III 8.00 20.00
6 Dan Herron 6.00 15.00
7 Doug Martin 10.00 25.00
8 Dwight Jones 6.00 15.00
9 Isaiah Pead 6.00 15.00
11 Jeff Fuller 6.00 15.00
12 Juron Criner 10.00 25.00
13 Kellen Moore 15.00 40.00
14 Kirk Cousins 25.00 60.00
15 Michael Floyd 40.00 100.00
16 Nick Foles 15.00 40.00
17 Nick Toon 6.00 15.00
18 Quinton Coples 10.00 25.00
19 Ryan Broyles 15.00 40.00
21 Ryan Tannehill 10.00 25.00
22 Andrew Luck EXCH 150.00 300.00

2013 Ultimate Collection

1-61 VETERAN PRINT RUN 175
62-160 ROOKIE PRINT RUN 99
161-192 ROOKIE AU PRINT RUN 199
EXCH EXPIRATION: 11/22/2015
1 Dan Marino 4.00 10.00
2 Joe Montana 5.00 12.00
3 Jim Kelly 2.00 5.00
4 Bart Starr 3.00 8.00
5 Billy Sims 1.50 4.00
6 John Elway 3.00 8.00
7 Jerry Rice 3.00 8.00
8 Ricky Watters 1.25 3.00
9 Jason White 1.25 3.00
10 Joe Theismann 2.00 5.00
11 Jerome Bettis 2.00 5.00
12 Anthony Carter 1.25 3.00
13 Charles White 1.25 3.00
14 Daryle Lamonica 1.25 3.00
15 Drew Bledsoe 1.50 4.00
16 George Rogers 1.25 3.00
17 Barry Sanders 3.00 8.00
18 Garrison Hearst 1.25 3.00
19 Charlie Ward 1.25 3.00
20 Dan Fouts 1.50 4.00
21 Roger Craig 1.50 4.00
22 Ken MacAfee 1.25 3.00
23 Al Toon 1.25 3.00
24 Joe Washington 1.25 3.00
25 Mike Rozier 1.25 3.00
26 Rodney Peete 1.25 3.00
27 Bo Jackson 2.50 6.00
28 Tommie Frazier 1.25 3.00
29 Alan Page 1.25 3.00
30 Bruce Smith 1.50 4.00
31 Vinny Testaverde 1.25 3.00
32 Billy Cannon 1.25 3.00
33 Nick Buoniconti 1.25 3.00
34 Steve Young 2.50 6.00
35 Gary Beban 1.25 3.00
36 Archie Griffin 1.25 3.00
37 Steve Owens 1.25 3.00
38 Aaron Rodgers 6.00 15.00
39 Jake Plummer 1.25 3.00
40 Keith Jackson 1.25 3.00
41 Paul Hornung 2.00 5.00
42 Andy Katzenmoyer 1.25 3.00
43 Robert Smith 1.25 3.00
44 Tedy Bruschi 1.50 4.00
45 Ronnie Lott 1.50 4.00
46 Joe Namath 2.50 6.00
47 Ozzie Newsome 1.50 4.00
48 Brian Bosworth 1.50 4.00
49 Doug Flutie 1.50 4.00
50 Ty Detmer 1.25 3.00
51 Warren Moon 2.00 5.00
52 Ray Guy 1.25 3.00
53 Earl Campbell 2.00 5.00
54 Roman Gabriel 1.25 3.00
55 Warren Sapp 1.50 4.00
56 John Hannah 2.00 5.00
57 Herschel Walker 2.00 5.00
58 Eddie George 1.50 4.00
59 Lawrence Taylor 2.00 5.00
60 Ron Dayne 1.50 4.00
61 Andrew Luck 3.00 8.00
62 Aaron Mellette 1.25 3.00
63 Alec Ogletree 1.25 3.00
64 Andre Ellington 1.25 3.00
65 Arthur Brown 1.25 3.00
66 Barkevious Mingo 1.25 3.00
67 Bjoern Werner 1.25 3.00
68 Blidi Wreh-Wilson 1.50 4.00
69 Datone Jones 1.25 3.00
70 Aaron Dobson 1.25 3.00
71 Chris Harper 1.25 3.00
72 Cierre Wood 1.25 3.00
73 Cobi Hamilton 1.25 3.00
74 Collin Klein 1.50 4.00
75 Braden Wilson 1.50 4.00
76 Cordarrelle Patterson 1.25 3.00
77 D.J. Fluker 1.25 3.00
78 D.J. Swearinger 1.25 3.00
79 Damontre Moore 1.25 3.00
80 Da'Rick Rogers 1.25 3.00
81 Dayne Crist 1.50 4.00
82 DeAndre Hopkins 3.00 8.00
83 Dee Milliner 1.25 3.00
84 Denard Robinson 1.25 3.00
85 Dennis Johnson 1.25 3.00
86 Desmond Trufant 1.25 3.00
87 Justin Pugh 1.25 3.00
88 Dion Jordan 1.25 3.00
89 Dion Sims 1.25 3.00
90 Eddie Lacy 1.25 3.00
91 EJ Manuel 1.25 3.00
92 Eric Fisher 1.25 3.00
93 Ezekiel Ansah 1.25 3.00
94 Gavin Escobar 1.25 3.00
95 Geno Smith 1.25 3.00
96 Giovani Bernard 1.25 3.00
97 Jarvis Jones 1.25 3.00
98 Jawan Jamison 1.25 3.00
99 Johnathan Franklin 1.25 3.00
100 Jon Bostic 1.25 3.00
101 Jordan Rodgers 1.50 4.00
102 Jordan Reed 2.00 5.00
103 Joseph Randle 1.25 3.00
104 Josh Boyce 1.25 3.00
105 Justin Hunter 1.25 3.00
106 Kawann Short 1.25 3.00
107 Keenan Allen 2.50 6.00
108 Kenjon Barner 1.25 3.00
109 Kenny Vaccaro 1.25 3.00
110 Kenny Stills 1.25 3.00
111 Kevin Minter 1.25 3.00
112 Kiko Alonso 1.50 4.00
113 Knile Davis 3.00 8.00
114 Landry Jones 1.25 3.00
115 Lane Johnson 1.50 4.00
116 Le'Veon Bell 4.00 10.00
117 Brad Sorensen 1.25 3.00
118 Luke Joeckel 1.25 3.00
119 Manti Te'o 1.50 4.00
120 Marcus Lattimore 1.25 3.00
121 B.J. Daniels 2.00 5.00
122 Markus Wheaton 1.25 3.00
123 Marquess Wilson 2.00 5.00
124 Marquise Goodwin 1.25 3.00
125 Matt Barkley 1.25 3.00
126 Matt Scott 1.25 3.00
127 Matt Elam 1.25 3.00
128 Mike Glennon 1.25 3.00
129 Mike Gillislee 1.25 3.00
130 Montee Ball 1.25 3.00
131 Chris Thompson 1.25 3.00
132 Rex Burkhead 6.00 15.00
133 Robert Woods 2.00 5.00
134 Eric Reid 1.50 4.00
135 Vance McDonald 1.50 4.00
136 Ryan Nassib 3.00 8.00
137 Ryan Swope 1.25 3.00
138 Sam Montgomery 1.25 3.00
139 Nick Kasa 1.25 3.00
140 Sharrif Floyd 1.25 3.00
141 Sheldon Richardson 1.25 3.00
142 Spencer Ware 1.25 3.00
143 Star Lotulelei 1.50 4.00
144 Stedman Bailey 1.25 3.00
145 Stepfan Taylor 1.25 3.00
146 Sylvester Williams 1.25 3.00
148 Tavarres King 1.25 3.00
149 Tavon Austin 1.50 4.00
150 Terrance Williams 1.25 3.00
151 Theo Riddick 1.25 3.00
153 Travis Kelce 3.00 8.00
154 Tyler Bray 1.25 3.00
155 Tyler Wilson 3.00 8.00
156 Tyler Eifert 1.25 3.00
157 Corey Fuller 1.25 3.00
158 Xavier Rhodes 1.25 3.00
159 Zac Dysert 1.25 3.00
160 Zach Ertz 2.50 6.00
161 Keenan Allen AU 8.00 20.00
162 Giovani Bernard AU 4.00 10.00
163 Stepfan Taylor AU 4.00 10.00
164 Mike Glennon AU 4.00 10.00
165 Ryan Nassib AU 8.00 20.00
166 Kenjon Barner AU 4.00 10.00
167 Ryan Swope AU 4.00 10.00
168 Le'Veon Bell AU 12.00 30.00
169 Montee Ball AU 4.00 10.00
170 Andre Ellington AU 8.00 20.00
171 Eddie Lacy AU 4.00 10.00
172 Josh Boyce AU 4.00 10.00
173 Joseph Randle AU 4.00 10.00
174 Marcus Lattimore AU 15.00 30.00
175 Zach Ertz AU 8.00 20.00
176 Tyler Wilson AU 4.00 10.00
177 Johnathan Franklin AU 4.00 10.00
178 Robert Woods AU 6.00 15.00
179 Justin Hunter AU 12.00 30.00
180 Terrance Williams AU 4.00 10.00
181 Aaron Dobson AU 4.00 10.00
182 Mike Gillislee AU 4.00 10.00
183 Denard Robinson AU 4.00 10.00
184 Markus Wheaton AU 4.00 10.00
185 Knile Davis AU 4.00 10.00
186 Tavarres King AU 4.00 10.00
187 Chris Harper AU 4.00 10.00
188 Kenny Stills AU 4.00 10.00
189 Stedman Bailey AU 4.00 10.00
190 Marquise Goodwin AU 4.00 10.00
191 Corey Fuller AU 4.00 10.00
192 Tyler Eifert AU 4.00 10.00
193 Tavon Austin AU/75 EXCH 6.00 15.00
194 Manti Te'o AU/75 6.00 15.00
196 EJ Manuel AU/75 5.00 12.00
197 DeAndre Hopkins AU/75 12.00 30.00
198 Cordarrelle Patterson AU/75 5.00 12.00
199 Matt Barkley AU/75 5.00 12.00
200 Geno Smith AU/75 5.00 12.00

2013 Ultimate Collection 1997 Legends Autographs

GROUP A ODDS 1:200
GROUP A ODDS 1:17
OVERALL ODDS 1:15
101 Al Toon B 4.00 10.00
102 Andy Katzenmoyer B 4.00 10.00
103 Joe Montana A
104 Bart Starr A
105 Bruce Smith A
106 Charlie Ward B 4.00 10.00
107 Marcus Lattimore B 4.00 10.00
108 Dan Fouts A
109 Don Maynard B 20.00 40.00
110 Drew Bledsoe A
111 Garrison Hearst B 4.00 10.00
112 Jake Plummer B 20.00 40.00
113 Jerome Bettis A
114 Joe Namath A
115 John Hannah B 4.00 10.00
116 Johnny Lattner B 4.00 10.00
117 Ken MacAfee B 15.00 40.00
118 Mike Rozier B 30.00 80.00
119 Nick Buoniconti B 15.00 30.00
120 Ray Guy B 20.00 40.00
122 Robert Smith B 15.00 30.00
123 Rodney Peete B 40.00 80.00
124 Ronnie Lott A
125 Tedy Bruschi A
126 Tommie Frazier B 4.00 10.00
127 Vinny Testaverde B 15.00 40.00
128 Warren Sapp A
130 Montee Ball B 4.00 10.00
131 Tavon Austin B 10.00 25.00
132 Eddie Lacy B 4.00 10.00
133 Tyler Wilson B 4.00 10.00
134 Geno Smith A
135 Matt Barkley B 8.00 20.00
136 Mike Glennon B 4.00 10.00
137 Justin Hunter B 4.00 10.00
138 Keenan Allen B 8.00 20.00
139 Ryan Nassib B 10.00 25.00
140 EJ Manuel A
141 Manti Te'o B 5.00 12.00
142 Collin Klein B EXCH 20.00 40.00

2013 Ultimate Collection Super Jerseys

*PATCH/25: .5X TO 1.2X BASIC JSY/35
USJAC Anthony Carter 6.00 15.00
USJAD Aaron Dobson 3.00 8.00
USJAE Andre Ellington 6.00 15.00
USJBA Montee Ball 3.00 8.00
USJBC Billy Cannon 5.00 12.00
USJBJ Bo Jackson 12.00 30.00
USJBT Tyler Bray 3.00 8.00
USJCP Cordarrelle Patterson 3.00 8.00
USJCW Charles White 5.00 12.00
USJDB Drew Bledsoe 8.00 20.00
USJDH DeAndre Hopkins 6.00 15.00
USJDL Daryle Lamonica 5.00 12.00
USJDR Denard Robinson 3.00 8.00
USJEC Earl Campbell 8.00 20.00
USJEG Eddie George 10.00 25.00
USJEL Eddie Lacy 10.00 25.00
USJEM EJ Manuel 3.00 8.00
USJGB Giovani Bernard 3.00 8.00
USJGM Mike Glennon 3.00 8.00
USJGS Geno Smith 8.00 20.00
USJHU Justin Hunter 3.00 8.00
USJHW Herschel Walker 8.00 20.00
USJJB Jerome Bettis 10.00 25.00
USJJE John Elway 12.00 30.00
USJJF Johnathan Franklin 3.00 8.00
USJJH John Hannah 8.00 20.00
USJJL Johnny Lattner 5.00 12.00
USJJN Joe Namath 20.00 50.00
USJJR Jerry Rice 12.00 30.00
USJJT Joe Theismann 8.00 20.00
USJKA Keenan Allen 8.00 20.00
USJKB Kenjon Barner 3.00 8.00
USJKJ Keith Jackson 5.00 12.00
USJLB Le'Veon Bell 8.00 20.00
USJLJ Landry Jones 3.00 8.00
USJMB Matt Barkley 3.00 8.00
USJMG Mike Gillislee 3.00 8.00
USJML Marcus Lattimore 3.00 8.00
USJMT Manti Te'o 4.00 10.00
USJMW Markus Wheaton 3.00 8.00
USJON Ozzie Newsome 6.00 15.00
USJPH Paul Hornung 8.00 20.00
USJRC Roger Craig 6.00 15.00
USJRD Ron Dayne 6.00 15.00
USJRG Roman Gabriel 5.00 12.00
USJRN Ryan Nassib 3.00 8.00
USJRW Robert Woods 5.00 12.00
USJSA Barry Sanders 12.00 30.00
USJSB Stedman Bailey 3.00 8.00
USJSO Steve Owens 5.00 12.00
USJTA Tavon Austin 4.00 10.00
USJTB Tedy Bruschi 6.00 15.00
USJTD Ty Detmer 5.00 12.00
USJTE Tyler Eifert 3.00 8.00
USJTK Tavarres King 4.00 10.00
USJTW Terrance Williams 3.00 8.00
USJVT Vinny Testaverde 6.00 15.00
USJWI Tyler Wilson 3.00 8.00
USJWM Warren Moon 8.00 20.00
USJZE Zach Ertz 6.00 15.00

2013 Ultimate Collection Ultimate Dual Jerseys

UJ2AA T.Austin/K.Allen 5.00 12.00
UJ2BK D.Bledsoe/J.Kelly 8.00 20.00
UJ2BT J.Bettis/J.Theismann
UJ2BW M.Barkley/R.Woods 4.00 10.00
UJ2CW E.Campbell/H.Walker 8.00 20.00
UJ2EM J.Elway/D.Marino 20.00 40.00
UJ2EN J.Elway/J.Namath 20.00 40.00
UJ2ER J.Elway/J.Rice 20.00 40.00
UJ2HL P.Hornung/D.Lamonica 8.00 20.00
UJ2HT P.Hornung/J.Theismann 8.00 20.00
UJ2JS B.Jackson/B.Sanders 15.00 40.00
UJ2KT J.Kelly/V.Testaverde 12.00 30.00
UJ2LB E.Lacy/M.Ball 2.50 6.00
UJ2LM L.Bell/M.Ball 8.00 20.00
UJ2MK D.Marino/J.Kelly 15.00 40.00
UJ2NS O.Newsome/B.Starr 12.00 30.00
UJ2OJ S.Owens/K.Jackson 5.00 12.00
UJ2RM J.Rice/D.Marino
UJ2RS J.Rice/B.Sanders 25.00 50.00
UJ2SA G.Smith/T.Austin 3.00 8.00
UJ2SB G.Smith/M.Barkley 2.50 6.00
UJ2SE B.Sanders/J.Elway 12.00 30.00
UJ2SW G.Smith/T.Wilson 2.50 6.00
UJ2WJ B.Jackson/H.Walker 20.00 40.00
UJ2WS B.Sims/C.White 6.00 15.00

2013 Ultimate Collection Ultimate Dual Patch

UJ2AA T.Austin/K.Allen 4.00 10.00
UJ2BK D.Bledsoe/J.Kelly 8.00 20.00
UJ2BT J.Bettis/J.Theismann 10.00 25.00
UJ2BW M.Barkley/R.Woods 3.00 8.00
UJ2CW H.Walker/E.Campbell 8.00 20.00
UJ2EM J.Elway/D.Marino 15.00 40.00
UJ2EN J.Elway/J.Namath 12.00 30.00
UJ2HL P.Hornung/D.Lamonica 8.00 20.00
UJ2HT P.Hornung/J.Theismann
UJ2JS B.Jackson/B.Sanders 15.00 40.00
UJ2KT V.Testaverde/J.Kelly 8.00 20.00
UJ2LB E.Lacy/M.Ball 2.00 5.00
UJ2LM L.Bell/M.Ball 6.00 15.00
UJ2MK J.Kelly/D.Marino 15.00 40.00
UJ2NS O.Newsome/B.Starr 10.00 25.00
UJ2OJ S.Owens/K.Jackson 8.00 20.00
UJ2RM J.Rice/D.Marino 15.00 40.00
UJ2RS J.Rice/B.Sanders 20.00 50.00
UJ2SA G.Smith/T.Austin 2.50 6.00
UJ2SB G.Smith/M.Barkley 2.00 5.00
UJ2SE J.Elway/B.Sanders 15.00 40.00
UJ2SW T.Wilson/G.Smith 2.00 5.00
UJ2WJ B.Jackson/H.Walker 12.00 30.00
UJ2WS B.Sims/C.White 6.00 15.00

2013 Ultimate Collection Ultimate Jerseys

*PATCH/60: .5X TO 1.2X BASIC JSY/50
UJAC Anthony Carter 6.00 15.00
UJAE Andre Ellington 5.00 12.00
UJBA Matt Barkley 5.00 12.00
UJBC Billy Cannon 6.00 15.00
UJBI Billy Sims 5.00 12.00
UJBJ Bo Jackson 15.00 40.00
UJBR Tedy Bruschi 5.00 12.00
UJBS Barry Sanders 12.00 30.00
UJCP Cordarrelle Patterson 2.50 6.00
UJCW Charles White 4.00 10.00
UJDB Drew Bledsoe 6.00 15.00
UJDH DeAndre Hopkins 4.00 10.00
UJDL Daryle Lamonica 4.00 10.00
UJDM Dan Marino 12.00 30.00
UJEC Earl Campbell 5.00 12.00
UJEL Eddie Lacy 10.00 25.00
UJEM EJ Manuel 3.00 8.00
UJGS Geno Smith 3.00 8.00
UJHW Herschel Walker 5.00 12.00
UJJA John Hannah 6.00 15.00
UJJB Jerome Bettis 6.00 15.00
UJJE John Elway 10.00 25.00
UJJH Justin Hunter 5.00 12.00
UJJK Jim Kelly 5.00 12.00
UJJL Johnny Lattner 4.00 10.00
UJJN Joe Namath 20.00 40.00
UJJR Jerry Rice 15.00 40.00
UJJT Joe Theismann 6.00 15.00
UJKA Keenan Allen 5.00 12.00
UJKJ Keith Jackson 3.00 8.00
UJLB Le'Veon Bell 5.00 12.00
UJLJ Landry Jones 2.50 6.00
UJMB Montee Ball 2.50 6.00
UJMG Mike Glennon 5.00 12.00
UJMT Manti Te'o 5.00 12.00
UJON Ozzie Newsome 4.00 10.00
UJPH Paul Hornung 6.00 15.00
UJRC Roger Craig 4.00 10.00
UJRG Roman Gabriel 5.00 12.00
UJRN Ryan Nassib 5.00 12.00
UJSO Steve Owens 5.00 12.00
UJST Bart Starr 8.00 20.00
UJTA Tavon Austin 5.00 12.00
UJTB Tyler Bray 2.50 6.00
UJTD Ty Detmer 3.00 8.00
UJTE Tyler Eifert 2.50 6.00
UJTW Terrance Williams 2.50 6.00
UJVT Vinny Testaverde 4.00 10.00
UJWI Tyler Wilson 2.50 6.00
UJZE Zach Ertz 5.00 12.00

2013 Ultimate Collection Ultimate Quad Jerseys

UJ4AHAP An/Hr/An/Pn 5.00 12.00
UJ4CJSW Cl/Jn/Ss/Wr 25.00 50.00
UJ4CWSC Cl/We/Ss/Cn 10.00 25.00
UJ4EMKB Ey/Mo/Ky/Be 20.00 50.00
UJ4ESMR Ey/Ss/Mo/Re 20.00 50.00
UJ4HTLB Hg/Tn/La/Bs 10.00 25.00
UJ4JGDW Ss/Jn/Cl/Wr 15.00 40.00
UJ4LBBE Ly/Bl/Bl/In 8.00 20.00
UJ4SBWJ Sh/By/Wn/Js 2.50 6.00
UJ4SGJW Ss/Ss/Jn/Wr 25.00 60.00

2013 Ultimate Collection Ultimate Signature Jerseys

SJAC Anthony Carter 4.00 10.00
SJAD Aaron Dobson 4.00 10.00
SJAE Andre Ellington 4.00 10.00
SJBA Matt Barkley 4.00 10.00
SJBC Billy Cannon 4.00 10.00
SJBJ Bo Jackson 40.00 80.00
SJBR Tedy Bruschi 15.00 30.00
SJBT Bart Starr 50.00 100.00
SJCP Cordarrelle Patterson 4.00 10.00
SJDB Drew Bledsoe 10.00 25.00
SJDL Daryle Lamonica 10.00 25.00
SJEC Earl Campbell 25.00 50.00
SJEG Eddie George 15.00 30.00
SJEL Eddie Lacy 25.00 50.00
SJEM EJ Manuel 4.00 10.00
SJGB Giovani Bernard
SJGM Mike Gillislee 4.00 10.00
SJGS Geno Smith 4.00 10.00
SJHA John Hannah 10.00 25.00
SJJB Jerome Bettis 40.00 80.00
SJJE John Elway 50.00 100.00
SJJH Justin Hunter 4.00 10.00
SJJL Johnny Lattner 10.00 25.00
SJJN Joe Namath 50.00 100.00
SJJR Jerry Rice 40.00 80.00
SJJT Joe Theismann 10.00 25.00
SJKB Kenjon Barner 4.00 10.00
SJKJ Keith Jackson 8.00 20.00
SJKS Kenny Stills 4.00 10.00
SJLB Le'Veon Bell 30.00 60.00
SJMB Montee Ball 4.00 10.00
SJMG Mike Glennon 4.00 10.00
SJML Marcus Lattimore 4.00 10.00
SJMT Manti Te'o 5.00 12.00
SJMW Marquess Wilson 6.00 15.00
SJON Ozzie Newsome 10.00 25.00
SJRC Roger Craig 10.00 25.00
SJRD Ron Dayne 5.00 12.00
SJRG Roman Gabriel 4.00 10.00
SJRN Ryan Nassib 4.00 10.00
SJRW Robert Woods 6.00 15.00
SJSA Barry Sanders 100.00 200.00
SJSO Steve Owens 25.00 50.00
SJTA Tavon Austin 5.00 12.00
SJTB Tyler Bray 4.00 10.00
SJTD Ty Detmer 10.00 25.00
SJTE Tyler Eifert 4.00 10.00
SJTK Tavarres King 4.00 10.00
SJVT Vinny Testaverde 10.00 25.00
SJWI Tyler Wilson 4.00 10.00
SJWM Markus Wheaton 4.00 10.00
SJZE Zach Ertz 8.00 20.00

2013 Ultimate Collection Ultimate Signatures Futures

UFSAD Aaron Dobson 4.00 10.00
UFSAE Andre Ellington 10.00 25.00
UFSBA Montee Ball 4.00 10.00
UFSCK Collin Klein
UFSCP Cordarrelle Patterson 4.00 10.00
UFSEL Eddie Lacy 4.00 10.00
UFSEM EJ Manuel 4.00 10.00
UFSGS Geno Smith 4.00 10.00
UFSJH Justin Hunter 8.00 20.00
UFSJJ Jawan Jamison 4.00 10.00
UFSLB Le'Veon Bell 12.00 30.00
UFSMB Matt Barkley 8.00 20.00
UFSMG Mike Glennon 4.00 10.00
UFSML Marcus Lattimore 4.00 10.00
UFSMT Manti Te'o 5.00 12.00
UFSRN Ryan Nassib 8.00 20.00
UFSRW Robert Woods 6.00 15.00
UFSTA Tavon Austin 5.00 12.00
UFSTW Tyler Wilson 4.00 10.00
UFSZE Zach Ertz 8.00 20.00

2013 Ultimate Collection Ultimate Signatures Legends

ULSBB Brian Bosworth/15 12.00 30.00
ULSEC Earl Campbell/15 15.00 40.00
ULSGH Garrison Hearst/15 10.00 25.00
ULSSI Billy Sims/15
ULSSO Steve Owens/15 12.00 30.00
ULSTD Ty Detmer/15 10.00 25.00
ULSVT Vinny Testaverde/15 10.00 25.00
ULSWS Warren Sapp/15

2013 Ultimate Collection Ultimate Triple Patch

UJ3AAP Astn/Pttrsn/Alln 6.00 15.00
UJ3BHT Btts/Hrnng/Thsmnn 25.00 60.00
UJ3EKM Elwy/Klly/Mrno 25.00 60.00
UJ3HTL Hrnng/Thsmnn/Lmnca 15.00 40.00
UJ3JCW Wlkr/Jcksn/Cmpbll
UJ3JWS Jcksn/Sms/Wlkr 12.00 30.00
UJ3LBB Lcy/Bll/Bll
UJ3SBG Smth/Brkly/Glnnn
UJ3SBW Brkly/Wlsn/Smth
UJ3SJC Sndrs/Jcksn/Cmpbll 25.00 60.00
UJ3SJW Sndrs/Jcksn/Wlkr 25.00 60.00
UJ3SWC Sms/Cnnn/Whte
UJ3WJS Sndrs/Whte/Jcksn

2013 Upper Deck Ultimate Collection Inserts

INSERTS IN 2013 UPPER DECK
STATED PRINT RUN 525 SER.#'d SETS
1 Tavon Austin 1.50 4.00
2 Collin Klein 1.50 4.00
3 Tyler Bray 1.25 3.00
4 Montee Ball 1.25 3.00
5 Tyler Wilson 1.25 3.00
6 Damontre Moore 1.25 3.00
7 Eddie Lacy 1.25 3.00
8 Knile Davis 1.25 3.00
9 Joseph Randle 1.25 3.00
10 Da'Rick Rogers 1.25 3.00
11 Luke Joeckel 1.25 3.00
12 Steptan Taylor 1.25 3.00
13 Kenny Stills 1.25 3.00
14 Matt Barkley 1.25 3.00
15 Ryan Nassib 1.25 3.00
16 Zac Dysert 1.25 3.00
17 Manti Te'o 1.50 4.00
18 Mike Glennon 1.25 3.00
19 Keenan Allen 2.00 5.00
21 Bjoern Werner 1.25 3.00
22 Corey Fuller 1.25 3.00
23 Dion Jordan 1.25 3.00
24 Dion Sims 1.25 3.00
25 Josh Boyce 1.25 3.00
26 Matt Scott 1.25 3.00
27 Marquess Wilson 2.00 5.00
28 Conner Vernon 1.25 3.00
29 Andre Ellington 1.25 3.00
30 Markus Wheaton 1.25 3.00
31 Cobi Hamilton 1.25 3.00
32 Kenjon Barner 1.25 3.00
33 Ryan Swope 1.25 3.00
34 Star Lotulelei 1.50 4.00
35 Dennis Johnson 1.25 3.00
36 Jarvis Jones 1.25 3.00
37 Tavarres King 1.25 3.00
38 Johnathan Franklin 1.25 3.00
39 Landry Jones 1.25 3.00
40 Justin Hunter 1.25 3.00
41 Dee Milliner 1.25 3.00
42 Zach Ertz 2.50 6.00
43 Jawan Jamison 1.25 3.00
44 DeAndre Hopkins 3.00 8.00
45 EJ Manuel 1.25 3.00
46 Geno Smith 1.25 3.00
47 Tyler Eifert 1.25 3.00
48 Marcus Lattimore 1.25 3.00
49 Theo Riddick 1.25 3.00
50 Cordarrelle Patterson 1.25 3.00
51 Robert Woods 2.00 5.00
52 Aaron Mellette 1.25 3.00
53 Terrance Williams 1.25 3.00
54 Le'Veon Bell 4.00 10.00
55 Erik Highsmith 1.50 4.00
56 Giovani Bernard 1.25 3.00
57 Stedman Bailey 1.25 3.00
58 Mike Gillislee 1.25 3.00
59 Denard Robinson 1.25 3.00
60 Aaron Dobson 1.25 3.00

2013 Upper Deck Ultimate Collection Rookie Autographs Inserts

UNPRICED GRP A ODDS 1:5166
GROUP B ODDS 1:3079
GROUP C ODDS 1:677
INSERTS IN 2013 UPPER DECK
3 Landry Jones C 15.00 40.00
4 EJ Manuel C 8.00 20.00
6 Mike Glennon B 10.00 25.00
8 Montee Ball C 15.00 40.00
9 Johnathan Franklin C 6.00 15.00
12 Mike Gillislee C 8.00 20.00
15 Aaron Dobson C 30.00 60.00
17 Aaron Mellette C 8.00 20.00
19 Denard Robinson C 8.00 20.00
20 Cobi Hamilton C 8.00 20.00
21 Markus Wheaton C 8.00 20.00

1991-92 Ultimate Promo Panel

1 6-card strip 1.25 3.00

2000 Ultimate Victory

Released as a 150-card set, Ultimate Victory features 90 veteran player cards and 60 rookie cards serial numbered to 2000. Base cards are all foil and have red foil highlights. Ultimate Victory was packaged in 24-pack boxes with five cards per pack and carried a suggested retail price of $2.99.

COMPLETE SET (150) 175.00 300.00
COMP.SET w/o SP's (90) 6.00 15.00
91-150 ROOKIE PRINT RUN 2000
1 Jake Plummer .12 .30
2 David Boston .12 .30
3 Frank Sanders .12 .30
4 Chris Chandler .15 .40
5 Jamal Anderson .15 .40
6 Shawn Jefferson .12 .30
7 Qadry Ismail .12 .30
8 Tony Banks .12 .30
9 Shannon Sharpe .15 .40
10 Peerless Price .15 .40
11 Rob Johnson .15 .40
12 Eric Moulds .12 .30
13 Muhsin Muhammad .12 .30
14 Steve Beuerlein .15 .40
15 Tim Biakabutuka .15 .40
16 Cade McNown .12 .30
17 Curtis Enis .12 .30
18 Marcus Robinson .15 .40
19 Akili Smith .12 .30
20 Corey Dillon .12 .30
21 Darnay Scott .15 .40
22 Tim Couch .15 .40
23 Kevin Johnson .12 .30
24 Errict Rhett .15 .40
25 Troy Aikman .25 .60
26 Emmitt Smith .30 .75
27 Rocket Ismail .15 .40
28 Joey Galloway .15 .40
29 Terrell Davis .15 .40
30 Olandis Gary .15 .40
31 Ed McCaffrey .15 .40
32 Charlie Batch .12 .30
33 Germane Crowell .12 .30
34 James Stewart .12 .30
35 Brett Favre .40 1.00
36 Antonio Freeman .15 .40
37 Dorsey Levens .15 .40
38 Peyton Manning .50 1.25
39 Edgerrin James .15 .40
40 Marvin Harrison .15 .40
41 Mark Brunell .15 .40
42 Fred Taylor .12 .30
43 Jimmy Smith .15 .40
44 Elvis Grbac .12 .30
45 Tony Gonzalez .15 .40
46 Derrick Alexander .12 .30
47 Tony Martin .15 .40
48 Damon Huard .12 .30
49 O.J. McDuffie .15 .40
50 Randy Moss .15 .40
51 Robert Smith .12 .30
52 Daunte Culpepper .15 .40
53 Drew Bledsoe .15 .40
54 Terry Glenn .15 .40
55 Ricky Williams .15 .40
56 Jake Reed .15 .40
57 Jeff Blake .15 .40
58 Kerry Collins .12 .30
59 Amani Toomer .12 .30
60 Ike Hilliard .12 .30
61 Ray Lucas .12 .30
62 Curtis Martin .15 .40
63 Vinny Testaverde .12 .30
64 Tim Brown .20 .50
65 Rich Gannon .15 .40
66 Tyrone Wheatley .12 .30
67 Duce Staley .12 .30
68 Donovan McNabb .15 .40
69 Troy Edwards .12 .30
70 Jerome Bettis .20 .50
71 Marshall Faulk .15 .40
72 Kurt Warner .30 .75
73 Isaac Bruce .20 .50
74 Curtis Conway .15 .40
75 Freddie Jones .12 .30
76 Jeff Graham .12 .30
77 Jeff Garcia .12 .30
78 Jerry Rice .50 1.25
79 Ricky Watters .15 .40
80 Jon Kitna .12 .30
81 Derrick Mayes .12 .30
82 Keyshawn Johnson .15 .40
83 Shaun King .12 .30
84 Mike Alstott .12 .30
85 Eddie George .15 .40
86 Steve McNair .15 .40
87 Jevon Kearse .12 .30
88 Brad Johnson .15 .40
89 Stephen Davis .12 .30
90 Michael Westbrook .12 .30
91 Anthony Becht RC 1.00 2.50
92 Anthony Lucas RC 1.00 2.50
93 Bashir Yamini RC 1.00 2.50
94 Brian Urlacher RC 5.00 12.00
95 Chad Morton RC 1.25 3.00
96 Chad Pennington RC 1.25 3.00
97 Chris Cole RC 1.25 3.00
98 Chris Hovan RC 1.25 3.00
99 Tim Rattay RC 1.25 3.00
100 Chris Redman RC 1.00 2.50
101 Chris Samuels RC 1.50 4.00
102 Corey Simon RC 1.25 3.00
103 Courtney Brown RC 1.25 3.00
104 Curtis Keaton RC 1.00 2.50
105 Danny Farmer RC 1.00 2.50
106 Erron Kinney RC 1.00 2.50
107 Darren Howard RC 1.00 2.50
108 Deltha O'Neal RC 1.00 2.50
109 Dennis Northcutt RC 1.00 2.50
110 Demario Brown RC 1.00 2.50
111 Dez White RC 1.00 2.50
112 Frank Murphy RC 1.00 2.50
113 Gari Scott RC 1.00 2.50
114 Giovanni Carmazzi RC 1.00 2.50
115 J.R. Redmond RC 1.00 2.50
116 JaJuan Dawson RC 1.00 2.50
117 Jamal Lewis RC 1.50 4.00
118 Leon Murray RC 1.00 2.50
119 Jerry Porter RC 1.50 4.00
120 Joe Hamilton RC 1.00 2.50
121 John Abraham RC 1.50 4.00
122 John Engelberger RC 1.00 2.50
123 Keith Bulluck RC 1.25 3.00
124 Kwame Cavil RC 1.00 2.50
125 Laveranues Coles RC 1.25 3.00
126 Marc Bulger RC 1.25 3.00
127 Marcus Knight RC 1.00 2.50
128 Mareno Philyaw RC 1.00 2.50
129 Michael Wiley RC 1.00 2.50
130 Na'il Diggs RC 1.00 2.50
131 Peter Warrick RC 1.00 2.50
132 Plaxico Burress RC 1.25 3.00
133 Raynoch Thompson RC 1.00 2.50
134 Reuben Droughns RC 1.00 2.50
135 Rob Morris RC 1.25 3.00
136 Ron Dayne RC 1.50 4.00
137 Ron Dugans RC 1.00 2.50
138 Sebastian Janikowski RC 1.50 4.00
139 Shaun Alexander RC 1.50 4.00
140 Sherrod Gideon RC 1.00 2.50
141 Sylvester Morris RC 1.00 2.50
142 Tee Martin RC 1.00 2.50
143 Thomas Jones RC 1.25 3.00
144 Todd Husak RC 1.00 2.50
145 Todd Pinkston RC 1.00 2.50
146 Tom Brady RC 100.00 200.00
147 Travis Prentice RC 1.00 2.50
148 Travis Taylor RC 1.00 2.50
149 Trevor Gaylor RC 1.00 2.50
150 Trung Canidate RC 1.00 2.50

2000 Ultimate Victory Parallel

*VETS 1-90: 3X TO 8X BASIC CARDS
1-90 VETERAN ODDS 1:11
*ROOKIES 91-150: .4X TO 1X
91-150 ROOKIE ODDS 1:23

2000 Ultimate Victory Parallel 100

*VETS 1-90: 8X TO 20X BASIC CARDS
*ROOKIES 91-150: 1X TO 2.5X
STATED PRINT RUN 100 SER.#'d SETS
146 Tom Brady 250.00 500.00

2000 Ultimate Victory Parallel 25

*VETS 1-90: 20X TO 50X BASIC CARDS
*ROOKIES 91-150: 2.5X TO 6X
STATED PRINT RUN 25 SER.#'d SETS
146 Tom Brady 600.00 1000.00

2000 Ultimate Victory Battle Ground

Randomly inserted in packs at the rate of one in 11, this 10-card set features full color action photography set against a red foil background. Cards contain gold foil highlights.

COMPLETE SET (10) 7.50 20.00
STATED ODDS 1:11
BG1 Eddie George .50 1.25
BG2 Edgerrin James .50 1.25
BG3 Terrell Davis .50 1.25
BG4 Jamal Anderson .50 1.25
BG5 Ricky Williams .50 1.25
BG6 Thomas Jones .50 1.25
BG7 Jamal Lewis .60 1.50
BG8 Ron Dayne .60 1.50
BG9 Shaun Alexander .60 1.50
BG10 Trung Canidate .40 1.00

2000 Ultimate Victory Competitors

Randomly inserted in packs at the rate of one in 11, this 10-card set features color player photography on an all-foil card stock with gold foil highlights.

COMPLETE SET (10) 6.00 15.00
STATED ODDS 1:11
UC1 Randy Moss .75 2.00
UC2 Peyton Manning 2.50 6.00
UC3 Stephen Davis .60 1.50
UC4 Cris Carter 1.00 2.50
UC5 Jevon Kearse .60 1.50
UC6 Peter Warrick .60 1.50
UC7 Plaxico Burress .75 2.00
UC8 Travis Taylor .60 1.50
UC9 Sylvester Morris .60 1.50
UC10 R.Jay Soward .60 1.50

2000 Ultimate Victory Crowning Glory

Randomly inserted in packs at the rate of one in 23, this 10-card set features color player photography set against a gold foil background and a purple left border. Cards contain gold foil highlights.

COMPLETE SET (10) 10.00 25.00
STATED ODDS 1:23
CG1 Peyton Manning 2.50 6.00
CG2 Edgerrin James .75 2.00
CG3 Randy Moss .75 2.00
CG4 Tim Couch .75 2.00
CG5 Eddie George .75 2.00
CG6 Terrell Davis .75 2.00
CG7 Marcus Robinson .75 2.00
CG8 Marvin Harrison .75 2.00
CG9 Charlie Batch .60 1.50
CG10 Shaun King .60 1.50

2000 Ultimate Victory Fabrics

Randomly inserted in packs at the rate of one in 239, the first six cards of this set feature swatches of game jerseys from Super Bowl XXXIV. The other three cards in the set are individually numbered and feature two or four Super Bowl

jersey swatches.
SINGLE JERSEY ODDS 1:239
AZ Az-Zahir Hakim 6.00 15.00
IB Isaac Bruce 10.00 25.00
KC Kevin Carter 6.00 15.00
KW Kurt Warner 15.00 40.00
MF Marshall Faulk 8.00 20.00
TH Torry Holt 8.00 20.00
THIB T.Holt/I.Bruce/100 25.00 60.00
MFKW M.Faulk/K.Warner/50 50.00 120.00
RAMS Warnr/Faulk/Bruc/Holt/10

2000 Ultimate Victory Legendary Fabrics

Randomly inserted in packs, this 4-card set features individual player cards with a swatch of game worn jersey sequentially numbered to 250, and a triple card with all three sequentially numbered to 100.
HL Howie Long/250 20.00 50.00
JM Joe Montana/250 30.00 80.00
RL Ronnie Lott/250 20.00 50.00
HOF Lott/Long/Montana/100 50.00 120.00

1992 Ultimate WLAF Promos

This set of unnumbered cards was issued to promote the 1992 Ultimate WLAF release. The cards include the basic cardfront but the cardback has an advertisement for the set and rules for their "Win $1,000,000" game except for Paul Palmer which features a cardback written in Spanish.
1 Tony Baker 1.50 4.00
2 Kerwin Bell 2.00 5.00
3 Stan Gelbaugh 2.00 5.00
4 Lee Morris 1.25 3.00
5 Pete Najarian 1.25 3.00
6 Mike Norseth 1.25 3.00
7 Eric Wilkerson 1.25 3.00
8 Paul Palmer 1.25 3.00
(Spanish cardback)

1992 Ultimate WLAF

The 1992 Ultimate WLAF football set consists of 200 standard-size cards. Twelve nine-card foil packs were packaged in each coliseum display box, and each box came with a mini-poster and one hologram card. There were ten different hologram cards produced, one for each WLAF team logo. In addition, each foil pack contained a giveaway game card, and the individual who collected all five letters to spell W-O-R-L-D would win one million dollars. The cards are checklisted alphabetically according to teams. The set closes with two topical subsets: How to Play the Game (180-192) and How To Collect Cards (193-200).
COMPLETE SET (200) 4.80 12.00
1 Barcelona Dragons .02 .10
2 Demetrius Davis .02 .10
3 Tim Egerton .01 .05
4 Scott Erney .01 .05
6 Anthony Greene .01 .05
7 Mike Hinnant UER .01 .05
8 Erik Naposki .01 .05
9 Paul Palmer .07 .20
10 Gene Taylor .01 .05
11 Thomas Woods .01 .05
12 Tony Rice .40 1.00
13 Terry O'Shea .01 .05
14 Brett Wiese .01 .05
15 Phil Alexander .01 .05
16 Eric Wilkerson .01 .05
17 Barcelona Dragons .01 .05
18 Barcelona Dragons .01 .05
19 Birmingham Fire .01 .05
20 Eric Jones QB .01 .05
21 Steven Avery .01 .05
22 Willie Bouyer .01 .05
23 Anthony Parker .07 .20
24 Elroy Harris .01 .05
25 James Henry .01 .05
26 John Holland .02 .10
27 Mark Hopkins .01 .05
28 Arthur Hunter .01 .05
29 Danny Lockett .01 .05
30 Kirk Maggio .01 .05
31 John Miller .01 .05
32 Ricky Shaw .01 .05
33 Phil Ross .01 .05
34 Mike Norseth .01 .05
35 Birmingham Fire .01 .05
36 Frankfurt Galaxy .01 .05
37 Anthony Wallace .01 .05
38 Lew Barnes .01 .05
39 Richard Buchanan .01 .05
40 Yepi Pau'u .01 .05
41 Pat McGuirk UER .01 .05
42 Tony Baker .20 .50
43 1992 TV Schedule 1 .01 .05
44 Tim Broady .01 .05
45 Lonnie Finch .01 .05
46 Chad Fortune .01 .05
47 Harry Jackson .01 .05
48 Jason Johnson .01 .05
49 Pat Moorer .01 .05
50 Mike Perez .02 .10
51 Mark Seals .01 .05
52 Cedric Stallworth .01 .05
53 Tom Whelihan .01 .05
54 Joe Johnson DB .10 .30
55 Frankfurt Galaxy .01 .05
56 London Monarchs .02 .10
1991 Team Statistics
Stan Gelbaugh
57 Stan Gelbaugh .02 .10
58 Jeff Alexander .01 .05
59 Dana Brinson .01 .05
60 Marlon Brown .01 .05
61 Dedrick Dodge .01 .05
62 Judd Garrett .02 .10
63 Greg Horne .01 .05
64 Jon Horton .01 .05
65 Danny Lockett .01 .05
66 Andre Riley .01 .05
67 Charlie Young .01 .05
68 David Smith RB .01 .05
69 Irvin Smith .01 .05
70 Rickey Williams .01 .05
71 Roland Smith .01 .05
72 William Kirksey .01 .05
73 Phil Alexander .01 .05
74 London Monarchs Team .02 .10
75 London Monarchs CL .01 .05
76 Montreal Machine .01 .05
1991 Team Statistics
77 Rollin Putzier .01 .05
78 Adam Bob .01 .05
79 K.D. Dunn .01 .05
80 Darryl Holmes .01 .05
81 Ricky Johnson .01 .05
82 Michael Finn .01 .05
83 Chris Mohr .02 .10
84 Don Murray .01 .05
85 Bjorn Nittmo .01 .05
86 Michael Proctor .01 .05
87 Broderick Sargent .01 .05
88 Richard Shelton .01 .05
89 Emanuel King .02 .10
90 Pete Mandley .02 .10
91 Kris McCall .01 .05
92 1992 TV Schedule 2 .01 .05
93 Montreal Machine .01 .05
94 NY .01 .05
NJ Knights
95 Andre Alexander .01 .05
96 Pat Marlatt .01 .05
97 Cecil Fletcher .01 .05
98 Lonnie Turner .01 .05
99 Monty Gilbreath .01 .05
100 Tony Jones UER .01 .05
101 Kip Lewis .01 .05
102 Bobby Lilljedahl .01 .05
103 Mark Moore .01 .05
104 Falanda Newton .01 .05
105 Anthony Parker UER .07 .20
106 Kendall Trainor .01 .05
107 Eric Wilkerson .01 .05
108 Tony Woods Okl. .07 .20
109 Reggie Slack .01 .05
110 Joey Banes .01 .05
111 Ron Sancho .01 .05
112 Mike Husar .01 .05
113 NY .01 .05
NJ Knights
114 Orlando Thunder .01 .05
115 Byron Williams UER .01 .05
116 Charlie Baumann .02 .10
117 Kerwin Bell .02 .10
118 Rodney Lossow .01 .05
119 Myron Jones .01 .05
120 Bruce Lasane .01 .05
121 Eric Mitchel .01 .05
122 Billy Owens .01 .05
123 1992 TV Schedule 3 .01 .05
124 Chris Roscoe .01 .05
125 Tommie Stowers .01 .05
126 Wayne Dickson UER .01 .05
127 Scott Mitchell .50 1.25
128 Karl Dunbar .01 .05
129 Dana Brinson .01 .05
130 Orlando Thunder .01 .05
131 Sacramento Surge .01 .05
132 1992 TV Schedule 4 .01 .05
133 Mike Adams .01 .05
134 Greg Coauette .01 .05
135 Mel Farr Jr. .02 .10
136 Victor Floyd .01 .05
137 Paul Frazier .01 .05
138 Tom Gerhart .01 .05
139 Pete Najarian .01 .05
140 John Nies .01 .05
141 Carl Parker .01 .05
142 Saute Sapolu .01 .05
143 George Bethune .01 .05
144 David Archer .50 1.25
145 John Buddenberg .01 .05
146 Jon Horton UER .01 .05
147 Sacramento Surge .01 .05
148 San Antonio Riders .01 .05
149 Ricky Blake .02 .10
150 Jim Gallery .01 .05
151 Jason Garrett 1.25 3.00
152 John Garrett .01 .05
153 Broderick Graves .01 .05
154 Bill Hess .01 .05
155 Mike Johnson QB .02 .10
156 Lee Morris .01 .05
157 Dwight Pickens .01 .05
158 Kent Sullivan .01 .05
159 Ken Watson .01 .05
160 Ronnie Williams .01 .05
161 Titus Dixon .01 .05
162 Mike Kiselak .01 .05
163 Greg Lee .01 .05
164 Judd Garrett UER .02 .10
165 San Antonio Riders .01 .05
166 Tenth Week Summaries .01 .05
167 Randy Bethel .01 .05
168 Melvin Patterson .01 .05
169 Eric Harmon .01 .05
170 Patrick Jackson .01 .05
171 Tim James .01 .05
172 George Koonce .07 .20
173 Babe Laufenberg .07 .20
174 Amir Rasul .01 .05
175 Stan Gelbaugh .08 .25
176 Jason Wallace .01 .05
177 Walter Wilson .01 .05
178 Power Meter Info .02 .10
179 Ohio Glory Checklist .01 .05
180 The Football Field .30 .75
Jim Kelly
181 Moving the Ball .30 .75
Jim Kelly
182 Defense: Back Field .10 .30
Cornerbacks and Safeties
Lawrence Taylor
183 Defense: Linebackers .10 .30
Lawrence Taylor
184 Defense: Defensive Line .10 .30
Defensive Tackles
and Ends
Lawrence Taylor
185 Offense: Offensive Line .30 .75
Centers, Guards,
Tackles and Tight Ends
Jim Kelly
186 Offense: Receivers .10 .30
Lawrence Taylor
187 Offense: Running Backs .30 .75
Jim Kelly
188 Offensive: Quarterback .30 .75
Jim Kelly
189 Special Teams .01 .05
190 Rules and Regulations .01 .05
WL Rules that differ
from NFL 1990 Rules
191 Defensive Overview .01 .05
Scoring Touchdowns
and Extra Points
192 Offensive Overview .01 .05
Scoring, Field Goals
and Safeties
193 How to Collect .10 .30
What is a Set
Lawrence Taylor
194 How to Collect .10 .30
What is a Wax Pack
Lawrence Taylor
195 How to Collect .10 .30
Premier Editions
Lawrence Taylor
196 How to Collect .10 .30
What Creates Value
Lawrence Taylor
197 How to Collect .30 .75
Rookie Cards
Jim Kelly
198 How to Collect .30 .75
Grading Your Cards
Jim Kelly
199 How to Collect .30 .75
Storing Your Cards
Jim Kelly
200 How to Collect .30 .75
Trading Your Cards
Jim Kelly

1992 Ultimate WLAF Logo Holograms

The 1992 Ultimate WLAF Team Logo Hologram set consists of ten standard-size cards. Twelve nine-card foil packs were packaged in each coliseum display box, and each box came with a mini-poster and one hologram card. There were ten different hologram cards produced, one for each WLAF team logo.
COMPLETE SET (10) 2.40 6.00
1 Barcelona Dragons .30 .75
2 Birmingham Fire .30 .75
3 Frankfurt Galaxy .30 .75
4 London Monarchs .30 .75
5 Montreal Machine .30 .75
6 NY .30 .75
NJ Knights
7 Ohio Glory .30 .75
8 Orlando Thunder .30 .75
9 Sacramento Surge .30 .75
10 San Antonio Riders .30 .75

1991 Ultra

The 1991 Ultra football set contains 300 standard-size cards. Cards were issued in 14-card packs. The cards are alphabetically within and according to teams. The last subset included in this set was Rookie Prospects (279-298). Rookie Cards in this set include Mike Croel, Brett Favre, Randal Hill, Russell Maryland, Herman Moore, Mike Pritchard and Ricky Watters.
COMPLETE SET (300) 7.50 20.00
1 Don Beebe .01 .05
2 Shane Conlan .01 .05
3 Pete Metzelaars .01 .05
4 Jamie Mueller .01 .05
5 Scott Norwood .01 .05
6 Andre Reed .02 .10
7 Leon Seals .01 .05
8 Bruce Smith .08 .25
9 Leonard Smith .01 .05
10 Thurman Thomas .08 .25
11 Lewis Billups .01 .05
12 Jim Breech .01 .05
13 James Brooks .02 .10
14 Eddie Brown .01 .05
15 Boomer Esiason .02 .10
16 David Fulcher .01 .05
17 Rodney Holman .01 .05
18 Bruce Kozerski .01 .05
19 Tim Krumrie .01 .05
20 Tim McGee .01 .05
21 Anthony Munoz .02 .10
22 Leon White .01 .05
23 Ickey Woods .01 .05
24 Carl Zander .01 .05
25 Brian Brennan .01 .05
26 Thane Gash .01 .05
27 Leroy Hoard .02 .10
28 Mike Johnson .01 .05
29 Reggie Langhorne .01 .05
30 Kevin Mack .01 .05
31 Clay Matthews .02 .10
32 Eric Metcalf .02 .10
33 Steve Atwater .01 .05
34 Melvin Bratton .01 .05
35 John Elway .50 1.25
36 Bobby Humphrey .01 .05
37 Mark Jackson .01 .05
38 Vance Johnson .01 .05
39 Ricky Nattiel .01 .05
40 Steve Sewell .01 .05
41 Dennis Smith .01 .05
42 David Treadwell .01 .05
43 Michael Young .01 .05
44 Ray Childress .01 .05
45 Cris Dishman RC .01 .05
46 William Fuller .02 .10
47 Ernest Givins .02 .10
48 John Grimsley UER .01 .05
49 Drew Hill .01 .05
50 Haywood Jeffires .02 .10
51 Sean Jones .02 .10
52 Johnny Meads .01 .05
53 Warren Moon .08 .25
54 Al Smith .01 .05
55 Lorenzo White .01 .05
56 Albert Bentley .01 .05
57 Duane Bickett .01 .05
58 Bill Brooks .01 .05
59 Jeff George .08 .25
60 Mike Prior .01 .05
61 Rohn Stark .01 .05
62 Jack Trudeau .01 .05
63 Clarence Verdin .01 .05
64 Steve DeBerg .01 .05
65 Emile Harry .01 .05
66 Albert Lewis .01 .05
67 Nick Lowery UER .01 .05
68 Todd McNair .01 .05
69 Christian Okoye .01 .05
70 Stephone Paige .01 .05
71 Kevin Porter UER .01 .05
72 Derrick Thomas .08 .25
73 Robb Thomas .01 .05
74 Barry Word .01 .05
75 Marcus Allen .08 .25
76 Eddie Anderson .01 .05
77 Tim Brown .08 .25
78 Mervyn Fernandez .01 .05
79 Willie Gault .02 .10
80 Ethan Horton .01 .05
81 Howie Long .08 .25
82 Vance Mueller .01 .05
83 Jay Schroeder .01 .05
84 Steve Smith .01 .05
85 Greg Townsend .01 .05
86 Mark Clayton .02 .10
87 Jim C. Jensen .01 .05
88 Dan Marino .50 1.25
89 Tim McKyer UER .01 .05
90 John Offerdahl .01 .05
91 Louis Oliver .01 .05
92 Reggie Roby .01 .05
93 Sammie Smith .01 .05
94 Hart Lee Dykes .01 .05
95 Irving Fryar .02 .10
96 Tommy Hodson .01 .05
97 Maurice Hurst .01 .05
98 John Stephens .01 .05
99 Andre Tippett .01 .05
100 Mark Boyer .01 .05
101 Kyle Clifton .01 .05
102 James Hasty .01 .05
103 Erik McMillan .01 .05
104 Rob Moore .08 .25
105 Joe Mott .01 .05
106 Ken O'Brien .01 .05
107 Ron Stallworth UER .01 .05
108 Al Toon .02 .10
109 Gary Anderson K .01 .05
110 Bubby Brister .01 .05
111 Thomas Everett .01 .05
112 Merril Hoge .01 .05
113 Louis Lipps .01 .05
114 Greg Lloyd .08 .25
115 Hardy Nickerson .02 .10
116 Dwight Stone .01 .05
117 Rod Woodson .08 .25
118 Tim Worley .01 .05
119 Rod Bernstine .01 .05
120 Marion Butts .02 .10
121 Gill Byrd .01 .05
122 Arthur Cox .01 .05
123 Burt Grossman .01 .05
124 Ronnie Harmon .01 .05
125 Anthony Miller .02 .10
126 Leslie O'Neal .02 .10
127 Gary Plummer .01 .05
128 Sam Seale .01 .05
129 Junior Seau .08 .25
130 Broderick Thompson .01 .05
131 Billy Joe Tolliver .01 .05
132 Brian Blades .02 .10
133 Jeff Bryant .01 .05
134 Derrick Fenner .01 .05
135 Jacob Green .01 .05
136 Andy Heck .01 .05
137 Patrick Hunter UER RC .01 .05
138 Norm Johnson .01 .05
139 Tommy Kane .01 .05
140 Dave Krieg .02 .10
141 John L. Williams .01 .05
142 Terry Wooden .01 .05
143 Steve Broussard .01 .05
144 Keith Jones .01 .05
145 Brian Jordan .02 .10
146 Chris Miller .02 .10
147 John Rade .01 .05
148 Andre Rison .02 .10
149 Mike Rozier .01 .05
150 Deion Sanders .15 .40
151 Neal Anderson .02 .10
152 Trace Armstrong .01 .05
153 Kevin Butler .01 .05
154 Mark Carrier DB .02 .10
155 Richard Dent .02 .10
156 Dennis Gentry .01 .05
157 Jim Harbaugh .08 .25
158 Brad Muster .01 .05
159 William Perry .02 .10
160 Mike Singletary .02 .10
161 Lemuel Stinson .01 .05
162 Troy Aikman .30 .75
163 Michael Irvin .08 .25
164 Mike Saxon .01 .05
165 Emmitt Smith 1.00 2.50
166 Jerry Ball .01 .05
167 Michael Cofer .01 .05
168 Rodney Peete .02 .10
169 Barry Sanders .50 1.25
170 Robert Brown .01 .05
171 Anthony Dilweg .01 .05
172 Tim Harris .01 .05
173 Johnny Holland .01 .05
174 Perry Kemp .01 .05
175 Don Majkowski .01 .05
176 Brian Noble .01 .05
177 Jeff Query .01 .05
178 Sterling Sharpe .08 .25
179 Charles Wilson .01 .05
180 Keith Woodside .01 .05
181 Flipper Anderson UER .01 .05
182 Bern Brostek .01 .05
183 Pat Carter RC .01 .05
184 Aaron Cox .01 .05
185 Henry Ellard .02 .10
186 Jim Everett .02 .10
187 Cleveland Gary .01 .05
188 Jerry Gray .01 .05
189 Kevin Greene .02 .10
190 Mike Wilcher .01 .05
191 Alfred Anderson .01 .05
192 Joey Browner .01 .05
193 Anthony Carter .02 .10
194 Chris Doleman .01 .05
195 Rick Fenney .01 .05
196 Darrell Fullington .01 .05
197 Rich Gannon .08 .25
198 Hassan Jones .01 .05
199 Steve Jordan .01 .05
200 Mike Merriweather .01 .05
201 Al Noga .01 .05
202 Herschel Walker .02 .10
203 Wade Wilson .02 .10
204 Morten Andersen .01 .05
205 Gene Atkins .01 .05
206 Toi Cook RC .01 .05
207 Craig Heyward .02 .10
208 Dalton Hilliard .01 .05
209 Vaughan Johnson .01 .05
210 Eric Martin .01 .05
211 Brett Perriman .08 .25
212 Pat Swilling .01 .05
213 Steve Walsh .01 .05
214 Ottis Anderson .02 .10
215 Carl Banks .01 .05
216 Maurice Carthon .01 .05
217 Mark Collins .01 .05
218 Rodney Hampton .08 .25
219 Erik Howard .01 .05
220 Mark Ingram .01 .05
221 Pepper Johnson .01 .05
222 Dave Meggett .02 .10
223 Phil Simms .02 .10
224 Lawrence Taylor .08 .25
225 Lewis Tillman .01 .05
226 Everson Walls .01 .05
227 Fred Barnett .08 .25
228 Jerome Brown .01 .05
229 Keith Byars .01 .05
230 Randall Cunningham .08 .25
231 Byron Evans .01 .05
232 Wes Hopkins .01 .05
233 Keith Jackson .02 .10
234 Heath Sherman .01 .05
235 Anthony Toney .01 .05
236 Reggie White .08 .25
237 Rich Camarillo .01 .05
238 Ken Harvey .02 .10
239 Eric Hill .01 .05
240 Johnny Johnson .01 .05
241 Ernie Jones .01 .05
242 Tim McDonald .01 .05
243 Timm Rosenbach .01 .05
244 Jay Taylor RC .01 .05
245 Dexter Carter .01 .05
246 Mike Cofer .01 .05
247 Kevin Fagan .01 .05
248 Don Griffin .01 .05
249 Charles Haley .02 .10
250 Brent Jones .08 .25
251 Joe Montana UER .50 1.25
252 Darryl Pollard .01 .05
253 Tom Rathman .01 .05
254 Jerry Rice .30 .75
255 John Taylor .02 .10
256 Steve Young .30 .75
257 Gary Anderson RB .01 .05
258 Mark Carrier WR .08 .25
259 Chris Chandler .08 .25
260 Reggie Cobb .01 .05
261 Reuben Davis .01 .05
262 Willie Drewrey .01 .05
263 Ron Hall .01 .05
264 Eugene Marve .01 .05
265 Winston Moss UER .01 .05
266 Vinny Testaverde .02 .10
267 Broderick Thomas .01 .05
268 Jeff Bostic .01 .05
269 Earnest Byner .01 .05
270 Gary Clark .08 .25
271 Darrell Green .01 .05
272 Jim Lachey .01 .05
273 Wilber Marshall .01 .05
274 Art Monk .02 .10
275 Gerald Riggs .01 .05
276 Mark Rypien .02 .10
277 Ricky Sanders .01 .05
278 Alvin Walton .01 .05
279 Nick Bell RC .01 .05
280 Eric Bieniemy RC .01 .05
281 Jarrod Bunch RC .01 .05
282 Mike Croel RC .08 .25
283 Brett Favre RC 5.00 10.00
284 Moe Gardner RC .01 .05
285 Pat Harlow RC .01 .05
286 Randal Hill RC .02 .10
287 Todd Marinovich RC .01 .05
288 Russell Maryland RC .08 .25
289 Dan McGwire RC .01 .05
290 Ernie Mills UER RC .02 .10
291 Herman Moore RC .08 .25
292 Godfrey Myles RC .01 .05
293 Browning Nagle RC .01 .05
294 Mike Pritchard RC .08 .25
295 Esera Tuaolo RC .01 .05
296 Mark Vander Poel RC .01 .05
297 Ricky Watters RC .60 1.50
298 Chris Zorich RC .08 .25
299 Checklist Card .02 .10
300 Checklist Card .02 .10

1991 Ultra All-Stars

The 1991 Ultra All-Stars set consists of 10 standard-size cards. The cards were issued as inserts into the regular 1991 Ultra packs that were sold (primarily to the hobby) in black boxes.
COMPLETE SET (10) 6.00 12.00
RANDOM INSERTS IN HOBBY PACKS
1 Barry Sanders 2.50 5.00
2 Keith Jackson .15 .40
3 Bruce Smith .40 1.00
4 Randall Cunningham .40 1.00
5 Dan Marino 2.50 5.00
6 Charles Haley .15 .40
7 John L. Williams .07 .20
8 Darrell Green .07 .20
9 Stephone Paige .07 .20
10 Kevin Greene .15 .40

1991 Ultra Performances

This ten-card standard-size set was produced by Fleer to showcase outstanding NFL football players. The front features a color action player photo, banded above and below by silver stripes but bleeding to the edge of the card on the sides. To highlight the featured player, the background and other players in the picture are washed out. Inside black and silver borders, the back presents player profile. The cards were issued as inserts into the regular 1991 Ultra packs that were sold primarily to the retail industry in green boxes.
COMPLETE SET (10) 5.00 12.00
RANDOM INSERTS IN RETAIL PACKS
1 Emmitt Smith 5.00 10.00
2 Andre Rison .20 .50
3 Derrick Thomas .60 1.25
4 Joe Montana 3.00 6.00
5 Warren Moon .60 1.25
6 Mike Singletary .20 .50
7 Thurman Thomas .60 1.25
8 Rod Woodson .60 1.25
9 Jerry Rice 2.00 4.00
10 Reggie White .60 1.25

1991 Ultra Update

This 100-card standard-size set was produced by Fleer and featured some of the leading rookies and players who switched franchises during the 1991 season. Rookie Cards include Lawrence Dawsey, Ricky Ervins, Jeff Graham, Merton Hanks, Michael Jackson, Neil O'Donnell, Stanley Richard, Leonard Russell, Jon Vaughn and Harvey Williams. The cards are numbered with a "U" prefix excpet for the Jerry Rice #99.
COMP.FACT.SET (100) 10.00 25.00
U1 Brett Favre 6.00 15.00
U2 Moe Gardner .02 .10
U3 Tim McKyer .02 .10
U4 Bruce Pickens RC .02 .10
U5 Mike Pritchard .15 .40
U6 Cornelius Bennett .07 .20
U7 Phil Hansen RC .02 .10
U8 Henry Jones RC .07 .20
U9 Mark Kelso .02 .10
U10 James Lofton .07 .20
U11 Anthony Morgan RC .02 .10
U12 Stan Thomas .02 .10
U13 Chris Zorich .07 .20
U14 Reggie Rembert .02 .10
U15 Alfred Williams RC .02 .10
U16 Michael Jackson WR RC .15 .40
U17 Ed King RC .02 .10
U18 Joe Morris .02 .10
U19 Vince Newsome .02 .10
U20 Tony Casillas .02 .10
U21 Russell Maryland .15 .40
U22 Jay Novacek .15 .40
U23 Mike Croel .02 .10
U24 Gaston Green .02 .10
U25 Kenny Walker RC .02 .10
U26 Melvin Jenkins RC .02 .10
U27 Herman Moore .15 .40
U28 Kelvin Pritchett RC .07 .20
U29 Chris Spielman .07 .20
U30 Vinnie Clark RC .02 .10
U31 Allen Rice .02 .10
U32 Vai Sikahema .02 .10
U33 Esera Tuaolo .02 .10
U34 Mike Dumas RC .02 .10
U35 John Flannery RC .02 .10
U36 Allen Pinkett .02 .10
U37 Tim Barnett RC .02 .10
U38 Dan Saleaumua .02 .10
U39 Harvey Williams RC .15 .40
U40 Nick Bell .02 .10
U41 Roger Craig .07 .20
U42 Ronnie Lott .07 .20
U43 Todd Marinovich .02 .10
U44 Robert Delpino .02 .10
U45 Todd Lyght RC .02 .10
U46 Robert Young RC .07 .20
U47 Aaron Craver RC .02 .10
U48 Mark Higgs RC .02 .10
U49 Vestee Jackson .02 .10
U50 Carl Lee .02 .10
U51 Felix Wright .02 .10
U52 Darrell Fullington .02 .10
U53 Pat Harlow .02 .10
U54 Eugene Lockhart .02 .10
U55 Hugh Millen RC .02 .10
U56 Leonard Russell RC .15 .40
U57 Jon Vaughn RC .02 .10
U58 Quinn Early .07 .20
U59 Bobby Hebert .02 .10
U60 Rickey Jackson .02 .10
U61 Sam Mills .07 .20
U62 Jarrod Bunch .02 .10
U63 John Elliott .02 .10
U64 Jeff Hostetler .07 .20
U65 Ed McCaffrey RC 2.50 6.00
U66 Kanavis McGhee RC .02 .10
U67 Mo Lewis RC .07 .20
U68 Browning Nagle .02 .10
U69 Blair Thomas .02 .10
U70 Antone Davis RC .02 .10
U71A Brad Goebel RC .02 .10
U71B Randal Hill UER .07 .20
U72 Jim McMahon .07 .20
U73 Clyde Simmons .02 .10
U75 Eric Swann RC .15 .40
U76 Tom Tupa .02 .10
U77 Jeff Graham RC .15 .40
U78 Eric Green .02 .10
U79 Neil O'Donnell RC .15 .40
U80 Huey Richardson RC .02 .10
U81 Eric Bieniemy .02 .10
U82 John Friesz .15 .40
U83 Eric Moten RC .02 .10
U84 Stanley Richard RC .02 .10
U85 Todd Bowles .08 .25
U86 Merton Hanks RC .15 .40
U87 Tim Harris .02 .10
U88 Pierce Holt .02 .10
U89 Ted Washington RC .02 .10
U90 John Kasay RC .07 .20
U91 Dan McGwire .02 .10
U92 Lawrence Dawsey RC .07 .20
U93 Charles McRae RC .02 .10
U94 Jesse Solomon .02 .10
U95 Robert Wilson RC .02 .10
U96 Ricky Ervins RC .07 .20
U97 Charles Mann .02 .10
U98 Bobby Wilson RC .02 .10
99 Jerry Rice PV .60 1.50
U100 N.Bell/J.McMahon CL .02 .10

1992 Ultra

This 450-card standard-size set features color action player photos. Cards were issued in 14-card packs. The cards are checklisted below alphabetically according to teams. The set closes with Draft Picks (417-446). Rookie Cards include Edgar Bennett, Steve Bono, Terrell Buckley, Amp Lee, Kevin Turner and Tommy Vardell.
COMPLETE SET (450) 6.00 15.00
1 Steve Broussard .02 .10
2 Rick Bryan .02 .10
3 Scott Case .02 .10
4 Darion Conner .02 .10
5 Bill Fralic .02 .10
6 Moe Gardner .02 .10
7 Tim Green .02 .10
8 Michael Haynes .07 .20
9 Chris Hinton .02 .10
10 Mike Kenn .02 .10
11 Tim McKyer .02 .10
12 Chris Miller .07 .20
13 Eric Pegram .07 .20
14 Mike Pritchard .07 .20
15 Andre Rison .07 .20
16 Jessie Tuggle .02 .10
17 Carlton Bailey RC .02 .10
18 Howard Ballard .02 .10
19 Cornelius Bennett .07 .20
20 Shane Conlan .02 .10
21 Kenneth Davis .02 .10
22 Kent Hull .02 .10
23 Mark Kelso .02 .10
24 James Lofton .07 .20
25 Keith McKeller .02 .10
26 Nate Odomes .02 .10
27 Jim Ritcher .02 .10
28 Leon Seals .02 .10
29 Darryl Talley .02 .10
30 Steve Tasker .07 .20
31 Thurman Thomas .15 .40
32 Will Wolford .02 .10
33 Jeff Wright .02 .10
34 Neal Anderson .02 .10
35 Trace Armstrong .02 .10
36 Mark Carrier DB .02 .10
37 Wendell Davis .02 .10
38 Richard Dent .07 .20
39 Shaun Gayle .02 .10
40 Jim Harbaugh .15 .40
41 Jay Hilgenberg .02 .10
42 Darren Lewis .02 .10
43 Steve McMichael .07 .20
44 Anthony Morgan .02 .10
45 Brad Muster .02 .10
46 William Perry .07 .20
47 John Roper .02 .10
48 Lemuel Stinson .02 .10
49 Tom Waddle .02 .10
50 Donnell Woolford .02 .10
51 Leo Barker RC .02 .10
52 Eddie Brown .02 .10
53 James Francis .02 .10
54 David Fulcher UER .02 .10
55 David Grant .02 .10
56 Harold Green .02 .10
57 Rodney Holman .02 .10
58 Lee Johnson .02 .10
59 Tim Krumrie .02 .10
60 Tim McGee .02 .10
61 Alonzo Mitz RC .02 .10
62 Anthony Munoz .07 .20
63 Alfred Williams .02 .10
64 Stephen Braggs .02 .10
65 Richard Brown RC .02 .10
66 Randy Hilliard RC .02 .10
67 Leroy Hoard .07 .20
68 Michael Jackson .07 .20
69 Mike Johnson .02 .10
70 James Jones DT .02 .10
71 Tony Jones T .02 .10
72 Ed King .02 .10
73 Kevin Mack .02 .10
74 Clay Matthews .07 .20
75 Eric Metcalf .07 .20
76 Vince Newsome .02 .10
77 Steve Beuerlein .07 .20
78 Larry Brown DB .02 .10
79 Tony Casillas .02 .10
80 Alvin Harper .07 .20
81 Issiac Holt .02 .10
82 Ray Horton .02 .10
83 Michael Irvin .15 .40
84 Daryl Johnston .15 .40
85 Kelvin Martin .02 .10
86 Ken Norton .07 .20
87 Jay Novacek .07 .20
88 Emmitt Smith 1.50 3.00
89 Vinson Smith RC .02 .10
90 Mark Stepnoski .07 .20
91 Tony Tolbert .02 .10
92 Alexander Wright .02 .10
93 Steve Atwater .02 .10
94 Tyrone Braxton .02 .10
95 Michael Brooks .02 .10
96 Mike Croel .02 .10
97 John Elway 1.00 2.50
98 Simon Fletcher .02 .10
99 Gaston Green .02 .10
100 Mark Jackson .02 .10
101 Keith Kartz .02 .10
102 Greg Kragen .02 .10
103 Greg Lewis .02 .10
104 Karl Mecklenburg .02 .10
105 Derek Russell .02 .10
106 Steve Sewell .02 .10
107 Dennis Smith .02 .10
108 David Treadwell .02 .10
109 Kenny Walker .02 .10
110 Michael Young .02 .10
111 Jerry Ball .02 .10
112 Bennie Blades .02 .10
113 Lomas Brown .02 .10
114 Scott Conover RC .02 .10
115 Ray Crockett .02 .10
116 Mel Gray .07 .20
117 Willie Green .02 .10
118 Erik Kramer .07 .20
119 Dan Owens .02 .10
120 Rodney Peete .07 .20
121 Brett Perriman .15 .40
122 Barry Sanders 1.00 2.50
123 Chris Spielman .07 .20
124 Marc Spindler .02 .10
125 William White .02 .10
126 Tony Bennett .02 .10
127 Matt Brock .02 .10
128 LeRoy Butler .02 .10
129 Chuck Cecil .02 .10
130 Johnny Holland .02 .10
131 Perry Kemp .02 .10
132 Don Majkowski .02 .10
133 Tony Mandarich .02 .10
134 Brian Noble .02 .10
135 Bryce Paup .15 .40
136 Sterling Sharpe .15 .40
137 Darrell Thompson .02 .10
138 Mike Tomczak .02 .10
139 Vince Workman .02 .10
140 Ray Childress .02 .10
141 Cris Dishman .02 .10
142 Curtis Duncan .02 .10
143 William Fuller .02 .10
144 Ernest Givins .07 .20
145 Haywood Jeffires .07 .20
146 Sean Jones .02 .10
147 Lamar Lathon .02 .10
148 Bruce Matthews .02 .10
149 Bubba McDowell .02 .10
150 Johnny Meads .02 .10
151 Warren Moon .15 .40
152 Mike Munchak .07 .20
153 Bo Orlando RC .02 .10
154 Al Smith .02 .10
155 Doug Smith .02 .10
156 Lorenzo White .02 .10
157 Chip Banks .02 .10
158 Duane Bickett .02 .10
159 Bill Brooks .02 .10
160 Eugene Daniel .02 .10
161 Jon Hand .02 .10
162 Jeff Herrod .02 .10
163 Jessie Hester .02 .10
164 Scott Radecic .02 .10
165 Rohn Stark .02 .10
166 Clarence Verdin .02 .10
167 John Alt .02 .10
168 Tim Barnett .02 .10
169 Tim Grunhard .02 .10
170 Dino Hackett .02 .10
171 Jonathan Hayes .02 .10
172 Bill Maas .02 .10
173 Chris Martin .02 .10
174 Christian Okoye .02 .10
175 Stephone Paige .02 .10
176 Jayice Pearson RC .02 .10
177 Kevin Porter .02 .10
178 Kevin Ross .02 .10
179 Dan Saleaumua .02 .10
180 Tracy Simien RC .02 .10
181 Neil Smith .15 .40
182 Derrick Thomas .15 .40
183 Robb Thomas .02 .10
184 Barry Word .02 .10
185 Marcus Allen .15 .40
186 Eddie Anderson .02 .10
187 Nick Bell .02 .10
188 Tim Brown .15 .40
189 Mervyn Fernandez .02 .10
190 Willie Gault .07 .20
191 Jeff Gossett .02 .10
192 Ethan Horton .02 .10
193 Jeff Jaeger .02 .10
194 Howie Long .15 .40
195 Ronnie Lott .07 .20
196 Todd Marinovich .02 .10
197 Don Mosebar .02 .10
198 Jay Schroeder .02 .10
199 Anthony Smith .02 .10
200 Greg Townsend .02 .10
201 Lionel Washington .02 .10
202 Steve Wisniewski .02 .10
203 Flipper Anderson .02 .10
204 Robert Delpino .02 .10
205 Henry Ellard .07 .20
206 Jim Everett .07 .20
207 Kevin Greene .07 .20
208 Darryl Henley .02 .10
209 Damone Johnson .02 .10
210 Larry Kelm .02 .10
211 Todd Lyght .02 .10
212 Jackie Slater .02 .10
213 Michael Stewart .02 .10
214 Pat Terrell .02 .10
215 Robert Young .02 .10
216 Mark Clayton .07 .20
217 Bryan Cox .07 .20
218 Jeff Cross .02 .10
219 Mark Duper .02 .10
220 Harry Galbreath .02 .10
221 David Griggs .02 .10
222 Mark Higgs .02 .10
223 Vestee Jackson .02 .10
224 John Offerdahl .02 .10
225 Louis Oliver .02 .10
226 Tony Paige .02 .10
227 Reggie Roby .02 .10
228 Pete Stoyanovich .02 .10
229 Richmond Webb .02 .10
230 Terry Allen .15 .40
231 Ray Berry .02 .10
232 Anthony Carter .07 .20
233 Cris Carter .30 .75
234 Chris Doleman .02 .10
235 Rich Gannon .15 .40
236 Steve Jordan .02 .10
237 Carl Lee .02 .10
238 Randall McDaniel .05 .15
239 Mike Merriweather .02 .10
240 Harry Newsome .02 .10
241 John Randle .07 .20
242 Henry Thomas .02 .10
243 Bruce Armstrong .02 .10
244 Vincent Brown .02 .10
245 Marv Cook .02 .10
246 Irving Fryar .07 .20
247 Pat Harlow .02 .10
248 Maurice Hurst .02 .10
249 Eugene Lockhart .02 .10
250 Greg McMurtry .02 .10
251 Hugh Millen .02 .10
252 Leonard Russell .07 .20
253 Chris Singleton .02 .10
254 Andre Tippett .02 .10
255 Jon Vaughn .02 .10
256 Morten Andersen .02 .10
257 Gene Atkins .02 .10
258 Wesley Carroll .02 .10
259 Jim Dombrowski .02 .10
260 Quinn Early .07 .20
261 Bobby Hebert .02 .10
262 Joel Hilgenberg .02 .10
263 Rickey Jackson .02 .10
264 Vaughan Johnson .02 .10
265 Eric Martin .02 .10
266 Brett Maxie .02 .10
267 Fred McAfee RC .02 .10
268 Sam Mills .02 .10
269 Pat Swilling .02 .10
270 Floyd Turner .02 .10
271 Steve Walsh .02 .10
272 Stephen Baker .02 .10
273 Jarrod Bunch .02 .10
274 Mark Collins .02 .10
275 John Elliott .02 .10
276 Myron Guyton .02 .10
277 Rodney Hampton .07 .20
278 Jeff Hostetler .07 .20
279 Mark Ingram .02 .10
280 Pepper Johnson .02 .10
281 Sean Landeta .02 .10
282 Leonard Marshall .02 .10
283 Kanavis McGhee .02 .10
284 Dave Meggett .07 .20
285 Bart Oates .02 .10
286 Phil Simms .07 .20
287 Reyna Thompson .02 .10
288 Lewis Tillman .02 .10
289 Brad Baxter .02 .10

290 Mike Brim RC .02 .10
291 Chris Burkett .02 .10
292 Kyle Clifton .02 .10
293 James Hasty .02 .10
294 Joe Kelly .02 .10
295 Jeff Lageman .02 .10
296 Mo Lewis .02 .10
297 Erik McMillan .02 .10
298 Scott Mersereau .02 .10
299 Rob Moore .07 .20
300 Tony Stargell .02 .10
301 Jim Sweeney .02 .10
302 Marvin Washington .02 .10
303 Lonnie Young .02 .10
304 Eric Allen .02 .10
305 Fred Barnett .15 .40
306 Keith Byars .02 .10
307 Byron Evans .02 .10
308 Wes Hopkins .02 .10
309 Keith Jackson .07 .20
310 James Joseph .02 .10
311 Seth Joyner .02 .10
312 Roger Ruzek .02 .10
313 Clyde Simmons .02 .10
314 William Thomas .02 .10
315 Reggie White .15 .40
316 Calvin Williams .07 .20
317 Rich Camarillo .02 .10
318 Jeff Faulkner .02 .10
319 Ken Harvey .02 .10
320 Eric Hill .02 .10
321 Johnny Johnson .02 .10
322 Ernie Jones .02 .10
323 Tim McDonald .02 .10
324 Freddie Joe Nunn .02 .10
325 Luis Sharpe .02 .10
326 Eric Swann .07 .20
327 Aeneas Williams .07 .20
328 Michael Zordich RC .02 .10
329 Gary Anderson K .02 .10
330 Bubby Brister .02 .10
331 Barry Foster .07 .20
332 Eric Green .02 .10
333 Bryan Hinkle .02 .10
334 Tunch Ilkin .02 .10
335 Carnell Lake .02 .10
336 Louis Lipps .02 .10
337 David Little .02 .10
338 Greg Lloyd .07 .20
339 Neil O'Donnell .07 .20
340 Rod Woodson .15 .40
341 Rod Bernstine .02 .10
342 Marion Butts .02 .10
343 Gill Byrd .02 .10
344 John Friesz .07 .20
345 Burt Grossman .02 .10
346 Courtney Hall .02 .10
347 Ronnie Harmon .02 .10
348 Shawn Jefferson .02 .10
349 Nate Lewis .02 .10
350 Craig McEwen RC .02 .10
351 Eric Moten .02 .10
352 Gary Plummer .02 .10
353 Henry Rolling .02 .10
354 Broderick Thompson .02 .10
355 Derrick Walker .02 .10
356 Harris Barton .02 .10
357 Steve Bono RC .15 .40
358 Todd Bowles .08 .25
359 Dexter Carter .02 .10
360 Michael Carter .02 .10
361 Keith DeLong .02 .10
362 Charles Haley .07 .20
363 Merton Hanks .07 .20
364 Tim Harris .02 .10
365 Brent Jones .07 .20
366 Guy McIntyre .02 .10
367 Tom Rathman .02 .10
368 Bill Romanowski .02 .10
369 Jesse Sapolu .02 .10
370 John Taylor .07 .20
371 Steve Young .60 1.50
372 Robert Blackmon .02 .10
373 Brian Blades .07 .20
374 Jacob Green .02 .10
375 Dwayne Harper .02 .10
376 Andy Heck .02 .10
377 Tommy Kane .02 .10
378 John Kasay .02 .10
379 Cortez Kennedy .07 .20
380 Bryan Millard .02 .10
381 Rufus Porter .02 .10
382 Eugene Robinson .02 .10
383 John L. Williams .02 .10
384 Terry Wooden .02 .10
385 Gary Anderson RB .02 .10
386 Ian Beckles .02 .10
387 Mark Carrier WR .07 .20
388 Reggie Cobb .02 .10
389 Tony Covington .02 .10
390 Lawrence Dawsey .07 .20
391 Ron Hall .02 .10
392 Keith McCants .02 .10
393 Charles McRae .02 .10
394 Tim Newton .02 .10
395 Jesse Solomon .02 .10
396 Vinny Testaverde .07 .20
397 Broderick Thomas .02 .10
398 Robert Wilson .02 .10
399 Earnest Byner .02 .10
400 Gary Clark .15 .40
401 Andre Collins .02 .10
402 Brad Edwards .02 .10
403 Kurt Gouveia .02 .10
404 Darrell Green .02 .10
405 Joe Jacoby .02 .10
406 Jim Lachey .02 .10
407 Chip Lohmiller .02 .10
408 Charles Mann .02 .10
409 Wilber Marshall .02 .10
410 Brian Mitchell .07 .20
411 Art Monk .07 .20
412 Mark Rypien .02 .10
413 Ricky Sanders .02 .10
414 Mark Schlereth RC .02 .10
415 Fred Stokes .02 .10
416 Bobby Wilson .02 .10
417 Corey Barlow RC .02 .10
418 Edgar Bennett RC .15 .40
419 Eddie Blake RC .02 .10
420 Terrell Buckley RC .02 .10
421 Willie Clay RC .02 .10
422 Rodney Culver RC .02 .10
423 Ed Cunningham RC .02 .10
424 Mark D'Onofrio RC .02 .10
425 Matt Darby RC .02 .10
426 Charles Davenport RC .02 .10
427 Will Furrer RC .02 .10
428 Keith Goganious RC .02 .10
429 Mario Bailey RC .02 .10
430 Chris Hakel RC .02 .10
431 Keith Hamilton RC .07 .20
432 Aaron Pierce RC .02 .10
433 Amp Lee RC .02 .10
434 Scott Lockwood RC .02 .10
435 Ricardo McDonald RC .02 .10
436 Dexter McNabb RC .02 .10
437 Chris Mims RC .02 .10
438 Mike Mooney RC .02 .10
439 Ray Roberts RC .02 .10
440 Patrick Rowe RC .02 .10
441 Leon Searcy RC .02 .10
442 Siran Stacy RC .02 .10
443 Kevin Turner RC .02 .10
444 Tommy Vardell RC .02 .10
445 Bob Whitfield RC .02 .10
446 Darryl Williams RC .02 .10
447 Checklist 1-110 .02 .10
448 Checklist 111-224 .02 .10
449 Checklist 230-340 UER .02 .10
450 Checklist 341-450 .02 .10
AD Super Bowl XXVII Strip .75 2.00

1992 Ultra Award Winners

This ten-card standard-size set was randomly inserted in 1992 Ultra foil packs. Each player featured was a recipient of an award for his performance during the 1991 season. The player photos are full-bleed except at the bottom where a diagonal gold foil stripe separates the picture from a black marbleized area. The player's name and the award won are printed in gold foil in this marbleized area, and a black emblem with "Award Winner" and a banner in gold foil is superimposed toward the lower right corner.

COMPLETE SET (10) 4.00 10.00
RANDOM INSERTS IN FOIL PACKS
1 Mark Rypien .10 .30
2 Cornelius Bennett .25 .60
3 Anthony Munoz .25 .60
4 Lawrence Dawsey .25 .60
5 Thurman Thomas .60 1.25
6 Michael Irvin .60 1.25
7 Mike Croel .10 .30
8 Barry Sanders 4.00 8.00
9 Pat Swilling .10 .30
10 Leonard Russell .25 .60

1992 Ultra Chris Miller

Randomly inserted in the foil packs, this ten-card standard-size set is part of Fleer's signature series. Miller signed over 2,000 of his subset cards. Card numbers 11-12 were available only by mail for ten '92 Ultra wrappers plus 2.00.

COMPLETE SET (10) 2.50 6.00
COMMON C.MILLER (1-10) .30 .75
COMMON SEND-OFF (11-12) .75 2.00
RANDOM INSERTS IN FOIL PACKS
AU Chris Miller AUTO 10.00 25.00

1992 Ultra Reggie White

Randomly inserted in foil packs, this ten-card standard-size set is part of Ultra's signature series. White signed over 2,000 of cards #1-10. Card numbers 11-12 were available only by mail for ten '92 Ultra wrappers plus 2.00. The fronts display color action player photos with a green inner border and a gray marbleized outer border. The player's name and the set title "Career Highlights" appear in gold foil lettering in the bottom border. On a gray marbleized background, the backs carry a color head shot and summary of White's football career. Card numbers 11-12 have rose-colored backs.

COMPLETE SET (10) 4.00 10.00
COMMON R.WHITE (1-10) .50 1.25
COMMON SEND-OFF (11-12) 1.00 2.50
RANDOM INSERTS IN FOIL PACKS

1992 Ultra Reggie White Autographs

COMMON CARD (1-10) 40.00 80.00

1993 Ultra

The 1993 Ultra set comprises 500 standard-size cards that were issued in 14 and 19-card packs. The cards are checklisted below alphabetically according to teams. Rookie Cards include Jerome Bettis, Drew Bledsoe, Vincent Brisby, Reggie Brooks, Curtis Conway, Troy Drayton, Garrison Hearst, Qadry Ismail, Terry Kirby, Leon Lett, O.J. McDuffie, Natrone Means, Glyn Milburn, Rick Mirer, Willie Roaf, Robert Smith and Dana Stubblefield.

COMPLETE SET (500) 7.50 20.00
1 Vinnie Clark .02 .10
2 Darion Conner .02 .10
3 Eric Dickerson .07 .20
4 Moe Gardner .02 .10
5 Tim Green .02 .10
6 Roger Harper RC .02 .10
7 Michael Haynes .07 .20
8 Bobby Hebert .02 .10
9 Chris Hinton .02 .10
10 Pierce Holt .02 .10
11 Mike Kenn .02 .10
12 Lincoln Kennedy RC .02 .10
13 Chris Miller .07 .20
14 Mike Pritchard .07 .20
15 Andre Rison .07 .20
16 Deion Sanders .30 .75
17 Tony Smith RB .02 .10
18 Jessie Tuggle .02 .10
19 Howard Ballard .02 .10
20 Don Beebe .02 .10
21 Cornelius Bennett .07 .20
22 Bill Brooks .02 .10
23 Kenneth Davis .02 .10
24 Phil Hansen .02 .10
25 Henry Jones .02 .10
26 Jim Kelly .15 .40
27 Nate Odomes .02 .10
28 John Parrella RC .02 .10
29 Andre Reed .07 .20
30 Frank Reich .07 .20
31 Jim Ritcher .02 .10
32 Bruce Smith .15 .40
33 Thomas Smith RC .07 .20
34 Darryl Talley .02 .10
35 Steve Tasker .07 .20
36 Thurman Thomas .15 .40
37 Jeff Wright .02 .10
38 Neal Anderson .02 .10
39 Trace Armstrong .02 .10
40 Mark Carrier DB .02 .10
41 Curtis Conway RC .30 .75
42 Wendell Davis .02 .10
43 Richard Dent .07 .20
44 Shaun Gayle .02 .10
45 Jim Harbaugh .15 .40
46 Craig Heyward .07 .20
47 Darren Lewis .02 .10
48 Steve McMichael .07 .20
49 William Perry .07 .20
50 Carl Simpson RC .02 .10
51 Alonzo Spellman .02 .10
52 Keith Van Horne .02 .10
53 Tom Waddle .02 .10
54 Donnell Woolford .02 .10
55 John Copeland RC .07 .20
56 Derrick Fenner .02 .10
57 James Francis .02 .10
58 Harold Green .02 .10
59 David Klingler .02 .10
60 Tim Krumrie .02 .10
61 Ricardo McDonald .02 .10
62 Tony McGee RC .07 .20
63 Carl Pickens .07 .20
64 Lamar Rogers .02 .10
65 Jay Schroeder .02 .10
66 Daniel Stubbs .02 .10
67 Steve Tovar RC .02 .10
68 Alfred Williams .02 .10
69 Darryl Williams .02 .10
70 Jerry Ball .02 .10
71 David Brandon .02 .10
72 Rob Burnett .02 .10
73 Mark Carrier WR .07 .20
74 Steve Everitt RC .02 .10
75 Dan Footman RC .02 .10
76 Leroy Hoard .07 .20
77 Michael Jackson .07 .20
78 Mike Johnson .02 .10
79 Bernie Kosar .07 .20
80 Clay Matthews .07 .20
81 Eric Metcalf .07 .20
82 Michael Dean Perry .07 .20
83 Vinny Testaverde .07 .20
84 Tommy Vardell .02 .10
85 Troy Aikman .60 1.50
86 Larry Brown DB .02 .10
87 Tony Casillas .02 .10
88 Thomas Everett .02 .10
89 Charles Haley .07 .20
90 Alvin Harper .07 .20
91 Michael Irvin .15 .40
92 Jim Jeffcoat .02 .10
93 Daryl Johnston .15 .40
94 Robert Jones .02 .10
95 Leon Lett RC .07 .20
96 Russell Maryland .02 .10
97 Nate Newton .07 .20
98 Ken Norton .07 .20
99 Jay Novacek .07 .20
100 Darrin Smith RC .07 .20
101 Emmitt Smith 1.25 3.00
102 Kevin Smith .07 .20
103 Mark Stepnoski .02 .10
104 Tony Tolbert .02 .10
105 Kevin Williams RC WR .15 .40
106 Steve Atwater .02 .10
107 Rod Bernstine .02 .10
108 Mike Croel .02 .10
109 Robert Delpino .02 .10
110 Shane Dronett .02 .10
111 John Elway 1.25 3.00
112 Simon Fletcher .02 .10
113 Greg Kragen .02 .10
114 Tommy Maddox .15 .40
115 Arthur Marshall RC .02 .10
116 Karl Mecklenburg .02 .10
117 Glyn Milburn RC .15 .40
118 Reggie Rivers RC .02 .10
119 Shannon Sharpe .15 .40
120 Dennis Smith .02 .10
121 Kenny Walker .02 .10
122 Dan Williams RC .02 .10
123 Bennie Blades .02 .10
124 Lomas Brown .02 .10
125 Bill Fralic .02 .10
126 Mel Gray .07 .20
127 Willie Green .02 .10
128 Jason Hanson .02 .10
129 Antonio London RC .02 .10
130 Ryan McNeil RC .15 .40
131 Herman Moore .15 .40
132 Rodney Peete .02 .10
133 Brett Perriman .15 .40
134 Kelvin Pritchett .02 .10
135 Barry Sanders 1.00 2.50
136 Tracy Scroggins .02 .10
137 Chris Spielman .07 .20
138 Pat Swilling .02 .10
139 Andre Ware .02 .10
140 Edgar Bennett .15 .40
141 Tony Bennett .02 .10
142 Matt Brock .02 .10
143 Terrell Buckley .02 .10
144 LeRoy Butler .02 .10
145 Mark Clayton .02 .10
146 Brett Favre 1.50 4.00
147 Jackie Harris .02 .10
148 Johnny Holland .02 .10
149 Bill Maas .02 .10
150 Brian Noble .02 .10
151 Bryce Paup .07 .20
152 Ken Ruettgers .02 .10
153 Sterling Sharpe .15 .40
154 Wayne Simmons RC .02 .10
155 John Stephens .02 .10
156 George Teague RC .07 .20
157 Reggie White .15 .40
158 Micheal Barrow RC .15 .40
159 Cody Carlson .02 .10
160 Ray Childress .02 .10
161 Cris Dishman .02 .10
162 Curtis Duncan .02 .10
163 William Fuller .02 .10
164 Ernest Givins .07 .20
165 Brad Hopkins RC .02 .10
166 Haywood Jeffires .07 .20
167 Lamar Lathon .02 .10
168 Wilber Marshall .02 .10
169 Bruce Matthews .02 .10
170 Bubba McDowell .02 .10
171 Warren Moon .15 .40
172 Mike Munchak .07 .20
173 Eddie Robinson .02 .10
174 Al Smith .02 .10
175 Lorenzo White .02 .10
176 Lee Williams .02 .10
177 Chip Banks .02 .10
178 John Baylor .02 .10
179 Duane Bickett .02 .10
180 Kerry Cash .02 .10
181 Quentin Coryatt .07 .20
182 Rodney Culver .02 .10
183 Steve Emtman .02 .10
184 Jeff George .15 .40
185 Jeff Herrod .02 .10
186 Jessie Hester .02 .10
187 Anthony Johnson .07 .20
188 Reggie Langhorne .02 .10
189 Roosevelt Potts RC .02 .10
190 Rohn Stark .02 .10
191 Clarence Verdin .02 .10
192 Will Wolford .02 .10
193 Marcus Allen .15 .40
194 John Alt .02 .10
195 Tim Barnett .02 .10
196 J.J.Birden .02 .10
197 Dale Carter .02 .10
198 Willie Davis .15 .40
199 Jaime Fields RC .02 .10
200 Dave Krieg .07 .20
201 Nick Lowery .02 .10
202 Charles Mincy RC .02 .10
203 Joe Montana 1.25 3.00
204 Christian Okoye .02 .10
205 Dan Saleaumua .02 .10
206 Will Shields RC .15 .40
207 Tracy Simien .02 .10
208 Neil Smith .15 .40
209 Derrick Thomas .15 .40
210 Harvey Williams .07 .20
211 Barry Word .02 .10
212 Eddie Anderson .02 .10
213 Patrick Bates RC .02 .10
214 Nick Bell .02 .10
215 Tim Brown .15 .40
216 Willie Gault .02 .10
217 Gaston Green .02 .10
218 Billy Joe Hobert RC .15 .40
219 Ethan Horton .02 .10
220 Jeff Hostetler .07 .20
221 James Lofton .07 .20
222 Howie Long .15 .40
223 Todd Marinovich .02 .10
224 Terry McDaniel .02 .10
225 Winston Moss .02 .10
226 Anthony Smith .02 .10
227 Greg Townsend .02 .10
228 Aaron Wallace .02 .10
229 Lionel Washington .02 .10
230 Steve Wisniewski .02 .10
231 Flipper Anderson .02 .10
232 Jerome Bettis RC 4.00 8.00
233 Marc Boutte .02 .10
234 Shane Conlan .02 .10
235 Troy Drayton RC .07 .20
236 Henry Ellard .07 .20
237 Jim Everett .07 .20
238 Cleveland Gary .02 .10
239 Sean Gilbert .07 .20
240 Darryl Henley .02 .10
241 David Lang .02 .10
242 Todd Lyght .02 .10
243 Anthony Newman .02 .10
244 Roman Phifer .02 .10
245 Gerald Robinson .02 .10
246 Henry Rolling .02 .10
247 Jackie Slater .02 .10
248 Keith Byars .02 .10
249 Marco Coleman .02 .10
250 Bryan Cox .02 .10
251 Jeff Cross .02 .10
252 Irving Fryar .07 .20
253 Mark Higgs .02 .10
254 Dwight Hollier RC .02 .10
255 Mark Ingram .02 .10
256 Keith Jackson .07 .20
257 Terry Kirby RC .15 .40
258 Dan Marino 1.25 3.00
259 O.J. McDuffie RC .15 .40
260 John Offerdahl .02 .10
261 Louis Oliver .02 .10
262 Pete Stoyanovich .02 .10
263 Troy Vincent .02 .10
264 Richmond Webb .02 .10
265 Jarvis Williams .02 .10
266 Terry Allen .15 .40
267 Anthony Carter .07 .20
268 Cris Carter .15 .40
269 Roger Craig .07 .20
270 Jack Del Rio .02 .10
271 Chris Doleman .02 .10
272 Qadry Ismail RC .15 .40
273 Steve Jordan .02 .10
274 Randall McDaniel .05 .15
275 Audray McMillian .02 .10
276 John Randle .07 .20
277 Sean Salisbury .02 .10
278 Todd Scott .02 .10
279 Robert Smith RC 1.00 2.50
280 Henry Thomas .02 .10
281 Ray Agnew .02 .10
282 Bruce Armstrong .02 .10
283 Drew Bledsoe RC 2.00 5.00
284 Vincent Brisby RC .15 .40
285 Vincent Brown .02 .10
286 Eugene Chung .02 .10
287 Marv Cook .02 .10
288 Pat Harlow .02 .10
289 Jerome Henderson .02 .10
290 Greg McMurtry .02 .10
291 Leonard Russell .07 .20
292 Chris Singleton .02 .10
293 Chris Slade RC .07 .20
294 Andre Tippett .02 .10
295 Brent Williams .02 .10
296 Scott Zolak .02 .10
297 Morten Andersen .02 .10
298 Gene Atkins .02 .10
299 Mike Buck .02 .10
300 Toi Cook .02 .10
301 Jim Dombrowski .02 .10
302 Vaughn Dunbar .02 .10
303 Quinn Early .07 .20
304 Joel Hilgenberg .02 .10
305 Dalton Hilliard .02 .10
306 Rickey Jackson .02 .10
307 Vaughan Johnson .02 .10
308 Reginald Jones .02 .10
309 Eric Martin .02 .10
310 Wayne Martin .02 .10
311 Sam Mills .02 .10
312 Brad Muster .02 .10
313 Willie Roaf RC .25 .60
314 Irv Smith RC .02 .10
315 Wade Wilson .02 .10
316 Carlton Bailey .02 .10
317 Michael Brooks .02 .10
318 Derek Brown TE .02 .10
319 Marcus Buckley RC .02 .10
320 Jarrod Bunch .02 .10
321 Mark Collins .02 .10
322 Eric Dorsey .02 .10
323 Rodney Hampton .07 .20
324 Mark Jackson .02 .10
325 Pepper Johnson .02 .10
326 Ed McCaffrey .15 .40
327 Dave Meggett .02 .10
328 Bart Oates .02 .10
329 Mike Sherrard .02 .10
330 Phil Simms .07 .20
331 Michael Strahan RC 1.25 3.00
332 Lawrence Taylor .15 .40
333 Brad Baxter .02 .10
334 Chris Burkett .02 .10
335 Kyle Clifton .02 .10
336 Boomer Esiason .07 .20
337 James Hasty .02 .10
338 Johnny Johnson .02 .10
339 Marvin Jones RC .02 .10
340 Jeff Lageman .02 .10
341 Mo Lewis .02 .10
342 Ronnie Lott .07 .20
343 Leonard Marshall .02 .10
344 Johnny Mitchell .02 .10
345 Rob Moore .07 .20
346 Browning Nagle .02 .10
347 Coleman Rudolph RC .02 .10
348 Blair Thomas .02 .10
349 Eric Thomas .02 .10
350 Brian Washington .02 .10
351 Marvin Washington .02 .10
352 Eric Allen .02 .10
353 Victor Bailey RC .02 .10
354 Fred Barnett .07 .20
355 Mark Bavaro .02 .10
356 Randall Cunningham .15 .40
357 Byron Evans .02 .10
358 Andy Harmon RC .07 .20
359 Tim Harris .02 .10
360 Lester Holmes .02 .10
361 Seth Joyner .02 .10
362 Keith Millard .02 .10
363 Leonard Renfro RC .02 .10
364 Heath Sherman .02 .10
365 Vai Sikahema .02 .10
366 Clyde Simmons .02 .10
367 William Thomas .02 .10
368 Herschel Walker .07 .20
369 Andre Waters .02 .10
370 Calvin Williams .07 .20
371 Johnny Bailey .02 .10
372 Steve Beuerlein .07 .20
373 Rich Camarillo .02 .10
374 Chuck Cecil .02 .10
375 Chris Chandler .07 .20
376 Gary Clark .07 .20
377 Ben Coleman RC .02 .10
378 Ernest Dye RC .02 .10
379 Ken Harvey .02 .10
380 Garrison Hearst RC .60 1.50
381 Randal Hill .02 .10
382 Robert Massey .02 .10
383 Freddie Joe Nunn .02 .10
384 Ricky Proehl .02 .10
385 Luis Sharpe .02 .10
386 Tyronne Stowe .02 .10
387 Eric Swann .07 .20
388 Aeneas Williams .02 .10
389 Chad Brown RC LB .07 .20
390 Dermontti Dawson .08 .20
391 Donald Evans .02 .10
392 Deon Figures RC .02 .10
393 Barry Foster .07 .20
394 Jeff Graham .07 .20
395 Eric Green .02 .10
396 Kevin Greene .07 .20
397 Carlton Haselrig .02 .10
398 Andre Hastings RC .07 .20
399 D.J. Johnson .02 .10
400 Carnell Lake .02 .10
401 Greg Lloyd .07 .20
402 Neil O'Donnell .15 .40
403 Darren Perry .02 .10
404 Mike Tomczak .02 .10
405 Rod Woodson .15 .40
406 Eric Bieniemy .02 .10
407 Marion Butts .02 .10
408 Gill Byrd .02 .10
409 Darren Carrington RC .02 .10
410 Darrien Gordon RC .02 .10
411 Burt Grossman .02 .10
412 Courtney Hall .02 .10
413 Ronnie Harmon .02 .10
414 Stan Humphries .07 .20
415 Nate Lewis .02 .10
416 Natrone Means RC .15 .40
417 Anthony Miller .07 .20
418 Chris Mims .02 .10
419 Leslie O'Neal .07 .20
420 Gary Plummer .02 .10
421 Stanley Richard .02 .10
422 Junior Seau .15 .40
423 Harry Swayne .02 .10
424 Jerrol Williams .02 .10
425 Harris Barton .02 .10
426 Steve Bono .07 .20
427 Kevin Fagan .02 .10
428 Don Griffin .02 .10
429 Dana Hall .02 .10
430 Adrian Hardy .02 .10
431 Brent Jones .07 .20
432 Todd Kelly RC .02 .10
433 Amp Lee .02 .10
434 Tim McDonald .02 .10
435 Guy McIntyre .02 .10
436 Tom Rathman .02 .10
437 Jerry Rice .75 2.00
438 Bill Romanowski .02 .10
439 Dana Stubblefield RC .15 .40
440 John Taylor .07 .20
441 Steve Wallace .02 .10
442 Michael Walter .02 .10
443 Ricky Watters .15 .40
444 Steve Young .60 1.50
445 Robert Blackmon .02 .10
446 Brian Blades .07 .20
447 Jeff Bryant .02 .10
448 Ferrell Edmunds .02 .10
449 Carlton Gray RC .02 .10
450 Dwayne Harper .02 .10
451 Andy Heck .02 .10
452 Tommy Kane .02 .10
453 Cortez Kennedy .07 .20
454 Kelvin Martin .02 .10
455 Dan McGwire .02 .10
456 Rick Mirer RC .15 .40
457 Rufus Porter .02 .10
458 Ray Roberts .02 .10
459 Eugene Robinson .02 .10
460 Chris Warren .07 .20
461 John L. Williams .02 .10
462 Gary Anderson RB .02 .10
463 Tyji Armstrong .02 .10
464 Reggie Cobb .02 .10
465 Eric Curry RC .02 .10
466 Lawrence Dawsey .02 .10
467 Steve DeBerg .02 .10
468 Santana Dotson .07 .20
469 Demetrius DuBose RC .02 .10
470 Paul Gruber .02 .10
471 Ron Hall .02 .10
472 Courtney Hawkins .02 .10
473 Hardy Nickerson .07 .20
474 Ricky Reynolds .02 .10
475 Broderick Thomas .02 .10
476 Mark Wheeler .02 .10
477 Jimmy Williams .02 .10
478 Carl Banks .02 .10
479 Reggie Brooks RC .07 .20
480 Earnest Byner .02 .10
481 Tom Carter RC .07 .20
482 Andre Collins .02 .10
483 Brad Edwards .02 .10
484 Ricky Ervins .02 .10
485 Kurt Gouveia .02 .10
486 Darrell Green .02 .10
487 Desmond Howard .07 .20
488 Jim Lachey .02 .10
489 Chip Lohmiller .02 .10
490 Charles Mann .02 .10
491 Tim McGee .02 .10
492 Brian Mitchell .07 .20
493 Art Monk .07 .20
494 Mark Rypien .02 .10
495 Ricky Sanders .02 .10
496 Checklist 1-126 .02 .10
497 Checklist 127-254 .02 .10
498 Checklist 255-382 .02 .10
499 Checklist 383-500 .02 .10
500 Inserts Checklist .02 .10

1993 Ultra All-Rookies

The 1993 Ultra All-Rookies set comprises 10 standard-size cards, randomly inserted in Ultra 14 and 19-card foil packs. The cards are arranged in alphabetical order and are numbered on the back "X of 10."

COMPLETE SET (10) 12.00 30.00
1 Patrick Bates .20 .50
2 Jerome Bettis 6.00 15.00
3 Drew Bledsoe 4.00 10.00
4 Curtis Conway 1.25 3.00
5 Garrison Hearst 2.50 6.00
6 Qadry Ismail .60 1.50
7 Marvin Jones .20 .50
8 Glyn Milburn .30 .75
9 Rick Mirer .60 1.50
10 Kevin Williams WR .30 .75

1993 Ultra Award Winners

The 1993 Ultra Award Winners set comprises ten standard size cards, randomly inserted in Fleer Ultra 14- and 19-card foil packs. The set spotlights MVP's of the AFC and NFC, Rookies of the Year and other awards. The cards are arranged in alphabetical order and numbered on the back "X of 10."

COMPLETE SET (10) 15.00 40.00
1 Troy Aikman 6.00 15.00
2 Dale Carter .40 1.00
3 Chris Doleman .40 1.00
4 Santana Dotson .60 1.50
5 Barry Foster .75 2.00
6 Jason Hanson .40 1.00
7 Cortez Kennedy .60 1.50
8 Carl Pickens .75 2.00
9 Steve Tasker .75 2.00
10 Steve Young 6.00 15.00

1993 Ultra Michael Irvin

Subtitled Performance Highlights and randomly inserted in 1993 Fleer packs at a rate of one in 12, these ten standard-size cards feature on their fronts color action shots of Irvin that are borderless, except at the bottom, where the card is edged with a black marbleized stripe that carries the set's subtitle in silver-foil lettering.

COMPLETE SET (10) 3.00 8.00
COMMON M.IRVIN (1-10) .40 1.00
STATED ODDS 1:12
COMMON SEND-OFF (11-12) .75 2.00
AU Michael Irvin AUTO 15.00 30.00

1993 Ultra League Leaders

The 1993 Ultra League Leaders set comprises ten standard size cards, randomly inserted in Ultra 14 and 19-card foil packs. The set spotlights players who led their respective conferences in specific defensive or offensive categories. The cards are arranged in alphabetical order and numbered on the back "X of 10."

COMPLETE SET (10) 20.00 50.00
1 Haywood Jeffires .75 2.00
2 Henry Jones .40 1.00
3 Audray McMillian .40 1.00
4 Warren Moon 1.50 4.00
5 Leslie O'Neal .75 2.00
6 Deion Sanders 3.00 8.00
7 Sterling Sharpe 1.50 4.00
8 Clyde Simmons .40 1.00
9 Emmitt Smith 10.00 25.00
10 Thurman Thomas 1.50 4.00

1993 Ultra Stars

The 1993 Ultra Stars set comprises ten standard-size cards, randomly inserted exclusively in Ultra 19-card jumbo packs. The cards are arranged in alphabetical order.

COMPLETE SET (10) 20.00 50.00
RANDOM INSERTS IN JUMBO PACKS
1 Brett Favre 12.00 30.00
2 Barry Foster .60 1.50
3 Michael Irvin 2.00 5.00
4 Cortez Kennedy .60 1.50
5 Deion Sanders 2.50 6.00
6 Junior Seau 1.50 4.00
7 Derrick Thomas 1.50 4.00
8 Ricky Watters 1.00 2.50
9 Reggie White 1.50 4.00
10 Steve Young 5.00 12.00

1993 Ultra Touchdown Kings

The 1993 Ultra Touchdown Kings set comprises ten standard-size cards, randomly inserted exclusively in Ultra 14 and 19-card packs. The set spotlights the NFL's best offensive players. The cards are arranged in alphabetical order.

COMPLETE SET (10) 15.00 40.00
1 Rodney Hampton .50 1.25
2 Dan Marino 4.00 10.00
3 Art Monk .75 2.00
4 Joe Montana 4.00 10.00
5 Jerry Rice 2.50 6.00
6 Andre Rison .75 2.00
7 Barry Sanders 3.00 8.00
8 Sterling Sharpe .75 2.00
9 Emmitt Smith 4.00 10.00
10 Thurman Thomas 1.50 4.00

1994 Ultra

Cards from this 525-card standard size set were issued in two series of 325 and 200. Cards were issued in 14, 17, and 20-card packs. Card fronts have full-bleed photos with the player's name, team, position and a helmet in gold foil at the bottom. The backs have three photos and statistics. The cards are grouped alphabetically within teams, and checklisted below alphabetically according to teams. Rookie Cards include Derrick Alexander, Mario Bates, Isaac Bruce, Lake Dawson, Trent Dilfer, Bert Emanuel, Marshall Faulk, William Floyd, Greg Hill, Charles Johnson, Bam Morris, Errict Rhett, Darnay Scott and Heath Shuler.

COMPLETE SET (525) 10.00 25.00
COMP.SERIES 1 (325) 5.00 12.00
COMP.SERIES 2 (200) 5.00 12.00
1 Steve Beuerlein .07 .20
2 Gary Clark .07 .20
3 Randal Hill .02 .10
4 Seth Joyner .02 .10
5 Jamir Miller RC .07 .20
6 Ronald Moore .02 .10
7 Luis Sharpe .02 .10
8 Clyde Simmons .02 .10
9 Eric Swann .07 .20
10 Aeneas Williams .02 .10
11 Chris Doleman .02 .10
12 Bert Emanuel RC .15 .40
13 Moe Gardner .02 .10
14 Jeff George .15 .40
15 Roger Harper .02 .10
16 Pierce Holt .02 .10
17 Lincoln Kennedy .02 .10
18 Erric Pegram .02 .10
19 Andre Rison .07 .20
20 Deion Sanders .30 .75
21 Jessie Tuggle .02 .10
22 Cornelius Bennett .07 .20
23 Bill Brooks .02 .10
24 Jeff Burris RC .07 .20
25 Kent Hull .02 .10
26 Henry Jones .02 .10
27 Jim Kelly .15 .40
28 Marvcus Patton .02 .10
29 Andre Reed .07 .20
30 Bruce Smith .15 .40
31 Thomas Smith .02 .10
32 Thurman Thomas .15 .40
33 Jeff Wright .02 .10
34 Trace Armstrong .02 .10
35 Mark Carrier DB .02 .10
36 Dante Jones .02 .10
37 Erik Kramer .07 .20
38 Terry Obee .02 .10
39 Alonzo Spellman .02 .10
40 John Thierry RC .02 .10
41 Tom Waddle .02 .10
42 Donnell Woolford .02 .10
43 Tim Worley .02 .10
44 Chris Zorich .02 .10
45 John Copeland .02 .10
46 Harold Green .02 .10
47 David Klingler .02 .10
48 Ricardo McDonald .02 .10
49 Tony McGee .02 .10
50 Louis Oliver .02 .10
51 Carl Pickens .07 .20
52 Darnay Scott RC .30 .75
53 Steve Tovar .02 .10
54 Dan Wilkinson RC .07 .20
55 Darryl Williams .02 .10
56 Derrick Alexander WR RC .15 .40
57 Michael Jackson .07 .20
58 Tony Jones T .02 .10
59 Antonio Langham RC .07 .20
60 Eric Metcalf .07 .20
61 Stevon Moore .02 .10
62 Michael Dean Perry .07 .20
63 Anthony Pleasant .02 .10
64 Vinny Testaverde .07 .20
65 Eric Turner .02 .10
66 Tommy Vardell .02 .10
67 Troy Aikman .60 1.50
68 Larry Brown DB .02 .10
69 Shante Carver RC .02 .10
70 Charles Haley .07 .20
71 Michael Irvin .15 .40
72 Leon Lett .02 .10
73 Nate Newton .02 .10
74 Jay Novacek .07 .20
75 Darrin Smith .02 .10
76 Emmitt Smith 1.00 2.50
77 Tony Tolbert .02 .10
78 Erik Williams .02 .10
79 Kevin Williams WR .07 .20
80 Steve Atwater .02 .10
81 Rod Bernstine .02 .10
82 Ray Crockett .02 .10
83 Mike Croel .02 .10
84 Shane Dronett .02 .10
85 Jason Elam .07 .20
86 John Elway 1.25 3.00
87 Simon Fletcher .02 .10
88 Glyn Milburn .07 .20
89 Anthony Miller .07 .20
90 Shannon Sharpe .07 .20
91 Gary Zimmerman .02 .10
92 Bennie Blades .02 .10
93 Lomas Brown .02 .10
94 Mel Gray .02 .10
95 Jason Hanson .02 .10
96 Ryan McNeil .02 .10
97 Scott Mitchell .07 .20
98 Herman Moore .15 .40
99 Johnnie Morton RC .60 1.50
100 Robert Porcher .02 .10
101 Barry Sanders 1.00 2.50
102 Chris Spielman .07 .20
103 Pat Swilling .02 .10
104 Edgar Bennett .15 .40
105 Terrell Buckley .02 .10
106 Reggie Cobb .02 .10
107 Brett Favre 1.25 3.00
108 Sean Jones .02 .10
109 Ken Ruettgers .02 .10
110 Sterling Sharpe .07 .20
111 Wayne Simmons .02 .10
112 Aaron Taylor RC .02 .10
113 George Teague .02 .10
114 Reggie White .15 .40
115 Micheal Barrow .02 .10
116 Gary Brown .02 .10
117 Cody Carlson .02 .10
118 Ray Childress .02 .10
119 Cris Dishman .02 .10
120 Henry Ford RC .02 .10
121 Haywood Jeffires .07 .20
122 Bruce Matthews .02 .10
123 Bubba McDowell .02 .10
124 Marcus Robertson .02 .10
125 Eddie Robinson .02 .10
126 Webster Slaughter .02 .10
127 Trev Alberts RC .07 .20
128 Tony Bennett .02 .10
129 Ray Buchanan .02 .10
130 Quentin Coryatt .02 .10
131 Eugene Daniel .02 .10
132 Steve Emtman .02 .10
133 Marshall Faulk RC 2.50 6.00
134 Jim Harbaugh .15 .40
135 Roosevelt Potts .02 .10
136 Rohn Stark .02 .10
137 Marcus Allen .15 .40
138 Donnell Bennett RC .15 .40
139 Dale Carter .02 .10
140 Tony Casillas .02 .10
141 Mark Collins .02 .10
142 Willie Davis .07 .20
143 Tim Grunhard .02 .10
144 Greg Hill RC .15 .40
145 Joe Montana 1.25 3.00
146 Tracy Simien .02 .10
147 Neil Smith .07 .20
148 Derrick Thomas .15 .40
149 Tim Brown .15 .40
150 James Folston RC .02 .10
151 Rob Fredrickson RC .07 .20
152 Jeff Hostetler .07 .20
153 Rocket Ismail .07 .20
154 James Jett .02 .10
155 Terry McDaniel .02 .10
156 Winston Moss .02 .10
157 Greg Robinson .02 .10
158 Anthony Smith .02 .10
159 Steve Wisniewski .02 .10
160 Flipper Anderson .02 .10
161 Jerome Bettis .25 .60
162 Isaac Bruce RC 2.00 4.00
163 Shane Conlan .02 .10
164 Wayne Gandy RC .02 .10
165 Sean Gilbert .02 .10
166 Todd Lyght .02 .10
167 Chris Miller .02 .10
168 Anthony Newman .02 .10
169 Roman Phifer .02 .10
170 Jackie Slater .02 .10
171 Gene Atkins .02 .10
172 Aubrey Beavers RC .02 .10
173 Tim Bowens RC .07 .20
174 J.B. Brown .02 .10
175 Marco Coleman .02 .10
176 Bryan Cox .02 .10
177 Irving Fryar .07 .20
178 Terry Kirby .15 .40
179 Dan Marino 1.25 3.00
180 Troy Vincent .02 .10
181 Richmond Webb .02 .10
182 Terry Allen .07 .20
183 Cris Carter .30 .75
184 Jack Del Rio .02 .10
185 Vencie Glenn .02 .10
186 Randall McDaniel .05 .15
187 Warren Moon .15 .40
188 David Palmer RC .15 .40
189 John Randle .07 .20
190 Todd Scott .02 .10
191 Todd Steussie RC .07 .20
192 Henry Thomas .02 .10
193 Dewayne Washington RC .07 .20
194 Bruce Armstrong .02 .10
195 Harlon Barnett .02 .10
196 Drew Bledsoe .40 1.00
197 Vincent Brisby .07 .20
198 Vincent Brown .02 .10
199 Marion Butts .02 .10
200 Ben Coates .07 .20
201 Todd Collins .02 .10
202 Maurice Hurst .02 .10
203 Willie McGinest RC .15 .40
204 Ricky Reynolds .02 .10
205 Chris Slade .02 .10
206 Mario Bates RC .15 .40
207 Derek Brown RBK .02 .10
208 Vince Buck .02 .10
209 Quinn Early .07 .20
210 Jim Everett .07 .20
211 Michael Haynes .07 .20

212 Tyrone Hughes .07 .20
213 Joe Johnson RC .02 .10
214 Vaughan Johnson .02 .10
215 Willie Roaf .02 .10
216 Renaldo Turnbull .02 .10
217 Michael Brooks .02 .10
218 Dave Brown .07 .20
219 Howard Cross .02 .10
220 Stacey Dillard .02 .10
221 Jumbo Elliott .02 .10
222 Keith Hamilton .02 .10
223 Rodney Hampton .07 .20
224 Thomas Lewis RC .07 .20
225 Dave Meggett .02 .10
226 Corey Miller .02 .10
227 Thomas Randolph RC .02 .10
228 Mike Sherrard .02 .10
229 Kyle Clifton .02 .10
230 Boomer Esiason .07 .20
231 Aaron Glenn RC .15 .40
232 James Hasty .02 .10
233 Bobby Houston .02 .10
234 Johnny Johnson .02 .10
235 Mo Lewis .02 .10
236 Ronnie Lott .07 .20
237 Rob Moore .07 .20
238 Marvin Washington .02 .10
239 Ryan Yarborough RC .02 .10
240 Eric Allen .02 .10
241 Victor Bailey .02 .10
242 Fred Barnett .07 .20
243 Mark Bavaro .02 .10
244 Randall Cunningham .15 .40
245 Byron Evans .02 .10
246 William Fuller .02 .10
247 Andy Harmon .02 .10
248 William Perry .07 .20
249 Herschel Walker .07 .20
250 Bernard Williams RC .02 .10
251 Dermontti Dawson .08 .20
252 Deon Figures .02 .10
253 Barry Foster .02 .10
254 Kevin Greene .07 .20
255 Charles Johnson RC .15 .40
256 Levon Kirkland .02 .10
257 Greg Lloyd .07 .20
258 Neil O'Donnell .15 .40
259 Darren Perry .02 .10
260 Dwight Stone .02 .10
261 Rod Woodson .07 .20
262 John Carney .02 .10
263 Isaac Davis RC .02 .10
264 Courtney Hall .02 .10
265 Ronnie Harmon .02 .10
266 Stan Humphries .07 .20
267 Vance Johnson .02 .10
268 Natrone Means .15 .40
269 Chris Mims .02 .10
270 Leslie O'Neal .02 .10
271 Stanley Richard .02 .10
272 Junior Seau .15 .40
273 Harris Barton .02 .10
274 Dennis Brown .02 .10
275 Eric Davis .02 .10
276 William Floyd RC .15 .40
277 John Johnson .02 .10
278 Tim McDonald .02 .10
279 Ken Norton Jr. .07 .20
280 Jerry Rice .60 1.50
281 Jesse Sapolu .02 .10
282 Dana Stubblefield .07 .20
283 Ricky Watters .07 .20
284 Bryant Young RC .25 .60
285 Steve Young .40 1.00
286 Sam Adams RC .07 .20
287 Brian Blades .07 .20
288 Ferrell Edmunds .02 .10
289 Patrick Hunter .02 .10
290 Cortez Kennedy .07 .20
291 Rick Mirer .15 .40
292 Nate Odomes .02 .10
293 Ray Roberts .02 .10
294 Eugene Robinson .02 .10
295 Rod Stephens .02 .10
296 Chris Warren .07 .20
297 Marty Carter .02 .10
298 Horace Copeland .02 .10
299 Eric Curry .02 .10
300 Santana Dotson .07 .20
301 Craig Erickson .02 .10
302 Paul Gruber .02 .10
303 Courtney Hawkins .02 .10
304 Martin Mayhew .02 .10
305 Hardy Nickerson .07 .20
306 Errict Rhett RC .15 .40
307 Vince Workman .02 .10
308 Reggie Brooks .07 .20
309 Tom Carter .02 .10
310 Andre Collins .02 .10
311 Brad Edwards .02 .10
312 Kurt Gouveia .02 .10
313 Darrell Green .02 .10
314 Ethan Horton .02 .10
315 Desmond Howard .07 .20
316 Tre Johnson RC .02 .10
317 Sterling Palmer RC .02 .10
318 Heath Shuler RC .15 .40
319 Tyronne Stowe .02 .10
320 NFL 75th Anniversary .02 .10
321 Checklist .02 .10
322 Checklist .02 .10
323 Checklist .02 .10
324 Checklist .02 .10
325 Checklist .02 .10
326 Garrison Hearst .15 .40
327 Eric Hill .02 .10
328 Seth Joyner .02 .10
329 Jim McMahon .07 .20
330 Jamir Miller .02 .10
331 Ricky Proehl .02 .10
332 Clyde Simmons .02 .10
333 Chris Doleman .02 .10
334 Bert Emanuel .15 .40
335 Jeff George .15 .40
336 D.J. Johnson .02 .10
337 Terance Mathis .07 .20
338 Clay Matthews .02 .10
339 Tony Smith RB .02 .10
340 Don Beebe .02 .10
341 Bucky Brooks RC .02 .10
342 Jeff Burris .07 .20
343 Kenneth Davis .02 .10
344 Phil Hansen .02 .10
345 Pete Metzelaars .02 .10
346 Darryl Talley .02 .10
347 Joe Cain .02 .10
348 Curtis Conway .15 .40
349 Shaun Gayle .02 .10
350 Chris Gedney .02 .10
351 Erik Kramer .07 .20
352 Vinson Smith .02 .10
353 John Thierry .02 .10
354 Lewis Tillman .02 .10
355 Mike Brim .02 .10
356 Derrick Fenner .02 .10
357 James Francis .02 .10
358 Louis Oliver .02 .10
359 Darnay Scott .15 .40
360 Dan Wilkinson .07 .20
361 Alfred Williams .02 .10
362 Derrick Alexander WR .15 .40
363 Rob Burnett .02 .10
364 Mark Carrier WR .07 .20
365 Steve Everitt .02 .10
366 Leroy Hoard .02 .10
367 Pepper Johnson .02 .10
368 Antonio Langham .07 .20
369 Shante Carver .02 .10
370 Alvin Harper .07 .20
371 Daryl Johnston .07 .20
372 Russell Maryland .02 .10
373 Kevin Smith .02 .10
374 Mark Stepnoski .02 .10
375 Darren Woodson .07 .20
376 Allen Aldridge RC .02 .10
377 Ray Crockett .02 .10
378 Karl Mecklenburg .02 .10
379 Anthony Miller .07 .20
380 Mike Pritchard .02 .10
381 Leonard Russell .02 .10
382 Dennis Smith .02 .10
383 Anthony Carter .07 .20
384 Van Malone RC .02 .10
385 Robert Massey .02 .10
386 Scott Mitchell .07 .20
387 Johnnie Morton .25 .60
388 Brett Perriman .07 .20
389 Tracy Scroggins .02 .10
390 Robert Brooks .15 .40
391 LeRoy Butler .02 .10
392 Reggie Cobb .02 .10
393 Sean Jones .02 .10
394 George Koonce .02 .10
395 Steve McMichael .07 .20
396 Bryce Paup .07 .20
397 Aaron Taylor .02 .10
398 Henry Ford .02 .10
399 Ernest Givins .07 .20
400 Jeremy Nunley RC .02 .10
401 Bo Orlando .02 .10
402 Al Smith .02 .10
403 Barron Wortham RC .02 .10
404 Trev Alberts .07 .20
405 Tony Bennett .02 .10
406 Kerry Cash .02 .10
407 Sean Dawkins RC .15 .40
408 Marshall Faulk .75 2.00
409 Jim Harbaugh .15 .40
410 Jeff Herrod .02 .10
411 Kimble Anders .07 .20
412 Donnell Bennett .07 .20
413 J.J. Birden .02 .10
414 Mark Collins .02 .10
415 Lake Dawson RC .07 .20
416 Greg Hill .15 .40
417 Charles Mincy .02 .10
418 Greg Biekert .02 .10
419 Rob Fredrickson .07 .20
420 Nolan Harrison .02 .10
421 Jeff Jaeger .02 .10
422 Albert Lewis .02 .10
423 Chester McGlockton .02 .10
424 Tom Rathman .02 .10
425 Harvey Williams .07 .20
426 Isaac Bruce .60 1.50
427 Troy Drayton .02 .10
428 Wayne Gandy .02 .10
429 Fred Stokes .02 .10
430 Robert Young .02 .10
431 Gene Atkins .02 .10
432 Aubrey Beavers .02 .10
433 Tim Bowens .07 .20
434 Keith Byars .02 .10
435 Jeff Cross .02 .10
436 Mark Ingram .02 .10
437 Keith Jackson .02 .10
438 Michael Stewart .02 .10
439 Chris Hinton .02 .10
440 Qadry Ismail .15 .40
441 Carlos Jenkins .02 .10
442 Warren Moon .15 .40
443 David Palmer .07 .20
444 Jake Reed .07 .20
445 Robert Smith .15 .40
446 Todd Steussie .07 .20
447 Dewayne Washington .07 .20
448 Marion Butts .02 .10
449 Tim Goad .02 .10
450 Myron Guyton .02 .10
451 Kevin Lee RC .02 .10
452 Willie McGinest .15 .40
453 Ricky Reynolds .02 .10
454 Michael Timpson .02 .10
455 Morten Andersen .02 .10
456 Jim Everett .07 .20
457 Michael Haynes .07 .20
458 Joe Johnson .02 .10
459 Wayne Martin .02 .10
460 Sam Mills .02 .10
461 Irv Smith .02 .10
462 Carlton Bailey .02 .10
463 Chris Calloway .02 .10
464 Mark Jackson .02 .10
465 Thomas Lewis .07 .20
466 Thomas Randolph .02 .10
467 Stevie Anderson RC .02 .10
468 Brad Baxter .02 .10
469 Aaron Glenn .07 .20
470 Jeff Lageman .02 .10
471 Johnny Mitchell .02 .10
472 Art Monk .07 .20
473 William Fuller .02 .10
474 Charlie Garner RC .50 1.25
475 Vaughn Hebron .02 .10
476 Bill Romanowski .02 .10
477 William Thomas .02 .10
478 Greg Townsend .02 .10
479 Bernard Williams .02 .10
480 Calvin Williams .07 .20
481 Eric Green .02 .10
482 Charles Johnson .15 .40
483 Carnell Lake .02 .10
484 Byron Bam Morris RC .07 .20
485 John L. Williams .02 .10
486 Darren Carrington .02 .10
487 Andre Coleman RC .02 .10
488 Isaac Davis .02 .10
489 Dwayne Harper .02 .10
490 Tony Martin .15 .40
491 Mark Seay RC .15 .40
492 Richard Dent .07 .20
493 William Floyd .15 .40
494 Rickey Jackson .02 .10
495 Brent Jones .07 .20
496 Ken Norton Jr. .07 .20
497 Gary Plummer .02 .10
498 Deion Sanders .30 .75
499 John Taylor .07 .20
500 Lee Woodall RC .02 .10
501 Bryant Young .25 .60
502 Sam Adams .07 .20
503 Howard Ballard .02 .10
504 Michael Bates .02 .10
505 Robert Blackmon .02 .10
506 John Kasay .02 .10
507 Kelvin Martin .02 .10
508 Kevin Mawae RC .15 .40
509 Rufus Porter .02 .10
510 Lawrence Dawsey .02 .10
611 Trent Dilfer RC .50 1.25
512 Thomas Everett .02 .10
513 Jackie Harris .02 .10
514 Errict Rhett .07 .20
515 Henry Ellard .07 .20
516 John Friesz .07 .20
517 Ken Harvey .02 .10
518 Ethan Horton .02 .10
519 Tre Johnson .02 .10
520 Jim Lachey .02 .10
521 Heath Shuler .15 .40
522 Tony Woods .02 .10
523 Checklist .02 .10
524 Checklist .02 .10
525 Checklist .02 .10

1994 Ultra Achievement Awards

Randomly inserted in packs, this 10-card standard-size set features top players including those homing in on career milestones. Full-bleed fronts have a player photo superimposed over multi-color backgrounds. The player's name and set logo are in gold foil. The card backs have a photo with a similar background and highlights. The set is sequenced in alphabetical order. A jumbo version of this set was issued one set per hobby case. Those cards are valued as a multiple of the cards listed below.

COMPLETE SET (10) 4.00 10.00
COMPLETE JUMBO SET (10) 10.00 25.00
*JUMBOS: 1X TO 2.5X BASIC INSERT
ONE JUMBO SET PER HOBBY CASE
1 Marcus Allen .15 .40
2 John Elway 1.50 3.00
3 Dan Marino 1.50 3.00
4 Joe Montana 1.50 3.00
5 Jerry Rice .75 1.50
6 Barry Sanders 1.25 2.50
7 Sterling Sharpe .07 .20
8 Emmitt Smith 1.25 2.50
9 Thurman Thomas .15 .40
10 Reggie White .15 .40

1994 Ultra Award Winners

Randomly inserted in packs, this five-card standard-size set has a full-bleed design. A player photo is surpimposed over a background of three small versions of the same photo. The backs have a player photo and a write-up about the award. The set is sequenced in alphabetical order.

COMPLETE SET (5) 1.50 4.00
1 Jerome Bettis .30 .75
2 Rick Mirer .20 .50
3 Emmitt Smith 1.50 3.00
4 Dana Stubblefield .08 .25
5 Rod Woodson .08 .25

1994 Ultra First Rounders

Randomly inserted in packs, this 20-card standard-size set depicts player selected in the first round of the 1994 NFL draft. Full-bleed fronts feature a player photo with a First Round logo at the bottom. The backs have a photo and information about the player's college career and why the team drafted him. The set is sequenced in alphabetical order.

COMPLETE SET (20) 2.50 6.00
1 Sam Adams .05 .15
2 Trev Alberts .05 .15
3 Shante Carver .02 .10
4 Marshall Faulk 2.50 5.00
5 William Floyd .10 .30
6 Rob Fredrickson .05 .15
7 Wayne Gandy .02 .10
8 Aaron Glenn .10 .30
9 Charles Johnson .10 .30
10 Joe Johnson .02 .10
11 Antonio Langham .05 .15
12 Willie McGinest .10 .30
13 Jamir Miller .05 .15
14 Johnnie Morton .60 1.25
15 Heath Shuler .10 .30
16 John Thierry .02 .10
17 Dewayne Washington .05 .15
18 Dan Wilkinson .05 .15
19 Bernard Williams .02 .10
20 Bryant Young .20 .50

1994 Ultra Flair Hot Numbers

Randomly inserted in second series packs, this 15-card standard-size set is comprised of top offensive players. Card fronts have a player photo superimposed over a multi-color background. The Hot Number logo at bottom left or right includes the player's uniform number. The backs have a solid color background consistent with that player's team colors and the player uniform number. There is a small photo in the center and a write-up. The set is sequenced in alphabetical order.

COMPLETE SET (15) 7.50 20.00
RANDOM INSERTS IN SER.2 PACKS
1 Troy Aikman 1.00 2.00
2 Jerome Bettis .30 .75
3 Tim Brown .20 .50
4 John Elway 2.00 4.00
5 Rodney Hampton .08 .25
6 Michael Irvin .20 .50
7 Dan Marino 2.00 4.00
8 Joe Montana 2.00 4.00
9 Jerry Rice 1.00 2.00
10 Andre Rison .08 .25
11 Barry Sanders 1.50 3.00
12 Sterling Sharpe .08 .25
13 Emmitt Smith 1.50 3.00
14 Thurman Thomas .20 .50
15 Steve Young .60 1.25

1994 Ultra Flair Scoring Power

Randomly inserted in second series packs, this six-card standard-size set features touchdown leaders from the running back and wide receiver positions. The fronts contain a player photo superimposed over a multi-color background that includes the words "Scoring Power". The backs have a photo and highlights. The set is sequenced in alphabetical order.

COMPLETE SET (6) 3.00 8.00
RANDOM INSERTS IN SER.2 PACKS
1 Marcus Allen .30 .75
2 Natrone Means .30 .75
3 Jerry Rice 1.50 3.00
4 Andre Rison .15 .40
5 Emmitt Smith 1.50 4.00
6 Ricky Watters .15 .40

1994 Ultra Flair Wave of the Future

Randomly inserted in second series, this six-card standard-size set focuses on top young players that could be household names for years to come. Card fronts feature a player photo superimposed over a solid color background that accentuates the uniform colors. The backs are similar and include highlights. The set is sequenced in alphabetical order.

COMPLETE SET (6) 1.50 4.00
RANDOM INSERTS IN SER.2 PACKS
1 Trent Dilfer .40 1.00
2 Marshall Faulk 1.25 3.00
3 Greg Hill .10 .30
4 Charles Johnson .10 .30
5 Heath Shuler .10 .30
6 Dan Wilkinson .05 .15

1994 Ultra Rick Mirer

This 12-card standard-size set chronicles the collegiate career and rookie season of Seattle's Rick Mirer. The cards were randonly inserted in packs. The card fronts have two photos including an action shot that stands out from a larger faded photo used as background. The backs take a look at each stage of Mirer's career. Certified autographed cards of Mirer were randomly inserted as well. A two-card Promo sheet was produced and priced below.

COMPLETE SET (12) 1.50 4.00
COMMON MIRER (1-10) .20 .50
1-10: RANDOM INSERTS IN PACKS
COMMON SEND-OFF (11-12) .60 1.50
11-12 ISSUED VIA MAIL REDEMPTION
P1 Promo Sheet .40 1.00

1994 Ultra Rick Mirer Autographs

COMMON AUTO 12.50 30.00

1994 Ultra Second Year Standouts

This 15-card standard-size set, honoring leading 1993 rookies, was randomly inserted into packs. The cards are arranged in alphabetical order.

COMPLETE SET (15) 2.00 5.00
1 Jerome Bettis .60 1.25
2 Drew Bledsoe 1.00 2.00
3 Reggie Brooks .15 .40
4 Tom Carter .07 .20
5 Eric Curry .07 .20
6 Jason Elam .15 .40
7 Tyrone Hughes .15 .40
8 James Jett .07 .20
9 Terry Kirby .30 .75
10 Natrone Means .30 .75
11 Rick Mirer .30 .75
12 Ronald Moore .07 .20
13 Willie Roaf .07 .20
14 Chris Slade .07 .20
15 Dana Stubblefield .15 .40

1994 Ultra Stars

Randomly inserted in 17-card packs, this nine-card standard-size set showcases top offensive players. Horizontally designed, the card fronts have a player photo superimposed over a glossy background that differs in color according to the player's team. The backs have a player photo and highlights.The set is sequenced in alphabetical order.

COMPLETE SET (9) 25.00 60.00
RANDOM INSERTS IN 17-CARD PACKS
1 Troy Aikman 4.00 10.00
2 Jerome Bettis 2.50 6.00
3 Tim Brown 1.50 4.00
4 Michael Irvin 1.50 4.00
5 Rick Mirer 1.00 2.50
6 Jerry Rice 5.00 12.00
7 Barry Sanders 6.00 15.00
8 Emmitt Smith 6.00 15.00
9 Rod Woodson 1.25 3.00

1994 Ultra Touchdown Kings

This nine-card standard-size set was randomly inserted in 14-card packs. Horizontally designed, the card fronts have two player photos over a glossy background that includes a football. The backs have a player photo with a write-up and a solid color background according to team. The set is sequenced in alphabetical order.

COMPLETE SET (9) 25.00 50.00
1 Marcus Allen .75 2.00
2 Dan Marino 6.00 15.00
3 Joe Montana 6.00 15.00
4 Jerry Rice 3.00 8.00
5 Andre Rison .40 1.00
6 Sterling Sharpe .40 1.00
7 Emmitt Smith 5.00 12.00
8 Ricky Watters .40 1.00
9 Steve Young 2.00 5.00

1995 Ultra

This standard-size set was printed in two series, which consisted of 550 standard-size cards. They were issued in 12 and 15 card packs with a suggested retail price of $2.29 and $2.99, respectively. Each pack comes with an insert card and a "Gold Medallion Edition" parallel set card. The series two set is also known as "Ultra Extra". Rookie cards include Ki-Jana Carter, Steve McNair, Michael Westbrook, Kerry Collins, Joey Galloway, J.J. Stokes, Tyrone Wheatley, Jeff Blake and Rashaan Salaam. The first series cards are grouped alphabetically within teams and checklisted below alphabetically according to teams. A Bam Morris prototype card was sent out as a promotion. It is very similar to the regular issue Morris, except that the prototype reads "1994 Steelers" instead of "1994 Pittsburgh" in the stat lines. A 4-card series two promo sheet was produced and priced below as an uncut sheet.

COMPLETE SET (550) 20.00 50.00
COMP.SERIES 1 (350) 10.00 25.00
COMP.SERIES 2 (200) 10.00 25.00
1 Michael Bankston .02 .10
2 Larry Centers .07 .20
3 Garrison Hearst .15 .40
4 Eric Hill .02 .10
5 Seth Joyner .02 .10
6 Lorenzo Lynch .02 .10
7 Jamir Miller .02 .10
8 Clyde Simmons .02 .10
9 Eric Swann .07 .20
10 Aeneas Williams .02 .10
11 Devin Bush RC .02 .10
12 Ron Davis RC .02 .10
13 Chris Doleman .02 .10
14 Bert Emanuel .15 .40
15 Jeff George .07 .20
16 Roger Harper .02 .10
17 Craig Heyward .07 .20
18 Pierce Holt .02 .10
19 D.J. Johnson .02 .10
20 Terance Mathis .07 .20
21 Chuck Smith .02 .10
22 Jessie Tuggle .02 .10
23 Cornelius Bennett .07 .20
24 Ruben Brown RC .15 .40
25 Jeff Burris .02 .10
26 Matt Darby .02 .10
27 Phil Hansen .02 .10
28 Henry Jones .02 .10
29 Jim Kelly .15 .40
30 Mark Maddox RC .02 .10
31 Andre Reed .07 .20
32 Bruce Smith .15 .40
33 Don Beebe .02 .10
34 Kerry Collins RC .75 2.00
35 Darion Conner .02 .10
36 Pete Metzelaars .02 .10
37 Sam Mills .07 .20
38 Tyrone Poole RC .15 .40
39 Joe Cain .02 .10
40 Mark Carrier DB .02 .10
41 Curtis Conway .15 .40
42 Jeff Graham .02 .10
43 Raymont Harris .02 .10
44 Erik Kramer .02 .10
45 Rashaan Salaam RC .07 .20
46 Lewis Tillman .02 .10
47 Donnell Woolford .02 .10
48 Chris Zorich .02 .10
49 Jeff Blake RC .30 .75
50 Mike Brim .02 .10
51 Ki-Jana Carter RC .15 .40
52 James Francis .02 .10
53 Carl Pickens .07 .20
54 Darnay Scott .07 .20
55 Steve Tovar .02 .10
56 Dan Wilkinson .07 .20
57 Alfred Williams .02 .10
58 Darryl Williams .02 .10
59 Derrick Alexander WR .15 .40
60 Rob Burnett .02 .10
61 Steve Everitt .02 .10
62 Leroy Hoard .02 .10
63 Michael Jackson .07 .20
64 Pepper Johnson .02 .10
65 Tony Jones T .02 .10
66 Antonio Langham .02 .10
67 Anthony Pleasant .02 .10
68 Craig Powell RC .02 .10
69 Vinny Testaverde .07 .20
70 Eric Turner .02 .10
71 Troy Aikman .60 1.50
72 Charles Haley .07 .20
73 Michael Irvin .15 .40
74 Daryl Johnston .07 .20
75 Robert Jones .02 .10
76 Leon Lett .02 .10
77 Russell Maryland .02 .10
78 Jay Novacek .07 .20
79 Darrin Smith .02 .10
80 Emmitt Smith 1.25 2.50
81 Kevin Smith .02 .10
82 Erik Williams .02 .10
83 Kevin Williams WR .07 .20
84 Sherman Williams RC .02 .10
85 Darren Woodson .07 .20
86 Elijah Alexander RC .02 .10
87 Steve Atwater .02 .10
88 Ray Crockett .02 .10
89 Shane Dronett .02 .10
90 Jason Elam .07 .20
91 John Elway 1.25 3.00
92 Simon Fletcher .02 .10
93 Glyn Milburn .02 .10
94 Anthony Miller .07 .20
95 Leonard Russell .02 .10
96 Shannon Sharpe .07 .20
97 Bennie Blades .02 .10
98 Lomas Brown .02 .10
99 Willie Clay .02 .10
100 Luther Elliss RC .02 .10
101 Mike Johnson .02 .10
102 Robert Massey .02 .10
103 Scott Mitchell .07 .20
104 Herman Moore .15 .40
105 Brett Perriman .07 .20
106 Robert Porcher .02 .10
107 Barry Sanders 1.00 2.50
108 Chris Spielman .07 .20
109 Edgar Bennett .07 .20
110 Robert Brooks .15 .40
111 LeRoy Butler .02 .10
112 Brett Favre 1.50 3.00
113 Sean Jones .02 .10
114 John Jurkovic .02 .10
115 George Koonce .02 .10
116 Wayne Simmons .02 .10
117 George Teague .02 .10
118 Reggie White .15 .40
119 Micheal Barrow .02 .10
120 Gary Brown .02 .10
121 Cody Carlson .02 .10
122 Ray Childress .02 .10
123 Cris Dishman .02 .10
124 Bruce Matthews .02 .10
125 Steve McNair RC 1.25 3.00
126 Marcus Robertson .02 .10
127 Webster Slaughter .02 .10
128 Al Smith .02 .10
129 Tony Bennett .02 .10
130 Ray Buchanan .02 .10
131 Quentin Coryatt .07 .20
132 Sean Dawkins .07 .20
133 Marshall Faulk .75 2.00
134 Stephen Grant RC .02 .10
135 Jim Harbaugh .07 .20
136 Jeff Herrod .02 .10
137 Ellis Johnson RC .02 .10
138 Tony Siragusa .02 .10
139 Steve Beuerlein .07 .20
140 Tony Boselli RC .15 .40
141 Darren Carrington .02 .10
142 Reggie Cobb .02 .10
143 Kelvin Martin .02 .10
144 Kelvin Pritchett .02 .10
145 Joel Smeenge .02 .10
146 James O. Stewart RC .50 1.25
147 Marcus Allen .15 .40
148 Kimble Anders .07 .20
149 Dale Carter .07 .20
150 Mark Collins .02 .10
151 Willie Davis .07 .20
152 Lake Dawson .07 .20
153 Greg Hill .07 .20
154 Trezelle Jenkins RC .02 .10
155 Darren Mickell RC .02 .10
156 Tracy Simien .02 .10
157 Neil Smith .07 .20
158 William White .02 .10
159 Joe Aska RC .02 .10
160 Greg Biekert .02 .10
161 Tim Brown .15 .40
162 Rob Fredrickson .02 .10
163 Andrew Glover RC .02 .10
164 Jeff Hostetler .07 .20
165 Rocket Ismail .07 .20
166 Napoleon Kaufman RC .50 1.25
167 Terry McDaniel .02 .10
168 Chester McGlockton .07 .20
169 Anthony Smith .02 .10
170 Harvey Williams .02 .10
171 Steve Wisniewski .02 .10
172 Gene Atkins .02 .10
173 Aubrey Beavers .02 .10
174 Tim Bowens .02 .10
175 Bryan Cox .02 .10
176 Jeff Cross .02 .10
177 Irving Fryar .07 .20
178 Dan Marino 1.25 3.00
179 O.J. McDuffie .15 .40
180 Billy Milner RC .02 .10
181 Bernie Parmalee .07 .20
182 Troy Vincent .02 .10
183 Richmond Webb .02 .10
184 Derrick Alexander DE RC .02 .10
185 Cris Carter .15 .40
186 Jack Del Rio .02 .10
187 Qadry Ismail .07 .20
188 Ed McDaniel .02 .10
189 Randall McDaniel .05 .15
190 Warren Moon .07 .20
191 John Randle .07 .20
192 Jake Reed .07 .20
193 Fuad Reveiz .02 .10
194 Korey Stringer RC .10 .30
195 Dewayne Washington .07 .20
196 Bruce Armstrong .02 .10
197 Drew Bledsoe .40 1.00
198 Vincent Brisby .02 .10
199 Vincent Brown .02 .10
200 Marion Butts .02 .10
201 Ben Coates .07 .20
202 Myron Guyton .02 .10
203 Maurice Hurst .02 .10
204 Mike Jones .02 .10
205 Ty Law RC .60 1.50
206 Willie McGinest .07 .20
207 Chris Slade .02 .10
208 Mario Bates .07 .20
209 Quinn Early .07 .20
210 Jim Everett .02 .10
211 Mark Fields RC .15 .40
212 Michael Haynes .07 .20
213 Tyrone Hughes .07 .20
214 Joe Johnson .02 .10
215 Wayne Martin .02 .10
216 Willie Roaf .02 .10
217 Irv Smith .02 .10
218 Jimmy Spencer .02 .10
219 Winfred Tubbs .02 .10
220 Renaldo Turnbull .02 .10
221 Michael Brooks .02 .10
222 Dave Brown .07 .20
223 Chris Calloway .02 .10
224 Howard Cross .02 .10
225 John Elliott .02 .10
226 Keith Hamilton .02 .10
227 Rodney Hampton .07 .20
228 Thomas Lewis .07 .20
229 Thomas Randolph .02 .10
230 Mike Sherrard .02 .10
231 Michael Strahan .15 .40
232 Tyrone Wheatley RC .50 1.25
233 Brad Baxter .02 .10
234 Kyle Brady RC .15 .40
235 Kyle Clifton .02 .10
236 Hugh Douglas RC .15 .40
237 Boomer Esiason .07 .20
238 Aaron Glenn .02 .10
239 Bobby Houston .02 .10
240 Johnny Johnson .02 .10
241 Mo Lewis .02 .10
242 Johnny Mitchell .02 .10
243 Marvin Washington .02 .10
244 Fred Barnett .07 .20
245 Randall Cunningham .15 .40
246 William Fuller .02 .10
247 Charlie Garner .15 .40
248 Andy Harmon .02 .10
249 Greg Jackson .02 .10
250 Mike Mamula RC .02 .10
251 Bill Romanowski .02 .10
252 Bobby Taylor RC .15 .40
253 William Thomas .02 .10
254 Calvin Williams .07 .20
255 Michael Zordich .02 .10
256 Chad Brown .07 .20
257 Mark Bruener RC .07 .20
258 Dermontti Dawson .15 .40
259 Barry Foster .07 .20
260 Kevin Greene .07 .20
261 Charles Johnson .07 .20
262 Carnell Lake .02 .10
263 Greg Lloyd .07 .20
264 Byron Bam Morris .02 .10
265 Neil O'Donnell .07 .20
266 Darren Perry .02 .10
267 Ray Seals .02 .10
268 Kordell Stewart RC .60 1.50
269 John L. Williams .02 .10
270 Rod Woodson .07 .20
271 Jerome Bettis .15 .40
272 Isaac Bruce .30 .75
273 Kevin Carter RC .15 .40
274 Shane Conlan .02 .10
275 Troy Drayton .02 .10
276 Sean Gilbert .07 .20
277 Todd Lyght .02 .10
278 Chris Miller .02 .10
279 Anthony Newman .02 .10
280 Roman Phifer .02 .10
281 Robert Young .02 .10
282 John Carney .02 .10
283 Andre Coleman .02 .10
284 Courtney Hall .02 .10
285 Ronnie Harmon .02 .10
286 Dwayne Harper .02 .10
287 Stan Humphries .07 .20
288 Shawn Jefferson .02 .10
289 Tony Martin .07 .20
290 Natrone Means .07 .20
291 Chris Mims .02 .10
292 Leslie O'Neal .07 .20
293 Junior Seau .15 .40
294 Mark Seay .07 .20
295 Eric Davis .02 .10
296 William Floyd .07 .20
297 Merton Hanks .02 .10
298 Brent Jones .02 .10
299 Ken Norton Jr. .07 .20
300 Gary Plummer .02 .10
301 Jerry Rice .60 1.50
302 Deion Sanders .40 1.00
303 Jesse Sapolu .02 .10
304 J.J. Stokes RC .15 .40
305 Dana Stubblefield .07 .20
306 John Taylor .02 .10
307 Steve Wallace .02 .10
308 Lee Woodall .02 .10
309 Bryant Young .07 .20
310 Steve Young .50 1.25
311 Sam Adams .02 .10
312 Howard Ballard .02 .10
313 Robert Blackmon .02 .10
314 Brian Blades .07 .20
315 Joey Galloway RC .60 1.50
316 Carlton Gray .02 .10
317 Cortez Kennedy .07 .20
318 Rick Mirer .07 .20
319 Eugene Robinson .02 .10
320 Chris Warren .07 .20
321 Terry Wooden .02 .10
322 Derrick Brooks RC .60 1.50
323 Lawrence Dawsey .02 .10
324 Trent Dilfer .15 .40
325 Santana Dotson .02 .10
326 Thomas Everett .02 .10
327 Paul Gruber .02 .10
328 Jackie Harris .02 .10
329 Courtney Hawkins .02 .10
330 Martin Mayhew .02 .10
331 Hardy Nickerson .02 .10
332 Errict Rhett .07 .20
333 Warren Sapp RC .60 1.50
334 Charles Wilson .02 .10
335 Reggie Brooks .07 .20
336 Tom Carter .02 .10
337 Henry Ellard .07 .20
338 Ricky Ervins .02 .10
339 Darrell Green .02 .10
340 Ken Harvey .02 .10
341 Brian Mitchell .02 .10
342 Cory Raymer RC .02 .10
343 Heath Shuler .07 .20
344 Michael Westbrook RC .15 .40
345 Tony Woods * .02 .10
346 Checklist .02 .10
347 Checklist .02 .10
348 Checklist .02 .10
349 Checklist .02 .10
350 Checklist .02 .10
351 Checklist .02 .10
352 Checklist .02 .10
353 Dave Krieg .02 .10
354 Rob Moore .07 .20
355 J.J. Birden .02 .10
356 Eric Metcalf .07 .20
357 Bryce Paup .07 .20
358 Willie Green .07 .20
359 Derrick Moore .02 .10
360 Michael Timpson .02 .10
361 Eric Bieniemy .02 .10
362 Keenan McCardell .15 .40
363 Andre Rison .07 .20
364 Lorenzo White .02 .10
365 Deion Sanders .40 1.00
366 Wade Wilson .02 .10
367 Aaron Craver .02 .10
368 Michael Dean Perry .02 .10
369 Rod Smith WR RC 5.00 12.00
370 Henry Thomas .02 .10
371 Mark Ingram .02 .10
372 Chris Chandler .07 .20
373 Mel Gray .02 .10
374 Flipper Anderson .02 .10
375 Craig Erickson .02 .10
376 Mark Brunell .40 1.00
377 Ernest Givins .02 .10
378 Randy Jordan .02 .10
379 Webster Slaughter .02 .10
380 Tamarick Vanover RC .15 .40
381 Gary Clark .02 .10
382 Steve Emtman .02 .10
383 Eric Green .02 .10
384 Louis Oliver .02 .10
385 Robert Smith .15 .40
386 Dave Meggett .02 .10
387 Eric Allen .02 .10
388 Wesley Walls .07 .20
389 Herschel Walker .07 .20
390 Ronald Moore .02 .10
391 Adrian Murrell .07 .20
392 Charles Wilson .02 .10
393 Derrick Fenner .02 .10
394 Pat Swilling .02 .10
395 Kelvin Martin .02 .10
396 Rodney Peete .02 .10
397 Ricky Watters .07 .20
398 Erric Pegram .07 .20
399 Leonard Russell .02 .10
400 Alexander Wright .02 .10
401 Darrien Gordon .02 .10
402 Alfred Pupunu .02 .10
403 Elvis Grbac .15 .40
404 Derek Loville .02 .10
405 Steve Broussard .02 .10
406 Ricky Proehl .02 .10
407 Bobby Joe Edmonds .02 .10
408 Alvin Harper .02 .10
409 Dave Moore RC .02 .10
410 Terry Allen .07 .20
411 Gus Frerotte .07 .20
412 Leslie Shepherd RC .07 .20
413 Stoney Case RC .02 .10
414 Frank Sanders RC .15 .40
415 Roell Preston RC .07 .20
416 Lorenzo Styles RC .02 .10
417 Justin Armour RC .02 .10
418 Todd Collins RC .50 1.25
419 Darick Holmes RC .07 .20
420 Kerry Collins .30 .75
421 Tyrone Poole .07 .20
422 Rashaan Salaam .07 .20
423 Todd Sauerbrun RC .02 .10
424 Ki-Jana Carter .15 .40
425 David Dunn RC .02 .10
426 Ernest Hunter RC .02 .10
427 Eric Zeier RC .15 .40
428 Eric Bjornson RC .02 .10
429 Sherman Williams .02 .10
430 Terrell Davis RC 1.00 2.50
431 Luther Elliss .02 .10
432 Kez McCorvey RC .02 .10
433 Antonio Freeman RC .50 1.25
434 Craig Newsome RC .02 .10
435 Steve McNair .60 1.50
436 Chris Sanders RC .07 .20
437 Zack Crockett RC .07 .20
438 Ellis Johnson .02 .10
439 Tony Boselli .15 .40
440 James O. Stewart .15 .40
441 Trezelle Jenkins .02 .10
442 Tamarick Vanover .15 .40
443 Derrick Alexander DE .02 .10
444 Chad May RC .02 .10
445 James A.Stewart RC .02 .10
446 Ty Law .15 .40
447 Curtis Martin RC 1.25 3.00
448 Will Moore RC .02 .10
449 Mark Fields .07 .20
450 Ray Zellars RC .07 .20
451 Charles Way RC .02 .10
452 Tyrone Wheatley .15 .40
453 Kyle Brady .15 .40
454 Wayne Chrebet RC 1.00 2.50
455 Hugh Douglas .07 .20
456 Chris T.Jones RC .02 .10
457 Mike Mamula .02 .10
458 Fred McCrary RC .02 .10
459 Bobby Taylor .15 .40
460 Mark Bruener .07 .20
461 Kordell Stewart .25 .60
462 Kevin Carter .07 .20
463 Lovell Pinkney RC .02 .10
464 Johnny Thomas WR RC .02 .10
465 Terrell Fletcher RC .02 .10
466 Jimmy Oliver RC .02 .10
467 J.J. Stokes .15 .40
468 Christian Fauria RC .07 .20
469 Joey Galloway .25 .60
470 Derrick Brooks .25 .60
471 Warren Sapp .15 .40
472 Michael Westbrook .15 .40
473 Garrison Hearst ES .15 .40
474 Jeff George ES .07 .20
475 Terance Mathis ES .07 .20
476 Andre Reed ES .07 .20
477 Bruce Smith ES .15 .40
478 Lamar Lathon ES .02 .10
479 Curtis Conway ES .15 .40
480 Jeff Blake ES .15 .40
481 Carl Pickens ES .07 .20
482 Eric Turner ES .02 .10
483 Troy Aikman ES .30 .75
484 Michael Irvin ES .15 .40
485 Emmitt Smith ES .50 1.25
486 John Elway ES .60 1.50
487 Shannon Sharpe ES .07 .20
488 Herman Moore ES .15 .40
489 Barry Sanders ES .50 1.25
490 Brett Favre ES .60 1.50
491 Reggie White ES .15 .40
492 Haywood Jeffires ES .02 .10
493 Sean Dawkins ES .02 .10
494 Marshall Faulk ES .40 1.00
495 Desmond Howard ES .07 .20
496 Steve Bono ES .07 .20
497 Derrick Thomas ES .15 .40
498 Irving Fryar ES .07 .20
499 Terry Kirby ES .07 .20
500 Dan Marino ES .60 1.50
501 O.J. McDuffie ES .15 .40
502 Cris Carter ES .15 .40
503 Warren Moon ES .07 .20
504 Jake Reed ES .07 .20
505 Drew Bledsoe ES .15 .40
506 Ben Coates ES .07 .20
507 Jim Everett ES .02 .10
508 Rodney Hampton ES .07 .20
509 Mo Lewis ES .02 .10
510 Tim Brown ES .15 .40
511 Jeff Hostetler ES .07 .20
512 Rocket Ismail ES .07 .20
513 Chester McGlockton ES .07 .20
514 Fred Barnett ES .07 .20
515 Greg Lloyd ES .07 .20
516 Byron Bam Morris ES .02 .10
517 Rod Woodson ES .07 .20
518 Jerome Bettis ES .15 .40
519 Isaac Bruce ES .15 .40
520 Stan Humphries ES .07 .20
521 Natrone Means ES .07 .20
522 Junior Seau ES .15 .40
523 William Floyd ES .07 .20
524 Jerry Rice ES .30 .75
525 Steve Young ES .25 .60
526 Cortez Kennedy ES .07 .20
527 Rick Mirer ES .07 .20
528 Chris Warren ES .07 .20
529 Trent Dilfer ES .15 .40
530 Errict Rhett ES .07 .20
531 Darrell Green ES .02 .10
532 Heath Shuler ES .07 .20

533 Stoney Case RO .02 .10
534 Eric Zeier RO .07 .20
535 Kerry Collins RO .15 .40
536 Steve McNair RO .50 1.25
537 Kordell Stewart RO .25 .60
538 Rob Johnson RO RC .40 1.00
539 Eric Ball EE .02 .10
540 Darrick Brownlow EE .02 .10
541 Paul Butcher EE .02 .10
542 Carlester Crumpler EE .02 .10
543 Maurice Douglas EE .02 .10
544 Keith Elias EE RC .02 .10
545 Kenneth Gant EE .02 .10
546 Corey Harris EE .02 .10
547 Andre Hastings EE .07 .20
548 Thomas Homco EE .02 .10
549 Lenny McGill EE .02 .10
550 Mark Pike EE .02 .10
P1 Promo Sheet .75 2.00
P264 Byron Bam Morris Prototype .40 1.00

1995 Ultra Gold Medallion

COMPLETE SET (550) 100.00 250.00
COMP.SERIES 1 (350) 60.00 150.00
COMP.SERIES 2 (200) 40.00 100.00
*STARS: 3X TO 6X BASIC CARDS
*RCs: 1.2X TO 3X BASIC CARDS
ONE PER PACK

1995 Ultra Achievements

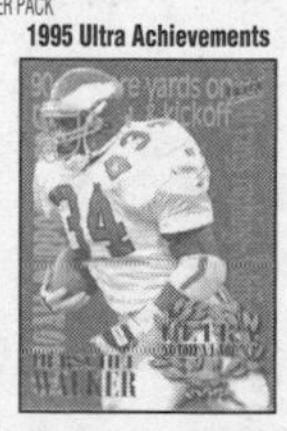

This 10-card set was randomly inserted into series one packs at a rate of one in seven packs and features outstanding achievements by individual players. This set also has a gold medallion parallel, which is identified by a gold seal on the front of the card.
COMPLETE SET (10) 4.00 10.00
STATED ODDS 1:7
*GOLD MED.: .8X TO 2X BASIC INSERTS
1 Drew Bledsoe .60 1.50
2 Cris Carter .25 .60
3 Ben Coates .10 .30
4 Mel Gray .05 .15
5 Jerry Rice 1.00 2.50
6 Barry Sanders 1.50 4.00
7 Deion Sanders .60 1.50
8 Herschel Walker .10 .30
9 Dewayne Washington .10 .30
10 Steve Young .75 2.00

1995 Ultra All-Rookie Team

Randomly inserted at a rate of one in 55 series two packs, this 10 card set is printed on plastic stock and features top rookies from the 1995 season. A parallel of this set also exists - the All-Rookie Team Hot Pack. This set came only as a complete set inserted in packs at a rate of one in 360 packs. Cards have a "Hot Pack" designation on both the front and the back against a flame background. A cover card was included in the hot pack sets.
COMPLETE SET (10) 20.00 50.00
SER.2 STATED ODDS 1:55
*HOT PACK: .2X TO .5X BASIC INSERTS
HP SET: SER.2 STATED ODDS 1:360
1 Michael Westbrook .75 2.00
2 Terrell Davis 5.00 12.00
3 Curtis Martin 6.00 15.00
4 Joey Galloway 3.00 8.00
5 Rashaan Salaam .40 1.00
6 J.J. Stokes .75 2.00
7 Napoleon Kaufman 2.50 6.00
8 Mike Mamula .20 .50
9 Kyle Brady .75 2.00
10 Hugh Douglas .75 2.00

1995 Ultra Award Winners

This six card set was randomly inserted into series one packs at a rate of one in five and features award-winning players from the 1994 season. A gold medallion parallel set also exists and is designated with a gold foil stamp on the front of the card.
COMPLETE SET (6) 3.00 8.00
SER.1 STATED ODDS 1:5
*GOLD MED.: .8X TO 2X BASIC INSERTS
1 Tim Bowens .02 .10
2 Marshall Faulk .75 2.00
3 Dan Marino 1.25 3.00
4 Barry Sanders 1.00 2.50
5 Deion Sanders .40 1.00
6 Steve Young .50 1.25

1995 Ultra First Rounders

This 20 card set was randomly inserted into series one packs at a rate of one in seven packs and features players who were chosen in the first round of the 1995 draft. This set contains a gold medallion parallel which is designated on the front with a gold foil logo.
COMPLETE SET (20) 10.00 25.00
SER.1 STATED ODDS 1:7
*GOLD MED: .8X TO 2X BASIC INSERTS
1 Derrick Alexander DE .05 .15
2 Tony Boselli .25 .60
3 Kyle Brady .25 .60
4 Mark Bruener .10 .30
5 Devin Bush .05 .15
6 Kevin Carter .25 .60
7 Ki-Jana Carter .25 .60
8 Kerry Collins 1.25 3.00
9 Mark Fields .25 .60
10 Joey Galloway 1.00 2.50
11 Napoleon Kaufman .75 2.00
12 Ty Law 1.00 2.50
13 Mike Mamula .05 .15
14 Steve McNair 2.00 5.00
15 Rashaan Salaam .10 .30
16 Warren Sapp 1.00 2.50
17 James O. Stewart .75 2.00
18 J.J.Stokes .25 .60
19 Michael Westbrook .25 .60
20 Tyrone Wheatley .75 2.00

1995 Ultra Magna Force

This 20 card set was randomly inserted into series two hobby packs at a rate of one in 20 packs. Card fronts feature the title "Magna Force" in block letters on a silver foil background with the player's name at the bottom. Card backs feature a background action shot and a headshot in the upper right corner. A commentary on the player is also included.
COMPLETE SET (20) 40.00 100.00
SER.2 STATED ODDS 1:20 HOBBY
1 Emmitt Smith 10.00 20.00
2 Jerry Rice 5.00 10.00
3 Drew Bledsoe 4.00 8.00
4 Marshall Faulk 7.50 15.00
5 Heath Shuler .75 1.50
6 Carl Pickens .75 1.50
7 Ben Coates .75 1.50
8 Terry Allen .75 1.50
9 Terance Mathis .75 1.50
10 Fred Barnett .75 1.50
11 O.J. McDuffie 1.50 3.00
12 Garrison Hearst 1.50 3.00
13 Deion Sanders 4.00 8.00
14 Reggie White 1.50 3.00
15 Herman Moore 1.50 3.00
16 Brett Favre 10.00 20.00
17 William Floyd .75 1.50
18 Curtis Martin 6.00 12.00
19 Joey Galloway 3.00 6.00
20 Tyrone Wheatley 2.50 5.00

1995 Ultra Overdrive

This 20 card set was randomly inserted into series two retail packs at a rate of one in 20. Card fronts feature a colored swirl background with the card name running along the right and the player's name and position at the bottom. Card backs feature a background action shot with the player's head "boxed" and in color. A brief commentary on the player is under the headshot.
COMPLETE SET (20) 20.00 50.00
SER.2 STATED ODDS 1:20 RETAIL
1 Barry Sanders 5.00 12.00
2 Troy Aikman 3.00 8.00
3 Natrone Means .40 1.00
4 Steve Young 2.50 6.00
5 Errict Rhett .40 1.00
6 Terrell Davis 2.00 5.00
7 Michael Westbrook .20 .50
8 Michael Irvin .75 2.00
9 Chris Warren .40 1.00
10 Tim Brown .75 2.00
11 Jerome Bettis .75 2.00
12 Ricky Watters .40 1.00
13 Derrick Thomas .75 2.00
14 Bruce Smith .75 2.00
15 Rashaan Salaam .20 .50
16 Jeff Blake .40 1.00
17 Alvin Harper .20 .50
18 Shannon Sharpe .40 1.00
19 Eric Swann .40 1.00
20 Andre Rison .40 1.00

1995 Ultra Rising Stars

This nine card set was randomly inserted into series one packs at a rate of one in 37 and features young players on a ultra-crystal design. A gold medallion parallel of this set exists and is designated by a gold foil stamp on the front of the card.
COMPLETE SET (9) 15.00 40.00
SER.1 STATED ODDS 1:37
*GOLD MED.: .6X TO 1.5X BASIC INSERTS
1 Jerome Bettis 1.25 3.00
2 Jeff Blake 1.00 2.50
3 Drew Bledsoe 3.00 8.00
4 Ben Coates .60 1.50
5 Marshall Faulk 6.00 15.00
6 Brett Favre 10.00 25.00
7 Natrone Means .60 1.50
8 Byron Bam Morris .30 .75
9 Eric Turner .30 .75

1995 Ultra Second Year Standouts

Randomly inserted into series one packs at a rate of one in five packs, this 15 card set focuses on 1994 rookies that made a big impact. A gold medallion parallel of this set exists and is designated with a gold foil stamp on the front of the card.
COMPLETE SET (15) 4.00 8.00
SER.1 STATED ODDS 1:5
*GOLD MED: .8X TO 2X BASIC INSERTS
1 Derrick Alexander WR .75 2.00
2 Mario Bates .40 1.00
3 Tim Bowens .20 .50
4 Bert Emanuel .75 2.00
5 Marshall Faulk 4.00 10.00
6 William Floyd .40 1.00
7 Rob Fredrickson .20 .50
8 Antonio Langham .20 .50
9 Byron Bam Morris .20 .50
10 Errict Rhett .40 1.00
11 Darnay Scott .40 1.00
12 Heath Shuler .40 1.00
13 Dewayne Washington .40 1.00
14 Dan Wilkinson .40 1.00
15 Bryant Young .40 1.00

1995 Ultra Stars

Randomly inserted into series one jumbo 17 card packs only at a rate of one in seven packs, this 10 card set features some of the most popular NFL superstars. Card fronts contain a multi-photo background with the player's name and card title in silver foil. Card backs contain a photo and commentary. A gold medallion parallel of this set exists and is designated with a gold foil stamp on the front of the card.
COMPLETE SET (10) 7.50 15.00
SER.1 STATED ODDS 1:7 JUMBO
*GOLD MED: .8X TO 2X BASIC INSERTS
1 Tim Brown .25 .60
2 Marshall Faulk 1.25 3.00
3 Irving Fryar .10 .30
4 Dan Marino 2.00 5.00
5 Natrone Means .10 .30
6 Jerry Rice 1.00 2.50
7 Barry Sanders 1.50 4.00
8 Deion Sanders .60 1.50
9 Emmitt Smith 1.50 4.00
10 Rod Woodson .10 .30

1995 Ultra Touchdown Kings

Randomly inserted into series one 12 card packs only at a rate of one in seven packs, this 10 card set features players with a knack for hitting pay dirt. Card fronts feature a colorful background with the letters "TD". The player's name and card title are located along the bottom in gold foil. Card backs feature a photo with commentary. A gold medallion parallel also exists and is designated by a gold foil stamp on the front of the card.
COMPLETE SET (10) 4.00 10.00
SER.1 STATED ODDS 1:7
*GOLD MED: .8X TO 2X BASIC INSERTS
1 Marshall Faulk 1.25 3.00
2 Terance Mathis .10 .30
3 Natrone Means .10 .30
4 Herman Moore .25 .60
5 Carl Pickens .10 .30
6 Jerry Rice 1.00 2.50
7 Andre Rison .10 .30
8 Emmitt Smith 1.50 4.00
9 Chris Warren .10 .30
10 Steve Young .75 2.00

1995 Ultra Ultrabilities

Randomly inserted into series two packs at a rate of one in five packs, this 30 card set is broken into three subsets: Blasts, Bolts and Guns. Blast card fronts contain an orange background with the title "Blasts" in gold foil and the player's name and team in white against an aqua background. Bolt card fronts contain an orange background with the title "Bolts" in gold foil and the player's name and team in white against a green background. Gun card fronts contain an orange swirl background with the title "Guns" in gold foil and the player's name and team in white against a red background. All card backs contain the player's name at the top followed by a brief commentary and a headshot.
COMPLETE SET (30) 25.00 50.00
SER.2 STATED ODDS 1:5
1 Dan Marino 4.00 8.00
2 Steve Young 1.50 3.00
3 Drew Bledsoe 1.25 2.50
4 Jeff Blake .60 1.25
5 Troy Aikman 2.00 4.00
6 John Elway 4.00 8.00
7 Trent Dilfer .40 1.00
8 Steve Bono .20 .50
9 Brett Favre 4.00 8.00
10 Kerry Collins 1.25 3.00
11 Barry Sanders 3.00 6.00
12 Errict Rhett .20 .50
13 Emmitt Smith 3.00 6.00
14 Chris Warren .20 .50
15 Irving Fryar .20 .50
16 Charlie Garner .40 1.00
17 Tim Brown .40 1.00
18 Eric Metcalf .20 .50
19 Herman Moore .40 1.00
20 Robert Smith .40 1.00
21 Natrone Means .20 .50
22 Derrick Thomas .40 1.00
23 Bruce Smith .40 1.00
24 Hugh Douglas .25 .60
25 Mike Mamula .05 .15
26 Jerome Bettis .40 1.00
27 Byron Bam Morris UER .08 .25
28 Tim Bowens .08 .25
29 William Floyd .20 .50
30 Daryl Johnston .20 .50

1996 Ultra

The 1996 Ultra set consists of 200 standard-size cards. The 12-card packs have a suggested retail priced of $2.49 each. Dealers had the option of purchasing either six, 12 or 30 box cases. Each case contained 24 packs per box with the 12 cards in the packs. The cards are grouped alphabetically within teams and checklisted below alphabetically according to teams. The following topical subsets are also part of the set: Rookies (164-178), First Impressions (179-188) and Secret Weapons (189-198). Rookie Cards include Tim Biakabutuka, Bobby Engram, Eddie George, Terry Glenn, Keyshawn Johnson, Leeland McElroy and Lawrence Phillips. A 3-card promo sheet was produced and priced below. Finally, some collectors have reported that the Ultra logo on the fronts can be found with either silver foil or bronze foil in addition to the intended gold foil.
COMPLETE SET (200) 10.00 25.00
1 Larry Centers .08 .25
2 Garrison Hearst .08 .25
3 Rob Moore .08 .25
4 Eric Swann .02 .10
5 Aeneas Williams .02 .10
6 Bert Emanuel .08 .25
7 Jeff George .08 .25
8 Craig Heyward .02 .10
9 Terance Mathis .02 .10
10 Eric Metcalf .02 .10
11 Cornelius Bennett .02 .10
12 Darick Holmes .02 .10
13 Jim Kelly .20 .50
14 Bryce Paup .02 .10
15 Bruce Smith .08 .25
16 Mark Carrier WR .02 .10
17 Kerry Collins .20 .50
18 Lamar Lathon .02 .10
19 Derrick Moore .02 .10
20 Tyrone Poole .02 .10
21 Curtis Conway .20 .50
22 Jeff Graham .02 .10
23 Raymont Harris .08 .25
24 Erik Kramer .02 .10
25 Rashaan Salaam .08 .25
26 Jeff Blake .20 .50
27 Ki-Jana Carter .08 .25
28 Carl Pickens .08 .25
29 Darnay Scott .08 .25
30 Dan Wilkinson .02 .10
31 Leroy Hoard .02 .10
32 Michael Jackson .08 .25
33 Andre Rison .08 .25
34 Vinny Testaverde .08 .25
35 Eric Turner .02 .10
36 Troy Aikman .50 1.25
37 Charles Haley .08 .25
38 Michael Irvin .20 .50
39 Daryl Johnston .08 .25
40 Jay Novacek .02 .10
41 Deion Sanders .30 .75
42 Emmitt Smith .75 2.00
43 Steve Atwater .02 .10
44 Terrell Davis .40 1.00
45 John Elway 1.00 2.50
46 Anthony Miller .08 .25
47 Shannon Sharpe .08 .25
48 Scott Mitchell .08 .25
49 Herman Moore .08 .25
50 Johnnie Morton .08 .25
51 Brett Perriman .02 .10
52 Barry Sanders .75 2.00
53 Chris Spielman .02 .10
54 Edgar Bennett .08 .25
55 Robert Brooks .20 .50
56 Mark Chmura .08 .25
57 Brett Favre 1.00 2.50
58 Reggie White .20 .50
59 Mel Gray .02 .10
60 Haywood Jeffires .02 .10
61 Steve McNair .40 1.00
62 Chris Sanders .08 .25
63 Rodney Thomas .02 .10
64 Quentin Coryatt .02 .10
65 Sean Dawkins .02 .10
66 Ken Dilger .08 .25
67 Marshall Faulk .25 .60
68 Jim Harbaugh .08 .25
69 Tony Boselli .02 .10
70 Mark Brunell .30 .75
71 Desmond Howard .08 .25
72 Jimmy Smith .20 .50
73 James O. Stewart .08 .25
74 Marcus Allen .20 .50
75 Steve Bono .02 .10
76 Lake Dawson .02 .10
77 Neil Smith .08 .25
78 Derrick Thomas .20 .50
79 Tamarick Vanover .08 .25
80 Bryan Cox .02 .10
81 Irving Fryar .08 .25
82 Eric Green .02 .10
83 Dan Marino 1.00 2.50
84 O.J. McDuffie .08 .25
85 Bernie Parmalee .02 .10
86 Cris Carter .20 .50
87 Qadry Ismail .08 .25
88 Warren Moon .08 .25
89 Jake Reed .08 .25
90 Robert Smith .08 .25
91 Drew Bledsoe .30 .75
92 Vincent Brisby .02 .10
93 Ben Coates .08 .25
94 Curtis Martin .40 1.00
95 Willie McGinest .02 .10
96 Dave Meggett .02 .10
97 Mario Bates .08 .25
98 Quinn Early .02 .10
99 Jim Everett .02 .10
100 Michael Haynes .02 .10
101 Renaldo Turnbull .02 .10
102 Dave Brown .02 .10
103 Rodney Hampton .08 .25
104 Mike Sherrard .02 .10
105 Phillippi Sparks .02 .10
106 Tyrone Wheatley .08 .25
107 Hugh Douglas .08 .25
108 Boomer Esiason .08 .25
109 Aaron Glenn .02 .10
110 Mo Lewis .02 .10
111 Johnny Mitchell .02 .10
112 Tim Brown .20 .50
113 Jeff Hostetler .02 .10
114 Rocket Ismail .02 .10
115 Chester McGlockton .02 .10
116 Harvey Williams .02 .10
117 Fred Barnett .02 .10
118 William Fuller .02 .10
119 Charlie Garner .08 .25
120 Ricky Watters .08 .25
121 Calvin Williams .02 .10
122 Kevin Greene .08 .25
123 Greg Lloyd .08 .25
124 Byron Bam Morris .02 .10
125 Neil O'Donnell .08 .25
126 Erric Pegram .02 .10
127 Kordell Stewart .20 .50
128 Yancey Thigpen .08 .25
129 Rod Woodson .08 .25
130 Jerome Bettis .20 .50
131 Isaac Bruce .20 .50
132 Troy Drayton .02 .10
133 Sean Gilbert .02 .10
134 Chris Miller .02 .10
135 Andre Coleman .02 .10
136 Ronnie Harmon .02 .10
137 Aaron Hayden RC .02 .10
138 Stan Humphries .08 .25
139 Natrone Means .08 .25
140 Junior Seau .20 .50
141 William Floyd .08 .25
142 Merton Hanks .02 .10
143 Brent Jones .02 .10
144 Derek Loville .02 .10
145 Jerry Rice .50 1.25
146 J.J. Stokes .20 .50
147 Steve Young .40 1.00
148 Brian Blades .02 .10
149 Joey Galloway .20 .50
150 Cortez Kennedy .02 .10
151 Rick Mirer .08 .25
152 Chris Warren .08 .25
153 Derrick Brooks .20 .50
154 Trent Dilfer .20 .50
155 Alvin Harper .02 .10
156 Jackie Harris .02 .10
157 Hardy Nickerson .02 .10
158 Errict Rhett .08 .25
159 Terry Allen .08 .25
160 Henry Ellard .02 .10
161 Brian Mitchell .02 .10
162 Heath Shuler .08 .25
163 Michael Westbrook .20 .50
164 Tim Biakabutuka RC .20 .50
165 Tony Brackens RC .20 .50
166 Rickey Dudley RC .20 .50
167 Bobby Engram RC .20 .50
168 Daryl Gardener RC .02 .10
169 Eddie George RC .60 1.50
170 Terry Glenn RC .50 1.25
171 Kevin Hardy RC .20 .50
172 Keyshawn Johnson RC .50 1.25
173 Cedric Jones RC .02 .10
174 Leeland McElroy RC .08 .25
175 Jonathan Ogden RC .50 1.25
176 Lawrence Phillips RC .20 .50
177 Simeon Rice RC .50 1.25
178 Regan Upshaw RC .02 .10
179 Justin Armour FI .02 .10
180 Kyle Brady FI .02 .10
181 Devin Bush FI .02 .10
182 Kevin Carter FI .02 .10
183 Wayne Chrebet FI .30 .75
184 Napoleon Kaufman FI .20 .50
185 Frank Sanders FI .08 .25
186 Warren Sapp FI .02 .10
187 Eric Zeier FI .02 .10
188 Ray Zellars FI .02 .10
189 Bill Brooks SW .02 .10
190 Chris Calloway SW .02 .10
191 Zack Crockett SW .02 .10
192 Antonio Freeman SW .20 .50
193 Tyrone Hughes SW .02 .10
194 Daryl Johnston SW .08 .25
195 Tony Martin SW .02 .10
196 Keenan McCardell SW .20 .50
197 Glyn Milburn SW .02 .10
198 David Palmer SW .02 .10
199 Checklist .02 .10
200 Checklist .02 .10
P1 Promo Sheet .75 2.00

1996 Ultra All-Rookie Die Cuts

This 10 card die-cut set contains some of the better 1996 rookies. The cards were inserted at the rate of 1 in 180 Ultra packs and are numbered as "X" of 10.
COMPLETE SET (10) 15.00 40.00
STATED ODDS 1:180
1 Bobby Engram 1.50 4.00
2 Daryl Gardener .30 .75
3 Eddie George 5.00 12.00
4 Terry Glenn 4.00 10.00
5 Kevin Hardy 1.50 4.00
6 Keyshawn Johnson 4.00 10.00
7 Cedric Jones .30 .75
8 Leeland McElroy .75 2.00
9 Jonathan Ogden 3.00 8.00
10 Simeon Rice 4.00 10.00

1996 Ultra Mr. Momentum

Randomly inserted in packs at a rate of one 10, this 20-card standard-size set features players who can dominate a game. The set is printed on special holographic-foil enhanced cards. The cards are sequenced in alphabetical order and numbered "X" of 20.
COMPLETE SET (20) 15.00 40.00
STATED ODDS 1:10
1 Robert Brooks .75 1.50
2 Isaac Bruce .75 1.50
3 Terrell Davis 1.50 3.00
4 John Elway 4.00 8.00
5 Marshall Faulk 1.00 2.00
6 Brett Favre 4.00 8.00
7 Joey Galloway .75 1.50
8 Dan Marino 4.00 8.00
9 Curtis Martin 1.50 3.00
10 Herman Moore .30 .75
11 Carl Pickens .30 .75
12 Jerry Rice 2.00 4.00
13 Barry Sanders 3.00 6.00
14 Chris Sanders .30 .75
15 Deion Sanders 1.25 2.50
16 Kordell Stewart .75 1.50
17 Tamarick Vanover .30 .75
18 Chris Warren .30 .75
19 Ricky Watters .30 .75
20 Steve Young 1.50 3.00

1996 Ultra Pulsating

Randomly inserted in packs at a rate of one in 20, this 10-card standard-size set featured offensive skill position players. The set is printed on foil-enhanced cards. The cards are sequenced in alphabetical order and are numbered "X" of 10.
COMPLETE SET (10) 12.50 30.00
STATED ODDS 1:20
1 Isaac Bruce .75 1.50
2 Brett Favre 4.00 8.00
3 Joey Galloway .75 1.50
4 Curtis Martin 1.50 3.00
5 Rashaan Salaam .30 .75
6 Barry Sanders 3.00 6.00
7 Deion Sanders 1.25 2.50
8 Emmitt Smith 3.00 6.00
9 Kordell Stewart .75 1.50
10 Chris Warren .30 .75

1996 Ultra Rookies

The cards in this thirty card gold-bordered standard-size insert set feature leading 1996 NFL draft picks. These cards were inserted at a ratio of 1 per 3 packs. The cards are sequenced in alphabetical order and were numbered as "X" of 30.
COMPLETE SET (30) 20.00 40.00
STATED ODDS 1:3
1 Karim Abdul-Jabbar 1.00 2.50
2 Mike Alstott 1.25 3.00
3 Marco Battaglia .30 .75
4 Tim Biakabutuka 1.00 2.50
5 Sean Boyd .30 .75
6 Tony Brackens .50 1.25
7 Duane Clemons .30 .75
8 Bobby Engram .50 1.25
9 Daryl Gardener .30 .75
10 Eddie George 1.50 4.00
11 Terry Glenn 1.25 3.00
12 Kevin Hardy .30 .75
13 Marvin Harrison 3.00 8.00
14 Dietrich Jells .30 .75
15 Keyshawn Johnson 1.25 3.00
16 Lance Johnstone .50 1.25
17 Cedric Jones .30 .75
18 Marcus Jones .30 .75
19 Danny Kanell .50 1.25
20 Markco Maddox .30 .75
21 Derrick Mayes .50 1.25
22 Leeland McElroy .50 1.25
23 Dell McGee .30 .75
24 Alex Molden .30 .75
25 Eric Moulds 1.50 4.00
26 Jonathan Ogden 2.00 5.00
27 Lawrence Phillips 1.00 2.50
28 Simeon Rice 1.25 3.00
29 Regan Upshaw .30 .75
30 Jerome Woods .30 .75

1996 Ultra Sledgehammer

Randomly inserted in hobby packs only at a rate of one in 15, this 10-card embossed standard-size set highlights powerful offensive or defensive players. The cards are numbered as "X" of 10 and are sequenced in alphabetical order.
COMPLETE SET (10) 7.50 20.00
STATED ODDS 1:15 HOBBY
1 Jeff Blake 1.00 2.50
2 Terrell Davis 2.00 5.00
3 Hugh Douglas .50 1.25
4 Marshall Faulk 1.25 3.00
5 Michael Irvin 1.00 2.50
6 Steve McNair 2.00 5.00
7 Natrone Means .50 1.25
8 Errict Rhett .50 1.25
9 Emmitt Smith 4.00 10.00
10 Rodney Thomas .20 .50

1997 Ultra

The 1997 Ultra set was released in two series totaling 350 cards with a large number of insert sets. Hobby packs of Series 1 and Series 2 also contained one Gold Medallion parallel card per pack with a Platinum Medallion parallel replacing the Gold version in 1:100 packs. The cardbacks were printed with a blue tinted back for NFC players and green for AFC players. An equally printed brown colored cardback variation was also produced for each series one veteran card. Series 2 packs also included randomly inserted "Lucky 13" redemptions (expiration date 12/1/98) good for various Dan Marino signed collectibles including an embossed series 1 Ultra card as listed below. The cards were distributed in 24-pack hobby boxes with 10 cards per pack (2 inserts per pack) and a suggested retail price of $2.49.
COMPLETE SET (350) 40.00 80.00
COMP.SERIES 1 (200) 15.00 30.00
COMP.SERIES 2 (150) 25.00 50.00
1 Brett Favre 1.00 2.50
2 Ricky Watters .15 .40
3 Dan Marino 1.00 2.50
4 Bryan Still .08 .25
5 Chester McGlockton .08 .25
6 Tim Biakabutuka .15 .40
7 Dave Brown .08 .25
8 Mike Alstott .25 .60
9 O.J. McDuffie .15 .40
10 Mark Brunell .30 .75
11 Michael Bates .08 .25
12 Tyrone Wheatley .15 .40
13 Eddie George .25 .60
14 Kevin Greene .15 .40
15 Jerris McPhail .08 .25
16 Harvey Williams .08 .25
17 Eric Swann .08 .25
18 Carl Pickens .15 .40
19 Terrell Davis .30 .75
20 Charles Way .08 .25
21 Jamie Asher .08 .25
22 Qadry Ismail .15 .40
23 Lawrence Phillips .08 .25
24 John Friesz .08 .25
25 Dorsey Levens .25 .60
26 Willie McGinest .08 .25
27 Chris T. Jones .08 .25
28 Cortez Kennedy .08 .25
29 Raymont Harris .08 .25
30 William Roaf .08 .25
31 Ted Johnson .08 .25
32 Tony Martin .15 .40
33 Jim Everett .08 .25
34 Ray Zellars .08 .25
35 Derrick Alexander WR .15 .40
36 Leonard Russell .08 .25
37 William Thomas .08 .25
38 Karim Abdul-Jabbar .15 .40
39 Kevin Turner .08 .25
40 Robert Brooks .15 .40
41 Kent Graham .08 .25
42 Tony Brackens .08 .25
43 Rodney Hampton .15 .40
44 Drew Bledsoe .30 .75
45 Barry Sanders .75 2.00
46 Tim Brown .25 .60
47 Reggie White .25 .60
48 Terry Allen .25 .60
49 Jim Harbaugh .15 .40
50 John Elway 1.00 2.50
51 William Floyd .15 .40
52 Michael Jackson .15 .40
53 Larry Centers .15 .40
54 Emmitt Smith .75 2.00
55 Bruce Smith .15 .40
56 Terrell Owens .30 .75
57 Deion Sanders .25 .60
58 Neil O'Donnell .15 .40
59 Kordell Stewart .25 .60
60 Bobby Engram .15 .40
61 Keenan McCardell .15 .40
62 Ben Coates .15 .40
63 Curtis Martin .30 .75
64 Hugh Douglas .08 .25
65 Eric Moulds .25 .60
66 Derrick Thomas .25 .60
67 Byron Bam Morris .08 .25
68 Bryan Cox .08 .25
69 Rob Moore .15 .40
70 Michael Haynes .08 .25
71 Brian Mitchell .08 .25
72 Alex Molden .08 .25
73 Steve Young .30 .75
74 Andre Reed .15 .40
75 Michael Westbrook .15 .40
76 Eric Metcalf .15 .40
77 Tony Banks .15 .40
78 Ken Dilger .08 .25
79 John Henry Mills RC .08 .25
80 Ashley Ambrose .08 .25
81 Jason Dunn .08 .25
82 Trent Dilfer .25 .60
83 Wayne Chrebet .25 .60
84 Ty Detmer .15 .40
85 Aeneas Williams .08 .25
86 Frank Wycheck .08 .25
87 Jessie Tuggle .08 .25
88 Steve McNair .30 .75
89 Chris Slade .08 .25
90 Anthony Johnson .08 .25
91 Simeon Rice .15 .40
92 Mike Tomczak .08 .25
93 Sean Jones .08 .25
94 Wesley Walls .15 .40
95 Thurman Thomas .25 .60
96 Scott Mitchell .15 .40
97 Desmond Howard .15 .40
98 Chris Warren .15 .40
99 Glyn Milburn .08 .25
100 Vinny Testaverde .15 .40
101 James O.Stewart .15 .40
102 Iheanyi Uwaezuoke .08 .25
103 Stan Humphries .15 .40
104 Terance Mathis .15 .40
105 Thomas Lewis .08 .25
106 Eddie Kennison .15 .40
107 Rashaan Salaam .08 .25
108 Curtis Conway .15 .40
109 Chris Sanders .08 .25
110 Marcus Allen .25 .60
111 Gilbert Brown .15 .40
112 Jason Sehorn .15 .40
113 Zach Thomas .25 .60
114 Bobby Hebert .08 .25
115 Herman Moore .15 .40
116 Ray Lewis .40 1.00
117 Darnay Scott .15 .40
118 Jamal Anderson .25 .60
119 Keyshawn Johnson .25 .60
120 Adrian Murrell .15 .40
121 Sam Mills .08 .25
122 Irving Fryar .15 .40
123 Ki-Jana Carter .08 .25
124 Gus Frerotte .08 .25
125 Terry Glenn .25 .60
126 Quentin Coryatt .08 .25
127 Robert Smith .15 .40
128 Jeff Blake .15 .40
129 Natrone Means .15 .40
130 Isaac Bruce .25 .60
131 Lamar Lathon .08 .25
132 Johnnie Morton .15 .40
133 Jerry Rice .50 1.25
134 Errict Rhett .08 .25
135 Junior Seau .25 .60
136 Joey Galloway .15 .40
137 Napoleon Kaufman .25 .60
138 Troy Aikman .50 1.25
139 Kevin Hardy .08 .25
140 Jimmy Smith .15 .40
141 Edgar Bennett .15 .40
142 Hardy Nickerson .08 .25
143 Greg Lloyd .08 .25
144 Dale Carter .08 .25
145 Jake Reed .15 .40
146 Cris Carter .25 .60
147 Todd Collins .08 .25
148 Mel Gray .08 .25
149 Lawyer Milloy .15 .40
150 Kimble Anders .15 .40
151 Darick Holmes .08 .25
152 Bert Emanuel .15 .40
153 Marshall Faulk .30 .75
154 Frank Sanders .15 .40
155 Leeland McElroy .08 .25
156 Rickey Dudley .15 .40
157 Tamarick Vanover .15 .40
158 Kerry Collins .25 .60
159 Jeff Graham .08 .25
160 Jerome Bettis .25 .60
161 Greg Hill .08 .25
162 John Mobley .08 .25
163 Michael Irvin .25 .60
164 Marvin Harrison .25 .60
165 Jim Schwantz RC .08 .25
166 Jermaine Lewis .25 .60
167 Levon Kirkland .08 .25
168 Nilo Silvan .08 .25
169 Ken Norton .08 .25
170 Yancey Thigpen .15 .40
171 Antonio Freeman .25 .60
172 Terry Kirby .15 .40
173 Brad Johnson .25 .60
174 Reidel Anthony RC .25 .60
175 Tiki Barber RC 2.00 5.00
176 Pat Barnes RC .25 .60
177 Michael Booker RC .08 .25
178 Peter Boulware RC .25 .60
179 Rae Carruth RC .08 .25
180 Troy Davis RC .15 .40
181 Corey Dillon RC 1.25 3.00
182 Jim Druckenmiller RC .15 .40
183 Warrick Dunn RC 1.00 2.50
184 James Farrior RC .25 .60
185 Yatil Green RC .15 .40
186 Walter Jones RC .40 1.00
187 Tom Knight RC .08 .25
188 Sam Madison RC .25 .60
189 Tyrus McCloud RC .08 .25
190 Orlando Pace RC .25 .60
191 Jake Plummer RC 1.25 3.00
192 Dwayne Rudd RC .25 .60
193 Darrell Russell RC .08 .25
194 Sedrick Shaw RC .15 .40
195 Shawn Springs RC .15 .40
196 Bryant Westbrook RC .08 .25
197 Danny Wuerffel RC .25 .60
198 Reinard Wilson RC .15 .40
199 Checklist .08 .25
200 Checklist .25 .60
201 Rick Mirer .08 .25
202 Torrance Small .08 .25
203 Ricky Proehl .08 .25
204 Will Blackwell RC .15 .40
205 Warrick Dunn .50 1.25
206 Rob Johnson .25 .60
207 Jim Schwantz .08 .25
208 Ike Hilliard RC .50 1.25
209 Chris Canty RC .08 .25
210 Chris Boniol .08 .25
211 Jim Druckenmiller .08 .25
212 Tony Gonzalez RC 1.25 3.00
213 Scottie Graham .08 .25
214 Byron Hanspard RC .15 .40
215 Gary Brown .08 .25
216 Darrell Russell .08 .25
217 Sedrick Shaw .15 .40
218 Boomer Esiason .15 .40
219 Peter Boulware .15 .40
220 Willie Green .08 .25
221 Dietrich Jells .08 .25
222 Freddie Jones RC .15 .40
223 Eric Metcalf .15 .40
224 John Henry Mills .08 .25
225 Michael Timpson .08 .25
226 Danny Wuerffel .25 .60
227 Daimon Shelton RC .08 .25
228 Henry Ellard .08 .25
229 Flipper Anderson .08 .25
230 Hunter Goodwin RC .08 .25
231 Jay Graham RC .15 .40
232 Duce Staley RC 2.50 6.00
233 Lamar Thomas .08 .25
234 Rod Woodson .15 .40
235 Zack Crockett .08 .25
236 Ernie Mills .08 .25
237 Kyle Brady .08 .25
238 Jesse Campbell .08 .25
239 Anthony Miller .08 .25
240 Michael Haynes .08 .25
241 Qadry Ismail .15 .40
242 Tom Knight .08 .25
243 Brian Manning RC .08 .25
244 Derrick Mayes .15 .40
245 Jamie Sharper RC .15 .40
246 Sherman Williams .08 .25
247 Yatil Green .15 .40
248 Howard Griffith .08 .25
249 Brian Blades .08 .25
250 Mark Chmura .15 .40
251 Chris Darkins .08 .25
252 Willie Davis .08 .25
253 Quinn Early .08 .25
254 Marc Edwards RC .08 .25
255 Charlie Jones .08 .25
256 Jake Plummer .60 1.50
257 Heath Shuler .08 .25
258 Fred Barnett .08 .25
259 William Henderson .15 .40
260 Michael Booker .08 .25
261 Chad Brown .08 .25
262 Garrison Hearst .15 .40
263 Leon Johnson RC .15 .40
264 Antowain Smith RC .75 2.00
265 Darnell Autry RC .15 .40
266 Craig Heyward .08 .25
267 Walter Jones .15 .40
268 Dexter Coakley RC .25 .60
269 Mercury Hayes .08 .25
270 Brett Perriman .08 .25
271 Chris Spielman .08 .25
272 Kevin Greene .15 .40
273 Kevin Lockett RC .15 .40
274 Troy Davis .15 .40
275 Brent Jones .08 .25
276 Chris Chandler .15 .40
277 Bryant Westbrook .08 .25
278 Desmond Howard .15 .40
279 Tyrone Hughes .08 .25
280 Kez McCorvey .08 .25
281 Stephen Davis .25 .60
282 Steve Everitt .08 .25
283 Andre Hastings .08 .25
284 Marcus Robinson RC 2.00 5.00
285 Donnell Woolford .08 .25
286 Mario Bates .08 .25
287 Corey Dillon .60 1.50
288 Jackie Harris .08 .25
289 Lorenzo Neal .08 .25
290 Anthony Pleasant .08 .25
291 Andre Rison .15 .40
292 Amani Toomer .15 .40
293 Eric Turner .08 .25
294 Elvis Grbac .15 .40
295 Cris Dishman .08 .25
296 Tom Carter .08 .25
297 Mark Carrier DB .08 .25
298 Orlando Pace .15 .40
299 Jay Riemersma RC .08 .25
300 Daryl Johnston .15 .40
301 Joey Kent RC .25 .60
302 Ronnie Harmon .08 .25
303 Rocket Ismail .15 .40
304 Terrell Davis .30 .75
305 Sean Dawkins .08 .25
306 Jeff George .15 .40
307 David Palmer .08 .25
308 Dwayne Rudd .08 .25
309 J.J. Stokes .15 .40
310 James Farrior .15 .40
311 William Fuller .08 .25
312 George Jones RC .15 .40
313 John Allred RC .08 .25
314 Tony Graziani RC .25 .60
315 Jeff Hostetler .08 .25
316 Keith Poole RC .25 .60
317 Neil Smith .15 .40
318 Steve Tasker .08 .25
319 Mike Vrabel RC 5.00 12.00
320 Pat Barnes .25 .60
321 James Hundon RC .25 .60
322 O.J. Santiago RC .15 .40
323 Billy Davis RC .08 .25
324 Shawn Springs .15 .40
325 Reinard Wilson .08 .25
326 Charles Johnson .15 .40
327 Micheal Barrow .08 .25
328 Derrick Mason RC 1.25 3.00
329 Muhsin Muhammad .15 .40
330 David LaFleur RC .08 .25
331 Reidel Anthony .15 .40
332 Tiki Barber .75 2.00
333 Ray Buchanan .08 .25
334 John Elway 1.00 2.50
335 Alvin Harper .08 .25
336 Damon Jones RC .08 .25
337 Dedric Ward RC .15 .40
338 Jim Everett .08 .25
339 Jon Harris .08 .25
340 Warren Moon .25 .60
341 Rae Carruth .08 .25
342 John Mobley .08 .25
343 Tyrone Poole .08 .25
344 Mike Cherry RC .08 .25
345 Horace Copeland .08 .25
346 Deon Figures .08 .25
347 Antwuan Wyatt RC .08 .25
348 Tommy Vardell .08 .25
349 Checklist (201-324) .08 .25
350 Checklist (325-350 inserts) .08 .25
S1A T.Davis Sample AU 40.00 80.00
AU3 Dan Marino AU 40.00 100.00
S1 Terrell Davis Sample 1.25 3.00

1997 Ultra Gold Medallion

COMPLETE SET (346) 200.00 400.00
COMP.SERIES 1 (198) 75.00 150.00
COMP.SERIES 2 (148) 125.00 250.00
*STARS: 1.5X TO 3X BASIC CARDS
*RCs: 1X TO 2X BASIC CARDS
ONE PER HOBBY PACK

1997 Ultra Platinum Medallion

*VETS: 15X TO 40X BASIC CARDS
*ROOKIES: 6X TO 15X BASIC RC
STATED ODDS 1:100 HOBBY
ANNOUNCED PRINT RUN UNDER 150

1997 Ultra All-Rookie Team

Randomly inserted in Ultra Series 2 packs at the rate of one in 18, this 12-card set features color action images of 1997's top rookie players showcased in what looks like a chunk of

gold encased in a screwdown protector, complete with facsimile signature.
COMPLETE SET (12) 12.50 30.00
STATED ODDS 1:18 SER.2
1 Antowain Smith 3.00 8.00
2 Jay Graham .60 1.50
3 Ike Hilliard 2.00 5.00
4 Warrick Dunn 4.00 10.00
5 Tony Gonzalez 5.00 12.00
6 David LaFleur .40 1.00
7 Reidel Anthony 1.00 2.50
8 Rae Carruth .40 1.00
9 Byron Hanspard .60 1.50
10 Joey Kent 1.00 2.50
11 Kevin Lockett .60 1.50
12 Jake Plummer 5.00 12.00

1997 Ultra Blitzkrieg

Randomly inserted in packs at a rate of one in 6, these cards feature top offensive players with a rainbow foil "blitzkrieg" logo running down the left side of the card front. A Die Cut parallel set was produced and randomly inserted at the rate of 1:36 packs.
COMPLETE SET (18) 20.00 50.00
STATED ODDS 1:6 SER.1
*DIE CUTS: 1X TO 2.5X BASIC INSERTS
DIE CUT ODDS 1:36 SER.1
1 Eddie George .75 2.00
2 Terry Glenn .75 2.00
3 Karim Abdul-Jabbar .50 1.25
4 Emmitt Smith 2.50 6.00
5 Dan Marino 3.00 8.00
6 Brett Favre 3.00 8.00
7 Keyshawn Johnson .75 2.00
8 Curtis Martin 1.00 2.50
9 Marvin Harrison .75 2.00
10 Barry Sanders 2.50 6.00
11 Jerry Rice 1.50 4.00
12 Terrell Davis 1.00 2.50
13 Troy Aikman 1.50 4.00
14 Drew Bledsoe 1.00 2.50
15 John Elway 3.00 8.00
16 Kordell Stewart .75 2.00
17 Kerry Collins .75 2.00
18 Steve Young 1.00 2.50

1997 Ultra Comeback Kids

Randomly inserted in Ultra Series 2 packs at the rate of one in eight, this 10-card set features action color images of top players printed on an irregularly die cut card with a facsimile autograph and a parchment paper background.
COMPLETE SET (10) 15.00 30.00
STATED ODDS 1:8 SER.2
1 Dan Marino 3.00 8.00
2 Barry Sanders 2.50 6.00
3 Jerry Rice 1.50 4.00
4 John Elway 3.00 8.00
5 Steve Young 1.00 2.50
6 Deion Sanders .75 2.00
7 Mark Brunell 1.00 2.50
8 Tim Biakabutuka .50 1.25
9 Tony Banks .50 1.25
10 Terry Allen .75 2.00

1997 Ultra First Rounders

Randomly inserted in Ultra Series 2 packs at the rate of one in four, this 12-card set features action color images of the top 1997 rookies on a football field background enhanced with silver rainbow holofoil.
COMPLETE SET (12) 3.00 8.00
STATED ODDS 1:4 SER.2
1 Antowain Smith 1.00 2.50
2 Rae Carruth .10 .30
3 Peter Boulware .30 .75
4 Shawn Springs .20 .50
5 Bryant Westbrook .10 .30
6 Orlando Pace .30 .75
7 Jim Druckenmiller .20 .50
8 Yatil Green .20 .50
9 Reidel Anthony .30 .75
10 Ike Hilliard .60 1.50
11 Darrell Russell .10 .30
12 Warrick Dunn 1.25 3.00

1997 Ultra Main Event

Randomly inserted in Ultra Series 2 packs at the rate of one in eight, this 10-card set features color action images of players who make headlines on the field printed on die-cut canvas cards.
COMPLETE SET (10) 15.00 30.00
STATED ODDS 1:8 SER.2
1 Dan Marino 3.00 8.00
2 Barry Sanders 2.50 6.00
3 Jerry Rice 1.50 4.00
4 Drew Bledsoe 1.00 2.50
5 John Elway 3.00 8.00
6 Troy Aikman 1.50 4.00
7 Deion Sanders .75 2.00
8 Joey Galloway .50 1.25
9 Steve McNair 1.00 2.50
10 Marshall Faulk 1.00 2.50

1997 Ultra Play of the Game

Cards from this set were randomly inserted in 1997 Ultra packs at the rate of 1:8. Each of these 10 cards feature a top offensive star with a short write-up about a great play or career game that player has had.
COMPLETE SET (10) 6.00 15.00
STATED ODDS 1:8 SER.1
1 Deion Sanders .75 2.00
2 Jerry Rice 1.50 4.00
3 Michael Westbrook .50 1.25
4 Steve McNair 1.00 2.50
5 Marshall Faulk 1.00 2.50
6 Terrell Davis 1.00 2.50
7 Mark Brunell 1.00 2.50
8 Isaac Bruce .75 2.00
9 Tony Banks .50 1.25
10 Jamal Anderson .75 2.00

1997 Ultra Reebok

Issued one per pack, these cards are essentially a parallel to 15-different 1997 Ultra cards featuring the company's spokesmen. The differentiating factor is the Reebok logo on the cardback along with the Reebok website address at the bottom of the cardback. The address was printed in five different colors each with different unannounced insertion ratios: Bronze (easiest to pull), Silver (next easiest), Gold (third easiest), and Red and Green (the toughest two). Therefore, each of the 15-cards has 5-different color variations.
COMP.REEBOK BRONZE (15) 1.50 4.00
*REEBOK GOLDS: 2X TO 5X BRONZES
*REEBOK GREENS: 25X TO 50X BRONZES
*REEBOK REDS: 12.5X TO 25X BRONZES
*REEBOK SILVERS: .75X TO 2X BRONZES
OVERALL REEBOK ODDS ONE PER PACK
202 Torrance Small .08 .25
207 Jim Schwantz .08 .25
210 Chris Boniol .08 .25
223 Eric Metcalf .15 .40
238 Jesse Campbell .08 .25
241 Qadry Ismail .15 .40
270 Brett Perriman .08 .25
271 Chris Spielman .08 .25
278 Desmond Howard .15 .40
282 Steve Everitt .08 .25
289 Lorenzo Neal .08 .25
317 Neil Smith .15 .40
310 Steve Tasker .15 .40
334 John Elway .50 1.25
343 Tyrone Poole .08 .25

1997 Ultra Rising Stars

Randomly inserted in Ultra Series 2 packs at the rate of one in four, this 10-card set features color action photos of rising [illegible]
COMPLETE SET (10) 6.00 12.00
STATED ODDS 1:4 SER.2
1 Keyshawn Johnson .60 1.50
2 Terrell Davis .75 2.00
3 Kordell Stewart .60 1.50
4 Kerry Collins .60 1.50
5 Joey Galloway .40 1.00
6 Steve McNair .75 2.00
7 Jamal Anderson .60 1.50
8 Michael Westbrook .40 1.00
9 Marshall Faulk .75 2.00
10 Isaac Bruce .60 1.50

1997 Ultra Rookies

Rookies inserts were randomly seeded at a rate of one in four. Each card was printed with the player's name and the Ultra logo in silver foil. A Gold Foil Embossed parallel version was also produced and randomly inserted at the rate of 1:18 packs.
COMPLETE SET (12) 4.00 10.00
STATED ODDS 1:4 SER.1
*GOLD EMBOSSED: 1.2X TO 3X BASIC INS.
GOLD EMBOSSED ODDS 1:18 SER.1
1 Darnell Autry .30 .75
2 Orlando Pace .20 .50
3 Peter Boulware .30 .75
4 Shawn Springs .30 .75
5 Bryant Westbrook .20 .50
6 Rae Carruth .20 .50
7 Jim Druckenmiller .60 1.50
8 Yatil Green .30 .75
9 James Farrior .20 .50
10 Dwayne Rudd .20 .50
11 Darrell Russell .20 .50
12 Warrick Dunn 2.00 5.00

1997 Ultra Specialists

Randomly inserted in Ultra Series two packs at the rate of one in six, this 18-card set features color action photos of players who are considered the best at their positions printed on a horizontal card which is die-cut like a file folder. An "Ultra" parallel version of each card was also produced and inserted at a rate of 1:36 packs. These parallel cards are a bi-fold version of each base insert.
COMPLETE SET (18) 35.00 80.00
STATED ODDS 1:6 SER.2
*ULTRA PARALL: .8X TO 2X BASIC INSERTS
ULTRA PARALLEL STATED ODDS 1:36 SER.2
1 Eddie George 1.25 3.00
2 Terry Glenn 1.25 3.00
3 Karim Abdul-Jabbar .75 2.00
4 Emmitt Smith 4.00 10.00
5 Brett Favre 5.00 12.00
6 Mark Brunell 1.50 4.00
7 Curtis Martin 1.50 4.00
8 Kerry Collins 1.25 3.00
9 Marvin Harrison 1.25 3.00
10 Jerry Rice 2.50 6.00
11 Tony Martin .75 2.00
12 Terrell Davis 1.50 4.00
13 Troy Aikman 2.50 6.00
14 Drew Bledsoe 1.50 4.00
15 John Elway 5.00 12.00
16 Kordell Stewart 1.25 3.00
17 Keyshawn Johnson 1.25 3.00
18 Steve Young 1.50 4.00

1997 Ultra Starring Role

This set was the toughest to pull of the non-parallel inserts in 1997 Ultra. Cards in this 10-card set were randomly inserted in packs at the rate of one in 288.
COMPLETE SET (10) 60.00 150.00
STATED ODDS 1:288 SER.1
1 Emmitt Smith 8.00 20.00
2 Barry Sanders 8.00 20.00
3 Curtis Martin 3.00 8.00
4 Dan Marino 10.00 25.00
5 Keyshawn Johnson 2.50 6.00
6 Marvin Harrison 2.50 6.00
7 Terry Glenn 2.50 6.00
8 Eddie George 2.50 6.00
9 Brett Favre 10.00 25.00
10 Karim Abdul-Jabbar 1.50 4.00

1997 Ultra Stars

Randomly inserted in Ultra Series 2 packs at the rate of one in 288, this 10-card set features color action images of top "immortal" stars of the game printed on a fireworks display background.
COMPLETE SET (10) 100.00 200.00
STATED ODDS 1:288 SER.1
1 Emmitt Smith 15.00 40.00
2 Barry Sanders 15.00 40.00
3 Curtis Martin 6.00 15.00
4 Dan Marino 20.00 50.00
5 Mark Brunell 6.00 15.00
6 Marvin Harrison 5.00 12.00
7 Terry Glenn 5.00 12.00
8 Eddie George 5.00 12.00
9 Brett Favre 20.00 50.00
10 Karim Abdul-Jabbar 3.00 8.00

1997 Ultra Sunday School

Randomly inserted in packs at a rate of one in 8, this 10-card set features an X's and O's type play diagram printed in silver foil on the card fronts.
COMPLETE SET (10) 12.50 25.00
STATED ODDS 1:8 SER.1
1 Marvin Harrison 1.00 2.50
2 Barry Sanders 3.00 8.00
3 Troy Aikman 2.00 5.00
4 Drew Bledsoe 1.25 3.00
5 John Elway 4.00 10.00
6 Kordell Stewart 1.00 2.50
7 Kerry Collins 1.00 2.50
8 Steve Young 1.25 3.00
9 Deion Sanders 1.00 2.50
10 Joey Galloway .60 1.50

1997 Ultra Talent Show

Randomly inserted in packs at a rate of one in 4, each card includes a player photo against a foil card stock background. The 10-card set focuses on up and coming NFL stars and includes gold foil lettering on the card fronts.
COMPLETE SET (10) 4.00 8.00
STATED ODDS 1:4 SER.1
1 Joey Galloway .50 1.25
2 Steve McNair 1.00 2.50
3 Marshall Faulk 1.00 2.50
4 Isaac Bruce .75 2.00
5 Michael Westbrook .50 1.25
6 Zach Thomas .75 2.00
7 Jamal Anderson .75 2.00
8 Mike Alstott .75 2.00
9 Mark Brunell 1.00 2.50
10 Eddie Kennison .50 1.25

1998 Ultra

The 1998 Ultra set was issued in two series totalling 425 cards and was distributed in 10-card packs with a suggested retail price of $2.69. The fronts feature borderless color player photos. The backs carry player information and career statistics. Series 1 contains a limited 25-card subset of rookies (#201-225) with an insertion rate of 1:3. Series 2 contains three subsets: Checklists (358-360), '98 Greats (361-385), and Rookies (386-425) with an insertion rate of 1:3. The basic hobby set includes a special card honoring the achievements of Reggie White. Also, 25-cards were randomly inserted in hobby packs which were redeemable for an autographed Reggie White mini-helmet.
COMPLETE SET (425) 50.00 120.00
COMP.SERIES 1 (225) 30.00 80.00
COMP.SERIES 2 (200) 25.00 50.00
1 Barry Sanders 1.00 2.50
2 Brett Favre 1.50 3.00
3 Napoleon Kaufman .30 .75
5 Terry Allen .30 .75
6 Vinny Testaverde .20 .50
7 William Floyd .10 .30
8 Carl Pickens .20 .50
9 Antonio Freeman .30 .75
10 Ben Coates .20 .50
11 Elvis Grbac .20 .50
12 Kerry Collins .20 .50
13 Orlando Pace .10 .30
14 Steve Broussard .10 .30
15 Terance Mathis .20 .50
16 Tiki Barber .30 .75
17 Cris Carter .30 .75
18 Eric Green .10 .30
19 Eric Metcalf .10 .30
20 Jeff George .20 .50
21 Leslie Shepherd .10 .30
22 Natrone Means .20 .50
23 Scott Mitchell .20 .50
24 Adrian Murrell .20 .50
25 Gilbert Brown .10 .30
26 Jimmy Smith .20 .50
27 Mark Bruener .10 .30
28 Troy Aikman .60 1.50
29 Warrick Dunn .30 .75
30 Jay Graham .10 .30
31 Craig Whelihan RC .10 .30
32 Ed McCaffrey .20 .50
33 Jamie Asher .10 .30
34 John Randle .20 .50
35 Michael Jackson .10 .30
36 Rickey Dudley .10 .30
37 Sean Dawkins .10 .30
38 Andre Rison .20 .50
39 Bert Emanuel .20 .50
40 Jeff Blake .20 .50
41 Curtis Conway .20 .50
42 Eddie Kennison .20 .50
43 James McKnight .30 .75
44 Rae Carruth .10 .30
45 Tito Wooten RC .10 .30
46 Cris Dishman .10 .30
47 Ernie Conwell .10 .30
48 Fred Lane .10 .30
49 Jamal Anderson .30 .75
50 Lake Dawson .10 .30
51 Michael Strahan .20 .50
52 Reggie White .30 .75
53 Trent Dilfer .30 .75
54 Troy Brown .20 .50
55 Wesley Walls .20 .50
56 Chidi Ahanotu .10 .30
57 Dwayne Rudd .10 .30
58 Jerry Rice .60 1.50
59 Johnnie Morton .20 .50
60 Sherman Williams .10 .30
61 Steve McNair .30 .75
62 Will Blackwell .10 .30
63 Chris Chandler .20 .50
64 Dexter Coakley .10 .30
65 Horace Copeland .10 .30
66 Jerald Moore .10 .30
67 Leon Johnson .10 .30
68 Mark Chmura .20 .50
69 Micheal Barrow .10 .30
70 Muhsin Muhammad .20 .50
71 Terry Glenn .30 .75
72 Tony Brackens .10 .30
73 Chad Scott .10 .30
74 Glenn Foley .20 .50
75 Keenan McCardell .20 .50
76 Peter Boulware .10 .30
77 Reidel Anthony .20 .50
78 William Henderson .20 .50
79 Tony Martin .20 .50
80 Tony Gonzalez .30 .75
81 Charlie Jones .10 .30
82 Chris Gedney .10 .30
83 Chris Calloway .10 .30
84 Dale Carter .10 .30
85 Ki-Jana Carter .10 .30
86 Shawn Springs .10 .30
87 Antowain Smith .30 .75
88 Eric Turner .10 .30
89 John Mobley .10 .30
90 Ken Dilger .10 .30
91 Bobby Hoying .20 .50
92 Curtis Martin .30 .75
93 Drew Bledsoe .50 1.25
94 Gary Brown .10 .30
95 Marvin Harrison .30 .75
96 Todd Collins .10 .30
97 Chris Warren .20 .50
98 Danny Kanell .20 .50
99 Tony McGee .10 .30
100 Rod Smith .20 .50
101 Frank Sanders .20 .50
102 Irving Fryar .20 .50
103 Marcus Allen .30 .75
104 Marshall Faulk .40 1.00
105 Bruce Smith .20 .50
106 Charlie Garner .20 .50
107 Paul Justin .10 .30
108 Randal Hill .10 .30
109 Erik Kramer .10 .30
110 Rob Moore .20 .50
111 Shannon Sharpe .20 .50
112 Warren Moon .30 .75
113 Zach Thomas .30 .75
114 Dan Marino 1.50 3.00
115 Duce Staley .40 1.00
116 Eric Swann .10 .30
117 Kenny Holmes .10 .30
118 Merton Hanks .10 .30
119 Raymont Harris .10 .30
120 Terrell Davis .30 .75
121 Thurman Thomas .30 .75
122 Wayne Martin .10 .30
123 Charles Way .10 .30
124 Chuck Smith .10 .30
125 Corey Dillon .30 .75
126 Darnell Autry .10 .30
127 Isaac Bruce .30 .75
128 Joey Galloway .20 .50
129 Kimble Anders .20 .50
130 Aeneas Williams .10 .30
131 Andre Hastings .10 .30
132 Chad Lewis .20 .50
133 J.J. Stokes .20 .50
134 John Elway 1.25 3.00
135 Karim Abdul-Jabbar .30 .75
136 Ken Harvey .10 .30
137 Robert Brooks .20 .50
138 Rodney Thomas .10 .30
139 James Stewart .20 .50
140 Billy Joe Hobert .10 .30
141 Frank Wycheck .10 .30
142 Jake Plummer .30 .75
143 Jerris McPhail .10 .30
144 Kordell Stewart .30 .75
145 Terrell Owens .30 .75
146 Willie Green .10 .30
147 Anthony Miller .10 .30
148 Courtney Hawkins .10 .30
149 Larry Centers .10 .30
150 Gus Frerotte .10 .30
151 O.J. McDuffie .20 .50
152 Ray Zellars .10 .30
153 Terry Kirby .10 .30
154 Tommy Vardell .10 .30
155 Willie Davis .10 .30
156 Chris Canty .10 .30
157 Byron Hanspard .10 .30
158 Chris Penn .10 .30
159 Damon Jones .10 .30
160 Derrick Mayes .20 .50
161 Emmitt Smith 1.25 2.50
162 Keyshawn Johnson .30 .75
163 Mike Alstott .30 .75
164 Tom Carter .10 .30
165 Tony Banks .20 .50
166 Bryant Westbrook .10 .30
167 Chris Sanders .10 .30
168 Deion Sanders .30 .75
169 Garrison Hearst .30 .75
170 Jason Taylor .20 .50
171 Jerome Bettis .30 .75
172 John Lynch .20 .50
173 Troy Davis .10 .30
174 Freddie Jones .10 .30
175 Herman Moore .20 .50
176 Jake Reed .20 .50
177 Mark Brunell .30 .75
178 Ray Lewis .30 .75
179 Stephen Davis .10 .30
180 Tim Brown .30 .75
181 Willie McGinest .10 .30
182 Andre Reed .20 .50
183 Darrien Gordon .10 .30
184 David Palmer .10 .30
185 James Jett .20 .50
186 Junior Seau .30 .75
187 Zack Crockett .10 .30
188 Brad Johnson .30 .75
189 Charles Johnson .10 .30
190 Eddie George .30 .75
191 Jermaine Lewis .20 .50
192 Michael Irvin .30 .75
193 Reggie Brown LB .10 .30
194 Steve Young .40 1.00
195 Warren Sapp .20 .50
196 Wayne Chrebet .30 .75
197 David Dunn .10 .30
198 Dorsey Levens CL .20 .50
199 Troy Aikman CL .30 .75
200 John Elway CL .30 .75
201 Peyton Manning RC 12.00 30.00
202 Ryan Leaf RC 1.25 3.00
203 Charles Woodson RC 2.50 6.00
204 Andre Wadsworth RC 1.00 2.50
205 Brian Simmons RC 1.00 2.50
206 Curtis Enis RC .60 1.50
207 Randy Moss RC 6.00 15.00
208 Germane Crowell RC 1.00 2.50
209 Greg Ellis RC .60 1.50
210 Kevin Dyson RC 1.25 3.00
211 Skip Hicks RC 1.00 2.50
212 Alonzo Mayes RC .60 1.50
213 Robert Edwards RC 1.00 2.50
214 Fred Taylor RC 2.00 5.00
215 Robert Holcombe RC 1.00 2.50
216 John Dutton RC .60 1.50
217 Vonnie Holliday RC 1.00 2.50
218 Tim Dwight RC 1.25 3.00
219 Tavian Banks RC 1.00 2.50
220 Marcus Nash RC .60 1.50
221 Jason Peter RC .60 1.50
222 Michael Myers RC .60 1.50
223 Takeo Spikes RC 1.25 3.00
224 Kivuusama Mays RC .60 1.50
225 Jacquez Green RC 1.00 2.50
226 Doug Flutie .30 .75
227 Ike Hilliard .20 .50
228 Craig Heyward .10 .30
229 Kevin Hardy .10 .30
230 Jason Dunn .10 .30
231 Billy Davis .10 .30
232 Chester McGlockton .10 .30
233 Sean Gilbert .10 .30
234 Bert Emanuel .20 .50
235 Keith Byars .10 .30
236 Tyrone Wheatley .20 .50
237 Ricky Proehl .10 .30
238 Michael Bates .10 .30
239 Derrick Alexander .20 .50
240 Harvey Williams .10 .30
241 Mike Pritchard .10 .30
242 Paul Justin .10 .30
243 Jeff Hostetler .10 .30
244 Eric Moulds .30 .75
245 Jeff Burris .10 .30
246 Gary Brown .10 .30
247 Anthony Johnson .10 .30
248 Dan Wilkinson .10 .30
249 Chris Warren .20 .50
250 Chris Darkins .10 .30
251 Eric Metcalf .10 .30
252 Pat Swilling .10 .30
253 Lamar Smith .20 .50
254 Quinn Early .10 .30
255 Carlester Crumpler .10 .30
256 Eric Bieniemy .10 .30
257 Aaron Bailey .10 .30
258 Neil O'Donnell .20 .50
259 Rod Woodson .20 .50
260 Ricky Whittle .10 .30
261 Iheanyi Uwaezuoke .10 .30
262 Heath Shuler .10 .30
263 Darren Sharper .30 .75
264 John Henry Mills .10 .30
265 Marco Battaglia .10 .30
266 Yancey Thigpen .10 .30
267 Irv Smith .10 .30
268 Jamie Sharper .10 .30
269 Marcus Robinson 2.00 5.00
270 Dorsey Levens .30 .75
271 Qadry Ismail .20 .50
272 Desmond Howard .20 .50
273 Webster Slaughter .10 .30
274 Eugene Robinson .10 .30
275 Bill Romanowski .10 .30
276 Vincent Brisby .10 .30
277 Errict Rhett .20 .50
278 Albert Connell .10 .30
279 Thomas Lewis .10 .30
280 John Farquhar RC .10 .30
281 Marc Edwards .10 .30
282 Tyrone Davis .10 .30
283 Eric Allen .10 .30
284 Aaron Glenn .10 .30
285 Roosevelt Potts .10 .30
286 Kez McCorvey .10 .30
287 Joey Kent .20 .50
288 Jim Druckenmiller .10 .30
289 Sean Dawkins .10 .30
290 Edgar Bennett .10 .30
291 Vinny Testaverde .20 .50
292 Chris Slade .10 .30
293 Lamar Lathon .10 .30
294 Jackie Harris .10 .30
295 Jim Harbaugh .20 .50
296 Rob Fredrickson .10 .30
297 Ty Detmer .20 .50
298 Karl Williams .10 .30
299 Troy Drayton .10 .30
300 Curtis Martin .30 .75
301 Tamarick Vanover .10 .30
302 Lorenzo Neal .10 .30
303 John Hall .10 .30
304 Kevin Greene .20 .50
305 Bryan Still .10 .30
306 Neil Smith .20 .50
307 Greg Lloyd .10 .30
308 Shawn Jefferson .10 .30
309 Aaron Taylor .10 .30
310 Sedrick Shaw .10 .30
311 O.J. Santiago .10 .30
312 Kevin Abrams .10 .30
313 Dana Stubblefield .10 .30
314 Daryl Johnston .20 .50
315 Bryan Cox .10 .30
316 Jeff Graham .10 .30
317 Mario Bates .20 .50
318 Adrian Murrell .20 .50
319 Greg Hill .10 .30
320 Jahine Arnold .10 .30
321 Justin Armour .10 .30
322 Ricky Watters .20 .50
323 Lamont Warren .10 .30
324 Mack Strong .30 .75
325 Darnay Scott .20 .50
326 Brian Mitchell .10 .30
327 Rob Johnson .20 .50
328 Kent Graham .10 .30
329 Hugh Douglas .10 .30
330 Simeon Rice .20 .50
331 Rick Mirer .10 .30
332 Randall Cunningham .30 .75
333 Steve Atwater .10 .30
334 Latario Rachal .10 .30
335 Tony Martin .20 .50
336 Leroy Hoard .10 .30
337 Howard Griffith .10 .30
338 Kevin Lockett .10 .30
339 William Floyd .10 .30
340 Jerry Ellison .10 .30
341 Kyle Brady .10 .30
342 Michael Westbrook .20 .50
343 Kevin Turner .10 .30
344 David LaFleur .10 .30
345 Robert Jones .10 .30
346 Dave Brown .10 .30
347 Kevin Williams .10 .30
348 Amani Toomer .20 .50
349 Amp Lee .10 .30
350 Bryce Paup .10 .30
351 Dewayne Washington .10 .30
352 Mercury Hayes .10 .30
353 Tim Biakabutuka .20 .50
354 Ray Crockett .10 .30
355 Ted Washington .10 .30
356 Pete Mitchell .10 .30
357 Billy Jenkins RC .10 .30
358 Troy Aikman CL .30 .75
359 Drew Bledsoe CL .30 .75
360 Steve Young CL .30 .75
361 Antonio Freeman NG .20 .50
362 Antowain Smith NG .20 .50
363 Barry Sanders NG .60 1.50
364 Bobby Hoying NG .10 .30
365 Brett Favre NG .75 2.00
366 Corey Dillon NG .20 .50
367 Dan Marino NG .75 2.00
368 Drew Bledsoe NG .30 .75
369 Eddie George NG .20 .50
370 Emmitt Smith NG .60 1.50
371 Herman Moore NG .20 .50
372 Jake Plummer NG .20 .50
373 Jerome Bettis NG .20 .50
374 Jerry Rice NG .40 1.00
375 Joey Galloway NG .20 .50
376 John Elway NG .75 2.00
377 Kordell Stewart NG .20 .50
378 Mark Brunell NG .30 .75
379 Keyshawn Johnson NG .20 .50
380 Steve Young NG .30 .75
381 Steve McNair NG .20 .50
382 Terrell Davis NG .30 .75
383 Tim Brown NG .20 .50
384 Troy Aikman NG .40 1.00
385 Warrick Dunn NG .30 .75
386 Ryan Leaf 1.25 3.00
387 Tony Simmons RC .75 2.00
388 Rodney Williams RC .50 1.25
389 John Avery RC .75 2.00
390 Shaun Williams RC .75 2.00
391 Anthony Simmons RC .75 2.00
392 Rashaan Shehee RC .75 2.00
393 Robert Holcombe .75 2.00
394 Larry Shannon RC .50 1.25
395 Skip Hicks .75 2.00
396 Rod Rutledge RC .50 1.25
397 Donald Hayes RC .75 2.00
398 Curtis Enis .50 1.25
399 Mikhael Ricks RC .75 2.00
400 Brian Griese RC 2.50 6.00
401 Michael Pittman RC 1.50 4.00
402 Jacquez Green .75 2.00
403 Jerome Pathon RC 1.25 3.00
404 Ahman Green RC 3.00 8.00
405 Marcus Nash .50 1.25
406 Randy Moss 5.00 12.00
407 Terry Fair RC .75 2.00
408 Jammi German RC .50 1.25
409 Stephen Alexander RC .75 2.00
410 Grant Wistrom RC .75 2.00
411 Charlie Batch RC 1.25 3.00
412 Fred Taylor 1.50 4.00
413 Pat Johnson RC .75 2.00
414 Robert Edwards .75 2.00
415 Keith Brooking RC 1.25 3.00
416 Peyton Manning 10.00 25.00
417 Duane Starks RC .50 1.25
418 Andre Wadsworth .75 2.00
419 Brian Alford RC .50 1.25
420 Brian Kelly RC .75 2.00
421 Joe Jurevicius RC 1.25 3.00
422 Tebucky Jones RC .50 1.25
423 R.W. McQuarters RC .75 2.00
424 Kevin Dyson 1.00 2.50
425 Charles Woodson 2.00 5.00
R1 Reggie White COMM .25 .60
P20 Jeff George Promo .30 .75

1998 Ultra Gold Medallion

COMPLETE SET (425) 500.00 1000.00
*GOLD MED.STARS: 1.2X TO 3X BASIC CARDS
*GOLD MED.RCs: .8X TO 2X BASIC CARDS
*GOLD MED.SER.2 DRAFT PICKS: 1.5X TO 4X
STATED ODDS 1:1 HOBBY

1998 Ultra Masterpiece

STATED PRINT RUN 1 SER.#'d SET

1998 Ultra Platinum Medallion

*PLAT.MED.STARS: 12X TO 30X HI COL.
*PLAT.MED.SER.1 RCs: 3X TO 8X
*PLAT.MED.SER.2 DRAFT PICKS: 5X TO 10X
1-200/226-385 PRINT RUN 98 SER.#'d SETS
201-225/386-425 PRINT RUN 66 SER.#'d SETS
HOBBY ONLY INSERTS
201P Peyton Manning 250.00 400.00
416P Peyton Manning 200.00 350.00

1998 Ultra Sensational Sixty

Inserted one per retail packs, this retail only 60-card set is a mini parallel version of the base set with blue foil highlights and a gold-foil 'sensational sixty' logo printed on the fronts.
COMPLETE SET (60) 15.00 40.00
ONE PER RETAIL PACK
1 Karim Abdul-Jabbar .40 1.00
2 Troy Aikman .75 2.00
3 Terry Allen .40 1.00
4 Mike Alstott .40 1.00
5 Tony Banks .25 .60
6 Jerome Bettis .40 1.00
7 Drew Bledsoe .60 1.50
8 Peter Boulware .15 .40
9 Robert Brooks .25 .60
10 Tim Brown .40 1.00
11 Isaac Bruce .40 1.00
12 Mark Brunell .40 1.00
13 Cris Carter .40 1.00
14 Kerry Collins .25 .60
15 Curtis Conway .25 .60
16 Terrell Davis .40 1.00
17 Troy Davis .15 .40
18 Trent Dilfer .40 1.00
19 Corey Dillon .40 1.00
20 Warrick Dunn .40 1.00
21 John Elway 1.50 4.00
22 Bert Emanuel .25 .60
23 Brett Favre 1.50 4.00
24 Antonio Freeman .40 1.00
25 Gus Frerotte .15 .40
26 Joey Galloway .25 .60
27 Eddie George .40 1.00
28 Jeff George .25 .60
29 Elvis Grbac .25 .60
30 Marvin Harrison .40 1.00
31 Bobby Hoying .25 .60
32 Michael Irvin .40 1.00
33 Brad Johnson .40 1.00
34 Keyshawn Johnson .40 1.00
35 Dan Marino 1.50 4.00
36 Curtis Martin .40 1.00
37 Tony Martin .25 .60
38 Keenan McCardell .25 .60
39 Steve McNair .40 1.00
40 Warren Moon .40 1.00
41 Herman Moore .25 .60
42 Johnnie Morton .25 .60
43 Terrell Owens .40 1.00
44 Carl Pickens .25 .60
45 Jake Plummer .40 1.00
46 Jerry Rice .75 2.00
47 Andre Rison .25 .60
48 Barry Sanders 1.25 3.00
49 Deion Sanders .40 1.00
50 Junior Seau .40 1.00
51 Shannon Sharpe .25 .60
52 Antowain Smith .40 1.00
53 Emmitt Smith 1.25 3.00
54 Jimmy Smith .25 .60
55 Robert Smith .40 1.00
56 Kordell Stewart .40 1.00
57 Jeff Blake .25 .60
58 Charles Way .15 .40
59 Reggie White .40 1.00
60 Steve Young .50 1.25

1998 Ultra Canton Classics

Randomly inserted in Series 1 packs at the rate of one in 288, this 10-card set features photos of future Hall of Fame prospects printed on cards enhanced with 23 kt. gold etching and embossing.
COMPLETE SET (10) 60.00 120.00
STATED ODDS 1:288
1 Terrell Davis 2.50 6.00
2 Brett Favre 10.00 25.00
3 John Elway 10.00 25.00
4 Barry Sanders 8.00 20.00
5 Eddie George 2.50 6.00
6 Jerry Rice 5.00 12.00
7 Emmitt Smith 8.00 20.00
8 Dan Marino 10.00 25.00
9 Troy Aikman 5.00 12.00
10 Marcus Allen 2.50 6.00

1998 Ultra Caught in the Draft

Randomly inserted in Series 2 packs at a rate of one in 24, this 15-card set features color action photos of the most impactful rookies of 1998. The backs carry player information.
COMPLETE SET (15) 30.00 60.00
STATED ODDS 1:24
1 Andre Wadsworth .50 1.25
2 Curtis Enis .30 .75
3 Germane Crowell .50 1.25
4 Peyton Manning 7.50 15.00
5 Tavian Banks .30 .75
6 Fred Taylor 1.00 2.50
7 John Avery .30 .75
8 Randy Moss 4.00 10.00
9 Robert Edwards .50 1.25
10 Charles Woodson 1.50 4.00
11 Ryan Leaf .50 1.25
12 Ahman Green 1.50 4.00
13 Robert Holcombe .30 .75
14 Jacquez Green .50 1.25
15 Skip Hicks .50 1.25

1998 Ultra Damage, Inc.

Randomly inserted in Series 2 packs at the rate of one in 72, this 15-card set features color images of top NFL players on a business card background.
COMPLETE SET (15) 50.00 100.00
STATED ODDS 1:72
1 Terrell Davis 2.00 5.00
2 Joey Galloway 1.25 3.00
3 Kordell Stewart 2.00 5.00
4 Troy Aikman 4.00 10.00
5 Barry Sanders 6.00 15.00
6 Ryan Leaf .60 1.50
7 Antonio Freeman 2.00 5.00
8 Keyshawn Johnson 2.00 5.00
9 Eddie George 2.00 5.00
10 Warrick Dunn 2.00 5.00
11 Drew Bledsoe 3.00 8.00
12 Peyton Manning 12.00 30.00
13 Antowain Smith 2.00 5.00
14 Brett Favre 8.00 20.00
15 Emmitt Smith 6.00 15.00

1998 Ultra Exclamation Points

Randomly inserted in Series 2 packs at the rate of one in 288, this 15-card set features color action photos of top NFL impact players printed on plastic and pattern holofoil cards.
COMPLETE SET (15) 150.00 300.00
STATED ODDS 1:288
1 Terrell Davis 5.00 12.00
2 Brett Favre 20.00 50.00
3 John Elway 20.00 50.00
4 Barry Sanders 15.00 40.00
5 Peyton Manning 25.00 50.00
6 Jerry Rice 10.00 25.00
7 Emmitt Smith 15.00 40.00
8 Dan Marino 20.00 50.00
9 Kordell Stewart 5.00 12.00
10 Mark Brunell 5.00 12.00
11 Ryan Leaf 2.00 5.00
12 Corey Dillon 5.00 12.00
13 Antowain Smith 5.00 12.00
14 Curtis Martin 5.00 12.00
15 Deion Sanders 5.00 12.00

1998 Ultra Flair Showcase Preview

Randomly inserted in Series 1 packs at the rate of one in 144, this 10-card set displays portraits and action photos of players featured in the Flair Showcase set and are printed on laminated 28-point stock in the Showcase version design.
COMPLETE SET (10) 75.00 150.00
STATED ODDS 1:144
1 Kordell Stewart 4.00 10.00
2 Mark Brunell 4.00 10.00
3 Terrell Davis 4.00 10.00
4 Brett Favre 15.00 40.00
5 Steve McNair 4.00 10.00
6 Curtis Martin 4.00 10.00
7 Warrick Dunn 4.00 10.00
8 Emmitt Smith 12.50 30.00
9 Dan Marino 15.00 40.00
10 Corey Dillon 4.00 10.00

1998 Ultra Indefensible

Randomly inserted in Series 2 packs at the rate of one in 144, this 10-card set features action color photos of top NFL players who can't be stopped printed on fold-out cards with embossed graphics.
COMPLETE SET (10) 50.00 100.00
STATED ODDS 1:144
1 Jake Plummer 2.50 6.00
2 Mark Brunell 2.50 6.00
3 Terrell Davis 2.50 6.00
4 Jerry Rice 5.00 12.00
5 Barry Sanders 8.00 20.00
6 Curtis Martin 2.50 6.00
7 Warrick Dunn 2.50 6.00
8 Emmitt Smith 8.00 20.00
9 Dan Marino 10.00 25.00
10 Corey Dillon 2.50 6.00

1998 Ultra Next Century

Randomly inserted in Series 1 packs at the rate of one in 72, this 15-card set features silhouetted action photos of future great players printed on 100% foil and sculpture embossed card stock. The photos are backed by graphic treatment of the logo of the team that drafted the pictured player.
COMPLETE SET (15) 40.00 80.00
STATED ODDS 1:72
1 Ryan Leaf 1.00 2.50
2 Peyton Manning 12.50 25.00
3 Charles Woodson 2.00 5.00
4 Randy Moss 6.00 15.00
5 Curtis Enis .50 1.25
6 Ahman Green 2.50 6.00
7 Skip Hicks .75 2.00
8 Andre Wadsworth .75 2.00
9 Germane Crowell .75 2.00
10 Robert Edwards .75 2.00
11 Tavian Banks .75 2.00
12 Takeo Spikes 1.00 2.50
13 Jacquez Green .75 2.00
14 Brian Simmons .75 2.00
15 Alonzo Mayes .50 1.25

1998 Ultra Rush Hour

Randomly inserted in Series 2 packs at the rate of one in six, this 20-card set features color action photos of players who "get it done in a hurry."
COMPLETE SET (20) 20.00 40.00
STATED ODDS 1:6
1 Robert Edwards .50 1.25
2 John Elway 3.00 8.00
3 Mike Alstott .75 2.00
4 Robert Holcombe .50 1.25
5 Mark Brunell .75 2.00
6 Deion Sanders .75 2.00
7 Curtis Martin .75 2.00
8 Curtis Enis .30 .75
9 Dorsey Levens .75 2.00
10 Fred Taylor 1.00 2.50
11 John Avery .40 1.00
12 Eddie George .75 2.00
13 Jake Plummer .75 2.00
14 Andre Wadsworth .50 1.25
15 Fred Lane .30 .75
16 Corey Dillon .75 2.00
17 Brett Favre 3.00 8.00
18 Kordell Stewart .75 2.00
19 Steve McNair .75 2.00
20 Warrick Dunn .75 2.00

1998 Ultra Shots

Randomly inserted in packs at the rate of one in six, this 20-card set features color photos of great moments in the NFL with a printed discussion by the photographers who captured them on film.
COMPLETE SET (20) 15.00 35.00
STATED ODDS 1:6
1 Deion Sanders .75 2.00
2 Corey Dillon .75 2.00
3 Mike Alstott .75 2.00
4 Jake Plummer .75 2.00
5 Antowain Smith .75 2.00
6 Kordell Stewart .75 2.00
7 Curtis Martin .75 2.00
8 Bobby Hoying .50 1.25
9 Kerry Collins .50 1.25
10 Herman Moore .50 1.25
11 Terry Glenn .75 2.00
12 Eddie George .75 2.00
13 Drew Bledsoe 1.25 3.00
14 Steve McNair .75 2.00
15 Jerry Rice 1.50 4.00
16 Trent Dilfer .75 2.00
17 Joey Galloway .50 1.25
18 Dan Marino 3.00 8.00
19 Barry Sanders 2.50 6.00
20 Warrick Dunn .75 2.00

1998 Ultra Top 30

Inserted one per Series 2 retail pack, this 30-card set is a retail only mini parallel version of the base set with blue foil highlights and a "Top 30" logo printed in gold foil on the fronts.
COMPLETE SET (30) 10.00 25.00
STATED ODDS: 1 PER RETAIL PACK
1 Warrick Dunn .30 .75
2 Troy Aikman .60 1.50
3 Trent Dilfer .30 .75
4 Tony Banks .20 .50
5 Tim Brown .30 .75
6 Terrell Davis .30 .75
7 Steve McNair .30 .75
8 Steve Young .40 1.00
9 Mark Brunell .30 .75
10 Kordell Stewart .30 .75
11 Keyshawn Johnson .30 .75
12 John Elway 1.25 3.00
13 Joey Galloway .20 .50
14 Jerry Rice .60 1.50
15 Jerome Bettis .30 .75
16 Jake Plummer .30 .75
17 Emmitt Smith 1.00 2.50
18 Eddie George .30 .75
19 Drew Bledsoe .50 1.25
20 Dan Marino 1.25 3.00
21 Curtis Martin .30 .75
22 Curtis Conway .20 .50
23 Cris Carter .30 .75
24 Corey Dillon .30 .75
25 Carl Pickens .20 .50
26 Brett Favre 1.25 3.00
27 Bobby Hoying .20 .50
28 Barry Sanders 1.00 2.50
29 Antowain Smith .30 .75
30 Antonio Freeman .30 .75

1998 Ultra Touchdown Kings

Randomly inserted in Series 1 packs at the rate of one in 24, this 15-card set highlights great players who regularly make touchdowns with a holofoil and sculptured embossed player image and a gallery-suitable frame design printed on a die-cut card.

COMPLETE SET (15) 50.00 100.00
STATED ODDS 1:24
1 Terrell Davis 2.00 5.00
2 Joey Galloway 1.25 3.00
3 Kordell Stewart 2.00 5.00
4 Corey Dillon 2.00 5.00
5 Barry Sanders 6.00 15.00
6 Cris Carter 2.00 5.00
7 Antonio Freeman 2.00 5.00
8 Mike Alstott 2.00 5.00
9 Eddie George 2.00 5.00
10 Warrick Dunn 2.00 5.00
11 Drew Bledsoe 3.00 8.00
12 Karim Abdul-Jabbar 2.00 5.00
13 Mark Brunell 2.00 5.00
14 Brett Favre 8.00 20.00
15 Emmitt Smith 6.00 15.00

1999 Ultra

This 300 card set was released in July, 1999. The cards were issued in 10 card packs with a SRP of $2.69. Subsets include 3 Checklist card (248-250), Super Bowl Highlights (251-260) and a Rookie Subset (261-300). The Rookie subset were seeded one every 4 packs. Notable Rookie Cards include Tim Couch, Edgerrin James and Ricky Williams. A couple of weeks before the product's release, a promo card of Fred Taylor was released. It is listed at the end of the Ultra set.

COMPLETE SET (300) 30.00 80.00
COMP.SET w/o SP's (250) 8.00 20.00
1 Terrell Davis .20 .50
2 Courtney Hawkins .15 .40
3 Cris Carter .25 .60
4 Darnay Scott .15 .40
5 Darrell Green .25 .60
6 Jimmy Smith .20 .50
7 Doug Flutie .25 .60
8 Michael Jackson .15 .40
9 Warren Sapp .20 .50
10 Greg Hill .15 .40
11 Karim Abdul-Jabbar .15 .40
12 Greg Ellis .15 .40
13 Dan Marino .50 1.25
14 Napoleon Kaufman .15 .40
15 Peyton Manning .75 2.00
16 Simeon Rice .15 .40
17 Tony Simmons .15 .40
18 Carlester Crumpler .15 .40
19 Charles Johnson .15 .40
20 Derrick Alexander .15 .40
21 Kent Graham .15 .40
22 Randall Cunningham .20 .50
23 Trent Green .15 .40
24 Chris Spielman .20 .50
25 Carl Pickens .20 .50
26 Bill Romanowski .20 .50
27 Jermaine Lewis .15 .40
28 Ahman Green .20 .50
29 Bryan Still .15 .40
30 Dorsey Levens .20 .50
31 Frank Wycheck .20 .50
32 Jerome Bettis .25 .60
33 Reidel Anthony .15 .40
34 Robert Jones .15 .40
35 Terry Glenn .20 .50
36 Tim Brown .25 .60
37 Eric Metcalf .15 .40
38 Kevin Greene .25 .60
39 Takeo Spikes .15 .40
40 Brian Mitchell .20 .50
41 Duane Starks .15 .40
42 Eddie George .20 .50
43 Joe Jurevicius .15 .40
44 Kimble Anders .15 .40
45 Kordell Stewart .15 .40
46 Leroy Hoard .15 .40
47 Rod Smith .20 .50
48 Terrell Owens .20 .50
49 Ty Detmer .15 .40
50 Charles Woodson .25 .60
51 Andre Rison .20 .50
52 Chris Slade .15 .40
53 Frank Sanders .15 .40
54 Michael Irvin .25 .60
55 Jerome Pathon .15 .40
56 Desmond Howard .20 .50
57 Billy Davis .15 .40
58 Anthony Simmons .15 .40
59 James Jett .15 .40
60 Jake Plummer .15 .40
61 John Avery .15 .40
62 Marvin Harrison .20 .50
63 Merton Hanks .15 .40
64 Ricky Proehl .15 .40
65 Steve Beuerlein .20 .50
66 Willie McGinest .20 .50
67 Bryce Paup .15 .40
68 Brett Favre .50 1.25
69 Brian Griese .15 .40
70 Curtis Martin .20 .50
71 Drew Bledsoe .20 .50
72 Jim Harbaugh .20 .50
73 Joey Galloway .20 .50
74 Natrone Means .20 .50
75 O.J. McDuffie .20 .50
76 Tiki Barber .20 .50
77 Wesley Walls .20 .50
78 Will Blackwell .15 .40
79 Bert Emanuel .20 .50
80 J.J. Stokes .15 .40
81 Steve McNair .20 .50
82 Adrian Murrell .15 .40
83 Dexter Coakley .15 .40
84 Jeff George .15 .40
85 Marshall Faulk .20 .50
86 Tim Biakabutuka .20 .50
87 Troy Drayton .15 .40
88 Ty Law .25 .60
89 Brian Simmons .15 .40
90 Eric Allen .20 .50
91 Jon Kitna .15 .40
92 Junior Seau .20 .50
93 Kevin Turner .15 .40
94 Larry Centers .15 .40
95 Robert Edwards .15 .40
96 Rocket Ismail .20 .50
97 Sam Madison .15 .40
98 Stephen Alexander .15 .40
99 Trent Dilfer .15 .40
100 Vonnie Holliday .15 .40
101 Charlie Garner .20 .50
102 Deion Sanders .20 .50
103 Jamal Anderson .20 .50
104 Mike Vanderjagt .15 .40
105 Aeneas Williams .15 .40
106 Daryl Johnston .20 .50
107 Hugh Douglas .20 .50
108 Torrance Small .15 .40
109 Amani Toomer .15 .40
110 Amp Lee .15 .40
111 Germane Crowell .15 .40
112 Marco Battaglia .15 .40
113 Michael Westbrook .15 .40
114 Randy Moss .20 .50
115 Ricky Watters .20 .50
116 Rob Johnson .20 .50
117 Tony Gonzalez .20 .50
118 Charles Way .15 .40
119 Chris Penn .15 .40
120 Eddie Kennison .20 .50
121 Elvis Grbac .15 .40
122 Eric Moulds .15 .40
123 Terry Fair .15 .40
124 Tony Banks .20 .50
125 Chris Chandler .20 .50
126 Emmitt Smith .40 1.00
127 Herman Moore .20 .50
128 Irv Smith .15 .40
129 Kyle Brady .15 .40
130 Lamont Warren .20 .50
131 Troy Davis .15 .40
132 Andre Reed .25 .60
133 Justin Armour .15 .40
134 James Hasty .15 .40
135 Johnnie Morton .20 .50
136 Reggie Barlow .15 .40
137 Robert Holcombe .15 .40
138 Sean Dawkins .15 .40
139 Steve Atwater .20 .50
140 Tim Dwight .20 .50
141 Wayne Chrebet .15 .40
142 Alonzo Mayes .15 .40
143 Mark Brunell .20 .50
144 Antowain Smith .15 .40
145 Byron Bam Morris .15 .40
146 Isaac Bruce .25 .60
147 Bryan Cox .20 .50
148 Bryant Westbrook .15 .40
149 Duce Staley .15 .40
150 Barry Sanders .40 1.00
151 La'Roi Glover RC .25 .60
152 Ray Crockett .15 .40
153 Tony Brackens .15 .40
154 Roy Barker .15 .40
155 Kerry Collins .15 .40
156 Andre Wadsworth .15 .40
157 Cameron Cleeland .15 .40
158 Koy Detmer .15 .40
159 Marcus Pollard .15 .40
160 Patrick Jeffers RC .25 .60
161 Aaron Glenn .15 .40
162 Andre Hastings .15 .40
163 Bruce Smith .20 .50
164 David Palmer .15 .40
165 Erik Kramer .20 .50
166 Orlando Pace .15 .40
167 Robert Brooks .20 .50
168 Shawn Springs .15 .40
169 Terance Mathis .15 .40
170 Chris Calloway .15 .40
171 Gilbert Brown .15 .40
172 Charlie Jones .15 .40
173 Curtis Enis .15 .40
174 Eugene Robinson .20 .50
175 Garrison Hearst .15 .40
176 Jason Elam .15 .40
177 John Randle .25 .60
178 Keith Poole .15 .40
179 Kevin Hardy .15 .40
180 Keyshawn Johnson .20 .50
181 O.J. Santiago .15 .40
182 Jacquez Green .15 .40
183 Bobby Engram .15 .40
184 Damon Jones .15 .40
185 Freddie Jones .15 .40
186 Jake Reed .20 .50
187 Jerry Rice .60 1.50
188 Joey Kent .15 .40
189 Lamar Smith .15 .40
190 John Elway .40 1.00
191 Leon Johnson .15 .40
192 Mark Chmura .15 .40
193 Peter Boulware .15 .40
194 Zach Thomas .20 .50
195 Marc Edwards .20 .50
196 Mike Alstott .15 .40
197 Yancey Thigpen .15 .40
198 Oronde Gadsden .15 .40
199 Rae Carruth .15 .40
200 Troy Aikman .30 .75
201 Shawn Jefferson .15 .40
202 Rob Moore .15 .40
203 Rickey Dudley .15 .40
204 Jason Taylor .20 .50
205 Curtis Conway .20 .50
206 Darrien Gordon .15 .40
207 Eric Green .15 .40
208 Jessie Armstead .20 .50
209 Keenan McCardell .20 .50
210 Robert Smith .15 .40
211 Mo Lewis .15 .40
212 Ryan Leaf .20 .50
213 Steve Young .30 .75
214 Tyrone Davis .15 .40
215 Chad Brown .15 .40
216 Ike Hilliard .15 .40
217 Jimmy Hitchcock .15 .40
218 Kevin Dyson .15 .40
219 Levon Kirkland .15 .40
220 Neil O'Donnell .20 .50
221 Ray Lewis .25 .60
222 Shannon Sharpe .20 .50
223 Skip Hicks .15 .40
224 Brad Johnson .20 .50
225 Charlie Batch .15 .40
226 Corey Dillon .15 .40
227 Dale Carter .15 .40
228 John Mobley .15 .40
229 Hines Ward .20 .50
230 Leslie Shepherd .15 .40
231 Michael Strahan .20 .50
232 R.W. McQuarters .15 .40
233 Mike Pritchard .15 .40
234 Antonio Freeman .20 .50
235 Ben Coates .20 .50
236 Michael Bates .15 .40
237 Ed McCaffrey .20 .50
238 Gary Brown .15 .40
239 Mark Bruener .15 .40
240 Mikhael Ricks .15 .40
241 Muhsin Muhammad .15 .40
242 Priest Holmes .15 .40
243 Stephen Davis .15 .40
244 Vinny Testaverde .15 .40
245 Warrick Dunn .15 .40
246 Derrick Mayes .15 .40
247 Fred Taylor .15 .40
248 Drew Bledsoe CL .15 .40
249 Eddie George CL .15 .40
250 Steve Young CL .25 .60
251 Jamal Anderson BB .25 .60
252 D.Gordon
Romanowski BB .25 .60
253 Shannon Sharpe BB .25 .60
254 Terrell Davis BB .25 .60
255 Rod Smith BB .25 .60
256 Rod Smith BB .25 .60
257 John Elway BB .50 1.25
258 Tim Dwight BB .25 .60
259 Elway .50 1.25
McC
Griff
Dav.BB
260 John Elway BB .50 1.25
261 Ricky Williams RC 1.00 2.50
262 Tim Couch RC .75 2.00
263 Chris Claiborne RC .60 1.50
264 Champ Bailey RC 1.25 3.00
265 Torry Holt RC 1.25 3.00
266 Donovan McNabb RC 5.00 12.00
267 David Boston RC .60 1.50
268 Chris McAlister RC .60 1.50
269 Brock Huard RC .60 1.50
270 Daunte Culpepper RC 1.00 2.50
271 Matt Stinchcomb RC .60 1.50
272 Edgerrin James RC 1.00 2.50
273 Jevon Kearse RC .75 2.00
274 Ebenezer Ekuban RC .60 1.50
275 Kris Farris RC .60 1.50
276 Chris Terry RC .60 1.50
277 Jerame Tuman RC .60 1.50
278 Akili Smith RC .60 1.50
279 Aaron Gibson RC .60 1.50
280 Rahim Abdullah RC .60 1.50
281 Peerless Price RC .60 1.50
282 Antoine Winfield RC .60 1.50
283 Antuan Edwards RC .60 1.50
284 Rob Konrad RC .60 1.50
285 Troy Edwards RC .60 1.50
286 John Thornton RC .60 1.50
287 James Johnson RC .60 1.50
288 Gary Stills RC .60 1.50
289 Mike Peterson RC .60 1.50
290 Kevin Faulk RC .60 1.50
291 Jared DeVries RC .60 1.50
292 Martin Gramatica RC .60 1.50
293 Montae Reagor RC .60 1.50
294 Andy Katzenmoyer RC .75 2.00
295 Sedrick Irvin RC .60 1.50
296 D'Wayne Bates RC .60 1.50
297 Amos Zereoue RC .60 1.50
298 Dre Bly RC 1.00 2.50
299 Kevin Johnson RC .75 2.00
300 Cade McNown RC .60 1.50
P247 Fred Taylor Promo .75 2.00

1999 Ultra Gold Medallion

COMPLETE SET (300) 200.00 400.00
*GOLD MED.STARS: 1.2X TO 3X HI COL.
*GOLD MED.RCs: .6X TO 1.5X
GOLD MED.VETERAN ODDS ONE PER PACK
GOLD MED.DRAFT PICK ODDS 1:25 PACKS
GOLD MED.BACK TO BACK ODDS 1:50
GOLD MED.DRAFT PICK ODDS 1:50

1999 Ultra Platinum Medallion

*PLAT.MED.STARS: 10X TO 25X HI COL.
*PLAT.MED.RCs: 2.5X TO 6X
PM VETS PRINT RUN 99 SER.#'d SETS
PM DRAFT PICK PRINT RUN 65 SER.#'d SETS
PM BACK/BACK PRINT RUN 40 SER.#'d SETS

1999 Ultra As Good As It Gets

Inserted one every 288 packs, these 15 cards feature the best players in football photographed on die-cut felt-sandwiched stock with silver holofoil and gold foil stamping.

COMPLETE SET (15) 60.00 150.00
STATED ODDS 1:288
1 Warrick Dunn 2.50 6.00
2 Terrell Davis 2.50 6.00
3 Robert Edwards 1.00 2.50
4 Randy Moss 6.00 15.00
5 Peyton Manning 8.00 20.00
6 Mark Brunell 2.50 6.00
7 John Elway 8.00 20.00
8 Jerry Rice 5.00 12.00
9 Jake Plummer 1.50 4.00
10 Fred Taylor 2.50 6.00
11 Emmitt Smith 5.00 12.00
12 Dan Marino 8.00 20.00
13 Charlie Batch 2.50 6.00
14 Brett Favre 8.00 20.00
15 Barry Sanders 8.00 20.00

1999 Ultra Caught In The Draft

Issued one every 18 packs, these 15 cards feature top 1999 rookies featured on silver pattern holofoil with the player's name in gold foil.

COMPLETE SET (15) 25.00 50.00
STATED ODDS 1:18
1 Ricky Williams 2.00 5.00
2 Tim Couch 1.00 2.50
3 Chris Claiborne .50 1.25
4 Champ Bailey 1.50 4.00
5 Torry Holt 2.50 6.00
6 Donovan McNabb 5.00 12.00
7 David Boston 1.00 2.50
8 Andy Katzenmoyer .75 2.00
9 Daunte Culpepper 4.00 10.00
10 Edgerrin James 4.00 10.00
11 Cade McNown .75 2.00
12 Troy Edwards .75 2.00
13 Akili Smith .75 2.00
14 Peerless Price 1.00 2.50
15 Amos Zereoue 1.00 2.50

1999 Ultra Counterparts

Issued one every 36 packs, these 15 cards feature leading duos from NFL teams with the cards embossed with silver holofoil stamping.

COMPLETE SET (15) 40.00 80.00
STATED ODDS 1:36
1 T.Aikman
M.Irvin 4.00 10.00
2 D.Bledsoe
B.Coates 2.50 6.00
3 T.Davis
H.Griffith 2.00 5.00
4 W.Dunn
M.Alstott 2.00 5.00
5 B.Favre
A.Freeman 6.00 15.00
6 J.Plummer
F.Sanders 1.25 3.00
7 R.Moss
R.Cunningham 5.00 12.00
8 E.George
S.McNair 2.00 5.00
9 K.Johnson
W.Chrebet 2.00 5.00
10 R.Leaf
M.Ricks 2.00 5.00
11 P.Manning
M.Faulk 6.00 15.00
12 B.Sanders
T.Vardell 6.00 15.00
13 C.Batch
H.Moore 2.00 5.00
14 E.Smith
D.Johnston 4.00 10.00
15 K.Stewart
J.Bettis 2.00 5.00

1999 Ultra Damage, Inc.

Inserted at a rate of one every 72 packs, these 15 cards feature players who can dominate a game on cards featuring sculpted silver foil cards.

COMPLETE SET (15) 50.00 120.00
STATED ODDS 1:72
1 Brett Favre 8.00 20.00
2 Dan Marino 8.00 20.00
3 John Elway 8.00 20.00
4 Mark Brunell 2.50 6.00
5 Peyton Manning 8.00 20.00
6 Robert Edwards 1.00 2.50
7 Terrell Davis 2.50 6.00
8 Troy Aikman 5.00 12.00
9 Randy Moss 6.00 15.00
10 Kordell Stewart 1.50 4.00
11 Jerry Rice 5.00 12.00
12 Fred Taylor 2.50 6.00
13 Emmitt Smith 5.00 12.00
14 Charlie Batch 2.50 6.00
15 Barry Sanders 8.00 20.00

1999 Ultra Over The Top

Inserted at a rate of one in six, these 20 foil stamped cards feature leading players.

COMPLETE SET (20) 10.00 20.00
STATED ODDS 1:6
1 Troy Aikman 1.00 2.50
2 Drew Bledsoe .60 1.50
3 Mark Brunell .60 1.26
4 Randall Cunningham .50 1.25
5 Jamal Anderson .50 1.25
6 Warrick Dunn .50 1.25
7 Robert Edwards .20 .50
8 John Elway 1.50 4.00
9 Eddie George .50 1.25
10 Eric Moulds .50 1.25
11 Keyshawn Johnson .50 1.25
12 Ryan Leaf .50 1.25
13 Dan Marino 1.50 4.00
14 Steve McNair .50 1.25
15 Jake Plummer .30 .75
16 Jerry Rice 1.00 2.50
17 Deion Sanders .50 1.25
18 Kordell Stewart .30 .75
19 Fred Taylor .50 1.25
20 Steve Young .60 1.50

2000 Ultra

leased as a 249-card set, 2000 Ultra is composed of 220 veteran cards and 29 prospect cards found one in four packs. Base cards contain full-color action photography and rainbow holofoil stamping. Ultra was packaged in 24-pack boxes with packs that contained 10 cards and carried a suggested retail price of $2.99. It is thought that card #240 was released only in small quantities early in the print run.

COMPLETE SET (249) 40.00 100.00
COMP.SET w/o RC's (220) 7.50 20.00
220-250 ROOKIE ODDS 1:4
1 Kurt Warner .40 1.00
2 Derrick Alexander .15 .40
3 Aaron Craver .15 .40
4 Kevin Faulk .15 .40
5 Marcus Robinson .20 .50
6 Tony Banks .15 .40
7 Jon Ritchie .15 .40
8 Torry Holt .20 .50
9 Joe Horn .20 .50
10 Eddie George .20 .50
11 Michael Westbrook .15 .40
12 Gus Frerotte .15 .40
13 Tim Brown .25 .60
14 Tamarick Vanover .15 .40
15 David Sloan .15 .40
16 Darnay Scott .20 .50
17 Junior Seau .20 .50
18 Warren Sapp .20 .50
19 Priest Holmes .15 .40
20 Jerry Rice .60 1.50
21 Cade McNown .15 .40
22 Johnnie Morton .20 .50
23 Vinny Testaverde .15 .40
24 James Jett .20 .50
25 Tony Gonzalez .20 .50
26 Charlie Batch .15 .40
27 Tony Simmons .15 .40
28 James Stewart .15 .40
29 Corey Dillon .15 .40
30 Ricky Williams .20 .50
31 Ryan Leaf .20 .50
32 Terry Allen .20 .50
33 Freddie Jones .15 .40
34 Terry Kirby .15 .40
35 Charles Johnson .15 .40
36 William Henderson .15 .40
37 Stephen Alexander .15 .40
38 Moe Williams .15 .40
39 David Boston .15 .40
40 Emmitt Smith .40 1.00
41 Ken Oxendine .15 .40
42 Byron Hanspard .15 .40
43 Dwight Stone .15 .40
44 Jim Harbaugh .20 .50
45 Curtis Enis .15 .40
46 Peerless Price .20 .50
47 Terance Mathis .15 .40
48 Mike Alstott .15 .40
49 Rod Smith .20 .50
50 Marshall Faulk .20 .50
51 Derrick Mayes .15 .40
52 Keenan McCardell .20 .50
53 Curtis Martin .20 .50
54 Bobby Engram .15 .40
55 Carl Pickens .20 .50
56 Robert Smith .15 .40
57 Ike Hilliard .15 .40
58 Reidel Anthony .15 .40
59 Jeff Graham .15 .40
60 Mark Brunell .20 .50
61 Joe Montgomery .15 .40
62 Ed McCaffrey .20 .50
63 Kenny Bynum .15 .40
64 Curtis Conway .20 .50
65 Trent Dilfer .15 .40
66 Jake Reed .20 .50
67 Jake Plummer .15 .40
68 Tony Martin .20 .50
69 Yatil Green .15 .40
70 Keyshawn Johnson .20 .50
71 Leroy Hoard .15 .40
72 Skip Hicks .15 .40
73 Marvin Harrison .20 .50
74 Steve Beuerlein .20 .50
75 Will Blackwell .15 .40
76 Derek Loville .15 .40
77 Warrick Dunn .15 .40
78 Amos Zereoue .15 .40
79 Ray Lucas .15 .40
80 Randy Moss .20 .50
81 Wesley Walls .15 .40
82 Jimmy Smith .20 .50
83 Kordell Stewart .15 .40
84 Brian Griese .15 .40
85 Martin Gramatica .15 .40
86 Chris Chandler .20 .50
87 Reggie Barlow .15 .40
88 Jeff George .20 .50
89 Tavian Banks .15 .40
90 Mushin Muhammad .15 .40
91 Steve McNair .20 .50
92 Hines Ward .20 .50
93 Brian Mitchell .15 .40
94 Daunte Culpepper .20 .50
95 Tim Dwight .20 .50
96 Terrence Wilkins .15 .40
97 Fred Lane .15 .40
98 Brett Favre .50 1.25
99 Richie Anderson .15 .40
100 Jamal Anderson .20 .50
101 Doug Flutie .20 .50
102 Charles Woodson .25 .60
103 Jacquez Green .15 .40
104 Olandis Gary .20 .50
105 Steve Young .30 .75
106 Wayne Chrebet .15 .40
107 Karim Abdul-Jabbar .15 .40
108 Andre Rison .20 .50
109 Eddie Kennison .15 .40
110 Jevon Kearse .15 .40
111 Tony Richardson RC .15 .40
112 Jake Delhomme RC .20 .50
113 Errict Rhett .20 .50
114 Akili Smith .15 .40
115 Tyrone Wheatley .15 .40
116 Corey Bradford .15 .40
117 J.J. Stokes .20 .50
118 Simeon Rice .20 .50
119 Brad Johnson .20 .50
120 Edgerrin James .20 .50
121 Amani Toomer .15 .40
122 O.J. McDuffie .20 .50
123 Az-Zahir Hakim .15 .40
124 Troy Edwards .15 .40
125 Tim Biakabutuka .20 .50
126 Jason Tucker .15 .40
127 Charles Way .15 .40
128 Terrell Davis .20 .50
129 Garrison Hearst .15 .40
130 Fred Taylor .15 .40
131 Robert Holcombe .15 .40
132 Frank Sanders .15 .40
133 Morten Andersen .15 .40
134 Cris Carter .25 .60
135 Patrick Jeffers .15 .40
136 Antonio Freeman .20 .50
137 Jonathan Linton .15 .40
138 Rashaan Shehee .15 .40
139 Luther Broughton RC .15 .40
140 Tim Couch .20 .50
141 Keith Poole .15 .40
142 Champ Bailey .20 .50
143 Yancey Thigpen .15 .40
144 Joey Galloway .20 .50
145 Mac Cody .15 .40
146 Damon Huard .15 .40
147 Dorsey Levens .20 .50
148 Donovan McNabb .20 .50
149 Jamie Asher .15 .40
150 Peyton Manning .60 1.50
151 Leslie Shepherd .15 .40
152 Charlie Rogers .15 .40
153 Tony Horne .15 .40
154 Jim Miller .15 .40
155 Richard Huntley .15 .40
156 Germane Crowell .15 .40
157 Natrone Means .20 .50
158 Justin Armour .15 .40
159 Drew Bledsoe .20 .50
160 Dedric Ward .15 .40
161 Allen Rossum .15 .40
162 Ricky Watters .20 .50
163 Kerry Collins .15 .40
164 James Johnson .15 .40
165 Elvis Grbac .15 .40
166 Larry Centers .15 .40
167 Rob Moore .15 .40
168 Jay Riemersma .15 .40
169 Bill Schroeder .20 .50
170 Deion Sanders .20 .50
171 Jerome Bettis .25 .60
172 Dan Marino .50 1.25
173 Terrell Owens .20 .50
174 Kevin Carter .15 .40
175 Lamar Smith .15 .40
176 Ken Dilger .15 .40
177 Napoleon Kaufman .20 .50
178 Kevin Williams .15 .40
179 Tremain Mack .15 .40
180 Troy Aikman .30 .75
181 Glyn Milburn .15 .40
182 Pete Mitchell .15 .40
183 Cameron Cleeland .15 .40
184 Qadry Ismail .15 .40
185 Michael Pittman .15 .40
186 Kevin Dyson .20 .50
187 Matt Hasselbeck .15 .40
188 Kevin Johnson .15 .40
189 Rich Gannon .20 .50
190 Stephen Davis .15 .40
191 Frank Wycheck .20 .50
192 Eric Moulds .15 .40
193 Jon Kitna .15 .40
194 Mario Bates .15 .40
195 Na Brown .15 .40
196 Jeff Blake .20 .50
197 Charles Evans .15 .40
198 Oronde Gadsden .20 .50
199 Donnell Bennett .15 .40
200 Isaac Bruce .25 .60
201 Olindo Mare .15 .40
202 Darnell McDonald .15 .40
203 Charlie Garner .20 .50
204 Shawn Jefferson .15 .40
205 Adrian Murrell .15 .40
206 Peter Boulware .15 .40
207 LeShon Johnson .15 .40
208 Herman Moore .15 .40
209 Duce Staley .15 .40
210 Sean Dawkins .15 .40
211 Antowain Smith .20 .50
212 Albert Connell .15 .40
213 Jeff Garcia .15 .40
214 Kimble Anders .15 .40
215 Shaun King .15 .40
216 Rocket Ismail .20 .50
217 Andrew Glover .15 .40
218 Rickey Dudley .15 .40
219 Michael Basnight .15 .40
220 Terry Glenn .20 .50
221 Peter Warrick RC .60 1.50
222 Ron Dayne RC 1.00 2.50
223 Thomas Jones RC .75 2.00
224 Joe Hamilton RC .60 1.50
225 Tim Rattay RC .75 2.00
226 Chad Pennington RC .75 2.00
227 Dennis Northcutt RC .60 1.50
228 Troy Walters RC .60 1.50
229 Travis Prentice RC .60 1.50
230 Shaun Alexander RC 1.00 2.50
231 J.R. Redmond RC .60 1.50
232 Chris Redman RC .60 1.50
233 Tee Martin RC .60 1.50
234 Tom Brady RC 40.00 80.00
235 Travis Taylor RC .60 1.50
236 R.Jay Soward RC .60 1.50
237 Jamal Lewis RC 1.00 2.50
238 Giovanni Carmazzi RC .60 1.50
239 Dez White RC .60 1.50
240 LaVar Arrington RC SP 25.00 60.00
241 Laveranues Coles RC .75 2.00
242 Sherrod Gideon RC .60 1.50
243 Trung Canidate RC .60 1.50
244 Michael Wiley RC .60 1.50
245 Anthony Lucas RC .60 1.50
246 Darrell Jackson RC .60 1.50
247 Plaxico Burress RC .75 2.00
248 Reuben Droughns RC .60 1.50
249 Marc Bulger RC .75 2.00
250 Danny Farmer RC .60 1.50

2000 Ultra Gold Medallion

COMPLETE SET (249) 100.00 200.00
*VETS 1-220: 1.2X TO 3X BASIC CARDS
1-220 STATED ODDS 1:1
*ROOKIES 221-250: .6X TO 1.5X
221-250 ROOKIE ODDS 1:4
234 Tom Brady 60.00 125.00
240 LaVar Arrington SP 60.00 120.00

2000 Ultra Masterpiece

ONE SET PRODUCED

2000 Ultra Platinum Medallion

*VETS 1-220: 20X TO 50X BASIC CARDS
1-220 VETERAN PRINT RUN 50
*ROOKIES 221-250: 6X TO 15X
221-250 ROOKIE PRINT RUN 25
234 Tom Brady 900.00 1500.00

2000 Ultra Dream Team

Randomly inserted in packs at the rate of one in 24, this 10-card set features some of the NFL's top stars on an all foil card with rainbow holofoil accents and stamping.

COMPLETE SET (10) 12.50 25.00
STATED ODDS 1:24
1 Terrell Davis .60 1.50
2 Brett Favre 1.50 4.00
3 Troy Aikman 1.00 2.50
4 Keyshawn Johnson .60 1.50
5 Edgerrin James .60 1.50
6 Randy Moss .60 1.50
7 Marvin Harrison .60 1.50
8 Kurt Warner 1.25 3.00
9 Fred Taylor .50 1.25
10 Ricky Williams .60 1.50

2000 Ultra Fast Lane

Randomly seeded in packs at the rate of one in three, this 15-card set features top receivers on a card highlighted with silver foil stamping. The card front also features the respective player's jersey number above the "Fast Lane" logo.

COMPLETE SET (15) 3.00 8.00
STATED ODDS 1:3
1 Jimmy Smith .30 .75
2 Cris Carter .40 1.00
3 Marvin Harrison .30 .75
4 Tim Brown .40 1.00
5 Mushin Muhammad .25 .60
6 Isaac Bruce .40 1.00
7 Bobby Engram .25 .60
8 Terance Mathis .25 .60
9 Randy Moss .30 .75
10 Rocket Ismail .30 .75
11 Keyshawn Johnson .30 .75
12 Terry Glenn .30 .75
13 Jerry Rice 1.00 2.50
14 Marcus Robinson .30 .75
15 Antonio Freeman .30 .75

2000 Ultra Head of the Class

Randomly seeded in packs at the rate of one in six, this 10-card set features full color portraits of top prospects from the 2000 draft on a rainbow holofoil "fleck" card.

COMPLETE SET (10) 5.00 12.00
STATED ODDS 1:6
1 Peter Warrick .20 .50
2 Ron Dayne .30 .75
3 Thomas Jones .25 .60
4 Chad Pennington .25 .60
5 Joe Hamilton .20 .50
6 Shaun Alexander .30 .75
7 J.R. Redmond .20 .50
8 Troy Walters .20 .50
9 Travis Prentice .20 .50
10 Chris Redman .20 .50

2000 Ultra Instant Three Play

Randomly inserted in packs at the rate of one in three, this 15-card set features a centered player action shot with three smaller action shots on a "film cell" on the right side of the card. Card fronts have silver foil stamping.

COMPLETE SET (15) 3.00 8.00
STATED ODDS 1:3
1 Peyton Manning 1.00 2.50
2 Curtis Enis .25 .60
3 Charlie Batch .25 .60
4 Fred Taylor .25 .60
5 Az-Zahir Hakim .25 .60
6 Randy Moss .30 .75
7 Jacquez Green .25 .60
8 Kevin Dyson .30 .75
9 Brian Griese .25 .60
10 Rashaan Shehee .25 .60
11 Tony Simmons .25 .60
12 Charles Woodson .40 1.00
13 Hines Ward .30 .75
14 Skip Hicks .25 .60
15 Tim Dwight .30 .75

2000 Ultra Millennium Monsters

Randomly inserted in packs at the rate of one in 12, this 10-card set features close up portrait photos of players on an embossed card with bronze foil highlights.

COMPLETE SET (10) 6.00 15.00
STATED ODDS 1:12
1 Tim Couch .40 1.00
2 Eddie George .40 1.00
3 Brian Griese .30 .75
4 Keyshawn Johnson .40 1.00
5 Peyton Manning 1.25 3.00
6 Randy Moss .40 1.00
7 Ricky Williams .40 1.00
8 Edgerrin James .40 1.00
9 Cade McNown .30 .75
10 Donovan McNabb .40 1.00

2000 Ultra Won by One

Randomly inserted in packs at the rate of one in 72, this 10-card set features full-color action shots on a die-cut rainbow holofoil card.

COMPLETE SET (10) 25.00 50.00
STATED ODDS 1:72
1 Peyton Manning 4.00 10.00
2 Randy Moss 1.25 3.00
3 Brett Favre 3.00 8.00
4 Terrell Davis 1.25 3.00
5 Dan Marino 3.00 8.00
6 Jake Plummer 1.00 2.50
7 Tim Couch 1.25 3.00
8 Eddie George 1.25 3.00
9 Brian Griese 1.00 2.50
10 Kurt Warner 2.50 6.00

2001 Ultra

Released as a 300-card set, 2001 Ultra is composed of 250 veteran cards and 60 rookie cards which are serial numbered to 2499. Base cards contain full-color action photography and rainbow holofoil stamping. Ultra was packaged in 24-pack boxes with packs that contained 10 cards and carried a suggested retail price of $2.99. Cards numbered U301 through U310 were issued later in the season and featured players who had an impact during the 2001 season.

COMP.SET w/o SP's (250) 10.00 25.00
251-310 ROOKIE PRINT RUN 2499
1 Daunte Culpepper .25 .60
2 Kurt Warner .50 1.25
3 Emmitt Smith .50 1.25
4 Eddie George .30 .75
5 Ron Dayne .25 .60
6 Zach Thomas .25 .60
7 Itula Mili .20 .50
8 Jake Reed .25 .60
9 James Stewart .20 .50
10 Terrence Wilkins .20 .50
11 Jeff Blake .25 .60
12 Kerry Collins .20 .50
13 Christian Fauria .20 .50
14 Jackie Harris .25 .60
15 Kevin Johnson .20 .50
16 Tony Martin .25 .60
17 Joey Galloway .25 .60
18 Junior Seau .25 .60
19 Jason Tucker .20 .50
20 Steve Beuerlein .25 .60
21 Mike Cloud .20 .50
22 Kevin Faulk .20 .50
23 Az-Zahir Hakim .20 .50
24 Charles Johnson .20 .50
25 Curtis Martin .25 .60
26 Eric Moulds .20 .50
27 Bill Schroeder .25 .60
28 Amani Toomer .20 .50
29 Obafemi Ayanbadejo .20 .50
30 Aaron Shea .20 .50
31 Ken Dilger .20 .50
32 Terry Glenn .25 .60
33 Rocket Ismail .25 .60
34 Dorsey Levens .25 .60
35 Brian Mitchell .25 .60
36 Tony Richardson .20 .50
37 Sam Madison .20 .50
38 Darren Sharper .25 .00
39 Derrick Alexander .20 .50
40 Aaron Brooks .20 .50
41 Casey Crawford .20 .50
42 Terrell Fletcher .20 .50
43 William Henderson .20 .50
44 Thomas Jones .20 .50
45 Keenan McCardell .25 .60
46 Chad Pennington .20 .50
47 Akili Smith .20 .50
48 Hines Ward .25 .60
49 Champ Bailey .25 .60
50 Cris Carter .30 .75
51 Corey Dillon .20 .50
52 Tony Gonzalez .25 .60
53 Darrell Jackson .25 .60
54 Chad Lewis .20 .50
55 Dave Moore .20 .50
56 Jay Riemersma .20 .50
57 J.J. Stokes .20 .50
58 Frank Wycheck .20 .50
59 Tiki Barber .25 .60
60 Tony Carter .20 .50
61 Rickey Dudley .20 .50
62 John Lynch .25 .60
63 Larry Foster .20 .50
64 Willie Jackson .20 .50
65 Jamal Lewis .30 .75
66 Herman Moore .20 .50
67 Andre Rison .25 .60
68 Michael Strahan .25 .60
69 Charlie Batch .20 .50
70 Larry Centers .20 .50
71 Ron Dugans .20 .50
72 Jeff Graham .20 .50
73 Edgerrin James .25 .60
74 Jermaine Lewis .20 .50
75 Charles Woodson .30 .75
76 Chris Redman .30 .75
77 Jon Ritchie .20 .50
78 Fred Taylor .20 .50
79 Jamal Anderson .25 .60
80 Isaac Bruce .30 .75
81 Terrell Davis .25 .60
82 Rich Gannon .25 .60
83 Joe Horn .20 .50
84 Eddie Kennison .25 .60
85 Steve McNair .25 .60
86 Travis Prentice .20 .50
87 Rod Smith .25 .60
88 Ricky Watters .25 .60
89 Michael Bates .20 .50
90 Byron Chamberlain .20 .50
91 Warrick Dunn .20 .50
92 Elvis Grbac .25 .60
93 Patrick Jeffers .20 .50
94 Ray Lewis .30 .75
95 Sammy Morris .20 .50
96 Marcus Robinson .25 .60
97 Travis Taylor .20 .50
98 Fred Beasley .20 .50
99 Chris Chandler .25 .60
100 Tim Dwight .25 .60
101 Ahman Green .25 .60
102 Shawn Jefferson .20 .50
103 Jeremy McDaniel .20 .50
104 Sylvester Morris .20 .50
105 John Randle .25 .60
106 Vinny Testaverde .20 .50
107 Anthony Becht .20 .50
108 Wayne Chrebet .20 .50
109 Stephen Boyd .20 .50
110 Jacquez Green .20 .50
111 MarTay Jenkins .20 .50
112 Jason Gildon .20 .50
113 Chad Morton .20 .50
114 Deion Sanders .25 .60
115 Yancey Thigpen .20 .50
116 Marty Booker .20 .50
117 Curtis Conway .25 .60
118 Jermaine Fazande .20 .50
119 Matthew Hatchette .20 .50
120 Pat Johnson .20 .50
121 Terance Mathis .20 .50
122 Terrell Owens .25 .60
123 Corey Simon .20 .50
124 Darrick Vaughn .20 .50
125 Drew Bledsoe .25 .60
126 Albert Connell .20 .50
127 Brett Favre .60 1.50
128 Marvin Harrison .25 .60
129 Keyshawn Johnson .25 .60
130 Derrick Mason .20 .50
131 Dennis Northcutt .20 .50
132 Shannon Sharpe .25 .60
133 Brian Urlacher .40 1.00
134 Mike Anderson .20 .50
135 Mark Bruener .25 .60
136 Sean Dawkins .20 .50
137 Jeff Garcia .20 .50
138 Tony Horne .20 .50
139 Shaun King .20 .50
140 Cade McNown .25 .60
141 Peerless Price .20 .50
142 R.Jay Soward .20 .50
143 Tyrone Wheatley .25 .60
144 Richie Anderson .20 .50
145 Mark Brunell .25 .60
146 JaJuan Dawson .20 .50
147 Charlie Garner .25 .60
148 Desmond Howard .25 .60
149 Jon Kitna .20 .50
150 Duane Starks .20 .50
151 J.R. Redmond .20 .50
152 Duce Staley .20 .50
153 Dez White .25 .60
154 David Boston .20 .50
155 Tim Couch .20 .50
156 Jay Fiedler .25 .60
157 Jessie Armstead .20 .50
158 Rob Johnson .25 .60
159 Brad Johnson .25 .60
160 Derrick Mayes .20 .50
161 Jerome Pathon .20 .50
162 David Sloan .20 .50
163 Wesley Walls .20 .50
164 Shaun Alexander .20 .50
165 Derrick Brooks .20 .50
166 Germane Crowell .20 .50
167 Doug Flutie .25 .60
168 Ike Hilliard .20 .50
169 Hugh Douglas .20 .50
170 Wane McGarity .20 .50
171 Michael Pittman .25 .60
172 Shawn Bryson .20 .50
173 Richard Huntley .20 .50
174 Darnell Autry .20 .50
175 Plaxico Burress .20 .50
176 Trent Dilfer .20 .50
177 Jeff George .25 .60
178 Qadry Ismail .20 .50
179 Ryan Leaf .20 .50
180 Jim Miller .25 .60
181 Jerry Rice .60 1.50
182 Kordell Stewart .20 .50
183 Ricky Williams .25 .60
184 James Allen .20 .50
185 Courtney Brown .20 .50
186 Reidel Anthony .20 .50
187 Bubba Franks .20 .50
188 Priest Holmes .20 .50
189 Napoleon Kaufman .20 .50
190 Trevor Pryce .20 .50
191 Jake Plummer .20 .50
192 Jimmy Smith .25 .60

193 Michael Wiley .20 .50
194 Brock Huard .20 .50
195 Troy Brown .20 .50
196 Stephen Davis .20 .50
197 Oronde Gadsden .20 .50
198 Brad Hoover .25 .60
199 La'Roi Glover .20 .50
200 Donovan McNabb .25 .60
201 Jerry Porter .20 .50
202 Robert Smith .20 .50
203 Justin Watson .20 .50
204 Tim Biakabutuka .20 .50
205 Laveranues Coles .25 .60
206 Marshall Faulk .25 .60
207 Jim Harbaugh .25 .60
208 Doug Johnson .20 .50
209 Tee Martin .25 .60
210 Muhsin Muhammad .20 .50
211 Darnay Scott .25 .60
212 Jeremiah Trotter .20 .50
213 Troy Aikman .40 1.00
214 Kyle Brady .20 .50
215 Sam Cowart .20 .50
216 Darren Howard .20 .50
217 Donald Hayes .20 .50
218 Freddie Jones .20 .50
219 Ed McCaffrey .25 .60
220 David Patten .20 .50
221 Brian Griese .20 .50
222 Dedric Ward .20 .50
223 Jerome Bettis .30 .75
224 Greg Clark .20 .50
225 Bobby Engram .20 .50
226 Matt Hasselbeck .20 .50
227 James Jett .20 .50
228 Peyton Manning .75 2.00
229 Randy Moss .25 .60
230 Warren Sapp .25 .60
231 James Thrash .25 .60
232 Mike Alstott .20 .50
233 Tim Brown .30 .75
234 Randall Cunningham .25 .60
235 Antonio Freeman .30 .75
236 Torry Holt .25 .60
237 Jevon Kearse .20 .50
238 James McKnight .20 .50
239 Marcus Pollard .20 .50
240 Lamar Smith .25 .60
241 Peter Warrick .20 .50
242 Donnell Bennett .20 .50
243 Joe Johnson .20 .50
244 Troy Edwards .20 .50
245 Trent Green .20 .50
246 Jason Taylor .30 .75
247 Aeneas Williams .20 .50
248 Johnnie Morton .25 .60
249 Frank Sanders .20 .50
250 Jason Sehorn .25 .60
251 Chris Weinke RC 1.50 4.00
252 Bobby Newcombe RC 1.50 4.00
253 LaDainian Tomlinson RC 6.00 15.00
254 Chad Johnson RC 2.00 5.00
255 Derrick Gibson RC 1.25 3.00
256 Sage Rosenfels RC 1.50 4.00
257 LaMont Jordan RC 2.00 5.00
258 Mike McMahon RC 1.50 4.00
259 Vinny Sutherland RC 1.25 3.00
260 Drew Brees RC 50.00 100.00
261 Deuce McAllister RC 2.00 5.00
262 Kevan Barlow RC 1.50 4.00
263 Jamar Fletcher RC 1.25 3.00
264 Gerard Warren RC 1.50 4.00
265 Todd Heap RC 1.50 4.00
266 Travis Henry RC 1.50 4.00
267 Quincy Morgan RC 1.50 4.00
268 Anthony Thomas RC 2.00 5.00
269 Andre Carter RC 1.50 4.00
270 Freddie Mitchell RC 1.25 3.00
271 Richard Seymour RC 2.00 5.00
272 Josh Booty RC 1.50 4.00
273 Robert Ferguson RC 2.00 5.00
274 Marques Tuiasosopo RC 1.50 4.00
275 Reggie Wayne RC 2.50 6.00
276 Jabari Holloway RC 1.25 3.00
277 Rudi Johnson RC 2.00 5.00
278 Michael Bennett RC 1.50 4.00
279 Snoop Minnis RC 1.25 3.00
280 Dan Morgan RC 1.50 4.00
281 Rod Gardner RC 1.50 4.00
282 Jesse Palmer RC 1.50 4.00
283 Michael Vick RC 3.00 8.00
284 Chris Chambers RC 1.25 3.00
285 James Jackson RC 1.25 3.00
286 David Terrell RC 1.50 4.00
287 Koren Robinson RC 1.50 4.00
288 Travis Minor RC 1.50 4.00
289 Santana Moss RC 2.00 5.00
290 Josh Heupel RC 2.00 5.00
291 Jamal Reynolds RC 1.25 3.00
292 Ken-Yon Rambo RC 1.25 3.00
293 Cedrick Wilson RC 1.50 4.00
294 Alge Crumpler RC 2.00 5.00
295 Fred Smoot RC 1.50 4.00
296 Dan Alexander RC 1.50 4.00
297 Tim Hasselbeck RC 1.50 4.00
298 Will Allen RC 2.00 5.00
299 Keith Adams RC 1.25 3.00
300 Heath Evans RC 1.50 4.00
U301 Quincy Carter RC 1.50 4.00
U302 Derrick Blaylock RC 1.50 4.00
U303 Correll Buckhalter RC 1.25 3.00
U304 A.J. Feeley RC 1.50 4.00
U305 Milton Wynn RC 1.25 3.00
U306 Kevin Kasper RC 1.25 3.00
U307 Justin McCareins RC 1.50 4.00
U308 Dave Dickenson RC 1.50 4.00
U309 Steve Smith RC 4.00 10.00
U310 Moran Norris RC 1.25 3.00

2001 Ultra Gold Medallion

*VETS 1-250: 4X TO 10X BASIC CARDS
VETERAN PRINT RUN 250
*ROOK.251-300: 1.2X TO 3X BASIC CARDS
ROOKIE PRINT RUN 100
260G Drew Brees 250.00 500.00

2001 Ultra Platinum Medallion

*VETS 1-250: 12X TO 30X BASIC CARDS
1-250 VETERAN PRINT RUN 50
*ROOKIE 251-300: 3X TO 8X BASIC CARDS
251-300 ROOKIE PRINT RUN 25
253P LaDainian Tomlinson 125.00 250.00
260P Drew Brees 400.00 800.00
283P Michael Vick 125.00 250.00

2001 Ultra Ball Hawks

Randomly inserted at a rate of 1:144 packs, this 24-card set [illegible] from the NFL with a swatch of a game used football.
STATED ODDS 1:144
1 Troy Aikman 5.00 12.00
2 Derrick Alexander 2.50 6.00
3 Jamal Anderson 3.00 8.00
4 Charlie Batch 2.50 6.00
5 Courtney Brown 2.50 6.00
6 Mark Brunell 3.00 8.00
7 Tim Couch 2.50 6.00
8 Eddie George 4.00 10.00
9 Tony Gonzalez 3.00 8.00
10 Elvis Grbac 3.00 8.00
11 Marvin Harrison 3.00 8.00
12 Edgerrin James 3.00 8.00
13 Kevin Johnson 2.50 6.00
14 Jevon Kearse 2.50 6.00
15 Donovan McNabb 3.00 8.00
16 Steve McNair 3.00 8.00
17 Cade McNown 3.00 8.00
18 Herman Moore 2.50 6.00
19 Travis Prentice 2.50 6.00
20 Marcus Robinson 3.00 8.00
21 Emmitt Smith 6.00 15.00
22 Jimmy Smith 3.00 8.00
23 Duce Staley 2.50 6.00
24 Brian Urlacher 5.00 12.00

2001 Ultra College Greats Previews

Randomly inserted at a rate of 1:22 packs, this 35 card set featued past and present NFL superstars in action in their college gear. The cardbacks had no numbers so they were arranged alphabetically for the checklist below.
COMPLETE SET (35) 40.00 80.00
STATED ODDS 1:22
1 Marcus Allen 1.50 4.00
2 Drew Brees 10.00 25.00
3 Tim Brown 1.50 4.00
4 Earl Campbell 1.50 4.00
5 John Cappelletti 1.00 2.50
6 Ron Dayne 1.00 2.50
7 Tony Dorsett 1.50 4.00
8 Tim Dwight 1.00 2.50
9 Doug Flutie 1.25 3.00
10 Eddie George 1.25 3.00
11 Brian Griese .75 2.00
12 Archie Griffin 1.00 2.50
13 Franco Harris 1.50 4.00
14 Bob Hayes 1.25 3.00
15 Josh Heupel 1.00 2.50
16 Paul Hornung 1.50 4.00
17 Bo Jackson 2.00 5.00
18 Thomas Jones .75 2.00
19 Jamal Lewis 1.25 3.00
20 Bob Lilly 1.25 3.00
21 Johnny Lujack 1.25 3.00
22 Donovan McNabb 1.00 2.50
23 Santana Moss 1.00 2.50
24 Jim Plunkett 1.25 3.00
25 Billy Sims 1.25 3.00
26 Roger Staubach 2.00 5.00
27 Pat Sullivan 1.00 2.50
28 David Terrell 1.00 2.50
29 LaDainian Tomlinson 3.00 8.00
30 Amani Toomer .75 2.00
31 Michael Vick 1.50 4.00
32 Herschel Walker 1.50 4.00
33 Chris Weinke 1.00 2.50
34 Ricky Williams 1.00 2.50
35 Steve Young 2.00 5.00

2001 Ultra College Greats Previews Autographs

Randomly inserted at a rate of 1:61 packs, this 35-card set was an autographed parallel to the base College Greats Preview set. Please note the entire set was issued as exchange cards. The exchange cards feature the actual card minus the autograph with the words "redemption card" on the bottom. The exchange card expiration date was June 1, 2002. Please note this is a skip numbered set.
STATED ODDS 1:61
1 Marcus Allen 12.00 30.00
2 Drew Brees 50.00 100.00
3 Tim Brown 20.00 40.00
4 Earl Campbell 12.00 30.00
5 John Cappelletti 8.00 20.00
6 Ron Dayne 10.00 25.00
7 Tony Dorsett 25.00 50.00
8 Tim Dwight 8.00 20.00
9 Doug Flutie 20.00 40.00
10 Eddie George 10.00 25.00
12 Archie Griffin 10.00 25.00
13 Franco Harris 20.00 40.00
14 Bob Hayes 60.00 120.00
15 Josh Heupel 10.00 25.00
16 Paul Hornung 12.00 30.00
17 Bo Jackson 60.00 120.00
19 Jamal Lewis 10.00 25.00
20 Bob Lilly 10.00 25.00
22 Donovan McNabb 15.00 40.00
23 Santana Moss 8.00 20.00
24 Jim Plunkett 12.00 30.00
26 Roger Staubach 50.00 100.00
27 Pat Sullivan 8.00 20.00
28 David Terrell 8.00 20.00
29 LaDainian Tomlinson 20.00 50.00
30 Amani Toomer 6.00 15.00
31 Michael Vick 20.00 50.00
33 Chris Weinke 8.00 20.00

2001 Ultra College Greats Previews Autograph Redemptions

*SINGLES: .6X TO 1.5X UNSIGNED INSERTS
1 Marcus Allen 2.50 6.00
2 Drew Brees 15.00 40.00
3 Tim Brown 2.50 6.00
4 Earl Campbell 2.50 6.00
5 John Cappelletti 1.50 4.00
6 Ron Dayne 1.50 4.00
7 Tony Dorsett 2.50 6.00
8 Tim Dwight 1.50 4.00
9 Doug Flutie 2.00 5.00
10 Eddie George 2.00 5.00
12 Archie Griffin 1.50 4.00
13 Franco Harris 2.50 6.00
14 Bob Hayes 2.00 5.00
15 Josh Heupel 1.50 4.00
16 Paul Hornung 2.50 6.00
17 Bo Jackson 3.00 8.00
19 Jamal Lewis 2.00 5.00
20 Bob Lilly 2.00 5.00
22 Donovan McNabb 1.50 4.00
23 Santana Moss 1.50 4.00
24 Jim Plunkett 2.00 5.00
26 Roger Staubach 3.00 8.00
27 Pat Sullivan 1.50 4.00
28 David Terrell 1.25 3.00
29 LaDainian Tomlinson 5.00 12.00
30 Amani Toomer 1.25 3.00
31 Michael Vick 2.50 6.00
33 Chris Weinke 1.25 3.00

2001 Ultra Ground Command

Randomly inserted at a rate of 1:22, this 10-card set featured the top running backs from the NFL in action. The cards were enhanced by holofoil design and some of their stats floating past in the background.
COMPLETE SET (10) 7.50 20.00
STATED ODDS 1:22
*GOLD MED/250: 1X TO 2.5X BASIC INSERT
GOLD MED.PRINT RUN 250 SER.#'d SETS
*PLAT.MED/50: 2.5X TO 6X BASIC INSERT
PLAT.MED.PRINT RUN 50 SER.#'d SETS
1 Emmitt Smith 1.00 2.50
2 Edgerrin James .50 1.25
3 Marshall Faulk .50 1.25
4 Jamal Lewis [illegible]
5 Mike Anderson .40 1.00
6 Duce Staley .40 1.00
7 Jamal Anderson .50 1.25
8 Ricky Williams .50 1.25
9 Corey Dillon .40 1.00
10 Terrell Davis .50 1.25

2001 Ultra Head of the Class

Randomly inserted in packs at a rate of 1:22, this 25-card set featured top players from the rookie class of 2000. The cards were enhanced with silver foil stamping.
COMPLETE SET (25) 20.00 50.00
STATED ODDS 1:22
1 Trung Canidate .60 1.50
2 Thomas Jones .60 1.50
3 Curtis Keaton .60 1.50
4 Courtney Brown .60 1.50
5 Chris Redman 1.00 2.50
6 Dennis Northcutt .60 1.50
7 Sylvester Morris .60 1.50
8 Shaun Alexander .60 1.50
9 Dez White .75 2.00
10 Laveranues Coles .75 2.00
11 R.Jay Soward .60 1.50
12 Jamal Lewis 1.00 2.50
13 J.R. Redmond .60 1.50
14 Travis Taylor .60 1.50
15 Plaxico Burress .60 1.50
16 Peter Warrick .60 1.50
17 Joe Hamilton .60 1.50
18 Ron Dugans .60 1.50
19 Tee Martin .75 2.00
20 Brian Urlacher 1.25 3.00
21 Ron Dayne .75 2.00
22 Travis Prentice .60 1.50
23 Chad Pennington .60 1.50
24 Corey Simon .60 1.50
25 Mike Anderson .60 1.50

2001 Ultra Head of the Class Player Worn Caps

Randomly inserted in packs, this 25-card set featured top players from the rookie class of 2000. The cards featured a swatch of a player worn sideline cap with each being enhanced with silver foil stamping.
STATED PRINT RUN 100 SER.#'d SETS
1 Trung Canidate 4.00 10.00
2 Thomas Jones 4.00 10.00
3 Curtis Keaton 4.00 10.00
4 Courtney Brown 4.00 10.00
5 Chris Redman 6.00 15.00
6 Dennis Northcutt 4.00 10.00
7 Sylvester Morris 4.00 10.00
8 Shaun Alexander 4.00 10.00
9 Dez White 5.00 12.00
10 Laveranues Coles 5.00 12.00
11 R.Jay Soward 4.00 10.00
12 Jamal Lewis 6.00 15.00
13 J.R. Redmond 4.00 10.00
14 Travis Taylor 4.00 10.00
15 Plaxico Burress 4.00 10.00
16 Peter Warrick 4.00 10.00
17 Joe Hamilton 4.00 10.00
18 Ron Dugans 4.00 10.00
19 Tee Martin 5.00 12.00
20 Brian Urlacher 8.00 20.00
21 Ron Dayne 5.00 12.00
22 Travis Prentice 4.00 10.00
23 Chad Pennington 4.00 10.00
24 Corey Simon 4.00 10.00
25 Mike Anderson 4.00 10.00

2001 Ultra Quick Strike

Randomly inserted in packs at a rate of 1:22, this 20-card set featured top players from the NFL that were instant scoing threats. The cards were enhanced with red foil stamping and contained an action photo of the featured player.
COMPLETE SET (20) 20.00 50.00
STATED ODDS 1:22
*GOLD.MED/250: .8X TO 2X BASIC INSERT
GOLD MED.PRINT RUN 250 SER.#'d SETS
*PLAT.MED/50: 2X TO 5X BASIC INSERT
PLAT.MED.PRINT RUN 50 SER.#'d SETS
1 Kurt Warner 1.50 4.00
2 Mark Brunell .75 2.00
3 Fred Taylor .60 1.50
4 Emmitt Smith 1.50 4.00
5 Jerry Rice 2.00 5.00
6 Eddie George 1.00 2.50
7 Cade McNown .75 2.00
8 Randy Moss .75 2.00
9 Donovan McNabb .75 2.00
10 Peyton Manning 2.50 6.00
11 Edgerrin James .75 2.00
12 Shaun King .60 1.50
13 Troy Aikman 1.25 3.00
14 Tim Couch .60 1.50
15 Jamal Lewis 1.00 2.50
16 Daunte Culpepper .75 2.00
17 Brett Favre 2.00 5.00
18 Drew Bledsoe .75 2.00
19 Terrell Davis .75 2.00
20 Marshall Faulk .75 2.00

2001 Ultra Sunday's Best Jerseys

Randomly inserted in packs at a rate of 1:63, this 28 card set featured top NFL superstars with a swatch of their Sunday attire. These were player worn jersey swatches from the previous NFL season.
STATED ODDS 1:63 HOB, 1:96 RETAIL
1 Jamal Anderson 2.50 6.00
2 Jerome Bettis 3.00 8.00
3 Drew Bledsoe 2.50 6.00
4 Isaac Bruce 3.00 8.00
5 Mark Brunell 2.50 6.00
6 Trung Canidate 2.00 5.00
7 Tim Couch 2.00 5.00
8 Stephen Davis 2.00 5.00
9 Ron Dayne 2.50 6.00
10 Warrick Dunn 2.00 5.00
11 Marshall Faulk 2.50 6.00
12 Doug Flutie 2.50 6.00
13 Antonio Freeman 3.00 8.00
14 Brian Griese 2.00 5.00
15 Kevin Johnson 2.00 5.00
16 Thomas Jones 2.00 5.00
17 Napoleon Kaufman 2.00 5.00
18 Curtis Martin 2.50 6.00
19 Keenan McCardell 2.50 6.00
20 Terrell Owens 2.50 6.00
21 Jake Plummer 2.00 5.00
22 Jerry Rice 6.00 15.00
23 Jimmy Smith 2.50 6.00
24 Rod Smith 2.50 6.00
25 R.Jay Soward 2.00 5.00
26 Fred Taylor 2.00 5.00
27 Brian Urlacher 4.00 10.00
28 [illegible] [illegible] 10.00

2001 Ultra Two Minute Thrill

Randomly inserted in packs at a rate of 1:22, this 20-card set featured NFL superstars who were the go to guys in the last two minutes of any game. These cards were printed on holofoil design with red foil stamping.
COMPLETE SET (20) 15.00 40.00
STATED ODDS 1:22
*GOLD.MED/250: .8X TO 2X BASIC INSERT
GOLD MED.PRINT RUN 250 SER.#'d SETS
*PLAT.MED/50: 2X TO 5X BASIC INSERT
PLAT.MED.PRINT RUN 50 SER.#'d SETS
1 Troy Aikman 1.25 3.00
2 Terrell Davis .75 2.00
3 Keyshawn Johnson .75 2.00
4 Peyton Manning 2.50 6.00
5 Donovan McNabb .75 2.00
6 Steve McNair .75 2.00
7 Cade McNown .75 2.00
8 Ricky Williams .75 2.00
9 Brett Favre 2.00 5.00
10 Edgerrin James .75 2.00
11 Tim Couch .60 1.50
12 Fred Taylor .60 1.50
13 Rich Gannon .75 2.00
14 Kurt Warner 1.50 4.00
15 Randy Moss .75 2.00
16 Peter Warrick .60 1.50
17 Ron Dayne .75 2.00
18 Mark Brunell .75 2.00
19 Daunte Culpepper .75 2.00
20 Marshall Faulk .75 2.00

2001 Ultra White Rose Die Cast

White Rose Collectibles, a division of Fleer, released these 1:58 scale die-cast PT Cruiser cars in 2001. Each blister pack included one die-cast piece along with a 2001 Ultra card of the featured player. The cards are essentially a parallel to the player's base Ultra card but have been re-numbered and include the White Rose logo on the cardbacks. We've included pricing below on just the cards.
COMPLETE SET (38) 20.00 50.00
1 Michael Vick .60 1.50
2 Brian Urlacher .60 1.50
3 Emmitt Smith .75 2.00
4 Charlie Batch .30 .75
5 Brett Favre 1.00 2.50
6 Kurt Warner .75 2.00
7 Marshall Faulk .40 1.00
8 Daunte Culpepper .40 1.00
9 Randy Moss .40 1.00
10 Ricky Williams .40 1.00
11 Ron Dayne .40 1.00
12 Tiki Barber .40 1.00
13 Donovan McNabb .40 1.00
14 Jake Plummer .30 .75
15 Jeff Garcia .30 .75
16 Keyshawn Johnson .40 1.00
17 Stephen Davis .30 .75
18 Rod Gardner .40 1.00
19 Eric Moulds .30 .75
20 Peter Warrick .30 .75
21 Jamal Lewis .50 1.25
22 Terrell Davis .40 1.00
23 Brian Griese .30 .75
24 Peyton Manning 1.25 3.00
25 Edgerrin James .40 1.00
26 Eddie George .50 1.25
27 Tony Gonzalez .40 1.00
28 Rich Gannon .40 1.00
29 Tim Brown .50 1.25
30 Zach Thomas .40 1.00
31 Drew Bledsoe .40 1.00
32 Santana Moss .40 1.00
33 Jerome Bettis .50 1.25
34 LaDainian Tomlinson 1.25 3.00
35 Koren Robinson .40 1.00
36 Fred Taylor .30 .75
37 Chris Weinke .40 1.00
38 Tim Couch .30 .75

2002 Ultra

This 240 card set was released in late July, 2002. It is composed of 200 veterans and 40 rookies. The rookies are seeded 1:4 packs. SRP for this product is $2.99. Boxes contain 24 packs, each with 10 cards per pack.
COMPLETE SET (240) 60.00 150.00
COMP.SET w/o SP's (200) 10.00 25.00
ROOKIE STATED ODDS 1:4
1 Donovan McNabb .25 .60
2 Chad Pennington .20 .50
3 Shaun Alexander .20 .50
4 Corey Dillon .20 .50
5 Kurt Warner .25 .60
6 Ed McCaffrey .25 .60
7 Hugh Douglas .20 .50
8 Tony Gonzalez .25 .60
9 Travis Taylor .20 .50
10 Tony Boselli .25 .60
11 Chad Scott .20 .50
12 Ernie Conwell .20 .50
13 Brad Johnson .25 .60
14 Donald Hayes .20 .50
15 Emmitt Smith .50 1.25
16 Jimmy Smith .25 .60
17 Anthony Becht .20 .50
18 Rod Gardner .20 .50
19 Muhsin Muhammad .20 .50
20 Troy Hambrick .20 .50
21 Keenan McCardell .25 .60
22 Laveranues Coles .25 .60
23 Kevin Dyson .25 .60
24 Grant Wistrom .20 .50
25 Eric Moulds .20 .50
26 Nate Clements .20 .50
27 Terrell Davis .25 .60
28 Aaron Glenn .20 .50
29 Eric Hicks .20 .50
30 Tiki Barber .25 .60
31 Jake Plummer .20 .50
32 Junior Seau .25 .60
33 Marshall Faulk .25 .60
34 Warrick Dunn .20 .50
35 Bill Gramatica .20 .50
36 Tim Couch .20 .50
37 Kabeer Gbaja-Biamila .20 .50
38 Kailee Wong .20 .50
39 David Patten .20 .50
40 Correll Buckhalter .20 .50
41 Troy Brown .20 .50
42 Drew Bledsoe .25 .60
43 Travis Henry .20 .50
44 Jim Miller .20 .50
45 Rod Smith .25 .60
46 Tai Streets .20 .50
47 Snoop Minnis .20 .50
48 Ron Dayne .25 .60
49 Tyrone Wheatley .25 .60
50 LaDainian Tomlinson .30 .75
51 Akili Smith .25 .60
52 Warren Sapp .25 .60
53 Adam Archuleta .20 .50
54 Chris Fuamatu-Ma'afala .20 .50
55 Marty Booker .20 .50
56 Trevor Pryce .20 .50
57 Peyton Manning .75 2.00
58 Lamar Smith .20 .50
59 Amani Toomer .20 .50
60 Greg Biekert .20 .50
61 Marcellus Wiley .20 .50
62 Ahmed Plummer .20 .50
63 Mike Alstott .20 .50
64 Gary Walker .20 .50
65 Champ Bailey .25 .60
66 Chris Redman .20 .50
67 David Terrell .20 .50
68 Mike McMahon .20 .50
69 Marvin Harrison .25 .60
70 Jay Fiedler .25 .60
71 JaJuan Dawson .20 .50
72 Charlie Garner .25 .60
73 Curtis Conway .25 .60
74 J.J. Stokes .20 .50
75 Ronde Barber .20 .50
76 Alge Crumpler .25 .60
77 Jamir Miller .20 .50
78 Brett Favre .60 1.50
79 Randy Moss .25 .60
80 Joe Horn .20 .50
81 Hines Ward .25 .60
82 Lawyer Milloy .20 .50
83 Aeneas Williams .20 .50
84 Chris McAlister .20 .50
85 Anthony Thomas .25 .60
86 Johnnie Morton .25 .60
87 Edgerrin James .25 .60
88 Chris Chambers .20 .50
89 Michael Strahan .25 .60
90 Charles Woodson .30 .75
91 Tim Dwight .20 .50
92 Kevan Barlow .20 .50
93 Donnie Abraham .20 .50
94 Peter Boulware .20 .50
95 Marcus Robinson .25 .60
96 Shaun Rogers .20 .50
97 Dominic Rhodes .20 .50
98 Zach Thomas .25 .60
99 Kerry Collins .20 .50
100 Tim Brown .30 .75
101 Garrison Hearst .20 .50
102 Steve McNair .25 .60
103 Fred Smoot .25 .60
104 Isaac Bruce .30 .75
105 Jamal Lewis .25 .60
106 Brian Urlacher .30 .75
107 Takeo Spikes .20 .50
108 Marcus Pollard .20 .50
109 Jason Taylor .25 .60
110 Deuce McAllister .25 .60
111 Jerry Rice .60 1.50
112 Terrell Owens .25 .60
113 Eddie George .25 .60
114 Rob Morris .20 .50
115 Mike Brown .20 .50
116 Joey Galloway .25 .60
117 Fred Taylor .20 .50
118 Rich Gannon .25 .60
119 Chris Chandler .25 .60
120 Koren Robinson .20 .50
121 Dan Morgan .20 .50
122 Rocket Ismail .25 .60
123 Mark Brunell .25 .60
124 John Abraham .25 .60
125 Stephen Davis .20 .50
126 Patrick Kerney .20 .50
127 Anthony Henry .20 .50
128 Scotty Anderson .20 .50
129 Oronde Gadsden .20 .50
130 Willie Jackson .20 .50
131 Kendrell Bell .20 .50
132 Ray Lewis .30 .75
133 Quincy Carter .20 .50
134 James Stewart .20 .50
135 Travis Minor .20 .50
136 Kyle Turley .20 .50
137 Jason Gildon .25 .60
138 David Boston .20 .50
139 Justin Smith .25 .60
140 Jamie Sharper .25 .60
141 Antowain Smith .25 .60
142 Freddie Mitchell .20 .50
143 Frank Sanders .20 .50
144 Kevin Johnson .20 .50
145 Darren Sharper .20 .50
146 Eric Johnson .20 .50
147 Ty Law .30 .75
148 James Thrash .25 .60
149 Matt Hasselbeck .20 .50
150 Peerless Price .20 .50
151 T.J. Houshmandzadeh .20 .50
152 Mike Anderson .20 .50
153 Jermaine Lewis .20 .50
154 Trent Green .20 .50
155 Ron Dixon .20 .50
156 Duce Staley .20 .50
157 Drew Brees .60 1.50
158 Torry Holt .25 .60
159 Keyshawn Johnson .25 .60
160 Michael Vick .25 .60
161 Benjamin Gay .20 .50
162 Bill Schroeder .20 .50
163 Byron Chamberlain .20 .50
164 Tedy Bruschi .25 .60
165 Kordell Stewart .20 .50
166 Deltha O'Neal .20 .50
167 Quincy Morgan .20 .50
168 Bubba Franks .20 .50
169 Daunte Culpepper .25 .60
170 Ricky Williams .25 .60
171 Plaxico Burress .20 .50
172 Trent Dilfer .20 .50
173 Steve Smith .30 .75
174 Greg Ellis .20 .50
175 Tony Brackens .20 .50
176 Santana Moss .25 .60
177 Frank Wycheck .20 .50
178 Michael Pittman .25 .60
179 Peter Warrick .20 .50
180 Antonio Freeman .30 .75
181 Tom Brady 1.50 4.00
182 Bobby Taylor .25 .60
183 Jeff Garcia .20 .50
184 Darrell Jackson .25 .60
185 Chris Weinke .20 .50
186 Darren Woodson .25 .60
187 Hardy Nickerson .20 .50
188 Wayne Chrebet .20 .50
189 Samari Rolle .20 .50
190 Jamal Anderson .25 .60
191 James Jackson .20 .50
192 Ahman Green .25 .60
193 Michael Bennett .20 .50
194 Aaron Brooks .20 .50
195 Jerome Bettis .30 .75
196 Jay Riemersma .20 .50
197 Brian Griese .20 .50
198 Priest Holmes .20 .50
199 Curtis Martin .25 .60
200 Derrick Mason .20 .50
201 Antonio Bryant RC 1.50 4.00
202 David Carr RC 1.00 2.50
203 Eric Crouch RC 1.50 4.00
204 Freddie Milons RC 1.00 2.50
205 Najeh Davenport RC 1.00 2.50
206 Rohan Davey RC 1.50 4.00
207 T.J. Duckett RC 1.00 2.50
208 DeShaun Foster RC 1.50 4.00
209 Jabar Gaffney RC 1.00 2.50
210 William Green RC 1.25 3.00
211 Joey Harrington RC 1.00 2.50
212 Travis Stephens RC 1.00 2.50
213 Julius Peppers RC 2.50 6.00
214 Adrian Peterson RC 1.25 3.00
215 Josh Reed RC 1.25 3.00
216 Mike Williams RC 1.00 2.50
217 Javon Walker RC 1.50 4.00
218 Marquise Walker RC 1.00 2.50
219 Patrick Ramsey RC 1.25 3.00
220 Lamar Gordon RC 1.25 3.00
221 David Garrard RC 1.25 3.00
222 Major Applewhite RC 1.50 4.00
223 Andre Davis RC 1.00 2.50
224 Roy Williams RC 1.00 2.50
225 Tim Carter RC 1.25 3.00
226 Ron Johnson RC 1.25 3.00
227 Randy Fasani RC 1.00 2.50
228 Ashley Lelie RC 1.00 2.50
229 Ladell Betts RC 1.50 4.00
230 Antwaan Randle El RC 1.25 3.00
231 Jonathan Wells RC 1.25 3.00
232 Brian Westbrook RC 2.00 5.00
233 Clinton Portis RC 1.50 4.00
234 Luke Staley RC 1.00 2.50
235 Cliff Russell RC 1.00 2.50
236 Jeremy Shockey RC 1.50 4.00
237 Donte Stallworth RC 1.50 4.00
238 Daniel Graham RC 1.25 3.00
239 Reche Caldwell RC 1.25 3.00
240 Ryan Sims RC 1.50 4.00

2002 Ultra Gold Medallion

*VETS 1-200: 1.5X TO 4X BASIC CARDS
OVERALL ODDS ONE PER PACK
*ROOKIES 201-240: 1.2X TO 3X
201-240 ROOKIE PRINT RUN 100

2002 Ultra League Leaders

This 27-card set was inserted at a rate of 1:6 and features some of the NFL's statistical leaders from the 2001 season.
COMPLETE SET (27) 15.00 40.00
STATED ODDS 1:6
1 Brett Favre 1.50 4.00
2 Kurt Warner .60 1.50
3 Marshall Faulk .60 1.50
4 Daunte Culpepper .60 1.50
5 LaDainian Tomlinson .75 2.00
6 Jeff Garcia .50 1.25
7 Terrell Owens .60 1.50
8 Zach Thomas .60 1.50
9 Brian Urlacher .75 2.00
10 Corey Dillon .50 1.25
11 David Boston .50 1.25
12 Donovan McNabb .60 1.50
13 Anthony Thomas .60 1.50
14 Priest Holmes .50 1.25
15 Torry Holt .60 1.50
16 Marvin Harrison .60 1.50
17 Stephen Davis .50 1.25
18 Michael Strahan .60 1.50
19 Rod Smith .60 1.50
20 Ray Lewis .75 2.00
21 Curtis Martin .60 1.50
22 Aaron Brooks .50 1.25
23 Antowain Smith .60 1.50
24 Eddie George .60 1.50
25 Emmitt Smith 1.25 3.00
26 Laveranues Coles .60 1.50
27 Ricky Williams .60 1.50

2002 Ultra League Leaders Memorabilia

This 18-card set is a partial parallel to the League Leaders set. Inserted at a rate of 1:20 packs, these cards each contain a piece of game used memorabilia. A Platinum Medallion version numbered of 25 also was produced.
STATED ODDS 1:20 HOB, 1:80 RET
*PLATINUM MED/25: 1.2X TO 3X BASIC JSY
PLATINUM MEDALLION PRINT RUN 25
1 Aaron Brooks 2.50 6.00
2 Laveranues Coles 3.00 8.00
3 Daunte Culpepper 3.00 8.00
4 Stephen Davis 2.50 6.00
5 Marshall Faulk 3.00 8.00
6 Jeff Garcia 2.50 6.00
7 Eddie George 3.00 8.00
8 Torry Holt 3.00 8.00
9 Curtis Martin 3.00 8.00
10 Donovan McNabb 3.00 8.00
11 Terrell Owens 3.00 8.00
12 Antowain Smith 3.00 8.00
13 Emmitt Smith 6.00 15.00
14 Anthony Thomas 3.00 8.00
15 LaDainian Tomlinson 4.00 10.00
16 Brian Urlacher 4.00 10.00
17 Kurt Warner 3.00 8.00
18 Ricky Williams 3.00 8.00

2002 Ultra LOGO Rhythm

This 22-card set features some of the NFL's best and brightest. Cards were inserted at a rate of 1:12 packs.
COMPLETE SET (22) 15.00 40.00
STATED ODDS 1:12
1 Brett Favre 2.00 5.00
2 Kurt Warner .75 2.00
3 Marshall Faulk .75 2.00
4 Daunte Culpepper .75 2.00
5 LaDainian Tomlinson 1.00 2.50
6 Jeff Garcia .60 1.50
7 Terrell Owens .75 2.00
8 Zach Thomas .75 2.00
9 Brian Urlacher 1.00 2.50
10 Drew Brees 2.00 5.00
11 Rich Gannon .75 2.00
12 Germane Crowell .60 1.50
13 Brian Griese .60 1.50
14 Mark Brunell .75 2.00
15 Ron Dayne .75 2.00
16 Jake Plummer .60 1.50
17 Ray Lewis 1.00 2.50
18 Corey Dillon .60 1.50
19 Kordell Stewart .60 1.50
20 Donovan McNabb .75 2.00
21 Michael Vick .75 2.00
22 Chad Pennington .60 1.50

2002 Ultra LOGO Rhythm Memorabilia

This 12-card set is a partial parallel to the Logo Rhythm set. Inserted at a rate of 1:96 packs, these cards each contain a piece of game used memorabilia.
STATED ODDS 1:96 HOB, 1:192 RET
1 Germane Crowell 2.50 6.00
2 Daunte Culpepper 3.00 8.00
3 Marshall Faulk 3.00 8.00
4 Jeff Garcia 2.50 6.00
5 Brian Griese 2.50 6.00
6 Donovan McNabb 3.00 8.00
7 Terrell Owens 3.00 8.00
8 Chad Pennington 2.50 6.00
9 LaDainian Tomlinson 4.00 10.00
10 Brian Urlacher 4.00 10.00
11 Michael Vick 3.00 8.00
12 Kurt Warner 3.00 8.00

2002 Ultra San Diego Bound

This 20-card set was inserted at a rate of 1:72, and gives you a sneak preview at some players who may appear in the 2003 Super Bowl in San Diego.
COMPLETE SET (20) 40.00 100.00
STATED ODDS 1:72
1 Brett Favre 4.00 10.00
2 Kurt Warner 1.50 4.00
3 Marshall Faulk 1.50 4.00
4 Daunte Culpepper 1.50 4.00
5 LaDainian Tomlinson 2.00 5.00
6 Jeff Garcia 1.25 3.00
7 Terrell Owens 1.50 4.00
8 Zach Thomas 1.50 4.00
9 Brian Urlacher 2.00 5.00
10 Drew Brees 4.00 10.00
11 Donovan McNabb 1.50 4.00
12 Brian Griese 1.25 3.00
13 Marvin Harrison 1.50 4.00
14 Tim Couch 1.25 3.00
15 Anthony Thomas 1.50 4.00
16 Tom Brady 10.00 25.00
17 Michael Vick 1.50 4.00
18 Fred Taylor 1.25 3.00
19 Chad Pennington 1.25 3.00
20 Trung Canidate 1.25 3.00

2002 Ultra San Diego Bound Memorabilia

This 15-card set is a partial parallel to the San Diego Bound set. Inserted at a rate of 1:48 packs, these cards each contain a piece of game used memorabilia. A Platinum Medallion version numbered of 25 also exists.
STATED ODDS 1:48 HOB, 1:96 RET
*PLATINUM MED: .8X TO 2X BASIC JSY
*PLATINUM MED: .6X TO 1.5X BASIC JSY SP
PLATINAM MEDALLION PRINT RUN 25
1 Tom Brady 20.00 50.00
2 Tim Couch 2.50 6.00
3 Daunte Culpepper 3.00 8.00
4 Marshall Faulk SP 4.00 10.00
5 Jeff Garcia 2.50 6.00
6 Brian Griese 2.50 6.00
7 Donovan McNabb 3.00 8.00
8 Terrell Owens 3.00 8.00
9 Chad Pennington 2.50 6.00
10 Fred Taylor 2.50 6.00
11 Anthony Thomas 3.00 8.00
12 LaDainian Tomlinson 4.00 10.00
13 Brian Urlacher 4.00 10.00
14 Michael Vick 3.00 8.00
15 Kurt Warner 3.00 8.00

2003 Ultra

This 198-card set was released in May, 2003. The set was issued in eight-card packs with an SRP of $2.99 and those packs were issued 24 to a box. The first 160 cards are veterans, while the final 38 cards are rookies. Those rookie cards were issued at a stated rate of one in four.
COMP.SET w/o SP's (160) 12.50 30.00
ROOKIE 161-198 ODDS 1:4
ROOKIE U199-U218 ODDS 1:4
1 Rich Gannon .25 .60
2 Warren Sapp .25 .60
3 Steve McNair .25 .60
4 Donovan McNabb .25 .60
5 Chad Pennington .20 .50
6 Michael Vick .25 .60
7 Hines Ward .25 .60
8 Terrell Owens .25 .60
9 Brett Favre .60 1.50
10 Jeremy Shockey .20 .50
11 William Green .20 .50
12 Marvin Harrison .25 .60
13 Mark Brunell .25 .60
14 Todd Heap .20 .50
15 Tim Couch .20 .50
16 Javon Walker .25 .60
17 Zach Thomas .25 .60
18 Brian Westbrook .20 .50
19 Matt Hasselbeck .20 .50
20 Jevon Kearse .20 .50
21 David Boston .20 .50
22 Michael Bennett .20 .50
23 James Mungro .20 .50
24 Antowain Smith .25 .60
25 Laveranues Coles .20 .50
26 Curtis Conway .20 .50
27 Peerless Price .20 .50
28 Michael Strahan .25 .60
29 Tommy Maddox .20 .50
30 Dennis Northcutt .20 .50
31 Rod Gardner .20 .50
32 Marcel Shipp .20 .50
33 Quincy Morgan .20 .50
34 Reggie Wayne .25 .60
35 Troy Brown .20 .50
36 John Abraham .25 .60
37 Tim Dwight .20 .50
38 Jamal Lewis .25 .60
39 Chad Hutchinson .20 .50
40 Jerramy Stevens .25 .60
41 Deion Branch .20 .50
42 Jake Plummer .20 .50
43 Junior Seau .25 .60
44 T.J. Duckett .20 .50
45 Emmitt Smith .50 1.25
46 Edgerrin James .25 .60
47 David Patten .20 .50
48 Charlie Garner .25 .60
49 Quentin Jammer .20 .50
50 Corey Dillon .20 .50
51 Rod Smith .25 .60
52 Marc Boerigter .20 .50
53 Michael Lewis .20 .50
54 Kendrell Bell .20 .50
55 Isaac Bruce .30 .75
56 Warrick Dunn .20 .50
57 Antonio Bryant .20 .50
58 Peyton Manning .75 2.00
59 Ty Law .30 .75
60 Jerry Rice .60 1.50
61 Jeff Garcia .20 .50
62 Joey Galloway .25 .60
63 Aaron Glenn .20 .50
64 Aaron Brooks .20 .50
65 Tim Brown .30 .75
66 David Terrell .20 .50
67 Fred Smoot .20 .50
68 Brian Finneran .20 .50
69 Roy Williams .20 .50
70 Corey Bradford .20 .50
71 Deuce McAllister .25 .60
72 Jerry Porter .20 .50
73 Kevan Barlow .20 .50
74 Keith Brooking .25 .60
75 Brian Urlacher .30 .75
76 Jabar Gaffney .20 .50
77 Randy Moss .25 .60
78 Charles Woodson .30 .75
79 Darrell Jackson .25 .60
80 John Lynch .25 .60
81 Chester Taylor .25 .60
82 Anthony Thomas .25 .60
83 Jonathan Wells .20 .50
84 Daunte Culpepper .25 .60
85 Phillip Buchanon .20 .50
86 Koren Robinson .25 .60
87 Ronde Barber .20 .50
88 Julius Peppers .30 .75
89 Clinton Portis .20 .50
90 Jay Fiedler .20 .50
91 Donte Stallworth .20 .50
92 Marc Bulger .20 .50
93 Joe Jurevicius .25 .60
94 Jon Kitna .20 .50
95 Ricky Williams .25 .60
96 Joe Horn .20 .50
97 Jerome Bettis .30 .75
98 Kurt Warner .25 .60
99 Travis Henry .20 .50
100 Ahman Green .25 .60
101 Jimmy Smith .25 .60
102 Curtis Martin .25 .60
103 Simeon Rice .20 .50
104 Patrick Ramsey .25 .60
105 Josh Reed .20 .50
106 James Stewart .20 .50
107 Trent Green .20 .50
108 Randy McMichael .20 .50
109 Amos Zereoue .20 .50
110 Keyshawn Johnson .30 .75
111 DeShaun Foster .25 .60
112 Kevin Johnson .20 .50
113 Dwight Freeney .20 .50
114 Tom Brady 1.25 3.00

115 Santana Moss .25 .60
116 LaDainian Tomlinson .30 .75
117 Joey Harrington .20 .50
118 Priest Holmes .20 .50
119 Amani Toomer .20 .50
120 Plaxico Burress .20 .50
121 Brad Johnson .25 .60
122 Champ Bailey .25 .60
123 Muhsin Muhammad .20 .50
124 Ashley Lelie .20 .50
125 Tony Gonzalez .25 .60
126 Kerry Collins .20 .50
127 Antwaan Randle El .20 .50
128 Torry Holt .25 .60
129 Ladell Betts .20 .50
130 Travis Taylor .20 .50
131 Marty Booker .20 .50
132 Patrick Surtain .20 .50
133 Duce Staley .20 .50
134 Shaun Alexander .20 .50
135 Eddie George .25 .60
136 Eric Moulds .20 .50
137 David Carr .20 .50
138 Fred Taylor .20 .50
139 Wayne Chrebet .20 .50
140 Bobby Taylor .25 .60
141 Derrick Brooks .20 .50
142 Stephen Davis .20 .50
143 Ray Lewis .30 .75
144 Kelly Holcomb .20 .50
145 Terry Glenn .25 .60
146 Jason Taylor .25 .60
147 Todd Pinkston .20 .50
148 Derrick Mason .20 .50
149 Chad Johnson .20 .50
150 Ed McCaffrey .25 .60
151 Tiki Barber .25 .60
152 Drew Brees .30 .75
153 Marshall Faulk .25 .60
154 Drew Bledsoe .25 .60
155 Andre Davis .20 .50
156 Donald Driver .25 .60
157 Chris Chambers .20 .50
158 Brian Dawkins .30 .75
159 Garrison Hearst .20 .50
160 Frank Wycheck .20 .50
161 Carson Palmer RC 2.00 5.00
162 Byron Leftwich RC 1.25 3.00
163 Charles Rogers RC 1.25 3.00
164 Andre Johnson RC 2.50 6.00
165 Chris Simms RC 1.00 2.50
166 Rex Grossman RC 1.25 3.00
167 Brandon Lloyd RC 1.50 4.00
168 Lee Suggs RC 1.00 2.50
169 Larry Johnson RC 1.25 3.00
170 Onterrio Smith RC 1.00 2.50
171 Dave Ragone RC 1.00 2.50
172 Taylor Jacobs RC 1.00 2.50
173 Kelley Washington RC 1.00 2.50
174 Bryant Johnson RC 1.50 4.00
175 Kyle Boller RC 1.00 2.50
176 Ken Dorsey RC 1.25 3.00
177 Kliff Kingsbury RC 1.50 4.00
178 Jason Gesser RC 1.25 3.00
179 Brian St.Pierre RC 1.00 2.50
180 Brad Banks RC 1.25 3.00
181 Seneca Wallace RC 1.25 3.00
182 Tony Romo RC 12.00 30.00
183 Terrell Suggs RC 1.25 3.00
184 Terence Newman RC 1.50 4.00
185 Willis McGahee RC 1.25 3.00
186 Justin Fargas RC 1.50 4.00
187 Musa Smith RC 1.00 2.50
188 Earnest Graham RC 1.50 4.00
189 Chris Brown RC 1.00 2.50
190 LaBrandon Toefield RC 1.00 2.50
191 Bennie Joppru RC 1.00 2.50
192 Jason Witten RC 4.00 10.00
193 Anquan Boldin RC 1.50 4.00
194 Talman Gardner RC 1.00 2.50
195 Justin Gage RC 1.25 3.00
196 Sam Aiken RC 1.25 3.00
197 Kevin Curtis RC 1.00 2.50
198 Terrence Edwards RC 1.00 2.50
U199 DeWayne Robertson RC 1.25 3.00
U200 Kevin Williams RC 1.50 4.00
U201 Marcus Trufant RC 1.25 3.00
U202 Jimmy Kennedy RC 1.25 3.00
U203 Ty Warren RC 1.25 3.00
U204 Michael Haynes RC 1.00 2.50
U205 Jerome McDougle RC 1.00 2.50
U206 Dallas Clark RC 1.50 4.00
U207 William Joseph RC 1.00 2.50
U208 Andre Woolfolk RC 1.00 2.50
U209 Bethel Johnson RC 1.00 2.50
U210 Teyo Johnson RC 1.25 3.00
U211 Tyrone Calico RC 1.00 2.50
U212 L.J. Smith RC 1.50 4.00
U213 Nate Burleson RC 1.25 3.00
U214 B.J. Askew RC 1.25 3.00
U215 Billy McMullen RC 1.00 2.50
U216 Domanick Davis RC 1.25 3.00
U217 Doug Gabriel RC 1.25 3.00
U218 Quentin Griffin RC 1.25 3.00

2003 Ultra Gold Medallion

*VETS 1-160: 1.5X TO 4X BASIC CARDS
*ROOKIES 161-198: .5X TO 1.2X
ONE GOLD MEDALLION PER PACK
182 Tony Romo 20.00 50.00

2003 Ultra Platinum Medallion

*VETS 1-160: 6X TO 15X BASIC CARDS
*ROOKIES 161-98: 2X TO 5X
STATED PRINT RUN 100 SER.#'d SETS
182 Tony Romo 60.00 150.00

2003 Ultra Autographs

Randomly inserted in packs, these four cards feature authentic autographs of leading NFL prospects. We have provided the stated print runs of the cards next to their names in our checklist. The print runs were provided by Fleer.
ANNOUNCED PRINT RUN 300-350
UAJ Andre Johnson/300* 25.00 60.00
UBL Byron Leftwich/300* 10.00 25.00
UCP Carson Palmer/300* 15.00 40.00
ULJ Larry Johnson/350* 10.00 25.00

2003 Ultra Award Winners

Inserted at a stated rate of one in 12, this 10-card set features players who won important NFL awards for the 2002 season.
COMPLETE SET (10) 7.50 20.00
STATED ODDS 1:12
1 Priest Holmes .60 1.50
2 Clinton Portis .60 1.50
3 Rich Gannon .75 2.00
4 Derrick Brooks .60 1.50
5 Michael Vick .75 2.00
6 Jeremy Shockey .60 1.50
7 Ricky Williams .75 2.00
8 Marvin Harrison .75 2.00
9 Chad Pennington .60 1.50
10 Tommy Maddox .60 1.50

2003 Ultra Award Winners Memorabilia

Inserted at a stated rate of one in 25, these 14 cards feature not only a major award winner but also a game-used memorabilia piece pertaining to that player's career.
STATED ODDS 1:25
*ULTRSWTCH/55-88: .8X TO 2X BASE JSY
*ULTRSWTCH/31-34: 1.2X TO 3X BASE JSY
*ULTRSWTCH/20-28: 1.5X TO 4X BASE JSY
ULTRASWATCH PRINT RUN 7-88
AWCP Clinton Portis 2.50 6.00
AWCP2 Chad Pennington 2.50 6.00
AWDB Derrick Brooks 2.50 6.00
AWDM Deuce McAllister 3.00 8.00
AWJS Jeremy Shockey 2.50 6.00
AWLT LaDainian Tomlinson 4.00 10.00
AWMF Marshall Faulk 3.00 8.00
AWMH Marvin Harrison 3.00 8.00
AWMV Michael Vick 3.00 8.00
AWPH Priest Holmes 2.50 6.00
AWRG Rich Gannon 3.00 8.00
AWRW Ricky Williams 3.00 8.00
AWTH Travis Henry 2.50 6.00
AWTO Terrell Owens 3.00 8.00

2003 Ultra Head of the Class

Randomly inserted in packs, these 16 cards featured some of the leading players selected in the 2003 NFL draft. These cards were issued to a stated print run of 599 serial numbered sets.
STATED PRINT RUN 599 SER.#'d SETS
1 Carson Palmer 2.00 5.00
2 Byron Leftwich 1.25 3.00
3 Charles Rogers 1.25 3.00
4 Andre Johnson 2.50 6.00
5 Chris Simms 1.00 2.50
6 Rex Grossman 1.25 3.00
7 Brandon Lloyd 1.50 4.00
8 Lee Suggs 1.00 2.50
9 Larry Johnson 1.25 3.00
10 Onterrio Smith 1.00 2.50
11 Dave Ragone 1.00 2.50
12 Taylor Jacobs 1.00 2.50
13 Kelley Washington 1.00 2.50
14 Bryant Johnson 1.50 4.00
15 Willis McGahee 1.25 3.00
NNO Carson Palmer JSY/1500 10.00 25.00

2003 Ultra Touchdown Kings

Issued at a stated rate of one in 24, these 15 cards feature players who are among the best in putting the ball in their opponents end zone.
COMPLETE SET (15) 25.00 50.00
STATED ODDS 1:24
1 Jerry Rice 3.00 8.00
2 Peyton Manning 4.00 10.00
3 Randy Moss 1.25 3.00
4 Tom Brady 6.00 15.00
5 Brett Favre 3.00 8.00
6 Drew Bledsoe 1.25 3.00
7 Steve McNair 1.25 3.00
8 Emmitt Smith 2.50 6.00
9 Priest Holmes 1.00 2.50
10 Michael Vick 1.25 3.00
11 Chad Pennington 1.00 2.50
12 Donovan McNabb 1.25 3.00
13 Shaun Alexander 1.00 2.50
14 Ricky Williams 1.25 3.00
15 Clinton Portis 1.00 2.50

2003 Ultra Touchdown Kings Memorabilia

Inserted at a stated rate of one in 26, these cards parallle the basic Touchdown Kings insert set. These cards contain a game-used memorabilia swatch on them.
STATED ODDS 1:26
*CAREER/326: .5X TO 1.2X BASE JSY
*CAREER/147-202: .6X TO 1.5X BASE JSY
*CAREER/60-103: .8X TO 2X BASE JSY
*CAREER/35-47: 1.2X TO 3X BASE JSY
*CAREER26-27: 1.5X TO 4X BASE JSY
CAREER PRINT RUN 17-326
*ULTRSWTCH/31-34: 1.2X TO 3X BASE JSY
*ULTRSWTCH/20-28: 1.5X TO 4X BASE JSY
ULTRASWATCH PRINT RUN 2-37
TKBF Brett Favre 8.00 20.00
TKCP Clinton Portis 2.50 6.00
TKCP2 Chad Pennington 2.50 6.00
TKDB Drew Bledsoe 3.00 8.00
TKDM Donovan McNabb 3.00 8.00
TKES Emmitt Smith 6.00 15.00
TKJR Jerry Rice 8.00 20.00
TKMV Michael Vick 3.00 8.00
TKPH Priest Holmes 2.50 6.00
TKPM Peyton Manning 10.00 25.00
TKRM Randy Moss 3.00 8.00
TKRW Ricky Williams 3.00 8.00
TKSA Shaun Alexander 2.50 6.00
TKSM Steve McNair 3.00 8.00
TKTB Tom Brady 15.00 40.00

2004 Ultra

Ultra released in May of 2004 and was Fleer's first football product of the year. The base set consists of 232-cards including 200-veterans and 32-rookies. Thirteen of the rookies were designated as "Lucky 13" with only 500-copies produced of each card. Mike Williams is part of the Lucky 13 although he was declared ineligible for the NFL Draft. Hobby and retail boxes both contained 24-packs of 8-cards with an SRP of $2.99 for hobby and $1.99 for retail packs. Two parallel sets and a large section of inserts with a variety of game-used versions can be found seeded in packs. Insert highlights include Season Crowns Autographs and a triple signed Manning Family Passing Kings card. A 20-card Update set was included in packs of 2004 Fleer Tradition. Each of these cards was seeded two-per rookie hot pack in the product with one hot pack in every box on average. Some signed cards were issued via mail-in exchange or redemption cards with a number of those EXCH cards not yet appearing live on the secondary market as of the printing of this book.
COMP.SET w/o L13's (218) 25.00 60.00
COMP.SET w/o SP's (200) 12.50 30.00
COMP.UPDATE SET (21) 15.00 40.00
201-213 L13 ROOKIE/500 ODDS 1:100H,1:530R
214-232 ROOKIE ODDS 1:4H,1:6R
U234-U254 ODDS 2:1 TRADITION HOT PACK
1 Michael Vick .25 .60
2 Kelley Washington .20 .50
3 Rex Grossman .20 .50
4 Boss Bailey .20 .50
5 Johnnie Morton .25 .60
6 Michael Strahan .25 .60
7 Joey Porter .25 .60
8 Keenan McCardell .20 .50
9 Quincy Carter .20 .50
10 Travis Henry .20 .50
11 Bertrand Berry .25 .60
12 Marvin Harrison .25 .60
13 Ty Law .30 .75
14 Phillip Buchanon .25 .60
15 Kevan Barlow .20 .50
16 Eddie George .25 .60
17 Drew Bledsoe .25 .60
18 Antonio Bryant .25 .60
19 Marcus Pollard .20 .50
20 Brian Russell RC .20 .50
21 Santana Moss .25 .60
22 Julian Peterson .25 .60
23 Justin McCareins .20 .50
24 Ed Reed .25 .60
25 Charles Tillman .25 .60
26 Dat Nguyen .20 .50
27 Ricky Manning .20 .50
28 Dwight Freeney .20 .50
29 Zach Thomas .25 .60
30 Tiki Barber .25 .60
31 Jay Riemersma .20 .50
32 Joe Jurevicius .20 .50
33 Marcel Shipp .20 .50
34 Justin Gage .25 .60
35 Charles Rogers .20 .50
36 Eddie Kennison .25 .60
37 Deion Branch .20 .50
38 Matt Hasselbeck .20 .50
39 L.J. Smith .25 .60
40 Jamal Lewis .25 .60
41 Muhsin Muhammad .20 .50
42 Terence Newman .25 .60
43 Jabar Gaffney .20 .50
44 Junior Seau .30 .75
45 Jeremy Shockey .20 .50
46 Hines Ward .25 .60
47 Brad Johnson .25 .60
48 Kyle Boller .20 .50
49 Steve Smith .30 .75
50 Quincy Morgan .20 .50
51 Corey Bradford .20 .50
52 Ricky Williams .25 .60
53 Amani Toomer .20 .50
54 Plaxico Burress .20 .50
55 Derrick Brooks .20 .50
56 Dre Bly .20 .50
57 Terrell Suggs .20 .50
58 DeShaun Foster .25 .60
59 Andre Davis .20 .50
60 Rod Smith .25 .60
61 Andre Johnson .25 .60
62 Randy McMichael .20 .50
63 Ike Hilliard .20 .50
64 Antwaan Randle El .20 .50
65 Warren Sapp .25 .60
66 LaBrandon Toefield .20 .50
67 Chad Johnson .20 .50
68 Javon Walker .20 .50
69 Jimmy Smith .25 .60
70 Donte Stallworth .20 .50
71 Brian Dawkins .20 .50
72 Leonard Little .20 .50
73 Ladell Betts .20 .50
74 Ray Lewis .30 .75
75 Stephen Davis .20 .50
76 Dennis Northcutt .20 .50
77 Ashley Lelie .20 .50
78 Billy Miller .20 .50
79 Chris Chambers .20 .50
80 John Abraham .20 .50
81 Quentin Jammer .20 .50
82 Isaac Bruce .30 .75
83 Peerless Price .20 .50
84 Jake Delhomme .20 .50
85 Lee Suggs .25 .60
86 Shannon Sharpe .25 .60
87 Domanick Davis .20 .50
88 Daunte Culpepper .25 .60
89 Shaun Ellis .20 .50
90 Drew Brees .30 .75
91 Torry Holt .25 .60
92 Alge Crumpler .25 .60
93 Mike Rucker .20 .50
94 Tim Couch .25 .60
95 Quentin Griffin .20 .50
96 David Carr .20 .50
97 Moe Williams .20 .50
98 Chad Pennington .20 .50
99 LaDainian Tomlinson .30 .75
100 Adam Archuleta .20 .50
101 Julius Peppers .25 .60
102 Clinton Portis .20 .50
103 Marcus Stroud .20 .50
104 Tom Brady 1.25 3.00
105 Teyo Johnson .20 .50
106 Terrell Owens .25 .60
107 Keith Bulluck .20 .50
108 Eric Moulds .20 .50
109 Jake Plummer .20 .50
110 Reggie Wayne .25 .60
111 Tedy Bruschi .25 .60
112 Rich Gannon .25 .60
113 Tony Parrish .20 .50
114 Steve McNair .25 .60
115 T.J. Duckett .20 .50
116 Peter Warrick .20 .50
117 Donald Driver .25 .60
118 Fred Taylor .20 .50
119 Joe Horn .20 .50
120 Jerry Porter .20 .50
121 Marc Bulger .20 .50
122 Trung Canidate .20 .50
123 Warrick Dunn .20 .50
124 Kelly Holcomb .20 .50
125 Robert Ferguson .20 .50
126 Byron Leftwich .20 .50
127 Michael Lewis .25 .60
128 Jerry Rice .60 1.50
129 Marshall Faulk .25 .60
130 Patrick Ramsey .25 .60
131 Josh McCown .25 .60
132 Anthony Thomas .25 .60
133 Joey Harrington .20 .50
134 Dante Hall .20 .50
135 Daniel Graham .20 .50
136 Richard Seymour .20 .50
137 Brandon Lloyd .25 .60
138 Anquan Boldin .20 .50
139 Jon Kitna .20 .50
140 Nick Barnett .20 .50
141 Priest Holmes .20 .50
142 Bethel Johnson .20 .50
143 Shaun Alexander .20 .50
144 Todd Heap .20 .50
145 Brian Urlacher .30 .75
146 Peyton Manning .75 2.00
147 Jason Taylor .25 .60
148 Kerry Collins .20 .50
149 Tommy Maddox .20 .50
150 Charles Lee .20 .50
151 Tim Rattay .20 .50
152 Carson Palmer .25 .60
153 Brett Favre .60 1.50
154 Trent Green .20 .50
155 Aaron Brooks .20 .50
156 Brian Westbrook .20 .50
157 Itula Mili .20 .50
158 Keith Brooking .20 .50
159 Rudi Johnson .20 .50
160 Najeh Davenport .20 .50
161 Kevin Johnson .20 .50
162 Boo Williams .20 .50
163 Corey Simon .25 .60
164 Darrell Jackson .25 .60
165 Darnerien McCants .20 .50
166 Willis McGahee .20 .50
167 Terry Glenn .25 .60
168 Dallas Clark .20 .50
169 Randy Moss .25 .60
170 Charles Woodson .30 .75
171 Jeff Garcia .20 .50
172 Chris Brown .20 .50
173 Emmitt Smith .50 1.25
174 Marty Booker .20 .50
175 Artose Pinner .20 .50
176 Tony Gonzalez .25 .60
177 Troy Brown .20 .50
178 Freddie Mitchell .20 .50
179 Marcus Trufant .20 .50
180 London Fletcher .25 .60
181 Roy Williams S .20 .50
182 Edgerrin James .25 .60
183 Michael Bennett .20 .50
184 Jerald Sowell .20 .50
185 David Boston .20 .50
186 Derrick Mason .20 .50
187 Bryant Johnson .20 .50
188 Corey Dillon .20 .50
189 Ahman Green .25 .60
190 Vonnie Holliday .20 .50
191 Deuce McAllister .25 .60
192 Donovan McNabb .25 .60
193 Koren Robinson .20 .50
194 Laveranues Coles .20 .50
195 Takeo Spikes .20 .50
196 Richie Anderson .20 .50
197 Onterrio Smith .20 .50
198 Curtis Martin .25 .60
199 Antonio Gates .30 .75
200 Champ Bailey .25 .60
201 Eli Manning L13 RC 15.00 40.00
202 Philip Rivers L13 RC 10.00 25.00
203 Roy Williams L13 RC 3.00 8.00
204 Drew Henson L13 RC 3.00 8.00
205 Chris Perry L13 RC 3.00 8.00
206 Larry Fitzgerald L13 RC 10.00 25.00
207 Rashaun Woods L13 RC 3.00 8.00
208 Reggie Williams L13 RC 3.00 8.00
209 Mike Williams L13 RC 4.00 10.00
210 Kellen Winslow L13 RC 3.00 8.00
211 Steven Jackson L13 RC 5.00 12.00
212 Kevin Jones L13 RC 4.00 10.00
213 Ben Roethlisberger L13 RC 20.00 50.00
214 Michael Turner RC .75 2.00
215 Tatum Bell RC .75 2.00
216 Quincy Wilson RC .75 2.00
217 Devery Henderson RC .75 2.00
218 Ernest Wilford RC 1.00 2.50
219 Cody Pickett RC .75 2.00
220 Ryan Dinwiddie RC .75 2.00
221 J.P. Losman RC .75 2.00
222 Derrick Knight RC .75 2.00
223 Michael Jenkins RC .75 2.00
224 Greg Jones RC .75 2.00
225 Cedric Cobbs RC .75 2.00
226 Will Poole RC 1.25 3.00
227 Michael Clayton RC 1.00 2.50
228 Sean Taylor RC 5.00 12.00
229 Will Smith RC 1.00 2.50
230 Jonathan Vilma RC 1.00 2.50
231 Lee Evans RC 1.25 3.00
232 Julius Jones RC .75 2.00
U234 D.J. Williams RC 1.25 3.00
U235 Mewelde Moore RC 1.00 2.50
U236 Ben Watson RC 1.00 2.50
U237 Robert Gallery RC 1.00 2.50
U238 DeAngelo Hall RC 1.25 3.00
U239 Luke McCown RC .75 2.00
U240 Ben Troupe RC .75 2.00
U241 Keary Colbert RC .75 2.00
U242 Matt Schaub RC .75 2.00
U243 Kenechi Udeze RC 1.00 2.50
U244 Jeff Smoker RC 1.00 2.50
U245 Derrick Hamilton RC .75 2.00
U246 Bernard Berrian RC .75 2.00
U247 Devard Darling RC .75 2.00
U248 Johnnie Morant RC .75 2.00
U249 Vince Wilfork RC 1.25 3.00
U250 Jerricho Cotchery RC 1.00 2.50
U251 Darius Watts RC .75 2.00
U252 Carlos Francis RC .75 2.00
U253 P.K. Sam RC .75 2.00

2004 Ultra Gold Medallion

*VETS: 1.5X TO 4X BASIC CARDS
*ROOKIES 201-213: .12X TO .3X
*ROOKIES 214-232: .4X TO 1X
OVERALL STATED ODDS 1:1H,1:3R
ROOKIE 201-232 ODDS 1:8H,1:12R
201 Eli Manning L13 12.00 30.00
213 Ben Roethlisberger L13 12.00 30.00

2004 Ultra Platinum Medallion

*VETS 1-200: 10X TO 25X BASIC CARDS
*ROOKIES 214-232: 2X TO 5X
1-200/214-232 PLAT/66 ODDS 1:45 HOB
1-200/214-232 PRINT RUN 66 #'d SETS
UNPRICED L13 201-213 ODDS 1:3650

2004 Ultra Update Draft Day

*DRAFT DAY/375: .6X TO 1.5X BASIC CARDS
STATED PRINT RUN 375 SER.#'d SETS

2004 Ultra Gridiron Producers

ATED ODDS 1:144H,1:288R
1GP Donovan McNabb 1.50 4.00
2GP Charles Rogers 1.25 3.00
3GP Daunte Culpepper 1.50 4.00
4GP Matt Hasselbeck 1.25 3.00
5GP Jerry Rice 4.00 10.00
6GP Tom Brady 8.00 20.00
7GP Byron Leftwich 1.25 3.00
8GP Ahman Green 1.50 4.00
9GP Stephen Davis 1.25 3.00
10GP LaDainian Tomlinson 2.00 5.00

2004 Ultra Gridiron Producers Game Used Copper

OVERALL GAME USED/AUTO ODDS 1:12
*GOLD/77: .6X TO 1.5X COPPER
GOLD PRINT RUN 77 SER.#'d SETS
UNPRICED PLATINUM PRINT RUN 9
*ULTRASWATCH/48-80: .6X TO 1.5X COPPER
*ULTRASWATCH/21-30: .8X TO 2X COPPER
*ULTRASWATCH/11-12: 1X TO 2.5X COPPER
ULTRASWATCH PRINT RUN 5-84
GPAG Ahman Green 4.00 10.00
GPBL Byron Leftwich 3.00 8.00
GPCR Charles Rogers 3.00 8.00
GPDC Daunte Culpepper 4.00 10.00
GPDM Donovan McNabb 4.00 10.00
GPJR Jerry Rice 10.00 25.00
GPLT LaDainian Tomlinson 5.00 12.00
GPMH Matt Hasselbeck 3.00 8.00
GPSD Stephen Davis 3.00 8.00
GPTB Tom Brady 15.00 40.00

2004 Ultra Hummer H2 In Package

These 6-cards were actually issued in a blister package with a 1:64 scale Hummer H2 die-cast vehicle. One of these Hummer/card packages were inserted in each 2004 Fleer Platinum hobby box. The cards appear at first glance to be base 2004 Ultra cards but differ in that they are not "Lucky 13" versions like the base cards not are they serial numbered. Prices below reflect that of single cards out of the packaging.
*SINGLE CARDS: .3X TO .8X PACKAGE
201 Eli Manning 6.00 12.00
202 Philip Rivers 3.00 8.00
204 Drew Henson 1.50 4.00
206 Larry Fitzgerald 3.00 6.00
210 Kellen Winslow 2.00 5.00
213 Ben Roethlisberger 6.00 12.00

2004 Ultra Passing Kings

COMPLETE SET (10) 12.00 30.00
OVERALL KINGS ODDS 1:12H,1:24R
*GOLD/50: 1.5X TO 4X BASIC INSERTS
GOLD PRINT RUN 50 SER.#'d SETS
1PA Brett Favre 2.50 6.00
2PA Donovan McNabb 1.00 2.50
3PA Peyton Manning 3.00 8.00
4PA Steve McNair 1.00 2.50
5PA Daunte Culpepper 1.00 2.50
6PA Tom Brady 5.00 12.00
7PA Byron Leftwich .75 2.00
8PA Joey Harrington .75 2.00
9PA Matt Hasselbeck .75 2.00
10PA Marc Bulger .75 2.00
NNO Manning Family AU/50 400.00 600.00

2004 Ultra Performers

COMPLETE SET (15) 12.50 30.00
STATED ODDS 1:6H,1:8R
*GOLD DIE CUT: .4X TO 1X BASIC INSERTS
ONE GOLD PER RETAIL PACK
1UP Tom Brady 3.00 8.00
2UP Clinton Portis .50 1.25
3UP Priest Holmes .50 1.25
4UP Marshall Faulk .60 1.50
5UP Randy Moss .60 1.50
6UP Marvin Harrison .60 1.50
7UP Donovan McNabb .60 1.50
8UP Ricky Williams .60 1.50
9UP Brett Favre 1.50 4.00
10UP Steve McNair .60 1.50
11UP Peyton Manning 2.00 5.00
12UP Shaun Alexander .50 1.25
13UP Edgerrin James .60 1.50
14UP Chad Johnson .50 1.25
15UP Torry Holt .60 1.50

2004 Ultra Performers Game Used Copper

OVERALL GAME USED/AUTO ODDS 1:12
*GOLD/89: .6X TO 1.5X COPPER
GOLD PRINT RUN 88 SER.# SETS
*PLATINUM: 1.2X TO 3X COPPER
PLATINUM PRINT RUN 19 #'d SETS
*ULTRASWATCH/81-88: .6X TO 1.5X COP
*ULTRASWATCH/26-37: .8X TO 2X COP
*ULTRASWATCH/12-18: 1X TO 2.5X COP
ULTRASWATCH PRINT RUN 4-88
UPBF Brett Favre 10.00 25.00
UPCJ Chad Johnson 3.00 8.00
UPCP Clinton Portis 3.00 8.00
UPDM Donovan McNabb 4.00 10.00
UPEJ Edgerrin James 4.00 10.00
UPMF Marshall Faulk 4.00 10.00
UPMH Marvin Harrison 4.00 10.00
UPPH Priest Holmes 3.00 8.00
UPPM Peyton Manning 12.00 30.00
UPRM Randy Moss 4.00 10.00
UPRW Ricky Williams 4.00 10.00
UPSA Shaun Alexander 3.00 8.00
UPSM Steve McNair 4.00 10.00
UPTB Tom Brady 20.00 50.00
UPTH Torry Holt 4.00 10.00

2004 Ultra Receiving Kings

MPLETE SET (10) 8.00 20.00
OVERALL KINGS ODDS 1:12H,1:24R
*GOLD/50: 2X TO 5X BASIC INSERTS
GOLD PRINT RUN 50 SER.#'d SETS
1RE Randy Moss .75 2.00
2RE Torry Holt .75 2.00
3RE Anquan Boldin .60 1.50
4RE Chad Johnson .60 1.50
5RE Derrick Mason .60 1.50
6RE Marvin Harrison .75 2.00
7RE Laveranues Coles .60 1.50
8RE Terrell Owens .75 2.00
9RE Charles Rogers .60 1.50
10RE Jerry Rice 2.00 5.00

2004 Ultra Rushing Kings

MPLETE SET (10) 10.00 25.00
OVERALL KINGS ODDS 1:12H,1:24R
*GOLD/50: 2X TO 5X BASIC INSERTS
GOLD PRINT RUN 50 SER.#'d SETS
1RU Clinton Portis .60 1.50
2RU Priest Holmes .60 1.50
3RU Stephen Davis .60 1.50
4RU Marshall Faulk .75 2.00
5RU LaDainian Tomlinson 1.00 2.50
6RU Shaun Alexander .60 1.50
7RU Deuce McAllister .75 2.00
8RU Ricky Williams .75 2.00
9RU Jamal Lewis .75 2.00
10RU Ahman Green .75 2.00

2004 Ultra Season Crowns Autographs

ATED PRINT RUN 25-150
GOLD STATED PRINT RUN 25
1 Kyle Boller/150 5.00 12.00
2 Plaxico Burress/150 5.00 12.00
3 David Carr/150 5.00 12.00
4 LaDainian Tomlinson/150 30.00 60.00
6 Donovan McNabb/25 30.00 80.00
7 Matt Hasselbeck/70 8.00 20.00
8 Philip Rivers/150 30.00 60.00
9 Roy Williams WR/150 5.00 12.00
10 Eli Manning/150 75.00 135.00
11 Dante Hall/150 5.00 12.00
12 Brian Westbrook/150 5.00 12.00
13 Jake Delhomme/150 5.00 12.00
14 Kelley Washington/150 5.00 12.00
15 Joe Jurevicius/150 5.00 12.00
16 Byron Leftwich/150 8.00 20.00
17 Shaun Alexander/150 8.00 20.00
18 Drew Henson/150 5.00 12.00
19 Deuce McAllister/150 6.00 15.00
21 Steven Jackson/150 8.00 20.00
22 Will Poole/150 8.00 20.00

2004 Ultra Season Crowns Game Used Copper

PPER PRINT RUN 349 SER.#'d SETS
*GOLD/99: .6X TO 1.5X COPPER
GOLD PRINT RUN 99 SER.#'d SETS
*PLATINUM/29: 1X TO 2.5X COPPER
PLATINUM PRINT RUN 29 SER.#'d SETS
*SILVER/149: .5X TO 1.2X COPPER
SILVER PRINT RUN 149 SER.#'d SETS
1 Rex Grossman 2.50 6.00
2 Julius Peppers 3.00 8.00
3 Antwaan Randle El 2.50 6.00
4 Charles Rogers 2.50 6.00
5 Brian Urlacher 4.00 10.00
6 Carson Palmer 3.00 8.00
7 Priest Holmes 2.50 6.00
8 Travis Henry 2.50 6.00
9 Andre Johnson 3.00 8.00
10 Marvin Harrison 3.00 8.00
11 Randy Moss 3.00 8.00
12 Corey Dillon 2.50 6.00
13 Ray Lewis 4.00 10.00
14 Ricky Williams 3.00 8.00
15 Peyton Manning Pants 10.00 25.00
16 Michael Bennett 2.50 6.00
17 Torry Holt 3.00 8.00
18 Deuce McAllister 3.00 8.00
19 Deion Branch 2.50 6.00
20 DeShaun Foster 3.00 8.00
21 Edgerrin James 3.00 8.00
22 Steve McNair 3.00 8.00
23 Brett Favre 8.00 20.00
24 Chad Pennington 2.50 6.00
25 Brad Johnson 3.00 8.00
26 Fred Taylor 2.50 6.00
27 Michael Vick 3.00 8.00
28 Derrick Brooks 2.50 6.00
29 LaDainian Tomlinson 4.00 10.00
30 Warren Sapp 3.00 8.00
31 Byron Leftwich 2.50 6.00
32 Donovan McNabb 3.00 8.00
33 Ahman Green 3.00 8.00
34 Emmitt Smith 6.00 15.00
35 Tommy Maddox 2.50 6.00
36 Shaun Alexander 2.50 6.00
37 Joey Harrington 2.50 6.00
38 Marshall Faulk 3.00 8.00
39 Jerry Rice 8.00 20.00
40 T.J. Duckett 2.50 6.00
41 Eric Moulds 2.50 6.00
42 Tom Brady 15.00 40.00
43 David Carr 2.50 6.00
44 Daunte Culpepper 3.00 8.00
45 Isaac Bruce 4.00 10.00
46 Chad Johnson 2.50 6.00
47 Jeremy Shockey 2.50 6.00
48 Eddie George 3.00 8.00
49 Quincy Carter 2.50 6.00
50 Aaron Brooks 2.50 6.00

2004 Ultra Three Kings Game Used

ATED PRINT RUN 33 SER.#'d SETS
FHB M.Faulk/Holt/Bulger 15.00 40.00
GMT A.Green/McAll/Tmlinsn 20.00 50.00
HHL Hassel/Harring/Leftwich 12.00 30.00
HMR M.Harris/R.Moss/Rice 40.00 80.00
HWF Holmes/Ri.Will/Faulk 20.00 50.00
JRB Ch.Johnson/Rogers/Boldin 12.00 30.00
LAD Jam.Lewis/S.Alex/St.Davis 15.00 40.00
MBF P.Manning/Brady/Favre 75.00 150.00
MMC McNair/McNbb/Culpep 20.00 50.00
ORM T.Owens/Rice/R.Moss 40.00 80.00

2005 Ultra

This 248-card set was released in January, 2006. This set was issued in the hobby in eight-card packs with an $2.99 SRP which came 24 packs to a box. The first 200 cards in the set feature veterans while cards numbered 201-213 featured 13 leading 2005 NFL rookies with cards numbered 214-248 being other NFL rookies. The cards 201-213 were issued to a stated print run of 599 serial numbered sets. For all the rookies, the stated odds on those cards were in four hobby and one in five retail.
COMP.SET w/o RC's (200) 12.50 30.00
201-213 L13 PRINT RUN 599 SER.#'d SETS
OVERALL ROOKIE ODDS 1:4 HOB, 1:5 RET
1 Peyton Manning .75 2.00
2 Brian Westbrook .20 .50
3 Daunte Culpepper .25 .60
4 Marvin Harrison .25 .60
5 Edgerrin James .25 .60
6 Reggie Wayne .25 .60
7 Michael Vick .25 .60
8 Donte Stallworth .20 .50
9 Brian Urlacher .30 .75
10 Hines Ward .25 .60
11 Charles Rogers .20 .50
12 Roy Williams WR .20 .50
13 Julius Peppers .25 .60
14 Eric Moulds .20 .50
15 Ray Lewis .30 .75
16 Byron Leftwich .20 .50
17 Fred Taylor .20 .50
18 Andre Johnson .25 .60
19 Travis Henry .20 .50
20 Tom Brady 1.25 3.00
21 Drew Bledsoe .25 .60
22 Tiki Barber .25 .60
23 Larry Fitzgerald .30 .75
24 Jeff Garcia .20 .50
25 Rex Grossman .20 .50
26 Larry Johnson .20 .50
27 Curtis Martin .25 .60
28 Chad Pennington .20 .50
29 Dwight Freeney .20 .50
30 Peerless Price .20 .50
31 Rich Gannon .25 .60
32 Matt Hasselbeck .20 .50
33 Clinton Portis .20 .50
34 Jerry Rice .60 1.50
35 Jeremy Shockey .20 .50
36 Tony Gonzalez .25 .60
37 Deuce McAllister .25 .60
38 Shaun Alexander .20 .50
39 Peter Warrick .20 .50
40 Isaac Bruce .30 .75
41 Antonio Bryant .20 .50
42 Mike Alstott .20 .50
43 Domanick Davis .20 .50
44 Jake Delhomme .20 .50
45 Santana Moss .25 .60
46 Ahman Green .25 .60
47 David Carr .20 .50
48 Kyle Boller .20 .50
49 Chris Chambers .20 .50
50 Quentin Griffin .20 .50
51 Donovan McNabb .25 .60
52 Eli Manning .50 1.25
53 Julius Jones .20 .50
54 Sean Taylor .30 .75
55 Javon Walker .20 .50
56 Randy Moss .25 .60
57 Thomas Jones .20 .50
58 Joey Harrington .20 .50
59 Michael Boulware .20 .50
60 Marshall Faulk .25 .60
61 Tony Parrish .20 .50
62 Bertrand Berry .20 .50
63 Alge Crumpler .25 .60
64 Aaron Brooks .20 .50
65 Muhsin Muhammad .20 .50
66 Simeon Rice .20 .50
67 Corey Dillon .20 .50
68 Willis McGahee .20 .50
69 Ben Roethlisberger .50 1.25
70 Chad Johnson .20 .50
71 Jamal Lewis .25 .60
72 Drew Brees .30 .75
73 LaDainian Tomlinson .30 .75
74 Reuben Droughns .20 .50
75 Priest Holmes .20 .50
76 Jerry Porter .20 .50
77 Chris Brown .20 .50
78 Steve McNair .25 .60
79 Troy Brown .20 .50
80 Jerome Bettis .30 .75
81 Patrick Kerney .20 .50
82 Terrell Owens .25 .60
83 Brett Favre .60 1.50
84 Carson Palmer .25 .60
85 Jake Plummer .20 .50
86 Tedy Bruschi .25 .60
87 Plaxico Burress .20 .50
88 Jonathan Vilma .20 .50
89 Ed Reed .25 .60
90 Brian Dawkins .30 .75
91 Anquan Boldin .20 .50
92 Vinny Testaverde .20 .50
93 David Givens .20 .50
94 Rudi Johnson .20 .50
95 Philip Rivers .30 .75
96 Jimmy Smith .25 .60
97 Emmitt Smith .60 1.50
98 Eric Johnson .20 .50
99 Jeremiah Trotter .20 .50
100 Duce Staley .20 .50
101 Warrick Dunn .20 .50
102 Nate Burleson .20 .50
103 Marc Bulger .20 .50
104 Joe Horn .20 .50
105 Rodney Harrison .20 .50
106 Zach Thomas .25 .60
107 Michael Clayton .20 .50
108 Derrick Brooks .20 .50
109 Michael Lewis .20 .50
110 Kurt Warner .25 .60
111 Jason Witten .25 .60
112 Roy Williams S .20 .50
113 Kabeer Gbaja-Biamila .20 .50
114 Torry Holt .25 .60
115 Tim Rattay .20 .50
116 Josh McCown .25 .60
117 Brian Griese .20 .50
118 Patrick Ramsey .25 .60
119 A.J. Feeley .20 .50
120 Kerry Collins .20 .50
121 Trent Green .20 .50
122 Billy Volek .20 .50
123 Travis Taylor .20 .50
124 T.J. Houshmandzadeh .20 .50
125 James Farrior .20 .50
126 Bryan Scott .20 .50
127 Lito Sheppard .25 .60
128 David Patten .20 .50
129 Antwaan Randle El .20 .50
130 Antonio Gates .30 .75
131 Brandon Stokley .20 .50
132 Keyshawn Johnson .25 .60
133 Amani Toomer .20 .50
134 Shawn Springs .20 .50
135 Eddie George .25 .60
136 Kevin Jones .20 .50
137 Darrell Jackson .20 .50
138 Ricky Manning .20 .50
139 Laveranues Coles .20 .50
140 Champ Bailey .25 .60
141 Rod Smith .25 .60
142 Ashley Lelie .20 .50
143 Charles Woodson .30 .75
144 Drew Bennett .25 .60
145 Derrick Mason .20 .50
146 Donovin Darius .20 .50
147 Dennis Northcutt .20 .50
148 Jamie Sharper .20 .50
149 Steven Jackson .20 .50
150 David Terrell .20 .50
151 Onterrio Smith .20 .50
152 Donald Driver .25 .60
153 Antoine Winfield .25 .60
154 Michael Pittman .20 .50
155 Dan Morgan .20 .50
156 Troy Polamalu .30 .75
157 Willie McGinest .25 .60
158 Justin McCareins .20 .50
159 Allen Rossum .20 .50
160 Deion Branch .20 .50
161 Deion Sanders .25 .60
162 Josh Reed .20 .50
163 Lee Evans .25 .60
164 Lee Suggs .20 .50
165 Dante Hall .20 .50
166 Eddie Kennison .20 .50
167 Ken Dorsey .20 .50
168 Andre Dyson .20 .50
169 Keith Bulluck .20 .50
170 Todd Pinkston .20 .50
171 Jevon Kearse .20 .50
172 Dunta Robinson .20 .50
173 Steve Smith .30 .75
174 Koren Robinson .20 .50
175 Freddie Mitchell .20 .50
176 L.J. Smith .25 .60
177 Kevin Curtis .25 .60
178 Marcus Robinson .20 .50
179 Kellen Winslow .20 .50
180 Reggie Williams .20 .50
181 Bubba Franks .20 .50
182 J.P. Losman .20 .50
183 Chris Perry .20 .50
184 Michael Jenkins .20 .50
185 T.J. Duckett .20 .50
186 Rashaun Woods .20 .50
187 Ben Watson .25 .60
188 Bryant Johnson .20 .50
189 Dallas Clark .20 .50
190 William Green .20 .50
191 Daniel Graham .25 .60
192 Jerramy Stevens .25 .60
193 DeShaun Foster .25 .60
194 Nick Goings .20 .50
195 Ronald Curry .20 .50
196 Kevan Barlow .20 .50
197 Kevin Faulk .20 .50
198 Eric Parker .20 .50
199 Keenan McCardell .25 .60
200 LaMont Jordan .25 .60
201 Alex Smith QB L13 RC 12.00 30.00
202 Aaron Rodgers L13 RC 40.00 80.00
203 Cedric Benson L13 RC 5.00 12.00
204 Braylon Edwards L13 RC 5.00 12.00
205 Ronnie Brown L13 RC 12.00 30.00
206 Cadillac Williams L13 RC 5.00 12.00
207 Troy Williamson L13 RC 5.00 12.00
208 Mark Clayton L13 RC 5.00 12.00
209 Charlie Frye L13 RC 5.00 12.00
210 Mike Williams L13 6.00 15.00
211 Marion Barber L13 RC 5.00 12.00
212 Eric Shelton L13 RC 5.00 12.00
213 Antrel Rolle L13 RC 8.00 20.00
214 Heath Miller RC 2.50 6.00
215 Dan Cody RC 1.25 3.00
216 Adam Jones RC 1.25 3.00
217 Derrick Johnson RC 1.50 4.00
218 Alex Smith TE RC 1.25 3.00
219 Kyle Orton RC 1.25 3.00
220 David Pollack RC 1.25 3.00
221 Erasmus James RC 1.25 3.00
222 Justin Tuck RC 1.50 4.00
223 Jason Campbell RC 1.25 3.00
224 Dan Orlovsky RC 1.25 3.00
225 Thomas Davis RC 1.25 3.00
226 J.J. Arrington RC 1.50 4.00
227 Roddy White RC 2.00 5.00
228 David Greene RC 1.25 3.00
229 Ciatrick Fason RC 1.25 3.00
230 Chris Henry RC 1.50 4.00
231 Reggie Brown RC 1.25 3.00
232 Vernand Morency RC 1.25 3.00
233 Carlos Rogers RC 2.00 5.00
234 Ryan Moats RC 1.25 3.00
235 Roscoe Parrish RC 1.25 3.00
236 Terrence Murphy RC 1.25 3.00
237 Shawne Merriman RC 2.00 5.00
238 Courtney Roby RC 1.25 3.00
239 Mark Bradley RC 1.25 3.00
240 Marcus Spears RC 1.25 3.00
241 Justin Miller RC 1.25 3.00
242 Matt Jones RC 1.25 3.00
243 DeMarcus Ware RC 4.00 10.00
244 Fabian Washington RC 1.25 3.00
245 Marlin Jackson RC 1.25 3.00
246 Corey Webster RC 1.50 4.00
247 Brandon Jacobs RC 1.50 4.00
248 Frank Gore RC 2.50 6.00

2005 Ultra Gold Medallion

ETERANS: 1.2X TO 3X BASIC CARDS
*ROOKIES L13 201-213: .15X TO .4X
*ROOK.214-248: .4X TO 1X BASIC CARDS
OVERALL STATED ODDS 1:1 HOB, 1:3 RET
ROOKIE STATED ODDS 1:8 HOB, 1:12 RET
202 Aaron Rodgers L13 25.00 60.00

2005 Ultra Platinum Medallion

*VETERANS: 6X TO 15X BASIC CARDS
1-200 STATED PRINT RUN 50 SER.#'d SETS
UNPRICED L13 201-213 PRINT RUN 13 SETS
*ROOKIES 214-248: 2X TO 5X BASIC CARDS
214-248 STATED PRINT RUN 25 SER.#'d SETS

2005 Ultra All-Ultra Team Autographs Gold

OVERALL AUTO STATED ODDS 1:384

UNPRICED MASTERPIECES #'d TO 1
BB Bernard Berrian/49 7.50 20.00
BB1 Boss Bailey/66 7.50 20.00
CC Chris Chambers/26 12.50 30.00
DH Dante Hall/26 15.00 30.00
DS Donte Stallworth/27 15.00 30.00
JJ Julius Jones/26 30.00 60.00
JM Josh McCown/64 15.00 30.00
LF Larry Fitzgerald/21 25.00 60.00
LM Luke McCown/64 7.50 20.00
PR Philip Rivers/29 30.00 60.00
RB Ronde Barber/34 25.00 50.00
RW1 Reggie Williams/64 10.00 25.00
TB2 Troy Brown/26 15.00 40.00
WP Will Poole/51 7.50 20.00

2005 Ultra All-Ultra Team Autographs Platinum

PLATINUM PRINT RUN 25 SER.#'d SETS
BB Bernard Berrian 12.50 30.00
CC Chris Chambers 12.50 30.00
CP Chad Pennington 20.00 50.00
DF Doug Flutie 20.00 50.00
DH Dante Hall 12.50 30.00
EM Eli Manning 75.00 135.00
JJ Julius Jones 30.00 60.00
JM Josh McCown 10.00 25.00
LF Larry Fitzgerald 25.00 60.00
PB Plaxico Burress 12.50 30.00
PR Philip Rivers 20.00 50.00
RB Ronde Barber 25.00 60.00
RW1 Reggie Williams 20.00 50.00
RW2 Roy Williams WR 20.00 50.00
TB1 Tiki Barber 20.00 50.00
WP Will Poole 10.00 25.00

2005 Ultra All-Ultra Team Jerseys Gold

ERALL JERSEY STATED ODDS 1:12
*PLATINUM: .8X TO 2X BASIC JERSEYS
PLATINUM PRINT RUN 50 SER.#'d SETS
AB Antonio Bryant 2.00 5.00
AJ Andre Johnson 2.50 6.00
BF Brett Favre 6.00 15.00
BL Byron Leftwich 2.00 5.00
BU Brian Urlacher 3.00 8.00
BW Brian Westbrook 2.00 5.00
CC Chris Chambers 2.00 5.00
CM Curtis Martin 2.50 6.00
CP1 Chad Pennington 2.00 5.00
CP2 Clinton Portis 2.00 5.00
CR Charles Rogers 2.00 5.00
DB Drew Bledsoe 2.50 6.00
DC1 David Carr 2.00 5.00
DC2 Daunte Culpepper 2.50 6.00
DD Domanick Davis 2.00 5.00
DF Dwight Freeney 2.00 5.00
DM Deuce McAllister 2.50 6.00
DS Donte Stallworth 2.00 5.00
EJ Edgerrin James 2.50 6.00
EM Eric Moulds 2.00 5.00
FT Fred Taylor 2.00 5.00
HW Hines Ward 2.50 6.00
JD Jake Delhomme 2.00 5.00
JG Jeff Garcia 2.00 5.00
JJ Julius Jones 2.00 5.00
JP Julius Peppers 2.50 6.00
JR Jerry Rice 6.00 15.00
JS Jeremy Shockey 2.00 5.00
KB Kyle Boller 2.00 5.00
LF Larry Fitzgerald 3.00 8.00
LJ Larry Johnson 2.00 5.00
MA Mike Alstott 2.00 5.00
MH1 Marvin Harrison 2.50 6.00
MH2 Matt Hasselbeck 2.00 5.00
MV Michael Vick 2.50 6.00
PM Peyton Manning 8.00 20.00
PP Peerless Price 2.00 5.00
PW Peter Warrick 2.00 5.00
QG Quentin Griffin 2.00 5.00
RG1 Rich Gannon 2.50 6.00
RG2 Rex Grossman 2.00 5.00
RL Ray Lewis 3.00 8.00
RW1 Reggie Wayne 2.50 6.00
RW2 Roy Williams WR 2.00 5.00
SA Shaun Alexander 2.00 5.00
SM Santana Moss 2.50 6.00
TB Tiki Barber 2.50 6.00
TG Tony Gonzalez 2.50 6.00
TH Travis Henry 2.00 5.00

2005 Ultra First Rounders

ATED ODDS 1:12 HOB, 1:15 RET
1 Michael Vick 1.25 3.00
2 LaDainian Tomlinson 1.50 4.00
3 Daunte Culpepper 1.25 3.00
4 Eli Manning 2.50 6.00
5 Randy Moss 1.25 3.00
6 Ben Roethlisberger 2.50 6.00
7 Carson Palmer 1.25 3.00
8 Joey Harrington 1.00 2.50
9 David Carr 1.00 2.50
10 Steve McNair 1.25 3.00
11 Edgerrin James 1.25 3.00
12 Philip Rivers 1.50 4.00
13 Willis McGahee 1.00 2.50
14 Kevin Jones 1.00 2.50
15 Larry Fitzgerald 1.50 4.00

2005 Ultra First Rounders Jerseys Copper

COPPER PRINT RUN 150 SER.#'d SETS
*PLATINUM: 1X TO 2.5X COPPER
PLATINUM PRINT RUN 25 SER.#'d SETS
UNPRICED ULTRASWATCH #'d TO DRAFT #
BR Ben Roethlisberger 7.50 20.00
CP Carson Palmer 4.00 10.00
DC David Carr 3.00 8.00
DC Daunte Culpepper 4.00 10.00
EM Eli Manning 7.50 20.00
JH Joey Harrington 4.00 10.00
LT LaDainian Tomlinson 5.00 12.00
MV Michael Vick 6.00 15.00
RM Randy Moss 4.00 10.00
SM Steve McNair 4.00 10.00

2005 Ultra Sensations

ATED ODDS 1:24 HOB, 1:48 RET
1 Drew Brees 2.00 5.00
2 Ben Roethlisberger 3.00 8.00
3 Aaron Brooks 1.25 3.00
4 Marc Bulger 1.25 3.00
5 Jerome Bettis 2.00 5.00
6 Santana Moss 1.50 4.00
7 Anquan Boldin 1.25 3.00
8 Michael Vick 1.50 4.00
9 Marvin Harrison 1.50 4.00
10 Randy Moss 1.50 4.00
11 Brian Westbrook 1.25 3.00
12 Julius Jones 1.25 3.00
13 Antonio Gates 2.00 5.00
14 Tom Brady 8.00 20.00
15 Donovan McNabb 1.50 4.00

2005 Ultra Sensations Jerseys Copper

PPER PRINT RUN 150 SER.#'d SETS
*PLATINUM: 1X TO 2.5X COPPER
PLATINUM PRINT RUN 25 SER.#'d SETS
*ULTRASWATCH/81-88: .8X TO 2X COPPER
ULTRASWATCH SER.#'d TO JER.NUMBER
AB Aaron Brooks 3.00 8.00
AB Anquan Boldin 3.00 8.00
BR Ben Roethlisberger 10.00 25.00
DB Drew Brees 4.00 10.00
JB Jerome Bettis 4.00 10.00
MB Marc Bulger 3.00 8.00
MH Marvin Harrison 4.00 10.00
MV Michael Vick 6.00 15.00
RM Randy Moss 4.00 10.00
SM Santana Moss 3.00 8.00
TB Tom Brady 7.50 20.00

2005 Ultra TD Kings

ATED ODDS 1:6
*DIE CUTS: .3X TO .8X BASIC INSERTS
DIE CUTS TWO PER TARGET RETAIL
1 Shaun Alexander .75 2.00
2 Terrell Owens 1.00 2.50
3 Clinton Portis .75 2.00
4 Ahman Green 1.00 2.50
5 Torry Holt 1.00 2.50
6 Priest Holmes .75 2.00
7 Michael Vick 1.00 2.50
8 Peyton Manning 3.00 8.00
9 Donovan McNabb 1.00 2.50
10 Willis McGahee .75 2.00
11 Chad Johnson .75 2.00
12 Jamal Lewis 1.00 2.50
13 Marshall Faulk 1.00 2.50
14 Emmitt Smith 2.50 6.00
15 Brett Favre 2.50 6.00
16 Jerome Bettis 1.25 3.00
17 LaDainian Tomlinson 1.25 3.00
18 Muhsin Muhammad .75 2.00
19 Marvin Harrison 1.00 2.50
20 Corey Dillon .75 2.00

2005 Ultra TD Kings Jerseys Copper

OVERALL JERSEY STATED ODDS 1:12
*GOLD/250: .5X TO 1.2X COPPER
*PLATINUM/99: .6X TO 1.5X COPPER
*RED: .4X TO 1X COPPER
*ULTRASWATCH/30: .8X TO 2X COPPER
*ULTRASWATCH/49: .6X TO 1.5X COPPER
AG Ahman Green 3.00 8.00
BF Brett Favre 8.00 20.00
CJ Chad Johnson 2.50 6.00
CP Clinton Portis 2.50 6.00
DM Donovan McNabb 3.00 8.00
ES Emmitt Smith 8.00 20.00
JL Jamal Lewis 3.00 8.00
MF Marshall Faulk 3.00 8.00
MV Michael Vick 3.00 8.00
PH Priest Holmes 2.50 6.00
PM Peyton Manning 10.00 25.00
SA Shaun Alexander 2.50 6.00
TH Torry Holt 3.00 8.00
TO Terrell Owens 3.00 8.00
WM Willis McGahee 2.50 6.00

2006 Ultra

This 263-card set was released in June, 2006. The set was issued into the hobby in eight-card packs, with an $2.99 SRP, which came 24 packs to a box. The first 200 cards in the set feature veterans in alphabetical team order while cards numbered 201-263 all feature 2006 rookies. Cards numbered 201-213 were considered to be the most influential rookies in that crop and those cards were issued to a stated print run of 500 serial numbered sets. The overall odds of getting any rookie from a pack was stated to be one in four.

COMP.SET w/o RC's (200) 12.50 30.00
201-213 L13 PRINT RUN 500 SER.#'d SETS
OVERALL ROOKIE ODDS 1:4
1 Larry Fitzgerald .25 .60
2 Anquan Boldin .20 .50
3 Kurt Warner .25 .60
4 Bryant Johnson .20 .50
5 Marcel Shipp .20 .50
6 J.J. Arrington .20 .50
7 Michael Vick .25 .60
8 Warrick Dunn .20 .50
9 T.J. Duckett .20 .50
10 Alge Crumpler .25 .60
11 Michael Jenkins .20 .50
12 DeAngelo Hall .20 .50
13 Kyle Boller .20 .50
14 Jamal Lewis .25 .60
15 Todd Heap .20 .50
16 Derrick Mason .20 .50
17 Ray Lewis .30 .75
18 Terrell Suggs .20 .50
19 J.P. Losman .25 .60
20 Willis McGahee .20 .50
21 Eric Moulds .20 .50
22 Lee Evans .25 .60
23 Roscoe Parrish .20 .50
24 Kelly Holcomb .20 .50
25 Jake Delhomme .20 .50
26 Steve Smith .30 .75
27 Stephen Davis .20 .50
28 Julius Peppers .25 .60
29 DeShaun Foster .25 .60
30 Keary Colbert .20 .50
31 Chris Gamble .20 .50
32 Kyle Orton .20 .50
33 Thomas Jones .20 .50
34 Rex Grossman .20 .50
35 Muhsin Muhammad .20 .50
36 Brian Urlacher .30 .75
37 Adrian Peterson .25 .60
38 Carson Palmer .25 .60
39 Chad Johnson .20 .50
40 Rudi Johnson .20 .50
41 Chris Perry .25 .60
42 T.J. Houshmandzadeh .20 .50
43 Chris Henry .20 .50
44 Deltha O'Neal .20 .50
45 Trent Dilfer .20 .50
46 Reuben Droughns .25 .60
47 Antonio Bryant .20 .50
48 Braylon Edwards .20 .50
49 Charlie Frye .25 .60
50 Dennis Northcutt .20 .50
51 Drew Bledsoe .25 .60
52 Julius Jones .20 .50
53 Keyshawn Johnson .25 .60
54 Jason Witten .25 .60
55 Roy Williams S .20 .50
56 Marion Barber .25 .60
57 Terry Glenn .25 .60
58 Jake Plummer .20 .50
59 Mike Anderson .20 .50
60 Champ Bailey .25 .60
61 Tatum Bell .20 .50
62 Rod Smith .25 .60
63 Ashley Lelie .20 .50
64 Joey Harrington .20 .50
65 Kevin Jones .20 .50
66 Roy Williams WR .20 .50
67 Mike Williams .20 .50
68 Marcus Pollard .20 .50
69 Jeff Garcia .20 .50
70 Brett Favre .60 1.50
71 Javon Walker .25 .60
72 Donald Driver .25 .60
73 Samkon Gado .20 .50
74 Najeh Davenport .20 .50
75 Robert Ferguson .20 .50
76 David Carr .20 .50
77 Domanick Davis .20 .50
78 Andre Johnson .25 .60
79 Jabar Gaffney .20 .50
80 Corey Bradford .20 .50
81 Dunta Robinson .20 .50
82 Peyton Manning .75 2.00
83 Edgerrin James .25 .60
84 Marvin Harrison .25 .60
85 Reggie Wayne .25 .60
86 Dallas Clark .20 .50
87 Dwight Freeney .20 .50
88 Cato June .25 .60
89 Byron Leftwich .20 .50
90 Fred Taylor .20 .50
91 Jimmy Smith .25 .60
92 Matt Jones .20 .50
93 Ernest Wilford .20 .50
94 Greg Jones .20 .50
95 Trent Green .20 .50
96 Priest Holmes .20 .50
97 Larry Johnson .20 .50
98 Tony Gonzalez .25 .60
99 Dante Hall .20 .50
100 Eddie Kennison .20 .50
101 Gus Frerotte .20 .50
102 Chris Chambers .20 .50
103 Ronnie Brown .25 .60
104 Ricky Williams .20 .50
105 Randy McMichael .20 .50
106 Zach Thomas .25 .60
107 Daunte Culpepper .25 .60
108 Nate Burleson .20 .50
109 Michael Bennett .20 .50
110 Mewelde Moore .20 .50
111 Troy Williamson .20 .50
112 Travis Taylor .20 .50
113 Jermaine Wiggins .20 .50
114 Tom Brady 1.00 2.50
115 Corey Dillon .20 .50
116 Deion Branch .20 .50
117 Tedy Bruschi .25 .60
118 David Givens .25 .60
119 Patrick Pass .20 .50
120 Aaron Brooks .20 .50
121 Deuce McAllister .25 .60
122 Joe Horn .20 .50
123 Donte Stallworth .20 .50
124 Antowain Smith .20 .50
125 Devery Henderson .20 .50
126 Eli Manning .25 .60
127 Tiki Barber .25 .60
128 Jeremy Shockey .20 .50
129 Plaxico Burress .20 .50
130 Amani Toomer .20 .50
131 Michael Strahan .25 .60
132 Chad Pennington .20 .50
133 Curtis Martin .25 .60
134 Jonathan Vilma .20 .50
135 Laveranues Coles .20 .50
136 Justin McCareins .20 .50
137 Ty Law .30 .75
138 Kerry Collins .20 .50
139 LaMont Jordan .25 .60
140 Randy Moss .25 .60
141 Jerry Porter .20 .50
142 Doug Gabriel .20 .50
143 Zack Crockett .20 .50
144 Donovan McNabb .25 .60
145 Brian Westbrook .20 .50
146 Terrell Owens .25 .60
147 Jevon Kearse .20 .50
148 L.J. Smith .20 .50
149 Greg Lewis .20 .50
150 Ben Roethlisberger .40 1.00
151 Willie Parker .25 .60
152 Hines Ward .25 .60
153 Jerome Bettis .30 .75
154 Antwaan Randle El .20 .50
155 Heath Miller .20 .50
156 Joey Porter .20 .50
157 Drew Brees .30 .75
158 LaDainian Tomlinson .30 .75
159 Antonio Gates .30 .75
160 Keenan McCardell .25 .60
161 Donnie Edwards .20 .50
162 Shawne Merriman .25 .60
163 Eric Parker .20 .50
164 Alex Smith .25 .60
165 Kevan Barlow .20 .50
166 Frank Gore .25 .60
167 Brandon Lloyd .20 .50
168 Eric Johnson .20 .50
169 Julian Peterson .20 .50
170 Matt Hasselbeck .20 .50
171 Shaun Alexander .20 .50
172 Darrell Jackson .25 .60
173 Joe Jurevicius .20 .50
174 Jerramy Stevens .25 .60
175 D.J. Hackett .20 .50
176 Marc Bulger .20 .50
177 Steven Jackson .20 .50
178 Torry Holt .25 .60
179 Isaac Bruce .30 .75
180 Kevin Curtis .25 .60
181 Marshall Faulk .25 .60
182 Chris Simms .20 .50
183 Cadillac Williams .25 .60
184 Michael Pittman .20 .50
185 Michael Clayton .20 .50
186 Joey Galloway .25 .60
187 Brian Griese .20 .50
188 Steve McNair .25 .60
189 Chris Brown .20 .50
190 Drew Bennett .25 .60
191 Travis Henry .20 .50
192 Ben Troupe .20 .50
193 Billy Volek .20 .50
194 Erron Kinney .20 .50
195 Mark Brunell .25 .60
196 Santana Moss .25 .60
197 Clinton Portis .20 .50
198 Chris Cooley .20 .50
199 Ladell Betts .20 .50
200 Sean Taylor .30 .75
201 Matt Leinart L13 RC 6.00 15.00
202 Vince Young L13 RC 6.00 15.00
203 Reggie Bush L13 RC 10.00 25.00
204 D'Brick Ferguson L13 RC 6.00 15.00
205 DeAngelo Williams L13 RC 8.00 20.00
206 Jay Cutler L13 RC 8.00 20.00
207 A.J. Hawk L13 RC 8.00 20.00
208 Mario Williams L13 RC 10.00 25.00
209 Santonio Holmes L13 RC 8.00 20.00
210 Chad Greenway L13 RC 10.00 25.00
211 Laurence Maroney L13 RC 6.00 15.00
212 LenDale White L13 RC 6.00 15.00
213 Sinorice Moss L13 RC 6.00 15.00
214 A.J. Nicholson RC 1.25 3.00
215 Abdul Hodge RC 1.25 3.00
216 Jeremy Bloom RC 1.25 3.00
217 Anthony Fasano RC 1.25 3.00
218 Bobby Carpenter RC 1.25 3.00
219 Brian Calhoun RC 1.25 3.00
220 Brodie Croyle RC 1.25 3.00
221 Chad Jackson RC 1.25 3.00
222 Charlie Whitehurst RC 1.25 3.00
223 Claude Wroten RC 1.25 3.00
224 Darnell Bing RC 1.50 4.00
225 Darrell Hackney RC 1.50 4.00
226 David Thomas RC 1.25 3.00
227 Demetrius Williams RC 1.25 3.00
228 Derek Hagan RC 1.50 4.00
229 Devin Hester RC 2.50 6.00
230 Dominique Byrd RC 1.25 3.00
231 D'Qwell Jackson RC 1.25 3.00
232 Elvis Dumervil RC 2.00 5.00
233 Haloti Ngata RC 1.50 4.00
234 Hank Baskett RC 1.25 3.00
235 Jason Avant RC 1.25 3.00
236 Jerome Harrison RC 1.25 3.00
237 Jimmy Williams RC 1.25 3.00
238 Joe Klopfenstein RC 1.25 3.00
239 Joseph Addai RC 1.25 3.00
240 Kellen Clemens RC 1.25 3.00
241 Cory Rodgers RC 1.25 3.00
242 Leon Washington RC 1.25 3.00
243 Leonard Pope RC 2.00 5.00
244 Marcedes Lewis RC 1.25 3.00
245 Martin Nance RC 1.25 3.00
246 Mathias Kiwanuka RC 2.00 5.00
247 Maurice Drew RC 2.00 5.00
248 Maurice Stovall RC 1.25 3.00
249 Michael Huff RC 1.50 4.00
250 Mike Hass RC 1.25 3.00
251 Omar Jacobs RC 1.25 3.00
252 Orien Harris RC 1.50 4.00
253 Owen Daniels RC 2.00 5.00
254 Reggie McNeal RC 1.25 3.00
255 DeMeco Ryans RC 1.50 4.00
256 Tamba Hali RC 2.00 5.00
257 Ernie Sims RC 1.25 3.00
258 Thomas Howard RC 1.25 3.00
259 Todd Watkins RC 1.25 3.00
260 Travis Wilson RC 1.25 3.00
261 Greg Lee RC 1.25 3.00
262 Tye Hill RC 1.25 3.00
263 Vernon Davis RC 1.50 4.00

2006 Ultra Gold Medallion

*VETS 1-200: 1.2X TO 3X BASIC CARDS
1-200 STATED ODDS 1:1
*ROOKIE L13: .25X TO .6X BASIC CARDS
201-213 L13 ROOKIE ODDS 1:288H,1:960R
*ROOKIE 214-263: .6X TO 1.5X BASIC CARDS
14-263 ROOKIE ODDS 1:24 H, 1:72 R

2006 Ultra Platinum Medallion

*VETS 1-200: 4X TO 10X BASIC CARDS
*ROOKIE 214-263: 1.5X TO 4X
1-200/214-263 PRINT 99 SER.#'d SETS
*ROOKIE L13: .6X TO 1.5X BASIC CARDS
201-213 ROOK.L13 PRINT 25 SER.#'d SETS
201 Matt Leinart L13 75.00 150.00
202 Vince Young L13 75.00 200.00
203 Reggie Bush L13 40.00 100.00
206 Jay Cutler L13 30.00 60.00
207 A.J. Hawk L13 60.00 120.00

2006 Ultra Achievements

COMPLETE SET (15) 6.00 15.00
STATED ODDS 1:6
UAAB Anquan Boldin .60 1.50
UACD Corey Dillon .60 1.50
UACM Curtis Martin .75 2.00
UADB Drew Bledsoe .75 2.00
UADC Daunte Culpepper .75 2.00
UAHW Hines Ward .75 2.00
UALF Larry Fitzgerald .75 2.00
UALT LaDainian Tomlinson 1.00 2.50
UAMF Marshall Faulk .75 2.00
UAMH Marvin Harrison .75 2.00
UAMV Michael Vick .75 2.00
UAPH Priest Holmes .60 1.50
UASA Shaun Alexander .60 1.50
UASM Steve McNair .75 2.00
UATB Tom Brady 3.00 8.00

2006 Ultra Achievements Jerseys

STATED ODDS 1:72 HOB, 1:144 RET
UAAB Anquan Boldin 2.50 6.00
UACD Corey Dillon 2.50 6.00
UACM Curtis Martin 3.00 8.00
UADB Drew Bledsoe 3.00 8.00
UADC Daunte Culpepper 3.00 8.00
UAHW Hines Ward 3.00 8.00
UALF Larry Fitzgerald 3.00 8.00
UALT LaDainian Tomlinson 4.00 10.00
UAMF Marshall Faulk 3.00 8.00
UAMH Marvin Harrison 3.00 8.00
UAMV Michael Vick 3.00 8.00
UAPH Priest Holmes 2.50 6.00
UASA Shaun Alexander 2.50 6.00
UASM Steve McNair 3.00 8.00
UATB Tom Brady 12.00 30.00

2006 Ultra Autographics

STATED ODDS 1:288 HOB, 1:960 RET
ULAJ A.J. Hawk SP
ULBF Brett Favre SP
ULBG Brad Smith
ULBQ Bruce Gradkowski 8.00 20.00
ULCG Chad Greenway 8.00 20.00
ULCP Carson Palmer SP
ULCR Cory Rodgers 8.00 20.00
ULDE Demetrius Williams 8.00 20.00
ULDF D'Brickashaw Ferguson 8.00 20.00
ULDH Derek Hagan 8.00 20.00
ULDO Drew Olson 8.00 15.00
ULDR DeMeco Ryans SP
ULDW DeAngelo Williams SP 25.00 60.00
ULEM Eli Manning SP 50.00 100.00
ULGR Gerald Riggs 8.00 20.00
ULHB Hank Baskett 8.00 20.00
ULJA Jason Avant 8.00 20.00
ULJN Jerious Norwood 12.00 30.00
ULKO Kyle Orton SP 8.00 20.00
ULLE LenDale White SP
ULLT LaDainian Tomlinson SP 50.00 100.00
ULMI Mike Bell 8.00 20.00
ULMK Mathias Kiwanuka 10.00 25.00
ULML Matt Leinart SP 25.00 60.00
ULMN Martin Nance 8.00 20.00
ULMO DonTrell Moore 6.00 15.00
ULMV Michael Vick SP
ULPH Paul Hornung SP 30.00 60.00
ULPM Peyton Manning SP
ULRB Reggie Bush SP 20.00 50.00
ULRJ Rudi Johnson SP 10.00 25.00
ULRM Reggie McNeal 8.00 20.00
ULRW Reggie Wayne SP
ULSI Sinorice Moss SP 10.00 25.00
ULTB Tiki Barber SP
ULTJ T.J. Houshmandzadeh SP
ULTR Travis Wilson 8.00 20.00
ULVD Vernon Davis SP

2006 Ultra Award Winners

COMPLETE SET (15) 6.00 15.00
STATED ODDS 1:6
UAAAB Anquan Boldin .60 1.50
UAABF Brett Favre 2.00 5.00
UAABR Ben Roethlisberger 1.25 3.00
UAACM Curtis Martin .75 2.00
UAACW Cadillac Williams .75 2.00
UAAER Ed Reed .75 2.00
UAAJV Jonathan Vilma .60 1.50
UAAKW Kurt Warner .75 2.00
UAAMB Marc Bulger .60 1.50
UAAMF Marshall Faulk .75 2.00
UAAPH Priest Holmes .60 1.50
UAARL Ray Lewis 1.00 2.50
UAARM Randy Moss .75 2.00
UAASM Steve McNair .75 2.00
UAATS Terrell Suggs .60 1.50

2006 Ultra Award Winners Jerseys

STATED ODDS 1:72 HOB, 1:144 RET
UAAAB Anquan Boldin 2.50 6.00
UAABF Brett Favre SP 8.00 20.00
UAABR Ben Roethlisberger 5.00 12.00
UAACM Curtis Martin 3.00 8.00
UAACW Cadillac Williams 3.00 8.00
UAAER Ed Reed 3.00 8.00
UAAJV Jonathan Vilma 2.50 6.00
UAAKW Kurt Warner 3.00 8.00
UAAMB Marc Bulger 2.50 6.00
UAAMF Marshall Faulk 3.00 8.00
UAAPH Priest Holmes 2.50 6.00
UAARL Ray Lewis 4.00 10.00
UAARM Randy Moss 3.00 8.00
UAASM Steve McNair 3.00 8.00
UAATS Terrell Suggs 2.50 6.00

2006 Ultra Campus Classics

STATED ODDS 1:12 HOB, 1:24 RET
CCAG Archie Griffin 1.00 2.50
CCBA Barry Sanders 2.50 6.00
CCBF Brett Favre 4.00 10.00
CCBO Bo Jackson 1.50 4.00
CCBS Billy Sims 1.00 2.50
CCCJ Chad Johnson 1.00 2.50
CCCP Carson Palmer 1.50 4.00
CCCW Charles White 1.00 2.50
CCDA Dan Fouts 1.00 2.50
CCDF Doug Flutie 1.00 2.50
CCDM Dan Marino 4.00 10.00
CCEC Earl Campbell 1.50 4.00
CCFT Fran Tarkenton 1.50 4.00
CCGR George Rogers 1.00 2.50
CCHW Herschel Walker 1.00 2.50
CCJH John Hannah .75 2.00
CCJK Joe Klecko .75 2.00
CCJP Jim Plunkett 1.00 2.50
CCJR Johnny Rodgers 1.50 4.00
CCJT Joe Theismann 1.50 4.00
CCKJ Keyshawn Johnson 1.00 2.50
CCKO Kyle Orton 1.00 2.50
CCLJ LaMont Jordan 1.00 2.50
CCMA Marcus Allen 1.50 4.00
CCMG Mike Garrett .75 2.00
CCMV Michael Vick 1.50 4.00
CCNM Nat Moore .75 2.00
CCPH Paul Hornung 1.00 2.50
CCPM Peyton Manning 3.00 8.00
CCRI Rocket Ismail 1.00 2.50
CCRJ Rudi Johnson 1.00 2.50
CCRS Roger Staubach 2.00 5.00
CCRW Reggie Wayne 1.00 2.50
CCSY Steve Young 2.00 5.00
CCTA Troy Aikman 2.00 5.00
CCTB Tiki Barber 1.00 2.50
CCTD Tony Dorsett 1.50 4.00
CCTJ T.J. Houshmandzadeh .75 2.00

2006 Ultra Campus Classics Autographs

STATED PRINT RUN 25 SER.#'d SETS
CCBA Barry Sanders 75.00 150.00
CCBF Brett Favre 150.00 250.00
CCBS Billy Sims 15.00 40.00
CCCP Carson Palmer 15.00 40.00
CCCW Charles White 15.00 40.00
CCDA Dan Fouts 25.00 60.00
CCDF Doug Flutie 20.00 50.00
CCDM Dan Marino 150.00 250.00
CCFT Fran Tarkenton 20.00 50.00
CCHW Herschel Walker 30.00 60.00
CCJH John Hannah 15.00 40.00
CCJK Joe Klecko
CCJR Johnny Rodgers 30.00 60.00
CCJT Joe Theismann 20.00 50.00
CCKJ Keyshawn Johnson
CCKO Kyle Orton 15.00 40.00
CCMV Michael Vick 30.00 60.00
CCNM Nat Moore
CCPH Paul Hornung
CCPM Peyton Manning 100.00 200.00
CCRI Rocket Ismail 20.00 50.00
CCRJ Rudi Johnson 12.00 30.00
CCRS Roger Staubach 60.00 120.00
CCSY Steve Young 30.00 80.00
CCTJ T.J. Houshmandzadeh 12.00 30.00

2006 Ultra Dream Team

TWO PER JUMBO PACK
UDTAC Alge Crumpler .60 1.50
UDTAG Antonio Gates .75 2.00
UDTBA Tiki Barber .60 1.50
UDTBD Brian Dawkins .75 2.00
UDTBF Brett Favre 1.50 4.00
UDTBR Ben Roethlisberger 1.00 2.50
UDTBS Bob Sanders .60 1.50
UDTBU Brian Urlacher .75 2.00
UDTCB Champ Bailey .60 1.50
UDTCJ Chad Johnson .50 1.25
UDTCP Carson Palmer .60 1.50
UDTDB Derrick Brooks .50 1.25
UDTDF Dwight Freeney .50 1.25
UDTDH DeAngelo Hall .50 1.25
UDTEJ Edgerrin James .60 1.50
UDTER Ed Reed .60 1.50
UDTGL Terry Glenn .60 1.50
UDTJP Joey Porter .50 1.25
UDTJS Jeremy Shockey .50 1.25
UDTJT Jason Taylor .60 1.50
UDTJV Jonathan Vilma .50 1.25
UDTLF Larry Fitzgerald .60 1.50
UDTLJ Larry Johnson .50 1.25
UDTLT LaDainian Tomlinson .75 2.00
UDTMS Michael Strahan .60 1.50
UDTMV Michael Vick .60 1.50
UDTNR Neil Rackers .50 1.25
UDTPE Julius Peppers .60 1.50
UDTPM Peyton Manning 2.00 5.00
UDTPO Clinton Portis .50 1.25
UDTRB Ronde Barber .50 1.25
UDTRL Ray Lewis .75 2.00
UDTRM Randy Moss .60 1.50
UDTRW Roy Williams S .50 1.25
UDTSA Shaun Alexander .50 1.25
UDTSM Santana Moss .60 1.50
UDTSS Steve Smith .75 2.00
UDTTA Lofa Tatupu .50 1.25
UDTTB Tom Brady 2.50 6.00
UDTTG Tony Gonzalez .60 1.50
UDTTH Torry Holt .60 1.50
UDTTP Troy Polamalu .75 2.00

2006 Ultra Head of the Class

STATED ODDS 1:4 WAL-MART PACKS
HCAF Anthony Fasano .75 2.00
HCAH A.J. Hawk 1.00 2.50
HCBC Brian Calhoun .75 2.00
HCCJ Chad Jackson .75 2.00
HCCR Brodie Croyle .75 2.00
HCCW Charlie Whitehurst .75 2.00
HCDA Devin Aromashodu .75 2.00
HCDB Dominique Byrd .75 2.00
HCDF D'Brickashaw Ferguson .75 2.00
HCDH Devin Hester 1.50 4.00
HCDW DeAngelo Williams 1.00 2.50
HCES Ernie Sims .75 2.00
HCGJ Greg Jennings 1.25 3.00
HCHA Mike Hass .75 2.00
HCHN Haloti Ngata 1.00 2.50
HCJA Joseph Addai .75 2.00
HCJB Jeremy Bloom .75 2.00
HCJC Jay Cutler 1.00 2.50
HCJH Jerome Harrison .75 2.00
HCJK Joe Klopfenstein .75 2.00
HCLE Marcedes Lewis .75 2.00
HCLM Laurence Maroney .75 2.00
HCLP Leonard Pope 1.25 3.00
HCLW LenDale White .75 2.00
HCMD Maurice Drew 1.25 3.00
HCMH Michael Huff 1.00 2.50
HCML Matt Leinart .75 2.00
HCMS Maurice Stovall .75 2.00
HCMV Marcus Vick .75 2.00
HCMW Mario Williams 1.25 3.00
HCOJ Omar Jacobs .75 2.00
HCRB Reggie Bush 1.25 3.00
HCRM Reggie McNeal .75 2.00
HCRO Cory Rodgers .75 2.00
HCSH Santonio Holmes 1.00 2.50
HCSM Sinorice Moss .75 2.00
HCTH Tye Hill .75 2.00
HCTW Todd Watkins .75 2.00
HCVD Vernon Davis 1.00 2.50
HCVY Vince Young .75 2.00
HCWA Leon Washington .75 2.00
HCWI Travis Wilson .75 2.00

2006 Ultra Kings of Defense

COMPLETE SET (15) 6.00 15.00
STATED ODDS 1:6
KDBU Brian Urlacher 1.00 2.50
KDCB Champ Bailey .75 2.00
KDDB Derrick Brooks .60 1.50
KDDF Dwight Freeney .60 1.50
KDJK Jevon Kearse .60 1.50
KDJP Julius Peppers .75 2.00
KDJT Jason Taylor .75 2.00
KDJV Jonathan Vilma .60 1.50
KDKB Kendrell Bell .60 1.50
KDRL Ray Lewis 1.00 2.50
KDRW Roy Williams S .60 1.50
KDTB Tedy Bruschi .75 2.00
KDTN Terence Newman .60 1.50
KDTS Terrell Suggs .60 1.50
KDWM Willie McGinest .60 1.50

2006 Ultra Kings of Defense Jerseys

STATED ODDS 1:72 HOB, 1:144 RET
KDBU Brian Urlacher 4.00 10.00
KDCB Champ Bailey 3.00 8.00
KDDB Derrick Brooks 2.50 6.00
KDDF Dwight Freeney 2.50 6.00
KDJK Jevon Kearse 2.50 6.00
KDJP Julius Peppers 3.00 8.00
KDJT Jason Taylor 3.00 8.00
KDJV Jonathan Vilma 2.50 6.00
KDKB Kendrell Bell 2.50 6.00
KDRL Ray Lewis 4.00 10.00
KDRW Roy Williams S 2.50 6.00
KDTB Tedy Bruschi 3.00 8.00
KDTN Terence Newman 2.50 6.00
KDTS Terrell Suggs 2.50 6.00
KDWM Willie McGinest 2.50 6.00

2006 Ultra Lucky 13 Autographs

STATED PRINT RUN 25 SER.#'d SETS
201 Matt Leinart 75.00 150.00
202 Vince Young 125.00 250.00
203 Reggie Bush 50.00 100.00
204 D'Brickashaw Ferguson 25.00 60.00
205 DeAngelo Williams 30.00 80.00
206 Jay Cutler 30.00 80.00
209 Santonio Holmes 30.00 80.00
210 Chad Greenway 40.00 100.00
211 Laurence Maroney 25.00 60.00
212 LenDale White 25.00 60.00
213 Sinorice Moss 25.00 60.00

2006 Ultra Postseason Performers

COMPLETE SET (15) 6.00 15.00
STATED ODDS 1:6
UPPBR Ben Roethlisberger 1.25 3.00
UPPBU Brian Urlacher 1.00 2.50
UPPCP Chad Pennington .60 1.50
UPPDB Drew Bledsoe .75 2.00
UPPDM Donovan McNabb .75 2.00
UPPEJ Edgerrin James .75 2.00
UPPJD Jake Delhomme .60 1.50
UPPJP Jake Plummer .60 1.50
UPPKW Kurt Warner .75 2.00
UPPMF Marshall Faulk .75 2.00
UPPMV Michael Vick .75 2.00
UPPRL Ray Lewis 1.00 2.50
UPPRM Randy Moss .75 2.00
UPPSM Steve McNair .75 2.00
UPPTE Tedy Bruschi .75 2.00

2006 Ultra Postseason Performers Jerseys

STATED ODDS 1:72 HOB, 1:144 RET
UPPBR Ben Roethlisberger 5.00 12.00
UPPBU Brian Urlacher 4.00 10.00
UPPCP Chad Pennington 2.50 6.00
UPPDB Drew Bledsoe 3.00 8.00
UPPDM Donovan McNabb 3.00 8.00
UPPEJ Edgerrin James 3.00 8.00
UPPJD Jake Delhomme 2.50 6.00
UPPJP Jake Plummer 2.50 6.00
UPPKW Kurt Warner 3.00 8.00
UPPMF Marshall Faulk 3.00 8.00
UPPMV Michael Vick 3.00 8.00
UPPRL Ray Lewis 4.00 10.00
UPPRM Randy Moss 3.00 8.00
UPPSM Steve McNair 3.00 8.00
UPPTE Tedy Bruschi 3.00 8.00

2006 Ultra Scoring Kings

COMPLETE SET (15) 5.00 12.00
STATED ODDS 1:6
SKCJ Chad Johnson .60 1.50
SKCP Carson Palmer .75 2.00
SKDC David Carr .60 1.50
SKDM Deuce McAllister .75 2.00
SKJH Joe Horn .60 1.50
SKJS Jeremy Shockey .60 1.50
SKKM Keenan McCardell .75 2.00
SKLJ LaMont Jordan .75 2.00
SKMA Matt Hasselbeck .60 1.50
SKPB Plaxico Burress .60 1.50
SKPH Priest Holmes .60 1.50
SKPO Clinton Portis .60 1.50
SKSS Steve Smith 1.00 2.50
SKTB Tiki Barber .75 2.00
SKWM Willis McGahee .60 1.50

2006 Ultra Scoring Kings Jerseys

STATED ODDS 1:72 HOB, 1:144 RET
SKCJ Chad Johnson 2.50 6.00
SKCP Carson Palmer 3.00 8.00
SKDC David Carr 2.50 6.00
SKDM Deuce McAllister 3.00 8.00
SKJH Joe Horn 2.50 6.00
SKJS Jeremy Shockey 2.50 6.00
SKKM Keenan McCardell 3.00 8.00
SKLJ LaMont Jordan 3.00 8.00
SKMA Matt Hasselbeck 2.50 6.00
SKPB Plaxico Burress 2.50 6.00
SKPH Priest Holmes 2.50 6.00
SKPO Clinton Portis 2.50 6.00
SKSS Steve Smith 4.00 10.00
SKTB Tiki Barber 3.00 8.00
SKWM Willis McGahee 2.50 6.00

2006 Ultra Stars

COMPLETE SET (15) 6.00 15.00
STATED ODDS 1:6
USBE Tatum Bell .60 1.50
USBL Byron Leftwich .60 1.50
USBW Brian Westbrook .60 1.50
USCP Carson Palmer .75 2.00
USDC Daunte Culpepper .75 2.00
USDD Domanick Davis .60 1.50
USGR Trent Green .60 1.50
USJH Joey Harrington .60 1.50
USLF Larry Fitzgerald .75 2.00
USMA Mark Brunell .75 2.00
USMB Marc Bulger .60 1.50
USSA Shaun Alexander .60 1.50
USTB Tom Brady 3.00 8.00
USTE Tedy Bruschi .75 2.00
USTG Tony Gonzalez .75 2.00

2006 Ultra Stars Jerseys

STATED ODDS 1:72 HOB, 1:144 RET
USBE Tatum Bell 2.50 6.00
USBL Byron Leftwich 2.50 6.00
USBW Brian Westbrook 2.50 6.00
USCP Carson Palmer 3.00 8.00
USDC Daunte Culpepper 3.00 8.00
USDD Domanick Davis 2.50 6.00
USGR Trent Green 2.50 6.00
USJH Joey Harrington 2.50 6.00
USLF Larry Fitzgerald 3.00 8.00
USMA Mark Brunell 3.00 8.00
USMB Marc Bulger 2.50 6.00
USSA Shaun Alexander 2.50 6.00
USTB Tom Brady 12.00 30.00
USTE Tedy Bruschi 3.00 8.00
USTG Tony Gonzalez 3.00 8.00

2006 Ultra Target Exclusive Rookies

*201-213 L13: .1X TO .25X BASIC L13 RCs
*214-263: .4X TO 1X BASIC RCs
201-213 L13 ODDS ONE PER TARGET BOX
214-263 ODDS SEVEN PER TARGET BOX
PRINTED WITHOUT FOIL ON FRONT
201 Matt Leinart L13 2.00 5.00
203 Reggie Bush L13 6.00 15.00

2007 Ultra

This 300-card set was released in July, 2007. The set was issued into the hobby in five-card packs, with a $20 SRP, which came 15 packs to a box. Cards numbered 1-200 feature veterans in their 2006 team alphabetical order while cards numbered 201-300 feature 2007 NFL rookies. Cards numbered 201-213 feature the 13 players expected to have the biggest impact as rookies during the 2007 season.

COMP.SET w/o RCs (200) 15.00 40.00
HOBBY PRODUCED WITH SILVER HOLOFOIL
1 Bryant Johnson .30 .75
2 Matt Leinart .30 .75
3 Edgerrin James .40 1.00
4 Larry Fitzgerald .40 1.00
5 Anquan Boldin .30 .75
6 Jerious Norwood .30 .75
7 Roddy White .30 .75
8 Keith Brooking .30 .75
9 DeAngelo Hall .30 .75
10 Michael Vick .40 1.00
11 Warrick Dunn .30 .75
12 Alge Crumpler .40 1.00
13 Terrell Suggs .30 .75
14 Derrick Mason .30 .75
15 Todd Heap .30 .75
16 Ray Lewis .50 1.25
17 Steve McNair .40 1.00
18 Willis McGahee .30 .75
19 Mark Clayton .30 .75
20 Aaron Schobel .30 .75
21 Terrence McGee .30 .75
22 J.P. Losman .30 .75
23 Anthony Thomas .30 .75
24 Lee Evans .40 1.00
25 Keyshawn Johnson .40 1.00
26 DeAngelo Williams .30 .75
27 Julius Peppers .40 1.00
28 Jake Delhomme .30 .75
29 DeShaun Foster .40 1.00
30 Steve Smith .40 1.00
31 Mark Anderson .40 1.00
32 Devin Hester .40 1.00
33 Bernard Berrian .30 .75
34 Muhsin Muhammad .30 .75
35 Rex Grossman .30 .75
36 Cedric Benson .30 .75
37 Brian Urlacher .50 1.25
38 Reggie Kelly .30 .75
39 Carson Palmer .40 1.00
40 Rudi Johnson .30 .75
41 Chad Johnson .30 .75
42 T.J. Houshmandzadeh .30 .75
43 Jamal Lewis .40 1.00
44 Charlie Frye .40 1.00
45 Braylon Edwards .30 .75
46 Kellen Winslow .30 .75
47 DeMarcus Ware .40 1.00
48 Roy Williams S .30 .75
49 Jason Witten .40 1.00
50 Marion Barber .40 1.00
51 Tony Romo .60 1.50
52 Julius Jones .30 .75
53 Terrell Owens .40 1.00
54 Terry Glenn .40 1.00
55 Rod Smith .40 1.00
56 Mike Bell .40 1.00
57 Jason Elam .30 .75
58 Jay Cutler .30 .75
59 Champ Bailey .40 1.00
60 Javon Walker .40 1.00
61 Tatum Bell .30 .75
62 Jason Hanson .30 .75
63 Jon Kitna .30 .75
64 Kevin Jones .30 .75
65 Roy Williams WR .30 .75
66 Mike Furrey .40 1.00
67 Charles Woodson .50 1.25
68 Aaron Kampman .40 1.00
69 Bubba Franks .30 .75
70 Brett Favre 1.00 2.50
71 Greg Jennings .30 .75
72 Donald Driver .40 1.00
73 Ron Dayne .40 1.00
74 DeMeco Ryans .40 1.00
75 Jeb Putzier .30 .75
76 Matt Schaub .30 .75
77 Ahman Green .40 1.00
78 Andre Johnson .40 1.00
79 Terrence Wilkins .30 .75
80 Bob Sanders .40 1.00
81 Dwight Freeney .30 .75
82 Dallas Clark .40 1.00
83 Adam Vinatieri .30 .75
84 Peyton Manning 1.25 3.00
85 Joseph Addai .30 .75
86 Marvin Harrison .40 1.00
87 Reggie Wayne .40 1.00
88 Rashean Mathis .30 .75
89 Matt Jones .40 1.00
90 Fred Taylor .30 .75
91 Byron Leftwich .30 .75
92 David Garrard .30 .75
93 Reggie Williams .40 1.00
94 Maurice Jones-Drew .30 .75
95 Damon Huard .40 1.00
96 Dante Hall .30 .75
97 Eddie Kennison .30 .75
98 Trent Green .30 .75
99 Larry Johnson .30 .75
100 Tony Gonzalez .40 1.00
101 Jason Taylor .40 1.00
102 Randy McMichael .30 .75
103 Zach Thomas .40 1.00
104 Daunte Culpepper .40 1.00
105 Ronnie Brown .30 .75
106 Chris Chambers .30 .75

107 Troy Williamson .30 .75
108 Tony Richardson .30 .75
109 Tarvaris Jackson .30 .75
110 Chester Taylor .30 .75
111 Travis Taylor .30 .75
112 Richard Seymour .30 .75
113 Reche Caldwell .30 .75
114 Tedy Bruschi .40 1.00
115 Ben Watson .30 .75
116 Tom Brady 1.50 4.00
117 Laurence Maroney .40 1.00
118 Asante Samuel .30 .75
119 Michael Lewis .30 .75
120 Devery Henderson .30 .75
121 Mike Karney .30 .75
122 Will Smith .30 .75
123 Drew Brees .50 1.25
124 Deuce McAllister .40 1.00
125 Reggie Bush .30 .75
126 Marques Colston .30 .75
127 Michael Strahan .40 1.00
128 Reuben Droughns .40 1.00
129 Jeremy Shockey .30 .75
130 Eli Manning .40 1.00
131 Brandon Jacobs .30 .75
132 Plaxico Burress .30 .75
133 Jonathan Vilma .30 .75
134 Jerricho Cotchery .30 .75
135 Thomas Jones .30 .75
136 Chad Pennington .30 .75
137 Leon Washington .30 .75
138 Laveranues Coles .30 .75
139 Dominic Rhodes .30 .75
140 Andrew Walter .30 .75
141 Randy Moss .40 1.00
142 Ronald Curry .30 .75
143 LaMont Jordan .40 1.00
144 Justin Fargas .30 .75
145 David Akers .30 .75
146 Correll Buckhalter .30 .75
147 Brian Dawkins .50 1.25
148 L.J. Smith .30 .75
149 Donovan McNabb .40 1.00
150 Brian Westbrook .30 .75
151 Reggie Brown .30 .75
152 Cedrick Wilson .30 .75
153 Aaron Smith .30 .75
154 Troy Polamalu .50 1.25
155 Ben Roethlisberger .50 1.25
156 Willie Parker .40 1.00
157 Hines Ward .40 1.00
158 Santonio Holmes .30 .75
159 Eric Parker .30 .75
160 Lorenzo Neal .30 .75
161 Shawne Merriman .30 .75
162 Philip Rivers .50 1.25
163 LaDainian Tomlinson .50 1.25
164 Antonio Gates .50 1.25
165 Walt Harris .30 .75
166 Vernon Davis .30 .75
167 Alex Smith QB .40 1.00
168 Frank Gore .40 1.00
169 Arnaz Battle .30 .75
170 Maurice Morris .30 .75
171 Julian Peterson .30 .75
172 D.J. Hackett .30 .75
173 Lofa Tatupu .30 .75
174 Darrell Jackson .30 .75
175 Matt Hasselbeck .30 .75
176 Shaun Alexander .30 .75
177 Deion Branch .30 .75
178 Tye Hill .30 .75
179 Isaac Bruce .50 1.25
180 Marc Bulger .30 .75
181 Steven Jackson .30 .75
182 Torry Holt .40 1.00
183 Drew Bennett .30 .75
184 Jeff Garcia .30 .75
185 Michael Clayton .30 .75
186 Derrick Brooks .30 .75
187 Cadillac Williams .40 1.00
188 Joey Galloway .40 1.00
189 Ronde Barber .30 .75
190 Chris Simms .30 .75
191 Keith Bulluck .30 .75
192 LenDale White .40 1.00
193 David Givens .30 .75
194 Vince Young .30 .75
195 Ladell Bells .30 .75
196 Chris Cooley .30 .75
197 Antwaan Randle El .30 .75
198 Jason Campbell .30 .75
199 Clinton Portis .30 .75
200 Santana Moss .40 1.00
201 JaMarcus Russell L13 RC 2.50 6.00
202 Brady Quinn L13 RC 2.50 6.00
203 Calvin Johnson L13 RC 10.00 25.00
204 Joe Thomas L13 RC 4.00 10.00
205 Adrian Peterson L13 RC 12.00 30.00
206 Marshawn Lynch L13 RC 5.00 12.00
207 Ted Ginn Jr. L13 RC 3.00 8.00
208 Leon Hall L13 RC 2.50 6.00
209 Dwayne Bowe L13 RC 2.50 6.00
210 Steve Smith USC L13 RC 2.50 6.00
211 Robert Meachem L13 RC 3.00 8.00
212 LaRon Landry L13 RC 4.00 10.00
213 Dwayne Jarrett L13 RC 3.00 8.00
214 Darius Walker RC 1.50 4.00
215 Chris Leak RC 1.50 4.00
216 Darrelle Revis RC 2.00 5.00
217 Paul Posluszny RC 1.50 4.00
218 Daymeion Hughes RC 1.50 4.00
219 LaMarr Woodley RC 3.00 8.00
220 Garrett Wolfe RC 1.50 4.00
221 DeShawn Wynn RC 1.50 4.00
222 Alan Branch RC 1.50 4.00
223 Greg Olsen RC 2.50 6.00
224 Tyler Palko RC 2.50 6.00
225 Jordan Palmer RC 2.00 5.00
226 Drew Stanton RC 1.50 4.00
227 Jamaal Anderson RC 2.00 5.00
228 Eric Wright RC 1.50 4.00
229 Quentin Moses RC 1.50 4.00
230 Patrick Willis RC 2.50 6.00
231 Troy Smith RC 1.50 4.00
232 Amobi Okoye RC 2.00 5.00
233 Lawrence Timmons RC 2.50 6.00
234 H.B. Blades RC 1.50 4.00
235 Jared Zabransky RC 1.50 4.00
236 John Beck RC 1.50 4.00
237 Kevin Kolb RC 2.00 5.00
238 Matt Moore RC 2.50 6.00
239 Trent Edwards RC 1.50 4.00
240 Antonio Pittman RC 1.50 4.00
241 Brandon Jackson RC 1.50 4.00
242 Chris Henry RC 1.50 4.00
243 Dwayne Wright RC 1.50 4.00
244 Brian Leonard RC 1.50 4.00
245 Kenneth Darby RC 1.50 4.00
246 Kenny Irons RC 1.50 4.00
247 Kolby Smith RC 1.50 4.00
248 Lorenzo Booker RC 2.00 5.00
249 Drew Tate RC 2.00 5.00
250 Tanard Jackson RC 1.50 4.00
251 Michael Bush RC 1.50 4.00
252 Selvin Young RC 1.50 4.00
253 Tony Hunt RC 1.50 4.00
254 Tyrone Moss RC 1.50 4.00
255 Reggie Nelson RC 1.50 4.00
256 Zach Miller RC 1.50 4.00
257 Anthony Gonzalez RC 1.50 4.00
258 Adam Carriker RC 1.50 4.00
259 Sidney Rice RC 2.00 5.00
260 Aundrae Allison RC 1.50 4.00
261 Chansi Stuckey RC 2.00 5.00
262 Courtney Taylor RC 1.50 4.00
263 Craig Buster Davis RC 1.50 4.00
264 Dallas Baker RC 1.50 4.00
265 David Clowney RC 1.50 4.00
266 David Ball RC 1.50 4.00
267 Jason Hill RC 1.50 4.00
268 Johnnie Lee Higgins RC 1.50 4.00
269 Rhema McKnight RC 1.50 4.00
270 Gaines Adams RC 2.00 5.00
271 Mike Walker RC 2.50 6.00
272 Steve Breaston RC 1.50 4.00
273 Gary Russell RC 2.00 5.00
274 Marcus McCauley RC 1.50 4.00
275 Jarvis Moss RC 1.50 4.00
276 Syvelle Newton RC 2.00 5.00
277 DeMarcus Tank Tyler RC 1.50 4.00
278 Alvin Banks RC 2.00 5.00
279 Joel Filani RC 1.50 4.00
280 Chris Davis RC 1.50 4.00
281 Matt Trannon RC 1.50 4.00
282 Ryan Kalil RC 1.50 4.00
283 Levi Brown RC 1.50 4.00
284 Anthony Spencer RC 2.00 5.00
285 Brandon Meriweather RC 2.00 5.00
286 Chris Houston RC 1.50 4.00
287 Michael Griffin RC 1.50 4.00
288 Jon Beason RC 1.50 4.00
289 Legedu Naanee RC 2.00 5.00
290 Eric Weddle RC 2.00 5.00
291 Isaiah Stanback RC 1.50 4.00
292 Aaron Ross RC 1.50 4.00
293 Sabby Piscitelli RC 1.50 4.00
294 Charles Johnson RC 1.50 4.00
295 Buster Davis RC 2.00 5.00
296 Justin Harrell RC 1.50 4.00
297 Stewart Bradley RC 1.50 4.00
298 A.J. Davis RC 1.50 4.00
299 David Irons RC 1.50 4.00
300 Scott Chandler RC 2.50 6.00

2007 Ultra Gold

*VETS: 1.5X TO 4X BASIC CARDS
*ROOKIE L13: .5X TO 1.2X BASIC CARDS
*ROOKIE 214-300: .5X TO 1.2X BASIC CARDS
ONE PER PACK

2007 Ultra Retail

COMPLETE SET (300) 25.00 50.00
*VETERANS 1-200: .25X TO .6X HOBBY
*ROOKIES 201-300: .3X TO .8X HOBBY
RETAIL PRODUCED WITH FLAT SILVER FOIL

2007 Ultra Autographics

STATED PRINT RUN 15-150
*RETAIL: .3X TO .8X BASIC AU/150
*RETAIL: .2X TO .5X BASIC AU/50
AB Anquan Boldin/50 6.00 15.00
BF Brett Favre/15 125.00 250.00
CH Chester Taylor/50 8.00 20.00
CJ Chad Johnson/50 6.00 15.00
CT Courtney Taylor/150 4.00 10.00
DB Drew Brees/50 40.00 80.00
DD Donald Driver/50 20.00 40.00
DH Daymeion Hughes/150 4.00 10.00
DR Darrelle Revis/150 12.50 25.00
EW Eric Wright/150 4.00 10.00
JT Joe Thomas/150 15.00 40.00
JT Joe Theismann/50 20.00 40.00
LE Lee Evans/50 8.00 20.00
MC Marques Colston/50 15.00 40.00
QM Quentin Moses/150 4.00 10.00
RB Ronnie Brown/50 10.00 25.00
TE Trent Edwards/150 4.00 10.00
TH Tony Hunt/150 4.00 10.00
ZM Zach Miller/150 4.00 10.00

2007 Ultra Comparisons

AP G.Adams/J.Peppers 1.00 2.50
AT J.Anderson/J.Taylor 1.00 2.50
AW A.Allison/H.Ward 1.25 3.00
BH D.Bowe/M.Harrison 1.00 2.50
BR J.Beck/T.Romo 1.50 4.00
CB D.Clowney/P.Burress .75 2.00
DC C.Davis/M.Colston .75 2.00
ER T.Edwards/P.Rivers 1.25 3.00
GB A.Gonzalez/A.Boldin .75 2.00
GH T.Ginn/T.Holt 1.00 2.50
HB L.Hall/C.Bailey 1.00 2.50
HJ T.Hunt/L.Johnson .75 2.00
HS C.Houston/A.Samuel .75 2.00
IW K.Irons/Cad.Williams 1.00 2.50
JF D.Jarrett/L.Fitzgerald 1.00 2.50
JG B.Jackson/F.Gore 1.00 2.50
JO Cal.Johnson/T.Owens 2.50 6.00
KB K.Kolb/M.Bulger 1.00 2.50
LJ M.Lynch/Jones-Drew 1.50 4.00
LM C.Leak/D.McNabb 1.00 2.50
LR L.Landry/E.Reed 1.25 3.00
MG Z.Miller/A.Gates 1.25 3.00
MV J.Moss/J.Vilma .75 2.00
MW Meachem/Ro.Williams WR 1.00 2.50
NP R.Nelson/T.Polamalu 1.25 3.00
OS G.Olsen/J.Shockey 1.25 3.00
OW A.Okoye/D.Ware 1.00 2.50
PA Antonio Pittman 1.25 3.00
Shaun Alexander
PL P.Posluszny/R.Lewis 1.25 3.00
PP J.Palmer/C.Palmer 1.00 2.50
PT A.Peterson/Tomlinson 2.50 6.00
QB B.Quinn/T.Brady 4.00 10.00
RJ S.Rice/Ch.Johnson 1.00 2.50
RY J.Russell/V.Young .75 2.00
SB Tr.Smith/D.Brees 1.25 3.00
SM D.Stanton/P.Manning 2.50 6.00
SS S.Smith WR/S.Smith USC 1.00 2.50
SW C.Stuckey/R.Wayne 1.00 2.50
TF J.Thomas/Ferguson 1.25 3.00
TM L.Timmons/Merriman 1.25 3.00
WJ D.Walker/Ju.Jones .75 2.00
WU P.Willis/B.Urlacher 1.25 3.00

2007 Ultra Dual Materials Gold

COMMON CARD/99 3.00 8.00
SEMISTARS/99 4.00 10.00
UNL.STARS/99 5.00 12.00
GOLD PRINT RUN 10-99
AG Ahman Green 4.00 10.00
AS Alex Smith QB 4.00 10.00
BF Brett Favre 10.00 25.00
BL Byron Leftwich 3.00 8.00
BR Ben Roethlisberger 5.00 12.00
BS Barry Sanders 12.00 30.00
CJ Chad Johnson 3.00 8.00
CP Carson Palmer 4.00 10.00
CP Clinton Portis 3.00 8.00
CS Chris Simms 3.00 8.00
DB Drew Brees 5.00 12.00
DM Dan Marino 15.00 40.00
EJ Edgerrin James 4.00 10.00
ES Emmitt Smith 12.00 30.00
HW Hines Ward 4.00 10.00
JH Joe Horn 3.00 8.00
JJ Julius Jones 3.00 8.00
JL Jamal Lewis 4.00 10.00
JN Joe Namath/25 30.00 80.00
JP Jake Plummer 3.00 8.00
JS Jeremy Shockey 3.00 8.00
JT Joe Theismann 8.00 20.00
LJ LaMont Jordan 4.00 10.00
LM Laurence Maroney 4.00 10.00
LT LaDainian Tomlinson 5.00 12.00
MA Marcus Allen 8.00 20.00
MB Marc Bulger/75 3.00 8.00
MF Marshall Faulk 4.00 10.00
ML Matt Leinart 3.00 8.00
MS Mike Singletary 8.00 20.00
MV Michael Vick 4.00 10.00
OW Terrell Owens/20 8.00 20.00
PA Carson Palmer 4.00 10.00
PE Chad Pennington/15 6.00 15.00
PM Peyton Manning 12.00 30.00
PM Priest Holmes 4.00 10.00
RG Rex Grossman/25 6.00 15.00
RJ Rudi Johnson/15 6.00 15.00
RL Ray Lewis/20 10.00 25.00
RS Rod Smith 4.00 10.00
RW Reggie Wayne 4.00 10.00
TG Trent Green 3.00 8.00
VY Vince Young 3.00 8.00
WM Willis McGahee 3.00 8.00
BF2 Brett Favre 10.00 25.00
CEB Cedric Benson 3.00 8.00
CHB Champ Bailey 4.00 10.00
CJ2 Chad Johnson 3.00 8.00
DEM Deuce McAllister 4.00 10.00
DM2 Donovan McNabb 4.00 10.00
DOM Donovan McNabb 4.00 10.00
LM2 Laurence Maroney 4.00 10.00
LT2 LaDainian Tomlinson 5.00 12.00
MH2 Marvin Harrison 4.00 10.00
MHK Matt Hasselbeck 3.00 8.00
MHN Marvin Harrison 4.00 10.00
MJ2 Maurice Jones-Drew 3.00 8.00
MJD Maurice Jones-Drew 3.00 8.00
ML2 Matt Leinart 3.00 8.00
PM2 Peyton Manning 12.00 30.00
RB2 Reggie Bush 3.00 8.00
REB Reggie Bush 3.00 8.00
RO2 Ben Roethlisberger 5.00 12.00
ROB Ronnie Brown 3.00 8.00
TB2 Tom Brady/50 20.00 50.00
TEB Tedy Bruschi 4.00 10.00
TOB Tom Brady 15.00 40.00
VY2 Vince Young 3.00 8.00

2007 Ultra Dual Materials Gold Patch

AB Anquan Boldin/30 8.00 20.00
AG Ahman Green 8.00 20.00
AL Marcus Allen 15.00 40.00
AS Alex Smith QB 8.00 20.00
BF1 Brett Favre 20.00 50.00
BL Byron Leftwich 6.00 15.00
BS Barry Sanders 25.00 60.00
CJ1 Chad Johnson 6.00 15.00
CP Carson Palmer 8.00 20.00
CP Clinton Portis 6.00 15.00
CS Chris Simms 6.00 15.00
DB Drew Brees 10.00 25.00
DM Dan Marino 30.00 80.00
EJ Edgerrin James 8.00 20.00
ES Emmitt Smith 25.00 60.00
GO Tony Gonzalez/20 10.00 25.00
HW Hines Ward 8.00 20.00
JH Joe Horn 6.00 15.00
JJ Julius Jones 6.00 15.00
JL Jamal Lewis 8.00 20.00
JP Jake Plummer 6.00 15.00
JS Jeremy Shockey 6.00 15.00
JT Joe Theismann 15.00 40.00
LJ LaMont Jordan 8.00 20.00
LM Laurence Maroney 8.00 20.00
LT LaDainian Tomlinson 10.00 25.00
MB Marc Bulger 6.00 15.00
MF Marshall Faulk 8.00 20.00
MH Marvin Harrison 8.00 20.00
ML Matt Leinart 6.00 15.00
MS Mike Singletary 15.00 40.00
MV Michael Vick 8.00 20.00
OW Terrell Owens/30 10.00 25.00
PA Carson Palmer 8.00 20.00
PE Chad Pennington 6.00 15.00
PH Priest Holmes 8.00 20.00
PM Peyton Manning 25.00 60.00
RG Rex Grossman 6.00 15.00
RJ Rudi Johnson 6.00 15.00
RL Ray Lewis 10.00 25.00
RM Randy Moss 8.00 20.00
RS Rod Smith 8.00 20.00
SA Shaun Alexander/30 8.00 20.00
SS Steve Smith 8.00 20.00
SY Steve Young 20.00 50.00
TE Tedy Bruschi 8.00 20.00
TG Trent Green 6.00 15.00
VY Vince Young 6.00 15.00
WA Reggie Wayne 8.00 20.00
WM Willis McGahee 6.00 15.00
WP Willie Parker/20 10.00 25.00
BF2 Brett Favre 20.00 50.00
CEB Cedric Benson 6.00 15.00
CHB Champ Bailey 8.00 20.00
CJ2 Chad Johnson 6.00 15.00
DEM Deuce McAllister 8.00 20.00
DM2 Donovan McNabb 8.00 20.00
DOM Donovan McNabb 8.00 20.00
HA2 Matt Hasselbeck/25 8.00 20.00
LM1 Laurence Maroney 8.00 20.00
LT2 LaDainian Tomlinson 10.00 25.00
MH2 Marvin Harrison 5.00 12.00
MJ2 Maurice Jones-Drew 6.00 15.00
MJD Maurice Jones-Drew 6.00 15.00
ML2 Matt Leinart 6.00 15.00
PM2 Peyton Manning 25.00 60.00
RB2 Reggie Bush 6.00 15.00
REB Reggie Bush 6.00 15.00
ROB Ronnie Brown 6.00 15.00
TAB Tatum Bell 6.00 15.00
TB2 Tom Brady 30.00 80.00
TOB Tom Brady 30.00 80.00
VY2 Vince Young 6.00 15.00

2007 Ultra Dual Materials Silver

AB Anquan Boldin/190 2.50 6.00
AG Ahman Green/199 3.00 8.00
AS Alex Smith QB/199 3.00 8.00
BF Brett Favre/199 8.00 20.00
BL Byron Leftwich/199 2.50 6.00
BS Barry Sanders/199 10.00 25.00
CP Carson Palmer/199 3.00 8.00
CP Clinton Portis/199 2.50 6.00
CS Chris Simms/199 2.50 6.00
DB Drew Brees/199 4.00 10.00
DM Dan Marino/199 12.00 30.00
EJ Edgerrin James/199 3.00 8.00
ES Emmitt Smith/199 10.00 25.00
GO Tony Gonzalez/40 5.00 12.00
HW Hines Ward/60 4.00 10.00
JH Joe Horn/199 2.50 6.00
JJ Julius Jones/199 2.50 6.00
JL Jamal Lewis/199 3.00 8.00
JN Joe Namath/50 15.00 40.00
JP Jake Plummer/199 2.50 6.00
JS Jeremy Shockey/199 2.50 6.00
JT Joe Theismann/199 6.00 15.00
LJ LaMont Jordan/199 3.00 8.00
MA Marcus Allen/199 6.00 15.00
MB Marc Bulger/90 3.00 8.00
MF Marshall Faulk/199 3.00 8.00
MS Mike Singletary/75 8.00 20.00
MV Michael Vick/199 3.00 8.00
OW Terrell Owens/30 5.00 12.00
PA Carson Palmer/199 3.00 8.00
PE Chad Pennington/199 2.50 6.00
PM Priest Holmes/199 3.00 8.00
RG Rex Grossman/199 2.50 6.00
RJ Rudi Johnson/60 3.00 8.00
RL Ray Lewis/75 5.00 12.00
RM Randy Moss/99 4.00 10.00
RS Rod Smith/199 3.00 8.00
RW Reggie Wayne/199 3.00 8.00
SA Shaun Alexander/40 4.00 10.00
SS Steve Smith/85 4.00 10.00
SY Steve Young/149 6.00 15.00
TG Trent Green/199 2.50 6.00
WM Willis McGahee/199 2.50 6.00
WP Willie Parker/20 6.00 15.00
BF2 Brett Favre/199 8.00 20.00
CEB Cedric Benson/199 2.50 6.00
CHB Champ Bailey/199 3.00 8.00
CJ1 Chad Johnson/199 2.50 6.00
CJ2 Chad Johnson/199 2.50 6.00
DEM Deuce McAllister/199 3.00 8.00
DM1 Donovan McNabb/60 4.00 10.00
DM2 Donovan McNabb/199 3.00 8.00
LM1 Laurence Maroney/199 3.00 8.00
LM2 Laurence Maroney/199 3.00 8.00
LT1 LaDainian Tomlinson/199 4.00 10.00
LT2 LaDainian Tomlinson/199 4.00 10.00
MH1 Marvin Harrison/199 3.00 8.00
MH2 Marvin Harrison/15 6.00 15.00
MHK Matt Hasselbeck/199 2.50 6.00
MJ1 Maurice Jones-Drew/199 2.50 6.00
MJ2 Maurice Jones-Drew/199 2.50 6.00
ML1 Matt Leinart/199 2.50 6.00
ML2 Matt Leinart/199 2.50 6.00
PM1 Peyton Manning/199 10.00 25.00
PM2 Peyton Manning/199 10.00 25.00
RB1 Reggie Bush/199 2.50 6.00
RB2 Reggie Bush/199 2.50 6.00
RO1 Ben Roethlisberger/199 4.00 10.00
RO2 Ben Roethlisberger/199 4.00 10.00
ROB Ronnie Brown/199 2.50 6.00
TAB Tatum Bell/55 3.00 8.00
TB1 Tom Brady/199 12.00 30.00
TB2 Tom Brady/199 12.00 30.00
TEB Tedy Bruschi/199 3.00 8.00
VY1 Vince Young/199 2.50 6.00
VY2 Vince Young/199 2.50 6.00

2007 Ultra Feel the Game

AG Ahman Green .75 2.00
AR Aaron Rodgers 2.50 6.00
AS Alex Smith QB .75 2.00
BD Brian Dawkins 1.00 2.50
BE Braylon Edwards .60 1.50
BL Byron Leftwich .60 1.50
BR Ben Roethlisberger 1.00 2.50
BW Brian Westbrook .60 1.50
CB Cedric Benson .60 1.50
CP Chad Pennington .60 1.50
CS Chris Simms .60 1.50
DM Donovan McNabb .75 2.00
EJ Edgerrin James .75 2.00
HW Hines Ward .75 2.00
JH Joe Horn .60 1.50
JJ Julius Jones .60 1.50
JL Jamal Lewis .75 2.00
JW Jason Witten .75 2.00
LT Lofa Tatupu .60 1.50
MV Michael Vick .75 2.00
RB Ronnie Brown .60 1.50
RG Rex Grossman .60 1.50
RL Ray Lewis 1.00 2.50
RW Roy Williams S .60 1.50
SJ Steven Jackson .60 1.50
TB Tedy Bruschi .75 2.00
JPE Julius Peppers .75 2.00
JPL Jake Plummer .60 1.50
LJN Larry Johnson .60 1.50
LJO LaMont Jordan .75 2.00

2007 Ultra Feel the Game Jerseys

AG Ahman Green 3.00 8.00
AR Aaron Rodgers 12.00 30.00
AS Alex Smith QB 3.00 8.00
BD Brian Dawkins 4.00 10.00
BE Braylon Edwards 2.50 6.00
BL Byron Leftwich 2.50 6.00
BR Ben Roethlisberger 4.00 10.00
BW Brian Westbrook 2.50 6.00
CB Cedric Benson 2.50 6.00
CP Chad Pennington 2.50 6.00
CS Chris Simms 2.50 6.00
DM Donovan McNabb 3.00 8.00
EJ Edgerrin James 3.00 8.00
HW Hines Ward 3.00 8.00
JH Joe Horn 2.50 6.00
JJ Julius Jones 2.50 6.00
JL Jamal Lewis 3.00 8.00
JW Jason Witten 4.00 10.00
LT Lofa Tatupu 2.50 6.00
MV Michael Vick 3.00 8.00
RB Ronnie Brown 2.50 6.00
RG Rex Grossman 2.50 6.00
RL Ray Lewis 4.00 10.00
RW Roy Williams S 2.50 6.00
SJ Steven Jackson 2.50 6.00
TB Tedy Bruschi 3.00 8.00
JPE Julius Peppers 3.00 8.00
JPL Jake Plummer 2.50 6.00
LJN Larry Johnson 2.50 6.00
LJO LaMont Jordan 3.00 8.00

2007 Ultra Field Generals

BF Brett Favre 2.00 5.00
BR Ben Roethlisberger 1.00 2.50
CP Carson Palmer .75 2.00
DB Drew Brees 1.00 2.50
DM Donovan McNabb .75 2.00
EM Eli Manning .75 2.00
JC Jay Cutler .60 1.50
JP Jake Plummer .60 1.50
MB Marc Bulger .60 1.50
ML Matt Leinart .60 1.50
MV Michael Vick .75 2.00
PM Peyton Manning 2.50 6.00
PR Philip Rivers 1.00 2.50
TB Tom Brady 3.00 8.00
VY Vince Young .60 1.50

2007 Ultra Field Generals Jerseys

BF Brett Favre 8.00 20.00
BR Ben Roethlisberger 4.00 10.00
CP Carson Palmer 3.00 8.00
DB Drew Brees 4.00 10.00
DM Donovan McNabb 3.00 8.00
EM Eli Manning 3.00 8.00
JC Jay Cutler 2.50 6.00
JP Jake Plummer 2.50 6.00
MB Marc Bulger 2.50 6.00
ML Matt Leinart 2.50 6.00
MV Michael Vick 3.00 8.00
PM Peyton Manning 10.00 25.00
PR Philip Rivers 4.00 10.00
TB Tom Brady 12.00 30.00
VY Vince Young 2.50 6.00

2007 Ultra Fresh Faces

TWO PER RETAIL FAT PACK
AB Alan Branch .60 1.50
AC Adam Carriker .60 1.50
AG Anthony Gonzalez .60 1.50
AR Aaron Ross .60 1.50
AS Anthony Spencer .75 2.00
BJ Brandon Jackson .60 1.50
BL Brian Leonard .60 1.50
BQ Brady Quinn .60 1.50
CH Chris Henry .60 1.50
CJ Calvin Johnson 2.00 5.00
CL Chris Leak .60 1.50
DB Dwayne Bowe .60 1.50
DH Daymeion Hughes .60 1.50
DJ Dwayne Jarrett .75 2.00
DR Darrelle Revis .75 2.00
DS Drew Stanton .60 1.50
DW Darius Walker .60 1.50
GA Gaines Adams .75 2.00
GO Greg Olsen 1.00 2.50
JA Jamaal Anderson .75 2.00
JP Jordan Palmer .75 2.00
JR JaMarcus Russell .60 1.50
JT Joe Thomas 1.00 2.50
LH Leon Hall .60 1.50
LL LaRon Landry 1.00 2.50
LT Lawrence Timmons 1.00 2.50
LW LaMarr Woodley 1.25 3.00
MB Michael Bush .60 1.50
ML Marshawn Lynch 1.25 3.00
PP Paul Posluszny .60 1.50
PW Patrick Willis 1.00 2.50
RM Robert Meachem .75 2.00
RN Reggie Nelson .60 1.50
SB Steve Breaston .60 1.50
SR Sidney Rice .75 2.00
SS Steve Smith USC .60 1.50
TG Ted Ginn Jr. .75 2.00
TS Troy Smith .60 1.50
APE Adrian Peterson 2.00 5.00
API Antonio Pittman .60 1.50
CHJ Charles Johnson .60 1.50
CHO Chris Houston .60 1.50

2007 Ultra Gridiron Legends

BJ Bo Jackson 3.00 8.00
BK Bernie Kosar 2.00 5.00
BS Barry Sanders 4.00 10.00
DM Dan Marino 5.00 12.00
ES Emmitt Smith 4.00 10.00
JN Joe Namath 3.00 8.00
JT Joe Theismann 2.50 6.00
MA Marcus Allen 2.50 6.00
MS Mike Singletary 2.50 6.00
SY Steve Young 3.00 8.00

2007 Ultra Gridiron Legends Autographs

*RETAIL UNNUMBERED: .3X TO .8X AU/99
BJ Bo Jackson/25 Red 50.00 100.00
DP Drew Pearson/99 20.00 40.00
JT Joe Theismann/99 15.00 30.00
LG L.C. Greenwood/99 15.00 30.00
PH Paul Hornung/99 20.00 40.00
RC Roger Craig/99 15.00 30.00

2007 Ultra Gridiron Legends Jerseys

BJ Bo Jackson 6.00 15.00
BS Barry Sanders 8.00 20.00
DM Dan Marino 10.00 25.00
ES Emmitt Smith 8.00 20.00
JN Joe Namath 8.00 20.00
JT Joe Theismann 5.00 12.00
MS Mike Singletary 5.00 12.00
SY Steve Young 6.00 15.00

2007 Ultra Paydirt

AG Antonio Gates 1.00 2.50
BW Brian Westbrook .60 1.50
CB Cedric Benson .60 1.50
CD Corey Dillon .60 1.50
CJ Chad Johnson .60 1.50
DM Deuce McAllister .75 2.00
LJ Larry Johnson .60 1.50
LT LaDainian Tomlinson 1.00 2.50
MH Marvin Harrison .75 2.00
RJ Rudi Johnson .60 1.50
SA Shaun Alexander .60 1.50
SJ Steven Jackson .60 1.50
TO Terrell Owens .75 2.00
WP Willie Parker .75 2.00
MJD Maurice Jones-Drew .60 1.50

2007 Ultra Paydirt Jerseys

AG Antonio Gates 4.00 10.00
BW Brian Westbrook 2.50 6.00
CB Cedric Benson 2.50 6.00
CD Corey Dillon 2.50 6.00
CJ Chad Johnson 2.50 6.00
DM Deuce McAllister 3.00 8.00
LJ Larry Johnson 2.50 6.00
LT LaDainian Tomlinson 4.00 10.00
MH Marvin Harrison 3.00 8.00
RJ Rudi Johnson 2.50 6.00
SA Shaun Alexander 2.50 6.00
SJ Steven Jackson 2.50 6.00
TO Terrell Owens 3.00 8.00
WP Willie Parker 3.00 8.00
MJD Maurice Jones-Drew 2.50 6.00

2007 Ultra Rookie Autographs

201 JaMarcus Russell L13/50 20.00 50.00
202 Brady Quinn L13/50 6.00 15.00
203 Calvin Johnson L13/50 75.00 150.00
204 Joe Thomas L13/150 15.00 40.00
205 Adrian Peterson L13/50 150.00 300.00
206 Marshawn Lynch L13/100 25.00 50.00
207 Ted Ginn Jr. L13/100 12.00 30.00
208 Leon Hall L13/150 10.00 25.00
209 Dwayne Bowe L13/150 30.00 60.00
210 Steve Smith USC L13/150 10.00 25.00
211 Robert Meachem L13/100 12.00 30.00
212 LaRon Landry L13/150 15.00 40.00
213 Dwayne Jarrett L13/150 12.00 30.00
214 Darius Walker 5.00 12.00
215 Chris Leak 5.00 12.00
216 Darrelle Revis 6.00 15.00
217 Paul Posluszny 5.00 12.00
218 Daymeion Hughes 5.00 12.00
219 LaMarr Woodley 10.00 25.00
220 Garrett Wolfe 5.00 12.00
221 DeShawn Wynn 5.00 12.00
222 Alan Branch 5.00 12.00
223 Greg Olsen 8.00 20.00
224 Tyler Palko 8.00 20.00
225 Jordan Palmer 6.00 15.00
226 Drew Stanton 5.00 12.00
227 Jamaal Anderson 6.00 15.00
228 Eric Wright 5.00 12.00
229 Quentin Moses 5.00 12.00
230 Patrick Willis 8.00 20.00
232 Amobi Okoye 6.00 15.00
233 Lawrence Timmons 8.00 20.00
234 H.B. Blades 5.00 12.00
235 Jared Zabransky 5.00 12.00
236 John Beck 5.00 12.00
237 Kevin Kolb 6.00 15.00
238 Matt Moore 12.00 30.00
239 Trent Edwards 5.00 12.00
240 Antonio Pittman 5.00 12.00
241 Brandon Jackson 5.00 12.00
242 Chris Henry 5.00 12.00
243 Dwayne Wright 5.00 12.00
244 Brian Leonard 5.00 12.00
245 Kenneth Darby 5.00 12.00
246 Kenny Irons 5.00 12.00
247 Kolby Smith 5.00 12.00
248 Lorenzo Booker 6.00 15.00
249 Drew Tate 6.00 15.00
251 Michael Bush 5.00 12.00
252 Selvin Young 10.00 25.00
253 Tony Hunt 5.00 12.00
254 Tyrone Moss 5.00 12.00
255 Reggie Nelson 5.00 12.00
256 Zach Miller 5.00 12.00
257 Anthony Gonzalez 12.00 30.00
258 Adam Carriker 5.00 12.00
259 Sidney Rice 6.00 15.00
260 Aundrae Allison 5.00 12.00
261 Chansi Stuckey 6.00 15.00
262 Courtney Taylor 5.00 12.00
263 Craig Buster Davis 5.00 12.00
264 Dallas Baker 5.00 12.00
265 David Clowney 5.00 12.00
266 David Ball 5.00 12.00
267 Jason Hill 5.00 12.00
268 Johnnie Lee Higgins 5.00 12.00
269 Rhema McKnight 5.00 12.00
270 Gaines Adams 6.00 15.00
273 Gary Russell 6.00 15.00
274 Marcus McCauley 5.00 12.00
279 Joel Filani 5.00 12.00
285 Brandon Meriweather 6.00 15.00
287 Michael Griffin 5.00 12.00
289 Legedu Naanee 6.00 15.00
291 Isaiah Stanback 5.00 12.00
295 Buster Davis 6.00 15.00
299 David Irons 5.00 12.00
300 Scott Chandler 8.00 20.00

2007 Ultra Signature Class Autographs

BQ Brady Quinn/25 8.00 20.00
DB Dallas Baker/150 8.00 20.00
DH Daymeion Hughes/150 6.00 15.00
GO Greg Olsen/150 10.00 25.00
GW Garrett Wolfe/250 8.00 20.00
HB H.B. Blades/150 6.00 15.00
JA Jamaal Anderson/150 8.00 20.00
JA Joseph Addai/50 10.00 25.00
JB John Beck/100 10.00 25.00
JC Jason Campbell/50 10.00 25.00
KK Kevin Kolb/50 12.00 30.00
KS Kolby Smith/250 8.00 20.00
LH Leon Hall/150 8.00 20.00
LJ Larry Johnson/50 12.00 30.00
LL LaRon Landry/100 10.00 25.00
LT LaDainian Tomlinson/25 40.00 100.00
LW LaMarr Woodley/250 10.00 25.00
MB Marc Bulger/50 8.00 20.00
MS Matt Schaub/150 8.00 20.00
PM Peyton Manning/50 60.00 120.00
PP Paul Posluszny/150 12.00 30.00
PR Philip Rivers/50 12.00 30.00
PW Patrick Willis/250 12.00 30.00
RB Ronnie Brown/50 10.00 25.00
RN Reggie Nelson/150 8.00 20.00
SC Scott Chandler/150 6.00 15.00
TH T.J. Houshmandzadeh/50 8.00 20.00
WP Willie Parker/50 10.00 25.00

2007 Ultra Signature Class Autographs Dual

BG D.Bowe/A.Gonzalez/50 20.00 50.00
BW A.Branch/L.Woodley/50 15.00 40.00
HW L.Hall/E.Wright/50 12.00 30.00
JP Jackson/Peterson/25 100.00 200.00
JR J.Campbell/Ro.Brown/25
JT Tomlinson/L.Johnson/25 40.00 100.00
JW Br.Jackson/D.Walker/75 12.00 30.00
LH M.Lynch/D.Hughes/75 20.00 50.00
LN C.Leak/R.Nelson/75 15.00 40.00
MO Z.Miller/G.Olsen/50 20.00 50.00
QS B.Quinn/D.Stanton/50 8.00 20.00
QW B.Quinn/D.Walker/50 8.00 20.00
RJ S.Rice/D.Jarrett/25 25.00 60.00
RL J.Russell/L.Landry/25 20.00 50.00
SA C.Stuckey/G.Adams/50 12.00 30.00
WB M.Bush/G.Wolfe/50 15.00 40.00
WP P.Willis/Posluszny/50 20.00 50.00

2007 Ultra Signature Class Autographs Triple

ABP Addai/Ro.Brwn/Parker/25 25.00 60.00
ATS Allison/Taylor/Stuckey/25 20.00 50.00
ELJ Edwards/Lynch/Jarrett/25 25.00 60.00
HBW L.Hall/Branch/Woodley/25 25.00 60.00
NHL R.Nelson/Hall/Landry/25 20.00 50.00
PWL Peterson/Walker/Lynch/25 125.00 250.00
SGJ C.Jhnsn/Ginn/Jarrett/25 75.00 150.00

2007 Ultra Stars

AB Anquan Boldin .60 1.50
AC Alge Crumpler .75 2.00
AG Antonio Gates 1.00 2.50
AJ Andre Johnson .75 2.00
BU Brian Urlacher 1.00 2.50
CB Champ Bailey .75 2.00
CJ Chad Johnson .60 1.50
EM Eli Manning .75 2.00
JS Jeremy Shockey .60 1.50
LE Lee Evans .75 2.00
LF Larry Fitzgerald .75 2.00
LT LaDainian Tomlinson 1.00 2.50
MH Matt Hasselbeck .60 1.50
ML Matt Leinart .60 1.50
PH Priest Holmes .75 2.00
RB Reggie Bush .60 1.50
RM Randy Moss .75 2.00
RS Rod Smith .75 2.00
SA Shaun Alexander .60 1.50
SJ Steven Jackson .60 1.50
SS Steve Smith .75 2.00
VY Vince Young .60 1.50
WM Willis McGahee .60 1.50
CPA Carson Palmer .75 2.00
CPO Clinton Portis .60 1.50
RWA Reggie Wayne .75 2.00
RWI Roy Williams WR .60 1.50
TBE Tatum Bell .60 1.50
TBR Tom Brady 3.00 8.00
TGO Tony Gonzalez .75 2.00
TGR Trent Green .60 1.50

2007 Ultra Stars Jerseys

AB Anquan Boldin 2.50 6.00
AC Alge Crumpler 3.00 8.00
AG Antonio Gates 4.00 10.00
AJ Andre Johnson 3.00 8.00
BU Brian Urlacher 4.00 10.00
CB Champ Bailey 3.00 8.00
CJ Chad Johnson 2.50 6.00
EM Eli Manning 3.00 8.00
JS Jeremy Shockey 2.50 6.00
LE Lee Evans 3.00 8.00
LF Larry Fitzgerald 3.00 8.00
LT LaDainian Tomlinson 4.00 10.00
MH Matt Hasselbeck 2.50 6.00
PH Priest Holmes 3.00 8.00
RB Reggie Bush 2.50 6.00
RM Randy Moss 3.00 8.00
RS Rod Smith 3.00 8.00
SA Shaun Alexander 2.50 6.00
SJ Steven Jackson 2.50 6.00
SS Steve Smith 3.00 8.00
VY Vince Young 2.50 6.00
WM Willis McGahee 2.50 6.00
CPA Carson Palmer 3.00 8.00
CPO Clinton Portis 2.50 6.00
RWA Reggie Wayne 3.00 8.00
RWI Roy Williams WR 2.50 6.00
TBE Tatum Bell 2.50 6.00
TBR Tom Brady 12.00 30.00
TGO Tony Gonzalez 3.00 8.00
TGR Trent Green 2.50 6.00

2007 Ultra Target Exclusive Rookies

*TARGET SILVER: .4X TO 1X BASIC CARDS
INSERTS IN SPECIAL TARGET RETAIL PACKS
TARGET VERSION FEATURES DIFFERENT PHOTOS

1996 Ultra Sensations

The 1996 Ultra Sensations set was issued in one series totalling 100 cards. The 12-card packs carried a suggested retail price of $2.49. Each card was produced in five different foil border colors with each inserted at various ratios. The Rainbow foil was the most difficult to pull (1% of total print run).

COMPLETE GOLD SET (101) 6.00 15.00
1 Leeland McElroy RC .07 .20
2 Frank Sanders .07 .20
3 Eric Swann .02 .10
4 Jeff George .07 .20
5 Terance Mathis .02 .10
6 Eric Metcalf .02 .10
7 Michael Jackson .07 .20
8 Eric Turner .02 .10
9 Jim Kelly .15 .40
10 Bryce Paup .02 .10
11 Bruce Smith .07 .20
12 Thurman Thomas .15 .40
13 Tim Biakabutuka RC .15 .40
14 Kerry Collins .15 .40
15 Muhsin Muhammad RC .40 1.00
16 Winslow Oliver RC .02 .10
17 Curtis Conway .15 .40
18 Bryan Cox .02 .10
19 Bobby Engram RC .15 .40
20 Erik Kramer .02 .10
21 Rashaan Salaam .07 .20
22 Jeff Blake .15 .40
23 Ki-Jana Carter .07 .20
24 Carl Pickens .07 .20
25 Troy Aikman .40 1.00
26 Michael Irvin .15 .40
27 Daryl Johnston .07 .20
28 Deion Sanders .30 .75
29 Emmitt Smith .60 1.50
30 Terrell Davis .30 .75
31 John Elway .75 2.00
32 Anthony Miller .07 .20
33 John Mobley RC .02 .10
34 Scott Mitchell .07 .20
35 Herman Moore .07 .20
36 Barry Sanders .60 1.50
37 Edgar Bennett .07 .20
38 Robert Brooks .15 .40
39 Brett Favre .75 2.00
40 Reggie White .15 .40
41 Eddie George RC .50 1.25
42 Steve McNair .30 .75
43 Chris Sanders .07 .20
44 Quentin Coryatt .02 .10
45 Marshall Faulk .20 .50
46 Jim Harbaugh .07 .20
47 Marvin Harrison RC 1.00 2.50
48 Mark Brunell .25 .60
49 Natrone Means .07 .20
50 Andre Rison .07 .20
51 Marcus Allen .15 .40
52 Steve Bono .02 .10
53 Greg Hill .07 .20
54 Tamarick Vanover .07 .20
55 Karim Abdul-Jabbar RC .15 .40
56 Dan Marino .75 2.00
57 O.J. McDuffie .07 .20
58 Zach Thomas RC .30 .75
59 Cris Carter .15 .40
60 Warren Moon .07 .20
61 Jake Reed .07 .20
62 Drew Bledsoe .25 .60
63 Ben Coates .07 .20
64 Terry Glenn RC .40 1.00
65 Curtis Martin .30 .75
66 Mario Bates .07 .20
67 Michael Haynes .02 .10
68 Dave Brown .02 .10
69 Rodney Hampton .07 .20
70 Amani Toomer RC .40 1.00
71 Tyrone Wheatley .07 .20
72 Keyshawn Johnson RC .40 1.00
73 Neil O'Donnell .07 .20
74 Tim Brown .15 .40
75 Rickey Dudley RC .15 .40
76 Napoleon Kaufman .15 .40
77 Chester McGlockton .02 .10
78 Charlie Garner .07 .20
79 Chris T. Jones .07 .20
80 Ricky Watters .07 .20
81 Jerome Bettis .15 .40
82 Kordell Stewart .15 .40
83 Rod Woodson .07 .20
84 Aaron Hayden .02 .10
85 Stan Humphries .07 .20
86 Junior Seau .15 .40
87 Tony Banks RC .15 .40
88 Isaac Bruce .15 .40
89 Lawrence Phillips RC .15 .40
90 Derek Loville .02 .10
91 Jerry Rice .40 1.00
92 J.J. Stokes .15 .40
93 Steve Young .30 .75
94 Joey Galloway .15 .40
95 Rick Mirer .07 .20
96 Chris Warren .07 .20
97 Trent Dilfer .15 .40
98 Errict Rhett .07 .20
99 Terry Allen .07 .20
100 Michael Westbrook .15 .40
NNO Brett Favre CL 1.25 2.50
NNO Promo Sheet 1.00 2.50
Favre

1996 Ultra Sensations Blue

*BLUE CARDS: .6X TO 1.5X BASIC CARDS

1996 Ultra Sensations Rainbow

*RAINBOW STARS: 6X TO 15X BASIC CARDS
*RAINBOW RCs: 3X TO 8X BASIC CARDS
RAINBOWS:RANDOM INS.IN PACKS

1996 Ultra Sensations Marble Gold

*STARS: .8X TO 2X BASIC CARDS
*RCs: .6X TO 1.5X BASIC CARDS

1996 Ultra Sensations Pewter

*PEWTER STARS: 1.5X TO 4X BASIC CARDS
*PEWTER RCs: 1.2X TO 3X BASIC CARDS
PEWTERS: RANDOM INS. IN PACKS

1996 Ultra Sensations Creative Chaos

Randomly inserted in packs at a rate of one in 12, each card features two top NFL stars. Ten different players were paired together in all possible combinations to produce this 100-card set.

COMPLETE SET (100) 400.00 800.00
STATED ODDS 1:12
1A E.Smith 6.00 15.00
E.Smith
1B E.Smith 7.50 20.00
B.Favre
1C E.Smith 5.00 12.00
C.Martin
1D E.Smith 5.00 12.00
C.Warren
1E E.Smith 5.00 12.00
D.Sanders
1F E.Smith 5.00 12.00
S.Young
1G E.Smith 5.00 12.00
J.Rice
1H E.Smith 5.00 12.00
T.Davis
1I E.Smith 5.00 12.00
C.Pickens
1J E.Smith 5.00 12.00
M.Faulk
2A B.Favre 7.50 20.00
E.Smith
2B B.Favre 10.00 20.00
B.Favre
2C B.Favre 6.00 15.00
C.Martin
2D B.Favre 5.00 12.00
C.Warren
2E B.Favre 5.00 12.00
D.Sanders
2F B.Favre 5.00 12.00

Card	Low	High
S.Young		
2G B.Favre	6.00	15.00
J.Rice		
2H B.Favre	6.00	15.00
T.Davis		
2I B.Favre	5.00	12.00
C.Pickens		
2J B.Favre	5.00	12.00
M.Faulk		
3A C.Martin	5.00	12.00
E.Smith		
3B C.Martin	6.00	15.00
B.Favre		
3C C.Martin	2.50	6.00
C.Martin		
3D C.Martin	4.00	10.00
C.Warren		
3E C.Martin	4.00	10.00
D.Sanders		
3F C.Martin	4.00	10.00
S.Young		
3G C.Martin	4.00	10.00
J.Rice		
3H C.Martin	4.00	10.00
T.Davis		
3I C.Martin	4.00	10.00
C.Pickens		
3J C.Martin	4.00	10.00
M.Faulk		
4A C.Warren	5.00	12.00
E.Smith		
4B C.Warren	5.00	12.00
B.Favre		
4C C.Warren	4.00	10.00
C.Martin		
4D C.Warren	1.50	4.00
C.Warren		
4E C.Warren	2.50	6.00
D.Sanders		
4F C.Warren	2.50	6.00
S.Young		
4G C.Warren	4.00	10.00
J.Rice		
4H C.Warren	4.00	10.00
T.Davis		
4I C.Warren	1.50	4.00
C.Pickens		
4J C.Warren	2.50	6.00
M.Faulk		
5A D.Sanders	5.00	12.00
E.Smith		
5B D.Sanders	5.00	12.00
B.Favre		
5C D.Sanders	4.00	10.00
C.Martin		
5D D.Sanders	2.50	6.00
C.Warren		
5E D.Sanders	2.50	6.00
D.Sanders		
5F D.Sanders	2.50	6.00
S.Young		
5G D.Sanders	4.00	10.00
J.Rice		
5H D.Sanders	4.00	10.00
T.Davis		
5I D.Sanders	2.50	6.00
C.Pickens		
5J D.Sanders	2.50	6.00
M.Faulk		
6A S.Young	5.00	12.00
E.Smith		
6B S.Young	5.00	12.00
B.Favre		
6C S.Young	4.00	10.00
C.Martin		
6D S.Young	2.50	6.00
C.Warren		
6E S.Young	2.50	6.00
D.Sanders		
6F S.Young	2.50	6.00
S.Young		
6G S.Young	4.00	10.00
J.Rice		
6H S.Young	4.00	10.00
T.Davis		
6I S.Young	2.50	6.00
C.Pickens		
6J S.Young	2.50	6.00
M.Faulk		
7A J.Rice	5.00	12.00
E.Smith		
7B J.Rice	6.00	15.00
B.Favre		
7C J.Rice	4.00	10.00
C.Martin		
7D J.Rice	4.00	10.00
C.Warren		
7E J.Rice	4.00	10.00
D.Sanders		
7F J.Rice	4.00	10.00
S.Young		
7G J.Rice	4.00	10.00
J.Rice		
7H J.Rice	4.00	10.00
T.Davis		
7I J.Rice	4.00	10.00
C.Pickens		
7J J.Rice	4.00	10.00
M.Faulk		
8A T.Davis	7.50	20.00
E.Smith		
8B T.Davis	6.00	15.00
B.Favre		
8C T.Davis	4.00	10.00
C.Martin		
8D T.Davis	4.00	10.00
C.Warren		
8E T.Davis	4.00	10.00
D.Sanders		
8F T.Davis	4.00	10.00
S.Young		
8G T.Davis	4.00	10.00
J.Rice		
8H T.Davis	4.00	10.00
T.Davis		
8I T.Davis	4.00	10.00
C.Pickens		
8J T.Davis	4.00	10.00
M.Faulk		
9A C.Pickens	5.00	12.00
E.Smith		
9B C.Pickens	5.00	12.00
B.Favre		
9C C.Pickens	4.00	10.00
C.Martin		
9D C.Pickens	1.50	4.00
C.Warren		
9E C.Pickens	2.50	6.00
D.Sanders		
9F C.Pickens	2.50	6.00
S.Young		
9G C.Pickens	4.00	10.00
J.Rice		
9H C.Pickens	4.00	10.00
T.Davis		
9I C.Pickens	1.50	4.00
C.Pickens		
9J C.Pickens	2.50	6.00
M.Faulk		
10A M.Faulk	5.00	12.00
E.Smith		
10B M.Faulk	5.00	12.00
B.Favre		
10C M.Faulk	4.00	10.00
C.Martin		
10D M.Faulk	2.50	6.00
C.Warren		
10E M.Faulk	2.50	6.00
D.Sanders		
10F M.Faulk	2.50	6.00
S.Young		
10G M.Faulk	4.00	10.00
J.Rice		
10H M.Faulk	4.00	10.00
T.Davis		
10I M.Faulk	2.50	6.00
C.Pickens		
10J M.Faulk	2.50	6.00
M.Faulk		

1996 Ultra Sensations Random Rookies

Randomly inserted in packs only at a rate of one in 48,each of these inserts features a top 1996 NFL rookie. Hobby packs contained cards numbered from 1-5, while cards numbered from 6-10 were inserted into retail packs. A Gold parallel version was also produced that comprised no more than 20 percent of the print run.

Card	Low	High
COMPLETE SET (10)	40.00	100.00
COMP.HOBBY SER.1 (5)	20.00	50.00
COMP.RETAIL SER.2 (5)	20.00	50.00
CARDS 1-5 STATED ODDS 1:48 HOBBY		
CARDS 6-10 STATED ODDS 1:48 RETAIL		
*GOLDS: 1X TO 2.5X BASIC INSERTS		
GOLDS STATED 20% OF PRINT RUN		
1 Keyshawn Johnson	3.00	8.00
2 Eddie George	4.00	10.00
3 Leeland McElroy	2.00	5.00
4 Eric Moulds	4.00	10.00
5 Lawrence Phillips	2.50	6.00
6 Marvin Harrison	7.50	20.00
7 Tim Biakabutuka	2.50	6.00
8 Terry Glenn	3.00	8.00
9 Rickey Dudley	2.00	5.00
10 Tony Banks	2.50	6.00

1957-59 Union Oil Booklets

These booklets were distributed by Union Oil. The front cover of each booklet features a drawing of the subject player. The booklets are numbered and were issued over several years beginning in 1957. These are 12-page pamphlets and are approximately 4" by 5 1/2". The set is subtitled "Family Sports Fun." This was apparently primarily a Southern California promotion.

Card	Low	High
COMPLETE SET (44)	200.00	400.00
1 Elroy Hirsch FB 57	10.00	20.00
2 Les Richter FB 57	2.00	4.00
3 Frankie Albert FB 57	7.50	15.00
4 Y.A. Tittle FB 57	10.00	20.00
27 Bob Waterfield FB 58	10.00	20.00
28 Pete Elliott FB 58	5.00	10.00
29 Elroy Hirsch FB 58	7.50	15.00
30 Frank Gifford FB 58	10.00	20.00

1991 Upper Deck

This 700-card standard size set was the first football card set produced by Upper Deck. The set was released in two series with the first series containing 500 cards and the high-number series containing 200 cards. Factory sets were produced for each series. A Darrell Green insert (SP1) and an insert card commemorating Don Shula's historic 300th NFL victory (SP2) were randomly inserted in first and second series packs respectively. Two Promo cards were released to preview the set. Series One cards can be found printed with three different Upper Deck anti-counterfeiting holograms on the back: the standard 1990 style with only the words "Upper Deck" visible, the 1991 hologram that includes "91" printed on it upside down, and the 1992 hologram that features a diamond shaped Upper Deck logo. Series Two cards can be found only with the 1992 hologram on back.

627370202

1991 Upper Deck

Card	Low	High
COMPLETE SET (700)	8.00	20.00
COMP.FACT.SET (700)	12.00	30.00
COMP.SERIES 1 SET (500)	6.00	15.00
COMP.SERIES 2 SET (200)	2.00	5.00
COMP.FACT.SERIES 2 (200)	4.00	10.00
1990 HOLOGRAM BACK: .4X TO 1X 1991 HOLO		
1992 HOLOGRAM BACK: .4X TO 1X 1991 HOLO		
1 Dan McGwire CL	.01	.05
2 Eric Bieniemy RC	.01	.05
3 Mike Dumas RC	.01	.05
4 Mike Croel RC	.01	.05
5 Russell Maryland RC	.08	.25
6 Charles McRae RC	.01	.05
7 Dan McGwire RC	.01	.05
8 Mike Pritchard RC	.08	.25
9 Ricky Watters RC	.60	1.50
10 Chris Zorich RC	.08	.25
11 Browning Nagle RC	.01	.05
12 Wesley Carroll RC	.01	.05
13 Brett Favre RC	5.00	10.00
14 Rob Carpenter RC	.01	.05
15 Eric Swann RC	.08	.25
16 Stanley Richard RC	.01	.05
17 Herman Moore RC	.08	.25
18 Todd Marinovich RC	.01	.05
19 Aaron Craver RC	.01	.05
20 Chuck Webb RC	.01	.05
21 Todd Lyght RC	.01	.05
22 Greg Lewis RC	.01	.05
23 Eric Turner RC	.02	.10
24 Alvin Harper RC	.08	.25
25 Jarrod Bunch RC	.01	.05
26 Bruce Pickens RC	.01	.05
27 Harvey Williams RC	.08	.25
28 Randal Hill RC	.02	.10
29 Nick Bell RC	.01	.05
30 Everett/Ellard AT	.02	.10
31 R.Cunningham/Jackson AT	.01	.05
32 S.DeBerg/Paige AT	.01	.05
33 W.Moon/D.Hill AT	.02	.10
34 D.Marino/M.Clayton AT	.20	.50
35 J.Montana/J.Rice AT	.20	.50
36 Percy Snow	.01	.05
37 Kelvin Martin	.01	.05
38 Scott Case	.01	.05
39 John Gesek RC	.01	.05
40 Barry Word	.01	.05
41 Cornelius Bennett	.02	.10
42 Mike Kenn	.01	.05
43 Andre Reed	.02	.10
44 Bobby Hebert	.01	.05
45 William Perry	.02	.10
46 Dennis Byrd	.01	.05
47 Martin Mayhew	.01	.05
48 Issiac Holt	.01	.05
49 William White	.01	.05
50 JoJo Townsell	.01	.05
51 Jarvis Williams	.01	.05
52 Joey Browner	.01	.05
53 Pat Terrell	.01	.05
54 Joe Montana 3X UER	.50	1.25
55 Jeff Herrod	.01	.05
56 Cris Carter	.20	.50
57 Jerry Rice	.30	.75
58 Brett Perriman	.08	.25
59 Kevin Fagan	.01	.05
60 Wayne Haddix	.01	.05
61 Tommy Kane	.01	.05
62 Pat Beach	.01	.05
63 Jeff Lageman	.01	.05
64 Hassan Jones	.01	.05
65 Bennie Blades	.01	.05
66 Tim McGee	.01	.05
67 Robert Blackmon	.01	.05
68 Fred Stokes RC	.01	.05
69 Barney Bussey RC	.01	.05
70 Eric Metcalf	.02	.10
71 Mark Kelso	.01	.05
72 Neal Anderson TC	.01	.05
73 Boomer Esiason TC	.01	.05
74 Thurman Thomas TC	.08	.25
75 John Elway TC	.20	.50
76 Eric Metcalf TC	.02	.10
77 Vinny Testaverde TC	.02	.10
78 Johnny Johnson TC	.01	.05
79 Anthony Miller TC	.02	.10
80 Derrick Thomas TC	.02	.10
81 Jeff George TC	.02	.10
82 Troy Aikman TC	.15	.40
83 Dan Marino TC	.20	.50
84 Randall Cunningham TC	.02	.10
85 Deion Sanders TC	.01	.05
86 Jerry Rice TC	.15	.40
87 Lawrence Taylor TC	.02	.10
88 Al Toon TC	.01	.05
89 Barry Sanders TC	.20	.50
90 Warren Moon TC	.02	.10
91 Don Majkowski TC	.01	.05
92 Andre Tippett TC	.01	.05
93 Bo Jackson TC	.10	.30
94 Jim Everett TC	.02	.10
95 Art Monk TC	.02	.10
96 Morten Andersen TC	.01	.05
97 John L. Williams TC	.01	.05
98 Rod Woodson TC	.02	.10
99 Herschel Walker TC	.02	.10
100 Checklist 1-100	.01	.05
101 Steve Young	.30	.75
102 Jim Lachey	.01	.05
103 Tom Rathman	.01	.05
104 Earnest Byner	.01	.05
105 Karl Mecklenburg	.01	.05
106 Wes Hopkins	.01	.05
107 Michael Irvin	.08	.25
108 Burt Grossman	.01	.05
109 Jay Novacek UER	.08	.25
110 Ben Smith	.01	.05
111 Rod Woodson	.08	.25
112 Ernie Jones	.01	.05
113 Bryan Hinkle	.01	.05
114 Vai Sikahema	.01	.05
115 Bubby Brister	.01	.05
116 Brian Blades	.02	.10
117 Don Majkowski	.01	.05
118 Rod Bernstine	.01	.05
119 Brian Noble	.01	.05
120 Eugene Robinson	.01	.05
121 John Taylor	.02	.10
122 Vance Johnson	.01	.05
123 Art Monk	.02	.10
124 John Elway	.50	1.25
125 Dexter Carter	.01	.05
126 Anthony Miller	.02	.10
127 Keith Jackson	.02	.10
128 Albert Lewis	.01	.05
129 Billy Ray Smith	.01	.05
130 Clyde Simmons	.01	.05
131 Merril Hoge	.01	.05
132 Ricky Proehl	.01	.05
133 Tim McDonald	.01	.05
134 Louis Lipps	.01	.05
135 Ken Harvey	.02	.10
136 Sterling Sharpe	.02	.10
137 Gill Byrd	.01	.05
138 Tim Harris	.01	.05
139 Derrick Fenner	.01	.05
140 Johnny Holland	.01	.05
141 Ricky Sanders	.01	.05
142 Bobby Humphrey	.01	.05
143 Roger Craig	.02	.10
144 Steve Atwater	.01	.05
145 Ickey Woods	.01	.05
146 Randall Cunningham	.08	.25
147 Marion Butts	.02	.10
148 Reggie White	.08	.25
149 Ronnie Harmon	.01	.05
150 Mike Saxon	.01	.05
151 Greg Townsend	.01	.05
152 Troy Aikman	.30	.75
153 Shane Conlan	.01	.05
154 Deion Sanders	.15	.40
155 Bo Jackson	.10	.30
156 Jeff Hostetler	.02	.10
157 Albert Bentley	.01	.05
158 James Williams	.01	.05
159 Bill Brooks	.01	.05
160 Nick Lowery	.01	.05
161 Ottis Anderson	.02	.10
162 Kevin Greene	.02	.10
163 Neil Smith	.08	.25
164 Jim Everett	.02	.10
165 Derrick Thomas	.08	.25
166 John L. Williams	.01	.05
167 Timm Rosenbach	.01	.05
168 Leslie O'Neal	.02	.10
169 Clarence Verdin	.01	.05
170 Dave Krieg	.02	.10
171 Steve Broussard	.01	.05
172 Emmitt Smith	1.00	2.50
173 Andre Rison	.02	.10
174 Bruce Smith	.08	.25
175 Mark Clayton	.02	.10
176 Christian Okoye	.01	.05
177 Duane Bickett	.01	.05
178 Stephone Paige	.01	.05
179 Fredd Young	.01	.05
180 Mervyn Fernandez	.01	.05
181 Phil Simms	.02	.10
182 Pete Holohan	.01	.05
183 Pepper Johnson	.01	.05
184 Jackie Slater	.01	.05
185 Stephen Baker	.01	.05
186 Frank Cornish	.01	.05
187 Dave Waymer	.01	.05
188 Terance Mathis	.02	.10
189 Darryl Talley	.01	.05
190 James Hasty	.01	.05
191 Jay Schroeder	.01	.05
192 Kenneth Davis	.01	.05
193 Chris Miller	.02	.10
194 Scott Davis	.01	.05
195 Tim Green	.01	.05
196 Dan Saleaumua	.01	.05
197 Rohn Stark	.01	.05
198 John Alt	.01	.05
199 Steve Tasker	.02	.10
200 Checklist 101-200	.01	.05
201 Freddie Joe Nunn	.01	.05
202 Jim Breech	.01	.05
203 Roy Green	.01	.05
204 Gary Anderson RB	.01	.05
205 Rich Camarillo	.01	.05
206 Mark Bortz	.01	.05
207 Eddie Brown	.01	.05
208 Brad Muster	.01	.05
209 Anthony Munoz	.02	.10
210 Dalton Hilliard	.01	.05
211 Erik McMillan	.01	.05
212 Perry Kemp	.01	.05
213 James Thornton	.01	.05
214 Anthony Dilweg	.01	.05
215 Cleveland Gary	.01	.05
216 Leo Goeas	.01	.05
217 Mike Merriweather	.01	.05
218 Courtney Hall	.01	.05
219 Wade Wilson	.02	.10
220 Billy Joe Tolliver	.01	.05
221 Harold Green	.02	.10
222 Al(Bubba) Baker	.02	.10
223 Carl Zander	.01	.05
224 Thane Gash	.01	.05
225 Kevin Mack	.01	.05
226 Morten Andersen	.01	.05
227 Dennis Gentry	.01	.05
228 Vince Buck	.01	.05
229 Mike Singletary	.02	.10
230 Rueben Mayes	.01	.05
231 Mark Carrier WR	.08	.25
232 Tony Mandarich	.01	.05
233 Al Toon	.02	.10
234 Renaldo Turnbull	.01	.05
235 Broderick Thomas	.01	.05
236 Anthony Carter	.02	.10
237 Flipper Anderson	.01	.05
238 Jerry Robinson	.01	.05
239 Vince Newsome	.01	.05
240 Keith Millard	.01	.05
241 Reggie Langhorne	.01	.05
242 James Francis	.01	.05
243 Felix Wright	.01	.05
244 Neal Anderson	.02	.10
245 Boomer Esiason	.02	.10
246 Pat Swilling	.02	.10
247 Richard Dent	.02	.10
248 Craig Heyward	.02	.10
249 Ron Morris	.01	.05
250 Eric Martin	.01	.05
251 Jim C. Jensen	.01	.05
252 Anthony Toney	.01	.05
253 Sammie Smith	.01	.05
254 Calvin Williams	.02	.10
255 Dan Marino	.50	1.25
256 Warren Moon	.08	.25
257 Tommie Agee	.01	.05
258 Haywood Jeffires	.02	.10
259 Eugene Lockhart	.01	.05
260 Drew Hill	.01	.05
261 Vinny Testaverde	.02	.10
262 Jim Arnold	.01	.05
263 Steve Christie	.01	.05
264 Chris Spielman	.02	.10
265 Reggie Cobb	.01	.05
266 John Stephens	.01	.05
267 Jay Hilgenberg	.01	.05
268 Brent Williams	.01	.05
269 Rodney Hampton	.08	.25
270 Irving Fryar	.02	.10
271 Terry McDaniel	.01	.05
272 Reggie Roby	.01	.05
273 Allen Pinkett	.01	.05
274 Tim McKyer	.01	.05
275 Bob Golic	.01	.05
276 Wilber Marshall	.01	.05
277 Ray Childress	.01	.05
278 Charles Mann	.01	.05
279 Cris Dishman RC	.01	.05
280 Mark Rypien	.02	.10
281 Michael Cofer	.01	.05
282 Keith Byars	.01	.05
283 Mike Rozier	.01	.05
284 Seth Joyner	.02	.10
285 Jessie Tuggle	.01	.05
286 Mark Bavaro	.01	.05
287 Eddie Anderson	.01	.05
288 Sean Landeta	.01	.05
289 H.Long/George Brett	.08	.25
290 Reyna Thompson	.01	.05
291 Ferrell Edmunds	.01	.05
292 Willie Gault	.02	.10
293 John Offerdahl	.01	.05
294 Tim Brown	.08	.25
295 Bruce Matthews	.02	.10
296 Kevin Ross	.01	.05
297 Lorenzo White	.01	.05
298 Dino Hackett	.01	.05
299 Curtis Duncan	.01	.05
300 Checklist 201-300	.01	.05
301 Andre Ware	.02	.10
302 David Little	.01	.05
303 Jerry Ball	.01	.05
304 Dwight Stone UER	.01	.05
305 Rodney Peete	.02	.10
306 Mike Baab	.01	.05
307 Tim Worley	.01	.05
308 Paul Farren	.01	.05
309 Carnell Lake	.01	.05
310 Clay Matthews	.02	.10
311 Alton Montgomery	.01	.05
312 Ernest Givins	.02	.10
313 Mike Horan	.01	.05
314 Sean Jones	.02	.10
315 Leonard Smith	.01	.05
316 Carl Banks	.01	.05
317 Jerome Brown	.01	.05
318 Everson Walls	.01	.05
319 Ron Heller	.01	.05
320 Mark Collins	.01	.05
321 Eddie Murray	.01	.05
322 Jim Harbaugh	.08	.25
323 Mel Gray	.02	.10
324 Keith Van Horne	.01	.05
325 Lomas Brown	.01	.05
326 Carl Lee	.01	.05
327 Ken O'Brien	.01	.05
328 Dermontti Dawson	.02	.10
329 Brad Baxter	.01	.05
330 Chris Doleman	.01	.05
331 Louis Oliver	.01	.05
332 Frank Stams	.01	.05
333 Mike Munchak	.02	.10
334 Fred Strickland	.01	.05
335 Mark Duper	.02	.10
336 Jacob Green	.01	.05
337 Tony Paige	.01	.05
338 Jeff Bryant	.01	.05
339 Lemuel Stinson	.01	.05
340 David Wyman	.01	.05
341 Lee Williams	.01	.05
342 Trace Armstrong	.01	.05
343 Junior Seau	.08	.25
344 John Roper	.01	.05
345 Jeff George	.08	.25
346 Herschel Walker	.02	.10
347 Sam Clancy	.01	.05
348 Steve Jordan	.01	.05
349 Nate Odomes	.01	.05
350 Martin Bayless	.01	.05
351 Brent Jones	.08	.25
352 Ray Agnew	.01	.05
353 Charles Haley	.02	.10
354 Andre Tippett	.01	.05
355 Ronnie Lott	.02	.10
356 Thurman Thomas	.08	.25
357 Fred Barnett	.08	.25
358 James Lofton	.02	.10
359 William Frizzell RC	.01	.05
360 Keith McKeller	.01	.05
361 Rodney Holman	.01	.05
362 Henry Ellard	.02	.10
363 David Fulcher	.01	.05
364 Jerry Gray	.01	.05
365 James Brooks	.02	.10
366 Tony Stargell	.01	.05
367 Keith McCants	.01	.05
368 Lewis Billups	.01	.05
369 Ervin Randle	.01	.05
370 Pat Leahy	.01	.05
371 Bruce Armstrong	.01	.05
372 Steve DeBerg	.01	.05
373 Guy McIntyre	.01	.05
374 Deron Cherry	.01	.05
375 Fred Marion	.01	.05
376 Michael Haddix	.01	.05
377 Kent Hull	.01	.05
378 Jerry Holmes	.01	.05
379 Jim Ritcher	.01	.05
380 Ed West	.01	.05
381 Richmond Webb	.01	.05
382 Mark Jackson	.01	.05
383 Tom Newberry	.01	.05
384 Ricky Nattiel	.01	.05
385 Keith Sims	.01	.05
386 Ron Hall	.01	.05
387 Ken Norton	.02	.10
388 Paul Gruber	.01	.05
389 Daniel Stubbs	.01	.05
390 Ian Beckles	.01	.05
391 Hoby Brenner	.01	.05
392 Tory Epps	.01	.05
393 Sam Mills	.01	.05
394 Chris Hinton	.01	.05
395 Steve Walsh	.01	.05
396 Simon Fletcher	.01	.05
397 Tony Bennett	.02	.10
398 Aundray Bruce	.01	.05
399 Mark Murphy	.01	.05
400 Checklist 301-400	.01	.05
401 Barry Sanders SL	.20	.50
402 Jerry Rice SL	.15	.40
403 Warren Moon SL	.02	.10
404 Derrick Thomas SL	.02	.10
405 Nick Lowery LL	.01	.05
406 Mark Carrier DB LL	.02	.10
407 Michael Carter	.01	.05
408 Chris Singleton	.01	.05
409 Matt Millen	.02	.10
410 Ronnie Lippett	.01	.05
411 E.J. Junior	.01	.05
412 Ray Donaldson	.01	.05
413 Keith Willis	.01	.05
414 Jessie Hester	.01	.05
415 Jeff Cross	.01	.05
416 Greg Jackson RC	.01	.05
417 Alvin Walton	.01	.05
418 Bart Oates	.01	.05
419 Chip Lohmiller	.01	.05
420 John Elliott	.01	.05
421 Randall McDaniel	.02	.10
422 Richard Johnson CB RC	.01	.05
423 Al Noga	.01	.05
424 Lamar Lathon	.01	.05
425 Rick Fenney	.01	.05
426 Jack Del Rio	.02	.10
427 Don Mosebar	.01	.05
428 Luis Sharpe	.01	.05
429 Steve Wisniewski	.01	.05
430 Jimmie Jones	.01	.05
431 Freeman McNeil	.01	.05
432 Ron Rivera	.01	.05
433 Hart Lee Dykes	.01	.05
434 Mark Carrier DB	.02	.10
435 Rob Moore	.08	.25
436 Gary Clark	.08	.25
437 Heath Sherman	.01	.05
438 Darrell Green	.01	.05
439 Jessie Small	.01	.05
440 Monte Coleman	.01	.05
441 Leonard Marshall	.01	.05
442 Richard Johnson	.01	.05
443 Dave Meggett	.02	.10
444 Barry Sanders	.50	1.25
445 Lawrence Taylor	.08	.25
446 Marcus Allen	.08	.25
447 Johnny Johnson	.01	.05
448 Aaron Wallace	.01	.05
449 Anthony Thompson	.01	.05
450 D.Marino/S.DeBerg CL	.15	.40
451 Andre Rison MVP	.02	.10
452 Thurman Thomas MVP	.02	.10
453 Neal Anderson MVP	.01	.05
454 Boomer Esiason MVP	.01	.05
455 Eric Metcalf MVP	.02	.10
456 Emmitt Smith MVP	.50	1.25
457 Bobby Humphrey MVP	.01	.05
458 Barry Sanders MVP	.20	.50
459 Sterling Sharpe MVP	.02	.10
460 Warren Moon MVP	.02	.10
461 Albert Bentley MVP	.01	.05
462 Steve DeBerg MVP	.01	.05
463 Greg Townsend MVP	.01	.05
464 Henry Ellard MVP	.02	.10
465 Dan Marino MVP	.20	.50
466 Anthony Carter MVP	.02	.10
467 John Stephens MVP	.01	.05
468 Pat Swilling MVP	.01	.05
469 Ottis Anderson MVP	.02	.10
470 Dennis Byrd MVP	.01	.05
471 Randall Cunningham MVP	.02	.10
472 Johnny Johnson MVP	.01	.05
473 Rod Woodson MVP	.02	.10
474 Anthony Miller MVP	.02	.10
475 Jerry Rice MVP	.15	.40
476 John L.Williams MVP	.01	.05
477 Wayne Haddix MVP	.01	.05
478 Earnest Byner MVP	.01	.05
479 Doug Widell	.01	.05
480 Tommy Hodson	.01	.05
481 Shawn Collins	.01	.05
482 Rickey Jackson	.01	.05
483 Tony Casillas	.01	.05
484 Vaughan Johnson	.01	.05
485 Floyd Dixon	.01	.05
486 Eric Green	.01	.05
487 Harry Hamilton	.01	.05
488 Gary Anderson K	.01	.05
489 Bruce Hill	.01	.05
490 Gerald Williams	.01	.05
491 Cortez Kennedy	.08	.25
492 Chet Brooks	.01	.05
493 Dwayne Harper RC	.01	.05
494 Don Griffin	.01	.05
495 Andy Heck	.01	.05
496 David Treadwell	.01	.05
497 Irv Pankey	.01	.05
498 Dennis Smith	.01	.05
499 Marcus Dupree	.08	.25
500 Checklist 401-500	.01	.05
501 Wendell Davis	.01	.05
502 Matt Bahr	.01	.05
503 Rob Burnett RC	.02	.10
504 Maurice Carthon	.01	.05
505 Donnell Woolford	.01	.05
506 Howard Ballard	.01	.05
507 Mark Boyer	.01	.05
508 Eugene Marve	.01	.05
509 Joe Kelly	.01	.05
510 Will Wolford	.01	.05
511 Robert Clark	.01	.05
512 Matt Brock RC	.01	.05
513 Chris Warren	.08	.25
514 Ken Willis	.01	.05
515 George Jamison RC	.01	.05
516 Rufus Porter	.01	.05
517 Mark Higgs RC	.01	.05
518 Thomas Everett	.01	.05
519 Robert Brown	.01	.05
520 Gene Atkins	.01	.05
521 Hardy Nickerson	.02	.10
522 Johnny Bailey	.01	.05
523 William Frizzell	.01	.05
524 Steve McMichael	.02	.10
525 Kevin Porter	.01	.05
526 Carwell Gardner	.01	.05
527 Eugene Daniel	.01	.05
528 Vestee Jackson	.01	.05
529 Chris Goode	.01	.05
530 Leon Seals	.01	.05
531 Darion Conner	.01	.05
532 Stan Brock	.01	.05
533 Kirby Jackson RC	.01	.05
534 Marv Cook	.01	.05
535 Bill Fralic	.01	.05
536 Keith Woodside	.01	.05
537 Hugh Green	.01	.05
538 Grant Feasel	.01	.05
539 Bubba McDowell	.01	.05
540 Vai Sikahema	.01	.05
541 Aaron Cox	.01	.05
542 Roger Craig	.02	.10
543 Robb Thomas	.01	.05
544 Ronnie Lott	.02	.10
545 Robert Delpino	.01	.05
546 Greg McMurtry	.01	.05
547 Jim Morrissey RC	.01	.05
548 Johnny Rembert	.01	.05
549 Markus Paul RC	.01	.05
550 Karl Wilson RC	.01	.05
551 Gaston Green	.01	.05
552 Willie Drewrey	.01	.05
553 Michael Young	.01	.05
554 Tom Tupa	.01	.05
555 John Friesz	.08	.25
556 Cody Carlson RC	.01	.05
557 Eric Allen	.01	.05
558 Thomas Benson	.01	.05
559 Scott Mersereau RC	.01	.05
560 Lionel Washington	.01	.05
561 Brian Brennan	.01	.05
562 Jim Jeffcoat	.01	.05
563 Jeff Jaeger	.01	.05
564 D.J. Johnson	.01	.05
565 Danny Villa	.01	.05
566 Don Beebe	.01	.05
567 Michael Haynes	.08	.25
568 Brett Faryniarz RC	.01	.05
569 Mike Prior	.01	.05
570 John Davis RC	.01	.05
571 Vernon Turner RC	.01	.05
572 Michael Brooks	.01	.05
573 Mike Gann	.01	.05
574 Ron Holmes	.01	.05
575 Gary Plummer	.01	.05
576 Bill Romanowski	.01	.05
577 Chris Jacke	.01	.05
578 Gary Reasons	.01	.05
579 Tim Jorden RC	.01	.05
580 Tim McKyer	.01	.05
581 Johnnie Jackson RC	.01	.05
582 Ethan Horton	.01	.05
583 Pete Stoyanovich	.01	.05
584 Jeff Query	.01	.05
585 Frank Reich	.02	.10
586 Riki Ellison	.01	.05
587 Eric Hill	.01	.05
588 Anthony Shelton RC	.01	.05
589 Steve Smith	.01	.05
590 Garth Jax RC	.01	.05
591 Greg Davis RC	.01	.05
592 Bill Maas	.01	.05
593 Henry Rolling RC	.01	.05
594 Keith Jones	.01	.05
595 Tootie Robbins	.01	.05
596 Brian Jordan	.02	.10
597 Derrick Walker RC	.01	.05
598 Jonathan Hayes	.01	.05
599 Nate Lewis RC	.01	.05
600 Checklist 501-600	.01	.05
601 Croel/Lewis/Tray/Walk CL	.01	.05
602 James Jones RC	.01	.05
603 Tim Barnett RC	.01	.05
604 Ed King RC	.01	.05
605 Shane Curry	.01	.05
606 Mike Croel	.01	.05
607 Bryan Cox RC	.08	.25
608 Shawn Jefferson RC	.02	.10
609 Kenny Walker RC	.01	.05
610 Michael Jackson WR RC	.08	.25
611 Jon Vaughn RC	.01	.05
612 Greg Lewis	.01	.05
613 Joe Valerio RC	.01	.05
614 Pat Harlow RC	.01	.05
615 Henry Jones RC	.02	.10
616 Jeff Graham RC	.08	.25
617 Darryll Lewis RC	.02	.10
618 Keith Traylor UER RC	.01	.05
619 Scott Miller RF	.01	.05
620 Nick Bell	.01	.05
621 John Flannery RC	.01	.05
622 Leonard Russell RC	.02	.10
623 Alfred Williams RC	.01	.05
624 Browning Nagle	.01	.05
625 Harvey Williams	.02	.10
626 Dan McGwire	.01	.05
627 Favre/Pritch/Pgrm CL	.20	.50
628 William Thomas RC	.01	.05
629 Lawrence Dawsey RC	.02	.10
630 Aeneas Williams RC	.50	1.25
631 Stan Thomas RF	.01	.05
632 Randal Hill	.01	.05
633 Moe Gardner RC	.01	.05
634 Alvin Harper	.02	.10
635 Esera Tuaolo RC	.01	.05
636 Russell Maryland	.02	.10
637 Anthony Morgan RC	.01	.05
638 Erric Pegram RC	.08	.25
639 Herman Moore	.08	.25
640 Ricky Ervins RC	.02	.10
641 Kelvin Pritchett RC	.02	.10
642 Roman Phifer RC	.01	.05
643 Antone Davis RC	.01	.05
644 Mike Pritchard	.02	.10
645 Vinnie Clark RC	.01	.05
646 Jake Reed RC	.20	.50
647 Brett Favre	1.50	4.00
648 Todd Lyght	.01	.05
649 Bruce Pickens	.01	.05
650 Darren Lewis RC	.01	.05
651 Wesley Carroll	.01	.05
652 James Joseph RC	.02	.10
653 R.Delpino/T.McDonald AR	.01	.05
654 D.Sanders/V.Glenn AR	.01	.05
655 J.Rice/T.McDaniels AR	.10	.30
656 B.Sanders/D.Thomas AR	.20	.50
657 K.Tippins/L.White AR	.01	.05
658 C.Okoye/J.Green AR	.01	.05
659 Rich Gannon	.08	.25
660 Johnny Meads	.01	.05
661 J.J. Birden RC	.02	.10
662 Bruce Kozerski	.01	.05
663 Felix Wright	.01	.05
664 Al Smith	.01	.05
665 Stan Humphries	.08	.25
666 Alfred Anderson	.01	.05
667 Nate Newton	.02	.10
668 Vince Workman RC	.02	.10
669 Ricky Reynolds	.01	.05
670 Bryce Paup RC	.08	.25
671 Gill Fenerty	.01	.05
672 Darrell Thompson	.01	.05
673 Anthony Smith	.01	.05
674 Darryl Henley RC	.01	.05
675 Brett Maxie	.01	.05
676 Craig Taylor RC	.01	.05
677 Steve Wallace	.02	.10
678 Jeff Feagles RC	.01	.05
679 James Washington RC	.01	.05
680 Tim Harris	.01	.05
681 Dennis Gibson	.01	.05
682 Toi Cook RC	.01	.05
683 Lorenzo Lynch	.01	.05
684 Brad Edwards RC	.01	.05
685 Ray Crockett RC	.01	.05
686 Harris Barton	.01	.05
687 Byron Evans	.01	.05
688 Eric Thomas	.01	.05
689 Jeff Criswell	.01	.05
690 Eric Ball	.01	.05
691 Brian Mitchell	.02	.10
692 Quinn Early	.02	.10
693 Aaron Jones	.01	.05
694 Jim Dombrowski	.01	.05
695 Jeff Bostic	.01	.05
696 Tony Casillas	.01	.05
697 Ken Lanier	.01	.05
698 Henry Thomas	.01	.05
699 Steve Beuerlein	.02	.10
700 Checklist 601-700	.01	.05
1P Joe Montana Promo	1.00	2.50
500P Barry Sanders Promo	.75	2.00
SP1 Darrell Green Fastest	.20	.50
SP2 Don Shula 300th Win	.30	.75

1991 Upper Deck Game Breaker Holograms

This nine-card hologram standard-size set spotlights outstanding NFL running backs. Holograms 1-6 were randomly inserted in Upper Deck low series wax packs, and holograms 7-9 were inserted in the high series.

Card	Low	High
COMPLETE SET (9)	3.00	8.00
GB1 Barry Sanders	1.00	2.50
GB2 Thurman Thomas	.20	.50
GB3 Bobby Humphrey	.07	.20
GB4 Earnest Byner	.07	.20
GB5 Emmitt Smith	2.00	5.00
GB6 Neal Anderson	.10	.30
GB7 Marion Butts	.10	.30
GB8 James Brooks	.10	.30
GB9 Marcus Allen	.20	.50

1991 Upper Deck Joe Montana Heroes

This ten-card Joe Montana standard-size set introduces Upper Deck's "Football Heroes" series, which were randomly inserted into 1991 Upper Deck first series foil packs. Montana personally autographed 2500 of these cards, which feature a diamond hologram as a sign of authenticity. Card number 9 features a portrait of Montana by noted sports artist Vernon Wells.

Card	Low	High
COMPLETE SET (10)	4.00	10.00
COMMON MONTANA (1-9)	.30	.75
RANDOM INSERTS IN LO SER		
AU Joe Montana AU	40.00	100.00
NNO Title Header Card SP	4.00	8.00

1991 Upper Deck Heroes Montana Box Bottoms

These eight oversized "cards" (approximately 5 1/4" by 7 1/4") were featured on the bottom of 1991 Upper Deck low series wax boxes. They are identical in design to the Montana Football Heroes insert cards, with the same color player photos in an oval frame. The backs are blank and the cards are unnumbered. We have checklisted them below according to their Heroes card numbering.

Card	Low	High
COMPLETE SET (8)	2.40	6.00
COMMON CARD (1-8)	.40	1.00

1991 Upper Deck Joe Namath Heroes

This ten-card Joe Namath standard-size set is the second part of Upper Deck's "Football Heroes" series, which were inserted in its High Number Series packs. Namath personally autographed 2,500 of these cards, and every 100th card was signed "Broadway Joe." Card number 18 features a portrait of Namath by noted sports artist Vernon Wells. The cards are numbered (10-18) in continuation of the Joe Montana Heroes set.

Card	Low	High
COMPLETE SET (10)	4.00	10.00
COMMON NAMATH (10-18)	.30	.75
RANDOM INSERTS IN HI SER		
18B Joe Namath AU/2500	60.00	120.00
NNO Title Header Card SP	4.00	8.00

1991 Upper Deck Heroes Namath Box Bottoms

These eight oversized "cards" (approximately 5 1/4" by 7 1/4") were featured on the bottom of 1991 Upper Deck high series wax boxes. They are identical in design to the Namath Football Heroes insert cards, with the same color player photos in an oval frame. The backs are blank and the cards are unnumbered. We have checklisted them below according to the numbering of the Heroes cards.

Card	Low	High
COMPLETE SET (8)	2.40	6.00
COMMON CARD (10-17)	.40	1.00

1991 Upper Deck Sheets

Upper Deck issued two football sheets in 1991. The 8 1/2" by 11" sheet to honor the Super Bowl XXV Champions features six Upper Deck Giants cards, which are listed as they appear counterclockwise beginning from the upper left corner. The background is a green football field design. At the top are the words, "Washington Redskins vs. New York Giants" and "The Upper Deck Company Salutes The Super Bowl XXV Champions" in yellow lettering. In the center are game highlights in red lettering. The sheet is bordered by two blue and one red stripe. The issue date appears in the lower right corner as do the production run and issue number, which appear in the Upper Deck gold foil stamp. The Rams sheet commemorated the 40th anniversary of the 1951 Rams championship team. 60,000 numbered Ram sheets were distributed. The backs of both sheets are blank.

Card	Low	High
COMPLETE SET (2)	4.00	10.00
1 Los Angeles Rams	2.00	5.00
2 New York Giants	2.00	5.00

1992 Upper Deck

The 1992 Upper Deck football set was issued in two series and totaled 620 standard-size cards. No low series cards were included in this year's second series packs. First series packs featured the following random insert sets: a ten-card Walter Payton "Football Heroes"; a 15-card Pro Bowl; and five Game Breaker holograms (GB1, GB3, GB4, GB6, and

GB8). Randomly inserted throughout series II foil packs were a ten-card Dan Marino "Football Heroes" subset, special cards of James Lofton (SP3) and Art Monk (SP4), and three Game Breaker holograms (GB2, GB5, and GB7). A 20-card "Coach's Report" insert set was featured only in hobby packs while ten "Fanimation" cards were included only in retail packs. Members of both NFL Properties and the NFL Players Association are included in the second series.

COMPLETE SET (620) 6.00 15.00
COMP.SERIES 1 (400) 4.00 10.00
COMP.SERIES 2 (220) 2.50 5.00
1 Bennett/Buckley/McNabb C .02 .10
2 Edgar Bennett RC .08 .25
3 Eddie Blake RC .01 .05
4 Brian Bollinger RC .01 .05
5 Joe Bowden RC .01 .05
6 Terrell Buckley RC .01 .05
7 Willie Clay RC .01 .05
8 Ed Cunningham RC .01 .05
9 Matt Darby RC .01 .05
10 Will Furrer RC .01 .05
11 Chris Hakel RC .01 .05
12 Carlos Huerta .01 .05
13 Amp Lee RC .01 .05
14 Ricardo McDonald RC .01 .05
15 Dexter McNabb RC .01 .05
16 Chris Mims RC .01 .05
17 Derrick Moore RC .02 .10
18 Mark D'Onofrio RC .01 .05
19 Patrick Rowe RC .01 .05
20 Leon Searcy RC .01 .05
21 Torrance Small RC .02 .10
22 Jimmy Smith RC 1.25 3.00
23 Tony Smith WR RC .01 .05
24 Siran Stacy RC .01 .05
25 Kevin Turner RC .01 .05
26 Tommy Vardell RC .01 .05
27 Bob Whitfield RC .01 .05
28 Darryl Williams RC .01 .05
29 Jeff Sydner RC .01 .05
30 Mike Croel/L.Russell CL .01 .05
31 Todd Marinovich ART .01 .05
32 Leonard Russell ART .01 .05
33 Nick Bell ART .01 .05
34 Alvin Harper ART .01 .05
35 Mike Pritchard ART .01 .05
36 Lawrence Dawsey AR .01 .05
37 Tim Barnett AR .01 .05
38 John Flannery AR .01 .05
39 Stan Thomas AR .01 .05
40 Ed King AR .01 .05
41 Charles McRae AR .01 .05
42 Eric Moten AR .01 .05
43 Moe Gardner AR .01 .05
44 Kenny Walker AR .01 .05
45 Esera Tuaolo AR .01 .05
46 Alfred Williams AR .01 .05
47 Bryan Cox AR .01 .05
48 Mo Lewis AR .01 .05
49 Mike Croel ART .01 .05
50 Stanley Richard AR .01 .05
51 Tony Covington AR .01 .05
52 Larry Brown DB AR .01 .05
53 Aeneas Williams AR .01 .05
54 John Kasay AR .01 .05
55 Jon Vaughn ART .01 .05
56 David Fulcher .01 .05
57 Barry Foster .02 .10
58 Terry Wooden .01 .05
59 Gary Anderson K .01 .05
60 Alfred Williams .01 .05
61 Robert Blackmon .01 .05
62 Brian Noble .01 .05
63 Terry Allen .08 .25
64 Darrell Green .01 .05
65 Darren Comeaux .01 .05
66 Rob Burnett .01 .05
67 Jarrod Bunch .01 .05
68 Michael Jackson .02 .10
69 Greg Lloyd .02 .10
70 Richard Brown RC .01 .05
71 Harold Green .01 .05
72 William Fuller .01 .05
73 Mark Carrier DB TC .01 .05
74 David Fulcher TC .01 .05
75 Cornelius Bennett TC .01 .05
76 Steve Atwater TC .01 .05
77 Kevin Mack TC .01 .05
78 Mark Carrier WR TC .01 .05
79 Tim McDonald TC .01 .05
80 Marion Butts TC .01 .05
81 Christian Okoye TC .01 .05
82 Jeff Herrod TC .01 .05
83 Emmitt Smith TC .25 .60
84 Mark Duper TC .01 .05
85 Keith Jackson TC .01 .05
86 Andre Rison TC .02 .10
87 John Taylor TC .01 .05
88 Rodney Hampton TC .02 .10
89 Rob Moore TC .01 .05
90 Chris Spielman TC .01 .05
91 Haywood Jeffires TC .01 .05
92 Sterling Sharpe TC .02 .10
93 Irving Fryar TC .01 .05
94 Marcus Allen TC .02 .10
95 Henry Ellard TC .01 .05
96 Mark Rypien TC .01 .05
97 Pat Swilling TC .01 .05
98 Brian Blades TC .01 .05
99 Eric Green TC .01 .05
100 Anthony Carter TC .01 .05
101 Burt Grossman .01 .05
102 Gary Anderson RB .01 .05
103 Neil Smith .08 .25
104 Jeff Feagles .01 .05
105 Shane Conlan .01 .05
106 Jay Novacek .02 .10
107 Bill Brooks .01 .05
108 Mark Ingram .01 .05
109 Anthony Munoz .02 .10
110 Wendell Davis .01 .05
111 Jim Everett .02 .10
112 Bruce Matthews .01 .05
113 Mark Higgs .01 .05
114 Chris Warren .02 .10
115 Brad Baxter .01 .05
116 Greg Townsend .01 .05
117 Al Smith .01 .05
118 Jeff Cross .01 .05
119 Terry McDaniel .01 .05
120 Ernest Givins .02 .10
121 Fred Barnett .02 .10
122 Flipper Anderson .01 .05
123 Floyd Turner .01 .05
124 Stephen Baker .01 .05
125 Tim Johnson .01 .05
126 Brent Jones .02 .10
127 Leonard Marshall .01 .05
128 Jim Price .01 .05
129 Jessie Hester .01 .05
130 Mark Carrier WR .02 .10
131 Bubba McDowell .01 .05
132 Andre Tippett .01 .05
133 James Hasty .01 .05
134 Mel Gray .02 .10
135 Christian Okoye .01 .05
136 Earnest Byner .01 .05
137 Ferrell Edmunds .01 .05
138 Henry Ellard .02 .10
139 Rob Moore .02 .10
140 Brian Jordan .02 .10
141 Clarence Verdin .01 .05
142 Cornelius Bennett .02 .10
143 John Taylor .02 .10
144 Derrick Thomas .08 .25
145 Thurman Thomas .08 .25
146 Warren Moon .08 .25
147 Vinny Testaverde .02 .10
148 Steve Bono RC .08 .25
149 Robb Thomas .01 .05
150 John Friesz .02 .10
151 Richard Dent .02 .10
152 Eddie Anderson .01 .05
153 Kevin Greene .02 .10
154 Marion Butts .01 .05
155 Barry Sanders .50 1.25
156 Andre Rison .02 .10
157 Ronnie Lott .02 .10
158 Eric Allen .01 .05
159 Mark Clayton .02 .10
160 Terance Mathis .02 .10
161 Darryl Talley .01 .05
162 Eric Metcalf .02 .10
163 Reggie Cobb .01 .05
164 Ernie Jones .01 .05
165 David Griggs .01 .05
166 Tom Rathman .01 .05
167 Bubby Brister .02 .10
168 Broderick Thomas .01 .05
169 Chris Doleman .01 .05
170 Charles Haley .02 .10
171 Michael Haynes .02 .10
172 Rodney Hampton .02 .10
173 Nick Bell .01 .05
174 Gene Atkins .01 .05
175 Mike Merriweather .01 .05
176 Reggie Roby .01 .05
177 Bennie Blades .01 .05
178 John L. Williams .01 .05
179 Rodney Peete .02 .10
180 Greg Montgomery .01 .05
181 Vince Newsome .01 .05
182 Andre Collins .01 .05
183 Erik Kramer .02 .10
184 Bryan Hinkle .01 .05
185 Reggie White .08 .25
186 Bruce Armstrong .01 .05
187 Anthony Carter .02 .10
188 Pat Swilling .01 .05
189 Robert Delpino .01 .05
190 Brent Williams .01 .05
191 Johnny Johnson .01 .05
192 Aaron Craver .01 .05
193 Vincent Brown .01 .05
194 Herschel Walker .02 .10
195 Tim McDonald .01 .05
196 Gaston Green .01 .05
197 Brian Blades .02 .10
198 Rod Bernstine .01 .05
199 Brett Perriman .02 .10
200 John Elway .50 1.25
201 Michael Carter .01 .05
202 Mark Carrier DB .01 .05
203 Cris Carter .20 .50
204 Kyle Clifton .01 .05
205 Alvin Wright .01 .05
206 Andre Ware .01 .05
207 Dave Waymer .01 .05
208 Darren Lewis .01 .05
209 Joey Browner .01 .05
210 Rich Miano .01 .05
211 Marcus Allen .08 .25
212 Steve Broussard .01 .05
213 Joel Hilgenberg .01 .05
214 Bo Orlando RC .01 .05
215 Clay Matthews .02 .10
216 Chris Hinton .01 .05
217 Al Edwards .01 .05
218 Tim Brown .08 .25
219 Sam Mills .01 .05
220 Don Majkowski .01 .05
221 James Francis .01 .05
222 Steve Hendrickson RC .01 .05
223 James Thornton .01 .05
224 Byron Evans .01 .05
225 Pepper Johnson .01 .05
226 Darryl Henley .01 .05
227 Simon Fletcher .01 .05
228 Hugh Millen .01 .05
229 Tim McGee .01 .05
230 Richmond Webb .01 .05
231 Tony Bennett .01 .05
232 Nate Odomes .01 .05
233 Scott Case .01 .05
234 Dalton Hilliard .01 .05
235 Paul Gruber .01 .05
236 Jeff Lageman .01 .05
237 Tony Mandarich .01 .05
238 Cris Dishman .01 .05
239 Steve Walsh .01 .05
240 Moe Gardner .01 .05
241 Bill Romanowski .01 .05
242 Chris Zorich .02 .10
243 Stephone Paige .01 .05
244 Mike Croel .01 .05
245 Leonard Russell .02 .10
246 Mark Rypien .01 .05
247 Aeneas Williams .02 .10
248 Steve Atwater .01 .05
249 Michael Stewart .01 .05
250 Pierce Holt .01 .05
251 Kevin Mack .01 .05
252 Sterling Sharpe .08 .25
253 Lawrence Dawsey .02 .10
254 Emmitt Smith .60 1.50
255 Todd Marinovich .01 .05
256 Neal Anderson .01 .05
257 Mo Lewis .01 .05
258 Vance Johnson .01 .05
259 Rickey Jackson .01 .05
260 Esera Tuaolo .01 .05
261 Wilber Marshall .01 .05
262 Keith Henderson .01 .05
263 William Thomas .01 .05
264 Rickey Dixon .01 .05
265 Dave Meggett .02 .10
266 Gerald Riggs .01 .05
267 Tim Harris .01 .05
268 Ken Harvey .01 .05
269 Clyde Simmons .01 .05
270 Irving Fryar .02 .10
271 Darion Conner .01 .05
272 Vince Workman .01 .05
273 Jim Harbaugh .08 .25
274 Lorenzo White .01 .05
275 Bobby Hebert .01 .05
276 Duane Bickett .01 .05
277 Jeff Bryant .01 .05
278 Scott Stephen .01 .05
279 Bob Golic .01 .05
280 Steve McMichael .02 .10
281 Jeff Graham .08 .25
282 Keith Jackson .02 .10
283 Howard Ballard .01 .05
284 Michael Brooks .01 .05
285 Freeman McNeil .02 .10
286 Rodney Holman .01 .05
287 Eric Bieniemy .01 .05
288 Seth Joyner .01 .05
289 Carwell Gardner .01 .05
290 Brian Mitchell .02 .10
291 Chris Miller .02 .10
292 Ray Berry .01 .05
293 Matt Brock .01 .05
294 Eric Thomas .01 .05
295 John Kasay .01 .05
296 Jay Hilgenberg .01 .05
297 Darrell Thompson .01 .05
298 Rich Gannon .08 .25
299 Steve Young .25 .60
300 Mike Kenn .01 .05
301 Emmitt Smith SL .25 .60
302 Haywood Jeffires SL .01 .05
303 Michael Irvin SL .08 .25
304 Warren Moon SL .02 .10
305 Chip Lohmiller SL .01 .05
306 Barry Sanders SL .20 .50
307 Ronnie Lott SL .02 .10
308 Pat Swilling SL .01 .05
309 Thurman Thomas SL .02 .10
310 Reggie Roby SL .01 .05
311 Moon/Irvin/T.Thomas CL .02 .10
312 Jacob Green .01 .05
313 Stephen Braggs .01 .05
314 Haywood Jeffires .02 .10
315 Freddie Joe Nunn .01 .05
316 Gary Clark .02 .10
317 Tim Barnett .01 .05
318 Mark Duper .01 .05
319 Eric Green .01 .05
320 Robert Wilson .01 .05
321 Michael Ball .01 .05
322 Eric Martin .01 .05
323 Alexander Wright .01 .05
324 Jessie Tuggle .01 .05
325 Ronnie Harmon .01 .05
326 Jeff Hostetler .02 .10
327 Eugene Daniel .01 .05
328 Ken Norton Jr. .02 .10
329 Reyna Thompson .01 .05
330 Jerry Ball .01 .05
331 Leroy Hoard .02 .10
332 Chris Martin .01 .05
333 Keith McKeller .01 .05
334 Brian Washington .01 .05
335 Eugene Robinson .01 .05
336 Maurice Hurst .01 .05
337 Dan Saleaumua .01 .05
338 Neil O'Donnell .02 .10
339 Dexter Davis .01 .05
340 Keith McCants .01 .05
341 Steve Beuerlein .02 .10
342 Roman Phifer .01 .05
343 Bryan Cox .02 .10
344 Art Monk .02 .10
345 Michael Irvin .08 .25
346 Vaughan Johnson .01 .05
347 Jeff Herrod .01 .05
348 Stanley Richard .01 .05
349 Michael Young .01 .05
350 R.Hampton/R.Cobb CL .02 .10
351 Jim Harbaugh MVP .02 .10
352 David Fulcher MVP .01 .05
353 Thurman Thomas MVP .02 .10
354 Gaston Green MVP .01 .05
355 Leroy Hoard MVP .01 .05
356 Reggie Cobb MVP .01 .05
357 Tim McDonald MVP .01 .05
358 Ronnie Harmon MVP UER .01 .05
359 Derrick Thomas MVP .02 .10
360 Jeff Herrod MVP .01 .05
361 Michael Irvin MVP .08 .25
362 Mark Higgs MVP .01 .05
363 Reggie White MVP .02 .10
364 Chris Miller MVP .01 .05
365 Steve Young MVP .10 .30
366 Rodney Hampton MVP .02 .10
367 Jeff Lageman MVP .01 .05
368 Barry Sanders MVP .20 .50
369 Haywood Jeffires MVP .01 .05
370 Tony Bennett MVP .01 .05
371 Leonard Russell MVP .01 .05
372 Jeff Jaeger MVP .01 .05
373 Robert Delpino MVP .01 .05
374 Mark Rypien MVP .01 .05
375 Pat Swilling MVP .01 .05
376 Cortez Kennedy MVP .02 .10
377 Eric Green MVP .01 .05
378 Cris Carter MVP .02 .10
379 John Roper .01 .05
380 Barry Word .01 .05
381 Shawn Jefferson .01 .05
382 Tony Casillas .01 .05
383 John Baylor RC .01 .05
384 Al Noga .01 .05
385 Charles Mann .01 .05
386 Gill Byrd .01 .05
387 Chris Singleton .01 .05
388 James Joseph .01 .05
389 Larry Brown DB .01 .05
390 Chris Spielman .02 .10
391 Anthony Thompson .01 .05
392 Karl Mecklenburg .01 .05
393 Joe Kelly .01 .05
394 Kanavis McGhee .01 .05
395 Bill Maas .01 .05
396 Marv Cook .01 .05
397 Louis Lipps .01 .05
398 Marty Carter RC .01 .05
399 Louis Oliver .01 .05
400 Eric Swann .02 .10
401 Troy Auzenne RC .01 .05
402 Kurt Barber .01 .05
403 Marc Boutte RC .01 .05
404 Dale Carter .02 .10
405 Marco Coleman .01 .05
406 Quentin Coryatt .01 .05
407 Shane Dronett RC .01 .05
408 Vaughn Dunbar .01 .05
409 Steve Emtman .01 .05
410 Dana Hall RC .01 .05
411 Jason Hanson RC .02 .10
412 Courtney Hawkins RC .02 .10
413 Terrell Buckley .01 .05
414 Robert Jones RC .01 .05
415 David Klingler .01 .05
416 Tommy Maddox .60 1.50
417 Johnny Mitchell RC .01 .05
418 Carl Pickens .02 .10
419 Tracy Scroggins .01 .05
420 Tony Sacca RC .01 .05
421 Kevin Smith DB .01 .05
422 Alonzo Spellman .02 .10
423 Troy Vincent RC .01 .05
424 Sean Gilbert RC .02 .10
425 Larry Webster RC .01 .05
426 C.Pickens/Klingler CL .02 .10
427 Bill Fralic .01 .05
428 Kevin Murphy .01 .05
429 Lemuel Stinson .01 .05
430 Harris Barton .01 .05
431 Dino Hackett .01 .05
432 John Stephens .01 .05
433 Keith Jennings RC .01 .05
434 Derrick Fenner .01 .05
435 Kenneth Gant RC .01 .05
436 Willie Gault .02 .10
437 Steve Jordan .01 .05
438 Charles Haley .02 .10
439 Keith Kartz .01 .05
440 Nate Lewis .01 .05
441 Doug Widell .01 .05
442 William White .01 .05
443 Eric Hill .01 .05
444 Melvin Jenkins .01 .05
445 David Wyman .01 .05
446 Ed West .01 .05
447 Brad Muster .01 .05
448 Ray Childress .01 .05
449 Kevin Ross .01 .05
450 Johnnie Jackson .01 .05
451 Tracy Simien RC .01 .05
452 Don Mosebar .01 .05
453 Jay Hilgenberg .01 .05
454 Wes Hopkins .01 .05
455 Jay Schroeder .01 .05
456 Jeff Bostic .01 .05
457 Bryce Paup .08 .25
458 Dave Waymer .01 .05
459 Toi Cook .01 .05
460 Anthony Smith .01 .05
461 Don Griffin .01 .05
462 Bill Hawkins .01 .05
463 Courtney Hall .01 .05
464 Jeff Uhlenhake .01 .05
465 Mike Sherrard .01 .05
466 James Jones DT .01 .05
467 Jerrol Williams .01 .05
468 Eric Ball .01 .05
469 Randall McDaniel .02 .10
470 Alvin Harper .02 .10
471 Tom Waddle .01 .05
472 Tony Woods .01 .05
473 Kelvin Martin .01 .05
474 Jon Vaughn .01 .05
475 Gill Fenerty .01 .05
476 Aundray Bruce .01 .05
477 Morten Andersen .01 .05
478 Lamar Lathon .01 .05
479 Steve DeOssie .01 .05
480 Marvin Washington .01 .05
481 Herschel Walker .02 .10
482 Howie Long .08 .25
483 Calvin Williams .02 .10
484 Brett Favre 1.25 2.50
485 Johnny Bailey .01 .05
486 Jeff Gossett .01 .05
487 Carnell Lake .01 .05
488 Michael Zordich RC .01 .05
489 Henry Rolling .01 .05
490 Steve Smith .01 .05
491 Vestee Jackson .01 .05
492 Ray Crockett .01 .05
493 Dexter Carter .01 .05
494 Nick Lowery .01 .05
495 Cortez Kennedy .02 .10
496 Cleveland Gary .01 .05
497 Kelly Stouffer .01 .05
498 Carl Carter .01 .05
499 Shannon Sharpe .08 .25
500 Roger Craig .02 .10
501 Willie Drewrey .01 .05
502 Mark Schlereth RC .01 .05
503 Tony Martin .02 .10
504 Tom Newberry .01 .05
505 Ron Hall .01 .05
506 Scott Miller .01 .05
507 Donnell Woolford .01 .05
508 Dave Krieg .02 .10
509 Erric Pegram .02 .10
510 Checklist 401-510 .01 .05
511 Barry Sanders SBK .25 .60
512 Thurman Thomas SBK .02 .10
513 Warren Moon SBK .02 .10
514 John Elway SBK .20 .50
515 Ronnie Lott SBK .02 .10
516 Emmitt Smith SBK .25 .60
517 Andre Rison SBK .02 .10
518 Steve Atwater SBK .01 .05
519 Steve Young SBK .10 .30
520 Mark Rypien SBK .01 .05
521 Rich Camarillo .01 .05
522 Mark Bavaro .01 .05
523 Brad Edwards .01 .05
524 Chad Hennings RC .02 .10
525 Tony Paige .01 .05
526 Shawn Moore .01 .05
527 Sidney Johnson RC .01 .05
528 Sanjay Beach RC .01 .05
529 Kelvin Pritchett .01 .05
530 Jerry Holmes .01 .05
531 Al Del Greco .01 .05
532 Bob Gagliano .01 .05
533 Drew Hill .01 .05
534 Donald Frank RC .01 .05
535 Pio Sagapolutele RC .01 .05
536 Jackie Slater .01 .05
537 Vernon Turner .01 .05
538 Bobby Humphrey .01 .05
539 Audray McMillian .01 .05
540 Gary Brown RC .08 .25
541 Wesley Carroll .01 .05
542 Nate Newton .01 .05
543 Vai Sikahema .01 .05
544 Chris Chandler .08 .25
545 Nolan Harrison RC .01 .05
546 Mark Green .01 .05
547 Ricky Watters .08 .25
548 J.J. Birden .01 .05
549 Cody Carlson .01 .05
550 Tim Green .01 .05
551 Mark Jackson .01 .05
552 Vince Buck .01 .05
553 George Jamison .01 .05
554 Anthony Pleasant .01 .05
555 Reggie Johnson .01 .05
556 John Jackson .01 .05
557 Ian Beckles .01 .05
558 Buford McGee .01 .05
559 Fuad Reveiz UER .01 .05
560 Joe Montana .50 1.25
561 Phil Simms .02 .10
562 Greg McMurtry .01 .05
563 Gerald Williams .01 .05
564 Dave Cadigan .01 .05
565 Rufus Porter .01 .05
566 Jim Kelly .08 .25
567 Deion Sanders .20 .50
568 Mike Singletary .02 .10
569 Boomer Esiason .02 .10
570 Andre Reed .02 .10
571 James Washington .01 .05
572 Jack Del Rio .01 .05
573 Gerald Perry .01 .05
574 Vinnie Clark .01 .05
575 Mike Piel .01 .05
576 Michael Dean Perry .02 .10
577 Ricky Proehl .01 .05
578 Leslie O'Neal .02 .10
579 Russell Maryland .01 .05
580 Eric Dickerson .02 .10
581 Fred Strickland .01 .05
582 Nick Lowery .01 .05
583 Joe Milinichik RC .01 .05
584 Mark Vlasic .01 .05
585 James Lofton .02 .10
586 Bruce Smith .08 .25
587 Harvey Williams .02 .10
588 Bernie Kosar .02 .10
589 Carl Banks .01 .05
590 Jeff George .08 .25
591 Fred Jones RC .01 .05
592 Todd Scott .01 .05
593 Keith Jones .01 .05
594A Tootie Robbins ERR .01 .05
594B Tootie Robbins COR .01 .05
595 Todd Philcox RC .01 .05
596 Browning Nagle .01 .05
597 Troy Aikman .30 .75
598 Dan Marino .50 1.25
599 Lawrence Taylor .08 .25
600 Webster Slaughter .01 .05
601 Aaron Cox .01 .05
602 Matt Stover .01 .05
603 Keith Sims .01 .05
604 Dennis Smith .01 .05
605 Kevin Porter .01 .05
606 Anthony Miller .02 .10
607 Ken O'Brien .01 .05
608 Randall Cunningham .08 .25
609 Timm Rosenbach .01 .05
610 Junior Seau .08 .25
611 Johnny Rembert .01 .05
612 Rick Tuten .01 .05
613 Willie Green .01 .05
614 Sean Salisbury UER RC .01 .05
615 Martin Bayless .01 .05
616 Jerry Rice .30 .75
617 Randal Hill .01 .05
618 Dan McGwire .01 .05
619 Merril Hoge .01 .05
620 Checklist 571-620 .01 .05
A560 Joe Montana Blowup UDA 6.00 15.00
A598 Dan Marino Blowup UDA 6.00 15.00
SP3 James Lofton Yardage .30 .75
SP4 Art Monk Catches .20 .50

1992 Upper Deck Gold

These 50 standard-size cards feature players licensed by NFL Properties. Each low series foil box contained one 15-card foil pack of these cards. Two Game Breaker holograms of Jerry Rice and Andre Reed were randomly inserted throughout these packs. On the Quarterback Club cards, the player's name is printed in a black stripe along the left edge, while the other cards have the player's name and position printed in different designs at the bottom. Though the backs of the Prospects cards feature a career summary, the backs of the remaining cards carry a color close-up photo as well as biography, statistics, or player profile. Two distinguishing features of the backs are a gold (instead of silver) Upper Deck hologram image and the NFL Properties logo. The cards are numbered on the back with a "G" prefix and subdivided into NFL Top Prospects (1-20), Quarterback Club (21-25), and veteran players (26-50). The key Rookie Cards in this set are Quentin Coryatt, Steve Emtman and Carl Pickens.

COMPLETE SET (50) 5.00 12.00
G1 Steve Emtman RC .02 .10
G2 Carl Pickens RC .10 .30
G3 Dale Carter RC .10 .30
G4 Greg Skrepenak RC .02 .10
G5 Kevin Smith RC .05 .15
G6 Marco Coleman RC .05 .15
G7 David Klingler RC .05 .15
G8 Phillippi Sparks RC .02 .10
G9 Tommy Maddox RC .60 1.50
G10 Quentin Coryatt RC .05 .15
G11 Ty Detmer .10 .30
G12 Vaughn Dunbar RC .02 .10
G13 Ashley Ambrose RC .10 .30
G14 Kurt Barber RC .02 .10
G15 Chester McGlockton RC .10 .30
G16 Todd Collins RC .02 .10
G17 Steve Israel RC .02 .10
G18 Marquez Pope RC .02 .10
G19 Alonzo Spellman RC .05 .15
G20 Tracy Scroggins RC .02 .10
G21 Jim Kelly QC .10 .30
G22 Troy Aikman QC .25 .60
G23 Randall Cunningham QC .10 .30
G24 Bernie Kosar QC .05 .15
G25 Dan Marino QC .40 1.00
G26 Andre Reed .05 .15
G27 Deion Sanders .20 .50
G28 Randal Hill .02 .10
G29 Eric Dickerson .05 .15
G30 Jim Kelly .10 .30
G31 Bernie Kosar .05 .15
G32 Mike Singletary .05 .15
G33 Anthony Miller .05 .15
G34 Harvey Williams .10 .30
G35 Randall Cunningham .10 .30
G36 Joe Montana .50 1.25
G37 Dan McGwire .02 .10
G38 Al Toon .05 .15
G39 Carl Banks .02 .10
G40 Troy Aikman .30 .75
G41 Junior Seau .10 .30
G42 Jeff George .10 .30
G43 Michael Dean Perry .05 .15
G44 Lawrence Taylor .10 .30
G45 Dan Marino .50 1.25
G46 Jerry Rice .30 .75
G47 Boomer Esiason .05 .15
G48 Bruce Smith .10 .30
G49 Leslie O'Neal .05 .15
G50 Checklist Card .02 .10

1992 Upper Deck Coach's Report

These 20 standard-size cards were randomly inserted throughout 1992 Upper Deck II hobby foil packs only. The set features Chuck Noll, former Steelers' head coach, analyzing 1992 rookies along with outstanding second-year players on their potential to achieve stardom in the NFL. The cards are numbered (with a "CR" prefix) on a white stripe that cuts across the top of the card.

COMPLETE SET (20) 6.00 15.00
RANDOM INSERTS IN SER.2 HOBBY PACKS
CR1 Mike Pritchard .05 .15
CR2 Will Furrer .05 .15
CR3 Alfred Williams .05 .15
CR4 Tommy Vardell .05 .15
CR5 Brett Favre 3.00 8.00
CR6 Alvin Harper .10 .30
CR7 Mike Croel .05 .15
CR8 Herman Moore .10 .30
CR9 Edgar Bennett .30 .75
CR10 Todd Marinovich .05 .15
CR11 Aeneas Williams .10 .30
CR12 Ricky Watters .30 .75
CR13 Amp Lee .05 .15
CR14 Terrell Buckley .05 .15
CR15 Tim Barnett .05 .15
CR16 Nick Bell .05 .15
CR17 Leonard Russell .10 .30
CR18 Lawrence Dawsey .10 .30
CR19 Robert Porcher .05 .15
CR20 Ricky Watters CL .10 .30

1992 Upper Deck Fanimation

These ten standard-size cards were randomly inserted throughout 1992 Upper Deck second series retail foil packs only and were the work of artists Jim Lee and Rob Liefeld. The cards feature on the fronts full-bleed color cartoon illustrations that are based on NFL stars. The "Fanimation" logo appears in one of the lower corners. On a background that shades from red to orange to yellow, the backs have a head shot, biography (including topics such as "Armament" and "Special Features"), and a discussion of the character's strengths. The cards are numbered on the back in the upper left corner with an "F" prefix. The player's nickname is mentioned in the listing below.

COMPLETE SET (10) 10.00 25.00
RANDOM INSERTS IN SER.2 RETAIL PACKS
F1 Jim Kelly .50 1.25
F2 Dan Marino 4.00 8.00
F3 Lawrence Taylor .50 1.25
F4 Deion Sanders 2.00 4.00
F5 Troy Aikman 3.00 6.00
F6 Junior Seau .50 1.25
F7 Mike Singletary .50 1.25
F8 Eric Dickerson .50 1.25
F9 Jerry Rice 3.00 6.00
F10 Jim Kelly 2.00 4.00
D.Marino CL

1992 Upper Deck Game Breaker Holograms

is nine-card hologram standard-size set showcases some of the NFL's standout wide receivers. Card numbers 1, 3, 4, 6, 8, and 9 were randomly inserted in 1992 Upper Deck first series packs while card numbers 2, 5, and 7 were found in the second series. The cards are numbered on the back with a "GB" prefix.

COMPLETE SET (9) 2.50 6.00
STATED ODDS 1:30 PACKS
GB2/GB5/GB7 ISSUED WITH SER.2
GB1 Art Monk .15 .40
GB2 Drew Hill .07 .20
GB3 Haywood Jeffires .15 .40
GB4 Andre Rison .15 .40
GB5 Mark Clayton .15 .40
GB6 Jerry Rice 1.50 3.00
GB7 Michael Haynes .15 .40
GB8 Andre Reed .15 .40
GB9 Michael Irvin .40 1.00

1992 Upper Deck Dan Marino Heroes

This ten-card standard-size set chronicles the collegiate and professional career of Dan Marino. The cards were randomly inserted in 1992 Upper Deck second series foil packs. The cards are numbered (28-36) in continuation of the Upper Deck Football Heroes set. Upper Deck Authenticated sold complete sets with the Header card signed by Marino and serial numbered of 2800-cards.

COMPLETE SET (10) 10.00 25.00
COMMON MARINO (28-36) 1.25 3.00
MARINO HEADER (NNO) 2.00 5.00
RANDOM INSERTS IN SER.2 PACKS
NNO D.Marino AU/2800 20.00 50.00

1992 Upper Deck Walter Payton Heroes

Randomly inserted in first series foil packs, this ten-card standard-size set depicts the former Chicago Bears running back Walter Payton during various stages of his career.The cards are numbered (19-27) as a continuation of Upper Deck's "Football Heroes" series. Upper Deck Authenticated sold complete sets with the Header card signed by Payton and serial numbered of 2800-cards.

COMPLETE SET (10) 8.00 20.00
COMMON PAYTON (19-27) 1.25 3.00
PAYTON HEADER (NNO) 2.00 5.00
RANDOM INSERTS IN SER.1 PACKS
NNO W.Payton Hdr AU/2800 125.00 250.00

1992 Upper Deck Heroes Payton Box Bottoms

These eight oversized "cards" (approximately 5 1/4" by 7 1/4") were featured on the bottoms of 1992 Upper Deck first series waxboxes. They are identical in design to the Payton Football Heroes insert cards, with the same color player photos in an oval picture frame. The backs are blank and the cards are unnumbered. We have checklisted them below according to the numbering of the Heroes cards.

COMPLETE SET (8) 2.40 6.00
COMMON CARD (19-26) .40 1.00

1992 Upper Deck Pro Bowl

Randomly inserted in series I foil packs, this 16-card standard-size set featured players from the 1992 Pro Bowl in Hawaii. The horizontal fronts carry two full-bleed player photos; the left one features an AFC Pro Bowl player, while the right one has a NFC Pro Bowl player. The photos are separated by a rainbow consisting of six different color bands and overprinted with "Pro Bowl" in silver foil lettering. When rotated under a light, the bands reflect light in different directions. This unique look was produced by a process called prismatic lithography. The player's name in silver foil lettering at the bottom rounds out the front. On two rainbow-colored panels, the horizontal backs present a career summary for each player. The cards are numbered on the back with a "PB" prefix.

COMPLETE SET (16) 7.50 20.00
STATED ODDS 1:30 SER.1 PACKS
PB1 M.Irvin .75 2.00
H.Jeffires
PB2 G.Clark .40 1.00
M.Clayton
PB3 A.Munoz J.Lachey .60 1.50
PB4 W.Moon .75 2.00
M.Rypien
PB5 B.Sanders 2.00 5.00
T.Thomas
PB6 E.Smith 2.50 6.00
M.Butts
PB7 R.White .75 2.00
G.Townsend
PB8 C.Bennett .40 1.00
S.Joyner
PB9 D.Thomas .75 2.00
P.Swilling
PB10 D.Talley .40 1.00
C.Spielman
PB11 R.Lott .60 1.50
M.Carrier DB
PB12 S.Atwater .40 1.00
S.Gayle
PB13 R.Woodson .60 1.50
D.Green
PB14 J.Gossett .40 1.00
C.Lohmiller
PB15 T.Brown .75 2.00
M.Gray
PB16 Checklist Card .75 2.00

1992 Upper Deck NFL Sheets

As an advertising promotion, Upper Deck released 8 1/2" by 11" commemorative sheets printed on card stock and picturing a series of Upper Deck cards. The fronts feature either captions indicating the event the sheet commemorates, or text advertising Upper Deck cards. The sheets have an Upper Deck stamp indicating the production run and serial number. The backs of the game sheets are blank. The backs of the advertising sheets are printed in black with the words "Upper Deck Limited Edition Commemorative Sheet." The AFC and NFC championship game commemorative sheets were distributed at Upper Deck's Super Bowl Card Show III and at the NFL Experience in Minneapolis. In the listing of sheets below, the players cards are listed beginning in the upper left corner of the sheet and moving toward the lower right corner. A sheet was also issued to promote Upper Deck's 1992 Comic Ball Comic Bowl IV cards. The front features a color photo of Lawrence Taylor, Jerry Rice, Thurman Thomas, Dan Marino, and various Looney Tunes characters set against a blue sky background. A green bottom border carries the issue number and production run in the Upper Deck gold foil stamp, the Looney Tunes logo, and product information. The Comic Ball logo overlaps the green border and the photo. The entire sheet is bordered by a thin black and wider white border.

COMPLETE SET (5) 10.00 25.00
1 AFC Championship 1.60 4.00
2 NFC Championship 1.60 4.00
3 Super Bowl XXVI 2.40 6.00
4 Super Bowl XXVI 1.60 4.00
5 Comic Ball IV 4.00 10.00

1992 Upper Deck SCD Sheets

Upper Deck produced eight different sheets for insertion into the Sept. 18, 1992, issue of Sports Collector's Digest. Reportedly 8,000 of each sheet were produced, and one was inserted into each SCD issue. Each 11" by 8 1/2" sheet features two rows of three cards each, on a speckled granite background. The backs are covered by the phrase "Upper Deck Limited Edition Commemorative Sheet." The sheets are numbered at the lower left corner "Version X of 8."

COMPLETE SET (8) 24.00 60.00
1 Marino 6.00 15.00
Aikman
2 Carl Pickens 1.60 4.00
3 Quentin Coryatt 1.60 4.00
4 Ty Detmer 1.60 4.00
5 Eric Dickerson 2.40 6.00
Deion
Kelly
6 Joe Montana 6.00 15.00
Cunning.
7 Aikman 4.00 10.00
Toon
J.George
8 Dan Marino 6.00 15.00
LT
Rice

1992-93 Upper Deck NFL Experience

This 50-card standard-size set commemorates the stars of previous Super Bowls and potential stars of tomorrow. The set was produced in conjunction with the NFL Experience, a theme park held January 28-31, 1993, at the Rose Bowl (Pasadena, California), the site of Super Bowl XXVII. The set was available only through hobby dealers and was introduced at the Super Bowl Card Show at the NFL Experience. The fronts of card numbers 1-20 have full-bleed color player photos that are edged on two sides by various border stripes, while the fronts of cards numbers 21-50 feature color player photos tilted slightly to the left and bordered in the remaining area by a ghosted background. Some cards are accented with silver foil highlights, with at least one set in every case having gold-foil highlights. The backs present a color close-up photo, player profile, game performance summary, or player quote. The set is subdivided as follows: Super Bowl MVPs (1-5), Super Bowl Moments (6-10), Future Champions (11-20), and Super Bowl Dreams (21-50).

COMPLETE SET (50) 4.00 8.00
*GOLDS: 1.2X TO 3X SILVERS
1 Joe Montana MVP 1.00 2.50
2 Roger Staubach MVP .20 .50
3 Bart Starr MVP .20 .50
4 Len Dawson MVP .07 .20
5 Fred Biletnikoff MVP .07 .20
6 Jim Plunkett .07 .20
7 Terry Bradshaw .20 .50
8 Jerry Rice .40 1.00
9 Doug Williams .02 .10
10 Dan Marino .80 2.00
11 David Klingler .07 .20
12 Steve Emtman .02 .10
13 Dale Carter .02 .10
14 Quentin Coryatt .07 .20
15 Tommy Maddox .10 .30
16 Vaughn Dunbar .02 .10
17 Marco Coleman .02 .10
18 Carl Pickens .07 .20
19 Sean Gilbert .07 .20
20 Tony Smith RB .02 .10
21 Jim Kelly .15 .40
22 Dan Marino .80 2.00
23 Boomer Esiason .07 .20
24 Bernie Kosar .02 .10
25 Ken O'Brien .02 .10
26 Deion Sanders .30 .75
27 Mike Singletary .07 .20
28 Andre Reed .07 .20
29 Michael Dean Perry .02 .10
30 Ricky Proehl .02 .10
31 Leslie O'Neal .02 .10
32 Jerry Rice .40 1.00
33 Eric Dickerson .07 .20
34 Troy Aikman .40 1.00
35 Bruce Smith .07 .20
36 Browning Nagle .02 .10
37 Carl Banks .02 .10
38 Harvey Williams .07 .20
39 Jeff George .07 .20
40 Lawrence Taylor .08 .25
41 Webster Slaughter .02 .10
42 Anthony Miller .07 .20
43 Randall Cunningham .07 .20
44 Timm Rosenbach .02 .10
45 Russell Maryland .02 .10
46 Randal Hill .02 .10
47 Dan McGwire .02 .10
48 Merril Hoge .02 .10
49 Kevin Fagan .02 .10
50 Junior Seau .07 .20

1993 Upper Deck

e 1993 Upper Deck football set was issued in a single series consisting of 530 standard-size cards. Cards were issued in 12-card hobby and retail packs and 22-card jumbo packs. Topical subsets featured are Star Rookies (1-29), All-Rookie Team (30-55), Hitmen (56-62), Team Checklists (63-90), Season Leaders (421-431), and Berman's Best (432-442). Rookie Cards include Jerome Bettis, Drew Bledsoe, Reggie Brooks, Curtis Conway, Garrison Hearst, Terry Kirby, O.J. McDuffie, Natrone Means and Rick Mirer. An Eric Dickerson Promo card was produced to preview the set. It can easily be differentiated from the regular issue card by the team (Raiders for the promo card, Falcons for the regular issue).

COMPLETE SET (530) 10.00 25.00
1 Mirer/Hearst/Con/Ken CL .08 .25
2 Eric Curry RC .01 .05
3 Rick Mirer RC .08 .25
4 Dan Williams RC .01 .05
5 Marvin Jones RC .01 .05
6 Willie Roaf RC .10 .30
7 Reggie Brooks RC .02 .10
8 Horace Copeland RC .02 .10
9 Lincoln Kennedy RC .01 .05
10 Curtis Conway RC .15 .40
11 Drew Bledsoe RC 1.00 2.50
12 Patrick Bates RC .01 .05
13 Wayne Simmons RC .01 .05
14 Irv Smith RC .01 .05
15 Robert Smith RC .50 1.25
16 O.J.McDuffie RC .08 .25
17 Darrien Gordon RC .01 .05
18 John Copeland RC .02 .10
19 Derek Brown RBK RC .01 .05
20 Jerome Bettis RC 2.50 5.00
21 Deon Figures RC .01 .05
22 Glyn Milburn RC .08 .25
23 Garrison Hearst RC .30 .75
24 Qadry Ismail RC .08 .25
25 Terry Kirby RC .08 .25
26 Lamar Thomas RC .01 .05
27 Tom Carter RC .02 .10
28 Andre Hastings RC .02 .10
29 George Teague RC .02 .10
30 Tommy Maddox CL .02 .10
31 David Klingler ART .01 .05
32 Tommy Maddox ART .02 .10
33 Vaughn Dunbar ART .01 .05
34 Rodney Culver ART .01 .05
35 Carl Pickens ART .02 .10
36 Courtney Hawkins ART .01 .05
37 Tyji Armstrong ART .01 .05
38 Ray Roberts ART .01 .05
39 Troy Auzenne ART .01 .05
40 Shane Dronett ART .01 .05
41 Chris Mims ART .01 .05
42 Sean Gilbert ART .01 .05
43 Steve Emtman ART .01 .05
44 Robert Jones ART .01 .05
45 Marco Coleman ART .01 .05
46 Ricardo McDonald ART .01 .05
47 Quentin Coryatt ART .02 .10
48 Dana Hall ART .01 .05
49 Darren Perry ART .01 .05
50 Darryl Williams ART .01 .05
51 Kevin Smith ART .01 .05
52 Terrell Buckley ART .01 .05
53 Troy Vincent ART .01 .05
54 Lin Elliott ART .01 .05
55 Dale Carter ART .01 .05

Card	Low	High
56 Steve Atwater HIT	.01	.05
57 Junior Seau HIT	.02	.10
58 Ronnie Lott HIT	.01	.05
59 Louis Oliver HIT	.01	.05
60 Cortez Kennedy HIT	.01	.05
61 Pat Swilling HIT	.01	.05
62 Hitmen Checklist	.01	.05
63 Curtis Conway TC	.08	.25
64 Alfred Williams TC	.01	.05
65 Jim Kelly TC	.02	.10
66 Simon Fletcher TC	.01	.05
67 Eric Metcalf TC	.01	.05
68 Lawrence Dawsey TC	.01	.05
69 Garrison Hearst TC	.08	.25
70 Anthony Miller TC	.01	.05
71 Neil Smith TC	.01	.05
72 Jeff George TC	.02	.10
73 Emmitt Smith TC	.30	.75
74 Dan Marino TC	.30	.75
75 Clyde Simmons TC	.01	.05
76 Deion Sanders TC	.08	.25
77 Ricky Watters TC	.02	.10
78 Rodney Hampton TC	.02	.10
79 Brad Baxter TC	.01	.05
80 Barry Sanders TC	.25	.60
81 Warren Moon TC	.02	.10
82 Brett Favre TC	.40	1.00
83 Drew Bledsoe TC	.50	1.25
84 Tim Brown TC	.02	.10
85 Jim Everett TC	.01	.05
86 Earnest Byner TC	.01	.05
87 Wayne Martin TC	.01	.05
88 Rick Mirer TC	.08	.25
89 Barry Foster TC	.01	.05
90 Terry Allen TC	.02	.10
91 Vinnie Clark	.01	.05
92 Howard Ballard	.01	.05
93 Eric Ball	.01	.05
94 Marc Boutte	.01	.05
95 Larry Centers RC	.08	.25
96 Gary Brown	.01	.05
97 Hugh Millen	.01	.05
98 Anthony Newman RC	.01	.05
99 Darrell Thompson	.01	.05
100 George Jamison	.01	.05
101 James Francis	.01	.05
102 Leonard Harris	.01	.05
103 Lomas Brown	.01	.05
104 James Lofton	.02	.10
105 Jamie Dukes	.01	.05
106 Quinn Early	.02	.10
107 Ernie Jones	.01	.05
108 Torrance Small	.01	.05
109 Michael Carter	.01	.05
110 Aeneas Williams	.01	.05
111 Renaldo Turnbull	.01	.05
112 Al Smith	.01	.05
113 Troy Auzenne	.01	.05
114 Stephen Baker	.01	.05
115 Daniel Stubbs	.01	.05
116 Dana Hall	.01	.05
117 Lawrence Taylor	.08	.25
118 Ron Hall	.01	.05
119 Derrick Fenner	.01	.05
120 Martin Mayhew	.01	.05
121 Jay Schroeder	.01	.05
122 Michael Zordich	.01	.05
123 Ed McCaffrey	.08	.25
124 John Stephens	.01	.05
125 Brad Edwards	.01	.05
126 Don Griffin	.01	.05
127 Broderick Thomas	.01	.05
128 Ted Washington	.01	.05
129 Haywood Jeffires	.02	.10
130 Gary Plummer	.01	.05
131 Mark Wheeler	.01	.05
132 Ty Detmer	.08	.25
133 Derrick Walker	.01	.05
134 Henry Ellard	.02	.10
135 Neal Anderson	.01	.05
136 Bruce Smith	.08	.25
137 Cris Carter	.08	.25
138 Vaughn Dunbar	.01	.05
139 Dan Marino	.60	1.50
140 Troy Aikman	.30	.75
141 Randall Cunningham	.08	.25
142 Daryl Johnston	.08	.25
143 Mark Clayton	.01	.05
144 Rich Gannon	.08	.25
145 Nate Newton	.02	.10
146 Willie Gault	.01	.05
147 Brian Washington	.01	.05
148 Fred Barnett	.02	.10
149 Gill Byrd	.01	.05
150 Art Monk	.02	.10
151 Stan Humphries	.02	.10
152 Charles Mann	.01	.05
153 Greg Lloyd	.02	.10
154 Marvin Washington	.01	.05
155 Bernie Kosar	.02	.10
156 Pete Metzelaars	.01	.05
157 Chris Hinton	.01	.05
158 Jim Harbaugh	.08	.25
159 Willie Davis	.08	.25
160 Leroy Thompson	.01	.05
161 Scott Miller	.01	.05
162 Eugene Robinson	.01	.05
163 David Little	.01	.05
164 Pierce Holt	.01	.05
165 James Hasty	.01	.05
166 Dave Krieg	.02	.10
167 Gerald Williams	.01	.05
168 Kyle Clifton	.01	.05
169 Bill Brooks	.01	.05
170 Vance Johnson	.01	.05
171 Greg Townsend	.01	.05
172 Jason Belser	.01	.05
173 Brett Perriman	.08	.25
174 Steve Jordan	.01	.05
175 Kelvin Martin	.01	.05
176 Greg Kragen	.01	.05
177 Kerry Cash	.01	.05
178 Chester McGlockton	.02	.10
179 Jim Kelly	.08	.25
180 Todd McNair	.01	.05
181 Leroy Hoard	.02	.10
182 Seth Joyner	.01	.05
183 Sam Gash RC	.08	.25
184 Joe Nash	.01	.05
185 Lin Elliott RC	.01	.05
186 Robert Porcher	.01	.05
187 Tommy Hodson	.01	.05
188 Greg Lewis	.01	.05
189 Dan Saleaumua	.01	.05
190 Chris Goode	.01	.05
191 Henry Thomas	.01	.05
192 Bobby Hebert	.01	.05
193 Clay Matthews	.02	.10
194 Mark Carrier WR	.02	.10
195 Anthony Pleasant	.01	.05
196 Eric Dorsey	.01	.05
197 Clarence Verdin	.01	.05
198 Marc Spindler	.01	.05
199 Tommy Maddox	.08	.25
200 Wendell Davis	.01	.05
201 John Fina	.01	.05
202 Alonzo Spellman	.01	.05
203 Darryl Williams	.01	.05
204 Mike Croel	.01	.05
205 Ken Norton Jr.	.02	.10
206 Mel Gray	.02	.10
207 Chuck Cecil	.01	.05
208 John Flannery	.01	.05
209 Chip Banks	.01	.05
210 Chris Martin	.01	.05
211 Dennis Brown	.01	.05
212 Vinny Testaverde	.02	.10
213 Nick Bell	.01	.05
214 Robert Delpino	.01	.05
215 Mark Higgs	.01	.05
216 Al Noga	.01	.05
217 Andre Tippett	.01	.05
218 Pat Swilling	.01	.05
219 Phil Simms	.02	.10
220 Ricky Proehl	.01	.05
221 William Thomas	.01	.05
222 Jeff Graham	.02	.10
223 Darion Conner	.01	.05
224 Mark Carrier DB	.01	.05
225 Willie Green	.01	.05
226 Reggie Rivers RC	.01	.05
227 Andre Reed	.02	.10
228 Deion Sanders	.20	.50
229 Chris Doleman	.01	.05
230 Jerry Ball	.01	.05
231 Eric Dickerson	.02	.10
232 Carlos Jenkins	.01	.05
233 Mike Johnson	.01	.05
234 Marco Coleman	.01	.05
235 Leslie O'Neal	.02	.10
236 Browning Nagle	.01	.05
237 Carl Pickens	.02	.10
238 Steve Emtman	.01	.05
239 Alvin Harper	.02	.10
240 Keith Jackson	.02	.10
241 Jerry Rice	.40	1.00
242 Cortez Kennedy	.02	.10
243 Tyji Armstrong	.01	.05
244 Troy Vincent	.01	.05
245 Randal Hill	.01	.05
246 Robert Blackmon	.01	.05
247 Junior Seau	.08	.25
248 Sterling Sharpe	.08	.25
249 Thurman Thomas	.08	.25
250 David Klingler	.01	.05
251 Jeff George	.08	.25
252 Anthony Miller	.02	.10
253 Earnest Byner	.01	.05
254 Eric Swann	.02	.10
255 Jeff Herrod	.01	.05
256 Eddie Robinson	.01	.05
257 Eric Allen	.01	.05
258 John Taylor	.02	.10
259 Sean Gilbert	.02	.10
260 Ray Childress	.01	.05
261 Michael Haynes	.02	.10
262 Greg McMurtry	.01	.05
263 Bill Romanowski	.01	.05
264 Todd Lyght	.01	.05
265 Clyde Simmons	.01	.05
266 Webster Slaughter	.01	.05
267 J.J. Birden	.01	.05
268 Aaron Wallace	.01	.05
269 Carl Banks	.01	.05
270 Ricardo McDonald	.01	.05
271 Michael Brooks	.01	.05
272 Dale Carter	.01	.05
273 Mike Pritchard	.02	.10
274 Derek Brown TE	.01	.05
275 Burt Grossman	.01	.05
276 Mark Schlereth	.01	.05
277 Karl Mecklenburg	.01	.05
278 Rickey Jackson	.01	.05
279 Ricky Ervins	.01	.05
280 Jeff Bryant	.01	.05
281 Eric Martin	.01	.05
282 Carlton Haselrig	.01	.05
283 Kevin Mack	.01	.05
284 Brad Muster	.01	.05
285 Kelvin Pritchett	.01	.05
286 Courtney Hawkins	.01	.05
287 Levon Kirkland	.01	.05
288 Steve DeBerg	.01	.05
289 Edgar Bennett	.08	.25
290 Michael Dean Perry	.02	.10
291 Richard Dent	.02	.10
292 Howie Long	.08	.25
293 Chris Mims	.01	.05
294 Kurt Barber	.01	.05
295 Wilber Marshall	.01	.05
296 Ethan Horton	.01	.05
297 Tony Bennett	.01	.05
298 Johnny Johnson	.01	.05
299 Craig Heyward	.02	.10
300 Steve Israel	.01	.05
301 Kenneth Gant	.01	.05
302 Eugene Chung	.01	.05
303 Harvey Williams	.02	.10
304 Jarrod Bunch	.01	.05
305 Darren Perry	.01	.05
306 Steve Christie	.01	.05
307 John Randle	.02	.10
308 Warren Moon	.08	.25
309 Charles Haley	.02	.10
310 Tony Smith RB	.01	.05
311 Steve Broussard	.01	.05
312 Alfred Williams	.01	.05
313 Terrell Buckley	.01	.05
314 Trace Armstrong	.01	.05
315 Brian Mitchell	.02	.10
316 Steve Atwater	.01	.05
317 Nate Lewis	.01	.05
318 Richard Brown	.01	.05
319 Rufus Porter	.01	.05
320 Pat Harlow	.01	.05
321 Anthony Smith	.01	.05
322 Jack Del Rio	.01	.05
323 Darryl Talley	.01	.05
324 Sam Mills	.01	.05
325 Chris Miller	.02	.10
326 Ken Harvey	.01	.05
327 Rod Woodson	.08	.25
328 Tony Tolbert	.01	.05
329 Todd Kinchen	.01	.05
330 Brian Noble	.01	.05
331 Dave Meggett	.01	.05
332 Chris Spielman	.02	.10
333 Barry Word	.01	.05
334 Jessie Hester	.01	.05
335 Michael Jackson	.02	.10
336 Mitchell Price	.01	.05
337 Michael Irvin	.08	.25
338 Simon Fletcher	.01	.05
339 Keith Jennings	.01	.05
340 Vai Sikahema	.01	.05
341 Roger Craig	.02	.10
342 Ricky Watters	.08	.25
343 Reggie Cobb	.01	.05
344 Kanavis McGhee	.01	.05
345 Barry Foster	.02	.10
346 Marion Butts	.01	.05
347 Bryan Cox	.01	.05
348 Wayne Martin	.01	.05
349 Jim Everett	.02	.10
350 Nate Odomes	.01	.05
351 Anthony Johnson	.02	.10
352 Rodney Hampton	.02	.10
353 Terry Allen	.08	.25
354 Derrick Thomas	.08	.25
355 Calvin Williams	.02	.10
356 Pepper Johnson	.01	.05
357 John Elway	.60	1.50
358 Steve Young	.30	.75
359 Emmitt Smith	.60	1.50
360 Brett Favre	.75	2.00
361 Cody Carlson	.01	.05
362 Vincent Brown	.01	.05
363 Gary Anderson RB	.01	.05
364 Jon Vaughn	.01	.05
365 Todd Marinovich	.01	.05
366 Carnell Lake	.01	.05
367 Kurt Gouveia	.01	.05
368 Lawrence Dawsey	.01	.05
369 Neil O'Donnell	.08	.25
370 Duane Bickett	.01	.05
371 Ronnie Harmon	.01	.05
372 Rodney Peete	.01	.05
373 Cornelius Bennett	.02	.10
374 Brad Baxter	.01	.05
375 Ernest Givins	.02	.10
376 Keith Byars	.01	.05
377 Eric Bieniemy	.01	.05
378 Mike Brim	.01	.05
379 Darren Lewis	.01	.05
380 Heath Sherman	.01	.05
381 Leonard Russell	.02	.10
382 Brent Jones	.02	.10
383 David Whitmore	.01	.05
384 Ray Roberts	.01	.05
385 John Offerdahl	.01	.05
386 Keith McCants	.01	.05
387 John Baylor	.01	.05
388 Amp Lee	.01	.05
389 Chris Warren	.02	.10
390 Herman Moore	.08	.25
391 Johnny Bailey	.01	.05
392 Tim Johnson	.01	.05
393 Eric Metcalf	.02	.10
394 Chris Chandler	.02	.10
395 Mark Rypien	.01	.05
396 Christian Okoye	.01	.05
397 Shannon Sharpe	.08	.25
398 Eric Hill	.01	.05
399 David Lang	.01	.05
400 Bruce Matthews	.01	.05
401 Harold Green	.01	.05
402 Mo Lewis	.01	.05
403 Terry McDaniel	.01	.05
404 Wesley Carroll	.01	.05
405 Richmond Webb	.01	.05
406 Andre Rison	.02	.10
407 Lonnie Young	.01	.05
408 Tommy Vardell	.01	.05
409 Gene Atkins	.01	.05
410 Sean Salisbury	.01	.05
411 Kenneth Davis	.01	.05
412 John L. Williams	.01	.05
413 Roman Phifer	.01	.05
414 Bennie Blades	.01	.05
415 Tim Brown	.08	.25
416 Lorenzo White	.01	.05
417 Tony Casillas	.01	.05
418 Tom Waddle	.01	.05
419 David Fulcher	.01	.05
420 Jessie Tuggle	.01	.05
421 Emmitt Smith SL	.30	.75
422 Clyde Simmons SL	.01	.05
423 Sterling Sharpe SL	.02	.10
424 Sterling Sharpe SL	.02	.10
425 Emmitt Smith SL	.30	.75
426 Dan Marino SL	.30	.75
427 H.Jones/A.McMillian SL	.01	.05
428 Thurman Thomas SL	.02	.10
429 Greg Montgomery SL	.01	.05
430 Pete Stoyanovich SL	.01	.05
431 Emmitt Smith CL	.15	.40
432 Steve Young BB	.15	.40
433 Jerry Rice BB	.20	.50
434 Ricky Watters BB	.02	.10
435 Barry Foster BB	.01	.05
436 Cortez Kennedy BB	.01	.05
437 Warren Moon BB	.02	.10
438 Thurman Thomas BB	.02	.10
439 Brett Favre BB	.40	1.00
440 Andre Rison BB	.02	.10
441 Barry Sanders BB	.25	.60
442 Chris Berman CL	.01	.05
443 Moe Gardner	.01	.05
444 Robert Jones	.01	.05
445 Reggie Langhorne	.01	.05
446 Flipper Anderson	.01	.05
447 James Washington	.01	.05
448 Aaron Craver	.01	.05
449 Jack Trudeau	.01	.05
450 Neil Smith	.08	.25
451 Chris Burkett	.01	.05
452 Russell Maryland	.01	.05
453 Drew Hill	.01	.05
454 Barry Sanders	.50	1.25
455 Jeff Cross	.01	.05
456 Bennie Thompson	.01	.05
457 Marcus Allen	.08	.25
458 Tracy Scroggins	.01	.05
459 LeRoy Butler	.01	.05
460 Joe Montana	.60	1.50
461 Eddie Anderson	.01	.05
462 Tim McDonald	.01	.05
463 Ronnie Lott	.02	.10
464 Gaston Green	.01	.05
465 Shane Conlan	.01	.05
466 Leonard Marshall	.01	.05
467 Melvin Jenkins	.01	.05
468 Don Beebe	.01	.05
469 Johnny Mitchell	.01	.05
470 Darryl Henley	.01	.05
471 Boomer Esiason	.02	.10
472 Mark Kelso	.01	.05
473 John Booty	.01	.05
474 Pete Stoyanovich	.01	.05
475 Thomas Smith RC	.02	.10
476 Carlton Gray RC	.01	.05
477 Dana Stubblefield RC	.08	.25
478 Ryan McNeil RC	.08	.25
479 Natrone Means RC	.08	.25
480 Carl Simpson RC	.01	.05
481 Robert O'Neal RC	.01	.05
482 Demetrius DuBose RC	.01	.05
483 Darrin Smith RC	.02	.10
484 Micheal Barrow RC	.08	.25
485 Chris Slade RC	.02	.10
486 Steve Tovar RC	.01	.05
487 Ron George RC	.01	.05
488 Steve Tasker	.02	.10
489 Will Furrer	.01	.05
490 Reggie White	.08	.25
491 Sean Jones	.01	.05
492 Gary Clark	.02	.10
493 Donnell Woolford	.01	.05
494 Steve Beuerlein	.02	.10
495 Anthony Carter	.02	.10
496 Louis Oliver	.01	.05
497 Chris Zorich	.01	.05
498 David Brandon	.01	.05
499 Bubba McDowell	.01	.05
500 Adrian Cooper	.01	.05
501 Bill Johnson	.01	.05
502 Shawn Jefferson	.01	.05
503 Siran Stacy	.01	.05
504 James Jones DT	.01	.05
505 Tom Rathman	.01	.05
506 Rob Moore	.02	.10
507 Kent Graham RC	.08	.25
508 Darren Carrington RC	.01	.05
509 Rickey Dixon	.01	.05
510 Toi Cook	.01	.05
511 Steve Smith	.01	.05
512 Eric Green	.01	.05
513 Phillippi Sparks	.01	.05
514 Lee Williams	.01	.05
515 Gary Reasons	.01	.05
516 Shane Dronett	.01	.05
517 Jay Novacek	.02	.10
518 Kevin Greene	.02	.10
519 Derek Russell	.01	.05
520 Quentin Coryatt	.02	.10
521 Santana Dotson	.02	.10
522 Donald Frank	.01	.05
523 Mike Prior	.01	.05
524 Dwight Hollier RC	.01	.05
525 Eric Davis	.01	.05
526 Dalton Hilliard	.01	.05
527 Rodney Culver	.01	.05
528 Jeff Hostetler	.02	.10
529 Ernie Mills	.01	.05
530 Craig Erickson	.02	.10
P231 Eric Dickerson Promo	.50	1.25

1993 Upper Deck America's Team

Randomly inserted in hobby foil packs at a rate of one in 25, this 15-card standard-size set showcases past and present Super Bowl champions from the Dallas Cowboys. Card numbers 1-6 feature Cowboys who participated in Super Bowl XII while card numbers 7-13 highlight Cowboys from Super Bowl XXVII. The cards are numbered on the back with an "AT" prefix. There is also a jumbo parallel version of this set inserted one per special retail blister pack. The Jumbo card set is only 14-cards with a slightly different checklist -- most notably the Troy Aikman cards were removed from the Jumbo set.

Card	Low	High
COMPLETE SET (15)	20.00	50.00
STATED ODDS 1:25 HOBBY		
JUMBOS:ONE PER SPEC.RETAIL BLISTER		
AT1 Roger Staubach	4.00	10.00
AT2 Chuck Howley	.75	2.00
AT3 Harvey Martin	.75	2.00
AT4 Randy White	1.25	3.00
AT5 Bob Lilly	1.25	3.00
AT6 Drew Pearson	1.25	3.00
AT7 Emmitt Smith	6.00	15.00
AT8 Troy Aikman	4.00	10.00
AT9 Ken Norton Jr.	1.25	3.00
AT10 Robert Jones	.75	2.00
AT11 Russell Maryland	.75	2.00
AT12 Jay Novacek	1.25	3.00
AT13 Michael Irvin	2.00	5.00
AT14 Troy Aikman CL	2.50	6.00
NNO Emmitt Smith HDR	4.00	10.00

1993 Upper Deck America's Team Jumbos

Card	Low	High
COMPLETE SET (15)	50.00	100.00
AT1 Roger Staubach	6.00	15.00
AT2 Chuck Howley	2.00	5.00
AT3 Harvey Martin	2.00	5.00
AT4 Randy White	2.50	6.00
AT5 Bob Lilly	2.50	6.00
AT6 Drew Pearson	2.50	6.00
AT7 Emmitt Smith	10.00	25.00
AT8 Bernie Kosar	2.00	5.00
AT9 Ken Norton Jr.	2.00	5.00
AT10 Robert Jones	2.00	5.00
AT11 Russell Maryland	2.00	5.00
AT12 Jay Novacek	3.00	8.00
AT13 Michael Irvin	4.00	10.00
AT14 Emmitt Smith CL	6.00	15.00
AT15 Emmitt Smith Hdr	6.00	15.00

1993 Upper Deck Future Heroes

Inserted at a rate of one in 20 foil packs and one per special retail pack, this ten-card standard-size set focuses on eight stars whose current performance may one day land them in the Pro Football Hall of Fame. The cards are numbered 37-45 in continuation of previous years "Football Heroes" series.

Card	Low	High
COMPLETE SET (10)	6.00	15.00
STATED ODDS 1:20 HOB/JUM		
ONE PER SPECIAL RETAIL PACK		
37 Barry Foster	.10	.30
38 Junior Seau	.30	.75
39 Emmitt Smith	2.50	5.00
40 Troy Aikman	1.25	2.50
41 David Klingler	.05	.15
42 Ricky Watters	.30	.75
43 Barry Sanders	2.00	4.00
44 Brett Favre	3.00	6.00
45 Emmitt Smith CL	.60	1.25
NNO Ricky Watters HDR	.30	.75

1993 Upper Deck Pro Bowl

Randomly inserted in retail foil packs at a rate of one in 25, this 15-card standard-size set highlights the top NFC and AFC participants in last year's Pro Bowl. Produced with Upper Deck's new "Electric" printing technology, the horizontal fronts display glossy color player photos that are full-bleed on the top and right and bordered on the left and bottom by holographic stripes. The cards are numbered on the back with a "PB" prefix.

Card	Low	High
COMPLETE SET (20)	20.00	50.00
STATED ODDS 1:25 RETAIL		
PB1 Andre Reed	.30	.75
PB2 Dan Marino	5.00	12.00
PB3 Warren Moon	.75	2.00
PB4 Anthony Miller	.30	.75
PB5 Barry Foster	.30	.75
PB6 Steve Atwater	.15	.40
PB7 Cortez Kennedy	.30	.75
PB8 Junior Seau	.75	2.00
PB9 Jerry Rice	3.00	8.00
PB10 Michael Irvin	.75	2.00
PB11 Sterling Sharpe	.75	2.00
PB12 Steve Young	2.50	6.00
PB13 Troy Aikman	2.50	6.00
PB14 Brett Favre	6.00	15.00
PB15 Emmitt Smith	5.00	12.00
PB16 Rodney Hampton	.30	.75
PB17 Barry Sanders	4.00	10.00
PB18 Ricky Watters	.75	2.00
PB19 Pat Swilling	.15	.40
PB20 Checklist Card	1.25	3.00

1993 Upper Deck Rookie Exchange

Produced by Upper Deck's "Electric" printing technology, this seven-card standard-size set was obtainable by redeeming the "Trade Upper Deck" card. The cards are numbered on the back with an "RE" prefix.

Card	Low	High
COMPLETE SET (6)	5.00	12.00
ONE SET PER TRADE CARD BY MAIL		
RE1 Trade Card Expired	.20	.50
RE1X Trade Card Punched	.20	.50
RE2 Drew Bledsoe UER	2.00	5.00
RE3 Rick Mirer	.20	.50
RE4 Garrison Hearst	.75	1.50
RE5 Marvin Jones	.02	.10
RE6 Curtis Conway	.30	.75
RE7 Jerome Bettis	3.00	8.00

1993 Upper Deck Team MVPs

Issued one per jumbo pack, this 29-card standard-size set spotlights the Most Valuable Player on each of the NFL's 28 teams. The cards are numbered on the back with a "TM" prefix.

Card	Low	High
COMPLETE SET (29)	12.50	25.00
ONE PER JUMBO PACK		
TM1 Neal Anderson	.07	.20
TM2 Harold Green	.07	.20
TM3 Thurman Thomas	.40	1.00
TM4 John Elway	3.00	6.00
TM5 Eric Metcalf	.15	.40
TM6 Reggie Cobb	.07	.20
TM7 Johnny Bailey	.07	.20
TM8 Junior Seau	.40	1.00
TM9 Derrick Thomas	.40	1.00
TM10 Steve Emtman	.07	.20
TM11 Troy Aikman	1.50	3.00
TM12 Dan Marino	3.00	6.00
TM13 Clyde Simmons	.07	.20
TM14 Andre Rison	.15	.40
TM15 Steve Young	1.50	3.00
TM16 Rodney Hampton	.15	.40
TM17 Rob Moore	.15	.40
TM18 Barry Sanders	2.50	5.00
TM19 Warren Moon	.40	1.00
TM20 Sterling Sharpe	.40	1.00
TM21 Jon Vaughn	.07	.20
TM22 Tim Brown	.40	1.00
TM23 Jim Everett	.15	.40
TM24 Gary Clark	.15	.40
TM25 Wayne Martin	.07	.20
TM26 Cortez Kennedy	.15	.40
TM27 Barry Foster	.15	.40
TM28 Terry Allen	.40	1.00
TM29 Checklist Card	.07	.20

1993 Upper Deck Team Chiefs

The 1993 Upper Deck Chiefs Team Set consists of 25 standard-size cards. The fronts display a color action player photo with white borders and two team color-coded stripes at the bottom. The player's name and position are printed in the top stripe. On the left side of the card, the team name is printed in a team color against a ghosted background. The backs carry a second photo alongside biographical and statistical information. The cards are numbered on the back with a "KC" prefix.

Card	Low	High
COMP.FACT SET (25)	3.20	8.00
KC1 Nick Lowery	.07	.20
KC2 Lonnie Marts	.07	.20
KC3 Marcus Allen	.30	.75
KC4 Bennie Thompson	.07	.20
KC5 Bryan Barker	.07	.20
KC6 Christian Okoye	.10	.30
KC7 Dale Carter	.10	.30
KC8 Dan Saleaumua	.07	.20
KC9 Dave Krieg	.10	.30
KC10 Derrick Thomas	.20	.50
KC11 Doug Terry	.07	.20
KC12 Fred Jones	.07	.20
KC13 Harvey Williams	.10	.30
KC14 J.J. Birden	.07	.20
KC15 Joe Montana	2.00	5.00
KC16 John Alt	.07	.20
KC17 Leonard Griffin	.07	.20
KC18 Matt Blundin	.07	.20
KC19 Neil Smith	.10	.30
KC20 Tim Barnett	.07	.20
KC21 Tim Grunhard	.07	.20
KC22 Todd McNair	.07	.20
KC23 Tracy Simien	.07	.20
KC24 Willie Davis	.10	.30
KC25 Joe Montana CL	.60	1.50

1993 Upper Deck Team Cowboys

The 1993 Upper Deck Cowboys Team Set consists of 25 standard-size cards. The fronts display a color action player photo with white borders and two team color-coded stripes at the bottom. The player's name and position are printed in the top stripe. On the left side of the card, the team name is printed in a team color against a ghosted background. The backs carry a second photo alongside biographical and statistical information. The cards are numbered on the back with a "D" prefix.

Card	Low	High
COMP.FACT SET (25)	3.20	8.00
D1 Alvin Harper	.07	.20
D2 Charles Haley	.10	.30
D3 Jimmy Smith	.20	.50
D4 Darrin Smith	.07	.20
D5 Jim Jeffcoat	.07	.20
D6 Daryl Johnston	.15	.40
D7 Dixon Edwards	.07	.20
D8 Emmitt Smith	1.60	4.00
D9 James Washington	.07	.20
D10 Jay Novacek	.10	.30
D11 Ken Norton Jr.	.07	.20
D12 Kenneth Gant	.07	.20
D13 Larry Brown DB	.07	.20
D14 Leon Lett	.07	.20
D15 Lin Elliott	.07	.20
D16 Mark Tuinei	.07	.20
D17 Michael Irvin	.25	.60
D18 Nate Newton	.07	.20
D19 Robert Jones	.07	.20
D20 Thomas Everett UER	.07	.20
D21 Tony Casillas	.07	.20
D22 Tony Tolbert	.07	.20
D23 Troy Aikman	.80	2.00
D24 Russell Maryland	.07	.20
D25 Troy Aikman CL	.40	1.00

1993 Upper Deck Team 49ers

The 1993 Upper Deck 49ers Team Set consists of 25 standard-size cards. The fronts display a color action player photo with white borders and two team color-coded stripes at the bottom. The player's name and position are printed in the top stripe. On the left side of the card, the team name is printed in a team color against a ghosted background. The backs carry a second photo alongside biographical and statistical information. The cards are numbered on the back with an "SF" prefix.

Card	Low	High
COMP.FACT SET (25)	3.20	8.00
SF1 Amp Lee	.07	.20
SF2 Bill Romanowski	.07	.20
SF3 Brent Jones	.10	.30
SF4 Dana Hall	.07	.20
SF5 Dana Stubblefield	.25	.60
SF6 Dennis Brown	.07	.20
SF7 Dexter Carter	.07	.20
SF8 Don Griffin	.07	.20
SF9 Eric Davis	.07	.20
SF10 Guy McIntyre	.07	.20
SF11 Jamie Williams	.07	.20
SF12 Jerry Rice	.80	2.00
SF13 John Taylor	.10	.30
SF14 Keith DeLong	.07	.20
SF15 Marc Logan	.07	.20
SF16 Michael Walter	.07	.20
SF17 Mike Cofer	.07	.20
SF18 Odessa Turner	.07	.20
SF19 Ricky Watters	.25	.60
SF20 Steve Bono	.10	.30
SF21 Steve Young	.60	1.50
SF22 Ted Washington	.07	.20
SF23 Tom Rathman	.10	.30
SF24 Jesse Sapolu	.07	.20
SF25 Steve Young CL	.30	.75

1993 Upper Deck 24K Gold

This eight card set was issued by Upper Deck only through their hobby channels. The black and gold fronts are horizontal and have the player's facsimile signature on the left with an etched portrait on the right. Although the cards are numbered on the back out of 2500, reportedly only 1500 of each card was produced. Six quarterbacks and two running backs are featured in this set.

Card	Low	High
COMPLETE SET (8)	100.00	200.00
1 Joe Montana	25.00	60.00
2 Emmitt Smith	20.00	50.00
3 Drew Bledsoe	15.00	40.00
4 Troy Aikman	12.50	30.00
5 Rick Mirer	4.00	10.00
6 Dan Marino	20.00	50.00
7 Steve Young	10.00	25.00
8 Thurman Thomas	6.00	15.00

1993-94 Upper Deck Miller Lite SB

onsored by Miller Lite Beer and Tombstone Pizza, the 1993 Upper Deck Super Bowl Showdown Series consists of five cards measuring approximately 5" by 3 1/2". One card was included in specially-marked half-cases of Miller Lite beer. Furthermore, the set could be obtained by mailing in the official certificate (included in each specially-marked case), along with three UPC symbols from three 24-packs (or case equivalents) of 12-ounce Miller Lite cans and the dated cash register receipt. All certificates must be received by March 18, 1994. All entries were entered in a random drawing for 1,000 sweepstakes prizes of a Joe Montana personally autographed collector sheet. The horizontal card fronts feature the starting quarterbacks from competing Super Bowl teams. On each side of the front is a color action player cut-out photo superimposed over a ghosted game photo. The quarterbacks' last names appear in the center of the card in white print above the Super Bowl depicted on the card, the final score, and the date all printed in gold foil lettering. A blue stripe intersects the lower portion of the left photo containing the words "Super Bowl," and "Showdowns" appears on a red stripe intersecting the right photo. A ghosted Super Bowl logo for the play-off depicted on the front, serves as a background for highlights of the quarterbacks' accomplishments during the game. The backs are bordered in team color-coded borders that fade to a metallic silver. Sponsor logos are printed on the lower edge. The cards are numbered on the front.

Card	Low	High
COMPLETE SET (5)	4.80	12.00
1 Troy Aikman J.Kelly	1.20	3.00
2 Jim Kelly Rypien	.80	2.00
3 John Elway Montana	1.60	4.00
4 John Elway Simms	1.20	3.00
5 Joe Montana Dan Marino	1.60	4.00

1994 Upper Deck Pro Bowl Samples

Measuring the standard-size, this six-card sample set spotlights players who participated in the Pro Bowl. The cards were originally passed out at the National Convention in Houston. On the left edge, the horizontal fronts have a purple stripe carrying the player's name, team name, and a holographic headshot framed by a black border. The rest of the front displays a full-bleed color action player photo with a metallic sheen. On a white screened background of a gray Upper Deck logos, the backs have the disclaimer "SAMPLE CARD" printed diagonally. The cards are unnumbered and checklisted below in alphabetical order.

Card	Low	High
COMPLETE SET (6)	14.00	35.00
1 Jerome Bettis	1.20	3.00
2 Brett Favre	4.80	12.00
3 John Elway	4.80	12.00
4 Thurman Thomas	1.20	3.00
5 Jerry Rice	2.40	6.00
6 Steve Young	2.00	5.00

1994 Upper Deck

This 330-card standard-size set was released in one series. They were issued in 12-card packs with a suggested retail price of $1.99. The following subsets include Rookies (1-30) and Heavy Weights (31-40). Rookie Cards include Isaac Bruce, Trent Dilfer, Marshall Faulk, William Floyd, Errict Rhett, and Heath Shuler. A Joe Montana Promo card was produced and priced below.

Card	Low	High
COMPLETE SET (330)	12.50	25.00
1 Dan Wilkinson RC	.07	.20
2 Antonio Langham RC	.07	.20
3 Derrick Alexander WR RC	.15	.40
4 Charles Johnson RC	.15	.40
5 Bucky Brooks RC	.02	.10
6 Trev Alberts RC	.07	.20
7 Marshall Faulk RC	2.50	6.00
8 Willie McGinest RC	.15	.40
9 Aaron Glenn RC	.15	.40
10 Ryan Yarborough RC	.02	.10
11 Greg Hill RC	.15	.40
12 Sam Adams RC	.07	.20
13 John Thierry RC	.02	.10
14 Johnnie Morton RC	.30	.75
15 LeShon Johnson RC	.07	.20
16 David Palmer RC	.15	.40
17 Trent Dilfer RC	.50	1.25
18 Jamir Miller RC	.07	.20
19 Thomas Lewis RC	.07	.20
20 Heath Shuler RC	.15	.40
21 Wayne Gandy	.02	.10
22 Isaac Bruce RC	2.00	4.00
23 Joe Johnson RC	.02	.10
24 Mario Bates RC	.15	.40
25 Bryant Young RC	.25	.60
26 William Floyd RC	.15	.40
27 Errict Rhett RC	.15	.40
28 Chuck Levy RC	.02	.10
29 Darnay Scott RC	.30	.75
30 Rob Fredrickson RC	.07	.20
31 Jamir Miller HW	.02	.10
32 Thomas Lewis HW	.02	.10
33 John Thierry HW	.02	.10
34 Sam Adams HW	.02	.10
35 Joe Johnson HW	.02	.10
36 Bryant Young HW	.10	.30
37 Wayne Gandy HW	.02	.10
38 LeShon Johnson HW	.02	.10
39 Mario Bates HW	.07	.20
40 Greg Hill HW	.07	.20
41 Andy Heck	.02	.10
42 Warren Moon	.15	.40
43 Jim Everett	.07	.20
44 Bill Romanowski	.02	.10
45 Michael Haynes	.07	.20
46 Chris Doleman	.02	.10
47 Merril Hoge	.02	.10
48 Chris Miller	.02	.10
49 Clyde Simmons	.02	.10
50 Jeff George	.15	.40
51 Jeff Burris RC	.07	.20
52 Ethan Horton	.02	.10
53 Scott Mitchell	.07	.20
54 Howard Ballard	.02	.10
55 Lewis Tillman	.02	.10
56 Marion Butts	.02	.10
57 Erik Kramer	.07	.20
58 Ken Norton Jr.	.07	.20
59 Anthony Miller	.07	.20
60 Chris Hinton	.02	.10
61 Ricky Proehl	.02	.10
62 Craig Heyward	.07	.20
63 Darryl Talley	.02	.10
64 Tim Worley	.02	.10
65 Derrick Fenner	.02	.10
66 Jerry Ball	.02	.10
67 Darrin Smith	.02	.10
68 Mike Croel	.02	.10
69 Ray Crockett	.02	.10
70 Tony Bennett	.02	.10
71 Webster Slaughter	.02	.10
72 Anthony Johnson	.07	.20
73 Charles Mincy	.02	.10
74 Calvin Jones RC	.02	.10
75 Henry Ellard	.07	.20
76 Troy Vincent	.02	.10
77 Sean Salisbury	.02	.10
78 Pat Harlow	.02	.10
79 James Williams RC	.02	.10
80 Dave Brown	.07	.20
81 Kent Graham	.07	.20
82 Seth Joyner	.02	.10
83 Deon Figures	.02	.10
84 Stanley Richard	.02	.10
85 Tom Rathman	.02	.10
86 Rod Stephens	.02	.10
87 Ray Seals	.02	.10
88 Andre Collins	.02	.10
89 Cornelius Bennett	.07	.20
90 Richard Dent	.07	.20
91 Louis Oliver	.02	.10
92 Rodney Peete	.02	.10
93 Jackie Harris	.02	.10
94 Tracy Simien	.02	.10
95 Greg Townsend	.02	.10
96 Michael Stewart	.02	.10
97 Irving Fryar	.07	.20
98 Todd Collins	.02	.10
99 Irv Smith	.02	.10
100 Chris Calloway	.02	.10
101 Kevin Greene	.07	.20
102 John Friesz	.07	.20
103 Steve Bono	.07	.20
104 Brian Blades	.07	.20
105 Reggie Cobb	.02	.10
106 Eric Swann	.07	.20
107 Mike Pritchard	.02	.10
108 Bill Brooks	.02	.10
109 Jim Harbaugh	.15	.40
110 David Whitmore	.02	.10
111 Eddie Anderson	.02	.10
112 Ray Crittenden RC	.02	.10
113 Mark Collins	.02	.10
114 Brian Washington	.02	.10
115 Barry Foster	.02	.10
116 Gary Plummer	.02	.10
117 Marc Logan	.02	.10
118 John L. Williams	.02	.10
119 Marty Carter	.02	.10
120 Kurt Gouveia	.02	.10
121 Ronald Moore	.02	.10
122 Pierce Holt	.02	.10
123 Henry Jones	.02	.10
124 Donnell Woolford	.02	.10
125 Steve Tovar	.02	.10
126 Anthony Pleasant	.02	.10
127 Jay Novacek	.07	.20
128 Dan Williams	.02	.10
129 Barry Sanders	1.00	2.50
130 Robert Brooks	.15	.40
131 Lorenzo White	.02	.10
132 Kerry Cash	.02	.10
133 Joe Montana	1.25	3.00
134 Jeff Hostetler	.07	.20
135 Jerome Bettis	.25	.60
136 Dan Marino	1.25	3.00
137 Vencie Glenn	.02	.10
138 Vincent Brown	.02	.10
139 Rickey Jackson	.02	.10
140 Carlton Bailey	.02	.10
141 Jeff Lageman	.02	.10
142 William Thomas	.02	.10
143 Neil O'Donnell	.15	.40
144 Shawn Jefferson	.02	.10
145 Steve Young	.40	1.00
146 Chris Warren	.07	.20
147 Courtney Hawkins	.02	.10
148 Brad Edwards	.02	.10
149 O.J.McDuffie	.15	.40
150 David Lang	.02	.10
151 Chuck Cecil	.02	.10
152 Norm Johnson	.02	.10
153 Pete Metzelaars	.02	.10
154 Shaun Gayle	.02	.10
155 Alfred Williams	.02	.10
156 Eric Turner	.02	.10
157A Emmitt Smith ERR 1900	1.00	2.50
157B Emmitt Smith COR	1.00	2.50
158 Steve Atwater	.02	.10
159 Robert Porcher	.02	.10
160 Edgar Bennett	.15	.40
161 Bubba McDowell	.02	.10
162 Jeff Herrod	.02	.10
163 Keith Cash	.02	.10
164 Patrick Bates	.02	.10
165 Todd Lyght	.02	.10
166 Mark Higgs	.02	.10
167 Carlos Jenkins	.02	.10
168 Drew Bledsoe	.40	1.00
169 Wayne Martin	.02	.10
170 Mike Sherrard	.02	.10
171 Ronnie Lott	.07	.20
172 Fred Barnett	.07	.20
173 Eric Green	.02	.10
174 Leslie O'Neal	.02	.10
175 Brent Jones	.07	.20
176 Jon Vaughn	.02	.10
177 Vince Workman	.02	.10
178 Ron Middleton	.02	.10
179 Terry McDaniel	.02	.10
180 Willie Davis	.07	.20
181 Gary Clark	.07	.20
182 Bobby Hebert	.02	.10
183 Russell Copeland	.02	.10
184 Chris Gedney	.02	.10
185 Tony McGee	.02	.10
186 Rob Burnett	.02	.10
187 Charles Haley	.07	.20
188 Shannon Sharpe	.07	.20
189 Mel Gray	.02	.10
190 George Teague	.02	.10
191 Ernest Givins	.07	.20
192 Ray Buchanan	.02	.10
193 J.J. Birden	.02	.10
194 Tim Brown	.15	.40
195 Tim Lester	.02	.10
196 Marco Coleman	.02	.10
197 Randall McDaniel	.05	.15
198 Bruce Armstrong	.02	.10
199 Willie Roaf	.02	.10
200 Greg Jackson	.02	.10
201 Johnny Mitchell	.02	.10
202 Calvin Williams	.07	.20
203 Jeff Graham	.02	.10
204 Darren Carrington	.02	.10
205 Jerry Rice	.60	1.50
206 Cortez Kennedy	.07	.20
207 Charles Wilson	.02	.10
208 James Jenkins RC	.02	.10
209 Ray Childress	.02	.10
210 LeRoy Butler	.02	.10
211 Randal Hill	.02	.10
212 Lincoln Kennedy	.02	.10
213 Kenneth Davis	.02	.10
214 Terry Obee	.02	.10

215 Ricardo McDonald .02 .10
216 Pepper Johnson .02 .10
217 Alvin Harper .07 .20
218 John Elway 1.25 3.00
219 Derrick Moore .02 .10
220 Terrell Buckley .02 .10
221 Haywood Jeffires .07 .20
222 Jessie Hester .02 .10
223 Kimble Anders .07 .20
224 Rocket Ismail .07 .20
225 Roman Phifer .02 .10
226 Bryan Cox .02 .10
227 Cris Carter .30 .75
228 Sam Gash .02 .10
229 Renaldo Turnbull .02 .10
230 Rodney Hampton .07 .20
231 Johnny Johnson .02 .10
232 Tim Harris .02 .10
233 Leroy Thompson .02 .10
234 Junior Seau .15 .40
235 Tim McDonald .02 .10
236 Eugene Robinson .02 .10
237 Lawrence Dawsey .02 .10
238 Tim Johnson .02 .10
239 Jason Elam .07 .20
240 Willie Green .02 .10
241 Larry Centers .15 .40
242 Erric Pegram .02 .10
243 Bruce Smith .15 .40
244 Alonzo Spellman .02 .10
245 Carl Pickens .07 .20
246 Michael Jackson .07 .20
247 Kevin Williams WR .07 .20
248 Glyn Milburn .07 .20
249 Herman Moore .15 .40
250 Brett Favre 1.25 3.00
251 Al Smith .02 .10
252 Roosevelt Potts .02 .10
253 Marcus Allen .15 .40
254 Anthony Smith .02 .10
255 Sean Gilbert .02 .10
256 Keith Byars .02 .10
257 Scottie Graham RC .07 .20
258 Leonard Russell .02 .10
259 Eric Martin .02 .10
260 Jarrod Bunch .02 .10
261 Rob Moore .07 .20
262 Herschel Walker .07 .20
263 Levon Kirkland .02 .10
264 Chris Mims .02 .10
265 Ricky Watters .07 .20
266 Rick Mirer .15 .40
267 Santana Dotson .07 .20
268 Reggie Brooks .07 .20
269 Garrison Hearst .15 .40
270 Thurman Thomas .15 .40
271 Johnny Bailey .02 .10
272 Andre Rison .07 .20
273 Jim Kelly .15 .40
274 Mark Carrier DB .02 .10
275 David Klingler .02 .10
276 Eric Metcalf .07 .20
277 Troy Aikman UER .60 1.50
278 Simon Fletcher .02 .10
279 Pat Swilling .02 .10
280 Sterling Sharpe .07 .20
281 Cody Carlson .02 .10
282 Steve Emtman .02 .10
283 Neil Smith .07 .20
284 James Jett .02 .10
285 Shane Conlan .02 .10
286 Keith Jackson .02 .10
287 Qadry Ismail .15 .40
288 Chris Slade .02 .10
289 Derek Brown RBK .02 .10
290 Phil Simms .07 .20
291 Boomer Esiason .07 .20
292 Eric Allen .02 .10
293 Rod Woodson .07 .20
294 Ronnie Harmon .02 .10
295 John Taylor .07 .20
296 Ferrell Edmunds .02 .10
297 Craig Erickson .02 .10
298 Brian Mitchell .02 .10
299 Dante Jones .02 .10
300 John Copeland .02 .10
301 Steve Beuerlein .07 .20
302 Deion Sanders .30 .75
303 Andre Reed .07 .20
304 Curtis Conway .15 .40
305 Harold Green .02 .10
306 Vinny Testaverde .07 .20
307 Michael Irvin .15 .40
308 Rod Bernstine .02 .10
309 Chris Spielman .07 .20
310 Reggie White .15 .40
311 Gary Brown .02 .10
312 Quentin Coryatt .02 .10
313 Derrick Thomas .15 .40
314 Greg Robinson .02 .10
315 Troy Drayton .02 .10
316 Terry Kirby .15 .40
317 John Randle .07 .20
318 Ben Coates .07 .20
319 Tyrone Hughes .07 .20
320 Corey Miller .02 .10
321 Brad Baxter .02 .10
322 Randall Cunningham .15 .40
323 Greg Lloyd .07 .20
324 Stan Humphries .07 .20
325 Dana Stubblefield .07 .20
326 Kelvin Martin .02 .10
327 Hardy Nickerson .07 .20
328 Desmond Howard .07 .20
329 Mark Carrier WR .07 .20
330 Daryl Johnston .07 .20
P19 Joe Montana Promo 1.00 2.50

1994 Upper Deck Electric Gold

*STARS: 6X TO 15X BASIC CARDS
*RCs: 3X TO 8X BASIC CARDS
ONE PER HOBBY BOX

1994 Upper Deck Electric Silver

COMPLETE SET (330) 40.00 100.00
*STARS: 1.2X TO 3X BASIC CARDS
*RCs: .8X TO 2X BASIC CARDS
STATED OODS 1:1 HOB, 2:1 SPEC.RETAIL

1994 Upper Deck Predictor Award Winners

Randomly inserted in Hobby packs at a rate of one in 20, this set was designed to include a potential league MVP and Rookie of the Year. The card of the player that won an award could have been redeemed for a special foil enhanced 20-card Predictor set including the league MVP (Longshot, Steve Young) and Rookie of the Year (Marshall Faulk) game cards. The card of a second place finisher (Barry Sanders MVP, several tied for Longshot ROY) could have been redeemed for a foil enhanced 10-card Predictor set for the category with which the player placed second. The offer expired March 31, 1995. The cards feature a color photo on front with the Predictor category on the left border that is broken into two solid colors. The player's name, team and position are at bottom right. The backs contain game rules. The cards are numbered with an "HP" prefix.

COMPLETE SET (20) 20.00 50.00
STATED ODDS 1:20 HOBBY
H PREFIX PRIZE SET (20) 12.50 30.00
*PRIZE CARDS: .15X TO .4X BASIC INSERTS
HP1 Emmitt Smith 3.00 8.00
HP2 Barry Sanders W-2 3.00 8.00
HP3 Jerome Bettis .75 2.00
HP4 Joe Montana 4.00 10.00
HP5 Dan Marino 4.00 10.00
HP6 Marshall Faulk 4.00 10.00
HP7 Dan Wilkinson .10 .30
HP8 Sterling Sharpe .25 .60
HP9 Thurman Thomas .50 1.25
HP10 Longshot W-1 S.Young .10 .30
HP11 Marshall Faulk W-1 4.00 10.00
HP12 Trent Dilfer .75 2.00
HP13 Heath Shuler .25 .60
HP14 David Palmer .25 .60
HP15 Charles Johnson .25 .60
HP16 Greg Hill .25 .60
HP17 Johnnie Morton .50 1.25
HP18 Errict Rhett .25 .60
HP19 Darnay Scott .50 1.25
HP20 ROY Longshot W-2 .10 .30

1994 Upper Deck Predictor League Leaders

Randomly inserted in Retail packs at a rate of one in 20, this 30-card standard-size set was designed to include potential top passers (1-9), rushers (11-19) and receivers (21-29). There are also three Longshot cards. If the players within a certain category did not finish first or second, the Longshot card could be redeemed. If one of the players included in either of the three categories finished first, that card could be redeemed for a special foil enhanced 30-card Predictor set which includes the Rushing, Passing and Receiving category game cards. Cards of second place finishers could be exchanged for a 10-card foil enhanced Predictor set for that category. Winning cards are noted below. The cardbacks contain the game rules and each card is numbered with an "RP" prefix.

COMPLETE SET (30) 20.00 50.00
STATED ODDS 1:20 RETAIL
R PREFIX PRIZE SET (30) 12.50 30.00
*PRIZE CARDS: .15X to .4X BASIC INSERTS
RP1 Troy Aikman 2.00 5.00
RP2 Steve Young 1.25 3.00
RP3 John Elway 4.00 10.00
RP4 Joe Montana 4.00 10.00
RP5 Brett Favre 4.00 10.00
RP6 Heath Shuler .25 .60
RP7 Dan Marino W-2 4.00 10.00
RP8 Rick Mirer .50 1.25
RP9 Drew Bledsoe W-1 1.25 3.00
RP10 The Longshot .10 .30
RP11 Emmitt Smith 3.00 8.00
RP12 Barry Sanders W-1 3.00 8.00
RP13 Jerome Bettis .75 2.00
RP14 Rodney Hampton .25 .60
RP15 Thurman Thomas .50 1.25
RP16 Marshall Faulk 4.00 10.00
RP17 Barry Foster .10 .30
RP18 Reggie Brooks .25 .60
RP19 Ricky Watters .25 .60
RP20 Longshot W-2 Warren .10 .30
RP21 Jerry Rice W-1 2.00 5.00
RP22 Sterling Sharpe .25 .60
RP23 Andre Rison .25 .60
RP24 Michael Irvin .50 1.25
RP25 Tim Brown .50 1.25
RP26 Shannon Sharpe .25 .60
RP27 Andre Reed .25 .60
RP28 Irving Fryar .25 .60
RP29 Charles Johnson .25 .60
RP30 Longshot W-2 Ellard .10 .30

1994 Upper Deck Pro Bowl

Randomly inserted in both Hobby and Retail packs, this 20-card standard-size set reflects on performers in the 1994 Pro Bowl. Horizontally designed cards feature the debut of Upper Deck's Holoview process. An action photo from the Pro Bowl covers most of the card front. The left side has a small hologram and the player's name and position. The back contains a photo, 1993 season highlights and a player quote. The backs are numbered with a "PB" prefix.

COMPLETE SET (20) 25.00 60.00
STATED ODDS 1:20
PB1 Jerome Bettis 1.50 4.00
PB2 Jay Novacek .50 1.25
PB3 Shannon Sharpe .50 1.25
PB4 Brent Jones .50 1.25
PB5 Andre Rison .50 1.25
PB6 Tim Brown 1.00 2.50
PB7 Anthony Miller .50 1.25
PB8 Jerry Rice 4.00 10.00
PB9 Brett Favre 8.00 20.00
PB10 Emmitt Smith 6.00 15.00
PB11 Steve Young 2.50 6.00
PB12 John Elway 8.00 20.00
PB13 Warren Moon 1.00 2.50
PB14 Thurman Thomas 1.00 2.50
PB15 Ricky Watters .50 1.25
PB16 Rod Woodson .50 1.25
PB17 Reggie White 1.00 2.50
PB18 Tyrone Hughes .50 1.25
PB19 Derrick Thomas 1.00 2.50
PB20 Checklist .50 1.25

1994 Upper Deck Rookie Jumbos

These cards are a 5" by 7" version of the first 30-cards in the basic issue set.

1 Dan Wilkinson .50 1.25
2 Antonio Langham .50 1.25
3 Derrick Alexander WR RC .60 1.50
4 Charles Johnson .60 1.50
5 Bucky Brooks .40 1.00
6 Trev Alberts .50 1.25
7 Marshall Faulk 3.00 8.00
8 Willie McGinest .60 1.50
9 Aaron Glenn .60 1.50
10 Ryan Yarborough .40 1.00
11 Greg Hill .60 1.50
12 Sam Adams .50 1.25
13 John Thierry .40 1.00
14 Johnnie Morton 1.00 2.50
15 LeShon Johnson .50 1.25
16 David Palmer .60 1.50
17 Trent Dilfer 1.25 3.00
18 Jamir Miller .50 1.25
19 Thomas Lewis .50 1.25
20 Heath Shuler .60 1.50
21 Wayne Gandy .40 1.00
22 Isaac Bruce 2.50 6.00
23 Joe Johnson .40 1.00
24 Mario Bates .60 1.50
25 Bryant Young .75 2.00
26 William Floyd .60 1.50
27 Errict Rhett .60 1.50
28 Chuck Levy .40 1.00
29 Darnay Scott 1.00 2.50
30 Rob Fredrickson .50 1.25

1994 Upper Deck Commemorative Cards

1 1994 Launch Tour/2000 2.00 5.00
Wayne Gretzky
Reggie Jackson
Michael Jordan
Joe Montana

1994-95 Upper Deck Sheets

These 11" by 8.5" sheets were issued by Upper Deck. The autograph sheet was given out during the 1995 Super Bowl Card Show VI for collectors to have signed by players appearing at the show. The Dan Marino was issued in 1995 to commemorate Marino's record breaking season.

COMPLETE SET (3) 12.00 30.00
NNO Rookie Class 1994 3.20 8.00
NNO Super Bowl XXIX 1.60 4.00
NNO Dan Marino 4.80 12.00
NNO Upper Deck Salutes Rams 3.20 8.00

1995 Upper Deck

This 300-card standard-size set was released in one series. They were issued in 12-card packs with a suggested retail price of $1.99. There is one subset, Rookies (1-30). Rookie Cards include Jeff Blake, Ki-Jana Carter, Kerry Collins, Joey Galloway, Curtis Martin, Steve McNair, Rashaan Salaam, J.J. Stokes, Michael Westbrook and Tyrone Wheatley. Joe Montana (#19) and Marshall Faulk (PB95) Promo cards were produced and listed at the end of our checklist.

COMPLETE SET (300) 12.50 30.00
1 Ki-Jana Carter RC .15 .40
2 Tony Boselli RC .15 .40
3 Steve McNair RC 1.50 4.00
4 Michael Westbrook RC .15 .40
5 Kerry Collins RC .75 2.00
6 Kevin Carter RC .15 .40
7 James A.Stewart RC .02 .10
8 Joey Galloway RC .75 2.00
9 Kyle Brady RC .15 .40
10 J.J. Stokes RC .15 .40
11 Derrick Alexander DE RC .02 .10
12 Warren Sapp RC .75 2.00
13 Mark Fields RC .15 .40
14 Tyrone Wheatley RC .60 1.50
15 Napoleon Kaufman RC .60 1.50
16 James O. Stewart RC .60 1.50
17 Luther Elliss RC .02 .10
18 Rashaan Salaam RC .07 .20
19 Jimmy Oliver RC .02 .10
20 Mark Bruener RC .07 .20
21 Derrick Brooks RC .75 2.00
22 Christian Fauria RC .07 .20
23 Ray Zellars RC .07 .20
24 Todd Collins RC .50 1.25
25 Sherman Williams RC .02 .10
26 Frank Sanders RC .15 .40
27 Rodney Thomas RC .07 .20
28 Rob Johnson RC .50 1.25
29 Steve Stenstrom RC .02 .10
30 Curtis Martin RC 1.50 4.00
31 Gary Clark .02 .10
32 Troy Aikman .60 1.50
33 Mike Sherrard .02 .10
34 Fred Barnett .07 .20
35 Henry Ellard .07 .20
36 Terry Allen .07 .20
37 Jeff Graham .02 .10
38 Herman Moore .15 .40
39 Brett Favre 1.25 3.00
40 Trent Dilfer .15 .40
41 Derek Brown RBK .02 .10
42 Andre Rison .07 .20
43 Flipper Anderson .02 .10
44 Jerry Rice .60 1.50
45 Andre Reed .07 .20
46 Sean Dawkins .07 .20
47 Irving Fryar .07 .20
48 Vincent Brisby .02 .10
49 Rob Moore .07 .20
50 Carl Pickens .07 .20
51 Vinny Testaverde .07 .20
52 Ray Childress .02 .10
53 Eric Green .02 .10
54 Anthony Miller .07 .20
55 Lake Dawson .07 .20
56 Tim Brown .15 .40
57 Stan Humphries .07 .20
58 Rick Mirer .07 .20
59 Randal Hill .02 .10
60 Charles Haley .07 .20
61 Chris Calloway .02 .10
62 Calvin Williams .07 .20
63 Ethan Horton .02 .10
64 Cris Carter .15 .40
65 Curtis Conway .15 .40
66 Scott Mitchell .07 .20
67 Edgar Bennett .07 .20
68 Craig Erickson .02 .10
69 Jim Everett .02 .10
70 Terance Mathis .07 .20
71 Robert Young .02 .10
72 Brent Jones .02 .10
73 Bill Brooks .07 .20
74 Marshall Faulk .75 2.00
75 O.J. McDuffie .15 .40
76 Ben Coates .07 .20
77 Johnny Mitchell .02 .10
78 Darnay Scott .07 .20
79 Derrick Alexander WR .15 .40
80 Lorenzo White .02 .10
81 Charles Johnson .07 .20
82 John Elway 1.25 3.00
83 Willie Davis .07 .20
84 James Jett .07 .20
85 Mark Seay .07 .20
86 Brian Blades .07 .20
87 Ronald Moore .02 .10
88 Alvin Harper .02 .10
89 Dave Brown .07 .20
90 Randall Cunningham .15 .40
91 Heath Shuler .07 .20
92 Jake Reed .07 .20
93 Donnell Woolford .02 .10
94 Barry Sanders 1.00 2.50
95 Reggie White .15 .40
96 Lawrence Dawsey .02 .10
97 Michael Haynes .07 .20
98 Bert Emanuel .15 .40
99 Troy Drayton .02 .10
100 Steve Young .50 1.25
101 Bruce Smith .15 .40
102 Roosevelt Potts .02 .10
103 Dan Marino 1.25 3.00
104 Michael Timpson .02 .10
105 Boomer Esiason .07 .20
106 David Klingler .07 .20
107 Eric Metcalf .07 .20
108 Gary Brown .02 .10
109 Neil O'Donnell .07 .20
110 Shannon Sharpe .07 .20
111 Joe Montana 1.25 3.00
112 Jeff Hostetler .07 .20
113 Ronnie Harmon .02 .10
114 Chris Warren .07 .20
115 Larry Centers .07 .20
116 Michael Irvin .15 .40
117 Rodney Hampton .07 .20
118 Herschel Walker .07 .20
119 Reggie Brooks .07 .20
120 Qadry Ismail .07 .20
121 Chris Zorich .02 .10
122 Chris Spielman .07 .20
123 Sean Jones .02 .10
124 Errict Rhett .07 .20
125 Tyrone Hughes .07 .20
126 Jeff George .07 .20
127 Chris Miller .02 .10
128 Ricky Watters .07 .20
129 Jim Kelly .15 .40
130 Tony Bennett .02 .10
131 Terry Kirby .07 .20
132 Drew Bledsoe .40 1.00
133 Johnny Johnson .02 .10
134 Dan Wilkinson .07 .20
135 Leroy Hoard .02 .10
136 Darryll Lewis .02 .10
137 Barry Foster .07 .20
138 Shane Dronett .02 .10
139 Marcus Allen .15 .40
140 Harvey Williams .02 .10
141 Tony Martin .07 .20
142 Rod Stephens .02 .10
143 Eric Swann .07 .20
144 Daryl Johnston .07 .20
145 Dave Meggett .02 .10
146 Charlie Garner .15 .40
147 Ken Harvey .02 .10
148 Warren Moon .07 .20
149 Steve Walsh .02 .10
150 Pat Swilling .02 .10
151 Terrell Buckley .02 .10
152 Courtney Hawkins .02 .10
153 Willie Roaf .02 .10
154 Chris Doleman .02 .10
155 Jerome Bettis .15 .40
156 Dana Stubblefield .07 .20
157 Cornelius Bennett .07 .20
158 Quentin Coryatt .07 .20
159 Bryan Cox .02 .10
160 Marion Butts .02 .10
161 Aaron Glenn .02 .10
162 Louis Oliver .02 .10
163 Eric Turner .02 .10
164 Cris Dishman .02 .10
165 John L. Williams .02 .10
166 Simon Fletcher .02 .10
167 Neil Smith .07 .20
168 Chester McGlockton .07 .20
169 Natrone Means .07 .20
170 Sam Adams .02 .10
171 Clyde Simmons .02 .10
172 Jay Novacek .07 .20
173 Keith Hamilton .02 .10
174 William Fuller .02 .10
175 Tom Carter .02 .10
176 John Randle .07 .20
177 Lewis Tillman .02 .10
178 Mel Gray .02 .10
179 George Teague .02 .10
180 Hardy Nickerson .02 .10
181 Mario Bates .07 .20
182 D.J. Johnson .02 .10
183 Sean Gilbert .07 .20
184 Bryant Young .07 .20
185 Jeff Burris .02 .10
186 Floyd Turner .02 .10
187 Troy Vincent .02 .10
188 Willie McGinest .07 .20
189 James Hasty .02 .10
190 Jeff Blake RC .40 1.00
191 Stevon Moore .02 .10
192 Ernest Givins .02 .10
193 Byron Bam Morris .02 .10
194 Ray Crockett .02 .10
195 Dale Carter .07 .20
196 Terry McDaniel .02 .10
197 Leslie O'Neal .07 .20
198 Cortez Kennedy .07 .20
199 Seth Joyner .02 .10
200 Emmitt Smith 1.00 2.50
201 Thomas Lewis .07 .20
202 Andy Harmon .02 .10
203 Ricky Ervins .02 .10
204 Fuad Reveiz .02 .10
205 John Thierry .02 .10
206 Bennie Blades .02 .10
207 LeShon Johnson .07 .20
208 Charles Wilson .02 .10
209 Joe Johnson .02 .10
210 Chuck Smith .02 .10
211 Roman Phifer .02 .10
212 Ken Norton Jr. .07 .20
213 Bucky Brooks .02 .10
214 Ray Buchanan .02 .10
215 Tim Bowens .02 .10
216 Vincent Brown .02 .10
217 Marcus Turner .02 .10
218 Derrick Fenner .02 .10
219 Antonio Langham .02 .10
220 Cody Carlson .02 .10
221 Greg Lloyd .07 .20
222 Steve Atwater .02 .10
223 Donnell Bennett .07 .20
224 Rocket Ismail .07 .20
225 John Carney .02 .10
226 Eugene Robinson .02 .10
227 Aeneas Williams .02 .10
228 Darrin Smith .02 .10
229 Phillippi Sparks .02 .10
230 Eric Allen .02 .10
231 Brian Mitchell .02 .10
232 David Palmer .07 .20
233 Mark Carrier DB .02 .10
234 Dave Krieg .02 .10
235 Robert Brooks .15 .40
236 Eric Curry .02 .10
237 Wayne Martin .02 .10
238 Craig Heyward .07 .20
239 Isaac Bruce .30 .75
240 Deion Sanders .40 1.00
241 Steve Tasker .07 .20
242 Jim Harbaugh .07 .20
243 Aubrey Beavers .02 .10
244 Chris Slade .02 .10
245 Mo Lewis .02 .10
246 Alfred Williams .02 .10
247 Michael Dean Perry .02 .10
248 Marcus Robertson .02 .10
249 Kevin Greene .07 .20
250 Leonard Russell .02 .10
251 Greg Hill .07 .20
252 Rob Fredrickson .02 .10
253 Junior Seau .15 .40
254 Rick Tuten .02 .10
255 Garrison Hearst .15 .40
256 Russell Maryland .02 .10
257 Michael Brooks .02 .10
258 Bernard Williams .02 .10
259 Reggie Roby .02 .10
260 Dewayne Washington .07 .20
261 Raymont Harris .02 .10
262 Brett Perriman .07 .20
263 LeRoy Butler .02 .10
264 Santana Dotson .02 .10
265 Irv Smith .02 .10
266 Ron George .02 .10
267 Marquez Pope .02 .10
268 William Floyd .07 .20
269 Matt Darby .02 .10
270 Jeff Herrod .02 .10
271 Bernie Parmalee .07 .20
272 Leroy Thompson .02 .10
273 Ronnie Lott .07 .20
274 Steve Tovar .02 .10
275 Michael Jackson .07 .20
276 Al Smith .02 .10
277 Rod Woodson .07 .20
278 Glyn Milburn .02 .10
279 Kimble Anders .07 .20
280 Anthony Smith .02 .10
281 Andre Coleman .02 .10
282 Terry Wooden .02 .10
283 Mickey Washington .02 .10
284 Steve Beuerlein .07 .20
285 Mark Brunell .40 1.00
286 Keith Goganious .02 .10
287 Desmond Howard .07 .20
288 Darren Carrington .02 .10
289 Derek Brown TE .02 .10
290 Reggie Cobb .02 .10
291 Jeff Lageman .02 .10
292 Lamar Lathon .02 .10
293 Sam Mills .07 .20
294 Carlton Bailey .02 .10
295 Mark Carrier WR .07 .20
296 Willie Green .07 .20
297 Frank Reich .02 .10
298 Don Beebe .02 .10
299 Tim McKyer .02 .10
300 Pete Metzelaars .02 .10
A19 Joe Montana 6.00 15.00
A103 Dan Marino 6.00 15.00
P1 Joe Montana Promo .75 2.00
P2 Joe Montana Promo .75 2.00
Numbered 19
P3 Marshall Faulk Promo .40 1.00

1995 Upper Deck Electric Gold

*STARS: 4X TO 10X BASIC CARDS
*RCs: 1.5X TO 4X BASIC CARDS
STATED ODDS 1:35

1995 Upper Deck Electric Silver

COMPLETE SET (300) 40.00 100.00
*STARS: 1X TO 2.5X BASIC CARDS
*RCs: .6X TO 1.5X BASIC CARDS
ONE PER PACK

1995 Upper Deck Joe Montana Trilogy

This 23 card standard size set was issued in three parts: part one (MT1-MT8) was in 1995 Collector's Choice, part two (MT9-MT16) was in 1995 Upper Deck and part three (MT17-MT21) was in 1995 SP. The cards come one in 12 packs in Collector's Choice and Upper Deck and one in 29 SP packs.

COMPLETE SET (23) 20.00 50.00
COMMON CC 1.50 3.00
MT1-MT8: COL. CHOICE STATED ODDS 1:12
COMMON UD 2.00 4.00
MT9-MT16: UP. DECK STATED ODDS 1:12
COMMON SP 2.50 5.00
MT17-MT21: SP STATED ODDS 1:29
CCH Coll.Choice Header 1.50 3.00
SPH SP Header 2.00 4.00
UDH Upper Deck Header 2.50 5.00

1995 Upper Deck Predictor Award Winners

This 20-card standard-size set was randomly inserted in hobby packs at a rate of one in 35. The first ten cards are NFL MVP Award predictors and the second ten are Rookie-of-the-Year Award predictors. The cardfronts have a color action photo with the player's name above and the set title and award category below the picture in copper foil. The backs contain the contest rules. If the player featured won, in the category included on the card, the collector could exchange his card (plus $3 postage) for a special foil enhanced parallel redemption prize set with all-new cardbacks. Each card is numbered with an "HP" for hobby predictor. The exchange cards expired 3/30/96.

COMPLETE SET (20) 25.00 60.00
STATED ODDS 1:35 HOBBY
*PRIZE STARS: .6X TO 1.5X BASE CARD HI
*PRIZE ROOKIES: .3X TO .8X BASE CARD HI
HP1 Dan Marino 4.00 10.00
HP2 Steve Young 1.50 4.00
HP3 Drew Bledsoe 1.50 4.00
HP4 Troy Aikman 2.00 5.00
HP5 Barry Sanders 3.00 8.00
HP6 Emmitt Smith 3.00 8.00
HP7 Jerry Rice W2 2.00 5.00
HP8 Steve McNair 2.50 6.00
HP9 Natrone Means .30 .75
HP10 The Longshot W1 .20 .50
HP11 Ki-Jana Carter .30 .75
HP12 Steve McNair 2.50 6.00
HP13 Michael Westbrook .30 .75
HP14 Kerry Collins 1.25 3.00
HP15 Joey Galloway 1.25 3.00
HP16 Kyle Brady .30 .75
HP17 Napoleon Kaufman 1.00 2.50
HP18 Tyrone Wheatley 1.00 2.50
HP19 Rashaan Salaam .20 .50
HP20 The Longshot W1 .20 .50

1995 Upper Deck Predictor League Leaders

This 30-card standard-size set was randomly inserted in retail packs at a rate of one in 30. The first ten cards are passing efficiency predictors, the second ten rushing yardage and the final ten receiving yardage predictors. The fronts contain a color action photo with the player's name above and the set title and category below the photo. Cardbacks contained the game rules. If the featured player finished first or second in the category included on the card, the collector could exchange his card (plus $3 postage) for a foil enhanced parallel prize set with all-new cardbacks. The exchange cards expired 3/30/96.

COMPLETE SET (30) 20.00 50.00
STATED ODDS 1:30 RET,1:17 SPEC.RET
*PRIZE STARS: .6X TO 1.5X BASE CARD HI
*PRIZE ROOKIES: .3X TO .8X BASE CARD HI
RP1 Dan Marino 4.00 10.00
RP2 Steve Young 1.50 4.00
RP3 Drew Bledsoe 1.50 4.00
RP4 Troy Aikman 2.00 5.00
RP5 John Elway 4.00 10.00
RP6 Brett Favre W2 4.00 10.00
RP7 Stan Humphries .30 .75
RP8 Jeff George .30 .75
RP9 Kerry Collins 1.25 3.00
RP10 The Longshot W1 .20 .50
RP11 Barry Sanders W2 3.00 8.00
RP12 Chris Warren .30 .75
RP13 Emmitt Smith W1 3.00 8.00
RP14 Natrone Means .30 .75
RP15 Rodney Hampton .30 .75
RP16 Marshall Faulk 3.00 8.00
RP17 Errict Rhett .30 .75
RP18 Napoleon Kaufman 1.00 2.50
RP19 Ki-Jana Carter .20 .50
RP20 The Longshot .20 .50
RP21 Jerry Rice W1 2.00 5.00
RP22 Ben Coates .30 .75
RP23 Cris Carter .60 1.50
RP24 Andre Reed .30 .75
RP25 Andre Rison .30 .75
RP26 Tim Brown .60 1.50
RP27 Michael Irvin .60 1.50
RP28 Irving Fryar .30 .75
RP29 Michael Westbrook .20 .50
RP30 The Longshot W2 .20 .50

1995 Upper Deck Pro Bowl

This 25 card standard-size set was randomly inserted in packs at a rate of one in 25. The set commemorates the players who went to the 1995 Pro Bowl. The fronts are laid out horizontally with a 3-D holoview image of the player and palm trees behind him. The backs have a color-action player photo in his Pro Bowl uniform with information on his 1994 season that got him to Hawaii. Card backs contain a "PB" prefix.

COMPLETE SET (25) 25.00 60.00
STATED ODDS 1:25
PB1 Barry Sanders 5.00 12.00
PB2 Brent Jones .20 .50
PB3 Cris Carter .75 2.00
PB4 Emmitt Smith 5.00 12.00
PB5 Jay Novacek .40 1.00
PB6 Jerome Bettis .75 2.00
PB7 Jerry Rice 3.00 8.00
PB8 Michael Irvin .75 2.00
PB9 Ricky Watters .40 1.00
PB10 Steve Young 2.50 6.00
PB11 Troy Aikman 3.00 8.00
PB12 Warren Moon .40 1.00
PB13 Terance Mathis .40 1.00
PB14 Ben Coates .40 1.00
PB15 Chris Warren .40 1.00
PB16 Dan Marino 6.00 15.00
PB17 Drew Bledsoe 2.00 5.00
PB18 Irving Fryar .40 1.00
PB19 Jeff Hostetler .40 1.00
PB20 John Elway 6.00 15.00
PB21 Leroy Hoard .20 .50
PB22 Marshall Faulk 4.00 10.00
PB23 Natrone Means .40 1.00
PB24 Tim Brown .75 2.00
PB25 Checklist .40 1.00

1995 Upper Deck Special Edition

This 90-card standard-size set was inserted in each hobby pack. The fronts have a full-bleed color photo. The words "Special Edition" with Upper Deck between them are in at the top of the card with the player's name at the bottom, all of which are in silver-foil. The backs have a small version of the picture from the front with the player's name above it and "Special Edition" above that in silver. Information and statistics are on the bottom of the card. A gold version of the set also exists and was inserted into packs at a rate of one in 35.

COMPLETE SET (90) 12.50 30.00
ONE SILVER PER HOBBY PACK
*GOLD SE STARS: 3X TO 8X BASE CARD HI
*GOLD SE ROOKIES: 1.5X TO 4X BASE CARD HI
GOLD STATED ODDS 1:35 HOBBY
SE1 Terry Kirby .10 .30
SE2 Marcus Allen .25 .60
SE3 Bernie Parmalee .10 .30
SE4 Vernon Turner .05 .15
SE5 Dolphin's Defense .05 .15
SE6 Kevin Turner .05 .15
SE7 Henry Thomas .05 .15
SE8 Barry Sanders 2.00 4.00
SE9 Marshall Faulk 1.50 3.00
SE10 Bill Bates .10 .30
SE11 Stan Humphries .10 .30
SE12 Barry Foster .10 .30
SE13 Shannon Sharpe .10 .30
SE14 Joe Montana 2.50 5.00
SE15 Bryan Cox .05 .15
SE16 Dale Carter .10 .30
SE17 Drew Bledsoe .75 1.50
SE18 Dan Marino 2.50 5.00
SE19 Ricky Watters .10 .30
SE20 Alvin Harper .05 .15
SE21 Harris Barton .05 .15
SE22 Dan Marino 2.50 5.00
SE23 Ronnie Harmon .05 .15
SE24 Michael Irvin .25 .60
SE25 Emmitt Smith 2.00 4.00
SE26 Jeff Christy .05 .15
SE27 Terry Allen .10 .30
SE28 Randall Cunningham .25 .60
SE29 Todd Steussie .05 .15
SE30 Warren Moon .10 .30
SE31 Vikings Defense .05 .15
SE32 Tony Tolbert .05 .15
SE33 William Fuller .05 .15
SE34 Bernard Williams .05 .15
SE35 Charlie Garner .25 .60
SE36 Troy Aikman 1.25 2.50
SE37 Alvin Harper .05 .15
SE38 Kenneth Gant .05 .15
SE39 Daryl Johnston .10 .30
SE40 Ben Coates .10 .30
SE41 Rickey Jackson .05 .15
SE42 O.J. McDuffie .25 .60
SE43 Marion Butts .05 .15
SE44 The Snap .05 .15
SE45 Kimble Anders .10 .30
SE46 Chief's Defense .10 .30
SE47 Richmond Webb .05 .15
SE48 Carlos Jenkins .05 .15
SE49 James Harris DE .05 .15
SE50 Dexter Carter .05 .15
SE51 Qadry Ismail .10 .30
SE52 Jeff Herrod .05 .15
SE53 Sean Jones .05 .15
SE54 Keith Sims .05 .15
SE55 William Floyd .10 .30
SE56 Don Majkowski .05 .15
SE57 Charger's Defense .05 .15
SE58 Byron Evans .05 .15
SE59 Chad Hennings .05 .15
SE60 Eric Allen .05 .15
SE61 Curtis Martin 1.50 3.00
SE62 Napoleon Kaufman .60 1.25
SE63 Kevin Carter .25 .60
SE64 Luther Elliss .05 .15
SE65 Frank Sanders .10 .30
SE66 Rob Johnson .40 1.00
SE67 Christian Fauria .10 .30
SE68 Kyle Brady .25 .60
SE69 Ray Zellars .10 .30
SE70 James A.Stewart .05 .15
SE71 Ty Law .05 .15
SE72 Rodney Thomas .10 .30
SE73 Jimmy Oliver .05 .15
SE74 James O. Stewart .60 1.25
SE75 Dave Barr .05 .15
SE76 Kordell Stewart .75 2.00
SE77 Michael Westbrook .10 .30
SE78 Bobby Taylor .05 .15
SE79 Mark Fields .25 .60
SE80 Kerry Collins .75 1.50
SE81 Natrone Means .10 .30
SE82 Mark Seay .10 .30
SE83 Deion Sanders .75 1.50
SE84 Dana Stubblefield .10 .30
SE85 49ers Defense .10 .30
SE86 Alfred Pupunu .05 .15
SE87 Tim Harris .05 .15
SE88 Jerry Rice 1.25 2.50
SE89 Steve Young 1.00 2.00
SE90 Steve Young 1.25 2.50
Jerry Rice

1995 Upper Deck Gold Signature/Electric Gold

COMPLETE GOLD SET (300) 350.00 700.00
COMP.GOLD SIG.SET (150) 200.00 400.00
COMP. ELE.GOLD SET (150) 150.00 300.00
*GOLD STARS: 8X TO 20X BASE CARDS

1995 Upper Deck GTE Phone Cards AFC

Upper Deck and GTE joined together to produce these 15 prepaid phone cards. Measuring approximately 3 3/8" by 2 1/8", the cards have rounded corners and carry 5 units of U.S. long distance calling. The fronts feature color action player photos of AFC football players, with the player's name, position and team in a team color-coded bar alongside the left. A red bar below the photo carries the words "Prepaid Calling Card, 5 Units". The backs have instructions on how to use the calling cards. The cards are unnumbered and checklisted below in alphabetical order. Just 2,500 of each card were produced, and they are individually numbered on the back. A special card with more detailed instructions was included with each set.

COMPLETE SET (15) 16.00 40.00
1 Marcus Allen 1.20 3.00
2 Drew Bledsoe 2.00 5.00
3 Gary Brown .40 1.00
4 Tim Brown 1.20 3.00
5 John Elway 4.80 12.00
6 Marshall Faulk 2.40 6.00
7 Barry Foster .40 1.00
8 Jim Kelly 1.20 3.00
9 Ronnie Lott .60 1.50
10 Dan Marino 4.80 12.00
11 Rick Mirer .60 1.50
12 Carl Pickens .60 1.50
13 Junior Seau .60 1.50
14 Vinny Testaverde .60 1.50
15 Title Card .40 1.00

1995 Upper Deck GTE Phone Cards NFC

Upper Deck and GTE joined together to produce these 15 prepaid phone cards. Measuring approximately 3 3/8" by 2 1/8", the cards have rounded corners and carry five units of U.S. long distance calling. The fronts feature color action player photos of NFC football players, with the player's name, position and team in a team color-coded bar alongside the left. A blue bar below the photo carries the words "Prepaid Calling Card, 5 Units". The backs have instructions on how to use the calling cards. They are unnumbered and checklisted below in alphabetical order. Only 2,500 of each card were produced, and they are individually numbered on the back. A special card with more detailed instructions was included with each set.

COMPLETE SET (15) 12.00 30.00
1 Jerome Bettis 1.20 3.00
2 Gary Clark .40 1.00
3 Curtis Conway .80 2.00
4 Randall Cunningham 1.20 3.00
5 Rodney Hampton .40 1.00
6 Michael Haynes .40 1.00
7 Michael Irvin 1.20 3.00
8 Warren Moon 1.20 3.00
9 Hardy Nickerson .40 1.00
10 Jerry Rice 2.40 6.00
11 Andre Rison .80 2.00
12 Barry Sanders 4.80 12.00
13 Sterling Sharpe .80 2.00
14 Heath Shuler .80 2.00
15 Title Card .40 1.00

1995 Upper Deck Joe Montana Box Set

This 45-card, boxed set summarizes the career of Joe Montana from the Pennsylvania Pee-Wee Leagues through his NFL career. On the fronts, the full-bleed photos are edged by a gold foil design and a black-and-red bar. The backs feature a second color photo and commentary summarizing various facets of his career. The set is subdivided as follows: The Early Years (1-5), Montana's Dominance (6-25), The New Chief (20-30), Joe's Numbers (31-40), and Teammates (41-45). The set includes one of four oversized (8 1/8" by 3 3/8") cards commemorating Montana's Super Bowls. Each of these oversized cards was serial numbered and, apparently, also sold separately by Upper Deck Authenticated through the catalog.

COMP.FACTORY SET (46) 8.00 20.00
COMMON CARD (1-45) .24 .60
41 Bill Walsh CO .25 .60
42 Russ Francis .25 .60
43 Roger Craig .25 .60
44 Jerry Rice .50 1.25
45 Dwight Clark .25 .60
JM16 Joe Montana Promo .60 1.50
NNO1 Super Bowl XVI 2.00 5.00
(numbered of 24,000)
NNO2 Super Bowl XIX 1.60 4.00
NNO3 Super Bowl XXIII 1.20 3.00
(numbered of 46,000)
NNO4 Super Bowl XXIV 2.40 6.00

1996 Upper Deck

The 1996 Upper Deck set was issued in one series totalling 300-cards. The 12-card packs originally retailed for $2.99 each. The set contains a 33-card Star Rookies subset and numerous insert sets. Also included as an insert, in both Collector's Choice and Upper Deck packs (1:4 packs), was a game piece for the Meet the Stars promotion. Each game piece featured multiple choice trivia questions about football. A collector could scratch of the box next to the answer that they felt best matched the question to determine if they won. Instant win game pieces were also inserted one in 72 packs. Winning game pieces could be sent to Upper Deck for prize drawings. The Grand Prize was a chance to meet Dan Marino. Prizes for 2nd through 4th were for Upper Deck Authenticated shopping sprees. The 5th prize was two special Dan Marino Meet the Stars cards. The blankbacked die cut cards measure roughly 5" X 7" and are entitled Dynamic Debut and Magic Memories. These two cards are priced at the bottom of the base set below.

COMPLETE SET (300) 12.50 30.00
1 Keyshawn Johnson RC .50 1.25
2 Kevin Hardy RC .20 .50
3 Simeon Rice RC .50 1.25
4 Jonathan Ogden RC .50 1.25
5 Cedric Jones RC .02 .10
6 Lawrence Phillips RC .20 .50
7 Tim Biakabutuka RC .20 .50
8 Terry Glenn RC .50 1.25
9 Rickey Dudley RC .20 .50
10 Willie Anderson RC .02 .10
11 Alex Molden RC .02 .10
12 Regan Upshaw RC .02 .10
13 Walt Harris RC .02 .10
14 Eddie George RC .60 1.50
15 John Mobley RC .02 .10
16 Duane Clemons RC .02 .10
17 Eddie Kennison RC .20 .50
18 Marvin Harrison RC 1.25 3.00
19 Daryl Gardener RC .02 .10
20 Leeland McElroy RC .08 .25
21 Eric Moulds RC .60 1.50
22 Alex Van Dyke RC .08 .25
23 Mike Alstott RC .50 1.25
24 Jeff Lewis RC .08 .25
25 Bobby Engram RC .20 .50
26 Derrick Mayes RC .20 .50
27 Karim Abdul-Jabbar RC .20 .50
28 Bobby Hoying RC .20 .50
29 Stepfret Williams RC .08 .25
30 Chris Darkins RC .02 .10
31 Stephen Davis RC .75 2.00
32 Danny Kanell RC .20 .50
33 Tony Brackens RC .20 .50
34 Leslie O'Neal .02 .10
35 Chris Doleman .02 .10
36 Larry Brown .02 .10
37 Ronnie Harmon .02 .10
38 Chris Spielman .02 .10
39 John Jurkovic .02 .10
40 Shawn Jefferson .02 .10
41 William Floyd .08 .25
42 Eric Davis .02 .10
43 Willie Clay .02 .10
44 Marco Coleman .02 .10
45 Lorenzo White .02 .10
46 Neil O'Donnell .08 .25
47 Natrone Means .08 .25
48 Cornelius Bennett .02 .10
49 Steve Walsh .02 .10
50 Jerome Bettis .20 .50
51 Boomer Esiason .08 .25
52 Glyn Milburn .02 .10
53 Kevin Greene .08 .25
54 Seth Joyner .02 .10
55 Jeff Graham .02 .10
56 Darren Woodson .08 .25
57 Dale Carter .02 .10
58 Lorenzo Lynch .02 .10
59 Tim Brown .20 .50
60 Jerry Rice .50 1.25
61 Garrison Hearst .08 .25
62 Eric Metcalf .02 .10
63 Leroy Hoard .02 .10
64 Thurman Thomas .20 .50
65 Sam Mills .02 .10
66 Curtis Conway .20 .50
67 Carl Pickens .08 .25
68 Deion Sanders .30 .75
69 Shannon Sharpe .08 .25
70 Herman Moore .08 .25
71 Robert Brooks .20 .50
72 Rodney Thomas .02 .10
73 Ken Dilger .08 .25
74 Mark Brunell .30 .75
75 Marcus Allen .20 .50
76 Dan Marino 1.00 2.50
77 Robert Smith .00 .25
78 Drew Bledsoe .30 .75
79 Jim Everett .02 .10

80 Rodney Hampton .08 .25
81 Adrian Murrell .08 .25
82 Daryl Hobbs RC .02 .10
83 Ricky Watters .08 .25
84 Yancey Thigpen .08 .25
85 Roman Phifer .02 .10
86 Tony Martin .08 .25
87 Dana Stubblefield .08 .25
88 Joey Galloway .20 .50
89 Errict Rhett .08 .25
90 Terry Allen .08 .25
91 Aeneas Williams .02 .10
92 Craig Heyward .02 .10
93 Vinny Testaverde .08 .25
94 Bryce Paup .02 .10
95 Kerry Collins .20 .50
96 Rashaan Salaam .08 .25
97 Dan Wilkinson .02 .10
98 Jay Novacek .02 .10
99 John Elway 1.00 2.50
100 Bennie Blades .02 .10
101 Edgar Bennett .08 .25
102 Darryll Lewis .02 .10
103 Marshall Faulk .25 .60
104 Bryan Schwartz .02 .10
105 Tamarick Vanover .08 .25
106 Terry Kirby .08 .25
107 John Randle .08 .25
108 Ted Johnson RC .20 .50
109 Mario Bates .08 .25
110 Phillippi Sparks .02 .10
111 Marvin Washington .02 .10
112 Terry McDaniel .02 .10
113 Bobby Taylor .02 .10
114 Carnell Lake .02 .10
115 Troy Drayton .02 .10
116 Darren Bennett .02 .10
117 J.J. Stokes .20 .50
118 Rick Mirer .08 .25
119 Jackie Harris .02 .10
120 Ken Harvey .02 .10
121 Rob Moore .08 .25
122 Jeff George .08 .25
123 Andre Rison .08 .25
124 Darick Holmes .02 .10
125 Tim McKyer .02 .10
126 Alonzo Spellman .02 .10
127 Jeff Blake .20 .50
128 Kevin Williams .02 .10
129 Anthony Miller .08 .25
130 Barry Sanders .75 2.00
131 Brett Favre 1.25 2.50
132 Steve McNair .40 1.00
133 Jim Harbaugh .08 .25
134 Desmond Howard .08 .25
135 Steve Bono .02 .10
136 Bernie Parmalee .02 .10
137 Warren Moon .08 .25
138 Curtis Martin .40 1.00
139 Irv Smith .02 .10
140 Thomas Lewis .02 .10
141 Kyle Brady .02 .10
142 Napoleon Kaufman .20 .50
143 Mike Mamula .02 .10
144 Erric Pegram .02 .10
145 Isaac Bruce .20 .50
146 Andre Coleman .02 .10
147 Merton Hanks .02 .10
148 Brian Blades .02 .10
149 Hardy Nickerson .02 .10
150 Michael Westbrook .20 .50
151 Larry Centers .08 .25
152 Morten Andersen .02 .10
153 Michael Jackson .08 .25
154 Bruce Smith .08 .25
155 Derrick Moore .02 .10
156 Mark Carrier DB .02 .10
157 John Copeland .02 .10
158 Emmitt Smith .75 2.00
159 Jason Elam .08 .25
160 Scott Mitchell .08 .25
161 Mark Chmura .08 .25
162 Blaine Bishop .02 .10
163 Tony Bennett .02 .10
164 Pete Mitchell .08 .25
165 Dan Saleaumua .02 .10
166 Pete Stoyanovich .02 .10
167 Cris Carter .20 .50
168 Vince Brisby .02 .10
169 Wayne Martin .02 .10
170 Tyrone Wheatley .08 .25
171 Mo Lewis .02 .10
172 Harvey Williams .02 .10
173 Calvin Williams .02 .10
174 Norm Johnson .02 .10
175 Mark Rypien .02 .10
176 Stan Humphries .08 .25
177 Derek Loville .02 .10
178 Christian Fauria .02 .10
179 Warren Sapp .02 .10
180 Henry Ellard .02 .10
181 Jamir Miller .02 .10
182 Jessie Tuggle .02 .10
183 Stevon Moore .02 .10
184 Jim Kelly .20 .50
185 Mark Carrier .02 .10
186 Chris Zorich .02 .10
187 Harold Green .02 .10
188 Chris Boniol .02 .10
189 Allen Aldridge .02 .10
190 Brett Perriman .02 .10
191 Chris Jacke .02 .10
192 Todd McNair .02 .10
193 Floyd Turner .02 .10
194 Jeff Lageman .02 .10
195 Derrick Thomas .20 .50
196 Eric Green .02 .10
197 Orlando Thomas .02 .10
198 Ben Coates .08 .25
199 Tyrone Hughes .02 .10
200 Dave Brown .02 .10
201 Brad Baxter .02 .10
202 Chester McGlockton .02 .10
203 Rodney Peete .02 .10
204 Willie Williams .02 .10
205 Kevin Carter .02 .10
206 Aaron Hayden RC .02 .10
207 Steve Young .40 1.00
208 Chris Warren .08 .25
209 Eric Curry .02 .10
210 Brian Mitchell .02 .10
211 Frank Sanders .08 .25
212 Terance Mathis UER .02 .10
213 Eric Turner .02 .10
214 Bill Brooks .02 .10
215 John Kasay .02 .10
216 Erik Kramer .02 .10
217 Darnay Scott .08 .25
218 Charles Haley .08 .25
219 Steve Atwater .02 .10
220 Jason Hanson .02 .10
221 LeRoy Butler .02 .10
222 Cris Dishman .02 .10
223 Sean Dawkins .02 .10
224 James O. Stewart .08 .25
225 Greg Hill .08 .25
226 Jeff Cross .02 .10
227 Qadry Ismail .08 .25
228 Dave Meggett .02 .10
229 Eric Allen .02 .10
230 Chris Calloway .02 .10
231 Wayne Chrebet .30 .75
232 Jeff Hostetler .02 .10
233 Andy Harmon .02 .10
234 Greg Lloyd .08 .25
235 Toby Wright .02 .10
236 Junior Seau .20 .50
237 Bryant Young .08 .25
238 Robert Blackmon .02 .10
239 Trent Dilfer .20 .50
240 Leslie Shepherd .02 .10
241 Eric Swann .02 .10
242 Bert Emanuel .08 .25
243 Antonio Langham .02 .10
244 Steve Christie .02 .10
245 Tyrone Poole .02 .10
246 Jim Flanigan .02 .10
247 Tony McGee .02 .10
248 Michael Irvin .20 .50
249 Byron Bam Morris .02 .10
250 Terrell Davis .40 1.00
251 Johnnie Morton .08 .25
252 Sean Jones .02 .10
253 Chris Sanders .08 .25
254 Quentin Coryatt .02 .10
255 Willie Jackson .08 .25
256 Mark Collins .02 .10
257 Randal Hill .02 .10
258 David Palmer .02 .10
259 Will Moore .02 .10
260 Michael Haynes .02 .10
261 Mike Sherrard .02 .10
262 William Thomas .02 .10
263 Kordell Stewart .20 .50
264 D'Marco Farr .02 .10
265 Terrell Fletcher .02 .10
266 Lee Woodall .02 .10
267 Eugene Robinson .02 .10
268 Alvin Harper .02 .10
269 Gus Frerotte .08 .25
270 Antonio Freeman .20 .50
271 Clyde Simmons .02 .10
272 Chuck Smith .02 .10
273 Steve Tasker .02 .10
274 Kevin Butler .02 .10
275 Steve Tovar .02 .10
276 Troy Aikman .50 1.25
277 Aaron Craver .02 .10
278 Henry Thomas .02 .10
279 Craig Newsome .02 .10
280 Brent Jones .02 .10
281 Micheal Barrow .02 .10
282 Ray Buchanan .02 .10
283 Jimmy Smith .20 .50
284 Neil Smith .08 .25
285 O.J. McDuffie .08 .25
286 Jake Reed .08 .25
287 Ty Law .20 .50
288 Torrance Small .02 .10
289 Hugh Douglas .08 .25
290 Pat Swilling .02 .10
291 Charlie Garner .08 .25
292 Ernie Mills .02 .10
293 John Carney .02 .10
294 Ken Norton .02 .10
295 Cortez Kennedy .02 .10
296 Derrick Brooks .20 .50
297 Heath Shuler .08 .25
298 Reggie White .20 .50
299 Kimble Anders .08 .25
300 Willie McGinest .02 .10
P96 Dan Marino Promo .75 2.00
MS1 Dan Marino 2.00 5.00
MS2 Dan Marino 2.00 5.00
P13 Dan Marino Promo 1.00 2.50

1996 Upper Deck Game Face

This 10 card standard-sized set was inserted one per pack in 1996 Upper Deck special retail packs.The front of the card has a photo of the player, his name, team, and positon, and a Game Face logo in the lower left hand corner of the card. The back of the card has a color photo in the upper right hand side of the card, with a short analysis of that player's skills.

COMPLETE SET (10) 4.00 10.00
ONE PER SPECIAL RETAIL PACK
GF1 Dan Marino 1.50 4.00
GF2 Barry Sanders 1.25 3.00
GF3 Jerry Rice .75 2.00
GF4 Stan Humphries .15 .40
GF5 Drew Bledsoe .50 1.25
GF6 Greg Lloyd .15 .40
GF7 Jim Harbaugh .15 .40
GF8 Rashaan Salaam .15 .40
GF9 Jeff Blake .30 .75
GF10 Reggie White .30 .75

1996 Upper Deck Game Jerseys

Randomly inserted in packs at a rate of one in 2500, this 10-card standard-sized insert set features an actual piece of a game-used jersey from the particular player featured on the card. The front of the card features a color picture of the player, the player's name, team, and the piece of jersey, with the insert name "Game Jersey" surrounding it.

STATED ODDS 1:2500 80.00
GJ1 Dan Marino Teal 60.00 120.00
GJ2 Jerry Rice Red 60.00 120.00
GJ3 Joe Montana 60.00 120.00
GJ4R Jerry Rice Red 60.00 120.00
GJ4W Jerry Rice White 60.00 120.00
GJ5 Rashaan Salaam 25.00 60.00
GJ6 Marshall Faulk 40.00 100.00
GJ7 Dan Marino White 60.00 120.00
GJ8 Steve Young 60.00 120.00
GJ9 Barry Sanders 75.00 150.00
GJ10 Mark Brunell 30.00 80.00

1996 Upper Deck Hot Properties

Randomly inserted in packs at a rate of one in 11, this 20-card standard-sized set featured two players on opposite sides of the card who were considered to be "hot" players within the NFL. The cards have a outlined player photo on both sides of the card, as well as name and position, with a "Hot Properties" logo in the bottom center of the card. The cards are numbered with a "HT" prefix. There is also a gold parallel version of this set that was inserted at a rate of 1:71 packs.

COMPLETE SET (20) 40.00 100.00
STATED ODDS 1:11
*GOLD CARDS: 1X TO 2X REDS
GOLD STATED ODDS 1:71
HT1 D.Marino 5.00 12.00
D.Bledsoe
HT2 J.Rice 4.00 8.00
J.J. Stokes
HT3 K.Stewart 2.50 6.00
D.Sanders
HT4 B.Favre 7.50 15.00
R.Mirer
HT5 J.Blake 2.50 6.00
S.McNair
HT6 E.Smith 6.00 12.00
E.Rhett
HT7 J.Elway 5.00 12.00
W.Moon
HT8 S.Young 4.00 8.00
M.Brunell
HT9 T.Aikman 3.00 8.00
K.Collins
HT10 J.Galloway 2.50 6.00
C.Sanders
HT11 H.Moore 2.50 6.00
C.Carter
HT12 R.Hampton 3.00 8.00
T.Davis
HT13 C.Pickens 2.00 4.00
I.Bruce
HT14 R.Salaam 2.00 4.00
M.Westbrook
HT15 M.Faulk 3.00 8.00
C.Martin
HT16 T.Vanover 1.00 2.50
E.Metcalf
HT17 K.Johnson 2.50 6.00
T.Glenn
HT18 L.Phillips 2.50 6.00
T.Biakabutuka
HT19 K.Hardy 3.00 8.00
Simeon Rice
HT20 B.Sanders 5.00 12.00
T.Thomas

1996 Upper Deck Predictors

The 1996 Upper Deck Predictors were randomly inserted in both hobby and retail packs at a rate of one in 23, with stated odds of 1:14 in some special retail packs. These otherwise standard-sized insert cards had a small concave die-cut into the ends of the card, which had a gold border surrounding a picture of the player. This interactive insert listed an accomplishment (I.e., 14 receptions in a game, 450 yards passing in a game, etc.) that the player pictured had to reach during the 1996 NFL season for the card to be redeemable for a "TV-Cel" upgrade of the particular card. The results listed after the player below by a W (winner) or L (loser) reflects their success in meeting those goals. The predictors inserted in hobby packs have a "PH" prefix, while the retail predictors have a "PR" prefix. The expiration date was 2/28/1997.

COMP.HOBBY SET (20) 30.00 60.00
COMP.RETAIL SET (20) 30.00 60.00
PH1-PH20: STATED ODDS 1:23 HOBBY
PR1-PR20: ODDS 1:23 RET, 1:14 SPEC.RET
PH1 Dan Marino 450 YDS L 3.00 8.00
PH2 S.Young 35 COMP L 1.25 3.00
PH3 B.Favre 375 YDS W 3.00 8.00
PH4 D.Bledsoe 35 COMP W 1.00 2.50
PH5 Jeff George 380 YDS L .30 .75
PH6 J.Elway 30 COMP W 3.00 8.00
PH7 Sanders 190 TO.YDS W 2.50 6.00
PH8 C.Martin 58 YD.PLAY L 1.25 3.00
PH9 M.Faulk 195 TOT.YDS L .75 2.00
PH10 E.Smith 75 YD.PLAY L 2.50 6.00
PH11 Ter.Davis 150 YDS W 1.25 3.00
PH12 E.Rhett 50 YD.PLAY L .30 .75
PH13 L.Phillips 55 YD.PLAY L .15 .40
PH14 Jerry Rice 14 REC L 1.50 4.00
PH15 M.Irvin 130 YDS W .60 1.50
PH16 J.Galloway 10 REC L .60 1.50
PH17 H.Moore 190 YDS L .30 .75
PH18 Isaac Bruce 12 REC L .60 1.50
PH19 C.Pickens 150 YDS W .30 .75
PH20 K.Johnson 11 REC L .60 1.50
PR1 Dan Marino 35 COMP L 3.00 8.00
PR2 Young 435 TOT.YDS W 1.25 3.00
PR3 Brett Favre 30 COMP L 3.00 8.00
PR4 D.Bledsoe 350 YDS W 1.00 2.50
PR5 Jeff George 35 COMP L .30 .75
PR6 John Elway 350 YDS W 3.00 8.00
PR7 B.Sanders 70 YD.PLAY L 2.50 6.00
PR8 C.Martin 160 YDS W 1.25 3.00
PR9 M.Faulk 75 YD.PLAY L .75 2.00
PR10 E.Smith 195 TOT.YDS L 2.50 6.00
PR11 T.Davis 59 YD.PLAY W 1.25 3.00
PR12 Errict Rhett 150 YDS L .30 .75
PR13 Law.Phillips 130 YDS L .15 .40
PR14 Jerry Rice 200 YDS L 1.50 4.00
PR15 Michael Irvin 12 REC W .60 1.50
PR16 Galloway 250 TOT.YDS L .60 1.50
PR17 Her.Moore 12 REC W .30 .75
PR18 Isaac Bruce 200 YDS W .60 1.50
PR19 Carl Pickens 10 REC W .30 .75
PR20 K.Johnson 140 YDS L .60 1.50

1996 Upper Deck Pro Bowl

This standard-sized set of 20 cards was inserted at a rate of 1:33 packs in 1996 Upper Deck hobby and retail issues. The front of the card features the player in Pro Bowl action with the words "Pro Bowl" prominently displayed on the left side of the card, and the player, position, and conference symbol listed at the bottom of the card. The card backs have a photo of the player in the center of the card, as well as a short biography on the player.

COMPLETE SET (20) 30.00 80.00
STATED ODDS 1:33
PB1 Warren Moon .75 2.00
PB2 Brett Favre 8.00 20.00
PB3 Steve Young 3.00 8.00
PB4 Barry Sanders 6.00 15.00
PB5 Emmitt Smith 6.00 15.00
PB6 Jerry Rice 4.00 10.00
PB7 Herman Moore .75 2.00
PB8 Michael Irvin 1.50 4.00
PB9 Mark Chmura .75 2.00
PB10 Reggie White 1.50 4.00
PB11 Jim Harbaugh .75 2.00
PB12 Jeff Blake 1.50 4.00
PB13 Curtis Martin 3.00 8.00
PB14 Marshall Faulk 2.00 5.00
PB15 Chris Warren .75 2.00
PB16 Bryan Cox .30 .75
PB17 Junior Seau 1.50 4.00
PB18 Carl Pickens .75 2.00
PB19 Yancey Thigpen .75 2.00
PB20 Ben Coates .75 2.00

1996 Upper Deck Proview

This 40 card set was inserted at a rate of one per each special edition retail Upper Deck Tech pack. The standard-sized cards have a player photo on the front, with a half-dollar sized player photo cel inserted on the upper right side of the card, with the player's name and position listed on the lower right-hand side of the card. The back of the card identifies the player and gives a short biography, and the cards are numbered with a "PV" prefix. These cards were also inserted in parallel silver (1:35 UD Tech packs) and gold (1:143 UD Tech packs).

COMPLETE SET (40) 40.00 100.00
ONE PER UD TECH RETAIL PACK
*SILVERS: 1.2X TO 3X BASIC INSERTS
SILVER ODDS 1:35 UD TECH PACKS
*GOLDS: 3X TO 8X BASIC INSERTS
GOLD ODDS 1:143 UD TECH PACKS
PV1 Warren Moon .30 .75
PV2 Jerry Rice 1.50 4.00
PV3 Brett Favre 3.00 8.00
PV4 Jim Harbaugh .30 .75
PV5 Junior Seau .60 1.50
PV6 Jeff Blake .60 1.50
PV7 John Elway 3.00 8.00
PV8 Troy Aikman 1.50 4.00
PV9 Steve Young 1.25 3.00
PV10 Kordell Stewart .60 1.50
PV11 Drew Bledsoe 1.00 2.50
PV12 Jim Kelly .60 1.50
PV13 Dan Marino 3.00 8.00
PV14 Kerry Collins .60 1.50
PV15 Jeff Hostetler .15 .40
PV16 Terry Allen .30 .75
PV17 Carl Pickens .30 .75
PV18 Mark Brunell 1.00 2.50
PV19 Keyshawn Johnson .60 1.50
PV20 Barry Sanders 2.50 6.00
PV21 Deion Sanders 1.00 2.50
PV22 Emmitt Smith 2.50 6.00
PV23 Curtis Conway .60 1.50
PV24 Herman Moore .30 .75
PV25 Joey Galloway .60 1.50
PV26 Robert Smith .30 .75
PV27 Eddie George .75 2.00
PV28 Curtis Martin 1.25 3.00
PV29 Marshall Faulk .75 2.00
PV30 Terrell Davis 1.25 3.00
PV31 Rashaan Salaam .30 .75
PV32 Jamal Anderson .15 .40
PV33 Karim Abdul-Jabbar .15 .40
PV34 Edgar Bennett .30 .75
PV35 Thurman Thomas .60 1.50
PV36 Jerome Bettis .60 1.50
PV37 Tim Brown .60 1.50
PV38 Chris Sanders .30 .75
PV39 Eddie Kennison .15 .40
PV40 Shannon Sharpe .30 .75

1996 Upper Deck Rookie Jumbos

These cards are a 5" by 7" version of the first 33-cards in the basic issue set.

*SINGLES: .2X TO .5X BASIC CARDS

1996 Upper Deck Team Trio

Randomly inserted in packs at a rate of one in 4, this 90-card set features die-cutting on 60 of the 90 cards as well as 30 standard-sized cards within the set. Each of the 30 NFL teams has 3 cards within the set, which when placed together forms the "Team Trio". The cards that would be on the left and right hand sides of the "Team Trio" have a rounded die-cut edge. The front of each card gives the player's name, position, and the insert name, while the backs give a snapshot photo and biography.

COMPLETE SET (90) 40.00 80.00
STATED ODDS 1:4 HOB/RET, 1:2 SPEC.RET
TT1 Curtis Conway .50 1.25
TT2 Darnay Scott .25 .60
TT3 Bryce Paup .08 .25
TT4 Terrell Davis 1.00 2.50
TT5 Hardy Nickerson .08 .25
TT6 Frank Sanders .25 .60
TT7 Stan Humphries .25 .60
TT8 Tamarick Vanover .25 .60
TT9 Sean Dawkins .08 .25
TT10 Deion Sanders .75 2.00
TT11 Dan Marino 2.50 6.00
TT12 Charlie Garner .25 .60
TT13 Eric Metcalf .08 .25
TT14 J.J. Stokes .50 1.25
TT15 Chris Calloway .08 .25
TT16 Pete Mitchell .25 .60
TT17 Wayne Chrebet .75 2.00
TT18 Herman Moore .25 .60
TT19 Steve McNair 1.00 2.50
TT20 Edgar Bennett .25 .60
TT21 Kerry Collins .50 1.25
TT22 Vincent Brisby .08 .25
TT23 Jeff Hostetler .08 .25
TT24 Kevin Carter .08 .25
TT25 Michael Jackson .25 .60
TT26 Michael Westbrook .50 1.25
TT27 Tyrone Hughes .08 .25
TT28 Joey Galloway .50 1.25
TT29 Byron Bam Morris .08 .25
TT30 Warren Moon .25 .60
TT31 Rashaan Salaam .25 .60
TT32 Jeff Blake .50 1.25
TT33 Thurman Thomas .50 1.25
TT34 John Elway 2.50 6.00
TT35 Errict Rhett .25 .60
TT36 Garrison Hearst .25 .60
TT37 Andre Coleman .08 .25
TT38 Steve Bono .08 .25
TT39 Marshall Faulk .60 1.50
TT40 Troy Aikman 1.25 3.00
TT41 Terry Kirby .25 .60
TT42 Rodney Peete .08 .25
TT43 Craig Heyward .08 .25
TT44 Steve Young 1.00 2.50
TT45 Rodney Hampton .25 .60
TT46 Mark Brunell .75 2.00
TT47 Kyle Brady .08 .25
TT48 Scott Mitchell .25 .60
TT49 Chris Sanders .25 .60
TT50 Brett Favre 2.50 6.00
TT51 Mark Carrier WR .08 .25
TT52 Drew Bledsoe .75 2.00
TT53 Napoleon Kaufman .50 1.25
TT54 Mark Rypien .08 .25
TT55 Andre Rison .25 .60
TT56 Terry Allen .25 .60
TT57 Jim Everett .08 .25
TT58 Chris Warren .25 .60
TT59 Kordell Stewart .50 1.25
TT60 Jake Reed .25 .60
TT61 Erik Kramer .08 .25
TT62 Carl Pickens .25 .60
TT63 Jim Kelly .50 1.25
TT64 Anthony Miller .25 .60
TT65 Trent Dilfer .50 1.25
TT66 Larry Centers .25 .60
TT67 Junior Seau .50 1.25
TT68 Marcus Allen .50 1.25
TT69 Jim Harbaugh .25 .60
TT70 Emmitt Smith 2.00 5.00
TT71 O.J.McDuffie .25 .60
TT72 Ricky Watters .25 .60
TT73 Jeff George .25 .60
TT74 Jerry Rice 1.25 3.00
TT75 Dave Brown .08 .25
TT76 James O. Stewart .25 .60
TT77 Adrian Murrell .25 .60
TT78 Barry Sanders 2.00 5.00
TT79 Rodney Thomas .08 .25
TT80 Robert Brooks .50 1.25
TT81 Derrick Moore .08 .25
TT82 Curtis Martin 1.00 2.50
TT83 Tim Brown .50 1.25
TT84 Isaac Bruce .50 1.25
TT85 Vinny Testaverde .25 .60
TT86 Henry Ellard .08 .25
TT87 Mario Bates .25 .60
TT88 Rick Mirer .25 .60
TT89 Yancey Thigpen .25 .60
TT90 Cris Carter .50 1.25

1996 Upper Deck TV-Cels

This 20 card insert set contains a "TV-Cel" in the middle of the card surrounded by gold border that identifies the player, and also, the fact that the card is a "TV-Cel" and has slightly concave die-cuts on the end of the card. If measured by the outside edges of the card, it is a standard-sized card. The distribution of these cards were as follows: A maximum of 500 TV-Cels of each player were inserted in 1996 Upper Deck packs, while in addition, these cards were also available as the redemption prizes for a particular players winning Predictor card. The amount of times that a player's predictor card won is listed after their name in the list below.

COMPLETE SET (20) 60.00 150.00
1 Dan Marino 15.00 40.00
2 Steve Young 1W 2.00 5.00
3 Brett Favre 1W 5.00 12.00
4 Drew Bledsoe 2W 1.50 4.00
5 Jeff George 2W 1.25 3.00
6 John Elway 2W 4.00 10.00
7 Barry Sanders 1W 3.00 8.00
8 Curtis Martin 1W 2.50 6.00
9 Marshall Faulk 4.00 10.00
10 Emmitt Smith 15.00 40.00
11 Terrell Davis 1W 2.50 6.00
12 Errict Rhett 2.00 5.00
13 Lawrence Phillips 3.00 8.00
14 Jerry Rice 10.00 25.00
15 Michael Irvin 1W 1.50 4.00
16 Joey Galloway 3.00 8.00
17 Herman Moore 1W 1.25 3.00
18 Isaac Bruce 1W 1.50 4.00
19 Carl Pickens 1W 1.25 3.00
20 Keyshawn Johnson 3.00 8.00

1996 Upper Deck A Cut Above Jumbos

This set includes parallels of some of the ten 1997 Collector's Choice A Cut Above insert cards on oversized (3-1/2" by 5") stock. Two other players were switched from the original checklist. The sets were released in box set form through Upper Deck Authenticated and some retail outlets.

COMPLETE SET (10) 4.00 10.00
1 Terrell Davis 1.20 3.00
2 Tim Biakabutuka .20 .50
3 Drew Bledsoe .50 1.25
4 Emmitt Smith .80 2.00
5 Marshall Faulk
6 Brett Favre 1.20 3.00
7 Keyshawn Johnson .40 1.00
8 Deion Sanders .30 .75
9 Curtis Martin .40 1.00
10 Jerry Rice .60 1.50

1996 Upper Deck Mini

This set was issued in early 1997 by Upper Deck. The cards follow the basic set design and use the photos from the 1996 Collector's Choice football set but carry only the Upper Deck logo on the fronts. The backs have a 1997 copyright date and a unique numbering system that is different from 1996 Collector's Choice. Finally, the cards measure slightly smaller than standard size: roughly 2 5/16" by 3 5/8" and the first six cards in the set were created in a foil format similar to SP products.

1 Brett Favre FOIL SP 5.00 12.00
2 Drew Bledsoe FOIL SP 1.25 3.00
3 Emmitt Smith FOIL SP 3.00 8.00
4 Terrell Davis FOIL SP 1.25 3.00
5 Steve Young FOIL SP 1.50 4.00
6 Dan Marino FOIL SP 4.00 10.00
7 Jerry Rice 2.50 6.00
8 Rashaan Salaam .60 1.50
9 Carl Pickens .60 1.50
10 Jim Kelly 1.50 4.00
11 John Elway 2.50 6.00
12 Errict Rhett .60 1.50
13 Eric Swann .50 1.25
14 Tony Martin .60 1.50
15 Marcus Allen .75 2.00
16 Marshall Faulk .75 2.00
17 Troy Aikman 2.00 5.00
18 Karim Abdul-Jabbar .50 1.25
19 Ricky Watters .60 1.50
20 Eric Metcalf .60 1.50
21 Rodney Hampton .60 1.50
22 Mark Brunell .60 1.50
23 Adrian Murrell .50 1.25
24 Barry Sanders 2.50 6.00
25 Steve McNair .75 2.00
26 Reggie White 1.00 2.50
27 Kerry Collins .75 2.00
28 Curtis Martin .75 2.00
29 Napoleon Kaufman .60 1.50
30 Isaac Bruce .75 2.00
31 Vinny Testaverde .60 1.50
32 Terry Allen .60 1.50
33 Jim Everett .60 1.50
34 Joey Galloway .60 1.50
35 Kordell Stewart .75 2.00
36 Cris Carter 1.00 2.50
37 Jeff Blake .60 1.50
38 Bruce Smith .75 2.00
39 Junior Seau .75 2.00
40 Derrick Thomas 1.00 2.50
41 Jim Harbaugh .60 1.50
42 Terance Mathis .50 1.25
43 Dave Brown .50 1.25
44 Henry Thomas .50 1.25
45 Tim Brown 1.00 2.50
46 Gus Frerotte .50 1.25
47 Mario Bates .50 1.25
48 Chris Warren .50 1.25

1996 Upper Deck Troy Aikman A Cut Above Jumbos

This set was released through Upper Deck Authenticated and some retail outlets and sold in box set form. Each card is oversized (3-1/2" by 5") and die cut. The card numbering resumes where other A Cut Above sets left off.

COMPLETE SET (10) 4.00 10.00
COMMON CARD CA11-CA20) .40 1.00

1996 Upper Deck Troy Aikman Chronicles Jumbos

Upper Deck issued this 10-card box set to highlight the career achievements of Troy Aikman. The set was distributed primarily by UDA. A signed Aikman card from the set could also be purchased originally for $100.

COMPLETE SET (10) 8.00 20.00
COMMON CARD (1-10) .80 2.00
TA10AU Troy Aikman AU/500 40.00 80.00

1996 Upper Deck 22K Gold Dan Marino

1 Dan Marino 6.00 15.00

1997 Upper Deck

The 1997 Upper Deck first series totals 300-cards and was distributed in 12-card packs with a suggested retail price of $2.49. The fronts feature color action player photos with player information on the backs. The set contains the topical subsets: Star Rookie (1-31), and Star Rookie Flashback (32-41).

COMPLETE SET (300) 20.00 40.00
1 Orlando Pace RC .25 .60
2 Darrell Russell RC .08 .25
3 Shawn Springs RC .15 .40
4 Bryant Westbrook RC .08 .25
5 Ike Hilliard RC .50 1.25
6 Peter Boulware RC .25 .60
7 Tom Knight RC .08 .25
8 Yatil Green RC .15 .40
9 Tony Gonzalez RC 1.25 3.00
10 Reidel Anthony RC .25 .60
11 Warrick Dunn RC 1.00 2.50
12 Kenny Holmes RC .25 .60
13 Jim Druckenmiller RC .15 .40
14 James Farrior RC .25 .60
15 David LaFleur RC .08 .25
16 Antowain Smith RC .75 2.00
17 Rae Carruth RC .08 .25
18 Dwayne Rudd RC .25 .60
19 Jake Plummer RC 1.25 3.00
20 Reinard Wilson RC .15 .40
21 Byron Hanspard RC .15 .40
22 Will Blackwell RC .15 .40
23 Troy Davis RC .15 .40
24 Corey Dillon RC 1.25 3.00
25 Joey Kent RC .25 .60
26 Renaldo Wynn RC .08 .25
27 Pat Barnes RC .25 .60
28 Kevin Lockett RC .15 .40
29 Darnell Autry RC .15 .40
30 Walter Jones RC .40 1.00
31 Trevor Pryce RC .25 .60
32 Dan Marino SRF .50 1.25
33 Steve Young SRF [illegible] [illegible]
34 John Elway SRF .50 1.25
35 Jerry Rice SRF .25 .60
36 Tim Brown SRF .25 .60
37 Deion Sanders SRF .25 .60
38 Troy Aikman SRF .25 .60
39 Barry Sanders SRF .40 1.00
40 Emmitt Smith SRF .40 1.00
41 Junior Seau SRF .25 .60
42 Neil Smith .15 .40
43 Brett Perriman .08 .25
44 Jim Everett .08 .25
45 Qadry Ismail .15 .40
46 Dana Stubblefield .08 .25
47 Bryant Young .08 .25
48 Ken Norton Jr. .08 .25
49 Terrell Owens .30 .75
50 Jerry Rice .50 1.25
51 Steve Young .30 .75
52 Terry Kirby .15 .40
53 Chris Doleman .08 .25
54 Lee Woodall .08 .25
55 Merton Hanks .08 .25
56 Garrison Hearst .15 .40
57 Rashaan Salaam .08 .25
58 Raymont Harris .08 .25
59 Curtis Conway .15 .40
60 Bobby Engram .15 .40
61 Bryan Cox .08 .25
62 Walt Harris .08 .25
63 Tyrone Hughes .08 .25
64 Rick Mirer .08 .25
65 Jeff Blake .15 .40
66 Carl Pickens .15 .40
67 Darnay Scott .15 .40
68 Tony McGee .08 .25
69 Ki-Jana Carter .08 .25
70 Ashley Ambrose .08 .25
71 Dan Wilkinson .08 .25
72 Chris Spielman .08 .25
73 Todd Collins .08 .25
74 Andre Reed .15 .40
75 Quinn Early .08 .25
76 Eric Moulds .25 .60
77 Darick Holmes .08 .25
78 Thurman Thomas .25 .60
79 Bruce Smith .15 .40
80 Bryce Paup .08 .25
81 John Elway 1.00 2.50
82 Terrell Davis .30 .75
83 Anthony Miller .08 .25
84 Shannon Sharpe .15 .40
85 Alfred Williams .08 .25
86 John Mobley .08 .25
87 Tory James .08 .25
88 Steve Atwater .08 .25
89 Darrien Gordon .08 .25
90 Mike Alstott .25 .60
91 Errict Rhett .08 .25
92 Trent Dilfer .25 .60
93 Courtney Hawkins .08 .25
94 Warren Sapp .15 .40
95 Regan Upshaw .08 .25
96 Hardy Nickerson .08 .25
97 Donnie Abraham RC .25 .60
98 Larry Centers .15 .40
99 Aeneas Williams .08 .25
100 Kent Graham UER .08 .25
101 Rob Moore .15 .40
102 Frank Sanders .15 .40
103 Leeland McElroy .08 .25
104 Eric Swann .08 .25
105 Simeon Rice .15 .40
106 Seth Joyner .08 .25
107 Stan Humphries .15 .40
108 Tony Martin .15 .40
109 Charlie Jones .08 .25
110 Andre Coleman UER 103 .08 .25
111 Terrell Fletcher .08 .25
112 Junior Seau .25 .60
113 Eric Metcalf .15 .40
114 Chris Penn .08 .25
115 Marcus Allen .25 .60
116 Greg Hill .08 .25
117 Tamarick Vanover .15 .40
118 Lake Dawson .08 .25
119 Derrick Thomas .25 .60
120 Dale Carter .08 .25
121 Elvis Grbac .15 .40
122 Aaron Bailey .08 .25
123 Jim Harbaugh .15 .40
124 Marshall Faulk .30 .75
125 Sean Dawkins .08 .25
126 Marvin Harrison .25 .60
127 Ken Dilger .08 .25
128 Tony Bennett .08 .25
129 Jeff Herrod .08 .25
130 Chris Gardocki .08 .25
131 Cary Blanchard .08 .25
132 Troy Aikman .50 1.25
133 Emmitt Smith .75 2.00
134 Sherman Williams .08 .25
135 Michael Irvin .25 .60
136 Eric Bjornson .08 .25
137 Herschel Walker .15 .40
138 Tony Tolbert .08 .25
139 Deion Sanders .25 .60
140 Daryl Johnston .15 .40
141 Dan Marino 1.00 2.50
142 O.J. McDuffie .15 .40
143 Troy Drayton .08 .25
144 Karim Abdul-Jabbar .15 .40
145 Stanley Pritchett .08 .25
146 Fred Barnett .08 .25
147 Zach Thomas .25 .60
148 Shawn Wooden RC .08 .25
149 Ty Detmer .15 .40
150 Derrick Witherspoon .08 .25
151 Ricky Watters .15 .40
152 Charlie Garner .15 .40
153 Chris T. Jones .08 .25
154 Irving Fryar .15 .40
155 Mike Mamula .08 .25
156 Troy Vincent .08 .25
157 Bobby Taylor .08 .25
158 Chris Boniol .08 .25
159 Devin Bush .08 .25
160 Bert Emanuel .15 .40
161 Jamal Anderson .25 .60
162 Terance Mathis .15 .40
163 Cornelius Bennett .08 .25
164 Ray Buchanan .08 .25
165 Chris Chandler .15 .40
166 Dave Brown .08 .25
167 Danny Kanell .08 .25
168 Rodney Hampton .15 .40
169 Tyrone Wheatley .15 .40
170 Amani Toomer .15 .40
171 Chris Calloway .08 .25
172 Thomas Lewis .08 .25
173 Phillippi Sparks .08 .25
174 Mark Brunell .30 .75
175 Keenan McCardell .15 .40
176 Willie Jackson .08 .25
177 Jimmy Smith .15 .40
178 Pete Mitchell .08 .25
179 Natrone Means .15 .40
180 Kevin Hardy .08 .25
181 Tony Brackens .08 .25
182 James O. Stewart .15 .40
183 Wayne Chrebet .25 .60
184 Keyshawn Johnson .25 .60
185 Adrian Murrell .15 .40
186 Neil O'Donnell .15 .40
187 Hugh Douglas .08 .25
188 Mo Lewis .08 .25
189 Marvin Washington .08 .25
190 Aaron Glenn .08 .25
191 Barry Sanders .75 2.00
192 Scott Mitchell .15 .40
193 Herman Moore .15 .40
194 Johnnie Morton .15 .40
195 Glyn Milburn .08 .25
196 Reggie Brown LB .15 .40
197 Jason Hanson .08 .25
198 Steve McNair .30 .75
199 Eddie George .25 .60
200 Ronnie Harmon .08 .25
201 Chris Sanders .08 .25
202 Willie Davis .08 .25
203 Frank Wycheck .08 .25
204 Darryll Lewis .08 .25
205 Blaine Bishop .08 .25
206 Robert Brooks .15 .40
207 Brett Favre 1.25 2.50
208 Edgar Bennett .15 .40
209 Dorsey Levens .25 .60
210 Derrick Mayes .15 .40
211 Antonio Freeman .25 .60
212 Mark Chmura .15 .40
213 Reggie White .25 .60
214 Gilbert Brown .15 .40
215 LeRoy Butler .08 .25
216 Craig Newsome .08 .25
217 Kerry Collins .25 .60
218 Wesley Walls .15 .40
219 Muhsin Muhammad .15 .40
220 Anthony Johnson .08 .25
221 Tim Biakabutuka .15 .40
222 Kevin Greene .15 .40
223 Sam Mills .08 .25
224 John Kasay .08 .25
225 Micheal Barrow .08 .25
226 Drew Bledsoe .30 .75
227 Curtis Martin .30 .75
228 Terry Glenn .25 .60
229 Ben Coates .15 .40
230 Shawn Jefferson .08 .25
231 Willie McGinest .08 .25
232 Ted Johnson .08 .25
233 Lawyer Milloy .15 .40
234 Ty Law .15 .40
235 Willie Clay .08 .25
236 Tim Brown .25 .60
237 Rickey Dudley .15 .40
238 Napoleon Kaufman .25 .60
239 Chester McGlockton .08 .25
240 Rob Fredrickson .08 .25
241 Terry McDaniel .08 .25
242 Desmond Howard .15 .40
243 Jeff George .15 .40
244 Isaac Bruce .25 .60
245 Tony Banks .15 .40
246 Lawrence Phillips UER 247 .08 .25
247 Kevin Carter .08 .25
248 Roman Phifer .08 .25
249 Keith Lyle .08 .25
250 Eddie Kennison .15 .40
251 Craig Heyward .08 .25
252 Vinny Testaverde .15 .40
253 Derrick Alexander WR .15 .40
254 Michael Jackson .15 .40
255 Byron Bam Morris .08 .25
256 Eric Green .08 .25
257 Ray Lewis .40 1.00
258 Antonio Langham .08 .25
259 Michael McCrary .08 .25
260 Gus Frerotte .08 .25
261 Terry Allen .25 .60
262 Brian Mitchell .08 .25
263 Michael Westbrook .15 .40
264 Sean Gilbert .08 .25
265 Rich Owens .08 .25
266 Ken Harvey .08 .25
267 Jeff Hostetler .08 .25
268 Michael Haynes .08 .25
269 Mario Bates .08 .25
270 Renaldo Turnbull UER 273 .08 .25
271 Ray Zellars .08 .25
272 Joe Johnson .08 .25
273 Eric Allen .08 .25
274 Heath Shuler .08 .25
275 Daryl Hobbs .08 .25
276 John Friesz .08 .25
277 Brian Blades .08 .25
278 Joey Galloway .15 .40
279 Chris Warren .15 .40
280 Lamar Smith .25 .60
281 Cortez Kennedy .08 .25
282 Chad Brown .08 .25
283 Warren Moon .25 .60
284 Jerome Bettis .25 .60
285 Charles Johnson .15 .40
286 Kordell Stewart .25 .60
287 Erric Pegram .08 .25
288 Norm Johnson .08 .25
289 Levon Kirkland .08 .25
290 Greg Lloyd .08 .25
291 Carnell Lake .08 .25
292 Brad Johnson .25 .60
293 Cris Carter .25 .60
294 Jake Reed .15 .40
295 Robert Smith .15 .40
296 Derrick Alexander DE .08 .25
297 John Randle .15 .40
298 Dixon Edwards .08 .25
299 Orlando Thomas .08 .25
300 Dewayne Washington .08 .25
DC Draw Your Own Card entry .20 .50

1997 Upper Deck Game Dated Moment Foils

STATED ODDS 1:1500
50 Jerry Rice 15.00 40.00
51 Steve Young 10.00 25.00
78 Thurman Thomas 8.00 20.00
81 John Elway 30.00 80.00
82 Terrell Davis 10.00 25.00
90 Mike Alstott 8.00 20.00
115 Marcus Allen 8.00 20.00
126 Marvin Harrison 8.00 20.00
132 Troy Aikman 15.00 40.00
133 Emmitt Smith 25.00 60.00
141 Dan Marino 30.00 80.00
151 Ricky Watters 5.00 12.00
154 Irving Fryar 5.00 12.00
174 Mark Brunell 10.00 25.00
184 Keyshawn Johnson 8.00 20.00
191 Barry Sanders 25.00 60.00
199 Eddie George 8.00 20.00
207 Brett Favre 30.00 80.00
217 Kerry Collins 8.00 20.00
224 John Kasay 3.00 8.00
226 Drew Bledsoe 10.00 25.00
227 Curtis Martin 10.00 25.00
228 Terry Glenn 8.00 20.00
236 Tim Brown 8.00 20.00
238 Napoleon Kaufman 8.00 20.00
250 Eddie Kennison 5.00 12.00
261 Terry Allen 8.00 20.00
278 Joey Galloway 5.00 12.00
284 Jerome Bettis 8.00 20.00
286 Kordell Stewart 8.00 20.00

1997 Upper Deck Game Jerseys

Randomly inserted in packs at a rate of one in 2600, this 10-card set features actual pieces of an NFL game worn jersey of the player pictured on the card. There were two different

Brett Favre cards produced.
COMPLETE SET (10) 400.00 800.00
MULTI-COLORED PATCH: .6X TO 1.5X
STATED ODDS 1:2600
GJ1 Warren Moon 30.00 80.00
GJ2 Joey Galloway 20.00 50.00
GJ3 Terrell Davis 30.00 80.00
GJ4 Brett Favre GRN 100.00 200.00
GJ5 Brett Favre WHT 100.00 200.00
GJ6 Reggie White 60.00 100.00
GJ7 John Elway 100.00 200.00
GJ8 Troy Aikman 60.00 120.00
GJ9 Carl Pickens 15.00 40.00
GJ10 Herman Moore 15.00 40.00

1997 Upper Deck Memorable Moments

This ten card standard-size set was issued one per special retail Collectors Choice pack. Ten leading offensive football players were featured in this set.
COMPLETE SET (10) 5.00 12.00
ONE PER SPECIAL RETAIL COLL.CHOICE
1 Steve Young .30 .75
2 Dan Marino 1.00 2.50
3 Terrell Davis .30 .75
4 Brett Favre 1.00 2.50
5 Ricky Watters .15 .40
6 Terry Glenn .25 .60
7 John Elway 1.00 2.50
8 Troy Aikman .50 1.25
9 Terry Allen .25 .60
10 Joey Galloway .15 .40

1997 Upper Deck MVPs

This 20-card set features color photos of some of NFL's brightest stars printed with gold Light F/X printing technology. Reported production was limited to 100 hand numbered sets.
STATED PRINT RUN 100 SERIAL #'d SETS
MP1 Jerry Rice 20.00 50.00
MP2 Carl Pickens 6.00 15.00
MP3 Terrell Davis 10.00 25.00
MP4 Mike Alstott 10.00 25.00
MP5 Vinny Testaverde 8.00 20.00
MP6 Junior Seau 10.00 25.00
MP7 Marcus Allen 10.00 25.00
MP8 Troy Aikman 20.00 50.00
MP9 Dan Marino 40.00 100.00
MP10 Ricky Watters 8.00 20.00
MP11 Mark Brunell 10.00 25.00
MP12 Barry Sanders 30.00 80.00
MP13 Eddie George 10.00 25.00
MP14 Brett Favre 40.00 100.00
MP15 Kerry Collins 8.00 20.00
MP16 Drew Bledsoe 10.00 25.00
MP17 Napoleon Kaufman 6.00 15.00
MP18 Isaac Bruce 10.00 25.00
MP19 Terry Allen 8.00 20.00
MP20 Jerome Bettis 10.00 25.00

1997 Upper Deck Star Attractions

Issued one per Collectors Choice retail jumbo pack, this 20 card set features 20 of the most popular NFL players. A gold version of this set was also issued, those cards were issued at a rate of one every 20 retail jumbo pack.
COMPLETE SET (20) 6.00 15.00
ONE PER COLL.CHOICE RETAIL JUMBO
*GOLD: .8X TO 2X BASIC INSERTS
GOLD ODDS 1:20 COLL.CHO.RET.JUMBO
SA1 Dan Marino 1.00 2.50
SA2 Emmitt Smith .75 2.00
SA3 John Elway 1.00 2.50
SA4 Kordell Stewart .25 .60
SA5 Napoleon Kaufman .25 .60
SA6 Curtis Martin .30 .75
SA7 Troy Aikman .50 1.25
SA8 Warrick Dunn 1.00 2.50
SA9 Antowain Smith .75 2.00
SA10 Reggie White .25 .60
SA11 Jeff George .15 .40
SA12 Brett Favre 1.00 2.50
SA13 Lawrence Phillips .08 .25
SA14 Rod Smith WR .15 .40
SA15 Steve Young .30 .75
SA16 Drew Bledsoe .30 .75
SA17 Barry Sanders .75 2.00
SA18 Terrell Davis .30 .75
SA19 Eddie George .25 .60
SA20 Deion Sanders .25 .60

1997 Upper Deck Star Crossed

Randomly inserted in packs at a rate of one in 23 hobby or 1:27 retail or special retail, this 30-card set features nine different cards inserted in hobby only packs (SC1-SC9), nine in special retail packs (SC10-SC18), and nine in standard retail packs (SC19-SC27). The fronts feature color player photos printed with light F/X technology on silver foil stock. A trade card good in exchange for a complete Star Crossed 27-card set was randomly inserted into each pack type and numbered SC28-SC30. The trade card actually pictured two players on the front and required $2 for postage and handling fees. Trade cards expired on June 8, 1998 and were inserted at the rate of 1:230 hobby, 1:270 retail or special retail packs.
COMPLETE SET (30) 12.50 30.00
SC1-SC9 STATED ODDS 1:23 HOBBY
SC10-SC18 STATED ODDS 1:27 SPEC.RETAIL
SC19-SC27 STATED ODDS 1:27 RETAIL
SC1 Dan Marino 2.00 5.00
SC2 Mark Brunell .60 1.50
SC3 Kerry Collins .50 1.25
SC4 Jerry Rice 1.00 2.50
SC5 Curtis Martin .60 1.50
SC6 Isaac Bruce .50 1.25
SC7 Eddie George .50 1.25
SC8 Kevin Greene .30 .75
SC9 Deion Sanders .50 1.25
SC10 Troy Aikman 1.00 2.50
SC11 John Elway 2.00 5.00
SC12 Steve Young .60 1.50
SC13 Barry Sanders 1.50 4.00
SC14 Jerome Bettis .50 1.25
SC15 Herman Moore .30 .75
SC16 Keyshawn Johnson .50 1.25
SC17 Simeon Rice .30 .75
SC18 Bruce Smith .30 .75
SC19 Drew Bledsoe .60 1.50
SC20 Kordell Stewart .50 1.25
SC21 Brett Favre 2.00 5.00
SC22 Emmitt Smith 1.50 4.00
SC23 Terrell Davis .60 1.50
SC24 Carl Pickens .30 .75
SC25 Terry Glenn .50 1.25
SC26 Reggie White .50 1.25
SC27 Rod Woodson .50 1.25
SC28 Trade Card .20 .50
SC29 Trade Card .20 .50
SC30 Trade Card .20 .50

1997 Upper Deck Team Mates

Randomly inserted in packs at a rate of 1:4 hobby and 1:2 retail, this 60-card set features color photos of two top players from each NFL team. The backs carry player information and stats. Each pair of cards is die cut so that they can be interlocked like a puzzle.
COMPLETE SET (60) 20.00 40.00
STATED ODDS 1:4 HOBBY, 1:2 RETAIL
TM1 Simeon Rice .25 .60
TM2 Eric Swann .15 .40
TM3 Terance Mathis .25 .60
TM4 Jamal Anderson .40 1.00
TM5 Vinny Testaverde .25 .60
TM6 Michael Jackson .25 .60
TM7 Thurman Thomas .40 1.00
TM8 Bruce Smith .25 .60
TM9 Kerry Collins .40 1.00
TM10 Anthony Johnson .16 .40
TM11 Bobby Engram .25 .60
TM12 Bryan Cox .15 .40
TM13 Carl Pickens .25 .60
TM14 Jeff Blake .25 .60
TM15 Troy Aikman .75 2.00
TM16 Emmitt Smith 1.25 3.00
TM17 John Elway 1.50 4.00
TM18 Terrell Davis .50 1.25
TM19 Herman Moore .25 .60
TM20 Barry Sanders 1.25 3.00
TM21 Brett Favre 1.50 4.00
TM22 Reggie White .40 1.00
TM23 Eddie George .40 1.00
TM24 Steve McNair .50 1.25
TM25 Marshall Faulk .50 1.25
TM26 Jim Harbaugh .25 .60
TM27 Mark Brunell .50 1.25
TM28 Keenan McCardell .25 .60
TM29 Marcus Allen .40 1.00
TM30 Derrick Thomas .40 1.00
TM31 Dan Marino 1.50 4.00
TM32 Karim Abdul-Jabbar .25 .60
TM33 Cris Carter .40 1.00
TM34 Jake Reed .25 .60
TM35 Curtis Martin .50 1.25
TM36 Drew Bledsoe .50 1.25
TM37 Mario Bates .15 .40
TM38 Ray Zellars .15 .40
TM39 Keyshawn Johnson .40 1.00
TM40 Adrian Murrell .25 .60
TM41 Tyrone Wheatley .25 .60
TM42 Rodney Hampton .25 .60
TM43 Napoleon Kaufman .40 1.00
TM44 Tim Brown .40 1.00
TM45 Ricky Watters .25 .60
TM46 Chris T. Jones .15 .40
TM47 Kordell Stewart .40 1.00
TM48 Jerome Bettis .40 1.00
TM49 Junior Seau .40 1.00
TM50 Tony Martin .25 .60
TM51 Steve Young .50 1.25
TM52 Jerry Rice .75 2.00
TM53 Joey Galloway .25 .60
TM54 Chris Warren .25 .60
TM55 Tony Banks .25 .60
TM56 Eddie Kennison .25 .60
TM57 Mike Alstott .40 1.00
TM58 Errict Rhett .15 .40
TM59 Terry Allen .40 1.00
TM60 Gus Frerotte .15 .40

1997 Upper Deck Crash the Game Super Bowl XXXI

This special Crash the Game set for Super Bowl XXXI in New Orleans was produced by Upper Deck and distributed primarily through the hobby publication SCD. Each of the eight cards carries the Super Bowl date (Jan. 26) on the cardfront in gold foil along with a player photo set against a purple colored background. The featured player must have scored a touchdown or passed for a touchdown in the game for the card to be exchangeable. Collectors could exchange those winners, along with $2 for postage, for a parallel complete set printed on foil stock. A header card was also included with the prize set. The contest cards expired on February 29, 1997.
COMPLETE SET (8) 3.00 8.00
COMP.FOIL PRIZE SET (9) 2.50 6.00
*FOIL PRIZES: .3X TO.8X
A1 Drew Bledsoe .60 1.50
A2 Curtis Martin .50 1.25
A3 Ben Coates .20 .50
A4 Terry Glenn .30 .75
N1 Brett Favre 1.20 3.00
N2 Edgar Bennett .20 .50
N3 Don Beebe .20 .50
N4 Antonio Freeman .50 1.25

1997 Upper Deck Mini

This set was issued in early 1998 by Upper Deck. The cards follow the basic set design and use the photos from the 1997 Collector's Choice football set but carry only the Upper Deck logo on the fronts. The backs have a 1998 copyright date and a unique numbering system that is different from 1997 Collector's Choice. Finally, the cards measure slightly smaller than standard size: roughly 2 5/16" by 3 5/8" and the first six cards in the set were created in a foil format similar to SP products.
COMPLETE SET (48) 30.00 60.00
1 Brett Favre FOIL SP 5.00 12.00
2 Drew Bledsoe FOIL SP 1.25 3.00
3 Emmitt Smith FOIL SP 3.00 8.00
4 Barry Sanders FOIL SP 2.50 6.00
5 Jerry Rice FOIL SP 2.50 6.00
6 Karim Abdul-Jabbar FOIL SP 1.00 2.50
7 Ken Norton .50 1.25
8 Curtis Conway .60 1.50
9 Rashaan Salaam .60 1.50
10 Jeff Blake .60 1.50
11 Jim Kelly 1.50 4.00
12 Bryce Paup .50 1.25
13 Terrell Davis 1.00 2.50
14 Errict Rhett .60 1.50
15 Simeon Rice .50 1.25
16 Junior Seau .75 2.00
17 Marcus Allen .75 2.00
18 Greg Hill .50 1.25
19 Jim Harbaugh .60 1.50
20 Deion Sanders 1.25 3.00
21 Michael Irvin 1.00 2.50
22 Zach Thomas .75 2.00
23 Bobby Taylor .60 1.50
24 Cornelius Bennett .60 1.50
25 Mark Brunell .60 1.50
26 Jimmy Smith .60 1.50
27 Keyshawn Johnson .60 1.50
28 Steve McNair .75 2.00
29 Frank Wycheck .60 1.50
30 Antonio Freeman .75 2.00
31 Reggie White 1.00 2.50
32 Kerry Collins .75 2.00
33 Kevin Greene .60 1.50
34 Terry Glenn .60 1.50
35 Ben Coates .60 1.50
36 Tim Brown 1.00 2.50
37 Chester McGlockton .50 1.25
38 Isaac Bruce .75 2.00
39 Vinny Testaverde .60 1.50
40 Antonio Langham .50 1.25
41 Michael Westbrook .50 1.25
42 Ken Harvey .50 1.25
43 Mario Bates .50 1.25
44 Joey Galloway .60 1.50
45 Jerome Bettis 1.00 2.50
46 Kordell Stewart .75 2.00
47 Greg Lloyd .50 1.25
48 Cris Carter 1.00 2.50

1997 Upper Deck Holiday Troy Drive

NNO Troy Aikman 2.00 5.00

1998 Upper Deck

The 1998 Upper Deck set was issued with 255 standard size cards. The 10-card packs retail for $2.49 each. The set contains the subset: Star Rookie (1-42) with those cards seeded at the rate of 1:4. The card fronts feature color action photos with a black and grey three-sided border. A bronze foil parallel version of this set was also produced and serial-numbered to 100.
COMPLETE SET (255) 75.00 150.00
COMP.SET w/o SP's (213) 12.50 25.00
1 Peyton Manning RC 15.00 40.00
2 Ryan Leaf RC 1.25 3.00
3 Andre Wadsworth RC 1.50 4.00
4 Charles Woodson RC 5.00 12.00
5 Curtis Enis RC 1.25 3.00
6 Grant Wistrom RC 1.00 2.50
7 Greg Ellis RC 1.25 3.00
8 Fred Taylor RC 2.00 5.00
9 Duane Starks RC 1.00 2.50
10 Keith Brooking RC 1.50 4.00
11 Takeo Spikes RC 1.25 3.00
12 Jason Peter RC 1.00 2.50
13 Anthony Simmons RC 1.00 2.50
14 Kevin Dyson RC 1.25 3.00
15 Brian Simmons RC 1.00 2.50
16 Robert Edwards RC 1.25 3.00
17 Randy Moss RC 8.00 20.00
18 John Avery RC 1.25 3.00
19 Marcus Nash RC 1.00 2.50
20 Jerome Pathon RC 1.25 3.00
21 Jacquez Green RC 1.25 3.00
22 Robert Holcombe RC 1.00 2.50
23 Pat Johnson RC 1.25 3.00
24 Germane Crowell RC 1.00 2.50
25 Joe Jurevicius RC 1.50 4.00
26 Skip Hicks RC 1.25 3.00
27 Ahman Green RC 2.00 5.00
28 Brian Griese RC 2.00 5.00
29 Hines Ward RC 8.00 20.00
30 Tavian Banks RC 1.25 3.00
31 Tony Simmons RC 1.25 3.00
32 Victor Riley RC 1.00 2.50
33 Rashaan Shehee RC 1.00 2.50
34 R.W. McQuarters RC 1.50 4.00
35 Flozell Adams RC 1.25 3.00
36 Tra Thomas RC 1.00 2.50
37 Greg Favors RC 1.00 2.50
38 Jon Ritchie RC 1.25 3.00
39 Jesse Haynes RC 1.00 2.50
40 Ryan Sutter RC 1.00 2.50
41 Mo Collins RC 1.00 2.50
42 Tim Dwight RC 1.50 4.00
43 Chris Chandler .20 .50
44 Byron Hanspard .15 .40
45 Jessie Tuggle .15 .40
46 Jamal Anderson .20 .50
47 Terance Mathis .15 .40
48 Morten Andersen .15 .40
49 Jake Plummer .15 .40
50 Mario Bates .15 .40
51 Frank Sanders .15 .40
52 Adrian Murrell .15 .40
53 Simeon Rice .20 .50
54 Aeneas Williams .15 .40
55 Eric Swann UER .15 .40
56 Jim Harbaugh .25 .60
57 Michael Jackson .15 .40
58 Peter Boulware .15 .40
59 Errict Rhett .20 .50
60 Jermaine Lewis .15 .40
61 Eric Zeier .15 .40
62 Rod Woodson .25 .60
63 Rob Johnson .20 .50
64 Antowain Smith .20 .50
65 Bruce Smith .20 .50
66 Eric Moulds .20 .50
67 Andre Reed .25 .60
68 Thurman Thomas .20 .50
69 Lonnie Johnson .15 .40
70 Kerry Collins .15 .40
71 Kevin Greene .25 .60
72 Fred Lane .15 .40
73 Rae Carruth .15 .40
74 Michael Bates .15 .40
75 William Floyd .15 .40
76 Sean Gilbert .15 .40
77 Erik Kramer .15 .40
78 Edgar Bennett .20 .50
79 Curtis Conway .20 .50
80 Darnell Autry .15 .40
81 Ryan Wetnight RC .15 .40
82 Walt Harris .15 .40
83 Bobby Engram .15 .40
84 Jeff Blake .20 .50
85 Carl Pickens .20 .50
86 Darnay Scott .20 .50
87 Corey Dillon .15 .40
88 Reinard Wilson .15 .40
89 Ashley Ambrose .15 .40
90 Troy Aikman .30 .75
91 Michael Irvin .25 .60
92 Emmitt Smith .40 1.00
93 Deion Sanders .20 .50
94 David LaFleur .15 .40
95 Chris Warren .20 .50
96 Darren Woodson .20 .50
97 John Elway .40 1.00
98 Terrell Davis .20 .50
99 Rod Smith .20 .50
100 Shannon Sharpe .20 .50
101 Ed McCaffrey .20 .50
102 Steve Atwater .20 .50
103 John Mobley .15 .40
104 Darrien Gordon .15 .40
105 Barry Sanders .40 1.00
106 Scott Mitchell .20 .50
107 Herman Moore .20 .50
108 Johnnie Morton .20 .50
109 Robert Porcher .15 .40
110 Bryant Westbrook .15 .40
111 Tommy Vardell .15 .40
112 Brett Favre .50 1.25
113 Dorsey Levens .20 .50
114 Reggie White .25 .60
115 Antonio Freeman .25 .60
116 Robert Brooks .20 .50
117 Mark Chmura .15 .40
118 Derrick Mayes .20 .50
119 Gilbert Brown .15 .40
120 Marshall Faulk .20 .50
121 Jeff Burris .15 .40
122 Marvin Harrison .20 .50
123 Quentin Coryatt .15 .40
124 Ken Dilger .15 .40
125 Zack Crockett .15 .40
126 Mark Brunell .20 .50
127 Bryce Paup .15 .40
128 Tony Brackens .15 .40
129 Renaldo Wynn .15 .40
130 Keenan McCardell .20 .50
131 Jimmy Smith .20 .50
132 Kevin Hardy .15 .40
133 Elvis Grbac .20 .50
134 Tamarick Vanover .15 .40
135 Chester McGlockton .15 .40
136 Andre Rison .20 .50
137 Derrick Alexander .20 .50
138 Tony Gonzalez .20 .50
139 Derrick Thomas .25 .60
140 Dan Marino .50 1.25
141 Karim Abdul-Jabbar .15 .40
142 O.J. McDuffie .20 .50
143 Yatil Green .15 .40
144 Charles Jordan .15 .40
145 Brock Marion .15 .40
146 Zach Thomas .20 .50
147 Brad Johnson .20 .50
148 Cris Carter .25 .60
149 Jake Reed .20 .50
150 Robert Smith .15 .40
151 John Randle .25 .60
152 Dwayne Rudd .15 .40
153 Randall Cunningham .20 .50
154 Drew Bledsoe .20 .50
155 Terry Glenn .20 .50
156 Ben Coates .20 .50
157 Willie Clay .15 .40
158 Chris Slade .15 .40
159 Derrick Cullors RC .15 .40
160 Ty Law .25 .60
161 Danny Wuerffel .20 .50
162 Andre Hastings .15 .40
163 Troy Davis .15 .40
164 Billy Joe Hobert .15 .40
165 Eric Guliford .15 .40
166 Mark Fields .15 .40
167 Alex Molden .15 .40
168 Danny Kanell .15 .40
169 Tiki Barber .20 .50
170 Charles Way .15 .40
171 Amani Toomer .15 .40
172 Michael Strahan .20 .50
173 Jessie Armstead .15 .40
174 Jason Sehorn .20 .50
175 Glenn Foley .15 .40
176 Curtis Martin .20 .50
177 Aaron Glenn .15 .40
178 Keyshawn Johnson .20 .50
179 James Farrior .15 .40
180 Wayne Chrebet .15 .40
181 Keith Byars .20 .50
182 Jeff George .20 .50
183 Napoleon Kaufman .15 .40
184 Tim Brown .25 .60
185 Darrell Russell .15 .40
186 Rickey Dudley .15 .40
187 James Jett .15 .40
188 Desmond Howard .20 .50
189 Bobby Hoying .20 .50
190 Charlie Garner .20 .50
191 Irving Fryar .20 .50
192 Chris T. Jones .15 .40
193 Mike Mamula .15 .40
194 Troy Vincent .20 .50
195 Kordell Stewart .15 .40
196 Jerome Bettis .25 .60
197 Will Blackwell .15 .40
198 Levon Kirkland .15 .40
199 Carnell Lake .15 .40
200 Charles Johnson .15 .40
201 Greg Lloyd .20 .50
202 Donnell Woolford .15 .40
203 Tony Banks .20 .50
204 Amp Lee .15 .40
205 Isaac Bruce .25 .60
206 Eddie Kennison .15 .40
207 Ryan McNeil .15 .40
208 Mike Jones .15 .40
209 Ernie Conwell .15 .40
210 Natrone Means .20 .50
211 Junior Seau .20 .50
212 Tony Martin .20 .50
213 Freddie Jones .15 .40
214 Bryan Still .15 .40
215 Rodney Harrison .15 .40
216 Steve Young .30 .75
217 Jerry Rice .60 1.50
218 Garrison Hearst .15 .40
219 J.J. Stokes .20 .50
220 Ken Norton .15 .40
221 Greg Clark .15 .40
222 Terrell Owens .20 .50
223 Bryant Young .20 .50
224 Warren Moon .25 .60
225 Jon Kitna .15 .40
226 Ricky Watters .20 .50
227 Chad Brown .15 .40
228 Joey Galloway .20 .50
229 Shawn Springs .15 .40
230 Cortez Kennedy .20 .50
231 Trent Dilfer .20 .50
232 Warrick Dunn .15 .40
233 Mike Alstott .15 .40
234 Warren Sapp .20 .50
235 Bert Emanuel .20 .50
236 Reidel Anthony .15 .40
237 Hardy Nickerson .15 .40
238 Derrick Brooks .25 .60
239 Steve McNair .20 .50
240 Yancey Thigpen .15 .40
241 Anthony Dorsett .15 .40
242 Blaine Bishop .15 .40
243 Kenny Holmes .15 .40
244 Eddie George .20 .50
245 Chris Sanders .15 .40
246 Gus Frerotte .15 .40
247 Terry Allen .20 .50
248 Dana Stubblefield .15 .40
249 Michael Westbrook .20 .50
250 Darrell Green .25 .60
251 Brian Mitchell .20 .50
252 Ken Harvey .15 .40
CL1 Troy Aikman CL .25 .60
CL2 Dan Marino CL .50 1.25
CL3 Herman Moore CL .15 .40

1998 Upper Deck Bronze

*BRONZE VETS/100: 12X TO 30X BASIC CARDS
*1-42 BRONZE ROOK/100: 1.5X TO 4X RC
BRONZE PRINT RUN 100 SER.#'d SETS
1 Peyton Manning 100.00 200.00

1998 Upper Deck Constant Threat

Randomly inserted in packs at a rate of one in 12, this 30-card set is a four-tiered insert set. The non-die cut base set includes blue foil highlights on the cardfronts. Three different die cut parallels were produced with each using a unique fol color and sequential numbering of 1000, 25, and 1.
COMPLETE SET (30) 50.00 100.00
STATED ODDS 1:12
*BRNZ.DC VETS: 10X TO 25X BASIC INSERTS
*BRONZE DC ROOKIES: 6X TO 15X
BRONZE DIE CUT PRINT RUN 25
*SILVER DC VETS: .8X TO 2X BAS.INSERTS
*SILVER DC ROOKIE: .6X TO 1.5X BAS.INSERTS
SILVER DIE CUT PRINT RUN 1000
CT1 Dan Marino 4.00 10.00
CT2 Peyton Manning 7.50 15.00
CT3 Randy Moss 4.00 10.00
CT4 Brett Favre 4.00 10.00
CT5 Mark Brunell 1.00 2.50
CT6 Keyshawn Johnson 1.00 2.50
CT7 John Elway 4.00 10.00
CT8 Troy Aikman 2.00 5.00
CT9 Steve Young 1.25 3.00
CT10 Kordell Stewart 1.00 2.50
CT11 Drew Bledsoe 1.50 4.00
CT12 Joey Galloway .60 1.50
CT13 Elvis Grbac .60 1.50
CT14 Marvin Harrison 1.00 2.50
CT15 Napoleon Kaufman 1.00 2.50
CT16 Ryan Leaf .60 1.50
CT17 Jake Plummer 1.00 2.50
CT18 Terrell Davis 1.00 2.50
CT19 Steve McNair 1.00 2.50
CT20 Barry Sanders 3.00 8.00
CT21 Deion Sanders 1.00 2.50
CT22 Emmitt Smith 3.00 8.00
CT23 Antowain Smith 1.00 2.50
CT24 Herman Moore .60 1.50
CT25 Curtis Martin 1.00 2.50
CT26 Jerry Rice 2.00 5.00
CT27 Eddie George 1.00 2.50
CT28 Warrick Dunn 1.00 2.50
CT29 Curtis Enis .60 1.50
CT30 Michael Irvin 1.00 2.50

1998 Upper Deck Define the Game

Randomly inserted in packs at a rate of one in 8, this 30-card set is a four-tiered insert. The base set includes top players printed with a foil enhanced cardfront in a non-die cut format. The three die cut parallel tiers are sequentially numbered of 1500, 50, and 1 with each group utilizing a different foil color.
COMPLETE SET (30) 30.00 60.00
STATED ODDS 1:8
*BRONZE DC VETS: 10X TO 25X BASIC INS.
*BRONZE DC ROOKIES: 6X TO 15X BASIC INS.
BRONZE DIE CUT PRINT RUN 50
*SILVER DIE CUTS: .8X TO 2X BASIC INSERTS
SILVER DIE CUT PRINT RUN 1500
DG1 Dan Marino 3.00 8.00
DG2 Curtis Enis .25 .60
DG3 Dorsey Levens .75 2.00
DG4 Charles Woodson 1.00 2.50
DG5 Junior Seau .75 2.00
DG6 Tiki Barber .75 2.00
DG7 Randy Moss 5.00 10.00
DG8 Troy Aikman 1.50 4.00
DG9 Jake Plummer .75 2.00
DG10 Corey Dillon .75 2.00
DG11 Jerry Rice 1.50 4.00
DG12 Emmitt Smith 2.50 6.00
DG13 Herman Moore .50 1.25
DG14 Brad Johnson .75 2.00
DG15 Gus Frerotte .30 .75
DG16 Ryan Leaf .50 1.25
DG17 Shannon Sharpe .50 1.25
DG18 Jermaine Lewis .50 1.25
DG19 Jerome Bettis .75 2.00
DG20 Barry Sanders 2.50 6.00
DG21 Terry Allen .75 2.00
DG22 Reidel Anthony .50 1.25
DG23 Isaac Bruce .75 2.00
DG24 Mike Alstott .75 2.00
DG25 Rae Carruth .30 .75
DG26 Tamarick Vanover .30 .75
DG27 Eddie George .75 2.00
DG28 Warrick Dunn .75 2.00
DG29 Tony Gonzalez .75 2.00
DG30 Keenan McCardell .50 1.25

1998 Upper Deck Game Jerseys

The first ten cards in the set were randomly inserted in hobby and retail packs at a rate of one in 2500 with the last ten being inserted exclusively in hobby packs at the rate of 1:288. Each of the 20-cards features a swatch cut from actual game-worn jersey.
1-10 STATED ODDS 1:2500
11-20 STATED ODDS 1:288 HOBBY
GJ1 Brett Favre 40.00 100.00
GJ2 Reggie White 30.00 80.00
GJ3 Barry Sanders 30.00 80.00
GJ4 John Elway 30.00 80.00
GJ5 Mark Brunell 15.00 40.00
GJ6 Mike Alstott 15.00 40.00
GJ7 Ryan Leaf 15.00 40.00
GJ8 Andre Wadsworth 12.00 30.00
GJ9 Robert Edwards 12.00 30.00
GJ10 Kevin Dyson 12.00 30.00
GJ11 Dan Marino 30.00 80.00
GJ12 Deion Sanders 15.00 40.00
GJ13 Steve Young 20.00 50.00
GJ14 Terrell Davis 12.00 30.00
GJ15 Tim Brown 12.00 30.00
GJ16 Peyton Manning 75.00 150.00
GJ17 Takeo Spikes 10.00 25.00
GJ18 Curtis Enis 8.00 20.00
GJ19 Fred Taylor 12.00 30.00
GJ20 John Avery 8.00 20.00

1998 Upper Deck Jumbos

This 10-card set was released one per special retail box of the 1998 Upper Deck product. Each card is essentially an enlarged parallel version of the base set card.
COMPLETE SET (10) 6.00 15.00
ONE PER SPECIAL RETAIL BOX
49 Jake Plummer .60 1.50
64 Antowain Smith .50 1.25
87 Corey Dillon .60 1.50
98 Terrell Davis .75 2.00
105 Barry Sanders 2.00 5.00
112 Brett Favre 2.00 5.00
126 Mark Brunell .60 1.50
136 Andre Rison .30 .75
195 Kordell Stewart .60 1.50
232 Warrick Dunn .50 1.25

1998 Upper Deck Super Powers

Randomly inserted in packs at a rate of 1:4 hobby and 1:2 retail packs, this 30-card set is a three-tiered insert. The base set is not die cut and includes bronze foil on the cardfronts. The tiered die cut sets have three levels of sequential numbering: 2000, 100, and 1. The fronts feature color action photos on a background of digital technology design. The backs offer a black-and-white photo against a bronze background.
COMPLETE SET (30) 20.00 50.00
STATED ODDS 1:4 HOB, 1:2 RET
*BRONZE DC/100: 6X TO 15X BASIC INSERTS
BRONZE DIE CUT PRINT RUN 100 SETS
*SILVER DC/2000: .8X TO 2X BASIC INSERTS
SILVER DIE CUT PRINT RUN 2000
S1 Dan Marino 1.25 3.00
S2 Jerry Rice 1.50 4.00
S3 Napoleon Kaufman .40 1.00
S4 Brett Favre 1.25 3.00
S5 Andre Rison .50 1.25
S6 Jerome Bettis .60 1.50
S7 John Elway 1.00 2.50
S8 Troy Aikman .75 2.00
S9 Steve Young .75 2.00
S10 Kordell Stewart .40 1.00
S11 Drew Bledsoe .50 1.25
S12 Antonio Freeman .60 1.50
S13 Mark Brunell .50 1.25
S14 Shannon Sharpe .50 1.25
S15 Trent Dilfer .50 1.25
S16 Peyton Manning 5.00 12.00
S17 Cris Carter .60 1.50
S18 Michael Irvin .60 1.50
S19 Terry Glenn .50 1.25
S20 Keyshawn Johnson .50 1.25
S21 Deion Sanders .50 1.25
S22 Emmitt Smith 1.00 2.50
S23 Marcus Allen .60 1.50
S24 Dorsey Levens .50 1.25
S25 Jake Plummer .40 1.00
S26 Eddie George .50 1.25
S27 Tim Brown .60 1.50
S28 Warrick Dunn .40 1.00
S29 Reggie White .60 1.50
S30 Terrell Davis .50 1.25

1999 Upper Deck

Released as a 270-card set, 1999 Upper Deck is comprised of 222 regular player cards, three checklists, and 45 star rookie cards seeded at one in four packs. Base cards have a bottom border that is enhanced with bronze foil and star rookies cards are bordered all the way around and are also enhanced with bronze foil. Packaged in 24 pack boxes, packs contained 10 cards and carried a suggested retail price of $2.99.
COMPLETE SET (270) 50.00 100.00
COMP.SET w/o SP's (225) 12.50 25.00
1 Jake Plummer .15 .40
2 Adrian Murrell .15 .40
3 Rob Moore .15 .40
4 Larry Centers .15 .40
5 Simeon Rice .15 .40
6 Andre Wadsworth .15 .40
7 Frank Sanders .15 .40
8 Tim Dwight .20 .50
9 Ray Buchanan .15 .40
10 Chris Chandler .20 .50
11 Jamal Anderson .20 .50
12 O.J. Santiago .15 .40
13 Danny Kanell .15 .40
14 Terance Mathis .15 .40
15 Priest Holmes .15 .40
16 Tony Banks .20 .50
17 Ray Lewis .25 .60
18 Patrick Johnson .15 .40
19 Michael Jackson .15 .40
20 Michael McCrary .15 .40
21 Jermaine Lewis .15 .40
22 Eric Moulds .15 .40
23 Doug Flutie .25 .60
24 Antowain Smith .15 .40
25 Rob Johnson .20 .50
26 Bruce Smith .20 .50
27 Andre Reed .25 .60
28 Thurman Thomas .20 .50
29 Fred Lane .15 .40
30 Wesley Walls .20 .50
31 Tim Biakabutuka .20 .50
32 Kevin Greene .25 .60
33 Steve Beuerlein .20 .50
34 Muhsin Muhammad .15 .40
35 Rae Carruth .15 .40
36 Bobby Engram .15 .40
37 Curtis Enis .15 .40
38 Edgar Bennett .20 .50
39 Erik Kramer .20 .50
40 Steve Stenstrom .15 .40
41 Alonzo Mayes .15 .40
42 Curtis Conway .20 .50
43 Tony McGee .15 .40
44 Darnay Scott .15 .40
45 Jeff Blake .20 .50
46 Corey Dillon .15 .40
47 Ki-Jana Carter .15 .40
48 Takeo Spikes .15 .40
49 Carl Pickens .20 .50
50 Ty Detmer .15 .40
51 Leslie Shepherd .15 .40
52 Terry Kirby .15 .40
53 Marquez Pope .15 .40
54 Antonio Langham .15 .40
55 Jamir Miller .15 .40
56 Derrick Alexander DT .15 .40
57 Troy Aikman .30 .75
58 Rocket Ismail .20 .50
59 Emmitt Smith .40 1.00
60 Michael Irvin .25 .60
61 David LaFleur .15 .40
62 Chris Warren .20 .50
63 Deion Sanders .20 .50
64 Greg Ellis .15 .40
65 John Elway .40 1.00
66 Bubby Brister .15 .40
67 Terrell Davis .20 .50
68 Ed McCaffrey .20 .50
69 John Mobley .15 .40
70 Bill Romanowski .20 .50
71 Rod Smith .20 .50
72 Shannon Sharpe .20 .50
73 Charlie Batch .15 .40
74 Germane Crowell .15 .40
75 Johnnie Morton .20 .50
76 Barry Sanders .40 1.00
77 Robert Porcher .15 .40
78 Stephen Boyd .15 .40
79 Herman Moore .20 .50
80 Brett Favre .50 1.25
81 Mark Chmura .15 .40
82 Antonio Freeman .20 .50
83 Robert Brooks .20 .50
84 Vonnie Holliday .15 .40
85 Bill Schroeder .20 .50
86 Dorsey Levens .20 .50
87 Santana Dotson .15 .40
88 Peyton Manning .75 2.00
89 Jerome Pathon .15 .40
90 Marvin Harrison .20 .50
91 Ellis Johnson .15 .40
92 Ken Dilger .15 .40
93 E.G. Green .15 .40
94 Jeff Burris .15 .40
95 Mark Brunell .20 .50
96 Fred Taylor .15 .40
97 Jimmy Smith .20 .50
98 James Stewart .15 .40
99 Kyle Brady .15 .40
100 Dave Thomas RC .20 .50
101 Keenan McCardell .20 .50
102 Elvis Grbac .15 .40
103 Tony Gonzalez .20 .50
104 Andre Rison .20 .50
105 Donnell Bennett .15 .40
106 Derrick Thomas .25 .60
107 Warren Moon .25 .60
108 Derrick Alexander WR .15 .40
109 Dan Marino .50 1.25
110 O.J. McDuffie .20 .50
111 Karim Abdul-Jabbar .15 .40
112 John Avery .15 .40
113 Sam Madison .15 .40
114 Jason Taylor .20 .50
115 Zach Thomas .20 .50
116 Randall Cunningham .20 .50
117 Randy Moss .20 .50
118 Cris Carter .25 .60
119 Jake Reed .20 .50
120 Matthew Hatchette .20 .50
121 John Randle .25 .60
122 Robert Smith .15 .40
123 Drew Bledsoe .20 .50
124 Ben Coates .20 .50
125 Terry Glenn .20 .50
126 Ty Law .25 .60
127 Tony Simmons .15 .40
128 Ted Johnson .15 .40
129 Tony Carter .15 .40
130 Willie McGinest .20 .50
131 Danny Wuerffel .20 .50
132 Cameron Cleeland .15 .40
133 Eddie Kennison .20 .50
134 Joe Johnson .15 .40
135 Andre Hastings .15 .40
136 La'Roi Glover RC .25 .60
137 Kent Graham .15 .40
138 Tiki Barber .20 .50
139 Gary Brown .15 .40
140 Ike Hilliard .15 .40
141 Jason Sehorn .20 .50
142 Michael Strahan .20 .50
143 Amani Toomer .15 .40
144 Kerry Collins .15 .40
145 Vinny Testaverde .15 .40
146 Wayne Chrebet .15 .40
147 Curtis Martin .20 .50
148 Mo Lewis .15 .40
149 Aaron Glenn .15 .40
150 Steve Atwater .20 .50
151 Keyshawn Johnson .20 .50
152 James Farrior .15 .40
153 Rich Gannon .20 .50
154 Tim Brown .25 .60
155 Darrell Russell .15 .40
156 Rickey Dudley .15 .40
157 Charles Woodson .25 .60
158 James Jett .15 .40
159 Napoleon Kaufman .15 .40
160 Duce Staley .15 .40
161 Doug Pederson .15 .40
162 Bobby Hoying .15 .40
163 Koy Detmer .15 .40
164 Kevin Turner .15 .40
165 Charles Johnson .15 .40
166 Mike Mamula .15 .40
167 Jerome Bettis .25 .60
168 Courtney Hawkins .15 .40
169 Will Blackwell .15 .40
170 Kordell Stewart .15 .40
171 Richard Huntley .15 .40
172 Levon Kirkland .15 .40
173 Hines Ward .20 .50
174 Trent Green .15 .40
175 Marshall Faulk .20 .50
176 Az-Zahir Hakim .15 .40
177 Amp Lee .15 .40
178 Robert Holcombe .15 .40
179 Isaac Bruce .25 .60
180 Kevin Carter .15 .40
181 Jim Harbaugh .20 .50
182 Junior Seau .20 .50
183 Natrone Means .20 .50
184 Ryan Leaf .20 .50
185 Charlie Jones .15 .40
186 Rodney Harrison .15 .40
187 Mikhael Ricks .15 .40
188 Steve Young .30 .75
189 Terrell Owens .20 .50
190 Jerry Rice .60 1.50
191 J.J. Stokes .15 .40
192 Irv Smith .15 .40
193 Bryant Young .20 .50
194 Garrison Hearst .15 .40
195 Jon Kitna .15 .40
196 Ahman Green .20 .50
197 Joey Galloway .20 .50
198 Ricky Watters .20 .50
199 Chad Brown .15 .40
200 Shawn Springs .15 .40
201 Mike Pritchard .15 .40
202 Trent Dilfer .15 .40
203 Reidel Anthony .15 .40
204 Bert Emanuel .20 .50
205 Warrick Dunn .15 .40
206 Jacquez Green .15 .40
207 Hardy Nickerson .15 .40
208 Mike Alstott .15 .40
209 Eddie George .20 .50
210 Steve McNair .20 .50
211 Kevin Dyson .15 .40
212 Frank Wycheck .20 .50
213 Jackie Harris .20 .50
214 Blaine Bishop .15 .40
215 Yancey Thigpen .15 .40
216 Brad Johnson .20 .50
217 Rodney Peete .20 .50
218 Michael Westbrook .15 .40
219 Skip Hicks .15 .40
220 Brian Mitchell .20 .50
221 Dan Wilkinson .20 .50
222 Dana Stubblefield .15 .40
223 Kordell Stewart CL .12 .30
224 Fred Taylor CL .12 .30
225 Warrick Dunn CL .12 .30
226 Champ Bailey RC 1.00 2.50
227 Chris McAlister RC .50 1.25
228 Jevon Kearse RC .60 1.50
229 Ebenezer Ekuban RC .50 1.25
230 Chris Claiborne RC .50 1.25
231 Andy Katzenmoyer RC .60 1.50
232 Tim Couch RC .60 1.50
233 Daunte Culpepper RC .75 2.00
234 Akili Smith RC .50 1.25
235 Donovan McNabb RC 4.00 10.00
236 Sean Bennett RC .50 1.25
237 Brock Huard RC .50 1.25
238 Cade McNown RC .50 1.25
239 Shaun King RC .50 1.25
240 Joe Germaine RC .60 1.50
241 Ricky Williams RC .75 2.00
242 Edgerrin James RC .75 2.00
243 Sedrick Irvin RC .50 1.25
244 Kevin Faulk RC .50 1.25
245 Rob Konrad RC .50 1.25
246 James Johnson RC .50 1.25
247 Amos Zereoue RC .50 1.25
248 Torry Holt RC 1.00 2.50
249 D'Wayne Bates RC .50 1.25
250 David Boston RC .50 1.25
251 Dameane Douglas RC .50 1.25
252 Troy Edwards RC .50 1.25
253 Kevin Johnson RC .60 1.50
254 Peerless Price RC .50 1.25
255 Antoine Winfield RC .50 1.25
256 Mike Cloud RC .50 1.25
257 Joe Montgomery RC .50 1.25
258 Jermaine Fazande RC .50 1.25
259 Scott Covington RC .50 1.25
260 Aaron Brooks RC .60 1.50
261 Patrick Kerney RC .50 1.25
262 Cecil Collins RC .50 1.25
263 Chris Greisen RC .50 1.25
264 Craig Yeast RC .50 1.25
265 Karsten Bailey RC .50 1.25
266 Reginald Kelly RC .50 1.25
267 Al Wilson RC .75 2.00
268 Jeff Paulk RC .50 1.25
269 Jim Kleinsasser RC .75 2.00
270 Darrin Chiaverini RC .50 1.25

1999 Upper Deck Exclusives 100

*1-225 VETS/100: 8X TO 20X BASIC CARDS
*226-270 ROOKIE/100: 2.5X TO 6X BASIC RC
EXC.SILVER PRINT RUN 100 SER.#'d SETS

1999 Upper Deck 21 TD Salute

Randomly inserted in packs at the rate of one in 23, this 10-card set pays tribute to Terrell Davis. Base cards a printed on an embossed all-foil holographic card stock. Card backs carry a "TD" prefix.
COMPLETE SET (10) 20.00 40.00
COMMON CARD (TD1-TD10) 2.00 5.00
STATED ODDS 1:23
*SILVER/100: 3X TO 8X BASIC INSERTS

1999 Upper Deck Game Jersey

Randomly inserted in Hobby and Retal packs at one in 2500 and the Hobby only versions at one in 288, this 21-card set offers all players in the Hobby version and select players in the Retail version Each card contains a swatch of a game-worn jersey with certain select players containing autographs also.
HOBBY (H) STATED ODDS 1:288
HOBBY/RETAIL ODDS 1:2500
BH Brock Huard H 10.00 25.00
BS Barry Sanders H 20.00 50.00
CM Cade McNown H 10.00 25.00
DB Drew Bledsoe H/R 12.00 30.00
DC Daunte Culpepper H 12.00 30.00
DF Doug Flutie H/R 15.00 40.00
DM Dan Marino H/R 30.00 80.00
DV David Boston H 10.00 25.00

EJ Edgerrin James H/R 20.00 50.00
EM Eric Moulds H 10.00 25.00
JA Jamal Anderson H/R 10.00 25.00
JE John Elway H 20.00 50.00
JR Jerry Rice H 12.00 30.00
KJ Keyshawn Johnson H/R 12.00 30.00
MC Donovan McNabb H 15.00 40.00
PM Peyton Manning H 15.00 40.00
RM Randy Moss H/R 15.00 40.00
SY Steve Young H/R 15.00 40.00
TA Troy Aikman H 12.00 30.00
TC Tim Couch H 10.00 25.00
TD Terrell Davis H/R 15.00 40.00
TDA T.Davis AUTO/30 H/R 75.00 150.00

1999 Upper Deck Game Jersey Patch

Randomly inserted in packs at the rate of one in 7500, this 19-card set features prime swatches of patches from a game-used jersey.

STATED ODDS 1:7500
BHP Brock Huard 20.00 50.00
BSP Barry Sanders 60.00 150.00
CMP Cade McNown 25.00 60.00
DBP Drew Bledsoe 30.00 80.00
DCP Daunte Culpepper 30.00 80.00
DFP Doug Flutie 30.00 80.00
DMP Dan Marino 75.00 200.00
DVP David Boston 20.00 50.00
EJP Edgerrin James 50.00 100.00
JAP Jamal Anderson 30.00 80.00
JEP John Elway 60.00 150.00
JRP Jerry Rice 60.00 150.00
MCP Donovan McNabb 50.00 120.00
PMP Peyton Manning 75.00 200.00
RMP Randy Moss 50.00 120.00
SYP Steve Young 50.00 120.00
TAP Troy Aikman 40.00 100.00
TCP Tim Couch 25.00 60.00
TDP Terrell Davis 30.00 80.00

1999 Upper Deck Highlight Zone

Randomly inserted in packs at the rate of one in 23, this 20-card set features superstar highlight photos. Card backs carry a "Z" prefix.

COMPLETE SET (20) 40.00 100.00
STATED ODDS 1:23
*SILVER/100: 2X TO 5X BASIC INSERTS
Z1 Terrell Davis 1.25 3.00
Z2 Ricky Williams 1.50 4.00
Z3 Akili Smith 1.00 2.50
Z4 Charlie Batch 1.00 2.50
Z5 Jake Plummer 1.00 2.50
Z6 Emmitt Smith 2.50 6.00
Z7 Dan Marino 3.00 8.00
Z8 Tim Couch 1.25 3.00
Z9 Randy Moss 1.25 3.00
Z10 Troy Aikman 2.00 5.00
Z11 Barry Sanders 2.50 6.00
Z12 Jerry Rice 4.00 10.00
Z13 Mark Brunell 1.25 3.00
Z14 Jamal Anderson 1.25 3.00
Z15 Peyton Manning 5.00 12.00
Z16 Jerome Bettis 1.50 4.00
Z17 Donovan McNabb 3.00 8.00
Z18 Steve Young 2.00 5.00
Z19 Keyshawn Johnson 1.25 3.00
Z20 Brett Favre 3.00 8.00

1999 Upper Deck Live Wires

Randomly inserted in packs at the rate of one in 10, this 15-card set features player with a printed statement of theirs made during a game. Card backs carry an "L" prefix.

COMPLETE SET (15) 10.00 25.00
STATED ODDS 1:10
*SILVER/100: 5X TO 12X BASIC INSERTS
L1 Jake Plummer .40 1.00
L2 Jamal Anderson .50 1.25
L3 Emmitt Smith 1.00 2.50
L4 John Elway 1.00 2.50
L5 Barry Sanders 1.00 2.50
L6 Brett Favre 1.25 3.00
L7 Mark Brunell .50 1.25
L8 Fred Taylor .40 1.00
L9 Randy Moss .50 1.25
L10 Drew Bledsoe .50 1.25
L11 Keyshawn Johnson .50 1.25
L12 Jerome Bettis .60 1.50
L13 Kordell Stewart .40 1.00
L14 Terrell Owens .50 1.25
L15 Eddie George .50 1.25

1999 Upper Deck PowerDeck Inserts

Randomly inserted in packs at the rate of one in 24 for the regular cards and one in 288 for the shortprint cards, this set is printed on CD's that contain actual footage, photos, interviews, and statistics.

COMPLETE SET (16) 125.00 250.00
STATED ODDS 1:24
SP STATED ODDS 1:288
1 Troy Aikman 3.00 8.00
2 Tim Couch SP 4.00 10.00
3 Daunte Culpepper SP 15.00 30.00
4 Terrell Davis 1.50 4.00
5 John Elway SP 20.00 40.00
6 Joe Germaine 1.00 2.50
7 Brock Huard 1.25 3.00
8 Shaun King 1.25 3.00
9 Dan Marino SP 20.00 40.00
10 Peyton Manning SP 15.00 40.00
11 Donovan McNabb 4.00 10.00
12 Cade McNown SP 6.00 15.00
13 Joe Montana 5.00 12.00
14 Randy Moss 4.00 10.00
15 Barry Sanders SP 20.00 40.00
16 Akili Smith SP 4.00 10.00

1999 Upper Deck Quarterback Class

Randomly seeded in packs at the rate of one in 10, this all-foil insert features both rookie and veteran quarterbacks. Cards are enhanced with red foil highlights and card backs carry a "QC" prefix.

COMPLETE SET (15) 15.00 30.00
STATED ODDS 1:10
*SILVER/100: 5X TO 12X BASIC INSERTS
QC1 Tim Couch .50 1.25
QC2 Akili Smith .40 1.00
QC3 Daunte Culpepper .60 1.50
QC4 Cade McNown .40 1.00
QC5 Donovan McNabb 1.25 3.00
QC6 Brock Huard .40 1.00
QC7 John Elway 1.00 2.50
QC8 Dan Marino 1.25 3.00
QC9 Brett Favre 1.25 3.00
QC10 Charlie Batch .40 1.00
QC11 Steve Young .75 2.00
QC12 Jake Plummer .40 1.00
QC13 Peyton Manning 2.00 5.00
QC14 Mark Brunell .50 1.25
QC15 Troy Aikman .75 2.00

1999 Upper Deck Strike Force

Randomly inserted in packs at the rate of one in four, this 30-card set pays tribute to some of the NFL's top scorers. Cards are all-foil and have copper foil highlights. Card backs carry an "SF" prefix.

COMPLETE SET (30) 12.00 30.00
STATED ODDS 1:4
*SILVER/100: 6X TO 15X BASIC INSERTS
SF1 Jamal Anderson .30 .75
SF2 Keyshawn Johnson .30 .75
SF3 Eddie George .30 .75
SF4 Steve Young .50 1.25
SF5 Emmitt Smith .60 1.50
SF6 Karim Abdul-Jabbar .25 .60
SF7 Kordell Stewart .25 .60
SF8 Cade McNown .25 .60
SF9 Tim Couch .30 .75
SF10 Corey Dillon .25 .60
SF11 Peyton Manning 1.25 3.00
SF12 Curtis Martin .30 .75
SF13 Jerome Bettis .40 1.00
SF14 Jon Kitna .25 .60
SF15 Dan Marino .75 2.00
SF16 Eric Moulds .25 .60
SF17 Charlie Batch .25 .60
SF18 Ricky Williams .30 .75
SF19 Terrell Owens .30 .75
SF20 Ty Detmer .25 .60
SF21 Curtis Enis .25 .60
SF22 Doug Flutie .40 1.00
SF23 Randall Cunningham .30 .75
SF24 Donovan McNabb .60 1.50
SF25 Steve McNair .30 .75
SF26 Terrell Davis .30 .75
SF27 Daunte Culpepper .30 .75
SF28 Warrick Dunn .25 .60
SF29 Akili Smith .25 .60
SF30 Barry Sanders .60 1.50

1999 Upper Deck Super Bowl XXXIII

This 25-card boxed set features color action photos of the top players from the Denver Broncos and the Atlanta Falcons, the two teams that played in the 1999 Super Bowl XXXIII. The backs carry player information. Cards 21-24 feature borderless color photos of four previous top Super Bowl players with facsimile autographs printed across the bottom half of the card.

COMPLETE SET (25) 6.00 15.00
1 Jamal Anderson .30 .75
2 Chris Chandler .15 .40
3 Terance Mathis .15 .40
4 Tony Martin .15 .40
5 O.J. Santiago .15 .40
6 Tim Dwight .30 .75
7 Chuck Smith .08 .25
8 Cornelius Bennett .08 .25
9 Lester Archambeau .08 .25
10 Ray Buchanan .08 .25
11 Steve Atwater .08 .25
12 Terrell Davis .75 2.00
13 John Elway 1.20 3.00
14 Ed McCaffrey .15 .40
15 John Mobley .08 .25
16 Bill Romanowski .08 .25
17 Shannon Sharpe UER .15 .40
18 Rod Smith .15 .40
19 Neil Smith .15 .40
20 Maa Tanuvasa .08 .25
21 Troy Aikman .75 2.00
22 Dan Marino 1.20 3.00
23 Jerry Rice .75 2.00
24 Joe Montana 1.20 3.00
25 Super Bowl XXXIII Logo .08 .25

2000 Upper Deck

Upper Deck features a 270-card base set comprised of 222 veteran cards 48 short-printed Rookie cards inserted in packs at the rate of one in four, and three checklist cards. Base cards feature a blue border along the right side of the card and bronze foil highlights. Upper Deck was packaged in 24-pack boxes with packs containing 10 cards and carried a suggested retail price of $2.99.

COMPLETE SET (1-270) 60.00 120.00
COMP.SET w/o RCs (225) 12.50 30.00
223-267 ROOKIE ODDS 1:4
1 Jake Plummer .20 .50
2 Michael Pittman .20 .50
3 Rob Moore .20 .50
4 David Boston .20 .50
5 Frank Sanders .20 .50
6 Aeneas Williams .20 .50
7 Kwamie Lassiter .20 .50
8 Rob Fredrickson .20 .50
9 Tim Dwight .25 .60
10 Chris Chandler .25 .60
11 Jamal Anderson .25 .60
12 Shawn Jefferson .20 .50
13 Ken Oxendine .20 .50
14 Terance Mathis .20 .50
15 Bob Christian .20 .50
16 Qadry Ismail .20 .50
17 Jermaine Lewis .20 .50
18 Rod Woodson .30 .75
19 Michael McCrary .20 .50
20 Tony Banks .20 .50
21 Peter Boulware .20 .50
22 Shannon Sharpe .25 .60
23 Peerless Price .25 .60
24 Rob Johnson .25 .60
25 Eric Moulds .20 .50
26 Doug Flutie .25 .60
27 Jay Riemersma .20 .50
28 Antowain Smith .25 .60
29 Jonathan Linton .20 .50
30 Muhsin Muhammad .20 .50
31 Patrick Jeffers .20 .50
32 Steve Beuerlein .25 .60
33 Natrone Means .25 .60
34 Tim Biakabutuka .25 .60
35 Michael Bates .20 .50
36 Chuck Smith .20 .50
37 Wesley Walls .20 .50
38 Cade McNown .20 .50
39 Curtis Enis .20 .50
40 Marcus Robinson .25 .60
41 Eddie Kennison .20 .50
42 Bobby Engram .20 .50
43 Glyn Milburn .20 .50
44 Marty Booker .20 .50
45 Akili Smith .20 .50
46 Corey Dillon .20 .50
47 Darnay Scott .25 .60
48 Tremain Mack .20 .50
49 Damon Griffin .20 .50
50 Takeo Spikes .20 .50
51 Tony McGee .20 .50
52 Tim Couch .25 .60
53 Kevin Johnson .20 .50
54 Darrin Chiaverini .20 .50
55 Jamir Miller .20 .50
56 Errict Rhett .25 .60
57 Terry Kirby .20 .50
58 Marc Edwards .20 .50
59 Troy Aikman .40 1.00
60 Emmitt Smith .50 1.25
61 Rocket Ismail .25 .60
62 Jason Tucker .20 .50
63 Dexter Coakley .20 .50
64 Joey Galloway .25 .60
65 Wane McGarity .20 .50
66 Terrell Davis .25 .60
67 Olandis Gary .25 .60
68 Brian Griese .20 .50
69 Gus Frerotte .20 .50
70 Byron Chamberlain .20 .50
71 Ed McCaffrey .25 .60
72 Rod Smith .25 .60
73 Al Wilson .20 .50
74 Charlie Batch .20 .50
75 Germane Crowell .20 .50
76 Sedrick Irvin .20 .50
77 Johnnie Morton .25 .60
78 Robert Porcher .20 .50
79 Herman Moore .20 .50
80 James Stewart .20 .50
81 Brett Favre .60 1.50
82 Antonio Freeman .25 .60
83 Bill Schroeder .25 .60
84 Dorsey Levens .25 .60
85 Corey Bradford .20 .50
86 De'Mond Parker .20 .50
87 Vonnie Holliday .20 .50
88 Peyton Manning .75 2.00
89 Edgerrin James .25 .60
90 Marvin Harrison .25 .60
91 Ken Dilger .20 .50
92 Terrence Wilkins .20 .50
93 Marcus Pollard .20 .50
94 Fred Lane .20 .50
95 Mark Brunell .25 .60
96 Fred Taylor .20 .50
97 Jimmy Smith .25 .60
98 Keenan McCardell .25 .60
99 Carnell Lake .20 .50
100 Tavian Banks .20 .50
101 Kyle Brady .20 .50
102 Hardy Nickerson .20 .50
103 Elvis Grbac .20 .50
104 Tony Gonzalez .25 .60
105 Derrick Alexander WR .20 .50
106 Donnell Bennett .20 .50
107 Mike Cloud .20 .50
108 Donnie Edwards .20 .50
109 Jay Fiedler .25 .60
110 James Johnson .20 .50
111 Tony Martin .25 .60
112 Damon Huard .20 .50
113 O.J. McDuffie .25 .60
114 Thurman Thomas .25 .60
115 Zach Thomas .25 .60
116 Oronde Gadsden .25 .60
117 Randy Moss .25 .60
118 Robert Smith .20 .50
119 Cris Carter .30 .75
120 Matthew Hatchette .20 .50
121 Daunte Culpepper .25 .60
122 Leroy Hoard .20 .50
123 Drew Bledsoe .25 .60
124 Terry Glenn .25 .60
125 Troy Brown .20 .50
126 Kevin Faulk .20 .50
127 Lawyer Milloy .20 .50
128 Ricky Williams .25 .60
129 Keith Poole .20 .50
130 Jake Reed .25 .60
131 Cam Cleeland .20 .50
132 Jeff Blake .25 .60
133 Andrew Glover .20 .50
134 Kerry Collins .20 .50
135 Amani Toomer .20 .50
136 Joe Montgomery .20 .50
137 Ike Hilliard .20 .50
138 Tiki Barber .25 .60
139 Pete Mitchell .20 .50
140 Ray Lucas .20 .50
141 Mo Lewis .20 .50
142 Curtis Martin .25 .60
143 Vinny Testaverde .20 .50
144 Wayne Chrebet .20 .50
145 Dedric Ward .20 .50
146 Tim Brown .30 .75
147 Rich Gannon .25 .60
148 Tyrone Wheatley .20 .50
149 Napoleon Kaufman .25 .60
150 Charles Woodson .30 .75
151 Darrell Russell .20 .50
152 James Jett .25 .60
153 Rickey Dudley .20 .50
154 Jon Ritchie .20 .50
155 Duce Staley .20 .50
156 Donovan McNabb .25 .60
157 Torrance Small .20 .50
158 Allen Rossum .20 .50
159 Mike Mamula .20 .50
160 Na Brown .20 .50
161 Charles Johnson .20 .50
162 Kent Graham .20 .50
163 Troy Edwards .20 .50
164 Jerome Bettis .30 .75
165 Hines Ward .25 .60
166 Kordell Stewart .20 .50
167 Levon Kirkland .20 .50
168 Richard Huntley .20 .50
169 Marshall Faulk .25 .60
170 Kurt Warner .50 1.25
171 Torry Holt .25 .60
172 Isaac Bruce .30 .75
173 Kevin Carter .20 .50
174 Az-Zahir Hakim .20 .50
175 Ricky Proehl .20 .50
176 Jermaine Fazande .20 .50
177 Curtis Conway .25 .60
178 Freddie Jones .20 .50
179 Junior Seau .25 .60
180 Jeff Graham .20 .50
181 Jim Harbaugh .25 .60
182 Rodney Harrison .20 .50
183 Steve Young .40 1.00
184 Jerry Rice .75 2.00
185 Charlie Garner .25 .60
186 Terrell Owens .25 .60
187 Jeff Garcia .20 .50
188 Fred Beasley .20 .50
189 J.J. Stokes .25 .60
190 Ricky Watters .25 .60
191 Jon Kitna .20 .50
192 Derrick Mayes .20 .50
193 Sean Dawkins .20 .50
194 Charlie Rogers .20 .50
195 Mike Pritchard .20 .50
196 Cortez Kennedy .25 .60
197 Christian Fauria .20 .50
198 Warrick Dunn .20 .50
199 Shaun King .20 .50
200 Mike Alstott .20 .50
201 Warren Sapp .25 .60
202 Jacquez Green .20 .50
203 Reidel Anthony .20 .50
204 Dave Moore .20 .50
205 Keyshawn Johnson .25 .60
206 Eddie George .25 .60
207 Steve McNair .25 .60
208 Kevin Dyson .25 .60
209 Jevon Kearse .20 .50
210 Yancey Thigpen .20 .50
211 Frank Wycheck .25 .60
212 Isaac Byrd .20 .50
213 Neil O'Donnell .20 .50
214 Brad Johnson .25 .60
215 Stephen Davis .20 .50
216 Michael Westbrook .20 .50
217 Albert Connell .20 .50
218 Brian Mitchell .20 .50
219 Bruce Smith .25 .60
220 Stephen Alexander .20 .50
221 Jeff George .25 .60
222 Adrian Murrell .20 .50
223 Courtney Brown RC 1.25 3.00
224 John Engelberger RC 1.00 2.50
225 Deltha O'Neal RC 1.00 2.50
226 Corey Simon RC 1.25 3.00
227 R.Jay Soward RC 1.00 2.50
228 Marc Bulger RC 1.25 3.00
229 Raynoch Thompson RC 1.00 2.50
230 Deon Grant RC 1.00 2.50
231 Darrell Jackson RC 1.00 2.50
232 Chris Cole RC 1.25 3.00
233 Trevor Gaylor RC 1.00 2.50
234 John Abraham RC 1.50 4.00
235 Chris Redman RC 1.00 2.50
236 Joe Hamilton RC 1.00 2.50
237 Chad Pennington RC 1.25 3.00
238 Tee Martin RC 1.00 2.50
239 Giovanni Carmazzi RC 1.00 2.50
240 Tim Rattay RC 1.25 3.00
241 Ron Dayne RC 1.50 4.00
242 Shaun Alexander RC 1.50 4.00
243 Thomas Jones RC 1.25 3.00
244 Reuben Droughns RC 1.00 2.50
245 Jamal Lewis RC 1.50 4.00
246 Michael Wiley RC 1.00 2.50
247 J.R. Redmond RC 1.00 2.50
248 Travis Prentice RC 1.00 2.50
249 Todd Husak RC 1.00 2.50
250 Trung Canidate RC 1.00 2.50
251 Brian Urlacher RC 5.00 12.00
252 Anthony Becht RC 1.00 2.50
253 Bubba Franks RC 1.00 2.50
254 Tom Brady RC 125.00 250.00
255 Peter Warrick RC 1.00 2.50
256 Plaxico Burress RC 1.25 3.00
257 Sylvester Morris RC 1.00 2.50
258 Dez White RC 1.00 2.50
259 Travis Taylor RC 1.00 2.50
260 Todd Pinkston RC 1.00 2.50
261 Dennis Northcutt RC 1.00 2.50
262 Jerry Porter RC 1.50 4.00
263 Laveranues Coles RC 1.25 3.00
264 Danny Farmer RC 1.00 2.50
265 Curtis Keaton RC 1.00 2.50
266 Sherrod Gideon RC 1.00 2.50
267 Ron Dugans RC 1.00 2.50
268 Steve McNair CL .20 .50
269 Jake Plummer CL .15 .40
270 Antonio Freeman CL .20 .50

2000 Upper Deck Exclusives Gold

*VETS 1-222: 15X TO 40X BASIC CARDS
*ROOKIES 223-267: 3X TO 8X
GOLD PRINT RUN 25 SER.#'d SETS
251 Brian Urlacher 100.00 200.00
254 Tom Brady 1250.00 2000.00

2000 Upper Deck Exclusives Silver

*VETS 1-222/268-270: 8X TO 20X
*ROOKIES 223-267: 1.5X TO 4X
SILVER PRINT RUN 100 SER.#'d SETS
254 Tom Brady 450.00 700.00

2000 Upper Deck e-Card

Randomly inserted at two per box, this six card set features all-foil cards with a validation number. Card numbers can be typed in at www.upperdeckdigital.com to see if they can be exchanged for a Game Used Ball e-Card, an Autograph e-Card, or an Autographed Game Jersey e-Card.

COMPLETE SET (6) 7.50 20.00
STATED ODDS TWO PER BOX
CP Chad Pennington 2.00 5.00
CR Chris Redman .50 1.25
JL Jamal Lewis 2.00 5.00
SA Shaun Alexander 2.50 6.00
TJ Thomas Jones 1.25 3.00
TT Travis Taylor .75 2.00

2000 Upper Deck e-Card Prizes

This set is comprised of the different cards sent to winners of the e-card redemption program. Each card features a memorabilia swatch, and autograph, or both, as well as serial numbering.

CPA Chad Pennington AU/200 15.00 40.00
CPB Chad Pennington Ball/300 10.00 25.00
CPJ C Pennington Jsy AU/50 25.00 60.00
CRA Chris Redman AU/200 7.50 20.00
CRB Chris Redman Ball/300 6.00 15.00
CRJ Chris Redman Jsy AU/50 20.00 50.00
JLA Jamal Lewis AU/200 15.00 40.00
JLB Jamal Lewis Ball/300 10.00 25.00
JLJ Jamal Lewis Jsy AU/50 15.00 40.00
SAA Shaun Alexander AU/200 20.00 50.00
SAB Shaun Alexander Ball/300 10.00 25.00
SAJ Sha Alexander Jsy AU/50 25.00 60.00
TJA Thomas Jones AU/200 12.50 30.00
TJB Thomas Jones Ball/300 7.50 20.00
TJJ Thomas Jones Jsy AU/50 40.00 80.00
TTB Travis Taylor Ball/300 6.00 15.00

2000 Upper Deck Game Jersey

ndomly inserted in Hobby packs at the rate of one in 287, this 38-card set features full color action player photography coupled with a swatch of a game worn jersey. A Brett Favre Promo card was issued late in the year to employees of the Sports Division at Krause Publications. Each of these was serial numbered to 60.

STATED ODDS 1:287 HOBBY
AF Antonio Freeman 6.00 15.00
BF Brett Favre 15.00 40.00
BG Brian Griese 5.00 12.00
BO David Boston 5.00 12.00
CB Courtney Brown 6.00 15.00
CM Curtis Martin 6.00 15.00
CR Chris Redman 5.00 12.00
DA Daunte Culpepper 6.00 15.00
DL Dorsey Levens 6.00 15.00
DO Donovan McNabb 6.00 15.00
EM Eric Moulds 5.00 12.00
ES Emmitt Smith 12.00 30.00
FA Danny Farmer 5.00 12.00
FR Bubba Franks 5.00 12.00
HM Herman Moore 5.00 12.00
JA Jamal Anderson 6.00 15.00
JJ J.J. Stokes 6.00 15.00
JL Jamal Lewis 8.00 20.00
JR Jerry Rice 20.00 50.00
MA Mike Alstott 5.00 12.00
OG Olandis Gary 6.00 15.00
PB Plaxico Burress 6.00 15.00
RJ R.Jay Soward 5.00 12.00
RL Ray Lucas 5.00 12.00
RW Ricky Williams 6.00 15.00
SK Shaun King 5.00 12.00
SL Sylvester Morris 5.00 12.00
SM Steve McNair 6.00 15.00
SY Steve Young 12.00 30.00
TB Tim Brown 8.00 20.00
TH Torry Holt 6.00 15.00
TJ Thomas Jones 6.00 15.00
TM Tee Martin 5.00 12.00
TO Terrell Owens 6.00 15.00
TT Travis Taylor 5.00 12.00
KPGJ Brett Favre/60 Promo 40.00 100.00

2000 Upper Deck Game Jersey Autographs Gold

Randomly inserted in Hobby packs at the rate of one in 287, this set features both a swatch of game worn jersey and an authentic player signature. Reportedly, each card was produced with a gold background and gold foil highlights. Some players were issued via redempton cards that expired on 4/5/2001.

STATED ODDS 1:287 HOBBY
CPA Chad Pennington 20.00 40.00
DBA Drew Bledsoe 30.00 60.00
DMA Dan Marino 75.00 150.00
EGA Eddie George 15.00 40.00
EJA Edgerrin James 15.00 40.00
IBA Isaac Bruce 20.00 50.00
JOA Kevin Johnson 12.00 30.00
KJA Keyshawn Johnson 15.00 40.00
KWA Kurt Warner 30.00 60.00
KWAX Kurt Warner EXCH 2.50 6.00
MBA Mark Brunell 15.00 40.00
MCA Cade McNown 12.00 30.00
MFA Marshall Faulk 15.00 40.00
MHA Marvin Harrison 15.00 40.00
PMA Peyton Manning 75.00 150.00
PWA Peter Warrick 8.00 20.00
RDA Ron Dayne 12.00 30.00
RMA Randy Moss 50.00 100.00
SAA Shaun Alexander 12.00 30.00
TAA Troy Aikman 50.00 120.00
TCA Tim Couch 12.00 30.00
TDA Terrell Davis 15.00 40.00

2000 Upper Deck Game Jersey Autographs Silver Numbered

Randomly inserted in packs, this set features cards with both swatches of game worn jerseys and authentic player autographs. Each card is also sequentially hand numbered to the featured player's jersey number. Reportedly, each card was produced with a silver colored background and silver foil highlights. Most cards were issued via exchange cards which expired on 4/5/2001.

STATED PRINT RUN 8-92
SER.#'d UNDER 25 NOT PRICED
BOA David Boston/80 15.00 40.00
CBA Courtney Brown/92 15.00 40.00
DLA Dorsey Levens/25 30.00 80.00
EGA Eddie George/27 30.00 80.00
EJA Edgerrin James/32 25.00 60.00
IBA Isaac Bruce/80 25.00 60.00
JAA Jamal Anderson/32 20.00 50.00
JOA Kevin Johnson/85 15.00 40.00
MFA Marshall Faulk/28 75.00 150.00
MHA Marvin Harrison/88 20.00 50.00
PWA Peter Warrick/80 15.00 40.00
RDA Ron Dayne/27 30.00 80.00
SAA Shaun Alexander/37 25.00 60.00
TBA Tim Brown/81 40.00 80.00
TDA Terrell Davis/30 25.00 60.00

2000 Upper Deck Game Jersey Greats Autographs

Each 2000 Upper Deck product included one Game Jersey Greats Autograph card with its release. The cards feature full color action photography, a swatch of a game worn jersey and an authentic player autograph. Note that Joe Namath and Bart Starr have two cards each that are virtually identical except for the card number. The Marino card was issued via mail redemptions that carried an expiration date of 2/28/2001.

STATED PRINT RUN 175-400
GJGBS1 Bart Starr/200 125.00 250.00
GJGBS2 Bart Starr/200 125.00 250.00
GJGDM Dan Marino/375 150.00 300.00
GJGJE John Elway/350 125.00 250.00
GJGJM Joe Montana 175.00 300.00
GJGJU Johnny Unitas/400 300.00 600.00
GJGJN1 Joe Namath/175 125.00 250.00
GJGJN2 Joe Namath/175 125.00 250.00
GJGRS Roger Staubach/400 75.00 150.00
GJGSY Steve Young/175 125.00 250.00
GJGTB Terry Bradshaw/400 100.00 200.00

2000 Upper Deck Game Jersey Patch

Randomly inserted in packs at the rate of one in 7500, this 30-card set features a premium swatch from the patch of an authentic game worn jersey.

STATED ODDS 1:7500
*SERIAL #'d/25: .5X TO 1.2X BASIC JSY
SERIAL #'d STATED PRINT RUN 25
AFP Antonio Freeman 15.00 40.00
BFP Brett Favre 40.00 100.00
BGP Brian Griese 12.00 30.00
BOP David Boston 12.00 30.00
CMP Curtis Martin 15.00 40.00
DAP Daunte Culpepper 15.00 40.00
DBP Drew Bledsoe 15.00 40.00
DLP Dorsey Levens 15.00 40.00
DMP Dan Marino 40.00 100.00
EGP Eddie George 15.00 40.00
EJP Edgerrin James 15.00 40.00
ESP Emmitt Smith 30.00 80.00
FTP Fred Taylor 12.00 30.00
JAP Jamal Anderson 15.00 40.00
JOP Kevin Johnson 12.00 30.00
KJP Keyshawn Johnson 15.00 40.00
MBP Mark Brunell 15.00 40.00
MCP Cade McNown 12.00 30.00
MFP Marshall Faulk 15.00 40.00
MHP Marvin Harrison 15.00 40.00
OGP Olandis Gary 15.00 40.00
PMP Peyton Manning 50.00 120.00
RLP Ray Lucas 12.00 30.00
RMP Randy Moss 15.00 40.00
SKP Shaun King 12.00 30.00
TBP Tim Brown 20.00 50.00
TCP Tim Couch 15.00 40.00
TDP Terrell Davis 15.00 40.00
THP Torry Holt 15.00 40.00
TOP Terrell Owens 15.00 40.00

2000 Upper Deck Game Jersey Patch Autographs

Randomly seeded in Hobby packs, this six-card set features both a premium swatch of an authentic game worn jersey patch and an authentic player signature. Cards are sequentially numbered to 25. The exchange cards expired on 4/5/2001.

STATED PRINT RUN 25 SERIAL #'d SETS
EGSP Eddie George 50.00 100.00
EJSP Edgerrin James 50.00 100.00
KWSP Kurt Warner 100.00 200.00
MFSP Marshall Faulk 50.00 120.00
RMSP Randy Moss EXCH 10.00 20.00
TCSP Tim Couch 25.00 60.00

2000 Upper Deck Headline Heroes

Randomly seeded in packs at the rate of one in 23, this 15-card set features an all foil card stock and features players from the highlight reel week after week.

COMPLETE SET (15) 12.50 30.00
STATED ODDS 1:23
HH1 Mark Brunell .75 2.00
HH2 Damon Huard .60 1.50
HH3 Ricky Williams .75 2.00
HH4 Jevon Kearse .60 1.50
HH5 Keyshawn Johnson .75 2.00
HH6 Ricky Watters .75 2.00
HH7 Michael Westbrook .60 1.50
HH8 Charlie Batch .60 1.50
HH9 Warren Sapp .75 2.00
HH10 Muhsin Muhammad .60 1.50
HH11 Brett Favre 2.00 5.00
HH12 Jeff George .75 2.00
HH13 Germane Crowell .60 1.50
HH14 Troy Aikman 1.25 3.00
HH15 Jimmy Smith .75 2.00

2000 Upper Deck Highlight Zone

Randomly inserted in packs at the rate of one in 11, this 10-card set features memorable individual highlights of the showcased player.

COMPLETE SET (10) 5.00 12.00
STATED ODDS 1:11
HZ1 Eddie George .50 1.25
HZ2 Steve McNair .50 1.25
HZ3 Kevin Dyson .50 1.25
HZ4 Kurt Warner 1.00 2.50
HZ5 Emmitt Smith 1.00 2.50
HZ6 Brad Johnson .50 1.25
HZ7 Curtis Martin .50 1.25
HZ8 Ray Lucas .40 1.00
HZ9 Akili Smith .40 1.00
HZ10 Jake Plummer .40 1.00

2000 Upper Deck New Guard

Randomly inserted in packs at the rate of one in 23, this 15-card all foil insert set showcases top 2000 draft picks to be the next group of marquee players in the NFL.

COMPLETE SET (15) 15.00 40.00
STATED ODDS 1:23
NG1 Tim Couch .75 2.00
NG2 Ricky Williams .75 2.00
NG3 Shaun King .60 1.50
NG4 Brian Griese .60 1.50
NG5 Rob Johnson .75 2.00
NG6 Marcus Robinson .75 2.00
NG7 Troy Edwards .60 1.50
NG8 Kevin Johnson .60 1.50
NG9 Cade McNown .60 1.50
NG10 Jon Kitna .60 1.50
NG11 Peyton Manning 2.50 6.00
NG12 Edgerrin James .75 2.00
NG13 Akili Smith .60 1.50
NG14 Donovan McNabb .75 2.00
NG15 Randy Moss .75 2.00

2000 Upper Deck Proving Ground

Randomly inserted in packs at the rate of one in 11, this 10-card all-foil insert set showcases rising young stars who have begun to prove their worth in the NFL.

COMPLETE SET (10) 3.00 8.00
STATED ODDS 1:11
PG1 Marcus Robinson .50 1.25
PG2 Stephen Davis .40 1.00
PG3 Daunte Culpepper .50 1.25
PG4 Jevon Kearse .40 1.00
PG5 Marshall Faulk .50 1.25
PG6 Marvin Harrison .50 1.25
PG7 Germane Crowell .40 1.00
PG8 Darnay Scott .50 1.25
PG9 Duce Staley .40 1.00
PG10 Warrick Dunn .40 1.00

2000 Upper Deck Strike Force

Randomly inserted in packs at the rate of one in four, this 15-card all-foil insert set features full color action photograpy of quick-strike NFL talents.

COMPLETE SET (15) 3.00 6.00
STATED ODDS 1:4
SF1 Fred Taylor .25 .60
SF2 Muhsin Muhammad .25 .60
SF3 Tony Gonzalez .30 .75
SF4 Marcus Robinson .30 .75
SF5 Charlie Garner .30 .75
SF6 Torry Holt .30 .75
SF7 Germane Crowell .25 .60
SF8 Amani Toomer .25 .60
SF9 Patrick Jeffers .25 .60
SF10 Albert Connell .25 .60
SF11 Olandis Gary .30 .75
SF12 Robert Smith .25 .60
SF13 Napoleon Kaufman .30 .75
SF14 Tim Biakabutuka .30 .75
SF15 Priest Holmes .25 .60

2000 Upper Deck Wired

Randomly inserted in packs at the rate of one in eight, this 15-card set showcases top NFL talents who made the biggest plays in 1999.

COMPLETE SET (15) 5.00 12.00
STATED ODDS 1:8
W1 Charlie Batch .40 1.00
W2 Terrell Davis .50 1.25
W3 Jake Plummer .40 1.00
W4 Cris Carter .60 1.50
W5 James Stewart .40 1.00
W6 Corey Dillon .40 1.00
W7 Ricky Watters .50 1.25
W8 Curtis Enis .40 1.00
W9 Errict Rhett .50 1.25
W10 Stephen Davis .40 1.00
W11 Mike Alstott .40 1.00
W12 Steve Beuerlein .50 1.25
W13 Michael Westbrook .40 1.00
W14 Terry Glenn .50 1.25
W15 Bill Schroeder .50 1.25

2000 Upper Deck 22K Gold John Elway

1 John Elway 8.00 20.00

2001 Upper Deck

In July of 2001 Upper Deck released this base brand in both retail and hobby packs. The set consisted of 280 cards and cards 181-280 were short printed rookies. The stated odds for the rookies were 1:4 packs. The base set design had a border on only the bottom of the card where the player's name and team were represented. The cardfronts were full color action photos and were highlighted with silver-foil lettering and logo.

COMPLETE SET (280) 150.00 300.00
COMP.SET w/o SP's (180) 10.00 25.00
ROOKIE STATED ODDS 1:4
1 Jake Plummer .20 .50
2 David Boston .20 .50
3 Thomas Jones .20 .50
4 Frank Sanders .20 .50
5 Eric Zeier .20 .50
6 Jamal Anderson .25 .60
7 Chris Chandler .25 .60
8 Shawn Jefferson .20 .50
9 Darrick Vaughn .20 .50
10 Terance Mathis .20 .50
11 Jamal Lewis .30 .75
12 Shannon Sharpe .25 .60
13 Elvis Grbac .25 .60
14 Ray Lewis .30 .75
15 Qadry Ismail .20 .50
16 Chris Redman .30 .75
17 Rob Johnson .25 .60
18 Eric Moulds .20 .50
19 Sammy Morris .20 .50
20 Shawn Bryson .20 .50
21 Jeremy McDaniel .20 .50
22 Muhsin Muhammad .20 .50
23 Brad Hoover .25 .60
24 Tim Biakabutuka .20 .50
25 Steve Beuerlein .25 .60
26 Jeff Lewis .20 .50
27 Wesley Walls .20 .50
28 Cade McNown .25 .60
29 James Allen .20 .50
30 Marcus Robinson .25 .60
31 Brian Urlacher .40 1.00
32 Bobby Engram .20 .50
33 Peter Warrick .20 .50
34 Corey Dillon .20 .50
35 Akili Smith .20 .50
36 Danny Farmer .20 .50
37 Ron Dugans .20 .50
38 Jon Kitna .20 .50
39 Tim Couch .20 .50
40 Kevin Johnson .20 .50
41 Travis Prentice .20 .50
42 Spergon Wynn .20 .50
43 Errict Rhett .25 .60
44 Dennis Northcutt .20 .50
45 Courtney Brown .20 .50
46 Tony Banks .20 .50
47 Emmitt Smith .50 1.25
48 Joey Galloway .25 .60
49 Rocket Ismail .25 .60
50 Randall Cunningham .25 .60
51 James McKnight .20 .50
52 Terrell Davis .25 .60
53 Mike Anderson .20 .50
54 Brian Griese .20 .50
55 Rod Smith .25 .60
56 Ed McCaffrey .25 .60
57 Eddie Kennison .25 .60
58 Olandis Gary .20 .50
59 Charlie Batch .20 .50
60 Germane Crowell .20 .50
61 James O. Stewart .20 .50
62 Johnnie Morton .25 .60
63 Brett Favre .60 1.50
64 Antonio Freeman .30 .75
65 Dorsey Levens .25 .60
66 Ahman Green .25 .60
67 Bill Schroeder .25 .60
68 Peyton Manning .75 2.00
69 Edgerrin James .25 .60
70 Marvin Harrison .25 .60
71 Jerome Pathon .20 .50
72 Ken Dilger .20 .50
73 Mark Brunell .25 .60
74 Fred Taylor .20 .50
75 Jimmy Smith .25 .60
76 Keenan McCardell .25 .60
77 R.Jay Soward .20 .50
78 Todd Collins .20 .50
79 Tony Gonzalez .25 .60
80 Derrick Alexander .20 .50
81 Tony Richardson .20 .50
82 Sylvester Morris .20 .50
83 Oronde Gadsden .20 .50
84 Lamar Smith .25 .60
85 Jay Fiedler .25 .60
86 Jason Taylor .30 .75
87 Ray Lucas .20 .50
88 O.J. McDuffie .20 .50
89 Randy Moss .25 .60
90 Cris Carter .30 .75
91 Daunte Culpepper .25 .60
92 Moe Williams .20 .50
93 Troy Walters .20 .50
94 Drew Bledsoe .25 .60
95 Terry Glenn .25 .60
96 Kevin Faulk .20 .50
97 J.R. Redmond .20 .50
98 Troy Brown .20 .50
99 Ricky Williams .25 .60
100 Jeff Blake .25 .60
101 Joe Horn .20 .50
102 Albert Connell .20 .50
103 Aaron Brooks .20 .50
104 Chad Morton .20 .50
105 Kerry Collins .20 .50
106 Amani Toomer .20 .50
107 Ron Dayne .25 .60
108 Tiki Barber .25 .60
109 Ike Hilliard .20 .50
110 Ron Dixon .20 .50
111 Jason Sehorn .25 .60
112 Vinny Testaverde .20 .50
113 Wayne Chrebet .20 .50
114 Curtis Martin .25 .60
115 Dedric Ward .20 .50
116 Laveranues Coles .25 .60
117 Windrell Hayes .20 .50
118 Tim Brown .30 .75
119 Rich Gannon .25 .60
120 Tyrone Wheatley .25 .60
121 Charlie Garner .25 .60
122 Andre Rison .25 .60
123 Charles Woodson .30 .75
124 Trace Armstrong .20 .50
125 Duce Staley .20 .50
126 Donovan McNabb .25 .60
127 Darnell Autry .20 .50
128 Charles Johnson .20 .50
129 Torrance Small .20 .50
130 Kordell Stewart .20 .50
131 Jerome Bettis .30 .75
132 Plaxico Burress .20 .50
133 Bobby Shaw .20 .50
134 Troy Edwards .20 .50
135 Marshall Faulk .25 .60
136 Kurt Warner .50 1.25
137 Isaac Bruce .30 .75
138 Torry Holt .25 .60
139 Trent Green .20 .50
140 Az-Zahir Hakim .20 .50
141 Junior Seau .25 .60
142 Curtis Conway .25 .60
143 Doug Flutie .25 .60
144 Jeff Graham .20 .50
145 Freddie Jones .20 .50
146 Marcellus Wiley .20 .50
147 Jeff Garcia .20 .50
148 Jerry Rice .60 1.50
149 Fred Beasley .20 .50
150 Terrell Owens .25 .60
151 J.J. Stokes .20 .50
152 Garrison Hearst .25 .60
153 Ricky Watters .25 .60
154 Shaun Alexander .20 .50
155 Matt Hasselbeck .20 .50
156 Brock Huard .20 .50
157 Darrell Jackson .25 .60
158 John Randle .25 .60
159 Warrick Dunn .20 .50
160 Shaun King .20 .50
161 Ryan Leaf .20 .50
162 Mike Alstott .20 .50
163 Jacquez Green .20 .50
164 Brad Johnson .25 .60
165 Keyshawn Johnson .25 .60
166 Eddie George .30 .75
167 Steve McNair .25 .60
168 Neil O'Donnell .25 .60
169 Derrick Mason .20 .50
170 Frank Wycheck .20 .50
171 Kevin Dyson .20 .50
172 Jevon Kearse .20 .50
173 Jeff George .25 .60
174 Stephen Davis .20 .50
175 Larry Centers .20 .50
176 Michael Westbrook .20 .50
177 Stephen Alexander .20 .50
178 Ron Dayne .25 .60
179 Donovan McNabb .25 .60
180 Jimmy Smith .25 .60
181 Adam Archuleta RC 1.00 2.50
182 A.J. Feeley RC 1.00 2.50
183 Alex Bannister RC .75 2.00
184 Alge Crumpler RC 1.25 3.00
185 Andre Carter RC 1.00 2.50
186 Andre Dyson RC .75 2.00
187 Anthony Thomas RC 1.25 3.00
188 Arther Love RC .75 2.00
189 Bobby Newcombe RC 1.00 2.50
190 Brandon Spoon RC 1.00 2.50
191 Carlos Polk RC .75 2.00
192 Casey Hampton RC 1.25 3.00
193 Cedrick Wilson RC 1.00 2.50
194 Chad Johnson RC 1.25 3.00
195 Chris Chambers RC .75 2.00
196 Chris Taylor RC .75 2.00
197 Chris Weinke RC 1.00 2.50
198 Correll Buckhalter RC .75 2.00
199 Damione Lewis RC 1.00 2.50
200 Dan Alexander RC 1.00 2.50
201 Dan Morgan RC 1.00 2.50
202 Willie Middlebrooks RC 1.00 2.50
203 David Terrell RC 1.00 2.50
204 Derrick Gibson RC .75 2.00
205 Deuce McAllister RC 1.25 3.00
206 Drew Brees RC 15.00 40.00

207 Edgerton Hartwell RC .75 2.00
208 Fred Smoot RC 1.00 2.50
209 Freddie Mitchell RC .75 2.00
210 Gary Baxter RC .75 2.00
211 Gerard Warren RC 1.00 2.50
212 Hakim Akbar RC .75 2.00
213 Heath Evans RC 1.00 2.50
214 Jabari Holloway RC .75 2.00
215 Jamal Reynolds RC .75 2.00
216 Jamar Fletcher RC .75 2.00
217 James Jackson RC .75 2.00
218 Jamie Winborn RC 1.00 2.50
219 Jesse Palmer RC 1.00 2.50
220 Josh Booty RC 1.00 2.50
221 Josh Heupel RC 1.25 3.00
222 Justin Smith RC 1.50 4.00
223 Karon Riley RC .75 2.00
224 Ken Lucas RC 1.00 2.50
225 Kenyatta Walker RC .75 2.00
226 Ken-Yon Rambo RC .75 2.00
227 Kevan Barlow RC 1.00 2.50
228 Kevin Kasper RC .75 2.00
229 Koren Robinson RC 1.00 2.50
230 LaDainian Tomlinson RC 4.00 10.00
231 LaMont Jordan RC 1.25 3.00
232 Leonard Davis RC 1.25 3.00
233 Marcus Stroud RC 1.00 2.50
234 Marques Tuiasosopo RC 1.00 2.50
235 Snoop Minnis RC .75 2.00
236 Michael Bennett RC 1.00 2.50
237 Michael Stone RC .75 2.00
238 Mike McMahon RC 1.00 2.50
239 Michael Vick RC 2.00 5.00
240 Moran Norris RC .75 2.00
241 Morlon Greenwood RC .75 2.00
242 Nate Clements RC 1.00 2.50
243 Orlando Huff RC .75 2.00
244 Quincy Morgan RC 1.00 2.50
245 Reggie Wayne RC 1.50 4.00
246 Richard Seymour RC 1.25 3.00
247 Robert Ferguson RC 1.25 3.00
248 Rod Gardner RC 1.00 2.50
249 Rudi Johnson RC 1.25 3.00
250 Sage Rosenfels RC 1.00 2.50
251 Santana Moss RC 1.25 3.00
252 Scotty Anderson RC .75 2.00
253 Sedrick Hodge RC .75 2.00
254 Shaun Rogers RC 1.25 3.00
255 Steve Hutchinson RC 2.00 5.00
256 T.J. Houshmandzadeh RC 1.00 2.50
257 Tay Cody RC .75 2.00
258 George Layne RC .75 2.00
259 Todd Heap RC 1.00 2.50
260 Tommy Polley RC .75 2.00
261 Tony Dixon RC .75 2.00
262 Brian Allen RC .75 2.00
263 Torrance Marshall RC .75 2.00
264 Travis Henry RC 1.00 2.50
265 Travis Minor RC 1.00 2.50
266 Vinny Sutherland RC .75 2.00
267 Will Allen RC 1.25 3.00
268 Derrick Blaylock RC 1.00 2.50
269 Zeke Moreno RC 1.00 2.50
270 Chris Barnes RC .75 2.00
271 Dee Brown RC .75 2.00
272 Reggie White RC .75 2.00
273 Derek Combs RC .75 2.00
274 Steve Smith RC 2.50 6.00
275 John Capel RC .75 2.00
276 Justin McCareins RC 1.00 2.50
277 Damerien McCants RC 1.00 2.50
278 Eddie Berlin RC .75 2.00
279 Francis St. Paul RC .75 2.00
280 Quincy Carter RC 1.00 2.50

2001 Upper Deck Gold

*VETS 1-180: 4X TO 10X BASIC CARDS
1-180 VETERAN PRINT RUN 100
*ROOKIES 181-280: 2X TO 5X
181-280 ROOKIE PRINT RUN 50

2001 Upper Deck Championship Threads

ndomly inserted in packs of 2001 Upper Deck at a rate of 1:144, this 15-card set featured swatches of game jerseys from some of the hottest stars in the NFL. The cards carried a 'CT' prefix for the card numbering.

STATED ODDS 1:144
CTAF Antonio Freeman 3.00 8.00
CTBF Brett Favre 6.00 15.00
CTDI Trent Dilfer 2.00 5.00
CTDL Dorsey Levens 2.50 6.00
CTEM Ed McCaffrey 2.50 6.00
CTIB Isaac Bruce 3.00 8.00
CTJL Jamal Lewis 3.00 8.00
CTJR Jerry Rice 6.00 15.00
CTKW Kurt Warner 5.00 12.00
CTMF Marshall Faulk 2.50 6.00
CTRL Ray Lewis 3.00 8.00
CTRS Rod Smith 2.50 6.00
CTSS Shannon Sharpe 2.50 6.00
CTTD Terrell Davis 2.50 6.00
CTTH Torry Holt 2.50 6.00

2001 Upper Deck Classic Drafts Jerseys

ndomly inserted in packs of 2001 Upper Deck at a rate of 1:288, this 10-card set featured swatches of game jerseys from some of the hottest stars in the NFL. The cards carried a 'CD' suffix for the card numbering.

STATED ODDS 1:288
BGCD Brian Griese 2.00 5.00
DBCD Drew Bledsoe 2.50 6.00
DCCD Daunte Culpepper 2.50 6.00
DMCD Dan Marino 6.00 15.00
FTCD Fred Taylor 2.00 5.00
JECD John Elway 5.00 12.00
JKCD Jim Kelly 3.00 8.00
KECD Jevon Kearse 2.00 5.00
MBCD Mark Brunell 2.50 6.00
TCCD Tim Couch 2.00 5.00

2001 Upper Deck Constant Threat

Constant Threats were inserted in packs of 2001 Upper Deck at a rate of 1:36. This 10-card set featured gold-foil highlights and a rainbow-holofoil background. The set featured some of the top players from the NFL. The cards carried a 'CT' prefix for the card numbering.

COMPLETE SET (10) 5.00 12.00
STATED ODDS 1:36
CT1 Aaron Brooks .50 1.25
CT2 Charlie Batch .50 1.25
CT3 Donovan McNabb .60 1.50
CT4 Mark Brunell .60 1.50
CT5 Akili Smith .50 1.25
CT6 Ray Lucas .50 1.25
CT7 Jake Plummer .50 1.25
CT8 Steve McNair .60 1.50
CT9 Trent Green .50 1.25
CT10 Doug Flutie .60 1.50

2001 Upper Deck e-Card

ndomly inserted in packs of 2001 Upper Deck at a rate of 1:12, the eCard set featured 6 rookies from the 2001 NFL Draft. Each card had a scratch off which would reveal a code to enter on upperdeck.com and the cards had an opportunity to e-volve into jersey and autograph cards. The cards carried an 'E' prefix for the card numbering.

COMPLETE SET (6) 10.00 25.00
STATED ODDS 1:12
ECW Chris Weinke .75 2.00
EDB Drew Brees 4.00 10.00
EFM Freddie Mitchell .60 1.50
ELT LaDainian Tomlinson 3.00 8.00
EMB Michael Bennett .75 2.00
EMV Michael Vick 1.50 4.00

2001 Upper Deck e-Card Prizes

These were the redemption cards for the eCards that were inserted in packs of 2001 Upper Deck at a rate of 1:12, the eCard set featured 6 rookies from the 2001 NFL Draft. Each card had a scratch off which would reveal a code to enter on upperdeck.com and the cards had an opportunity to e-volve into jersey and autograph cards. The cards carried an 'E' prefix for the card numbering.

JSY STATED PRINT RUN 300 SER.#'d SETS
AU STATED PRINT RUN 100 SER.#'d SETS
EACW Chris Weinke AU 10.00 25.00
EADB Drew Brees AU 60.00 120.00
EAFM Freddie Mitchell AU 8.00 20.00
EALT LaDainian Tomlinson AU 30.00 60.00
EAMB Michael Bennett AU 10.00 25.00
EAMV Michael Vick AU 50.00 100.00
EJCW Chris Weinke JSY 5.00 12.00
EJDB Drew Brees JSY 20.00 40.00
EJFM Freddie Mitchell JSY 4.00 10.00
EJLT LaDainian Tomlinson JSY 12.50 30.00
EJMB Michael Bennett JSY 5.00 12.00
EJMV Michael Vick JSY 15.00 40.00

2001 Upper Deck Game Jersey Autographs

me Jersey Autographs were randomly inserted in packs of 2001 Upper Deck at a rate of 1:288. This set featured a swatch of a game jersey from one of the top players from the NFL. Please note that the Jeff Garcia and Kurt Warner were originally issued as an exchange cards at the time the packs were released and Kurt Warner signed cards never were released.

STATED ODDS 1:288
BJAJ Brad Johnson 15.00 40.00
DCAJ Daunte Culpepper 10.00 25.00
IBAJ Isaac Bruce 15.00 40.00
JGAJ Jeff Garcia 10.00 25.00
JGAJX Jeff Garcia EXCH 2.00 5.00
JLAJ Jamal Lewis 15.00 40.00
JPAJ Jake Plummer 12.00 30.00
MAAJ Mike Alstott 12.00 30.00
PMAJ Peyton Manning 75.00 150.00
RMAJ Randy Moss 50.00 100.00

2001 Upper Deck Lettermen Patches

ttermen Patches were randomly inserted in packs of 2001 Upper Deck. The cards were serial numbered to 50 and contained two swatches of jersey, one college and one pro. The cards carried an 'LP' suffix for the card numbering.

STATED PRINT RUN 50 SER.#'d SETS
CWLP Chris Weinke 12.00 30.00
DMLP Deuce McAllister 15.00 40.00
FMLP Freddie Mitchell 10.00 25.00
MBLP Michael Bennett 12.00 30.00
MTLP Marques Tuiasosopo 12.00 30.00
MVLP Michael Vick 25.00 60.00

2001 Upper Deck Power Surge

wer Surge was inserted in packs of 2001 Upper Deck at a rate of 1:36. The 10-card set was highlighted with gold-foil lettering and had a rainbow holofoil background. The cards carried a 'PS' prefix for the card numbering.

COMPLETE SET (10) 7.50 20.00
STATED ODDS 1:36
PS1 Eddie George 1.00 2.50
PS2 Cris Carter 1.00 2.50
PS3 Curtis Martin .75 2.00
PS4 Jerry Rice 2.00 5.00
PS5 Jamal Anderson .75 2.00
PS6 Keyshawn Johnson .75 2.00
PS7 Ricky Williams .75 2.00
PS8 Randy Moss .75 2.00
PS9 Marvin Harrison .75 2.00
PS10 Corey Dillon .60 1.50

2001 Upper Deck Premium Patches

Premium Patches were inserted in packs of 2001 Upper Deck at a rate of 1:5000. This set features jersey swatches with premium patches highlighting them. The cards carried a 'PP' suffix along with the initials of the player's name for the card numbering.

STATED ODDS 1:5000
AFPP Drew Bledsoe 8.00 20.00
BFPP Brett Favre 20.00 50.00
BGPP Brian Griese 6.00 15.00
DLPP Dorsey Levens 8.00 20.00
EGPP Eddie George 10.00 25.00
EMPP Ed McCaffrey 8.00 20.00
FTPP Fred Taylor 6.00 15.00
IBPP Isaac Bruce 10.00 25.00
JLPP Jamal Lewis 10.00 25.00
JRPP Jerry Rice 20.00 50.00
KWPP Kurt Warner 15.00 40.00
MBPP Mark Brunell 8.00 20.00
MFPP Marshall Faulk 8.00 20.00
RSPP Rod Smith 8.00 20.00
SMPP Steve McNair 8.00 20.00
SSPP Shannon Sharpe 8.00 20.00
TAPP Troy Aikman 12.00 30.00
TCPP Tim Couch 6.00 15.00
THPP Torry Holt 8.00 20.00
TDPP Terrell Davis 8.00 20.00

2001 Upper Deck Proving Ground

ndomly inserted in packs of 2001 Upper Deck at a rate of 1:9, this 20-card set featured nsome of the top players in the NFL. The cards feature players from the NFL that have proved that their prior accomplishments were no fluke. The cards carried a 'PG' prefix to the cards numbering.

COMPLETE SET (20) 6.00 15.00
STATED ODDS 1:9
PG1 Mike Anderson .30 .75
PG2 Tim Couch .30 .75
PG3 Donovan McNabb .40 1.00
PG4 Aaron Brooks .30 .75
PG5 Trent Dilfer .30 .75
PG6 Brian Griese .30 .75
PG7 Kevin Johnson .30 .75
PG8 Ahman Green .40 1.00
PG9 Sylvester Morris .30 .75
PG10 Peter Warrick .30 .75
PG11 Tiki Barber .40 1.00
PG12 Torry Holt .40 1.00
PG13 Trent Green .30 .75
PG14 Ed McCaffrey .40 1.00
PG15 Joe Horn .30 .75
PG16 Muhsin Muhammad .30 .75
PG17 Kerry Collins .30 .75
PG18 Edgerrin James .40 1.00
PG19 Brad Hoover .40 1.00
PG20 Ron Dayne .40 1.00

2001 Upper Deck Rookie Threads

ndomly inserted in packs of 2001 Upper Deck at a rate of 1:144, this 15-card set featured swatches of game jerseys from some of the top picks from the 2001 NFL Draft. The cards carried a 'RT' suffix for the card numbering. Please note there were 2 short printed cards.

STATED ODDS 1:144
RTCC Chris Chambers 2.00 5.00
RTCJ Chad Johnson/102 SP 15.00 40.00
RTCW Chris Weinke 2.50 6.00
RTDB Drew Brees 25.00 50.00
RTDM Deuce McAllister 3.00 8.00
RTFM Freddie Mitchell 2.00 5.00
RTKB Kevan Barlow 2.50 6.00
RTKR Koren Robinson 2.50 6.00
RTLT LaDainian Tomlinson/50 SP 30.00 60.00
RTMB Michael Bennett 2.50 6.00
RTMV Michael Vick 5.00 12.00
RTRF Robert Ferguson 3.00 8.00
RTRG Rod Gardner 2.50 6.00
RTRW Reggie Wayne 4.00 10.00
RTTH Travis Henry 2.50 6.00

2001 Upper Deck Running Wild

Running Wild was randomly inserted in packs of 2001 Upper Deck at a rate of 1:24. This 15-card set featured some of the top running backs in the NFL. The cards had gold-foil highlights and a rainbow holofoil background. The cards carried a 'RW' prefix for the card numbering.

COMPLETE SET (15) 10.00 25.00
STATED ODDS 1:24
RW1 Eddie George 1.00 2.50
RW2 Corey Dillon .60 1.50
RW3 Edgerrin James .75 2.00
RW4 Charlie Garner .75 2.00
RW5 Jamal Anderson .75 2.00
RW6 Emmitt Smith 1.50 4.00
RW7 Terrell Davis .75 2.00
RW8 Mike Anderson .60 1.50
RW9 James O. Stewart .60 1.50
RW10 Ricky Watters .75 2.00
RW11 Lamar Smith .75 2.00
RW12 Curtis Martin .75 2.00
RW13 Ricky Williams .75 2.00
RW14 Stephen Davis .60 1.50
RW15 Jerome Bettis 1.00 2.50

2001 Upper Deck Starstruck

ndomly inserted in packs of 2001 Upper Deck at a rate of 1:24, this 15-card set featured top stars from the NFL. The cardfronts were highlighted with gold-foil. The cardbacks featured a gold Upper Deck hologram and the card numbers contained an 'S' prefix.

COMPLETE SET (15) 7.50 20.00
STATED ODDS 1:24
S1 Curtis Martin .60 1.50
S2 Keyshawn Johnson .60 1.50
S3 Tim Brown .75 2.00
S4 Terrell Owens .60 1.50
S5 Duce Staley .50 1.25
S6 Rich Gannon .60 1.50
S7 Mike Anderson .50 1.25
S8 Stephen Davis .50 1.25
S9 Emmitt Smith 1.25 3.00
S10 Steve McNair .60 1.50
S11 Ricky Williams .60 1.50
S12 Marcus Robinson .60 1.50
S13 Vinny Testaverde .50 1.25
S14 Rod Smith .60 1.50
S15 Drew Bledsoe .60 1.50

2001 Upper Deck Teammates Jerseys

ammate Jerseys were inserted in packs of 2001 Upper Deck at a rate of 1:144. The cards featured two jersey swatches, one for each player featured on the card. The cards featured two teammates from the NFL. The card numbers carried a 'T' suffix.

STATED ODDS 1:144
AST T.Aikman/E.Smith 8.00 20.00
BMT C.Batch/H.Moore 3.00 8.00
CMT D.Culpepper/R.Moss 4.00 10.00
DBT R.Dayne/T.Barber 4.00 10.00
FLT B.Favre/D.Levens 10.00 25.00
GOT J.Garcia/T.Owens 4.00 10.00
KJT S.King/Key.Johnson 4.00 10.00
MHT P.Manning/M.Harrison 12.00 30.00
MJT P.Manning/E.James 12.00 30.00
WFT K.Warner/M.Faulk 8.00 20.00

2002 Upper Deck

Released in September 2002, this set features 180 veterans, 30 Sunday Stars, and 100 rookies. Note that Ed Reed was intended to be card #222, but was misnumbered 310. Therefore, no cad #222 was produced and two #310 cards were issued. The Sunday Stars were inserted at a rate of 1:12, and the rookies were inserted at a rate of 1:4. Each box contained 24 packs of 8 cards. SRP was $2.99 per pack.

COMP.SET w/o SP's (180) 10.00 25.00
211-310 ROOKIE STATED ODDS 1:4
1 Jake Plummer .20 .50
2 Marcel Shipp .20 .50
3 David Boston .20 .50
4 Arnold Jackson .20 .50
5 Frank Sanders .20 .50
6 Freddie Jones .20 .50
7 Michael Vick .25 .60
8 Jamal Anderson .25 .60
9 Warrick Dunn .20 .50
10 Maurice Smith .20 .50
11 Shawn Jefferson .20 .50
12 Chris Redman .20 .50
13 Jeff Blake .25 .60
14 Jamal Lewis .25 .60
15 Travis Taylor .20 .50
16 Ray Lewis .30 .75
17 Chris McAlister .20 .50
18 Drew Bledsoe .25 .60
19 Travis Henry .20 .50
20 Larry Centers .20 .50
21 Eric Moulds .20 .50
22 Reggie Germany .20 .50
23 Peerless Price .20 .50
24 Chris Weinke .20 .50
25 Lamar Smith .20 .50
26 Nick Goings .20 .50
27 Muhsin Muhammad .20 .50
28 Isaac Byrd .20 .50
29 Wesley Walls .25 .60
30 Jim Miller .20 .50
31 Anthony Thomas .25 .60
32 Dez White .20 .50
33 David Terrell .20 .50
34 Marty Booker .20 .50
35 Brian Urlacher .30 .75
36 Jon Kitna .20 .50
37 Corey Dillon .20 .50
38 Peter Warrick .20 .50
39 Darnay Scott .25 .60
40 Chad Johnson .20 .50
41 Tim Couch .20 .50
42 James Jackson .20 .50
43 JaJuan Dawson .20 .50
44 Kevin Johnson .20 .50
45 Quincy Morgan .20 .50
46 Courtney Brown .20 .50
47 Quincy Carter .20 .50
48 Emmitt Smith .50 1.25
49 Joey Galloway .25 .60
50 Rocket Ismail .25 .60
51 Ken-Yon Rambo .20 .50
52 Brian Griese .20 .50
53 Terrell Davis .25 .60
54 Mike Anderson .20 .50
55 Shannon Sharpe .25 .60
56 Ed McCaffrey .25 .60
57 Rod Smith .25 .60
58 Mike McMahon .20 .50
59 James Stewart .20 .50
60 Az-Zahir Hakim .20 .50
61 Desmond Howard .25 .60
62 Germane Crowell .20 .50
63 Brett Favre .60 1.50
64 Ahman Green .25 .60
65 Antonio Freeman .30 .75
66 Terry Glenn .25 .60
67 Kabeer Gbaja-Biamila .20 .50
68 Kent Graham .20 .50
69 James Allen .20 .50
70 Corey Bradford .20 .50
71 Jermaine Lewis .20 .50
72 Jamie Sharper .25 .60
73 Peyton Manning .75 2.00
74 Edgerrin James .25 .60
75 Dominic Rhodes .20 .50
76 Marvin Harrison .25 .60
77 Qadry Ismail .20 .50
78 Mark Brunell .25 .60
79 Fred Taylor .20 .50
80 Stacey Mack .20 .50
81 Jimmy Smith .25 .60
82 Keenan McCardell .25 .60
83 Trent Green .20 .50
84 Priest Holmes .20 .50
85 Derrick Alexander .20 .50
86 Johnnie Morton .25 .60
87 Snoop Minnis .20 .50
88 Tony Gonzalez .25 .60
89 Jay Fiedler .25 .60
90 Ricky Williams .25 .60
91 Chris Chambers .20 .50
92 Oronde Gadsden .20 .50
93 Zach Thomas .25 .60
94 Daunte Culpepper .25 .60
95 Michael Bennett .20 .50
96 Randy Moss .25 .60
97 Sean Dawkins .25 .60
98 Tom Brady 1.50 4.00
99 Antowain Smith .25 .60
100 David Patten .20 .50
101 Troy Brown .20 .50
102 Adam Vinatieri .20 .50
103 Aaron Brooks .20 .50
104 Deuce McAllister .25 .60
105 Jake Reed .25 .60
106 Jerome Pathon .20 .50
107 Joe Horn .20 .50
108 Kyle Turley .20 .50
109 Kerry Collins .20 .50
110 Ron Dayne .25 .60
111 Tiki Barber .25 .60
112 Amani Toomer .20 .50
113 Ike Hilliard .20 .50
114 Michael Strahan .25 .60
115 Vinny Testaverde .20 .50
116 Chad Pennington .20 .50
117 Curtis Martin .25 .60
118 Santana Moss .25 .60
119 Laveranues Coles .25 .60
120 Wayne Chrebet .20 .50
121 Rich Gannon .25 .60
122 Charlie Garner .25 .60
123 Jerry Rice .60 1.50
124 Tim Brown .30 .75
125 Charles Woodson .30 .75
126 Donovan McNabb .25 .60
127 Duce Staley .20 .50
128 Correll Buckhalter .20 .50
129 Freddie Mitchell .20 .50
130 James Thrash .25 .60
131 Todd Pinkston .20 .50
132 Kordell Stewart .20 .50
133 Jerome Bettis .30 .75
134 Chris Fuamatu-Ma'afala .20 .50
135 Hines Ward .25 .60
136 Plaxico Burress .20 .50
137 Kendrell Bell .20 .50
138 Doug Flutie .25 .60
139 Drew Brees .60 1.50
140 LaDainian Tomlinson .30 .75
141 Curtis Conway .25 .60
142 Tim Dwight .20 .50
143 Junior Seau .25 .60
144 Jeff Garcia .20 .50
145 Garrison Hearst .20 .50
146 Kevan Barlow .20 .50
147 Terrell Owens .25 .60
148 J.J. Stokes .20 .50
149 Trent Dilfer .20 .50
150 Shaun Alexander .20 .50
151 Ricky Watters .25 .60
152 Bobby Engram .20 .50
153 Koren Robinson .20 .50
154 Kurt Warner .25 .60
155 Marshall Faulk .25 .60
156 Isaac Bruce .30 .75
157 Ricky Proehl .25 .60
158 Terrence Wilkins .20 .50
159 Torry Holt .25 .60
160 Brad Johnson .25 .60
161 Shaun King .20 .50
162 Rob Johnson .25 .60
163 Mike Alstott .20 .50
164 Michael Pittman .25 .60
165 Keyshawn Johnson .25 .60
166 Steve McNair .25 .60
167 Eddie George .25 .60
168 Derrick Mason .20 .50
169 Kevin Dyson .25 .60
170 Frank Wycheck .20 .50
171 Jevon Kearse .20 .50
172 Danny Wuerffel .25 .60
173 Stephen Davis .20 .50
174 Michael Westbrook .20 .50
175 Rod Gardner .20 .50
176 Champ Bailey .25 .60
177 Darrell Green .30 .75
178 Kurt Warner CL .20 .50
179 Brett Favre CL .50 1.25
180 Randy Moss CL .20 .50
181 David Boston SS .75 2.00
182 Jake Plummer SS .75 2.00
183 Michael Vick SS 1.00 2.50
184 Drew Bledsoe SS 1.00 2.50
185 Anthony Thomas SS 1.00 2.50
186 Tim Couch SS .75 2.00
187 Emmitt Smith SS 2.00 5.00
188 Ahman Green SS 1.00 2.50
189 Brett Favre SS 2.50 6.00
190 Edgerrin James SS 1.00 2.50
191 Peyton Manning SS 3.00 8.00
192 Mark Brunell SS 1.00 2.50
193 Daunte Culpepper SS 1.00 2.50
194 Randy Moss SS 1.00 2.50
195 Tom Brady SS 6.00 15.00
196 Aaron Brooks SS .75 2.00
197 Ricky Williams SS 1.00 2.50
198 Curtis Martin SS 1.00 2.50
199 Jerry Rice SS 2.50 6.00
200 Donovan McNabb SS 1.00 2.50
201 Jerome Bettis SS 1.25 3.00
202 Kordell Stewart SS .75 2.00
203 LaDainian Tomlinson SS 1.25 3.00
204 Jeff Garcia SS .75 2.00
205 Terrell Owens SS 1.00 2.50
206 Shaun Alexander SS .75 2.00
207 Kurt Warner SS 1.00 2.50
208 Marshall Faulk SS 1.00 2.50
209 Keyshawn Johnson SS 1.00 2.50
210 Steve McNair SS 1.00 2.50
211 Damien Anderson RC 1.25 3.00
212 Jason McAddley RC 1.50 4.00
213 Josh McCown RC 2.00 5.00
214 Josh Scobey RC 1.50 4.00
215 Preston Parsons RC 1.25 3.00
216 Dusty Bonner RC 1.25 3.00
217 Kahlil Hill RC 1.25 3.00
218 Kurt Kittner RC 1.25 3.00
219 T.J. Duckett RC 1.25 3.00
220 Chester Taylor RC 2.00 5.00
221 Kalimba Edwards RC 1.50 4.00
223 Ron Johnson RC 1.50 4.00
224 Tellis Redmon RC 1.25 3.00
225 Wes Pate RC 1.25 3.00
226 David Priestley RC 1.25 3.00
227 Josh Reed RC 1.50 4.00
228 Mike Williams RC 1.25 3.00
229 Ryan Denney RC 1.25 3.00
230 DeShaun Foster RC 2.00 5.00
231 Julius Peppers RC 3.00 8.00
232 Randy Fasani RC 1.25 3.00
233 Adrian Peterson RC 1.50 4.00
234 Alex Brown RC 2.00 5.00
235 Gavin Hoffman RC 1.25 3.00
236 Levi Jones RC 1.25 3.00
237 Andra Davis RC 1.25 3.00
238 Andre Davis RC 1.25 3.00
239 William Green RC 1.50 4.00
240 Antonio Bryant RC 2.00 5.00
241 Chad Hutchinson RC 1.25 3.00
242 Roy Williams RC 1.25 3.00
243 Woody Dantzler RC 1.50 4.00
244 Ashley Lelie RC 1.25 3.00
245 Clinton Portis RC 2.00 5.00
246 Lamont Thompson RC 1.50 4.00
247 James Mungro RC 2.00 5.00
248 Joey Harrington RC 1.25 3.00
249 Luke Staley RC 1.25 3.00
250 Craig Nall RC 1.50 4.00
251 Javon Walker RC 2.00 5.00
252 Najeh Davenport RC 1.25 3.00
253 David Carr RC 1.25 3.00
254 Saleem Rasheed RC 1.25 3.00
255 Mike Rumph RC 1.25 3.00
256 Jabar Gaffney RC 1.25 3.00
257 Jonathan Wells RC 1.50 4.00
258 Dwight Freeney RC 2.50 6.00
259 Larry Tripplett RC 1.25 3.00
260 David Garrard RC 1.50 4.00
261 John Henderson RC 1.50 4.00
262 Ryan Sims RC 2.00 5.00
263 Leonard Henry RC 1.25 3.00
264 Brian Allen RC 1.50 4.00
265 Atrews Bell RC 1.25 3.00
266 Bryant McKinnie RC 1.25 3.00
267 Kelly Campbell RC 1.50 4.00
268 Raonall Smith RC 1.25 3.00
269 Antwoine Womack RC 1.25 3.00
270 Daniel Graham RC 1.50 4.00
271 Deion Branch RC 2.00 5.00
272 Sam Simmons RC 1.25 3.00
273 Rohan Davey RC 2.00 5.00
274 Charles Grant RC 2.00 5.00
275 Derrick Lewis RC 1.25 3.00
276 Donte Stallworth RC 2.00 5.00
277 J.T. O'Sullivan RC 1.50 4.00
278 Keyuo Craver RC 1.25 3.00
279 Ricky Williams RC 1.50 4.00
280 Bryan Thomas RC 1.25 3.00
281 Jeremy Shockey RC 2.00 5.00
282 Tim Carter RC 1.50 4.00
283 Larry Ned RC 1.25 3.00
284 Napoleon Harris RC 1.50 4.00
285 Phillip Buchanon RC 2.00 5.00
286 Ronald Curry RC 1.25 3.00
287 Brian Westbrook RC 2.50 6.00
288 Freddie Milons RC 1.25 3.00
289 Lito Sheppard RC 2.00 5.00
290 Antwaan Randle El RC 1.50 4.00
291 Lee Mays RC 1.25 3.00
292 Daryl Jones RC 1.25 3.00
293 Justin Peelle RC 1.25 3.00
294 Quentin Jammer RC 2.00 5.00
295 Reche Caldwell RC 1.50 4.00
296 Seth Burford RC 1.25 3.00
297 Terry Charles RC 1.25 3.00
298 Brandon Doman RC 1.25 3.00
299 Maurice Morris RC 1.50 4.00
300 Eric Crouch RC 2.00 5.00
301 Lamar Gordon RC 1.50 4.00
302 Marquise Walker RC 1.25 3.00
303 Tracey Wistrom RC 1.50 4.00
304 Travis Stephens RC 1.25 3.00
305 Herb Haygood RC 1.25 3.00
306 Albert Haynesworth RC 2.00 5.00
307 Rocky Calmus RC 1.50 4.00
308 Cliff Russell RC 1.25 3.00
309 Ladell Betts RC 2.00 5.00
310A Patrick Ramsey RC 1.50 4.00
310B Ed Reed RC 6.00 15.00

2002 Upper Deck Battle-Worn

Inserted at a rate of 1:144, this set features a piece of game worn jersey of top NFL stars cut out in the shape of the NFL shield.

STATED ODDS 1:144
*GOLD/75: .8X TO 2X BASIC JSY
GOLD PRINT RUN 75 SER.#'d SETS
BWAT Anthony Thomas SP 4.00 10.00
BWBG Brian Griese SP 3.00 8.00
BWBU Brian Urlacher 4.00 10.00
BWJK Jevon Kearse 2.50 6.00
BWJS Junior Seau 3.00 8.00
BWMS Michael Strahan 3.00 8.00
BWRH Rodney Harrison 2.50 6.00
BWRL Ray Lewis 4.00 10.00
BWTB Tiki Barber 3.00 8.00
BWTD Terrell Davis 3.00 8.00

2002 Upper Deck Blitz Brigade

Inserted at a rate of 1:12, this set focuses on some of the NFL's best defenders.

COMPLETE SET (14) 6.00 15.00
STATED ODDS 1:12 HOB/RET
BB1 Ray Lewis .75 2.00
BB2 Brian Urlacher .75 2.00
BB3 Kabeer Gbaja-Biamila .50 1.25
BB4 Zach Thomas .60 1.50
BB5 Michael Strahan .60 1.50
BB6 Charles Woodson .75 2.00
BB7 Kendrell Bell .50 1.25
BB8 Junior Seau .60 1.50
BB9 Rodney Harrison .50 1.25
BB10 Levon Kirkland .50 1.25
BB11 Warren Sapp .60 1.50
BB12 Jevon Kearse .50 1.25
BB13 Bruce Smith .60 1.50
BB14 Champ Bailey .60 1.50

2002 Upper Deck Buy Back Autographs

Randomly inserted in packs, this set features previously released cards that were bought back and then hand signed and numbered to various quantities. Most cards were issued via mail redemption cards in packs. When known, we have published the stated print run next to the player's name in our checklist. Note that all cards were issued with a separate certificate with matching serial numbers on the card and certificate beginning with the letters "AAA."

STATED PRINT RUN 1-100
SERIAL #'d UNDER 20 NOT PRICED
AG A.Green 01UDTT/22 15.00 40.00
JG J.Garcia 01UDTT/23 10.00 25.00
KS K.Stewart 99UD/33 8.00 20.00
BJ1 B.Johnson 00UDL/48 8.00 20.00
PM1 Manning 99UDMVP/26 75.00 150.00
PM2 Manning 99UDPOH/25 75.00 150.00
PM3 P.Manning 99SPA/100 50.00 100.00
PM4 P.Manning 99UD/39 60.00 120.00
PM6 P.Manning 00UD/21 75.00 150.00
PM7 Manning 00UDMVP/32 75.00 150.00
PM11 P.Manning 01UDTT/39 60.00 120.00
TC1 T.Couch 00UD/29 10.00 25.00
TC2 T.Couch 01UDTT/27 10.00 25.00
TG2 T.Gonzalez 01LEG/21 15.00 40.00

2002 Upper Deck First Team Fabrics

Inserted in packs at rate of 1 in 144, this set features game used jersey swatches cut out in the form of the number 1.

STATED ODDS 1:144 HOB/RET
*GOLD/150: .6X TO 1.5X BASIC JERSEY
GOLD PRINT RUN 150 SER.#'d SETS
FTCD Corey Dillon 2.50 6.00
FTDB David Boston 2.50 6.00
FTES Emmitt Smith 6.00 15.00
FTJP Jake Plummer 2.00 6.00
FTJS Jimmy Smith 3.00 8.00
FTKJ Keyshawn Johnson 3.00 8.00
FTMH Marvin Harrison 3.00 8.00
FTRS Rod Smith 3.00 8.00
FTTB Tom Brady 20.00 50.00
FTTC Tim Couch 2.50 6.00

2002 Upper Deck Flight Suits Jerseys

serted in packs at a rate of 1:288, this set features a swatch of game used jersey.

STATED ODDS 1:288
*GOLD/25: .8X TO 2X BASIC JERSEY
GOLD PRINT RUN 25 SER.#'d SETS
FSBF Brett Favre 10.00 25.00
FSDC Daunte Culpepper 4.00 10.00
FSDM Donovan McNabb 4.00 10.00
FSKS Kordell Stewart 3.00 8.00
FSMV Michael Vick 4.00 10.00
FSTB Tom Brady 25.00 60.00

2002 Upper Deck Fourth Quarter Fabrics

serted in packs at a rate of 1:288, this set features a swatch of game worn jersey cut out in the shape of the number 4.

STATED ODDS 1:288 HOB/RET
*GOLD: .6X TO 1.5X BASIC JERSEYS
*GOLD/150: .4X TO 1X BASIC JSY SP
GOLD PRINT RUN 150 SER.#'d SETS
FQBF Brett Favre 10.00 25.00
FQBG Brian Griese 3.00 8.00
FQJR Jerry Rice SP 12.00 30.00
FQKW Kurt Warner 4.00 10.00
FQMF Marshall Faulk SP 5.00 12.00
FQPM Peyton Manning 12.00 30.00
FQRM Randy Moss 4.00 10.00

2002 Upper Deck Ground Shakers Jerseys

serted in packs at a rate of 1:288, this set features a piece of game used jersey on each card.

STATED ODDS 1:288
*GOLD/25: .8X TO 2X BASIC JERSEY
GOLD PRINT RUN 25 SER.#'d SETS
GSAT Anthony Thomas 4.00 10.00
GSCM Curtis Martin 4.00 10.00
GSES Emmitt Smith 8.00 20.00
GSLT LaDainian Tomlinson 5.00 12.00
GSTD Terrell Davis 4.00 10.00

2002 Upper Deck Kick-Off Classics Jerseys

serted in packs at a rate of 1:288, this set features a swatch of game used jersey cut out in the shape of the letter "C".

STATED ODDS 1:288 HOB/RET
*GOLD/150: .5X TO 1.2X BASIC JSY
GOLD PRINT RUN 150 SER.#'d SETS
KOBF Brett Favre 8.00 20.00
KOCC Chris Chambers 2.50 6.00
KODM Donovan McNabb 3.00 8.00
KOEJ Edgerrin James 3.00 8.00
KOLT LaDainian Tomlinson 4.00 10.00

2002 Upper Deck NFL Patches

Randomly inserted into packs, this one of a kind set features a game used NFL logo patch. Each card is serial #'d to 1. As the print run is one serial numbered card, no pricing is available due to market scarcity.

STATED PRINT RUN 1 SER.#'d SET

2002 Upper Deck Pigskin Patches

Inserted in packs at a rate of 1:2500, this set features top NFL quarterbacks and recievers with a swatch of game worn jersey cut out in the shape of the letter "P" on the card front. Some cards were issued in hobby packs only as noted below.

STATED ODDS 1:2500 HOB/RET
PPAB Aaron Brooks 12.00 30.00
PPAT Anthony Thomas II 15.00 40.00
PPBF Brett Favre 40.00 100.00
PPDC Daunte Culpepper H 15.00 40.00
PPDF Doug Flutie H 15.00 40.00
PPDM Donovan McNabb H 12.00 30.00
PPEJ Edgerrin James 15.00 40.00
PPES Emmitt Smith 30.00 80.00
PPJB Jerome Bettis 40.00 80.00
PPJG Jeff Garcia 12.00 30.00
PPJR Jerry Rice 40.00 100.00
PPKW Kurt Warner 15.00 40.00
PPLT LaDainian Tomlinson H
PPMF Marshall Faulk H 15.00 40.00
PPMV Michael Vick H 15.00 40.00
PPPM Peyton Manning 50.00 120.00
PPRG Rich Gannon H 15.00 40.00
PPRM Randy Moss 15.00 40.00
PPRW Ricky Williams H 15.00 40.00
PPTB Tom Brady H 100.00 250.00

2002 Upper Deck Playbooks Jerseys

Randomly inserted in packs, cards from this set feature a fold-out design including a swatch of game-worn jersey. According to Upper Deck, a total of 200-cards were produced.

PBAB Aaron Brooks 12.00 30.00
PBAG Ahman Green 15.00 40.00
PBAT Anthony Thomas 15.00 40.00
PBBF Brett Favre 40.00 100.00
PBBO David Boston 12.00 30.00
PBCM Curtis Martin 15.00 40.00
PBDC Daunte Culpepper 15.00 40.00
PBDM Donovan McNabb 15.00 40.00
PBJB Jerome Bettis 20.00 50.00
PBKW Kurt Warner 15.00 40.00
PBLT LaDainian Tomlinson 20.00 50.00
PBMF Marshall Faulk 15.00 40.00
PBPM Peyton Manning 50.00 120.00
PBRS Rod Smith 15.00 40.00
PBTB Tom Brady 100.00 250.00

2002 Upper Deck Power Surge

Inserted at a rate of 1:12, this set features top players in the NFL. The cards have the words "Power Surge" in both small and large print on the fronts.

COMPLETE SET (14) 12.50 30.00
STATED ODDS 1:12 HOB/RET
PS1 Michael Vick .75 2.00
PS2 Anthony Thomas .75 2.00
PS3 Emmitt Smith 1.50 4.00
PS4 Terrell Davis .75 2.00
PS5 Brett Favre 2.00 5.00
PS6 Edgerrin James .75 2.00
PS7 Peyton Manning 2.50 6.00
PS8 Ricky Williams .75 2.00
PS9 Curtis Martin .75 2.00
PS10 Jerome Bettis 1.00 2.50
PS11 LaDainian Tomlinson 1.00 2.50
PS12 Shaun Alexander .60 1.50
PS13 Kurt Warner .75 2.00
PS14 Marshall Faulk .75 2.00

2002 Upper Deck Rookie Futures Jersey

Inserted at a rate of 1:72, this set features event used memorabilia from some of the NFL's top 2002 rookies.

STATED ODDS 1:72
*GOLD/150: .5X TO 1.5X BASIC JSY
GOLD PRINT RUN 150 SER.#'d SETS
RFAL Ashley Lelie 2.50 6.00
RFCP Clinton Portis 4.00 10.00
RFDC David Carr 2.50 6.00
RFDF DeShaun Foster 4.00 10.00
RFDS Donte Stallworth 4.00 10.00
RFEL Antwaan Randle El 3.00 8.00
RFJH Joey Harrington 2.50 6.00
RFJR Josh Reed 3.00 8.00
RFPR Patrick Ramsey 3.00 8.00
RFWG William Green 3.00 8.00

2002 Upper Deck Stadium Swatches

Inserted in packs at a rate of 1:144, this set features a swatch of game used jersey cut out in the shape of an "S".

STATED ODDS 1:144
*GOLD/75: .6X TO 1.5X BASIC JSY
GOLD PRINT RUN 75 SER.#'d SETS
SSDF Doug Flutie 4.00 10.00
SSEG Eddie George 4.00 10.00
SSMB Mark Brunell SP 4.00 10.00
SSMB Michael Bennett 3.00 8.00
SSPW Peter Warrick 3.00 8.00
SSQC Quincy Carter SP 3.00 8.00

2002 Upper Deck Synchronicity

Inserted at a rate of 1:12, this set features the games best quarterback/receiver duos.

COMPLETE SET (14) 10.00 25.00
STATED ODDS 1:12 HOB/RET
SY1 J.Plummer/D.Boston .50 1.25
SY2 M.Vick/W.Dunn .60 1.50
SY3 D.Bledsoe/J.Reed .60 1.50
SY4 T.Couch/A.Davis .50 1.25
SY5 B.Favre/J.Walker 1.50 4.00
SY6 P.Manning/M.Harrison 2.00 5.00
SY7 M.Brunell/J.Smith .60 1.50
SY8 D.Culpepper/R.Moss .60 1.50
SY9 T.Brady/T.Brown 4.00 10.00
SY10 A.Brooks/D.Stallworth .75 2.00
SY11 K.Warner/I.Bruce .75 2.00
SY12 D.McNabb/F.Mitchell .60 1.50
SY13 K.Stewart/P. Burress .50 1.25
SY14 J.Garcia/T.Owens .60 1.50

2002 Upper Deck Uniforms

serted in packs at a rate of 1:72,this set features a swatch of game used jersey cut out in the shape of a "U" on card front.

STATED ODDS 1:72 HOB/RET
*GOLD/150: .6X TO 1.5X BASIC JSY
GOLD PRINT RUN 150 SER.#'d SETS
UDUBG Brian Griese 2.50 6.00
UDUBJ Brad Johnson 3.00 8.00
UDUCC Chris Chambers 2.50 6.00
UDUDB Drew Brees 8.00 20.00
UDUFT Fred Taylor 2.50 6.00
UDUIB Isaac Bruce 4.00 10.00
UDUJG Jeff Garcia 2.50 6.00
UDUJP Jerome Pathon 2.50 6.00
UDUMB Mark Brunell 3.00 8.00
UDUPM Peyton Manning 10.00 25.00
UDUQM Quincy Morgan 2.50 6.00
UDURD Ron Dayne 3.00 8.00
UDUSS Shannon Sharpe 3.00 8.00
UDUTB Tim Brown 4.00 10.00
UDUTH Travis Henry 2.50 6.00

2002 Upper Deck Wildcard Jerseys

Inserted in packs at a rate of 1:144, this set features a swatch of game used jersey.

STATED ODDS 1:144 HOB/RET
*GOLD/150: .5X TO 1.2X BASIC JSY
GOLD PRINT RUN 150 SER.#'d SETS
WCAG Ahman Green 4.00 10.00
WCCD Corey Dillon 3.00 8.00
WCDT David Terrell 3.00 8.00
WCIB Isaac Bruce 5.00 12.00
WCJP Jerome Pathon 3.00 8.00
WCMB Michael Bennett 3.00 8.00
WCMV Michael Vick 4.00 10.00
WCPW Peter Warrick 3.00 8.00
WCRM Randy Moss 4.00 10.00
WCTO Terrell Owens 4.00 10.00

2002 Upper Deck Twizzlers

7 Donovan McNabb 1.25 3.00
8 Donovan McNabb 1.25 3.00

2003 Upper Deck

Released in August of 2003, this set consists of 285 cards, including 180 veterans, 30 short prints (inserted 1:12), and 75 rookies. Rookies 211-240 were inserted at a rate of 1:4, and rookies 241-285 were inserted at a rate of 1:8. Boxes contained 24 packs of 8 cards, with an SRP of $2.99.

COMPLETE SET (285) 60.00 120.00
COMP.SET w/o SP's (180) 10.00 25.00
1 Brad Johnson .25 .60
2 Derrick Brooks .20 .50
3 Simeon Rice .20 .50
4 Warren Sapp .25 .60
5 Thomas Jones .20 .50
6 Mike Alstott .20 .50
7 Michael Pittman .20 .50
8 Tim Brown .30 .75
9 Rich Gannon .25 .60
10 Charlie Garner .25 .60
11 Jerry Porter .20 .50
12 Phillip Buchanon .20 .50
13 Charles Woodson .30 .75
14 James Thrash .20 .50
15 Duce Staley .20 .50
16 Brian Westbrook .20 .50
17 Correll Buckhalter .20 .50
18 Koy Detmer .20 .50
19 Brian Dawkins .30 .75
20 Jon Ritchie .20 .50
21 Ahman Green .25 .60
22 Donald Driver .25 .60
23 Bubba Franks .25 .60
24 Javon Walker .25 .60
25 Kabeer Gbaja-Biamila .20 .50
26 Robert Ferguson .20 .50
27 Eddie George .25 .60
28 Jevon Kearse .20 .50
29 Billy Volek .25 .60
30 Frank Wycheck .20 .50
31 Derrick Mason .20 .50
32 Tommy Maddox .20 .50
33 Jerome Bettis .30 .75
34 Antwaan Randle El .20 .50
35 Amos Zereoue .20 .50
36 Hines Ward .25 .60
37 Jeff Garcia .20 .50
38 Terrell Owens .25 .60
39 Tim Rattay .20 .50
40 Brandon Doman .20 .50
41 Tai Streets .20 .50
42 Garrison Hearst .20 .50
43 Kerry Collins .20 .50
44 Tiki Barber .25 .60
45 Amani Toomer .20 .50
46 Jesse Palmer .20 .50
47 Tim Carter .20 .50
48 Michael Strahan .25 .60
49 Ike Hilliard .20 .50
50 Marvin Harrison .25 .60
51 Peyton Manning .75 2.00
52 Marcus Pollard .20 .50
53 James Mungro .20 .50
54 Reggie Wayne .25 .60
55 Peerless Price .20 .50
56 Warrick Dunn .20 .50
57 T.J. Duckett .20 .50
58 Keith Brooking .25 .60
59 Doug Johnson .20 .50
60 Brian Finneran .20 .50

61 Chad Pennington .20 .50
62 Curtis Martin .25 .60
63 Marvin Jones .20 .50
64 Wayne Chrebet .20 .50
65 LaMont Jordan .25 .60
66 Curtis Conway .20 .50
67 Vinny Testaverde .20 .50
68 Tim Couch .20 .50
69 William Green .20 .50
70 Andre Davis .20 .50
71 Quincy Morgan .20 .50
72 Dennis Northcutt .20 .50
73 Kelly Holcomb .20 .50
74 Jake Plummer .20 .50
75 Mike Anderson .20 .50
76 Ashley Lelie .20 .50
77 Ed McCaffrey .25 .60
78 Shannon Sharpe .25 .60
79 Rod Smith .25 .60
80 Terrell Davis .25 .60
81 Antowain Smith .25 .60
82 Kevin Faulk .20 .50
83 David Patten .20 .50
84 Deion Branch .20 .50
85 Troy Brown .20 .50
86 Rohan Davey .20 .50
87 Jay Fiedler .20 .50
88 Randy McMichael .20 .50
89 Derrius Thompson .20 .50
90 Jason Taylor .25 .60
91 Zach Thomas .25 .60
92 Ricky Williams .25 .60
93 Deuce McAllister .25 .60
94 Donte Stallworth .20 .50
95 Jerome Pathon .20 .50
96 Michael Lewis .20 .50
97 Joe Horn .20 .50
98 Priest Holmes .20 .50
99 Johnnie Morton .25 .60
100 Eddie Kennison .20 .50
101 Dante Hall .20 .50
102 Tony Gonzalez .25 .60
103 Marc Boerigter .20 .50
104 Drew Brees .30 .75
105 David Boston .20 .50
106 Reche Caldwell .20 .50
107 Tim Dwight .20 .50
108 Doug Flutie .25 .60
109 Drew Bledsoe .25 .60
110 Eric Moulds .20 .50
111 Alex Van Pelt .20 .50
112 Charles Johnson .20 .50
113 Takeo Spikes .20 .50
114 Josh Reed .20 .50
115 Ladell Betts .20 .50
116 Laveranues Coles .20 .50
117 Champ Bailey .25 .60
118 Trung Canidate .20 .50
119 Kenny Watson .20 .50
120 Rod Gardner .20 .50
121 Kurt Warner .25 .60
122 Lamar Gordon .20 .50
123 Shaun McDonald RC .30 .75
124 Marc Bulger .20 .50
125 Isaac Bruce .30 .75
126 Torry Holt .25 .60
127 Matt Hasselbeck .20 .50
128 Maurice Morris .20 .50
129 Bobby Engram .20 .50
130 Darrell Jackson .25 .60
131 Koren Robinson .25 .60
132 Chris Redman .20 .50
133 Todd Heap .20 .50
134 Travis Taylor .20 .50
135 Ron Johnson .20 .50
136 Ray Lewis .30 .75
137 Jake Delhomme .20 .50
138 Muhsin Muhammad .20 .50
139 Stephen Davis .20 .50
140 Julius Peppers .30 .75
141 Rodney Peete .20 .50
142 Mark Brunell .25 .60
143 Jimmy Smith .25 .60
144 Kyle Brady .20 .50
145 Kevin Lockett .20 .50
146 David Garrard .20 .50
147 Fred Taylor .20 .50
148 Michael Bennett .20 .50
149 Ronald Bellamy RC .30 .75
150 Randy Moss .25 .60
151 D'Wayne Bates .20 .50
152 Josh McCown .25 .60
153 Marquise Walker .20 .50
154 Jeff Blake .25 .60
155 Freddie Jones .20 .50
156 Marcel Shipp .20 .50
157 Troy Hambrick .20 .50
158 Joey Galloway .25 .60
159 Terry Glenn .25 .60
160 Roy Williams .20 .50
161 Antonio Bryant .20 .50
162 Quincy Carter .20 .50
163 Anthony Thomas .25 .60
164 Marty Booker .20 .50
165 Dez White .20 .50
166 Adrian Peterson .20 .50
167 Kordell Stewart .20 .50
168 David Terrell .20 .50
169 Jabar Gaffney .20 .50
170 Bennie Joppru RC .25 .60
171 Corey Bradford .20 .50
172 David Carr .20 .50
173 James Stewart .20 .50
174 Ty Detmer .20 .50
175 Az-Zahir Hakim .20 .50
176 Bill Schroeder .20 .50
177 Jon Kitna .20 .50
178 Chad Johnson .20 .50
179 Ron Dugans .20 .50
180 Peter Warrick .20 .50
181 Brett Favre SS 2.50 6.00
182 Emmitt Smith SS 2.00 5.00
183 LaDainian Tomlinson SS 1.25 3.00
184 Joey Harrington SS .75 2.00
185 Brian Urlacher SS 1.25 3.00
186 Daunte Culpepper SS 1.00 2.50
187 Jamal Lewis SS 1.00 2.50
188 Shaun Alexander SS .75 2.00
189 Marshall Faulk SS 1.00 2.50
190 Travis Henry SS .75 2.00
191 Trent Green SS .75 2.00
192 Aaron Brooks SS .75 2.00
193 Chris Chambers SS .75 2.00
194 Tom Brady SS 5.00 12.00
195 Clinton Portis SS .75 2.00
196 Kevin Johnson SS .75 2.00
197 Santana Moss SS 1.00 2.50
198 Michael Vick SS 1.00 2.50
199 Edgerrin James SS 1.00 2.50
200 Jeremy Shockey SS .75 2.00
201 Kevan Barlow SS .75 2.00
202 Plaxico Burress SS .75 2.00
203 Steve McNair SS 1.00 2.50
204 Donovan McNabb SS 1.00 2.50
205 Jerry Rice SS 2.50 6.00
206 Keyshawn Johnson SS 1.25 3.00
207 Patrick Ramsey SS 1.00 2.50
208 Stephen Davis SS .75 2.00
209 Corey Dillon SS .75 2.00
210 Chad Hutchinson SS .75 2.00
211 Brad Banks RC 1.50 4.00
212 Kliff Kingsbury RC 2.00 5.00
213 Jason Gesser RC 1.50 4.00
214 Jason Johnson RC 1.25 3.00
215 Brian St.Pierre RC 1.25 3.00
216 Ken Dorsey RC 1.50 4.00
217 Seneca Wallace RC 1.50 4.00
218 Brooks Bollinger RC 1.50 4.00
219 Chris Brown RC 1.25 3.00
220 B.J Askew RC 1.50 4.00
221 Earnest Graham RC 2.00 5.00
222 Quentin Griffin RC 1.50 4.00
223 Musa Smith RC 1.25 3.00
224 Artose Pinner RC 1.25 3.00
225 Domanick Davis RC 1.50 4.00
226 Anquan Boldin RC 2.00 5.00
227 Talman Gardner RC 1.25 3.00
228 Brandon Lloyd RC 2.00 5.00
229 Bryant Johnson RC 2.00 5.00
230 Kareem Kelly RC 1.25 3.00
231 Arnaz Battle RC 2.00 5.00
232 Keenan Howry RC 1.25 3.00
233 Justin Gage RC 1.50 4.00
234 Tyrone Calico RC 1.25 3.00
235 Teyo Johnson RC 1.50 4.00
236 Malaefou MacKenzie RC 1.25 3.00
237 Terence Newman RC 2.00 5.00
238 Marcus Trufant RC 1.50 4.00
239 Mike Doss RC 2.00 5.00
240 Terrell Suggs RC 1.50 4.00
241 Carson Palmer RC 4.00 10.00
242 Byron Leftwich RC 2.50 6.00
243 Rex Grossman RC 2.50 6.00
244 Kyle Boller RC 2.00 5.00
245 Dave Ragone RC 2.00 5.00
246 Chris Simms RC 2.00 5.00
247 Larry Johnson RC 2.50 6.00
248 Lee Suggs RC 2.00 5.00
249 Justin Fargas RC 3.00 8.00
250 Onterrio Smith RC 2.00 5.00
251 Willis McGahee RC 2.50 6.00
252 Charles Rogers RC 2.50 6.00
253 Andre Johnson RC 5.00 12.00
254 Taylor Jacobs RC 2.00 5.00
255 Kelley Washington RC 2.00 5.00
256 Tony Romo RC 10.00 25.00
257 Jerel Myers RC 1.50 4.00
258 Kirk Farmer RC 2.00 5.00
259 Kevin Walter RC 4.00 10.00
260 Gibran Hamdan RC 1.50 4.00
261 Juston Wood RC 1.50 4.00
262 Travis Anglin RC 1.50 4.00
263 Marquel Blackwell RC 1.50 4.00
264 Jason Thomas RC 1.50 4.00
265 Carl Ford RC 1.50 4.00
266 Walter Young RC 1.50 4.00
267 Sultan McCullough RC 1.50 4.00
268 Dahrran Diedrick RC 1.50 4.00
269 Cecil Sapp RC 1.50 4.00
270 Doug Gabriel RC 2.00 5.00
271 LaBrandon Toefield RC 1.50 4.00
272 Adrian Madise RC 1.50 4.00
273 J.R. Tolver RC 2.00 5.00
274 Kevin Curtis RC 1.50 4.00
275 Bobby Wade RC 2.00 5.00
276 Sam Aiken RC 2.00 5.00
277 Mike Bush RC 1.50 4.00
278 Billy McMullen RC 1.50 4.00
279 Bethel Johnson RC 1.50 4.00
280 David Kircus RC 2.00 5.00
281 Zuriel Smith RC 1.50 4.00
282 LaTarence Dunbar RC 1.50 4.00
283 Nate Burleson RC 2.00 5.00
284 Antwone Savage RC 1.50 4.00
285 Terrence Edwards RC 1.50 4.00

2003 Upper Deck Gold

*VETS 1-180: 8X TO 20X BASIC CARDS
*SS 181-210: 2X TO 5X
*ROOKIES 211-240: 1.2X TO 3X
*ROOKIES 241-255: .8X TO 2X
*ROOKIES 256-285: 1X TO 2.5X
STATED PRINT RUN 50 SER.#'d SETS
256 Tony Romo 30.00 80.00

2003 Upper Deck Game Jerseys

is set features authentic game worn jersey swatches. Group 1 was inserted at a rate of 1:48 hobby packs and 1:96 retail packs. Group 2 was inserted at a rate of 1:72 hobby packs and 1:144 retail packs. A gold parallel version also exists, with each card serial numbered to 99. Finally, Logo, Names, and Numbers versions for some cards were produced, but all are too scarce to establish pricing for.

GROUP 1 STATED ODDS 1:48HOB, 1:96RET
GROUP 2 STATED ODDS 1:72 HOB, 1:144 RET
*GOLD/99: .8X TO 2X BASIC JSY
GOLD PRINT RUN 99 SER.#'d SETS
GJAB Aaron Brooks 2 3.00 8.00
GJAL Ashley Lelie 1 3.00 8.00
GJAT Amani Toomer 1 3.00 8.00
GJBF Brett Favre 2 10.00 25.00
GJBG Brian Griese 1 3.00 8.00
GJBJ Brad Johnson 1 4.00 10.00
GJBR Antonio Bryant 2 3.00 8.00
GJCB1 Champ Bailey 1 4.00 10.00
GJCB2 Correll Buckhalter 1 3.00 8.00
GJCJ Chad Johnson 1 3.00 8.00
GJCP Clinton Portis 2 3.00 8.00
GJCW Charles Woodson 1 5.00 12.00
GJDC David Carr 2 3.00 8.00
GJDS Duce Staley 1 3.00 8.00
GJEM Eric Moulds 1 3.00 8.00
GJJB Jerome Bettis 2 5.00 12.00
GJJK Jevon Kearse 1 3.00 8.00
GJJL Jamal Lewis 2 4.00 10.00
GJJS Jeremy Shockey 2 3.00 8.00
GJKJ Kevin Johnson 2 3.00 8.00
GJKS Kordell Stewart 1 3.00 8.00
GJKW Kurt Warner 2 6.00 15.00
GJMA Mike Alstott 1 3.00 8.00
GJMB Mark Brunell 2 4.00 10.00
GJMF Marshall Faulk 2 4.00 10.00
GJMS Michael Strahan 1 4.00 10.00
GJMV Michael Vick 2 4.00 10.00
GJOG Olandis Gary 1 3.00 8.00
GJPM Peyton Manning 2 12.00 30.00
GJPW Peter Warrick 1 3.00 8.00
GJQJ Quentin Jammer 1 3.00 8.00
GJRG Rich Gannon 2 4.00 10.00
GJRL Ray Lewis 1 5.00 12.00
GJRM Randy Moss 2 4.00 10.00
GJRW Roy Williams 1 3.00 8.00
GJSE Junior Seau 2 4.00 10.00
GJSM Steve McNair 2 4.00 10.00
GJTH Torry Holt 2 4.00 10.00
GJWC Wayne Chrebet 1 3.00 8.00
GJWS Warren Sapp 1 4.00 10.00
GJZT Zach Thomas 1 4.00 10.00

2003 Upper Deck Game Jerseys Autographs

Randomly inserted into packs, this set features authentic game worn jersey swatches along with a genuine autograph. Each card is serial numbered to various quantities.

STATED PRINT RUN 5-99
GJAAB Antonio Bryant/99 12.00 30.00
GJAAL Ashley Lelie/99 12.00 30.00
GJACP Clinton Portis/26 30.00 80.00
GJADC David Carr/99 12.00 30.00
GJADF DeShaun Foster/99 15.00 40.00
GJAJS Jeremy Shockey/99 12.00 30.00
GJAKK Kurt Kittner/45 12.00 30.00
GJARW Roy Williams/99 12.00 30.00
GJAWD Woody Dantzler/99 12.00 30.00

2003 Upper Deck Game Jerseys Logos

Inserted into packs at a rate of 1:5000 hobby and retail, this set features authentic jersey swatches cut from jersey logos. Upper Deck announced print runs of 4 for David Carr, and 24 for Ricky Williams, though neither card is serial numbered.

STATED ODDS 1:5000 HOB, RET
PLODC David Carr/4*
PLOJG Jeff Garcia 20.00 50.00
PLOLT LaDainian Tomlinson 30.00 80.00
PLOMF Marshall Faulk 25.00 60.00
PLORW Ricky Williams/24*

2003 Upper Deck Game Jerseys Names

Inserted into packs at a rate of 1:7500 hobby and retail, this set features authentic jersey swatches cut from jersey nameplates. Upper Deck announced print runs of 11 for Michael Vick, and 18 for Edgerrin James, though neither card is serial numbered.

STATED ODDS 1:7500 HOB, RET
PNABF Brett Favre
PNACP Chad Pennington 15.00 40.00
PNADEM Deuce McAllister 20.00 50.00
PNADOM Donovan McNabb 20.00 50.00
PNAEJ Edgerrin James/18*
PNAKW Kurt Warner 30.00 80.00
PNAMV Michael Vick/11*
PNARM Randy Moss 20.00 50.00
PNATB Tom Brady 100.00 250.00
PNATO Terrell Owens 20.00 50.00

2003 Upper Deck Game Jerseys Numbers

Inserted into packs at a rate of 1:2500 hobby and retail, this set features authentic jersey swatches cut from jersey numbers. Cards are not serial numbered, and print runs were not released by Upper Deck.

STATED ODDS 1:2500 HOB, RET
PNUAG Ahman Green 15.00 40.00
PNUBR Drew Brees 20.00 50.00
PNUCP Clinton Portis 12.00 30.00
PNUDB Drew Bledsoe 15.00 40.00
PNUDC Daunte Culpepper 15.00 40.00
PNUEG Eddie George 15.00 40.00
PNUJB Jerome Bettis 20.00 50.00
PNUJS Jeremy Shockey 12.00 30.00
PNUMH Marvin Harrison 15.00 40.00
PNUTC Tim Couch 12.00 30.00

2003 Upper Deck Game Jerseys Duals

Inserted into packs at a rate of 1:144 hobby packs, and 1:288 retail packs, this set features two swatches of authentic game worn jerseys behind a geometric shaped die-cut area. A gold parallel also exists, where each card is serial numbered to 99.

STATED ODDS 1:144HOB, 1:288RET
*GOLD/99: .6X TO 1.5X BASIC DUAL JSY
GOLD STATED PRINT RUN 99 SER.#'d SETS
DGJBM D.Bledsoe/W.McGahee 5.00 12.00
DGJBS N.Burleson/O.Smith 4.00 10.00
DGJBT D.Brees/L.Tomlinson 6.00 15.00
DGJCJ T.Couch/K.Johnson 6.00 15.00
DGJCR D.Carr/D.Ragone 4.00 10.00
DGJCS K.Collins/J.Shockey 4.00 10.00
DGJCW C.Palmer/K.Washington 6.00 15.00
DGJDM D.Culpepper/R.Moss 5.00 12.00
DGJFC J.Fiedler/C.Chambers 4.00 10.00
DGJFG B.Favre/A.Green 12.00 30.00
DGJGR R.Gannon/J.Rice 10.00 25.00
DGJJB B.Johnson/A.Boldin 5.00 12.00
DGJJG T.Jacobs/R.Gardner 4.00 10.00
DGJKJ Keyshawn Johnson 6.00 15.00
DGJMC P.Manning/D.Clark 15.00 40.00
DGJPC C.Pennington/W.Chrebet 4.00 10.00
DGJWH K.Warner/T.Holt 5.00 12.00

2003 Upper Deck Power Surge

COMPLETE SET (18) 12.50 30.00
STATED ODDS 1:8
PS1 Marshall Faulk .75 2.00
PS2 LaDainian Tomlinson 1.00 2.50
PS3 Ricky Williams .75 2.00
PS4 Edgerrin James .75 2.00
PS5 Deuce McAllister .75 2.00
PS6 Jerome Bettis 1.00 2.50
PS7 Ahman Green .75 2.00
PS8 Jeremy Shockey .60 1.50
PS9 Steve McNair .75 2.00
PS10 William Green .60 1.50
PS11 Daunte Culpepper .75 2.00
PS12 Terrell Owens .75 2.00
PS13 Jerry Rice 2.00 5.00
PS14 Brad Johnson .75 2.00
PS15 Priest Holmes .60 1.50
PS16 Clinton Portis .60 1.50
PS17 Brian Urlacher 1.00 2.50
PS18 Rod Gardner .60 1.50

2003 Upper Deck Rookie Future Jerseys

Inserted into packs at a rate of 1:24 hobby packs, and 1:48 retail packs, this set features event-worn swatches taken from the 2003 Rookie Photo Shoot. A gold parallel also exists, where each card is serial numbered to 99.

STATED ODDS 1:24 HOB, 1:48 RET
*GOLD/99: .8X TO 2X BASIC JSY
GOLD STATED PRINT RUN 99 SER.#'d SETS
RFAB Anquan Boldin 4.00 10.00
RFAJ Andre Johnson 6.00 15.00
RFAP Artose Pinner 2.50 6.00
RFBE Bethel Johnson 2.50 6.00
RFBJ Bryant Johnson 4.00 10.00
RFBL Byron Leftwich 3.00 8.00
RFBS Brian St.Pierre 2.50 6.00
RFCB Chris Brown 2.50 6.00
RFCP Carson Palmer 10.00 25.00
RFDC Dallas Clark 4.00 10.00
RFDR Dave Ragone 2.50 6.00
RFJF Justin Fargas 4.00 10.00
RFKB Kyle Boller 2.50 6.00
RFKC Kevin Curtis 2.50 6.00
RFKK Kliff Kingsbury 4.00 10.00
RFKW Kelley Washington 2.50 6.00
RFLJ Larry Johnson 3.00 8.00
RFMS Musa Smith 2.50 6.00
RFMT Marcus Trufant 3.00 8.00
RFNB Nate Burleson 3.00 8.00
RFOS Onterrio Smith 2.50 6.00
RFRG Rex Grossman 3.00 8.00
RFRM Ricky Manning 3.00 8.00
RFRO DeWayne Robertson EXCH 3.00 8.00
RFSW Seneca Wallace 3.00 8.00
RFTE Teyo Johnson 3.00 8.00
RFTG Tyrone Calico 2.50 6.00
RFTJ Taylor Jacobs 2.50 6.00
RFTN Terence Newman 4.00 10.00
RFTS Terrell Suggs 3.00 8.00
RFWM Willis McGahee 6.00 15.00
RFWP Willie Pile 2.50 6.00

2003 Upper Deck Rookie Future Jerseys Autographs

Randomly inserted into packs, this features swatches of Rookie Photo Shoot jerseys, along with an authentic player autograph. Each card is serial numbered to various quantities.

SERIAL #'d UNDER 21 NOT PRICED
RFAKW Kelley Washington/87 12.50 30.00
RFALJ Larry Johnson/34 20.00 50.00
RFARO DeWayne Robertson/63 15.00 40.00

2003 Upper Deck Rookie Premiere

COMPLETE SET (30) 15.00 40.00
STATED ODDS 1:1 RETAIL
RP1 Carson Palmer .75 2.00
RP2 Byron Leftwich .50 1.25
RP3 Kyle Boller .40 1.00
RP4 Rex Grossman .50 1.25
RP5 Dave Ragone .40 1.00
RP6 Kliff Kingsbury .60 1.50
RP7 Seneca Wallace .50 1.25
RP8 Brian St.Pierre .40 1.00
RP9 Dallas Clark .60 1.50
RP10 Willis McGahee .50 1.25
RP11 Larry Johnson .50 1.25
RP12 Musa Smith .40 1.00
RP13 Chris Brown .40 1.00
RP14 Justin Fargas .60 1.50
RP15 Artose Pinner .40 1.00
RP16 Onterrio Smith .40 1.00
RP17 Nate Burleson .50 1.25
RP18 Andre Johnson 1.00 2.50
RP19 Bryant Johnson .60 1.50
RP20 Taylor Jacobs .40 1.00
RP21 Bethel Johnson .40 1.00
RP22 Anquan Boldin .60 1.50
RP23 Tyrone Calico .40 1.00
RP24 Teyo Johnson .50 1.25
RP25 Kelley Washington .40 1.00
RP26 Kevin Curtis .40 1.00
RP27 Terence Newman .60 1.50
RP28 Marcus Trufant .50 1.25
RP29 Terrell Suggs .50 1.25
RP30 DeWayne Robertson .50 1.25

2003 Upper Deck Super Powers

COMPLETE SET (12) 10.00 25.00
STATED ODDS 1:12
SP1 Kurt Warner .60 1.50
SP2 Aaron Brooks .50 1.25
SP3 Joey Harrington .50 1.25
SP4 Brett Favre 1.50 4.00
SP5 Donovan McNabb .60 1.50
SP6 Emmitt Smith 1.25 3.00
SP7 Michael Vick .60 1.50
SP8 David Carr .50 1.25
SP9 Drew Brees .75 2.00
SP10 Chad Pennington .50 1.25
SP11 Drew Bledsoe .60 1.50
SP12 Tom Brady 3.00 8.00

2003 Upper Deck UD Promos

*UD PROMO: .8X TO 2X BASIC CARD

2000 Upper Deck Plays of the Week

Released through Upper Deck's Collectors Club, this 38-card set was comprised of cards that measure 3 1/2"x5" and highlight 34 (2-per week) of the 1999 season's top plays. The cardfronts feature a "film cell" design showcasing full color action photos, while card backs contain a brief write-up of the featured play. The cards are not numbered, therefore they appear in order by week with the four tribute cards appearing in alphabetical order at the end of the set. NFL Plays of the Week was a mail-order set through the Upper Deck Collectors Club and was originally sold for $14.99.

COMPLETE SET (38) 7.50 20.00
1 Drew Bledsoe .25 .60
2 Troy Aikman .40 1.00
3 James Stewart .20 .50
4 Lance Schulters .20 .50
5 Brett Favre .60 1.50
6 Darryll Lewis .20 .50
7 Az-Zahir Hakim .20 .50
8 Neil O'Donnell .20 .50
9 Doug Pederson .20 .50
10 Dan Marino .60 1.50
11 Cade McNown .20 .50
12 Ed McCaffrey .25 .60
13 Kent Graham .20 .50
14 Tony Gonzalez .25 .60
15 Doug Flutie .25 .60
16 Marshall Faulk .25 .60
17 Kurt Warner .50 1.25
18 Keyshawn Johnson .25 .60
19 Jim Miller .20 .50
20 Peyton Manning .75 2.00
21 Donnie Abraham .20 .50
22 Edgerrin James .25 .60
23 Jake Plummer .20 .50
24 Cris Dishman .20 .50
25 Mike Vanderjagt .20 .50
26 Keith McKenzie .20 .50
27 Steve Beuerlein .25 .60
28 Jeff Blake .25 .60
29 Frank Wycheck .25 .60
30 Eric Bjornson .20 .50
31 Robert Smith .20 .50
32 Steve McNair .25 .60
33 Kenny Shedd .20 .50
34 Randy Moss .25 .60
35 John Elway GL .40 1.00
36 Walter Payton GL 1.00 2.50
37 F.Wycheck .25 .60
K.Dyson
38 Rams Super Bowl Champs .30 .75

2000 Upper Deck PowerDeck Super Bowl XXXIV

This Joe Montana card was distributed at Super Bowl XXXIV in Atlanta. One card was inserted per seat cushion. The CD-ROM card was issued attached to a larger cardboard backer.

1 Joe Montana 10.00 20.00

2000 Upper Deck Super Bowl XXXIV Black Diamond

This 14-card set was released at the 2000 Super Bowl Card Show in Atlanta. Each card measures roughly 3 1/2" by 5" and features a top 1999 NFL rookie along with the Super Bowl XXXIV logo on the cardfronts. The #1 card was pulled from the set before its release, but there have been a few reports of some copies of the card in circulation.

COMPLETE SET (13) 10.00 25.00
1 Cecil Collins SP
2 Cade McNown .60 1.50
3 James Johnson .60 1.50
4 Champ Bailey .75 2.00
5 Tim Couch .75 2.00
6 Peerless Price .75 2.00
7 David Boston .60 1.50
8 Ricky Williams .75 2.00
9 Edgerrin James .75 2.00
10 Donovan McNabb .75 2.00
11 Torry Holt .75 2.00
12 Daunte Culpepper .75 2.00
13 Jevon Kearse .60 1.50
14 Akili Smith .60 1.50

2000 Upper Deck Super Bowl XXXIV Special Moments

These oversized cards (roughly 3 1/2" by 5") were distributed at the 2000 Super Bowl Card Show in Atlanta. Each features a special moment and player from a past Super Bowl with serial numbering of 2000-sets produced on the cardfronts.

COMPLETE SET (10) 8.00 20.00
1 Jerry Rice 1.50 4.00
2 Terrell Davis .50 1.25
3 Brett Favre 1.25 3.00
4 Joe Namath 1.25 3.00
5 Jamal Anderson .50 1.25
6 Chris Chandler .50 1.25
7 Steve Young .75 2.00
8 Joe Montana 2.00 5.00
9 Antonio Freeman .50 1.25
10 Emmitt Smith 1.00 2.50

2001 Upper Deck e-Card Manning

This single card was issued to attendees of the 2001 NFL Experience Super Bowl Card Show in Tampa, Florida through the Upper Deck corporate booth. The card features a scratch off area in which collector's would enter the revealed ID number at upperdeckdigital.com to have a chance to "digitize" the card into an autographed card or jersey card of Manning. The expiration date for enhancing the card on the website is July 1, 2002.

1 Peyton Manning 3.00 5.00
1J Peyton Manning JSY/200 12.50 30.00

2001 Upper Deck Super Bowl XXXV Black Diamond

These jumbo (roughly 3 1/2" by 5") cards were issued through the Upper Deck booth during the 2001 NFL Experience Super Bowl Card Show in Tampa, Florida. Each is essentially an enlarged version of the player's base 2000 Black Diamond Rookie Card along with a Super Bowl XXXV logo and a facsimile jersey swatch on the cardfronts. The cardbacks were re-written to reflect events from the 2000 season.

COMPLETE SET (10) 20.00 50.00
1 Courtney Brown 2.00 5.00
2 Ron Dayne 2.50 6.00
3 Shaun Alexander 2.00 5.00
4 Thomas Jones 2.00 5.00
5 Jamal Lewis 3.00 8.00
6 J.R. Redmond 2.00 5.00
7 Peter Warrick 2.00 5.00
8 Plaxico Burress 2.00 5.00
9 Sylvester Morris 2.00 5.00
10 Laveranues Coles 2.50 6.00

2001 Upper Deck Super Bowl XXXV Box Set

This 21-card set was issued to traditional retailers and the hobby to commemorate the Giants and Ravens in Super Bowl XXXV.

COMPLETE SET (21) 6.00 15.00
1 Trent Dilfer .40 1.00
2 Tony Banks .40 1.00
3 Rod Woodson .60 1.50
4 Jamal Lewis .60 1.50
5 Priest Holmes .40 1.00
6 Ray Lewis .60 1.50
7 Shannon Sharpe .50 1.25
8 Jermaine Lewis .40 1.00
9 Qadry Ismail .40 1.00
10 Travis Taylor .40 1.00
11 Tiki Barber .50 1.25
12 Kerry Collins .40 1.00
13 Ron Dayne .50 1.25
14 Ron Dixon .40 1.00
15 Ike Hilliard .40 1.00
16 Joe Jurevicious .40 1.00
17 Pete Mitchell .40 1.00
18 Amani Toomer .40 1.00
19 Jessie Armstead .40 1.00
20 Michael Strahan .50 1.25
NNO Jumbo Cover Card .40 1.00

2001 Upper Deck Super Bowl XXXV Box Set Game Jersey Jumbos

These six oversized cards were issued one per special factory set of the 2001 Upper Deck Super Bowl XXXV Box Set. These special sets were primarily issued through Shop at Home and retailed for $79.99 per set.

MF Marshall Faulk 10.00 25.00
PM Peyton Manning 30.00 80.00
RD Ron Dayne 10.00 25.00
RM Randy Moss 10.00 25.00
TB Tim Brown 12.00 30.00
WD Warrick Dunn 8.00 20.00

2001 Upper Deck Super Bowl XXXV Special Moments

Some attendees to the 2001 NFL Experience Super Bowl Card Show in Tampa, Florida could receive one-card from this set by visiting the Upper Deck booth. Each card is oversized (roughly 3 1/2" by 5") and highlights one player and his outstanding performance in a Super Bowl game. All were serial numbered of 2001-sets produced.

COMPLETE SET (6) 8.00 20.00
BF Brett Favre 2.00 5.00
EG Eddie George 1.00 2.50
JA Jamal Anderson .75 2.00
MF Marshall Faulk .75 2.00
TA Troy Aikman 1.25 3.00
TD Terrell Davis .75 2.00

2002 Upper Deck Super Bowl Card Show

These cards were available via a wrapper redemption contest at the 2002 Super Bowl Card Show in New Orleans. In order to receive a card one had to open a box of 2002 Upper Deck product at their booth to receive a pack which contained one of the 6 cards in the set.

8 Archie Manning/2002 .50 1.25
8 Archie Manning AU/100 15.00 40.00
18 Peyton Manning AU/500 50.00 100.00
18 Peyton Manning/2002 1.50 4.00
SBAP Peyton Manning 1.50 4.00
Archie Manning/2002
SBAP Peyton Manning AU/36
Archie Manning AU

2003 Upper Deck Magazine

As a bonus to buyers of the Upper Deck magazine produced by Krause Publications late in 2003, a nine-card perforated sheet featuring players basically signed to Upper Deck exclusives was included. When the cards were perforated, these cards measured the standard size. Please note that all of these cards have a "UD" prefix.

COMPLETE SET (9) 8.00 20.00
UD6 Michael Vick 1.00 2.50

2003 Upper Deck Super Bowl Card Show

COMPLETE SET (10) 6.00 12.00
1 Tom Brady 1.50 4.00
2 Kurt Warner .30 .75
3 Brett Favre .75 2.00
4 Drew Bledsoe .30 .75
5 Joey Harrington .25 .60
6 Jeff Garcia .25 .60
7 Michael Vick .30 .75
8 Peyton Manning 1.00 2.50
9 Donovan McNabb .30 .75
10 David Carr .25 .60

2004 Upper Deck

Upper Deck was initially released in mid-September 2004. The base set consists of 275-cards including 25-short printed rookies and 50-rookies issued one per pack. Hobby boxes contained 24-packs of 8-cards and carried an S.R.P. of $2.99 per pack. Two parallel sets and a variety of inserts can be found seeded in packs highlighted by the Signature Sensations autographed inserts.

COMPLETE SET (275) 75.00 135.00
COMP.SET w/o SP's (250) 30.00 60.00
COMP.SET w/o RC's (200) 10.00 25.00
201-225 ROOKIE STATED ODDS 1:8
226-275 ROOKIE STATED ODDS 1:1
UNPRICED PRINT PLATE PRINT RUN 1 SET
1 Anquan Boldin .20 .50
2 Josh McCown .25 .60
3 Emmitt Smith .50 1.25
4 Freddie Jones .20 .50
5 Marcel Shipp .20 .50
6 Shaun King .20 .50
7 Michael Vick .25 .60
8 T.J. Duckett .20 .50
9 Peerless Price .20 .50
10 Warrick Dunn .20 .50
11 Keith Brooking .20 .50
12 Brian Finneran .20 .50
13 Anthony Wright .20 .50
14 Kyle Boller .20 .50
15 Jamal Lewis .25 .60
16 Todd Heap .20 .50
17 Ray Lewis .30 .75
18 Terrell Suggs .20 .50
19 Travis Taylor .20 .50
20 Drew Bledsoe .25 .60
21 Willis McGahee .20 .50
22 Eric Moulds .20 .50
23 Travis Henry .20 .50
24 Takeo Spikes .20 .50
25 Josh Reed .20 .50
26 Lawyer Milloy .20 .50
27 Stephen Davis .20 .50
28 Jake Delhomme .20 .50
29 Steve Smith .30 .75
30 DeShaun Foster .25 .60
31 Dan Morgan .25 .60
32 Julius Peppers .25 .60
33 Rod Smart .25 .60
34 Rex Grossman .20 .50
35 Thomas Jones .20 .50
36 Marty Booker .20 .50
37 Anthony Thomas .25 .60
38 Brian Urlacher .30 .75
39 Justin Gage .25 .60
40 Chad Johnson .20 .50
41 Carson Palmer .25 .60
42 Peter Warrick .20 .50
43 Jon Kitna .20 .50
44 Kelley Washington .20 .50
45 Rudi Johnson .20 .50
46 Jeff Garcia .20 .50
47 Dennis Northcutt .20 .50
48 Lee Suggs .25 .60
49 Andre Davis .20 .50
50 Quincy Morgan .20 .50
51 Kelly Holcomb .20 .50
52 Keyshawn Johnson .25 .60
53 Quincy Carter .20 .50
54 Antonio Bryant .25 .60
55 Terry Glenn .25 .60
56 Terence Newman .25 .60
57 Roy Williams S .20 .50
58 Champ Bailey .25 .60
59 Jake Plummer .20 .50
60 Quentin Griffin .20 .50
61 John Lynch .25 .60
62 Rod Smith .25 .60
63 Ashley Lelie .20 .50
64 Joey Harrington .20 .50
65 Az-Zahir Hakim .20 .50
66 Charles Rogers .20 .50
67 Tai Streets .20 .50
68 Shawn Bryson .20 .50
69 Artose Pinner .20 .50
70 Brett Favre .60 1.50
71 Nick Barnett .20 .50
72 Ahman Green .25 .60
73 Kabeer Gbaja-Biamila .20 .50
74 Javon Walker .20 .50
75 Donald Driver .25 .60
76 Tim Couch .25 .60
77 David Carr .20 .50
78 Corey Bradford .20 .50
79 J.J. Moses .20 .50
80 Domanick Davis .20 .50
81 Jabar Gaffney .20 .50
82 Andre Johnson .25 .60
83 Marvin Harrison .25 .60
84 Peyton Manning .75 2.00
85 Dallas Clark .20 .50
86 Edgerrin James .25 .60
87 Reggie Wayne .25 .60
88 Dwight Freeney .20 .50
89 Byron Leftwich .20 .50
90 LaBrandon Toefield .20 .50
91 Fred Taylor .20 .50
92 Troy Edwards .20 .50
93 Jimmy Smith .25 .60
94 Kyle Brady .20 .50
95 Trent Green .20 .50
96 Tony Gonzalez .25 .60
97 Dante Hall .20 .50
98 Priest Holmes .20 .50
99 Eddie Kennison .25 .60
100 Johnnie Morton .25 .60
101 Jay Fiedler .20 .50
102 Junior Seau .30 .75
103 Ricky Williams .25 .60
104 Chris Chambers .20 .50
105 Zach Thomas .25 .60
106 David Boston .20 .50
107 A.J. Feeley .20 .50
108 Daunte Culpepper .25 .60
109 Onterrio Smith .20 .50
110 Randy Moss .25 .60
111 Moe Williams .20 .50
112 Michael Bennett .20 .50
113 Jim Kleinsasser .20 .50
114 Tom Brady 1.25 3.00
115 Kevin Faulk .20 .50
116 Deion Branch .20 .50
117 Corey Dillon .20 .50
118 Troy Brown .20 .50
119 Adam Vinatieri .20 .50
120 Tedy Bruschi .25 .60
121 Aaron Brooks .20 .50
122 Deuce McAllister .25 .60
123 Donte' Stallworth .20 .50
124 Joe Horn .20 .50
125 Jerome Pathon .20 .50
126 Boo Williams .20 .50
127 Jeremy Shockey .20 .50
128 Kurt Warner .25 .60
129 Amani Toomer .20 .50
130 Tiki Barber .25 .60
131 Ike Hilliard .20 .50
132 Michael Strahan .25 .60
133 Chad Pennington .20 .50
134 Santana Moss .25 .60
135 Wayne Chrebet .20 .50
136 Curtis Martin .25 .60
137 LaMont Jordan .25 .60
138 Justin McCareins .20 .50
139 Jerry Rice .60 1.50
140 Rich Gannon .25 .60
141 Tim Brown .30 .75
142 Jerry Porter .20 .50
143 Warren Sapp .25 .60
144 Charles Woodson .30 .75
145 Donovan McNabb .25 .60
146 Brian Westbrook .20 .50
147 Todd Pinkston .20 .50
148 Jevon Kearse .20 .50
149 Freddie Mitchell .20 .50
150 Correll Buckhalter .20 .50
151 Terrell Owens .25 .60
152 Tommy Maddox .20 .50
153 Duce Staley .20 .50
154 Plaxico Burress .20 .50
155 Hines Ward .25 .60
156 Antwaan Randle El .20 .50
157 Jerome Bettis .30 .75
158 Kendrell Bell .20 .50
159 LaDainian Tomlinson .30 .75
160 Doug Flutie .25 .60
161 Quentin Jammer .20 .50
162 Drew Brees .30 .75
163 Reche Caldwell .25 .60
164 Tim Dwight .20 .50
165 Tim Rattay .20 .50
166 Kevan Barlow .20 .50
167 Brandon Lloyd .25 .60
168 Cedrick Wilson .20 .50
169 Julian Peterson .25 .60
170 Ahmed Plummer .20 .50
171 Matt Hasselbeck .20 .50
172 Koren Robinson .20 .50
173 Shaun Alexander .20 .50
174 Darrell Jackson .25 .60
175 Marcus Trufant .20 .50
176 Bobby Engram .20 .50
177 Marc Bulger .20 .50
178 Torry Holt .25 .60
179 Marshall Faulk .25 .60
180 Orlando Pace .20 .50
181 Isaac Bruce .30 .75
182 Kyle Turley .20 .50
183 Brad Johnson .25 .60
184 Charlie Garner .25 .60
185 Keenan McCardell .20 .50
186 Mike Alstott .20 .50
187 Derrick Brooks .20 .50
188 Brian Griese .20 .50
189 Steve McNair .25 .60
190 Chris Brown .20 .50
191 Eddie George .25 .60
192 Tyrone Calico .25 .60
193 Derrick Mason .20 .50
194 Drew Bennett .25 .60
195 Mark Brunell .25 .60
196 LaVar Arrington .20 .50
197 Clinton Portis .20 .50
198 Laveranues Coles .20 .50
199 Patrick Ramsey .25 .60
200 Rod Gardner .20 .50
201 Eli Manning RC 10.00 25.00
202 Larry Fitzgerald RC 5.00 12.00
203 Michael Jenkins RC 1.25 3.00
204 Ben Roethlisberger RC 10.00 25.00
205 Philip Rivers RC 4.00 10.00
206 Kellen Winslow RC 1.25 3.00
207 Kevin Jones RC 1.50 4.00
208 Steven Jackson RC 2.00 5.00
209 Reggie Williams RC 1.25 3.00
210 Chris Perry RC 1.25 3.00
211 Roy Williams RC 1.25 3.00
212 Rashaun Woods RC 1.25 3.00
213 Chris Gamble RC 1.25 3.00
214 Sean Taylor RC 8.00 20.00
215 Robert Gallery RC 1.50 4.00
216 Ben Troupe RC 1.25 3.00
217 Lee Evans RC 2.00 5.00
218 Michael Clayton RC 1.50 4.00
219 J.P. Losman RC 1.25 3.00
220 Devery Henderson RC 1.25 3.00
221 Drew Henson RC 1.25 3.00
222 DeAngelo Hall RC 2.00 5.00
223 Julius Jones RC 1.25 3.00
224 Ben Watson RC 1.50 4.00
225 Greg Jones RC 1.25 3.00
226 D.J. Williams RC .60 1.50
227 Tommie Harris RC .50 1.25
228 Shawn Andrews RC .50 1.25
229 Vince Wilfork RC .60 1.50
230 Dunta Robinson RC .40 1.00
231 Will Smith RC .50 1.25
232 Jonathan Vilma RC .50 1.25
233 Ricardo Colclough RC .40 1.00
234 Ahmad Carroll RC .40 1.00
235 Karlos Dansby RC .50 1.25
236 Matt Ware RC .60 1.50
237 Jim Sorgi RC .50 1.25
238 Will Poole RC .60 1.50
239 Derrick Strait RC .40 1.00
240 Andy Hall RC .40 1.00
241 Nathan Vasher RC .60 1.50
242 D.J. Hackett RC .40 1.00
243 Jason Babin RC .60 1.50
244 Derrick Hamilton RC .40 1.00
245 Michael Boulware RC .60 1.50
246 Michael Turner RC .40 1.00
247 Sean Jones RC .40 1.00
248 Ernest Wilford RC .50 1.25
249 Cedric Cobbs RC .40 1.00
250 Tatum Bell RC .40 1.00
251 Bernard Berrian RC .40 1.00
252 Vernon Carey RC .40 1.00
253 Kenechi Udeze RC .50 1.25
254 P.K. Sam RC .40 1.00
255 Ben Hartsock RC .40 1.00
256 Chris Cooley RC .50 1.25
257 Josh Harris RC .40 1.00
258 Cody Pickett RC .40 1.00
259 Carlos Francis RC .40 1.00
260 Devard Darling RC .40 1.00
261 Johnnie Morant RC .40 1.00
262 John Navarre RC .40 1.00
263 Kris Wilson RC .50 1.25
264 Jerricho Cotchery RC .50 1.25
265 Darius Watts RC .40 1.00
266 Quincy Wilson RC .40 1.00
267 Maurice Mann RC .40 1.00
268 Samie Parker RC .40 1.00
269 B.J. Symons RC .40 1.00
270 Matt Schaub RC .40 1.00
271 Jeff Smoker RC .50 1.25
272 Craig Krenzel RC .40 1.00
273 Luke McCown RC .40 1.00
274 Mewelde Moore RC .50 1.25
275 Keary Colbert RC .40 1.00

2004 Upper Deck UD Exclusive

*VETS 1-200: 6X TO 15X BASIC CARDS
*ROOKIES 201-225: 1X TO 2.5X
*ROOKIES 226-275: 3X TO 8X
STATED PRINT RUN 50 SER.#'d SETS
UNPRICED VINTAGE PRINT RUN 10 SET
UNPRICED VINT.PRINT PLATE PRINT RUN 1

2004 Upper Deck UD Promos

*UD PROMO: .8X TO 2X BASIC CARDS

2004 Upper Deck Game Jerseys

STATED ODDS 1:32 HOB, 1:28 RET
ABGJ Anquan Boldin 2.50 6.00
AJGJ Andre Johnson 3.00 8.00

BFGJ Brett Favre 8.00 20.00
CDGJ Corey Dillon 2.50 6.00
CJGJ Chad Johnson 2.50 6.00
CPGJ Clinton Portis 2.50 6.00
DCGJ Daunte Culpepper 3.00 8.00
DDGJ Domanick Davis 2.50 6.00
DMGJ Deuce McAllister 3.00 8.00
DOGJ Donovan McNabb 3.00 8.00
JDGJ Jake Delhomme 2.50 6.00
KBGJ Kyle Boller SP 3.00 8.00
LTGJ LaDainian Tomlinson 4.00 10.00
MVGJ Michael Vick 3.00 8.00
PHGJ Priest Holmes 2.50 6.00
PMGJ Peyton Manning 10.00 25.00
RMGJ Randy Moss 3.00 8.00
SAGJ Shaun Alexander 2.50 6.00
SMGJ Steve McNair 3.00 8.00
TBGJ Tom Brady 15.00 40.00
TSGJ Terrell Suggs SP 3.00 8.00

2004 Upper Deck Game Jersey Duals

STATED ODDS 1:480
BD2J T.Brady/J.Delhomme 30.00 80.00
FM2J B.Favre/P.Manning 20.00 50.00
HF2J P.Holmes/M.Faulk 6.00 15.00
MH2J R.Moss/M.Harrison 6.00 15.00
SR2J E.Smith/J.Rice 15.00 40.00
TP2J L.Tomlinson/C.Portis 8.00 20.00
US2J B.Urlacher/J.Seau 8.00 20.00
VM2J M.Vick/D.McNabb 6.00 15.00

2004 Upper Deck Game Jersey Patch Logos

PATCH LOGO STATED ODDS 1:2500
PLOAG Ahman Green 10.00 25.00
PLOBL Byron Leftwich 8.00 20.00
PLOBU Brian Urlacher 12.00 30.00
PLOCL Clinton Portis 8.00 20.00
PLOCP Chad Pennington 8.00 20.00
PLOHW Hines Ward 10.00 25.00
PLOJH Joe Horn 8.00 20.00
PLOMV Michael Vick 10.00 25.00
PLOPH Priest Holmes 8.00 20.00
PLORM Randy Moss 10.00 25.00
PLOTH Todd Heap 8.00 20.00

2004 Upper Deck Game Jersey Patch Names

PATCH NAMES ODDS 1:5000
PNAEJ Edgerrin James SP 15.00 40.00
PNALT LaDainian Tomlinson 15.00 40.00
PNAMS Michael Strahan 12.00 30.00
PNASA Santana Moss 12.00 30.00
PNASM Steve McNair 12.00 30.00
PNATB Tom Brady 60.00 150.00
PNATH Torry Holt 12.00 30.00
PNATO Terrell Owens 12.00 30.00

2004 Upper Deck Game Jersey Patch Numbers

PATCH NUMBER ODDS 1:1500
PNUBF Brett Favre 20.00 50.00
PNUCC Chris Chambers 6.00 15.00
PNUCJ Chad Johnson 6.00 15.00
PNUCP Clinton Portis 6.00 15.00
PNUDC Daunte Culpepper 8.00 20.00
PNUDH Dante Hall 6.00 15.00
PNUDM Deuce McAllister 8.00 20.00
PNUJL Jamal Lewis 8.00 20.00
PNUJR Jerry Rice 20.00 50.00
PNUMB Marc Bulger 6.00 15.00
PNUPM Peyton Manning 25.00 60.00
PNURG Rex Grossman 6.00 15.00

2004 Upper Deck Rewind to 1997 Jerseys

STATED ODDS 1:480
97BF Brett Favre 10.00 25.00
97CD Corey Dillon 3.00 8.00
97CM Curtis Martin 4.00 10.00
97DF Doug Flutie 4.00 10.00
97EM Eric Moulds 3.00 8.00
97ES Emmitt Smith SP 8.00 20.00
97JB Jerome Bettis 5.00 12.00
97JP Jake Plummer 3.00 8.00
97JR Jerry Rice SP 10.00 25.00
97JS Junior Seau 5.00 12.00
97MF Marshall Faulk 4.00 10.00
97TB Tim Brown SP 5.00 12.00
97TG Tony Gonzalez 4.00 10.00
97WD Warrick Dunn 3.00 8.00

2004 Upper Deck Rookie Futures Jerseys

STATED ODDS 1:24
RFBB Bernard Berrian 2.50 6.00
RFBR Ben Roethlisberger 20.00 50.00
RFBT Ben Troupe 2.50 6.00
RFBW Ben Watson 3.00 8.00
RFCC Cedric Cobbs 2.50 6.00
RFCP Chris Perry 2.50 6.00
RFDD Devard Darling 2.50 6.00
RFDE Devery Henderson 2.50 6.00
RFDK Derrick Hamilton 2.50 6.00
RFDR Dunta Robinson 2.50 6.00
RFDW Darius Watts 2.50 6.00
RFEM Eli Manning 8.00 20.00
RFGJ Greg Jones 2.50 6.00
RFHA DeAngelo Hall 4.00 10.00
RFJJ Julius Jones 2.50 6.00
RFJP J.P. Losman 2.50 6.00
RFKC Keary Colbert 2.50 6.00
RFKJ Kevin Jones 3.00 8.00
RFKW Kellen Winslow Jr. 2.50 6.00
RFLE Lee Evans 4.00 10.00
RFLF Larry Fitzgerald 8.00 20.00
RFLM Luke McCown 2.50 6.00
RFMI Michael Clayton 3.00 8.00
RFMJ Michael Jenkins 2.50 6.00
RFMM Mewelde Moore 3.00 8.00
RFMS Matt Schaub 2.50 6.00
RFPR Philip Rivers 12.00 30.00
RFRA Rashaun Woods 2.50 6.00
RFRG Robert Gallery 3.00 8.00
RFRO Roy Williams WR 2.50 6.00
RFRW Reggie Williams 2.50 6.00
RFSJ Steven Jackson 4.00 10.00
RFTB Tatum Bell 2.50 6.00

2004 Upper Deck Rookie Prospects

COMPLETE SET (30) 15.00 40.00
ONE PER RETAIL PACK
RPBR Ben Roethlisberger 2.50 6.00
RPBT Ben Troupe .30 .75
RPBW Ben Watson .40 1.00
RPCC Cedric Cobbs .30 .75
RPCP Chris Perry .30 .75
RPDD Devard Darling .30 .75
RPDE Devery Henderson .30 .75
RPDH Derrick Hamilton .30 .75
RPDR Drew Henson .30 .75
RPDW Darius Watts .30 .75
RPEM Eli Manning 2.50 6.00
RPGJ Greg Jones .30 .75
RPJJ Julius Jones .30 .75
RPJP J.P. Losman .30 .75
RPKC Keary Colbert .30 .75
RPKJ Kevin Jones .40 1.00
RPKW Kellen Winslow Jr. .30 .75
RPLE Lee Evans .50 1.25
RPLF Larry Fitzgerald 1.25 3.00
RPLM Luke McCown .30 .75
RPMI Michael Clayton .40 1.00
RPMJ Michael Jenkins .30 .75
RPMM Mewelde Moore .40 1.00
RPMS Matt Schaub .30 .75
RPPR Philip Rivers 1.00 2.50
RPRA Rashaun Woods .30 .75
RPRO Roy Williams WR .30 .75
RPRW Reggie Williams .30 .75
RPSJ Steven Jackson .50 1.25
RPTB Tatum Bell .30 .75

2004 Upper Deck Rookie Review Jerseys

STATED ODDS 1:480
RRAB Anquan Boldin 2.50 6.00
RRAJ Andre Johnson 3.00 8.00
RRAP Artose Pinner 2.50 6.00
RRBJ Bethel Johnson 2.50 6.00
RRBL Byron Leftwich 2.50 6.00
RRCB Chris Brown 2.50 6.00
RRCP Carson Palmer 3.00 8.00
RRDC Dallas Clark 2.50 6.00
RRJF Justin Fargas 3.00 8.00
RRKB Kyle Boller 2.50 6.00
RRKW Kelley Washington 2.50 6.00
RRLJ Larry Johnson 2.50 6.00
RRMT Marcus Trufant 2.50 6.00
RROS Onterrio Smith 2.50 6.00
RRRG Rex Grossman 2.50 6.00
RRTC Tyrone Calico 3.00 8.00
RRTJ Teyo Johnson 2.50 6.00
RRTN Terence Newman 3.00 8.00
RRTS Terrell Suggs 2.50 6.00
RRWM Willis McGahee 2.50 6.00

2004 Upper Deck Signature Sensations

SIGN SENSATION PRINT RUN 4-88
CARDS SER.#'d UNDER 20 NOT PRICED
SSBE Ben Watson/84 12.50 30.00
SSBL Brandon Lloyd/85 10.00 25.00
SSBS Barry Sanders/20 100.00 175.00
SSBT Ben Troupe/86 15.00 40.00
SSBW Brian Westbrook/36
SSCC Cedric Cobbs/34 15.00 40.00
SSCP Chris Perry/26 15.00 40.00
SSDD Domanick Davis/37
SSDH DeAngelo Hall/21 15.00 40.00
SSDM Deuce McAllister/26 15.00 40.00
SSGJ Greg Jones/33 15.00 40.00
SSHA Dante Hall/82 12.50 30.00
SSJG Jon Gruden/60 12.00 30.00
SSJH Joe Horn/87 10.00 25.00
SSJJ Jimmy Johnson/60 15.00 40.00
SSJU Julius Jones/21
SSKC Keary Colbert/85 12.50 30.00
SSKJ Kevin Jones/34 15.00 40.00
SSKW Kellen Winslow Jr./81 10.00 25.00
SSLE Lee Evans/83 12.00 30.00
SSLT LaDainian Tomlinson/21 25.00 60.00
SSMI Michael Clayton/80 10.00 25.00
SSRA Rashaun Woods/81 10.00 25.00
SSRG Robert Gallery/74 12.00 30.00
SSRJ Rudi Johnson/32 12.00 30.00
SSRW Roy Williams S/31
SSSJ Steven Jackson/39 15.00 40.00
SSTA Tatum Bell/26 15.00 40.00
SSTG Tony Gonzalez/88 10.00 25.00
SSWI Kellen Winslow Sr./80 12.00 30.00
SSWM Willis McGahee/21 15.00 40.00

2004 Upper Deck Earl Campbell Promo

This promo card was issued at the 2004 Super Bowl XXXVIII Card Show in Houston. It features Earl Campbell along with the notation "The Tyler Rose" on the cardfront as well as serial numbering of 1000-cards produced. Note that the copyright line on the back designates the year as 2003.
EC Earl Campbell 2.00 5.00

2004 Upper Deck Pepsi Get Out There and Play

NNO Donovan McNabb 1.25 3.00

2005 Upper Deck

This 275-card set was released in August, 2005. The set was issued into the hobby in eight-card packs with an $2.99 SRP which came 24 packs to a box. Cards numbered 1-193 were sequenced in team alphabetical order based on where the player pictured played in 2004. In addition, cards numbered 201-275 featured 2005 rookies. Cards numbered 201-225 were inserted at a stated rate of one in eight and cards numbered 226-275 were inserted at a stated rate of one per pack.

COMPLETE SET (275) 100.00 200.00
COMP.SET w/o SP's (250) 30.00 60.00
COMP.SET w/o RC's (200) 12.50 30.00
201-225 ROOKIE STATED ODDS 1:8
226-275 ROOKIE STATED ODDS 1:1
1 Larry Fitzgerald .30 .75
2 Anquan Boldin .20 .50
3 Kurt Warner .25 .60
4 Josh McCown .25 .60
5 Bryant Johnson .20 .50
6 Duane Starks .20 .50
7 Michael Vick .25 .60
8 Warrick Dunn .20 .50
9 T.J. Duckett .20 .50
10 Peerless Price .20 .50
11 Alge Crumpler .25 .60
12 Patrick Kerney .20 .50
13 Ed Reed .25 .60
14 Ray Lewis .30 .75
15 Kyle Boller .20 .50
16 Ma'Ake Kemoeatu RC .20 .50
17 Jamal Lewis .25 .60
18 Derrick Mason .20 .50
19 J.P. Losman .20 .50
20 Willis McGahee .20 .50
21 Lawyer Milloy .20 .50
22 Lee Evans .25 .60
23 Eric Moulds .20 .50
24 Takeo Spikes .20 .50
25 Jake Delhomme .20 .50
26 DeShaun Foster .25 .60
27 Keary Colbert .20 .50
28 Stephen Davis .20 .50
29 Nick Goings .20 .50
30 Julius Peppers .25 .60
31 Rex Grossman .20 .50
32 Brian Urlacher .30 .75
33 Thomas Jones .20 .50
34 Muhsin Muhammad .20 .50
35 Anthony Thomas .20 .50
36 Bernard Berrian .20 .50
37 Carson Palmer .25 .60
38 Chad Johnson .20 .50
39 Peter Warrick .20 .50
40 T.J. Houshmandzadeh .20 .50
41 Rudi Johnson .20 .50
42 Justin Smith .25 .60
43 Jeff Garcia .20 .50
44 Lee Suggs .20 .50
45 William Green .20 .50
46 Kellen Winslow .20 .50
47 Dennis Northcutt .20 .50
48 Antonio Bryant .20 .50
49 Julius Jones .20 .50
50 Drew Bledsoe .25 .60
51 Keyshawn Johnson .25 .60
52 Al Johnson .20 .50
53 Jason Witten .25 .60
54 Roy Williams S .20 .50
55 Jake Plummer .20 .50
56 Champ Bailey .25 .60
57 Tatum Bell .20 .50
58 Reuben Droughns .20 .50
59 Ashley Lelie .20 .50
60 Rod Smith .25 .60
61 Kevin Jones .20 .50
62 Roy Williams WR .20 .50
63 Charles Rogers .20 .50
64 Joey Harrington .20 .50
65 Az-Zahir Hakim .20 .50
66 Dre Bly .20 .50
67 Brett Favre .60 1.50
68 Javon Walker .20 .50
69 Ahman Green .25 .60
70 Donald Driver .25 .60
71 Robert Ferguson .20 .50
72 Nick Barnett .20 .50
73 David Carr .20 .50
74 Domanick Davis .20 .50
75 Andre Johnson .25 .60
76 Jabar Gaffney .20 .50
77 Dunta Robinson .20 .50
78 Jamie Sharper .20 .50
79 Peyton Manning .75 2.00
80 Edgerrin James .25 .60
81 Marvin Harrison .25 .60
82 Reggie Wayne .25 .60
83 Brandon Stokley .20 .50
84 Dwight Freeney .20 .50
85 Byron Leftwich .20 .50
86 Fred Taylor .20 .50
87 Jimmy Smith .25 .60
88 Greg Jones .20 .50
89 Donovin Darius .20 .50
90 Reggie Williams .20 .50
91 Priest Holmes .20 .50
92 Larry Johnson .20 .50
93 Tony Gonzalez .25 .60
94 Trent Green .20 .50
95 Eddie Kennison .20 .50
96 Johnnie Morton .25 .60
97 Jason Taylor .25 .60
98 A.J. Feeley .20 .50
99 Sammy Morris .20 .50
100 Chris Chambers .20 .50
101 Randy McMichael .20 .50
102 Zach Thomas .25 .60
103 Antoine Winfield .25 .60
104 Daunte Culpepper .25 .60
105 Michael Bennett .20 .50
106 Nate Burleson .20 .50
107 Onterrio Smith .20 .50
108 Marcus Robinson .20 .50
109 Tom Brady 1.25 3.00
110 Corey Dillon .20 .50
111 David Givens .20 .50
112 David Patten .20 .50
113 Adam Vinatieri .20 .50
114 Troy Brown .20 .50
115 Aaron Brooks .20 .50
116 Deuce McAllister .25 .60
117 Joe Horn .20 .50
118 Donte Stallworth .20 .50
119 Charles Grant .20 .50
120 Jerome Pathon .20 .50
121 Eli Manning .50 1.25
122 Tiki Barber .25 .60
123 Amani Toomer .20 .50
124 Jeremy Shockey .20 .50
125 Michael Strahan .25 .60
126 Plaxico Burress .20 .50
127 Chad Pennington .20 .50
128 Curtis Martin .25 .60
129 Laveranues Coles .20 .50
130 Wayne Chrebet .20 .50
131 Jonathan Vilma .20 .50
132 Justin McCareins .20 .50
133 Kerry Collins .20 .50
134 Jerry Porter .20 .50
135 LaMont Jordan .25 .60
136 Randy Moss .25 .60
137 Barry Sims .20 .50
138 Warren Sapp .25 .60
139 Donovan McNabb .25 .60
140 Brian Westbrook .20 .50
141 Terrell Owens .25 .60
142 Jevon Kearse .20 .50
143 Brian Dawkins .30 .75
144 Ben Roethlisberger .50 1.25
145 Jerome Bettis .30 .75
146 Duce Staley .20 .50
147 Cedrick Wilson .20 .50
148 Hines Ward .25 .60
149 Antwaan Randle El .20 .50
150 Troy Polamalu .30 .75
151 Philip Rivers .30 .75
152 Drew Brees .30 .75
153 LaDainian Tomlinson .30 .75
154 Antonio Gates .30 .75
155 Reche Caldwell .20 .50
156 Eric Parker .20 .50
157 Kevan Barlow .20 .50
158 Tim Rattay .20 .50
159 Eric Johnson .20 .50
160 Rashaun Woods .20 .50
161 Brandon Lloyd .20 .50
162 Julian Peterson .20 .50
163 Matt Hasselbeck .20 .50
164 Shaun Alexander .20 .50
165 Michael Boulware .20 .50
166 Darrell Jackson .20 .50
167 Koren Robinson .20 .50
168 Marcus Trufant .20 .50
169 Marc Bulger .20 .50
170 Steven Jackson .20 .50
171 Marshall Faulk .25 .60
172 Isaac Bruce .30 .75
173 Torry Holt .25 .60
174 Michael Clayton .20 .50
175 Michael Pittman .20 .50
176 Brian Griese .20 .50
177 Joey Galloway .25 .60
178 Derrick Brooks .20 .50
179 Josh Savage RC .20 .50
180 Steve McNair .25 .60
181 Chris Brown .30 .75
182 Billy Volek .20 .50
183 Ben Troupe .20 .50
184 Drew Bennett .25 .60
185 Clinton Portis .20 .50
186 Mark Brunell .25 .60
187 Patrick Ramsey .25 .60
188 Sean Taylor .30 .75
189 LaVar Arrington .20 .50
190 Santana Moss .25 .60
191 David Terrell .20 .50
192 Deion Branch .20 .50
193 Chester Taylor .25 .60
194 Derrick Blaylock .20 .50
195 Shaun Ellis .20 .50
196 Terrell Suggs .20 .50
197 Charles Woodson .30 .75
198 Jason Elam .20 .50
199 Lawrence Tynes RC .25 .60
200 David Akers .20 .50
201 Alex Smith QB RC 6.00 15.00
202 Aaron Rodgers RC 15.00 30.00
203 Ronnie Brown RC 2.00 5.00
204 Cadillac Williams RC 1.50 4.00
205 Braylon Edwards RC 1.50 4.00
206 Antrel Rolle RC 2.50 6.00
207 Cedric Benson RC 1.50 4.00
208 Troy Williamson RC 1.50 4.00
209 Mark Clayton RC 1.50 4.00
210 Matt Jones RC 1.50 4.00
211 Reggie Brown RC 1.50 4.00
212 Charlie Frye RC 1.50 4.00
213 Heath Miller RC 3.00 8.00
214 Vincent Jackson RC 2.50 6.00
215 Andrew Walter RC 1.50 4.00
216 Roddy White RC 2.50 6.00
217 Adam Jones RC 1.50 4.00
218 J.J. Arrington RC 2.00 5.00
219 Eric Shelton RC 1.50 4.00
220 Terrence Murphy RC 1.50 4.00
221 Frank Gore RC 3.00 8.00
222 Roscoe Parrish RC 1.50 4.00
223 Jason Campbell RC 1.50 4.00
224 Carlos Rogers RC 2.50 6.00
225 Mike Williams 2.00 5.00
226 Erasmus James RC .50 1.25
227 Travis Johnson RC .50 1.25
228 Dan Cody RC .50 1.25
229 Thomas Davis RC .50 1.25
230 David Pollack RC .50 1.25
231 David Greene RC .50 1.25
232 Alex Smith TE RC .50 1.25
233 Ryan Moats RC .50 1.25
234 Ciatrick Fason RC .50 1.25
235 Vernand Morency RC .60 1.50
236 Fred Gibson RC .50 1.25
237 Craphonso Thorpe RC .50 1.25
238 Kevin Everett RC .75 2.00
239 Kyle Orton RC .50 1.25
240 Derek Anderson RC .60 1.50
241 Derrick Johnson RC .60 1.50
242 Mark Bradley RC .50 1.25
243 Chris Henry RC .60 1.50
244 DeMarcus Ware RC 1.50 4.00
245 Luis Castillo RC .60 1.50
246 Mike Patterson RC .50 1.25
247 Brodney Pool RC .75 2.00
248 Barrett Ruud RC .60 1.50
249 Darren Sproles RC .75 2.00
250 Stefan LeFors RC .50 1.25
251 Josh Bullocks RC .60 1.50
252 Kevin Burnett RC .60 1.50
253 Lofa Tatupu RC .60 1.50
254 Matt Roth RC .50 1.25
255 Shaun Cody RC .60 1.50
256 Shawne Merriman RC .75 2.00
257 Corey Webster RC .60 1.50
258 Channing Crowder RC .60 1.50
259 Justin Miller RC .50 1.25
260 Eric Green RC .50 1.25
261 Marcus Spears RC .50 1.25
262 Marlin Jackson RC .50 1.25
263 Odell Thurman RC .75 2.00
264 Mike Nugent RC .60 1.50
265 Marion Barber RC .50 1.25
266 Anttaj Hawthorne RC .50 1.25
267 Dan Orlovsky RC .50 1.25
268 Fabian Washington RC .50 1.25
269 Justin Tuck RC .60 1.50
270 Jerome Mathis RC .75 2.00
271 Ronald Bartell RC .60 1.50
272 Kirk Morrison RC .75 2.00
273 Adrian McPherson RC .50 1.25
274 Matt Cassel RC .50 1.25
275 Maurice Clarett .60 1.50

2005 Upper Deck UD Exclusive

*VETS: 5X TO 12X BASE CARD HI
*ROOKIES 201-225: 1.2X TO 3X BASE CARD HI
*ROOKIES 226-275: 4X TO 10X BASE CARD HI
STATED PRINT RUN 50 SER.#'d SETS
202 Aaron Rodgers 125.00 200.00

2005 Upper Deck UD Exclusive Spectrum

UNPRICED SPECTRUM PRINT RUN 10 SETS

2005 Upper Deck Barry Sanders Heroes

COMPLETE SET (10) 10.00 25.00
COMMON CARD 1.25 3.00
STATED ODDS 1:12 HOB, 1:24 RET
UNPRICED AUTOGRAPH PRINT RUN 5

2005 Upper Deck Barry Sanders Heroes Jerseys

COMMON CARD 40.00 80.00
STATED PRINT RUN 25 SER.#'d SETS

2005 Upper Deck Game Jerseys

GAME JSY/ROOK.FUTURE JSY ODDS 1:8 H
STATED ODDS 1:24 RETAIL
*PATCHES: 1X TO 2.5X BASIC JERSEYS
PATCH STATED ODDS 1:288H, 1:960R
AH Ahman Green 3.00 8.00
BL Byron Leftwich 2.50 6.00
BR Ben Roethlisberger 8.00 20.00
DB Drew Bledsoe 3.00 8.00
DC Daunte Culpepper 3.00 8.00
DE Deuce McAllister 3.00 8.00
DM Donovan McNabb 3.00 8.00
DR David Carr 2.50 6.00
DS Duce Staley 2.50 6.00
EJ Edgerrin James 3.00 8.00
EM Eli Manning 6.00 15.00
ER Eric Moulds 2.50 6.00
JB Jerome Bettis 5.00 12.00
JH Joey Harrington 2.50 6.00
JJ Julius Jones 2.50 6.00
JL Jamal Lewis 3.00 8.00
JP Jake Plummer 2.50 6.00
JR Jerry Rice 8.00 20.00
JS Jeremy Shockey 2.50 6.00
JU Julius Peppers 3.00 8.00
KE Keyshawn Johnson 3.00 8.00
KJ Kevin Jones 2.50 6.00
LF Larry Fitzgerald 4.00 10.00
LT LaDainian Tomlinson 4.00 10.00
MB Marc Bulger 2.50 6.00
MF Marshall Faulk 3.00 8.00
MH Matt Hasselbeck 2.50 6.00
MS Michael Strahan 3.00 8.00
MV Michael Vick 3.00 8.00
OS Onterrio Smith 2.50 6.00
PM Peyton Manning 10.00 25.00
PR Philip Rivers 4.00 10.00
RG Rod Gardner 2.50 6.00
RL Ray Lewis 5.00 12.00
RM Randy Moss 3.00 8.00
SA Shaun Alexander 2.50 6.00
SM Steve McNair 3.00 8.00
TB Tom Brady 10.00 25.00
TG Trent Green 2.50 6.00
TI Tiki Barber 3.00 8.00
TY Tony Gonzalez 3.00 8.00
WM Willis McGahee 2.50 6.00

2005 Upper Deck MVP Predictors

STATED ODDS 1:12 HOB/RET
MVP1 Anquan Boldin 1.50 4.00
MVP2 Larry Fitzgerald 1.50 4.00
MVP3 Michael Vick 2.50 5.00
MVP4 Warrick Dunn 1.50 4.00
MVP5 Jamal Lewis 1.50 4.00
MVP6 Kyle Boller 1.50 4.00
MVP7 Willis McGahee 1.50 4.00
MVP8 J.P. Losman 1.50 4.00
MVP9 Jake Delhomme 1.50 4.00
MVP10 Stephen Davis 1.25 3.00
MVP11 Mushin Muhammad 1.25 3.00
MVP12 Rex Grossman 1.00 2.50
MVP13 Carson Palmer 1.50 4.00
MVP14 Rudi Johnson 1.25 3.00
MVP15 Chad Johnson 1.50 4.00
MVP16 Jeff Garcia 1.25 3.00
MVP17 Lee Suggs 1.00 2.50
MVP18 Julius Jones 1.50 4.00
MVP19 Drew Bledsoe 1.50 4.00
MVP20 Jake Plummer 1.50 4.00
MVP21 Reuben Droughns 1.25 3.00
MVP22 Ashley Lelie 1.00 2.50
MVP23 Roy Williams WR 1.50 4.00
MVP24 Kevin Jones 1.50 4.00
MVP25 Joey Harrington 1.50 4.00
MVP26 Brett Favre 3.00 8.00
MVP27 Ahman Green 1.50 4.00
MVP28 Javon Walker 1.25 3.00
MVP29 David Carr 1.50 4.00
MVP30 Andre Johnson 1.00 2.50
MVP31 Domanick Davis 1.25 3.00
MVP32 Peyton Manning 2.50 6.00
MVP33 Edgerrin James 1.50 4.00
MVP34 Marvin Harrison 1.25 3.00
MVP35 Byron Leftwich 1.50 4.00
MVP36 Fred Taylor 1.25 3.00
MVP37 Trent Green 1.50 4.00
MVP38 Priest Holmes 1.50 4.00
MVP39 Chris Chambers 1.00 2.50
MVP40 Daunte Culpepper 1.50 4.00
MVP41 Randy Moss 1.50 4.00
MVP42 Tom Brady 3.00 8.00
MVP43 Corey Dillon 1.50 4.00
MVP44 Aaron Brooks 1.50 4.00
MVP45 Joe Horn 1.00 2.50
MVP46 Deuce McAllister 1.50 4.00
MVP47 Eli Manning 2.50 6.00
MVP48 Tiki Barber 1.50 4.00
MVP49 Chad Pennington 1.50 4.00
MVP50 Laveranues Coles 1.00 2.50
MVP51 Curtis Martin 1.50 4.00
MVP52 Jerry Porter 1.00 2.50
MVP53 Kerry Collins 1.50 4.00
MVP54 Donovan McNabb 2.00 5.00
MVP55 Terrell Owens 1.50 4.00
MVP56 Brian Westbrook 1.25 3.00
MVP57 Ben Roethlisberger 3.00 8.00
MVP58 Hines Ward 1.50 4.00
MVP59 Drew Brees 1.50 4.00
MVP60 LaDainian Tomlinson 1.50 4.00
MVP61 Kevan Barlow 1.00 2.50
MVP62 Shaun Alexander WIN 30.00 60.00
MVP63 Matt Hasselbeck 1.50 4.00
MVP64 Darrell Jackson 1.00 2.50
MVP65 Marc Bulger 1.50 4.00
MVP66 Torry Holt 1.25 3.00
MVP67 Marshall Faulk 1.50 4.00
MVP68 Michael Pittman 1.00 2.50
MVP69 Michael Clayton 1.25 3.00
MVP70 Brian Griese 1.50 4.00
MVP71 Steve McNair 1.50 4.00
MVP72 Chris Brown 1.25 3.00
MVP73 Clinton Portis 1.50 4.00
MVP74 Patrick Ramsey 1.25 3.00
MVP75 J.J. Arrington 1.50 4.00
MVP76 Alex Smith QB 2.00 5.00
MVP77 Ronnie Brown 2.00 5.00
MVP78 Cadillac Williams 1.25 3.00
MVP79 Ciatrick Fason 1.50 4.00
MVP80 Matt Jones 1.25 3.00
MVP81 Braylon Edwards 1.50 4.00
MVP82 Troy Williamson 1.50 4.00
MVP83 Mark Clayton 1.50 4.00
MVP84 Roddy White 1.25 3.00
MVP85 Reggie Brown 1.50 4.00
MVP86 Stefan LeFors 1.00 2.50
MVP87 Frank Gore 2.00 5.00
MVP88 Charlie Frye 1.50 4.00
MVP89 Jason Campbell 1.50 4.00
MVP90 Wild Card 1.25 3.00

2005 Upper Deck Rookie Futures Jerseys

GAME JSY/ROOKIE FUT.JSY ODDS 1:8 HOB
STATED ODDS 1:24 RETAIL
AJ Adam Jones 2.50 6.00
AN Antrel Rolle 4.00 10.00
AS Alex Smith QB 10.00 25.00
AW Andrew Walter 2.50 6.00
BE Braylon Edwards 2.50 6.00
CA Carlos Rogers 4.00 10.00
CF Charlie Frye 2.50 6.00
CI Ciatrick Fason 2.50 6.00
CR Courtney Roby 2.50 6.00
CW Cadillac Williams 2.50 6.00
ES Eric Shelton 2.50 6.00
FG Frank Gore 5.00 12.00
JC Jason Campbell 2.50 6.00
JJ J.J. Arrington 3.00 8.00
KO Kyle Orton 2.50 6.00
MB Mark Bradley 2.50 6.00
MC Mark Clayton 2.50 6.00
MJ Matt Jones 2.50 6.00
MO Maurice Clarett 2.50 6.00
RB Ronnie Brown 3.00 8.00
RE Reggie Brown 2.50 6.00
RM Ryan Moats 2.50 6.00
RP Roscoe Parrish 2.50 6.00
RW Roddy White 4.00 10.00
SL Stefan LeFors 2.50 6.00
TM Terrence Murphy 2.50 6.00
TW Troy Williamson 2.50 6.00
VJ Vincent Jackson 4.00 10.00
VM Vernand Morency 2.50 6.00

2005 Upper Deck Rookie Futures Dual Jerseys

STATED ODDS 1:288
AR J.Arrington/A.Rolle 8.00 20.00
CB M.Clayton/M.Bradley 5.00 12.00
CW J.Campbell/C.Williams 5.00 12.00
FE B.Edwards/C.Frye 5.00 12.00
FO C.Frye/K.Orton 5.00 12.00
GS F.Gore/A.Smith QB 15.00 40.00
LS S.LeFors/E.Shelton 5.00 12.00
MM V.Morency/R.Moats 5.00 12.00
RB Ron.Brown/C.Rogers 8.00 20.00
RP A.Rolle/R.Parrish 8.00 20.00
WB Ron.Brown/C.Williams 6.00 15.00
WE B.Edwards/T.Williamson 5.00 12.00
WR Re.Brown/R.White 8.00 20.00

2005 Upper Deck Rookie Predictor Autographs

These cards were issued as prizes for the Upper Deck Rookie Debut Rookie of the Year Predictor contest. Since Cadillac Williams won the NFL's Offensive Rookie of the Year Award, collectors who mailed-in that winning predictor card to Upper Deck were awarded one of these signed cards at random. Each card is a basic 2005 Upper Deck rookie card with a clear sticker autograph applied on front and a special hologram on back with a serial number that matches one on an accompaning authentication card typical of Upper Deck "buy back" cards. Each one is hand serial numbered on the front.

PRIZES FOR UD DEBUT ROY PREDICTOR
202 Aaron Rodgers/25 250.00 400.00
204 Cadillac Williams/25 60.00 120.00
205 Braylon Edwards/25 30.00 80.00
206 Antrel Rolle/100
207 Cedric Benson/25
208 Troy Williamson/25
209 Mark Clayton/25
211 Reggie Brown/100
212 Charlie Frye/100
213 Heath Miller/100 20.00 40.00
214 Vincent Jackson/100
215 Andrew Walter/100
216 Roddy White/100
217 Adam Jones/100
218 J.J. Arrington/100 10.00 25.00
219 Eric Shelton/100 8.00 20.00
220 Terrence Murphy/50 8.00 20.00
221 Frank Gore/100 30.00 60.00
223 Jason Campbell/50 35.00 60.00
224 Carlos Rogers/40
225 Mike Williams/25 15.00 40.00

2005 Upper Deck Rookie Prospects

COMPLETE SET (30) 15.00 30.00
ONE PER RETAIL PACK
RPAJ Adam Jones .40 1.00
RPAN Antrel Rolle .60 1.50
RPAS Alex Smith QB 1.50 4.00
RPAW Andrew Walter .40 1.00
RPBE Braylon Edwards .40 1.00
RPCA Carlos Rogers .60 1.50
RPCF Charlie Frye .40 1.00
RPCR Courtney Roby .40 1.00
RPCT Ciatrick Fason .40 1.00
RPCW Cadillac Williams .40 1.00
RPES Eric Shelton .40 1.00
RPFG Frank Gore .75 2.00
RPJA J.J. Arrington .50 1.25
RPJC Jason Campbell .40 1.00
RPKO Kyle Orton .40 1.00
RPMB Mark Bradley .40 1.00
RPMC Mark Clayton .40 1.00
RPMJ Matt Jones .40 1.00
RPMO Maurice Clarett .40 1.00
RPMW Mike Williams .50 1.25
RPRB Ronnie Brown .50 1.25
RPRE Reggie Brown .40 1.00
RPRM Ryan Moats .40 1.00
RPRP Roscoe Parrish .40 1.00
RPRW Roddy White .60 1.50
RPSL Stefan LeFors .40 1.00
RPTM Terrence Murphy .40 1.00
RPTW Troy Williamson .40 1.00
RPVJ Vincent Jackson .60 1.50
RPVM Vernand Morency .40 1.00

2005 Upper Deck Signature Sensations

CARDS SER.#'d TO PLAYER'S JERSEY NO.
AB Aaron Brooks
AD Anthony Davis/28 12.50 30.00
AG Antonio Gates/85 12.50 30.00
AH Ahman Green/30 20.00 40.00
AN Anttaj Hawthorne/77 10.00 25.00
AQ Anquan Boldin/81 10.00 25.00
AR Antrel Rolle
BA Barrett Ruud/38 20.00 40.00
BF Brett Favre
BJ Brandon Jacobs/27 50.00 100.00
BL Byron Leftwich
CB Chris Brown/27 10.00 25.00
CD Cedric Benson/32 25.00 60.00
CE Chris Berman/25 12.50 30.00
CJ Chad Johnson/85 10.00 25.00
CW Cadillac Williams/24
DD Domanick Davis/37 12.50 30.00
DE Deuce McAllister/26 12.50 30.00
DI Deion Sanders/37 40.00 80.00
DO Dan Orlovsky
DP David Pollack/47 25.00 50.00
DS Darren Sproles/47 25.00 50.00
EJ Erasmus James/90 12.50 30.00
ES Eric Shelton/32 12.50 30.00
FG Fred Gibson/82 10.00 25.00
FT Fred Taylor/28 12.50 30.00
HM Heath Miller/89 20.00 50.00
JA J.J. Arrington/30 15.00 40.00
JB James Butler/22
JH Joe Horn/87 7.50 20.00
JJ Julius Jones/21 7.50 20.00
JO J.P. Losman
KC Keary Colbert/83 10.00 25.00
LE Lee Evans/83 10.00 25.00
LJ Larry Johnson/34 12.00 30.00
MAO Marion Barber/21
MB Marc Bulger
MI Michael Clayton/80 10.00 25.00
MM Muhsin Muhammad/87 7.50 20.00
MV Michael Vick
NB Nate Burleson/81 12.50 30.00
RB Ronnie Brown/23 10.00 25.00
RJ Rudi Johnson/32 15.00 40.00
RM Ryan Moats/20
RW Roy Williams WR
RY Reggie Wayne/87 12.50 30.00
SJ Steven Jackson/39 30.00 60.00
TM T.A. McLendon/44 12.50 30.00
TS Taylor Stubblefield/21
TW Troy Williamson/82 15.00 40.00
VJ Vincent Jackson/81 10.00 25.00
VM Vernand Morency/33 12.50 30.00
WR Walter Reyes/39 10.00 25.00

2005 Upper Deck Troy Aikman Heroes

COMPLETE SET (10) 10.00 25.00
COMMON CARD 1.25 3.00
STATED ODDS 1:12 HOB, 1:24 RET
UNPRICED AUTOGRAPH PRINT RUN 5

2005 Upper Deck Troy Aikman Heroes Jerseys

COMMON CARD 40.00 80.00
STATED PRINT RUN 25 SER.#'d SETS

2005 Upper Deck LAPD

These cards were produced by Upper Deck but issued by the Los Angeles Police Department during the 2005 NFL season. Each card appears to be a standard issue 2005 Upper Deck card on the front but the cardback has been re-created to include a safety message, a new card number, and the LAPD logo. Each NFL team is represented in the set by one player.

COMPLETE SET (32) 12.50 25.00
1 Anquan Boldin .30 .75
2 DeAngelo Hall .30 .75
3 Eric Moulds .30 .75
4 Steve Smith .50 1.25
5 Rex Grossman .30 .75
6 Chad Johnson .30 .75
7 Roy Williams S .50 1.25
8 John Lynch .30 .75
9 Kevin Jones .60 1.50
10 Javon Walker .30 .75
11 Domanick Davis .30 .75
12 Peyton Manning 1.00 2.50
13 Byron Leftwich .50 1.25
14 Priest Holmes .50 1.25
15 Ronnie Brown 1.50 4.00
16 Daunte Culpepper .50 1.25
17 Adam Vinatieri .50 1.25
18 Joe Horn .30 .75
19 Jeremy Shockey .50 1.25
20 Jevon Kearse .30 .75
21 Jerome Bettis .50 1.25
22 Torry Holt .30 .75
23 Drew Brees .30 .75
24 Alex Smith QB 1.50 4.00
25 Matt Hasselbeck .30 .75
26 Joey Galloway .30 .75
27 Clinton Portis .50 1.25
28 Kyle Boller .30 .75
29 Steve McNair .50 1.25
30 Kerry Collins .30 .75
31 Jonathan Vilma .30 .75
32 Braylon Edwards .75 2.00

2005 Upper Deck Rookies National Convention

Upper Deck produced this set and distributed it at the 2005 National Sport Collectors Convention in Chicago. The set includes the top-6 2005 NFL draft picks along with the title "The National" printed on the cardfronts. The company made the cards available to collectors via a wrapper redemption program at their show booth and each card was serial numbered to 750-copies. Each player also signed just 5-cards.

COMPLETE SET (6) 20.00 40.00
UNPRICED AUTOS SER.#'d TO 5
NFL1 Alex Smith QB 4.00 10.00
NFL2 Braylon Edwards 4.00 10.00
NFL3 Cedric Benson 3.00 8.00
NFL4 Aaron Rodgers 6.00 15.00
NFL5 Ronnie Brown 4.00 10.00
NFL6 Cadillac Williams 3.00 8.00

2005 Upper Deck UD Promos

*UD PROMOS: .8X TO 2X BASIC CARDS

2006 Upper Deck

This 275-card set was released in August, 2006. The set was issued into the hobby in eight card packs, with an $2.99 SRP, which came 24 packs to a box. Cards numbered 1-200 are veteran players sequenced in alphabetical team order while cards 201-275 are all rookies. The rookies are broken into two subsets, both of which are in first name alphabetical order: Cards numbered 201-225 were inserted at a stated rate of one in eight while cards numbered 226-275 were inserted at a stated rate of one per pack.

COMPLETE SET (275) 150.00 300.00
COMP.SET w/o SP's (250) 30.00 60.00
COMP.SET w/o RC's (200) 12.00 30.00
201-225 ROOKIE ODDS 1:8
226-275 ROOKIE ODDS 1:1
1 Larry Fitzgerald .25 .60
2 Anquan Boldin .20 .50
3 J.J. Arrington .20 .50
4 Kurt Warner .25 .60
5 Neil Rackers .20 .50
6 Edgerrin James .25 .60
7 Michael Vick .25 .60
8 Alge Crumpler .25 .60
9 Warrick Dunn .20 .50
10 Michael Jenkins .20 .50
11 Roddy White .20 .50
12 DeAngelo Hall .20 .50
13 Jamal Lewis .25 .60
14 Derrick Mason .20 .50
15 Todd Heap .20 .50
16 Kyle Boller .20 .50
17 Ray Lewis .30 .75
18 Ed Reed .25 .60
19 Willis McGahee .20 .50
20 Lee Evans .25 .60
21 J.P. Losman .25 .60
22 Rashad Baker .20 .50
23 Takeo Spikes .20 .50
24 Aaron Schobel .20 .50
25 Steve Smith .30 .75
26 Jake Delhomme .20 .50
27 DeShaun Foster .25 .60
28 Keary Colbert .20 .50
29 Julius Peppers .25 .60
30 Ma'Ake Kemoeatu .20 .50
31 Rex Grossman .20 .50
32 Muhsin Muhammad .20 .50
33 Brian Urlacher .30 .75
34 Thomas Jones .20 .50
35 Cedric Benson .20 .50
36 Nathan Vasher .20 .50
37 Rudi Johnson .20 .50
38 Chad Johnson .20 .50
39 T.J. Houshmandzadeh .20 .50
40 Chris Henry .20 .50
41 Deltha O'Neal .20 .50
42 Odell Thurman .20 .50
43 Carson Palmer .25 .60
44 Charlie Frye .25 .60
45 Reuben Droughns .25 .60
46 Braylon Edwards .20 .50
47 Kellen Winslow Jr. .20 .50
48 Steve Heiden .20 .50
49 Joe Jurevicius .20 .50
50 Drew Bledsoe .25 .60
51 Julius Jones .20 .50
52 Terrell Owens .25 .60
53 Terry Glenn .25 .60
54 Jason Witten .25 .60
55 DeMarcus Ware .25 .60
56 Roy Williams S .20 .50
57 Jake Plummer .20 .50
58 Tatum Bell .20 .50
59 Al Wilson .20 .50
60 Rod Smith .25 .60
61 Ashley Lelie .20 .50
62 Champ Bailey .25 .60
63 Javon Walker .25 .60
64 Jon Kitna .20 .50
65 Kevin Jones .20 .50
66 Roy Williams WR .20 .50
67 Mike Williams .20 .50
68 Marcus Pollard .20 .50
69 Dre Bly .20 .50
70 Brett Favre .60 1.50
71 Ahman Green .25 .60
72 Donald Driver .25 .60
73 Robert Ferguson .20 .50
74 Bubba Franks .20 .50
75 Kabeer Gbaja-Biamila .20 .50
76 David Carr .20 .50
77 Domanick Davis .20 .50
78 Andre Johnson .25 .60
79 Eric Moulds .20 .50
80 Jeb Putzier .20 .50
81 Dunta Robinson .20 .50
82 Peyton Manning .75 2.00
83 Dominic Rhodes .20 .50
84 Reggie Wayne .25 .60
85 Marvin Harrison .25 .60
86 Dallas Clark .20 .50
87 Dwight Freeney .20 .50
88 Bob Sanders .25 .60
89 Byron Leftwich .20 .50
90 Fred Taylor .20 .50
91 Greg Jones .20 .50
92 Ernest Wilford .20 .50
93 John Henderson .20 .50
94 Matt Jones .20 .50

95 Trent Green .20 .50
96 Larry Johnson .20 .50
97 Priest Holmes .20 .50
98 Eddie Kennison .20 .50
99 Tony Gonzalez .25 .60
100 Dante Hall .20 .50
101 Daunte Culpepper .25 .60
102 Ronnie Brown .25 .60
103 Marty Booker .20 .50
104 Chris Chambers .20 .50
105 Randy McMichael .20 .50
106 Zach Thomas .25 .60
107 Brad Johnson .25 .60
108 Chester Taylor .25 .60
109 Antoine Winfield .20 .50
110 Koren Robinson .20 .50
111 Travis Taylor .20 .50
112 Darren Sharper .20 .50
113 Tom Brady 1.00 2.50
114 Corey Dillon .20 .50
115 Deion Branch .20 .50
116 Reche Caldwell .20 .50
117 Ben Watson .20 .50
118 Tedy Bruschi .25 .60
119 Rodney Harrison .20 .50
120 Drew Brees .30 .75
121 Deuce McAllister .25 .60
122 Joe Horn .20 .50
123 Donte Stallworth .20 .50
124 Devery Henderson .20 .50
125 Will Smith .20 .50
126 Eli Manning .25 .60
127 Tiki Barber .25 .60
128 Plaxico Burress .20 .50
129 Amani Toomer .20 .50
130 Jeremy Shockey .20 .50
131 Michael Strahan .25 .60
132 Osi Umenyiora .20 .50
133 Chad Pennington .20 .50
134 Curtis Martin .25 .60
135 Justin McCareins .20 .50
136 Laveranues Coles .20 .50
137 Jonathan Vilma .20 .50
138 Shaun Ellis .20 .50
139 Aaron Brooks .20 .50
140 LaMont Jordan .25 .60
141 Randy Moss .25 .60
142 Jerry Porter .20 .50
143 Doug Gabriel .20 .50
144 Derrick Burgess .20 .50
145 Donovan McNabb .25 .60
146 Brian Westbrook .20 .50
147 Jevon Kearse .20 .50
148 Reggie Brown .20 .50
149 L.J. Smith .20 .50
150 Brian Dawkins .30 .75
151 Ben Roethlisberger .40 1.00
152 Willie Parker .25 .60
153 Hines Ward .25 .60
154 Cedrick Wilson .20 .50
155 Heath Miller .20 .50
156 Joey Porter .20 .50
157 Troy Polamalu .30 .75
158 Philip Rivers .30 .75
159 LaDainian Tomlinson .30 .75
160 Keenan McCardell .25 .60
161 Eric Parker .20 .50
162 Antonio Gates .30 .75
163 Shawne Merriman .25 .60
164 Donnie Edwards .20 .50
165 Alex Smith QB .25 .60
166 Frank Gore .25 .60
167 Antonio Bryant .20 .50
168 Eric Johnson .20 .50
169 Arnaz Battle .20 .50
170 Bryant Young .20 .50
171 Matt Hasselbeck .20 .50
172 Shaun Alexander .20 .50
173 Darrell Jackson .25 .60
174 Etric Pruitt .20 .50
175 Julian Peterson .20 .50
176 Lofa Tatupu .20 .50
177 Marc Bulger .20 .50
178 Steven Jackson .20 .50
179 Torry Holt .25 .60
180 Kevin Curtis .25 .60
181 Isaac Bruce .30 .75
182 Leonard Little .20 .50
183 Chris Simms .20 .50
184 Cadillac Williams .25 .60
185 Joey Galloway .25 .60
186 Michael Clayton .20 .50
187 Derrick Brooks .20 .50
188 Ronde Barber .20 .50
189 Billy Volek .20 .50
190 Chris Brown .20 .50
191 Drew Bennett .25 .60
192 Ben Troupe .20 .50
193 David Givens .25 .60
194 Adam Jones .20 .50
195 Mark Brunell .25 .60
196 Clinton Portis .20 .50
197 Santana Moss .25 .60
198 Chris Cooley .20 .50
199 Antwaan Randle El .20 .50
200 Sean Taylor .30 .75
201 A.J. Hawk RC 2.00 5.00
202 Anthony Fasano RC 1.50 4.00
203 Brian Calhoun RC 1.50 4.00
204 Chad Greenway RC 2.50 6.00
205 Chad Jackson RC 1.50 4.00
206 DeAngelo Williams RC 2.00 5.00
207 D'Brickashaw Ferguson RC 1.50 4.00
208 Brodie Croyle RC 1.50 4.00
209 Haloti Ngata RC 2.00 5.00
210 Jay Cutler RC 2.00 5.00
211 Joseph Addai RC 1.50 4.00
212 Laurence Maroney RC 1.50 4.00
213 LenDale White RC 1.50 4.00
214 Maurice Drew RC 2.50 6.00
215 Mario Williams RC 2.50 6.00
216 Matt Leinart RC 1.50 4.00
217 Maurice Stovall RC 1.50 4.00
218 Michael Huff RC 2.00 5.00
219 Reggie Bush RC 2.50 6.00
220 Santonio Holmes RC 2.00 5.00
221 Sinorice Moss RC 1.50 4.00
222 Kellen Clemens RC 1.50 4.00
223 Tarvaris Jackson RC 1.50 4.00
224 Vernon Davis RC 2.00 5.00
225 Vince Young RC 1.50 4.00
226 Donte Whitner RC .75 2.00
227 Antonio Cromartie RC .75 2.00
228 Ashton Youboty RC .60 1.50
229 Bobby Carpenter RC .60 1.50
230 Brad Smith RC .75 2.00
231 Brandon Williams RC .60 1.50
232 Dominique Byrd RC .60 1.50
233 Brodrick Bunkley RC .75 2.00
234 Charlie Whitehurst RC .60 1.50
235 Demetrius Williams RC .60 1.50
236 Cory Rodgers RC .60 1.50
237 Daniel Bullocks RC .60 1.50
238 Manny Lawson RC .75 2.00
239 Darrell Hackney RC .75 2.00
240 Darryl Tapp RC .75 2.00
241 David Thomas RC .60 1.50
242 DeMeco Ryans RC .75 2.00
243 Derek Hagan RC .75 2.00
244 Devin Hester RC 1.25 3.00
245 D'Qwell Jackson RC .60 1.50
246 Brandon Marshall RC 1.25 3.00
247 Ernie Sims RC .60 1.50
248 Gabe Watson RC .60 1.50
249 Jason Allen RC .75 2.00
250 Greg Jennings RC 1.00 2.50
251 Marcus Vick RC .60 1.50
252 Jason Avant RC .60 1.50
253 Jeremy Bloom RC .60 1.50
254 Jerome Harrison RC .60 1.50
255 Joe Klopfenstein RC .60 1.50
256 Johnathan Joseph RC .75 2.00
257 Jimmy Williams RC .60 1.50
258 Kamerion Wimbley RC .75 2.00
259 Leon Washington RC .60 1.50
260 Marcedes Lewis RC .60 1.50
261 Marcus McNeill RC .60 1.50
262 Mathias Kiwanuka RC 1.00 2.50
263 Leonard Pope RC 1.00 2.50
264 Tamba Hali RC 1.00 2.50
265 Mike Hass RC .60 1.50
266 Omar Jacobs RC .60 1.50
267 Jerious Norwood RC .60 1.50
268 Owen Daniels RC 1.00 2.50
269 P.J. Daniels RC .60 1.50
270 Ray Edwards RC 1.00 2.50
271 Michael Robinson RC .60 1.50
272 Rocky McIntosh RC .60 1.50
273 Travis Wilson RC .60 1.50
274 Tye Hill RC .60 1.50
275 Thomas Howard RC .60 1.50

2006 Upper Deck Exclusive Edition Rookies

These cards were inserted 30-per special 2006 Upper Deck Rookie Exclusive Fat Pack. Each is a parallel of the basic issue rookie subset with the addition of the set name "Rookie Exclusive Edition" on the cardfronts.
*EXCLUSIVE EDITION: .1X TO .25X
30-PER ROOKIE EDITION FAT PACK

2006 Upper Deck Target Exclusive Rookies

*SINGLES: .25X TO .6X BASIC CARDS
TWO PER SPECIAL TARGET PACKS
TARGET VERSION PHOTOS DIFFER

2006 Upper Deck Target Exclusive Rookies Autographs

NDOM INSERTS IN TARGET PACKS
GOLD FOIL PRINTED ON FRONT
202 Anthony Fasano
210 Jay Cutler 20.00 50.00
211 Joseph Addai 75.00 150.00
216 Matt Leinart SP
219 Reggie Bush SP
225 Vince Young SP
232 Dominique Byrd
234 Charlie Whitehurst
235 Demetrius Williams
236 Cory Rodgers
239 Darrell Hackney
242 DeMeco Ryans
243 Derek Hagan
246 Brandon Marshall
247 Ernie Sims
250 Greg Jennings
254 Jerome Harrison
257 Jimmy Williams
259 Leon Washington
263 Leonard Pope
268 Owen Daniels

2006 Upper Deck UD Exclusive Gold

*VETS 1-200: 4X TO 10X BASIC CARDS
*ROOKIES 201-225: 1X TO 2.5X BASIC CARDS
*ROOKIES 226-275: 2.5X TO 6X BASIC CARDS
STATED PRINT RUN 100 SER.#'d SETS
219 Reggie Bush 6.00 15.00

2006 Upper Deck UD Exclusive Silver

*VETERANS 1-200: 6X TO 15X BASIC CARDS
*ROOKIES 201-225: 1.5X TO 4X BASIC CARDS
*ROOKIES 226-275: 4X TO 10X BASIC CARDS
STATED PRINT RUN 50 SER.#'d SETS
219 Reggie Bush 10.00 25.00

2006 Upper Deck 10 Sack Club

COMPLETE SET (10) 2.50 6.00
STATED ODDS 1:6
10SDB Derrick Burgess .50 1.25
10SDF Dwight Freeney .50 1.25
10SJP Joey Porter .50 1.25
10SJT Jason Taylor .60 1.50
10SKG Kabeer Gbaja-Biamila .50 1.25
10SMS Michael Strahan .60 1.50
10SOU Osi Umenyiora .50 1.25
10SPE Julius Peppers .60 1.50
10SSM Shawne Merriman .60 1.50
10SSR Simeon Rice .50 1.25

2006 Upper Deck 1000 Yard Receiving Club

MPLETE SET (15) 4.00 10.00
STATED ODDS 1:6
1KREAB Anquan Boldin .50 1.25
1KRECC Chris Chambers .50 1.25
1KRECJ Chad Johnson .50 1.25
1KREHW Hines Ward .60 1.50
1KREJG Joey Galloway .60 1.50
1KREJW Javon Walker .60 1.50
1KRELF Larry Fitzgerald .60 1.50
1KREMH Marvin Harrison .60 1.50
1KREPB Plaxico Burress .50 1.25
1KRERM Randy Moss .60 1.50
1KRERW Reggie Wayne .60 1.50
1KRESM Santana Moss .60 1.50
1KRESS Steve Smith .75 2.00
1KRETH Torry Holt .60 1.50
1KRETO Terrell Owens .60 1.50

2006 Upper Deck 1000 Yard Rushing Club

COMPLETE SET (20) 8.00 20.00
STATED ODDS 1:4.5
1KRAG Ahman Green .60 1.50
1KRCD Corey Dillon .50 1.25
1KRCM Curtis Martin .60 1.50
1KRCP Clinton Portis .50 1.25
1KRCW Cadillac Williams .60 1.50
1KRDM Deuce McAllister .60 1.50
1KREJ Edgerrin James .60 1.50
1KRJL Jamal Lewis .60 1.50
1KRJO LaMont Jordan .60 1.50
1KRKJ Kevin Jones .50 1.25
1KRLJ Larry Johnson .50 1.25
1KRLT LaDainian Tomlinson .75 2.00
1KRPH Priest Holmes .50 1.25
1KRRJ Rudi Johnson .50 1.25
1KRSA Shaun Alexander .50 1.25
1KRSJ Steven Jackson .50 1.25
1KRTB Tiki Barber .60 1.50
1KRWD Warrick Dunn .50 1.25
1KRWM Willis McGahee .50 1.25
1KRWP Willie Parker .60 1.50

2006 Upper Deck 3000 Yard Passing Club

COMPLETE SET (20) 8.00 20.00
STATED ODDS 1:4.5
3KPAB Aaron Brooks .50 1.25
3KPBF Brett Favre 1.50 4.00
3KPBR Drew Brees .75 2.00
3KPBU Marc Bulger .50 1.25
3KPCA David Carr .50 1.25
3KPCP Carson Palmer .60 1.50
3KPDB Drew Bledsoe .60 1.50
3KPDC Daunte Culpepper .60 1.50
3KPDM Donovan McNabb .60 1.50
3KPEM Eli Manning .60 1.50
3KPJD Jake Delhomme .50 1.25
3KPJH Joey Harrington .50 1.25
3KPJP Jake Plummer .50 1.25
3KPKW Kurt Warner .60 1.50
3KPMB Mark Brunell .60 1.50
3KPMH Matt Hasselbeck .50 1.25
3KPPM Peyton Manning 2.00 5.00
3KPSM Steve McNair .60 1.50
3KPTB Tom Brady 2.50 6.00
3KPTG Trent Green .50 1.25

2006 Upper Deck All Upper Deck Team

TWO PER RETAIL FAT PACK
AC Alge Crumpler .60 1.50
AG Antonio Gates .75 2.00
AW Al Wilson .50 1.25
BA Tiki Barber .60 1.50
BF Brett Favre 1.50 4.00
BR Ben Roethlisberger 1.00 2.50
BS Bob Sanders .60 1.50
BU Brian Urlacher .75 2.00
CB Champ Bailey .60 1.50
CJ Chad Johnson .50 1.25
CP Carson Palmer .60 1.50
DB Derrick Brooks .50 1.25
DF Dwight Freeney .50 1.25
DM Donovan McNabb .60 1.50
EJ Edgerrin James .60 1.50
JM Jerome Mathis .50 1.25
JP Julius Peppers .60 1.50
JS Jeremy Shockey .50 1.25
LB Lance Briggs .60 1.50
LF Larry Fitzgerald .60 1.50
LJ Larry Johnson .50 1.25
LT LaDainian Tomlinson .75 2.00
MS Mack Strong .40 1.00
MV Michael Vick .60 1.50
NR Neil Rackers .50 1.25
NV Nathan Vasher .50 1.25
OU Osi Umenyiora .50 1.25
OW Terrell Owens .60 1.50
PM Peyton Manning 2.00 5.00
PO Clinton Portis .50 1.25
RB Ronde Barber .50 1.25
RJ Rudi Johnson .50 1.25
RM Randy Moss .60 1.50
RS Richard Seymour .50 1.25
SA Shaun Alexander .50 1.25
SM Santana Moss .60 1.50
SS Steve Smith .75 2.00
ST Sean Taylor .75 2.00
TB Tom Brady 2.50 6.00
TG Tony Gonzalez .60 1.50
TH Torry Holt .60 1.50
TP Troy Polamalu .75 2.00

2006 Upper Deck Collect The Rookies Game

1 Reggie Bush .25 .60
2 Jay Cutler .20 .50
3 Santonio Holmes .20 .50
4 Matt Leinart .15 .40
5 DeAngelo Williams .20 .50
6 Vince Young .15 .40

2006 Upper Deck Fantasy Top 25

COMPLETE SET (25) 15.00 40.00
STATED ODDS 1:4
F25AB Anquan Boldin .60 1.50
F25BR Tom Brady 3.00 8.00
F25CJ Chad Johnson .60 1.50
F25CP Carson Palmer .75 2.00
F25CW Cadillac Williams .75 2.00
F25DM Donovan McNabb .75 2.00
F25DW DeAngelo Williams .50 1.25
F25EJ Edgerrin James .75 2.00
F25EM Eli Manning .75 2.00
F25HA Matt Hasselbeck .60 1.50
F25JO LaMont Jordan .75 2.00
F25LF Larry Fitzgerald .75 2.00
F25LJ Larry Johnson .60 1.50
F25LT LaDainian Tomlinson 1.00 2.50
F25MH Marvin Harrison .75 2.00
F25PM Peyton Manning 2.50 6.00
F25PO Clinton Portis .60 1.50
F25RB Reggie Bush .60 1.50
F25RJ Rudi Johnson .60 1.50
F25RM Randy Moss .75 2.00
F25SA Shaun Alexander .60 1.50
F25SS Steve Smith 1.00 2.50
F25TB Tiki Barber .75 2.00
F25TG Trent Green .60 1.50
F25TH Torry Holt .75 2.00

2006 Upper Deck Game Jerseys

STATED ODDS 1:24
GJAB Aaron Brooks 3.00 8.00
GJAC Alge Crumpler 3.00 8.00
GJBA Tiki Barber 4.00 10.00
GJBD Brian Dawkins 4.00 10.00
GJBE Braylon Edwards 4.00 10.00
GJBL Drew Bledsoe 4.00 10.00
GJBR Tom Brady 6.00 15.00
GJBU Brian Urlacher 4.00 10.00
GJCA David Carr 3.00 8.00
GJCD Corey Dillon 3.00 8.00
GJCF Charlie Frye 3.00 8.00
GJCW Cadillac Williams 3.00 8.00
GJDB Drew Brees 4.00 10.00
GJDC Daunte Culpepper 4.00 10.00
GJDM Deuce McAllister 4.00 10.00
GJEM Eli Manning 6.00 15.00
GJER Ed Reed 3.00 8.00
GJJJ Julius Jones 4.00 10.00
GJJO LaMont Jordan 3.00 8.00
GJJP Julius Peppers 3.00 8.00
GJJS Jeremy Shockey 4.00 10.00
GJKJ Kevin Jones 4.00 10.00
GJKO Kyle Orton 3.00 8.00
GJLE Byron Leftwich 4.00 10.00
GJLF Larry Fitzgerald 3.00 8.00
GJLJ Larry Johnson 5.00 12.00
GJMB Marc Bulger SP 10.00 25.00
GJMH Matt Hasselbeck 4.00 10.00
GJMW Mike Williams 3.00 8.00
GJPB Plaxico Burress 3.00 8.00
GJPH Priest Holmes 3.00 8.00
GJPL Jake Plummer 3.00 8.00
GJPM Peyton Manning 6.00 15.00
GJRB Ronnie Brown 4.00 10.00
GJRJ Rudi Johnson 3.00 8.00
GJSJ Steven Jackson 4.00 10.00
GJSS Steve Smith 4.00 10.00
GJTB Tatum Bell 3.00 8.00
GJTG Tony Gonzalez 3.00 8.00
GJTO Terrell Owens 4.00 10.00
GJTW Troy Williamson 3.00 8.00
GJWM Willis McGahee 4.00 10.00

2006 Upper Deck Gridiron Debut

RANDOM INSERTS IN WAL-MART PACKS
GDAF Anthony Fasano .60 1.50
CDAH A.J. Hawk .75 2.00
GDAV Jason Avant .60 1.50
GDBB Brodrick Bunkley .75 2.00
GDBC Brian Calhoun .60 1.50
GDBM Brandon Marshall 1.25 3.00
GDBW Brandon Williams .60 1.50
GDCJ Chad Jackson .60 1.50
GDCR Brodie Croyle .60 1.50
GDCW Charlie Whitehurst .60 1.50
GDDB Dominique Byrd .60 1.50
GDDF D'Brickashaw Ferguson .60 1.50
GDDW DeAngelo Williams .75 2.00
GDES Ernie Sims .60 1.50
GDHA Derek Hagan .75 2.00
GDHN Haloti Ngata .75 2.00
GDJA Joseph Addai .60 1.50
GDJC Jay Cutler .75 2.00
GDJK Joe Klopfenstein .60 1.50
GDJN Jerious Norwood .60 1.50
GDKC Kellen Clemens .60 1.50
GDKW Kamerion Wimbley .75 2.00
GDLE Marcedes Lewis .60 1.50
GDLM Laurence Maroney .60 1.50
GDLP Leonard Pope 1.00 2.50
GDLW LenDale White .60 1.50
GDMD Maurice Drew 1.00 2.50
GDMH Michael Huff .75 2.00
GDML Matt Leinart .60 1.50
GDMR Michael Robinson .60 1.50
GDMS Maurice Stovall .60 1.50
GDMW Mario Williams 1.00 2.50
GDOJ Omar Jacobs .60 1.50
GDRB Reggie Bush 1.00 2.50
GDSH Santonio Holmes .75 2.00
GDSM Sinorice Moss .60 1.50
GDTJ Tarvaris Jackson .60 1.50
GDTW Travis Wilson .60 1.50
GDVD Vernon Davis .75 2.00
GDVY Vince Young .60 1.50
GDWA Leon Washington .60 1.50
GDWI Demetrius Williams .60 1.50

2006 Upper Deck Joe Theismann Heroes

COMPLETE SET (10) 12.00 30.00
COMMON CARD 1.50 4.00
STATED ODDS 1:24
UNPRICED AUTOS SER.#'d TO 5

2006 Upper Deck Joe Theismann Heroes Jerseys

MMON CARD 35.00 60.00
STATED PRINT RUN 25 SER.#'d SETS

2006 Upper Deck Roger Staubach Heroes

COMPLETE SET (10) 12.00 30.00
COMMON CARD 1.50 4.00
STATED ODDS 1:24
UNPRICED AUTOS SER.#'d TO 5

2006 Upper Deck Roger Staubach Heroes Jerseys

COMMON CARD 40.00 80.00
STATED PRINT RUN 25 SER.#'d SETS

2006 Upper Deck Rookie Exclusive Rookie Photo Shoot Flashback

AB Anquan Boldin .25 .60
AJ Adam Jones .25 .60
AR Antrel Rolle .25 .60
AW Andrew Walter .25 .60
BL Byron Leftwich .25 .60
BU Brian Urlacher .40 1.00
CJ Chad Johnson .25 .60
CP Carson Palmer .30 .75
CR Carlos Rogers .25 .60
CW Cadillac Williams .30 .75
DB Drew Brees .40 1.00
DC Daunte Culpepper .30 .75
DM Donovan McNabb .30 .75
EJ Edgerrin James .30 .75
EM Eli Manning .30 .75
FG Frank Gore .30 .75
HW Hines Ward .30 .75
JC Jason Campbell .25 .60
JG Joey Galloway .30 .75
JJ Julius Jones .25 .60
JL Jamal Lewis .30 .75
JP Jake Plummer .25 .60
KJ Kevin Jones .25 .60
KW Kellen Winslow .25 .60
LE Lee Evans .30 .75
LF Larry Fitzgerald .30 .75
LJ Larry Johnson .25 .60
LT LaDainian Tomlinson .40 1.00
MC Mark Clayton .25 .60
MH Marvin Harrison .30 .75
MJ Matt Jones .25 .60
MJ Michael Jenkins .25 .60
MV Michael Vick .30 .75
PB Plaxico Burress .25 .60
PM Peyton Manning 1.00 2.50
PR Philip Rivers .40 1.00
RB Ronnie Brown .30 .75
RB Reggie Brown .25 .60
RJ Rudi Johnson .25 .60
RO Ben Roethlisberger .50 1.25
RW Reggie Wayne .30 .75
SA Shaun Alexander .25 .60
SJ Steven Jackson .25 .60
SM Santana Moss .30 .75
TH Torry Holt .30 .75
TW Troy Williamson .25 .60
WD Warrick Dunn .25 .60
WH Roddy White .25 .60
WI Reggie Williams .30 .75
WM Willis McGahee .25 .60

2006 Upper Deck Rookie Futures Jerseys

ATED ODDS 1:24 HOB
RFAH A.J. Hawk 3.00 8.00
RFBC Brian Calhoun 2.50 6.00
RFBM Brandon Marshall 5.00 12.00
RFBW Brandon Williams 2.50 6.00
RFCJ Chad Jackson 2.50 6.00
RFCW Charlie Whitehurst 2.50 6.00
RFDH Derek Hagan 3.00 8.00
RFDW DeAngelo Williams 3.00 8.00
RFJA Jason Avant 2.50 6.00
RFJK Joe Klopfenstein 2.50 6.00
RFJN Jerious Norwood 2.50 6.00
RFKC Kellen Clemens 2.50 6.00
RFLE Marcedes Lewis 2.50 6.00
RFLM Laurence Maroney 2.50 6.00
RFLW LenDale White 2.50 6.00
RFMD Maurice Drew 4.00 10.00
RFML Matt Leinart 2.50 6.00
RFMR Michael Robinson 2.50 6.00
RFMS Maurice Stovall 2.50 6.00
RFMW Mario Williams 4.00 10.00
RFOJ Omar Jacobs 2.50 6.00
RFRB Reggie Bush 4.00 10.00
RFSH Santonio Holmes 3.00 8.00
RFSM Sinorice Moss 2.50 6.00
RFTJ Tarvaris Jackson 2.50 6.00
RFTW Travis Wilson 2.50 6.00
RFVD Vernon Davis 3.00 8.00
RFVY Vince Young 2.50 6.00
RFWA Leon Washington 2.50 6.00
RFWI Demetrius Williams 2.50 6.00

2006 Upper Deck Rookie Futures Jerseys Dual

BL M.Leinart/R.Bush SP 15.00 40.00
BW L.White/R.Bush SP 20.00 50.00
CJ K.Clemens/O.Jacobs 8.00 20.00
DL M.Lewis/M.Drew 10.00 25.00
DR M.Robinson/V.Davis 6.00 15.00
HH A.Hawk/S.Holmes 12.00 30.00
HW D.Hagan/T.Wilson 8.00 20.00
JM C.Jackson/S.Moss 8.00 20.00
LY M.Leinart/V.Young SP 10.00 25.00
MW B.Williams/B.Marshall 10.00 25.00
NC B.Calhoun/J.Norwood 8.00 20.00
WM D.Williams/L.Maroney 12.00 30.00

2006 Upper Deck Rookie Futures Jersey Autographs

STATED PRINT RUN 10-100
RFAH A.J. Hawk/100 12.00 30.00
RFBC Brian Calhoun/100 10.00 25.00
RFBM Brandon Marshall/100 20.00 50.00
RFBW Brandon Williams/100 10.00 25.00
RFCJ Chad Jackson/100 10.00 25.00
RFCW Charlie Whitehurst/100 10.00 25.00
RFDH Derek Hagan/100 12.00 30.00
RFDW DeAngelo Williams/100 12.00 30.00
RFJA Jason Avant/100 10.00 25.00
RFJK Joe Klopfenstein/100 10.00 25.00
RFJN Jerious Norwood/100 10.00 25.00
RFKC Kellen Clemens/100 10.00 25.00
RFLE Marcedes Lewis/25 15.00 40.00
RFLM Laurence Maroney/100 10.00 25.00
RFLW LenDale White/100 10.00 25.00
RFMD Maurice Drew/100 15.00 40.00
RFML Matt Leinart/25 20.00 50.00
RFMR Michael Robinson/100 10.00 25.00
RFMS Maurice Stovall/100 10.00 25.00
RFMW Mario Williams/35 20.00 50.00
RFOJ Omar Jacobs/100 10.00 25.00
RFRB Reggie Bush/10
RFSH Santonio Holmes/100 12.00 30.00
RFSM Sinorice Moss/100 10.00 25.00
RFTJ Tarvaris Jackson/100 10.00 25.00
RFTW Travis Wilson/100 10.00 25.00
RFVD Vernon Davis/100 12.00 30.00
RFVY Vince Young/50 12.00 30.00
RFWA Leon Washington/100 10.00 25.00
RFWI Demetrius Williams/100 10.00 25.00

2006 Upper Deck Rookie Futures Jersey Dual Autographs

STATED PRINT RUN 10-50
SERIAL #'d UNDER 25 NOT PRICED
BW L.White/R.Bush/25 40.00 100.00
CJ Clemens/Jacobs/50 15.00 40.00
DL M.Lewis/M.Drew/25 30.00 80.00
DR Robinson/V.Davis/50 20.00 50.00
HH A.Hawk/S.Holmes/50 50.00 120.00
HW Hagan/T.Wilson/50 15.00 40.00
JM C.Jackson/S.Moss/50 20.00 50.00
LY M.Leinart/V.Young/25 40.00 100.00
MW B.Williams/Marshall/50 40.00 80.00
NC Calhoun/J.Norwood/50 20.00 50.00
WM D.Williams/Maroney/50 40.00 100.00

2006 Upper Deck XL Jerseys

TAIL PACK STATED ODDS 1:288
AUTO PATCHES TOO SCARCE TO PRICE
XLAG Antonio Gates 5.00 12.00
XLBA Tiki Barber 4.00 10.00
XLBD Brian Dawkins 5.00 12.00
XLBE Braylon Edwards 3.00 8.00
XLBF Brett Favre 10.00 25.00
XLBL Drew Bledsoe 4.00 10.00
XLBR Ben Roethlisberger 6.00 15.00
XLCP Carson Palmer 4.00 10.00
XLCW Cadillac Williams 4.00 10.00
XLDB Drew Brees 5.00 12.00
XLDF DeShaun Foster 4.00 10.00
XLDG David Givens 4.00 10.00
XLEM Eli Manning 4.00 10.00
XLGJ Greg Jones 3.00 8.00
XLHO T.J. Houshmandzadeh 3.00 8.00
XLHW Hines Ward 4.00 10.00
XLJJ Julius Jones 3.00 8.00
XLJO LaMont Jordan 4.00 10.00
XLJP Julius Peppers 4.00 10.00
XLKC Kevin Curtis 4.00 10.00
XLKJ Keyshawn Johnson 4.00 10.00
XLKO Kyle Orton 3.00 8.00
XLKW Kurt Warner 4.00 10.00
XLLE Byron Leftwich 3.00 8.00
XLLJ Larry Johnson 3.00 8.00
XLLT LaDainian Tomlinson 5.00 12.00
XLMV Michael Vick 4.00 10.00
XLPL Jake Plummer 3.00 8.00
XLPM Peyton Manning 12.00 30.00
XLPR Philip Rivers 5.00 12.00
XLRB Ronnie Brown 4.00 10.00
XLRO Ronde Barber 3.00 8.00
XLRW Reggie Wayne 4.00 10.00
XLTB Tom Brady 15.00 40.00
XLTE Tedy Bruschi 4.00 10.00
XLTW Troy Williamson 3.00 8.00

2006 Upper Deck Employee Quad Jerseys

LJDJSCRB James/Jeter/Crosby/Bush 20.00 40.00

2006 Upper Deck National NFL

MPLETE SET (6) 5.00 10.00
NFL1 Peyton Manning 1.50 4.00
NFL2 Ben Roethlisberger .75 2.00
NFL3 Brett Favre 1.25 3.00
NFL4 Tom Brady 2.00 5.00
NFL5 Alex Smith QB .50 1.25
NFL6 Donovan McNabb .50 1.25

2006 Upper Deck National NFL VIP

COMPLETE SET (6) 6.00 12.00
1 Cedric Benson .60 1.50
2 Michael Vick .75 2.00
3 Tom Brady 3.00 8.00
4 Shaun Alexander .60 1.50
5 Cadillac Williams .75 2.00
6 Aaron Rodgers 2.50 6.00

2006 Upper Deck National Southern California

COMPLETE SET (6) 5.00 12.00
SoCal3 LaDainian Tomlinson .75 2.00
SoCal4 Philip Rivers .75 2.00

2006 Upper Deck Tuff Stuff

Please note that both David Wright and Jered Weaver are card #24 in this set.
1 Reggie Bush 1.25 3.00
2 Matt Leinart .75 2.00
3 Vince Young 1.00 2.50
4 Jay Cutler .75 2.00
13 Tom Brady .60 1.50
14 Ben Roethlisberger .60 1.50
15 Peyton Manning .75 2.00
16 Brett Favre .75 2.00
17 Santonio Holmes .60 1.50
18 Mario Williams .40 1.00
19 DeAngelo Williams .75 2.00
20 Laurence Maroney .75 2.00
29 Kellen Clemens .40 1.00
30 Vernon Davis .60 1.50
31 Joseph Addai .75 2.00
32 Chad Jackson .50 1.25
33 Greg Jennings .40 1.00
34 A.J. Hawk .75 2.00
35 Maurice Drew .75 2.00
36 Devin Hester .60 1.50
41 LaDainian Tomlinson .50 1.25
42 Tony Romo 1.00 2.50
43 Drew Brees .40 1.00
44 Larry Johnson .40 1.00

2007 Upper Deck

This 300-card set was released in August, 2007. The set was issued into the hobby in fifteen-card packs, with an $2.99 SRP, which came 16 packs to a box. Cards numbered 1-200 feature veterans while cards 201-300 feature 2007 NFL rookies. Those Rookie Cards were inserted at stated rates of one per hobby pack and one per eight retail packs.
COMPLETE SET (300) 150.00 250.00
COMP.SET w/o RC's (200) 12.50 30.00
ROOKIE ODDS 1:1 HOB, 1:8 RET
1 Karlos Dansby .20 .50
2 Edgerrin James .25 .60
3 Matt Leinart .20 .50
4 Larry Fitzgerald .25 .60
5 Anquan Boldin .20 .50
6 Joe Horn .20 .50
7 Michael Jenkins .20 .50
8 Michael Vick .25 .60
9 Warrick Dunn .20 .50
10 Alge Crumpler .25 .60
11 Derrick Mason .20 .50
12 Ed Reed .25 .60
13 Willis McGahee .20 .50
14 Steve McNair .25 .60
15 Mark Clayton .20 .50
16 Todd Heap .20 .50
17 Ray Lewis .30 .75
18 J.P. Losman .20 .50
19 Peerless Price .20 .50
20 Lee Evans .25 .60
21 Anthony Thomas .20 .50
22 David Carr .20 .50
23 DeAngelo Williams .20 .50
24 Julius Peppers .25 .60
25 Jake Delhomme .20 .50
26 DeShaun Foster .25 .60
27 Steve Smith .25 .60
28 Muhsin Muhammad .20 .50
29 Rex Grossman .20 .50
30 Desmond Clark .20 .50
31 Devin Hester .25 .60
32 Cedric Benson .20 .50
33 Bernard Berrian .20 .50
34 Brian Urlacher .30 .75
35 Justin Smith .25 .60
36 T.J. Houshmandzadeh .20 .50
37 Carson Palmer .25 .60
38 Rudi Johnson .20 .50
39 Chad Johnson .20 .50
40 Kamerion Wimbley .20 .50
41 Charlie Frye .25 .60
42 Tim Carter .20 .50
43 Jamal Lewis .25 .60
44 Kellen Winslow .20 .50
45 Braylon Edwards .20 .50
46 Roy Williams S .20 .50
47 Marion Barber .25 .60
48 Jason Witten .25 .60
49 Terry Glenn .25 .60
50 Demarcus Ware .25 .60
51 Tony Romo .40 1.00
52 Julius Jones .20 .50
53 Terrell Owens .25 .60
54 Mike Bell .25 .60
55 John Lynch .25 .60
56 Rod Smith .25 .60
57 Travis Henry .25 .60
58 Jay Cutler .20 .50
59 Javon Walker .25 .60
60 Champ Bailey .25 .60
61 Tatum Bell .20 .50
62 Mike Furrey .25 .60
63 Jon Kitna .20 .50
64 Kevin Jones .20 .50
65 Roy Williams WR .20 .50
66 Bubba Franks .20 .50
67 Charles Woodson .30 .75
68 Brett Favre .60 1.50
69 Donald Driver .25 .60
70 A.J. Hawk .20 .50
71 Ahman Green .25 .60
72 DeMeco Ryans .25 .60
73 Matt Schaub .20 .50
74 Andre Johnson .25 .60
75 Mario Williams .25 .60
76 Ron Dayne .25 .60
77 Dwight Freeney .20 .50
78 Dallas Clark .25 .60
79 Peyton Manning .75 2.00
80 Marvin Harrison .25 .60
81 Reggie Wayne .25 .60
82 Joseph Addai .20 .50
83 Matt Jones .25 .60
84 David Garrard .20 .50
85 Ernest Wilford .20 .50
86 Reggie Williams .25 .60
87 Maurice Jones-Drew .20 .50
88 Fred Taylor .20 .50
89 Byron Leftwich .20 .50
90 Eddie Kennison .20 .50
91 Samie Parker .20 .50
92 Derrick Johnson .20 .50
93 Trent Green .20 .50
94 Larry Johnson .20 .50
95 Tony Gonzalez .25 .60
96 Damon Huard .25 .60
97 Zach Thomas .25 .60
98 Daunte Culpepper .25 .60
99 Ronnie Brown .20 .50
100 Jason Taylor .25 .60
101 Chris Chambers .20 .50
102 Antoine Winfield .20 .50
103 Ryan Longwell .20 .50
104 Chester Taylor .20 .50
105 Tarvaris Jackson .20 .50
106 Troy Williamson .20 .50
107 Rodney Harrison .20 .50
108 Randy Moss .25 .60
109 Stephen Gostkowski .30 .75
110 Donte Stallworth .25 .60
111 Tom Brady 1.00 2.50
112 Laurence Maroney .25 .60
113 Ben Watson .20 .50
114 Tedy Bruschi .25 .60
115 Charles Grant .20 .50
116 Michael Lewis .20 .50
117 Drew Brees .30 .75
118 Marques Colston .20 .50
119 Reggie Bush .20 .50
120 Deuce McAllister .25 .60
121 Amani Toomer .20 .50
122 Reuben Droughns .25 .60
123 Michael Strahan .25 .60
124 Plaxico Burress .20 .50
125 Osi Umenyiora .20 .50
126 Eli Manning .25 .60
127 Jeremy Shockey .20 .50
128 Brandon Jacobs .20 .50
129 Jonathan Vilma .20 .50
130 Jerricho Cotchery .20 .50
131 Chris Baker .20 .50
132 Chad Pennington .20 .50
133 Leon Washington .20 .50
134 Laveranues Coles .20 .50
135 Nnamdi Asomugha .20 .50
136 Dominic Rhodes .20 .50
137 Warren Sapp .25 .60
138 Justin Fargas .20 .50
139 Ronald Curry .20 .50
140 Brian Dawkins .30 .75
141 L.J. Smith .20 .50
142 Mike Patterson .20 .50
143 Brian Westbrook .20 .50
144 Reggie Brown .20 .50
145 Donovan McNabb .25 .60
146 Hines Ward .25 .60
147 James Farrior .20 .50
148 Ike Taylor .20 .50
149 Santonio Holmes .20 .50
150 Ben Roethlisberger .30 .75
151 Willie Parker .25 .60
152 Troy Polamalu .30 .75
153 Michael Turner .20 .50
154 Vincent Jackson .20 .50
155 Nate Kaeding .20 .50
156 Philip Rivers .30 .75
157 Antonio Gates .30 .75
158 Shawne Merriman .20 .50
159 LaDainian Tomlinson .30 .75
160 Arnaz Battle .20 .50
161 Nate Clements .20 .50
162 Ashley Lelie .25 .60
163 Alex Smith QB .25 .60
164 Frank Gore .25 .60
165 Vernon Davis .20 .50
166 Mack Strong .20 .50
167 Lofa Tatupu .20 .50
168 Maurice Morris .20 .50
169 Bobby Engram .20 .50
170 Matt Hasselbeck .20 .50
171 Shaun Alexander .20 .50
172 Deion Branch .20 .50
173 Leonard Little .20 .50
174 Pisa Tinoisamoa .20 .50
175 Drew Bennett .20 .50
176 Steven Jackson .20 .50
177 Marc Bulger .20 .50
178 Torry Holt .25 .60
179 Isaac Bruce .30 .75
180 Ronde Barber .20 .50
181 Chris Simms .20 .50
182 Mike Alstott .20 .50
183 Derrick Brooks .20 .50
184 Cadillac Williams .25 .60
185 Michael Clayton .20 .50
186 Joey Galloway .25 .60
187 Brandon Jones .20 .50
188 Keith Bulluck .20 .50
189 Nick Harper .20 .50
190 David Givens .20 .50
191 Vince Young .20 .50
192 LenDale White .25 .60
193 Mark Brunell .25 .60
194 Sean Taylor .30 .75
195 Chris Cooley .20 .50
196 Brandon Lloyd .20 .50
197 Jason Campbell .20 .50
198 Clinton Portis .20 .50
199 Santana Moss .25 .60
200 Antwaan Randle El .20 .50
201 Levi Brown RC 1.00 2.50
202 Alan Branch RC 1.00 2.50
203 Buster Davis RC 1.25 3.00
204 Steve Breaston RC 1.00 2.50
205 Justin Blalock RC 1.00 2.50
206 Chris Houston RC 1.00 2.50
207 Laurent Robinson RC 1.50 4.00
208 Ben Grubbs RC 1.25 3.00
209 Troy Smith RC 1.00 2.50
210 Yamon Figurs RC 1.00 2.50
211 Le'Ron McClain RC 1.50 4.00
212 Trent Edwards RC 1.00 2.50
213 Dwayne Wright RC 1.00 2.50
214 Jon Beason RC 1.00 2.50
215 Ryan Kalil RC 1.00 2.50
216 Dan Bazuin RC 1.25 3.00
217 Garrett Wolfe RC 1.00 2.50
218 Michael Okwo RC 1.25 3.00
219 Chris Leak RC 1.00 2.50
220 Leon Hall RC 1.00 2.50
221 Jeff Rowe RC 1.00 2.50
222 Eric Wright RC 1.00 2.50
223 Isaiah Stanback RC 1.00 2.50
224 Anthony Spencer RC 1.25 3.00
225 Jarvis Moss RC 1.00 2.50
226 Tim Crowder RC 1.25 3.00
227 Ikaika Alama-Francis RC 1.50 4.00
228 Justin Harrell RC 1.00 2.50
229 Brandon Jackson RC 1.00 2.50
230 James Jones RC 1.00 2.50
231 Jacoby Jones RC 1.00 2.50
232 Tony Ugoh RC 1.00 2.50
233 Daymeion Hughes RC 1.00 2.50
234 Reggie Nelson RC 1.00 2.50
235 Justin Durant RC 1.50 4.00
236 Turk McBride RC 1.25 3.00
237 DeMarcus Tank Tyler RC 1.00 2.50
238 Kolby Smith RC 1.00 2.50
239 Lorenzo Booker RC 1.25 3.00
240 Marcus McCauley RC 1.00 2.50
241 Brandon Meriweather RC 1.25 3.00
242 Antonio Pittman RC 1.00 2.50
243 Usama Young RC 1.25 3.00
244 Aaron Ross RC 1.00 2.50
245 Zak DeOssie RC 1.25 3.00
246 Darrelle Revis RC 1.25 3.00
247 David Harris RC 1.00 2.50
248 Zach Miller RC 1.00 2.50
249 Johnnie Lee Higgins RC 1.00 2.50
250 Michael Bush RC 1.00 2.50
251 Quentin Moses RC 1.00 2.50
252 Victor Abiamiri RC 1.00 2.50
253 Tony Hunt RC 1.00 2.50
254 Stewart Bradley RC 1.00 2.50
255 Lawrence Timmons RC 1.50 4.00
256 LaMarr Woodley RC 2.00 5.00
257 Matt Spaeth RC 1.50 4.00
258 Eric Weddle RC 1.25 3.00
259 Scott Chandler RC 1.50 4.00
260 Anthony Waters RC 1.25 3.00
261 Joe Staley RC 1.25 3.00
262 Jason Hill RC 1.00 2.50
263 Josh Wilson RC 1.25 3.00
264 Brandon Mebane RC 1.25 3.00
265 Adam Carriker RC 1.00 2.50
266 Jonathan Wade RC 1.00 2.50
267 Arron Sears RC 1.25 3.00
268 Sabby Piscitelli RC 1.00 2.50
269 Quincy Black RC 1.50 4.00
270 Michael Griffin RC 1.00 2.50
271 Chris Henry RB RC 1.00 2.50
272 Paul Williams RC 1.00 2.50
273 Chris Davis RC 1.00 2.50
274 H.B. Blades RC 1.00 2.50
275 Jordan Palmer RC 1.25 3.00
276 JaMarcus Russell RC 1.00 2.50
277 Calvin Johnson RC 3.00 8.00
278 Brady Quinn RC 1.00 2.50
279 Adrian Peterson RC 4.00 10.00
280 Marshawn Lynch RC 2.00 5.00

281 Ted Ginn Jr. RC 1.25 3.00
282 LaRon Landry RC 1.50 4.00
283 Jamaal Anderson RC 1.25 3.00
284 Amobi Okoye RC 1.25 3.00
285 Dwayne Bowe RC 1.00 2.50
286 Greg Olsen RC 1.50 4.00
287 Gaines Adams RC 1.25 3.00
288 Patrick Willis RC 1.50 4.00
289 Drew Stanton RC 1.00 2.50
290 Kevin Kolb RC 1.25 3.00
291 John Beck RC 1.00 2.50
292 Anthony Gonzalez RC 1.00 2.50
293 Sidney Rice RC 1.25 3.00
294 Robert Meachem RC 1.25 3.00
295 Joe Thomas RC 1.50 4.00
296 Dwayne Jarrett RC 1.25 3.00
297 Kenny Irons RC 1.00 2.50
298 Brian Leonard RC 1.00 2.50
299 Craig Buster Davis RC 1.00 2.50
300 Steve Smith USC RC 1.00 2.50

2007 Upper Deck Exclusive Edition Rookies

COMPLETE SET (100) 15.00 40.00
*SINGLES: .1X TO .25X BASIC CARDS
30-PER ROOKIE EDITION FAT PACK

2007 Upper Deck Gold Predictor Edition

COMPLETE SET (300) 100.00 200.00
*VETS: .4X TO 1X BASIC CARDS
*ROOKIES: .3X TO .8X BASIC CARDS
ISSUED AS PRIZE FOR PREDICTOR WINNERS

2007 Upper Deck Silver

*VETS 1-200: 4X TO 10X BASIC CARDS
*ROOKIES 201-300: .8X TO 2X BASIC CARDS
STATED PRINT RUN 99 SER.#'d SETS
STATED ODDS 1:16

2007 Upper Deck 1964 Philadelphia

OVERALL INSERT ODDS 1:4 H, 1:12 R
UNPRICED AUTO PRINT RUN 5
OVERALL AUTO ODDS 1:16 H, 1:2500 R
1 Matt Leinart 1.00 2.50
2 Larry Fitzgerald 1.25 3.00
3 Anquan Boldin 1.00 2.50
4 Edgerrin James 1.25 3.00
5 Jerious Norwood 1.00 2.50
6 Michael Vick 1.25 3.00
7 Alge Crumpler 1.25 3.00
8 Warrick Dunn 1.00 2.50
9 Steve McNair 1.25 3.00
10 Ray Lewis 1.50 4.00
11 Mark Clayton 1.00 2.50
12 Todd Heap 1.00 2.50
13 Jake Delhomme 1.00 2.50
14 Steve Smith 1.25 3.00
15 Julius Peppers 1.25 3.00
16 Brian Urlacher 1.50 4.00
17 Devin Hester 1.25 3.00
18 Bernard Berrian 1.00 2.50
19 Mike Singletary 2.50 6.00
20 Chad Johnson 1.00 2.50
21 T.J. Houshmandzadeh 1.00 2.50
22 Carson Palmer 1.25 3.00
23 Tony Romo 2.00 5.00
24 Terrell Owens 1.25 3.00
25 Roy Williams S 1.00 2.50
26 Marion Barber 1.50 4.00
27 Drew Pearson 2.00 5.00
28 Champ Bailey 1.25 3.00
29 Javon Walker 1.25 3.00
30 John Lynch 1.25 3.00
31 Jay Cutler 1.00 2.50
32 Brandon Marshall 1.25 3.00
33 Kevin Jones 1.00 2.50
34 Roy Williams WR 1.00 2.50
35 Brett Favre 3.00 8.00
36 Donald Driver 1.25 3.00
37 Paul Hornung 2.50 6.00
38 Andre Johnson 1.25 3.00
39 Matt Schaub 1.00 2.50
40 Ahman Green 1.25 3.00
41 Marvin Harrison 1.25 3.00
42 Joseph Addai 1.00 2.50
43 Peyton Manning 4.00 10.00
44 Reggie Wayne 1.25 3.00
45 Dwight Freeney 1.00 2.50
46 Maurice Jones-Drew 1.00 2.50
47 Fred Taylor 1.00 2.50
48 Larry Johnson 1.00 2.50
49 Tony Gonzalez 1.25 3.00
50 Ronnie Brown 1.00 2.50
51 Zach Thomas 1.25 3.00
52 Chester Taylor 1.00 2.50
53 Tarvaris Jackson 1.00 2.50
54 Tom Brady 5.00 12.00
55 Tedy Bruschi 1.25 3.00
56 Laurence Maroney 1.25 3.00
57 Drew Brees 1.50 4.00
58 Marques Colston 1.00 2.50
59 Reggie Bush 1.00 2.50
60 Eli Manning 1.25 3.00
61 Plaxico Burress 1.00 2.50
62 Jeremy Shockey 1.00 2.50
63 Michael Strahan 1.25 3.00
64 Curtis Martin 1.25 3.00
65 Chad Pennington 1.00 2.50
66 Laveranues Coles 1.00 2.50
67 Jerricho Cotchery 1.00 2.50
68 Ronald Curry 1.00 2.50
69 Marcus Allen 2.50 6.00
70 Donovan McNabb 1.25 3.00
71 Brian Westbrook 1.00 2.50
72 L.J. Smith 1.00 2.50
73 Willie Parker 1.25 3.00
74 Ben Roethlisberger 1.50 4.00
75 Santonio Holmes 1.00 2.50
76 L.C. Greenwood 1.50 4.00
77 Philip Rivers 1.50 4.00
78 LaDainian Tomlinson 1.50 4.00
79 Shawne Merriman 1.00 2.50
80 Frank Gore 1.25 3.00
81 Vernon Davis 1.00 2.50
82 Roger Craig 2.00 5.00
83 Alex Smith QB 1.25 3.00
84 Deion Branch 1.00 2.50
85 Matt Hasselbeck 1.00 2.50
86 Shaun Alexander 1.00 2.50
87 Lofa Tatupu 1.00 2.50
88 Marc Bulger 1.00 2.50
89 Steven Jackson 1.00 2.50
90 Torry Holt 1.25 3.00
91 Isaac Bruce 1.50 4.00
92 Cadillac Williams 1.25 3.00
93 Ronde Barber 1.00 2.50
94 Joey Galloway 1.25 3.00
95 Michael Clayton 1.00 2.50
96 Vince Young 1.00 2.50
97 Jason Campbell 1.00 2.50
98 Santana Moss 1.25 3.00
99 Antwaan Randle El 1.00 2.50
100 Joe Theismann 2.50 6.00

2007 Upper Deck College to Pros

OVERALL INSERT ODDS 1:4 H, 1:12 R
AJ Andre Johnson 1.00 2.50
BA Marion Barber 1.25 3.00
BE Braylon Edwards .75 2.00
BF Brett Favre 2.50 6.00
BR Ben Roethlisberger 1.25 3.00
CB Champ Bailey 1.00 2.50
CJ Chad Johnson .75 2.00
CP Carson Palmer 1.00 2.50
CW Charles Woodson 1.25 3.00
DB Drew Brees 1.25 3.00
DH Devin Hester 1.00 2.50
DM Donovan McNabb 1.00 2.50
EM Eli Manning 1.00 2.50
ES Emmitt Smith 2.50 6.00
FG Frank Gore 1.00 2.50
HW Hines Ward 1.00 2.50
JG Joey Galloway 1.00 2.50
JM Joe Montana 5.00 12.00
LF Larry Fitzgerald 1.00 2.50
LJ Larry Johnson .75 2.00
LT LaDainian Tomlinson 1.25 3.00
MB Marc Bulger .75 2.00
MC Steve McNair 1.00 2.50
MH Matt Hasselbeck .75 2.00
ML Matt Leinart .75 2.00
MS Matt Schaub .75 2.00
MV Michael Vick 1.00 2.50
PE Chad Pennington .75 2.00
PM Peyton Manning 3.00 8.00
PO Clinton Portis .75 2.00
PR Philip Rivers 1.25 3.00
RB Reggie Bush .75 2.00
RM Randy Moss 1.00 2.50
RO Ronnie Brown .75 2.00
RW Roy Williams WR .75 2.00
SA Shaun Alexander .75 2.00
SJ Steven Jackson .75 2.00
SM Santana Moss 1.00 2.50
TB Tom Brady 4.00 10.00
TG Tony Gonzalez 1.00 2.50
TH T.J. Houshmandzadeh .75 2.00
VY Vince Young .75 2.00
WA Reggie Wayne 1.00 2.50
WD Warrick Dunn .75 2.00
WI Cadillac Williams 1.00 2.50

2007 Upper Deck College to Pros Autographs

STATED PRINT RUN 10-25
NTNBA Marion Barber/25 15.00 40.00
NTNDB Drew Brees 40.00 100.00
NTNLJ Larry Johnson/25 12.00 30.00
NTNMB Marc Bulger/25 12.00 30.00
NTNML Matt Leinart/25 12.00 30.00
NTNPM Peyton Manning/25 60.00 120.00
NTNPR Philip Rivers/25 20.00 50.00
NTNRO Ronnie Brown/25 12.00 30.00
NTNVY Vince Young/25 12.00 30.00
NTNWA Reggie Wayne 15.00 40.00

2007 Upper Deck Football Heroes

OVERALL INSERT ODDS 1:4 H, 1:12 R
FH73 JaMarcus Russell .50 1.25
FH74 JaMarcus Russell .50 1.25
FH75 JaMarcus Russell .50 1.25
FH76 JaMarcus Russell .50 1.25
FH77 JaMarcus Russell .50 1.25
FH78 Calvin Johnson 1.50 4.00
FH79 Calvin Johnson 1.50 4.00
FH80 Calvin Johnson 1.50 4.00
FH81 Calvin Johnson 1.50 4.00
FH82 Calvin Johnson 1.50 4.00
FH83 Adrian Peterson 1.50 4.00
FH84 Adrian Peterson 1.50 4.00
FH85 Adrian Peterson 1.50 4.00
FH86 Adrian Peterson 1.50 4.00
FH87 Adrian Peterson 1.50 4.00
FH88 Brady Quinn .50 1.25
FH89 Brady Quinn .50 1.25
FH90 Brady Quinn .50 1.25
FH91 Brady Quinn .50 1.25
FH92 Brady Quinn .50 1.25
FH93 Marshawn Lynch 1.00 2.50
FH94 Marshawn Lynch 1.00 2.50
FH95 Marshawn Lynch 1.00 2.50
FH96 Marshawn Lynch 1.00 2.50
FH97 Marshawn Lynch 1.00 2.50
FH98 Ted Ginn Jr. .60 1.50
FH99 Ted Ginn Jr. .60 1.50
FH100 Ted Ginn Jr. .60 1.50
FH101 Ted Ginn Jr. .60 1.50
FH102 Ted Ginn Jr. .60 1.50
FH103 Gaines Adams .60 1.50
FH104 Gaines Adams .60 1.50
FH105 Gaines Adams .60 1.50
FH106 Gaines Adams .60 1.50
FH107 Gaines Adams .60 1.50
FH108 Joe Thomas .75 2.00
FH109 Joe Thomas .75 2.00
FH110 Joe Thomas .75 2.00
FH111 Joe Thomas .75 2.00
FH112 Joe Thomas .75 2.00
FH113 Dwayne Bowe .50 1.25
FH114 Dwayne Bowe .50 1.25
FH115 Dwayne Bowe .50 1.25
FH116 Dwayne Bowe .50 1.25
FH117 Dwayne Bowe .50 1.25

2007 Upper Deck Game Jerseys

OVERALL MEMORABILIA ODDS 1:8H, 1:288R
BF Brett Favre 8.00 20.00
BL Byron Leftwich 2.50 6.00
CB Chris Brown 2.50 6.00
CE Cedric Benson 2.50 6.00
CF Charlie Frye 3.00 8.00
CJ Chad Johnson 2.50 6.00
CR Charles Rogers 2.50 6.00
CS Chris Simms 2.50 6.00
CW Cadillac Williams Red 3.00 8.00
CW2 Cadillac Williams Wht 3.00 8.00
DC Daunte Culpepper Teal 3.00 8.00
DC2 Daunte Culpepper Wht 3.00 8.00
DE Deuce McAllister 3.00 8.00
DM Dan Marino 12.00 30.00
DW Domanick Williams 2.50 6.00
EJ Edgerrin James 3.00 8.00
EJ2 Edgerrin James 3.00 8.00
ES Emmitt Smith
FT Fred Taylor 2.50 6.00
HW Hines Ward 3.00 8.00
JS Jeremy Shockey 2.50 6.00
KB Kyle Boller 2.50 6.00
KO Kyle Orton 2.50 6.00
KW Kurt Warner 3.00 8.00
LA Larry Johnson 2.50 6.00
LJ LaMont Jordan 3.00 8.00
LT LaDainian Tomlinson
MB Marc Bulger 2.50 6.00
MC Donovan McNabb 3.00 8.00
MH Marvin Harrison 3.00 8.00
MM Muhsin Muhammad 2.50 6.00
MV Michael Vick Red 3.00 8.00
MV2 Michael Vick Wht 3.00 8.00
MW Mike Williams 2.50 6.00
NB Nate Burleson 2.50 6.00
PM Peyton Manning 10.00 25.00
RW Reggie Wayne 3.00 8.00
SM Steve McNair 3.00 8.00
TG Trent Green 2.50 6.00
TH Torry Holt 3.00 8.00
WM Willis McGahee 2.50 6.00
WM2 Willis McGahee 2.50 6.00

2007 Upper Deck Inkredible

OVERALL AUTO ODDS 1:16 H, 1:2500 R
UNPRICED RED INK SER.#'d TO 10
INKAB Anquan Boldin 6.00 15.00
INKAD Joseph Addai 15.00 40.00
INKAO Amobi Okoye 6.00 15.00
INKCT Chester Taylor 6.00 15.00
INKFG Frank Gore 8.00 20.00
INKGA Gaines Adams 6.00 15.00
INKGR Gary Russell 6.00 15.00
INKJA Jamaal Anderson 6.00 15.00
INKJC Jason Campbell 8.00 20.00
INKKI Kenny Irons 6.00 15.00
INKKK Kevin Kolb 6.00 15.00
INKLE Lee Evans 6.00 15.00
INKLL LaRon Landry 8.00 20.00
INKMB Marc Bulger 8.00 20.00
INKRB Reggie Bush 30.00 80.00
INKRM Robert Meachem 8.00 20.00
INKSR Sidney Rice 12.50 25.00
INKZM Zach Miller 8.00 20.00

2007 Upper Deck MVP Predictor

OVERALL PREDICTOR ODDS 1:16H, 1:64R
MVPAJ Andre Johnson 1.50 4.00
MVPBF Brett Favre 4.00 10.00
MVPBU Reggie Bush 1.25 3.00
MVPCB Cedric Benson 1.25 3.00
MVPCJ Chad Johnson 1.25 3.00
MVPCP Carson Palmer 1.50 4.00
MVPCT Chester Taylor 1.25 3.00
MVPCW Cadillac Williams 1.50 4.00
MVPDB Drew Brees 2.00 5.00
MVPDM Donovan McNabb 1.50 4.00
MVPEJ Edgerrin James 1.50 4.00
MVPEM Eli Manning 1.50 4.00
MVPFG Frank Gore 1.50 4.00
MVPFT Fred Taylor 1.25 3.00
MVPJC Jay Cutler 1.25 3.00
MVPLE Lee Evans 1.50 4.00
MVPLJ Larry Johnson 1.25 3.00
MVPLT LaDainian Tomlinson 2.00 5.00
MVPMB Marc Bulger 1.25 3.00
MVPML Matt Leinart 1.25 3.00
MVPMO Santana Moss 1.50 4.00
MVPMV Michael Vick 1.50 4.00
MVPPE Chad Pennington 1.25 3.00
MVPPM Peyton Manning 5.00 12.00
MVPRB Ronnie Brown 1.25 3.00
MVPRW Roy Williams WR 1.25 3.00
MVPSA Shaun Alexander 1.25 3.00
MVPSJ Steven Jackson 1.25 3.00
MVPSM Steve McNair 1.50 4.00
MVPSS Steve Smith 1.50 4.00
MVPTB Tom Brady 30.00 80.00
MVPTR Tony Romo 2.50 6.00
MVPVY Vince Young 1.25 3.00
MVPWP Willie Parker 1.50 4.00

2007 Upper Deck NFL Ink

OVERALL AUTO ODDS 1:16H, 1:2500R
UNPRICED RED INK SER.#'d TO 10
AP Adrian Peterson
BQ Brady Quinn 8.00 20.00
CD Craig Buster Davis 6.00 15.00
CJ Calvin Johnson 60.00 125.00
CW Cadillac Williams 8.00 20.00
DB Dwayne Bowe 12.00 30.00
DJ Dwayne Jarrett 8.00 20.00
EM Eli Manning
EW Eric Wright 6.00 15.00
JF Joel Filani 6.00 15.00
JP Jordan Palmer 6.00 15.00
JT Joe Theismann
LB Lorenzo Booker 8.00 20.00
LF Larry Fitzgerald 8.00 20.00
LJ Larry Johnson 15.00 40.00
LL LaRon Landry 8.00 20.00
MB Marion Barber 12.00 30.00
MG Michael Griffin 6.00 15.00
MI Matt Leinart 40.00 80.00
RB Ronnie Brown 8.00 20.00
RN Reggie Nelson 8.00 20.00
TG Ted Ginn Jr.
TP Tyler Palko 6.00 15.00
TR Tony Romo
WP Willie Parker 12.00 30.00

2007 Upper Deck Rookie Bonus

RELEASED IN RETAIL FACTORY SET
BC1 Adrian Peterson .60 1.50
BC2 Brady Quinn .20 .50
BC6 JaMarcus Russell .20 .50

2007 Upper Deck Rookie Exclusive Photo Shoot Flashback

RPS1 Alex Smith QB .30 .75
RPS2 Andre Johnson .30 .75
RPS3 Anquan Boldin .25 .60
RPS4 Ben Roethlisberger .40 1.00
RPS5 Brian Urlacher .40 1.00
RPS6 Cadillac Williams .30 .75
RPS7 Carson Palmer .30 .75
RPS8 Chad Johnson .25 .60
RPS9 Donovan McNabb .30 .75
RPS10 Drew Brees .40 1.00
RPS11 Eli Manning .30 .75
RPS12 Frank Gore .30 .75
RPS13 Julius Peppers .30 .75
RPS14 LaDainian Tomlinson .40 1.00
RPS15 Larry Fitzgerald .30 .75
RPS16 Larry Johnson .25 .60
RPS17 Lee Evans .30 .75
RPS18 Matt Leinart .25 .60
RPS19 Maurice Jones-Drew .25 .60
RPS20 Peyton Manning 1.00 2.50
RPS21 Philip Rivers .40 1.00
RPS22 Hines Ward .30 .75
RPS23 Reggie Bush .25 .60
RPS24 Reggie Wayne .30 .75
RPS25 Ronnie Brown .25 .60
RPS26 Roy Williams WR .25 .60
RPS27 Shaun Alexander .25 .60
RPS28 Steven Jackson .25 .60
RPS29 Torry Holt .30 .75
RPS30 Vince Young .25 .60

2007 Upper Deck Rookie Fantasy Team

TWO PER TARGET RETAIL RACK PACKS
RFTAA Aundrae Allison .50 1.25
RFTAG Anthony Gonzalez .50 1.25
RFTAP Adrian Peterson 1.50 4.00
RFTBA Dallas Baker .50 1.25
RFTBJ Brandon Jackson .50 1.25
RFTBL Brian Leonard .50 1.25
RFTBQ Brady Quinn .50 1.25
RFTCD Chris Davis .50 1.25
RFTCH Chris Henry RB .50 1.25
RFTDA Craig Buster Davis .50 1.25
RFTDB Dwayne Bowe .50 1.25
RFTDC David Clowney .50 1.25
RFTDJ Dwayne Jarrett .60 1.50
RFTDS Drew Stanton .50 1.25
RFTDW Dwayne Wright .50 1.25
RFTGO Greg Olsen .75 2.00
RFTGW Garrett Wolfe .50 1.25
RFTHI Johnnie Lee Higgins .50 1.25
RFTIS Isaiah Stanback .50 1.25
RFTJB John Beck .50 1.25
RFTJH Jason Hill .50 1.25
RFTJJ Jacoby Jones .50 1.25
RFTJO James Jones .50 1.25
RFTJP Jordan Palmer .60 1.50
RFTJR JaMarcus Russell .50 1.25
RFTKI Kenny Irons .50 1.25
RFTKK Kevin Kolb .60 1.50
RFTKS Kolby Smith .50 1.25
RFTLB Lorenzo Booker .60 1.50
RFTLM Le'Ron McClain .75 2.00
RFTLR Laurent Robinson .75 2.00
RFTMB Michael Bush .50 1.25
RFTML Marshawn Lynch 1.00 2.50
RFTMM Martrez Milner .50 1.25
RFTMS Matt Spaeth .75 2.00
RFTMW Mike Walker .75 2.00
RFTPI Antonio Pittman .50 1.25
RFTPW Paul Williams .50 1.25
RFTRM Robert Meachem .60 1.50
RFTRR Ryne Robinson .60 1.50
RFTSB Steve Breaston .50 1.25
RFTSC Scott Chandler .75 2.00
RFTSR Sidney Rice .60 1.50
RFTSS Steve Smith USC .50 1.25
RFTTE Trent Edwards .50 1.25
RFTTG Ted Ginn Jr. .60 1.50
RFTTH Tony Hunt .50 1.25
RFTTS Troy Smith .50 1.25
RFTYF Yamon Figurs .50 1.25
RFTZM Zach Miller .50 1.25

2007 Upper Deck Rookie Ink

OVERALL AUTO ODDS 1:16H, 1:2500R
UNPRICED RED INK SER.#'d TO 10
RIAP Antonio Pittman 5.00 12.00
RIBL Brian Leonard 5.00 12.00
RICD Craig Buster Davis 5.00 12.00
RIDB Dwayne Bowe 5.00 12.00
RIDH Daymeion Hughes 5.00 12.00
RIDR Darrelle Revis 6.00 15.00
RIDS Drew Stanton 5.00 12.00
RIDW DeShawn Wynn 5.00 12.00
RIGO Greg Olsen 8.00 20.00
RIHB H.B. Blades 5.00 12.00
RIHI Johnnie Lee Higgins 5.00 12.00
RIJB John Beck 5.00 12.00
RIJH Jason Hill 5.00 12.00
RIJT Joe Thomas 8.00 20.00
RILH Leon Hall 5.00 12.00
RILT Lawrence Timmons 8.00 20.00
RIML Marshawn Lynch SP 15.00 30.00
RIPP Paul Posluszny 5.00 12.00
RIPW Patrick Willis 8.00 20.00
RIRN Reggie Nelson 5.00 12.00
RISS Steve Smith USC 5.00 12.00
RITE Trent Edwards 5.00 12.00
RITG Ted Ginn Jr. 6.00 15.00
RITM Tyrone Moss 5.00 12.00
RIWR Dwayne Wright 5.00 12.00

2007 Upper Deck Rookie Jerseys

OVERALL MEMORABILIA ODDS 1:8H, 1:288R
AG Anthony Gonzalez 2.50 6.00
AP Adrian Peterson 15.00 40.00
BJ Brandon Jackson 2.50 6.00
BL Brian Leonard 2.50 6.00
BQ Brady Quinn 2.50 6.00
CH Chris Henry RB 2.50 6.00
CJ Calvin Johnson 8.00 20.00
DB Dwayne Bowe 6.00 15.00
DJ Dwayne Jarrett 3.00 8.00
DS Drew Stanton 2.50 6.00
GA Gaines Adams 3.00 8.00
GO Greg Olsen 4.00 10.00
GW Garrett Wolfe 2.50 6.00
JB John Beck 2.50 6.00
JH Jason Hill 2.50 6.00
JL Johnnie Lee Higgins 2.50 6.00
JR JaMarcus Russell 2.50 6.00
JT Joe Thomas 4.00 10.00
KI Kenny Irons 2.50 6.00
KK Kevin Kolb 3.00 8.00
MB Michael Bush 2.50 6.00
ML Marshawn Lynch 5.00 12.00
PW Patrick Willis 6.00 15.00
RM Robert Meachem 3.00 8.00
SR Sidney Rice 3.00 8.00
SS Steve Smith USC 2.50 6.00
TE Trent Edwards 2.50 6.00
TG Ted Ginn Jr. 3.00 8.00
TH Tony Hunt 2.50 6.00
TS Troy Smith 2.50 6.00
WI Paul Williams 2.50 6.00
YF Yamon Figurs 2.50 6.00

2007 Upper Deck Rookie Tandem Materials

OVERALL MEMORABILIA ODDS 1:8H, 1:288R
AT G.Adams/J.Thomas 8.00 20.00
RR J.Russell/D.Bowe 15.00 40.00
EL T.Edwards/M.Lynch 10.00 25.00
GG T.Ginn Jr./A.Gonzalez 8.00 20.00
GS T.Ginn Jr./T.Smith 8.00 20.00
HL C.Henry RB/M.Lynch 10.00 25.00
IJ B.Jackson/K.Irons 8.00 20.00
JR C.Johnson/J.Russell 15.00 40.00
JS D.Jarrett/S.Smith USC 8.00 20.00
KH K.Kolb/T.Hunt 8.00 20.00
LB B.Leonard/M.Bush 10.00 25.00
PL A.Peterson/M.Lynch 20.00 50.00
PR A.Peterson/S.Rice 15.00 40.00
QR B.Quinn/J.Russell 15.00 40.00
QT B.Quinn/J.Thomas 15.00 40.00
SP T.Smith/A.Pittman 8.00 20.00

2007 Upper Deck ROY Predictor

OVERALL PREDICTOR ODDS 1:16H, 1:64R
ROYAG Anthony Gonzalez 1.25 3.00
ROYAO Amobi Okoye 1.50 4.00
ROYAP Adrian Peterson 40.00 80.00
ROYBJ Brandon Jackson 1.25 3.00
ROYBL Brian Leonard 1.25 3.00
ROYBQ Brady Quinn 1.25 3.00
ROYCD Craig Buster Davis 1.25 3.00
ROYCJ Calvin Johnson 4.00 10.00
ROYCL Chris Leak 1.25 3.00
ROYDB Dwayne Bowe 1.25 3.00
ROYDJ Dwayne Jarrett 1.50 4.00
ROYDR Darrelle Revis 1.50 4.00
ROYDS Drew Stanton 1.25 3.00
ROYGA Gaines Adams 1.50 4.00
ROYGO Greg Olsen 2.00 5.00
ROYJB John Beck 1.25 3.00
ROYJH Jason Hill 1.25 3.00
ROYJJ James Jones 1.25 3.00
ROYJR JaMarcus Russell 1.25 3.00
ROYKI Kenny Irons 1.25 3.00
ROYKK Kevin Kolb 1.50 4.00
ROYLB Lorenzo Booker 1.50 4.00
ROYLR Laurent Robinson 2.00 5.00
ROYMB Michael Bush 1.25 3.00
ROYML Marshawn Lynch 2.50 6.00
ROYPW Paul Williams 1.25 3.00
ROYRM Robert Meachem 1.50 4.00
ROYSB Steve Breaston 1.25 3.00
ROYSR Sidney Rice 1.50 4.00
ROYSS Steve Smith USC 1.25 3.00
ROYTE Trent Edwards 1.25 3.00
ROYTG Ted Ginn Jr. 1.50 4.00
ROYTH Tony Hunt 1.25 3.00
ROYZM Zach Miller 1.25 3.00

2007 Upper Deck Signature Sensations

OVERALL AUTO ODDS 1:16H, 1:2500R
UNPRICED RED INK SER.#'d TO 10
SSAB Alan Branch 5.00 12.00
SSBJ Brandon Jackson 8.00 20.00
SSBM Brandon Meriweather 6.00 15.00
SSCJ Chad Johnson 8.00 20.00
SSCL Chris Leak 12.00 30.00
SSCT Chester Taylor 6.00 15.00
SSGW Garrett Wolfe 8.00 20.00
SSHU Tony Hunt 5.00 12.00
SSIS Isaiah Stanback 8.00 20.00
SSJZ Jared Zabransky 6.00 15.00
SSLG L.C. Greenwood 20.00 40.00
SSLW LaMarr Woodley 10.00 25.00
SSMB Michael Bush 8.00 20.00
SSMM Marcus McCauley 6.00 15.00
SSRW Reggie Wayne 10.00 25.00
SSSN Syvelle Newton 5.00 12.00
SSTH T.J. Houshmandzadeh 6.00 15.00

2007 Upper Deck Super Bowl Predictor

OVERALL PREDICTOR ODDS 1:16H, 1:64R
SBP1 James/Fitzgerald/Leinart 2.00 5.00
SBP2 Vick/Dunn/Jenkins 1.25 3.00
SBP3 Lewis/McNair/Clayton 1.50 4.00
SBP4 Thomas/Evans/Losman 1.25 3.00
SBP5 Delhomme/Peppers/Smith 1.50 4.00
SBP6 Urlacher/Grossman/Hester 2.00 5.00
SBP7 Johnson/Johnson/Palmer 2.00 5.00
SBP8 Lewis/Edwards/Winslow 1.25 3.00
SBP9 Glenn/Owens/Romo 5.00 12.00
SBP10 Bailer/Walker/Cutler 2.00 5.00
SBP11 Kitna/Williams WR/Jones 1.25 3.00
SBP12 Favre/Driver/Jennings 5.00 12.00
SBP13 Green/Johnson/Schaub 1.25 3.00
SBP14 Harrison/Manning/Addai 3.00 8.00
SBP15 Taylor/Leftwich/Jones-Drew 1.50 4.00
SBP16 Johnson/Gonzalez/Huard 2.00 5.00
SBP17 Chambers/Taylor/Brown 1.50 4.00
SBP18 Taylor/Williamson/Jackson 1.50 4.00
SBP19 Brady/Bruschi/Maroney 4.00 10.00
SBP20 Brees/McAllister/Bush 2.50 6.00
SBP21 Brrss/Shcky/Mnnng 40.00 80.00
SBP22 Pennington/Coles/Washington 1.50 4.00
SBP23 Jordan/Curry/Asomugha 1.25 3.00
SBP24 McNabb/Brown/Westbrook 2.00 5.00
SBP25 Wrd/Rthlsbrgr/Prkr 3.00 8.00
SBP26 Tomlinson/Gates/Rivers 3.00 8.00
SBP27 Gore/Smith QB/Davis 2.00 5.00
SBP28 Alexander/Hasselbeck/Branch 2.00 5.00
SBP29 Holt/Bulger/Jackson 2.00 5.00
SBP30 Galloway/Simms/Williams 1.50 4.00
SBP31 Givens/White/Young 2.50 6.00
SBP32 Moss/Portis/Campbell 1.50 4.00

2007 Upper Deck Target Exclusive Rookies

*ROOKIES: .4X TO 1X BASIC CARDS
FEATURES NEW PHOTO AND GRAY BORDER

2007 Upper Deck Target Exclusive Rookies Autographs

AUTO/5 TOO SCARCE TO PRICE

2007 Upper Deck Alumni Greats

These cards were packaged one at a time with a 1:64 die-cast car and offered at a retail price of $12.99. Each card follows the format of the base 2007 Upper Deck Football set but includes the player in his college uniform.

DCCU3 Julius Peppers 1.50 4.00
DCCU4 Lee Evans 1.50 4.00
DCCU5 Shawne Merriman 1.25 3.00
DCCU6 Jared Lorenzen 1.25 3.00
DCCU7 Shaun Alexander 1.25 3.00
DCCU8 Ronnie Brown 1.25 3.00
DCCU9 Warrick Dunn 1.25 3.00
DCCU10 Champ Bailey 1.50 4.00
DCCU11 Joseph Addai 1.25 3.00
DCCU12 Willis McGahee 1.25 3.00
DCCU13 Braylon Edwards 1.25 3.00
DCCU14 Ahman Green 1.50 4.00
DCCU15 Mark Clayton 1.25 3.00
DCCU16 Larry Johnson 1.25 3.00
DCCU17 Peyton Manning 5.00 12.00
DCCU18 Ryan Fowler 1.25 3.00

2007 Upper Deck Prilosec Brett Favre

This 6-card set was sponsored by Prilosec and produced by Upper Deck. It pays tribute to the career of Brett Favre from his high school days through to the NFL.

COMPLETE SET (6) 6.00 15.00
COMMON FAVRE 1.25 3.00

2008 Upper Deck

COMPLETE SET (325) 125.00 250.00
COMP.SET w/o SP's (300) 25.00 50.00
COMP.SET w/o RC's (200) 10.00 25.00
ROOKIE ODDS 4:1 HOB, 2:1 RET
1 Edgerrin James .20 .50
2 Matt Leinart .15 .40
3 Larry Fitzgerald .20 .50
4 Anquan Boldin .15 .40
5 Antrel Rolle .15 .40
6 Joe Horn .15 .40
7 Warrick Dunn .15 .40
8 Alge Crumpler .15 .40
9 Jerious Norwood .15 .40
10 Michael Jenkins .15 .40
11 Derrick Mason .15 .40
12 Ed Reed .20 .50
13 Willis McGahee .15 .40
14 Steve McNair .20 .50
15 Todd Heap .15 .40
16 Ray Lewis .25 .60
17 Terrell Suggs .15 .40
18 Trent Edwards .15 .40
19 Lee Evans .20 .50
20 Roscoe Parrish .15 .40
21 Marshawn Lynch .20 .50
22 Stacy Andrews .15 .40
23 DeAngelo Williams .15 .40
24 Julius Peppers .20 .50
25 Steve Smith .20 .50
26 Jake Delhomme .15 .40
27 Lance Briggs .20 .50
28 Rex Grossman .15 .40
29 Devin Hester .20 .50
30 Bernard Berrian .15 .40
31 Brian Urlacher .25 .60
32 Cedric Benson .15 .40
33 Greg Olsen .20 .50
34 T.J. Houshmandzadeh .15 .40
35 Carson Palmer .20 .50
36 Rudi Johnson .15 .40
37 Chad Johnson .15 .40
38 Kurt Warner .20 .50
39 Kamerion Wimbley .15 .40
40 Josh Cribbs .15 .40
41 Jamal Lewis .20 .50
42 Kellen Winslow .15 .40
43 Braylon Edwards .15 .40
44 Eric Wright .15 .40
45 Anthony Henry .15 .40
46 Roy Williams S .15 .40
47 Marion Barber .15 .40
48 Jason Witten .20 .50
49 DeMarcus Ware .20 .50
50 Tony Romo .20 .50
51 Julius Jones .15 .40
52 Terrell Owens .20 .50
53 Greg Ellis .15 .40
54 Patrick Crayton .20 .50
55 John Lynch .20 .50
56 Brandon Marshall .20 .50
57 Travis Henry .15 .40
58 Jay Cutler .15 .40
59 Dre Bly .15 .40
60 Javon Walker .20 .50
61 Champ Bailey .20 .50
62 Tatum Bell .15 .40
63 Calvin Johnson .25 .60
64 Jon Kitna .15 .40
65 Roy Williams WR .15 .40
66 Ernie Sims .15 .40
67 Aaron Kampman .20 .50
68 Bubba Franks .15 .40
69 Charles Woodson .25 .60
70 Brett Favre .50 1.25
71 Donald Driver .20 .50
72 A.J. Hawk .15 .40
73 Ahman Green .20 .50
74 DeMeco Ryans .20 .50
75 Andre Johnson .20 .50
76 Mario Williams .20 .50
77 Ron Dayne .15 .40
78 Dwight Freeney .15 .40
79 Dallas Clark .15 .40
80 Peyton Manning .60 1.50
81 Marvin Harrison .20 .50
82 Reggie Wayne .20 .50
83 Joseph Addai .15 .40
84 Matt Jones .20 .50
85 David Garrard .15 .40
86 Ernest Wilford .15 .40
87 Reggie Williams .20 .50
88 Maurice Jones-Drew .15 .40
89 Fred Taylor .15 .40
90 Reggie Nelson .15 .40
91 Dwayne Bowe .20 .50
92 Samie Parker .15 .40
93 Derrick Johnson .15 .40
94 Larry Johnson .15 .40
95 Brodie Croyle .20 .50
96 Tony Gonzalez .20 .50
97 Jared Allen .15 .40
98 Zach Thomas .20 .50
99 Ronnie Brown .15 .40
100 Jason Taylor .20 .50
101 Ted Ginn Jr. .15 .40
102 John Beck .15 .40
103 Antoine Winfield .15 .40
104 Adrian Peterson .25 .60
105 Bob Sanders .20 .50
106 Sidney Rice .15 .40
107 Chester Taylor .15 .40
108 Wes Welker .20 .50
109 Rodney Harrison .15 .40
110 Randy Moss .20 .50
111 Donte Stallworth .15 .40
112 Tom Brady .75 2.00
113 Laurence Maroney .20 .50
114 Ben Watson .15 .40
115 Tedy Bruschi .20 .50
116 Mike Vrabel .15 .40
117 Charles Grant .15 .40
118 Drew Brees .25 .60
119 Marques Colston .15 .40
120 Reggie Bush .15 .40
121 Deuce McAllister .20 .50
122 Mike McKenzie .15 .40
123 Amani Toomer .15 .40
124 Michael Strahan .20 .50
125 Plaxico Burress .15 .40
126 Osi Umenyiora .15 .40
127 Eli Manning .20 .50
128 Jeremy Shockey .15 .40
129 Brandon Jacobs .15 .40
130 Antonio Pierce .15 .40
131 Jonathan Vilma .15 .40
132 Jerricho Cotchery .15 .40
133 Kellen Clemens .15 .40
134 Leon Washington .15 .40
135 Thomas Jones .15 .40
136 Kirk Morrison .15 .40
137 Nnamdi Asomugha .15 .40
138 Derrick Burgess .15 .40
139 Justin Fargas .15 .40
140 Ronald Curry .15 .40
141 JaMarcus Russell .15 .40
142 Brian Dawkins .25 .60
143 Brian Westbrook .15 .40
144 Reggie Brown .15 .40
145 Donovan McNabb .20 .50
146 Hines Ward .20 .50
147 Santonio Holmes .15 .40
148 Ben Roethlisberger .25 .60
149 Willie Parker .20 .50
150 Troy Polamalu .25 .60
151 James Farrior .15 .40
152 Heath Miller .15 .40
153 Chris Chambers .15 .40
154 Philip Rivers .25 .60
155 Antonio Gates .20 .50
156 Shawne Merriman .15 .40
157 LaDainian Tomlinson .25 .60
158 Antonio Cromartie .15 .40
159 Shaun Phillips .15 .40
160 Jamal Williams .15 .40
161 Arnaz Battle .15 .40
162 Nate Clements .15 .40
163 Alex Smith QB .20 .50
164 Frank Gore .20 .50
165 Vernon Davis .15 .40
166 Patrick Willis .20 .50
167 Lofa Tatupu .15 .40
168 Patrick Kerney .15 .40
169 Bobby Engram .15 .40
170 Matt Hasselbeck .15 .40
171 Shawn Andrews .15 .40
172 Deion Branch .15 .40
173 D.J. Hackett .15 .40
174 Leonard Little .15 .40
175 Pisa Tinoisamoa .15 .40
176 Steven Jackson .15 .40
177 Marc Bulger .15 .40
178 Torry Holt .20 .50
179 Isaac Bruce .25 .60
180 Randy McMichael .15 .40
181 Ronde Barber .15 .40
182 Cadillac Williams .20 .50
183 Derrick Brooks .15 .40
184 Michael Clayton .15 .40
185 Jeff Garcia .15 .40
186 Joey Galloway .20 .50
187 Gaines Adams .15 .40
188 Keith Bulluck .15 .40
189 Nick Harper .15 .40
190 David Givens .15 .40
191 Vince Young .15 .40
192 LenDale White .15 .40
193 Eric Moulds .20 .50
194 Jason Campbell .15 .40
195 Randall Godfrey .15 .40
196 Chris Cooley .15 .40
197 Brandon Lloyd .15 .40
198 Clinton Portis .15 .40
199 Santana Moss .15 .40
200 London Fletcher .20 .50
201 Will Franklin RC .60 1.50
202 Jerome Felton RC .50 1.25
203 Adrian Arrington RC .50 1.25
204 Alex Brink RC .60 1.50
205 Allen Patrick RC .50 1.25
206 Andre Caldwell RC .50 1.25
207 Anthony Morelli RC .50 1.25
208 Antoine Cason RC .60 1.50
209 Aqib Talib RC .75 2.00
210 Ben Moffitt RC .50 1.25
211 Caleb Campbell RC .75 2.00
212 T.C. Ostrander RC .60 1.50
213 Bruce Davis RC .60 1.50
214 Calais Campbell RC .60 1.50
215 Chris Williams RC .50 1.25
216 Chad Henne RC .60 1.50
217 Chevis Jackson RC .50 1.25
218 Chris Ellis RC .50 1.25
219 Chris Johnson RC .60 1.50
220 Cory Boyd RC .50 1.25
221 Craig Steltz RC .50 1.25
222 DJ Hall RC .50 1.25
223 Chauncey Washington RC .60 1.50
224 Darius Reynaud RC .50 1.25
225 Davone Bess RC .60 1.50
226 DeJuan Tribble RC .50 1.25
227 DeMario Pressley RC .60 1.50
228 Dennis Keyes RC .50 1.25
229 Derrick Harvey RC .50 1.25
230 Donnie Avery RC .60 1.50
231 Xavier Omon RC .50 1.25
232 Dre Moore RC .50 1.25
233 Dustin Keller RC .60 1.50
234 Earl Bennett RC .75 2.00
235 Erik Ainge RC .50 1.25
236 Erin Henderson RC .60 1.50
237 Curtis Lofton RC .60 1.50
238 Felix Jones RC .50 1.25
239 Josh Barrett RC .50 1.25
240 Gosder Cherilus RC .60 1.50
241 Harry Douglas RC .60 1.50
242 Colt Brennan RC .60 1.50
243 J Leman RC .50 1.25
244 Jack Ikegwuonu RC .50 1.25
245 Jacob Hester RC .50 1.25
246 Jacob Tamme RC .60 1.50
247 Jamaal Charles RC .75 2.00
248 James Hardy RC .50 1.25
249 Jermichael Finley RC .50 1.25
250 Jerod Mayo RC .75 2.00
251 Joe Flacco RC 1.00 2.50
252 John Carlson RC .50 1.25
253 John David Booty RC .50 1.25
254 Jonathan Goff RC .50 1.25
255 Jonathan Hefney RC .50 1.25
256 Jordon Dizon RC .50 1.25
257 Jordy Nelson RC 1.50 4.00
258 Josh Johnson RC .50 1.25
259 Justin Forsett RC .60 1.50
260 Kalvin McRae RC .50 1.25
261 Keenan Burton RC .50 1.25
262 Kellen Davis RC .50 1.25
263 Kentwan Balmer RC .50 1.25
264 Keon Lattimore RC .60 1.50
265 Kevin O'Connell RC .50 1.25
266 Kevin Smith RC .50 1.25
267 Thomas DeCoud RC .50 1.25
268 Malcolm Kelly RC .50 1.25
269 Marcus Monk RC .60 1.50
270 Mario Manningham RC .50 1.25
271 Mario Urrutia RC .50 1.25
272 Martellus Bennett RC .60 1.50
273 Martin Rucker RC .50 1.25
274 Matt Flynn RC .50 1.25
275 Matt Forte RC .75 2.00
276 Owen Schmitt RC .50 1.25
277 Paul Hubbard RC .50 1.25
278 Paul Smith RC .50 1.25
279 Philip Wheeler RC .60 1.50
280 Quentin Groves RC .60 1.50
281 Quintin Demps RC .60 1.50
282 Rashard Mendenhall RC .50 1.25
283 Ray Rice RC .50 1.25
284 Ryan Clady RC .60 1.50
285 Ryan Grice-Mullen RC .50 1.25
286 Ryan Torain RC .60 1.50
287 Spencer Larsen RC .50 1.25
288 Marcus Thomas RC .60 1.50
289 Shawn Crable RC .50 1.25
290 Frank Okam RC .50 1.25
291 Tashard Choice RC .50 1.25
292 Terrell Thomas RC .50 1.25
293 Thomas Brown RC .50 1.25
294 Tom Zbikowski RC .60 1.50
295 Simeon Castille RC .50 1.25
296 Trevor Laws RC .50 1.25
297 Vernon Gholston RC .50 1.25
298 Vince Hall RC .50 1.25
299 Xavier Adibi RC .50 1.25
300 Yvenson Bernard RC .75 2.00
301 Andre Woodson SP RC 1.50 4.00
302 Brian Brohm SP RC 1.50 4.00
303 Devin Thomas SP RC 1.50 4.00
304 Dennis Dixon SP RC 1.50 4.00
305 Matt Ryan SP RC 5.00 12.00
306 Darren McFadden SP RC 1.50 4.00
307 Jonathan Stewart SP RC 2.50 6.00
308 Mike Hart SP RC 1.50 4.00
309 DeSean Jackson SP RC 3.00 8.00
310 Early Doucet SP RC 1.50 4.00
311 Lavelle Hawkins SP RC 2.00 5.00
312 Limas Sweed SP RC 1.50 4.00
313 Jake Long SP RC 2.50 6.00
314 Sam Baker SP RC 1.50 4.00
315 Glenn Dorsey SP RC 1.50 4.00
316 Sedrick Ellis SP RC 1.50 4.00
317 Chris Long SP RC 2.00 5.00
318 Lawrence Jackson SP RC 1.50 4.00
319 Ali Highsmith SP RC 1.50 4.00
320 Dan Connor SP RC 1.50 4.00
321 Kenny Phillips SP RC 1.50 4.00
322 Keith Rivers SP RC 1.50 4.00
323 Justin King SP RC 2.00 5.00
324 Mike Jenkins SP RC 1.50 4.00
325 Fred Davis SP RC 1.50 4.00

2008 Upper Deck College to Pros

UNPRICED AUTO PRINT RUN 5
CP1 Donnie Avery .60 1.50
CP2 Earl Bennett .75 2.00
CP3 John David Booty .50 1.25
CP4 Brian Brohm .50 1.25
CP5 Andre Caldwell .50 1.25
CP6 Jamaal Charles .75 2.00
CP7 Glenn Dorsey .50 1.25
CP8 Early Doucet .50 1.25
CP9 Harry Douglas .60 1.50
CP10 Joe Flacco 1.00 2.50
CP11 Matt Forte .75 2.00
CP12 James Hardy .50 1.25
CP13 Chad Henne .60 1.50
CP14 DeSean Jackson 1.00 2.50
CP15 Chris Johnson .60 1.50
CP16 Felix Jones .50 1.25
CP17 Devin Thomas .50 1.25
CP18 Dexter Jackson .75 2.00
CP19 Dustin Keller .60 1.50
CP20 Malcolm Kelly .50 1.25
CP21 Jake Long .75 2.00
CP22 Darren McFadden .50 1.25
CP23 Rashard Mendenhall .50 1.25
CP24 Kevin O'Connell .50 1.25
CP25 Mario Manningham .50 1.25
CP26 Ray Rice .50 1.25
CP27 Eddie Royal .50 1.25
CP28 Matt Ryan 1.50 4.00
CP29 Jerome Simpson .60 1.50
CP30 Steve Slaton .50 1.25
CP31 Kevin Smith .50 1.25
CP32 Jonathan Stewart .75 2.00
CP33 Limas Sweed .60 1.50
CP34 Jordy Nelson 1.50 4.00

2008 Upper Deck Excell Rookie Cards

ERCAC Andre Caldwell .60 1.50
ERCBB Brian Brohm .60 1.50
ERCCH Chad Henne .75 2.00
ERCDA Donnie Avery .75 2.00
ERCDJ DeSean Jackson 1.25 3.00
ERCDK Dustin Keller .75 2.00
ERCDM Darren McFadden .60 1.50
ERCDT Devin Thomas .60 1.50
ERCER Eddie Royal .60 1.50
ERCFJ Felix Jones .60 1.50
ERCHD Harry Douglas .75 2.00
ERCJA Dexter Jackson 1.00 2.50
ERCJB John David Booty .60 1.50
ERCJC Jamaal Charles 1.00 2.50
ERCJF Joe Flacco 1.25 3.00
ERCJH James Hardy .60 1.50
ERCJL Jake Long 1.00 2.50
ERCJN Jordy Nelson 2.00 5.00
ERCJS Jerome Simpson .75 2.00
ERCKO Kevin O'Connell .60 1.50
ERCKS Kevin Smith .60 1.50
ERCLS Limas Sweed .60 1.50
ERCMF Matt Forte 1.00 2.50
ERCMK Malcolm Kelly .60 1.50
ERCMM Mario Manningham .60 1.50
ERCMR Matt Ryan 2.00 5.00
ERCRM Rashard Mendenhall .60 1.50
ERCRR Ray Rice .60 1.50
ERCSS Steve Slaton .60 1.50
ERCST Jonathan Stewart 1.00 2.50

2008 Upper Deck Game Jerseys

*GOLD/200: .5X TO 1.2X SILVER JSY
GOLD/200 INSERTED IN HOT BOXES
OVERALL MEMORABILIA ODDS 1:8
UDGJAC Antonio Cromartie 2.50 6.00
UDGJAK Aaron Kampman 3.00 8.00
UDGJAS Alex Smith QB 3.00 8.00
UDGJBD Brian Dawkins 4.00 10.00
UDGJBE Braylon Edwards 2.50 6.00
UDGJBJ Brandon Jacobs 2.50 6.00
UDGJBR Ben Roethlisberger 4.00 10.00
UDGJBU Brian Urlacher 4.00 10.00
UDGJCJ Chad Johnson 2.50 6.00
UDGJCP Carson Palmer 3.00 8.00
UDGJDB Drew Brees 4.00 10.00
UDGJDG David Garrard 2.50 6.00
UDGJEM Eli Manning 3.00 8.00
UDGJFT Fred Taylor 2.50 6.00
UDGJGJ Greg Jennings 2.50 6.00
UDGJJA Joseph Addai 2.50 6.00
UDGJJC Jason Campbell 2.50 6.00
UDGJJG Jeff Garcia 2.50 6.00
UDGJJV Jonathan Vilma 2.50 6.00
UDGJLE Lee Evans 3.00 8.00
UDGJMB Marion Barber 5.00 12.00
UDGJMH Matt Hasselbeck 2.50 6.00
UDGJRL Ray Lewis 4.00 10.00
UDGJSJ Steven Jackson 2.50 6.00
UDGJSM Shawne Merriman 2.50 6.00
UDGJSR Sidney Rice 2.50 6.00
UDGJSS Steve Smith 3.00 8.00
UDGJTE Trent Edwards 2.50 6.00
UDGJTR Tony Romo 3.00 8.00
UDGJVY Vince Young 2.50 6.00

2008 Upper Deck Green Bay Gamers

1 A.J. Hawk 1.50 4.00
2 Greg Jennings 1.50 4.00
3 Brady Poppinga 1.50 4.00
4 Chad Clifton 1.50 4.00
5 Nick Collins 1.50 4.00
6 Mason Crosby 1.50 4.00
7 Ryan Grant 2.00 5.00
8 Aaron Rodgers 5.00 12.00
9 Mark Tauscher 1.50 4.00
10 Donald Lee 2.00 5.00
11 Will Blackmon 1.50 4.00
12 Scott Wells 1.50 4.00
13 Aaron Kampman 2.00 5.00
14 Al Harris 1.50 4.00
15 Donald Driver 2.00 5.00
16 Brian Brohm 1.50 4.00
17 Brandon Jackson 2.00 5.00
18 Ruvell Martin 1.50 4.00
19 Jordy Nelson 5.00 12.00
20 Matt Flynn 1.50 4.00
21 Charles Woodson 2.50 6.00
22 Nick Barnett 1.50 4.00
23 James Jones 1.50 4.00
24 Kabeer Gbaja-Biamila 1.50 4.00

2008 Upper Deck Masterpieces Preview

COMPLETE SET (10) 12.00 30.00
STATED ODDS 1:8
MPP1 Franco Harris 1.50 4.00
MPP2 Dwight Clark 1.25 3.00
MPP3 Alan Ameche 1.00 2.50
MPP4 Vince Lombardi 2.50 6.00
MPP5 Adrian Peterson 1.25 3.00
MPP6 Gale Sayers 1.50 4.00
MPP7 Walter Payton 3.00 8.00
MPP8 Tom Brady 4.00 10.00
MPP9 Red Grange 2.00 5.00
MPP10 Johnny Unitas 2.50 6.00

2008 Upper Deck Mystery Iconic Cuts Redemption

Cards from this set were issued via a redemption card inserted in to 2008 Upper Deck football packs. The generic EXCH card was good for a randomly selected cut autograph. Many of the autographs feature famous football players and coaches, with a slant towards vintage college football, while others feature different sports like golf or horse racing or even non-sport subjects. Of the non-sport subjects, a large percentage are actors or musicians with a few politicians and military heroes mixed in. All cards feature just the subject's cut autograph on the front, along with a hand written serial number, without any photo.

STATED PRINT RUN 1-66
SERIAL #'d UNDER 20 NOT PRICED
IC5 Arnie Weinmeister/26 40.00 80.00
IC14 Bill Willis/56 30.00 60.00
IC41 Dick Lane/24 75.00 150.00
IC44 Doak Walker/22 75.00 150.00
IC51 Dutch Clark/20 60.00 120.00
IC55 Eddie Arcaro/25 50.00 100.00
IC59 Eleanor Powell/26 20.00 50.00
IC60 Elizabeth Montgomery/43 50.00 100.00
IC61 Elroy Hirsch/55 30.00 60.00
IC63 Ernie Stautner/53 20.00 50.00
IC66 Frank Gatski/60 40.00 80.00
IC73 George Connor/70 20.00 50.00
IC75 George Musso/20 50.00 100.00
IC81 Glenn Ford/37 20.00 50.00
IC91 J. Paul Getty/28 50.00 100.00
IC93 Jack Haley/35 40.00 80.00
IC95 Jack Lord/34 40.00 80.00
IC100 Jim Parker/26 30.00 60.00
IC122 Lucille Ball/26 100.00 175.00
IC129 Mel Torme/66 25.00 60.00
IC131 Mike Webster/25 75.00 125.00
IC133 Red Badgro/30 80.00 80.00
IC136 Otto Graham/54 30.00 60.00
IC138 Paul Brown/62 50.00 100.00
IC142 Ray Flaherty/24 25.00 50.00
IC143 Ray Nitschke/26 75.00 150.00
IC144 Red Buttons/30 40.00 80.00
IC154 Roosevelt Brown/66 15.00 40.00
IC155 Rory Calhoun/42 20.00 50.00
IC162 Sid Gillman/22 50.00 100.00
IC173 Tony Canadeo/51 30.00 60.00
IC178 Vincent Price/38 60.00 100.00
IC182 Weeb Ewbank/30 40.00 80.00

2008 Upper Deck Potential Unlimited

TWO PER RACK PACK
PU1 John David Booty .50 1.25
PU2 Andre Woodson .50 1.25
PU3 Antoine Cason .60 1.50
PU4 Brady Quinn .50 1.25
PU5 Brian Brohm .50 1.25
PU6 Calais Campbell .60 1.50
PU7 Chris Ellis .50 1.25
PU8 Chris Long .60 1.50
PU9 Colt Brennan .60 1.50
PU10 Dan Connor .50 1.25
PU11 Darren McFadden .50 1.25
PU12 DeSean Jackson 1.00 2.50
PU13 Glenn Dorsey .50 1.25
PU14 Jake Long .75 2.00
PU15 JaMarcus Russell .50 1.25
PU16 Jonathan Stewart .75 2.00
PU17 Rashard Mendenhall .50 1.25
PU18 Joe Flacco 1.00 2.50
PU19 Jordy Nelson 1.50 4.00
PU20 Keith Rivers .50 1.25
PU21 Kenny Phillips .50 1.25
PU22 Limas Sweed .50 1.25
PU23 Justin King .60 1.50
PU24 Mario Manningham .50 1.25
PU25 Mario Urrutia .50 1.25
PU26 Martin Rucker .50 1.25
PU27 Matt Ryan 1.50 4.00
PU28 Mike Hart .50 1.25
PU29 Ray Rice .50 1.25
PU30 Sam Baker .50 1.25
PU31 Sedrick Ellis .50 1.25
PU32 Chris Johnson .60 1.50
PU33 Trent Edwards .50 1.25

2008 Upper Deck Record Breakers

COMPLETE SET (6) 6.00 15.00
ISSUED AT THE 2008 NFL EXPERIENCE IN AZ
RB1 Brett Favre 1.50 4.00
RB2 Tom Brady 2.50 6.00
RB3 Adrian Peterson .75 2.00
RB4 Tony Gonzalez .60 1.50
RB5 Randy Moss .60 1.50
RB6 Devin Hester .60 1.50

2008 Upper Deck Rookie Autographs

OVERALL AUTO ODDS 1:16
201-300 PRINT RUN 35 SER.#'d SETS
201 Will Franklin 8.00 20.00
202 Jerome Felton 6.00 15.00
203 Adrian Arrington 6.00 15.00
204 Alex Brink 8.00 20.00
205 Allen Patrick 6.00 15.00
206 Andre Caldwell 6.00 15.00
207 Anthony Morelli 6.00 15.00
208 Antoine Cason 8.00 20.00
209 Aqib Talib 10.00 25.00
210 Ben Moffitt 6.00 15.00
213 Bruce Davis 8.00 20.00
214 Calais Campbell 8.00 20.00
215 Chris Williams 6.00 15.00
216 Chad Henne 12.00 30.00
217 Chevis Jackson 6.00 15.00
218 Chris Ellis 6.00 15.00
219 Chris Johnson 8.00 20.00
220 Cory Boyd 6.00 15.00
221 Craig Steltz 6.00 15.00
222 DJ Hall 6.00 15.00
224 Darius Reynaud 6.00 15.00
225 Davone Bess 8.00 20.00
226 DeJuan Tribble 6.00 15.00
227 DeMario Pressley 8.00 20.00
228 Dennis Keyes 6.00 15.00
229 Derrick Harvey 6.00 15.00
230 Donnie Avery 8.00 20.00
231 Xavier Omon 6.00 15.00
232 Dre Moore 6.00 15.00
233 Dustin Keller 8.00 20.00
235 Erik Ainge 6.00 15.00
236 Erin Henderson 8.00 20.00
237 Curtis Lofton 8.00 20.00
238 Felix Jones 6.00 15.00
239 Josh Barrett 6.00 15.00
240 Gosder Cherilus 8.00 20.00
241 Harry Douglas 8.00 20.00
242 Colt Brennan 8.00 20.00
243 J Leman 6.00 15.00
244 Jack Ikegwuonu 6.00 15.00
245 Jacob Hester 6.00 15.00
246 Jacob Tamme 8.00 20.00
247 Jamaal Charles 20.00 50.00
248 James Hardy 6.00 15.00
249 Jermichael Finley 6.00 15.00
251 Joe Flacco 30.00 80.00
252 John Carlson 6.00 15.00
253 John David Booty 6.00 15.00
255 Jonathan Hefney 6.00 15.00
256 Jordon Dizon 6.00 15.00
257 Jordy Nelson 25.00 50.00
258 Josh Johnson 6.00 15.00
259 Justin Forsett 8.00 20.00
260 Kalvin McRae 6.00 15.00
261 Keenan Burton 6.00 15.00
262 Kellen Davis 6.00 15.00
263 Kentwan Balmer 6.00 15.00
264 Keon Lattimore 8.00 20.00
265 Kevin O'Connell 6.00 15.00
267 Thomas DeCoud 6.00 15.00
268 Malcolm Kelly 6.00 15.00
269 Marcus Monk 8.00 20.00
270 Mario Manningham 6.00 15.00
271 Mario Urrutia 6.00 15.00
272 Martellus Bennett 8.00 20.00
273 Martin Rucker 6.00 15.00
274 Matt Flynn 6.00 15.00
275 Matt Forte 25.00 60.00
276 Owen Schmitt 6.00 15.00
277 Paul Hubbard 6.00 15.00
278 Paul Smith 6.00 15.00
279 Philip Wheeler 8.00 20.00
280 Quentin Groves 8.00 20.00
281 Quintin Demps 8.00 20.00
282 Rashard Mendenhall 6.00 15.00
283 Ray Rice 12.00 30.00
284 Ryan Clady 8.00 20.00
286 Ryan Torain 8.00 20.00
287 Spencer Larsen 6.00 15.00
288 Marcus Thomas 8.00 20.00
289 Shawn Crable 6.00 15.00
290 Frank Okam 6.00 15.00
291 Tashard Choice 6.00 15.00
292 Terrell Thomas 6.00 15.00
293 Thomas Brown 6.00 15.00
294 Tom Zbikowski 8.00 20.00
296 Trevor Laws 6.00 15.00
297 Vernon Gholston 6.00 15.00
298 Vince Hall 6.00 15.00
299 Xavier Adibi 6.00 15.00
300 Yvenson Bernard 10.00 25.00

2008 Upper Deck Rookie Jerseys

OLD/350: .5X TO 1.2X SILVER JSY
GOLD/350 INSERTED IN HOT BOXES
OVERALL MEMORABILIA ODDS 1:8
UDRJBB Brian Brohm 1.50 4.00
UDRJCH Chad Henne 2.00 5.00
UDRJCJ Chris Johnson 2.00 5.00
UDRJDA Donnie Avery 2.00 5.00
UDRJDJ Dexter Jackson 2.50 6.00
UDRJDK Dustin Keller 2.00 5.00
UDRJDM Darren McFadden 1.50 4.00
UDRJDT Devin Thomas 1.50 4.00
UDRJEB Earl Bennett 2.50 6.00
UDRJED Early Doucet 1.50 4.00
UDRJFJ Felix Jones 1.50 4.00
UDRJGD Glenn Dorsey 1.50 4.00
UDRJJA DeSean Jackson 3.00 8.00
UDRJJF Joe Flacco 3.00 8.00
UDRJJL Jake Long 2.50 6.00
UDRJJN Jordy Nelson 5.00 12.00
UDRJJS Jonathan Stewart 2.50 6.00
UDRJKO Kevin O'Connell 1.50 4.00
UDRJLS Limas Sweed 1.50 4.00
UDRJMF Matt Forte 2.50 6.00
UDRJMK Malcolm Kelly 1.50 4.00
UDRJMM Mario Manningham 1.50 4.00
UDRJMR Matt Ryan 8.00 20.00
UDRJRR Ray Rice 1.50 4.00
UDRJSS Steve Slaton 1.50 4.00

2008 Upper Deck Same Day Signatures

SERTS IN VARIOUS UD BRANDS
SDS1 Donnie Avery 8.00 20.00
SDS2 Earl Bennett 10.00 25.00
SDS3 John David Booty
SDS4 Brian Brohm 6.00 15.00
SDS5 Andre Caldwell 6.00 15.00
SDS6 Jamaal Charles 12.00 30.00
SDS7 Glenn Dorsey
SDS8 Early Doucet
SDS9 Harry Douglas
SDS10 Joe Flacco 30.00 80.00
SDS11 Matt Forte 10.00 25.00
SDS12 James Hardy
SDS13 Chad Henne
SDS14 DeSean Jackson 12.00 30.00
SDS15 Dexter Jackson 10.00 25.00
SDS16 Chris Johnson 8.00 20.00
SDS17 Felix Jones
SDS18 Dustin Keller 25.00 50.00
SDS19 Malcolm Kelly
SDS20 Chris Long
SDS21 Jake Long
SDS22 Mario Manningham
SDS23 Darren McFadden 6.00 15.00
SDS24 Rashard Mendenhall 6.00 15.00
SDS25 Jordy Nelson 30.00 60.00
SDS26 Kevin O'Connell 6.00 15.00
SDS27 Ray Rice 6.00 15.00
SDS28 Eddie Royal 6.00 15.00
SDS29 Matt Ryan 100.00 200.00
SDS30 Jerome Simpson
SDS31 Steve Slaton
SDS32 Kevin Smith
SDS33 Jonathan Stewart 10.00 25.00
SDS34 Limas Sweed 12.00 30.00
SDS35 Devin Thomas 6.00 15.00
SDS36 Erik Ainge
SDS37 Martellus Bennett
SDS38 Colt Brennan
SDS39 Keenan Burton
SDS40 John Carlson
SDS41 Tashard Choice
SDS42 Fred Davis
SDS43 Dennis Dixon
SDS44 Jordon Dizon
SDS45 Vernon Gholston
SDS46 Mike Hart
SDS47 Derrick Harvey
SDS48 Lavelle Hawkins
SDS49 Jacob Hester
SDS50 Josh Johnson
SDS51 Jerod Mayo
SDS52 Leodis McKelvin
SDS53 Kenny Phillips
SDS54 Keith Rivers
SDS55 Andre Woodson
SDS56 J.Flacco/M.Ryan
SDS57 C.Henne/J.Long
SDS58 McFadden/F.Jones
SDS59 J.Nelson/D.Thomas 25.00 50.00
SDS60 Mendenhall/L.Sweed 6.00 15.00

2008 Upper Deck Signature Shots

OVERALL AUTO ODDS 1:16
SS1 Adrian Peterson 75.00 150.00
SS2 Andre Woodson 4.00 10.00
SS3 Dwayne Bowe 6.00 15.00
SS4 Antoine Cason 5.00 12.00
SS5 Aqib Talib 6.00 15.00
SS6 Paul Posluszny 5.00 12.00
SS7 Brandon Marshall 6.00 15.00
SS8 Brett Favre
SS9 John Beck 5.00 12.00
SS10 Michael Huff 5.00 12.00
SS11 Calais Campbell 5.00 12.00
SS12 Wes Welker 20.00 40.00
SS13 Jamal Lewis 6.00 15.00
SS14 Chris Long 5.00 12.00
SS15 Clinton Portis 5.00 12.00
SS16 Colt Brennan 5.00 12.00
SS17 Dan Connor 4.00 10.00
SS18 Sidney Rice 5.00 12.00
SS19 Darrell Jackson 5.00 12.00
SS20 Darren McFadden
SS21 Kolby Smith 5.00 12.00
SS22 DeSean Jackson 8.00 20.00
SS23 Early Doucet 4.00 10.00
SS24 Chad Henne 5.00 12.00
SS25 Frank Gore 12.00 30.00
SS26 Fred Davis 4.00 10.00
SS27 Glenn Dorsey 4.00 10.00
SS28 Tony Hunt 6.00 15.00
SS29 Jake Long 6.00 15.00
SS30 Shawn Crable 5.00 12.00
SS31 Jerious Norwood 5.00 12.00
SS32 Ben Watson 5.00 12.00
SS33 Joe Flacco 8.00 20.00
SS34 John Carlson 4.00 10.00
SS35 Jonathan Stewart 8.00 30.00
SS36 Joseph Addai 5.00 12.00
SS38 Brandon Jacobs 5.00 12.00
SS39 Lawrence Jackson 4.00 10.00
SS40 Limas Sweed 4.00 10.00
SS41 Justin King 5.00 12.00
SS42 Marion Barber 5.00 12.00
SS43 Mark Clayton 5.00 12.00
SS44 Matt Ryan 40.00 80.00
SS45 Jeff Garcia 5.00 12.00
SS46 Mike Hart 4.00 10.00
SS47 Dennis Dixon
SS48 Peyton Manning 60.00 120.00
SS49 Lorenzo Booker 5.00 12.00
SS50 Ray Rice 4.00 10.00
SS51 Sam Baker 4.00 10.00
SS52 Sedrick Ellis 4.00 10.00
SS53 Tashard Choice 4.00 10.00
SS54 Tom Zbikowski 5.00 12.00
SS55 Brandon Meriweather 5.00 12.00
SS56 Tony Romo 40.00 80.00
SS57 Marcus McCauley 5.00 12.00
SS58 Vince Hall
SS59 Dwayne Wright 5.00 12.00
SS60 Xavier Adibi 4.00 10.00

2008 Upper Deck StarQuest Silver Board

SILVER ANNOUNCED ODDS 1:2
*RAINBOW BLACK: .6X TO 1.5X SILVER
BLACK ANNOUNCED ODDS 1:16 HOB
*RAINBOW BLUE: .4X TO 1X SILVER
BLUE ANNOUNCED ODDS 1:4
*RAINBOW GOLD: .8X TO 2X SILVER
GOLD ANNOUNCED ODDS 1:24
*RAINBOW GREEN: .6X TO 1.5X SILVER
GREEN ANNOUNCED ODDS 1:16
*RAINBOW RED: .5X TO 1.2X SILVER
RED ANNOUNCED ODDS 1:6
OVERALL STAR QUEST ODDS 1:16
SQ1 Adrian Peterson 1.00 2.50
SQ2 Andre Woodson .50 1.25
SQ3 Antonio Cromartie .50 1.25
SQ4 Ben Roethlisberger 1.00 2.50
SQ5 Brian Westbrook .60 1.50
SQ6 Carson Palmer .75 2.00
SQ7 Chris Long .60 1.50
SQ8 Darren McFadden .50 1.25
SQ9 DeSean Jackson 1.00 2.50
SQ10 Drew Brees 1.00 2.50
SQ11 Early Doucet .50 1.25
SQ12 Ed Reed .75 2.00
SQ13 Ernie Sims .60 1.50
SQ14 Fred Taylor .60 1.50
SQ15 Glenn Dorsey .50 1.25
SQ16 Shawn Crable .50 1.25
SQ17 Joseph Addai .60 1.50
SQ18 Kenny Phillips .50 1.25
SQ19 LaDainian Tomlinson 1.00 2.50
SQ20 Larry Fitzgerald .75 2.00
SQ21 Matt Hasselbeck .60 1.50
SQ22 Matt Ryan 1.50 4.00
SQ23 Osi Umenyiora .60 1.50
SQ24 Patrick Willis .75 2.00
SQ25 Peyton Manning 2.50 6.00
SQ26 Randy Moss .75 2.00
SQ27 Sam Baker .50 1.25
SQ28 Terrell Owens .75 2.00
SQ29 Tom Brady 3.00 8.00
SQ30 Tony Romo .75 2.00

2008 Upper Deck Superstar

UNPRICED AUTO PRINT RUN 5
UDSSAP Adrian Peterson 1.25 3.00
UDSSBR Ben Roethlisberger 1.25 3.00
UDSSCP Clinton Portis .75 2.00
UDSSEM Eli Manning 1.00 2.50
UDSSLT LaDainian Tomlinson 1.25 3.00
UDSSML Marshawn Lynch 1.00 2.50
UDSSPM Peyton Manning 3.00 8.00
UDSSRM Randy Moss 1.00 2.50
UDSSTB Tom Brady 4.00 10.00
UDSSTR Tony Romo 1.00 2.50

2008 Upper Deck Superstar Autographs

UNPRICED AUTO PRINT RUN 5

2008 Upper Deck Target Exclusive Rookies

UNPRICED AUTO PRINT RUN 5
1 Alex Brink 1.25 3.00
2 Andre Woodson 1.00 2.50
3 Antoine Cason 1.25 3.00
4 Brian Brohm 1.00 2.50
5 Calais Campbell 1.25 3.00
6 Chris Ellis 1.00 2.50
7 Chris Long 1.25 3.00
8 Colt Brennan 1.25 3.00
9 Dan Connor 1.00 2.50
10 Darren McFadden 1.00 2.50
11 DeSean Jackson 2.00 5.00
12 Glenn Dorsey 1.00 2.50
13 Jake Long 1.50 4.00
14 Shawn Crable 1.00 2.50
15 J Leman 1.00 2.50
16 Joe Flacco 2.00 5.00
17 John Carlson 1.00 2.50
18 Jordy Nelson 3.00 8.00
19 Keith Rivers 1.00 2.50
20 Kenny Phillips 1.00 2.50
21 Limas Sweed 1.00 2.50
22 Justin King 1.25 3.00
23 Mario Manningham 1.00 2.50
24 Mario Urrutia 1.00 2.50
25 Martin Rucker 1.00 2.50
26 Matt Ryan 3.00 8.00
27 Mike Hart 1.00 2.50
28 Sam Baker 1.00 2.50
29 Sedrick Ellis 1.00 2.50
30 Chris Johnson 1.25 3.00

2008 Upper Deck Team Colors Jerseys

*GOLD/299: .5X TO 1.2X SILVER JSY
GOLD/299 INSERTED IN HOT BOXES
OVERALL MEMORABILIA ODDS 1:8
TCAP Adrian Peterson 3.00 8.00
TCBE Braylon Edwards 3.00 8.00
TCBF Brett Favre 6.00 15.00
TCCB Cedric Benson 2.00 5.00
TCCJ Calvin Johnson 3.00 8.00
TCCP Carson Palmer 2.50 6.00
TCDB Dwayne Bowe 2.50 6.00
TCDG David Garrard 2.00 5.00
TCEM Eli Manning 2.50 6.00
TCJC Jay Cutler 4.00 10.00
TCMB Marion Barber 5.00 12.00
TCML Marshawn Lynch 2.50 6.00
TCPM Peyton Manning 8.00 20.00
TCPR Philip Rivers 3.00 8.00
TCRB Reggie Bush 2.00 5.00
TCSA Shaun Alexander 2.00 5.00
TCTB Tedy Bruschi 2.50 6.00
TCTO Terrell Owens 4.00 10.00
TCWM Willis McGahee 2.00 5.00
TCWP Willie Parker 4.00 10.00

2008 Upper Deck 20th Anniversary

Upper Deck produced this 80-card set featuring past and present athletes from baseball, football, basketball and hockey and issued them through their Certified Diamond Dealers program. Eight cards were released every month from March through December 2008. By entering in all 80 unique codes from the back of the cards on the company's website by December 31, 2008, collectors had a chance to win a trip to four major sporting events.

UD16 Joe Montana .75 2.00
UD17 Brett Favre .75 2.00
UD18 Reggie Bush .40 1.00
UD19 Ben Roethlisberger .50 1.25
UD20 Tom Brady .60 1.50
UD21 Peyton Manning .60 1.50
UD22 Randy Moss .30 .75
UD23 Dan Marino 1.00 2.50
UD24 Walter Payton 1.25 3.00
UD25 LaDainian Tomlinson .40 1.00
UD26 Tony Romo .75 2.00
UD27 Joseph Addai .30 .75
UD28 Vince Young .30 .75
UD29 Matt Leinart .30 .75
UD30 Adrian Peterson .75 2.00
UD66 Darren McFadden .75 2.00
UD67 Matt Ryan 1.50 4.00
UD68 Brian Brohm .30 .75
UD69 Felix Jones .50 1.25
UD70 Rashard Mendenhall .50 1.25

2009 Upper Deck

COMPLETE SET (325) 60.00 120.00
COMP.SET w/o SP's (300) 25.00 50.00
COMP.SET w/o RC's (200) 10.00 25.00
FOUR ROOKIES PER HOBBY PACK
1 Kurt Warner .20 .50
2 Tim Hightower .15 .40
3 Larry Fitzgerald .20 .50
4 Anquan Boldin .15 .40
5 Steve Breaston .20 .50
6 Matt Leinart .15 .40
7 Adrian Wilson .15 .40
8 Michael Turner .15 .40
9 Jerious Norwood .15 .40
10 Roddy White .15 .40
11 Michael Jenkins .15 .40
12 Matt Ryan .20 .50
13 John Abraham .15 .40
14 Ed Reed .20 .50
15 Willis McGahee .15 .40
16 Ray Rice .15 .40
17 Le'Ron McClain .20 .50
18 Derrick Mason .15 .40
19 Joe Flacco .20 .50
20 Ray Lewis .25 .60
21 Mark Clayton .15 .40
22 Lee Evans .20 .50
23 Marshawn Lynch .20 .50
24 Leodis McKelvin .15 .40
25 Trent Edwards .15 .40
26 Terrell Owens .20 .50
27 Roscoe Parrish .15 .40
28 DeAngelo Williams .15 .40
29 Jonathan Stewart .15 .40
30 Steve Smith .20 .50
31 Muhsin Muhammad .15 .40
32 Jake Delhomme .15 .40
33 Jon Beason .15 .40
34 Julius Peppers .20 .50
35 Brian Urlacher .25 .60
37 Matt Forte .15 .40
38 Tommie Harris .15 .40
39 Lance Briggs .20 .50
40 Devin Hester .20 .50
41 Olin Kreutz .15 .40
42 Leon Hall .15 .40
43 Cedric Benson .15 .40
44 Reggie Kelly .15 .40
45 Carson Palmer .20 .50
46 Chad Johnson .15 .40
47 Laveranues Coles .15 .40
48 Jamal Lewis .20 .50
49 Braylon Edwards .15 .40
50 Derek Anderson .15 .40
51 Joe Thomas .20 .50
52 Brady Quinn .15 .40
53 Marion Barber .20 .50
54 Jason Witten .20 .50
55 Bradie James .15 .40
56 Tony Romo .20 .50
57 DeMarcus Ware .20 .50
58 Felix Jones .15 .40
59 Roy Williams WR .15 .40
60 Brandon Marshall .20 .50
61 Eddie Royal .15 .40
62 Michael Pittman .15 .40
63A Jay Cutler .15 .40
63B Kyle Orton .15 .40
64 Champ Bailey .20 .50
65 Daunte Culpepper .20 .50
66 Kevin Smith .15 .40
67 Calvin Johnson .25 .60
68 Jason Hanson .15 .40
69 Rudi Johnson .15 .40
70 Ryan Grant .20 .50
71 Greg Jennings .15 .40
72 Donald Driver .20 .50
73 Aaron Rodgers .50 1.25
74 Aaron Kampman .20 .50
75 Charles Woodson .25 .60
76 Will Blackmon .15 .40
77 A.J. Hawk .15 .40
78 Steve Slaton .15 .40
79 Andre Johnson .20 .50
80 Kevin Walter .20 .50
81 Kris Brown .15 .40
82 Matt Schaub .15 .40
83 DeMeco Ryans .20 .50
84 Mario Williams .20 .50
85 Peyton Manning .60 1.50
86 Joseph Addai .15 .40
87 Reggie Wayne .20 .50
88 Anthony Gonzalez .15 .40
89 Dallas Clark .15 .40
90 Adam Vinatieri .15 .40
91 Dwight Freeney .15 .40
92 Bob Sanders .20 .50
93 Maurice Jones-Drew .15 .40
94 Marcedes Lewis .15 .40
95 Justin Durant .15 .40
96 Rashean Mathis .15 .40
97 David Garrard .15 .40
98 Tony Gonzalez .20 .50
99 Larry Johnson .15 .40
100 Dwayne Bowe .20 .50
101 Matt Cassel .15 .40
102 Tyler Thigpen .15 .40
103 Ronnie Brown .15 .40
104 Ricky Williams .20 .50
105 Greg Camarillo .20 .50
106 Ted Ginn Jr. .15 .40
107 Chad Pennington .15 .40
108 Joey Porter .20 .50
109 Adrian Peterson .25 .60
110 Visanthe Shiancoe .20 .50
111 Bernard Berrian .15 .40
112A Sage Rosenfels .15 .40
112B Brett Favre 125.00 200.00
112C Brett Favre passing 40.00 100.00
113 Jared Allen .15 .40
114 Chester Taylor .15 .40
115 Tom Brady .75 2.00
116 Wes Welker .20 .50
117 Stephen Gostkowski .25 .60
118 Randy Moss .20 .50
119 Kevin Faulk .15 .40
120 Sammy Morris .15 .40
121 Reggie Bush .15 .40
122 Drew Brees .25 .60
123 Pierre Thomas .15 .40
124 Lance Moore .15 .40
125 Marques Colston .15 .40
126 Jeremy Shockey .15 .40
127 Eli Manning .20 .50
128 Brandon Jacobs .15 .40
129 Domenik Hixon .15 .40
130 Ahmad Bradshaw .15 .40
131 Steve Smith USC .20 .50
132 Thomas Jones .15 .40
133 Bart Scott .15 .40
134 Dustin Keller .15 .40
135 Kellen Clemens .15 .40
136 Leon Washington .15 .40
137 Jerricho Cotchery .15 .40
138 Johnnie Lee Higgins .15 .40
139 Justin Fargas .15 .40
140 Darren McFadden .25 .60
141 JaMarcus Russell .15 .40
142 Kirk Morrison .15 .40
143 Brian Westbrook .15 .40
144 DeSean Jackson .20 .50
145 Donovan McNabb .20 .50
146 Shawn Andrews .15 .40
147 Asante Samuel .15 .40
148 Reggie Brown .15 .40
149 Willie Parker .15 .40
150 Hines Ward .20 .50
151 Santonio Holmes .15 .40
152 Ben Roethlisberger .25 .60
153 James Harrison .25 .60
154 Troy Polamalu .25 .60
155 Rashard Mendenhall .15 .40
156 LaDainian Tomlinson .25 .60
157 Vincent Jackson .15 .40
158 Antonio Gates .20 .50
159 Philip Rivers .25 .60
160 Shawne Merriman .15 .40
161 Antonio Cromartie .15 .40
162 Chris Chambers .15 .40
163 Darren Sproles .20 .50
164 Frank Gore .20 .50
165 Isaac Bruce .25 .60
166 Alex Smith .25 .60
167 Patrick Willis .20 .50
168 Josh Morgan .15 .40
169 Shaun Hill .15 .40
170 Vernon Davis .15 .40
171 Julius Jones .15 .40
172 Matt Hasselbeck .15 .40
173 Lofa Tatupu .15 .40
174 Deion Branch .15 .40
175 T.J. Houshmandzadeh .15 .40
176 Steven Jackson .15 .40
177 Antonio Pittman .15 .40
178 Donnie Avery .15 .40
179 Marc Bulger .15 .40
180 Oshiomogho Atogwe .15 .40
181 Warrick Dunn .15 .40
182 Kellen Winslow .15 .40
183 Barrett Ruud .15 .40
184 Michael Clayton .15 .40
185 Aqib Talib .15 .40
186 Ronde Barber .15 .40
187 Cadillac Williams .20 .50
188 Chris Johnson .15 .40
189 LenDale White .15 .40
190 Bo Scaife .15 .40
191 Kerry Collins .15 .40
192 Cortland Finnegan .15 .40
193 Vince Young .15 .40
194 Clinton Portis .15 .40
195 Santana Moss .20 .50
196 Chris Cooley .15 .40
197 Antwaan Randle El .15 .40
198 Jason Campbell .15 .40
199 London Fletcher .20 .50
200 Albert Haynesworth .15 .40
201 Morgan Trent RC .60 1.50
202 Everette Brown RC .50 1.25
203 Clay Matthews RC 2.00 5.00
204 Eben Britton RC .60 1.50
205 Andre Brown RC .60 1.50
206 DeAngelo Smith RC .60 1.50
207 Glen Coffee RC .50 1.25
208 Jairus Byrd RC .75 2.00
209 Sherrod Martin RC .50 1.25
210 Victor Harris RC .60 1.50
211 Sen'Derrick Marks RC .50 1.25
212 Shawn Nelson RC .50 1.25
213 Captain Munnerlyn RC .60 1.50
214 D.J. Moore RC .60 1.50
215 Gerald McRath RC .60 1.50
216 Alphonso Smith RC .50 1.25
217 Darius Butler RC .60 1.50
218 Chase Coffman RC .50 1.25
219 Mike Goodson RC .60 1.50
220 Ron Brace RC .60 1.50
221 William Beatty RC .50 1.25
222 Michael Hamlin RC .50 1.25
223 Marcus Freeman RC .50 1.25
224 Michael Oher RC .75 2.00
225 Patrick Chung RC .50 1.25
226 Larry English RC .60 1.50
227 Connor Barwin RC .60 1.50
228 Eric Wood RC .50 1.25
229 Peria Jerry RC .50 1.25
230 Clint Sintim RC .50 1.25
231 Fili Moala RC .50 1.25
232 Keenan Lewis RC .75 2.00
233 Derrick Williams RC .50 1.25
234 Kaluka Maiava RC .50 1.25
235 Rhett Bomar RC .50 1.25
236 Sean Smith RC .50 1.25
237 Antoine Caldwell RC .50 1.25
238 Cody Brown RC .50 1.25
239 Travis Beckum RC .50 1.25
240 William Moore RC .50 1.25
241 Brian Robiskie RC .50 1.25
242 Curtis Painter RC .50 1.25
243 Vontae Davis RC .50 1.25
244 Richard Quinn RC .60 1.50
245 Robert Ayers RC .50 1.25
246 Brandon Gibson RC .60 1.50
247 Alex Mack RC .50 1.25
248 Asher Allen RC .50 1.25
249 Max Unger RC .75 2.00
250 Herman Johnson RC .60 1.50
251 Jamon Meredith RC .50 1.25
252 Jonathan Luigs RC .50 1.25
253 Phil Loadholt RC .60 1.50
254 Sebastian Vollmer RC .60 1.50
255 Michael Mitchell RC .50 1.25
256 Javon Ringer RC .50 1.25
257 Nate Davis RC .50 1.25
258 Rudy Carpenter RC .60 1.50
259 Paul Kruger RC .75 2.00
260 Stephen McGee RC .50 1.25
261 Ian Johnson RC .50 1.25
262 Mike Wallace RC .75 2.00
263 Brian Hartline RC .75 2.00
264 Devin Moore RC .50 1.25
265 Jared Cook RC .60 1.50
266 Sammie Stroughter RC .50 1.25
267 Quan Cosby RC .50 1.25
268 Brooks Foster RC .50 1.25
269 Anthony Hill RC .50 1.25
270 Mike Thomas RC .50 1.25
271 Eugene Monroe RC .50 1.25
272 Rodney Ferguson RC .60 1.50
273 Rey Maualuga RC .75 2.00
274 Tony Fiammetta RC .50 1.25
275 Michael Johnson RC .50 1.25
276 Evander Hood RC .75 2.00
277 Austin Collie RC .50 1.25
278 Jason Phillips RC .60 1.50
279 Ramses Barden RC .50 1.25
280 Louis Delmas RC .60 1.50
281 James Davis RC .50 1.25
282 Demetrius Byrd RC .60 1.50
283 Frank Summers RC .75 2.00
284 Juaquin Iglesias RC .50 1.25
285 Jasper Brinkley RC .60 1.50
286 Louis Murphy RC .50 1.25
287 Kevin Barnes RC .50 1.25
288 Gartrell Johnson RC .50 1.25
289 Matt Shaughnessy RC .60 1.50
290 Patrick Turner RC .50 1.25
291 Cornelius Ingram RC .50 1.25
292 Jarron Gilbert RC .60 1.50
293 James Casey RC .60 1.50
294 Rashad Jennings RC .60 1.50
295 Deon Butler RC .50 1.25
296 James Laurinaitis RC .50 1.25
297 Brandon Tate RC .60 1.50
298 Nic Harris RC .60 1.50
299 Brian Cushing RC .50 1.25
300 Alex Magee RC .60 1.50
301 Andre Smith RC 1.25 3.00
302 Shonn Greene RC 1.25 3.00
303 Pat White RC 1.50 4.00
304 Malcolm Jenkins RC 1.25 3.00
305 Matthew Stafford RC 6.00 15.00
306 Michael Crabtree RC 2.00 5.00
307 Tyson Jackson RC 1.25 3.00
308 Brandon Pettigrew RC 1.25 3.00
309 Brian Orakpo RC 1.50 4.00
310 Jeremy Maclin RC 1.50 4.00
311 Jason Smith RC 1.25 3.00
312 Chris Wells RC 1.25 3.00
313 Aaron Curry RC 2.00 5.00
314 Mark Sanchez RC 1.25 3.00
315 Aaron Maybin RC 1.50 4.00
316 B.J. Raji RC 1.50 4.00
317 Kenny Britt RC 2.00 5.00
318 Mohamed Massaquoi RC 1.25 3.00
319 Knowshon Moreno RC 1.25 3.00
320 Percy Harvin RC 1.25 3.00
321 Hakeem Nicks RC 1.50 4.00
322 LeSean McCoy RC 3.00 8.00
323 Darrius Heyward-Bey RC 2.00 5.00
324 Josh Freeman RC 1.25 3.00
325 Donald Brown RC 1.25 3.00
0 Michael Vick 12.00 30.00

2009 Upper Deck 3D Stars

ATED ODDS 1:8
3D1 T.Brady/R.Moss 2.00 5.00
3D2 Adrian Peterson 2.50 6.00
3D3 Randy Moss 2.00 5.00
3D4 Devin Hester 2.00 5.00
3D5 D.Clark/P.Manning 6.00 15.00
3D6 Chad Johnson 1.50 4.00
3D7 Michael Turner 1.50 4.00
3D8 Matt Ryan 2.00 5.00
3D9 Larry Fitzgerald 2.00 5.00
3D10 Kurt Warner 2.00 5.00
3D11 Tony Romo 2.00 5.00
3D12 Wes Welker 2.00 5.00
3D13 Andre Johnson 2.00 5.00
3D14 Reggie Wayne 2.00 5.00
3D15 Willie Parker 1.50 4.00
3D16 Carson Palmer 2.00 5.00
3D17 Calvin Johnson 2.50 6.00
3D18 Terrell Owens 2.00 5.00
3D19 J.Delhomme/S.Smith 2.00 5.00
3D20 Marion Barber 2.00 5.00
3D21 Reggie Bush 1.50 4.00
3D22 Lee Evans 2.00 5.00
3D23 Maurice Jones-Drew 1.50 4.00
3D24 Frank Gore 2.00 5.00
3D25 Ben Roethlisberger 2.50 6.00
3D26 D.Tyree/E.Manning 2.00 5.00
3D27 Brian Westbrook 1.50 4.00
3D28 Clinton Portis 1.50 4.00
3D29 Steven Jackson 1.50 4.00
3D30 Drew Brees 2.50 6.00
3D31 Philip Rivers 2.50 6.00
3D32 Michael Crabtree 1.50 4.00
3D33 Chris Wells 1.00 2.50
3D34 Mark Sanchez 1.00 2.50
3D35 LeSean McCoy 2.50 6.00
3D36 Josh Freeman 1.00 2.50
3D37 Hakeem Nicks 1.25 3.00
3D38 Shonn Greene 1.00 2.50
3D39 Matthew Stafford 5.00 12.00
3D40 Donald Brown 1.00 2.50
3D41 Kenny Britt 1.50 4.00
3D42 Aaron Curry 1.50 4.00
3D43 Pat White 1.25 3.00
3D44 Percy Harvin 1.00 2.50
3D45 Knowshon Moreno 1.00 2.50
3D46 Brandon Pettigrew 1.00 2.50
3D47 Darrius Heyward-Bey 1.50 4.00
3D48 Jeremy Maclin 1.25 3.00
3D49 Mohamed Massaquoi 1.00 2.50
3D50 Barack Obama 6.00 15.00

2009 Upper Deck America's Team

RANDOM INSERTS IN 2009 UD BOXES
ONE FIVE CARD PACK PER SPECIAL BLASTER
1 Miles Austin 1.00 2.50
2 Andre Gurode 1.00 2.50
3 Anthony Spencer 1.25 3.00
4 Benny Barnes 1.00 2.50
5 Bill Bates 1.00 2.50
6 Billy Joe Dupree 1.00 2.50
7 Bobby Carpenter 1.00 2.50
8 Bob Breunig 1.00 2.50
9 Marc Colombo 1.00 2.50
10 Bob Lilly 1.25 3.00
11 Leonard Davis 1.00 2.50
12 Martellus Bennett 1.00 2.50
13 Andre Gurode 1.00 2.50
14 Charlie Waters 1.25 3.00
15 Chuck Howley 1.25 3.00
16 Cliff Harris 1.25 3.00
17 Cornell Green 1.00 2.50
18 Benny Barnes 1.00 2.50
19 D.D. Lewis 1.00 2.50
20 Dan Reeves 1.25 3.00
21 Danny White 1.25 3.00
22 Bill Bates 1.00 2.50
23 Daryl Johnston 1.25 3.00
24 Billy Joe Dupree 1.00 2.50
25 Bob Breunig 1.00 2.50
26 Bob Lilly 1.25 3.00
27 DeMarcus Ware 1.25 3.00
28 Charlie Waters 1.25 3.00
29 Cliff Harris 1.25 3.00
30 Cornell Green 1.00 2.50
31 D.D. Lewis 1.00 2.50
32 Dan Reeves 1.25 3.00
33 Drew Pearson 1.25 3.00
34 Danny White 1.25 3.00
35 Ed Too Tall Jones 1.25 3.00
36 John Niland 1.00 2.50
37 Eddie LeBaron 1.50 4.00
38 Emmitt Smith 2.50 6.00
39 Drew Pearson 1.25 3.00
40 Everson Walls 1.00 2.50
41 Felix Jones 1.00 2.50
42 Flozell Adams 1.00 2.50
43 Ed Too Tall Jones 1.25 3.00
44 George Andrie 1.00 2.50
45 Miles Austin 1.00 2.50
46 Greg Ellis 1.00 2.50
47 Harvey Martin 1.00 2.50
48 Everson Walls 1.00 2.50
49 Felix Jones 1.00 2.50
50 Jackie Smith 1.00 2.50
51 Jason Witten 1.25 3.00
52 Jay Novacek 1.25 3.00
53 George Andrie 1.00 2.50
54 Jethro Pugh 1.00 2.50
55 Jim Jeffcoat 1.00 2.50
56 Jimmy Johnson 1.25 3.00
57 John Fitzgerald 1.00 2.50
58 Greg Ellis 1.00 2.50
59 Bobby Carpenter 1.00 2.50
60 Jason Witten 1.25 3.00
61 Jay Novacek 1.25 3.00
62 Larry Cole 1.00 2.50
63 Jethro Pugh 1.00 2.50
64 Jim Jeffcoat 1.00 2.50
65 Marion Barber 1.25 3.00
66 Mark Stepnoski 1.00 2.50
67 Mark Tuinei 1.00 2.50
68 Mel Renfro 1.25 3.00
69 Michael Downs 1.00 2.50
70 Marc Colombo 1.00 2.50
71 John Fitzgerald 1.00 2.50
72 Larry Cole 1.00 2.50
73 Marion Barber 1.25 3.00
74 Nick Folk 1.00 2.50
75 Pat Donovan 1.00 2.50
76 Mark Stepnoski 1.00 2.50
77 Patrick Crayton 1.00 2.50
78 Leonard Davis 1.00 2.50
79 Martellus Bennett 1.00 2.50
80 Mel Renfro 1.25 3.00
81 Randy White 1.50 4.00
82 Michael Downs 1.00 2.50
83 Nick Folk 1.00 2.50
84 Roger Staubach 2.00 5.00
85 Roy Williams WR 1.00 2.50
86 Pat Donovan 1.00 2.50
87 Scott Laidlaw 1.00 2.50
88 Terence Newman 1.00 2.50
89 Terrell Owens 1.25 3.00
90 Roger Staubach 2.00 5.00
91 Thomas Henderson 1.00 2.50
92 Troy Aikman 2.00 5.00
93 Tom Rafferty 1.00 2.50
94 Tony Romo 1.25 3.00
95 Roy Williams WR 1.00 2.50
96 Terence Newman 1.00 2.50

97 Tony Romo 1.25 3.00
98 Tony Tolbert 1.00 2.50
99 Troy Aikman 2.00 5.00
100 Thomas Henderson 1.00 2.50

2009 Upper Deck America's Team Autographs

RANDOM INSERTS IN 2009 UD BOXES
ONE FIVE CARD PACK PER SPECIAL BLASTER
4 Benny Barnes 20.00 40.00
5 Bill Bates 25.00 50.00
6 Billy Joe Dupree 25.00 50.00
8 Bob Breunig 25.00 50.00
10 Bob Lilly 50.00 100.00
14 Charlie Waters 25.00 60.00
15 Chuck Howley 30.00 80.00
16 Cliff Harris
17 Cornell Green 25.00 50.00
19 D.D. Lewis 25.00 50.00
20 Dan Reeves 30.00 60.00
21 Danny White 25.00 60.00
23 Daryl Johnston 30.00 60.00
33 Drew Pearson 20.00 50.00
35 Ed Too Tall Jones 30.00 80.00
36 John Niland 25.00 50.00
37 Eddie LeBaron 50.00 100.00
38 Emmitt Smith 250.00 400.00
40 Everson Walls 25.00 50.00
44 George Andrie 25.00 50.00
50 Jackie Smith 20.00 40.00
52 Jay Novacek 25.00 50.00
54 Jethro Pugh 25.00 50.00
55 Jim Jeffcoat 25.00 50.00
56 Jimmy Johnson 30.00 80.00
57 John Fitzgerald 15.00 40.00
62 Larry Cole 25.00 50.00
66 Mark Stepnoski 25.00 50.00
68 Mel Renfro 25.00 50.00
69 Michael Downs 15.00 40.00
75 Pat Donovan 25.00 50.00
81 Randy White 30.00 60.00
84 Roger Staubach 125.00 200.00
87 Scott Laidlaw 25.00 50.00
91 Thomas Henderson 30.00 60.00
93 Tom Rafferty 25.00 50.00
94 Tony Romo 125.00 200.00
98 Tony Tolbert 25.00 50.00
99 Troy Aikman

2009 Upper Deck America's Team Jerseys

23 Daryl Johnston 10.00 25.00
38 Emmitt Smith 12.00 30.00
41 Felix Jones 8.00 20.00
51 Jason Witten SP 30.00 60.00
65 Marion Barber 8.00 20.00
84 Roger Staubach 12.00 30.00
89 Terrell Owens 6.00 15.00
94 Tony Romo 12.00 30.00
99 Troy Aikman 12.00 30.00

2009 Upper Deck Game Day Gear

SERTS IN VARIOUS 2009 UD PRODUCTS
AC Andre Caldwell 2.50 6.00
AG Anthony Gonzalez 2.50 6.00
AJ Jason Avant 2.50 6.00
AR Aaron Ross 2.50 6.00
AS Aaron Schobel 2.50 6.00
AV Adam Vinatieri 2.50 6.00
BB Brian Brohm 2.50 6.00
BE Bernard Berrian 2.50 6.00
BJ Brandon Jacobs 2.50 6.00
BO John David Booty 3.00 8.00
BQ Brady Quinn 2.50 6.00
BR Deion Branch 2.50 6.00
BW Ben Watson 2.50 6.00
CC Chris Chambers 2.50 6.00
CH Chris Henry 2.50 6.00
CJ Chris Johnson 2.50 6.00
CR Antonio Cromartie 2.50 6.00
CT Chester Taylor 2.50 6.00
DA Donnie Avery 2.50 6.00
DB Dre Bly 2.50 6.00
DC Dexter Jackson 2.50 6.00
DE DeSean Jackson 3.00 8.00
DJ Dwayne Jarrett 2.50 6.00
DK Dustin Keller 2.50 6.00
DM Deuce McAllister 3.00 8.00
DS Drew Stanton 4.00 10.00
DT Devin Thomas 2.50 6.00
EA Earl Bennett 3.00 8.00
ED Early Doucet 3.00 8.00
ER Eddie Royal 2.50 6.00
FJ Felix Jones 2.50 6.00
FO Matt Forte 2.50 6.00
GD Glenn Dorsey 2.50 6.00
GJ Greg Jones 2.50 6.00
HD Harry Douglas 2.50 6.00
HE Chad Henne 3.00 8.00
HM Heath Miller 2.50 6.00
IB Isaac Bruce 4.00 10.00
JA Jared Allen 2.50 6.00
JC Jamaal Charles 3.00 8.00
FL Joe Flacco 3.00 8.00
JG Jeff Garcia 2.50 6.00
JH James Hardy 3.00 8.00
JL Jake Long 2.50 6.00
JN Jerious Norwood 2.50 6.00
JS Jonathan Stewart 2.50 6.00
KO Kevin O'Connell 2.50 6.00
KS Kevin Smith 2.50 6.00
LE Marcedes Lewis 2.50 6.00
LM Laurence Maroney 3.00 8.00
LS Limas Sweed 3.00 8.00
ME Rashard Mendenhall 2.50 6.00
MH Michael Huff 2.50 6.00
MJ Michael Jenkins 2.50 6.00
MK Malcolm Kelly 2.50 6.00
ML Matt Leinart 2.50 6.00
MM Mario Manningham 2.50 6.00
MO Randy Moss 3.00 8.00
MR Matt Ryan 3.00 8.00
MS Matt Schaub 2.50 6.00
MV Mike Vrabel 2.50 6.00
NE Jordy Nelson 3.00 8.00
RJ Rudi Johnson 2.50 6.00
RM Robert Meachem 2.50 6.00
RR Ray Rice 2.50 6.00
RW Roy Williams WR 2.50 6.00
SA Asante Samuel 2.50 6.00
SI Jerome Simpson 2.50 6.00
SL Steve Slaton 2.50 6.00
SM Sinorice Moss 3.00 8.00
SR Sidney Rice 2.50 6.00
SU Terrell Suggs 2.50 6.00
TB Tedy Bruschi 3.00 8.00
TH Todd Heap 2.50 6.00
TS Troy Smith 3.00 8.00
TW Travis Wilson 2.50 6.00
VD Vernon Davis 2.50 6.00
VY Vince Young 2.50 6.00
WD Warrick Dunn 2.50 6.00

2009 Upper Deck Game Jersey

OVERALL MEMORABILIA ODDS 3:16
GJAB Anquan Boldin 2.50 6.00
GJAG Antonio Gates 3.00 8.00
GJAJ Andre Johnson 3.00 8.00
GJAR Aaron Rodgers 12.00 30.00
GJAS Alex Smith 4.00 10.00
GJBQ Brady Quinn 2.50 6.00
GJBR Ben Roethlisberger 4.00 10.00
GJBU Brian Urlacher 4.00 10.00
GJCB Champ Bailey 3.00 8.00
GJCD Craig Davis 2.50 6.00
GJCP Carson Palmer 3.00 8.00
GJDB Drew Brees 4.00 10.00
GJDM Donovan McNabb 3.00 8.00
GJDW DeAngelo Williams 2.50 6.00
GJEJ Edgerrin James 3.00 8.00
GJFG Frank Gore 3.00 8.00
GJHW Hines Ward 3.00 8.00
GJJA Jared Allen 2.50 6.00
GJJC Jay Cutler 2.50 6.00
GJJP Julius Peppers 3.00 8.00
GJJW Javon Walker 2.50 6.00
GJLE Lee Evans 3.00 8.00
GJLT LaDainian Tomlinson 4.00 10.00
GJMC Marques Colston 2.50 6.00
GJMH Marvin Harrison 3.00 8.00
GJMJ Maurice Jones-Drew 2.50 6.00
GJML Marshawn Lynch 3.00 8.00
GJRB Ronnie Brown 2.50 6.00
GJRL Ray Lewis 4.00 10.00
GJRM Randy Moss 3.00 8.00

2009 Upper Deck Mystery Iconic Cuts Redemption

AUTOS ISSUED VIA EXCH CARD
EXCH EXCH Card
ICCB Cliff Battles/22 50.00 100.00
ICCC Charley Conerly/32 20.00 50.00
ICDL Dick Lane/21 40.00 80.00
ICDT Danny Thomas/41 30.00 60.00
ICDW Doak Walker/72 60.00 120.00
ICEH Elroy Hirsch/50 15.00 40.00
ICES Ernie Stautner/43 15.00 40.00
ICEW Weeb Ewbank/30 15.00 40.00
ICGC George Connor/45 15.00 40.00
ICGD Glenn Davis/75 20.00 50.00
ICGU Gene Upshaw/48 20.00 50.00
ICJB Jay Berwanger/22 15.00 40.00
ICJP Jim Parker/31 20.00 50.00
ICJR Jim Ringo/18 20.00 50.00
ICLA Dante Lavelli/52 15.00 40.00
ICLG Lou Groza/26 40.00 80.00
ICLH Lamar Hunt/22 50.00 100.00
ICMH Mel Hein/17 20.00 50.00
ICMM George McAfee/66 15.00 40.00
ICOG Otto Graham/31 20.00 50.00
ICRB Roosevelt Brown/62 15.00 40.00
ICSB Sammy Baugh/75 40.00 80.00
ICTC Tony Canadeo/28 40.00 80.00
ICTF Tom Fears/70 15.00 40.00

2009 Upper Deck Premier Rookie Jersey Autographs

ROOKIE JSY AUTO PRINT RUN 5-40
RPAB Andre Brown/40 12.00 30.00
RPAC Aaron Curry/40 15.00 40.00
RPBO Rhett Bomar/40 10.00 25.00
RPBP Brandon Pettigrew/40 10.00 25.00
RPBR Brian Robiskie/40 10.00 25.00
RPBU Deon Butler/40 10.00 25.00
RPCW Chris Wells/40 10.00 25.00
RPDB Donald Brown/40 10.00 25.00
RPDH Darrius Heyward-Bey/40 15.00 40.00
RPDW Derrick Williams/40 10.00 25.00
RPGC Glen Coffee/40 10.00 25.00
RPHN Hakeem Nicks/40 12.00 30.00
RPJF Josh Freeman/40 10.00 25.00
RPJI Juaquin Iglesias/40 10.00 25.00
RPJM Jeremy Maclin/40 12.00 30.00
RPJR Javon Ringer/40 10.00 25.00
RPJS Jason Smith/40
RPKB Kenny Britt/40 15.00 40.00
RPKM Knowshon Moreno/25 12.00 30.00
RPLM LeSean McCoy/40 25.00 60.00
RPMC Michael Crabtree/25 20.00 50.00
RPMM Mohamed Massaquoi/40 10.00 25.00
RPMW Mike Wallace/40 16.00 40.00
RPND Nate Davis/40 10.00 25.00
RPPH Percy Harvin/40 10.00 25.00
RPPT Patrick Turner/40 10.00 25.00
RPPW Pat White/40 12.00 30.00
RPRB Ramses Barden/40 10.00 25.00
RPSG Shonn Greene/40 10.00 25.00
RPSM Stephen McGee/40 10.00 25.00
RPTJ Tyson Jackson/40 10.00 25.00

2009 Upper Deck Rookie Jersey

OVERALL MEMORABILIA ODDS 3:16
RJAC Aaron Curry 2.50 6.00
RJBO Rhett Bomar 1.50 4.00
RJBP Brandon Pettigrew 1.50 4.00
RJBR Brian Robiskie 1.50 4.00
RJCW Chris Wells 1.50 4.00
RJDB Donald Brown 1.50 4.00
RJDE Deon Butler 1.50 4.00
RJDH Darrius Heyward-Bey 2.50 6.00
RJDW Derrick Williams 1.50 4.00
RJGC Glen Coffee 1.50 4.00
RJHN Hakeem Nicks 2.00 5.00
RJJF Josh Freeman 1.50 4.00
RJJI Juaquin Iglesias 1.50 4.00
RJJM Jeremy Maclin 2.00 5.00
RJJR Javon Ringer 1.50 4.00
RJJS Jason Smith 1.50 4.00
RJKB Kenny Britt 2.50 6.00
RJKM Knowshon Moreno 5.00 12.00
RJLM LeSean McCoy 4.00 10.00
RJMC Michael Crabtree 5.00 12.00
RJMM Mohamed Massaquoi 1.50 4.00
RJMS Mark Sanchez 1.50 4.00
RJND Nate Davis 1.50 4.00
RJPH Percy Harvin 1.50 4.00
RJPT Patrick Turner 1.50 4.00
RJPW Pat White 2.00 5.00
RJRB Ramses Barden 1.50 4.00
RJSG Shonn Greene 1.50 4.00
RJST Matthew Stafford 6.00 15.00
RJTJ Tyson Jackson 1.50 4.00

2009 Upper Deck Rookie Sensations

TWO PER RETAIL RACK PACK
RSAC Aaron Curry .60 1.50
RSAM Aaron Maybin .50 1.25
RSBC Brian Cushing .40 1.00
RSBO Brian Orakpo .50 1.25
RSBR Brian Robiskie .40 1.00
RSBU Deon Butler .40 1.00
RSCW Chris Wells .40 1.00
RSDB Donald Brown .40 1.00
RSDH Darrius Heyward-Bey .60 1.50
RSDW Derrick Williams .40 1.00
RSEM Eugene Monroe .40 1.00
RSGC Glen Coffee .40 1.00
RSHN Hakeem Nicks .50 1.25
RSJF Josh Freeman .40 1.00
RSJI Juaquin Iglesias .40 1.00
RSJM Jeremy Maclin .50 1.25
RSJR Javon Ringer .40 1.00
RSJS Jason Smith .40 1.00
RSKB Kenny Britt .60 1.50
RSKM Knowshon Moreno .40 1.00
RSLM LeSean McCoy 1.00 2.50
RSMC Michael Crabtree .60 1.50
RSMJ Malcolm Jenkins .40 1.00
RSMM Mohamed Massaquoi .40 1.00
RSMO Michael Oher .60 1.50
RSMS Mark Sanchez .40 1.00
RSND Nate Davis .40 1.00
RSPH Percy Harvin .40 1.00
RSPW Pat White .50 1.25
RSSG Shonn Greene .40 1.00
RSSM Andre Smith .40 1.00
RSST Matthew Stafford 2.00 5.00
RSTJ Tyson Jackson .40 1.00

2009 Upper Deck Same Day Signatures

OVERALL AUTO ODDS 1:16 HOB
SDAB Andre Brown 8.00 20.00
SDAC Aaron Curry 10.00 25.00
SDBA Ramses Barden 6.00 15.00
SDBP Brandon Pettigrew 6.00 15.00
SDBU Deon Butler 6.00 15.00
SDCW Chris Wells 25.00 60.00
SDDB Donald Brown 6.00 15.00
SDDH Darrius Heyward-Bey 10.00 25.00
SDDW Derrick Williams 6.00 15.00
SDGC Glen Coffee 6.00 15.00
SDHN Hakeem Nicks 8.00 20.00
SDJF Josh Freeman 6.00 15.00
SDJI Juaquin Iglesias 6.00 15.00
SDJM Jeremy Maclin 15.00 40.00
SDJR Javon Ringer 6.00 15.00
SDJS Jason Smith 6.00 15.00
SDKB Kenny Britt 10.00 25.00
SDKM Knowshon Moreno 6.00 15.00
SDLM LeSean McCoy 20.00 50.00
SDMC Michael Crabtree 40.00 80.00
SDMM Mohamed Massaquoi 6.00 15.00
SDMS Mark Sanchez 50.00 120.00
SDMT Mike Thomas 6.00 15.00
SDMW Mike Wallace 10.00 25.00
SDND Nate Davis 6.00 15.00
SDPH Percy Harvin 6.00 15.00
SDPT Patrick Turner 6.00 15.00
SDPW Pat White 20.00 50.00
SDRB Rhett Bomar 6.00 15.00
SDRO Brian Robiskie 6.00 15.00
SDSG Shonn Greene 15.00 40.00
SDSM Stephen McGee 6.00 15.00
SDST Matthew Stafford 40.00 100.00
SDTJ Tyson Jackson 6.00 15.00

2009 Upper Deck Signature Shots

OVERALL AUTO ODDS 1:16 HOB
SSAB Ahmad Bradshaw 8.00 20.00
SSAC Aaron Curry 6.00 15.00
SSAG Anthony Gonzalez 8.00 20.00
SSAH A.J. Hawk 5.00 12.00
SSAL Alex Smith 10.00 25.00
SSAN Derek Anderson 5.00 12.00
SSAP Adrian Peterson
SSAR Aaron Rodgers 100.00 175.00
SSAS Andre Smith 4.00 10.00
SSAW Andre Woodson 5.00 12.00
SSBB Bernard Berrian 5.00 12.00
SSBC Brian Cushing 4.00 10.00
SSBE Braylon Edwards 8.00 20.00
SSBJ Brandon Jacobs 5.00 12.00
SSBM Brandon Marshall 6.00 15.00
SSBO Anquan Boldin 5.00 12.00
SSBR Brian Brohm 5.00 12.00
SSCB Colt Brennan 8.00 20.00
SSCC Chase Coffman 4.00 10.00
SSCD Craig Davis 5.00 12.00
SSCH Chad Henne 6.00 15.00
SSCJ Calvin Johnson 20.00 50.00
SSCL Chris Long 6.00 15.00
SSCP Clinton Portis 12.50 25.00
SSCS Chansi Stuckey 5.00 12.00
SSCW Chris Wells 4.00 10.00
SSDA Donnie Avery 5.00 12.00
SSDB Donald Brown 10.00 25.00
SSDH Darrius Heyward-Bey 6.00 15.00
SSDJ DeSean Jackson 6.00 15.00
SSDK Dustin Keller 5.00 12.00
SSDL Donald Lee 5.00 12.00
SSDM Darren McFadden 25.00 50.00
SSDW Dwayne Bowe 6.00 15.00
SSED Early Doucet 6.00 15.00
SSEM Eugene Monroe 4.00 10.00
SSER Eddie Royal 8.00 20.00
SSEW Eric Weddle 5.00 12.00
SSFG Frank Gore 6.00 15.00
SSFL Joe Flacco 25.00 50.00
SSFM Fili Moala 4.00 10.00
SSGH Graham Harrell 10.00 25.00
SSGM Gerald McRath 5.00 12.00
SSGW Garrett Wolfe 5.00 12.00
SSHA DJ Hall 5.00 12.00
SSHD Harry Douglas 5.00 12.00
SSHE Chris Henry 5.00 12.00
SSHN Hakeem Nicks 5.00 12.00
SSJA Joseph Addai 5.00 12.00
SSJB John David Booty 6.00 15.00
SSJC Chad Johnson 5.00 12.00
SSJE Malcolm Jenkins 6.00 15.00
SSJF Josh Freeman 4.00 10.00
SSJI Juaquin Iglesias 4.00 10.00
SSJJ Josh Johnson 5.00 12.00
SSJL James Laurinaitis 10.00 25.00
SSJM Jeremy Maclin 5.00 12.00
SSJN Jerious Norwood 5.00 12.00
SSJO Chris Johnson 5.00 12.00
SSJR JaMarcus Russell 5.00 12.00
SSJS Jonathan Stewart 8.00 20.00
SSKM Knowshon Moreno 4.00 10.00
SSKS Kevin Smith 5.00 12.00
SSLM LeSean McCoy 12.00 30.00
SSLT LaDainian Tomlinson
SSLY Marshawn Lynch 12.00 30.00
SSMC Michael Crabtree 20.00 50.00
SSME Rashard Mendenhall 5.00 12.00
SSMF Matt Forte 4.00 10.00
SSMJ Michael Johnson 4.00 10.00
SSML Matt Leinart 5.00 12.00
SSMO Michael Oher 10.00 25.00
SSMR Matt Ryan 25.00 50.00
SSMS Matthew Stafford 40.00 100.00
SSMW Mike Walker 6.00 15.00
SSND Nate Davis 8.00 20.00
SSNE Jordy Nelson 8.00 20.00
SSOR Brian Orakpo 5.00 12.00
SSPH Percy Harvin 4.00 10.00
SSPW Patrick Willis 6.00 15.00
SSQD Quintin Demps 5.00 12.00
SSRI Javon Ringer 4.00 10.00
SSRM Rey Maualuga 6.00 15.00
SSRW Reggie Wayne 8.00 20.00
SSSA Mark Sanchez 20.00 50.00
SSSM Alphonso Smith 4.00 10.00
SSSS Sean Smith 4.00 10.00
SSST Steve Smith USC 6.00 16.00
SSTB Thomas Brown 5.00 12.00
SSTG Ted Ginn Jr. 5.00 12.00
SSTR Tony Romo 40.00 80.00
SSTT Tyler Thigpen 5.00 12.00
SSVD Vontae Davis 4.00 10.00
SSVH Victor Harris 5.00 12.00
SSVJ Vincent Jackson 5.00 12.00
SSVY Vince Young 8.00 20.00
SSWM William Moore 5.00 12.00

2009 Upper Deck Franchise Super Bowl XLIII

This set was issued at the Upper Deck booth during the 2009 Super Bowl Card Show in Tampa, Florida. A complete set was given to any collector that opened a specified number of football card packs at the booth during the show.
COMPLETE SET (6) 5.00 10.00
FRA1 Chris Johnson .50 1.25
FRA2 Darren McFadden .75 2.00
FRA3 Joe Flacco .60 1.50
FRA4 Jonathan Stewart .50 1.25
FRA5 Matt Forte .50 1.25
FRA6 Matt Ryan .60 1.50

2009 Upper Deck Limited Edition Brett Favre

ISSUED AS BONUS VIA MAIL REDEMPTION
BF1 Brett Favre 8.00 20.00
BF2 Brett Favre 8.00 20.00
BF3 Brett Favre 8.00 20.00
BF4 Brett Favre 8.00 20.00
BF5 Brett Favre 8.00 20.00
BF6 Brett Favre 8.00 20.00

2010-11 Upper Deck College Colors

COMPLETE SET (15) 6.00 15.00
6 Barry Sanders .50 1.25
7 Bo Jackson .40 1.00
8 Peyton Manning .50 1.25
9 Adrian Peterson .60 1.50
10 Tim Tebow 1.00 2.50
11 Chris Wells .30 .75
12 Shonn Greene .30 .75
13 John Elway .50 1.25

2011 Upper Deck

COMP.SET w/o ROOKIES (50) 5.00 12.00
201-209 RANDOM INSERTS IN HOBBY
210-218 RANDOM INSERTS IN RETAIL
1 Jack Youngblood .20 .50
2 Thurman Thomas .25 .60
3 Steve Young .40 1.00
4 Jack Ham .25 .60
5 Troy Aikman .40 1.00
6 Herman Moore .20 .50
7 Rocket Ismail .25 .60
8 Roman Gabriel .20 .50
9 Bob Griese .30 .75
10 Mike Alstott .20 .50
11 Alan Page .20 .50
12 Bo Jackson .40 1.00
13 Steve Largent .30 .75
14 John Elway .50 1.25
15 Paul Hornung .30 .75
16 Craig Morton .20 .50
17 Greg Pruitt .20 .50
18 Jerry Rice .50 1.25
19 Lee Roy Selmon .20 .50
20 Lee Roy Jordan .20 .50
21 George Rogers .25 .60
22 Tim Brown .30 .75
23 Thurman Thomas .25 .60
24 Doug Flutie .25 .60
25 Barry Sanders .50 1.25
26 John Cappelletti .20 .50
27 Kellen Winslow Sr. .25 .60
28 Jim Kelly .30 .75
29 Roger Craig .25 .60
30 Floyd Little .20 .50
31 Bernie Kosar .25 .60
32 Rocky Bleier .25 .60
33 Brian Bosworth .25 .60
34 Charles White .20 .50
35 Earl Campbell .30 .75
36 Doug Flutie .25 .60
37 Ron Yary .20 .50
38 Keith Jackson .20 .50
39 Billy Sims .25 .60
40 Mike Singletary .30 .75
41 Daryl Johnston .25 .60
42 Bubba Smith .20 .50
43 Steve Young .40 1.00
44 Troy Aikman .40 1.00
45 John Elway .50 1.25
46 Jerry Rice .50 1.25
47 Tim Brown .30 .75
48 Barry Sanders .50 1.25
49 Earl Campbell .30 .75
50 Jim Kelly .30 .75
51 Ronald Johnson SP 2.00 5.00
52 Adrian Clayborn SP 2.00 5.00
53 Niles Paul SP 4.00 10.00
54 Mark Herzlich SP 2.00 5.00
55 Stephen Paea SP 2.00 5.00
56 Colin Kaepernick SP 3.00 8.00
57 Allen Bailey SP 2.00 5.00
58 Torrey Smith SP 2.00 5.00
59 Evan Royster SP 2.00 5.00
60 DeMarco Murray SP 4.00 10.00
61 Titus Young SP 2.00 5.00
62 Noel Devine SP 3.00 8.00
63 Jeremy Beal SP 2.50 6.00
64 Pat Devlin SP 3.00 8.00
65 Greg Little SP 2.50 6.00
66 Cameron Heyward SP 2.50 6.00
67 Armon Binns SP 2.50 6.00
68 Greg Jones SP 2.50 6.00
69 Jake Locker SP 2.00 5.00
70 Vincent Brown SP 2.00 5.00
71 Andy Dalton SP 4.00 10.00
72 Jeremy Kerley SP 3.00 8.00
73 Jerrel Jernigan SP 2.00 5.00
74 Daniel Thomas SP 2.00 5.00
75 Prince Amukamara SP 2.00 5.00
76 Von Miller SP 3.00 8.00
77 Delone Carter SP 2.00 5.00
78 Graig Cooper SP 2.50 6.00
79 Deunta Williams .75 2.00
80 Mike Pouncey SP 3.00 8.00
81 T.J. Yates SP 2.00 5.00
82 Jimmy Smith SP 2.00 5.00
83 Jamie Harper .60 1.50
84 Ras-I Dowling SP 2.00 5.00
85 Chimdi Chekwa .75 2.00
86 Greg Salas .60 1.50
87 Anthony Allen SP 2.00 5.00
88 Kendall Hunter SP 2.00 5.00
89 Bruce Carter SP 2.00 5.00
90 Marvin Austin SP 2.00 5.00
91 Pierre Allen 1.00 2.50
92 Rashad Carmichael SP 2.50 6.00
93 Quan Sturdivant SP 2.50 6.00
94 Vai Taua .60 1.50
95 Austin Pettis SP 2.00 5.00
96 Cecil Shorts SP 2.00 5.00
97 DeAndre McDaniel SP 2.00 5.00
98 Ross Homan .75 2.00
99 Anthony Castonzo SP 2.00 5.00
100 Nathan Enderle .60 1.50
101 Tandon Doss SP 2.00 5.00
102 Kelvin Sheppard SP 2.00 5.00
103 Ryan Kerrigan SP 2.50 6.00
104 Dane Sanzenbacher SP 2.00 5.00
105 D.J. Williams SP 2.00 5.00
106 Adrian Taylor SP 2.50 6.00
107 Cam Acho SP 2.00 5.00
108 Terrence Toliver .75 2.00
109 Marcus Cannon SP 2.00 5.00
110 Colin McCarthy .75 2.00
111 Roy Helu .60 1.50
112 Ricky Stanzi SP 2.00 5.00
113 Mason Foster SP 2.00 5.00
114 Brooks Reed .75 2.00
115 James Cleveland SP 2.00 5.00
116 Brandon Saine SP 3.00 8.00
117 Jabaal Sheard SP 2.00 5.00
118 Drake Nevis SP 2.00 5.00
119 Armando Allen SP 3.00 8.00
120 Corey Liuget SP 2.00 5.00
121 Luke Stocker .60 1.50
122 Dwayne Harris SP 2.00 5.00
123 Ahmad Black .75 2.00
124 Nate Solder .60 1.50
125 Jerrod Johnson SP 2.50 6.00
126 Cameron Jordan SP 2.50 6.00
127 Stefen Wisniewski SP 3.00 8.00
128 Tyrod Taylor SP 4.00 10.00
129 Lance Kendricks SP 2.00 5.00
130 Alex Wujciak SP 2.50 6.00
131 Christian Ponder SP 5.00 12.00
132 Jeff Maehl SP 2.00 5.00
133 Phil Taylor .60 1.50
134 Eric Hagg 1.00 2.50
135 Darvin Adams .60 1.50
136 Shaun Chapas .60 1.50
137 Adam Weber .60 1.50
138 Damien Berry .75 2.00
139 Aldon Smith .60 1.50
140 Lawrence Wilson .75 2.00
141 Lee Ziemba .60 1.50
142 Bilal Powell .75 2.00
143 Kendric Burney .60 1.50
144 Taylor Potts .60 1.50
145 Ryan Bartholomew .60 1.50
146 Lestar Jean .60 1.50
147 Tyron Smith .75 2.00
148 Zack Pianalto .75 2.00
149 Scott Lutrus .60 1.50
150 Jason Pinkston .60 1.50
151 Brandon Hogan .60 1.50
152 Ryan Whalen .60 1.50
153 Jarvis Williams .60 1.50
154 Kyle Adams .60 1.50
155 Chykie Brown .60 1.50
156 Derrick Locke .75 2.00
157 Davon House .60 1.50
158 Stevan Ridley .60 1.50
159 Armand Robinson .75 2.00
160 Mario Butler .60 1.50
161 Charles Clay .60 1.50
162 Jarvis Jenkins .60 1.50
163 Kris Durham .60 1.50
164 Joe Lefeged .75 2.00
165 Chris Carter .75 2.00
166 Korey Lindsey-Woods .60 1.50
167 Allen Bradford .60 1.50
168 Stephen Burton .60 1.50
169 Virgil Green .60 1.50
170 Jock Sanders .75 2.00
171 Rob Housler .60 1.50
172 Matt Szczur 1.00 2.50
173 Ian Williams .75 2.00
174 Brandon Burton .75 2.00
175 Orlando Franklin .75 2.00
176 Ryan Mallett .60 1.50
177 Akeem Ayers .60 1.50
178 Marcell Dareus .60 1.50
179 Jacquizz Rodgers .60 1.50
180 Blaine Gabbert .60 1.50
181 Shane Vereen .75 2.00
182 Casey Matthews .60 1.50
183 Jonathan Baldwin .60 1.50
184 Dion Lewis .75 2.00
185 John Clay 1.00 2.50
186 Justin Houston .75 2.00
187 Jordan Todman .60 1.50
188 J.J. Watt 3.00 8.00
189 Sione Fua .60 1.50
190 Randall Cobb 1.00 2.50
191 Nick Fairley .60 1.50
192 Mark Ingram 1.00 2.50
193 Da'Quan Bowers .60 1.50
194 Aaron Williams .60 1.50
195 Julio Jones 2.00 5.00
196 Rahim Moore .60 1.50
197 A.J. Green 1.50 4.00
198 Cam Newton 3.00 8.00
199 Ryan Williams .60 1.50
200 Kyle Rudolph .60 1.50
201 Blaine Gabbert 2.50 6.00
202 Courtney Smith 8.00 20.00
203 Daniel Thomas 6.00 15.00
204 Leonard Hankerson 8.00 20.00
205 Julio Jones 8.00 20.00
206 Mark Ingram 15.00 30.00
207 Ryan Mallett 2.50 6.00
208 Mario Fannin 5.00 12.00
209 Torrey Smith 2.50 6.00
210 A.J. Green 15.00 40.00
211 Cam Newton 15.00 40.00
212 DeMarco Murray 5.00 12.00
213 Jake Locker 2.50 6.00
214 Jonathan Baldwin 15.00 30.00
215 Mikel Leshoure 10.00 25.00
216 Ryan Williams 10.00 25.00
217 Edmond Gates 6.00 15.00
218 Von Miller 4.00 10.00

2011 Upper Deck 15 Stripe

*ROOKIES: 2.5X TO 6X BASIC CARDS
*ROOKIES: 1.2X TO 3X BASIC SP
EACH REDEEMABLE FOR 15 BASE CARDS

2011 Upper Deck 25 Stripe

*ROOKIES: 4X TO 10X BASIC CARDS
*ROOKIES: 2X TO 5X BASIC SP
EACH REDEEMABLE FOR 25 BASE CARDS

2011 Upper Deck 100 Stripe

*ROOKIES: 6X TO 15X BASIC CARDS
*ROOKIES: 3X TO 8X BASIC SP
EACH REDEEMABLE FOR 100 BASE CARDS

2011 Upper Deck 20th Anniversary

STATED ODDS 1:2 HOBBY
20A1 Jack Youngblood .75 2.00
20A2 Bubba Smith .75 2.00
20A3 Steve Young 1.50 4.00
20A4 Jack Ham 1.00 2.50
20A5 Troy Aikman 1.50 4.00
20A6 Herman Moore .75 2.00
20A7 Rocket Ismail 1.00 2.50
20A8 Roman Gabriel .75 2.00
20A9 Bob Griese 1.25 3.00
20A10 Mike Alstott .75 2.00
20A11 Alan Page .75 2.00
20A12 Bo Jackson 1.50 4.00
20A13 Steve Largent 1.25 3.00
20A14 John Elway 2.00 5.00
20A15 Paul Hornung 1.25 3.00
20A16 Craig Morton .75 2.00
20A17 Greg Pruitt .75 2.00
20A18 Jerry Rice 2.00 5.00
20A19 Lee Roy Selmon .75 2.00
20A20 Lee Roy Jordan .75 2.00
20A21 George Rogers 1.00 2.50
20A22 Tim Brown 1.25 3.00
20A23 Thurman Thomas 1.00 2.50
20A24 Doug Flutie 1.00 2.50
20A25 Barry Sanders 2.00 5.00
20A26 John Cappelletti .75 2.00
20A27 Kellen Winslow Sr. 1.00 2.50
20A28 Jim Kelly 1.25 3.00
20A29 Roger Craig 1.00 2.50
20A30 Floyd Little .75 2.00
20A31 Bernie Kosar 1.00 2.50
20A32 Rocky Bleier 1.00 2.50
20A33 Brian Bosworth 1.00 2.50
20A34 Charles White .75 2.00
20A35 Earl Campbell 1.25 3.00
20A36 Daryl Johnston 1.00 2.50
20A37 Ron Yary .75 2.00
20A38 Keith Jackson .75 2.00
20A39 Billy Sims 1.00 2.50
20A40 Mike Singletary 1.25 3.00
20A41 Mario Butler .75 2.00
20A42 Justin Houston 1.00 2.50
20A43 Marcell Dareus .75 2.00
20A44 Tandon Doss .75 2.00
20A45 Tyron Smith 1.00 2.50
20A46 Evan Royster .75 2.00
20A47 Charles Clay .75 2.00
20A48 Colin McCarthy 1.00 2.50
20A49 Adrian Taylor 1.00 2.50
20A50 Niles Paul .75 2.00
20A51 Chimdi Chekwa 1.00 2.50
20A52 Ricky Stanzi .75 2.00
20A53 Orlando Franklin 1.00 2.50
20A54 Von Miller 1.25 3.00
20A55 Jeff Maehl .75 2.00
20A56 Colin Kaepernick 1.25 3.00
20A57 Tyrod Taylor 1.50 4.00
20A58 Ahmad Black 1.00 2.50
20A59 Christian Ponder .75 2.00
20A60 Scott Lutrus .75 2.00
20A61 Armon Binns 1.00 2.50
20A62 Anthony Castonzo .75 2.00
20A63 Lawrence Wilson 1.00 2.50
20A64 Brooks Reed 1.00 2.50
20A65 Torrey Smith .75 2.00
20A66 Jarvis Williams .75 2.00
20A67 Delone Carter .75 2.00
20A68 Adam Weber .75 2.00
20A69 Daniel Thomas .75 2.00
20A70 Ross Homan 1.00 2.50
20A71 Sam Acho .75 2.00
20A72 Greg Little 1.00 2.50
20A73 Adrian Clayborn .75 2.00
20A74 Jeremy Kerley 1.25 3.00
20A75 Taylor Potts .75 2.00
20A76 Virgil Green .75 2.00
20A77 Damien Berry 1.00 2.50
20A78 Kyle Adams .75 2.00
20A79 Andy Dalton 3.00 8.00
20A80 Dane Sanzenbacher .75 2.00
20A81 Stevan Ridley .75 2.00
20A82 Sione Fua .75 2.00
20A83 Greg Salas .75 2.00
20A84 Vai Taua .75 2.00
20A85 Anthony Allen .75 2.00
20A86 James Cleveland .75 2.00
20A87 Jason Pinkston .75 2.00
20A88 Roy Helu .75 2.00
20A89 Ryan Bartholomew .75 2.00
20A90 Austin Pettis .75 2.00
20A91 Nate Solder .75 2.00
20A92 Bilal Powell 1.00 2.50
20A93 Stefen Wisniewski 1.25 3.00
20A94 Terrence Toliver 1.00 2.50
20A95 Jock Sanders 1.00 2.50
20A96 Zack Pianalto 1.00 2.50
20A97 Jake Locker .75 2.00
20A98 Korey Lindsey-Woods .75 2.00
20A99 Ras-I Dowling .75 2.00
20A100 Jeremy Beal 1.00 2.50
20A101 Luke Stocker .75 2.00
20A102 J.J. Watt 4.00 10.00
20A103 Stephen Paea .75 2.00
20A104 Greg Jones 1.00 2.50
20A105 Brandon Saine 1.25 3.00
20A106 Bruce Carter .75 2.00
20A107 Corey Liuget .75 2.00
20A108 Ian Williams 1.00 2.50
20A109 Pierre Allen 1.25 3.00
20A110 Titus Young .75 2.00
20A111 Jabaal Sheard .75 2.00
20A112 Nathan Enderle .75 2.00
20A113 Akeem Ayers .75 2.00
20A114 Jimmy Smith .75 2.00
20A115 Cameron Jordan 1.00 2.50
20A116 Pat Devlin 1.25 3.00
20A117 D.J. Williams .75 2.00
20A118 Quan Sturdivant 1.00 2.50
20A119 Jerrel Jernigan .75 2.00
20A120 Davon House .75 2.00
20A121 Allen Bailey .75 2.00
20A122 Rahim Moore .75 2.00
20A123 Alex Wujciak 1.00 2.50
20A124 Shaun Chapas .75 2.00
20A125 Kelvin Sheppard .75 2.00
20A126 Marvin Austin .75 2.00
20A127 Armando Allen 1.25 3.00
20A128 Jerrod Johnson 1.00 2.50
20A129 Mark Herzlich .75 2.00
20A130 Drake Nevis .75 2.00
20A131 Ronald Johnson .75 2.00
20A132 Ryan Kerrigan 1.00 2.50
20A133 Mike Pouncey 1.25 3.00
20A134 Noel Devine 1.25 3.00
20A135 Allen Bradford .75 2.00
20A136 Cameron Heyward 1.00 2.50
20A137 Dwayne Harris .75 2.00
20A138 Da'Quan Bowers .75 2.00
20A139 Joe Lefeged 1.00 2.50
20A140 Prince Amukamara .75 2.00
20A141 T.J. Yates .75 2.00
20A142 Kendall Hunter .75 2.00
20A143 Darvin Adams .75 2.00
20A144 DeMarco Murray 1.50 4.00
20A145 Randall Cobb 1.25 3.00
20A146 Vincent Brown .75 2.00
20A147 Cecil Shorts .75 2.00
20A148 DeAndre McDaniel .75 2.00
20A149 Kris Durham .75 2.00
20A150 Lance Kendricks .75 2.00
20A151 Derrick Locke 1.00 2.50
20A152 Matt Szczur 1.25 3.00
20A153 Chris Carter 1.00 2.50
20A154 Graig Cooper 1.00 2.50
20A155 Aaron Williams .75 2.00
20A156 Jamie Harper .75 2.00
20A157 Casey Matthews .75 2.00
20A158 Ryan Mallett .75 2.00
20A159 A.J. Green 2.00 5.00
20A160 Julio Jones 2.50 6.00
20A161 Jonathan Baldwin .75 2.00
20A162 Blaine Gabbert .75 2.00
20A163 Lee Ziemba .75 2.00
20A164 Cam Newton 4.00 10.00
20A165 Mark Ingram 1.25 3.00
20A166 Rob Housler .75 2.00
20A167 Dion Lewis 1.00 2.50
20A168 Nick Fairley .75 2.00
20A169 Shane Vereen 1.00 2.50
20A170 John Clay 1.25 3.00
20A171 Jacquizz Rodgers .75 2.00
20A172 Jordan Todman .75 2.00
20A173 Ryan Williams .75 2.00
20A174 Kyle Rudolph .75 2.00

2011 Upper Deck Class Of

COMPLETE SET (20) 6.00 15.00
RANDOM INSERTS IN PACKS
CO1 Tim Brown .60 1.50
CO2 Jerry Rice 1.00 2.50
CO3 Bo Jackson .75 2.00
CO4 Charles White .40 1.00
CO5 John Elway 1.00 2.50
CO6 Earl Campbell .60 1.50
CO7 Doug Flutie .50 1.25
CO8 Troy Aikman .75 2.00
CO9 George Rogers .50 1.25
CO10 Keith Jackson .40 1.00
CO11 John Cappelletti .40 1.00
CO12 Kellen Winslow Sr. .50 1.25
CO13 Paul Hornung .60 1.50
CO14 Thurman Thomas .50 1.25
CO15 Floyd Little .40 1.00
CO16 Lee Roy Selmon .40 1.00
CO17 Bob Griese .60 1.50
CO18 Jake Locker .40 1.00
CO19 Daniel Thomas .40 1.00
CO20 DeMarco Murray .75 2.00

2011 Upper Deck Conference Clashes

COMPLETE SET (20) 5.00 12.00
RANDOM INSERTS IN PACKS
CC1 G.Pruitt/B.Sanders 1.00 2.50
CC2 J.Elway/T.Aikman 1.00 2.50
CC3 T.Thomas/G.Pruitt .50 1.25
CC4 B.Sanders/B.Sims 1.00 2.50
CC5 C.White/J.Elway 1.00 2.50
CC6 M.Ingram/C.Newton 2.00 5.00
CC7 C.White/T.Aikman .75 2.00
CC8 R.Craig/K.Winslow Sr. .50 1.25
CC9 R.Williams/T.Smith .40 1.00
CC10 B.Gabbert/D.Murray .75 2.00
CC11 J.Locker/J.Elway 1.00 2.50
CC12 J.Baldwin/N.Devine .60 1.50
CC13 K.Hunter/D.Murray .75 2.00
CC14 D.Murray/D.Thomas .75 2.00
CC15 A.Green/M.Ingram 1.00 2.50
CC16 M.Ingram/B.Jackson .75 2.00
CC17 J.Rodgers/J.Locker .40 1.00
CC18 M.Ingram/R.Mallett .60 1.50
CC19 J.Jones/A.Green 1.25 3.00
CC20 A.Green/C.Newton 2.00 5.00

2011 Upper Deck Dream Tandems

COMPLETE SET (20) 6.00 15.00
RANDOM INSERTS IN PACKS
DT1 T.Brown/T.Aikman .75 2.00
DT2 J.Elway/J.Rice 1.00 2.50
DT3 L.Selmon/A.Page .40 1.00
DT4 B.Sanders/J.Rice 1.00 2.50
DT5 J.Rice/T.Aikman 1.00 2.50
DT6 T.Brown/R.Ismail .60 1.50
DT7 S.Largent/S.Young .75 2.00
DT8 T.Brown/K.Winslow Sr. .60 1.50
DT9 B.Jackson/D.Flutie .75 2.00
DT10 B.Jackson/C.Newton 2.00 5.00
DT11 B.Sanders/J.Elway 1.00 2.50
DT12 G.Rogers/F.Little .50 1.25
DT13 B.Bosworth/M.Singletary .60 1.50
DT14 M.Ingram/C.Newton 2.00 5.00
DT15 B.Gabbert/A.Green 1.00 2.50
DT16 B.Sanders/T.Aikman 1.00 2.50
DT17 B.Bosworth/L.Selmon .50 1.25
DT18 J.Locker/D.Thomas .40 1.00
DT19 A.Green/J.Jones 1.25 3.00
DT20 M.Ingram/B.Gabbert .60 1.50

2011 Upper Deck Evolution Video Cards

ANNOUNCED ODDS 1:HOBBY CASE
UDVC1 Adrian Peterson red 25.00 60.00
UDVC2 Adrian Peterson wht 25.00 60.00
UDVC6 DeSean Jackson 15.00 40.00
UDVC7 Patrick Willis 20.00 50.00
UDVC9 Tony Romo 15.00 40.00

2011 Upper Deck Historical Programs

COMPLETE SET (25) 8.00 20.00
RANDOM INSERTS IN PACKS
HP1 Jack Youngblood .40 1.00
HP2 Steve Young .75 2.00
HP3 Troy Aikman .75 2.00
HP4 Herman Moore .40 1.00
HP5 Bob Griese .60 1.50
HP6 Bo Jackson .75 2.00
HP7 John Elway 1.00 2.50
HP8 Craig Morton .40 1.00
HP9 Lee Roy Jordan .40 1.00
HP10 Doug Flutie .50 1.25
HP11 Tim Brown .60 1.50
HP12 Kellen Winslow Sr .50 1.25
HP13 Jim Kelly .60 1.50
HP14 Roger Craig .50 1.25
HP15 Barry Sanders 1.00 2.50
HP16 John Cappelletti .40 1.00
HP17 Floyd Little .40 1.00
HP18 Charles White .40 1.00
HP19 Earl Campbell .60 1.50
HP20 Billy Sims .50 1.25
HP21 Jake Locker .40 1.00
HP22 Ryan Williams .40 1.00
HP23 Christian Ponder .40 1.00
HP24 Ryan Mallett .40 1.00
HP25 A.J. Green 1.00 2.50

2011 Upper Deck Rookie Autographs

EXCH EXPIRATION: 3/9/2013
51 Ronald Johnson 4.00 10.00
52 Adrian Clayborn 4.00 10.00
53 Niles Paul 4.00 10.00
54 Mark Herzlich 4.00 10.00
55 Stephen Paea 4.00 10.00
56 Colin Kaepernick 6.00 15.00
57 Allen Bailey 4.00 10.00
58 Torrey Smith 4.00 10.00
59 Evan Royster 4.00 10.00
60 DeMarco Murray 8.00 20.00
61 Titus Young 4.00 10.00
62 Noel Devine 6.00 15.00
63 Jeremy Beal 5.00 12.00
64 Pat Devlin 6.00 15.00
65 Greg Little 5.00 12.00
66 Cameron Heyward 5.00 12.00
67 Armon Binns 5.00 12.00
68 Greg Jones 5.00 12.00
69 Jake Locker 4.00 10.00
70 Vincent Brown 4.00 10.00
71 Andy Dalton 8.00 20.00
72 Jeremy Kerley 6.00 15.00
73 Jerrel Jernigan 4.00 10.00
74 Daniel Thomas 4.00 10.00
75 Prince Amukamara EXCH 15.00 40.00
76 Von Miller 10.00 25.00
77 Delone Carter 4.00 10.00
78 Graig Cooper 5.00 12.00
79 Deunta Williams 5.00 12.00
80 Mike Pouncey 6.00 15.00
81 T.J. Yates 4.00 10.00
82 Jimmy Smith 4.00 10.00
83 Jamie Harper 4.00 10.00
84 Ras-I Dowling 4.00 10.00
85 Chimdi Chekwa 5.00 12.00
86 Greg Salas 4.00 10.00
87 Anthony Allen 4.00 10.00
88 Kendall Hunter 4.00 10.00

89 Bruce Carter	4.00	10.00
91 Pierre Allen	6.00	15.00
92 Rashad Carmichael	5.00	12.00
93 Quan Sturdivant	5.00	12.00
94 Vai Taua	4.00	10.00
95 Austin Pettis	4.00	10.00
96 Cecil Shorts	4.00	10.00
97 DeAndre McDaniel	4.00	10.00
98 Ross Homan	5.00	12.00
99 Anthony Castonzo	4.00	10.00
100 Nathan Enderle	4.00	10.00
101 Tandon Doss	4.00	10.00
102 Kelvin Sheppard	4.00	10.00
103 Ryan Kerrigan	5.00	12.00
104 Dane Sanzenbacher	4.00	10.00
105 D.J. Williams	4.00	10.00
106 Adrian Taylor	5.00	12.00
107 Sam Acho	4.00	10.00
108 Terrence Toliver	5.00	12.00
109 Marcus Cannon	4.00	10.00
110 Colin McCarthy	5.00	12.00
111 Roy Helu	4.00	10.00
112 Ricky Stanzi	4.00	10.00
113 Mason Foster	4.00	10.00
114 Brooks Reed	5.00	12.00
115 James Cleveland	4.00	10.00
116 Brandon Saine	6.00	15.00
117 Jabaal Sheard	4.00	10.00
118 Drake Nevis	4.00	10.00
119 Armando Allen	6.00	15.00
120 Corey Liuget	4.00	10.00
121 Luke Stocker	4.00	10.00
122 Dwayne Harris	4.00	10.00
123 Ahmad Black	5.00	12.00
124 Nate Solder	4.00	10.00
125 Jerrod Johnson	5.00	12.00
126 Cameron Jordan	10.00	25.00
127 Stefen Wisniewski	6.00	15.00
128 Tyrod Taylor	8.00	20.00
129 Lance Kendricks	4.00	10.00
130 Alex Wujciak	5.00	12.00
131 Christian Ponder	4.00	10.00
132 Jeff Maehl	4.00	10.00
133 Phil Taylor	4.00	10.00
134 Eric Hagg	6.00	15.00
135 Darvin Adams	4.00	10.00
136 Shaun Chapas	4.00	10.00
137 Adam Weber	4.00	10.00
138 Damien Berry	5.00	12.00
139 Aldon Smith	4.00	10.00
140 Lawrence Wilson	5.00	12.00
141 Lee Ziemba	4.00	10.00
142 Bilal Powell	5.00	12.00
143 Kendric Burney	4.00	10.00
144 Taylor Potts	4.00	10.00
145 Ryan Bartholomew	4.00	10.00
146 Lestar Jean	4.00	10.00
147 Tyron Smith	5.00	12.00
148 Zack Pianalto	5.00	12.00
149 Scott Lutrus	4.00	10.00
150 Jason Pinkston	4.00	10.00
151 Brandon Hogan	4.00	10.00
152 Ryan Whalen	4.00	10.00
153 Jarvis Williams	4.00	10.00
154 Kyle Adams	4.00	10.00
155 Chykie Brown	4.00	10.00
156 Derrick Locke	5.00	12.00
157 Davon House	4.00	10.00
158 Stevan Ridley	4.00	10.00
159 Armand Robinson	5.00	12.00
160 Mario Butler	4.00	10.00
161 Charles Clay	4.00	10.00
162 Jarvis Jenkins	4.00	10.00
163 Kris Durham	4.00	10.00
164 Joe Lefeged	5.00	12.00
165 Chris Carter	5.00	12.00
166 Korey Lindsey-Woods	4.00	10.00
167 Allen Bradford	4.00	10.00
168 Stephen Burton	4.00	10.00
169 Virgil Green	4.00	10.00
170 Jock Sanders	5.00	12.00
171 Rob Housler	4.00	10.00
172 Matt Szczur	6.00	15.00
173 Ian Williams	5.00	12.00
174 Brandon Burton	5.00	12.00
175 Orlando Franklin	5.00	12.00
176 Ryan Mallett	4.00	10.00
177 Akeem Ayers	4.00	10.00
178 Marcell Dareus	4.00	10.00
179 Jacquizz Rodgers	12.00	30.00
180 Blaine Gabbert	4.00	10.00
181 Shane Vereen	5.00	12.00
182 Casey Matthews	4.00	10.00
183 Jonathan Baldwin	4.00	10.00
184 Dion Lewis	5.00	12.00
185 John Clay	6.00	15.00
186 Justin Houston	5.00	12.00
187 Jordan Todman	4.00	10.00
188 J.J. Watt	30.00	60.00
189 Sione Fua	4.00	10.00
190 Randall Cobb	15.00	40.00
192 Mark Ingram	30.00	60.00
193 Da'Quan Bowers	8.00	20.00
194 Aaron Williams	4.00	10.00
195 Julio Jones	40.00	80.00
196 Rahim Moore	4.00	10.00
197 A.J. Green	15.00	40.00
198 Cam Newton	50.00	100.00
199 Ryan Williams	4.00	10.00
200 Kyle Rudolph	4.00	10.00

2011 Upper Deck Rookie Letterman Autographs

ANNOUNCED PRINT RUN 210-800
EXCH EXPIRATION: 3/9/2013

RSLAB Allen Bailey/500*	6.00	15.00
RSLAD Andy Dalton/550*	12.00	30.00
RSLAG A.J. Green/280*	25.00	60.00
RSLAP Austin Pettis/700*	12.00	30.00
RSLBC Bruce Carter/600*	6.00	15.00
RSLBE Jeremy Beal/700*	6.00	15.00
RSLBG Blaine Gabbert/300*	6.00	15.00
RSLBI Armon Binns/800*	6.00	15.00
RSLBS Brandon Saine/600*	10.00	25.00
RSLCH Cameron Heyward/800*	10.00	25.00
RSLCP Christian Ponder/315*	15.00	40.00
RSLDH Dwayne Harris/700*	10.00	25.00
RSLDM DeMarco Murray/350*	12.00	30.00
RSLDT Daniel Thomas/400*	12.00	30.00
RSLER Evan Royster/420*	6.00	15.00
RSLGC Graig Cooper/500*	8.00	20.00
RSLGL Greg Little/600*	8.00	20.00
RSLJB Jonathan Baldwin/280*	6.00	15.00
RSLJC John Clay/245*	10.00	25.00
RSLJJ Jerrel Jernigan/700*	8.00	20.00
RSLJK Jeremy Kerley/550*	10.00	25.00
RSLJL Jake Locker/245*	6.00	15.00
RSLJO Jerrod Johnson/600*	8.00	20.00
RSLJU Julio Jones/275*	20.00	50.00
RSLKA Colin Kaepernick/600*	10.00	25.00
RSLKH Kendall Hunter/700*	10.00	25.00
RSLLS Luke Stocker/750*	6.00	15.00
RSLMH Mark Herzlich/600*	6.00	15.00
RSLMI Mark Ingram/275*	20.00	50.00
RSLND Noel Devine/600*	12.00	30.00
RSLNE Nathan Enderle/700*	8.00	20.00
RSLNP Niles Paul/550*	10.00	25.00
RSLPD Pat Devlin/600*	10.00	25.00
RSLRH Roy Helu/550*	6.00	15.00
RSLRJ Ronald Johnson/700*	8.00	20.00
RSLRK Ryan Kerrigan/600*	10.00	25.00
RSLRM Ryan Mallett/250*	6.00	15.00
RSLRO Jacquizz Rodgers/245*	10.00	25.00
RSLRW Ryan Williams/210*	12.00	30.00
RSLTT Terrence Toliver/600*	8.00	20.00
RSLTY Titus Young/700*	6.00	15.00
RSLVB Vincent Brown/600*	6.00	15.00
RSLVM Von Miller/600*	15.00	40.00

2011 Upper Deck Saturday in Action

COMPLETE SET (15)	6.00	15.00
RANDOM INSERTS IN PACKS		
SIA1 Troy Aikman	.75	2.00
SIA2 John Elway	1.00	2.50
SIA3 Rocket Ismail	.50	1.25
SIA4 Barry Sanders	1.00	2.50
SIA5 Bo Jackson	.75	2.00
SIA6 Thurman Thomas	.50	1.25
SIA7 Floyd Little	.40	1.00
SIA8 Charles White	.40	1.00
SIA9 Doug Flutie	.50	1.25
SIA10 Jerry Rice	1.00	2.50
SIA11 Jim Kelly	.60	1.50
SIA12 Steve Young	.75	2.00
SIA13 Cam Newton	2.00	5.00
SIA14 Mark Ingram	.60	1.50
SIA15 A.J. Green	1.00	2.50

2011 Upper Deck Ultimate Rookie Signatures

RANDOM INSERTS IN PACKS
EXCH EXPIRATION: 3/9/2013

1 Allen Bailey	8.00	20.00
2 Cameron Heyward	10.00	25.00
4 Mark Herzlich	12.00	30.00
5 Jake Locker	8.00	20.00
6 Von Miller	20.00	50.00
7 Christian Ponder	40.00	100.00
8 Pat Devlin	12.00	30.00
9 Daniel Thomas	8.00	20.00
10 DeMarco Murray	15.00	40.00
11 Evan Royster	8.00	20.00
12 Noel Devine	12.00	30.00
13 Kendall Hunter	8.00	20.00
14 Greg Little	10.00	25.00
15 Armon Binns	10.00	25.00
16 Terrence Toliver	10.00	25.00
17 Niles Paul	8.00	20.00
18 Ronald Johnson	8.00	20.00
19 Austin Pettis	8.00	20.00
20 Titus Young	8.00	20.00

2012 Upper Deck

COMP.SET w/o ROOK (50)	5.00	12.00
COMP.SET w/o SP's (150)	20.00	50.00
248-272 INSERTED IN HOBBY PACKS		
273-297 INSERTED IN RETAIL PACKS		
1 Adrian Peterson	.30	.75
2 Alan Page	.20	.50
3 Andre Ware	.25	.60
4 Anthony Carter	.20	.50
5 Archie Griffin	.20	.50
6 Barry Sanders	.50	1.25
7 Bernie Kosar	.25	.60
8 Billy Cannon	.20	.50
9 Billy Sims	.25	.60
10 Bo Jackson	.40	1.00
11 Brian Bosworth	.25	.60
12 Charles White	.20	.50
13 Dan Marino	.60	1.50
14 Danny Wuerffel	.20	.50
15 Dave Casper	.20	.50
16 Doug Flutie	.25	.60
17 Drew Bledsoe	.25	.60
18 Drew Brees	.30	.75
19 Earl Campbell	.30	.75
20 Eddie George	.25	.60
21 Gale Sayers	.30	.75
22 Gary Beban	.20	.50
23 George Rogers	.20	.50
24 Gino Torretta	.20	.50
25 Herschel Walker	.30	.75
26 Jason White	.25	.60
27 Jim McMahon	.25	.60
28 Jim Plunkett	.25	.60
29 John Cappelletti	.20	.50
30 Johnny Rodgers	.25	.60
31 Kellen Winslow Sr.	.25	.60
32 Ken Stabler	.30	.75
33 Lawrence Taylor	.25	.60
34 Lee Roy Jordan	.20	.50
35 Marques Colston	.20	.50
36 Mike Singletary	.30	.75
37 Paul Hornung	.30	.75
38 Rocket Ismail	.25	.60
39 Rod Woodson	.25	.60
40 Roman Gabriel	.20	.50
41 Ron Dayne	.20	.50
42 Steve Young	.40	1.00
43 Thurman Thomas	.25	.60
44 Tim Brown	.30	.75
45 Todd Marinovich	.20	.50
46 Tony Dorsett	.30	.75
47 Troy Aikman	.40	1.00
48 Ty Detmer	.20	.50
49 Warren Moon	.30	.75
50 William Perry	.20	.50
51 Bobby Massie	.40	1.00
52 Alameda Ta'amu	.50	1.25
53 Alfred Morris	.40	1.00
54 Michael Brockers	.40	1.00
55 Zach Brown	.40	1.00
56 Antwon Bailey	.50	1.25
57 Audie Cole	.40	1.00
58 Emil Igwenagu	.50	1.25
59 B.J. Cunningham	.40	1.00
60 Tyler Hansen	.40	1.00
61 Ryan Steed	.40	1.00
62 Brandon Weeden	.40	1.00
63 Brian Reader	.50	1.25
64 Bryce Beall	.40	1.00
65 David Molk	.60	1.50
66 Cam Johnson	.60	1.50
67 Case Keenum	.75	2.00
68 Casey Hayward	.40	1.00
69 Duane Bennett	.50	1.25
70 Winston Guy	.40	1.00
71 Cliff Harris	.60	1.50
72 Cody Johnson	.50	1.25
73 Coryell Judie	.40	1.00
74 Courtney Upshaw	.50	1.25
75 Tim Benford	.40	1.00
76 Da'Jon McKnight	.50	1.25
77 Dan Persa	.50	1.25
78 Coby Fleener	.40	1.00
79 David DeCastro	.40	1.00
80 David Paulson	.60	1.50
81 Amini Silatolu	.40	1.00
82 Derek Moye	.60	1.50
83 Devon Still	.50	1.25
84 Devon Wylie	.40	1.00
85 Evan Rodriguez	.50	1.25
86 George Iloka	.40	1.00
87 Greg Childs	.40	1.00
88 Tyler Shoemaker	.50	1.25
89 Harrison Smith	.40	1.00
90 Jared Crick	.40	1.00
91 Jarrett Lee	.60	1.50
92 Jason Ford	.40	1.00
93 Jeff Fuller	.40	1.00
94 Jermaine Kearse	.60	1.50
95 Jake Bequette	.60	1.50
96 Josh Chapman	.40	1.00
97 Junior Hemingway	.60	1.50
98 Justin Blackmon	.40	1.00
99 Keenan Robinson	.50	1.25
100 Kellen Moore	.50	1.25
101 Bobby Wagner	.60	1.50
102 Kentrell Lockett	.40	1.00
103 Keshawn Martin	.50	1.25
104 Micanor Regis	.40	1.00
105 Kirk Cousins	1.50	4.00
106 Brock Osweiler	.40	1.00
107 LaMichael James	.40	1.00
108 Lavasier Tuinei	.60	1.50
109 Jeremy Ebert	.40	1.00
110 Marc Tyler	.40	1.00
111 Marcus Forston	.40	1.00
112 Markelle Martin	.50	1.25
113 Marquis Maze	.40	1.00
114 Nelson Rosario	.40	1.00
115 Matt Kalil	.40	1.00
116 Rodney Stewart	.50	1.25
117 Michael Egnew	.40	1.00
118 Michael Floyd	.40	1.00
119 Brandon Washington	.40	1.00
120 Mike Harris	.40	1.00
121 Mike Willie	.60	1.50
122 Darrell Scott	.50	1.25
123 Mychal Kendricks	.60	1.50
124 Robert Blanton	.50	1.25
125 Nick Foles	1.00	2.50
126 Nick Toon	.40	1.00
127 Shea McClellin	.50	1.25
128 Rhett Ellison	.50	1.25
129 Quinton Coples	.40	1.00
130 James-Michael Johnson	.50	1.25
131 Darron Thomas	1.00	2.50
132 William Vlachos	.50	1.25
133 Rueben Randle	.40	1.00
134 Russell Wilson	3.00	8.00
135 Ryan Broyles	.40	1.00
136 Fletcher Cox	.60	1.50
137 Ryan Tannehill	.60	1.50
138 Sean Spence	.50	1.25
139 Stephfon Green	.60	1.50
140 Brian Linthicum	.50	1.25
141 Mike Martin	.50	1.25
142 Tony Dye	.40	1.00
143 Travis Benjamin	.40	1.00
144 Trent Richardson	.40	1.00
145 Trenton Robinson	.50	1.25
146 Ladarius Green	.40	1.00
147 Kelechi Osemele	.40	1.00
148 Vinny Curry	.50	1.25
149 Shaun Prater	.60	1.50
150 Zebrie Sanders	.40	1.00
151 A.J. Jenkins	2.00	5.00
152 Whitney Mercilus	2.00	5.00
153 Alfonzo Dennard	2.00	5.00
154 Andre Branch	2.00	5.00
155 Lucas Nix	2.00	5.00
156 Antonio Allen	2.00	5.00
157 Billy Winn	3.00	8.00
158 Brandon Bolden	2.00	5.00
159 Brandon Boykin	2.50	6.00
160 Thomas Mayo	2.00	5.00
161 Brandon Thompson	2.50	6.00
162 Joe Looney	2.50	6.00
163 Chandler Harnish	2.00	5.00
164 Olivier Vernon	3.00	8.00
165 Keith Tandy	2.50	6.00
166 Kevin Koger	3.00	8.00
167 Cordy Glenn	2.50	6.00
168 Cyrus Gray	2.00	5.00
169 Dan Herron	2.00	5.00
170 Darius Reynolds	2.50	6.00
171 Davin Meggett	2.00	5.00
172 Dominique Davis	2.50	6.00
173 Donnie Fletcher	2.00	5.00
174 Dont'a Hightower	3.00	8.00
175 Doug Martin	3.00	8.00
176 Dwayne Allen	2.00	5.00
177 Dwight Jones	2.00	5.00
178 Gerell Robinson	2.00	5.00
179 Isaiah Pead	2.00	5.00
180 Jarius Wright	2.00	5.00
181 Jarrett Boykin	5.00	12.00
182 Jayron Hosley	3.00	8.00
183 Jamell Fleming	2.00	5.00
184 Jermaine Thomas	2.50	6.00
185 Joe Adams	2.00	5.00
186 Kyle Wilber	3.00	8.00
187 Jordan Jefferson	2.50	6.00
188 Jordan White	2.50	6.00
189 Juron Criner	2.00	5.00
190 Kendall Reyes	2.00	5.00
191 Kendall Wright	2.00	5.00
192 Tommy Streeter	2.00	5.00
193 Laron Byrd	2.50	6.00
194 Lavonte David	3.00	8.00
195 Levy Adcock	2.00	5.00
196 Darius Hanks	3.00	8.00
197 Marvin Jones	2.00	5.00
198 Marvin McNutt	2.00	5.00
199 Melvin Ingram	2.00	5.00
200 Bradie Ewing	2.50	6.00
201 Nigel Bradham	2.50	6.00
202 Riley Reiff	5.00	12.00
203 Ronnell Lewis	2.00	5.00
204 Ryan Lindley	2.00	5.00
205 Stephon Gilmore	4.00	10.00
206 Tank Carder	3.00	8.00
207 Tauren Poole	2.00	5.00
208 Eric Page	2.50	6.00
209 Travis Lewis	2.50	6.00
210 Vontaze Burfict	2.50	6.00
211 Aaron Corp	2.00	5.00
212 Alshon Jeffery	6.00	15.00
213 Bernard Pierce	2.00	5.00
214 Bobby Rainey	2.00	5.00
215 Chris Galippo	2.50	6.00
216 Brian Quick	2.00	5.00
217 Mike Daniels	4.00	10.00
218 Eddie Whitley	2.50	6.00
219 DeVier Posey	2.00	5.00
220 Dontari Poe	2.00	5.00
221 Dre Kirkpatrick	2.00	5.00
222 Edwin Baker	2.50	6.00
223 Fozzy Whittaker	2.00	5.00
224 Trevor Guyton	2.50	6.00
225 Jacory Harris	2.50	6.00
226 Janoris Jenkins	2.50	6.00
227 Jerry Franklin	2.50	6.00
228 Jonathan Martin	2.00	5.00
229 Chris Givens	2.00	5.00
230 Lamar Miller	3.00	8.00
231 Lance Lewis	2.50	6.00
232 Brandon Carswell	2.50	6.00
233 Lennon Creer	2.00	5.00
234 Leonard Johnson	2.50	6.00
235 Luke Kuechly	5.00	12.00
236 Josh Norman	2.50	6.00
237 Marshall Lobbestael	2.50	6.00
238 Mohamed Sanu	3.00	8.00
239 T.Y. Hilton	4.00	10.00
240 T.J. Graham	2.00	5.00
241 Orson Charles	2.00	5.00
242 Patrick Edwards	2.50	6.00
243 Rishard Matthews	2.00	5.00
244 Robert Griffin III	2.50	6.00
245 Ronnie Hillman	2.00	5.00
246 Stephen Garcia	3.00	8.00
247 Stephen Hill	2.00	5.00
248 Quinton Coples	3.00	8.00
249 Robert Griffin III	4.00	10.00
250A Trent Richardson	15.00	40.00
250B Andrew Luck	25.00	60.00
251 Alfonzo Dennard	3.00	8.00
252 Alshon Jeffery	6.00	15.00
253 Brandon Bolden	3.00	8.00
254 Brandon Thompson	4.00	10.00
255 Case Keenum	6.00	15.00
256 Stephen Hill	3.00	8.00
257 Cyrus Gray	3.00	8.00
258 DeVier Posey	3.00	8.00
259 Doug Martin	5.00	12.00
260 Isaiah Pead	3.00	8.00
261 Jarius Wright	3.00	8.00
262 Rueben Randle	3.00	8.00
263 Joe Adams	3.00	8.00
264 Kendall Wright	3.00	8.00
265 Kirk Cousins	12.00	30.00
266 Darron Thomas	8.00	20.00
267 Marc Tyler	3.00	8.00
268 Marquis Maze	3.00	8.00
269 Chris Givens	3.00	8.00
270 Michael Egnew	3.00	8.00
271 Mohamed Sanu	5.00	12.00
272 Nick Toon	3.00	8.00
273 Ryan Lindley	5.00	12.00
274 Ryan Tannehill	8.00	20.00
275 Tauren Poole	5.00	12.00
276 Lamar Miller	8.00	20.00
277 B.J. Cunningham	5.00	12.00
278 Brandon Weeden	5.00	12.00
279 Brian Quick	5.00	12.00
280 Dwayne Allen	15.00	30.00
281 Courtney Upshaw	6.00	15.00
282 Dan Herron	5.00	12.00
283 Dwight Jones	5.00	12.00
284 Gerell Robinson	5.00	12.00
285 Jarrett Boykin	12.00	30.00
286 Brock Osweiler	5.00	12.00
287 Jeff Fuller	5.00	12.00
288 Juron Criner	5.00	12.00
289 Justin Blackmon	5.00	12.00
290 Kellen Moore	6.00	15.00
291 LaMichael James	5.00	12.00
292 Marvin McNutt	5.00	12.00
293 Michael Floyd	5.00	12.00
294 Bernard Pierce	5.00	12.00
295 Nick Foles	12.00	30.00
296 Russell Wilson	30.00	60.00
297 Ryan Broyles	5.00	12.00
NNO QB Draft Trade/Luck	40.00	80.00

2012 Upper Deck 1993 SP Inserts

SP STATED ODDS 1:5		
93SP1 Alameda Ta'amu	1.25	3.00
93SP2 Alfonzo Dennard	1.00	2.50
93SP3 Alshon Jeffery	2.00	5.00
93SP4 Lamar Miller	1.50	4.00
93SP5 B.J. Cunningham	1.00	2.50
93SP6 Brandon Bolden	1.00	2.50
93SP7 Brandon Thompson	1.25	3.00
93SP8 Brandon Weeden	1.00	2.50
93SP9 Brian Quick	1.00	2.50
93SP10 Brock Osweiler	1.00	2.50
93SP11 Case Keenum	2.00	5.00
93SP12 Chandler Harnish	1.00	2.50
93SP13 Marvin Jones	1.00	2.50
93SP14 Darron Thomas	2.50	6.00
93SP15 Bernard Pierce	1.00	2.50
93SP16 Dwayne Allen	1.00	2.50
93SP17 Courtney Upshaw	1.25	3.00
93SP18 Cyrus Gray	1.00	2.50
93SP19 Dan Herron	1.00	2.50
93SP20 Davin Meggett	1.00	2.50
93SP21 DeVier Posey	1.00	2.50
93SP22 Doug Martin	1.50	4.00
93SP23 Dwight Jones	1.00	2.50
93SP24 Rueben Randle	1.00	2.50
93SP25 Gerell Robinson	1.00	2.50
93SP26 Greg Childs	1.00	2.50
93SP27 Isaiah Pead	1.00	2.50
93SP28 Dre Kirkpatrick	1.00	2.50
93SP29 Jared Crick	1.00	2.50
93SP30 Jarius Wright	1.00	2.50
93SP31 Jarrett Boykin	2.50	6.00
93SP32 Eric Page	1.25	3.00
93SP33 Jeff Fuller	1.00	2.50
93SP34 Jermaine Kearse	1.50	4.00
93SP35 Joe Adams	1.00	2.50
93SP36 Juron Criner	1.00	2.50
93SP37 Justin Blackmon	1.00	2.50
93SP38 Kellen Moore	1.25	3.00
93SP39 Kendall Wright	1.00	2.50
93SP40 Keshawn Martin	1.25	3.00
93SP41 Kirk Cousins	4.00	10.00
93SP42 LaMichael James	1.00	2.50
93SP43 Chris Givens	1.00	2.50
93SP44 Marc Tyler	1.00	2.50
93SP45 Marquis Maze	1.00	2.50
93SP46 Marvin McNutt	2.00	5.00
93SP47 Ronnie Hillman	1.00	2.50
93SP48 Melvin Ingram	1.00	2.50
93SP49 Michael Egnew	1.00	2.50
93SP50 Michael Floyd	5.00	12.00
93SP51 Mohamed Sanu	1.50	4.00
93SP52 Luke Kuechly	2.50	6.00
93SP53 Nick Foles	2.50	6.00
93SP54 Nick Toon	1.00	2.50
93SP55 Quinton Coples	1.00	2.50
93SP56 Rishard Matthews	1.00	2.50
93SP57 Robert Griffin III	1.25	3.00
93SP58 Russell Wilson	6.00	15.00
93SP59 Ryan Broyles	1.00	2.50
93SP60 Ryan Lindley	1.00	2.50
93SP61 Ryan Tannehill	1.50	4.00
93SP62 Tauren Poole	1.00	2.50
93SP63 Tommy Streeter	1.00	2.50
93SP64 Trent Richardson	1.00	2.50
93SP65 Stephen Hill	1.00	2.50
93SP66 Thurman Thomas	1.00	2.50
93SP67 Antonio Freeman	.75	2.00
93SP68 Johnny Rodgers	1.00	2.50
93SP69 Billy Cannon	.75	2.00
93SP70 Bo Jackson	1.50	4.00
93SP71 Bob Lilly	1.00	2.50
93SP72 Charles White	.75	2.00
93SP73 Chris Spielman	.75	2.00
93SP74 Danny Wuerffel	.75	2.00
93SP75 Dave Casper	.75	2.00
93SP76 Drew Brees	1.25	3.00
93SP77 Earl Campbell	1.25	3.00
93SP78 Eric Metcalf	.75	2.00
93SP79 Floyd Little	.75	2.00
93SP80 Gary Beban	.75	2.00
93SP81 Gino Torretta	.75	2.00
93SP82 Harry Carson	.75	2.00
93SP83 Herman Moore	.75	2.00
93SP84 Jason White	1.00	2.50
93SP85 Bernie Kosar	1.00	2.50
93SP86 Billy Sims	1.00	2.50
93SP87 Kellen Winslow Sr.	1.00	2.50
93SP88 Lawrence Taylor	1.00	2.50
93SP89 Marques Colston	.75	2.00
93SP90 Ozzie Newsome	1.00	2.50
93SP91 Randy White	1.00	2.50
93SP92 Roger Staubach	1.50	4.00
93SP93 Roman Gabriel	.75	2.00
93SP94 Ron Dayne	.75	2.00
93SP95 Ron Yary	.75	2.00
93SP96 Steve Young	1.50	4.00
93SP97 Todd Marinovich	.75	2.00
93SP98 Troy Aikman	1.50	4.00
93SP99 Ty Detmer	.75	2.00
93SP100 Warren Moon	1.25	3.00

2012 Upper Deck 1993 SP Inserts Autographs

93SP1 Alameda Ta'amu	10.00	25.00
93SP2 Alfonzo Dennard	8.00	20.00
93SP3 Alshon Jeffery	30.00	60.00
93SP5 B.J. Cunningham	8.00	20.00
93SP6 Brandon Bolden	20.00	50.00
93SP7 Brandon Thompson	10.00	25.00
93SP8 Brandon Weeden	15.00	40.00
93SP9 Brian Quick	15.00	40.00
93SP10 Brock Osweiler	8.00	20.00
93SP11 Case Keenum	15.00	40.00
93SP12 Chandler Harnish	8.00	20.00
93SP13 Marvin Jones	8.00	20.00
93SP15 Bernard Pierce	8.00	20.00
93SP16 Dwayne Allen	8.00	20.00
93SP17 Courtney Upshaw	12.00	30.00
93SP18 Cyrus Gray	8.00	20.00
93SP19 Dan Herron	12.00	30.00
93SP20 Davin Meggett	10.00	25.00
93SP21 DeVier Posey	12.00	30.00
93SP22 Doug Martin	12.00	30.00
93SP23 Dwight Jones	8.00	20.00
93SP24 Rueben Randle		
93SP25 Gerell Robinson	8.00	20.00
93SP26 Greg Childs	8.00	20.00
93SP27 Isaiah Pead	8.00	20.00
93SP28 Dre Kirkpatrick	25.00	50.00
93SP29 Jared Crick	12.00	30.00
93SP30 Jarius Wright	8.00	20.00
93SP31 Jarrett Boykin	20.00	50.00
93SP32 Eric Page	10.00	25.00
93SP33 Jeff Fuller	8.00	20.00
93SP34 Jermaine Kearse	12.00	30.00
93SP35 Joe Adams	8.00	20.00
93SP37 Justin Blackmon	25.00	60.00
93SP38 Kellen Moore	25.00	60.00
93SP39 Kendall Wright	12.00	30.00
93SP40 Keshawn Martin	15.00	40.00
93SP41 Kirk Cousins	20.00	50.00
93SP42 LaMichael James	15.00	40.00
93SP44 Marc Tyler	8.00	20.00
93SP45 Marquis Maze	8.00	20.00
93SP46 Marvin McNutt	25.00	50.00
93SP47 Ronnie Hillman	8.00	20.00
93SP48 Melvin Ingram	15.00	30.00
93SP49 Michael Egnew	12.00	30.00
93SP50 Michael Floyd	60.00	100.00
93SP51 Mohamed Sanu	12.00	30.00
93SP52 Luke Kuechly	20.00	40.00
93SP53 Nick Foles	20.00	50.00
93SP54 Nick Toon	30.00	60.00
93SP55 Quinton Coples	8.00	20.00
93SP56 Rishard Matthews	8.00	20.00
93SP57 Robert Griffin III	40.00	80.00
93SP58 Russell Wilson	75.00	125.00
93SP59 Ryan Broyles	25.00	50.00
93SP60 Ryan Lindley	8.00	20.00
93SP61 Ryan Tannehill	12.00	30.00
93SP62 Tauren Poole	8.00	20.00
93SP64 Trent Richardson	40.00	100.00
93SP65 Stephen Hill	8.00	20.00
93SP66 Thurman Thomas	20.00	40.00
93SP67 Antonio Freeman	20.00	40.00
93SP68 Johnny Rodgers	15.00	30.00
93SP70 Bo Jackson		
93SP71 Bob Lilly	30.00	60.00
93SP74 Danny Wuerffel		
93SP75 Dave Casper		
93SP76 Drew Brees	60.00	120.00
93SP78 Eric Metcalf		
93SP79 Floyd Little	15.00	30.00
93SP81 Gino Torretta	10.00	25.00
93SP83 Herman Moore		
93SP84 Jason White		
93SP87 Kellen Winslow Sr.	10.00	25.00
93SP88 Lawrence Taylor	15.00	40.00
93SP89 Marques Colston	25.00	50.00
93SP90 Ozzie Newsome	10.00	25.00
93SP91 Randy White	20.00	50.00
93SP92 Roger Staubach		
93SP93 Roman Gabriel	12.00	30.00
93SP94 Ron Dayne	20.00	40.00
93SP96 Steve Young	40.00	80.00
93SP98 Troy Aikman		
93SP99 Ty Detmer	25.00	50.00
93SP100 Warren Moon	20.00	40.00

2012 Upper Deck College Mascot Manufactured Patch

GROUP A ODDS 1:99 HOB
GROUP B ODDS 1:158 HOB
GROUP C ODDS 1:1752 HOB
GROUP D ODDS 1:7595 HOB
OVERALL STATED ODDS 1:40 HOBBY

CM1 Big Al A	15.00	40.00
CM2 Sparky B	6.00	15.00
CM3 Willie the Wildcat B	6.00	15.00
CM4 Tusk A	10.00	25.00
CM5 Black Jack C	25.00	60.00
CM6 War Eagle C	40.00	100.00
CM7 Aubie A	8.00	20.00
CM8 Bruiser B	8.00	20.00
CM9 Buster Bronco B	8.00	20.00
CM10 Baldwin the Eagle B	6.00	15.00
CM11 Cosmo A	6.00	15.00
CM12 Oski A	8.00	20.00
CM13 Knightro B	8.00	20.00
CM14 Ralphie B	8.00	20.00
CM15 YoUDee C	15.00	40.00
CM16 PeeDee B	8.00	20.00
CM17 Albert E. Gator A	12.00	30.00
CM18 Uga D	250.00	350.00
CM19 Hairy Dawg A	10.00	25.00
CM20 Buzz A	6.00	15.00
CM21 Herky Hawk A	10.00	25.00
CM22 The Wildcat B	8.00	20.00
CM23 Mike the Tiger D	250.00	350.00
CM24 Mike the Tiger A	12.00	30.00
CM25 Sebastian the Ibis C	30.00	80.00
CM26 Sparty A	10.00	25.00
CM27 Goldy Gopher B	6.00	15.00
CM28 Bully A	8.00	20.00
CM29 Truman the Tiger A	8.00	20.00
CM30 Monte B	6.00	15.00
CM31 Herbie Husker A	10.00	25.00
CM32 Lil Red D	100.00	175.00
CM33 Rameses B	10.00	25.00
CM34 The Leprechaun A	15.00	30.00
CM35 Brutus Buckeye A	20.00	50.00
CM36 Sooner Schooner A	10.00	25.00
CM37 Pistol Pete A	8.00	20.00
CM38 The Duck A	20.00	40.00
CM39 Benny Beaver C	25.00	50.00
CM40 Roc the Panther A	6.00	15.00
CM41 The Clemson Tiger A	10.00	25.00
CM42 Purdue Pete A	8.00	20.00
CM43 Cocky B	8.00	20.00
CM44 Rocky D. Bull B	6.00	15.00
CM45 Super Frog B	6.00	15.00
CM46 Smokey A	10.00	25.00
CM47 Reveille A	10.00	25.00
CM48 Bevo D	125.00	200.00
CM49 Hook Em A	8.00	20.00
CM50 Raider Red A	6.00	15.00
CM51 Joe and Josephine Bruin A	8.00	20.00
CM52 Traveler D	150.00	250.00
CM53 Trojan Warrior A	8.00	20.00
CM54 CavMan A	6.00	15.00
CM55 HukieBird A	8.00	20.00
CM56 Demon Deacon A	8.00	20.00
CM57 Harry the Husky A	8.00	20.00
CM58 Big Red A	8.00	20.00
CM59 Bucky Badger A	10.00	25.00
CM60 Handsome Dan A	8.00	20.00

2012 Upper Deck Rookie Autographs

51 Bobby Massie	4.00	10.00
52 Alameda Ta'amu	8.00	20.00
53 Alfred Morris	4.00	10.00
54 Michael Brockers	10.00	25.00
56 Antwon Bailey	5.00	12.00
57 Audie Cole	4.00	10.00
58 Emil Igwenagu	4.00	10.00
59 B.J. Cunningham	10.00	25.00
60 Tyler Hansen	4.00	10.00
61 Ryan Steed	4.00	10.00
62 Brandon Weeden	12.00	30.00
63 Brian Reader	5.00	12.00
64 Bryce Beall	4.00	10.00
65 David Molk	6.00	15.00
66 Cam Johnson	6.00	15.00
67 Case Keenum	12.00	30.00
68 Casey Hayward	4.00	10.00
69 Duane Bennett	5.00	12.00
70 Winston Guy	4.00	10.00
71 Cliff Harris	8.00	20.00
72 Cody Johnson	5.00	12.00
73 Coryell Judie	4.00	10.00
74 Courtney Upshaw	5.00	12.00
75 Tim Benford	4.00	10.00
76 Da'Jon McKnight	5.00	12.00
77 Dan Persa	5.00	12.00
78 Coby Fleener	4.00	10.00
80 David Paulson	8.00	20.00
81 Amini Silatolu	4.00	10.00
82 Derek Moye	8.00	20.00
84 Devon Wylie	4.00	10.00
85 Evan Rodriguez	5.00	12.00
86 George Iloka	4.00	10.00
87 Greg Childs	4.00	10.00
88 Tyler Shoemaker	5.00	12.00
89 Harrison Smith	8.00	20.00
90 Jared Crick	8.00	20.00
91 Jarrett Lee	8.00	20.00
92 Jason Ford	4.00	10.00
93 Jeff Fuller	4.00	10.00
94 Jermaine Kearse	8.00	20.00
95 Jake Bequette	6.00	15.00
96 Josh Chapman	4.00	10.00
97 Junior Hemingway	8.00	20.00
98 Justin Blackmon	8.00	20.00
99 Keenan Robinson	5.00	12.00
100 Kellen Moore	15.00	40.00
101 Bobby Wagner	6.00	15.00
102 Kentrell Lockett	4.00	10.00
103 Keshawn Martin	5.00	12.00
104 Micanor Regis	4.00	10.00
105 Kirk Cousins	15.00	40.00
106 Brock Osweiler	4.00	10.00
107 LaMichael James	12.00	30.00
108 Lavasier Tuinei	6.00	15.00
109 Jeremy Ebert	4.00	10.00
110 Marc Tyler	4.00	10.00
112 Markelle Martin	5.00	12.00
113 Marquis Maze	15.00	30.00
114 Nelson Rosario	4.00	10.00
115 Matt Kalil	8.00	20.00
116 Rodney Stewart	5.00	12.00
117 Michael Egnew	4.00	10.00
118 Michael Floyd	20.00	40.00
121 Mike Willie	6.00	15.00
123 Mychal Kendricks	6.00	15.00
124 Robert Blanton	5.00	12.00
125 Nick Foles	10.00	25.00
126 Nick Toon	15.00	30.00
127 Shea McClellin	8.00	20.00
128 Rhett Ellison	5.00	12.00
129 Quinton Coples	6.00	15.00
130 James-Michael Johnson	5.00	12.00
132 William Vlachos	5.00	12.00
133 Rueben Randle	10.00	25.00
134 Russell Wilson	60.00	120.00
135 Ryan Broyles	12.00	30.00
137 Ryan Tannehill	6.00	15.00
139 Stephfon Green	10.00	25.00
140 Brian Linthicum	5.00	12.00
141 Mike Martin	5.00	12.00
142 Tony Dye	4.00	10.00
143 Travis Benjamin	4.00	10.00
144 Trent Richardson	20.00	50.00
145 Trenton Robinson	5.00	12.00
146 Ladarius Green	4.00	10.00
147 Kelechi Osemele	4.00	10.00
149 Shaun Prater	6.00	15.00
151 A.J. Jenkins	10.00	25.00
152 Whitney Mercilus	4.00	10.00
153 Alfonzo Dennard	8.00	20.00
154 Andre Branch	4.00	10.00
155 Lucas Nix	4.00	10.00
157 Billy Winn	6.00	15.00
158 Brandon Bolden	4.00	10.00
160 Thomas Mayo	4.00	10.00
161 Brandon Thompson	5.00	12.00
162 Joe Looney	5.00	12.00
163 Chandler Harnish	4.00	10.00
165 Keith Tandy	5.00	12.00
166 Kevin Koger	6.00	15.00
168 Cyrus Gray	4.00	10.00
169 Dan Herron	8.00	20.00
171 Davin Meggett	6.00	15.00
172 Dominique Davis	5.00	12.00
173 Donnie Fletcher	4.00	10.00
174 Dont'a Hightower	12.00	30.00
175 Doug Martin	15.00	40.00
176 Dwayne Allen	4.00	10.00
177 Dwight Jones	4.00	10.00
178 Gerell Robinson	5.00	12.00
179 Isaiah Pead	8.00	20.00
180 Jarius Wright	8.00	20.00
181 Jarrett Boykin	8.00	20.00
182 Jayron Hosley	6.00	15.00
183 Jamell Fleming	6.00	15.00
184 Jermaine Thomas	5.00	12.00
185 Joe Adams	6.00	15.00
186 Kyle Wilber	6.00	15.00
187 Jordan Jefferson	5.00	12.00
188 Jordan White	6.00	15.00
190 Kendall Reyes	4.00	10.00
191 Kendall Wright	4.00	10.00
193 Laron Byrd	5.00	12.00
194 Lavonte David	6.00	15.00
195 Levy Adcock	4.00	10.00
196 Darius Hanks	8.00	20.00
197 Marvin Jones	8.00	20.00
198 Marvin McNutt	10.00	25.00
199 Melvin Ingram	8.00	20.00
200 Bradie Ewing	5.00	12.00
201 Nigel Bradham	5.00	12.00
202 Riley Reiff	20.00	40.00
203 Ronnell Lewis	10.00	25.00
204 Ryan Lindley	4.00	10.00
205 Stephon Gilmore	6.00	15.00
206 Tank Carder	6.00	15.00
207 Tauren Poole	8.00	20.00
208 Eric Page	5.00	12.00
209 Travis Lewis	5.00	12.00
210 Vontaze Burfict	5.00	12.00
212 Alshon Jeffery	20.00	40.00
213 Bernard Pierce	4.00	10.00
214 Bobby Rainey	8.00	20.00
215 Chris Galippo	5.00	12.00
216 Brian Quick	4.00	10.00
217 Mike Daniels	8.00	20.00
218 Eddie Whitley	6.00	15.00
219 DeVier Posey	8.00	20.00
220 Dontari Poe	4.00	10.00
221 Dre Kirkpatrick	12.00	30.00
222 Edwin Baker	5.00	12.00
223 Fozzy Whittaker	4.00	10.00
224 Trevor Guyton	5.00	12.00
226 Janoris Jenkins	6.00	15.00
227 Jerry Franklin	5.00	12.00
228 Jonathan Martin	4.00	10.00
232 Brandon Carswell	5.00	12.00
233 Lennon Creer	4.00	10.00
234 Leonard Johnson	5.00	12.00
235 Luke Kuechly	15.00	30.00
236 Josh Norman	5.00	12.00
237 Marshall Lobbestael	5.00	12.00
238 Mohamed Sanu	8.00	20.00
240 T.J. Graham	4.00	10.00
241 Orson Charles	8.00	20.00
242 Patrick Edwards	5.00	12.00
243 Rishard Matthews	4.00	10.00
244 Robert Griffin III	60.00	120.00
245 Ronnie Hillman	4.00	10.00
246 Stephen Garcia	6.00	15.00
247 Stephen Hill	10.00	25.00
250 Andrew Luck	250.00	400.00

2012 Upper Deck Rookie Exclusives

RANDOM INSERTS IN PACKS		
REAJ Alshon Jeffery	1.00	2.50
REBW Brandon Weeden	.50	1.25
REJB Justin Blackmon	.50	1.25
REKW Kendall Wright	.50	1.25
RELJ LaMichael James	.50	1.25
RELM Lamar Miller	.75	2.00
REMF Michael Floyd	.50	1.25
RENF Nick Foles	1.25	3.00
RERG Robert Griffin III	.60	1.50
RETR Trent Richardson	.50	1.25

2012 Upper Deck Rookie Lettermen Autographs

SERIAL #'d 5-45, TOTAL PRINT RUNS 100-405		
RLAD Alfonzo Dennard/275*	6.00	15.00
RLAJ1 Alshon Jeffery/200*	25.00	50.00
RLAJ2 Alshon Jeffery C/10	25.00	50.00
RLAT Alameda Ta'amu/315*	8.00	20.00
RLBB Brandon Bolden/270*	8.00	20.00
RLBC B.J. Cunningham/360*	6.00	15.00
RLBO Jarrett Boykin/270*	15.00	40.00
RLBQ Brian Quick/300*	6.00	15.00
RLBT Brandon Thompson/270*	8.00	20.00
RLBW Brandon Weeden/315*	10.00	25.00
RLCG Cyrus Gray/270*	6.00	15.00
RLCH Chandler Harnish/315*	6.00	15.00
RLCK Case Keenum/315*	12.00	30.00
RLCU Courtney Upshaw/275*	8.00	20.00
RLDA Davin Meggett/405*	6.00	15.00
RLDH Dan Herron/360*	6.00	15.00
RLDJ Dwight Jones/360*	6.00	15.00
RLDM Doug Martin/315*	10.00	25.00
RLDP DeVier Posey/360*	6.00	15.00
RLGC1 Greg Childs/315*	6.00	15.00
RLGC2 Greg Childs Z/15	6.00	15.00
RLGR Gerell Robinson/405*	6.00	15.00
RLIP Isaiah Pead/360*	6.00	15.00
RLJA Joe Adams/350*	6.00	15.00
RLJB1 Justin Blackmon/150*	15.00	40.00
RLJB2 Justin Blackmon O/10	15.00	40.00
RLJC Jared Crick/275*	12.00	30.00
RLJF1 Jeff Fuller/175*	6.00	15.00
RLJF2 Jeff Fuller G/15	6.00	15.00
RLJJ Janoris Jenkins/225*	8.00	20.00
RLJK Jermaine Kearse/315*	10.00	25.00
RLJU1 Juron Criner/245*	6.00	15.00
RLJU2 Juron Criner C/15	15.00	30.00
RLKC1 Kirk Cousins/245*	25.00	60.00
RLKC2 Kirk Cousins/15	25.00	60.00
RLKM Keshawn Martin/360*	8.00	20.00
RLLA1 LaMichael James/100*	15.00	40.00
RLLA2 LaMichael James U/10	150.00	300.00
RLLK Luke Kuechly/270*	25.00	50.00
RLMC Marvin McNutt/360*	12.00	30.00
RLME Michael Egnew/270*	6.00	15.00
RLMF1 Michael Floyd/300*	20.00	50.00
RLMF2 Michael Floyd I/10	30.00	80.00
RLMI Melvin Ingram/405*	12.00	30.00
RLMM Marquis Maze/385*	12.00	30.00
RLMO1 Kellen Moore/210*	15.00	40.00
RLMO2 Kellen Moore B/15	25.00	60.00
RLMS Mohamed Sanu/210*	12.00	30.00
RLMT Marc Tyler/315*	6.00	15.00
RLNF Nick Foles/280*	15.00	40.00
RLNT Nick Toon/245*	12.00	30.00
RLQC Quinton Coples/360*	6.00	15.00
RLRB Ryan Broyles/315*	6.00	15.00
RLRG Robert Griffin III/225*	50.00	100.00
RLRL Ryan Lindley/210*	6.00	15.00
RLRT Ryan Tannehill/210*	10.00	25.00
RLRW Russell Wilson/315*	50.00	100.00
RLTP Tauren Poole/350*	6.00	15.00
RLTR1 Trent Richardson/150*	12.00	30.00
RLTR2 Trent Richardson T/5		

2012 Upper Deck Tim Tebow

COMPLETE SET (10)	15.00	40.00
COMMON TEBOW (TT1-TT10)	1.00	2.50
INSERTED IN UD RACK PACKS		
TT4 Tim Tebow	5.00	12.00
TT7 Tim Tebow	5.00	12.00

2013 Upper Deck

MP.SET w/o SP's (150)	20.00	50.00
215-275 INSERTED IN HOBBY PACKS		
276-300 INSERTED IN RETAIL PACKS		
1 Vinny Testaverde	.20	.50
2 Ronnie Lott	.25	.60
3 Daryle Lamonica	.20	.50
4 Paul Hornung	.30	.75
5 Steve Young	.40	1.00
6 Don Maynard	.25	.60
7 Roger Craig	.25	.60
8 Bart Starr	.50	1.25
9 Anthony Carter	.20	.50
10 Ken MacAfee	.20	.50
11 Jake Plummer	.20	.50
12 Archie Griffin	.20	.50
13 John Elway	.50	1.25
14 Jerry Rice	.50	1.25
15 Warren Sapp	.25	.60
16 Joe Namath	.40	1.00
17 Charles White	.20	.50
18 Ken Stabler	.30	.75
19 Dan Fouts	.25	.60
20 George Rogers	.20	.50
21 Ozzie Newsome	.25	.60
22 Bo Jackson	.40	1.00
23 Bruce Smith	.25	.60
24 Al Toon	.20	.50
25 Nick Buoniconti	.20	.50
26 Keith Jackson	.20	.50
27 Billy Cannon	.20	.50
28 Warren Moon	.30	.75
29 Rich Gannon	.20	.50
30 Archie Manning	.25	.60
31 Robert Smith	.20	.50
32 Johnny Lattner	.20	.50

33 Jim Kelly .30 .75
34 Billy Sims .25 .60
35 Tedy Bruschi .25 .60
36 Rodney Peete .20 .50
37 Mike Rozier .20 .50
38 Jerome Bettis .30 .75
39 Drew Bledsoe .25 .60
40 Chris Weinke .20 .50
41 Dan Marino .60 1.50
42 Ty Detmer .20 .50
43 Joe Theismann .30 .75
44 Brian Bosworth .25 .60
45 Tommie Frazier .20 .50
46 Doug Flutie .25 .60
47 Garrison Hearst .20 .50
48 Andre Ware .20 .50
49 Barry Sanders .50 1.25
50 Charlie Ward .20 .50
51 Marquess Wilson .60 1.50
52 Philip Lutzenkirchen .60 1.50
53 Jordan Hill .60 1.50
54 Mitchell Gale .40 1.00
55 Marcus Davis .40 1.00
56 DeVonte Holloman .50 1.25
57 Marquise Goodwin .40 1.00
58 Kenny Stills .40 1.00
59 Datone Jones .40 1.00
60 Da'Rick Rogers .40 1.00
61 Emory Blake .40 1.00
62 Keith Pough .40 1.00
63 Kwame Geathers .40 1.00
64 Cameron Marshall .40 1.00
65 Knile Davis .40 1.00
66 Xavier Rhodes .40 1.00
67 Dion Jordan .40 1.00
68 Rex Burkhead .50 1.25
69 B.W. Webb .50 1.25
70 Terry Hawthorne .50 1.25
71 Duke Williams .40 1.00
72 Justin Hunter .40 1.00
73 Mike Gillislee .40 1.00
74 Dan Buckner .40 1.00
75 Keenan Davis .60 1.50
76 Trevardo Williams .50 1.25
77 Chris Harper .40 1.00
78 Gerald Hodges .50 1.25
79 Gavin Escobar .40 1.00
80 Margus Hunt .40 1.00
81 Eric Reid .50 1.25
82 Le'Veon Bell 1.25 3.00
83 Erik Highsmith .50 1.25
84 Travis Kelce 1.00 2.50
85 DeAndre Hopkins 1.00 2.50
86 Barrett Jones .40 1.00
87 Johnny Adams .40 1.00
88 Nick Kasa .40 1.00
89 Spencer Ware .40 1.00
90 Dee Milliner .40 1.00
91 Geno Smith .40 1.00
92 Sean Porter .40 1.00
93 Chris Thompson .40 1.00
94 D.J. Harper .50 1.25
95 T.J. Moe .50 1.25
96 Oday Aboushi .40 1.00
97 Zach Boren .50 1.25
98 Ryan Swope .40 1.00
99 Dayne Crist .50 1.25
100 Jordan Reed .60 1.50
101 D.J. Fluker .40 1.00
102 Aaron Dobson .40 1.00
103 Malliciah Goodman .40 1.00
104 Josh Boyce .40 1.00
105 Sheldon Richardson .40 1.00
106 Chase Thomas .40 1.00
107 Andre Ellington .40 1.00
108 John Wetzel .50 1.25
109 Blidi Wreh-Wilson .50 1.25
110 Cobi Hamilton .40 1.00
111 Logan Ryan .50 1.25
112 Manti Te'o .50 1.25
113 Lonnie Pryor .40 1.00
114 Kawann Short .40 1.00
115 Mike Shanahan .50 1.25
116 Khaled Holmes .40 1.00
117 Zac Dysert .40 1.00
118 Kiko Alonso .50 1.25
119 EJ Manuel .40 1.00
120 Roy Roundtree 1.00 2.50
121 Matt McGloin 6.00 12.00
122 Theo Riddick .40 1.00
123 Conner Vernon .40 1.00
124 Ricky Wagner .40 1.00
125 T.J. McDonald .40 1.00
126 Matt Elam .40 1.00
127 Eddie Lacy .40 1.00
128 Eric Fisher .40 1.00
129 Robert Alford .40 1.00
130 Braden Wilson .50 1.25
131 Terrance Williams .40 1.00
132 Sanders Commings .40 1.00
133 Greg Reid .60 1.50
134 Chuck Jacobs .40 1.00
135 Michael Williams .50 1.25
136 Robert Lester .40 1.00
137 Brandon Ford .50 1.25
138 Mike Glennon .40 1.00
139 Michael Mauti .60 1.50
140 Damontre Moore .40 1.00
141 Joseph Fauria .40 1.00
142 Drew Terrell .40 1.00
143 Menelik Watson .60 1.50
144 D.J. Swearinger .40 1.00
145 Josh Johnson .40 1.00
146 Tyler Bray .40 1.00
147 Justin Pugh .40 1.00
148 Bjoern Werner .40 1.00
149 Braxston Cave .60 1.50
150 Joseph Randle .40 1.00
151 Dyrell Roberts SP 3.00 8.00
152 Lavar Edwards SP 3.00 8.00
153 Tavon Austin SP 3.00 8.00
154 John Simon SP 4.00 10.00
155 Russell Shepard SP 2.50 6.00
156 Josh Jarboe SP 2.50 6.00
157 Michael Clay SP 4.00 10.00
158 Ryan Lacy SP 3.00 8.00
159 Akeem Spence SP 2.50 6.00
160 Corey Fuller SP 2.50 6.00
161 Dion Sims SP 2.50 6.00
162 Marc Anthony SP 2.50 6.00
163 Sharrif Floyd SP 2.50 6.00
164 Jon Bostic SP 6.00 15.00
165 Collin Klein SP 3.00 8.00
166 Zaviar Gooden SP 3.00 8.00
167 Uzoma Nwachukwu SP 3.00 8.00
168 Curtis McNeal SP 3.00 8.00
169 Jarvis Jones SP 2.50 6.00
170 Brandon Jenkins SP 3.00 8.00
171 Leon McFadden SP 3.00 8.00
172 Seth Doege SP 4.00 10.00
173 Steve Greer SP 2.50 6.00
174 John Boyett SP 3.00 8.00
175 Sylvester Williams SP 2.50 6.00
176 Vince Williams SP 4.00 10.00
177 Jeff Tuel SP 2.50 6.00
178 Bacarri Rambo SP 3.00 8.00
179 Brandon McGee SP 2.50 6.00
180 Brad Sorensen SP 2.50 6.00
181 Ray Graham SP 2.50 6.00
182 Ryan Nassib SP 5.00 12.00
183 Khaseem Greene SP 2.50 6.00
184 Ryan Otten SP 2.50 6.00
185 Kevin Reddick SP 2.50 6.00
186 Jesse Williams SP 4.00 10.00
187 Jack Doyle SP 2.50 6.00
188 Michael Buchanan SP 4.00 10.00
189 Dallas Thomas SP 4.00 10.00
190 Onterio McCalebb SP 3.00 8.00
191 Matt Barkley SP 15.00 30.00
192 Kevin Minter SP 2.50 6.00
193 Tommy Bohanon SP 3.00 8.00
194 Stefphon Jefferson SP 3.00 8.00
195 Jordan Rodgers SP 3.00 8.00
196 Jordan Poyer SP 2.50 6.00
197 Desmond Trufant SP 2.50 6.00
198 Arthur Brown SP 2.50 6.00
199 B.J. Daniels SP 4.00 10.00
200 Stedman Bailey SP 2.50 6.00
201 Travis Howard SP 3.00 8.00
202 Stepfan Taylor SP 2.50 6.00
203 Vance McDonald SP 3.00 8.00
204 Everett Dawkins SP 2.50 6.00
205 Lane Johnson SP 3.00 8.00
206 Cordarrelle Patterson SP 2.50 6.00
207 Shamarko Thomas SP 5.00 12.00
208 Skye Dawson SP 3.00 8.00
209 Cierre Wood SP 2.50 6.00
210 Montee Ball SP 2.50 6.00
211 Alex Okafor SP 3.00 8.00
212 Jelani Jenkins SP 4.00 10.00
213 Daimion Stafford SP 6.00 15.00
214 Star Lotulelei SP 4.00 10.00
215 Zach Ertz SP 6.00 15.00
216 Zach Line SP 3.00 8.00
217 Alec Ogletree SP 3.00 8.00
218 Bennie Logan SP 4.00 10.00
219 Lerentee McCray SP 3.00 8.00
220 Tyler Eifert SP 3.00 8.00
221 Aaron Mellette SP 3.00 8.00
222 Landry Jones SP 3.00 8.00
223 Rodney Smith SP 3.00 8.00
224 Robert Woods SP 5.00 12.00
225 Jawan Jamison SP 3.00 8.00
226 Giovani Bernard SP 3.00 8.00
227 Tyler Wilson SP 3.00 8.00
228 Robbie Rouse SP 3.00 8.00
229 Brandon Kaufman SP 3.00 8.00
230 David Amerson SP 3.00 8.00
231 Denard Robinson SP 3.00 8.00
232 Tavarres King SP 3.00 8.00
233 Ezekiel Ansah SP 3.00 8.00
234 Kenny Vaccaro SP 6.00 15.00
235 Barkevious Mingo SP 3.00 8.00
236 Sheldon Price SP 3.00 8.00
237 Sam Montgomery SP 3.00 8.00
238 Luke Joeckel SP 3.00 8.00
239 Nico Johnson SP 4.00 10.00
240 Markus Wheaton SP 3.00 8.00
241 Matt Scott SP 3.00 8.00
242 Dennis Johnson SP 3.00 8.00
243 Keenan Allen SP 6.00 15.00
244 Zach Maynard SP 4.00 10.00
245 Tyrone Goard SP 3.00 8.00
246 Will Davis SP 3.00 8.00
247 Tony Jefferson SP 5.00 12.00
248 Johnathan Franklin SP 3.00 8.00
249 Marcus Lattimore SP 3.00 8.00
250 Kenjon Barner SP 3.00 8.00
251 Mike Gillislee SP 5.00 12.00
252 Barkevious Mingo SP 5.00 12.00
253 Luke Joeckel SP 20.00 40.00
254 Da'Rick Rogers SP 5.00 12.00
255 Mike Glennon SP 5.00 12.00
256 Theo Riddick SP 5.00 12.00
257 Stedman Bailey SP 5.00 12.00
258 Aaron Dobson SP 5.00 12.00
259 Giovani Bernard SP 5.00 12.00
260 Geno Smith SP 5.00 12.00
261 Landry Jones SP 5.00 12.00
262 Tavon Austin SP 6.00 15.00
263 Markus Wheaton SP 5.00 12.00
264 EJ Manuel SP 5.00 12.00
265 Keenan Allen SP 10.00 25.00
266 Knile Davis SP 5.00 12.00
267 Montee Ball SP 5.00 12.00
268 Zach Ertz SP 10.00 25.00
269 DeAndre Hopkins SP 12.00 30.00
270 Eddie Lacy SP 5.00 12.00
271 Justin Hunter SP 5.00 12.00
272 Ryan Swope SP 5.00 12.00
273 Zac Dysert SP 5.00 12.00
274 Manti Te'o SP 6.00 15.00
275 Cordarrelle Patterson SP 5.00 12.00
276 Tyler Wilson SP 5.00 12.00
277 Cobi Hamilton SP 5.00 12.00
278 Joseph Randle SP 5.00 12.00
279 Kenjon Barner SP 10.00 25.00
280 Tyler Bray SP 12.00 30.00
281 Le'Veon Bell SP 15.00 40.00
282 Terrance Williams SP 5.00 12.00
283 Matt Barkley SP 15.00 40.00
284 Johnathan Franklin SP 5.00 12.00
285 Corey Fuller SP 8.00 20.00
286 Marquess Wilson SP 8.00 20.00
287 Collin Klein SP 6.00 15.00
288 Denard Robinson SP 5.00 12.00
289 Andre Ellington SP 5.00 12.00
290 Bjoern Werner SP 5.00 12.00
291 Stepfan Taylor SP 5.00 12.00
292 Tyler Eifert SP 5.00 12.00
293 Jawan Jamison SP 5.00 12.00
294 Dennis Johnson SP 5.00 12.00
295 Aaron Mellette SP 5.00 12.00
296 Ryan Nassib SP 5.00 12.00
297 Star Lotulelei SP 6.00 15.00
298 Tavarres King SP 12.00 30.00
299 Matt Scott SP 5.00 12.00
300 Robert Woods SP 12.00 30.00

2013 Upper Deck 1995 SP Inserts

SP1 Al Toon .75 2.00
95SP2 Jason White .75 2.00
95SP3 Ken MacAfee .75 2.00
95SP4 Brian Bosworth 1.00 2.50
95SP5 Bart Starr 2.00 5.00
95SP6 Nick Buoniconti .75 2.00
95SP7 Charlie Ward .75 2.00
95SP8 Rodney Peete .75 2.00
95SP9 Ken Stabler 1.25 3.00
95SP10 Steve Young 1.50 4.00
95SP11 Troy Aikman 1.50 4.00
95SP12 Paul Hornung 1.25 3.00
95SP13 Drew Bledsoe 1.00 2.50
95SP14 Herschel Walker 1.25 3.00
95SP15 Roger Craig 1.00 2.50
95SP16 Archie Griffin .75 2.00
95SP17 Garrison Hearst .75 2.00
95SP18 Don Maynard 1.00 2.50
95SP19 John Elway 2.00 5.00
95SP20 Bruce Smith 1.00 2.50
95SP21 Johnny Lattner .75 2.00
95SP22 Joe Theismann 1.25 3.00
95SP23 Rich Gannon .75 2.00
95SP24 Tedy Bruschi 1.00 2.50
95SP25 Andre Ware .75 2.00
95SP26 Keith Jackson .75 2.00
95SP27 Charles White .75 2.00
95SP28 Daryle Lamonica .75 2.00
95SP29 Jim Kelly 1.25 3.00
95SP30 Chris Weinke .75 2.00
95SP31 Archie Manning 1.00 2.50
95SP32 Doug Flutie 1.00 2.50
95SP33 Joe Namath 1.50 4.00
95SP34 Billy Cannon .75 2.00
95SP35 Dan Fouts 1.00 2.50
95SP36 Dan Marino 2.50 6.00
95SP37 Bo Jackson 1.50 4.00
95SP38 Jake Plummer .75 2.00
95SP39 Barry Sanders 2.00 5.00
95SP40 George Rogers .75 2.00
95SP41 Joe Washington .75 2.00
95SP42 Earl Campbell 1.25 3.00
95SP43 Billy Sims 1.00 2.50
95SP44 Ozzie Newsome 1.00 2.50
95SP45 Jerome Bettis 1.25 3.00
95SP46 Mike Rozier .75 2.00
95SP47 Robert Smith .75 2.00
95SP48 Gary Beban .75 2.00
95SP49 Anthony Carter .75 2.00
95SP50 Jerry Rice 2.00 5.00
95SP51 Mike Gillislee PP 1.00 2.50
95SP52 Zac Dysert PP 1.00 2.50
95SP53 Matt Barkley PP 1.00 2.50
95SP54 Robert Woods PP 1.50 4.00
95SP55 Denard Robinson PP 1.00 2.50
95SP56 Ryan Nassib PP 1.00 2.50
95SP57 Dion Sims PP 1.00 2.50
95SP58 Cordarrelle Patterson PP 1.00 2.50
95SP59 Montee Ball PP 1.00 2.50
95SP60 Le'Veon Bell PP 3.00 8.00
95SP61 Tyler Eifert PP 1.00 2.50
95SP62 Da'Rick Rogers PP 1.00 2.50
95SP63 Aaron Mellette PP 1.00 2.50
95SP64 Luke Joeckel PP 1.00 2.50
95SP65 Jarvis Jones PP 1.00 2.50
95SP66 Knile Davis PP 1.00 2.50
95SP67 Justin Hunter PP 1.00 2.50
95SP68 EJ Manuel PP 1.00 2.50
95SP69 Terrance Williams PP 1.00 2.50
95SP70 Mike Glennon PP 1.00 2.50
95SP71 Tavarres King PP 1.00 2.50
95SP72 Zach Ertz PP 2.00 5.00
95SP73 Geno Smith PP 1.00 2.50
95SP74 Jawan Jamison PP 1.00 2.50
95SP75 Manti Te'o PP 1.25 3.00
95SP76 Conner Vernon PP 1.00 2.50
95SP77 Johnathan Franklin PP 1.00 2.50
95SP78 Kenjon Barner PP 1.00 2.50
95SP79 Corey Fuller PP 1.00 2.50
95SP80 Giovani Bernard PP 1.00 2.50
95SP81 Landry Jones PP 1.00 2.50
95SP82 Markus Wheaton PP 1.00 2.50
95SP83 Tyler Wilson PP 1.00 2.50
95SP84 Stedman Bailey PP 1.00 2.50
95SP85 Kenny Stills PP 1.00 2.50
95SP86 Tavon Austin PP 1.25 3.00
95SP87 Joseph Randle PP 1.00 2.50
95SP88 Ryan Swope PP 1.00 2.50
95SP89 Collin Klein PP 1.25 3.00
95SP90 DeAndre Hopkins PP 2.50 6.00
95SP91 Dion Jordan PP 1.00 2.50
95SP92 Cobi Hamilton PP 1.00 2.50
95SP93 Tyler Bray PP 1.00 2.50
95SP94 Keenan Allen PP 2.00 5.00
95SP95 Marcus Lattimore PP 1.00 2.50
95SP96 Aaron Dobson PP 1.00 2.50
95SP97 Matt Scott PP 1.00 2.50
95SP98 Andre Ellington PP 1.00 2.50
95SP99 Eddie Lacy PP 1.00 2.50
95SP100 Marquess Wilson PP 1.50 4.00

2013 Upper Deck 1995 SP Inserts Autographs

UNPRICED RETIRED GRP A ODDS 1:4549
UNPRICED RETIRED GRP B ODDS 1:3349
RETIRED GROUP C ODDS 1:390
RETIRED GROUP D ODDS 1:762
UNPRICED ROOKIE GRP A ODDS 1:6773
UNPRICED ROOKIE GRP B ODDS 1:2032
ROOKIE GROUP C ODDS 1:1033
ROOKIE GROUP D ODDS 1:462
OVERALL AUTO ODDS 6:20
95SP1 Al Toon D 6.00 15.00
95SP2 Jason White C 6.00 15.00
95SP3 Ken MacAfee D 6.00 15.00
95SP7 Charlie Ward D 6.00 15.00
95SP8 Rodney Peete C 6.00 15.00
95SP17 Garrison Hearst C 6.00 15.00
95SP21 Johnny Lattner C 6.00 15.00
95SP25 Andre Ware C 8.00 20.00
95SP26 Keith Jackson C 6.00 15.00
95SP27 Charles White D 6.00 15.00
95SP30 Chris Weinke C 6.00 15.00
95SP38 Jake Plummer C 6.00 15.00
95SP40 George Rogers C 8.00 20.00
95SP43 Billy Sims C 8.00 20.00
95SP46 Mike Rozier C 6.00 15.00
95SP47 Robert Smith C 8.00 20.00
95SP48 Gary Beban C 6.00 15.00
95SP49 Anthony Carter C 8.00 20.00
95SP51 Mike Gillislee PP D 12.00 30.00
95SP55 Denard Robinson PP D 6.00 15.00
95SP57 Dion Sims PP D 6.00 15.00
95SP61 Tyler Eifert PP C
95SP63 Aaron Mellette PP D 6.00 15.00
95SP65 Jarvis Jones PP C
95SP66 Knile Davis PP D 6.00 15.00
95SP71 Tavarres King PP D 6.00 15.00
95SP72 Zach Ertz PP C 12.00 30.00
95SP74 Jawan Jamison PP D 6.00 15.00
95SP76 Conner Vernon PP D 6.00 15.00
95SP77 Johnathan Franklin PP C 6.00 15.00
95SP78 Kenjon Barner PP C 6.00 15.00
95SP84 Stedman Bailey PP C 25.00 50.00
95SP85 Kenny Stills PP C 6.00 15.00
95SP87 Joseph Randle PP C
95SP88 Ryan Swope PP D 12.00 30.00
95SP89 Collin Klein PP C
95SP91 Dion Jordan PP C 6.00 15.00
95SP92 Cobi Hamilton PP C
95SP95 Marcus Lattimore PP C 12.00 30.00
95SP97 Matt Scott PP D 6.00 15.00
95SP98 Andre Ellington PP C 6.00 15.00
95SP100 Marquess Wilson PP D 10.00 25.00

2013 Upper Deck Barry Sanders Heroes

COMPLETE SET (11) 12.00 30.00
COMP.SET w/o SP's (10) 6.00 15.00
COMMON SANDERS 1.25 3.00
HERO HEADER ODDS 1:480
UNPRICED HERO AU ODDS 1:7500
OVERALL HEROES ODDS 1:5
CFHBS Barry Sanders Hdr CL 6.00 15.00

2013 Upper Deck College Mascot Manufactured Patch

61-90 GROUP D ODDS 1:49
91-105 GROUP C ODDS 1:227
106-115 GRP B ODDS 1:782
116-120 UNPRICED GRP A ODDS 1:6513
OVERALL ODDS 1:40
CM61 Smokey D 8.00 20.00
CM62 Rocky D 6.00 15.00
CM63 Dubs D 8.00 20.00
CM64 Wilbur D 6.00 15.00
CM65 Bearcat D 8.00 20.00
CM66 Champ D 8.00 20.00
CM67 Renegade D 10.00 25.00
CM68 Alphie D 6.00 15.00
CM69 Shasta D 6.00 15.00
CM70 Joe Vandal D 6.00 15.00
CM71 Big Jay and Baby Jay D 10.00 25.00
CM72 Louie D 6.00 15.00
CM73 Marco D 6.00 15.00
CM74 Testudo D 6.00 15.00
CM75 Paydirt Pete D 6.00 15.00
CM76 Big House D 20.00 40.00
CM77 Bill The Goat D 6.00 15.00
CM78 Mr. Wuf D 8.00 20.00
CM79 Willie D 6.00 15.00
CM80 Rufus D 8.00 20.00
CM81 Rebel Black Bear D 8.00 20.00
CM82 Scarlet Knight D 8.00 20.00
CM83 Peruna D 8.00 20.00
CM84 Otto D 8.00 20.00
CM85 T-Roy D 6.00 15.00
CM86 Hey Reb D 6.00 15.00
CM87 Utah Swoop D 6.00 15.00
CM88 Butch T. Cougar D 8.00 20.00
CM89 Mountaineer D 20.00 40.00
CM90 Pistol Pete D 6.00 15.00
CM91 General Scott C 8.00 20.00
CM92 Albert&Alberta Gator C 12.00 30.00
CM93 Ramblin Wreck C 8.00 20.00
CM94 Boomer and Sooner C 10.00 25.00
CM95 Bird C 8.00 20.00
CM96 CAM C 8.00 20.00
CM97 Sammy Spartan C 8.00 20.00
CM98 Benny C 8.00 20.00
CM99 Cy the Cardinal C 12.00 30.00
CM100 Big Blue C 8.00 20.00
CM101 Lobo Louie C 12.00 30.00
CM102 Pouncer C 8.00 20.00
CM103 Sammy C 8.00 20.00
CM104 Blue Devil C 12.00 30.00
CM105 Hooter C 10.00 25.00
CM106 Big Red B 12.00 30.00
CM107 Purdue Pete B 12.00 30.00
CM108 Freddie Falcon B 12.00 30.00
CM109 EM Swoop B 12.00 30.00
CM110 Mr. C B 15.00 40.00
CM111 Louie the Lumberjack B 15.00 40.00
CM112 Jack the Bulldog B 15.00 40.00
CM113 Seymour D'Campus B 15.00 40.00
CM114 Captain Cane B 15.00 40.00
CM115 Oregon Duck B 15.00 40.00

2013 Upper Deck Robert Griffin Heroes

COMPLETE SET (10) 8.00 20.00
COMMON GRIFFIN (RG1-RG10) 1.25 3.00
OVERALL HEROES ODDS 1:5
*FAT PACK: .25X TO .6X BASIC INSERT

2013 Upper Deck Rookie Autographs

51-150 UNPRICED GRP A ODDS 1:12,192
51-150 GROUP B ODDS 1:847
51-150 GROUP C ODDS 1:368
51-150 GROUP D ODDS 1:78
51-150 GROUP E ODDS 1:16
151-210 GROUP A ODDS 1:6096
151-210 GROUP B ODDS 1:93
151-210 GROUP C ODDS 1:83
211-250 GROUP A ODDS 1:1804
211-250 GROUP B ODDS 1:321
211-250 GROUP C ODDS 1:191
OVERALL AUTO ODDS 6:20
*51-150 HOLOFOIL/15: .6X TO 1.5X GRP D-E
*51-150 HOLOFOIL/15: .5X TO 1.2X GRP B-C
*51-150 HOLOFOIL/15: .4X TO 1X GRP A
*151-210 HOLOFOIL/15: .5X TO 1.2X GRP B-C
*211-250 HOLOFOIL/15: .5X TO 1.2X GRP C
*211-250 HOLOFOIL/15: .4X TO 1X GRP B
*211-250 HOLOFOIL/15: .25X TO .6X GRP A
51 Marquess Wilson E 6.00 15.00
52 Philip Lutzenkirchen E 6.00 15.00
53 Jordan Hill E 6.00 15.00
54 Mitchell Gale E 4.00 10.00
55 Marcus Davis D 4.00 10.00
56 DeVonte Holloman E 5.00 12.00
57 Marquise Goodwin D 4.00 10.00
58 Kenny Stills E 8.00 20.00
59 Datone Jones E 4.00 10.00
60 Da'Rick Rogers D 4.00 10.00
61 Emory Blake C 5.00 12.00
62 Keith Pough C 5.00 12.00
63 Kwame Geathers D 4.00 10.00
64 Cameron Marshall D 4.00 10.00
65 Knile Davis D 4.00 10.00
66 Xavier Rhodes E 4.00 10.00
67 Dion Jordan D 4.00 10.00
68 Rex Burkhead D 5.00 12.00
69 B.W. Webb E 5.00 12.00
70 Terry Hawthorne E 5.00 12.00
71 Duke Williams E 4.00 10.00
72 Justin Hunter C 5.00 12.00
73 Mike Gillislee D 4.00 10.00
74 Dan Buckner E 4.00 10.00
75 Keenan Davis E 6.00 15.00
76 Trevardo Williams E 5.00 12.00
77 Chris Harper E 4.00 10.00
78 Gerald Hodges D 5.00 12.00
79 Gavin Escobar E 4.00 10.00
80 Margus Hunt E 4.00 10.00
82 Le'Veon Bell D 20.00 40.00
83 Erik Highsmith E 5.00 12.00
84 Travis Kelce E 10.00 25.00
85 DeAndre Hopkins C 15.00 40.00
86 Barrett Jones B 5.00 12.00
87 Johnny Adams E 4.00 10.00
88 Nick Kasa E 4.00 10.00
89 Spencer Ware E 4.00 10.00
90 Dee Milliner D 4.00 10.00
91 Geno Smith C 5.00 12.00
92 Sean Porter E 4.00 10.00
93 Chris Thompson E 4.00 10.00
94 D.J. Harper E 5.00 12.00
95 T.J. Moe E 5.00 12.00
96 Oday Aboushi E 4.00 10.00
97 Zach Boren E 5.00 12.00
98 Ryan Swope C 5.00 12.00
99 Dayne Crist E 5.00 12.00
100 Jordan Reed E 6.00 15.00
101 D.J. Fluker E 4.00 10.00
102 Aaron Dobson D 4.00 10.00
103 Malliciah Goodman E 4.00 10.00
104 Josh Boyce E 4.00 10.00
106 Chase Thomas E 4.00 10.00
107 Andre Ellington D 4.00 10.00
109 Blidi Wreh-Wilson E 5.00 12.00
110 Cobi Hamilton D 4.00 10.00
111 Logan Ryan E 5.00 12.00
112 Manti Te'o B 6.00 15.00
113 Lonnie Pryor E 4.00 10.00
114 Kawann Short E 4.00 10.00
115 Mike Shanahan E 5.00 12.00
116 Khaled Holmes E 4.00 10.00
117 Zac Dysert D 4.00 10.00
118 Kiko Alonso D 5.00 12.00
119 EJ Manuel C 5.00 12.00
120 Roy Roundtree E 10.00 25.00
122 Theo Riddick E 4.00 10.00
123 Conner Vernon E 4.00 10.00
124 Ricky Wagner E 4.00 10.00
125 T.J. McDonald E 4.00 10.00
126 Matt Elam E 4.00 10.00
127 Eddie Lacy B 5.00 12.00
128 Eric Fisher E 8.00 20.00
129 Robert Alford E 4.00 10.00
130 Braden Wilson C 6.00 15.00
131 Terrance Williams D 4.00 10.00
132 Sanders Commings E 4.00 10.00
133 Greg Reid E 6.00 15.00
134 Chuck Jacobs E 4.00 10.00
135 Michael Williams E 5.00 12.00
136 Robert Lester E 4.00 10.00
137 Brandon Ford E 5.00 12.00
138 Mike Glennon B 5.00 12.00
139 Michael Mauti E 6.00 15.00
140 Damontre Moore D 4.00 10.00
141 Joseph Fauria E 4.00 10.00
142 Drew Terrell E 4.00 10.00
143 Menelik Watson E 6.00 15.00
144 D.J. Swearinger B 10.00 25.00
145 Josh Johnson E 4.00 10.00
146 Tyler Bray B 8.00 20.00
147 Justin Pugh E 4.00 10.00
148 Bjoern Werner A 15.00 40.00
149 Braxston Cave E 6.00 15.00
150 Joseph Randle D 4.00 10.00
151 Dyrell Roberts SP B 6.00 15.00
152 Lavar Edwards SP B 6.00 15.00
153 Tavon Austin SP B 6.00 15.00
154 John Simon SP C 8.00 20.00
155 Russell Shepard SP B 5.00 12.00
156 Josh Jarboe SP B 5.00 12.00
157 Michael Clay SP B 8.00 20.00
159 Akeem Spence SP B 5.00 12.00
160 Corey Fuller SP C 5.00 12.00
161 Dion Sims SP C 5.00 12.00
162 Marc Anthony SP C 5.00 12.00
163 Sharrif Floyd SP C 5.00 12.00
164 Jon Bostic SP C 5.00 12.00
165 Collin Klein SP C 6.00 15.00
166 Zaviar Gooden SP B 6.00 15.00
167 Uzoma Nwachukwu SP A 10.00 25.00
168 Curtis McNeal SP B 6.00 15.00
169 Jarvis Jones SP B 10.00 25.00
170 Brandon Jenkins SP B 6.00 15.00
171 Leon McFadden SP B 6.00 15.00
172 Seth Doege SP C 8.00 20.00
173 Steve Greer SP B 5.00 12.00
174 John Boyett SP B 6.00 15.00
175 Sylvester Williams SP C 5.00 12.00
176 Vince Williams SP C 8.00 20.00
177 Jeff Tuel SP C 5.00 12.00
178 Bacarri Rambo SP B 6.00 15.00
179 Brandon McGee SP B 5.00 12.00
180 Brad Sorensen SP B 5.00 12.00
181 Ray Graham SP C 5.00 12.00
182 Ryan Nassib SP C 8.00 20.00
183 Khaseem Greene SP B 5.00 12.00
184 Ryan Otten SP B 5.00 12.00
185 Kevin Reddick SP C 5.00 12.00
186 Jesse Williams SP C 8.00 20.00
187 Jack Doyle SP B 5.00 12.00
188 Michael Buchanan B 8.00 20.00
190 Onterio McCalebb SP C 6.00 15.00
191 Matt Barkley SP B 5.00 12.00
192 Kevin Minter SP B 5.00 12.00
193 Tommy Bohanon SP B 6.00 15.00
194 Stefphon Jefferson SP B 6.00 15.00
195 Jordan Rodgers SP C 6.00 15.00
196 Jordan Poyer SP C 5.00 12.00
197 Desmond Trufant SP B 5.00 12.00
198 Arthur Brown SP C 5.00 12.00
199 B.J. Daniels SP B 8.00 20.00
200 Stedman Bailey SP B 5.00 12.00
201 Travis Howard SP B 6.00 15.00
202 Stepfan Taylor SP B 5.00 12.00
203 Vance McDonald SP B 6.00 15.00
204 Everett Dawkins SP C 5.00 12.00
205 Lane Johnson SP B 6.00 15.00
206 Cordarrelle Patterson SP C 5.00 12.00
207 Shamarko Thomas SP C 12.00 20.00
208 Skye Dawson SP C 6.00 15.00
209 Cierre Wood SP B 5.00 12.00
210 Montee Ball SP C 12.00 30.00
211 Alex Okafor SP A 8.00 20.00
212 Jelani Jenkins SP C 6.00 15.00
213 Daimion Stafford SP C 6.00 15.00
214 Star Lotulelei SP C 6.00 15.00
215 Zach Ertz SP B 12.00 30.00
216 Zach Line SP C 5.00 12.00
218 Bennie Logan SP C 6.00 15.00
219 Lerentee McCray SP C 5.00 12.00
220 Tyler Eifert SP B 12.00 30.00
221 Aaron Mellette SP B 6.00 15.00
222 Landry Jones SP C 10.00 25.00
223 Rodney Smith SP C 5.00 12.00
224 Robert Woods SP C 8.00 20.00
225 Jawan Jamison SP A 10.00 25.00
226 Giovani Bernard SP B 6.00 15.00
227 Tyler Wilson SP B 6.00 15.00
228 Robbie Rouse SP C 5.00 12.00
229 Brandon Kaufman SP C 5.00 12.00
230 David Amerson SP C 5.00 12.00
231 Denard Robinson SP A 10.00 25.00
232 Tavarres King SP B 6.00 15.00
233 Ezekiel Ansah SP A 10.00 25.00
234 Kenny Vaccaro SP B 12.00 30.00
235 Barkevious Mingo SP B 6.00 15.00
236 Sheldon Price SP C 5.00 12.00
237 Sam Montgomery SP B 6.00 15.00
238 Luke Joeckel SP B 6.00 15.00
239 Nico Johnson SP C 6.00 15.00
240 Markus Wheaton SP B 6.00 15.00
241 Matt Scott SP B 6.00 15.00
242 Dennis Johnson SP B 6.00 15.00
243 Keenan Allen SP C 10.00 25.00
244 Zach Maynard SP C 6.00 15.00
245 Tyrone Goard SP C 5.00 12.00
246 Will Davis SP A 10.00 25.00
247 Tony Jefferson SP C 8.00 20.00
248 Johnathan Franklin SP B 6.00 15.00
249 Marcus Lattimore SP B 12.00 30.00
250 Kenjon Barner SP B 6.00 15.00

2013 Upper Deck Rookie Exclusives

ONE PER SPECIAL RETAIL PACK
REAE Andre Ellington .60 1.50
REBA Montee Ball .60 1.50
REEL Eddie Lacy .60 1.50
REEM EJ Manuel .60 1.50
REGB Giovani Bernard .60 1.50
REGS Geno Smith .60 1.50
REJH Justin Hunter .60 1.50
REJR Joseph Randle .60 1.50
REKA Keenan Allen 1.25 3.00
REKD Knile Davis .60 1.50
RELB Le'Veon Bell 2.00 5.00
RELJ Landry Jones .60 1.50
REMB Matt Barkley .60 1.50
REMG Mike Glennon .60 1.50
REMW Marquess Wilson 1.00 2.50
RERN Ryan Nassib .60 1.50
RERW Robert Woods 1.00 2.50
RETA Tavon Austin .75 2.00
RETW Tyler Wilson .60 1.50
REWI Terrance Williams .60 1.50

2013 Upper Deck Rookie Lettermen Autographs

SER.#'d 15-75, TOTAL PRINT RUNS 105-675
RLAD Aaron Dobson/350* 15.00 40.00
RLAE Andre Ellington/300* 20.00 40.00
RLAO Alex Okafor/450* 6.00 15.00
RLBA Montee Ball/175* 12.00 30.00
RLBJ Brandon Jenkins/675* 8.00 20.00
RLCH Cobi Hamilton/500* 6.00 15.00
RLCK Collin Klein/400* 8.00 20.00
RLDB Dan Buckner/400* 6.00 15.00
RLDJ Dion Jordan/250* 6.00 15.00
RLDR Denard Robinson/250* 6.00 15.00
RLEB Emory Blake/450* 8.00 20.00
RLEH Erik Highsmith/400* 6.00 15.00
RLEM EJ Manuel/225* 6.00 15.00
RLGI Mike Gillislee/450* 12.00 30.00
RLGO Marquise Goodwin/450* 12.00 30.00
RLGS Geno Smith/180* 6.00 15.00
RLJF Johnathan Franklin/450* 6.00 15.00
RLJH Justin Hunter/150* 30.00 80.00
RLJO Dennis Johnson/500* 8.00 20.00
RLKA Keenan Allen/165* 12.00 30.00
RLKD Keenan Davis/400* 10.00 25.00
RLKR Kevin Reddick/600* 6.00 15.00
RLKV Kenny Vaccaro/675* 12.00 30.00
RLLJ Landry Jones/350* 6.00 15.00
RLMB Matt Barkley/105* 20.00 50.00
RLMD Marcus Davis/150* 6.00 15.00
RLME Aaron Mellette/350* 6.00 15.00
RLMG Mike Glennon/400* 6.00 15.00
RLML Marcus Lattimore/135* 40.00 80.00
RLMS Matt Scott/600* 10.00 25.00
RLMT Manti Te'o/650* 8.00 20.00
RLMW Markus Wheaton/350* 6.00 15.00
RLOM Onterio McCalebb/300* 8.00 20.00
RLRB Rex Burkhead/550* 20.00 50.00
RLRG Ray Graham/400* 6.00 15.00
RLRN Ryan Nassib/300* 15.00 40.00
RLRO Dyrell Roberts/300* 8.00 20.00
RLRR Roy Roundtree/500* 15.00 40.00
RLRS Ryan Swope/300* 12.00 30.00
RLRW Robert Woods/105* 12.00 30.00
RLSH Russell Shepard/300* 6.00 15.00
RLSL Star Lotulelei/300* 8.00 20.00
RLSM Rodney Smith/450* 6.00 15.00
RLSW Sylvester Williams/400* 6.00 15.00
RLTA Tavon Austin/300* 8.00 20.00
RLTK Tavarres King/400* 6.00 15.00
RLTR Theo Riddick/325* 12.00 30.00
RLTW Tyler Wilson/250* 15.00 40.00
RLWI Terrance Williams/125* 6.00 15.00
RLZD Zac Dysert/400* 6.00 15.00

2014 Upper Deck

COMP.SET w/o SP's (150) 25.00 50.00
51-150 ROOKIE ODDS 2:1
151-210 ROOKIE ODDS 1:12 H/R/BL
211-250 ROOK.SP ODDS 1:120 H/R/BL
251-275 ROOK.SP ODDS 1:120 HOB
276-300 ROOK.SP ODDS 1:120 RET/BL
1 Andrew Luck .40 1.00
2 Tim Brown .30 .75
3 Steve Young .40 1.00
4 Terrell Davis .12 .30
5 Jerry Rice .50 1.25
6 LaDainian Tomlinson .25 .60
7 Eric Dickerson .25 .60
8 Joe Theismann .30 .75
9 Jerome Bettis .30 .75
10 Peyton Manning .60 1.50
11 Warren Moon .30 .75
12 Charlie Ward .20 .50
13 Eddie George .25 .60
14 Drew Bledsoe .25 .60
15 Joe Montana .75 2.00
16 Earl Campbell .30 .75
17 Tedy Bruschi .25 .60
18 Thurman Thomas .25 .60
19 Bart Starr .50 1.25
20 John Elway .50 1.25
21 Roman Gabriel .20 .50
22 Garrison Hearst .20 .50
23 Jim Kelly .30 .75
24 Kordell Stewart .20 .50
25 Barry Sanders .50 1.25
26 Ickey Woods .20 .50
27 Craig Krenzel .20 .50
28 Johnny Rodgers .20 .50
29 Mike Alstott .25 .60
30 Dan Marino .60 1.50
31 Chris Weinke .20 .50
32 Bernie Kosar .25 .60
33 Ozzie Newsome .25 .60
34 George Rogers .20 .50
35 Drew Brees .30 .75
36 Rick Mirer .20 .50
37 Irving Fryar .20 .50
38 Bo Jackson .40 1.00
39 Billy Sims .25 .60
40 Ben Roethlisberger .30 .75
41 Randall Cunningham .25 .60
42 Archie Griffin .20 .50
43 Paul Hornung .30 .75
44 Charley Taylor .20 .50
45 Dan Fouts .25 .60
46 Jim Plunkett .25 .60
47 Joe Namath .40 1.00
48 Roger Craig .25 .60
49 Lawrence Taylor .30 .75
50 Doug Flutie .25 .60
51 Teddy Bridgewater .60 1.50
52 Kevin Norwood .40 1.00
53 Arthur Lynch .40 1.00
54 Anthony Barr .40 1.00
55 Jason Verrett .40 1.00
56 Lache Seastrunk .40 1.00
57 Taylor Lewan .40 1.00
58 James White .75 2.00
59 Louis Nix III .40 1.00
60 Marqise Lee .50 1.25
61 Tom Savage .40 1.00
62 Jimmy Garoppolo 3.00 8.00
63 Timmy Jernigan .40 1.00
64 Tyler Gaffney .40 1.00
65 Jalen Saunders .40 1.00
66 Ricardo Allen .40 1.00
67 Pierre Desir .40 1.00
68 Marcus Smith .40 1.00
69 Lamarcus Joyner .50 1.25
70 Jarvis Landry .75 2.00
71 Lorenzo Taliaferro .40 1.00
72 Andre Williams .40 1.00
73 TJ Jones .60 1.50
74 Logan Thomas .40 1.00
75 Carl Bradford .40 1.00
76 Dion Bailey .40 1.00
77 Jordan Lynch .50 1.25
78 Bryn Renner .40 1.00
79 Terrance Mitchell .60 1.50
80 Johnny Manziel .60 1.50
81 Jace Amaro .40 1.00
82 Christian Jones .50 1.25
83 Quintin Payton .40 1.00
84 Josh Mauro .40 1.00
85 Ka'Deem Carey .40 1.00
86 Weston Richburg .40 1.00
87 Keith Wenning .50 1.25
88 Stanley Jean-Baptiste .75 2.00
89 Morgan Breslin .60 1.50
90 Blake Bortles .50 1.25
91 Rob Blanchflower .40 1.00
92 Bradley Roby .40 1.00
93 Noel Grigsby .40 1.00
94 Kyle Fuller .40 1.00
95 Tevin Reese .40 1.00
96 Brendon Kay .50 1.25
97 DaQuan Jones .50 1.25
98 Keith Price .60 1.50
99 Shayne Skov .40 1.00
100 Odell Beckham Jr. 1.00 2.50
101 Calvin Barnett .40 1.00
102 Ahmad Dixon .40 1.00
103 Tracy Moore .50 1.25
104 Adrian Hubbard .50 1.25
105 Ryan Grant .40 1.00
106 Kelcy Quarles .50 1.25
107 Trevor Reilly .40 1.00
108 Trey Watts .40 1.00
109 Chris Smith .40 1.00
110 Eric Ward .50 1.25
111 Jacob Pedersen .50 1.25
112 Jaylen Watkins .40 1.00
113 Matt Hazel .40 1.00
114 Jackson Jeffcoat .50 1.25
115 De'Anthony Thomas .40 1.00
116 Xavier Su'a-Filo .50 1.25
117 Calvin Pryor .40 1.00
118 David Fluellen .40 1.00
119 Deone Bucannon .40 1.00
120 Bene Benwikere .40 1.00
121 J.C. Copeland .60 1.50
122 Kapri Bibbs .50 1.25
123 Ryan Lankford .40 1.00
124 Isaiah Crowell .50 1.25
125 Paul Richardson .50 1.25
126 Richard Rodgers .60 1.50
127 Alfred Blue .40 1.00
128 Jay Prosch .60 1.50
129 Aaron Donald 1.00 2.50
130 Marcus Lucas .50 1.25
131 George Atkinson III .40 1.00
132 Taylor Hart .50 1.25
133 Colt Lyerla .60 1.50
134 Greg Blair .40 1.00
135 Marion Grice .40 1.00
136 Vinnie Sunseri .60 1.50
137 Quincy Enunwa .60 1.50
138 Dominique Easley .40 1.00
139 Ben Malena .50 1.25
140 Stephen Morris .40 1.00
141 Erik Lora .40 1.00
142 John Urschel .50 1.25
143 Jerick Mckinnon .50 1.25
144 Telvin Smith .40 1.00
145 Jeremy Gallon .75 2.00
146 Devonta Freeman .60 1.50
147 Crockett Gillmore .50 1.25
148 Donte Moncrief .40 1.00
149 Aaron Lynch .40 1.00
150 Victor Hampton .50 1.25
151 Kelvin Benjamin SP 6.00 15.00
152 Ra'Shede Hageman SP 2.50 6.00
153 Sammy Watkins SP 4.00 10.00
154 Justin Gilbert SP 2.50 6.00
155 Casey Pachall SP 4.00 10.00
156 Scott Crichton SP 4.00 10.00
157 Eric Ebron SP 3.00 8.00
158 Mike Flacco SP 2.50 6.00
159 Bishop Sankey SP 5.00 12.00
160 Aaron Murray SP 2.50 6.00
161 Yawin Smallwood SP 2.50 6.00
162 Deandre Coleman SP 3.00 8.00
163 Davante Adams SP 5.00 12.00
164 Tommy Rees SP 3.00 8.00
165 Brett Smith SP 2.50 6.00
166 Rajion Neal SP 2.50 6.00
167 Cassius Marsh SP 3.00 8.00
168 Jeremy Hill SP 3.00 8.00
169 Kenny Shaw SP 4.00 10.00
170 David Fales SP 2.50 6.00
171 Antonio Richardson SP 4.00 10.00
172 Daniel McCullers SP 3.00 8.00
173 Chris Borland SP 2.50 6.00
174 Derel Walker SP 3.00 8.00
175 Bruce Ellington SP 2.50 6.00
176 Cyril Richardson SP 4.00 10.00
177 Austin Franklin SP 3.00 8.00
178 Antone Exum SP 2.50 6.00
179 Zach Mettenberger SP 2.50 6.00
180 Cody Latimer SP 3.00 8.00
181 Keith McGill SP 2.50 6.00
182 Chase Rettig SP 2.50 6.00
183 Silas Redd SP 3.00 8.00
184 Ryan Shazier SP 4.00 10.00
185 Mike Davis SP 2.50 6.00
186 Martavis Bryant SP 3.00 8.00
187 Shaquelle Evans SP 2.50 6.00
188 Timothy Flanders SP 2.50 6.00
189 Damian Copeland SP 3.00 8.00
190 Troy Niklas SP 2.50 6.00
191 Jeff Janis SP 2.50 6.00
192 Zack Martin SP 3.00 8.00
193 Ryan Hewitt SP 2.50 6.00
194 Terrence Brooks SP 2.50 6.00
195 Brandon Coleman SP 2.50 6.00
196 Kyle Van Noy SP 3.00 8.00
197 Rashaad Reynolds SP 2.50 6.00
198 Isaiah Burse SP 2.50 6.00
199 Will Sutton SP 3.00 8.00
200 James Franklin SP 3.00 8.00
201 Josh Stewart SP 4.00 10.00
202 Trent Murphy SP 2.50 6.00
203 Carlos Hyde SP 3.00 8.00
204 Louchiez Purifoy SP 2.50 6.00
205 Derek Carr SP 6.00 15.00
206 Kony Ealy SP 3.00 8.00
207 Jared Abbrederis SP 6.00 15.00
208 Trey Burton SP 2.50 6.00
209 Damien Williams SP 2.50 6.00
210 Max Bullough SP 4.00 10.00
211 Tajh Boyd SP 3.00 8.00
212 Charles Sims SP 3.00 8.00
213 Austin Seferian-Jenkins SP 3.00 8.00
214 Marcus Roberson SP 4.00 10.00
215 Devin Street SP 3.00 8.00
216 Ego Ferguson SP 3.00 8.00
217 Mike Evans SP 8.00 20.00
218 Roderick McDowell SP 3.00 8.00
219 James Wilder Jr. SP 4.00 10.00
220 C.J. Mosley SP 6.00 15.00
221 Storm Johnson SP 3.00 8.00
222 Xavier Grimble SP 4.00 10.00
223 Dri Archer SP 3.00 8.00
224 Darqueze Dennard SP 5.00 12.00
225 Terrance West SP 3.00 8.00
226 LaDarius Perkins SP 3.00 8.00
227 Josh Huff SP 4.00 10.00
228 A.C. Leonard SP 3.00 8.00
229 Stephon Tuitt SP 5.00 12.00
230 Jake Matthews SP 3.00 8.00
231 Lamin Barrow SP 5.00 12.00
232 Allen Robinson SP 5.00 12.00
233 E.J. Gaines SP 3.00 8.00
234 Bashaud Breeland SP 3.00 8.00
235 Shayne Skov SP 3.00 8.00
236 Marcel Jensen SP 3.00 8.00
237 Robert Herron SP 3.00 8.00
238 Khalil Mack SP 8.00 20.00
239 Tre Mason SP 8.00 20.00
240 Brandin Cooks SP 5.00 12.00
241 Jerome Smith SP 3.00 8.00
242 Ha Ha Clinton-Dix SP 4.00 10.00
243 Michael Sam SP 3.00 8.00
244 Dee Ford SP 3.00 8.00
245 Jeff Mathews SP 4.00 10.00
246 Aaron Colvin SP 3.00 8.00
247 Antonio Andrews SP 3.00 8.00
248 Cody Hoffman SP 3.00 8.00
249 Ross Cockrell SP 3.00 8.00
250 Travis Swanson SP 3.00 8.00
251 Johnny Manziel SP 8.00 20.00
252 Teddy Bridgewater SP 8.00 20.00
253 Aaron Murray SP 5.00 12.00
254 Jimmy Garoppolo SP 20.00 50.00
255 Tajh Boyd SP 5.00 12.00
256 David Fales SP 10.00 25.00
257 Zach Mettenberger SP 5.00 12.00
258 Sammy Watkins SP 8.00 20.00
259 Marqise Lee SP 12.00 30.00
260 Mike Evans SP 12.00 30.00
261 Allen Robinson SP 8.00 20.00
262 Davante Adams SP 10.00 25.00
263 Odell Beckham Jr. SP 40.00 80.00
264 Ka'Deem Carey SP 5.00 12.00
265 Carlos Hyde SP 6.00 15.00
266 Tre Mason SP 5.00 12.00
267 Jeremy Hill SP 6.00 15.00
268 Bishop Sankey SP 5.00 12.00
269 Devonta Freeman SP 8.00 20.00
270 Eric Ebron SP 6.00 15.00
271 Austin Seferian-Jenkins SP 10.00 25.00
272 Ha Ha Clinton-Dix SP 6.00 15.00
273 C.J. Mosley SP 6.00 15.00
274 Justin Gilbert SP 5.00 12.00
275 Darqueze Dennard SP 6.00 15.00
276 Blake Bortles SP 8.00 20.00
277 Derek Carr SP 20.00 40.00
278 Brett Smith SP 6.00 15.00
279 Stephen Morris SP 10.00 25.00
280 Logan Thomas SP 6.00 15.00
281 Lache Seastrunk SP 6.00 15.00
282 Charles Sims SP 12.00 30.00
283 Terrance West SP 6.00 15.00

284 De'Anthony Thomas SP 6.00 15.00
285 Marion Grice SP 10.00 25.00
286 James Wilder Jr. SP 8.00 20.00
287 Kelvin Benjamin SP 20.00 50.00
288 Brandin Cooks SP 25.00 50.00
289 Jarvis Landry SP 15.00 40.00
290 Martavis Bryant SP 8.00 20.00
291 Paul Richardson SP 10.00 25.00
292 Jared Abbrederis SP 15.00 30.00
293 TJ Jones SP 10.00 25.00
294 Donte Moncrief SP 6.00 15.00
295 Jace Amaro SP 15.00 40.00
296 Jason Verrett SP 12.00 30.00
297 Louis Nix III SP 6.00 15.00
298 Anthony Barr SP 6.00 15.00
299 Jake Matthews SP 10.00 25.00
300 Khalil Mack SP 15.00 40.00

2014 Upper Deck '94 UD Tribute

941-9440 ODDS 1:10 H,1:40 R,1:20 B,1:15 F
9441-94100 ODDS 1:7 H,1:27 R,1:13 B,1:10 F
941 Andrew Luck 1.25 3.00
942 Tim Brown 1.00 2.50
943 Steve Young 1.25 3.00
944 Terrell Davis .40 1.00
945 Jerry Rice 1.50 4.00
946 LaDainian Tomlinson .75 2.00
947 Eric Dickerson .75 2.00
948 Joe Theismann 1.00 2.50
949 Jerome Bettis 1.00 2.50
9410 Peyton Manning 2.00 5.00
9411 Warren Moon 1.00 2.50
9412 Eddie George .75 2.00
9413 Joe Montana 2.50 6.00
9414 Earl Campbell 1.00 2.50
9415 Tedy Bruschi .75 2.00
9416 Thurman Thomas .75 2.00
9417 Bart Starr 1.50 4.00
9418 John Elway 1.50 4.00
9419 Garrison Hearst .60 1.50
9420 Jim Kelly 1.00 2.50
9421 Kordell Stewart .60 1.50
9422 Barry Sanders 1.50 4.00
9423 Craig Krenzel .60 1.50
9424 Dan Marino 2.00 5.00
9425 Bernie Kosar .75 2.00
9426 Ozzie Newsome .75 2.00
9427 George Rogers .60 1.50
9428 Drew Brees 1.00 2.50
9429 Rick Mirer .60 1.50
9430 Bo Jackson 1.25 3.00
9431 Ben Roethlisberger 1.00 2.50
9432 Randall Cunningham .75 2.00
9433 Archie Griffin .60 1.50
9434 Paul Hornung 1.00 2.50
9435 Charley Taylor .60 1.50
9436 Dan Fouts .75 2.00
9437 Jim Plunkett .75 2.00
9438 Roger Craig .75 2.00
9439 Joe Namath 1.25 3.00
9440 Doug Flutie .75 2.00
9441 Johnny Manziel 1.00 2.50
9442 Sammy Watkins 1.00 2.50
9443 Josh Huff .75 2.00
9444 Bishop Sankey .60 1.50
9445 Zach Mettenberger .60 1.50
9446 Eric Ebron .75 2.00
9447 Brandin Cooks 1.00 2.50
9448 Anthony Barr .60 1.50
9449 Charles Sims .60 1.50
9450 Tajh Boyd .60 1.50
9451 C.J. Mosley .75 2.00
9452 Jarvis Landry 1.25 3.00
9453 De'Anthony Thomas .60 1.50
9454 Brett Smith .60 1.50
9455 Bruce Ellington .60 1.50
9456 Davante Adams 1.00 2.50
9457 Carlos Hyde .75 2.00
9458 Ha Ha Clinton-Dix .75 2.00
9459 Aaron Murray .60 1.50
9460 Mike Evans 1.50 4.00
9461 Jace Amaro .60 1.50
9462 Jake Matthews .60 1.50
9463 Calvin Pryor .60 1.50
9464 Lache Seastrunk .60 1.50
9465 Jason Verrett .60 1.50
9466 Teddy Bridgewater 1.00 2.50
9467 Devonta Freeman 1.00 2.50
9468 Donte Moncrief .60 1.50
9469 James White 1.25 3.00
9470 Marqise Lee .75 2.00
9471 Marion Grice .60 1.50
9472 Justin Gilbert .60 1.50
9473 Austin Seferian-Jenkins .60 1.50
9474 Martavis Bryant .75 2.00
9475 Troy Niklas .60 1.50
9476 Blake Bortles .75 2.00
9477 James Wilder Jr. .75 2.00
9478 Andre Williams .60 1.50
9479 David Fales .60 1.50
9480 Allen Robinson 1.00 2.50
9481 Jeremy Hill .75 2.00
9482 Louis Nix III .60 1.50
9483 Taylor Lewan .60 1.50
9484 Kelvin Benjamin 1.00 2.50
9485 Jared Abbrederis .60 1.50
9486 Mike Davis .60 1.50
9487 Terrance West .60 1.50
9488 Logan Thomas .60 1.50
9489 Derek Carr 4.00 10.00
9490 Kony Ealy .75 2.00
9491 Ka'Deem Carey .60 1.50
9492 Odell Beckham Jr. 1.50 4.00
9493 Robert Herron .60 1.50
9494 Bradley Roby .60 1.50
9495 Stephen Morris .60 1.50
9496 Paul Richardson .75 2.00
9497 Tre Mason .60 1.50
9498 Darqueze Dennard .75 2.00
9499 Jimmy Garoppolo 5.00 12.00
94100 Khalil Mack 2.50 6.00

2014 Upper Deck '94 UD Tribute Autographs

ATED ODDS 1:360 HOB
LEGENDS TOO SCARCE TO PRICE
945 Jerry Rice 50.00 100.00
946 LaDainian Tomlinson 30.00 60.00
949 Jerome Bettis 30.00 60.00
9428 Drew Brees 40.00 80.00
9439 Joe Namath 40.00 80.00
9441 Johnny Manziel 8.00 20.00
9442 Sammy Watkins 8.00 20.00
9443 Josh Huff 6.00 15.00
9444 Bishop Sankey 5.00 12.00
9445 Zach Mettenberger 5.00 12.00
9446 Eric Ebron 6.00 15.00
9447 Brandin Cooks 20.00 40.00
9448 Anthony Barr 5.00 12.00
9449 Charles Sims 5.00 12.00
9450 Tajh Boyd 5.00 12.00
9452 Jarvis Landry 10.00 25.00
9453 De'Anthony Thomas 5.00 12.00
9454 Brett Smith 5.00 12.00
9455 Bruce Ellington 5.00 12.00
9456 Davante Adams 10.00 25.00
9457 Carlos Hyde 6.00 15.00
9458 Ha Ha Clinton-Dix 6.00 15.00
9459 Aaron Murray 5.00 12.00
9460 Mike Evans 20.00 40.00
9461 Jace Amaro 5.00 12.00
9462 Jake Matthews 5.00 12.00
9463 Calvin Pryor 5.00 12.00
9464 Lache Seastrunk 5.00 12.00
9465 Jason Verrett 3.00 12.00
9466 Teddy Bridgewater 12.00 30.00
9467 Devonta Freeman
9468 Donte Moncrief 5.00 12.00
9469 James White 10.00 25.00
9470 Marqise Lee
9471 Marion Grice 5.00 12.00
9473 Austin Seferian-Jenkins 5.00 12.00
9474 Martavis Bryant 6.00 15.00
9475 Troy Niklas 5.00 12.00
9476 Blake Bortles 6.00 15.00
9477 James Wilder Jr. 6.00 15.00
9478 Andre Williams 8.00 20.00
9479 David Fales 5.00 12.00
9480 Allen Robinson 8.00 20.00
9481 Jeremy Hill 6.00 15.00
9482 Louis Nix III 5.00 12.00
9483 Taylor Lewan 15.00 40.00
9484 Kelvin Benjamin 8.00 20.00
9485 Jared Abbrederis 8.00 20.00
9486 Mike Davis
9487 Terrance West 5.00 12.00
9488 Logan Thomas 5.00 12.00
9489 Derek Carr 50.00 100.00
9490 Kony Ealy 6.00 15.00
9491 Ka'Deem Carey 5.00 12.00
9492 Odell Beckham Jr. 50.00 80.00
9493 Robert Herron 5.00 12.00
9495 Stephen Morris 5.00 12.00
9496 Paul Richardson 12.00 30.00
9498 Darqueze Dennard 6.00 15.00
9499 Jimmy Garoppolo 40.00 100.00
94100 Khalil Mack 20.00 50.00

2014 Upper Deck 70s and 80s Football Heroes

12 STATED ODDS 1:10
HEADER STATED ODDS 1:480
MONTANA/MARINO ODDS 1:480
CFHAG Archie Griffin .50 1.25
CFHBJ Bo Jackson 1.00 2.50
CFHBS Barry Sanders 1.25 3.00
CFHDF Dan Fouts .60 1.50
CFHDM Dan Marino 1.50 4.00
CFHEC Earl Campbell .75 2.00
CFHHW Herschel Walker .75 2.00
CFHJE John Elway 1.25 3.00
CFHJM Joe Montana 2.00 5.00
CFHJR Jerry Rice 1.25 3.00
CFHON Ozzie Newsome .60 1.50
CFHTT Thurman Thomas .60 1.50
CFHART J.Montana/D.Marino 8.00 20.00
NNO Header Card CL 5.00 12.00

2014 Upper Deck Authentics Rookies

1 Blake Bortles 1.25 3.00
UA2 Sammy Watkins 1.50 4.00
UA3 Bishop Sankey 1.00 2.50
UA4 Eric Ebron 1.25 3.00
UA5 Johnny Manziel 1.50 4.00
UA6 C.J. Mosley 1.25 3.00
UA7 Mike Evans 2.50 6.00
UA8 Lache Seastrunk 1.00 2.50
UA9 Josh Huff 1.25 3.00
UA10 Kelvin Benjamin 1.50 4.00
UA11 Carlos Hyde 1.25 3.00
UA12 Devin Street 1.00 2.50
UA13 James Wilder Jr. 1.25 3.00
UA14 Allen Robinson 1.50 4.00
UA15 Zach Mettenberger 1.00 2.50
UA16 Marqise Lee 1.25 3.00
UA17 Jared Abbrederis 1.00 2.50
UA18 Jeremy Hill 1.25 3.00
UA19 Jace Amaro 1.00 2.50
UA20 Devonta Freeman 1.50 4.00
UA21 Tom Savage 1.00 2.50
UA22 Martavis Bryant 1.25 3.00
UA23 Ha Ha Clinton-Dix 1.25 3.00
UA24 Brandin Cooks 1.50 4.00
UA25 Derek Carr 6.00 15.00
UA26 Jalen Saunders 1.00 2.50
UA27 Anthony Barr 1.00 2.50
UA28 Aaron Murray 1.00 2.50
UA29 Austin Seferian-Jenkins 1.00 2.50
UA30 Tajh Boyd 1.00 2.50
UA31 Ka'Deem Carey 1.00 2.50
UA32 Teddy Bridgewater 1.50 4.00
UA33 Bradley Roby 1.00 2.50
UA34 Marion Grice 1.00 2.50
UA35 Donte Moncrief 1.00 2.50
UA36 Louis Nix III 1.00 2.50
UA37 Charles Sims 1.00 2.50
UA38 Brandon Coleman 1.00 2.50
UA39 Jeff Mathews 1.25 3.00
UA40 Stephen Morris 1.00 2.50
UA41 Bruce Ellington 1.00 2.50
UA42 Jason Verrett 1.00 2.50
UA43 Mike Davis 1.00 2.50
UA44 Ryan Grant 1.00 2.50
UA45 Brett Smith 1.00 2.50
UA46 TJ Jones 1.50 4.00
UA47 De'Anthony Thomas 1.00 2.50
UA48 Troy Niklas 1.00 2.50
UA49 Robert Herron 1.00 2.50
UA50 David Fales 1.00 2.50
UA51 Jarvis Landry 2.00 5.00
UA52 Paul Richardson 1.25 3.00
UA53 Jake Matthews 1.00 2.50
UA54 Tre Mason 1.00 2.50
UA55 Jimmy Garoppolo 8.00 20.00
UA56 James White 2.00 5.00
UA57 Odell Beckham Jr. 2.50 6.00
UA58 Logan Thomas 1.00 2.50
UA59 Davante Adams 1.50 4.00
UA60 Andre Williams 1.00 2.50

2014 Upper Deck Authentics Rookies Autographs

STATED ODDS 1:480
UAS1 Sammy Watkins 10.00 25.00
UAS2 Johnny Manziel 10.00 25.00
UAS3 Zach Mettenberger 6.00 15.00
UAS5 Teddy Bridgewater 30.00 60.00
UAS6 Allen Robinson 10.00 25.00
UAS7 Carlos Hyde 8.00 20.00
UAS8 Kelvin Benjamin
UAS9 Marqise Lee
UAS10 Tajh Boyd 6.00 15.00
UAS11 Ka'Deem Carey 6.00 15.00
UAS12 Jimmy Garoppolo 20.00 40.00
UAS13 Mike Evans 15.00 40.00
UAS14 Odell Beckham Jr. 50.00 100.00
UAS15 Lache Seastrunk
UAS16 Jace Amaro
UAS17 Blake Bortles 8.00 20.00
UAS18 Eric Ebron 8.00 20.00
UAS19 Aaron Murray 6.00 15.00
UAS20 Derek Carr
UAS21 Bishop Sankey 6.00 15.00

2014 Upper Deck College Football Heroes Andrew Luck

COMPLETE SET (10) 6.00 15.00
COMMON LUCK (AL1-AL10) .75 2.00
TWO PER FAT PACK

2014 Upper Deck College Football Heroes Bo Jackson

COMPLETE SET (10) 12.50 25.00
COMMON BO (CFHBJ1-CFHBJ10) 1.25 3.00
STATED ODDS 1:8 RET, 1:8 BL

2014 Upper Deck College Tribute Patch Logos

CM121-CM155 GRP D ODDS 1:80
CM156-CM167 STATED ODDS 1:340
CM168-CM175 STATED ODDS 1:960
CM170-CM180 STATED ODDS 1:3400
OVERALL ODDS 1:60H, 1:120R, 1:120B
CM121 Bryant- Denny Stadium D 15.00 30.00
CM122 Bear Down D 6.00 15.00
CM123 Razorback Stadium D 8.00 20.00
CM124 Army Marching In D 8.00 20.00
CM125 Ben Hill Griffin Stadium D 8.00 20.00
CM126 Tomahawk D 8.00 20.00
CM127 Dawg Walk D 8.00 20.00
CM128 The Haka War Dance D 6.00 15.00
CM129 Kinnick Stadium D 8.00 20.00
CM130 Cyhawk Trophy D 6.00 15.00
CM131 The Smoke D 10.00 25.00
CM132 Hail to the Victors Song D 12.00 30.00
CM133 TCF Bank Stadium D 6.00 15.00
CM134 The Grove D 8.00 20.00
CM135 Rock M D 6.00 15.00
CM136 Memorial Stadium D 10.00 25.00
CM137 Irish Guard D 8.00 20.00
CM138 Skull Session D 15.00 30.00
CM139 Oklahoma Memorial Stadium D 6.00 15.00
CM140 The Waving Song D 6.00 15.00
CM141 Autzen Stadium D 15.00 30.00
CM142 Reser Stadium D 8.00 20.00
CM143 White Out D 8.00 20.00
CM144 Sweet Caroline D 8.00 20.00
CM145 Stanford Stadium D 6.00 15.00
CM146 Carrier Dome D 8.00 20.00
CM147 Vol Walk D 8.00 20.00
CM148 Running Through the T D 8.00 20.00
CM149 Hook 'em Horns D 8.00 20.00
CM150 Corps of Cadets March D 8.00 20.00
CM151 Sword in Stone D 8.00 20.00
CM152 L.A. Memorial Coliseum D 15.00 30.00
CM153 Utah Student Fan Club D 6.00 15.00
CM154 Husky Stadium D 8.00 20.00
CM155 The Beer Song D 6.00 15.00
CM156 Denny Chimes C 12.00 30.00
CM157 Keg of Nails C 8.00 20.00
CM158 Navy Marching In C 8.00 20.00
CM159 Death Valley C 12.00 30.00
CM160 Testudo Statue C 8.00 20.00
CM161 Sparty C 12.00 30.00
CM162 Paul Bunyan's Axe C 10.00 25.00
CM163 Buckeye Helmet Sticker C 12.00 30.00
CM164 Corral C 8.00 20.00
CM165 Fremont Cannon C 8.00 20.00
CM166 Jump Around C 12.00 30.00
CM167 Johnny Unitas Statue C 12.00 30.00
CM168 Tightwad Hill B 10.00 25.00
CM169 Howard's Rock B 25.00 50.00
CM170 Sod Cemetery B 15.00 30.00
CM171 Between The Hedges B 20.00 40.00
CM172 The Cowbell B 15.00 30.00
CM173 Black Shirts Defense B 75.00 135.00
CM174 Riff Ram Bah Zoo B 10.00 25.00
CM175 12th Man B 30.00 60.00
CM176 Blue Turf A 15.00 40.00
CM177 Word of Life Mural A 100.00 175.00
CM178 World's Largest Drum A 25.00 50.00
CM179 Cockaboose Railroad A 30.00 60.00
CM180 Lunch Pail A 25.00 50.00

2014 Upper Deck Johnny Manziel Career Highlights

FIVE PER FAT PACK

2014 Upper Deck Predictor First QB Drafted

OVERALL PREDICTOR ODDS 1:1440
QBP1 Teddy Bridgewater EXCH 2.00 5.00
QBP2 Blake Bortles Win EXCH 1.50 4.00
QBP3 Johnny Manziel EXCH 8.00 20.00
QBP4 Derek Carr EXCH 8.00 20.00
QBP5 Zach Mettenberger EXCH 1.25 3.00
QBP6 Wild Card EXCH 2.00 5.00

2014 Upper Deck Predictor First RB Drafted

OVERALL PREDICTOR ODDS 1:1440
EXCH EXPIRATION: 3/31/2015
RBP1 Bishop Sankey Win EXCH 50.00 80.00
RBP2 Tre Mason EXCH 1.25 3.00
RBP3 Lache Seastrunk EXCH 1.25 3.00
RBP4 Ka'Deem Carey EXCH 1.25 3.00
RBP5 Carlos Hyde EXCH 1.50 4.00
RBP6 Wild Card EXCH 2.00 5.00

2014 Upper Deck Predictor First WR Drafted

OVERALL PREDICTOR ODDS 1:1440
EXCH EXPIRATION: 3/31/2015
WRP1 Marqise Lee EXCH 1.50 4.00
WRP2 Sammy Watkins Win EXCH 90.00 150.00
WRP3 Mike Evans EXCH 3.00 8.00
WRP4 Kelvin Benjamin EXCH 2.00 5.00
WRP5 Odell Beckham Jr. EXCH 3.00 8.00
WRP6 Wild Card EXCH 2.00 5.00

2014 Upper Deck Rookie Autographs

-150 ODDS 1:16H,1:48R,1:120B,1:45F
151-210 ODDS 1:64H,1:80R,1:200B,1:75F
211-250 ODDS 1:160H,1:120R,1:300B,1:112F
51 Teddy Bridgewater 6.00 15.00
52 Kevin Norwood 4.00 10.00
53 Arthur Lynch 4.00 10.00
54 Anthony Barr 4.00 10.00
55 Jason Verrett 4.00 10.00
56 Lache Seastrunk 4.00 10.00
57 Taylor Lewan 8.00 20.00
58 James White 8.00 20.00
59 Louis Nix III 4.00 10.00
60 Marqise Lee 5.00 12.00
61 Tom Savage 15.00 40.00
62 Jimmy Garoppolo 30.00 60.00
63 Timmy Jernigan 4.00 10.00
64 Tyler Gaffney 4.00 10.00
65 Jalen Saunders 4.00 10.00
66 Ricardo Allen 4.00 10.00
67 Pierre Desir 4.00 10.00
68 Marcus Smith 4.00 10.00
69 Lamarcus Joyner 5.00 12.00
70 Jarvis Landry 8.00 20.00
71 Lorenzo Taliaferro 15.00 30.00
72 Andre Williams 4.00 10.00
73 TJ Jones 8.00 20.00
74 Logan Thomas 4.00 10.00
75 Carl Bradford 4.00 10.00
76 Dion Bailey 4.00 10.00
77 Jordan Lynch 5.00 12.00
78 Bryn Renner 4.00 10.00
79 Terrance Mitchell 6.00 15.00
80 Johnny Manziel 15.00 40.00
81 Jace Amaro 4.00 10.00
82 Christian Jones 5.00 12.00
83 Quintin Payton 4.00 10.00
84 Josh Mauro 4.00 10.00
85 Ka'Deem Carey 4.00 10.00
86 Weston Richburg 4.00 10.00
88 Stanley Jean-Baptiste 8.00 20.00
89 Morgan Breslin 6.00 15.00
90 Blake Bortles 5.00 12.00
91 Rob Blanchflower 5.00 12.00
93 Noel Grigsby 4.00 10.00
94 Kyle Fuller 4.00 10.00
95 Tevin Reese 4.00 10.00
96 Brendon Kay 8.00 20.00
97 DaQuan Jones 5.00 12.00
98 Keith Price 6.00 15.00
99 Shayne Skov 4.00 10.00
100 Odell Beckham Jr. UER 50.00 80.00
101 Calvin Dernott UER 4.00 10.00
102 Ahmad Dixon 8.00 20.00
103 Tracy Moore 5.00 12.00
104 Adrian Hubbard 6.00 15.00
105 Ryan Grant 4.00 10.00
106 Kelcy Quarles 5.00 12.00
107 Trevor Reilly 4.00 10.00
108 Trey Watts 4.00 10.00
109 Chris Smith 4.00 10.00
110 Eric Ward 5.00 12.00
111 Jacob Pedersen 5.00 12.00
112 Jaylen Watkins 4.00 10.00
113 Matt Hazel 4.00 10.00
114 Jackson Jeffcoat 5.00 12.00
115 De'Anthony Thomas 4.00 10.00
116 Xavier Su'a-Filo 5.00 12.00
117 Calvin Pryor 4.00 10.00
118 David Fluellen 4.00 10.00
119 Deone Bucannon 4.00 10.00
120 Bene Benwikere 4.00 10.00
121 J.C. Copeland 6.00 15.00
122 Kapri Bibbs 5.00 12.00
123 Ryan Lankford 4.00 10.00
124 Isaiah Crowell 5.00 12.00
125 Paul Richardson 8.00 20.00
126 Richard Rodgers 6.00 15.00
127 Alfred Blue 4.00 10.00
129 Aaron Donald 10.00 25.00
130 Marcus Lucas 5.00 12.00
131 George Atkinson III 4.00 10.00
132 Taylor Hart 5.00 12.00
133 Colt Lyerla 10.00 25.00
134 Greg Blair 4.00 10.00
135 Marion Grice 4.00 10.00
136 Vinnie Sunseri 6.00 15.00
137 Quincy Enunwa 6.00 15.00
138 Dominique Easley 4.00 10.00
139 Ben Malena 5.00 12.00
140 Stephen Morris 4.00 10.00
141 Erik Lora 4.00 10.00
142 John Urschel 5.00 12.00
143 Jerick Mckinnon 5.00 12.00
144 Telvin Smith 4.00 10.00
145 Jeremy Gallon 8.00 20.00
146 Devonta Freeman 6.00 15.00
147 Crockett Gillmore 5.00 12.00
148 Donte Moncrief 4.00 10.00
149 Aaron Lynch 5.00 12.00
150 Victor Hampton 5.00 12.00
151 Kelvin Benjamin SP 8.00 20.00
152 Ra'Shede Hageman SP 5.00 12.00
153 Sammy Watkins SP 8.00 20.00
155 Casey Pachall SP 8.00 20.00
156 Scott Crichton SP 5.00 12.00
157 Eric Ebron SP 6.00 15.00
158 Mike Flacco SP 5.00 12.00
159 Bishop Sankey SP 15.00 30.00
160 Aaron Murray SP 5.00 12.00
161 Yawin Smallwood SP 5.00 12.00
162 Deandre Coleman SP 6.00 15.00
163 Davante Adams SP 12.00 30.00
164 Tommy Rees SP 10.00 25.00
165 Brett Smith SP 5.00 12.00
166 Rajion Neal SP 5.00 12.00
167 Cassius Marsh SP 6.00 15.00
168 Jeremy Hill SP 6.00 15.00
169 Kenny Shaw SP 8.00 20.00
170 David Fales SP 10.00 25.00
171 Antonio Richardson SP 8.00 20.00
172 Daniel McCullers SP 8.00 20.00
173 Chris Borland SP 5.00 12.00
174 Derel Walker SP 6.00 15.00
175 Bruce Ellington SP 5.00 12.00
176 Cyril Richardson SP 5.00 12.00
177 Austin Franklin SP 6.00 15.00
178 Antone Exum SP 5.00 12.00
179 Zach Mettenberger SP 15.00 40.00
180 Cody Latimer SP 10.00 25.00
181 Keith McGill SP 5.00 12.00
182 Chase Rettig SP 5.00 12.00
183 Silas Redd SP 6.00 15.00
184 Ryan Shazier SP 8.00 20.00
185 Mike Davis SP 5.00 12.00
186 Martavis Bryant SP 6.00 15.00
187 Shaquelle Evans SP 5.00 12.00
188 Timothy Flanders SP 5.00 12.00
189 Damian Copeland SP 6.00 15.00
190 Troy Niklas SP 5.00 12.00
191 Jeff Janis SP 8.00 20.00
192 Zack Martin SP 12.50 25.00
193 Ryan Hewitt SP 5.00 12.00
194 Terrence Brooks SP 5.00 12.00
195 Brandon Coleman SP 5.00 12.00
196 Kyle Van Noy SP 6.00 15.00
197 Rashaad Reynolds SP 5.00 12.00
198 Isaiah Burse SP 5.00 12.00
199 Will Sutton SP 10.00 25.00
200 James Franklin SP 6.00 15.00
201 Josh Stewart SP 8.00 20.00
202 Trent Murphy SP 5.00 12.00
203 Carlos Hyde SP 6.00 15.00
204 Louchiez Purifoy SP 5.00 12.00
205 Derek Carr SP 25.00 60.00
206 Kony Ealy SP 6.00 15.00
207 Jared Abbrederis SP 5.00 12.00
208 Trey Burton SP 5.00 12.00
209 Damien Williams SP 5.00 12.00
210 Max Bullough SP 8.00 20.00
211 Tajh Boyd SP 5.00 12.00
212 Charles Sims SP 5.00 12.00
213 Austin Seferian-Jenkins SP 5.00 12.00
214 Marcus Roberson SP 6.00 15.00
215 Devin Street SP 8.00 20.00
216 Ego Ferguson SP 6.00 15.00
217 Mike Evans SP 25.00 50.00
218 Roderick McDowell SP 5.00 12.00
219 James Wilder Jr. SP 6.00 15.00
221 Storm Johnson SP 5.00 12.00
222 Xavier Grimble SP 6.00 15.00
223 Dri Archer SP 15.00 40.00
224 Darqueze Dennard SP 6.00 15.00
225 Terrance West SP 5.00 12.00
226 LaDarius Perkins SP 5.00 12.00
227 Josh Huff SP 12.00 30.00
228 A.C. Leonard SP 5.00 12.00
229 Stephon Tuitt SP 10.00 25.00
230 Jake Matthews SP 5.00 12.00
231 Lamin Barrow SP 8.00 20.00
232 Allen Robinson SP 8.00 20.00
233 E.J. Gaines SP 5.00 12.00
234 Bashaud Breeland SP 8.00 20.00
235 Shayne Skov SP 8.00 20.00
236 Marcel Jensen SP 5.00 12.00
237 Robert Herron SP 5.00 12.00
238 Khalil Mack SP 20.00 50.00
240 Brandin Cooks SP 8.00 20.00
241 Jerome Smith SP 5.00 12.00
242 Ha Ha Clinton-Dix SP 6.00 15.00
243 Michael Sam SP 8.00 20.00
244 Dee Ford SP 10.00 25.00
245 Jeff Mathews SP 6.00 15.00
246 Aaron Colvin SP 5.00 12.00
247 Antonio Andrews SP 5.00 12.00
249 Ross Cockrell SP 5.00 12.00
250 Travis Swanson SP 5.00 12.00

2014 Upper Deck Rookie Exclusives

FIVE PER BLASTER BOX
RE1 Johnny Manziel 6.00 15.00
RE2 Brett Smith .50 1.25
RE3 Teddy Bridgewater .75 2.00
RE4 Mike Evans 1.25 3.00
RE5 Blake Bortles .60 1.50
RE6 Tre Mason .50 1.25
RE7 Lache Seastrunk .50 1.25
RE8 Marqise Lee .60 1.50
RE9 Aaron Murray .50 1.25
RE10 Sammy Watkins .75 2.00
RE11 Ka'Deem Carey .50 1.25
RE12 Kelvin Benjamin .75 2.00
RE13 Allen Robinson .75 2.00
RE14 Bishop Sankey .50 1.25
RE15 Zach Mettenberger .50 1.25
RE16 Odell Beckham Jr. 1.25 3.00
RE17 Jimmy Garoppolo 4.00 10.00
RE18 Carlos Hyde .60 1.50
RE19 Tajh Boyd .50 1.25
RE20 Derek Carr 3.00 8.00

2014 Upper Deck Rookie Letterman Autographs

STATED ODDS 1:20 H, 1:960 R/BL
RLAF Alfred Blue/450* 5.00 12.00
RLAM Aaron Murray/200* 6.00 15.00
RLBC Brandon Coleman/210* 6.00 15.00
RLBS Bishop Sankey/105* 20.00 50.00
RLBT Tajh Boyd/150* 8.00 20.00
RLCH Carlos Hyde/600* 10.00 25.00
RLCJ Christian Jones/675* 5.00 12.00
RLCS Charles Sims/300* 6.00 15.00
RLDA Dri Archer/975* 8.00 20.00
RLDC Derek Carr/120* 40.00 80.00
RLDF David Fales/400* 10.00 25.00
RLDM Donte Moncrief/150* 8.00 20.00
RLDS Devin Street/400* 8.00 20.00
RLDT De'Anthony Thomas/75* 8.00 20.00
RLDW Damien Williams/525* 4.00 10.00
RLEW Eric Ward/500* 5.00 12.00
RLHE Robert Herron/525* 4.00 10.00
RLJA Jared Abbrederis/350* 12.00 30.00
RLJG Jeremy Gallon/750* 8.00 20.00
RLJH Josh Huff/375* 8.00 20.00
RLJM Johnny Manziel/150* 20.00 50.00
RLJS Jalen Saunders/175* 6.00 15.00
RLJV Jason Verrett/550* 4.00 10.00
RLJW James White/525* 8.00 20.00
RLLN Louis Nix III/195* 6.00 15.00
RLLP LaDarius Perkins/600* 4.00 10.00
RLLS Lache Seastrunk/75* 15.00 40.00
RLLT Logan Thomas/375* 6.00 15.00
RLMD Mike Davis/450* 5.00 12.00
RLME Mike Evans/90* 40.00 80.00
RLMG Marion Grice/450* 5.00 12.00
RLMJ Jake Matthews/300* 6.00 15.00
RLML Marqise Lee/105* 10.00 25.00
RLMT Tracy Moore/525* 5.00 12.00
RLRG Ryan Grant/675* 6.00 15.00
RLRH Ra'Shede Hageman/650* 4.00 10.00
RLRM Roderick McDowell/300* 6.00 15.00
RLSE Shaquelle Evans/450* 5.00 12.00
RLSM Stephen Morris/250* 10.00 25.00
RLSR Silas Redd/350* 6.00 15.00
RLSW Sammy Watkins/90* 12.00 30.00
RLTB Teddy Bridgewater/135* 12.00 30.00
RLTJ TJ Jones/975* 6.00 15.00
RLTL Taylor Lewan/500* 8.00 20.00
RLTM Trent Murphy/600* 4.00 10.00
RLTR Tevin Reese/250* 8.00 20.00
RLZM Zach Mettenberger/300* 6.00 15.00

2015 Upper Deck

COMP.SET w/o SP's (145) 15.00 40.00
46-145 ROOKIE ODDS TWO PER PACK
146-185 ROOKIE ODDS 1:12 HOB/RET/BL
186-215 ROOKIE ODDS 1:120 HOB/RET/BL
216-235 ROOKIE ODDS 1:120 HOB
236-255 ROOKIE ODDS 1:120 RET/BL
1 Troy Aikman .40 1.00
2 Marcus Allen .30 .75
3 Jerry Rice .50 1.25
4 Mike Ditka .30 .75
5 Donovan McNabb .25 .60
6 Emmitt Smith .50 1.25
7 Tim Brown .30 .75
8 Jim Kelly .30 .75
9 Steve Young .40 1.00
10 Barry Sanders .50 1.25
11 Peter Warrick .20 .50
12 LaDainian Tomlinson .25 .60
13 Ken Anderson .25 .60
14 Jerome Bettis .30 .75
15 Chris Cooley .20 .50
16 Ahman Green .25 .60
17 Jeff Garcia .20 .50
18 Tiki Barber .25 .60
19 Rod Woodson .25 .60
20 Terrell Davis .25 .60
21 John Elway .50 1.25
22 Brian Westbrook .20 .50
23 Hines Ward .25 .60
24 Steve Slaton .20 .50
25 Joey Harrington .20 .50
26 Thurman Thomas .25 .60
27 Brandon Jacobs .20 .50
28 Chuck Foreman .20 .50
29 Bart Starr .50 1.25
30 Trent Green .20 .50
31 Eddie George .25 .60
32 James Lofton .20 .50
33 Kellen Winslow .25 .60
34 Tim Couch .20 .50
35 Kurt Warner .25 .60
36 Eric Dickerson .25 .60
37 Bernie Kosar .25 .60
38 Earl Campbell .30 .75
39 Vinny Testaverde .20 .50
40 Bert Jones .25 .60
41 Joe Theismann .30 .75
42 Donnie Shell .25 .60
43 Lawrence Taylor .30 .75
44 Ronde Barber .20 .50
45 Nick Saban .30 .75
46 Jameis Winston .75 2.00
47 Ameer Abdullah .50 1.25
48 Ben Koyack .50 1.25
49 Leonard Williams .30 .75
50 Kevin White .40 1.00
51 Landon Collins .40 1.00
52 Ezell Ruffin .30 .75
53 Ifo Ekpre-Olomu .30 .75
54 Jahwan Edwards .40 1.00
55 Marcus Mariota 1.25 3.00
56 Brandon Scherff .50 1.25
57 Laken Tomlinson .30 .75
58 Dylan Thompson .30 .75
59 Maxx Williams .30 .75
60 Jaelen Strong .40 1.00
61 Shaq Thompson .40 1.00
62 Quinten Rollins .60 1.50
63 Arik Armstead .30 .75
64 Tevin Coleman .40 1.00
65 Shane Carden .30 .75
66 Eddie Goldman .30 .75
67 Wes Saxton .40 1.00
68 Quandre Diggs .30 .75
69 Eric Kendricks .30 .75
70 Kurtis Drummond .40 1.00
71 Preston Smith .40 1.00
72 Rakeem Cato .50 1.25
73 Kevin White CB .40 1.00
74 T.J. Yeldon .30 .75
75 Sean Mannion .30 .75
76 Andrus Peat .30 .75
77 Dante Fowler Jr. .50 1.25
78 Blake Bell .50 1.25
79 Danielle Hunter .40 1.00
80 Austin Hill .30 .75
81 Craig Mager .30 .75
82 Christian Jones .40 1.00
83 Byron Jones .50 1.25
84 Jaquiski Tartt .30 .75
85 Brandon Bridge .30 .75
86 Mike Davis .30 .75
87 Kwon Alexander .40 1.00
88 Michael Bennett RB .50 1.25
89 Justin Coleman .30 .75
90 Tyler Lockett .50 1.25
91 Chris Hackett .30 .75
92 Malcom Brown .30 .75
93 Eric Rowe .30 .75
94 Paul Dawson .40 1.00
95 Henry Anderson .40 1.00
96 David Cobb .30 .75
97 Nick Montana .50 1.25
98 Nick Boyle .30 .75
99 Lorenzo Mauldin .30 .75
100 Jaxon Shipley .30 .75
101 Josh Shaw .50 1.25
102 Brett Hundley .30 .75
103 Michael Dyer .50 1.25
104 Jalston Fowler .40 1.00
105 Bryan Bennett .30 .75
106 Nick Marshall .50 1.25
107 Hroniss Grasu .40 1.00
108 Christian Covington .30 .75
109 La'el Collins .40 1.00
110 Rannell Hall .30 .75
111 Gabe Wright .30 .75
112 Mike Hull .50 1.25
113 Cedric Reed .30 .75
114 Terrance Magee .50 1.25
115 Adrian Amos .40 1.00
116 Jordan Phillips .30 .75
117 Doran Grant .50 1.25
118 Ramik Wilson .40 1.00
119 Blake Sims .30 .75
120 Jamison Crowder .40 1.00
121 Randy Gregory .30 .75
122 Xavier Cooper .30 .75
123 Denzel Perryman .30 .75
124 Jesse James .40 1.00
125 Hutson Mason .30 .75
126 Cameron Artis-Payne .30 .75
127 Devante Davis .40 1.00
128 Anthony Harris .30 .75
129 Lorenzo Doss .30 .75
130 Vince Mayle .40 1.00
131 MyCole Pruitt .30 .75
132 Geneo Grissom .30 .75
133 Julian Wilson .40 1.00
134 Dominique Brown .30 .75
135 Kaelin Clay .30 .75
136 Marcus Peters .50 1.25
137 Jarrod West .40 1.00
138 Cameron Erving .40 1.00
139 Rory Anderson .40 1.00
140 Titus Davis .40 1.00
141 Jeff Heuerman .40 1.00
142 Matt Miller .30 .75
143 Marcus Murphy .30 .75
144 A.J. Cann .40 1.00
145 Anthony Boone .30 .75
146 Jordon James SP 2.00 5.00
147 Todd Gurley SP 6.00 15.00
148 Jordan Taylor SP 2.00 5.00
149 Nick O'Leary SP 1.50 4.00
150 Amari Cooper SP 5.00 12.00
151 P.J. Williams SP 2.00 5.00
152 Jalen Collins SP 1.50 4.00
153 Derron Smith SP 1.50 4.00
154 Danny Shelton SP 1.50 4.00
155 Nate Orchard SP 1.50 4.00
156 Jay Ajayi SP 2.50 6.00
157 Darious Cummings SP 1.50 4.00
158 Ben Heeney SP 1.50 4.00
159 Cam Thomas SP 1.50 4.00
160 Dorial Green-Beckham SP 1.50 4.00
161 Owamagbe Odighizuwa SP 2.00 5.00
162 Devin Gardner SP 2.50 6.00
163 Jacoby Glenn SP 1.50 4.00
164 Cody Fajardo SP 2.00 5.00
165 Jeremy Langford SP 1.50 4.00
166 E.J. Bibbs SP 2.00 5.00
167 Carl Davis SP 2.00 5.00
168 Nelson Agholor SP 2.00 5.00
169 Steven Nelson SP 1.50 4.00
170 Hayes Pullard SP 2.50 6.00
171 Eric Tomlinson SP 2.00 5.00
172 Malcolm Brown SP 2.00 5.00
173 Gerald Christian SP 2.00 5.00
174 Alvin Dupree SP 2.00 5.00
175 Stefon Diggs SP 4.00 10.00
176 Ty Sambrailo SP 1.50 4.00
177 Taylor Kelly SP 2.00 5.00
178 Malcolm Agnew SP 1.50 4.00
179 Levi Norwood SP 1.50 4.00
180 Gary Nova SP 1.50 4.00
181 Corey Grant SP 2.50 6.00
182 Shane Ray SP 1.50 4.00
183 Phillip Dorsett SP 1.50 4.00
184 Devin Smith SP 1.50 4.00
185 Reese Dismukes SP 2.00 5.00
186 Cole Stoudt SP 4.00 10.00
187 Devante Parker SP 4.00 10.00
188 Melvin Gordon III SP 15.00 30.00
189 Cedric Ogbuehi SP 2.50 6.00
190 Kenny Bell SP 4.00 10.00
191 David Johnson SP 6.00 15.00
192 Devin Funchess SP 4.00 10.00
193 Trae Waynes SP 2.50 6.00
194 Bryce Petty SP 2.50 6.00
195 Sammie Coates SP 3.00 8.00
196 Benardrick Mckinney SP 2.50 6.00
197 Ronald Darby SP 2.50 6.00
198 Tony Lippett SP 2.50 6.00
199 Bo Wallace SP 2.50 6.00
200 Justin Hardy SP 2.50 6.00
201 Taylor Heinicke SP 4.00 10.00
202 Josh Harper SP 2.50 6.00
203 Duke Johnson SP 4.00 10.00
204 Charles Gaines SP 4.00 10.00
205 Antwan Goodley SP 2.50 6.00
206 JaCorey Shepherd SP 2.50 6.00
207 Rashad Greene SP 2.50 6.00
208 Javorius Allen SP 3.00 8.00
209 Tre McBride SP 2.50 6.00
210 Vic Beasley SP 3.00 8.00
211 Dres Anderson SP 2.50 6.00
212 Trey DePriest SP 2.50 6.00
213 Karlos Williams SP 2.50 6.00
214 Cam Worthy SP 2.50 6.00
215 Garrett Grayson SP 2.50 6.00
216 Jameis Winston SP 40.00 80.00
217 Amari Cooper SP 12.00 30.00
218 Melvin Gordon III SP 15.00 30.00
219 Tyler Lockett SP 8.00 20.00
220 Brett Hundley SP 2.50 6.00
221 Devin Funchess SP 10.00 25.00
222 Ameer Abdullah SP 4.00 10.00
223 Jaelen Strong SP 3.00 8.00
224 Tony Lippett SP 10.00 25.00
225 Leonard Williams SP 2.50 6.00
226 T.J. Yeldon SP 2.50 6.00
227 Devante Parker SP 4.00 10.00
228 Shane Carden SP 2.50 6.00
229 Rashad Greene SP 8.00 20.00
230 Mike Davis SP 2.50 6.00
231 Maxx Williams SP 2.50 6.00
232 Cody Fajardo SP 3.00 8.00
233 Brandon Bridge SP 2.50 6.00
234 Javorius Allen SP 3.00 8.00
235 Jamison Crowder SP 6.00 15.00
236 Marcus Mariota SP 20.00 50.00
237 Kevin White SP 6.00 15.00
238 Todd Gurley SP 20.00 50.00
239 Blake Sims SP 5.00 12.00
240 Taylor Heinicke SP
241 Tevin Coleman SP 6.00 15.00
242 Sammie Coates SP 6.00 15.00
243 Dres Anderson SP 10.00 25.00
244 Bryce Petty SP 5.00 12.00
245 Duke Johnson SP 8.00 20.00
246 Josh Harper SP 5.00 12.00
247 Devin Smith SP 5.00 12.00
248 Garrett Grayson SP 5.00 12.00
249 David Cobb SP 5.00 12.00
250 Jay Ajayi SP 8.00 20.00
251 Nelson Agholor SP
252 Sean Mannion SP 5.00 12.00
253 Jeremy Langford SP 12.00 30.00
254 Dorial Green-Beckham SP 5.00 12.00
255 Bo Wallace SP 5.00 12.00

2015 Upper Deck A Cut Above

ACA1-ACA20 ODDS 1:16 HOB,1:67 RET,1:54 BL
ACA11-ACA60 ODDS 1:7 HOB,1:30 RET,1:20 BL
ACA1 Emmitt Smith 1.50 4.00
ACA2 Hines Ward .75 2.00
ACA3 Jerry Rice 1.50 4.00
ACA4 Eric Dickerson .75 2.00
ACA5 John Elway 1.50 4.00
ACA6 Rod Woodson .75 2.00
ACA7 Brian Westbrook .60 1.50
ACA8 James Lofton .60 1.50
ACA9 Joe Namath 1.25 3.00
ACA10 Tiki Barber .75 2.00
ACA11 Kurt Warner .75 2.00
ACA12 Lawrence Taylor 1.00 2.50
ACA13 Barry Sanders 1.50 4.00
ACA14 Donovan McNabb .75 2.00
ACA15 Marcus Allen 1.00 2.50
ACA16 Jerome Bettis 1.00 2.50
ACA17 Troy Aikman 1.25 3.00
ACA18 Thurman Thomas .75 2.00
ACA19 Tim Brown 1.00 2.50
ACA20 Mike Ditka 1.00 2.50
ACA21 Marcus Mariota 6.00 15.00
ACA22 Amari Cooper 2.00 5.00
ACA23 Melvin Gordon III 1.50 4.00
ACA24 Ifo Ekpre-Olomu .60 1.50
ACA25 Blake Sims .60 1.50
ACA26 Dorial Green-Beckham .60 1.50
ACA27 Ameer Abdullah 1.00 2.50
ACA28 Bo Wallace .60 1.50
ACA29 Devin Funchess 1.00 2.50
ACA30 Bryce Petty .60 1.50
ACA31 Devin Smith .60 1.50
ACA32 Duke Johnson 1.00 2.50
ACA33 Antwan Goodley .60 1.50
ACA34 Nelson Agholor .75 2.00
ACA35 Garrett Grayson .60 1.50
ACA36 Sammie Coates .75 2.00
ACA37 T.J. Yeldon .60 1.50
ACA38 Trae Waynes .60 1.50
ACA39 Nick O'Leary .60 1.50
ACA40 Jameis Winston 1.50 4.00
ACA41 Devante Parker 1.00 2.50
ACA42 Todd Gurley 2.50 6.00
ACA43 Josh Harper .60 1.50
ACA44 Jay Ajayi 1.00 2.50
ACA45 Brett Hundley .60 1.50
ACA46 Tony Lippett .60 1.50
ACA47 Tevin Coleman .75 2.00
ACA48 Cody Fajardo .75 2.00
ACA49 Ben Koyack 1.00 2.50
ACA50 Maxx Williams .60 1.50
ACA51 Kevin White .75 2.00
ACA52 Javorius Allen .75 2.00
ACA53 Rashad Greene .60 1.50
ACA54 Taylor Heinicke 1.00 2.50
ACA55 Shane Carden .60 1.50
ACA56 Jaelen Strong .75 2.00
ACA57 Mike Davis .60 1.50
ACA58 P.J. Williams .75 2.00
ACA59 Dres Anderson .60 1.50
ACA60 Sean Mannion .60 1.50

2015 Upper Deck A Cut Above Autographs

ACA1-ACA19 ODDS 1:360 HOB, 1:2500 RET/BL
ACA21-ACA60 ODDS 1:96 HOB, 1:2500 RET/BL
EXCH EXPIRATION: 3/12/2017
ACA1 Emmitt Smith
ACA2 Hines Ward
ACA3 Jerry Rice
ACA4 Eric Dickerson
ACA5 John Elway
ACA6 Rod Woodson
ACA7 Brian Westbrook
ACA8 James Lofton
ACA9 Joe Namath
ACA10 Tiki Barber
ACA11 Kurt Warner
ACA12 Lawrence Taylor
ACA13 Barry Sanders
ACA14 Donovan McNabb
ACA15 Marcus Allen
ACA16 Jerome Bettis
ACA17 Troy Aikman
ACA18 Thurman Thomas
ACA19 Tim Brown EXCH
ACA21 Marcus Mariota 50.00 100.00
ACA22 Amari Cooper 20.00 50.00
ACA23 Melvin Gordon III 25.00 50.00
ACA24 Ifo Ekpre-Olomu 4.00 10.00
ACA25 Blake Sims 4.00 10.00
ACA26 Dorial Green-Beckham 4.00 10.00
ACA27 Ameer Abdullah 6.00 15.00
ACA28 Bo Wallace 4.00 10.00
ACA29 Devin Funchess 6.00 15.00
ACA30 Bryce Petty 4.00 10.00
ACA31 Devin Smith 4.00 10.00
ACA32 Duke Johnson 6.00 15.00
ACA34 Nelson Agholor 5.00 12.00
ACA35 Garrett Grayson 4.00 10.00
ACA36 Sammie Coates EXCH 20.00 40.00
ACA37 T.J. Yeldon 4.00 10.00
ACA38 Trae Waynes 4.00 10.00
ACA39 Nick O'Leary 4.00 10.00
ACA40 Jameis Winston 60.00 120.00
ACA41 Devante Parker 6.00 15.00
ACA42 Todd Gurley 30.00 60.00
ACA43 Josh Harper
ACA44 Jay Ajayi 12.00 30.00
ACA45 Brett Hundley 15.00 40.00
ACA46 Tony Lippett 4.00 10.00
ACA47 Tevin Coleman 5.00 12.00
ACA48 Cody Fajardo 5.00 12.00
ACA49 Ben Koyack 6.00 15.00
ACA50 Maxx Williams 4.00 10.00
ACA51 Kevin White 20.00 50.00
ACA52 Javorius Allen 5.00 12.00
ACA53 Rashad Greene 4.00 10.00
ACA54 Taylor Heinicke 6.00 15.00
ACA55 Shane Carden EXCH 4.00 10.00
ACA56 Jaelen Strong 5.00 12.00
ACA57 Mike Davis 8.00 20.00
ACA58 P.J. Williams 5.00 12.00
ACA60 Sean Mannion 4.00 10.00

2015 Upper Deck Authentics Rookies

UA1 Marcus Mariota 12.00 30.00
UA2 Melvin Gordon III 2.00 5.00
UA3 Sammie Coates 1.00 2.50
UA4 Trae Waynes .75 2.00
UA5 Brett Hundley .75 2.00
UA6 Tevin Coleman 1.00 2.50
UA7 Amari Cooper 2.50 6.00
UA8 Ben Koyack 1.25 3.00
UA9 Nelson Agholor 1.00 2.50
UA10 Bo Wallace .75 2.00
UA11 Cameron Artis-Payne .75 2.00
UA12 Kevin White 1.00 2.50
UA13 Ifo Ekpre-Olomu .75 2.00
UA14 Justin Hardy .75 2.00
UA15 Cody Fajardo 1.00 2.50
UA16 Duke Johnson 1.25 3.00

UA17 Alvin Dupree 1.00 2.50
UA18 Nick Marshall 1.25 3.00
UA19 Tony Lippett .75 2.00
UA20 Garrett Grayson .75 2.00
UA21 David Johnson 2.00 5.00
UA22 Dorial Green-Beckham .75 2.00
UA23 Marcus Peters 1.25 3.00
UA24 Devin Smith .75 2.00
UA25 Shane Carden .75 2.00
UA26 T.J. Yeldon .75 2.00
UA27 Kenny Bell 1.25 3.00
UA28 Devin Funchess 1.25 3.00
UA29 Leonard Williams .75 2.00
UA30 Jameis Winston 10.00 25.00
UA31 Todd Gurley 3.00 8.00
UA32 Dres Anderson .75 2.00
UA33 Connor Halliday 1.25 3.00
UA34 Phillip Dorsett .75 2.00
UA35 Bryce Petty 1.00 2.50
UA36 Jeremy Langford .75 2.00
UA37 Rashad Greene .75 2.00
UA38 David Cobb .75 2.00
UA39 Jeff Heuerman 1.00 2.50
UA40 Sean Mannion .75 2.00
UA41 Mike Davis .75 2.00
UA42 Jamison Crowder 1.00 2.50
UA43 Brandon Scherff 1.25 3.00
UA44 Stefon Diggs 2.00 5.00
UA45 Tyler Lockett 1.25 3.00
UA46 Maxx Williams .75 2.00
UA47 Nick O'Leary .75 2.00
UA48 Austin Hill .75 2.00
UA49 Benardrick Mckinney .75 2.00
UA50 Brandon Bridge .75 2.00
UA51 Ameer Abdullah 1.25 3.00
UA52 Devante Parker 1.25 3.00
UA53 P.J. Williams 1.00 2.50
UA54 Karlos Williams .75 2.00
UA55 Blake Sims .75 2.00
UA56 Jay Ajayi 1.25 3.00
UA57 Josh Harper .75 2.00
UA58 Taylor Kelly 1.00 2.50
UA59 Quinten Rollins 1.50 4.00
UA60 Landon Collins 1.00 2.50
UA61 Javorius Allen 1.00 2.50
UA62 Jaelen Strong 1.00 2.50
UA63 Jalen Collins .75 2.00
UA64 Vince Mayle 1.00 2.50
UA65 Taylor Heinicke 1.25 3.00

2015 Upper Deck Authentics Rookies Signatures

STATED ODDS 1:480 HOB
EXCH EXPIRATION: 3/12/2017
UAS1 Todd Gurley 40.00 80.00
UAS2 Ameer Abdullah 6.00 15.00
UAS3 Bryce Petty 4.00 10.00
UAS4 Devante Parker 6.00 15.00
UAS5 Connor Halliday 6.00 15.00
UAS6 Sammie Coates EXCH 5.00 12.00
UAS7 Shane Carden 4.00 10.00
UAS8 Amari Cooper 30.00 60.00
UAS9 Tevin Coleman 5.00 12.00
UAS10 Brett Hundley 20.00 40.00
UAS11 Melvin Gordon III 25.00 50.00
UAS12 Jameis Winston 100.00 200.00
UAS13 Devin Funchess 6.00 15.00
UAS14 Jaelen Strong
UAS15 Sean Mannion 4.00 10.00
UAS16 Leonard Williams 4.00 10.00
UAS17 Dorial Green-Beckham 4.00 10.00
UAS18 Maxx Williams 4.00 10.00
UAS19 Kevin White 20.00 50.00
UAS20 Blake Sims 4.00 10.00
UAS21 T.J. Yeldon 4.00 10.00
UAS22 Garrett Grayson 4.00 10.00
UAS23 Marcus Mariota 50.00 100.00
UAS24 Duke Johnson 6.00 15.00
UAS25 Josh Harper 8.00 20.00

2015 Upper Deck College Football Heroes

STATED ODDS 1:16 HOB/RET
CFHBJ Brandon Jacobs .60 1.50
CFHBW Brian Westbrook .60 1.50
CFHDM Donovan McNabb .75 2.00
CFHEG Eddie George .75 2.00
CFHES Emmitt Smith 1.50 4.00
CFHHW Hines Ward .75 2.00
CFHJB Jerome Bettis 1.00 2.50
CFHJG Jeff Garcia .60 1.50
CFHKW Kurt Warner .75 2.00
CFHTB Tiki Barber .75 2.00

2015 Upper Deck College Football Heroes Autographs

STATED ODDS 1:4080 HOB
CFHBJ Brandon Jacobs
CFHBW Brian Westbrook
CFHDM Donovan McNabb
CFHEG Eddie George 50.00 100.00
CFHES Emmitt Smith
CFHHW Hines Ward 40.00 80.00
CFHJB Jerome Bettis 50.00 100.00
CFHJG Jeff Garcia
CFHKW Kurt Warner 75.00 125.00
CFHTB Tiki Barber

2015 Upper Deck College Football Heroes Rookies

COMPLETE SET (10) 12.50 25.00
COMMON WINSTON (JW1-JW5) 1.25 3.00
COMMON MARIOTA (MM6-MM10) 1.50 4.00
TWO PER FAT PACK

2015 Upper Deck College Tribute Patches

CM181-CM214 STATED ODDS 1:80 HOB
CM215-CM226 STATED ODDS 1:340 HOB
CM227-CM234 STATED ODDS 1:960 HOB
CM235-CM239 UNPRICED ODDS 1:3400 HOB
OVERALL ODDS 1:60 HOB, 1:120 RET/BL
CM181 Bryce Petty 3.00 8.00
CM182 Notre Dame Stadium 10.00 25.00
CM183 Commander in Chief Trophy 8.00 20.00
CM184 Neyland Stadium 10.00 25.00
CM185 Tiger Walk 8.00 20.00
CM186 Unconquered Statue 20.00 40.00
CM187 Georgia-Florida Rivalry 15.00 30.00
CM188 Arizona Stadium 6.00 15.00
CM189 Go Blue 20.00 40.00
CM190 Old Oaken Bucket 8.00 20.00
CM191 Camp Randall Stadium 12.00 30.00
CM192 Enter Sandman Song 8.00 20.00
CM193 Sea of Red 20.00 40.00
CM194 Spartan Stadium 10.00 25.00
CM195 Mascot Memorial 8.00 20.00
CM196 Stanford Marching Band 8.00 20.00
CM197 Centennial Cup 6.00 15.00
CM198 Jordan-Hare Stadium 8.00 20.00
CM199 Calling the Hogs 8.00 20.00
CM200 Kyle Field 8.00 20.00
CM201 Beaver Stadium 8.00 20.00
CM202 Cardinal Express 8.00 20.00
CM203 Boone Pickens Stadium 6.00 15.00
CM204 Gator Chomp 10.00 25.00
CM205 Little Brown Jug 8.00 20.00
CM206 Stadium Stampede 8.00 20.00
CM207 Song Girls 8.00 20.00
CM208 Vol Navy 10.00 25.00
CM209 Floyd of Rosedale 8.00 20.00
CM210 Williams-Brice Stadium 8.00 20.00
CM211 Hat and Cane Toss
CM212 Lane Stadium 8.00 20.00
CM213 Amon G. Carter Stadium 6.00 15.00
CM214 Sundevil Stadium 8.00 20.00
CM215 Devante Parker 6.00 15.00
CM216 Red River Showdown 10.00 25.00
CM217 Ohio Stadium 15.00 40.00
CM218 Heroes Trophy 30.00 60.00
CM219 Sanford Stadium 10.00 25.00
CM220 Ryan Field 8.00 20.00
CM221 Doak Campbell Stadium 10.00 25.00
CM222 Paul Bunyan Trophy 12.00 30.00
CM223 Gamecock Walk 8.00 20.00
CM224 Y Mountain 8.00 20.00
CM225 Walk of Champions 30.00 60.00
CM226 Play Like A Champion 12.00 30.00
CM227 Brett Hundley 20.00 40.00
CM228 Todd Gurley 20.00 50.00
CM229 Ameer Abdullah 8.00 20.00
CM230 Amari Cooper 30.00 80.00
CM231 Johnny Manziel 15.00 40.00
CM232 Teddy Bridgewater 10.00 25.00
CM233 Blake Bortles 8.00 20.00
CM234 Sammy Watkins 12.00 30.00
CM235 Jameis Winston 125.00 200.00
CM236 Marcus Mariota 50.00 125.00
CM237 Barry Sanders 60.00 100.00
CM238 Troy Aikman
CM239 Jerry Rice 60.00 100.00

2015 Upper Deck Predictor First QB Drafted

OVERALL PREDICTOR ODDS 1:1440
EXCH EXPIRATION: 4/1/2016
QBP1 Brett Hundley EXCH 1.25 3.00
QBP2 Bryce Petty EXCH 1.25 3.00
QBP3 Garrett Grayson EXCH 1.25 3.00
QBP4 Marcus Mariota EXCH 15.00 40.00
QBP5 Jameis Winston EXCH 60.00 100.00

2015 Upper Deck Predictor First RB Drafted

OVERALL PREDICTOR ODDS 1:1440
EXCH EXPIRATION: 4/1/2016
RBP1 Todd Gurley EXCH 12.00 30.00
RBP2 Melvin Gordon III EXCH 15.00 30.00
RBP3 Ameer Abdullah EXCH 2.00 5.00
RBP4 Tevin Coleman EXCH 1.50 4.00
RBP5 Duke Johnson EXCH 2.00 5.00

2015 Upper Deck Predictor First WR Drafted

OVERALL PREDICTOR ODDS 1:1440
EXCH EXPIRATION: 4/1/2016
WRP1 Amari Cooper EXCH 40.00 80.00
WRP2 Kevin White EXCH 25.00 60.00
WRP3 Devante Parker EXCH 2.00 5.00
WRP4 Jaelen Strong EXCH 1.50 4.00
WRP5 Dorial Green-Beckham EXCH 1.25 3.00

2015 Upper Deck Rookie Lettermen Autographs

STATED ODDS 1:20 HOB, 1:960 RET/BLST
EXCH EXPIRATION: 3/12/2017
RLAA Ameer Abdullah/275* 8.00 20.00
RLAC Amari Cooper/165* 30.00 60.00
RLAD Alvin Dupree/600* 10.00 25.00
RLAH Austin Hill/400* 4.00 10.00
RLBE D.Green-Beckham/175* 5.00 12.00
RLBH Brett Hundley/150* 6.00 15.00
RLBK Ben Koyack/650* 8.00 20.00
RLBP Bryce Petty/125* 10.00 25.00
RLBW Bo Wallace/300* 5.00 12.00
RLCD Carl Davis/200* 12.00 30.00
RLCR Cody Riggs/650* 6.00 15.00
RLCS Shane Carden/350* 5.00 12.00
RLDA Dres Anderson/600* 5.00 12.00
RLDB Dominique Brown/450* 4.00 10.00
RLDG Devin Gardner/500* 6.00 15.00
RLDP Devante Parker/450* 6.00 15.00
RLGO Markus Golden/300* 5.00 12.00
RLGR Doran Grant/600* 8.00 20.00
RLHA Justin Hardy/350* 12.00 30.00
RLHE Jeff Heuerman/600* 5.00 12.00
RLHM Hutson Mason/600* 4.00 10.00
RLIO Ifo Ekpre-Olomu/250* 12.00 30.00
RLJC Jamison Crowder/250* 12.00 30.00
RLJH Josh Harper/400* 4.00 10.00
RLJL Jeremy Langford/400* 8.00 20.00
RLJR Jake Ryan/750* 10.00 25.00
RLJS Jaelen Strong/135* EXCH 8.00 20.00
RLJW Jameis Winston/135* 100.00 200.00
RLKB Kenny Bell/550* 6.00 15.00
RLKW Karlos Williams/225* 5.00 12.00
RLLW Leonard Williams/350* 5.00 12.00
RLMR Malcolm Brown/450* 5.00 12.00
RLMG Melvin Gordon III/175* 25.00 50.00
RLMM Marcus Mariota/125* 60.00 125.00
RLNO Nick O'Leary/135* 6.00 15.00
RLPE Denzel Perryman/500* 4.00 10.00
RLRG Rashad Greene/225* 5.00 12.00
RLRW Ramik Wilson/600* 5.00 12.00
RLSC Sammie Coates/90* EXCH 8.00 20.00
RLSH Josh Shaw/175* 8.00 20.00
RLSM Sean Mannion/350* 5.00 12.00
RLST Cole Stoudt/150* 12.00 30.00
RLTF Trey Flowers/250* 8.00 20.00
RLTG Todd Gurley/120* 40.00 80.00
RLTK Taylor Kelly/675* 5.00 12.00
RLTL Tyler Lockett/600* 6.00 15.00
RLTW Tony Washington/125* 8.00 20.00
RLVB Vic Beasley/300* 12.00 30.00
RLWK Kevin White/600* 5.00 12.00

2015 Upper Deck Star Rookies Autographs

46-145 ODDS 1:16 HOB, 1:48 RET, 1:120 BL
146-184 ODDS 1:64 HOB, 1:80 RET, 1:200 BL
186-215 ODDS 1:160 HOB, 1:120 RET, 1:300 BL
EXCH EXPIRATION: 3/12/2017
46 Jameis Winston 90.00 150.00
47 Ameer Abdullah 5.00 12.00
48 Ben Koyack 5.00 12.00
49 Leonard Williams 3.00 8.00
50 Kevin White 15.00 40.00
51 Landon Collins 4.00 10.00
52 Ezell Ruffin 3.00 8.00
53 Ifo Ekpre-Olomu 8.00 20.00
54 Jahwan Edwards 4.00 10.00
55 Marcus Mariota 60.00 125.00
56 Brandon Scherff 5.00 12.00
57 Laken Tomlinson 3.00 8.00
58 Dylan Thompson 3.00 8.00
59 Maxx Williams
60 Jaelen Strong EXCH 4.00 10.00
61 Shaq Thompson 4.00 10.00
62 Quinten Rollins 6.00 15.00
63 Arik Armstead 8.00 20.00
64 Tevin Coleman 4.00 10.00
65 Shane Carden 3.00 8.00
67 Wes Saxton 4.00 10.00
68 Quandre Diggs 3.00 8.00
69 Eric Kendricks 3.00 8.00
70 Kurtis Drummond 4.00 10.00
72 Rakeem Cato 5.00 12.00
73 Kevin White CB 8.00 20.00
74 T.J. Yeldon 3.00 8.00
75 Sean Mannion 3.00 8.00
78 Blake Bell 6.00 15.00
80 Austin Hill 3.00 8.00
81 Craig Mager 3.00 8.00
84 Jaquiski Tartt 3.00 8.00
85 Brandon Bridge 3.00 8.00
86 Mike Davis 8.00 20.00
88 Michael Bennett RB 6.00 15.00
89 Justin Coleman 4.00 10.00
90 Tyler Lockett 5.00 12.00
92 Malcom Brown 3.00 8.00
93 Eric Rowe 3.00 8.00
94 Paul Dawson 4.00 10.00
96 David Cobb 3.00 8.00
97 Nick Montana 5.00 12.00
98 Nick Boyle 3.00 8.00
101 Josh Shaw 5.00 12.00
102 Brett Hundley 3.00 8.00
103 Michael Dyer 5.00 12.00
104 Jalston Fowler 6.00 15.00
105 Bryan Bennett 3.00 8.00
106 Nick Marshall 5.00 12.00
107 Hroniss Grasu 5.00 12.00
109 La'el Collins 4.00 10.00
110 Rannell Hall 3.00 8.00
113 Cedric Reed 3.00 8.00
114 Terrance Magee 5.00 12.00
115 Adrian Amos 4.00 10.00
116 Jordan Phillips 3.00 8.00
117 Doran Grant 8.00 20.00
118 Ramik Wilson 4.00 10.00
119 Blake Sims 3.00 8.00
120 Jamison Crowder 6.00 15.00
121 Randy Gregory 3.00 8.00
122 Xavier Cooper 3.00 8.00
123 Denzel Perryman 3.00 8.00
124 Jesse James 4.00 10.00
125 Hutson Mason 3.00 8.00
126 Cameron Artis-Payne 3.00 8.00
127 Devante Davis 4.00 10.00
128 Anthony Harris 3.00 8.00
130 Vince Mayle 4.00 10.00
132 Geneo Grissom 3.00 8.00
133 Julian Wilson 4.00 10.00
134 Dominique Brown 3.00 8.00
135 Kaelin Clay 3.00 8.00
136 Marcus Peters 5.00 12.00
138 Cameron Erving 4.00 10.00
139 Rory Anderson 3.00 8.00
140 Titus Davis 4.00 10.00
141 Jeff Heuerman 4.00 10.00
142 Matt Miller 3.00 8.00
144 A.J. Cann 4.00 10.00
145 Anthony Boone 3.00 8.00
146 Jordon James SP 5.00 12.00
147 Todd Gurley SP 40.00 80.00
148 Jordan Taylor SP 5.00 12.00
149 Nick O'Leary SP 4.00 10.00
150 Amari Cooper SP 25.00 50.00
151 P.J. Williams SP 5.00 12.00
152 Jalen Collins SP 6.00 15.00
153 Derron Smith SP 4.00 10.00
154 Danny Shelton SP 8.00 20.00
155 Nate Orchard SP 4.00 10.00
156 Jay Ajayi SP 6.00 15.00
157 Darious Cummings SP 4.00 10.00
158 Ben Heeney SP 4.00 10.00
159 Cam Thomas SP 4.00 10.00
160 Dorial Green-Beckham SP 4.00 10.00
161 Owamagbe Odighizuwa SP 5.00 12.00
162 Devin Gardner SP 6.00 15.00
163 Jacoby Glenn SP 4.00 10.00
164 Cody Fajardo SP 5.00 12.00
165 Jeremy Langford SP 4.00 10.00
166 E.J. Bibbs SP 5.00 12.00
167 Carl Davis SP 6.00 15.00
168 Nelson Agholor SP 5.00 12.00
169 Steven Nelson SP 4.00 10.00
170 Hayes Pullard SP 6.00 15.00
171 Eric Tomlinson SP 5.00 12.00
172 Malcolm Brown SP 5.00 12.00
174 Alvin Dupree SP 5.00 12.00
175 Stefon Diggs SP 10.00 25.00
176 Ty Sambrailo SP 4.00 10.00
177 Taylor Kelly SP 5.00 12.00
178 Malcolm Agnew SP 4.00 10.00
179 Levi Norwood SP 4.00 10.00
180 Gary Nova SP 4.00 10.00
181 Corey Grant SP 8.00 20.00
182 Shane Ray SP 8.00 20.00
183 Phillip Dorsett SP 4.00 10.00
184 Devin Smith SP 4.00 10.00
186 Cole Stoudt SP 6.00 15.00
187 Devante Parker SP 6.00 15.00
188 Melvin Gordon III SP 15.00 40.00
189 Cedric Ogbuehi SP 4.00 10.00
190 Kenny Bell SP 6.00 15.00
191 David Johnson SP 10.00 25.00
192 Devin Funchess SP 6.00 15.00
193 Trae Waynes SP 4.00 10.00
194 Bryce Petty SP 8.00 20.00
195 Sammie Coates SP
196 Benardrick Mckinney SP 4.00 10.00
197 Ronald Darby SP 4.00 10.00
198 Tony Lippett SP 4.00 10.00
199 Bo Wallace SP 4.00 10.00
200 Justin Hardy SP 8.00 20.00
201 Taylor Heinicke SP 6.00 15.00
202 Josh Harper SP 4.00 10.00
203 Duke Johnson SP 6.00 15.00
207 Rashad Greene SP 4.00 10.00
208 Javorius Allen SP 5.00 12.00
209 Tre McBride SP 4.00 10.00
210 Vic Beasley SP 5.00 12.00
213 Karlos Williams SP 4.00 10.00
215 Garrett Grayson SP 4.00 10.00

2015 Upper Deck Sweet Spot

ONE PER BLASTER BOX
*VARIATIONS: .6X TO 1.5X BASIC HELMET
SSAA Ameer Abdullah 8.00 20.00
SSAC Amari Cooper jer.# 4.00 10.00
SSAG Antwan Goodley white 2.50 6.00
SSAH Austin Hill 2.50 6.00
SSAP Andrus Peat black 2.50 6.00
SSBA Javorius Allen red 1.50 4.00
SSBH Brett Hundley 8.00 20.00
SSBK Ben Koyack blue 5.00 12.00
SSBM Benardrick Mckinney white 2.50 6.00
SSBP Bryce Petty 1.25 3.00
SSBS Barry Sanders white 10.00 25.00
SSBW Bo Wallace blue 5.00 12.00
SSCA Shane Carden purple 3.00 8.00
SSCF Cody Fajardo 3.00 8.00
SSCO Cedric Ogbuehi 3.00 8.00
SSDB Dorial Green-Beckham 1.25 3.00
SSDF Devin Funchess 2.00 5.00
SSDG Devin Gardner blue 2.00 5.00
SSDJ Duke Johnson white 2.00 5.00
SSDM Donovan McNabb 3.00 8.00
SSGR Rashad Greene 1.25 3.00
SSHE Jeff Heuerman 1.50 4.00
SSHJ Justin Hardy purple 1.25 3.00
SSHM Hutson Mason 1.25 3.00
SSHW Hines Ward 6.00 15.00
SSIO Ifo Ekpre-Olomu green 6.00 15.00
SSJA Jay Ajayi blue 5.00 12.00
SSJB Jerome Bettis 8.00 20.00
SSJE John Elway black 6.00 15.00
SSJH Josh Harper 2.50 6.00
SSJL Jeremy Langford 1.25 3.00
SSJR Jerry Rice white 6.00 15.00
SSJS Jaelen Strong fork 1.50 4.00
SSJW Jameis Winston arrow 15.00 30.00
SSLC Landon Collins jer.# 1.50 4.00
SSLN Levi Norwood white 2.50 6.00
SSLW Leonard Williams red 1.25 3.00
SSMA Marcus Allen red 5.00 12.00
SSMD Mike Davis white 3.00 8.00
SSMG Melvin Gordon white 3.00 8.00
SSMM Marcus Mariota green 20.00 40.00
SSMP Marcus Peters 3.00 8.00
SSNA Nelson Agholor 3.00 8.00
SSPD Devante Parker red 2.00 5.00
SSRG Randy Gregory 6.00 15.00
SSSC Sammie Coates 5.00 12.00
SSSD Stefon Diggs 3.00 8.00
SSSM Sean Mannion black 1.25 3.00
SSSY Steve Young 6.00 15.00
SSTA Troy Aikman 6.00 15.00
SSTC Tevin Coleman white 1.50 4.00
SSTG Todd Gurley 8.00 20.00
SSTL Tony Lippett 3.00 8.00
SSTW Trae Waynes 4.00 10.00
SSTY T.J. Yeldon 10.00 25.00
SSVB Vic Beasley orange 1.50 4.00
SSWI Karlos Williams 1.25 3.00
SSWK Kevin White 8.00 20.00

2009 Upper Deck 20th Anniversary

CARDS ISSUED IN FIVE CARD RUNS
EACH PRICED EQUALLY WITHIN RUNS
6 Notre Dame Fighting Irish .20 .50
7 Notre Dame Fighting Irish .20 .50
8 Notre Dame Fighting Irish .20 .50
9 Notre Dame Fighting Irish .20 .50
10 Notre Dame Fighting Irish .20 .50
31 San Francisco 49ers .20 .50
32 San Francisco 49ers .20 .50
33 San Francisco 49ers .20 .50
34 San Francisco 49ers .20 .50
35 San Francisco 49ers .20 .50
41 Dallas Cowboys .40 1.00
42 Dallas Cowboys .40 1.00
43 Dallas Cowboys .40 1.00
44 Dallas Cowboys .40 1.00
45 Dallas Cowboys .40 1.00
141 Louisiana Super Bowl .20 .50
142 Louisiana Super Bowl .20 .50
143 Louisiana Super Bowl .20 .50
144 Louisiana Super Bowl .20 .50
145 Louisiana Super Bowl .20 .50
221 Miami Hurricanes .20 .50
222 Miami Hurricanes .20 .50
223 Miami Hurricanes .20 .50
224 Miami Hurricanes .20 .50
225 Miami Hurricanes .20 .50
311 Georgia Tech/Colorado .20 .50
312 Georgia Tech/Colorado .20 .50
313 Georgia Tech/Colorado .20 .50
314 Georgia Tech/Colorado .20 .50
315 Georgia Tech/Colorado .20 .50
436 Washington Redskins .20 .50
437 Washington Redskins .20 .50
438 Washington Redskins .20 .50
439 Washington Redskins .20 .50
440 Washington Redskins .20 .50
496 Univ.of Washington/Univ.of Miami .20 .50
497 Univ.of Washington/Univ.of Miami .20 .50
498 Univ.of Washington/Univ.of Miami .20 .50
499 Univ.of Washington/Univ.of Miami .20 .50
500 Univ.of Washington/Univ.of Miami .20 .50
596 NCAA Football Champions/Alabama .20 .50
597 NCAA Football Champions/Alabama .20 .50
598 NCAA Football Champions/Alabama .20 .50
599 NCAA Football Champions/Alabama .20 .50
600 NCAA Football Champions/Alabama .20 .50
611 Final Game in Cleveland Stadium .20 .50
612 Final Game in Cleveland Stadium .20 .50
613 Final Game in Cleveland Stadium .20 .50
614 Final Game in Cleveland Stadium .20 .50
615 Final Game in Cleveland Stadium .20 .50
796 Carolina Panthers/Collins .20 .50
797 Carolina Panthers .20 .50
798 Carolina Panthers .20 .50
799 Carolina Panthers .20 .50
800 Carolina Panthers .20 .50
801 Jacksonville Jaguars .20 .50
802 Jacksonville Jaguars .20 .50
803 Jacksonville Jaguars .20 .50
804 Jacksonville Jaguars .20 .50
805 Jacksonville Jaguars .20 .50
901 Dallas Cowboys .40 1.00
902 Dallas Cowboys .40 1.00
903 Dallas Cowboys .40 1.00
904 Dallas Cowboys .40 1.00
905 Dallas Cowboys .40 1.00
961 NCAA Football Champions/Nebraska .20 .50
962 NCAA Football Champions/Nebraska .20 .50
963 NCAA Football Champions/Nebraska .20 .50
964 NCAA Football Champions/Nebraska .20 .50
965 NCAA Football Champions/Nebraska .20 .50
1016 Green Bay Packers .30 .75
1017 Green Bay Packers .30 .75
1018 Green Bay Packers .30 .75
1019 Green Bay Packers .30 .75
1020 Green Bay Packers .30 .75
1086 NCAA Football Champions .20 .50
1087 NCAA Football Champions .20 .50
1088 NCAA Football Champions .20 .50
1089 NCAA Football Champions .20 .50
1090 NCAA Football Champions .20 .50
1136 Denver Broncos .20 .50
1137 Denver Broncos .20 .50
1138 Denver Broncos .20 .50
1139 Denver Broncos .20 .50
1140 Denver Broncos .20 .50
1176 NCAA Football Champions .20 .50
1177 NCAA Football Champions .20 .50
1178 NCAA Football Champions .20 .50
1179 NCAA Football Champions .20 .50
1180 NCAA Football Champions .20 .50
1181 Peyton Manning .75 2.00
1182 Peyton Manning .75 2.00
1183 Peyton Manning .75 2.00
1184 Peyton Manning .75 2.00
1185 Peyton Manning .75 2.00
1261 Denver Broncos .20 .50
1262 Denver Broncos .20 .50
1263 Denver Broncos .20 .50
1264 Denver Broncos .20 .50
1265 Denver Broncos .20 .50
1396 St. Louis Rams .20 .50
1397 St. Louis Rams .20 .50
1398 St. Louis Rams .20 .50
1399 St. Louis Rams .20 .50
1400 St. Louis Rams .20 .50
1516 Baltimore Ravens .20 .50
1517 Baltimore Ravens .20 .50
1518 Baltimore Ravens .20 .50
1519 Baltimore Ravens .20 .50
1520 Baltimore Ravens .20 .50
1626 New England Patriots .20 .50
1627 New England Patriots .20 .50
1628 New England Patriots .20 .50
1629 New England Patriots .20 .50
1630 New England Patriots .20 .50
1656 Ed Reed .25 .60
1657 Ed Reed .25 .60
1658 Ed Reed .25 .60
1659 Ed Reed .25 .60
1660 Ed Reed .25 .60
1686 Tom Brady .75 2.00
1687 Tom Brady .75 2.00
1688 Tom Brady .75 2.00
1689 Tom Brady .75 2.00
1690 Tom Brady .75 2.00
1691 Brian Westbrook .40 1.00
1692 Brian Westbrook .40 1.00
1693 Brian Westbrook .40 1.00
1694 Brian Westbrook .40 1.00
1695 Brian Westbrook .40 1.00
1706 Clinton Portis .40 1.00
1707 Clinton Portis .40 1.00
1708 Clinton Portis .40 1.00
1709 Clinton Portis .40 1.00
1710 Clinton Portis .40 1.00
1716 Tuck Rule NFL Playoff Game .20 .50
1717 Tuck Rule NFL Playoff Game .20 .50
1718 Tuck Rule NFL Playoff Game .20 .50
1719 Tuck Rule NFL Playoff Game .20 .50
1720 Tuck Rule NFL Playoff Game .20 .50
1751 Troy Polamalu .40 1.00
1752 Troy Polamalu .40 1.00
1753 Troy Polamalu .40 1.00
1754 Troy Polamalu .40 1.00
1755 Troy Polamalu .40 1.00
1771 Tampa Bay Buccaneers .20 .50
1772 Tampa Bay Buccaneers .20 .50
1773 Tampa Bay Buccaneers .20 .50
1774 Tampa Bay Buccaneers .20 .50
1775 Tampa Bay Buccaneers .20 .50
1856 Tony Romo .75 2.00
1857 Tony Romo .75 2.00
1858 Tony Romo .75 2.00
1859 Tony Romo .75 2.00
1860 Tony Romo .75 2.00
1911 Eli Manning .40 1.00
1912 Eli Manning .40 1.00
1913 Eli Manning .40 1.00
1914 Eli Manning .40 1.00
1915 Eli Manning .40 1.00
1916 New England Patriots .20 .50
1917 New England Patriots .20 .50
1918 New England Patriots .20 .50
1919 New England Patriots .20 .50
1920 New England Patriots .20 .50
1971 Ben Roethlisberger .50 1.25
1972 Ben Roethlisberger .50 1.25
1973 Ben Roethlisberger .50 1.25
1974 Ben Roethlisberger .50 1.25
1975 Ben Roethlisberger .50 1.25
1986 Peyton Manning .75 2.00
1987 Peyton Manning .75 2.00
1988 Peyton Manning .75 2.00
1989 Peyton Manning .75 2.00
1990 Peyton Manning .75 2.00
2051 NFL Game Played in Mexico .20 .50
2052 NFL Game Played in Mexico .20 .50
2053 NFL Game Played in Mexico .20 .50
2054 NFL Game Played in Mexico .20 .50
2055 NFL Game Played in Mexico .20 .50
2056 New England Patriots .20 .50
2057 New England Patriots .20 .50
2058 New England Patriots .20 .50
2059 New England Patriots .20 .50
2060 New England Patriots .20 .50
2136 Pittsburgh Steelers .20 .50
2137 Pittsburgh Steelers .20 .50
2138 Pittsburgh Steelers .20 .50
2139 Pittsburgh Steelers .20 .50
2140 Pittsburgh Steelers .20 .50
2321 Adrian Peterson 1.00 2.50
2322 Adrian Peterson 1.00 2.50
2323 Adrian Peterson 1.00 2.50
2324 Adrian Peterson 1.00 2.50
2325 Adrian Peterson 1.00 2.50
2341 Indianapolis Colts .20 .50
2342 Indianapolis Colts .20 .50
2343 Indianapolis Colts .20 .50
2344 Indianapolis Colts .20 .50
2345 Indianapolis Colts .20 .50
2396 New York Giants .20 .50
2397 New York Giants .20 .50
2398 New York Giants .20 .50
2399 New York Giants .20 .50
2400 New York Giants .20 .50
2406 Brett Favre 1.25 3.00
2407 Brett Favre 1.25 3.00
2408 Brett Favre 1.25 3.00
2409 Brett Favre 1.25 3.00
2410 Brett Favre 1.25 3.00
2461 Brett Favre 1.00 2.50
2462 Brett Favre 1.00 2.50
2463 Brett Favre 1.00 2.50
2464 Brett Favre 1.00 2.50
2465 Brett Favre 1.00 2.50
2466 Matt Ryan .60 1.50
2467 Matt Ryan .60 1.50
2468 Matt Ryan .60 1.50
2469 Matt Ryan .60 1.50
2470 Matt Ryan .60 1.50
2496 Chris Johnson .40 1.00
2497 Chris Johnson .40 1.00
2498 Chris Johnson .40 1.00
2499 Chris Johnson .40 1.00
2500 Chris Johnson .40 1.00

2009 Upper Deck 20th Anniversary Memorabilia

NFLAP Adrian Peterson 10.00 25.00
NFLBF Brett Favre 20.00 50.00
NFLBU Brian Urlacher 4.00 10.00
NFLCP Carson Palmer 5.00 12.00
NFLDG David Garrard 3.00 8.00
NFLDH Devin Hester 4.00 10.00
NFLDW DeAngelo Williams 3.00 8.00
NFLEJ Edgerrin James 4.00 10.00
NFLJP Julius Peppers 4.00 10.00
NFLMC Donovan McNabb 5.00 12.00
NFLPM Peyton Manning 8.00 20.00
NFLRM Randy Moss 6.00 15.00
NFLTR Tony Romo 8.00 20.00

2014 Upper Deck 25th Anniversary Promos

UD25PM Peyton Manning 2.50 6.00

2014 Upper Deck 25th Anniversary

2 Barry Sanders .60 1.50
5 Bart Starr .60 1.50
7 John Elway .60 1.50
8 Steve Young .60 1.50
13 Billy Sims .40 1.00
16 Joe Montana 1.00 2.50
18 Peyton Manning 1.00 2.50
21 Ickey Woods .40 1.00
34 Thurman Thomas .50 1.25
35 Ben Roethlisberger .50 1.25
36 George Rogers .40 1.00
41 Tiki Barber .40 1.00
45 Archie Griffin .40 1.00
52 Ty Detmer .30 .75
58 Johnny Rodgers .30 .75
70 Jerome Bettis .50 1.25
80 Jerry Rice .75 2.00
83 Tim Couch .30 .75
84 Bo Jackson .75 2.00
89 Kordell Stewart .30 .75
90 LaDainian Tomlinson .50 1.25
91 Keenan Allen .40 1.00
95 Rick Mirer .30 .75
98 Garrison Hearst .40 1.00
107 Doug Flutie .40 1.00
109 Drew Brees .50 1.25
110 Joe Namath .60 1.50
111 Ha Ha Clinton-Dix .60 1.50
113 Blake Bortles .75 2.00
114 Teddy Bridgewater 1.25 3.00
118 Marqise Lee .50 1.25
119 Eric Ebron .60 1.50
121 Calvin Pryor .40 1.00
123 Bishop Sankey .50 1.25
125 Odell Beckham Jr 1.50 4.00
126 Jake Matthews .40 1.00
131 Johnny Manziel 1.00 2.50
132 Carlos Hyde .50 1.25
133 Khalil Mack .40 1.00
135 Tajh Boyd .40 1.00
136 Aaron Murray .50 1.25
138 Ka'Deem Carey .40 1.00
141 Mike Evans .60 1.50
148 Darqueze Dennard .40 1.00

2014 Upper Deck 25th Anniversary Silver

*SILVER/230: 1.2X TO 3X BASIC CARDS

2014 Upper Deck 25th Anniversary Autographs

11 Elvin Hayes/25 6.00 15.00
21 Ickey Woods/25
36 George Rogers/25
41 Tiki Barber/25
52 Ty Detmer/25
58 Johnny Rodgers/25
83 Tim Couch/125 5.00 12.00
91 Keenan Allen/25
95 Rick Mirer/25
98 Garrison Hearst/125 5.00 12.00
101 Antoine Walker/25
107 Doug Flutie/25
111 Ha Ha Clinton-Dix/25
118 Marqise Lee/25
119 Eric Ebron/25
123 Bishop Sankey/25
125 Odell Beckham Jr/25
126 Jake Matthews/25
132 Carlos Hyde/25
133 Khalil Mack/25
135 Tajh Boyd/25
136 Aaron Murray/25
138 Ka'Deem Carey/25
141 Mike Evans/25

2009 Upper Deck Own the Rookies

This set was distributed directly to hobby shops and dealers in December 2009. Each features the top ten rookies of the 2009 season and was issued in a sealed cellophane wrapper as a set.

COMPLETE SET (10) 3.00 8.00
RW1 Mark Sanchez .15 .40
RW2 Donald Brown .15 .40
RW3 Matthew Stafford .75 2.00
RW4 Mohamed Massaquoi .15 .40
RW5 Jeremy Maclin .20 .50
RW6 Hakeem Nicks .20 .50
RW7 Shonn Greene .15 .40
RW8 Percy Harvin .15 .40
RW9 Josh Freeman .15 .40
RW10 Chris Wells .15 .40

2009 Upper Deck Prominent Cuts

COMPLETE SET (60) 30.00 60.00
14 Steve Largent .40 1.00

2011 Upper Deck Signature Icons Las Vegas Summit Promos

UNPRICED AUTO PRINT RUN 4-15
LVBJ Bo Jackson/15
LVSY Steve Young/10

1993 Upper Deck Adventures in Toon World

IT'S WAY COOLER! This new Upper Deck produced set definitely builds the success of the 'Comic Ball' series on. Indeed, nothing creates funnier stories than pairing Looney Tune characters with respected professional athletes. The base set is divided into 9-card subsets: 'Act 1' (A1S1-A1S9) through 'Act 10' (A10S1-A10S9); each of 18 scenes and with each card being double-sided with two different scenes.

COMPLETE SET (91) 10.00 25.00
COMMON CARD (1-90) .20 .50

1993 Upper Deck Adventures in Toon World Bugs Bunny Hare-os

BBH1 Joe Montana with Bugs (comic art)
BBH5 Michael Jordan Wayne Gretzky Joe Montana Reggie Jackson with Bugs (comic art)

1993 Upper Deck Adventures in Toon World Holograms

3 Joe Montana with Elmer Fudd
4 Joe Montana with Yosemite Sam
5 Michael Jordan Wayne Gretzky Joe Montana Reggie Jackson with Bugs and Toonimator

2005 Upper Deck AFL

COMPLETE SET (90) 20.00 40.00
1 Hunkie Cooper .30 .75
2 Siaha Burley .30 .75
3 Sherdrick Bonner .30 .75
4 Bo Kelly .20 .50
5 Evan Hlavacek .20 .50
6 Tacoma Fontaine .20 .50
7 Troy Bergeron .40 1.00
8 Darrin Chiaverini .30 .75
9 Bobby Pesavento .20 .50
10 Tom Pace .20 .50
11 Raymond Philyaw .30 .75
12 Bob McMillen .30 .75
13 Etu Molden .30 .75
14 Jeremy McDaniel .30 .75
15 Todd Hammel .30 .75
16 John Dutton .30 .75
17 Damian Harrell .40 1.00
18 Kevin McKenzie .20 .50
19 Willis Marshall .20 .50
20 Rashad Floyd .20 .50
21 Andy McCullough .20 .50
22 Damien Groce .30 .75
23 Chad Salisbury .20 .50
24 Sedrick Robinson .20 .50
25 Cornelius White .20 .50
26 Wilmont Perry .20 .50
27 Clint Stoerner .75 2.00
28 Will Pettis .30 .75
29 Bobby Sippio .30 .75
30 Jason Shelley .20 .50
31 Duke Pettijohn .20 .50
32 Robert Thomas .20 .50
33 Jim Kubiak .30 .75
34 Dialleo Burks .30 .75
35 Matt Nagy .60 1.50
36 Kevin Gaines .20 .50
37 Josh Bush .20 .50
38 Michael Bishop .40 1.00
39 Anthony Hines .20 .50
40 Chris Jackson .30 .75
41 Jerome Riley .20 .50
42 Josh Jeffries .20 .50
43 Clint Dolezel .40 .75
44 Marcus Nash .40 1.00
45 Coco Blalock .30 .75
46 Cornelius Bonner .20 .50
47 Frank Carter .20 .50
48 John Kaleo .30 .75
49 Kevin Ingram .20 .50
50 Greg Hopkins .30 .75
51 Lonnie Ford .20 .50
52 Brian Sump .20 .50
53 Leon Murray .20 .50
54 Darryl Hammond .20 .50
55 Fred Coleman .20 .50
56 Ahmad Hawkins .20 .50
57 Gabe Amey .20 .50
58 Andy Kelly .30 .75
59 Chris Pointer .20 .50
60 Aaron Bailey .30 .75
61 Dan Curran .20 .50
62 Lamont Moore .20 .50
63 Thabiti Davis .30 .75
64 Aaron Garcia .40 1.00
65 Lincoln DuPree .20 .50
66 William Holder .20 .50
67 Chris Anthony .20 .50
68 Markeith Cooper .20 .50
69 Cory Fleming .30 .75
70 Kenny McEntyre .30 .75
71 Bret Cooper .20 .50
72 Travis McGriff .30 .75
73 Joe Hamilton .30 .75
74 Tony Graziani .40 1.00
75 Takuya Furutani .20 .50
76 Chris Ryan .20 .50
77 Joseph Todd .20 .50
78 Sean Scott .30 .75
79 Mark Grieb .40 1.00
80 James Hundon .30 .75
81 James Roe .30 .75
82 Omarr Smith .30 .75
83 Rashied Davis .30 .75
84 Calvin Schexnayder .20 .50
85 Shane Stafford .40 .75
86 Lawrence Samuels .30 .75
87 T.T. Toliver .20 .50
88 Freddie Solomon .30 .75
89 Cliff Dell .20 .50
90 Rich Young .20 .50

2005 Upper Deck AFL Gold

*GOLD: 5X TO 12X BASIC CARDS
GOLD PRINT RUN 100 SER.#'d SETS

2005 Upper Deck AFL Arena Action

STATED ODDS 1:10
AA1 Kenny McEntyre 1.50 4.00
AA2 Cory Fleming 1.50 4.00
AA3 Marcus Nash 2.00 5.00
AA4 Hunkie Cooper 1.50 4.00
AA5 Tony Graziani 2.00 5.00
AA6 Kevin Ingram 1.00 2.50
AA7 Dan Curran 1.00 2.50
AA8 Mark Grieb 2.00 5.00
AA9 Joe Hamilton 1.50 4.00
AA10 Will Pettis 1.50 4.00
AA11 Damian Harrell 2.00 5.00
AA12 Rashad Floyd 1.00 2.50
AA13 Etu Molden 1.50 4.00
AA14 Lincoln DuPree 1.00 2.50
AA15 Kevin McKenzie 1.00 2.50
AA16 James Roe 1.50 4.00
AA17 T.T. Toliver 1.00 2.50
AA18 Sedrick Robinson 1.00 2.50
AA19 Rashied Davis 1.50 4.00
AA20 Clint Dolezel 1.50 4.00
AA21 Chris Jackson 1.50 4.00
AA22 Thabiti Davis 1.50 4.00
AA23 Aaron Bailey 1.50 4.00
AA24 Freddie Solomon 1.50 4.00
AA25 Bobby Sippio 1.50 4.00
AA26 Lawrence Samuels 1.50 4.00
AA27 Siaha Burley 1.50 4.00
AA28 Markeith Cooper 1.00 2.50
AA29 Aaron Garcia 2.00 5.00
AA30 Cornelius White 1.00 2.50

2005 Upper Deck AFL ArenaBowl Archives

COMPLETE SET (18) 12.50 25.00
STATED ODDS 1:20
AB1 Arena Bowl I .75 2.00
AB2 Arena Bowl II .75 2.00
AB3 Arena Bowl III .75 2.00
AB4 Arena Bowl IV .75 2.00
AB5 Arena Bowl V .75 2.00
AB6 Arena Bowl VI .75 2.00
AB7 Arena Bowl VII .75 2.00
AB8 Arena Bowl VIII .75 2.00
AB9 Arena Bowl IX .75 2.00
AB10 Arena Bowl X .75 2.00
AB11 Arena Bowl XI .75 2.00
AB12 Arena Bowl XII .75 2.00
AB13 Arena Bowl XIII .75 2.00
AB14 Arena Bowl XIV .75 2.00
AB15 Arena Bowl XV .75 2.00
AB16 Arena Bowl XVI .75 2.00
AB17 Arena Bowl XVII .75 2.00
AB18 Arena Bowl XVIII .75 2.00

2005 Upper Deck AFL Arenagraphs

STATED ODDS 1:24 HOB, 1:48 RET
ABA Aaron Bailey 10.00 25.00
AGA Aaron Garcia 12.50 30.00
AMA Adrian McPherson 30.00 80.00
BMA Bob McMillen 10.00 25.00
CDA Clint Dolezel 12.50 30.00
CFA Cory Fleming 12.50 30.00
CJA Chris Jackson 10.00 25.00
DBA David Baker 7.50 20.00
DHA Damian Harrell 12.50 30.00
EMA Etu Molden 10.00 25.00
HCA Hunkie Cooper 12.50 30.00
JEA John Elway SP 125.00 200.00
JHA James Hundon
JJA Jerry Jones
KEA Kevin McKenzie 7.50 20.00
KIA Kevin Ingram 7.50 20.00
KMA Kenny McEntyre 10.00 25.00
LSA Lawrence Samuels 10.00 - 25.00
MDA Mike Ditka SP 50.00 100.00
MGA Mark Grieb 12.50 30.00
MNA Marcus Nash 12.50 30.00
OSA Omarr Smith 10.00 25.00
RDA Rashied Davis 10.00 25.00
SBA Siaha Burley 7.50 20.00
SRA Sedrick Robinson 10.00 25.00
TFA Tacoma Fontaine 12.50 30.00
TGA Tony Graziani 12.50 30.00
TMA Tim McGraw SP 125.00 200.00
TTA T.T. Toliver 7.50 20.00
WPA Will Pettis 10.00 25.00

2005 Upper Deck AFL Arenagraphs Duals

STATED PRINT RUN 50 SER.#'d SETS
BBA2 Aaron Bailey/Coco Blalock 15.00 40.00
BFA2 Siaha Burley/Tacoma Fontaine 15.00 40.00
DNA2 Clint Dolezel/Marcus Nash 20.00 50.00
EHA2 John Elway/Damian Harrell/25 150.00 300.00
FMA2 Cory Fleming/Kenny McEntyre 15.00 40.00
GGA2 Tony Graziani/Aaron Garcia 25.00 60.00
GHA2 Mark Grieb/James Hundon
GIA2 Tony Graziani/Kevin Ingram 20.00 50.00
HMA2 Damian Harrell/Kevin McKenzie 15.00 40.00
MBA2 Tim McGraw/David Baker/25 100.00 175.00
MMA2 Bob McMillen/Etu Molden 15.00 40.00
RPA2 Sedrick Robinson/Will Pettis 15.00 40.00
SDA2 Omarr Smith/Rashied Davis 15.00 40.00
STA2 Lawrence Samuels/T.T. Toliver 15.00 40.00
TCA2 Robert Thomas/Hunkie Cooper 20.00 50.00

2005 Upper Deck AFL Dance Team Stars

COMPLETE SET (10) 15.00 40.00
STATED ODDS 1:36
DTS1 Crystal 2.00 5.00
DTC2 Cina 2.00 5.00
DTS3 Katie 2.00 5.00

DTS4 Christina 2.00 5.00
DTS5 Heather 2.00 5.00
DTS6 Lisa 2.00 5.00
DTS7 Gloria 2.00 5.00
DTS8 Kelli 2.00 5.00
DTS9 Bridget 2.00 5.00
DTS10 Katie 2.00 5.00

2005 Upper Deck AFL Jerseys

STATED ODDS 1:12
AGJ Aaron Garcia 8.00 20.00
BSJ Bobby Sippio 5.00 12.00
CAJ Chris Anthony 4.00 10.00
CDJ Clint Dolezel 5.00 12.00
CJJ Chris Jackson 5.00 12.00
CRJ Chris Ryan 4.00 10.00
CSJ Corey Sawyer
DHJ Damian Harrell 8.00 20.00
HCJ Hunkie Cooper 5.00 12.00
JHJ James Hundon 8.00 20.00
JRJ James Roe 5.00 12.00
KEJ Kevin McKenzie 4.00 10.00
KIJ Kevin Ingram 4.00 10.00
LSJ Lawrence Samuels 5.00 12.00
MGJ Mark Grieb 8.00 20.00
MNJ Marcus Nash 8.00 20.00
MRJ Mark Ricks
OSJ Omarr Smith 5.00 12.00
RDJ Rashied Davis 5.00 12.00
RRJ Ricky Ross 4.00 10.00
SBJ Siaha Burley 5.00 12.00
SRJ Sedrick Robinson 4.00 10.00
TFJ Tacoma Fontaine 4.00 10.00
TGJ Tony Graziani 8.00 20.00
THJ Todd Hammel 5.00 12.00
TTJ T.T. Toliver 4.00 10.00
WPJ Will Pettis 5.00 12.00

2005 Upper Deck AFL League Luminaries

STATED ODDS 1:24
LL1 Tommy Maddox 2.50 6.00
LL2 David Baker 2.00 5.00
LL3 Kurt Warner 2.50 6.00
LL4 John Elway OWN 5.00 12.00
LL5 Danny White CO 2.50 6.00
LL6 Tim McGraw OWN 4.00 10.00
LL7 Adrian McPherson 7.50 20.00
LL8 Marcus Nash 2.50 6.00
LL9 Tony Graziani 3.00 8.00
LL10 Cory Fleming 2.50 6.00
LL11 Mike Ditka OWN 5.00 12.00
LL12 Jay Gruden 2.00 5.00
LL13 Tim Marcum CO 2.00 5.00
LL14 Kevin Swayne 2.00 5.00
LL15 Barry Wagner 2.00 5.00

2005 Upper Deck AFL Timeline

STATED ODDS 1:30
AFL1 Barry Wagner 2.00 5.00
AFL2 Sherdrick Bonner 2.00 5.00
AFL3 Jerry Jones OWN 3.00 8.00
AFL4 Tim McGraw OWN 4.00 10.00
AFL5 John Elway OWN 5.00 12.00
AFL6 Jay Gruden 2.00 5.00
AFL7 Tim Marcum 2.00 5.00
AFL8 Mike Ditka OWN 5.00 12.00
AFL9 Jim Kubiak 2.50 6.00
AFL10 David Baker COM 2.00 5.00
AFL11 Aaron Garcia 2.50 6.00
AFL12 2004 Attendance Record 2.00 5.00

2006 Upper Deck AFL

This 190-card set was released in February, 2006. The set was issued into the hobby in eight-card packs which came 24 packs to a box.
COMPLETE SET (190) 30.00 60.00
1 Sherdrick Bonner .30 .75
2 Clarence Coleman .20 .50
3 Randy Gatewood .20 .50
4 Tom Pace .20 .50
5 Vince Amey .20 .50
6 Evan Hlavacek .20 .50
7 Josh Jeffries .20 .50
8 Gary Kral .20 .50
9 Bo Kelly .20 .50
10 Clarence Lawson .20 .50
11 Damien Groce .30 .75
12 John Fitzgerald .20 .50
13 Kevin Nickerson .30 .75
14 Tom Briggs .20 .50
15 Darrin Chiaverini .30 .75
16 Ira Gooch .20 .50
17 Tacoma Fontaine .30 .75
18 Lindsay Fleshman .20 .50
19 Tim Seder .20 .50
20 Henry Bryant .20 .50
21 Sedrick Robinson .20 .50
22 Damon Mason .20 .50
23 Raymond Philyaw .30 .75
24 John Moyer .20 .50
25 Etu Molden .30 .75
26 Henry Douglas .20 .50
27 Bob McMillen .30 .75
28 Todd Hammel .30 .75
29 Jeremy McDaniel .30 .75
30 Keith Gispert .20 .50
31 Russell Shaw .20 .50
32 C.J. Johnson .20 .50
33 Cornelius White .20 .50
34 John Dutton .30 .75
35 Damian Harrell .40 1.00
36 Willis Marshall .20 .50
37 Clay Rush .20 .50
38 Andy McCullough .30 .75
39 Kevin McKenzie .20 .50
40 Rich Young .20 .50
41 Ahmad Hawkins .20 .50
42 Rashad Floyd .20 .50
43 Delvin Hughley .20 .50
44 Saul Patu .20 .50
45 Matt D'Orazio .30 .75
46 Lenzie Jackson .20 .50
47 B.J. Barre .20 .50
48 Mike Sutton .20 .50
49 Gillis Wilson .20 .50
50 Randall Lane .20 .50
51 Frank Carter .20 .50
52 Bobby Olive .20 .50
53 Jamarr Ward .20 .50
54 Thabiti Davis .30 .75
55 John Kaleo .30 .75
56 Clint Dolezel .40 1.00
57 Jason Shelley .20 .50
58 Will Pettis .30 .75
59 Hamin Milligan .20 .50
60 Duke Pettijohn .20 .50
61 Carlos Martinez .20 .50
62 Lucas Yarnell .20 .50
63 Jermaine Lewis .20 .50
64 Joe Minucci .20 .50
65 Jermaine Jones .20 .50
66 Scottie Montgomery .20 .50
67 Jim Kubiak .30 .75
68 Matt Nagy .40 1.00
69 Troy Bergeron .40 1.00
70 Chris Jackson .30 .75
71 Derek Lee .40 1.00
72 Rubert Thomas .20 .50
73 Kevin Aldridge .20 .50
74 Nelson Garner .20 .50
75 Nick Ward .20 .50
76 Ricky Parker .20 .50
77 Willie Gary .20 .50
78 Michael Bishop .40 1.00
79 Anthony Hines .30 .75
80 Chris Avery .30 .75
81 Josh Bush .20 .50
82 Rupert Grant .20 .50
83 Bryant Shaw .20 .50
84 Dennison Robinson .20 .50
85 Kahlil Carter .20 .50
86 Chris Ryan .20 .50
87 Marvin Taylor .20 .50
88 Timon Marshall .20 .50
89 Traco Rachal .20 .50
90 Marcus Nash .40 1.00
91 Coco Blalock .30 .75
92 Joe Douglass .20 .50
93 Ricky Ross .20 .50
94 Sunungura Rusununguko .20 .50
95 Marlion Jackson .20 .50
96 Jerome Riley .20 .50
97 Wilky Bazile .20 .50
98 Dameon Porter .20 .50
99 Rodney Filer .20 .50
100 Cornelius Bonner .20 .50
101 Brian Mann .20 .50
102 Silas Demary .30 .75
103 Tony Locke .20 .50
104 Kevin Ingram .20 .50
105 Lonnie Ford .20 .50
106 Greg Hopkins .30 .75
107 Remy Hamilton .20 .50
108 Brian Sump .20 .50
109 Antuan Simmons .20 .50
110 Jerald Brown .20 .50
111 Anthony Derricks .20 .50
112 Leon Murray .20 .50
113 James Baron .20 .50
114 Clint Stoerner .50 1.25
115 T.T. Toliver .30 .75
116 Jarrick Hillery .20 .50
117 Darryl Hammond .20 .50
118 Tony Dodson .20 .50
119 Hardy Mitchell .20 .50
120 Levelle Brown .20 .50
121 DeRon Jenkins .20 .50
122 Cory Fleming .30 .75
123 Andy Kelly .30 .75
124 Aaron Bailey .30 .75
125 B.J. Cohen .20 .50
126 Carl Bond .20 .50
127 Nyle Wiren .20 .50
128 Jermaine Miles .20 .50
129 Stacy Evans .20 .50
130 Terrance Joseph .20 .50
131 Nikia Adderson .20 .50
132 Calvin Spears .20 .50
133 Chris Pointer .20 .50
134 Steve Smith .20 .50
135 Aaron Garcia .40 1.00
136 Mike Horacek .30 .75
137 Chris Anthony .20 .50
138 Ernest Certain .20 .50
139 Josh White .20 .50
140 Rob Bironas .20 .50
141 Lynaris Elpheage .20 .50
142 Corey Johnson .20 .50
143 Marcus Owen .20 .50
144 Sir Mawn Wilson .20 .50
145 Chris Angel .20 .50
146 Billy Parker .20 .50
147 Joe Hamilton .30 .75
148 E.J. Burt .20 .50
149 Jimmy Fryzel .20 .50
150 Wes Ours .20 .50
151 Idris Price .20 .50
152 Kenny McEntyre .30 .75
153 Chris Sanders .20 .50
154 Jerrian James .20 .50
155 Jonathan Ordway .20 .50
156 Tony Graziani .40 1.00
157 Marcus Knight .30 .75
158 Sean Scott .30 .75
159 Kevin Gaines .20 .50
160 Tyronne Jones .20 .50
161 Rob Milanese .20 .50
162 Chris Brown .20 .50
163 Eddie Moten .20 .50
164 Calvin Coleman .20 .50
165 Mark Grieb .40 1.00
166 James Roe .30 .75
167 Rashied Davis .30 .75
168 James Hundon .30 .75
169 Barry Wagner .20 .50
170 Rodney Wright .20 .50
171 Shalon Baker .20 .50
172 Dan Frantz .20 .50
173 Calvin Schexnayder .20 .50
174 Clevan Thomas .20 .50
175 Fred Coleman .20 .50
176 Shane Stafford .40 1.00
177 Lawrence Samuels .30 .75
178 Freddie Solomon .30 .75
179 Ronney Daniels .20 .50
180 Bobby Sippio .30 .75
181 Matt George .20 .50
182 Jarrod Penright .20 .50
183 Demetris Bendross .20 .50
184 Tramain Jones .20 .50
185 Khori Ivy .20 .50
186 Kelvin Hunter .20 .50
187 Siaha Burley .30 .75
188 Justin Skaggs .20 .50
189 Orshawante Bryant .20 .50
190 Joe Germaine .30 .75

2006 Upper Deck AFL Gold

*GOLD: 5X TO 12X BASIC CARDS
GOLD PRINT RUN 100 SER.#'d SETS

2006 Upper Deck AFL Arena Action

AA1 Jarrick Hillery 1.00 2.50
AA2 Derek Lee 2.00 5.00
AA3 Troy Bergeron 2.00 5.00
AA4 Andy McCullough 1.50 4.00
AA5 Cliff Dell 1.50 4.00
AA6 Cornelius White 1.00 2.50
AA7 Anthony Derricks 1.00 2.50
AA8 Thabiti Davis 1.50 4.00
AA9 Ira Gooch 1.00 2.50
AA10 R.Floyd/A.Hawkins 1.00 2.50
AA11 Chris Jackson 1.50 4.00
AA12 Tacoma Fontaine 1.00 2.50
AA13 Anthony Hines 1.50 4.00
AA14 Jimmy Fryzel 1.00 2.50
AA15 Kevin Ingram 1.00 2.50
AA16 Damian Harrell 2.00 5.00
AA17 Marcus Nash 2.00 5.00
AA18 Siaha Burley 1.50 4.00
AA19 Coco Blalock 1.50 4.00
AA20 Aaron Bailey 1.50 4.00
AA21 Dialleo Burks 1.50 4.00
AA22 Sean Scott 1.50 4.00
AA23 Darryl Hammond 1.00 2.50

2006 Upper Deck AFL Arena Award Winners

COMPLETE SET (10) 10.00 20.00
AAW1 Kevin Ingram .75 2.00
AAW2 Damian Harrell 1.50 4.00
AAW3 Silas Demary 1.25 3.00
AAW4 Doug Plank .75 2.00
AAW5 Troy Bergeron 1.50 4.00
AAW6 Silas Demary 1.25 3.00
AAW7 Remy Hamilton .75 2.00
AAW8 Cory Fleming 1.25 3.00
AAW9 Marcus Nash 1.50 4.00
AAW10 Kenny McEntyre 1.25 3.00

2006 Upper Deck AFL ArenaBowl Recap

COMPLETE SET (10) 8.00 20.00
AB1 ArenaBowl XIX Logo .75 2.00
AB2 Siaha Burley 1.25 3.00
AB3 John Kaleo 1.25 3.00
AB4 Mike Dailey .75 2.00
AB5 Kevin McKenzie .75 2.00
AB6 Derek Lee 1.50 4.00
AB7 Chris Jackson 1.25 3.00
AB8 Clay Rush .75 2.00
AB9 Colorado Crush .75 2.00
AB10 John Dutton 1.25 3.00

2006 Upper Deck AFL Arenagraphs

OVERALL AUTO ODDS 1:12
AB Aaron Bailey 10.00 25.00
AG Aaron Garcia 12.50 30.00
AK Andy Kelly 10.00 25.00
BM Bob McMillen 12.50 30.00
CB Coco Blalock 8.00 20.00
CD Clint Dolezel 12.50 30.00
CF Cory Fleming 10.00 25.00
CJ Chris Jackson 10.00 25.00
CS Clint Stoerner 25.00 50.00
DB David Baker SP 15.00 40.00
DG Damien Groce 8.00 20.00
DH Damian Harrell 12.50 30.00
DL Derek Lee 10.00 25.00
DP Doug Plank 8.00 20.00
EM Etu Molden 12.50 30.00
GR Jay Gruden 10.00 25.00
HC Hunkie Cooper 10.00 25.00
JD John Dutton 10.00 25.00
JF John Fitzgerald 8.00 20.00
JG Joe Germaine 12.50 30.00
JH Joe Hamilton 12.50 30.00
JK John Kaleo 10.00 25.00
JR James Roe 12.50 30.00
KE Kenny McEntyre 10.00 25.00
KI Kevin Ingram 8.00 20.00
KM Kevin McKenzie 8.00 20.00
LS Lawrence Samuels 8.00 20.00
MA Marcus Nash 12.50 30.00
MB Michael Bishop 12.50 30.00
MD Mike Ditka 40.00 80.00
MG Mark Grieb 12.50 30.00
MN Matt Nagy 12.50 30.00
OS Omarr Smith 10.00 25.00
RJ Ron Jaworski SP 15.00 40.00
RP Raymond Philyaw 10.00 25.00
RT Robert Thomas 8.00 20.00
SB Siaha Burley 10.00 25.00
SD Silas Demary 8.00 20.00
SH Shane Stafford 12.50 30.00
SS Sean Scott 10.00 25.00
TB Troy Bergeron 12.50 30.00
TF Tacoma Fontaine 10.00 25.00
TG Tony Graziani 12.50 30.00
TM Tim McGraw SP 75.00 150.00
TT T.T. Toliver 8.00 20.00
WP Will Pettis 8.00 20.00
DGI Dancer: Gina 12.50 30.00
DHE Dancer: Heidi 12.50 30.00
DHY Dancer: Holly 12.50 30.00
DJS Dancer: Jessica 12.50 30.00
DKR Dancer: Kara 12.50 30.00
DNI Dancer: Nikki 12.50 30.00
DRA Dancer: Rachel 12.50 30.00
DSU Dancer: Susan 12.50 30.00
DVI Dancer: Victoria 12.50 30.00

2006 Upper Deck AFL Arenagraphs Duals

BD M.Bishop/C.Dolezel 25.00 60.00
BG S.Burley/J.Germaine
BK A.Bailey/A.Kelly 30.00 60.00
BL T.Bergeron/D.Lee 30.00 60.00
BM D.Baker/M.Ditka 50.00 100.00
GG A.Garcia/T.Graziani 40.00 80.00
GJ T.Graziani/R.Jaworski 30.00 60.00
HD D.Harrell/J.Dutton 30.00 60.00
HF J.Hamilton/C.Fleming
KI J.Kaleo/K.Ingram 30.00 60.00
NB M.Nash/C.Blalock 30.00 60.00
PG D.Plank/J.Gruden 30.00 60.00
PM R.Philyaw/E.Molden 30.00 60.00
SP C.Stoerner/W.Pettis 40.00 80.00
SS S.Stafford/L.Samuels 30.00 60.00

2006 Upper Deck AFL Arenagraphs Triples

UNPRICED TRIPLE SER.#'d TO 10

2006 Upper Deck AFL Dream Team Dancers

COMPLETE SET (16) 25.00 50.00
DT1 Erin 2.00 5.00
DT2 Kara 2.00 5.00
DT3 Gina 2.00 5.00
DT4 Heidi 2.00 5.00
DT5 Holly 2.00 5.00
DT6 Jessica 2.00 5.00
DT7 Susan 2.00 5.00
DT8 Karen 2.00 5.00
DT9 Meghan 2.00 5.00
DT10 Laverne 2.00 5.00
DT11 Layne 2.00 5.00
DT12 Michelle 2.00 5.00
DT13 Michelle 2.00 5.00
DT14 Nikki 2.00 5.00
DT15 Rachel 2.00 5.00
DT16 Victoria 2.00 5.00

2006 Upper Deck AFL Fabrics

STATED ODDS 1:12
FAAB Aaron Bailey 5.00 12.00
FAAG Aaron Garcia 8.00 20.00
FAAK Andy Kelly 8.00 20.00
FACD Clint Dolezel 8.00 20.00
FACH Charlie Davidson 4.00 10.00
FACR Clay Rush 4.00 10.00
FACS Clint Stoerner 10.00 25.00
FADB David Baker 10.00 25.00
FADG Damien Groce 5.00 12.00
FADH Damian Harrell 8.00 20.00
FAJD John Dutton 8.00 20.00
FAJK John Kaleo 5.00 12.00
FAJR James Roe 5.00 12.00
FAKI Kevin Ingram 4.00 10.00
FAKM Kevin McKenzie 4.00 10.00
FAKN Kevin Nickerson 4.00 10.00
FALM Leon Murray 5.00 12.00
FALS Lawrence Samuels 5.00 12.00
FAMA Marcus Nash 5.00 12.00
FAMG Mark Grieb 8.00 20.00
FAMH Mike Horacek 5.00 12.00
FAMK Marcus Knight 5.00 12.00
FARD Rashied Davis 8.00 20.00
FARP Raymond Philyaw 5.00 12.00
FASB Siaha Burley 5.00 12.00
FASD Silas Demary 4.00 10.00
FASH Shane Stafford 8.00 20.00
FASK Steve Konopka 4.00 10.00
FASS Sean Scott 5.00 12.00
FAST Steve Smith 4.00 10.00
FATB Tom Briggs 4.00 10.00
FATG Tony Graziani 8.00 20.00
FATT T.T. Toliver 4.00 10.00

2006 Upper Deck AFL League Leaders

COMPLETE SET (10) 15.00 40.00
LL1 Mark Grieb 2.50 6.00
LL2 Andy Kelly 2.00 5.00
LL3 Marcus Nash 2.50 6.00
LL4 Siaha Burley 2.00 5.00
LL5 Michael Bishop 2.50 6.00
LL6 Michael Bishop 2.50 6.00
LL7 Siaha Burley 2.00 5.00
LL8 Remy Hamilton 1.50 4.00
LL9 Silas Demary 2.00 5.00
LL10 Billy Parker 1.50 4.00

2012 Upper Deck All-Time Greats

STATED PRINT RUN 99 SER. #'d SETS
16 Dan Marino 4.00 10.00
17 Dan Marino 4.00 10.00
18 Dan Marino 4.00 10.00
19 Dan Marino 4.00 10.00
20 Dan Marino 4.00 10.00
21 Jerry Rice 4.00 10.00
22 Jerry Rice 4.00 10.00
23 Jerry Rice 4.00 10.00
24 Jerry Rice 4.00 10.00
25 Jerry Rice 4.00 10.00
49 Barry Sanders 4.00 10.00
50 Barry Sanders 4.00 10.00
51 Barry Sanders 4.00 10.00
52 Barry Sanders 4.00 10.00
53 Barry Sanders 4.00 10.00
75 Bo Jackson 5.00 12.00
76 Bo Jackson 5.00 12.00
77 Bo Jackson 5.00 12.00
78 Bo Jackson 5.00 12.00
79 Bo Jackson 5.00 12.00
96 Troy Aikman 3.00 8.00
97 Troy Aikman 3.00 8.00
98 Troy Aikman 3.00 8.00
99 Troy Aikman 3.00 8.00
100 Troy Aikman 3.00 8.00

2012 Upper Deck All-Time Greats Bronze

*BRONZE/65: .5X TO 1.2X BASIC CARDS

2012 Upper Deck All-Time Greats Silver

*SILVER/35: .6X TO 1.5X BASIC CARDS

2012 Upper Deck All-Time Greats Athletes of the Century Booklet Autographs

STATED PRINT RUN 5-35
ACBJ Bo Jackson/25
ACBS Barry Sanders/20 75.00 150.00
ACDM Dan Marino/15
ACJR Jerry Rice/15
ACTA Troy Aikman/25 50.00 100.00

2012 Upper Deck All-Time Greats Letterman Autographs

PRINT RUN 7-140
LBJ Bo Jackson/140 30.00 60.00
LBS Barry Sanders/70 75.00 150.00
LDM Dan Marino/24
LJR Jerry Rice/20
LTA Troy Aikman/60 50.00 100.00

2012 Upper Deck All-Time Greats Shining Moments Autographs

PRINT RUN 2-30
SMBJ1 Bo Jackson/10
SMBJ2 Bo Jackson/10
SMBJ3 Bo Jackson/10
SMBJ4 Bo Jackson/10
SMBJ5 Bo Jackson/10
SMBJ6 Bo Jackson/10
SMBS1 Barry Sanders/10 75.00 150.00
SMBS2 Barry Sanders/10 75.00 150.00
SMBS3 Barry Sanders/10 75.00 150.00
SMBS4 Barry Sanders/10 75.00 150.00
SMBS5 Barry Sanders/10 75.00 150.00
SMDM1 Dan Marino/5
SMDM2 Dan Marino/5
SMDM3 Dan Marino/5
SMDM4 Dan Marino/5
SMDM5 Dan Marino/5
SMJR1 Jerry Rice/5
SMJR2 Jerry Rice/5
SMJR3 Jerry Rice/5
SMJR4 Jerry Rice/5
SMJR5 Jerry Rice/5
SMTA1 Troy Aikman/10 30.00 60.00
SMTA2 Troy Aikman/10 30.00 60.00
SMTA3 Troy Aikman/10 30.00 60.00
SMTA4 Troy Aikman/10 30.00 60.00
SMTA5 Troy Aikman/10
SMTA6 Troy Aikman/10

2012 Upper Deck All-Time Greats Signatures

PRINT RUN 3-70
GABJ1 Bo Jackson/20 40.00 80.00
GABJ2 Bo Jackson/20 40.00 80.00
GABJ3 Bo Jackson/20 40.00 80.00
GABJ4 Bo Jackson/20 40.00 80.00
GABJ5 Bo Jackson/20 40.00 80.00
GABS1 Barry Sanders/5 200.00 300.00
GABS2 Barry Sanders/5 200.00 300.00
GABS3 Barry Sanders/5 200.00 300.00
GABS4 Barry Sanders/5 200.00 300.00
GABS5 Barry Sanders/5 200.00 300.00
GADM1 Dan Marino/6
GADM2 Dan Marino/6
GADM3 Dan Marino/6
GADM4 Dan Marino/6
GADM5 Dan Marino/6
GAJR1 Jerry Rice/5
GAJR2 Jerry Rice/5
GAJR3 Jerry Rice/5
GAJR4 Jerry Rice/5
GAJR5 Jerry Rice/5
GATA1 Troy Aikman/10 40.00 80.00
GATA2 Troy Aikman/10 40.00 80.00
GATA3 Troy Aikman/10 40.00 80.00
GATA4 Troy Aikman/10 40.00 80.00
GATA5 Troy Aikman/10 40.00 80.00
GATA6 Troy Aikman/10 40.00 80.00

2012 Upper Deck All-Time Greats Signatures Silver

*SILVER: X TO X BASIC CARDS
PRINT RUN 2-25

2012 Upper Deck All-Time Greats SPx All-Time Dual Forces Autographs

PRINT RUN 1-25
ATF2AJ B.Jackson/T.Aikman/15
ATF2AM Troy Aikman
Dan Marino/10
ATF2HA T.Aikman/H.Hogan/25
ATF2SJ Bo Jackson
Barry Sanders/10
ATF2TJ B.Jackson/M.Tyson/20

2012 Upper Deck All-Time Greats SPx All-Time Forces Autographs

PRINT RUN 1-30
ATFBJ Bo Jackson/25 40.00 80.00
ATFBS Barry Sanders/20
ATFDM Dan Marino/15
ATFJR Jerry Rice/15
ATFTA Troy Aikman/25

1993-97 Upper Deck Authenticated Commemorative Cards

Upper Deck Authenticated, in addition to its line of certified autograph products, produced a continuing series of over-sized (4" by 6") unsigned cards commemorating various events, players and teams. These are often referred to as "C-Cards." These cards typically are serially numbered and encased in clear plastic holders. The print number is noted at the end of the card description when known. Most of these cards are unnumbered but have been assigned numbers below for cataloging purposes.
1 1993 Draft Picks/7500 3.00 8.00
2 Montana
Marino/20,000 4.00 10.00
3 1994 Rookies/10,000 3.00 8.00
4 Joe Montana ND/10,000 5.00 12.00
5 Joe Montana SAL/10,000 5.00 12.00
6 Dallas Cowboys/5000 2.50 6.00
7 Jerry Rice/5000 4.00 10.00
8 Troy Aikman/4500* 4.00 10.00
8AU Troy Aikman AU/500 50.00 100.00
9 Troy Aikman/2500 4.00 10.00
10 Terrell Davis/2500 4.00 10.00
11 Reggie White/5000 1.50 4.00
A133 Joe Montana Blowup '94 6.00 15.00
A139 Dan Marino Blowup '93 6.00 15.00
A140 Troy Aikman Blowup '93 5.00 12.00
A460 Joe Montana Blowup '93 6.00 15.00

1994-96 Upper Deck Authenticated Dan Marino Jumbos

These oversized (roughly 4" by 6") cards were issued only through Upper Deck Authenticated. UDA, through their contract with Dan Marino, was able to issue special cards to honor his record breaking career over a number of years. Each is generally serial numbered and was originally distributed within a plastic card holder.
COMPLETE SET (7) 30.00 60.00
COMMON CARD (1-7) 5.00 12.00
1 Dan Marino 1994 SP
A136 Dan Marino Blowup '94 6.00 15.00

1995 Upper Deck Authenticated Dan Marino 24K Gold

Upper Deck Authenticated issued these 24K Cards in 1995 to honor Dan Marino's record breaking season. The cards measures the standard size and are sculpted using the "Metaltech" process where 24K gold and a nickle-silver combination are embossed onto stainless steel. Each card comes with a screw-down lucite block and black jeweler's pouch.
COMPLETE SET (4) 40.00 100.00
COMMON MARINO (1-4) 12.00 30.00

1995 Upper Deck Authenticated Joe Montana Jumbos

Upper Deck released this 4-card set through it's Upper Deck Authenticated catalog. The cards of the 49ers' great quarterback measure approximately 5" by 3 1/2" and feature color action photos of Joe Montana playing in four Super Bowls. Each card came packaged in its own snap together plastic holder. The backs carry regular and post season statistics as well as the card's number.
COMPLETE SET (4) 16.00 40.00
COMMON CARD (1-4) 4.00 10.00

1999 Upper Deck Century Legends

This 173-card features color action photos of some of the league's all-time great players along with top rookies from the 1999 NFL Draft class. The set contains two subsets and two different Walter Payton signed inserts. Cards 4, 6, 14, 26, 31, 38, and 43 were never released. Two cards, #168B Eric Dickerson CM and #172B John Riggins, were inserted in packs with each featuring an embossed player image that was used to help identify the cards for removal during the pack-out process. Most copies of these two cards were pulled from production before pack-out.
COMPLETE SET (173) 20.00 50.00
1 Jim Brown .50 1.25
2 Jerry Rice .75 2.00
3 Joe Montana 1.00 2.50
5 Johnny Unitas .75 2.00
7 Otto Graham .25 .60
8 Walter Payton 1.25 3.00
9 Dick Butkus .40 1.00
10 Bob Lilly .25 .60
11 Sammy Baugh .30 .75
12 Barry Sanders .50 1.25
13 Deacon Jones .25 .60
15 Gino Marchetti .20 .50
16 John Elway .50 1.25
17 Anthony Munoz .25 .60
18 Ray Nitschke .40 1.00
19 Dick Lane .20 .50
20 John Hannah .20 .50
21 Gale Sayers .30 .75
22 Reggie White .30 .75
23 Ronnie Lott .25 .60
24 Jim Parker .20 .50
25 Merlin Olsen .20 .50
27 Dan Marino .60 1.50
28 Forrest Gregg .20 .50
29 Roger Staubach .40 1.00
30 Jack Lambert .30 .75
32 Marion Motley .25 .60
33 Earl Campbell .30 .75
34 Alan Page .20 .50
35 Bronko Nagurski .30 .75
36 Mel Blount .25 .60
37 Deion Sanders .25 .60
39 Sid Luckman .25 .60
40 Raymond Berry .25 .60
41 Bart Starr .75 2.00
42 Willie Lanier .20 .50
44 Terry Bradshaw .75 2.00
45 Herb Adderley .25 .60
46 Steve Largent .30 .75
47 Jack Ham .30 .75
48 John Mackey .20 .50
49 Bill George .20 .50
50 Willie Brown .20 .50
51 Jerry Rice .75 2.00
52 Barry Sanders .50 1.25
53 John Elway .50 1.25
54 Reggie White .30 .75
55 Dan Marino .60 1.50
56 Deion Sanders .25 .60
57 Bruce Smith .25 .60
58 Steve Young .40 1.00
59 Emmitt Smith .50 1.25
60 Brett Favre .60 1.50
61 Rod Woodson .30 .75
62 Troy Aikman .40 1.00
63 Terrell Davis .25 .60
64 Michael Irvin .30 .75
65 Andre Rison .25 .60
66 Warren Moon .30 .75
67 Thurman Thomas .25 .60
68 Randall Cunningham .25 .60
69 Jerome Bettis .30 .75
70 Junior Seau .25 .60
71 Drew Bledsoe .25 .60
72 Andre Reed .30 .75
73 Tim Brown .30 .75
74 Derrick Thomas .30 .75
75 Jake Plummer .20 .50
76 Kordell Stewart .20 .50
77 Herman Moore .25 .60
78 Shannon Sharpe .25 .60
79 Antonio Freeman .25 .60
80 Ricky Walters .25 .60
81 Warrick Dunn .20 .50
82 Mark Brunell .25 .60
83 Randy Moss .25 .60
84 Fred Taylor .20 .50
85 Curtis Martin .25 .60
86 Keyshawn Johnson .25 .60
87 Eddie George .25 .60
88 Marshall Faulk .25 .60
89 Joey Galloway .25 .60
90 Vinny Testaverde .20 .50
91 Garrison Hearst .20 .50
92 Jimmy Smith .25 .60
93 Doug Flutie .30 .75
94 Napoleon Kaufman .20 .50
95 Natrone Means .25 .60
96 Peyton Manning 1.00 2.50
97 Steve McNair .25 .60
98 Corey Dillon .20 .50
99 Terrell Owens .25 .60
100 Charlie Batch .20 .50
101 Brett Favre APR .50 1.25
102 Terrell Davis APR .20 .50
103 Roger Staubach APR .30 .75
104 Terry Bradshaw APR .60 1.50
105 Fran Tarkenton APR .25 .60
106 Walter Payton APR 1.00 2.50
107 Mark Brunell APR .20 .50
108 Jim Brown APR .40 1.00
109 Kordell Stewart APR .15 .40
110 Bart Starr APR .60 1.50
111 Steve Largent APR .25 .60
112 Raymond Berry APR .20 .50
113 Emmitt Smith APR .40 1.00
114 Forrest Gregg APR .15 .40
115 Drew Bledsoe APR .20 .50
116 Dick Butkus APR .30 .75
117 Johnny Unitas APR .60 1.50
118 Joe Montana APR .75 2.00
119 Deacon Jones APR .20 .50
120 Steve Young APR .30 .75
121 Bob Lilly APR .20 .50
122 Troy Aikman APR .30 .75
123 Alan Page APR .15 .40
124 Earl Campbell APR .25 .60
125 Deion Sanders APR .20 .50
126 Ronnie Lott APR .20 .50
127 Reggie White APR .25 .60
128 Marshall Faulk APR .20 .50
129 Gale Sayers APR .25 .60
130 Dick Lane APR .15 .40
131 Ricky Williams RC .40 1.00
132 Tim Couch RC .30 .75
133 Donovan McNabb RC .75 2.00
134 Daunte Culpepper RC .40 1.00
135 Edgerrin James RC .40 1.00
136 Cade McNown RC .25 .60
137 Torry Holt RC .50 1.25
138 David Boston RC .25 .60
139 Champ Bailey RC .50 1.25
140 Peerless Price RC .25 .60
141 D'Wayne Bates RC .25 .60
142 Joe Germaine RC .30 .75
143 Brock Huard RC .25 .60
144 Chris Claiborne RC .25 .60
145 Jevon Kearse RC .30 .75
146 Troy Edwards RC .25 .60
147 Amos Zereoue RC .25 .60
148 Aaron Brooks RC .30 .75
149 Andy Katzenmoyer RC .30 .75
150 Kevin Faulk RC .25 .60
151 Shaun King RC .25 .60
152 Kevin Johnson RC .30 .75
153 Dameane Douglas RC .25 .60
154 Mike Cloud RC .25 .60
155 Sedrick Irvin RC .25 .60
156 Akili Smith RC .25 .60
157 Rob Konrad RC .25 .60
158 Scott Covington RC .25 .60
159 Jeff Paulk RC .25 .60
160 Shawn Bryson RC .25 .60
161 Joe Montana CM .75 2.00
162 John Elway CM .40 1.00
163 Joe Namath CM .50 1.25
164 Jerry Rice CM .60 1.50
165 Terry Bradshaw CM .60 1.50
166 Jim Brown CM .40 1.00
167 Paul Warfield CM .25 .60
168A Herman Moore CM .20 .50
168B Eric Dickerson CM ERR 25.00 50.00
169 Walter Payton CM 1.00 2.50
170 Roger Staubach CM .30 .75
171 Ken Stabler CM .30 .75
172A Steve Young CM .30 .75
172B John Riggins CM ERR 20.00 50.00
173 Troy Aikman CM .30 .75
174 Fran Tarkenton CM .25 .60
175 Doug Williams CM .20 .50
176 Steve Largent CM .25 .60
177 Marcus Allen CM .25 .60
178 Mike Singletary CM .25 .60
179 Earl Campbell CM .25 .60
180 Dan Fouts CM .20 .50
WPAC Walter Payton AU/50 450.00 700.00
WPCL W.Payton Jsy AU/34 1000.00 1500.00

1999 Upper Deck Century Legends Century Collection

*VETS/100: 8X TO 20X BASIC CARDS
*ROOKIES/100: 5X TO 12X BASIC RC
STATED PRINT RUN 100 SER.#'d SETS

1999 Upper Deck Century Legends 20th Century Superstars

Randomly inserted in packs at the rate on one in 11, this 10-card set features current NFL superstars. Full color action photos are segmented by a radius of points that eminate from behind the player. Card backs carry an "S" prefix.
COMPLETE SET (10) 8.00 20.00
STATED ODDS 1:11
S1 Tim Couch .50 1.25
S2 Ricky Williams .60 1.50
S3 Akili Smith .40 1.00
S4 Donovan McNabb 1.25 3.00
S5 Jake Plummer .40 1.00
S6 Brett Favre 1.25 3.00
S7 Steve Young .75 2.00
S8 Randy Moss .50 1.25
S9 Kordell Stewart .40 1.00
S10 Peyton Manning 2.00 5.00

1999 Upper Deck Century Legends Epic Milestones

Randomly inserted in packs at the rate of one in 11, this 10-card set highlights 10 of the most impressive NFL milestones ever reached. Players range from Walter Payton to Randy Moss. Card backs carry an "EM" prefix.
COMPLETE SET (10) 20.00 40.00
STATED ODDS 1:11
EM1 John Elway 2.50 6.00
EM2 Joe Montana 4.00 10.00
EM3 Randy Moss 2.00 5.00
EM4 Terrell Davis .75 2.00
EM5 Dan Marino 2.50 6.00
EM6 Jamal Anderson .75 2.00
EM7 Jerry Rice 1.50 4.00
EM8 Barry Sanders 2.50 6.00
EM9 Emmitt Smith 1.50 4.00
EM10 Walter Payton 4.00 10.00

1999 Upper Deck Century Legends Epic Signatures

Randomly seeded in packs at the rate of one in 23, this 30-card set features authentic autographs of NFL legends. Featured players include Earl Campbell, Joe Montana and Gale Sayers. A gold parallel version of this set was released also.
STATED ODDS 1:23
*GOLD/100: .6X TO 1.5X BASIC AU
*GOLD/100: .4X TO 1X BASIC AU SP
AM Art Monk 15.00 40.00
CC Cris Carter 12.00 30.00
CJ Charlie Joiner 8.00 20.00
DB Dick Butkus 30.00 60.00
DF Dan Fouts 15.00 40.00
DM Dan Marino 100.00 200.00
DR Dan Reeves 8.00 20.00
DW Doug Williams 12.00 30.00
EC Earl Campbell 20.00 50.00
FL Floyd Little 8.00 20.00
FT Fran Tarkenton 20.00 50.00
GS Gale Sayers 25.00 60.00
HC Harold Carmichael 6.00 15.00
JM Joe Montana 75.00 150.00
JN Joe Namath 50.00 100.00
JR Jerry Rice SP 125.00 200.00
JU Johnny Unitas 200.00 350.00
JY Jack Youngblood 8.00 20.00
LD Len Dawson 12.00 30.00
MS Mike Singletary 10.00 25.00
MY Don Maynard 10.00 25.00
ON Ozzie Newsome 8.00 20.00
PW Paul Warfield 8.00 20.00
RB Raymond Berry 6.00 15.00
RM Randy Moss 50.00 100.00
RS Roger Staubach 50.00 100.00
SL Steve Largent 12.00 30.00
TA Troy Aikman 50.00 100.00
TB Terry Bradshaw 50.00 100.00
TD Terrell Davis 12.00 30.00

1999 Upper Deck Century Legends Jerseys of the Century

Randomly inserted in packs at the rate of one in 418, this 9-card set features pieces of game-used jerseys from some of the NFL's greats. Card number GJ9 was never released.
STATED ODDS 1:418
GJ1 Jerry Rice 25.00 60.00
GJ2 Roger Staubach 20.00 50.00
GJ3 Warren Moon 10.00 25.00
GJ4 Ken Stabler 20.00 50.00
GJ5 Reggie White 20.00 50.00
GJ6 Dan Marino 30.00 80.00
GJ7 Doug Flutie 15.00 40.00
GJ8 Bob Lilly 10.00 25.00
GJ10 Jim Brown 25.00 60.00

1999 Upper Deck Century Legends Tour de Force

Randomly inserted in packs at the rate of one in 23, this 10-card set features current NFL superstars on a silver boardered card with gold foil highlights. Card backs carry an "A" prefix.
COMPLETE SET (10) 15.00 40.00
STATED ODDS 1:23
A1 Tim Couch 1.00 2.50
A2 Ricky Williams 1.25 3.00
A3 Peyton Manning 4.00 10.00
A4 Troy Aikman 1.50 4.00
A5 Jake Plummer .75 2.00
A6 Jamal Anderson 1.00 2.50
A7 Terrell Davis 1.00 2.50
A8 Barry Sanders 2.00 5.00
A9 Fred Taylor .75 2.00
A10 Keyshawn Johnson 1.00 2.50

2009-10 Upper Deck Champ's Hall of Legends Memorabilia

STATED ODDS 1:160
HLBO Bo Jackson 20.00 50.00
HLDM Dan Marino 25.00 60.00
HLEW John Elway 25.00 50.00
HLFH Franco Harris 12.00 30.00
HLJR Jerry Rice 15.00 40.00
HLWM Warren Moon 10.00 25.00

2009-10 Upper Deck Champ's Signatures

STATED ODDS 1:15
CSDF Doug Flutie 25.00 60.00
CSES Emmitt Smith
CSJR Jerry Rice 75.00 150.00
CSSA Barry Sanders
CSWM Warren Moon 60.00 120.00

2002 Upper Deck Collector's Club

This set was issued directly to members of the Upper Deck Collector's Club. Each member could choose a set of cards from one sport only. The cards are highlighted with silver foil on the fronts along with the "club exclusive" notation on both front and back. One of two different jersey cards was issued with each set.
COMPLETE SET (20) 12.50 25.00
NFL1 Peyton Manning 1.25 3.00
NFL2 Aaron Brooks .30 .75
NFL3 Brett Favre 1.00 2.50
NFL4 Daunte Culpepper .40 1.00
NFL5 Donovan McNabb .40 1.00
NFL6 Eddie George .40 1.00
NFL7 Edgerrin James .40 1.00
NFL8 Emmitt Smith .75 2.00
NFL9 Jerome Bettis .50 1.25
NFL10 Jerry Rice 1.00 2.50
NFL11 Kerry Collins .30 .75
NFL12 Kurt Warner .40 1.00
NFL13 LaDainian Tomlinson .50 1.25
NFL14 Marshall Faulk .40 1.00
NFL15 Michael Vick .40 1.00
NFL16 Ahman Green .40 1.00
NFL17 Randy Moss .40 1.00
NFL18 Ricky Williams .40 1.00
NFL19 Shaun Alexander .30 .75
NFL20 Terrell Davis .40 1.00
PMJ Peyton Manning JSY 15.00 40.00
MVJ Michael Vick JSY 5.00 12.00

2014 Upper Deck College Colors

COMPLETE SET (26)
4 Joe Montana FB 1.00 2.50
9 Peyton Manning FB 1.00 2.50
13 John Elway FB .75 2.00
16 Ha Ha Clinton- Dix FB .60 1.50
17 Khalil Mack FB .60 1.50
18 Carlos Hyde FB .60 1.50
19 Bishop Sankey FB .40 1.00
21 Johnny Manziel FB 1.25 3.00
22 Teddy Bridgewater FB 1.25 3.00
23 Jake Matthews FB .40 1.00
24 Odell Beckham Jr FB 2.00 5.00

2011 Upper Deck College Legends

COMPLETE SET (100) 8.00 20.00
1 Keith Jackson .20 .50
2 Tommy McDonald .25 .60
3 Willie Buchanon .20 .50
4 Ron Yary .20 .50
5 Tony Casillas .20 .50
6 Steve Young .40 1.00
7 Jason White .20 .50
8 Daryl Johnston .25 .60
9 Troy Aikman .40 1.00
10 Rocket Ismail .25 .60
11 Bubba Smith .20 .50
12 Roman Gabriel .20 .50
13 Bob Griese .30 .75
14 Alan Page .20 .50
15 Mike Alstott .20 .50
16 Craig Morton .20 .50
17 Bo Jackson .40 1.00
18 John Elway .50 1.25
19 Paul Hornung .30 .75
20 Greg Pruitt .20 .50
21 Jerry Rice .50 1.25
22 Lee Roy Selmon .20 .50
23 George Rogers .25 .60
24 Lee Roy Jordan .20 .50
25 Doug Flutie .25 .60
26 Tim Brown .30 .75
27 Barry Sanders .50 1.25
28 Jim Kelly .30 .75

29 Kellen Winslow Sr. .25 .60
30 Bernie Kosar .25 .60
31 John Cappelletti .20 .50
32 Roger Craig .25 .60
33 Rocky Bleier .25 .60
34 Floyd Little .20 .50
35 Brian Bosworth .25 .60
36 Charles White .20 .50
37 Earl Campbell .30 .75
38 Mike Singletary .30 .75
39 Thurman Thomas .25 .60
40 Eddie George .25 .60
41 Danny Wuerffel .20 .50
42 Billy Cannon .20 .50
43 Rod Woodson .25 .60
44 Dave Casper .20 .50
45 Ozzie Newsome .25 .60
46 Archie Griffin .25 .60
47 Andre Rison .20 .50
48 Chris Spielman .20 .50
49 Antonio Freeman .20 .50
50 Tony Mandarich .20 .50
51 Daryle Lamonica .20 .50
52 Herman Moore .20 .50
53 Cris Carter .30 .75
54 Dwight Stephenson .20 .50
55 Ken Stabler .30 .75
56 Gary Beban .20 .50
57 Gino Torretta .20 .50
58 Anthony Carter .20 .50
59 Ron Dayne .25 .60
60 Andre Ware .25 .60
61 Eric Metcalf .20 .50
62 Steve Owens .20 .50
63 Jim Plunkett .25 .60
64 Ty Detmer .20 .50
65 Herschel Walker .30 .75
66 Todd Marinovich .20 .50
67 Warren Moon .30 .75
68 Gale Sayers .30 .75
69 William Perry .20 .50
70 Dan Marino .60 1.50
71 Tom Rathman .20 .50
72 Joe Theismann .30 .75
73 Billy Sims .25 .60
74 Jim McMahon .25 .60
75 Johnny Rodgers .20 .50
76 Tony Dorsett .30 .75
77 Adrian Peterson .30 .75
78 Drew Brees .30 .75
79 Aaron Rodgers .50 1.25
80 Steven Jackson .20 .50
81 Jake Locker .20 .50
82 Pat Devlin .30 .75
83 Christian Ponder .20 .50
84 Colin Kaepernick .30 .75
85 Prince Amukamara .20 .50
86 DeMarco Murray .40 1.00
87 Kendall Hunter .20 .50
88 Noel Devine .30 .75
89 Daniel Thomas .20 .50
90 Greg Little .25 .60
91 Leonard Hankerson .20 .50
92 Ronald Johnson .20 .50
93 Titus Young .20 .50
94 Blaine Gabbert .20 .50
95 Cam Newton 1.00 2.50
96 Ryan Mallett .20 .50
97 Andy Dalton .40 1.00
98 Mark Ingram .30 .75
99 A.J. Green .50 1.25
100 Julio Jones .60 1.50

2011 Upper Deck College Legends All-Americans

AAAC Anthony Carter .40 1.00
AAAP Adrian Peterson .60 1.50
AABB Brian Bosworth .50 1.25
AABC Billy Cannon .40 1.00
AABG Bob Griese .60 1.50
AABJ Bo Jackson .75 2.00
AABS Barry Sanders 1.00 2.50
AACN Cam Newton 2.00 5.00
AACS Chris Spielman .40 1.00
AACW Charles White .40 1.00
AADF Doug Flutie .50 1.25
AADW Danny Wuerffel .40 1.00
AAEC Earl Campbell .60 1.50
AAGB Gary Beban .40 1.00
AAGP Greg Pruitt .40 1.00
AAGR George Rogers .50 1.25
AAGS Gale Sayers .60 1.50
AAJC John Cappelletti .40 1.00
AAJE John Elway 1.00 2.50
AAJT Joe Theismann .60 1.50
AAJW Jason White .40 1.00
AAKW Kellen Winslow Sr. .50 1.25
AALS Lee Roy Selmon .40 1.00
AAMI Mark Ingram .60 1.50
AAPA Alan Page .40 1.00
AAPH Paul Hornung .60 1.50
AASI Billy Sims .50 1.25
AASM Bubba Smith .40 1.00
AASO Steve Owens .40 1.00
AASY Steve Young .75 2.00
AATA Troy Aikman .75 2.00
AATB Tim Brown .60 1.50
AATC Tony Casillas .40 1.00
AATM Tommy McDonald .50 1.25
AATT Thurman Thomas .50 1.25

2011 Upper Deck College Legends All-Americans Autographs

STATED PRINT RUN 5-70
AAAC Anthony Carter/70 10.00 25.00
AACW Charles White/70 10.00 25.00
AAGP Greg Pruitt/70 10.00 25.00
AAGR George Rogers/70 12.00 30.00
AAJC John Cappelletti/70 12.00 30.00
AAJW Jason White/70 10.00 25.00
AAPA Alan Page/25 12.00 30.00
AASI Billy Sims/70 12.00 30.00
AASO Steve Owens/70 10.00 25.00
AATC Tony Casillas/70 10.00 25.00
AATM Tommy McDonald/70 12.00 30.00

2011 Upper Deck College Legends Autographs

OVERALL AUTO ODDS 3:20
SOME SPs TOO SCARCE TO PRICE
EXCH EXPIRATION: 5/1/2014
1 Keith Jackson 6.00 15.00
2 Tommy McDonald 8.00 20.00
3 Willie Buchanon 6.00 15.00
4 Ron Yary 6.00 15.00
5 Tony Casillas 6.00 15.00
6 Steve Young SP 100.00 200.00
7 Jason White 6.00 15.00
8 Daryl Johnston 8.00 20.00
9 Troy Aikman SP 175.00 300.00
10 Rocket Ismail 12.00 30.00
12 Roman Gabriel 6.00 15.00
13 Bob Griese SP 50.00 100.00
14 Alan Page 6.00 15.00
15 Mike Alstott 8.00 20.00
16 Craig Morton 6.00 15.00
17 Bo Jackson SP 40.00 80.00
18 John Elway SP
19 Paul Hornung 12.00 30.00
20 Greg Pruitt 6.00 15.00
21 Jerry Rice SP
23 George Rogers 8.00 20.00
24 Lee Roy Jordan 6.00 15.00
25 Doug Flutie SP 15.00 40.00
26 Tim Brown SP 25.00 60.00
27 Barry Sanders SP 125.00 250.00
28 Jim Kelly SP 75.00 150.00
29 Kellen Winslow Sr. SP 20.00 40.00
30 Bernie Kosar SP 25.00 60.00
31 John Cappelletti 6.00 15.00
32 Roger Craig 8.00 20.00
33 Rocky Bleier 8.00 20.00
34 Floyd Little 6.00 15.00
35 Brian Bosworth 12.00 30.00
36 Charles White 6.00 15.00
37 Earl Campbell SP 50.00 100.00
38 Mike Singletary 10.00 25.00
39 Thurman Thomas 30.00 80.00
40 Eddie George SP
41 Danny Wuerffel SP 20.00 40.00
42 Billy Cannon SP 15.00 40.00
43 Rod Woodson SP 150.00 300.00
44 Dave Casper SP 10.00 25.00
45 Ozzie Newsome SP 15.00 40.00
46 Archie Griffin SP
48 Chris Spielman 20.00 50.00
49 Antonio Freeman 6.00 15.00
50 Tony Mandarich 10.00 25.00
51 Daryle Lamonica SP 20.00 50.00
52 Herman Moore 6.00 15.00
53 Cris Carter SP 20.00 50.00
54 Dwight Stephenson 8.00 20.00
55 Ken Stabler SP 30.00 60.00
56 Gary Beban SP 10.00 25.00
57 Gino Torretta 8.00 20.00
58 Anthony Carter 6.00 15.00
59 Ron Dayne 8.00 20.00
60 Andre Ware SP 12.00 30.00
61 Eric Metcalf 8.00 20.00
62 Steve Owens 6.00 15.00
64 Ty Detmer SP 10.00 25.00
65 Herschel Walker SP 20.00 50.00
66 Todd Marinovich SP 12.00 30.00
67 Warren Moon SP 20.00 40.00
68 Gale Sayers 20.00 50.00
69 William Perry 6.00 15.00
70 Dan Marino SP
71 Tom Rathman 6.00 15.00
72 Joe Theismann 10.00 25.00
73 Billy Sims 8.00 20.00
74 Jim McMahon 40.00 100.00
75 Johnny Rodgers SP 12.00 30.00
76 Tony Dorsett SP 100.00 200.00
77 Adrian Peterson SP
78 Drew Brees SP
79 Aaron Rodgers SP 400.00 800.00
80 Steven Jackson SP 40.00 100.00
81 Jake Locker 5.00 12.00
82 Pat Devlin 5.00 12.00
83 Christian Ponder 15.00 40.00
84 Colin Kaepernick 8.00 20.00
85 Prince Amukamara 5.00 12.00
86 DeMarco Murray 10.00 25.00
87 Kendall Hunter 6.00 15.00
88 Noel Devine 5.00 12.00
89 Daniel Thomas 5.00 12.00
90 Greg Little 6.00 15.00
91 Leonard Hankerson 5.00 12.00
92 Ronald Johnson 5.00 12.00
93 Titus Young 5.00 12.00
94 Blaine Gabbert SP 15.00 40.00
95 Cam Newton SP 60.00 120.00
96 Ryan Mallett 5.00 12.00
97 Andy Dalton 10.00 25.00
98 Mark Ingram 8.00 20.00
99 A.J. Green SP 40.00 100.00
100 Julio Jones SP 30.00 80.00

2011 Upper Deck College Legends Bowl Game Heroes

HAC Anthony Carter .40 1.00
BGHAP Adrian Peterson .60 1.50
BGHAR Aaron Rodgers 1.00 2.50
BGHBB Brian Bosworth .50 1.25
BGHBJ Bo Jackson .75 2.00
BGHBK Bernie Kosar .50 1.25
BGHBS Barry Sanders 1.00 2.50
BGHCN Cam Newton 2.00 5.00
BGHCW Charles White .40 1.00
BGHDB Drew Brees .60 1.50
BGHDF Doug Flutie .50 1.25
BGHDJ Daryl Johnston .50 1.25
BGHDM Dan Marino 1.25 3.00
BGHDW Danny Wuerffel .40 1.00
BGHEC Earl Campbell .60 1.50
BGHGB Gary Beban .40 1.00
BGHGP Greg Pruitt .40 1.00
BGHJK Jim Kelly .60 1.50
BGHJM Jim McMahon .50 1.25
BGHJP Jim Plunkett .50 1.25
BGHMI Mark Ingram .60 1.50
BGHRD Ron Dayne .50 1.25
BGHSI Billy Sims .50 1.25
BGHTT Thurman Thomas .50 1.25
BGHWM Warren Moon .60 1.50

2011 Upper Deck College Legends Bowl Game Heroes Autographs

STATED PRINT RUN 5-75
BGHAC Anthony Carter/75 10.00 25.00
BGHBB Brian Bosworth/30 30.00 60.00
BGHCN Cam Newton/75 50.00 120.00
BGHCW Charles White/75 8.00 20.00
BGHDJ Daryl Johnston/75 12.00 30.00
BGHDW Danny Wuerffel/30 12.00 30.00
BGHGB Gary Beban/75 8.00 20.00
BGHGP Greg Pruitt/75 10.00 25.00
BGHSI Billy Sims/75 12.00 30.00
BGHWM Warren Moon/30 25.00 60.00

2011 Upper Deck College Legends Decades Best

AC Anthony Carter .40 1.00
DBAG Archie Griffin .50 1.25
DBAP Adrian Peterson .60 1.50
DBBB Brian Bosworth .50 1.25
DBBG Bob Griese .60 1.50
DBBJ Bo Jackson .75 2.00
DBBK Bernie Kosar .50 1.25
DBBS Barry Sanders 1.00 2.50
DBCC Cris Carter .60 1.50
DBCM Craig Morton .40 1.00
DBCW Charles White .40 1.00
DBDF Doug Flutie .50 1.25
DBDM Dan Marino 1.25 3.00
DBEC Earl Campbell .60 1.50
DBEG Eddie George .50 1.25
DBFL Floyd Little .40 1.00
DBGP Greg Pruitt .40 1.00
DBGR George Rogers .50 1.25
DBGS Gale Sayers .60 1.50
DBJC John Cappelletti .40 1.00
DBJE John Elway 1.00 2.50
DBJR Jerry Rice 1.00 2.50
DBJT Joe Theismann .60 1.50
DBJW Jason White .40 1.00
DBKW Kellen Winslow Sr. .50 1.25
DBLS Lee Roy Selmon .40 1.00
DBMS Mike Singletary .60 1.50
DBPA Alan Page .40 1.00
DBPH Paul Hornung .60 1.50
DBRD Ron Dayne .50 1.25
DBRG Roman Gabriel .40 1.00
DBRY Ron Yary .40 1.00
DBSI Billy Sims .50 1.25
DBSM Bubba Smith .40 1.00
DBSO Steve Owens .40 1.00
DBSY Steve Young .75 2.00
DBTA Troy Aikman .75 2.00
DBTB Tim Brown .60 1.50
DBTM Tommy McDonald .50 1.25
DBTT Thurman Thomas .50 1.25

2011 Upper Deck College Legends Decades Best Autographs

STATED PRINT RUN 5-80
DBAC Anthony Carter
DBAG Archie Griffin/15 15.00 40.00
DBAP Adrian Peterson
DBBB Brian Bosworth/15 40.00 100.00
DBBG Bob Griese
DBBJ Bo Jackson
DBBK Bernie Kosar
DBBS Barry Sanders
DBCC Cris Carter
DBCM Craig Morton/80 10.00 25.00
DBCW Charles White/80 8.00 20.00
DBDF Doug Flutie
DBDM Dan Marino
DBEC Earl Campbell/15 15.00 40.00
DBEG Eddie George/5
DBFL Floyd Little/80 10.00 25.00
DBGP Greg Pruitt/80 10.00 25.00
DBGR George Rogers/80 12.00 30.00
DBGS Gale Sayers/5
DBJC John Cappelletti/80 10.00 25.00
DBJE John Elway/5
DBJR Jerry Rice/5
DBJT Joe Theismann
DBJW Jason White/80 12.00 30.00
DBKW Kellen Winslow Sr.
DBMS Mike Singletary/15 40.00 80.00
DBPA Alan Page/15 12.00 30.00
DBPH Paul Hornung
DBRD Ron Dayne
DBRG Roman Gabriel/15 12.00 30.00
DBRY Ron Yary/80 10.00 25.00
DBSI Billy Sims/80 12.00 30.00
DBSO Steve Owens
DBSY Steve Young/5
DBTA Troy Aikman
DBTB Tim Brown
DBTM Tommy McDonald/80 12.00 30.00
DBTT Thurman Thomas

2011 Upper Deck College Legends Inscriptions

STATED PRINT RUN 5-99
CIAC Anthony Carter/25 30.00 60.00
CIAG Archie Griffin/5
CIAM Prince Amukamara
CIAP Adrian Peterson
CIAW Andre Ware/25 15.00 40.00
CIBB Brian Bosworth/25 40.00 80.00
CIBC Billy Cannon/25 15.00 40.00
CIBG Bob Griese
CIBJ Bo Jackson
CIBK Bernie Kosar
CIBS Barry Sanders
CICK Colin Kaepernick/99 10.00 25.00
CICM Craig Morton/99 10.00 25.00
CICN Cam Newton/25 75.00 150.00
CICP Christian Ponder/25 12.00 30.00
CICS Chris Spielman/25 15.00 40.00
CICW Charles White/99 10.00 25.00
CIDF Doug Flutie/5
CIDM DeMarco Murray/99 12.00 30.00
CIDW Danny Wuerffel/25 15.00 40.00
CIEC Earl Campbell
CIEG Eddie George
CIEM Eric Metcalf/25 12.00 30.00
CIFL Floyd Little/99 12.00 30.00
CIGA Blaine Gabbert/99 6.00 15.00
CIGB Gary Beban/25 12.00 30.00
CIGL Greg Little/99 8.00 20.00
CIGP Greg Pruitt/99 10.00 25.00
CIGR George Rogers/99 12.00 30.00
CIGS Gale Sayers
CIJC John Cappelletti/99 10.00 25.00
CIJL Jake Locker/99 6.00 15.00
CIJR Johnny Rodgers
CIJT Joe Theismann/99 15.00 40.00
CIJW Jason White/99 15.00 40.00
CIKH Kendall Hunter/99 6.00 15.00
CIKW Kellen Winslow Sr.
CILH Leonard Hankerson/99 8.00 20.00
CIMA Tony Mandarich/25 15.00 40.00
CIMI Mark Ingram/25 12.00 30.00
CIND Noel Devine/99 8.00 20.00
CION Ozzie Newsome/25 15.00 40.00
CIPA Alan Page/99 10.00 25.00
CIPH Paul Hornung/99 15.00 40.00
CIRB Rocky Bleier/99 15.00 40.00
CIRD Ron Dayne/25 20.00 50.00
CIRG Roman Gabriel/25 12.00 30.00
CIRJ Ronald Johnson/99 6.00 15.00
CIRY Ron Yary/99 10.00 25.00
CISI Billy Sims/99 12.00 30.00
CISO Steve Owens
CITB Tim Brown/5
CITC Tony Casillas/99 10.00 25.00
CITM Tommy McDonald/99 12.00 30.00
CITR Tom Rathman/99 12.00 30.00
CITY Titus Young/99 10.00 25.00
CIWP William Perry/25 12.00 30.00

1992 Upper Deck Comic Ball 4

This 198-card set of Upper Deck's animation-style trading cards contains ten 18-card stories; 16 special cards featuring Marino, Taylor, Rice and Thomas with their Looney Toons teammates, and two checklist cards. We've listed below only the cards which feature NFL players. Packs also contained nine holograms featuring NFL standouts Dan Marino, Lawrence Taylor, Jerry Rice and Thurman Thomas with Looney Toons characters such as Bugs Bunny, Daffy Duck, Elmer Fudd, Porky Pig, The Tasmanian Devil, Sylvester and Tweety.

COMPLETE SET (198) 10.00 20.00
1 Pop Goes The Martian .20 .50
5 Pop Goes The Martian .08 .25
6 Pop Goes The Martian .08 .25
10 Pop Goes The Martian .30 .75
11 Pop Goes The Martian .30 .75
15 Pop Goes The Martian .30 .75
16 Pop Goes The Martian .30 .75
19 Hang Time .20 .50
24 Hang Time .08 .25
25 Hang Time .08 .25
27 Hang Time .30 .75
31 Hang Time .30 .75
36 Hang Time .30 .75
37 Run and Shout .20 .50
39 Run and Shout .08 .25
44 Run and Shout .08 .25
46 Run and Shout .08 .25
47 Run and Shout .08 .25
48 Run and Shout .08 .25
49 Run and Shout .08 .25
50 Run and Shout .08 .25
51 Run and Shout .08 .25
52 Run and Shout .08 .25
55 I Get a Kick Out of You .20 .50
57 I Get a Kick Out of You .20 .50
58 I Get a Kick Out of You .20 .50
59 I Get a Kick Out of You .20 .50
60 I Get a Kick Out of You .30 .75
72 I Get a Kick Out of You .30 .75
73 Zee Smell of Victory .20 .50
74 Zee Smell of Victory .08 .25
75 Zee Smell of Victory .08 .25
80 Zee Smell of Victory .08 .25
82 Zee Smell of Victory .08 .25
83 Zee Smell of Victory .08 .25
84 Zee Smell of Victory .08 .25
85 Zee Smell of Victory .08 .25
86 Zee Smell of Victory .08 .25
91 Half Time .30 .75
92 Half Time .30 .75
93 Half Time .20 .50
94 Half Time .20 .50
95 Half Time .20 .50
96 Half Time .08 .25
97 Half Time .08 .25
98 Half Time .08 .25
100 Crowd Control .20 .50
109 Crowd Control .08 .25
110 Crowd Control .08 .25
111 Crowd Control .08 .25
112 Crowd Control .08 .25
113 Crowd Control .08 .25
116 Crowd Control .08 .25
117 Crowd Control .08 .25
118 Repeat Defender .20 .50
120 Repeat Defender .08 .25
125 Repeat Defender .08 .25
126 Repeat Defender .08 .25
127 Repeat Defender .08 .25
129 Repeat Defender .08 .25
131 Repeat Defender .08 .25
132 Repeat Defender .20 .50
136 Hoppin' Half Time .20 .50
137 Hoppin' Half Time .30 .75
142 Hoppin' Half Time .30 .75
147 Hoppin' Half Time .30 .75
149 Hoppin' Half Time .30 .75
151 Hoppin' Half Time .30 .75
152 Hoppin' Half Time .20 .50
153 Hoppin' Half Time .30 .75
154 Martian Touchdown .20 .50
155 Martian Touchdown .08 .25
159 Martian Touchdown .08 .25
160 Martian Touchdown .08 .25
169 Martian Touchdown .30 .75
170 Martian Touchdown .30 .75
171 Martian Touchdown .30 .75
172 Gut-Check Time .20 .50
174 Gut-Check Time .30 .75
175 Gut-Check Time .30 .75
176 Gut-Check Time .30 .75
177 Gut-Check Time .30 .75
178 Gut-Check Time .30 .75
179 Gut-Check Time .30 .75
180 Gut-Check Time .30 .75
190 Half Time .08 .25
191 Half Time .08 .25
192 Half Time .20 .50
193 Half Time .20 .50
194 Half Time .30 .75
195 Half Time .30 .75
196 Half Time .08 .25
197 Half Time .30 .75

1992 Upper Deck Comic Ball 4 Holograms

1 Dan Marino 2.00 5.00
2 Dan Marino 2.00 5.00
3 Jerry Rice 1.25 3.00
4 Jerry Rice 1.25 3.00
with Taz
5 Jerry Rice 1.25 3.00
with Yosemite Sam
6 Lawrence Taylor .75 2.00
7 Lawrence Taylor .75 2.00
with Sylvester
8 Thurman Thomas 1.00 2.50
with K-9
9 Thurman Thomas 1.00 2.50

2014 Upper Deck Conference Greats

COMPLETE SET (160) 40.00 80.00
COMP.SET w/o SP's (100) 10.00 25.00
101-140 STATED ODDS 1:6 HOBBY
141-160 STATED ODDS 1:12 HOBBY
*PEWTER: .5X TO 1.2X BASIC CARDS
*COPPER: 1.5X TO 4X BASIC CARDS
1 Joe Namath .25 .60
2 Bart Starr .30 .75
3 Andrew Zow .12 .30
4 Ozzie Newsome .15 .40
5 Steve Sloan .12 .30
6 Cornelius Bennett .12 .30
7 Nick Saban .20 .50
8 Kevin Norwood .12 .30
9 Alabama Team Schedule .12 .30
10 Carlos Alvarez .12 .30
11 John Reaves .12 .30
12 Danny Wuerffel .12 .30
13 Ike Hilliard .12 .30
14 Chris Doering .12 .30
15 Shane Matthews .12 .30
16 Lomas Brown .12 .30
17 Doug Johnson .12 .30
18 Loucheiz Purifoy .12 .30
19 Dominique Easley .12 .30
20 Trey Burton .12 .30
21 Florida Team Schedule .12 .30
22 Anthony Lucas .12 .30
23 Clint Stoerner .12 .30
24 Marcus Monk .12 .30
25 James Rouse .12 .30
26 Shawn Andrews .12 .30
27 Travis Swanson .12 .30
28 Arkansas Team Schedule .12 .30
29 Garrison Hearst .12 .30
30 Thomas Brown .12 .30
31 Hines Ward .15 .40
32 David Greene .12 .30
33 D.J. Shockley .12 .30
34 Joe Cox .12 .30
35 Matthew Stafford .15 .40
36 Fred Gibson .12 .30
37 Eric Zeier .12 .30
38 Rodney Hampton .12 .30
39 Terrell Davis .07 .20
40 Aaron Murray .12 .30
41 Georgia Team Schedule .12 .30
42 Bo Jackson .25 .60
43 Frank Thomas .40 1.00
44 Tyrone Goodson .12 .30
45 Auburn Team Schedule .12 .30
46 Babe Parilli .12 .30
47 Jared Lorenzen .12 .30
48 Craig Yeast .12 .30
49 George Adams .12 .30
50 Dermontti Dawson .12 .30
51 Oliver Barnett .12 .30
52 Tim Couch .12 .30
53 Kentucky Team Schedule .12 .30
54 Kevin Faulk .12 .30
55 Charles Alexander .12 .30
56 Josh Reed .12 .30
57 Jeff Wickersham .12 .30
58 David LaFleur .12 .30
59 Wendell Davis .12 .30
60 Zach Mettenberger .12 .30
61 Odell Beckham Jr. .30 .75
62 Jeremy Hill .15 .40
63 Jarvis Landry .25 .60
64 J.C. Copeland .20 .50
65 Lamin Barrow .20 .50
66 LSU Team Schedule .12 .30
67 Duce Staley .12 .30
68 Andrew Pinnock .12 .30
69 Steve Taneyhill .12 .30
70 George Rogers .12 .30
71 Robert Brooks .15 .40
72 Todd Ellis .12 .30
73 Bruce Ellington .12 .30
74 Victor Hampton .15 .40
75 South Carolina Team Schedule .12 .30
76 Deuce McAllister .15 .40
77 Jeff Herrod .12 .30
78 Donte Moncrief .12 .30
79 Mississippi Team Schedule .12 .30
80 Peyton Manning .40 1.00
81 Anthony Miller .20 .50
82 Phillip Fulmer .12 .30
83 Daniel McCullers .15 .40
84 Rajion Neal .12 .30
85 Tennessee Team Schedule .12 .30
86 Derrick Taite .12 .30
87 Eric Moulds .12 .30
88 Jerious Norwood .12 .30
89 Mississippi State Team Schedule .12 .30
90 Alan Young .12 .30
91 Greg Zolman .12 .30
92 Vanderbilt Team Schedule .12 .30
93 Johnny Manziel .20 .50
94 Derel Walker .15 .40
95 Ben Malena .15 .40
96 Mike Evans .30 .75
97 Texas A&M Team Schedule .12 .30
98 Michael Sam .12 .30
99 E.J. Gaines .12 .30
100 Missouri Team Schedule .12 .30
101 Peyton Manning S .75 2.00
102 Antonio Langham S .25 .60
103 Fred Weary S .25 .60
104 Kenny Irons S .25 .60
105 Erik Ainge S .25 .60
106 Matthew Stafford S .30 .75
107 Eric Martin S .25 .60
108 Jevan Snead S .25 .60
109 Terrence Edwards S .25 .60
110 Dan Stricker S .25 .60
111 Nick Saban S .40 1.00
112 Wayne Madkin S .25 .60
113 Quincy Carter S .25 .60
114 Billy Ray Smith S .25 .60
115 Brandon Bennett S .25 .60
116 Bo Jackson S .50 1.25
117 Freddie Milons S .25 .60
118 Andre Woodson S .25 .60
119 Michael Clayton S .25 .60
120 Hines Ward S .30 .75
121 Johnny Manziel R .40 1.00
122 Marcus Lucas R .30 .75
123 Ha Ha Clinton-Dix R .30 .75
124 Alfred Blue R .25 .60
125 Aaron Murray R .25 .60
126 Jake Matthews R .25 .60
127 Jay Prosch R .40 1.00
128 Chris Davis R .25 .60
129 Odell Beckham Jr. R .60 1.50
130 Kony Ealy R .30 .75
131 C.J. Mosley R .30 .75
132 LaDarius Perkins R .25 .60
133 Zach Mettenberger R .25 .60
134 L'Damian Washington R .30 .75
135 Dee Ford R .25 .60
136 Jaylen Watkins R .25 .60
137 Mike Evans R .60 1.50
138 James Franklin R .30 .75
139 Arthur Lynch R .25 .60
140 Vinnie Sunseri R .40 1.00
141 George Rogers MM .40 1.00
142 Peyton Manning MM 1.25 3.00
143 Matthew Stafford MM .50 1.25
144 Bo Jackson MM .75 2.00
145 Joe Namath MM .75 2.00
146 Hines Ward MM .50 1.25
147 Danny Wuerffel MM .40 1.00
148 Nick Saban MM .60 1.50
149 Johnny Manziel MM .60 1.50
150 Chris Davis MM .40 1.00
151 D.Wuerffel/C.Alvarez AS .40 1.00
152 M.Stafford/A.Murray AS .50 1.25
153 P.Manning/P.Fulmer AS 2.50 6.00
154 E.Zeier/G.Hearst AS .40 1.00
155 N.Saban/J.Namath AS .75 2.00
156 T.Couch/J.Lorenzen AS .40 1.00
157 D.Staley/G.Rogers AS .40 1.00
158 M.Stafford/H.Ward AS .50 1.25
159 J.Manziel/M.Evans AS 1.00 2.50
160 Z.Mettenberger/O.Beckham Jr. AS 1.00 2.50

2014 Upper Deck Conference Greats Autographs

1 Joe Namath A 40.00 80.00
2 Bart Starr A 40.00 80.00
3 Andrew Zow C 3.00 8.00
4 Ozzie Newsome C 10.00 25.00
5 Steve Sloan C 3.00 8.00
6 Cornelius Bennett C 3.00 8.00
7 Nick Saban A EXCH 100.00 200.00
8 Kevin Norwood C 3.00 8.00
10 Carlos Alvarez C 8.00 20.00
11 John Reaves C 12.00 30.00
12 Danny Wuerffel C 12.00 30.00
13 Ike Hilliard C 12.00 30.00
14 Chris Doering C 3.00 8.00
15 Shane Matthews B 6.00 15.00
17 Doug Johnson B 6.00 15.00
18 Loucheiz Purifoy C 3.00 8.00
19 Dominique Easley C 3.00 8.00
20 Trey Burton C 3.00 8.00
22 Anthony Lucas C 3.00 8.00
23 Clint Stoerner C 6.00 15.00
24 Marcus Monk C 3.00 8.00
25 James Rouse C 8.00 20.00
30 Thomas Brown C 3.00 8.00
31 Hines Ward A 15.00 40.00
32 David Greene C 3.00 8.00
33 D.J. Shockley C 3.00 8.00
34 Joe Cox C 3.00 8.00
35 Matthew Stafford A 25.00 50.00
36 Fred Gibson C 3.00 8.00
37 Eric Zeier C 3.00 8.00
38 Rodney Hampton C 3.00 8.00
39 Terrell Davis A 8.00 20.00
40 Aaron Murray C 3.00 8.00
42 Bo Jackson A 75.00 150.00
43 Frank Thomas A
44 Tyrone Goodson C 3.00 8.00
46 Babe Parilli C 3.00 8.00
47 Jared Lorenzen C 3.00 8.00
48 Craig Yeast C 3.00 8.00
50 Dermontti Dawson C 8.00 20.00
51 Oliver Barnett C 3.00 8.00
52 Tim Couch C 3.00 8.00
54 Kevin Faulk C 3.00 8.00
55 Charles Alexander C 20.00 40.00
57 Jeff Wickersham C 3.00 8.00
58 David LaFleur C 3.00 8.00
59 Wendell Davis C 3.00 8.00
60 Zach Mettenberger C 3.00 8.00
61 Odell Beckham Jr. C EXCH 40.00 80.00
62 Jeremy Hill C 4.00 10.00
63 Jarvis Landry C 6.00 15.00
65 Lamin Barrow C 5.00 12.00
67 Duce Staley B 12.00 30.00
69 Steve Taneyhill C 3.00 8.00
70 George Rogers C 10.00 25.00
71 Robert Brooks C 6.00 15.00
72 Todd Ellis B 6.00 15.00
73 Bruce Ellington C 3.00 8.00
74 Victor Hampton C 4.00 10.00
77 Jeff Herrod C 3.00 8.00
78 Donte Moncrief C 3.00 8.00
80 Peyton Manning A 150.00 250.00
81 Anthony Miller C 5.00 12.00
83 Daniel McCullers B 8.00 20.00
84 Rajion Neal C 3.00 8.00
86 Derrick Taite C 3.00 8.00
87 Eric Moulds C 3.00 8.00
88 Jerious Norwood C 3.00 8.00
90 Alan Young C 3.00 8.00
91 Greg Zolman C 3.00 8.00
93 Johnny Manziel A 20.00 50.00
94 Derel Walker C 4.00 10.00
95 Ben Malena C 4.00 10.00
96 Mike Evans A 30.00 80.00
98 Michael Sam C 3.00 8.00
99 E.J. Gaines B 10.00 25.00
101 Peyton Manning S A 50.00 125.00
102 Antonio Langham S B
103 Fred Weary S B
104 Kenny Irons S B
105 Erik Ainge S B
106 Matthew Stafford S A
107 Eric Martin S B
108 Jevan Snead S B
109 Terrence Edwards S B
110 Dan Stricker S B
111 Nick Saban S A EXCH 200.00 300.00
112 Wayne Madkin S B
113 Quincy Carter S B
114 Billy Ray Smith S B
115 Brandon Bennett S B
116 Bo Jackson S A
117 Freddie Milons S B
118 Andre Woodson S B
120 Hines Ward S A
121 Johnny Manziel R A
122 Marcus Lucas R B
123 Ha Ha Clinton-Dix R B 8.00 20.00
124 Alfred Blue R B 6.00 15.00
125 Aaron Murray R B 6.00 15.00
126 Jake Matthews R B 6.00 15.00
127 Jay Prosch R B 20.00 40.00
128 Chris Davis R B 6.00 15.00
129 Odell Beckham Jr. R A
130 Kony Ealy R B 8.00 20.00
131 C.J. Mosley R B 8.00 20.00
132 LaDarius Perkins R B 6.00 15.00
133 Zach Mettenberger R B 10.00 25.00
135 Dee Ford R A
137 Mike Evans R A
138 James Franklin R B
139 Arthur Lynch R B
141 George Rogers MM B
142 Peyton Manning MM A
143 Matthew Stafford MM A 40.00 80.00
144 Bo Jackson MM A 40.00 80.00
145 Joe Namath MM A 40.00 80.00
146 Hines Ward MM B
147 Danny Wuerffel MM B 12.00 30.00
148 Nick Saban MM A EXCH
149 Johnny Manziel MM A 25.00 60.00
150 Chris Davis MM B 12.00 30.00
151 D.Wuerffel/C.Alvarez
152 M.Stafford/A.Murray
154 E.Zeier/G.Hearst
155 N.Saban/J.Namath
156 T.Couch/J.Lorenzen
157 D.Staley/G.Rogers
158 M.Stafford/H.Ward
159 J.Manziel/M.Evans 25.00 60.00
160 Z.Mettenberger/O.Beckham Jr.

2014 Upper Deck Conference Greats Jersey Autographs

14 Chris Doering/25 6.00 15.00
15 Shane Matthews/25 6.00 15.00
33 D.J. Shockley/25 6.00 15.00
34 Joe Cox/25 6.00 15.00
37 Eric Zeier/25 6.00 15.00
40 Aaron Murray/25 6.00 15.00
47 Jarod Lorenzen/25 6.00 15.00
52 Tim Couch/25 6.00 15.00
58 David LaFleur/25 6.00 15.00
60 Zach Mettenberger/25
62 Jeremy Hill/25 EXCH 8.00 20.00
63 Jarvis Landry/25
73 Bruce Ellington/25 EXCH 6.00 15.00
78 Donte Moncrief/25
87 Eric Moulds/25 6.00 15.00
98 Michael Sam/25

2014 Upper Deck Conference Greats Jerseys

1 Joe Namath 10.00 25.00
2 Bart Starr 8.00 20.00
4 Ozzie Newsome 6.00 15.00
6 Cornelius Bennett 4.00 10.00
10 Carlos Alvarez 3.00 8.00
12 Danny Wuerffel 3.00 8.00
13 Ike Hilliard 3.00 8.00
14 Chris Doering 3.00 8.00
15 Shane Matthews 3.00 8.00
29 Garrison Hearst 3.00 8.00
31 Hines Ward 4.00 10.00
33 D.J. Shockley 3.00 8.00
34 Joe Cox 3.00 8.00
37 Eric Zeier 3.00 8.00
39 Terrell Davis 2.00 5.00
40 Aaron Murray 2.00 5.00
42 Bo Jackson 6.00 15.00
46 Babe Parilli 3.00 8.00
47 Jared Lorenzen 3.00 8.00
52 Tim Couch 3.00 8.00
58 David LaFleur 3.00 8.00
60 Zach Mettenberger 2.00 5.00
61 Odell Beckham Jr. 5.00 12.00
62 Jeremy Hill 2.50 6.00
63 Jarvis Landry 4.00 10.00
70 George Rogers 3.00 8.00
73 Bruce Ellington 2.00 5.00
78 Donte Moncrief 2.00 5.00
80 Peyton Manning 10.00 25.00
87 Eric Moulds 3.00 8.00
93 Johnny Manziel 3.00 8.00
96 Mike Evans 5.00 12.00
98 Michael Sam 2.00 5.00

2014 Upper Deck Conference Greats Jumbos

ONE PER HOBBY BOX
BT1 Johnny Manziel .50 1.25
BT2 Jarvis Landry .60 1.50
BT3 Kevin Norwood .30 .75
BT4 Aaron Murray .30 .75
BT5 Donte Moncrief .30 .75
BT6 C.J. Mosley .40 1.00
BT7 Mike Evans .75 2.00
BT8 Michael Sam .30 .75
BT9 Arthur Lynch .30 .75
BT10 Zach Mettenberger .30 .75
BT11 Bruce Ellington .30 .75
BT12 Chris Davis .30 .75
BT13 Odell Beckham Jr. .75 2.00
BT14 Ha Ha Clinton-Dix .40 1.00
BT15 Jeremy Hill .40 1.00
BT16 Joe Namath 5.00 12.00
BT17 Peyton Manning 15.00 30.00
BT18 Hines Ward .40 1.00
BT19 Danny Wuerffel .30 .75
BT20 Matthew Stafford .40 1.00
BT21 Bo Jackson 4.00 10.00

2014 Upper Deck Conference Greats Manufactured Patches

PRIMARY STATED ODDS 1:94 HOBBY
SECONDARY STATED ODDS 1:165 HOBBY
RIVALRY STATED ODDS 1:578 HOBBY
STARS STATED ODDS 1:1540 HOBBY
P1 Alabama Primary Logo 20.00 40.00
P2 Auburn Primary Logo 8.00 20.00
P3 Vanderbilt Primary Logo 4.00 10.00
P4 Tennessee Primary Logo 8.00 20.00
P5 Mississippi Primary Logo 4.00 10.00
P6 Mississippi State Primary Logo 4.00 10.00
P7 Texas A&M Primary Logo 8.00 20.00
P8 Georgia Primary Logo 10.00 25.00
P9 Louisiana State Primary Logo 6.00 15.00
P10 Florida Primary Logo 10.00 25.00
P11 Arkansas Primary Logo 6.00 15.00
P12 Kentucky Primary Logo 4.00 10.00
P13 Missouri Primary Logo
P14 South Carolina Primary Logo 5.00 12.00
P15 Alabama Secondary Logo 75.00 125.00
P16 Auburn Secondary Logo
P17 Louisiana St. Secondary Logo 8.00 20.00
P18 Florida Secondary Logo 15.00 40.00
P19 Georgia Secondary Logo 15.00 40.00
P20 Texas A&M Secondary Logo 12.00 30.00
P21 Vanderbilt Secondary Logo
P22 Tennessee Secondary Logo 30.00 60.00
P23 Mississippi Secondary Logo 6.00 15.00
P24 Mississippi Secondary Logo 6.00 15.00
P25 S.C. Secondary Logo 8.00 20.00
P26 Kentucky Secondary Logo
P27 Arkansas Secondary Logo 10.00 25.00
P28 Missouri Secondary Logo
P29 Iron Bowl Trophy R
P30 Tiger Bowl R 15.00 40.00
P31 Magnolia Bowl Trophy R
P32 Egg Bowl Trophy R
P33 The Mayors Cup R 10.00 25.00
P34 The Golden Boot Trophy R 12.00 30.00
P35 Southwest Classic Trophy R 10.00 25.00
P36 Okefenokee Oar Trophy R
P37 Nick Saban P
P39 Bo Jackson P
P40 Johnny Manziel P 20.00 50.00
P41 Peyton Manning P 75.00 125.00
P42 Matthew Stafford P

2008 Upper Deck Draft Edition

COMPLETE SET (250) 25.00 60.00
COMP.RC SET (100) 15.00 30.00
101-200: TWO PER PACK
201-250: ONE PER PACK
1 Anthony Morelli RC .30 .75
2 Adarius Bowman RC .40 1.00
3 Ali Highsmith RC .30 .75
4 Andre Woodson RC .30 .75
5 Allen Patrick RC .30 .75
6 Antoine Cason RC .40 1.00
7 Aqib Talib RC .50 1.25
8 Ben Moffitt RC .30 .75
9 Gosder Cherilus RC .40 1.00
10 Brian Brohm RC .30 .75
11 Calais Campbell RC .40 1.00
12 Chad Henne RC .40 1.00
13 Chevis Jackson RC .30 .75
14 Davone Bess RC .40 1.00
15 Justin Forsett RC .40 1.00
16 Chris Ellis RC .30 .75
17 Chris Long RC .40 1.00
18 Colt Brennan RC .40 1.00
19 Craig Steltz RC .30 .75
20 DJ Hall RC .30 .75
21 Dan Connor RC .30 .75
22 Darren McFadden RC .30 .75
23 DeMario Pressley RC .40 1.00
24 Dennis Dixon RC .30 .75
25 Derrick Harvey RC .30 .75
26 DeSean Jackson RC .60 1.50
27 D.Rodgers-Cromartie RC .40 1.00
28 Donnie Avery RC .40 1.00
29 Dorien Bryant RC .40 1.00
30 Dre Moore RC .30 .75
31 Kellen Davis RC .30 .75
32 DaJuan Morgan RC .40 1.00
33 Earl Bennett RC .50 1.25
34 Early Doucet RC .30 .75
35 Kentwan Balmer RC .30 .75
36 Erik Ainge RC .30 .75
37 Felix Jones RC .30 .75
38 Frank Okam RC .30 .75
39 Fred Davis RC .30 .75
40 Glenn Dorsey RC .30 .75
41 Harry Douglas RC .40 1.00
42 Jack Ikegwuonu RC .30 .75
43 Bruce Davis RC .40 1.00
44 Jacob Tamme RC .40 1.00
45 Jake Long RC .50 1.25
46 Jamaal Charles RC .50 1.25
47 James Hardy RC .30 .75
48 Erin Henderson RC .40 1.00
49 J Leman RC .30 .75
50 Joe Flacco RC .60 1.50
51 John Carlson RC .30 .75
52 John David Booty RC .30 .75
53 Jonathan Hefney RC .30 .75
54 Jonathan Stewart RC .50 1.25
55 Jordy Nelson RC 1.00 2.50
56 Josh Johnson RC .30 .75
57 Jacob Hester RC .30 .75
58 Keenan Burton RC .30 .75
59 Keith Rivers RC .30 .75
60 Kenny Phillips RC .30 .75
61 Kevin Smith RC .30 .75
62 Lavelle Hawkins RC .40 1.00
63 Lawrence Jackson RC .30 .75
64 Limas Sweed RC .30 .75
65 Adrian Arrington RC .30 .75
66 Malcolm Kelly RC .30 .75
67 Martellus Bennett RC .40 1.00
68 Marcus Monk RC .40 1.00
69 Mario Manningham RC .30 .75
70 Mario Urrutia RC .30 .75
71 Martin Rucker RC .30 .75
72 Matt Flynn RC .30 .75
73 Matt Forte RC .50 1.25
74 Matt Ryan RC 1.00 2.50
75 Mike Hart RC .30 .75
76 Mike Jenkins RC .30 .75
77 Vernon Gholston RC .30 .75
78 Owen Schmitt RC .30 .75
79 Jonathan Goff RC .30 .75
80 Shawn Crable RC .30 .75
81 Justin King RC .40 1.00
82 Philip Wheeler RC .40 1.00
83 Paul Smith RC .30 .75
84 Rashard Mendenhall RC .30 .75
85 Ray Rice RC .30 .75
86 Ryan Clady RC .40 1.00
87 Ryan Torain RC .40 1.00
88 Sam Baker RC .30 .75
89 Quintin Demps RC .40 1.00
90 Sam Keller RC .30 .75
91 Phillip Merling RC .30 .75
92 Steve Slaton RC .30 .75
93 Tashard Choice RC .30 .75
94 Terrell Thomas RC .30 .75
95 Thomas Brown RC .30 .75
96 Tom Zbikowski RC .40 1.00
97 DeJuan Tribble RC .30 .75
98 Trevor Laws RC .30 .75
99 Vince Hall RC .30 .75
100 Xavier Adibi RC .30 .75
101 Edgerrin James .25 .60
102 Matt Leinart .20 .50
103 Larry Fitzgerald .25 .60
104 Joe Horn .20 .50
105 Warrick Dunn .20 .50
106 Jerious Norwood .20 .50
107 Ed Reed .25 .60
108 Willis McGahee .20 .50
109 Steve McNair .25 .60
110 Ray Lewis .30 .75
111 J.P. Losman .20 .50
112 Lee Evans .25 .60
113 Marshawn Lynch .25 .60
114 Eric Moulds .25 .60

115 Julius Peppers .25 .60
116 Steve Smith .25 .60
117 DeShaun Foster .20 .50
118 Devin Hester .25 .60
119 Bernard Berrian .20 .50
120 Cedric Benson .20 .50
121 Thomas Jones .20 .50
122 T.J. Houshmandzadeh .20 .50
123 Carson Palmer .25 .60
124 Chad Johnson .20 .50
125 Derek Anderson .20 .50
126 Kellen Winslow .20 .50
127 Braylon Edwards .20 .50
128 Anthony Henry .20 .50
129 Marion Barber .20 .50
130 DeMarcus Ware .25 .60
131 Tony Romo .25 .60
132 Brandon Marshall .25 .60
133 Jay Cutler .20 .50
134 Champ Bailey .25 .60
135 Tatum Bell .20 .50
136 Calvin Johnson .30 .75
137 Jon Kitna .20 .50
138 Ernie Sims .20 .50
139 Aaron Kampman .25 .60
140 Charles Woodson .30 .75
141 A.J. Hawk .20 .50
142 DeMeco Ryans .25 .60
143 Andre Johnson .25 .60
144 Mario Williams .25 .60
145 Dwight Freeney .20 .50
146 Dallas Clark .20 .50
147 Joseph Addai .20 .50
148 David Garrard .20 .50
149 Reggie Nelson .20 .50
150 Maurice Jones-Drew .20 .50
151 Dwayne Bowe .25 .60
152 Derrick Johnson .20 .50
153 Brodie Croyle .25 .60
154 Ronnie Brown .20 .50
155 Ted Ginn Jr. .20 .50
156 Channing Crowder .20 .50
157 Antoine Winfield .20 .50
158 Adrian Peterson .30 .75
159 Sidney Rice .20 .50
160 Wes Welker .25 .60
161 Laurence Maroney .25 .60
162 Ben Watson .20 .50
163 Drew Brees .30 .75
164 Reggie Bush .20 .50
165 Marques Colston .20 .50
166 Amani Toomer .20 .50
167 Osi Umenyiora .20 .50
168 Eli Manning .25 .60
169 Jonathan Vilma .20 .50
170 Kellen Clemens .20 .50
171 Kirk Morrison .20 .50
172 Nnamdi Asomugha .20 .50
173 JaMarcus Russell .20 .50
174 Brian Westbrook .20 .50
175 Reggie Brown .20 .50
176 Brian Dawkins .30 .75
177 Hines Ward .25 .60
178 Santonio Holmes .20 .50
179 Ben Roethlisberger .30 .75
180 Shawne Merriman .20 .50
181 LaDainian Tomlinson .30 .75
182 Antonio Cromartie .20 .50
183 Shaun Phillips .20 .50
184 Patrick Willis .25 .60
185 Alex Smith QB .25 .60
186 Frank Gore .25 .60
187 Lofa Tatupu .20 .50
188 Bobby Engram .20 .50
189 Deion Branch .20 .50
190 Steven Jackson .20 .50
191 Pisa Tinoisamoa .20 .50
192 Torry Holt .25 .60
193 Cadillac Williams .25 .60
194 Michael Clayton .20 .50
195 Gaines Adams .20 .50
196 Vince Young .20 .50
197 LenDale White .20 .50
198 Chris Cooley .20 .50
199 Clinton Portis .20 .50
200 Santana Moss .20 .50
201 B.Brohm/M.Urrutia .40 1.00
202 D.McFadden/F.Jones .40 1.00
203 D.Tribble/M.Ryan 1.25 3.00
204 E.Doucet/G.Dorsey .40 1.00
205 J.Long/M.Hart .60 1.50
206 C.Brennan/D.Bess .50 1.25
207 J.Booty/F.Davis .40 1.00
208 D.Anderson/S.Jackson .50 1.25
209 T.Brady/B.Edwards 2.50 6.00
210 R.Bush/M.Leinart .50 1.25
211 A.Highsmith/J.Leman .40 1.00
212 A.Cason/D.Tribble .50 1.25
213 C.Brennan/D.Dixon .40 1.00
214 D.McFadden/M.Hart .40 1.00
215 F.Davis/M.Rucker .40 1.00
216 J.Hefney/C.Steltz .40 1.00
217 L.Sweed/M.Manningham .40 1.00
218 S.Baker/J.Long .60 1.50
219 K.Balmer/G.Dorsey .40 1.00
220 S.Slaton/R.Rice .40 1.00
221 A.Highsmith/D.Connor .40 1.00
222 A.Cason/T.Thomas .50 1.25
223 B.Brohm/A.Woodson .40 1.00
224 C.Long/Q.Groves .50 1.25
225 C.Steltz/K.Phillips .40 1.00
226 F.Davis/J.Carlson .40 1.00
227 G.Dorsey/S.Ellis .40 1.00
228 J.Long/S.Baker .60 1.50
229 L.Sweed/E.Doucet .40 1.00
230 T.Choice/D.McFadden .40 1.00
231 A.Highsmith/C.Jackson .40 1.00
232 C.Henne/M.Manningham .50 1.25
233 L.Hawkins/D.Jackson .75 2.00
234 E.Henderson/D.Moore .50 1.25
235 M.Kelly/A.Patrick .40 1.00
236 M.Urrutia/H.Douglas .50 1.25
237 M.Rucker/A.Spieker .40 1.00
238 F.Jones/P.Hillis .60 1.50
239 J.Hefney/E.Ainge .40 1.00
240 V.Hall/X.Adibi .40 1.00
241 C.Brennan/D.Lowery .50 1.25
242 D.Dixon/K.Rivers .40 1.00
243 H.Douglas/M.Jenkins .50 1.25
244 J.Hester/K.Phillips .40 1.00
245 J.Hefney/D.Hall .40 1.00
246 M.Kelly/F.Okam .40 1.00
247 J.Leman/M.Manningham .40 1.00
248 M.Ryan/C.Long 1.25 3.00
249 J.Booty/A.Cason .50 1.25
250 S.Keller/A.Patrick .40 1.00

2008 Upper Deck Draft Edition Blue

*ROOKIES 1-100: .6X TO 1.5X BASIC CARDS
*SINGLES 201-250: .5X TO 1.2X BASIC CARDS
APPROXIMATE ODDS 1:8

2008 Upper Deck Draft Edition Bronze

*ROOKIES 1-100: 1X TO 2.5X BASIC CARDS
*SINGLES 201-250: .6X TO 1.5X BASIC CARDS
STATED PRINT RUN 175 SER.#'d SETS

2008 Upper Deck Draft Edition Gold

*ROOKIES 1-100: 4X TO 10X BASIC CARDS
*SINGLES 201-250: 2.5X TO 6X BASIC CARDS
STATED PRINT RUN 25 SER.#'d SETS

2008 Upper Deck Draft Edition Green

*ROOKIES 1-100: .6X TO 1.5X BASIC CARDS
*SINGLES 201-250: .4X TO 1X BASIC CARDS
RANDOM INSERTS IN RETAIL PACKS

2008 Upper Deck Draft Edition Red

*ROOKIES 1-100: .5X TO 1.2X BASIC CARDS
*SINGLES 201-250: .4X TO 1X BASIC CARDS
APPROXIMATE ODDS 1:2

2008 Upper Deck Draft Edition Silver

*ROOKIES 1-100: 1.2X TO 3X BASIC CARDS
*SINGLES 201-250: .8X TO 2X BASIC CARDS
STATED PRINT RUN 100 SER.#'d SETS

2008 Upper Deck Draft Edition Autographs

201-250 PRINT RUN 25
UNPRICED PLATINUM PRINT RUN 1
1 Anthony Morelli 3.00 8.00
2 Adarius Bowman 4.00 10.00
4 Andre Woodson 3.00 8.00
6 Antoine Cason 4.00 10.00
60C Antoine Cason on-card 10.00 25.00
7 Aqib Talib 5.00 12.00
9 Gosder Cherilus 4.00 10.00
10 Brian Brohm 3.00 8.00
11 Calais Campbell 4.00 10.00
12 Chad Henne 4.00 10.00
13 Chevis Jackson 3.00 8.00
14 Davone Bess 4.00 10.00
15 Justin Forsett 4.00 10.00
16 Chris Ellis 3.00 8.00
17 Chris Long 4.00 10.00
18 Colt Brennan SP 4.00 10.00
19 Craig Steltz 3.00 8.00
20 DJ Hall 3.00 8.00
21 Dan Connor 3.00 8.00
22 Darren McFadden SP 25.00 50.00
23 DeMario Pressley 4.00 10.00
24 Dennis Dixon 3.00 8.00
25 Derrick Harvey 3.00 8.00
26 DeSean Jackson 6.00 15.00
27 D.Rodgers-Cromartie SP 8.00 20.00
28 Donnie Avery 4.00 10.00
29 Dorien Bryant 4.00 10.00
30 Dre Moore 3.00 8.00
31 Kellen Davis 3.00 8.00
32 DaJuan Morgan 4.00 10.00
34 Early Doucet 3.00 8.00
35 Kentwan Balmer 3.00 8.00
36 Erik Ainge 3.00 8.00
37 Felix Jones EXCH
38 Frank Okam 3.00 8.00
39 Fred Davis 3.00 8.00
40 Glenn Dorsey 3.00 8.00
42 Jack Ikegwuonu 3.00 8.00
43 Bruce Davis 4.00 10.00
44 Jacob Tamme 4.00 10.00
45 Jake Long 5.00 12.00
46 Jamaal Charles 5.00 12.00
47 James Hardy 3.00 8.00
48 Erin Henderson 4.00 10.00
49 J Leman 3.00 8.00
50 Joe Flacco 6.00 15.00
51 John Carlson 3.00 8.00
52 John David Booty 3.00 8.00
53 Jonathan Hefney 3.00 8.00
54 Jonathan Stewart 5.00 12.00
56 Josh Johnson 3.00 8.00
57 Jacob Hester 3.00 8.00
58 Keenan Burton 3.00 8.00
59 Keith Rivers 3.00 8.00
60 Kenny Phillips 3.00 8.00
61 Kevin Smith 3.00 8.00
62 Lavelle Hawkins 4.00 10.00
63 Lawrence Jackson 3.00 8.00
64 Limas Sweed 3.00 8.00
65 Adrian Arrington 3.00 8.00
66 Malcolm Kelly EXCH
70 Mario Urrutia 3.00 8.00
71 Martin Rucker 3.00 8.00
72 Matt Flynn 3.00 8.00
73 Matt Forte 5.00 12.00
74 Matt Ryan 15.00 40.00
75 Mike Hart 3.00 8.00
76 Mike Jenkins EXCH
77 Vernon Gholston 3.00 8.00
78 Owen Schmitt 3.00 8.00
80 Shawn Crable 3.00 8.00
81 Justin King EXCH
82 Philip Wheeler 4.00 10.00
83 Paul Smith 3.00 8.00
84 Rashard Mendenhall 3.00 8.00
85 Ray Rice 3.00 8.00
86 Ryan Clady 4.00 10.00
88 Sam Baker 3.00 8.00
89 Quintin Demps
90 Sam Keller 3.00 8.00
91 Phillip Merling 3.00 8.00
93 Tashard Choice 3.00 8.00
94 Terrell Thomas 3.00 8.00
95 Thomas Brown 3.00 8.00
96 Tom Zbikowski 4.00 10.00
97 DeJuan Tribble 3.00 8.00
98 Trevor Laws 3.00 8.00
100 Xavier Adibi 3.00 8.00
201 B.Brohm/M.Urrutia 20.00 50.00
202 McFadden/Jones 15.00 40.00
203 D.Tribble/M.Ryan 20.00 50.00
204 E.Doucet/G.Dorsey 20.00 50.00
205 J.Long/M.Hart 20.00 50.00
206 Brennan/Bess 10.00 25.00
207 J.Booty/F.Davis 6.00 15.00
212 A.Cason/D.Tribble 12.00 30.00
213 Brennan/Dixon 15.00 40.00
214 D.McFadden/M.Hart 40.00 100.00
215 F.Davis/M.Rucker 15.00 40.00
216 J.Hefney/C.Steltz 12.00 30.00
218 S.Baker/J.Long 20.00 50.00
219 K.Balmer/G.Dorsey 20.00 50.00
222 A.Cason/T.Thomas 12.00 30.00
223 B.Brohm/A.Woodson 12.00 30.00
225 C.Steltz/K.Phillips 15.00 40.00
226 F.Davis/J.Carlson 12.00 30.00
227 G.Dorsey/S.Ellis 15.00 40.00
228 J.Long/S.Baker 20.00 50.00
229 L.Sweed/E.Doucet 20.00 50.00
230 T.Choice/D.McFadden 40.00 100.00
233 L.Hawkins/D.Jackson 12.00 30.00
234 E.Henderson/D.Moore 12.00 30.00
238 F.Jones/P.Hillis 15.00 40.00
239 J.Hefney/E.Ainge 15.00 40.00
242 D.Dixon/K.Rivers 15.00 40.00
244 J.Hester/K.Phillips 20.00 50.00
245 J.Hefney/D.Hall 12.00 30.00
248 M.Ryan/C.Long 60.00 120.00
249 J.Booty/A.Cason 8.00 20.00

2008 Upper Deck Draft Edition Autographs Bronze

*BRONZE/50: .6X TO 1.5X BASIC AUTO
BRONZE PRINT RUN 50 SER.#'d SETS
66 Malcolm Kelly 5.00 12.00
74 Matt Ryan 25.00 60.00

2008 Upper Deck Draft Edition Autographs Blue

*BLUE/75: .6X TO 1.5X BASIC AUTO
BLUE PRINT RUN 75 SER.#'d SETS
74 Matt Ryan 25.00 60.00

2008 Upper Deck Draft Edition Autographs Gold

*GOLD/25: .8X TO 2X BASIC AUTO
1-100 GOLD PRINT RUN 25
UNPRICED 201-250 GOLD PRINT RUN 10
66 Malcolm Kelly 6.00 15.00
74 Matt Ryan 30.00 80.00

2008 Upper Deck Draft Edition Autographs Red

*RED/125: .5X TO 1.2X BASIC AUTO
RED PRINT RUN 125 SER.#'d SETS
74 Matt Ryan 20.00 50.00

2008 Upper Deck Draft Edition College Greats

COMPLETE SET (10) 6.00 15.00
RANDOM INSERTS IN RETAIL PACKS
CG1 Brian Brohm .30 .75
CG2 Matt Ryan 1.00 2.50
CG3 Darren McFadden .30 .75
CG4 DeSean Jackson .60 1.50
CG5 Early Doucet .30 .75
CG6 Keith Rivers .30 .75
CG7 Limas Sweed .30 .75
CG8 Marcus Monk .40 1.00
CG9 Mike Hart .30 .75
CG10 Antoine Cason .40 1.00

2008 Upper Deck Draft Edition Stars of the Draft

COMPLETE SET (10) 10.00 25.00
RANDOM INSERTS IN RETAIL PACKS
SOD1 Brian Brohm .50 1.25
SOD2 Matt Ryan 1.50 4.00
SOD3 Darren McFadden .50 1.25
SOD4 DeSean Jackson 1.00 2.50
SOD5 Early Doucet .50 1.25
SOD6 Limas Sweed .50 1.25
SOD7 Keith Rivers .50 1.25
SOD8 Antoine Cason .60 1.50
SOD9 Mike Hart .50 1.25
SOD10 Dan Connor .50 1.25

2009 Upper Deck Draft Edition

COMPLETE SET (295) 50.00 100.00
COMP.SET w/o SP's (200) 25.00 50.00
1 Curtis Painter RC .25 .60
2 DeAngelo Smith RC .30 .75
3 Matthew Stafford RC 1.25 3.00
4 Chris Wells RC .25 .60
5 Michael Johnson RC .25 .60
6 Percy Harvin RC .25 .60
7 Michael Crabtree RC .40 1.00
8 Knowshon Moreno RC .25 .60
9 Jason Smith RC .25 .60
10 James Laurinaitis RC .25 .60
11 Rey Maualuga RC .40 1.00
12 Hunter Cantwell RC .25 .60
13 Chase Daniel RC .30 .75
14 Alphonso Smith RC .25 .60
15 Jason Phillips RC .30 .75
16 Pat White RC .30 .75
17 Peria Jerry RC .25 .60
18 Graham Harrell RC .25 .60
19 Sammie Stroughter RC .25 .60
20 James Davis RC .25 .60
21 Javon Ringer RC .25 .60
22 D.J. Moore RC .30 .75
23 Nate Davis RC .25 .60
24 P.J. Hill RC .25 .60
25 Kevin Barnes RC .25 .60
26 Darrius Heyward-Bey RC .40 1.00
28 Glen Coffee RC .25 .60
29 Jaison Williams RC .30 .75
30 Brian Robiskie RC .25 .60
31 Derrick Williams RC .25 .60
32 Darius Passmore RC .25 .60
33 Chase Coffman RC .25 .60
34 Cornelius Ingram RC .25 .60
35 Travis Beckum RC .25 .60
36 Brandon Pettigrew RC .25 .60
37 Louis Delmas RC .30 .75
38 Alex Mack RC .25 .60
39 Duke Robinson RC .25 .60
40 Jarett Dillard RC .25 .60
41 Kraig Urbik RC .30 .75
42 Herman Johnson RC .30 .75
43 Otis Wiley RC .25 .60
44 Michael Oher RC .40 1.00
45 Phil Loadholt RC .30 .75
46 Alex Boone RC .40 1.00
47 Max Unger RC .40 1.00
48 Andre Smith RC .25 .60
49 Fili Moala RC .25 .60
52 Terrance Taylor RC .30 .75
53 Sen'Derrick Marks RC .25 .60
54 Tyson Jackson RC .25 .60
55 Captain Munnerlyn RC .30 .75
56 Ian Campbell RC .30 .75
57 Asher Allen RC .25 .60
58 Brandon Tate RC .30 .75
59 Darry Beckwith RC .25 .60
60 Jasper Brinkley RC .30 .75
61 Brian Cushing RC .25 .60
62 Dannell Ellerbe RC .30 .75
63 Marcus Freeman RC .25 .60
64 Maurice Crum RC .30 .75
65 Anthony Heygood RC .25 .60
66 Patrick Chung RC .25 .60
67 Jeremy Maclin RC .30 .75
68 Troy Kropog RC .25 .60
69 William Moore RC .25 .60
70 Kevin Ellison RC .25 .60
71 Malcolm Jenkins RC .25 .60
72 Victor Harris RC .30 .75
73 Vontae Davis RC .25 .60
74 Matt Shaughnessy RC .30 .75
75 Mike Mickens RC .25 .60
76 LeSean McCoy RC .60 1.50
77 Rudy Carpenter RC .30 .75
78 Arian Foster RC .60 1.50
79 Devin Moore RC .25 .60
80 Tyrell Sutton RC .25 .60
81 Ian Johnson RC .25 .60
82 James Casey RC .30 .75
83 Paul Kruger RC .40 1.00
84 Kenny Britt RC .40 1.00
85 Josh Freeman RC .25 .60
86 Louis Murphy RC .25 .60
87 Demetrius Byrd RC .30 .75
88 Brandon Gibson RC .30 .75
89 Aaron Kelly RC .25 .60
90 Keenan Lewis RC .40 1.00
91 Nathan Brown RC .30 .75
92 Connor Barwin RC .30 .75
93 B.J. Raji RC .30 .75
94 Tom Brandstater RC .30 .75
95 Shonn Greene RC .25 .60
96 Brannan Southerland RC .30 .75
97 Eben Britton RC .30 .75
98 Jairus Byrd RC .40 1.00
99 Nic Harris RC .30 .75
100 Ryan Purvis RC .25 .60
101 Clay Matthews RC 1.00 2.50
102 Mark Sanchez RC .25 .60
103 Brian Orakpo RC .30 .75
104 Tim Jamison RC .30 .75
105 Jonathan Luigs RC .25 .60
106 Darius Butler RC .30 .75
107 Eugene Monroe RC .25 .60
108 Xavier Fulton RC .25 .60
109 Andrew Gardner RC .25 .60
110 Jamon Meredith RC .25 .60
111 Jason Watkins RC .30 .75
112 Fenuki Tupou RC .25 .60
113 Juaquin Iglesias RC .25 .60
114 Marko Mitchell RC .25 .60
115 Kenny McKinley RC .25 .60
116 Ramses Barden RC .25 .60
117 Jeremy Childs RC .25 .60
119 Tiquan Underwood RC .25 .60
120 Quan Cosby RC .25 .60
121 David Veikune RC .30 .75
122 Brennan Marion RC .30 .75
123 Morgan Trent RC .30 .75
124 Larry English RC .30 .75
125 Mohamed Massaquoi RC .25 .60
126 Aaron Curry RC .40 1.00
127 Rashad Jennings RC .30 .75
128 Jeremiah Johnson RC .25 .60
129 Michael Hamlin RC .25 .60
130 Andre Brown RC .30 .75
132 Keegan Herring RC .30 .75
133 Willie Tuitama RC .30 .75
134 Cedric Peerman RC .25 .60
135 Gerald McRath RC .30 .75
136 Jared Cook RC .30 .75
137 Austin Collie RC .25 .60
138 Garrett Reynolds RC .30 .75
139 Cullen Harper RC .25 .60
140 Donald Brown RC .25 .60
141 John Parker Wilson RC .25 .60
142 Derek Pegues RC .25 .60
143 Rhett Bomar RC .25 .60
144 Mike Reilly RC .25 .60
145 Clint Sintim RC .25 .60
146 Courtney Greene RC .25 .60
147 Sean Smith RC .25 .60
148 Shawn Nelson RC .25 .60
149 Hakeem Nicks RC .30 .75
150 Bear Pascoe RC .30 .75
151 Clinton Portis .20 .50
152 Brett Favre .60 1.50
153 Drew Brees .30 .75
154 Peyton Manning .75 2.00
155 Eli Manning .25 .60
156 Tony Romo .25 .60
157 Jay Cutler .20 .50
158 Brandon Marshall .25 .60
159 LaDainian Tomlinson .30 .75
160 Michael Turner .20 .50
161 Darren McFadden .30 .75
162 Devin Hester .25 .60
163 Marion Barber .25 .60
164 Troy Polamalu .30 .75
165 Ben Roethlisberger .30 .75
166 Chris Johnson .20 .50
167 Matt Forte .20 .50
168 Matt Ryan .25 .60
169 Aaron Rodgers .60 1.50
170 Greg Jennings .20 .50
171 Brian Westbrook .20 .50
172 Adrian Peterson .30 .75
173 Larry Fitzgerald .25 .60
174 Reggie Wayne .25 .60
175 Trent Edwards .20 .50
176 Marshawn Lynch .25 .60
177 Brian Urlacher .30 .75
178 Jason Campbell .20 .50
179 Ronnie Brown .20 .50
180 Anquan Boldin .20 .50
181 Brady Quinn .20 .50
182 Roddy White .20 .50
183 Felix Jones .20 .50
184 Jason Witten .25 .60
185 Andre Johnson .25 .60
186 Calvin Johnson .30 .75
187 Tom Brady 1.00 2.50
188 A.J. Hawk .20 .50
189 Patrick Willis .25 .60
190 Philip Rivers .30 .75
191 Chris Cooley .20 .50
192 Dwayne Bowe .25 .60
193 Mario Williams .25 .60
194 DeMarcus Ware .25 .60
195 Joey Porter .25 .60
196 Hines Ward .25 .60
197 Lance Briggs .25 .60
198 Frank Gore .25 .60
199 Nnamdi Asomugha .20 .50
200 Donovan McNabb .25 .60
201 Chris Wells SR .25 .60
202 Mark Sanchez SR .25 .60
203 Curtis Painter SR .25 .60
204 Michael Crabtree SR .40 1.00
205 Knowshon Moreno SR .25 .60
206 LeSean McCoy SR .60 1.50
207 Shonn Greene SR .25 .60
208 Matthew Stafford SR 1.25 3.00
209 Josh Freeman SR .25 .60
210 Pat White SR .30 .75
211 Aaron Curry SR .40 1.00
212 Alphonso Smith SR .25 .60
213 Darrius Heyward-Bey SR .40 1.00
214 Percy Harvin SR .25 .60
215 James Laurinaitis SR .25 .60
216 Brian Robiskie SR .25 .60
217 Jeremy Maclin SR .30 .75
218 William Moore SR .25 .60
219 Chase Coffman SR .25 .60
220 Brandon Pettigrew SR .25 .60
221 Hakeem Nicks SR .30 .75
222 Michael Johnson SR .25 .60
223 Fili Moala SR .25 .60
224 Rey Maualuga SR .40 1.00
225 Brian Cushing SR .25 .60
226 Donald Brown SR .25 .60
227 Malcolm Jenkins SR .25 .60
228 Vontae Davis SR .25 .60
229 Patrick Chung SR .25 .60
230 Sen'Derrick Marks SR .25 .60
231 T.Polamalu/R.Maualuga AA .40 1.00
232 J.Wilson/An.Smith AA .25 .60
233 M.Crabtree/W.Welker AA .40 1.00
234 H.Ward/M.Stafford AA 1.25 3.00
235 M.Stafford/K.Moreno AA 1.25 3.00
236 J.Laurinaitis/A.Hawk AA .25 .60
237 C.Harper/J.Davis AA .25 .60
238 A.Peterson/J.Iglesias AA .40 1.00
239 D.Brees/C.Painter AA .25 .60
240 G.Harrell/M.Crabtree AA .40 1.00
241 P.Jerry/P.Willis AA .30 .75
242 C.Johnson/M.Johnson AA .40 1.00
243 M.Sanchez/A.Munoz AA .30 .75
244 E.Brown/A.Boldin AA .25 .60
245 R.Maualuga/B.Cushing AA .25 .60
246 C.Sintim/E.Monroe AA .25 .60
247 P.Harvin/L.Murphy AA .25 .60
248 L.McCoy/L.Fitzgerald AA .60 1.50
249 J.Campbell/S.Marks AA .25 .60
250 Massaquoi/K.Moreno AA .25 .60
251 J.Wilson/M.Stafford CC 1.25 3.00
252 M.Johnson/E.Brown CC .25 .60
253 W.Moore/G.Harrell CC .25 .60
254 J.Ringer/C.Wells CC .25 .60
255 B.Robiskie/D.Williams CC .25 .60
256 Heyward-Bey/A.Kelly CC .40 1.00
257 D.Byrd/P.Harvin CC .25 .60
258 S.Marks/K.Moreno CC .25 .60
259 M.Jenkins/V.Davis CC .25 .60
260 B.Pettigrew/C.Coffman CC .25 .60
261 B.Orakpo/G.Harrell CC .30 .75
262 A.Smith/M.Oher CC .40 1.00
263 Laurinaitis/S.Greene CC .25 .60
264 T.Jackson/A.Smith CC .25 .60
265 B.Gibson/R.Maualuga CC .40 1.00
266 C.Wells/S.Greene CC .25 .60
267 M.Crabtree/J.Maclin CC .40 1.00
268 M.Sanchez/R.Carpenter CC .30 .75
269 Q.Cosby/M.Crabtree CC .40 1.00
270 P.Hill/J.Ringer CC .25 .60
271 Knowshon Moreno AA .25 .60
272 Michael Crabtree AA .40 1.00
273 Herman Johnson AA .30 .75
274 Fili Moala AA .25 .60
275 James Laurinaitis AA .25 .60
276 Jeremy Maclin AA .30 .75
277 Chase Coffman AA .25 .60
278 Jarett Dillard AA .25 .60
279 Michael Oher AA .40 1.00
280 Javon Ringer AA .25 .60
281 Aaron Maybin AA .30 .75
282 Andre Smith AA .25 .60
283 Rey Maualuga AA .40 1.00
284 Malcolm Jenkins AA .25 .60
285 Shonn Greene AA .25 .60
286 Adrian Peterson AA .50 1.25
287 Peyton Manning AA 1.25 3.00
288 Calvin Johnson AA .50 1.25
289 Darren McFadden AA .50 1.25
290 A.J. Hawk AA .30 .75
291 Roeth/Rivers/Eli DC .50 1.25
292 Forte/McFdd/C.Jhnsn DC .50 1.25
293 Tomlin/Brees/Wayne DC .50 1.25
294 J.Kelly/Craig/D.Green DC .50 1.25
295 M.Willi/V.Young/Bush DC .40 1.00
296 J.Cmpbll/Rodgrs/Barbr DC 1.00 2.50
297 Ryan/McFadd/Flacco DC .50 1.25
298 C.Wdson/Ward/P.Mann DC 1.25 3.00
299 D.Hester/Hawk/Cutler DC .40 1.00
300 Cooley/Fitzg/Roeth DC .50 1.25

2009 Upper Deck Draft Edition Blue 50

*ROOKIES 1-150: 2.5X TO 6X BASIC CARDS
*VETS 151-200: 5X TO 12X BASIC CARDS
*SR 201-230: 2X TO 5X BASIC CARDS
*DUAL 231-270: 2X TO 5X BASIC CARDS
*AA 271-285: 2X TO 5X BASIC CARDS
*VETS 286-300: 3X TO 8X BASIC CARDS
BLUE PRINT RUN 50 SER.#'d SETS

2009 Upper Deck Draft Edition Burgundy 75

*ROOKIES 1-150: 2X TO 5X BASIC CARDS
*VETS 151-200: 4X TO 10X BASIC CARDS
*SR 201-230: 1.5X TO 4X BASIC CARDS
*DUAL 231-270: 1.5X TO 4X BASIC CARDS
*AA 271-285: 1.5X TO 4X BASIC CARDS
*VETS 286-300: 2.5X TO 6X BASIC CARDS
BURGUNDY PRINT RUN 75 SER.#'d SETS

2009 Upper Deck Draft Edition Copper 25

*ROOKIES 1-150: 4X TO 10X BASIC CARDS
*VETS 151-200: 8X TO 20X BASIC CARDS
*SR 201-230: 3X TO 8X BASIC CARDS
*DUAL 231-270: 3X TO 8X BASIC CARDS
*AA 271-285: 3X TO 8X BASIC CARDS
*VETS 286-300: 5X TO 12X BASIC CARDS
COPPER PRINT RUN 25 SER.#'d SETS

2009 Upper Deck Draft Edition Dark Green

*ROOKIES 1-150: .8X TO 2X BASIC CARDS
*VETS 151-200: 1.5X TO 4X BASIC CARDS
*SR 201-230: .4X TO 1.5X BASIC CARDS
*DUAL 231-270: .6X TO 1.5X BASIC CARDS
*AA 271-285: .6X TO 1.5X BASIC CARDS
*VETS 286-300: 1X TO 2.5X BASIC CARDS
RANDOM INSERTS IN RETAIL PACKS

2009 Upper Deck Draft Edition Green 350

*ROOKIES 1-150: 1.2X TO 3X BASIC CARDS
*VETS 151-200: 2.5X TO 6X BASIC CARDS
*SR 201-230: 1X TO 2.5X BASIC CARDS
*DUAL 231-270: 1X TO 2.5X BASIC CARDS
*AA 271-285: 1X TO 2.5X BASIC CARDS
*VETS 286-300: 1.5X TO 4X BASIC CARDS
GREEN PRINT RUN 350-351

2009 Upper Deck Draft Edition Bronze 125

*ROOKIES 1-150: 1.5X TO 4X BASIC CARDS
*VETS 151-200: 3X TO 8X BASIC CARDS
*SR 201-230: 1.2X TO 3X BASIC CARDS
*DUAL 231-270: 1.2X TO 3X BASIC CARDS
*AA 271-285: 1.2X TO 3X BASIC CARDS
*VETS 286-300: 2X TO 5X BASIC CARDS
BRONZE PRINT RUN 125 SER.#'d SETS

2009 Upper Deck Draft Edition Brown

*ROOKIES 1-150: .8X TO 2X BASIC CARDS
*VETS 151-200: 1.5X TO 4X BASIC CARDS
*SR 201-230: .4X TO 1.5X BASIC CARDS
*DUAL 231-270: .6X TO 1.5X BASIC CARDS
*AA 271-285: .6X TO 1.5X BASIC CARDS
*VETS 286-300: 1X TO 2.5X BASIC CARDS
RANDOM INSERTS IN HOBBY PACKS

2009 Upper Deck Draft Edition Autographs Blue

*1-150 BLUE/25: .5X TO 1.2X COPPER AU
1-150 BLUE ROOKIE PRINT RUN 25
151-200 BLUE UNPRICED VET PRINT RUN 3
3 Matthew Stafford 30.00 80.00
7 Michael Crabtree 15.00 40.00
8 Knowshon Moreno 6.00 15.00
102 Mark Sanchez 30.00 80.00

2009 Upper Deck Draft Edition Autographs Copper

1-150 COPPER PRINT RUN 50
151-198 UNPRICED COPPER PRINT RUN 5
201-230 COPPER SR PRINT RUN 25
232-270 COPPER DUAL PRINT RUN 50
271-290 COPPER AA PRINT RUN 25
291-295 UNPRICED COPPER PRINT RUN 10
OVERALL AUTO ODDS 5:16
1 Curtis Painter 5.00 12.00
3 Matthew Stafford 25.00 60.00
4 Chris Wells 5.00 12.00
5 Michael Johnson 5.00 12.00
6 Percy Harvin 5.00 12.00
7 Michael Crabtree 12.00 30.00
8 Knowshon Moreno 5.00 12.00
9 Jason Smith 5.00 12.00
10 James Laurinaitis 5.00 12.00
11 Rey Maualuga 8.00 20.00
12 Hunter Cantwell 5.00 12.00
14 Alphonso Smith 5.00 12.00
16 Pat White 6.00 15.00
17 Peria Jerry 5.00 12.00
18 Graham Harrell 5.00 12.00
20 James Davis 5.00 12.00
21 Javon Ringer 5.00 12.00
22 D.J. Moore 6.00 15.00
24 P.J. Hill 5.00 12.00
25 Kevin Barnes 5.00 12.00
26 Darrius Heyward-Bey 8.00 20.00
29 Jaison Williams 6.00 15.00
31 Derrick Williams 5.00 12.00
33 Chase Coffman 5.00 12.00
34 Cornelius Ingram 5.00 12.00
35 Travis Beckum 5.00 12.00
36 Brandon Pettigrew 5.00 12.00
39 Duke Robinson 5.00 12.00
40 Jarett Dillard 5.00 12.00
41 Kraig Urbik 6.00 15.00
42 Herman Johnson 6.00 15.00
43 Otis Wiley 5.00 12.00
44 Michael Oher 15.00 40.00
45 Phil Loadholt 6.00 15.00
46 Alex Boone 8.00 20.00
47 Max Unger 8.00 20.00
48 Andre Smith 5.00 12.00
49 Fili Moala 5.00 12.00
52 Terrance Taylor 6.00 15.00
53 Sen'Derrick Marks 5.00 12.00
54 Tyson Jackson 5.00 12.00
56 Ian Campbell 6.00 15.00
59 Darry Beckwith 5.00 12.00
60 Jasper Brinkley 6.00 15.00
61 Brian Cushing 5.00 12.00
63 Marcus Freeman 5.00 12.00
64 Maurice Crum 6.00 15.00
65 Anthony Heygood 5.00 12.00
67 Jeremy Maclin 6.00 15.00
68 Troy Kropog 5.00 12.00
69 William Moore 5.00 12.00
71 Malcolm Jenkins 5.00 12.00
72 Victor Harris 6.00 15.00
73 Vontae Davis 5.00 12.00
74 Matt Shaughnessy 6.00 15.00
75 Mike Mickens 5.00 12.00
76 LeSean McCoy 12.00 30.00
77 Rudy Carpenter EXCH 5.00 12.00
78 Arian Foster 12.00 30.00
79 Devin Moore 5.00 12.00
80 Tyrell Sutton 5.00 12.00
83 Paul Kruger 8.00 20.00
84 Kenny Britt 8.00 20.00
87 Demetrius Byrd 6.00 15.00
88 Brandon Gibson 6.00 15.00
89 Aaron Kelly 5.00 12.00
90 Keenan Lewis 8.00 20.00
91 Nathan Brown 6.00 15.00
93 B.J. Raji 6.00 15.00
94 Tom Brandstater 6.00 15.00
95 Shonn Greene 5.00 12.00
96 Brannan Southerland 6.00 15.00
99 Nic Harris 6.00 15.00
100 Ryan Purvis 6.00 15.00
102 Mark Sanchez 25.00 60.00
103 Brian Orakpo 6.00 15.00
104 Tim Jamison 6.00 15.00
105 Jonathan Luigs 5.00 12.00
107 Eugene Monroe 5.00 12.00
108 Xavier Fulton 5.00 12.00
109 Andrew Gardner 5.00 12.00
110 Jamon Meredith 5.00 12.00
111 Jason Watkins 5.00 12.00
112 Fenuki Tupou 5.00 12.00
113 Juaquin Iglesias 6.00 15.00
114 Marko Mitchell 5.00 12.00
115 Kenny McKinley 6.00 15.00
116 Ramses Barden 5.00 12.00
117 Mike Thomas 5.00 12.00
119 Tiquan Underwood 5.00 12.00
120 Quan Cosby 5.00 12.00
121 David Veikune 6.00 15.00
122 Brennan Marion 6.00 15.00
123 Morgan Trent 6.00 15.00
124 Deon Butler 5.00 12.00
125 Mohamed Massaquoi 5.00 12.00
126 Aaron Curry 8.00 20.00
127 Rashad Jennings 6.00 15.00
128 Jeremiah Johnson 5.00 12.00
129 Michael Hamlin 5.00 12.00
130 Andre Brown 6.00 15.00
131 Brad Lester 5.00 12.00
132 Keegan Herring 6.00 15.00
133 Willie Tuitama 6.00 15.00
135 Gerald McRath 6.00 15.00
136 Jared Cook 6.00 15.00
137 Austin Collie 6.00 15.00
138 Garrett Reynolds 6.00 15.00
140 Donald Brown 5.00 12.00
141 John Parker Wilson 5.00 12.00
142 Derek Pegues 5.00 12.00
143 Rhett Bomar 5.00 12.00
144 Mike Reilly 5.00 12.00
145 Clint Sintim 6.00 15.00
148 Shawn Nelson 6.00 15.00
149 Hakeem Nicks 6.00 15.00
150 Bear Pascoe 6.00 15.00
201 Chris Wells SR/25 6.00 15.00
202 Mark Sanchez SR/25 25.00 60.00
203 Curtis Painter SR/25 6.00 15.00
204 Michael Crabtree SR/25 15.00 40.00
205 Knowshon Moreno SR/25 15.00 40.00
206 LeSean McCoy SR/25 15.00 40.00
207 Shonn Greene SR/25 6.00 15.00
208 Matthew Stafford SR/25 30.00 80.00
210 Pat White SR/25 8.00 20.00
211 Aaron Curry SR/25 10.00 25.00
212 Alphonso Smith SR/25 6.00 15.00
213 Darrius Heyward-Bey SR/25 10.00 25.00
214 Percy Harvin SR/25 15.00 40.00
215 James Laurinaitis SR/25 6.00 15.00
217 Jeremy Maclin SR/25 8.00 20.00
218 William Moore SR/25 6.00 15.00
219 Chase Coffman SR/25 6.00 15.00
220 Brandon Pettigrew SR/25 6.00 15.00
221 Hakeem Nicks SR/25 8.00 20.00
222 Michael Johnson SR/25 6.00 15.00
223 Fili Moala SR/25 6.00 15.00
224 Rey Maualuga SR/25 10.00 25.00
225 Brian Cushing SR/25 6.00 15.00
226 Donald Brown SR/25 6.00 15.00
227 Malcolm Jenkins SR/25 6.00 15.00
228 Vontae Davis SR/25 6.00 15.00
229 Patrick Chung SR/25 6.00 15.00
230 Sen'Derrick Marks SR/25 6.00 15.00
232 Wilson/Smith AA 10.00 25.00
235 M.Stafford/K.Moreno AA 30.00 80.00
236 J.Laurinaitis/A.Hawk AA 20.00 50.00
237 C.Harper/J.Davis AA 12.00 30.00
238 A.Peterson/J.Iglesias AA 60.00 100.00
239 D.Brees/C.Painter AA 30.00 60.00
240 G.Harrell/M.Crabtree AA 20.00 50.00
241 P.Jerry/P.Willis AA 12.00 30.00
242 C.Johnson/M.Johnson AA 25.00 50.00
243 Sanchez/Munoz AA 30.00 80.00
245 R.Maualuga/B.Cushing AA 12.00 30.00
246 C.Sintim/E.Monroe AA 12.00 30.00
248 L.McCoy/L.Fitzgerald AA 40.00 80.00
249 J.Campbell/S.Marks AA 12.00 30.00
250 Massaquoi/K.Moreno AA 20.00 50.00
251 J.Wilson/M.Stafford CC 20.00 50.00
253 W.Moore/G.Harrell CC 15.00 40.00
254 J.Ringer/C.Wells CC 6.00 15.00
256 Heyward-Bey/A.Kelly CC 10.00 25.00
257 D.Byrd/P.Harvin CC 8.00 20.00
258 S.Marks/K.Moreno CC 30.00 80.00
259 M.Jenkins/V.Davis CC 12.00 30.00
260 Pettigrew/Coffman CC EXCH 12.00 30.00
261 Orakpo/G.Harrell CC EXCH 15.00 40.00
262 A.Smith/M.Oher CC 20.00 50.00
263 Laurinaitis/S.Greene CC 20.00 50.00
264 T.Jackson/A.Smith CC 12.00 30.00
265 B.Gibson/R.Maualuga CC 12.00 30.00
266 C.Wells/S.Greene CC 20.00 50.00
267 M.Crabtree/J.Maclin CC 20.00 50.00
268 Sanchez/Carpenter CC 25.00 60.00
269 Q.Cosby/M.Crabtree CC 20.00 50.00
270 P.Hill/J.Ringer CC 6.00 15.00
271 Knowshon Moreno AA/25 8.00 20.00
272 Michael Crabtree AA/25 25.00 60.00
273 Herman Johnson AA/25 8.00 20.00
274 Fili Moala AA/25 0.00 15.00
275 James Laurinaitis AA/25 8.00 20.00
276 Jeremy Maclin AA/25 8.00 20.00
277 Chase Coffman AA/25 6.00 15.00
278 Jarett Dillard AA/25 6.00 15.00
279 Michael Oher AA/25 25.00 60.00
280 Javon Ringer AA/25 6.00 15.00
282 Andre Smith AA/25 6.00 15.00
283 Rey Maualuga AA/25 10.00 25.00
284 Malcolm Jenkins AA/25 6.00 15.00
285 Shonn Greene AA/25 6.00 15.00
286 Adrian Peterson AA/25 50.00 100.00
287 Peyton Manning AA/25 50.00 100.00
288 Calvin Johnson AA/25 30.00 60.00
289 Darren McFadden AA/25 30.00 60.00
290 A.J. Hawk AA/25 10.00 25.00

2009 Upper Deck Draft Edition Autographs Green

*GREEN: .3X TO .8X BRONZE AUTO

2009 Upper Deck Draft Edition Autographs Silver

*1-150 SILVER: .3X TO .8X COPPER AUTO
151-200 DRAFT HISTORY VETS NOT PRICED
201-230 SCOUTING REPORT/5 NOT PRICED
232-270 DUAL AUTO/15 NOT PRICED
271-285 ROOKIE ALL AMER/5 NOT PRICED
286-290 VETERAN AA/5 NOT PRICED
292-295 DRAFT CLASS/5 NOT PRICED

2009-10 Upper Deck Draft Edition Alma Mater

COMPLETE SET (24) 25.00 50.00
RANDOM INSERTS IN PACKS
*BLUE: .6X TO 1.5X BASE HI
BLUE PRINT RUN 99 SER.#'d SETS
AMMR Matt Ryan 2.00 5.00
AMTB Terry Bradshaw 1.00 2.50

2009-10 Upper Deck Draft Edition Alma Mater Green

*GREEN: .75X TO 2X BASE HI
GREEN PRINT RUN 50 SER.#'d SETS

2009-10 Upper Deck Draft Edition Alma Mater Autographs

STATED PRINT RUN 10 TO 99 SER.#'d SETS
SOME UNPRICED DUE TO SCARCITY
AMMR Matt Ryan/25 50.00 100.00

2009-10 Upper Deck Draft Edition Alma Mater Red

*RED: 2X TO 5X BASE HI
RED PRINT RUN 25 SER.#'d SETS

1998 Upper Deck Encore

he 1998 Upper Deck Encore set was issued in one series totalling 150 cards and distributed in six-card packs with a suggested retail price of $3.99. The set features color player photos printed on cards with a special rainbow-foil treatment and contains the following subset with an insertion rate of 1:4 packs: Star Rookies (1-30).

COMPLETE SET (150) 75.00 150.00
1 Peyton Manning RC 12.00 30.00
2 Ryan Leaf RC 1.00 2.50
3 Andre Wadsworth RC 1.25 3.00
4 Charles Woodson RC 4.00 10.00
5 Curtis Enis RC 1.00 2.50
6 Fred Taylor RC 1.50 4.00
7 Duane Starks RC .75 2.00
8 Keith Brooking RC 1.25 3.00
9 Takeo Spikes RC 1.00 2.50
10 Kevin Dyson RC 1.00 2.50
11 Robert Edwards RC 1.00 2.50
12 Randy Moss RC 6.00 15.00
13 John Avery RC 1.00 2.50
14 Marcus Nash RC .75 2.00
15 Jerome Pathon RC 1.00 2.50
16 Jacquez Green RC 1.00 2.50
17 Robert Holcombe RC .75 2.00
18 Pat Johnson RC 1.00 2.50
19 Skip Hicks RC 1.00 2.50
20 Ahman Green RC 1.50 4.00
21 Brian Griese RC 1.50 4.00
22 Hines Ward RC 6.00 15.00
23 Tavian Banks RC 1.00 2.50
24 Tony Simmons RC 1.00 2.50
25 Rashaan Shehee RC .75 2.00
26 R.W. McQuarters RC 1.25 3.00
27 Jon Ritchie RC 1.00 2.50
28 Ryan Sutter RC .75 2.00
29 Tim Dwight RC 1.25 3.00
30 Charlie Batch RC 1.25 3.00
31 Chris Chandler .25 .60
32 Jamal Anderson .25 .60
33 Terance Mathis .20 .50
34 Jake Plummer .20 .50
35 Mario Bates .20 .50
36 Frank Sanders .20 .50
37 Adrian Murrell .20 .50
38 Jim Harbaugh .30 .75
39 Michael Jackson .20 .50
40 Jermaine Lewis .20 .50
41 Doug Flutie .30 .75
42 Rob Johnson .25 .60
43 Antowain Smith .25 .60
44 Eric Moulds .25 .60
45 Thurman Thomas .25 .60
46 Kevin Greene .30 .75
47 Fred Lane .20 .50
48 Rae Carruth .20 .50
49 William Floyd .20 .50
50 Erik Kramer .20 .50
51 Edgar Bennett .25 .60
52 Curtis Conway .25 .60
53 Bobby Engram .20 .50
54 Jeff Blake .25 .60
55 Carl Pickens .25 .60
56 Darnay Scott .25 .60
57 Corey Dillon .20 .50
58 Troy Aikman .40 1.00
59 Michael Irvin .30 .75
60 Emmitt Smith .50 1.25
61 Deion Sanders .25 .60
62 John Elway .50 1.25
63 Terrell Davis .25 .60
64 Rod Smith WR .25 .60
65 Shannon Sharpe .25 .60
66 Ed McCaffrey .25 .60
67 Barry Sanders .50 1.25
68 Scott Mitchell .25 .60
69 Herman Moore .25 .60
70 Johnnie Morton .25 .60
71 Brett Favre .60 1.50
72 Dorsey Levens .25 .60
73 Reggie White .30 .75
74 Antonio Freeman .30 .75
75 Robert Brooks .25 .60
76 Marshall Faulk .25 .60
77 Marvin Harrison .25 .60
78 Mark Brunell .25 .60
79 Keenan McCardell .25 .60
80 Jimmy Smith .25 .60
81 Elvis Grbac .25 .60
82 Andre Rison .25 .60
83 Tony Gonzalez .25 .60
84 Derrick Thomas .30 .75
85 Dan Marino .60 1.50
86 Karim Abdul-Jabbar .20 .50
87 O.J. McDuffie .25 .60
88 Zach Thomas .25 .60
89 Brad Johnson .25 .60
90 Cris Carter .30 .75
91 Jake Reed .25 .60
92 Robert Smith .20 .50
93 John Randle .30 .75
94 Randall Cunningham .25 .60
95 Drew Bledsoe .25 .60
96 Terry Glenn .25 .60
97 Ben Coates .25 .60
98 Danny Wuerffel .25 .60
99 Andre Hastings .20 .50

100 Troy Davis .20 .50
101 Danny Kanell .20 .50
102 Tiki Barber .25 .60
103 Amani Toomer .20 .50
104 Vinny Testaverde .20 .50
105 Glenn Foley .20 .50
106 Curtis Martin .25 .60
107 Keyshawn Johnson .25 .60
108 Wayne Chrebet .20 .50
109 Jeff George .25 .60
110 Napoleon Kaufman .20 .50
111 Tim Brown .30 .75
112 James Jett .20 .50
113 Bobby Hoying .25 .60
114 Charlie Garner .25 .60
115 Irving Fryar .25 .60
116 Kordell Stewart .20 .50
117 Jerome Bettis .30 .75
118 Will Blackwell .20 .50
119 Charles Johnson .20 .50
120 Tony Banks .25 .60
121 Amp Lee .20 .50
122 Isaac Bruce .30 .75
123 Eddie Kennison .20 .50
124 Natrone Means .25 .60
125 Junior Seau .25 .60
126 Bryan Still .20 .50
127 Steve Young .40 1.00
128 Jerry Rice .75 2.00
129 Garrison Hearst .20 .50
130 J.J. Stokes .25 .60
131 Terrell Owens .25 .60
132 Warren Moon .30 .75
133 Jon Kitna .20 .50
134 Ricky Watters .25 .60
135 Joey Galloway .25 .60
136 Trent Dilfer .25 .60
137 Warrick Dunn .20 .50
138 Mike Alstott .20 .50
139 Bert Emanuel .25 .60
140 Reidel Anthony .20 .50
141 Steve McNair .25 .60
142 Yancey Thigpen .20 .50
143 Eddie George .25 .60
144 Chris Sanders .20 .50
145 Gus Frerotte .20 .50
146 Terry Allen .25 .60
147 Michael Westbrook .25 .60
148 Troy Aikman CL .30 .75
149 Dan Marino CL .60 1.50
150 Randy Moss CL 1.00 2.50

1998 Upper Deck Encore F/X

*F/X VETS/125: 8X TO 20X BASIC CARDS
*F/X ROOKIES/125: 1.5X TO 4X BASIC RC
STATED PRINT RUN 125 SER.#'d SETS
1 Peyton Manning 100.00 175.00

1998 Upper Deck Encore Constant Threat

Randomly inserted in packs at the rate of one in 11, this 15-card set features color action photos of high-impact players who can affect the outcome of a game in the blink of an eye.
COMPLETE SET (15) 40.00 80.00
STATED ODDS 1:11
CT1 Dan Marino 4.00 10.00
CT2 Peyton Manning 10.00 20.00
CT3 Randy Moss 5.00 12.00
CT4 Brett Favre 4.00 10.00
CT5 Mark Brunell 1.00 2.50
CT6 John Elway 4.00 10.00
CT7 Ryan Leaf .75 2.00
CT8 Jake Plummer 1.00 2.50
CT9 Terrell Davis 1.00 2.50
CT10 Barry Sanders 3.00 8.00
CT11 Emmitt Smith 3.00 8.00
CT12 Curtis Martin 1.00 2.50
CT13 Eddie George 1.00 2.50
CT14 Warrick Dunn 1.00 2.50
CT15 Curtis Enis .40 1.00

1998 Upper Deck Encore Driving Forces

Randomly inserted into packs at the rate of one in 23, this 14-card set features color action photos of offensive superstars, including the top quarterbacks, running backs and wide receivers. A limited-edition paralell set was also produced with a special "Encore F/X" call-out on the card fronts and backs and sequentially number to 1500.
COMPLETE SET (14) 30.00 60.00
STATED ODDS 1:23
*F/X GOLD/1500: .8X TO 2X BASIC INSERTS
F1 Terrell Davis 1.50 4.00
F2 Barry Sanders 5.00 12.00
F3 Doug Flutie 1.50 4.00
F4 Mark Brunell 1.50 4.00
F5 Garrison Hearst 1.50 4.00
F6 Jamal Anderson 1.50 4.00
F7 Jerry Rice 3.00 8.00
F8 John Elway 6.00 15.00
F9 Robert Smith 1.50 4.00
F10 Kordell Stewart 1.50 4.00
F11 Eddie George 1.50 4.00
F12 Antonio Freeman 1.50 4.00
F13 Dan Marino 6.00 15.00
F14 Steve Young 2.00 5.00

1998 Upper Deck Encore Milestones

Randomly inserted into packs, this eight-card set features color action player photos with a special "UD Milestones" stamp printed on gold foil cards. Each card is sequentially numberd to the pictured player's specific milestone number.
1 Peyton Manning/26 250.00 500.00
12 Randy Moss/17 125.00 250.00
60 Emmitt Smith/124 30.00 60.00
62 John Elway/50 40.00 100.00
63 Terrell Davis/30 15.00 40.00
67 Barry Sanders/100 40.00 80.00
85 Dan Marino/400 15.00 40.00
128 Jerry Rice/184 8.00 20.00

1998 Upper Deck Encore Rookie Encore

Randomly inserted in packs at the rate of one in 23, this 10-card set features color photos of the season's top first-year players. A limited edition parallel version of this set was also produced with a special "Encore F/X" call-out on the card fronts and backs and sequentially numbered to 500.
COMPLETE SET (10) 40.00 80.00
STATED ODDS 1:23
*F/X GOLD/500: 1.2X TO 3X BASIC INSERTS
RE1 Randy Moss 5.00 12.00
RE2 Peyton Manning 12.50 25.00
RE3 Charlie Batch 1.00 2.50
RE4 Fred Taylor 1.25 3.00
RE5 Robert Edwards .75 2.00
RE6 Curtis Enis .75 2.00
RE7 Robert Holcombe .60 1.50
RE8 Ryan Leaf .75 2.00
RE9 John Avery .75 2.00
RE10 Tim Dwight 1.00 2.50

1998 Upper Deck Encore Super Powers

Randomly inserted into packs at the rate of one in 11, this 15-card set features color action photos of the season's hot players who are in pursuit of a Super Bowl ring.
COMPLETE SET (15) 40.00 80.00
STATED ODDS 1:11
S1 Dan Marino 2.00 5.00
S2 Napoleon Kaufman .60 1.50
S3 Brett Favre 2.00 5.00
S4 John Elway 1.50 4.00
S5 Randy Moss 4.00 10.00
S6 Kordell Stewart .60 1.50
S7 Mark Brunell .75 2.00
S8 Peyton Manning 10.00 20.00
S9 Emmitt Smith 1.50 4.00
S10 Jake Plummer .60 1.50
S11 Eddie George .75 2.00
S12 Warrick Dunn .60 1.50
S13 Jerome Bettis 1.00 2.50
S14 Terrell Davis .75 2.00
S15 Fred Taylor 1.00 2.50

1998 Upper Deck Encore Superstar Encore

Randomy inserted into packs at the rate of one in 23, this six-card set features color action photos of the league's premier players. A limited edtion parallel version of this set was produced with a special "Encore F/X" call-out on the card fronts and backs and sequentially numbered to 25.
COMPLETE SET (6) 20.00 50.00
STATED ODDS 1:23
*F/X VETS/25: 12X TO 30X BASIC INSERTS
*F/X ROOKIES/25: 6X TO 15X
RR1 Brett Favre 4.00 10.00
RR2 Barry Sanders 3.00 8.00
RR3 Mark Brunell 1.00 2.50
RR4 Emmitt Smith 3.00 8.00
RR5 Randy Moss 6.00 15.00
RR6 Terrell Davis 1.00 2.50

1998 Upper Deck Encore UD Authentics

Randomly inserted in packs at the rate of one in 288, this five-card set features color player photos of five NFL superstars with their autographs. Some were issued via mail redemption cards that carried an expiration date of 1/8/2000. An unpriced Red Ink signature version was produced for each player and limited in production to the player's jersey number (although they were not serial numbered).
STATED ODDS 1:288
DM2 Dan Marino 60.00 120.00
JM2 Joe Montana 49ers 50.00 100.00
MB1 Mark Brunell blue 10.00 25.00
RM Randy Moss 90.00 150.00
TD Terrell Davis 15.00 40.00

1999 Upper Deck Encore

Released as a 225-card set, the 1999 Upper Deck Encore set is comprised of 180 regular player cards and 45 short printed Star Rookies cards found one in every eight packs. The base set parallels the regular issue 1999 Upper Deck set with an enhanced rainbow holo-foil card stock. Encore was packaged in 24-pack boxes with six cards per pack and carried a suggested retail price of $3.99.
COMPLETE SET (225) 50.00 120.00
COMP.SET w/o SP's (180) 15.00 40.00
1 Jake Plummer .20 .50
2 Adrian Murrell .20 .50
3 Rob Moore .20 .50
4 Simeon Rice .20 .50
5 Andre Wadsworth .20 .50
6 Frank Sanders .20 .50
7 Tim Dwight .25 .60
8 Chris Chandler .25 .60
9 Jamal Anderson .25 .60
10 O.J. Santiago .20 .50
11 Tony Graziani .20 .50
12 Terance Mathis .20 .50
13 Priest Holmes .20 .50
14 Stoney Case .20 .50
15 Ray Lewis .30 .75
16 Peter Boulware .20 .50
17 Errict Rhett .20 .50
18 Jermaine Lewis .20 .50
19 Eric Moulds .20 .50
20 Doug Flutie .30 .75
21 Antowain Smith .20 .50
22 Rob Johnson .25 .60
23 Bruce Smith .25 .60
24 Andre Reed .30 .75
25 Wesley Walls .25 .60
26 Tim Biakabutuka .25 .60
27 Fred Lane .20 .50
28 Steve Beuerlein .25 .60
29 Muhsin Muhammad .20 .50
30 Rae Carruth .20 .50
31 Bobby Engram .20 .50
32 Curtis Enis .20 .50
33 Edgar Bennett .25 .60
34 Curtis Conway .25 .60
35 Shane Matthews .20 .50
36 Tony McGee .20 .50
37 Darnay Scott .20 .50
38 Jeff Blake .25 .60
39 Corey Dillon .20 .50
40 Ki-Jana Carter .20 .50
41 Ty Detmer .20 .50
42 Leslie Shepherd .20 .50
43 Terry Kirby .20 .50
44 Antonio Langham .20 .50
45 Jamir Miller .20 .50
46 Marc Edwards .25 .60
47 Troy Aikman .40 1.00
48 Rocket Ismail .25 .60
49 Emmitt Smith .50 1.25
50 Michael Irvin .30 .75
51 Deion Sanders .25 .60
52 Greg Ellis .20 .50
53 Bubby Brister .20 .50
54 Terrell Davis .25 .60
55 Ed McCaffrey .25 .60
56 Rod Smith .25 .60
57 Shannon Sharpe .25 .60
58 Brian Griese .20 .50
59 Charlie Batch .20 .50
60 Germane Crowell .20 .50
61 Johnnie Morton .25 .60
62 Robert Porcher .20 .50
63 Ron Rivers .20 .50
64 Herman Moore .25 .60
65 Brett Favre .60 1.50
66 Bill Schroeder .25 .60
67 Antonio Freeman .25 .60
68 Dorsey Levens .25 .60
69 Desmond Howard .25 .60
70 Vonnie Holliday .20 .50
71 Peyton Manning 1.00 2.50
72 Jerome Pathon .20 .50
73 Marvin Harrison .25 .60
74 Ken Dilger .20 .50
75 E.G. Green .20 .50
76 Cornelius Bennett .25 .60
77 Mark Brunell .25 .60
78 Fred Taylor .20 .50
79 Jimmy Smith .25 .60
80 James Stewart .20 .50
81 Keenan McCardell .25 .60
82 Carnell Lake .25 .60
83 Elvis Grbac .20 .50
84 Tony Gonzalez .25 .60
85 Andre Rison .25 .60
86 Derrick Thomas .30 .75
87 Warren Moon .30 .75
88 Derrick Alexander WR .20 .50
89 Dan Marino .60 1.50
90 O.J. McDuffie .25 .60
91 Karim Abdul-Jabbar .20 .50
92 Sam Madison .20 .50
93 Zach Thomas .25 .60
94 Tony Martin .25 .60
95 Randall Cunningham .25 .60
96 Randy Moss .25 .60
97 Cris Carter .30 .75
98 Jake Reed .25 .60
99 John Randle .30 .75
100 Robert Smith .20 .50
101 Drew Bledsoe .25 .60
102 Ben Coates .25 .60
103 Terry Glenn .25 .60
104 Tony Simmons .20 .50
105 Terry Allen .25 .60
106 Danny Wuerffel .25 .60
107 Cameron Cleeland .20 .50
108 Eddie Kennison .25 .60
109 Billy Joe Hobert .20 .50
110 Andre Hastings .20 .50
111 Kent Graham .20 .50
112 Tiki Barber .25 .60
113 Gary Brown .20 .50
114 Ike Hilliard .20 .50
115 Jason Sehorn .25 .60
116 Kerry Collins .20 .50
117 Vinny Testaverde .20 .50
118 Wayne Chrebet .20 .50
119 Curtis Martin .25 .60
120 Rick Mirer .25 .60
121 Aaron Glenn .20 .50
122 Keyshawn Johnson .25 .60
123 Rich Gannon .25 .60
124 Tim Brown .30 .75
125 Darrell Russell .20 .50
126 Tyrone Wheatley .25 .60
127 Charles Woodson .30 .75
128 Napoleon Kaufman .20 .50
129 Duce Staley .20 .50
130 Doug Pederson .20 .50
131 Kevin Turner .20 .50
132 Charles Johnson .20 .50
133 Jerome Bettis .30 .75
134 Courtney Hawkins .20 .50
135 Kordell Stewart .20 .50
136 Richard Huntley .20 .50
137 Levon Kirkland .20 .50
138 Hines Ward .25 .60
139 Kurt Warner RC 5.00 12.00
140 Marshall Faulk .25 .60
141 Az-Zahir Hakim .20 .50
142 Amp Lee .20 .50
143 Isaac Bruce .30 .75
144 Kevin Carter .20 .50
145 Jim Harbaugh .25 .60
146 Junior Seau .25 .60
147 Natrone Means .25 .60
148 Rodney Harrison .20 .50
149 Mikhael Ricks .20 .50
150 Erik Kramer .25 .60
151 Steve Young .40 1.00
152 Terrell Owens .25 .60
153 Jerry Rice .75 2.00
154 J.J. Stokes .20 .50
155 Jeff Garcia RC 3.00 8.00
156 Lawrence Phillips .25 .60
157 Jon Kitna .20 .50
158 Derrick Mayes .20 .50
159 Ricky Watters .25 .60
160 Chad Brown .20 .50
161 Shawn Springs .20 .50
162 Sean Dawkins .20 .50
163 Trent Dilfer .20 .50
164 Reidel Anthony .20 .50
165 Bert Emanuel .25 .60
166 Warrick Dunn .20 .50
167 Jacquez Green .20 .50
168 Mike Alstott .20 .50
169 Eddie George .25 .60
170 Steve McNair .25 .60
171 Kevin Dyson .20 .50
172 Frank Wycheck .25 .60
173 Blaine Bishop .20 .50
174 Yancey Thigpen .20 .50
175 Brad Johnson .25 .60
176 Michael Westbrook .20 .50
177 Skip Hicks .20 .50
178 Brian Mitchell .25 .60
179 Dana Stubblefield .20 .50
180 Stephen Davis .20 .50
181 Champ Bailey RC 1.50 4.00
182 Chris McAlister RC .75 2.00
183 Jevon Kearse RC 1.00 2.50
184 Ebenezer Ekuban RC .75 2.00
185 Chris Claiborne RC .75 2.00
186 Andy Katzenmoyer RC 1.00 2.50
187 Tim Couch RC 1.00 2.50
188 Daunte Culpepper RC 1.25 3.00
189 Akili Smith RC .75 2.00
190 Donovan McNabb RC 2.50 6.00
191 Sean Bennett RC .75 2.00
192 Brock Huard RC .75 2.00
193 Cade McNown RC .75 2.00
194 Shaun King RC .75 2.00
195 Joe Germaine RC 1.00 2.50
196 Ricky Williams RC 1.25 3.00
197 Edgerrin James RC 1.25 3.00
198 Sedrick Irvin RC .75 2.00
199 Kevin Faulk RC .75 2.00
200 Rob Konrad RC .75 2.00
201 James Johnson RC .75 2.00
202 Amos Zereoue RC .75 2.00
203 Torry Holt RC 1.50 4.00
204 D'Wayne Bates RC .75 2.00
205 David Boston RC .75 2.00
206 Dameane Douglas RC .75 2.00
207 Troy Edwards RC .75 2.00
208 Kevin Johnson RC 1.00 2.50
209 Peerless Price RC .75 2.00
210 Antoine Winfield RC .75 2.00
211 Mike Cloud RC .75 2.00
212 Joe Montgomery RC .75 2.00
213 Jermaine Fazande RC .75 2.00
214 Scott Covington RC .75 2.00
215 Aaron Brooks RC 1.00 2.50
216 Terry Jackson RC .75 2.00
217 Cecil Collins RC .75 2.00
218 Olandis Gary RC 1.25 3.00
219 Craig Yeast RC .75 2.00
220 Karsten Bailey RC .75 2.00
221 Reginald Kelly RC .75 2.00
222 Travis McGriff RC .75 2.00
223 Jeff Paulk RC .75 2.00
224 Jim Kleinsasser RC 1.25 3.00
225 Jason Tucker RC 1.00 2.50
WPE W.Payton Jsy AU/34 1000.00 1500.00

1999 Upper Deck Encore F/X

*STARS: 8X TO 20X HI COL.
*RCs: 1X TO 2.5X
STATED PRINT RUN 100 SER.#'d SETS

1999 Upper Deck Encore F/X Gold

STATED PRINT RUN 1 SER.#'d SET

1999 Upper Deck Encore Electric Currents

Randomly seeded in packs at the rate of one in six, this 20-card set features some of the NFL's premier offensive stars on an all-foil insert card. Card backs carry an "EC" prefix.
COMPLETE SET (20) 10.00 20.00
STATED ODDS 1:6
EC1 Steve Young 1.00 2.50
EC2 Doug Flutie .75 2.00
EC3 Jon Kitna .75 2.00
EC4 Randall Cunningham .75 2.00
EC5 Curtis Enis .30 .75
EC6 Jerry Rice 1.50 4.00
EC7 Antonio Freeman .75 2.00
EC8 Keyshawn Johnson .75 2.00
EC9 Steve McNair .75 2.00
EC10 Kordell Stewart .50 1.25
EC11 Drew Bledsoe 1.00 2.50
EC12 Corey Dillon .75 2.00
EC13 Vinny Testaverde .50 1.25
EC14 Tim Brown .75 2.00
EC15 Antowain Smith .75 2.00
EC16 Charlie Batch .75 2.00
EC17 Stephen Davis .75 2.00
EC18 Isaac Bruce .75 2.00
EC19 Curtis Martin .75 2.00
EC20 Ricky Watters .50 1.25

1999 Upper Deck Encore Game Used Helmets

Randomly inserted in packs at the rate of one in 575, this 20-card set features swatches of game-used helmets for the veterans and shoot-used helmets, obtained from the NFL Premier Rookie Photo Shoot in May 1999, for the rookies.
COMPLETE SET (20) 300.00 600.00
STATED ODDS 1:575
HAS Akili Smith 10.00 25.00
HBF Brett Favre 40.00 100.00
HBH Brock Huard 10.00 25.00
HCB Champ Bailey 12.50 30.00
HCC Cecil Collins 10.00 25.00
HCM Cade McNown 10.00 25.00
HDB David Boston 10.00 25.00
HDC Daunte Culpepper 30.00 80.00
HDM Dan Marino 40.00 100.00
HDW D'Wayne Bates 10.00 25.00
HEJ Edgerrin James 25.00 60.00
HJR Jerry Rice 25.00 60.00
HKF Kevin Faulk 10.00 25.00
HKJ Kevin Johnson 10.00 25.00
HMB Mark Brunell 10.00 25.00
HMC Donovan McNabb 30.00 80.00
HTC Tim Couch 10.00 25.00
HTD Terrell Davis 10.00 25.00
HTE Troy Edwards 10.00 25.00
HTH Torry Holt 20.00 50.00

1999 Upper Deck Encore Live Wires

Randomly inserted in packs at the rate of one in 11, this 15-card set features some of the NFL's top superstars and includes a short biography of each player. Card backs carry an "L" prefix.
COMPLETE SET (15) 20.00 40.00
STATED ODDS 1:11
L1 Jake Plummer .60 1.50
L2 Jamal Anderson 1.00 2.50
L3 Emmitt Smith 2.00 5.00
L4 John Elway 3.00 8.00
L5 Barry Sanders 3.00 8.00
L6 Brett Favre 3.00 8.00
L7 Mark Brunell 1.00 2.50
L8 Fred Taylor 1.00 2.50
L9 Randy Moss 2.00 5.00
L10 Drew Bledsoe 1.25 3.00
L11 Keyshawn Johnson 1.00 2.50
L12 Jerome Bettis 1.00 2.50
L13 Kordell Stewart .60 1.50
L14 Terrell Owens 1.00 2.50
L15 Eddie George 1.00 2.50

1999 Upper Deck Encore Seize the Game

Randomly seeded in packs, this 30-card set highlights game-breakers like Edgerring James, Eddie George and Keyshawn Johnson. The set is divided up into two tiers. Tier one cards, 1-20, are seeded at one in 20 packs, and tier two cards, 21-30, are seeded at one in 23 packs. Card backs carry an "SG" prefix. A gold one of one parallel of this set was released also.
COMPLETE SET (30) 50.00 100.00
SG1-SG20 STATED ODDS 1:20
SG21-SG30 STATED ODDS 1:23
*SG1-SG20 GOLD/250: 1X TO 2.5X
*SG21-SG30 GOLD/250: 1.2X TO 3X
SG1 Donovan McNabb 3.00 8.00
SG2 Keyshawn Johnson 1.50 4.00
SG3 Eddie George 1.50 4.00
SG4 Randall Cunningham 1.50 4.00
SG5 Charlie Batch 1.50 4.00
SG6 Curtis Martin 1.50 4.00
SG7 Edgerrin James 2.50 6.00
SG8 Jake Plummer 1.00 2.50
SG9 Drew Bledsoe 2.00 5.00
SG10 Marshall Faulk 2.00 5.00
SG11 Fred Taylor 1.50 4.00
SG12 Terrell Owens 1.50 4.00
SG13 Jerome Bettis 1.50 4.00
SG14 Antonio Freeman 1.50 4.00
SG15 Corey Dillon 1.50 4.00
SG16 Jerry Rice 3.00 8.00
SG17 Curtis Enis .60 1.50
SG18 Warrick Dunn 1.50 4.00
SG19 Kordell Stewart 1.00 2.50
SG20 Jamal Anderson 1.50 4.00
SG21 Terrell Davis 1.25 3.00
SG22 Randy Moss 2.50 6.00
SG23 Troy Aikman 2.50 6.00
SG24 Dan Marino 4.00 10.00
SG25 Ricky Williams 1.00 2.50
SG26 Peyton Manning 3.00 8.00
SG27 Steve Young 1.50 4.00
SG28 Tim Couch .60 1.50
SG29 Emmitt Smith 2.50 6.00
SG30 Brett Favre 4.00 10.00

1999 Upper Deck Encore UD Authentics

Randomly seeded in packs at the rate of one in 144, this 15-card set features authentic autographs of NFL superstars including Kurt Warner, Edgerrin James and Randy Moss. Shaun King was issued as a redemption card with an expiration date of 8/7/2000 but he never signed for the set.
STATED ODDS 1:144
BH Brock Huard 7.50 20.00
CM Cade McNown 7.50 20.00
DB David Boston 7.50 20.00
EJ Edgerrin James 20.00 50.00
JN Joe Namath 50.00 120.00
KF Kevin Faulk 10.00 25.00
KW Kurt Warner 40.00 80.00
MB Mark Brunell 10.00 25.00
PM Peyton Manning 60.00 120.00
RM Randy Moss 30.00 80.00
SK Shaun King EXCH 1.25 3.00
TA Troy Aikman 30.00 80.00
TC Tim Couch 7.50 20.00
TE Troy Edwards 7.50 20.00
TH Torry Holt 12.50 30.00

1999 Upper Deck Encore Upper Realm

Randomly inserted in packs at the rate of one in 12, this 10-card set pays tribute to 10 of the NFL's current superstars. Card backs carry a "UR" prefix.
COMPLETE SET (10) 12.50 30.00
STATED ODDS 1:12
UR1 Randy Moss 1.50 4.00
UR2 Warrick Dunn .75 2.00
UR3 Stephen Davis .75 2.00
UR4 Peyton Manning 2.00 5.00
UR5 Tim Biakabutuka .50 1.25
UR6 Steve Young 1.00 2.50
UR7 Kurt Warner 4.00 10.00
UR8 Steve McNair .75 2.00
UR9 Dan Marino 2.50 6.00
UR10 Jake Plummer .50 1.25

2000 Upper Deck Encore

Released in early December 2000, Encore features a 270-card set consisting of 222 regular issue cards, 45 Star Rookie cards inserted at the rate of one in 6, and three checklist cards. The base card design parallels that of the regular issue Upper Deck set from earlier this year with cards enhanced with gold foil highlights and a rainbow holofoil card stock. Encore was packaged in 24-pack boxes with packs containing five cards each and carried a suggested retail price of $4.99. An Update set of 13-cards was issued in April 2001 as part of 3-card packs distributed directly to Upper Deck hobby accounts.
COMPLETE SET (270) 50.00 120.00
COMP.SET w/o SP's (225) 6.00 15.00
223-267 ROOKIE ODDS 1:6
1 Jake Plummer .15 .40
2 Michael Pittman .15 .40
3 Rob Moore .15 .40
4 David Boston .15 .40
5 Frank Sanders .15 .40
6 Aeneas Williams .15 .40
7 Kwamie Lassiter .15 .40
8 Rob Fredrickson .15 .40
9 Tim Dwight .20 .50
10 Chris Chandler .20 .50
11 Jamal Anderson .20 .50
12 Shawn Jefferson .15 .40
13 Brian Finneran RC .25 .60
14 Terance Mathis .15 .40
15 Bob Christian .15 .40
16 Qadry Ismail .15 .40
17 Jermaine Lewis .15 .40
18 Rod Woodson .25 .60
19 Michael McCrary .15 .40
20 Tony Banks .15 .40
21 Peter Boulware .15 .40
22 Shannon Sharpe .20 .50
23 Peerless Price .20 .50
24 Rob Johnson .20 .50
25 Eric Moulds .15 .40
26 Doug Flutie .20 .50
27 Jeremy McDaniel .15 .40
28 Antowain Smith .20 .50
29 Shawn Bryson .15 .40
30 Muhsin Muhammad .15 .40
31 Donald Hayes .15 .40
32 Steve Beuerlein .20 .50
33 Reggie White .25 .60
34 Tim Biakabutuka .20 .50
35 Michael Bates .15 .40
36 Chuck Smith .15 .40
37 Wesley Walls .15 .40
38 Cade McNown .15 .40
39 Curtis Enis .15 .40
40 Marcus Robinson .20 .50
41 Eddie Kennison .15 .40
42 Bobby Engram .15 .40
43 Glyn Milburn .15 .40
44 Marty Booker .15 .40
45 Akili Smith .15 .40
46 Corey Dillon .15 .40
47 James Allen .15 .40
48 Tremain Mack .15 .40
49 Damon Griffin .15 .40
50 Takeo Spikes .15 .40
51 Tony McGee .15 .40
52 Tim Couch .20 .50
53 Kevin Johnson .15 .40
54 Darrin Chiaverini .15 .40
55 Jamir Miller .15 .40
56 Errict Rhett .20 .50
57 Aaron Shea RC .20 .50
58 Kevin Thompson RC .15 .40
59 Troy Aikman .30 .75
60 Emmitt Smith .40 1.00
61 Rocket Ismail .20 .50
62 Jason Tucker .15 .40
63 Chris Brazzell RC .15 .40
64 Joey Galloway .20 .50
65 Wane McGarity .15 .40
66 Terrell Davis .20 .50
67 Olandis Gary .20 .50
68 Brian Griese .15 .40
69 Gus Frerotte .15 .40
70 Byron Chamberlain .15 .40
71 Ed McCaffrey .20 .50
72 Rod Smith .20 .50
73 Al Wilson .15 .40
74 Charlie Batch .15 .40
75 Germane Crowell .15 .40
76 Sedrick Irvin .15 .40
77 Johnnie Morton .20 .50
78 Robert Porcher .15 .40
79 Herman Moore .15 .40
80 James Stewart .15 .40
81 Brett Favre .50 1.25
82 Antonio Freeman .20 .50
83 Bill Schroeder .20 .50
84 Dorsey Levens .20 .50
85 Herbert Goodman RC .15 .40
86 Ahman Green .20 .50
87 Matt Hasselbeck .15 .40
88 Peyton Manning .60 1.50
89 Edgerrin James .20 .50
90 Marvin Harrison .20 .50
91 Basil Mitchell .15 .40
92 Terrence Wilkins .15 .40
93 Karim Abdul-Jabbar .15 .40
94 Ken Dilger .15 .40
95 Mark Brunell .20 .50
96 Fred Taylor .15 .40
97 Jimmy Smith .20 .50
98 Keenan McCardell .20 .50
99 Stacey Mack .15 .40
100 Jonathan Quinn .15 .40
101 Kyle Brady .15 .40
102 Hardy Nickerson .15 .40
103 Elvis Grbac .15 .40
104 Tony Gonzalez .20 .50
105 Derrick Alexander WR .15 .40
106 Tony Richardson RC .15 .40
107 Michael Cloud .15 .40
108 Donnie Edwards .15 .40
109 Jay Fiedler .20 .50
110 James Johnson .15 .40
111 Tony Martin .20 .50
112 Damon Huard .15 .40
113 Lamar Smith .15 .40
114 Thurman Thomas .20 .50
115 Mike Quinn .15 .40
116 Oronde Gadsden .20 .50
117 Randy Moss .20 .50
118 Robert Smith .15 .40
119 Cris Carter .25 .60
120 Matthew Hatchette .15 .40
121 Daunte Culpepper .20 .50
122 Moe Williams .15 .40
123 Drew Bledsoe .20 .50
124 Terry Glenn .20 .50
125 Troy Brown .15 .40
126 Kevin Faulk .15 .40
127 Lawyer Milloy .15 .40
128 Ricky Williams .20 .50
129 Keith Poole .15 .40
130 Jake Reed .20 .50
131 Jake Delhomme RC .20 .50
132 Jeff Blake .20 .50
133 Andrew Glover .15 .40
134 Kerry Collins .15 .40
135 Amani Toomer .15 .40
136 Joe Montgomery .15 .40
137 Ike Hilliard .15 .40
138 Tiki Barber .20 .50
139 Pete Mitchell .15 .40
140 Ray Lucas .15 .40
141 Mo Lewis .15 .40
142 Curtis Martin .20 .50
143 Vinny Testaverde .15 .40
144 Wayne Chrebet .15 .40
145 Dedric Ward .15 .40
146 Tim Brown .25 .60
147 Rich Gannon .20 .50
148 Tyrone Wheatley .15 .40
149 Napoleon Kaufman .20 .50
150 Charles Woodson .25 .60
151 Darrell Russell .15 .40
152 James Jett .20 .50
153 Rickey Dudley .15 .40
154 Jon Ritchie .15 .40
155 Duce Staley .15 .40
156 Donovan McNabb .20 .50
157 Torrance Small .15 .40
158 Ron Powlus RC .25 .60
159 Mike Mamula .15 .40
160 Dameane Douglas .15 .40
161 Charles Johnson .15 .40
162 Kent Graham .15 .40
163 Troy Edwards .15 .40
164 Jerome Bettis .25 .60
165 Hines Ward .20 .50
166 Kordell Stewart .15 .40
167 Levon Kirkland .15 .40
168 Bobby Shaw RC .15 .40
169 Marshall Faulk .20 .50
170 Kurt Warner .40 1.00
171 Torry Holt .20 .50
172 Isaac Bruce .25 .60
173 Kevin Carter .15 .40
174 Az-Zahir Hakim .15 .40
175 Ricky Proehl .15 .40
176 Robert Chancey .15 .40
177 Curtis Conway .20 .50
178 Freddie Jones .15 .40
179 Junior Seau .20 .50
180 Jeff Graham .15 .40
181 Reggie Jones RC .15 .40
182 Rodney Harrison .15 .40
183 Rick Mirer .15 .40
184 Jerry Rice .60 1.50
185 Charlie Garner .20 .50
186 Terrell Owens .20 .50
187 Jeff Garcia .15 .40
188 Fred Beasley .15 .40
189 J.J. Stokes .20 .50
190 Ricky Watters .20 .50
191 Jon Kitna .15 .40
192 Derrick Mayes .15 .40
193 Sean Dawkins .15 .40
194 Charlie Rogers .15 .40
195 Brock Huard .15 .40
196 Cortez Kennedy .20 .50
197 Christian Fauria .15 .40
198 Warrick Dunn .15 .40
199 Shaun King .15 .40
200 Mike Alstott .20 .50
201 Warren Sapp .15 .40
202 Jacquez Green .15 .40
203 Reidel Anthony .15 .40
204 Dave Moore .15 .40
205 Keyshawn Johnson .20 .50
206 Eddie George .20 .50
207 Steve McNair .20 .50
208 Billy Volek RC .25 .60
209 Jevon Kearse .15 .40
210 Yancey Thigpen .15 .40
211 Frank Wycheck .20 .50
212 Carl Pickens .20 .50
213 Neil O'Donnell .15 .40
214 Brad Johnson .20 .50
215 Stephen Davis .15 .40
216 Michael Westbrook .15 .40
217 Albert Connell .15 .40
218 Aaron Stecker RC .15 .40
219 Bruce Smith .20 .50
220 Stephen Alexander .15 .40
221 Jeff George .20 .50
222 Adrian Murrell .15 .40
223 Courtney Brown RC .75 2.00
224 John Engelberger RC .60 1.50
225 Deltha O'Neal RC .60 1.50
226 Corey Simon RC .75 2.00
227 R.Jay Soward RC .60 1.50
228 Chris Samuels RC 1.00 2.50
229 Avion Black RC .60 1.50
230 Doug Chapman RC .60 1.50
231 Darrell Jackson RC .60 1.50
232 Chris Cole RC .75 2.00
233 Trevor Gaylor RC .60 1.50
234 Chad Morton RC .75 2.00
235 Chris Redman RC .60 1.50
236 Joe Hamilton RC .60 1.50
237 Chad Pennington RC .75 2.00
238 Tee Martin RC .60 1.50
239 Giovanni Carmazzi RC .60 1.50
240 Tim Rattay RC .75 2.00
241 Ron Dayne RC 1.00 2.50
242 Shaun Alexander RC 1.00 2.50
243 Thomas Jones RC .75 2.00
244 Reuben Droughns RC .60 1.50
245 Jamal Lewis RC 1.00 2.50
246 Michael Wiley RC .60 1.50
247 J.R. Redmond RC .60 1.50
248 Travis Prentice RC .60 1.50
249 Todd Husak RC .60 1.50
250 Trung Canidate RC .60 1.50
251 Brian Urlacher RC 3.00 8.00
252 Anthony Becht RC .60 1.50
253 Bubba Franks RC .60 1.50
254 Tom Brady RC 75.00 150.00
255 Peter Warrick RC .60 1.50
256 Plaxico Burress RC .75 2.00
257 Sylvester Morris RC .60 1.50
258 Dez White RC .60 1.50
259 Travis Taylor RC .60 1.50
260 Todd Pinkston RC .60 1.50
261 Dennis Northcutt RC .60 1.50
262 Jerry Porter RC 1.00 2.50
263 Laveranues Coles RC .75 2.00
264 Danny Farmer RC .60 1.50
265 Curtis Keaton RC .60 1.50
266 Windrell Hayes RC .60 1.50
267 Ron Dugans RC .60 1.50
268 Steve McNair CL .15 .40
269 Jake Plummer CL .12 .30
270 Antonio Freeman CL .15 .40
271 Brad Hoover RC .75 2.00
272 Charles Lee RC .60 1.50
273 Deon Dyer RC .60 1.50
274 Doug Johnson RC .60 1.50
275 JaJuan Dawson RC .60 1.50
276 Jarious Jackson RC .75 2.00
277 Larry Foster RC .60 1.50
278 Mike Anderson RC .60 1.50
279 Ron Dixon RC .60 1.50
280 Sammy Morris RC .60 1.50
281 Shyrone Stith RC .60 1.50
282 Spergon Wynn RC .60 1.50
283 Troy Walters RC .60 1.50

2000 Upper Deck Encore Highlight Zone

Randomly seeded in packs at the rate of one in seven, this 10-card set features top NFL Players on an all foil insert card with three player photos. In the upper left corner is a small action shot, centered is a large action photo, and in the lower right corner a player portrait style photo appears. Cards are highlighted with gold foil.
COMPLETE SET (10) 3.00 8.00
STATED ODDS 1:7
HZ1 Eddie George .40 1.00
HZ2 Steve McNair .40 1.00
HZ3 Kevin Dyson .40 1.00
HZ4 Kurt Warner .75 2.00
HZ5 Emmitt Smith .75 2.00
HZ6 Brad Johnson .40 1.00
HZ7 Curtis Martin .40 1.00
HZ8 Ray Lucas .30 .75
HZ9 Akili Smith .30 .75
HZ10 Jake Plummer .30 .75

2000 Upper Deck Encore Proving Ground

Randomly inserted in packs at the rate of one in seven, this 10-card set features full color action photography on an all foil card with red border alond the left side of the card and gold foil highlights.
COMPLETE SET (10) 2.50 6.00
STATED ODDS 1:7
PG1 Marcus Robinson .40 1.00
PG2 Stephen Davis .30 .75
PG3 Daunte Culpepper .40 1.00
PG4 Jevon Kearse .30 .75
PG5 Marshall Faulk .40 1.00
PG6 Marvin Harrison .40 1.00
PG7 Germane Crowell .30 .75
PG8 Darnay Scott .40 1.00
PG9 Duce Staley .30 .75
PG10 Warrick Dunn .30 .75

2000 Upper Deck Encore Rookie Combo Jerseys

Randomly seeded in packs at the rate of one in 287, this nine card set pairs top rookies and showcases an authentic game jersey swatch of each. The last three cards in the set have three players on the front and three jersey swatches respectively.
STATED ODDS 1:287
RC1 D.White/B.Urlacher 20.00 50.00
RC2 T.Martin/P.Burress 8.00 20.00
RC3 J.Porter/Syl.Morris 10.00 25.00
RC4 P.Warrick/C.Brown 8.00 20.00
RC5 P.Warrick/C.Keaton 6.00 15.00
RC6 T.Prentice/D.Northcutt 6.00 15.00
RC7 Taylor/Lewis/Redman 10.00 25.00
RC8 Dayne/T.Jones/Alexander 10.00 25.00
RC9 Pennington/Coles/Becht 8.00 20.00

2000 Upper Deck Encore Rookie Helmets

Randomly inserted in packs at the rate of one in 287, this 28-card set features top 2000 rookies in action with a swatch of a game worn helmet. An Autographed version for 13 of the cards was also produced with each serial numbered to 25.
STATED ODDS 1:287
HAS Shaun Alexander 6.00 15.00
HBF Bubba Franks 4.00 10.00
HBU Brian Urlacher 20.00 50.00
HCB Courtney Brown 5.00 12.00
HCK Curtis Keaton 4.00 10.00
HCP Chad Pennington 5.00 12.00
HCR Chris Redman 4.00 10.00
HCS Corey Simon 5.00 12.00
HDF Danny Farmer 4.00 10.00
HDN Dennis Northcutt 4.00 10.00
HDR Reuben Droughns 4.00 10.00
HDU Ron Dugans 4.00 10.00
HDW Dez White 4.00 10.00
HJL Jamal Lewis 6.00 15.00
HJP Jerry Porter 6.00 15.00
HJR J.R. Redmond 4.00 10.00
HLC Laveranues Coles 5.00 12.00
HPB Plaxico Burress 5.00 12.00
HPI Todd Pinkston 4.00 10.00
HPW Peter Warrick 4.00 10.00
HRD Ron Dayne 6.00 15.00
HRJ R.Jay Soward 4.00 10.00
HSM Sylvester Morris 4.00 10.00
HTJ Thomas Jones 5.00 12.00
HTM Tee Martin 4.00 10.00
HTP Travis Prentice 4.00 10.00
HTT Travis Taylor 4.00 10.00
HTW Anthony Becht 4.00 10.00

2000 Upper Deck Encore Rookie Helmets Autographs

Randomly inserted in packs, this 13-card set features player action photography and both a swatch of a game used helmet and an authentic player autograph. Each card is sequentially numbered to 25.
STATED PRINT RUN 25 SER.#'d SETS
AHBU Brian Urlacher 100.00 200.00
AHCB Courtney Brown 15.00 40.00
AHCP Chad Pennington 15.00 40.00
AHCR Chris Redman 12.00 30.00
AHDF Danny Farmer 12.00 30.00
AHDN Dennis Northcutt 12.00 30.00
AHDU Ron Dugans 12.00 30.00
AHDW Dez White 12.00 30.00
AHLC Laveranues Coles 15.00 40.00
AHPB Plaxico Burress 15.00 40.00
AHRD Ron Dayne 20.00 50.00
AHSA Shaun Alexander 20.00 50.00
AHSM Sylvester Morris 12.00 30.00
AHTP Travis Prentice 12.00 30.00

2000 Upper Deck Encore UD Authentics

Randomly inserted in packs at the rate of one in 23, this set features top rookies with both action and portrait style photos coupled with an authentic player autograph. Cards are mainly gold with blue highlights. Some were issued via mail redemption cards that carried an expiration date of 8/14/2001.
STATED ODDS 1:23
BU Brian Urlacher 20.00 50.00
CB Courtney Brown 5.00 12.00
CC Chris Coleman 4.00 10.00
CM Corey Moore 4.00 10.00
CP Chad Pennington 5.00 12.00
CR Chris Redman 4.00 10.00
DF Danny Farmer 4.00 10.00
DJ Darrell Jackson 4.00 10.00
DN Dennis Northcutt 4.00 10.00
DU Ron Dugans 4.00 10.00
DW Dez White 4.00 10.00
DX Ron Dixon 4.00 10.00
JO Doug Johnson 4.00 10.00
KC Kwame Cavil 4.00 10.00
LC Laveranues Coles 5.00 12.00
LCX Laveranues Coles EXCH 1.25 3.00
MA Mike Anderson 4.00 10.00
MW Michael Wiley 4.00 10.00
PB Plaxico Burress 5.00 12.00
RD Ron Dayne 6.00 15.00
SA Shaun Alexander 10.00 25.00
SG Sherrod Gideon 4.00 10.00
SM Sylvester Morris 4.00 10.00
TC Trung Canidate 4.00 10.00
TG Trevor Gaylor 4.00 10.00
TM Tee Martin 4.00 10.00
TP Travis Prentice 4.00 10.00
TR Tim Rattay 5.00 12.00
TW Troy Walters 4.00 10.00

2005 Upper Deck ESPN

This 160-card set was released through Upper Deck's retail channels in September, 2005. The set was issued in nine-card packs with an $2.99 SRP which came 24 packs to a box. Cards numbered 1-100 feature veterans in team alphabetical order while cards numbered 101-160 feature 2005 rookies. Those rookies were inserted into packs at a stated rate of one in four.
COMP.SET w/o RC's (100) 10.00 25.00
DRAFT PICK STATED ODDS 1:4
1 Larry Fitzgerald .30 .75
2 Josh McCown .25 .60
3 Anquan Boldin .20 .50
4 Michael Vick .25 .60
5 Warrick Dunn .20 .50
6 Peerless Price .20 .50
7 Alge Crumpler .25 .60
8 Jamal Lewis .25 .60
9 Kyle Boller .20 .50
10 Derrick Mason .20 .50

11 Willis McGahee .20 .50
12 J.P. Losman .20 .50
13 Eric Moulds .20 .50
14 Jake Delhomme .20 .50
15 Steve Smith .30 .75
16 DeShaun Foster .25 .60
17 Muhsin Muhammad .20 .50
18 Thomas Jones .20 .50
19 Rex Grossman .20 .50
20 Chad Johnson .20 .50
21 Carson Palmer .25 .60
22 Rudi Johnson .20 .50
23 Lee Suggs .20 .50
24 Kellen Winslow .20 .50
25 Luke McCown .20 .50
26 Julius Jones .20 .50
27 Keyshawn Johnson .25 .60
28 Drew Bledsoe .25 .60
29 Tatum Bell .20 .50
30 Jake Plummer .20 .50
31 Rod Smith .25 .60
32 Roy Williams WR .20 .50
33 Kevin Jones .20 .50
34 Joey Harrington .20 .50
35 Jeff Garcia .20 .50
36 Brett Favre .60 1.50
37 Javon Walker .20 .50
38 Ahman Green .25 .60
39 David Carr .20 .50
40 Andre Johnson .25 .60
41 Domanick Davis .20 .50
42 Peyton Manning .75 2.00
43 Edgerrin James .25 .60
44 Marvin Harrison .25 .60
45 Byron Leftwich .20 .50
46 Fred Taylor .20 .50
47 Jimmy Smith .25 .60
48 Priest Holmes .20 .50
49 Trent Green .20 .50
50 Tony Gonzalez .25 .60
51 Larry Johnson .20 .50
52 Chris Chambers .20 .50
53 A.J. Feeley .20 .50
54 Randy McMichael .20 .50
55 Daunte Culpepper .25 .60
56 Nate Burleson .20 .50
57 Michael Bennett .20 .50
58 Tom Brady 1.25 3.00
59 Deion Branch .20 .50
60 Corey Dillon .20 .50
61 Aaron Brooks .20 .50
62 Deuce McAllister .25 .60
63 Joe Horn .20 .50
64 Eli Manning .50 1.25
65 Jeremy Shockey .20 .50
66 Tiki Barber .25 .60
67 Plaxico Burress .20 .50
68 Chad Pennington .20 .50
69 Curtis Martin .25 .60
70 Laveranues Coles .20 .50
71 Jerry Porter .20 .50
72 Randy Moss .25 .60
73 Kerry Collins .20 .50
74 Donovan McNabb .25 .60
75 Brian Westbrook .20 .50
76 Terrell Owens .25 .60
77 Ben Roethlisberger .50 1.25
78 Jerome Bettis .30 .75
79 Hines Ward .25 .60
80 Drew Brees .30 .75
81 LaDainian Tomlinson .30 .75
82 Antonio Gates .30 .75
83 Tim Rattay .20 .50
84 Eric Johnson .20 .50
85 Rashaun Woods .20 .50
86 Matt Hasselbeck .20 .50
87 Shaun Alexander .20 .50
88 Darrell Jackson .20 .50
89 Marc Bulger .20 .50
90 Marshall Faulk .25 .60
91 Torry Holt .25 .60
92 Brian Griese .20 .50
93 Michael Pittman .20 .50
94 Michael Clayton .20 .50
95 Steve McNair .25 .60
96 Chris Brown .20 .50
97 Drew Bennett .25 .60
98 Clinton Portis .20 .50
99 Patrick Ramsey .25 .60
100 Santana Moss .25 .60
101 Aaron Rodgers RC 6.00 15.00
102 Alex Smith QB RC 2.00 5.00
103 Charlie Frye RC .50 1.25
104 Andrew Walter RC .50 1.25
105 David Greene RC .50 1.25
106 Dan Orlovsky RC .50 1.25
107 Derek Anderson RC .60 1.50
108 Cadillac Williams RC .50 1.25
109 Ronnie Brown RC .60 1.50
110 Ciatrick Fason RC .50 1.25
111 Cedric Benson RC .50 1.25
112 Vincent Jackson RC .75 2.00
113 Eric Shelton RC .50 1.25
114 Frank Gore RC 1.00 2.50
115 Braylon Edwards RC .50 1.25
116 Roddy White RC .75 2.00
117 Troy Williamson RC .50 1.25
118 Craphonso Thorpe RC .50 1.25
119 Mark Clayton RC .50 1.25
120 Fred Gibson RC .50 1.25
121 Reggie Brown RC .50 1.25
122 Matt Jones RC .50 1.25
123 David Pollack RC .50 1.25
124 Derrick Johnson RC .60 1.50
125 Erasmus James RC .50 1.25
126 Antrel Rolle RC .75 2.00
127 Thomas Davis RC .50 1.25
128 Adam Jones RC .60 1.50
129 Corey Webster RC .60 1.50
130 Marlin Jackson RC .50 1.25
131 Brodney Pool RC .75 2.00
132 Mark Bradley RC .50 1.25
133 Stefan LeFors RC .50 1.25
134 Alex Smith TE RC .50 1.25
135 Heath Miller RC 1.00 2.50
136 Jason Campbell RC .50 1.25
137 Kyle Orton RC .50 1.25
138 Vernand Morency RC .60 1.50
139 Carlos Rogers RC .75 2.00
140 J.J. Arrington RC .60 1.50
141 Ryan Moats RC .60 1.50
142 Chris Henry RC .60 1.50
143 Terrence Murphy RC .50 1.25
144 Fabian Washington RC .50 1.25
145 Roscoe Parrish RC .50 1.25
146 Kevin Everett RC .75 2.00
147 Travis Johnson RC .50 1.25
148 Mike Williams .60 1.50
149 Maurice Clarett .60 1.50
150 Channing Crowder RC .60 1.50
151 Odell Thurman RC .75 2.00
152 DeMarcus Ware RC 1.50 4.00
153 Shawne Merriman RC .75 2.00
154 Jerome Mathis RC .75 2.00
155 Marcus Spears RC .50 1.25
156 Luis Castillo RC .60 1.50
157 Darren Sproles RC .75 2.00
158 Marion Barber RC .50 1.25
159 Justin Tuck RC .60 1.50
160 Courtney Roby RC .50 1.25

2005 Upper Deck ESPN Holofoil

*VETERANS: 3X TO 8X BASIC CARDS
*ROOKIES: 1X TO 2.5X BASIC CARDS
STATED ODDS 1:24
STATED PRINT RUN 199 SER.#'d SETS

2005 Upper Deck ESPN ESPY Award Winners

COMPLETE SET (20) 12.50 30.00
BASIC INSERTS ONE PER PACK OVERALL
*HOLOFOIL: 3X TO 8X BASIC INSERTS
HOLOFOIL PRINT RUN 25 SER.#'d SETS
EA1 Michael Vick .60 1.50
EA2 Tom Brady 3.00 8.00
EA3 Daunte Culpepper .60 1.50
EA4 Kurt Warner .60 1.50
EA5 Randy Moss .60 1.50
EA6 Michael Vick .60 1.50
EA7 Marshall Faulk .60 1.50
EA8 Marshall Faulk .60 1.50
EA9 Brett Favre 1.50 4.00
EA10 Brett Favre 1.50 4.00
EA11 Peyton Manning 2.00 5.00
EA12 Peyton Manning 2.00 5.00
EA13 Barry Sanders 1.25 3.00
EA14 Jerry Rice 1.50 4.00
EA15 Brett Favre 1.50 4.00
EA16 Donte Stallworth .50 1.25
EA17 Brett Favre 1.50 4.00
EA18 Tommy Maddox .50 1.25
EA19 Steve McNair .60 1.50
EA20 Antonio Freeman .60 1.50

2005 Upper Deck ESPN Ink

AUTO OVERALL STATED ODDS 1:480
AN Antrel Rolle 10.00 25.00
AR Aaron Rodgers 175.00 300.00
AS Alex Smith QB 30.00 60.00
AW Andrew Walter 12.50 30.00
BE Braylon Edwards
BR Ben Roethlisberger 60.00 120.00
CB Chris Berman 12.50 30.00
CE Cedric Benson 10.00 25.00
DA David Pollack 12.50 30.00
DD Domanick Davis 7.50 20.00
DP Dan Patrick
JP J.P. Losman 12.50 30.00
JT Joe Theismann
JW Jason White 10.00 25.00
KM Kenny Mayne 10.00 25.00
KO Kyle Orton
LC Linda Cohn
MA Mark Clayton
MB Marc Bulger 10.00 25.00
MC Maurice Clarett
MI Michael Clayton 10.00 25.00
PM Peyton Manning
RB Ronnie Brown 40.00 80.00
RW Reggie Wayne
SS Stuart Scott 25.00 50.00
TD Thomas Davis 7.50 20.00
VM Vernand Morency
WR Walter Reyes 7.50 20.00

2005 Upper Deck ESPN Insider Playmakers

COMPLETE SET (8) 3.00 8.00
ONE PER PACK
BF Brett Favre .75 2.00
CD Corey Dillon .25 .60
DM Donovan McNabb .30 .75
EJ Edgerrin James .30 .75
JS Jeremy Shockey .25 .60
LT LaDainian Tomlinson .40 1.00
MV Michael Vick .30 .75
TO Terrell Owens .30 .75

2005 Upper Deck ESPN Magazine Covers

COMPLETE SET (20) 12.50 30.00
BASIC INSERTS ONE PER PACK OVERALL
*HOLOFOIL: 3X TO 8X BASIC INSERTS
HOLOFOIL PRINT RUN 25 SER.#'d SETS
TM1 LaDainian Tomlinson .75 2.00
TM2 Corey Dillon .50 1.25
TM3 T.Owens/D.McNabb .60 1.50
TM4 Randy Moss .60 1.50
TM5 Dante Hall .50 1.25
TM6 Tom Brady 3.00 8.00
TM7 Steve McNair .60 1.50
TM8 Mike Vanderjagt .50 1.25
TM9 Jeremy Shockey .50 1.25
TM10 Derrick Brooks .50 1.25
TM11 Michael Vick .60 1.50
TM12 Terrell Owens .60 1.50
TM13 J.Rice/T.Brown 1.50 4.00
TM14 Donovan McNabb .60 1.50
TM15 Marshall Faulk .60 1.50
TM16 Ben Roethlisberger 1.25 3.00
TM17 Randy Moss .60 1.50
TM18 Daunte Culpepper .60 1.50
TM19 Edgerrin James .60 1.50
TM20 Brett Favre 1.50 4.00

2005 Upper Deck ESPN Plays of the Week

COMPLETE SET (30) 15.00 40.00
BASIC INSERTS ONE PER PACK OVERALL
*HOLOFOIL: 3X TO 8X BASIC INSERTS
HOLOFOIL PRINT RUN 25 SER.#'d SETS
PW1 Michael Vick .60 1.50
PW2 Donovan McNabb .60 1.50
PW3 Roy Williams S .50 1.25
PW4 Ben Roethlisberger 1.25 3.00
PW5 Brian Urlacher .75 2.00
PW6 Jerome Bettis .75 2.00
PW7 Julius Jones .50 1.25
PW8 Ed Reed .60 1.50
PW9 Randy Moss .60 1.50
PW10 Peyton Manning 2.00 5.00
PW11 Brett Favre 1.50 4.00
PW12 Santana Moss .60 1.50
PW13 Deion Branch .50 1.25
PW14 Dante Hall .50 1.25
PW15 Rodney Harrison .50 1.25
PW16 Byron Leftwich .50 1.25
PW17 Larry Fitzgerald .75 2.00
PW18 Chad Johnson .50 1.25
PW19 Kevin Jones .50 1.25
PW20 Willis McGahee .50 1.25
PW21 Steven Jackson .50 1.25
PW22 Eli Manning 1.25 3.00
PW23 Marvin Harrison .60 1.50
PW24 Terrell Owens .60 1.50
PW25 Daunte Culpepper .60 1.50
PW26 Joe Horn .50 1.25
PW27 Ahman Green .60 1.50
PW28 LaDainian Tomlinson .75 2.00
PW29 Carson Palmer .60 1.50
PW30 Marc Bulger .50 1.25

2005 Upper Deck ESPN Sports Center Swatches

STATED ODDS 1:12
AG Ahman Green 3.00 8.00
AJ Andre Johnson 2.50 6.00
BF Brett Favre 7.50 20.00
BR Ben Roethlisberger 7.50 20.00
BU Brian Urlacher 3.00 8.00
CP Chad Pennington 3.00 8.00
DA David Carr 3.00 8.00
DC Daunte Culpepper 3.00 8.00
DF DeShaun Foster 2.50 6.00
DR Drew Brees 2.50 6.00
DS Donte Stallworth 2.50 6.00
EJ Edgerrin James 3.00 8.00
EM Eli Manning 6.00 15.00
HW Hines Ward 3.00 8.00
JE Jerry Porter 2.50 6.00
JH Joey Harrington 3.00 8.00
JJ Julius Jones 4.00 10.00
JL Jamal Lewis 3.00 8.00
JR Jerry Rice 6.00 15.00
JS Jeremy Shockey 3.00 8.00
KJ Kevin Jones 3.00 8.00
LF Larry Fitzgerald 3.00 8.00
LS Lee Suggs 2.50 6.00
LT LaDainian Tomlinson 3.00 8.00
MB Marc Bulger 2.50 6.00
MF Marshall Faulk 3.00 8.00
MH Marvin Harrison 3.00 8.00
MV Michael Vick 4.00 10.00
PH Priest Holmes 3.00 8.00
PM Peyton Manning 5.00 12.00
PR Philip Rivers 3.00 8.00
RG Rex Grossman 3.00 8.00
SA Shaun Alexander 4.00 10.00
SM Steve McNair 2.50 6.00
TB Tom Brady 7.50 20.00
TG Trent Green 2.50 6.00
TH Todd Heap 2.00 5.00
TI Tiki Barber SP 6.00 15.00
TJ T.J. Duckett 2.50 6.00
TN Terrence Newman 2.50 6.00
TO Terrell Owens 3.00 8.00
TY Tony Gonzalez 2.50 6.00

2005 Upper Deck ESPN Sports Century

COMPLETE SET (10) 10.00 25.00
BASIC INSERTS ONE PER PACK OVERALL
*HOLOFOIL: 3X TO 8X BASIC INSERTS
HOLOFOIL PRINT RUN 25 SER.#'d SETS
SCBJ Bo Jackson 1.25 3.00
SCBS Barry Sanders 2.00 5.00
SCDB Dick Butkus 1.50 4.00
SCDM Dan Marino 2.50 6.00
SCDS Deion Sanders 1.25 3.00
SCGS Gale Sayers 1.25 3.00
SCJB Jim Brown 1.50 4.00
SCJM Joe Montana 3.00 8.00
SCLT Lawrence Taylor 1.25 3.00
SCWP Walter Payton 3.00 8.00

2005 Upper Deck ESPN Sports Century Signatures

AUTO OVERALL STATED ODDS 1:480
AD Art Donovan 15.00 40.00
CJ Charlie Joiner 10.00 25.00
CT Charley Taylor 10.00 25.00
DC Dave Casper 12.50 30.00
DD Dan Dierdorf 10.00 25.00
DM Don Maynard
HA Herb Adderley 12.50 30.00
JL James Lofton
LC L.C. Greenwood 15.00 30.00
MA Marcus Allen
MO Merlin Olsen 15.00 40.00
OA Ottis Anderson 10.00 25.00
ON Ozzie Newsome 15.00 40.00
RB Raymond Berry

2005 Upper Deck ESPN This Day in Football History

COMPLETE SET (20) 12.50 30.00
BASIC INSERTS ONE PER PACK OVERALL
*HOLOFOIL: 3X TO 8X BASIC INSERTS
HOLOFOIL PRINT RUN 25 SER.#'d SETS
1 Drew Bledsoe .75 2.00
2 Jerry Rice 1.25 3.00
3 Jamal Lewis .75 2.00
4 Jerry Rice 1.25 3.00
5 Johnny Unitas 1.50 4.00
6 Walter Payton 3.00 8.00
7 Corey Dillon .75 2.00
8 Eddie George .60 1.50
9 Tom Dempsey .50 1.25
10 Derrick Thomas .75 2.00
11 Dan Marino 2.50 6.00
12 Jim Brown 1.50 4.00
13 David Carr .75 2.00
14 Dan Marino 2.50 6.00
15 Eric Dickerson .60 1.50
16 Steve Largent .75 2.00
17 Marvin Harrison .75 2.00
18 Terrell Owens .75 2.00
19 Barry Sanders 2.00 5.00
20 Franco Harris .75 2.00

2003 Upper Deck Finite

Released in December of 2003, this set contains 300 cards, including 191 veterans and 109 rookies. Cards 1-100 are serial numbered to 2350. Cards 101-160 make up the Major Factors (MF) subset and are serial numbered to 750. Cards 161-185 make up the Prominent Powers (PP) subset and are serial numbered to 500. Cards 186-200 make up the First Class Finite (FCF) subset and are serial numbered to 100. FCF cards were inserted at a rate of 1:84. Finite Rookies Tier 1 (201-250) are serial numbered to 999, Rookies Tier 2 (251-285) are serial numbered to 500, and Rookies Tier 3 (286-300) are serial numbered to 100. Boxes contained 10 packs of 3 cards.

COMP.SET w/o SP's (100) 35.00 60.00
201-250 ROOKIE PRINT RUN 999
251-285 ROOKIE PRINT RUN 500
286-300 ROOKIE PRINT RUN 100
1 Peyton Manning 1.50 4.00
2 Aaron Brooks .40 1.00
3 Joey Harrington .40 1.00
4 Brett Favre 1.25 3.00
5 Donovan McNabb .50 1.25
6 Steve McNair .50 1.25
7 Michael Vick .50 1.25
8 David Carr .40 1.00
9 Drew Brees .60 1.50
10 Chad Pennington .40 1.00
11 Daunte Culpepper .50 1.25
12 Tom Brady 2.50 6.00
13 Kurt Warner .50 1.25
14 Brad Johnson .50 1.25
15 Drew Bledsoe .50 1.25
16 Jake Plummer .40 1.00
17 Jeff Garcia .40 1.00
18 Mark Brunell .50 1.25
19 Josh McCown .50 1.25
20 Travis Henry .40 1.00
21 LaDainian Tomlinson .60 1.50
22 Emmitt Smith 1.00 2.50
23 Michael Bennett .40 1.00
24 Brian Westbrook .40 1.00
25 Curtis Martin .50 1.25
26 Clinton Portis .40 1.00
27 Eddie George .50 1.25
28 Marshall Faulk .50 1.25
29 Deuce McAllister .50 1.25
30 Ahman Green .50 1.25
31 LaMont Jordan .50 1.25
32 Edgerrin James .50 1.25
33 Jamel White .40 1.00
34 Ricky Williams .50 1.25
35 Anthony Thomas .50 1.25
36 Amos Zereoue .40 1.00
37 Ladell Betts .40 1.00
38 Stephen Davis .40 1.00
39 T.J. Duckett .40 1.00
40 Troy Hambrick .40 1.00
41 Maurice Morris .40 1.00
42 James Jackson .40 1.00
43 Correll Buckhalter .40 1.00
44 Keith Brooking .50 1.25
45 Michael Strahan .50 1.25
46 Jason Taylor .50 1.25
47 Kendrell Bell .40 1.00
48 Jevon Kearse .40 1.00
49 Chris Horn RC .50 1.25
50 Quentin Jammer .40 1.00
51 Phillip Buchanon .40 1.00
52 Charles Woodson .60 1.50
53 Rod Woodson .50 1.25
54 Simeon Rice .40 1.00
55 Derrick Brooks .40 1.00
56 Warren Sapp .50 1.25
57 John Lynch .50 1.25
58 Champ Bailey .50 1.25
59 Reggie Wayne .50 1.25
60 Darrell Jackson .50 1.25
61 Derrick Mason .40 1.00
62 Travis Minor .40 1.00
63 Eric Parker RC .60 1.50
64 Ron Johnson .40 1.00
65 Dante Hall .40 1.00
66 David Terrell .40 1.00
67 Daniel Graham .40 1.00
68 Randy McMichael .40 1.00
69 Jeremy Shockey .40 1.00
70 J.J. Stokes .40 1.00
71 Johnnie Morton .50 1.25
72 Dennis Northcutt .40 1.00
73 Peter Warrick .40 1.00
74 Rod Smith .50 1.25
75 Javon Walker .50 1.25
76 Tim Carter .40 1.00
77 Wayne Chrebet .40 1.00
78 Corey Bradford .40 1.00
79 Deion Branch .40 1.00
80 Jerry Rice 1.25 3.00
81 Terrell Owens .50 1.25
82 Josh Reed .40 1.00
83 Ed McCaffrey .50 1.25
84 Randy Moss .50 1.25
85 Chad Johnson .40 1.00
86 Hines Ward .50 1.25
87 Rod Gardner .40 1.00
88 Tony Gonzalez .50 1.25
89 David Boston .40 1.00
90 Jerry Porter .40 1.00
91 Kevin Johnson .40 1.00
92 Rohan Davey .40 1.00
93 Tim Rattay .40 1.00
94 Jon Kitna .40 1.00
95 Jay Fiedler .40 1.00
96 Doug Flutie .50 1.25
97 Quincy Carter .40 1.00
98 Vinny Testaverde .40 1.00
99 Kelly Holcomb .40 1.00
100 Marc Bulger .40 1.00
101 Patrick Ramsey MF 1.25 3.00
102 Tim Couch MF 1.00 2.50
103 Tommy Maddox MF 1.00 2.50
104 Chad Hutchinson MF 1.00 2.50
105 Trent Green MF 1.00 2.50
106 Kerry Collins MF 1.00 2.50
107 Will Heller MF RC 1.50 4.00
108 Brian Griese MF 1.00 2.50
109 Kordell Stewart MF 1.00 2.50
110 Jake Delhomme MF 1.00 2.50
111 Chris Redman MF 1.00 2.50
112 Mike Anderson MF 1.00 2.50
113 Olandis Gary MF 1.00 2.50
114 Antonio Gates MF RC 20.00 40.00
115 Garrison Hearst MF 1.00 2.50
116 Fred Taylor MF 1.00 2.50
117 Casey Fitzsimmons MF RC 1.50 4.00
118 Tiki Barber MF 1.25 3.00
119 Mike Alstott MF 1.00 2.50
120 Kevan Barlow MF 1.00 2.50
121 Jamal Lewis MF 1.25 3.00
122 Mike Banks MF RC 1.25 3.00
123 Jimmy Farris MF RC 1.25 3.00
124 Warrick Dunn MF 1.00 2.50
125 Jerome Bettis MF 1.50 4.00
126 Antonio Chatman MF RC 2.00 5.00
127 Bubba Franks MF 1.25 3.00
128 Todd Heap MF 1.00 2.50
129 Shannon Sharpe MF 1.25 3.00
130 Donald Driver MF 1.25 3.00
131 Antonio Freeman MF 1.25 3.00
132 Joey Galloway MF 1.25 3.00
133 Marc Boerigter MF 1.00 2.50
134 Torry Holt MF 1.25 3.00
135 Amani Toomer MF 1.00 2.50
136 Marty Booker MF 1.00 2.50
137 Santana Moss MF 1.25 3.00
138 Jimmy Smith MF 1.25 3.00
139 Jabar Gaffney MF 1.00 2.50
140 Isaac Bruce MF 1.50 4.00
141 Laveranues Coles MF 1.00 2.50
142 Quincy Morgan MF 1.00 2.50
143 Peerless Price MF 1.00 2.50
144 Eric Moulds MF 1.00 2.50
145 Troy Brown MF 1.00 2.50
146 Plaxico Burress MF 1.00 2.50
147 Chris Chambers MF 1.00 2.50
148 Tim Brown MF 1.50 4.00
149 Antonio Brown MF RC 1.25 3.00
150 Koren Robinson MF 1.25 3.00
151 David Boston MF 1.00 2.50
152 C.J. Jones MF RC 1.25 3.00
153 Marvin Harrison MF 1.25 3.00
154 Keyshawn Johnson MF 1.50 4.00
155 J.J. Moses MF RC 1.25 3.00
156 Antwaan Randle El MF 1.00 2.50
157 Ashley Lelie MF 1.00 2.50
158 Andre Davis MF 1.00 2.50
159 Donte Stallworth MF 1.00 2.50
160 Antonio Bryant MF 1.00 2.50
161 Tom Brady PP 8.00 20.00
162 Drew Bledsoe PP 1.50 4.00
163 Rich Gannon PP 1.50 4.00
164 David Carr PP 1.25 3.00
165 Drew Brees PP 2.00 5.00
166 Aaron Brooks PP 1.25 3.00
167 Joey Harrington PP 1.25 3.00
168 Matt Hasselbeck PP 1.25 3.00
169 Jake Plummer PP 1.25 3.00
170 Edgerrin James PP 1.50 4.00
171 Ahman Green PP 1.50 4.00
172 Deuce McAllister PP 1.50 4.00
173 Priest Holmes PP 1.25 3.00
174 Travis Henry PP 1.25 3.00
175 William Green PP 1.25 3.00
176 Corey Dillon PP 1.25 3.00
177 Shaun Alexander PP 1.25 3.00
178 Jeremy Shockey PP 1.25 3.00
179 Brian Dawkins PP 2.00 5.00
180 Roy Williams PP 1.25 3.00
181 Julius Peppers PP 2.00 5.00
182 Ray Lewis PP 2.00 5.00
183 Junior Seau PP 1.50 4.00
184 Zach Thomas PP 1.50 4.00
185 Brian Urlacher PP 2.00 5.00
186 Michael Vick FCF 2.50 6.00
187 Jeff Garcia FCF 2.00 5.00
188 Daunte Culpepper FCF 2.50 6.00
189 Steve McNair FCF 2.50 6.00
190 Chad Pennington FCF 2.00 5.00
191 LaDainian Tomlinson FCF 3.00 8.00
192 Clinton Portis FCF 2.00 5.00
193 Ricky Williams FCF 2.50 6.00
194 Donovan McNabb FCF 2.50 6.00
195 Peyton Manning FCF 8.00 20.00
196 Marshall Faulk FCF 2.50 6.00
197 Kurt Warner FCF 2.50 6.00
198 Emmitt Smith FCF 5.00 12.00
199 Jerry Rice FCF 6.00 15.00
200 Brett Favre FCF 6.00 15.00
201 Carson Palmer RC 2.50 6.00
202 Kyle Boller RC 1.25 3.00
203 Kliff Kingsbury RC 2.00 5.00
204 Brooks Bollinger RC 1.50 4.00
205 Mike Doss RC 2.00 5.00
206 Dewayne White RC 1.25 3.00
207 Roderick Babers RC 1.25 3.00
208 Seneca Wallace RC 1.50 4.00
209 Nate Hybl RC 1.50 4.00
210 Jason Gesser RC 1.50 4.00
211 Willis McGahee RC 1.50 4.00
212 George Wrighster RC 1.25 3.00
213 Drayton Florence RC 2.00 5.00
214 L.J. Smith RC 2.00 5.00
215 B.J. Askew RC 1.50 4.00
216 Adewale Ogunleye RC 2.50 6.00
217 Ahmaad Galloway RC 1.50 4.00
218 Dwone Hicks RC 1.25 3.00
219 Travaris Robinson RC 1.25 3.00
220 William Joseph RC 1.25 3.00
221 Terrence Kiel RC 1.50 4.00
222 Marcus Trufant RC 1.50 4.00
223 Terence Newman RC 2.00 5.00
224 Nnamdi Asomugha RC 2.00 5.00
225 Troy Polamalu RC 15.00 30.00
226 Terrell Suggs RC 1.50 4.00
227 Boss Bailey RC 1.50 4.00
228 Dan Klecko RC 1.50 4.00
229 Jerome McDougle RC 1.25 3.00
230 Johnathan Sullivan RC 1.25 3.00
231 Mike Seidman RC 1.25 3.00
232 Dallas Clark RC 2.00 5.00
233 Tony Romo RC 12.00 30.00
234 Reggie Newhouse RC 1.25 3.00
235 David Tyree RC 1.50 4.00
236 Andre Woolfolk RC 1.25 3.00
237 Domanick Davis RC 1.50 4.00
238 Zuriel Smith RC 1.25 3.00
239 Tommy Jones RC 1.25 3.00
240 Arnaz Battle RC 2.00 5.00
241 Kassim Osgood RC 2.00 5.00
242 Gerald Hayes RC 1.50 4.00
243 Keenan Howry RC 1.25 3.00
244 Bobby Wade RC 1.50 4.00
245 Brock Forsey RC 1.50 4.00
246 Walter Young RC 1.25 3.00
247 Shaun McDonald RC 1.50 4.00
248 Nate Burleson RC 1.50 4.00
249 Anquan Boldin RC 2.00 5.00
250 Taylor Jacobs RC 1.25 3.00
251 Chris Simms RC 1.50 4.00
252 Rex Grossman RC 2.00 5.00
253 Arlen Harris RC 1.50 4.00
254 Dave Ragone RC 1.50 4.00
255 Chris Brown RC 1.50 4.00
256 Musa Smith RC 1.50 4.00
257 Artose Pinner RC 1.50 4.00
258 Sammy Davis RC 2.00 5.00
259 DeWayne Robertson RC 2.00 5.00
260 Tony Hollings RC 2.00 5.00
261 LaBrandon Toefield RC 1.50 4.00
262 Cortez Hankton RC 2.00 5.00
263 Justin Griffith RC 2.00 5.00
264 Jeremi Johnson RC 1.50 4.00
265 E.J. Henderson RC 2.00 5.00
266 Casey Moore RC 1.50 4.00
267 Ken Hamlin RC 2.50 6.00
268 Nick Barnett RC 2.50 6.00
269 Vishante Shiancoe RC 2.50 6.00
270 Aaron Walker RC 2.00 5.00
271 Bennie Joppru RC 1.50 4.00
272 Terrence Edwards RC 1.50 4.00
273 Willie Ponder RC 1.50 4.00
274 Pisa Tinoisamoa RC 2.50 6.00
275 Doug Gabriel RC 2.00 5.00
276 Kerry Carter RC 1.50 4.00
277 Avon Cobourne RC 1.50 4.00
278 Sam Aiken RC 2.00 5.00
279 Brandon Lloyd RC 2.50 6.00
280 LaTarence Dunbar RC 1.50 4.00
281 J.R. Tolver RC 2.00 5.00
282 Kevin Curtis RC 1.50 4.00
283 Tyrone Calico RC 1.50 4.00
284 Bryant Johnson RC 2.50 6.00
285 Charles Rogers RC 2.00 5.00
286 Teyo Johnson RC 6.00 15.00
287 Jason Witten RC 20.00 50.00
288 Kelley Washington RC 5.00 12.00
289 Billy McMullen RC 5.00 12.00
290 Adrian Madise RC 5.00 12.00
291 Justin Gage RC 6.00 15.00
292 Andre Johnson RC 12.00 30.00
293 Bethel Johnson RC 5.00 12.00
294 Lee Suggs RC 5.00 12.00
295 Larry Johnson RC 6.00 15.00
296 Justin Fargas RC 8.00 20.00
297 Onterrio Smith RC 5.00 12.00
298 Ken Dorsey RC 6.00 15.00
299 Brian St.Pierre RC 5.00 12.00
300 Byron Leftwich RC 6.00 15.00

2003 Upper Deck Finite Gold

*VETS 1-100: 2.5X TO 6X BASIC CARDS
*VET MF 101-160: 1.2X TO 3X
*ROOKIE MF 101-160: 1X TO 2.5X
*VET PP 161-185: 1X TO 2.5X
*VET FCF 186-200: .6X TO 1.5X
*ROOKIES 201-250: 1.2X TO 3X
*ROOKIES 251-285: 1X TO 2.5X
*ROOKIES 286-300: .3X TO .8X
GOLD/50 ODDS 1:10
STATED PRINT RUN 50 SER.#'d SETS
233 Tony Romo 50.00 120.00

2003 Upper Deck Finite Autographs

This set features authentic player autographs imbedded in the card fronts. The Peyton Manning/1254 (PM2) and DeShaun Foster/651 (DF2) cards feature player autographs on silver foil stickers. Please note that Dewayne Robertson and Taylor Jacobs were issued as exchange cards in packs. The exchange deadline is 03/15/2007.

OVERALL AUTO STATED ODDS 1:10
AB Antonio Bryant/100 8.00 20.00
AD Andre Davis/263 6.00 15.00
AL Mike Alstott/175 12.00 30.00
AP Artose Pinner/396 6.00 15.00
AQ Anquan Boldin/396 20.00 50.00
AZ Az-Zahir Hakim/186 6.00 15.00
BB Brad Banks/1000 6.00 15.00
BD Brandon Doman/262 6.00 15.00
BR Bryant Johnson/396 10.00 25.00
BS Brian St.Pierre/720 5.00 12.00
CB Chris Brown/396 6.00 15.00
CJ Chad Johnson/815 5.00 12.00
CP Clinton Portis/70 30.00 80.00
CS Chris Simms/80 20.00 40.00
DC Dallas Clark/396 10.00 25.00
DF DeShaun Foster/207 8.00 20.00
DF2 DeShaun Foster/651 6.00 15.00
EC Eric Crouch/263 10.00 25.00
EG Earnest Graham/800 8.00 20.00
JA Jason Johnson/205 6.00 15.00
JB Jeff Blake/35 12.00 30.00
JF Justin Fargas/396 10.00 25.00
JG Jabar Gaffney/260 6.00 15.00
JJ James Jackson/300 6.00 15.00
JS Jeremy Shockey/93 15.00 40.00
KA Kareem Kelly/1300 5.00 12.00
KB Kevan Barlow/107 8.00 20.00
KC Kelly Campbell/262 6.00 15.00
KC Kevin Curtis/396 6.00 15.00
KK Kurt Kittner/55 10.00 25.00
KL Kliff Kingsbury/396 10.00 25.00
KM Keenan McCardell/30 12.00 30.00
KW Kelley Washington/1058 5.00 12.00
LJ Larry Johnson/396 8.00 20.00
LS Luke Staley/263 6.00 15.00
MB Marc Bulger/35 10.00 25.00
MS Musa Smith/396 6.00 15.00
MT Marcus Trufant/396 8.00 20.00
NB Nate Burleson/396 8.00 20.00
NH Napoleon Harris/262 6.00 15.00
PM1 Peyton Manning/1280 50.00 100.00
PM2 Peyton Manning/1254 50.00 100.00
PR Patrick Ramsey/190 8.00 20.00
QG Quentin Griffin/447 8.00 20.00
RC Reche Caldwell/261 6.00 15.00
RD Rohan Davey/262 6.00 15.00
RJ Ron Johnson/263 6.00 15.00
RW Roy Williams/151 25.00 50.00
SU Lee Suggs/30 10.00 25.00
SW Seneca Wallace/414 8.00 20.00
TA Taylor Jacobs/409 6.00 15.00
TG Tony Gonzalez/46 12.00 30.00
TH Todd Heap/63 10.00 25.00
TM Travis Minor/364 6.00 15.00
TS Terrell Suggs/950 10.00 25.00
VT Vinny Testaverde/212 6.00 15.00
WD Woody Dantzler/207 6.00 15.00

2003 Upper Deck Finite Autographs Gold

AB Antonio Bryant 12.00 30.00
AD Andre Davis 12.00 30.00
AL Mike Alstott 12.00 30.00
AL Ashley Lelie 12.00 30.00
AP Artose Pinner 12.00 30.00
AQ Anquan Boldin 40.00 100.00
AZ Az-Zahir Hakim 12.00 30.00
BB Brad Banks 15.00 40.00
BD Brandon Doman 12.00 30.00
BR Bryant Johnson 20.00 50.00
BS Brian St.Pierre 12.00 30.00
CB Chris Brown 12.00 30.00
CJ Chad Johnson 12.00 30.00
CP Clinton Portis 12.00 30.00
CS Chris Simms 12.00 30.00
DC David Carr 12.00 30.00
DC Dallas Clark 20.00 50.00
DF DeShaun Foster 15.00 40.00
DF2 DeShaun Foster 15.00 40.00
EC Eric Crouch 20.00 50.00
EG Earnest Graham 20.00 50.00
JA Jason Johnson
JB Jeff Blake
JF Justin Fargas 20.00 50.00
JG Jabar Gaffney 12.00 30.00
JJ James Jackson
JS Jeremy Shockey 12.00 30.00
KA Kareem Kelly
KB Kevan Barlow
KC Kelly Campbell
KC Kevin Curtis 12.00 30.00
KK Kurt Kittner 12.00 30.00
KL Kliff Kingsbury 20.00 50.00
KM Keenan McCardell 15.00 40.00
KW Kelley Washington
LJ Larry Johnson 15.00 40.00
LS Luke Staley 12.00 30.00
MB Marc Bulger
MM Maurice Morris 12.00 30.00
MS Musa Smith
MT Marcus Trufant 15.00 40.00
NB Nate Burleson 15.00 40.00
NH Napoleon Harris 12.00 30.00
PM1 Peyton Manning 75.00 150.00
PM2 Peyton Manning 75.00 150.00
PR Patrick Ramsey 15.00 40.00
QG Quentin Griffin 15.00 40.00
RC Reche Caldwell 12.00 30.00
RD Rohan Davey 12.00 30.00
RJ Ron Johnson
RW Roy Williams 12.00 30.00
SU Lee Suggs 12.00 30.00
SW Seneca Wallace 15.00 40.00
TA Taylor Jacobs 12.00 30.00
TG Tony Gonzalez 15.00 40.00
TH Todd Heap 12.00 30.00
TM Travis Minor 12.00 30.00
TS Terrell Suggs 30.00 60.00
VT Vinny Testaverde 12.00 30.00
WD Woody Dantzler

2003 Upper Deck Finite Jerseys

This set features jersey swatches of promising rookies and established NFL stars. There is a Black and a Gold parallel of this set. Cards in the Finite Jerseys Black set feature black highlights and are serial numbered to 99. Cards in the Finite Jerseys Gold set feature gold highlights and are serial numbered to 25.

OVERALL JERSEY STATED ODDS 1:4
*BLACK/99: .8X TO 2X BASIC JSY
BLACK PRINT RUN 99 SER.#'d SETS
*GOLD/25: 1.2X TO 3X BASIC JSY
GOLD PRINT RUN 25 SER.#'d SETS
FJAB Anquan Boldin 2.50 6.00
FJAG Ahman Green 3.00 8.00
FJAJ Andre Johnson 4.00 10.00
FJAP Artose Pinner 2.50 6.00
FJBE Bethel Johnson 2.50 6.00
FJBF Brett Favre 8.00 20.00
FJBJ Bryant Johnson 4.00 10.00
FJBL Byron Leftwich 2.00 5.00
FJBS Brian St.Pierre 2.50 6.00
FJCB Chris Brown 2.50 6.00
FJCP Carson Palmer 3.00 8.00
FJCU Daunte Culpepper 3.00 8.00
FJDA Dallas Clark 4.00 10.00
FJDC David Carr 2.50 6.00
FJDR DeWayne Robertson 3.00 8.00
FJDR Dave Ragone 2.50 6.00
FJES Emmitt Smith 6.00 15.00
FJGA Rich Gannon 3.00 8.00
FJJF Justin Fargas 4.00 10.00
FJKB Kyle Boller 1.50 4.00
FJKC Kevin Curtis 1.50 4.00
FJKK Kliff Kingsbury 4.00 10.00
FJKW Kelley Washington 2.50 6.00
FJLJ Larry Johnson 2.00 5.00
FJMC Donovan McNabb 3.00 8.00
FJMS Musa Smith 2.50 6.00
FJMT Marcus Trufant 2.00 5.00
FJMV Michael Vick SP 5.00 12.00
FJNB Nate Burleson 3.00 8.00
FJOS Onterrio Smith 2.50 6.00
FJPE Chad Pennington 2.50 6.00
FJPH Priest Holmes 2.50 6.00
FJPM Peyton Manning 10.00 25.00
FJPO Clinton Portis 2.50 6.00
FJRG Rex Grossman 2.00 5.00
FJSW Seneca Wallace 3.00 8.00
FJTA Taylor Jacobs 2.50 6.00
FJTC Tyrone Calico 2.50 6.00
FJTJ Teyo Johnson 3.00 8.00
FJTN Terence Newman 2.50 6.00
FJTS Terrell Suggs 2.00 5.00
FJWM Willis McGahee 2.00 5.00

2004 Upper Deck Finite HG

Upper Deck Finite HG was initially released in late November 2004. The base set consists of 278-cards including 65-rookies serial numbered to 275 and 13-rookies numbered to 99. Hobby boxes contained 10-packs of 3-cards each. One parallel set and a variety of game jersey and autograph inserts can be found seeded in packs.

COMP.SET w/o SP's (100) 12.50 30.00
101-265 ROOKIE PRINT RUN 275
266-278 ROOKIE PRINT RUN 99
1 Emmitt Smith .75 2.00
2 Anquan Boldin .30 .75
3 Josh McCown .40 1.00
4 Michael Vick .40 1.00
5 Peerless Price .30 .75
6 Warrick Dunn .30 .75
7 Todd Heap .30 .75
8 Jamal Lewis .40 1.00
9 Kyle Boller .30 .75
10 Drew Bledsoe .40 1.00
11 Travis Henry .30 .75
12 Eric Moulds .30 .75
13 Jake Delhomme .30 .75
14 Steve Smith .50 1.25
15 Stephen Davis .30 .75
16 Rex Grossman .30 .75
17 Brian Urlacher .50 1.25
18 Thomas Jones .30 .75
19 Rudi Johnson .30 .75
20 Carson Palmer .40 1.00
21 Chad Johnson .30 .75
22 Jeff Garcia .30 .75
23 Andre Davis .30 .75
24 Lee Suggs .40 1.00
25 Keyshawn Johnson .40 1.00
26 Eddie George .40 1.00
27 Vinny Testaverde .30 .75
28 Quentin Griffin .30 .75
29 Champ Bailey .40 1.00
30 Jake Plummer .30 .75
31 Az-Zahir Hakim .30 .75
32 Joey Harrington .30 .75
33 Charles Rogers .30 .75
34 Javon Walker .30 .75
35 Ahman Green .40 1.00
36 Brett Favre 1.00 2.50
37 Domanick Davis .30 .75
38 David Carr .30 .75
39 Andre Johnson .40 1.00
40 Edgerrin James .40 1.00
41 Marvin Harrison .40 1.00
42 Reggie Wayne .40 1.00
43 Peyton Manning 1.25 3.00
44 Fred Taylor .30 .75
45 Jimmy Smith .40 1.00
46 Byron Leftwich .30 .75
47 Dante Hall .30 .75
48 Tony Gonzalez .40 1.00
49 Trent Green .30 .75
50 Priest Holmes .30 .75
51 Zach Thomas .40 1.00
52 A.J. Feeley .30 .75
53 Chris Chambers .30 .75
54 Randy McMichael .30 .75
55 Randy Moss .40 1.00
56 Onterrio Smith .30 .75
57 Daunte Culpepper .40 1.00
58 Tom Brady 2.00 5.00
59 Deion Branch .30 .75
60 Corey Dillon .30 .75
61 Donte' Stallworth .30 .75
62 Deuce McAllister .40 1.00
63 Aaron Brooks .30 .75
64 Amani Toomer .30 .75
65 Jeremy Shockey .30 .75
66 Kurt Warner .40 1.00
67 Curtis Martin .40 1.00
68 Chad Pennington .30 .75
69 Santana Moss .40 1.00
70 Jerry Porter .30 .75
71 Jerry Rice 1.00 2.50
72 Rich Gannon .40 1.00
73 Justin Fargas .40 1.00
74 Terrell Owens .40 1.00
75 Brian Westbrook .30 .75
76 Donovan McNabb .40 1.00
77 Tommy Maddox .30 .75
78 Hines Ward .40 1.00
79 Plaxico Burress .30 .75
80 Antonio Gates .50 1.25
81 LaDainian Tomlinson .50 1.25
82 Drew Brees .50 1.25
83 Brandon Lloyd .40 1.00
84 Tim Rattay .30 .75
85 Kevan Barlow .30 .75
86 Koren Robinson .30 .75
87 Shaun Alexander .30 .75
88 Matt Hasselbeck .30 .75
89 Torry Holt .40 1.00
90 Marc Bulger .30 .75
91 Marshall Faulk .40 1.00
92 Chris Simms .30 .75
93 Keenan McCardell .30 .75
94 Derrick Brooks .30 .75
95 Steve McNair .40 1.00
96 Chris Brown .30 .75
97 Derrick Mason .30 .75
98 Mark Brunell .40 1.00
99 Laveranues Coles .30 .75
100 Clinton Portis .30 .75
101 Michael Jenkins RC 2.50 6.00
102 Ryan Krause RC 2.50 6.00
103 Darnell Dockett RC 4.00 10.00
104 Quincy Wilson RC 2.50 6.00
105 Nate Lawrie RC 2.50 6.00
106 Joey Thomas RC 2.50 6.00
107 Junior Siavii RC 2.50 6.00
108 Landon Johnson RC 2.50 6.00
109 Michael Waddell RC 2.50 6.00
110 Lee Evans RC 4.00 10.00
111 Jason David RC 2.50 6.00
112 Chris Collins RC 2.50 6.00
113 Troy Fleming RC 2.50 6.00
114 Tim Euhus RC 2.50 6.00
115 Sean Jones RC 2.50 6.00
116 Jason Babin RC 4.00 10.00
117 Jorge Cordova RC 2.50 6.00
118 Josh Scobee RC 3.00 8.00
119 Luke McCown RC 2.50 6.00
120 Darius Watts RC 2.50 6.00
121 Clarence Moore RC 2.50 6.00
122 Randy Starks RC 2.50 6.00
123 Brandon Miree RC 2.50 6.00
124 Gibril Wilson RC 4.00 10.00
125 Jeremy LeSueur RC 2.50 6.00
126 Dwan Edwards RC 2.50 6.00
127 Richard Seigler RC 2.50 6.00
128 Stanford Samuels RC 2.50 6.00
129 Casey Clausen RC 3.00 8.00
130 Erik Coleman RC 3.00 8.00
131 Donnell Washington RC 3.00 8.00
132 Jammal Lord RC 2.50 6.00
133 Chris Cooley RC 3.00 8.00
134 Shawntae Spencer RC 2.50 6.00
135 Marcus Tubbs RC 2.50 6.00
136 Caleb Miller RC 2.50 6.00
137 Jeff Shoate RC 2.50 6.00
138 Bradlee Van Pelt RC 3.00 8.00
139 D.J. Hackett RC 2.50 6.00
140 Greg Brooks RC 2.50 6.00
141 Thomas Tapeh RC 3.00 8.00
142 Ben Hartsock RC 2.50 6.00
143 Madieu Williams RC 2.50 6.00
144 Vince Wilfork RC 4.00 10.00

145 Marquis Cooper RC	2.50	6.00
146 Nate Kaeding RC	3.00	8.00
147 B.J. Symons RC	2.50	6.00
148 Maurice Mann RC	2.50	6.00
149 Tim Anderson RC	3.00	8.00
150 Michael Turner RC	2.50	6.00
151 Kris Wilson RC	3.00	8.00
152 Keiwan Ratliff RC	2.50	6.00
153 Kenechi Udeze RC	3.00	8.00
154 Courtney Watson RC	2.50	6.00
155 Stacy Andrews RC	2.50	6.00
156 Jeff Smoker RC	3.00	8.00
157 Carlos Francis RC	2.50	6.00
158 Derek Abney RC	2.50	6.00
159 Dexter Wynn RC	2.50	6.00
160 Jason Wright RC	2.50	6.00
161 Dunta Robinson RC	2.50	6.00
162 Nathan Vasher RC	4.00	10.00
163 Karlos Dansby RC	3.00	8.00
164 Jake Grove RC	2.50	6.00
165 Matt Mauck RC	2.50	6.00
166 Johnnie Morant RC	2.50	6.00
167 Justin Jenkins RC	2.50	6.00
168 Cedric Cobbs RC	2.50	6.00
169 Ben Troupe RC	2.50	6.00
170 Bob Sanders RC	5.00	12.00
171 Will Smith RC	3.00	8.00
172 Michael Boulware RC	4.00	10.00
173 Nat Dorsey RC	2.50	6.00
174 Casey Bramlet RC	2.50	6.00
175 Ernest Wilford RC	3.00	8.00
176 Kendrick Starling RC	2.50	6.00
177 Mewelde Moore RC	3.00	8.00
178 Ben Watson RC	3.00	8.00
179 Ricardo Colclough RC	2.50	6.00
180 Tommie Harris RC	3.00	8.00
181 Dontarrious Thomas RC	3.00	8.00
182 Keith Lewis RC	2.50	6.00
183 John Navarre RC	2.50	6.00
184 Samie Parker RC	2.50	6.00
185 B.J. Johnson RC	2.50	6.00
186 Tatum Bell RC	2.50	6.00
187 Mike Karney RC	3.00	8.00
188 Ahmad Carroll RC	2.50	6.00
189 Will Allen RC	3.00	8.00
190 Teddy Lehman RC	2.50	6.00
191 Justin Smiley RC	3.00	8.00
192 Cody Pickett RC	2.50	6.00
193 Jerricho Cotchery RC	3.00	8.00
194 Tramon Douglas RC	2.50	6.00
195 Greg Jones RC	2.50	6.00
196 Kellen Winslow RC	2.50	6.00
197 Chris Gamble RC	2.50	6.00
198 Dexter Reid RC	2.50	6.00
199 Daryl Smith RC	2.50	6.00
200 Max Starks RC	3.00	8.00
201 J.P. Losman RC	2.50	6.00
202 Rashaun Woods RC	2.50	6.00
203 Triandos Luke RC	2.50	6.00
204 Rashad Washington RC	2.50	6.00
205 Derrick Ward RC	4.00	10.00
206 Matt Kranchick RC	3.00	8.00
207 Keith Smith RC	2.50	6.00
208 Travis LaBoy RC	3.00	8.00
209 Demorrio Williams RC	4.00	10.00
210 Jason Shivers RC	2.50	6.00
211 Craig Krenzel RC	2.50	6.00
212 Keary Colbert RC	2.50	6.00
213 Mark Jones RC	2.50	6.00
214 Shawn Johnson RC	2.50	6.00
215 Jarrett Payton RC	3.00	8.00
216 Michael Gaines RC	2.50	6.00
217 Matt Ware RC	4.00	10.00
218 Antwan Odom RC	2.50	6.00
219 Brandon Chillar RC	3.00	8.00
220 Michael Clayton RC	3.00	8.00
221 Jamaar Taylor RC	2.50	6.00
222 George Wilson RC	3.00	8.00
223 Tony Hargrove RC	2.50	6.00
224 Sean Ryan RC	2.50	6.00
225 Stuart Schweigert RC	3.00	8.00
226 Igor Olshansky RC	3.00	8.00
227 Keyaron Fox RC	3.00	8.00
228 Glenn Earl RC	2.50	6.00
229 Bruce Thornton RC	2.50	6.00
230 Derrick Hamilton RC	2.50	6.00
231 Sloan Thomas RC	3.00	8.00
232 Matthias Askew RC	2.50	6.00
233 Ran Carthon RC	2.50	6.00
234 Ben Utecht RC	3.00	8.00
235 Kendyll Pope RC	2.50	6.00
236 Marquise Hill RC	2.50	6.00
237 Shawn Andrews RC	3.00	8.00
238 Jim Sorgi RC	3.00	8.00
239 Devard Darling RC	2.50	6.00
240 Patrick Crayton RC	4.00	10.00
241 Ryan McGuffey RC	2.50	6.00
242 Darrion Scott RC	3.00	8.00
243 DeAngelo Hall RC	4.00	10.00
244 Alex Lewis RC	2.50	6.00
245 D.J. Williams RC	4.00	10.00
246 Chris Snee RC	6.00	15.00
247 Matt Schaub RC	2.50	6.00
248 Devery Henderson RC	2.50	6.00
249 Jeris McIntyre RC	2.50	6.00
250 Wes Welker RC	12.00	30.00
251 Bruce Perry RC	2.50	6.00
252 Jeff Dugan RC	2.50	6.00
253 Derrick Strait RC	2.50	6.00
254 Terry Johnson RC	2.50	6.00
255 Niko Koutouvides RC	2.50	6.00
256 Von Hutchins RC	2.50	6.00
257 Josh Harris RC	2.50	6.00
258 Bernard Berrian RC	2.50	6.00
259 Roderick Green RC	2.50	6.00
260 Romar Crenshaw RC	2.50	6.00
261 Jacob Rogers RC	4.00	10.00
262 Sean Taylor RC	15.00	40.00
263 J.R. Reed RC	2.50	6.00
264 Jonathan Vilma RC	3.00	8.00
265 Stephen Peterman RC	4.00	10.00
266 Eli Manning RC	25.00	50.00
267 Philip Rivers RC	50.00	100.00
268 Larry Fitzgerald RC	12.00	30.00
269 Ben Roethlisberger RC	50.00	100.00
270 Kevin Jones RC	4.00	10.00
271 Steven Jackson RC	5.00	12.00
272 Roy Williams RC	3.00	8.00
273 Julius Jones RC	3.00	8.00
274 Reggie Williams RC	3.00	8.00
275 Chris Perry RC	3.00	8.00
276 Robert Gallery RC	4.00	10.00
277 Kellen Winslow RC	3.00	8.00
278 Drew Henson RC	3.00	8.00

2004 Upper Deck Finite HG Radiance

*VETS 1-100: 10X TO 25X BASIC CARDS
*ROOKIES 101-265: 5X TO 12X BASIC RC
*ROOKIES 266-278: 3X TO 8X BASIC RC
RADIANCE PRINT RUN 15 SETS

2004 Upper Deck Finite HG Fabrics

STATED ODDS 1:10
*RADIANCE/25: 1.2X TO 3X BASIC JSY
*RADIANCE/25: 1X TO 2.5X JSY SP
RADIANCE PRINT RUN 25 SER.#'d SETS

FFBA Barry Sanders SP	10.00	25.00
FFBF Brett Favre	8.00	20.00
FFBU Brian Urlacher	4.00	10.00
FFCP Clinton Portis	2.50	6.00
FFCR Charles Rogers	2.50	6.00
FFCW Charles Woodson	4.00	10.00
FFDA David Boston	2.50	6.00
FFDB Drew Bledsoe	3.00	8.00
FFDC Daunte Culpepper	3.00	8.00
FFDE Deuce McAllister	3.00	8.00
FFDM Dan Marino SP	12.00	30.00
FFEM Eric Moulds	2.50	6.00
FFES Emmitt Smith	6.00	15.00
FFFT Fred Taylor	2.50	6.00
FFIB Isaac Bruce	4.00	10.00
FFJB Jerome Bettis	4.00	10.00
FFJE John Elway	8.00	20.00
FFJK Jevon Kearse	2.50	6.00
FFJM Joe Montana SP	20.00	50.00
FFJP Jake Plummer	2.50	6.00
FFJU Johnny Unitas	12.00	30.00
FFKC Kerry Collins	2.50	6.00
FFKE Kellen Winslow Sr. SP	6.00	15.00
FFKW Kurt Warner	3.00	8.00
FFLA LaVar Arrington	4.00	10.00
FFLD Len Dawson SP	8.00	20.00
FFLT LaDainian Tomlinson	4.00	10.00
FFMA Mark Brunell	3.00	8.00
FFMB Marc Bulger	2.50	6.00
FFMV Michael Vick	3.00	8.00
FFPM Peyton Manning	10.00	25.00
FFRM Randy Moss	3.00	8.00
FFRS Roger Staubach SP	8.00	20.00
FFSM Santana Moss	3.00	8.00
FFST Steve McNair	3.00	8.00
FFTA Troy Aikman SP	8.00	20.00
FFTB Tom Brady	15.00	40.00
FFTG Tony Gonzalez	3.00	8.00
FFTM Tommy Maddox	2.50	6.00
FFTO Terrell Owens	3.00	8.00
FFWS Warren Sapp	3.00	8.00
FFZT Zach Thomas	3.00	8.00

2004 Upper Deck Finite HG Fabrics Duals

STATED ODDS 1:30

AS T.Aikman/Staubach SP	15.00	40.00
BB M.Bulger/I.Bruce	5.00	12.00
BM D.Boston/E.Moulds	3.00	8.00
BP M.Brunell/C.Portis	4.00	10.00
BW T.Brady/K.Warner	20.00	50.00
EM J.Elway/D.Marino	20.00	50.00
FW L.Fitzgerald/R.Williams	8.00	20.00
JJ J.Jones/K.Jones	2.50	6.00
LR J.Losman/B.Roethlisberger	15.00	40.00
MB T.Maddox/J.Bettis	8.00	20.00
MM P.Manning/S.McNair	12.00	30.00
PA C.Portis/L.Arrington	3.00	8.00
RM P.Rivers/E.Manning	15.00	40.00
UD J.Unitas/L.Dawson SP	20.00	50.00
WS C.Woodson/W.Sapp	5.00	12.00

2004 Upper Deck Finite HG Fabrics Triples

STATED ODDS 1:40

BRB Bruce/C.Rogers/Boston	8.00	20.00
BVB Bulger/Vick/Brunell	6.00	15.00
JJJ Jones/Jones/Jones	6.00	15.00
MMF Manning/Montana/Favre	40.00	80.00
MRR Manning/Rivers/Roeth	25.00	60.00
NAM Namath/Aikman/Marino SP	25.00	60.00
OMM Owens/Moss/Moss SP	6.00	15.00
PBM Plummer/Bledsoe/McNair	6.00	15.00
PST Portis/Emmitt/Tomlinson	12.00	30.00
SPT Sanders/Perry/Tomlinson	15.00	40.00
UAT Urlacher/Arrington/Thomas	8.00	20.00
USE Unitas/Staubach/Elway SP	30.00	80.00
WFW Williams/Fitz/Winslow	12.00	30.00
WMF Williams/Moss/Fitz	12.00	30.00
WWG Winslow/Winslow/Gonzalez	8.00	20.00

2004 Upper Deck Finite HG Rookie Fabrics

STATED ODDS 1:10

BB Bernard Berrian	2.50	6.00
BR Ben Roethlisberger	15.00	40.00
BT Ben Troupe	2.50	6.00
CP Chris Perry	2.50	6.00
DH Devery Henderson	2.50	6.00
DW Darius Watts	2.50	6.00
EM Eli Manning	12.00	30.00
GJ Greg Jones	2.50	6.00
JJ Julius Jones	2.50	6.00
JP J.P. Losman	2.50	6.00
KC Keary Colbert	2.50	6.00
KJ Kevin Jones	3.00	8.00
KW Kellen Winslow Jr.	2.50	6.00
LE Lee Evans	4.00	10.00
LF Larry Fitzgerald	8.00	20.00
LM Luke McCown	2.50	6.00
MC Michael Clayton	3.00	8.00
MJ Michael Jenkins	2.50	6.00
PR Philip Rivers	10.00	25.00
RA Rashaun Woods	2.50	6.00
RE Reggie Williams	2.50	6.00
RG Robert Gallery	3.00	8.00
RW Roy Williams WR	2.50	6.00
SJ Steven Jackson	4.00	10.00
TB Tatum Bell	2.50	6.00

2004 Upper Deck Finite HG Signatures

STATED ODDS 1:10

FSAN Andy Reid SP	20.00	50.00
FSAR Antwaan Randle El	5.00	12.00
FSBC Brandon Chillar	6.00	15.00
FSBE Ben Watson	6.00	15.00
FSBH Ben Hartsock	5.00	12.00
FSBL Brandon Lloyd	6.00	15.00
FSBR Ben Roethlisberger SP	100.00	175.00
FSBS Barry Sanders SP	60.00	120.00
FSBT Ben Troupe	5.00	12.00
FSBW Brian Westbrook	5.00	12.00
FSCC Casey Clausen	6.00	15.00
FSCE Cedric Cobbs	5.00	12.00
FSCF Clarence Farmer	5.00	12.00
FSCO Cody Pickett	5.00	12.00
FSCP Chad Pennington	5.00	12.00
FSDB Drew Bledsoe SP	8.00	20.00
FSDD Devard Darling	5.00	12.00
FSDE Deuce McAllister	6.00	15.00
FSDH Devery Henderson	5.00	12.00
FSDR Drew Henson SP	5.00	12.00
FSDW Darius Watts	5.00	12.00
FSEM Eli Manning	75.00	150.00
FSGA Robert Gallery	6.00	15.00
FSGR Jon Gruden SP	10.00	25.00
FSHA DeAngelo Hall	8.00	20.00
FSJC Jerricho Cotchery	6.00	15.00
FSJF John Fox SP	5.00	12.00
FSJG Joey Galloway	6.00	15.00
FSJJ Julius Jones	5.00	12.00
FSJM Johnnie Morant	5.00	12.00
FSJN John Navarre	5.00	12.00
FSJO Joe Montana SP	100.00	200.00
FSJP J.P. Losman	5.00	12.00
FSJS Josh McCown	6.00	15.00
FSJT Joe Theismann SP	10.00	25.00
FSJV Jonathan Vilma	6.00	15.00
FSKC Keary Colbert	5.00	12.00
FSKE Kelley Washington	5.00	12.00
FSKJ Kevin Jones	6.00	15.00
FSLE Lee Evans	8.00	20.00
FSMS Matt Schaub	5.00	12.00
FSMV Michael Vick SP	20.00	50.00
FSNA Joe Namath	40.00	100.00
FSPM Peyton Manning SP	50.00	100.00
FSPR Philip Rivers	25.00	60.00
FSQW Quincy Wilson	5.00	12.00
FSRE Reggie Williams	5.00	12.00
FSRG Rex Grossman	5.00	12.00
FSRJ Rudi Johnson	5.00	12.00
FSRW Roy Williams WR	5.00	12.00
FSSJ Steven Jackson	8.00	20.00
FSSP Samie Parker	5.00	12.00
FSTB Tatum Bell	5.00	12.00
FSTH Tommie Harris	6.00	15.00
FSTR Travis Henry	5.00	12.00
FSWM Willis McGahee	5.00	12.00

2004 Upper Deck Finite HG Signatures Radiance

*RADIANCE: .8X TO 2X BASIC SIGS
RADIANCE PRINT RUN 25 SER.#'d SETS

FSAN Andy Reid	30.00	80.00
FSBR Ben Roethlisberger	125.00	250.00
FSBS Barry Sanders	125.00	250.00
FSEM Eli Manning	125.00	250.00
FSJO Joe Montana	125.00	250.00
FSMV Michael Vick	25.00	60.00
FSPM Peyton Manning	125.00	200.00
FSPR Philip Rivers	50.00	120.00

2007 Upper Deck First Edition

This 200-card set was released in July, 2007. The set was issued through Upper Deck's retail channels and contained 10 cards with an 99 cent SRP which came 36 packs to a box. Cards numbered 1-100 feature veterans in team alphabetical order while cards numbered 101-200 feature 2007 NFL rookies.

COMPLETE SET (200)	20.00	40.00
COMP.SET w/o RCs (100)	8.00	20.00
1 Matt Leinart	.10	.25
2 Larry Fitzgerald	.12	.30
3 Anquan Boldin	.10	.25
4 Michael Vick	.12	.30
5 Warrick Dunn	.10	.25
6 Alge Crumpler	.12	.30
7 Steve McNair	.12	.30
8 Mark Clayton	.10	.25
9 Todd Heap	.10	.25
10 Ray Lewis	.15	.40
11 J.P. Losman	.10	.25
12 Lee Evans	.12	.30
13 Anthony Thomas	.10	.25
14 Jake Delhomme	.10	.25
15 DeShaun Foster	.12	.30
16 Steve Smith	.12	.30
17 Cedric Benson	.10	.25
18 Bernard Berrian	.10	.25
19 Brian Urlacher	.15	.40
20 Carson Palmer	.12	.30
21 Rudi Johnson	.10	.25
22 Chad Johnson	.10	.25
23 Kellen Winslow	.10	.25
24 Braylon Edwards	.10	.25
25 Tony Romo	.20	.50
26 Julius Jones	.10	.25
27 Terrell Owens	.12	.30
28 Jay Cutler	.10	.25
29 Javon Walker	.12	.30
30 Champ Bailey	.12	.30
31 Jon Kitna	.10	.25
32 Kevin Jones	.10	.25
33 Roy Williams WR	.10	.25
34 Brett Favre	.30	.75
35 Donald Driver	.12	.30
36 A.J. Hawk	.10	.25
37 Andre Johnson	.12	.30
38 Mario Williams	.12	.30
39 Ron Dayne	.12	.30
40 Peyton Manning	.40	1.00
41 Marvin Harrison	.12	.30
42 Reggie Wayne	.12	.30
43 Joseph Addai	.10	.25
44 Maurice Jones-Drew	.10	.25
45 Fred Taylor	.10	.25
46 Byron Leftwich	.10	.25
47 Larry Johnson	.10	.25
48 Tony Gonzalez	.12	.30
49 Damon Huard	.12	.30
50 Ronnie Brown	.10	.25
51 Jason Taylor	.12	.30
52 Chris Chambers	.10	.25
53 Chester Taylor	.10	.25
54 Tarvaris Jackson	.10	.25
55 Troy Williamson	.10	.25
56 Tom Brady	.50	1.25
57 Laurence Maroney	.12	.30
58 Ben Watson	.10	.25
59 Asante Samuel	.10	.25
60 Chad Pennington	.10	.25
61 Leon Washington	.10	.25
62 Laveranues Coles	.10	.25
63 Eli Manning	.12	.30
64 Jeremy Shockey	.10	.25
65 Brandon Jacobs	.10	.25
66 Drew Brees	.15	.40
67 Marques Colston	.10	.25
68 Reggie Bush	.10	.25
69 Deuce McAllister	.12	.30
70 Jerry Porter	.12	.30
71 Justin Fargas	.10	.25
72 Randy Moss	.12	.30
73 Brian Westbrook	.10	.25
74 Reggie Brown	.10	.25
75 Donovan McNabb	.12	.30
76 Ben Roethlisberger	.15	.40
77 Willie Parker	.12	.30
78 Troy Polamalu	.15	.40
79 Antonio Gates	.15	.40
80 Shawne Merriman	.10	.25
81 LaDainian Tomlinson	.15	.40
82 Alex Smith QB	.12	.30
83 Frank Gore	.12	.30
84 Vernon Davis	.10	.25
85 Steven Jackson	.10	.25
86 Marc Bulger	.10	.25
87 Torry Holt	.12	.30
88 Isaac Bruce	.15	.40
89 Matt Hasselbeck	.10	.25
90 Shaun Alexander	.10	.25
91 Deion Branch	.10	.25
92 Cadillac Williams	.12	.30
93 Michael Clayton	.10	.25
94 Joey Galloway	.12	.30
95 Vince Young	.10	.25
96 LenDale White	.12	.30
97 Jason Campbell	.10	.25
98 Clinton Portis	.10	.25
99 Santana Moss	.12	.30
100 Antwaan Randle El	.10	.25
101 JaMarcus Russell RC	.40	1.00
102 Brady Quinn RC	.40	1.00
103 Calvin Johnson RC	1.25	3.00
104 Adrian Peterson RC	1.25	3.00
105 Joe Thomas RC	.60	1.50
106 Levi Brown RC	.40	1.00
107 Gaines Adams RC	.50	1.25
108 Adam Carriker RC	.40	1.00
109 Ted Ginn Jr. RC	.50	1.25
110 Anthony Gonzalez RC	.40	1.00
111 Troy Smith RC	.40	1.00
112 Leon Hall RC	.40	1.00
113 LaMarr Woodley RC	.75	2.00
114 Alan Branch RC	.40	1.00
115 Patrick Willis RC	.60	1.50
116 Reggie Nelson RC	.40	1.00
117 Paul Posluszny RC	.40	1.00
118 Dwayne Bowe RC	.40	1.00
119 Steve Smith RC	.40	1.00
120 Dwayne Jarrett RC	.50	1.25
121 Marshawn Lynch RC	.75	2.00
122 Darius Walker RC	.40	1.00
123 Daymeion Hughes RC	.40	1.00
124 LaRon Landry RC	.60	1.50
125 Jon Beason RC	.40	1.00
126 Lawrence Timmons RC	.60	1.50
127 Drew Stanton RC	.40	1.00
128 Trent Edwards RC	.40	1.00
129 John Beck RC	.40	1.00
130 Kevin Kolb RC	.50	1.25
131 Amobi Okoye RC	.50	1.25
132 Michael Bush RC	.40	1.00
133 Darrelle Revis RC	.50	1.25
134 H.B. Blades RC	.40	1.00
135 Jamaal Anderson RC	.50	1.25
136 Robert Meachem RC	.50	1.25
137 Sidney Rice RC	.50	1.25
138 Craig Davis RC	.40	1.00
139 Paul Williams RC	.40	1.00
140 Greg Olsen RC	.60	1.50
141 Jarvis Moss RC	.40	1.00
142 Justin Harrell RC	.40	1.00
143 DeMarcus Tank Tyler RC	.40	1.00
144 Aaron Ross RC	.40	1.00
145 Chris Houston RC	.40	1.00
146 Brandon Meriweather RC	.50	1.25
147 Eric Weddle RC	.50	1.25
148 Lorenzo Booker RC	.50	1.25
149 Buster Davis RC	.50	1.25
150 Antonio Pittman RC	.40	1.00
151 Chris Henry RC	.40	1.00
152 Kenny Irons RC	.40	1.00
153 Brandon Jackson RC	.40	1.00
154 Tony Hunt RC	.40	1.00
155 Brian Leonard RC	.40	1.00
156 Garrett Wolfe RC	.40	1.00
157 Yamon Figurs RC	.40	1.00
158 Johnnie Lee Higgins RC	.40	1.00
159 Jordan Palmer RC	.50	1.25
160 Chris Leak RC	.40	1.00
161 Rhema McKnight RC	.40	1.00
162 Dwayne Wright RC	.40	1.00
163 Matt Moore RC	.60	1.50
164 Jeff Rowe RC	.40	1.00
165 Zach Miller RC	.40	1.00
166 Ben Patrick RC	.50	1.25
167 Joe Staley RC	.50	1.25
168 Eric Wright RC	.40	1.00
169 Aundrae Allison RC	.40	1.00
170 Steve Breaston RC	.40	1.00
171 David Harris RC	.40	1.00
172 Brandon Siler RC	.40	1.00
173 Tim Shaw RC	.50	1.25
174 Selvin Young RC	.40	1.00
175 Michael Griffin RC	.40	1.00
176 Kenneth Darby RC	.40	1.00
177 Anthony Spencer RC	.50	1.25
178 Charles Johnson RC	.40	1.00
179 Quentin Moses RC	.40	1.00
180 DeShawn Wynn RC	.40	1.00
181 Scott Chandler RC	.60	1.50
182 Stewart Bradley RC	.40	1.00
183 Ahmad Bradshaw RC	.60	1.50
184 Matt Spaeth RC	.60	1.50
185 Ray McDonald RC	.50	1.25
186 Ben Grubbs RC	.50	1.25
187 Jon Abbate RC	.40	1.00
188 Victor Abiamiri RC	.40	1.00
189 Courtney Taylor RC	.40	1.00
190 A.J. Davis RC	.40	1.00
191 Nate Harris RC	.50	1.25
192 Jonathan Wade RC	.40	1.00
193 Tim Crowder RC	.50	1.25
194 Legedu Naanee RC	.50	1.25
195 Quinn Pitcock RC	.50	1.25
196 Marcus McCauley RC	.40	1.00
197 Sabby Piscitelli RC	.40	1.00
198 Tanard Jackson RC	.40	1.00
199 Josh Gattis RC	.40	1.00
200 Rufus Alexander RC	.40	1.00

2007 Upper Deck First Edition Gold

*VETS: 1.5X TO 4X BASIC CARDS
*ROOKIES: .6X TO 1.5X BASIC CARDS

2007 Upper Deck First Edition 1st and Goal

FGBJ Brandon Jacobs	.50	1.25
FGBR Ronnie Brown	.50	1.25
FGCP Clinton Portis	.50	1.25
FGCT Chester Taylor	.50	1.25
FGCW Cadillac Williams	.60	1.50
FGDM Deuce McAllister	.60	1.50
FGEJ Edgerrin James	.60	1.50
FGFG Frank Gore	.60	1.50
FGJA Joseph Addai	.50	1.25
FGKJ Kevin Jones	.50	1.25
FGLJ Larry Johnson	.50	1.25
FGLT LaDainian Tomlinson	.75	2.00
FGMB Marion Barber	.60	1.50
FGMJ Maurice Jones-Drew	.50	1.25
FGRB Reggie Bush	.50	1.25
FGRJ Rudi Johnson	.50	1.25
FGSA Shaun Alexander	.50	1.25
FGSJ Steven Jackson	.50	1.25
FGTJ Thomas Jones	.50	1.25
FGWP Willie Parker	.60	1.50

2007 Upper Deck First Edition Autographs

RANDOM INSERTS IN PACKS

SEAO Amobi Okoye	5.00	12.00
SEBA Dallas Baker	5.00	12.00
SEBL Brian Leonard	4.00	10.00
SEBU Marc Bulger	4.00	10.00
SECD Craig Davis	5.00	12.00
SECT Chester Taylor	3.00	8.00
SEDB David Ball	4.00	10.00
SEDH Daymeion Hughes	3.00	8.00
SEDW Dwayne Wright	3.00	8.00
SEGA Gaines Adams	5.00	12.00
SEGW Garrett Wolfe	5.00	12.00
SEHB H.B. Blades	4.00	10.00
SEHI Johnnie Lee Higgins	4.00	10.00
SEHO T.J. Houshmandzadeh	4.00	10.00
SEJB John Beck	3.00	8.00
SEJH Jason Hill	5.00	12.00
SEJP Jordan Palmer	5.00	12.00
SEJT Joe Thomas	5.00	12.00
SEKD Kenneth Darby	5.00	12.00
SEKS Kolby Smith	3.00	8.00
SELH Leon Hall	5.00	12.00
SELN Legedu Naanee	4.00	10.00
SELT Lawrence Timmons	5.00	12.00
SELW LaMarr Woodley	8.00	20.00
SEMM Matt Moore	5.00	12.00
SEQM Quentin Moses	4.00	10.00
SERM Rhema McKnight	4.00	10.00
SERN Reggie Nelson	5.00	12.00
SESC Scott Chandler	4.00	10.00
SESY Selvin Young	8.00	20.00
SETP Tyler Palko	4.00	10.00
SEZM Zach Miller	4.00	10.00

2007 Upper Deck First Edition Freshman Phenoms

FPAO Amobi Okoye	.60	1.50
FPAP Adrian Peterson	1.50	4.00
FPBJ Brandon Jackson	.50	1.25
FPBQ Brady Quinn	.50	1.25
FPCJ Calvin Johnson	1.50	4.00
FPDB Dwayne Bowe	.50	1.25
FPDJ Dwayne Jarrett	.60	1.50
FPDS Drew Stanton	.50	1.25
FPDW Darius Walker	.50	1.25
FPGA Gaines Adams	.60	1.50
FPGO Greg Olsen	.75	2.00
FPJR JaMarcus Russell	.50	1.25
FPLH Leon Hall	.50	1.25
FPLL LaRon Landry	.75	2.00
FPML Marshawn Lynch	1.00	2.50
FPPP Paul Posluszny	.50	1.25
FPRM Robert Meachem	.60	1.50
FPRN Reggie Nelson	.50	1.25
FPSS Steve Smith USC	.50	1.25
FPTG Ted Ginn Jr.	.60	1.50

2007 Upper Deck First Edition Passing Grade

PGAS Alex Smith QB	.60	1.50
PGBF Brett Favre	1.50	4.00
PGBR Ben Roethlisberger	.75	2.00
PGCP Carson Palmer	.60	1.50
PGDB Drew Brees	.75	2.00
PGDM Donovan McNabb	.60	1.50
PGEM Eli Manning	.60	1.50
PGJD Jake Delhomme	.50	1.25
PGJL J.P. Losman	.50	1.25
PGMB Marc Bulger	.50	1.25
PGMH Matt Hasselbeck	.50	1.25
PGML Matt Leinart	.50	1.25
PGMV Michael Vick	.60	1.50
PGPE Chad Pennington	.50	1.25
PGPM Peyton Manning	2.00	5.00
PGRG Rex Grossman	.50	1.25
PGSM Steve McNair	.60	1.50
PGTB Tom Brady	2.50	6.00
PGTR Tony Romo	1.00	2.50
PGVY Vince Young	.50	1.25

2007 Upper Deck First Edition Sophomore Sensations

SSAF Anthony Fasano	.50	1.25
SSAH A.J. Hawk	.50	1.25
SSDH Devin Hester	.60	1.50
SSDW DeAngelo Williams	.50	1.25
SSJA Joseph Addai	.50	1.25
SSJC Jay Cutler	.50	1.25
SSJN Jerious Norwood	.50	1.25
SSLM Laurence Maroney	.60	1.50
SSLW Leon Washington	.50	1.25
SSMA Mark Anderson	.60	1.50
SSMC Marques Colston	.50	1.25
SSMH Michael Huff	.60	1.50
SSMJ Maurice Jones-Drew	.50	1.25
SSML Matt Leinart	.50	1.25
SSMW Mario Williams	.60	1.50
SSRB Reggie Bush	.50	1.25
SSSH Santonio Holmes	.50	1.25
SSTJ Tarvaris Jackson	.50	1.25
SSVD Vernon Davis	.50	1.25
SSVY Vince Young	.50	1.25

2007 Upper Deck First Edition Speed 2 Burn

SBBR Ronnie Brown	.50	1.25
SBBW Brian Westbrook	.50	1.25
SBCB Champ Bailey	.60	1.50
SBCJ Chad Johnson	.50	1.25
SBDH Devin Hester	.60	1.50
SBFG Frank Gore	.60	1.50
SBFT Fred Taylor	.50	1.25
SBLJ Larry Johnson	.50	1.25
SBLT LaDainian Tomlinson	.75	2.00
SBMV Michael Vick	.60	1.50
SBRB Reggie Bush	.50	1.25
SBRW Reggie Wayne	.60	1.50
SBSA Shaun Alexander	.50	1.25
SBSJ Steven Jackson	.50	1.25
SBSM Santana Moss	.60	1.50
SBSS Steve Smith	.60	1.50
SBTO Terrell Owens	.60	1.50
SBVY Vince Young	.50	1.25
SBWI Roy Williams WR	.50	1.25
SBWP Willie Parker	.60	1.50

2008 Upper Deck First Edition

This set was released on September 8, 2008. The base set consists of 225 cards. Cards 1-150 feature veterans, and cards 151-225 are rookies.

COMPLETE SET (225)	20.00	40.00
COMP.FACT.SET (226)	25.00	40.00
1 Edgerrin James	.12	.30
2 Matt Leinart	.10	.25
3 Larry Fitzgerald	.12	.30
4 Anquan Boldin	.10	.25
5 Antrel Rolle	.10	.25
6 Joe Horn	.10	.25
7 Warrick Dunn	.10	.25
8 Jerious Norwood	.10	.25
9 Michael Jenkins	.10	.25
10 Ed Reed	.12	.30
11 Willis McGahee	.10	.25
12 Steve McNair	.12	.30
13 Todd Heap	.10	.25
14 Ray Lewis	.15	.40
15 Terrell Suggs	.10	.25
16 Trent Edwards	.10	.25
17 Lee Evans	.12	.30
18 Roscoe Parrish	.10	.25
19 Marshawn Lynch	.12	.30
20 DeAngelo Williams	.10	.25
21 Julius Peppers	.12	.30
22 Steve Smith	.12	.30
23 Cedric Benson	.10	.25
24 Greg Olsen	.12	.30
25 Lance Briggs	.12	.30
26 Rex Grossman	.10	.25
27 Devin Hester	.12	.30
28 Brian Urlacher	.15	.40
29 T.J. Houshmandzadeh	.10	.25
30 Carson Palmer	.12	.30
31 Rudi Johnson	.10	.25
32 Chad Johnson	.10	.25
33 Stacy Andrews	.12	.30
34 Kamerion Wimbley	.10	.25
35 Joshua Cribbs	.10	.25
36 Jamal Lewis	.12	.30
37 Kellen Winslow	.10	.25
38 Braylon Edwards	.10	.25
39 Marion Barber	.10	.25
40 Jason Witten	.12	.30
41 DeMarcus Ware	.12	.30
42 Tony Romo	.12	.30
43 Terrell Owens	.12	.30
44 John Lynch	.12	.30
45 Brandon Marshall	.12	.30
46 Jay Cutler	.10	.25
47 Dre Bly	.10	.25
48 Champ Bailey	.12	.30
49 Tatum Bell	.10	.25
50 Calvin Johnson	.15	.40
51 Jon Kitna	.10	.25
52 Roy Williams WR	.10	.25
53 Ernie Sims	.10	.25
54 Aaron Kampman	.12	.30
55 Charles Woodson	.15	.40
56 Brett Favre	.30	.75
57 Donald Driver	.12	.30
58 A.J. Hawk	.10	.25
59 DeMeco Ryans	.12	.30
60 Andre Johnson	.12	.30
61 Mario Williams	.12	.30
62 Ron Dayne	.10	.25
63 Dwight Freeney	.10	.25
64 Dallas Clark	.10	.25
65 Peyton Manning	.40	1.00
66 Marvin Harrison	.12	.30
67 Reggie Wayne	.12	.30
68 Matt Jones	.12	.30
69 David Garrard	.10	.25
70 Reggie Williams	.12	.30
71 Maurice Jones-Drew	.10	.25
72 Fred Taylor	.10	.25
73 Dwayne Bowe	.12	.30
74 Derrick Johnson	.10	.25
75 Larry Johnson	.10	.25
76 Tony Gonzalez	.12	.30
77 Ronnie Brown	.10	.25
78 Jason Taylor	.12	.30
79 Ted Ginn Jr.	.10	.25
80 John Beck	.10	.25
81 Adrian Peterson	.15	.40
82 Sidney Rice	.10	.25
83 Chester Taylor	.10	.25
84 Bernard Berrian	.10	.25
85 Wes Welker	.12	.30
86 Randy Moss	.12	.30
87 Tom Brady	.50	1.25
88 Laurence Maroney	.12	.30
89 Mike Vrabel	.10	.25
90 Drew Brees	.15	.40
91 Marques Colston	.10	.25
92 Reggie Bush	.10	.25
93 Mike McKenzie	.10	.25
94 Michael Strahan	.12	.30
95 Plaxico Burress	.10	.25
96 Eli Manning	.12	.30
97 Jeremy Shockey	.10	.25
98 Brandon Jacobs	.10	.25
99 Jerricho Cotchery	.10	.25
100 Kellen Clemens	.10	.25
101 Leon Washington	.10	.25
102 Thomas Jones	.10	.25
103 Kirk Morrison	.10	.25
104 Nnamdi Asomugha	.10	.25
105 Derrick Burgess	.10	.25
106 Ronald Curry	.10	.25
107 JaMarcus Russell	.10	.25
108 Brian Dawkins	.15	.40
109 Brian Westbrook	.10	.25
110 Reggie Brown	.10	.25
111 Donovan McNabb	.12	.30
112 Hines Ward	.12	.30
113 Santonio Holmes	.10	.25
114 Ben Roethlisberger	.15	.40
115 Willie Parker	.12	.30
116 Troy Polamalu	.15	.40
117 Philip Rivers	.15	.40
118 Antonio Gates	.12	.30
119 Shawne Merriman	.10	.25
120 LaDainian Tomlinson	.15	.40
121 Antonio Cromartie	.10	.25
122 Alex Smith QB	.12	.30
123 Frank Gore	.12	.30
124 Vernon Davis	.10	.25
125 Patrick Willis	.12	.30
126 Lofa Tatupu	.10	.25
127 Patrick Kerney	.10	.25
128 Bobby Engram	.10	.25
129 Matt Hasselbeck	.10	.25
130 Deion Branch	.10	.25
131 Pisa Tinoisamoa	.10	.25
132 Steven Jackson	.10	.25
133 Marc Bulger	.10	.25
134 Torry Holt	.12	.30
135 Randy McMichael	.10	.25
136 Ronde Barber	.10	.25
137 Cadillac Williams	.12	.30
138 Joey Galloway	.12	.30
139 Jeff Garcia	.10	.25
140 Gaines Adams	.10	.25
141 Keith Bulluck	.10	.25
142 Nick Harper	.10	.25
143 Vince Young	.10	.25
144 LenDale White	.10	.25
145 Alge Crumpler	.10	.25
146 Jason Campbell	.10	.25
147 Chris Cooley	.10	.25
148 Brandon Lloyd	.10	.25
149 Clinton Portis	.10	.25
150 Santana Moss	.10	.25
151 Alex Brink RC	.50	1.25
152 Anthony Morelli RC	.40	1.00
153 Antoine Cason RC	.50	1.25
154 Aqib Talib RC	.60	1.50
155 Calais Campbell RC	.50	1.25
156 Erin Henderson RC	.50	1.25
157 Chris Johnson RC	.50	1.25
158 DJ Hall RC	.40	1.00
159 DeJuan Tribble RC	.40	1.00
160 Derrick Harvey RC	.40	1.00
161 Mike Jenkins RC	.40	1.00
162 Dustin Keller RC	.50	1.25
163 Erik Ainge RC	.40	1.00
164 Felix Jones RC	.40	1.00
165 Gosder Cherilus RC	.50	1.25
166 Jack Ikegwuonu RC	.40	1.00
167 Jacob Hester RC	.40	1.00
168 Chauncey Washington RC	.50	1.25
169 J Leman RC	.40	1.00
170 Joe Flacco RC	.75	2.00
171 John David Booty RC	.40	1.00
172 Jordy Nelson RC	1.25	3.00
173 Josh Johnson RC	.40	1.00
174 Kenny Phillips RC	.40	1.00
175 Malcolm Kelly RC	.40	1.00
176 Marcus Monk RC	.50	1.25
177 Mario Manningham RC	.40	1.00
178 Mario Urrutia RC	.40	1.00
179 Martin Rucker RC	.40	1.00
180 Matt Flynn RC	.40	1.00
181 Matt Forte RC	.60	1.50
182 Jerome Felton RC	.40	1.00
183 Owen Schmitt RC	.40	1.00
184 Ryan Grice-Mullen RC	.40	1.00
185 Paul Hubbard RC	.40	1.00
186 Quentin Groves RC	.50	1.25
187 Ray Rice RC	.40	1.00
188 Ryan Clady RC	.50	1.25
189 Ryan Torain RC	.50	1.25
190 Adrian Arrington RC	.40	1.00
191 Shawn Crable RC	.40	1.00
192 Allen Patrick RC	.40	1.00
193 Tashard Choice RC	.40	1.00
194 Terrell Thomas RC	.40	1.00
195 Thomas Brown RC	.40	1.00
196 Tom Zbikowski RC	.50	1.25
197 Jermichael Finley RC	.40	1.00
198 Trevor Laws RC	.40	1.00
199 Vince Hall RC	.40	1.00
200 Xavier Adibi RC	.40	1.00
201 Ali Highsmith RC	.40	1.00
202 Andre Woodson RC	.40	1.00
203 Brian Brohm RC	.40	1.00
204 Chad Henne RC	.50	1.25
205 Chris Long RC	.50	1.25
206 Colt Brennan RC	.50	1.25
207 Dan Connor RC	.40	1.00
208 Darren McFadden RC	.40	1.00
209 Dennis Dixon RC	.40	1.00
210 DeSean Jackson RC	.75	2.00
211 Early Doucet RC	.40	1.00
212 Fred Davis RC	.40	1.00
213 Glenn Dorsey RC	.40	1.00
214 Jake Long RC	.60	1.50
215 Jonathan Stewart RC	.60	1.50
216 Justin King RC	.50	1.25
217 Keith Rivers RC	.40	1.00
218 Lavelle Hawkins RC	.50	1.25
219 Lawrence Jackson RC	.40	1.00
220 Limas Sweed RC	.40	1.00
221 Matt Ryan RC	1.25	3.00
222 Mike Hart RC	.40	1.00
223 Earl Bennett RC	.60	1.50
224 Sam Baker RC	.40	1.00
225 Sedrick Ellis RC	.40	1.00

2008 Upper Deck First Edition Jerseys

ONE PER FACTORY SET

FGJAB Anquan Boldin	2.00	5.00
FGJAC Alge Crumpler	2.00	5.00
FGJAG Antonio Gates	2.50	6.00
FGJAJ Andre Johnson	2.50	6.00
FGJAL Shaun Alexander	2.00	5.00
FGJAP Adrian Peterson	3.00	8.00
FGJAR Aaron Rodgers	6.00	15.00
FGJAS Alex Smith QB	2.50	6.00
FGJBB Bernard Berrian	2.00	5.00
FGJBC Brodie Croyle	2.50	6.00
FGJBE Braylon Edwards	2.00	5.00
FGJBF Brett Favre	6.00	15.00
FGJBJ Brandon Jacobs	2.00	5.00
FGJBQ Brady Quinn	2.00	5.00
FGJBR Drew Brees	3.00	8.00
FGJBS Bob Sanders	2.50	6.00
FGJBW Ben Watson	2.00	5.00
FGJCA Jason Campbell	2.00	5.00
FGJCB Champ Bailey	2.50	6.00
FGJCJ Calvin Johnson	3.00	8.00
FGJCL Michael Clayton	2.00	5.00
FGJCO Jerricho Cotchery	2.00	5.00
FGJCP Carson Palmer	2.50	6.00
FGJCW Cadillac Williams	2.50	6.00
FGJDA Derek Anderson	2.00	5.00
FGJDB Dwayne Bowe	2.50	6.00
FGJDC Dallas Clark	2.00	5.00
FGJDD Donald Driver	2.50	6.00
FGJDF DeShaun Foster	2.00	5.00
FGJDG David Garrard	2.00	5.00
FGJDH Devin Hester	2.50	6.00
FGJDM Derrick Mason	2.00	5.00
FGJDO Donovan McNabb	2.50	6.00
FGJDW DeMarcus Ware	2.50	6.00
FGJEJ Edgerrin James	2.50	6.00
FGJEM Eli Manning	2.50	6.00
FGJER Ed Reed	2.50	6.00
FGJES Ernie Sims	2.00	5.00
FGJFG Frank Gore	2.50	6.00
FGJFT Fred Taylor	2.00	5.00
FGJGJ Greg Jennings	2.00	5.00
FGJGO Greg Olsen	2.50	6.00
FGJHM Heath Miller	3.00	8.00
FGJHO Torry Holt	2.50	6.00
FGJHU Michael Huff	2.00	5.00
FGJHW Hines Ward	2.50	6.00
FGJIB Isaac Bruce	3.00	8.00
FGJJA Jason Witten	2.50	6.00
FGJJC Jay Cutler	2.00	5.00
FGJJG Joey Galloway	2.50	6.00
FGJJN Jerious Norwood	2.00	5.00
FGJJP Julius Peppers	2.50	6.00
FGJJR JaMarcus Russell	2.00	5.00
FGJJT Jason Taylor	2.50	6.00
FGJJV Jonathan Vilma	2.00	5.00
FGJJW Javon Walker	2.50	6.00
FGJKJ Kevin Jones	2.00	5.00
FGJKM Kirk Morrison	2.00	5.00
FGJKW Kellen Winslow	2.00	5.00
FGJLE Lee Evans	2.50	6.00
FGJLF Larry Fitzgerald	2.50	6.00
FGJLJ Larry Johnson	2.00	5.00
FGJLM Laurence Maroney	2.50	6.00
FGJLT LaDainian Tomlinson	3.00	8.00
FGJLW LenDale White	2.00	5.00
FGJLY Marshawn Lynch	2.50	6.00
FGJMA Marques Colston	2.00	5.00
FGJMB Marc Bulger	2.00	5.00
FGJMC Deuce McAllister	2.50	6.00
FGJMH Marvin Harrison	2.50	6.00
FGJMJ Maurice Jones-Drew	2.00	5.00
FGJML Matt Leinart	2.00	5.00
FGJMS Matt Schaub	2.00	5.00
FGJMV Mike Vrabel	2.00	5.00
FGJPB Plaxico Burress	2.00	5.00
FGJPM Peyton Manning	8.00	20.00
FGJPO Clinton Portis	2.00	5.00
FGJPW Patrick Willis	2.50	6.00
FGJRB Reggie Bush	2.00	5.00
FGJRG Ryan Grant	2.50	6.00
FGJRJ Rudi Johnson	2.00	5.00
FGJRL Ray Lewis	3.00	8.00
FGJRM Randy Moss	2.50	6.00
FGJRO Ronnie Brown	2.00	5.00
FGJRW Roy Williams WR	2.00	5.00
FGJSA Asante Samuel	2.00	5.00
FGJSM Shawne Merriman	2.00	5.00
FGJSS Steve Smith	2.50	6.00
FGJTA Tatum Bell	2.00	5.00
FGJTB Tedy Bruschi	2.50	6.00
FGJTG Tony Gonzalez	2.50	6.00
FGJTH Todd Heap	2.00	5.00
FGJTS Terrell Suggs	2.00	5.00
FGJVY Vince Young	2.00	5.00
FGJWA Kurt Warner	2.50	6.00
FGJWE Brian Westbrook	2.00	5.00
FGJWI DeAngelo Williams	2.00	5.00
FGJWM Willis McGahee	2.00	5.00
FGJWO Charles Woodson	3.00	8.00
FGJZT Zach Thomas	2.50	6.00

2008 Upper Deck First Edition StarQuest

SQ1 Adrian Peterson	1.25	3.00
SQ2 Andre Woodson	.50	1.25
SQ3 Antonio Cromartie	.75	2.00
SQ4 Ben Roethlisberger	1.25	3.00
SQ5 Brian Westbrook	.75	2.00
SQ6 Carson Palmer	1.00	2.50
SQ7 Chris Long	.60	1.50
SQ8 Darren McFadden	.50	1.25
SQ9 DeSean Jackson	1.00	2.50
SQ10 Drew Brees	1.25	3.00
SQ11 Early Doucet	.50	1.25
SQ12 Ed Reed	1.00	2.50
SQ13 Ernie Sims	.75	2.00
SQ14 Fred Taylor	.75	2.00
SQ15 Glenn Dorsey	.50	1.25
SQ16 Shawn Crable	.50	1.25
SQ17 Joseph Addai	.75	2.00
SQ18 Kenny Phillips	.50	1.25
SQ19 LaDainian Tomlinson	1.25	3.00
SQ20 Larry Fitzgerald	1.00	2.50
SQ21 Matt Hasselbeck	.75	2.00
SQ22 Matt Ryan	1.50	4.00
SQ23 Osi Umenyiora	.75	2.00
SQ24 Patrick Willis	1.00	2.50
SQ25 Peyton Manning	3.00	8.00
SQ26 Randy Moss	1.00	2.50
SQ27 Sam Baker	.60	1.50
SQ28 Terrell Owens	1.00	2.50
SQ29 Tom Brady	4.00	10.00
SQ30 Tony Romo	1.00	2.50

2009 Upper Deck First Edition

COMPLETE SET (200)	20.00	40.00
1 Kurt Warner	.12	.30
2 Tim Hightower	.10	.25
3 Larry Fitzgerald	.12	.30
4 Anquan Boldin	.10	.25
5 Steve Breaston	.12	.30
6 Matt Ryan	.12	.30
7 Michael Jenkins	.10	.25
8 Jerious Norwood	.10	.25
9 Roddy White	.10	.25
10 Michael Turner	.10	.25

11 Ed Reed .12 .30
12 Willis McGahee .10 .25
13 Joe Flacco .12 .30
14 Ray Lewis .15 .40
15 Derrick Mason .10 .25
16 Lee Evans .12 .30
17 Marshawn Lynch .12 .30
18 Trent Edwards .10 .25
19 Leodis McKelvin .10 .25
20 Terrell Owens .12 .30
21 DeAngelo Williams .10 .25
22 Steve Smith .12 .30
23 Muhsin Muhammad .10 .25
24 Jonathan Stewart .10 .25
25 Jake Delhomme .10 .25
26 Devin Hester .12 .30
27 Matt Forte .10 .25
28 Lance Briggs .12 .30
29 Jay Cutler .10 .25
30 Brian Urlacher .15 .40
31 Carson Palmer .12 .30
32 Chad Johnson .10 .25
33 Laveranues Coles .10 .25
34 Cedric Benson .10 .25
35 Jamal Lewis .12 .30
36 Derek Anderson .10 .25
37 Brady Quinn .10 .25
38 Braylon Edwards .10 .25
39 Felix Jones .10 .25
40 Jason Witten .12 .30
41 Roy Williams WR .10 .25
42 DeMarcus Ware .12 .30
43 Tony Romo .12 .30
44 Marion Barber .12 .30
45 Kyle Orton .10 .25
46 Eddie Royal .10 .25
47 Champ Bailey .12 .30
48 Brandon Marshall .12 .30
49 Jason Hanson .10 .25
50 Calvin Johnson .15 .40
51 Kevin Smith .12 .30
52 Daunte Culpepper .12 .30
53 A.J. Hawk .10 .25
54 Aaron Rodgers .30 .75
55 Donald Driver .12 .30
56 Greg Jennings .10 .25
57 Ryan Grant .12 .30
58 Matt Schaub .10 .25
59 Andre Johnson .12 .30
60 Steve Slaton .10 .25
61 Mario Williams .12 .30
62 DeMeco Ryans .12 .30
63 Peyton Manning .40 1.00
64 Joseph Addai .10 .25
65 Reggie Wayne .12 .30
66 Anthony Gonzalez .10 .25
67 Dallas Clark .10 .25
68 Bob Sanders .12 .30
69 Maurice Jones-Drew .10 .25
70 David Garrard .10 .25
71 Marcedes Lewis .10 .25
72 Rashean Mathis .10 .25
73 Justin Durant .10 .25
74 Larry Johnson .10 .25
75 Matt Cassel .10 .25
76 Tyler Thigpen .10 .25
77 Dwayne Bowe .12 .30
78 Ronnie Brown .10 .25
79 Greg Camarillo .12 .30
80 Ted Ginn Jr. .10 .25
81 Chad Pennington .10 .25
82 Joey Porter .12 .30
83 Adrian Peterson .15 .40
84 Bernard Berrian .10 .25
85 Jared Allen .10 .25
86 Chester Taylor .10 .25
87 Visanthe Shiancoe .12 .30
88 Tom Brady .50 1.25
89 Wes Welker .12 .30
90 Randy Moss .12 .30
91 Kevin Faulk .10 .25
92 Sammy Morris .10 .25
93 Reggie Bush .10 .25
94 Drew Brees .15 .40
95 Lance Moore .10 .25
96 Pierre Thomas .10 .25
97 Marques Colston .10 .25
98 Brandon Jacobs .10 .25
99 Ahmad Bradshaw .10 .25
100 Steve Smith USC .12 .30
101 Eli Manning .12 .30
102 Domenik Hixon .10 .25
103 Thomas Jones .10 .25
104 Jerricho Cotchery .10 .25
105 Kellen Clemens .10 .25
106 Dustin Keller .10 .25
107 Leon Washington .10 .25
108 Darren McFadden .15 .40
109 JaMarcus Russell .10 .25
110 Johnnie Lee Higgins .10 .25
111 Justin Fargas .10 .25
112 Asante Samuel .10 .25
113 Brian Westbrook .10 .25
114 DeSean Jackson .12 .30
115 Donovan McNabb .12 .30
116 Shawn Andrews .10 .25
117 Troy Polamalu .15 .40
118 Willie Parker .10 .25
119 Ben Roethlisberger .15 .40
120 Santonio Holmes .10 .25
121 Hines Ward .12 .30
122 James Harrison .15 .40
123 Darren Sproles .12 .30
124 LaDainian Tomlinson .15 .40
125 Philip Rivers .15 .40
126 Antonio Gates .12 .30
127 Vincent Jackson .10 .25
128 Patrick Willis .12 .30
129 Frank Gore .12 .30
130 Vernon Davis .10 .25
131 Julius Jones .10 .25
132 Matt Hasselbeck .10 .25
133 Deion Branch .10 .25
134 Lofa Tatupu .10 .25
135 Marc Bulger .10 .25
136 Donnie Avery .10 .25
137 Steven Jackson .10 .25
138 Kellen Winslow .10 .25
139 Cadillac Williams .12 .30
140 Michael Clayton .10 .25
141 Ronde Barber .10 .25
142 Kerry Collins .10 .25
143 Chris Johnson .10 .25
144 LenDale White .10 .25
145 Bo Scaife .10 .25
146 Clinton Portis .10 .25
147 Jason Campbell .10 .25
148 Santana Moss .12 .30
149 Antwaan Randle El .10 .25
150 Albert Haynesworth .10 .25
151 Ramses Barden RC .30 .75
152 Andre Brown RC .40 1.00
153 Patrick Turner RC .30 .75
154 Mike Wallace RC .50 1.25
155 Derrick Williams RC .30 .75
156 Deon Butler RC .30 .75
157 Juaquin Iglesias RC .30 .75
158 Stephen McGee RC .30 .75
159 Patrick Chung RC .30 .75
160 Darius Butler RC .40 1.00
161 Alex Mack RC .30 .75
162 Glen Coffee RC .30 .75
163 Nate Davis RC .30 .75
164 Chase Coffman RC .30 .75
165 Evander Hood RC .50 1.25
166 James Laurinaitis RC .30 .75
167 Vontae Davis RC .30 .75
168 Brian Robiskie RC .30 .75
169 Eugene Monroe RC .30 .75
170 Javon Ringer RC .30 .75
171 Clay Matthews RC 1.25 3.00
172 Rey Maualuga RC .50 1.25
173 Brian Cushing RC .30 .75
174 Michael Oher RC .50 1.25
175 Brandon Tate RC .40 1.00
176 Andre Smith RC .30 .75
177 Shonn Greene RC .30 .75
178 Pat White RC .40 1.00
179 Malcolm Jenkins RC .30 .75
180 Matthew Stafford RC 2.00 5.00
181 Michael Crabtree RC .50 1.25
182 Tyson Jackson RC .30 .75
183 Brandon Pettigrew RC .30 .75
184 Brian Orakpo RC .40 1.00
185 Jeremy Maclin RC .40 1.00
186 Jason Smith RC .30 .75
187 Chris Wells RC .30 .75
188 Aaron Curry RC .50 1.25
189 Mark Sanchez RC .30 .75
190 Aaron Maybin RC .40 1.00
191 B.J. Raji RC .40 1.00
192 Kenny Britt RC .50 1.25
193 Mohamed Massaquoi RC .30 .75
194 Knowshon Moreno RC .30 .75
195 Percy Harvin RC .30 .75
196 Hakeem Nicks RC .40 1.00
197 LeSean McCoy RC .75 2.00
198 Darrius Heyward-Bey RC .50 1.25
199 Josh Freeman RC .30 .75
200 Donald Brown RC .30 .75

2009 Upper Deck First Edition Silver

*VETS: 1.5X TO 4X BASIC CARDS
*ROOKIES: .6X TO 1.5X BASIC CARDS
ONE SILVER PER PACK

2009 Upper Deck First Edition Bombs Away

OVERALL INSERT ODDS 1:1
BA1 Kurt Warner .60 1.50
BA2 Drew Brees .75 2.00
BA3 Carson Palmer .60 1.50
BA4 Tom Brady 2.50 6.00
BA5 Ben Roethlisberger .75 2.00
BA6 Marc Bulger .50 1.25
BA7 Philip Rivers .75 2.00
BA8 Jay Cutler .50 1.25
BA9 Trent Edwards .50 1.25
BA10 Joe Flacco .60 1.50
BA11 Kyle Orton .50 1.25
BA12 Peyton Manning 2.00 5.00
BA13 Jake Delhomme .50 1.25
BA14 Chad Pennington .50 1.25
BA15 David Garrard .50 1.25
BA16 Kerry Collins .50 1.25
BA17 Donovan McNabb .60 1.50
BA18 Eli Manning .60 1.50
BA19 Aaron Rodgers 1.50 4.00
BA20 Matt Schaub .50 1.25
BA21 Matt Ryan .60 1.50
BA22 Tony Romo .60 1.50
BA23 Matt Hasselbeck .50 1.25
BA24 Matt Cassel .50 1.25
BA25 Jason Campbell .50 1.25

2009 Upper Deck First Edition Crunch Time

OVERALL INSERT ODDS 1:1
CT1 Albert Haynesworth .50 1.25
CT2 Ray Lewis .75 2.00
CT3 Brian Urlacher .75 2.00
CT4 Asante Samuel .50 1.25
CT5 Ed Reed .60 1.50
CT6 Troy Polamalu .75 2.00
CT7 Shawne Merriman .50 1.25
CT8 James Harrison .75 2.00
CT9 Dwight Freeney .50 1.25
CT10 Lance Briggs .60 1.50
CT11 Nnamdi Asomugha .50 1.25
CT12 A.J. Hawk .50 1.25
CT13 Bob Sanders .60 1.50
CT14 Keith Bulluck .50 1.25
CT15 Antrel Rolle .50 1.25
CT16 Adrian Wilson .50 1.25
CT17 Julius Peppers .60 1.50
CT18 DeMarcus Ware .60 1.50
CT19 Patrick Willis .60 1.50
CT20 DeMeco Ryans .60 1.50
CT21 Jared Allen .50 1.25
CT22 Lofa Tatupu .50 1.25
CT23 Nick Collins .50 1.25
CT24 Chris Hope .50 1.25
CT25 Jerod Mayo .60 1.50

2009 Upper Deck First Edition Speed to Burn

OVERALL INSERT ODDS 1:1
SB1 Darren McFadden .75 2.00
SB2 Steven Jackson .50 1.25
SB3 Chris Johnson .50 1.25
SB4 Devin Hester .60 1.50
SB5 Reggie Wayne .60 1.50
SB6 Randy Moss .60 1.50
SB7 Ted Ginn Jr. .50 1.25
SB8 Darren Sproles .60 1.50
SB9 Reggie Bush .50 1.25
SB10 Steve Smith .60 1.50
SB11 Santana Moss .60 1.50
SB12 Larry Fitzgerald .60 1.50
SB13 Lee Evans .60 1.50
SB14 Chad Johnson .50 1.25
SB15 Willie Parker .50 1.25
SB16 Willis McGahee .50 1.25
SB17 DeSean Jackson .60 1.50
SB18 Santonio Holmes .50 1.25
SB19 Eddie Royal .50 1.25
SB20 Calvin Johnson .75 2.00
SB21 Roy Williams .50 1.25
SB22 Brian Dawkins .50 1.25
SB23 Ed Reed .60 1.50
SB24 Michael Turner .50 1.25
SB25 Terrell Owens .60 1.50

2009 Upper Deck First Edition Star Attractions

OVERALL INSERT ODDS 1:1
SA1 Matt Ryan .60 1.50
SA2 Adrian Peterson .75 2.00
SA3 Chris Johnson .50 1.25
SA4 Randy Moss .60 1.50
SA5 Kurt Warner .60 1.50
SA6 Michael Turner .50 1.25
SA7 Thomas Jones .50 1.25
SA8 Steve Smith .60 1.50
SA9 Peyton Manning 2.00 5.00
SA10 Anquan Boldin .50 1.25
SA11 DeAngelo Williams .50 1.25
SA12 Andre Johnson .60 1.50
SA13 Donovan McNabb .60 1.50
SA14 Brian Westbrook .50 1.25
SA15 Ben Roethlisberger .75 2.00
SA16 Larry Fitzgerald .60 1.50
SA17 Clinton Portis .50 1.25
SA18 Marion Barber .60 1.50
SA19 Eli Manning .60 1.50
SA20 Frank Gore .60 1.50
SA21 Ray Lewis .75 2.00
SA22 Tom Brady 2.50 6.00
SA23 Shawne Merriman .50 1.25
SA24 Calvin Johnson .75 2.00
SA25 Troy Polamalu .75 2.00

2004 Upper Deck Foundations

Upper Deck Foundations was initially released in late September 2004. The base set consists of 263-cards including 140-rookies serial numbered to 250, 17 rookie jersey cards numbered to 1299 and 6-rookie jersey cards numbered to 499. Hobby boxes contained 24-packs of 5-cards and carried an S.R.P. of $4.99 per pack. Two parallel sets and a variety of inserts can be found seeded in packs highlighted by the Dual Endorsements autograph and Signature Foundations inserts.

COMP.SET w/o SP's (100) 7.50 20.00
101-240 ROOKIE PRINT RUN 350
241-257 ROOKIE JSY PRINT RUN 1299
258-263 ROOKIE JSY PRINT RUN 499
1 Josh McCown .25 .60
2 Emmitt Smith .50 1.25
3 Anquan Boldin .20 .50
4 T.J. Duckett .20 .50
5 Peerless Price .20 .50
6 Michael Vick .25 .60
7 Todd Heap .20 .50
8 Kyle Boller .20 .50
9 Jamal Lewis .25 .60
10 Travis Henry .20 .50
11 Eric Moulds .20 .50
12 Drew Bledsoe .25 .60
13 Steve Smith .30 .75
14 Stephen Davis .20 .50
15 Jake Delhomme .20 .50
16 Rex Grossman .20 .50
17 Brian Urlacher .30 .75
18 Anthony Thomas .25 .60
19 Rudi Johnson .20 .50
20 Chad Johnson .20 .50
21 Carson Palmer .25 .60
22 Quincy Morgan .20 .50
23 Jeff Garcia .20 .50
24 Andre Davis .20 .50
25 Roy Williams S .20 .50
26 Eddie George .25 .60
27 Keyshawn Johnson .25 .60
28 Jake Plummer .20 .50
29 Champ Bailey .25 .60
30 Ashley Lelie .20 .50
31 Joey Harrington .20 .50
32 Charles Rogers .20 .50
33 Az-Zahir Hakim .20 .50
34 Javon Walker .20 .50
35 Brett Favre .60 1.50
36 Ahman Green .25 .60
37 Domanick Davis .20 .50
38 David Carr .20 .50
39 Andre Johnson .25 .60
40 Peyton Manning .75 2.00
41 Marvin Harrison .25 .60
42 Edgerrin James .25 .60
43 Jimmy Smith .25 .60
44 Fred Taylor .20 .50
45 Byron Leftwich .20 .50
46 Trent Green .20 .50
47 Tony Gonzalez .25 .60
48 Priest Holmes .20 .50
49 Dante Hall .20 .50
50 Ricky Williams .25 .60
51 David Boston .20 .50
52 Chris Chambers .20 .50
53 A.J. Feeley .20 .50
54 Randy Moss .25 .60
55 Michael Bennett .20 .50
56 Daunte Culpepper .25 .60
57 Troy Brown .20 .50
58 Tom Brady 1.25 3.00
59 Corey Dillon .20 .50
60 Donte' Stallworth .20 .50
61 Deuce McAllister .25 .60
62 Aaron Brooks .20 .50
63 Kurt Warner .25 .60
64 Jeremy Shockey .20 .50
65 Santana Moss .25 .60
66 Curtis Martin .25 .60
67 Chad Pennington .20 .50
68 Amani Toomer .20 .50
69 Tim Brown .30 .75
70 Rich Gannon .25 .60
71 Jerry Rice .60 1.50
72 Jerry Porter .20 .50
73 Terrell Owens .25 .60
74 Jevon Kearse .20 .50
75 Donovan McNabb .25 .60
76 Tommy Maddox .20 .50
77 Plaxico Burress .20 .50
78 Hines Ward .25 .60
79 Duce Staley .20 .50
80 LaDainian Tomlinson .30 .75
81 Drew Brees .30 .75
82 Donnie Edwards .25 .60
83 Tim Rattay .20 .50
84 Kevan Barlow .20 .50
85 Brandon Lloyd .25 .60
86 Shaun Alexander .20 .50
87 Matt Hasselbeck .20 .50
88 Koren Robinson .20 .50
89 Torry Holt .25 .60
90 Marshall Faulk .25 .60
91 Marc Bulger .20 .50
92 Keenan McCardell .20 .50
93 Derrick Brooks .20 .50
94 Brad Johnson .25 .60
95 Steve McNair .25 .60
96 Derrick Mason .20 .50
97 Chris Brown .20 .50
98 Mark Brunell .25 .60
99 LaVar Arrington .20 .50
100 Clinton Portis .20 .50
101 Brandon Chillar RC 2.50 6.00
102 Mike Karney RC 2.50 6.00
103 Jamaar Taylor RC 2.00 5.00
104 Casey Clausen RC 2.50 6.00
105 Drew Carter RC 2.50 6.00
106 Travis LaBoy RC 2.50 6.00
107 Jonathan Vilma RC 2.50 6.00
108 Tramon Douglas RC 2.00 5.00
109 Bob Sanders RC 4.00 10.00
110 Mewelde Moore RC 2.50 6.00
111 Randy Starks RC 2.00 5.00
112 Tank Johnson RC 2.00 5.00
113 Triandos Luke RC 2.00 5.00
114 Dexter Reid RC 2.00 5.00
115 Cedric Cobbs RC 2.00 5.00
116 Darius Watts RC 2.00 5.00
117 Ryan Krause RC 2.00 5.00
118 Igor Olshansky RC 2.50 6.00
119 Adimchinobe Echemandu RC 2.50 6.00
120 Jason Fife RC 2.00 5.00
121 Justin Smiley RC 2.50 6.00
122 Marcus Tubbs RC 2.00 5.00
123 Nathan Vasher RC 3.00 8.00
124 Troy Fleming RC 2.00 5.00
125 Ben Troupe RC 2.00 5.00
126 Jammal Lord RC 2.00 5.00
127 Jared Lorenzen RC 2.50 6.00
128 Shawntae Spencer RC 2.00 5.00
129 Darnell Dockett RC 3.00 8.00
130 Derrick Strait RC 2.00 5.00
131 Clarence Moore RC 2.00 5.00
132 Jason Babin RC 3.00 8.00
133 Jerricho Cotchery RC 2.50 6.00
134 Karlos Dansby RC 2.50 6.00
135 Marquise Hill RC 2.00 5.00
136 Niko Koutouvides RC 2.00 5.00
137 Andy Hall RC 2.00 5.00
138 Teddy Lehman RC 2.00 5.00
139 Will Smith RC 2.50 6.00
140 Bernard Berrian RC 2.00 5.00
141 Chris Cooley RC 2.50 6.00
142 Landon Johnson RC 2.00 5.00
143 Devard Darling RC 2.00 5.00
144 Mark Jones RC 2.00 5.00
145 Jake Grove RC 2.00 5.00
146 John Navarre RC 2.00 5.00
147 Keary Colbert RC 2.00 5.00
148 Gilbert Gardner RC 2.00 5.00
149 P.K. Sam RC 2.00 5.00
150 Richard Seigler RC 2.00 5.00
151 Marquis Cooper RC 2.00 5.00
152 Tommie Harris RC 2.50 6.00
153 Thomas Tapeh RC 2.50 6.00
154 Ben Utecht RC 2.50 6.00
155 Chris Gamble RC 2.00 5.00
156 Daryl Smith RC 2.00 5.00
157 Sean Taylor RC 12.00 30.00
158 Caleb Miller RC 2.00 5.00
159 Johnnie Morant RC 2.00 5.00
160 Keith Smith RC 2.00 5.00
161 Matt Mauck RC 2.00 5.00
162 Matt Ware RC 3.00 8.00
163 Quincy Wilson RC 2.00 5.00
164 Samie Parker RC 2.00 5.00
165 Kendrick Starling RC 2.00 5.00
166 Antwan Odom RC 2.00 5.00
167 Brandon Miree RC 2.00 5.00
168 Casey Bramlet RC 2.00 5.00
169 Cody Pickett RC 2.00 5.00
170 Demorrio Williams RC 3.00 8.00
171 Dunta Robinson RC 2.00 5.00
172 D.J. Hackett RC 2.00 5.00
173 Josh Harris RC 2.00 5.00
174 Kenechi Udeze RC 2.50 6.00
175 Michael Boulware RC 3.00 8.00
176 Ricardo Colclough RC 2.00 5.00
177 Shawn Andrews RC 2.50 6.00
178 Jeris McIntyre RC 2.00 5.00
179 Jim Sorgi RC 2.50 6.00
180 Clarence Farmer RC 2.00 5.00
181 Courtney Watson RC 2.00 5.00
182 Derek Abney RC 2.00 5.00
183 Dwan Edwards RC 2.00 5.00
184 Ryan Dinwiddie RC 2.00 5.00
185 B.J. Johnson RC 2.00 5.00
186 Ben Watson RC 2.50 6.00
187 Kris Wilson RC 2.50 6.00
188 Michael Turner RC 2.00 5.00
189 Derrick Ward RC 3.00 8.00
190 Jonathan Smith RC 2.50 6.00
191 Vernon Carey RC 2.00 5.00
192 Ben Hartsock RC 2.00 5.00
193 Rich Gardner RC 2.50 6.00
194 D.J. Williams RC 3.00 8.00
195 Derrick Hamilton RC 2.00 5.00
196 Drew Henson RC 2.00 5.00
197 Jeff Smoker RC 2.50 6.00
198 Joey Thomas RC 2.00 5.00
199 Keyaron Fox RC 2.50 6.00
200 Nate Lawrie RC 2.00 5.00
201 Sloan Thomas RC 2.50 6.00
202 Justin Jenkins RC 2.00 5.00
203 Stuart Schweigert RC 2.50 6.00
204 Ran Carthon RC 2.00 5.00
205 Ahmad Carroll RC 2.00 5.00
206 Bradlee Van Pelt RC 2.50 6.00
207 Patrick Crayton RC 3.00 8.00
208 Chris Snee RC 6.00 15.00
209 Fred Russell RC 2.50 6.00
210 Dontarrious Thomas RC 2.50 6.00
211 Will Poole RC 3.00 8.00
212 Jarrett Payton RC 2.50 6.00
213 Keiwan Ratliff RC 2.00 5.00
214 Nate Kaeding RC 2.50 6.00
215 Tim Euhus RC 2.00 5.00
216 Sean Jones RC 2.00 5.00
217 Will Allen RC 2.50 6.00
218 B.J. Symons RC 2.00 5.00
219 Carlos Francis RC 2.00 5.00
220 Craig Krenzel RC 2.00 5.00
221 Andrae Thurman RC 2.00 5.00
222 Ernest Wilford RC 2.50 6.00
223 Glenn Earl RC 2.00 5.00
224 Jeremy LeSueur RC 2.00 5.00
225 Junior Siavii RC 2.00 5.00
226 Maurice Mann RC 2.00 5.00
227 Michael Waddell RC 2.00 5.00
228 Jason Wright RC 2.00 5.00
229 Sean Ryan RC 2.00 5.00
230 Vince Wilfork RC 3.00 8.00
231 Matt Kegel RC 3.00 8.00
232 Chris Collins RC 2.00 5.00
233 Jonathan Smith RC 2.00 5.00
234 Renaldo Works RC 2.00 5.00
235 Matt Kranchick RC 2.50 6.00
236 J.R. Reed RC 2.00 5.00
237 Jason Shivers RC 2.00 5.00
238 Donnell Washington RC 2.50 6.00
239 Jorge Cordova RC 2.00 5.00
240 Wes Welker RC 10.00 25.00
241 Robert Gallery JSY RC 2.00 5.00
242 Luke McCown JSY RC 1.50 4.00
243 Roy Williams JSY RC 1.50 4.00
244 Julius Jones JSY RC 1.50 4.00
245 Tatum Bell JSY RC 1.50 4.00
246 Steven Jackson JSY RC 2.50 6.00
247 Reggie Williams JSY RC 1.50 4.00
248 Devery Henderson JSY RC 1.50 4.00
249 DeAngelo Hall JSY RC 2.50 6.00
250 Rashaun Woods JSY RC 1.50 4.00
251 Chris Perry JSY RC 1.50 4.00
252 Matt Schaub JSY RC 1.50 4.00
253 Lee Evans JSY RC 2.50 6.00
254 Michael Jenkins JSY RC 1.50 4.00
255 J.P. Losman JSY RC 1.50 4.00
256 Kevin Jones JSY RC 2.00 5.00
257 Michael Clayton JSY RC 2.00 5.00
258 Eli Manning JSY RC 10.00 25.00
259 Roethlisberger JSY RC 12.00 30.00
260 Larry Fitzgerald JSY RC 6.00 15.00
261 Philip Rivers JSY RC 8.00 20.00
262 Greg Jones JSY RC 1.50 4.00
263 Kellen Winslow JSY RC 1.50 4.00

2004 Upper Deck Foundations Exclusive Gold

*1-100 VETS/100: 4X TO 10X BASE CARD HI
*101-240 ROOKIES/100: .5X TO 1.2X
STATED PRINT RUN 100 SER.#'d SETS

2004 Upper Deck Foundations Exclusive Rainbow Silver

*VETS/100: 5X TO 12X BASIC CARDS
*ROOKIES/100: .6X TO 1.5X BASIC CARDS
RAINBOW SILVER PRINT RUN 100 SETS

2004 Upper Deck Foundations Dual Endorsements

STATED ODDS 1:96
DEBH T.Brady/D.Henson SP 125.00 250.00
DEBL D.Bledsoe/J.P.Losman 15.00 40.00
DEBR K.Boller/P.Rivers 15.00 40.00
DEBW T.Bell/D.Watts 12.00 30.00
DECH Clayton/D.Henderson 15.00 40.00
DEEW L.Evans/J.P.Losman 20.00 50.00
DEFW Re.Will/Ro.Williams WR 12.00 30.00
DEHJ D.Hall/M.Jenkins 20.00 50.00
DEHW J.Horn/Ro.Williams WR 12.00 30.00
DEJH J.Jones/Henson/50* 12.00 30.00
DEJJ K.Jones/S.Jackson 15.00 40.00
DEMM P.Manning/E.Manning 150.00 300.00
DEMP D.McAllister/C.Perry SP 15.00 40.00
DEMR E.Mann/Roethlisberger 175.00 300.00
DERR Roethlisberger/Rivers 100.00 200.00
DEVM Vick/E.Manning SP 75.00 150.00
DEWJ Ro.Will.WR/K.Jones 15.00 40.00
DEWW Wins.Sr./Wins.Jr. SP 20.00 50.00

2004 Upper Deck Foundations Patches

STATED PRINT RUN 50 SER.#'d SETS
FPAB Antonio Bryant 8.00 20.00
FPAL Ashley Lelie 6.00 15.00
FPAN Anthony Thomas 8.00 20.00
FPAT Amani Toomer 6.00 15.00
FPBF Brett Favre 20.00 50.00
FPBL Byron Leftwich 6.00 15.00
FPCB Champ Bailey 8.00 20.00
FPCC Chris Chambers 6.00 15.00
FPCD Corey Dillon 6.00 15.00
FPCJ Chad Johnson 6.00 15.00
FPCM Curtis Martin 8.00 20.00
FPCW Charles Woodson 10.00 25.00
FPDB David Boston 6.00 15.00
FPDC Daunte Culpepper 8.00 20.00
FPDS Duce Staley 6.00 15.00
FPEM Eric Moulds 6.00 15.00
FPFT Fred Taylor 6.00 15.00
FPIB Isaac Bruce 10.00 25.00
FPJG Jeff Garcia 6.00 15.00
FPJH Joey Harrington 6.00 15.00
FPJK Jevon Kearse 6.00 15.00
FPJL Jamal Lewis 8.00 20.00
FPJR Jerry Rice 20.00 50.00
FPJS Junior Seau 10.00 25.00
FPKB Kyle Boller 6.00 15.00
FPKJ Keyshawn Johnson 8.00 20.00
FPKM Keenan McCardell 6.00 15.00
FPMB Mark Brunell 8.00 20.00
FPMF Marshall Faulk 8.00 20.00
FPMH Marvin Harrison 8.00 20.00
FPPP Peerless Price 6.00 15.00
FPRL Ray Lewis 10.00 25.00
FPRM Randy Moss 8.00 20.00
FPRW Ricky Williams 8.00 20.00
FPTB Tiki Barber 8.00 20.00
FPTH Travis Henry 6.00 15.00
FPTI Tim Brown 10.00 25.00
FPTO Terrell Owens 8.00 20.00
FPWD Warrick Dunn 6.00 15.00
FPWS Warren Sapp 8.00 20.00
FPZT Zach Thomas 8.00 20.00

2004 Upper Deck Foundations Rookie Foundations Patch

*ROOKIE PATCH/25: 1.5X TO 4X BASIC JSY
STATED PRINT RUN 25 SER.#'d SETS

2004 Upper Deck Foundations Rookie Foundations Patch Autographs

STATED PRINT RUN 25 SER.#'d SETS
241AP Robert Gallery 15.00 40.00
242AP Luke McCown 12.00 30.00
243AP Roy Williams WR 12.00 30.00
244AP Julius Jones 12.00 30.00
245AP Tatum Bell 12.00 30.00
246AP Steven Jackson 20.00 50.00
247AP Reggie Williams 12.00 30.00
248AP Devery Henderson 12.00 30.00
249AP DeAngelo Hall 30.00 80.00
250AP Rashaun Woods 12.00 30.00
251AP Chris Perry 12.00 30.00
252AP Matt Schaub 12.00 30.00
253AP Lee Evans 20.00 50.00
254AP Michael Jenkins 12.00 30.00
255AP J.P. Losman 12.00 30.00
256AP Kevin Jones 15.00 40.00
257AP Michael Clayton 15.00 40.00
258AP Eli Manning 200.00 400.00
259AP Ben Roethlisberger 250.00 400.00
260AP Larry Fitzgerald 100.00 200.00
261AP Philip Rivers 125.00 250.00
262AP Greg Jones 12.00 30.00
263AP Kellen Winslow Jr. 12.00 30.00

2004 Upper Deck Foundations Signature Foundations

STATED ODDS 1:12
SFBB Bernard Berrian 5.00 12.00
SFBC Brandon Chillar 6.00 15.00
SFBH Ben Hartsock SP 5.00 12.00
SFBJ B.J. Symons 5.00 12.00
SFBR Ben Roethlisberger SP 100.00 200.00
SFBW Ben Watson 6.00 15.00
SFCC Casey Clausen 6.00 15.00
SFCO Cody Pickett 5.00 12.00
SFCP Chris Perry SP 5.00 12.00
SFDA Devard Darling 5.00 12.00
SFDE DeAngelo Hall 8.00 20.00
SFDH Dante Hall SP 5.00 12.00
SFDR Drew Henson SP 5.00 12.00
SFDV Devery Henderson 5.00 12.00
SFDW Darius Watts 5.00 12.00
SFEM Eli Manning SP 75.00 150.00
SFEW Ernest Wilford 6.00 15.00
SFGJ Greg Jones 5.00 12.00
SFJC Jerricho Cotchery 6.00 15.00
SFJJ Julius Jones SP 5.00 12.00
SFJN John Navarre 5.00 12.00
SFJO Johnnie Morant 5.00 12.00
SFJP J.P. Losman SP 5.00 12.00
SFJS Jeff Smoker 6.00 15.00
SFJV Jonathan Vilma 6.00 15.00
SFKC Keary Colbert 5.00 12.00
SFKE Kellen Winslow Jr. SP 5.00 12.00
SFKJ Kevin Jones SP 6.00 15.00
SFKU Kenechi Udeze 6.00 15.00
SFLE Lee Evans SP 8.00 20.00
SFLM Luke McCown 5.00 12.00
SFLT LaDainian Tomlinson SP 30.00 60.00
SFMI Michael Clayton 6.00 15.00
SFMJ Michael Jenkins 5.00 12.00
SFMS Matt Schaub 5.00 12.00
SFMV Michael Vick/100* 15.00 40.00
SFPM Peyton Manning SP 50.00 100.00
SFPR Philip Rivers SP 25.00 60.00
SFQW Quincy Wilson 5.00 12.00
SFRE Reggie Williams 5.00 12.00
SFRG Robert Gallery 6.00 15.00
SFRO Roy Williams WR 5.00 12.00
SFRW Rashaun Woods SP 5.00 12.00
SFSJ Steven Jackson SP 8.00 20.00
SFTB Tatum Bell SP 5.00 12.00
SFTH Todd Heap SP 5.00 12.00
SFTO Tommie Harris 6.00 15.00
SFVW Vince Wilfork 12.50 25.00
SFWS Will Smith 6.00 15.00

2005 Upper Deck Foundations

This 258-card set was released in November, 2005. The set was issued through the hobby in five-card packs with an $4.00 SRP which came 24 packs to a box. Cards numbered 1-100 feature veterans sequenced by alphabetical team order while cards numbered 101-260 feature rookie. In the rookie grouping, cards numbered 201-260 were all autographed. Cards numbered 101-200 were issued to a stated print run of 399 serial numbered sets while cards numbered 201-260 were issued to stated print runs between 575 and 699 serial numbered copies. Those signed rookies were inserted into packs at a stated rate of one in 12. Please note that no cards number 233 or 257 were released.

COMP.SET w/o RCs (100) 7.50 20.00
101-200 RC PRINT RUN 399 SER.#'d SETS
ROOKIE AU STATED ODDS 1:12
UNPRICED ROOKIE FOUNDATIONS #'d TO 1
1 Larry Fitzgerald .30 .75
2 Anquan Boldin .20 .50
3 Kurt Warner .25 .60
4 Michael Vick .25 .60
5 T.J. Duckett .20 .50
6 Peerless Price .20 .50
7 Todd Heap .20 .50
8 Jamal Lewis .25 .60
9 Kyle Boller .20 .50
10 Derrick Mason .20 .50
11 J.P. Losman .20 .50
12 Willis McGahee .20 .50
13 Lee Evans .25 .60
14 Eric Moulds .20 .50
15 Jake Delhomme .20 .50
16 Keary Colbert .20 .50
17 DeShaun Foster .25 .60
18 Brian Urlacher .30 .75
19 Rex Grossman .20 .50
20 Muhsin Muhammad .20 .50
21 Carson Palmer .25 .60
22 Rudi Johnson .20 .50
23 Chad Johnson .20 .50
24 Julius Jones .20 .50
25 Keyshawn Johnson .25 .60
26 Drew Bledsoe .25 .60
27 Tatum Bell .20 .50
28 Jake Plummer .20 .50
29 Ashley Lelie .20 .50
30 Roy Williams WR .20 .50
31 Kevin Jones .20 .50
32 Jeff Garcia .20 .50
33 Brett Favre .60 1.50
34 Ahman Green .25 .60
35 Javon Walker .20 .50
36 David Carr .20 .50
37 Andre Johnson .25 .60
38 Domanick Davis .20 .50
39 Peyton Manning .75 2.00
40 Reggie Wayne .25 .60
41 Edgerrin James .25 .60
42 Marvin Harrison .25 .60
43 Byron Leftwich .20 .50
44 Fred Taylor .20 .50
45 Jimmy Smith .25 .60
46 Priest Holmes .20 .50
47 Tony Gonzalez .25 .60
48 Trent Green .20 .50
49 A.J. Feeley .20 .50
50 Chris Chambers .20 .50
51 Randy McMichael .20 .50
52 Daunte Culpepper .25 .60
53 Michael Bennett .20 .50
54 Nate Burleson .20 .50
55 Tom Brady 1.25 3.00
56 Corey Dillon .20 .50
57 Deion Branch .20 .50
58 Richard Seymour .20 .50
59 Aaron Brooks .20 .50
60 Deuce McAllister .25 .60
61 Joe Horn .20 .50
62 Eli Manning .50 1.25
63 Jeremy Shockey .20 .50
64 Tiki Barber .25 .60
65 Chad Pennington .20 .50
66 Curtis Martin .25 .60
67 Laveranues Coles .20 .50
68 Kerry Collins .20 .50
69 LaMont Jordan .25 .60
70 Randy Moss .25 .60
71 Donovan McNabb .25 .60
72 Terrell Owens .25 .60
73 Jeremiah Trotter .20 .50
74 Brian Westbrook .20 .50
75 Ben Roethlisberger .50 1.25
76 Jerome Bettis .30 .75
77 Hines Ward .25 .60
78 Antwaan Randle El .20 .50
79 Drew Brees .30 .75
80 LaDainian Tomlinson .30 .75
81 Antonio Gates .30 .75
82 Tim Rattay .20 .50
83 Brandon Lloyd .20 .50
84 Eric Johnson .20 .50
85 Shaun Alexander .20 .50
86 Darrell Jackson .20 .50
87 Matt Hasselbeck .20 .50
88 Marc Bulger .20 .50
89 Steven Jackson .20 .50
90 Marshall Faulk .25 .60
91 Torry Holt .25 .60
92 Joey Galloway .25 .60
93 Brian Griese .20 .50
94 Michael Clayton .20 .50
95 Steve McNair .25 .60
96 Drew Bennett .25 .60
97 Chris Brown .20 .50
98 Clinton Portis .20 .50
99 Patrick Ramsey .25 .60
100 Santana Moss .25 .60
101 Gino Guidugli RC 1.50 4.00
102 James Kilian RC 1.50 4.00
103 Matt Cassel RC 1.50 4.00
104 Adrian McPherson RC 1.50 4.00
105 Timmy Chang RC 1.50 4.00
106 Chris Rix RC 2.00 5.00
107 Lionel Gates RC 1.50 4.00
108 Alvin Pearman RC 1.50 4.00
109 Damien Nash RC 2.00 5.00
110 Noah Herron RC 1.50 4.00
111 Steve Savoy RC 1.50 4.00
112 Craig Bragg RC 1.50 4.00
113 Larry Brackins RC 1.50 4.00
114 Nick Collins RC 2.50 6.00
115 Josh Davis RC 1.50 4.00
116 Chad Owens RC 1.50 4.00
117 Dante Ridgeway RC 1.50 4.00
118 Airese Currie RC 1.50 4.00
119 Chauncey Stovall RC 1.50 4.00
120 Harry Williams RC 2.00 5.00
121 Alex Smith TE RC 1.50 4.00
122 Jerome Collins RC 2.00 5.00
123 Rick Razzano RC 1.50 4.00
124 Derrick Johnson RC 2.00 5.00
125 Mike Patterson RC 1.50 4.00
126 Jonathan Babineaux RC 1.50 4.00
127 Matt Roth RC 1.50 4.00
128 Shaun Cody RC 2.00 5.00
129 Justin Tuck RC 2.00 5.00
130 Vincent Burns RC 1.50 4.00
131 DeMarcus Ware RC 5.00 12.00
132 Jerome Mathis RC 2.50 6.00
133 Darryl Blackstock RC 1.50 4.00
134 Robert McCune RC 2.00 5.00
135 Channing Crowder RC 2.00 5.00
136 Odell Thurman RC 2.50 6.00
137 Marcus Maxwell RC 1.50 4.00
138 Lance Mitchell RC 2.00 5.00
139 Jordan Beck RC 2.00 5.00
140 Alfred Fincher RC 2.00 6.00
141 Kirk Morrison RC 2.50 6.00
142 Kelvin Hayden RC 2.00 5.00
143 Justin Miller RC 1.50 4.00
144 Bryant McFadden RC 2.00 5.00
145 Eric Green RC 1.50 4.00
146 Fabian Washington RC 1.50 4.00
147 Ellis Hobbs RC 2.50 6.00
148 Ronald Bartell RC 2.00 5.00
149 Brodney Pool RC 2.00 5.00
150 Josh Bullocks RC 2.00 5.00
151 Vincent Fuller RC 2.00 5.00
152 Donte Nicholson RC 1.50 4.00
153 Sean Considine RC 1.50 4.00
154 Oshiomogho Atogwe RC 2.00 5.00
155 Dustin Fox RC 2.00 5.00
156 Mike Nugent RC 2.00 5.00
157 Shane Boyd RC 1.50 4.00
158 Ryan Fitzpatrick RC 2.50 6.00
159 Brock Berlin RC 1.50 4.00
160 Bryan Randall RC 2.00 5.00
161 Matt Jones RC 1.50 4.00
162 Todd Mortensen RC 1.50 4.00
163 Darian Durant RC 1.50 4.00
164 Stanley Wilson RC 2.00 5.00
165 Nehemiah Broughton RC 2.00 5.00
166 Manuel White RC 2.00 5.00
167 Zach Tuiasosopo RC 1.50 4.00
168 Deandra Cobb RC 1.50 4.00
169 Charles Frederick 1.50 4.00
170 Efrem Hill RC 1.50 4.00
171 Jason Anderson RC 1.50 4.00
172 Rasheed Marshall RC 2.00 5.00
173 Tab Perry RC 1.50 4.00
174 Paris Warren RC 2.00 5.00
175 Roydell Williams RC 2.00 5.00
176 Fred Amey RC UER 1.50 4.00
177 Kerry Wright RC 2.00 5.00
178 Joel Dreessen RC 2.00 5.00
179 Bo Scaife RC 2.00 5.00
180 Alex Barron RC 1.50 4.00
181 Jammal Brown RC 2.50 6.00
182 Michael Roos RC 1.50 4.00
183 Khalif Barnes RC 1.50 4.00
184 Logan Mankins RC 2.50 6.00
185 Elton Brown RC 1.50 4.00
186 David Baas RC 1.50 4.00
187 Chris Spencer RC 2.50 6.00
188 Marcus Spears RC 1.50 4.00
189 Trent Cole RC 2.50 6.00
190 Luis Castillo RC 2.00 5.00
191 Bill Swancutt RC 1.50 4.00
192 Jesse Lumsden RC 1.50 4.00
193 Lofa Tatupu RC 2.00 5.00
194 Boomer Grigsby RC 2.50 6.00
195 Domonique Foxworth RC 2.00 5.00
196 Travis Daniels RC 2.00 5.00
197 Darrent Williams RC 2.50 6.00
198 Kerry Rhodes RC 2.00 5.00
199 Mark Bradley RC 1.50 4.00
200 Bobby Purify RC 2.00 5.00
201 Dan Orlovsky AU/699 RC 3.00 8.00
202 David Greene AU/699 RC 3.00 8.00
203 Anthony Davis AU/699 RC 3.00 8.00
204 Taylor Stubblefield AU/699 RC 3.00 8.00
205 Walter Reyes AU/699 RC 3.00 8.00
206 Darren Sproles AU/699 RC 5.00 12.00
207 Courtney Roby AU/375 RC 4.00 10.00
208 Marlin Jackson AU/699 RC 3.00 8.00
209 Corey Webster AU/699 RC 4.00 10.00
210 Ryan Moats AU/699 RC 3.00 8.00
211 Marion Barber AU/375 RC 12.00 30.00
212 Frank Gore AU/699 RC 10.00 25.00
213 Kay-Jay Harris AU/699 RC 3.00 8.00
214 Anttaj Hawthorne AU/699 RC 3.00 8.00
215 Adam Jones AU/699 RC 3.00 8.00
216 Stefan LeFors AU/375 RC 4.00 10.00
217 Barrett Ruud AU/699 RC 4.00 10.00
218 Kevin Burnett AU/699 RC 4.00 10.00
219 T.A. McLendon AU/699 RC 3.00 8.00
220 James Butler AU/699 RC 4.00 10.00
221 J.R. Russell AU/699 RC 3.00 8.00
222 Vincent Jackson AU/300 RC 6.00 15.00
223 J.J. Arrington AU/699 RC 4.00 10.00
224 Maurice Clarett AU/175 6.00 15.00
225 Brandon Jacobs AU/699 RC 4.00 10.00
226 Craphonso Thorpe AU/699 RC 3.00 8.00
227 Fred Gibson AU/575 RC 3.00 8.00
228 Travis Johnson AU/699 RC 3.00 8.00
229 Kyle Orton AU/575 RC 8.00 20.00
230 Jason White AU/575 RC 5.00 12.00
231 Terrence Murphy AU/575 RC 3.00 8.00
232 Mark Clayton AU/375 RC 4.00 10.00
234 David Pollack AU/575 RC 3.00 8.00
235 Erasmus James AU/575 RC 3.00 8.00
236 Dan Cody AU/575 RC 3.00 8.00
237 Thomas Davis AU/575 RC 3.00 8.00
238 Carlos Rogers AU/575 RC 5.00 12.00
239 Derek Anderson AU/699 RC 4.00 10.00
240 Antrel Rolle AU/575 RC 5.00 12.00
241 Shawne Merriman AU/575 RC 5.00 12.00
242 Reggie Brown AU/699 RC 3.00 8.00
243 Heath Miller AU/699 RC 6.00 15.00
244 Roscoe Parrish AU/375 RC 4.00 10.00
245 Roddy White AU/375 RC 5.00 12.00
246 Eric Shelton AU/699 RC 3.00 8.00
247 Vernand Morency AU/575 RC 3.00 8.00
248 Ciatrick Fason AU/375 RC 4.00 10.00
249 Andrew Walter AU/375 RC 4.00 10.00
250 Jason Campbell AU/375 RC 15.00 40.00
251 Charles Frederick AU/699 RC 3.00 8.00
252 Troy Williamson AU/175 RC 6.00 15.00
253 Braylon Edwards AU/175 RC 6.00 15.00
254 Mike Williams AU/175 8.00 20.00
255 Cedric Benson AU/50 RC 20.00 50.00
256 Cadillac Williams AU/175 RC 6.00 15.00
258 Charlie Frye AU/175 RC 6.00 15.00
259 Alex Smith QB AU/175 RC 20.00 50.00
260 Aaron Rodgers AU/175 RC 200.00 400.00
P1 Ben Roethlisberger Promo 2.50 6.00

2005 Upper Deck Foundations Exclusive Gold

*VETERANS 1-100: 3X TO 8X BASIC CARDS
*ROOKIES 101-200: .5X TO 1.2X BASIC CARDS
1-200 PRINT RUN 99 SER.#'d SETS
*ROOKIE AU: 1.2X TO 3X BASE AU/575-699
*ROOKIE AU: 1X TO 2.5X BASE AU/300-375
*ROOK.AU/252-259: .6X TO 1.5X AU/175
*ROOK.AU/252-259: .4X TO 1X AU/50
ROOKIE AUTO PRINT RUN 25 SER.#'d SETS
OVERALL GOLD STATED ODDS 1:24
260 Aaron Rodgers AU 400.00 600.00

2005 Upper Deck Foundations Signature Foundations Silver

SILVER STATED ODDS 1:24
UNPRICED PLATINUM #'d TO 1
SFAA Aaron Brooks 3.00 8.00
SFAB Anquan Boldin SP 6.00 15.00
SFAD Anthony Davis 3.00 8.00
SFAG Ahman Green SP 7.50 20.00
SFAH Anttaj Hawthorne 3.00 8.00
SFAJ A.J. Feeley 4.00 10.00
SFAN Antrel Rolle 4.00 10.00
SFAP Alan Page SP 7.50 20.00
SFAR Aaron Rodgers SP 175.00 300.00
SFAS Alex Smith QB SP 50.00 100.00
SFAW Andrew Walter 4.00 10.00
SFBA Marion Barber 6.00 15.00
SFBD Brian Dawkins 15.00 30.00
SFBE Braylon Edwards SP 15.00 40.00
SFBJ Brandon Jacobs 6.00 15.00
SFBL Byron Leftwich SP 10.00 25.00
SFBR Barrett Ruud 6.00 15.00
SFBS Barry Sanders SP 60.00 120.00
SFCA Carlos Rogers 4.00 10.00
SFCC Cris Collinsworth SP 7.50 20.00
SFCF Charlie Frye SP 6.00 15.00
SFCI Ciatrick Fason SP
SFCJ Chad Johnson 6.00 15.00
SFCK Charles Frederick 3.00 8.00

SFCN Chuck Noll SP 12.50 30.00
SFCO Corey Webster 3.00 8.00
SFCR Chris Brown SP
SFCT Craphonso Thorpe 3.00 8.00
SFCW Cadillac Williams SP 10.00 25.00
SFDA Derek Anderson 6.00 15.00
SFDB Drew Bennett 3.00 8.00
SFDC Dave Casper SP
SFDD Domanick Davis SP
SFDG David Greene 4.00 10.00
SFDM Deuce McAllister SP 10.00 25.00
SFDO Dan Orlovsky 4.00 10.00
SFDP David Pollack 4.00 10.00
SFDS Darren Sproles 10.00 25.00
SFDW Dwight Clark SP 10.00 25.00
SFEJ Erasmus James 3.00 8.00
SFEM Eli Manning SP 60.00 100.00
SFFG Frank Gore 15.00 30.00
SFFR Fred Gibson 3.00 8.00
SFFT Fred Taylor 4.00 10.00
SFHM Heath Miller 6.00 15.00
SFJA J.J. Arrington 4.00 10.00
SFJB James Butler 3.00 8.00
SFJC Jason Campbell 15.00 30.00
SFJH Joe Horn SP 10.00 25.00
SFJW Jason White 4.00 10.00
SFKC Keary Colbert 3.00 8.00
SFKJ Kay-Jay Harris 3.00 8.00
SFKO Kyle Orton 6.00 15.00
SFKS Ken Stabler SP 25.00 50.00
SFLJ Larry Johnson 8.00 20.00
SFLT LaDainian Tomlinson SP 20.00 50.00
SFMA Dan Marino SP 60.00 120.00
SFMB Marc Bulger SP 10.00 25.00
SFMC Mark Clayton SP 6.00 15.00
SFMJ Marlin Jackson SP
SFMM Muhsin Muhammad 6.00 15.00
SFMW Mike Williams SP 6.00 15.00
SFNB Nate Burleson 6.00 15.00
SFPM Peyton Manning SP 60.00 100.00
SFRB Ronnie Brown SP 10.00 25.00
SFRC Roger Craig SP 7.50 20.00
SFRE Reggie Brown 5.00 12.00
SFRG Reggie Wayne 6.00 15.00
SFRJ Rudi Johnson 6.00 15.00
SFRM Ryan Moats 4.00 10.00
SFRW Roy Williams WR SP 10.00 25.00
SFTB Tiki Barber SP
SFTE Terrence Murphy 4.00 10.00
SFTM T.A. McLendon 3.00 8.00
SFTS Taylor Stubblefield 3.00 8.00
SFTW Troy Williamson SP
SFVM Vernand Morency 6.00 15.00
SFWR Walter Reyes 3.00 8.00

2005 Upper Deck Foundations Signature Foundations Gold

*GOLD/20: 1X TO 2.5X BASIC AU
*GOLD/20: .6X TO 1.5X BASIC AU SP
GOLD PRINT RUN 20 SETS
SFAR Aaron Rodgers 400.00 600.00

2005 Upper Deck Foundations Dual Endorsements

STATED ODDS 1:288
DEAG D.Anderson/D.Greene/75 12.50 30.00
DEBT A.Boldin/C.Thorpe/50 10.00 25.00
DEBW Ro.Brown/C.Williams/75 15.00 40.00
DECD Ch.Johnson/De.Ander/50 12.50 30.00
DECN D.Casper/O.Newsome/50 15.00 40.00
DECR J.Campbell/C.Rogers/75 15.00 40.00
DECW Mi.Clay/Ro.Will.WR/50 12.50 30.00
DEDH Ant.Davis/K.Harris/75 7.50 20.00
DEEW Edwards/Mi.Will/75 15.00 40.00
DEGB F.Gibson/Re.Brown/75 12.50 30.00
DEGC A.Gates/A.Crumpler/50 20.00 50.00
DEGD T.Green/Len Dawson/15 75.00 150.00
DEGJ A.Green/Ju.Jones/15 25.00 50.00
DFHF C.Henry/C.Frederick/75 12.50 30.00
DEHM J.Horn/D.McAllister/50 10.00 25.00
DEJB Bo Jackson/Ro.Brown/15 100.00 200.00
DEJH Er.James/Hawthorne/75 7.50 20.00
DEKB K.Colbert/A.Boldin/50 7.50 20.00
DELL S.Largent/J.Lofton/15 75.00 150.00
DELR B.Leftwich/Roeth/15 75.00 150.00
DEMB R.Moats/M.Barber/50 12.50 30.00
DEMF P.Manning/B.Favre/15 250.00 500.00
DEMH T.Murphy/C.Henry/50 12.50 30.00
DEMM E.Manning/D.Marino/15 100.00 200.00
DEMO J.McMahon/K.Orton/75 25.00 60.00
DEOD M.Olsen/A.Donovan/50 15.00 40.00
DEOS Orton/Stubblefield/75 12.50 30.00
DERA R.Moats/J.Arrington/75 12.50 30.00
DERB A.Smith QB/Ro.Brown/15 15.00 40.00
DERD Ca.Rogers/Th.Davis/75 7.50 20.00
DERF Roeth/B.Favre/15 150.00 300.00
DERS A.Rodgers/A.Smith QB/15 200.00 400.00
DERT C.Roby/C.Thorpe/50
DESM E.Shelton/V.Morency/50 10.00 25.00
DETF F.Taylor/C.Fason/50 12.50 30.00
DEVR M.Vick/A.Smith QB/15 25.00 50.00
DEWB R.Wayne/D.Bennett/50 12.50 30.00
DEWG Ja.White/D.Greene/50 12.50 30.00
DEWM Williamson/Mi.Will/75 12.50 30.00
DEWO J.White/D.Orlovsky/75 12.50 30.00
DEWP Ro.White/R.Parrish/75 6.00 15.00

2005 Upper Deck Foundations Three Star Signatures

ATED PRINT RUN 75 SER.#'d SETS
CPJ Cody/Pick/T.Jhnsn 15.00 40.00
DHJ A.Davis/Hawthrn/Er.James 12.50 30.00
EMC Edwards/Murphy/Clayton 30.00 80.00
FWJ Fason/Willmsn/Er.James 15.00 40.00
HPT C.Henry/Parrish/Thorpe 15.00 40.00
HWB C.Henry/White/Bradley 15.00 40.00
LEP Losman/Evans/Parrish 15.00 40.00
MBB Merriman/Burnett/Th.Davis 12.00 30.00
MJW P.Mann/M.Jcksn/Wayne 90.00 150.00
MSB Moats/Sproles/Barber 30.00 50.00
PJJ Pollck/Ru.Jhnsn/Ch.Jhnsn 30.00 60.00
RDJ Rolle/A.Jones/Rogers 12.50 30.00
RGP Rolle/Gore/Parrish 15.00 40.00
RSF Rodgers/Smith QB/Cmpbll 150.00 300.00

2005 Upper Deck Foundations Four Star Signatures

RICED PRINT RUN 20 SER.#'d SETS

2005 Upper Deck Foundations Five Star Signatures

UNPRICED PRINT RUN 15 SER.#'d SETS

2005 Upper Deck Foundations Six Star Signatures

UNPRICED PRINT RUN 10 SER.#'d SETS

2005 Upper Deck Foundations Eight Star Signatures

UNPRICED PRINT RUN 5 SER.#'d SETS

2005 Upper Deck Foundations UD Promos

*UD PROMOS: .8X TO 2X BASIC CARDS

2000 Upper Deck Gold Reserve

Released in Late November 2000 as a 222-card set, Gold Reserve features 177 veteran player cards and 41 rookie cards. Shortly before it's release, card numbers 220, 221, and 222 were pulled from the set, therefore Gold Reserve is numbered up to 225. Gold Reserve was released primarily as a retail product and was packaged in 24-pack boxes with packs containing 10 cards and carried a suggested retail price of $2.99.

COMP.SET w/o RC's (180) 10.00 25.00
RC STATED PRINT RUN 2500 SER.#'d SETS
1 Jake Plummer .20 .50
2 Rob Moore .20 .50
3 David Boston .20 .50
4 Frank Sanders .20 .50
5 Chris Chandler .25 .60
6 Jamal Anderson .25 .60
7 Shawn Jefferson .20 .50
8 Terance Mathis .20 .50
9 Qadry Ismail .20 .50
10 Jermaine Lewis .20 .50
11 Tony Banks .20 .50
12 Peter Boulware .20 .50
13 Shannon Sharpe .25 .60
14 Peerless Price .25 .60
15 Rob Johnson .25 .60
16 Eric Moulds .20 .50
17 Doug Flutie .25 .60
18 Antowain Smith .25 .60
19 Muhsin Muhammad .20 .50
20 Patrick Jeffers .20 .50
21 Steve Beuerlein .25 .60
22 Natrone Means .25 .60
23 Tim Biakabutuka .25 .60
24 Wesley Walls .20 .50
25 Cade McNown .20 .50
26 Curtis Enis .20 .50
27 Marcus Robinson .25 .60
28 Eddie Kennison .20 .50
29 Bobby Engram .20 .50
30 Akili Smith .20 .50
31 Corey Dillon .20 .50
32 Damon Griffin .20 .50
33 Takeo Spikes .20 .50
34 Tony McGee .20 .50
35 Tim Couch .25 .60
36 Kevin Johnson .20 .50
37 Darrin Chiaverini .20 .50
38 Errict Rhett .25 .60
39 Troy Aikman .40 1.00
40 Emmitt Smith .50 1.25
41 Rocket Ismail .25 .60
42 Jason Tucker .20 .50
43 Joey Galloway .25 .60
44 Wane McGarity .20 .50
45 Terrell Davis .25 .60
46 Olandis Gary .25 .60
47 Brian Griese .20 .50
48 Gus Frerotte .20 .50
49 Ed McCaffrey .25 .60
50 Rod Smith .25 .60
51 Charlie Batch .20 .50
52 Germane Crowell .20 .50
53 Johnnie Morton .25 .60
54 Robert Porcher .20 .50
55 Herman Moore .20 .50
56 James Stewart .20 .50
57 Brett Favre .60 1.50
58 Antonio Freeman .25 .60
59 Bill Schroeder .25 .60
60 Dorsey Levens .25 .60
61 Corey Bradford .20 .50
62 Vonnie Holliday .20 .50
63 Peyton Manning .75 2.00
64 Edgerrin James .25 .60
65 Marvin Harrison .25 .60
66 Ken Dilger .20 .50
67 Terrence Wilkins .20 .50
68 Marcus Pollard .20 .50
69 Mark Brunell .25 .60
70 Fred Taylor .20 .50
71 Jimmy Smith .25 .60
72 Keenan McCardell .25 .60
73 Carnell Lake .20 .50
74 Kyle Brady .20 .50
75 Hardy Nickerson .20 .50
76 Elvis Grbac .20 .50
77 Tony Gonzalez .25 .60
78 Derrick Alexander .20 .50
79 Donnell Bennett .20 .50
80 Mike Cloud .20 .50
81 Donnie Edwards .20 .50
82 Jay Fiedler .25 .60
83 James Johnson .20 .50
84 Tony Martin .25 .60
85 Damon Huard .20 .50
86 O.J. McDuffie .25 .60
87 Thurman Thomas .25 .60
88 Oronde Gadsden .25 .60
89 Randy Moss .25 .60
90 Robert Smith .20 .50
91 Cris Carter .30 .75
92 Daunte Culpepper .25 .60
93 Matthew Hatchette .20 .50
94 Drew Bledsoe .25 .60
95 Terry Glenn .25 .60
96 Troy Brown .20 .50
97 Kevin Faulk .20 .50
98 Lawyer Milloy .20 .50
99 Ricky Williams .25 .60
100 Keith Poole .20 .50
101 Jake Reed .25 .60
102 Jeff Blake .25 .60
103 Andrew Glover .20 .50
104 Kerry Collins .20 .50
105 Amani Toomer .20 .50
106 Joe Montgomery .20 .50
107 Ike Hilliard .20 .50
108 Tiki Barber .25 .60
109 Ray Lucas .20 .50
110 Mo Lewis .20 .50
111 Curtis Martin .25 .60
112 Vinny Testaverde .20 .50
113 Wayne Chrebet .20 .50
114 Dedric Ward .20 .50
115 Tim Brown .30 .75
116 Rich Gannon .25 .60
117 Tyrone Wheatley .20 .50
118 Napoleon Kaufman .25 .60
119 Charles Woodson .30 .75
120 James Jett .25 .60
121 Rickey Dudley .20 .50
122 Duce Staley .20 .50
123 Donovan McNabb .25 .60
124 Torrance Small .20 .50
125 Allen Rossum .20 .50
126 Na Brown .20 .50
127 Charles Johnson .20 .50
128 Kent Graham .20 .50
129 Troy Edwards .20 .50
130 Jerome Bettis .30 .75
131 Hines Ward .25 .60
132 Kordell Stewart .20 .50
133 Richard Huntley .20 .50
134 Marshall Faulk .25 .60
135 Kurt Warner .50 1.25
136 Torry Holt .25 .60
137 Isaac Bruce .30 .75
138 Kevin Carter .20 .50
139 Az-Zahir Hakim .20 .50
140 Jermaine Fazande .20 .50
141 Curtis Conway .25 .60
142 Freddie Jones .20 .50
143 Junior Seau .25 .60
144 Jeff Graham .20 .50
145 Jim Harbaugh .25 .60
146 Jerry Rice .75 2.00
147 Charlie Garner .25 .60
148 Terrell Owens .25 .60
149 Jeff Garcia .20 .50
150 J.J. Stokes .25 .60
151 Ricky Watters .25 .60
152 Jon Kitna .20 .50
153 Derrick Mayes .20 .50
154 Sean Dawkins .20 .50
155 Charlie Rogers .20 .50
156 Cortez Kennedy .25 .60
157 Warrick Dunn .20 .50
158 Shaun King .20 .50
159 Mike Alstott .20 .50
160 Warren Sapp .25 .60
161 Jacquez Green .20 .50
162 Reidel Anthony .20 .50
163 Keyshawn Johnson .25 .60
164 Eddie George .25 .60
165 Steve McNair .25 .60
166 Kevin Dyson .25 .60
167 Jevon Kearse .20 .50
168 Yancey Thigpen .20 .50
169 Isaac Byrd .20 .50
170 Neil O'Donnell .20 .50
171 Brad Johnson .25 .60
172 Stephen Davis .20 .50
173 Michael Westbrook .20 .50
174 Albert Connell .20 .50
175 Bruce Smith .25 .60
176 Stephen Alexander .20 .50
177 Jeff George .25 .60
178 Bubba Franks RC 1.00 2.50
179 Brian Urlacher RC 5.00 12.00
180 Chad Pennington RC 1.25 3.00
181 Tim Rattay RC 1.25 3.00
182 Chris Redman RC 1.00 2.50
183 Corey Simon RC 1.25 3.00
184 Courtney Brown RC 1.25 3.00
185 Curtis Keaton RC 1.00 2.50
186 Danny Farmer RC 1.00 2.50
187 Erron Kinney RC 1.00 2.50
188 Deltha O'Neal RC 1.00 2.50
189 Dennis Northcutt RC 1.00 2.50
190 Dez White RC 1.00 2.50
191 Frank Murphy RC 1.00 2.50
192 Gari Scott RC 1.00 2.50
193 Giovanni Carmazzi RC 1.00 2.50
194 J.R. Redmond RC 1.00 2.50
195 JaJuan Dawson RC 1.00 2.50
196 Jamal Lewis RC 1.50 4.00
197 Jerry Porter RC 1.50 4.00
198 Joe Hamilton RC 1.00 2.50
199 Laveranues Coles RC 1.25 3.00
200 Michael Wiley RC 1.00 2.50
201 Peter Warrick RC 1.00 2.50
202 Plaxico Burress RC 1.25 3.00
203 R.Jay Soward RC 1.00 2.50
204 Reuben Droughns RC 1.00 2.50
205 Rob Morris RC 1.25 3.00
206 Ron Dayne RC 1.50 4.00
207 Ron Dugans RC 1.00 2.50
208 Sebastian Janikowski RC 1.50 4.00
209 Shaun Alexander RC 1.50 4.00
210 Sylvester Morris RC 1.00 2.50
211 Tee Martin RC 1.00 2.50
212 Thomas Jones RC 1.25 3.00
213 Todd Husak RC 1.00 2.50
214 Todd Pinkston RC 1.00 2.50
215 Tom Brady RC 200.00 400.00
216 Travis Prentice RC 1.00 2.50
217 Travis Taylor RC 1.00 2.50
218 Trevor Gaylor RC 1.00 2.50
219 Trung Canidate RC 1.00 2.50
223 Peyton Manning CL .60 1.50
224 Randy Moss CL .20 .50
225 Kurt Warner CL .40 1.00

2000 Upper Deck Gold Reserve Face Masks

Randomly inserted in packs, this 15-card set features swatches from authentic game worn helmet face masks. Each card is sequentially numbered to 100.

STATED PRINT RUN 100 SER.#'d SETS
*GOLD/25: .6X TO 1.5X FACE MASK/100
GOLD STATED PRINT RUN 25 SETS
FMCB Courtney Brown 10.00 25.00
FMCK Curtis Keaton 8.00 20.00
FMCP Chad Pennington 10.00 25.00
FMCR Chris Redman 8.00 20.00
FMDR Reuben Droughns 8.00 20.00
FMJL Jamal Lewis 12.00 30.00
FMJR J.R. Redmond 8.00 20.00
FMPB Plaxico Burress 10.00 25.00
FMPW Peter Warrick 8.00 20.00
FMRD Ron Dayne 12.00 30.00
FMRJ R.Jay Soward 8.00 20.00
FMSA Shaun Alexander 12.00 30.00
FMSM Sylvester Morris 8.00 20.00
FMTJ Thomas Jones 10.00 25.00
FMTT Travis Taylor 8.00 20.00

2000 Upper Deck Gold Reserve Gold Mine

ndomly inserted in packs at the rate of one in 12, this 12-card set features portrait style photography framed by purple borders with gold foil highlights.

COMPLETE SET (12) 6.00 15.00
STATED ODDS 1:12
GM1 Dez White .40 1.00
GM2 Peter Warrick .40 1.00
GM3 Plaxico Burress .50 1.25
GM4 Bubba Franks .40 1.00
GM5 Jamal Lewis .60 1.50
GM6 Travis Taylor .40 1.00
GM7 Chris Redman .40 1.00
GM8 Sylvester Morris .40 1.00
GM9 Courtney Brown .50 1.25
GM10 Shaun Alexander .60 1.50
GM11 Trung Canidate .40 1.00
GM12 J.R. Redmond .40 1.00

2000 Upper Deck Gold Reserve Gold Strike

ndomly inserted in packs at the rate of one in 12, this 12-card set features a framed action shot with three borders solid white and the border along the left side in gold. Card contain gold foil highlights.

COMPLETE SET (12) 6.00 15.00
STATED ODDS 1:12
GS1 Eddie George .50 1.25
GS2 Edgerrin James .50 1.25
GS3 Terrell Davis .50 1.25
GS4 Jamal Anderson .50 1.25
GS5 Ricky Williams .50 1.25
GS6 Marshall Faulk .50 1.25
GS7 Keyshawn Johnson .50 1.25
GS8 Brett Favre 1.25 3.00
GS9 Cade McNown .40 1.00
GS10 Emmitt Smith 1.00 2.50
GS11 Peyton Manning 1.50 4.00
GS12 Kurt Warner 1.00 2.50

2000 Upper Deck Gold Reserve Setting the Standard

ndomly inserted in packs at the rate of one in 12, this 12-card set features a gold background framed by white with full color player action shots. Cards contain gold borders and gold foil highlights.

COMPLETE SET (12) 6.00 15.00
STATED ODDS 1:12
SS1 Randy Moss .50 1.25
SS2 Peyton Manning 1.50 4.00
SS3 Stephen Davis .40 1.00
SS4 Cris Carter .60 1.50
SS5 Jevon Kearse .40 1.00
SS6 Jerry Rice 1.50 4.00
SS7 Troy Aikman .75 2.00
SS8 Edgerrin James .50 1.25
SS9 Daunte Culpepper .50 1.25
SS10 Shaun King .40 1.00
SS11 Mark Brunell .50 1.25
SS12 Fred Taylor .40 1.00

2000 Upper Deck Gold Reserve Solid Gold Gallery

Randomly inserted in packs at the rate of one in 23, this six card set features posed action shots set on a gold backgroud that fades to white along the borders.

COMPLETE SET (6) 6.00 15.00
STATED ODDS 1:23
SG1 Jamal Lewis .75 2.00
SG2 Peter Warrick .50 1.25
SG3 Ron Dayne .75 2.00
SG4 Chad Pennington .60 1.50
SG5 Thomas Jones .60 1.50
SG6 Plaxico Burress .60 1.50

2000 Upper Deck Gold Reserve UD Authentics

ndomly inserted in packs at the rate of one in 160, this set features authentic player signatures on cards showing full color player action photography and a gold and white background. Some were issued via mail redemption cards that carried an expiration date of 7/25/2001.

STATED ODDS 1:160
*GOLD/25: 1.2X TO 3X BASIC AUTO
GOLD STATED PRINT RUN 25
CC Chris Coleman 4.00 10.00
CCX Chris Coleman EXCH .40 1.00
CP Chad Pennington 5.00 12.00
CR Chris Redman 4.00 10.00
DF Doug Flutie 8.00 20.00
DUX Ron Dugans EXCH .40 1.00
DW Dez White 4.00 10.00
FAX Danny Farmer EXCH .40 1.00
JHX Joe Hamilton EXCH .40 1.00
KC Kwame Cavil 4.00 10.00
MW Michael Wiley 4.00 10.00
RD Ron Dayne 8.00 20.00
SA Shaun Alexander 12.00 30.00
SG Sherrod Gideon 4.00 10.00
SJX Sebastian Janikowski EXCH .40 1.00
SKX Shaun King EXCH .40 1.00
TA Troy Aikman 30.00 60.00
TJX Thomas Jones EXCH .40 1.00
TM Tee Martin 4.00 10.00
TR Tim Rattay 5.00 12.00
TW Troy Walters 4.00 10.00

2009 Upper Deck Goodwin Champions

MMON CARD (1-150) .15 .40
COMMON NIGHT 5.00 12.00
COMMON SP (151-190) 1.25 3.00
151-190 STATED ODDS 1:2 HOBBY
COMMON SUPER SP (191-210) 1.50 4.00
SUPER SP MINORS 1.50 4.00
SUPER SP SEMIS 1.50 4.00
SUPER SP UNLISTED 1.50 4.00
191-210 STATED ODDS 1:10 HOBBY
PLATES RANDOMLY INSERTED
PLATE PRINT RUN 1 SET PER COLOR
BLACK-CYAN-MAGENTA-YELLOW ISSUED
NO PLATE PRICING DUE TO SCARCITY
45 Peyton Manning .50 1.25
57 Eli Manning .40 1.00
68 Matt Ryan .40 1.00
94 Adrian Peterson .60 1.50
99 Ben Roethlisberger .50 1.25
125 Chris Johnson .40 1.00

2009 Upper Deck Goodwin Champions Mini

MPLETE SET (192) 75.00 150.00
*MINI 1-150: 1X TO 2.5X BASIC
APPX.MINI ODDS ONE PER PACK
PLATES RANDOMLY INSERTED
PLATE PRINT RUN 1 SET PER COLOR
BLACK-CYAN-MAGENTA-YELLOW ISSUED
NO PLATE PRICING DUE TO SCARCITY

2009 Upper Deck Goodwin Champions Mini Black Border

*MINI BLK 1-150: 1.5X TO 4X BASE
*MINI BLK 211-252: .75X TO 2X MINI
RANDOM INSERTS IN PACKS

2009 Upper Deck Goodwin Champions Mini Foil

*MINI FOIL 1-150: 3X TO 8X BASE
*MINI FOIL 211-252: 1.5X TO 4X MINI
RANDOM INSERTS IN PACKS
ANNCD PRINT RUN OF 88 TOTAL SETS

2011 Upper Deck Goodwin Champions

COMP.SET w/o VAR (210) 40.00 80.00
COMP.SET w/o SP's (150) 10.00 25.00
COMMON SP (151-190) 1.00 2.50
151-190 SP ODDS 1:3 HOBBY
COMMON SP (191-210) 1.50 4.00
191-210 SP ODDS 1:12 HOBBY
COMMON VARIATION SP 4.00 10.00
15 Bo Jackson .30 .75
20 Dan Marino .50 1.25
36 Jake Locker .40 1.00
40 Troy Aikman .30 .75
48 Drew Brees .25 .60
57 Barry Sanders .40 1.00
65 Mark Ingram .60 1.50
71A John Elway .40 1.00
71B Elway Lightning SP 4.00 10.00
78 Cam Newton 1.00 2.50
80 Aaron Rodgers .30 .75
82 Earl Campbell .25 .60
83 Jerry Rice .40 1.00
86 Von Miller .30 .75
102 Billy Sims .20 .50
104 Steve Young .30 .75
109 Julio Jones .50 1.25
113A A.J. Green .50 1.25
113B Green Lightning SP 6.00 15.00
206 Walter Camp SP 1.50 4.00

2011 Upper Deck Goodwin Champions Mini

*1-150 MINI: 1X TO 2.5X BASIC
1-150 MINI ODDS 1:4 HOBBY
COMMON CARD (211-231) .60 1.50
211-231 MINI ODDS 1:13 HOBBY
PRINTING PLATES RANDOMLY INSERTED
PLATE PRINT RUN 1 SET PER COLOR
BLACK-CYAN-MAGENTA-YELLOW ISSUED
NO PLATE PRICING DUE TO SCARCITY

2011 Upper Deck Goodwin Champions Mini Black

*1-150 MINI BLACK: 1.2X TO 3X BASIC
1-150 MINI BLACK ODDS 1:13 HOBBY
*211-231 MINI BLK: .6X TO 1.5X BASIC MINI
211-231 MINI BLACK ODDS 1:46 HOBBY

2011 Upper Deck Goodwin Champions Mini Foil

*1-150 MINI FOIL: 2.5X TO 6X BASIC
1-150 ANNCD PRINT RUN OF 89
*211-231 MINI FOIL : 1X TO 2.5X BASIC MINI
211-231 ANNCD PRINT RUN OF 178
PRINT RUNS PROVIDED BY UD

2011 Upper Deck Goodwin Champions Autographs

Please note that the Dwayne De Rosario card in this set was issued in the 2014 Upper Deck Goodwin Champions product.

GROUP A ODDS 1:1577 HOBBY
GROUP B ODDS 1:729 HOBBY
GROUP C ODDS 1:339 HOBBY
GROUP D ODDS 1:246 HOBBY
GROUP E ODDS 1:72 HOBBY
GROUP F ODDS 1:35 HOBBY
OVERALL AUTO ODDS 1:20 HOBBY
EXCHANGE DEADLINE 6/7/2013
BS Billy Sims F 5.00 12.00
JA Bo Jackson B 50.00 100.00

2011 Upper Deck Goodwin Champions Figures of Sport

COMP.SET. w/o SP's (14) 10.00 25.00
COMMON CARD (1-14) .60 1.50
1-14 STATED ODDS 1:21 HOBBY
15-18 SP ODDS 1:300 HOBBY
FS2 Jerry Rice 1.50 4.00
FS8 Cam Newton 2.00 5.00

2011 Upper Deck Goodwin Champions Memorabilia

GROUP A ODDS 1:14,613 HOBBY
GROUP B ODDS 1:179 HOBBY
GROUP C ODDS 1:31 HOBBY
GROUP D ODDS 1:22 HOBBY
AI Troy Aikman C 3.00 8.00
BJ Bo Jackson D 4.00 10.00
BS Barry Sanders C 6.00 15.00
EH Earl Campbell C 3.00 8.00
JE John Elway C 5.00 12.00
JR Jerry Rice C 4.00 10.00
YO Steve Young C 4.00 10.00

2011 Upper Deck Goodwin Champions Memorabilia Dual

GROUP A ODDS 1:87,680 HOBBY
GROUP B ODDS 1:8768 HOBBY
GROUP C ODDS 1:2923 HOBBY
GROUP D ODDS 1:877 HOBBY
GROUP E ODDS 1:585 HOBBY
NO GROUP A PRICING AVAILABLE
JE John Elway D 6.00 15.00

2011 Upper Deck Goodwin Champions Sport Royalty Autographs

RANDOM INSERTS IN PACKS
NO PRICING DUE TO SCARCITY
SRABG Bob Griese 30.00 60.00
SRACP Clinton Portis 20.00 40.00
SRAJE John Elway
SRAPM Peyton Manning
SRAWP William Perry

2012 Upper Deck Goodwin Champions

MP.SET w/o VAR (210) 25.00 50.00
COMP.SET w/o SP's (150) 10.00 25.00
151-190 SP ODDS 1:3 HOBBY, BLASTER
191-210 SP ODDS 1:12 HOBBY, BLASTER
3 Herschel Walker .30 .75
10 Lawrence Taylor .20 .50
13 Knute Rockne .25 .60
19 Dan Marino .50 1.25
26 Jim McMahon .25 .60
34 Troy Aikman .30 .75
35 John Elway .40 1.00
39 Jerry Rice .40 1.00
48 Colin Kaepernick .40 1.00
51 Justin Blackmon .60 1.50
52 Robert Griffin III 1.25 3.00
56 Bo Jackson .30 .75
71 Charles White .20 .50
73 Steven Jackson .15 .40
86 Kellen Winslow Sr. .15 .40
87A Jim Kelly .30 .75
87B Jim Kelly Horizontal SP 4.00 10.00
96 Trent Richardson .60 1.50
99 Barry Sanders .40 1.00
117 Gale Sayers .30 .75
130 Marques Colston .15 .40
131 Aaron Rodgers .30 .75
132 Brian Bosworth .20 .50
136 Doug Flutie .20 .50
137 Blaine Gabbert .20 .50
141 Thurman Thomas .20 .50
144 Adrian Peterson .30 .75
148 Christian Ponder .20 .50
149 Warren Moon .25 .60
150 Tim Brown .20 .50
161 Prince Amukamara SP 1.00 2.50
173 Marcell Dareus SP 1.00 2.50
200 John Heisman SP 1.50 4.00

2012 Upper Deck Goodwin Champions Mini

*1-150 MINI: 1X TO 2.5X BASIC CARDS
1-150 MINI STATED ODDS 1:2 HOBBY, BLASTER
211-231 MINI ODDS 1:2 HOBBY, BLASTER

2012 Upper Deck Goodwin Champions Mini Foil

*1-150 MINI FOIL: 2.5X TO 6X BASIC
1-150 MINI FOIL ANNCD. PRINT RUN 99
*211-231 MINI FOIL: 1X TO 2.5X BASIC MINI
211-231 MINI FOIL ANNCD. PRINT RUN 199

2012 Upper Deck Goodwin Champions Mini Green

*1-150 MINI GREEN: 1.25X TO 3X BASIC
*211-231 MINI GREEN: .6X TO 1.5X BASIC MINI
TWO MINI GREEN PER HOBBY BOX
ONE MINI GREEN PER BLASTER

2012 Upper Deck Goodwin Champions Mini Green Blank Back

UNPRICED DUE TO SCARCITY

2012 Upper Deck Goodwin Champions Autographs

GROUP A ODDS 1:1,977
GROUP B ODDS 1:353
GROUP C ODDS 1:264
GROUP D ODDS 1:185
GROUP E ODDS 1:82
GROUP F ODDS 1:36
OVERALL AUTO ODDS 1:20
EXCHANGE DEADLINE 7/12/2014
ABG Blaine Gabbert B 4.00 10.00
ACW Charles White F 4.00 10.00
ADM Dan Marino A 75.00 150.00
AGR Robert Griffin III B 40.00 100.00
ALT Lawrence Taylor B 10.00 25.00
AMC Marques Colston A 15.00 40.00
APA Prince Amukamara D 4.00 10.00
APO Christian Ponder C 10.00 25.00
ATR Trent Richardson B 16.00 10.00

2012 Upper Deck Goodwin Champions Memorabilia

GROUP A ODDS 1:10,631
GROUP B ODDS 1:4,784
GROUP C ODDS 1:302
GROUP D ODDS 1:118
GROUP E ODDS 1:36
GROUP F ODDS 1:23
MAP Adrian Peterson E 5.00 12.00
MAR Aaron Rodgers D 8.00 20.00
MBB Brian Bosworth F 4.00 10.00
MBG Blaine Gabbert F 3.00 8.00
MBJ Bo Jackson F 5.00 12.00
MBR Tim Brown C 3.00 8.00
MCK Colin Kaepernick F 4.00 10.00
MDF Doug Flutie E 3.00 8.00
MDM Dan Marino D 10.00 25.00
MGS Gale Sayers E 4.00 10.00
MJE John Elway E 4.00 10.00
MJK Jim Kelly E 3.00 8.00
MJM Jim McMahon F 3.00 8.00
MJR Jerry Rice D 5.00 12.00
MKW Kellen Winslow Sr. E 3.00 8.00
MLT Lawrence Taylor E 3.00 8.00
MMC Marques Colston F 3.00 8.00
MPO Christian Ponder F 3.00 8.00
MSA Barry Sanders C 5.00 12.00
MSJ Steven Jackson C 3.00 8.00
MTA Troy Aikman E 4.00 10.00
MTT Thurman Thomas F 3.00 8.00
MWM Warren Moon F 3.00 8.00

2012 Upper Deck Goodwin Champions Memorabilia Dual

GROUP A ODDS 1:95,680
GROUP B ODDS 1:31,893
GROUP C ODDS 1:2,514
GROUP D ODDS 1:1,306
GROUP E ODDS 1:520
NO PRICING ON GROUP A
M2AP Adrian Peterson E 6.00 15.00
M2BG Blaine Gabbert E 6.00 15.00
M2DM Dan Marino E 10.00 25.00
M2GS Gale Sayers E 8.00 20.00

2012 Upper Deck Goodwin Champions Sport Royalty Autographs

GROUP A ODDS 1:15,947
GROUP B ODDS 1:7,973
GROUP C ODDS 1:4,932
AGS Gale Sayers C 25.00 50.00
ARY Ron Yary B

2013 Upper Deck Goodwin Champions

COMP. SET w/o VAR (210) 25.00 60.00
COMP. SET w/o SPs (150) 8.00 20.00
151-190 SP ODDS 1:3 HOBBY,BLASTER
191-210 SP ODDS 1:12 HOBBY,BLASTER
OVERALL VARIATION ODDS 1:320 H, 1:1,200 B
GROUP A ODDS 1:4,800
GROUP B ODDS 1:2,400
GROUP C ODDS 1:1,400
3 Bo Jackson .30 .75
10 Joe Namath .40 1.00
13 Ray Guy .15 .40
19 Paul Hornung .25 .60
26 Archie Griffin .15 .40
34A Nick Buoniconti .20 .50
34B N.Buoniconti/J.Nicklaus SP 5.00 12.00
35 Steve Young .30 .75
36A Manti Te'o 1.00 2.50
36B Manti Te'o Horizontal SP B 6.00 15.00
37 Tim Tebow .40 1.00
39 Bruce Smith .20 .50
48A Ronnie Lott .25 .60
48B R.Lott/J.Namath SP 30.00 60.00
52 Dan Fouts .20 .50
55 Eddie Lacy .75 2.00
65 George Gipp .15 .40
67 Roman Gabriel .20 .50
69 Aaron Rodgers .30 .75
80 Barry Sanders .40 1.00
81 Daryle Lamonica .15 .40
89 Don Maynard .20 .50
98 Cordarrelle Patterson .60 1.50
105 Ken Stabler .20 .50
109 Dan Marino .40 1.00
114A Jerry Rice .40 1.00
114B J.Rice/S.Young SP 6.00 15.00
117 John Elway .40 1.00
121A Bart Starr .30 .75
121B B.Starr/J.Unitas SP 6.00 15.00
123 Geno Smith 1.00 2.50
126B K.Lofton/W.Moon SP 12.00 30.00
127 Dave Casper .15 .40
144 Tony Dorsett .30 .75
145 Matt Barkley .60 1.50
146 Ozzie Newsome .25 .60
147 Alan Page .20 .50
173A Roger Staubach SP 1.00 2.50
173B R.Staubach/R.Reagan SP 50.00 100.00
184 Rudy Ruettiger SP 1.00 2.50

2013 Upper Deck Goodwin Champions Mini

-150 MINI: 1X TO 2.5X BASIC CARDS
7 MINIS PER HOBBY BOX, 4 MINIS PER BLASTER

2013 Upper Deck Goodwin Champions Mini Canvas

-150 MINI CANVAS: 2.5X TO 6X BASIC CARDS
1-150 MINI CANVAS ANNCD. PRINT RUN 99
*211-225 MINI CANVAS: 1X TO 2.5 BASIC MINI
211-225 MINI CANVAS ANNCD. PRINT RUN 198

2013 Upper Deck Goodwin Champions Mini Green

ATED ODDS 1:12 HOBBY, 1:15 BLASTER
STATED SP ODDS 1:60 HOBBY, 1:72 BLASTER

2013 Upper Deck Goodwin Champions Autographs

ERALL ODDS 1:20
GROUP A ODDS 1:7,517
GROUP B ODDS 1:1,224
GROUP C ODDS 1:489
GROUP D ODDS 1:142
GROUP E ODDS 1:206
GROUP F ODDS 1:28
ABS Bruce Smith B 10.00 25.00
ABU Nick Buoniconti E 8.00 20.00
ADF Dan Fouts B 20.00 50.00
AEL Eddie Lacy D 12.00 30.00
AGA Roman Gabriel E 6.00 15.00
AJN Joe Namath A 60.00 120.00
AMB Matt Barkley B 2014 10.00 25.00
AMT Manti Te'o 2014 6.00 15.00
APA Cordarelle Patterson 2014 8.00 20.00
ARG Ray Guy F 4.00 10.00
AST Bart Starr C 35.00 70.00

2013 Upper Deck Goodwin Champions Memorabilia

OVERALL ODDS 1:12
GROUP A ODDS 1:23,082
GROUP B ODDS 1:5,970
GROUP C ODDS 1:104
GROUP D ODDS 1:22
GROUP E ODDS 1:37
MAP Alan Page D 4.00 10.00
MBJ Bo Jackson D 5.00 12.00
MBS Bart Starr C 5.00 12.00
MBS Barry Sanders D 5.00 12.00
MDC Dave Casper D 3.00 8.00
MDL Daryle Lamonica D 3.00 8.00
MDM Dan Marino D 6.00 15.00
MJE John Elway D 4.00 10.00
MJN Joe Namath D 6.00 15.00
MKS Ken Stabler D 3.00 8.00
MMT Manti Te'o D 4.00 10.00
MPH Paul Hornung D 4.00 10.00
MRG Roman Gabriel D 3.00 8.00
MRL Ronnie Lott D 3.00 8.00
MRS Roger Staubach D 5.00 12.00
MTD Tony Dorsett D 3.00 8.00
MTT Tim Tebow E 4.00 10.00

2013 Upper Deck Goodwin Champions Sport Royalty Autographs

OVERALL ODDS 1:1,161
GROUP A ODDS 1:7,473
GROUP B ODDS 1:4,171
GROUP C ODDS 1:2,050
SRABJ Bo Jackson C 30.00 80.00
SRAJR Jerry Rice A
SRASY Steve Young B 40.00 80.00

2013 Upper Deck Goodwin Champions Sport Royalty Memorabilia

OVERALL ODDS 1:350
GROUP A ODDS 1:2,391
GROUP B ODDS 1:957
GROUP C ODDS 1:717
SRMJR Jerry Rice B 8.00 20.00
SRMSY Steve Young B 6.00 15.00

2013 Upper Deck Goodwin Champions Sport Royalty Memorabilia Dual

OVERALL ODDS 1:3,986
GROUP A ODDS 1:11,957
GROUP B ODDS 1:5,979
SRM2JR Jerry Rice B
SRM2SY Steve Young B

2014 Upper Deck Goodwin Champions

COMPLETE SET w/o AU's(180) 40.00 100.00
COMPLETE SET w/o SP's(155) 12.00 30.00
131-155 SP ODDS 1:3 HOBBY,BLAST
156-180 SP ODDS 1:12 HOB/1:12 BLAST
AU ODDS 1:60 HOB/1:720 BLAST
NOLA AU ODDS 1:860 '15 PACKS
NOLA AU ISSUED IN '15 GOODWIN
3 Earl Campbell .25 .60
5A LaDainian Tomlinson .20 .50
5B Tomlinson/Brees SP 4.00 10.00
11 Peyton Manning .60 1.50
18 Joe Theismann .25 .60
24 Ben Roethlisberger .25 .60
37 Bernie Kosar .20 .50
44 Blake Bortles 1.00 2.50
45 John Elway .40 1.00
46 Jim Plunkett .20 .50
50 Giovani Bernard .20 .50
52 Jerome Bettis .25 .60
53 Jerry Rice .40 1.00
56A Mike Evans .50 1.25
56B Evans/Manziel SP 6.00 15.00
57 Dan Marino .50 1.25
65 Warren Moon .25 .60
68 Johnny Manziel 1.25 3.00
70 Joe Montana .60 1.50
76 Drew Brees .25 .60
Barack Obama
79 Ickey Woods .15 .40
81 Bo Jackson .30 .75
82A Eric Dickerson .20 .50
82B Dickerson/Marino SP 4.00 10.00
84A Terrell Davis .20 .50
84B Davis/Sanders SP 4.00 10.00
85 Joe Namath .30 .75
90 Kordell Stewart .15 .40
92 Charley Taylor .15 .40
94 Tim Brown .20 .50
95 Tedy Bruschi .25 .60
96 Teddy Bridgewater .75 2.00
97 Jim Kelly .25 .60
105 Doug Flutie .20 .50
107 Barry Sanders .75 2.00
114B Lemieux/Bettis SP 12.00 30.00
118A Sammy Watkins .75 2.00
118B Watkins/Boyd SP 10.00 25.00
119 Bart Starr .40 1.00

2014 Upper Deck Goodwin Champions Mini

*1-130 MINI: .75X TO 2X BASIC
COMMON CARD (131-180) .50 1.25
7 MINIS PER HOBBY 4 PER BLASTER

2014 Upper Deck Goodwin Champions Mini Canvas

*1-130 MINI CANVAS: 2X TO 5X BASIC
COMMON CARD (131-180) 1.25 3.00
RANDOM INSERTS IN PACKS
11 Peyton Manning 8.00 20.00
81 Bo Jackson 5.00 12.00
85 Joe Namath 10.00 25.00

2014 Upper Deck Goodwin Champions Mini Green

*1-130 MINI GREEN: 1X TO 2.5X BASIC
COMMON CARD (131-180) .60 1.50
STATED ODDS 1:10 HOB/1:12 BLAST

2014 Upper Deck Goodwin Champions Autographs

GROUP A ODDS 1:54,400 HOBBY
GROUP B ODDS 1:6590 HOBBY
GROUP C ODDS 1:17,525 HOBBY
GROUP D ODDS 1:1280 HOBBY
GROUP E ODDS 1:410 HOBBY
GROUP F ODDS 1:135 HOBBY
GROUP G ODDS 1:42 HOBBY
'16 STATED ODDS 1:4352 HOBBY
ABJ Bo Jackson D 30.00 60.00
AED Eric Dickerson C 12.00 30.00
AGB Giovani Bernard E 4.00 10.00
AIW Ickey Woods F 4.00 10.00
AJM Joe Montana B 75.00 200.00
ALT LaDainian Tomlinson C 15.00 40.00
APM Peyton Manning B

2014 Upper Deck Goodwin Champions Goudey

COMPLETE SET (52) 25.00 60.00
BB ODDS 1:13 HOB/1:32 BLAST
BK ODDS 1:25 HOB/1:60 BLAST
FB ODDS 1:25 HOB/1:60 BLAST
HK ODDS 1:33 HOB/1:80 BLAST
GOLF ODDS 1:33 HOB/1:80 BLAST
MISC SPORT ODDS 1:100 HOB/1:240 BLAST
HISTORY ODDS 1:40 HOB/1:96 BLAST
19 Earl Campbell .60 1.50
20 Jerry Rice 1.00 2.50
21 Peyton Manning 1.50 4.00
22 Joe Montana 1.50 4.00
23 Dan Marino 1.25 3.00
24 LaDainian Tomlinson .50 1.25
25 Roman Gabriel .50 1.25
26 John Elway 1.00 2.50

2014 Upper Deck Goodwin Champions Goudey Autographs

GROUP A ODDS 1:7200 HOBBY
GROUP B ODDS 1:4800 HOBBY
GROUP C ODDS 1:1650 HOBBY
GROUP D ODDS 1:1200 HOBBY
'16 GROUP A ODDS 1:21,760 HOBBY
'16 GROUP B ODDS 1:8369 HOBBY
20 Jerry Rice A
21 Peyton Manning A 350.00 500.00
24 LaDainian Tomlinson A
25 Roman Gabriel C 12.00 30.00
26 John Elway A

2014 Upper Deck Goodwin Champions Memorabilia

GROUP A ODDS 1:5140
GROUP B ODDS 1:685
GROUP C ODDS 1:80
GROUP D ODDS 1:18
MBJ Bo Jackson D 3.00 8.00
MBK Bernie Kosar D 3.00 8.00
MBS Barry Sanders C 5.00 12.00
MDF Doug Flutie B 2.50 6.00
MDM Dan Marino C 4.00 10.00
MEC Earl Campbell D 2.50 6.00
MED Eric Dickerson D 3.00 8.00
MGB Giovani Bernard D 4.00 10.00
MJE John Elway C 4.00 10.00
MJM Joe Montana D 8.00 20.00
MJN Joe Namath D 6.00 15.00
MJT Joe Theismann D 4.00 10.00
MKE Jim Kelly D 2.50 6.00
MLT LaDainian Tomlinson D 3.00 8.00
MPM Peyton Manning C 8.00 20.00
MRI Jerry Rice A 6.00 15.00
MTB Tedy Bruschi C 3.00 8.00
MWM Warren Moon D 4.00 10.00

2014 Upper Deck Goodwin Champions Memorabilia Dual

GROUP A ODDS 1:2055 HOBBY
GROUP B ODDS 1:1285 HOBBY
GROUP C ODDS 1:860 HOBBY
GROUP D ODDS 1:1285 HOBBY
M2DF Doug Flutie B 3.00 8.00
M2DM Dan Marino A 10.00 25.00
M2WM Warren Moon C 5.00 12.00

2014 Upper Deck Goodwin Champions Memorabilia Premium

*PREMIUM: .75X TO 2X BASIC
RANDOM INSERTS IN PACKS
PRINT RUNS B/WN 10-50 COPIES PER
NO PRICING ON QTY 15 OR LESS
MKE Jim Kelly/25

2014 Upper Deck Goodwin Champions Sport Royalty Memorabilia

GROUP A ODDS 1:3425 HOBBY
GROUP B ODDS 1:5140 HOBBY
GROUP C ODDS 1:495 HOBBY
GROUP D ODDS 1:285 HOBBY
SRMJE John Elway C 5.00 12.00
SRMJM Joe Montana C 15.00 40.00
SRMJN Joe Namath C 12.00 30.00
SRMJR Jerry Rice A
SRMPM Peyton Manning C 8.00 20.00

2015 Upper Deck Goodwin Champions

COMPLETE SET w/o AU's(150) 25.00 60.00
COMPLETE SET w/o SP's(100) 6.00 15.00
131-155 SP ODDS APPX. 1:3 PACKS
156-180 SP ODDS 1:8 PACKS
GROUP A AU ODDS 1:755 PACKS
GROUP B AU ODDS 1:65 PACKS
PRINTING PLATES RANDOMLY INSERTED
PLATE PRINT RUN 1 SET PER COLOR
BLACK-CYAN-MAGENTA-YELLOW ISSUED
NO PLATE PRICING DUE TO SCARCITY
EXCHNAGE DEADLINE 6/10/2017
2 Aaron Murray .25 .60
6 Rod Woodson .25 .60
7 Steve Slaton .15 .40
12 Cornelius Bennett .15 .40
17 John Elway .40 1.00
18 Marcus Allen .25 .60
21 Nelson Agholor .30 .75
22 Ronde Barber .15 .40
24 Kurt Warner .25 .60
26 Vinny Testaverde .20 .50
27 Barry Sanders .40 1.00
28 Jerry Rice .40 1.00
29 Kellen Winslow Sr. .20 .50
30 Mike Evans .25 .60
33 Brett Hundley .50 1.25
37 Mike Ditka .20 .50
40 Eric Dickerson .20 .50
42 Devante Parker .50 1.25
43 Eddie George .20 .50
50 Amari Cooper .60 1.50
52 Michael Pinball Clemons .15 .40
53 Lawrence Taylor .25 .60
65 Ameer Abdullah .50 1.25
69 Donte Moncrief .20 .50
73 Tiki Barber .20 .50
74 Melvin Gordon III .60 1.50
75 Todd Gurley .60 1.50
86 Nick Marshall .40 1.00
87 Emmitt Smith .40 1.00
91 Jerome Bettis .25 .60
94 Teddy Bridgewater .25 .60
96 Terrell Davis .20 .50
103 Eric Dickerson SP .60 1.50
107 Lawrence Taylor SP .75 2.00
108 Earl Campbell SP .75 2.00
111 Barry Sanders SP 1.25 3.00
112 John Elway SP 1.25 3.00
113 Emmitt Smith SP 1.25 3.00
117 Marcus Allen SP .75 2.00
118 Peyton Manning SP 1.50 4.00
124 Mike Ditka SP .60 1.50
135 Jerry Rice SP 1.50 4.00
138 Kurt Warner SP 1.00 2.50
141 Ben Roethlisberger SP 1.00 2.50

2015 Upper Deck Goodwin Champions Mini

*MINI 1-100: 1X TO 2.5X BASIC
*MINI 101-125: .3X TO .75X BASIC
*MINI 126-150: .25X TO .6X BASIC
STATED ODDS THREE PER BOX

2015 Upper Deck Goodwin Champions Mini Canvas

*CANVAS 1-100: 2X TO 5X BASIC
*CANVAS 101-125: .6X TO 1.5X BASIC
*CANVAS 126-150: .5X TO 1.2X BASIC
RANDOM INSERTS IN PACKS
ANNCD PRINT RUN OF 99 COPIES PER

2015 Upper Deck Goodwin Champions Mini Cloth Lady Luck

*LUCK 1-100: 2.5X TO 6X BASIC
*LUCK 101-125: .75X TO 2X BASIC
*LUCK 126-150: .6X TO 1.5X BASIC
RANDOM INSERTS IN PACKS
STATED PRINT RUN 50 SER.#'d SETS

2015 Upper Deck Goodwin Champions Mini Leather Magician

*MAGICIAN 1-100: 6X TO 15X BASIC
*MAGICIAN 101-125: 2X TO 5X BASIC
*MAGICIAN 126-150: 1.5X TO 4X BASIC
RANDOM INSERTS IN PACKS
STATED PRINT RUN 15 SER.#'d SETS

2015 Upper Deck Goodwin Champions Autographs

GROUP A ODDS 1:6830 PACKS
GROUP B ODDS 1:780 PACKS
GROUP C ODDS 1:685 PACKS
GROUP D ODDS 1:350 PACKS
GROUP E ODDS 1:150 PACKS
GROUP F ODDS 1:65 PACKS
'16 GROUP A ODDS 1:14,836 PACKS
'16 GROUP B ODDS 1:1106 PACKS
EXCHANGE DEADLINE 6/10/2017
AAM Aaron Murray F 2.50 6.00
ACB Cornelius Bennett E 2.50 6.00
ADM Donte Moncrief E 2.50 6.00
AJB Jerome Bettis B 20.00 50.00
AKW Kurt Warner B 12.00 30.00
ALT Lawrence Taylor A 75.00 200.00
AMA Marcus Allen B 10.00 25.00
AME Mike Evans C 5.00 12.00
APC Michael Pinball Clemons F 2.50 6.00
ASS Steve Slaton D 2.50 6.00
ATB Teddy Bridgewater B 50.00 100.00

2015 Upper Deck Goodwin Champions Autographs Inscriptions

RANDOM INSERTS IN PACKS
PRINT RUNS B/WN 2-298 COPIES PER
NO PRICING ON QTY 16 OR LESS
EXCHANGE DEADLINE 6/10/2017
AAM Aaron Murray 5.00 12.00
Go Dawgs/30
ACB Cornelius Bennett 6.00 15.00
Roll Tide/30
ASS Steve Slaton 4.00 10.00
Go Argos/30

2015 Upper Deck Goodwin Champions Goudey

COMPLETE SET (60) 15.00 40.00
1-40 STATED ODDS 1:5 PACKS
41-60 STATED ODDS 1:20 PACKS
5 Marcus Allen .60 1.50
10 Mike Ditka .50 1.25
13 Donovan McNabb .50 1.25
17 Earl Campbell .60 1.50
18 Eric Dickerson .50 1.25
19 Joe Theismann .60 1.50
21 Lawrence Taylor .60 1.50
22 Peyton Manning 1.25 3.00
36 Kurt Warner .60 1.50
37 Ben Roethlisberger .60 1.50
38 Jerry Rice 1.00 2.50
39 Emmitt Smith 1.00 2.50

2015 Upper Deck Goodwin Champions Goudey Memorabilia

GROUP A ODDS 1:750 PACKS
GROUP B ODDS 1:240 PACKS
GROUP C ODDS 1:145 PACKS
OVERALL GOUDEY MEM 1:80 PACKS
GMDM Donovan McNabb Jsy C 2.50 6.00
GMEC Earl Campbell Jsy C 2.50 6.00
GMED Eric Dickerson Jsy C 2.50 6.00
GMJT Joe Theismann Jsy C 2.50 6.00
GMLT Lawrence Taylor Jsy C 2.50 6.00
GMMA Marcus Allen Jsy B 2.50 6.00
GMPM Peyton Manning Jsy B 4.00 10.00

2015 Upper Deck Goodwin Champions Goudey Memorabilia Premium Series

*PREMIUM: .6X TO 1.5X BASIC
RANDOM INSERTS IN PACKS
PRINT RUNS B/WN 10-50 COPIES PER
NO PRICING ON QTY 10
EXCHANGE DEADLINE 6/10/2017
GMPM Peyton Manning Patch/25 20.00 50.00

2015 Upper Deck Goodwin Champions Goudey Sport Royalty Dual Memorabilia

GROUP A ODDS 1:16,215 PACKS
GROUP B ODDS 1:3040 PACKS
OVERAL SR DUAL 1:2560 PACKS
SRM2ER Elway/Rice B 15.00 40.00
SRM2SA Sanders/Allen B 15.00 40.00

2015 Upper Deck Goodwin Champions Goudey Sport Royalty Memorabilia

OVERAL SR MEM ODDS 1:320 PACKS
SRMBS Barry Sanders Jsy 10.00 25.00
SRMJE John Elway Jsy 5.00 12.00
SRMJR Jerry Rice Jsy 5.00 12.00
SRMMA Marcus Allen Jsy 4.00 10.00

2015 Upper Deck Goodwin Champions Goudey Sport Royalty Memorabilia Premium Series

*PREMIUM: .6X TO 1.5X BASIC
RANDOM INSERTS IN PACKS
PRINT RUNS B/WN 5-25 COPIES PER
NO PRICING ON QTY 10 OR LESS

2015 Upper Deck Goodwin Champions Memorabilia

GROUP A ODDS 1:1420 PACKS
GROUP B ODDS 1:175 PACKS
GROUP C ODDS 1:28 PACKS
MAM Aaron Murray Jsy C 2.50 6.00
MBA Tiki Barber Jsy C 2.50 6.00
MCB Cornelius Bennett Jsy C 2.50 6.00
MDM Donte Moncrief Jsy C 2.50 6.00
MEG Eddie George Jsy C 2.50 6.00
MEV Mike Evans Jsy C 2.50 6.00
MJB Jerome Bettis Jsy C 3.00 8.00
MKW Kurt Warner Jsy C 2.50 6.00
MMA Marcus Allen Jsy B 2.50 6.00
MSS Steve Slaton Jsy C 2.50 6.00
MTB Teddy Bridgewater Jsy B 2.50 6.00

2015 Upper Deck Goodwin Champions Memorabilia Black and White

GROUP A ODDS 1:3970 PACKS
GROUP B ODDS 1:400 PACKS
OVERAL B/W MEM ODDS 1:360 PACKS
BWMBS Barry Sanders Jsy B 5.00 12.00
BWMED Eric Dickerson Jsy B 3.00 8.00
BWMLT Lawrence Taylor Jsy B 3.00 8.00
BWMPM Peyton Manning Jsy B 6.00 15.00

2015 Upper Deck Goodwin Champions Memorabilia Black and White Premium Series

*PREMIUM: .6X TO 1.5X BASIC
RANDOM INSERTS IN PACKS
PRINT RUNS B/WN 5-25 COPIES PER
NO PRICING ON QTY 10 OR LESS

2015 Upper Deck Goodwin Champions Goudey Autographs

GROUP A ODDS 1:1:16,535 PACKS
GROUP B ODDS 1:15,260 PACKS
GROUP C ODDS 1:1585 PACKS
GROUP D ODDS 1:1340 PACKS
OVERALL GOUDEY ODDS 1:660 PACKS
EXCHANGE DEADLINE 6/10/2017
GADM Donovan McNabb D 6.00 15.00
GAES Emmitt Smith A EXCH
GAMA Marcus Allen C 10.00 25.00

2015 Upper Deck Goodwin Champions Memorabilia Premium Series

*PREMIUM: .6X TO 1.5X BASIC
RANDOM INSERTS IN PACKS
PRINT RUNS B/WN 10-75 COPIES PER
NO PRICING ON QTY 15 OR LESS

2007 Upper Deck Goudey Sport Royalty

ONE PER HOBBY BOX LOADER
ES Emmitt Smith 4.00 10.00
JN Joe Namath 6.00 15.00
LT LaDainian Tomlinson 3.00 8.00
PM Peyton Manning 5.00 12.00

2007 Upper Deck Goudey Sport Royalty Autographs

STATED ODDS TWO PER CASE
FOUND IN HOBBY BOX LOADER PACKS
EXCH DEADLINE 8/8/2009
LT LaDainian Tomlinson 40.00 80.00
PM Peyton Manning 100.00 175.00

2008 Upper Deck Goudey

MP.SET w/o HIGH #s (200) 20.00 50.00
COMMON CARD (1-200) .20 .50
COMMON ROOKIE (1-200) .30 .75
COMMON SP (201-230) 2.00 5.00
COMMON SP (231-250) 1.50 4.00
COMMON SP (251-270) 2.00 5.00
COMMON CARD (271-300) 2.00 5.00
COMMON CARD (301-330) 3.00 8.00
275 Brett Favre SR SP 4.00 10.00
278 Barry Sanders SR SP 3.00 8.00
289 Emmitt Smith SR SP 3.00 8.00
295 John Elway SR SP 3.00 8.00
302 Tom Brady SR SP 6.00 15.00
304 Dan Marino SR SP 6.00 15.00
327 Terry Bradshaw SR SP 4.00 10.00

2008 Upper Deck Goudey Mini Black Backs

*BLACK 1-200: .75X TO 2X GRN 1-200
*BLACK RC 1-200: .75X TO 2X GRN RC 1-200
*BLACK SP 201-250: .75X TO 2X GRN 201-250
*BLACK SP 251-270: .5X TO 1.2X GRN 251-270
*BLACK SR 271-330: .5X TO 1.2X GRN 271-330
RANDOM INSERTS IN PACKS
STATED PRINT RUN 34 SER.#'d SETS
278 Barry Sanders SR 10.00 25.00

2008 Upper Deck Goudey Mini Blue Backs

LUE 1-200: 1.5X TO 4X BASIC 1-200
*BLUE RC 1-200: 1X TO 2.5X BASIC RC 1-200
*BLUE 201-270: .6X TO 1.5X BASIC SP 201-270
*BLUE 271-330: .6X TO 1.5X BASIC SR 201-270
RANDOM INSERTS IN PACKS

2008 Upper Deck Goudey Mini Green Backs

NDOM INSERTS IN PACKS
STATED PRINT RUN 88 SER.#'d SETS
275 Brett Favre SR 5.00 12.00
278 Barry Sanders SR 4.00 10.00
289 Emmitt Smith SR 4.00 10.00
295 John Elway SR 6.00 15.00
302 Tom Brady 10.00 25.00
304 Dan Marino 5.00 12.00
327 Terry Bradshaw 3.00 8.00

2008 Upper Deck Goudey Mini Red Backs

*RED 1-200: 1X TO 2.5X BASIC 1-200
*RED RC 1-200: .75X TO 2X BASIC RC 1-200
*RED 201-270: .5X TO 1.2X BASIC SP 201-270
*RED 271-330: .5X to 1.2X BASIC SR 271-330
RANDOM INSERTS IN PACKS

2008 Upper Deck Goudey Hit Parade of Champions

RANDOM INSERTS IN PACKS
3 Ben Roethlisberger .75 2.00
9 Emmitt Smith 1.25 3.00
11 Joe Montana 1.25 3.00
12 Joe Namath .75 2.00
15 LaDainian Tomlinson .75 2.00
24 Peyton Manning .75 2.00
27 Roger Staubach .75 2.00
29 Tom Brady 1.00 2.50

2008 Upper Deck Goudey Sport Royalty Autographs

OVERALL AUTO ODDS 1:18 HOBBY
ASTERISK EQUALS PARTIAL EXCHANGE
EXCHANGE DEADLINE 7/17/2010
TB Terry Bradshaw SP 60.00 120.00

2009 Upper Deck Goudey

COMPLETE SET (300) 200.00 300.00
COMP.SET w/o SP's (200) 20.00 50.00
COMMON CARD (1-200) .20 .50
COMMON RC (1-200) .40 1.00
COMMON SP (201-300) 2.00 5.00
APPX.SP ODDS 201-220 1:9 HOBBY
APPX.SP ODDS 221-260 1:6 HOBBY
APPX.SP ODDS 261-300 1:6 HOBBY
251 Adrian Peterson SR SP 4.00 10.00

2009 Upper Deck Goudey Mini Green Back

*GREEN 1-200: 1.2X TO 3X BASIC
*GREEN RC 1-200: .6X TO 1.5X BASIC
COMMON CARD (201-300) .75 2.00
APPROX.ODDS 1:6 HOBBY
251 Adrian Peterson SR 4.00 10.00

2009 Upper Deck Goudey Mini Navy Blue Back

*BLUE 1-200: 1.5X TO 4X BASIC
*BLUE RC 1-200: .75X TO 2X BASIC
*BLUE: 201-300: .6X TO 1.5X MINI GREEN
APPROX.ODDS 1:9 HOBBY

2000 Upper Deck Hawaii

These cards were issued by Upper Deck and given away at the Kit Young annual conference in Hawaii in 2000. These cards feature autographs of four athletes Upper Deck brought over to the conference. Each player signed a card serial numbered to 500. The card featuring all four players signed was not included in the factory set, but 100 cards featuring all four players were also signed and distributed. Two Kit Young cards were also included with the factory sets.

COMPLETE SET (6) 160.00 400.00
JN Joe Namath AU 40.00 100.00
GAU Julius Erving AU/100 200.00 500.00
Gordie Howe AU
Joe Namath AU
Tom Seaver AU

2006 Upper Deck Hawaii Trade Conference Signature Dual Jumbos

In its entirety this set contains 10 cards, five of which feature baseball players and the remaining five feature football players. The jumbo sized cards were issued within attractive cherry wood boxes (one per box) of which were given to attendees of the 2006 Hawaii Trade Conference held the last week of February, 2006. The cards are serial-numbered in blue ink with only 10 copies of each produced. The lone anomaly to this rule is the Carnell Williams/Ronnie Brown card of which only eight copies were produced. The cards are not priced due to scarcity

UNPRICED AUTO PRINT RUN 8-15

2006 Upper Deck Hawaii Trade Conference Signature Jumbos

In its entirety this set contains 15 cards, seven of which feature baseball players and the remaining eight feature football players. The jumbo sized cards were issued within attractive cherry wood boxes (one per box) of which were given to attendees of the 2006 Hawaii Trade Conference held the last week of February, 2006. The cards are serial-numbered in blue ink with only 15 copies of each produced. The lone anomaly to this rule is the Ken Griffey Jr. card of which only nine copies were produced. The cards are not priced due to scarcity.

UNPRICED AUTO PRINT RUN 9-15

2007 Upper Deck Hawaii Trade Conference

COMPLETE SET (13) 15.00 40.00
1 Daisuke Matsuzaka 1.25 3.00
2 Kei Igawa .40 1.00
3 Akinori Iwamura .40 1.00
4 Ken Griffey Jr. 2.00 5.00
5 Cal Ripken Jr. 4.00 10.00
6 Derek Jeter 2.50 6.00
7 Delmon Young .60 1.50
8 Joaquin Arias .40 1.00
9 Troy Tulowitzki .60 1.50
10 Peyton Manning 1.50 4.00
11 Sidney Crosby 1.50 4.00
12 LeBron James 3.00 8.00
13 Michael Jordan 5.00 12.00

2008 Upper Deck Heroes

This set was released on July 8, 2008. The base set consists of 266 skip-numbered cards. Each subject in the set has between 2-4 different cards. Cards #1-100 feature veterans, cards 101-200 are rookies, cards 201-245 are legends, and cards 246-269 are miscellaneous subjects from track and field and famous guitarists.

COMPLETE SET (266) 25.00 60.00
UNPRICED PRINT PLATE PRINT RUN 1
UNPRICED BLACK PRINT RUN 1
EACH HAS MULTIPLE CARDS: EQUAL VALUE
1 Adrian Peterson .30 .75
2 Adrian Peterson .30 .75
3 Adrian Peterson .30 .75
4 Adrian Peterson .30 .75
5 Brett Favre .60 1.50
6 Brett Favre .60 1.50
7 Brett Favre .60 1.50
8 Brett Favre .60 1.50
9 Braylon Edwards .20 .50
10 Braylon Edwards .20 .50
11 Braylon Edwards .20 .50
12 Braylon Edwards .20 .50
13 Brodie Croyle .25 .60
14 Brodie Croyle .25 .60
15 Brodie Croyle .25 .60
16 Brodie Croyle .25 .60
17 Bob Sanders .25 .60
18 Bob Sanders .25 .60
19 Bob Sanders .25 .60
20 Bob Sanders .25 .60
21 Chad Johnson .20 .50
22 Chad Johnson .20 .50
23 Chad Johnson .20 .50
24 Chad Johnson .20 .50
25 DeMarcus Ware .25 .60
26 DeMarcus Ware .25 .60
27 DeMarcus Ware .25 .60
28 DeMarcus Ware .25 .60
29 Derek Anderson .20 .50
30 Derek Anderson .20 .50
31 Derek Anderson .20 .50
32 Derek Anderson .20 .50
33 Devin Hester .25 .60
34 Devin Hester .25 .60
35 Devin Hester .25 .60
36 Devin Hester .25 .60
37 Dwayne Bowe .25 .60
38 Dwayne Bowe .25 .60
39 Dwayne Bowe .25 .60
40 Dwayne Bowe .25 .60
41 Eli Manning .25 .60
42 Eli Manning .25 .60
43 Eli Manning .25 .60
44 Eli Manning .25 .60
45 Jason Campbell .20 .50
46 Jason Campbell .20 .50
47 Jason Campbell .20 .50
48 Jason Campbell .20 .50
49 Joseph Addai .20 .50
50 Joseph Addai .20 .50
51 Joseph Addai .20 .50
52 Joseph Addai .20 .50
53 LenDale White .20 .50
54 LenDale White .20 .50
55 LenDale White .20 .50
56 LenDale White .20 .50
57 LaDainian Tomlinson .30 .75
58 LaDainian Tomlinson .30 .75
59 LaDainian Tomlinson .30 .75
60 LaDainian Tomlinson .30 .75
61 Marion Barber .20 .50
62 Marion Barber .20 .50
63 Marion Barber .20 .50
64 Marion Barber .20 .50
65 Marshawn Lynch .25 .60
66 Marshawn Lynch .25 .60
67 Marshawn Lynch .25 .60
68 Marshawn Lynch .25 .60
69 Greg Jennings .20 .50
70 Greg Jennings .20 .50
71 Greg Jennings .20 .50
72 Greg Jennings .20 .50
73 Patrick Willis .25 .60
74 Patrick Willis .25 .60
75 Patrick Willis .25 .60
76 Patrick Willis .25 .60
77 Peyton Manning .75 2.00
78 Peyton Manning .75 2.00
79 Peyton Manning .75 2.00
80 Peyton Manning .75 2.00
81 David Garrard .20 .50
82 David Garrard .20 .50
83 David Garrard .20 .50
84 David Garrard .20 .50
85 Ryan Grant .25 .60
86 Ryan Grant .25 .60
87 Ryan Grant .25 .60
88 Ryan Grant .25 .60
89 Tony Romo .25 .60
90 Tony Romo .25 .60
91 Tony Romo .25 .60
92 Tony Romo .25 .60
93 Wes Welker .25 .60
94 Wes Welker .25 .60
95 Wes Welker .25 .60
96 Wes Welker .25 .60
97 Willie Parker .25 .60
98 Willie Parker .25 .60
99 Willie Parker .25 .60
100 Willie Parker .25 .60
101 Adarius Bowman RC .40 1.00
102 Adarius Bowman RC .40 1.00
103 Ali Highsmith RC .30 .75
104 Ali Highsmith RC .30 .75
105 Andre Woodson RC .30 .75
106 Andre Woodson RC .30 .75
107 Antoine Cason RC .40 1.00
108 Antoine Cason RC .40 1.00
109 Aqib Talib RC .50 1.25
110 Aqib Talib RC .50 1.25
111 Ben Moffitt RC .30 .75
112 Ben Moffitt RC .30 .75
113 Brian Brohm RC .30 .75
114 Brian Brohm RC .30 .75
115 Calais Campbell RC .40 1.00
116 Calais Campbell RC .40 1.00
117 Chad Henne RC .40 1.00
118 Chad Henne RC .40 1.00
119 Chevis Jackson RC .30 .75
120 Chevis Jackson RC .30 .75
121 Chris Long RC .40 1.00
122 Chris Long RC .40 1.00
123 Colt Brennan RC .40 1.00
124 Colt Brennan RC .40 1.00
125 Craig Steltz RC .30 .75
126 Craig Steltz RC .30 .75
127 DJ Hall RC .30 .75
128 DJ Hall RC .30 .75
129 Dan Connor RC .30 .75
130 Dan Connor RC .30 .75
131 Darren McFadden RC .30 .75
132 Darren McFadden RC .30 .75
133 Dennis Dixon RC .30 .75
134 Dennis Dixon RC .30 .75
135 Derrick Harvey RC .30 .75
136 Derrick Harvey RC .30 .75
137 DeSean Jackson RC .60 1.50
138 DeSean Jackson RC .60 1.50
139 Dwight Lowery RC .40 1.00
140 Dwight Lowery RC .40 1.00
141 Early Doucet RC .30 .75
142 Early Doucet RC .30 .75
143 Felix Jones RC .30 .75
144 Felix Jones RC .30 .75
145 Fred Davis RC .30 .75
146 Fred Davis RC .30 .75
147 Glenn Dorsey RC .30 .75
148 Glenn Dorsey RC .30 .75
149 Jacob Tamme RC .40 1.00
150 Jacob Tamme RC .40 1.00
151 Jake Long RC .50 1.25
152 Jake Long RC .50 1.25
153 Shawn Crable RC .30 .75
154 Shawn Crable RC .30 .75
155 J Leman RC .30 .75
156 J Leman RC .30 .75
157 Joe Flacco RC .60 1.50
158 Joe Flacco RC .60 1.50
159 John Carlson RC .30 .75
160 John Carlson RC .30 .75
161 Jonathan Hefney RC .30 .75
162 Jonathan Hefney RC .30 .75
163 Jonathan Stewart RC .50 1.25
164 Jonathan Stewart RC .50 1.25
165 Keith Rivers RC .30 .75
166 Keith Rivers RC .30 .75
167 Lavelle Hawkins RC .40 1.00
168 Lavelle Hawkins RC .40 1.00
169 Lawrence Jackson RC .30 .75
170 Lawrence Jackson RC .30 .75
171 Limas Sweed RC .30 .75
172 Limas Sweed RC .30 .75
173 Justin King RC .40 1.00
174 Justin King RC .40 1.00
175 Malcolm Kelly RC .30 .75
176 Malcolm Kelly RC .30 .75
177 Mario Manningham RC .30 .75
178 Mario Manningham RC .30 .75
179 Matt Ryan RC 1.00 2.50
180 Matt Ryan RC 1.00 2.50
181 Mike Hart RC .30 .75
182 Mike Hart RC .30 .75
183 Mike Jenkins RC .30 .75
184 Mike Jenkins RC .30 .75
185 Ray Rice RC .30 .75
186 Ray Rice RC .30 .75
187 Rashard Mendenhall RC .30 .75
188 Rashard Mendenhall RC .30 .75
189 Sam Baker RC .30 .75
190 Sam Baker RC .30 .75
191 Sedrick Ellis RC .30 .75
192 Sedrick Ellis RC .30 .75
193 Tashard Choice RC .30 .75
194 Tashard Choice RC .30 .75
195 Terrell Thomas RC .30 .75
196 Terrell Thomas RC .30 .75
197 Tom Zbikowski RC .40 1.00
198 Tom Zbikowski RC .40 1.00
199 Xavier Adibi RC .30 .75
200 Xavier Adibi RC .30 .75
201 Barry Sanders .75 2.00
202 Barry Sanders .75 2.00
203 Barry Sanders .75 2.00
204 Billy Sims .40 1.00
205 Billy Sims .40 1.00
206 Billy Sims .40 1.00
207 Bo Jackson .75 2.00
208 Bo Jackson .75 2.00
209 Bo Jackson .75 2.00
210 Dan Marino 1.00 2.50
211 Dan Marino 1.00 2.50
212 Dan Marino 1.00 2.50
213 Fran Tarkenton .50 1.25
214 Fran Tarkenton .50 1.25
215 Fran Tarkenton .50 1.25
216 Franco Harris .50 1.25
217 Franco Harris .50 1.25
218 Franco Harris .50 1.25
219 Mel Blount .40 1.00
220 Mel Blount .40 1.00
221 Mel Blount .40 1.00
222 Paul Hornung .50 1.25
223 Paul Hornung .50 1.25
224 Paul Hornung .50 1.25
225 Jim Brown .60 1.50
226 Jim Brown .60 1.50
227 Jim Brown .60 1.50
228 Jim McMahon .50 1.25
229 Jim McMahon .50 1.25
230 Jim McMahon .50 1.25
231 John Elway .75 2.00
232 John Elway .75 2.00
233 John Elway .75 2.00
234 Ken Stabler .50 1.25
235 Ken Stabler .50 1.25
236 Ken Stabler .50 1.25
237 Ken Anderson .40 1.00
238 Ken Anderson .40 1.00
239 Ken Anderson .40 1.00
240 Roger Craig .40 1.00
241 Roger Craig .40 1.00
242 Roger Craig .40 1.00
243 Gale Sayers .50 1.25
244 Gale Sayers .50 1.25
245 Gale Sayers .50 1.25
246 Michael Johnson .40 1.00
247 Michael Johnson .40 1.00
248 Michael Johnson .40 1.00
249 Steve Vai .40 1.00
250 Steve Vai .40 1.00
251 Steve Vai .40 1.00
252 Tom Morello .40 1.00
253 Tom Morello .40 1.00
254 Tom Morello .40 1.00
255 Justin Hayward .75 2.00
256 Justin Hayward .75 2.00
257 Justin Hayward .75 2.00
258 Rulon Gardner .40 1.00
259 Rulon Gardner .40 1.00
260 Rulon Gardner .40 1.00
264 Tony Iommi .40 1.00
265 Tony Iommi .40 1.00
266 Tony Iommi .40 1.00
267 Jackie Joyner-Kersee .40 1.00
268 Jackie Joyner-Kersee .40 1.00
269 Jackie Joyner-Kersee .40 1.00

2008 Upper Deck Heroes Blue

*VETS 1-100: 2.5X TO 6X BASIC CARDS
*ROOKIES 101-200: 1X TO 2.5X BASIC CARDS
*LEGENDS 201-269: 2X TO 5X BASIC CARDS
STATED PRINT RUN 125 SER.#'d SETS

2008 Upper Deck Heroes Bronze

*VETS 1-100: 3X TO 8X BASIC CARDS
*ROOKIES 101-200: 1.2X TO 3X BASIC CARDS
*LEGENDS 201-269: 2.5X TO 6X BASIC CARDS
STATED PRINT RUN 75 SER.#'d SETS

2008 Upper Deck Heroes Gold

*VETS 1-100: 4X TO 10X BASIC CARDS
*ROOKIES 101-200: 2X TO 5X BASIC CARDS
*LEGENDS 201-269: 3X TO 8X BASIC CARDS
STATED PRINT RUN 25 SER.#'d SETS

2008 Upper Deck Heroes Green

ETS: 2X TO 5X BASIC CARDS
*ROOKIES: .8X TO 2X BASIC CARDS
*LEGENDS: 1.5X TO 4X BASIC CARDS
STATED PRINT RUN 350 SER.#'d SETS

2008 Upper Deck Heroes Platinum

ETS 1-100: 8X TO 20X BASIC CARDS
*ROOKIES 101-200: 3X TO 8X BASIC CARDS
*LEGENDS/10 201-269: 6X TO 15X BASIC CARDS
PLATINUM PRINT RUN 1-10

2008 Upper Deck Heroes Autograph Jerseys

ATED PRINT RUN 15 SER.#'d SETS
UNPRICED PATCH AU PRINT RUN 5
1 Adrian Peterson 50.00 100.00
5 Brett Favre 125.00 200.00
17 Bob Sanders 40.00 80.00
41 Eli Manning 50.00 120.00
57 L.Tomlinson EXCH 50.00 100.00
77 Peyton Manning 75.00 150.00
81 David Garrard 30.00 60.00
89 Tony Romo 60.00 120.00
93 Wes Welker 40.00 80.00

2008 Upper Deck Heroes Autographs Blue

COMMON CARD 3.00 8.00
SEMISTARS 4.00 10.00
UNLISTED STARS 5.00 12.00
BLUE PRINT RUN 150-350
UNPRICED BLACK PRINT RUN 1
UNPRICED CUT AUTO PRINT RUN 1
UNPRICED PLATINUM PRINT RUN 5-15
101 Adarius Bowman/250 4.00 10.00
103 Ali Highsmith/250 3.00 8.00
105 Andre Woodson/150 3.00 8.00
107 Antoine Cason/250 4.00 10.00
109 Aqib Talib/250 5.00 12.00
113 Brian Brohm/150 3.00 8.00
115 Calais Campbell/250 4.00 10.00
117 Chad Henne/250 4.00 10.00
119 Chevis Jackson/250 3.00 8.00
121 Chris Long/250 4.00 10.00
123 Colt Brennan/150 4.00 10.00
125 Craig Steltz/250 3.00 8.00
127 DJ Hall/250 3.00 8.00
129 Dan Connor/250 3.00 8.00
131 Darren McFadden/150 3.00 8.00
133 Dennis Dixon/250 3.00 8.00
135 Derrick Harvey/350 3.00 8.00
137 DeSean Jackson/150 6.00 15.00
139 Dwight Lowery/250 4.00 10.00
141 Early Doucet/250 3.00 8.00
143 Felix Jones/250 3.00 8.00
145 Fred Davis/250 3.00 8.00
147 Glenn Dorsey/250 3.00 8.00
149 Jacob Tamme/250 4.00 10.00
151 Jake Long/250 5.00 12.00
153 Shawn Crable/350 3.00 8.00
155 J Leman/250 3.00 8.00
157 Joe Flacco/250 6.00 15.00
159 John Carlson/250 3.00 8.00
161 Jonathan Hefney/250 3.00 8.00
163 Jonathan Stewart/250 5.00 12.00
165 Keith Rivers/250 3.00 8.00
167 Lavelle Hawkins/250 4.00 10.00
169 Lawrence Jackson/250 3.00 8.00
171 Limas Sweed/250 3.00 8.00
173 Justin King/250 4.00 10.00
175 Malcolm Kelly/250 3.00 8.00
179 Matt Ryan/150 40.00 80.00
181 Mike Hart/250 3.00 8.00
183 Mike Jenkins/250 3.00 8.00
185 Ray Rice/250 3.00 8.00
187 Rashard Mendenhall/350 3.00 8.00
189 Sam Baker/350 3.00 8.00
191 Sedrick Ellis/350 3.00 8.00
193 Tashard Choice/250 3.00 8.00
195 Terrell Thomas/250 3.00 8.00
199 Xavier Adibi/350 3.00 8.00

2008 Upper Deck Heroes Autographs Bronze

RONZE/50-75: .5X TO 1.2X BLUE AUTO
*BRONZE/25: .6X TO 1.5X BLUE AUTO
BRONZE STATED PRINT RUN 25-75
131 Darren McFadden/25 5.00 12.00
179 Matt Ryan/25 75.00 150.00

2008 Upper Deck Heroes Autographs Gold

*101-200 GOLD ROOKIES: .6X TO 1.5X BLUE AU
GOLD STATED PRINT RUN 10-40
SERIAL #'d OF 10 NOT PRICED
EACH HAS MULTIPLE CARDS: EQUAL VALUE
1 Adrian Peterson/25 50.00 120.00
5 Brett Favre/25 125.00 200.00
9 Braylon Edwards/25 12.00 30.00
13 Brodie Croyle/25 10.00 25.00
17 Bob Sanders/25 15.00 40.00
21 Chad Johnson/25 8.00 20.00
25 DeMarcus Ware/25 12.00 30.00
29 Derek Anderson/25 12.00 30.00
37 Dwayne Bowe/25 12.00 30.00
41 Eli Manning/25 40.00 80.00
45 Jason Campbell/25 8.00 20.00
49 Joseph Addai/25 8.00 20.00
57 L.Tomlinson/25 EXCH 40.00 80.00
61 Marion Barber/25 8.00 20.00
65 Marshawn Lynch/25 10.00 25.00
73 Patrick Willis/25 12.00 30.00
77 Peyton Manning/25 60.00 120.00
81 David Garrard/25 8.00 20.00
89 Tony Romo/25 60.00 120.00
93 Wes Welker/25 25.00 60.00
204 Billy Sims/40 8.00 20.00
207 Bo Jackson/25 40.00 80.00
213 Fran Tarkenton/25 25.00 50.00
216 Franco Harris/25 25.00 50.00
219 Mel Blount/40 EXCH
222 Paul Hornung/40 15.00 40.00
234 Ken Stabler/25 30.00 60.00
237 Ken Anderson/40 8.00 20.00
240 Roger Craig/40 10.00 25.00
246 Michael Johnson/25 40.00 80.00
258 Rulon Gardner/25 8.00 20.00
267 Jackie Joyner-Kersee/25 15.00 30.00

2008 Upper Deck Heroes Jerseys Blue

UE PRINT RUN 125-175
*BRONZE/75: .5X TO 1.2X BLUE
BRONZE PRINT RUN 75 SER.#'d SETS
*GREEN RETAIL: .4X TO 1X BLUE
UNPRICED BLACK PATCH PRINT RUN 5
EACH HAS MULTIPLE CARDS: EQUAL VALUE
1 Adrian Peterson/175 8.00 20.00
5 Brett Favre/175 8.00 20.00
9 Braylon Edwards/125 2.50 6.00
13 Brodie Croyle/125 3.00 8.00
17 Bob Sanders/125 4.00 10.00
21 Chad Johnson/175 2.50 6.00
25 DeMarcus Ware/175 3.00 8.00
29 Derek Anderson/175 2.50 6.00
33 Devin Hester/175 3.00 8.00
37 Dwayne Bowe/125 3.00 8.00
41 Eli Manning/125 3.00 8.00
45 Jason Campbell/175 2.50 6.00
49 Joseph Addai/175 2.50 6.00
53 LenDale White/175 2.50 6.00
57 LaDainian Tomlinson/175 4.00 10.00
61 Marion Barber/175 2.50 6.00
65 Marshawn Lynch/175 3.00 8.00
69 Greg Jennings/125 2.50 6.00
73 Patrick Willis/125 3.00 8.00
77 Peyton Manning/175 10.00 25.00
81 David Garrard/125 2.50 6.00
85 Ryan Grant/125 5.00 12.00
89 Tony Romo/175 6.00 15.00
93 Wes Welker/125 3.00 8.00
97 Willie Parker/125 3.00 8.00

2008 Upper Deck Heroes Jerseys Gold

*GOLD 1-100: .6X TO 1.5X BLUE
1-100 GOLD PRINT RUN 35
201-245 GOLD PRINT RUN 25
SUBJECTS HAVE MULTIPLE CARDS OF EQUAL VALUE
*PLAT.PATCH 1-100: .8X TO 2X BLUE
*PLAT.PATCH 201-245: .6X TO 1.5X GOLD
1-100 PLATINUM PATCH PRINT RUN 25
201-245 PLAT.PATCH PRINT RUN 10
201 Barry Sanders 15.00 40.00
204 Billy Sims 8.00 20.00
207 Bo Jackson 15.00 40.00
210 Dan Marino 20.00 50.00
213 Fran Tarkenton 10.00 25.00
216 Franco Harris 10.00 25.00
219 Mel Blount 10.00 25.00
222 Paul Hornung 10.00 25.00
225 Jim Brown 12.00 30.00
228 Jim McMahon 10.00 25.00
231 John Elway 15.00 40.00
234 Ken Stabler 12.00 30.00
237 Ken Anderson 10.00 25.00
240 Roger Craig 8.00 20.00
243 Gale Sayers 10.00 25.00

2009 Upper Deck Heroes

is set was released on June 16, 2009 and was issued in 8-card packs with 24-packs per box at an SRP of $1.59 per pack. The base set consists of 416 skip-numbered cards and each subject in the set has between 2-4 different cards. Cards #1-100 feature veterans, cards 101-198 are rookies, 201-300 are NFL legends, 301-340 feature miscellaneous subjects from track and field, tennis, volleyball and ice skating, 341-360 feature famous historical figures, 361-384 are famous guitarists, 401-470 are artist's renderings of various subjects in the set, and 471-489 feature dual player cards including some hockey players. Finally, cards #301-489 were short printed.

1 Brett Favre .60 1.50
2 Brett Favre .60 1.50
3 LaDainian Tomlinson .30 .75
4 LaDainian Tomlinson .30 .75
5 LaDainian Tomlinson .30 .75
6 LaDainian Tomlinson .30 .75
7 Jay Cutler .20 .50
8 Jay Cutler .20 .50
9 Jay Cutler .20 .50
10 Jay Cutler .20 .50
11 Drew Brees .30 .75
12 Drew Brees .30 .75
13 Drew Brees .30 .75
14 Drew Brees .30 .75
15 Matt Forte .20 .50
16 Matt Forte .20 .50
17 Matt Forte .20 .50
18 Matt Forte .20 .50
19 Darren McFadden .30 .75
20 Darren McFadden .30 .75
21 Darren McFadden .30 .75
22 Darren McFadden .30 .75
23 Ben Roethlisberger .30 .75
24 Ben Roethlisberger .30 .75
25 Ben Roethlisberger .30 .75
26 Ben Roethlisberger .30 .75
27 Brett Favre .60 1.50
28 Brett Favre .60 1.50
29 Peyton Manning .75 2.00
30 Peyton Manning .75 2.00
31 Peyton Manning .75 2.00
32 Peyton Manning .75 2.00
33 Tony Romo .25 .60
34 Tony Romo .25 .60
35 Tony Romo .25 .60
36 Tony Romo .25 .60
37 Devin Hester .25 .60
38 Devin Hester .25 .60
39 Devin Hester .25 .60
40 Devin Hester .25 .60
41 Eli Manning .25 .60
42 Eli Manning .25 .60
43 Eli Manning .25 .60
44 Eli Manning .25 .60
45 A.J. Hawk .20 .50
46 A.J. Hawk .20 .50
47 A.J. Hawk .20 .50
48 A.J. Hawk .20 .50
49 Adrian Peterson .30 .75
50 Adrian Peterson .30 .75
51 Adrian Peterson .30 .75
52 Adrian Peterson .30 .75
53 Dallas Clark .20 .50
54 Dallas Clark .20 .50
55 Dallas Clark .20 .50
56 Dallas Clark .20 .50
57 Larry Fitzgerald .25 .60
58 Larry Fitzgerald .25 .60
59 Larry Fitzgerald .25 .60
60 Larry Fitzgerald .25 .60
61 Philip Rivers .30 .75
62 Philip Rivers .30 .75
63 Philip Rivers .30 .75
64 Philip Rivers .30 .75
65 Brian Westbrook .20 .50
66 Brian Westbrook .20 .50
67 Brian Westbrook .20 .50
68 Brian Westbrook .20 .50
69 Tom Brady 1.00 2.50
70 Tom Brady 1.00 2.50
71 Tom Brady 1.00 2.50
72 Tom Brady 1.00 2.50
73 Clinton Portis .20 .50
74 Clinton Portis .20 .50
75 Clinton Portis .20 .50
76 Clinton Portis .20 .50
77 Marvin Harrison .25 .60
78 Marvin Harrison .25 .60
79 Marvin Harrison .25 .60
80 Marvin Harrison .25 .60
81 Aaron Rodgers .60 1.50
82 Aaron Rodgers .60 1.50
83 Aaron Rodgers .60 1.50
84 Aaron Rodgers .60 1.50
85 Kurt Warner .25 .60
86 Kurt Warner .25 .60
87 Kurt Warner .25 .60
88 Kurt Warner .25 .60
89 Steven Jackson .20 .50
90 Steven Jackson .20 .50
91 Steven Jackson .20 .50
92 Steven Jackson .20 .50
93 Reggie Wayne .25 .60
94 Reggie Wayne .25 .60
95 Reggie Wayne .25 .60
96 Reggie Wayne .25 .60
97 Calvin Johnson .30 .75
98 Calvin Johnson .30 .75
99 Calvin Johnson .30 .75
100 Calvin Johnson .30 .75
101 LeSean McCoy RC .75 2.00
102 LeSean McCoy RC .75 2.00
103 Michael Crabtree RC .50 1.25
104 Michael Crabtree RC .50 1.25
105 Jeremy Maclin RC .40 1.00
106 Jeremy Maclin RC .40 1.00
107 Chris Wells RC .30 .75
108 Chris Wells RC .30 .75
109 Nate Davis RC .30 .75
110 Nate Davis RC .30 .75
111 Percy Harvin RC .30 .75

112 Percy Harvin RC .30 .75
113 Knowshon Moreno RC .30 .75
114 Knowshon Moreno RC .30 .75
115 Curtis Painter RC .30 .75
116 Curtis Painter RC .30 .75
117 Matthew Stafford RC 1.50 4.00
118 Matthew Stafford RC 1.50 4.00
119 Chase Coffman RC .30 .75
120 Chase Coffman RC .30 .75
121 Shonn Greene RC .30 .75
122 Shonn Greene RC .30 .75
123 Marcus Freeman RC .30 .75
124 Marcus Freeman RC .30 .75
125 Brian Robiskie RC .30 .75
126 Brian Robiskie RC .30 .75
127 James Laurinaitis RC .30 .75
128 James Laurinaitis RC .30 .75
129 Pat White RC .40 1.00
130 Pat White RC .40 1.00
131 James Davis RC .30 .75
132 James Davis RC .30 .75
133 Darrius Heyward-Bey RC .50 1.25
134 Darrius Heyward-Bey RC .50 1.25
135 Everette Brown RC .30 .75
136 Everette Brown RC .30 .75
137 Sean Smith RC .30 .75
138 Sean Smith RC .30 .75
139 Fili Moala RC .30 .75
140 Fili Moala RC .30 .75
141 Juaquin Iglesias RC .30 .75
142 Juaquin Iglesias RC .30 .75
143 Mark Sanchez RC .30 .75
144 Mark Sanchez RC .30 .75
145 Derrick Williams RC .30 .75
146 Derrick Williams RC .30 .75
147 Brandon Gibson RC .40 1.00
148 Brandon Gibson RC .40 1.00
149 Brandon Pettigrew RC .30 .75
150 Brandon Pettigrew RC .30 .75
151 Donald Brown RC .30 .75
152 Donald Brown RC .30 .75
153 Josh Freeman RC .30 .75
154 Josh Freeman RC .30 .75
155 Andre Smith RC .30 .75
156 Andre Smith RC .30 .75
157 Hakeem Nicks RC .40 1.00
158 Hakeem Nicks RC .40 1.00
161 Keenan Lewis RC .50 1.25
162 Keenan Lewis RC .50 1.25
163 Louis Murphy RC .30 .75
164 Louis Murphy RC .30 .75
165 Demetrius Byrd RC .40 1.00
166 Demetrius Byrd RC .40 1.00
167 Malcolm Jenkins RC .30 .75
168 Malcolm Jenkins RC .30 .75
169 Brian Cushing RC .30 .75
170 Brian Cushing RC .30 .75
171 Vontae Davis RC .30 .75
172 Vontae Davis RC .30 .75
173 Rey Maualuga RC .50 1.25
174 Rey Maualuga RC .50 1.25
175 Michael Johnson RC .30 .75
176 Michael Johnson RC .30 .75
177 Jonathan Luigs RC .30 .75
178 Jonathan Luigs RC .30 .75
179 D.J. Moore RC .40 1.00
180 D.J. Moore RC .40 1.00
181 William Moore RC .30 .75
182 William Moore RC .30 .75
183 Brian Orakpo RC .40 1.00
184 Brian Orakpo RC .40 1.00
185 Aaron Curry RC .50 1.25
186 Aaron Curry RC .50 1.25
187 Michael Oher RC .50 1.25
188 Michael Oher RC .50 1.25
189 Darius Butler RC .40 1.00
190 Darius Butler RC .40 1.00
191 Sen'Derrick Marks RC .30 .75
192 Sen'Derrick Marks RC .30 .75
193 Javon Ringer RC .30 .75
194 Javon Ringer RC .30 .75
195 Tyson Jackson RC .30 .75
196 Tyson Jackson RC .30 .75
197 Graham Harrell RC .30 .75
198 Graham Harrell RC .30 .75
201 Paul Hornung .50 1.25
202 Paul Hornung .50 1.25
203 Paul Hornung .50 1.25
204 Paul Hornung .50 1.25
205 Paul Hornung .50 1.25
206 Bob Griese .50 1.25
207 Bob Griese .50 1.25
208 Bob Griese .50 1.25
209 Bob Griese .50 1.25
210 Bob Griese .50 1.25
211 Jerry Kramer .40 1.00
212 Jerry Kramer .40 1.00
213 Jerry Kramer .40 1.00
214 Jerry Kramer .40 1.00
215 Jerry Kramer .40 1.00
216 Merlin Olsen .30 .75
217 Merlin Olsen .30 .75
218 Merlin Olsen .30 .75
219 Merlin Olsen .30 .75
220 Mike Singletary .50 1.25
221 Mike Singletary .50 1.25
222 Mike Singletary .50 1.25
223 Mike Singletary .50 1.25
224 Don Maynard .40 1.00
225 Don Maynard .40 1.00
226 Don Maynard .40 1.00
227 Don Maynard .40 1.00
232 Terry Bradshaw .60 1.50
233 Terry Bradshaw .60 1.50
234 Emmitt Smith .75 2.00
235 Emmitt Smith .75 2.00
236 Bob Lilly .40 1.00
237 Bob Lilly .40 1.00
238 Bob Lilly .40 1.00
239 Bob Lilly .40 1.00
240 Thurman Thomas .40 1.00
241 Thurman Thomas .40 1.00
242 Thurman Thomas .40 1.00
243 Thurman Thomas .40 1.00
247 Jack Ham .40 1.00
248 Jack Ham .40 1.00
249 Jack Ham .40 1.00
250 Mike Ditka .50 1.25
251 Mike Ditka .50 1.25
252 Troy Aikman .60 1.50
253 Troy Aikman .60 1.50
254 Roger Staubach .60 1.50
255 Roger Staubach .60 1.50
261 Bart Starr .75 2.00
262 Bart Starr .75 2.00
266 Steve Young .60 1.50
267 Steve Young .60 1.50
268 Steve Young .60 1.50
269 Darrell Green .40 1.00
270 Darrell Green .40 1.00
271 Darrell Green .40 1.00
272 Earl Campbell .50 1.25
273 Earl Campbell .50 1.25
274 Earl Campbell .50 1.25
275 Fred Biletnikoff .50 1.25
276 Fred Biletnikoff .50 1.25
277 Fred Biletnikoff .50 1.25
278 Fred Biletnikoff .50 1.25
279 Alex Karras .40 1.00
280 Alex Karras .40 1.00
281 Alex Karras .40 1.00
282 Alex Karras .40 1.00
283 Lawrence Taylor .50 1.25
284 Lawrence Taylor .50 1.25
285 Lawrence Taylor .50 1.25
286 Jim Kelly .50 1.25
287 Jim Kelly .50 1.25
288 Jim Kelly .50 1.25
289 Phil Simms .40 1.00
290 Phil Simms .40 1.00
291 Phil Simms .40 1.00
292 Phil Simms .40 1.00
297 Alan Page .30 .75
298 Alan Page .30 .75
299 Alan Page .30 .75
300 Alan Page .30 .75
301 Kristi Yamaguchi .40 1.00
302 Kristi Yamaguchi .40 1.00
303 Kristi Yamaguchi .40 1.00
304 Kristi Yamaguchi .40 1.00
305 Peggy Fleming .40 1.00
306 Peggy Fleming .40 1.00
307 Peggy Fleming .40 1.00
308 Peggy Fleming .40 1.00
325 Michael Johnson Track .50 1.25
326 Michael Johnson Track .50 1.25
327 Michael Johnson Track .50 1.25
328 Michael Johnson Track .50 1.25
329 Laird Hamilton .40 1.00
330 Laird Hamilton .40 1.00
331 Laird Hamilton .40 1.00
332 Laird Hamilton .40 1.00
333 Lindsay Davenport .40 1.00
334 Lindsay Davenport .40 1.00
335 Lindsay Davenport .40 1.00
336 Lindsay Davenport .40 1.00
337 Phil Dalhausser .40 1.00
338 Phil Dalhausser .40 1.00
339 Phil Dalhausser .40 1.00
340 Phil Dalhausser .40 1.00
341 Pablo Picasso .40 1.00
342 Vincent Van Gogh .40 1.00
343 Thomas Edison .40 1.00
344 George Washington .40 1.00
345 Mount Rushmore .40 1.00
346 Paul Revere .40 1.00
347 Sitting Bull .40 1.00
348 Sir Isaac Newton .40 1.00
349 Wolfgang Mozart .40 1.00
350 Ludwig Beethoven .40 1.00
351 Woodstock Anniv. .40 1.00
352 Wyatt Earp .40 1.00
353 Benjamin Franklin .40 1.00
354 Christopher Columbus .40 1.00
355 Florence Nightingale .40 1.00
356 Johnny Appleseed .40 1.00
357 William Wallace .40 1.00
358 Frederick Douglass .40 1.00
359 Davy Crockett .40 1.00
360 Daniel Boone .40 1.00
361 Pete Best .50 1.25
362 Pete Best .50 1.25
363 Pete Best .50 1.25
364 Pete Best .50 1.25
373 Justin Hayward .50 1.25
374 Justin Hayward .50 1.25
375 Justin Hayward .50 1.25
376 Steve Vai .50 1.25
377 Steve Vai .50 1.25
378 Steve Vai .50 1.25
379 Tony Iommi .50 1.25
380 Tony Iommi .50 1.25
381 Tony Iommi .50 1.25
382 Tom Morello .50 1.25
383 Tom Morello .50 1.25
384 Tom Morello .50 1.25
401 Brett Favre ART 1.50 4.00
402 Peyton Manning ART 2.00 5.00
403 Tony Romo ART .60 1.50
404 Devin Hester ART .60 1.50
405 Eli Manning ART .60 1.50
406 Ben Roethlisberger ART .75 2.00
407 Calvin Johnson ART .75 2.00
408 LaDainian Tomlinson ART .75 2.00
409 Larry Fitzgerald ART .60 1.50
410 Philip Rivers ART .75 2.00
411 Brian Westbrook ART .50 1.25
412 Tom Brady ART 2.50 6.00
413 Plaxico Burress ART .50 1.25
414 Marvin Harrison ART .60 1.50
415 Aaron Rodgers ART 1.50 4.00
416 Carson Palmer ART .60 1.50
417 Jay Cutler ART .50 1.25
418 Drew Brees ART .75 2.00
419 Darren McFadden ART .75 2.00
420 Matt Forte ART .50 1.25
421 Paul Hornung ART .75 2.00
422 Bob Griese ART .75 2.00
423 Jerry Kramer ART .60 1.50
425 Mike Singletary ART .75 2.00
426 Don Maynard ART .60 1.50
429 Emmitt Smith ART 1.25 3.00
430 Bob Lilly ART .60 1.50
431 Thurman Thomas ART .60 1.50
432 Tony Dorsett ART .75 2.00
433 Jack Ham ART .60 1.50
434 Mike Ditka ART .75 2.00
436 Alex Karras ART .60 1.50
437 Troy Aikman ART 1.00 2.50
438 Alan Page ART .50 1.25
439 Fred Biletnikoff ART .75 2.00
440 Earl Campbell ART .75 2.00
441 Kristi Yamaguchi ART .60 1.50
442 Peggy Fleming ART .60 1.50
447 Laird Hamilton ART .60 1.50
448 Lindsay Davenport ART .60 1.50
449 Michael Johnson Trck ART .60 1.50
450 Phil Dalhausser ART .60 1.50
451 Pablo Picasso ART .60 1.50
452 Vincent Van Gogh ART .60 1.50
453 Thomas Edison ART .60 1.50
454 George Washington ART .60 1.50
455 Mount Rushmore ART .60 1.50
456 Paul Revere ART .60 1.50
457 Sitting Bull ART .60 1.50
458 Wolfgang Mozart ART .60 1.50
459 Ludwig Beethoven ART .60 1.50
460 Woodstock Anniv. ART .60 1.50
461 Wyatt Earp ART .60 1.50
462 Benjamin Franklin ART .60 1.50
463 Christopher Columbus ART .60 1.50
464 Florence Nightingale ART .60 1.50
465 Johnny Appleseed ART .60 1.50
466 William Wallace ART .60 1.50
467 Frederick Douglass ART .60 1.50
468 Davy Crockett ART .60 1.50
469 Daniel Boone ART .60 1.50
470 Sir Isaac Newton ART .60 1.50
471 B.Favre/J.Namath 2.00 5.00
472 E.Manning/Manning 2.50 6.00
473 Maynard/Biletnikoff 1.00 2.50
474 E.Manning/T.Brady 3.00 8.00
475 M.Harrison/R.Wayne .75 2.00
476 T.Romo/T.Aikman 1.25 3.00
478 Roethlis/C.Palmer 1.00 2.50
479 E.Manning/T.Romo .75 2.00
480 L.Tomlinson/P.Rivers 1.00 2.50
481 B.Sanders/G.Howe HH 1.50 4.00
483 R.Bourque/T.Brady HH 3.00 8.00
484 E.Manning/M.Messier HH 1.50 4.00
485 Roethlis/E.Malkin HH 1.00 2.50
486 Lemieux/Bradshaw HH 3.00 8.00
488 M.Modano/T.Romo HH .75 2.00
489 B.Hull/M.Ditka HH 1.00 2.50

2009 Upper Deck Heroes Blue

*1-100 VETS: 2.5X TO 6X BASIC INSERTS
*101-198 ROOKIES: 1X TO 2.5X
*201-300 LEGENDS: 1.5X TO 4X
*301-384 MISC: 1.5X TO 4X
*401-440 ART NFL: 1.2X TO 3X
*441-470 ART MISC: 1.2X TO 3X
*471-489 ART DUAL: 1X TO 2.5X
BLUE PRINT RUN 99 SER.#'d SETS

2009 Upper Deck Heroes Orange

-100 VETS: 4X TO 10X BASIC INSERTS
*101-198 ROOKIES: 1.5X TO 4X
*201-300 LEGENDS: 2.5X TO 6X
*301-384 MISC: 2.5X TO 6X
*401-440 ART NFL: 2X TO 5X
*441-470 ART MISC: 2X TO 5X
*471-489 ART DUAL: 1.5X TO 4X
STATED PRINT RUN 35 SER.#'d SETS

2009 Upper Deck Heroes Purple

*1-100 VETS: 8X TO 20X BASIC INSERTS
*101-198 ROOKIES: 4X TO 10X
*201-300 LEGENDS: 5X TO 12X
*301-384 MISC: 5X TO 12X
*401-440 ART NFL: 4X TO 10X
*441-470 ART MISC: 4X TO 10X
*471-489 ART DUAL: 3X TO 8X
STATED PRINT RUN 10 SER.#'d SETS

2009 Upper Deck Heroes Autographs Gold

01-198 ROOK/25: .6X TO 1.5X SILVER/199
*101-198 ROOK/25: .5X TO 1.2X SILVER/99
101-198 ROOKIE PRINT RUN 10-25
402-440 ART NFL PRINT RUN 9-50
441-450 ART MISC PRINT RUN 25
472-488 ART DUAL PRINT RUN 40
420 Matt Forte ART/22 12.00 30.00
421 Paul Hornung ART/25 15.00 40.00
426 Don Maynard ART/25 15.00 30.00
430 Bob Lilly ART/25 10.00 25.00
431 Thurman Thomas ART/25 20.00 40.00
436 Alex Karras ART/25 12.00 30.00
438 Alan Page ART/25 12.00 30.00
439 Fred Biletnikoff ART/25 20.00 40.00
440 Earl Campbell ART/25 20.00 40.00
442 P.Fleming ART/25 EXCH 10.00 25.00
450 P.Dalhausser ART/25 EXCH 15.00 40.00
472 Eli/P.Mann.HH/20 100.00 175.00
473 Maynard/Biletnik HH/20 20.00 40.00
479 Eli/Romo HH/40 EXCH 75.00 150.00
481 Sndrs/Howe HH/40 EXCH 150.00 250.00

2009 Upper Deck Heroes Autographs Silver

3-96 VET PRINT RUN 4-25
101-198 ROOKIE PRINT RUN 50-199
201-300 NFL LEGEND PRINT RUN 5-35
301-400 MISC LEGEND PRINT RUN 20-51
EACH HAS MULTIPLE CARDS EQUAL VALUE
SERIAL #'d UNDER 15 NOT PRICED
29 Peyton Manning/25 60.00 100.00
30 Peyton Manning/25 60.00 100.00
31 Peyton Manning/25 60.00 100.00
32 Peyton Manning/25 60.00 100.00
53 Dallas Clark/15 8.00 20.00
54 Dallas Clark/15 8.00 20.00
55 Dallas Clark/15 8.00 20.00
56 Dallas Clark/15 8.00 20.00
73 Clinton Portis/15 8.00 20.00
74 Clinton Portis/15 8.00 20.00
75 Clinton Portis/15 8.00 20.00
76 Clinton Portis/15 8.00 20.00
93 Reggie Wayne/25 10.00 25.00
94 Reggie Wayne/25 10.00 25.00
95 Reggie Wayne/25 10.00 25.00
96 Reggie Wayne/25 10.00 25.00
101 LeSean McCoy/199 8.00 20.00
102 LeSean McCoy/199 8.00 20.00
103 Michael Crabtree/50 30.00 80.00
104 Michael Crabtree/50 30.00 80.00
105 Jeremy Maclin/99 5.00 12.00
106 Jeremy Maclin/99 5.00 12.00
107 Chris Wells/50 20.00 50.00
108 Chris Wells/50 20.00 50.00
111 Percy Harvin/99 4.00 10.00
112 Percy Harvin/99 4.00 10.00
113 Knowshon Moreno/50 12.00 30.00
114 Knowshon Moreno/50 12.00 30.00
115 Curtis Painter/199 3.00 8.00
116 Curtis Painter/199 3.00 8.00
117 Matthew Stafford/50 40.00 100.00
118 Matthew Stafford/50 25.00 60.00
119 Chase Coffman/199 3.00 8.00
120 Chase Coffman/199 3.00 8.00
121 Shonn Greene/99 4.00 10.00
122 Shonn Greene/99 4.00 10.00
123 Marcus Freeman/199 3.00 8.00
124 Marcus Freeman/199 3.00 8.00
125 Brian Robiskie/199 3.00 8.00
126 Brian Robiskie/199 3.00 8.00
127 James Laurinaitis/199 3.00 8.00
128 James Laurinaitis/199 3.00 8.00
129 Pat White/199 4.00 10.00
130 Pat White/199 4.00 10.00
131 James Davis/199 3.00 8.00
132 James Davis/199 3.00 8.00
133 Darrius Heyward-Bey/199 5.00 12.00
134 Darrius Heyward-Bey/199 5.00 12.00
139 Fili Moala/199 3.00 8.00
140 Fili Moala/199 3.00 8.00
141 Juaquin Iglesias/199 3.00 8.00
142 Juaquin Iglesias/199 3.00 8.00
143 Mark Sanchez/50 30.00 80.00
144 Mark Sanchez/50 30.00 80.00
145 Derrick Williams/199 3.00 8.00
146 Derrick Williams/199 3.00 8.00
147 Brandon Gibson/199 4.00 10.00
148 Brandon Gibson/199 4.00 10.00
149 Brandon Pettigrew/199 3.00 8.00
150 Brandon Pettigrew/199 3.00 8.00
151 Donald Brown/199 3.00 8.00
152 Donald Brown/199 3.00 8.00
153 Josh Freeman/99 4.00 10.00
154 Josh Freeman/99 4.00 10.00
155 Andre Smith/199 3.00 8.00
161 Keenan Lewis/199 5.00 12.00
162 Keenan Lewis/199 5.00 12.00
165 Demetrius Byrd/199 4.00 10.00
166 Demetrius Byrd/199 4.00 10.00
167 Malcolm Jenkins/199 3.00 8.00
168 Malcolm Jenkins/199 3.00 8.00
169 Brian Cushing/199 3.00 8.00
170 Brian Cushing/199 3.00 8.00
171 Vontae Davis/199 3.00 8.00
172 Vontae Davis/199 3.00 8.00
173 Rey Maualuga/199 5.00 12.00
174 Rey Maualuga/199 5.00 12.00
175 Michael Johnson/199 3.00 8.00
176 Michael Johnson/199 3.00 8.00
177 Jonathan Luigs/199 3.00 8.00
178 Jonathan Luigs/199 3.00 8.00
179 D.J. Moore/199 4.00 10.00
180 D.J. Moore/199 4.00 10.00
181 William Moore/199 3.00 8.00
182 William Moore/199 3.00 8.00
183 Brian Orakpo/199 4.00 10.00
184 Brian Orakpo/199 4.00 10.00
185 Aaron Curry/199 5.00 12.00
186 Aaron Curry/199 5.00 12.00
189 Darius Butler/199 4.00 10.00
190 Darius Butler/199 4.00 10.00
191 Sen'Derrick Marks/199 3.00 8.00
192 Sen'Derrick Marks/199 3.00 8.00
195 Tyson Jackson/199 3.00 8.00
196 Tyson Jackson/199 3.00 8.00
197 Graham Harrell/199 8.00 20.00
198 Graham Harrell/199 8.00 20.00
201 Paul Hornung/25 12.50 30.00
202 Paul Hornung/25 12.50 30.00
203 Paul Hornung/25 12.50 30.00
204 Paul Hornung/25 12.50 30.00
205 Paul Hornung/25 12.50 30.00
211 Jerry Kramer/25 8.00 20.00
212 Jerry Kramer/25 8.00 20.00
213 Jerry Kramer/25 8.00 20.00
214 Jerry Kramer/25 8.00 20.00
215 Jerry Kramer/25 8.00 20.00
216 Merlin Olsen/25 15.00 30.00
217 Merlin Olsen/25 15.00 30.00
218 Merlin Olsen/25 15.00 30.00
219 Merlin Olsen/25 15.00 30.00
224 Don Maynard/25 8.00 20.00
225 Don Maynard/25 8.00 20.00
226 Don Maynard/25 8.00 20.00
227 Don Maynard/25 8.00 20.00
236 Bob Lilly/25 8.00 20.00
237 Bob Lilly/25 8.00 20.00
238 Bob Lilly/25 8.00 20.00
239 Bob Lilly/25 8.00 20.00
240 Thurman Thomas/25 12.00 30.00
241 Thurman Thomas/25 12.00 30.00
242 Thurman Thomas/25 12.00 30.00
243 Thurman Thomas/25 12.00 30.00
247 Jack Ham/25 15.00 40.00
248 Jack Ham/25 15.00 40.00
249 Jack Ham/25 15.00 40.00
275 Fred Biletnikoff/25 15.00 40.00
276 Fred Biletnikoff/25 15.00 40.00
277 Fred Biletnikoff/25 15.00 40.00
278 Fred Biletnikoff/25 15.00 40.00
279 Alex Karras/25 10.00 25.00
280 Alex Karras/25 10.00 25.00
281 Alex Karras/25 10.00 25.00
282 Alex Karras/25 10.00 25.00
297 Alan Page/25 10.00 25.00
298 Alan Page/25 10.00 25.00
299 Alan Page/25 10.00 25.00
300 Alan Page/25 10.00 25.00
301 Kristi Yamaguchi/10 25.00 50.00
302 Kristi Yamaguchi/10 25.00 50.00
303 Kristi Yamaguchi/10 25.00 50.00
304 Kristi Yamaguchi/10 25.00 50.00
305 Peggy Fleming/20 EXCH 10.00 25.00
306 Peggy Fleming/20 EXCH 10.00 25.00
307 Peggy Fleming/20 EXCH 10.00 25.00
308 Peggy Fleming/20 EXCH 10.00 25.00
325 M.Johnson Trk/20 EXCH 12.00 30.00
326 M.Johnson Trk/20 EXCH 12.00 30.00
327 M.Johnson Trk/20 EXCH 12.00 30.00
328 M.Johnson Trk/20 EXCH 12.00 30.00
329 Laird Hamilton/20 EXCH 20.00 40.00
330 Laird Hamilton/20 EXCH 20.00 40.00
331 Laird Hamilton/20 EXCH 20.00 40.00
332 Laird Hamilton/20 EXCH 20.00 40.00
337 Phil Dalhausser/20 EXCH 20.00 40.00
338 Phil Dalhausser/20 EXCH 20.00 40.00
339 Phil Dalhausser/20 EXCH 20.00 40.00
340 Phil Dalhausser/20 EXCH 20.00 40.00
373 Justin Hayward/48 20.00 50.00
374 Justin Hayward/51 20.00 50.00
375 Justin Hayward/51 20.00 50.00
376 Steve Vai/45 30.00 60.00
377 Steve Vai/50 30.00 60.00
378 Steve Vai/46 30.00 60.00
379 Tony Iommi/50 30.00 60.00
380 Tony Iommi/50 30.00 60.00
382 Tom Morello/40 20.00 50.00
384 Tom Morello/35 20.00 50.00

2009 Upper Deck Heroes Jerseys Gold Patch

*2-100 GOLD VET/15: .6X TO 1.5X PURP/50
2-100 GOLD PATCH VET PRINT RUN 15
201-292 UNPRICED GOLD LEG PRINT RUN 5
EACH HAS MULTIPLE CARDS EQUAL VALUE
49 Adrian Peterson/15 8.00 20.00

2009 Upper Deck Heroes Jerseys Purple

100 PURPLE VET PRINT RUN 50
402-420 UNPRICED VET ART PRINT RUN 15
421-440 UNPRICED LEG ART PRINT RUN 5
472-480 DUAL ART PRINT RUN 25
481-488 DUAL ART PRINT RUN 150
*7-98 GREEN VET/150: .3X TO .8X PURPLE/50
7-98 GREEN VET PRINT RUN 150
3-100 UNPRICED SILVER VET PRINT RUN 10
201-292 UNPRICED SILVER LEG PRINT RUN 15
PLAYERS HAVE MULTIPLE CARDS OF EQUAL VALUE
1 Brett Favre 10.00 25.00
2 Brett Favre 10.00 25.00
3 LaDainian Tomlinson 5.00 12.00
4 LaDainian Tomlinson 5.00 12.00
5 LaDainian Tomlinson 5.00 12.00
6 LaDainian Tomlinson 5.00 12.00
7 Jay Cutler 3.00 8.00
8 Jay Cutler 3.00 8.00
9 Jay Cutler 3.00 8.00
10 Jay Cutler 3.00 8.00
11 Drew Brees 5.00 12.00
12 Drew Brees 5.00 12.00
13 Drew Brees 5.00 12.00
14 Drew Brees 5.00 12.00
15 Matt Forte 3.00 8.00
16 Matt Forte 3.00 8.00
17 Matt Forte 3.00 8.00
18 Matt Forte 3.00 8.00
19 Darren McFadden 5.00 12.00
20 Darren McFadden 5.00 12.00
21 Darren McFadden 5.00 12.00
22 Darren McFadden 5.00 12.00
23 Ben Roethlisberger 5.00 12.00
24 Ben Roethlisberger 5.00 12.00
27 Brett Favre 10.00 25.00
29 Peyton Manning 12.00 30.00
30 Peyton Manning 12.00 30.00
31 Peyton Manning 12.00 30.00
32 Peyton Manning 12.00 30.00
33 Tony Romo 4.00 10.00
34 Tony Romo 4.00 10.00
35 Tony Romo 4.00 10.00
36 Tony Romo 4.00 10.00
37 Devin Hester 4.00 10.00
38 Devin Hester 4.00 10.00
39 Devin Hester 4.00 10.00
40 Devin Hester 4.00 10.00
41 Eli Manning 4.00 10.00
42 Eli Manning 4.00 10.00
43 Eli Manning 4.00 10.00
44 Eli Manning 4.00 10.00
45 A.J. Hawk 3.00 8.00
46 A.J. Hawk 3.00 8.00
47 A.J. Hawk 3.00 8.00
48 A.J. Hawk 3.00 8.00
53 Dallas Clark 3.00 8.00
54 Dallas Clark 3.00 8.00
55 Dallas Clark 3.00 8.00
56 Dallas Clark 3.00 8.00
57 Larry Fitzgerald 4.00 10.00
58 Larry Fitzgerald 4.00 10.00
59 Larry Fitzgerald 4.00 10.00
60 Larry Fitzgerald 4.00 10.00
61 Philip Rivers 5.00 12.00
62 Philip Rivers 5.00 12.00
63 Philip Rivers 5.00 12.00
64 Philip Rivers 5.00 12.00
65 Brian Westbrook 3.00 8.00
68 Brian Westbrook 3.00 8.00
69 Tom Brady 15.00 40.00
70 Tom Brady 15.00 40.00
71 Tom Brady 15.00 40.00
72 Tom Brady 15.00 40.00
76 Clinton Portis 3.00 8.00
77 Marvin Harrison 4.00 10.00
78 Marvin Harrison 4.00 10.00
79 Marvin Harrison 4.00 10.00
80 Marvin Harrison 4.00 10.00
81 Aaron Rodgers 10.00 25.00
82 Aaron Rodgers 10.00 25.00
83 Aaron Rodgers 10.00 25.00
84 Aaron Rodgers 10.00 25.00
89 Steven Jackson 3.00 8.00
90 Steven Jackson 3.00 8.00
91 Steven Jackson 3.00 8.00
92 Steven Jackson 3.00 8.00
93 Reggie Wayne 4.00 10.00
94 Reggie Wayne 4.00 10.00
95 Reggie Wayne 4.00 10.00
96 Reggie Wayne 4.00 10.00
97 Calvin Johnson 5.00 12.00
98 Calvin Johnson 5.00 12.00
99 Calvin Johnson 5.00 12.00
100 Calvin Johnson 5.00 12.00
402 Peyton Manning ART/15
404 Devin Hester ART/15
405 Eli Manning ART/15
407 Calvin Johnson ART/15
408 LaDainian Tomlinson ART/15
413 Plaxico Burress ART/15
417 Jay Cutler ART/15
418 Drew Brees ART/15
420 Matt Forte ART/15
421 Paul Hornung ART/5
423 Jerry Kramer ART/5
425 Mike Singletary ART/5
426 Don Maynard ART/5
429 Emmitt Smith ART/5
433 Jack Ham ART/5
437 Troy Aikman ART/5
440 Earl Campbell ART/5
471 B.Favre/J.Namath/25 30.00 60.00
472 E.Manning/Manning/25 20.00 40.00
474 E.Manning/T.Brady/25 15.00 40.00
475 M.Harrison/R.Wayne/25 8.00 20.00
476 T.Romo/T.Aikman/25 15.00 40.00
479 E.Manning/T.Romo/25 10.00 25.00
480 L.Tomlinson/P.Rivers/25 8.00 20.00
481 B.Sanders/G.Howe/150 12.00 30.00
483 T.Brady/R.Bourque/150 10.00 25.00
484 E.Manning/M.Messier/150 10.00 25.00
485 Roethlis/E.Malkin/150 12.00 30.00
486 Bradshaw/M.Lemieux/150 15.00 40.00
488 T.Romo/M.Modano/150 8.00 20.00

2009 Upper Deck Heroes Jerseys Retail Blue

RANDOM INSERTS IN RETAIL PACKS
RJAC Andre Caldwell 2.50 6.00
RJAG Anthony Gonzalez 2.50 6.00
RJAS Alex Smith 4.00 10.00
RJBE Braylon Edwards 2.50 6.00
RJBQ Brady Quinn 2.50 6.00
RJCH Chad Henne 3.00 8.00
RJCJ Chris Johnson 2.50 6.00
RJDA Donnie Avery 2.50 6.00
RJDC DeSean Jackson 3.00 8.00
RJDK Dustin Keller 2.50 6.00
RJDM Darren McFadden 4.00 10.00
RJDS Dexter Jackson 2.50 6.00
RJDT Devin Thomas 2.50 6.00
RJED Early Doucet 3.00 8.00
RJER Eddie Royal 2.50 6.00
RJGD Glenn Dorsey 2.50 6.00
RJJC Jamaal Charles 3.00 8.00
RJJF Joe Flacco 3.00 8.00
RJJH James Hardy 3.00 8.00
RJJL Jake Long 2.50 6.00
RJJN Jordy Nelson 3.00 8.00
RJJR JaMarcus Russell 2.50 6.00
RJJS Jerome Simpson 2.50 6.00
RJJT Jonathan Stewart 2.50 6.00
RJKK Kevin Kolb 2.50 6.00
RJKS Kevin Smith 2.50 6.00
RJLS Limas Sweed 3.00 8.00
RJMF Matt Forte 2.50 6.00
RJMK Malcolm Kelly 2.50 6.00
RJMM Mario Manningham 2.50 6.00
RJRR Ray Rice 2.50 6.00
RJSS Steve Slaton 2.50 6.00
RJTE Trent Edwards 2.50 6.00
RJTJ Tarvaris Jackson 3.00 8.00
RJTS Troy Smith 3.00 8.00
RJVY Vince Young 2.50 6.00

1999 Upper Deck HoloGrFX

Released as a 89-card set, 1999 Upper Deck HoloGrFX was comprised of 60-veteran cards and 29-rookies seeded one every two packs. Base cards are all-foil and feature a laser-etching effect in the background. Card #90 (Michael Bishop) was not released in packs, but at least one copy surfaced in the marketplace after the intitial release. It has an embossed image of a face that was added as part of the method used by the printer to identify cards to be pulled from the pack-out process.

COMPLETE SET (89) 12.50 30.00
1 Jake Plummer .15 .40
2 Jamal Anderson .20 .50
3 Priest Holmes .15 .40
4 Antowain Smith .15 .40
5 Doug Flutie .25 .60
6 Tim Biakabutuka .20 .50
7 Curtis Enis .15 .40
8 Corey Dillon .15 .40
9 Darnay Scott .15 .40
10 Leslie Shepherd .15 .40
11 Troy Aikman .30 .75
12 Emmitt Smith .40 1.00
13 Michael Irvin .25 .60
14 Terrell Davis .20 .50
15 Shannon Sharpe .20 .50
16 Rod Smith .20 .50
17 Barry Sanders .40 1.00
18 Charlie Batch .15 .40
19 Herman Moore .20 .50
20 Brett Favre .50 1.25
21 Dorsey Levens .20 .50
22 Antonio Freeman .20 .50
23 Peyton Manning .75 2.00
24 Mark Brunell .20 .50
25 Fred Taylor .15 .40
26 Jimmy Smith .20 .50
27 Andre Rison .20 .50
28 Tony Gonzalez .20 .50
29 Dan Marino .50 1.25
30 Karim Abdul-Jabbar .15 .40
31 Randy Moss .20 .50
32 Randall Cunningham .20 .50
33 Drew Bledsoe .20 .50
34 Terry Glenn .20 .50
35 Cameron Cleeland .15 .40
36 Andre Hastings .15 .40
37 Amani Toomer .15 .40
38 Kent Graham .15 .40
39 Curtis Martin .20 .50
40 Keyshawn Johnson .20 .50
41 Vinny Testaverde .15 .40
42 Napoleon Kaufman .15 .40
43 Tim Brown .25 .60
44 Duce Staley .15 .40
45 Kordell Stewart .15 .40
46 Jerome Bettis .25 .60
47 Marshall Faulk .20 .50
48 Natrone Means .20 .50
49 Ryan Leaf .20 .50
50 Steve Young .30 .75
51 Jerry Rice .60 1.50
52 Terrell Owens .20 .50
53 Joey Galloway .20 .50
54 Ricky Watters .20 .50
55 Jon Kitna .15 .40
56 Warrick Dunn .15 .40
57 Trent Dilfer .15 .40
58 Steve McNair .20 .50
59 Eddie George .20 .50
60 Brad Johnson .20 .50
61 Tim Couch RC .50 1.25
62 Donovan McNabb RC 2.50 6.00
63 Akili Smith RC .40 1.00
64 Edgerrin James RC .60 1.50
65 Ricky Williams RC .60 1.50
66 Torry Holt RC .75 2.00
67 Champ Bailey RC .75 2.00
68 David Boston RC .40 1.00
69 Daunte Culpepper RC .60 1.50
70 Cade McNown RC .40 1.00
71 Troy Edwards RC .40 1.00
72 Kevin Johnson RC .50 1.25
73 James Johnson RC .40 1.00
74 Rob Konrad RC .40 1.00
75 Kevin Faulk RC .40 1.00
76 Shaun King RC .40 1.00
77 Peerless Price RC .40 1.00
78 Mike Cloud RC .40 1.00
79 Jermaine Fazande RC .40 1.00
80 D'Wayne Bates RC .40 1.00
81 Brock Huard RC .40 1.00
82 Marty Booker RC .40 1.00
83 Karsten Bailey RC .40 1.00
84 Al Wilson RC .60 1.50
85 Joe Germaine RC .50 1.25
86 Dameane Douglas RC .40 1.00
87 Sedrick Irvin RC .40 1.00
88 Aaron Brooks RC .50 1.25
89 Cecil Collins RC .40 1.00
90 Michael Bishop SP

1999 Upper Deck HoloGrFX Ausome

MPLETE SET (89) 75.00 150.00
*AUSOME STARS: 1.5X TO 4X HI COL.
AUSOME VETERAN STATED ODDS 1:8
*AUSOME RCs: .6X TO 1.5X
AUSOME DRAFT PICK STATED ODDS 1:17

1999 Upper Deck HoloGrFX 24/7

ndomly inserted in packs at the rate of one in three, this 15-card set features quarterbacks, speed burners and touchdown makers. Card fronts are holographic and feature the 24/7 logo. A gold parallel version of this set was relelased also.

COMPLETE SET (15) 12.50 30.00
STATED ODDS 1:3
*GOLD CARDS: 3X TO 8X HI COL.
GOLD STATED ODDS 1:105
N1 Jake Plummer .25 .60
N2 Emmitt Smith 1.25 3.00
N3 Terrell Davis .40 1.00
N4 Peyton Manning 2.00 5.00
N5 Drew Bledsoe .75 2.00
N6 Troy Aikman 1.25 3.00
N7 Ricky Williams 1.00 2.50
N8 Keyshawn Johnson .40 1.00
N9 Akili Smith .30 .75
N10 Eddie George .40 1.00
N11 Edgerrin James 2.00 5.00
N12 David Boston .40 1.00
N13 Cade McNown .30 .75
N14 Jerome Bettis .40 1.00
N15 Herman Moore .25 .60

1999 Upper Deck HoloGrFX Future Fame

ndomly inserted in packs at the rate of one in 34, this 6-card set features NFL players on a unique holographic patterned background. A gold parallel version of this set was relelased also.

COMPLETE SET (6) 15.00 40.00
STATED ODDS 1:34
*GOLD CARDS: 1.2X TO 3X BASIC INSERTS
GOLD STATED ODDS 1:431
FF1 John Elway 4.00 10.00
FF2 Dan Marino 4.00 10.00
FF3 Emmitt Smith 2.50 6.00
FF4 Randy Moss 3.00 8.00
FF5 Tim Brown .75 2.00
FF6 Barry Sanders 4.00 10.00

1999 Upper Deck HoloGrFX Star View

ndomly inserted in packs at the rate of one in 17, this 9-card set showcases marquee football players on a holographic card stock. A gold parallel version of this set was relelased also.

COMPLETE SET (9) 15.00 30.00
STATED ODDS 1:17
*GOLD: 1.2X TO 3X BASIC INSERTS
GOLD STATED ODDS 1:210
S1 Dan Marino 2.50 6.00
S2 Brett Favre 2.50 6.00
S3 Barry Sanders 2.50 6.00
S4 Terrell Davis .50 1.25
S5 Mark Brunell .50 1.25
S6 Eddie George .50 1.25
S7 Fred Taylor .50 1.25
S8 Tim Couch .50 1.25
S9 Randy Moss 2.00 5.00

1999 Upper Deck HoloGrFX UD Authentics

ndomly inserted in packs at the rate of one in 432, this 19-card set features player photos paired with an authentic autograph on the card front.

STATED ODDS 1:432
AS Akili Smith 10.00 25.00
BH Brock Huard 10.00 25.00
CM Cade McNown 12.00 30.00
DC Daunte Culpepper 10.00 25.00
DM Donovan McNabb 25.00 60.00
EG Eddie George 12.00 30.00
EJ Edgerrin James 15.00 40.00
EM Eric Moulds 10.00 25.00
JA Jamal Anderson 12.00 30.00
JP Jake Plummer 12.00 30.00
JR Jerry Rice 60.00 120.00
PM Peyton Manning 50.00 100.00
RW Ricky Williams 15.00 40.00
SK Shaun King 10.00 25.00
SY Steve Young 30.00 80.00
TA Troy Aikman 50.00 100.00
TC Tim Couch 12.00 30.00
TD Terrell Davis 15.00 40.00
TH Torry Holt 10.00 25.00

2002 Upper Deck Honor Roll

Released in late-October 2002 as a retail only product, this set contains 90 veterans and 150 rookies. The rookies were serial #'d to 1375.

COMP.SET w/o SP's (90) 10.00 25.00
91-180 ROOKIE PRINT RUN 1375
1 Jake Plummer .15 .40
2 David Boston .15 .40
3 Michael Vick .20 .50
4 Warrick Dunn .15 .40
5 Jamal Lewis .20 .50
6 Chris Redman .15 .40
7 Drew Bledsoe .20 .50
8 Travis Henry .15 .40
9 Chris Weinke .15 .40
10 Anthony Thomas .20 .50
11 Marty Booker .15 .40
12 Corey Dillon .15 .40
13 Michael Westbrook .15 .40
14 Tim Couch .15 .40
15 Emmitt Smith .40 1.00
16 Quincy Carter .15 .40
17 Brian Griese .15 .40
18 Terrell Davis .20 .50
19 Az-Zahir Hakim .15 .40
20 Brett Favre .50 1.25
21 Ahman Green .20 .50
22 Corey Bradford .15 .40
23 Edgerrin James .20 .50
24 Peyton Manning .60 1.50
25 Stacey Mack .15 .40
26 Mark Brunell .20 .50
27 Trent Green .15 .40
28 Priest Holmes .15 .40
29 Ricky Williams .20 .50
30 Jay Fiedler .20 .50
31 Daunte Culpepper .20 .50
32 Randy Moss .20 .50
33 Antowain Smith .20 .50
34 Tom Brady 1.25 3.00
35 Aaron Brooks .15 .40
36 Deuce McAllister .20 .50
37 Kerry Collins .15 .40
38 Ron Dayne .20 .50
39 Curtis Martin .20 .50
40 Vinny Testaverde .15 .40
41 Jerry Rice .50 1.25
42 Rich Gannon .20 .50
43 Donovan McNabb .20 .50
44 Duce Staley .15 .40
45 Jerome Bettis .25 .60
46 Kordell Stewart .15 .40
47 Doug Flutie .20 .50
48 LaDainian Tomlinson .25 .60
49 Jeff Garcia .15 .40
50 Terrell Owens .20 .50
51 Darrell Jackson .20 .50
52 Shaun Alexander .15 .40
53 Kurt Warner .20 .50
54 Marshall Faulk .20 .50
55 Keyshawn Johnson .20 .50
56 Brad Johnson .20 .50
57 Eddie George .20 .50
58 Steve McNair .20 .50
59 Stephen Davis .15 .40
60 Rod Gardner .15 .40
61 Plummer/T.Jones/Boston .12 .30
62 Vick/Dunn/Jefferson .15 .40
63 Redman/J.Lewis/Taylor .15 .40
64 Bledsoe/Henry/Price .15 .40
65 Miller/A.Thomas/Booker .15 .40
66 Kitna/Dillon/Warrick .12 .30
67 Couch/J.White/K.Johnson .12 .30
68 Carter/Smith/Ismail .30 .75
69 Griese/T.Davis/R.Smith .15 .40
70 McMahon/Stewart/Hakim .12 .30
71 Favre/Green/Glenn .40 1.00
72 Manning/James/Harrison .50 1.25
73 Brunell/F.Taylor/J.Smith .15 .40
74 T.Green/Holmes/Morton .15 .40
75 Fiedler/R.Williams/Chambers .15 .40
76 Culpepper/Bennett/R.Moss .15 .40
77 Brady/Smith/Brown 1.00 2.50
78 Brooks/McAllister/J.Horn .15 .40
79 Collins/Dayne/Toomer .15 .40
80 Testaverde/Martin/Coles .15 .40
81 Gannon/Brown/Rice .40 1.00
82 McNabb/Staley/Thrash .15 .40
83 K.Stewart/Bettis/H.Ward .20 .50
84 Brees/Tomlinson/Conway .40 1.00
85 Garcia/Hearst/Owens .15 .40
86 Dilfer/Alexander/D.Jackson .15 .40
87 Warner/Faulk/Bruce .20 .50
88 B.Johnson/Pittman/K.Johnson .15 .40
89 McNair/George/D.Mason .15 .40
90 Matthews/S.Davis/Gardner .12 .30
91 Adrian Peterson RC 1.50 4.00
92 Albert Haynesworth RC 2.00 5.00
93 Alex Brown RC 2.00 5.00
94 Andre Davis RC 1.25 3.00
95 Antwoine Womack RC 1.25 3.00
96 Antonio Bryant RC 2.00 5.00
97 Antwaan Randle El RC 1.50 4.00
98 Ashley Lelie RC 1.25 3.00
99 Ed Reed RC 5.00 12.00
100 Brandon Doman RC 1.25 3.00
101 Brian Allen RC 1.25 3.00
102 Najeh Davenport RC 1.25 3.00
103 Brian Westbrook RC 2.50 6.00
104 Chad Hutchinson RC 1.25 3.00
105 Chester Taylor RC 2.00 5.00
106 Cliff Russell RC 1.25 3.00
107 Clinton Portis RC 2.00 5.00
108 Craig Nall RC 1.50 4.00
109 Javin Hunter RC 1.25 3.00
110 Bryan Thomas RC 1.25 3.00
111 Daniel Graham RC 1.50 4.00
112 Daryl Jones RC 1.25 3.00
113 David Carr RC 1.25 3.00
114 David Garrard RC 1.50 4.00
115 Shaun Hill RC 2.00 5.00
116 Deion Branch RC 2.00 5.00
117 Derrick Lewis RC 1.25 3.00
118 DeShaun Foster RC 2.00 5.00
119 Jeff Kelly RC 1.25 3.00
120 Donte Stallworth RC 2.00 5.00
121 Levi Jones RC 1.25 3.00
122 Dwight Freeney RC 2.50 6.00
123 Eric Crouch RC 2.00 5.00
124 Freddie Milons RC 1.25 3.00
125 Jamin Elliott RC 1.25 3.00
126 Herb Haygood RC 1.25 3.00
127 J.T. O'Sullivan RC 1.50 4.00
128 Jabar Gaffney RC 1.25 3.00
129 Jake Schifino RC 1.25 3.00
130 Jason McAddley RC 1.50 4.00
131 Javon Walker RC 2.00 5.00
132 Jeremy Shockey RC 2.00 5.00
133 Jerramy Stevens RC 2.00 5.00
134 Joey Harrington RC 1.25 3.00
135 John Henderson RC 1.50 4.00
136 Jonathan Wells RC 1.50 4.00
137 Josh McCown RC 2.00 5.00
138 Josh Reed RC 1.50 4.00
139 Josh Scobey RC 1.50 4.00
140 Julius Peppers RC 3.00 8.00
141 Kalimba Edwards RC 1.50 4.00
142 Kelly Campbell RC 1.50 4.00
143 Keyuo Craver RC 1.25 3.00
144 Kurt Kittner RC 1.25 3.00
145 Ladell Betts RC 2.00 5.00
146 Lamar Gordon RC 1.50 4.00
147 Larry Ned RC 1.25 3.00
148 Lee Mays RC 1.25 3.00
149 Leonard Henry RC 1.25 3.00
150 Lito Sheppard RC 2.00 5.00
151 Luke Staley RC 1.25 3.00
152 Marquise Walker RC 1.25 3.00
153 Maurice Morris RC 1.50 4.00
154 Darrell Hill RC 1.25 3.00
155 Napoleon Harris RC 1.50 4.00
156 Patrick Ramsey RC 1.50 4.00
157 Kevin Curtis RC 1.25 3.00
158 Phillip Buchanon RC 2.00 5.00
159 Kendall Newson RC 1.25 3.00

160 Quentin Jammer RC	2.00	5.00
161 Randy Fasani RC	1.25	3.00
162 Reche Caldwell RC	1.50	4.00
163 Ricky Williams RC	1.50	4.00
164 Rocky Calmus RC	1.50	4.00
165 Rohan Davey RC	2.00	5.00
166 Ron Johnson RC	1.50	4.00
167 Ronald Curry RC	1.25	3.00
168 Roy Williams RC	1.25	3.00
169 Ryan Sims RC	2.00	5.00
170 Sam Simmons RC	1.25	3.00
171 Seth Burford RC	1.25	3.00
172 T.J. Duckett RC	1.25	3.00
173 Tellis Redmon RC	1.25	3.00
174 Tim Carter RC	1.50	4.00
175 Travis Stephens RC	1.25	3.00
176 Wendell Bryant RC	1.25	3.00
177 Lamont Thompson RC	1.50	4.00
178 William Green RC	1.50	4.00
179 Dennis Johnson RC	1.25	3.00
180 Michael Lewis RC	1.50	4.00

2002 Upper Deck Honor Roll Gold

*VETS 1-90: 15X TO 40X BASIC CARDS
*ROOKIES 91-180: 2.5X TO 6X
STATED PRINT RUN 25 SER.#'d SETS

2002 Upper Deck Honor Roll Clutch Performers Jerseys

Inserted at a rate of 1:72, this set focuses on the top clutch performers in the NFL.
STATED ODDS 1:72

CPBO David Boston	3.00	8.00
CPCC Cris Carter	5.00	12.00
CPCD Corey Dillon	3.00	8.00
CPEJ Edgerrin James	4.00	10.00
CPJP Jake Plummer	3.00	8.00
CPMH Marvin Harrison	4.00	10.00
CPPM Peyton Manning	12.00	30.00
CPRM Randy Moss	4.00	10.00
CPVT Vinny Testaverde	3.00	8.00

2002 Upper Deck Honor Roll Dean's List

serted at a rate of 1:24, this set is composed of three smaller sets - quarterbacks, runningbacks, and wide receivers. In addition, there is a gold parallel version serial #'d to 25.

COMPLETE SET (30)	25.00	60.00

*GOLD/25: 2X TO 5X BASIC INSERTS
GOLD PRINT RUN 25 SER.#'d SETS

DLQ1 Jake Plummer	.60	1.50
DLQ2 Donovan McNabb	.75	2.00
DLQ3 Kurt Warner	.75	2.00
DLQ4 Brett Favre	2.00	5.00
DLQ5 Peyton Manning	2.50	6.00
DLQ6 Rich Gannon	.75	2.00
DLQ7 Daunte Culpepper	.75	2.00
DLQ8 Drew Bledsoe	.75	2.00
DLQ9 Vinny Testaverde	.60	1.50
DLQ10 Jeff Garcia	.60	1.50
DLR1 Marshall Faulk	.75	2.00
DLR2 Edgerrin James	.75	2.00
DLR3 Curtis Martin	.75	2.00
DLR4 Stephen Davis	.60	1.50
DLR5 Eddie George	.75	2.00
DLR6 Ricky Williams	.75	2.00
DLR7 Jerome Bettis	1.00	2.50
DLR8 Terrell Davis	.75	2.00
DLR9 Emmitt Smith	1.50	4.00
DLR10 Warrick Dunn	.60	1.50
DLW1 Randy Moss	.75	2.00
DLW2 Wayne Chrebet	.60	1.50
DLW3 Marvin Harrison	.75	2.00
DLW4 Jimmy Smith	.75	2.00
DLW5 Jerry Rice	2.00	5.00
DLW6 Tim Brown	1.00	2.50
DLW7 Keyshawn Johnson	.75	2.00
DLW8 David Boston	.60	1.50
DLW9 Terrell Owens	.75	2.00
DLW10 Isaac Bruce	1.00	2.50

2002 Upper Deck Honor Roll Field Generals Dual Jerseys

Inserted at a rate of 1:240, this set features dual player cards with two jersey swatches.
STATED ODDS 1:240

FGCH D.Carr/J.Harrington	3.00	8.00
FGDC R.Davey/D.Carr	5.00	12.00
FGHM J.Harrington/J.McCown	5.00	12.00
FGHR J.Harrington/P.Ramsey	4.00	10.00
FGMG J.McCown/D.Garrard	5.00	12.00

2002 Upper Deck Honor Roll Great Connections Dual Jerseys

Inserted at a rate of 1:240, this set features dual player cards with two jersey swatches. Each set of players are teammates who make great connections on and off the field.
STATED ODDS 1:240

GCBF D.Flutie/D.Brees	10.00	25.00
GCCJ L.Jordan/W.Chrebet	4.00	10.00
GCGM J.Morton/T.Green	4.00	10.00
GCRB L.Betts/P.Ramsey	5.00	12.00
GCSF D.Flutie/J.Seau	4.00	10.00

2002 Upper Deck Honor Roll Letterman Autographs

Inserted at a rate of 1:480, this set features authentic autographs from many of the NFL's best young players.
STATED ODDS 1:480

HRLAT Anthony Thomas	12.00	30.00
HRLBR Drew Brees	30.00	80.00
HRLCW Chris Weinke	10.00	25.00
HRLLT LaDainian Tomlinson	15.00	40.00
HRLLLP Luke Petitgout	10.00	25.00
HRLMV Michael Vick	20.00	50.00
HRLPM Peyton Manning	50.00	100.00
HRLRC Rosevelt Colvin	15.00	40.00
HRLRW Roy Williams	8.00	20.00

2002 Upper Deck Honor Roll Offensive Threats Dual Jerseys

Inserted at a rate of 1:240, this set features dual player cards with two jersey swatches.
STATED ODDS 1:240

OTBF B.Favre/M.Brunell	10.00	25.00
OTFC C.Conway/D.Flutie	4.00	10.00
OTGS J.Stokes/J.Garcia	3.00	8.00
OTMB M.Brunell/P.Manning	12.00	30.00
OTRW C.Woodson/J.Rice	10.00	25.00

2002 Upper Deck Honor Roll Rookie Honor Roll Jerseys

This set features top rookies from the 2002 class along with jersey swatches. Cards were inserted at a rate of 1:72.
STATED ODDS 1:72

RHRAL Ashley Lelie	2.50	6.00
RHRDC David Carr	2.50	6.00
RHRDG David Garrard	3.00	8.00
RHRDS Donte Stallworth	4.00	10.00
RHREL Antwaan Randle El	3.00	8.00
RHRJH Joey Harrington	2.50	6.00
RHRJM Josh McCown	4.00	10.00
RHRPR Patrick Ramsey	3.00	8.00
RHRRD Rohan Davey	4.00	10.00

2002 Upper Deck Honor Roll Sophomore Standouts

Inserted at a rate of 1:24, this set is composed of three smaller sets - quarterbacks, runningbacks, and wide receivers. There is also a gold parallel version #'d to 25.

COMPLETE SET (30)	12.00	30.00

SSQ1-SSQ10 STATED ODDS 1:24
SSR1-SSR10 STATED ODDS 1:24
SSW1-SSW10 STATED ODDS 1:24
*GOLD/25: 2.5X TO 6X BASIC INSERTS
GOLD STATED PRINT RUN 25 SER.#'d SETS

SSQ1 Michael Vick	.75	2.00
SSQ2 Tom Brady	5.00	12.00
SSQ3 Chris Redman	.60	1.50
SSQ4 Quincy Carter	.60	1.50
SSQ5 Mike McMahon	.60	1.50
SSQ6 Chris Weinke	.60	1.50
SSQ7 Aaron Brooks	.60	1.50
SSQ8 Drew Brees	2.00	5.00
SSQ9 Chad Pennington	.60	1.50
SSQ10 Sage Rosenfels	.75	2.00
SSR1 LaDainian Tomlinson	1.00	2.50
SSR2 Anthony Thomas	.75	2.00
SSR3 Shaun Alexander	.60	1.50
SSR4 James Jackson	.60	1.50
SSR5 Dominic Rhodes	.60	1.50
SSR6 Thomas Jones	.60	1.50
SSR7 Michael Bennett	.60	1.50
SSR8 Elvis Joseph	.60	1.50
SSR9 Travis Henry	.60	1.50
SSR10 Kevan Barlow	.60	1.50
SSW1 Chris Chambers	.60	1.50
SSW2 Snoop Minnis	.60	1.50
SSW3 Plaxico Burress	.60	1.50
SSW4 Quincy Morgan	.60	1.50
SSW5 Robert Ferguson	.75	2.00
SSW6 Travis Taylor	.60	1.50
SSW7 Santana Moss	.75	2.00
SSW8 Rod Gardner	.60	1.50
SSW9 David Terrell	.60	1.50
SSW10 Freddie Mitchell	.60	1.50

2002 Upper Deck Honor Roll Students of the Game

Inserted at a rate of 1:24, this set consists of three smaller sets featuring rookie quarterbacks, running backs, and wide receivers. There is also a gold parallel that is serial #'d to 25.

COMPLETE SET (30)	12.00	30.00

SGQ1-SGQ10 STATED ODDS 1:24
SGR1-SGR10 STATED ODDS 1:24
SGW1-SGW10 STATED ODDS 1:24
*GOLD/25: 2.5X TO 6X BASIC INSERTS
GOLD PRINT RUN 25 SER.#'d SETS

SGQ1 David Carr	.50	1.25
SGQ2 Joey Harrington	.50	1.25
SGQ3 Patrick Ramsey	.60	1.50
SGQ4 Josh McCown	.75	2.00
SGQ5 Kurt Kittner	.50	1.25
SGQ6 Randy Fasani	.50	1.25
SGQ7 J.T. O'Sullivan	.60	1.50
SGQ8 Rohan Davey	.75	2.00
SGQ9 Chad Hutchinson	.50	1.25
SGQ10 David Garrard	.60	1.50
SGR1 William Green	.60	1.50
SGR2 T.J. Duckett	.50	1.25
SGR3 DeShaun Foster	.75	2.00
SGR4 Clinton Portis	.75	2.00
SGR5 Maurice Morris	.60	1.50
SGR6 Travis Stephens	.50	1.25
SGR7 Jonathan Wells	.60	1.50
SGR8 Lamar Gordon	.60	1.50
SGR9 LaDell Betts	.75	2.00
SGR10 Brian Westbrook	1.00	2.50
SGW1 Ashley Lelie	.50	1.25
SGW2 Donte Stallworth	.75	2.00
SGW3 Javon Walker	.75	2.00
SGW4 Josh Reed	.60	1.50
SGW5 Jabar Gaffney	.50	1.25
SGW6 Reche Caldwell	.60	1.50
SGW7 Antonio Bryant	.75	2.00
SGW8 Tim Carter	.60	1.50
SGW9 Marquise Walker	.50	1.25
SGW10 Ron Johnson	.60	1.50

2002 Upper Deck Honor Roll Up and Coming Jerseys

Inserted at a rate of 1:72, this set features some of the NFL's young superstars along with a jersey swatch.
STATED ODDS 1:72

UCBO David Boston	2.50	6.00
UCBR Drew Brees	8.00	20.00
UCLC Laveranues Coles	3.00	8.00
UCRD Ron Dayne	3.00	8.00
UCRM Randy Moss	3.00	8.00
UCSM Santana Moss	3.00	8.00
UCTC Tim Couch	2.50	6.00
UCTJ Thomas Jones	2.50	6.00

2003 Upper Deck Honor Roll

Released in September of 2003, this set contains 190 cards including 100 base cards, 30 short prints, and 60 rookies. The short prints were inserted at a rate of 1:6. Please note that rookie cards can be found in both the base cards and the short prints. Rookies 131-190 are serial numbered to 2003. Boxes contained 24 packs of 5 cards. Pack SRP was $2.99.

COMP.SET w/o SP's (100)	10.00	25.00

131-190 ROOKIE/2003 ODDS 1:8

1 Corey Dillon	.20	.50
2 Kelley Washington RC	.25	.60
3 Peter Warrick	.20	.50
4 Joey Harrington	.20	.50
5 Az-Zahir Hakim	.20	.50
6 David Kircus RC	.30	.75
7 Jabar Gaffney	.20	.50
8 Domanick Davis RC	.30	.75
9 Dave Ragone RC	.25	.60
10 Kordell Stewart	.20	.50
11 Justin Gage RC	.30	.75
12 Bobby Wade RC	.30	.75
13 Anthony Thomas	.25	.60
14 Chad Hutchinson	.20	.50
15 Antonio Bryant	.20	.50
16 Bradie James RC	.40	1.00
17 Josh McCown	.25	.60
18 Jeff Blake	.25	.60
19 Kenny King RC	.30	.75
20 Daunte Culpepper	.25	.60
21 Michael Bennett	.20	.50
22 Randy Moss	.25	.60
23 Onterrio Smith RC	.25	.60
24 Mark Brunell	.25	.60
25 George Wrighster RC	.25	.60
26 Fred Taylor	.20	.50
27 Jake Delhomme	.20	.50
28 Mike Seidman RC	.25	.60
29 Walter Young RC	.25	.60
30 Chris Redman	.20	.50
31 Jamal Lewis	.25	.60
32 Ovie Mughelli RC	.30	.75
33 Koren Robinson	.25	.60
34 Shaun Alexander	.20	.50
35 Taco Wallace RC	.25	.60
36 Kurt Warner	.25	.60
37 Kevin Curtis RC	.25	.60
38 Torry Holt	.25	.60
39 Patrick Ramsey	.25	.60
40 Laveranues Coles	.20	.50
41 Gibran Hamdan RC	.25	.60
42 Drew Bledsoe	.25	.60
43 Jerel Myers RC	.25	.60
44 Eric Moulds	.20	.50
45 Drew Brees	.30	.75
46 David Boston	.20	.50
47 LaDainian Tomlinson	.30	.75
48 Reche Caldwell	.20	.50
49 Priest Holmes	.20	.50
50 Tony Gonzalez	.25	.60
51 Mike Pinkard RC	.25	.60
52 Aaron Brooks	.20	.50
53 Deuce McAllister	.25	.60
54 Montrae Holland RC	.30	.75
55 Jay Fiedler	.20	.50
56 Junior Seau	.25	.60
57 Chris Chambers	.20	.50
58 Ricky Williams	.25	.60
59 Tom Brady	1.25	3.00
60 Troy Brown	.20	.50
61 Antowain Smith	.25	.60
62 Jake Plummer	.20	.50
63 Cecil Sapp RC	.25	.60
64 Adrian Madise RC	.25	.60
65 Tim Couch	.20	.50
66 William Green	.20	.50
67 Kelly Holcomb	.20	.50
68 Chad Pennington	.20	.50
69 Santana Moss	.25	.60
70 Curtis Martin	.25	.60
71 Michael Vick	.25	.60
72 LaTarence Dunbar RC	.25	.60
73 Peerless Price	.20	.50
74 Marvin Harrison	.25	.60
75 Peyton Manning	.75	2.00
76 Edgerrin James	.25	.60
77 Jeremy Shockey	.20	.50
78 Tiki Barber	.25	.60
79 Kevin Walter RC	.60	1.50
80 Jeff Garcia	.20	.50
81 Terrell Owens	.25	.60
82 Andrew Williams RC	.25	.60
83 Tommy Maddox	.20	.50
84 Plaxico Burress	.20	.50
85 Brian St.Pierre RC	.25	.60
86 Steve McNair	.25	.60
87 Eddie George	.25	.60
88 Derrick Mason	.20	.50
89 Brett Favre	.60	1.50
90 Ahman Green	.25	.60
91 Donald Driver	.25	.60
92 Donovan McNabb	.25	.60
93 Brian Dawkins	.30	.75
94 Norman LeJeune RC	.25	.60
95 Jerry Rice	.60	1.50
96 Rich Gannon	.25	.60
97 Siddeeq Shabazz RC	.25	.60
98 DeWayne White RC	.25	.60
99 Brad Johnson	.25	.60
100 Keyshawn Johnson	.30	.75
101 Chad Johnson SP	.60	1.50
102 Artose Pinner SP RC	.75	2.00
103 David Carr SP	.60	1.50
104 Brian Urlacher SP	1.00	2.50
105 Jason Witten SP RC	3.00	8.00
106 Emmitt Smith SP	1.50	4.00
107 Nate Burleson SP RC	1.00	2.50
108 LaBrandon Toefield SP RC	.75	2.00
109 Julius Peppers SP	1.00	2.50
110 Musa Smith SP RC	.75	2.00
111 Seneca Wallace SP RC	1.00	2.50
112 Marshall Faulk SP	.75	2.00
113 Brad Banks SP RC	1.00	2.50
114 Travis Henry SP	.60	1.50
115 Mike Scifres SP RC	.75	2.00
116 J.R. Tolver SP RC	1.00	2.50
117 Kliff Kingsbury SP RC	1.25	3.00
118 Clinton Portis SP	.60	1.50
119 Kevin Johnson SP	.60	1.50
120 Brooks Bollinger SP RC	1.00	2.50
121 Terrence Edwards SP RC	.75	2.00
122 Steve Sciullo SP RC	.75	2.00
123 Ken Dorsey SP RC	1.00	2.50
124 Jerome Bettis SP	1.00	2.50
125 Chris Brown SP RC	.75	2.00
126 Carl Ford SP RC	.75	2.00
127 Billy McMullen SP RC	.75	2.00
128 Doug Gabriel SP RC	1.00	2.50
129 Earnest Graham SP RC	1.25	3.00
130 Chris Simms SP RC	1.50	4.00
131 Carson Palmer RC	2.00	5.00
132 Charles Rogers RC	1.25	3.00
133 Andre Johnson RC	2.50	6.00
134 DeWayne Robertson RC	1.25	3.00
135 Terence Newman RC	1.50	4.00
136 Johnathan Sullivan RC	1.00	2.50
137 Byron Leftwich RC	1.25	3.00
138 Jordan Gross RC	1.00	2.50
139 Kevin Williams RC	1.50	4.00
140 Terrell Suggs RC	1.25	3.00
141 Marcus Trufant RC	1.25	3.00
142 Jimmy Kennedy RC	1.25	3.00
143 Ty Warren RC	1.25	3.00
144 Michael Haynes RC	1.00	2.50
145 Jerome McDougle RC	1.00	2.50
146 J.T. Wall RC	1.00	2.50
147 Bryant Johnson RC	1.50	4.00
148 Calvin Pace RC	1.00	2.50
149 Kyle Boller RC	1.00	2.50
150 Quentin Griffin RC	1.25	3.00
151 Lee Suggs RC	1.00	2.50
152 Rex Grossman RC	1.25	3.00
153 Willis McGahee RC	1.25	3.00
154 Dallas Clark RC	1.50	4.00
155 William Joseph RC	1.00	2.50
156 Kwame Harris RC	1.00	2.50
157 Larry Johnson RC	1.25	3.00
158 Andre Woolfolk RC	1.00	2.50
159 Nick Barnett RC	1.50	4.00
160 Dahrran Diedrick RC	1.00	2.50
161 Teyo Johnson RC	1.25	3.00
162 Justin Fargas RC	1.50	4.00
163 Eric Steinbach RC	1.00	2.50
164 Boss Bailey RC	1.25	3.00
165 Charles Tillman RC	5.00	12.00
166 Eugene Wilson RC	1.50	4.00
167 Jonathan Stinchcomb RC	1.25	3.00
168 Al Johnson RC	1.25	3.00
169 Rashean Mathis RC	1.00	2.50
170 Keenan Howry RC	1.00	2.50
171 Ben Joppru RC	1.00	2.50
172 Rashad Moore RC	1.00	2.50
173 Shaun McDonald RC	1.25	3.00
174 Taylor Jacobs RC	1.00	2.50
175 Bethel Johnson RC	1.00	2.50
176 Matt Wilhelm RC	1.25	3.00
177 Kawika Mitchell RC	1.50	4.00
178 Chris Kelsay RC	1.25	3.00
179 Lon Sheriff RC	1.00	2.50
180 Ricky Manning RC	1.25	3.00
181 Terry Pierce RC	1.00	2.50
182 Chaun Thompson RC	1.00	2.50
183 Victor Hobson RC	1.00	2.50
184 Anquan Boldin RC	1.50	4.00
185 Justin Griffith RC	1.25	3.00
186 Osi Umenyiora RC	2.00	5.00
187 Brandon Lloyd RC	1.50	4.00
188 Michael Doss RC	1.50	4.00
189 Alonzo Jackson RC	1.00	2.50
190 Tyrone Calico RC	1.00	2.50

2003 Upper Deck Honor Roll Gold

*VETS 1-100: 12X TO 30X BASIC CARDS
*ROOKIES 1-100: 10X TO 25X
*VETS 101-130: 4X TO 10X BASIC CARDS
*ROOKIES 101-130: 3X TO 8X
*ROOKIES 131-190: 2.5X TO 6X
STATED PRINT RUN 25 SERIAL #'d SETS

2003 Upper Deck Honor Roll Silver

*VETS 1-100: 3X TO 8X BASIC CARDS
*ROOKIES 1-100: 2.5X TO 6X
*VETS 101-130: 1X TO 2.5X BASIC CARDS
*ROOKIES 101-130: .8X TO 2X
*ROOKIES 131-190: .6X TO 1.5X
OVERALL PARALLEL ODDS 1:24
SILVER PRINT RUN 200 SER.#'d SETS

2003 Upper Deck Honor Roll Dean's List

STATED ODDS 1:13
*SILVER/200: .5X TO 1.2X BASIC JSY
SILVER PRINT RUN 200 SER.#'d SETS
*GOLD/25: 1X TO 2.5X BASIC JSY
GOLD PRINT RUN 25 SER.#'d SETS

DLAN Mike Anderson	2.50	6.00
DLBL Byron Leftwich	2.00	5.00
DLBO Kyle Boller	2.50	6.00
DLBS Brandon Stokley	2.50	6.00
DLCB Champ Bailey SP	3.00	8.00
DLCJ Chad Johnson	2.50	6.00
DLCM Chris McAlister	3.00	8.00
DLCS Chris Samuels	2.50	6.00
DLCU Curtis Martin	3.00	8.00
DLDC Dallas Clark	4.00	10.00
DLDM Damerian McCants	2.50	6.00
DLDR Dave Ragone	2.50	6.00
DLDW Dez White SP	2.50	6.00
DLJB Josh Booty	2.50	6.00
DLJK Jevon Kearse SP	2.50	6.00
DLKB Kendrell Bell	2.50	6.00
DLKC Kerry Collins	2.50	6.00
DLKW Kevin Ware	2.50	6.00
DLMA Mike Alstott	2.50	6.00
DLMB Marty Booker	2.50	6.00
DLMC Donovan McNabb SP	3.00	8.00
DLMM Michael McCrary	2.50	6.00
DLMR Marcus Robinson	3.00	8.00
DLMV Michael Vick SP	3.00	8.00
DLOG Olandis Gary	2.50	6.00
DLOP Orlando Pace	2.50	6.00
DLPB Plaxico Burress SP	2.50	6.00
DLPM Peyton Manning SP	10.00	25.00
DLQJ Quentin Jammer	2.50	6.00
DLRG Rex Grossman	2.00	5.00
DLRO DeWayne Robertson	3.00	8.00
DLRW Reggie Wayne	3.00	8.00
DLSA Shaun Alexander	2.50	6.00
DLSC Carson Palmer	3.00	8.00
DLSH Jeremy Shockey	2.50	6.00
DLSI Corey Simon	3.00	8.00
DLSM Sammy Morris	2.50	6.00
DLTB Tiki Barber	3.00	8.00
DLTH Torry Holt	3.00	8.00
DLZT Zach Thomas	3.00	8.00

2003 Upper Deck Honor Roll Letterman Autographs

Inserted into packs at an overall rate of 1:240, this set features authentic player autographs. Please note that James Jackson was issued in packs as an exchange card. A gold parallel version also exists, with each card serial numbered to 25.
OVERALL AUTOGRAPH ODDS 1:240
*GOLD/25: .8X TO 2X BASE AUTO
GOLD PRINT RUN 25 SER.#'d SETS

HRLCJ Chad Johnson	6.00	15.00
HRLDM Deuce McAllister	8.00	20.00
HRLHE Travis Henry	6.00	15.00
HRLJJ James Jackson	6.00	15.00
HRLKB Kevan Barlow	6.00	15.00
HRLMM Snoop Minnis	6.00	15.00
HRLPM Peyton Manning	40.00	80.00
HRLRJ Rudi Johnson	6.00	15.00
HRLTH Todd Heap	6.00	15.00
HRLTM Travis Minor	6.00	15.00

2008 Upper Deck Icons

This set was released on August 27, 2008. The base set consists of 248 cards. Cards 1-100 feature veterans, while cards 101-200 are rookies serial numbered of 750 and cards 201-250 are rookies serial numbered of 999.

COMP.SET w/o RC's (100)	8.00	20.00

ROOKIE/750 PRINT RUN 750 SER.#'d SETS
ROOKIE/999 PRINT RUN 999 SER.#'d SETS

1 Edgerrin James	.25	.60
2 Larry Fitzgerald	.25	.60
3 Matt Leinart	.20	.50
4 Jamal Lewis	.25	.60
5 Aaron Rodgers	.60	1.50
6 Steve McNair	.25	.60
7 Ray Lewis	.30	.75
8 Todd Heap	.20	.50
9 Willis McGahee	.20	.50
10 Marshawn Lynch	.25	.60
11 Roscoe Parrish	.20	.50
12 Trent Edwards	.20	.50
13 DeShaun Foster	.20	.50
14 Julius Peppers	.25	.60
15 Thomas Jones	.20	.50
16 Brian Urlacher	.30	.75
17 Devin Hester	.25	.60
18 Rex Grossman	.20	.50
19 Carson Palmer	.25	.60
20 T.J. Houshmandzadeh	.20	.50
21 Rudi Johnson	.20	.50
22 Derek Anderson	.20	.50
23 Kellen Winslow	.20	.50
24 Braylon Edwards	.20	.50
25 Tony Romo	.25	.60
26 Terrell Owens	.25	.60
27 Marion Barber	.20	.50
28 Brandon Marshall	.25	.60
29 Travis Henry	.20	.50
30 Champ Bailey	.25	.60
31 Calvin Johnson	.30	.75
32 Joseph Addai	.20	.50
33 Jon Kitna	.20	.50
34 Brett Favre	.60	1.50
35 Donald Driver	.25	.60
36 Ryan Grant	.25	.60
37 Greg Jennings	.20	.50
38 DeMeco Ryans	.25	.60
39 Andre Johnson	.25	.60
40 Matt Schaub	.20	.50
41 Peyton Manning	.75	2.00
42 Reggie Wayne	.25	.60
43 Bob Sanders	.25	.60
44 David Garrard	.20	.50
45 Maurice Jones-Drew	.20	.50
46 Matt Jones	.25	.60
47 Fred Taylor	.20	.50
48 Tony Gonzalez	.25	.60
49 Derrick Johnson	.20	.50
50 Dwayne Bowe	.25	.60
51 Larry Johnson	.20	.50
52 Ronnie Brown	.20	.50
53 Ted Ginn Jr.	.20	.50
54 Jason Taylor	.25	.60
55 Tarvaris Jackson	.20	.50
56 Adrian Peterson	.30	.75
57 Ben Roethlisberger	.30	.75
58 Tom Brady	1.00	2.50
59 Randy Moss	.25	.60
60 Laurence Maroney	.25	.60
61 Wes Welker	.25	.60
62 Drew Brees	.30	.75
63 Marques Colston	.20	.50
64 Reggie Bush	.20	.50
65 Eli Manning	.25	.60
66 Antonio Pierce	.20	.50
67 Plaxico Burress	.20	.50
68 Jeremy Shockey	.20	.50
69 Jonathan Vilma	.20	.50
70 JaMarcus Russell	.20	.50
71 Kirk Morrison	.20	.50
72 Ronald Curry	.20	.50
73 Brian Westbrook	.20	.50
74 Brian Dawkins	.30	.75
75 Donovan McNabb	.25	.60
76 Santonio Holmes	.20	.50
77 Willie Parker	.25	.60
78 Troy Polamalu	.30	.75
79 LaDainian Tomlinson	.30	.75
80 Shawne Merriman	.20	.50
81 Antonio Cromartie	.20	.50
82 Antonio Gates	.25	.60
83 Alex Smith QB	.25	.60
84 Frank Gore	.25	.60
85 Patrick Willis	.25	.60
86 Matt Hasselbeck	.20	.50
87 Shaun Alexander	.20	.50
88 Deion Branch	.20	.50
89 Steven Jackson	.20	.50
90 Torry Holt	.25	.60
91 Marc Bulger	.20	.50
92 Jeff Garcia	.20	.50
93 Cadillac Williams	.25	.60
94 Joey Galloway	.25	.60
95 Vince Young	.20	.50
96 LenDale White	.20	.50
97 Albert Haynesworth	.20	.50
98 Jason Campbell	.20	.50
99 Chris Cooley	.20	.50
100 Clinton Portis	.20	.50
101 Earl Bennett RC	1.25	3.00
102 Adrian Arrington RC	.75	2.00
103 Ali Highsmith RC	.75	2.00
104 Allen Patrick RC	.75	2.00
105 Andre Caldwell RC	.75	2.00
106 Andre Woodson RC	.75	2.00
107 Antoine Cason RC	1.00	2.50
108 Aqib Talib RC	1.25	3.00
109 Ben Moffitt RC	.75	2.00
110 Brian Brohm RC	.75	2.00
111 Bruce Davis RC	1.00	2.50
112 Calais Campbell RC	1.00	2.50
113 Chad Henne RC	1.00	2.50
114 Chevis Jackson RC	.75	2.00
115 Chris Ellis RC	.75	2.00
116 Chris Johnson RC	1.00	2.50
117 Chris Long RC	1.00	2.50
118 Colt Brennan RC	1.00	2.50
119 Craig Steltz RC	.75	2.00
120 DJ Hall RC	.75	2.00
121 Dan Connor RC	.75	2.00
122 Darren McFadden RC	.75	2.00
123 Davone Bess RC	1.00	2.50
124 DeMario Pressley RC	1.00	2.50
125 Dennis Dixon RC	.75	2.00
126 DeSean Jackson RC	1.50	4.00
127 Donnie Avery RC	1.00	2.50
128 Jerome Simpson RC	1.00	2.50
129 Dre Moore RC	.75	2.00
130 Dwight Lowery RC	1.00	2.50
131 Early Doucet RC	.75	2.00
132 Erik Ainge RC	.75	2.00
133 Felix Jones RC	.75	2.00
134 Fred Davis RC	.75	2.00
135 Glenn Dorsey RC	.75	2.00
136 Harry Douglas RC	1.00	2.50
137 Eddie Royal RC	.75	2.00
138 Jack Ikegwuonu RC	.75	2.00
139 Jacob Hester RC	.75	2.00
140 Jacob Tamme RC	1.00	2.50
141 Jake Long RC	1.25	3.00
142 Jamaal Charles RC	1.25	3.00
143 James Hardy RC	.75	2.00
144 J Leman RC	.75	2.00
145 Joe Flacco RC	1.50	4.00
146 John Carlson RC	.75	2.00
147 John David Booty RC	.75	2.00
148 Jonathan Goff RC	.75	2.00
149 Jonathan Hefney RC	.75	2.00
150 Jonathan Stewart RC	1.25	3.00
151 Jordy Nelson RC	2.50	6.00
152 Josh Johnson RC	.75	2.00
153 Justin Forsett RC	1.00	2.50
154 Justin King RC	1.00	2.50
155 Keenan Burton RC	.75	2.00
156 Keith Rivers RC	.75	2.00
157 Kenny Phillips RC	.75	2.00
158 Kentwan Balmer RC	.75	2.00
159 Kevin O'Connell RC	.75	2.00
160 Kevin Smith RC	.75	2.00
161 Alex Brink RC	1.00	2.50
162 Lavelle Hawkins RC	1.00	2.50
163 Lawrence Jackson RC	.75	2.00
164 Limas Sweed RC	.75	2.00
165 Malcolm Kelly RC	.75	2.00
166 Marcus Monk RC	1.00	2.50
167 Mario Manningham RC	.75	2.00
168 Mario Urrutia RC	.75	2.00
169 Martellus Bennett RC	1.00	2.50
170 Martin Rucker RC	.75	2.00
171 Matt Flynn RC	.75	2.00
172 Matt Forte RC	1.25	3.00
173 Matt Ryan RC	2.50	6.00
174 Mike Hart RC	.75	2.00
175 Mike Jenkins RC	.75	2.00
176 Owen Schmitt RC	.75	2.00
177 Paul Smith RC	.75	2.00
178 Philip Wheeler RC	1.00	2.50
179 Quentin Groves RC	1.00	2.50
180 Quintin Demps RC	1.00	2.50
181 Rashard Mendenhall RC	.75	2.00
182 Ray Rice RC	.75	2.00
183 Ryan Clady RC	1.00	2.50
184 Ryan Torain RC	1.00	2.50
185 Sam Baker RC	.75	2.00
186 Anthony Morelli RC	.75	2.00
187 Sedrick Ellis RC	.75	2.00
188 Dexter Jackson RC	1.25	3.00
189 Shawn Crable RC	.75	2.00
190 Steve Slaton RC	.75	2.00
191 Tashard Choice RC	.75	2.00
192 Terrell Thomas RC	.75	2.00
193 Thomas Brown RC	.75	2.00
194 Tom Zbikowski RC	1.00	2.50
195 Gosder Cherilus RC	1.00	2.50
196 Trevor Laws RC	.75	2.00
197 Vernon Gholston RC	.75	2.00
198 Vince Hall RC	.75	2.00
199 Xavier Adibi RC	.75	2.00
200 Yvenson Bernard RC	1.25	3.00
201 Jerome Felton RC	.75	2.00
202 Simeon Castille RC	.75	2.00
203 Craig Stevens RC	.75	2.00
204 Barry Richardson RC	.75	2.00
205 Beau Bell RC	1.00	2.50
206 Caleb Campbell RC	1.25	3.00
207 T.C. Ostrander RC	1.00	2.50
208 Brad Cottam RC	.75	2.00
209 Brandon Flowers RC	1.00	2.50
211 Chauncey Washington RC	1.00	2.50
212 Chris Williams RC	.75	2.00
213 Cory Boyd RC	.75	2.00
214 Will Franklin RC	1.00	2.50
215 Jo-Lonn Dunbar RC	1.00	2.50
216 Xavier Omon RC	.75	2.00
217 Darius Reynaud RC	.75	2.00
218 Dantrell Savage RC	1.00	2.50
219 DeJuan Tribble RC	.75	2.00
220 Dennis Keyes RC	.75	2.00
221 Devin Thomas RC	.75	2.00
222 Marcus Griffin RC	.75	2.00
223 Drew Radovich RC	1.00	2.50
224 Marcus Thomas RC	1.00	2.50
225 Frank Okam RC	.75	2.00
226 Brian Bonner RC	.75	2.00
227 Jamie Silva RC	1.00	2.50
228 Jehuu Caulcrick RC	1.00	2.50
229 Jermichael Finley RC	.75	2.00
230 Jerod Mayo RC	1.25	3.00
231 Brandon McAnderson RC	1.00	2.50
232 Jordon Dizon RC	.75	2.00
233 Josh Barrett RC	.75	2.00
234 Kalvin McRae RC	.75	2.00
235 Kellen Davis RC	.75	2.00
236 Keon Lattimore RC	1.00	2.50
237 Leodis McKelvin RC	1.00	2.50
239 Curtis Lofton RC	1.00	2.50
240 Paul Hubbard RC	.75	2.00
241 Titus Brown RC	.75	2.00
242 Ryan Grice-Mullen RC	.75	2.00
243 Spencer Larsen RC	.75	2.00
244 Thomas DeCoud RC	.75	2.00
245 Erin Henderson RC	1.00	2.50
246 Tracy Porter RC	1.00	2.50
247 Trae Williams RC	.75	2.00
248 Trevor Scott RC	1.00	2.50
249 Wesley Woodyard RC	1.25	3.00
250 Xavier Lee RC	1.00	2.50

2008 Upper Deck Icons Blue Die Cut

ETS/70-99: 4X TO 10X BASIC CARDS
*ROOKIES/70-99: .8X TO 2X BASIC CARDS
*VETS/45-69: 5X TO 12X BASIC CARDS
*ROOKIES/45-69: 1X TO 2.5X BASIC CARDS
*VETS/30-44: 6X TO 15X BASIC CARDS
*ROOKIES/30-44: 1.2X TO 3X BASIC CARDS
*VETS/20-29: 8X TO 20X BASIC CARDS
*ROOKIES/20-29: 1.5X TO 4X BASIC CARDS
*VETS/10-19: 10X TO 25X BASIC CARDS
*ROOKIES/10-19: 2X TO 5X BASIC CARDS
STATED PRINT RUN 1-98

122 Darren McFadden/20	3.00	8.00

2008 Upper Deck Icons Gold Die Cut

*VETS 1-100: 4X TO 10X BASIC CARDS
*ROOKIES 101-250: .8X TO 2X BASIC CARDS
STATED PRINT RUN 75 SER.#'d SETS

2008 Upper Deck Icons Rainbow Foil

*VETS: 1.5X TO 4X BASIC CARDS
RANDOM INSERTS IN RETAIL PACKS

2008 Upper Deck Icons Silver Die Cut

*VETS 1-100: 3X TO 8X BASIC CARDS
*ROOKIES 101-250: .6X TO 1.5X BASIC CARDS
STATED PRINT RUN 150 SER.#'d SETS

2008 Upper Deck Icons Class of 2008 Silver

SILVER PRINT RUN 750 SER.#'d SETS
*BLUE/250: .5X TO 1.2X SILVER/750
BLUE PRINT RUN 250 SER.#'d SETS
*GOLD/99: .6X TO 1.5X SILVER/750
GOLD PRINT RUN 99 SER.#'d SETS

CO1 Darren McFadden	.50	1.25
CO2 DeSean Jackson	1.00	2.50
CO3 Brian Brohm	.50	1.25
CO4 Matt Ryan	1.50	4.00
CO5 Devin Thomas	.50	1.25
CO6 Jonathan Stewart	.75	2.00
CO7 Jake Long	.75	2.00
CO8 Chad Henne	.60	1.50
CO9 Chris Johnson	.60	1.50
CO10 Chris Long	.60	1.50
CO11 Earl Bennett	.75	2.00
CO12 Rashard Mendenhall	.50	1.25
CO13 Glenn Dorsey	.50	1.25
CO14 Early Doucet	.50	1.25
CO15 Andre Caldwell	.50	1.25
CO16 Felix Jones	.50	1.25
CO17 Dustin Keller	.60	1.50
CO18 Jamaal Charles	.75	2.00
CO19 Joe Flacco	1.00	2.50
CO20 John David Booty	.50	1.25
CO21 Jordy Nelson	1.50	4.00
CO22 Jerome Simpson	.60	1.50
CO23 Kevin Smith	.50	1.25
CO24 Limas Sweed	.50	1.25
CO25 Donnie Avery	.60	1.50
CO26 Malcolm Kelly	.50	1.25
CO27 Mario Manningham	.50	1.25
CO28 James Hardy	.50	1.25
CO29 Matt Forte	.75	2.00
CO30 Dexter Jackson	.75	2.00
CO31 Eddie Royal	.50	1.25
CO32 Ray Rice	.50	1.25
CO33 Steve Slaton	.50	1.25
CO34 Harry Douglas	.60	1.50
CO35 Kevin O'Connell	.50	1.25

2008 Upper Deck Icons Class of 2008 Jersey Silver

STATED PRINT RUN 199 SER.#'d SETS
*GOLD/75: .5X TO 1.2X SILVER/199
GOLD PRINT RUN 75 SER.#'d SETS

CO1 Darren McFadden	1.50	4.00
CO2 DeSean Jackson	3.00	8.00
CO3 Brian Brohm	1.50	4.00
CO4 Matt Ryan	5.00	12.00
CO5 Devin Thomas	1.50	4.00
CO6 Jonathan Stewart	5.00	12.00
CO7 Jake Long	2.50	6.00
CO8 Chad Henne	2.00	5.00
CO9 Chris Johnson	2.00	5.00
CO10 Chris Long	2.00	5.00
CO11 Earl Bennett	2.50	6.00
CO12 Rashard Mendenhall	1.50	4.00
CO13 Glenn Dorsey	1.50	4.00
CO14 Early Doucet	1.50	4.00
CO15 Andre Caldwell	1.50	4.00
CO16 Felix Jones	1.50	4.00
CO17 Dustin Keller	2.00	5.00
CO18 Jamaal Charles	2.50	6.00
CO19 Joe Flacco	3.00	8.00
CO20 John David Booty	1.50	4.00
CO21 Jordy Nelson	5.00	12.00
CO22 Jerome Simpson	2.00	5.00
CO23 Kevin Smith	1.50	4.00
CO24 Limas Sweed	1.50	4.00
CO25 Donnie Avery	2.00	5.00
CO26 Malcolm Kelly	1.50	4.00
CO27 Mario Manningham	1.50	4.00
CO28 James Hardy	1.50	4.00
CO29 Matt Forte	2.50	6.00
CO30 Dexter Jackson	2.50	6.00
CO31 Eddie Royal	1.50	4.00
CO32 Ray Rice	1.50	4.00
CO33 Steve Slaton	1.50	4.00
CO34 Harry Douglas	2.00	5.00
CO35 Kevin O'Connell	1.50	4.00

2008 Upper Deck Icons Future Foundations Silver

SILVER PRINT RUN 750 SER.#'d SETS
*BLUE/250: .5X TO 1.2X SILVER/750
BLUE PRINT RUN 250 SER.#'d SETS
*GOLD/99: .6X TO 1.5X SILVER/750
GOLD PRINT RUN 99 SER.#'d SETS

FF1 A.J. Hawk	1.00	2.50
FF2 Anquan Boldin	1.00	2.50
FF3 Ben Roethlisberger	1.50	4.00
FF4 Bob Sanders	1.25	3.00
FF5 Brady Quinn	1.00	2.50
FF6 Brian Brohm	.50	1.25
FF7 Calvin Johnson	1.50	4.00
FF8 Chad Henne	.60	1.50
FF9 Chad Johnson	1.00	2.50
FF10 Darren McFadden	.50	1.25
FF11 Derek Anderson	1.00	2.50
FF12 Early Doucet	.50	1.25
FF13 Felix Jones	.50	1.25
FF14 Dustin Keller	.60	1.50
FF15 JaMarcus Russell	1.00	2.50
FF16 Joe Flacco	1.00	2.50
FF17 Jonathan Stewart	.75	2.00
FF18 Jerome Simpson	.60	1.50
FF19 Kevin Smith	.50	1.25
FF20 Malcolm Kelly	.50	1.25
FF21 Marshawn Lynch	1.25	3.00
FF22 Matt Forte	.75	2.00
FF23 Matt Ryan	1.50	4.00
FF24 Rashard Mendenhall	.50	1.25
FF25 Vince Young	1.00	2.50

2008 Upper Deck Icons Future Foundations Jersey Silver

LVER PRINT RUN 199 SER.#'d SETS
*GOLD/75: .5X TO 1.2X SILVER/199
GOLD PRINT RUN 75 SER.#'d SETS

FF1 A.J. Hawk	2.50	6.00
FF2 Anquan Boldin	2.50	6.00
FF3 Ben Roethlisberger	4.00	10.00
FF4 Bob Sanders	4.00	10.00
FF5 Brady Quinn	2.50	6.00
FF6 Brian Brohm	1.50	4.00
FF7 Calvin Johnson	4.00	10.00
FF8 Chad Henne	2.00	5.00
FF9 Chad Johnson	2.50	6.00
FF10 Darren McFadden	1.50	4.00
FF11 Derek Anderson	2.50	6.00
FF12 Early Doucet	1.50	4.00
FF13 Felix Jones	1.50	4.00
FF14 Dustin Keller	2.00	5.00
FF15 JaMarcus Russell	2.50	6.00
FF16 Joe Flacco	3.00	8.00
FF17 Jonathan Stewart	5.00	12.00
FF18 Jerome Simpson	2.00	5.00
FF19 Kevin Smith	1.50	4.00
FF20 Malcolm Kelly	1.50	4.00
FF21 Marshawn Lynch	3.00	8.00
FF22 Matt Forte	2.50	6.00
FF23 Matt Ryan	5.00	12.00
FF24 Rashard Mendenhall	1.50	4.00
FF25 Vince Young	2.50	6.00

2008 Upper Deck Icons Future Stars Materials

FSM1 Adrian Peterson	4.00	10.00
FSM2 Dwayne Bowe	3.00	8.00
FSM3 Brady Quinn	2.50	6.00
FSM4 Darren McFadden	1.50	4.00
FSM5 DeSean Jackson	3.00	8.00
FSM6 Brian Brohm	1.50	4.00
FSM7 Matt Ryan	5.00	12.00
FSM8 Earl Bennett	2.50	6.00
FSM9 Jonathan Stewart	5.00	12.00
FSM10 Kevin O'Connell	1.50	4.00
FSM11 Chad Henne	2.00	5.00
FSM12 Chris Johnson	2.00	5.00
FSM13 Glenn Dorsey	1.50	4.00
FSM14 Rashard Mendenhall	1.50	4.00
FSM15 Dexter Jackson	2.50	6.00
FSM16 Early Doucet	1.50	4.00
FSM17 Eddie Royal	1.50	4.00
FSM18 Felix Jones	1.50	4.00
FSM19 Dustin Keller	2.00	5.00
FSM20 Jamaal Charles	2.50	6.00
FSM21 Joe Flacco	3.00	8.00
FSM22 John David Booty	1.50	4.00
FSM23 Jerome Simpson	2.00	5.00
FSM24 Kevin Smith	1.50	4.00
FSM25 Limas Sweed	1.50	4.00
FSM26 Steve Slaton	1.50	4.00
FSM27 Malcolm Kelly	1.50	4.00
FSM28 Mario Manningham	1.50	4.00
FSM29 Matt Forte	2.50	6.00
FSM30 Jordy Nelson	5.00	12.00
FSM31 Devin Thomas	1.50	4.00
FSM32 Ray Rice	1.50	4.00
FSM33 Andre Caldwell	1.50	4.00

2008 Upper Deck Icons Immortal Lettermen

INT RUNS 20-97 PER LETTER
TOTAL PRINT RUNS 306-630
*PARALLEL: .4X TO 1X BASIC INSERTS
PARAL.PRINT RUNS 25-99 PER LETTER
PARALLEL TOTAL PRINT RUNS 306-636

AROY Chris Johnson ROY/1485*	8.00	20.00
BB19 Brian Bosworth/624*	8.00	20.00
BF1 Brett Favre/1612*	12.00	30.00
BF2 Brett Favre/1397*	12.00	30.00
BJ18 Bo Jackson/546*	20.00	50.00
BN4 Bronko Nagurski/488*	8.00	20.00
BS16 Barry Sanders/497*	20.00	50.00
DB21 Dick Butkus/462*	10.00	25.00
DM20 Dan Marino/366*	20.00	50.00
FH23 Franco Harris/306*	8.00	20.00
FT22 Fran Tarkenton/342*	10.00	25.00
GS3 Gale Sayers/528*	10.00	25.00
JB26 Jim Brown/485*	10.00	25.00
JL25 Jack Lambert/630*	10.00	25.00
JT7 Jim Thorpe/318*	12.00	30.00
JU2 Johnny Unitas/528*	15.00	40.00
KS28 Ken Stabler/504*	10.00	25.00
LA14 Lance Alworth/560*	6.00	15.00
NROY Matt Ryan/1485*	12.00	30.00
OG9 Otto Graham/480*	6.00	15.00
RG1 Red Grange/306*	10.00	25.00
RS15 Roger Staubach/512*	10.00	25.00
SI17 Billy Sims/320*	5.00	12.00
SL10 Sid Luckman/560*	8.00	20.00
TL5 Tom Landry/528*	10.00	25.00
WE13 Weeb Ewbank/540*	5.00	12.00
WP8 Walter Payton/384*	20.00	50.00
YT12 Y.A. Tittle/480*	6.00	15.00

2008 Upper Deck Icons Immortal Lettermen Autographs

TOTAL AUTO PRINT RUNS 72-270
AUTO STATED PRINT RUNS 12-42

BB19 Brian Bosworth/162*	25.00	50.00
BJ18 Bo Jackson/126*	50.00	100.00
BS16 Barry Sanders/140*	90.00	175.00
DB21 Dick Butkus/132*	40.00	80.00
DM20 Dan Marino/96*	125.00	250.00
FH23 Franco Harris/156*	30.00	80.00
FT22 Fran Tarkenton/270*	25.00	60.00
JB26 Jim Brown/72*	40.00	80.00
JL25 Jack Lambert/100*	40.00	80.00
KS28 Ken Stabler/128*	40.00	80.00
SI17 Billy Sims/168*	15.00	30.00

2008 Upper Deck Icons Legendary Icons Silver

LVER PRINT RUN 799 SER.#'d SETS
*BLUE/250: .5X TO 1.2X SILVER/799
BLUE PRINT RUN 250 SER.#'d SETS
*GOLD/99: .6X TO 1.5X SILVER/799
GOLD PRINT RUN 99 SER.#'d SETS

LI1 Barry Sanders	2.50	6.00
LI2 Billy Sims	1.25	3.00
LI3 Bo Jackson	2.00	5.00
LI4 Brian Bosworth	1.50	4.00
LI5 Dan Marino	3.00	8.00
LI6 Dick Butkus	2.00	5.00
LI7 Emmitt Smith	2.50	6.00
LI8 Bert Jones	1.00	2.50
LI9 Jack Lambert	1.50	4.00
LI10 Jim Brown	2.00	5.00
LI11 Joe Theismann	1.50	4.00
LI12 Ken Anderson	1.25	3.00
LI13 Lynn Swann	1.50	4.00
LI14 Roger Craig	1.25	3.00
LI15 Ottis Anderson	1.00	2.50

2008 Upper Deck Icons Legendary Icons Autographs

STATED PRINT RUN 25 SER.#'d SETS

LI1 Barry Sanders	60.00	120.00
LI2 Billy Sims	15.00	30.00
LI3 Bo Jackson	30.00	60.00
LI4 Brian Bosworth	20.00	40.00
LI5 Dan Marino	90.00	150.00

LI6 Dick Butkus EXCH 30.00 60.00
LI7 Emmitt Smith 90.00 150.00
LI8 Bert Jones
LI9 Jack Lambert 30.00 60.00
LI10 Jim Brown 40.00 80.00
LI11 Joe Theismann 15.00 30.00
LI12 Ken Anderson 20.00 40.00
LI13 Lynn Swann
LI14 Roger Craig 25.00 50.00
LI15 Ottis Anderson

2008 Upper Deck Icons Legendary Icons Jersey Silver

SILVER PRINT RUN 150 SER.#'d SETS
*GOLD/25: .6X TO 1.5X SILVER/150
GOLD PRINT RUN 25 SER.#'d SETS
*PATCH/15: 1.2X TO 3X SILVER/150
PATCH PRINT RUN 15 SER.#'d SETS
LI1 Barry Sanders 8.00 20.00
LI2 Billy Sims 4.00 10.00
LI3 Bo Jackson 8.00 20.00
LI4 Brian Bosworth 5.00 12.00
LI5 Dan Marino 10.00 25.00
LI6 Dick Butkus 6.00 15.00
LI7 Emmitt Smith 8.00 20.00
LI8 Bert Jones 3.00 8.00
LI9 Jack Lambert 5.00 12.00
LI10 Jim Brown 6.00 15.00
LI11 Joe Theismann 5.00 12.00
LI12 Ken Anderson 4.00 10.00
LI13 Lynn Swann 5.00 12.00
LI14 Roger Craig 4.00 10.00
LI15 Ottis Anderson 3.00 8.00

2008 Upper Deck Icons Movie Icons

STATED PRINT RUN 999 SER.#'d SETS
*SILVER DC/99: .6X TO 1.5X BASIC INSERTS
SILVER DIE CUT PRINT RUN 99 SER.#'d SETS
*GOLD DIE CUT/75: .8X TO 2X BASIC INSERTS
GOLD DIE CUT PRINT RUN 75 SER.#'d SETS
*BLUE DIE CUT/35: 1.2X TO 3X BASIC INSERTS
BLUE DIE CUT PRINT RUN 35 SER.#'d SETS
MI3 Billy Dee Williams .40 1.00
MI4 Burt Reynolds .40 1.00
MI9 Ed O'Neill .40 1.00

2008 Upper Deck Icons Movie Icons Lettermen

STATED PRINT RUN 47-68 EACH LETTER
TOTAL PRINT RUNS 272-378
*PARALLEL: .4X TO 1X BASIC INSERTS
PARALLEL PRINT RUNS 30-47 EACH LETTER
TOTAL PARALLEL PRINT RUNS 240-480
BR5 Burt Reynolds/376* 5.00 12.00
BW4 Billy Dee Williams/376* 5.00 12.00
EO11 Ed O'Neill/378* 5.00 12.00
HA13 Goldie Hawn/272* 5.00 12.00

2008 Upper Deck Icons Movie Icons Lettermen Autographs

TOTAL AUTO PRINT RUNS 63--120
BW Billy Dee Williams/120* 15.00 40.00
BR Burt Reynolds/63* 20.00 50.00
EO Ed O'Neill/96* 30.00 60.00

2008 Upper Deck Icons NFL Chronology Silver

SILVER PRINT RUN 750 SER.#'d SETS
*BLUE/250: .5X TO 1.2X SILVER/750
BLUE PRINT RUN 250 SER.#'d SETS
*GOLD/99: .6X TO 1.5X SILVER/750
GOLD PRINT RUN 99 SER.#'d SETS
CHR2 Jim Brown 2.00 5.00
CHR4 Joe Namath 2.00 5.00
CHR5 Franco Harris 1.50 4.00
CHR7 Jack Lambert 1.50 4.00
CHR8 Walter Payton 3.00 8.00
CHR9 Joe Montana 5.00 12.00
CHR10 Dan Marino 3.00 8.00
CHR13 Walter Payton 3.00 8.00
CHR14 Bo Jackson 2.00 5.00
CHR15 Barry Sanders 2.50 6.00
CHR16 Brett Favre 3.00 8.00
CHR17 Rod Woodson 1.25 3.00
CHR18 Jerry Rice 3.00 8.00
CHR19 Emmitt Smith 2.50 6.00
CHR20 Brett Favre 3.00 8.00
CHR21 Barry Sanders 2.50 6.00
CHR23 John Elway 2.50 6.00
CHR25 Terrell Owens 1.25 3.00
CHR26 Terrell Owens 1.25 3.00
CHR27 Jerry Rice 3.00 8.00
CHR28 Emmitt Smith 2.50 6.00
CHR29 Marvin Harrison 1.25 3.00
CHR30 Clinton Portis 1.00 2.50
CHR31 Jerry Rice 3.00 8.00
CHR32 Anquan Boldin 1.00 2.50
CHR33 Peyton Manning 4.00 10.00
CHR34 Devin Hester 1.25 3.00
CHR35 LaDainian Tomlinson 1.50 4.00
CHR36 Antonio Cromartie 1.00 2.50
CHR37 Tony Gonzalez 1.25 3.00
CHR38 Adrian Peterson 1.50 4.00
CHR39 Tom Brady 5.00 12.00
CHR40 Randy Moss 1.25 3.00

2008 Upper Deck Icons NFL Chronology Jersey Silver

SILVER PRINT RUN 150 SER.#'d SETS
*GOLD/50: .5X TO 1.2X SILVER/150
GOLD PRINT RUN 50 SER.#'d SETS
CHR2 Jim Brown 6.00 15.00
CHR4 Joe Namath 8.00 20.00
CHR5 Franco Harris 6.00 15.00
CHR7 Jack Lambert 5.00 12.00
CHR8 Walter Payton 10.00 25.00
CHR9 Joe Montana 15.00 40.00
CHR10 Dan Marino 10.00 25.00
CHR13 Walter Payton 10.00 25.00
CHR14 Bo Jackson 8.00 20.00
CHR15 Barry Sanders 8.00 20.00
CHR16 Brett Favre 8.00 20.00
CHR17 Rod Woodson 4.00 10.00
CHR18 Jerry Rice 10.00 25.00
CHR19 Emmitt Smith 8.00 20.00
CHR20 Brett Favre 8.00 20.00
CHR21 Barry Sanders 8.00 20.00
CHR23 John Elway 8.00 20.00
CHR25 Terrell Owens 3.00 8.00
CHR26 Terrell Owens 3.00 8.00
CHR27 Jerry Rice 10.00 25.00
CHR28 Emmitt Smith 8.00 20.00
CHR29 Marvin Harrison 3.00 8.00
CHR30 Clinton Portis/200 2.50 6.00
CHR31 Jerry Rice 10.00 25.00
CHR32 Anquan Boldin 2.50 6.00
CHR33 Peyton Manning 10.00 25.00
CHR34 Devin Hester 3.00 8.00
CHR35 LaDainian Tomlinson 4.00 10.00
CHR36 Antonio Cromartie/200 2.50 6.00
CHR37 Tony Gonzalez/200 3.00 8.00
CHR38 Adrian Peterson 4.00 10.00
CHR39 Tom Brady 12.00 30.00
CHR40 Randy Moss 3.00 8.00

2008 Upper Deck Icons NFL Icons Silver

SILVER PRINT RUN 799 SER.#'d SETS
*BLUE/250: .5X TO 1.2X SILVER/799
BLUE PRINT RUN 250 SER.#'d SETS
*GOLD/99: .6X TO 1.5X SILVER/799
GOLD PRINT RUN 99 SER.#'d SETS
NFL1 Adrian Peterson 1.50 4.00
NFL2 Aaron Schobel 1.00 2.50
NFL3 Brandon Marshall 1.25 3.00
NFL4 Ben Roethlisberger 1.50 4.00
NFL5 A.J. Hawk 1.00 2.50
NFL6 Bob Sanders 1.25 3.00
NFL7 DeMarcus Ware 1.25 3.00
NFL8 Brett Favre 3.00 8.00
NFL9 Jamal Lewis 1.25 3.00
NFL10 Brady Quinn 1.00 2.50
NFL11 Cadillac Williams 1.25 3.00
NFL12 Chad Johnson 1.00 2.50
NFL13 Aaron Rodgers 3.00 8.00
NFL14 Clinton Portis 1.00 2.50
NFL15 David Garrard 1.00 2.50
NFL16 Derek Anderson 1.00 2.50
NFL17 Dallas Clark 1.00 2.50
NFL18 Donald Lee 1.25 3.00
NFL19 Dwayne Bowe 1.25 3.00
NFL20 Roy Williams WR 1.00 2.50
NFL21 Eli Manning 1.25 3.00
NFL22 Frank Gore 1.25 3.00
NFL23 Marques Colston 1.00 2.50
NFL24 Brodie Croyle 1.25 3.00
NFL25 Jason Campbell 1.00 2.50
NFL26 Jeff Garcia 1.00 2.50
NFL27 Jeremy Shockey 1.00 2.50
NFL28 Joseph Addai 1.00 2.50
NFL29 Kellen Winslow 1.00 2.50
NFL30 LaDainian Tomlinson 1.50 4.00
NFL31 Larry Johnson 1.00 2.50
NFL32 Marc Bulger 1.00 2.50
NFL33 Marion Barber 1.00 2.50
NFL34 Marshawn Lynch 1.25 3.00
NFL35 Kurt Warner 1.25 3.00
NFL36 Matt Schaub 1.00 2.50
NFL37 Michael Huff 1.00 2.50
NFL38 Mike Vrabel 1.00 2.50
NFL39 Patrick Willis 1.25 3.00
NFL40 Peyton Manning 4.00 10.00
NFL41 Philip Rivers 1.50 4.00
NFL42 Randy Moss 1.25 3.00
NFL43 Jerricho Cotchery 1.00 2.50
NFL44 Tom Brady 5.00 12.00
NFL45 Ben Watson 1.00 2.50
NFL46 Tony Romo 1.25 3.00
NFL47 Troy Polamalu 1.50 4.00
NFL48 Trent Edwards 1.00 2.50
NFL49 Wes Welker 1.25 3.00
NFL50 Braylon Edwards 1.00 2.50

2008 Upper Deck Icons NFL Icons Autographs

STATED PRINT RUN 35-56
NFL1 Adrian Peterson 90.00 150.00
NFL2 Aaron Schobel 6.00 15.00
NFL3 Brandon Marshall
NFL4 Ben Roethlisberger 40.00 100.00
NFL5 A.J. Hawk 10.00 25.00
NFL6 Bob Sanders 20.00 50.00
NFL7 DeMarcus Ware 10.00 25.00
NFL8 Brett Favre 100.00 200.00
NFL9 Jamal Lewis
NFL10 Brady Quinn 25.00 50.00
NFL11 Cadillac Williams 8.00 20.00
NFL12 Chad Johnson 8.00 20.00
NFL13 Aaron Rodgers 125.00 200.00
NFL14 Clinton Portis 10.00 25.00
NFL15 David Garrard 10.00 25.00
NFL16 Derek Anderson 10.00 25.00
NFL17 Dallas Clark 10.00 25.00
NFL18 Donald Lee
NFL19 Dwayne Bowe 8.00 20.00
NFL20 Roy Williams WR
NFL21 Eli Manning 35.00 60.00
NFL22 Frank Gore 10.00 25.00
NFL23 Marques Colston 20.00 40.00
NFL24 Brodie Croyle 8.00 20.00
NFL25 Jason Campbell 10.00 25.00
NFL26 Jeff Garcia 8.00 20.00
NFL27 Jeremy Shockey EXCH 20.00 40.00
NFL28 Joseph Addai 15.00 30.00
NFL29 Kellen Winslow
NFL30 LaDainian Tomlinson 35.00 60.00
NFL31 Larry Johnson 10.00 25.00
NFL32 Marc Bulger
NFL33 Marion Barber 15.00 30.00
NFL34 Marshawn Lynch 12.00 30.00
NFL35 Kurt Warner 25.00 50.00
NFL36 Matt Schaub/56 10.00 25.00
NFL37 Michael Huff
NFL39 Patrick Willis/56 10.00 25.00
NFL40 Peyton Manning 60.00 100.00
NFL41 Philip Rivers 15.00 30.00
NFL43 Jerricho Cotchery 8.00 20.00
NFL44 Tom Brady 125.00 200.00
NFL45 Ben Watson 6.00 15.00
NFL46 Tony Romo 60.00 120.00
NFL48 Trent Edwards/56
NFL49 Wes Welker
NFL50 Braylon Edwards

2008 Upper Deck Icons NFL Icons Jersey Silver

SILVER PRINT RUN 150 SER.#'d SETS
*GOLD/50: .5X TO 1.2X SILVER/150
GOLD PRINT RUN 50 SER.#'d SETS
*PATCH/25: 1X TO 2.5X SILVER/150
PATCH PRINT RUN 25 SER.#'d SETS
NFL1 Adrian Peterson 4.00 10.00
NFL2 Aaron Schobel 2.50 6.00
NFL3 Brandon Marshall 3.00 8.00
NFL4 Ben Roethlisberger 4.00 10.00
NFL5 A.J. Hawk 2.50 6.00
NFL6 Bob Sanders 3.00 8.00
NFL7 DeMarcus Ware 3.00 8.00
NFL8 Brett Favre 8.00 20.00
NFL9 Jamal Lewis 3.00 8.00
NFL10 Brady Quinn 2.50 6.00
NFL11 Cadillac Williams 3.00 8.00
NFL12 Chad Johnson 2.50 6.00
NFL13 Aaron Rodgers 12.00 30.00
NFL14 Clinton Portis 2.50 6.00
NFL15 David Garrard 2.50 6.00
NFL16 Derek Anderson 2.50 6.00
NFL17 Dallas Clark 2.50 6.00
NFL18 Donald Lee 3.00 8.00
NFL19 Dwayne Bowe 3.00 8.00
NFL20 Roy Williams WR 2.50 6.00
NFL21 Eli Manning 3.00 8.00
NFL22 Frank Gore 3.00 8.00
NFL23 Marques Colston 2.50 6.00
NFL24 Brodie Croyle 3.00 8.00
NFL25 Jason Campbell 2.50 6.00
NFL26 Jeff Garcia 2.50 6.00
NFL27 Jeremy Shockey 2.50 6.00
NFL28 Joseph Addai 2.50 6.00
NFL29 Kellen Winslow 2.50 6.00
NFL30 LaDainian Tomlinson 4.00 10.00
NFL31 Larry Johnson 2.50 6.00
NFL32 Marc Bulger 2.50 6.00
NFL33 Marion Barber 2.50 6.00
NFL34 Marshawn Lynch 3.00 8.00
NFL35 Kurt Warner 3.00 8.00
NFL36 Matt Schaub 2.50 6.00
NFL37 Michael Huff 2.50 6.00
NFL38 Mike Vrabel 2.50 6.00
NFL39 Patrick Willis 3.00 8.00
NFL40 Peyton Manning 12.00 30.00
NFL41 Philip Rivers 4.00 10.00
NFL42 Randy Moss 3.00 8.00
NFL43 Jerricho Cotchery 2.50 6.00
NFL44 Tom Brady 12.00 30.00
NFL45 Ben Watson 2.50 6.00
NFL46 Tony Romo 3.00 8.00
NFL47 Troy Polamalu 4.00 10.00
NFL48 Trent Edwards 2.50 6.00
NFL49 Wes Welker 3.00 8.00
NFL50 Braylon Edwards 2.50 6.00

2008 Upper Deck Icons NFL Legends

STATED PRINT RUN 999 SER.#'d SETS
*SILVER DC/150: .6X TO 1.5X BASIC INSERTS
SILVER DIE CUT PRINT RUN 150 SER.#'d SETS
*GOLD DIE CUT/75: .8X TO 2X BASIC INSERTS
GOLD DIE CUT PRINT RUN 75 SER.#'d SETS
*BLUE DC/88: .6X TO 1.5X BASIC INSERTS
*BLUE DC/47-58: .8X TO 2X BASIC INSERTS
*BLUE DC/32-34: 1X TO 2.5X BASIC INSERTS
*BLUE DC/10-20: 1.5X TO 4X BASIC INSERTS
BLUE DIE CUT PRINT RUN 7-88
LEG1 Barry Sanders 2.50 6.00
LEG2 Billy Sims 1.25 3.00
LEG3 Bo Jackson 2.00 5.00
LEG4 Bob Griese 1.50 4.00
LEG5 Brian Bosworth 1.50 4.00
LEG6 Dan Marino 3.00 8.00
LEG7 Daryl Johnston 1.25 3.00
LEG8 Emmitt Smith 2.50 6.00
LEG9 Fran Tarkenton 1.50 4.00
LEG10 Herschel Walker 1.50 4.00
LEG11 Jack Lambert 1.50 4.00
LEG12 Jim Brown 2.00 5.00
LEG13 Jim McMahon 1.50 4.00
LEG14 Joe Montana 5.00 12.00
LEG15 Joe Namath 2.00 5.00
LEG16 Joe Theismann 1.50 4.00
LEG17 John Elway 2.50 6.00
LEG18 Ken Stabler 1.50 4.00
LEG20 Lynn Swann 1.50 4.00
LEG21 Mel Blount 1.25 3.00
LEG22 Roger Craig 1.25 3.00
LEG24 Sonny Jurgensen 1.25 3.00
LEG25 Y. A. Tittle 1.50 4.00

2008 Upper Deck Icons Presidential Icons Lettermen

PL1 Barack Obama/229 12.00 30.00
PL2 Barack Obama/127 12.00 30.00

2008 Upper Deck Icons Rookie Autographs Rainbow

STATED PRINT RUN 135-155
101 Earl Bennett 5.00 12.00
102 Adrian Arrington 3.00 8.00
103 Ali Highsmith 3.00 8.00
104 Allen Patrick 3.00 8.00
105 Andre Caldwell 3.00 8.00
106 Andre Woodson 3.00 8.00
107 Antoine Cason 4.00 10.00
108 Aqib Talib 5.00 12.00
109 Ben Moffitt 3.00 8.00
110 Brian Brohm/100 3.00 8.00
111 Bruce Davis 4.00 10.00
112 Calais Campbell 4.00 10.00
113 Chad Henne 4.00 10.00
114 Chevis Jackson 3.00 8.00
115 Chris Ellis 3.00 8.00
116 Chris Johnson 4.00 10.00
117 Chris Long 4.00 10.00
118 Colt Brennan/100 4.00 10.00
119 Craig Steltz 3.00 8.00
120 DJ Hall 3.00 8.00
121 Dan Connor 3.00 8.00
122 Darren McFadden/100 3.00 8.00
123 Davone Bess 4.00 10.00
124 DeMario Pressley/155 4.00 10.00
125 Dennis Dixon 3.00 8.00
126 DeSean Jackson 6.00 15.00
127 Donnie Avery 4.00 10.00
128 Jerome Simpson 4.00 10.00
129 Dre Moore/155 3.00 8.00
130 Dwight Lowery 4.00 10.00
131 Early Doucet 3.00 8.00
132 Erik Ainge 3.00 8.00
133 Felix Jones 3.00 8.00
134 Fred Davis 3.00 8.00
136 Harry Douglas 4.00 10.00
138 Jack Ikegwuonu 3.00 8.00
139 Jacob Hester 3.00 8.00
140 Jacob Tamme 4.00 10.00
141 Jake Long 5.00 12.00
142 Jamaal Charles 12.00 30.00
143 James Hardy 3.00 8.00
145 Joe Flacco 6.00 15.00
146 John Carlson 3.00 8.00
147 John David Booty 3.00 8.00
149 Jonathan Hefney/155 3.00 8.00
150 Jonathan Stewart/100 12.00 30.00
151 Jordy Nelson 10.00 25.00
152 Josh Johnson 3.00 8.00
153 Justin Forsett 4.00 10.00
154 Justin King 4.00 10.00
155 Keenan Burton 3.00 8.00
156 Keith Rivers 3.00 8.00
157 Kenny Phillips 3.00 8.00
159 Kevin O'Connell 3.00 8.00
160 Kevin Smith 3.00 8.00
161 Alex Brink 4.00 10.00
162 Lavelle Hawkins 4.00 10.00
163 Lawrence Jackson 3.00 8.00
164 Limas Sweed 3.00 8.00
165 Malcolm Kelly 3.00 8.00
166 Marcus Monk 4.00 10.00
167 Mario Manningham 3.00 8.00
168 Mario Urrutia 3.00 8.00
169 Martellus Bennett 4.00 10.00
170 Martin Rucker 3.00 8.00
171 Matt Flynn 3.00 8.00
172 Matt Forte 15.00 40.00
173 Matt Ryan/100 25.00 60.00
174 Mike Hart 3.00 8.00
175 Mike Jenkins/155 3.00 8.00
176 Owen Schmitt/155 3.00 8.00
177 Paul Smith 3.00 8.00
178 Philip Wheeler 4.00 10.00
179 Quentin Groves/155 4.00 10.00
180 Quintin Demps 4.00 10.00
181 Rashard Mendenhall 3.00 8.00
182 Ray Rice 3.00 8.00
183 Ryan Clady 4.00 10.00
184 Ryan Torain 4.00 10.00
185 Sam Baker 3.00 8.00
186 Anthony Morelli 3.00 8.00
187 Sedrick Ellis 3.00 8.00
188 Dexter Jackson 5.00 12.00
190 Steve Slaton 3.00 8.00
191 Tashard Choice 3.00 8.00
192 Terrell Thomas 3.00 8.00
193 Thomas Brown 3.00 8.00
194 Tom Zbikowski 4.00 10.00
195 Gosder Cherilus 4.00 10.00
196 Trevor Laws 3.00 8.00
197 Vernon Gholston 3.00 8.00
199 Xavier Adibi 3.00 8.00

2008 Upper Deck Icons Rookie Autographs Rainbow Die Cut

IE CUT/25: .6X TO 1.5X AU/135-155
DIE CUT PRINT RUN 25 SER.#'d SETS
145 Joe Flacco 10.00 25.00
173 Matt Ryan 40.00 100.00

2008 Upper Deck Icons Rookie Brilliance Silver

SILVER PRINT RUN 799 SER.#'d SETS
*BLUE/250: .5X TO 1.2X SILVER/799
BLUE PRINT RUN 250 SER.#'d SETS
*GOLD/99: .6X TO 1.5X SILVER/799
GOLD PRINT RUN 99 SER.#'d SETS
RB1 Donnie Avery .60 1.50
RB2 Jake Long .75 2.00
RB3 Brian Brohm .50 1.25
RB4 Chad Henne .60 1.50
RB5 Chris Johnson .60 1.50
RB6 Chris Long .60 1.50
RB7 Devin Thomas .50 1.25
RB8 Darren McFadden .50 1.25
RB9 Earl Bennett .75 2.00
RB10 Glenn Dorsey .50 1.25
RB11 DeSean Jackson 1.00 2.50
RB12 Harry Douglas .60 1.50
RB13 Early Doucet .50 1.25
RB14 Andre Caldwell .50 1.25
RB15 Felix Jones .50 1.25
RB16 Dustin Keller .60 1.50
RB17 Jamaal Charles .75 2.00
RB18 Joe Flacco 1.00 2.50
RB19 John David Booty .50 1.25
RB20 Jonathan Stewart .75 2.00
RB21 Jordy Nelson 1.50 4.00
RB22 Jerome Simpson .60 1.50
RB23 Kevin Smith .50 1.25
RB24 Limas Sweed .50 1.25
RB25 Malcolm Kelly .50 1.25
RB26 Mario Manningham .50 1.25
RB27 James Hardy .50 1.25
RB28 Matt Forte .75 2.00
RB29 Matt Ryan 1.50 4.00
RB30 Dexter Jackson .75 2.00
RB31 Eddie Royal .50 1.25
RB32 Rashard Mendenhall .50 1.25
RB33 Ray Rice .50 1.25
RB34 Steve Slaton .50 1.25
RB35 Kevin O'Connell .50 1.25

2008 Upper Deck Icons Rookie Brilliance Autographs

STATED PRINT RUN 125-199
RB1 Donnie Avery/165 4.00 10.00
RB2 Jake Long/199 5.00 12.00
RB3 Brian Brohm/125 3.00 8.00
RB4 Chad Henne/165 4.00 10.00
RB5 Chris Johnson/165 4.00 10.00
RB6 Chris Long/165 4.00 10.00
RB7 Devin Thomas/165 3.00 8.00
RB8 Darren McFadden/125 3.00 8.00
RB9 Earl Bennett/165 5.00 12.00
RB10 Glenn Dorsey/165 3.00 8.00
RB11 DeSean Jackson/165 6.00 15.00
RB12 Harry Douglas/199 4.00 10.00
RB13 Early Doucet/199 3.00 8.00
RB14 Andre Caldwell/165 3.00 8.00
RB15 Felix Jones/165 3.00 8.00
RB16 Dustin Keller/199 4.00 10.00
RB17 Jamaal Charles/165 12.00 30.00
RB18 Joe Flacco/165 6.00 15.00
RB19 John David Booty/165 3.00 8.00
RB20 Jonathan Stewart/125 15.00 40.00
RB21 Jordy Nelson/165 10.00 25.00
RB22 Jerome Simpson/165 4.00 10.00
RB23 Kevin Smith/165 3.00 8.00
RB24 Limas Sweed/165 3.00 8.00
RB25 Malcolm Kelly/165 3.00 8.00
RB26 Mario Manningham/166 3.00 8.00
RB27 James Hardy/165 3.00 8.00
RB28 Matt Forte/165 12.00 30.00
RB29 Matt Ryan/125 30.00 80.00
RB30 Dexter Jackson/165 5.00 12.00
RB31 Eddie Royal/165 3.00 8.00
RB32 Rashard Mendenhall/165 3.00 8.00
RB33 Ray Rice/165 3.00 8.00
RB34 Steve Slaton/165 3.00 8.00
RB35 Kevin O'Connell/165 3.00 8.00

2008 Upper Deck Icons Rookie Brilliance Jersey Silver

SILVER PRINT RUN 199 SER.#'d SETS
*GOLD/99: .5X TO 1.2X SILVER/199
GOLD PRINT RUN 99 SER.#'d SETS
*PATCH/35: 1X TO 2.5X SILVER/199
PATCH PRINT RUN 35 SER.#'d SETS
RB1 Donnie Avery 2.00 5.00
RB2 Jake Long 2.50 6.00
RB3 Brian Brohm 1.50 4.00
RB4 Chad Henne 2.00 5.00
RB5 Chris Johnson 2.00 5.00
RB6 Chris Long 2.00 5.00
RB7 Devin Thomas 1.50 4.00
RB8 Darren McFadden 1.50 4.00
RB9 Earl Bennett 2.50 6.00
RB10 Glenn Dorsey 1.50 4.00
RB11 DeSean Jackson 3.00 8.00
RB12 Harry Douglas 2.00 5.00
RB13 Early Doucet 1.50 4.00
RB14 Andre Caldwell 1.50 4.00
RB15 Felix Jones 1.50 4.00
RB16 Dustin Keller 2.00 5.00
RB17 Jamaal Charles 2.50 6.00
RB18 Joe Flacco 3.00 8.00
RB19 John David Booty 1.50 4.00
RB20 Jonathan Stewart 5.00 12.00
RB21 Jordy Nelson 5.00 12.00
RB22 Jerome Simpson 2.00 5.00
RB23 Kevin Smith 1.50 4.00
RB24 Limas Sweed 1.50 4.00
RB25 Malcolm Kelly 1.50 4.00
RB26 Mario Manningham 1.50 4.00
RB27 James Hardy 1.50 4.00
RB28 Matt Forte 2.50 6.00
RB29 Matt Ryan 5.00 12.00
RB30 Dexter Jackson 2.50 6.00
RB31 Eddie Royal 1.50 4.00
RB32 Rashard Mendenhall 1.50 4.00
RB33 Ray Rice 1.50 4.00
RB34 Steve Slaton 1.50 4.00
RB35 Kevin O'Connell 1.50 4.00

2009 Upper Deck Icons

MP.SET w/o SP's (100) 8.00 20.00
101-170 ROOKIE PRINT RUN 599
171-200 LEGEND PRINT RUN 599
1 Tony Romo .25 .60
2 Marion Barber .25 .60
3 Terrell Owens .25 .60
4 Jason Witten .25 .60
5 DeMarcus Ware .25 .60
6 Eli Manning .25 .60
7 Brandon Jacobs .20 .50
8 Antonio Pierce .20 .50
9 Donovan McNabb .25 .60
10 Brian Westbrook .20 .50
11 DeSean Jackson .25 .60
12 Chris Cooley .20 .50
13 Jason Campbell .20 .50
14 Clinton Portis .20 .50
15 Santana Moss .25 .60
16 Tim Hightower .20 .50
17 Larry Fitzgerald .25 .60
18 Anquan Boldin .20 .50
19 Kurt Warner .25 .60
20 Frank Gore .25 .60
21 Patrick Willis .25 .60
22 Isaac Bruce .30 .75
23 Julius Jones .20 .50
24 Steven Jackson .20 .50
25 Matt Forte .20 .50
26 Brian Urlacher .30 .75
27 Kyle Orton .20 .50
28 Calvin Johnson .30 .75
29 Aaron Rodgers .60 1.50
30 Ryan Grant .25 .60
31 Greg Jennings .20 .50
32 A.J. Hawk .20 .50
33 Aaron Kampman .25 .60
34 Adrian Peterson .30 .75
35 Matt Ryan .25 .60
36 Michael Turner .20 .50
37 Jake Delhomme .20 .50
38 Steve Smith .25 .60
39 DeAngelo Williams .20 .50
40 Drew Brees .30 .75
41 Reggie Bush .20 .50
42 Marques Colston .20 .50
43 Jonathan Vilma .20 .50
44 Earnest Graham .20 .50
45 Jeff Garcia .20 .50
46 Trent Edwards .20 .50
47 Marshawn Lynch .25 .60
48 Lee Evans .25 .60
49 Chad Pennington .20 .50
50 Ronnie Brown .20 .50
51 Joey Porter .25 .60
52 Tom Brady 1.00 2.50
53 Randy Moss .25 .60
54 Wes Welker .25 .60
55 Bart Scott .20 .50
56 Thomas Jones .20 .50
57 Laveranues Coles .20 .50
58 Jerricho Cotchery .20 .50
59 Jay Cutler .20 .50
60 Brandon Marshall .25 .60
61 Eddie Royal .20 .50
62 Tyler Thigpen .20 .50
63 Larry Johnson .20 .50
64 Dwayne Bowe .25 .60
65 Tony Gonzalez .25 .60
66 JaMarcus Russell .20 .50
67 Darren McFadden .30 .75
68 Philip Rivers .30 .75
69 LaDainian Tomlinson .30 .75
70 Antonio Gates .25 .60
71 Vincent Jackson .20 .50
72 Derrick Mason .20 .50
73 Ray Lewis .30 .75
74 Joe Flacco .25 .60
75 Carson Palmer .25 .60
76 Chad Johnson .20 .50
77 T.J. Houshmandzadeh .20 .50
78 Keith Rivers .20 .50
79 Jamal Lewis .25 .60
80 Brady Quinn .20 .50
81 Braylon Edwards .20 .50
82 Ben Roethlisberger .30 .75
83 Willie Parker .20 .50
84 Hines Ward .25 .60
85 Troy Polamalu .30 .75
86 James Harrison .30 .75
87 Steve Slaton .20 .50
88 Matt Schaub .20 .50
89 Andre Johnson .25 .60
90 Peyton Manning .75 2.00
91 Joseph Addai .20 .50
92 Reggie Wayne .25 .60
93 Bob Sanders .25 .60
94 David Garrard .20 .50
95 John Henderson .20 .50
96 Maurice Jones-Drew .20 .50
97 LenDale White .20 .50
98 Chris Johnson .20 .50
99 Albert Haynesworth .20 .50
100 Roddy White .20 .50
101 Matthew Stafford RC 5.00 12.00
102 Mark Sanchez RC 1.00 2.50
103 Eben Britton RC 1.25 3.00
104 Josh Freeman RC 1.00 2.50
105 Chris Wells RC 1.00 2.50
106 Javon Ringer RC 1.00 2.50
107 Knowshon Moreno RC 1.00 2.50
108 James Davis RC 1.00 2.50
109 Victor Harris RC 1.25 3.00
110 P.J. Hill RC 1.00 2.50
111 Michael Crabtree RC 1.50 4.00
112 Darrius Heyward-Bey RC 1.50 4.00
113 Jeremy Maclin RC 1.25 3.00
114 Percy Harvin RC 1.00 2.50
115 Brian Robiskie RC 1.00 2.50
116 Aaron Kelly RC 1.00 2.50
117 Kenny Britt RC 1.50 4.00
118 Ramses Barden RC 1.00 2.50
119 Alphonso Smith RC 1.00 2.50
120 Demetrius Byrd RC 1.25 3.00
121 Chase Coffman RC 1.00 2.50
122 Brandon Pettigrew RC 1.00 2.50
123 Clay Matthews RC 4.00 10.00
124 Fili Moala RC 1.00 2.50
125 Michael Oher RC 1.50 4.00
126 Andre Smith RC 1.00 2.50
127 Derek Pegues RC 1.00 2.50
128 Jason Smith RC 1.00 2.50
129 Duke Robinson RC 1.00 2.50
130 Max Unger RC 1.50 4.00
131 Hakeem Nicks RC 1.25 3.00
132 Alex Mack RC 1.00 2.50
133 Nate Davis RC 1.00 2.50
134 Andre Brown RC 1.25 3.00
135 Eugene Monroe RC 1.00 2.50
136 Alex Boone RC 1.50 4.00
137 Graham Harrell RC 1.00 2.50
138 Jonathan Luigs RC 1.00 2.50
139 Brian Orakpo RC 1.25 3.00
140 Patrick Chung RC 1.00 2.50
141 Austin Collie RC 1.00 2.50
142 Tyson Jackson RC 1.00 2.50
143 Michael Johnson RC 1.00 2.50
144 Devin Moore RC 1.00 2.50
145 Juaquin Iglesias RC 1.00 2.50
146 Quan Cosby RC 1.00 2.50
147 D.J. Moore RC 1.25 3.00
148 LeSean McCoy RC 2.50 6.00
149 Sean Smith RC 1.00 2.50
150 B.J. Raji RC 1.25 3.00
151 Jared Cook RC 1.25 3.00
152 Everette Brown RC 1.00 2.50
153 Cedric Peerman RC 1.00 2.50
154 James Laurinaitis RC 1.00 2.50
155 Rey Maualuga RC 1.50 4.00
156 Brandon Tate RC 1.25 3.00
157 Aaron Curry RC 1.50 4.00
158 Brian Cushing RC 1.00 2.50
159 Rashad Jennings RC 1.25 3.00
160 Marcus Freeman RC 1.00 2.50
161 Malcolm Jenkins RC 1.00 2.50
162 Vontae Davis RC 1.00 2.50
163 Mike Mickens RC 1.00 2.50
164 Derrick Williams RC 1.00 2.50
165 William Moore RC 1.00 2.50
166 Shonn Greene RC 1.00 2.50
167 Mohamed Massaquoi RC 1.00 2.50
168 Aaron Maybin RC 1.25 3.00
169 Donald Brown RC 1.00 2.50
170 Darius Butler RC 1.25 3.00
171 Bob Griese 2.00 5.00
172 Jack Youngblood 1.25 3.00
173 Thurman Thomas 1.50 4.00
174 Rocky Bleier 1.50 4.00
175 Jack Ham 1.50 4.00
176 Darrell Green 1.50 4.00
177 Paul Hornung 2.00 5.00
178 Ken Anderson 1.50 4.00
179 Joe Theismann 2.00 5.00
180 Barry Sanders 3.00 8.00
181 Bob Lilly 1.50 4.00
182 Merlin Olsen UER 1.25 3.00
183 Fred Biletnikoff 2.00 5.00
184 Earl Campbell 2.00 5.00
185 Jim Kelly 2.00 5.00
186 Daryl Johnston 1.50 4.00
187 Mike Ditka 2.00 5.00
188 Lem Barney 1.25 3.00
189 Mike Singletary 2.00 5.00
190 Don Maynard 1.50 4.00
191 Anthony Munoz 1.50 4.00
192 Ron Yary 1.25 3.00
193 John Elway 3.00 8.00
194 Terry Bradshaw 2.50 6.00
195 Billy Sims 1.50 4.00
196 Bubba Smith 1.25 3.00
197 Jerry Kramer 1.50 4.00
198 Alan Page 1.25 3.00
199 Tom Rathman 1.25 3.00
200 Alex Karras 1.50 4.00

2009 Upper Deck Icons Gold Holofoil Die Cut

*VETS 1-100: 4X TO 10X BASIC CARDS
1-100 STATED PRINT RUN 75
*ROOKIES 101-170: .8X TO 2X
101-170 STATED PRINT RUN 50
*LEGENDS 171-200: 1.2X TO 3X
171-200 STATED PRINT RUN 25

2009 Upper Deck Icons Gold Foil

ETS 1-100: 3X TO 8X BASIC CARDS
1-100 STATED PRINT RUN 125
*ROOKIES 101-170: .6X TO 1.5X
*LEGENDS 171-200: .6X TO 1.5X
101-200 STATED PRINT RUN 99

2009 Upper Deck Icons Rainbow Foil

*VETS: 1.5X TO 4X BASIC CARDS
RANDOM INSERTS IN RETAIL PACKS

2009 Upper Deck Icons Autographs

1-170 ROOKIE PRINT RUN 75-150
171-200 LEGEND PRINT RUN 5-25
101 Matthew Stafford/75 30.00 80.00
102 Mark Sanchez/75 20.00 50.00
103 Eben Britton 4.00 10.00
104 Josh Freeman/75 3.00 8.00
105 Chris Wells/75 15.00 40.00
106 Javon Ringer 3.00 8.00
107 Knowshon Moreno/75 3.00 8.00
108 James Davis 3.00 8.00
109 Victor Harris 4.00 10.00
110 P.J. Hill 3.00 8.00
111 Michael Crabtree/75 12.00 30.00
112 Darrius Heyward-Bey 5.00 12.00
113 Jeremy Maclin 4.00 10.00
114 Percy Harvin 3.00 8.00
115 Brian Robiskie 3.00 8.00
116 Aaron Kelly 3.00 8.00
117 Kenny Britt 5.00 12.00
118 Ramses Barden 3.00 8.00
119 Alphonso Smith 3.00 8.00
120 Demetrius Byrd 4.00 10.00
121 Chase Coffman 3.00 8.00
122 Brandon Pettigrew 3.00 8.00
123 Clay Matthews 25.00 50.00
124 Fili Moala 3.00 8.00
125 Michael Oher 15.00 40.00
126 Andre Smith 6.00 15.00
127 Derek Pegues 3.00 8.00
128 Jason Smith 3.00 8.00
129 Duke Robinson 3.00 8.00
130 Max Unger 5.00 12.00
131 Hakeem Nicks 4.00 10.00
132 Alex Mack 5.00 12.00
133 Nate Davis 3.00 8.00
134 Andre Brown 4.00 10.00
135 Eugene Monroe 3.00 8.00
136 Alex Boone 5.00 12.00
137 Graham Harrell 8.00 20.00
138 Jonathan Luigs 3.00 8.00
139 Brian Orakpo 4.00 10.00
140 Patrick Chung 6.00 15.00
141 Austin Collie 2.50 6.00
142 Tyson Jackson 3.00 8.00
143 Michael Johnson 3.00 8.00
144 Devin Moore 3.00 8.00
145 Juaquin Iglesias 3.00 8.00
146 Quan Cosby 3.00 8.00
147 D.J. Moore 4.00 10.00
148 LeSean McCoy 8.00 20.00
149 Sean Smith 5.00 12.00
150 B.J. Raji 4.00 10.00
151 Jared Cook 4.00 10.00
153 Cedric Peerman 3.00 8.00
154 James Laurinaitis 3.00 8.00
155 Rey Maualuga 5.00 12.00
156 Brandon Tate 4.00 10.00
157 Aaron Curry 5.00 12.00
158 Brian Cushing 3.00 8.00
159 Rashad Jennings 4.00 10.00
160 Marcus Freeman 3.00 8.00
161 Malcolm Jenkins 3.00 8.00
162 Vontae Davis 3.00 8.00
163 Mike Mickens 3.00 8.00
164 Derrick Williams 3.00 8.00
165 William Moore 3.00 8.00
166 Shonn Greene 3.00 8.00
167 Mohamed Massaquoi 3.00 8.00
169 Donald Brown/75 10.00 25.00
170 Darius Butler 6.00 15.00
174 Rocky Bleier/25 20.00 40.00
178 Ken Anderson/25 20.00 40.00
181 Bob Lilly/25 12.00 30.00
188 Lem Barney/25 12.00 30.00
191 Anthony Munoz/25 12.00 30.00
198 Alan Page/25 12.00 30.00
199 Tom Rathman/25 12.00 30.00
200 Alex Karras/25 12.00 30.00

2009 Upper Deck Icons Class of 2009 Silver

LVER PRINT RUN 450 SER.#'d SETS
*GOLD/130: .5X TO 1.2X SILVER/450
AC Aaron Curry 1.00 2.50
AS Andre Smith .60 1.50
BC Brian Cushing .60 1.50
BO Brian Orakpo .75 2.00
BP Brandon Pettigrew .60 1.50
BR Brian Robiskie .60 1.50
CC Chase Coffman .60 1.50
CM Clay Matthews 2.50 6.00
CW Chris Wells .60 1.50
DB Donald Brown .60 1.50
DH Darrius Heyward-Bey 1.00 2.50
DW Derrick Williams .60 1.50
EB Everette Brown .60 1.50
HN Hakeem Nicks .75 2.00
JD James Davis .60 1.50
JF Josh Freeman .60 1.50
JI Juaquin Iglesias .60 1.50
JL James Laurinaitis .60 1.50
JM Jeremy Maclin .75 2.00
JO Michael Johnson .60 1.50
JR Javon Ringer .60 1.50
KB Kenny Britt 1.00 2.50
KM Knowshon Moreno .60 1.50
LM LeSean McCoy 1.50 4.00
MC Michael Crabtree 1.00 2.50
MJ Malcolm Jenkins .60 1.50
MS Mark Sanchez .60 1.50
MU Louis Murphy .60 1.50
ND Nate Davis .60 1.50
PH Percy Harvin .60 1.50
RJ Rashad Jennings .75 2.00
RM Rey Maualuga 1.00 2.50
SG Shonn Greene .60 1.50
ST Matthew Stafford 3.00 8.00
VD Vontae Davis .60 1.50

2009 Upper Deck Icons Class of 2009 Autographs

STATED PRINT RUN 50-99
AC Aaron Curry/99 5.00 12.00
AS Andre Smith/99 3.00 8.00
BC Brian Cushing/99 3.00 8.00
BO Brian Orakpo/99 4.00 10.00
BP Brandon Pettigrew/99 3.00 8.00
BR Brian Robiskie/99 3.00 8.00
CC Chase Coffman/99 3.00 8.00
CM Clay Matthews/99 25.00 50.00
CW Chris Wells/50 12.00 30.00
DB Donald Brown/50 3.00 8.00
DH Darrius Heyward-Bey/50 5.00 12.00
DW Derrick Williams/99 3.00 8.00
HN Hakeem Nicks/99 4.00 10.00
JD James Davis/99 3.00 8.00
JF Josh Freeman/50 3.00 8.00
JI Juaquin Iglesias/99 3.00 8.00
JL James Laurinaitis/99 3.00 8.00
JM Jeremy Maclin/50 4.00 10.00
JO Michael Johnson/99 4.00 10.00
JR Javon Ringer/99 3.00 8.00
KB Kenny Britt/99 5.00 12.00
KM Knowshon Moreno/50 3.00 8.00
LM LeSean McCoy/99 8.00 20.00
MC Michael Crabtree/50 12.00 30.00
MJ Malcolm Jenkins/99 3.00 8.00
MS Mark Sanchez/50 15.00 40.00
ND Nate Davis/99 3.00 8.00
PH Percy Harvin/99 3.00 8.00
RJ Rashad Jennings/99 4.00 10.00
RM Rey Maualuga/99 5.00 12.00
SG Shonn Greene/99 3.00 8.00
ST Matthew Stafford/50 30.00 80.00
VD Vontae Davis/99 3.00 8.00

2009 Upper Deck Icons Decade of Dominance Silver

LVER PRINT RUN 450 SER.#'d SETS
*GOLD/130: .6X TO 1.5X SILVER/450
DDAP Adrian Peterson 1.50 4.00
DDBR Ben Roethlisberger 1.50 4.00
DDBU Brian Urlacher 1.50 4.00
DDBW Brian Westbrook 1.00 2.50
DDCJ Calvin Johnson 1.50 4.00
DDCP Clinton Portis 1.00 2.50
DDCU Jay Cutler 1.00 2.50
DDDB Derrick Brooks 1.00 2.50
DDDC Dallas Clark 1.00 2.50
DDDF Dwight Freeney 1.00 2.50
DDDH Devin Hester 1.25 3.00
DDDS Darren Sharper 1.00 2.50
DDDW DeMarcus Ware 1.25 3.00
DDEM Eli Manning 1.25 3.00
DDER Ed Reed 1.25 3.00
DDFA Brett Favre 3.00 8.00
DDFG Frank Gore 1.25 3.00
DDGJ Greg Jennings 1.00 2.50
DDHO T.J. Houshmandzadeh 1.00 2.50
DDHW Hines Ward 1.25 3.00
DDJA Jared Allen 1.00 2.50
DDJH James Harrison 1.50 4.00
DDJP Joey Porter 1.25 3.00
DDJW Jason Witten 1.25 3.00
DDLB Lance Briggs 1.25 3.00
DDLF Larry Fitzgerald 1.25 3.00
DDMB Marion Barber 1.25 3.00
DDMJ Maurice Jones-Drew 1.00 2.50
DDMW Mario Williams 1.25 3.00
DDNA Nnamdi Asomugha 1.00 2.50
DDPM Peyton Manning 4.00 10.00
DDPR Philip Rivers 1.50 4.00
DDPW Patrick Willis 1.25 3.00
DDRW Reggie Wayne 1.25 3.00
DDSJ Steven Jackson 1.00 2.50
DDTB Tom Brady 5.00 12.00
DDTO LaDainian Tomlinson 1.50 4.00
DDTP Troy Polamalu 1.50 4.00
DDTR Tony Romo 1.25 3.00
DDWJ Walter Jones 1.00 2.50

2009 Upper Deck Icons Decade of Dominance Jerseys

STATED PRINT RUN 150-199
DDBR Ben Roethlisberger/199 4.00 10.00
DDBU Brian Urlacher/199 4.00 10.00
DDBW Brian Westbrook/199 2.50 6.00
DDCP Clinton Portis/199 2.50 6.00
DDCU Jay Cutler/199 2.50 6.00
DDDC Dallas Clark/199 2.50 6.00
DDDH Devin Hester/199 3.00 8.00
DDDW DeMarcus Ware/199 3.00 8.00
DDEM Eli Manning/199 3.00 8.00
DDFA Brett Favre/199 8.00 20.00
DDFG Frank Gore/199 3.00 8.00
DDHO T.J. Houshmandzadeh/199 2.50 6.00
DDHW Hines Ward/199 4.00 10.00
DDJA Jared Allen/199 4.00 10.00
DDJW Jason Witten/150 3.00 8.00
DDLF Larry Fitzgerald/199 3.00 8.00
DDMJ Maurice Jones-Drew/199 2.50 6.00
DDPM Peyton Manning/199 10.00 25.00
DDPR Philip Rivers/150 4.00 10.00
DDPW Patrick Willis/199 3.00 8.00
DDRW Reggie Wayne/199 3.00 8.00
DDSJ Steven Jackson/199 2.50 6.00
DDTB Tom Brady/199 8.00 20.00
DDTO LaDainian Tomlinson/199 4.00 10.00
DDTP Troy Polamalu/199 6.00 15.00
DDTR Tony Romo/199 3.00 8.00

2009 Upper Deck Icons Greats of the Game Silver

SILVER PRINT RUN 450 SER.#'d SETS
*DIE CUT/40: 1X TO 2.5X SILVER/450
*GOLD/199: .5X TO 1.2X SILVER/450
GGBG Bob Griese 1.50 4.00
GGBJ Bo Jackson 2.00 5.00
GGBS Barry Sanders 2.50 6.00
GGDB Dick Butkus 2.00 5.00
GGDJ Daryl Johnston 1.25 3.00
GGES Emmitt Smith 2.50 6.00
GGFH Franco Harris 1.50 4.00
GGGS Gale Sayers 1.50 4.00
GGJE John Elway 2.50 6.00
GGJH Jack Ham 1.25 3.00
GGJT Joe Theismann 1.50 4.00
GGKW Kellen Winslow Sr. 1.25 3.00
GGMD Mike Ditka 1.50 4.00
GGPH Paul Hornung 1.50 4.00
GGRS Roger Staubach 2.00 5.00
GGSI Billy Sims 1.25 3.00
GGST Bart Starr 2.50 6.00
GGSY Steve Young 2.00 5.00
GGTA Troy Aikman 2.00 5.00
GGTB Terry Bradshaw 2.00 5.00

2009 Upper Deck Icons Greats of the Game Jerseys

STATED PRINT RUN 99 SER.#'d SETS
GGBG Bob Griese 6.00 15.00
GGBJ Bo Jackson 8.00 20.00
GGBS Barry Sanders 10.00 25.00
GGDB Dick Butkus 8.00 20.00

GGDJ Daryl Johnston 10.00 25.00
GGES Emmitt Smith 10.00 25.00
GGFH Franco Harris 6.00 15.00
GGGS Gale Sayers 6.00 15.00
GGJE John Elway 10.00 25.00
GGJT Joe Theismann 6.00 15.00
GGKW Kellen Winslow Sr. 5.00 12.00
GGPH Paul Hornung 6.00 15.00
GGRS Roger Staubach 10.00 25.00
GGSI Billy Sims 5.00 12.00
GGSY Steve Young 8.00 20.00
GGTA Troy Aikman 8.00 20.00
GGTB Terry Bradshaw 8.00 20.00

2009 Upper Deck Icons Immortal Lettermen

TAL PRINT RUNS 430-630
STATED PRINT RUNS 62-150
ILAK Alex Karras/525* 5.00 12.00
ILAP Alan Page/532* 8.00 20.00
ILBG Bob Griese/600* 8.00 20.00
ILBL Bobby Layne/430* 6.00 15.00
ILBP Brian Piccolo/600* 8.00 20.00
ILBT Bulldog Turner/430* 6.00 15.00
ILCB Chuck Bednarik/528* 5.00 12.00
ILCH Chuck Howley/525* 6.00 15.00
ILCR Roger Craig/525* 5.00 12.00
ILDJ Deacon Jones/524* 5.00 12.00
ILDM Don Maynard/524* 5.00 12.00
ILEC Earl Campbell/594* 6.00 15.00
ILED Eric Dickerson/600* 6.00 15.00
ILEJ Ed Jones/525* 5.00 12.00
ILFB Fred Biletnikoff/609* 10.00 25.00
ILFH Franco Harris/592* 8.00 20.00
ILGH George Halas/430* 8.00 20.00
ILGS Gale Sayers/600* 8.00 20.00
ILHC Harry Carson/522* 5.00 12.00
ILJG Joe Greene/592* 8.00 20.00
ILJK Jerry Kramer/532* 5.00 12.00
ILJR Jerry Rice/620* 15.00 40.00
ILJU Johnny Unitas/630* 10.00 25.00
ILJZ Jim Zorn/520* 8.00 20.00
ILKW Kellen Winslow Sr./568* 5.00 12.00
ILMD Mike Ditka/600* 10.00 25.00
ILMO Merlin Olsen/524* 5.00 12.00
ILMS Mike Singletary/575* 8.00 20.00
ILPS Phil Simms/594* 5.00 12.00
ILRB Rocky Bleier/520* 6.00 15.00
ILRC Randall Cunningham/594* 8.00 20.00
ILRG Roman Gabriel/524* 6.00 15.00
ILTB Terry Bradshaw/600* 10.00 25.00
ILTT Thurman Thomas/600* 6.00 15.00
ILVL Vince Lombardi/434* 8.00 20.00
ILYT Y.A. Tittle/624* 6.00 15.00
ILBL1 Bob Lilly/525* 8.00 20.00
ILPH1 Paul Hornung/574* 8.00 20.00

2009 Upper Deck Icons Immortal Lettermen Autographs

TOTAL AUTO PRINT RUNS 24-104
AUTO STATED PRINT RUNS 3-25
ILAK Alex Karras/100* 15.00 40.00
ILAP Alan Page/98* 25.00 60.00
ILBL Bob Lilly/98* 15.00 40.00
ILCH Chuck Howley/98* 25.00 50.00
ILCR Roger Craig/100* 12.00 30.00
ILDJ Deacon Jones/100* 12.00 30.00
ILDM Don Maynard/100* 15.00 40.00
ILEC Earl Campbell/24* 25.00 50.00
ILEJ Ed Jones/98* 15.00 40.00
ILFH Franco Harris/24* 40.00 80.00
ILHC Harry Carson/102* 12.00 30.00
ILJK Jerry Kramer/98* 20.00 50.00
ILJZ Jim Zorn/96* 12.00 30.00
ILKW Kellen Winslow Sr./48* 25.00 50.00
ILGS Gale Sayers/25* 25.00 50.00
ILMO Merlin Olsen/100* 15.00 40.00
ILPH Paul Hornung/49* 20.00 50.00
ILPS Phil Simms/24* 40.00 80.00
ILRB Rocky Bleier/104* 30.00 60.00
ILRC Randall Cunningham/30* 30.00 60.00
ILRG Roman Gabriel/100* 15.00 40.00
ILTT Thurman Thomas/25* 30.00 60.00

2009 Upper Deck Icons Movie Lettermen

TOTAL PRINT RUNS 216-555
STATED PRINT RUNS 20-111
MLAH Anthony Michael Hall/540* 4.00 10.00
MLBB Beau Bridges/539* 4.00 10.00
MLCH Corey Haim/555* 4.00 10.00
MLEB Ernest Borgnine/546* 4.00 10.00
MLHW Henry Winkler/220* 4.00 10.00
MLLH Lauren Holley/220* 5.00 12.00
MLMR Mickey Rourke/91/146 4.00 10.00
MLSA Sean Astin/224* 4.00 10.00
MLSB Scott Bakula/216* 5.00 12.00
MMBJ Bruce Jenner/220* 4.00 10.00
MMCS Charlie Sheen/222* 4.00 10.00

2009 Upper Deck Icons Movie Lettermen Autographs

TOTAL AUTO PRINT RUN 100
AUTO STATED PRINT RUNS 10-20
MLAH Anthony Michael Hall EXCH 12.50 25.00
MLCH Corey Haim/100* 90.00 150.00
MLEB Ernest Borgnine EXCH 15.00 30.00
MLHW Henry Winkler/100* 20.00 40.00
MLMR Mickey Rourke EXCH 15.00 30.00
MLSA Sean Astin/100*

2009 Upper Deck Icons NFL Icons Silver

LVER PRINT RUN 450 SER.#'d SETS
*GOLD/199: .5X TO 1.2X SILVER/450
*DIE CUT/40: .8X TO 2X SILVER/450
ICAG Antonio Gates 1.25 3.00
ICAP Adrian Peterson 1.50 4.00
ICBA Brandon Jacobs 1.00 2.50
ICBD Brian Dawkins 1.00 2.50
ICBF Brett Favre 3.00 8.00
ICBH Braylon Edwards 1.00 2.50
ICBM Brandon Marshall 1.25 3.00
ICBR Drew Brees 1.50 4.00
ICCB Champ Bailey 1.25 3.00
ICCC Chris Cooley 1.00 2.50
ICCJ Chad Johnson 1.00 2.50
ICCP Clinton Portis 1.00 2.50
ICDB Deion Branch 1.00 2.50
ICDC Dallas Clark 1.00 2.50
ICDD Donald Driver 1.25 3.00
ICDG David Garrard 1.00 2.50
ICDI DeAngelo Williams 1.00 2.50
ICDM Donovan McNabb 1.25 3.00
ICDW DeMarcus Ware 1.25 3.00
ICEJ Edgerrin James 1.25 3.00
ICFG Frank Gore 1.25 3.00
ICHW Hines Ward 1.25 3.00
ICJA Joseph Addai 1.00 2.50
ICJC Jay Cutler 1.00 2.50
ICJL Jamal Lewis 1.25 3.00
ICJP Julius Peppers 1.25 3.00
ICJT Jason Taylor 1.25 3.00
ICKW Kellen Winslow Jr. 1.00 2.50
ICLE Lee Evans 1.25 3.00
ICLJ Larry Johnson 1.00 2.50
ICLT LaDainian Tomlinson 1.50 4.00
ICMB Marc Bulger 1.00 2.50
ICMC Marques Colston 1.00 2.50
ICMH Marvin Harrison 1.25 3.00
ICMJ Maurice Jones-Drew 1.00 2.50
ICMK Matt Hasselbeck 1.00 2.50
ICML Marshawn Lynch 1.25 3.00
ICPM Peyton Manning 4.00 10.00
ICPW Patrick Willis 1.25 3.00
ICRB Ronde Barber 1.00 2.50
ICRL Ray Lewis 1.50 4.00
ICRR Ronnie Brown 1.00 2.50
ICRU Reggie Bush 1.00 2.50
ICSH Santonio Holmes 1.00 2.50
ICSJ Steven Jackson 1.00 2.50
ICSS Steve Smith 1.25 3.00
ICTB Tom Brady 5.00 12.00
ICTG Tony Gonzalez 1.25 3.00
ICVJ Vincent Jackson 1.00 2.50
ICWP Willie Parker 1.00 2.50

2009 Upper Deck Icons NFL Icons Jerseys

STATED PRINT RUN 299 SER.#'d SETS
ICAG Antonio Gates 3.00 8.00
ICBA Brandon Jacobs 2.50 6.00
ICBD Brian Dawkins 2.50 6.00
ICBF Brett Favre 8.00 20.00
ICBH Braylon Edwards 2.50 6.00
ICBM Brandon Marshall 3.00 8.00
ICBR Drew Brees 4.00 10.00
ICCB Champ Bailey 3.00 8.00
ICCJ Chad Johnson 2.50 6.00
ICCP Clinton Portis 2.50 6.00
ICDB Deion Branch 2.50 6.00
ICDC Dallas Clark 2.50 6.00
ICDD Donald Driver 3.00 8.00
ICDG David Garrard 2.50 6.00
ICDI DeAngelo Williams 2.50 6.00
ICDM Donovan McNabb 3.00 8.00
ICDW DeMarcus Ware 3.00 8.00
ICEJ Edgerrin James 3.00 8.00
ICFG Frank Gore 3.00 8.00
ICHW Hines Ward 3.00 8.00
ICJA Joseph Addai 2.50 6.00
ICJC Jay Cutler 2.50 6.00
ICJL Jamal Lewis 3.00 8.00
ICJP Julius Peppers 3.00 8.00
ICJT Jason Taylor 3.00 8.00
ICKW Kellen Winslow Jr. 2.50 6.00
ICLE Lee Evans 3.00 8.00
ICLJ Larry Johnson 2.50 6.00
ICLT LaDainian Tomlinson 4.00 10.00
ICMB Marc Bulger 2.50 6.00
ICMC Marques Colston 2.50 6.00
ICMH Marvin Harrison 3.00 8.00
ICMJ Maurice Jones-Drew 2.50 6.00
ICMK Matt Hasselbeck 2.50 6.00
ICML Marshawn Lynch 3.00 8.00
ICPM Peyton Manning 10.00 25.00
ICPW Patrick Willis 3.00 8.00
ICRB Ronde Barber 2.50 6.00
ICRL Ray Lewis 4.00 10.00
ICRR Ronnie Brown 2.50 6.00
ICRU Reggie Bush 2.50 6.00
ICSH Santonio Holmes 2.50 6.00
ICSJ Steven Jackson 2.50 6.00
ICSS Steve Smith 3.00 8.00
ICTB Tom Brady 12.00 30.00
ICTG Tony Gonzalez 3.00 8.00
ICVJ Vincent Jackson 2.50 6.00
ICWP Willie Parker 2.50 6.00

2009 Upper Deck Icons NFL Reflections Silver

SILVER PRINT RUN 450 SER.#'d SETS
*GOLD/199: .5X TO 1.2X SILVER/450
*DIE CUT/40: .8X TO 2X SILVER/450
RFAP J.Addai/W.Parker 1.00 2.50
RFBB C.Bailey/R.Barber 1.25 3.00
RFBE B.Edwards/D.Branch 1.00 2.50
RFBJ M.Jones-Drew/R.Brown 1.00 2.50
RFBV M.Vrabel/T.Bruschi 1.25 3.00
RFCE L.Evans/M.Colston 1.25 3.00
RFDJ A.Johnson/D.Driver 1.25 3.00
RFDS A.Schobel/V.Davis 1.00 2.50
RFGC A.Gates/D.Clark 1.25 3.00
RFGH J.Garcia/M.Hasselbeck 1.00 2.50
RFGY D.Garrard/V.Young 1.00 2.50
RFHH D.Hester/S.Holmes 1.25 3.00
RFJC M.Jenkins/R.Curry 1.00 2.50
RFJG E.James/F.Gore 1.25 3.00
RFJL B.Jacobs/J.Lewis 1.25 3.00
RFJM D.McAllister/L.Johnson 1.25 3.00
RFLW De.Williams/M.Lynch 1.25 3.00
RFMC D.McNabb/J.Cutler 1.25 3.00
RFMS D.Sproles/L.Maroney 1.25 3.00
RFMW B.Watson/H.Miller 1.00 2.50
RFQS B.Quinn/M.Schaub 1.00 2.50
RFRH A.Ross/M.Huff 1.00 2.50
RFSJ S.Smith/V.Jackson 1.00 2.50
RFSP A.Smith/C.Palmer 1.50 4.00
RFTP J.Taylor/J.Peppers 1.25 3.00

2009 Upper Deck Icons NFL Reflections Jerseys

STATED PRINT RUN 99 SER.#'d SETS
RFAP J.Addai/W.Parker 4.00 10.00
RFBB C.Bailey/R.Barber 5.00 12.00
RFBE B.Edwards/D.Branch 4.00 10.00
RFBJ M.Jones-Drew/R.Brown 4.00 10.00
RFBV M.Vrabel/T.Bruschi 5.00 12.00
RFCE L.Evans/M.Colston 5.00 12.00
RFDJ A.Johnson/D.Driver 5.00 12.00
RFDS A.Schobel/V.Davis 4.00 10.00
RFGC A.Gates/D.Clark 5.00 12.00
RFGH J.Garcia/M.Hasselbeck 4.00 10.00
RFGY D.Garrard/V.Young 4.00 10.00
RFHH D.Hester/S.Holmes 5.00 12.00
RFJC M.Jenkins/R.Curry 4.00 10.00
RFJG E.James/F.Gore 5.00 12.00
RFJL B.Jacobs/J.Lewis 5.00 12.00
RFJM D.McAllister/L.Johnson 5.00 12.00
RFLW De.Williams/M.Lynch 5.00 12.00
RFMC D.McNabb/J.Cutler 5.00 12.00
RFMS D.Sproles/L.Maroney 5.00 12.00
RFMW B.Watson/H.Miller 4.00 10.00
RFQS B.Quinn/M.Schaub 4.00 10.00
RFRH A.Ross/M.Huff 4.00 10.00
RFSJ S.Smith/V.Jackson 4.00 10.00
RFSP A.Smith/C.Palmer 6.00 15.00
RFTP J.Taylor/J.Peppers 5.00 12.00

2009 Upper Deck Icons Sophomore Sensations Silver

SILVER PRINT RUN 450 SER.#'d SETS
*GOLD/130: .5X TO 1.2X SILVER/450
SSBB Brian Brohm 1.00 2.50
SSCJ Chris Johnson 1.00 2.50
SSDA Donnie Avery 1.00 2.50
SSDJ DeSean Jackson 1.25 3.00
SSDK Dustin Keller 1.00 2.50
SSDM Darren McFadden 1.50 4.00
SSEB Earl Bennett 1.25 3.00
SSED Early Doucet 1.25 3.00
SSER Eddie Royal 1.00 2.50
SSFJ Felix Jones 1.00 2.50
SSHD Harry Douglas 1.00 2.50
SSJB John David Booty 1.25 3.00
SSJC Jamaal Charles 1.25 3.00
SSJF Joe Flacco 1.25 3.00
SSJH James Hardy 1.25 3.00
SSJN Jordy Nelson 1.25 3.00
SSJS Jonathan Stewart 1.00 2.50
SSKS Kevin Smith 1.00 2.50
SSLS Limas Sweed 1.25 3.00
SSMF Matt Forte 1.00 2.50
SSMK Malcolm Kelly 1.00 2.50
SSMR Matt Ryan 1.25 3.00

2009 Upper Deck Icons Sophomore Sensations Jerseys

STATED PRINT RUN 299 SER.#'d SETS
SSBB Brian Brohm 2.50 6.00
SSCJ Chris Johnson 2.50 6.00
SSDA Donnie Avery 2.50 6.00
SSDJ DeSean Jackson 3.00 8.00
SSDK Dustin Keller 2.50 6.00
SSDM Darren McFadden 4.00 10.00
SSEB Earl Bennett 3.00 8.00
SSER Eddie Royal 2.50 6.00
SSFJ Felix Jones 2.50 6.00
SSHD Harry Douglas 2.50 6.00
SSJB John David Booty 3.00 8.00
SSJC Jamaal Charles 3.00 8.00
SSJF Joe Flacco 3.00 8.00
SSJH James Hardy 3.00 8.00
SSJN Jordy Nelson 3.00 8.00
SSJS Jonathan Stewart 2.50 6.00
SSKS Kevin Smith 2.50 6.00
SSLS Limas Sweed 3.00 8.00
SSMF Matt Forte 2.50 6.00
SSMK Malcolm Kelly 2.50 6.00
SSMR Matt Ryan 3.00 8.00

2009 Upper Deck Icons Sophomore Sensations Autographs

STATED PRINT RUN 50 SER.#'d SETS
SSBB Brian Brohm/50 8.00 20.00
SSCJ Chris Johnson/50 8.00 20.00
SSDA Donnie Avery/50 8.00 20.00
SSDJ DeSean Jackson/50 10.00 25.00
SSDK Dustin Keller/50 8.00 20.00
SSEB Earl Bennett/50 10.00 25.00
SSED Early Doucet/50 10.00 25.00
SSER Eddie Royal/50 8.00 20.00
SSFJ Felix Jones/50 12.00 30.00
SSHD Harry Douglas/50 8.00 20.00
SSJB John David Booty/50 10.00 25.00
SSJC Jamaal Charles/50 10.00 25.00
SSJF Joe Flacco/50 10.00 25.00
SSJH James Hardy/50 10.00 25.00
SSJN Jordy Nelson/50 10.00 25.00
SSJS Jonathan Stewart/30 12.00 30.00
SSKS Kevin Smith/50 8.00 20.00
SSLS Limas Sweed/50 10.00 25.00
SSMF Matt Forte/50 8.00 20.00
SSMK Malcolm Kelly/50 8.00 20.00

2009 Upper Deck Icons Sports Lettermen

TOTAL PRINT RUNS 250-297
STATED PRINT RUNS 25-43
SLKY Kristi Yamaguchi/297* 5.00 12.00
SLLD Lindsay Davenport/33 4.00 10.00
(Letters spell out DAVENPORT
Total print run 297)
SLLH Laird Hamilton/296* 5.00 12.00
SLMJ Michael Johnson track/294* 5.00 12.00
SLPD Phil Dalhausser/250* 5.00 12.00
SLPF Peggy Fleming/294* 4.00 10.00

2009 Upper Deck Icons Sports Lettermen Autographs

SLKY Kristi Yamaguchi/27* 50.00 100.00
SLMJ Michael Johnson track EXCH 20.00 40.00
SLPD Phil Dalhausser EXCH 15.00 30.00
SLPF Peggy Fleming EXCH 20.00 40.00

2009 Upper Deck Icons Sweet Spot Icons Autographs

SSIAH Anthony Michael Hall 15.00 30.00
SSIAM Archie Manning/98 30.00 60.00
SSIBS Billy Sims EXCH
SSICF Carrie Fisher EXCH
SSICH Corey Haim/120 60.00 100.00
SSIJP Jeremy Piven/50 40.00 80.00
SSIKA Ken Anderson/60 20.00 40.00
SSIKK Kim Kardashian/55 40.00 100.00
SSIPB Pete Best/100 40.00 80.00
SSIRC Roger Craig/60 20.00 40.00
SSIRK Mickey Rourke/50 25.00 50.00
SSISS Scottie Schwartz/100 12.50 25.00
SSITR Tom Rathman/100 20.00 40.00

2012 Upper Deck Industry Summit Signature Icons Autographs

LAS VEGAS INDUSTRY SUMMIT EXCLUSIVE
LVGS Gale Sayers/25

2015 Upper Deck Inscriptions

EXCH EXPIRATION: 2/23/2017
AA Ameer Abdullah SP 4.00 10.00
AB Anthony Boone
AC Amari Cooper SP 25.00 60.00
AD Alvin Dupree 3.00 8.00
AG Antwan Goodley SP
AH Anthony Harris EXCH
AM Malcolm Agnew 2.50 6.00
AN Andre Davis 2.50 6.00
AU Austin Hill 2.50 6.00
BB Brandon Bridge SP 5.00 12.00
BE Michael Bennett RB 4.00 10.00
BH Brett Hundley SP 20.00 40.00
BJ Byron Jones 4.00 10.00
BK Ben Koyack 4.00 10.00
BL Blake Bell 4.00 10.00
BP Bryce Petty SP 8.00 20.00
BW Bo Wallace 2.50 6.00
CE Cameron Erving 3.00 8.00
CF Cody Fajardo SP
CH Connor Halliday 4.00 10.00
CJ Christion Jones 2.50 6.00
CO Cedric Ogbuehi 2.50 6.00
CP Cameron Artis-Payne 6.00 15.00
CR Cody Riggs 4.00 10.00
CS Cole Stoudt 4.00 10.00
DA Dres Anderson 2.50 6.00
DB Dorial Green-Beckham SP EXCH 30.00 60.00
DC David Cobb 2.50 6.00
DD Devante Davis 3.00 8.00
DE Devante Parker SP 4.00 10.00
DF Devin Funchess SP 4.00 10.00
DG Devin Gardner 4.00 10.00
DJ Duke Johnson SP 4.00 10.00
DL Deon Long 3.00 8.00
DO Dominique Brown 2.50 6.00
DS Devin Smith 2.50 6.00
DW DeAndrew White 4.00 10.00
DY Michael Dyer 4.00 10.00
GE Terrance Magee EXCH
GG Garrett Grayson 2.50 6.00
GN Gary Nova 2.50 6.00
HA Justin Hardy 2.50 6.00
JE Jeff Heuerman 3.00 8.00
HM Hutson Mason 2.50 6.00
IO Ifo Ekpre-Olomu 2.50 6.00
IP Jaxon Shipley 2.50 6.00
JA Jay Ajayi SP EXCH 8.00 20.00
JB Javorius Allen 3.00 8.00
JC Jamison Crowder 3.00 8.00
JE Jahwan Edwards 3.00 8.00
JH Josh Harper 2.50 6.00
JM Justin McCay 3.00 8.00
JO David Johnson 10.00 25.00
JS Jaelen Strong SP 3.00 8.00
JT Jordan Taylor 10.00 25.00
JW Jameis Winston SP 75.00 200.00
KA Karlos Williams EXCH 8.00 20.00
KB Kenny Bell 4.00 10.00
KP Kevin Parks 2.50 6.00
KW Kevin White SP 12.00 30.00
LC La'el Collins 3.00 8.00
LM Lorenzo Mauldin 2.50 6.00
LN Levi Norwood 2.50 6.00
LO Tyler Lockett 4.00 10.00
LW Leonard Williams 2.50 6.00
MA Venric Mark 3.00 8.00
MB Malcolm Brown
MD Mike Davis SP
MG Melvin Gordon III SP 10.00 25.00
MI Matt Miller 2.50 6.00
MM Marcus Mariota SP 30.00 60.00
MO Nick Montana 4.00 10.00
NA Nelson Agholor SP EXCH 3.00 8.00
NM Nick Marshall EXCH 4.00 10.00
NO Nick O'Leary EXCH 2.50 6.00
OS Josh Shaw 4.00 10.00
PD Phillip Dorsett 2.50 6.00
PE Denzel Perryman 2.50 6.00
RC Rakeem Cato 4.00 10.00
RG Rashad Greene SP 2.50 6.00
RH Rannell Hall 2.50 6.00
SC Sammie Coates SP
SH Shane Carden SP
SM Sean Mannion SP 2.50 6.00
SN Steven Nelson EXCH
TC Tevin Coleman 3.00 8.00
TD Titus Davis EXCH
TG Todd Gurley SP 15.00 40.00
TH Taylor Heinicke 4.00 10.00
TJ Terris Jones-Grigsby 3.00 8.00
TK Taylor Kelly SP
TL Tony Lippett 2.50 6.00
TY T.J. Yeldon SP 10.00 25.00
VB Vic Beasley 3.00 8.00
VE Marcus Murphy 2.50 6.00
VM Vince Mayle 3.00 8.00
WA Jake Waters 3.00 8.00
WE Jarrod West 3.00 8.00
WS Wes Saxton 3.00 8.00

2015 Upper Deck Inscriptions Black

*BLACK/25: 1X TO 2.5X BASIC AU
*BLACK/25: .8X TO 2X BASIC AU SP
AC Amari Cooper 100.00 200.00
DB Dorial Green-Beckham EXCH 60.00 100.00
DJ Duke Johnson 25.00 60.00
JA Jay Ajayi EXCH 25.00 50.00
JW Jameis Winston
KB Kenny Bell 25.00 60.00
TG Todd Gurley 40.00 100.00

2015 Upper Deck Inscriptions Red

*RED/149: .5X TO 1.2X BASIC AUTO
*RED/75: .6X TO 1.5X BASIC AUTO
*RED/49: .8X TO 2X BASIC AUTO
DJ Duke Johnson/75 30.00 60.00
JW Jameis Winston/49 125.00 250.00

2008 Upper Deck Kellogg's Autographs

JB Jerome Bettis 20.00 50.00
JR Jerry Rice 30.00 60.00
JT Joe Theismann 8.00 20.00

2005 Upper Deck Kickoff

This 135-card set was released through Upper Deck retail channels in August, 2005. The set was issued in six-card packs which came 24 packs to a box. Cards numbered 1-100 feature veteran players in team alphabetical order while cards numbered 91-135 featured 2005 rookies. Those rookies were inserted at a stated rate of one per pack.

COMPLETE SET (135) 20.00 50.00
COMP.SET w/o RC's (90) 7.50 20.00
ONE DRAFT PICK PER PACK
1 Larry Fitzgerald .20 .50
2 Anquan Boldin .12 .30
3 Josh McCown .15 .40
4 Michael Vick .15 .40
5 Alge Crumpler .15 .40
6 Peerless Price .12 .30
7 Ray Lewis .20 .50
8 Kyle Boller .12 .30
9 Derrick Mason .12 .30
10 J.P. Losman .12 .30
11 Willis McGahee .12 .30
12 Eric Moulds .12 .30
13 Jake Delhomme .12 .30
14 DeShaun Foster .15 .40
15 Steve Smith .20 .50
16 Thomas Jones .12 .30
17 Rex Grossman .12 .30
18 Muhsin Muhammad .12 .30
19 Carson Palmer .15 .40
20 Rudi Johnson .12 .30
21 Chad Johnson .12 .30
22 Julius Jones .12 .30
23 Keyshawn Johnson .15 .40
24 Drew Bledsoe .15 .40
25 Tatum Bell .12 .30
26 Jake Plummer .12 .30
27 Ashley Lelie .12 .30
28 Roy Williams WR .12 .30
29 Kevin Jones .12 .30
30 Joey Harrington .12 .30
31 Brett Favre .40 1.00
32 Ahman Green .15 .40
33 Javon Walker .12 .30
34 David Carr .12 .30
35 Andre Johnson .15 .40
36 Domanick Davis .12 .30
37 Peyton Manning .50 1.25
38 Reggie Wayne .15 .40
39 Marvin Harrison .15 .40
40 Byron Leftwich .12 .30
41 Fred Taylor .12 .30
42 Jimmy Smith .15 .40
43 Priest Holmes .12 .30
44 Larry Johnson .12 .30
45 Trent Green .12 .30
46 A.J. Feeley .12 .30
47 Chris Chambers .12 .30
48 Randy McMichael .12 .30
49 Daunte Culpepper .15 .40
50 Michael Bennett .12 .30
51 Nate Burleson .12 .30
52 Tom Brady .75 2.00
53 Corey Dillon .12 .30
54 Deion Branch .12 .30
55 Aaron Brooks .12 .30
56 Deuce McAllister .15 .40
57 Joe Horn .12 .30
58 Eli Manning .30 .75
59 Jeremy Shockey .12 .30
60 Tiki Barber .15 .40
61 Chad Pennington .12 .30
62 Curtis Martin .15 .40
63 Kerry Collins .12 .30
64 Jerry Porter .12 .30
65 Randy Moss .15 .40
66 Donovan McNabb .15 .40
67 Terrell Owens .15 .40
68 Brian Westbrook .12 .30
69 Ben Roethlisberger .30 .75
70 Jerome Bettis .20 .50
71 Hines Ward .15 .40
72 Drew Brees .20 .50
73 LaDainian Tomlinson .20 .50
74 Antonio Gates .20 .50
75 Kevan Barlow .12 .30
76 Eric Johnson .12 .30
77 Shaun Alexander .12 .30
78 Matt Hasselbeck .12 .30
79 Marc Bulger .12 .30
80 Steven Jackson .12 .30
81 Torry Holt .15 .40
82 Michael Pittman .12 .30
83 Brian Griese .12 .30
84 Michael Clayton .12 .30
85 Steve McNair .15 .40
86 Drew Bennett .15 .40
87 Chris Brown .12 .30
88 Clinton Portis .12 .30
89 Patrick Ramsey .15 .40
90 Santana Moss .15 .40
91 Aaron Rodgers RC 7.50 15.00
92 Alex Smith QB RC 1.25 3.00
93 Charlie Frye RC .30 .75
94 Andrew Walter RC .30 .75
95 Jason Campbell RC .30 .75
96 Derek Anderson RC .40 1.00
97 David Greene RC .30 .75
98 Ronnie Brown RC .40 1.00
99 Cadillac Williams RC .30 .75
100 Cedric Benson RC .30 .75
101 Ciatrick Fason RC .30 .75
102 Vernand Morency RC .40 1.00
103 Matt Jones RC .30 .75
104 Maurice Clarett .40 1.00
105 Mike Williams .40 1.00
106 Braylon Edwards RC .30 .75
107 Mark Clayton RC .30 .75
108 Reggie Brown RC .30 .75
109 Troy Williamson RC .30 .75
110 Roddy White RC .50 1.25
111 Jerome Mathis RC .50 1.25
112 Heath Miller RC .60 1.50
113 Antrel Rolle RC .50 1.25
114 Adam Jones RC .40 1.00
115 Vincent Jackson RC .50 1.25
116 Alex Smith TE RC .30 .75
117 Marcus Spears RC .30 .75
118 Courtney Roby RC .30 .75
119 Stefan LeFors RC .30 .75
120 Derrick Johnson RC .40 1.00
121 Shawne Merriman RC .50 1.25
122 Thomas Davis RC .30 .75
123 Marlin Jackson RC .30 .75
124 Ryan Moats RC .40 1.00
125 Dan Orlovsky RC .30 .75
126 Kyle Orton RC .30 .75
127 Adrian McPherson RC .30 .75
128 Eric Shelton RC .30 .75
129 Chris Henry RC .40 1.00
130 Carlos Rogers RC .50 1.25
131 Roscoe Parrish RC .30 .75
132 J.J. Arrington RC .40 1.00
133 Mark Bradley RC .30 .75
134 Frank Gore RC .60 1.50
135 Terrence Murphy RC .30 .75

2005 Upper Deck Kickoff Autographs

UNPRICED AUTO STATED ODDS 1:480
KSAW Andrew Walter 8.00 20.00
KSCF Ciatrick Fason 8.00 20.00
KSCJ Chad Johnson
KSCW Corey Webster
KSDA Derek Anderson 8.00 20.00
KSDD Domanick Davis
KSDO Dan Orlovsky 8.00 20.00
KSEJ Erasmus James
KSEM Eli Manning SP
KSFG Fred Gibson 6.00 15.00
KSJA J.J. Arrington 8.00 20.00
KSJB James Butler
KSJH Joe Horn
KSJJ Julius Jones SP
KSJW Jason White 8.00 20.00
KSKC Keary Colbert
KSKH Kay-Jay Harris
KSKO Kyle Orton
KSMB Marc Bulger SP
KSMC Michael Clayton SP
KSMJ Marlin Jackson
KSMM Muhsin Muhammad
KSNB Nate Burleson
KSRB Ronnie Brown SP
KSRJ Rudi Johnson 10.00 25.00
KSRP Roscoe Parrish
KSRW Reggie Wayne
KSTA T.A. McLendon
KSTM Terrence Murphy 8.00 20.00
KSVM Vernand Morency

2005 Upper Deck Kickoff Game Jerseys

STATED ODDS 1:24
KJAD Andre Davis 2.50 6.00
KJBL Byron Leftwich 4.00 10.00
KJBU Brian Urlacher 4.00 10.00
KJBW Brian Westbrook 3.00 8.00
KJCD Corey Dillon 4.00 10.00
KJCH Chad Pennington 4.00 10.00
KJCR Charles Rogers 3.00 8.00
KJDA David Carr 4.00 10.00
KJDB Drew Bledsoe 4.00 10.00
KJDC Daunte Culpepper 4.00 10.00
KJDM Derrick Mason 3.00 8.00
KJDS Donte Stallworth 3.00 8.00
KJEJ Edgerrin James 4.00 10.00
KJFM Freddie Mitchell 2.50 6.00
KJHW Hines Ward 4.00 10.00
KJIB Isaac Bruce 3.00 8.00
KJJH Joey Harrington 4.00 10.00
KJJL Jamal Lewis 4.00 10.00
KJJP Jerry Porter 3.00 8.00
KJJS Jeremy Shockey 4.00 10.00
KJJT Jason Taylor 2.50 6.00
KJKW Kelley Washington 2.50 6.00
KJMC Deuce McAllister 4.00 10.00
KJMS Michael Strahan 3.00 8.00
KJPP Peerless Price 2.50 6.00
KJRM Randy Moss 4.00 10.00
KJSM Jimmy Smith 3.00 8.00
KJST Steve McNair 3.00 8.00
KJTH Torry Holt 4.00 10.00
KJTP Todd Heap 2.50 6.00

1997 Upper Deck Legends

This 208-card set was distributed in packs with a suggested retail price of $4.99 and features color action photos of some of the league's all-time great players. The set contains the following two subsets: Legendary Leaders, which honors ten great coaches, and Super Bowl Memories, which features photographs by Walter Iooss, Jr., of behind the scenes of the Super Bowl.

COMPLETE SET (208) 30.00 80.00
1 Bart Starr 1.00 2.50
2 Jim Brown 1.00 2.50
3 Joe Namath 1.25 3.00
4 Walter Payton 2.00 5.00
5 Terry Bradshaw 1.25 3.00
6 Franco Harris .25 .60
7 Dan Fouts .25 .60
8 Steve Largent .25 .60
9 Johnny Unitas 1.00 2.50
10 Gale Sayers .60 1.50
11 Roger Staubach 1.25 3.00
12 Tony Dorsett .25 .60
13 Fran Tarkenton .60 1.50
14 Charley Taylor .15 .40
15 Ray Nitschke .25 .60
16 Jim Ringo .15 .40
17 Dick Butkus .60 1.50
18 Fred Biletnikoff .25 .60
19 Lenny Moore .15 .40
20 Len Dawson .25 .60
21 Lance Alworth .15 .40
22 Chuck Bednarik .15 .40
23 Raymond Berry .15 .40
24 Donnie Shell .10 .30
25 Mel Blount .15 .40
26 Willie Brown .15 .40
27 Ken Houston .10 .30
28 Larry Csonka .25 .60
29 Mike Ditka .50 1.25
30 Art Donovan .15 .40
31 Sam Huff .15 .40
32 Lem Barney .10 .30
33 Hugh McElhenny .15 .40
34 Otto Graham .30 .75
35 Joe Greene .25 .60
36 Mike Rozier .10 .30
37 Lou Groza .15 .40
38 Ted Hendricks .10 .30
39 Elroy Hirsch .15 .40
40 Paul Hornung .30 .75
41 Charlie Joiner .15 .40
42 Deacon Jones .15 .40
43 Bill Bradley .10 .30
44 Floyd Little .10 .30
45 Willie Lanier .10 .30
46 Bob Lilly .15 .40
47 Sid Luckman .15 .40
48 John Mackey .10 .30
49 Don Maynard .15 .40
50 Mike McCormack .10 .30
51 Bobby Mitchell .15 .40
52 Ron Mix .15 .40
53 Marion Motley .10 .30
54 Leo Nomellini .15 .40
55 Mark Duper .10 .30
56 Mel Renfro .10 .30
57 Jim Otto .15 .40
58 Alan Page .15 .40
59 Joe Perry .15 .40
60 Andy Robustelli .10 .30
61 Lee Roy Selmon .15 .40
62 Jackie Smith .15 .40
63 Art Shell .15 .40
64 Jan Stenerud .10 .30
65 Gene Upshaw .15 .40
66 Y.A. Tittle .25 .60
67 Paul Warfield .25 .60
68 Kellen Winslow .15 .40
69 Randy White .15 .40
70 Larry Wilson .10 .30
71 Willie Wood .15 .40
72 Jack Ham .15 .40
73 Jack Youngblood .10 .30
74 Dan Abramowicz .10 .30
75 Dick Anderson .10 .30
76 Ken Anderson .15 .40
77 Steve Bartkowski .10 .30
78 Bill Bergey .10 .30
79 Rocky Bleier .15 .40
80 Cliff Branch .15 .40
81 John Brodie .10 .30
82 Bobby Bell .10 .30
83 Billy Cannon .10 .30
84 Gino Cappelletti .10 .30
85 Harold Carmichael .10 .30
86 Dave Casper .10 .30
87 Wes Chandler .10 .30
88 Todd Christensen .10 .30
89 Dwight Clark .15 .40
90 Mark Clayton .10 .30
91 Cris Collinsworth .10 .30
92 Roger Craig .15 .40
93 Randy Cross .10 .30
94 Isaac Curtis .10 .30
95 Mike Curtis .10 .30
96 Ben Davidson .10 .30
97 Fred Dean .10 .30
98 Tom Dempsey .10 .30
99 Eric Dickerson .15 .40
100 Lynn Dickey .10 .30
101 John McKay LL .10 .30
102 Carl Eller .10 .30
103 Chuck Foreman .10 .30
104 Russ Francis .10 .30
105 Joe Gibbs LL .15 .40
106 Gary Garrison .10 .30
107 Randy Gradishar .10 .30
108 L.C. Greenwood .15 .40
109 Rosey Grier .10 .30
110 Steve Grogan .10 .30
111 Ray Guy .10 .30
112 John Hadl .10 .30
113 Jim Hart .10 .30
114 George Halas LL .15 .40
115 Mike Haynes .10 .30
116 Charlie Hennigan .10 .30
117 Chuck Howley .10 .30
118 Harold Jackson .10 .30
119 Tom Jackson .10 .30
120 Ron Jaworski .10 .30
121 John Jefferson .10 .30
122 Billy Johnson .10 .30
123 Ed Too Tall Jones .15 .40
124 Jack Kemp .60 1.50
125 Jim Kiick .10 .30
126 Billy Kilmer .15 .40
127 Jerry Kramer .15 .40
128 Paul Krause .10 .30
129 Daryle Lamonica .10 .30
130 Bill Walsh LL .15 .40
131 James Lofton .10 .30
132 Hank Stram LL .10 .30
133 Archie Manning .15 .40
134 Jim Marshall .10 .30
135 Harvey Martin .10 .30
136 Tommy McDonald .10 .30
137 Max McGee .15 .40
138 Reggie McKenzie .10 .30
139 Karl Mecklenburg .10 .30
140 Tom Landry LL .25 .60
141 Terry Metcalf .10 .30
142 Matt Millen .10 .30
143 Earl Morrall .10 .30
144 Mercury Morris .10 .30
145 Chuck Noll LL .15 .40
146 Joe Morris .10 .30
147 Mark Moseley .10 .30
148 Haven Moses .10 .30
149 Chuck Muncie .10 .30
150 Anthony Munoz .15 .40
151 Tommy Nobis .10 .30
152 Babe Parilli .10 .30
153 Drew Pearson .15 .40
154 Ozzie Newsome .10 .30
155 Jim Plunkett .15 .40
156 William Perry .10 .30
157 Johnny Robinson .10 .30
158 Ahmad Rashad .15 .40
159 George Rogers .10 .30
160 Sterling Sharpe .15 .40
161 Billy Sims .15 .40
162 Sid Gillman LL .10 .30
163 Mike Singletary .25 .60
164 Charlie Sanders .10 .30
165 Bubba Smith .10 .30
166 Ken Stabler .75 2.00
167 Freddie Solomon .10 .30
168 John Stallworth .15 .40
169 Dwight Stephenson .15 .40
170 Vince Lombardi LL .40 1.00
171 Weeb Ewbank LL .10 .30
172 Lionel Taylor .10 .30
173 Otis Taylor .10 .30
174 Joe Theismann .25 .60
175 Bob Trumpy .10 .30
176 Mike Webster .10 .30
177 Jim Zorn .10 .30
178 Joe Montana 2.00 5.00
179 Packers Superbowl SM .15 .40
180 B.Starr/D.Lamonica .50 1.25
181 Max McGee SM .15 .40
182 Joe Namath SM .60 1.50
183 Johnny Unitas SM .50 1.25
184 Len Dawson SM .15 .40
185 Chuck Howley SM .10 .30
186 R.Staubach/T.Landry .60 1.50
187 Paul Warfield SM .15 .40
188 Larry Csonka SM .15 .40
189 Fran Tarkenton SM .25 .60
190 T.Bradshaw/F.Harris .60 1.50
191 Ken Stabler SM .30 .75
192 K.Stabler/F.Biletnikoff .15 .40
193 C.Foreman/F.Tarkenton .10 .30
194 Harvey Martin SM .10 .30
195 Tony Dorsett SM .15 .40
196 Terry Bradshaw SM .60 1.50
197 John Stallworth SM .10 .30
198 Franco Harris SM .15 .40
199 Ken Anderson SM .10 .30
200 Joe Theismann SM .15 .40
201 Jim Plunkett SM .10 .30
202 Roger Craig SM .10 .30
203 William Perry SM .10 .30
204 S.Grogan/W.Payton .10 .30
205 J.Montana/D.Clark 1.00 2.50
206 R.Francis/J.Montana .10 .30
207 Joe Montana SM 1.00 2.50
208 Joe Montana SM 1.00 2.50

1997 Upper Deck Legends Autographs

Randomly inserted in retail packs at the rate of one in five foil and one in 10 magazine/retail packs, this set is a partial parallel version of the main set with an actual player autograph on 162-different regular issue cards. Some were available only via a mail-in redemption that carried an expiration date of 10/15/98. Although Billy Johnson, Fred Dean, Russ Francis, Sid Luckman, Bob Trumpy, Willie Wood, and Mike Webster did have redemption cards inserted in packs, none of those players returned any cards signed to Upper Deck. Therefore, Upper Deck substituted other autographs for those players. Mike Webster, Fred Dean and Russ Francis authentic signed cards appeared on the secondary market at a later date. There has been speculatation that they released the signed cards themselves, but forged signatures of Fred Dean seem to be fairly common. The Sid Luckman EXCH card apparently is in the most demand with sales well above $100.

STATED ODDS 1:5H, 1:7 SPEC.RET,1:10R
AL1 Bart Starr SP 500.00 800.00
AL2 Jim Brown SP 800.00 1200.00
AL3 Joe Namath SP 600.00 1000.00
AL4 Walter Payton SP 1500.00 2000.00
AL5 Terry Bradshaw SP 500.00 800.00
AL6 Franco Harris SP 400.00 700.00
AL7 Dan Fouts 15.00 40.00
AL8 Steve Largent 15.00 40.00
AL9 Johnny Unitas SP 1200.00 2000.00
AL10 Gale Sayers 25.00 50.00
AL11 Roger Staubach 125.00 200.00
AL12 Tony Dorsett SP 250.00 350.00
AL13 Fran Tarkenton 20.00 50.00
AL14 Charley Taylor 10.00 25.00
AL15 Ray Nitschke 60.00 120.00
AL16 Jim Ringo 20.00 50.00
AL17 Dick Butkus SP 600.00 1000.00
AL18 Fred Biletnikoff 15.00 40.00
AL19 Lenny Moore 8.00 20.00
AL20 Len Dawson 20.00 50.00
AL21 Lance Alworth SP 60.00 125.00
AL22 Chuck Bednarik 12.00 30.00
AL23 Raymond Berry 12.00 30.00
AL24 Donnie Shell 8.00 20.00
AL25 Mel Blount 12.00 30.00
AL26 Willie Brown 12.00 30.00
AL27 Ken Houston 10.00 25.00
AL28 Larry Csonka SP 175.00 300.00
AL29 Mike Ditka 30.00 60.00
AL30 Art Donovan 10.00 25.00
AL31 Sam Huff 12.00 30.00
AL32 Lem Barney 8.00 20.00
AL33 Hugh McElhenny 12.00 30.00
AL34 Otto Graham 35.00 60.00
AL35 Joe Greene SP 125.00 250.00
AL36 Mike Rozier 12.00 30.00
AL37 Lou Groza 15.00 40.00
AL38 Ted Hendricks 10.00 25.00
AL39 Elroy Hirsch 15.00 40.00
AL40 Paul Hornung 20.00 50.00
AL41 Charlie Joiner 10.00 25.00
AL42 Deacon Jones 15.00 40.00
AL43 Bill Bradley 8.00 20.00
AL44 Floyd Little 10.00 25.00
AL45 Willie Lanier 12.00 30.00
AL46 Bob Lilly 15.00 40.00
AL47 Sid Luckman EXCH 100.00 200.00
AL48 John Mackey 8.00 20.00
AL49 Don Maynard 8.00 20.00
AL50 Mike McCormack 12.00 30.00
AL51 Bobby Mitchell 10.00 25.00
AL52 Ron Mix 8.00 20.00
AL53 Marion Motley 25.00 50.00
AL54 Leo Nomellini 15.00 40.00
AL55 Mark Duper 6.00 15.00
AL56 Mel Renfro 15.00 40.00
AL57 Jim Otto 15.00 40.00
AL58 Alan Page 12.00 30.00
AL59 Joe Perry 15.00 40.00
AL60 Andy Robustelli 15.00 40.00
AL61 Lee Roy Selmon 20.00 50.00
AL62 Jackie Smith 8.00 20.00
AL63 Art Shell SP 50.00 100.00
AL64 Jan Stenerud 10.00 25.00
AL65 Gene Upshaw 15.00 40.00
AL66 Y.A. Tittle 15.00 40.00
AL67 Paul Warfield 15.00 40.00
AL68 Kellen Winslow 20.00 50.00
AL69 Randy White 8.00 20.00
AL70 Larry Wilson 8.00 20.00
AL71 Willie Wood EXCH 4.00 10.00
AL72 Jack Ham 15.00 40.00
AL73 Jack Youngblood 10.00 25.00
AL74 Danny Abramowicz 8.00 20.00
AL75 Dick Anderson 8.00 20.00
AL76 Ken Anderson 10.00 25.00
AL77 Steve Bartkowski 8.00 20.00
AL78 Bill Bergey 10.00 25.00
AL79 Rocky Bleier 12.00 30.00
AL80 Cliff Branch 8.00 20.00
AL81 John Brodie 12.00 30.00
AL82 Bobby Bell 10.00 25.00
AL83 Billy Cannon SP 30.00 80.00
AL84 Gino Cappelletti 10.00 25.00
AL85 Harold Carmichael 8.00 20.00
AL86 Dave Casper 10.00 25.00
AL87 Wes Chandler 8.00 20.00
AL88 Todd Christensen 12.00 30.00
AL89 Dwight Clark 10.00 25.00
AL90 Mark Clayton 10.00 25.00
AL91 Cris Collinsworth 8.00 20.00
AL92 Roger Craig 12.00 30.00
AL93 Randy Cross 12.00 30.00
AL94 Isaac Curtis 8.00 20.00
AL95 Mike Curtis 12.00 30.00
AL96 Ben Davidson 8.00 20.00
AL97X Fred Dean EXCH 4.00 10.00
AL98 Tom Dempsey 8.00 20.00

AL99 Eric Dickerson 12.00 30.00
AL100 Lynn Dickey 15.00 40.00
AL102 Carl Eller 25.00 60.00
AL103 Chuck Foreman 8.00 20.00
AL104 Russ Francis SP 50.00 100.00
AL104X Russ Francis EXCH 4.00 10.00
AL106 Gary Garrison 8.00 20.00
AL107 Randy Gradishar 8.00 20.00
AL108 L.C. Greenwood 12.00 30.00
AL109 Rosey Grier 15.00 40.00
AL110 Steve Grogan 12.00 30.00
AL111 Ray Guy 10.00 25.00
AL112 John Hadl 8.00 20.00
AL113 Jim Hart 8.00 20.00
AL115 Mike Haynes 12.00 30.00
AL116 Charlie Hennigan 10.00 25.00
AL117 Chuck Howley 10.00 25.00
AL118 Harold Jackson 8.00 20.00
AL119 Tom Jackson 12.00 30.00
AL120 Ron Jaworski 12.00 30.00
AL121 John Jefferson 10.00 25.00
AL122 Billy Johnson EXCH 4.00 10.00
AL123 Ed Too Tall Jones 12.00 30.00
AL124 Jack Kemp 25.00 60.00
AL125 Jim Kiick 10.00 25.00
AL126 Billy Kilmer 8.00 20.00
AL127 Jerry Kramer 12.00 30.00
AL128 Paul Krause 10.00 25.00
AL129 Daryle Lamonica 12.00 30.00
AL131 James Lofton 12.00 30.00
AL133 Archie Manning 15.00 40.00
AL134 Jim Marshall 10.00 25.00
AL135 Harvey Martin 12.00 30.00
AL136 Tommy McDonald 8.00 20.00
AL137 Max McGee 25.00 60.00
AL138 Reggie McKenzie 10.00 25.00
AL139 Karl Mecklenburg 8.00 20.00
AL141 Terry Metcalf 8.00 20.00
AL142 Matt Millen SP 30.00 80.00
AL143 Earl Morrall 12.00 30.00
AL144 Mercury Morris 10.00 25.00
AL146 Joe Morris 8.00 20.00
AL147 Mark Moseley 8.00 20.00
AL148 Haven Moses 8.00 20.00
AL149 Chuck Muncie 8.00 20.00
AL150 Anthony Munoz 10.00 25.00
AL151 Tommy Nobis 8.00 20.00
AL152 Babe Parilli 8.00 20.00
AL153 Drew Pearson 10.00 25.00
AL154 Ozzie Newsome 8.00 20.00
AL155 Jim Plunkett 12.00 30.00
AL156 William Perry 12.00 30.00
AL157 Johnny Robinson 12.00 30.00
AL158 Ahmad Rashad 12.00 30.00
AL159 George Rogers 10.00 25.00
AL160 Sterling Sharpe 10.00 25.00
AL161 Billy Sims 10.00 25.00
AL163 Mike Singletary 15.00 40.00
AL164 Charlie Sanders 8.00 20.00
AL165 Bubba Smith SP 125.00 250.00
AL166 Ken Stabler 50.00 100.00
AL167 Freddie Solomon 8.00 20.00
AL168 John Stallworth 15.00 40.00
AL169 Dwight Stephenson 10.00 25.00
AL172 Lionel Taylor 8.00 20.00
AL173 Otis Taylor SP 60.00 120.00
AL174 Joe Theismann 12.00 30.00
AL175 Bob Trumpy EXCH 4.00 10.00
AL176 Mike Webster SP 60.00 125.00
AL177 Jim Zorn 8.00 20.00
AL178 Joe Montana 300.00 600.00

1997 Upper Deck Legends Big Game Hunters

Randomly inserted in packs at the rate of one in 75 (or 1:58 special retail packs), this 20-card set features color action oval-shaped photos of some of the top quarterbacks of all-time.

COMPLETE SET (20) 125.00 250.00
STATED ODDS 1:75, 1:58 SPEC.RETAIL
B1 Joe Montana 8.00 20.00
B2 Bart Starr 8.00 20.00
B3 Roger Staubach 8.00 20.00
B4 Johnny Unitas 10.00 25.00
B5 Terry Bradshaw 6.00 15.00
B6 Ken Stabler 7.50 20.00
B7 Jim Plunkett 3.00 8.00
B8 Len Dawson 6.00 15.00
B9 Fran Tarkenton 7.50 20.00
B10 Dan Fouts 6.00 15.00
B11 Daryle Lamonica 3.00 8.00
B12 Y.A. Tittle 4.00 10.00
B13 Joe Namath 12.50 30.00
B14 Ken Anderson 4.00 10.00
B15 John Brodie 3.00 8.00
B16 Billy Kilmer 4.00 10.00
B17 Earl Morrall 3.00 8.00
B18 Jack Kemp 7.50 20.00
B19 Steve Grogan 3.00 8.00
B20 Joe Theismann 6.00 15.00

1997 Upper Deck Legends Marquee Matchups

Randomly inserted in packs at the rate of one in 17 (or 1:8 special retail packs), this 30-card set features Light F/X action photos of two great NFL players printed to resemble pairing off against each other.

COMPLETE SET (30) 40.00 100.00
STATED ODDS 1:17, 1:8 SPEC.RETAIL
MM1 J.Namath/D.Fouts 2.50 6.00
MM2 J.Unitas/J.Namath 3.00 8.00
MM3 L.Dawson/B.Starr 2.50 6.00
MM4 R.Staubach/F.Tarkenton 2.50 6.00
MM5 T.Bradshaw/K.Stabler 2.50 6.00
MM6 J.Montana/K.Anderson 4.00 10.00
MM7 B.Starr/J.Unitas 3.00 8.00
MM8 J.Greene/J.Kiick 2.00 5.00
MM9 F.Harris/W.Payton 4.00 10.00
MM10 K.Stabler/D.Fouts 2.50 6.00
MM11 C.Joiner/S.Largent 1.25 3.00
MM12 J.Lofton/D.Pearson 1.25 3.00
MM13 J.Brodie/D.Jones 1.25 3.00
MM14 F.Biletnikoff/D.Maynard 2.00 5.00
MM15 J.Brown/C.Bednarik 2.50 6.00
MM16 R.Nitschke/G.Sayers 2.50 6.00
MM17 P.Hornung/D.Butkus 2.50 6.00
MM18 J.Montana/E.Dickerson 4.00 10.00
MM19 T.Dorsett/M.Singletary 2.00 5.00
MM20 B.Sims/C.Foreman .75 2.00
MM21 L.Dawson/W.Brown 1.25 3.00
MM22 J.Robinson/L.Wilson .75 2.00
MM23 M.Motley/R.Berry 1.25 3.00
MM24 R.Mix/J.Otto .75 2.00
MM25 R.Staubach/T.Bradshaw 3.00 8.00
MM26 B.Lilly/B.Kilmer 2.00 5.00
MM27 T.Hendricks/R.Francis .75 2.00
MM28 B.Parilli/J.Kemp 2.00 5.00
MM29 D.Jones/A.Page 2.00 5.00
MM30 D.Butkus/R.Nitschke 2.50 6.00

1997 Upper Deck Legends Sign of the Times

Randomly inserted in packs, this 10-card set features color images of ten of the greatest NFL players on a leather-look background with an authentic autograph printed in a football-shaped area beside the image. Uppe Deck announced that only 100 of each card was available.

STATED PRINT RUN 100 SETS
ST1 Joe Montana 200.00 350.00
ST2 Fran Tarkenton 60.00 120.00
ST3 Johnny Unitas 350.00 600.00
ST3X Johnny Unitas EXCH 4.00 10.00
ST4 Joe Namath 250.00 500.00
ST5 Terry Bradshaw 125.00 250.00
ST6 Jim Brown 200.00 350.00
ST7 Franco Harris 125.00 200.00
ST8 Walter Payton 600.00 1000.00
ST9 Steve Largent 75.00 125.00
ST10 Bart Starr 250.00 400.00

2000 Upper Deck Legends

Released in late September 2000, Upper Deck NFL Legends was comprised of 132 cards. The set was divided up into 90 Veteran Player cards, 12 20th Century Legends cards sequentially numbered to 2500, and 30 Generation Y2K Rookie cards. Base cards have a blue border along the bottom card edge and silver foil highlights. NFL Legends was packaged in 24-pack boxes with packs containing five cards and carried a suggested retail price of $4.99.

COMPLETE SET (132) 200.00 400.00
COMP.SET w/o SP's (90) 7.50 20.00
1 Jake Plummer .15 .40
2 Jamal Anderson .20 .50
3 Doug Flutie .20 .50
4 Jim Kelly .25 .60
5 Dick Butkus .30 .75
6 Mike Singletary .25 .60
7 Gale Sayers .25 .60
8 Boomer Esiason .25 .60
9 Anthony Munoz .20 .50
10 Otto Graham .20 .50
11 Jim Brown .30 .75
12 Ozzie Newsome .15 .40
13 Bob Lilly .20 .50
14 Troy Aikman .30 .75
15 Emmitt Smith .40 1.00
16 Roger Staubach .30 .75
17 Deion Sanders .20 .50
18 Tony Dorsett .25 .60
19 Terrell Davis .20 .50
20 John Elway .40 1.00
21 Charlie Batch .15 .40
22 Brett Favre .50 1.25
23 Bart Starr .60 1.50
24 Reggie White .25 .60
25 Earl Campbell .25 .60
26 Peyton Manning .60 1.50
27 Edgerrin James .20 .50
28 Johnny Unitas .60 1.50
29 Marvin Harrison .20 .50
30 Mark Brunell .20 .50
31 Fred Taylor .15 .40
32 Len Dawson .25 .60
33 Dan Marino .50 1.25
34 Bob Griese .25 .60
35 Mark Duper .20 .50
36 Thurman Thomas .20 .50
37 Fran Tarkenton .25 .60
38 Randy Moss .20 .50
39 Cris Carter .25 .60
40 Gary Anderson .15 .40
41 John Randle .25 .60
42 Drew Bledsoe .20 .50
43 Archie Manning .20 .50
44 Ricky Williams .20 .50
45 Frank Gifford .25 .60
46 Kerry Collins .15 .40
47 Phil Simms .25 .60
48 Vinny Testaverde .15 .40
49 Curtis Martin .20 .50
50 Keyshawn Johnson .20 .50
51 Joe Namath .50 1.25
52 Marcus Allen .25 .60
53 Bruce Smith .20 .50
54 Ken Stabler .30 .75
55 Fred Biletnikoff .25 .60
56 Howie Long .25 .60
57 Ron Jaworski .20 .50
58 Harold Carmichael .15 .40
59 Kordell Stewart .15 .40
60 Levon Kirkland .15 .40
61 Mel Blount .20 .50
62 Jerome Bettis .25 .60
63 John Stallworth .20 .50
64 Franco Harris .25 .60
65 Jim Harbaugh .20 .50
66 Kellen Winslow .20 .50
67 Charlie Joiner .15 .40
68 Junior Seau .20 .50
69 Jerry Rice .60 1.50
70 Steve Young .30 .75
71 Joe Montana .75 2.00
72 Roger Craig .20 .50
73 Ronnie Lott .25 .60
74 Jon Kitna .15 .40
75 Steve Largent .25 .60
76 Ricky Watters .20 .50
77 Kurt Warner .40 1.00
78 Marshall Faulk .20 .50
79 Isaac Bruce .25 .60
80 Merlin Olsen .15 .40
81 Lee Roy Selmon .15 .40
82 Tim Brown .25 .60
83 Tim Couch .20 .50
84 Mike Alstott .15 .40
85 Eddie George .20 .50
86 Steve McNair .20 .50
87 Brad Johnson .20 .50
88 Sonny Jurgensen .25 .60
89 Art Monk .25 .60
90 Joe Theismann .25 .60
91 Ray Nitschke TCL 4.00 10.00
92 Doak Walker TCL 3.00 8.00
93 Thurman Thomas TCL 2.50 6.00
94 Jim Brown TCL 4.00 10.00
95 Sammy Baugh TCL 3.00 8.00
96 Reggie White TCL 3.00 8.00
97 Eric Dickerson TCL 2.50 6.00
98 Paul Hornung TCL 3.00 8.00
99 Deion Sanders TCL 2.50 6.00
100 Bronko Nagurski TCL 3.00 8.00
101 Walter Payton TCL 12.00 30.00
102 Jim Thorpe TCL 5.00 12.00
103 Ron Dayne RC 2.00 5.00
104 Tim Rattay RC 1.50 4.00
105 Brian Urlacher RC 6.00 15.00
106 Bubba Franks RC 1.25 3.00
107 Chad Pennington RC 1.50 4.00
108 Chris Cole RC 1.50 4.00
109 Chris Redman RC 1.25 3.00
110 Courtney Brown RC 1.50 4.00
111 Curtis Keaton RC 1.25 3.00
112 Dennis Northcutt RC 1.25 3.00
113 Dez White RC 1.25 3.00
114 Giovanni Carmazzi RC 1.25 3.00
115 J.R. Redmond RC 1.25 3.00
116 JaJuan Dawson RC 1.25 3.00
117 Jamal Lewis RC 2.00 5.00
118 Jerry Porter RC 2.00 5.00
119 Laveranues Coles RC 1.50 4.00
120 Peter Warrick RC 1.25 3.00
121 Plaxico Burress RC 1.50 4.00
122 R.Jay Soward RC 1.25 3.00
123 Reuben Droughns RC 1.25 3.00
124 Ron Dixon RC 1.25 3.00
125 Ron Dugans RC 1.25 3.00
126 Shaun Alexander RC 2.00 5.00
127 Sylvester Morris RC 1.25 3.00
128 Thomas Jones RC 1.50 4.00
129 Todd Pinkston RC 1.25 3.00
130 Travis Prentice RC 1.25 3.00
131 Travis Taylor RC 1.25 3.00
132 Trung Canidate RC 1.25 3.00

2000 Upper Deck Legends Autographs

Randomly inserted in packs at the rate of one in 47, this 68-card set features authentic autographs on the base card stock. This is a skip-numbered set. Some of the cards were issued via mail redemption cards.

STATED ODDS 1:47
AM Archie Manning 10.00 25.00
AZ Anthony Munoz 10.00 25.00
BE Boomer Esiason 12.00 30.00
BG Bob Griese 12.00 30.00
BJ Brad Johnson 10.00 25.00
BL Drew Bledsoe 25.00 50.00
BL2 Bob Lilly 10.00 25.00
BR Mark Brunell 10.00 25.00
BS Bart Starr 75.00 150.00
CC Cris Carter 12.00 30.00
CJ Charlie Joiner 8.00 20.00
DA Terrell Davis 10.00 25.00
DB Dick Butkus 15.00 40.00
DF Doug Flutie 10.00 25.00
DM Dan Marino 125.00 250.00
EC Earl Campbell 25.00 50.00
EG Eddie George 12.00 30.00
EJ Edgerrin James 10.00 25.00
FB Fred Biletnikoff 12.00 30.00
FG Frank Gifford 30.00 60.00
FH Franco Harris 25.00 50.00
FT Fran Tarkenton 20.00 50.00
GS Gale Sayers 25.00 50.00
HC Harold Carmichael 8.00 20.00
HL Howie Long 15.00 40.00
IB Isaac Bruce 12.00 30.00
JA Jamal Anderson 10.00 25.00
JB Jerome Bettis 60.00 120.00
JB2 Jim Brown 40.00 100.00
JK Jim Kelly 12.00 30.00
JM Joe Montana 50.00 120.00
JN Joe Namath 50.00 100.00
JP Jake Plummer 8.00 20.00
JS John Stallworth 10.00 25.00
JT Joe Theismann 12.00 30.00
JU Johnny Unitas 250.00 400.00
KI Jon Kitna 8.00 20.00
KJ Keyshawn Johnson 10.00 25.00
KS Ken Stabler 15.00 40.00
KW Kellen Winslow 10.00 25.00
LD Len Dawson 15.00 40.00
LS Lee Roy Selmon 8.00 20.00
MA Marcus Allen 12.00 30.00
MB Mel Blount 10.00 25.00
MD Mark Duper 10.00 25.00
MH Marvin Harrison 25.00 50.00
MK Art Monk 15.00 40.00
MS Mike Singletary 12.00 30.00
OG Otto Graham 20.00 50.00
ON Ozzie Newsome 8.00 20.00
PM Peyton Manning 75.00 150.00
PS Phil Simms 15.00 40.00
RC Roger Craig 10.00 25.00
RI Ricky Watters 10.00 25.00
RJ Ron Jaworski 10.00 25.00
RL Ronnie Lott SP 300.00 450.00
RM Randy Moss 30.00 60.00
RS Roger Staubach 75.00 135.00
RW Ricky Williams EXCH 1.50 4.00
SJ Sonny Jurgensen 12.00 30.00
SL Steve Largent 12.00 30.00
SY Steve Young 30.00 60.00
TA Troy Aikman 40.00 100.00
TB Tim Brown 12.00 30.00
TC Tim Couch 10.00 25.00
TD Tony Dorsett 30.00 60.00
VT Vinny Testaverde 8.00 20.00
WA Kurt Warner 30.00 60.00

2000 Upper Deck Legends Autographs Gold

*GOLD/25: .8X TO 2X BASIC AUTO
GOLD PRINT RUN 25 SER.#'d SETS
BS Bart Starr 125.00 250.00
DM Dan Marino 250.00 400.00
JU Johnny Unitas 500.00 750.00
PM Peyton Manning 125.00 250.00
RL Ronnie Lott 200.00 400.00
RW Ricky Williams 4.00 8.00

2000 Upper Deck Legends Canton Calling

Randomly inserted in packs at the rate of one in 18, this six card set features players most likely to have a place in Canton reserved for them upon their retirement.

COMPLETE SET (6) 6.00 12.00
STATED ODDS 1:18
CC1 Peyton Manning 2.00 5.00
CC2 Steve Young 1.00 2.50
CC3 Jerry Rice 2.00 5.00
CC4 Randy Moss .60 1.50
CC5 Cris Carter .75 2.00
CC6 Emmitt Smith 1.25 3.00

2000 Upper Deck Legends Defining Moments

Randomly inserted in packs at the rate of one in nine, this 10-card set features ten of the most exciting moments in football history.

COMPLETE SET (10) 7.50 20.00
STATED ODDS 1:9
DM1 Terrell Davis .40 1.00
DM2 Troy Aikman .60 1.50
DM3 Jerry Rice 1.25 3.00
DM4 Walter Payton 2.00 5.00
DM5 Joe Namath 1.00 2.50
DM6 Emmitt Smith .75 2.00
DM7 Steve Young .60 1.50
DM8 Franco Harris .60 1.25
DM9 Kurt Warner .75 2.00
DM10 Brett Favre 1.00 2.50

1997 Upper Deck Legends Jumbos

These cards measure roughly 5" 7" and are essentially a jumbo version of a basic issue card. They were inserted as a box topper in special retail boxes.

COMPLETE SET (10) 10.00 25.00
*JUMBOS: 3X TO 8X BASIC CARDS
ONE PER SPECIAL RETAIL PACK
101 John McKay LL 1.00 2.50
105 Joe Gibbs LL 1.25 3.00
114 George Halas LL
130 Bill Walsh LL 1.25 3.00
132 Hank Stram LL 1.00 2.50
140 Tom Landry LL 2.00 5.00
145 Chuck Noll LL
162 Sid Gillman LL 1.00 2.50
170 Vince Lombardi LL 3.00 8.00
171 Weeb Ewbank LL 1.00 2.50

2000 Upper Deck Legends Legendary Jerseys

Randomly inserted in packs at the rate of one in 23, this set features swatches of authentic game-worn jerseys on an all-white card front with a portrait player photo centered along the top card edge. Please note that Marcus Allen and Ted Hendrincks have a second card version with the words Special Edition printed on the front. These cards often featured swatches other than jerseys (such as pants) due to short supployof jersey swatches.

STATED ODDS 1:23
LJBF Brett Favre 15.00 40.00
LJBL Bob Lilly 8.00 20.00
LJCB Cliff Branch 6.00 15.00
LJCH Charles Haley 10.00 25.00
LJDB Drew Bledsoe 8.00 20.00
LJDF Doug Flutie 8.00 20.00
LJDJ Daryl Johnston 8.00 20.00
LJDM Dan Marino 12.00 30.00
LJDS Deion Sanders 8.00 20.00
LJED Eric Dickerson 8.00 20.00
LJEM J.Elway/D.Marino 60.00 150.00
LJES Emmitt Smith 12.00 30.00
LJFB Fred Biletnikoff 10.00 25.00
LJFT Fran Tarkenton 10.00 25.00
LJGU Gene Upshaw 6.00 15.00
LJHL Howie Long 10.00 25.00
LJHW Herschel Walker 10.00 25.00
LJJA Jamal Anderson 8.00 20.00
LJJB John Brodie 10.00 25.00
LJJE John Elway 12.00 30.00
LJJM Joe Montana 20.00 50.00
LJJN Joe Namath 12.00 30.00
LJJP Jim Plunkett 8.00 20.00
LJJR Jerry Rice 12.00 30.00
LJKN Ken Norton Jr. 6.00 15.00
LJKS Ken Stabler 12.00 30.00
LJKW Kurt Warner 12.00 30.00
LJMA1 Marcus Allen 10.00 25.00
LJMA2 Marcus Allen SE 10.00 25.00
LJMB Mark Brunell 8.00 20.00
LJMF Marshall Faulk 8.00 20.00
LJMI Michael Irvin 10.00 25.00
LJNO Jay Novacek 8.00 20.00
LJOS Otis Sistrunk 6.00 15.00
LJPM Peyton Manning 15.00 40.00
LJRL Ronnie Lott 10.00 25.00
LJRM Randy Moss 6.00 15.00
LJRS Roger Staubach 15.00 40.00
LJRW Reggie White 12.00 30.00
LJSM Bruce Smith 8.00 20.00
LJSY Steve Young 10.00 25.00
LJTA Troy Aikman 12.00 30.00
LJTC Todd Christensen 6.00 15.00
LJTD Terrell Davis 8.00 20.00
LJTH1 Ted Hendricks 8.00 20.00
LJTH2 Ted Hendricks SE 8.00 20.00
LJVE Mark Van Eeghen 6.00 15.00
LJWM Warren Moon 10.00 25.00
LJWP Walter Payton 20.00 50.00

2000 Upper Deck Legends Millennium QBs

Randomly inserted in packs at the rate of one in five, this 10-card set features ten of the NFL's best quarterbacks on a card with foil stamping highlights.

COMPLETE SET (10) 6.00 15.00
STATED ODDS 1:5
M1 Joe Montana 1.25 3.00
M2 Dan Marino .75 2.00
M3 John Elway .60 1.50
M4 Fran Tarkenton .40 1.00
M5 Sammy Baugh .40 1.00
M6 Joe Namath .75 2.00
M7 Warren Moon .40 1.00
M8 Mark Brunell .30 .75
M9 Brett Favre .75 2.00
M10 Drew Bledsoe .30 .75

2000 Upper Deck Legends Reflections in Time

Randomly inserted in packs at the rate of one in 11, this 10-card set features dual player cards linking a player from the past to a player of today.

COMPLETE SET (10) 6.00 15.00
STATED ODDS 1:11
R1 E.Campbell .75 2.00
E.George
R2 M.Singletary .75 2.00
J.Seau
R3 D.Walker .75 2.00
R.Williams
R4 A.Manning 2.00 5.00
P.Manning
R5 R.White .75 2.00
J.Kearse
R6 H.Carmichael .60 1.50
R.Moss
R7 G.Sayers .75 2.00
E.James
R8 W.Moon .75 2.00
D.Culpepper
R9 R.Staubach 1.00 2.50
T.Aikman
R10 T.Thomas .60 1.50
M.Faulk

2000 Upper Deck Legends Rookie Gallery

Randomly inserted in packs at the rate of one in 21, this 10-card set features this year's top rookie prospects.

COMPLETE SET (10) 10.00 25.00
STATED ODDS 1:21
RG1 Peter Warrick .60 1.50
RG2 Chris Redman .60 1.50
RG3 Courtney Brown .75 2.00
RG4 Thomas Jones .75 2.00
RG5 Chad Pennington .75 2.00
RG6 Jamal Lewis 1.00 2.50
RG7 Plaxico Burress .75 2.00
RG8 Ron Dayne 1.00 2.50
RG9 Sylvester Morris .60 1.50
RG10 Shaun Alexander 1.00 2.50

2001 Upper Deck Legends

This 180 card set featured a mix of veterans, retired players and 2001 NFL rookies. Cards numbered 91 through 180 were released in a lesser quantity than the other first 90 card in the set. Those cards were printed to a quantity of 750.

COMP.SET w/o SP's (90) 10.00 25.00
91-180 ROOKIE PRINT RUN 750
1 Jake Plummer .20 .50
2 Jamal Anderson .25 .60
3 Ray Lewis .30 .75
4 Johnny Unitas .75 2.00
5 Jamal Lewis .30 .75
6 Andre Reed .30 .75
7 Jim Kelly .40 1.00
8 Thurman Thomas .25 .60
9 Rob Johnson .25 .60
10 Brian Urlacher .40 1.00
11 Dick Butkus .50 1.25
12 Gale Sayers .40 1.00
13 James Allen .20 .50
14 Corey Dillon .20 .50
15 Jim Brown .50 1.25
16 Tim Couch .20 .50
17 Joey Galloway .25 .60
18 Emmitt Smith .50 1.25
19 Randy White .40 1.00
20 Roger Staubach .50 1.25
21 Troy Aikman .40 1.00
22 Tony Dorsett .40 1.00
23 Brian Griese .20 .50
24 Floyd Little .25 .60
25 John Elway .60 1.50
26 Mike Anderson .20 .50
27 Terrell Davis .25 .60
28 Barry Sanders .50 1.25
29 Charlie Batch .20 .50
30 Bart Starr .75 2.00
31 Paul Hornung .40 1.00
32 Reggie White .40 1.00
33 Warren Moon .40 1.00
34 Edgerrin James .25 .60
35 Peyton Manning .75 2.00
36 Mark Brunell .25 .60
37 Tony Gonzalez .25 .60
38 Eric Dickerson .30 .75
39 Jack Youngblood .25 .60
40 Jay Fiedler .25 .60
41 Lamar Smith .25 .60
42 Dan Marino .75 2.00
43 Oronde Gadsden .20 .50
44 Cris Carter .30 .75
45 Fran Tarkenton .40 1.00
46 Daunte Culpepper .25 .60
47 Randy Moss .25 .60
48 Robert Smith .20 .50
49 Drew Bledsoe .25 .60
50 Archie Manning .30 .75
51 Jeff Blake .25 .60
52 Ricky Williams .25 .60
53 Kerry Collins .20 .50
54 Ron Dayne .25 .60
55 Lawrence Taylor .40 1.00
56 Wayne Chrebet .20 .50
57 Vinny Testaverde .20 .50
58 Joe Namath .60 1.50
59 Jim Plunkett .30 .75
60 George Blanda .30 .75
61 Tim Brown .30 .75
62 Jerry Rice .60 1.50
63 Ken Stabler .50 1.25
64 Marcus Allen .40 1.00
65 Donovan McNabb .25 .60
66 Harold Carmichael .25 .60
67 Franco Harris .40 1.00
68 Jerome Bettis .30 .75
69 Terry Bradshaw .50 1.25
70 Doug Flutie .25 .60
71 Lance Alworth .30 .75
72 Junior Seau .25 .60
73 Kellen Winslow .30 .75
74 Dan Fouts .30 .75
75 Joe Montana 1.25 3.00
76 Terrell Owens .25 .60
77 Jeff Garcia .20 .50
78 Steve Young .50 1.25
79 Matt Hasselbeck .20 .50
80 Kurt Warner .50 1.25
81 Marshall Faulk .25 .60
82 Brad Johnson .25 .60
83 Eddie George .30 .75
84 Charley Taylor .25 .60
85 Stephen Davis .20 .50
86 Jeff George .25 .60
87 John Riggins .30 .75
88 Joe Theismann .40 1.00
89 Michael Westbrook .20 .50
90 Sonny Jurgensen .40 1.00
91 Andre Carter RC 2.00 5.00
92 Cedrick Wilson RC 2.00 5.00
93 Kevan Barlow RC 2.00 5.00
94 Anthony Thomas RC 2.50 6.00
95 David Terrell RC 2.00 5.00
96 Chad Johnson RC 2.50 6.00
97 Justin Smith RC 3.00 8.00
98 Rudi Johnson RC 2.50 6.00
99 T.J. Houshmandzadeh RC 2.00 5.00
100 Brandon Spoon RC 2.00 5.00
101 Nate Clements RC 2.00 5.00
102 Travis Henry RC 2.00 5.00
103 Kevin Kasper RC 1.50 4.00
104 Willie Middlebrooks RC 2.00 5.00
105 Gerard Warren RC 2.00 5.00
106 James Jackson RC 1.50 4.00
107 Quincy Morgan RC 2.00 5.00
108 Bobby Newcombe RC 2.00 5.00
109 Arnold Jackson RC 1.50 4.00
110 Carlos Polk RC 1.50 4.00
111 Drew Brees RC 10.00 25.00
112 LaDainian Tomlinson RC 8.00 20.00
113 Tay Cody RC 1.50 4.00
114 Zeke Moreno RC 2.00 5.00
115 Snoop Minnis RC 1.50 4.00
116 George Layne RC 1.50 4.00
117 Derrick Blaylock RC 2.00 5.00
118 Reggie Wayne RC 3.00 8.00
119 Tony Dixon RC 1.50 4.00
120 Quincy Carter RC 2.00 5.00
121 Chris Chambers RC 1.50 4.00
122 Jamar Fletcher RC 1.50 4.00
123 Josh Heupel RC 2.50 6.00
124 Travis Minor RC 2.00 5.00
125 A.J. Feeley RC 2.00 5.00
126 Correll Buckhalter RC 1.50 4.00
127 Freddie Mitchell RC 1.50 4.00
128 Alge Crumpler RC 2.50 6.00
129 Michael Vick RC 4.00 10.00
130 Vinny Sutherland RC 1.50 4.00
131 Marcus Stroud RC 2.00 5.00
132 Mike McMahon RC 2.00 5.00
133 Scotty Anderson RC 1.50 4.00
134 Shaun Rogers RC 2.50 6.00
135 Jesse Palmer RC 2.00 5.00
136 Will Allen RC 2.50 6.00
137 LaMont Jordan RC 2.50 6.00
138 Santana Moss RC 2.50 6.00
139 Reggie White RC 1.50 4.00
140 Jamal Reynolds RC 1.50 4.00
141 Robert Ferguson RC 2.50 6.00
142 Torrance Marshall RC 1.50 4.00
143 Chris Weinke RC 2.00 5.00
144 Dan Morgan RC 2.00 5.00
145 Steve Smith RC 5.00 12.00
146 Dee Brown RC 1.50 4.00
147 Arther Love RC 1.50 4.00
148 Hakim Akbar RC 1.50 4.00
149 Jabari Holloway RC 1.50 4.00
150 Derek Combs RC 1.50 4.00
151 Derrick Gibson RC 1.50 4.00
152 Ken-Yon Rambo RC 1.50 4.00
153 Marques Tuiasosopo RC 2.00 5.00
154 Adam Archuleta RC 2.00 5.00
155 Tommy Polley RC 1.50 4.00
156 Brian Allen RC 1.50 4.00
157 Milton Wynn RC 1.50 4.00
158 Francis St.Paul RC 1.50 4.00
159 Edgerton Hartwell RC 1.50 4.00
160 Gary Baxter RC 1.50 4.00
161 Todd Heap RC 2.00 5.00
162 Chris Barnes RC 1.50 4.00
163 Fred Smoot RC 2.00 5.00
164 Rod Gardner RC 2.00 5.00
165 Sage Rosenfels RC 2.00 5.00
166 Damerien McCants RC 2.00 5.00
167 Deuce McAllister RC 2.50 6.00
168 Moran Norris RC 1.50 4.00
169 Sedrick Hodge RC 1.50 4.00
170 Alex Bannister RC 1.50 4.00
171 Heath Evans RC 2.00 5.00
172 Josh Booty RC 2.00 5.00
173 Ken Lucas RC 2.00 5.00
174 Koren Robinson RC 2.00 5.00
175 Chris Taylor RC 1.50 4.00
176 Andre Dyson RC 1.50 4.00
177 Dan Alexander RC 2.00 5.00
178 Justin McCareins RC 2.00 5.00
179 Eddie Berlin RC 1.50 4.00
180 Michael Bennett RC 2.00 5.00

2001 Upper Deck Legends Autographs

serted at a rate of one in 54 packs, these 51-cards feature autographs of a mix of NFL legends and current players. Stated print runs on some cards were provided by Upper Deck. Finally, some cards were issued in packs via mail redemption cards that carried an expiration date of 10/22/2004.

STATED ODDS 1:54
PRINT RUNS ANNC'd BY UPPER DECK
AM Archie Manning 15.00 40.00
AR Andre Reed 15.00 40.00
BS1 Barry Sanders 50.00 100.00
BS2 Bart Starr 100.00 200.00
BU Brian Urlacher 25.00 50.00
CT Charley Taylor 10.00 25.00
DB Dick Butkus 25.00 60.00
DC Daunte Culpepper SP/50* 25.00 60.00
DF1 Dan Fouts 15.00 40.00
DF2 Doug Flutie SP/50* 50.00 100.00
DM Dan Marino 125.00 200.00
ED Eric Dickerson 30.00 60.00
FH Franco Harris 20.00 50.00
FT Fran Tarkenton 25.00 50.00
GS Gale Sayers 20.00 50.00
HC Harold Carmichael 6.00 15.00
JB1 Jeff Blake 6.00 15.00
JB2 Jim Brown SP/50* 150.00 300.00
JE John Elway 100.00 200.00
JG1 Jeff Garcia SP/50* 40.00 80.00
JG2 Jeff George SP/50* 40.00 80.00
JK Jim Kelly SP/100* 150.00 250.00
JM Joe Montana 60.00 120.00
JN Joe Namath 50.00 100.00
JP1 Jake Plummer SP/50* 50.00 100.00
JP2 Jim Plunkett 15.00 40.00
JR John Riggins 20.00 50.00
JT Joe Theismann UER 15.00 40.00
JU Johnny Unitas 75.00 150.00
JY Jack Youngblood 10.00 25.00
KS Ken Stabler 25.00 50.00
KW1 Kellen Winslow 15.00 40.00
KW2 Kurt Warner 25.00 50.00
LA Lance Alworth SP/100* 50.00 100.00
LT Lawrence Taylor SP/100* 50.00 100.00
MA Marcus Allen 15.00 40.00
PH Paul Hornung 20.00 50.00
PM Peyton Manning 60.00 125.00
RM Randy Moss SP/50* 60.00 120.00
RS Roger Staubach 60.00 120.00
RW Ricky Williams SP/50* 40.00 80.00
TA Troy Aikman 50.00 100.00
TB1 Terry Bradshaw 50.00 100.00
TB2 Tim Brown 15.00 40.00
TD Tony Dorsett SP/100* 60.00 120.00
TT Thurman Thomas 15.00 40.00
VT Vinny Testaverde 50.00 100.00
WC Wayne Chrebet 6.00 15.00
WM Warren Moon 25.00 60.00

2001 Upper Deck Legends Legendary Artwork

sued at a rate of one in 18, these 15 cards feature drawings of some of the all-time NFL legends. The artist whose drawings were used was noted sports artist James Fiorentino.

COMPLETE SET (15) 30.00 60.00
STATED ODDS 1:18
LA1 Jim Thorpe 2.00 5.00
LA2 Jerry Rice 2.50 6.00
LA3 Bart Starr 3.00 8.00
LA4 Fran Tarkenton 1.50 4.00
LA5 Barry Sanders 2.00 5.00
LA6 Jim Brown 2.00 5.00
LA7 Joe Montana 5.00 12.00
LA8 Joe Namath 2.50 6.00
LA9 John Elway 2.00 5.00
LA10 Johnny Unitas 3.00 8.00
LA11 Roger Staubach 2.00 5.00
LA12 Terry Bradshaw 2.00 5.00
LA13 Walter Payton 4.00 10.00
LA14 Dan Marino 2.50 6.00
LA15 Dick Butkus 2.00 5.00

2001 Upper Deck Legends Legendary Cuts

Randomly inserted in packs, these cards feature signed cuts of 17 different NFL Hall of Famers. Upper Deck announced that a sum total of 330 cuts were inserted into this product.

STATED PRINT RUN 1-113
330 TOTAL CARDS AVAILABLE
LCBN Bronko Nagurski/28 250.00 450.00
LCEN Ernie Nevers/63 150.00 250.00
LCET Emlen Tunnell/22 100.00 200.00
LCGH George Halas/113 350.00 600.00

2001 Upper Deck Legends Memorable Materials

Inserted at a rate of one in 36, these 12 cards feature game-worn memorabilia of NFL players past and present.

STATED ODDS 1:36
MMBS Barry Sanders 5.00 12.00
MMCB Charlie Batch 2.00 5.00
MMDB Drew Bledsoe 2.50 6.00
MMDF Doug Flutie 2.50 6.00
MMDM Dan Marino 6.00 15.00
MMED Eric Dickerson SP/150* 4.00 10.00
MMIB Isaac Bruce UER 3.00 8.00
MMJE John Elway 5.00 12.00
MMMB Mark Brunell 2.50 6.00
MMMF Marshall Faulk 2.50 6.00
MMSM Steve McNair 2.50 6.00
MMWP Walter Payton SP/150* 12.00 30.00

2001 Upper Deck Legends Past Patterns Jerseys

Inserted at a rate of one in 18, this 37 card set features a mix of active and retired NFL greats and swatches of game-worn uniforms.

STATED ODDS 1:18
PPAM Archie Manning 8.00 20.00
PPAR Andre Reed 6.00 15.00
PPBF Brett Favre 8.00 20.00
PPCC Cris Carter 6.00 15.00
PPDF Doug Flutie 5.00 12.00
PPDM Dan Marino 10.00 25.00
PPES Emmitt Smith 15.00 40.00
PPFT Fred Taylor 3.00 8.00
PPGB George Blanda 5.00 12.00
PPJG Jeff George 4.00 10.00
PPJK Jim Kelly 6.00 15.00
PPJM Joe Montana SP/150 25.00 60.00
PPJN Joe Namath SP/150 15.00 40.00
PPJP Jim Plunkett 5.00 12.00
PPJR Jerry Rice 10.00 25.00
PPJS Junior Seau 4.00 10.00
PPJTA John Taylor 4.00 10.00
PPKC Kerry Collins 3.00 8.00
PPKN Ken Norton 4.00 8.00
PPLT Lawrence Taylor 6.00 15.00
PPMA Mike Alstott 3.00 8.00
PPPH Paul Hornung 10.00 25.00
PPPM Peyton Manning 12.00 30.00
PPRS Roger Staubach SP/95 25.00 50.00
PPRSM Robert Smith 3.00 8.00
PPRW1 Reggie White 8.00 20.00
PPRW2 Rod Woodson 5.00 12.00
PPSD Stephen Davis 3.00 8.00
PPSJ Sonny Jurgensen 6.00 15.00
PPSK Shaun King 4.00 10.00
PPSS Shannon Sharpe SP 5.00 12.00
PPSY Steve Young 8.00 20.00
PPTA Troy Aikman 6.00 15.00
PPTB Terry Bradshaw SP/150 25.00 50.00
PPTC Tim Couch 4.00 8.00
PPWD Warrick Dunn 3.00 8.00
PPWM Warren Moon 6.00 15.00

2001 Upper Deck Legends Timeless Tributes Jersey

Inserted at a rate of one in 36, this 11-card set honors some of the best NFL players past and present along with a swatch of game worn jersey on each card.

STATED ODDS 1:36
TTBS Bruce Smith 4.00 10.00
TTDG Darrell Green 5.00 12.00
TTDT Derrick Thomas 15.00 40.00
TTHM Harvey Martin 4.00 10.00
TTJB Jerome Bettis 5.00 12.00
TTJM Joe Montana 15.00 40.00
TTKN Ken Norton Jr. 3.00 8.00
TTLT Lawrence Taylor 5.00 12.00
TTRW Randy White 5.00 12.00
TTTT Thurman Thomas 4.00 10.00
TTWS Warren Sapp 4.00 10.00

2004 Upper Deck Legends

Upper Deck Legends was initially released in mid-January 2005. The base set consists of 190-cards including 20-Legends numbered of 1299 and 80-rookies serial numbered to 650. Hobby boxes contained 24-packs of 5-cards and carried an S.R.P. of $4.99 per pack. One parallel set and a variety of autograph and jersey inserts can be found seeded in packs highlighted by one of the more actively traded autographed inserts of the year in Legendary Signatures.

COMP.SET w/o SP's (90) 7.50 20.00
91-110 LEGENDS/1250 ODDS 1:24
111-190 ROOKIE/650 ODDS 1:12
UNPRICED PRINT PLATE PRINT RUN 1
1 Josh McCown .20 .50
2 Emmitt Smith .40 1.00
3 Michael Vick .20 .50
4 Peerless Price .15 .40
5 Ray Lewis .25 .60
6 Kyle Boller .15 .40
7 Deion Sanders .20 .50
8 Drew Bledsoe .20 .50
9 Travis Henry .15 .40
10 Eric Moulds .15 .40
11 Steve Smith .25 .60
12 Stephen Davis .15 .40
13 Jake Delhomme .15 .40
14 Rex Grossman .15 .40
15 Brian Urlacher .25 .60
16 Thomas Jones .15 .40
17 Chad Johnson .15 .40
18 Rudi Johnson .15 .40
19 Carson Palmer .20 .50
20 William Green .15 .40
21 Andre Davis .15 .40
22 Jeff Garcia .15 .40
23 Roy Williams S .15 .40
24 Eddie George .20 .50
25 Keyshawn Johnson .20 .50
26 Reuben Droughns .20 .50
27 Jake Plummer .15 .40
28 Champ Bailey .20 .50
29 Charles Rogers .15 .40
30 Joey Harrington .15 .40
31 Ahman Green .20 .50
32 Brett Favre .50 1.25
33 Javon Walker .15 .40
34 David Carr .15 .40
35 Domanick Davis .15 .40
36 Andre Johnson .20 .50
37 Marvin Harrison .20 .50
38 Edgerrin James .20 .50
39 Peyton Manning .60 1.50
40 Byron Leftwich .15 .40
41 Fred Taylor .15 .40
42 Trent Green .15 .40
43 Tony Gonzalez .20 .50
44 Priest Holmes .15 .40
45 Zach Thomas .20 .50
46 Chris Chambers .15 .40
47 Jay Fiedler .15 .40
48 Daunte Culpepper .20 .50
49 Randy Moss .20 .50
50 Onterrio Smith .15 .40
51 Tom Brady 1.00 2.50
52 Deion Branch .15 .40
53 Corey Dillon .15 .40
54 Deuce McAllister .20 .50
55 Aaron Brooks .15 .40
56 Joe Horn .15 .40
57 Tiki Barber .20 .50
58 Kurt Warner .20 .50
59 Jeremy Shockey .15 .40
60 Chad Pennington .15 .40
61 Santana Moss .20 .50
62 Curtis Martin .20 .50
63 Kerry Collins .15 .40
64 Jerry Rice .50 1.25
65 Jerry Porter .15 .40
66 Terrell Owens .20 .50
67 Jevon Kearse .15 .40
68 Donovan McNabb .20 .50
69 Hines Ward .20 .50
70 Plaxico Burress .15 .40
71 Duce Staley .15 .40
72 Drew Brees .25 .60
73 LaDainian Tomlinson .25 .60
74 Tim Rattay .15 .40
75 Brandon Lloyd .20 .50
76 Kevan Barlow .15 .40
77 Shaun Alexander .15 .40
78 Koren Robinson .15 .40
79 Matt Hasselbeck .15 .40
80 Marshall Faulk .20 .50
81 Torry Holt .20 .50
82 Marc Bulger .15 .40
83 Brian Griese .15 .40
84 Derrick Brooks .15 .40
85 Steve McNair .20 .50
86 Derrick Mason .15 .40
87 Chris Brown .15 .40
88 Mark Brunell .20 .50
89 Laveranues Coles .15 .40
90 Clinton Portis .15 .40
91 Dick Butkus 2.00 5.00
92 Gale Sayers 1.50 4.00
93 Mike Ditka 1.50 4.00
94 Jim Brown 2.00 5.00
95 Roger Staubach 2.00 5.00
96 Troy Aikman 2.00 5.00
97 John Elway 2.50 6.00
98 Barry Sanders 2.50 6.00
99 Bart Starr 4.00 10.00
100 Paul Hornung 1.50 4.00
101 Len Dawson 1.50 4.00
102 Dan Marino 3.00 8.00
103 Fran Tarkenton 1.50 4.00
104 Archie Manning 1.25 3.00
105 Joe Namath 2.50 6.00
106 Ken Stabler 2.00 5.00
107 Lynn Swann 2.00 5.00
108 Terry Bradshaw 2.00 5.00
109 Joe Montana 5.00 12.00
110 Joe Theismann 1.50 4.00
111 Bernard Berrian RC 1.25 3.00
112 Ben Hartsock RC 1.25 3.00
113 Karlos Dansby RC 1.50 4.00
114 Thomas Tapeh RC 1.50 4.00
115 Keary Colbert RC 1.25 3.00
116 Ben Troupe RC 1.25 3.00
117 Jonathan Vilma RC 1.50 4.00
118 Jamaar Taylor RC 1.25 3.00
119 Ben Roethlisberger RC 10.00 25.00
120 Samie Parker RC 1.25 3.00
121 Dunta Robinson RC 1.25 3.00
122 Dontarrious Thomas RC 1.50 4.00
123 Adimchinobe Echemandu RC 1.50 4.00
124 Darius Watts RC 1.25 3.00
125 Ben Watson RC 1.50 4.00
126 Terry Johnson RC 1.25 3.00
127 D.J. Hackett RC 1.25 3.00
128 Devery Henderson RC 1.25 3.00
129 Kellen Winslow Jr. RC 1.25 3.00
130 Travis LaBoy RC 1.50 4.00
131 Maurice Mann RC 1.25 3.00
132 Rashaun Woods RC 1.25 3.00
133 Michael Turner RC 1.25 3.00

134 Junior Siavii RC 1.25 3.00
135 Johnnie Morant RC 1.25 3.00
136 Larry Fitzgerald RC 5.00 12.00
137 Kevin Jones RC 1.50 4.00
138 Will Smith RC 1.50 4.00
139 Robert Gallery RC 1.50 4.00
140 Michael Jenkins RC 1.25 3.00
141 Cedric Cobbs RC 1.25 3.00
142 Igor Olshansky RC 1.50 4.00
143 Josh Harris RC 1.25 3.00
144 Michael Clayton RC 1.50 4.00
145 Mewelde Moore RC 1.50 4.00
146 Jason Babin RC 2.00 5.00
147 Cody Pickett RC 1.25 3.00
148 Lee Evans RC 2.00 5.00
149 Greg Jones RC 1.25 3.00
150 Marcus Tubbs RC 1.25 3.00
151 Craig Krenzel RC 1.25 3.00
152 Roy Williams RC 1.25 3.00
153 Tatum Bell RC 1.25 3.00
154 Kenechi Udeze RC 1.50 4.00
155 Shawn Andrews RC 1.50 4.00
156 Reggie Williams RC 1.25 3.00
157 Julius Jones RC 1.25 3.00
158 Vince Wilfork RC 2.00 5.00
159 Vernon Carey RC 1.25 3.00
160 Eli Manning RC 10.00 25.00
161 Devard Darling RC 1.25 3.00
162 Sean Taylor RC 8.00 20.00
163 Teddy Lehman RC 1.25 3.00
164 Jammal Lord RC 1.25 3.00
165 J.P. Losman RC 1.25 3.00
166 Jerricho Cotchery RC 1.50 4.00
167 Ahmad Carroll RC 1.25 3.00
168 Michael Boulware RC 2.00 5.00
169 Quincy Wilson RC 1.25 3.00
170 Derrick Hamilton RC 1.25 3.00
171 Kris Wilson RC 1.50 4.00
172 D.J. Williams RC 2.00 5.00
173 P.K. Sam RC 1.25 3.00
174 Matt Schaub RC 1.25 3.00
175 Ernest Wilford RC 1.50 4.00
176 Chris Gamble RC 1.25 3.00
177 Courtney Watson RC 1.25 3.00
178 Drew Henson RC 1.25 3.00
179 Chris Perry RC 1.25 3.00
180 Tommie Harris RC 1.50 4.00
181 Marquis Cooper RC 1.25 3.00
182 Philip Rivers RC 4.00 10.00
183 Carlos Francis RC 1.25 3.00
184 DeAngelo Hall RC 2.00 5.00
185 Daryl Smith RC 1.25 3.00
186 Troy Fleming RC 1.25 3.00
187 Luke McCown RC 1.25 3.00
188 Steven Jackson RC 2.00 5.00
189 Ricardo Colclough RC 1.25 3.00
190 Gilbert Gardner RC 1.25 3.00

2004 Upper Deck Legends Gold

*GOLD VETS: 10X TO 25X BASIC CARDS
*GOLD LEGENDS: 25X TO 5X
*GOLD ROOKIES: 1.5X TO 4X
GOLD/25 STATED ODDS 1:192

2004 Upper Deck Legends Future Legends Jersey

STATED ODDS 1:24
FLBR Ben Roethlisberger 12.00 30.00
FLCP Chris Perry 2.00 5.00
FLEM Eli Manning 6.00 15.00
FLGJ Greg Jones 2.00 5.00
FLJJ Julius Jones 2.00 5.00
FLJP J.P. Losman 2.00 5.00
FLKJ Kevin Jones 2.50 6.00
FLKW Kellen Winslow Jr. 2.00 5.00
FLLE Lee Evans 3.00 8.00
FLLF Larry Fitzgerald 8.00 20.00
FLMC Michael Clayton 2.50 6.00
FLMJ Michael Jenkins 2.00 5.00
FLPR Philip Rivers 8.00 20.00
FLRE Reggie Williams 2.00 5.00
FLRG Robert Gallery 2.50 6.00
FLRW Roy Williams WR 2.00 5.00
FLSJ Steven Jackson 3.00 8.00
FLTB Tatum Bell 2.00 5.00

2004 Upper Deck Legends Future Legends Throwback Jersey

STATED ODDS 1:192
FLTBB Bernard Berrian 2.50 6.00
FLTBR Ben Roethlisberger 20.00 50.00
FLTBT Ben Troupe 2.50 6.00
FLTBW Ben Watson 3.00 8.00
FLTCC Cedric Cobbs 2.50 6.00
FLTCP Chris Perry 2.50 6.00
FLTDE Devery Henderson 2.50 6.00
FLTDH DeAngelo Hall 4.00 10.00
FLTDW Darius Watts 2.50 6.00
FLTEM Eli Manning 25.00 50.00
FLTGJ Greg Jones 2.50 6.00
FLTHA Derrick Hamilton 2.50 6.00
FLTJJ Julius Jones 2.50 6.00
FLTJP J.P. Losman 2.50 6.00
FLTKC Keary Colbert 2.50 6.00
FLTKJ Kevin Jones 3.00 8.00
FLTKW Kellen Winslow Jr. 2.50 6.00
FLTLE Lee Evans 4.00 10.00
FLTLF Larry Fitzgerald 10.00 25.00
FLTLM Luke McCown 2.50 6.00
FLTMC Michael Clayton 3.00 8.00
FLTMJ Michael Jenkins 2.50 6.00
FLTMS Matt Schaub 2.50 6.00
FLTPR Philip Rivers 12.00 30.00
FLTRA Rashaun Woods 2.50 6.00
FLTRE Reggie Williams 2.50 6.00
FLTRG Robert Gallery 3.00 8.00
FLTRW Roy Williams WR 2.50 6.00
FLTSJ Steven Jackson 4.00 10.00
FLTTB Tatum Bell 2.50 6.00

2004 Upper Deck Legends Immortal Inscriptions

STATED PRINT RUN 45 SER.#'d SETS
IIAM Archie Manning 20.00 50.00
IIBS Barry Sanders 75.00 150.00
IIDB Dick Butkus 60.00 120.00
IIDM Dan Marino 100.00 200.00
IIFH Franco Harris 30.00 80.00
IIFT Fran Tarkenton 25.00 60.00
IIGS Gale Sayers 50.00 100.00
IIHL Howie Long 50.00 100.00
IIJB Jim Brown 60.00 120.00
IIJE John Elway 100.00 200.00
IIJM Joe Montana 75.00 150.00
IIJN Joe Namath 60.00 120.00
IIJT Joe Theismann 20.00 50.00
IIKS Ken Stabler 30.00 80.00
IIKW Kellen Winslow Sr. 20.00 50.00
IIPH Paul Hornung 15.00 40.00
IIRS Roger Staubach 60.00 120.00
IITA Troy Aikman 60.00 100.00
IITB Terry Bradshaw 50.00 120.00

2004 Upper Deck Legends Legendary Jerseys

LEGENDARY JERSEY/99 ODDS 1:384
LJAM Archie Manning 8.00 20.00
LJBS Barry Sanders 20.00 50.00
LJDM Dan Marino 30.00 60.00
LJFT Fran Tarkenton 10.00 25.00
LJGS Gale Sayers 10.00 25.00
LJHL Howie Long 12.00 30.00
LJJE John Elway 20.00 50.00
LJJM Joe Montana 30.00 60.00
LJJN Joe Namath 15.00 40.00
[illegible]
LJJU Johnny Unitas 15.00 40.00
LJKS Ken Stabler 12.00 30.00
LJKW Kellen Winslow Sr. 10.00 25.00
LJLD Len Dawson 10.00 25.00
LJLS Lynn Swann 25.00 60.00
LJON Ozzie Newsome 8.00 20.00
LJRS Roger Staubach 12.00 30.00
LJTA Troy Aikman 12.00 30.00
LJTB Terry Bradshaw 12.00 30.00
LJWP Walter Payton 30.00 80.00

2004 Upper Deck Legends Legendary Lines of Defense Autographs

STATED PRINT RUN 75 SER.#'d SETS
HGL Ham/Greene/Lambert 125.00 250.00
JGW T.Jcksn/Grdshr/Wright 30.00 60.00
PEM Page/Eller/Marshall 60.00 120.00
SHD Single/Hmptn/Dent 75.00 150.00
YYJ Ji.Yng/Jk.Yng/D.Jones 40.00 80.00

2004 Upper Deck Legends Legendary Signatures

STATED ODDS 1:8
LSAK Alex Karras 10.00 25.00
LSAM Archie Manning SP 30.00 80.00
LSAN Andy Russell 8.00 20.00
LSAP Alan Page 5.00 12.00
LSBB Bill Bergey 5.00 12.00
LSBE Raymond Berry 8.00 20.00
LSBG Bob Griese 15.00 40.00
LSBI Billy Sims 6.00 15.00
LSBJ Bert Jones 6.00 15.00
LSBK Billy Kilmer 8.00 20.00
LSBL Bob Lilly 8.00 20.00
LSBS Barry Sanders SP 125.00 250.00
LSBY Billy Johnson 5.00 12.00
LSCB Cliff Branch 5.00 12.00
LSCE Carl Eller 5.00 12.00
LSCF Chuck Foreman 5.00 12.00
LSCJ Charlie Joiner 5.00 12.00
LSCM Craig Morton 6.00 15.00
LSCT Charley Taylor 6.00 15.00
LSDA Doug Atkins 8.00 20.00
LSDB Dick Butkus SP 125.00 250.00
LSDC Dave Casper 8.00 20.00
LSDF Dan Fouts SP 40.00 80.00
LSDH Dan Hampton 10.00 25.00
LSDI Dick Anderson SP 10.00 25.00
LSDJ Deacon Jones SP 25.00 50.00
LSDL Daryle Lamonica 8.00 20.00
LSDM Dan Marino SP 150.00 300.00
LSDO Don Maynard 6.00 15.00
LSDP Drew Pearson 6.00 15.00
LSEC Earl Campbell SP 40.00 80.00
LSED Eric Dickerson SP 15.00 40.00
LSEJ Ed Too Tall Jones 5.00 12.00
LSFG Frank Gifford SP 30.00 60.00
LSFT Fran Tarkenton SP 60.00 120.00
LSGA Roman Gabriel 10.00 25.00
LSGS Gale Sayers SP 60.00 120.00
LSHA Chris Hanburger 8.00 20.00
LSHC Harold Carmichael 5.00 12.00
LSHL Howie Long SP 40.00 80.00
LSHN John Hannah 6.00 15.00
LSHT Jim Hart 5.00 12.00
LSIC Isaac Curtis 5.00 12.00
LSJB Jim Brown SP 125.00 250.00
LSJE John Elway SP 60.00 125.00
LSJG Joe Greene SP 125.00 250.00
LSJH Jack Ham SP 125.00 200.00
LSJI Jim Marshall 8.00 20.00
LSJK Jerry Kramer 12.00 30.00
LSJL Jack Lambert SP 40.00 80.00
LSJM Joe Montana SP 125.00 250.00
LSJN Joe Namath SP 300.00 500.00
LSJO John Taylor 6.00 15.00
LSJP Jim Plunkett 8.00 20.00
LSJT Joe Theismann SP 15.00 40.00
LSJY Jim Youngblood 5.00 12.00
LSKA Ken Anderson 8.00 20.00
LSKI Jim Kiick 5.00 12.00
LSKS Ken Stabler SP 40.00 80.00
LSKW Kellen Winslow Sr. SP 12.00 30.00
LSLC L.C. Greenwood SP 15.00 40.00
LSLD Len Dawson SP 20.00 50.00
LSLW Louis Wright 5.00 12.00
LSMA Mark Duper 6.00 15.00
LSMC Mark Clayton 5.00 12.00
LSMD Mike Ditka SP 20.00 50.00
LSMF Manny Fernandez 5.00 12.00
LSMI Mike Curtis 5.00 12.00
LSMM Mercury Morris 5.00 12.00
LSMR Mel Renfro 6.00 15.00
LSMS Mike Singletary SP 60.00 120.00
LSMU Anthony Munoz 6.00 15.00
LSOM Ollie Matson 25.00 50.00
LSON Ozzie Newsome 6.00 15.00
LSPH Paul Hornung SP 60.00 120.00
LSPK Paul Krause 6.00 15.00
LSRA Ray Guy 6.00 15.00
LSRB Robert Brazile 25.00 60.00
LSRC Roger Craig 8.00 20.00
LSRD Richard Dent 12.00 30.00
LSRG Randy Gradishar 5.00 12.00
LSRJ Ron Jaworski 8.00 20.00
LSRO Roger Wehrli 6.00 15.00
LSRW Randy White 12.00 30.00
LSSB Steve Bartkowski 6.00 15.00
LSSH Sam Huff 12.00 30.00
LSSJ Sonny Jurgensen SP 15.00 40.00
LSSS Steve Spurrier SP 15.00 40.00
LSTA Troy Aikman SP 75.00 135.00
LSTB Terry Bradshaw/20* 200.00 400.00
LSTD Tony Dorsett/45* 150.00 300.00
LSVG Vencie Glenn 5.00 12.00
LSWB Willie Brown 5.00 12.00
LSWM Wilbert Montgomery 6.00 15.00
LSYO Jack Youngblood 6.00 15.00

2004 Upper Deck Legends Link to the Future Autographs

STATED PRINT RUN 25-50
LFBL D.Bledsoe/J.Losman/50 12.00 30.00
LFBM K.Boller/L.McCown/50 12.00 30.00
LFBR D.Bledsoe/P.Rivers/25 40.00 100.00
LFCC Chambers/Colbert/25 15.00 40.00
LFDK McAllister/Ke.Jones/25 25.00 60.00
LFGB A.Green/T.Bell/50 12.00 30.00
LFGC J.Galloway/M.Clayton/50 12.00 30.00
LFGW Gonzal/Winslow Jr./50 15.00 40.00
LFHE D.Hall/L.Evans/50 15.00 40.00
LFHH Horn/Henderson/50 12.00 30.00
LFHT T.Heap/B.Troupe/50 12.00 30.00
LFJW C.Johnson/Re.Williams/50 15.00 40.00
LFMJ McAllister/S.Jackson/25 20.00 50.00
LFMM P.Manning/Eli/25 250.00 400.00
LFMW Mason/Ro.Will.WR/50 20.00 50.00
LFPS Pennington/Schaub/50 25.00 60.00
LFRJ Ro.Will.S/J.Jones/50 25.00 60.00
LFTE T.Brady/E.Manning/25 250.00 400.00
LFTJ Tomlinson/J.Jones/25 25.00 60.00
LFVR Vick/Roethlisberger/25 125.00 250.00
LFWJ B.Westbrook/G.Jones/50 15.00 40.00

2004 Upper Deck Legends Link to the Past Autographs

STATED PRINT RUN 25-50
LPBM T.Brady/J.Montana/25 250.00 400.00
LPBS M.Brunell/K.Stabler/50 25.00 60.00
LPCC C.Chambers/M.Clayton/50 20.00 50.00
LPCT Clppr/Trkntn/50
LPDC D.Davis/E.Campbell/50 20.00 50.00
LPDP Marino/P.Manning/25 250.00 400.00
LPFT L.Fitzgerald/C.Taylor/25 30.00 80.00
LPGT Grossman/Theismann/50 20.00 50.00
[illegible] 20.00 50.00
LPHS Henson/Staubach/25 40.00 100.00
LPJD Ju.Jones/T.Dorsett/50 25.00 60.00
LPJE S.Jack/E.Dicker/50 15.00 40.00
LPJH G.Jones/F.Harris/50 25.00 60.00
LPJS Ke.Jones/B.Sanders/25 75.00 150.00
LPMJ McNabb/Jaworski/50 25.00 60.00
LPMM E.Mann/A.Mann/50 175.00 300.00
LPPA P.Mann/A.Mann/25 150.00 300.00
LPPN Penning/Namath/25 40.00 100.00
LPRB Roeth/Bradshaw/25 200.00 350.00
LPRF P.Rivers/D.Fouts/50 60.00 100.00
LPUE K.Udeze/C.Eller/50 15.00 40.00
LPVA M.Vick/T.Aikman/50 40.00 100.00
LPWW Winslow Jr./Wins.Sr./50 25.00 60.00

2005 Upper Deck Legends

This 195-card set was released in August, 2005. The set was issued in five-card packs with an $4.99 SRP which also came 24 packs to a box. The set features mainly retired greats except for Brett Favre (card #7) and 2005 rookies (101-165, 191-195). In addition there are subsets featuring checklists (96-100) and Legends of the Hall (166-190). All of the rookies were issued to a stated print run of 725 serial numbered copies while the Legends of the Hall were issued to a stated print run of 1,025 copies.

COMP SET w/o SP's (100) 7.50 20.00
ROOKIE PRINT RUN 725 SER.#'d SETS
166-195 LEG.PRINT RUN 1025 SER.#'d SETS
1 Charley Taylor .25 .60
2 Roger Craig .30 .75
3 Ozzie Newsome .25 .60
4 Rocky Bleier .25 .60
5 Russ Francis .20 .50
6 Jerry Rice .60 1.50
7 Pat Haden .20 .50
8 Brett Favre .60 1.50
9 Joe Ferguson .20 .50
10 Ed Jones .25 .60
11 Joe Washington .20 .50
12 John Brodie .20 .50
13 Peyton Manning .75 2.00
14 Mark Van Eeghen .20 .50
15 William Perry .20 .50
16 Bob Brown .20 .50
17 Herb Adderley .25 .60
18 Deion Sanders .25 .60
19 Lenny Moore .20 .50
20 Tom Mack .20 .50
21 Jim McMahon .30 .75
22 Bobby Mitchell .25 .60
23 John Mackey .20 .50
24 Curtis Martin .25 .60
25 Junior Seau .25 .60
26 Harold Jackson .20 .50
27 Jim Zorn .20 .50
28 Chuck Foreman .20 .50
29 Willie Brown .20 .50
30 Cliff Branch .20 .50
31 Jerry Kramer .25 .60
32 Harry Carson .20 .50
33 Chuck Noll .25 .60
34 Len Hauss .20 .50
35 Jim Plunkett .25 .60
36 Ollie Matson .25 .60
37 Billy Kilmer .25 .60
38 Jim Marshall .20 .50
39 Dan Dierdorf .20 .50
40 Jim Kelly .30 .75
41 Vince Ferragamo .20 .50
42 Ottis Anderson .20 .50
43 Charlie Joiner .20 .50
44 George Blanda .25 .60
45 Drew Pearson .25 .60
46 Andre Reed .25 .60
47 Merlin Olsen .20 .50
48 Paul Warfield .25 .60
49 James Lofton .20 .50
50 Art Donovan .20 .50
51 Dwight Clark .25 .60
52 Raymond Berry .25 .60
53 L.C. Greenwood .20 .50
54 Dave Casper .20 .50
55 Don Maynard .25 .60
56 Bud Grant .20 .50
57 Roman Gabriel .20 .50
58 Cris Collinsworth .25 .60
59 Joe Theismann .30 .75
60 Paul Hornung .30 .75
61 Alan Page .20 .50
62 Deacon Jones .25 .60
63 Steve Largent .30 .75
64 Phil Simms .25 .60
65 Floyd Little .20 .50
66 Archie Manning .25 .60
67 Ken Stabler .40 1.00
68 Fran Tarkenton .30 .75
69 Len Dawson .30 .75
70 Mike Ditka .30 .75
71 Conrad Dobler .20 .50
72 Jack Lambert .30 .75
73 Marcus Allen .30 .75
74 Bo Jackson .40 1.00
75 Jerome Bettis .30 .75
76 Jack Ham .25 .60
77 Marshall Faulk .25 .60
78 Mike Singletary .30 .75
79 Bob Griese .30 .75
80 Dick Butkus .40 1.00
81 Gale Sayers .30 .75
82 Earl Campbell .30 .75
83 Dan Fouts .25 .60
84 Franco Harris .30 .75
85 Steve Young .40 1.00
86 Tony Dorsett .30 .75
87 Jim Brown .40 1.00
88 Roger Staubach .40 1.00
89 Troy Aikman .40 1.00
90 Barry Sanders .50 1.25
91 Bernie Kosar .25 .60
92 Dan Marino .60 1.50
93 John Elway .50 1.25
94 Randy Moss .25 .60
95 Joe Montana 1.00 2.50
96 Joe Montana CL .60 1.50
97 Dan Marino CL .40 1.00
98 John Elway CL .30 .75
99 Gale Sayers CL .20 .50
100 Paul Hornung CL .20 .50
101 Aaron Rodgers RC 25.00 50.00
102 Alex Smith QB RC 4.00 10.00
103 Cadillac Williams RC 1.00 2.50
104 Ronnie Brown RC 1.25 3.00
105 Ciatrick Fason RC 1.00 2.50
106 Charlie Frye RC 1.00 2.50
107 Derek Anderson RC 1.25 3.00
108 Braylon Edwards RC 1.00 2.50
109 Roddy White RC 1.50 4.00
110 Thomas Davis RC 1.00 2.50
111 Jason Campbell RC 1.00 2.50
112 Andrew Walter RC 1.00 2.50
113 Kyle Orton RC 1.00 2.50
114 David Greene RC 1.00 2.50
115 Cedric Benson RC 1.00 2.50
116 Vernand Morency RC 1.25 3.00
117 Eric Shelton RC 1.00 2.50
118 Maurice Clarett 1.25 3.00
119 Brandon Jacobs RC 1.25 3.00
120 Anthony Davis RC 1.00 2.50
121 Marion Barber RC 1.00 2.50
122 J.J. Arrington RC 1.25 3.00
123 Ryan Moats RC 1.25 3.00
124 Frank Gore RC 2.00 5.00
125 Stefan LeFors RC 1.00 2.50
126 Darren Sproles RC 1.50 4.00
127 Cedric Houston RC 1.50 4.00
128 Troy Williamson RC 1.00 [illegible]
129 Mark Clayton RC 1.00 2.50
130 Chris Henry RC 1.25 3.00
131 Fred Gibson RC 1.00 2.50
132 Craphonso Thorpe RC 1.00 2.50
133 Terrence Murphy RC 1.00 2.50
134 Dan Orlovsky RC 1.00 2.50
135 Roscoe Parrish RC 1.00 2.50
136 Reggie Brown RC 1.00 2.50
137 Craig Bragg RC 1.00 2.50
138 Larry Brackins RC 1.00 2.50
139 Adrian McPherson RC 1.00 2.50
140 Matt Jones RC 1.00 2.50
141 Heath Miller RC 2.00 5.00
142 Alex Smith TE RC 1.00 2.50
143 Kevin Everett RC 1.50 4.00
144 Jerome Mathis RC 1.50 4.00
145 Travis Johnson RC 1.00 2.50
146 Channing Crowder RC 1.25 3.00
147 Mike Williams 1.25 3.00
148 Barrett Ruud RC 1.25 3.00
149 Marcus Spears RC 1.00 2.50
150 Derrick Johnson RC 1.25 3.00
151 Shawne Merriman RC 1.50 4.00
152 Kevin Burnett RC 1.25 3.00
153 Erasmus James RC 1.00 2.50
154 Dan Cody RC 1.00 2.50
155 David Pollack RC 1.00 2.50
156 Antrel Rolle RC 1.50 4.00
157 Adam Jones RC 1.25 3.00
158 Mark Bradley RC 1.00 2.50
159 Carlos Rogers RC 1.50 4.00
160 Vincent Jackson RC 1.50 4.00
161 DeMarcus Ware RC 3.00 8.00
162 Corey Webster RC 1.25 3.00
163 Justin Miller RC 1.00 2.50
164 Eric Green RC 1.00 2.50
165 Marlin Jackson RC 1.00 2.50
166 Herb Adderley LH 1.50 4.00
167 Fran Tarkenton LH 2.00 5.00
168 Troy Aikman LH 2.50 6.00
169 Charlie Joiner LH 1.25 3.00
170 George Blanda LH 1.50 4.00
171 Jim Kelly LH 2.00 5.00
172 Joe Montana LH 6.00 15.00
173 Jack Ham LH 1.50 4.00
174 Marcus Allen LH 2.00 5.00
175 Tony Dorsett LH 2.00 5.00
176 Barry Sanders LH 3.00 8.00
177 Paul Warfield LH 1.50 4.00
178 Dan Marino LH 4.00 10.00
179 John Elway LH 3.00 8.00
180 Franco Harris LH 2.00 5.00
181 Mike Singletary LH 2.00 5.00
182 Gale Sayers LH 2.00 5.00
183 Bob Griese LH 2.00 5.00
184 Dan Fouts LH 1.50 4.00
185 Earl Campbell LH 2.00 5.00
186 Jim Brown LH 2.50 6.00
187 Dick Butkus LH 2.50 6.00
188 Paul Hornung LH 2.00 5.00
189 Roger Staubach LH 2.50 6.00
190 Steve Largent LH 2.00 5.00
191 Ryan Fitzpatrick RC 1.50 4.00
192 Alvin Pearman RC 1.00 2.50
193 Courtney Roby RC 1.00 2.50
194 Chase Lyman RC 1.00 2.50
195 Roydell Williams RC 1.25 3.00

2005 Upper Deck Legends Dream Teammates Autographs

UNPRICED PRINT RUN 10 SER.#'d SETS

2005 Upper Deck Legends Future Legends Jersey

STATED ODDS 1:24 HOB, 1:48 RET
AJ Adam Jones 3.00 8.00
AN Antrel Rolle 3.00 8.00
AS Alex Smith QB 10.00 25.00
AW Andrew Walter 3.00 8.00
BE Braylon Edwards 7.50 20.00
CA Carlos Rogers 3.00 8.00
CF Charlie Frye 3.00 8.00
CI Ciatrick Fason 3.00 8.00
CR Courtney Roby 3.00 8.00
CW Cadillac Williams 6.00 15.00
ES Eric Shelton 3.00 8.00
FG Frank Gore 5.00 12.00
JA J.J. Arrington 3.00 8.00
JC Jason Campbell 5.00 12.00
KO Kyle Orton 3.00 8.00
MB Mark Bradley 3.00 8.00
MC Mark Clayton 3.00 8.00
MJ Matt Jones 4.00 10.00
MO Maurice Clarett 3.00 8.00
RB Ronnie Brown 10.00 25.00
RE Reggie Brown 3.00 8.00
RM Ryan Moats 3.00 8.00
RP Roscoe Parrish 3.00 8.00
RW Roddy White 3.00 8.00
SL Stefan LeFors 3.00 8.00
TM Terrence Murphy 3.00 8.00
TW Troy Williamson 3.00 8.00
VJ Vincent Jackson 4.00 10.00
VM Vernand Morency 3.00 8.00

2005 Upper Deck Legends Legendary Cuts Timeless Tandems

NOT PRICED DUE TO SCARCITY

2005 Upper Deck Legends Legendary Heritage Autographs

UNPRICED HERITAGE SER.#'d TO 5

2005 Upper Deck Legends Legendary Jerseys

STATED PRINT RUN 60 SER.#'d SETS
BA Barry Sanders 25.00 50.00
BJ Bo Jackson 20.00 40.00
BK Bernie Kosar 7.50 20.00
DM Dan Marino 40.00 80.00
FT Fran Tarkenton 12.50 30.00
GS Gale Sayers 20.00 50.00
HA Herb Adderley UER 7.50 20.00
JB John Brodie 12.50 30.00
JE John Elway 25.00 50.00
JI Jim Marshall 12.50 30.00
JK Jim Kelly 15.00 40.00
JM Joe Montana 40.00 80.00
JT Joe Theismann 12.50 30.00
JU Johnny Unitas 30.00 60.00
KS Ken Stabler 15.00 40.00
LT Lawrence Taylor 15.00 40.00
MA Marcus Allen 12.50 30.00
MO Merlin Olsen 12.50 30.00
ON Ozzie Newsome 7.50 20.00
PS Phil Simms 12.50 30.00
RL Ronnie Lott 15.00 40.00
RS Roger Staubach 15.00 40.00
SL Steve Largent 12.50 30.00
SY Steve Young 15.00 40.00
TA Troy Aikman 15.00 40.00
WP Walter Payton 40.00 100.00

2005 Upper Deck Legends Legendary Signatures

STATED ODDS 1:8 HOB, 1:24 RET
AD Art Donovan 12.50 25.00
AM Archie Manning SP 20.00 50.00
AP Alan Page 10.00 25.00
BB Bob Brown 8.00 20.00
BE Bob Griese SP 60.00 120.00
DC Dud Grant 25.00 60.00
BI Billy Kilmer 6.00 15.00
BJ Bo Jackson SP 50.00 100.00
BK Bernie Kosar SP 25.00 50.00
BM Bobby Mitchell 8.00 20.00
[illegible] 150.00 300.00
CB Cliff Branch 8.00 20.00
CC Cris Collinsworth 8.00 20.00
CD Conrad Dobler 5.00 12.00
CF Chuck Foreman 8.00 20.00
CJ Charlie Joiner 5.00 12.00
CN Chuck Noll 25.00 50.00
CT Charley Taylor 5.00 12.00
DA Dave Casper 8.00 20.00
DB Dick Butkus SP 75.00 150.00
DC Dwight Clark 8.00 20.00
DD Dan Dierdorf 8.00 20.00
DF Dan Fouts SP 50.00 100.00
DJ Deacon Jones SP 15.00 30.00
DM Don Maynard SP 30.00 50.00
DO Dan Marino SP 250.00 500.00
DR Drew Pearson SP 10.00 25.00
EC Earl Campbell SP 30.00 80.00
EJ Ed Jones 10.00 25.00
FH Franco Harris SP 40.00 100.00
FL Floyd Little 5.00 12.00
FT Fran Tarkenton SP 30.00 60.00
GB George Blanda SP 25.00 60.00
GS Gale Sayers SP 30.00 80.00
HA Herb Adderley 10.00 25.00
HC Harry Carson 8.00 20.00
HJ Harold Jackson 5.00 12.00
JB John Brodie 8.00 20.00
JC Jack Lambert SP 75.00 135.00
JE John Elway SP 50.00 120.00
JF Joe Ferguson 8.00 20.00
JH Jack Ham SP 40.00 80.00
JI Jim Brown 75.00 150.00
JK Jerry Kramer 8.00 20.00
JL James Lofton 8.00 20.00
JM Joe Montana SP 125.00 250.00
JP Jim Plunkett 10.00 25.00
JR Jim Marshall 8.00 20.00
JT Joe Theismann 10.00 25.00
JW Joe Washington 5.00 12.00
JY John Mackey 12.00 30.00
JZ Jim Zorn 8.00 20.00
KE Jim Kelly SP 25.00 60.00
KS Ken Stabler SP 40.00 80.00
LA Andre Reed 10.00 25.00
LD Len Dawson SP 25.00 60.00
LG L.C. Greenwood 15.00 30.00
LH Len Hauss 5.00 12.00
LM Lenny Moore 8.00 20.00
MA Marcus Allen SP 50.00 100.00
MC Jim McMahon 20.00 40.00
MD Mike Ditka SP 25.00 50.00
MO Merlin Olsen SP 30.00 60.00
MS Mike Singletary SP 30.00 60.00
MV Mark Van Eeghan 8.00 20.00
OA Ottis Anderson 8.00 20.00
OM Ollie Matson 20.00 40.00
ON Ozzie Newsome 5.00 12.00
PA Paul Hornung 15.00 40.00
PH Pat Haden 6.00 15.00
PW Paul Warfield 8.00 20.00
RB Rocky Bleier 10.00 25.00
RG Roger Craig 8.00 20.00
RO Roman Gabriel 10.00 25.00
RS Russ Francis 5.00 12.00
RU Roger Staubach SP 75.00 150.00
RY Raymond Berry 8.00 20.00
SL Steve Largent SP 20.00 40.00
TA Troy Aikman SP 30.00 80.00
TD Tony Dorsett SP 30.00 80.00
TM Tom Mack 6.00 15.00
VF Vince Ferragamo 8.00 20.00
WB Willie Brown 6.00 15.00
WP William Perry 8.00 20.00

2005 Upper Deck Legends Legends of the Hall Autographs

STATED PRINT RUN 25 SER.#'d SETS
BG Bob Griese 40.00 80.00
BS Barry Sanders 100.00 175.00
CJ Charlie Joiner 20.00 40.00
DB Dick Butkus 60.00 120.00
DF Dan Fouts 40.00 80.00
DM Dan Marino 150.00 300.00
EC Earl Campbell 25.00 50.00
FH Franco Harris 40.00 80.00
FT Fran Tarkenton 30.00 60.00
GB George Blanda 40.00 80.00
GS Gale Sayers 40.00 80.00
HA Herb Adderley 20.00 40.00
JB Jim Brown 75.00 135.00
JE John Elway 125.00 200.00
JH Jack Ham 35.00 60.00
JK Jim Kelly 40.00 80.00
JM Joe Montana 125.00 250.00
MA Marcus Allen 30.00 80.00
MS Mike Singletary 25.00 50.00
PH Paul Hornung 40.00 80.00
PW Paul Warfield 20.00 40.00
RS Roger Staubach 60.00 120.00
SL Steve Largent 30.00 60.00
TA Troy Aikman 60.00 120.00
TD Tony Dorsett 30.00 80.00

2005 Upper Deck Legends Link to the Future Autographs

UNPRICED PRINT RUN 20 SER.#'d SETS

2005 Upper Deck Legends Link to the Past Autographs

COMMON CARD/20 15.00 40.00
UNL.STARS/20 20.00 50.00
BA T.Barber/O.Anderson 20.00 50.00
BC Ch.Brown/E.Campbell 20.00 50.00
FG A.Feeley/Bo.Griese 15.00 40.00
FH B.Favre/P.Hornung 150.00 250.00
GD T.Green/L.Dawson 20.00 50.00
GN A.Gates/O.Newsome 15.00 40.00
GS A.Green/G.Sayers 15.00 40.00
JA La.Johnson/M.Allen 15.00 40.00
JC Ch.Johnson/C.Collinsworth 15.00 40.00
LA B.Leftwich/T.Aikman 40.00 80.00
LK J.Losman/J.Kelly 30.00 60.00
MJ D.McAllister/Bo Jackson 40.00 80.00
MM P.Manning/J.Montana 300.00 600.00
MT E.Manning/F.Tarkenton 60.00 120.00
PK C.Palmer/B.Kosar 12.00 30.00
TS L.Tomlinson/Ba.Sanders 150.00 250.00
VF M.Vick/F.Tarkenton 30.00 60.00

2005 Upper Deck Legends Touchdown Tandems Autographs

UNPRICED TANDEMS SER.#'d TO 20

2006 Upper Deck Legends

This 200-card set was released in August, 2006. The set was issued into the hobby in five-card packs with an $4.99 SRP which came 24 packs to a box. The first 100 cards (with a fex exceptions) featured retired greats while cards 101-200 featured rookies. Cards numbered 101-200 were issued to a stated print run of 750 serial numbered sets.

COMP.SET w/o RC's (100) 8.00 20.00
101-200 ROOKIE PRINT RUN 750
1 Marshall Faulk .25 .60
2 John Elway .50 1.25
3 Barry Sanders .50 1.25
4 Dan Marino .60 1.50
5 Troy Aikman .40 1.00
6 Roger Staubach .40 1.00
7 Curtis Martin .25 .60
8 O.J. McDuffie .25 .60
9 Steve Young .40 1.00
10 Jim Kelly .30 .75
11 Dan Fouts .25 .60
12 Franco Harris .30 .75
13 Christian Okoye .25 .60
14 Craig Morton .20 .50
15 Doug Flutie .25 .60
16 Gale Sayers .30 .75
17 Bob Griese .30 .75
18 Jim Plunkett .25 .60
19 Marvin Harrison .25 .60
20 L.C. Greenwood .20 .50
21 Len Dawson .30 .75
22 Ken Stabler .40 1.00
23 Fran Tarkenton .30 .75
24 Herman Moore .20 .50
25 Joe Theismann .30 .75
26 Paul Hornung .30 .75
27 Herschel Walker .30 .75
28 Randy Moss .25 .60
29 Drew Pearson .25 .60
30 Don Maynard .25 .60
31 Dwight Clark .25 .60
32 Golden Richards .20 .50
33 Wesley Walker .25 .60
34 Greg Landry .20 .50
35 Mick Tingelhoff .20 .50
36 Ken O'Brien .20 .50
37 Emerson Boozer .20 .50
38 Reggie McKenzie .20 .50
39 Wally Hilgenberg .20 .50
40 Jan Stenerud .20 .50
41 Roger Craig .30 .75
42 Joe Cribbs .25 .60
43 Reggie Rucker .20 .50
44 Louis Lipps .20 .50
45 Rick Upchurch .20 .50
46 Ben Roethlisberger .40 1.00
47 Rocket Ismail .25 .60
48 Gary Clark .25 .60
50 Dwight Stephenson .20 .50
51 Joe Klecko .20 .50
52 John Hannah .20 .50
53 John Cappelletti .20 .50
54 Tiki Barber .25 .60
55 Coy Bacon .20 .50
56 A.J. Duhe .20 .50
57 Brett Favre .60 1.50
58 Jon Kolb .20 .50
59 Rich Saul .20 .50
60A Antonio Freeman .25 .60
60B Diron Talbert .20 .50
61 John Taylor .25 .60
62 Ron McDole .20 .50
63 Jethro Pugh .20 .50
64 Joe Jacoby .20 .50
65 Steve Smith .30 .75
66 Terrell Owens .25 .60
67 Charle Young .20 .50
68 Roy Jefferson .20 .50
69 Gary Fencik .20 .50
70 Terry Metcalf .20 .50
71 Johnny Rodgers .20 .50
72 Charles White .20 .50
73 Billy Sims .25 .60
74 Neal Anderson .20 .50
75 Marlin Briscoe .20 .50
76 Edgerrin James .25 .60
77 LaDainian Tomlinson .30 .75
78 Steve DeBerg .20 .50
79 Randy Grossman .20 .50
80 Ickey Woods .20 .50
81 Donovan McNabb .25 .60
82 Ron Mix .20 .50
83 Gerald Riggs Sr. .20 .50
84 Curt Warner .20 .50
85 Everson Walls .20 .50
86 Mike Quick .20 .50
87 Shaun Alexander .20 .50
88 Al Toon .20 .50
89 Nat Moore .20 .50
90 Michael Vick .25 .60
91 Carson Palmer .25 .60
92 Tom Brady 1.00 2.50
93 Gary Garrison .20 .50
94 Fred Dean .20 .50
95 Bob Trumpy .20 .50
96 Doug Cosbie .20 .50
97 Tommy Kramer .20 .50
98 Peyton Manning .75 2.00
99 John Brockington .20 .50
100 Stanley Morgan .25 .60
101 A.J. Hawk RC 2.00 5.00
102 Abdul Hodge RC 1.50 4.00
103 Antonio Cromartie RC 2.00 5.00
104 Anthony Fasano RC 1.50 4.00
105 Brandon Marshall RC 3.00 8.00
106 Ben Obomanu RC 2.00 5.00
107 Bobby Carpenter RC 1.50 4.00
108 Brad Smith RC 2.00 5.00
109 Erik Meyer RC 1.50 4.00
110 Brandon Williams RC 1.50 4.00
111 Brian Calhoun RC 1.50 4.00
112 Brodie Croyle RC 1.50 4.00
113 Frostee Rucker RC 2.00 5.00
114 Bruce Eugene RC 2.00 5.00
115 Bruce Gradkowski RC 2.00 5.00
116 Cedric Humes RC 1.50 4.00
117 Chad Greenway RC 2.50 6.00
118 Chad Jackson RC 1.50 4.00
119 Charles Davis RC 2.00 5.00
120 Charlie Whitehurst RC 1.50 4.00
121 Jason Allen RC 2.00 5.00
122 Cory Rodgers RC 1.50 4.00
123 Cory Ross RC 2.50 6.00
124 D.J. Shockley RC 2.00 5.00
125 Darnell Bing RC 2.00 5.00
126 Darrell Hackney RC 2.00 5.00
127 D'Brickashaw Ferguson RC 1.50 4.00
128 DeAngelo Williams RC 2.00 5.00
129 DeMeco Ryans RC 2.00 5.00
130 Demetrius Williams RC 1.50 4.00
131 Derek Hagan RC 2.00 5.00
132 Devin Aromashodu RC 1.50 4.00
133 Devin Hester RC 3.00 8.00
134 Dominique Byrd RC 1.50 4.00
135 Donte Whitner RC 2.00 5.00
136 DonTrell Moore RC 2.00 5.00
137 D'Qwell Jackson RC 1.50 4.00
138 Ernie Sims RC 1.50 4.00
139 John McCargo RC 1.50 4.00
140 Gerald Riggs Jr. RC 2.00 5.00
141 Greg Jennings RC 2.50 6.00
142 Greg Lee RC 1.50 4.00
143 Haloti Ngata RC 2.00 5.00
144 Johnathan Joseph RC 2.00 5.00
145 Jason Avant RC 1.50 4.00
146 Jay Cutler RC 2.00 5.00
147 Jeff King RC 2.00 5.00
148 Jeff Webb RC 2.00 5.00
149 Jeremy Bloom RC 1.50 4.00
150 Jerious Norwood RC 1.50 4.00
151 Jerome Harrison RC 1.50 4.00
152 Jimmy Williams RC 1.50 4.00
153 Joe Klopfenstein RC 1.50 4.00
154 Jonathan Orr RC 2.00 5.00
155 Joseph Addai RC 1.50 4.00
156 Josh Betts RC 2.00 5.00
157 Matt Baker RC 2.50 6.00
158 Kamerion Wimbley RC 2.00 5.00
159 Kellen Clemens RC 1.50 4.00
160 Ko Simpson RC 2.00 5.00
161 Laurence Maroney RC 1.50 4.00
162 Lawrence Vickers RC 2.00 5.00
163 LenDale White RC 1.50 4.00
164 Leon Washington RC 1.50 4.00
165 Leonard Pope RC 2.50 6.00
166 Marcedes Lewis RC 1.50 4.00
167 Marcus Vick RC 1.50 4.00
168 Mario Williams RC 2.50 6.00
169 Marques Hagans RC 1.50 4.00
170 Martin Nance RC 1.50 4.00
171 Mathias Kiwanuka RC 2.50 6.00
172 Matt Bernstein RC 1.50 4.00
173 Matt Leinart RC 1.50 4.00
174 Maurice Drew RC 2.50 6.00
175 Maurice Stovall RC 1.50 4.00
176 Michael Huff RC 2.00 5.00
177 Michael Robinson RC 1.50 4.00
178 Mike Hass RC 1.50 4.00
179 Miles Austin RC 2.00 5.00
180 Omar Jacobs RC 1.50 4.00
181 Owen Daniels RC 2.50 6.00
182 P.J. Daniels RC 1.50 4.00
183 Quinton Ganther RC 1.50 4.00
184 Reggie Bush RC 4.00 10.00
185 Reggie McNeal RC 1.50 4.00
186 Santonio Holmes RC 2.00 5.00
187 Sinorice Moss RC 1.50 4.00
188 Skyler Green RC 1.50 4.00
189 T.J. Williams RC 2.50 6.00
190 Tamba Hali RC 2.50 6.00
191 Manny Lawson RC 2.00 5.00
192 Tarvaris Jackson RC 1.50 4.00
193 Travis Wilson RC 1.50 4.00
194 Tye Hill RC 1.50 4.00
195 Vernon Davis RC 2.00 5.00
196 Vince Young RC 1.50 4.00
197 Wali Lundy RC 1.50 4.00
198 Wendell Mathis RC 2.00 5.00
199 Will Blackmon RC 1.50 4.00
200 Willie Reid RC 2.00 5.00

2006 Upper Deck Legends Canton Classics Autographs

UNPRICED CANTON AUTO SER.#'d TO 5

2006 Upper Deck Legends Franchise Signatures

UNPRICED FRANCHISE SIGS SER.#'d TO 5

2006 Upper Deck Legends Legendary Signatures

STATED ODDS 1:4
2 John Elway SP 50.00 120.00
3 Barry Sanders SP 75.00 150.00
4 Dan Marino SP 250.00 400.00
5 Troy Aikman SP 50.00 120.00
6 Roger Staubach SP 40.00 100.00
8 O.J. McDuffie 5.00 12.00
9 Steve Young SP 50.00 120.00
10 Jim Kelly SP 25.00 60.00
11 Dan Fouts SP 30.00 60.00
12 Franco Harris SP 75.00 150.00
13 Christian Okoye 6.00 15.00
14 Craig Morton 8.00 20.00
15 Doug Flutie SP 15.00 40.00
16 Gale Sayers SP 90.00 150.00
17 Bob Griese SP 30.00 60.00
18 Jim Plunkett 8.00 20.00
20 L.C. Greenwood SP 15.00 40.00
21 Len Dawson SP 20.00 50.00
22 Ken Stabler SP 20.00 50.00
23 Fran Tarkenton SP 30.00 60.00
24 Herman Moore 5.00 12.00
25 Joe Theismann 15.00 40.00
26 Paul Hornung 15.00 40.00
27 Herschel Walker SP 15.00 40.00
29 Drew Pearson 8.00 20.00
30 Don Maynard SP 20.00 40.00
31 Dwight Clark 8.00 20.00
32 Golden Richards 8.00 20.00
33 Wesley Walker 5.00 12.00
34 Greg Landry 6.00 15.00
35 Mick Tingelhoff 12.00 30.00
36 Ken O'Brien 5.00 12.00
37 Emerson Boozer 6.00 15.00
39 Wally Hilgenberg 5.00 12.00
40 Jan Stenerud 5.00 12.00
41 Roger Craig 5.00 12.00
42 Joe Cribbs 5.00 12.00
43 Reggie Rucker 5.00 12.00
44 Louis Lipps 6.00 15.00
45 Rick Upchurch 5.00 12.00
47 Rocket Ismail SP 8.00 20.00
48 Gary Clark 8.00 20.00
50 Dwight Stephenson 6.00 15.00
51 Joe Klecko 5.00 12.00
52 John Hannah 6.00 15.00
53 John Cappelletti 6.00 15.00
55 Coy Bacon 5.00 12.00
56 A.J. Duhe 5.00 12.00
59 Rich Saul 5.00 12.00
60 Antonio Freeman 6.00 15.00
60 Diron Talbert 5.00 12.00
61 John Taylor 6.00 15.00
62 Ron McDole 5.00 12.00
63 Jethro Pugh 6.00 15.00
64 Joe Jacoby 5.00 12.00
67 Charle Young 5.00 12.00
68 Roy Jefferson 6.00 15.00
69 Gary Fencik 6.00 15.00
70 Terry Metcalf 6.00 15.00
71 Johnny Rodgers 8.00 20.00
72 Charles White 6.00 15.00
73 Billy Sims 8.00 20.00
74 Neal Anderson 6.00 15.00
75 Marlin Briscoe 5.00 12.00
78 Steve DeBerg 5.00 12.00
79 Randy Grossman 6.00 15.00
80 Ickey Woods 6.00 15.00
82 Ron Mix 6.00 15.00
83 Gerald Riggs Sr. 5.00 12.00
84 Curt Warner 6.00 15.00
85 Everson Walls 8.00 20.00
86 Mike Quick 6.00 15.00
88 Al Toon 6.00 15.00
89 Nat Moore 6.00 15.00
93 Gary Garrison 5.00 12.00
94 Fred Dean 8.00 20.00
95 Bob Trumpy 5.00 12.00
96 Doug Cosbie 8.00 20.00
97 Tommy Kramer 6.00 15.00
99 John Brockington 8.00 20.00
100 Stanley Morgan 6.00 15.00

2006 Upper Deck Legends Signature Generations

UNPRICED SIG GENERATION SER.#'d TO 5

2006 Upper Deck Legends Time Passages Autographs

STATED PRINT RUN 5 SER.#'d SETS

2006 Upper Deck Legends Trophy Tandems Autographs

UNPRICED TROPHY TANDEM SER.#'d TO 5

2000 Upper Deck Montana Master Collection

Released as a continuation in the production of Master Collection sets, this product focused on Joe Montana's career achievements. Reportedly, a total of 250 numbered

Master Collection sets were produced and initially offered at $4000 each. Each card comes in an individual card holder and the set is packaged in a wooden box. Each factory set contained 16-regular cards (each numbered to 250), one game jersey card (numbered to 50), one Autograph card (numbered to 50), one signed mini-helmet numbered to 50, and one mystery pack that contained one of the following: a Montana Jersey card, a Montana Autographed card, a Combo Jersey card of Montana, Rice, Lott or any dual combination, a Combo Autograph card of the same assortment as the Jerseys, or a one of one version of the base set cards.

COMPLETE SET (16) 40.00 80.00
COMMON CARD/250 3.00 8.00

2000 Upper Deck Montana Master Collection Autographs

Inserted at one in each Master Collection, a total of five different Montana Autograph cards were released. Each is sequentially numbered to 50.

COMMON AUTO/50 75.00 150.00

2000 Upper Deck Montana Master Collection Game Jerseys

Inserted at one in each Master Collection, a total of five different Game Jersey cards were released. Each card contains a swatch of a game worn jersey and is sequentially numbered to 50.

COMMON CARD/50 25.00 60.00

1999 Upper Deck MVP Promos

These four cards were distributed at the 1998 Hawaii Trade Conference as well as other locations to promote the new Upper Deck brand. Dan Marino and Joe Montana signed a limited number of ProSign Promos.

COMPLETE SET (4) 80.00 200.00
54 Dan Marino 1.25 3.00
54SS Dan Marino Silver Sig. 2.00 5.00
DM Dan Marino AUTO 60.00 120.00
JM Joe Montana AUTO 50.00 125.00
NNO Cover Card .02 .10

1999 Upper Deck MVP

The 1999 Upper Deck MVP set was issued in one series for a total of 220 cards and was distributed in packs with a suggested retail price of $1.59. The fronts feature color action player photos with player information on the backs.

COMPLETE SET (220) 10.00 25.00
1 Jake Plummer .12 .30
2 Adrian Murrell .12 .30
3 Larry Centers .12 .30
4 Frank Sanders .12 .30
5 Andre Wadsworth .12 .30
6 Rob Moore .12 .30
7 Simeon Rice .12 .30
8 Jamal Anderson .15 .40
9 Chris Chandler .15 .40
10 Chuck Smith .12 .30
11 Terance Mathis .12 .30
12 Tim Dwight .15 .40
13 Ray Buchanan .12 .30
14 O.J. Santiago .12 .30
15 Eric Zeier .12 .30
16 Priest Holmes .12 .30
17 Michael Jackson .12 .30
18 Jermaine Lewis .12 .30
19 Michael McCrary .12 .30
20 Rob Johnson .15 .40
21 Antowain Smith .12 .30
22 Thurman Thomas .15 .40
23 Doug Flutie .20 .50
24 Eric Moulds .12 .30
25 Bruce Smith .15 .40
26 Andre Reed UER .20 .50
27 Fred Lane .12 .30
28 Tim Biakabutuka .15 .40
29 Rae Carruth .12 .30
30 Wesley Walls .15 .40
31 Steve Beuerlein .15 .40
32 Muhsin Muhammad .12 .30
33 Erik Kramer .15 .40
34 Edgar Bennett .15 .40
35 Curtis Conway .15 .40
36 Curtis Enis .12 .30
37 Bobby Engram .12 .30
38 Alonzo Mayes .12 .30
39 Corey Dillon .12 .30
40 Jeff Blake .15 .40
41 Carl Pickens .15 .40
42 Darnay Scott .12 .30
43 Tony McGee .12 .30
44 Ki-Jana Carter .12 .30
45 Ty Detmer .12 .30
46 Terry Kirby .12 .30
47 Justin Armour .12 .30
48 Freddie Solomon .12 .30
49 Marquez Pope .12 .30
50 Antonio Langham .12 .30
51 Troy Aikman .25 .60
52 Emmitt Smith .30 .75
53 Deion Sanders .15 .40
54 Rocket Ismail .15 .40
55 Michael Irvin .20 .50
56 Chris Warren .15 .40
57 Greg Ellis .12 .30
58 John Elway .30 .75
59 Terrell Davis .15 .40
60 Rod Smith .15 .40
61 Shannon Sharpe .15 .40
62 Ed McCaffrey .15 .40
63 John Mobley .12 .30
64 Bill Romanowski .15 .40
65 Barry Sanders .30 .75
66 Johnnie Morton .15 .40
67 Herman Moore .15 .40
68 Charlie Batch .12 .30
69 Germane Crowell .12 .30
70 Robert Porcher .12 .30
71 Brett Favre .40 1.00
72 Antonio Freeman .15 .40
73 Dorsey Levens .15 .40
74 Mark Chmura .12 .30
75 Vonnie Holliday .12 .30
76 Bill Schroeder .15 .40
77 Marshall Faulk .15 .40
78 Marvin Harrison .15 .40
79 Peyton Manning .60 1.50
80 Jerome Pathon .12 .30
81 E.G. Green .12 .30
82 Ellis Johnson .12 .30
83 Mark Brunell .15 .40
84 Jimmy Smith .15 .40
85 Keenan McCardell .15 .40
86 Fred Taylor .12 .30
87 James Stewart .12 .30
88 Kevin Hardy .12 .30
89 Elvis Grbac .12 .30
90 Andre Rison .15 .40
91 Derrick Alexander WR .12 .30
92 Tony Gonzalez .15 .40
93 Donnell Bennett .12 .30
94 Derrick Thomas .20 .50
95 Tamarick Vanover .15 .40
96 Dan Marino .40 1.00
97 Karim Abdul-Jabbar .12 .30
98 Zach Thomas .15 .40
99 O.J. McDuffie .15 .40
100 John Avery .12 .30
101 Sam Madison .12 .30
102 Randall Cunningham .15 .40
103 Cris Carter .20 .50
104 Robert Smith .12 .30
105 Randy Moss .15 .40
106 Jake Reed .15 .40
107 Matthew Hatchette .15 .40
108 John Randle .20 .50
109 Drew Bledsoe .15 .40
110 Terry Glenn .15 .40
111 Ben Coates .15 .40
112 Ty Law .20 .50
113 Tony Simmons .12 .30
114 Ted Johnson .12 .30
115 Danny Wuerffel .15 .40
116 Lamar Smith .12 .30
117 Sean Dawkins .12 .30
118 Cameron Cleeland .12 .30
119 Joe Johnson .12 .30
120 Andre Hastings .12 .30
121 Kent Graham .12 .30
122 Gary Brown .12 .30
123 Amani Toomer .12 .30
124 Tiki Barber .15 .40
125 Ike Hilliard .12 .30
126 Jason Sehorn .15 .40
127 Vinny Testaverde .12 .30
128 Curtis Martin .15 .40
129 Keyshawn Johnson .15 .40
130 Wayne Chrebet .12 .30
131 Mo Lewis .12 .30
132 Steve Atwater .15 .40
133 Donald Hollas .12 .30
134 Napoleon Kaufman .12 .30
135 Tim Brown .20 .50
136 Darrell Russell .12 .30
137 Rickey Dudley .12 .30
138 Charles Woodson .15 .40
139 Koy Detmer .12 .30
140 Duce Staley .12 .30
141 Charlie Garner .15 .40
142 Doug Pederson .12 .30
143 Jeff Graham .12 .30
144 Charles Johnson .12 .30
145 Kordell Stewart .12 .30
146 Jerome Bettis .20 .50
147 Hines Ward .15 .40
148 Courtney Hawkins .12 .30
149 Will Blackwell .12 .30
150 Richard Huntley .12 .30
151 Levon Kirkland .12 .30
152 Trent Green .12 .30
153 Tony Banks .15 .40
154 Isaac Bruce .20 .50
155 Eddie Kennison .15 .40
156 Az-Zahir Hakim .12 .30
157 Amp Lee .12 .30
158 Robert Holcombe .12 .30
159 Ryan Leaf .15 .40
160 Natrone Means .15 .40
161 Jim Harbaugh .15 .40
162 Junior Seau .15 .40
163 Charlie Jones .12 .30
164 Rodney Harrison .12 .30
165 Steve Young .25 .60
166 Jerry Rice .50 1.25
167 Garrison Hearst .12 .30
168 Terrell Owens .15 .40
169 J.J. Stokes .12 .30
170 Bryant Young .15 .40
171 Ricky Watters .15 .40
172 Joey Galloway .15 .40
173 Jon Kitna .12 .30
174 Ahman Green .15 .40
175 Mike Pritchard .12 .30
176 Chad Brown .12 .30
177 Warrick Dunn .12 .30
178 Trent Dilfer .12 .30
179 Mike Alstott .12 .30
180 Reidel Anthony .12 .30
181 Bert Emanuel .15 .40
182 Jacquez Green .12 .30
183 Hardy Nickerson .12 .30
184 Steve McNair .15 .40
185 Eddie George .15 .40
186 Yancey Thigpen .12 .30
187 Frank Wycheck .15 .40
188 Kevin Dyson .12 .30
189 Jackie Harris .15 .40
190 Blaine Bishop .12 .30
191 Skip Hicks .12 .30
192 Michael Westbrook .12 .30
193 Stephen Alexander .12 .30
194 Leslie Shepherd .12 .30
195 Jeff Hostetler .15 .40
196 Brian Mitchell .15 .40
197 Dan Wilkinson .15 .40
198 Terrell Davis CL .12 .30
199 Troy Aikman CL .20 .50
200 Tim Couch CL .12 .30
201 Ricky Williams RC .30 .75
202 Tim Couch RC .25 .60
203 Akili Smith RC .20 .50
204 Daunte Culpepper RC .30 .75
205 Torry Holt RC .40 1.00
206 Edgerrin James RC .30 .75
207 David Boston RC .20 .50
208 Peerless Price RC .20 .50
209 Chris Claiborne RC .20 .50
210 Champ Bailey RC .40 1.00
211 Cade McNown RC .20 .50
212 Jevon Kearse RC .25 .60
213 Joe Germaine RC .25 .60
214 D'Wayne Bates RC .20 .50
215 Dameane Douglas RC .20 .50
216 Troy Edwards RC .20 .50
217 Sedrick Irvin RC .20 .50
218 Brock Huard RC .20 .50
219 Amos Zereoue RC .20 .50
220 Donovan McNabb RC 1.25 3.00

1999 Upper Deck MVP Gold Script

*1-200 VETS/100: 15X TO 40X BASIC CARDS
*201-220 ROOKIES/100: 10X TO 25X BASIC RC
GOLD SCRIPT PRINT RUN 100 SER.#'d SETS

1999 Upper Deck MVP Silver Script

MPLETE SET (217) 60.00 120.00
*1-200 VETS: 2X TO 5X BASIC CARDS
*201-220 ROOKIES: 1.2X TO 3X
STATED ODDS 1:2

1999 Upper Deck MVP Super Script

*1-200 VETS/25: 30X TO 80X BASIC CARDS
*201-220 ROOKIE/25: 20X TO 50X BASIC RC
STATED PRINT RUN 25 SERIAL #'d SETS

1999 Upper Deck MVP Draw Your Own Card

rds form this set were randomly inserted in packs at the rate of 1:6. Each features an artist's rendering of an NFL player from winners of the 1998 Upper Deck Draw Your Card contest. Cards #1-10 feature winners in the age 5-8 bracket, #W11-W20 were from ages 9-14, and #W21-W30 were winners over the age of 15.

COMPLETE SET (30) 7.50 20.00
STATED ODDS 1:6
W1 Brett Favre .75 2.00
W2 Emmitt Smith .50 1.25
W3 John Elway .75 2.00
W4 Emmitt Smith .50 1.25
W5 Randy Moss .60 1.50
W6 Terrell Davis .25 .60
W7 Steve Young .30 .75
W8 Drew Bledsoe .30 .75
W9 Troy Aikman .50 1.25
W10 Terry Allen .08 .25
W11 Warrick Dunn .25 .60
W12 Kimble Anders .08 .25
W13 Joey Galloway .15 .40
W14 Barry Sanders .75 2.00
W15 Mark Brunell .25 .60
W16 Bruce Smith .15 .40
W17 Randy Moss .60 1.60
W18 Jerome Bettis .25 .60
W19 John Elway .75 2.00
W20 Jerome Bettis .25 .60
W21 Brett Favre .75 2.00
W22 Troy Aikman .50 1.25
W23 Cris Carter .25 .60
W24 Jason Gildon .08 .25
W25 Randall Cunningham .25 .60
W26 Thurman Thomas .15 .40
W27 Jerry Rice .50 1.25
W28 Jerome Bettis .25 .60
W29 Steve Young .30 .75
W30 Reggie White .25 .60

1999 Upper Deck MVP Drive Time

Randomly inserted into packs at the rate of one in six, this 14-card set features color action photos of star players who led the best offensive drives during the 1998 season.

COMPLETE SET (14) 3.00 8.00
STATED ODDS 1:6
DT1 Steve Young .50 1.25
DT2 Kordell Stewart .25 .60
DT3 Eric Moulds .40 1.00
DT4 Corey Dillon .40 1.00
DT5 Doug Flutie .40 1.00
DT6 Charlie Batch .40 1.00
DT7 Curtis Martin .40 1.00
DT8 Marshall Faulk .50 1.25
DT9 Terrell Owens .40 1.00
DT10 Antowain Smith .40 1.00
DT11 Troy Aikman .75 2.00
DT12 Drew Bledsoe .50 1.25
DT13 Keyshawn Johnson .40 1.00
DT14 Steve McNair .40 1.00

1999 Upper Deck MVP Dynamics

Randomly inserted into packs at the rate of one in 28, this 15-card set features color action photos of some of the most collectible players in the league today.

COMPLETE SET (15) 30.00 60.00
STATED ODDS 1:28
D1 John Elway 5.00 12.00
D2 Steve Young 2.00 5.00
D3 Jake Plummer 1.00 2.50
D4 Fred Taylor 1.50 4.00
D5 Mark Brunell 1.50 4.00
D6 Joey Galloway 1.00 2.50
D7 Terrell Davis 1.50 4.00
D8 Randy Moss 4.00 10.00
D9 Charlie Batch 1.50 4.00
D10 Peyton Manning 5.00 12.00
D11 Barry Sanders 5.00 12.00
D12 Eddie George 1.50 4.00
D13 Warrick Dunn 1.50 4.00
D14 Jamal Anderson 1.50 4.00
D15 Brett Favre 5.00 12.00

1999 Upper Deck MVP Game Used Souvenirs

Randomly inserted into packs at the rate of one in 130, this 22-card set features color action player photos with actual pieces of game used memorabilia embedded in the cards.

COMPLETE SET (22) 200.00 500.00
STATED ODDS 1:130
ASS Akili Smith 6.00 15.00
BFS Brett Favre 20.00 50.00
BHS Brock Huard 6.00 15.00
BSS Barry Sanders 15.00 40.00
CBS Champ Bailey 7.50 20.00
CMS Cade McNown 6.00 15.00
DBS David Boston 6.00 15.00
DCS Daunte Culpepper 12.50 30.00
DFS Doug Flutie 6.00 15.00
DMS Dan Marino 20.00 50.00
EJS Edgerrin James 12.50 30.00
ESS Emmitt Smith 15.00 40.00
JAS Jamal Anderson 6.00 15.00
JES John Elway 15.00 40.00
JPS Jake Plummer 6.00 15.00
KJS Keyshawn Johnson 6.00 15.00
MCS Donovan McNabb 15.00 40.00
PMS Peyton Manning 12.50 30.00
RMA Randy Moss AU/84 75.00 150.00
RMS Randy Moss 12.50 30.00
TCS Tim Couch 6.00 15.00
TDA Terrell Davis AU/30 50.00 120.00
TDS Terrell Davis 6.00 15.00
THS Torry Holt 6.00 15.00

1999 Upper Deck MVP Jumbos

This 10-card set features a postcard-sized enlarged version of the featured player's base Upper Deck MVP card. The Jumbos were inserted one per special retail box.

COMPLETE SET (10) 20.00 40.00
ONE PER SPECIAL RETAIL BOX
201 Ricky Williams 1.00 2.50
202 Tim Couch .40 1.00
203 Akili Smith .30 .75
204 Daunte Culpepper 2.00 5.00
205 Torry Holt 1.25 3.00
206 Edgerrin James 2.00 5.00
207 David Boston .40 1.00
211 Cade McNown .30 .75
218 Brock Huard .40 1.00
220 Donovan McNabb 2.50 6.00

1999 Upper Deck MVP Power Surge

Randomly inserted into packs at the rate of one in nine, this 15-card set features color action photos that highlight some of the game's most impressive talents.

COMPLETE SET (15) 10.00 20.00
STATED ODDS 1:9
PS1 Jerome Bettis .75 2.00
PS2 Eddie George .75 2.00
PS3 Karim Abdul-Jabbar .50 1.25
PS4 Curtis Martin .75 2.00
PS5 Antowain Smith .75 2.00
PS6 Kordell Stewart .50 1.25
PS7 Curtis Enis .30 .75
PS8 Joey Galloway .50 1.25
PS9 Mark Brunell .75 2.00
PS10 Peyton Manning 2.50 6.00
PS11 Antonio Freeman .75 2.00
PS12 Jerry Rice 1.50 4.00
PS13 Eric Moulds .75 2.00
PS14 Drew Bledsoe 1.00 2.50
PS15 Fred Taylor .75 2.00

1999 Upper Deck MVP ProSign

ndomly inserted in retail packs only at the rate of one in 216, this 34-card set features autographed color action photos of today's superstars and future stars. Some cards were issued via mail redemptions. We've priced below only the signed cards that are most commonly traded. The Randy Moss, Ricky Williams and Daunte Culpepper cards reportedly exist but are too thinly traded to price.

STATED ODDS 1:216 RETAIL
AG Ahman Green 12.00 30.00
AM Adrian Murrell 5.00 12.00
AS Akili Smith 5.00 12.00
AS2 Antowain Smith 8.00 20.00
BH Brock Huard 6.00 15.00
CB Charlie Batch 5.00 12.00
CC Curtis Conway 6.00 15.00
CM Cade McNown SP 12.00 30.00
DC Daunte Culpepper SP 20.00 40.00
DM Donovan McNabb 40.00 80.00
EM Ed McCaffrey 8.00 20.00
EM2 Eric Moulds 6.00 15.00
FT Fred Taylor 12.00 30.00
GH Greg Hill 5.00 12.00
JA Jamal Anderson 8.00 20.00
JM John Mobley 5.00 12.00
JS Jimmy Smith 8.00 20.00
KAJ Karim Abdul-Jabbar 5.00 12.00
MB Michael Bishop 6.00 15.00
MF Marshall Faulk 20.00 40.00
MM Muhsin Muhammad 8.00 20.00
PH Priest Holmes 10.00 25.00
RE Robert Edwards 5.00 12.00
RL Ray Lewis 40.00 80.00
RM Randy Moss SP 100.00 200.00
RW Ricky Watters 8.00 20.00
RW2 Ricky Williams SP 25.00 60.00
SK Shaun King 5.00 12.00
SS Shannon Sharpe 12.00 30.00
TC Tim Couch 6.00 15.00
TD Terrell Davis 15.00 40.00
TG Trent Green 8.00 20.00
TH Torry Holt SP 15.00 40.00
TR Troy Drayton 5.00 12.00

1999 Upper Deck MVP Strictly Business

Randomly inserted into packs at the rate of one in 14, this 13-card set features color action photos of top players printed on cards utilizing strong graphics-led technology.

COMPLETE SET (13) 20.00 40.00
STATED ODDS 1:14
SB1 Eddie George 1.00 2.50
SB2 Curtis Martin 1.00 2.50
SB3 Fred Taylor 1.00 2.50
SB4 Steve Young 1.25 3.00
SB5 Kordell Stewart .60 1.50
SB6 Corey Dillon 1.00 2.50
SB7 Dan Marino 3.00 8.00
SB8 Jake Plummer .60 1.50
SB9 Jerry Rice 2.00 5.00
SB10 Warrick Dunn 1.00 2.50
SB11 Jerome Bettis 1.00 2.50
SB12 John Elway 3.00 8.00
SB13 Randy Moss 2.50 6.00

1999 Upper Deck MVP Theatre

ndomly inserted into packs at the rate of one in nine, this 15-card set features spectacular action photos of some of the most collectible NFL players.

COMPLETE SET (15) 12.50 25.00
STATED ODDS 1:9
M1 Terrell Davis .60 1.50
M2 Corey Dillon .60 1.50
M3 Brett Favre 2.00 5.00
M4 Jerry Rice 1.25 3.00
M5 Emmitt Smith 1.25 3.00
M6 Dan Marino 2.00 5.00
M7 Jerome Bettis .60 1.50
M8 Napoleon Kaufman .60 1.50
M9 Keyshawn Johnson .60 1.50
M10 Warrick Dunn .60 1.50
M11 Barry Sanders 2.00 5.00
M12 Troy Aikman 1.25 3.00
M13 Jamal Anderson .60 1.50
M14 Randall Cunningham .60 1.50
M15 Doug Flutie .60 1.50

2000 Upper Deck MVP

Released as both a Hobby and Retail product, Upper Deck MVP contains 187-veteran player cards, 29-prospect cards, and three checklists. Base cards are white-bordered and have gold foil highlights. Also inserted into this set was a Joe Montana tribute jersey card limited to just 350 copies. Card number 189 LaVar Arrington was not initially released as a full card, but instead packaged as a portion of a card with the center cut out. Card #220 Donovan Mcnabb CL was issued in two versions -- one with an embossed stamping on the front and one without. Like the Arrington, this card was supposed to have been pulled during the collation process but some copies did make the packout. MVP was packaged in boxes containing 28 packs of 10 cards each and carried a suggested retail price of $1.59.

COMPLETE SET (218) 10.00 25.00
1 Jake Plummer .10 .25
2 Michael Pittman .10 .25
3 Rob Moore .10 .25
4 David Boston .10 .25
5 Frank Sanders .10 .25
6 Aeneas Williams .10 .25
7 Kwamie Lassiter .10 .25
8 Tim Dwight .12 .30
9 Chris Chandler .12 .30
10 Jamal Anderson .12 .30
11 Shawn Jefferson .10 .25
12 Qadry Ismail .10 .25
13 Jermaine Lewis .10 .25
14 Rod Woodson .15 .40
15 Michael McCrary .10 .25
16 Tony Banks .10 .25
17 Peter Boulware .10 .25
18 Shannon Sharpe .12 .30
19 Peerless Price .12 .30
20 Rob Johnson .12 .30
21 Eric Moulds .10 .25
22 Doug Flutie .12 .30
23 Muhsin Muhammad .10 .25
24 Patrick Jeffers .10 .25
25 Steve Beuerlein .12 .30
26 Tim Biakabutuka .12 .30
27 Michael Bates .10 .25
28 Cade McNown .10 .25
29 Curtis Enis .10 .25
30 Marcus Robinson .12 .30
31 Shane Matthews .10 .25
32 Bobby Engram .10 .25
33 Glyn Milburn .10 .25
34 Akili Smith .10 .25
35 Corey Dillon .10 .25
36 Darnay Scott .12 .30
37 Tremain Mack .10 .25
38 Tim Couch .12 .30
39 Kevin Johnson .10 .25
40 Darrin Chiaverini .10 .25
41 Jamir Miller .10 .25
42 Errict Rhett .12 .30
43 Troy Aikman .20 .50
44 Emmitt Smith .25 .60
45 Rocket Ismail .12 .30
46 Jason Tucker .10 .25
47 Dexter Coakley .10 .25
48 Joey Galloway .12 .30
49 Greg Ellis .10 .25
50 Terrell Davis .12 .30
51 Olandis Gary .12 .30
52 Brian Griese .10 .25
53 Ed McCaffrey .12 .30
54 Rod Smith .12 .30
55 Trevor Pryce .10 .25
56 Charlie Batch .10 .25
57 Germane Crowell .10 .25
58 Johnnie Morton .12 .30
59 Robert Porcher .10 .25
60 Luther Elliss .10 .25
61 James Stewart .10 .25
62 Brett Favre .30 .75
63 Antonio Freeman .12 .30
64 Bill Schroeder .12 .30
65 Dorsey Levens .12 .30
66 Peyton Manning .40 1.00
67 Edgerrin James .12 .30
68 Marvin Harrison .12 .30
69 Ken Dilger .10 .25
70 Terrence Wilkins .10 .25
71 Mark Brunell .12 .30
72 Fred Taylor .10 .25
73 Jimmy Smith .12 .30
74 Keenan McCardell .12 .30
75 Carnell Lake .10 .25
76 Tony Brackens .10 .25
77 Kevin Hardy .10 .25
78 Hardy Nickerson .10 .25
79 Elvis Grbac .10 .25
80 Tony Gonzalez .12 .30
81 Derrick Alexander .10 .25
82 Donnell Bennett .10 .25
83 James Hasty .10 .25
84 Jay Fiedler .12 .30
85 James Johnson .10 .25
86 Tony Martin .12 .30
87 Damon Huard .10 .25
88 O.J. McDuffie .12 .30
89 Oronde Gadsden .12 .30
90 Zach Thomas .12 .30
91 Sam Madison .10 .25
92 Jeff George .12 .30
93 Randy Moss .12 .30
94 Robert Smith .10 .25
95 Cris Carter .15 .40
96 Matthew Hatchette .10 .25
97 Drew Bledsoe .12 .30
98 Terry Glenn .12 .30
99 Troy Brown .10 .25
100 Kevin Faulk .10 .25
101 Lawyer Milloy .10 .25
102 Ricky Williams .12 .30
103 Keith Poole .10 .25
104 Jake Reed .12 .30
105 Cam Cleeland .10 .25
106 Jeff Blake .12 .30
107 Andrew Glover .10 .25
108 Kerry Collins .10 .25
109 Amani Toomer .10 .25
110 Joe Montgomery .10 .25
111 Ike Hilliard .10 .25
112 Michael Strahan .12 .30
113 Jessie Armstead .10 .25
114 Ray Lucas .10 .25
115 Keyshawn Johnson .12 .30
116 Curtis Martin .12 .30
117 Vinny Testaverde .10 .25
118 Wayne Chrebet .10 .25
119 Dedric Ward .10 .25
120 Tim Brown .15 .40
121 Rich Gannon .12 .30
122 Tyrone Wheatley .10 .25
123 Napoleon Kaufman .12 .30
124 Charles Woodson .15 .40
125 Darrell Russell .10 .25
126 Duce Staley .10 .25
127 Donovan McNabb .12 .30
128 Torrance Small .10 .25
129 Allen Rossum .10 .25
130 Brian Dawkins .15 .40
131 Troy Vincent .10 .25
132 Troy Edwards .10 .25
133 Jerome Bettis .15 .40
134 Hines Ward .12 .30
135 Kordell Stewart .10 .25
136 Levon Kirkland .10 .25
137 Kent Graham .10 .25
138 Marshall Faulk .12 .30
139 Kurt Warner .25 .60
140 Torry Holt .12 .30
141 Isaac Bruce .15 .40
142 Kevin Carter .10 .25
143 Az-Zahir Hakim .10 .25
144 Todd Lyght .10 .25
145 Jermaine Fazande .10 .25
146 Curtis Conway .12 .30
147 Freddie Jones .10 .25
148 Junior Seau .12 .30
149 Jeff Graham .10 .25
150 Ryan Leaf .12 .30
151 Rodney Harrison .10 .25
152 Steve Young .20 .50
153 Jerry Rice .40 1.00
154 Charlie Garner .12 .30
155 Terrell Owens .12 .30
156 Jeff Garcia .10 .25
157 Bryant Young .10 .25
158 Lance Schulters .10 .25
159 Ricky Watters .12 .30
160 Jon Kitna .10 .25
161 Derrick Mayes .10 .25
162 Sean Dawkins .10 .25
163 Cortez Kennedy .12 .30
164 Chad Brown .10 .25
165 Warrick Dunn .10 .25
166 Shaun King .10 .25
167 Mike Alstott .10 .25
168 Warren Sapp .12 .30
169 Jacquez Green .10 .25
170 Derrick Brooks .10 .25
171 John Lynch .12 .30
172 Donnie Abraham .10 .25
173 Eddie George .12 .30
174 Steve McNair .12 .30
175 Kevin Dyson .12 .30
176 Jevon Kearse .10 .25
177 Yancey Thigpen .10 .25
178 Frank Wycheck .12 .30
179 Eddie Robinson .10 .25
180 Samari Rolle .10 .25
181 Brad Johnson .12 .30
182 Stephen Davis .10 .25
183 Michael Westbrook .10 .25
184 Albert Connell .10 .25
185 Brian Mitchell .10 .25
186 Bruce Smith .12 .30
187 Stephen Alexander .10 .25
188 Peter Warrick RC .15 .40
189C Cutout Card Arrington 3.00 8.00
190 Chris Redman RC .15 .40
191 Courtney Brown RC .20 .50
192 Brian Urlacher RC .75 2.00
193 Plaxico Burress RC .20 .50
194 Corey Simon RC .20 .50
195 Bubba Franks RC .15 .40
196 Deon Grant RC .15 .40
197 Michael Wiley RC .15 .40
198 Tim Rattay RC .20 .50
199 Ron Dayne RC .25 .60
200 Sylvester Morris RC .15 .40
201 Shaun Alexander RC .25 .60
202 Dez White RC .15 .40
203 Thomas Jones RC .20 .50
204 Reuben Droughns RC .15 .40
205 Travis Taylor RC .15 .40
206 Trevor Gaylor RC .15 .40
207 Jamal Lewis RC .25 .60
208 Chad Pennington RC .20 .50
209 J.R. Redmond RC .15 .40
210 Laveranues Coles RC .20 .50
211 Travis Prentice RC .15 .40
212 R.Jay Soward RC .15 .40
213 Todd Pinkston RC .15 .40
214 Dennis Northcutt RC .15 .40
215 Shyrone Stith RC .15 .40
216 Tee Martin RC .15 .40
217 Giovanni Carmazzi RC .15 .40
218 Drew Bledsoe CL .10 .25
219 Steve Young CL .15 .40
220A Donovan McNabb CL SP 15.00 30.00
220B D.McNabb CL SP Emb. 15.00 30.00

2000 Upper Deck MVP Gold Script

*VETS 1-220: 12X TO 30X BASIC CARDS
*ROOKIE 188-217: 8X TO 20X BASIC CARD
GOLD SCRIPT PRINT RUN 100 SER.#'d SETS

2000 Upper Deck MVP Silver Script

COMPLETE SET (218) 40.00 100.00
*VETS 1-220: 1.2X TO 3X BASIC CARDS
*ROOKIE 188-217: .8X TO 2X BASIC CARD
SILVER SCRIPT ODDS 1:2
189 LaVar Arrington 75.00 150.00
189C Cutout Card Arrington 12.00 30.00
220 Donovan McNabb CL 50.00 100.00

2000 Upper Deck MVP Super Script

*VETS 1-220: 25X TO 60X BASIC CARDS
*ROOKIE 188-216: 15X TO 40X BASIC CARD
SUPER SCRIPT PRINT RUN 25 SER.#'d SETS
189 LaVar Arrington 12.00 30.00

2000 Upper Deck MVP Air Show

ndomly inserted in packs at the rate of one in 14, this 10-card set features top NFL quarterbacks. Card backs carry an "AS" prefix.

COMPLETE SET (10) 5.00 12.00
STATED ODDS 1:14
AS1 Brian Griese .50 1.25
AS2 Drew Bledsoe .60 1.50
AS3 Rob Johnson .60 1.50
AS4 Jeff Garcia .50 1.25
AS5 Ray Lucas .50 1.25
AS6 Jon Kitna .50 1.25
AS7 Jeff George .60 1.50
AS8 Shaun King .50 1.25
AS9 Troy Aikman 1.00 2.50
AS10 Steve Beuerlein .60 1.50

2000 Upper Deck MVP Game Used Souvenirs

ndomly inserted in Hobby packs at the rate of one in 229, this 22-card set pairs players with a swatch of an authentic game-used football.

STATED ODDS 1:229 HOBBY
AS Akili Smith 4.00 10.00
BF Brett Favre 15.00 40.00
BG Brian Griese 4.00 10.00
BJ Brad Johnson 5.00 12.00
CB Charlie Batch 4.00 10.00
CC Cris Carter 6.00 15.00
CM Cade McNown 4.00 10.00
DF Doug Flutie 5.00 12.00
DM Donovan McNabb 5.00 12.00
DM Dan Marino 12.00 30.00
EG Eddie George SB/40 60.00 100.00
EJ Edgerrin James 5.00 12.00
ES Emmitt Smith 10.00 25.00
FT Fred Taylor 4.00 10.00
JK Jon Kitna 4.00 10.00
JP Jake Plummer 4.00 10.00
JR Jerry Rice 15.00 40.00
KE Keyshawn Johnson 5.00 12.00
KJ Kevin Johnson 4.00 10.00
KW Kurt Warner SB/40 60.00 150.00
MA Mike Alstott 4.00 10.00
MB Mark Brunell 5.00 12.00
MF Marshall Faulk 5.00 12.00
PM Peyton Manning 15.00 40.00
RM Randy Moss 5.00 12.00
RW Ricky Williams 5.00 12.00
SD Stephen Davis 4.00 10.00
SK Shaun King 4.00 10.00
TA Troy Aikman 8.00 20.00
TC Tim Couch 5.00 12.00
TD Terrell Davis 5.00 12.00

2000 Upper Deck MVP Game Used Souvenirs Autographs

Randomly inserted in Hobby packs, this 22-card set parallels the base Game-Used Souvenirs insert set with cards that feature authentic autographs. Each card is sequentially numbered to 25.

AUTO PRINT RUN 25 SER.#'d SETS
ASA Akili Smith 20.00 50.00
BGA Brian Griese 20.00 50.00
BJA Brad Johnson 25.00 60.00
CBA Charlie Batch 20.00 50.00
CCA Cris Carter 30.00 80.00
DFA Doug Flutie 25.00 60.00
DMA Dan Marino 200.00 400.00
EJA Edgerrin James 25.00 60.00
JKA Jon Kitna 20.00 50.00
JPA Jake Plummer 20.00 50.00
KEA Keyshawn Johnson 25.00 60.00
KWA Kurt Warner 75.00 125.00
MBA Mark Brunell 25.00 60.00
MFA Marshall Faulk 25.00 60.00
PMA Peyton Manning 150.00 250.00
RMA Randy Moss 25.00 60.00
SDA Stephen Davis 20.00 50.00
TAA Troy Aikman 125.00 250.00
TCA Tim Couch 25.00 60.00
TDA Terrell Davis 25.00 60.00

2000 Upper Deck MVP Headliners

ndomly inserted in packs at the rate of one in six, this 10-card set highlights 10 of the NFL's top headline makers. Card backs carry an "H" prefix.

COMPLETE SET (10) 2.50 6.00
STATED ODDS 1:6
H1 Isaac Bruce .50 1.25
H2 Michael Westbrook .30 .75
H3 James Stewart .30 .75
H4 Keyshawn Johnson .40 1.00
H5 Marcus Robinson .40 1.00
H6 Charlie Batch .30 .75
H7 Marvin Harrison .40 1.00
H8 Olandis Gary .40 1.00
H9 Curtis Martin .40 1.00
H10 Jevon Kearse .30 .75

2000 Upper Deck MVP Highlight Reel

ndomly inserted in packs at the rate of one in 28, this 7-card set focuses on today's most recognized players. Background features portrait player shots with a full color action photo in the foreground. Card backs carry an "HR" prefix.

COMPLETE SET (7) 5.00 12.00
STATED ODDS 1:28
HR1 Marvin Harrison 1.00 2.50
HR2 Isaac Bruce 1.25 3.00
HR3 Cris Carter 1.25 3.00
HR4 Ray Lucas .75 2.00
HR5 Muhsin Muhammad .75 2.00
HR6 Eddie George 1.00 2.50
HR7 Ricky Williams 1.00 2.50

2000 Upper Deck MVP Prolifics

Randomly inserted in packs at the rate of one in 28, this 7-card set highlights some of today's most prolific players. Card backs carry a "P" prefix.

COMPLETE SET (7) 10.00 25.00
STATED ODDS 1:28
P1 Brett Favre 2.00 5.00
P2 Marshall Faulk .75 2.00
P3 Edgerrin James .75 2.00
P4 Peyton Manning 2.50 6.00
P5 Tim Couch .75 2.00
P6 Dan Marino 2.00 5.00
P7 Kurt Warner 1.50 4.00

2000 Upper Deck MVP ProSign

ndomly inserted in Retail packs at the rate of one in 215, this 27-card set features authentic player autographs. Dan Marino signed for the ProSign Gold version only.

STATED ODDS 1:215 RETAIL
BG Brian Griese 8.00 20.00
CB Charlie Batch 8.00 20.00
CP Chad Pennington 8.00 20.00
CR Chris Redman 6.00 15.00
DW Dez White 6.00 15.00
EJ Edgerrin James 10.00 25.00
HT Ron Dayne 12.00 30.00
IB Isaac Bruce 12.00 30.00
JK Jon Kitna 8.00 20.00
JL Jamal Lewis 10.00 25.00
JP Jake Plummer 8.00 20.00
KC Kwame Cavil 8.00 20.00
KJ Keyshawn Johnson 10.00 25.00
KW Kurt Warner 20.00 50.00
MB Mark Brunell 10.00 25.00
MF Marshall Faulk 10.00 25.00
PM Peyton Manning 50.00 100.00
PW Peter Warrick EXCH 10.00 25.00
RD Ron Dugans 8.00 20.00
RM Randy Moss 30.00 60.00
SA Shaun Alexander 10.00 25.00
TC Tim Couch 10.00 25.00
TH Torry Holt 10.00 25.00
TJ Thomas Jones 8.00 20.00
TM Tee Martin 6.00 15.00
TT Travis Taylor 6.00 15.00
RW Ricky Williams 8.00 20.00

2000 Upper Deck MVP ProSign Gold

OLD/25: .8X TO 2X BASIC AUTO
DM Dan Marino 175.00 300.00

2000 Upper Deck MVP Theatre

ndomly inserted in packs at the rate of one in six, this 10-card set highlights top performers on from the 1999 season. Card backs carry an "M" prefix.

COMPLETE SET (10) 3.00 8.00
STATED ODDS 1:6
M1 Troy Edwards .30 .75
M2 Ed McCaffrey .40 1.00
M3 Stephen Davis .30 .75
M4 Corey Dillon .30 .75
M5 Steve McNair .40 1.00
M6 Jimmy Smith .40 1.00
M7 Fred Taylor .30 .75
M8 Terrell Davis .40 1.00
M9 Jon Kitna .30 .75
M10 Germane Crowell .30 .75

2001 Upper Deck MVP

Released as both a Hobby and Retail product, Upper Deck MVP contains 280-veteran player cards, 45-prospect cards, and five checklists. Base cards are white-bordered with players team color trim and have silver foil highlights. MVP was packaged in boxes containing 24 packs of 8 cards each and carried a suggested retail price of $1.99.

COMPLETE SET (330) 20.00 50.00
1 Jake Plummer .10 .25
2 David Boston .10 .25
3 Thomas Jones .10 .25
4 Michael Pittman .12 .30
5 Frank Sanders .10 .25
6 MarTay Jenkins .10 .25
7 Pat Tillman RC 10.00 25.00
8 Tywan Mitchell .10 .25
9 Jamal Anderson .12 .30
10 Doug Johnson .10 .25
11 Ephraim Salaam RC .10 .25
12 Chris Chandler .12 .30
13 Shawn Jefferson .10 .25
14 Tim Dwight .12 .30
15 Terance Mathis .10 .25
16 Jamal Lewis .15 .40
17 Shannon Sharpe .12 .30
18 Trent Dilfer .10 .25
19 Ray Lewis .15 .40
20 Qadry Ismail .10 .25
21 Travis Taylor .10 .25
22 Chris Redman .15 .40
23 Priest Holmes .10 .25
24 Rod Woodson .15 .40
25 Jamie Sharper .10 .25
26 Doug Flutie .12 .30
27 Rob Johnson .12 .30
28 Eric Moulds .10 .25
29 Sammy Morris .10 .25
30 Shawn Bryson .10 .25
31 Antowain Smith .12 .30
32 Jeremy McDaniel .10 .25
33 Sam Cowart .10 .25
34 Muhsin Muhammad .10 .25
35 Brad Hoover .12 .30
36 Tim Biakabutuka .10 .25
37 Steve Beuerlein .12 .30
38 Donald Hayes .10 .25
39 Jeff Lewis .10 .25
40 Dameyune Craig .10 .25
41 Wesley Walls .10 .25
42 Isaac Byrd .10 .25
43 Cade McNown .12 .30
44 James Allen .10 .25
45 Marcus Robinson .12 .30
46 Brian Urlacher .20 .50
47 Jim Miller .12 .30
48 Curtis Enis .10 .25
49 Eddie Kennison .12 .30
50 Marty Booker .10 .25
51 Bobby Engram .10 .25
52 Peter Warrick .10 .25
53 Corey Dillon .10 .25
54 Akili Smith .10 .25
55 Danny Farmer .10 .25
56 Brandon Bennett .10 .25
57 Curtis Keaton .10 .25
58 Ron Dugans .10 .25
59 Takeo Spikes .10 .25
60 Scott Mitchell .10 .25
61 Tim Couch .10 .25
62 Kevin Johnson .10 .25
63 Travis Prentice .10 .25
64 Spergon Wynn .10 .25
65 Errict Rhett .12 .30
66 David Patten .10 .25
67 Dennis Northcutt .10 .25
68 Aaron Shea .10 .25
69 Courtney Brown .10 .25
70 Troy Aikman .20 .50
71 Emmitt Smith .25 .60
72 Joey Galloway .12 .30
73 Rocket Ismail .12 .30
74 Randall Cunningham .12 .30
75 Anthony Wright .10 .25
76 James McKnight .10 .25
77 Dexter Coakley .10 .25
78 Terrell Davis .12 .30
79 Mike Anderson .10 .25
80 Brian Griese .10 .25
81 Rod Smith .12 .30
82 Ed McCaffrey .12 .30
83 Olandis Gary .10 .25
84 Trevor Pryce .10 .25
85 John Mobley .10 .25
86 Charlie Batch .10 .25
87 Germane Crowell .10 .25
88 James O. Stewart .10 .25
89 Johnnie Morton .12 .30
90 Herman Moore .10 .25
91 Mario Bates .10 .25
92 Desmond Howard .12 .30
93 Stephen Boyd .10 .25

94 Chris Claiborne .10 .25
95 Kurt Schulz .10 .25
96 Brett Favre .30 .75
97 Antonio Freeman .15 .40
98 Dorsey Levens .12 .30
99 Ahman Green .12 .30
100 Matt Hasselbeck .10 .25
101 De'Mond Parker .10 .25
102 Bill Schroeder .12 .30
103 Bubba Franks .10 .25
104 Donald Driver .12 .30
105 Darren Sharper .12 .30
106 Peyton Manning .40 1.00
107 Edgerrin James .12 .30
108 Marvin Harrison .12 .30
109 Jerome Pathon .10 .25
110 Terrence Wilkins .10 .25
111 Ken Dilger .10 .25
112 Marcus Pollard .10 .25
113 Brad Scioli RC .10 .25
114 Mark Brunell .12 .30
115 Fred Taylor .10 .25
116 Jimmy Smith .12 .30
117 Jamie Martin .10 .25
118 Keenan McCardell .12 .30
119 Kyle Brady .10 .25
120 R.Jay Soward .10 .25
121 Alvis Whitted .10 .25
122 Brant Boyer RC .10 .25
123 Elvis Grbac .12 .30
124 Tony Gonzalez .12 .30
125 Derrick Alexander .10 .25
126 Tony Richardson .10 .25
127 Frank Moreau .10 .25
128 Sylvester Morris .10 .25
129 Kevin Lockett .10 .25
130 Donnie Edwards .10 .25
131 Oronde Gadsden .10 .25
132 Lamar Smith .12 .30
133 Jay Fiedler .12 .30
134 James Johnson .10 .25
135 Thurman Thomas .12 .30
136 Leslie Shepherd .10 .25
137 Tony Martin .12 .30
138 O.J. McDuffie .10 .25
139 Zach Thomas .12 .30
140 Randy Moss .12 .30
141 Bubby Brister .10 .25
142 Cris Carter .15 .40
143 Daunte Culpepper .12 .30
144 Moe Williams .10 .25
145 Troy Walters .10 .25
146 Chris Walsh RC .10 .25
147 Matthew Hatchette .10 .25
148 Kailee Wong .10 .25
149 Robert Griffith .10 .25
150 Drew Bledsoe .12 .30
151 Terry Glenn .12 .30
152 Kevin Faulk .10 .25
153 J.R. Redmond .10 .25
154 Tony Carter .10 .25
155 Patrick Pass .10 .25
156 Troy Brown .10 .25
157 Tony Simmons .10 .25
158 Michael Bishop .12 .30
159 Lawyer Milloy .10 .25
160 Ricky Williams .12 .30
161 Jeff Blake .12 .30
162 Joe Horn .10 .25
163 Aaron Brooks .10 .25
164 La'Roi Glover .10 .25
165 Chad Morton .10 .25
166 Keith Mitchell RC .10 .25
167 Willie Jackson .10 .25
168 Robert Wilson .10 .25
169 Jake Reed .12 .30
170 Kerry Collins .10 .25
171 Amani Toomer .10 .25
172 Ron Dayne .12 .30
173 Tiki Barber .12 .30
174 Greg Comella .10 .25
175 Ike Hilliard .10 .25
176 Joe Jurevicius .10 .25
177 Ron Dixon .10 .25
178 Jason Sehorn .12 .30
179 Michael Strahan .12 .30
180 Vinny Testaverde .10 .25
181 Wayne Chrebet .10 .25
182 Curtis Martin .12 .30
183 Richie Anderson .10 .25
184 Dedric Ward .10 .25
185 Laveranues Coles .12 .30
186 Windrell Hayes .10 .25
187 Chad Pennington .10 .25
188 Tim Brown .15 .40
189 Rich Gannon .12 .30
190 Tyrone Wheatley .12 .30
191 Napoleon Kaufman .10 .25
192 Jon Ritchie .10 .25
193 James Jett .10 .25
194 Rickey Dudley .10 .25
195 Andre Rison .12 .30
196 Eric Allen .12 .30
197 Charles Woodson .15 .40
198 Duce Staley .10 .25
199 Donovan McNabb .12 .30
200 Darnell Autry .10 .25
201 Chad Lewis .10 .25
202 Charles Johnson .10 .25
203 Torrance Small .10 .25
204 Todd Pinkston .10 .25
205 Brian Mitchell .12 .30
206 Hugh Douglas .10 .25
207 David Akers RC .10 .25
208 Kordell Stewart .10 .25
209 Jerome Bettis .15 .40
210 Bobby Shaw .10 .25
211 Hines Ward .12 .30
212 Plaxico Burress .10 .25
213 Courtney Hawkins .10 .25
214 Troy Edwards .10 .25
215 Earl Holmes .10 .25
216 Richard Huntley .10 .25
217 Marshall Faulk .12 .30
218 Kurt Warner .25 .60
219 Isaac Bruce .15 .40
220 Torry Holt .12 .30
221 Trent Green .10 .25
222 Justin Watson .10 .25
223 Trung Canidate .10 .25
224 Az-Zahir Hakim .10 .25
225 Ricky Proehl .10 .25
226 Dexter McCleon .10 .25
227 London Fletcher .12 .30
228 Junior Seau .12 .30
229 Curtis Conway .12 .30
230 Rodney Harrison .10 .25
231 Jeff Graham .10 .25
232 Freddie Jones .10 .25
233 Reggie Jones .10 .25
234 Ronney Jenkins .10 .25
235 Trevor Gaylor .10 .25
236 Jeff Garcia .10 .25
237 Jerry Rice .30 .75
238 Charlie Garner .12 .30
239 Terrell Owens .12 .30
240 J.J. Stokes .10 .25
241 Fred Beasley .10 .25
242 Tim Rattay .10 .25
243 Garrison Hearst .12 .30
244 Ricky Watters .12 .30
245 Shaun Alexander .10 .25
246 Jon Kitna .10 .25
247 Brock Huard .10 .25
248 Darrell Jackson .12 .30
249 James Williams WR .10 .25
250 Sean Dawkins .10 .25
251 John Hilliard RC .10 .25
252 Warrick Dunn .10 .25
253 Shaun King .10 .25
254 Ryan Leaf .10 .25
255 Mike Alstott .10 .25
256 Jacquez Green .10 .25
257 Reidel Anthony .10 .25
258 Derrick Brooks .10 .25
259 John Lynch .12 .30
260 Warren Sapp .12 .30
261 Eddie George .15 .40
262 Steve McNair .12 .30
263 Rodney Thomas .10 .25
264 Derrick Mason .10 .25
265 Yancey Thigpen .10 .25
266 Frank Wycheck .10 .25
267 Chris Sanders .10 .25
268 Carl Pickens .12 .30
269 Kevin Dyson .10 .25
270 Jevon Kearse .10 .25
271 Jeff George .12 .30
272 Stephen Davis .10 .25
273 Brad Johnson .12 .30
274 Albert Connell .10 .25
275 James Thrash .12 .30
276 Michael Westbrook .10 .25
277 Stephen Alexander .10 .25
278 Deion Sanders .12 .30
279 Champ Bailey .12 .30
280 Todd Husak .10 .25
281 Dan Morgan RC .30 .75
282 Josh Booty RC .30 .75
283 Michael Vick RC 2.50 6.00
284 Mike McMahon RC .30 .75
285 Reggie White RC .25 .60
286 Chris Weinke RC .30 .75
287 Drew Brees RC 12.00 30.00
288 Sage Rosenfels RC .30 .75
289 Marques Tuiasosopo RC .30 .75
290 Josh Heupel RC .40 1.00
291 David Rivers RC .25 .60
292 Kevin Kasper RC .25 .60
293 Jesse Palmer RC .30 .75
294 LaDainian Tomlinson RC 2.50 6.00
295 Deuce McAllister RC .40 1.00
296 Kevan Barlow RC .30 .75
297 LaMont Jordan RC .40 1.00
298 James Jackson RC .25 .60
299 Anthony Thomas RC .40 1.00
300 Correll Buckhalter RC .25 .60
301 Travis Henry RC .30 .75
302 Dan Alexander RC .30 .75
303 Travis Minor RC .30 .75
304 Derrick Gibson RC .25 .60
305 Rudi Johnson RC .40 1.00
306 Michael Bennett RC .30 .75
307 Alge Crumpler RC .40 1.00
308 Todd Heap RC .30 .75
309 Snoop Minnis RC .25 .60
310 Santana Moss RC .40 1.00
311 Reggie Wayne RC .50 1.25
312 Koren Robinson RC .30 .75
313 Chris Chambers RC .25 .60
314 David Terrell RC .30 .75
315 Rod Gardner RC .30 .75
316 Quincy Morgan RC .30 .75
317 Ken-Yon Rambo RC .25 .60
318 Vinny Sutherland RC .25 .60
319 David Allen RC .25 .60
320 Bobby Newcombe RC .30 .75
321 Ronney Daniels RC .25 .60
322 T.J. Houshmandzadeh RC .30 .75
323 Chad Johnson RC .40 1.00
324 Freddie Mitchell RC .25 .60
325 Moran Norris RC .25 .60
326 Ron Dayne CL .10 .25
327 Mike Anderson CL .07 .20
328 Jamal Lewis CL .12 .30
329 Brian Urlacher CL .15 .40
330 Darren Howard CL .10 .25

2001 Upper Deck MVP Campus Classics Game Jerseys

Randomly inserted at a rate of one in 144 packs, this 19-card set features NFL stars pictured in their college uniforms with a swatch of their college jersey. The jersey is planted inside the cut-out shape of a football with two black pieces of card that represent the stripes on the football. Most of the cards were issued in an Autographed version with each being serial numbered to 25.

STATED ODDS 1:144 HOB.
CCAT Anthony Thomas 8.00 20.00
CCCM Cade McNown 6.00 15.00
CCCW Chris Weinke 6.00 15.00
CCDB Drew Brees 15.00 40.00
CCDM Deuce McAllister 8.00 20.00
CCFM Freddie Mitchell 5.00 12.00
CCJF Jamar Fletcher 5.00 12.00
CCKJ Keyshawn Johnson 6.00 15.00
CCLT LaDainian Tomlinson 12.00 30.00
CCMB Michael Bennett 6.00 15.00
CCMF Marshall Faulk 6.00 15.00
CCMT Marques Tuiasosopo 6.00 15.00
CCMV Michael Vick 8.00 20.00
CCPM Peyton Manning 25.00 60.00
CCRD Ron Dayne 6.00 15.00
CCTA Troy Aikman 15.00 40.00

2001 Upper Deck MVP Campus Classics Game Jerseys Autographs

Randomly inserted in packs, this set features NFL stars pictured in their college uniforms with a swatch of their college jersey. The jersey is planted inside the cut-out shape of a football with two black pieces of card that represent the stripes on the football. The signatures are clear and cards are serial numbered to 25.

STATED PRINT RUN 25 SER.#'d SETS
CCSAT Anthony Thomas 30.00 80.00
CCSCM Cade McNown 25.00 60.00
CCSCW Chris Weinke 25.00 60.00
CCSDB Drew Brees 250.00 450.00
CCSDM Deuce McAllister 30.00 80.00
CCSFM Freddie Mitchell 20.00 50.00
CCSJF Jamar Fletcher 20.00 50.00
CCSLT LaDainian Tomlinson 125.00 250.00
CCSMB Michael Bennett 25.00 60.00
CCSMF Marshall Faulk 25.00 60.00
CCSMT Marques Tuiasosopo 25.00 60.00
CCSMV Michael Vick 60.00 120.00
CCSPM Peyton Manning 125.00 250.00
CCSRD Ron Dayne 25.00 60.00
CCSTA Troy Aikman 100.00 200.00

2001 Upper Deck MVP Souvenirs

Randomly inserted at a rate of one in 48 hobby packs and one in 96 retail packs, this 30-card set features a swatch of a football and the card is dated as to when it was used, some are from photo shoots and some are from actual games. Some of the cards were issued in an Autographed version with each being serial numbered to 25.

STATED ODDS 1:48 HOB, 1:96 RET
AB Aaron Brooks 2.00 5.00
BF Brett Favre 6.00 15.00
BU Brian Urlacher 4.00 10.00
BW A.Brooks/K.Warner 6.00 15.00
CB Charlie Batch 2.00 5.00
CM D.Culpepper/R.Moss 3.00 8.00
DC Daunte Culpepper 2.50 6.00
DM Donovan McNabb 2.50 6.00
EJ Edgerrin James 2.50 6.00
FM B.Favre/D.McNabb 8.00 20.00
GB R.Gannon/T.Brown 4.00 10.00
GD J.George/S.Davis 3.00 8.00
GR J.Garcia/J.Rice 8.00 20.00
JL Jamal Lewis 3.00 8.00
JR Jerry Rice 6.00 15.00
KJ Keyshawn Johnson 2.50 6.00
KW Kurt Warner 5.00 12.00
MC D.McNabb/D.Culpepper 3.00 8.00
MJ P.Manning/E.James 10.00 25.00
MR C.McNown/M.Robinson 3.00 8.00
PM Peyton Manning 8.00 20.00
PW Peter Warrick 2.00 5.00
RD Ron Dayne 2.50 6.00
RE J.R. Redmond 2.00 5.00
RM Randy Moss 2.50 6.00
SD Stephen Davis 2.00 5.00
TB S.King/K.Johnson 3.00 8.00
TJ Thomas Jones 2.00 5.00
TM V.Testaverde/C.Martin 3.00 8.00
WF K.Warner/M.Faulk 6.00 15.00

2001 Upper Deck MVP Souvenirs Autographs

Randomly inserted in packs, this set features a swatch of a football and the card is dated as to when it was used, some are from photo shoots and some are from actual games. These cards were hand-numbered to 25 and are highlighted by a gold background.

STATED PRINT RUN 25 SER.#'d SETS
ABS Aaron Brooks 20.00 50.00
BUS Brian Urlacher 75.00 150.00
BWS A.Brooks/K.Warner 40.00 100.00
CBS Charlie Batch 20.00 50.00
CMS D.Culpepper/R.Moss 75.00 150.00
DCS Daunte Culpepper 25.00 60.00
EJS Edgerrin James 25.00 60.00
GBS R.Gannon/T.Brown 30.00 80.00
GDS J.George/S.Davis 25.00 60.00
GRS J.Garcia/J.Rice 175.00 300.00
JRS Jerry Rice 175.00 300.00
KWS Kurt Warner 40.00 100.00
MJS P.Manning/E.James 150.00 250.00
MRS C.McNown/M.Robinson 25.00 60.00
PMS Peyton Manning 125.00 200.00
RDS Ron Dayne 25.00 60.00
RMS Randy Moss 75.00 150.00
SDS Stephen Davis 20.00 50.00
WFS K.Warner/M.Faulk 100.00 200.00

2001 Upper Deck MVP Team MVP

Randomly inserted in packs at a rate of one in six, this 20-card set features top players from the NFL. The set was highlighted with gold and silver foil trim and had an action photo of the featured player.

COMPLETE SET (20) 5.00 12.00
STATED ODDS 1:6
MVP1 Brian Griese .40 1.00
MVP2 Rich Gannon .50 1.25
MVP3 Marshall Faulk .50 1.25
MVP4 Edgerrin James .50 1.25
MVP5 Eddie George .60 1.50
MVP6 Mike Anderson .40 1.00
MVP7 Ed McCaffrey .50 1.25
MVP8 Marvin Harrison .50 1.25
MVP9 Isaac Bruce .60 1.50
MVP10 Eric Moulds .40 1.00
MVP11 Tony Gonzalez .50 1.25
MVP12 Mike Alstott .40 1.00
MVP13 Ray Lewis .60 1.50
MVP14 Junior Seau .50 1.25
MVP15 Warren Sapp .50 1.25
MVP16 La'Roi Glover .40 1.00
MVP17 Derrick Brooks .40 1.00
MVP18 Charles Woodson .60 1.50
MVP19 Champ Bailey .50 1.25
MVP20 John Lynch .50 1.25

2001 Upper Deck MVP Top 10 Performers

Randomly inserted in packs at a rate of one in 13, this 10-card set highlights the top 10 single game performances from the 2000 football season. The set design had an action photo of the featured player along with gold and silver foil lettering.

COMPLETE SET (10) 4.00 10.00
STATED ODDS 1:13
TOP1 Mike Anderson .40 1.00
TOP2 Vinny Testaverde .40 1.00
TOP3 Terrell Owens .50 1.25
TOP4 Aaron Brooks .40 1.00
TOP5 Jamal Lewis .60 1.50
TOP6 Fred Taylor .40 1.00
TOP7 Randy Moss .50 1.25
TOP8 Ricky Williams .50 1.25
TOP9 Jason Sehorn .50 1.25
TOP10 Shannon Sharpe .50 1.25

2002 Upper Deck MVP

Released in July, 2002. There are 8 cards per pack and 24 packs per box. The set contains 255 veteran and 45 rookie cards.

COMPLETE SET (300) 20.00 50.00
1 Arnold Jackson .12 .30
2 Dave Brown .12 .30
3 David Boston .12 .30
4 Frank Sanders .12 .30
5 Jake Plummer .12 .30
6 MarTay Jenkins .12 .30
7 Freddie Jones .12 .30
8 Jamal Anderson .15 .40
9 Keith Brooking .12 .30
10 Michael Vick .15 .40
11 Rodney Thomas .15 .40
12 Shawn Jefferson .12 .30
13 Tony Martin .15 .40
14 Warrick Dunn .12 .30
15 Brandon Stokley .12 .30
16 Chris McAlister .12 .30
17 Chris Redman .12 .30
18 Ray Lewis .20 .50
19 Sam Gash .12 .30
20 Travis Taylor .12 .30
21 Terry Allen .15 .40
22 Drew Bledsoe .15 .40
23 Alex Van Pelt .12 .30
24 Eric Moulds .12 .30
25 Kenyatta Wright .12 .30
26 Larry Centers .12 .30
27 Peerless Price .12 .30
28 Shawn Bryson .12 .30
29 Travis Henry .12 .30
30 Chris Weinke .12 .30
31 Lamar Smith .12 .30
32 Isaac Byrd .12 .30
33 Muhsin Muhammad .12 .30
34 Nick Goings .12 .30
35 Richard Huntley .12 .30
36 Tim Biakabutuka .15 .40
37 Wesley Walls .15 .40
38 Anthony Thomas .15 .40
39 Brian Urlacher .20 .50
40 David Terrell .12 .30
41 Dez White .12 .30
42 Jim Miller .12 .30
43 Larry Whigham .12 .30
44 Marty Booker .12 .30
45 Chris Chandler .15 .40
46 Corey Dillon .12 .30
47 Darnay Scott .15 .40
48 Jon Kitna .12 .30
49 Peter Warrick .12 .30
50 Ron Dugans .12 .30
51 Scott Mitchell .15 .40
52 Chad Johnson .12 .30
53 Courtney Brown .12 .30
54 JaJuan Dawson .12 .30
55 [illegible]
56 Kevin Johnson .12 .30
57 Quincy Morgan .12 .30
58 Rickey Dudley .12 .30
59 Tim Couch .12 .30
60 Chris Sanders .12 .30
61 Emmitt Smith .30 .75
62 Joey Galloway .15 .40
63 Ken-Yon Rambo .12 .30
64 La'Roi Glover .12 .30
65 Quincy Carter .12 .30
66 Rocket Ismail .15 .40
67 Darren Woodson .15 .40
68 Ryan Leaf .12 .30
69A Chester McGlockton .12 .30
69B Tony Carter UER .15 .40
70 Brian Griese .12 .30
71 Shannon Sharpe .15 .40
72 Kevin Kasper .12 .30
73 Mike Anderson .12 .30
74 Olandis Gary .15 .40
75 Rod Smith .15 .40
76 Terrell Davis .15 .40
78 Az-Zahir Hakim .12 .30
79 Charlie Batch .12 .30
80 Chris Claiborne .12 .30
81 Cory Schlesinger .12 .30
82 Desmond Howard .15 .40
83 Germane Crowell .12 .30
84 James Stewart .12 .30
85 Mike McMahon .12 .30
86 Bill Schroeder .12 .30
87 Ahman Green .15 .40
88 Brett Favre .40 1.00
89 Bubba Franks .12 .30
90 Antonio Freeman .20 .50
91 Donald Driver .15 .40
92 Kabeer Gbaja-Biamila .12 .30
93 William Henderson .12 .30
94 Corey Bradford .12 .30
95 Jamie Sharper .15 .40
96 Jermaine Lewis .12 .30
97 Kailee Wong .12 .30
98 Matt Stevens .12 .30
99 Tony Boselli .15 .40
100 James Allen .12 .30
101 Aaron Glenn .12 .30
102 Edgerrin James .15 .40
103 Dominic Rhodes .12 .30
104 Marcus Pollard .12 .30
105 Marvin Harrison .15 .40
106 Peyton Manning .50 1.25
107 Qadry Ismail .12 .30
108 Reggie Wayne .15 .40
109 Stacey Mack .12 .30
110 Elvis Joseph .12 .30
111 Fred Taylor .12 .30
112 Jimmy Smith .15 .40
113 Jonathan Quinn .12 .30
114 Keenan McCardell .15 .40
115 Mark Brunell .15 .40
116 Trent Green .12 .30
117 Derrick Alexander .12 .30
118 Johnnie Morton .15 .40
119 Snoop Minnis .12 .30
120 Mike Cloud .12 .30
121 Priest Holmes .12 .30
122 Tony Gonzalez .15 .40
123 Tony Richardson .12 .30
124 Ricky Williams .15 .40
125 Chris Chambers .12 .30
126 James McKnight .12 .30
127 Jay Fiedler .15 .40
128 Zach Thomas .15 .40
129 Oronde Gadsden .12 .30
130 Ray Lucas .12 .30
131 Randy Moss .15 .40
132 Spergon Wynn .12 .30
133 Cris Carter .20 .50
134 Daunte Culpepper .15 .40
135 Doug Chapman .12 .30
136 Michael Bennett .12 .30
137 Tom Brady 1.00 2.50
138 Troy Brown .12 .30
139 Adam Vinatieri .12 .30
140 Antowain Smith .15 .40
141 David Patten .12 .30
142 Donald Hayes .12 .30
143 J.R. Redmond .12 .30
144 Willie Jackson .12 .30
145 Jerome Pathon .12 .30
146 Jake Reed .15 .40
147 Aaron Brooks .12 .30
148 John Carney .12 .30
149 Deuce McAllister .15 .40
150 Joe Horn .12 .30
151 Kyle Turley .12 .30
152 Robert Wilson .12 .30
153 Tiki Barber .15 .40
154 Amani Toomer .12 .30
155 Ike Hilliard .12 .30
156 Jason Sehorn .15 .40
157 Joe Jurevicius .12 .30
158 Kerry Collins .12 .30
159 Michael Strahan .15 .40
160 Ron Dayne .15 .40
161 Wayne Chrebet .12 .30
162 Chad Pennington .12 .30
163 Curtis Martin .15 .40
164 LaMont Jordan .15 .40
165 Laveranues Coles .15 .40
166 Marvin Jones .12 .30
167 Santana Moss .15 .40
168 Vinny Testaverde .12 .30
169 Tyrone Wheatley .15 .40
170 Charles Woodson .20 .50
171 Charlie Garner .15 .40
172 Jerry Rice .40 1.00
173 John Parrella .12 .30
174 Jon Ritchie .12 .30
175 Rich Gannon .15 .40
176 Tim Brown .20 .50
177 Todd Pinkston .12 .30
178 Correll Buckhalter .12 .30
179 Donovan McNabb .15 .40
180 Duce Staley .12 .30
181 Freddie Mitchell .12 .30
182 Hugh Douglas .12 .30
183 James Thrash .15 .40
184 Koy Detmer .15 .40
185 Troy Edwards .12 .30
186 Chris Fuamatu-Ma'afala .12 .30
187 Hines Ward .15 .40
188 Jerome Bettis .20 .50
189 Kendrell Bell .12 .30
190 Kordell Stewart .12 .30
191 Mark Bruener .15 .40
192 Plaxico Burress .12 .30
193 Tim Dwight .12 .30
194 Curtis Conway .15 .40
195 Doug Flutie .15 .40
196 Drew Brees .40 1.00
197 Junior Seau .15 .40
198 LaDainian Tomlinson .20 .50
199 Marcellus Wiley .12 .30
200 Rodney Harrison .12 .30
201 Stephen Alexander .12 .30
202 Terrell Owens .15 .40
203 Andre Carter .12 .30
204 Cedrick Wilson .15 .40
205 Fred Beasley .12 .30
206 Garrison Hearst .12 .30
207 J.J. Stokes .12 .30
208 Jeff Garcia .12 .30
209 Kevan Barlow .12 .30
210 Tai Streets .12 .30
211 Doug Evans .12 .30
212 Bobby Engram .12 .30
213 Darrell Jackson .15 .40
214 James Williams .12 .30
215 John Randle .15 .40
216 Koren Robinson .12 .30
217 Matt Hasselbeck .12 .30
218 Shaun Alexander .12 .30
219 Trent Dilfer .12 .30
220 Aeneas Williams .12 .30
221 Isaac Bruce .20 .50
222 Kurt Warner .15 .40
223 Marshall Faulk .15 .40
224 Ricky Proehl .15 .40
225 Torry Holt .15 .40
226 Trung Canidate .12 .30
227 Terrence Wilkins .12 .30
228 John Lynch .15 .40
229 Keyshawn Johnson .15 .40
230 Michael Pittman .15 .40
231 Mike Alstott .12 .30
232 Rob Johnson .15 .40
233 Shaun King .12 .30
234 Warren Sapp .15 .40
235 Brad Johnson .15 .40
236 Derrick Mason .12 .30
237 Eddie George .15 .40
238 Frank Wycheck .12 .30
239 Jevon Kearse .12 .30
240 Kevin Dyson .15 .40
241 Steve McNair .15 .40
242 Chris Coleman .12 .30
243 Darrell Green .20 .50
244 Jacquez Green .12 .30
245 Ki-Jana Carter .15 .40
246 Michael Westbrook .12 .30
247 Rod Gardner .12 .30
248 Stephen Davis .12 .30
249 Tony Banks .12 .30
250 Champ Bailey .15 .40
251 David Carr RC .25 .60
252 DeShaun Foster RC .40 1.00
253 Antonio Bryant RC .40 1.00
254 Joey Harrington RC .25 .60
255 William Green RC .30 .75
256 Josh Reed RC .30 .75
257 Patrick Ramsey RC .30 .75
258 Clinton Portis RC .40 1.00
259 Jabar Gaffney RC .25 .60
260 Rohan Davey RC .40 1.00
261 T.J. Duckett RC .25 .60
262 Ashley Lelie RC .25 .60
263 Kurt Kittner RC .25 .60
264 Luke Staley RC .25 .60
265 Ron Johnson RC .30 .75
266 Antwaan Randle El RC .30 .75
267 Travis Stephens RC .25 .60
268 Marquise Walker RC .25 .60
269 Julius Peppers RC .60 1.50
270 Chad Hutchinson RC .25 .60
271 Maurice Morris RC .30 .75
272 Reche Caldwell RC .30 .75
273 Randy Fasani RC .25 .60
274 Lamar Gordon RC .30 .75
275 Donte Stallworth RC .40 1.00
276 Brandon Doman RC .25 .60
277 Damien Anderson RC .25 .60
278 Roy Williams RC .25 .60
279 J.T. O'Sullivan RC .30 .75
280 Leonard Henry RC .25 .60
281 Javon Walker RC .40 1.00
282 David Garrard RC .30 .75
283 Chester Taylor RC .40 1.00
284 Andre Davis RC .25 .60
285 Josh McCown RC .40 1.00
286 Adrian Peterson RC .30 .75
287 Seth Burford RC .25 .60
288 Deion Branch RC .40 1.00
289 Jonathan Wells RC .30 .75
290 Ladell Betts RC .40 1.00
291 Cliff Russell RC .25 .60
292 Eric Crouch RC .40 1.00
293 Dusty Bonner RC .25 .60
294 Tim Carter RC .30 .75
295 Brian Westbrook RC .50 1.25
296 Quentin Jammer RC .40 1.00
297 Brian Poli-Dixon RC .25 .60
298 Donovan McNabb CL .10 .25
299 Curtis Martin CL .10 .25
300 Tom Brady CL .60 1.50

2002 Upper Deck MVP Gold

*VETS: 20X TO 50X BASIC CARDS
*ROOKIES: 10X TO 25X BASIC CARDS
STATED PRINT RUN 25 SER.#'d SETS

2002 Upper Deck MVP Silver

*VETS: 6X TO 15X BASIC CARDS
*ROOKIES: 3X TO 8X BASIC CARDS
STATED PRINT RUN 100 SER.#'d SETS

2002 Upper Deck MVP ProSign

Randomly inserted into packs, these cards feature autographs of some of the NFL's best and brightest young players. Cards are serial numbered to 127.

STATED PRINT RUN 127 SER.#'d SETS
PSAT Anthony Thomas 12.00 30.00
PSCC Chris Chambers 10.00 25.00
PSCW Chris Weinke 10.00 25.00
PSDB Drew Brees 30.00 60.00
PSEC Eric Crouch 12.00 30.00
PSFM Freddie Mitchell 10.00 25.00
PSJR Josh Reed 12.00 30.00
PSMMC Mike McMahon 10.00 25.00
PSMW Marquise Walker 10.00 25.00
PSPM Peyton Manning 50.00 100.00
PSRJ Ron Johnson 12.00 30.00
PSWG William Green 12.00 30.00

2002 Upper Deck MVP Souvenirs

Randomly inserted in packs at a rate of 1:48. These cards feature a swatch of game used material.

STATED ODDS 1:48 HOB/RET
SSAB Anthony Becht 3.00 8.00
SSAT Anthony Thomas 4.00 10.00
SSBF Brett Favre 10.00 25.00
SSCB Champ Bailey 4.00 10.00
SSCC Curtis Conway 4.00 10.00
SSCG Charlie Garner 4.00 10.00
SSCP Chad Pennington 3.00 8.00
SSCW Charles Woodson 5.00 12.00
SSDB Drew Brees 10.00 25.00
SSDF Doug Flutie 4.00 10.00
SSDS Duce Staley 3.00 8.00
SSDT David Terrell 3.00 8.00
SSEM Eric Moulds 3.00 8.00
SSFS Frank Sanders 3.00 8.00
SSFT Fred Taylor 3.00 8.00
SSJA Jessie Armstead 3.00 8.00
SSJG Jeff Garcia 3.00 8.00
SSJJ J.J. Stokes 3.00 8.00
SSJS Junior Seau 4.00 10.00
SSMB Mark Brunell 4.00 10.00
SSRG Rod Gardner 3.00 8.00
SSSD Stephen Davis 3.00 8.00

2002 Upper Deck MVP Souvenirs Doubles

Randomly inserted in packs at a rate of 1:48. These cards feature two swatches of game used memorabilia. Mark Brunell and Jerry Rice have cards by themselves with two different types of swatches on them.

STATED ODDS 1:48
SDBB Mark Brunell 5.00 12.00
SDBG C.Bailey/D.Green 6.00 15.00
SDBT D.Brees/L.Tomlinson 12.00 30.00
SDCA K.Collins/I.Hilliard 4.00 10.00
SDCJ T.Couch/Kev.Johnson 4.00 10.00
SDDA W.Dunn/M.Alstott 4.00 10.00
SDGF J.Garcia/D.Flutie 5.00 12.00
SDJF F.Jones/D.Flutie 5.00 12.00
SDLS Jer.Lewis/J.Sharper 5.00 12.00
SDMH P.Manning/M.Harrison 15.00 40.00
SDMJ Q.Morgan/J.Jackson 4.00 10.00
SDMT J.Miller/D.Terrell 4.00 10.00
SDPJ L.Jordan/C.Pennington 5.00 12.00
SDPS J.Plummer/F.Sanders 4.00 10.00
SDRR Jerry Rice 12.00 30.00
SDSM D.Staley/D.McNabb 5.00 12.00
SDTM V.Testaverde/C.Martin 5.00 12.00
SDTT A.Thomas/L.Tomlinson 6.00 15.00
SDUS B.Urlacher/J.Seau 6.00 15.00

2002 Upper Deck MVP Team MVP

Randomly inserted in packs at a rate of 1:6. This set features some of the top players from the 2001 season.

COMPLETE SET (20) 10.00 25.00
STATED ODDS 1:6 HOB/RET
TM1 Jake Plummer .50 1.25
TM2 Michael Vick .60 1.50
TM3 Corey Dillon .50 1.25
TM4 Tim Couch .50 1.25
TM5 Rod Smith .60 1.50
TM6 Brett Favre 1.50 4.00
TM7 Peyton Manning 2.00 5.00
TM8 Mark Brunell .60 1.50
TM9 Randy Moss .60 1.50
TM10 Ricky Williams .60 1.50
TM11 Curtis Martin .60 1.50
TM12 Donovan McNabb .60 1.50
TM13 Kordell Stewart .50 1.25
TM14 LaDainian Tomlinson .75 2.00
TM15 Jeff Garcia .50 1.25
TM16 Terrell Owens .60 1.50
TM17 Shaun Alexander .50 1.25
TM18 Isaac Bruce .75 2.00
TM19 Keyshawn Johnson .60 1.50
TM20 Eddie George .60 1.50

2002 Upper Deck MVP Top 10 Performers

Randomly inserted in packs at a rate of 1:12. This set showcases the top performers at many of the skill positions.

COMPLETE SET (10) 7.50 20.00
STATED ODDS 1:12 HOB/RET
TT1 Anthony Thomas .60 1.50
TT2 Priest Holmes .50 1.25
TT3 Tom Brady 4.00 10.00
TT4 Michael Strahan .60 1.50
TT5 Jerry Rice 1.50 4.00
TT6 Rich Gannon .60 1.50
TT7 Emmitt Smith 1.25 3.00
TT8 Jerome Bettis .75 2.00
TT9 Kurt Warner .60 1.50
TT10 Marshall Faulk .60 1.50

2003 Upper Deck MVP

Issued in July of 2003, this set consists of 440 cards, including 330 veterans and 100 rookies. The rookie cards were issued approximately two per pack. Boxes featured 24 packs, each with 8 cards.

COMPLETE SET (440) 30.00 60.00
1 Brad Johnson .15 .40
2 Dexter Jackson RC .20 .50
3 Derrick Brooks .12 .30
4 Simeon Rice .12 .30
5 Warren Sapp .15 .40
6 John Lynch .15 .40
7 Joe Jurevicius .15 .40
8 Ronde Barber .12 .30
9 Mike Alstott .12 .30
10 Michael Pittman .12 .30
11 Keyshawn Johnson .20 .50
12 Jerry Rice .40 1.00
13 Tim Brown .20 .50
14 Rich Gannon .15 .40
15 Charlie Garner .15 .40
16 Jerry Porter .12 .30
17 Sebastian Janikowski .12 .30
18 Zack Crockett .15 .40
19 Tyrone Wheatley .15 .40
20 Bill Romanowski .15 .40
21 Charles Woodson .20 .50
22 Rod Woodson .15 .40
23 Donovan McNabb .15 .40
24 James Thrash .12 .30
25 Duce Staley .12 .30
26 Brian Westbrook .12 .30
27 A.J. Feeley .12 .30
28 Koy Detmer .12 .30
29 Brian Dawkins .20 .50
30 Dorsey Levens .15 .40
31 Jon Ritchie .12 .30
32 Todd Pinkston .12 .30
33 Chad Lewis .15 .40
34 Brett Favre .40 1.00
35 Ahman Green .15 .40
36 Donald Driver .15 .40
37 Bubba Franks .15 .40
38 Javon Walker .15 .40
39 Kabeer Gbaja-Biamila .12 .30
40 Robert Ferguson .12 .30
41 Tony Fisher .12 .30
42 Marques Anderson .12 .30
43 Ryan Longwell .15 .40
44 Craig Nall .12 .30
45 Steve McNair .15 .40
46 Eddie George .15 .40
47 Jevon Kearse .12 .30
48 Kevin Carter .12 .30
49 Samari Rolle .15 .40
50 Keith Bulluck .12 .30
51 Joe Nedney .12 .30
52 Robert Holcombe .12 .30
53 Drew Bennett .15 .40
54 Frank Wycheck .12 .30
55 Derrick Mason .12 .30
56 Tommy Maddox .12 .30
57 Jerome Bettis .20 .50
58 Plaxico Burress .12 .30
59 Antwaan Randle El .12 .30
60 Amos Zereoue .12 .30
61 Chris Fuamatu-Ma'afala .15 .40
62 Jason Gildon .15 .40
63 Kendrell Bell .12 .30
64 Dewayne Washington .12 .30
65 Jeff Reed RC .40 1.00
66 Hines Ward .15 .40
67 Jeff Garcia .12 .30
68 Terrell Owens .15 .40
69 Andre Carter .12 .30
70 Tai Streets .12 .30
71 Tim Rattay .12 .30
72 Eric Johnson .15 .40
73 Cedrick Wilson .12 .30
74 Brandon Doman .12 .30
75 Kevan Barlow .12 .30
76 Bryant Young .12 .30
77 Garrison Hearst .12 .30
78 Kerry Collins .12 .30
79 Daryl Jones .12 .30
80 Tiki Barber .15 .40
81 Amani Toomer .12 .30
82 Tim Carter .12 .30
83 Michael Strahan .15 .40
84 Ike Hilliard .12 .30
85 Brian Mitchell .12 .30
86 Ron Dixon .12 .30
87 Jeremy Shockey .12 .30
88 Marvin Harrison .15 .40
89 Peyton Manning .50 1.25
90 Edgerrin James .15 .40
91 Dominic Rhodes [illegible]
92 Brock Huard .12 .30
93 Marcus Pollard .12 .30
94 James Mungro .12 .30
95 Dwight Freeney .12 .30
96 Reggie Wayne .15 .40
97 Rob Morris .12 .30
98 Michael Vick .15 .40
99 Warrick Dunn .12 .30
100 T.J. Duckett .12 .30
101 Keith Brooking .15 .40
102 Ray Buchanan .12 .30
103 Alge Crumpler .15 .40
104 Quentin McCord .12 .30
105 Doug Johnson .12 .30
106 Brian Finneran .12 .30
107 Peerless Price .12 .30
108 Chad Pennington .12 .30
109 Curtis Martin .15 .40
110 Laveranues Coles .12 .30
111 Wayne Chrebet .12 .30
112 LaMont Jordan .15 .40
113 Anthony Becht .12 .30
114 Marvin Jones .12 .30
115 Mo Lewis .12 .30
116 Sam Cowart .12 .30
117 Vinnie Testaverde .12 .30
118 Santana Moss .15 .40
119 Tim Couch .12 .30
120 William Green .12 .30
121 Andre Davis .12 .30
122 Quincy Morgan .12 .30
123 Kevin Johnson .12 .30
124 James Jackson .12 .30
125 Jamel White .12 .30
126 Robert Griffith .12 .30
127 Dennis Northcutt .12 .30
128 Josh Booty .12 .30
129 Kelly Holcomb .12 .30
130 Jake Plummer .12 .30
131 Olandis Gary .12 .30
132 Clinton Portis .12 .30
133 Mike Anderson .12 .30
134 Ashley Lelie .12 .30
135 Ed McCaffrey .15 .40
136 Shannon Sharpe .15 .40
137 Rod Smith .15 .40
138 John Mobley .12 .30
139 Jason Elam .12 .30
140 Terrell Davis .15 .40
141 Tom Brady .75 2.00
142 Christian Fauria .12 .30
143 Antowain Smith .15 .40
144 Kevin Faulk .12 .30
145 Ty Law .20 .50
146 Lawyer Milloy .12 .30
147 David Patten .12 .30
148 Deion Branch .12 .30
149 Troy Brown .12 .30
150 Rohan Davey .12 .30
151 Adam Vinatieri .12 .30
152 Jay Fiedler .12 .30
153 Chris Chambers .12 .30
154 Randy McMichael .12 .30
155 Rob Konrad .12 .30
156 Morlon Greenwood .12 .30
157 Derrius Thompson .12 .30
158 Travis Minor .12 .30
159 Olindo Mare .12 .30
160 Jason Taylor .15 .40
161 Zach Thomas .15 .40
162 Ricky Williams .15 .40
163 Aaron Brooks .12 .30
164 Deuce McAllister .15 .40
165 Donte Stallworth .12 .30
166 Jerome Pathon .12 .30
167 J.T. O'Sullivan .20 .50
168 Darrin Smith .12 .30
169 Michael Lewis .12 .30
170 John Carney .12 .30
171 Kyle Turley .12 .30
172 Joe Horn .12 .30
173 Trent Green .12 .30
174 Priest Holmes .12 .30
175 Johnnie Morton .15 .40
176 Eddie Kennison .12 .30
177 Marvcus Patton .12 .30
178 Omar Easy .12 .30
179 Derrick Blaylock .12 .30
180 Snoop Minnis .12 .30
181 Dante Hall .12 .30
182 Tony Gonzalez .15 .40
183 Marc Boerigter .12 .30
184 Drew Brees .20 .50
185 David Boston .12 .30
186 Stephen Alexander .12 .30
187 Quentin Jammer .12 .30
188 Donnie Edwards .12 .30
189 LaDainian Tomlinson .20 .50
190 Junior Seau .15 .40
191 Reche Caldwell .12 .30
192 Lorenzo Neal .12 .30
193 Tim Dwight .12 .30
194 Doug Flutie .15 .40
195 Drew Bledsoe .15 .40
196 Travis Henry .12 .30
197 Eric Moulds .12 .30
198 Alex Van Pelt .12 .30
199 Charles Johnson .12 .30
200 Nate Clements .15 .40
201 Takeo Spikes .12 .30
202 Bobby Shaw .12 .30
203 London Fletcher .15 .40
204 Sammy Morris .12 .30
205 Josh Reed .12 .30
206 Patrick Ramsey .15 .40
207 Ladell Betts .12 .30
208 Chad Morton .12 .30
209 Trung Canidate .12 .30
210 Kenny Watson .12 .30
211 Jessie Armstead .12 .30
212 Fred Smoot .12 .30
213 Champ Bailey .15 .40
214 Bruce Smith .15 .40
215 Rod Gardner .12 .30
216 Kurt Warner .15 .40
217 Troy Edwards .12 .30
218 Adam Archuleta .12 .30
219 Grant Wistrom .12 .30
220 Marshall Faulk .15 .40
221 Jeff Wilkins .12 .30
222 Aeneas Williams .12 .30
223 Lamar Gordon .12 .30
224 Marc Bulger .12 .30
225 Isaac Bruce .20 .50
226 Torry Holt .15 .40
227 Matt Hasselbeck .12 .30
228 Maurice Morris .12 .30
229 Bobby Engram .12 .30
230 Darrell Jackson .15 .40
231 James Williams .12 .30
232 Chad Brown .12 .30
233 Anthony Simmons .12 .30
234 Shaun Alexander .12 .30
235 Koren Robinson .15 .40
236 Chris Redman .12 .30
237 Jamal Lewis .15 .40
238 Brandon Stokley .12 .30
239 Peter Boulware .15 .40
240 Randy Hymes RC .12 .30
241 Todd Heap .12 .30
242 Travis Taylor .12 .30
243 Ron Johnson .12 .30
244 Ray Lewis .20 .50
[illegible]

246 DeShaun Foster .15 .40
247 Dee Brown .12 .30
248 Steve Smith .20 .50
249 Kevin Dyson .12 .30
250 Muhsin Muhammad .12 .30
251 Stephen Davis .12 .30
252 Julius Peppers .20 .50
253 Rodney Peete .12 .30
254 Mark Brunell .15 .40
255 Jimmy Smith .15 .40
256 Kyle Brady .12 .30
257 Kevin Lockett .12 .30
258 Quinn Gray .15 .40
259 Tony Brackens .12 .30
260 Marco Coleman .12 .30
261 David Garrard .12 .30
262 Fred Taylor .12 .30
263 Daunte Culpepper .15 .40
264 Michael Bennett .12 .30
265 D'Wayne Bates .12 .30
266 Cedric James .12 .30
267 Kelly Campbell .12 .30
268 Derrick Alexander .12 .30
269 Byron Chamberlain .12 .30
270 Shaun Hill .20 .50
271 Randy Moss .15 .40
272 Josh McCown .15 .40
273 Thomas Jones .12 .30
274 Wendell Bryant .12 .30
275 Kevin Kasper .12 .30
276 Jason McAddley .12 .30
277 Emmitt Smith .30 .75
278 Preston Parsons .12 .30
279 Freddie Jones .12 .30
280 Marcel Shipp .12 .30
281 Chad Hutchinson .12 .30
282 Troy Hambrick .12 .30
283 Dat Nguyen .12 .30
284 Michael Wiley .12 .30
285 Joey Galloway .15 .40
286 Terry Glenn .15 .40
287 La'Roi Glover .12 .30
288 Roy Williams .12 .30
289 Antonio Bryant .12 .30
290 Quincy Carter .12 .30
291 Anthony Thomas .15 .40
292 Marty Booker .12 .30
293 Dez White .12 .30
294 Marcus Robinson .15 .40
295 Kordell Stewart .12 .30
296 David Terrell .12 .30
297 John Davis .12 .30
298 Mike Brown .12 .30
299 Brian Urlacher .20 .50
300 Jabar Gaffney .12 .30
301 Jonathan Wells .12 .30
302 JaJuan Dawson .12 .30
303 Corey Bradford .12 .30
304 Frank Murphy .12 .30
305 Billy Miller .12 .30
306 Aaron Glenn .12 .30
307 Avion Black .12 .30
308 David Carr .12 .30
309 Joey Harrington .12 .30
310 James Stewart .12 .30
311 Ty Detmer .12 .30
312 Jason Hanson .12 .30
313 Bill Schroeder .12 .30
314 Mikhael Ricks .12 .30
315 Scotty Anderson .12 .30
316 Robert Porcher .12 .30
317 Az-Zahir Hakim .12 .30
318 Jon Kitna .12 .30
319 Ron Dugans .12 .30
320 Chad Johnson .12 .30
321 Brandon Bennett .12 .30
322 T.J. Houshmandzadeh .12 .30
323 Rudi Johnson .12 .30
324 Kevin Hardy .12 .30
325 Corey Dillon .12 .30
326 Peter Warrick .12 .30
327 Carson Palmer RC .50 1.25
328 Byron Leftwich RC .30 .75
329 Rex Grossman RC .30 .75
330 Kyle Boller RC .25 .60
331 Dave Ragone RC .25 .60
332 Chris Simms RC .25 .60
333 Brad Banks RC .30 .75
334 Kliff Kingsbury RC .40 1.00
335 Jason Gesser RC .30 .75
336 Jason Johnson RC .25 .60
337 Brian St.Pierre RC .25 .60
338 Ken Dorsey RC .30 .75
339 Seneca Wallace RC .30 .75
340 Seth Marler RC .25 .60
341 Tony Romo RC 10.00 25.00
342 J.T. Wall RC .25 .60
343 Kirk Farmer RC .30 .75
344 Ricky Manning RC .30 .75
345 B.J. Askew RC .30 .75
346 Juston Wood RC .25 .60
347 Jeremi Johnson RC .25 .60
348 Tom Lopienski RC .25 .60
349 Justin Griffith RC .30 .75
350 Ovie Mughelli RC .30 .75
351 Bradie James RC .40 1.00
352 Larry Johnson RC .30 .75
353 Lee Suggs RC .25 .60
354 Justin Fargas RC .40 1.00
355 Chris Brown RC .25 .60
356 Onterrio Smith RC .25 .60
357 Willis McGahee RC .30 .75
358 Claude Diggs RC .25 .60
359 Lance Briggs RC 1.25 3.00
360 Earnest Graham RC .40 1.00
361 Quentin Griffin RC .30 .75
362 Michael Haynes RC .25 .60
363 Musa Smith RC .25 .60
364 Artose Pinner RC .25 .60
365 Domanick Davis RC .30 .75
366 LaBrandon Toefield RC .25 .60
367 Bethel Johnson RC .25 .60
368 Sultan McCullough RC .25 .60
369 Dahrran Diedrick RC .25 .60
370 Soloman Bates RC .25 .60
371 Andrew Pinnock RC .30 .75
372 Charles Rogers RC .30 .75
373 Andre Johnson RC .60 1.50
374 Taylor Jacobs RC .25 .60
375 Anquan Boldin RC .40 1.00
376 Talman Gardner RC .25 .60
377 Brandon Lloyd RC .40 1.00
378 Bryant Johnson RC .40 1.00
379 Kelley Washington RC .25 .60
380 Kareem Kelly RC .25 .60
381 Arnaz Battle RC .40 1.00
382 Billy McMullen RC .25 .60
383 Kennan Howry RC .25 .60
384 Nate Burleson RC .30 .75
385 Doug Gabriel RC .30 .75
386 J.R. Tolver RC .30 .75
387 Wayne Hunter RC .25 .60
388 Teyo Johnson RC .30 .75
389 Eric Steinbach RC .25 .60
390 Kevin Curtis RC .25 .60
391 Bobby Wade RC .30 .75
392 Sam Aiken RC .30 .75
393 Willie Pile RC .25 .60
394 Jerel Myers RC .25 .60
395 Tyrone Calico RC .25 .60
396 Terrence Edwards RC .25 .60
397 Travis Anglin RC .25 .60
398 Antwone Savage RC .25 .60
399 Cato June RC .50 1.25
400 Charles Drake RC .25 .60
401 Ronald Bellamy RC .30 .75
402 Justin Gage RC .30 .75
403 Mat McBriar RC .40 1.00
404 Kevin Garrett RC .25 .60
405 Kenny Peterson RC .30 .75
406 L.J. Smith RC .40 1.00
407 Jason Witten RC 1.00 2.50
408 Dallas Clark RC .40 1.00
409 DeWayne White RC .25 .60
410 Mike Seidman RC .25 .60
411 Aaron Walker RC .30 .75
412 Bennie Joppru RC .25 .60
413 Mike Pinkard RC .25 .60
414 Danny Curley RC .25 .60
415 Trent Smith RC .30 .75
416 George Wrighster RC .25 .60
417 Terrell Suggs RC .30 .75
418 Tully Banta-Cain RC .40 1.00
419 Jerome McDougle RC .25 .60
420 William Joseph RC .25 .60
421 DeWayne Robertson RC .30 .75
422 Jimmy Kennedy RC .30 .75
423 Chris Kelsay RC .30 .75
424 Kevin Williams RC .40 1.00
425 Boss Bailey RC .30 .75
426 Terry Pierce RC .25 .60
427 Terence Newman RC .40 1.00
428 Marcus Trufant RC .30 .75
429 Mike Doss RC .40 1.00
430 Dennis Weathersby RC .25 .60
431 Matt Wilhelm RC .30 .75
432 Andre Woolfolk RC .25 .60
433 Shane Walton RC .25 .60
434 DeJuan Groce RC .40 1.00
435 Antwoine Sanders RC .25 .60
436 Julian Battle RC .30 .75
437 Brett Favre CL .25 .60
438 Chad Pennington CL .07 .20
439 David Carr CL .07 .20
440 Drew Brees CL .12 .30

2003 Upper Deck MVP Silver

*VETS 1-326: 3X TO 8X BASIC CARDS
*ROOKIES 327-440: 1.5X TO 4X
STATED ODDS 1:12
341 Tony Romo 15.00 40.00

2003 Upper Deck MVP Future MVP

COMPLETE SET (42) 20.00 50.00
STATED ODDS 1:4
QB1 Carson Palmer .60 1.50
QB2 Byron Leftwich .40 1.00
QB3 Dave Ragone .30 .75
QB4 Kyle Boller .30 .75
QB5 Chris Simms .30 .75
QB6 Kliff Kingsbury .50 1.25
QB7 Jason Gesser .40 1.00
QB8 Brad Banks .40 1.00
QB9 Ken Dorsey .40 1.00
QB10 Rex Grossman .40 1.00
QB11 Jason Johnson .30 .75
QB12 Tony Romo 5.00 12.00
QB13 Brian St.Pierre .30 .75
QB14 Seneca Wallace .40 1.00
RB1 Larry Johnson .40 1.00
RB2 Lee Suggs .30 .75
RB3 Onterrio Smith .30 .75
RB4 Willis McGahee .40 1.00
RB5 Justin Fargas .50 1.25
RB6 Chris Brown .30 .75
RB7 Domanick Davis .40 1.00
RB8 LaBrandon Toefield .30 .75
RB9 Earnest Graham .50 1.25
RB10 Musa Smith .30 .75
RB11 Artose Pinner .30 .75
RB12 Sultan McCullough .30 .75
RB13 Dahrran Diedrick .30 .75
RB14 Quentin Griffin .40 1.00
WR1 Charles Rogers .40 1.00
WR2 Andre Johnson .75 2.00
WR3 Taylor Jacobs .30 .75
WR4 Anquan Boldin .50 1.25
WR5 Brandon Lloyd .50 1.25
WR6 Bryant Johnson .50 1.25
WR7 Kelley Washington .30 .75
WR8 Kareem Kelly .30 .75
WR9 Talman Gardner .30 .75
WR10 Arnaz Battle .50 1.25
WR11 Tyrone Calico .30 .75
WR12 Billy McMullen .30 .75
WR13 Keenan Howry .30 .75
WR14 Teyo Johnson .40 1.00

2003 Upper Deck MVP ProSign

Inserted at a rate of 1:480 packs, this set features authentic player autographs from several NFL superstars and youngsters. Please note that Byron Leftwich, Carson Palmer, Chris Simms, Kyle Boller, Larry Johnson, Rex Grossman, and Willis McGahee were only available in boxes as redemptions. According to Upper Deck, each redemption player signed less than 40 cards.
STATED ODDS 1:480
SP ANNOUNCED PRINT RUN 40 OR LESS
PSBL Byron Leftwich SP 15.00 40.00
PSCP Carson Palmer SP 30.00 80.00
PSCS Chris Simms SP 15.00 40.00
PSEL Elvis Grbac
PSJM Jim Miller 5.00 12.00
PSJT J.T. O'Sullivan 8.00 20.00
PSKD Ken Dorsey SP
PSKK Kurt Kittner 5.00 12.00
PSKL Kliff Kingsbury SP 12.00 30.00
PSLP Luke Petitgout 5.00 12.00
PSPM Peyton Manning 60.00 120.00
PSQM Quincy Morgan 5.00 12.00
PSRC Reche Caldwell 5.00 12.00
PSRF Randy Fasani 5.00 12.00
PSRG Rex Grossman SP 25.00 60.00
PSRJ Ron Johnson 5.00 12.00
PSWM Willis McGahee SP 20.00 50.00
PSLJ Larry Johnson SP 15.00 40.00

2003 Upper Deck MVP Souvenirs

Inserted at a rate of 1:96, this set features swatches of game used football. Each card was printed on thick stock, to accommodate the ball swatch.
STATED ODDS 1:96
GBAG Ahman Green 5.00 12.00
GBBF Brett Favre 12.00 30.00
GBBU Brian Urlacher 6.00 15.00
GBCP Chad Pennington 4.00 10.00
GBCR Chris Redman 4.00 10.00
GBDA David Carr 4.00 10.00
GBDB Drew Brees 6.00 15.00
GBDC Daunte Culpepper 5.00 12.00
GBDM Deuce McAllister 5.00 12.00
GBEJ Edgerrin James 5.00 12.00
GBJH Joey Harrington 4.00 10.00
GBJL Jamal Lewis 5.00 12.00
GBJR Jerry Rice 12.00 30.00
GBKB Kevan Barlow 4.00 10.00
GBKJ Keyshawn Johnson 6.00 15.00
GBKW Kurt Warner 5.00 12.00
GBLC Laveranues Coles SP 4.00 10.00
GBLT LaDainian Tomlinson SP 6.00 15.00
GBMB Michael Bennett SP 4.00 10.00
GBMC Donovan McNabb 5.00 12.00
GBMO Santana Moss 5.00 12.00
GBMV Michael Vick 5.00 12.00
GBPB Plaxico Burress 4.00 10.00
GBPM Peyton Manning 15.00 40.00
GBPO Clinton Portis 4.00 10.00
GBRG Rich Gannon SP 5.00 12.00
GBRM Randy Moss 5.00 12.00
GBSA Shaun Alexander 4.00 10.00
GBSD Stephen Davis SP 4.00 10.00
GBSM Steve McNair SP 5.00 12.00
GBTB1 Tim Brown 6.00 15.00
GBTB2 Tom Brady SP 25.00 60.00
GBTC Tim Couch 4.00 10.00
GBTH Travis Henry 4.00 10.00
GBTO Terrell Owens 5.00 12.00

2003 Upper Deck MVP Talk of the Town

COMPLETE SET (90) 25.00 60.00
STATED ODDS 1:3
TT1 Peyton Manning 2.00 5.00
TT2 Aaron Brooks .50 1.25
TT3 Joey Harrington .50 1.25
TT4 Brett Favre 1.50 4.00
TT5 Donovan McNabb .60 1.50
TT6 Tim Couch .50 1.25
TT7 Michael Vick .60 1.50
TT8 David Carr .50 1.25
TT9 Drew Brees .75 2.00
TT10 Chad Pennington .50 1.25
TT11 Daunte Culpepper .60 1.50
TT12 Tom Brady 3.00 8.00
TT13 Kurt Warner .60 1.50
TT14 Brad Johnson .60 1.50
TT15 Rich Gannon .60 1.50
TT16 Jake Plummer .50 1.25
TT17 Jeff Garcia .50 1.25
TT18 Drew Bledsoe .60 1.50
TT19 Steve McNair .60 1.50
TT20 Mark Brunell .60 1.50
TT21 Dave Ragone .50 1.25
TT22 Kordell Stewart .50 1.25
TT23 Jay Fiedler .50 1.25
TT24 Tommy Maddox .50 1.25
TT25 Chris Redman .50 1.25
TT26 Jon Kitna .50 1.25
TT27 Trent Green .50 1.25
TT28 Kerry Collins .50 1.25
TT29 Patrick Ramsey .60 1.50
TT30 Chad Hutchinson .50 1.25
TT31 Rodney Peete .50 1.25
TT32 Josh McCown .60 1.50
TT33 Matt Hasselbeck .50 1.25
TT34 Kelly Holcomb .50 1.25
TT35 Marc Bulger .50 1.25
TT36 Carson Palmer .75 2.00
TT37 Byron Leftwich .50 1.25
TT38 Kyle Boller .50 1.25
TT39 Chris Simms .40 1.00
TT40 Rex Grossman .50 1.25
TT41 Marshall Faulk .60 1.50
TT42 LaDainian Tomlinson .75 2.00
TT43 Emmitt Smith 1.25 3.00
TT44 Ricky Williams .60 1.50
TT45 Edgerrin James .60 1.50
TT46 Deuce McAllister .60 1.50
TT47 Eddie George .60 1.50
TT48 Ahman Green .60 1.50
TT49 Clinton Portis .50 1.25
TT50 Anthony Thomas .60 1.50
TT51 Priest Holmes .50 1.25
TT52 Curtis Martin .60 1.50
TT53 Michael Bennett .50 1.25
TT54 Shaun Alexander .50 1.25
TT55 Jerome Bettis .75 2.00
TT56 Fred Taylor .50 1.25
TT57 Travis Henry .50 1.25
TT58 Garrison Hearst .50 1.25
TT59 Charlie Garner .60 1.50
TT60 Kevan Barlow .50 1.25
TT61 Corey Dillon .50 1.25
TT62 Duce Staley .50 1.25
TT63 Jamal Lewis .60 1.50
TT64 William Green .50 1.25
TT65 Jerry Rice 1.50 4.00
TT66 Terrell Owens .60 1.50
TT67 Randy Moss .60 1.50
TT68 David Boston .50 1.25
TT69 Marvin Harrison .60 1.50
TT70 Isaac Bruce .75 2.00
TT71 Torry Holt .60 1.50
TT72 Plaxico Burress .50 1.25
TT73 Keyshawn Johnson .75 2.00
TT74 Chris Chambers .50 1.25
TT75 Rod Smith .60 1.50
TT76 Tim Brown .75 2.00
TT77 Rod Gardner .50 1.25
TT78 Peerless Price .50 1.25
TT79 Jabar Gaffney .50 1.25
TT80 Antonio Bryant .50 1.25
TT81 Troy Brown .50 1.25
TT82 Jimmy Smith .60 1.50
TT83 Donald Driver .60 1.50
TT84 Eric Moulds .50 1.25
TT85 Kevin Johnson .50 1.25
TT86 Charles Rogers .60 1.50
TT87 Andre Johnson 1.00 2.50
TT88 Taylor Jacobs .50 1.25
TT89 Tony Gonzalez .60 1.50
TT90 Jeremy Shockey .50 1.25

2002 Upper Deck National Convention

N6 Peyton Manning .75 2.00
N7 Michael Vick .60 1.50

2004 Upper Deck National Convention

STATED PRINT RUN 500 SER.#'d SETS
TN11 Tom Brady 1.50 4.00
TN12 Eli Manning 3.00 8.00
TN16 Michael Vick .75 2.00

2005 Upper Deck National Convention

Upper Deck produced this set and distributed it at the 2005 National Sport Collectors Convention in Chicago. The set includes famous Chicago area athletes from a variety of sports with the title "The National" printed on the cardfronts. The company made the cards available to collectors via a wrapper redemption program at their show booth and each card was serial numbered to 750-copies. Some players also signed just 5-cards which are not priced due to scarcity.
STATED PRINT RUN 750 SER.#'d SETS
UNPRICED AUTO PRINT RUN 5
CL4 Walter Payton 3.00 8.00
CL5 Gale Sayers 2.00 5.00
CL6 Mike Ditka 2.00 5.00

2005 Upper Deck National Convention VIP

Upper Deck produced this set and distributed it to special VIP package members attending the 2005 National Sport Collectors Convention in Chicago. The set includes famous athletes from a variety of sports with the title "The National" printed on the cardfronts along with a "VIP" stamp.
VIP5 Peyton Manning 4.00 10.00
VIP6 Donovan McNabb 3.00 8.00

2007 Upper Deck National Convention

NTL8 Reggie Bush 1.00 2.50
NTL9 Vince Young 1.00 2.50
NTL10 Peyton Manning 1.25 3.00
NTL11 Matt Leinart .60 1.50

2007 Upper Deck National Convention VIP

VIP8 Reggie Bush 1.25 3.00
VIP9 Vince Young 1.25 3.00
VIP10 Peyton Manning 2.00 5.00
VIP11 Matt Leinart .75 2.00

2008 Upper Deck National Convention

NAT3 Devin Hester .50 1.25
NAT7 Peyton Manning .75 2.00
NAT12 Tom Brady .75 2.00
NAT16 Brian Urlacher .50 1.25
NAT18 LaDainian Tomlinson .60 1.50
NAT19 Randy Moss .50 1.25

2008 Upper Deck National Convention VIP

CARDS FEATURE VIP LOGO ON FRONT
NAT3 Devin Hester 1.50 4.00
NAT7 Peyton Manning 2.50 6.00
NAT12 Tom Brady 2.50 6.00
NAT16 Brian Urlacher 1.50 4.00
NAT18 LaDainian Tomlinson 2.00 5.00
NAT19 Randy Moss 1.50 4.00

2009 Upper Deck National Convention

NC2 Brady Quinn .50 1.25
NC9 Adrian Peterson 1.00 2.50
NC11 Ben Roethlisberger .60 1.50
NC19 Larry Fitzgerald .50 1.25
NC20 Matt Ryan .60 1.50
NC23 Peyton Manning .75 2.00

2009 Upper Deck National Convention VIP

VIP9 Peyton Manning 2.50 6.00

2010 Upper Deck National Convention

COMPLETE SET (20) 15.00 40.00
NSC2 Anquan Boldin 1.25 3.00
NSC4 Joe Flacco 1.50 4.00
NSC8 Ray Rice 1.25 3.00
NSC12 Ray Lewis 1.25 3.00
NSC15 Vernon Davis 1.25 3.00
NSC18 Michael Oher 1.25 3.00

2010 Upper Deck National Convention Autographs

STATED PRINT RUN 9-90
NAJF Joe Flacco/54 30.00 60.00
NARR Ray Rice/90 25.00 50.00

2010 Upper Deck National Convention VIP

COMPLETE SET (6) 6.00 15.00
VIP4 Joe Flacco 1.25 3.00

2011 Upper Deck National Convention

NSCC11 Mike Singletary .75 2.00
NSCC18 Jake Locker 2.00 5.00

2011 Upper Deck National Convention Autographs

NSCCJL Jake Locker/18

2012 Upper Deck National Convention

NSCC4 Roger Staubach 1.25 3.00
NSCC7 Robert Griffin III 3.00 8.00
NSCC15 Trent Richardson 2.00 5.00

2012 Upper Deck National Convention Autographs

STATED PRINT RUN 1-35

2015 Upper Deck National Convention

NSCC5 Joe Theismann .30 .75
NSCC10 Tim Brown .30 .75

2015 Upper Deck National Convention Autographs

NSCC5 Tim Brown/10
NSCC9 Joe Theismann/20

2015 Upper Deck National Convention VIP

VIP2 Jerome Bettis 1.00 2.50

1999 Upper Deck Ovation

The 1999 Upper Deck Ovation set was released in mid-September as a 90-card base set containing 60 veteran cards and a 30 card Rookie Ovation subset listed at one in four packs. Full color action photos are set against an embossed football background. Upper Deck Ovation was released in 20-pack boxes containing five cards each and carried a suggested retail price of $3.99 per pack.
COMPLETE SET (90) 50.00 120.00
COMP.SET w/o SP's (60) 10.00 20.00
1 Jake Plummer .20 .50
2 Adrian Murrell .20 .50
3 Jamal Anderson .25 .60
4 Chris Chandler .25 .60
5 Tony Banks .25 .60
6 Antowain Smith .20 .50
7 Doug Flutie .30 .75
8 Tim Biakabutuka .25 .60
9 Steve Beuerlein .25 .60
10 Curtis Conway .25 .60
11 Curtis Enis .20 .50
12 Corey Dillon .20 .50
13 Jeff Blake .25 .60
14 Ty Detmer .20 .50
15 Troy Aikman .40 1.00
16 Emmitt Smith .50 1.25
17 Terrell Davis .25 .60
18 Bubby Brister .20 .50
19 Barry Sanders .50 1.25
20 Charlie Batch .20 .50
21 Brett Favre .60 1.50
22 Dorsey Levens .25 .60
23 Peyton Manning 1.00 2.50
24 Marvin Harrison .25 .60
25 Mark Brunell .25 .60
26 Fred Taylor .20 .50
27 Elvis Grbac .20 .50
28 Andre Rison .25 .60
29 Dan Marino .60 1.50
30 Karim Abdul-Jabbar .20 .50
31 Randall Cunningham .25 .60
32 Randy Moss .25 .60
33 Drew Bledsoe .25 .60
34 Terry Glenn .25 .60
35 Danny Wuerffel .25 .60
36 Cam Cleeland .20 .50
37 Kerry Collins .20 .50
38 Amani Toomer .20 .50
39 Curtis Martin .25 .60
40 Keyshawn Johnson .25 .60
41 Napoleon Kaufman .20 .50
42 Tim Brown .30 .75
43 Doug Pederson .20 .50
44 Charles Johnson .20 .50
45 Kordell Stewart .20 .50
46 Jerome Bettis .30 .75
47 Trent Green .20 .50
48 Marshall Faulk .25 .60
49 Natrone Means .25 .60
50 Jim Harbaugh .25 .60
51 Steve Young .40 1.00
52 Jerry Rice .75 2.00
53 Joey Galloway .25 .60
54 Jon Kitna .20 .50
55 Warrick Dunn .20 .50
56 Trent Dilfer .20 .50
57 Steve McNair .25 .60
58 Eddie George .25 .60
59 Brad Johnson .25 .60
60 Skip Hicks .20 .50
61 Tim Couch RC .75 2.00
62 Donovan McNabb RC 4.00 10.00
63 Akili Smith RC .60 1.50
64 Edgerrin James RC 1.00 2.50
65 Ricky Williams RC 1.00 2.50
66 Torry Holt RC 1.25 3.00
67 Champ Bailey RC 1.25 3.00
68 David Boston RC .60 1.50
69 Daunte Culpepper RC 1.00 2.50
70 Cade McNown RC .60 1.50
71 Troy Edwards RC .60 1.50
72 Kevin Johnson RC .75 2.00
73 James Johnson RC .60 1.50
74 Rob Konrad RC .60 1.50
75 Kevin Faulk RC .60 1.50
76 Shaun King RC .60 1.50
77 Peerless Price RC .60 1.50
78 Mike Cloud RC .60 1.50
79 Jermaine Fazande RC .60 1.50
80 D'Wayne Bates RC .60 1.50
81 Brock Huard RC .60 1.50
82 Marty Booker RC .60 1.50
83 Karsten Bailey RC .60 1.50
84 Al Wilson RC 1.00 2.50
85 Joe Germaine RC .75 2.00
86 Dameane Douglas RC .60 1.50
87 Sedrick Irvin RC .60 1.50
88 Amos Zereoue RC .60 1.50
89 Cecil Collins RC .60 1.50
90 Ebenezer Ekuban RC .60 1.50
WPO W.Payton Jsy AU/34 1000.00 1500.00

1999 Upper Deck Ovation Standing Ovation

*STARS: 15X TO 40X BASE CARD HI
*ROOKIES: 5X TO 12X BASE CARD HI
STATED PRINT RUN 50 SER.#'d SETS

1999 Upper Deck Ovation A Piece of History

Randomly inserted in packs, this 13-card set features an actual piece of a game-used football on the card front. Total print run for this set is 4560 cards.
COMPLETE SET (13) 500.00 1000.00
STATED PRINT RUN 4560 TOTAL CARDS
ASH Akili Smith 5.00 12.00
BFH Brett Favre 20.00 50.00
BHH Brock Huard 5.00 12.00
CMH Cade McNown 5.00 12.00
DCH Daunte Culpepper 15.00 40.00
DMH Dan Marino 25.00 60.00
EJH Edgerrin James 15.00 40.00
JGH Joe Germaine 5.00 12.00
JRH Jerry Rice 10.00 25.00
MCH Donovan McNabb 20.00 50.00
RWA Ricky Williams AU/34 100.00 200.00
RWH Ricky Williams 7.50 20.00
SYH Steve Young 10.00 25.00
THH Torry Holt 10.00 25.00

1999 Upper Deck Ovation Center Stage

Randomly inserted in packs, this 24-card set is divided up into three tiers containing 8 cards each. Tier one, card numbers CS1-CS8, are seeded at one in nine, Tier two, card numbers CS9-CS16, are seeded at one in twenty-five and Tier three, card numbers CS17-CS24, are seeded at one in ninety-nine packs. Card front features an action photo foreground set against a silhouette background.
COMPLETE SET (24) 100.00 200.00
CS1-CS8 STATED ODDS 1:9
CS9-CS16 STATED ODDS 1:25
CS17-CS24 STATED ODDS 1:99
CS1 Walter Payton 1.50 4.00
CS2 Barry Sanders 2.00 5.00
CS3 Emmitt Smith 1.25 3.00
CS4 Terrell Davis .60 1.50
CS5 Jamal Anderson .60 1.50
CS6 Fred Taylor .60 1.50
CS7 Ricky Williams 1.00 2.50
CS8 Edgerrin James 2.00 5.00
CS9 Walter Payton 3.00 8.00
CS10 Barry Sanders 4.00 10.00
CS11 Emmitt Smith 2.50 6.00
CS12 Terrell Davis 1.25 3.00
CS13 Jamal Anderson 1.25 3.00
CS14 Fred Taylor 1.25 3.00
CS15 Ricky Williams 2.00 5.00
CS16 Edgerrin James 4.00 10.00
CS17 Walter Payton 7.50 20.00
CS18 Barry Sanders 10.00 25.00
CS19 Emmitt Smith 6.00 15.00
CS20 Terrell Davis 3.00 8.00
CS21 Jamal Anderson 3.00 8.00
CS22 Fred Taylor 3.00 8.00
CS23 Ricky Williams 5.00 12.00
CS24 Edgerrin James 10.00 25.00

1999 Upper Deck Ovation Curtain Calls

Randomly inserted in packs at one in four. This 30 card set showcases a high point in the featured players 1999 season. Color photos are set on an all foil stock and card back carrys a "CC" prefix.
COMPLETE SET (30) 40.00 80.00
STATED ODDS 1:4
CC1 Peyton Manning 3.00 8.00
CC2 Fred Taylor 1.00 2.50
CC3 Randy Moss 2.50 6.00
CC4 Cris Carter 1.00 2.50
CC5 Troy Aikman 2.00 5.00
CC6 Randall Cunningham 1.00 2.50
CC7 Mark Brunell 1.00 2.50
CC8 Jon Kitna 1.00 2.50
CC9 Steve McNair 1.00 2.50
CC10 Jake Plummer .60 1.50
CC11 Jerry Rice 2.00 5.00
CC12 Kordell Stewart .60 1.50
CC13 Warrick Dunn 1.00 2.50
CC14 Emmitt Smith 2.00 5.00
CC15 Jerome Bettis 1.00 2.50
CC16 Terrell Owens 1.00 2.50
CC17 Antonio Freeman 1.00 2.50
CC18 Joey Galloway .60 1.50
CC19 Curtis Martin 1.00 2.50
CC20 Tim Brown 1.00 2.50
CC21 Charlie Batch 1.00 2.50
CC22 Doug Flutie 1.00 2.50
CC23 Barry Sanders 3.00 8.00
CC24 Drew Bledsoe 1.25 3.00
CC25 Corey Dillon 1.00 2.50
CC26 Eddie George 1.00 2.50
CC27 Keyshawn Johnson 1.00 2.50
CC28 Steve Young 1.25 3.00
CC29 Brett Favre 3.00 8.00
CC30 Terrell Davis 1.00 2.50

1999 Upper Deck Ovation Spotlight

Randomly inserted in packs at one in nine. This 15 card set depicts the top players from the 1999 NFL Draft. The card back carrys an "OS" prefix.
COMPLETE SET (15) 40.00 80.00
STATED ODDS 1:9
OS1 Tim Couch 1.00 2.50
OS2 Donovan McNabb 5.00 12.00
OS3 Akili Smith .75 2.00
OS4 Edgerrin James 4.00 10.00
OS5 Ricky Williams 2.00 5.00
OS6 Torry Holt 2.50 6.00
OS7 Champ Bailey 1.25 3.00
OS8 David Boston 1.00 2.50
OS9 Daunte Culpepper 4.00 10.00
OS10 Cade McNown .75 2.00
OS11 Troy Edwards .75 2.00
OS12 Kevin Johnson 1.00 2.50
OS13 Joe Germaine .75 2.00
OS14 Brock Huard 1.00 2.50
OS15 Kevin Faulk 1.00 2.50

1999 Upper Deck Ovation Star Performers

Randomly inserted in packs at one in thirty-nine, this 15 card die-cut set features the top stars in the NFL in action photos. Card back carries a 'SP' prefix.
COMPLETE SET (15) 60.00 120.00
STATED ODDS 1:39
SP1 Terrell Davis 2.50 6.00
SP2 Peyton Manning 8.00 20.00
SP3 Brett Favre 8.00 20.00
SP4 Dan Marino 8.00 20.00
SP5 Barry Sanders 8.00 20.00
SP6 Jamal Anderson 2.50 6.00
SP7 Mark Brunell 2.50 6.00
SP8 Jerome Bettis 2.50 6.00
SP9 Charlie Batch 2.50 6.00
SP10 Antowain Smith 2.50 6.00
SP11 Jake Plummer 1.50 4.00
SP12 Joey Galloway 1.50 4.00
SP13 Randy Moss 6.00 15.00
SP14 Steve Young 3.00 8.00
SP15 Warrick Dunn 2.50 6.00

1999 Upper Deck Ovation Super Signatures Gold

GOLD PRINT RUN 150 SER.#'d SETS
JM Joe Montana 125.00 250.00
JN Joe Namath 100.00 200.00
WP Walter Payton 500.00 750.00

1999 Upper Deck Ovation Super Signatures Silver

Randomly inserted in packs, this three-tiered insert set features autographs from Joe Namath, Joe Montana, and Walter Payton. Each player has signed three different levels of 'Super Signature' cards. Level 1 (silver foil) numbered to 300, Level 2 (gold foil), numbered to 150, and Level 3 (rainbow foil), numbered to 10.
SILVER PRINT RUN 300 SER.#'d SETS
JM Joe Montana 75.00 150.00
JN Joe Namath 50.00 120.00
WP Walter Payton 400.00 600.00

2000 Upper Deck Ovation

Released as a 90-card set, Upper Deck Ovation features 60 veteran players and 30 World Premier rookie cards sequentially numbered to 2500. Base cards have embossed white borders along the top, bottom and right side of the card in the texture of a football, and are enhanced with gold foil stamping. A special Joe Namath Autographed Jersey card sequentially numbered to 175 was also randomly inserted in packs. Ovation was packaged in 20-pack boxes with packs containing five cards and carried a suggested retail price of $3.99
COMPLETE SET (90) 125.00 250.00
COMP.SET w/o RC's (60) 7.50 20.00
61-90 ROOKIE PRINT RUN 2500
1 Jake Plummer .15 .40
2 Frank Sanders .15 .40
3 Chris Chandler .20 .50
4 Jamal Anderson .20 .50
5 Qadry Ismail .15 .40
6 Eric Moulds .15 .40
7 Muhsin Muhammad .15 .40
8 Steve Beuerlein .20 .50
9 Cade McNown .15 .40
10 Marcus Robinson .20 .50
11 Akili Smith .15 .40
12 Corey Dillon .15 .40
13 Tim Couch .20 .50
14 Kevin Johnson .15 .40
15 Troy Aikman .30 .75
16 Emmitt Smith .40 1.00
17 Terrell Davis .20 .50
18 Olandis Gary .20 .50
19 Charlie Batch .15 .40
20 Germane Crowell .15 .40
21 Brett Favre .50 1.25
22 Antonio Freeman .20 .50
23 Peyton Manning .60 1.50
24 Edgerrin James .20 .50
25 Mark Brunell .20 .50
26 Fred Taylor .15 .40
27 Elvis Grbac .15 .40
28 Tony Gonzalez .20 .50
29 Tony Martin .20 .50
30 Damon Huard .15 .40
31 Randy Moss .20 .50
32 Daunte Culpepper .20 .50
33 Drew Bledsoe .20 .50
34 Terry Glenn .20 .50
35 Ricky Williams .20 .50
36 Jeff Blake .20 .50
37 Kerry Collins .15 .40
38 Amani Toomer .15 .40
39 Curtis Martin .20 .50
40 Vinny Testaverde .15 .40
41 Tim Brown .25 .60
42 Rickey Dudley .15 .40
43 Duce Staley .15 .40
44 Donovan McNabb .20 .50
45 Troy Edwards .15 .40
46 Jerome Bettis .25 .60
47 Marshall Faulk .20 .50
48 Kurt Warner .40 1.00
49 Freddie Jones .15 .40
50 Junior Seau .20 .50
51 Jerry Rice .60 1.50
52 Steve Young .30 .75
53 Ricky Watters .20 .50
54 Jon Kitna .15 .40
55 Shaun King .15 .40
56 Keyshawn Johnson .20 .50
57 Eddie George .20 .50
58 Steve McNair .20 .50
59 Brad Johnson .20 .50
60 Stephen Davis .15 .40
61 Courtney Brown RC 1.25 3.00
62 Corey Simon RC 1.25 3.00
63 R.Jay Soward RC 1.00 2.50
64 Anthony Becht RC 1.00 2.50
65 Chris Redman RC 1.00 2.50
66 Chad Pennington RC 1.25 3.00
67 Tee Martin RC 1.00 2.50
68 Giovanni Carmazzi RC 1.00 2.50
69 Ron Dayne RC 1.50 4.00
70 Shaun Alexander RC 1.50 4.00
71 Thomas Jones RC 1.25 3.00
72 Reuben Droughns RC 1.00 2.50
73 Jamal Lewis RC 1.50 4.00
74 J.R. Redmond RC 1.00 2.50
75 Travis Prentice RC 1.00 2.50
76 Trung Canidate RC 1.00 2.50
77 Brian Urlacher RC 5.00 12.00
78 Bubba Franks RC 1.00 2.50
79 Peter Warrick RC 1.00 2.50
80 Plaxico Burress RC 1.25 3.00
81 Sylvester Morris RC 1.00 2.50
82 Dez White RC 1.00 2.50
83 Travis Taylor RC 1.00 2.50
84 Todd Pinkston RC 1.00 2.50
85 Dennis Northcutt RC 1.00 2.50
86 Jerry Porter RC 1.50 4.00
87 Laveranues Coles RC 1.25 3.00
88 Danny Farmer RC 1.00 2.50
89 Curtis Keaton RC 1.00 2.50
90 Ron Dugans RC 1.00 2.50

2000 Upper Deck Ovation Standing Ovation

*VETS 1-60: 12X TO 30X BASIC CARDS
*ROOKIES 61-90: 2X TO 5X
STATED PRINT RUN 50 SER.#'d SETS

2000 Upper Deck Ovation A Piece of History

Randomly inserted in packs, this 22-card set features player photos coupled with a swatch of a game used memorabilia. A total of 4800-cards were printed for the entire set. The football swatches on cards of the 2000 draft picks are from the 2000 NFL Rookie Photo Shoot. Five cards were issued in a signed version serial numbered to 25.
BFB Brett Favre 12.00 30.00
CPB Chad Pennington 4.00 10.00
CPH Chad Pennington Helmet 4.00 10.00
CRB Chris Redman 4.00 10.00
CRH Chris Redman Helmet 4.00 10.00
DCB Daunte Culpepper 5.00 12.00
DMB Dan Marino 12.00 30.00
EJB Edgerrin James 5.00 12.00
IBH Isaac Bruce Helmet 6.00 15.00
JRB Jerry Rice 15.00 40.00
KWH Kurt Warner Helmet 10.00 25.00
PMB Peyton Manning 15.00 40.00
PWB Peter Warrick 4.00 10.00
PWH Peter Warrick Helmet 4.00 10.00
RDB Ron Dayne 6.00 15.00
RDH Ron Dayne Helmet 6.00 15.00
RMB Randy Moss 5.00 12.00
SKH Shaun King Helmet 5.00 12.00
TCB Tim Couch 5.00 12.00
TJB Thomas Jones 4.00 10.00
TJH Thomas Jones Helmet 4.00 10.00

2000 Upper Deck Ovation A Piece of History Autographs

Randomly inserted in packs, this five card set features player photos, swatches of authentic game used memorabilia, and authentic player autographs. Each card is sequentially numbered to 25.
STATED PRINT RUN 25 SER.#'d SETS
CPA Chad Pennington Helmet 20.00 50.00
CRA Chris Redman Helmet 15.00 40.00
PMA Peyton Manning 125.00 225.00
PWA Peter Warrick 15.00 40.00
RMA Randy Moss 60.00 120.00
TJA Thomas Jones 20.00 50.00

2000 Upper Deck Ovation Center Stage

Randomly inserted in packs at the rate of one in 19, this 10-card set features top veterans and rookies. Each card contains an action photo and is enhanced with silver foil highlights.
COMPLETE SET (10) 8.00 20.00
STATED ODDS 1:19
*ACT 2: .8X TO 2X BASIC INSERTS
ACT 2 STATED ODDS 1:79
*ACT 3/50: 3X TO 8X BASIC INSERTS
ACT 3 STATED PRINT RUN 50
CS1 Tim Couch .60 1.50
CS2 Fred Taylor .50 1.25
CS3 Kurt Warner 1.25 3.00
CS4 Edgerrin James .60 1.50
CS5 Ron Dayne .75 2.00
CS6 Jamal Lewis .75 2.00
CS7 Thomas Jones .60 1.50
CS8 Peter Warrick .50 1.25
CS9 Plaxico Burress .60 1.50
CS10 Chad Pennington .60 1.50

2000 Upper Deck Ovation Curtain Calls

Randomly inserted in packs at the rate of one in three, this 15-card set highlights the most memorable moments from the 1999 football season.
COMPLETE SET (15) 3.00 8.00
STATED ODDS 1:3
CC1 Eddie George .40 1.00
CC2 Muhsin Muhammad .30 .75
CC3 Marvin Harrison .40 1.00
CC4 Marcus Robinson .40 1.00
CC5 Duce Staley .30 .75
CC6 Isaac Bruce .50 1.25
CC7 Germane Crowell .30 .75
CC8 Amani Toomer .30 .75
CC9 Fred Taylor .30 .75
CC10 Michael Westbrook .30 .75
CC11 Olandis Gary .40 1.00
CC12 Stephen Davis .30 .75
CC13 Cade McNown .30 .75
CC14 Priest Holmes .30 .75
CC15 Corey Dillon .30 .75

2000 Upper Deck Ovation Spotlight

ndomly inserted in packs at the rate of one in nine, this 15-card set pictures top young players expected to capture the spotlight in 2000. Cards have white borders along the left side and bottom and are enhanced with silver foil highlights.
COMPLETE SET (15) 6.00 15.00
STATED ODDS 1:9
OS1 Edgerrin James .50 1.25
OS2 Rob Johnson .50 1.25
OS3 Jake Plummer .40 1.00
OS4 Jamal Anderson .50 1.25
OS5 James Stewart .40 1.00
OS6 Shaun King .40 1.00
OS7 Jon Kitna .40 1.00
OS8 Ricky Williams .50 1.25
OS9 Errict Rhett .50 1.25
OS10 Stephen Davis .40 1.00
OS11 Daunte Culpepper .50 1.25
OS12 Donovan McNabb .50 1.25
OS13 Kevin Johnson .40 1.00
OS14 Akili Smith .40 1.00
OS15 Cade McNown .40 1.00

2000 Upper Deck Ovation Star Performers

ndomly seeded in packs at the rate of one in nine, this 15-card set features player action photography and foil highlights.
COMPLETE SET (15) 10.00 25.00
STATED ODDS 1:9
SP1 Mark Brunell .60 1.50
SP2 Eddie George .60 1.50
SP3 Brad Johnson .60 1.50
SP4 Vinny Testaverde .50 1.25
SP5 Marshall Faulk .60 1.50
SP6 Tim Couch .60 1.50
SP7 Brett Favre 1.50 4.00
SP8 Ricky Williams .60 1.50
SP9 Peyton Manning 2.00 5.00
SP10 Keyshawn Johnson .60 1.50
SP11 Emmitt Smith 1.25 3.00
SP12 Jerry Rice 2.00 5.00
SP13 Tim Brown .75 2.00
SP14 Randy Moss .60 1.50
SP15 Jamal Anderson .60 1.50

2000 Upper Deck Ovation Super Signatures Silver

Randomly inserted in packs, this eight card set features authentic autographs from some of today and yesterday's NFL stars. Each card is sequentially numbered to either 10 or 100 and features silver foil highlights. The exchange cards expired on 4/27/2001.
SILVER PRINT RUN 10-100
*GOLD/50: .5X TO 1.2X SILVER/100
GOLD PRINT RUN 50
UNPRICED RAINBOW PRINT RUN 10
EG Eddie George 20.00 50.00
JB Jim Brown 75.00 150.00
JN Joe Namath 50.00 120.00
MB Mark Brunell 20.00 50.00

MF Marshall Faulk 20.00 50.00
PM Peyton Manning 75.00 150.00
RM Randy Moss 30.00 80.00
TD Terrell Davis 20.00 50.00

2001 Upper Deck Ovation

Issued in five card packs, this 150 card set features a mix of active players and 2001 NFL rookies. The first 90 cards are NFL vets while the final 60 cards were printed in lesser quantities. Cards numbered 91 through 115 had a stated print run of 700 sets, while card numbered from 116 through 135 had a stated print run of 425 sets and cards 136 through 150 had a stated print run of 250 sets.

COMP.SET w/o SP's (90) 10.00 25.00
91-115 ROOKIE PRINT RUN 700
135-150 ROOKIE PRINT RUN 250
1 Jake Plummer .15 .40
2 Thomas Jones .15 .40
3 Frank Sanders .15 .40
4 Jamal Anderson .20 .50
5 Chris Chandler .20 .50
6 Terance Mathis .15 .40
7 Jamal Lewis .25 .60
8 Elvis Grbac .20 .50
9 Travis Taylor .15 .40
10 Shawn Bryson .15 .40
11 Rob Johnson .20 .50
12 Eric Moulds .15 .40
13 Muhsin Muhammad .15 .40
14 Donald Hayes .15 .40
15 Tim Biakabutuka .15 .40
16 Cade McNown .20 .50
17 Marcus Robinson .20 .50
18 Brian Urlacher .30 .75
19 Akili Smith .15 .40
20 Peter Warrick .15 .40
21 Corey Dillon .15 .40
22 Kevin Johnson .15 .40
23 Spergon Wynn .15 .40
24 Tim Couch .15 .40
25 Tony Banks .15 .40
26 Emmitt Smith .40 1.00
27 Anthony Wright .15 .40
28 Terrell Davis .20 .50
29 Mike Anderson .15 .40
30 Brian Griese .15 .40
31 Ed McCaffrey .20 .50
32 Charlie Batch .15 .40
33 Germane Crowell .15 .40
34 Johnnie Morton .20 .50
35 Brett Favre .50 1.25
36 Antonio Freeman .25 .60
37 Dorsey Levens .20 .50
38 Ahman Green .20 .50
39 Peyton Manning .60 1.50
40 Edgerrin James .20 .50
41 Marvin Harrison .20 .50
42 Mark Brunell .20 .50
43 Fred Taylor .15 .40
44 Jimmy Smith .20 .50
45 Tony Gonzalez .20 .50
46 Trent Green .15 .40
47 Derrick Alexander .15 .40
48 Oronde Gadsden .15 .40
49 Tony Martin .20 .50
50 Lamar Smith .20 .50
51 Randy Moss .20 .50
52 Cris Carter .25 .60
53 Daunte Culpepper .20 .50
54 Drew Bledsoe .20 .50
55 Terry Glenn .20 .50
56 Ricky Williams .20 .50
57 Jeff Blake .20 .50
58 Aaron Brooks .15 .40
59 Kerry Collins .15 .40
60 Tiki Barber .20 .50
61 Ron Dayne .20 .50
62 Vinny Testaverde .15 .40
63 Wayne Chrebet .15 .40
64 Curtis Martin .20 .50
65 Tim Brown .25 .60
66 Rich Gannon .20 .50
67 Jerry Rice .50 1.25
68 Duce Staley .15 .40
69 Donovan McNabb .20 .50
70 Kordell Stewart .15 .40
71 Jerome Bettis .25 .60
72 Marshall Faulk .20 .50
73 Kurt Warner .40 1.00
74 Isaac Bruce .25 .60
75 Doug Flutie .20 .50
76 Junior Seau .20 .50
77 Jeff Garcia .15 .40
78 Garrison Hearst .20 .50
79 Terrell Owens .20 .50
80 Ricky Watters .20 .50
81 Matt Hasselbeck .15 .40
82 Keyshawn Johnson .20 .50
83 Warrick Dunn .15 .40
84 Mike Alstott .15 .40
85 Kevin Dyson .15 .40
86 Eddie George .25 .60
87 Steve McNair .20 .50
88 Jeff George .20 .50
89 Michael Westbrook .15 .40
90 Stephen Davis .15 .40
91 Milton Wynn RC 1.50 4.00
92 Dan Alexander RC 2.00 5.00
93 Rudi Johnson RC 2.50 6.00
94 Ken-Yon Rambo RC 1.50 4.00
95 Alex Bannister RC 1.50 4.00
96 Adam Archuleta RC 2.00 5.00
97 Andre Dyson RC 1.50 4.00
98 Cedrick Wilson RC 2.00 5.00
99 Chris Taylor RC 1.50 4.00
100 Eddie Berlin RC 1.50 4.00
101 Gary Baxter RC 1.50 4.00
102 Heath Evans RC 2.00 5.00
103 Jabari Holloway RC 1.50 4.00
104 Jamal Reynolds RC 1.50 4.00
105 Jamar Fletcher RC 1.50 4.00
106 Justin Smith RC 3.00 8.00
107 Kevin Kasper RC 1.50 4.00
108 Moran Norris RC 1.50 4.00
109 Nate Clements RC 2.00 5.00
110 Scotty Anderson RC 1.50 4.00
111 T.J. Houshmandzadeh RC 2.00 5.00
112 Travis Minor RC 2.00 5.00
113 Vinny Sutherland RC 1.50 4.00
114 Will Allen RC 2.50 6.00
115 Derrick Gibson RC 1.50 4.00
116 Kevan Barlow RC 2.50 6.00
117 LaMont Jordan RC 3.00 8.00
118 Todd Heap RC 2.50 6.00
119 Quincy Morgan RC 2.50 6.00
120 Dan Morgan RC 2.50 6.00
121 Gerard Warren RC 2.50 6.00
122 Mike McMahon RC 2.50 6.00
123 Sage Rosenfels RC 2.50 6.00
124 Marques Tuiasosopo RC 2.50 6.00
125 Josh Heupel RC 3.00 8.00
126 Jesse Palmer RC 2.50 6.00
127 Quincy Carter RC 2.50 6.00
128 Josh Booty RC 2.50 6.00
129 Correll Buckhalter RC 2.00 5.00
130 Travis Henry RC 2.50 6.00
131 Algo Crumpler RC 3.00 8.00
132 Snoop Minnis RC 2.00 5.00
133 Bobby Newcombe RC 2.50 6.00
134 Robert Ferguson RC 3.00 8.00
135 James Jackson RC 2.00 5.00
136 Michael Bennett RC 3.00 8.00
137 Drew Brees RC 100.00 200.00
138 Chris Chambers RC 2.50 6.00
139 Rod Gardner RC 3.00 8.00
140 Chad Johnson RC 4.00 10.00
141 Freddie Mitchell RC 2.50 6.00
142 Deuce McAllister RC 4.00 10.00
143 Santana Moss RC 4.00 10.00
144 Koren Robinson RC 3.00 8.00
145 David Terrell RC 3.00 8.00
146 LaDainian Tomlinson RC 12.00 30.00
147 Anthony Thomas RC 4.00 10.00
148 Reggie Wayne RC 5.00 12.00
149 Michael Vick RC 6.00 15.00
150 Chris Weinke RC 3.00 8.00

2001 Upper Deck Ovation Black and White Rookies

*ROOKIES: .3X TO .8X BASIC CARDS
91-115 ROOKIE PRINT RUN 700
116-135 ROOKIE PRINT RUN 425
136-150 ROOKIE PRINT RUN 250

2001 Upper Deck Ovation Embossed Rookies

*EMBOSSED: .4X TO 1X BASIC CARDS

2001 Upper Deck Ovation Rookie Autographs

ATED PRINT RUN 250 SER.#'d SETS
136 Michael Bennett 8.00 20.00
137 Drew Brees 500.00 1000.00
138 Chris Chambers 6.00 15.00
139 Rod Gardner 8.00 20.00
140 Chad Johnson 10.00 25.00
141 Freddie Mitchell 6.00 15.00
142 Deuce McAllister 10.00 25.00
143 Santana Moss 10.00 25.00
144 Koren Robinson 8.00 20.00
145 David Terrell 8.00 20.00
146 LaDainian Tomlinson 40.00 100.00
147 Anthony Thomas 10.00 25.00
148 Reggie Wayne 12.00 30.00
149 Michael Vick 50.00 120.00
150 Chris Weinke 8.00 20.00

2001 Upper Deck Ovation Rookie Gear

Issued at a rate of one in 20, this 13 card set featured leading 2001 NFL rookies along with a game-worn uniform swatch.

STATED ODDS 1:20
RCC Chris Chambers 2.50 6.00
RCW Chris Weinke 3.00 8.00
RDB Drew Brees 15.00 40.00
RDM Deuce McAllister 4.00 10.00
RJJ James Jackson 2.50 6.00
RKB Kevan Barlow 3.00 8.00
RKR Koren Robinson 3.00 8.00
RMB Michael Bennett 3.00 8.00
RMV Michael Vick 6.00 15.00
RQM Quincy Morgan 3.00 8.00
RRF Robert Ferguson 4.00 10.00
RRG Rod Gardner 3.00 8.00
RSM Santana Moss 4.00 10.00

2001 Upper Deck Ovation Train for the Game Jerseys

Issued at a rate of one in 120, these six cards feature leading NFL players with 2 game-worn swatches on them.

STATED ODDS 1:120
TGBF Brett Favre 15.00 40.00
TGDF Doug Flutie SP 25.00 50.00
TGJA Jessie Armstead 6.00 15.00
TGJS Junior Seau 8.00 20.00
TGMB Mark Brunell 8.00 20.00
TGRD Ron Dayne 8.00 20.00

2001 Upper Deck Ovation Training Gear

sued at a rate of one in 20, these 29 cards feature these NFL veterans as well as a piece of game-used memorabilia.

STATED ODDS 1:20
TAS Akili Smith 4.00 10.00
TBF Brett Favre 10.00 25.00
TBO David Boston 4.00 10.00
TCC Curtis Conway 5.00 12.00
TCD Corey Dillon 4.00 10.00
TCG Charlie Garner 5.00 12.00
TCK Curtis Keaton 4.00 10.00
TCW Charles Woodson 6.00 15.00
TDB Drew Brees 15.00 40.00
TEG Elvis Grbac 5.00 12.00
TFS Frank Sanders 4.00 10.00
TFT Fred Taylor 4.00 10.00
TJG Jeff Garcia 4.00 10.00
TJJ J.J. Stokes 4.00 10.00
TJP Jake Plummer 4.00 10.00
TJR Jerry Rice 12.00 30.00
TJS Jason Sehorn 5.00 12.00
TKM Keenan McCardell 5.00 12.00
TMB Mark Brunell 5.00 12.00
TMP Michael Pittman 5.00 12.00
TPW Peter Warrick 4.00 10.00
TRD Ron Dayne 5.00 12.00
TRG Rich Gannon 5.00 12.00
TTB Tiki Barber 5.00 12.00
TTC Tim Couch 4.00 10.00
TTJ Thomas Jones 4.00 10.00
TTO Terrell Owens 5.00 12.00
TTW Tyrone Wheatley 5.00 12.00
TJRS Junior Seau 5.00 12.00

2001 Upper Deck Ovation Training Gear Trios

Inserted at a rate of one in 240, these seven cards feature uniform swatches from three teammates using training camp uniforms.

STATED ODDS 1:240
TTA Plummer/Jones/Boston 10.00 25.00
TTC A.Smith/Dillon/Warrick 10.00 25.00
TTJ Brunell/Taylor/McCardell 10.00 25.00
TTO Gannon/Wheatley/Rice 25.00 60.00
TTGB Garcia/Owens/Stokes 15.00 40.00
TTNY Armstead/Barber/Dayne 12.00 30.00
TTSD Seau/Brees/Flutie 20.00 50.00

2002 Upper Deck Ovation

Released in August, 2002, this set contains 90 veterans and 30 rookies making a total of 120 cards. The rookie cards are sequentially #'d to 1985, and on average you get one rookie per box.

COMPLETE SET (120) 75.00 125.00
COMP.SET w/o SP's (90) 10.00 25.00
91-120 ROOKIE PRINT RUN 1985
1 David Boston .15 .40
2 Jake Plummer .15 .40
3 Warrick Dunn .15 .40
4 Michael Vick .20 .50
5 Jamal Anderson .20 .50
6 Travis Taylor .15 .40
7 Ray Lewis .25 .60
8 Alex Van Pelt .15 .40
9 Travis Henry .15 .40
10 Drew Bledsoe .20 .50
11 Muhsin Muhammad .15 .40
12 Chris Weinke .15 .40
13 Lamar Smith .15 .40
14 Marty Booker .15 .40
15 Jim Miller .15 .40
16 Anthony Thomas .20 .50
17 Peter Warrick .15 .40
18 Jon Kitna .15 .40
19 Corey Dillon .15 .40
20 Quincy Morgan .15 .40
21 Tim Couch .15 .40
22 Rocket Ismail .20 .50
23 Quincy Carter .15 .40
24 Emmitt Smith .40 1.00
25 Shannon Sharpe .20 .50
26 Brian Griese .15 .40
27 Terrell Davis .20 .50
28 Mike McMahon .15 .40
29 James Stewart .15 .40
30 Az-Zahir Hakim .15 .40
31 Terry Glenn .20 .50
32 Brett Favre .50 1.25
33 Ahman Green .20 .50
34 James Allen .15 .40
35 Jermaine Lewis .15 .40
36 Marvin Harrison .20 .50
37 Peyton Manning .60 1.50
38 Edgerrin James .20 .50
39 Jimmy Smith .20 .50
40 Mark Brunell .20 .50
41 Johnnie Morton .20 .50
42 Trent Green .15 .40
43 Priest Holmes .15 .40
44 Jay Fiedler .20 .50
45 Chris Chambers .15 .40
46 Ricky Williams .20 .50
47 Randy Moss .20 .50
48 Michael Bennett .15 .40
49 Daunte Culpepper .20 .50
50 Troy Brown .15 .40
51 Tom Brady 1.25 3.00
52 Antowain Smith .20 .50
53 Joe Horn .15 .40
54 Aaron Brooks .15 .40
55 Deuce McAllister .20 .50
56 Amani Toomer .15 .40
57 Kerry Collins .15 .40
58 Ron Dayne .20 .50
59 Vinny Testaverde .15 .40
60 Curtis Martin .20 .50
61 Santana Moss .20 .50
62 Tim Brown .25 .60
63 Jerry Rice .50 1.25
64 Rich Gannon .20 .50
65 Donovan McNabb .20 .50
66 Duce Staley .15 .40
67 Freddie Mitchell .15 .40
68 Plaxico Burress .15 .40
69 Kordell Stewart .15 .40
70 Jerome Bettis .25 .60
71 Doug Flutie .20 .50
72 LaDainian Tomlinson .25 .60
73 Drew Brees .50 1.25
74 Terrell Owens .20 .50
75 Jeff Garcia .15 .40
76 Garrison Hearst .15 .40
77 Shaun Alexander .15 .40
78 Trent Dilfer .15 .40
79 Kurt Warner .20 .50
80 Marshall Faulk .20 .50
81 Isaac Bruce .25 .60
82 Keyshawn Johnson .20 .50
83 Brad Johnson .20 .50
84 Mike Alstott .15 .40
85 Rob Johnson .20 .50
86 Steve McNair .20 .50
87 Eddie George .20 .50
88 Jessie Armstead .15 .40
89 Rod Gardner .15 .40
90 Stephen Davis .15 .40
91 Andre Davis RC 1.25 3.00
92 Antonio Bryant RC 2.00 5.00
93 Antwaan Randle El RC 1.50 4.00
94 Ashley Lelie RC 1.25 3.00
95 Cliff Russell RC 1.25 3.00
96 Clinton Portis RC 2.00 5.00
97 Daniel Graham RC 1.50 4.00
98 David Carr RC 1.25 3.00
99 David Garrard RC 1.50 4.00
100 DeShaun Foster RC 2.00 5.00
101 Reche Caldwell RC 1.50 4.00
102 Donte Stallworth RC 2.00 5.00
103 Jabar Gaffney RC 1.25 3.00
104 Javon Walker RC 2.00 5.00
105 Jeremy Shockey RC 2.00 5.00
106 Joey Harrington RC 1.25 3.00
107 Josh McCown RC 2.00 5.00
108 Josh Reed RC 1.50 4.00
109 Julius Peppers RC 3.00 8.00
110 Marquise Walker RC 1.25 3.00
111 Maurice Morris RC 1.50 4.00
112 Patrick Ramsey RC 1.50 4.00
113 Quentin Jammer RC 2.00 5.00
114 Rohan Davey RC 2.00 5.00
115 Ron Johnson RC 1.50 4.00
116 Roy Williams RC 1.25 3.00
117 T.J. Duckett RC 1.25 3.00
118 Tim Carter RC 1.50 4.00
119 Travis Stephens RC 1.25 3.00
120 William Green RC 1.50 4.00

2002 Upper Deck Ovation Gold

*VETS: 15X TO 40X BASIC CARDS
STATED PRINT RUN 25 SER.#'d SETS

2002 Upper Deck Ovation Silver

*VETS: 5X TO 12X BASIC CARDS
STATED PRINT RUN 100 SER.#'d SETS

2002 Upper Deck Ovation Bound for Glory Jerseys

This set features game used jersey swatches, with each card inserted at a rate of 1:72.

STATED ODDS 1:72 HOB/RET
*GOLD/25: 1X TO 2.5X BASIC JSY
GOLD PRINT RUN 25 SER.#'d SETS
BGCW Charles Woodson 5.00 12.00
BGDS Duce Staley 3.00 8.00
BGDT David Terrell 3.00 8.00
BGJH Joey Harrington 3.00 8.00
BGJJ James Jackson SP 3.00 8.00
BGLT LaDainian Tomlinson/75* 5.00 12.00
BGMB Michael Bennett 3.00 8.00
BGMW Michael Westbrook 3.00 8.00
BGPP Peerless Price 3.00 8.00
BGQM Quincy Morgan 3.00 8.00
BGRD Ron Dayne 4.00 10.00
BGRG Rod Gardner 3.00 8.00
BGTB Tom Brady 25.00 60.00
BGTB Tiki Barber 4.00 10.00
BGTH Travis Henry 3.00 8.00

2002 Upper Deck Ovation Jerseys

This set features game used jersey swatches, with each card inserted at a rate of 1:72.

STATED ODDS 1:72 HOB/RET
*GOLD/25: 1X TO 2.5X BASIC JSY
GOLD PRINT RUN 25 SER.#'d SETS
OJAB Aaron Brooks 3.00 8.00
OJDC Daunte Culpepper 4.00 10.00
OJDF DeShaun Foster 5.00 12.00
OJDM Donovan McNabb SP 4.00 10.00
OJES Emmitt Smith 8.00 20.00
OJID Isaac Bruce 5.00 12.00
OJJF Jay Fiedler 4.00 10.00
OJMB Mark Brunell SP 4.00 10.00
OJMF Marshall Faulk 4.00 10.00
OJPM Peyton Manning 12.00 30.00
OJRW Ricky Williams 4.00 10.00
OJTC Tim Couch 3.00 8.00
OJWS Warren Sapp 4.00 10.00

2002 Upper Deck Ovation Lead Performers

Inserted at a rate of 1:12, this 30-card set highlights some of the NFL's top performers from 2001.

COMPLETE SET (30) 15.00 40.00
STATED ODDS 1:12 HOB/RET
LP1 Jake Plummer .50 1.25
LP2 Warrick Dunn .50 1.25
LP3 Michael Vick .60 1.50
LP4 Travis Henry .50 1.25
LP5 David Terrell .50 1.25
LP6 Brian Urlacher .75 2.00
LP7 Tim Couch .50 1.25
LP8 Brett Favre 1.50 4.00
LP9 Peyton Manning 2.00 5.00
LP10 Jimmy Smith .60 1.50
LP11 Mark Brunell .60 1.50
LP12 Trent Green .50 1.25
LP13 Chris Chambers .50 1.25
LP14 Jay Fiedler .60 1.50
LP15 Ricky Williams .60 1.50
LP16 Daunte Culpepper .60 1.50
LP17 Michael Bennett .50 1.25
LP18 Randy Moss .60 1.50
LP19 Antowain Smith .60 1.50
LP20 Tom Brady 4.00 10.00
LP21 Aaron Brooks .50 1.25
LP22 Deuce McAllister .60 1.50
LP23 Kerry Collins .50 1.25
LP24 Ron Dayne .60 1.50
LP25 Duce Staley .50 1.25
LP26 Kordell Stewart .50 1.25
LP27 Jerome Bettis .75 2.00
LP28 Drew Brees 1.50 4.00
LP29 Isaac Bruce .75 2.00
LP30 Steve McNair .60 1.50

2002 Upper Deck Ovation Milestones

Inserted at a rate of 1:12, this set highlights players who achieved a personal milestone during the 2001 season.

COMPLETE SET (30) 15.00 40.00
STATED ODDS 1:12 HOB/RET
OM1 David Boston .50 1.25
OM2 Jamal Anderson .60 1.50
OM3 Tony Martin .60 1.50
OM4 Ray Lewis .75 2.00
OM5 Anthony Thomas .60 1.50
OM6 Corey Dillon .50 1.25
OM7 Emmitt Smith 1.25 3.00
OM8 Terrell Davis .60 1.50
OM9 Brett Favre 1.50 4.00
OM10 Edgerrin James .60 1.50
OM11 Peyton Manning 2.00 5.00
OM12 James Stewart .50 1.25
OM13 Mark Brunell .60 1.50
OM14 Priest Holmes .50 1.25
OM15 Randy Moss .60 1.50
OM16 Tom Brady 4.00 10.00
OM17 Drew Bledsoe .60 1.50
OM18 Curtis Martin .60 1.50
OM19 Michael Strahan .60 1.50
OM20 Vinny Testaverde .50 1.25
OM21 Jerry Rice 1.50 4.00
OM22 Rich Gannon .60 1.50
OM23 Tim Brown .75 2.00
OM24 Jerome Bettis .75 2.00
OM25 Kendrell Bell .50 1.25
OM26 Terrell Owens .60 1.50
OM27 Kurt Warner .60 1.50
OM28 Marshall Faulk .60 1.50
OM29 Eddie George .60 1.50
OM30 Darrell Green .75 2.00

2002 Upper Deck Ovation Standing O

Inserted at a rate of 1:12, this set showcases players with outstanding stats during the 2001 season.

COMPLETE SET (30) 15.00 40.00
STATED ODDS 1:12 HOB/RET
SO1 David Boston .50 1.25
SO2 Michael Vick .60 1.50
SO3 Jamal Lewis .60 1.50
SO4 Chris Weinke .50 1.25
SO5 Anthony Thomas .60 1.50
SO6 Jim Miller .50 1.25
SO7 Marty Booker .50 1.25
SO8 Peter Warrick .50 1.25
SO9 Emmitt Smith 1.25 3.00
SO10 Quincy Carter .50 1.25
SO11 Brian Griese .50 1.25
SO12 Mike Anderson .50 1.25
SO13 Rod Smith .60 1.50
SO14 Mike McMahon .50 1.25
SO15 Ahman Green .60 1.50
SO16 Edgerrin James .60 1.50
SO17 Marvin Harrison .60 1.50
SO18 Peyton Manning 2.00 5.00
SO19 Donovan McNabb .60 1.50
SO20 Freddie Mitchell .50 1.25
SO21 Jerome Bettis .75 2.00
SO22 Plaxico Burress .50 1.25
SO23 Doug Flutie .60 1.50
SO24 LaDainian Tomlinson .75 2.00
SO25 Garrison Hearst .50 1.25
SO26 Jeff Garcia .50 1.25
SO27 Terrell Owens .60 1.50
SO28 Shaun Alexander .50 1.25
SO29 Keyshawn Johnson .60 1.50
SO30 Rod Gardner .50 1.25

2002 Upper Deck Ovation Tried and True Jerseys

is set features game used jersey swatches, with each card inserted at a rate of 1:72.

STATED ODDS 1:72 HOB/RET
*GOLD/25: 1X TO 2.5X BASIC JSY
GOLD PRINT RUN 25 SER.#'d SETS
TTAT Amani Toomer 3.00 8.00
TTBF Brett Favre 10.00 25.00
TTBS Bruce Smith 4.00 10.00
TTCD Corey Dillon/57* 3.00 8.00
TTDM Dan Marino 10.00 25.00
TTEJ Edgerrin James 4.00 10.00
TTJB Jerome Bettis 5.00 12.00
TTJE John Elway 8.00 20.00
TTJR Jerry Rice SP 10.00 25.00
TTKW Kurt Warner 4.00 10.00
TTMH Marvin Harrison 4.00 10.00
TTMW Michael Westbrook 3.00 8.00
TTRM Randy Moss 4.00 10.00
TTTH Torry Holt 4.00 10.00

1999 Upper Deck PowerDeck

Realeased in mid October of 1999, The Powerdeck set features 60 cards. 30 of the cards were made on an actual CD ROM which features audio and video footage of both stars and rookies. Also within the set were autographed CD ROM cards which were signed by each respective player and hand nubered to on 50 of each on the card front. Also available were the autographed Walter Payton Game Jersey cards which featured a game used jersey swatch and an authentic autograph on the card front and hand numbered to only 34 of each made exclusively for the Powerdeck Product. CD ROM cards were available at a rate of 1 per pack. Also included was a one of one gold auxillary power cards done in gold foil.

COMPLETE SET (30) 25.00 60.00
PD1 Troy Aikman 1.25 3.00
PD2 Drew Bledsoe .75 2.00
PD3 Randy Moss .75 2.00
PD4 Barry Sanders 1.50 4.00
PD5 Brett Favre 2.00 5.00
PD6 Terrell Davis .75 2.00
PD7 Peyton Manning 3.00 8.00
PD8 Emmitt Smith 1.50 4.00
PD9 Dan Marino 2.00 5.00
PD10 Jake Plummer .60 1.50
PD11 Eddie George .75 2.00
PD12 Jerry Rice 2.50 6.00
PD13 Steve Young 1.25 3.00
PD14 Mark Brunell .75 2.00
PD15 Kordell Stewart .60 1.50
PD16 Keyshawn Johnson .75 2.00
PD17 Fred Taylor .60 1.50
PD18 Jamal Anderson .75 2.00
PD19 Cecil Collins .60 1.50
PD20 Ricky Williams 1.00 2.50
PD21 Tim Couch .75 2.00
PD22 Donovan McNabb 2.00 5.00
PD23 Akili Smith .60 1.50
PD24 Edgerrin James 1.00 2.50
PD25 Daunte Culpepper 1.00 2.50
PD26 Brock Huard .60 1.50
PD27 Torry Holt 1.25 3.00
PD28 David Boston .60 1.50
PD29 Cade McNown .60 1.50
PD30 Champ Bailey 1.25 3.00
CHKL Checklist Card .08 .25
WPPD W.Payton Jsy AU/34 1000.00 1500.00

1999 Upper Deck PowerDeck Auxiliary

ndomly inserted at a rate of aproximately two per pack, This is the parallel "paper card" sot to the CD ROM set which features full color action shots with key rookies such as Tim Couch and Cade Mcnown.

COMPLETE SET (30) 10.00 25.00
AUX1 Troy Aikman .50 1.25
AUX2 Drew Bledsoe .30 .75
AUX3 Randy Moss .30 .75
AUX4 Barry Sanders .60 1.50
AUX5 Brett Favre .75 2.00
AUX6 Terrell Davis .30 .75
AUX7 Peyton Manning 1.25 3.00
AUX8 Emmitt Smith .60 1.50
AUX9 Dan Marino .75 2.00
AUX10 Jake Plummer .25 .60
AUX11 Eddie George .30 .75
AUX12 Jerry Rice 1.00 2.50
AUX13 Steve Young .50 1.25
AUX14 Mark Brunell .30 .75
AUX15 Kordell Stewart .25 .60
AUX16 Keyshawn Johnson .30 .75
AUX17 Fred Taylor .25 .60
AUX18 Jamal Anderson .30 .75
AUX19 Cecil Collins .30 .75
AUX20 Ricky Williams .50 1.25
AUX21 Tim Couch .40 1.00
AUX22 Donovan McNabb 2.00 5.00
AUX23 Akili Smith .30 .75
AUX24 Edgerrin James .50 1.25
AUX25 Daunte Culpepper .50 1.25
AUX26 Brock Huard .30 .75
AUX27 Torry Holt .60 1.50
AUX28 David Boston .30 .75
AUX29 Cade McNown .30 .75
AUX30 Champ Bailey .60 1.50

1999 Upper Deck PowerDeck Auxiliary Gold

STATED PRINT RUN 1 SET

1999 Upper Deck PowerDeck Autographs

Randomly inserted in packs, This 13 card set fatures actual hand signed cards on an actual CD ROM card. Cards were hand numbered on card front to only 50 of each player made. Cards came with the Upper Deck hologram on the card front and a matching hologram on the certificate of authenticity. Key players who signed for this set include Dan Marino and Troy Aikman.

STATED PRINT RUN 50 SER.#'d SETS
AS Akili Smith 20.00 50.00
BH Brock Huard 20.00 50.00
CB Champ Bailey 50.00 100.00
CM Cade McNown 20.00 50.00
DC Daunte Culpepper 30.00 80.00
DM Dan Marino 100.00 200.00
EJ Edgerrin James 40.00 100.00
JP Jake Plummer 25.00 60.00
TA Troy Aikman 75.00 150.00
TC Tim Couch 25.00 60.00
TH Torry Holt 40.00 100.00

1999 Upper Deck PowerDeck Most Valuable Performances

ndomly inserted in packs at a rate of one in 287 packs, This 7 disc insert set features star players who have had MVP performances.

COMPLETE SET (7) 60.00 150.00
STATED ODDS 1:287
*AUXILIARY CARDS: .25X TO .6X CD-ROMS
AUXILIARY STATED ODDS 1:287
M1 Brett Favre 20.00 50.00
M2 Joe Montana 25.00 60.00
M3 John Elway 20.00 50.00
M4 Emmitt Smith 12.50 30.00
M5 Jamal Anderson 6.00 15.00
M6 Randy Moss 15.00 40.00
M7 Terrell Davis 6.00 15.00

1999 Upper Deck PowerDeck Powerful Moments

ndomly inserted at a rate of 1 in 23 packs, This 6 card set was done on an actual CD ROM and showcased key stars such as Dan Marino and Emmitt Smith.

COMPLETE SET (6) 25.00 60.00
STATED ODDS 1:23
*AUXILIARY CARDS: .25X TO .6X CD-ROMS
AUXILIARY STATED ODDS 1:23
P1 Joe Montana 7.50 20.00
P2 Terrell Davis 2.00 5.00
P3 John Elway 6.00 15.00
P4 Randy Moss 5.00 12.00
P5 Dan Marino 6.00 15.00
P6 Emmitt Smith 4.00 10.00

1999 Upper Deck PowerDeck Time Capsule

Randomly inserted in packs at a rate of 1 in 7 packs, This CD ROM cards insert set features color action shots of such stars as Emmitt Smith, Dan Marino and Tim Couch.

COMPLETE SET (6) 15.00 40.00
STATED ODDS 1:7
*AUXILIARY CARDS: .25X TO .6X CD's
AUXILIARY STATED ODDS 1:7
T1 Edgerrin James 6.00 15.00
T2 Barry Sanders 5.00 12.00
T3 Terrell Davis 1.50 4.00
T4 Emmitt Smith 3.00 8.00
T5 Dan Marino 5.00 12.00
T6 Tim Couch .75 2.00

1999 Upper Deck PowerDeck Athletes of the Century

These CD-Rom cards featuring four of the most prominent athletes of the 20th century were issued by Upper Deck in one boxed set. The cards are inserted into a computer and display various highlights of the player's career and his stats and other information.

COMPLETE SET (4) 8.00 20.00
3 Joe Montana 2.00 5.00

2004 Upper Deck Power Up

Upper Deck Power Up was initially released in mid-August 2004 as a retail-only product. The base set consists of 100-cards with no rookie cards. Boxes contained 24-packs of 6-cards and carried an S.R.P. of $1.99 per pack. Four parallel sets and two inserts can be found seeded in packs.

COMPLETE SET (100) 10.00 25.00
1 Emmitt Smith .40 1.00
2 Anquan Boldin .15 .40
3 Josh McCown .20 .50
4 Michael Vick .20 .50
5 Peerless Price .15 .40
6 Warrick Dunn .15 .40
7 Jamal Lewis .20 .50
8 Kyle Boller .15 .40
9 Ray Lewis .25 .60
10 Drew Bledsoe .20 .50
11 Travis Henry .15 .40
12 Eric Moulds .15 .40
13 Jake Delhomme .15 .40
14 Steve Smith .25 .60
15 Stephen Davis .15 .40
16 Anthony Thomas .20 .50
17 Marty Booker .15 .40
18 Rex Grossman .15 .40
19 Chad Johnson .15 .40
20 Rudi Johnson .15 .40
21 Jon Kitna .15 .40
22 Andre Davis .15 .40
23 Jeff Garcia .15 .40
24 William Green .15 .40
25 Antonio Bryant .20 .50
26 Quincy Carter .15 .40
27 Keyshawn Johnson .20 .50
28 Champ Bailey .20 .50
29 Jake Plummer .15 .40
30 Ashley Lelie .15 .40
31 Charles Rogers .15 .40
32 Joey Harrington .15 .40
33 Az-Zahir Hakim .15 .40
34 Brett Favre .50 1.25
35 Javon Walker .15 .40
36 Ahman Green .20 .50
37 David Carr .15 .40
38 Domanick Davis .15 .40
39 Andre Johnson .20 .50
40 Peyton Manning .60 1.50
41 Marvin Harrison .20 .50
42 Edgerrin James .20 .50
43 Byron Leftwich .15 .40
44 Fred Taylor .15 .40
45 Jimmy Smith .20 .50
46 Priest Holmes .15 .40
47 Trent Green .15 .40
48 Dante Hall .15 .40
49 Tony Gonzalez .20 .50
50 Ricky Williams .20 .50
51 Jay Fiedler .15 .40
52 Chris Chambers .15 .40
53 Daunte Culpepper .20 .50
54 Randy Moss .20 .50
55 Onterrio Smith .15 .40
56 Troy Brown .15 .40
57 Deion Branch .15 .40
58 Tom Brady 1.00 2.50
59 Deuce McAllister .20 .50
60 Aaron Brooks .15 .40
61 Joe Horn .15 .40
62 Jeremy Shockey .15 .40
63 Amani Toomer .15 .40
64 Tiki Barber .20 .50
65 Chad Pennington .15 .40
66 Santana Moss .20 .50
67 Curtis Martin .20 .50
68 Rich Gannon .20 .50
69 Jerry Rice .50 1.25
70 Tim Brown .25 .60
71 Jerry Porter .15 .40
72 Donovan McNabb .20 .50
73 Terrell Owens .20 .50
74 Jevon Kearse .15 .40
75 Hines Ward .20 .50
76 Jerome Bettis .25 .60
77 Tommy Maddox .15 .40
78 Plaxico Burress .15 .40
79 LaDainian Tomlinson .25 .60
80 Antonio Gates .25 .60
81 Drew Brees .25 .60
82 Tim Rattay .15 .40
83 Brandon Lloyd .20 .50
84 Kevan Barlow .15 .40
85 Matt Hasselbeck .15 .40
86 Shaun Alexander .15 .40
87 Koren Robinson .15 .40
88 Marshall Faulk .20 .50
89 Torry Holt .20 .50
90 Marc Bulger .15 .40
91 Isaac Bruce .25 .60
92 Brad Johnson .20 .50
93 Charlie Garner .20 .50
94 Keenan McCardell .15 .40
95 Steve McNair .20 .50
96 Eddie George .20 .50
97 Derrick Mason .15 .40
98 Mark Brunell .20 .50
99 Laveranues Coles .15 .40
100 Clinton Portis .15 .40

2004 Upper Deck Power Up Blue

*BLUE: 6X TO 15X BASIC CARDS
OVERALL PARALLEL STATED ODDS 1:4
BLUE WORTH 1000 POINTS EACH

2004 Upper Deck Power Up Green

*GREENS: 2X TO 5X BASIC CARDS
OVERALL PARALLEL STATED ODDS 1:4
GREEN WORTH 100 POINTS EACH

2004 Upper Deck Power Up Orange

RANGE: 3X TO 8X BASIC CARDS
OVERALL PARALLEL STATED ODDS 1:4
ORANGE WORTH 250 POINTS EACH

2004 Upper Deck Power Up Red

EDS: 5X TO 12X BASIC CARDS
OVERALL PARALLEL STATED ODDS 1:4
RED WORTH 500 POINTS EACH

2004 Upper Deck Power Up Shining Through

COMPLETE SET (30) 7.50 20.00
STATED ODDS 1:1
ST1 Anquan Boldin .25 .60
ST2 Michael Vick .30 .75
ST3 Jamal Lewis .30 .75
ST4 Aaron Brooks .25 .60
ST5 DeShaun Foster .30 .75
ST6 Rex Grossman .25 .60
ST7 Rudi Johnson .25 .60
ST8 Andre Davis .25 .60
ST9 Antonio Bryant .30 .75
ST10 Clinton Portis .25 .60
ST11 Brett Favre .75 2.00
ST12 David Carr .25 .60
ST13 Marvin Harrison .30 .75
ST14 Byron Leftwich .25 .60
ST15 Priest Holmes .25 .60
ST16 Dante Hall .25 .60
ST17 Chris Chambers .25 .60
ST18 Daunte Culpepper .30 .75
ST19 Tom Brady 1.50 4.00
ST20 Deuce McAllister .30 .75
ST21 Jeremy Shockey .25 .60
ST22 Santana Moss .30 .75
ST23 Jerry Rice .75 2.00
ST24 Donovan McNabb .30 .75
ST25 Plaxico Burress .25 .60
ST26 LaDainian Tomlinson .40 1.00
ST27 Koren Robinson .25 .60
ST28 Ahman Green .30 .75
ST29 Steve McNair .30 .75
ST30 Laveranues Coles .25 .60

2004 Upper Deck Power Up Stickers

MPLETE SET (30) 20.00 50.00
STATED ODDS 1:6
PU1 Emmitt Smith 1.25 3.00
PU2 Michael Vick .60 1.50
PU3 Kyle Boller .50 1.25
PU4 Drew Bledsoe .60 1.50
PU5 Jake Delhomme .50 1.25
PU6 Brian Urlacher .75 2.00
PU7 Carson Palmer .60 1.50
PU8 Quincy Carter .50 1.25
PU9 Jake Plummer .50 1.25
PU10 Joey Harrington .50 1.25
PU11 Brett Favre 1.50 4.00
PU12 David Carr .50 1.25
PU13 Peyton Manning 2.00 5.00
PU14 Byron Leftwich .50 1.25
PU15 Priest Holmes .50 1.25
PU16 Ricky Williams .60 1.50
PU17 Randy Moss .60 1.50
PU18 Tom Brady 3.00 8.00
PU19 Deuce McAllister .60 1.50
PU20 Chad Pennington .50 1.25
PU21 Jeremy Shockey .50 1.25
PU22 Jerry Rice 1.50 4.00
PU23 Donovan McNabb .60 1.50
PU24 Hines Ward .60 1.50
PU25 LaDainian Tomlinson .75 2.00
PU26 Kevan Barlow .50 1.25
PU27 Matt Hasselbeck .50 1.25
PU28 Marshall Faulk .60 1.50
PU29 Steve McNair .60 1.50
PU30 Clinton Portis .50 1.25

2007 Upper Deck Premier

This 162-card set was released in September, 2007. The set was issued into the hobby in a pack (box) with a $300 SRP. Cards numbered 1-100 feature veterans which were issued to a stated print run of 225 serial numbered sets while cards numbered 101-163 feature 2007 NFL Rookies. Within that grouping, cards numbered 101-130 were signed and those cards were issued to a stated print run of 225 serial numbered sets and cards numbered 131-163 had both a signature and a player-worn jersey swatch and those cards were issued to a stated print run of 199 serial numbered sets. Card number 135 was not issued in this set.

STATED PRINT RUN 225 SER.#'d SETS
JSY AU RC PRINT RUN 55-199
1 Matt Leinart 2.00 5.00
2 Anquan Boldin 2.00 5.00
3 Larry Fitzgerald 2.50 6.00
4 Edgerrin James 2.50 6.00
5 Michael Vick 2.50 6.00
6 Warrick Dunn 2.00 5.00
7 Alge Crumpler 2.50 6.00
8 Steve McNair 2.50 6.00
9 Mark Clayton 2.00 5.00
10 Ray Lewis 3.00 8.00
11 J.P. Losman 2.00 5.00
12 Lee Evans 2.50 6.00
13 Anthony Thomas 2.00 5.00
14 Jake Delhomme 2.00 5.00
15 Steve Smith 2.50 6.00
16 Julius Peppers 2.50 6.00
17 Brian Urlacher 3.00 8.00
18 Cedric Benson 2.00 5.00
19 Rex Grossman 2.00 5.00
20 Carson Palmer 2.50 6.00
21 Chad Johnson 2.00 5.00
22 Rudi Johnson 2.00 5.00
23 Charlie Frye 2.50 6.00
24 Braylon Edwards 2.00 5.00
25 Jamal Lewis 2.50 6.00
26 Tony Romo 4.00 10.00
27 Terrell Owens 2.50 6.00
28 Julius Jones 2.00 5.00
29 Marion Barber 2.50 6.00
30 Jay Cutler 2.00 5.00
31 Javon Walker 2.50 6.00
32 Champ Bailey 2.50 6.00
33 Roy Williams WR 2.00 5.00
34 Jon Kitna 2.00 5.00
35 Tatum Bell 2.00 5.00
36 Greg Jennings 2.00 5.00
37 Brett Favre 6.00 15.00
38 Donald Driver 2.50 6.00
39 Matt Schaub 2.00 5.00
40 Andre Johnson 2.50 6.00
41 Ahman Green 2.50 6.00
42 Peyton Manning 8.00 20.00
43 Marvin Harrison 2.50 6.00
44 Reggie Wayne 2.50 6.00
45 Joseph Addai 2.00 5.00
46 Fred Taylor 2.00 5.00
47 Maurice Jones-Drew 2.00 5.00
48 Byron Leftwich 2.00 5.00
49 Damon Huard 2.50 6.00
50 Larry Johnson 2.00 5.00
51 Tony Gonzalez 2.50 6.00
52 Zach Thomas 2.50 6.00
53 Ronnie Brown 2.00 5.00
54 Chris Chambers 2.00 5.00
55 Tarvaris Jackson 2.00 5.00
56 Chester Taylor 2.00 5.00
57 Troy Williamson 2.00 5.00
58 Tom Brady 10.00 25.00
59 Donte Stallworth 2.50 6.00
60 Laurence Maroney 2.50 6.00
61 Reggie Bush 2.00 5.00
62 Deuce McAllister 2.50 6.00
63 Drew Brees 3.00 8.00
64 Marques Colston 2.00 5.00
65 Eli Manning 2.50 6.00
66 Plaxico Burress 2.00 5.00
67 Brandon Jacobs 2.00 5.00
68 Chad Pennington 2.00 5.00
69 Thomas Jones 2.00 5.00
70 Laveranues Coles 2.00 5.00
71 LaMont Jordan 2.50 6.00
72 Ronald Curry 2.00 5.00
73 Dominic Rhodes 2.00 5.00
74 Donovan McNabb 2.50 6.00
75 Brian Westbrook 2.00 5.00
76 Reggie Brown 2.00 5.00
77 Ben Roethlisberger 3.00 8.00
78 Hines Ward 2.50 6.00
79 Willie Parker 2.50 6.00
80 LaDainian Tomlinson 3.00 8.00
81 Philip Rivers 3.00 8.00
82 Antonio Gates 3.00 8.00
83 Frank Gore 2.50 6.00
84 Alex Smith QB 2.50 6.00
85 Ashley Lelie 2.50 6.00
86 Matt Hasselbeck 2.00 5.00
87 Shaun Alexander 2.00 5.00
88 Deion Branch 2.00 5.00
89 Marc Bulger 2.00 5.00
90 Torry Holt 2.50 6.00
91 Steven Jackson 2.00 5.00
92 Cadillac Williams 2.50 6.00
93 Chris Simms 2.00 5.00
94 Joey Galloway 2.50 6.00
95 Vince Young 2.00 5.00
96 David Givens 2.00 5.00
97 LenDale White 2.50 6.00
98 Jason Campbell 2.00 5.00
99 Santana Moss 2.50 6.00
100 Clinton Portis 2.00 5.00
101 Craig Buster Davis AU RC 5.00 12.00
102 Amobi Okoye AU RC 6.00 15.00
103 Aundrae Allison AU RC 5.00 12.00
104 Chansi Stuckey AU RC 6.00 15.00
105 LaRon Landry AU RC 8.00 20.00
106 Brandon Meriweather AU RC 6.00 15.00
107 Courtney Taylor AU RC 5.00 12.00
108 Dallas Baker AU RC 5.00 12.00
109 Darius Walker AU RC 5.00 12.00
110 David Ball AU RC 5.00 12.00
111 Darrelle Revis AU RC 6.00 15.00
112 David Clowney AU RC 5.00 12.00
113 David Irons AU RC 5.00 12.00
114 Daymeion Hughes AU RC 5.00 12.00

115 Jamaal Anderson AU RC 6.00 15.00
116 Dwayne Wright AU RC 5.00 12.00
117 Jordan Palmer AU RC 6.00 15.00
118 Eric Wright AU RC 5.00 12.00
119 Gary Russell AU RC 6.00 15.00
120 Joel Filani AU RC 5.00 12.00
121 Kenneth Darby AU RC 5.00 12.00
122 Legedu Naanee AU RC 6.00 15.00
123 Marcus McCauley AU RC 5.00 12.00
124 Paul Posluszny AU RC 5.00 12.00
125 Quentin Moses AU RC 5.00 12.00
126 Jeff Rowe AU RC 5.00 12.00
127 Matt Moore AU RC 8.00 20.00
128 Rhema McKnight AU RC 5.00 12.00
129 Scott Chandler AU RC 8.00 20.00
130 Tyrone Moss AU RC 5.00 12.00
131 A.Peterson JSY AU/55 RC 150.00 300.00
132 Patrick Willis JSY AU RC 10.00 25.00
133 Anthony Gonzalez JSY AU RC 6.00 15.00
134 Antonio Pittman JSY AU RC 6.00 15.00
136 Brady Quinn JSY AU RC 6.00 15.00
137 Brandon Jackson JSY AU RC 6.00 15.00
138 Brian Leonard JSY AU/125 RC 6.00 15.00
139 Calvin Johnson JSY AU RC 60.00 125.00
140 Paul Williams JSY AU RC 6.00 15.00
141 Johnnie Lee Higgins JSY AU RC 6.00 15.00
142 Trent Edwards JSY AU RC 6.00 15.00
143 Greg Olsen JSY AU RC 10.00 25.00
144 Drew Stanton JSY AU RC 6.00 15.00
145 Dwayne Bowe JSY AU RC 6.00 15.00
146 Dwayne Jarrett JSY AU RC 8.00 20.00
147 Yamon Figurs JSY AU RC 6.00 15.00
148 Chris Henry RB JSY AU RC 6.00 15.00
149 JaMarcus Russell JSY AU RC 6.00 15.00
150 Joe Thomas JSY AU RC 10.00 25.00
151 Gaines Adams JSY AU RC 8.00 20.00
152 Lorenzo Booker JSY AU RC 8.00 20.00
153 Kenny Irons JSY AU RC 6.00 15.00
154 Kevin Kolb JSY AU RC 8.00 20.00
155 John Beck JSY AU RC 6.00 15.00
156 Garrett Wolfe JSY AU RC 6.00 15.00
157 Marshawn Lynch JSY AU RC 20.00 40.00
158 Michael Bush JSY AU RC 6.00 15.00
159 Robert Meachem JSY AU RC 8.00 20.00
160 Sidney Rice JSY AU RC 8.00 20.00
161 Steve Smith JSY AU RC 6.00 15.00
162 Ted Ginn Jr. JSY AU RC 8.00 20.00
163 Tony Hunt JSY AU RC 6.00 15.00

2007 Upper Deck Premier Rookie Autographed Materials Blue

LUE/99: .5X TO 1.2X BASIC RCs
BLUE PRINT RUN 99 SER.#'d SETS
131 Adrian Peterson 125.00 250.00

2007 Upper Deck Premier Rookie Autographed Materials Bronze

*BRONZE/125: .4X TO 1X BASIC RCs
BRONZE PRINT RUN 125 SER.#'d SETS
131 Adrian Peterson 100.00 200.00

2007 Upper Deck Premier Rookie Autographed Materials Gold

GOLD PRINT RUN 175 SER.#'d SETS
UNPRICED NFL LOGO PRINT RUN 1
131 Adrian Peterson 100.00 200.00

2007 Upper Deck Premier Rookie Autographed Materials Green Patches

*PATCH/50: .5X TO 1.2X BASIC RCs
PATCHES PRINT RUN 50 SER.#'d SETS
131 Adrian Peterson 150.00 300.00

2007 Upper Deck Premier Foursomes Autographs

FOURSOME AUTO PRINT RUN 15
1 Gonz/Mclnn/Dvls/Bowe 15.00 40.00
2 Jhnsn/Tmlin/Ptrsn/Lynch 150.00 300.00
3 Single/Grnwd/Willis/Timm 50.00 100.00
4 P.Mann/Rivrs/Qnn/Russ 75.00 150.00
5 Jhnsn/Clstn/Jhnsn/Jarrett
6 Brees/Eli/Cmpbl/A.Smith 75.00 150.00
7 Namth/Mntn/Mrino/Theis 200.00 350.00
8 Stntn/Bck/Kolb/Edwrds
9 Andr/Adms/Okoye/Crrikr
10 Nelson/Hall/Revis/Griffin 12.00 30.00

2007 Upper Deck Premier Impressions Autographs Gold

GOLD PRINT RUN 25-99
*BRONZE/75: .5X TO 1.2X BASIC AU/99
*BRONZE/25: .5X TO 1.2X BASIC AU/50
BRONZE PRINT RUN 10-75
UNPRICED GOLD HOLOFOIL PRINT RUN 1
PIBF Brett Favre/25 125.00 200.00
PIBL Brian Leonard/99 5.00 12.00
PIBU Reggie Bush/50 8.00 20.00
PICW Cadillac Williams/50 10.00 25.00
PIDB David Ball/99 5.00 12.00
PIDC David Clowney/99 5.00 12.00
PIDS Drew Stanton/99 5.00 12.00
PIDW Dwayne Wright/99 5.00 12.00
PIES Emmitt Smith/25 100.00 200.00
PIGW Garrett Wolfe/99 5.00 12.00
PIJA Joseph Addai/50 8.00 20.00
PIJF Joel Filani/99 5.00 12.00
PIJP Jordan Palmer/99 6.00 15.00
PIJR JaMarcus Russell/50 8.00 20.00
PIKD Kenneth Darby/99 5.00 12.00
PILJ Larry Johnson/50 8.00 20.00
PILW LaMarr Woodley/99 10.00 25.00
PIMB Marc Bulger/50 8.00 20.00
PIPW Patrick Willis/99 8.00 20.00
PIRB Reggie Brown/99 5.00 12.00
PISY Selvin Young/99 5.00 12.00
PITE Trent Edwards/99 5.00 12.00
PITH Tony Hunt/99 5.00 12.00
PITP Tyler Palko/99 8.00 20.00
PIZM Zach Miller/99 5.00 12.00

2007 Upper Deck Premier Insignias Autographs Gold

LD PRINT RUN 10-99
*BRONZE/75: .5X TO 1.2X BASIC AU/99
*BRONZE/25: .5X TO 1.2X BASIC AU/50
BRONZE PRINT RUN 5-75
INAG Anthony Gonzalez/99 5.00 12.00
INBE Drew Bennett/99 5.00 12.00
INBJ Bo Jackson/25 60.00 120.00
INBR Drew Brees/25 50.00 100.00
INCJ Calvin Johnson/10 150.00 300.00
INCS Chansi Stuckey/99 6.00 15.00
INDB Dallas Baker/99 5.00 12.00
INDH Daymeion Hughes/99 5.00 12.00
INDW Darius Walker/99 5.00 12.00
INEM Eli Manning/25 50.00 80.00
INGA Gaines Adams/99 6.00 15.00
INIS Isaiah Stanback/99 5.00 12.00
INJA Jamaal Anderson/99 6.00 15.00
INJB John Beck/99 5.00 12.00
INJC Jerricho Cotchery/99 5.00 12.00
INJH Johnnie Lee Higgins/99 5.00 12.00
INMM Marcus McCauley/99 5.00 12.00
INMO Matt Moore/99 8.00 20.00
INMS Matt Schaub/50 12.00 30.00
INQM Quentin Moses/99 5.00 12.00
INRB Reggie Bush/50 25.00 60.00
INSC Scott Chandler/99 8.00 20.00
INSI Mike Singletary/50 15.00 40.00
INWY DeShawn Wynn/99 5.00 12.00

2007 Upper Deck Premier Noteworthy Autographs Gold

GOLD PRINT RUN 25-99
*BRONZE/75: .5X TO 1.2X GOLD AU/99
*BRONZE/25: .5X TO 1.2X GOLD AU/50
*BRONZE/15: .5X TO 1.2X GOLD AU/25
NAA Aundrae Allison 6.00 15.00
NAB Alan Branch 6.00 15.00
NAP Adrian Peterson/25 125.00 250.00
NAS Alex Smith QB/25 12.00 30.00
NBM Brandon Meriweather 6.00 15.00
NCH Chris Henry RB 8.00 20.00
NCJ Chad Johnson/50 10.00 25.00
NCT Chester Taylor 6.00 15.00
NDB David Ball 5.00 12.00
NDD Donald Driver 15.00 30.00
NDP Drew Pearson 8.00 20.00
NEW Eric Wright 5.00 12.00
NJR Jeff Rowe 5.00 12.00
NJT Joe Thomas 8.00 20.00
NKK Kevin Kolb 6.00 15.00
NLL LaRon Landry 8.00 20.00
NLN Legedu Naanee 6.00 15.00
NLT L.Tomlinson/50 EXCH 25.00 60.00
NMG Michael Griffin 8.00 20.00
NML Matt Leinart/50 10.00 25.00
NRC Roger Craig 8.00 20.00
NSR Sidney Rice 10.00 25.00
NTH T.J. Houshmandzadeh/50 8.00 20.00
NTM Tyrone Moss 5.00 12.00
NWP Willie Parker/50 10.00 25.00

2007 Upper Deck Premier Octographs Autographs

UNPRICED OCTOGRAPHS PRINT RUN 5

2007 Upper Deck Premier Pairings Autographs

STATED PRINT RUN 25 SER.#'d SETS
1 J.Anderson/A.Carriker 12.00 30.00
2 G.Adams/A.Okoye 12.00 30.00
3 A.Allison/C.Stuckey 12.00 30.00
4 R.Brown/D.Bennett 12.00 30.00
6 R.Brown/B.Leonard 12.00 30.00
7 D.Brees/E.Manning 60.00 120.00
8 M.Bulger/J.Palmer 12.00 30.00
9 R.Craig/F.Gore 15.00 40.00
10 D.Clowney/J.Higgins 12.00 30.00
11 M.Colston/D.Jarrett
12 J.Campbell/C.Taylor 15.00 40.00
13 C.Davis/D.Bowe 20.00 50.00
14 C.Davis/L.Naanee 15.00 40.00
15 K.Darby/S.Young 15.00 40.00
17 T.Ginn Jr./T.Smith
18 L.Greenwood/L.Timmons 15.00 40.00
19 L.Hall/A.Branch 12.00 30.00
20 T.Houshmandzadeh/J.Filani 12.00 30.00
21 L.Hall/D.Revis 15.00 40.00
22 K.Irons/D.Irons 12.00 30.00
23 L.Johnson/M.Bush 20.00 50.00
24 D.Jackson/D.Driver 20.00 50.00
25 C.Johnson/R.Meachem 15.00 40.00
26 D.Jarrett/S.Smith USC 20.00 50.00
27 K.Kolb/T.Edwards 12.00 30.00
28 C.Leak/D.Baker 15.00 40.00
29 L.Landry/M.Griffin 15.00 40.00
30 C.Leak/T.Smith
31 R.Meachem/S.Rice 20.00 50.00
32 R.Nelson/B.Meriweather 10.00 25.00
33 G.Olsen/Z.Miller 10.00 25.00
34 W.Parker/L.Booker 15.00 40.00
35 A.Pittman/A.Gonzalez 15.00 40.00
36 R.Bush/M.Lynch 30.00 80.00
37 B.Quinn/J.Russell 40.00 100.00
38 B.Quinn/D.Walker 25.00 60.00
40 D.Stanton/J.Beck 25.00 50.00
43 C.Taylor/B.Jackson 12.00 30.00
44 I.Timmons/L.Woodley 20.00 50.00
45 R.Wayne/J.Addai 25.00 60.00
46 P.Williams/Y.Figurs 12.00 30.00
47 C.Williams/T.Hunt 15.00 40.00
48 E.Wright/M.McCauley 10.00 25.00
49 P.Willis/P.Posluszny 20.00 50.00
50 J.Zabransky/L.Naanee 15.00 40.00

2007 Upper Deck Premier Patches Dual

STATED PRINT RUN 35-99
*GOLD/75: .4X TO 1X BASIC INSERTS
GOLD PRINT RUN 15-75
*PLATINUM/15-25: .6X TO 15X BASIC INSERTS
PLATINUM PRINT RUN 15-25
UNPRICED MASTERPIECE PRINT RUN
PP2AB Anquan Boldin 5.00 12.00
PP2AG Ahman Green 6.00 15.00
PP2AP Adrian Peterson 8.00 20.00
PP2BF Brett Favre 15.00 40.00
PP2BL Brian Leonard 2.50 6.00
PP2BO Dwayne Bowe 2.50 6.00
PP2BQ Brady Quinn 2.50 6.00
PP2BU Brian Urlacher 10.00 25.00
PP2CJ Calvin Johnson 8.00 20.00
PP2CP Chad Pennington 5.00 12.00
PP2CT Chester Taylor 5.00 12.00
PP2DB Drew Brees 8.00 20.00
PP2DC David Carr 5.00 12.00
PP2DJ Dwayne Jarrett 3.00 8.00
PP2DM Deuce McAllister 6.00 15.00
PP2DS Drew Stanton 2.50 6.00
PP2DW DeAngelo Williams/35 6.00 15.00
PP2EJ Edgerrin James 6.00 15.00
PP2EV Lee Evans 6.00 15.00
PP2FT Fred Taylor 5.00 12.00
PP2GI Ted Ginn Jr. 3.00 8.00
PP2GO Anthony Gonzalez 2.50 6.00
PP2GR Trent Green 5.00 12.00
PP2HW Hines Ward 6.00 15.00
PP2JC Jay Cutler/35 6.00 15.00
PP2JH Joe Horn 5.00 12.00
PP2JO Chad Johnson 5.00 12.00
PP2JR JaMarcus Russell 2.50 6.00
PP2JS Jeremy Shockey 5.00 12.00
PP2LA LaMont Jordan 6.00 15.00
PP2LE Byron Leftwich 5.00 12.00
PP2LJ Larry Johnson 5.00 12.00
PP2LT LaDainian Tomlinson 8.00 20.00
PP2LY Marshawn Lynch 5.00 12.00
PP2MB Michael Bush 2.50 6.00
PP2MC Donovan McNabb 6.00 15.00
PP2MD Maurice Jones-Drew 5.00 12.00
PP2MH Matt Hasselbeck 5.00 12.00
PP2ML Matt Leinart 5.00 12.00
PP2PB Plaxico Burress 5.00 12.00
PP2PH Priest Holmes 6.00 15.00
PP2PR Philip Rivers 8.00 20.00
PP2RB Ronnie Brown 5.00 12.00
PP2RM Robert Meachem 3.00 8.00
PP2SJ Steven Jackson 5.00 12.00
PP2SR Sidney Rice 3.00 8.00
PP2TB Tom Brady 12.00 30.00
PP2TG Tony Gonzalez 6.00 15.00
PP2TH Tony Hunt 5.00 12.00
PP2TO Terrell Owens 6.00 15.00

2007 Upper Deck Premier Patches Dual Autographs

STATED PRINT RUN 25 SER.#'d SETS
PP2AB Anquan Boldin 12.00 30.00
PP2AP Adrian Peterson 125.00 250.00
PP2BF Brett Favre 125.00 250.00
PP2BL Brian Leonard 12.00 30.00
PP2BO Dwayne Bowe 15.00 40.00
PP2BQ Brady Quinn 12.00 30.00
PP2CJ Calvin Johnson 90.00 150.00
PP2CT Chester Taylor 12.00 30.00
PP2DB Drew Brees 50.00 100.00
PP2DJ Dwayne Jarrett 15.00 40.00
PP2DS Drew Stanton 12.00 30.00
PP2EV Lee Evans 15.00 40.00
PP2GI Ted Ginn Jr. 15.00 40.00
PP2GO Anthony Gonzalez 12.00 30.00
PP2JO Chad Johnson 12.00 30.00
PP2JR JaMarcus Russell 12.00 30.00
PP2LJ Larry Johnson 12.00 30.00
PP2LT LaDainian Tomlinson 40.00 80.00
PP2LY Marshawn Lynch 50.00 120.00
PP2MB Michael Bush 12.00 30.00
PP2MC Donovan McNabb
PP2ML Matt Leinart 12.00 30.00
PP2RB Ronnie Brown 12.00 30.00
PP2RM Robert Meachem 15.00 40.00
PP2SR Sidney Rice 15.00 40.00
PP2TB Tom Brady

2007 Upper Deck Premier Patches Triple

STATED PRINT RUN 99 SER.#'d SETS
*GOLD/75: .4X TO 1X BASIC INSERTS
GOLD PRINT RUN 75 SER.#'d SETS
*PLATINUM/10: .8X TO 2X BASIC INSERTS
PLATINUM PRINT RUN 10 SER.#'d SETS
UNPRICED MASTERPIECE PRINT RUN 1
PP3AP Adrian Peterson 8.00 20.00
PP3AS Alex Smith QB 6.00 15.00
PP3BJ Brandon Jackson 2.50 6.00
PP3BO Dwayne Bowe 2.50 6.00
PP3BQ Brady Quinn 2.50 6.00
PP3BR Ben Roethlisberger 10.00 25.00
PP3CB Champ Bailey 6.00 15.00
PP3CJ Chad Johnson 5.00 12.00
PP3CM Curtis Martin 6.00 15.00
PP3CP Carson Palmer 6.00 15.00
PP3DB Drew Brees 8.00 20.00
PP3DC Daunte Culpepper 6.00 15.00
PP3DJ Dwayne Jarrett 3.00 8.00
PP3DM Deuce McAllister 6.00 15.00
PP3EJ Edgerrin James 6.00 15.00
PP3EM Eli Manning 6.00 15.00
PP3FG Frank Gore 6.00 15.00
PP3GA Gaines Adams 5.00 12.00
PP3JA Joseph Addai 5.00 12.00
PP3JL Jamal Lewis 6.00 15.00
PP3JO Calvin Johnson 8.00 20.00
PP3JR JaMarcus Russell 2.50 6.00
PP3JS Jeremy Shockey 5.00 12.00
PP3LT LaDainian Tomlinson 8.00 20.00
PP3MB Marc Bulger 5.00 12.00
PP3MC Donovan McNabb 6.00 15.00
PP3MF Marshall Faulk 6.00 15.00
PP3MH Marvin Harrison 6.00 15.00
PP3ML Marshawn Lynch 5.00 12.00
PP3MV Michael Vick 6.00 15.00
PP3PE Chad Pennington 5.00 12.00
PP3PM Peyton Manning 20.00 50.00
PP3PO Clinton Portis 5.00 12.00
PP3RB Reggie Bush 5.00 12.00
PP3RJ Rudi Johnson 5.00 12.00
PP3RM Robert Meachem 3.00 8.00
PP3SA Shaun Alexander 5.00 12.00
PP3SH Santonio Holmes 5.00 12.00
PP3SM Shawne Merriman 5.00 12.00
PP3SR Sidney Rice 3.00 8.00
PP3SS Steve Smith USC 2.50 6.00
PP3TB Tom Brady 12.00 30.00
PP3TE Trent Edwards 2.50 6.00
PP3TG Ted Ginn Jr. 3.00 8.00
PP3TH Torry Holt 6.00 15.00
PP3TR Tony Romo 10.00 25.00
PP3TS Troy Smith 2.50 6.00
PP3VY Vince Young 5.00 12.00
PP3WM Willis McGahee 5.00 12.00
PP3WP Willie Parker 6.00 15.00

2007 Upper Deck Premier Patches Triple Autographs

TRIPLE PATCH AU PRINT RUN 5-15
PP3BQ Brady Quinn 12.00 30.00
PP3DB Drew Brees 50.00 100.00
PP3EM Eli Manning 50.00 100.00
PP3JA Joseph Addai 15.00 40.00
PP3JO Calvin Johnson 40.00 100.00
PP3JR JaMarcus Russell 12.00 30.00
PP3PM Peyton Manning 60.00 120.00
PP3RB Reggie Bush 15.00 40.00

2007 Upper Deck Premier Penmanship Autographs Gold

*BRONZE/50-75: .5X TO 1.2X BASIC AU/99
*BRONZE/25: .5X TO 1.2X BASIC AU/50
*BRONZE/15: .5X TO 1.2X BASIC AU/25
*GOLD HOLO/50: .6X TO 1.5X GOLD AU/99
*GOLD HOLO/25: .8X TO 2X GOLD AU/99
PPAA Aundrae Allison/99 5.00 12.00
PPAB Alan Branch/99 5.00 12.00
PPAD Joseph Addai/50 8.00 20.00
PPAG Anthony Gonzalez/99 5.00 12.00
PPAN Anquan Boldin/50 8.00 20.00
PPAO Amobi Okoye/99 6.00 15.00
PPAP Adrian Peterson/50 75.00 150.00
PPBA David Ball/99 5.00 12.00
PPBF Brett Favre/25 100.00 200.00
PPBJ Brandon Jackson/99 5.00 12.00
PPBL Brian Leonard/99 5.00 12.00
PPBO Bo Jackson/25 40.00 80.00
PPBQ Brady Quinn/25 6.00 15.00
PPBR Drew Brees/25
PPBU Marc Bulger/50 8.00 20.00
PPCB Champ Bailey/99 8.00 20.00
PPCD Craig Buster Davis/99 5.00 12.00
PPCH Chris Henry RB/99 5.00 12.00
PPCL Chris Leak/99 5.00 12.00
PPCM Curtis Martin/50
PPCS Chansi Stuckey/99 6.00 15.00
PPCT Courtney Taylor/99 5.00 12.00
PPCW Cadillac Williams/50
PPDB Dallas Baker/99 5.00 12.00
PPDC David Clowney/99 5.00 12.00
PPDD Donald Driver/99 15.00 40.00
PPDH Daymeion Hughes/99 5.00 12.00
PPDJ Dwayne Jarrett/99 6.00 15.00
PPDM Dan Marino/50 75.00 150.00
PPDP Drew Pearson/99 10.00 25.00
PPDR Darrelle Revis/99 10.00 25.00
PPDS Drew Stanton/99 5.00 12.00
PPDW Darius Walker/99 5.00 12.00
PPES Emmitt Smith/25 100.00 200.00
PPEW Eric Wright/99 5.00 12.00
PPFG Frank Gore/50 10.00 25.00
PPGA Gaines Adams/99 6.00 15.00
PPGO Greg Olsen/99 8.00 20.00
PPGW Garrett Wolfe/99 5.00 12.00
PPHI Johnnie Lee Higgins/99 5.00 12.00
PPHO T.J. Houshmandzadeh/50 8.00 20.00
PPIS Isaiah Stanback/99 5.00 12.00
PPJA Jamaal Anderson/99 6.00 15.00
PPJB John Beck/99 5.00 12.00
PPJC Jason Campbell/99 8.00 20.00
PPJF Joel Filani/99 5.00 12.00
PPJH Jason Hill/99 5.00 12.00
PPJO Chad Johnson/50 8.00 20.00
PPJP Jordan Palmer/99 6.00 15.00
PPJR Jeff Rowe/99 5.00 12.00
PPJT Joe Thomas/99 8.00 20.00
PPJZ Jared Zabransky/99 5.00 12.00
PPKD Kenneth Darby/99 5.00 12.00
PPKI Kenny Irons/99 5.00 12.00
PPKK Kevin Kolb/99 6.00 15.00
PPKS Kolby Smith/99 5.00 12.00
PPLB Lorenzo Booker/99 6.00 15.00
PPLE Lee Evans/50 10.00 25.00
PPLG L.C. Greenwood/99 10.00 25.00
PPLH Leon Hall/99 5.00 12.00
PPLJ Larry Johnson/50 8.00 20.00
PPLL LaRon Landry/99 8.00 20.00
PPLT Lawrence Timmons/99 8.00 20.00
PPLW LaMarr Woodley/99 10.00 25.00
PPMA Matt Leinart/50 8.00 20.00
PPMB Michael Bush/99 5.00 12.00
PPMC Marques Colston/99
PPME Robert Meachem/75 6.00 15.00
PPMG Michael Griffin/99 5.00 12.00
PPML Marshawn Lynch/50 15.00 40.00
PPMS Matt Schaub/50 8.00 20.00
PPPH Paul Hornung/50 12.00 30.00
PPPI Antonio Pittman/99 5.00 12.00
PPPM Peyton Manning/50 60.00 120.00
PPPP Paul Posluszny/99 5.00 12.00
PPPR Philip Rivers/50 12.00 30.00
PPPW Patrick Willis/99 8.00 20.00
PPRB Ronnie Brown/50 8.00 20.00
PPRC Roger Craig/99 6.00 15.00
PPRM Rhema McKnight/99 5.00 12.00
PPRN Reggie Nelson/99 5.00 12.00
PPRW Reggie Wayne/50 10.00 25.00
PPSC Scott Chandler/99 8.00 20.00
PPSI Mike Singletary/50 15.00 40.00
PPSR Sidney Rice/99 6.00 15.00
PPSS Steve Smith USC/99 5.00 12.00
PPSY Steve Young/50 20.00 50.00
PPTA Chester Taylor/99 5.00 12.00
PPTE Trent Edwards/99 5.00 12.00
PPTH Tony Hunt/99 5.00 12.00
PPTJ Joe Theismann/99 8.00 20.00
PPTM Tyrone Moss/99 5.00 12.00
PPTS Troy Smith/50
PPVY Vince Young/50 8.00 20.00
PPWI Paul Williams/99 5.00 12.00
PPWR Dwayne Wright/99 5.00 12.00
PPWY DeShawn Wynn/99 5.00 12.00
PPYF Yamon Figurs/99 5.00 12.00
PPZM Zach Miller/99 5.00 12.00

2007 Upper Deck Premier Preeminence Autographs Gold

GOLD PRINT RUN 25-99
*BRONZE/75: .5X TO 1.2X BASIC AU/99
*BRONZE/25: .5X TO 1.2X BASIC AU/50
*BRONZE/15: .5X TO 1.2X BASIC AU/25
BRONZE PRINT RUN 15-75
UNPRICED GOLD HOLOFOIL PRINT RUN 1
PREAB Anquan Boldin/50 10.00 25.00
PREAC Adam Carriker 6.00 15.00
PREAO Amobi Okoye 8.00 20.00
PREAP Antonio Pittman 6.00 15.00
PREBJ Brandon Jackson 10.00 25.00
PRECL Chris Leak 6.00 15.00
PRECT Courtney Taylor 6.00 15.00
PREDR Darrelle Revis 10.00 25.00
PREDT Drew Tate 8.00 20.00
PREFG Frank Gore/50 12.00 30.00
PREGO Greg Olsen 8.00 20.00
PREJC Jason Campbell 12.00 30.00
PREJZ Jared Zabransky 8.00 20.00
PRELE Lee Evans/50 10.00 25.00
PRELG L.C. Greenwood 12.00 30.00
PRELT Lawrence Timmons 8.00 20.00
PREMC Marques Colston
PREPH Paul Hornung/50 12.00 30.00
PREPP Paul Posluszny 8.00 20.00
PREPR Philip Rivers/50 12.00 30.00
PRERM Rhema McKnight/50 8.00 20.00
PRERN Reggie Nelson 5.00 12.00
PRERW Reggie Wayne/50 10.00 25.00
PRESN Syvelle Newton 6.00 15.00
PREVY Vince Young/25 30.00 80.00

2007 Upper Deck Premier Rare Patches Dual

STATED PRINT RUN 50 SER.#'d SETS
*GOLD/25: .5X TO 1.2X BASIC JSY/50
GOLD PRINT RUN 25 SER.#'d SETS
*PLAT.HOLOFOIL/10: .8X TO 2X BASIC JSY/50
PLATINUM HOLOFOIL PRINT RUN 10
UNPRICED GOLD HOLOFOIL PRINT RUN 1
AJ S.Alexander/S.Jackson 6.00 15.00
BD W.Dunn/L.Booker 8.00 20.00
BM P.Manning/T.Brady 30.00 80.00
BR D.Brees/T.Romo 30.00 80.00
CH C.Chambers/T.Houshmandzadeh 6.00 15.00
CO A.Crumpler/G.Olsen 10.00 25.00
CP C.Portis/J.Campbell 6.00 15.00
DD D.McNabb/D.Culpepper 8.00 20.00
DJ D.Driver/G.Jennings 8.00 20.00
DM C.Dillon/L.Maroney 8.00 20.00
FB A.Boldin/L.Fitzgerald 8.00 20.00
GG T.Ginn Jr./A.Gonzalez 4.00 10.00
HB I.Bruce/T.Holt 10.00 25.00
JB J.Jones/M.Barber 12.00 30.00
JD E.James/M.Jones-Drew 8.00 20.00
JE A.Johnson/L.Evans 8.00 20.00
JJ C.Johnson/D.Jarrett 10.00 25.00
JK J.Shockey/K.Winslow 6.00 15.00
LT J.Lewis/C.Taylor 8.00 20.00
MB P.Burress/E.Manning 8.00 20.00
MC D.McAllister/M.Colston 8.00 20.00
ML R.Lewis/S.Merriman 10.00 25.00
OG T.Glenn/T.Owens 8.00 20.00
PC C.Pennington/L.Coles 6.00 15.00
PL A.Peterson/M.Lynch 10.00 25.00
RB S.Rice/D.Bowe 4.00 10.00
RG A.Gates/P.Rivers 10.00 25.00
RP B.Roethlisberger/W.Parker 15.00 40.00
RQ B.Quinn/J.Russell 3.00 8.00
RW R.Williams S/E.Reed 8.00 20.00
SG F.Gore/A.Smith QB 8.00 20.00
SJ C.Johnson/S.Smith 8.00 20.00
SU M.Singletary/B.Urlacher 12.00 30.00
SW C.Simms/C.Williams 8.00 20.00
TJ L.Johnson/L.Tomlinson 10.00 25.00
TP J.Taylor/J.Peppers 8.00 20.00
TT T.Green/T.Gonzalez 8.00 20.00
VT Z.Thomas/J.Vilma 10.00 25.00
VY M.Vick/V.Young 8.00 20.00
WS R.Smith/J.Walker 8.00 20.00

2007 Upper Deck Premier Rare Patches Triple

STATED PRINT RUN 25 SER.#'d SETS
*GOLD/10: .5X TO 1.2X BASIC JSY/25
GOLD PRINT RUN 10 SER.#'d SETS
UNPRICED PLATINUM PRINT RUN 5
UNPRICED MASTERPIECE PRINT RUN
AHW Harrison/Wayne/Addai 12.00 30.00
BBC Brees/Bulger/Cutler 15.00 40.00
BTB Brooks/Thomas/Bruschi 12.00 30.00
FMB Favre/Manning/Brady 50.00 120.00
FST Strahan/Taylor/Freeney 12.00 30.00
IJL Jackson/Leonard/Irons 5.00 12.00
JGJ Johnson/Ginn Jr./Jarrett 15.00 40.00
JJG Johnson/Jackson/Gore 12.00 30.00
JSB Smith/Barber/Jackson
LRS Lewis/Reed/Suggs 25.00 60.00
MNM Namath/Montana/Marino
PLB Palmer/Leinart/Bush 12.00 30.00
PLH Peterson/Lynch/Hunt 15.00 40.00
PSA Sanders/Allen/Payton 50.00 125.00
RCB Brown/Rice/Carter
RQS Quinn/Russell/Stanton 5.00 12.00
SGP Smith/Pittman/Gonzalez 5.00 12.00
TAF Alexander/Faulk/Tomlinson 15.00 40.00
TSL Lott/Taylor/Singletary

2007 Upper Deck Premier Rare Remnants Quad

STATED PRINT RUN 25 SER.#'d SETS
*GOLD/10: .5X TO 1.2X BASIC JSY/25
GOLD PRINT RUN 10 SER.#'d SETS
UNPRICED PLATINUM PRINT RUN 5
UNPRICED MASTERPIECE PRINT RUN 1
BDMB Brady/Brusc/Stall/Mrny 25.00 60.00
BJHC Bruce/Holt/Blger/Jcksn 15.00 40.00
BRDB Dawk/Bley/Brbr/Reed 12.00 30.00
BYLC Cutlr/Lnart/Bush/Young 20.00 50.00
CGBJ Gore/Camp/Jcbs/Barber 15.00 40.00
FHDJ Favre/Driver/Hwk/Jenn 20.00 80.00
FMAT Alex/Fvre/Mann/Tomlin 30.00 80.00
GGGG Glen/Gllw/Ginn/A.Gnz 12.00 30.00
JGJR C.Jhnsn/Ginn/Jrrt/Rce 12.00 30.00
LJFB Jmes/Bldin/Fitzg/Lnart 15.00 40.00
MAWH Hrrsn/Mann/Wyn/Addai 25.00 60.00
MWWE Will.WR/Evns/Eli/Wnslw 15.00 40.00
PJMJ L.Jhn/A.Jhn/Plmr/McGa 15.00 40.00
PLBH Ptrsn/Lynch/Bush/Hunt 60.00 150.00
PMWC Penn/Mrtin/Cols/Wshin 15.00 40.00
RQSS Quinn/Rssll/Stntn/Smith 5.00 12.00
RTGM Toml/Gtes/Rivrs/Merrim 20.00 50.00
TMPA Tylr/Pprs/Merrim/Adams 15.00 40.00
TYSF Emmt/Faulk/S.Yng/Theis 30.00 80.00
YRBD Dun/Bldin/Roeth/V.Yng 20.00 50.00

2007 Upper Deck Premier Rare Remnants Triple

STATED PRINT RUN 50 SER.#'d SETS
*GOLD/25: .5X TO 1.2X BASIC JSY/50
GOLD PRINT RUN 25 SER.#'d SETS
*PLATINUM/10: .8X TO 2X BASIC JSY/50
PLATINUM PRINT RUN 10 SER.#'d SETS
UNPRICED MASTERPIECE PRINT RUN 1
ARB Addai/Russell/Bowe 12.00 30.00
AWM Manning/Wayne/Addai 20.00 50.00
BDS Brees/Delhomme/Simms 10.00 25.00
BJH Holt/Bulger/Jackson 12.00 30.00
BLW White/Leinart/Bush 15.00 40.00
BRH Rice/Bowe/Hill 10.00 25.00
CBC Chambers/Culpepper/Brown 10.00 25.00
DNA Andersen/Dunn/Norwood 10.00 25.00
DWS Delhomme/Williams/Smith 12.00 30.00
FAT Alexander/Faulk/Tomlinson 15.00 40.00
FMT Favre/Manning/Tomlinson 25.00 60.00
FWH Higgins/Williams/Figurs 8.00 20.00
HAB Alexander/Hassel/Branch 10.00 25.00
HBL Leonard/Booker/Hunt 8.00 20.00
HJC Holmes/Jennings/Colston 12.00 30.00
JGJ Johnson/Ginn Jr./Jarrett 15.00 40.00
JMB Johnson/Meachem/Bowe 15.00 40.00
JMG James/McGahee/Gore 12.00 30.00
JWW Wayne/Johnson/Will.WR 10.00 25.00
LIM Peterson/Lynch/Irons 50.00 120.00
MGU Manning/Urlacher/Grssmn 12.00 30.00
MJS Shockey/Manning/Jacobs 12.00 30.00
MRC McNabb/Romo/Campbell 25.00 60.00
MTG Green/McAllister/Taylor 10.00 25.00
MWW Williams/Maroney/White 12.00 30.00
PJJ Johnson/Johnson/Palmer 12.00 30.00
PLJ Peterson/Jackson/Lynch 50.00 120.00
PMW Penning/Martin/Washing 12.00 30.00
PPC Crumpler/Peppers/Parker 12.00 30.00
PRL Lewis/Peppers/Reed 12.00 30.00
ROG Glenn/Owens/Romo 25.00 60.00
RQS Quinn/Russell/Stanton 4.00 10.00
RWH Ward/Roethlisbrgr/Holmes 15.00 40.00
SPG Smith/Pittman/Gonzalez 10.00 25.00
SWO Franks/Shockey/Winslow 10.00 25.00
TBM Bailey/Taylor/Merriman 10.00 25.00
TJG Johnson/Tomlinson/Gore 15.00 40.00
VRL Vick/Leftwich/Roethlis 15.00 40.00
WBC Coles/Walker/Boldin 10.00 25.00
WPJ Portis/Westbrook/Jacobs 10.00 25.00

2007 Upper Deck Premier Remnants Quad

STATED PRINT RUN 99 SER.#'d SETS
*GOLD/75: .4X TO 1X BASIC JSY/99
GOLD PRINT RUN 75 SER.#'d SETS
*PLATINUM/10: .8X TO 2X BASIC JSY/99
PLATINUM PRINT RUN 10 SER.#'d SETS
UNPRICED MASTERPIECE PRINT RUN 1
UNPRICED QUAD AU PRINT RUN 15
PR4AC Alge Crumpler 8.00 20.00
PR4AP Adrian Peterson 10.00 25.00
PR4AS Alex Smith QB 8.00 20.00
PR4BF Brett Favre 20.00 50.00
PR4BJ Brandon Jacobs 6.00 15.00
PR4BQ Brady Quinn 3.00 8.00
PR4BR Ronnie Brown 6.00 15.00
PR4BU Brian Urlacher 10.00 25.00
PR4BW Brian Westbrook 6.00 15.00
PR4CJ Calvin Johnson 10.00 25.00
PR4CP Chad Pennington 6.00 15.00
PR4DB Dwayne Bowe 3.00 8.00
PR4DC David Carr 6.00 15.00
PR4DD Donald Driver 8.00 20.00
PR4DJ Dwayne Jarrett 4.00 10.00
PR4EJ Edgerrin James 8.00 20.00
PR4ER Ed Reed 8.00 20.00
PR4FG Frank Gore 8.00 20.00
PR4GO Tony Gonzalez 8.00 20.00
PR4HO Torry Holt 8.00 20.00
PR4HW Hines Ward 8.00 20.00
PR4JA Joseph Addai 6.00 15.00
PR4JN Jerious Norwood 6.00 15.00
PR4JP Julius Peppers 8.00 20.00
PR4JR JaMarcus Russell 3.00 8.00
PR4JT Jason Taylor 8.00 20.00
PR4KW Kellen Winslow 6.00 15.00
PR4LE Lee Evans 8.00 20.00
PR4LJ Larry Johnson 6.00 15.00
PR4LT LaDainian Tomlinson 10.00 25.00
PR4LW Leon Washington 6.00 15.00
PR4MB Marion Barber 10.00 25.00
PR4MD Maurice Jones-Drew 6.00 15.00
PR4MH Marvin Harrison 8.00 20.00
PR4ML Marshawn Lynch 6.00 15.00
PR4MV Michael Vick 8.00 20.00
PR4PB Plaxico Burress 6.00 15.00
PR4PM Peyton Manning 25.00 60.00
PR4RB Reggie Bush 6.00 15.00
PR4RL Ray Lewis 10.00 25.00
PR4RM Robert Meachem 4.00 10.00
PR4SH Santonio Holmes 6.00 15.00
PR4SJ Steven Jackson 6.00 15.00
PR4SR Sidney Rice 4.00 10.00
PR4TG Ted Ginn Jr. 4.00 10.00
PR4TH T.J. Houshmandzadeh 6.00 15.00
PR4TO Terrell Owens 8.00 20.00
PR4TR Tony Romo 12.00 30.00
PR4VY Vince Young 6.00 15.00
PR4WD Warrick Dunn 6.00 15.00

2007 Upper Deck Premier Remnants Quad Autographs

UNPRICED QUAD AU PRINT RUN 15

2007 Upper Deck Premier Remnants Triple

STATED PRINT RUN 99 SER.#'d SETS
*GOLD/75: .4X TO 1X BASIC JSY/99
GOLD PRINT RUN 75 SER.#'d SETS
*PLATINUM/25: .6X TO 1.5X BASIC JSY/99
PLATINUM PRINT RUN 25 SER.#'d SETS
UNPRICED MASTERPIECE PRINT RUN 1
PR3AB Anquan Boldin 5.00 12.00
PR3AG Antonio Gates 8.00 20.00
PR3AP Adrian Peterson 15.00 40.00
PR3AV Adam Vinatieri 5.00 12.00
PR3BF Brett Favre 15.00 40.00
PR3BQ Brady Quinn 2.50 6.00
PR3BR Ben Roethlisberger 8.00 20.00
PR3BW Brian Westbrook 5.00 12.00
PR3CB Champ Bailey 6.00 15.00
PR3CJ Chad Johnson 5.00 12.00
PR3CO Marques Colston 5.00 12.00
PR3CP Carson Palmer 6.00 15.00
PR3CT Chester Taylor 5.00 12.00
PR3CU Jay Cutler 5.00 12.00
PR3DB Drew Brees 8.00 20.00
PR3DJ Dwayne Jarrett 3.00 8.00
PR3DM Deuce McAllister 6.00 15.00
PR3EM Eli Manning 6.00 15.00
PR3EV Lee Evans 6.00 15.00
PR3FG Frank Gore 6.00 15.00
PR3JC Jason Campbell 5.00 12.00
PR3JO Calvin Johnson 8.00 20.00
PR3JR JaMarcus Russell 2.50 6.00
PR3LC Laveranues Coles 5.00 12.00
PR3LE Matt Leinart 5.00 12.00
PR3LF Larry Fitzgerald 6.00 15.00
PR3LJ Larry Johnson 5.00 12.00
PR3LM Laurence Maroney 6.00 15.00
PR3LT LaDainian Tomlinson 8.00 20.00
PR3MB Marc Bulger 5.00 12.00
PR3MC Donovan McNabb 6.00 15.00
PR3ML Marshawn Lynch 5.00 12.00
PR3MV Michael Vick 6.00 15.00
PR3PM Peyton Manning 20.00 50.00
PR3PR Philip Rivers 8.00 20.00
PR3RB Reggie Bush 5.00 12.00
PR3RG Rex Grossman 5.00 12.00
PR3RW Reggie Wayne 6.00 15.00
PR3SA Shaun Alexander 5.00 12.00
PR3SJ Steven Jackson 5.00 12.00
PR3SM Shawne Merriman 5.00 12.00
PR3SS Steve Smith 6.00 15.00
PR3TB Tom Brady 12.00 30.00
PR3TG Ted Ginn Jr. 3.00 8.00
PR3TO Terrell Owens 6.00 15.00
PR3TR Tony Romo 10.00 25.00
PR3VY Vince Young 5.00 12.00
PR3WI Roy Williams WR 5.00 12.00
PR3WM Willis McGahee 5.00 12.00
PR3WP Willie Parker 6.00 15.00

2007 Upper Deck Premier Remnants Triple Autographs

STATED PRINT RUN 25 SER.#'d SETS
PR3AB Anquan Boldin 15.00 40.00
PR3AG Antonio Gates 25.00 60.00
PR3AP Adrian Peterson 125.00 250.00
PR3BF Brett Favre 150.00 250.00
PR3CB Champ Bailey 20.00 50.00
PR3CJ Chad Johnson 15.00 40.00
PR3CO Marques Colston 15.00 40.00
PR3CT Chester Taylor 15.00 40.00
PR3DB Drew Brees 40.00 80.00
PR3DJ Dwayne Jarrett 20.00 50.00
PR3EM Eli Manning 50.00 100.00
PR3FG Frank Gore 20.00 50.00
PR3JC Jason Campbell 15.00 40.00
PR3JR JaMarcus Russell 15.00 40.00
PR3LE Matt Leinart 15.00 40.00
PR3LF Larry Fitzgerald 40.00 80.00
PR3LJ Larry Johnson 15.00 40.00
PR3LT LaDainian Tomlinson 40.00 80.00
PR3ML Marshawn Lynch 50.00 100.00
PR3PM Peyton Manning 100.00 200.00
PR3PR Philip Rivers 25.00 60.00
PR3SS Steve Smith 20.00 50.00
PR3TG Ted Ginn Jr. 20.00 50.00
PR3VY Vince Young 15.00 40.00
PR3WP Willie Parker 15.00 40.00

2007 Upper Deck Premier Six Autographs

PRICED SIX AU PRINT RUN 10

2007 Upper Deck Premier Stitchings Team Logo/NFL Draft

STATED PRINT RUN 75 SER.#'d SETS
*VARIATION/75: .4X TO 1X BASIC INSERTS
VARIATION PRINT RUN 75 SER.#'d SETS
*GOLD/40-50: .5X TO 1.2X BASIC INSERTS
*GOLD/20: .6X TO 1.5X BASIC INSERTS
GOLD PRINT RUN 20-50
*VARIATION PLAT.HOLO/40-50: .5X TO 1.2X
*VARIATION PLAT.HOLO/20: .6X TO 1.5X
VARIATION PLAT.HOLO.PRINT RUN 20-50
UNPRICED PLATINUM PRINT RUN 5
UNPRICED PLAT.VARIATION PRINT RUN 5
PS1 LaDainian Tomlinson 07MVP 8.00 20.00
PS2 Chris Leak 2.50 6.00
PS3 Adrian Peterson 8.00 20.00
PS4 Antonio Pittman 2.50 6.00
PS5 Brady Quinn 2.50 6.00
PS6 Brandon Jackson 2.50 6.00
PS7 Calvin Johnson 8.00 20.00
PS8 Jason Hill 2.50 6.00
PS9 Patrick Willis 4.00 10.00
PS10 Drew Stanton 2.50 6.00
PS11 Dwayne Bowe 2.50 6.00
PS12 Dwayne Jarrett 3.00 8.00
PS13 Lorenzo Booker 3.00 8.00
PS14 Garrett Wolfe 2.50 6.00
PS15 JaMarcus Russell 2.50 6.00
PS16 Kenny Irons 2.50 6.00
PS17 Marshawn Lynch 5.00 12.00
PS18 Michael Bush 2.50 6.00
PS19 Robert Meachem 3.00 8.00
PS20 Sidney Rice 3.00 8.00
PS21 Ted Ginn Jr. 3.00 8.00
PS22 Tony Hunt 2.50 6.00
PS23 Trent Edwards 2.50 6.00
PS24 Troy Smith 2.50 6.00
PS25 Chris Henry RB 2.50 6.00
PS26 Anthony Gonzalez 2.50 6.00
PS27 Brian Leonard 2.50 6.00
PS28 Greg Olsen 4.00 10.00
PS29 Yamon Figurs 2.50 6.00
PS30 Gaines Adams 3.00 8.00
PS31 Kevin Kolb 3.00 8.00
PS32 John Beck 2.50 6.00
PS33 Joe Thomas 4.00 10.00
PS34 Steve Smith USC 2.50 6.00
PS35 Frank Gore 6.00 15.00
PS36 Steve Young 10.00 25.00
PS37 Mike Singletary 8.00 20.00
PS38 Brian Urlacher 8.00 20.00
PS40 Gale Sayers 8.00 20.00
PS41 Walter Payton 15.00 40.00
PS42 Devin Hester 10.00 25.00
PS43 Carson Palmer 6.00 15.00
PS44 Chad Johnson 5.00 12.00
PS45 Jay Cutler 5.00 12.00
PS46 Champ Bailey 6.00 15.00
PS48 Kellen Winslow 5.00 12.00
PS49 Cadillac Williams 6.00 15.00
PS50 Larry Fitzgerald 6.00 15.00
PS51 Tony Gonzalez 6.00 15.00
PS52 Joseph Addai 5.00 12.00
PS53 Marvin Harrison 6.00 15.00
PS54 Marion Barber 8.00 20.00
PS55 Emmitt Smith 12.00 30.00
PS56 Tony Romo 10.00 25.00
PS58 Terrell Owens 6.00 15.00
PS59 Jason Taylor 6.00 15.00
PS60 Dan Marino 15.00 40.00
PS61 Donovan McNabb 6.00 15.00
PS62 Brian Westbrook 5.00 12.00
PS64 Jeremy Shockey 5.00 12.00
PS65 Eli Manning 6.00 15.00
PS66 Lawrence Taylor 8.00 20.00
PS67 Brett Favre 15.00 40.00
PS68 Vince Lombardi 12.00 30.00
PS69 Maurice Jones-Drew 5.00 12.00
PS70 Joe Namath 10.00 25.00
PS71 Barry Sanders 12.00 30.00
PS72 Roy Williams WR 5.00 12.00
PS74 Paul Hornung 8.00 20.00
PS75 Steve Smith 6.00 15.00
PS76 Bo Jackson 12.00 30.00
PS77 Marcus Allen 8.00 20.00
PS79 Steven Jackson 5.00 12.00
PS80 Torry Holt 6.00 15.00
PS81 Steve McNair 6.00 15.00
PS82 Willis McGahee 5.00 12.00
PS83 Reggie Bush 5.00 12.00
PS84 Marques Colston 5.00 12.00
PS85 Drew Brees 8.00 20.00
PS86 Shaun Alexander 5.00 12.00
PS87 L.C. Greenwood 5.00 12.00
PS88 Ben Roethlisberger 8.00 20.00
PS89 Willie Parker 6.00 15.00
PS90 Franco Harris 8.00 20.00
PS91 Hines Ward 6.00 15.00
PS92 Peyton Manning COLTS 15.00 40.00
PS93 Peyton Manning LOGO 15.00 40.00
PS94 Joe Montana SJ 25.00 60.00
PS96 Matt Leinart 5.00 12.00
PS97 Shawne Merriman 5.00 12.00
PS98 Larry Johnson 5.00 12.00
PS99 Tom Brady 15.00 40.00
PS100 Vince Young 5.00 12.00

2007 Upper Deck Premier Stitchings Autographs

STATED PRINT RUN 10-25
UNPRICED CUT AUTO PRINT RUN 1
PS1 LaDainian Tomlinson 40.00 80.00
PS2 Chris Leak 10.00 25.00
PS3 Adrian Peterson 175.00 300.00
PS4 Antonio Pittman 10.00 25.00
PS5 Brady Quinn 10.00 25.00
PS6 Brandon Jackson 10.00 25.00
PS7 Calvin Johnson 75.00 150.00
PS8 Jason Hill 10.00 25.00
PS9 Patrick Willis 30.00 60.00
PS10 Drew Stanton 10.00 25.00
PS11 Dwayne Bowe 15.00 40.00
PS14 Garrett Wolfe 10.00 25.00
PS15 JaMarcus Russell 10.00 25.00
PS17 Marshawn Lynch 30.00 60.00
PS18 Michael Bush 10.00 25.00
PS19 Robert Meachem 12.00 30.00
PS20 Sidney Rice 12.00 30.00
PS21 Ted Ginn Jr. 12.00 30.00
PS22 Tony Hunt 10.00 25.00
PS23 Trent Edwards/20 10.00 25.00
PS26 Anthony Gonzalez 10.00 25.00
PS27 Brian Leonard 10.00 25.00
PS28 Greg Olsen 15.00 40.00
PS29 Yamon Figurs/20 10.00 25.00
PS30 Gaines Adams 12.00 30.00
PS31 Kevin Kolb 12.00 30.00
PS33 Joe Thomas 15.00 40.00
PS35 Frank Gore 15.00 40.00
PS36 Steve Young 40.00 80.00
PS40 Gale Sayers 30.00 60.00
PS44 Chad Johnson 12.00 30.00
PS49 Cadillac Williams 15.00 40.00
PS50 Larry Fitzgerald 15.00 40.00
PS52 Joseph Addai 12.00 30.00
PS54 Marion Barber 15.00 40.00
PS65 Eli Manning 50.00 100.00
PS74 Paul Hornung 25.00 60.00
PS83 Reggie Bush 12.00 30.00
PS85 Drew Brees 40.00 80.00
PS94 Joe Montana 100.00 200.00
PS96 Matt Leinart 12.00 30.00
PS98 Larry Johnson 12.00 30.00
PS99 Tom Brady 250.00 400.00

2007 Upper Deck Premier Stitchings Cut Autographs

PRICED CUT AU PRINT RUN 1

2007 Upper Deck Premier Trios Autographs

ATED PRINT RUN 20 SER.#'d SETS
1 Anderson/Adams/Okoye 15.00 40.00
2 Johnson/Thomas/Russell 125.00 250.00
3 Willis/Posluszny/Timmons 25.00 60.00
4 Smith/Tomlin/Ptrsn 250.00 400.00
5 Gonzalez/Davis/Smith USC 25.00 60.00
6 Nelson/Landry/Meriweather 15.00 40.00
8 Eli/Smith QB/Leinart 50.00 100.00
9 Bulger/Schaub/Campbell 25.00 60.00
10 Bailey/Hall/Revis 25.00 60.00
11 Henry/Filani/Williams 15.00 40.00
12 Brown/Driver/Evans 25.00 60.00
13 Mann/Wayne/Addai 75.00 150.00
14 Stanton/Beck/Edwards 25.00 60.00
15 Jackson/Lynch/Irons 30.00 80.00
16 Gore/Smith QB/Hill
18 Bush/Miller/Higgins 25.00 60.00
19 Ch.John/Pearson/Jarrett 25.00 60.00
20 Nelson/Leak/Baker 20.00 50.00

2008 Upper Deck Premier

1-135 JSY AU PRINT RUN 199-375
136-160 ROOKIE AU PRINT RUN 199
UNPRICED GOLD PRINT RUN 1
1 Adrian Peterson 3.00 8.00
2 Hines Ward 2.50 6.00
3 Alex Smith QB 2.50 6.00
4 Andre Johnson 2.50 6.00
5 Anquan Boldin 2.00 5.00
6 Antonio Cromartie 2.00 5.00
7 Antonio Gates 2.50 6.00
8 Antonio Pierce 2.00 5.00
9 Barry Sanders 5.00 12.00
10 Ben Roethlisberger 3.00 8.00
11 Billy Sims 2.50 6.00
12 Bo Jackson 4.00 10.00
13 Bob Sanders 2.50 6.00
14 Brandon Marshall 2.50 6.00
15 Braylon Edwards 2.00 5.00
16 Brett Favre 6.00 15.00
17 Brian Bosworth 3.00 8.00
18 Brian Dawkins 3.00 8.00
19 Brian Urlacher 3.00 8.00
20 Brian Westbrook 2.00 5.00
21 Calvin Johnson 3.00 8.00
22 Cadillac Williams 2.50 6.00
23 Carson Palmer 2.50 6.00
24 Chad Johnson 2.00 5.00
25 Champ Bailey 2.50 6.00
26 Chris Cooley 2.00 5.00
27 Dallas Clark 2.00 5.00
28 David Garrard 2.00 5.00
29 Deion Branch 2.00 5.00
30 DeMarcus Ware 2.50 6.00
31 Tom Brady 10.00 25.00
32 Derek Anderson 2.00 5.00
33 Randy Moss 2.50 6.00
34 Devin Hester 2.50 6.00
35 Dick Butkus 4.00 10.00
36 Donovan McNabb 2.50 6.00
37 Drew Brees 3.00 8.00
38 Dwayne Bowe 2.50 6.00
39 Ed Reed 2.50 6.00
40 Edgerrin James 2.50 6.00
41 Eli Manning 2.50 6.00
42 Ernie Sims 2.00 5.00
43 Frank Gore 2.50 6.00
44 Fred Taylor 2.00 5.00
45 Greg Jennings 2.00 5.00
46 Jack Lambert 3.00 8.00
47 JaMarcus Russell 2.00 5.00
48 Jason Campbell 2.00 5.00
49 Jason Taylor 2.50 6.00
50 Jay Cutler 2.00 5.00
51 Jeff Garcia 2.00 5.00
52 Brandon Jacobs 2.00 5.00
53 Joey Galloway 2.50 6.00
54 John Elway 5.00 12.00
55 Jonathan Vilma 2.00 5.00
56 Chad Pennington 2.00 5.00
57 Kellen Winslow Jr. 2.00 5.00
58 Ken Stabler 3.00 8.00
59 Aaron Rodgers 6.00 15.00
60 LaDainian Tomlinson 3.00 8.00
61 LaRon Landry 2.50 6.00
62 Kellen Winslow Sr. 2.50 6.00

63 Larry Fitzgerald 2.50 6.00
64 Larry Johnson 2.00 5.00
65 LenDale White 2.00 5.00
66 Lofa Tatupu 2.00 5.00
67 Marc Bulger 2.00 5.00
68 Marion Barber 2.00 5.00
69 Marques Colston 2.00 5.00
70 Marshawn Lynch 2.50 6.00
71 Matt Hasselbeck 2.00 5.00
72 Matt Leinart 2.00 5.00
73 Maurice Jones-Drew 2.00 5.00
74 Patrick Willis 2.50 6.00
75 Peyton Manning 8.00 20.00
76 Philip Rivers 3.00 8.00
77 Plaxico Burress 2.00 5.00
78 Reggie Bush 2.00 5.00
79 Reggie Wayne 2.50 6.00
80 Ronnie Brown 2.00 5.00
81 Roscoe Parrish 2.00 5.00
82 Roy Williams WR 2.00 5.00
83 Ryan Grant 2.50 6.00
84 Santonio Holmes 2.00 5.00
85 Shawne Merriman 2.00 5.00
86 Sidney Rice 2.00 5.00
87 Steve McNair 2.50 6.00
88 Steve Smith 2.50 6.00
89 Steven Jackson 2.00 5.00
90 Tarvaris Jackson 2.00 5.00
91 Terrell Owens 2.50 6.00
92 Thomas Jones 2.00 5.00
93 Tony Gonzalez 2.50 6.00
94 Tony Romo 2.50 6.00
95 Torry Holt 2.50 6.00
96 Trent Edwards 2.00 5.00
97 Troy Polamalu 3.00 8.00
98 Vince Young 2.00 5.00
99 Warrick Dunn 2.00 5.00
100 Willis McGahee 2.00 5.00
101 Donnie Avery JSY AU/275 RC 6.00 15.00
102 Harry Douglas JSY AU/375 RC 6.00 15.00
103 Brian Brohm JSY AU/199 RC 5.00 12.00
104 Chad Henne JSY AU/275 RC 6.00 15.00
105 C.Johnson JSY AU/275 RC 6.00 15.00
107 D.Thomas JSY AU/275 RC 5.00 12.00
108 D.McFadden JSY AU/199 RC 5.00 12.00
109 E.Bennett JSY AU/275 RC 8.00 20.00
111 DeS.Jackson JSY AU/275 RC 10.00 25.00
112 J.Long JSY AU/375 RC 8.00 20.00
113 E.Doucet JSY AU/375 RC 5.00 12.00
114 A.Caldwell JSY AU/375 RC 5.00 12.00
115 F.Jones JSY AU/275 RC 5.00 12.00
116 D.Keller JSY AU/375 RC 6.00 15.00
117 J.Charles JSY AU/275 RC 15.00 40.00
118 J.Flacco JSY AU/275 RC 10.00 25.00
119 J.Booty JSY AU/275 RC 5.00 12.00
120 J.Stewart JSY AU/199 RC 15.00 40.00
121 J.Nelson JSY AU/275 RC 25.00 50.00
122 J.Simpson JSY AU/275 RC 6.00 15.00
123 K.Smith JSY AU/275 RC 5.00 12.00
124 L.Sweed JSY AU/275 RC 5.00 12.00
125 M.Kelly JSY AU/275 RC 5.00 12.00
126 Mnnnghm JSY AU/275 RC 12.00 30.00
127 J.Hardy JSY AU/275 RC 5.00 12.00
128 M.Forte JSY AU/375 RC 15.00 40.00
129 M.Ryan JSY AU/199 RC 50.00 100.00
130 D.Jackson JSY AU/275 RC 8.00 20.00
131 E.Royal JSY AU/275 RC 5.00 12.00
132 R.Mendenhall JSY AU/275 RC 5.00 12.00
133 R.Rice JSY AU/275 RC 5.00 12.00
134 S.Slaton JSY AU/275 RC 5.00 12.00
135 K.O'Connell JSY AU/275 RC 5.00 12.00
137 Dennis Dixon AU RC 4.00 10.00
138 Ali Highsmith AU RC 4.00 10.00
139 Allen Patrick AU RC 4.00 10.00
140 Antoine Cason AU RC 5.00 12.00
141 Aqib Talib AU RC 6.00 15.00
142 Ben Moffitt AU RC 4.00 10.00
143 Anthony Morelli AU RC 4.00 10.00
144 Bruce Davis AU RC 5.00 12.00
145 Calais Campbell AU RC 5.00 12.00
146 Chevis Jackson AU RC 4.00 10.00
147 Chris Ellis AU RC 4.00 10.00
148 Craig Steltz AU RC 4.00 10.00
149 DJ Hall AU RC 4.00 10.00
150 Dan Connor AU RC 4.00 10.00
151 DeMario Pressley AU RC 5.00 12.00
152 Derrick Harvey AU RC 4.00 10.00
153 D.Rodgers-Cromartie AU RC 5.00 12.00
155 Fred Davis AU RC 4.00 10.00
156 Dwight Lowery RC 5.00 12.00
157 Chris Long AU RC 5.00 12.00
158 Leodis McKelvin AU RC 5.00 12.00
160 Keith Rivers AU RC 4.00 10.00

2008 Upper Deck Premier Silver

ETS: .5X TO 1.2X BASIC CARDS
*RETIRED: .6X TO 1.5X BASIC CARDS
*ROOKIE JSY AU: .4X TO 1X BASIC CARDS
1-100 VETERAN PRINT RUN 35
101-135 ROOKIE JSY AU PRINT RUN 60

2008 Upper Deck Premier Emerging Stars Autographs Dual Gold

ATED PRINT RUN 10-100
UNPRICED SILVER SPECTRUM PRINT RUN 1
ES2 C.Brennan/D.Bess/50 8.00 20.00
ES3 C.Campbell/B.Davis/100 6.00 15.00
ES4 J.King/A.Cason/100 6.00 15.00
ES5 J.Flacco/D.Anderson/50 12.00 30.00
ES7 C.Henne/A.Arrington/50 12.00 30.00
ES8 D.Bowe/E.Doucet/50 12.00 30.00
ES10 K.Rivers/A.Hawk/50 10.00 25.00
ES11 B.Croyle/A.Woodson/50 10.00 25.00
ES12 J.Charles/C.Johnson/50 25.00 60.00
ES13 J.Long/C.Long/50 10.00 25.00
ES14 J.Long/S.Baker/50 10.00 25.00
ES15 M.Hart/R.Rice/25 25.00 50.00
ES16 D.Dixon/J.Johnson/90 5.00 12.00
ES17 D.Jackson/M.Lynch/50 25.00 50.00
ES18 D.Jackson/L.Hawkins/50 15.00 40.00
ES19 M.Rucker/F.Davis/100 5.00 12.00
ES22 E.Ainge/M.Flynn/50 6.00 15.00
ES24 J.Stewart/D.Dixon/50 25.00 50.00

2008 Upper Deck Premier Equipment 25

STATED PRINT RUN 25 SER.#'d SETS
PARALLELS #'d TO 10 AND 1/1 NOT PRICED
PEBF Brett Favre 20.00 50.00
PEBS Barry Sanders 25.00 60.00
PECJ Calvin Johnson 10.00 25.00
PEDB Dwayne Bowe 8.00 20.00
PEDM Dan Marino 30.00 80.00
PEEM Eli Manning 8.00 20.00
PEER Ed Reed 8.00 20.00
PEGJ Greg Jennings 6.00 15.00
PEJC Jay Cutler 6.00 15.00
PEJE John Elway 25.00 60.00
PEJO Chad Johnson 6.00 15.00
PEJR JaMarcus Russell 6.00 15.00
PEKW Kellen Winslow Jr. 6.00 15.00
PELM Laurence Maroney 8.00 20.00
PELT LaDainian Tomlinson 10.00 25.00
PEMJ Maurice Jones-Drew 6.00 15.00
PEPM Peyton Manning 25.00 60.00
PETB Tom Brady 30.00 80.00
PETR Tony Romo 8.00 20.00
PEWP Willie Parker 8.00 20.00

2008 Upper Deck Premier Five Jersey 30

STATED PRINT RUN 30 SER.#'d SETS
PARALLELS #'d TO 10 AND 1/1 NOT PRICED
BMJPR New York Giants 10.00 25.00
BWEJB Veteran WR's 10.00 25.00
EMMSM Retired QB's 40.00 100.00
FMBGP Veteran QB's 1 40.00 100.00
HBGSS Veteran QB's 2 10.00 25.00
HRPHS Pittsburgh Steelers 20.00 50.00
JTPJL Veteran RB's 12.00 30.00
MBWVM New England Patriots 40.00 100.00
PHSMJ Running Backs 25.00 60.00
PTWLB Bush/Whit/Lein/Plmr/Tat 10.00 25.00
SFTMP San/LT/Mar/Favre/Ptrsn 25.00 60.00
SMTMH Emm/LT/Pytn/Mar/Hrng 30.00 80.00
SORWB Dallas Cowboys 30.00 80.00
SSPHS Retired RB's 25.00 60.00

2008 Upper Deck Premier Foursome Jersey 35

STATED PRINT RUN 35 SER.#'d SETS
PARALLELS #'d TO 15 AND 1/1 NOT PRICED
AHGS Garr/Andr/Schaub/Hass 5.00 12.00
EMFM Mont/Elway/Favre/Peyton 30.00 80.00
FCJM Cutler/Mrshl/Jenn/Favre 15.00 40.00
FYMN Favre/Young/Mont/Namath 25.00 60.00
GGPL Peterson/Lynch/Grant/Gore 8.00 20.00
JPBL Bold/Jhnsn/Leinart/Palmer 6.00 15.00
JTJB LT/Bush/LJ/J-Drew 8.00 20.00
LWWB Willis/Lambrt/Ware/Boz 8.00 20.00
MJJB Jhnsn/Jhnsn/Bowe/Moss 8.00 20.00
MMBS Brady/Moss/Peyton/Sndrs 25.00 60.00
STML Sndrs/Lynch/McGah/LT 12.00 30.00
VWSH Hawk/Sims/Ware/Vrabel 6.00 15.00
WWSJ Jenn/ Wdsn/Welkr/Samuel 8.00 20.00

2008 Upper Deck Premier Foursome Patch 45

STATED PRINT RUN 45 SER.#'d SETS
*PATCH/15: .5X TO 1.2X PATCH/45
PARALLEL #'d 1/1 NOT PRICED
AJBG Jcbs/Grnt/Brber/Alxndr 6.00 15.00
AJHJ Anderson/Johnson/Jackson/Housh 5.00 12.00
CCJB Bowe/Calvin Johnson/Cotchery/Colston 8.00 20.00
CHEH Housh/Holmes
Braylon Edwards/Clayton 5.00 12.00
EMSM Mrino/Mntn/Elwy/Stblr 30.00 80.00
FHRM Eli/Favre/Romo/Hass 25.00 60.00
FUJP Fvre/Ptrsn/Urlchr/Jhnsn 15.00 40.00
GRPJ Grrard/Roeth/J-Drw/Prkr 8.00 20.00
GSGW Watson/Gates/Tony Gonzalez/Shockey 6.00 15.00
GWYW Willis/Frank Gore/Vince Young/White 6.00 15.00
HBRB Brnch/Hass/Romo/Brbr 6.00 15.00
JBBS Jhnsn/Lynn Swann/Deion Branch/Bowe 8.00 20.00
JHJS Smith QB/Hassel/Steven Jackson/James 6.00 15.00
JWMG McGahee/Edgerrin James
Frank Gore/Wayne 6.00 15.00
MBGR Brdy/Rvrs/Mann/Grrard 25.00 60.00
MFBP Brdy/Moss/Favre/Ptrsn 25.00 60.00
MMBM Brdy/Mntn/Mann/Mrino 50.00 100.00
MMGM Eli/Mann/Grant/Mrny 20.00 50.00
MRRQ Rivrs/Eli/Roeth/Quinn 8.00 20.00
MTCW Moss/Chris Chambers
Reggie Wayne/Taylor 6.00 15.00
OBBJ Burress/Greg Jennings
Terrell Owens/Branch 6.00 15.00
PWRM Eli/Romo/Wstbrk/Prtis 6.00 15.00
RCCR Cutler/Philip Rivers
JaMarcus Russell/Croyle 8.00 20.00
RPSS Sanders/Asante Samuel
Ed Reed/Polamalu 8.00 20.00
SMTB Sndrs/Tmlin/Mntna/Brdy 30.00 80.00
SSFK Freeney/Aaron Schobel
Kampman/Strahan 6.00 15.00
TAMJ Mrney/Tmlin/Addai/J-Drw 8.00 20.00
TGWC Cromartie/Tony Gonzalez
Fred Taylor/Welker 6.00 15.00
WGAL Williams/Frank Gore
Joseph Addai/Lynch 6.00 15.00
WHBY Yng/Huff/Bush/White 5.00 12.00
WJBC Johnson/Cromartie
Plaxico Burress/Woodson 8.00 20.00
WMJB Welker/Dwayne Bowe
Calvin Johnson/Marshall 8.00 20.00
WSWH Willis/DeMarcus Ware
AJ Hawk/Ernie Sims 6.00 15.00

2008 Upper Deck Premier Foursomes Autographs

FOURSOME AUTO PRINT RUN 15
3 Woodson/Tamme/Flynn/Hester 25.00 50.00
4 Tomlinson/LJ/McFadd/Stewart 5.00 12.00
5 Anderson/Garcia/Romo/Bulger 50.00 100.00
6 Flacco/Henne/Brohm/Ryan 40.00 100.00
9 McFadd/Jones/Stewart/Menden 5.00 12.00
10 Peterson/Rice/Slaton/Lynch 100.00 200.00

2008 Upper Deck Premier Highlights Autographs Gold

GOLD PRINT RUN 25
UNPRICED SILVER SPECTRUM PRINT RUN 1
SH3 Jake Long 6.00 15.00
SH4 Adrian Peterson 75.00 150.00
SH5 Chad Johnson 8.00 20.00
SH6 Peyton Manning 50.00 100.00
SH7 Wes Welker 25.00 60.00
SH8 Kurt Warner 20.00 40.00
SH9 Eli Manning 30.00 60.00
SH10 Bob Sanders 20.00 50.00
SH11 Barry Sanders 75.00 150.00
SH12 Jeremy Shockey 8.00 20.00
SH13 LaDainianTomlinson 30.00 60.00
SH14 Jeff Garcia 8.00 20.00
SH15 Tom Brady 100.00 200.00

2008 Upper Deck Premier Inscriptions Autographs Gold

GOLD STATED PRINT RUN 15-35
UNPRICED GOLD SPECTRUM PRINT RUN 1
UNPRICED SILVER SPECTRUM PRINT RUN 5
INSCJ Chad Johnson/25 8.00 20.00
INSCL Chris Long/35 5.00 12.00
INSDB Dwayne Bowe/25 10.00 25.00
INSDJ Daryl Johnston/25 20.00 50.00
INSFJ Felix Jones/25 6.00 15.00
INSJL Jake Long/25 6.00 15.00
INSKS Ken Stabler/25 15.00 40.00
INSLT L.Tomlinson/15 EXCH 40.00 80.00
INSML Marshawn Lynch/25 10.00 25.00
INSPW Patrick Willis/35 10.00 25.00
INSWW Wes Welker/25 25.00 60.00

2008 Upper Deck Premier Legends Autographs Gold

PRICED GOLD SPECTRUM PRINT RUN 1
UNPRICED SILVER SPECTRUM PRINT RUN 5
SERIAL #'d UNDER 25 NOT PRICED
PLBG Bob Griese/25 15.00 40.00
PLBS Billy Sims25 12.00 30.00
PLDJ Daryl Johnston/25 12.00 30.00
PLDM Don Maynard/25 12.00 30.00
PLDM Dan Marino/25 75.00 150.00
PLFT Fran Tarkenton/25 20.00 50.00
PLJA Bo Jackson/25 30.00 60.00
PLJB Jim Brown/25 40.00 80.00
PLJT Joe Theismann/25 15.00 40.00
PLLH Lester Hayes/45 12.00 30.00
PLPH Paul Hornung/25 15.00 40.00
PLRC Roger Craig/50 10.00 25.00
PLSY Steve Young/25 30.00 60.00
PLYT Y.A. Tittle/25 15.00 40.00

2008 Upper Deck Premier Milestones Autographs Gold

GOLD STATED PRINT RUN 15-40
UNPRICED GOLD SPECTRUM PRINT RUN 1
UNPRICED SILVER SPECTRUM PRINT RUN 5
PMAP Adrian Peterson/25 50.00 120.00
PMBF Brett Favre/15 100.00 200.00
PMBS Bob Sanders/30 20.00 50.00
PMDM Dan Marino/15 100.00 200.00
PMEM Eli Manning/25 30.00 60.00
PMFA Brett Favre/15 100.00 200.00
PMJB Jim Brown/25 30.00 60.00
PMJE John Elway/15 60.00 120.00
PMLT LaDainian Tomlinson/25 30.00 60.00
PMPE Adrian Peterson/25 100.00 175.00
PMPH Paul Hornung/35 12.00 30.00
PMPM Peyton Manning/25 50.00 100.00
PMPW Patrick Willis/40 8.00 20.00
PMTB Tom Brady/25 125.00 250.00
PMWW Wes Welker/35 25.00 50.00

2008 Upper Deck Premier Octographs

UNPRICED OCTOGRAPHS PRINT RUN 8

2008 Upper Deck Premier Pairings Autographs

STATED PRINT RUN 30-50
1 A.Peterson/J.Addai/30 50.00 100.00
2 D.Jackson/D.Jackson 8.00 20.00
3 A.Schobel/C.Long/42 8.00 20.00
4 D.Ware/C.Campbell 6.00 15.00
5 C.Jackson/A.Cason 4.00 10.00
6 D.Thomas/J.Nelson 10.00 25.00
7 D.Anderson/J.Flacco 10.00 25.00
8 J.Garcia/B.Croyle 8.00 20.00
10 F.Jones/C.Johnson 5.00 12.00
11 L.Johnson/M.Forte 15.00 40.00
12 K.Phillips/F.Gore 8.00 20.00
13 Y.Tittle/E.Manning 40.00 80.00
15 R.Rice/R.Mendenhall 4.00 10.00
16 O.Schmitt/J.Hester 3.00 8.00
17 D.Dixon/J.Johnson 3.00 8.00
18 D.Garrard/C.Johnson 5.00 12.00
19 B.Brohm/M.Urrutia 3.00 8.00
20 L.Jackson/P.Merling 5.00 12.00
21 W.Welker/B.Watson 12.00 30.00
22 B.Brohm/J.Nelson 15.00 40.00
24 J.Carlson/T.Zbikowski 8.00 20.00
26 B.Sanders/K.Phillips 15.00 40.00
27 P.Manning/D.Clark 60.00 120.00
28 F.Davis/M.Rucker 3.00 8.00
29 S.Baker/R.Clady 5.00 12.00
30 S.Crable/C.Henne 5.00 12.00
31 C.Williams/J.Campbell/30 15.00 30.00
32 L.Sweed/J.Charles 10.00 25.00
33 D.Dixon/B.Roethlisberger/30 50.00 100.00
34 L.McKelvin/D.Rodgers-Cromartie 4.00 10.00

2008 Upper Deck Premier Penmanship Autographs Bronze

BRONZE PRINT RUN 30-65
*GOLD/25: .5X TO 1.2X BRONZE/30-65
GOLD PRINT RUN 25
UNPRICED GOLD SPECTRUM PRINT RUN 1
PP1 Aaron Schobel/65 6.00 15.00
PP2 Kurt Warner/40 15.00 40.00
PP3 Andre Caldwell/65 3.00 8.00
PP4 Andre Woodson/65 3.00 8.00
PP5 Trent Edwards/65 6.00 15.00
PP6 Reggie Wayne/65 8.00 20.00
PP7 Ben Roethlisberger/35 50.00 100.00
PP8 Ben Watson/65 6.00 15.00
PP10 Don Maynard/65 10.00 25.00
PP11 Bo Jackson/99 25.00 50.00
PP12 Derek Anderson/65 6.00 15.00
PP13 Brian Bosworth/65 EXCH
PP14 Brian Brohm/40 3.00 8.00
PP15 Paul Hornung/65 12.00 30.00
PP16 Brodie Croyle/65 8.00 20.00
PP17 Bruce Davis/99 4.00 10.00
PP18 Dan Marino/35 75.00 150.00
PP19 Y.A. Tittle/65 12.00 30.00
PP20 Cadillac Williams/40 8.00 20.00
PP21 Chad Henne/65 4.00 10.00
PP22 Chris Johnson/65 4.00 10.00
PP23 Chris Long/65 4.00 10.00
PP24 Clinton Portis/40 6.00 15.00
PP25 Colt Brennan/65 4.00 10.00
PP26 Dan Connor/65 3.00 8.00
PP27 Darren McFadden/35 3.00 8.00
PP28 Daryl Johnston/65 10.00 25.00
PP29 David Garrard/65 6.00 15.00
PP30 John Elway/35 60.00 120.00
PP31 DeMarcus Ware/65 8.00 20.00
PP32 Dennis Dixon/65 6.00 15.00
PP33 DeSean Jackson/65 6.00 15.00
PP34 Kolby Smith/32 6.00 15.00
PP36 Dallas Clark/99 6.00 15.00
PP37 Dwayne Bowe/65 8.00 20.00
PP38 Early Doucet/99 3.00 8.00
PP39 Aaron Rodgers/40 EXCH
PP40 Erik Ainge/65 3.00 8.00
PP41 Marion Barber/40 6.00 15.00
PP42 Felix Jones/65 3.00 8.00
PP43 Fran Tarkenton/40 15.00 40.00
PP44 Frank Gore/40 8.00 20.00
PP45 Fred Davis/99 3.00 8.00
PP47 Tom Rathman/65 10.00 25.00
PP48 Herschel Walker/65 EXCH
PP49 Jamaal Charles/65 5.00 12.00
PP50 Josh Johnson/99 3.00 8.00
PP51 John Beck/65 6.00 15.00
PP53 Jason Campbell/65 6.00 15.00
PP54 Joe Flacco/65 6.00 15.00
PP55 John David Booty/65 3.00 8.00
PP56 John Lynch/99 8.00 20.00
PP57 Jonathan Stewart/40 15.00 40.00
PP58 Jordy Nelson/65 10.00 25.00
PP59 Joseph Addai/35 6.00 15.00
PP60 Keith Rivers/65 3.00 8.00
PP61 Kellen Winslow Sr/65 10.00 25.00
PP62 Ken Stabler/40 12.00 30.00
PP63 Kenny Phillips/65 3.00 8.00
PP64 Kevin Smith/65 3.00 8.00
PP65 LaDainian Tomlinson/35 25.00 50.00
PP66 Larry Johnson/40 6.00 15.00
PP67 Lavelle Hawkins/99 4.00 10.00
PP68 Limas Sweed/99 3.00 8.00
PP69 Lawrence Jackson/65 3.00 8.00
PP70 Malcolm Kelly/65 3.00 8.00
PP71 Marc Bulger/40 6.00 15.00
PP72 Devin Thomas/65 3.00 8.00
PP73 Tom Brady/65 125.00 200.00
PP75 Matt Forte/99 15.00 40.00
PP77 Matt Ryan/35 50.00 100.00
PP78 Ottis Anderson/65 8.00 20.00
PP80 Mike Hart/65 3.00 8.00
PP81 Mike Jenkins/65 3.00 8.00
PP82 Sedrick Ellis/65 3.00 8.00
PP83 Patrick Willis/99 8.00 20.00
PP84 Paul Smith/119 3.00 8.00
PP85 Bob Griese/35 12.00 30.00
PP86 Philip Rivers/30 12.00 30.00
PP87 Ryan Torain/99 4.00 10.00
PP88 Rashard Mendenhall/65 3.00 8.00
PP89 Ray Rice/99 3.00 8.00
PP90 Roger Craig/65 10.00 25.00
PP91 Roman Gabriel/65 8.00 20.00
PP92 Sam Baker/65 3.00 8.00
PP93 Steve Slaton/65 3.00 8.00
PP94 Tashard Choice/65 3.00 8.00
PP95 Kevin Boss/65 6.00 15.00
PP96 Tony Romo/65 30.00 80.00
PP97 Leodis McKelvin/65 4.00 10.00
PP98 Marshawn Lynch/40 8.00 20.00
PP99 Wes Welker/65 20.00 40.00
PP100 Jerry Kramer/65 15.00 30.00

2008 Upper Deck Premier Rare Materials Dual 65

STATED PRINT RUN 65 SER.#'d SETS
*PATCH/25: .6X TO 1.5X DUAL/65
*TRIPLE/50: .5X TO 1.2X DUAL/65
*TRIPLE PATCH/15: .8X TO 2X DUAL/65
PP2AR Anquan Boldin 3.00 8.00
PP2AP Adrian Peterson 5.00 12.00
PP2AS Aaron Schobel 3.00 8.00
PP2BB Brian Bosworth 8.00 20.00
PP2BC Brodie Croyle 4.00 10.00
PP2BE Bernard Berrian 3.00 8.00
PP2BJ Bo Jackson 10.00 25.00
PP2BS Billy Sims 6.00 15.00
PP2BW Ben Watson 3.00 8.00
PP2CA Jason Campbell 3.00 8.00
PP2CB Champ Bailey 4.00 10.00
PP2CJ Chad Johnson 3.00 8.00
PP2CP Clinton Portis 3.00 8.00
PP2CW Carnell Williams 4.00 10.00
PP2DB Dwayne Bowe 4.00 10.00
PP2DG David Garrard 3.00 8.00
PP2DH Devin Hester 4.00 10.00
PP2DM Dan Marino 15.00 40.00
PP2DW DeMarcus Ware 4.00 10.00
PP2ED Braylon Edwards 3.00 8.00
PP2EM Eli Manning 4.00 10.00
PP2ER Ed Reed 4.00 10.00
PP2ES Ernie Sims 3.00 8.00
PP2FG Frank Gore 4.00 10.00
PP2FT Fred Taylor 3.00 8.00
PP2HW Herschel Walker 8.00 20.00
PP2JA Joseph Addai 3.00 8.00
PP2JC Jay Cutler 3.00 8.00
PP2JM Joe Montana 25.00 60.00
PP2JN Jerious Norwood 3.00 8.00
PP2KS Ken Stabler 8.00 20.00
PP2KW Kellen Winslow Jr. 3.00 8.00
PP2LS Lynn Swann 10.00 25.00
PP2MB Marion Barber 3.00 8.00
PP2MC Jim McMahon 8.00 20.00
PP2MH Michael Huff 3.00 8.00
PP2ML Marshawn Lynch 4.00 10.00
PP2MS Matt Schaub 3.00 8.00
PP2MV Mike Vrabel 3.00 8.00
PP2PR Philip Rivers 5.00 12.00
PP2PW Patrick Willis 4.00 10.00
PP2RC Roger Craig 6.00 15.00
PP2RG Ryan Grant 4.00 10.00
PP2RW Roy Williams WR 3.00 8.00
PP2SA Asante Samuel 3.00 8.00
PP2SM Emmitt Smith 12.00 30.00
PP2SY Steve Young 10.00 25.00
PP2WE Brian Westbrook 3.00 8.00
PP2WI Kellen Winslow Sr. 5.00 12.00
PP2WM Willis McGahee 3.00 8.00

2008 Upper Deck Premier Remnants Quad 40

STATED PRINT RUN 40
UNPRICED AUTO PRINT RUN 9-15
PARALLELS #'d TO 10 AND 1/1 NOT PRICED
PR4AP Adrian Peterson 6.00 15.00
PR4AS Aaron Schobel 4.00 10.00
PR4BB Brian Bosworth 10.00 25.00
PR4BC Brodie Croyle 5.00 12.00
PR4BF Brett Favre 12.00 30.00
PR4BJ Bo Jackson 12.00 30.00
PR4BM Brian Brohm 2.50 6.00
PR4BR Ben Roethlisberger 6.00 15.00
PR4BS Bob Sanders 5.00 12.00
PR4BU Marc Bulger 4.00 10.00
PR4CA Jason Campbell 4.00 10.00
PR4CJ Chad Johnson 4.00 10.00
PR4CP Clinton Portis 4.00 10.00
PR4CW Cadillac Williams 5.00 12.00
PR4DA Darren McFadden 2.50 6.00
PR4DB Dwayne Bowe 5.00 12.00
PR4DC Dallas Clark 4.00 10.00
PR4DE Derek Anderson 4.00 10.00
PR4DG David Garrard 4.00 10.00
PR4DM Dan Marino 20.00 50.00
PR4DT Devin Thomas 2.50 6.00
PR4EM Eli Manning 5.00 12.00
PR4FG Frank Gore 5.00 12.00
PR4FJ Felix Jones 2.50 6.00
PR4JF Joe Flacco 5.00 12.00
PR4JG Jeff Garcia 4.00 10.00
PR4JI Jim McMahon 10.00 25.00
PR4JL Jack Lambert 10.00 25.00
PR4JM Joe Montana 30.00 80.00
PR4KS Ken Stabler 10.00 25.00
PR4KW Kellen Winslow Jr. 4.00 10.00
PR4LE Jamal Lewis 5.00 12.00
PR4LJ Larry Johnson 4.00 10.00
PR4LS Lynn Swann 10.00 25.00
PR4LT LaDainian Tomlinson 6.00 15.00
PR4MB Marion Barber 4.00 10.00
PR4MH Michael Huff 4.00 10.00
PR4ML Marshawn Lynch 5.00 12.00
PR4MR Matt Ryan 8.00 20.00
PR4PW Patrick Willis 5.00 12.00
PR4RC Roger Craig 8.00 20.00
PR4RM Rashard Mendenhall 2.50 6.00
PR4SI Billy Sims 8.00 20.00
PR4SM Kevin Smith 2.50 6.00
PR4WA Kurt Warner 5.00 12.00
PR4WI Kellen Winslow Sr. 6.00 15.00
PR4PM1 Peyton Manning 15.00 40.00
PR4PM2 Peyton Manning 15.00 40.00

2008 Upper Deck Premier Remnants Triple NFL

NFL STATED PRINT RUN 65
*JSY NO/25: .5X TO 1.2X NFL/65
JERSEY NUMBER PRINT RUN 25
UNPRICED HELMET DC PRINT RUN 1
PR3AD Joseph Addai 3.00 8.00
PR3AP Adrian Peterson 5.00 12.00
PR3AS Aaron Schobel 3.00 8.00
PR3BB Brian Bosworth 8.00 20.00
PR3BC Brodie Croyle 4.00 10.00
PR3BF Brett Favre 10.00 25.00
PR3BJ Bo Jackson 10.00 25.00
PR3BM Brian Brohm 2.00 5.00
PR3BO Bob Sanders 4.00 10.00
PR3BR Ben Roethlisberger 5.00 12.00
PR3BS Billy Sims 6.00 15.00
PR3BU Marc Bulger 3.00 8.00
PR3CJ Chad Johnson 3.00 8.00
PR3CP Clinton Portis 3.00 8.00
PR3CW Cadillac Williams 4.00 10.00
PR3DA Darren McFadden 2.00 5.00
PR3DB Dwayne Bowe 4.00 10.00
PR3DC Dallas Clark 3.00 8.00
PR3DE Derek Anderson 3.00 8.00
PR3DG David Garrard 3.00 8.00
PR3DK Dustin Keller 2.50 6.00
PR3DM Dan Marino 15.00 40.00
PR3DT Devin Thomas 2.00 5.00
PR3EM Eli Manning 4.00 10.00
PR3FG Frank Gore 4.00 10.00
PR3FJ Felix Jones 2.00 5.00
PR3JC Jason Campbell 3.00 8.00
PR3JF Joe Flacco 4.00 10.00
PR3JG Jeff Garcia 3.00 8.00
PR3JL Jack Lambert 8.00 20.00
PR3JM Joe Montana 25.00 60.00
PR3KS Ken Stabler 8.00 20.00
PR3LE Jamal Lewis 4.00 10.00
PR3LJ Larry Johnson 3.00 8.00
PR3LS Lynn Swann 8.00 20.00
PR3LT LaDainian Tomlinson 5.00 12.00
PR3MB Marion Barber 3.00 8.00
PR3MH Michael Huff 3.00 8.00
PR3ML Marshawn Lynch 4.00 10.00
PR3MR Matt Ryan 6.00 15.00
PR3MS Matt Schaub 3.00 8.00
PR3PW Patrick Willis 4.00 10.00
PR3RC Roger Craig 6.00 15.00
PR3RM Rashard Mendenhall 2.00 5.00
PR3SM Kevin Smith 2.00 5.00
PR3SY Steve Young 10.00 25.00
PR3WA Kurt Warner 4.00 10.00
PR3WI Kellen Winslow Sr. 5.00 12.00
PR3PM1 Peyton Manning 12.00 30.00
PR3PM2 Peyton Manning 12.00 30.00

2008 Upper Deck Premier Remnants Triple Autographs NFL

STATED PRINT RUN 15-45
UNPRICED QUAD AUTO PRINT RUN 9-15
AD Joseph Addai/25 10.00 25.00
AP Adrian Peterson/25 100.00 200.00
BC Brodie Croyle/25 12.00 30.00
BJ Bo Jackson/25 40.00 80.00
BM Brian Brohm/25 5.00 12.00
BO Bob Sanders/25 20.00 40.00
BR Ben Roethlisberger/25 60.00 120.00
BS Billy Sims/25 15.00 40.00
BU Marc Bulger/25 10.00 25.00
CJ Chad Johnson/25 10.00 25.00
CP Clinton Portis/25 10.00 25.00
CW Cadillac Williams/25 12.00 30.00
DA Darren McFadden/25 5.00 12.00
DB Dwayne Bowe/25 12.00 30.00
DC Dallas Clark/25 10.00 25.00
DE Derek Anderson/25 10.00 25.00
DG David Garrard/25 10.00 25.00
DK Dustin Keller/25 6.00 15.00
DM Dan Marino/25 100.00 200.00
DT Devin Thomas/35 5.00 12.00
EM Eli Manning/25 40.00 80.00
FG Frank Gore/25 12.00 30.00
FJ Felix Jones/45 5.00 12.00
JC Jason Campbell/25 10.00 25.00
JF Joe Flacco/25 20.00 50.00
JL Jack Lambert/25 40.00 80.00
JM Joe Montana/15 75.00 150.00
KS Ken Stabler/25 20.00 50.00
LJ Larry Johnson/25 10.00 25.00
LT LaDainian Tomlinson/25 30.00 80.00
MB Marion Barber/25 10.00 25.00
ML Marshawn Lynch/25 12.00 30.00
MR Matt Ryan/25 50.00 120.00
PW Patrick Willis/25 12.00 30.00
RC Roger Craig/25 15.00 40.00
RM Rashard Mendenhall/25 5.00 12.00
SM Kevin Smith/25 5.00 12.00
SY Steve Young/25 40.00 80.00
WA Kurt Warner/25 25.00 50.00
WI Kellen Winslow Sr./25 12.00 30.00
PM1 Peyton Manning/25 60.00 120.00
PM2 Peyton Manning/25 75.00 135.00

2008 Upper Deck Premier Rookie Autographed Patches Gold 30

*GOLD PATCH/30: .8X TO 2X BASIC CARD
GOLD PATCH PRINT RUN 30
GOLD PATCH 10 PARALLEL UNPRICED
GOLD PATCH 1/1 PARALLEL UNPRICED
105 Chris Johnson JSY AU 12.00 30.00
118 Joe Flacco JSY AU 20.00 50.00
129 Matt Ryan JSY AU 60.00 120.00

2008 Upper Deck Premier Signatures Gold

GOLD PRINT RUN 15-99
UNPRICED GOLD SPECTRUM PRINT RUN 1
UNPRICED SILVER SPECTRUM PRINT RUN 5
SP1 A.J. Hawk/65 6.00 15.00
SP2 Aaron Schobel/65 6.00 15.00
SP5 Don Maynard/65 EXCH 10.00 25.00
SP6 Ben Watson/99 6.00 15.00
SP7 Trent Edwards/35 6.00 15.00
SP8 Jason Campbell/65 6.00 15.00
SP9 Brodie Croyle/65 8.00 20.00
SP11 Chad Henne/99 4.00 10.00
SP12 Chad Johnson/35 6.00 15.00
SP13 Chris Johnson/99 4.00 10.00
SP14 Chris Long/65 4.00 10.00
SP15 Clinton Portis/35 6.00 15.00
SP16 Darren McFadden/15 15.00 40.00
SP17 David Garrard/35 6.00 15.00
SP18 Paul Hornung/65 12.00 30.00
SP19 Dennis Dixon/65 6.00 15.00
SP20 Derek Anderson/65 6.00 15.00
SP21 DeSean Jackson/99 6.00 15.00
SP22 Kurt Warner/35 15.00 40.00
SP23 DeMarcus Ware/65 10.00 25.00
SP24 Early Doucet/65 3.00 8.00
SP25 Erik Ainge/75 3.00 8.00
SP26 Felix Jones/99 3.00 8.00
SP27 Fred Davis/65 3.00 8.00
SP28 Jeremy Shockey/25 8.00 20.00
SP29 Jamaal Charles/65 12.00 30.00
SP30 Y.A. Tittle/65 12.00 30.00
SP31 Joe Flacco/65 6.00 15.00
SP32 John David Booty/65 3.00 8.00
SP33 Jordy Nelson/99 15.00 40.00
SP34 Kenny Phillips/65 3.00 8.00
SP35 Kevin Smith/99 3.00 8.00
SP36 Larry Johnson/35 6.00 15.00
SP37 Devin Thomas/80 3.00 8.00
SP38 Marshawn Lynch/20 10.00 25.00
SP39 Matt Flynn/65 EXCH 3.00 8.00
SP40 Matt Forte/95 20.00 50.00
SP41 Matt Ryan/35 50.00 120.00
SP42 Mike Hart/99 3.00 8.00
SP43 Mike Jenkins/65 3.00 8.00
SP44 Rashard Mendenhall/65 3.00 8.00
SP45 Ray Rice/85 3.00 8.00
SP46 Eli Manning/65 25.00 50.00
SP47 Steve Slaton/99 3.00 8.00
SP48 Peyton Manning/65 40.00 80.00
SP49 Tony Romo/65 50.00 100.00
SP50 Bob Sanders/65 25.00 50.00

2008 Upper Deck Premier Significant Stars Autographs Dual Gold

GOLD DUAL PRINT RUN 15-35
UNPRICED SILVER SPECTRUM PRINT RUN 1
AP A.Peterson/J.Addai/25 60.00 120.00
BH D.Butkus/A.Hawk/25 50.00 100.00
BL D.Butkus/J.Lambert/25 60.00 120.00
BW M.Bulger/K.Warner/25 20.00 50.00
DJ D.Garrard/J.Campbell/25 20.00 50.00
FL T.Edwards/M.Lynch/25 15.00 40.00
HM R.Mendenhall/F.Harris/25 30.00 80.00
JA K.Anderson/C.Johnson/25
JM B.Jackson/D.McFadden/15 40.00 80.00
LH J.Long/C.Henne/35 25.00 60.00
RB M.Barber/T.Romo/25 40.00 100.00
RW Croyle/Welker/25 25.00 60.00
SC Bob Sanders/D.Clark/25 40.00 80.00
SR B.Sanders/R.Craig/15 75.00 150.00
TA Tittle/Anderson/25 15.00 40.00
TS Tomlinson/G.Sayers/25 50.00 100.00

2008 Upper Deck Premier Six Autographs

UNPRICED SIX AUTO PRINT RUN 6

2008 Upper Deck Premier Stitchings Autographs

STATED PRINT RUN 20 SER.#'d SETS
PSAD Joseph Addai 6.00 15.00
PSAH A.J. Hawk 10.00 25.00
PSAP Adrian Peterson 100.00 175.00
PSAV Donnie Avery 8.00 20.00
PSAW Andre Woodson 6.00 15.00
PSBB Brian Brohm 6.00 15.00
PSBC Brodie Croyle 8.00 20.00
PSBF Brett Favre 3MVP 100.00 200.00
PSBO Dwayne Bowe 8.00 20.00
PSBS Barry Sanders 90.00 150.00
PSCH Chad Henne 8.00 20.00
PSCJ Chad Johnson 10.00 25.00
PSCL Chris Long 8.00 20.00
PSCO Colt Brennan 8.00 20.00
PSCP Clinton Portis 10.00 25.00
PSDA Derek Anderson 6.00 15.00
PSDB Dick Butkus 40.00 80.00
PSDD Dennis Dixon 6.00 15.00
PSDE DeSean Jackson 12.00 30.00
PSDG David Garrard 10.00 25.00
PSDJ Daryl Johnston 25.00 50.00
PSDM Dan Marino 100.00 200.00
PSDW DeMarcus Ware 12.00 30.00
PSEA Erik Ainge 6.00 15.00
PSED Early Doucet 6.00 15.00
PSEM Eli Manning 40.00 80.00
PSFA Brett Favre 100.00 200.00
PSFG Frank Gore 8.00 20.00
PSFH Franco Harris 30.00 60.00
PSFJ Felix Jones 6.00 15.00
PSFT Fran Tarkenton 25.00 50.00
PSGS Gale Sayers 20.00 50.00
PSHA Mike Hart 6.00 15.00
PSHE Jacob Hester 6.00 15.00
PSJA Bo Jackson 50.00 100.00
PSJB John David Booty 6.00 15.00
PSJC Jason Campbell 6.00 15.00
PSJE John Elway 50.00 100.00
PSJF Joe Flacco 8.00 20.00
PSJH Jack Ham 25.00 50.00
PSJK Jerry Kramer 20.00 40.00
PSJL Jack Lambert 30.00 60.00
PSJR Jerry Rice 75.00 150.00
PSJS Jonathan Stewart 10.00 25.00
PSJT Joe Theismann 20.00 50.00
PSKA Ken Anderson 15.00 40.00
PSKS Ken Stabler 20.00 50.00
PSLO Jake Long 10.00 25.00
PSLT LaDainian Tomlinson 30.00 60.00
PSMB Marion Barber 8.00 20.00
PSMC Darren McFadden 8.00 20.00
PSMF Matt Flynn 6.00 15.00
PSMK Malcolm Kelly 6.00 15.00
PSML Marshawn Lynch 12.00 30.00
PSMO Joe Montana 100.00 175.00
PSMR Matt Ryan 60.00 120.00
PSOA Ottis Anderson 12.00 30.00
PSPA Allen Patrick 6.00 15.00
PSPH Paul Hornung 20.00 50.00
PSPM Peyton Manning 90.00 150.00
PSPR Philip Rivers 15.00 40.00
PSPW Patrick Willis 12.00 30.00
PSRA Rashard Mendenhall 6.00 15.00
PSRC Roger Craig 15.00 40.00
PSRG Roman Gabriel 25.00 50.00
PSRO Tony Romo 75.00 150.00
PSRR Ray Rice 6.00 15.00
PSSA Bob Sanders 25.00 50.00
PSSI Billy Sims 15.00 40.00
PSSM Kevin Smith 6.00 15.00
PSSS Steve Slaton 6.00 15.00
PSTB Terry Bradshaw 60.00 120.00
PSTO Tom Brady 100.00 200.00
PSTR Tom Rathman 15.00 40.00
PSWE Wes Welker 25.00 50.00
PSWW Wes Welker 25.00 50.00
PSYT Y.A. Tittle 20.00 50.00

2008 Upper Deck Premier Stitchings Cut Signatures

STATED PRINT RUN 2-31
SER.#'d UNDER 14 NOT PRICED
PSCDS Dinah Shore/31 25.00 50.00
PSCGB George Burns/28 75.00 125.00
PSCLB1 Lucille Ball/16 175.00 300.00
PSCLB2 Lucille Ball/14 175.00 300.00

2008 Upper Deck Premier Stitchings Team Logo/NFL Draft Silver

SILVER PRINT RUN 30
*GOLD/15: .5X TO 1.2X SILVER/30
GOLD TEAM LOGO/DRAFT PRINT RUN 15
*COLL.LOGO/VAR GOLD/15: .5X TO 1.2X
GOLD COLL.LOGO/VAR PRINT RUN 15
*COLL.LOGO/VAR SLVR/30: .4X TO 1X
SILVER COLL.LOGO/VAR PRINT RUN 30
*GOLD VARIATION/15: .5X TO 1.2X SIL/30
GOLD VARIATION PRINT RUN 15
*SILVER VARIATION/30: .4X TO 1X SIL/30
SILVER VARIATION PRINT RUN 30
UNPRICED SILVER SPECTRUMS PRINT RUN 1
PSAD Joseph Addai 4.00 10.00
PSAH A.J. Hawk 4.00 10.00
PSAP Adrian Peterson 10.00 25.00
PSAV Donnie Avery 3.00 8.00
PSAW Andre Woodson 2.50 6.00
PSBB Brian Brohm 2.50 6.00
PSBC Brodie Croyle 5.00 12.00
PSBF Brett Favre 12.00 30.00
PSBJ Bert Jones 6.00 15.00
PSBL Mel Blount 8.00 20.00
PSBO Dwayne Bowe 5.00 12.00
PSBR Brandon Jacobs 4.00 10.00
PSBS Barry Sanders 15.00 40.00
PSBW Brian Bosworth BOZ 10.00 25.00
PSCB Champ Bailey 5.00 12.00
PSCH Chad Henne 3.00 8.00
PSCJ Chad Johnson 4.00 10.00
PSCL Chris Long 3.00 8.00
PSCO Colt Brennan 3.00 8.00
PSCP Clinton Portis 4.00 10.00
PSDA Derek Anderson 4.00 10.00
PSDB Dick Butkus 12.00 30.00
PSDD Dennis Dixon 2.50 6.00
PSDE DeSean Jackson 5.00 12.00
PSDG David Garrard 4.00 10.00
PSDJ Daryl Johnston 10.00 25.00
PSDM Dan Marino 20.00 50.00
PSDO Dorien Bryant 3.00 8.00
PSDW DeMarcus Ware 5.00 12.00
PSEA Erik Ainge 2.50 6.00
PSED Early Doucet 2.50 6.00
PSEM Eli Manning 5.00 12.00
PSER Ed Reed 5.00 12.00
PSFA Brett Favre MVP 12.00 30.00
PSFG Frank Gore 5.00 12.00
PSFH Franco Harris 10.00 25.00
PSFJ Felix Jones 2.50 6.00
PSFT Fran Tarkenton 10.00 25.00
PSGD Glenn Dorsey 2.50 6.00
PSGJ Greg Jennings 4.00 10.00
PSGS Gale Sayers 10.00 25.00
PSHA Mike Hart 2.50 6.00
PSHE Jacob Hester 2.50 6.00
PSJA Bo Jackson 12.00 30.00
PSJB John David Booty 2.50 6.00
PSJC Jason Campbell 4.00 10.00
PSJE John Elway 15.00 40.00
PSJF Joe Flacco 5.00 12.00
PSJH Jack Ham 8.00 20.00
PSJK Jerry Kramer 8.00 20.00
PSJL Jack Lambert 10.00 25.00
PSJM Jim McMahon 10.00 25.00
PSJR Jerry Rice 20.00 50.00
PSJS Jonathan Stewart 8.00 20.00
PSJT Joe Theismann 10.00 25.00
PSKA Ken Anderson 8.00 20.00
PSKS Ken Stabler 12.00 30.00
PSLE Matt Leinart 4.00 10.00
PSLO Jake Long 4.00 10.00
PSLS Lynn Swann 10.00 25.00
PSLT LaDainian Tomlinson 6.00 15.00
PSLY John Lynch 5.00 12.00
PSMB Marion Barber 4.00 10.00
PSMC Darren McFadden 2.50 6.00
PSME Don Meredith 10.00 25.00
PSMF Matt Flynn 2.50 6.00
PSMH Michael Huff 2.50 6.00
PSMK Malcolm Kelly 2.50 6.00
PSML Marshawn Lynch 5.00 12.00
PSMO Joe Montana 30.00 80.00
PSMR Matt Ryan 8.00 20.00
PSMS Matt Schaub 4.00 10.00
PSOA Ottis Anderson 6.00 15.00
PSPA Allen Patrick 2.50 6.00
PSPH Paul Hornung 10.00 25.00
PSPM Peyton Manning 15.00 40.00
PSPR Philip Rivers 6.00 15.00
PSPW Patrick Willis 5.00 12.00
PSRA Rashard Mendenhall 2.50 6.00
PSRC Roger Craig 8.00 20.00
PSRG Roman Gabriel 6.00 15.00
PSRM Randy Moss 5.00 12.00
PSRO Tony Romo 5.00 12.00
PSRR Ray Rice 2.50 6.00
PSRW Randy White 8.00 20.00
PSSA Bob Sanders 5.00 12.00
PSSB Sammy Baugh 10.00 25.00
PSSI Billy Sims 8.00 20.00
PSSJ Sonny Jurgensen 8.00 20.00
PSSM Kevin Smith 2.50 6.00
PSSS Steve Slaton 2.50 6.00
PSTB Terry Bradshaw 12.00 30.00
PSTG Tony Gonzalez 5.00 12.00
PSTO Tom Brady 20.00 50.00
PSTP Troy Polamalu 6.00 15.00
PSTR Tom Rathman 8.00 20.00
PSVY Vince Young 4.00 10.00
PSWE Wes Welker 112 REC 5.00 12.00
PSWW Wes Welker 5.00 12.00
PSYT Y.A. Tittle 10.00 25.00

2008 Upper Deck Premier Teams Jersey Team Logo

STATED PRINT RUN 65 SER.#'d SETS
*TEAM INITIAL/25: .5X TO 1.2X TEAM/65
TEAM INITIALS PRINT RUN 25
UNPRICED AFC/NFC PRINT RUN 1
AWE Edwards/Andrsn/Winslw 4.00 10.00
BBC Bush/Brees/Colston 6.00 15.00
BBL Brdshw/Blount/Lmbrt 12.00 30.00
BFL Leinart/Fitzg/Boldin 5.00 12.00
BMJ Eli/Jacobs/Burress 5.00 12.00
CBM Cutler/Bailey/Marshall 5.00 12.00
FJH Favre/Jennings/Hawk 12.00 30.00
GSW Smith/Gore/Willis 5.00 12.00
HBT Hassel/Branch/Tatupu 4.00 10.00
JGC Croyle/LJ/Gonzalez 5.00 12.00
JHP Johnson/Palmer/Housh 5.00 12.00
LEW Lewis/Edwrds/Winslw 5.00 12.00
MBW Moss/Brady/Welker 20.00 50.00
MWS Mann/Wyne/Sanders 15.00 40.00
PRP Parker/Roeth/Polamalu 6.00 15.00
RWB Romo/Barber/Ware 5.00 12.00
TGC Tomlin/Cromartie/Gates 6.00 15.00
TGJ Taylor/Garrard/J-Drew 4.00 10.00
UBH Hester/Forte/Urlacher 5.00 12.00
YWJ Young/White/Johnson 5.00 12.00

2008 Upper Deck Premier Trios Autographs

STATED PRINT RUN 15-25
2 Jcksn/Smp/Jcksn/25
3 McKlvn/R-Crom/Jnkns/25
4 Wtsn/Keller/F.Dvis/25 12.00 30.00
5 Avry/D.Thom/Nelsn/25 12.00 30.00
6 Ch.Jhn/Andrsn/Brmrd/25
8 C.Jhn/F.Jns/K.Smith/25 20.00 50.00
9 Garr/Flacco/Henne/25 15.00 40.00
10 Ware/Calais/B.Dvis/25 12.00 30.00
11 Cmpbll/Garr/Bulger/25 25.00 60.00
12 Long/Clady/Baker/25 15.00 40.00
13 Croyle/Bowe/LJ/25 30.00 60.00
16 Hart/Henne/Arring/25 20.00 50.00
17 Peyton/Addai/Clrk/25 75.00 150.00
18 Ellis/Booty/T.Thms/25
19 Brady/Namath/Elway/15 175.00 300.00

2008 Upper Deck Premier Trios Jersey 40

TRIOS JERSEY PRINT RUN 40
*TRIO JSY/25: .5X TO 1.2X TRIOS/40
TRIOS JERSEY 1/1 NOT PRICED
AJJ Jackson/Johnson/Anderson 4.00 10.00
EMM Elway/Marino/Montana 30.00 80.00
FMB Brady/Peyton/Favre 20.00 50.00
FRR Roeth/Favre/Rivers 12.00 30.00
FWP Will.WR/Favre/Peterson 12.00 30.00
GGW Gates/Gonzalez/Winslow 5.00 12.00
GPG Parker/Grant/Gore 5.00 12.00
HJL Hester/J-Drew/Lynch 5.00 12.00
HSL Leinart/Schaub/Hassel 4.00 10.00
JBJ Johnson/Johnson/Boldin 6.00 15.00
JBL James/Boldin/Leinart 5.00 12.00
JJB Jennings/Johnson/Bowe 6.00 15.00
JMG Gore/McGahee/James 5.00 12.00
JMJ McAllister/Jacobs/LJ 5.00 12.00
JMW McGahee/White/LJ 4.00 10.00
JPL Lynch/LJ/Peterson 6.00 15.00
JTM Tomlin/LJ/Maroney 6.00 15.00
MBC McAllister/Bush/Colston 5.00 12.00
MMW Eli/Willis/McAllister 5.00 12.00
MOJ Moss/TO/Ch.Johnson 5.00 12.00
MPJ McGahee/Lewis/Parker 5.00 12.00
MRR Rivers/Roeth/Eli 6.00 15.00
PLB Leinart/Palmer/Bush 5.00 12.00
RBJ Johnston/Barber/Romo 5.00 12.00
RPS Bob Sand/Reed/Polamalu 6.00 15.00
SCC Smith QB/Cutler/Croyle 5.00 12.00
SHS Swann/Sweed/Holmes 10.00 25.00
SMR Russell/Stabler/McFadden 4.00 10.00
SRA Smith QB/Rodgers/Anderson 12.00 30.00
STS B.Sanders/Tomlin/Sayers 15.00 40.00
TBM Barber/Maroney/Tomlins 6.00 15.00
WBE Brady/Edwards/Woodson 20.00 50.00
WBY Young/White/Bush 4.00 10.00
WPL Wdsn/Leinart/Palmer 6.00 15.00
WSH Hawk/Ware/Sims 5.00 12.00

2008 Upper Deck Premier Trios Patch 75

TRIOS PATCH PRINT RUN 75
*TRIO PATCH/25: .5X TO 1.2X TRIO PATCH/75
TRIOS PATCH 1/1 NOT PRICED
AGC Grrard/Andrsn/Croyle 5.00 12.00
AJJ Jcksn/Jhnsn/Andrsn 4.00 10.00
AWE Edwards/Andrsn/Winslow 4.00 10.00
BBJ Jennings/Burr/Branch 4.00 10.00
BGR Grrard/Roeth/Brdshw 12.00 30.00

BMJ Eli/Burress/Jacobs 5.00 12.00
BMS Brdshaw/Eli/Smith QB 12.00 30.00
BPP Parker/Brdshw/Pola 12.00 30.00
BRC Cutler/Bulger/Roeth 6.00 15.00
BVM Brady/Vrabel/Marney 20.00 50.00
EBB Elway/Brdshw/Brady 30.00 80.00
EJB Jenn/Edwards/Bowe 5.00 12.00
FHM Favre/Hassel/Eli 12.00 30.00
FWG Favre/Wdson/Grant 12.00 30.00
GCB Croyle/Gonza/Bowe 5.00 12.00
GPR Palmer/Roeth/Grrard 6.00 15.00
GRC Rivers/Gates/Crmrtie 6.00 15.00
GSG Gates/Shockey/Gonz 5.00 12.00
GSW Watson/Gonz/Shcky 5.00 12.00
HWP Wstbrk/Harris/Parker 10.00 25.00
JBW Jhnsn/Bailey/Williams 5.00 12.00
JMB Mrshll/Bowe/Jennings 5.00 12.00
JTJ LT/LJ/Jacobs 6.00 15.00
MBM Brady/Peyton/Eli 20.00 50.00
MBR Brady/Rivers/Peyton 12.00 30.00
MCQ Moss/Croyle/Quinn 5.00 12.00
MFM McMah/Mont/Favre 40.00 80.00
MJJ Moss/Jhnsn/Jhnsn 6.00 15.00
MWA Peyton/Wayne/Addai 15.00 40.00
OHB Holmes/Bowe/TO 5.00 12.00
PLB Palmer/Leinart/Bush 5.00 12.00
RSH Huff/Reed/Sanders 5.00 12.00
SMR Russell/McFad/Stabler 4.00 10.00
TGJ Taylor/J-Drew/Garrard 4.00 10.00
TJP Peterson/LT/J-Drew 6.00 15.00
TSG LT/Sayers/Grant 10.00 25.00
VWH Vrabel/Ware/Hawk 5.00 12.00
WAP Petrsn/Wstbrk/Addai 6.00 15.00
WEH Wlkr/Edwrds/Holms 5.00 12.00
WPJ Wstbrk/J-Drew/Prkr 5.00 12.00
WSC Samuel/Wdson/Crom 6.00 15.00
WSH Hawk/Sims/Ware 5.00 12.00

2008 Upper Deck Premier Vital Signs Autographs Gold

GOLD STATED PRINT RUN 10-35
VT1 Ben Watson/35 6.00 15.00
VT2 Jerome Simpson/35 5.00 12.00
VT4 Devin Thomas/35 4.00 10.00
VT5 David Garrard/15 8.00 20.00
VT6 Brodie Croyle/35 8.00 20.00
VT7 Matt Flynn/35 4.00 10.00
VT8 DeSean Jackson/35 8.00 20.00
VT9 Jeff Garcia/35 6.00 15.00
VT10 Colt Brennan/35 5.00 12.00
VT11 Jonathan Stewart/15 10.00 25.00
VT12 Andre Woodson/35 4.00 10.00
VT13 Chad Henne/35 12.00 30.00
VT14 Chris Long/35 5.00 12.00
VT15 Rashard Mendenhall/35 4.00 10.00
VT16 Dennis Dixon/35 8.00 20.00
VT17 Early Doucet/35 4.00 10.00
VT18 Erik Ainge/35 4.00 10.00
VT19 Jamaal Charles/35 10.00 25.00
VT20 Joe Flacco/35 8.00 20.00
VT21 Felix Jones/50 4.00 10.00
VT22 Mike Hart/35 4.00 10.00
VT23 Steve Slaton/35 4.00 10.00
VT24 Harry Douglas/55 5.00 12.00
VT25 Mike Jenkins/55 4.00 10.00
VT26 Adrian Arrington/35 4.00 10.00
VT27 Calais Campbell/50 5.00 12.00
VT28 Dan Connor/35 4.00 10.00
VT29 Bruce Davis/35 5.00 12.00
VT30 Bob Sanders/35 25.00 60.00
VT31 Aaron Schobel/35 6.00 15.00
VT32 Ben Roethlisberger/15 50.00 100.00
VT35 Kenny Phillips/55 4.00 10.00

2000 Upper Deck Pros and Prospects

Released as a 126-card base set, the 2000 Upper Deck Pros and Prospects set is comprised of 84 regular cards and 42 draft picks-each sequentially numbered to 1000. Base cards have a white border that clouds into a full color action shot and card fronts are enhanced with bronze foil highlights. Pros and Prospects was packaged in 24-pack boxes containing five cards each pack and carried a suggested retail price of $4.99. An Update set of 26-cards was issued in April 2001 as part of 3-card packs distributed directly to Upper Deck hobby accounts.

COMPLETE SET (126) 300.00 600.00
COMP.SET w/o SP's (84) 7.50 20.00
85-152 ROOKIE PRINT RUN 1000
1 Jake Plummer .12 .30
2 Michael Pittman .12 .30
3 Tim Dwight .15 .40
4 Chris Chandler .15 .40
5 Qadry Ismail .12 .30
6 Shannon Sharpe .15 .40
7 Peerless Price .15 .40
8 Rob Johnson .15 .40
9 Eric Moulds .12 .30
10 Muhsin Muhammad .12 .30
11 Patrick Jeffers .12 .30
12 Steve Beuerlein .15 .40
13 Cade McNown .12 .30
14 Curtis Enis .12 .30
15 Marcus Robinson .15 .40
16 Akili Smith .12 .30
17 Corey Dillon .12 .30
18 Tim Couch .15 .40
19 Kevin Johnson .12 .30
20 Errict Rhett .15 .40
21 Troy Aikman .25 .60
22 Emmitt Smith .30 .75
23 Rocket Ismail .15 .40
24 Terrell Davis .15 .40
25 Olandis Gary .15 .40
26 Brian Griese .12 .30
27 Ed McCaffrey .15 .40
28 Charlie Batch .12 .30
29 Germane Crowell .12 .30
30 James O. Stewart .12 .30
31 Brett Favre .40 1.00
32 Antonio Freeman .15 .40
33 Dorsey Levens .15 .40
34 Peyton Manning .50 1.25
35 Edgerrin James .15 .40
36 Marvin Harrison .15 .40
37 Mark Brunell .15 .40
38 Fred Taylor .12 .30
39 Jimmy Smith .15 .40
40 Elvis Grbac .12 .30
41 Tony Gonzalez .15 .40
42 Damon Huard .12 .30
43 James Johnson .12 .30
44 Jay Fiedler .15 .40
45 Randy Moss .15 .40
46 Robert Smith .12 .30
47 Cris Carter .20 .50
48 Drew Bledsoe .15 .40
49 Terry Glenn .15 .40
50 Ricky Williams .15 .40
51 Jeff Blake .15 .40
52 Keith Poole .12 .30
53 Kerry Collins .12 .30
54 Amani Toomer .12 .30
55 Vinny Testaverde .12 .30
56 Keyshawn Johnson .15 .40
57 Curtis Martin .15 .40
58 Tim Brown .20 .50
59 Rich Gannon .15 .40
60 Tyrone Wheatley .12 .30
61 Duce Staley .12 .30
62 Donovan McNabb .15 .40
63 Troy Edwards .12 .30
64 Jerome Bettis .20 .50
65 Marshall Faulk .15 .40
66 Kurt Warner .30 .75
67 Torry Holt .15 .40
68 Isaac Bruce .20 .50
69 Junior Seau .15 .40
70 Jeff Graham .12 .30
71 Steve Young .25 .60
72 Jerry Rice .50 1.25
73 Charlie Garner .15 .40
74 Ricky Watters .15 .40
75 Jon Kitna .12 .30
76 Warrick Dunn .12 .30
77 Shaun King .12 .30
78 Mike Alstott .12 .30
79 Eddie George .15 .40
80 Steve McNair .15 .40
81 Kevin Dyson .15 .40
82 Brad Johnson .15 .40
83 Stephen Davis .12 .30
84 Michael Westbrook .12 .30
85 Peter Warrick RC 2.50 6.00
86 LaVar Arrington RC 5.00 12.00
87 Chris Redman RC 2.50 6.00
88 Courtney Brown RC 3.00 8.00
89 Plaxico Burress RC 3.00 8.00
90 Corey Simon RC 3.00 8.00
91 Bubba Franks RC 2.50 6.00
92 Deon Grant RC 2.50 6.00
93 Brian Urlacher RC 12.00 30.00
94 Ron Dayne RC 4.00 10.00
95 Sylvester Morris RC 2.50 6.00
96 Shaun Alexander RC 4.00 10.00
97 Dez White RC 2.50 6.00
98 Thomas Jones RC 3.00 8.00
99 Travis Taylor RC 2.50 6.00
100 Kwame Cavil RC 2.50 6.00
101 Jamal Lewis RC 4.00 10.00
102 Chad Pennington RC 3.00 8.00
103 J.R. Redmond RC 2.50 6.00
104 Sebastian Janikowski RC 4.00 10.00
105 Anthony Lucas RC 2.50 6.00
106 Travis Prentice RC 2.50 6.00
107 Danny Farmer RC 2.50 6.00
108 Sherrod Gideon RC 2.50 6.00
109 Todd Pinkston RC 2.50 6.00
110 Dennis Northcutt RC 2.50 6.00
111 Tim Rattay RC 3.00 8.00
112 Troy Walters RC 2.50 6.00
113 Michael Wiley RC 2.50 6.00
114 R.Jay Soward RC 2.50 6.00
115 Trung Canidate RC 2.50 6.00
116 Reuben Droughns RC 2.50 6.00
117 Rondell Mealey RC 2.50 6.00
118 Chris Coleman RC 2.50 6.00
119 Giovanni Carmazzi RC 2.50 6.00
120 Trevor Insley RC 2.50 6.00
121 Shyrone Stith RC 2.50 6.00
122 Gari Scott RC 2.50 6.00
123 Tee Martin RC 2.50 6.00
124 Tom Brady RC 300.00 600.00
125 Marcus Knight RC 2.50 6.00
126 Jerry Porter RC 4.00 10.00
127 Brad Hoover RC 2.50 6.00
128 Chad Morton RC 2.50 6.00
129 Charles Lee RC 2.00 5.00
130 Damon Hodge RC 2.50 6.00
131 Darrell Jackson RC 2.00 5.00
132 Doug Johnson RC 2.00 5.00
133 Frank Moreau RC 2.00 5.00
134 JaJuan Dawson RC 2.00 5.00
135 Jake Delhomme RC 2.50 6.00
136 Jarious Jackson RC 2.50 6.00
137 Joe Hamilton RC 2.00 5.00
138 Larry Foster RC 2.00 5.00
139 Laveranues Coles RC 2.50 6.00
140 Aaron Shea RC 2.50 6.00
141 Matt Lytle RC 2.00 5.00
142 Mike Anderson RC 2.00 5.00
143 Ron Dixon RC 2.00 5.00
144 Ronney Jenkins RC 2.00 5.00
145 Sammy Morris RC 2.00 5.00
146 Shockmain Davis RC 2.00 5.00
147 Spergon Wynn RC 2.00 5.00
148 Todd Husak RC 2.00 5.00
149 Trevor Gaylor RC 2.00 5.00
150 Tywan Mitchell RC 2.00 5.00
151 Windrell Hayes RC 2.00 5.00
152 Bobby Shaw RC 2.00 5.00

2000 Upper Deck Pros and Prospects Future Fame

Randomly inserted in packs at the rate of one in six, this 10-card set focuses on this year's rookie crop that is most likely to leave an impression on the NFL right form the start. Card fronts contain holo-foil and gold foil highlights and card backs carry an "FF" prefix.

COMPLETE SET (10) 6.00 15.00
STATED ODDS 1:6
FF1 Peter Warrick .40 1.00
FF2 LaVar Arrington .75 2.00
FF3 Courtney Brown .50 1.25
FF4 Travis Taylor .40 1.00
FF5 Plaxico Burress .50 1.25
FF6 Ron Dayne .60 1.50
FF7 Jamal Lewis .60 1.50
FF8 Thomas Jones .50 1.25
FF9 Chad Pennington .50 1.25
FF10 Chris Redman .40 1.00

2000 Upper Deck Pros and Prospects Mirror Image

Randomly inserted in packs at the rate of one in 12, this 10-card set pairs rookies with a veteran player that plays the same style of game. Card front are silver foil with one picture of each player. Card backs carry an "M" prefix.

COMPLETE SET (10) 7.50 20.00
STATED ODDS 1:12
M1 T.Jones / F.Taylor .50 1.25
M2 R.Dayne / J.Bettis .60 1.50
M3 P.Burress / R.Moss .50 1.25
M4 P.Warrick / M.Harrison .50 1.25
M5 T.Martin / P.Manning 1.50 4.00
M6 C.Redman / B.Favre 1.25 3.00
M7 L.Arrington / J.Seau .75 2.00
M8 D.White / J.Smith .50 1.25
M9 C.Pennington / K.Warner 1.00 2.50
M10 S.Alexander / M.Faulk .60 1.50

2000 Upper Deck Pros and Prospects ProMotion

Randomly seeded in packs at the rate of one in six, this 10-card set features some of the most exciting veterans in the game. Card fronts are highlighted with silver and gold foil and card backs carry a "P" prefix.

COMPLETE SET (10) 5.00 12.00
STATED ODDS 1:6
P1 Kurt Warner .75 2.00
P2 Eddie George .40 1.00
P3 Marshall Faulk .40 1.00
P4 Keyshawn Johnson .40 1.00
P5 Emmitt Smith .75 2.00
P6 Randy Moss .40 1.00
P7 Marvin Harrison .40 1.00
P8 Mark Brunell .40 1.00
P9 Curtis Martin .40 1.00
P10 Brett Favre 1.00 2.50

2000 Upper Deck Pros and Prospects Report Card

Randomly inserted in packs at the rate of one in 12, this 12-card set recaps the 1999 rookie crop and issues a final grade for their rookie year performances. Card backs carry an "RC" prefix.

COMPLETE SET (12) 7.50 20.00
STATED ODDS 1:12
RC1 Edgerrin James .60 1.50
RC2 Tim Couch .60 1.50
RC3 Cade McNown .50 1.25
RC4 Champ Bailey .60 1.50
RC5 Donovan McNabb .60 1.50
RC6 Kevin Johnson .50 1.25
RC7 Shaun King .50 1.25
RC8 Peerless Price .60 1.50
RC9 David Boston .50 1.25
RC10 Ricky Williams .60 1.50
RC11 Akili Smith .50 1.25
RC12 Jevon Kearse .50 1.25

2000 Upper Deck Pros and Prospects Signature Piece 1

ndomly inserted in packs at the rate of one in 96, this set features both a swatch of a game-used jersey and the respective players autograph.

STATED ODDS 1:96
*SIG 2 BRONZE: .4X TO 1X SIG.PIECE 1
*GOLD/80-88: .5X TO 1.2X SIG.PIECE 1
*GOLD/32-50: .8X TO 2X SIG.PIECE 1
*GOLD/22-28: 1X TO 2.5X SIG.PIECE 1
GOLD STATED PRINT RUN 6-88
SPBG Brian Griese 8.00 20.00
SPCB Champ Bailey 10.00 25.00
SPCC Chris Claiborne 8.00 20.00
SPDB Drew Bledsoe 25.00 50.00
SPDF Danny Farmer 8.00 20.00
SPDL Dorsey Levens 10.00 25.00
SPDM Dan Marino 100.00 200.00
SPEG Edgerrin James 10.00 25.00
SPIB Isaac Bruce 15.00 40.00
SPKJ Kevin Johnson 8.00 20.00
SPKW Kurt Warner 30.00 60.00
SPMB Mark Brunell 12.00 30.00
SPMF Marshall Faulk 10.00 25.00
SPMH Marvin Harrison 10.00 25.00
SPOG Olandis Gary 10.00 25.00
SPPM Peyton Manning 75.00 150.00
SPRD Ron Dayne 12.00 30.00
SPRL Ray Lucas 8.00 20.00
SPRM Randy Moss 10.00 25.00
SPTA Troy Aikman 50.00 100.00
SPTH Torry Holt 12.00 30.00
SPTO Terrell Owens 10.00 25.00
SPWR Keyshawn Johnson 12.00 30.00

2001 Upper Deck Pros and Prospects

Released as a 140-card base set, the 2001 Upper Deck Pros and Prospects set is comprised of 90 regular cards and 50 draft picks-each sequentially numbered to 1000. Base cards have a white border that clouds into a full color action shot and card fronts are enhanced with bronze foil highlights. Pros and Prospects were packaged in 24-pack boxes containing five cards each pack.

COMP.SET w/o SP's (90) 6.00 15.00
91-140 ROOKIE PRINT RUN 1000
1 Jake Plummer .12 .30
2 David Boston .12 .30
3 Jamal Anderson .15 .40
4 Doug Johnson .12 .30
5 Maurice Smith .12 .30
6 Jamal Lewis .20 .50
7 Shannon Sharpe .15 .40
8 Trent Dilfer .12 .30
9 Doug Flutie .15 .40
10 Rob Johnson .15 .40
11 Eric Moulds .12 .30
12 Muhsin Muhammad .12 .30
13 Brad Hoover .15 .40
14 Tim Biakabutuka .12 .30
15 Cade McNown .15 .40
16 James Allen .12 .30
17 Marcus Robinson .15 .40
18 Brian Urlacher .25 .60
19 Peter Warrick .12 .30
20 Corey Dillon .12 .30
21 Tim Couch .12 .30
22 Kevin Johnson .12 .30
23 Travis Prentice .12 .30
24 Troy Aikman .25 .60
25 Emmitt Smith .30 .75
26 Terrell Davis .15 .40
27 Mike Anderson .12 .30
28 Brian Griese .12 .30
29 Charlie Batch .12 .30
30 Germane Crowell .12 .30
31 James Stewart .12 .30
32 Brett Favre .40 1.00
33 Antonio Freeman .20 .50
34 Dorsey Levens .15 .40
35 Ahman Green .15 .40
36 Peyton Manning .50 1.25
37 Edgerrin James .15 .40
38 Marvin Harrison .15 .40
39 Mark Brunell .15 .40
40 Fred Taylor .12 .30
41 Jimmy Smith .15 .40
42 Elvis Grbac .15 .40
43 Tony Gonzalez .15 .40
44 Derrick Alexander .12 .30
45 Oronde Gadsden .12 .30
46 Lamar Smith .15 .40
47 Jay Fiedler .15 .40
48 Randy Moss .15 .40
49 Moe Williams .12 .30
50 Cris Carter .20 .50
51 Daunte Culpepper .15 .40
52 Drew Bledsoe .15 .40
53 Terry Glenn .15 .40
54 Ricky Williams .15 .40
55 Jeff Blake .15 .40
56 Joe Horn .12 .30
57 Aaron Brooks .12 .30
58 La'Roi Glover .12 .30
59 Kerry Collins .12 .30
60 Amani Toomer .12 .30
61 Ron Dayne .15 .40
62 Vinny Testaverde .12 .30
63 Wayne Chrebet .12 .30
64 Curtis Martin .15 .40
65 Tim Brown .20 .50
66 Rich Gannon .15 .40
67 Tyrone Wheatley .15 .40
68 Duce Staley .12 .30
69 Donovan McNabb .15 .40
70 Kordell Stewart .12 .30
71 Jerome Bettis .20 .50
72 Marshall Faulk .15 .40
73 Kurt Warner .30 .75
74 Isaac Bruce .20 .50
75 Junior Seau .15 .40
76 Curtis Conway .15 .40
77 Jeff Garcia .12 .30
78 Jerry Rice .40 1.00
79 Charlie Garner .15 .40
80 Terrell Owens .15 .40
81 Ricky Watters .15 .40
82 Shaun Alexander .12 .30
83 Warrick Dunn .12 .30
84 Shaun King .12 .30
85 Derrick Brooks .12 .30
86 Eddie George .20 .50
87 Steve McNair .15 .40
88 Brad Johnson .15 .40
89 Jeff George .15 .40
90 Stephen Davis .12 .30
91 Jamal Reynolds RC 2.00 5.00
92 Justin Smith RC 4.00 10.00
93 Dan Morgan RC 2.50 6.00
94 Deuce McAllister RC 3.00 8.00
95 Drew Brees RC 40.00 80.00
96 Josh Booty RC 2.50 6.00
97 Mike McMahon RC 2.50 6.00
98 Sage Rosenfels RC 2.50 6.00
99 Marques Tuiasosopo RC 2.50 6.00
100 Josh Heupel RC 3.00 8.00
101 Heath Evans RC 2.50 6.00
102 Reggie White RC 2.00 5.00
103 Tim Hasselbeck RC 2.50 6.00
104 LaDainian Tomlinson RC 10.00 25.00
105 Kevan Barlow RC 2.50 6.00
106 LaMont Jordan RC 3.00 8.00
107 James Jackson RC 2.00 5.00
108 Anthony Thomas RC 3.00 8.00
109 Correll Buckhalter RC 2.00 5.00
110 Travis Henry RC 2.50 6.00
111 Dan Alexander RC 2.50 6.00
112 Travis Minor RC 2.50 6.00
113 Rudi Johnson RC 3.00 8.00
114 Michael Bennett RC 2.50 6.00
115 Todd Heap RC 2.50 6.00
116 Snoop Minnis RC 2.00 5.00
117 Santana Moss RC 3.00 8.00
118 Reggie Wayne RC 4.00 10.00
119 Koren Robinson RC 2.50 6.00
120 Chris Chambers RC 2.00 5.00
121 David Terrell RC 2.50 6.00
122 Rod Gardner RC 2.50 6.00
123 Quincy Morgan RC 2.50 6.00
124 Ken-Yon Rambo RC 2.00 5.00
125 Ronney Daniels RC 2.00 5.00
126 Ja'Mar Toombs RC 2.00 5.00
127 Bobby Newcombe RC 2.50 6.00
128 Cedrick Wilson RC 2.50 6.00
129 Chad Johnson RC 3.00 8.00
130 Shaun Rogers RC 3.00 8.00
131 Robert Ferguson RC 3.00 8.00
132 Kevin Kasper RC 2.00 5.00
133 Chris Weinke JSY RC 5.00 12.00
134 Freddie Mitchell JSY RC 4.00 10.00
135 Michael Vick JSY RC 15.00 40.00
136 Chris Taylor RC 2.00 5.00
137 Vinny Sutherland RC 2.00 5.00
138 Gerard Warren RC 2.50 6.00
139 Torrance Marshall RC 2.00 5.00
140 Jesse Palmer RC 2.50 6.00

2001 Upper Deck Pros and Prospects A Piece of History Autographs

Randomly inserted at a rate of one in 192 packs this 9-card set featured legendary players from the NFL's past. The card design included gold foil lettering on a silver and white background highlighted by a swatch of game used jersey and a signature. A Gold background version serial numbered to 50 was also produced.

STATED ODDS 1:192
BSAJ Bart Starr 75.00 150.00
CTAJ Charley Taylor 12.00 30.00
FTAJ Fran Tarkenton 25.00 60.00
JKAJ Jim Kelly 40.00 100.00
JTAJ Joe Theismann 15.00 40.00
JUAJ Johnny Unitas 300.00 450.00
JYAJ Jack Youngblood 12.00 30.00
RSAJ Roger Staubach 50.00 100.00
SYAJ Steve Young 60.00 120.00

2001 Upper Deck Pros and Prospects Centerpiece

ndomly inserted at a rate of one in 22 packs, this 6-card set featured some of the NFL's biggest playmakers. Card fronts were highlighted with gold foil and card backs carried a "C" prefix.

COMPLETE SET (6) 6.00 15.00
STATED ODDS 1:22
C1 Randy Moss .60 1.50
C2 Donovan McNabb .60 1.50
C3 Kurt Warner 1.25 3.00
C4 Jamal Lewis .75 2.00
C5 Eddie George .75 2.00
C6 Mike Anderson .50 1.25

2001 Upper Deck Pros and Prospects Future Fame

Randomly inserted in packs at the rate of one in 22, this 6-card set focuses on this year's rookie crop that is most likely to leave an impression on the NFL right from the start of their career. Card fronts contain holo-foil and gold foil highlights and card backs carry an "F" prefix.

COMPLETE SET (6) 10.00 25.00
STATED ODDS 1:22
F1 Michael Vick 1.25 3.00
F2 Deuce McAllister .75 2.00
F3 Drew Brees 8.00 20.00
F4 LaDainian Tomlinson 2.50 6.00
F5 Chris Weinke .60 1.50
F6 Santana Moss .75 2.00

2001 Upper Deck Pros and Prospects Game Jersey

Randomly inserted at a rate of one in 23 packs this 37-card set featured only the hottest players in the game. The card design included gold foil lettering and highlighted by a swatch of game used jersey.

STATED ODDS 1:23
*GOLD/50: .8X TO 2X BASIC JSY
GOLD/50 RANDOM INSERTS IN PACKS
GOLD PRINT RUN 50 SER.#'d SETS
ANJ Mike Anderson 2.50 6.00
BAJ Tiki Barber 3.00 8.00
BFJ Brett Favre 8.00 20.00
CDJ Corey Dillon 2.50 6.00
DCJ Daunte Culpepper 3.00 8.00
DLJ Dorsey Levens 3.00 8.00
EJJ Edgerrin James 3.00 8.00
ESJ Emmitt Smith 6.00 15.00
FTJ Fred Taylor 2.50 6.00
JEJ John Elway 6.00 15.00
JGJ Jeff Garcia 2.50 6.00
JMJ Joe Montana 12.00 30.00
JNJ Joe Namath 6.00 15.00
JPJ Jake Plummer 2.50 6.00
JRJ Jerry Rice 8.00 20.00
JSJ Junior Seau 3.00 8.00
KCJ Kerry Collins 2.50 6.00
KJJ Keyshawn Johnson 3.00 8.00
KMJ Keenan McCardell 3.00 8.00
KSJ Kordell Stewart 2.50 6.00
KWJ Kurt Warner 6.00 15.00
MAJ Marcus Allen 4.00 10.00
MBJ Mark Brunell 3.00 8.00
MFJ Marshall Faulk 3.00 8.00
PHJ Paul Hornung 4.00 10.00
PLJ Jim Plunkett 3.00 8.00
PMJ Peyton Manning 10.00 25.00
PSJ Phil Simms 3.00 8.00
RDJ Ron Dayne 3.00 8.00
RMJ Randy Moss 3.00 8.00
SKJ Shaun King 2.50 6.00
TAJ Troy Aikman 5.00 12.00
TBJ Terry Bradshaw 5.00 12.00
THJ Torry Holt 3.00 8.00
TJJ Thomas Jones 2.50 6.00
WDJ Warrick Dunn 2.50 6.00
WPJ Walter Payton 10.00 25.00

2001 Upper Deck Pros and Prospects A Piece of History Autographs Gold

*GOLD/50: .6X TO 1.5X BASIC JSY AU
JUAJ Johnny Unitas 400.00 700.00

2001 Upper Deck Pros and Prospects Game Jersey Combos

Randomly inserted into packs this 7-card set featured the hottest players in the game and some legends from the NFL's past. The card design included gold foil lettering and highlighted by a swatch of game used jersey from both players. These cards were serial numbered to 25.

STATED PRINT RUN 25 SER.#'d SETS
ASC T.Aikman/E.Smith 60.00 125.00
FWC M.Faulk/K.Warner 40.00 80.00
JMC E.James/P.Manning 40.00 80.00
MCC D.Culpepper/R.Moss 25.00 50.00
MYC J.Montana/S.Young 40.00 80.00
SBC T.Bradshaw/R.Staubach 40.00 80.00
SUC B.Starr/J.Unitas 125.00 250.00

2001 Upper Deck Pros and Prospects ProActive

Randomly seeded in packs at the rate of one in 15, this 9-card set features NFL veterans poised to make an impact in 2001. The cardfronts were highlighted with gold foil and the cardbacks carry a "PA" card number prefix.

COMPLETE SET (9) 6.00 15.00
STATED ODDS 1:15
PA1 Kurt Warner 1.25 3.00
PA2 Eddie George .75 2.00
PA3 Marshall Faulk .60 1.50
PA4 Corey Dillon .50 1.25
PA5 Emmitt Smith 1.25 3.00
PA6 Randy Moss .60 1.50
PA7 Marvin Harrison .60 1.50
PA8 Rich Gannon .60 1.50
PA9 Brett Favre 1.50 4.00

2001 Upper Deck Pros and Prospects ProMotion

Randomly seeded in packs at the rate of one in 15, this 9-card set features rookies who should make a big impact on the game. Card fronts are highlighted with gold foil and card backs carry a "PM" prefix.

COMPLETE SET (9) 10.00 25.00
STATED ODDS 1:15
PM1 Michael Vick 1.25 3.00
PM2 Michael Bennett .60 1.50
PM3 Reggie Wayne 1.00 2.50
PM4 Chad Johnson .75 2.00
PM5 Chris Chambers .50 1.25
PM6 David Terrell .60 1.50
PM7 Snoop Minnis .50 1.25
PM8 Koren Robinson .60 1.50
PM9 Rod Gardner .60 1.50

2003 Upper Deck Pros and Prospects

This 190-card set was released in May, 2003. It was issued in five-card packs. The first 90 cards of this set featured veterans while cards 91 through 120 are veteran cards which were short printed at a stated rate of one in six. Cards numbered 121 through 190 feature rookies paired with a veteran player. Those cards were issued to a stated print run of 1800 serial numbered cards. A few of those cards were autographed and not every player returned their cards in time for pack-out. Those exchange cards could be redeemed until May 16, 2006.

COMP.SET w/o SP's (90) 7.50 20.00
ROOKIE PRINT RUN 1800
ROOKIE AU PRINT RUN 250-2000
1 Jake Plummer .20 .50
2 David Boston .20 .50
3 Warrick Dunn .20 .50
4 T.J. Duckett .20 .50
5 Chris Redman .20 .50
6 Jamal Lewis .25 .60
7 Drew Bledsoe .25 .60
8 Travis Henry .20 .50
9 Eric Moulds .20 .50
10 Peerless Price .20 .50
11 Rodney Peete .20 .50
12 Julius Peppers .30 .75
13 Anthony Thomas .25 .60
14 Brian Urlacher .30 .75
15 Marty Booker .20 .50
16 David Terrell .20 .50
17 Corey Dillon .20 .50
18 Peter Warrick .20 .50
19 Jon Kitna .20 .50
20 Tim Couch .20 .50
21 Andre Davis .20 .50
22 Quincy Morgan .20 .50
23 Dennis Northcutt .20 .50
24 Roy Williams .20 .50
25 Emmitt Smith .50 1.25
26 Joey Galloway .25 .60
27 Antonio Bryant .20 .50
28 Brian Griese .20 .50
29 Clinton Portis .20 .50
30 Shannon Sharpe .25 .60
31 Joey Harrington .20 .50
32 Az-Zahir Hakim .20 .50
33 Brett Favre .60 1.50
34 Robert Ferguson .20 .50
35 Donald Driver .25 .60
36 David Carr .20 .50
37 Jabar Gaffney .20 .50
38 Edgerrin James .25 .60
39 Marvin Harrison .25 .60
40 Reggie Wayne .25 .60
41 Mark Brunell .25 .60
42 Fred Taylor .20 .50
43 Priest Holmes .20 .50
44 Trent Green .20 .50
45 Marc Boerigter .20 .50
46 Jay Fiedler .20 .50
47 Chris Chambers .20 .50
48 Randy McMichael .20 .50
49 Randy Moss .25 .60
50 Daunte Culpepper .25 .60
51 Michael Bennett .20 .50
52 Antowain Smith .25 .60
53 David Patten .20 .50
54 Troy Brown .20 .50
55 Aaron Brooks .20 .50
56 Joe Horn .20 .50
57 Donte Stallworth .20 .50
58 Amani Toomer .20 .50
59 Kerry Collins .20 .50
60 Tiki Barber .25 .60
61 Santana Moss .25 .60
62 Curtis Martin .25 .60
63 Wayne Chrebet .20 .50
64 Rich Gannon .25 .60
65 Charlie Garner .25 .60
66 Tim Brown .30 .75
67 Donovan McNabb .25 .60
68 Duce Staley .20 .50
69 Hines Ward .25 .60
70 Antwaan Randle El .20 .50
71 Plaxico Burress .20 .50
72 Jerome Bettis .30 .75
73 Junior Seau .25 .60
74 LaDainian Tomlinson .30 .75
75 Tai Streets .20 .50
76 Kevan Barlow .20 .50
77 Garrison Hearst .20 .50
78 Jeff Garcia .20 .50
79 Shaun Alexander .20 .50
80 Matt Hasselbeck .20 .50
81 Marshall Faulk .25 .60
82 Marc Bulger .20 .50
83 Torry Holt .25 .60
84 Isaac Bruce .30 .75
85 Brad Johnson .25 .60
86 Keyshawn Johnson .30 .75
87 Steve McNair .25 .60
88 Kevin Dyson .20 .50
89 Patrick Ramsey .25 .60
90 Ladell Betts .20 .50
91 Marcel Shipp SP .60 1.50
92 Michael Vick SP .75 2.00
93 Ray Lewis SP 1.00 2.50
94 Josh Reed SP .60 1.50
95 Josh McCown SP .75 2.00
96 Kelly Holcomb SP .60 1.50
97 William Green SP .60 1.50
98 Chad Hutchinson SP .60 1.50
99 Rod Smith SP .75 2.00
100 James Stewart SP .60 1.50
101 Ahman Green SP .75 2.00
102 Peyton Manning SP 2.50 6.00
103 Jimmy Smith SP .75 2.00
104 Tony Gonzalez SP .75 2.00
105 Ricky Williams SP .75 2.00
106 Jason Taylor SP .75 2.00
107 Tom Brady SP 4.00 10.00
108 Deuce McAllister SP .75 2.00
109 Jeremy Shockey SP .60 1.50
110 Chad Pennington SP .60 1.50
111 Jerry Rice SP 2.00 5.00
112 A.J. Feeley SP .60 1.50
113 Tommy Maddox SP .60 1.50
114 Drew Brees SP 1.00 2.50
115 Terrell Owens SP .75 2.00
116 Maurice Morris SP .60 1.50
117 Kurt Warner SP .75 2.00
118 Derrick Brooks SP .60 1.50
119 Eddie George SP .75 2.00
120 Rod Gardner SP .60 1.50
121 Leftwich AU RC/Pnn.AU/250 20.00 50.00
122 Dorsey AU RC/Test/2000 8.00 20.00
123 Palmer AU RC/Mnn.AU/250 60.00 120.00
124 Simms AU RC/Bru.AU/250 25.00 50.00
125 A.Johnson RC/S.Moss 3.00 8.00
126 Banks AU RC/Brks.AU/250 8.00 20.00
127 J.R. Tolver RC/Hakim 1.50 4.00
128 J.Myers RC/J.Reed 1.25 3.00
129 R.Bellamy RC/A.Toomer 1.50 4.00
130 J.Gesser RC/D.Bledsoe 1.50 4.00
131 Kingsbury AU RC/S.Baugh 10.00 25.00
132 K.Boller RC/Brees AU/500 25.00 60.00
133 L.Johnson RC/Thomas AU 8.00 20.00
134 K.Kelly AU RC/Morton/2000 8.00 20.00
135 B.Johnson RC/Gard.AU/500 10.00 25.00
136 Johnson RC/Couch AU/500 6.00 15.00
137 T.Suggs AU RC/Nmll/2000 12.00 30.00
138 Ragone RC/Brnll AU/500 8.00 20.00
139 M.Smith RC/C.Trippi 1.25 3.00
140 J.Wood RC/J.Harrington 1.25 3.00
141 J.Thomas RC/M.Vick 2.00 5.00
142 Graham AU RC/E.Smt/2000 8.00 20.00
143 McGahee AU RC/Jms/2000 12.00 30.00
144 R.Lee RC/Alexander AU/500 10.00 25.00
145 A.Boldin RC/J.Walker 2.00 5.00
146 Jacobs AU RC/Cald AU/250 6.00 15.00
147 T.Gardner RC/L.Coles 1.25 3.00
148 B.Wade RC/D.Northcutt 1.50 4.00
149 McMullen RC/Bruce AU/500 10.00 25.00
150 A.Cobourne RC/A.Zereoue 1.25 3.00
151 B.James RC/F.Kinard 2.00 5.00
152 Washing AU RC/Prc/2000 6.00 15.00
153 E.Steinbach RC/J.Parker 1.25 3.00
154 J.Kennedy RC/E.Stautner 1.50 4.00
155 R.Long RC/A.Weinmeister 1.25 3.00
156 C.Brown AU RC/Andr/2000 6.00 15.00
157 T.Johnson RC/T.Gonzalez 1.50 4.00
158 O.Smith RC/M.Morris 1.25 3.00
159 Fargas AU RC/Portis/2000 10.00 25.00
160 S.Wallace RC/A.Randle El 1.50 4.00
161 St.Pierre RC/Mann AU/500 30.00 80.00
162 Toefield RC/Tmln AU/500 25.00 60.00
163 M.Blackwell RC/Culpepper 1.50 4.00
164 K.Howry RC/A.J.Feeley 1.25 3.00
165 J.Gage RC/K.Farmer RC 1.50 4.00
166 S.Witten RC/A.Davis 1.25 3.00
167 Weathersby RC/A.Williams 1.25 3.00
168 B.Bailey RC/C.Bailey 1.50 4.00
169 B.Lloyd RC/K.Kittner 2.00 5.00
170 D.Gabriel RC/C.Chambers 1.50 4.00
171 A.Gbaja-Biamila RC/KGB 1.50 4.00
172 D.Diedrick RC/A.Green 1.50 4.00
173 K.Curtis RC/K.Dyson 1.25 3.00
174 McCull RC/McAll.AU/500 8.00 20.00
175 M.Bush RC/M.Trufant RC 1.50 4.00
176 Z.Hilton RC/S.Aiken RC 1.50 4.00
177 Newman RC/Woolfolk RC 2.00 5.00
178 T.Calico RC/K.Holcomb 1.25 3.00
179 J.T. Wall RC/T.Edwards RC 1.25 3.00
180 C.Paus RC/M.Seidman RC 1.25 3.00
181 L.J. Smith RC/M.Battaglia 2.00 5.00
182 Griffin AU RC/Sav.RC/2000 8.00 20.00
183 L.Suggs RC/M.Vick 2.00 5.00
184 B.Askew RC/B.Joppru RC 1.50 4.00
185 M.Pinkard RC/Todd Heap 1.25 3.00
186 A.Battle RC/Tim Brown 2.00 5.00
187 C.Rogers RC/P.Burress 1.50 4.00
188 A.Pinnock RC/D.Staley 1.50 4.00
189 Grossman RC/Mnn.AU/500 50.00 100.00
190 G.Wrighster RC/J.Peelle 1.25 3.00
KBBF K.Boller/B.Favre AU/25 100.00 200.00
RGBF Grossman/Favre AU/25 100.00 200.00

2003 Upper Deck Pros and Prospects Gold

NSIGNED: 1.2X TO 3X BASIC CARDS
*AUTO/50: .8X TO 2X BASE AU/250
*AUTO/50: 1X TO 2.5X BASE AU/500
*AUTO/50: 1X TO 2.5X BASE AU/2000
STATED PRINT RUN 50 SER.#'d SETS

2003 Upper Deck Pros and Prospects Game Day Jerseys

Randomly inserted into packs, these 29 cards feature a game-used jersey swatch. Each of these cards were issued to a stated print run of 350 serial numbered sets.

STATED PRINT RUN 350 SER.#'d SETS
*GOLD/50: .8X TO 2X BASIC JSY
GOLD STATED PRINT RUN 50
*BRONZE/75: .6X TO 1.5X BASIC JSY
BRONZE STATED PRINT RUN 75
JCAC Avon Cobourne 2.50 6.00
JCAG Antonio Gilbert 2.50 6.00
JCAP Andrew Pinnock 3.00 8.00
JCBL Byron Leftwich 3.00 8.00
JCBS Brian St.Pierre 2.50 6.00
JCCP Carson Palmer 5.00 12.00
JCDR Dave Ragone 2.50 6.00
JCGA Justin Gage 3.00 8.00
JCJG Jason Gesser 3.00 8.00
JCJJ Jason Johnson 2.50 6.00
JCJS Jeremy Shockey 2.50 6.00
JCJT J.R. Tolver 3.00 8.00
JCJW Juston Wood 2.50 6.00
JCKD Ken Dorsey 3.00 8.00
JCKH Keenan Howry 2.50 6.00
JCKI Kliff Kingsbury 4.00 10.00
JCKJ Keyshawn Johnson 4.00 10.00
JCKK Kareem Kelly 2.50 6.00
JCLS Lee Suggs 2.50 6.00
JCMD Mike Doss 4.00 10.00
JCMF Marshall Faulk 3.00 8.00
JCPM Peyton Manning 10.00 25.00
JCRB Ronald Bellamy 3.00 8.00
JCSM Sultan McCullough 2.50 6.00
JCST J.J. Stokes 2.50 6.00
JCSW Seneca Wallace 3.00 8.00
JCTI Jason Thomas 2.50 6.00
JCTS Terrell Suggs 3.00 8.00
JCZH Zach Hilton 3.00 8.00

2003 Upper Deck Pros and Prospects Game Day Jersey Duals

Randomly inserted into packs, these 26-card feature two players as well as game-used memorabilia swatches with each player. Each of these cards were issued to a stated print run of 350 serial numbered sets.

STATED PRINT RUN 350 SER.#'d SETS
*GOLD/50: .8X TO 2X BASIC DUAL
GOLD STATED PRINT RUN 50
*BRONZE/75: .6X TO 1.5X BASIC DUAL
BRONZE STATED PRINT RUN 75
DJCBT R.Bellamy/A.Thomas 4.00 10.00
DJCCD C.Palmer/K.Dorsey 6.00 15.00
DJCDS K.Dorsey/J.Shockey 5.00 12.00
DJCDT K.Dorsey/V.Testaverde 5.00 12.00
DJCGB J.Gesser/D.Bledsoe 5.00 12.00
DJCHH K.Howry/J.Harrington 4.00 10.00
DJCJF J.Stokes/D.Foster 5.00 12.00
DJCJT J.Johnson/J.Thomas 4.00 10.00
DJCKG K.Dorsey/J.Gesser 5.00 12.00
DJCKM K.Kelly/S.McCullough 4.00 10.00
DJCLD B.Leftwich/K.Dorsey 5.00 12.00
DJCLP B.Leftwich/C.Pennington 5.00 12.00
DJCPJ C.Palmer/K.Johnson 6.00 15.00
DJCPK C.Palmer/K.Kelly 6.00 15.00
DJCPL C.Palmer/B.Leftwich 6.00 15.00
DJCPW B.St.Pierre/J.Wood 4.00 10.00
DJCRK D.Ragone/K.Kingsbury 6.00 15.00
DJCRU D.Ragone/J.Unitas 20.00 50.00
DJCSB T.Suggs/W.Bryant 5.00 12.00
DJCSF B.St.Pierre/D.Flutie 5.00 12.00
DJCSS T.Suggs/W.Sapp 5.00 12.00
DJCSV L.Suggs/M.Vick 5.00 12.00
DJCTD M.Trufact/M.Doss 6.00 15.00
DJCTF J.Tolver/M.Faulk 5.00 12.00
DJCWJ J.Woord/J.Johnson 4.00 10.00
DJCWR S.Wallace/A.Randle El 5.00 12.00

2003 Upper Deck Pros and Prospects The Power and the Potential

ndomly inserted into packs, this 30-card set features a leading prospect paired with an established veteran at the same position. Each of these cards were issued to a stated print run of 1700 serial numbered sets.

COMPLETE SET (30) 20.00 50.00
STATED PRINT RUN 1700 SER.#'d SETS
PP1 D.Carr/T.Brady 3.00 8.00
PP2 J.Harrington/B.Favre 1.50 4.00
PP3 P.Ramsey/T.Couch .60 1.50
PP4 D.Garrard/S.McNair .60 1.50
PP5 K.Kittner/P.Manning 2.00 5.00
PP6 J.McCown/D.Bledsoe .60 1.50
PP7 R.Davey/D.Culpepper .60 1.50
PP8 C.Portis/E.James .60 1.50
PP9 W.Green/G.Hearst .50 1.25
PP10 T.J.Duckett/J.Bettis .75 2.00
PP11 M.Morris/S.Alexander .50 1.25
PP12 J.Wells/E.George .60 1.50
PP13 L.Gordon/M.Faulk .60 1.50
PP14 L.Betts/M.Alstott .50 1.25
PP15 B.Westbrook/D.Staley .50 1.25
PP16 D.Stallworth/J.Horn .50 1.25
PP17 A.Randle El/P.Burress .50 1.25
PP18 A.Lelie/R.Smith .60 1.50
PP19 J.Walker/D.Driver .60 1.50
PP20 J.Reed/E.Moulds .50 1.25
PP21 J.Gaffney/J.Smith .60 1.50
PP22 R.Caldwell/M.Harrison .60 1.50
PP23 A.Bryant/J.Galloway .60 1.50
PP24 D.Branch/T.Brown .50 1.25
PP25 M.Walker/Key.Johnson .75 2.00
PP26 C.Russell/R.Gardner .50 1.25
PP27 C.Hutchinson/C.Pennington .50 1.25
PP28 J.Peppers/W.Sapp .75 2.00
PP29 A.Davis/Q.Morgan .50 1.25
PP30 J.Shockey/T.Gonzalez .60 1.50

2013 Upper Deck Quantum

Aaron Rodgers 5.00 12.00
2 Barry Sanders 5.00 12.00
3 Jake Plummer 2.00 5.00
4 Rodney Peete 2.00 5.00
5 John Hannah 2.00 5.00
6 Billy Sims 2.50 6.00
7 Bo Jackson 5.00 12.00
8 Ronnie Lott 2.50 6.00
9 Dan Fouts 2.50 6.00
10 Al Toon 2.00 5.00
11 Dan Marino 6.00 15.00
12 Alan Page 2.00 5.00
13 Steve Young 4.00 10.00
14 Drew Brees 3.00 8.00
15 Earl Campbell 3.00 8.00
16 Lawrence Taylor 3.00 8.00
17 Natrone Means 2.00 5.00
18 Herschel Walker 3.00 8.00
19 Jason White 2.00 5.00
20 Jerry Rice 5.00 12.00
21 Vinny Testaverde 2.00 5.00
22 Tommie Frazier 2.00 5.00
23 Joe Theismann 3.00 8.00
24 Doug Flutie 2.50 6.00
25 Mike Rozier 2.00 5.00
26 John Elway 5.00 12.00
27 Brian Bosworth 2.50 6.00
28 Tedy Bruschi 2.50 6.00
29 Warren Sapp 2.50 6.00
30 Bruce Smith 2.50 6.00
31 Ray Guy 2.00 5.00
32 Ozzie Newsome 2.50 6.00
33 Paul Hornung 3.00 8.00
34 Nick Buoniconti 2.00 5.00
35 Roger Craig 2.50 6.00
36 Billy Cannon 2.00 5.00
37 Roman Gabriel 2.00 5.00
38 Ickey Woods 2.00 5.00
39 Steve Owens 2.00 5.00
40 Ron Dayne 2.50 6.00
41 Eddie George 2.50 6.00
42 Joe Namath 6.00 15.00
43 Archie Griffin 2.00 5.00
44 Ty Detmer 2.00 5.00
45 Warren Moon 3.00 8.00
46 Dion Jordan 1.50 4.00
47 Kenjon Barner 1.50 4.00
48 Matt Barkley 1.50 4.00
49 Ezekiel Ansah 1.50 4.00
50 Cobi Hamilton 1.50 4.00
51 Tavon Austin 2.00 5.00
52 Cordarrelle Patterson 1.50 4.00
53 Jawan Jamison 1.50 4.00
54 Giovani Bernard 1.50 4.00
55 Keenan Allen 3.00 8.00
56 Kenny Stills 1.50 4.00

57 Landry Jones 1.50 4.00
58 Le'Veon Bell 5.00 12.00
59 Manti Te'o 2.00 5.00
60 Corey Fuller 1.50 4.00
61 Mike Glennon 1.50 4.00
62 Ryan Nassib 1.50 4.00
63 Theo Riddick 1.50 4.00
64 Zac Dysert 1.50 4.00
65 Aaron Dobson 1.50 4.00
66 Tyler Wilson 1.50 4.00
67 Chris Harper 1.50 4.00
68 Dee Milliner 1.50 4.00
69 Denard Robinson 1.50 4.00
70 EJ Manuel 1.50 4.00
71 Justin Hunter 1.50 4.00
72 Marquess Wilson 2.50 6.00
73 Gavin Escobar 1.50 4.00
74 Montee Ball 1.50 4.00
75 Ryan Swope 1.50 4.00
76 Robert Woods 2.50 6.00
77 Andre Ellington 1.50 4.00
78 Josh Boyce 1.50 4.00
79 Eddie Lacy 1.50 4.00
80 Tavarres King 1.50 4.00
81 Chris Thompson 1.50 4.00
82 Geno Smith 1.50 4.00
83 Marquise Goodwin 1.50 4.00
84 Markus Wheaton 1.50 4.00
85 Stedman Bailey 1.50 4.00
86 Zach Ertz 3.00 8.00
87 Barkevious Mingo 1.50 4.00
88 Joseph Randle 1.50 4.00
89 Knile Davis 1.50 4.00
90 Marcus Lattimore 1.50 4.00
91 Tyler Eifert 1.50 4.00
92 Johnathan Franklin 1.50 4.00
93 Mike Gillislee 1.50 4.00
94 Star Lotulelei 2.00 5.00
95 Stepfan Taylor 1.50 4.00
96 Aaron Mellette 1.50 4.00
97 Collin Klein 2.00 5.00
98 Tyler Bray 1.50 4.00
99 Terrance Williams 1.50 4.00
100 DeAndre Hopkins 4.00 10.00

2013 Upper Deck Quantum '14 Draft Picks

ILVER/25: .6X TO 1.5X BASIC INSERT/175
XRC1 Sammy Watkins 8.00 20.00
XRC2 Johnny Manziel 3.00 8.00
XRC3 Tre Mason
XRC4 Eric Ebron 4.00 10.00
XRC5 Aaron Murray 4.00 10.00
XRC6 Lache Seastrunk 1.50 4.00
XRC7 Mike Evans 5.00 12.00
XRC8 Devonta Freeman 2.50 6.00
XRC9 Jarvis Landry 3.00 8.00
XRC10 Teddy Bridgewater 3.00 8.00
XRC11 Carlos Hyde 5.00 12.00
XRC12 Brandin Cooks 5.00 12.00
XRC13 Jace Amaro 1.50 4.00
XRC14 Martavis Bryant 5.00 12.00
XRC15 Blake Bortles 5.00 12.00
XRC16 Kelvin Benjamin 5.00 12.00
XRC17 Jeremy Hill 3.00 8.00
XRC18 David Fales 2.50 6.00
XRC19 Allen Robinson 3.00 8.00
XRC20 Tajh Boyd 3.00 8.00
XRC21 Bishop Sankey 4.00 10.00
XRC22 Davante Adams 4.00 10.00
XRC23 Derek Carr 6.00 15.00
XRC24 Odell Beckham Jr. 8.00 20.00
XRC25 Jimmy Garoppolo 10.00 25.00
XRC26 Marqise Lee 3.00 8.00
XRC27 Brett Smith 2.50 6.00
XRC28 Ka'Deem Carey 2.50 6.00
XRC29 Charles Sims 2.50 6.00
XRC30 Zach Mettenberger

2013 Upper Deck Quantum All Time Greats Letterman

GAP Alan Page/20*
ATGAR Aaron Rodgers/21* EXCH
ATGAT Al Toon/20*
ATGBB Brian Bosworth/40* 20.00 40.00
ATGBC Billy Cannon/30* 15.00 40.00
ATGBJ Bo Jackson/21* 60.00 120.00
ATGBS Billy Sims/20*
ATGDB Drew Brees/25* 40.00 80.00
ATGDF Dan Fouts/25* 15.00 40.00
ATGDH DeAndre Hopkins/35* 20.00 50.00
ATGDM Dan Marino/18* 150.00 250.00
ATGEC Earl Campbell/24*
ATGEG Eddie George/18*
ATGEL Eddie Lacy/20* 10.00 25.00
ATGEM EJ Manuel/30* 50.00 100.00
ATGGS Geno Smith/15*
ATGGU Ray Guy/15*
ATGJE John Elway/15* 100.00 175.00
ATGJM Joe Montana/21*
ATGJN Joe Namath/12*
ATGJR Jerry Rice/12*
ATGJT Joe Theismann/27* 20.00 50.00
ATGJW Jason White/25* 15.00 40.00
ATGMB Matt Barkley/21* 10.00 25.00
ATGMT Manti Te'o/15* 12.00 30.00
ATGON Ozzie Newsome/21* 12.00 30.00
ATGPL Jake Plummer/35* 25.00 50.00
ATGRG Roman Gabriel/35* 8.00 20.00
ATGSA Barry Sanders/18* 125.00 200.00
ATGSY Steve Young/15* 40.00 80.00
ATGTA Tavon Austin/30* 10.00 25.00
ATGTD Ty Detmer/30* 10.00 25.00
ATGTF Tommie Frazier/35*
ATGVT Vinny Testaverde/50* 8.00 20.00
ATGWS Warren Sapp/20* 15.00 40.00

2013 Upper Deck Quantum Autographs

1-45 UNPRICED VET PRINT RUN 10
46-100 ROOKIE PRINT RUN 35
46 Dion Jordan/35 5.00 12.00
47 Kenjon Barner/35 5.00 12.00
48 Matt Barkley/35 5.00 12.00
49 Ezekiel Ansah/35 5.00 12.00
50 Cobi Hamilton/35 5.00 12.00
51 Tavon Austin/35 6.00 15.00
52 Cordarrelle Patterson/35 5.00 12.00
53 Jawan Jamison/35 5.00 12.00
54 Giovani Bernard/35 5.00 12.00
55 Keenan Allen/35 10.00 25.00
56 Kenny Stills/35 5.00 12.00
57 Landry Jones/35
58 Le'Veon Bell/35
59 Manti Te'o/35 6.00 15.00
60 Corey Fuller/35 5.00 12.00
61 Mike Glennon/35 5.00 12.00
62 Ryan Nassib/35 5.00 12.00
63 Theo Riddick/35 5.00 12.00
64 Zac Dysert/35 12.00 30.00
65 Aaron Dobson/35 5.00 12.00
66 Tyler Wilson/35 5.00 12.00
67 Chris Harper/35 5.00 12.00
68 Dee Milliner/35
69 Denard Robinson/35 5.00 12.00
70 EJ Manuel/35 5.00 12.00
71 Justin Hunter/35 5.00 12.00
72 Marquess Wilson/35
73 Gavin Escobar/35 5.00 12.00
74 Montee Ball/35 5.00 12.00
75 Ryan Swope/35 5.00 12.00
76 Robert Woods/35 8.00 20.00
77 Andre Ellington/35 5.00 12.00
78 Josh Boyce/35
79 Eddie Lacy/35 5.00 12.00
80 Tavarres King/35 5.00 12.00
81 Chris Thompson/35 5.00 12.00
82 Geno Smith/35
83 Marquise Goodwin/35 5.00 12.00
84 Markus Wheaton/35 5.00 12.00
85 Stedman Bailey/35 5.00 12.00
86 Zach Ertz/35
87 Barkevious Mingo/35 5.00 12.00
88 Joseph Randle/35 5.00 12.00
89 Knile Davis/35 5.00 12.00
90 Marcus Lattimore/35 5.00 12.00
91 Tyler Eifert/35 5.00 12.00
92 Johnathan Franklin/35 5.00 12.00
93 Mike Gillislee/35 5.00 12.00
94 Star Lotulelei/35
95 Stepfan Taylor/35
96 Aaron Mellette/35
97 Collin Klein/35
98 Tyler Bray/35 5.00 12.00
99 Terrance Williams/35 5.00 12.00
100 DeAndre Hopkins/35 12.00 30.00

2013 Upper Deck Quantum Jersey Collection

BB Brian Bosworth 4.00 10.00
LCBC Billy Cannon 3.00 8.00
LCBJ Bo Jackson 10.00 25.00
LCBS Barry Sanders 8.00 20.00
LCDB Drew Bledsoe 6.00 15.00
LCDE Ty Detmer 3.00 8.00
LCDF Doug Flutie 4.00 10.00
LCDM Dan Marino 12.00 30.00
LCEC Earl Campbell 6.00 15.00
LCEG Eddie George 4.00 10.00
LCHW Herschel Walker 5.00 12.00
LCJE John Elway 8.00 20.00
LCJH John Hannah 3.00 8.00
LCJM Joe Montana 20.00 40.00
LCJN Joe Namath 20.00 40.00
LCJR Jerry Rice 8.00 20.00
LCJT Joe Theismann 5.00 12.00
LCJW Jason White 3.00 8.00
LCKJ Keith Jackson 3.00 8.00
LCON Ozzie Newsome 4.00 10.00
LCPH Paul Hornung 5.00 12.00
LCRC Roger Craig 5.00 12.00
LCRD Ron Dayne 5.00 12.00
LCRG Roman Gabriel 3.00 8.00
LCSI Billy Sims
LCSO Steve Owens 4.00 10.00
LCTB Tedy Bruschi 4.00 10.00
LCTT Tim Tebow 8.00 20.00
LCVT Vinny Testaverde 3.00 8.00
LCWM Warren Moon 5.00 12.00
RCAD Aaron Dobson 1.50 4.00
RCBM Montee Ball 1.50 4.00
RCCP Cordarrelle Patterson 1.50 4.00
RCDH DeAndre Hopkins 4.00 10.00
RCDR Denard Robinson 1.50 4.00
RCEL Eddie Lacy 1.50 4.00
RCEM EJ Manuel 1.50 4.00
RCGB Giovani Bernard 1.50 4.00
RCGS Geno Smith 1.50 4.00
RCJF Johnathan Franklin 1.50 4.00
RCJH Justin Hunter 1.50 4.00
RCJR Joseph Randle 1.50 4.00
RCKA Keenan Allen 3.00 8.00
RCKS Kenny Stills 1.50 4.00
RCLB Le'Veon Bell 4.00 10.00
RCLJ Landry Jones 1.50 4.00
RCMB Matt Barkley 1.50 4.00
RCMG Mike Glennon 1.50 4.00
RCML Marcus Lattimore 1.50 4.00
RCMT Manti Te'o 2.00 5.00
RCRN Ryan Nassib 1.50 4.00
RCRW Robert Woods 2.50 6.00
RCSB Stedman Bailey 1.50 4.00
RCTA Tavon Austin 2.00 5.00
RCTE Tyler Eifert 1.50 4.00
RCTK Tavarres King 2.00 5.00
RCTW Tyler Wilson 1.50 4.00
RCWM Markus Wheaton 1.50 4.00
RCWT Terrance Williams 1.50 4.00
RCZE Zach Ertz 3.00 8.00

2013 Upper Deck Quantum Legacy Autograph Jerseys

LJBB Brian Bosworth
LJBC Billy Cannon 25.00 50.00
LJBJ Bo Jackson
LJBS Barry Sanders 90.00 150.00
LJDE Ty Detmer 10.00 25.00
LJDF Doug Flutie
LJDM Dan Marino 100.00 200.00
LJEC Earl Campbell
LJJE John Elway
LJJH John Hannah 10.00 25.00
LJJN Joe Namath 100.00 175.00
LJJP Jim Plunkett
LJJR Jerry Rice 60.00 120.00
LJJT Joe Theismann
LJJW Jason White 10.00 25.00
LJKJ Keith Jackson 10.00 25.00
LJON Ozzie Newsome
LJRC Roger Craig 12.00 30.00
LJRD Ron Dayne 12.00 30.00
LJRG Roman Gabriel 10.00 25.00
LJSI Billy Sims 12.00 30.00
LJSO Steve Owens
LJTA Eddie George 50.00 100.00
LJTB Tedy Bruschi 20.00 50.00
LJTH Thurman Thomas
LJTT Tim Tebow
LJVT Vinny Testaverde 10.00 25.00

2013 Upper Deck Quantum Moments in Time Dual Autographs

LGG E.George/A.Griffin/75 60.00 120.00
MTRAB T.Austin/S.Bailey/75 6.00 15.00
MTRBB L.Bell/M.Ball/75 15.00 40.00
MTRBP T.Bray/C.Patterson/75 5.00 12.00
MTRBW M.Barkley/R.Woods/15 10.00 25.00
MTRDB B.Mingo/D.Jordan/75 5.00 12.00
MTREH A.Ellington/D.Hopkins/15 25.00 50.00
MTREM M.Ball/E.Lacy/15 6.00 15.00
MTRGL G.Bernard/L.Bell/15 50.00 100.00
MTRHP C.Patterson/J.Hunter/75 5.00 12.00
MTRMT T.Wilson/M.Barkley/15
MTRNB R.Nassib/J.Boyce/75 5.00 12.00
MTRNS R.Nassib/B.Sorensen/75 5.00 12.00
MTRWB G.Smith/T.Austin/15 8.00 20.00
MTRTM T.Williams/M.Wheaton/15 6.00 15.00
MTRWG M.Glennon/T.Wilson/15 6.00 15.00
MTRWH T.Wilson/C.Hamilton/75 10.00 25.00
MTRWW T.Williams/R.Woods/75 8.00 20.00

2013 Upper Deck Quantum Monumental Dual Signatures

MDRBB L.Bell/G.Bernard/25 30.00 80.00
MDRBD L.Bell/K.Davis/25 30.00 60.00
MDRBG G.Bernard/M.Gillislee/25 15.00 40.00
MDRBW M.Barkley/R.Woods/25 10.00 25.00
MDREE Z.Ertz/T.Eifert/25
MDREH A.Ellington/D.Hopkins/25
MDRLB E.Lacy/M.Ball/25 6.00 15.00
MDRLF M.Lattimore/J.Franklin/25 6.00 15.00
MDRNG R.Nassib/M.Glennon/25 6.00 15.00
MDRPH C.Patterson/J.Hunter/25 6.00 15.00
MDRSB G.Smith/M.Barkley/25
MDRWP R.Woods/C.Patterson/25 10.00 25.00

2013 Upper Deck Quantum New Generation Autograph Jerseys

JAD Aaron Dobson/85 4.00 10.00
NGJBM Montee Ball/85 4.00 10.00
NGJCH Cobi Hamilton/85 4.00 10.00
NGJCP Cordarrelle Patterson/15
NGJDH DeAndre Hopkins/85 10.00 25.00
NGJEL Eddie Lacy/15 6.00 15.00
NGJEM EJ Manuel/15
NGJGB Giovani Bernard/85 4.00 10.00
NGJGM Mike Gillislee/85 4.00 10.00
NGJJF Johnathan Franklin/15 6.00 15.00
NGJJH Justin Hunter/15
NGJJR Joseph Randle/85 4.00 10.00
NGJKA Keenan Allen/15 10.00 25.00
NGJKS Kenny Stills/85 4.00 10.00
NGJLB Le'Veon Bell/85 12.00 30.00
NGJMB Matt Barkley/15
NGJMG Mike Glennon/15 6.00 15.00
NGJML Marcus Lattimore/85 12.00 30.00
NGJMT Manti Te'o/15
NGJRD Denard Robinson/85 4.00 10.00
NGJRN Ryan Nassib/85 10.00 25.00
NGJRW Robert Woods/85 6.00 15.00
NGJSB Tyler Eifert/85 4.00 10.00
NGJTA Tavon Austin/15 8.00 20.00
NGJTW Tyler Wilson/15 6.00 15.00
NGJWM Markus Wheaton/85 4.00 10.00
NGJWT Terrance Williams/85 4.00 10.00

2013 Upper Deck Quantum Renditions Signatures

RAD Aaron Dobson/99 4.00 10.00
RAE Andre Ellington/99 10.00 25.00
RAU Tavon Austin/75 5.00 12.00
RCH Cobi Hamilton/75 4.00 10.00
RDA Da'Rick Rogers/99 4.00 10.00
REJ EJ Manuel/75 4.00 10.00
RGB Giovani Bernard/75 4.00 10.00
RJH Justin Hunter/99 4.00 10.00
RJN Joe Namath/99
RJR Johnny Rodgers/99
RKA Keenan Allen/75 10.00 25.00
RKB Kenjon Barner/99 4.00 10.00
RKS Kenny Stills/99 4.00 10.00
RML Marcus Lattimore/75 4.00 10.00
RRW Robert Woods/75 6.00 15.00
RSI Billy Sims/99 8.00 20.00

2013 Upper Deck Quantum Signature Numbers

AE Andre Ellington/23 6.00 15.00
SNAG Archie Griffin/45 15.00 40.00
SNAK Andy Katzenmoyer/45 8.00 20.00
SNAP Alan Page/81 6.00 15.00
SNAT Al Toon/87 8.00 20.00
SNBB Brian Bosworth/44 10.00 25.00
SNBC Billy Cannon/20 15.00 40.00
SNBJ Bo Jackson/34 60.00 100.00
SNBM Barkevious Mingo/49 5.00 12.00
SNBS Billy Sims/20 12.00 30.00
SNBW Bjoern Werner/95 4.00 10.00
SNCP Cordarrelle Patterson/84 4.00 10.00
SNCT Chris Thompson/24 6.00 15.00
SNDB Drew Brees/15 40.00 80.00
SNDJ Dion Jordan/96 4.00 10.00
SNDR Denard Robinson/16 10.00 25.00
SNEC Earl Campbell/20 20.00 40.00
SNEF Eric Fisher/79 4.00 10.00
SNEG Eddie George/27 60.00 100.00
SNEL Eddie Lacy/42 5.00 12.00
SNFD Doug Flutie/22 12.00 30.00
SNGA Gary Beban/16 10.00 25.00
SNGB Giovani Bernard/26 6.00 15.00
SNIW Ickey Woods/30 8.00 20.00
SNJA Jason White/18 10.00 25.00
SNJB Josh Boyce/82 4.00 10.00
SNJF Johnathan Franklin/23 6.00 15.00
SNJH John Hannah/73 6.00 15.00
SNJO Jarvis Jones/29 6.00 15.00
SNJP Jim Plunkett/16 10.00 25.00
SNKA Keenan Allen/21 12.00 30.00
SNKB Kenjon Barner/24 6.00 15.00
SNKJ Keith Jackson/88 6.00 15.00
SNKM Ken MacAfee/81 6.00 15.00
SNLU Luke Joeckel/76
SNMI Mike Gillislee/23 6.00 15.00
SNML Marcus Lattimore/21 6.00 15.00
SNMO Montee Ball/28 6.00 15.00
SNNB Nick Buoniconti/64 10.00 25.00
SNNM Natrone Means/20 10.00 25.00
SNON Ozzie Newsome/82 8.00 20.00
SNPJ Jake Plummer/16 10.00 25.00
SNRC Roger Craig/21
SNRD Ron Dayne/33 10.00 25.00
SNRG Roman Gabriel/18 10.00 25.00
SNRP Rodney Peete/16 10.00 25.00
SNRS Robert Smith/35 8.00 20.00
SNSA Barry Sanders/21 60.00 120.00
SNSM Bruce Smith/78 15.00 40.00
SNSO Steve Owens/36 12.00 30.00
SNST Stepfan Taylor/33
SNTB Tedy Bruschi/68 8.00 20.00
SNTF Tommie Frazier/15 25.00 50.00
SNTT Thurman Thomas/34 10.00 25.00
SNTY Tyler Eifert/80 4.00 10.00
SNWS Warren Sapp/76 10.00 25.00

2013 Upper Deck Quantum Signature Patches

EXCH EXPIRATION: 4/8/2016
101 Barry Sanders/30 100.00 200.00
102 Joe Namath/30 75.00 150.00
103 Billy Cannon/30 15.00 40.00
104 Billy Sims/30 12.00 30.00
105 Bo Jackson/30 50.00 100.00
106 Dan Marino/30 75.00 150.00
107 John Hannah/30 10.00 25.00
108 Ron Dayne/30 15.00 40.00
109 Brian Bosworth/30 15.00 40.00
110 Doug Flutie/30 12.00 30.00
111 Earl Campbell/30 25.00 50.00
113 Jason White/30 10.00 25.00
114 Jim Plunkett/30 12.00 30.00
115 Joe Theismann/30 15.00 40.00
116 Steve Owens/30 10.00 25.00
117 Eddie George/30 12.00 30.00
118 John Elway/30 60.00 120.00
119 Keith Jackson/30 10.00 25.00
120 Jerry Rice/30 50.00 100.00
121 Archie Griffin/30 10.00 25.00
122 Ozzie Newsome/30 12.00 30.00
123 Paul Hornung/30
124 Roger Craig/30 12.00 30.00
125 Roman Gabriel/30 10.00 25.00
126 Thurman Thomas/30 12.00 30.00
127 Tedy Bruschi/30 12.00 30.00
128 Vinny Testaverde/30 10.00 25.00
129 Ty Detmer/30 10.00 25.00
130 Warren Moon/30 15.00 40.00
131 Kenjon Barner/265 5.00 12.00
132 Robert Woods/265 8.00 20.00
133 Aaron Dobson/265 5.00 12.00
134 Marcus Lattimore/265 5.00 12.00
135 Tyler Wilson/265 5.00 12.00
136 Le'Veon Bell/265 15.00 40.00
137 Keenan Allen/265 10.00 25.00
138 Johnathan Franklin/265 5.00 12.00
139 Montee Ball/265 5.00 12.00
140 Ryan Nassib/265 5.00 12.00
141 Terrance Williams/265 5.00 12.00
142 Tavarres King/265 5.00 12.00
143 Denard Robinson/265 5.00 12.00
144 Tyler Eifert/265 5.00 12.00
145 Eddie Lacy/265 5.00 12.00
147 Kenny Stills/265 5.00 12.00
148 Markus Wheaton/265 5.00 12.00
149 Justin Hunter/265 5.00 12.00
150 Joseph Randle/265 5.00 12.00
151 Geno Smith/99 EXCH 6.00 15.00
152 Matt Barkley/99 6.00 15.00
153 DeAndre Hopkins/99 15.00 40.00
154 Cordarrelle Patterson/99 6.00 15.00
155 Mike Glennon/99 6.00 15.00
156 Tavon Austin/99 8.00 20.00
157 Manti Te'o/99 8.00 20.00
159 Giovani Bernard/99 6.00 15.00
160 EJ Manuel/99 6.00 15.00

1999 Upper Deck Retro

e 1999 Upper Deck Retro Set was issued in mid October and featured a 165 card set with a colored background with a white border. Set features the top players of the 1999 draft such as Edgerrin James and Tim Couch as well as past NFL superstars such as Joe Montana and Roger Staubach. Cards were distributed in a "lunchbox" style container which featured one Inkredible hand signed autographed card per sealed lunchbox of packs.

COMPLETE SET (165) 15.00 40.00
1 Jake Plummer .15 .40
2 Adrian Murrell .15 .40
3 Rob Moore .15 .40
4 Frank Sanders .15 .40
5 David Boston RC .25 .60
6 Tim Dwight .20 .50
7 Chris Chandler .20 .50
8 Jamal Anderson .20 .50
9 O.J. Santiago .15 .40
10 Terance Mathis .15 .40
11 Priest Holmes .15 .40
12 Tony Banks .20 .50
13 Patrick Johnson .15 .40
14 Scott Mitchell .15 .40
15 Jermaine Lewis .15 .40
16 Eric Moulds .15 .40
17 Doug Flutie .25 .60
18 Antowain Smith .15 .40
19 Thurman Thomas .20 .50
20 Peerless Price RC .25 .60
21 Fred Lane .15 .40
22 Tim Biakabutuka .20 .50
23 Steve Beuerlein .20 .50
24 Muhsin Muhammad .15 .40
25 Rae Carruth .15 .40
26 Curtis Enis .15 .40
27 Walter Payton 1.50 4.00
28 Bobby Engram .15 .40
29 Cade McNown RC .25 .60
30 Curtis Conway .20 .50
31 Darnay Scott .15 .40
32 Jeff Blake .20 .50
33 Corey Dillon .15 .40
34 Akili Smith RC .25 .60
35 Carl Pickens .20 .50
36 Tim Couch RC .30 .75
37 Ty Detmer .15 .40
38 Jim Brown UER .60 1.50
39 Kevin Johnson RC .30 .75
40 Ozzie Newsome .20 .50
41 Troy Aikman .30 .75
42 Rocket Ismail .20 .50
43 Emmitt Smith .40 1.00
44 Michael Irvin .25 .60
45 Deion Sanders .20 .50
46 Roger Staubach .50 1.25
47 John Elway .40 1.00
48 Bubby Brister .15 .40
49 Terrell Davis .20 .50
50 Ed McCaffrey .20 .50
51 Rod Smith .20 .50
52 Shannon Sharpe .20 .50
53 Charlie Batch .15 .40
54 Johnnie Morton .20 .50
55 Barry Sanders .40 1.00
56 Sedrick Irvin RC .25 .60
57 Herman Moore .20 .50
58 Brett Favre .50 1.25
59 Mark Chmura .15 .40
60 Antonio Freeman .20 .50
61 Robert Brooks .20 .50
62 Dorsey Levens .20 .50
63 Peyton Manning .75 2.00
64 Jerome Pathon .15 .40
65 Marvin Harrison .20 .50
66 Edgerrin James RC .40 1.00
67 Ken Dilger .15 .40
68 Mark Brunell .20 .50
69 Fred Taylor .15 .40
70 Jimmy Smith .20 .50
71 James Stewart .15 .40
72 Keenan McCardell .20 .50
73 Elvis Grbac .15 .40
74 Mike Cloud RC .25 .60
75 Andre Rison .20 .50
76 Tony Gonzalez .20 .50
77 Warren Moon .25 .60
78 Derrick Alexander WR .15 .40
79 Dan Marino .50 1.25
80 O.J. McDuffie .20 .50
81 James Johnson RC .25 .60
82 Paul Warfield .40 1.00
83 Cecil Collins RC .25 .60
84 Randall Cunningham .30 .75
85 Randy Moss .20 .50
86 Cris Carter .25 .60
87 Fran Tarkenton .40 1.00
88 Daunte Culpepper RC .40 1.00
89 Robert Smith .15 .40
90 Drew Bledsoe .20 .50
91 Terry Glenn .20 .50
92 Kevin Faulk RC .25 .60
93 Tony Simmons .15 .40
94 Ben Coates .20 .50
95 Billy Joe Hobert .15 .40
96 Cameron Cleeland .15 .40
97 Eddie Kennison .20 .50
98 Andre Hastings .15 .40
99 Ricky Williams RC .40 1.00
100 Kerry Collins .15 .40
101 Joe Montgomery RC .25 .60
102 Gary Brown .15 .40
103 Ike Hilliard .15 .40
104 Amani Toomer .15 .40
105 Vinny Testaverde .15 .40
106 Wayne Chrebet .15 .40
107 Curtis Martin .20 .50
108 Joe Namath .75 2.00
109 Keyshawn Johnson .20 .50
110 Don Maynard .20 .50
111 Rich Gannon .20 .50
112 Tim Brown .25 .60
113 Charles Woodson .25 .60
114 Rickey Dudley .15 .40
115 Darrell Russell .15 .40
116 Napoleon Kaufman .15 .40
117 Donovan McNabb RC 2.00 5.00
118 Doug Pederson .15 .40
119 Duce Staley .15 .40
120 Torrance Small .15 .40
121 Charles Johnson .15 .40
122 Jerome Bettis .25 .60
123 Courtney Hawkins .15 .40
124 Kordell Stewart .15 .40
125 Troy Edwards RC .25 .60
126 Amos Zereoue RC .25 .60
127 Trent Green .15 .40
128 Marshall Faulk .20 .50
129 Az Zahir Hakim .15 .40
130 Joe Germaine RC .30 .75
131 Torry Holt RC .50 1.25
132 Isaac Bruce .25 .60
133 Jim Harbaugh .20 .50
134 Junior Seau .20 .50
135 Natrone Means .20 .50
136 Ryan Leaf .20 .50
137 Dan Fouts .30 .75
138 Mikhael Ricks .15 .40
139 Steve Young .30 .75
140 Terrell Owens .20 .50
141 Jerry Rice .60 1.50
142 J.J. Stokes .15 .40
143 Lawrence Phillips .20 .50
144 Joe Montana 1.25 3.00
145 Jon Kitna .15 .40
146 Ahman Green .20 .50
147 Joey Galloway .20 .50
148 Ricky Watters .20 .50
149 Brock Huard RC .25 .60
150 Steve Largent .40 1.00
151 Trent Dilfer .15 .40
152 Reidel Anthony .15 .40
153 Warrick Dunn .15 .40
154 Mike Alstott .15 .40
155 Shaun King RC .25 .60
156 Eddie George .20 .50
157 Steve McNair .20 .50
158 Kevin Dyson .15 .40
159 Frank Wycheck .20 .50
160 Yancey Thigpen .15 .40
161 Brad Johnson .20 .50
162 Rodney Peete .20 .50
163 Michael Westbrook .15 .40
164 Skip Hicks .15 .40
165 Champ Bailey RC .50 1.25
WP1 Walter Payton AU 400.00 600.00
WPR W.Payton Jsy AU/34 1000.00 1500.00

1999 Upper Deck Retro Gold

COMPLETE SET (165) 300.00 600.00
*GOLD STARS: 5X TO 12X HI COL.
*GOLD RCs: 2.5X TO 6X
GOLD STATED PRINT RUN 175 SER.#'d SETS

1999 Upper Deck Retro Inkredible

Randomly inserted at a rate of 1 in 32 packs, this 25 card insert set features hand signed cards of past and present stars. Some of the key cards signed include Ricky Williams, Tim Couch, Joe Montana and Joe Namath. Some cards were issued via mail redemptions that carried an expiration date of 8/4/2000.

ONE PER BOX
AK Akili Smith 5.00 12.00
AM Adrian Murrell 5.00 12.00
AS Antowain Smith 6.00 15.00
BH Brock Huard 5.00 12.00
CC Cris Carter 10.00 25.00
CM Cade McNown 5.00 12.00
DB David Boston 5.00 12.00
DC Daunte Culpepper 10.00 25.00
DF Dan Fouts 15.00 40.00
DL Dorsey Levens 7.50 20.00
FT Fran Tarkenton 15.00 40.00
GH Garrison Hearst 6.00 15.00
JK Jon Kitna 7.50 20.00
JM Joe Montana 60.00 120.00
JN Joe Namath 50.00 100.00
MC Donovan McNabb 20.00 50.00
OZ Ozzie Newsome 8.00 20.00
PW Paul Warfield 8.00 20.00
RG Roger Staubach 60.00 120.00
RM Randy Moss 50.00 100.00
RS Rod Smith 7.50 20.00
RW Ricky Williams 12.00 30.00
SK Shaun King 5.00 12.00
SL Steve Largent 12.00 30.00
TC Tim Couch 6.00 15.00
TD Terrell Davis 15.00 30.00
TH Torry Holt 12.00 30.00
TO Terrell Owens 15.00 40.00
WC Wayne Chrebet 7.50 20.00
WP Walter Payton 400.00 600.00

1999 Upper Deck Retro Inkredible Gold

Ranomly inserted in packs this Autographed set is a 30 card parallel to the base Inkredible set. Cards are hand signed to each respective players jersey number.

STATED PRINT RUN 2-89
AM Adrian Murrell/29 12.00 30.00
AS Antowain Smith/23 15.00 40.00
CC Cris Carter/80 12.00 30.00
DB David Boston/89 8.00 20.00
DL Dorsey Levens/25 30.00 80.00
GH Garrison Hearst/20 15.00 40.00
OZ Ozzie Newsome/82 12.00 30.00
PW Paul Warfield/42 12.00 30.00
RM Randy Moss/84 50.00 120.00
RS Rod Smith/80 12.00 30.00
RW Ricky Williams/34 25.00 60.00
SL Steve Largent/80 15.00 40.00
TD Terrell Davis/30 30.00 80.00
TH Torry Holt/88 25.00 60.00
TO Terrell Owens/81 25.00 60.00
WC Wayne Chrebet/80 12.00 30.00
WP Walter Payton/34 800.00 1200.00

1999 Upper Deck Retro Legends of the Fall

Randomly inserted at a rate of 1 in 11 packs, this insert set features color action shots of both past and present stars including Emmitt Smith and Randy Moss.

COMPLETE SET (30) 20.00 40.00
STATED ODDS 1:11
*SILVER CARDS: 7X TO 20X BASIC INSERTS
SILVER PRINT RUN 75 SER.#'d SETS
L1 Jake Plummer .40 1.00
L2 Corey Dillon .60 1.50
L3 Curtis Martin .60 1.50
L4 Vinny Testaverde .40 1.00
L5 Brett Favre 2.00 5.00
L6 Randy Moss 1.50 4.00
L7 John Elway 2.00 5.00
L8 Jerry Rice 1.25 3.00
L9 Troy Aikman 1.25 3.00
L10 Ricky Watters .40 1.00
L11 Keyshawn Johnson .60 1.50
L12 Mark Brunell .60 1.50
L13 Dorsey Levens .60 1.50
L14 Steve McNair .60 1.50
L15 Emmitt Smith 1.25 3.00
L16 Marshall Faulk .75 2.00
L17 Priest Holmes 1.00 2.50
L18 Steve Young .75 2.00
L19 Skip Hicks .25 .60
L20 Eddie George .60 1.50
L21 Garrison Hearst .40 1.00
L22 Drew Bledsoe .75 2.00
L23 Warrick Dunn .60 1.50
L24 Eric Moulds .60 1.50
L25 Joey Galloway .40 1.00
L26 Tim Brown .60 1.50
L27 Chris Chandler .40 1.00
L28 Peyton Manning 2.00 5.00
L29 Antonio Freeman .60 1.50
L30 Deion Sanders .60 1.50

1999 Upper Deck Retro Lunchboxes

These lunchboxes were used to carry the individual wax packs and contained a picture on the lunchbox with either a single player only or a dual player design. The dual Player design Lunchbox was done a a rate of 1 per case.

COMPLETE SET (16) 150.00 250.00
ONE DUAL PLAYER BOX PER CASE
1 Joe Montana 12.50 25.00
2 Ricky Williams 3.00 8.00
3 Randy Moss 6.00 12.00
4 Barry Sanders 7.50 15.00
5 John Elway 7.50 15.00
6 Terrell Davis 4.00 10.00
7 Dan Marino 7.50 15.00
8 Joe Namath 7.50 15.00
9 J.Montana / J.Elway 12.50 25.00
10 J.Montana / D.Marino 12.50 25.00
11 J.Elway / D.Marino 12.50 25.00
12 J.Montana / J.Namath 12.50 25.00
13 R.Williams / T.Couch 4.00 10.00
14 J.Namath / D.Marino 12.50 25.00
15 T.Couch / J.Montana 12.50 25.00
16 B.Sanders / T.Davis 5.00 12.00

1999 Upper Deck Retro Old School/New School

Randomly inserted in packs, this 30-card set pairs a young star with a standout veteran of the same position. Cards are sequentially numbered to 1000 and backs carry an "ON" prefix.

STATED PRINT RUN 1000 SER.#'d SETS
*LEVEL 2/50: 2X TO 5X BASIC INSERT
ON1 T.Davis/R.Williams 2.00 5.00
ON2 J.Montana/J.Plummer 6.00 15.00
ON3 C.Carter/R.Moss 2.00 5.00
ON4 R.Cunningham/D.Culpepper 2.00 5.00
ON5 B.Favre/J.Kitna 4.00 10.00
ON6 E.Smith/F.Taylor 3.00 8.00
ON7 M.Brunell/B.Huard 1.50 4.00
ON8 J.Elway/P.Manning 6.00 15.00
ON9 S.Young/C.McNown 2.50 6.00
ON10 D.Maynard/K.Johnson 1.50 4.00
ON11 D.Marino/T.Couch 4.00 10.00
ON12 J.Rice/T.Owens 5.00 12.00
ON13 M.Faulk/E.James 2.00 5.00
ON14 D.Fouts/A.Smith 1.50 4.00
ON15 B.Sanders/J.Anderson 3.00 8.00
ON16 T.Glenn/D.Boston 1.50 4.00
ON17 D.Sanders/C.Bailey 1.50 4.00
ON18 A.Reed/E.Moulds 2.00 5.00
ON19 J.Seau/C.Claiborne 1.50 4.00
ON20 S.Largent/J.Galloway 2.00 5.00
ON21 K.Stewart/S.King 1.25 3.00
ON22 R.Watters/K.Faulk 1.50 4.00
ON23 T.Thomas/W.Dunn 1.50 4.00
ON24 T.Brown/T.Edwards 2.00 5.00
ON25 J.Bettis/C.Collins 2.00 5.00
ON26 I.Bruce/T.Holt 2.50 6.00
ON27 F.Tarkenton/D.McNabb 4.00 10.00
ON28 W.Moon/C.Batch 2.00 5.00
ON29 H.Moore/D.Bates 1.50 4.00
ON30 R.Staubach/T.Aikman 2.50 6.00

1999 Upper Deck Retro Smashmouth

ndomly inserted at a rate of 1 in 8 packs, this 15 card set features the hardest hitting stars in the NFL.

COMPLETE SET (15) 7.50 20.00
STATED ODDS 1:8
*LEVEL 2/100: 3X TO 8X BASIC INSERTS
S1 Fred Taylor .40 1.00
S2 Jamal Anderson .50 1.25
S3 John Elway 1.00 2.50
S4 Brock Huard .40 1.00
S5 Daunte Culpepper .60 1.50
S6 Charlie Batch .40 1.00
S7 Steve McNair .50 1.25
S8 Corey Dillon .40 1.00
S9 Natrone Means .50 1.25
S10 Randall Cunningham .50 1.25
S11 Drew Bledsoe .50 1.25
S12 Jerome Bettis .60 1.50
S13 Antowain Smith .40 1.00
S14 Steve Young .75 2.00
S15 Eddie George .50 1.25

1999 Upper Deck Retro Throwback Attack

Randomly inserted at a rate of 1 in 5 packs, this insert set features players who show a resemblence to past NFL greats.

COMPLETE SET (15) 10.00 25.00
GOLD STATED ODDS 1:5
*SILVER/500: 2X TO 5X BASIC INSERTS
T1 Brett Favre 1.00 2.50
T2 Herman Moore .40 1.00
T3 Troy Aikman .60 1.50
T4 Eric Moulds .30 .75
T5 Tim Couch .40 1.00
T6 Terrell Owens .40 1.00
T7 Champ Bailey .60 1.50
T8 Kordell Stewart .30 .75
T9 Mark Brunell .40 1.00
T10 Curtis Martin .40 1.00
T11 Torry Holt .60 1.50
T12 David Boston .30 .75
T13 Doug Flutie .50 1.25
T14 Edgerrin James .50 1.25
T15 Akili Smith .30 .75

2005 Upper Deck Rookie Debut

Upper Deck Rookie Debut was initially released in early-June 2005. The base set consists of 200-cards including 100-rookies inserted at the rate of 1:3 packs. Hobby boxes contained 28-packs of 6-cards and carried an S.R.P. of $2.99 per pack. Three parallel sets and a variety of inserts can be found seeded in packs highlighted by the Debut Ink and Draft Generations Autographs inserts.

COMP.SET w/o SP's (100) 10.00 20.00
ROOKIE STATED ODDS 1:3
1 Larry Fitzgerald .30 .75
2 Kurt Warner .25 .60
3 Anquan Boldin .20 .50
4 Michael Vick .25 .60
5 Warrick Dunn .20 .50
6 Peerless Price .20 .50
7 Jamal Lewis .25 .60
8 Derrick Mason .20 .50
9 Kyle Boller .20 .50
10 Willis McGahee .20 .50
11 J.P. Losman .20 .50
12 Eric Moulds .20 .50
13 Stephen Davis .20 .50
14 Jake Delhomme .20 .50
15 Steve Smith .30 .75
16 Thomas Jones .20 .50
17 Brian Urlacher .30 .75
18 Rex Grossman .20 .50
19 Carson Palmer .25 .60
20 Rudi Johnson .20 .50
21 Chad Johnson .20 .50
22 Kellen Winslow .20 .50
23 Luke McCown .20 .50
24 Loo Suggo .20 .50
25 Drew Bledsoe .25 .60
26 Keyshawn Johnson .25 .60
27 Julius Jones .20 .50
28 Roy Williams S .20 .50
29 Jake Plummer .20 .50
30 Tatum Bell .20 .50
31 Rod Smith .25 .60
32 Roy Williams WR .20 .50
33 Joey Harrington .20 .50
34 Kevin Jones .20 .50
35 Brett Favre .60 1.50
36 Javon Walker .20 .50
37 Ahman Green .25 .60
38 David Carr .20 .50
39 Andre Johnson .25 .60
40 Domanick Davis .20 .50
41 Peyton Manning .75 2.00
42 Marvin Harrison .25 .60
43 Edgerrin James .25 .60
44 Reggie Wayne .25 .60
45 Byron Leftwich .20 .50
46 Jimmy Smith .25 .60
47 Fred Taylor .20 .50
48 Priest Holmes .20 .50
49 Trent Green .20 .50
50 Tony Gonzalez .25 .60
51 Chris Chambers .20 .50
52 Sammy Morris .20 .50
53 A.J. Feeley .20 .50
54 Daunte Culpepper .25 .60
55 Nate Burleson .20 .50
56 Michael Bennett .20 .50
57 Tom Brady 1.25 3.00
58 David Givens .20 .50
59 Corey Dillon .20 .50
60 Ty Law .30 .75
61 Aaron Brooks .20 .50
62 Joe Horn .20 .50
63 Deuce McAllister .25 .60
64 Eli Manning .50 1.25
65 Tiki Barber .25 .60
66 Amani Toomer .20 .50
67 Chad Pennington .20 .50
68 Curtis Martin .25 .60
69 Santana Moss .25 .60
70 Jerry Porter .20 .50
71 Randy Moss .25 .60
72 Kerry Collins .20 .50
73 Donovan McNabb .25 .60
74 Terrell Owens .25 .60
75 Brian Westbrook .20 .50
76 Ben Roethlisberger .50 1.25
77 Hines Ward .25 .60
78 Jerome Bettis .30 .75
79 Duce Staley .20 .50
80 Drew Brees .30 .75
81 LaDainian Tomlinson .30 .75
82 Antonio Gates .30 .75
83 Tim Rattay .20 .50
84 Kevan Barlow .20 .50
85 Eric Johnson .20 .50
86 Matt Hasselbeck .20 .50
87 Shaun Alexander .20 .50
88 Darrell Jackson .20 .50
89 Marc Bulger .20 .50
90 Marshall Faulk .25 .60
91 Torry Holt .25 .60
92 Chris Simms .20 .50
93 Michael Clayton .20 .50
94 Michael Pittman .20 .50
95 Steve McNair .25 .60
96 Drew Bennett .25 .60
97 Chris Brown .20 .50
98 Clinton Portis .20 .50
99 Patrick Ramsey .25 .60
100 Laveranues Coles .20 .50
101 Gino Guidugli RC .75 2.00
102 Kyle Orton RC .75 2.00
103 David Greene RC .75 2.00
104 Charlie Frye RC .75 2.00
105 Andrew Walter RC .75 2.00
106 Dan Orlovsky RC .75 2.00
107 Jason White RC 1.25 3.00
108 Sonny Cumbie RC .75 2.00
109 Ronnie Brown RC 1.00 2.50
110 Cadillac Williams RC .75 2.00
111 Anthony Davis RC .75 2.00
112 Kay-Jay Harris RC .75 2.00
113 Walter Reyes RC .75 2.00
114 Darren Sproles RC 1.25 3.00
115 Mark Clayton RC .75 2.00
116 Braylon Edwards RC .75 2.00
117 Charles Frederick RC .75 2.00
118 Fred Gibson RC .75 2.00
119 Craphonso Thorpe RC .75 2.00
120 Terrence Murphy RC .75 2.00
121 Antrel Rolle RC 1.25 3.00
122 Marlin Jackson RC .75 2.00
123 Corey Webster RC 1.00 2.50
124 Travis Johnson RC .75 2.00
125 Shawne Merriman RC 1.25 3.00
126 Aaron Rodgers RC 12.50 25.00
127 Alex Smith QB RC 3.00 8.00
128 T.A. McLendon RC .75 2.00
129 Troy Williamson RC .75 2.00
130 Ryan Moats RC .75 2.00
131 Vernand Morency RC .75 2.00
132 Brock Berlin RC .75 2.00
133 J.J. Arrington RC 1.00 2.50
134 Frank Gore RC 1.50 4.00
135 Chris Henry RC 1.00 2.50
136 Roscoe Parrish RC .75 2.00
137 Alex Smith TE RC .75 2.00
138 Ciatrick Fason RC .75 2.00
139 Marion Barber RC .75 2.00
140 J.R. Russell RC .75 2.00
141 Heath Miller RC 1.50 4.00
142 Marcus Spears RC .75 2.00
143 Alvin Pearman RC .75 2.00
144 David Pollack RC .75 2.00
145 Erasmus James RC .75 2.00
146 Noah Herron RC .75 2.00
147 Dan Cody RC .75 2.00
148 Eric Shelton RC .75 2.00
149 Anttaj Hawthorne RC .75 2.00
150 Steve Savoy RC .75 2.00
151 Mike Patterson RC .75 2.00
152 Kirk Morrison RC 1.25 3.00
153 Airese Currie RC .75 2.00
154 Derrick Johnson RC 1.00 2.50
155 Darryl Blackstock RC .75 2.00
156 Mike Williams 1.00 2.50
157 Ernest Shazor RC 1.00 2.50
158 James Butler RC 1.00 2.50
159 Thomas Davis RC .75 2.00
160 Carlos Rogers RC 1.25 3.00
161 Mark Bradley RC .75 2.00
162 Jerome Mathis RC 1.25 3.00
163 Justin Miller RC .75 2.00
164 Donte Nicholson RC .75 2.00
165 Derek Anderson RC 1.00 2.50
166 Brandon Browner RC 1.25 3.00
167 Domonique Foxworth RC 1.00 2.50
168 Kevin Burnett RC 1.00 2.50
169 Lorenzo Alexander RC .75 2.00
170 Oshiomogho Atogwe RC 1.00 2.50
171 Dustin Fox RC 1.00 2.50
172 Jamaal Brimmer RC .75 2.00
173 Ryan Fitzpatrick RC 1.25 3.00
174 Bill Swancutt RC .75 2.00
175 Barrett Ruud RC 1.00 2.50
176 Channing Crowder RC 1.00 2.50
177 Timmy Chang RC .75 2.00
178 Chris Rix RC 1.00 2.50
179 Justin Tuck RC 1.00 2.50
180 Adam Jones RC .75 2.00
181 Bryant McFadden RC 1.00 2.50
182 Taylor Stubblefield RC .75 2.00
183 Vincent Jackson RC 1.25 3.00

184 Craig Bragg RC .75 2.00
185 Reggie Brown RC .75 2.00
186 Roddy White RC 1.25 3.00
187 Jason Campbell RC .75 2.00
188 Derek Cameron Wake RC 10.00 25.00
189 Josh Davis RC .75 2.00
190 Mike Nugent RC 1.00 2.50
191 Maurice Clarett .75 2.00
192 Brandon Jacobs RC 1.00 2.50
193 Matt Jones RC .75 2.00
194 Chad Owens RC .75 2.00
195 Paris Warren RC 1.00 2.50
196 Tab Perry RC .75 2.00
197 Jovan Haye RC .75 2.00
198 Cedric Benson RC .75 2.00
199 Bobby Purify RC 1.00 2.50
200 Stefan LeFors RC .75 2.00

2005 Upper Deck Rookie Debut Blue

*VETERANS: 12X TO 30X BASIC CARDS
*ROOKIES: 3X TO 8X BASIC CARDS
BLUE STATED PRINT RUN 15 SETS

2005 Upper Deck Rookie Debut Gold 100

*VETERANS: 5X TO 12X BASIC CARDS
*ROOKIES: 1.2X TO 3X BASIC CARDS
GOLD/100 INSERTED IN HOBBY PACKS

2005 Upper Deck Rookie Debut Gold 150

*VETERANS: 5X TO 12X BASIC CARDS
*ROOKIES: 1.2X TO 3X BASIC CARDS
GOLD/150 INSERTED IN RETAIL PACKS

2005 Upper Deck Rookie Debut Gold Spectrum

*VETS: 8X TO 20X BASIC CARDS
*ROOKIES: 2X TO 5X BASIC CARDS
GOLD SPECTRUM PRINT RUN 50 SER.#'d SETS

2005 Upper Deck Rookie Debut All-Pros

MPLETE SET (30) 12.50 30.00
STATED ODDS 1:4
*BLUE/15: 2.5X TO 6X BASIC INSERTS
BLUE PRINT RUN 15 SETS
*GOLD/100: .8X TO 2X BASIC INSERTS
GOLD PRINT RUN 100 SER.#'d SETS
*GOLD SPECT/50: 1.2X TO 3X BASIC INSERTS
GOLD SPECTRUM PRINT RUN 50 SETS
AP1 Peyton Manning 2.50 6.00
AP2 Donovan McNabb .75 2.00
AP3 Michael Vick .75 2.00
AP4 Tom Brady 4.00 10.00
AP5 Daunte Culpepper .75 2.00
AP6 Drew Brees 1.00 2.50
AP7 Tiki Barber .75 2.00
AP8 Brian Westbrook .60 1.50
AP9 Ahman Green .75 2.00
AP10 Rudi Johnson .60 1.50
AP11 LaDainian Tomlinson 1.00 2.50
AP12 Jerome Bettis 1.00 2.50
AP13 Hines Ward .75 2.00
AP14 Torry Holt .75 2.00
AP15 Joe Horn .60 1.50
AP16 Muhsin Muhammad .60 1.50
AP17 Marvin Harrison .75 2.00
AP18 Antonio Gates 1.00 2.50
AP19 Tony Gonzalez .75 2.00
AP20 Javon Walker .60 1.50
AP21 Jason Witten .75 2.00
AP22 Alge Crumpler .75 2.00
AP23 Andre Johnson .75 2.00
AP24 Ed Reed .75 2.00
AP25 Champ Bailey .75 2.00
AP26 Takeo Spikes .60 1.50
AP27 Allen Rossum .60 1.50
AP28 Terrence McGee .75 2.00
AP29 Troy Polamalu 1.00 2.50
AP30 Roy Williams S .60 1.50

2005 Upper Deck Rookie Debut Ink

STATED ODDS 1:28 HOB, 1:168 RET
*LIMITED: .6X TO 1.5X BASIC AU
*LIMITED: .5X TO 1.2X BASIC AU SP
LIMITEDD ODDS 6:1008 H, 6:3024 R
DIAD Anthony Davis 5.00 12.00
DIAH Anttaj Hawthorne SP 6.00 15.00
DIAN Antrel Rolle 8.00 20.00
DIAR Aaron Rodgers SP 125.00 250.00
DIAS Alex Smith QB SP 25.00 60.00
DIAW Andrew Walter 5.00 12.00
DIBE Braylon Edwards SP 15.00 40.00
DIBJ Brandon Jacobs 6.00 15.00
DIBR Barrett Ruud 6.00 15.00
DICB Cedric Benson SP 10.00 25.00
DICD Charles Frederick 5.00 12.00
DICF Charlie Frye 5.00 12.00
DICH Chris Henry SP 8.00 20.00
DICI Ciatrick Fason 5.00 12.00
DICO Corey Webster 6.00 15.00
DICR Carlos Rogers 8.00 20.00
DICT Craphonso Thorpe 5.00 12.00
DICW Cadillac Williams 8.00 20.00
DIDC Dan Cody 5.00 12.00
DIDG David Greene SP 6.00 15.00
DIDO Dan Orlovsky
DIDP David Pollack SP 6.00 15.00
DIDS Darren Sproles SP 10.00 25.00
DIEJ Erasmus James 5.00 12.00
DIFG Fred Gibson 5.00 12.00
DIFR Frank Gore 10.00 25.00
DIJA J.J. Arrington 6.00 15.00
DIJB James Butler 6.00 15.00
DIJR J.R. Russell 5.00 12.00
DIJW Jason White 8.00 20.00
DIKH Kay-Jay Harris 5.00 12.00
DIKO Kyle Orton 5.00 12.00
DIMB Marion Barber 5.00 12.00
DIMC Mark Clayton 5.00 12.00
DIMJ Marlin Jackson 5.00 12.00
DIMW Mike Williams 6.00 15.00
DIRB Ronnie Brown SP 15.00 40.00
DIRM Ryan Moats 5.00 12.00
DIRP Roscoe Parrish
DIRW Roddy White SP 10.00 25.00
DISC Sonny Cumbie 5.00 12.00
DITA T.A. McLendon 5.00 12.00
DITD Thomas Davis 5.00 12.00
DITM Terrence Murphy 5.00 12.00
DITS Taylor Stubblefield 5.00 12.00
DITW Troy Williamson SP 6.00 15.00
DIVM Vernand Morency 5.00 12.00
DIWR Walter Reyes 5.00 12.00

2005 Upper Deck Rookie Debut Draft Generations Autographs

UNPRICED PRINT RUN 10 SER.#'d SETS

2005 Upper Deck Rookie Debut Rookie of the Year Predictors

STATED ODDS 1:14
ROY1 Mike Williams .50 1.25
ROY2 Jerome Mathis .60 1.50
ROY3 Brandon Jacobs .50 1.25
ROY4 Andrew Walter .40 1.00
ROY5 Aaron Rodgers 7.50 15.00
ROY6 Cadillac Williams WIN 12.00 30.00
ROY7 Kyle Orton .40 1.00
ROY8 Ronnie Brown .50 1.25
ROY9 Troy Williamson .40 1.00
ROY10 Craphonso Thorpe .40 1.00
ROY11 Mark Clayton .40 1.00
ROY12 Charlie Frye .40 1.00
ROY13 David Greene .40 1.00
ROY14 Vernand Morency .40 1.00
ROY15 Chris Henry .50 1.25
ROY16 Dan Orlovsky .40 1.00
ROY17 Anthony Davis .40 1.00
ROY18 Kay-Jay Harris .40 1.00
ROY19 Walter Reyes .40 1.00
ROY20 Darren Sproles .60 1.50
ROY21 Fred Gibson .40 1.00
ROY22 Terrence Murphy .40 1.00
ROY23 Alex Smith QB 1.50 4.00
ROY24 Ryan Moats .40 1.00
ROY25 Marion Barber .40 1.00
ROY26 Frank Gore .75 2.00
ROY27 Taylor Stubblefield .40 1.00
ROY28 Alex Smith TE .40 1.00
ROY29 Charles Frederick .40 1.00
ROY30 Roscoe Parrish .40 1.00
ROY31 Roddy White .60 1.50
ROY32 Ciatrick Fason .40 1.00
ROY33 T.A. McLendon .40 1.00
ROY34 J.J. Arrington .50 1.25
ROY35 Derek Anderson .50 1.25
ROY36 Stefan LeFors .40 1.00
ROY37 Reggie Brown .40 1.00
ROY38 Craig Bragg .40 1.00
ROY39 J.R. Russell .40 1.00
ROY40 Heath Miller .75 2.00
ROY41 Jason Campbell .40 1.00
ROY42 Offensive Field .40 1.00

2005 Upper Deck Rookie Debut Saturday Swatches

STATED ODDS 1:28
*LIMITED: .5X TO 1.2X BASIC JSY
LIMITED ODDS 4:168H, 4:504R
*PATCH/50: 1X TO 2.5X BASIC JSY
SAAN Antrel Rolle 4.00 10.00
SABP Bobby Purify 3.00 8.00
SACO Chad Owens 2.50 6.00
SACR Carlos Rogers 4.00 10.00
SACW Cadillac Williams 2.50 6.00
SADA Derek Anderson 3.00 8.00
SADN Donte Nicholson 2.50 6.00
SADO Dan Orlovsky 2.50 6.00
SAES Ernest Shazor 3.00 8.00
SAFR Frank Gore 5.00 12.00
SAJR J.R. Russell 2.50 6.00
SAKO Kyle Orton 2.50 6.00
SAMC Mark Clayton 2.50 6.00
SAMS Marcus Spears 2.50 6.00
SAPW Paris Warren 3.00 8.00
SARB Ronnie Brown 3.00 8.00
SARM Ryan Moats 2.50 6.00
SARP Roscoe Parrish 2.50 6.00
SASL Stefan LeFors 2.50 6.00
SAST Santonio Thomas 2.50 6.00
SATC Timmy Chang 2.50 6.00
SATP Tab Perry 2.50 6.00
SATS Taylor Stubblefield 2.50 6.00
SAVM Vernand Morency 2.50 6.00

2005 Upper Deck Rookie Debut Sunday Swatches

STATED ODDS 1:28
SUAB Aaron Brooks 2.50 6.00
SUAL Ashley Lelie 2.50 6.00
SUAQ Anquan Boldin 2.50 6.00
SUBL Byron Leftwich 2.50 6.00
SUBR Ben Roethlisberger 6.00 15.00
SUCG Chad Pennington 2.50 6.00
SUCL Clinton Portis 2.50 6.00
SUCM Curtis Martin 3.00 8.00
SUCP Carson Palmer 3.00 8.00
SUCR Charles Rogers 2.50 6.00
SUDC David Carr 2.50 6.00
SUDM Derrick Mason 2.50 6.00
SUDU Daunte Culpepper 3.00 8.00
SUHW Hines Ward 3.00 8.00
SUJH Joey Harrington 2.50 6.00
SUJL Jamal Lewis 3.00 8.00
SUJS Jeremy Shockey 2.50 6.00
SUJW Javon Walker 2.50 6.00
SULT LaDainian Tomlinson 4.00 10.00
SUMA Matt Hasselbeck 2.50 6.00
SUMH Marvin Harrison 3.00 8.00
SUMV Michael Vick 3.00 8.00
SUPH Priest Holmes 2.50 6.00
SUPM Peyton Manning 10.00 25.00
SUPP Peerless Price 2.50 6.00
SURG Rex Grossman 2.50 6.00
SURW Roy Williams S 2.50 6.00
SUTB Tom Brady 15.00 40.00
SUTH Torry Holt 3.00 8.00
SUTO Terrell Owens 3.00 8.00

2006 Upper Deck Rookie Debut

This 260-card set was released in October, 2006. The set was issued into the hobby in six-card packs which came 28 packs to a box. The first 100 cards in the set feature veterans in team alphabetical order while cards numbered 201-260 feature 2006 rookies. Within the rookie subset, cards numbered 101-200 were issued at a stated rate of one per pack, and cards numbered 201-260 were signed by the player and issued to a stated rate of one in 28. A few players in the autograph subset signed fewer cards than the rest of the players and those production numbers, for those specific players, which Upper Deck released are notated in our checklist.

COMP.SET w/o RC's (100) 10.00 25.00
101-200 ROOKIES ONE PER PACK
201-260 AU ROOKIE ODDS 1:28
1 Anquan Boldin .20 .50
2 Larry Fitzgerald .25 .60
3 Edgerrin James .25 .60
4 Warrick Dunn .20 .50
5 Alge Crumpler .25 .60
6 Michael Vick .25 .60
7 Jamal Lewis .25 .60
8 Derrick Mason .20 .50
9 Steve McNair .25 .60
10 Willis McGahee .20 .50
11 Lee Evans .25 .60
12 J.P. Losman .25 .60
13 Steve Smith .30 .75
14 Jake Delhomme .20 .50
15 DeShaun Foster .25 .60
16 Rex Grossman .20 .50
17 Brian Urlacher .30 .75
18 Thomas Jones .20 .50
19 Carson Palmer .25 .60
20 Chad Johnson .20 .50
21 T.J. Houshmandzadeh .20 .50
22 Rudi Johnson .20 .50
23 Charlie Frye .25 .60
24 Reuben Droughns .25 .60
25 Braylon Edwards .20 .50
26 Terrell Owens .25 .60
27 Julius Jones .20 .50
28 Drew Bledsoe .25 .60
29 Terry Glenn .25 .60
30 Jake Plummer .20 .50
31 Tatum Bell .20 .50
32 Javon Walker .25 .60
33 Kevin Jones .20 .50
34 Roy Williams WR .20 .50
35 Jon Kitna .20 .50
36 Brett Favre .60 1.50
37 Donald Driver .25 .60
38 Ahman Green .25 .60
39 David Carr .20 .50
40 Domanick Davis .20 .50
41 Andre Johnson .25 .60
42 Peyton Manning .75 2.00
43 Reggie Wayne .25 .60
44 Marvin Harrison .25 .60
45 Byron Leftwich .20 .50
46 Greg Jones .20 .50
47 Ernest Wilford .20 .50
48 Trent Green .20 .50
49 Larry Johnson .20 .50
50 Tony Gonzalez .25 .60
51 Daunte Culpepper .25 .60
52 Ronnie Brown .25 .60
53 Chris Chambers .20 .50
54 Brad Johnson .25 .60
55 Chester Taylor .25 .60
56 Troy Williamson .20 .50
57 Tom Brady 1.00 2.50
58 Deion Branch .20 .50
59 Corey Dillon .20 .50
60 Drew Brees .30 .75
61 Deuce McAllister .25 .60
62 Joe Horn .20 .50
63 Eli Manning .25 .60
64 Tiki Barber .25 .60
65 Plaxico Burress .20 .50
66 Michael Strahan .25 .60
67 Chad Pennington .20 .50
68 Curtis Martin .25 .60
69 Jonathan Vilma .20 .50
70 Aaron Brooks .20 .50
71 Randy Moss .25 .60
72 LaMont Jordan .25 .60
73 Donovan McNabb .25 .60
74 Brian Westbrook .20 .50
75 L.J. Smith .20 .50
76 Ben Roethlisberger .40 1.00
77 Hines Ward .25 .60
78 Willie Parker .25 .60
79 LaDainian Tomlinson .30 .75
80 Philip Rivers .30 .75
81 Antonio Gates .30 .75
82 Alex Smith QB .25 .60
83 Antonio Bryant .20 .50
84 Frank Gore .25 .60
85 Matt Hasselbeck .20 .50
86 Shaun Alexander .20 .50
87 Nate Burleson .20 .50
88 Julian Peterson .20 .50
89 Torry Holt .25 .60
90 Marc Bulger .20 .50
91 Steven Jackson .20 .50
92 Cadillac Williams .25 .60
93 Chris Simms .20 .50
94 Joey Galloway .25 .60
95 Drew Bennett .25 .60
96 David Givens .25 .60
97 Chris Brown .20 .50
98 Clinton Portis .20 .50
99 Santana Moss .25 .60
100 Antwaan Randle El .20 .50
101 Todd Watkins RC .60 1.50
102 Damarius Bilbo RC .75 2.00
103 Troy Bergeron RC .75 2.00
104 Jerious Norwood RC .60 1.50
105 Adam Jennings RC .75 2.00
106 Haloti Ngata RC .75 2.00
107 Ed Hinkel RC 1.00 2.50
108 P.J. Daniels RC .60 1.50
109 Quinn Sypniewski RC .75 2.00
110 Donte Whitner RC .75 2.00
111 John McCargo RC .60 1.50
112 Chris Denney RC .60 1.50
113 Richard Marshall RC .60 1.50
114 Brett Basanez RC 1.00 2.50
115 Nate Salley RC .75 2.00
116 Jeff King RC .75 2.00
117 Danieal Manning RC 1.00 2.50
118 Devin Hester RC 1.25 3.00
119 P.J. Pope RC 1.00 2.50
120 Johnathan Joseph RC .75 2.00
121 Andrew Whitworth RC .60 1.50
122 Ethan Kilmer RC .75 2.00
123 Bennie Brazell RC .75 2.00
124 Erik Meyer RC .60 1.50
125 J.D. Runnels RC .75 2.00
126 Kamerion Wimbley RC .75 2.00
127 D'Qwell Jackson RC .60 1.50
128 Lawrence Vickers RC .75 2.00
129 Bobby Carpenter RC .60 1.50
130 Demetrius Summers RC .60 1.50
131 Tony Scheffler RC 1.00 2.50
132 Domenik Hixon RC 1.00 2.50
133 Daniel Bullocks RC .60 1.50
134 Joe Klopfenstein RC .60 1.50
135 Joel Klatt RC .75 2.00
136 Daryn Colledge RC 1.00 2.50
137 Brandon Marshall RC 1.25 3.00
138 Brandon Williams RC .60 1.50
139 Ingle Martin RC .75 2.00
140 Matt Baker RC 1.00 2.50
141 David Anderson RC .75 2.00
142 Charles Spencer RC .60 1.50
143 Wali Lundy RC .60 1.50
144 Mario Williams RC 1.00 2.50
145 David Kirtman RC .75 2.00
146 Tamba Hali RC 1.00 2.50
147 Bernard Pollard RC .75 2.00
148 Derrick Ross RC .75 2.00
149 Jeff Webb RC .75 2.00
150 De'Arrius Howard RC 1.00 2.50
151 Chris Hannon RC .75 2.00
152 Jason Allen RC .75 2.00
153 Devin Aromashodu RC .60 1.50
154 Cedric Griffin RC .75 2.00
155 Ryan Cook RC .75 2.00
156 Jason Carter RC .75 2.00
157 Barrick Nealy RC .75 2.00
158 Wendell Mathis RC .75 2.00
159 David Thomas RC .60 1.50
160 Garrett Mills RC .75 2.00
161 Roman Harper RC .75 2.00
162 Marques Colston RC 1.00 2.50
163 Travis Wilson RC .60 1.50
164 Anthony Mix RC .75 2.00
165 Nick Mangold RC .75 2.00
166 Brett Elliott RC 1.00 2.50
167 Antonio Cromartie RC .75 2.00
168 Kevin McMahan RC .75 2.00
169 Derek Hagan RC .75 2.00
170 Marcedes Lewis RC .60 1.50
171 Kent Smith RC 1.00 2.50
172 John Madsen RC .75 2.00
173 Charlie Whitehurst RC .60 1.50
174 Deuce Lutui RC .75 2.00
175 Jeremy Bloom RC .60 1.50
176 Cedric Humes RC .60 1.50
177 Jason Avant RC .60 1.50
178 Brodie Croyle RC .60 1.50
179 Marcus McNeill RC .60 1.50
180 Manny Lawson RC .75 2.00
181 Delanie Walker RC 1.25 3.00
182 Kelly Jennings RC .75 2.00
183 Darryl Tapp RC .75 2.00
184 Ben Obomanu RC .75 2.00
185 Travis Lulay RC .75 2.00
186 Matt Henshaw RC .75 2.00
187 Clinton Solomon RC .75 2.00
188 Marques Hagans RC .60 1.50
189 Davin Joseph RC .75 2.00
190 Jeremy Trueblood RC .75 2.00
191 T.J. Williams RC 1.00 2.50
192 Alan Zemaitis RC .60 1.50
193 Quinton Ganther RC .60 1.50
194 Cody Hodges RC .75 2.00
195 Jesse Mahelona RC .75 2.00
196 Rocky McIntosh RC .60 1.50
197 Mike Espy RC .75 2.00
198 Willie Reid RC .75 2.00
199 Jonathan Orr RC .75 2.00
200 Joe Rubin RC .75 2.00
201 A.J. Hawk AU/200* RC 15.00 40.00
202 Anthony Fasano AU RC 4.00 10.00
203 Ashton Youboty AU RC 4.00 10.00
204 Brad Smith AU RC 5.00 12.00
205 Thomas Howard AU RC 4.00 10.00
206 Will Blackmon AU RC 4.00 10.00
207 Brian Calhoun AU/200* RC 6.00 15.00
208 Terrence Whitehead AU RC 5.00 12.00
209 Brodrick Bunkley AU RC 5.00 12.00
210 Bruce Gradkowski AU RC 5.00 12.00
211 Chad Greenway AU RC 6.00 15.00
212 Chad Jackson AU/200* RC 6.00 15.00
213 Mike Bell AU RC 4.00 10.00
214 Clint Ingram AU RC 6.00 15.00
215 Josh Betts AU RC 5.00 12.00
216 D.J. Shockley AU RC 5.00 12.00
217 D.Ferguson AU RC 4.00 10.00
218 DeA.Williams AU/25* RC 60.00 120.00
219 DeMeco Ryans AU RC 5.00 12.00
220 Demetrius Williams AU RC 4.00 10.00
221 Martin Nance AU RC 4.00 10.00
222 Dominique Byrd AU RC 4.00 10.00
223 Drew Olson AU RC 4.00 10.00
224 Ernie Sims AU RC 4.00 10.00
225 Gerald Riggs AU RC 5.00 12.00
226 Greg Jennings AU RC 6.00 15.00
227 Greg Lee AU RC 4.00 10.00
228 Hank Baskett AU RC 4.00 10.00
229 Jay Cutler AU/50* RC 75.00 150.00
230 DonTrell Moore AU RC 5.00 12.00
231 Jerome Harrison AU RC 4.00 10.00
232 Jimmy Williams AU RC 4.00 10.00
233 Darnell Bing AU RC 5.00 12.00
234 Joseph Addai AU RC 4.00 10.00
235 Kellen Clemens AU/200* RC 6.00 15.00
236 Maroney AU/50* RC 15.00 40.00
237 LenDale White AU/200* RC 6.00 15.00
238 Leon Washington AU RC 4.00 10.00
239 Leonard Pope AU RC 6.00 15.00
240 Cory Rodgers AU RC 4.00 10.00
241 Darrell Hackney AU RC 5.00 12.00
242 Mathias Kiwanuka AU RC 6.00 15.00
243 Matt Leinart AU/50* RC 12.00 30.00
244 Maurice Drew AU/300* RC 15.00 40.00
245 Maurice Stovall AU/300* RC 6.00 15.00
246 Michael Huff AU/300* RC 8.00 20.00
247 Michael Robinson AU RC 4.00 10.00
248 Mike Hass AU RC 4.00 10.00
249 Omar Jacobs AU RC 4.00 10.00
250 Owen Daniels AU RC 6.00 15.00
251 Reggie Bush AU/25* RC 40.00 100.00
252 Reggie McNeal AU RC 4.00 10.00
253 S.Holmes AU/120* RC 12.00 30.00
254 Sinorice Moss AU/240* RC 6.00 15.00
255 Tarvaris Jackson AU/300* RC 6.00 15.00
256 Andre Hall AU RC 5.00 12.00
257 Tye Hill AU RC 4.00 10.00
259 Vince Young AU/25* RC 30.00 80.00
260 Winston Justice AU RC 5.00 12.00

2006 Upper Deck Rookie Debut Holofoil

*VETERANS: 2.5X TO 6X BASIC CARDS
*ROOKIES: .8X TO 2X BASIC CARDS
HOLOFOIL/325 ODDS 1:28

2006 Upper Deck Rookie Debut Gold

*GOLD VETS: 5X TO 12X BASIC CARDS
*GOLD ROOKIES: 1.5X TO 4X BASIC CARDS
GOLD/99 INSERTED IN HOT BOXES
GOLD PRINT RUN 99 SER.#'d SETS

2006 Upper Deck Rookie Debut Draft Link

STATED ODDS 1:18 HOB, 1:36 RET
1 J.Elway/P.Manning 4.00 10.00
2 B.Sanders/R.Bush 6.00 15.00
3 Roethlisberger/Cutler 3.00 8.00
4 Crumpler/Klopfenstein 1.25 3.00
5 R.Barber/A.Youboty 1.50 4.00
6 D.Foster/L.White 1.50 4.00
7 C.Simms/C.Whitehurst 1.25 3.00
8 C.Chambers/A.Fasano 1.25 3.00
9 K.Curtis/B.Calhoun 1.25 3.00
10 D.Mason/B.Marshall 2.00 5.00
11 D.Bledsoe/E.Manning 2.00 5.00
12 K.Johnson/C.Palmer 1.50 4.00
13 G.Jones/M.Drew 1.50 4.00
14 J.Witten/L.Pope 1.25 3.00
15 T.Jones/B.Leftwich 1.25 3.00
16 L.Jordan/J.Jones 1.50 4.00
17 T.Brady/M.Bulger 2.50 6.00
18 L.Tatupu/D.Ryans 1.50 4.00
19 L.Johnson/D.Williams 2.50 6.00
20 M.Williams/M.Leinart 3.00 8.00
21 Muhammad/C.Jackson 1.50 4.00
22 N.Burleson/T.Wilson 1.25 3.00
23 R.Wayne/J.Addai 1.25 3.00
24 R.Brown/S.Moss 1.50 4.00
25 R.Moats/B.Calhoun 1.25 3.00
26 Housh/D.Givens 1.25 3.00
27 P.Rivers/C.Benson 1.50 4.00
28 L.Tomlinson/C.Williams 1.50 4.00
29 B.Edwards/V.Young 3.00 8.00
30 K.Orton/M.Robinson 1.50 4.00
31 M.Muhammad/L.White 1.50 4.00
32 B.Lloyd/D.Williams 1.25 3.00
33 M.Clayton/T.Hill 1.25 3.00
34 R.Brown/R.Bush 5.00 12.00
35 D.Marino/D.Williams 3.00 8.00
36 T.Bruschi/C.Ingram 1.50 4.00
37 P.Hornung/J.Plunkett 1.50 4.00
38 L.Dawson/A.Hawk 2.00 5.00
39 G.Sayers/B.Griese 2.00 5.00
40 J.Hannah/D.Ferguson 1.25 3.00
41 Justice/D.Stephenson 1.25 3.00
42 D.Fouts/C.Whitehurst 1.50 4.00
43 R.Ismail/J.Avant 1.50 4.00
44 K.Stabler/K.Clemens 1.50 4.00
45 R.Craig/L.White 1.50 4.00
46 B.Dawkins/J.Williams 1.50 4.00
47 R.Johnson/Washington 1.50 4.00
48 T.Barber/M.Drew 1.50 4.00
49 M.Stovall/S.Smith 1.50 4.00
50 P.Manning/M.Vick 2.50 6.00
51 L.Tatupu/D.Bing 1.50 4.00
52 T.Jones/T.Barber 1.50 4.00
53 R.Wayne/S.Moss 1.50 4.00
54 R.Brown/L.Pope 1.25 3.00
55 M.Clayton/J.Addai 1.00 2.50
56 M.Clayton/T.Wilson 1.25 3.00
57 L.Johnson/F.Harris 2.00 5.00
58 M.Muhammad/D.Mason 1.25 3.00
59 C.Simms/V.Young 3.00 8.00
60 L.Jordan/V.Davis 1.25 3.00
61 L.Arrington/J.Peppers 1.50 4.00
62 M.Faulk/D.McNabb 1.50 4.00
63 D.Carr/A.Smith QB 1.50 4.00
64 K.Jones/H.Miller 1.50 4.00
65 A.Johnson/L.Fitzgerald 1.50 4.00
66 T.Polamalu/J.Allen 1.50 4.00
67 J.Losman/R.Grossman 1.25 3.00
68 J.Plummer/D.Brees 1.25 3.00
69 C.Portis/T.Bell 1.50 4.00
70 D.McAllister/W.McGahee 1.50 4.00
71 C.Martin/A.Green 1.50 4.00
72 Droughns/Westbrook 1.25 3.00
73 E.James/C.Woodson 1.50 4.00
74 W.Dunn/K.Brooking 1.25 3.00
75 E.Reed/S.Jackson 1.50 4.00
76 Alexander/Harrison 1.50 4.00
77 J.Seau/J.Lewis 1.50 4.00
78 F.Taylor/B.Urlacher 1.50 4.00
79 T.Glenn/R.Williams WR 1.50 4.00
80 R.Moss/M.Jones 1.50 4.00
81 T.Holt/R.Seymour 1.25 3.00
82 H.Ward/T.Owens 1.50 4.00
83 J.Galloway/P.Burress 1.25 3.00
84 D.Driver/R.Curry 1.25 3.00
85 S.Moss/J.Peterson 1.25 3.00
86 C.Johnson/A.Boldin 1.25 3.00
87 B.Franks/J.Shockey 1.50 4.00
88 T.Gonzalez/L.Evans 1.25 3.00
89 J.Vilma/S.Merriman 1.25 3.00
90 C.Bailey/T.Williamson 1.25 3.00
91 D.Culpepper/D.Freeney 1.50 4.00
92 R.Williams S/D.Hall 1.25 3.00
93 B.Edwards/J.Avant 1.50 4.00
94 M.Hasselbeck/T.Brady 2.50 6.00
95 D.Branch/G.Jennings 1.50 4.00
96 S.McNair/V.Young 3.00 8.00
97 J.Walker/W.Reid 1.50 4.00
98 O.McDuffie/S.Holmes 1.50 4.00
99 Pennington/Kennison 1.25 3.00
100 P.Rivers/M.Williams 1.50 4.00

2006 Upper Deck Rookie Debut Draft Link Autographs

3 Roethlisberger/Cutler 60.00 120.00
4 Crumpler/Klopfenstein 10.00 25.00
5 R.Barber/A.Youboty
6 D.Foster/L.White 12.00 30.00
7 C.Simms/C.Whitehurst
9 K.Curtis/B.Calhoun
10 D.Mason/B.Marshall 12.00 30.00
11 D.Bledsoe/E.Manning 40.00 80.00
12 K.Johnson/C.Palmer 12.00 30.00
13 G.Jones/M.Drew 15.00 40.00
14 J.Witten/L.Pope 15.00 30.00
15 T.Jones/B.Leftwich 12.00 30.00
16 L.Jordan/J.Jones 10.00 25.00
18 L.Tatupu/D.Ryans 10.00 25.00
19 L.Johnson/D.Williams 20.00 50.00
20 M.Williams/M.Leinart 15.00 40.00
21 Muhammad/C.Jackson 10.00 25.00
22 N.Burleson/T.Wilson
23 R.Wayne/J.Addai 20.00 50.00
24 R.Brown/S.Moss 10.00 25.00
25 R.Moats/B.Calhoun 10.00 25.00
27 P.Rivers/C.Benson 20.00 50.00
28 L.Tomlinson/C.Williams 30.00 80.00
30 K.Orton/M.Robinson 10.00 25.00
31 M.Muhammad/L.White 10.00 25.00
33 M.Clayton/T.Hill 8.00 20.00
34 R.Brown/R.Bush 30.00 60.00
46 B.Dawkins/J.Williams 12.00 30.00
47 R.Johnson/Washington
48 T.Barber/M.Drew 35.00 60.00
49 M.Stovall/S.Smith 12.00 30.00
50 P.Manning/M.Vick 90.00 150.00
51 L.Tatupu/D.Bing
52 T.Jones/T.Barber 15.00 40.00
53 R.Wayne/S.Moss 12.00 30.00
54 R.Brown/L.Pope 10.00 25.00
55 M.Clayton/J.Addai 12.00 30.00
56 M.Clayton/T.Wilson 12.00 30.00
58 Muhammad/D.Mason
59 C.Simms/V.Young 15.00 40.00
60 L.Jordan/V.Davis
93 Edwards/Avant 15.00 40.00
100 P.Rivers/M.Williams

2006 Upper Deck Rookie Debut Future Star Materials Silver

SILVER STATED ODDS 1:28 HOBBY
*GOLD/125: .5X TO 1.2X SILVER JSYs
GOLD PRINT RUN 125 SER.#'d SETS
FSMBC Brian Calhoun 3.00 8.00
FSMBM Brandon Marshall 4.00 10.00
FSMBW Brandon Williams 3.00 8.00
FSMCJ Chad Jackson 3.00 8.00
FSMCW Charlie Whitehurst 3.00 8.00
FSMDH Derek Hagan 3.00 8.00
FSMDW Demetrius Williams 3.00 8.00
FSMJA Jason Avant 3.00 8.00
FSMJK Joe Klopfenstein 3.00 8.00
FSMJN Jerious Norwood 4.00 10.00
FSMKC Kellen Clemens 3.00 8.00
FSMLW Leon Washington 4.00 10.00
FSMML Matt Leinart 6.00 15.00
FSMMR Michael Robinson 3.00 8.00
FSMMS Maurice Stovall 3.00 8.00
FSMOJ Omar Jacobs 3.00 8.00
FSMRB Reggie Bush 6.00 15.00
FSMSM Sinorice Moss 3.00 8.00
FSMTJ Tarvaris Jackson 3.00 10.00
FSMTW Travis Wilson 3.00 8.00
FSMVY Vince Young 8.00 20.00

2006 Upper Deck Rookie Debut Game Dated

ATED ODDS 1:7 HOB, 1:14 RET
GDDAG Antonio Gates 1.50 4.00
GDDBA Ronde Barber 1.00 2.50
GDDBD Brian Dawkins 1.50 4.00
GDDBE Braylon Edwards 1.00 2.50
GDDBF Brett Favre 3.00 8.00
GDDBL Byron Leftwich 1.00 2.50
GDDBR Ben Roethlisberger 2.00 5.00
GDDCB Cedric Benson 1.00 2.50
GDDCF Charlie Frye 1.25 3.00
GDDCS Chris Simms 1.00 2.50
GDDDB Drew Bennett 1.25 3.00
GDDDF DeShaun Foster 1.25 3.00
GDDDG David Givens 1.25 3.00
GDDDM Derrick Mason 1.00 2.50
GDDEM Eli Manning 1.25 3.00
GDDJJ Julius Jones 1.00 2.50
GDDJO LaMont Jordan 1.25 3.00
GDDJW Jason Witten 1.25 3.00
GDDKC Kevin Curtis 1.25 3.00
GDDKJ Keyshawn Johnson 1.25 3.00
GDDKO Kyle Orton 1.00 2.50
GDDLJ Larry Johnson 1.00 2.50
GDDLT LaDainian Tomlinson 1.50 4.00
GDDMB Marc Bulger 1.00 2.50
GDDMM Muhsin Muhammad 1.00 2.50
GDDMO Ryan Moats 1.00 2.50
GDDMW Mike Williams 1.00 2.50
GDDNB Nate Burleson 1.00 2.50
GDDPM Peyton Manning 4.00 10.00
GDDPR Philip Rivers 1.50 4.00
GDDRB Reggie Brown 1.00 2.50
GDDRJ Rudi Johnson 1.00 2.50
GDDRM Randy Moss 1.25 3.00
GDDRO Ronnie Brown 1.25 3.00
GDDRW Reggie Wayne 1.25 3.00
GDDSS Steve Smith 1.50 4.00
GDDTA Lofa Tatupu 1.00 2.50
GDDTB Tedy Bruschi 1.25 3.00
GDDTH T.J. Houshmandzadeh 1.00 2.50
GDDTI Tiki Barber 1.25 3.00
GDDTJ Thomas Jones 1.00 2.50
GDDWP Willie Parker 1.25 3.00

2006 Upper Deck Rookie Debut Game Dated Autographs

ATED PRINT RUN 40 SER.#'d SETS
GDDAG Antonio Gates 15.00 40.00
GDDBA Ronde Barber 12.50 30.00
GDDBD Brian Dawkins 20.00 50.00
GDDBL Byron Leftwich 10.00 25.00
GDDBR Ben Roethlisberger 60.00 120.00
GDDCB Cedric Benson 12.50 30.00
GDDCF Charlie Frye 10.00 25.00
GDDCS Chris Simms 10.00 25.00
GDDDB Drew Bennett 8.00 20.00
GDDDF DeShaun Foster 10.00 25.00
GDDDG David Givens 12.50 30.00
GDDDM Derrick Mason 10.00 25.00
GDDEM Eli Manning 50.00 100.00
GDDJJ Julius Jones 12.50 30.00
GDDJO LaMont Jordan 10.00 25.00
GDDJW Jason Witten 30.00 60.00
GDDKC Kevin Curtis 10.00 25.00
GDDKJ Keyshawn Johnson 10.00 25.00
GDDKO Kyle Orton 10.00 25.00
GDDLJ Larry Johnson 12.50 30.00
GDDLT LaDainian Tomlinson 60.00 120.00
GDDMB Marc Bulger 10.00 25.00
GDDMM Muhsin Muhammad 8.00 20.00
GDDMO Ryan Moats 10.00 25.00
GDDMW Mike Williams 12.50 30.00
GDDNB Nate Burleson 10.00 25.00
GDDPM Peyton Manning 60.00 120.00
GDDPR Philip Rivers 15.00 40.00
GDDRB Reggie Brown 10.00 25.00
GDDRO Ronnie Brown 12.50 30.00
GDDRW Reggie Wayne 12.50 30.00
GDDTA Lofa Tatupu 12.50 30.00
GDDTJ Thomas Jones 10.00 25.00

2006 Upper Deck Rookie Debut Rookie Jerseys

INSERTS IN TARGET RETAIL PACKS
63TE A.J. Hawk 3.00 8.00
64TE Brian Calhoun 2.50 6.00
65TE Brandon Marshall 5.00 12.00
66TE Brandon Williams 2.50 6.00
67TE Chad Jackson 2.50 6.00
68TE Charlie Whitehurst 2.50 6.00
69TE Derek Hagan 3.00 8.00
70TE DeAngelo Williams 3.00 8.00
71TE Jason Avant 2.50 6.00
72TE Joe Klopfenstein 2.50 6.00
73TE Jerious Norwood 2.50 6.00
74TE Kellen Clemens 2.50 6.00
75TE Marcedes Lewis 2.50 6.00
76TE Laurence Maroney 2.50 6.00
77TE LenDale White 2.50 6.00
78TE Maurice Drew 4.00 10.00
79TE Michael Huff 3.00 8.00
80TE Matt Leinart 2.50 6.00
81TE Michael Robinson 2.50 6.00
82TE Maurice Stovall 2.50 6.00
83TE Mario Williams 4.00 10.00
84TE Omar Jacobs 2.50 6.00
85TE Reggie Bush 4.00 10.00
86TE Santonio Holmes 3.00 8.00
87TE Sinorice Moss 2.50 6.00
88TE Tarvaris Jackson 2.50 6.00
89TE Travis Wilson 2.50 6.00
90TE Vernon Davis 3.00 8.00
91TE Vince Young 2.50 6.00
92TE Leon Washington 2.50 6.00
93TE Demetrius Williams 2.50 6.00

2006 Upper Deck Rookie Debut Rookie Photo Shoot Flashback Silver

SILVER ODDS 1:4 HOB, 1:7 RET
*GOLD/99: .6X TO 1.5X SILVER INSERTS
GOLD/99 INSERTED IN HOT BOXES
RPF1 Ahman Green 1.00 2.50
RPF2 Alex Smith QB 1.00 2.50
RPF3 James Farrior .75 2.00
RPF4 Andre Johnson 1.00 2.50
RPF5 Anquan Boldin .75 2.00
RPF6 Antonio Bryant .75 2.00
RPF7 Antwaan Randle El .75 2.00
RPF8 Ben Roethlisberger 1.50 4.00
RPF9 Bobby Engram .75 2.00
RPF10 Keith Brooking .75 2.00
RPF11 Braylon Edwards .75 2.00
RPF12 Brian Urlacher 1.25 3.00
RPF13 Byron Leftwich .75 2.00
RPF14 Cadillac Williams 1.00 2.50
RPF15 Carson Palmer 1.00 2.50
RPF16 Chad Johnson .75 2.00
RPF17 Chad Pennington .75 2.00
RPF18 Champ Bailey 1.00 2.50
RPF19 Brian Griese .75 2.00
RPF20 Chris McAlister .75 2.00
RPF21 Chris Chambers .75 2.00
RPF22 Takeo Spikes .75 2.00
RPF23 Corey Dillon .75 2.00
RPF24 Curtis Martin 1.00 2.50
RPF25 Dallas Clark .75 2.00
RPF26 Bubba Franks .75 2.00
RPF27 Daunte Culpepper 1.00 2.50
RPF28 Antoine Winfield .75 2.00
RPF29 David Garrard .75 2.00
RPF30 DeAngelo Hall .75 2.00
RPF31 Dan Morgan .75 2.00
RPF32 DeShaun Foster 1.00 2.50
RPF33 Deuce McAllister 1.00 2.50
RPF34 Dewayne Robertson .75 2.00
RPF35 Kevan Barlow .75 2.00
RPF36 Donovan McNabb 1.00 2.50
RPF37 Donte Stallworth .75 2.00
RPF38 Drew Brees 1.25 3.00
RPF39 Eddie Kennison .75 2.00
RPF40 Edgerrin James 1.00 2.50
RPF41 Eli Manning 1.00 2.50
RPF42 Eric Moulds .75 2.00
RPF43 Fred Taylor .75 2.00
RPF44 Greg Jones .75 2.00
RPF45 Hines Ward 1.00 2.50
RPF46 J.P. Losman 1.00 2.50
RPF47 Jake Plummer .75 2.00
RPF48 Jamal Lewis 1.00 2.50
RPF49 Javon Walker 1.00 2.50
RPF50 Jeremy Shockey .75 2.00
RPF51 Jerry Porter .75 2.00
RPF52 Joey Galloway 1.00 2.50
RPF53 Jonathan Ogden 1.00 2.50
RPF54 Julius Jones .75 2.00
RPF55 Julius Peppers 1.00 2.50
RPF56 Kevin Curtis 1.00 2.50
RPF57 Kevin Jones .75 2.00
RPF58 Kyle Boller .75 2.00
RPF59 LaDainian Tomlinson 1.25 3.00
RPF60 Corey Simon .60 1.50
RPF61 Larry Fitzgerald 1.00 2.50
RPF62 Larry Johnson .75 2.00
RPF63 Jevon Kearse .75 2.00
RPF64 Laveranues Coles .75 2.00
RPF65 Todd Pinkston .75 2.00
RPF66 Marvin Harrison 1.00 2.50
RPF67 Michael Vick 1.00 2.50
RPF68 Mike Alstott .75 2.00
RPF69 Nate Burleson .75 2.00
RPF70 Orlando Pace .75 2.00
RPF71 Peyton Manning 3.00 8.00
RPF72 Philip Rivers 1.25 3.00
RPF73 Plaxico Burress .75 2.00
RPF74 Kyle Orton .75 2.00
RPF75 Reggie Wayne 1.00 2.50
RPF76 Reuben Droughns 1.00 2.50
RPF77 Rex Grossman .75 2.00
RPF78 Richard Seymour .75 2.00
RPF79 Ronnie Brown 1.00 2.50
RPF80 Roy Williams WR .75 2.00
RPF81 Roy Williams S .75 2.00
RPF82 Rudi Johnson .75 2.00
RPF83 Santana Moss 1.00 2.50
RPF84 Koren Robinson .75 2.00
RPF85 Shaun Alexander .75 2.00
RPF86 Simeon Rice .75 2.00
RPF87 Stephen Davis .75 2.00
RPF88 Joe Jurevicius .75 2.00
RPF89 Steven Jackson .75 2.00
RPF90 T.J. Duckett .75 2.00
RPF91 Tatum Bell .75 2.00
RPF92 Terrell Suggs .75 2.00
RPF93 Terry Glenn 1.00 2.50
RPF94 Thomas Jones .75 2.00
RPF95 Todd Heap .75 2.00
RPF96 Tony Gonzalez 1.00 2.50
RPF97 Torry Holt 1.00 2.50
RPF98 Walter Jones .75 2.00
RPF99 Warrick Dunn .75 2.00
RPF100 Willis McGahee .75 2.00

2006 Upper Deck Rookie Debut Star Materials Silver

SILVER ODDS 1:28 HOBBY
*GOLD/125: .5X TO 1.2X SILVER JSYs
GOLD/125 INSERTED IN HOT BOXES
SMBE Cedric Benson 3.00 8.00
SMBR Mark Brunell 3.00 8.00
SMCB Chris Brown 3.00 8.00
SMCJ Chad Johnson 3.00 8.00
SMCP Clinton Portis 4.00 10.00
SMCS Chris Simms 3.00 8.00
SMDC Daunte Culpepper 4.00 10.00
SMDD Domanick Davis 3.00 8.00
SMDM Donovan McNabb 4.00 10.00
SMDS Donte Stallworth 3.00 8.00
SMFT Fred Taylor 3.00 8.00
SMJH Joe Horn 3.00 8.00
SMJJ Julius Jones 4.00 10.00
SMJL Jamal Lewis 3.00 8.00
SMKB Kyle Boller 3.00 8.00
SMMB Marc Bulger 3.00 8.00
SMMH Marvin Harrison 4.00 10.00
SMRE Antwaan Randle El 3.00 8.00
SMRW Reggie Wayne 3.00 8.00
SMSH Jeremy Shockey 4.00 10.00
SMWM Willis McGahee 3.00 8.00

2008 Upper Deck Rookie Exclusives

COMPLETE SET (100) 12.50 30.00
RE1 Curtis Lofton .12 .30
RE2 Ryan Clady .12 .30
RE3 Allen Patrick .10 .25
RE4 Kevin O'Connell .10 .25
RE5 Aqib Talib .15 .40
RE6 Davone Bess .12 .30
RE7 Bruce Davis .12 .30
RE8 Kalvin McRae .10 .25
RE9 Chevis Jackson .10 .25
RE10 Chris Johnson .12 .30
RE11 Craig Steltz .10 .25
RE12 Alex Brink .12 .30
RE13 DaJuan Morgan .12 .30
RE14 DeMario Pressley .12 .30
RE15 Chauncey Washington .12 .30
RE16 Jacob Hester .10 .25
RE17 Dustin Keller .12 .30
RE18 Erik Ainge .10 .25
RE19 Frank Okam .10 .25
RE20 Kevin Smith .10 .25
RE21 Harry Douglas .12 .30
RE22 Kellen Davis .10 .25
RE23 J Leman .10 .25
RE24 Jamaal Charles .15 .40
RE25 Jermichael Finley .10 .25
RE26 Joe Flacco .20 .50
RE27 John David Booty .10 .25
RE28 Jonathan Hefney .10 .25
RE29 Jerome Felton .10 .25
RE30 Justin Forsett .12 .30
RE31 Keenan Burton .10 .25
RE32 Geno Hayes .10 .25
RE33 Keon Lattimore .12 .30
RE34 Josh Johnson .10 .25
RE35 Marcus Monk .12 .30
RE36 Mario Urrutia .10 .25
RE37 Martin Rucker .10 .25
RE38 Matt Forte .15 .40
RE39 Paul Hubbard .10 .25
RE40 Phillip Merling .10 .25
RE41 Quintin Demps .12 .30
RE42 Ray Rice .10 .25
RE43 Ryan Grice-Mullins .10 .25
RE44 Anthony Morelli .10 .25
RE45 Shawn Crable .10 .25
RE46 Tashard Choice .10 .25
RE47 Thomas Brown .10 .25
RE48 Adrian Arrington .10 .25
RE49 Quentin Groves .12 .30
RE50 Xavier Adibi .10 .25
RE51 Jordy Nelson .30 .75
RE52 Derrick Harvey .10 .25
RE53 Andre Caldwell .10 .25
RE54 Antoine Cason .12 .30
RE55 Dominique Rodgers-Cromartie .12 .30
RE56 Leodis McKelvin .12 .30
RE57 Calais Campbell .12 .30
RE58 Chad Henne .12 .30
RE59 Chris Ellis .10 .25
RE60 Vernon Gholston .10 .25
RE61 Jerome Simpson .12 .30
RE62 Dexter Jackson .15 .40
RE63 DeJuan Tribble .10 .25
RE64 Dennis Keyes .10 .25
RE65 Donnie Avery .12 .30
RE66 Dre Moore .10 .25
RE67 Earl Bennett .15 .40
RE68 Eddie Royal .10 .25
RE69 Felix Jones .10 .25
RE70 Gosder Cherilus .12 .30
RE71 Colt Brennan .12 .30
RE72 Jack Ikegwuonu .10 .25
RE73 Jacob Tamme .12 .30
RE74 James Hardy .10 .25
RE75 Jerod Mayo .15 .40
RE76 Andre Woodson .30 .75
RE77 Brian Brohm .30 .75
RE78 Devin Thomas .30 .75
RE79 Mike Jenkins .30 .75
RE80 Matt Ryan 1.00 2.50
RE81 Darren McFadden .30 .75
RE82 Jonathan Stewart .50 1.25
RE83 Mike Hart .30 .75
RE84 DeSean Jackson .60 1.50
RE85 Early Doucet .30 .75
RE86 Lavelle Hawkins .40 1.00
RE87 Limas Sweed .30 .75
RE88 Jake Long .50 1.25
RE89 Sam Baker .30 .75
RE90 Glenn Dorsey .30 .75
RE91 Sedrick Ellis .30 .75
RE92 Chris Long .40 1.00
RE93 Lawrence Jackson .30 .75
RE94 Ali Highsmith .30 .75
RE95 Dan Connor .30 .75
RE96 Kenny Phillips .30 .75
RE97 Keith Rivers .30 .75
RE98 Justin King .40 1.00
RE99 Dennis Dixon .30 .75
RE100 Fred Davis .30 .75

2008 Upper Deck Rookie Exclusives Photo Shoot Flashbacks

MPLETE SET (30) 5.00 12.00
STATED ODDS 2:1
1 Carson Palmer .30 .75
2 Matt Leinart .25 .60
3 Plaxico Burress .25 .60
4 Brian Urlacher .40 1.00
5 Drew Brees .40 1.00
6 LaDainian Tomlinson .40 1.00
7 Julius Peppers .30 .75
8 Antwaan Randle El .25 .60
9 Jeremy Shockey .25 .60
10 Terrell Suggs .25 .60
11 Dallas Clark .25 .60
12 Willis McGahee .25 .60
13 Larry Johnson .25 .60
14 Anquan Boldin .25 .60
15 Philip Rivers .40 1.00
16 Steven Jackson .25 .60
17 Eli Manning .30 .75

18 Ben Roethlisberger .40 1.00
19 Kellen Winslow .25 .60
20 Ronnie Brown .25 .60
21 Braylon Edwards .25 .60
22 Adrian Peterson .40 1.00
23 Frank Gore .30 .75
24 Clinton Portis .25 .60
25 Santonio Holmes .25 .60
26 Reggie Bush .25 .60
27 Vince Young .25 .60
28 Gaines Adams .25 .60
29 Calvin Johnson .40 1.00
30 JaMarcus Russell .25 .60

2009 Upper Deck Rookie Exclusives

1 Alex Magee .12 .30
2 Rashad Johnson .10 .25
3 Cody Brown .10 .25
4 Clint Sintim .10 .25
5 Cornelius Ingram .10 .25
6 Roy Miller .10 .25
7 Kevin Barnes .10 .25
8 DeAngelo Smith .12 .30
9 Asher Allen .10 .25
10 Bradley Fletcher .10 .25
11 Patrick Turner .10 .25
12 Travis Beckum .10 .25
13 Sherrod Martin .10 .25
14 Paul Kruger .15 .40
15 Jairus Byrd .15 .40
16 Alphonso Smith .10 .25
17 Jason Williams .12 .30
18 Larry English .12 .30
19 David Veikune .12 .30
20 Connor Barwin .12 .30
21 B.J. Raji .12 .30
22 Richard Quinn .12 .30
23 Jarett Dillard .10 .25
24 Johnny Knox .12 .30
25 Austin Collie .10 .25
26 Quinn Johnson .10 .25
27 Gartrell Johnson .10 .25
28 Andre Brown .12 .30
29 Mike Goodson .12 .30
30 Tom Brandstater .12 .30
31 Louis Delmas .12 .30
32 Stephen McGee .10 .25
33 Ron Brace .12 .30
34 Brian Hartline .15 .40
35 Mike Wallace .15 .40
36 Mike Thomas .10 .25
37 Juaquin Iglesias .10 .25
38 Nate Davis .10 .25
39 Javon Ringer .10 .25
40 Robert Ayers .10 .25
41 Evander Hood .15 .40
42 James Laurinaitis .10 .25
43 Rey Maualuga .15 .40
44 Eben Britton .12 .30
45 Eric Wood .10 .25
46 Louis Murphy .10 .25
47 Mohamed Massaquoi .10 .25
48 Kenny McKinley .10 .25
49 Glen Coffee .10 .25
50 Deon Butler .10 .25
51 Vontae Davis .10 .25
52 Tony Fiammetta .10 .25
53 Fili Moala .10 .25
54 Derrick Williams .10 .25
55 Sean Smith .10 .25
56 Peria Jerry .10 .25
57 Chase Coffman .10 .25
58 Brandon Tate .12 .30
59 Everette Brown .10 .25
60 Rhett Bomar .10 .25
61 Max Unger .15 .40
62 Alex Mack .10 .25
63 D.J. Moore .12 .30
64 Ramses Barden .10 .25
65 Brandon Hughes .10 .25
66 William Moore .10 .25
67 Michael Johnson .10 .25
68 Jared Cook .12 .30
69 Jarron Gilbert .12 .30
70 Brian Robiskie .10 .25
71 Darius Butler .12 .30
72 Anthony Hill .10 .25
73 Malcolm Jenkins .10 .25
74 Michael Oher .15 .40
75 Patrick Chung .10 .25
76 Knowshon Moreno SP .30 .75
77 Matthew Stafford SP 1.50 4.00
78 Michael Crabtree SP .50 1.25
79 Mark Sanchez SP .30 .75
80 Aaron Curry SP .50 1.25
81 Jeremy Maclin SP .40 1.00
82 Chris Wells SP .30 .75
83 Donald Brown SP .30 .75
84 Josh Freeman SP .30 .75
85 Jason Smith SP .30 .75
86 Eugene Monroe SP .30 .75
87 Darrius Heyward-Bey SP .50 1.25
88 Kenny Britt SP .50 1.25
89 Hakeem Nicks SP .40 1.00
90 Pat White SP .40 1.00
91 Aaron Maybin SP .40 1.00
92 Brian Cushing SP .30 .75
93 Brandon Pettigrew SP .30 .75
94 Brian Orakpo SP .40 1.00
95 Percy Harvin SP .30 .75
96 Andre Smith SP .30 .75
97 Tyson Jackson SP .30 .75
98 Clay Matthews SP 1.25 3.00
99 LeSean McCoy SP .75 2.00
100 Shonn Greene SP .30 .75

2009 Upper Deck Rookie Exclusives College to Pros

AP Adrian Peterson .40 1.00
AR Aaron Rodgers .75 2.00
BR Ben Roethlisberger .40 1.00
BU Brian Urlacher .40 1.00
CB Champ Bailey .30 .75
CJ Chris Johnson .25 .60
CP Carson Palmer .30 .75
DM Donovan McNabb .30 .75
EM Eli Manning .30 .75
FG Frank Gore .30 .75
JC Jerricho Cotchery .25 .60
JJ Julius Jones .25 .60
JO Calvin Johnson .40 1.00
JR JaMarcus Russell .25 .60
LE Lee Evans .30 .75
LF Larry Fitzgerald .30 .75
MJ Maurice Jones-Drew .25 .60
MR Matt Ryan .30 .75
PM Peyton Manning 1.00 2.50
PO Clinton Portis .25 .60
PR Philip Rivers .40 1.00
RB Reggie Bush .25 .60
RL Ray Lewis .40 1.00
RO Ronnie Brown .25 .60
SJ Steven Jackson .25 .60
SL Steve Slaton .25 .60
SS Steve Smith .30 .75
TB Tom Brady 1.25 3.00
TP Troy Polamalu .40 1.00
TR Tony Romo .30 .75

2001 Upper Deck Rookie F/X

This 225 card set was issued in February, 2002. The cards were issued in five card packs which came 24 packs to a box and 16 boxes to a case. The SRP on the packs were $3.99. Rookie players were reproduced from earlier released products including Upper Deck Victory, Upper Deck Vintage, Upper Deck MVP, and base Upper Deck using a new foil card front and serial numbered to 750 of each brand reproduced. Rookie players were also featured on an all new F/X version also numbered to 750.

COMP.SET w/o SP's (225) 20.00 40.00
226-338 PRINT RUN 750 SER.#'d SETS
1 Jake Plummer .20 .50
2 Thomas Jones .20 .50
3 David Boston .20 .50
4 Jamal Anderson .25 .60
5 Chris Chandler .25 .60
6 Tony Martin .25 .60
7 Jamal Lewis .30 .75
8 Elvis Grbac .25 .60
9 Ray Lewis .30 .75
10 Rob Johnson .25 .60
11 Eric Moulds .20 .50
12 Muhsin Muhammad .20 .50
13 Tim Biakabutuka .20 .50
14 James Allen .20 .50
15 Marcus Robinson .25 .60
16 Brian Urlacher .40 1.00
17 Jon Kitna .20 .50
18 Peter Warrick .20 .50
19 Corey Dillon .20 .50
20 Kevin Johnson .20 .50
21 Dennis Northcutt .20 .50
22 Tim Couch .20 .50
23 Rocket Ismail .25 .60
24 Emmitt Smith .50 1.25
25 Joey Galloway .25 .60
26 Terrell Davis .25 .60
27 Rod Smith .25 .60
28 Brian Griese .20 .50
29 Mike Anderson .20 .50
30 Charlie Batch .20 .50
31 James O. Stewart .20 .50
32 Germane Crowell .20 .50
33 Brett Favre .60 1.50
34 Antonio Freeman .30 .75
35 Ahman Green .25 .60
36 Peyton Manning .75 2.00
37 Edgerrin James .25 .60
38 Marvin Harrison .25 .60
39 Jerome Pathon .20 .50
40 Mark Brunell .25 .60
41 Fred Taylor .20 .50
42 Jimmy Smith .25 .60
43 Tony Gonzalez .25 .60
44 Priest Holmes .20 .50
45 Trent Green .20 .50
46 Oronde Gadsden .20 .50
47 Jay Fiedler .25 .60
48 Lamar Smith .25 .60
49 Randy Moss .25 .60
50 Cris Carter .30 .75
51 Daunte Culpepper .25 .60
52 Drew Bledsoe .25 .60
53 Antowain Smith .25 .60
54 Tom Brady 40.00 80.00
55 Ricky Williams .25 .60
56 Joe Horn .20 .50
57 Aaron Brooks .20 .50
58 Kerry Collins .20 .50
59 Tiki Barber .25 .60
60 Ron Dayne .25 .60
61 Vinny Testaverde .20 .50
62 Wayne Chrebet .20 .50
63 Curtis Martin .25 .60
64 Tyrone Wheatley .25 .60
65 Rich Gannon .25 .60
66 Jerry Rice .60 1.50
67 Duce Staley .20 .50
68 Donovan McNabb .25 .60
69 Kordell Stewart .20 .50
70 Jerome Bettis .30 .75
71 Marshall Faulk .25 .60
72 Kurt Warner .50 1.25
73 Torry Holt .25 .60
74 Doug Flutie .25 .60
75 Freddie Jones .20 .50
76 Jeff Garcia .20 .50
77 Garrison Hearst .25 .60
78 Terrell Owens .25 .60
79 Tai Streets .20 .50
80 Ricky Watters .25 .60
81 Matt Hasselbeck .20 .50
82 Darrell Jackson .25 .60
83 Brad Johnson .25 .60
84 Warrick Dunn .20 .50
85 Keyshawn Johnson .25 .60
86 Eddie George .30 .75
87 Steve McNair .25 .60
88 Tony Banks .20 .50
89 Michael Westbrook .20 .50
90 Stephen Davis .20 .50
91 Bob Christian .20 .50
92 Brian Finneran .25 .60
93 Brandon Stokley .20 .50
94 Jeremy McDaniel .20 .50
95 Brad Hoover .25 .60
96 Donald Hayes .20 .50
97 Jim Miller .25 .60
98 Danny Farmer .20 .50
99 Anthony Wright .20 .50
100 Jackie Harris .25 .60
101 Howard Griffith .20 .50
102 Desmond Howard .25 .60
103 Bill Schroeder .25 .60
104 Terrence Wilkins .20 .50
105 Todd Collins .20 .50
106 Sylvester Morris .20 .50
107 Zach Thomas .25 .60
108 Robert Griffith .20 .50
109 Kevin Faulk .20 .50
110 Willie Jackson .20 .50
111 Ron Dixon .20 .50
112 Michael Strahan .25 .60
113 Richie Anderson .20 .50
114 Chad Pennington .20 .50
115 Charles Woodson .30 .75
116 Chad Lewis .20 .50
117 Az-Zahir Hakim .20 .50
118 Rodney Harrison .20 .50
119 Mike Alstott .20 .50
120 Jevon Kearse .20 .50
121 Martay Jenkins .20 .50
122 Pat Tillman RC 10.00 25.00
123 Rod Woodson .30 .75
124 Marty Booker .20 .50
125 Scott Mitchell .20 .50
126 John Mobley .20 .50
127 Stephen Boyd .20 .50
128 Kurt Schulz .20 .50
129 Kyle Brady .20 .50
130 Donnie Edwards .20 .50
131 J.J. Johnson .20 .50
132 Chris Walsh RC .20 .50
133 J.R. Redmond .20 .50
134 Keith Mitchell .20 .50
135 Joe Jurevicius .20 .50
136 Eric Allen .25 .60
137 Todd Pinkston .20 .50
138 Bobby Shaw .20 .50
139 Hines Ward .25 .60
140 Ricky Proehl .20 .50
141 London Fletcher .25 .60
142 Jeff Graham .20 .50
143 Tim Rattay .20 .50
144 Fred Beasley .20 .50
145 James Williams .20 .50
146 Derrick Brooks .20 .50
147 Warren Sapp .25 .60
148 Derrick Mason .20 .50
149 Kevin Dyson .20 .50
150 Champ Bailey .25 .60
151 Michael Pittman .25 .60
152 Kwamie Lassiter .20 .50
153 Maurice Smith .20 .50
154 Keith Brooking .25 .60
155 Travis Taylor .20 .50
156 Tony Siragusa .25 .60
157 Alex Van Pelt .20 .50
158 Shane Matthews .20 .50
159 Darnay Scott .25 .60
160 Aaron Shea .20 .50
161 JaJuan Dawson .20 .50
162 Clint Stoerner .25 .60
163 Dat Nguyen .20 .50
164 Bill Romanowski .25 .60
165 Robert Porcher .20 .50
166 Bubba Franks .20 .50
167 Rob Morris .20 .50
168 Stacey Mack .20 .50
169 Chris Hovan .20 .50
170 Lawyer Milloy .20 .50
171 La'Roi Glover .20 .50
172 Jessie Armstead .20 .50
173 Mo Lewis .20 .50
174 Jon Ritchie .20 .50
175 James Thrash .25 .60
176 Trung Canidate .20 .50
177 Grant Wistrom .20 .50
178 Curtis Conway .25 .60
179 Ronney Jenkins .20 .50
180 John Lynch .25 .60
181 Frank Sanders .20 .50
182 Shawn Jefferson .20 .50
183 Darrick Vaughn .20 .50
184 Terance Mathis .20 .50
185 Shannon Sharpe .25 .60
186 Qadry Ismail .20 .50
187 Sammy Morris .20 .50
188 Shawn Bryson .20 .50
189 Wesley Walls .20 .50
190 Akili Smith .20 .50
191 Ron Dugans .20 .50
192 Travis Prentice .20 .50
193 Courtney Brown .20 .50
194 Ed McCaffrey .25 .60
195 Olandis Gary .20 .50
196 Johnnie Morton .25 .60
197 Dorsey Levens .25 .60
198 Ken Dilger .20 .50
199 Keenan McCardell .25 .60
200 Derrick Alexander .20 .50
201 Tony Richardson .20 .50
202 Jason Taylor .30 .75
203 O.J. McDuffie .20 .50
204 Troy Walters .20 .50
205 Troy Brown .20 .50
206 Jeff Blake .25 .60
207 Albert Connell .20 .50
208 Amani Toomer .20 .50
209 Ike Hilliard .20 .50
210 Jason Sehorn .25 .60
211 Laveranues Coles .25 .60
212 Tim Brown .30 .75
213 Charlie Garner .25 .60
214 Plaxico Burress .20 .50
215 Troy Edwards .20 .50
216 Isaac Bruce .30 .75
217 Junior Seau .25 .60
218 Marcellus Wiley .20 .50
219 J.J. Stokes .20 .50
220 Shaun Alexander .20 .50
221 John Randle .25 .60
222 Jacquez Green .20 .50
223 Neil O'Donnell .25 .60
224 Frank Wycheck .20 .50
225 Stephen Alexander .20 .50
226F A.J. Feeley F X RC 1.00 2.50
226U A.J. Feeley UD .75 2.00
226VN A.J. Feeley VINT .75 2.00
227U Adam Archuleta UD .75 2.00
227VC Adam Archuleta VICT .75 2.00
227VN Adam Archuleta VINT .75 2.00
228U Willie Middlebrooks UD .75 2.00
228VN Willie Middlebrooks VINT .75 2.00
229U Alex Bannister UD .60 1.50
229VC Alex Bannister VICT .60 1.50
230M Alge Crumpler MVP 1.00 2.50
230U Alge Crumpler UD 1.00 2.50
230VC Alge Crumpler VICT 1.00 2.50
230VN Alge Crumpler VINT 1.00 2.50
231U Andre Carter UD .75 2.00
231VN Andre Carter VINT .75 2.00
232U Andre Dyson UD .60 1.50
233F Anthony Thomas F/X RC 1.25 3.00
233M Anthony Thomas MVP 1.00 2.50
233U Anthony Thomas UD 1.00 2.50
233VC Anthony Thomas VICT 1.00 2.50
233VN Anthony Thomas VINT 1.00 2.50
234U Arther Love UD .60 1.50
235M Bobby Newcombe MVP .75 2.00
235U Bobby Newcombe UD .75 2.00
235VC Bobby Newcombe VICT .75 2.00
235VN Bobby Newcombe VINT .75 2.00
236U Zeke Moreno UD .75 2.00
237U Brandon Spoon UD .75 2.00
238U Brian Allen UD .60 1.50
239U Carlos Polk UD .60 1.50
240U Casey Hampton UD 1.00 2.50
241F Cedrick Wilson F/X RC 1.00 2.50
241U Cedrick Wilson UD .75 2.00
241VC Cedrick Wilson VICT .75 2.00
242F Chad Johnson F/X RC 1.25 3.00
242M Chad Johnson MVP 1.00 2.50
242U Chad Johnson UD 1.00 2.50
242VC Chad Johnson VICT 1.00 2.50
242VN Chad Johnson VINT 1.00 2.50
243U Chris Barnes UD .60 1.50
243VC Chris Barnes VICT .60 1.50
243VN Chris Barnes VINT .60 1.50
244F Chris Chambers F/X RC .75 2.00
244M Chris Chambers MVP .60 1.50
244U Chris Chambers UD .60 1.50
244VC Chris Chambers VICT .60 1.50
244VN Chris Chambers VINT .60 1.50
245U Chris Taylor UD .60 1.50
246F Chris Weinke F/X RC 1.00 2.50
246M Chris Weinke MVP .75 2.00
246U Chris Weinke UD .75 2.00
246VC Chris Weinke VICT .75 2.00
246VN Chris Weinke VINT .75 2.00
247F Correll Buckhalter F/X RC .75 2.00
247M Correll Buckhalter MVP .60 1.50
247U Correll Buckhalter UD .60 1.50
247VC Correll Buckhalter VICT .60 1.50
247VN Correll Buckhalter VINT .60 1.50
248U Damione Lewis UD .75 2.00
249M Dan Alexander MVP .75 2.00
249U Dan Alexander UD .75 2.00
249VC Dan Alexander VICT .75 2.00
250F Dan Morgan F/X RC 1.00 2.50
250M Dan Morgan MVP .75 2.00
250U Dan Morgan UD .75 2.00
250VC Dan Morgan VICT .75 2.00
250VN Dan Morgan VINT .75 2.00
251U Damerien McCants UD .75 2.00
252VN Dave Dickenson VINT .75 2.00
253M David Allen MVP .60 1.50
253VN David Allen VINT .60 1.50
254M David Rivers MVP .60 1.50
255F David Terrell F/X RC 1.00 2.50
255M David Terrell MVP .75 2.00
255U David Terrell UD .75 2.00
255VC David Terrell VICT .75 2.00
255VN David Terrell VINT .75 2.00
256U Dee Brown UD .60 1.50
257U Derek Combs UD .60 1.50
258U Derrick Blaylock UD .75 2.00
259M Derrick Gibson MVP .60 1.50
259U Derrick Gibson UD .60 1.50
259VC Derrick Gibson VICT .60 1.50
260F Deuce McAllister F/X RC 1.25 3.00
260M Deuce McAllister MVP 1.00 2.50
260U Deuce McAllister UD 1.00 2.50
260VC Deuce McAllister VICT 1.00 2.50
260VN Deuce McAllister VINT 1.00 2.50
261F Dominic Rhodes F/X RC 1.00 2.50
262F Drew Bennett F/X RC 2.00 5.00
263F Drew Brees F/X RC 50.00 100.00
263M Drew Brees MVP 30.00 80.00
263U Drew Brees UD 30.00 80.00
263VC Drew Brees VICT 30.00 80.00
263VN Drew Brees VINT 30.00 80.00
264VN Dustin McClintock VINT .75 2.00
265U Eddie Berlin UD .60 1.50
265VC Eddie Berlin VICT .60 1.50
266U Edgerton Hartwell UD .60 1.50
267U Francis St.Paul UD .60 1.50
268U Fred Smoot UD .75 2.00
269F Freddie Mitchell F/X RC .75 2.00
269M Freddie Mitchell MVP .60 1.50
269U Freddie Mitchell UD .60 1.50
269VC Freddie Mitchell VICT .60 1.50
269VN Freddie Mitchell VINT .60 1.50
270U Gary Baxter UD .60 1.50
270VC Gary Baxter VICT .60 1.50
271U George Layne UD .60 1.50
272U Gerard Warren UD .75 2.00
272VC Gerard Warren VICT .75 2.00
272VN Gerard Warren VINT .75 2.00
273U Hakim Akbar UD .60 1.50
273VN Hakim Akbar VINT .60 1.50
274U Heath Evans UD .75 2.00
274VC Heath Evans VICT .75 2.00
275U Jabari Holloway UD .60 1.50
275VC Jabari Holloway VICT .60 1.50
276U Jamal Reynolds UD .60 1.50
276VC Jamal Reynolds VICT .60 1.50
276VN Jamal Reynolds VINT .60 1.50
277U Jamar Fletcher UD .60 1.50
277VC Jamar Fletcher VICT .60 1.50
278F James Jackson F/X RC .75 2.00
278M James Jackson MVP .60 1.50
278U James Jackson UD .60 1.50
278VC James Jackson VICT .60 1.50
278VN James Jackson VINT .60 1.50
279U Jamie Winborn UD .75 2.00
280F Jesse Palmer F/X RC 1.00 2.50
280M Jesse Palmer MVP .75 2.00
280U Jesse Palmer UD .75 2.00
280VC Jesse Palmer VICT .75 2.00
280VN Jesse Palmer VINT .75 2.00
281U John Capel UD .60 1.50
282F Josh Booty F/X RC 1.00 2.50
282M Josh Booty MVP .75 2.00
282U Josh Booty UD .75 2.00
282VC Josh Booty VICT .75 2.00
282VN Josh Booty VINT .75 2.00
283M Josh Heupel MVP 1.00 2.50
283U Josh Heupel UD 1.00 2.50
283VC Josh Heupel VICT 1.00 2.50
283VN Josh Heupel VINT 1.00 2.50
284F Justin McCareins F/X RC 1.00 2.50
284U Justin McCareins UD .75 2.00
285U Justin Smith UD 1.25 3.00
285VC Justin Smith VICT 1.25 3.00
285VN Justin Smith VINT 1.25 3.00
286U Karon Riley UD .60 1.50
287U Ken Lucas UD .75 2.00
288M Ken-Yon Rambo MVP .60 1.50
288U Ken-Yon Rambo UD .60 1.50
288VC Ken-Yon Rambo VICT .60 1.50
289U Kenyatta Walker UD .60 1.50
290F Kevan Barlow F/X RC 1.00 2.50
290M Kevan Barlow MVP .75 2.00
290U Kevan Barlow UD .75 2.00
290VC Kevan Barlow VICT .75 2.00
290VN Kevan Barlow VINT .75 2.00
291F Kevin Kasper F/X RC .75 2.00
291M Kevin Kasper MVP .60 1.50
291U Kevin Kasper UD .60 1.50
291VC Kevin Kasper VICT .60 1.50
291VN Kevin Kasper VINT .60 1.50
292F Koren Robinson F/X RC 1.00 2.50
292M Koren Robinson MVP .75 2.00
292U Koren Robinson UD .75 2.00
292VC Koren Robinson VICT .75 2.00
292VN Koren Robinson VINT .75 2.00
293F L.Tomlinson F/X RC 4.00 10.00
293M LaDainian Tomlinson MVP 3.00 8.00
293U LaDainian Tomlinson UD 3.00 8.00
293VC LaDainian Tomlinson VICT 3.00 8.00
293VN LaDainian Tomlinson VINT 3.00 8.00
294F LaMont Jordan F/X RC 1.25 3.00
294M LaMont Jordan MVP 1.00 2.50
294U LaMont Jordan UD 1.00 2.50
294VC LaMont Jordan VICT 1.00 2.50
294VN LaMont Jordan VINT 1.00 2.50
295U Leonard Davis UD 1.00 2.50
295VN Leonard Davis VINT 1.00 2.50
296U Marcus Stroud UD .75 2.00
296VN Marcus Stroud VINT .75 2.00
297F Marques Tuiasosopo F/X RC 1.00 2.50
297M Marques Tuiasosopo MVP .75 2.00
297U Marques Tuiasosopo UD .75 2.00
297VC Marques Tuiasosopo VICT .75 2.00
297VN Marques Tuiasosopo VINT .75 2.00
298F Snoop Minnis F/X RC .75 2.00
298M Snoop Minnis MVP .60 1.50
298U Snoop Minnis UD .60 1.50
298VC Snoop Minnis VICT .60 1.50
298VN Snoop Minnis VINT .60 1.50
299F Michael Bennett F/X RC 1.00 2.50
299M Michael Bennett MVP .75 2.00
299U Michael Bennett UD .75 2.00
299VC Michael Bennett VICT .75 2.00
299VN Michael Bennett VINT .75 2.00
300U Michael Stone UD .60 1.50
301F Michael Vick F/X RC 2.00 5.00
301M Michael Vick MVP 1.50 4.00
301U Michael Vick UD 1.50 4.00
301VN Michael Vick VINT 1.50 4.00
302F Mike McMahon F/X RC 1.00 2.50
302M Mike McMahon MVP .75 2.00
302U Mike McMahon UD .75 2.00
302VC Mike McMahon VICT .75 2.00
302VN Mike McMahon VINT .75 2.00
303M Moran Norris MVP .60 1.50
303U Moran Norris UD .60 1.50
303VC Moran Norris VICT .60 1.50
303VN Moran Norris VINT .60 1.50
304U Morlon Greenwood UD .60 1.50
305U Nate Clements UD .75 2.00
305VC Nate Clements VICT .75 2.00
305VN Nate Clements VINT .75 2.00
306F Nick Goings F/X RC 1.25 3.00
307U Orlando Huff UD .60 1.50
308F Quincy Carter F/X RC 1.00 2.50
308U Quincy Carter UD .75 2.00
308VC Quincy Carter VICT .75 2.00
308VN Quincy Carter VINT .75 2.00
309F Quincy Morgan F/X RC 1.00 2.50
309M Quincy Morgan MVP .75 2.00
309U Quincy Morgan UD .75 2.00
309VC Quincy Morgan VICT .75 2.00
309VN Quincy Morgan VINT .75 2.00
310F Reggie Wayne F/X RC 1.50 4.00
310M Reggie Wayne MVP 1.25 3.00
310U Reggie Wayne UD 1.25 3.00
310VC Reggie Wayne VICT 1.25 3.00
310VN Reggie Wayne VINT 1.25 3.00
311M Reggie White MVP .60 1.50
311U Reggie White UD .60 1.50
312U Richard Seymour UD 1.00 2.50
312VN Richard Seymour VINT 1.00 2.50
313F Robert Ferguson F/X RC 1.25 3.00
313U Robert Ferguson UD 1.00 2.50
313VC Robert Ferguson VICT 1.00 2.50
313VN Robert Ferguson VINT 1.00 2.50
314F Rod Gardner F/X RC 1.00 2.50
314M Rod Gardner MVP .75 2.00
314U Rod Gardner UD .75 2.00
314VC Rod Gardner VICT .75 2.00
314VN Rod Gardner VINT .75 2.00
315M Ronney Daniels MVP .60 1.50
316F Rudi Johnson F/X RC 1.25 3.00
316M Rudi Johnson MVP 1.00 2.50
316U Rudi Johnson UD 1.00 2.50
316VC Rudi Johnson VICT 1.00 2.50
316VN Rudi Johnson VINT 1.00 2.50
317M Sage Rosenfels MVP .75 2.00
317U Sage Rosenfels UD .75 2.00
317VC Sage Rosenfels VICT .75 2.00
317VN Sage Rosenfels VINT .75 2.00
318F Santana Moss F/X RC 1.25 3.00
318M Santana Moss MVP 1.00 2.50
318U Santana Moss UD 1.00 2.50
318VC Santana Moss VICT 1.00 2.50
318VN Santana Moss VINT 1.00 2.50
319U Scotty Anderson UD .60 1.50
319VC Scotty Anderson VICT .60 1.50
320U Sedrick Hodge UD .60 1.50
321U Shaun Rogers UD 1.00 2.50
321VN Shaun Rogers VINT 1.00 2.50
322U Steve Hutchinson UD 1.50 4.00
323F Steve Smith F/X RC 2.50 6.00
323U Steve Smith UD 2.00 5.00
323VC Steve Smith VICT 2.00 5.00
324M T.J. Houshmandzadeh MVP .75 2.00
324U T.J. Houshmandzadeh UD .75 2.00
324VC T.J. Houshmandzadeh VICT .75 2.00
324VN T.J. Houshmandzadeh VINT .75 2.00
325U Tay Cody UD .60 1.50
326VC Tim Hasselbeck VICT .75 2.00
326VN Tim Hasselbeck VINT .75 2.00
327F Todd Heap F/X RC 1.00 2.50
327M Todd Heap MVP .75 2.00
327U Todd Heap UD .75 2.00
327VC Todd Heap VICT .75 2.00
327VN Todd Heap VINT .75 2.00
328U Tommy Polley UD .60 1.50
329U Tony Dixon UD .60 1.50
329VN Tony Dixon VINT .60 1.50
330U Torrance Marshall UD .60 1.50
331F Travis Henry F/X RC 1.00 2.50
331M Travis Henry MVP .75 2.00
331U Travis Henry UD .75 2.00
331VC Travis Henry VICT .75 2.00
331VN Travis Henry VINT .75 2.00
332F Travis Minor F/X RC 1.00 2.50
332M Travis Minor MVP .75 2.00
332U Travis Minor UD .75 2.00
332VC Travis Minor VICT .75 2.00
332VN Travis Minor VINT .75 2.00
333M Vinny Sutherland MVP .60 1.50
333U Vinny Sutherland UD .60 1.50
333VC Vinny Sutherland VICT .60 1.50
333VN Vinny Sutherland VINT .60 1.50
334U Will Allen UD 1.00 2.50
334VC Will Allen VICT 1.00 2.50
334VN Will Allen VINT 1.00 2.50
335VN Jason Brookins VINT RC 1.25 3.00
336VN Dominic Rhodes VINT RC 1.00 2.50
337VN Benjamin Gay VINT RC 1.00 2.50
338VC Troy Hambrick VICT RC 1.00 2.50
338VN Troy Hambrick VINT RC 1.00 2.50

2001 Upper Deck Rookie F/X Heroes of Football Jerseys

Randomly inserted in packs at a rate of one in 48, this 15 card set features game used jersey swatches of past NFL supertars.The jersey swatches were placed into an "H" cutout area on card front.

STATED ODDS 1:48
HFDM Dan Marino 8.00 20.00
HFDW Danny White 3.00 8.00
HFHA Herb Adderley 3.00 8.00
HFJE John Elway 6.00 15.00
HFJK Jim Kelly 8.00 20.00
HFJR John Riggins 3.00 8.00
HFJT Jim Taylor 4.00 10.00
HFMA Jim Marshall 2.50 6.00
HFON Ozzie Newsome 3.00 8.00
HFRL Ronnie Lott 3.00 8.00
HFRW Reggie White 4.00 10.00
HFSY Steve Young 5.00 12.00
HFTM Tom Mack 2.50 6.00
HFTT Thurman Thomas 3.00 8.00
HFWM Warren Moon 4.00 10.00

2001 Upper Deck Rookie F/X Legendary Combos Jerseys

Randomly inserted in packs, This seven card set features dual game jersey swatches of two teammates on the card front. Cards were serial numbered to 100 on card back.

STATED PRINT RUN 100 SER.#'d SETS
LCDB R.Dayne/T.Barber 6.00 15.00
LCFG B.Favre/A.Green 15.00 40.00
LCGM B.Griese/E.McCaffrey 5.00 12.00
LCMH P.Manning/M.Harrison 20.00 50.00
LCTB L.Tomlinson/D.Brees 25.00 60.00
LCWF K.Warner/M.Faulk 12.00 30.00
LCYR S.Young/J.Rice 15.00 40.00

2001 Upper Deck Rookie F/X Legendary Cuts

ndomly inserted in packs at a rate of one in 788, this 20 card set features all-time NFL greats cut signatures inside a full color card front. Each player has a different amount of serial numbered cards available and we have notated that in our checklist.

STATED ODDS 1:788
LCBN Bronko Nagurski/50 200.00 300.00
LCDT Derrick Thomas/37 400.00 600.00
LCRB Red Badgro/65 75.00 135.00
LCVL Vince Lombardi/221 500.00 800.00
LCWE Weeb Ewbank/38 125.00 200.00

2001 Upper Deck Rookie F/X Legends In The Making Jerseys

ndomly inserted in packs at a rate of one in 48, this 20 card set features game worn jersey swatches on card front of current NFL superstars who might become legends over time.

STATED ODDS 1:48
LMBF Brett Favre 5.00 12.00
LMDB Drew Bledsoe 2.00 5.00
LMDBR Drew Brees 25.00 50.00
LMEG1 Eddie George 2.50 6.00
LMEG2 Elvis Grbac 2.00 5.00
LMJA Jamal Anderson 2.00 5.00
LMJR Jerry Rice 5.00 12.00
LMJRS Junior Seau 2.00 5.00
LMJS Jimmy Smith 2.00 5.00
LMKC Kerry Collins 1.50 4.00
LMLT LaDainian Tomlinson 8.00 20.00
LMPM Peyton Manning 6.00 15.00
LMTB Tim Brown 2.50 6.00
LMTC Tim Couch 1.50 4.00
LMTD Terrell Davis 2.00 5.00
LMWS Warren Sapp 2.00 5.00

2001 Upper Deck Rookie F/X PatchPlay Combos

Randomly inserted in packs, this 15 card set features dual players from the same team with two game worn jersey patches on the card front. The cards are serial numbered in gold on card front to a stated print run of 45 sets.

STATED PRINT RUN 45 SER.#'d SETS
ABP B.Favre/A.Freeman 30.00 80.00
BHP I.Bruce/T.Holt 15.00 40.00
BSP K.Stewart/J.Bettis 15.00 40.00
BTP M.Brunell/F.Taylor 12.00 30.00
CHP K.Collins/I.Hilliard 10.00 25.00
CMP C.Carter/R.Moss 15.00 40.00
FHP M.Faulk/A.Hakim 12.00 30.00
GMP B.Griese/E.McCaffrey 10.00 25.00
GOP T.Owens/J.Garcia 12.00 30.00
GPP D.Bledsoe/T.Glenn 12.00 30.00
MHP P.Manning/M.Harrison 40.00 100.00
SBP F.Sanders/D.Boston 10.00 25.00
TUP B.Urlacher/D.Terrell 20.00 50.00
WBP K.Warner/I.Bruce 25.00 60.00
WFP K.Warner/M.Faulk 25.00 60.00

2005 Upper Deck Rookie Materials

This 130-card set was released through Upper Deck's retail outlets in September, 2005. The set was issued in nine-card packs which came 24 packs to a box. Cards numbered 1-90 feature veterans in team alphabetical order while cards numbered 91-130 feature 2005 rookies. Those rookies were issued at a stated rate of one in three.

COMP.SET w/o RC's (90) 10.00 25.00
DRAFT PICK STATED ODDS 1:3
1 Larry Fitzgerald .30 .75
2 Kurt Warner .25 .60
3 Michael Vick .25 .60
4 Peerless Price .20 .50
5 Todd Heap .20 .50
6 Jamal Lewis .25 .60
7 Kyle Boller .20 .50
8 J.P. Losman .20 .50
9 Willis McGahee .20 .50
10 Lee Evans .25 .60
11 Eric Moulds .20 .50
12 Jake Delhomme .20 .50
13 Keary Colbert .20 .50
14 DeShaun Foster .25 .60
15 Brian Urlacher .30 .75
16 Rex Grossman .20 .50
17 Muhsin Muhammad .20 .50
18 Carson Palmer .25 .60
19 Rudi Johnson .20 .50
20 Chad Johnson .20 .50
21 Julius Jones .20 .50
22 Keyshawn Johnson .25 .60
23 Drew Bledsoe .25 .60
24 Tatum Bell .20 .50
25 Jake Plummer .20 .50
26 Ashley Lelie .20 .50
27 Roy Williams WR .20 .50
28 Kevin Jones .20 .50
29 Jeff Garcia .20 .50
30 Brett Favre .60 1.50
31 Ahman Green .25 .60
32 Javon Walker .20 .50
33 David Carr .20 .50
34 Andre Johnson .25 .60
35 Domanick Davis .20 .50
36 Peyton Manning .75 2.00
37 Edgerrin James .25 .60
38 Marvin Harrison .25 .60
39 Byron Leftwich .20 .50
40 Fred Taylor .20 .50
41 Jimmy Smith .25 .60
42 Priest Holmes .20 .50
43 Tony Gonzalez .25 .60
44 Trent Green .20 .50
45 A.J. Feeley .20 .50
46 Chris Chambers .20 .50
47 Randy McMichael .20 .50
48 Daunte Culpepper .25 .60
49 Michael Bennett .20 .50
50 Nate Burleson .20 .50
51 Tom Brady 1.25 3.00
52 Corey Dillon .20 .50
53 Deion Branch .20 .50
54 Aaron Brooks .20 .50
55 Deuce McAllister .25 .60
56 Joe Horn .20 .50
57 Eli Manning .50 1.25
58 Jeremy Shockey .20 .50
59 Tiki Barber .25 .60
60 Chad Pennington .20 .50
61 Curtis Martin .25 .60
62 Laveranues Coles .20 .50
63 Kerry Collins .20 .50
64 LaMont Jordan .25 .60
65 Randy Moss .25 .60
66 Donovan McNabb .25 .60
67 Terrell Owens .25 .60
68 Brian Westbrook .20 .50
69 Ben Roethlisberger .50 1.25
70 Jerome Bettis .30 .75
71 Hines Ward .25 .60
72 Drew Brees .30 .75
73 LaDainian Tomlinson .30 .75
74 Antonio Gates .30 .75
75 Tim Rattay .20 .50
76 Eric Johnson .20 .50
77 Shaun Alexander .20 .50
78 Darrell Jackson .20 .50
79 Matt Hasselbeck .20 .50
80 Marc Bulger .20 .50
81 Steven Jackson .20 .50
82 Torry Holt .25 .60
83 Joey Galloway .25 .60
84 Brian Griese .20 .50
85 Michael Clayton .20 .50
86 Steve McNair .25 .60
87 Chris Brown .20 .50
88 Clinton Portis .20 .50
89 Patrick Ramsey .25 .60
90 Santana Moss .25 .60
91 Aaron Rodgers RC 15.00 30.00
92 Alex Smith QB RC 3.00 8.00
93 Jason Campbell RC .75 2.00
94 Charlie Frye RC .75 2.00
95 David Greene RC .75 2.00
96 Dan Orlovsky RC .75 2.00
97 Adrian McPherson RC .75 2.00
98 Kyle Orton RC .75 2.00
99 Andrew Walter RC .75 2.00
100 [illegible] RC .75 2.00
101 Cadillac Williams RC .75 2.00
102 Ronnie Brown RC 1.00 2.50
103 Vernand Morency RC .75 2.00
104 Ciatrick Fason RC .75 2.00
105 Maurice Clarett .75 2.00
106 Eric Shelton RC .75 2.00
107 J.J. Arrington RC 1.00 2.50
108 Frank Gore RC 1.50 4.00
109 Stefan LeFors RC .75 2.00
110 Troy Williamson RC .75 2.00
111 Braylon Edwards RC .75 2.00
112 Mike Williams 1.00 2.50
113 Vincent Jackson RC 1.25 3.00
114 Courtney Roby RC .75 2.00
115 Roddy White RC 1.25 3.00
116 Matt Jones RC .75 2.00
117 Ryan Moats RC .75 2.00
118 Mark Bradley RC .75 2.00
119 Mark Clayton RC .75 2.00
120 Terrence Murphy RC .75 2.00
121 Roscoe Parrish RC .75 2.00
122 Carlos Rogers RC 1.25 3.00
123 Antrel Rolle RC 1.25 3.00
124 Adam Jones RC .75 2.00
125 Heath Miller RC 1.50 4.00
126 Reggie Brown RC .75 2.00
127 Shawne Merriman RC 1.25 3.00
128 Marcus Spears RC .75 2.00
129 DeMarcus Ware RC 2.50 6.00
130 Mike Nugent RC 1.00 2.50

2005 Upper Deck Rookie Materials Icons

COMPLETE SET (15) 10.00 25.00
STATED ODDS 1:4
IC1 Brett Favre 2.00 5.00
IC2 Peyton Manning 2.50 6.00
IC3 Michael Vick .75 2.00
IC4 Donovan McNabb .75 2.00
IC5 Tom Brady 4.00 10.00
IC6 LaDainian Tomlinson 1.00 2.50
IC7 Priest Holmes .60 1.50
IC8 Clinton Portis .60 1.50
IC9 Ahman Green .75 2.00
IC10 Shaun Alexander .60 1.50
IC11 Randy Moss .75 2.00
IC12 Terrell Owens .75 2.00
IC13 Marvin Harrison .75 2.00
IC14 Torry Holt .75 2.00
IC15 Tony Gonzalez .75 2.00

2005 Upper Deck Rookie Materials Rookie Jerseys

STATED ODDS 1:8
R10 Braylon Edwards 4.00 10.00
R11 Cadillac Williams 8.00 20.00
R12 Courtney Roby 2.50 6.00
R13 Adam Jones 2.50 6.00
R14 J.J. Arrington 2.50 6.00
R15 Stefan LeFors 2.50 6.00
R16 Eric Shelton 2.50 6.00
R17 Frank Gore 5.00 12.00
R18 Andrew Walter 2.50 6.00
R19 Ryan Moats 2.50 6.00

2005 Upper Deck Rookie Materials Stars of Tomorrow

COMPLETE SET (15) 12.50 30.00
STATED ODDS 1:4
ST1 Alex Smith QB 1.50 4.00
ST2 Aaron Rodgers 8.00 20.00
ST3 Jason Campbell .40 1.00
ST4 Charlie Frye .40 1.00
ST5 David Greene .40 1.00
ST6 Ronnie Brown .50 1.25
ST7 Cedric Benson .40 1.00
ST8 Cadillac Williams .40 1.00
ST9 Eric Shelton .40 1.00
ST10 Ciatrick Fason .40 1.00
ST11 J.J. Arrington .50 1.25
ST12 Braylon Edwards .40 1.00
ST13 Troy Williamson .40 1.00
ST14 Mike Williams .50 1.25
ST15 Matt Jones .40 1.00

2004 Upper Deck Rookie Premiere

This set was issued as a 30-card factory box set in August 2004. Each factory set also included one gold foil parallel card. Each card includes front and back photos of the player taken at the NFL Rookie Premiere photo shoot.

COMPLETE SET (30) 15.00 30.00
1 Eli Manning 2.00 5.00
2 Ben Roethlisberger 2.00 5.00
3 Philip Rivers .75 2.00
4 Roy Williams WR .25 .60
5 Larry Fitzgerald 1.00 2.50
6 Tatum Bell .25 .60
7 J.P. Losman .25 .60
8 Steven Jackson .40 1.00
9 Ben Watson .30 .75
10 Devery Henderson .25 .60
11 Kevin Jones .30 .75
12 Chris Perry .25 .60
13 Kellen Winslow Jr. .25 .60
14 Lee Evans .40 1.00
15 Reggie Williams .25 .60
16 Ben Troupe .25 .60
17 Michael Clayton .30 .75
18 Michael Jenkins .25 .60
19 Rashaun Woods .25 .60
20 DeAngelo Hall .40 1.00
21 Cedric Cobbs .25 .60
22 Luke McCown .25 .60
23 Robert Gallery .30 .75
24 Julius Jones .25 .60
25 Matt Schaub .25 .60
26 Keary Colbert .25 .60
27 Bernard Berrian .25 .60
28 Greg Jones .25 .60
29 Darius Watts .25 .60
30 Checklist Card .25 .60

2004 Upper Deck Rookie Premiere Gold

COMPLETE SET (30) 20.00 50.00
*GOLD: 1X TO 2.5X BASIC CARDS
ONE GOLD PER FACTORY SET

2004 Upper Deck Rookie Premiere Autographs

BB Bernard Berrian 10.00 25.00
BR Ben Roethlisberger 175.00 300.00
BT Ben Troupe 10.00 25.00
BW Ben Watson 12.00 30.00
CC Cedric Cobbs 10.00 25.00
CP Chris Perry 10.00 25.00
DD Devard Darling 10.00 25.00
DH DeAngelo Hall 15.00 40.00
DH2 Devery Henderson 10.00 25.00
DW Darius Watts 10.00 25.00
EM Eli Manning 175.00 300.00
GJ Greg Jones 10.00 25.00
JJ Julius Jones 10.00 25.00
KC Keary Colbert 10.00 25.00
KJ Kevin Jones 12.00 30.00
LE Lee Evans 15.00 40.00

LF Larry Fitzgerald 60.00 100.00
LM Luke McCown 10.00 25.00
MC Michael Clayton 12.00 30.00
MJ Michael Jenkins 10.00 25.00
MS Matt Schaub 10.00 25.00
PR Philip Rivers 60.00 120.00
RG Robert Gallery 12.00 30.00
RW Rashaun Woods 10.00 25.00
RW2 Reggie Williams 10.00 25.00
RW3 Roy Williams WR 10.00 25.00
JL J.P. Losman 10.00 25.00

2005 Upper Deck Rookie Premiere

This set was issued as a 30-card factory box set with an $9.99 SRP in August 2005. Each factory set included one gold foil parallel card. Each base set card includes front and back photos of the player taken at the NFL Rookie Premiere photo shoot.

COMPLETE SET (30) 10.00 20.00
1 Ciatrick Fason .20 .50
2 Alex Smith QB .75 2.00
3 Antrel Rolle .30 .75
4 Cadillac Williams .20 .50
5 Ronnie Brown .25 .60
6 Charlie Frye .20 .50
7 Roddy White .30 .75
8 Braylon Edwards .20 .50
9 Mark Bradley .20 .50
10 Vincent Jackson .30 .75
11 Matt Jones .20 .50
12 Stefan LeFors .20 .50
13 Kyle Orton .20 .50
14 Troy Williamson .20 .50
15 Mark Clayton .20 .50
16 Aaron Rodgers 6.00 15.00
17 Cedric Benson .20 .50
18 Mike Williams .25 .60
19 Adam Jones .20 .50
20 Reggie Brown .20 .50
21 J.J. Arrington .25 .60
22 Andrew Walter .20 .50
23 David Greene .20 .50
24 Roscoe Parrish .20 .50
25 Terrence Murphy .20 .50
26 Jason Campbell .20 .50
27 Maurice Clarett .20 .50
28 Frank Gore .40 1.00
29 Ryan Moats .20 .50
30 Checklist Card .30 .75

2005 Upper Deck Rookie Premiere Gold

COMPLETE SET (30) 30.00 80.00
*SINGLES: 1.2X TO 3X BASIC CARDS
ONE GOLD OR PLATINUM PER FACT.SET

2005 Upper Deck Rookie Premiere Platinum

COMPLETE SET (30) 30.00 80.00
*SINGLES: 1.2X TO 3X BASIC CARDS
ONE GOLD OR PLATINUM PER FACT.SET

2005 Upper Deck Rookie Premiere Autographs

STATED ODDS 1:24 FACTORY SETS
RSAJ Adam Jones 8.00 20.00
RSAN Antrel Rolle 12.00 30.00
RSAR Aaron Rodgers 150.00 300.00
RSAS Alex Smith QB 90.00 150.00
RSAW Andrew Walter 8.00 20.00
RSBE Braylon Edwards 40.00 100.00
RSCB Cedric Benson 20.00 40.00
RSCF Charlie Frye 8.00 20.00
RSCI Ciatrick Fason 8.00 20.00
RSCW Cadillac Williams 40.00 120.00
RSDG David Greene 8.00 20.00
RSFG Frank Gore 20.00 50.00
RSJA J.J. Arrington 10.00 25.00
RSJC Jason Campbell 20.00 50.00
RSKO Kyle Orton 15.00 40.00
RSMB Mark Bradley 8.00 20.00
RSMC Mark Clayton 8.00 20.00
RSMJ Matt Jones
RSMO Maurice Clarett
RSMW Mike Williams 10.00 25.00
RSRB Ronnie Brown 60.00 120.00
RSRE Reggie Brown 8.00 20.00
RSRM Ryan Moats 8.00 20.00
RSRP Roscoe Parrish 8.00 20.00
RSRW Roddy White 12.00 30.00
RSSL Stefan LeFors 8.00 20.00
RSTM Terrence Murphy 8.00 20.00
RSTW Troy Williamson 8.00 20.00
RSVJ Vincent Jackson 12.00 30.00

2005 Upper Deck Rookie Premiere Match-Ups

STATED ODDS 1:24 FACTORY SETS
RM1 C.Williams/Ron.Brown 1.50 4.00
RM2 A.Smith QB/S.LeFors 4.00 10.00
RM3 V.Jackson/M.Bradley 2.00 5.00
RM4 B.Edwards/C.Frye 1.25 3.00
RM5 R.Parrish/A.Rolle 2.00 5.00
RM6 Reg.Brown/R.Moats 1.25 3.00
RM7 A.Rodgers/T.Murphy 6.00 15.00
RM8 C.Benson/K.Orton 1.25 3.00
RM9 M.Jones/T.Williamson 1.25 3.00
RM10 B.Edwards/M.Williams 1.50 4.00

2006 Upper Deck Rookie Premiere

This 30-card set was released in factory set form in August, 2006. This set featured the leading 30 players who particpated in the yearly NFL rookie photo shoot. The set is sequenced in alphabetical order.

COMPLETE SET (30) 10.00 20.00
1 Jason Avant .25 .60
2 Reggie Bush .40 1.00
3 Brian Calhoun .25 .60
4 Kellen Clemens .25 .60
5 Vernon Davis .30 .75
6 Maurice Drew .40 1.00
7 Derek Hagan .30 .75
8 A.J. Hawk .30 .75
9 Santonio Holmes .30 .75
10 Michael Huff .30 .75
11 Chad Jackson .25 .60
12 Tarvaris Jackson .25 .60
13 Omar Jacobs .25 .60
14 Joe Klopfenstein .25 .60
15 Matt Leinart .25 .60
16 Marcedes Lewis .25 .60
17 Laurence Maroney .25 .60
18 Brandon Marshall .50 1.25
19 Sinorice Moss .25 .60
20 Jerious Norwood .25 .60
21 Maurice Stovall .25 .60
22 Leon Washington .25 .60
23 LenDale White .25 .60
24 Charlie Whitehurst .25 .60
25 Brandon Williams .25 .60
26 DeAngelo Williams .30 .75
27 Demetrius Williams .25 .60
28 Mario Williams .40 1.00
29 Travis Wilson .25 .60
30 Vince Young .25 .60

2006 Upper Deck Rookie Premiere Autographs

ONE AUTO PER 24-SET CASE
1 Jason Avant 5.00 12.00
2 Reggie Bush SP 100.00 200.00
3 Brian Calhoun 5.00 12.00
4 Kellen Clemens 5.00 12.00
5 Vernon Davis 6.00 15.00
6 Maurice Drew 8.00 20.00
7 Derek Hagan 6.00 15.00
8 A.J. Hawk SP 8.00 20.00
9 Santonio Holmes 20.00 50.00
10 Michael Huff 6.00 15.00
11 Chad Jackson 5.00 12.00
12 Tarvaris Jackson 10.00 25.00
13 Omar Jacobs 5.00 12.00
14 Joe Klopfenstein 5.00 12.00
15 Matt Leinart SP 50.00 120.00
16 Marcedes Lewis
17 Laurence Maroney 5.00 12.00
18 Brandon Marshall 20.00 40.00
19 Sinorice Moss 5.00 12.00
20 Jerious Norwood 5.00 12.00
21 Maurice Stovall 5.00 12.00
22 Leon Washington 5.00 12.00
23 LenDale White 5.00 12.00
24 Charlie Whitehurst 5.00 12.00
25 Brandon Williams 5.00 12.00
26 DeAngelo Williams SP 50.00 120.00
27 Demetrius Williams 5.00 12.00
28 Mario Williams 30.00 60.00
29 Travis Wilson 5.00 12.00
30 Vince Young SP 100.00 200.00

2007 Upper Deck Rookie Premiere

This 30-card set was released in factory set form in August, 2007. This set featured players who attended the 2007 NFL rookie photo shoot and the set is sequenced in alphabetical order.

COMPLETE SET (30) 7.50 15.00
1 Gaines Adams .25 .60
2 John Beck .20 .50
3 Lorenzo Booker .25 .60
4 Dwayne Bowe .20 .50
5 Michael Bush .20 .50
6 Yamon Figurs .20 .50
7 Ted Ginn .25 .60
8 Anthony Gonzalez .20 .50
9 Chris Henry .20 .50
10 Jason Hill .20 .50
11 Tony Hunt .20 .50
12 Kenny Irons .20 .50
13 Brandon Jackson .20 .50
14 Dwayne Jarrett .25 .60
15 Calvin Johnson .60 1.50
16 Kevin Kolb .25 .60
17 Brian Leonard .20 .50
18 Marshawn Lynch .40 1.00
19 Robert Meachem .25 .60
20 Greg Olsen .30 .75
21 Adrian Peterson 3.00 8.00
22 Antonio Pittman .20 .50
23 Brady Quinn .20 .50
24 Sidney Rice .25 .60
25 JaMarcus Russell .20 .50
26 Joe Thomas .30 .75
27 Steve Smith .20 .50
28 Troy Smith .20 .50
29 Drew Stanton .20 .50
30 Patrick Willis .30 .75

2007 Upper Deck Rookie Premiere Autographs

1 Gaines Adams 12.00 30.00
2 John Beck 10.00 25.00
3 Lorenzo Booker 12.00 30.00
4 Dwayne Bowe 10.00 25.00
5 Michael Bush 10.00 25.00
6 Yamon Figurs 10.00 25.00
7 Ted Ginn
8 Anthony Gonzalez 10.00 25.00
9 Chris Henry 10.00 25.00
10 Jason Hill 10.00 25.00
11 Tony Hunt
12 Kenny Irons 10.00 25.00
13 Brandon Jackson 10.00 25.00
14 Dwayne Jarrett 12.00 30.00
15 Calvin Johnson 100.00 200.00
16 Kevin Kolb 12.00 30.00
17 Brian Leonard 10.00 25.00
18 Marshawn Lynch 20.00 50.00
19 Robert Meachem 12.00 30.00
20 Greg Olsen 15.00 40.00
21 Adrian Peterson 250.00 400.00
22 Antonio Pittman 10.00 25.00
23 Brady Quinn 10.00 25.00
24 Sidney Rice 12.00 30.00
25 JaMarcus Russell
26 Joe Thomas 15.00 40.00
27 Steve Smith 10.00 25.00
28 Troy Smith 10.00 25.00
29 Drew Stanton 10.00 25.00
30 Patrick Willis 15.00 40.00

2008 Upper Deck Rookie Premiere

COMPLETE SET (30) 7.50 15.00
1 Darren McFadden .20 .50
2 DeSean Jackson .40 1.00
3 Brian Brohm .20 .50
4 Matt Ryan .60 1.50
5 Jonathan Stewart .30 .75
6 Jerome Simpson .25 .60
7 Chad Henne .25 .60
8 Chris Johnson .25 .60
9 Team Photo Checklist .60 1.50
10 Rashard Mendenhall .20 .50
11 Earl Bennett .30 .75
12 Early Doucet .20 .50
13 Kevin O'Connell .20 .50
14 Felix Jones .20 .50
15 Dustin Keller .25 .60
16 Jamaal Charles .30 .75
17 Joe Flacco .40 1.00
18 John David Booty .20 .50
19 Jordy Nelson .60 1.50
20 Kevin Smith .20 .50
21 Limas Sweed .20 .50
22 Dexter Jackson .30 .75
23 Malcolm Kelly .20 .50
24 Jake Long .30 .75
25 Eddie Royal .20 .50
26 Matt Forte .30 .75
27 Donnie Avery .25 .60
28 Ray Rice .20 .50
29 Harry Douglas .25 .60
30 Devin Thomas .20 .50

2008 Upper Deck Rookie Premiere Autographs

1 Darren McFadden 5.00 12.00
2 DeSean Jackson 10.00 25.00
3 Brian Brohm 5.00 12.00
4 Matt Ryan 30.00 80.00
5 Jonathan Stewart 8.00 20.00
6 Jerome Simpson 6.00 15.00
7 Chad Henne 6.00 15.00
8 Chris Johnson 6.00 15.00
10 Rashard Mendenhall
11 Earl Bennett 8.00 20.00
12 Early Doucet 5.00 12.00
13 Kevin O'Connell 5.00 12.00
14 Felix Jones 5.00 12.00
15 Dustin Keller 6.00 15.00
16 Jamaal Charles 8.00 20.00
17 Joe Flacco 25.00 60.00
18 John David Booty 5.00 12.00
19 Jordy Nelson 25.00 50.00
20 Kevin Smith 5.00 12.00
21 Limas Sweed 5.00 12.00
22 Dexter Jackson 8.00 20.00
23 Malcolm Kelly 5.00 12.00
24 Jake Long 8.00 20.00
25 Eddie Royal 5.00 12.00
26 Matt Forte 20.00 50.00
27 Donnie Avery
28 Ray Rice 5.00 12.00
29 Harry Douglas 6.00 15.00
30 Devin Thomas 5.00 12.00

2009 Upper Deck Rookie Premiere

COMPLETE SET (30) 7.50 15.00
1 Aaron Curry .30 .75
2 Brandon Pettigrew .20 .50
3 Brian Robiskie .20 .50
4 Chris Wells .20 .50
5 Darrius Heyward-Bey .30 .75
6 Deon Butler .20 .50
7 Derrick Williams .20 .50
8 Donald Brown .20 .50
9 Hakeem Nicks .25 .60
10 Jason Smith .20 .50
11 Javon Ringer .20 .50
12 Jeremy Maclin .25 .60
13 Josh Freeman .20 .50
14 Juaquin Iglesias .20 .50
15 Kenny Britt .30 .75
16 Knowshon Moreno .20 .50
17 LeSean McCoy .50 1.25
18 Mark Sanchez .20 .50
19 Matthew Stafford 1.00 2.50
20 Michael Crabtree .30 .75
21 Mohamed Massaquoi .20 .50
22 Nate Davis .20 .50
23 Pat White .25 .60
24 Patrick Turner .20 .50
25 Percy Harvin .20 .50
26 Ramses Barden .20 .50
27 Rhett Bomar .20 .50
28 Shonn Greene .20 .50
29 Tyson Jackson .20 .50
30 Checklist Card .25 .60

2009 Upper Deck Rookie Premiere Autographs

RANDOM INSERTS IN FACTORY SETS
1 Aaron Curry
2 Brandon Pettigrew 5.00 12.00
3 Brian Robiskie 5.00 12.00
4 Chris Wells 5.00 12.00
5 Darrius Heyward-Bey
6 Deon Butler 5.00 12.00
7 Derrick Williams 5.00 12.00
8 Donald Brown 5.00 12.00
9 Hakeem Nicks 6.00 15.00
10 Jason Smith 5.00 12.00
11 Javon Ringer 5.00 12.00
12 Jeremy Maclin 6.00 15.00
13 Josh Freeman 5.00 12.00
14 Juaquin Iglesias 5.00 12.00
15 Kenny Britt 8.00 20.00
16 Knowshon Moreno 5.00 12.00
17 LeSean McCoy 12.00 30.00
18 Mark Sanchez 5.00 12.00
19 Matthew Stafford
20 Michael Crabtree
21 Mohamed Massaquoi 5.00 12.00
22 Nate Davis 5.00 12.00
23 Pat White 6.00 15.00
24 Patrick Turner 5.00 12.00
25 Percy Harvin 5.00 12.00
26 Ramses Barden 5.00 12.00
27 Rhett Bomar
28 Shonn Greene 5.00 12.00
29 Tyson Jackson 5.00 12.00

1996 Upper Deck Silver

The 1996 Upper Deck Silver set was issued only through Upper Deck's hobby channels. The set was issued in one series totalling 225 standard-size cards. The 10-card packs had a suggested retail price of $2.49 each. 28 packs were in a box and 20 boxes made up a case. The set contains the topical subset Season Leaders (211-225).

COMPLETE SET (225) 7.50 20.00
1 Larry Centers .07 .20
2 Terance Mathis .02 .10
3 Justin Armour .02 .10
4 Kerry Collins .15 .40
5 Jim Flanigan UER .02 .10
6 Dan Wilkinson .02 .10
7 Eric Zeier .02 .10
8 Deion Sanders .20 .50
9 Steve Atwater .02 .10
10 Johnnie Morton .07 .20
11 Craig Newsome .02 .10
12 Broncos Offensive Line .02 .10
13 Ken Dilger .07 .20
14 Mark Brunell .25 .60
15 Tamarick Vanover .07 .20
16 Bernie Parmalee .02 .10
17 Orlando Thomas .02 .10
18 Will Moore .02 .10
19 Mark Fields .02 .10
20 Tyrone Wheatley .07 .20
21 Kyle Brady .02 .10
22 Napoleon Kaufman .15 .40
23 Mike Mamula .02 .10
24 Erric Pegram .02 .10
25 Brent Jones .02 .10
26 Aaron Hayden RC .02 .10
27 Christian Fauria .02 .10
28 Cowboys Offensive Line .07 .20
29 Derrick Brooks .15 .40
30 Brian Mitchell .02 .10
31 Garrison Hearst .07 .20
32 Devin Bush .02 .10
33 Andre Reed .07 .20
34 Derrick Moore .02 .10
35 Erik Kramer .02 .10
36 Jeff Blake .15 .40
37 Andre Rison .07 .20
38 Troy Aikman .40 1.00
39 Anthony Miller .07 .20
40 Scott Mitchell .07 .20
41 Reggie White .15 .40
42 Chris Sanders .07 .20
43 Ellis Johnson .02 .10
44 Willie Jackson .07 .20
45 Steve Bono .02 .10
46 Terry Kirby .07 .20
47 Jake Reed .07 .20
48 Vincent Brisby .02 .10
49 Quinn Early .02 .10
50 Thomas Lewis .02 .10
51 Wayne Chrebet .25 .60
52 Pat Swilling .02 .10
53 Bobby Taylor .02 .10
54 Mark Bruener .02 .10
55 Jerry Rice .40 1.00
56 Natrone Means .07 .20
57 Rick Mirer .07 .20
58 Kevin Carter .02 .10
59 Hardy Nickerson .02 .10
60 Lions Offensive Line .02 .10
61 Eric Swann .02 .10
62 Eric Metcalf .02 .10
63 Russell Copeland .02 .10
64 Pete Metzelaars .02 .10
65 Curtis Conway .15 .40
66 Darnay Scott .07 .20
67 Leroy Hoard .02 .10
68 Darren Woodson .07 .20
69 John Elway .75 2.00
70 Brett Perriman .02 .10
71 Mark Chmura .07 .20
72 Chris Chandler .07 .20
73 Marshall Faulk .20 .50
74 Pete Mitchell .07 .20
75 Willie Davis .02 .10
76 Irving Fryar .07 .20
77 Robert Smith .07 .20
78 Drew Bledsoe .25 .60
79 Mario Bates .07 .20
80 Chris Calloway .02 .10
81 Boomer Esiason .07 .20
82 Harvey Williams .02 .10
83 Fred Barnett .02 .10
84 Neil O'Donnell .07 .20
85 Lee Woodall .02 .10
86 Junior Seau .15 .40
87 Brian Blades .02 .10
88 Chris Miller .02 .10
89 Warren Sapp .02 .10
90 Terry Allen .07 .20
91 Dave Krieg .02 .10
92 Bert Emanuel .07 .20
93 Jim Kelly .15 .40
94 Mark Carrier WR .02 .10
95 Jeff Graham .02 .10
96 Tony McGee .02 .10
97 Vinny Testaverde .07 .20
98 Michael Irvin .15 .40
99 Shannon Sharpe .07 .20
100 Chris Spielman .02 .10
101 Edgar Bennett .07 .20
102 Haywood Jeffires .02 .10
103 Quentin Coryatt .02 .10
104 Jeff Lageman .02 .10
105 Neil Smith .07 .20
106 O.J. McDuffie .07 .20
107 Warren Moon .07 .20
108 Ben Coates .07 .20
109 Michael Haynes .02 .10
110 Mike Sherrard .02 .10
111 Adrian Murrell .07 .20
112 Jeff Hostetler .02 .10
113 Charlie Garner .07 .20
114 Yancey Thigpen .07 .20
115 Steve Young .25 .60
116 Tony Martin .07 .20
117 49ers Offensive Line .02 .10
118 Jerome Bettis .15 .40
119 Alvin Harper .02 .10
120 Heath Shuler .07 .20
121 Rob Moore .07 .20
122 Chris Doleman .02 .10
123 Bruce Smith .07 .20
124 Sam Mills .02 .10
125 Donnell Woolford .02 .10
126 Harold Green .02 .10
127 Antonio Langham .02 .10
128 Charles Haley .07 .20
129 Aaron Craver .02 .10
130 Barry Sanders .60 1.50
131 Sean Jones .02 .10
132 Steve McNair .30 .75
133 Tony Bennett .02 .10
134 Dolphins Offensive Line .15 .40
135 Greg Hill .07 .20
136 Eric Green .02 .10
137 John Randle .07 .20
138 Dave Meggett .02 .10
139 Irv Smith .02 .10
140 Dave Brown .02 .10
141 Raiders Offensive Line .02 .10
142 Rocket Ismail .02 .10
143 Rodney Peete .02 .10
144 Kevin Greene .07 .20
145 Derek Loville .02 .10
146 Leslie O'Neal .02 .10
147 Cortez Kennedy .02 .10
148 Sean Gilbert .02 .10
149 Jackie Harris .02 .10
150 Henry Ellard .02 .10
151 Frank Sanders .07 .20
152 Jeff George .07 .20
153 Darick Holmes .02 .10
154 Tyrone Poole .02 .10
155 Rashaan Salaam .07 .20
156 Carl Pickens .07 .20
157 Eric Turner .02 .10
158 Jay Novacek .02 .10
159 Terrell Davis .30 .75
160 Herman Moore .07 .20
161 Robert Brooks .15 .40
162 Rodney Thomas .02 .10
163 Sean Dawkins .02 .10
164 James O. Stewart .07 .20
165 Marcus Allen .15 .40
166 Dan Marino .75 2.00
167 Cris Carter .15 .40
168 Curtis Martin .30 .75
169 Tyrone Hughes .02 .10
170 Rodney Hampton .07 .20
171 Hugh Douglas .07 .20
172 Tim Brown .15 .40
173 Ricky Watters .07 .20
174 Kordell Stewart .15 .40
175 Stan Humphries .07 .20
176 J.J. Stokes .15 .40
177 Joey Galloway .15 .40
178 Isaac Bruce .15 .40
179 Errict Rhett .07 .20
180 Michael Westbrook .15 .40
181 Steelers Offensive Line .02 .10
182 Craig Heyward .02 .10
183 Bryce Paup .02 .10
184 Brett Maxie .02 .10
185 Kevin Butler .02 .10
186 John Copeland .02 .10
187 Keenan McCardell .15 .40
188 Emmitt Smith .60 1.50
189 Glyn Milburn .02 .10
190 Jason Hanson .02 .10
191 Brett Favre .75 2.00
192 Darryll Lewis UER .02 .10
193 Jim Harbaugh .07 .20
194 Desmond Howard .07 .20
195 Derrick Thomas .15 .40
196 Bryan Cox .02 .10
197 Amp Lee .02 .10
198 Ty Law .15 .40
199 Jim Everett .02 .10
200 Vencie Glenn .02 .10
201 Charles Wilson .02 .10
202 Terry McDaniel .02 .10
203 Calvin Williams .02 .10
204 Greg Lloyd .07 .20
205 Merton Hanks .02 .10
206 Andre Coleman .02 .10
207 Chris Warren .07 .20
208 D'Marco Farr .02 .10
209 Trent Dilfer .15 .40
210 Ken Harvey .02 .10
211 Jim Harbaugh SL .07 .20
212 Brett Favre SL .40 1.00
213 Curtis Martin SL .15 .40
214 Carl Pickens SL .07 .20
215 Norm Johnson SL .02 .10
216 Bryce Paup SL .02 .10
217 Herman Moore SL .07 .20
218 Jerry Rice SL .20 .50
219 Orlando Thomas SL .02 .10
220 Emmitt Smith SL .30 .75
221 Tyrone Hughes SL .02 .10
222 Tamarick Vanover SL .07 .20
223 Rick Tuten SL .02 .10
224 49ers Defense SL .02 .10
225 Lions Offensive Line SL .02 .10
DM13 Dan Marino Promo 1.00 2.50

1996 Upper Deck Silver All-NFL

Randomly inserted in packs at a rate of one in 5, this 20-card set highlights some of the top players selected to the Upper Deck All-NFL Team. The cards feature Light F/X Technology and a die-cut design with a football type texture. The cards are numbered with an "AN" prefix.

COMPLETE SET (20) 12.50 30.00
STATED ODDS 1:5
AN1 Herman Moore .40 1.00
AN2 Isaac Bruce .75 2.00
AN3 Jerry Rice 2.00 5.00
AN4 Michael Irvin .75 2.00
AN5 Eric Metcalf .20 .50
AN6 Ben Coates .40 1.00
AN7 Brett Favre 4.00 10.00
AN8 Jim Harbaugh .40 1.00
AN9 Emmitt Smith 3.00 8.00
AN10 Barry Sanders 3.00 8.00
AN11 Chris Warren .40 1.00
AN12 Curtis Martin 1.50 4.00
AN13 Hugh Douglas .40 1.00
AN14 Neil Smith .40 1.00
AN15 Reggie White .75 2.00
AN16 Bryce Paup .20 .50
AN17 Greg Lloyd .40 1.00
AN18 Carnell Lake .20 .50
AN19 Merton Hanks .20 .50
AN20 Tamarick Vanover .40 1.00

1996 Upper Deck Silver All-Rookie Team

Randomly inserted in packs at a rate of one in 18, this 20-card set features some of the top rookies selected to the Upper Deck All-Rookie Team. These cards also showcase Light F/X Technology and a die-cut design with a unique football texture. The cards differentiate from the All-NFL cards in that these cards have a golden color to them. The cards are numbered with an "AR" prefix.

COMPLETE SET (20) 50.00 100.00
STATED ODDS 1:18
AR1 Joey Galloway 2.00 5.00
AR2 Chris Sanders 1.00 2.50
AR3 J.J. Stokes 2.00 5.00
AR4 Ken Dilger 1.00 2.50
AR5 Pete Mitchell 1.00 2.50
AR6 Kordell Stewart 2.00 5.00
AR7 Kerry Collins 2.00 5.00
AR8 Tony Boselli .50 1.25
AR9 Terrell Davis 4.00 10.00
AR10 Rodney Thomas .50 1.25
AR11 Rashaan Salaam 1.00 2.50
AR12 Curtis Martin 4.00 10.00
AR13 Napoleon Kaufman 2.00 5.00
AR14 Hugh Douglas 1.00 2.50
AR15 Ellis Johnson .50 1.25
AR16 Kevin Carter .50 1.25
AR17 Derrick Brooks 2.00 5.00
AR18 Craig Newsome .50 1.25
AR19 Orlando Thomas .50 1.25
AR20 Tamarick Vanover 1.00 2.50

1996 Upper Deck Silver Helmet Cards

Randomly inserted in packs at a rate of one in 18, this 30-card standard-size set features double front Light F/X technology with each of the 30 NFL teams helmets on one side and two top stars on the other. We have sequenced this set below in alphabetical order within division order.

COMPLETE SET (30) 100.00 200.00
STATED ODDS 1:23
AC1 J.Blake D.Dunn 1.50 4.00
AC2 Testaverde E.Zeier 1.25 3.00
AC3 R.Thomas C.Sanders 1.25 3.00
AC4 M.Brunell J.O.Stewart 4.00 10.00
AC5 G.Lloyd K.Stewart 2.50 6.00
AE1 M.Faulk K.Dilger 3.00 8.00
AE2 W.Chrebet H.Douglas 4.00 10.00
AE3 D.Marino B.Milner 15.00 30.00
AE4 J.Kelly D.Holmes 2.50 6.00
AE5 D.Bledsoe C.Martin 7.50 20.00
AW1 S.Bono Vanover UER 1.50 4.00
AW2 C.Warren J.Galloway 2.50 6.00
AW3 N.Means A.Hayden 1.50 4.00
AW4 T.Brown N.Kaufman 2.50 6.00
AW5 J.Elway T.Davis 20.00 40.00
NC1 E.Kramer H.Salaam 1.50 4.00
NC2 H.Moore L.Elliss 1.50 4.00
NC3 C.Carter O.Thomas 2.50 6.00
NC4 E.Rhett D.Brooks 2.50 6.00
NC5 R.Brooks C.Newsome 2.50 6.00
NE1 G.Hearst F.Sanders 1.50 4.00
NE2 R.Hampton T.Wheatley 1.25 3.00
NE3 R.Watters M.Mamula 1.50 4.00
NE4 M.Westbrook T.Allen 2.50 6.00
NE5 E.Smith Sh.Williams 15.00 30.00
NW1 J.George D.Bush 1.50 4.00
NW2 S.Mills K.Collins 2.50 6.00
NW3 M.Bates M.Fields 1.25 3.00
NW4 I.Bruce Kev.Carter 1.50 4.00
NW5 J.Rice J.J.Stokes 10.00 20.00

1996 Upper Deck Silver Dan Marino

Randomly inserted in packs at a rate of one in 81, this 4-card standard-size set commemorates Dan's record breaking performances from the previous NFL season. The cards are numberded with an "RS" prefix.

COMPLETE SET (4) 25.00 60.00
COMMON CARD (RS1-RS4) 6.00 15.00
STATED ODDS 1:81

1996 Upper Deck Silver Prime Choice Rookies

This standard sized redemption set was available by returning a trade card randomly inserted in 1996 Upper Deck Silver. The cards contain an inset photo of the player and a full length foil accented shot of the player with "Prime Choice Rookie" placed in the upper left hand corner of the card with the player's name in the lower left hand corner. The backs contain a short biography with a color picture of the player. The redemption expired 8/30/96.

COMPLETE SET (20) 20.00 40.00
SET AVAILABLE VIA MAIL REDEMPTION
REDEMPT.CARD STATED ODDS 1:103
1 Keyshawn Johnson 2.00 5.00
2 Kevin Hardy .20 .50
3 Simeon Rice .60 1.50
4 Tim Biakabutuka .50 1.25
5 Terry Glenn 2.00 5.00
6 Rickey Dudley .30 .75
7 Alex Molden .20 .50
8 Regan Upshaw .20 .50
9 Eddie George 2.50 6.00
10 John Mobley .20 .50
11 Eddie Kennison .50 1.25
12 Marvin Harrison 5.00 12.00
13 Leeland McElroy .30 .75
14 Eric Moulds 2.50 6.00
15 Mike Alstott 2.00 5.00
16 Bobby Engram .30 .75
17 Derrick Mayes .30 .75
18 Karim Abdul-Jabbar .50 1.25
19 Stepfret Williams .20 .50
20 Jeff Lewis .30 .75

2004 Upper Deck Sportsfest

These cards were issued in groups of five over the course of three days at the 2004 Sportsfest card show in Chicago. Collectors would receive a group of 5 each day in exchange for 10 Upper Deck card wrappers that carried and SRP valued of $2.99 or higher. A 16th card was issued as an exchange card good for the first pick in the 2004 NBA draft.

STATED PRINT RUN 500 SER.#'d SETS
SF11 Tom Brady 1.00 2.50
SF12 Eli Manning 2.50 6.00

2005 Upper Deck Sportsfest

These cards were issued at the 2005 Sportsfest card show in Chicago. Collectors would receive a group of cards in exchange for a variety of Upper Deck card wrappers opened at Upper Deck's booth. Each card was serial numbered of 750.

COMPLETE SET (6) 12.50 25.00
NFL1 Michael Vick 1.00 2.50
NFL2 Tom Brady 2.50 6.00
NFL3 Eli Manning 3.00 8.00
NFL4 Peyton Manning 2.00 5.00
NFL5 Donovan McNabb 1.25 3.00
NFL6 Rex Grossman 1.00 2.50

2006 Upper Deck Sportsfest

UNPRICED AUTOS SER.#'d TO 5
NFL1 Peyton Manning 2.50 6.00
NFL2 Ben Roethlisberger 1.25 3.00
NFL4 Tom Brady 3.00 8.00
NFL5 Cedric Benson .60 1.50
NFL6 Shaun Alexander .60 1.50

2008 Upper Deck Sportsfest

COMPLETE SET (12) 15.00 40.00
UNPRICED AUTO PRINT RUN 5 SETS
SF3 Peyton Manning 1.00 2.50
SF6 Brian Urlacher .60 1.50
SF10 Devin Hester .60 1.50

2003 Upper Deck Standing O

Released in October of 2003, this retail only set consists of 84 cards, all of them veterans. Boxes contained 24 packs of 4 cards.

COMPLETE SET (84) 10.00 25.00
1 Michael Vick .25 .60
2 Tim Couch .20 .50
3 Joey Harrington .20 .50
4 Brett Favre .60 1.50
5 Donovan McNabb .25 .60
6 Jeff Garcia .20 .50
7 Chris Redman .20 .50
8 David Carr .20 .50
9 Steve McNair .25 .60
10 Chad Pennington .20 .50
11 Daunte Culpepper .25 .60
12 Tom Brady 1.25 3.00
13 Kurt Warner .25 .60
14 Brad Johnson .25 .60
15 Aaron Brooks .20 .50
16 Mark Brunell .25 .60
17 Drew Brees .30 .75
18 Peyton Manning .75 2.00
19 Drew Bledsoe .25 .60
20 Rich Gannon .25 .60
21 Kordell Stewart .20 .50
22 Josh McCown .25 .60
23 Chad Hutchinson .20 .50
24 Jake Delhomme .20 .50
25 Patrick Ramsey .25 .60
26 Jay Fiedler .20 .50
27 Trent Green .20 .50
28 Jake Plummer .20 .50
29 Tommy Maddox .20 .50
30 Matt Hasselbeck .20 .50
31 Kerry Collins .20 .50
32 Marshall Faulk .25 .60
33 Edgerrin James .25 .60
34 Ricky Williams .25 .60
35 Emmitt Smith .50 1.25
36 Deuce McAllister .25 .60
37 Ahman Green .25 .60
38 LaDainian Tomlinson .30 .75
39 Priest Holmes .20 .50
40 Curtis Martin .25 .60
41 Travis Henry .20 .50
42 Anthony Thomas .25 .60
43 Fred Taylor .20 .50
44 Jamal Lewis .25 .60
45 Michael Bennett .20 .50
46 Shaun Alexander .20 .50
47 Garrison Hearst .20 .50
48 Kevan Barlow .20 .50
49 Charlie Garner .25 .60
50 Clinton Portis .20 .50
51 Eddie George .25 .60
52 Corey Dillon .20 .50
53 Jerome Bettis .30 .75
54 Jeremy Shockey .20 .50
55 Tony Gonzalez .25 .60
56 Jerry Rice .60 1.50
57 Tim Brown .30 .75
58 Terrell Owens .25 .60
59 Randy Moss .25 .60
60 Keyshawn Johnson .30 .75
61 Marvin Harrison .25 .60
62 Peerless Price .20 .50
63 Chris Chambers .20 .50
64 David Boston .20 .50
65 Laveranues Coles .20 .50
66 Rod Gardner .20 .50
67 Isaac Bruce .30 .75
68 Torry Holt .25 .60
69 Troy Brown .20 .50
70 Antonio Bryant .20 .50
71 Plaxico Burress .20 .50
72 Antwaan Randle El .20 .50
73 Rod Smith .25 .60
74 Ashley Lelie .20 .50
75 Eric Moulds .20 .50
76 Chad Johnson .20 .50
77 Kevin Johnson .20 .50
78 Jevon Kearse .20 .50
79 Zach Thomas .25 .60
80 Roy Williams .20 .50
81 Julius Peppers .30 .75
82 Junior Seau .25 .60
83 Ray Lewis .30 .75
84 Brian Urlacher .30 .75

2003 Upper Deck Standing O Die Cuts

COMPLETE SET (84) 25.00 60.00
*DIE CUTS: 1X TO 2.5X BASIC CARDS
ONE PER PACK

2003 Upper Deck Standing O Rookies

Inserted at a rate of 1:4, this set highlights the NFL's best rookies from 2003.

COMPLETE SET (42) 60.00 150.00
STATED ODDS 1:4
*EMBOSSED: .8X TO 2X BASIC INSERTS
EMBOSSED STATED ODDS 1:24
*EMBOSSED DIE CUT: 2X TO 5X
EMBOSSED DIE CUT ODDS 1:480
1 Carson Palmer 1.50 4.00
2 Byron Leftwich 1.00 2.50
3 Kyle Boller .75 2.00
4 Rex Grossman 1.00 2.50
5 Dave Ragone .75 2.00
6 Chris Simms .75 2.00
7 Seneca Wallace 1.00 2.50
8 Brian St.Pierre .75 2.00
9 Brooks Bollinger 1.00 2.50
10 Kliff Kingsbury 1.25 3.00
11 Gibran Hamdan .75 2.00
12 Ken Dorsey 1.00 2.50
13 Willis McGahee 1.00 2.50
14 Larry Johnson 1.00 2.50
15 Musa Smith .75 2.00
16 B.J. Askew 1.00 2.50
17 Chris Brown .75 2.00
18 Justin Fargas 1.25 3.00
19 Artose Pinner .75 2.00
20 Domanick Davis 1.00 2.50
21 Onterrio Smith .75 2.00
22 Quentin Griffin 1.00 2.50
23 Charles Rogers 1.00 2.50
24 Andre Johnson 2.00 5.00
25 Bryant Johnson 1.25 3.00
26 Taylor Jacobs .75 2.00
27 Bethel Johnson .75 2.00
28 Anquan Boldin 1.25 3.00
29 Tyrone Calico .75 2.00
30 Teyo Johnson 1.00 2.50
31 Kelley Washington .75 2.00
32 Nate Burleson 1.00 2.50
33 Kevin Curtis .75 2.00
34 Billy McMullen .75 2.00
35 Dallas Clark 1.25 3.00
36 Ben Joppru .75 2.00
37 L.J. Smith 1.25 3.00
38 DeWayne Robertson 1.00 2.50
39 Marcus Trufant 1.00 2.50
40 Boss Bailey 1.00 2.50
41 Troy Polamalu 12.00 30.00
42 Terence Newman 1.25 3.00

2003 Upper Deck Standing O Signatures

Inserted at a rate of 1:480, this set features authentic player cut signatures. The print runs listed below were provided by Upper Deck.

STATED ODDS 1:480
SIAB Antonio Bryant/164* 6.00 15.00
SIAD Andre Davis/141* 6.00 15.00
SIAL Ashley Lelie/86* 6.00 15.00
SIAM Archie Manning/95* 15.00 30.00
SIBD Brandon Doman/141* 6.00 15.00
SIDC David Carr/86* 6.00 15.00
SIDF DeShaun Foster/95* 8.00 20.00
SIEC Eric Crouch/141* 10.00 25.00
SIJG Jabar Gaffney/141* 6.00 15.00
SIKC Kelly Campbell/141* 6.00 15.00
SIKK Kurt Kittner/86* 6.00 15.00
SILS Luke Staley/85* 6.00 15.00
SINH Napoleon Harris/141* 6.00 15.00
SIPM Peyton Manning/95* 60.00 100.00
SIRC Reche Caldwell/141* 6.00 15.00
SIRD Rohan Davey/141* 6.00 15.00
SIRJ Ron Johnson/141* 6.00 15.00
SIRW Roy Williams/149* 6.00 15.00

2003 Upper Deck Standing O Swatches

Inserted at a rate of 1:72, this set features game worn jersey swatches.

STATED ODDS 1:72
SWAB Antonio Bryant 3.00 8.00
SWAD Andre Davis 3.00 8.00
SWAR Antwaan Randle El 3.00 8.00
SWBJ Brad Johnson 4.00 10.00
SWBU Marc Bulger 3.00 8.00
SWCP Clinton Portis 3.00 8.00
SWIB Isaac Bruce 5.00 12.00
SWJB Jeff Blake 4.00 10.00
SWJG Jeff Garcia 3.00 8.00
SWJH Joey Harrington 3.00 8.00
SWJM Josh McCown 4.00 10.00
SWJP Jerry Porter 3.00 8.00
SWJS Jeremy Shockey 3.00 8.00
SWKM Keenan McCardell 4.00 10.00
SWMB Mark Brunell 4.00 10.00
SWMH Matt Hasselbeck 3.00 8.00
SWMV Michael Vick 4.00 10.00
SWPE Julius Peppers 5.00 12.00
SWPR Patrick Ramsey 4.00 10.00
SWRS Rod Smith 4.00 10.00
SWTB Tom Brady 20.00 50.00

2003 Upper Deck Star Rookie Sportsfest

is 6-card set was distributed by Upper Deck at the 2003 Sportsfest in Chicago. Collectors were required to open specific boxes of Upper Deck product at the booth in order to receive the set.

COMPLETE SET (6) 5.00 12.00
AJ Andre Johnson .75 2.00
BL Byron Leftwich .40 1.00
CP Carson Palmer .60 1.50
KB Kyle Boller .30 .75
RG Rex Grossman .40 1.00
WM Willis McGahee .40 1.00

2014 Upper Deck Star Rookies

COMPLETE SET (42) 6.00 15.00
COMP.FACT SET (42) 8.00 20.00
1 Johnny Manziel .30 .75
2 Marqise Lee .25 .60
3 Ka'Deem Carey .20 .50
4 Eric Ebron .25 .60
5 Teddy Bridgewater .30 .75
6 Sammy Watkins .30 .75
7 Carlos Hyde .25 .60
8 Tajh Boyd .20 .50
9 Donte Moncrief .20 .50
10 Derek Carr 1.25 3.00
11 Odell Beckham Jr. .50 1.25
12 Bishop Sankey .20 .50
13 Troy Niklas .20 .50
14 Martavis Bryant .25 .60
15 Jimmy Garoppolo 1.50 4.00
16 Brandin Cooks .30 .75
17 Jeremy Hill .25 .60
18 Logan Thomas .20 .50
19 Mike Davis .20 .50
20 Zach Mettenberger .20 .50
21 Kelvin Benjamin .30 .75
22 Charles Sims .20 .50
23 Austin Seferian-Jenkins .20 .50
24 Bruce Ellington .20 .50
25 David Fales .20 .50
26 Allen Robinson .30 .75
27 Devonta Freeman .30 .75
28 Jarvis Landry .40 1.00
29 Robert Herron .20 .50
30 Blake Bortles .25 .60
31 Mike Evans .50 1.25
32 Terrance West .20 .50
33 Josh Huff .25 .60
34 Ryan Grant .20 .50
35 Aaron Murray .20 .50
36 Davante Adams .30 .75
37 Lache Seastrunk .20 .50
38 Jace Amaro .20 .50

39 Jared Abbrederis .20 .50
40 Brett Smith .20 .50
41 Paul Richardson .25 .60
42 De'Anthony Thomas .20 .50

2014 Upper Deck Star Rookies Autographs

STATED ODDS 1:24 FACTORY SET
1 Johnny Manziel 15.00 40.00
2 Marqise Lee
3 Ka'Deem Carey 4.00 10.00
4 Eric Ebron
5 Teddy Bridgewater 6.00 15.00
6 Sammy Watkins 6.00 15.00
7 Carlos Hyde 5.00 12.00
8 Tajh Boyd
9 Donte Moncrief 4.00 10.00
10 Derek Carr 25.00 60.00
11 Odell Beckham Jr. 50.00 100.00
12 Bishop Sankey 4.00 10.00
13 Troy Niklas
14 Martavis Bryant 5.00 12.00
15 Jimmy Garoppolo 30.00 60.00
16 Brandin Cooks 6.00 15.00
17 Jeremy Hill 5.00 12.00
18 Logan Thomas 4.00 10.00
19 Mike Davis 4.00 10.00
20 Zach Mettenberger 4.00 10.00
21 Kelvin Benjamin 6.00 15.00
22 Charles Sims 4.00 10.00
23 Austin Seferian-Jenkins 4.00 10.00
24 Bruce Ellington 4.00 10.00
25 David Fales 4.00 10.00
26 Allen Robinson 6.00 15.00
27 Devonta Freeman 6.00 15.00
28 Jarvis Landry 8.00 20.00
29 Robert Herron
30 Blake Bortles 5.00 12.00
31 Mike Evans 10.00 25.00
32 Terrance West 4.00 10.00
33 Josh Huff
34 Ryan Grant 4.00 10.00
35 Aaron Murray 4.00 10.00
36 Davante Adams
37 Lache Seastrunk
38 Jace Amaro
39 Jared Abbrederis 4.00 10.00
40 Brett Smith
41 Paul Richardson
42 De'Anthony Thomas 4.00 10.00

2001 Upper Deck Top Tier

This 280 card set was issued in five-card packs. The first 180 cards in the set are NFL veterans while cards 181 through 280 feature Rookie Cards. The Rookie Cards were issued either in a stated print run of 1500, 2000 or 2500.

COMP.SET w/o SP's (180) 20.00 40.00
1 Jake Plummer .25 .60
2 David Boston .25 .60
3 Thomas Jones .25 .60
4 Frank Sanders .25 .60
5 Tony Martin .30 .75
6 Jamal Anderson .30 .75
7 Chris Chandler .30 .75
8 Shawn Jefferson .25 .60
9 Jammi German .25 .60
10 Terance Mathis .25 .60
11 Jamal Lewis .40 1.00
12 Shannon Sharpe .30 .75
13 Elvis Grbac .30 .75
14 Ray Lewis .40 1.00
15 Qadry Ismail .25 .60
16 Sam Gash .25 .60
17 Rob Johnson .30 .75
18 Eric Moulds .25 .60
19 Sammy Morris .25 .60
20 Shawn Bryson .25 .60
21 Jeremy McDaniel .25 .60
22 Muhsin Muhammad .25 .60
23 Brad Hoover .30 .75
24 Tim Biakabutuka .25 .60
25 Donald Hayes .25 .60
26 Dameyune Craig .25 .60
27 Wesley Walls .25 .60
28 Cade McNown .30 .75
29 James Allen .25 .60
30 Marcus Robinson .30 .75
31 Brian Urlacher .50 1.25
32 Bobby Engram .25 .60
33 Shane Matthews .25 .60
34 Peter Warrick .25 .60
35 Corey Dillon .25 .60
36 Akili Smith .25 .60
37 Scott Mitchell .25 .60
38 Jon Kitna .25 .60
39 Tim Couch .25 .60
40 Kevin Johnson .25 .60
41 Travis Prentice .25 .60
42 Spergon Wynn .25 .60
43 Jamel White .25 .60
44 JaJuan Dawson .25 .60
45 Courtney Brown .25 .60
46 Tony Banks .25 .60
47 Emmitt Smith .60 1.50
48 Joey Galloway .30 .75
49 Rocket Ismail .30 .75
50 Anthony Wright .25 .60
51 Darren Woodson .30 .75
52 Terrell Davis .30 .75
53 Mike Anderson .25 .60
54 Brian Griese .25 .60
55 Rod Smith .30 .75
56 Ed McCaffrey .30 .75
57 Eddie Kennison .30 .75
58 Olandis Gary .25 .60
59 Charlie Batch .25 .60
60 Germane Crowell .25 .60
61 James O. Stewart .25 .60
62 Johnnie Morton .30 .75
63 Desmond Howard .30 .75
64 Brett Favre .75 2.00
65 Antonio Freeman .40 1.00
66 Dorsey Levens .30 .75
67 Ahman Green .30 .75
68 Bill Schroeder .30 .75
69 Bubba Franks .25 .60
70 Peyton Manning 1.00 2.50
71 Edgerrin James .30 .75
72 Marvin Harrison .30 .75
73 Jerome Pathon .25 .60
74 Lennox Gordon .25 .60
75 Terrence Wilkins .25 .60
76 Mark Brunell .30 .75
77 Fred Taylor .25 .60
78 Jimmy Smith .30 .75
79 Keenan McCardell .30 .75
80 Kevin Hardy .25 .60
81 Stacey Mack .25 .60
82 Tony Gonzalez .30 .75
83 Derrick Alexander .25 .60
84 Priest Holmes .25 .60
85 Trent Green .25 .60
86 Tony Horne .25 .60
87 Oronde Gadsden .25 .60
88 Lamar Smith .30 .75
89 Jay Fiedler .30 .75
90 Zach Thomas .30 .75
91 Ray Lucas .25 .60
92 O.J. McDuffie .25 .60
93 Randy Moss .30 .75
94 Cris Carter .40 1.00
95 Daunte Culpepper .30 .75
96 Robert Griffith .25 .60
97 Jake Reed .30 .75
98 Drew Bledsoe .30 .75
99 Terry Glenn .30 .75
100 Kevin Faulk .25 .60
101 Michael Bishop .30 .75
102 Troy Brown .25 .60
103 Ricky Williams .30 .75
104 Jeff Blake .30 .75
105 Joe Horn .25 .60
106 Willie Jackson .25 .60
107 Aaron Brooks .25 .60
108 Albert Connell .25 .60
109 Kerry Collins .25 .60
110 Amani Toomer .25 .60
111 Ron Dayne .30 .75
112 Tiki Barber .30 .75
113 Ike Hilliard .25 .60
114 Ron Dixon .25 .60
115 Michael Strahan .30 .75
116 Vinny Testaverde .25 .60
117 Wayne Chrebet .25 .60
118 Curtis Martin .30 .75
119 Richie Anderson .25 .60
120 Laveranues Coles .30 .75
121 Chad Pennington .25 .60
122 Tim Brown .40 1.00
123 Rich Gannon .30 .75
124 Tyrone Wheatley .30 .75
125 Charlie Garner .30 .75
126 Jerry Rice .75 2.00
127 Charles Woodson .40 1.00
128 Duce Staley .25 .60
129 Donovan McNabb .30 .75
130 Todd Pinkston .25 .60
131 Chad Lewis .25 .60
132 Brian Mitchell .30 .75
133 Kordell Stewart .25 .60
134 Jerome Bettis .40 1.00
135 Plaxico Burress .25 .60
136 Bobby Shaw .25 .60
137 Hines Ward .30 .75
138 Marshall Faulk .30 .75
139 Kurt Warner .60 1.50
140 Isaac Bruce .40 1.00
141 Torry Holt .30 .75
142 Justin Watson .25 .60
143 Az-Zahir Hakim .25 .60
144 Junior Seau .30 .75
145 Curtis Conway .30 .75
146 Doug Flutie .30 .75
147 Jeff Graham .25 .60
148 Freddie Jones .25 .60
149 Rodney Harrison .25 .60
150 Jeff Garcia .25 .60
151 Tai Streets .25 .60
152 Terrell Owens .30 .75
153 J.J. Stokes .25 .60
154 Garrison Hearst .30 .75
155 Paul Smith .25 .60
156 Ricky Watters .30 .75
157 Shaun Alexander .25 .60
158 Matt Hasselbeck .25 .60
159 Brock Huard .25 .60
160 Darrell Jackson .30 .75
161 Karsten Bailey .25 .60
162 Warrick Dunn .25 .60
163 Shaun King .25 .60
164 Reidel Anthony .25 .60
165 Mike Alstott .25 .60
166 Jacquez Green .25 .60
167 Brad Johnson .30 .75
168 Keyshawn Johnson .30 .75
169 Eddie George .40 1.00
170 Steve McNair .30 .75
171 Neil O'Donnell .30 .75
172 Derrick Mason .25 .60
173 Frank Wycheck .25 .60
174 Chris Sanders .25 .60
175 Jevon Kearse .25 .60
176 Jeff George .30 .75
177 Stephen Davis .25 .60
178 Kevin Lockett .25 .60
179 Michael Westbrook .25 .60
180 Stephen Alexander .25 .60
181 Arnold Jackson/2000 RC 1.00 2.50
182 Bobby Newcombe/2000 RC 1.25 3.00
183 Vinny Sutherland/2000 RC 1.00 2.50
184 Michael Vick/1500 RC 3.00 8.00
185 Quentin McCord/2500 RC 1.00 2.50
186 Todd Heap/1500 RC 1.50 4.00
187 Chris Barnes/2000 RC 1.00 2.50
188 Travis Henry/1500 RC 1.50 4.00
189 Reggie Germany/2500 RC .75 2.00
190 Tim Hasselbeck/2000 RC 1.25 3.00
191 Dan Morgan/2500 RC 1.00 2.50
192 Dee Brown/2000 RC 1.00 2.50
193 Chris Weinke/2000 RC 1.25 3.00
194 David Terrell/1500 RC 1.50 4.00
195 Anthony Thomas/1500 RC 2.00 5.00
196 Rudi Johnson/2500 RC 1.25 3.00
197 Chad Johnson/1500 RC 2.00 5.00
198 Quincy Morgan/2500 RC 1.00 2.50
199 James Jackson/1500 RC 1.25 3.00
200 Quincy Carter/2000 RC 1.25 3.00
201 Kevin Kasper/2500 RC .75 2.00
202 Scotty Anderson/2000 RC 1.00 2.50
203 Mike McMahon/1500 RC 1.50 4.00
204 Robert Ferguson/1500 RC 2.00 5.00
205 David Martin/2000 RC 1.00 2.50
206 Reggie Wayne/2000 RC 2.00 5.00
207 K.Gbaja-Biamila/2500 RC 1.25 3.00
208 Snoop Minnis/2000 RC 1.00 2.50
209 Derrick Blaylock/1500 RC 1.50 4.00
210 Josh Heupel/2500 RC 1.25 3.00
211 Travis Minor/2000 RC 1.25 3.00
212 Chris Chambers/2000 RC 1.00 2.50
213 Michael Bennett/1500 RC 1.50 4.00
214 Justin Smith/1500 RC 2.50 6.00
215 Deuce McAllister/2000 RC 1.50 4.00
216 Moran Norris/2500 RC .75 2.00
217 Onome Ojo/2500 RC .75 2.00
218 Jesse Palmer/1500 RC 1.50 4.00
219 Santana Moss/2000 RC 1.50 4.00
220 LaMont Jordan/2000 RC 1.50 4.00
221 Marq Tuiasosopo/2000 RC 1.25 3.00
222 A.J. Feeley/1500 RC 1.50 4.00
223 Correll Buckhalter/1500 RC 1.25 3.00
224 Freddie Mitchell/2000 RC 1.00 2.50
225 Chris Taylor/2500 RC .75 2.00
226 Drew Brees/1500 RC 40.00 80.00
227 LaDain Tomlinson/1500 RC 6.00 15.00
228 Dave Dickenson/2000 RC 1.25 3.00
229 Kevan Barlow/2000 RC 1.25 3.00
230 Andre Carter/2000 RC 1.25 3.00
231 Cedrick Wilson/2000 RC 1.25 3.00
232 David Allen/2500 RC .75 2.00
233 Alex Bannister/1500 RC 1.25 3.00
234 Josh Booty/2000 RC 1.25 3.00
235 Koren Robinson/2500 RC 1.00 2.50
236 Damione Lewis/2000 RC 1.25 3.00
237 Eddie Berlin/2500 RC .75 2.00
238 Damerien McCants/1500 RC 1.50 4.00
239 Sage Rosenfels/2500 RC 1.00 2.50
240 Rod Gardner/1500 RC 1.50 4.00
241 Billy Baber/2500 RC .75 2.00
242 Dan Alexander/2000 RC 1.25 3.00
243 Reggie White/2500 RC .75 2.00
244 Adam Archuleta/2000 RC 1.25 3.00
245 Derrick Gibson/2500 RC .75 2.00
246 Hakim Akbar/2000 RC 1.00 2.50
247 Bra Manumaleuna/2500 RC 1.00 2.50
248 Andre King/2500 RC .75 2.00
249 Corey Alston/2500 RC .75 2.00
250 Fred Smoot/1500 RC 1.50 4.00
251 Kyle Vanden Bosch/2500 RC 1.25 3.00
252 Richard Seymour/1500 RC 2.00 5.00
253 Derek Combs/2000 RC 1.00 2.50
254 Ken-Yon Rambo/2500 RC .75 2.00
255 Joey Getherall/2000 RC 1.00 2.50
256 Jonathan Carter/1500 RC 1.25 3.00
257 Gerard Warren/1500 RC 1.50 4.00
258 Carlos Polk/2000 RC 1.00 2.50
259 Milton Wynn/2500 RC .75 2.00
260 Ronney Daniels/2000 RC 1.00 2.50
261 Edgerton Hartwell/1500 RC 1.25 3.00
262 Steve Smith/2000 RC 3.00 8.00
263 T.J. Houshmanza/1500 RC 1.50 4.00
264 Alge Crumpler/2000 RC 1.50 4.00
265 Torrance Marshall/1500 RC 1.25 3.00
266 Tommy Polley/2000 RC 1.00 2.50
267 Sedrick Hodge/2000 RC 1.00 2.50
268 Kendrell Bell/2500 RC 1.25 3.00
269 Jamie Winborn/1500 RC 1.50 4.00
270 Brian Allen/2000 RC 1.00 2.50
271 Brandon Spoon/1500 RC 1.50 4.00
272 Paul Toviessa/2000 RC 1.00 2.50
273 Aaron Schobel/2500 RC 1.25 3.00
274 Will Allen/2500 RC 1.25 3.00
275 Jamar Fletcher/1500 RC 1.25 3.00
276 Andre Dyson/2000 RC 1.00 2.50
277 Nate Clements/2500 RC 1.00 2.50
278 Willie Middlebrooks/2500 RC 1.00 2.50
279 Ken Lucas/2500 RC 1.00 2.50
280 Jamal Reynolds/2000 RC 1.00 2.50

2001 Upper Deck Top Tier Home and Away Jerseys

Inserted at a rate of one in 239, these cards feature 2001 NFL rookies and two game-worn uniform swatches. One swatch features the players home jersey and the other swatch features the road jersey.

OVERALL JSY or BALL ODDS 1:239
HACC Chris Chambers 2.50 6.00
HADB Drew Brees 15.00 40.00
HADM Dan Morgan 3.00 8.00
HAFM Freddie Mitchell 2.50 6.00
HAJH Josh Heupel 4.00 10.00
HAJJ James Jackson 2.50 6.00
HAJP Jesse Palmer 3.00 8.00
HAKB Kevan Barlow 3.00 8.00
HAKR Koren Robinson 3.00 8.00
HAMB Michael Bennett 3.00 8.00
HAMC Deuce McAllister 4.00 10.00
HAMM Mike McMahon 3.00 8.00
HAMT Marques Tuiasosopo 3.00 8.00
HAMV Michael Vick 6.00 15.00
HAQM Quincy Morgan 3.00 8.00
HARF Robert Ferguson 4.00 10.00
HARG Rod Gardner 3.00 8.00
HARJ Rudi Johnson 4.00 10.00
HARW Reggie Wayne 5.00 12.00
HASM Santana Moss 4.00 10.00
HATH Travis Henry 3.00 8.00
HATM Travis Minor 3.00 8.00

2001 Upper Deck Top Tier Rookie Duos Footballs

sued at a rate of one in 239, these cards feature a pair of NFL rookies along with two pieces of game ball swatches.

OVERALL JSY or BALL ODDS 1:239
RDBT D.Brees/L.Tomlinson 15.00 40.00
RDHC J.Heupel/C.Chambers 4.00 10.00
RDJJ C.Johnson/R.Johnson 4.00 10.00
RDMJ Q.Morgan/J.Jackson 3.00 8.00
RDMW R.Wayne/S.Moss 5.00 12.00
RDRG K.Robinson/R.Gardner 3.00 8.00
RDTT A.Thomas/D.Terrell 4.00 10.00
RDVB M.Vick/D.Brees 15.00 40.00
RDWM C.Weinke/D.Morgan 3.00 8.00

2001 Upper Deck Top Tier Then and Now Jerseys

sued at a rate of one in 239, these seven cards feature the player as well as two game-worn uniform swatches. One swatch is taken from a college uniform and the other is taken from their NFL's team uniform.

OVERALL JSY or BALL ODDS 1:239
TNDM Deuce McAllister 4.00 10.00
TNFM Freddie Mitchell 2.50 6.00
TNJJ J.J. Stokes 2.50 6.00
TNJS Junior Seau UER 3.00 8.00
(Sothern California on back)
TNRD Ron Dayne 3.00 8.00
TNTA Troy Aikman 5.00 12.00

2001 Upper Deck Top Tier Tri-Stars Footballs

This 8-card set, issued at a rate of one in 239, featured either three teammates or three players with something in common along with a piece of a game ball.

OVERALL JSY or BALL ODDS 1:239
3SCH McNown/Urlacher/Terrell 5.00 12.00
3SGB Favre/Green/Freeman 8.00 20.00
3SIC James/Manning/Harrison 10.00 25.00
3SMD Heupel/Minor/Chambers 4.00 10.00
3SMV Culpepper/Moss/Carter 4.00 10.00
3SNO Brooks/Williams/Horn 3.00 8.00
3SSF Garcia/Owens/Stokes 3.00 8.00
3STB Dunn/Alstott/Key.Johnson 2.50 6.00

2001 Upper Deck Top Tier Two of a Kind Footballs

sued at a rate in one in 239, these 9 cards feature two NFL players along a piece of a NFL game ball.

OVERALL JSY or BALL ODDS 1:239
2KCV D.Culpepper/M.Vick 6.00 15.00
2KDB R.Dayne/M.Bennett 3.00 8.00
2KFF B.Favre/R.Ferguson 8.00 20.00
2KJJ K.Johnson/C.Johnson 4.00 10.00
2KJT E.James/L.Tomlinson 12.00 30.00
2KMT R.Moss/D.Terrell 3.00 8.00
2KNO R.Williams/D.McAllister 4.00 10.00
2KUM B.Urlacher/D.Morgan 5.00 12.00
2KWM P.Warrick/S.Minnis 2.50 6.00

2007 Upper Deck Trilogy

This 184-card set was released in October, 2007. The set was issued into the hobby in three-card packs, with a $30 SRP, which came nine packs to a box. Cards number 1-100 feature veterans in alphabetical team order while cards number 101-184 feature 2007 NFL rookies that were issued to a stated print run of 399 serial numbered sets.

1 Matt Leinart .50 1.25
2 Anquan Boldin .50 1.25
3 Larry Fitzgerald .60 1.50
4 Edgerrin James .60 1.50
5 Michael Vick .60 1.50
6 Warrick Dunn .50 1.25
7 Joe Horn .50 1.25
8 Steve McNair .60 1.50
9 Willis McGahee .50 1.25
10 Mark Clayton .50 1.25
11 J.P. Losman .50 1.25
12 Lee Evans .60 1.50
13 Anthony Thomas .50 1.25
14 Jake Delhomme .50 1.25
15 DeAngelo Williams .50 1.25
16 Steve Smith .60 1.50
17 Rex Grossman .50 1.25
18 Cedric Benson .50 1.25
19 Brian Urlacher .75 2.00
20 Carson Palmer .60 1.50
21 Rudi Johnson .50 1.25
22 Chad Johnson .50 1.25
23 Charlie Frye .60 1.50
24 Braylon Edwards .50 1.25
25 Kellen Winslow .50 1.25
26 Tony Romo 1.00 2.50
27 Julius Jones .50 1.25
28 Terrell Owens .60 1.50
29 Jay Cutler .50 1.25
30 Travis Henry .60 1.50
31 Javon Walker .60 1.50
32 Jon Kitna .50 1.25
33 Roy Williams WR .50 1.25
34 Tatum Bell .50 1.25
35 Brett Favre 1.50 4.00
36 Donald Driver .60 1.50
37 Greg Jennings .50 1.25
38 Matt Schaub .50 1.25
39 Ahman Green .60 1.50
40 Andre Johnson .60 1.50
41 Peyton Manning 2.00 5.00
42 Joseph Addai .50 1.25
43 Marvin Harrison .60 1.50
44 Reggie Wayne .60 1.50
45 Byron Leftwich .50 1.25
46 Maurice Jones-Drew .50 1.25
47 Fred Taylor .50 1.25
48 Damon Huard .60 1.50
49 Larry Johnson .50 1.25
50 Tony Gonzalez .60 1.50
51 Daunte Culpepper .60 1.50
52 Ronnie Brown .50 1.25
53 Chris Chambers .50 1.25
54 Tarvaris Jackson .50 1.25
55 Chester Taylor .50 1.25
56 Troy Williamson .50 1.25
57 Tom Brady 2.50 6.00
58 Laurence Maroney .60 1.50
59 Randy Moss .60 1.50
60 Drew Brees .75 2.00
61 Reggie Bush .50 1.25
62 Deuce McAllister .60 1.50
63 Marques Colston .50 1.25
64 Eli Manning .60 1.50
65 Brandon Jacobs .50 1.25
66 Plaxico Burress .50 1.25
67 Chad Pennington .50 1.25
68 Thomas Jones .50 1.25
69 Laveranues Coles .50 1.25
70 Nnamdi Asomugha .50 1.25
71 LaMont Jordan .60 1.50
72 Ronald Curry .50 1.25
73 Donovan McNabb .60 1.50
74 Brian Westbrook .50 1.25
75 Reggie Brown .50 1.25
76 Ben Roethlisberger .75 2.00
77 Willie Parker .60 1.50
78 Hines Ward .60 1.50
79 Philip Rivers .75 2.00
80 LaDainian Tomlinson .75 2.00
81 Antonio Gates .75 2.00
82 Shawne Merriman .50 1.25
83 Alex Smith QB .60 1.50
84 Frank Gore .60 1.50
85 Vernon Davis .50 1.25
86 Matt Hasselbeck .50 1.25
87 Shaun Alexander .50 1.25
88 Deion Branch .50 1.25
89 Marc Bulger .50 1.25
90 Steven Jackson .50 1.25
91 Torry Holt .60 1.50
92 Chris Simms .50 1.25
93 Cadillac Williams .60 1.50
94 Joey Galloway .60 1.50
95 Vince Young .50 1.25
96 LenDale White .60 1.50
97 David Givens .50 1.25
98 Jason Campbell .50 1.25
99 Clinton Portis .50 1.25
100 Ladell Betts .50 1.25
101 JaMarcus Russell RC 1.50 4.00
102 Brady Quinn RC 1.50 4.00
103 Adrian Peterson RC 15.00 40.00
104 Marshawn Lynch RC 3.00 8.00
105 Anthony Gonzalez RC 1.50 4.00
106 Brian Leonard RC 1.50 4.00
107 Calvin Johnson RC 10.00 25.00
108 Darrelle Revis RC 2.00 5.00
109 Drew Stanton RC 1.50 4.00
110 Dwayne Bowe RC 1.50 4.00
111 Dwayne Jarrett RC 2.00 5.00
112 Kenny Irons RC 1.50 4.00
113 Kevin Kolb RC 2.00 5.00
114 LaRon Landry RC 2.50 6.00
115 Leon Hall RC 1.50 4.00
116 Robert Meachem RC 2.00 5.00
117 Sidney Rice RC 2.00 5.00
118 Steve Smith USC RC 1.50 4.00
119 Ted Ginn Jr. RC 2.00 5.00
120 Troy Smith RC 1.50 4.00
121 Adam Carriker RC 1.50 4.00
122 Alan Branch RC 1.50 4.00
123 Amobi Okoye RC 2.00 5.00
124 Antonio Pittman RC 1.50 4.00
125 Aundrae Allison RC 1.50 4.00
126 Brandon Jackson RC 1.50 4.00
127 Brandon Meriweather RC 2.00 5.00
128 Chansi Stuckey RC 2.00 5.00
129 Chris Henry RB RC 1.50 4.00
130 Chris Leak RC 1.50 4.00
131 Courtney Taylor RC 1.50 4.00
132 Craig Buster Davis RC 1.50 4.00
133 Dallas Baker RC 1.50 4.00
134 Darius Walker RC 1.50 4.00
135 David Ball RC 1.50 4.00
136 David Clowney RC 1.50 4.00
137 David Irons RC 1.50 4.00
138 Daymeion Hughes RC 1.50 4.00
139 DeShawn Wynn RC 1.50 4.00
140 Drew Tate RC 2.00 5.00
141 Dwayne Wright RC 1.50 4.00
142 Eric Wright RC 1.50 4.00
143 Gaines Adams RC 2.00 5.00
144 Garrett Wolfe RC 1.50 4.00
145 Gary Russell RC 2.00 5.00
146 Greg Olsen RC 2.50 6.00
147 H.B. Blades RC 1.50 4.00
148 Isaiah Stanback RC 1.50 4.00
149 Jamaal Anderson RC 2.00 5.00
150 Jared Zabransky RC 1.50 4.00
151 Jason Hill RC 1.50 4.00
152 Jeff Rowe RC 1.50 4.00
153 Joe Thomas RC 2.50 6.00
154 Joel Filani RC 1.50 4.00
155 John Beck RC 1.50 4.00
156 Johnnie Lee Higgins RC 1.50 4.00
157 Jordan Palmer RC 2.00 5.00
158 Kenneth Darby RC 1.50 4.00
159 Kolby Smith RC 1.50 4.00
160 LaMarr Woodley RC 3.00 8.00
161 Lawrence Timmons RC 2.50 6.00
162 Legedu Naanee RC 2.00 5.00
163 Lorenzo Booker RC 2.00 5.00
164 Marcus McCauley RC 1.50 4.00
165 Matt Moore RC 2.50 6.00
166 Michael Bush RC 1.50 4.00
167 Michael Griffin RC 1.50 4.00
168 Patrick Willis RC 2.50 6.00
169 Paul Posluszny RC 1.50 4.00
170 Paul Williams RC 1.50 4.00
171 Quentin Moses RC 1.50 4.00
172 Reggie Nelson RC 1.50 4.00
173 Rhema McKnight RC 1.50 4.00
174 Scott Chandler RC 2.50 6.00
175 Selvin Young RC 1.50 4.00
176 Syvelle Newton RC 2.00 5.00
177 Tony Hunt RC 1.50 4.00
178 Trent Edwards RC 1.50 4.00
179 Tyler Palko RC 2.50 6.00
180 Tyrone Moss RC 1.50 4.00
181 Yamon Figurs RC 1.50 4.00
182 Zach Miller RC 1.50 4.00
183 Laurent Robinson RC 2.50 6.00
184 James Jones RC 1.50 4.00

2007 Upper Deck Trilogy Gold

ETS 1-100: 2X TO 5X BASIC CARDS
VETERAN PRINT RUN 99 SER.#'d SETS
*ROOKIES 101-184: 1X TO 2.5X BASIC CARDS
ROOKIE PRINT RUN 33 SER.#'d SETS
103 Adrian Peterson 100.00 200.00

2007 Upper Deck Trilogy Platinum

UNPRICED PLATINUM PRINT RUN 3

2007 Upper Deck Trilogy America's Game Signatures

STATED PRINT RUN 33-199
AA Aundrae Allison/199 3.00 8.00
AB Alan Branch/199 3.00 8.00
AG Anthony Gonzalez/133 3.00 8.00
BM Brandon Meriweather/199 4.00 10.00
DB Dallas Baker/199 3.00 8.00
DJ Dwayne Jarrett/199 4.00 10.00
DT Drew Tate/199 4.00 10.00
GR Gary Russell/199 4.00 10.00
IS Isaiah Stanback/199 3.00 8.00
JF Joel Filani/199 3.00 8.00
JH Jason Hill/133 3.00 8.00
JR Jeff Rowe/199 3.00 8.00
JZ Jared Zabransky/199 3.00 8.00
KK Kevin Kolb/199 4.00 10.00
MM Marcus McCauley/199 3.00 8.00
PM Peyton Manning/33 75.00 150.00
RC Roger Craig/169 8.00 20.00
RM Robert Meachem/199 4.00 10.00
SN Syvelle Newton/199 4.00 10.00
TM Tyrone Moss/199 3.00 8.00
WI Paul Williams/199 3.00 8.00
YF Yamon Figurs/199 3.00 8.00

2007 Upper Deck Trilogy Auto Focus Autographs

STATED PRINT RUN 9-99
SERIAL #'d UNDER 25 NOT PRICED
AB Anquan Boldin/33 10.00 25.00
BF Brett Favre/33 125.00 250.00
BQ Brady Quinn/33 6.00 15.00
CL Chris Leak/99 6.00 15.00
GJ Greg Jennings/33 10.00 25.00
JA Joseph Addai/33 15.00 40.00
JH Johnnie Lee Higgins/99 6.00 15.00
JO Chad Johnson/33 10.00 25.00
JR JaMarcus Russell/33 12.00 30.00
JZ Jared Zabransky/99 6.00 15.00
MB Marc Bulger/33 10.00 25.00
ML Marshawn Lynch/33 15.00 40.00
PP Paul Posluszny/99 10.00 25.00
RB Reggie Brown/33 10.00 25.00
RW Reggie Wayne/33 EXCH 12.00 30.00
TE Trent Edwards/99 10.00 25.00
TG Ted Ginn/33 12.00 30.00
TH T.J. Houshmandzadeh/33 10.00 25.00
VY Vince Young/33 15.00 40.00

2007 Upper Deck Trilogy Crystal Clear Combos Autographs

ATED PRINT RUN 99 SER.#'d SETS
HB L.Hall/A.Branch 5.00 12.00
LB C.Leak/D.Baker 5.00 12.00

2007 Upper Deck Trilogy Crystal Clear Trios Autographs

PRICED TRIO AU PRINT RUN 9

2007 Upper Deck Trilogy Graphiti Autographs

STATED PRINT RUN 10-199
AA Aundrae Allison/199 3.00 8.00
AB Alan Branch/199 3.00 8.00
AG Anthony Gonzalez/199 3.00 8.00
AO Amobi Okoye/33 8.00 20.00
BA David Ball/199 3.00 8.00
CH Chris Henry RB/199 3.00 8.00
CS Chansi Stuckey/199 4.00 10.00
DA Darius Walker/199 3.00 8.00
DB Dallas Baker/199 3.00 8.00
DC David Clowney/199 3.00 8.00
DT Drew Tate/199 4.00 10.00
DW DeShawn Wynn/199 3.00 8.00
GR Gary Russell/199 4.00 10.00
IS Isaiah Stanback/199 3.00 8.00
JF Joel Filani/199 3.00 8.00
JR Jeff Rowe/199 3.00 8.00
JS Jared Zabransky/199 3.00 8.00
KD Kenneth Darby/199 3.00 8.00
KK Kevin Kolb/199 4.00 10.00
MM Marcus McCauley/199 3.00 8.00
PP Paul Posluszny/199 3.00 8.00
PW Paul Williams/199 3.00 8.00
QM Quentin Moses/199 3.00 8.00
SN Syvelle Newton/199 4.00 10.00
TM Tyrone Moss/199 3.00 8.00
YF Yamon Figurs/199 3.00 8.00
ZM Zach Miller/199 3.00 8.00

2007 Upper Deck Trilogy Materials Silver

STATED PRINT RUN 199 SER.#'d SETS
*GOLD/33: .6X TO 1.5X SILVER/199
GOLD PRINT RUN 33 SER.#'d SETS
UNPRICED PLATINUM PRINT RUN 3
*PATCH/79: .6X TO 1.5X SILVER/199
PATCH PRINT RUN 79 SER.#'d SETS
*PATCH HOLOGOLD/33: .8X TO 2X SLV/199
PATCH HOLOGOLD PRINT RUN 33 SER.#'d SETS
AB Anquan Boldin 2.50 6.00
AP Adrian Peterson 20.00 50.00
BJ Brandon Jacobs 2.50 6.00
BL Byron Leftwich 2.50 6.00
BQ Brady Quinn 1.50 4.00
CH Chris Henry RB 1.50 4.00
CJ Chad Johnson 2.50 6.00
CP Chad Pennington 2.50 6.00
DB Drew Bennett 2.50 6.00
DD Donald Driver 3.00 8.00
DF DeShaun Foster 3.00 8.00
JB John Beck 1.50 4.00
JC Jay Cutler 2.50 6.00
JP Julius Peppers 3.00 8.00
JR JaMarcus Russell 1.50 4.00
JS Jeremy Shockey 2.50 6.00
LF Larry Fitzgerald 3.00 8.00
MB Marion Barber 5.00 12.00
ML Marshawn Lynch 3.00 8.00
PB Plaxico Burress 2.50 6.00
PM Peyton Manning 10.00 25.00
RG Rex Grossman 2.50 6.00
RM Robert Meachem 2.00 5.00
RW Roy Williams WR 2.50 6.00
SH Santonio Holmes 2.50 6.00
SR Sidney Rice 2.00 5.00
TG Ted Ginn Jr. 2.00 5.00
VY Vince Young 2.50 6.00
WD Warrick Dunn 2.50 6.00
WM Willis McGahee 2.50 6.00

2007 Upper Deck Trilogy Rookie Autographed Patches

ATED PRINT RUN 33 SER.#'d SETS
AG Anthony Gonzalez 12.00 30.00
AP Adrian Peterson 200.00 400.00
BJ Brandon Jackson 12.00 30.00
BL Brian Leonard 12.00 30.00
BQ Brady Quinn 15.00 40.00
CH Chris Henry RB 12.00 30.00
CJ Calvin Johnson 100.00 200.00
DD Dwayne Bowe 20.00 50.00
DJ Dwayne Jarrett 15.00 40.00
DS Drew Stanton 12.00 30.00
GO Greg Olsen 20.00 50.00
GW Garrett Wolfe 12.00 30.00
HI Johnnie Lee Higgins 12.00 30.00
JB John Beck 12.00 30.00
JH Jason Hill 12.00 30.00
JR JaMarcus Russell 15.00 40.00
JT Joe Thomas 20.00 50.00
KI Kenny Irons 12.00 30.00
KK Kevin Kolb 15.00 40.00
LB Lorenzo Booker 15.00 40.00
MB Michael Bush 12.00 30.00
ML Marshawn Lynch 30.00 80.00
PI Antonio Pittman 12.00 30.00
PW Patrick Willis 40.00 80.00
RM Robert Meachem 15.00 40.00
SR Sidney Rice 15.00 40.00
SS Steve Smith USC 12.00 30.00
TE Trent Edwards 15.00 40.00
TG Ted Ginn Jr. 15.00 40.00
TH Tony Hunt 12.00 30.00
WI Paul Williams 12.00 30.00
YF Yamon Figurs 12.00 30.00

2007 Upper Deck Trilogy Rookie Autographs

STATED PRINT RUN 99-133
101 JaMarcus Russell/99 8.00 20.00
102 Brady Quinn/99 5.00 12.00
104 Marshawn Lynch/99 30.00 60.00
105 Anthony Gonzalez/99 5.00 12.00
106 Brian Leonard/99 5.00 12.00
107 Calvin Johnson/99 50.00 120.00
109 Drew Stanton/99 5.00 12.00
110 Dwayne Bowe/99 5.00 12.00
111 Dwayne Jarrett/99 6.00 15.00
113 Kevin Kolb/99 6.00 15.00
114 LaRon Landry/99 8.00 20.00
115 Leon Hall/99 5.00 12.00
116 Robert Meachem/99 6.00 15.00
117 Sidney Rice/99 6.00 15.00
118 Steve Smith USC/99 5.00 12.00
119 Ted Ginn Jr./99 6.00 15.00
122 Alan Branch/133 4.00 10.00
123 Amobi Okoye/132 5.00 12.00
124 Antonio Pittman/133 4.00 10.00
125 Aundrae Allison/133 4.00 10.00
127 Brandon Meriweather/133 5.00 12.00
128 Chansi Stuckey/133 5.00 12.00
129 Chris Henry RB/133 4.00 10.00
130 Chris Leak/133 4.00 10.00
131 Courtney Taylor/133 4.00 10.00
133 Dallas Baker/133 4.00 10.00
134 Darius Walker/133 4.00 10.00
135 David Ball/133 4.00 10.00
136 David Clowney/133 4.00 10.00
137 David Irons/133 4.00 10.00
139 DeShawn Wynn/133 4.00 10.00
140 Drew Tate/133 5.00 12.00
141 Dwayne Wright/99 5.00 12.00
142 Eric Wright/133 4.00 10.00
144 Garrett Wolfe/133 4.00 10.00
145 Gary Russell/133 5.00 12.00
146 Greg Olsen/133 6.00 15.00
148 Isaiah Stanback/133 4.00 10.00
150 Jared Zabransky/133 4.00 10.00
151 Jason Hill/133 4.00 10.00
152 Jeff Rowe/133 4.00 10.00
153 Joe Thomas/133 6.00 15.00
154 Joel Filani/133 4.00 10.00
156 Johnnie Lee Higgins/133 4.00 10.00
158 Kenneth Darby/133 4.00 10.00
159 Kolby Smith/133 4.00 10.00
160 LaMarr Woodley/133 8.00 20.00
161 Lawrence Timmons/133 6.00 15.00
162 Legedu Naanee/133 5.00 12.00
163 Lorenzo Booker/133 5.00 12.00
164 Marcus McCauley/133 4.00 10.00
165 Matt Moore/133 6.00 15.00
168 Patrick Willis/133 6.00 15.00
169 Paul Posluszny/133 4.00 10.00
170 Paul Williams/133 4.00 10.00
171 Quentin Moses/133 4.00 10.00
172 Reggie Nelson/133 4.00 10.00
173 Rhema McKnight/133 4.00 10.00
174 Scott Chandler/133 6.00 15.00
175 Selvin Young/133 4.00 10.00
176 Syvelle Newton/133 5.00 12.00
178 Trent Edwards/133 4.00 10.00
179 Tyler Palko/133 6.00 15.00
180 Tyrone Moss/133 4.00 10.00
181 Yamon Figurs/133 4.00 10.00
182 Zach Miller/133 4.00 10.00

2007 Upper Deck Trilogy Signature Future Autographs

ATED PRINT RUN 9-99
SERIAL #'d UNDER 33 NOT PRICED
AA Aundrae Allison/99 4.00 10.00
AB Alan Branch/99 4.00 10.00
AO Amobi Okoye/33 8.00 20.00
AP Adrian Peterson/99 125.00 250.00
BA David Ball/99 4.00 10.00
BM Brandon Meriweather/99 5.00 12.00
BQ Brady Quinn/99 4.00 10.00
CH Chris Henry RB/99 4.00 10.00
CS Chansi Stuckey/99 5.00 12.00
CT Courtney Taylor/99 4.00 10.00
DB Dallas Baker/99 4.00 10.00
DC David Clowney/99 4.00 10.00
DI David Irons/99 4.00 10.00
DT Drew Tate/99 5.00 12.00
DW DeShawn Wynn/99 4.00 10.00
GR Gary Russell/99 5.00 12.00
IS Isaiah Stanback/99 4.00 10.00
JF Joel Filani/99 4.00 10.00
JH Jason Hill/80 4.00 10.00
JR JaMarcus Russell/99 10.00 25.00
JZ Jared Zabransky/99 4.00 10.00
KS Kolby Smith/99 4.00 10.00
ML Marshawn Lynch/99 20.00 50.00
MM Marcus McCauley/99 4.00 10.00
MO Matt Moore/99 6.00 15.00
PP Paul Posluszny/99 Red Ink 4.00 10.00
QM Quentin Moses/99 4.00 10.00
RM Robert Meachem/99 5.00 12.00
RN Reggie Nelson/90 4.00 10.00
RO Jeff Rowe/99 4.00 10.00
SN Syvelle Newton/99 5.00 12.00
SY Selvin Young/99 4.00 10.00
TG Ted Ginn/99 5.00 12.00
TM Tyrone Moss/99 4.00 10.00
TP Tyler Palko/99 6.00 15.00
WA Darius Walker/99 4.00 10.00
WI Paul Williams/99 4.00 10.00
YF Yamon Figurs/99 4.00 10.00

2007 Upper Deck Trilogy Signature Numbers Autographs

ATED PRINT RUN 4-89
SERIAL #'d UNDER 20 NOT PRICED
BJ Brandon Jacobs/32 12.00 30.00
CW Cadillac Williams/24
ES Emmitt Smith/22 125.00 250.00
FG Frank Gore/21 15.00 40.00
JA Joseph Addai/29 30.00 60.00
JC Jerricho Cotchery/89 5.00 12.00
LE Lee Evans/83 6.00 15.00
LT LaDainian Tomlinson/21
WP Willie Parker/39 12.00 30.00

2007 Upper Deck Trilogy Signature Past Autographs

UNPRICED PRINT RUN 9 SER.#'d SETS

2007 Upper Deck Trilogy Signature Present Autographs

ATED PRINT RUN 33 SER.#'d SETS
BB Bernard Berrian 8.00 20.00
BJ Brandon Jacobs 10.00 25.00
BR Ronnie Brown 10.00 25.00
CB Champ Bailey 10.00 25.00
CJ Chad Johnson 10.00 25.00
CL Mark Clayton 10.00 25.00
CO Jerricho Cotchery 8.00 20.00
CT Chester Taylor 8.00 20.00
DJ Darrell Jackson 10.00 25.00
EM Eli Manning 35.00 60.00
FG Frank Gore 12.00 30.00
GJ Greg Jennings 10.00 25.00
JA Joseph Addai 30.00 60.00
JC Jason Campbell 10.00 25.00
JL John Lynch 10.00 25.00
LF Larry Fitzgerald 15.00 40.00
PM Peyton Manning 75.00 150.00
PR Philip Rivers 12.00 30.00
RB Reggie Brown 8.00 20.00
TH T.J. Houshmandzadeh 10.00 25.00
VJ Vincent Jackson 8.00 20.00
WP Willie Parker 10.00 25.00

2007 Upper Deck Trilogy Sunday Best Jersey Silver

LVER PRINT RUN 199 SER.#'d SETS
*GOLD/33: .6X TO 1.5X SILVER/199
GOLD PRINT RUN 33 SER.#'d SETS
UNPRICED PLATINUM PRINT RUN 3
*PATCH/79: .6X TO 1.5X SILVER/199
PATCH PRINT RUN 79 SER.#'d SETS
*PATCH HOLOGOLD/33: .8X TO 2X SILVER/199
PATCH HOLOGOLD PRINT RUN 33 SER.#'d SETS
AG Anthony Gonzalez 1.50 4.00
AJ Andre Johnson 3.00 8.00
BJ Brandon Jackson 2.50 6.00
BR Ben Roethlisberger 4.00 10.00
BU Brian Urlacher 4.00 10.00
CJ Calvin Johnson 5.00 12.00
CP Carson Palmer 3.00 8.00
DB Dwayne Bowe 1.50 4.00
DS Drew Stanton 1.50 4.00
EM Eli Manning 3.00 8.00
FG Frank Gore 3.00 8.00
HW Hines Ward 3.00 8.00
JA Joseph Addai 2.50 6.00
JR JaMarcus Russell 1.50 4.00
KK Kevin Kolb 2.00 5.00
LE Lee Evans 3.00 8.00
LJ Larry Johnson 2.50 6.00
LT LaDainian Tomlinson 4.00 10.00
MH Marvin Harrison 3.00 8.00
MJ Maurice Jones-Drew 2.50 6.00
ML Matt Leinart 2.50 6.00
PM Peyton Manning 10.00 25.00
PR Philip Rivers 4.00 10.00
SJ Steven Jackson 2.50 6.00
SM Shawne Merriman 2.50 6.00
SS Steve Smith 3.00 8.00
TB Tom Brady 12.00 30.00
TE Trent Edwards 1.50 4.00
TO Terrell Owens 3.00 8.00
TS Troy Smith 1.50 4.00

2007 Upper Deck Trilogy Supernova Swatches Silver

LVER PRINT RUN 199 SER.#'d SETS
*GOLD/33: .6X TO 1.5X SILVER/199
GOLD PRINT RUN 33 SER.#'d SETS
UNPRICED PLATINUM PRINT RUN 3
*PATCH/79: .6X TO 1.5X SILVER/199
PATCH PRINT RUN 79 SER.#'d SETS
*PATCH HOLOGOLD/33: .8X TO 2X SLV/199
PATCH HOLOGOLD PRINT RUN 33 SER.#'d SETS
AC Alge Crumpler 3.00 8.00
AG Antonio Gates 4.00 10.00
AP Adrian Peterson 20.00 50.00
BL Brian Leonard 1.50 4.00
BO Dwayne Bowe 1.50 4.00
BQ Brady Quinn 1.50 4.00
BW Brian Westbrook 2.50 6.00
CJ Calvin Johnson 5.00 12.00
CT Chester Taylor 2.50 6.00
DB Drew Brees 4.00 10.00
DJ Dwayne Jarrett 2.00 5.00
ER Ed Reed 3.00 8.00
GJ Greg Jennings 2.50 6.00
JC Jason Campbell 2.50 6.00
KI Kenny Irons 1.50 4.00
KW Kellen Winslow 2.50 6.00
LC Laveranues Coles 2.50 6.00
LM Laurence Maroney 3.00 8.00
LT LaDainian Tomlinson 4.00 10.00
MB Marc Bulger 2.50 6.00
MC Marques Colston 2.50 6.00
ML Marshawn Lynch 3.00 8.00
RB Reggie Bush 2.50 6.00
RL Ray Lewis 4.00 10.00
RM Robert Meachem 2.00 5.00
SA Shaun Alexander 2.50 6.00
SS Steve Smith USC 1.50 4.00
TG Trent Green 2.50 6.00
TR Tony Romo 5.00 12.00
WP Willie Parker 3.00 8.00

2007 Upper Deck Trilogy Trilojerseys

ATED PRINT RUN 33 SER.#'d SETS
BBC Brees/Bush/Colston 10.00 25.00
BGB Ginn Jr./Beck/Booker 8.00 20.00
BJH Holt/Bulger/Jackson 8.00 20.00
CEJ Coles/Johnson/Evans 8.00 20.00
ELE Evans/Edwards/Lynch 12.00 30.00
FMB Favre/Manning/Brady 40.00 100.00
GBW Benson/Grossman/Wolfe 6.00 15.00
GSW Shockey/Gates/Winslow 10.00 25.00
HSB Holt/Boldin/Smith 8.00 20.00
JGB Johnson/Ginn Jr./Bowe 15.00 40.00
LBF Boldin/Fitzgerald/Leinart 8.00 20.00
LBS Leinart/Bush/Smith 6.00 15.00
LTW Lewis/Thomas/Willis 10.00 25.00
MAJ Addai/Maroney/Jns-Drew 8.00 20.00
MAW Manning/Wayne/Addai 15.00 40.00
MFB Montana/Favre/Brady 40.00 100.00
MJB Burress/Manning/Jacobs 8.00 20.00
MLS Lewis/McGahee/Smith 10.00 25.00
MLY Manning/Leftwich/Young 20.00 50.00
MPR Manning/Palmer/Russell 15.00 40.00
MRR Manning/Roeth/Rivers 10.00 25.00
PCV Pennington/Coles/Vilma 6.00 15.00
PJI Johnson/Palmer/Irons 8.00 20.00
PLI Peterson/Lynch/Irons 30.00 80.00
PMA Peppers/Merriman/Adams 8.00 20.00
PTR Taylor/Peterson/Rice 30.00 80.00
QWT Winslow/Quinn/Thomas 10.00 25.00
RBO Owens/Romo/Barber 20.00 50.00
RHB Russell/Bush/Higgins 6.00 15.00
RPW Ward/Roeth/Parker 10.00 25.00
RQK Quinn/Russell/Kolb 10.00 25.00
RTG Tomlinson/Gates/Rivers 10.00 25.00
SBP Sayers/Bush/Peterson 40.00 100.00
SGG Ginn Jr./Smith/Gonzalez 8.00 20.00
SJF Foster/Smith/Jarrett 8.00 20.00
SJH Harrison/Johnson/Smith 8.00 20.00
SSS Smith/Sanders/Sayers 30.00 80.00
SUG Urlacher/Sayers/Grossman 10.00 25.00
TJG Johnson/Tomlinson/Gore 10.00 25.00
VDC Crumpler/Vick/Dunn 8.00 20.00
WJB Williams WR/Bell/Johnson 15.00 40.00
YLC Cutler/Leinart/Young 6.00 15.00

1999 Upper Deck Victory

is 440 card set was issued in 12 card packs with a SRP of 99 cents and was released in August, 1999. Subsets include All-Victory (281 through 310), Season Leaders (311 through 340), Victory Parade (341 through 360), Rookie Flasback (361 through 380) and a shortprinted 99 Rookie Class subset (381-440). The Rookie Subset cards were issued one per pack.

COMPLETE SET (440) 30.00 60.00
COMP. SET w/o SP's (380) 5.00 10.00
1 Arizona Cardinals CL .07 .20
2 Jake Plummer .10 .25
3 Adrian Murrell .10 .25
4 Michael Pittman .10 .25
5 Frank Sanders .10 .25
6 Andre Wadsworth .10 .25
7 Rob Moore .10 .25
8 Simeon Rice .10 .25
9 Kwamie Lassiter RC .10 .25
10 Mario Bates .10 .25
11 Atlanta Falcons CL .07 .20
12 Jamal Anderson .12 .30
13 Chris Chandler .12 .30
14 Chuck Smith .10 .25
15 Terance Mathis .10 .25
16 Tim Dwight .12 .30
17 Ray Buchanan .10 .25
18 O.J. Santiago .10 .25
19 Lester Archambeau .10 .25
20 Baltimore Ravens CL .07 .20
21 Tony Banks .12 .30
22 Priest Holmes .10 .25
23 Michael Jackson .10 .25
24 Jermaine Lewis .10 .25
25 Michael McCrary .10 .25
26 Rod Woodson .15 .40
27 Buffalo Bills CL .07 .20
28 Rob Johnson .12 .30
29 Antowain Smith .10 .25
30 Thurman Thomas .12 .30
31 Doug Flutie .15 .40
32 Eric Moulds .10 .25
33 Bruce Smith .12 .30
34 Andre Reed .15 .40
35 Phil Hansen .10 .25
36 Carolina Panthers CL .07 .20
37 Fred Lane .10 .25
38 Tim Biakabutuka .12 .30
39 Rae Carruth .10 .25
40 Wesley Walls .12 .30
41 Steve Beuerlein .12 .30
42 Muhsin Muhammad .10 .25
43 Kevin Greene .15 .40
44 Chicago Bears CL .07 .20
45 Erik Kramer .12 .30
46 Edgar Bennett .12 .30
47 Curtis Conway .12 .30
48 Curtis Enis .10 .25
49 Bobby Engram .10 .25
50 Alonzo Mayes .10 .25
51 Tony Parrish .10 .25
52 Glyn Milburn .10 .25
53 Cincinnati Bengals CL .07 .20
54 Corey Dillon .10 .25
55 Jeff Blake .12 .30
56 Carl Pickens .12 .30
57 Darnay Scott .10 .25
58 Tony McGee .10 .25
59 Ki-Jana Carter .10 .25
60 Takeo Spikes .10 .25
61 Cleveland Browns CL .07 .20
62 Ty Detmer .10 .25
63 Terry Kirby .10 .25
64 Derrick Alexander DT .10 .25
65 Leslie Shepherd .10 .25
66 Marquez Pope .10 .25
67 Antonio Langham .10 .25
68 Marc Edwards .12 .30
69 Dallas Cowboys CL .07 .20
70 Troy Aikman .20 .50
71 Emmitt Smith .25 .60
72 Deion Sanders .12 .30
73 Rocket Ismail .12 .30
74 Michael Irvin .15 .40
75 Chris Warren .12 .30
76 Greg Ellis .10 .25
77 Kavika Pittman .10 .25
78 David LaFleur .10 .25
79 Denver Broncos CL .07 .20
80 John Elway .25 .60
81 Terrell Davis .12 .30
82 Rod Smith .12 .30
83 Shannon Sharpe .12 .30
84 Ed McCaffrey .12 .30
85 John Mobley .10 .25
86 Bill Romanowski .12 .30
87 Jason Elam .10 .25
88 Howard Griffith .10 .25
89 Detroit Lions CL .07 .20
90 Barry Sanders .25 .60
91 Johnnie Morton .12 .30
92 Herman Moore .12 .30
93 Charlie Batch .10 .25
94 Germane Crowell .10 .25
95 Robert Porcher .10 .25
96 Stephen Boyd .10 .25
97 Green Bay Packers CL .07 .20
98 Brett Favre .30 .75
99 Antonio Freeman .12 .30
100 Dorsey Levens .12 .30
101 Mark Chmura .10 .25
102 Vonnie Holliday .10 .25
103 Bill Schroeder .12 .30
104 LeRoy Butler .12 .30
105 William Henderson .10 .25
106 Indianapolis Colts CL .07 .20
107 Peyton Manning .50 1.25
108 Marvin Harrison .12 .30
109 Ken Dilger .10 .25
110 Jerome Pathon .10 .25
111 E.G. Green .10 .25
112 Ellis Johnson .10 .25
113 Jeff Burris .10 .25
114 Jacksonville Jaguars CL .07 .20
115 Mark Brunell .12 .30
116 Jimmy Smith .12 .30
117 Keenan McCardell .12 .30
118 Fred Taylor .10 .25
119 James Stewart .10 .25
120 Dave Thomas .12 .30
121 Kyle Brady .10 .25
122 Bryce Paup .10 .25
123 Kansas City Chiefs CL .07 .20
124 Elvis Grbac .10 .25
125 Andre Rison .12 .30
126 Derrick Alexander WR .10 .25
127 Tony Gonzalez .12 .30
128 Donnell Bennett .10 .25
129 Derrick Thomas .15 .40
130 Tamarick Vanover .12 .30
131 Donnie Edwards .10 .25
132 Miami Dolphins CL .07 .20
133 Dan Marino .30 .75
134 Karim Abdul-Jabbar .10 .25
135 Zach Thomas .12 .30
136 O.J. McDuffie .12 .30
137 John Avery .10 .25
138 Sam Madison .10 .25
139 Terrell Buckley .12 .30
140 Jason Taylor .12 .30
141 Oronde Gadsden .10 .25
142 Minnesota Vikings CL .07 .20
143 Randall Cunningham .12 .30
144 Cris Carter .15 .40
145 Robert Smith .10 .25
146 Randy Moss .12 .30
147 Jake Reed .12 .30
148 Leroy Hoard .10 .25
149 Matthew Hatchette .12 .30
150 John Randle .15 .40
151 Gary Anderson .10 .25
152 New England Patriots CL .07 .20
153 Drew Bledsoe .12 .30
154 Terry Glenn .12 .30
155 Ben Coates .12 .30
156 Ty Law .15 .40
157 Tony Simmons .10 .25
158 Ted Johnson .10 .25
159 Willie McGinest .12 .30
160 Tony Carter .10 .25
161 Shawn Jefferson .10 .25
162 New Orleans Saints CL .07 .20
163 Danny Wuerffel .12 .30
164 Lamar Smith .10 .25
165 Keith Poole .10 .25
166 Cameron Cleeland .10 .25
167 Joe Johnson .10 .25
168 Andre Hastings .10 .25
169 La'Roi Glover RC .15 .40
170 Aaron Craver .10 .25
171 New York Giants FB CL .07 .20
172 Kent Graham .10 .25
173 Gary Brown .10 .25
174 Amani Toomer .10 .25
175 Tiki Barber .12 .30
176 Ike Hilliard .10 .25
177 Jason Sehorn .12 .30
178 Michael Strahan .12 .30
179 Charles Way .10 .25
180 New York Jets CL .07 .20
181 Vinny Testaverde .10 .25
182 Curtis Martin .12 .30
183 Keyshawn Johnson .12 .30
184 Wayne Chrebet .10 .25
185 Mo Lewis .10 .25
186 Steve Atwater .12 .30
187 Leon Johnson .10 .25
188 Bryan Cox .12 .30
189 Oakland Raiders CL .07 .20
190 Rich Gannon .12 .30
191 Napoleon Kaufman .10 .25
192 Tim Brown .15 .40
193 Darrell Russell .10 .25
194 Rickey Dudley .10 .25
195 Charles Woodson .15 .40
196 Harvey Williams .10 .25
197 James Jett .10 .25
198 Philadelphia Eagles CL .07 .20
199 Koy Detmer .10 .25
200 Duce Staley .10 .25
201 Bobby Taylor .12 .30
202 Doug Pederson .10 .25
203 Karl Hankton .10 .25
204 Charles Johnson .10 .25
205 Kevin Turner .10 .25
206 Hugh Douglas .12 .30
207 Pittsburgh Steelers CL .07 .20
208 Kordell Stewart .10 .25
209 Jerome Bettis .15 .40
210 Hines Ward .12 .30
211 Courtney Hawkins .10 .25
212 Will Blackwell .10 .25
213 Richard Huntley .10 .25
214 Levon Kirkland .10 .25
215 Jason Gildon .12 .30
216 St. Louis Rams CL .07 .20
217 Trent Green .10 .25
218 Isaac Bruce .15 .40
219 Az-Zahir Hakim .10 .25
220 Amp Lee .10 .25
221 Robert Holcombe .10 .25
222 Ricky Proehl .10 .25
223 Kevin Carter .10 .25
224 Marshall Faulk .12 .30
225 San Diego Chargers CL .07 .20
226 Ryan Leaf .12 .30
227 Natrone Means .12 .30
228 Jim Harbaugh .12 .30
229 Junior Seau .12 .30
230 Charlie Jones .10 .25
231 Rodney Harrison .10 .25
232 Terrell Fletcher .10 .25
233 Tremayne Stephens .10 .25
234 San Francisco 49ers CL .07 .20
235 Steve Young .20 .50
236 Jerry Rice .40 1.00
237 Garrison Hearst .10 .25
238 Terrell Owens .12 .30
239 J.J. Stokes .10 .25
240 Bryant Young .12 .30
241 Tim McDonald .10 .25
242 Merton Hanks .10 .25
243 Travis Jervey .12 .30
244 Seattle Seahawks CL .07 .20
245 Ricky Watters .12 .30
246 Joey Galloway .12 .30
247 Jon Kitna .10 .25
248 Ahman Green .12 .30
249 Mike Pritchard .10 .25
250 Chad Brown .10 .25
251 Christian Fauria .10 .25
252 Michael Sinclair .10 .25
253 Tampa Bay Buccaneers CL .07 .20
254 Warrick Dunn .10 .25
255 Trent Dilfer .10 .25
256 Mike Alstott .10 .25
257 Reidel Anthony .10 .25
258 Bert Emanuel .12 .30
259 Jacquez Green .10 .25
260 Hardy Nickerson .10 .25
261 Derrick Brooks .15 .40
262 Dave Moore .10 .25
263 Tennessee Titans CL .07 .20
264 Steve McNair .12 .30
265 Eddie George .12 .30
266 Yancey Thigpen .10 .25
267 Frank Wycheck .12 .30
268 Kevin Dyson .10 .25
269 Jackie Harris .12 .30
270 Blaine Bishop .10 .25
271 Willie Davis .10 .25
272 Washington Redskins CL .07 .20
273 Skip Hicks .10 .25
274 Michael Westbrook .10 .25
275 Stephen Alexander .10 .25
276 Dana Stubblefield .10 .25
277 Brad Johnson .12 .30
278 Brian Mitchell .12 .30
279 Dan Wilkinson .12 .30
280 Stephen Davis .10 .25
281 John Elway AV .20 .50
282 Dan Marino AV .25 .60
283 Troy Aikman AV .15 .40
284 Vinny Testaverde AV .07 .20
285 Corey Dillon AV .07 .20
286 Steve Young AV .15 .40
287 Randy Moss AV .10 .25
288 Drew Bledsoe AV .10 .25
289 Jerome Bettis AV .12 .30
290 Antonio Freeman AV .10 .25
291 Fred Taylor AV .07 .20
292 Doug Flutie AV .12 .30
293 Jerry Rice AV .30 .75
294 Peyton Manning AV .40 1.00
295 Brett Favre AV .25 .60
296 Barry Sanders AV .20 .50
297 Keyshawn Johnson AV .10 .25
298 Mark Brunell AV .10 .25
299 Jamal Anderson AV .10 .25
300 Terrell Davis AV .10 .25
301 Randall Cunningham AV .10 .25
302 Kordell Stewart AV .07 .20
303 Warrick Dunn AV .07 .20
304 Jake Plummer AV .07 .20
305 Junior Seau AV .10 .25
306 Antowain Smith AV .07 .20
307 Charlie Batch AV .07 .20
308 Eddie George AV .10 .25
309 Michael Irvin AV .12 .30
310 Joey Galloway AV .10 .25
311 Randall Cunningham SL .10 .25
312 Vinny Testaverde SL .07 .20
313 Steve Young SL .15 .40
314 Chris Chandler SL .10 .25
315 John Elway SL .20 .50
316 Steve Young SL .15 .40
317 Randall Cunningham SL .10 .25
318 Brett Favre SL .25 .60
319 Vinny Testaverde SL .07 .20
320 Peyton Manning SL .40 1.00
321 Terrell Davis SL .10 .25
322 Jamal Anderson SL .10 .25
323 Garrison Hearst SL .07 .20
324 Barry Sanders SL .20 .50
325 Emmitt Smith SL .20 .50
326 Terrell Davis SL .10 .25
327 Fred Taylor SL .07 .20
328 Jamal Anderson SL .10 .25
329 Emmitt Smith SL .20 .50
330 Ricky Watters SL .10 .25
331 O.J. McDuffie SL .10 .25
332 Frank Sanders SL .07 .20
333 Rod Smith SL .10 .25
334 Marshall Faulk SL .10 .25
335 Antonio Freeman SL .10 .25
336 Randy Moss SL .10 .25
337 Antonio Freeman SL .10 .25
338 Terrell Owens SL .10 .25
339 Cris Carter SL .12 .30
340 Terance Mathis SL .07 .20
341 Jake Plummer VP .07 .20
342 Steve McNair VP .10 .25
343 Randy Moss VP .10 .25
344 Peyton Manning VP .40 1.00
345 Mark Brunell VP .10 .25
346 Terrell Owens VP .10 .25
347 Antowain Smith VP .07 .20
348 Jerry Rice VP .30 .75
349 Troy Aikman VP .15 .40
350 Fred Taylor VP .07 .20
351 Charlie Batch VP .07 .20
352 Dan Marino VP .25 .60
353 Eddie George VP .10 .25
354 Drew Bledsoe VP .10 .25
355 Kordell Stewart VP .07 .20
356 Doug Flutie VP .12 .30
357 Deion Sanders VP .10 .25
358 Keyshawn Johnson VP .10 .25
359 Jerome Bettis VP .12 .30
360 Warrick Dunn VP .07 .20
361 John Elway RF .20 .50
362 Dan Marino RF .25 .60
363 Brett Favre RF .25 .60
364 Andre Rison RF .10 .25
365 Rod Woodson RF .12 .30
366 Jerry Rice RF .30 .75
367 Barry Sanders RF .20 .50
368 Thurman Thomas RF .10 .25
369 Troy Aikman RF .15 .40
370 Ricky Watters RF .10 .25
371 Jerome Bettis RF .12 .30
372 Reggie White RF .12 .30
373 Junior Seau RF .10 .25
374 Deion Sanders RF .10 .25
375 Chris Chandler RF .10 .25
376 Curtis Martin RF .10 .25
377 Kordell Stewart RF .07 .20
378 Mark Brunell RF .10 .25
379 Cris Carter RF .12 .30
380 Emmitt Smith RF .20 .50
381 Tim Couch RC .40 1.00
382 Donovan McNabb RC 2.00 5.00
383 Akili Smith RC .30 .75
384 Edgerrin James RC .50 1.25
385 Ricky Williams RC .50 1.25
386 Torry Holt RC .60 1.50
387 Champ Bailey RC .60 1.50
388 David Boston RC .30 .75
389 Chris Claiborne RC .30 .75
390 Chris McAlister RC .30 .75
391 Daunte Culpepper RC .50 1.25
392 Cade McNown RC .30 .75
393 Troy Edwards RC .30 .75
394 John Tait RC .30 .75
395 Anthony McFarland RC .40 1.00
396 Jevon Kearse RC .40 1.00
397 Damien Woody RC .30 .75
398 Matt Stinchcomb RC .30 .75
399 Luke Petitgout RC .30 .75
400 Ebenezer Ekuban RC .30 .75
401 L.J. Shelton RC .30 .75
402 Daylon McCutcheon RC .30 .75
403 Antoine Winfield RC .30 .75
404 Scott Covington RC .30 .75
405 Antuan Edwards RC .30 .75
406 Fernando Bryant RC .30 .75
407 Aaron Gibson RC .30 .75
408 Andy Katzenmoyer RC .40 1.00
409 Dimitrius Underwood RC .30 .75
410 Patrick Kerney RC .30 .75
411 Al Wilson RC .50 1.25
412 Kevin Johnson RC .40 1.00
413 Joel Makovicka RC .30 .75
414 Reginald Kelly RC .30 .75
415 Jeff Paulk RC .30 .75
416 Brandon Stokley RC .40 1.00
417 Peerless Price RC .30 .75
418 D'Wayne Bates RC .30 .75
419 Travis McGriff RC .30 .75
420 Sedrick Irvin RC .30 .75
421 Aaron Brooks RC .40 1.00
422 Mike Cloud RC .30 .75
423 Joe Montgomery RC .30 .75
424 Shaun King RC .30 .75
425 Dameane Douglas RC .30 .75
426 Joe Germaine RC .40 1.00
427 James Johnson RC .30 .75
428 Michael Bishop RC .40 1.00
429 Karsten Bailey RC .30 .75
430 Craig Yeast RC .30 .75
431 Jim Kleinsasser RC .50 1.25
432 Martin Gramatica RC .30 .75
433 Jermaine Fazande RC .30 .75
434 Dre Bly RC .50 1.25
435 Brock Huard RC .30 .75
436 Rob Konrad RC .30 .75
437 Tony Bryant RC .30 .75
438 Sean Bennett RC .30 .75
439 Kevin Faulk RC .30 .75
440 Amos Zereoue RC .30 .75

2000 Upper Deck Victory

Released as a 330-card set, Victory contains 195 base veteran cards, 20 Season Leaders, 25 All Victory Team Checklists, 30 Big Play Makers, 60 short printed Rookie Cards inserted at the rate of one in one, and a special Web Card inserted in every pack. Each Web Card has a number that can be checked on the Upper Deck Web site to see if it is a winner of one of 100 Peyton Manning autographed jerseys. Victory was packaged in 36-pack boxes with packs containing 12 cards each and carried a suggested retail price of $.99.

COMPLETE SET (330) 25.00 50.00
COMP.SET w/o RCs (270) 5.00 10.00
271-330 ROOKIE ODDS 1:1
1 Jake Plummer .10 .25
2 Michael Pittman .10 .25
3 Rob Moore .10 .25
4 David Boston .10 .25
5 Frank Sanders .10 .25
6 Aeneas Williams .10 .25
7 Tim Dwight .12 .30
8 Chris Chandler .12 .30
9 Jamal Anderson .12 .30
10 Shawn Jefferson .10 .25
11 Ken Oxendine .10 .25
12 Terance Mathis .10 .25
13 Qadry Ismail .10 .25
14 Jermaine Lewis .10 .25
15 Rod Woodson .15 .40
16 Michael McCrary .10 .25
17 Tony Banks .10 .25
18 Peter Boulware .10 .25
19 Shannon Sharpe .12 .30
20 Peerless Price .12 .30
21 Rob Johnson .12 .30
22 Eric Moulds .10 .25
23 Doug Flutie .12 .30
24 Jay Riemersma .10 .25
25 Antowain Smith .12 .30
26 Sam Cowart .10 .25
27 Muhsin Muhammad .10 .25
28 Patrick Jeffers .10 .25
29 Steve Beuerlein .12 .30
30 Natrone Means .12 .30
31 Tim Biakabutuka .12 .30
32 Michael Bates .10 .25
33 Wesley Walls .10 .25
34 Cade McNown .10 .25
35 Curtis Enis .10 .25
36 Marcus Robinson .12 .30
37 Bobby Engram .10 .25
38 Glyn Milburn .10 .25
39 Marty Booker .10 .25
40 Akili Smith .10 .25
41 Corey Dillon .10 .25
42 Darnay Scott .12 .30
43 Tremain Mack .10 .25
44 Michael Bankston .10 .25
45 Tony McGee .10 .25
46 Tim Couch .12 .30
47 Kevin Johnson .10 .25
48 Darrin Chiaverini .10 .25
49 Jamir Miller .10 .25
50 Errict Rhett .12 .30
51 Ty Detmer .10 .25
52 Terry Kirby .10 .25
53 Troy Aikman .20 .50
54 Emmitt Smith .25 .60
55 Rocket Ismail .12 .30
56 Chris Warren .10 .25
57 Joey Galloway .12 .30
58 Terrell Davis .12 .30
59 Olandis Gary .12 .30
60 Brian Griese .10 .25
61 Gus Frerotte .10 .25
62 Glenn Cadrez .10 .25
63 Ed McCaffrey .12 .30
64 Rod Smith .12 .30
65 Charlie Batch .10 .25
66 Germane Crowell .10 .25
67 Stephen Boyd .10 .25
68 Johnnie Morton .12 .30
69 Robert Porcher .10 .25
70 James Stewart .10 .25
71 Brett Favre .30 .75
72 Antonio Freeman .12 .30
73 Bill Schroeder .12 .30
74 Dorsey Levens .12 .30
75 Darren Sharper .10 .25
76 Peyton Manning .40 1.00
77 Edgerrin James .12 .30
78 Marvin Harrison .12 .30
79 Ken Dilger .10 .25
80 Terrence Wilkins .10 .25
81 Cornelius Bennett .10 .25
82 E.G. Green .10 .25
83 Mark Brunell .12 .30
84 Fred Taylor .10 .25
85 Jimmy Smith .12 .30
86 Keenan McCardell .12 .30
87 Carnell Lake .10 .25
88 Kevin Hardy .10 .25
89 Elvis Grbac .10 .25
90 Tony Gonzalez .12 .30
91 Derrick Alexander .10 .25
92 Donnell Bennett .10 .25
93 James Hasty .10 .25
94 Kevin Lockett .10 .25
95 Trace Armstrong .10 .25
96 Terrell Buckley .10 .25
97 Tony Martin .12 .30
98 Damon Huard .10 .25
99 O.J. McDuffie .12 .30
100 Brock Marion .10 .25
101 Zach Thomas .12 .30
102 Randy Moss .12 .30
103 Robert Smith .10 .25
104 Cris Carter .15 .40
105 Bubby Brister .10 .25
106 Daunte Culpepper .12 .30
107 John Randle .15 .40
108 Drew Bledsoe .12 .30
109 Terry Glenn .12 .30
110 Willie McGinest .12 .30
111 Kevin Faulk .10 .25
112 Tedy Bruschi .25 .60
113 Ricky Williams .12 .30
114 Keith Poole .10 .25
115 Jake Reed .12 .30
116 Mark Fields .10 .25
117 Jeff Blake .12 .30
118 Andrew Glover .10 .25
119 Kerry Collins .10 .25
120 Amani Toomer .10 .25
121 Jessie Armstead .10 .25
122 Ike Hilliard .10 .25
123 Ray Lucas .10 .25
124 Curtis Martin .12 .30
125 Vinny Testaverde .10 .25
126 Wayne Chrebet .10 .25
127 Dedric Ward .10 .25
128 Tim Brown .15 .40
129 Rich Gannon .12 .30
130 Tyrone Wheatley .10 .25
131 Napoleon Kaufman .12 .30
132 Charles Woodson .15 .40
133 Greg Biekert .10 .25
134 Rickey Dudley .10 .25
135 Duce Staley .10 .25
136 Donovan McNabb .12 .30
137 Torrance Small .10 .25
138 Mike Mamula .10 .25
139 Brian Dawkins .15 .40
140 Troy Vincent .10 .25
141 Kent Graham .10 .25
142 Troy Edwards .10 .25
143 Jerome Bettis .15 .40
144 Hines Ward .12 .30
145 Kordell Stewart .10 .25
146 Levon Kirkland .10 .25
147 Richard Huntley .10 .25
148 Marshall Faulk .12 .30
149 Kurt Warner .25 .60
150 Torry Holt .12 .30
151 Isaac Bruce .15 .40
152 Kevin Carter .10 .25
153 Az-Zahir Hakim .10 .25
154 Todd Lyght .10 .25
155 Jermaine Fazande .10 .25
156 Curtis Conway .12 .30
157 Freddie Jones .10 .25
158 Junior Seau .12 .30
159 Jeff Graham .10 .25
160 Moses Moreno .10 .25
161 Rodney Harrison .10 .25
162 Steve Young .20 .50
163 Jerry Rice .40 1.00
164 Ken Norton .10 .25
165 Terrell Owens .12 .30
166 Jeff Garcia .10 .25
167 Ricky Watters .12 .30
168 Jon Kitna .10 .25
169 Derrick Mayes .10 .25
170 Sean Dawkins .10 .25
171 Chad Brown .10 .25
172 Warrick Dunn .10 .25
173 Keyshawn Johnson .12 .30
174 Shaun King .10 .25
175 Mike Alstott .10 .25
176 Warren Sapp .12 .30
177 Jacquez Green .10 .25
178 Derrick Brooks .10 .25
179 John Lynch .12 .30
180 Eddie George .12 .30
181 Steve McNair .12 .30
182 Kevin Dyson .12 .30
183 Jevon Kearse .10 .25
184 Yancey Thigpen .10 .25
185 Frank Wycheck .12 .30
186 Eddie Robinson .10 .25
187 Jeff George .12 .30
188 Brad Johnson .12 .30
189 Stephen Davis .10 .25
190 Michael Westbrook .10 .25
191 Albert Connell .10 .25
192 Brian Mitchell .10 .25
193 Bruce Smith .12 .30
194 Champ Bailey .12 .30
195 Sam Shade .10 .25
196 Marvin Harrison SL .10 .25
197 Jimmy Smith SL .10 .25
198 Randy Moss SL .10 .25
199 Marcus Robinson SL .10 .25
200 Tim Brown SL .12 .30
201 Jimmy Smith SL .10 .25
202 Marvin Harrison SL .10 .25
203 Muhsin Muhammad SL .07 .20
204 Tim Brown SL .12 .30
205 Cris Carter SL .12 .30
206 Edgerrin James SL .10 .25
207 Curtis Martin SL .10 .25
208 Stephen Davis SL .07 .20
209 Emmitt Smith SL .20 .50
210 Marshall Faulk SL .10 .25
211 Kurt Warner SL .20 .50
212 Steve Beuerlein SL .10 .25
213 Jeff George SL .10 .25
214 Peyton Manning SL .30 .75
215 Brad Johnson SL .10 .25
216 Kurt Warner CL .20 .50
217 Peyton Manning CL .30 .75
218 Edgerrin James CL .10 .25
219 Marshall Faulk CL .10 .25
220 Randy Moss CL .10 .25
221 Jimmy Smith CL .10 .25
222 Tony Gonzalez CL .10 .25
223 Tony Boselli CL .10 .25
224 Orlando Pace CL .07 .20
225 Larry Allen CL .12 .30
226 Randall McDaniel CL .10 .25
227 Tom Nalen CL .07 .20
228 Kevin Carter CL .07 .20
229 Jevon Kearse CL .07 .20
230 Warren Sapp CL .10 .25
231 Darrell Russell CL .07 .20
232 Derrick Brooks CL .07 .20
233 Peter Boulware CL .07 .20
234 Junior Seau CL .10 .25
235 Sam Madison CL .07 .20
236 Charles Woodson CL .12 .30
237 John Lynch CL .10 .25
238 Carnell Lake CL .07 .20
239 Mitch Berger CL RC .10 .25
240 Jason Hanson CL .07 .20
241 Randy Moss PM .10 .25
242 Kurt Warner PM .20 .50
243 Peyton Manning PM .30 .75
244 Marshall Faulk PM .10 .25
245 Edgerrin James PM .10 .25
246 Eddie George PM .10 .25
247 Stephen Davis PM .07 .20
248 Keyshawn Johnson PM .10 .25
249 Brad Johnson PM .10 .25
250 Ricky Williams PM .10 .25
251 Jimmy Smith PM .10 .25
252 Isaac Bruce PM .12 .30
253 Muhsin Muhammad PM .07 .20
254 Marcus Robinson PM .10 .25
255 Kevin Johnson PM .07 .20
256 Tim Couch PM .10 .25
257 Curtis Martin PM .10 .25
258 Charlie Batch PM .07 .20
259 Tim Brown PM .12 .30
260 Jerry Rice PM .30 .75
261 Drew Bledsoe PM .10 .25
262 Brett Favre PM .25 .60
263 Mark Brunell PM .10 .25
264 Fred Taylor PM .07 .20
265 Troy Edwards PM .07 .20
266 Marvin Harrison PM .10 .25
267 Germane Crowell PM .07 .20
268 Terry Glenn PM .10 .25
269 Qadry Ismail PM .07 .20
270 Jake Plummer PM .07 .20
271 Anthony Becht RC .20 .50
272 Anthony Lucas RC .20 .50
273 Bashir Yamini RC .20 .50
274 Brian Urlacher RC 1.00 2.50
275 Chad Morton RC .25 .60
276 Chad Pennington RC .25 .60
277 Chris Cole RC .25 .60
278 Chris Hovan RC .25 .60
279 Tim Rattay RC .25 .60
280 Chris Redman RC .20 .50
281 Chris Samuels RC .30 .75
282 Corey Simon RC .25 .60
283 Courtney Brown RC .25 .60
284 Curtis Keaton RC .20 .50
285 Danny Farmer RC .20 .50
286 Erron Kinney RC .20 .50
287 Darren Howard RC .20 .50
288 Deltha O'Neal RC .20 .50
289 Dennis Northcutt RC .20 .50
290 Demario Brown RC .20 .50
291 Dez White RC .20 .50
292 Frank Murphy RC .20 .50
293 Garl Scott RC .20 .50
294 Giovanni Carmazzi RC .20 .50
295 J.R. Redmond RC .20 .50
296 JaJuan Dawson RC .20 .50
297 Jamal Lewis RC .30 .75
298 Leon Murray RC .20 .50
299 Jerry Porter RC .30 .75
300 Joe Hamilton RC .20 .50
301 John Abraham RC .30 .75
302 John Engelberger RC .20 .50
303 Keith Bulluck RC .25 .60
304 Kwame Cavil RC .20 .50
305 Laveranues Coles RC .25 .60
306 Marc Bulger RC .25 .60
307 Marcus Knight RC .20 .50
308 Mareno Philyaw RC .20 .50
309 Michael Wiley RC .20 .50
310 Na'il Diggs RC .20 .50
311 Peter Warrick RC .20 .50
312 Plaxico Burress RC .25 .60
313 Raynoch Thompson RC .20 .50
314 Reuben Droughns RC .20 .50
315 Rob Morris RC .25 .60
316 Ron Dayne RC .30 .75
317 Ron Dugans RC .20 .50
318 Sebastian Janikowski RC .30 .75
319 Shaun Alexander RC .30 .75
320 Sherrod Gideon RC .20 .50
321 Sylvester Morris RC .20 .50
322 Tee Martin RC .20 .50
323 Thomas Jones RC .25 .60
324 Todd Husak RC .20 .50
325 Todd Pinkston RC .20 .50
326 Tom Brady RC 50.00 100.00
327 Travis Prentice RC .20 .50
328 Travis Taylor RC .20 .50
329 Trevor Gaylor RC .20 .50
330 Trung Canidate RC .20 .50

2001 Upper Deck Victory

This set was issued as a 440-card set including 370 veterans, 60 rookies, and 10 checklist cards. Each card features a full color photo with white borders. There were 10 cards per pack, 36 packs per box.

COMPLETE SET (440) 30.00 60.00
1 Jake Plummer .10 .25
2 David Boston .10 .25
3 Thomas Jones .10 .25
4 Michael Pittman .12 .30
5 Frank Sanders .10 .25
6 Joel Makovicka .10 .25
7 Corey Chavous .10 .25
8 Kwamie Lassiter .10 .25
9 Rob Moore .10 .25
10 Jamal Anderson .12 .30
11 Tony Martin .12 .30
12 Travis Jervey .10 .25
13 Chris Chandler .12 .30
14 Shawn Jefferson .10 .25
15 Rodney Thomas .10 .25
16 Terance Mathis .10 .25
17 Jessie Tuggle .10 .25
18 Ashley Ambrose .10 .25
19 Brian Finneran .12 .30
20 Maurice Smith .10 .25
21 Keith Brooking .12 .30
22 Jamal Lewis .15 .40
23 Shannon Sharpe .12 .30
24 Brandon Stokley .10 .25
25 Ray Lewis .15 .40
26 Qadry Ismail .10 .25
27 Travis Taylor .10 .25
28 Chris Redman .15 .40
29 Rod Woodson .15 .40
30 Pat Johnson .10 .25
31 Jermaine Lewis .10 .25
32 Elvis Grbac .12 .30
33 Tony Siragusa .12 .30
34 Larry Centers .10 .25
35 Rob Johnson .12 .30
36 Eric Moulds .10 .25
37 Sammy Morris .10 .25
38 Shawn Bryson .10 .25
39 Alex Van Pelt .10 .25
40 Jeremy McDaniel .10 .25
41 Sam Cowart .10 .25
42 Peerless Price .10 .25
43 Avion Black .10 .25
44 Phil Hansen .10 .25
45 Muhsin Muhammad .10 .25
46 Brad Hoover .12 .30
47 Tim Biakabutuka .10 .25
48 Wesley Walls .10 .25
49 Donald Hayes .10 .25
50 Jeff Lewis .10 .25
51 Dameyune Craig .10 .25
52 Mike Minter RC .12 .30
53 Isaac Byrd .10 .25
54 Patrick Jeffers .10 .25
55 Cade McNown .12 .30
56 James Allen .10 .25
57 Marcus Robinson .12 .30
58 Brian Urlacher .20 .50
59 Shane Matthews .10 .25
60 Glyn Milburn .10 .25
61 Scott Dragos RC .10 .25
62 Marty Booker .10 .25
63 Bobby Engram .10 .25
64 Kaseem Sinceno .10 .25
65 Ted Washington .10 .25
66 Peter Warrick .10 .25
67 Corey Dillon .10 .25
68 Akili Smith UER .10 .25
69 Danny Farmer .10 .25
70 Scott Mitchell .10 .25
71 Darryl Williams .10 .25
72 Ron Dugans .10 .25
73 Takeo Spikes .10 .25
74 Jon Kitna .10 .25
75 Darnay Scott .12 .30
76 Tony McGee .10 .25
77 Tim Couch .10 .25
78 Kevin Johnson .10 .25
79 Travis Prentice .10 .25
80 Spergon Wynn .10 .25
81 Errict Rhett .12 .30
82 Ty Detmer .10 .25
83 Dennis Northcutt .10 .25
84 Aaron Shea .10 .25
85 Courtney Brown .10 .25
86 JaJuan Dawson .10 .25
87 Rickey Dudley .10 .25
88 Jamir Miller .10 .25
89 Clint Stoerner .12 .30
90 Emmitt Smith .25 .60
91 Joey Galloway .12 .30
92 Rocket Ismail .12 .30
93 Ebenezer Ekuban .10 .25
94 Anthony Wright .10 .25
95 David LaFleur .10 .25
96 Dexter Coakley .10 .25
97 Jackie Harris .12 .30
98 Michael Wiley .10 .25
99 Wane McGarity .10 .25
100 Dat Nguyen .10 .25
101 Terrell Davis .12 .30
102 Mike Anderson .10 .25
103 Brian Griese .10 .25
104 Rod Smith .12 .30
105 Ed McCaffrey .12 .30
106 Olandis Gary .10 .25
107 Kavika Pittman .10 .25
108 Bill Romanowski .12 .30
109 Gus Frerotte .10 .25
110 Howard Griffith .10 .25
111 Eddie Kennison .12 .30
112 Charlie Batch .10 .25
113 Germane Crowell .10 .25
114 James O. Stewart .10 .25
115 Johnnie Morton .12 .30
116 Herman Moore .10 .25
117 Larry Foster .10 .25
118 Desmond Howard .12 .30
119 Cory Schlesinger .10 .25
120 Robert Porcher .10 .25
121 Sedrick Irvin .10 .25
122 David Sloan .10 .25
123 Jim Harbaugh .12 .30
124 Brett Favre .30 .75
125 Antonio Freeman .15 .40
126 Dorsey Levens .12 .30
127 Ahman Green .12 .30
128 LeRoy Butler .12 .30
129 De'Mond Parker .10 .25
130 Bill Schroeder .12 .30
131 Bubba Franks .10 .25
132 Donald Driver .12 .30
133 Darren Sharper .12 .30
134 Corey Bradford .10 .25
135 Charles Lee .10 .25
136 Peyton Manning .40 1.00
137 Edgerrin James .12 .30
138 Marvin Harrison .12 .30
139 E.G. Green .10 .25
140 Terrence Wilkins .10 .25
141 Ken Dilger .10 .25
142 Jerome Pathon .10 .25
143 Rob Morris .10 .25
144 Lennox Gordon .10 .25
145 Chad Bratzke .10 .25
146 Mark Brunell .12 .30
147 Fred Taylor .10 .25
148 Jimmy Smith .12 .30
149 Jamie Martin .10 .25
150 Keenan McCardell .12 .30
151 Kyle Brady .10 .25
152 R.Jay Soward .10 .25
153 Alvis Whitted .10 .25
154 Stacey Mack .10 .25
155 Damon Jones .10 .25
156 Carnell Lake .10 .25
157 Kevin Hardy .10 .25
158 Trent Green .10 .25
159 Tony Gonzalez .12 .30
160 Derrick Alexander .10 .25
161 Tony Richardson .10 .25
162 Frank Moreau .10 .25
163 Sylvester Morris .10 .25
164 Priest Holmes .10 .25
165 Donnie Edwards .10 .25
166 Marvcus Patton .10 .25
167 Larry Parker .10 .25
168 Tony Horne .10 .25
169 Bubby Brister .10 .25
170 Oronde Gadsden .10 .25
171 Lamar Smith .12 .30
172 Jay Fiedler .12 .30
173 James Johnson .10 .25
174 Rob Konrad .10 .25
175 James McKnight .10 .25
176 Dedric Ward .10 .25
177 O.J. McDuffie .10 .25
178 Zach Thomas .12 .30
179 Ray Lucas .10 .25
180 Sam Madison .10 .25
181 Randy Moss .12 .30
182 Jake Reed .12 .30
183 Cris Carter .15 .40
184 Daunte Culpepper .12 .30
185 Moe Williams .10 .25
186 Troy Walters .10 .25
187 Todd Bouman .10 .25
188 Jim Kleinsasser .12 .30
189 Ed McDaniel .10 .25
190 Robert Griffith .10 .25
191 Byron Chamberlain .10 .25
192 Chris Hovan .10 .25
193 Drew Bledsoe .12 .30
194 Terry Glenn .12 .30
195 Kevin Faulk .10 .25
196 J.R. Redmond .10 .25
197 Antowain Smith .12 .30
198 Bert Emanuel .10 .25
199 Troy Brown .10 .25
200 Tony Simmons .10 .25
201 Michael Bishop .12 .30
202 Lawyer Milloy .10 .25
203 Torrance Small .10 .25
204 Ty Law .15 .40
205 Charles Johnson .10 .25
206 Willie McGinest .10 .25
207 Ricky Williams .12 .30
208 Jeff Blake .12 .30
209 Joe Horn .10 .25
210 Aaron Brooks .10 .25
211 La'Roi Glover .10 .25
212 Chad Morton .10 .25
213 Keith Mitchell .10 .25
214 Willie Jackson .10 .25
215 Robert Wilson .10 .25
216 Norman Hand .10 .25
217 Albert Connell .10 .25
218 Joe Johnson .10 .25
219 Kerry Collins .10 .25
220 Amani Toomer .10 .25
221 Ron Dayne .12 .30
222 Tiki Barber .12 .30
223 Greg Comella .10 .25
224 Ike Hilliard .10 .25
225 Joe Jurevicius .10 .25
226 Ron Dixon .10 .25
227 Jason Sehorn .12 .30
228 Michael Strahan .12 .30
229 Jessie Armstead .10 .25
230 Michael Barrow .10 .25
231 Jason Garrett .15 .40
232 Vinny Testaverde .10 .25
233 Wayne Chrebet .10 .25
234 Curtis Martin .12 .30
235 Richie Anderson .10 .25
236 Mo Lewis .10 .25
237 Laveranues Coles .12 .30
238 Windrell Hayes .10 .25
239 Chad Pennington .10 .25
240 Matthew Hatchette .10 .25
241 Anthony Becht .10 .25
242 Marvin Jones .10 .25
243 Tim Brown .15 .40
244 Rich Gannon .12 .30
245 Tyrone Wheatley .12 .30
246 Charlie Garner .12 .30
247 Jon Ritchie .10 .25
248 James Jett .10 .25
249 Roland Williams .10 .25
250 Jerry Porter .10 .25
251 Darrell Russell .10 .25
252 Charles Woodson .15 .40
253 Jerry Rice .30 .75
254 Greg Biekert .10 .25
255 Duce Staley .10 .25
256 Donovan McNabb .12 .30
257 Darnell Autry .10 .25
258 Chad Lewis .10 .25
259 Na Brown .10 .25
260 Koy Detmer .10 .25
261 Todd Pinkston .10 .25
262 Brian Mitchell .12 .30
263 Hugh Douglas .10 .25
264 James Thrash .12 .30
265 Ron Powlus .12 .30
266 Corey Simon .10 .25
267 Kordell Stewart .10 .25
268 Jerome Bettis .15 .40
269 Bobby Shaw .10 .25
270 Hines Ward .12 .30

271 Plaxico Burress	.10	.25
272 Courtney Hawkins	.10	.25
273 Troy Edwards	.10	.25
274 Earl Holmes	.10	.25
275 Richard Huntley	.10	.25
276 Kent Graham	.12	.30
277 Tee Martin	.12	.30
278 Jon Witman	.10	.25
279 Marshall Faulk	.12	.30
280 Kurt Warner	.25	.60
281 Isaac Bruce	.15	.40
282 Torry Holt	.12	.30
283 Joe Germaine	.10	.25
284 Ernie Conwell	.10	.25
285 Trung Canidate	.10	.25
286 Az-Zahir Hakim	.10	.25
287 Ricky Proehl	.10	.25
288 Grant Wistrom	.10	.25
289 London Fletcher	.12	.30
290 Paul Justin	.10	.25
291 Robert Holcombe	.10	.25
292 Junior Seau	.12	.30
293 Curtis Conway	.12	.30
294 Rodney Harrison	.10	.25
295 Jeff Graham	.10	.25
296 Freddie Jones	.10	.25
297 Reggie Jones	.10	.25
298 Ronney Jenkins	.10	.25
299 Trevor Gaylor	.10	.25
300 Tim Dwight	.12	.30
301 Fred McCrary	.10	.25
302 Terrell Fletcher	.10	.25
303 Doug Flutie	.12	.30
304 Dave Dickenson RC	.12	.30
305 Marcellus Wiley	.10	.25
306 Jeff Garcia	.10	.25
307 Jonas Lewis	.10	.25
308 Tai Streets	.10	.25
309 Terrell Owens	.12	.30
310 J.J. Stokes	.10	.25
311 Fred Beasley	.10	.25
312 Tim Rattay	.10	.25
313 Garrison Hearst	.12	.30
314 Giovanni Carmazzi	.10	.25
315 Bryant Young	.12	.30
316 Ricky Watters	.12	.30
317 Shaun Alexander	.10	.25
318 Matt Hasselbeck	.10	.25
319 Brock Huard	.10	.25
320 Darrell Jackson	.12	.30
321 James Williams	.10	.25
322 Charlie Rogers UER	.10	.25
323 Christian Fauria	.10	.25
324 Karsten Bailey	.10	.25
325 Travis Brown RC	.10	.25
326 Chad Brown	.10	.25
327 John Randle	.12	.30
328 Warrick Dunn	.10	.25
329 Shaun King	.10	.25
330 Rabih Abdullah	.10	.25
331 Mike Alstott	.10	.25
332 Jacquez Green	.10	.25
333 Reidel Anthony	.10	.25
334 Derrick Brooks	.10	.25
335 John Lynch	.12	.30
336 Warren Sapp	.12	.30
337 Brad Johnson	.12	.30
338 Keyshawn Johnson	.12	.30
339 Mark Royals	.10	.25
340 Dave Moore	.10	.25
341 Simeon Rice	.12	.30
342 Ronde Barber	.10	.25
343 Eddie George	.15	.40
344 Steve McNair	.12	.30
345 Samari Rolle	.10	.25
346 Derrick Mason	.10	.25
347 Randall Godfrey	.10	.25
348 Frank Wycheck	.10	.25
349 Chris Sanders	.10	.25
350 Neil O'Donnell	.12	.30
351 Kevin Dyson	.10	.25
352 Jevon Kearse	.10	.25
353 Chris Coleman	.10	.25
354 Mike Green	.10	.25
355 Blaine Bishop	.10	.25
356 Eddie Robinson	.10	.25
357 Jeff George	.12	.30
358 Stephen Davis	.10	.25
359 Donnell Bennett	.10	.25
360 Kevin Lockett	.10	.25
361 Derrius Thompson	.10	.25
362 Michael Westbrook	.10	.25
363 Stephen Alexander	.10	.25
364 Ki-Jana Carter	.10	.25
365 Champ Bailey	.12	.30
366 Todd Husak	.10	.25
367 Dan Wilkinson	.10	.25
368 Darrell Green	.15	.40
369 Sam Shade	.10	.25
370 Bruce Smith	.12	.30
371 Bobby Newcombe RC	.25	.60
372 Vinny Sutherland RC	.20	.50
373 Alge Crumpler RC	.30	.75
374 Michael Vick RC	3.00	8.00
375 Gary Baxter RC	.20	.50
376 Todd Heap RC	.25	.60
377 Nate Clements RC	.25	.60
378 Travis Henry RC	.25	.60
379 Dan Morgan RC	.25	.60
380 Chris Weinke RC	.25	.60
381 David Terrell RC	.25	.60
382 Anthony Thomas RC	.30	.75
383 Rudi Johnson RC	.30	.75
384 Justin Smith RC	.40	1.00
385 T.J. Houshmandzadeh RC	.25	.60
386 Chad Johnson RC	.30	.75
387 Quincy Morgan RC	.25	.60
388 Gerard Warren RC	.25	.60
389 James Jackson RC	.20	.50
390 Quincy Carter RC	.25	.60
391 Kevin Kasper RC	.20	.50
392 Scotty Anderson RC	.20	.50
393 Mike McMahon RC	.25	.60
394 Jamal Reynolds RC	.20	.50
395 Robert Ferguson RC	.30	.75
396 Reggie Wayne RC	.40	1.00
397 Snoop Minnis RC	.20	.50
398 Chris Chambers RC	.20	.50
399 Jamar Fletcher RC	.20	.50
400 Travis Minor RC	.25	.60
401 Josh Heupel RC	.30	.75
402 Michael Bennett RC	.25	.60
403 Jabari Holloway RC	.20	.50
404 Moran Norris RC	.20	.50
405 Deuce McAllister RC	.30	.75
406 Will Allen RC	.30	.75
407 Jesse Palmer RC	.25	.60
408 LaMont Jordan RC	.30	.75
409 Santana Moss RC	.30	.75
410 Ken-Yon Rambo RC	.20	.50
411 Derrick Gibson RC	.20	.50
412 Marques Tuiasosopo RC	.25	.60
413 Correll Buckhalter RC	.20	.50
414 Freddie Mitchell RC	.20	.50
415 Drew Brees RC	10.00	25.00
416 LaDainian Tomlinson RC	3.00	8.00
417 Cedrick Wilson RC	.25	.60
418 Kevan Barlow RC	.25	.60
419 Alex Bannister RC	.20	.50
420 Heath Evans RC	.25	.60
421 Josh Booty RC	.25	.60
422 Koren Robinson RC	.25	.60
423 Adam Archuleta RC	.25	.60
424 Dan Alexander RC	.25	.60
425 Eddie Berlin RC	.20	.50
426 Rod Gardner RC	.25	.60
427 Sage Rosenfels RC	.25	.60
428 Steve Smith RC	.60	1.50
429 Chris Barnes RC	.20	.50
430 Tim Hasselbeck RC	.25	.60
431 Peyton Manning CL	.25	.60
432 Mike Anderson CL	.10	.25
433 Jamal Lewis CL	.10	.25
434 Randy Moss CL	.07	.20
435 Donovan McNabb CL	.07	.20
436 Daunte Culpepper CL	.07	.20
437 Kurt Warner CL	.15	.40
438 Eddie George CL	.10	.25
439 Marshall Faulk CL	.07	.20
440 Brett Favre CL	.20	.50

2001 Upper Deck Victory Gold

*1-440 VETS: 2X TO 5X BASIC CARDS
*371-440 ROOKIES: 1X TO 2.5X
GOLD STATED ODDS 1:2

2000 Upper Deck Vintage Previews

Sent out as a bonus to those redeeming autographed redemption cards, these two card preview packs contain serial numberd versions of the Upper Deck Vintage football set. The packs contain one regular card, numbered to 900 and one rookie card numbered to 1,500, 1,000 or 500. The regular cards and rookie cards make up a 90-card set.
21-40 ROOKIE TRIO PRINT RUN 1500

1 Jamal Lewis	5.00	12.00
2 Sammy Morris	3.00	8.00
3 Peter Warrick	3.00	8.00
4 Travis Prentice	3.00	8.00
5 Mike Anderson	3.00	8.00
6 Sylvester Morris	3.00	8.00
7 Ron Dayne	5.00	12.00
8 Chad Pennington	4.00	10.00
9 Plaxico Burress	4.00	10.00
10 Laveranues Coles	4.00	10.00
11 S.Wynn D.Northcutt	1.50	4.00
12 C.Brown J.Dawson	2.00	5.00
13 R.Thompson T.Jones	2.00	5.00
14 T.Brady J.R.Redmond	40.00	80.00
15 J.Abraham W.Hayes	2.50	6.00
16 T.Husak C.Samuels	2.50	6.00
17 G.Carmazzi T.Rattay	2.00	5.00
18 S.Alexander D.Jackson	2.50	6.00
19 R.Morris K.McDougal	2.00	5.00
20 B.Urlacher D.White	8.00	20.00
21 Johnson Vaughn Simoneau	1.25	3.00
22 Redman J.Jones T.Taylor	1.25	3.00
23 Cavil Moore Flowers	1.25	3.00
24 Green Towns Hoover	1.50	4.00
25 Keaton Farmer Dugans	1.25	3.00
26 Mntgmry Coleman O'Neal	1.25	3.00
27 Franks Diggs C.Lee	1.25	3.00
28 Walters Hovan Chapman	1.50	4.00
29 Morton Howard T.Smith	1.50	4.00
30 G.Scott Pinkston Simon	1.50	4.00
31 Coleman Bulluck Kinney	1.50	4.00
32 Simon Volek Yamini	2.00	5.00
33 Webster A.Plummer Peterson	1.25	3.00
34 S.Davis Pass A.Harris	1.25	3.00
35 Soward Stith Slaughter	1.25	3.00
36 Gaylor Jenkins Beckett	1.25	3.00
37 Martin Hamilton J.Jackson	1.50	4.00
38 Cole Dixon Williams	1.50	4.00
39 Droughns Canidate Moreau	1.25	3.00
40 M.Brown Porter Wiley	2.00	5.00
41 Jake Plummer	.50	1.25
42 Jamal Anderson	.60	1.50
43 Qadry Ismail	.50	1.25
44 Doug Flutie	.60	1.50
45 Rob Johnson	.60	1.50
46 Steve Beuerlein	.60	1.50
47 Marcus Robinson	.60	1.50
48 Cade McNown	.50	1.25
49 Tim Couch	.60	1.50
50 Corey Dillon	.50	1.25
51 Troy Aikman	1.00	2.50
52 Emmitt Smith	1.25	3.00
53 Charlie Batch	.50	1.25
54 Brian Griese	.50	1.25
55 Terrell Davis	.60	1.50
56 Brett Favre	1.50	4.00
57 Antonio Freeman	.60	1.50
58 Peyton Manning	2.00	5.00
59 Edgerrin James	.60	1.50
60 Marvin Harrison	.60	1.50
61 Mark Brunell	.60	1.50
62 Fred Taylor	.50	1.25
63 Elvis Grbac	.50	1.25
64 Derrick Alexander	.50	1.25
65 Lamar Smith	.50	1.25
66 Daunte Culpepper	.60	1.50
67 Randy Moss	.60	1.50
68 Drew Bledsoe	.60	1.50
69 Vinny Testaverde	.50	1.25
70 Curtis Martin	.60	1.50
71 Kerry Collins	.50	1.25
72 Amani Toomer	.50	1.25
73 Jeff Blake	.60	1.50
74 Ricky Williams	.60	1.50
75 Rich Gannon	.60	1.50
76 Tim Brown	.75	2.00
77 Jerome Bettis	.75	2.00
78 Kurt Warner	1.25	3.00
79 Marshall Faulk	.60	1.50
80 Junior Seau	.60	1.50
81 Jeff Garcia	.50	1.25
82 Terrell Owens	.60	1.50
83 Jerry Rice	2.00	5.00
84 Ricky Watters	.60	1.50
85 Shaun King	.50	1.25
86 Keyshawn Johnson	.60	1.50
87 Steve McNair	.60	1.50
88 Eddie George	.60	1.50
89 Stephen Davis	.50	1.25
90 Brad Johnson	.60	1.50

2001 Upper Deck Vintage

Upper Deck released its Vintage set in August of 2001. The card design in that of the 2000 Upper Deck Vintage Preview set but this set is missing the serial numbers. The cards have either blue, red, or split blue and red borders, with the exception of the 10 season leader cards which had a white border. The cards are on greyback cardstock to give this set the vintage look. The rookies were on the split blue and red borders.

COMPLETE SET (290)	20.00	40.00
1 Jake Plummer	.12	.30
2 David Boston	.12	.30
3 Thomas Jones	.12	.30
4 Frank Sanders	.12	.30
5 Bob Christian	.12	.30
6 Jamal Anderson	.15	.40
7 Chris Chandler	.15	.40
8 Shawn Jefferson	.12	.30
9 Brian Finneran	.15	.40
10 Terance Mathis	.12	.30
11 Jamal Lewis	.20	.50
12 Shannon Sharpe	.15	.40
13 Elvis Grbac	.15	.40
14 Ray Lewis	.20	.50
15 Qadry Ismail	.12	.30
16 Brandon Stokley	.12	.30
17 Rob Johnson	.15	.40
18 Eric Moulds	.12	.30
19 Sammy Morris	.12	.30
20 Shawn Bryson	.12	.30
21 Jeremy McDaniel	.12	.30
22 Muhsin Muhammad	.12	.30
23 Brad Hoover	.15	.40
24 Tim Biakabutuka	.12	.30
25 Donald Hayes	.12	.30
26 Jeff Lewis	.12	.30
27 Wesley Walls	.12	.30
28 Cade McNown	.15	.40
29 James Allen	.12	.30
30 Marcus Robinson	.15	.40
31 Brian Urlacher	.25	.60
32 Jim Miller	.15	.40
33 Peter Warrick	.12	.30
34 Corey Dillon	.12	.30
35 Akili Smith	.12	.30
36 Danny Farmer	.12	.30
37 Ron Dugans	.12	.30
38 Jon Kitna	.12	.30
39 Tim Couch	.12	.30
40 Kevin Johnson	.12	.30
41 Travis Prentice	.12	.30
42 Spergon Wynn	.12	.30
43 Errict Rhett	.15	.40
44 Dennis Northcutt	.12	.30
45 Courtney Brown	.12	.30
46 Tony Banks	.12	.30
47 Emmitt Smith	.30	.75
48 Joey Galloway	.15	.40
49 Rocket Ismail	.15	.40
50 Anthony Wright	.12	.30
51 Jackie Harris	.15	.40
52 Terrell Davis	.15	.40
53 Mike Anderson	.12	.30
54 Brian Griese	.12	.30
55 Rod Smith	.15	.40
56 Ed McCaffrey	.15	.40
57 Howard Griffith	.12	.30
58 Olandis Gary	.12	.30
59 Charlie Batch	.12	.30
60 Germane Crowell	.12	.30
61 James O. Stewart	.12	.30
62 Johnnie Morton	.15	.40
63 Desmond Howard	.15	.40
64 Brett Favre	.40	1.00
65 Antonio Freeman	.20	.50
66 Dorsey Levens	.15	.40
67 Ahman Green	.15	.40
68 Bill Schroeder	.15	.40
69 Bubba Franks	.12	.30
70 Peyton Manning	.50	1.25
71 Edgerrin James	.15	.40
72 Marvin Harrison	.15	.40
73 Jerome Pathon	.12	.30
74 Ken Dilger	.12	.30
75 Terrence Wilkins	.12	.30
76 Mark Brunell	.15	.40
77 Fred Taylor	.12	.30
78 Jimmy Smith	.15	.40
79 Keenan McCardell	.15	.40
80 R. Jay Soward	.12	.30
81 Todd Collins	.12	.30
82 Tony Gonzalez	.15	.40
83 Derrick Alexander	.12	.30
84 Trent Green	.12	.30
85 Sylvester Morris	.12	.30
86 Oronde Gadsden	.12	.30
87 Lamar Smith	.15	.40
88 Jay Fiedler	.15	.40
89 Zach Thomas	.15	.40
90 Ray Lucas	.12	.30
91 O.J. McDuffie	.12	.30
92 Randy Moss	.15	.40
93 Cris Carter	.20	.50
94 Daunte Culpepper	.15	.40
95 Robert Griffith	.12	.30
96 Jake Reed	.15	.40
97 Drew Bledsoe	.15	.40
98 Terry Glenn	.15	.40
99 Kevin Faulk	.12	.30
100 Michael Bishop	.15	.40
101 Troy Brown	.12	.30
102 Ricky Williams	.15	.40
103 Jeff Blake	.15	.40
104 Joe Horn	.12	.30
105 Willie Jackson	.12	.30
106 Aaron Brooks	.12	.30
107 Keith Poole	.12	.30
108 Kerry Collins	.12	.30
109 Amani Toomer	.12	.30
110 Ron Dayne	.15	.40
111 Tiki Barber	.15	.40
112 Ike Hilliard	.12	.30
113 Ron Dixon	.12	.30
114 Michael Strahan	.15	.40
115 Vinny Testaverde	.12	.30
116 Wayne Chrebet	.12	.30
117 Curtis Martin	.15	.40
118 Richie Anderson	.12	.30
119 Laveranues Coles	.15	.40
120 Chad Pennington	.12	.30
121 Tim Brown	.20	.50
122 Rich Gannon	.15	.40
123 Tyrone Wheatley	.15	.40
124 Charlie Garner	.15	.40
125 Andre Rison	.15	.40
126 Charles Woodson	.20	.50
127 Jon Ritchie	.12	.30
128 Duce Staley	.12	.30
129 Donovan McNabb	.15	.40
130 Darnell Autry	.12	.30
131 Chad Lewis	.12	.30
132 Brian Mitchell	.15	.40
133 Kordell Stewart	.12	.30
134 Jerome Bettis	.20	.50
135 Plaxico Burress	.12	.30
136 Bobby Shaw	.12	.30
137 Hines Ward	.15	.40
138 Marshall Faulk	.15	.40
139 Kurt Warner	.30	.75
140 Isaac Bruce	.20	.50
141 Torry Holt	.15	.40
142 Justin Watson	.12	.30
143 Az-ZahirHakim	.12	.30
144 Junior Seau	.15	.40
145 Curtis Conway	.15	.40
146 Doug Flutie	.15	.40
147 Jeff Graham	.12	.30
148 Freddie Jones	.12	.30
149 Rodney Harrison	.12	.30
150 Jeff Garcia	.12	.30
151 Jerry Rice	.40	1.00
152 Jonas Lewis	.12	.30
153 Terrell Owens	.15	.40
154 J.J. Stokes	.12	.30
155 Garrison Hearst	.15	.40
156 Ricky Watters	.15	.40
157 Shaun Alexander	.12	.30
158 Matt Hasselbeck	.12	.30
159 Brock Huard	.12	.30
160 Darrell Jackson	.15	.40
161 Itula Mili	.12	.30
162 Warrick Dunn	.12	.30
163 Shaun King	.12	.30
164 Reidel Anthony	.12	.30
165 Mike Alstott	.12	.30
166 Jacquez Green	.12	.30
167 Brad Johnson	.15	.40
168 Keyshawn Johnson	.15	.40
169 Eddie George	.20	.50
170 Steve McNair	.15	.40
171 Neil O'Donnell	.15	.40
172 Derrick Mason	.12	.30
173 Frank Wycheck	.12	.30
174 Chris Sanders	.12	.30
175 Jevon Kearse	.12	.30
176 Jeff George	.15	.40
177 Stephen Davis	.12	.30
178 Skip Hicks	.12	.30
179 Michael Westbrook	.12	.30
180 Stephen Alexander	.12	.30
181 Vinny Testaverde SH	.12	.30
182 Trent Green SH	.12	.30
183 Brian Griese SH	.12	.30
184 Kerry Collins SH	.12	.30
185 Aaron Brooks SH	.12	.30
186 Jamal Lewis SH	.20	.50
187 Jeff Garcia SH	.12	.30
188 Warrick Dunn SH	.12	.30
189 Mike Anderson SH	.12	.30
190 Lamar Smith SH	.15	.40
191 Daunte Culpepper SL	.15	.40
192 Darren Sharper SL	.15	.40
193 Marvin Harrison SL	.15	.40
194 Torry Holt SL	.15	.40
195 Trent Green SL	.12	.30
196 Peyton Manning SL	.50	1.25
197 Muhsin Muhammad SL	.12	.30
198 La'Roi Glover SL	.12	.30
199 Brian Griese SL	.12	.30
200 Darrick Vaughn SL	.12	.30
201 Bobby Newcombe RC	.40	1.00
202 Leonard Davis RC	.50	1.25
203 Alge Crumpler RC	.50	1.25
204 Michael Vick RC	.75	2.00
205 Vinny Sutherland RC	.30	.75
206 Chris Barnes RC	.30	.75
207 Todd Heap RC	.40	1.00
208 Travis Henry RC	.40	1.00
209 Tim Hasselbeck RC	.40	1.00
210 Nate Clements RC	.40	1.00
211 Chris Weinke RC	.40	1.00
212 Dan Morgan RC	.40	1.00
213 Anthony Thomas RC	.50	1.25
214 David Terrell RC	.40	1.00
215 Chad Johnson RC	.50	1.25
216 Justin Smith RC	.60	1.50
217 Rudi Johnson RC	.50	1.25
218 T.J. Houshmandzadeh RC	.40	1.00
219 Gerard Warren RC	.40	1.00
220 James Jackson RC	.30	.75
221 Quincy Morgan RC	.40	1.00
222 Quincy Carter RC	.40	1.00
223 Tony Dixon RC	.30	.75
224 Kevin Kasper RC	.30	.75
225 Willie Middlebrooks RC	.40	1.00
226 Mike McMahon RC	.40	1.00
227 Shaun Rogers RC	.50	1.25
228 Jamal Reynolds RC	.30	.75
229 Robert Ferguson RC	.50	1.25
230 Reggie Wayne RC	.60	1.50
231 Marcus Stroud RC	.40	1.00
232 Dustin McClintock RC	.40	1.00
233 Snoop Minnis RC	.30	.75
234 Chris Chambers RC	.30	.75
235 Josh Heupel RC	.50	1.25
236 Travis Minor RC	.40	1.00
237 Michael Bennett RC	.40	1.00
238 Richard Seymour RC	.50	1.25
239 Hakim Akbar RC	.30	.75
240 Deuce McAllister RC	.50	1.25
241 Moran Norris RC	.30	.75
242 Jesse Palmer RC	.40	1.00
243 Will Allen RC	.50	1.25
244 LaMont Jordan RC	.50	1.25
245 Santana Moss RC	.50	1.25
246 Marques Tuiasosopo RC	.40	1.00
247 Correll Buckhalter RC	.30	.75
248 Freddie Mitchell RC	.30	.75
249 A.J. Feeley RC	.40	1.00
250 Dave Dickenson RC	.40	1.00
251 Drew Brees RC	15.00	40.00
252 LaDainian Tomlinson RC	4.00	10.00
253 David Allen RC	.30	.75
254 Andre Carter RC	.40	1.00
255 Kevan Barlow RC	.40	1.00
256 Josh Booty RC	.40	1.00
257 Koren Robinson RC	.40	1.00
258 Adam Archuleta RC	.40	1.00
259 Rod Gardner RC	.40	1.00
260 Sage Rosenfels RC	.40	1.00
261 R.Germany/K.Rambo RC	.30	.75
262 E.Hartwell/G.Baxter RC	.30	.75
263 A.Schobel/B.Spoon RC	.50	1.25
264 J.Capel/K.Riley RC	.30	.75
265 B.Baber/D.Blaylock RC	.40	1.00
266 J.Fletcher/M.Greenwood RC	.30	.75
267 A.King/R.Daniels RC	.30	.75
268 A.Love/J.Holloway RC	.30	.75
269 J.Jennings RC/K.Walker RC	.30	.75
270 B.Hamilton/P.Toviessa RC	.30	.75
271 C.Taylor/J.Getherall RC	.30	.75
272 C.Hampton/K.Bell RC	.50	1.25
273 C.Wilson/J.Winborn RC	.40	1.00
274 A.Bannister/H.Evans RC	.40	1.00
275 D.Lewis/R.Pickett RC	.40	1.00
276 T.Polley/B.Allen RC	.30	.75
277 J.Henderson/R.White RC	.40	1.00
278 E.Berlin/J.McCareins RC	.40	1.00
279 A.Dyson/D.Alexander RC	.40	1.00
280 Q.McCord/R.Garza RC	.40	1.00
281 Anderson/Kelly/Howard RC	.30	.75
282 Jue/Martin/Marshall RC	.40	1.00
283 St.Smith/D.Brown/Cooper RC	1.00	2.50
284 Grant/Combs/Gibson RC	.30	.75
285 Polk/Cody/Moreno RC	.40	1.00
286 Rivers/St.Paul/Wynn RC	.30	.75
287 Davis/Smith/Hodge RC	.30	.75
288 Lucas/Huff/Hutchinson RC	.75	2.00
289 Rivers/Burgess/Driver RC	.50	1.25
290 McCants/Smoot/Cerimele RC	.40	1.00

2001 Upper Deck Vintage Franchise Players

Franchise Players were inserted into packs of 2001 Uppcr Deck Vintage at a rate of 1:24. This 7-card set featured some of the top players from the NFL. The cards had a white border and the words 'Franchise Players down the left side of the card. The cards used an 'FP' prefix for the card numbers.

COMPLETE SET (7)	6.00	15.00
STATED ODDS 1:24		
FP1 Charlie Batch	.60	1.50
FP2 Ricky Williams	.75	2.00
FP3 Brett Favre	2.00	5.00
FP4 Emmitt Smith	1.50	4.00
FP5 Terrell Davis	.75	2.00
FP6 Jerome Bettis	1.00	2.50
FP7 Eddie George	1.00	2.50

2001 Upper Deck Vintage Matinee Idols

tinee Idols were randomly inserted in packs of 2001 Upper Deck Vintage at a rate of 1:18.This 10-card set featured some of the top players from the NFL. The card design featured a full color shot of the player and a black and white shot of him on the side of the card. The card numbers had an 'M' preceding them.

COMPLETE SET (10)	6.00	15.00
STATED ODDS 1:18		
M1 Stephen Davis	.60	1.50
M2 Mike Alstott	.60	1.50
M3 Ricky Williams	.75	2.00
M4 Ricky Watters	.75	2.00
M5 Donovan McNabb	.75	2.00
M6 Charlie Batch	.60	1.50
M7 Jamal Lewis	1.00	2.50
M8 Drew Bledsoe	.75	2.00
M9 Aaron Brooks	.60	1.50
M10 Vinny Testaverde	.60	1.50

2001 Upper Deck Vintage Old School Attitude

d School Attitude was inserted in packs of 2001 Upper Deck Vintage at a rate of 1:18. The cards featured veterans from the NFL who played with a throwback style. The card numbers featured an 'OS' prefix.

COMPLETE SET (10)	6.00	15.00
STATED ODDS 1:18		
OS1 Tim Brown	1.00	2.50
OS2 Peyton Manning	2.50	6.00
OS3 Jamal Anderson	.75	2.00
OS4 Doug Flutie	.75	2.00
OS5 Emmitt Smith	1.50	4.00
OS6 Cris Carter	1.00	2.50
OS7 Ed McCaffrey	.75	2.00
OS8 Fred Taylor	.60	1.50
OS9 Curtis Martin	.75	2.00
OS10 Tim Couch	.60	1.50

2001 Upper Deck Vintage Signatures

Randomly inserted in packs of 2001 Upper Deck Vintage at a rate of 1:144, this 25-card set featured the top players from the NFL. Please note there were 4 cards which were issued as exchange cards at the time of the product's release. They had an expiration date of August 7, 2004.

STATED ODDS 1:144 HOBBY		
ABVS Aaron Brooks	6.00	15.00
CBVS Charlie Batch	6.00	15.00
CDVS Corey Dillon	6.00	15.00
DFVS Doug Flutie	8.00	20.00
DIVS Trent Dilfer	6.00	15.00
EJVS Edgerrin James	8.00	20.00
IBVS Isaac Bruce	10.00	25.00
JBVS Jim Brown	75.00	150.00
JNVS Joe Namath	60.00	120.00
JRVS John Riggins	30.00	80.00
JSVS Junior Seau	25.00	50.00
MAVS Mike Anderson	6.00	15.00
MBVS Mark Brunell	12.00	30.00
MFVS Marshall Faulk	12.00	30.00
MRVS Marcus Robinson	8.00	20.00
NOVS Jeff Blake	8.00	20.00
PHVS Paul Hornung	15.00	30.00
PMVS Peyton Manning	50.00	100.00
TBVS Terry Bradshaw	50.00	120.00
TCVS Tim Couch	6.00	15.00
TDVS Terrell Davis	8.00	20.00
TGVS Tony Gonzalez	8.00	20.00
TOVS Terrell Owens	15.00	40.00
VTVS Vinny Testaverde	6.00	15.00
WCVS Wayne Chrebet	6.00	15.00

2001 Upper Deck Vintage Smashmouth

Randomly inserted in packs of 2001 Upper Deck Vintage at a rate of 1:12, this 15-card set featured active players with a smashmouth style of play. The cards carried an 'S' prefix for the card numbers. The cardfronts had a photo of the featured player on about half of the card and the other half was a white border with what the words 'Smashmouth' covering most of the border. Please note the words above the photo appear to be cut off, but this was done intentionally.

COMPLETE SET (15)	6.00	15.00
STATED ODDS 1:12		
S1 Ray Lewis	1.00	2.50
S2 Junior Seau	.75	2.00
S3 Eddie George	1.00	2.50
S4 Jerome Bettis	1.00	2.50
S5 Ricky Williams	.75	2.00
S6 Terrell Owens	.75	2.00
S7 Warren Sapp	.75	2.00
S8 John Lynch	.75	2.00
S9 Brian Urlacher	1.25	3.00
S10 Zach Thomas	.75	2.00
S11 Tyrone Wheatley	.75	2.00
S12 Stephen Davis	.60	1.50
S13 Mike Alstott	.60	1.50
S14 Fred Taylor	.60	1.50
S15 Cris Carter	1.00	2.50

2001 Upper Deck Vintage Threads

ndomly inserted in packs of 2001 Upper Deck Vintage at a rate of 1:144, this 25-card set featured the top players from the NFL. Each card had a small swatch of the featured player's game used jersey. The card numbers carried a 'VT' suffix on them.

STATED ODDS 1:144		
ASVT Akili Smith	2.50	6.00
BEVT Michael Bennett	3.00	8.00
BFVT Brett Favre	8.00	20.00
CDVT Corey Dillon	2.50	6.00
CJVT Chad Johnson	4.00	10.00
CWVT Chris Weinke	3.00	8.00
DMVT Deuce McAllister	4.00	10.00
DRVT Drew Brees	15.00	40.00
FMVT Freddie Mitchell	2.50	6.00
IHVT Ike Hilliard	2.50	6.00
JGVT Jeff Garcia	2.50	6.00
JJVT James Jackson	2.50	6.00
JRVT Jerry Rice	8.00	20.00
KBVT Kevan Barlow	3.00	8.00
KRVT Koren Robinson	3.00	8.00
KWVT Kurt Warner	8.00	20.00
LTVT LaDainian Tomlinson	12.00	30.00
MBVT Mark Brunell	3.00	8.00
MVVT Michael Vick	6.00	15.00
PWVT Peter Warrick	2.50	6.00
QMVT Quincy Morgan	3.00	8.00
RDVT Ron Dayne	3.00	8.00
RGVT Rod Gardner	3.00	8.00
RLVT Ray Lewis	4.00	10.00
RMVT Randy Moss	3.00	8.00
RWVT Reggie Wayne	5.00	12.00
SMVT Santana Moss	4.00	10.00
TAVT Troy Aikman	5.00	12.00
WSVT Warren Sapp	3.00	8.00
ZTVT Zach Thomas	3.00	8.00

2001 Upper Deck Vintage Threads Autographs

ndomly inserted in packs of 2001 Upper Deck Vintage, this 14-card set featured an authentic swatch of a player worn jersey along with a certified autograph. The cards carried an 'SVT' suffix for the card numbers. Each card was serial numbered to 100.

STATED PRINT RUN 100 SER.#'d SETS		
CDSVT Corey Dillon	15.00	40.00
DBSVT Drew Bledsoe	20.00	50.00
DCSVT Daunte Culpepper	20.00	50.00
JGSVT Jeff Garcia	15.00	40.00
JMSVT Joe Montana	150.00	300.00
JRSVT Jerry Rice	75.00	150.00
KWSVT Kurt Warner	40.00	100.00
MASVT Mike Alstott	15.00	40.00
MBSVT Mark Brunell	20.00	50.00
PMSVT Peyton Manning	60.00	120.00
RMSVT Randy Moss	50.00	100.00
SDSVT Stephen Davis	15.00	40.00
TASVT Troy Aikman	50.00	100.00
TCSVT Tim Couch	15.00	40.00

2001 Upper Deck Vintage Threads Combos

ndomly inserted in packs of 2001 Upper Deck Vintage, this 14-card set featured 2 authentic swatches of player worn jerseys from the 2 featured players. The cards carried a 'VTC' suffix for the card numbers. Each card was serial numbered to 50.

STATED PRINT RUN 50 SER.#'d SETS		
AMVTC T.Aikman/C.McNown	8.00	20.00
BDVTC T.Barber/R.Dayne	5.00	12.00
BFVTC M.Brunell/B.Favre	12.00	30.00
DBVTC R.Dayne/M.Bennett	5.00	12.00
FJVTC M.Faulk/E.James	5.00	12.00
FMVTC M.Faulk/D.McAllister	5.00	12.00
GSVTC D.Green/D.Sanders	6.00	15.00
MCVTC D.McNabb/D.Culpepper	5.00	12.00
MJVTC P.Manning/E.James	15.00	40.00
MRVTC R.Moss/J.Rice	12.00	30.00
WHVTC K.Warner/T.Holt	10.00	25.00

2011 Upper Deck World of Sports

COMPLETE SET (400)	75.00	150.00
COMP.SET w/o SPs (300)	25.00	60.00
89 Adrian Peterson	.40	1.00
90 Armon Binns	.15	.40
91 Rocket Ismail	.15	.40
92 Floyd Little	.25	.60
93 Greg Pruitt	.15	.40
94 Mikel Leshoure	.15	.40
95 Tim Brown	.15	.40
96 Kendall Hunter	.40	1.00
97 Doug Flutie	.15	.40
98 John Cappelletti	.15	.40
99 Bernie Kosar	.15	.40
100 Leonard Hankerson	.15	.40
101 Brian Bosworth	.15	.40
102 Andy Dalton	.75	2.00
103 Eric Metcalf	.15	.40
104 Christian Ponder	.60	1.50
105 Aaron Williams	.15	.40
106 Aldon Smith	.15	.40
107 Randall Cobb	.25	.60
108 Nick Fairley	.15	.40
109 Prince Amukamara	.25	.60
110 Ryan Mallett	.60	1.50
111 Titus Young	.15	.40
112 Daniel Thomas	.25	.60
113 Jonathan Baldwin	.15	.40
114 DeMarco Murray	.60	1.50
115 Colin Kaepernick	.75	2.00
116 Noel Devine	.25	.60
117 Kyle Rudolph	.40	1.00
118 Ryan Kerrigan	.40	1.00
119 Torrey Smith	.40	1.00
120 Adrian Clayborn	.15	.40
121 Justin Houston	.30	.75
122 Akeem Ayers	.15	.40
123 Ryan Williams	.15	.40
124 Greg Little	.15	.40
125 Charles White	.15	.40
126 Evan Royster	.15	.40
127 Allen Bradford	.15	.40
128 Rahim Moore	.15	.40
129 Da'Quan Bowers	.25	.60
130 Corey Liuget	.15	.40
131 Terrelle Pryor	.40	1.00
132 Vincent Brown	.15	.40
133 Bo Jackson	.40	1.00
134 Terrence Toliver	.15	.40
135 Ricky Stanzi	2.00	.50
136 Jaiquawn Jarrett	.15	.40
137 Adam Weber	.15	.40
138 Bruce Carter	.15	.40
139 Rod Woodson	.25	.60
140 Drew Brees	.40	1.00
141 Dan Marino	.40	1.00
142 Greg Salas	.40	1.00
310 Bo Jackson SP	1.50	4.00
330 Archie Griffin SP	1.00	2.50
331 Blaine Gabbert SP	1.25	3.00
332 Von Miller SP	1.00	2.50
333 Aaron Rodgers SP	1.50	4.00
334 Tony Dorsett SP	1.00	2.50
335 John Elway SP	1.25	3.00
336 Bubba Smith SP	1.00	2.50
337 Barry Sanders SP	1.00	2.50
338 Earl Campbell SP	1.00	2.50
339 Gale Sayers SP	1.00	2.50
340 Troy Aikman SP	1.00	2.50
341 A.J. Green SP	1.00	2.50
342 Cam Newton SP	1.50	4.00
343 Jake Locker SP	1.25	3.00
344 Julio Jones SP	1.00	2.50
345 Billy Sims SP	1.00	2.50
346 Mark Ingram SP	1.00	2.50
347 Herschel Walker SP	1.00	2.50

2011 Upper Deck World of Sports All-Sport Apparel Memorabilia

OVERALL AUTO/MEM ODDS 3 PER BOX		
ASAG A.J. Green	4.00	10.00
ASBG Blaine Gabbert	3.00	8.00
ASCK Colin Kaepernick	6.00	15.00
ASCN Cam Newton	10.00	25.00
ASJL Jake Locker	5.00	12.00
ASMI Mark Ingram	0.00	15.00
ASPO Christian Ponder	4.00	10.00
ASTS Torrey Smith	3.00	8.00
ASTT Terrence Toliver	3.00	8.00
AWJJ Julio Jones	8.00	20.00

2011 Upper Deck World of Sports All-Sport Apparel Memorabilia Autographs

ASAG A.J. Green/10		
ASBG Blaine Gabbert/10		
ASCK Colin Kaepernick/15	40.00	80.00
ASCN Cam Newton/5		
ASMI Mark Ingram/15	40.00	80.00
ASPO Christian Ponder/20		
ASTS Torrey Smith/10		
ASTT Terrence Toliver/20		
AWJJ Julio Jones/10		

2011 Upper Deck World of Sports Athletes of the World Autographs

OVERALL AUTO/MEM ODDS 3 PER BOX		
AWDM Darren McFadden	8.00	20.00
AWFL Joe Flacco	10.00	25.00
AWMR Ryan Mathews	6.00	15.00
AWRM Rashard Mendenhall	6.00	15.00
AWST Jonathan Stewart		

2011 Upper Deck World of Sports Autographs

89 Adrian Peterson A		
90 Armon Binns B	4.00	10.00
91 Rocket Ismail B		
92 Floyd Little B	8.00	20.00
93 Greg Pruitt A		
94 Mikel Leshoure B		
95 Tim Brown B		
96 Kendall Hunter C	6.00	15.00
99 Bernie Kosar B		
100 Leonard Hankerson B	4.00	10.00
101 Brian Bosworth B		
102 Andy Dalton C	8.00	20.00
104 Christian Ponder B	12.00	30.00
105 Aaron Williams B	4.00	10.00
107 Randall Cobb B		
109 Prince Amukamara C	5.00	12.00
110 Ryan Mallett B	12.00	30.00
111 Titus Young B	4.00	10.00
112 Daniel Thomas C	5.00	12.00
114 DeMarco Murray B		
115 Colin Kaepernick C	20.00	50.00
116 Noel Devine B		
117 Kyle Rudolph C	6.00	15.00
118 Ryan Kerrigan C	6.00	15.00
119 Torrey Smith B	6.00	15.00
121 Justin Houston C	5.00	12.00
123 Ryan Williams B		
124 Greg Little C	4.00	10.00
125 Charles White C		
126 Evan Royster B		
127 Allen Bradford C	4.00	10.00
128 Rahim Moore C	4.00	10.00
129 Da'Quan Bowers C	5.00	12.00
130 Corey Liuget C	4.00	10.00
131 Terrelle Pryor A		
132 Vincent Brown C	4.00	10.00
133 Bo Jackson B	30.00	60.00
134 Terrence Toliver C	4.00	10.00
135 Ricky Stanzi C	8.00	20.00
136 Jaiquawn Jarrett C		
137 Adam Weber C	4.00	10.00
138 Bruce Carter B		
139 Rod Woodson B	20.00	40.00
140 Drew Brees A	30.00	60.00
141 Dan Marino A		
142 Greg Salas B	6.00	15.00
310 Bo Jackson A	30.00	60.00
331 Blaine Gabbert A		
332 Von Miller B	12.00	30.00
334 Tony Dorsett A		
335 John Elway A		
336 Bubba Smith A	15.00	30.00
337 Barry Sanders A		
338 Earl Campbell A		
339 Gale Sayers A		
341 A.J. Green A		
342 Cam Newton A	50.00	100.00
343 Jake Locker A		
344 Julio Jones A	25.00	50.00
345 Billy Sims A		
346 Mark Ingram A	25.00	50.00

2002 Upper Deck XL

Released in June, 2002, this set contains 100-rookies and 500-veterans making a total of 600-cards. This was one of the most ambitious efforts in recent years from any card company in terms of player selection, hence the name "XL." The rookie cards were inserted at a stated rate of one every two packs.

COMPLETE SET (600)	75.00	150.00
COMP.SET w/o SP's (500)	25.00	60.00
ROOKIE STATED ODDS 1:2		
1 David Boston	.15	.40
2 Dave Brown	.15	.40
3 Frank Sanders	.15	.40
4 Jake Plummer	.15	.40
5 Joel Makovicka	.15	.40
6 Kwamie Lassiter	.15	.40
7 MarTay Jenkins	.15	.40
8 Michael Pittman	.20	.50
9 Raynoch Thompson	.15	.40
10 Rob Fredrickson	.15	.40
11 Ronald McKinnon	.15	.40
12 Steve Bush	.15	.40
13 Thomas Jones	.15	.40
14 Tywan Mitchell	.15	.40
15 Alvis Whitted	.15	.40
16 Ashley Ambrose	.15	.40
17 Bob Christian	.15	.40
18 Brady Smith	.15	.40
19 Brian Finneran	.15	.40
20 Chris Chandler	.20	.50
21 Chris Draft RC	.15	.40
22 Darrien Gordon	.15	.40
23 Doug Johnson	.15	.40
24 Ephraim Salaam	.15	.40
25 Jamal Anderson	.20	.50
26 Keith Brooking	.15	.40
27 Maurice Smith	.15	.40
28 Michael Vick	.20	.50
29 Ray Buchanan	.15	.40
30 Shawn Jefferson	.15	.40
31 Terance Mathis	.15	.40
32 Tony Martin	.20	.50
33 Brandon Stokley	.15	.40
34 Chris McAlister	.15	.40
35 Chris Redman	.15	.40
36 Elvis Grbac	.15	.40
37 Jonathan Ogden	.20	.50
38 Moe Williams	.15	.40
39 Obafemi Ayanbadejo	.15	.40
40 Peter Boulware	.15	.40
41 Qadry Ismail	.15	.40
42 Randall Cunningham	.20	.50
43 Ray Lewis	.25	.60
44 Rod Woodson	.25	.60
45 Sam Adams	.15	.40
46 Shannon Sharpe	.20	.50
47 Terry Allen	.20	.50
48 Todd Heap	.20	.50
49 Tony Siragusa	.20	.50
50 Travis Taylor	.15	.40
51 Alex Van Pelt	.15	.40
52 Antoine Winfield	.15	.40
53 Eric Moulds	.15	.40
54 Jay Foreman RC	.15	.40
55 Jay Riemersma	.15	.40
56 Jeremy McDaniel	.15	.40
57 Keith Newman	.15	.40
58 Kenyatta Wright	.15	.40
59 Larry Centers	.15	.40
60 Peerless Price	.15	.40

61 Rob Johnson .20 .50
62 Ruben Brown .15 .40
63 Shawn Bryson .15 .40
64 Travis Brown .15 .40
65 Travis Henry .15 .40
66 Brad Hoover .15 .40
67 Brentson Buckner .15 .40
68 Chris Weinke .15 .40
69 Dameyune Craig .15 .40
70 Deon Grant .15 .40
71 Donald Hayes .15 .40
72 Doug Evans .15 .40
73 Isaac Byrd .15 .40
74 Jay Williams RC .15 .40
75 Lester Towns .15 .40
76 Muhsin Muhammad .15 .40
77 Richard Huntley .15 .40
78 Steve Smith .25 .60
79 Tim Biakabutuka .20 .50
80 Todd Sauerbrun .15 .40
81 Wesley Walls .20 .50
82 Anthony Thomas .20 .50
83 Brian Urlacher .25 .60
84 Daimon Shelton .15 .40
85 David Terrell .15 .40
86 Dez White .15 .40
87 Fred Baxter .15 .40
88 James Allen .15 .40
89 James Williams .15 .40
90 Jim Miller .15 .40
91 Keith Traylor .15 .40
92 Larry Whigham .15 .40
93 Marcus Robinson .20 .50
94 Marty Booker .15 .40
95 Mike Brown .15 .40
96 Olin Kreutz RC .30 .75
97 R.W. McQuarters .15 .40
98 Rosevelt Colvin RC .30 .75
99 Shane Matthews .15 .40
100 Ted Washington .15 .40
101 Akili Smith .20 .50
102 Brandon Bennett .15 .40
103 Brian Simmons .15 .40
104 Chad Johnson .15 .40
105 Corey Dillon .15 .40
106 Darnay Scott .20 .50
107 Jon Kitna .15 .40
108 Lorenzo Neal .15 .40
109 Peter Warrick .15 .40
110 Ron Dugans .15 .40
111 Scott Mitchell .20 .50
112 Takeo Spikes .15 .40
113 Tony McGee .20 .50
114 Brant Boyer .15 .40
115 Corey Fuller .15 .40
116 Courtney Brown .15 .40
117 Dwayne Rudd .15 .40
118 JaJuan Dawson .15 .40
119 Jamel White .15 .40
120 James Jackson .15 .40
121 Jamir Miller .15 .40
122 Josh Booty .15 .40
123 Kelly Holcomb .20 .50
124 Kevin Johnson .15 .40
125 Lenoy Jones RC .15 .40
126 Quincy Morgan .15 .40
127 Raymond Jackson RC .15 .40
128 Rickey Dudley .15 .40
129 Tim Couch .15 .40
130 Darren Woodson .20 .50
131 Dat Nguyen .15 .40
132 Dexter Coakley .15 .40
133 Duane Hawthorne .15 .40
134 Emmitt Smith .40 1.00
135 Jackie Harris .20 .50
136 Joey Galloway .20 .50
137 Ken-Yon Rambo .15 .40
138 Larry Allen .25 .60
139 Mike Lucky .15 .40
140 Quincy Carter .15 .40
141 Rocket Ismail .20 .50
142 Reggie Swinton .15 .40
143 Robert Thomas .15 .40
144 Ryan Leaf .15 .40
145 Troy Hambrick .15 .40
146 Al Wilson .20 .50
147 Bill Romanowski .20 .50
148 Brian Griese .15 .40
149 Chester McGlockton .15 .40
150 Chris Cole .15 .40
151 Deltha O'Neal .15 .40
152 Desmond Clark .15 .40
153 Dwayne Carswell .15 .40
154 Ian Gold .15 .40
155 Jarious Jackson .15 .40
156 Jason Elam .15 .40
157 Keith Burns .15 .40
158 Mike Anderson .15 .40
159 Olandis Gary .20 .50
160 Rod Smith .20 .50
161 Scottie Montgomery .15 .40
162 Terrell Davis .20 .50
163 Trevor Pryce .15 .40
164 Charlie Batch .15 .40
165 Chris Claiborne .15 .40
166 Cory Schlesinger .15 .40
167 David Sloan .15 .40
168 Desmond Howard .20 .50
169 Germane Crowell .15 .40
170 James Stewart .15 .40
171 Johnnie Morton .20 .50
172 Lamont Warren .15 .40
173 Larry Foster .15 .40
174 Mike McMahon .15 .40
175 Robert Porcher .15 .40
176 Shaun Rogers .15 .40
177 Todd Lyght .15 .40
178 Ty Detmer .15 .40
179 Ahman Green .20 .50
180 Antonio Freeman .25 .60
181 Bhawoh Jue .15 .40
182 Bill Schroeder .15 .40
183 Brett Favre .50 1.25
184 Bubba Franks .15 .40
185 Corey Bradford .15 .40
186 Darren Sharper .15 .40
187 Donald Driver .20 .50
188 Dorsey Levens .20 .50
189 Doug Pederson .15 .40
190 Kabeer Gbaja-Biamila .15 .40
191 William Henderson .15 .40
192 Aaron Glenn .15 .40
193 Danny Wuerffel .20 .50
194 Gary Walker .15 .40
195 Jamie Sharper .20 .50
196 Jermaine Lewis .15 .40
197 Matt Stevens .15 .40
198 Seth Payne RC .15 .40
199 Tony Boselli .20 .50
200 Dominic Rhodes .15 .40
201 Edgerrin James .20 .50
202 Jerome Pathon .15 .40
203 Ken Dilger .15 .40
204 Kevin McDougal .15 .40
205 Marcus Pollard .15 .40
206 Mark Rypien .20 .50
207 Marvin Harrison .20 .50
208 Peyton Manning .60 1.50
209 Reggie Wayne .20 .50
210 Terrence Wilkins .15 .40
211 Donovin Darius .15 .40
212 Elvis Joseph .15 .40
213 Fred Taylor .15 .40
214 Hardy Nickerson .15 .40
215 Jimmy Smith .20 .50
216 Jonathan Quinn .15 .40
217 Keenan McCardell .20 .50
218 Kevin Hardy .15 .40
219 Kyle Brady .15 .40
220 Mark Brunell .20 .50
221 Patrick Washington .15 .40
222 Sean Dawkins .20 .50
223 Stacey Mack .15 .40
224 Tony Brackens .15 .40
225 Derrick Alexander .15 .40
226 Donnie Edwards .15 .40
227 Eric Hicks .15 .40
228 Kendall Gammon RC .15 .40
229 Snoop Minnis .15 .40
230 Mike Cloud .15 .40
231 Priest Holmes .15 .40
232 Todd Collins .20 .50
233 Tony Gonzalez .20 .50
234 Tony Richardson .15 .40
235 Trent Green .15 .40
236 Will Shields .15 .40
237 Brock Marion .15 .40
238 Chris Chambers .15 .40
239 Dedric Ward .15 .40
240 Hunter Goodwin .15 .40
241 James McKnight .15 .40
242 Jay Fiedler .20 .50
243 Kenny Mixon .15 .40
244 Lamar Smith .15 .40
245 Oronde Gadsden .15 .40
246 Patrick Surtain .15 .40
247 Ray Lucas .15 .40
248 Sam Madison .15 .40
249 Travis Minor .15 .40
250 Zach Thomas .20 .50
251 Byron Chamberlain .15 .40
252 Chris Walsh .15 .40
253 Cris Carter .25 .60
254 Daunte Culpepper .20 .50
255 Doug Chapman .15 .40
256 Gary Anderson .15 .40
257 Jake Reed .20 .50
258 Jim Kleinsasser .25 .60
259 Kailee Wong .15 .40
260 Matt Birk .15 .40
261 Michael Bennett .15 .40
262 Randy Moss .20 .50
263 Robert Tate .15 .40
264 Spergon Wynn .15 .40
265 Antowain Smith .20 .50
266 Bryan Cox .20 .50
267 David Patten .15 .40
268 Drew Bledsoe .20 .50
269 Adam Vinatieri .15 .40
270 J.R. Redmond .15 .40
271 Jermaine Wiggins .15 .40
272 Kevin Faulk .15 .40
273 Lawyer Milloy .15 .40
274 Marc Edwards .15 .40
275 Tedy Bruschi .20 .50
276 Tom Brady 1.25 3.00
277 Troy Brown .15 .40
278 Ty Law .25 .60
279 Willie McGinest .20 .50
280 Aaron Brooks .15 .40
281 Albert Connell .15 .40
282 Boo Williams .15 .40
283 Charlie Clemons RC .15 .40
284 Deuce McAllister .20 .50
285 Jay Bellamy .15 .40
286 Jeff Blake .20 .50
287 Joe Horn .15 .40
288 John Carney .15 .40
289 Kyle Turley .15 .40
290 La'Roi Glover .15 .40
291 Norman Hand .15 .40
292 Ricky Williams .20 .50
293 Robert Wilson .15 .40
294 Sammy Knight .15 .40
295 Terrelle Smith .15 .40
296 Willie Jackson .15 .40
297 Amani Toomer .15 .40
298 Anthony Becht .15 .40
299 Chad Pennington .15 .40
300 Curtis Martin .20 .50
301 Dan Campbell .15 .40
302 Dave Thomas .15 .40
303 Greg Comella .15 .40
304 Ike Hilliard .15 .40
305 James Farrior .15 .40
306 Jason Garrett .20 .50
307 Jason Sehorn .20 .50
308 Jessie Armstead .15 .40
309 Joe Jurevicius .15 .40
310 John Abraham .20 .50
311 Kerry Collins .15 .40
312 Kevin Mawae .15 .40
313 LaMont Jordan .20 .50
314 Laveranues Coles .20 .50
315 Marvin Jones .15 .40
316 Matthew Hatchette .15 .40
317 Michael Strahan .20 .50
318 Michael Barrow .15 .40
319 Morten Andersen .15 .40
320 Richie Anderson .15 .40
321 Ron Dayne .20 .50
322 Ron Dixon .15 .40
323 Ron Stone RC .15 .40
324 Santana Moss .20 .50
325 Tiki Barber .20 .50
326 Vinny Testaverde .15 .40
327 Wayne Chrebet .15 .40
328 Anthony Dorsett .15 .40
329 Charles Woodson .25 .60
330 Charlie Garner .20 .50
331 Regan Upshaw .15 .40
332 Jerry Porter .15 .40
333 Jerry Rice .50 1.25
334 Jon Ritchie .15 .40
335 Lincoln Kennedy .15 .40
336 Marques Tuiasosopo .15 .40
337 Rich Gannon .20 .50
338 Roland Williams .15 .40
339 Sebastian Janikowski .15 .40
340 Barry Sims RC .15 .40
341 Terry Kirby .15 .40
342 Tim Brown .25 .60
343 Tyrone Wheatley .20 .50
344 Zack Crockett .15 .40
345 A.J. Feeley .15 .40
346 Brian Dawkins .25 .60
347 Cecil Martin .15 .40
348 Chad Lewis .15 .40
349 Corey Simon .15 .40
350 Correll Buckhalter .15 .40
351 David Akers .15 .40
352 Donovan McNabb .20 .50
353 Duce Staley .15 .40
354 Freddie Mitchell .15 .40
355 Hugh Douglas .15 .40
356 James Thrash .20 .50
357 Brian Mitchell .20 .50
358 Koy Detmer .20 .50
359 Todd Pinkston .15 .40
360 Tra Thomas .15 .40
361 Troy Vincent .20 .50
362 Alan Faneca RC 30.00 80.00
363 Amos Zereoue .15 .40
364 Bobby Shaw .15 .40
365 Chris Fuamatu-Ma'afala .15 .40
366 Dan Kreider RC 3.00 8.00
367 Hines Ward .20 .50
368 Jason Gildon .20 .50
369 Jerome Bettis .25 .60
370 Jon Witman .15 .40
371 Kendrell Bell .15 .40
372 Kordell Stewart .15 .40
373 Mark Bruener .20 .50
374 Plaxico Burress .15 .40
375 Tommy Maddox .15 .40
376 Troy Edwards .15 .40
377 Curtis Conway .20 .50
378 Darren Bennett .15 .40
379 Doug Flutie .20 .50
380 Drew Brees .50 1.25
381 Fred McCrary .15 .40
382 Freddie Jones .15 .40
383 Jeff Graham .15 .40
384 John Parrella .15 .40
385 Junior Seau .20 .50
386 LaDainian Tomlinson .25 .60
387 Marcellus Wiley .15 .40
388 Tay Cody .15 .40
389 Raylee Johnson .15 .40
390 Rodney Harrison .15 .40
391 Ronney Jenkins .15 .40
392 Ryan McNeil .15 .40
393 Orlando Ruff .15 .40
394 Terrell Fletcher .15 .40
395 Tim Dwight .15 .40
396 Ahmed Plummer .15 .40
397 Andre Carter .15 .40
398 Bryant Young .15 .40
399 Dana Stubblefield .15 .40
400 Eric Johnson .15 .40
401 Fred Beasley .15 .40
402 Garrison Hearst .15 .40
403 J.J. Stokes .15 .40
404 Jeff Garcia .15 .40
405 Jeremy Newberry RC .15 .40
406 Junior Bryant .15 .40
407 Justin Swift .15 .40
408 Kevan Barlow .15 .40
409 Ray Brown .15 .40
410 Tai Streets .15 .40
411 Terrell Owens .20 .50
412 Terry Jackson .15 .40
413 Tim Rattay .20 .50
414 Bobby Engram .15 .40
415 Chad Brown .15 .40
416 Christian Fauria .15 .40
417 Darrell Jackson .20 .50
418 James Williams .15 .40
419 John Randle .20 .50
420 Koren Robinson .15 .40
421 Levon Kirkland .15 .40
422 Mack Strong .15 .40
423 Matt Hasselbeck .15 .40
424 Ricky Watters .20 .50
425 Shaun Alexander .15 .40
426 Shawn Springs .15 .40
427 Trent Dilfer .15 .40
428 Walter Jones .15 .40
429 Adam Timmerman .20 .50
430 Aeneas Williams .15 .40
431 Az-Zahir Hakim .15 .40
432 Dre Bly .15 .40
433 Ernie Conwell .15 .40
434 Isaac Bruce .25 .60
435 James Hodgins .15 .40
436 Jamie Martin .20 .50
437 Kurt Warner .20 .50
438 Leonard Little .20 .50
439 London Fletcher .20 .50
440 Marshall Faulk .20 .50
441 O.J. Brigance .15 .40
442 Orlando Pace .15 .40
443 Ricky Proehl .20 .50
444 Torry Holt .20 .50
445 Trung Canidate .15 .40
446 Aaron Stecker .15 .40
447 Brad Johnson .20 .50
448 Dave Moore .15 .40
449 Derrick Brooks .15 .40
450 Jacquez Green .15 .40
451 John Lynch .20 .50
452 Karl Williams .15 .40
453 Kenyatta Walker .15 .40
454 Keyshawn Johnson .20 .50
455 Mark Royals .15 .40
456 Mike Alstott .15 .40
457 Rabih Abdullah .15 .40
458 Reidel Anthony .15 .40
459 Ronde Barber .15 .40
460 Shaun King .15 .40
461 Simeon Rice .15 .40
462 Warren Sapp .20 .50
463 Warrick Dunn .15 .40
464 Bruce Matthews .15 .40
465 Chris Sanders .15 .40
466 Derrick Mason .15 .40
467 Eddie George .20 .50
468 Erron Kinney .15 .40
469 Frank Wycheck .15 .40
470 Jevon Kearse .15 .40
471 Kevin Dyson .20 .50
472 Mike Green .15 .40
473 Neil O'Donnell .20 .50
474 Perry Phenix RC .15 .40
475 Skip Hicks .15 .40
476 Steve McNair .20 .50
477 Champ Bailey .20 .50
478 Chris Samuels .15 .40
479 Dan Wilkinson .15 .40
480 Darrell Green .25 .60
481 Donnell Bennett .15 .40
482 Donovan Greer RC .15 .40
483 Ethan Albright RC .15 .40
484 Fred Smoot .20 .50
485 Kent Graham .15 .40
486 Kevin Lockett .15 .40
487 Ki-Jana Carter .20 .50
488 Michael Bates .15 .40
489 Michael Westbrook .15 .40
490 Rod Gardner .15 .40
491 Shawn Barber .15 .40
492 Stephen Alexander .15 .40
493 Stephen Davis .15 .40
494 Tony Banks .15 .40
495 Jeremiah Trotter .15 .40
496 Jerome Bettis .25 .60
497 Kurt Warner .20 .50
498 Marshall Faulk .20 .50
499 Randy Moss .20 .50
500 Tom Brady 1.25 3.00
501 Joey Harrington RC .50 1.25
502 David Carr RC .50 1.25
503 Rohan Davey RC .75 2.00
504 Brandon Doman RC .50 1.25
505 Woody Dantzler RC .60 1.50
506 Kurt Kittner RC .50 1.25
507 Donte Stallworth RC .75 2.00
508 Major Applewhite RC .75 2.00
509 Eric Crouch RC .75 2.00
510 Justin Peelle RC .50 1.25
511 J.T. O'Sullivan RC .60 1.50
512 Jason McAddley RC .60 1.50
513 Patrick Ramsey RC .60 1.50
514 Randy Fasani RC .50 1.25
515 Antwaan Randle El RC .60 1.50
516 DeShaun Foster RC .75 2.00
517 T.J. Duckett RC .50 1.25
518 William Green RC .60 1.50
519 Travis Stephens RC .50 1.25
520 Luke Staley RC .50 1.25
521 Leonard Henry RC .50 1.25
522 Najeh Davenport RC .50 1.25
523 Ricky Williams RC .60 1.50
524 Maurice Morris RC .60 1.50
525 Anthony Weaver RC .50 1.25
526 Jeremy Allen RC .50 1.25
527 Chester Taylor RC .75 2.00
528 Clinton Portis RC .75 2.00
529 Damien Anderson RC .50 1.25
530 Larry Ned RC .50 1.25
531 Jonathan Wells RC .60 1.50
532 Antwoine Womack RC .50 1.25
533 Adrian Peterson RC .60 1.50
534 Lamar Gordon RC .60 1.50
535 Chad Hutchinson RC .50 1.25
536 Antonio Bryant RC .75 2.00
537 Josh Reed RC .60 1.50
538 Jabar Gaffney RC .50 1.25
539 Ashley Lelie RC .50 1.25
540 Ron Johnson RC .60 1.50
541 Marquise Walker RC .50 1.25
542 Kelly Campbell RC .60 1.50
543 Andre Davis RC .50 1.25
544 Deion Branch RC .75 2.00
545 James Mungro RC .75 2.00
546 Brian Poli-Dixon RC .50 1.25
547 Kahlil Hill RC .50 1.25
548 Reche Caldwell RC .60 1.50
549 Jeremy Shockey RC .75 2.00
550 Julius Peppers RC 1.25 3.00
551 Wendell Bryant RC .50 1.25
552 John Henderson RC .60 1.50
553 Quentin Jammer RC .75 2.00
554 Roy Williams RC .50 1.25
555 Daniel Graham RC .60 1.50
556 Charles Grant RC .75 2.00
557 Verron Haynes RC .50 1.25
558 Ed Reed RC 3.00 8.00
559 Pete Rebstock RC .50 1.25
560 Tellis Redmon RC .50 1.25
561 Javon Walker RC .75 2.00
562 Larry Tripplett RC .50 1.25
563 Cliff Russell RC .50 1.25
564 Rocky Calmus RC .60 1.50
565 Tim Carter RC .60 1.50
566 Josh Scobey RC .60 1.50
567 Kyle Johnson RC .50 1.25
568 Brian Westbrook RC 1.00 2.50
569 Zak Kustok RC .50 1.25
570 Ronald Curry RC .50 1.25
571 Atrews Bell RC .50 1.25
572 Levar Fisher RC .50 1.25
573 Dicenzo Miller RC .50 1.25
574 Phillip Buchanon RC .75 2.00
575 Freddie Milons RC .50 1.25
576 Kalimba Edwards RC .60 1.50
577 Raonall Smith RC .50 1.25
578 Dameon Hunter RC .50 1.25
579 Lee Mays RC .50 1.25
580 Mike Rumph RC .50 1.25
581 Josh McCown RC .75 2.00
582 Napoleon Harris RC .60 1.50
583 David Garrard RC .60 1.50
584 Wes Pate RC .50 1.25
585 Lito Sheppard RC .75 2.00
586 Gavin Hoffman RC .50 1.25
587 David Priestley RC .50 1.25
588 Dwight Freeney RC 1.00 2.50
589 Dusty Bonner RC .50 1.25
590 Eric McCoo RC .50 1.25
591 Robert Thomas RC .50 1.25
592 Delvon Flowers RC .50 1.25
593 LaDell Betts RC .75 2.00
594 Jamar Martin RC .60 1.50
595 Seth Burford RC .50 1.25
596 Mike Williams RC .50 1.25
597 Bryant McKinnie RC .50 1.25
598 Ryan Sims RC .75 2.00
599 Albert Haynesworth RC .75 2.00
600 Craig Nall RC .60 1.50

2002 Upper Deck XL Holofoil

*VETS 1-500: 12X TO 30X BASIC CARDS
*ROOKIES 501-600: 4X TO 10X
STATED PRINT RUN 65 SER.#'d SETS
362 Alan Faneca 125.00 300.00
366 Dan Kreider 20.00 50.00

2002 Upper Deck XL Big Time Jerseys

This set features game used jersey swatches with each card serial numbered of either 250 or 500. A Grey Background parallel version was also produced for each card. These Grey card were serial numbered of either 100 or 50-copies.

STATED PRINT RUN 250-500
*GREY BACKGROUND/50-100: .6X TO 1.5X
BTBG Brian Griese/500 2.50 6.00
BTBJ Brad Johnson/500 3.00 8.00
BTCC Curtis Conway/500 3.00 8.00
BTDB Drew Brees/500 8.00 20.00
BTDG Darrell Green/500 4.00 10.00
BTDM Donovan McNabb/500 3.00 8.00
BTDS Duce Staley/500 2.50 6.00
BTDT David Terrell/250 3.00 8.00
BTEM Eric Moulds/250 3.00 8.00
BTFJ Freddie Jones/500 2.50 6.00
BTGA Rod Gardner/500 2.50 6.00
BTIK Ike Hilliard/500 2.50 6.00
BTJA Jamal Anderson/250 4.00 10.00
BTJD JaJuan Dawson/500 2.50 6.00
BTJF Jay Fiedler/500 3.00 8.00
BTJG Jeff Graham/500 2.50 6.00
BTJH Joey Harrington/500 2.50 6.00
BTKC Kerry Collins/500 2.50 6.00
BTKK Kurt Kittner/500 2.50 6.00
BTKW Kurt Warner/250 4.00 10.00
BTMF Marshall Faulk/500 3.00 8.00
BTMP Michael Pittman/250 4.00 10.00
BTPM Peyton Manning/500 10.00 25.00
BTPW Peter Warrick/250 3.00 8.00
BTRG Rich Gannon/250 4.00 10.00
BTRW Ricky Williams/500 3.00 8.00
BTSM Santana Moss/500 3.00 8.00
BTWS Warren Sapp/250 4.00 10.00
BTZT Zach Thomas/250 4.00 10.00

2002 Upper Deck XL Super Swatch Jerseys

is set features game used jersey swatches with each card serial numbered of either 800 or 75. A Grey Background parallel version (numbered of either 400 or 25) was also produced.

STATED PRINT RUN 75-800
*GREY BACKGROUND/400: .5X TO 1.2X
*GREY BACKGROUND/25: .6X TO 1.5X
SSAB Anthony Becht/800 2.50 6.00
SSAR Antwaan Randle El/800 3.00 8.00
SSAT Anthony Thomas/75 6.00 15.00
SSBR Mark Brunell/800 3.00 8.00
SSCM Curtis Martin/75 6.00 15.00
SSDB Drew Bledsoe/800 3.00 8.00
SSDC Daunte Culpepper/75 6.00 15.00
SSDF Doug Flutie/800 3.00 8.00
SSDR Drew Brees/800 8.00 20.00
SSDS DeShaun Foster/800 4.00 10.00
SSEM Eric Moulds/800 2.50 6.00
SSJJ James Jackson/800 2.50 6.00
SSJO Kevin Johnson/800 2.50 6.00
SSJP Jake Plummer/75 5.00 12.00
SSJR Jerry Rice/75 15.00 40.00
SSJS Junior Seau/800 3.00 8.00
SSKJ Keyshawn Johnson/800 3.00 8.00
SSLT LaDainian Tomlinson/800 4.00 10.00
SSMA Mike Alstott/800 2.50 6.00
SSMB Marty Booker/75 5.00 12.00
SSMM Maurice Morris/800 3.00 8.00
SSPM Peyton Manning/800 10.00 25.00
SSRD Ron Dayne/75 6.00 15.00
SSRM Randy Moss/75 6.00 15.00
SSSA Stephen Alexander/800 2.50 6.00
SSSD Stephen Davis/800 2.50 6.00
SSTB Tony Banks/800 2.50 6.00
SSTC Tim Couch/75 5.00 12.00
SSTH Travis Henry/800 2.50 6.00
SSWC Wayne Chrebet/800 2.50 6.00

2008 Upper Deck Yankee Stadium Legacy Collection Historical Moments

473 Notre Dame v. Army 1.50 4.00
2835 1958 NFL Championship 1.50 4.00

1990 U-Seal-It Stickers

is set was released in 1990 by U-Seal-It. Each NFL team was represented by a package of three-stickers measuring 2 standard card size. One blankbacked sticker (1989 copyright date) contained an assortment of metallic helmet stickers and a small team name banner. Another blankbacked sticker (1988 copyright date) featured a comical team mascot called a Hot Shot. Finally, the third sticker (1983 copyright date) featured the NFL Properties Huddle character with a UPC and team checklist on the cardback.

COMPLETE SET (84) 50.00 125.00
1 Atlanta Falcons Helmets .60 1.50
2 Atlanta Falcons Hot Shot .60 1.50
3 Atlanta Falcons Huddle .60 1.50
4 Buffalo Bills Helmets .80 2.00
5 Buffalo Bills Hot Shot .80 2.00
6 Buffalo Bills Huddle .80 2.00
7 Chicago Bears Helmets .80 2.00
8 Chicago Bears Hot Shot .80 2.00
9 Chicago Bears Huddle .80 2.00
10 Cleveland Browns Helmets .80 2.00
11 Cleveland Browns Hot Shot .80 2.00
12 Cleveland Browns Huddle .80 2.00
13 Cincinnati Bengals Helmets .60 1.50
14 Cincinnati Bengals Hot Shot .60 1.50
15 Cincinnati Bengals Huddle .60 1.50
16 Dallas Cowboys Helmets 1.20 3.00
17 Dallas Cowboys Hot Shot 1.20 3.00
18 Dallas Cowboys Huddle 1.20 3.00
19 Denver Broncos Helmets .80 2.00
20 Denver Broncos Hot Shot .80 2.00
21 Denver Broncos Huddle .80 2.00
22 Detroit Lions Helmets .60 1.50
23 Detroit Lions Hot Shot .60 1.50
24 Detroit Lions Huddle .60 1.50
25 Green Bay Packers Helmets 1.20 3.00
26 Green Bay Packers Hot Shot 1.20 3.00
27 Green Bay Packers Huddle 1.20 3.00
28 Houston Oilers Helmets .60 1.50
29 Houston Oilers Hot Shot .60 1.50
30 Houston Oilers Huddle .60 1.50
31 Indianapolis Colts Helmets .60 1.50
32 Indianapolis Colts Hot Shot .60 1.50
33 Indianapolis Colts Huddle .60 1.50
34 Kansas City Chiefs Helmets .60 1.50
35 Kansas City Chiefs Hot Shot .60 1.50
36 Kansas City Chiefs Huddle .60 1.50
37 Los Angeles Raiders Helmets 1.20 3.00
38 Los Angeles Raiders Hot Shot 1.20 3.00
39 Los Angeles Raiders Huddle 1.20 3.00
40 Los Angeles Rams Helmets .60 1.50
41 Los Angeles Rams Hot Shot .60 1.50
42 Los Angeles Rams Huddle .60 1.50
43 Miami Dolphins Helmets 1.20 3.00
44 Miami Dolphins Hot Shot 1.20 3.00
45 Miami Dolphins Huddle 1.20 3.00
46 Minnesota Vikings Helmets .80 2.00
47 Minnesota Vikings Hot Shot .80 2.00
48 Minnesota Vikings Huddle .80 2.00
49 New England Patriots Helmets .60 1.50
50 New England Patriots Hot Shot .60 1.50
51 New England Patriots Huddle .60 1.50
52 New Orleans Saints Helmets .60 1.50
53 New Orleans Saints Hot Shot .60 1.50
54 New Orleans Saints Huddle .60 1.50
55 New York Giants Helmets .80 2.00
56 New York Giants Hot Shot .80 2.00
57 New York Giants Huddle .80 2.00
58 New York Jets Helmets .80 2.00
59 New York Jets Hot Shot .80 2.00
60 New York Jets Huddle .80 2.00
61 Philadelphia Eagles Helmets .60 1.50
62 Philadelphia Eagles Hot Shot .60 1.50
63 Philadelphia Eagles Huddle .60 1.50
64 Phoenix Cardinals Helmets .60 1.50
65 Phoenix Cardinals Hot Shot .60 1.50
66 Phoenix Cardinals Huddle .60 1.50
67 Pittsburgh Steelers Helmets 1.20 3.00
68 Pittsburgh Steelers Hot Shot 1.20 3.00
69 Pittsburgh Steelers Huddle 1.20 3.00
70 San Diego Chargers Helmets .60 1.50
71 San Diego Chargers Hot Shot .60 1.50
72 San Diego Chargers Huddle .60 1.50
73 San Francisco 49ers Helmets 1.20 3.00
74 San Francisco 49ers Hot Shot 1.20 3.00
75 San Francisco 49ers Huddle 1.20 3.00
76 Seattle Seahawks Helmets .60 1.50
77 Seattle Seahawks Hot Shot .60 1.50
78 Seattle Seahawks Huddle .60 1.50
79 Tampa Bay Bucs Helmets .60 1.50
80 Tampa Bay Bucs Hot Shot .60 1.50
81 Tampa Bay Bucs Huddle .60 1.50
82 Washington Redskins Helmets .80 2.00
83 Washington Redskins Hot Shot .80 2.00
84 Washington Redskins Huddle .80 2.00

1993 U.S. Playing Cards Ditka's Picks

Part of the Bicycle Sports Collection, these 56 playing cards, featuring Mike Ditka's NFL player picks, measure the standard-size and have rounded corners. The set is checklisted below in playing card order by suits and assigned numbers to Aces (1), Jacks (11), Queens (12), and Kings (13).

COMPLETE SET (56) 2.00 5.00
1C Steve Young .20 .50
1D Joe Montana .60 1.50
1H Dan Marino .50 1.25
1S Troy Aikman .30 .75
2C Jim Lachey .01 .05
2D Richmond Webb .01 .05
2H Wilber Marshall .01 .05
2S Ronnie Lott .02 .10
3C Sean Gilbert .01 .05
3D Clay Matthews .02 .10
3H Jeff Lageman .01 .05
3S Audray McMillian .01 .05
4C Morten Andersen .01 .05
4D Pete Stoyanovich .01 .05
4H Rohn Stark .01 .05
4S Sean Landeta .01 .05
5C Broderick Thomas .01 .05
5D James Francis .01 .05
5H Derrick Thomas .07 .20
5S Tony Bennett .01 .05
6C Seth Joyner .01 .05
6D Percy Snow .01 .05
6H Junior Seau .07 .20
6S Chris Spielman .01 .05
7C Pierce Holt .01 .05
7D Rod Woodson .07 .20
7H Ray Childress .01 .05
7S Deion Sanders .15 .40
8C Jay Novacek .02 .10
8D Eric Green .01 .05
8H Marv Cook .01 .05
8S Brent Jones .01 .05
9C Randall McDaniel .02 .10
9D Mike Munchak .02 .10
9H Bruce Matthews .01 .05
9S Mark Stepnoski .01 .05
10C Harris Barton .01 .05
10D Steve Atwater .01 .05
10H Henry Jones .01 .05
10S Chuck Cecil .01 .05
11C Sterling Sharpe .07 .20
11D Anthony Miller .02 .10
11H Haywood Jeffires .02 .10
11S Jerry Rice .30 .75
12C Reggie White .07 .20
12D Howie Long .02 .10
12H Cortez Kennedy .02 .10
12S Chris Doleman .01 .05
13C Emmitt Smith .40 1.00
13D Thurman Thomas .07 .20
13H Barry Foster .01 .05
13S Barry Sanders .50 1.25
WILD Tom Waddle .01 .05
WILD Steve Wisniewski .01 .05
NNO Ditka's AFC Picks .02 .10
NNO Ditka's NFC Picks .02 .10

1994 U.S. Playing Cards Ditka's Picks

Part of the Bicycle Sports Collection, these 56 playing cards, featuring Mike Ditka's NFL player picks, measure the standard size and have rounded corners. The set is checklisted below in playing card order by suits, with numbers assigned to Aces (1), Jacks (11), Queens (12), and Kings (13).

COMPLETE SET (56) 1.60 4.00
1C Sterling Sharpe .02 .10
1D Rickey Jackson .01 .05
1H Emmitt Smith .50 1.25
1S Rod Woodson .02 .10
2C Marcus Robertson .01 .05
2D Rohn Stark .01 .05
2H Dave Cadigan .01 .05
2S Kevin Williams .02 .10
3C John Kasay .01 .05
3D Carlton Haselrig .01 .05
3H Donnell Woolford .01 .05
3S Dan Wilkinson .02 .10
4C Marshall Faulk .80 2.00
4D Greg Montgomery .01 .05
4H Leslie O'Neal .01 .05
4S Eric Curry .01 .05
5C Eric Turner .01 .05
5D Rick Mirer .02 .10
5H Kevin Smith .01 .05
5S Troy Vincent .01 .05
6C Cornelius Bennett .02 .10
6D Seth Joyner .02 .10
6H Gary Zimmerman .01 .05
6S LeRoy Butler .01 .05
7C Tommy Vardell .01 .05
7D Richmond Webb .01 .05
7H Ben Coates .02 .10
7S Steve Everitt .01 .05
8C Tom Rathman .01 .05
8D Ray Childress .01 .05
8H Tim Brown .07 .20
8S Mark Bavaro .01 .05
9C Bennie Blades .01 .05
9D John(Jumbo) Elliott .01 .05
9H Jim Lachey .01 .05
9S Neil Smith .02 .10
10C Sean Gilbert .01 .05
10D Steve Tasker .01 .05
10H Chris Zorich .01 .05
10S Haywood Jeffires .02 .10
11C Troy Aikman .30 .75
11D Jeff Hostetler .02 .10
11H Junior Seau .02 .10
11S Mark Stepnoski .01 .05
12C Chris Spielman .01 .05
12D Marcus Allen .07 .20
12H Reggie White .07 .20
12S Harris Barton .01 .05
13C Andre Rison .02 .10
13D Randall McDaniel .02 .10
13H Cortez Kennedy .01 .05
13S Norm Johnson .01 .05
WILD Heath Shuler .15 .40
WILD Shannon Sharpe .02 .10
NNO Ditka's AFC Picks .02 .10
NNO Ditka's NFC Picks .02 .10

1995 U.S. Playing Cards Ditka's Picks

Part of the Bicycle Sports Collection, these 56 playing cards, featuring Mike Ditka's NFL player picks, measure the standard size and have rounded corners. The set is checklisted below in playing card order by suits with numbers assigned to Aces (1), Jacks (11), Queens (12), and Kings (13).

COMPLETE SET (56) 1.60 4.00
1C Randall McDaniel .02 .10
1D Dan Marino .50 1.25
1H Drew Bledsoe .30 .75
1S Steve Young .20 .50
2C Renaldo Turnbull .01 .05
2D Tony Boselli .01 .05
2H Ki-Jana Carter .02 .10
2S Todd Sauerbrun .01 .05
3C Aeneas Williams .01 .05
3D Bruce Smith .02 .10
3H Shawn Jefferson .01 .05
3S Andy Harmon .01 .05
4C Donnell Woolford .01 .05
4D Ronnie Lott .02 .10
4H Tim Brown .07 .20
4S Charles Haley .01 .05
5C Merton Hanks .01 .05
5D Eric Turner .01 .05
5H Ben Coates .01 .05
5S Brian Williams OL .01 .05
6C Eric Metcalf .01 .05
6D Dave Meggett .01 .05
6H Neil Smith .02 .10
6S Ian Beckles .01 .05
7C Herman Moore .02 .10
7D Mel Gray .01 .05
7H Ray Childress .01 .05
7S Jim Lachey .01 .05
8C Bennie Blades .01 .05
8D Kevin Greene .01 .05
8H Gary Zimmerman .01 .05
8S William Roaf .01 .05
9C Bryant Young .01 .05
9D Bruce Matthews .01 .05
9H Richmond Webb .01 .05
9S Howard Cross .01 .05
10C Seth Joyner .01 .05
10D Marshall Faulk .30 .75
10H Jeff Dellenbach .01 .05
10S Cris Carter .07 .20
11C Sean Gilbert .01 .05
11D John Carney .01 .05
11H Rohn Stark .01 .05
11S Jerry Rice .30 .75
12C Reggie White .02 .10
12D Terry McDaniel .01 .05
12H Rod Woodson .02 .10
12S Daryl Johnston .02 .10
13C Norm Johnson .01 .05
13D Cortez Kennedy .01 .05
13H Cornelius Bennett .02 .10
13S Barry Sanders .50 1.25
WILD Chris Spielman .01 .05
WILD Junior Seau .02 .10
NNO Ditka's AFC Picks .02 .10
NNO Ditka's NFC Picks .02 .10

2006 Utah Blaze AFL

These blankbacked cards were sponsored by Zions Bank and issued by the team to fill fan requests for photos and for use at player signings. Each measures roughly 5" by 7" and includes a black and white image of the player on the front with the team logo and player name below the image. The backs are blank.

COMPLETE SET (23) 10.00 20.00
1 Orshaswante Bryant .40 1.00
2 Siaha Burley .40 1.00
3 Kevin Clemens .40 1.00
4 John Culp .40 1.00
5 Ryan Dennard .40 1.00
6 Joe Germaine .50 1.25
7 Jason Gesser .60 1.50
8 Ernest Grant .40 1.00
9 Aaron Hamilton .40 1.00
10 Kelvin Hunter .40 1.00
11 Craig Kobel .40 1.00
12 Kautai Oleveo .40 1.00
13 Hans Olsen .40 1.00
14 Tom Pace .50 1.25
15 Scott Pospisal .40 1.00
16 Lewis Powell .40 1.00
17 Chris Robinson .40 1.00
18 Justin Skaggs .40 1.00
19 Garrett Smith .40 1.00
20 Justin Taplin .40 1.00
21 Steve Videtich .40 1.00
22 Ronnie Washburn .40 1.00
23 Thal Woods .40 1.00

2007 Utah Blaze AFL

MPLETE SET (28) 6.00 12.00
1 Aaron Boone .20 .50
2 Manaia Brown .20 .50
3 Orshawante Bryant .20 .50
4 Thaddeus Bullard .20 .50
5 Siaha Burley .30 .75
6 Frank Carter .20 .50
7 Valentine Chude .20 .50
8 John Culp .20 .50
9 Ryan Dennard .20 .50
10 Joe Germaine .40 1.00
11 Jason Gesser .40 1.00
12 Ernest Grant .20 .50
13 Chris Janek .20 .50
14 Steve Konopka .20 .50
15 Clarence Lawson .20 .50
16 Kautai Olevao .20 .50
17 Hans Olsen .20 .50
18 Tom Pace .20 .50
19 Chris Robinson .20 .50
20 Jacoby Shepherd .20 .50
21 Dahnel Singfield .20 .50
22 Justin Skaggs .20 .50
23 Garrett Smith .20 .50
24 Leroy Smith .20 .50
25 Myniya Smith .20 .50
26 Steve Videtich .20 .50
27 Danny White CO .30 .75
28 Big Budah (Emcee) .20 .50

2008 Utah Blaze afl

MPLETE SET (38) 7.50 15.00
1 Aaron Boone .20 .50
2 E.J. Burt .20 .50
3 Eddie Canonico .20 .50
4 Corey Dodds .20 .50
5 Rodney Filer .20 .50
6 Rob Gatrell .20 .50
7 Joe Germaine .30 .75
8 Chris Janek .20 .50
9 J'Shatlon Jones .20 .50
10 Vaka Manupuna .20 .50
11 Damon Mason .20 .50
12 J.J. McKelvey .20 .50
13 Dwayne Missouri .20 .50
14 Kelvin Morris .20 .50
15 Kautai Olevao .20 .50
16 Tom Pace .20 .50
17 Tupe Peko .20 .50
18 Myniya Smith .20 .50
19 Steve Videtich .20 .50
20 Danny White CO .40 1.00
21 Huey Whittaker .20 .50
22 Devin Wyman .20 .50
23 Big Budah ANN. .20 .50
24 Chief - Mascot .20 .50
25 Blaze Dancer: Alecia .20 .50
26 Blaze Dancer: Ami .20 .50
27 Blaze Dancer: Brittany .20 .50
28 Blaze Dancer: Caitlin .20 .50
29 Blaze Dancer: Chanelle .20 .50
30 Blaze Dancer: Juliet .20 .50
31 Blaze Dancer: Kate .20 .50
32 Blaze Dancer: Kristina .20 .50
33 Blaze Dancer: Melissa .20 .50
34 Blaze Dancer: Nichole .20 .50
35 Blaze Dancer: Nicole .20 .50
36 Blaze Dancer: Randi .20 .50
37 Blaze Dancer: Stephanie .20 .50
38 Blaze Dancer: Tamy .20 .50

2000 Vanguard

sued as a 150-card set, Vanguard is comprised of 125 veteran player cards and 25 rookie cards which are sequentially numbered to 762. Base cards feature a red background with a black player name plate and white border along the bottom of the card. Player action photos are surrounded by a holofoil outline that fades into the red background. Rookie cards feature the same card design set against a green background. Vanguard was packaged in 24-pack boxes with packs containing four cards each.

COMP.SET w/o RCs (125) 15.00 30.00
UNPRICED PROOF PRINT RUN 1
1 Tony Banks .25 .60
2 Priest Holmes .25 .60
3 Qadry Ismail .25 .60
4 Doug Flutie .30 .75
5 Rob Johnson .30 .75
6 Eric Moulds .25 .60
7 Peerless Price .30 .75
8 Antowain Smith .30 .75
9 Corey Dillon .25 .60
10 Darnay Scott .30 .75
11 Akili Smith .25 .60
12 Tim Couch .30 .75
13 Kevin Johnson .25 .60
14 Terry Kirby .25 .60
15 Terrell Davis .30 .75
16 Olandis Gary .30 .75
17 Brian Griese .25 .60
18 Ed McCaffrey .30 .75
19 Rod Smith .30 .75
20 Marvin Harrison .30 .75
21 Edgerrin James .30 .75
22 Peyton Manning 1.00 2.50
23 Terrence Wilkins .25 .60
24 Mark Brunell .30 .75
25 Keenan McCardell .30 .75
26 Jimmy Smith .30 .75
27 Fred Taylor .25 .60
28 Derrick Alexander .25 .60
29 Donnell Bennett .25 .60
30 Tony Gonzalez .30 .75
31 Elvis Grbac .25 .60

32 Damon Huard .25 .60
33 James Johnson .25 .60
34 Dan Marino .75 2.00
35 Tony Martin .30 .75
36 O.J. McDuffie .30 .75
37 Drew Bledsoe .30 .75
38 Kevin Faulk .25 .60
39 Terry Glenn .30 .75
40 Wayne Chrebet .25 .60
41 Ray Lucas .25 .60
42 Curtis Martin .30 .75
43 Vinny Testaverde .25 .60
44 Tim Brown .40 1.00
45 Rich Gannon .30 .75
46 Napoleon Kaufman .30 .75
47 Tyrone Wheatley .25 .60
48 Jerome Bettis .40 1.00
49 Troy Edwards .25 .60
50 Richard Huntley .25 .60
51 Kordell Stewart .25 .60
52 Jermaine Fazande .25 .60
53 Jim Harbaugh .30 .75
54 Mikhael Ricks .25 .60
55 Junior Seau .30 .75
56 Brock Huard .25 .60
57 Jon Kitna .25 .60
58 Derrick Mayes .25 .60
59 Ricky Watters .30 .75
60 Eddie George .30 .75
61 Jevon Kearse .25 .60
62 Steve McNair .30 .75
63 Yancey Thigpen .25 .60
64 David Boston .25 .60
65 Rob Moore .25 .60
66 Jake Plummer .25 .60
67 Frank Sanders .25 .60
68 Jamal Anderson .30 .75
69 Chris Chandler .30 .75
70 Tim Dwight .30 .75
71 Terance Mathis .25 .60
72 Steve Beuerlein .30 .75
73 Tim Biakabutuka .30 .75
74 Patrick Jeffers .25 .60
75 Muhsin Muhammad .25 .60
76 Bobby Engram .25 .60
77 Curtis Enis .25 .60
78 Cade McNown .25 .60
79 Marcus Robinson .30 .75
80 Troy Aikman .50 1.25
81 Rocket Ismail .30 .75
82 Emmitt Smith .60 1.50
83 Jason Tucker .25 .60
84 Chris Warren .25 .60
85 Charlie Batch .25 .60
86 Germane Crowell .25 .60
87 Herman Moore .25 .60
88 Johnnie Morton .30 .75
89 Barry Sanders .60 1.50
90 Brett Favre .75 2.00
91 Antonio Freeman .30 .75
92 Dorsey Levens .30 .75
93 Bill Schroeder .30 .75
94 Cris Carter .40 1.00
95 Daunte Culpepper .30 .75
96 Randy Moss .30 .75
97 Robert Smith .25 .60
98 Cam Cleeland .25 .60
99 Keith Poole .25 .60
100 Ricky Williams .30 .75
101 Tiki Barber .30 .75
102 Kerry Collins .25 .60
103 Ike Hilliard .25 .60
104 Amani Toomer .25 .60
105 Charles Johnson .25 .60
106 Donovan McNabb .30 .75
107 Torrance Small .25 .60
108 Duce Staley .25 .60
109 Isaac Bruce .40 1.00
110 Marshall Faulk .30 .75
111 Torry Holt .30 .75
112 Kurt Warner .60 1.50
113 Charlie Garner .30 .75
114 Terrell Owens .30 .75
115 Jerry Rice 1.00 2.50
116 J.J. Stokes .30 .75
117 Steve Young .50 1.25
118 Mike Alstott .25 .60
119 Reidel Anthony .25 .60
120 Warrick Dunn .25 .60
121 Jacquez Green .25 .60
122 Shaun King .25 .60
123 Stephen Davis .25 .60
124 Brad Johnson .30 .75
125 Michael Westbrook .25 .60
126 Thomas Jones RC 2.50 6.00
127 Jamal Lewis RC 3.00 8.00
128 Chris Redman RC 2.00 5.00
129 Travis Taylor RC 2.00 5.00
130 Dez White RC 2.00 5.00
131 Ron Dugans RC 2.00 5.00
132 Peter Warrick RC 2.00 5.00
133 Dennis Northcutt RC 2.00 5.00
134 Travis Prentice RC 2.00 5.00
135 Reuben Droughns RC 2.00 5.00
136 R.Jay Soward RC 2.00 5.00
137 Sylvester Morris RC 2.00 5.00
138 Troy Walters RC 2.00 5.00
139 Tom Brady RC 250.00 500.00
140 J.R. Redmond RC 2.00 5.00
141 Marc Bulger RC 2.50 6.00
142 Ron Dayne RC 3.00 8.00
143 Laveranues Coles RC 2.50 6.00
144 Chad Pennington RC 2.50 6.00
145 Jerry Porter RC 3.00 8.00
146 Plaxico Burress RC 2.50 6.00
147 Trung Canidate RC 2.00 5.00
148 Giovanni Carmazzi RC 2.00 5.00
149 Shaun Alexander RC 3.00 8.00
150 Todd Husak RC 2.00 5.00
S1 Jon Kitna Sample 1.00 2.50

2000 Vanguard Gold

*GOLD/122: 5X TO 12X BASIC CARDS
GOLD RETAIL PRINT RUN 122 SER.#'d SETS

2000 Vanguard Premiere Date

REM.DATE/138: 5X TO 12X BASIC CARDS
PREMIERE DATE PRINT RUN 138

2000 Vanguard Purple

URPLE/138: 5X TO 12X BASIC CARDS
PURPLE HOBBY PRINT RUN 138 SER.#'d SETS

2000 Vanguard Cosmic Force

ndomly inserted in packs at the rate of one in 73, this 10-card set features color player portrait photos set against a player silhouette on an "outer space" background.

COMPLETE SET (10) 20.00 50.00
STATED ODDS 1:73
1 Tim Couch 1.00 2.50
2 Troy Aikman 1.50 4.00
3 Emmitt Smith 2.00 5.00
4 Terrell Davis 1.00 2.50
5 Barry Sanders 2.00 5.00
6 Brett Favre 2.50 6.00
7 Edgerrin James 1.00 2.50
8 Peyton Manning 3.00 8.00
9 Randy Moss 1.00 2.50
10 Kurt Warner 2.00 5.00

2000 Vanguard Game Worn Jerseys

ndomly inserted in packs, this 14-card set features player action photography set on an all foil background coupled with an authentic circular swatch of a game worn jersey. Player photos appear on the left while jersey swatches are on the right.

1 Cris Carter 8.00 20.00
2 Randall Cunningham 6.00 15.00
3 Randy Moss 6.00 15.00
4 Ricky Williams 6.00 15.00
5 Wayne Chrebet 5.00 12.00
6 Koy Detmer 5.00 12.00
7 Donovan McNabb 6.00 15.00
8 Torrance Small 5.00 12.00
9 Duce Staley 5.00 12.00
10 Jerome Bettis 8.00 20.00
11 Kordell Stewart 5.00 12.00
12 Jerry Rice 20.00 50.00
13 Steve Young 12.00 30.00
14 Steve McNair 6.00 15.00

2000 Vanguard Game Worn Jersey Duals

Randomly inserted in Hobby packs, this 6-card set pairs two top NFL stars of either the same team or same position and contains two swatches of game worn jerseys on the card front. Each card is sequentially numbered to 200.

STATED PRINT RUN 200 SER.#'d SETS
1 C.Carter/R.Moss 20.00 50.00
2 R.Williams/J.Bettis 12.00 30.00
3 D.Staley/D.McNabb 10.00 25.00
4 J.Bettis/K.Stewart 12.00 30.00
5 J.Rice/R.Moss 15.00 40.00
6 S.Young/S.McNair 15.00 40.00

2000 Vanguard Game Worn Jersey Dual Patches

Randomly inserted in Hobby packs at the rate of one in 5000, this six card set pairs two players of either the same team or same position and features dual premium swatches of authentic player worn jerseys. Each card is sequentially numbered from 12-35.

1 O.Gary/R.Williams/12 50.00 100.00
2 M.Brunell/S.Young/15 50.00 120.00
3 C.Carter/R.Moss/25 60.00 150.00
4 J.Bettis/K.Stewart/35 50.00 120.00
5 J.Rice/R.Moss/19 75.00 150.00
6 S.McNair/D.McNabb/25 30.00 80.00

2000 Vanguard Gridiron Architects

Randomly inserted in packs at the rate of one in 25, this 20-card set features full color player action shots set agains a blueprint of each respective player's home stadium.

COMPLETE SET (20) 20.00 50.00
STATED ODDS 1:25
1 Jake Plummer .60 1.50
2 Cade McNown .60 1.50
3 Tim Couch .75 2.00
4 Troy Aikman 1.25 3.00
5 Emmitt Smith 1.50 4.00
6 Terrell Davis .75 2.00
7 Brett Favre 2.00 5.00
8 Edgerrin James .75 2.00
9 Peyton Manning 2.50 6.00
10 Fred Taylor .60 1.50
11 Dan Marino 2.00 5.00
12 Randy Moss .75 2.00
13 Drew Bledsoe .75 2.00
14 Curtis Martin .75 2.00
15 Terrell Owens .75 2.00
16 Marshall Faulk .75 2.00
17 Kurt Warner 1.50 4.00
18 Shaun King .60 1.50
19 Eddie George .75 2.00
20 Stephen Davis .60 1.50

2000 Vanguard High Voltage

Inserted in packs at the rate of one in one, this 36-card set features top player and rookie action shots set against a colored background with lightning bolts. Several colored foil parallel sets were produced as well: Gold (199-sets), Green (99-sets), Red (299-sets), and Holographic Silver (10-sets).

COMPLETE SET (36) 8.00 20.00
OVERALL ODDS ONE PER PACK
*GOLD/199: 3X TO 8X BASIC INSERTS
*GREEN/99: 4X TO 10X BASIC INSERTS
*HOLO GOLD: 6X TO 15X BASIC INSERTS
*HOLO SILVER/10: 20X TO 50X
*RED/299: 2X TO 5X BASIC INSERTS
1 Thomas Jones .20 .50
2 Jamal Lewis .25 .60
3 Eric Moulds .15 .40
4 Marcus Robinson .20 .50
5 Corey Dillon .15 .40
6 Peter Warrick .15 .40
7 Tim Couch .20 .50
8 Kevin Johnson .15 .40
9 Emmitt Smith .40 1.00
10 Olandis Gary .20 .50
11 Brian Griese .15 .40
12 Charlie Batch .15 .40
13 Antonio Freeman .20 .50
14 Marvin Harrison .20 .50
15 Edgerrin James .20 .50
16 Mark Brunell .20 .50
17 Fred Taylor .15 .40
18 Damon Huard .15 .40
19 Cris Carter .25 .60
20 Daunte Culpepper .20 .50
21 Randy Moss .20 .50
22 Ron Dayne .25 .60
23 Curtis Martin .20 .50
24 Chad Pennington .20 .50
25 Jerome Bettis .25 .60
26 Plaxico Burress .20 .50
27 Isaac Bruce .25 .60
28 Marshall Faulk .20 .50
29 Kurt Warner .40 1.00
30 Giovanni Carmazzi .15 .40
31 Shaun Alexander .25 .60
32 Jon Kitna .15 .40
33 Eddie George .20 .50
34 Warrick Dunn .15 .40
35 Shaun King .15 .40
36 Stephen Davis .15 .40

2000 Vanguard Press Hobby

Randomly inserted in Hobby packs at the rate of two in 25, this 10-card set features AFC players on a card stock set to resemble the front page of a newspaper.

COMPLETE SET (10) 4.00 10.00
STATED ODDS 2:25 HOBBY
1 Peter Warrick .20 .50
2 Tim Couch .30 .75
3 Terrell Davis .30 .75
4 Edgerrin James .30 .75
5 Peyton Manning 1.00 2.50
6 Fred Taylor .25 .60
7 Drew Bledsoe .30 .75
8 Chad Pennington .25 .60
9 Jon Kitna .25 .60
10 Eddie George .30 .75

2000 Vanguard Press Retail

Randomly inserted in Retail packs at the rate of two in 25, this 10-card set features NFC players on a card stock set to resemble the front page of a newspaper.

COMPLETE SET (10) 6.00 15.00
STATED ODDS 2:25 RETAIL
1 Thomas Jones .30 .75
2 Cade McNown .30 .75
3 Troy Aikman .60 1.50
4 Emmitt Smith .75 2.00
5 Brett Favre 1.00 2.50
6 Ron Dayne .40 1.00
7 Randy Moss .40 1.00
8 Marshall Faulk .40 1.00
9 Kurt Warner .75 2.00
10 Stephen Davis .30 .75

2001 Vanguard

This 150 card set was issued in October, 2001. The cards were issued in four card packs which had an SRP of $3.99 per pack and there were 24 packs in a box. The last 50 cards in the set are all Rookie Cards with a stated print run of 450 cards. A highlight of these cards featured Pacific's "Vision-Glow" Technology which utilized chromium stryene card stock.

COMP.SET w/o SP's (100) 12.50 30.00
1 David Boston .25 .60
2 Thomas Jones .25 .60
3 Jake Plummer .25 .60
4 Jamal Anderson .30 .75
5 Chris Chandler .30 .75
6 Elvis Grbac .30 .75
7 Jamal Lewis .40 1.00
8 Shannon Sharpe .30 .75
9 Rob Johnson .30 .75
10 Eric Moulds .25 .60
11 Peerless Price .25 .60
12 Tim Biakabutuka .25 .60
13 Muhsin Muhammad .25 .60
14 James Allen .25 .60
15 Cade McNown .30 .75
16 Marcus Robinson .30 .75
17 Corey Dillon .25 .60
18 Akili Smith .25 .60
19 Peter Warrick .25 .60
20 Tim Couch .25 .60
21 Kevin Johnson .25 .60
22 Travis Prentice .25 .60
23 Rocket Ismail .30 .75
24 Emmitt Smith .60 1.50
25 Mike Anderson .25 .60
26 Terrell Davis .30 .75
27 Brian Griese .25 .60
28 Ed McCaffrey .30 .75
29 Rod Smith .30 .75
30 Charlie Batch .25 .60
31 Johnnie Morton .30 .75
32 James Stewart .25 .60
33 Brett Favre .75 2.00
34 Antonio Freeman .40 1.00
35 Ahman Green .30 .75
36 Bill Schroeder .30 .75
37 Marvin Harrison .30 .75
38 Edgerrin James .30 .75
39 Peyton Manning 1.00 2.50
40 Terrence Wilkins .25 .60
41 Mark Brunell .30 .75
42 Keenan McCardell .30 .75
43 Jimmy Smith .30 .75
44 Fred Taylor .25 .60
45 Derrick Alexander .25 .60
46 Tony Gonzalez .30 .75
47 Sylvester Morris .25 .60
48 Jay Fiedler .30 .75
49 Oronde Gadsden .25 .60
50 Lamar Smith .30 .75
51 Cris Carter .40 1.00
52 Daunte Culpepper .30 .75
53 Randy Moss .30 .75
54 Drew Bledsoe .30 .75
55 Terry Glenn .30 .75
56 Charles Johnson .25 .60
57 J.R. Redmond .25 .60
58 Jeff Blake .30 .75
59 Joe Horn .25 .60
60 Ricky Williams .30 .75
61 Tiki Barber .30 .75
62 Kerry Collins .25 .60
63 Ron Dayne .30 .75
64 Amani Toomer .25 .60
65 Wayne Chrebet .25 .60
66 Curtis Martin .30 .75
67 Vinny Testaverde .25 .60
68 Tim Brown .40 1.00
69 Rich Gannon .30 .75
70 Jerry Rice .75 2.00
71 Tyrone Wheatley .30 .75
72 Donovan McNabb .30 .75
73 Duce Staley .25 .60
74 Jerome Bettis .40 1.00
75 Kordell Stewart .25 .60
76 Hines Ward .30 .75
77 Isaac Bruce .40 1.00
78 Marshall Faulk .30 .75
79 Torry Holt .30 .75
80 Kurt Warner .60 1.50
81 Curtis Conway .30 .75
82 Tim Dwight .30 .75
83 Doug Flutie .30 .75
84 Junior Seau .30 .75
85 Jeff Garcia .25 .60
86 Terrell Owens .30 .75
87 Shaun Alexander .25 .60
88 Matt Hasselbeck .25 .60
89 Darrell Jackson .30 .75
90 Mike Alstott .25 .60
91 Warrick Dunn .25 .60
92 Keyshawn Johnson .30 .75
93 Brad Johnson .30 .75
94 Kevin Dyson .25 .60
95 Eddie George .40 1.00
96 Derrick Mason .25 .60
97 Steve McNair .30 .75
98 Stephen Davis .25 .60
99 Jeff George .30 .75
100 Michael Westbrook .25 .60
101 Bobby Newcombe RC 2.00 5.00
102 Alge Crumpler RC 2.50 6.00
103 Vinny Sutherland RC 1.50 4.00
104 Michael Vick RC 4.00 10.00
105 Todd Heap RC 2.00 5.00
106 Nate Clements RC 2.00 5.00
107 Travis Henry RC 2.00 5.00
108 Dan Morgan RC 2.00 5.00
109 Chris Weinke RC 2.00 5.00
110 David Terrell RC 2.00 5.00
111 Anthony Thomas RC 2.50 6.00
112 T.J. Houshmandzadeh RC 2.00 5.00
113 Chad Johnson RC 2.50 6.00
114 Rudi Johnson RC 2.50 6.00
115 James Jackson RC 1.50 4.00
116 Quincy Morgan RC 2.00 5.00
117 Quincy Carter RC 2.00 5.00
118 Scotty Anderson RC 1.50 4.00
119 Mike McMahon RC 2.00 5.00
120 Robert Ferguson RC 2.50 6.00
121 Reggie Wayne RC 3.00 8.00
122 Snoop Minnis RC 1.50 4.00
123 Chris Chambers RC 1.50 4.00
124 Jamar Fletcher RC 1.50 4.00
125 Josh Heupel RC 2.50 6.00
126 Travis Minor RC 2.00 5.00
127 Michael Bennett RC 2.00 5.00
128 Deuce McAllister RC 2.50 6.00
129 Will Allen RC 2.50 6.00
130 Jesse Palmer RC 2.00 5.00
131 LaMont Jordan RC 2.50 6.00
132 Santana Moss RC 2.50 6.00
133 Ken-Yon Rambo RC 1.50 4.00
134 Marques Tuiasosopo RC 2.00 5.00
135 Correll Buckhalter RC 1.50 4.00
136 A.J. Feeley RC 2.00 5.00
137 Freddie Mitchell RC 1.50 4.00
138 Chris Taylor RC 1.50 4.00
139 Adam Archuleta RC 2.00 5.00
140 Drew Brees RC 10.00 25.00
141 LaDainian Tomlinson RC 8.00 20.00
142 Kevan Barlow RC 2.00 6.00
143 Cedrick Wilson RC 2.00 5.00
144 Alex Bannister RC 1.50 4.00
145 Josh Booty RC 2.00 5.00
146 Heath Evans RC 2.00 5.00
147 Koren Robinson RC 2.00 5.00
148 Dan Alexander RC 2.00 5.00
149 Rod Gardner RC 2.00 5.00
150 Sage Rosenfels RC 2.00 5.00

2001 Vanguard Blue

*1-100 VETS: 3X TO 8X BASIC CARDS
*101-150 ROOKIES: .3X TO .8X
STATED PRINT RUN 299 SER.#'d SETS

2001 Vanguard Gold

*1-100 VETS: 5X TO 12X BASIC CARDS
*101-150 ROOKIES: .5X TO 1.2X
STATED PRINT RUN 99 SER.#'d SETS

2001 Vanguard Premiere Date

*1-100 VETS: 5X TO 12X BASIC CARDS
*101-150 ROOKIES: .5X TO 1.2X
STATED PRINT RUN 115 SER.#'d SETS

2001 Vanguard Red

*VETS/80-89: 5X TO 12X BASIC CARDS
*VETS/40-55: 6X TO 15X BASIC CARDS
*VETS/30-38: 8X TO 20X BASIC CARDS
*VETS/20-29: 10X TO 35X BASIC CARDS
*VETS/10-19: 12X TO 30X BASIC CARDS
1-100 VETERANS PRINT RUN 2-89
UNPRICED 101-150 ROOKIE PRINT RUN 10

2001 Vanguard Bombs Away

This 30 card insert set, serial numbered to 999, featured a mix of 15 leading quarterbacks and 15 leading receivers. The card features the players photo set against a target background. An interesting aspect of this set is that the quarterback cards were inserted in hobby packs and the receivers were inserted in retail packs.

COMPLETE SET (30) 30.00 80.00
STATED PRINT RUN 999 SER.#'d SETS
QUARTERBACKS FOUND IN HOBBY PACKS
RECEIVERS FOUND IN RETAIL PACKS
1 Michael Vick 1.50 4.00
2 Chris Weinke 1.00 2.50
3 Tim Couch .75 2.00
4 Brian Griese .75 2.00
5 Brett Favre 2.50 6.00
6 Peyton Manning 3.00 8.00
7 Mark Brunell 1.00 2.50
8 Daunte Culpepper 1.00 2.50
9 Drew Bledsoe 1.00 2.50
10 Rich Gannon 1.00 2.50
11 Donovan McNabb 1.00 2.50
12 Kurt Warner 2.00 5.00
13 Drew Brees 4.00 10.00
14 Jeff Garcia .75 2.00
15 Steve McNair 1.00 2.50
16 Eric Moulds .75 2.00
17 David Terrell 1.00 2.50
18 Peter Warrick .75 2.00
19 Marvin Harrison 1.00 2.50
20 Jimmy Smith 1.00 2.50
21 Cris Carter 1.25 3.00
22 Santana Moss 1.00 2.50
23 Tim Brown 1.25 3.00
24 Jerry Rice 2.50 6.00
25 Freddie Mitchell .75 2.00
26 Isaac Bruce 1.25 3.00
27 Torry Holt 1.00 2.50
28 Terrell Owens 1.00 2.50
29 Koren Robinson 1.00 2.50
30 Rod Gardner 1.00 2.50

2001 Vanguard Double Sided Jerseys

This 50 card set set, featuring a jersey swatch on each side were inserted at an announced rate of two in 25 in hobby packs and one in 49 for retail packs. Each card had two different players from the same team represented.

STATED ODDS 2:25 HOB, 1:49 RET
*PATCH/50: .6X TO 1.5X BASIC INSERTS
*PATCH/25: .8X TO 2X BASIC INSERTS
1 Plummer/Boston/270 2.50 6.00
2 R.Moore/F.Sanders 2.50 6.00
3 T.Jones/M.Pittman 3.00 8.00
4 C.Gedney/E.Conwell 2.50 6.00
5 C.Griesen/N.O'Donnell 3.00 8.00
6 C.Chandler/T.Mathis 3.00 8.00
7 R.Cunningham/A.Wright 3.00 8.00
8 T.Biaka/S.Beuerlein 3.00 8.00
9 B.Hoover/Moe Williams 3.00 8.00
10 Weinke/Mitchell/270 3.00 8.00
11 P.Jeffers/T.Dwight 3.00 8.00
12 Reg.White/J.Kearse 4.00 10.00
13 W.Walls/F.Wycheck 2.50 6.00
14 B.Engram/D.White 3.00 8.00
15 C.McNown/J.Allen 3.00 8.00
16 S.Matthews/J.Miller 3.00 8.00
17 B.Urlacher/Z.Thomas 5.00 12.00
18 A.Thomas/Tomlinson/270 12.00 30.00
19 C.Dillon/P.Warrick/255 2.50 6.00
20 R.Dugans/D.Farmer 2.50 6.00
21 T.Aikman/E.Smith/265 6.00 15.00
22 W.McGarity/J.McKnight 2.50 6.00
23 J.Tucker/R.Proehl 2.50 6.00
24 C.Pickens/K.Dyson 3.00 8.00
25 B.Griese/O.Gary/265 2.50 6.00
26 D.Carswell/B.Chamberlain 2.50 6.00
27 Anderson/Davis/260 3.00 8.00
28 G.Frerotte/M.Hasselbeck 2.50 6.00
29 H.Moore/J.Morton 3.00 8.00
30 J.Stewart/L.Foster 2.50 6.00
31 D.Howard/Tony Martin 3.00 8.00
32 A.Green/H.Goodman 3.00 8.00
33 B.Favre/A.Freeman/260 8.00 20.00
34 D.Levens/D.Parker 3.00 8.00
35 Ty.Davis/B.Franks 2.50 6.00
36 W.Henderson/G.Comella 2.50 6.00
37 A.Denson/Jam.Johnson 2.50 6.00
38 C.Walsh/T.Walters 2.50 6.00
39 C.Carter/Rob.Smith/265 4.00 10.00
40 Culpepper/R.Moss/265 3.00 8.00
41 D.Huard/B.Emanuel 3.00 8.00
42 J.Blake/W.Jackson 3.00 8.00
43 K.Collins/J.Jurevicius 2.50 6.00
44 T.Barber/R.Dayne/275 3.00 8.00
45 J.Sehorn/A.Williams 3.00 8.00
46 A.Toomer/C.Sanders 2.50 6.00
47 T.Wheatley/N.Kaufman 3.00 8.00
48 Tuiasop/D.Brees/265 15.00 40.00
49 K.Warner/M.Faulk/260 6.00 15.00
50 George/McNair/265 4.00 10.00

2001 Vanguard In Focus

Randomly inserted in packs, these cards honoring 15 leading offensive threats had a stated print run of 99 sets.

COMPLETE SET (15) 60.00 120.00
STATED PRINT RUN 99 SER. #'d SETS
1 Jamal Lewis 3.00 8.00
2 Emmitt Smith 5.00 12.00
3 Mike Anderson 2.00 5.00
4 Terrell Davis 2.50 6.00
5 Brett Favre 6.00 15.00
6 Edgerrin James 2.50 6.00
7 Peyton Manning 8.00 20.00
8 Mark Brunell 2.50 6.00
9 Daunte Culpepper 2.50 6.00
10 Randy Moss 2.50 6.00
11 Ricky Williams 2.50 6.00
12 Jerry Rice 6.00 15.00
13 Donovan McNabb 2.50 6.00
14 Marshall Faulk 2.50 6.00
15 Kurt Warner 5.00 12.00

2001 Vanguard Prime Prospects Bronze

These cards, featuring 36-leading 2001 rookies, were inserted one per hobby or retail pack. The words "Prime Prospects" are viewed on the left side while the players position and team are on the right side. These words frame an action photo of the player. The hobby version cards were printed with bronze foil and the silver foil retail version was serial numbered on the back to 300.

COMPLETE SET (36) 12.00 30.00
ONE BRONZE PER HOBBY PACK
*SILVER/300: .8X TO 2X BRONZE
SILVER STATED PRINT RUN 300
1 Michael Vick .75 2.00
2 Travis Henry .40 1.00
3 Dan Morgan .40 1.00
4 Chris Weinke .40 1.00
5 David Terrell .40 1.00
6 Anthony Thomas .50 1.25
7 Chad Johnson .50 1.25
8 James Jackson .30 .75
9 Quincy Morgan .40 1.00
10 Quincy Carter .40 1.00
11 Mike McMahon .40 1.00
12 Robert Ferguson .50 1.25
13 Reggie Wayne .60 1.50
14 Snoop Minnis .30 .75
15 Chris Chambers .30 .75
16 Josh Heupel .50 1.25
17 Travis Minor .40 1.00
18 Michael Bennett .40 1.00
19 Deuce McAllister .50 1.25
20 Jesse Palmer .40 1.00
21 LaMont Jordan .50 1.25
22 Santana Moss .50 1.25
23 Ken-Yon Rambo .30 .75
24 Marques Tuiasosopo .40 1.00
25 Correll Buckhalter .30 .75
26 Freddie Mitchell .30 .75
27 Adam Archuleta .40 1.00
28 Drew Brees 2.00 5.00
29 LaDainian Tomlinson 1.50 4.00
30 Kevan Barlow .40 1.00
31 Cedrick Wilson .40 1.00
32 Alex Bannister .30 .75
33 Koren Robinson .40 1.00
34 Dan Alexander .40 1.00
35 Rod Gardner .40 1.00
36 Sage Rosenfels .40 1.00

2001 Vanguard V-Team

Randomly inserted in packs, this 25 card set was serial numbered to 499. The horizontal cards have the words "V Team" in the upper left with the player's photo on the right. The serial numbers are also on the front along with the player's name.

COMPLETE SET (25) 40.00 80.00
STATED PRINT RUN 1499 SER. #'d SETS
1 Jamal Lewis 1.50 4.00
2 Corey Dillon 1.00 2.50
3 Peter Warrick 1.00 2.50
4 Tim Couch 1.00 2.50
5 Emmitt Smith 2.50 6.00
6 Mike Anderson 1.00 2.50
7 Terrell Davis 1.25 3.00
8 Brian Griese 1.00 2.50
9 Marvin Harrison 1.25 3.00
10 Edgerrin James 1.25 3.00
11 Peyton Manning 4.00 10.00
12 Mark Brunell 1.25 3.00
13 Fred Taylor 1.00 2.50
14 Cris Carter 1.50 4.00
15 Randy Moss 1.25 3.00
16 Drew Bledsoe 1.25 3.00
17 Ricky Williams 1.25 3.00
18 Ron Dayne 1.25 3.00
19 Jerry Rice 3.00 8.00
20 Donovan McNabb 1.25 3.00
21 Kurt Warner 2.50 6.00
22 Marshall Faulk 1.25 3.00
23 Jeff Garcia 1.00 2.50
24 Eddie George 1.50 4.00
25 Steve McNair 1.25 3.00

2001 Vanguard V-Team Rookies

Randomly inserted in packs, this 30 card set featuring leading 2001 rookies are serial numbered to 999. The horizontal cards have the words "V Team Rookies" in the upper left with the player's photo on the right. The serial numbers are also on the front along with the player's name.

COMPLETE SET (30) 50.00 100.00
STATED PRINT RUN 999 SER. #'d SETS
1 Michael Vick 1.50 4.00
2 Travis Henry .75 2.00
3 Chris Weinke .75 2.00
4 David Terrell .75 2.00
5 Anthony Thomas 1.00 2.50
6 Chad Johnson 1.00 2.50
7 James Jackson .60 1.50
8 Quincy Morgan .75 2.00
9 Quincy Carter .75 2.00
10 Mike McMahon .75 2.00
11 Robert Ferguson 1.00 2.50
12 Reggie Wayne 1.25 3.00
13 Snoop Minnis .60 1.50
14 Chris Chambers .60 1.50
15 Josh Heupel 1.00 2.50
16 Travis Minor .75 2.00
17 Michael Bennett .75 2.00
18 Deuce McAllister 1.00 2.50
19 Jesse Palmer .75 2.00
20 LaMont Jordan 1.00 2.50
21 Santana Moss 1.00 2.50
22 Marques Tuiasosopo .75 2.00
23 Correll Buckhalter .60 1.50
24 A.J. Feeley .75 2.00
25 Freddie Mitchell .60 1.50
26 Drew Brees 4.00 10.00
27 LaDainian Tomlinson 3.00 8.00
28 Koren Robinson .75 2.00
29 Rod Gardner .75 2.00
30 Sage Rosenfels .75 2.00

1966 Van Heusen Photos

1 Len Dawson 20.00 40.00

2001 Verigraph Crystal Cards

BF Brett Favre 15.00 30.00
BG Brian Griese 6.00 12.00
CD Corey Dillon 6.00 12.00
ES Emmitt Smith 12.50 25.00
JB Jerome Bettis 10.00 20.00
JE John Elway 12.50 25.00
KW Kurt Warner 7.50 15.00
LT LaDainian Tomlinson 7.50 15.00
MV Michael Vick 7.50 15.00
PM Peyton Manning 15.00 30.00
TB Tom Brady SB MVP 15.00 30.00
TC Tim Couch 6.00 12.00
WP Walter Payton 15.00 30.00

1961 Vikings Team Issue

These large photos measure approximately 5" by 7" and feature black-and-white player photos. The set was issued in "Picture Pak" form in its own envelope by the team. Each has a large white border below the player photo with his position (initials), name, and team (Minnesota) printed in the border. The player photos carry a brief bio on the backs with stats when applicable; the coaches photos are blankbacked. The cards are unnumbered and checklisted below in alphabetical order.

COMPLETE SET (48) 300.00 600.00
1 Grady Alderman 6.00 12.00
2 Bill Bishop 6.00 12.00
3 Darrel Brewster CO 6.00 12.00
4 Jamie Caleb 6.00 12.00
5 Ed Culpepper 6.00 12.00
6 Bob Denton 6.00 12.00
7 Paul Dickson 6.00 12.00
8 Billy Gault 6.00 12.00
9 Harry Gilmer CO 7.50 15.00
10 Dick Grecni 6.00 12.00
11 Dick Haley 6.00 12.00
12 Rip Hawkins 6.00 12.00
13 Raymond Hayes 6.00 12.00
14 Gerry Huth 6.00 12.00
15 Gene Johnson 6.00 12.00
16 Don Joyce 6.00 12.00
17 Bill Lapham 6.00 12.00
18 Jim Leo 6.00 12.00
19 Jim Marshall 10.00 20.00
20 Tommy Mason 7.50 15.00
21 Doug Mayberry 6.00 12.00
22 Hugh McElhenny 10.00 20.00
23 Mike Mercer 6.00 12.00
24 Dave Middleton 6.00 12.00
25 Jack Morris 6.00 12.00
26 Rich Mostardo 6.00 12.00
27 Fred Murphy 6.00 12.00
28 Clancy Osborne 6.00 12.00
29 Dick Pesonen 6.00 12.00
30 Ken Petersen 6.00 12.00
31 Jim Prestel 6.00 12.00
32 Mike Rabold 6.00 12.00
33 Jerry Reichow 6.00 12.00
34 Karl Rubke 6.00 12.00
35 Bob Schnelker 6.00 12.00
36 Ed Sharockman 6.00 12.00
37 George Shaw 7.50 15.00
38 Willard Sherman 6.00 12.00
39 Lebron Shields 6.00 12.00
40 Gordon Smith 6.00 12.00
41 Charlie Sumner 6.00 12.00
42 Fran Tarkenton 20.00 40.00
43 Mel Triplett 6.00 12.00
44 Norm Van Brocklin CO 7.50 15.00
45 Stan West CO 6.00 12.00
46 A.D. Wiliams 6.00 12.00
47 Frank Youso 6.00 12.00
48 Walt Yowarsky CO 6.00 12.00

1963-64 Vikings Team Issue

This 20-card set of the Minnesota Vikings measures approximately 5" by 7" and features black-and-white borderless player portraits with the players position, name and team in a bar at the card bottom. The photos were likely issued over a number of years. Either a Vikings or Minnesota name can be found on the cardfronts.The backs are blank. The cards are unnumbered and checklisted below in alphabetical order.

COMPLETE SET (20) 100.00 200.00
1 Jim Battle 6.00 12.00
2 Larry Bowie 6.00 12.00
3 Bill Butler 6.00 12.00
4 Lee Calland 6.00 12.00
5 John Campbell 6.00 12.00
6 Leon Clarke 6.00 12.00
7 Paul Dickson 6.00 12.00
8 Terry Dillon 6.00 12.00
9 Paul Flatley 6.00 12.00
10 Tom Franckhauser 6.00 12.00
11 Rip Hawkins 6.00 12.00
12 Don Hultz 6.00 12.00
13 Errol Linden 6.00 12.00
14 Mike Mercer 6.00 12.00
15 Ray Poage 6.00 12.00
16 Jim Prestel 6.00 12.00
17 Jerry Reichow 6.00 12.00
18 Ed Sharockman 6.00 12.00
19 Gordon Smith 6.00 12.00
20 Tom Wilson 6.00 12.00

1965 Vikings Team Issue

This set of photos from the Minnesota Vikings measures approximately 4 1/4" by 5 1/2" and features black-and-white player portraits with the players position (appreviated), name and team "Vikings" in a bar at the card bottom. Most of the players in the set are shown wearing their white jersey and most include a facsimile autograph. Some photos were issued with variations on the placement of the facsimilie signature on the front. The photos were likely issued over a number of years and vary slightly in text style and size. The cardbacks are blank; each is unnumbered and checklisted below in alphabetical order.

COMPLETE SET (27) 150.00 300.00
1 Larry Bowie 6.00 12.00
2 Bill Brown 7.50 15.00
3 Fred Cox 10.00 20.00
(with Fran Tarkenton holding)
4 Doug Davis 6.00 12.00
(facsimile sig in upper right)
5 Paul Dickson 6.00 12.00
(facsimile sig in upper right)
6 Carl Eller 7.50 15.00
8 Dale Hackbart 6.00 12.00
8 Paul Flatley 6.00 12.00
(facsimile sig in upper right)
9 Rip Hawkins 6.00 12.00
10 Jeff Jordan 6.00 12.00
(facsimile sig in upper left)
11 Karl Kassulke 6.00 12.00
(no facsimilie sig)
12 Phil King 6.00 12.00
(facsimile sig in upper left)
13 John Kirby 6.00 12.00
(facsimile sig in upper left)
14 Gary Larsen 6.00 12.00
(facsimile sig in upper left)
15 Jim Lindsey 6.00 12.00
(facsimile sig in upper right)
16 Jim Marshall 7.50 15.00
(facsimile sig in upper left)
17 Tommy Mason 6.00 12.00
18A Jim Phillips 6.00 12.00
(facsimile sig in upper right)
18B Jim Phillips 6.00 12.00
(facsimile sig in upper left)
19 Ed Sharockman 6.00 12.00
20 Milt Sunde 6.00 12.00
(facsimile sig in upper right)
21 Fran Tarkenton 12.50 25.00
22 Mick Tingelhoff 7.50 15.00
no facsimile, small type size)
23 Norm Van Brocklin CO 7.50 15.00
24 Ron Vanderkelen 6.00 12.00
25 Bobby Walden 6.00 12.00
(facsimile sig in upper left)
26 Lonnie Warwick 6.00 12.00
27 Roy Winston 6.00 12.00

1966 Vikings Team Issue

These large photo cards are approximately 8" by 10" and feature black-and-white player photos. Each has a white border and was printed on thick glossy stock. The cards are unnumbered and checklisted below in alphabetical order. They are very similar to the 1967 and 1968 issues, but can be differentiated by the player's position, name, and then team name spread out across the border below the photo. Any additions to the checklist below are appreciated.

COMPLETE SET (3) 15.00 30.00
1 Larry Bowie 6.00 12.00
2 Dave Tobey 6.00 12.00
3 Ron Vanderkelen 6.00 12.00

1967 Vikings Team Issue

These large photo cards are approximately 8" by 10" and feature black-and-white player photos. Each has a white border and was printed on thick glossy stock. The cards are unnumbered and checklisted below in alphabetical order. They are very similar to the 1966 and 1968 issues, but can be differentiated by the player's name, postion, and team name tightly arranged in the border below the photo.

COMPLETE SET (23) 100.00 200.00
1 Grady Alderman 7.50 15.00
2 John Beasley 6.00 12.00
3 Bob Berry 6.00 12.00
4 Doug Davis 6.00 12.00
5 Paul Dickson 6.00 12.00
6 Paul Flatley 6.00 12.00
7 Bob Grim 6.00 12.00
8 Dale Hackbart 6.00 12.00
9 Don Hansen 6.00 12.00
10 Jim Hargrove 6.00 12.00
11 Clint Jones 6.00 12.00
12 Jeff Jordan 6.00 12.00
13 Joe Kapp 7.50 15.00
14 John Kirby 6.00 12.00
15 Gary Larsen 6.00 12.00
16 Earsell Mackbee 6.00 12.00
17 Marlin McKeever 6.00 12.00
18 Milt Sunde 6.00 12.00
19 Jim Vellone 6.00 12.00
20 Bobby Walden 6.00 12.00
21 Lonnie Warwick 6.00 12.00
22 Gene Washington 6.00 12.00
23 Roy Winston 6.00 12.00

1968 Vikings Team Issue

These large photo cards are approximately 8" by 10" and feature black-and-white player photos. Each has a white border and was printed on thick glossy stock. The cards are unnumbered and checklisted below in alphabetical order. They are very similar to the 1966 and 1967 issues, but can be differentiated by the player's name, postion (initial), and team name loosely arranged in the border below the photo.

COMPLETE SET (3) 15.00 30.00
1 Grady Alderman 6.00 12.00
2 Gary Cuozzo 6.00 12.00
3 Gene Washington 6.00 12.00

1969 Vikings Team Issue

This 27-card set of the Minnesota Vikings measures approximately 5" by 6 7/8" and features black-and-white borderless player portraits with the players name, position and team in a wide bar at the bottom. The backs are blank. Although similar to earlier Vikings' team issues, these photos can be differentiated by the order in which the player details are listed at the bottom of the card. The cards are unnumbered and checklisted below in alphabetical order.

COMPLETE SET (27) 100.00 200.00
1 Bookie Bolin 5.00 10.00
2 Bobby Bryant 5.00 10.00
3 John Beasley 5.00 10.00
4 Gary Cuozzo 6.00 12.00
5 Doug Davis 5.00 10.00
6 Paul Dickson 5.00 10.00
7 Bob Grim 5.00 10.00
8 Dale Hackbart 5.00 10.00
9 Jim Hargrove 5.00 10.00
10 John Henderson 5.00 10.00
11 Wally Hilgenberg 5.00 10.00
12 Clinton Jones 5.00 10.00
13 Karl Kassulke 5.00 10.00
14 Kent Kramer 5.00 10.00
15 Gary Larsen 5.00 10.00
16 Bob Lee 5.00 10.00
17 Jim Lindsey 5.00 10.00
18 Earsell Mackbee 5.00 10.00
19 Mike McGill 5.00 10.00
20 Oscar Reed 5.00 10.00
21 Ed Sharockman 5.00 10.00
22 Steve Smith 5.00 10.00
23 Milt Sunde 5.00 10.00
24 Jim Vellone 5.00 10.00
25 Lonnie Warwick 5.00 10.00
26 Gene Washington 5.00 10.00
27 Charlie West 5.00 10.00

1970-71 Vikings Team Issue

This 17-card set of the Minnesota Vikings measures approximately 5" by 7" and features black-and-white borderless player portraits with the players name and team name only in a wide bar at the bottom. The backs are blank. The photos were likely issued over a number of years due to the different type styles used on the photo's text. The cards are unnumbered and checklisted below in alphabetical order. Any additions to this checklist would be greatly appreciated.

COMPLETE SET (17) 60.00 120.00
1 John Beasley 5.00 10.00
2 Doug Davis 5.00 10.00
3 Paul Dickson 5.00 10.00
4 Bob Grim 5.00 10.00
5 Jim Hargrove 5.00 10.00
6 John Henderson 5.00 10.00
7 Clint Jones 5.00 10.00
8 Bob Lee 5.00 10.00
9 Jim Lindsey 5.00 10.00
10 Oscar Reed 5.00 10.00
11 Ed Sharockman 5.00 10.00
12 Steve Smith 5.00 10.00
13 Milt Sunde 5.00 10.00
14 Dave Tobey 5.00 10.00
15 Jim Vellone 5.00 10.00
16 John Ward 5.00 10.00
17 Charlie West 5.00 10.00

1971 Vikings Color Photos

Issued in the late summer of 1971 (preseason), this team-issued set consists of 49 four-color close-up photos printed on thin paper stock. Each photo measures approximately 5" by 7 7/16". The player's name, position, and team name appear in a white bottom border. The backs are blank. The cards are unnumbered and checklisted below in alphabetical order.

COMPLETE SET (52) 175.00 300.00
1 Grady Alderman 4.00 8.00
2 Neill Armstrong CO 3.00 6.00
3 John Beasley 3.00 6.00
4 Bill Brown 4.00 8.00
5 Bob Brown 3.00 6.00
6 Bobby Bryant 4.00 8.00
7 Jerry Burns CO 3.00 6.00
8 Fred Cox 4.00 8.00
9 Gary Cuozzo 4.00 8.00
10 Doug Davis 3.00 6.00
11 Al Denson 3.00 6.00
12 Paul Dickson 3.00 6.00
13 Carl Eller 5.00 10.00
14 Bud Grant CO 7.50 15.00
15 Bob Grim 3.00 6.00
16 Leo Hayden 3.00 6.00
17 John Henderson 3.00 6.00
18 Wally Hilgenberg 4.00 8.00
19 Noel Jenke 3.00 6.00
20 Clint Jones 3.00 6.00
21 Karl Kassulke 3.00 6.00
22 Paul Krause 5.00 10.00
23 Gary Larsen 4.00 8.00
24 Bob Lee 3.00 6.00
25 Jim Lindsey 3.00 6.00
26 Jim Marshall 5.00 10.00
27 Bus Mertes CO 3.00 6.00
28 John Michels CO 3.00 6.00
29 Jocko Nelson CO 3.00 6.00
30 Dave Osborn 4.00 8.00
31 Alan Page 7.50 15.00
32 Jack Patera CO 3.00 6.00
33 Jerry Patton 3.00 6.00
34 Pete Perreault 3.00 6.00
35 Oscar Reed 3.00 6.00
36 Ed Sharockman 3.00 6.00
37 Norm Snead 4.00 8.00
38 Milt Sunde 3.00 6.00
39 Doug Sutherland 3.00 6.00
40 Mick Tingelhoff 4.00 8.00
41 Stu Voigt 3.00 6.00

42 John Ward 3.00 6.00
43 Lonnie Warwick 3.00 6.00
44 Gene Washington 4.00 8.00
45 Charlie West 3.00 6.00
46 Ed White 4.00 8.00
47 Carl Winfrey 3.00 6.00
48 Roy Winston 4.00 8.00
49 Jeff Wright S 3.00 6.00
50 Nate Wright 4.00 8.00
51 Ron Yary 4.00 8.00
52 Godfrey Zaunbrecher 3.00 6.00

1971 Vikings Color Postcards

This 19-card set measures roughly 5" by 7 1/2" and features posed color close-up photos on the fronts. These cards were issued after the season had begun and may have been sold at the stadium. The player's name, position, and team name appear in a white bottom border. As with a postcard, the horizontal backs are divided into two sections by a thin black stripe. Brief biographical information is given at the upper left corner, while a box for the stamp is printed at the upper right corner. The cards are unnumbered and checklisted below in alphabetical order.

COMPLETE SET (19) 75.00 125.00
1 Grady Alderman 4.00 8.00
2 Neill Armstrong CO 3.00 6.00
3 John Beasley 3.00 6.00
4 Paul Dickson 3.00 6.00
5 Bud Grant CO 7.50 15.00
6 Wally Hilgenberg 4.00 8.00
7 Noel Jenke 3.00 6.00
8 Paul Krause 5.00 10.00
9 Gary Larsen 4.00 8.00
10 Dave Osborn 4.00 8.00
11 Alan Page 7.50 15.00
12 Jerry Patton 3.00 6.00
13 Doug Sutherland 4.00 8.00
14 Mick Tingelhoff 5.00 10.00
15 Lonnie Warwick 3.00 6.00
16 Charlie West 3.00 6.00
17 Jeff Wright S 3.00 6.00
18 Nate Wright 4.00 8.00
19 Godfrey Zaunbrecher 3.00 6.00

1972 Vikings Color Postcards

Cards in this set measure roughly 4" by 5 7/8" and feature color close-up player photos. These cards were issued after the season had begun and likely were sold at the stadium. The player's name, position, and team name appear in a white bottom border. The backs included a typical postcard format although some have been found without the postcard format. The cards are unnumbered and checklisted below in alphabetical order.

COMPLETE SET ()
1 John Beasley 3.00 6.00
2 Fran Tarkenton 7.50 15.00
3 Godfrey Zaunbrecher 3.00 6.00
(blank backed)

1973 Vikings Team Issue

This 17-card set of the Minnesota Vikings measures roughly 5" by 7". The fronts feature white bordered black-and-white player portraits with the player's name and team in the bottom wide margin. The backs are blank. The photos can be differentiated from previous Vikings Team Issues by the distinctive white borders and scripted team name on the card fronts. The cards are unnumbered and checklisted below in alphabetical order.

COMPLETE SET (17) 50.00 100.00
1 John Beasley 4.00 8.00
2 Bob Berry 4.00 8.00
3 Terry Brown 4.00 8.00
4 Bobby Bryant 4.00 8.00
5 Larry Dibbles 4.00 8.00
6 Mike Eischeid 4.00 8.00
7 Charles Goodrum 4.00 8.00
8 Neil Graff 4.00 8.00
9 Wally Hilgenberg 4.00 8.00
10 Amos Martin 4.00 8.00
11 Brent McClanahan 4.00 8.00
12 John Michels 4.00 8.00
13 Oscar Reed 4.00 8.00
14 John Ward 4.00 8.00
15 Charlie West 4.00 8.00
16 Jeff Wright 4.00 8.00
17 Nate Wright 4.00 8.00

1974 Vikings Team Issue

These all-color blankbacked photos were released by the Vikings around 1974 presumably to fans via mail. Each includes the player's name and team name below the photo.

COMPLETE SET (11) 50.00 100.00
1 Bobby Bryant 4.00 8.00
2 Carl Eller 5.00 10.00
3 Chuck Foreman 5.00 10.00
4 John Gilliam 4.00 8.00
5 Paul Krause 5.00 10.00
6 Jim Marshall 5.00 10.00
7 Alan Page 6.00 12.00
8 Fran Tarkenton 7.50 15.00
9 Mick Tingelhoff 4.00 8.00
10 Ed White 4.00 8.00
11 Ron Yary 5.00 10.00

1975 Vikings Team Sheets

The Vikings issued these black and white player photo sheets for use in publicity opportunities. Each sheet features a number of small player images along with vital information about the player. Each sheet measures roughly 8" by 10" and is blankbacked.

COMPLETE SET (4) 20.00 40.00
1 Players A-H 5.00 10.00
2 Players H-R 5.00 10.00
3 Players K-M 5.00 10.00
4 Players O-Y 7.50 15.00

1976 Vikings Team Sheets

The Vikings issued these black and white player photo sheets for use in publicity opportunities and to fill media requests. Each sheet features a group of small player/coach images along with vital information about the player below the image. Each sheet measures roughly 8" by 10" and is blankbacked.

COMPLETE SET (3) 20.00 35.00
1 Sheet 1 5.00 10.00
2 Sheet 2 5.00 10.00
3 Sheet 3 7.50 15.00

1978 Vikings Country Kitchen

This seven-card set was sponsored by Country Kitchen Restaurants and measures approximately 5" by 7". The front features a black and white head shot of the player. The card backs have biographical and statistical information. The cards are unnumbered and hence are listed alphabetically below.

COMPLETE SET (7) 25.00 50.00
1 Bobby Bryant 3.00 6.00
2 Tommy Kramer 5.00 10.00
3 Paul Krause 5.00 10.00
4 Ahmad Rashad 7.50 15.00
5 Jeff Siemon 3.00 6.00
6 Mick Tingelhoff 4.00 8.00
7 Sammie White 4.00 8.00

1979 Vikings SuperAmerica

The 1979 SuperAmerica Vikings set was distributed through the SuperAmerica convenience stores with a fill-up of gasoline. These 10" by 12" unnumbered sepia posters display watercolor art of the player in action, with a write-up about his career in the top third of the poster. The bottom third of the poster shows a watercolor close-up of the particular player along with a descriptive cutline for the poster. The posters are cataloged in alphabetical order below. There are seven known posters.

COMPLETE SET (7) 40.00 80.00
1 Bill Brown 5.00 10.00
2 Karl Kassulke 4.00 8.00
3 Jim Marshall 7.50 15.00
4 Hugh McElhenny 10.00 20.00
5 Dave Osborn 4.00 8.00
6 Fran Tarkenton 15.00 30.00
7 Gene Washington 5.00 10.00

1983 Vikings Police

The 1983 Minnesota Vikings set contains 17 numbered cards. The cards measure approximately 2 5/8" by 4 1/8". This first Viking police set is sponsored by Pillsbury, Minnesota Crime Prevention Officers Association, Green Giant, and Burger King. In addition to the Vikings' logo, logos of all five organizations appear on the backs. The fronts contain a Vikings logo.

COMPLETE SET (17) 4.00 10.00
1 Checklist Card .30 .75
2 Tommy Kramer .40 1.00
3 Ted Brown .20 .50
4 Joe Senser .20 .50
5 Sammie White .40 1.00
6 Doug Martin .20 .50
7 Matt Blair .30 .75
8 Bud Grant CO .75 2.00
9 Scott Studwell .30 .75
10 Greg Coleman .20 .50
11 John Turner .20 .50
12 Jim Hough .20 .50
13 Joey Browner .40 1.00
14 Dennis Swilley .20 .50
15 Darrin Nelson .30 .75
16 Mark Mullaney .20 .50
17 Fran Tarkenton 1.50 4.00

1984 Vikings Police

This numbered 18-card set features the Minnesota Vikings. Cards measure approximately 2 5/8" by 4 1/8" and are dated in the lower right corner of the reverse. The set was printed on thick card stock. Logos on the card backs are printed in color. The set was sponsored by Pillsbury, Burger King, and the Minnesota Crime Prevention Officers Association.

COMPLETE SET (18) 3.00 8.00
1 Checklist Card .25 .60
2 Keith Nord .15 .40
3 Joe Senser .15 .40
4 Tommy Kramer .30 .75
5 Darrin Nelson .25 .60
6 Tim Irwin .15 .40
7 Mark Mullaney .15 .40
8 Les Steckel CO .15 .40
9 Greg Coleman .15 .40
10 Tommy Hannon .15 .40
11 Curtis Rouse .15 .40
12 Scott Studwell .25 .60
13 Steve Jordan .30 .75
14 Willie Teal .15 .40
15 Ted Brown .25 .60
16 Sammie White .30 .75
17 Matt Blair .25 .60
18 Jim Marshall .75 2.00

1985 Vikings Police

This 16-card set of Minnesota Vikings is numbered on the back. Cards measure approximately 2 5/8" by 4 1/8" and the backs contain a "Crime Prevention Tip". The set was sponsored by Frito-Lay, Pepsi-Cola, KS95-FM, and local area law enforcement agencies. Card backs are written in red and blue on white card stock. The set commemorates the 25th (Silver) Anniversary Season for the Vikings. The checklist card tells which week each card was available.

COMPLETE SET (16) 3.00 8.00
1 Checklist Card .25 .60
2 Bud Grant CO .50 1.25
3 Matt Blair .25 .60
4 Alfred Anderson .15 .40
5 Fred McNeill .15 .40
6 Tommy Kramer .30 .75
7 Jan Stenerud .40 1.00
8 Sammie White .30 .75
9 Doug Martin .15 .40
10 Greg Coleman .15 .40
11 Steve Riley .15 .40
12 Walker Lee Ashley .15 .40
13 Tim Irwin .15 .40
14 Scott Studwell .15 .40
15 Darrin Nelson .25 .60
16 Mick Tingelhoff .30 .75

1986 Vikings Police

This 14-card set of Minnesota Vikings is numbered on the back. Cards measure approximately 2 5/8" by 4 1/8" and the backs contain a "Crime Prevention Tip". The checklist for the set is on the back of the head coach card.

COMPLETE SET (14) 3.00 8.00
1 Jerry Burns CO .15 .40
2 Darrin Nelson .25 .60
3 Tommy Kramer .30 .75
4 Anthony Carter .60 1.50
5 Scott Studwell .15 .40
6 Chris Doleman .60 1.50
7 Joey Browner .30 .75
8 Steve Jordan .30 .75
9 David Howard .15 .40
10 Tim Newton .15 .40
11 Leo Lewis .15 .40
12 Keith Millard .30 .75
13 Doug Martin .15 .40
14 Bill Brown .25 .60

1987 Vikings Police

This 14-card set of Minnesota Vikings is numbered on the back. Cards measure approximately 2 5/8" by 4 1/8" and are in full color on the front. The backs contain a "Crime Prevention Tip". The checklist for the set is on the back of the first card. Purple Power '87 is actually an action montage by artist Cliff Spohn. Reportedly 2.1 million cards were distributed during the 14-week promotion. The set was sponsored by the Vikings, Frito-Lay, Campbell's Soup, and KSTP-FM in cooperation with the Minnesota Crime Prevention Officers Association.

COMPLETE SET (14) 3.00 8.00
1 Vikings Theme Art .25 .60
2 Jerry Burns CO .25 .60
3 Scott Studwell .15 .40
4 Tommy Kramer .30 .75
5 Gerald Robinson .15 .40
6 Wade Wilson .40 1.00
7 Anthony Carter .60 1.50
8 Terry Tausch .15 .40
9 Leo Lewis .15 .40
10 Keith Millard .30 .75
11 Carl Lee .15 .40
12 Steve Jordan .25 .60
13 D.J. Dozier .25 .60
14 Alan Page ATG .60 1.50

1988 Vikings Police

The 1988 Police Minnesota Vikings set contains 12 numbered cards measuring approximately 2 5/8" by 4 1/8". There are nine cards of current players, plus one checklist card, one "Vikings Defense" card, and one of "All-Time Great" Paul Krause.

COMPLETE SET (12) 2.50 6.00
1 Vikings Offense .25 .60
2 Jesse Solomon .15 .40
3 Kirk Lowdermilk .15 .40
4 Darrin Nelson .25 .60
5 Chris Doleman .30 .75
6 D.J. Dozier .25 .60
7 Gary Zimmerman .40 1.00
8 Allen Rice .15 .40
9 Joey Browner .25 .60
10 Anthony Carter .40 1.00
11 Vikings Defense .25 .60
12 Paul Krause .40 1.00

1989 Vikings Police

The 1989 Police Minnesota Vikings set contains ten standard-size cards. The fronts have gray borders and color action photos; the horizontally oriented backs have safety tips, bios, and career highlights. It has been reported that 175,000 cards of each player were given away by the police officers in the state of Minnesota.

COMPLETE SET (10) 2.50 6.00
1 Team Card .25 .60
2 Henry Thomas .40 1.00
3 Rick Fenney .15 .40
4 Chuck Nelson .15 .40
5 Jim Gustafson .15 .40
6 Wade Wilson .30 .75
7 Randall McDaniel .50 1.25
8 Jesse Solomon .15 .40
9 Anthony Carter .40 1.00
10 Joe Kapp .30 .75

1989 Vikings Taystee Discs

The 1989 Taystee Minnesota Vikings set contains 12 white-bordered, approximately 2 3/4" diameter discs. The fronts have helmetless color mug shots; the backs are white and have sparse bio and stats. One disc was included in each specially-marked Taystee product, distributed only in the Minnesota area.

COMPLETE SET (12) 5.00 10.00
1 Chris Doleman .50 1.25
2 Joey Browner .40 1.00
3 Anthony Carter .50 1.25
4 Steve Jordan .30 .75
5 Scott Studwell .30 .75
6 Wade Wilson .40 1.00
7 Kirk Lowdermilk .30 .75
8 Tommy Kramer .40 1.00
9 Keith Millard .30 .75
10 Rick Fenney .30 .75
11 Gary Zimmerman .40 1.00
12 Darrin Nelson .30 .75

1990 Vikings Police

This ten-card standard-size set was issued to promote safety in the Minneapolis area by using members of the 1990 Minnesota Vikings. The card photos have posed action shots on the front along with an advertisement for Gatorade on the front and a crime prevention tip on the back. We have checklisted the cards in this set in alphabetical order.

COMPLETE SET (10) 2.00 5.00
1 Chris Doleman .30 .75
2 Ray Berry .14 .35
3 Mike Merriweather .20 .50
4 Rick Fenney .14 .35
5 Wade Wilson .30 .75
6 Carl Lee .14 .35
7 Hassan Jones .20 .50
8 Scott Studwell .14 .35
9 Anthony Carter .40 1.00
10 Herschel Walker .50 1.25

1991 Vikings Police

This ten-card standard-size set was sponsored by Gatorade. The cards were distributed by participating Minnesota police departments, one per week, beginning on Aug. 23 with Rick Fenney, and concluding on Oct. 27 with Chris Doleman. Card fronts display an action player photo enclosed in a purple border, while player's name is printed at the top in a gray rectangle. Gatorade's logo appears at the bottom of the picture. The first card's back lists the Vikings' game schedule. The horizontally oriented backs of the remaining cards feature a black and white close-up of the player and a biographical sketch on the left portion. Player's name, position, and jersey number appear in a black box at the top right, while the Vikadontis Rex mascot appears below. A crime prevention tip appears under the card number, while sponsor logos of Super Bowl XXVI, KFAN Sports Radio, and K102 Radio round out the back design.

COMPLETE SET (10) 2.00 5.00
1 Rick Fenney .14 .35
2 Wade Wilson .30 .75
3 Mike Merriweather .20 .50
4 Hassan Jones .14 .35
5 Rich Gannon .40 1.00
6 Mark Dusbabek .14 .35
7 Sean Salisbury .20 .50
8 Reggie Rutland .20 .50
9 Tim Irwin .14 .35
10 Chris Doleman .30 .75

1992 Vikings Police

This ten-card standard size set was primarily sponsored by Gatorade. The card fronts display an action color player photo framed by a purple border, while the player's name and team name appear in a gray rectangle at the top. The Gatorade logo appears at the bottom of the picture. The horizontally oriented backs carry a black-and-white close-up of the player and biographical information within a black outline box on the left side of the card. The player's name and position appear in a black bar at the top. Below are Vikadontis Rex (the team mascot), a crime prevention tip, and other sponsor logos (KFAN Sports Radio AM 1130 and K102).

COMPLETE SET (10) 2.40 6.00
1 Dennis Green CO .20 .50
2 John Randle .20 .50
3 Todd Scott .14 .35
4 Anthony Carter .30 .75
5 Steve Jordan .20 .50
6 Terry Allen .80 2.00
7 Brian Habib .14 .35
8 Fuad Reveiz .14 .35
9 Roger Craig .20 .50
10 Cris Carter .80 2.00

1993 Vikings Police

This ten-card standard-size set was primarily sponsored by Gatorade, and the cards feature on their fronts purple-bordered color player photos. The player's name and team name appear within a gray rectangle at the top, and the Gatorade logo is displayed at the bottom. The white and horizontal back carries a black-and-white player headshot in the upper left, with his biography shown below. His name, position, and uniform number appear in the black stripe at the top. Below are Vikadontis Rex (the team mascot), a crime prevention tip, and other sponsor logos (KFAN Sports Radio and K102).

COMPLETE SET (10) 2.00 5.00
1 Dennis Green CO .20 .50
2 Henry Thomas .20 .50
3 Todd Scott .10 .30
4 Jack Del Rio .20 .50
5 Vencie Glenn .10 .30
6 Fuad Reveiz .10 .30
7 Cris Carter .60 1.50
8 Terry Allen .40 1.00
9 Roger Craig .30 .75
10 Carlos Jenkins .10 .30

1994 Vikings Police

This ten-card set was primarily sponsored by Gatorade. Each standard sized card featured a purple border and full color player photos on glossy card stock. The player's and team name appear within a gray rectangle at the top of the card, and the Gatorade logo, as well as the NFL 75th team anniversary logo are positioned near the bottom corners of the card. The cardbacks contain a player bio and are numbered directly over a crime prevention tip.

COMPLETE SET (10) 2.00 5.00
1 Dennis Green CO CL .10 .30
2 Randall McDaniel .20 .50
3 Vencie Glenn .10 .30
4 Jack Del Rio .20 .50
5 Cris Carter .50 1.25
6 Bernard Dafney .10 .30
7 Scottie Graham .20 .50
8 John Randle .30 .75
9 Warren Moon .40 1.00
10 Bud Grant CO .30 .75

1995 Vikings Police

This ten-card set was primarily sponsered by Gatorade, and these standard sized cards feature on the front purple-bordered player photos. The player's and team name appear within a gray rectangle at the top of the card, and the Gatorade logo, as well as an 35th team anniversary logo are positioned at the bottom corners of the card. The white and horizontal back features a black and white headshot with the players biography below the photo. The players name, position, and number are in a black stripe on the top of the back of the card. Below are Vikadontis Rex (the team mascot), a crime prevention tip, and other sponsor logos (KFAN Sports Radio and K102) The cards are numbered on the back directly over the crime prevention tip.

COMPLETE SET (10) 2.40 6.00
1 Warren Moon CL .40 1.00
2 Randall McDaniel .20 .50
3 Jake Reed .30 .75
4 Jack Del Rio .20 .50
5 Cris Carter .50 1.25
6 Fuad Reveiz .10 .30
7 Amp Lee .10 .30
8 John Randle .30 .75
9 Andrew Jordan .10 .30
10 DeWayne Washington .20 .50

1996 Vikings Police

This ten-card set was primarily sponsered by EF Johnson. The standard-sized cards feature a purple and yellow border with full-color player photos on the fronts. The player's name and team logo appear at the top of the card. The horizontal back features a black and white headshot with the player's biography below the photo. The cards are numbered on the back directly over a crime prevention tip.

COMPLETE SET (10) 2.00 5.00
1 Randall McDaniel .20 .50
2 Qadry Ismail .20 .50
3 Andrew Jordan .10 .30
4 Cris Carter .50 1.25
5 Vikadontis Rex Mascot .10 .30
6 Jake Reed .30 .75
7 Ed McDaniel .10 .30
8 Mike Morris .10 .30
9 Dixon Edwards .10 .30
10 John Randle .30 .75

1997 Vikings Police

This set of Vikings cards was distributed one game at a time during the 1997 NFL season. Each card was produced with a distinctive purple cardfront and sponsored by General Security Services Corp.

COMPLETE SET (8) 2.40 6.00
1 Cris Carter .60 1.50
Jake Reed
2 Robert Smith .40 1.00
3 Jeff Brady .30 .75
4 Brad Johnson .60 1.50
5 Robert Griffith .30 .75
6 Randall McDaniel .30 .75
7 Leroy Hoard .30 .75
8 John Randle .40 1.00

1998 Vikings Pizza Hut

This set of unnumbered cards was distributed through participating Pizza Hut stores during the 1998 NFL season. Each card was printed on light plastic coated stock, featured rounded corners, and measured roughly 2 1/8" by 3 3/8".

COMPLETE SET (3) 10.00 18.00
1 Bud Grant CO 2.00 5.00
2 Paul Krause 2.00 5.00
3 Fran Tarkenton 3.00 8.00

1998 Vikings Police

This set of Vikings cards was sponsored by GSSC and produced with a yellow border and color player photo on the cardfronts. Each card measures standard size.

COMPLETE SET (8) 2.40 6.00
1 Brad Johnson .60 1.50
2 Todd Steussie .30 .75
3 Dwayne Rudd .30 .75
4 Cris Carter .60 1.50
5 Randall Cunningham .60 1.50
6 Stalin Colinet .30 .75
7 Robert Smith .40 1.00
8 John Randle .40 1.00

1999 Vikings Burger King

This set was sponsored and distributed by Burger King stores in the Minneapolis area during the 1999 NFL season. The cards were distributed in 4-card packs over 9-weeks of the season. Each pack contained three-player cards and one coupon/checklist card. Each card features a full-color front and back player photo with a purple border.

COMPLETE SET (36) 4.80 12.00
1 Cris Carter .60 1.50
2 Stalin Colinet .08 .25
3 Tony Williams DT .08 .25
4 Gary Anderson K .08 .25
5 Mike Morris .08 .25
6 Randall McDaniel .15 .40
7 Randall Cunningham .50 1.25
8 Matthew Hatchette .08 .25
9 Mitch Berger .08 .25
10 Ed McDaniel .08 .25
11 David Palmer .15 .40
12 Kailee Wong .08 .25
13 Randy Moss 1.60 4.00
14 Todd Steussie .08 .25
15 Jeff Christy .08 .25
16 John Randle .30 .75
17 Jimmy Hitchcock .08 .25
18 Chris Walsh .08 .25
19 Jake Reed .08 .25
20 Andrew Glover .08 .25
21 Orlando Thomas .08 .25
22 Dwayne Rudd .08 .25
23 Leroy Hoard .08 .25
24 Korey Stringer .08 .25
25 Robert Smith .30 .75
26 Daunte Culpepper 1.60 4.00
27 Robert Griffith .08 .25
CL1 Checklist Week 1 .08 .25
CL2 Checklist Week 2 .08 .25
CL3 Checklist Week 3 .08 .25
CL4 Checklist Week 4 .08 .25
CL5 Checklist Week 5 .08 .25
CL6 Checklist Week 6 .08 .25
CL7 Checklist Week 7 .08 .25
CL8 Checklist Week 8 .08 .25
CL9 Checklist Week 9 .08 .25

1999 Vikings Police

This set of Vikings cards was produced with a purple border and color player photo on the cardfronts. Randy Moss was included for the first time in the, now traditional, Vikings Police issue. Each card measures standard size.

COMPLETE SET (8) 3.20 8.00
1 Randall Cunningham .50 1.25
2 Cris Carter .60 1.50
3 John Randle .40 1.00
4 Randy Moss 1.60 4.00
5 Jeff Christy .20 .50
6 Robert Smith .40 1.00
7 Gary Anderson K .20 .50
8 Robert Griffith .20 .50

2000 Vikings Police

This set was sponsered by Card Connection, the American Society for Industrial Security and the MCPA. Each measures roughly 2 5/8" by 3 5/8." The Vikings 40th team anniversary logo is positioned at the upper right hand corner of the card. The cardbacks feature a crime prevention tip along with a black and white player photo. The cards are numbered by the crime prevention tip on the backs.

COMPLETE SET (9) 3.00 8.00
1 Daunte Culpepper 1.00 2.50
2 Mitch Berger .20 .50
3 Robert Smith .40 1.00
4 Randy Moss 1.25 3.00
5 John Randle .40 1.00
6 Ed McDaniel .20 .50
7 Dwayne Rudd .20 .50
8 Cris Carter .60 1.50
NNO Cover Card .60 1.50

2001 Vikings Police

This set of Vikings cards was produced in standard card size with the typical color player photo on the cardfronts. The set featured the title "Autumn Heroes" at the top of the cards. This marked the 19th consecutive year for a Vikings Police-sponsored card set.

COMPLETE SET (10) 3.00 8.00
1 Kailee Wong .20 .50
2 Mitch Berger .20 .50
3 Cris Carter .60 1.50
4 Robert Griffith .20 .50
5 Randy Moss 1.25 3.00
6 Michael Bennett .75 2.00
7 Matt Birk .20 .50
8 Daunte Culpepper .75 2.00
9 Jake Reed .40 1.00
NNO Cover Card .40 1.00
Daunte Culpepper

2001 Vikings Upper Deck

This set was given away to the first 50,000 fans who attended the August 16, 2001 Vikings game. Each card includes a color photo player on front with the Upper Deck logo and a typical cardback.

COMPLETE SET (12) 4.00 10.00
1 Cris Carter .50 1.25
2 Daunte Culpepper .60 1.50
3 Randy Moss 1.00 2.50
4 Michael Bennett 1.00 2.50
5 Gary Anderson .20 .50
6 Robert Griffith .20 .50
7 Talance Sawyer .20 .50
8 Lance Johnstone .20 .50
9 Eric Kelly .20 .50
10 Matt Birk .20 .50
11 Todd Bouman .30 .75
12 Mick Tingelhoff .30 .75

2002 Vikings Police

This set of Vikings cards was produced in standard card size with the typical color player photo on the cardfronts. The set featured the "Purple Pride" Vikings logo at the top of the cards. The cards are numbered by the safety tip on the back beginning with card #9.

COMPLETE SET (8) 4.00 8.00
9 Michael Bennett .75 2.00
10 Mike Tice CO .40 1.00
11 Chris Hovan .50 1.25
12 Daunte Culpepper 1.00 2.50
13 Randy Moss 1.25 3.00
14 Matt Birk .40 1.00
15 Jim Kleinsasser .50 1.25
16 Byron Chamberlain .50 1.25

2002 Vikings Score

This six-card set was given away at a Vikings home game during the 2002 season. Each card follows the design of the 200 Score set, but has been re-numbered 1-6. An additional Carl Eller card sponsored by US Link was issued at a later date.

COMPLETE SET (6) 3.00 8.00
1 Chris Hovan .50 1.25
2 Moe Williams .50 1.25
3 Michael Bennett .75 2.00
4 Daunte Culpepper 1.00 2.50
5 Jim Kleinsasser .50 1.25
6 Matt Birk .40 1.00
CE Carl Eller .75 2.00

2005 Vikings Activa Medallions

COMPLETE SET (22) 30.00 60.00
1 Fran Tarkentnn 1.50 4.00
2 Alan Page 1.25 3.00
3 Scott Studwell 1.25 3.00
4 Carl Eller 1.25 3.00
5 Bill Brown 1.25 3.00
6 Cris Carter 1.50 4.00
7 Bud Grant 1.25 3.00
8 Chris Doleman 1.25 3.00
9 Mick Tingelhoff 1.25 3.00
10 Chuck Forman 1.25 3.00
11 Steve Jordan 1.25 3.00
12 Paul Krause 1.25 3.00
13 Carl Lee 1.25 3.00
14 45th Anniversary Logo 1.00 2.50
15 Randall McDaniel 1.25 3.00
16 Matt Blair 1.25 3.00
17 John Randle 1.25 3.00
18 Ahmad Rashad 1.25 3.00
19 Joey Browner 1.25 3.00
20 Ron Yary 1.25 3.00
21 Jerry Burns 1.25 3.00
22 Jim Marshall 1.25 3.00

2006 Vikings Topps

COMPLETE SET (12) 3.00 5.00
MIN1 Travis Taylor .25 .60
MIN2 Troy Williamson .25 .60
MIN3 Mewelde Moore .25 .60
MIN4 Marcus Robinson .25 .60
MIN5 Fred Smoot .25 .60
MIN6 Darren Sharper .25 .60
MIN7 Koren Robinson .25 .60
MIN8 Chester Taylor .30 .75
MIN9 Brad Johnson .30 .75
MIN10 Erasmus James .25 .60
MIN11 Chad Greenway .40 1.00
MIN12 Steve Hutchinson .30 .75

2007 Vikings Topps

COMPLETE SET (12) 4.00 10.00
1 Chester Taylor .25 .60
2 Tarvaris Jackson .25 .60
3 Troy Williamson .25 .60
4 Mewelde Moore .25 .60
5 Adrian Peterson 1.00 2.50
6 Antoine Winfield .25 .60
7 Steve Hutchinson .30 .75
8 Darren Sharper .25 .60
9 Kevin Williams .25 .60
10 E.J. Henderson .25 .60
11 Ryan Longwell .25 .60
12 Sidney Rice .30 .75

2008 Vikings Topps

COMPLETE SET (12) 2.50 5.00
1 Chester Taylor .20 .50
2 Adrian Peterson .40 1.00
3 Tarvaris Jackson .20 .50
4 Bernard Berrian .25 .60
5 Sidney Rice .25 .60
6 Bobby Wade .20 .50
7 Kevin Williams .20 .50
8 Pat Williams .20 .50
9 Darren Sharper .25 .60
10 Jared Allen .25 .60
11 John David Booty .25 .60
12 Tyrell Johnson .25 .60

1925-31 W590 Athletes

Issued over a period of years, this set (which measure approximately 1 3/8" by 2 1/2") features some of the leading athletes from the 1920's. The fronts have a B&W photo with the players name, position and team on the bottom for the baseball players and sport and additional short bio info on the other athletes. The backs are blank and as these cards are unnumbered we have sequenced them in alphabetical order within sport. They were initally issued in strips and panels and can often be found intact. A number of the baseball players were re-issued from year-to-year with updated team information.

60 Red Grange FB 350.00 600.00
61 Walter Koppisch FB 60.00 100.00

1986 Waddingtons Game

This boxed set of 40 oversized (3 1/2" by 5 11/16") playing cards was produced in England and comes complete with a plastic tray and game rules. The object of the game is to play all of one's cards onto a central pattern based on typical movements in an American Football Game. The fronts feature colorful illustrations of five of the most famous teams in the NFL. Each team is portrayed on seven cards; moreover, there are five interception cards, which show merely the NFL logo. The backs of all the cards are printed in two colors of blue and have an oversized NFL logo. The cards have been checklisted below alphabetically according to teams, with the interception cards listed at the end. We've included the names of recognizable but unidentified players on the card fronts. Most of the art was apparently produced in the early 1980s based on the players featured.

COMPLETE SET (40) 50.00 80.00
1 Bears 10 2.00 5.00
Walter Payton
2 Bears 20 2.00 5.00
Walter Payton
3 Bears 40 2.00 5.00
Walter Payton
4 Bears 50 2.00 5.00
Walter Payton
5 Bears First Down 2.00 5.00
Walter Payton
6 Bears Punt 2.00 5.00
Walter Payton
7 Bears Touchdown 2.00 5.00
Walter Payton
8 Cowboys 10 .50 1.25
Danny White
Tony Dorsett
9 Cowboys 20 .50 1.25
Danny White
Tony Dorsett
10 Cowboys 40 .50 1.25
Danny White
Tony Dorsett
11 Cowboys 50 .50 1.25
Danny White
Tony Dorsett
12 Cowboys First Down .50 1.25
Danny White
Tony Dorsett
13 Cowboys Punt .50 1.25
Danny White
Tony Dorsett
14 Cowboys Touchdown .50 1.25
Danny White
Tony Dorsett
15 Dolphins 10 .30 .75
Lorenzo Hampton
16 Dolphins 20 .30 .75
Lorenzo Hampton
17 Dolphins 40 .30 .75
Lorenzo Hampton
18 Dolphins 50 .30 .75
Lorenzo Hampton
19 Dolphins First Down .30 .75
Lorenzo Hampton
20 Dolphins Punt .30 .75
Lorenzo Hampton
21 Dolphins Touchdown .30 .75
Lorenzo Hampton
22 Redskins 10 .50 1.25
John Riggins
Joe Theismann
23 Redskins 20 .50 1.25
John Riggins
Joe Theismann
24 Redskins 40 .50 1.25
John Riggins
Joe Theismann
25 Redskins 50 .50 1.25
John Riggins
Joe Theismann
26 Redskins First Down .50 1.25
John Riggins
Joe Theismann
27 Redskins Punt .50 1.25
John Riggins
Joe Theismann
28 Redskins Touchdown .50 1.25
John Riggins
Joe Theismann
29 Steelers 10 1.25 2.50
Terry Bradshaw
Lynn Swann
30 Steelers 20 1.25 2.50
Terry Bradshaw
Lynn Swann
31 Steelers 40 1.25 2.50
Terry Bradshaw
Lynn Swann
32 Steelers 50 1.25 2.50
Terry Bradshaw
Lynn Swann
33 Steelers First Down 1.25 2.50
Terry Bradshaw
Lynn Swann
34 Steelers Punt 1.25 2.50
Terry Bradshaw
Lynn Swann
35 Steelers Touchdown 1.25 2.50
Terry Bradshaw
Lynn Swann
36 Interception Card .30 .75
37 Interception Card .30 .75
38 Interception Card .30 .75
39 Interception Card .30 .75
40 Interception Card .30 .75

1987 Wagon Wheel

This attractive set of eight large cards was issued in the United Kingdom by Burtons as an insert in a box of Chocolate Biscuits (cookies). Players in the set are recognizable but not explicitly identified on the card. The theme of the set is the explanation of American football to the British. The cards measure approximately 6 5/16" by 4 5/16" and are unnumbered. The card backs provide information on related mail order products available until May 31, 1988.

COMPLETE SET (8) 40.00 100.00
1 Defensive Back 5.00 12.00
2 Defensive Lineman 5.00 12.00
3 Kicker 3.00 8.00
4 Linebacker 3.00 8.00
5 Offensive Lineman 20.00 50.00
6 Quarterback 15.00 40.00
7 Receiver 8.00 20.00
8 Running Back 5.00 12.00

1988 Walter Payton Commemorative

Each of the 132 standard-size cards in this set pictures and features Walter Payton in some aspect of his great career. Cards listed below are generally listed by the title on the card back. Each set was packaged inside its own numbered (of 16,726) dark blue plastic box. Card fronts carry the NFL logo in the upper left corner and the Bears logo in the lower right corner. The set was issued in conjunction with a soft-cover book, "Sweetness".

COMPLETE SET (132) 16.00 40.00
COMMON CARD (1-132) .20 .50
1 Leading Scorer in .40 1.00
89 Ditka On Payton .60 1.50
132 Last Few Moments .40 1.00

1935 Wheaties All-Americans of 1934

This set of cards is very similar to the 1934 Fancy Frames issue and is often referred to as "Wheaties FB2." They are differentiated by the printed "All American...1934" title line. Each features a blue and white photo of the player surrounded by a blue frame border design which is often referred to as "fancy frames." The cardbacks are blank and each measures roughly 6" by 6 1/4" when cut around the frame border. The George Barclay and William Shepherd cards are thought to be the toughest to find.

COMPLETE SET (12) 1500.00 2500.00
1 George Barclay 100.00 175.00
2 Charles Hartwig 100.00 175.00
3 Dixie Howell 175.00 300.00
4 Don Hutson 350.00 600.00
5 Stan Kostka 100.00 175.00
6 Frank Larson 100.00 175.00
7 Bill Lee 100.00 175.00
8 George Maddox 100.00 175.00
9 Regis Monahan 100.00 175.00
10 John J. Robinson 100.00 175.00
11 William Shepherd 100.00 175.00
12 Cotton Warburton 100.00 175.00

1935 Wheaties Fancy Frames

Cards from this set could be cut from boxes of Wheaties cereals in the 1930s and are commonly found mis-cut. Each features a blue and white photo of a famous player or coach surrounded by a blue frame border design. The cards are often called "Wheaties FB1" as well as "Fancy Frames." In appearance they are very similar to the 1935 All-Americans issue, except for the player's name written in script on the cardfront. The cardbacks are blank and each measures roughly 6" by 6 1/4" when cut around the frame border. The Benny Friedman and Pop Warner cards are thought to be slightly tougher to find.

COMPLETE SET (8) 1500.00 2200.00
1 Jack Armstrong 75.00 150.00
2 Chris Cagle 100.00 175.00
3 Benny Friedman 175.00 300.00
4 Red Grange 500.00 800.00
5 Howard Jones CO 100.00 175.00
6 Harry Kipke 100.00 175.00
7 Ernie Nevers 250.00 400.00
8 Pop Warner CO 175.00 300.00

1936 Wheaties All-Americans of 1935

This set is often referred to as "Wheaties FB3" or the "All American of 1935" set due to that title line appearing on the cardfronts. As was the case with most Wheaties cards, the fronts were printed in blue and white on an orange background. Bernie Bierman is thought to be tougher to find than the rest.

COMPLETE SET (12) 1800.00 2800.00
1 Sheldon Beise 150.00 250.00
2 Bernie Bierman SP 175.00 300.00
3 Darrell Lester TX 150.00 250.00
4 Eddie Michaels 150.00 250.00
5 Wayne Millner 250.00 400.00
6 Monk Moscrip 150.00 250.00
7 Andy Pilney 150.00 250.00
8 Dick Smith 150.00 250.00
9 Riley Smith 150.00 250.00
10 Truman Spain 150.00 250.00
11 Charles Wasicek 150.00 250.00
12 Bobby Wilson 150.00 250.00

1936 Wheaties Coaches

ese cards are actually advertising panels cut from the backs of Wheaties cereal boxes. Unlike many of the other Wheaties cards from the era, they do not offer instructions on how or where to cut the cards from the boxes. Each includes a famous coach's picture along with a short quote and measures roughly 6" by 8 1/4" when cut cleanly. The Harry Stuhldreher is thought to be the toughest panel to find.

COMPLETE SET (7) 600.00 1200.00
1 Bernie Bierman 100.00 175.00
2 Jim Crowley 125.00 200.00
3 Red Dawson 100.00 175.00
4 Andy Kerr 100.00 175.00
5 Bo McMillin 100.00 175.00
6 Harry Stuhldreher 150.00 250.00
7 Lynn Waldorf 100.00 175.00

1936 Wheaties Six-Man

Famous coaches are featured on this set of Wheaties box panels discussing the unique rules and strategy involved with 6-man football. Each measures roughly 6" by 8 1/4" when cut from the box and was printed with the familiar blue and orange color scheme. The Red Dawson and Ossie Solem cards are thought to be the toughest to find.

COMPLETE SET (6) 800.00 1200.00
1 Bernie Bierman 150.00 250.00
2 Red Dawson 125.00 200.00
3 Tiny Hollingsberry 125.00 200.00
4 Andy Kerr 125.00 200.00
5 Ossie Solem 125.00 200.00
6 Tiny Thornhill 150.00 250.00

1937 Wheaties Big Ten Football

These Wheaties cards are actually advertisements cut from the backs of Wheaties cereal boxes. Each features a popular pro football player touting the "Big Ten Football Game" offered for sale on the box back. There was also a football field game board as part of the set that could be used to play a form of game with a football radio broadcast. The cards were printed in blue, white, and orange and each measures roughly 6" by 8 1/4" when cut cleanly from the box.

COMPLETE SET (5) 1200.00 1800.00
1 Ed Danowski 125.00 200.00
2 Arnie Herber 175.00 300.00
3 Ralph Kercheval 125.00 200.00
4 Ed Manske 125.00 200.00
5 Bronko Nagurski 600.00 1000.00
6 Football Game Board 175.00 300.00

1940 Wheaties M4

This set is referred to as the "Champs in the USA" The cards measure about 6" 8 1'4" and are numbered. The drawing portion (inside the dotted lines) measures approximately 6" X 6". There is a Baseball player on each card and they are joined by football players, football coaches, race car drivers, airline pilots, a circus clown, ice skater, hockey star and golfers. Each athlete appears in what looks like a stamp with a serrated edge. The stamps appear one above the other with a brief block of copy describing his or her achievements. There appears to have been three printings, resulting in some variation panels. The full panels tell the cereal buyer to look for either 27, 39, or 63 champ stamps. The first nine panels apparently were printed more than once, since all the unknown variations occur with those numbers.

COMPLETE SET (20) 400.00 800.00
3 J. Foxx/B. Dickey 35.00 60.00
4 M. Arnovich/D. Clark 15.00 25.00
5 Joe Medwick 15.00 25.00
Matty Bell
Ab Jenkins
6A J. Mize/D. O'Brien/Ralph Guldahl/(27 stamp 15.00
25.00
6C G. Hartnett/D. O'Brien/Ralph Guldahl/(unk 15.00 25.00
7A J. Cronin/Byron Nelson/(27 stamp 15.00 25.00
7C P. Derringer/Byron Nelson/(unkno 15.00 25.00
8A J. Manders/E. Lombardi/George I. Myers/(27 15.00
25.00
10 A. Inge/B. Herman 15.00 25.00
11 Dolph Camilli 15.00 25.00
Antoinette Concello
Wallace Wade

1941 Wheaties M5

This set is also referred to as "Champs of the U.S.A." These numbered cards made up the back of the Wheaties box; the whole panel measures 6" X 8 1/4" but the drawing portion (inside the dotted lines) is apparently 6" X 6". Each athlete appears in what looks like a stamp with a serrated edge. The stamps appear one above the other with a brief block of copy describing his or her achievements. The format is the same as the previous M4 set -- even the numbering system continues where the M4 set stops.

COMPLETE SET (8) 175.00 350.00
15 B. Bierman/B. Feller/Jessie McLeod 20.00 40.00
16 Hank Greenberg 20.00 40.00
Lowell Red Dawson
J.W. Stoker

1951 Wheaties

The cards in this six-card set measure approximately 2 1/2" by 3 1/4". Cards of the 1951 Wheaties set are actually the backs of small individual boxes of Wheaties. The cards are waxed and depict three baseball players, one football player, one basketball player, and one golfer. They are occasionally found as complete boxes, which are worth 50 percent more than the prices listed below. The catalog designation for this set is F272-3. The cards are blank-backed and unnumbered; they are numbered below in alphabetical order for convenience.

COMPLETE SET (6) 300.00 600.00
2 Johnny Lujack 40.00 80.00

1952 Wheaties

The cards in this 60-card set measure 2" by 2 3/4". The 1952 Wheaties set of orange, blue and white, unnumbered cards was issued in panels of eight or ten cards on the backs of Wheaties cereal boxes. Each player appears in an action pose, designated in the checklist with an "A", and as a portrait, listed in the checklist with a "B". The catalog designation is F272-4. The cards are blank-backed and unnumbered, but have been assigned numbers below using a sport prefix (BB- baseball, BK- basketball, FB- football, G- Golf, OT- other).

COMPLETE SET (60) 600.00 1000.00
FB1A Glenn Davis Action 4.00 8.00
FB1B Glenn Davis Portrait 4.00 8.00
FB2A Tom Fears Action 4.00 8.00
FB2B Tom Fears Portrait 4.00 8.00
FB3A Otto Graham Action 10.00 20.00
FB3B Otto Graham Portrait 10.00 20.00
FB4A Johnny Lujack Action 4.00 8.00
FB4B Johnny Lujack Portrait 4.00 8.00
FB5A Doak Walker Action 7.50 15.00
FB5B Doak Walker Portrait 7.50 15.00
FB6A Bob Waterfield Action 12.50 25.00
FB6B Bob Waterfield Portrait 12.50 25.00

1964 Wheaties Stamps

This set of 74 stamps was issued perforated within a 48-page album. There were 70 players and four team logo stamps bound into the album as six pages of 12 stamps each plus two stamps attached to the inside front cover. In fact, they are typically found this way, still bound into the album. The stamps measure approximately 2 1/2" by 2 3/4" and are unnumbered. The album itself measures approximately 8 1/8" by 11" and is entitled "Pro Bowl Football Player Stamp Album". The stamp list below has been alphabetized for convenience. Each player stamp has a facsimile autograph on the front. Note that there are no spaces in the album for Joe Schmidt, Y.A.Tittle, or the four team emblem stamps.

COMPLETE SET (74) 175.00 300.00
1 Herb Adderley 5.00 10.00
2 Grady Alderman 1.50 3.00
3 Doug Atkins 4.00 8.00
4 Sam Baker 1.50 3.00
5 Erich Barnes 1.50 3.00
6 Terry Barr 1.50 3.00
7 Dick Bass 2.00 4.00
8 Maxie Baughan 1.50 3.00
9 Raymond Berry 5.00 10.00
10 Charley Bradshaw 1.50 3.00
11 Jim Brown 20.00 40.00
12 Roger Brown 1.50 3.00
13 Timmy Brown 2.00 4.00
14 Gail Cogdill 1.50 3.00
15 Tommy Davis 1.50 3.00
16 Willie Davis 5.00 10.00
17 Bob DeMarco 1.50 3.00
18 Darrell Dess 1.50 3.00
19 Buddy Dial 1.50 3.00
20 Mike Ditka 10.00 20.00
21 Galen Fiss 1.50 3.00
22 Lee Folkins 1.50 3.00
23 Joe Fortunato 1.50 3.00
24 Bill Glass 1.50 3.00
25 John Gordy 1.50 3.00
26 Ken Gray 1.50 3.00
27 Forrest Gregg 4.00 8.00
28 Rip Hawkins 1.50 3.00
29 Charley Johnson 2.00 4.00
30 John Henry Johnson 4.00 8.00
31 Hank Jordan 4.00 8.00
32 Jim Katcavage 1.50 3.00
33 Jerry Kramer 4.00 8.00
34 Joe Krupa 1.50 3.00
35 John LoVetere 1.50 3.00
36 Dick Lynch 1.50 3.00
37 Gino Marchetti 4.00 8.00
38 Joe Marconi 1.50 3.00
39 Tommy Mason 2.00 4.00
40 Dale Meinert 1.50 3.00
41 Lou Michaels 2.00 4.00
42 Minnesota Vikings 1.50 3.00
43 Bobby Mitchell 4.00 8.00
44 John Morrow 1.50 3.00
45 New York Giants 1.50 3.00
46 Merlin Olsen 6.00 12.00
47 Jack Pardee 2.00 4.00
48 Jim Parker 3.00 6.00
49 Bernie Parrish 1.50 3.00
50 Don Perkins 3.00 6.00
51 Richie Petitbon 1.50 3.00
52 Vince Promuto 1.50 3.00
53 Myron Pottios 1.50 3.00
54 Mike Pyle 1.50 3.00
55 Pete Retzlaff 2.00 4.00
56 Jim Ringo 4.00 8.00
57 Joe Rutgens 1.50 3.00
58 St. Louis Cardinals 1.50 3.00
59 San Francisco 49ers 1.50 3.00
60 Dick Schafrath 1.50 3.00
61 Joe Schmidt 4.00 8.00
62 Del Shofner 2.00 4.00
63 Norm Snead 2.00 4.00
64 Bart Starr 18.00 30.00
65 Jim Taylor 10.00 20.00
66 Roosevelt Taylor 2.00 4.00
67 Clendon Thomas 1.50 3.00
68 Y.A. Tittle 7.50 15.00
69 Johnny Unitas 20.00 35.00
70 Bill Wade 2.00 4.00
71 Wayne Walker 1.50 3.00
72 Jesse Whittenton 1.50 3.00
73 Larry Wilson 3.00 6.00
74 Abe Woodson 1.50 3.00
NNO Stamp Album 10.00 20.00

1987 Wheaties Mini Posters

This set was distributed one per box in specially marked packages of Wheaties cereal in 1987. Each mini poster (measuring roughly 5" by 7") came folded inside a thin cellophane wrapper. Individual player information and statistics are printed in black and white on the card backs. The cards are numbered on the back in the upper left corner. This project was organized by Mike Schechter Associates and produced by Starline Inc. in conjunction with the NFL Players Association. Bernie Kosar and Lawrence Taylor are difficult to find and were not listed in the set the checklist Wheaties provided on the cereal box.

COMPLETE SET (26) 60.00 150.00
1 Tony Dorsett 5.00 12.00
2 Herschel Walker 1.25 3.00
3 Marcus Allen 5.00 12.00
4 Eric Dickerson 1.50 4.00
5 Walter Payton 10.00 25.00
6 Phil Simms 2.00 5.00
7 Tommy Kramer 1.00 2.50
8 Joe Morris 1.00 2.50
9 Roger Craig 2.00 5.00
10 Curt Warner 1.25 3.00
11 Andre Tippett 1.25 3.00
12 Joe Montana 10.00 25.00
13 Jim McMahon 2.00 5.00
14 Bernie Kosar SP 6.00 15.00
15 Jay Schroeder 1.00 2.50
16 Al Toon 1.00 2.50
17 Mark Gastineau 1.00 2.50
18 Kenny Easley 1.00 2.50
19 Howie Long 4.00 10.00
20 Dan Marino 10.00 25.00
21 Karl Mecklenburg 1.00 2.50
22 John Elway 10.00 25.00
23 Boomer Esiason 1.50 4.00
24 Dan Fouts 2.00 5.00
25 Jim Kelly 6.00 15.00
26 Louis Lipps 1.00 2.50
27 Lawrence Taylor SP 15.00 40.00

1991 Wild Card Prototypes

This six-card Wild Card Prototype set measures the standard-size. The front design features glossy color action player photos, on a black card face with yellow highlighting around the picture and different color numbers appearing in the top and right borders. A football icon with the words "NFL Premier Edition" overlays the lower left corner of the picture. The backs shade from black to yellow and have a color headshot, biography, and statistics for the last three years. The cards are numbered in the upper right corner.

COMPLETE SET (6) 2.40 6.00
1 Troy Aikman .40 1.00
2 Barry Sanders .80 2.00
3 Thurman Thomas .20 .50
4 Emmitt Smith 1.00 2.50
5 Jerry Rice .40 1.00
6 Lawrence Taylor .20 .50

1991 Wild Card

The Wild Card NFL contains 160 standard-size cards. Reportedly, production quantities were limited to 30,000 numbered ten-box cases. The series included three bonus cards (Wild Card Case Card, Wild Card Box Card, and Wild Card Hot Card) that were redeemable for the item pictured. Surprise wild card number 126 could be exchanged for a ten-card NFL Experience set, featuring five players each from the Washington Redskins and the Buffalo Bills. This set resembles that given away at the Super Bowl Show, except that the cards bear no date. The secondary market value of the striped cards did not prove to be as strong as Wild Card anticipated. Rookie Cards in this set include Ricky Ervins, Alvin Harper, Randal Hill, Michael Jackson, Herman Moore, Neil O'Donnell, Mike Pritchard, and Leonard Russell.

COMPLETE SET (160) 2.50 6.00
*5 STRIPES: 1.2X TO 3X BASIC CARDS
*10 STRIPES: 2X TO 5X
*20 STRIPES: 3X TO 8X
*50 STRIPES: 6X TO 15X
*100 STRIPE: 15X TO 40X
*1000 STRIPE: 50X TO 120X
1 Jeff George .02 .10
2 Sean Jones .02 .10
3 Duane Bickett .01 .05
4 John Elway .40 1.00
5 Christian Okoye .02 .10
6 Steve Atwater .01 .05
7 Anthony Munoz .02 .10
8 Dave Krieg .02 .10
9 Nick Lowery .01 .05
10 Albert Bentley .01 .05
11 Mark Jackson .01 .05
12 Jeff Bryant .01 .05
13 Johnny Hector .01 .05
14 John L. Williams .01 .05
15 Jim Everett .02 .10
16 Mark Duper .02 .10
17 Drew Hill UER .02 .10
18 Randal Hill RC .02 .10
19 Ernest Givins .02 .10
20 Ken O'Brien .01 .05
21 Blair Thomas .02 .10
22 Derrick Thomas .07 .20
23 Harvey Williams RC .02 .10
24 Simon Fletcher .01 .05
25 Stephone Paige .01 .05
26 Barry Word .01 .05
27 Warren Moon .02 .10
28 Derrick Fenner .01 .05
29 Shane Conlan .01 .05
30 Karl Mecklenburg .01 .05
31 Gary Anderson RB .01 .05
32 Sammie Smith .01 .05
33 Steve DeBerg .02 .10
34 Dan McGwire RC .01 .05
35 Roger Craig .02 .10
36 Tom Tupa .01 .05
37 Rod Woodson .07 .20
38 Junior Seau .07 .20
39 Bruce Pickens RC .01 .05
40 Greg Townsend .01 .05
41 Gary Clark .02 .10
42 Broderick Thomas .01 .05
43 Charles Mann .02 .10
44 Browning Nagle RC .01 .05
45 James Joseph RC .02 .10
46 Emmitt Smith UER .75 2.00
47 Cornelius Bennett .02 .10
48 Maurice Hurst .01 .05
49 Art Monk .02 .10
50 Louis Lipps .02 .10
51 Mark Rypien .02 .10
52 Bubby Brister .02 .10
53 John Stephens .01 .05
54 Merril Hoge .01 .05
55 Kevin Mack .01 .05
56 Al Toon .02 .10
57 Ronnie Lott .02 .10
58 Eric Metcalf .02 .10
59 Vinny Testaverde .02 .10
60 Darrell Green .01 .05
61 Randall Cunningham .07 .20
62 Charles Haley .02 .10
63 Mark Carrier DB .02 .10
64 Jim Harbaugh .02 .10
65 Richard Dent .02 .10
66 Stan Thomas .01 .05
67 Neal Anderson .02 .10
68 Troy Aikman .20 .50
69 Mike Pritchard RC .02 .10
70 Deion Sanders .10 .30
71 Andre Rison .02 .10
72 Keith Millard .01 .05
73 Jerry Rice .20 .50
74 Johnny Johnson .01 .05
75 Tim McDonald .01 .05
76 Leonard Russell RC .02 .10
77 Keith Jackson .02 .10
78 Keith Byars .02 .10
79 Ricky Proehl .01 .05
80 Dexter Carter .01 .05
81 Alvin Harper RC .02 .10
82 Irving Fryar .02 .10
83 Marion Butts .02 .10
84 Alfred Williams RC .01 .05
85 Timm Rosenbach .01 .05
86 Steve Young .20 .50
87 Albert Lewis .01 .05
88 Rodney Peete .02 .10
89 Barry Sanders .40 1.00
90 Bennie Blades .01 .05
91 Chris Spielman .02 .10
92 John Friesz .01 .05
93 Jerome Brown .01 .05
94 Reggie White .07 .20
95 Michael Irvin .07 .20
96 Keith McCants .01 .05
97 Vinnie Clark RC .02 .10
98 Louis Oliver .01 .05
99 Mark Clayton .02 .10
100 John Offerdahl .01 .05
101 Michael Carter .01 .05
102 John Taylor .02 .10
103 William Perry .02 .10
104 Gill Byrd .01 .05
105 Burt Grossman .01 .05
106 Herman Moore RC .07 .20
107 Howie Long .07 .20
108 Bo Jackson .08 .25
109 Kelvin Pritchett RC .01 .05
110 Jacob Green .01 .05
111 Chris Doleman .02 .10
112 Herschel Walker .02 .10
113 Russell Maryland RC .02 .10
114 Anthony Carter .02 .10
115 Joey Browner .01 .05
116 Tony Mandarich .01 .05
117 Don Majkowski .01 .05
118 Ricky Ervins RC .02 .10
119 Sterling Sharpe .02 .10
120 Tim Harris .01 .05
121 Hugh Millen RC .01 .05
122 Mike Rozier .01 .05
123 Chris Miller .02 .10
124 Morten Andersen .01 .05
125 Neil O'Donnell RC .07 .20
126 Surprise Wild Card .01 .05
127 Eddie Brown .01 .05
128 James Francis .01 .05
129 James Brooks .01 .05
130 David Fulcher .01 .05
131 Michael Jackson WR RC .07 .20
132 Clay Matthews .02 .10
133 Scott Norwood .01 .05
134 Wesley Carroll RC .01 .05
135 Thurman Thomas .07 .20
136 Mark Ingram .02 .10
137 Bobby Hebert .02 .10
138 Bobby Wilson RC .01 .05
139 Craig Heyward .01 .05
140 Dalton Hilliard .01 .05
141 Jeff Hostetler .02 .10
142 Dave Meggett .02 .10
143 Cris Dishman RC .01 .05
144 Lawrence Taylor .02 .10
145 Leonard Marshall .01 .05
146 Pepper Johnson .01 .05
147 Todd Marinovich RC .01 .05
148 Mike Croel RC .01 .05
149 Erik McMillan .01 .05
150 Flipper Anderson .01 .05
151 Cleveland Gary .01 .05
152 Henry Ellard .02 .10
153 Kevin Greene .02 .10
154 Michael Cofer .01 .05
155 Todd Lyght RC .02 .10
156 Bruce Smith .02 .10
157 Checklist 1 .01 .05
158 Checklist 2 .01 .05
159 Checklist 3 .01 .05
160 Checklist 4 .01 .05

1991 Wild Card NFL Experience Redemption

This ten-card standard-size set commemorates Super Bowl XXVI and features five players from each team. These cards were exchanged for 1991 Wild Card surprise card number 126, and thus they are numbered 126A-126J. In design, these redemption cards are nearly identical to the 1991 Wild Card NFL Super Bowl Promos/NFL Experience set, but carry a different card numbering on back. The copyright date on the backs is 1992.

COMPLETE SET (10) 1.25 3.00
*10 STRIPE: .6X TO 1.5X BASIC CARDS
*20 STRIPE: .8X TO 2X BASIC CARDS
*50 STRIPE: 1X TO 2.5X BASIC CARDS
*100 STRIPE: 2X TO 5X BASIC CARDS
*1000 STRIPE: 5X TO 12X BASIC CARDS
126A Mark Rypien .15 .40
126B Ricky Ervins .10 .30
126C Darrell Green .20 .50
126D Charles Mann .10 .30
126E Art Monk .20 .50
126F Thurman Thomas .30 .75
126G Bruce Smith .20 .50
126H Cornelius Bennett .20 .50
126I Scott Norwood .10 .30
126J Shane Conlan .10 .30

1991 Wild Card NFL Experience Super Bowl Promos

This ten-card standard-size set commemorates Super Bowl XXVI and features five players from each team. The cards were given away during the SuperBowl Card Show III by Wild Card, a corporate sponsor of the show. Prominently displayed on the card front is the "NFL Experience" logo and the backs carry a 1992 copyright date.

COMPLETE SET (10) 1.20 3.00
1 Mark Rypien .08 .25
2 Ricky Ervins .08 .25
3 Darrell Green .08 .25
4 Charles Mann .08 .25
5 Art Monk .15 .40
6 Thurman Thomas .40 1.00
7 Bruce Smith .15 .40
8 Cornelius Bennett .15 .40
9 Scott Norwood .08 .25
10 Shane Conlan .08 .25

1992 Wild Card NFL Prototypes

This 12-card Wild Card Prototype set features cards measuring the standard-size. The front design is the samer as the regular issue 1992 Wild Card NFL cards. The cards are numbered in the upper right corner of the reverse with a "P" prefix. The set numbering starts where the 1991 Wild Card Prototypes set left off.

COMPLETE SET (12) 2.00 5.00
P7 Barry Sanders .60 1.50
P8 John Taylor .07 .20
P9 John Elway .60 1.50
P10 Erik Kramer .07 .20
P11 Christian Okoye .07 .20
P12 Leonard Russell .07 .20
P13 Barry Sanders .60 1.50
P14 Earnest Byner .07 .20
P15 Warren Moon .20 .50
P16 Ronnie Lott .10 .30
P17 Michael Irvin .20 .50
P18 Haywood Jeffires .07 .20

1992 Wild Card

The 1992 Wild Card NFL set contains 460 standard-size cards issued in two series of 250 and 210 cards, respectively. It is reported that the first series production run was limited to 30,000 ten-box numbered foil cases. One hundred "case cards" and one thousand box cards were randomly inserted into the foil packs. Also cards from the Red Hot Rookie set were inserted in the packs. The first series is checklisted by teams. Subsets include Draft Picks (223-239) and League Leaders (240-245). Through a mail-in offer, the surprise card could be exchanged for a four-card cello pack featuring a P1 Barry Sanders (with first series Surprise Card 1) or P2 Emmitt Smith (with second series Surprise Card 251) Stat Smasher foil card, a Red Hot Rookie card, a Field Force card, and either a silver or gold Field Force card. Every jumbo pack included ten Series I cards, ten Series II cards, one Stat Smasher, one gold or silver foil Red Hot Rookie, and one gold or silver foil Running Wild. Rookie Cards include Edgar Bennett, Steve Bono, Terrell Buckley and Rob Johnson (his only Rookie Card). A Barry Sanders promo card was produced and distributed at the 1992 National Sports Collectors Convention. The card contains The National logo and was issued in striped values of 5, 10, 20, 50 and 100.

COMPLETE SET (460) 6.00 15.00
COMP.SERIES 1 (250) 2.00 5.00
COMP.SERIES 2 (210) 5.00 12.00
1 Surprise Card .01 .05
2 Marcus Dupree .08 .25
3 Jackie Slater .01 .05
4 Robert Delpino .01 .05
5 Jerry Gray .01 .05
6 Jim Everett .02 .10
7 Roman Phifer .01 .05
8 Alvin Wright .01 .05
9 Todd Lyght .01 .05
10 Reggie White .08 .25
11 Randal Hill .01 .05
12 Keith Byars .01 .05
13 Clyde Simmons .01 .05
14 Keith Jackson .02 .10
15 Seth Joyner .01 .05
16 James Joseph .01 .05
17 Eric Allen .01 .05
18 Sammie Smith .01 .05
19 Mark Clayton .01 .05
20 Aaron Craver .01 .05
21 Hugh Green .01 .05
22 John Offerdahl .01 .05
23 Jeff Cross .01 .05
24 Ferrell Edmunds .01 .05
25 Mark Duper .01 .05
26 Ronnie Harmon .01 .05
27 Derrick Walker .01 .05
28 Gary Plummer .01 .05
29 Rod Bernstine .01 .05
30 Burt Grossman .01 .05
31 Donnie Elder .01 .05
32 John Friesz .02 .10
33 Billy Ray Smith .01 .05
34 Luis Sharpe .01 .05
35 Aeneas Williams .02 .10
36 Ken Harvey .01 .05
37 Johnny Johnson .01 .05
38 Eric Swann .02 .10
39 Tom Tupa .01 .05
40 Anthony Thompson .01 .05
41 Broderick Thomas .01 .05
42 Vinny Testaverde .02 .10
43 Mark Carrier WR .02 .10
44 Gary Anderson RB .01 .05
45 Keith McCants .01 .05
46 Reggie Cobb .01 .05
47 Lawrence Dawsey .01 .05
48 Kevin Murphy .01 .05
49 Keith Woodside .01 .05
50 Darrell Thompson .01 .05
51 Vinnie Clark .01 .05
52 Sterling Sharpe .08 .25
53 Mike Tomczak .01 .05
54A Don Majkowski ERR .02 .10
54B Don Majkowski COR .02 .10
55 Tony Mandarich .01 .05
56 Mark Murphy .01 .05
57 Dexter McNabb RC .01 .05
58 Rick Fenney .01 .05
59 Cris Carter .08 .25
60 Wade Wilson .01 .05
61 Mike Merriweather .01 .05
62 Rich Gannon .08 .25
63 Herschel Walker .02 .10
64 Chris Doleman .02 .10
65 Al Noga UER .01 .05
66 Chris Mims RC .01 .05
67 Ed Cunningham RC .01 .05
68 Marcus Allen .08 .25
69 Kevin Turner RC .01 .05
70 Howie Long .08 .25
71 Tim Brown .08 .25
72 Nick Bell .01 .05
73 Todd Marinovich .01 .05
74 Jay Schroeder .01 .05
75 Mervyn Fernandez .01 .05
76 Tony Smith WR RC .01 .05
77 John Alt .01 .05
78 Christian Okoye .01 .05
79 Nick Lowery .01 .05
80 Derrick Thomas .02 .10
81 Bill Maas .01 .05
82 Dino Hackett .01 .05
83 Deron Cherry .01 .05
84 Barry Word .01 .05
85 Mike Mooney RC .01 .05
86 Cris Dishman .01 .05
87 Bruce Matthews .01 .05
88 Tony Jones T .01 .05
89 William Fuller .01 .05
90 Ray Childress .01 .05
91 Warren Moon .08 .25
92 Lorenzo White .01 .05
93 Joe Bowden RC .01 .05
94 Tom Rathman .01 .05
95 Keith Henderson .01 .05
96 Jesse Sapolu .01 .05
97 Charles Haley .02 .10
98 Steve Young .25 .60
99 John Taylor .02 .10
100 Tim Harris .01 .05
101 Scott Davis .01 .05
102 Steve Bono RC .08 .25
103 Mike Kenn .01 .05
104 Mike Farr .01 .05
105 Rodney Peete .02 .10
106 Jerry Ball .01 .05
107 Chris Spielman .02 .10
108 Barry Sanders .50 1.25
109 Bennie Blades .01 .05
110 Herman Moore .08 .25
111 Erik Kramer .02 .10
112 Vance Johnson .01 .05
113 Mike Croel .01 .05
114 Mark Jackson .01 .05
115 Steve Atwater .01 .05
116 Gaston Green .01 .05
117 John Elway .50 1.25
118 Simon Fletcher .01 .05
119 Karl Mecklenburg .01 .05
120 Hart Lee Dykes .01 .05
121 Jerome Henderson .01 .05
122 Chris Singleton .01 .05
123 Marv Cook .01 .05
124 Leonard Russell .01 .05
125 Hugh Millen .01 .05
126 Pat Harlow .01 .05
127 Andre Tippett .01 .05
128 Bruce Armstrong .01 .05
129 Gary Clark .02 .10
130 Art Monk .02 .10
131 Darrell Green .01 .05
132 Wilber Marshall .01 .05
133 Jim Lachey .01 .05
134 Earnest Byner .01 .05
135 Chip Lohmiller .01 .05
136 Mark Rypien .01 .05
137 Ricky Sanders .01 .05
138 Stan Thomas .01 .05
139 Neal Anderson .01 .05
140 Trace Armstrong .01 .05
141 Kevin Butler .01 .05
142 Mark Carrier DB .01 .05
143 Dennis Gentry .01 .05
144 Jim Harbaugh .02 .10
145 Richard Dent .02 .10
146 Andre Rison .02 .10
147 Bruce Pickens .01 .05
148 Chris Hinton UER .01 .05
149 Brian Jordan .02 .10
150 Chris Miller .01 .05
151 Moe Gardner .01 .05
152 Bill Fralic .01 .05
153 Michael Haynes .02 .10
154 Mike Pritchard .02 .10
155 Dean Biasucci .01 .05
156 Clarence Verdin .01 .05
157 Donnell Thompson .01 .05
158 Duane Bickett .01 .05
159 Jon Hand .01 .05
160 Sam Graddy RC .01 .05
161 Emmitt Smith .60 1.50
162 Michael Irvin .08 .25
163 Danny Noonan .01 .05
164 Jack Del Rio .01 .05
165 Jim Jeffcoat .01 .05
166 Alexander Wright .01 .05
167 Frank Minnifield .01 .05
168 Ed King .01 .05
169 Reggie Langhorne .01 .05
170 Mike Baab .01 .05
171 Eric Metcalf .02 .10
172 Clay Matthews .01 .05
173 Kevin Mack .01 .05
174 Mike Johnson .01 .05
175 Jeff Lageman .01 .05
176 Freeman McNeil .02 .10
177 Erik McMillan .01 .05
178 James Hasty .01 .05
179 Kyle Clifton .01 .05
180 Joe Kelly .01 .05
181 Phil Simms .02 .10
182 Everson Walls .01 .05
183 Jeff Hostetler .02 .10
184 Dave Meggett .02 .10
185 Matt Bahr .01 .05
186 Mark Ingram .01 .05
187 Rodney Hampton .02 .10
188 Kanavis McGhee .01 .05
189 Tim McGee .01 .05
190 Eddie Brown .01 .05
191 Rodney Holman .01 .05
192 Harold Green .01 .05
193 James Francis .01 .05
194 Anthony Munoz .02 .10
195 David Fulcher .01 .05
196 Tim Krumrie .01 .05
197 Bubby Brister .02 .10
198 Rod Woodson .08 .25
199 Louis Lipps .01 .05
200 Carnell Lake .01 .05
201 Don Beebe .01 .05
202 Thurman Thomas .08 .25
203 Cornelius Bennett .02 .10
204 Mark Kelso .01 .05
205 James Lofton .02 .10
206 Darryl Talley .01 .05
207 Morten Andersen .01 .05
208 Vince Buck .01 .05
209 Wesley Carroll .01 .05
210 Bobby Hebert .01 .05
211 Craig Heyward .02 .10
212 Dalton Hilliard .01 .05
213 Rickey Jackson .01 .05
214 Eric Martin .01 .05
215 Pat Swilling .01 .05
216 Steve Walsh .01 .05
217 Torrance Small RC .02 .10
218 Jacob Green .01 .05
219 Cortez Kennedy .02 .10
220 John L. Williams .01 .05
221 Terry Wooden .01 .05
222 Grant Feasel .01 .05
223 Siran Stacy RC .01 .05
224 Chris Hakel RC .01 .05
225 Todd Harrison RC .01 .05
226 Bob Whitfield RC .01 .05
227 Eddie Blake RC .01 .05
228 Keith Hamilton RC .02 .10
229 Darryl Williams RC .01 .05
230 Ricardo McDonald RC .01 .05
231 Alan Haller RC .01 .05
232 Leon Searcy RC .01 .05
233 Patrick Rowe RC .01 .05
234 Edgar Bennett RC .08 .25
235 Terrell Buckley RC .01 .05
236 Will Furrer RC .01 .05
237 Amp Lee RC .01 .05
238 Jimmy Smith RC 1.00 2.50
239 Tommy Vardell RC .01 .05
240 Leonard Russell O-ROY .01 .05
241 Mike Croel D-ROY .01 .05
242 Warren Moon LL .02 .10
243 Mark Rypien LL .01 .05
244 Thurman Thomas LL .02 .10
245 Emmitt Smith LL .30 .75
246 Checklist 1-50 .01 .05
247 Checklist 51-100 .01 .05
248 Checklist 101-150 .01 .05
249 Checklist 151-200 .01 .05
250 Checklist 201-250 .01 .05
251 Surprise Card .01 .05
252 Eric Pegram .02 .10
253 Anthony Carter .02 .10
254 Roger Craig .02 .10
255 Hassan Jones .01 .05
256 Steve Jordan .01 .05
257 Randall McDaniel .02 .10
258 Henry Thomas .01 .05
259 Carl Lee .01 .05
260 Ray Agnew .01 .05
261 Irving Fryar .02 .10
262 Tom Waddle .01 .05
263 Greg McMurtry .01 .05
264 Stephen Baker .01 .05
265 Mark Collins .01 .05
266 Howard Cross .01 .05
267 Pepper Johnson .01 .05
268 Fred Barnett .02 .10
269 Heath Sherman .01 .05
270 William Thomas .01 .05
271 Bill Bates .02 .10
272 Issiac Holt .01 .05
273 Emmitt Smith .60 1.50
274 Eric Bieniemy .01 .05
275 Marion Butts .01 .05
276 Gill Byrd .01 .05
277 Robert Blackmon .01 .05
278 Brian Blades .02 .10
279 Joe Nash .01 .05
280 Bill Brooks .01 .05
281 Mel Gray .01 .05
282 Andre Ware .02 .10
283 Steve McMichael .01 .05
284 Brad Muster .01 .05
285 Ron Rivera .01 .05
286 Chris Zorich .02 .10
287 Chris Burkett .01 .05
288 Irv Eatman .01 .05
289 Rob Moore .02 .10
290 Joe Mott .01 .05
291 Brian Washington .01 .05
292 Michael Carter .01 .05
293 Dexter Carter .01 .05
294 Don Griffin .01 .05
295 John Taylor .02 .10
296 Ted Washington .01 .05
297 Monte Coleman .01 .05
298 Andre Collins .01 .05
299 Charles Mann .01 .05
300 Shane Conlan .01 .05
301 Keith McKeller .01 .05
302 Nate Odomes .01 .05
303 Riki Ellison .01 .05
304 Willie Gault .02 .10
305 Bob Golic .01 .05
306 Ethan Horton .01 .05
307 Ronnie Lott .02 .10
308 Don Mosebar .01 .05
309 Aaron Wallace .01 .05
310 Wymon Henderson .01 .05
311 Vance Johnson .01 .05
312 Ken Lanier .01 .05
313 Steve Sewell .01 .05
314 Dennis Smith .01 .05
315 Kenny Walker .01 .05
316 Chris Martin .01 .05
317 Albert Lewis .01 .05
318 Todd McNair .01 .05
319 Tracy Simien RC .01 .05
320 Percy Snow .01 .05
321 Mark Rypien .01 .05
322 Bryan Hinkle .01 .05
323 David Little .01 .05
324 Dwight Stone .01 .05
325 Van Waiters RC .01 .05
326 Pio Sagapolutele RC .01 .05
327 Michael Jackson .02 .10
328 Vestee Jackson .01 .05
329 Tony Paige .01 .05
330 Reggie Roby .01 .05
331 Haywood Jeffires .02 .10
332 Lamar Lathon .01 .05
333 Bubba McDowell .01 .05
334 Doug Smith .01 .05
335 Dean Steinkuhler .01 .05
336 Jessie Tuggle .01 .05
337 Freddie Joe Nunn .01 .05
338 Pat Terrell .01 .05
339 Tom McHale RC .01 .05
340 Sam Mills .01 .05
341 John Tice .01 .05
342 Brent Jones .02 .10
343 Robert Porcher RC .08 .25
344 Mark D'Onofrio RC .01 .05
345 David Tate .01 .05
346 Courtney Hawkins RC .02 .10
347 Ricky Watters .08 .25
348 Amp Lee .01 .05
349 Steve Young .25 .60
350 Natu Tuatagaloa RC .01 .05
351 Alfred Williams .01 .05
352 Derek Brown TE RC .01 .05
353 Marco Coleman RC .01 .05
354 Tommy Maddox RC .60 1.50
355 Siran Stacy .01 .05
356 Greg Lewis .01 .05
357 Paul Gruber .01 .05
358 Troy Vincent RC .01 .05
359 Robert Wilson .01 .05
360 Jessie Hester .01 .05
361 Shaun Gayle .01 .05
362 Deron Cherry .01 .05
363 Wendell Davis .01 .05
364 David Klingler RC .01 .05
365 Jason Hanson RC .02 .10
366 Marquez Pope RC .01 .05
367 Robert Williams RC .01 .05
368 Kelvin Pritchett .01 .05
369 Dana Hall RC .01 .05
370 David Brandon RC .01 .05
371 Tim McKyer .01 .05
372 Darion Conner .01 .05
373 Derrick Fenner .01 .05
374 Hugh Millen .01 .05
375 Bill Jones RC .01 .05
376 J.J. Birden .01 .05
377 Ty Detmer .08 .25
378 Alonzo Spellman RC .02 .10
379 Sammie Smith .01 .05
380 Al Smith .01 .05
381 Louis Clark RC .01 .05
382 Vernice Smith RC .01 .05
383 Tony Martin .02 .10
384 Willie Green .01 .05
385 Sean Gilbert RC .02 .10
386 Eugene Chung RC .01 .05
387 Toi Cook .01 .05
388 Brett Maxie .01 .05
389 Steve Israel RC .01 .05
390 Mike Mularkey .01 .05
391 Barry Foster .02 .10
392 Hardy Nickerson .02 .10
393 Johnny Mitchell RC .01 .05
394 Thurman Thomas .08 .25
395 Tony Smith RC .01 .05
396 Keith Goganious RC .01 .05
397 Matt Darby RC .01 .05
398 Nate Turner RC .01 .05
399 Keith Jennings RC .01 .05
400 Mitchell Benson RC .01 .05
401 Kurt Barber RC .01 .05
402 Tony Sacca RC .01 .05
403 Steve Hendrickson RC .01 .05
404 Johnny Johnson .01 .05
405 Lorenzo Lynch .01 .05
406 Luis Sharpe .01 .05
407 Jim Everett .02 .10
408 Neal Anderson .01 .05
409 Ashley Ambrose RC .08 .25
410 George Williams RC .01 .05
411 Clarence Kay .01 .05
412 Dave Krieg .02 .10
413 Terrell Buckley .01 .05
414 Ricardo McDonald .01 .05
415 Kelly Stouffer .01 .05
416 Barney Bussey .01 .05
417 Ray Roberts RC .01 .05
418 Fred McAfee RC .01 .05
419 Fred Banks .01 .05
420 Tim McDonald .01 .05
421 Darryl Williams .01 .05
422 Bobby Abrams RC .01 .05
423 Tommy Vardell .01 .05
424 William White .01 .05
425 Billy Ray Smith .01 .05
426 Lemuel Stinson .01 .05
427 Brad Johnson RC 2.50 6.00
428 Herschel Walker .02 .10
429 Eric Thomas .01 .05
430 Anthony Thompson .01 .05
431 Ed West .01 .05
432 Edgar Bennett .08 .25
433 Warren Powers .01 .05
434 Byron Evans .01 .05
435 Rodney Culver RC .01 .05
436 Ray Horton .01 .05
437 Richmond Webb .01 .05
438 Mark McMillian RC .01 .05
439 Subset Checklist .01 .05
440 Lawrence Pete RC .01 .05
441 Rod Smith DB RC .01 .05
442 Mark Rodenhauser RC .01 .05
443 Scott Lockwood RC .01 .05
444 Charles Davenport RC .01 .05
445 Terry McDaniel .01 .05
446 Darren Perry RC .01 .05
447 Darrick Owens RC .01 .05
448 Alvin Wright .01 .05
449 Frank Stams .01 .05
450 Santana Dotson RC .02 .10
451 Mark Carrier DB .01 .05
452 Kevin Murphy .01 .05
453 Jeff Bryant .01 .05
454 Eric Allen .01 .05
455 Brian Bollinger RC .01 .05
456 Elston Ridgle RC .01 .05
457 Jim Riggs RC .01 .05
458 Checklist 251-320 .01 .05
459 Checklist 321-391 .01 .05
460 Checklist 392-460 .01 .05
P1 Barry Sanders Promo .40 1.00
P2 Barry Sanders Promo Sheet .75 2.00

1992 Wild Card 5 Stripe

*5 STRIPE: 1.2X TO 3X BASIC CARDS

1992 Wild Card 10 Stripe

*10 STRIPE: 2X TO 5X BASIC CARDS

1992 Wild Card 20 Stripe

*20 STRIPE: 3X TO 8X BASIC CARDS

1992 Wild Card 50 Stripe

*50 STRIPE: 6X TO 15X BASIC CARDS

1992 Wild Card 100 Stripe

00 STRIPE: 15X TO 40X BASIC CARDS
427 Brad Johnson 60.00 150.00

1992 Wild Card 1000 Stripe

*1000 STRIPE: 50X TO 120X BASIC CARDS
238 Jimmy Smith 60.00 150.00
427 Brad Johnson 60.00 150.00

1992 Wild Card Class Back Attack

is five-card standard-size set was randomly inserted in 1992 Wild Card WLAF foil packs. A football icon at the lower left is printed with the words "Class Back Attack" (1-4) or "Red Hot Rookie" (5). The player's name and position appear in the lower right corner. The backs are green and sport a close-up shot and biographical information. A pale green box with a red border contains an explanation of the odds of getting a wild card in packs or boxes. David Klingler was redeemable for a Surprise Card.

COMPLETE SET (5) 2.80 7.00
SP1 Vaughn Dunbar .20 .50
SP2 Barry Sanders 1.20 3.00
SP3 Emmitt Smith 1.20 3.00
SP4 Thurman Thomas .40 1.00
SP5 David Klingler .20 .50

1992 Wild Card Field Force

This 30-card standard-size set was randomly inserted in 1992 Wild Card NFL series 2 foil packs. Gold and silver foil versions of each card were also produced and randomly inserted in packs. The Golds were the toughest version to pull.

COMPLETE SET (30) 6.00 15.00
*5 STRIPES: .8X to 2X BASIC INSERTS
*10 STRIPES: 1X to 2.5X BASIC INSERTS
*20 STRIPES: 1.5X to 4X BASIC INSERTS
*50 STRIPES: 2.5X to 6X BASIC INSERTS
*100 STRIPES: 4X to 10X BASIC INSERTS
*1000 STRIPES: 30X to 80X BASIC INSERTS
*SILVERS: .8X to 2X BASIC INSERTS
*GOLDS: 1.2X to 3X BASIC INSERTS
RANDOM INSERTS IN SER.2 PACKS
1 Joe Montana 1.00 2.50
2 Quentin Coryatt .10 .30
3 Tommy Vardell .10 .30
4 Jim Kelly .20 .50
5 John Elway 1.00 2.50
6 Ricky Watters .15 .40
7 Vinny Testaverde .15 .40
8 Randal Hill .10 .30
9 Amp Lee .10 .30
10 Vaughn Dunbar .10 .30
11 Troy Aikman .50 1.25
12 Deion Sanders .30 .75
13 Rodney Hampton .10 .30
14 Brett Favre 1.00 2.50
15 Warren Moon .20 .50
16 Browning Nagle .10 .30
17 Terrell Buckley .10 .30
18 Barry Sanders .75 2.00
19 Dan Marino 1.00 2.50
20 Carl Pickens .15 .40
21 Herschel Walker .15 .40
22 Ronnie Lott .20 .50
23 Steve Emtman .10 .30
24 Mark Rypien .10 .30
25 Bobby Hebert .10 .30
26 Dan McGwire .10 .30
27 Neil O'Donnell .10 .30
28 Cris Carter .20 .50
29 Randall Cunningham .20 .50
30 Jerry Rice .60 1.50

1992 Wild Card Pro Picks

This eight-card standard-size set was randomly inserted one per retail jumbo packs.

COMPLETE SET (8) 3.00 8.00
ONE PER RETAIL JUMBO PACK
1 Emmitt Smith 1.00 2.50
2 Mark Rypien .02 .10
3 Warren Moon .15 .40
4 Leonard Russell .02 .10
5 Thurman Thomas .15 .40
6 John Elway .75 2.00
7 Barry Sanders .75 2.00
8 Steve Young .40 1.00

1992 Wild Card Red Hot Rookies

This 30-card standard-size set was randomly inserted in 1992 Wild Card NFL second series foil packs. The fronts feature glossy color player photos inside black inner borders. The outer borders shade from red to white and then to black as one moves from left to right across the card face, and the customary series of colored numbers (1000, 100, 50, 20, 10, and 5) form a right angle at the upper right corner of the photo. Gold and Silver parallel versions were also available one per jumbo pack.

COMPLETE SET (30) 5.00 12.00
COMP.SERIES 1 (10) 2.00 4.00
COMP.SERIES 2 (20) 3.00 6.00
*5 STRIPES: .6X to 1.5X BASIC INSERTS
*10 STRIPES: .8X to 2X BASIC INSERTS
*20 STRIPES: 1.2X to 3X BASIC INSERTS
*50 STRIPES: 2.5X to 6X BASIC INSERTS
*100 STRIPES: 4X to 10X BASIC INSERTS
*1000 STRIPES: 25X to 60X BASIC INSERTS
*GOLDS: .4X to 1X BASIC INSERTS
*SILVERS: .3X to .8X BASIC INSERTS
RANDOM INSERTS IN FOIL PACKS
ONE GOLD OR SILVER CARD PER JUMBO PACK
1 Darryl Williams .10 .30
2 Amp Lee .10 .30
3 Will Furrer .10 .30
4 Edgar Bennett .25 .60
5 Terrell Buckley .15 .40
6 Bob Whitfield .10 .30
7 Siran Stacy .10 .30
8 Jimmy Smith 1.25 3.00
9 Kevin Turner .10 .30

10 Tommy Vardell .15 .40
11 Surprise Card .10 .30
12 Derek Brown TE .10 .30
13 Marco Coleman .10 .30
14 Quentin Coryatt .10 .30
15 Rodney Culver .10 .30
16 Ty Detmer .25 .60
17 Vaughn Dunbar .10 .30
18 Steve Emtman .15 .40
19 Sean Gilbert .15 .40
20 Courtney Hawkins .15 .40
21 David Klingler .15 .40
22 Amp Lee .10 .30
23 Tommy Maddox .75 2.00
24 Johnny Mitchell .10 .30
25 Darren Perry .10 .30
26 Carl Pickens .25 .60
27 Robert Porcher .15 .40
28 Tony Smith RB .10 .30
29 Alonzo Spellman .15 .40
30 Troy Vincent .10 .30

1992 Wild Card Running Wild

is 40-card standard-size set was inserted one card per pack in 1992 Wild Card NFL series two jumbo packs. A parallel Gold foil version was also randomly inserted in packs. Those cards are slightly tougher to find.

COMPLETE SET (40) 6.00 15.00
*5 STRIPES: .6X TO 1.5X BASIC INSERTS
*10 STRIPES: .8X TO 2X BASIC INSERTS
*20 STRIPES: 1.2X TO 3X BASIC INSERTS
*50 STRIPES: 2.5X TO 6X BASIC INSERTS
*100 STRIPES: 4X TO 10X BASIC INSERTS
*1000 STRIPES: 25X TO 60X BASIC INSERTS
*GOLDS: .6X to 1.5X SILVERS
ONE PER SERIES 2 JUMBO
1 Terry Allen .15 .40
2 Neal Anderson .07 .20
3 Eric Ball .07 .20
4 Nick Bell .07 .20
5 Edgar Bennett .40 1.00
6 Rod Bernstine .07 .20
7 Marion Butts .07 .20
8 Keith Byars .07 .20
9 Earnest Byner .07 .20
10 Reggie Cobb .07 .20
11 Roger Craig .15 .40
12 Rodney Culver .07 .20
13 Barry Foster .15 .40
14 Cleveland Gary .07 .20
15 Harold Green .07 .20
16 Gaston Green .07 .20
17 Rodney Hampton .15 .40
18 Mark Higgs .07 .20
19 Dalton Hilliard .07 .20
20 Bobby Humphrey UER .07 .20
21 Amp Lee .07 .20
22 Kevin Mack .07 .20
23 Eric Metcalf .15 .40
24 Brad Muster .07 .20
25 Christian Okoye .07 .20
26 Tom Rathman .07 .20
27 Leonard Russell .07 .20
28 Barry Sanders 2.00 5.00
29 Heath Sherman .07 .20
30 Emmitt Smith 2.50 6.00
31 Blair Thomas .07 .20
32 Thurman Thomas .40 1.00
33 Tommy Vardell .07 .20
34 Herschel Walker .15 .40
35 Chris Warren .15 .40
36 Ricky Watters .40 1.00
37 Lorenzo White .07 .20
38 John L. Williams .07 .20
39 Barry Word .07 .20
40 Vince Workman .07 .20

1992 Wild Card Stat Smashers

is 52-card insert standard-size set was randomly inserted in 1992 Wild Card NFL packs. Card numbers 1-16 were randomly inserted in 1992 Wild Card NFL II foil packs, while card numbers 17-52 were inserted one per pack in second series jumbo packs. The collector could also obtain a Barry Sanders Stat Smasher card through a mail-in offer in exchange for the surprise card in series one. The second series surprise card could be exchanged for an Emmitt Smith SS promo (P2). The cards are numbered on the back with an "SS" prefix.

COMPLETE SET (52) 12.00 30.00
COMP.SERIES 1 (16) 6.00 15.00
COMP.SERIES 2 (36) 6.00 15.00
*5 STRIPES: .8X to 2X BASIC INSERTS
*10 STRIPES: 1X to 2.5X BASIC INSERTS
*20 STRIPES: 1.5X to 4X BASIC INSERTS
*50 STRIPES: 3X to 8X BASIC INSERTS
*100 STRIPES: 6X to 15X BASIC INSERTS
*1000 STRIPES: 15X to 40X BASIC INSERTS
SS1 Barry Sanders 1.25 3.00
SS2 Leonard Russell .10 .30
SS3 Thurman Thomas .20 .50
SS4 John Elway 1.50 4.00
SS5 Steve Young .60 1.50
SS6 Warren Moon .30 .75
SS7 Terrell Buckley .10 .30
SS8 Randall Cunningham .30 .75
SS9 Steve Emtman .10 .30
SS10 Dan Marino 1.50 4.00
SS11 Joe Montana 1.50 4.00
SS12 Carl Pickens .20 .50
SS13 Jerry Rice .75 2.00
SS14 Deion Sanders .40 1.00
SS15 Tommy Vardell .10 .30
SS16 Ricky Watters .20 .50
SS17 Troy Aikman .75 2.00
SS18 Dale Carter .10 .30
SS19 Quentin Coryatt .10 .30
SS20 Vaughn Dunbar .10 .30
SS21 Mark Duper .10 .30
SS22 Eric Metcalf .10 .30
SS23 Brett Favre 1.50 4.00
SS24 Barry Foster .10 .30
SS25 Jeff George .20 .50
SS26 Sean Gilbert UER .10 .30
SS27 Jim Harbaugh .20 .50
SS28 Courtney Hawkins .10 .30
SS29 Charles Haley .10 .30
SS30 Bobby Hebert .10 .30
SS31 Stan Humphries .20 .50
SS32 Michael Irvin .30 .75
SS33 Jim Kelly .30 .75
SS34 David Klingler .10 .30
SS35 Ronnie Lott .20 .50
SS36 Tommy Maddox .30 .75
SS37 Todd Marinovich .10 .30
SS38 Hugh Millen .10 .30
SS39 Art Monk .20 .50
SS40 Browning Nagle .10 .30
SS41 Neil O'Donnell .10 .30
SS42 Tom Rathman .10 .30
SS43 Andre Rison .20 .50
SS44 Mike Singletary .20 .50
SS45 Tony Smith RB .10 .30
SS46 Emmitt Smith 1.50 4.00
SS47 Pete Stoyanovich .10 .30
SS48 John Taylor .10 .30
SS49 Troy Vincent .10 .30
SS50 Herschel Walker .20 .50
SS51 Lorenzo White .10 .30
SS52 Rodney Culver .10 .30
P1 Barry Sanders PROMO 1.25 3.00
P2 Emmitt Smith PROMO 1.25 3.00

1992 Wild Card NASDAM

ese five promo standard-size cards were given away at the NASDAM trade show in Orlando in the spring of 1992. Team color-coded stripes form a right angle at the lower left corner, while the customary series of colored numbers (1000, 100, 50, 20, 10, and 5) form a right angle at the upper right corner of the photo.

COMPLETE SET (5) .80 2.00
1 Edgar Bennett .30 .75
2 Amp Lee .10 .30
3 Terrell Buckley .20 .50
4 Tony Smith RB .10 .30
5 Will Furrer UER .10 .30

1992 Wild Card NASDAM/SCAI Miami

clusively featuring Miami Dolphins, this six-card standard-size set was given out at the NASDAM/SCAI annual conference in Miami during November, 1992. The team color-coded stripes form a right angle at the lower left corner, while the customary series of colored numbers (1000, 100, 50, 20, 10, and 5) form a right angle at the upper right corner of the photo.

COMPLETE SET (6) 1.20 3.00
1 Mark Clayton .30 .75
2 Aaron Craver .20 .50
3 Tony Paige .20 .50
4 Mark Duper .30 .75
5 Tony Martin .30 .75
6 Reggie Roby .20 .50

1992 Wild Card Sacramento CardFest

is six-card standard-size set (of San Francisco 49ers) features color action player photos with thin black borders. A Sacramento CardFest icon is superimposed on the photo at the lower left. The player's name and position appear in the lower right corner.

COMPLETE SET (6) .80 2.00
1 Tom Rathman .10 .30
2 Steve Young .40 1.00
3 Steve Bono .20 .50
4 Brent Jones .10 .30
5 Ricky Watters .20 .50
6 Amp Lee .10 .30

1992 Wild Card WLAF

The Wild Card WLAF Football set contains 150 standard-size cards. It is reported that the production run was limited to 6,000 numbered ten-box cases, and that no factory sets were produced. The cards are checklisted according to teams.

COMPLETE SET (150) 2.40 6.00
*5 STRIPES: .6X TO 1.5X BASIC CARDS
*10 STRIPES: .8X TO 2X BASIC CARDS
*20 STRIPES: 1X TO 2.5X BASIC CARDS
*50 STRIPES: 2X TO 5X BASIC CARDS
*100 STRIPES: 4X TO 10X BASIC CARDS
*1000 STRIPES: 30X TO 80X BASIC CARDS
1 World Bowl Champs .02 .10
2 Pete Mandley .01 .05
3 Steve Williams WR .01 .05
4 Dee Thomas .01 .05
5 Emanuel King .01 .05
6 Anthony Dilweg .02 .10
7 Ben Brown .01 .05
8 Darryl Harris .01 .05
9 Aaron Emanuel .01 .05
10 Andre Brown .01 .05
11 Reggie McKenzie .02 .10
12 Darryl Holmes .01 .05
13 Michael Proctor .01 .05
14 Ricky Johnson .01 .05
15 Ray Savage .01 .05
16 George Searcy .01 .05
17 Titus Dixon .01 .05
18 Willie Fears .01 .05
19 Terrence Cooks .01 .05
20 Ivory Lee Brown .01 .05
21 Mike Johnson QB .01 .05
22 Doug Williams T .01 .05
23 Brad Goebel .02 .10
24 Tony Boles .01 .05
25 Cisco Richard .01 .05
26 Robb White .01 .05
27 Darrell Colbert .01 .05
28 Wayne Walker WR .01 .05
29 Ronnie Williams .01 .05
30 Erik Norgard .01 .05
31 Darren Willis .01 .05
32 Kent Wells .01 .05
33 Phil Logan .01 .05
34 Pat O'Hara .01 .05
35 Melvin Patterson .01 .05
36 Amir Rasul .01 .05
37 Tom Rouen .01 .05
38 Chris Cochrane .01 .05
39 Randy Bethel .01 .05
40 Eric Harmon .01 .05
41 Archie Herring .01 .05
42 Tim James .01 .05
43 Babe Laufenberg .02 .10
44 Herb Welch .01 .05
45 Stefon Adams .01 .05
46 Tony Burse .01 .05
47 Carl Parker .01 .05
48 Mike Prugle .01 .05
49 Mike Jones LB .02 .10
50 David Archer .30 .75
51 Corian Freeman .01 .05
52 Eddie Brown .01 .05
53 Paul Green .01 .05
54 Basil Proctor .01 .05
55 Michael Sinclair .02 .10
56 Louis Riddick .01 .05
57 Roman Matuez .01 .05
58 Darryl Clack .01 .05
59 Willie Davis WR .20 .50
60 Glen Rodgers .01 .05
61 Grantis Bell .01 .05
62 Joe Howard-Johnson .01 .05
63 Rocen Keeton .01 .05
64 Dean Witkowski .01 .05
65 Stacey Simmons .01 .05
66 Roger Vick .01 .05
67 Scott Mitchell .40 1.00
68 Todd Krumm .01 .05
69 Kerwin Bell .07 .20
70 Richard Carey .01 .05
71 Kip Lewis .01 .05
72 Andre Alexander .01 .05
73 Reggie Slack .01 .05
74 Falanda Newton .01 .05
75 Tony Woods Okl. .07 .20
76 Chris McLemore .01 .05
77 Eric Wilkerson .01 .05
78 Cornell Burbage .01 .05
79 Doug Pederson 1.20 3.00
80 Brent Pease .01 .05
81 Monty Gilbreath .01 .05
82 Wes Pritchett .01 .05
83 Byron Williams .01 .05
84 Ron Sancho .01 .05
85 Tony Jones .07 .20
86 Anthony Wallace .01 .05
87 Mike Perez .01 .05
88 Steve Bartalo .01 .05
89 Teddy Garcia .01 .05
90 Joe Greenwood .01 .05
91 Tony Baker .07 .20
92 Glenn Cobb .01 .05
93 Mark Tucker .01 .05
94 Lyneil Mayo .01 .05
95 Alex Espinoza .01 .05
96 Mike Norseth .01 .05
97 Steven Avery .01 .05
98 John Brantley .01 .05
99 Eddie Britton .01 .05
100 Philip Doyle .01 .05
101 Elroy Harris .01 .05
102 John R. Holland .01 .05
103 Mark Hopkins .01 .05
104 Arthur Hunter .01 .05
105 Paul McGowan .01 .05
106 John Miller .01 .05
107 Shawn Moore .01 .05
108 Phil Ross .01 .05
109 Eugene Rowell .01 .05
110 Joe Valerio .01 .05
111 Harvey Wilson .01 .05
112 Irvin Smith .01 .05
113 Tony Sargent .01 .05
114 Ricky Shaw .01 .05
115 Curtis Moore .01 .05
116 Fred McNair .01 .05
117 Danny Lockett .01 .05
118 William Kirksey .01 .05
119 Stan Gelbaugh .07 .20
120 Judd Garrett .02 .10
121 Dedrick Dodge .01 .05
122 Dan Crossman .01 .05
123 Jeff Alexander .01 .05
124 Lew Barnes .01 .05
125 Willie Don Wright .01 .05
126 Johnny Thomas CB .01 .05
127 Richard Buchanan .01 .05
128 Chad Fortune .01 .05
129 Eric Lindstrom .01 .05
130 Ron Goetz .01 .05
131 Bruce Clark .01 .05
132 Anthony Greene .01 .05
133 Demetrius Davis .01 .05
134 Mike Roth .01 .05
135 Tony Moss .01 .05
136 Scott Erney .01 .05
137 Brad Henke .01 .05
138 Malcolm Frank .01 .05
139 Sean Foster .01 .05
140 Michael Titley .01 .05
141 Rickey Williams .01 .05
142 Karl Dunbar .01 .05
143 Carl Bax .01 .05
144 Willie Bouyer .01 .05
145 Howard Feggins .01 .05
146 David Smith RB .01 .05
147 Bernard Ford .01 .05
148 Checklist 1 .01 .05
149 Checklist 2 .01 .05
150 Checklist 3 .01 .05
NNO Box Card .01 .05

1992-93 Wild Card San Francisco

Exclusively featuring San Francisco 49ers, this six-card, standard-size set was originally given out at the Sports Collectors Card Expo held in San Francisco in September, 1992 and then reissued (with a slightly different show logo, different individual card numbers, and two replacement players) at the Spring National Sports Collectors Convention in San Francisco in March 1993. The two sets are indistinguishable except for the different show logo in the lower left corner of each obverse and the card numbering. The two sets are valued equally. The team color-coded stripes form a right angle at the lower left corner, while the customary series of colored numbers (1000, 100, 50, 20, 10, and 5) form a right angle at the upper right corner of the photo. The cards are numbered on the back; cards designated below as A are from the original 1992 set, whereas the B versions are from the 1993 reissue set. The complete set below applies to either set.

COMPLETE SET (6) 1.60 4.00
1A John Taylor .10 .30
1B Tom Rathman .10 .30
2A Amp Lee .10 .30
2B Steve Young .30 .75
3A Steve Bono .20 .50
3B Steve Bono .20 .50
4A Steve Young .30 .75
4B Brent Jones .10 .30
5A Tom Rathman .10 .30
5B Ricky Watters .20 .50
6A Don Griffin .10 .30
6B Amp Lee .10 .30

1993 Wild Card Prototypes

ese six promo cards were given away at the 1993 National Sports Collectors Convention in Chicago, Ill. The cards are numbered on the back with a "P" prefix. The set numbering starts where the 1992 Wild Card Prototypes left off. A Superchrome version was also produced of each card. These were actually re-numbered (#SCP1 SCP6) but have been priced below using a multiplier.

COMPLETE SET (6) 1.60 4.00
P19 Emmitt Smith .80 2.00
P20 Ricky Watters .15 .40
P21 Drew Bledsoe .60 1.50
P22 Garrison Hearst .30 .75
P23 Barry Foster .15 .40
P24 Rick Mirer .30 .75

1993 Wild Card Prototypes Superchrome

These six standard-size promo cards feature on their fronts borderless metallic color player action shots, with the player's name, team, and position appearing within the jagged gold stripe at the bottom. The borderless horizontal back carries the player's name, team, and position at the top, followed by biography, statistics, and, on the right, another color player action shot. The cards are numbered on the back with an "SCP" prefix. Each card was also produced in a "Hobby Reserve" parallel version and distributed directly to dealer accounts. These cards are marked "Hobby Reserve" on the fronts.

COMPLETE SET (6) 3.00 7.50
*HOBBY RESERVE CARDS: .6X TO 1.5X
SCP1 Emmitt Smith 1.20 3.00
SCP2 Ricky Watters .30 .75
SCP3 Drew Bledsoe 1.00 2.50
SCP4 Garrison Hearst .20 .50
SCP5 Barry Foster .20 .50
SCP6 Rick Mirer .40 1.00

1993 Wild Card

e 1993 Wild Card NFL football set consists of 260 standard-size cards. The first series cards are checklisted according to teams. Randomly inserted in early 1993 Wild Card packs were cards from the 1993 Stat Smashers, Field Force, and Red Hot Rookies sets. A different packaging scheme begun early in 1994 featured six Superchrome counterparts to the regular cards inserted in special Superchrome 15-card low-series and 13-card high-series hobby packs, and are valued at four to nine times the value of the regular issue cards. One of ten Superchrome Back-to-Back inserts, featuring a Field Force player on the front and a Red Hot Rookie on the back, was inserted in each 18-pack box. Also, special striped cards were randomly inserted into regular Wild Card packs. These cards came in varying "denominations" of stripes, ranging from five to 1,000, and the corresponding values for them are noted in the header below. Rookie Cards include Jerome Bettis, Drew Bledsoe, Reggie Brooks, Derek Brown, Garrison Hearst, O.J. McDuffie and Rick Mirer.

COMPLETE SET (260) 5.00 10.00
COMP.SERIES 1 (200) 3.00 6.00
COMP.SERIES 2 (60) 2.00 4.00
*5 STRIPES: 1X TO 2.5X HI COL.
*10 STRIPES: 1.5X TO 3.5X HI COL.
*20 STRIPES: 2X TO 5X HI COL.
*50 STRIPE VETS: 5X TO 12X HI COL.
*50 STRIPE RCs: 3X TO 8X HI COL.
*100 STRIPE VETS: 10X TO 25X HI COL.
*100 STRIPE RCs: 8X TO 20X HI COL.
*1000 STRIPE VETS: 50X TO 120X HI COL.
*1000 STRIPE RCs: 50X TO 120X HI COL.
1 Surprise Card .01 .05
2 Steve Young .30 .75
3 John Taylor .02 .10
4 Jerry Rice .40 1.00
5 Brent Jones .02 .10
6 Ricky Watters .02 .10
7 Elvis Grbac RC .60 1.50
8 Amp Lee .01 .05
9 Steve Bono .02 .10
10 Wendell Davis .01 .05
11 Mark Carrier DB .01 .05
12 Jim Harbaugh .02 .10
13 Curtis Conway RC .15 .40
14 Neal Anderson .01 .05
15 Tom Waddle .01 .05
16 Jeff Query .01 .05
17 David Klingler .01 .05
18 Eric Ball .01 .05
19 Derrick Fenner .01 .05
20 Steve Tovar RC .01 .05
21 Carl Pickens .02 .10
22 Ricardo McDonald .01 .05
23 Harold Green .01 .05
24 Keith McKeller .01 .05
25 Steve Christie .01 .05
26 Andre Reed .02 .10
27 Kenneth Davis .01 .05
28 Frank Reich .01 .05
29 Jim Kelly .08 .25
30 Bruce Smith .02 .10
31 Thurman Thomas .08 .25
32 Glyn Milburn RC .02 .10
33 John Elway .60 1.50
34 Vance Johnson .01 .05
35 Greg Lewis .01 .05
36 Steve Atwater .01 .05
37 Shannon Sharpe .02 .10
38 Mike Croel .01 .05
39 Kevin Mack .01 .05
40 Lawyer Tillman .01 .05
41 Tommy Vardell .01 .05
42 Bernie Kosar .02 .10
43 Eric Metcalf .02 .10
44 Clay Matthews .01 .05
45 Keith McCants .01 .05
46 Broderick Thomas .01 .05
47 Lawrence Dawsey .01 .05
48 Reggie Cobb .01 .05
49 Lamar Thomas RC .01 .05
50 Courtney Hawkins .02 .10
51 Ivory Lee Brown RC .01 .05
52 Ernie Jones .01 .05
53 Freddie Joe Nunn .01 .05
54 Chris Chandler .02 .10
55 Randal Hill .01 .05
56 Lorenzo Lynch .01 .05
57 Garrison Hearst RC .30 .75
58 Marion Butts .01 .05
59 Anthony Miller .02 .10
60 Eric Bieniemy .01 .05
61 Ronnie Harmon .01 .05
62 Junior Seau .08 .25
63 Gill Byrd .01 .05
64 Stan Humphries .02 .10
65 John Friesz .01 .05
66 J.J. Birden .02 .10
67 Joe Montana .60 1.50
68 Christian Okoye .02 .10
69 Dale Carter .01 .05
70 Barry Word .01 .05
71 Derrick Thomas .08 .25
72 Todd McNair .01 .05
73 Harvey Williams .01 .05
74 Jack Trudeau .01 .05
75 Rodney Culver .01 .05
76 Anthony Johnson .01 .05
77 Steve Emtman .01 .05
78 Quentin Coryatt .02 .10
79 Kerry Cash .01 .05
80 Jeff George .02 .10
81 Darrin Smith RC .01 .05
82 Jay Novacek .02 .10
83 Michael Irvin .08 .25
84 Alvin Harper .02 .10
85 Kevin Williams RC WR .02 .10
86 Troy Aikman .30 .75
87 Emmitt Smith .60 1.50
88 O.J.McDuffie RC .08 .25
89 Mike Williams WR RC .01 .05
90 Dan Marino .60 1.50
91 Aaron Craver .01 .05
92 Troy Vincent .01 .05
93 Keith Jackson .02 .10
94 Marco Coleman .01 .05
95 Mark Higgs .01 .05
96 Fred Barnett .02 .10
97 Wes Hopkins .01 .05
98 Randall Cunningham .08 .25
99 Heath Sherman .01 .05
100 Vai Sikahema .01 .05
101 Tony Smith RB .01 .05
102 Andre Rison .02 .10
103 Chris Miller .01 .05
104 Deion Sanders .20 .50
105 Mike Pritchard .02 .10
106 Steve Broussard .01 .05
107 Stephen Baker .01 .05
108 Carl Banks .01 .05
109 Jarrod Bunch .01 .05
110 Phil Simms .02 .10
111 Rodney Hampton .02 .10
112 Dave Meggett .01 .05
113 Pepper Johnson .01 .05
114 Coleman Rudolph RC .01 .05
115 Boomer Esiason .02 .10
116 Browning Nagle .01 .05
117 Rob Moore .02 .10
118 Marvin Jones RC .01 .05
119 Herman Moore .08 .25
120 Bennie Blades .01 .05
121 Erik Kramer .01 .05
122 Mel Gray .01 .05
123 Rodney Peete .01 .05
124 Barry Sanders .50 1.25
125 Chris Spielman .01 .05
126 Lamar Lathon .01 .05
127 Ernest Givins .02 .10
128 Lorenzo White .02 .10
129 Micheal Barrow RC .08 .25
130 Warren Moon .02 .10
131 Cody Carlson .01 .05
132 Reggie White .08 .25
133 Terrell Buckley .01 .05
134 Ed West .01 .05
135 Mark Brunell RC .60 1.50
136 Brett Favre .75 2.00
137 Edgar Bennett .02 .10
138 Sterling Sharpe .02 .10
139 George Teague RC .01 .05
140 Leonard Russell .02 .10
141 Drew Bledsoe RC 1.00 2.50
142 Eugene Chung .01 .05
143 Walter Stanley .01 .05
144 Scott Zolak .01 .05
145 Jon Vaughn .01 .05
146A Andre Tippett ERR Tippet .02 .10
146B Andre Tippett COR .02 .10
147 Alexander Wright .01 .05
148 Billy Joe Hobert RC .08 .25
149 Terry McDaniel .01 .05
150 Tim Brown .08 .25
151 Willie Gault .01 .05
152 Howie Long .08 .25
153 Todd Marinovich .01 .05
154 Jim Everett .02 .10
155 David Lang .01 .05
156 Henry Ellard .02 .10
157 Cleveland Gary .01 .05
158 Steve Israel .01 .05
159 Jerome Bettis RC 1.50 4.00
160 Jackie Slater .01 .05
161 Art Monk .02 .10
162 Ricky Sanders .01 .05
163 Brian Mitchell .01 .05
164 Reggie Brooks RC .01 .05
165 Mark Rypien .01 .05
166 Earnest Byner .01 .05
167 Andre Collins .01 .05
168 Quinn Early .02 .10
169 Fred McAfee .01 .05
170 Wesley Carroll .01 .05
171 Gene Atkins .01 .05
172 Derek Brown RBK UER RC .02 .10
173 Vaughn Dunbar .01 .05
174A R.Jackson ERR Ricky .01 .05
174B Rickey Jackson COR .01 .05
175 John L. Williams .01 .05
176 Carlton Gray RC .01 .05
177 Cortez Kennedy .02 .10
178 Kelly Stouffer .01 .05
179 Rick Mirer RC .08 .25
180 Dan McGwire .01 .05
181 Chris Warren .02 .10
182 Barry Foster .02 .10
183 Merril Hoge .01 .05
184 Darren Perry .01 .05
185 Deon Figures RC .01 .05
186A J.Graham WR ERR Grahm .02 .10
186B Jeff Graham WR COR .02 .10
187 Dwight Stone .01 .05
188 Neil O'Donnell .02 .10
189 Rod Woodson .08 .25
190 Alex Van Pelt RC 1.00 2.50
191 Steve Jordan .01 .05
192 Roger Craig .02 .10
193 Qadry Ismail UER RC .08 .25
194 Robert Smith RC .50 1.25
195 Gino Torretta RC .02 .10
196 Anthony Carter .02 .10
197 Terry Allen .02 .10
198 Rich Gannon .08 .25
199 Checklist 1-100 .01 .05
200 Checklist 101-200 .01 .05
201 Victor Bailey RC .01 .05
202 Micheal Barrow .01 .05
203 Patrick Bates RC .01 .05
204 Jerome Bettis .75 2.00
205 Drew Bledsoe .50 1.25
206 Vincent Brisby RC .08 .25
207 Reggie Brooks .02 .10
208 Derek Brown RBK .02 .10
209 Keith Byars .01 .05
210 Tom Carter RC .01 .05
211 Curtis Conway .08 .25
212 Russell Copeland RC .02 .10
213 John Copeland RC .02 .10
214 Eric Curry RC .02 .10
215 Troy Drayton RC .02 .10
216 Jason Elam RC .08 .25
217 Steve Everitt RC .01 .05
218 Deon Figures .01 .05
219 Irving Fryar .02 .10
220 Darrien Gordon RC .01 .05
221 Carlton Gray .01 .05
222 Kevin Greene .02 .10
223 Andre Hastings RC .02 .10
224 Michael Haynes .02 .10
225 Garrison Hearst .15 .40
226 Bobby Hebert .01 .05
227 Lester Holmes .01 .05
228 Jeff Hostetler .02 .10
229 Desmond Howard .02 .10
230 Tyronc Hughes RC .02 .10
231 Qadry Ismail .02 .10
232 Rocket Ismail .02 .10
233 James Jett RC .08 .25
234 Marvin Jones .01 .05
235 Todd Kelly RC .01 .05
236 Lincoln Kennedy RC .01 .05
237 Terry Kirby RC .02 .10
238 Bernie Kosar Cowboys .02 .10
239 Derrick Lassic RC .01 .05
240 Wilber Marshall .01 .05
241 O.J.McDuffie .08 .25
242 Ryan McNeil RC .08 .25
243 Natrone Means RC .08 .25
244 Glyn Milburn .02 .10
245 Rick Mirer .08 .25
246 Scott Mitchell .08 .25
247 Ronald Moore RC .02 .10
248 Lorenzo Neal RC .01 .05
249 Erric Pegram .02 .10
250 Roosevelt Potts RC .01 .05
251 Leonard Renfro RC .01 .05
252 Greg Robinson RC .01 .05
253 Wayne Simmons RC .01 .05
254 Chris Slade RC .02 .10
255 Irv Smith RC .02 .10
256 Robert Smith .20 .50
257 Dana Stubblefield RC .08 .25
258 George Teague .01 .05
259 Kevin Williams WR .02 .10
260 Checklist 201-260 .01 .05

1993 Wild Card Bomb Squad

One of these 30 standard-size cards was inserted in each 1993 Wild Card high-number (201-260) pack. Reportedly, 10,000 Bomb Squad sets were produced. The cards feature on their metallic fronts embossed color action photos of the NFL's top receivers within lined silver and bronze borders. The player's name, team, and position appear at the bottom. The orangeish back carries the player's name, team, and position at the top, followed below by biography, a horizontal stat table, and player action shot.

COMPLETE SET (30) 3.00 8.00
ONE PER JUMBO PACK
1 Jerry Rice 1.00 2.50
2 John Taylor .08 .25
3 J.J. Birden .08 .25
4 Stephen Baker .05 .15
5 Victor Bailey .05 .15
6 O.J.McDuffie .25 .60
7 Haywood Jeffires .05 .15
8 Eric Green .05 .15
9 Johnny Mitchell .05 .15
10 Art Monk .08 .25
11 Quinn Early .08 .25
12 Troy Drayton .08 .25
13 Vincent Brisby .25 .60
14 Courtney Hawkins .08 .25
15 Tom Waddle .05 .15
16 Curtis Conway .25 .60
17 Andre Reed .08 .25
18 Carl Pickens .08 .25
19 Sterling Sharpe .08 .25
20 Shannon Sharpe .08 .25
21 Qadry Ismail .08 .25
22 Rocket Ismail .08 .25
23 Andre Rison .08 .25
24 Michael Haynes .08 .25
25 Alvin Harper .08 .25
26 Michael Irvin .25 .60
27 Michael Jackson .05 .15
28 Herman Moore .25 .60
29 Anthony Miller .08 .25
30 Gary Clark .08 .25

1993 Wild Card Bomb Squad Back to Back

These 15 standard-size cards are double-front (two-player) versions of the 30-card Bomb Squad set. One was randomly inserted in each 20-pack box of 1993 Wild Card high-number jumbo packs. Reportedly, 1,000 of these double-sided sets were made. The cards' designs are identical to the fronts of the regular Bomb Squad cards. The cards are numbered on one side.

COMPLETE SET (15) 6.00 15.00
RANDOM INSERTS IN JUMBO PACKS
1 J.Rice J.Taylor 2.50 6.00
2 T.Waddle C.Conway .60 1.50
3 A.Reed C.Pickens .25 .60
4 St.Sharpe Sh.Sharp .25 .60
5 Q.Ismail R.Ismail .25 .60
6 A.Rison M.Haynes .25 .60
7 M.Irvin A.Harper .60 1.50
8 M.Jackson H.Moore .60 1.50
9 A.Miller G.Clark .25 .60
10 J.J.Birden S.Baker .25 .60
11 V.Bailey O.J.McDuffie .60 1.50
12 H.Jeffires E.Green .10 .30
13 J.Mitchell A.Monk .25 .60
14 Q.Early T.Drayton .25 .60
15 V.Brisby C.Hawkins .10 .30

1993 Wild Card Field Force

ndomly inserted in foil packs, this 90-card standard-size set was issued in three 30-card series based on Division alignments. Gold and Silver parallel cards were also randomly inserted in packs. Cards 31-60 are numbered on the back with a "WFF" prefix. Cards 61-90 are numbered with an "EFF" prefix and cards 91-120 with a "CFF" prefix. Early in 1994, Superchrome counterparts to 10 Field Force cards were randomly inserted in Wild Card Superchrome foil packs.

COMPLETE SET (90) 12.00 30.00
COMPLETE WEST SET (30) 4.00 10.00
COMPLETE EAST SET (30) 4.00 10.00
*SILVERS: .5X to 1.2X BASIC INSERTS
*GOLDS: .6X to 1.5X BASIC INSERTS
31-60: RANDOM INSERTS IN WEST PACKS
61-90: RANDOM INSERTS IN EAST PACKS
91-120: RANDOM INS.IN CENTRAL PACKS
31 Jerry Rice .75 2.00
32 Ricky Watters .07 .20
33 Steve Bono .07 .20
34 Amp Lee .02 .10
35 Steve Young .60 1.50
36 Tommy Maddox .02 .10
37 Cleveland Gary .02 .10
38 John Elway 1.25 3.00
39 Glyn Milburn .07 .20
40 Stan Humphries .07 .20
41 Junior Seau .20 .50
42 Natrone Means .20 .50
43 Dale Carter .02 .10
44 Joe Montana 1.25 3.00
45 Christian Okoye .07 .20
46 Deion Sanders .40 1.00
47 Roger Harper .02 .10
48 Steve Broussard .02 .10
49 Todd Marinovich .02 .10
50 Billy Joe Hobert .20 .50
51 Patrick Bates .02 .10
52 Jerome Bettis 1.50 4.00
53 Flipper Anderson .02 .10
54 Irv Smith .07 .20
55 Quinn Early .07 .20
56 Vaughn Dunbar .02 .10
57 Rick Mirer .20 .50
58 Carlton Gray .02 .10
59 Chris Warren .07 .20
60 Dan McGwire .02 .10
61 Pete Metzelaars .02 .10
62 Kenneth Davis .02 .10
63 Thurman Thomas .20 .50
64 Chris Chandler .07 .20
65 Garrison Hearst .30 .75
66 Ricky Proehl .02 .10
67 Steve Emtman .02 .10
68 Jeff George .07 .20
69 Clarence Verdin .02 .10
70 Troy Aikman .60 1.50
71 Emmitt Smith 1.25 3.00
72 Alvin Harper .07 .20
73 Michael Irvin .20 .50
74 O.J.McDuffie .20 .50
75 Troy Vincent .02 .10
76 Keith Jackson .07 .20
77 Dan Marino 1.25 3.00
78 Leonard Renfro .02 .10
79 Heath Sherman .02 .10
80 Derek Brown TE .02 .10
81 Rodney Hampton .07 .20
82 James Hasty .02 .10
83 Johnny Mitchell .02 .10
84 Brad Baxter .02 .10
85 Leonard Russell .07 .20
86 Marv Cook .02 .10
87 Drew Bledsoe 1.00 2.50
88 Ricky Ervins .02 .10
89 Art Monk .07 .20
90 Earnest Byner .02 .10
91 Tom Waddle .02 .10
92 Neal Anderson .02 .10
93 Curtis Conway .20 .50
94 Harold Green .02 .10
95 Jeff Query .02 .10
96 Carl Pickens .07 .20
97 David Klingler .02 .10
98 Michael Jackson .07 .20
99 Eric Metcalf .07 .20
100 Courtney Hawkins .07 .20
101 Eric Curry .07 .20
102 Reggie Cobb .02 .10
103 Mel Gray .02 .10
104 Barry Sanders 1.00 2.50
105 Rodney Peete .02 .10
106 Haywood Jeffires .07 .20
107 Cody Carlson .02 .10
108 Curtis Duncan .02 .10
109 Edgar Bennett .07 .20
110 George Teague .02 .10
111 Terrell Buckley .02 .10
112 Brett Favre 1.50 4.00
113 Deon Figures .02 .10
114 Rod Woodson .20 .50
115 Neil O'Donnell .07 .20
116 Barry Foster .07 .20
117 Cris Carter .20 .50
118 Gino Torretta .07 .20
119 Terry Allen .07 .20
120 Qadry Ismail .07 .20

1993 Wild Card Red Hot Rookies

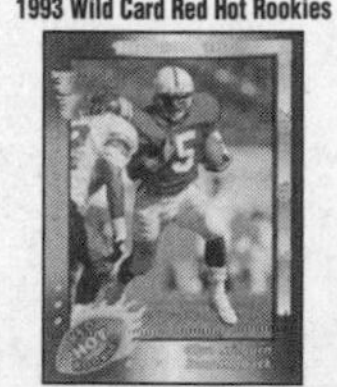

Randomly inserted in foil packs, this 30-card standard-size set is divided into three 10-card subsets based on divisional alignment. The fronts feature bordered glossy color player action photos. Cards 31-40 are numbered on the back with a "WRHR" prefix. Cards 41-50 are numbered with a "ERHR" prefix and cards 51-60 with a "CRHR" prefix. Early in 1994, Superchrome counterparts to 10 Red Hot Rookies cards were randomly inserted in Wild Card Superchrome foil packs.

COMPLETE SET (30) 4.00 10.00
COMPLETE WEST SET (10) 2.00 5.00
COMPLETE EAST SET (10) 2.00 5.00
31-40: RANDOM INSERTS IN WEST PACKS
41-50: RANDOM INSERTS IN EAST PACKS
51-60: RANDOM INS.IN CENTRAL PACKS
31 Dana Stubblefield .15 .40
32 Todd Kelly .02 .10
33 Dan Williams .02 .10
34 Glyn Milburn .05 .15
35 Natrone Means .15 .40
36 Lincoln Kennedy .02 .10
37 Patrick Bates .02 .10
38 Jerome Bettis 2.50 6.00
39 Irv Smith .05 .15
40 Rick Mirer .15 .40
41 Garrison Hearst .50 1.25
42 Kevin Williams WR .05 .15
43 Terry Kirby .05 .15
44 O.J.McDuffie .15 .40
45 Leonard Renfro .02 .10
46 Victor Bailey .02 .10
47 Marvin Jones .02 .10
48 Drew Bledsoe 1.50 4.00
49 Reggie Brooks .02 .10
50 Tom Carter .02 .10
51 Curtis Conway .25 .60
52 Dan Footman .02 .10
53 Lamar Thomas .02 .10
54 Eric Curry .05 .15
55 Ryan McNeil .15 .40
56 Micheal Barrow .15 .40
57 Wayne Simmons .02 .10
58 George Teague .02 .10
59 Robert Smith .75 2.00
60 Qadry Ismail .15 .40

1993 Wild Card Stat Smashers

Randomly inserted in foil packs, this 60-card standard-size set was issued in three subsets of 20 cards based on divisional alignment.

COMPLETE SET (60) 12.00 30.00
COMP.WEST SET (20) 4.00 10.00
53-72: RANDOM INSERTS IN WEST PACKS
73-92: RANDOM INSERTS IN EAST PACKS
93-112: RANDOM INS.IN CENTRAL PACKS
*GOLD CARDS: SAME PRICE
GOLD CARDS INSERTED IN RETAIL PACKS
53 Ricky Watters .07 .20
54 Jerry Rice .75 2.00
55 Steve Young .60 1.50
56 Shannon Sharpe .07 .20
57 John Elway 1.25 3.00
58 Glyn Milburn .07 .20
59 Marion Butts .02 .10
60 Junior Seau .20 .50
61 Natrone Means .20 .50
62 Joe Montana 1.25 3.00
63 J.J.Birden .07 .20
64 Michael Haynes .07 .20
65 Deion Sanders .40 1.00
66 Billy Joe Hobert .20 .50
67 Nick Bell .02 .10
68 Jerome Bettis 1.50 4.00
69 Vaughn Dunbar .02 .10
70 Quinn Early .07 .20
71 Dan McGwire .02 .10
72 Rick Mirer .20 .50
73 Kenneth Davis .02 .10
74 Thurman Thomas .20 .50
75 Garrison Hearst .30 .75
76 Ricky Proehl .02 .10
77 Jeff George .07 .20
78 Rodney Culver .02 .10
79 Troy Aikman .60 1.50
80 Emmitt Smith 1.25 3.00
81 Michael Irvin .20 .50
82 O.J.McDuffie .20 .50
83 Keith Jackson .07 .20
84 Dan Marino 1.25 3.00
85 Heath Sherman .02 .10
86 Fred Barnett .07 .20
87 Rodney Hampton .07 .20
88 Marvin Jones .02 .10
89 Brad Baxter .02 .10
90 Drew Bledsoe 1.00 2.50
91 Ricky Ervins .02 .10
92 Art Monk .07 .20
93 Neal Anderson .02 .10
94 Curtis Conway .20 .50
95 John Copeland .07 .20
96 Carl Pickens .07 .20
97 David Klingler .02 .10
98 Michael Jackson .07 .20
99 Kevin Mack .02 .10
100 Eric Curry .07 .20
101 Reggie Cobb .02 .10
102 Willie Green .02 .10
103 Barry Sanders 1.00 2.50
104 Haywood Jeffires .02 .10
105 Lorenzo White .07 .20
106 Sterling Sharpe .07 .20
107 Brett Favre 1.50 4.00
108 Neil O'Donnell .07 .20
109 Barry Foster .07 .20
110 Rich Gannon .20 .50
111 Robert Smith .40 1.00
112 Qadry Ismail .07 .20

1993 Wild Card Stat Smashers Rookies

is 52-card standard-size set was issued in gold or silver form. These cards (either type) were inserted one per jumbo pack.This set features an assortment of 1993 NFL rookies.

COMPLETE SET (52) 6.00 15.00
*GOLDS: .6X to 1.5X BASIC INSERTS
ONE GOLD OR SILVER PER JUMBO PACK
1 Todd Kelly .05 .15
2 Dana Stubblefield .30 .75
3 Curtis Conway .30 .75
4 John Copeland .10 .30
5 Russell Copeland .10 .30
6 Thomas Smith .05 .15
7 Glyn Milburn .10 .30
8 Jason Elam .30 .75
9 Steve Everitt .05 .15
10 Eric Curry .10 .30
11 Horace Copeland .05 .15
12 Ronald Moore .10 .30
13 Garrison Hearst .50 1.25
14 Natrone Means .30 .75

15 Darrien Gordon .05 .15
16 Roosevelt Potts .05 .15
17 Kevin Williams WR .10 .30
18 Derrick Lassic .05 .15
19 O.J.McDuffie .30 .75
20 Terry Kirby .10 .30
21 Scott Mitchell .30 .75
22 Victor Bailey .05 .15
23 Vaughn Hebron .05 .15
24 Lincoln Kennedy .05 .15
25 Michael Strahan .10 .30
26 Marvin Jones .05 .15
27 Tony McGee .05 .15
28 Ryan McNeil .30 .75
29 Micheal Barrow .05 .15
30 Wayne Simmons .05 .15
31 George Teague .05 .15
32 Vincent Brisby .30 .75
33 Drew Bledsoe 1.50 4.00
34 Rocket Ismail .10 .30
35 Patrick Bates .05 .15
36 James Jett .30 .75
37 Jerome Bettis 2.50 6.00
38 Troy Drayton .10 .30
39 Tom Carter .05 .15
40 Reggie Brooks .10 .30
41 Lorenzo Neal .05 .15
42 Derek Brown RBK .10 .30
43 Tyrone Hughes .10 .30
44 Rick Mirer .30 .75
45 Carlton Gray .05 .15
46 Andre Hastings .10 .30
47 Deon Figures .05 .15
48 Qadry Ismail .10 .30
49 Robert Smith .60 1.50
50 Irv Smith .10 .30
51 Chris Slade .10 .30
52 Willie Roaf .20 .50

1993 Wild Card Superchrome

The Superchrome set was distributed in its own packaging, but is essentially a parallel to the base 1993 Wild Card set. The cards feature a metallized foil look and included many of the same inserts as the base product.

COMPLETE SET (260) 8.00 20.00
COMP.SERIES 1 (200) 4.00 10.00
COMP.SERIES 2 (60) 4.00 10.00
1 Surprise Card .02 .10
2 Steve Young .40 1.00
3 John Taylor .05 .15
4 Jerry Rice .50 1.25
5 Brent Jones .05 .15
6 Ricky Watters .05 .15
7 Elvis Grbac RC .75 2.00
8 Amp Lee .02 .10
9 Steve Bono .05 .15
10 Wendell Davis .02 .10
11 Mark Carrier DB .02 .10
12 Jim Harbaugh .05 .15
13 Curtis Conway RC .20 .50
14 Neal Anderson .02 .10
15 Tom Waddle .02 .10
16 Jeff Query .02 .10
17 David Klingler .02 .10
18 Eric Ball .02 .10
19 Derrick Fenner .02 .10
20 Steve Tovar RC .02 .10
21 Carl Pickens .05 .15
22 Ricardo McDonald .02 .10
23 Harold Green .02 .10
24 Keith McKeller .02 .10
25 Steve Christie .02 .10
26 Andre Reed .05 .15
27 Kenneth Davis .02 .10
28 Frank Reich .02 .10
29 Jim Kelly .10 .30
30 Bruce Smith .05 .15
31 Thurman Thomas .10 .30
32 Glyn Milburn RC .05 .15
33 John Elway .75 2.00
34 Vance Johnson .02 .10
35 Greg Lewis .02 .10
36 Steve Atwater .02 .10
37 Shannon Sharpe .05 .15
38 Mike Croel .02 .10
39 Kevin Mack .02 .10
40 Lawyer Tillman .02 .10
41 Tommy Vardell .02 .10
42 Bernie Kosar .05 .15
43 Eric Metcalf .05 .15
44 Clay Matthews .02 .10
45 Keith McCants .02 .10
46 Broderick Thomas .02 .10
47 Lawrence Dawsey .02 .10
48 Reggie Cobb .02 .10
49 Lamar Thomas RC .02 .10
50 Courtney Hawkins .05 .15
51 Ivory Lee Brown RC .02 .10
52 Ernie Jones .02 .10
53 Freddie Joe Nunn .02 .10
54 Chris Chandler .05 .15
55 Randal Hill .02 .10
56 Lorenzo Lynch .02 .10
57 Garrison Hearst RC .40 1.00
58 Marion Butts .02 .10
59 Anthony Miller .05 .15
60 Eric Bieniemy .02 .10
61 Ronnie Harmon .02 .10
62 Junior Seau .10 .30
63 Gill Byrd .02 .10
64 Stan Humphries .05 .15
65 John Friesz .02 .10
66 J.J. Birden .05 .15
67 Joe Montana .75 2.00
68 Christian Okoye .05 .15
69 Dale Carter .02 .10
70 Barry Word .02 .10
71 Derrick Thomas .10 .30
72 Todd McNair .02 .10
73 Harvey Williams .02 .10
74 Jack Trudeau .02 .10
75 Rodney Culver .02 .10
76 Anthony Johnson .02 .10
77 Steve Emtman .02 .10
78 Quentin Coryatt .05 .15
79 Kerry Cash .02 .10
80 Jeff George .05 .15
81 Darrin Smith RC .02 .10
82 Jay Novacek .05 .15
83 Michael Irvin .10 .30
84 Alvin Harper .05 .15
85 Kevin Williams RC WR .05 .15
86 Troy Aikman .40 1.00
87 Emmitt Smith .75 2.00
88 O.J.McDuffie RC .10 .30
89 Mike Williams WR RC .02 .10
90 Dan Marino .75 2.00
91 Aaron Craver .02 .10
92 Troy Vincent .02 .10
93 Keith Jackson .05 .15
94 Marco Coleman .02 .10
95 Mark Higgs .02 .10
96 Fred Barnett .05 .15
97 Wes Hopkins .02 .10
98 Randall Cunningham .10 .30
99 Heath Sherman .02 .10
100 Vai Sikahema .02 .10
101 Tony Smith RB .02 .10
102 Andre Rison .05 .15
103 Chris Miller .02 .10
104 Deion Sanders .25 .60
105 Mike Pritchard .05 .15
106 Steve Broussard .02 .10
107 Stephen Baker .02 .10
108 Carl Banks .02 .10
109 Jarrod Bunch .02 .10
110 Phil Simms .05 .15
111 Rodney Hampton .05 .15
112 Dave Meggett .02 .10
113 Pepper Johnson .02 .10
114 Coleman Rudolph RC .02 .10
115 Boomer Esiason .05 .15
116 Browning Nagle .02 .10
117 Rob Moore .05 .15
118 Marvin Jones RC .02 .10
119 Herman Moore .10 .30
120 Bennie Blades .02 .10
121 Erik Kramer .02 .10
122 Mel Gray .02 .10
123 Rodney Peete .02 .10
124 Barry Sanders .60 1.50
125 Chris Spielman .02 .10
126 Lamar Lathon .02 .10
127 Ernest Givins .05 .15
128 Lorenzo White .05 .15
129 Micheal Barrow RC .10 .30
130 Warren Moon .05 .15
131 Cody Carlson .02 .10
132 Reggie White .10 .30
133 Terrell Buckley .02 .10
134 Ed West .02 .10
135 Mark Brunell RC .75 2.00
136 Brett Favre 1.00 2.50
137 Edgar Bennett .05 .15
138 Sterling Sharpe .05 .15
139 George Teague RC .02 .10
140 Leonard Russell .05 .15
141 Drew Bledsoe RC 1.25 3.00
142 Eugene Chung .02 .10
143 Walter Stanley .02 .10
144 Scott Zolak .02 .10
145 Jon Vaughn .02 .10
146 Andre Tippett .02 .10
147 Alexander Wright .02 .10
148 Billy Joe Hobert RC .10 .30
149 Terry McDaniel .02 .10
150 Tim Brown .10 .30
151 Willie Gault .02 .10
152 Howie Long .05 .15
153 Todd Marinovich .02 .10
154 Jim Everett .05 .15
155 David Lang .02 .10
156 Henry Ellard .05 .15
157 Cleveland Gary .02 .10
158 Steve Israel .02 .10
159 Jerome Bettis RC 2.00 5.00
160 Jackie Slater .02 .10
161 Art Monk .05 .15
162 Ricky Sanders .02 .10
163 Brian Mitchell .02 .10
164 Reggie Brooks RC .02 .10
165 Mark Rypien .02 .10
166 Earnest Byner .02 .10
167 Andre Collins .02 .10
168 Quinn Early .05 .15
169 Fred McAfee .02 .10
170 Wesley Carroll .02 .10
171 Gene Atkins .02 .10
172 Derek Brown RBK UER RC .05 .15
173 Vaughn Dunbar .02 .10
174 Rickey Jackson UER .02 .10
175 John L. Williams .02 .10
176 Carlton Gray RC .02 .10
177 Cortez Kennedy .05 .15
178 Kelly Stouffer .02 .10
179 Rick Mirer RC .10 .30
180 Dan McGwire .02 .10
181 Chris Warren .05 .15
182 Barry Foster .05 .15
183 Merril Hoge .02 .10
184 Darren Perry .02 .10
185 Deon Figures RC .05 .15
186A Jeff Graham WR ERR Grahm .05 .15
186B Jeff Graham WR COR .05 .15
187 Dwight Stone .02 .10
188 Neil O'Donnell .05 .15
189 Rod Woodson .10 .30
190 Alex Van Pelt RC 1.25 3.00
191 Steve Jordan .02 .10
192 Roger Craig .05 .15
193 Qadry Ismail UER RC .10 .30
194 Robert Smith RC .60 1.50
195 Gino Torretta RC .05 .15
196 Anthony Carter .05 .15
197 Terry Allen .05 .15
198 Rich Gannon .10 .30
199 Checklist 1-100 .02 .10
200 Checklist 101-200 .02 .10
201 Victor Bailey RC .02 .10
202 Micheal Barrow .10 .30
203 Patrick Bates RC .02 .10
204 Jerome Bettis 1.00 2.50
205 Drew Bledsoe .60 1.50
206 Vincent Brisby RC .10 .30
207 Reggie Brooks .05 .15
208 Derek Brown RBK .05 .15
209 Keith Byars .02 .10
210 Tom Carter RC .02 .10
211 Curtis Conway .10 .30
212 Russell Copeland RC .05 .15
213 John Copeland RC .05 .15
214 Eric Curry RC .05 .15
215 Troy Drayton RC .05 .15
216 Jason Elam RC .10 .30
217 Steve Everitt RC .02 .10
218 Deon Figures .05 .15
219 Irving Fryar .05 .15
220 Darrien Gordon RC .02 .10
221 Carlton Gray .02 .10
222 Kevin Greene .05 .15
223 Andre Hastings RC .05 .15
224 Michael Haynes .05 .15
225 Garrison Hearst .10 .30
226 Bobby Hebert .02 .10
227 Lester Holmes .02 .10
228 Jeff Hostetler .05 .15
229 Desmond Howard .05 .15
230 Tyrone Hughes RC .05 .15
231 Qadry Ismail .05 .15
232 Rocket Ismail .05 .15
233 James Jett RC .25 .60
234 Marvin Jones .02 .10
235 Todd Kelly RC .02 .10
236 Lincoln Kennedy RC .02 .10
237 Terry Kirby RC .05 .15
238 Bernie Kosar Cowboys .05 .15
239 Derrick Lassic RC .02 .10
240 Wilber Marshall .02 .10
241 O.J.McDuffie .10 .30
242 Ryan McNeil RC .10 .30
243 Natrone Means RC .10 .30
244 Glyn Milburn .05 .15
245 Rick Mirer .10 .30
246 Scott Mitchell .10 .30
247 Ronald Moore RC .05 .15
248 Lorenzo Neal RC .02 .10
249 Erric Pegram .05 .15
250 Roosevelt Potts RC .02 .10
251 Leonard Renfro RC .02 .10
252 Greg Robinson RC .02 .10
253 Wayne Simmons RC .02 .10
254 Chris Slade RC .05 .15
255 Irv Smith RC .05 .15
256 Robert Smith .25 .60
257 Dana Stubblefield RC .10 .30
258 George Teague .02 .10
259 [illegible] .05 .15
260 Checklist 201-260 .05 .15

1993 Wild Card Superchrome Field Force

ese 10 standard-size cards are Superchrome counterparts to selected cards from the 1993 Wild Card Field Force set. They were randomly inserted in 1993 Wild Card Superchrome foil packs. Aside from their special foil finish and the "SCF" prefix on their numbered (1-10) backs, they are otherwise identical to the regular Field Force cards. Twenty high-number Superchrome Field Force cards could be obtained by sending 29.95 to Wild Card. According to information on Superchrome foil packs, production of the high-number set was limited to 10,000 sets.

COMPLETE SET (10) 5.00 12.00
SCF1 Jerry Rice .60 1.50
SCF2 Glyn Milburn .07 .20
SCF3 Joe Montana 1.00 2.50
SCF4 Rick Mirer .15 .40
SCF5 Troy Aikman .50 1.25
SCF6 Emmitt Smith 1.00 2.50
SCF7 Dan Marino 1.00 2.50
SCF8 Drew Bledsoe .75 2.00
SCF9 Barry Sanders .75 2.00
SCF10 Brett Favre 1.25 3.00

1993 Wild Card Superchrome FF/RHR Back to Back

is set is frequently called "Red Hot Rookies and Field Force - - Back to Back." Measuring the standard-size, these cards were randomly inserted in Superchrome series two packs. The cards are double-sided, with a Red Hot Rookies on one side and a Field Force on the other. The cards are unnumbered and checklisted below alphabetically by the Field Force player.

COMPLETE SET (10) 6.00 15.00
RANDOM INS.IN SUPERCHROME SER.2
ONE FIELD FORCE/RED HOT ROOKIE PER CARD
1 T.Aikman .50 1.25
D.Stubblefield
2 Drew Bledsoe Combo .75 2.00
3 B.Favre 1.25 3.00
T.Kirby
4 D.Marino 1.00 2.50
R.Brooks
5 G.Milburn .15 .40
R.Mirer
6 R.Mirer .15 .40
G.Milburn
7 J.Montana 1.00 2.50
J.Bettis
8 J.Rice .60 1.50
G.Hearst
9 B.Sanders .75 2.00
V.Bailey
10 E.Smith 1.00 2.50
Q.Ismail

1993 Wild Card Superchrome Red Hot Rookies

These 10 standard-size cards are Superchrome counterparts to selected cards from the 1993 Wild Card Red Hot Rookies set. They were randomly inserted in 1993 Wild Card Superchrome foil packs. Aside from their special foil finish and the "SCR" prefix on their numbered (1-10) backs, they are otherwise identical to the regular Red Hot Rookies cards.

COMPLETE SET (10) 5.00 12.00
1 Dana Stubblefield .30 .75
2 Glyn Milburn .15 .40
3 Jerome Bettis 5.00 12.00
4 Rick Mirer .30 .75
5 Garrison Hearst 1.00 2.50
6 Terry Kirby .15 .40
7 Victor Bailey .08 .25
8 Drew Bledsoe 3.00 8.00
9 Reggie Brooks .08 .25
10 Qadry Ismail .30 .75

1993 Wild Card Superchrome Rookies Promos

ese five standard-size promo cards feature on their fronts metallic purple-bordered color player action shots set within gold elliptical inner borders. The cards are numbered on the back with a "P" prefix.

COMPLETE SET (6) 2.00 5.00
P1 Rick Mirer .30 .75
P2 Reggie Brooks .20 .50
P3 Glyn Milburn .20 .50
P4 Drew Bledsoe 1.00 2.50
P5 Jerome Bettis .60 1.50
P6 O.J. McDuffie .30 .75

1993 Wild Card Superchrome Rookies

These 50 standard-size cards issued early in 1994 were inserted, six per pack, in each special Superchrome Rookies 15-card foil pack. (The remaining cards in the pack were regular 1993 Wild Cards.) The set is sequenced in team order. Scott Mitchell is the only non-rookie in this set.

COMPLETE SET (50) 5.00 12.00
1 Dana Stubblefield .20 .50
2 Todd Kelly .05 .15
3 Curtis Conway .20 .50
4 John Copeland .08 .25
5 Tony McGee .05 .15
6 Russell Copeland .08 .25
7 Thomas Smith .05 .15
8 Jason Elam .20 .50
9 Glyn Milburn .08 .25
10 Steve Everitt .05 .15
11 Demetrius DuBose .05 .15
12 Eric Curry .08 .25
13 Garrison Hearst .20 .50
14 Ronald Moore .08 .25
15 Darrien Gordon .05 .15
16 Natrone Means .20 .50
17 Roosevelt Potts .05 .15
18 Derrick Lassic .05 .15
19 Kevin Williams WR .08 .25
20 Scott Mitchell .20 .50
21 O.J.McDuffie .20 .50
22 Terry Kirby .08 .25
23 Vaughn Hebron .05 .15
24 Victor Bailey .05 .15
25 Lincoln Kennedy .05 .15
26 Michael Strahan .05 .15
27 Marvin Jones .05 .15
28 Will Shields .05 .15
29 Ryan McNeil .20 .50
30 Micheal Barrow .20 .50
31 George Teague .05 .15
32 Wayne Simmons .05 .15
33 Vincent Brisby .20 .50
34 Drew Bledsoe 1.00 2.50
35 Patrick Bates .05 .15
36 James Jett .40 1.00
37 Rocket Ismail .08 .25
38 Troy Drayton .08 .25
39 Jerome Bettis 1.50 4.00
40 Tom Carter .05 .15
41 Reggie Brooks .08 .25
42 Tyrone Hughes .08 .25
43 Derek Brown RBK .08 .25
44 Willie Roaf .20 .50
45 Carlton Gray .05 .15
46 Rick Mirer .20 .50
47 Andre Hastings .08 .25
48 Deon Figures .08 .25
49 Qadry Ismail .08 .25
50 Robert Smith .40 1.00

1993 Wild Card Superchrome Rookies Back to Back

Randomly inserted in 1993 Wild Card Superchrome Rookies foil packs, these 25 standard-size cards feature on both metallic sides embossed color action shots of NFL rookies in their NFL uniforms within purple, black, blue, and gold borders. The player's name, team, and position appear above the photo within the card gold inner ... unnumbered and checklisted below in alphabetical order.

COMPLETE SET (25) 8.00 20.00
RANDOM INS.IN SUPERCHROME ROOKIES
1 V.Bailey .08 .25
V.Hebron
2 M.Barrow .30 .75
R.McNeil
3 P.Bates .30 .75
V.Brisby
4 J.Bettis .30 .75
N.Means
5 D.Bledsoe 3.00 8.00
R.Mirer
6 R.Brooks .15 .40
G.Milburn
7 D.Brown RBK .15 .40
T.Hughes
8 T.Carter .30 .75
J.Elam
9 C.Conway .50 1.25
S.Everitt
10 J.Copeland .15 .40
T.McGee
11 R.Copeland .08 .25
T.Smith
12 E.Curry .15 .40
D.DuBose
13 T.Drayton .08 .25
D.Gordon
14 D.Figures .15 .40
A.Hastings
15 C.Gray .30 .75
W.Roaf
16 G.Hearst 1.00 2.50
R.Moore
17 Q.Ismail .30 .75
R.Ismail
18 J.Jett 1.50 4.00
R.Smith
19 M.Jones .08 .25
W.Shields
20 T.Kelly .30 .75
D.Stubblefield
21 L.Kennedy .10 .25
M.Strahan
22 T.Kirby .30 .75
O.J.McDuffie
23 D.Lassic .15 .40
K.Williams WR
24 S.Mitchell .08 .25
R.Potts
25 W.Simmons .08 .25
G.Teague

1966 Williams Portraits Packers

This set consists of charcoal portraits of Green Bay Packers players with each portrait measuring approximately 8" by 10" This set preceded the complete NFL Williams Portraits released in 1967. The prints look very similar to the 1967 set, with each including the player's name and position beneath the charcoal portrait with blankbacks. The 1966 set is distinguished primarily by the lack of a year on the copyright line. The portraits are unnumbered and have been checklisted below alphabetically. An album was also produced to house the complete set.

COMPLETE SET (34) 175.00 300.00
1 Herb Adderley 10.00 15.00
2 Lionel Aldridge 5.00 8.00
3 Donny Anderson 6.00 10.00
4 Ken Bowman 5.00 8.00
5 Zeke Bratkowski 6.00 10.00
6 Bob Brown SP 6.00 10.00
7 Tom Brown 5.00 8.00
8 Lee Roy Caffey 5.00 8.00
9 Don Chandler 5.00 8.00
10 Tommy Crutcher 5.00 8.00
11 Bill Curry SP
12 Carroll Dale 6.00 10.00
13 Willie Davis 8.00 12.00
14 Boyd Dowler 6.00 10.00
15 Marv Fleming 6.00 10.00
16 Gale Gillingham SP 5.00 8.00
17 Jim Grabowski 5.00 8.00
18 Forrest Gregg 8.00 12.00
19 Doug Hart SP 5.00 8.00
20 Paul Hornung 15.00 25.00
21 Bob Jeter 5.00 8.00
22 Hank Jordan 8.00 12.00
23 Ron Kostelnik 5.00 8.00
24 Jerry Kramer 8.00 12.00
25 Bob Long 5.00 8.00
26 Max McGee 6.00 10.00
27 Ray Nitschke 15.00 25.00
28 Elijah Pitts 5.00 8.00
29 Dave Robinson 7.50 15.00
30 Bob Skoronski 5.00 8.00
31 Bart Starr 25.00 40.00
32 Jim Taylor 12.00 20.00
33 Fuzzy Thurston 8.00 12.00
34 Steve Wright SP 5.00 8.00
35 Willie Wood 8.00 12.00

1967 Williams Portraits

This set consists of charcoal art portraits of NFL players. Each portrait measures approximately 8" by 10", and they were sold in sets of eight for $1 along with the end flap from Velveeta, or a front label from Kraft Deluxe Slices or Singles, Cracker Barrel Cheddar or Kraft Sliced Natural Cheese. There were four eight-portrait groups for each of the 16 NFL teams. Moreover, an official NFL portrait album which would hold 32 portraits was offered for $2. The player's name and position were printed beneath the charcoal portrait. The backs are blank. The portraits are unnumbered and have been checklisted below alphabetically according to team. A checklist sheet (8" by 10") was produced, but is not considered a card. The Redskins and Packers sets appear to be the easiest to find. Popular players issued in their Rookie Card year include Leroy Kelly, Tommy Nobis, Dan Reeves and Jackie Smith. Players issued before their Rookie Card year include Lem Barney, Brian Piccolo, Bubba Smith and Steve Spurrier. It is believed that six players on this checklist did not have portraits produced while several other player listed are incorrect. Several players apparently were switched out for new players in their respective sets: Chuck Walton replaced Mike Alford and Bob Pickens replaced Bob Jones as examples. Lastly, a Vince Lombardi Williams Portrait was issued for a Downtown Businessman's function for the Green Bay Chamber of Commerce on August 7, 1968. We price this photo below as well although it is not considered part of the complete set.

COMPLETE SET (512) 5000.00 8000.00
1 Taz Anderson 10.00 20.00
2 Gary Barnes 10.00 20.00
3 Lee Calland 10.00 20.00
4 Junior Coffey 10.00 20.00
5 Ed Cook 10.00 20.00
6 Perry Lee Dunn 10.00 20.00
7 Dan Grimm 10.00 20.00
8 Alex Hawkins 12.50 25.00
9 Randy Johnson 10.00 20.00
10 Lou Kirouac 10.00 20.00
11 Errol Linden 10.00 20.00
12 Billy Lothridge 10.00 20.00
13 Frank Marchlewski 10.00 20.00
14 Rich Marshall 10.00 20.00
15 Billy Martin E 10.00 20.00
16 Tom Moore 12.50 25.00
17 Tommy Nobis 15.00 30.00
18 Jim Norton 10.00 20.00
19 Nick Rassas 10.00 20.00
20 Ken Reaves 10.00 20.00
21 Bobby Richards 10.00 20.00
22 Jerry Richardson 10.00 20.00
23 Bob Riggle 10.00 20.00
24 Karl Rubke 10.00 20.00
25 Marion Rushing 10.00 20.00
26 Chuck Sieminski 10.00 20.00
27 Steve Sloan 10.00 20.00
28 Ron Smith 10.00 20.00
29 Don Talbert 10.00 20.00
30 Ernie Wheelwright 10.00 20.00
31 Sam Williams 10.00 20.00
32 Jim Wilson 10.00 20.00
33 Sam Ball 10.00 20.00
34 Raymond Berry 20.00 40.00
35 Bob Boyd DB 10.00 20.00
36 Ordell Braase 10.00 20.00
37 Barry Brown 10.00 20.00
38 Bill Curry 10.00 20.00
39 Mike Curtis 12.50 25.00
40 Alvin Haymond 10.00 20.00
41 Jerry Hill 10.00 20.00
42 David Lee 10.00 20.00
43 Jerry Logan 10.00 20.00
44 Tony Lorick 10.00 20.00
45 Lenny Lyles 10.00 20.00
46 John Mackey 15.00 30.00
47 Tom Matte 12.50 25.00
48 Lou Michaels 12.50 25.00
49 Fred Miller 10.00 20.00
50 Lenny Moore 20.00 40.00
51 Jimmy Orr 10.00 20.00
52 Jim Parker 15.00 30.00
53 Glenn Ressler 10.00 20.00
54 Willie Richardson 10.00 20.00
55 Don Shinnick 10.00 20.00
56 Billy Ray Smith 10.00 20.00
57 Bubba Smith 15.00 30.00
58 Dan Sullivan 10.00 20.00
59 Dick Szymanski 10.00 20.00
60 Johnny Unitas 60.00 100.00
61 Bob Vogel 10.00 20.00
62 Rick Volk 10.00 20.00
63 Jim Welch 10.00 20.00
64 Butch Wilson 10.00 20.00
65 Charlie Bivins 12.50 25.00
66 Charlie Brown DB 12.50 25.00
67 Doug Buffone 12.50 25.00
68 Rudy Bukich 12.50 25.00
69 Ronnie Bull 12.50 25.00
70 Dick Butkus 40.00 75.00
71 Jim Cadile 12.50 25.00
72 Jack Concannon 12.50 25.00
73 Frank Cornish DT 12.50 25.00
74 Don Croftcheck 12.50 25.00
75 Dick Evey 12.50 25.00
76 Joe Fortunato 12.50 25.00
77 Curtis Gentry 12.50 25.00
78 Bobby Joe Green 12.50 25.00
79 John Johnson DT 12.50 25.00
80 Jimmy Jones 12.50 25.00
81 Ralph Kurek 12.50 25.00
82 Roger LeClerc 12.50 25.00
83 Andy Livingston 12.50 25.00
84 Bennie McRae 12.50 25.00
85 Johnny Morris 12.50 25.00
86 Richie Petitbon 12.50 25.00
87 Loyd Phillips 12.50 25.00
88 Brian Piccolo 40.00 75.00
89 Bob Pickens 12.50 25.00
90 Jim Purnell 12.50 25.00
91 Mike Pyle 12.50 25.00
92 Mike Reilly 12.50 25.00
93 Gale Sayers 40.00 75.00
94 George Seals 12.50 25.00
95 Roosevelt Taylor 15.00 30.00
96 Bob Wetoska 12.50 25.00
97 Erich Barnes 10.00 20.00
98 Johnny Brewer 10.00 20.00
99 Monte Clark 10.00 20.00
100 Gary Collins 12.50 25.00
101 Larry Conjar 10.00 20.00
102 Vince Costello 10.00 20.00
103 Ross Fichtner 10.00 20.00
104 Bill Glass 10.00 20.00
105 Ernie Green 10.00 20.00
106 Jack Gregory 10.00 20.00
107 Charlie Harraway 10.00 20.00
108 Gene Hickerson 10.00 20.00
109 Fred Hoaglin 10.00 20.00
110 Jim Houston 10.00 20.00
111 Mike Howell 10.00 20.00
112 Joe Bob Isbell 10.00 20.00
113 Walter Johnson 10.00 20.00
114 Jim Kanicki 10.00 20.00
115 Ernie Kellerman 10.00 20.00
116 Leroy Kelly 15.00 30.00
117 Dale Lindsey 10.00 20.00
118 Clifton McNeil 10.00 20.00
119 Milt Morin 10.00 20.00
120 Nick Pietrosante 10.00 20.00
121 Frank Ryan 12.50 25.00
122 Dick Schafrath 10.00 20.00
123 Randy Schultz 10.00 20.00
124 Ralph Smith 10.00 20.00
125 Carl Ward 10.00 20.00
126 Paul Warfield 15.00 30.00
127 Paul Wiggin 10.00 20.00
128 John Wooten 10.00 20.00
129 George Andrie 12.50 25.00
130 Jim Boeke 12.50 25.00
131 Frank Clarke 15.00 30.00
132 Mike Connelly 12.50 25.00
133 Buddy Dial 12.50 25.00
134 Leon Donohue 12.50 25.00
135 Dave Edwards 12.50 25.00
136 Mike Gaechter 12.50 25.00
137 Walt Garrison 15.00 30.00
138 Pete Gent 12.50 25.00
139 Cornell Green 15.00 30.00
140 Bob Hayes 20.00 40.00
141 Chuck Howley 20.00 40.00
142 Lee Roy Jordan 20.00 40.00
143 Bob Lilly 35.00 60.00
144 Tony Liscio 12.50 25.00
145 Warren Livingston 12.50 25.00
146 Dave Manders 12.50 25.00
147 Don Meredith 40.00 75.00
148 Ralph Neely 12.50 25.00
149 John Niland 12.50 25.00
150 Pettis Norman 12.50 25.00
151 Don Perkins 15.00 30.00
152 Jethro Pugh 12.50 25.00
153 Dan Reeves 25.00 50.00
154 Mel Renfro 20.00 40.00
155 Jerry Rhome 12.50 25.00
156 Les Shy 12.50 25.00
157 J.D. Smith 12.50 25.00
158 Willie Townes 12.50 25.00
159 Danny Villanueva 12.50 25.00
160 John Wilbur 12.50 25.00
161 Lem Barney 15.00 30.00
162 Charley Bradshaw 10.00 20.00
163 Roger Brown 12.50 25.00
164 Ernie Clark 10.00 20.00
165 Gail Cogdill 10.00 20.00
166 Nick Eddy 10.00 20.00
167 Mel Farr 10.00 20.00
168 Bobby Felts 10.00 20.00
169 Ed Flanagan 10.00 20.00
170 Jim Gibbons 12.50 25.00
171 John Gordy 10.00 20.00
172 Larry Hand 10.00 20.00
173 Wally Hilgenberg 10.00 20.00
174 Alex Karras 20.00 40.00
175 Bob Kowalkowski 10.00 20.00
176 Ron Kramer 10.00 20.00
177 Mike Lucci 10.00 20.00
178 Bruce Maher 10.00 20.00
179 Amos Marsh 10.00 20.00
180 Darris McCord 10.00 20.00
181 Tom Nowatzke 10.00 20.00
182 Milt Plum 12.50 25.00
183 Wayne Rasmussen 10.00 20.00
184 Roger Shoals 10.00 20.00
185 Pat Studstill 10.00 20.00
186 Karl Sweetan 10.00 20.00
187 Bobby Thompson DB 10.00 20.00
188 Doug Van Horn 10.00 20.00
189 Wayne Walker 10.00 20.00
190 Tommy Watkins 10.00 20.00
191 Chuck Walton 10.00 20.00
192 Garo Yepremian 12.50 25.00
193 Herb Adderley 10.00 20.00
194 Lionel Aldridge 5.00 10.00
195 Donny Anderson 6.00 12.00
196 Ken Bowman 5.00 10.00
197 Zeke Bratkowski 6.00 12.00
198 Bob Brown DT 5.00 10.00
199 Tom Brown 5.00 10.00
200 Lee Roy Caffey 5.00 10.00
201 Don Chandler 6.00 12.00
202 Tommy Crutcher 5.00 10.00
203 Carroll Dale 6.00 12.00
204 Willie Davis 7.50 15.00
205 Boyd Dowler 6.00 12.00
206 Marv Fleming 6.00 12.00
207 Gale Gillingham 5.00 10.00
208 Jim Grabowski 5.00 10.00
209 Forrest Gregg 10.00 20.00
210 Doug Hart 5.00 10.00
211 Bob Jeter 5.00 10.00
212 Hank Jordan 7.50 15.00
213 Ron Kostelnik 5.00 10.00
214 Jerry Kramer 7.50 15.00
215 Bob Long 5.00 10.00
216 Max McGee 6.00 12.00
217 Ray Nitschke 12.50 25.00
218 Elijah Pitts 6.00 12.00
219 Dave Robinson 6.00 12.00
220 Bob Skoronski 5.00 10.00
221 Bart Starr 25.00 50.00
222 Fred Thurston 7.50 15.00
223 Willie Wood 10.00 20.00
224 Steve Wright 5.00 10.00
225 Dick Bass 12.50 25.00
226 Maxie Baughan 10.00 20.00
227 Joe Carollo 10.00 20.00
228 Bernie Casey 10.00 20.00
229 Don Chuy 10.00 20.00
230 Charlie Cowan 10.00 20.00
231 Irv Cross 10.00 20.00
232 Willie Ellison 10.00 20.00
233 Roman Gabriel 15.00 30.00
234 Bruce Gossett 10.00 20.00
235 Roosevelt Grier 12.50 25.00
236 Tony Guillory 10.00 20.00
237 Ken Iman 10.00 20.00
238 Deacon Jones 20.00 40.00
239 Les Josephson 10.00 20.00
240 Jon Kilgore 10.00 20.00
241 Chuck Lamson 10.00 20.00
242 Lamar Lundy 12.50 25.00
243 Tom Mack 15.00 30.00
244 Tommy Mason 12.50 25.00
245 Tommy McDonald 12.50 25.00
246 Ed Meador 10.00 20.00
247 Bill Munson 10.00 20.00
248 Bob Nichols 10.00 20.00
249 Merlin Olsen 20.00 40.00
250 Jack Pardee 12.50 25.00
251 Bucky Pope 10.00 20.00
252 Joe Scibelli 10.00 20.00
253 Jack Snow 12.50 25.00
254 Billy Truax 10.00 20.00
255 Clancy Williams 10.00 20.00
256 Doug Woodlief 10.00 20.00
257 Grady Alderman 12.50 25.00
258 John Beasley 10.00 20.00
259 Bob Berry 10.00 20.00
260 Larry Bowie 10.00 20.00
261 Bill Brown 12.50 25.00
262 Fred Cox 12.50 25.00
263 Doug Davis 10.00 20.00
264 Paul Dickson 10.00 20.00
265 Carl Eller 15.00 30.00
266 Paul Flatley 10.00 20.00
267 Dale Hackbart 10.00 20.00
268 Don Hansen 10.00 20.00
269 Clint Jones 10.00 20.00
270 Jeff Jordan 10.00 20.00
271 Karl Kassulke 10.00 20.00
272 John Kirby 10.00 20.00
273 Gary Larsen 10.00 20.00
274 Jim Lindsey 10.00 20.00
275 Earsell Mackbee 10.00 20.00
276 Jim Marshall 15.00 30.00
277 Marlin McKeever 10.00 20.00
278 Dave Osborn 10.00 20.00
279 Jim Phillips 10.00 20.00
280 Ed Sharockman 10.00 20.00
281 Jerry Shay 10.00 20.00
282 Milt Sunde 10.00 20.00
283 Archie Sutton 10.00 20.00
284 Mick Tingelhoff 12.50 25.00
285 Ron VanderKelen 10.00 20.00
286 Jim Vellone 10.00 20.00
287 Lonnie Warwick 10.00 20.00
288 Roy Winston 10.00 20.00
289 Doug Atkins 15.00 30.00
290 Vern Burke 10.00 20.00
291 Bruce Cortez 10.00 20.00
292 Gary Cuozzo 12.50 25.00
293 Ted Davis 10.00 20.00
294 John Douglas 10.00 20.00
295 Jim Garcia 10.00 20.00
296 Tom Hall 10.00 20.00
297 Jim Heidel 10.00 20.00
298 Leslie Kelley 10.00 20.00
299 Billy Kilmer 12.50 25.00
300 Kent Kramer 10.00 20.00
301 Jake Kupp 10.00 20.00
302 Earl Leggett 10.00 20.00
303 Obert Logan 10.00 20.00
304 Tom McNeill 10.00 20.00
305 John Morrow 10.00 20.00
306 Ray Ogden 10.00 20.00
307 Ray Rissmiller 10.00 20.00
308 George Rose 10.00 20.00
309 Dave Rowe 10.00 20.00
310 Brian Schweda 10.00 20.00
311 Dave Simmons 10.00 20.00
312 Jerry Simmons 10.00 20.00
313 Steve Stonebreaker 10.00 20.00
314 Jim Taylor 20.00 40.00
315 Mike Tilleman 10.00 20.00
316 Phil Vandersea 10.00 20.00
317 Joe Wendryhoski 10.00 20.00
318 Dave Whitsell 10.00 20.00
319 Fred Whittingham 10.00 20.00
320 Gary Wood 10.00 20.00
321 Ken Avery 10.00 20.00
322 Bookie Bolin 10.00 20.00
323 Henry Carr 12.50 25.00
324 Pete Case 10.00 20.00
325 Clarence Childs 10.00 20.00
326 Mike Ciccolella 10.00 20.00
327 Glen Condren 10.00 20.00
328 Bob Crespino 10.00 20.00
329 Don Davis 10.00 20.00
330 Tucker Frederickson 12.50 25.00
331 Charlie Harper 10.00 20.00
332 Phil Harris 10.00 20.00
333 Allen Jacobs 10.00 20.00
334 Homer Jones 10.00 20.00
335 Jim Katcavage 10.00 20.00
336 Tom Kennedy 10.00 20.00
337 Ernie Koy 10.00 20.00
338 Greg Larson 10.00 20.00
339 Spider Lockhart 10.00 20.00
340 Chuck Mercein 10.00 20.00
341 Jim Moran 10.00 20.00
342 Earl Morrall 12.50 25.00
343 Joe Morrison 10.00 20.00
344 Francis Peay 10.00 20.00
345 Del Shofner 12.50 25.00
346 Jeff Smith LB 10.00 20.00
347 Fran Tarkenton 30.00 60.00
348 Aaron Thomas 10.00 20.00
349 Larry Vargo 10.00 20.00
350 Freeman White 10.00 20.00
351 Sidney Williams 10.00 20.00
352 Willie Young 10.00 20.00
353 Sam Baker 10.00 20.00
354 Gary Ballman 10.00 20.00
355 Randy Beisler 10.00 20.00
356 Bob Brown OT 12.50 25.00
357 Timmy Brown 12.50 25.00
358 Mike Ditka 40.00 75.00
359 Dave Graham 10.00 20.00
360 Ben Hawkins 10.00 20.00
361 Fred Hill 10.00 20.00
362 King Hill 10.00 20.00
363 Lynn Hoyem 10.00 20.00
364 Don Hultz 10.00 20.00
365 Dwight Kelley 10.00 20.00
366 Israel Lang 10.00 20.00
367 Dave Lloyd 10.00 20.00
368 Aaron Martin 10.00 20.00
369 Ron Medved 10.00 20.00
370 John Meyers 10.00 20.00
371 Mike Morgan LB 10.00 20.00
372 Al Nelson 10.00 20.00
373 Jim Nettles 10.00 20.00
374 Floyd Peters 10.00 20.00
375 Gary Pettigrew 10.00 20.00
376 Ray Poage 10.00 20.00
377 Nate Ramsey 10.00 20.00
378 Dave Recher 10.00 20.00
379 Jim Ringo 10.00 20.00
380 Joe Scarpati 10.00 20.00
381 Jim Skaggs 10.00 20.00
382 Norm Snead 12.50 25.00
383 Harold Wells 10.00 20.00
384 Tom Woodeshick 10.00 20.00
385 Bill Asbury 12.50 25.00
386 John Baker 12.50 25.00
387 Jim Bradshaw 12.50 25.00
388 Rod Breedlove 12.50 25.00
389 John Brown 12.50 25.00
390 Amos Bullocks 12.50 25.00
391 Jim Butler 12.50 25.00
392 John Campbell 12.50 25.00
393 Mike Clark 12.50 25.00
394 Larry Gagner 12.50 25.00
395 Earl Gros 12.50 25.00
396 John Hilton 12.50 25.00
397 Dick Hoak 12.50 25.00
398 Roy Jefferson 12.50 25.00
399 Tony Jeter 12.50 25.00
400 Brady Keys 12.50 25.00
401 Ken Kortas 12.50 25.00
402 Ray Mansfield 12.50 25.00
403 Paul Martha 12.50 25.00
404 Ben McGee 12.50 25.00
405 Bill Nelsen 15.00 30.00
406 Kent Nix 12.50 25.00
407 Fran O'Brien 12.50 25.00
408 Andy Russell 15.00 30.00
409 Bill Saul 12.50 25.00
410 Don Shy 12.50 25.00
411 Clendon Thomas 12.50 25.00
412 Bruce Van Dyke 12.50 25.00
413 Lloyd Voss 12.50 25.00
414 Ralph Wenzel 12.50 25.00
415 J.R. Wilburn 12.50 25.00
416 Marv Woodson 12.50 25.00
417 Jim Bakken 10.00 20.00
418 Don Brumm 10.00 20.00
419 Vidal Carlin 10.00 20.00
420 Bobby Joe Conrad 10.00 20.00
421 Willis Crenshaw 10.00 20.00
422 Bob DeMarco 10.00 20.00
423 Pat Fischer 12.50 25.00
424 Billy Gambrell 10.00 20.00
425 Prentice Gautt 10.00 20.00
426 Ken Gray 10.00 20.00
427 Jerry Hillebrand 10.00 20.00
428 Charley Johnson 12.50 25.00
429 Bill Koman 10.00 20.00
430 Dave Long 10.00 20.00
431 Ernie McMillan 10.00 20.00
432 Dave Meggysey 10.00 20.00
433 Dale Meinert 10.00 20.00
434 Mike Melinkovich 10.00 20.00
435 Dave O'Brien 10.00 20.00
436 Sonny Randle 10.00 20.00
437 Bob Reynolds 10.00 20.00
438 Joe Robb 10.00 20.00
439 Johnny Roland 10.00 20.00
440 Roy Shivers 10.00 20.00
441 Sam Silas 10.00 20.00
442 Jackie Smith 15.00 30.00
443 Rick Sortun 10.00 20.00
444 Jerry Stovall 10.00 20.00
445 Chuck Walker 10.00 20.00
446 Bobby Williams 10.00 20.00
447 Dave Williams 10.00 20.00
448 Larry Wilson 15.00 30.00
449 Kermit Alexander 10.00 20.00
450 Cas Banaszek 10.00 20.00
451 Bruce Bosley 10.00 20.00
452 John Brodie 20.00 40.00
453 Joe Cerne 10.00 20.00
454 John David Crow 12.50 25.00
455 Tommy Davis 10.00 20.00
456 Bob Harrison 10.00 20.00
457 Matt Hazeltine 10.00 20.00
458 Stan Hindman 10.00 20.00
459 Charlie Johnson DT 10.00 20.00
460 Jim Johnson 12.50 25.00
461 Dave Kopay 10.00 20.00
462 Charlie Krueger 10.00 20.00
463 Roland Lakes 10.00 20.00
464 Gary Lewis 10.00 20.00
465 Dave McCormick 10.00 20.00
466 Kay McFarland 10.00 20.00
467 Clark Miller 10.00 20.00
468 George Mira 10.00 20.00
469 Howard Mudd 10.00 20.00
470 Frank Nunley 10.00 20.00
471 Dave Parks 10.00 20.00
472 Walter Rock 10.00 20.00
473 Len Rohde 10.00 20.00
474 Steve Spurrier 30.00 60.00
475 Monty Stickles 10.00 20.00
476 John Thomas 10.00 20.00
477 Bill Tucker 10.00 20.00
478 Dave Wilcox 12.50 25.00
479 Ken Willard 10.00 20.00
480 Dick Witcher 10.00 20.00
481 Willie Adams 6.00 12.00
482 Walt Barnes DL 6.00 12.00
483 Jim Carroll 6.00 12.00
484 Dave Crossan 6.00 12.00
485 Charlie Gogolak 6.00 12.00
486 Tom Goosby 6.00 12.00

487 Chris Hanburger	7.50	15.00
488 Rickie Harris	6.00	12.00
489 Len Hauss	6.00	12.00
490 Sam Huff	12.50	25.00
491 Steve Jackson LB	6.00	12.00
492 Mitch Johnson	6.00	12.00
493 Sonny Jurgensen	12.50	25.00
494 Carl Kammerer	6.00	12.00
495 Paul Krause	10.00	20.00
496 Joe Don Looney	7.50	15.00
497 Ray McDonald	6.00	12.00
498 Bobby Mitchell	10.00	20.00
499 Jim Ninowski	6.00	12.00
500 Brig Owens	6.00	12.00
501 Vince Promuto	6.00	12.00
502 Pat Richter	6.00	12.00
503 Joe Rutgens	6.00	12.00
504 Lonnie Sanders	6.00	12.00
505 Ray Schoenke	6.00	12.00
506 Jim Shorter	6.00	12.00
507 Jerry Smith	6.00	12.00
508 Ron Snidow	6.00	12.00
509 Jim Snowden	6.00	12.00
510 Charley Taylor	10.00	20.00
511 Steve Thurlow	6.00	12.00
512 A.D. Whitfield	6.00	12.00
513 Vince Lombardi CO	60.00	100.00
514 Portrait Album	30.00	50.00

1948 Wilson Advisory Staff

These glossy black and white photos measure roughly 8 1/8" by 10" and were likely issued over a number of years. Each features a top player or coach photo with the Wilson advisory staff line of text below the picture. They also include facsimile autographs.

COMPLETE SET (5)	100.00	200.00
1 Paul Christman	20.00	40.00
2 Johnny Lujack	37.50	75.00
3 Clark Shaughnessy	15.00	30.00
4 Charley Trippi	25.00	50.00
5 Lynn Waldorf	15.00	30.00

1962-66 Wilson Advisory Staff

These 8X10 glossy photos were likely issued over a number of years in the 1960s. Each features a top player or coach photo printed in black and white with the Wilson advisory staff line of text below the picture. Some also include facsimile autographs.

COMPLETE SET (4)	45.00	90.00
1 Bernie Bierman	7.50	15.00
2 Boyd Dowler	10.00	20.00
3 Hugh McElhenny	12.50	25.00
4 Gale Sayers	20.00	40.00

1999 Winner's Circle Die Cast

Hasbro and Winner's Circle released these die cast pieces featuring NFL players. Each package includes a die cast 1999 Mustang (NFC players) or 1999 Corvette (AFC players) along with an oversized cardboard stand featuring a photo of the player. The player's photo is also included on the hood of the die cast car. Prices below reflect that of unopened blister packs.

COMPLETE SET (14)	25.00	50.00
1 Troy Aikman	2.50	5.00
2 Drew Bledsoe	2.00	4.00
3 Mark Brunell	2.00	4.00
4 Randall Cunningham	2.00	4.00
5 Terrell Davis	2.50	5.00
6 Warrick Dunn	2.00	4.00
7 John Elway	3.00	6.00
8 Brett Favre	3.00	6.00
9 Doug Flutie	2.00	4.00
10 Keyshawn Johnson	2.00	4.00
11 Dan Marino	3.00	6.00
12 Randy Moss	2.50	5.00
13 Barry Sanders	2.50	5.00
14 Deion Sanders	2.00	4.00

1974 Wonder Bread

The 1974 Wonder Bread Football set features 30 standard-size cards with colored borders and color photographs of the players on the front. Season by season records are given on the back of the cards as well as a particular football technique. A "Topps Chewing Gum, Inc." copyright appears on the reverse. A parallel version of the cards was also distributed by Town Talk Bread.

COMPLETE SET (30)	25.00	50.00
1 Jim Bakken	.60	1.50
2 Forrest Blue	.60	1.50
3 Bill Bradley	.60	1.50
4 Willie Brown	1.00	2.50
5 Larry Csonka	3.00	6.00
6 Ken Ellis	.60	1.50
7 Bruce Gossett	.60	1.50
8 Bob Griese	3.00	6.00
9 Chris Hanburger	.60	1.50
10 Winston Hill	.60	1.50
11 Jim Johnson	.75	2.00
12 Paul Krause	.75	2.00
13 Ted Kwalick	.60	1.50
14 Willie Lanier	1.00	2.50
15 Tom Mack	.75	2.00
16 Jim Otto	1.00	2.50
17 Alan Page	1.00	2.50
18 Frank Pitts	.60	1.50
19 Jim Plunkett	1.00	2.50
20 Mike Reid	.75	2.00
21 Paul Smith	.60	1.50
22 Bob Tucker	.60	1.50
23 Jim Tyrer	.60	1.50
24 Gene Upshaw	1.00	2.50
25 Phil Villapiano	.60	1.50
26 Paul Warfield	1.50	4.00
27 Dwight White	.75	2.00
28 Steve Owens	.75	2.00
29 Jerrel Wilson	.60	1.50
30 Ron Yary	.75	2.00

1974 Wonder Bread/Town Talk

The 1974 Town Talk Bread set features 30 standard-size cards with colored borders and color photographs of the players on the front. The cards are essentially a parallel version of the 1974 Wonder Bread release, but were distributed through Town Talk Bread products. A "Topps Chewing Gum, Inc." copyright appears on the reverse. These Town Talk cards are more difficult to find and are priced using the multiplier line given below. They are distinguished from the Wonder Bread issue by the absence of a credit line at the top of the cardback.

COMPLETE SET (30)	125.00	250.00
*TOWN TALK: 3X TO 6X BASIC CARDS		

1975 Wonder Bread

The 1975 Wonder Bread Football card set contains 24 standard-size cards with either blue (7-18) or red (1-6 and 19-24) borders. The backs feature several questions (about the player and the game of football) whose answers could be determined by turning the card upside down and reading the answers to the corresponding questions. The words "Topps Chewing Gum, Inc." appears at the bottom of the reverse of the card. Wonder Bread also produced a saver sheet and album for this set. A parallel version of the cards was also produced by Town Talk Bread.

COMPLETE SET (24)	20.00	40.00
1 Alan Page	.75	2.00
2 Emmitt Thomas	.60	1.50
3 John Mendenhall	.50	1.25
4 Ken Houston	.60	1.50
5 Jack Ham	1.50	4.00
6 L.C. Greenwood	.75	2.00
7 Tom Mack	.60	1.50
8 Winston Hill	.50	1.25
9 Isaac Curtis	.50	1.25
10 Terry Owens	.50	1.25
11 Drew Pearson	1.25	3.00
12 Don Cockroft	.50	1.25
13 Bob Griese	2.00	5.00
14 Riley Odoms	.50	1.25
15 Chuck Foreman	.60	1.50
16 Forrest Blue	.50	1.25
17 Franco Harris	2.50	6.00
18 Larry Little	.60	1.50
19 Bill Bergey	.50	1.25
20 Ray Guy	.60	1.50
21 Ted Hendricks	.75	2.00
22 Levi Johnson	.50	1.25
23 Jack Mildren	.50	1.25
24 Mel Tom	.50	1.25

1975 Wonder Bread/Town Talk

The 1975 Town Talk Bread card set contains 24 standard-size cards with either blue (7-18) or red (1-6 and 19-24) borders. The cards are essentially a parallel to the Wonder Bread issue. The words "Topps Chewing Gum, Inc." appears at the bottom of the cardback. These Town Talk cards are more difficult to find and are priced using the multiplier line given below. They are distinguished by the different "Town Talk" credit line at the top of the cardback.

COMPLETE SET (24)	125.00	250.00
*TOWN TALK: 4X TO 8X BASIC CARDS		

1976 Wonder Bread

The 1976 Wonder Bread Football Card set features 24 colored standard-size cards with red or blue frame lines and white borders. The first 12 cards (1-12) in the set feature offensive players with a blue frame and the last 12 cards (13-24) feature defensive players with a red frame. The backs feature one of coach Hank Stram's favorite plays, with a football diagram and a text listing each offensive player's assignments of the particular play. The "Topps Chewing Gum, Inc." copyright appears at the bottom on the cardback. A parallel version of the cards was also produced by Town Talk Bread.

COMPLETE SET (24)	2.50	5.00
1 Craig Morton	.25	.50
2 Chuck Foreman	.15	.40
3 Franco Harris	.50	1.25
4 Mel Gray	.15	.40
5 Charley Taylor	.30	.75
6 Richard Caster	.10	.30
7 George Kunz	.10	.30
8 Rayfield Wright	.10	.30
9 Gene Upshaw	.25	.50
10 Tom Mack	.15	.40
11 Len Hauss	.10	.30
12 Garo Yepremian	.10	.30
13 Cedrick Hardman	.10	.30
14 Jack Youngblood	.25	.50
15 Wally Chambers	.10	.30
16 Jerry Sherk	.10	.30
17 Bill Bergey	.10	.30
18 Jack Ham	.30	.75
19 Fred Carr	.10	.30
20 Jack Tatum	.15	.40
21 Cliff Harris	.25	.50
22 Emmitt Thomas	.10	.30
23 Ken Riley	.10	.30
24 Ray Guy	.25	.50

1976 Wonder Bread/Town Talk

The 1976 Town Talk Bread football card set features 24 colored standard-size cards with red or blue frame lines and white borders. The cards are essentially a parallel version to the Wonder Bread release. The "Topps Chewing Gum, Inc." copyright appears at the bottom on the cardback. These Town Talk cards are more difficult to find than the Wonder Bread issue and are priced using the multiplier line given below. They are distinguished by the different credit line at the top of the cardback.

COMPLETE SET (24)	50.00	100.00
*TOWN TALK: 6X TO 12X BASIC CARDS		

1964 Yuban Coffee Canvas Premiums

These large portraits were issued by Yuban Coffee around 1964. Each features a current NFL star in a painting format printed on canvas. The backs are blank. Any additions to this list are appreciated.

COMPLETE SET (17)	2500.00	4000.00
1 Gary Ballman	100.00	200.00
2 Jim Brown	500.00	800.00
3 Gail Cogdill	100.00	200.00
4 Bill George	125.00	250.00
5 Frank Gifford	125.00	250.00
6 Matt Hazeltine	100.00	200.00
7 Paul Hornung	200.00	400.00
8 Charley Johnson	100.00	200.00
9 Don Meredith	200.00	350.00
10 Bobby Mitchell	125.00	250.00
11 Earl Morrall	125.00	250.00
12 Jack Pardee	100.00	200.00
13 Nick Pietrosante	100.00	200.00
14 Pete Retzlaff	125.00	250.00
15 Fran Tarkenton	250.00	500.00
16 Y.A. Tittle	200.00	400.00
17 Johnny Unitas	400.00	800.00

1995 Zenith Promos

mmemorating the 1994 achievements of three Future Hall of Famers, this 4-card promo set was issued to herald the release of the 1995 Pinnacle Zenith series. Measuring the standard size, the cards are printed on 24-point card stock utilizing Pinnacle's all-foil metalized printing technology. The fronts display color action cutouts on a brown geometric design and bronze metallized brick design. The horizontal backs carry a color closeup photo and 1994 statistics presented on a football field graphic. The disclaimer "PROMO" is printed diagonally across the backs.

COMPLETE SET (4)	5.00	12.00
1 Emmitt Smith	2.00	5.00
94 Steve Young	1.20	3.00
97 Dan Marino	2.40	6.00
NNO Title Card	.10	.30

1995 Zenith

This 150-card standard-size set was issued by Pinnacle to honor some of the top NFL players. The cards are printed on 24-point card stock untilizing Pinnacle's all-foil metalized printing technology. The fronts display color action photos superimposed over a brown geometric design and bronze metalized printing technology. The horizontal backs carry a color close-up and 1994 statistics presented on a football field graphic. The only key Rookie Card is Jeff Blake.

COMPLETE SET (150)	7.50	20.00
Z1 Emmitt Smith	.75	2.00
Z2 Chris Spielman	.08	.25
Z3 Johnny Mitchell	.05	.15
Z4 Boomer Esiason	.08	.25
Z5 Jackie Harris	.05	.15
Z6 Warren Moon	.08	.25
Z7 Harvey Williams	.05	.15
Z8 Steve Walsh	.05	.15
Z9 Cris Carter	.15	.40
Z10 Natrone Means	.08	.25
Z11 Art Monk	.08	.25
Z12 Leslie O'Neal	.08	.25
Z13 Adrian Murrell	.08	.25
Z14 John Elway	1.00	2.50
Z15 Larry Centers	.08	.25
Z16 Ricky Ervins	.05	.15
Z17 Jeff Graham	.05	.15
Z18 Ricky Watters	.08	.25
Z19 Eric Green	.05	.15
Z20 Curtis Conway	.15	.40
Z21 Jake Reed	.08	.25
Z22 Michael Timpson	.05	.15
Z23 Marcus Allen	.15	.40
Z24 Andre Rison	.08	.25
Z25 Terry Kirby	.08	.25
Z26 Reggie White	.15	.40
Z27 Randall Cunningham	.15	.40
Z28 Jim Kelly	.15	.40
Z29 Robert Brooks	.15	.40
Z30 Terance Mathis	.08	.25
Z31 Anthony Miller	.08	.25
Z32 Neil O'Donnell	.08	.25
Z33 Jeff Hostetler	.08	.25
Z34 Drew Bledsoe	.30	.75
Z35 Irving Spikes	.08	.25
Z36 Keith Byars	.05	.15
Z37 Rod Woodson	.08	.25
Z38 Rob Moore	.08	.25
Z39 Scott Mitchell	.08	.25
Z40 Cody Carlson	.05	.15
Z41 Alvin Harper	.05	.15
Z42 Chris Warren	.08	.25
Z43 Ben Coates	.08	.25
Z44 Jim Everett	.05	.15
Z45 Vinny Testaverde	.08	.25
Z46 Glyn Milburn	.05	.15
Z47 Calvin Williams	.08	.25
Z48 Fred Barnett	.08	.25
Z49 Tim Brown	.15	.40
Z50 Lorenzo White	.05	.15
Z51 Brent Jones	.05	.15
Z52 Henry Ellard	.08	.25
Z53 Rick Mirer	.08	.25
Z54 Junior Seau	.15	.40
Z55 Jeff Blake RC	.40	1.00
Z56 Desmond Howard	.08	.25
Z57 Jerry Rice	.50	1.25
Z58 Lewis Tillman	.05	.15
Z59 Roosevelt Potts	.05	.15
Z60 Rocket Ismail	.08	.25
Z61 Eric Hill	.05	.15
Z62 Brett Favre	1.00	2.50
Z63 Haywood Jeffires	.05	.15
Z64 Barry Foster	.08	.25
Z65 Flipper Anderson	.05	.15
Z66 Troy Aikman	.50	1.25
Z67 Herschel Walker	.08	.25
Z68 Sean Dawkins	.08	.25
Z69 Erric Pegram	.08	.25
Z70 Irving Fryar	.08	.25
Z71 Thurman Thomas	.15	.40
Z72 Eric Metcalf	.08	.25
Z73 John Taylor	.05	.15
Z74 Jeff George	.08	.25
Z75 Courtney Hawkins	.05	.15
Z76 Carl Pickens	.08	.25
Z77 Mike Sherrard	.05	.15
Z78 Rodney Hampton	.08	.25
Z79 Joe Montana	1.00	2.50
Z80 Willie Davis	.08	.25
Z81 Chris Penn	.05	.15
Z82 Dave Brown	.08	.25
Z83 Gary Brown	.05	.15
Z84 Andre Reed	.08	.25
Z85 Michael Irvin	.15	.40
Z86 Vincent Brisby	.05	.15
Z87 Barry Sanders	.75	2.00
Z88 Qadry Ismail	.08	.25
Z89 Reggie Brooks	.08	.25
Z90 Bruce Smith	.15	.40
Z91 David Klingler	.08	.25
Z92 Michael Haynes	.08	.25
Z93 Derek Russell	.05	.15
Z94 Steve Young	.40	1.00
Z95 Terry Allen	.08	.25
Z96 Mark Seay	.08	.25
Z97 Dan Marino	1.00	2.50
Z98 Jerry Rice RW	.50	1.25
Z99 Cris Carter RW	.15	.40
Z100 Art Monk RW	.08	.25
Z101 Cortez Kennedy	.08	.25
Z102 Stan Humphries	.08	.25
Z103 Herman Moore	.15	.40
Z104 Ronald Moore	.05	.15
Z105 Greg Lloyd	.08	.25
Z106 Jerome Bettis	.15	.40
Z107 Craig Erickson	.05	.15
Z108 Keith Jackson	.05	.15
Z109 Sterling Sharpe	.08	.25
Z110 Ronnie Harmon	.05	.15
Z111 Deion Sanders	.30	.75
Z112 Charles Haley	.08	.25
Z113 Bernie Parmalee	.08	.25
Z114 Leroy Hoard	.05	.15
Z115 O.J. McDuffie	.15	.40
Z116 Garrison Hearst	.15	.40
Z117 Kevin Greene	.08	.25
Z118 Derek Brown	.05	.15
Z119 Mark Brunell	.30	.75
Z120 Kevin Williams	.08	.25
Z121 Dan Wilkinson	.08	.25
Z122 Chuck Levy	.05	.15
Z123 Derrick Alexander WR	.15	.40
Z124 Aaron Bailey RC	.05	.15
Z125 Thomas Lewis	.08	.25
Z126 Antonio Langham	.05	.15
Z127 Bryan Reeves	.05	.15
Z128 William Floyd	.08	.25
Z129 Lake Dawson	.08	.25
Z130 Bert Emanuel	.15	.40
Z131 Marshall Faulk	.60	1.50
Z132 Heath Shuler	.08	.25
Z133 David Palmer	.08	.25
Z134 Willie McGinest	.08	.25
Z135 Mario Bates	.08	.25
Z136 Byron Bam Morris	.05	.15
Z137 Tim Bowens	.05	.15
Z138 Errict Rhett	.08	.25
Z139 Charlie Garner	.15	.40
Z140 Darnay Scott	.08	.25
Z141 Greg Hill	.08	.25
Z142 LeShon Johnson	.08	.25
Z143 Charles Johnson	.08	.25
Z144 Trent Dilfer	.15	.40
Z145 Gus Frerotte	.08	.25
Z146 Johnnie Morton	.08	.25
Z147 Glenn Foley	.05	.15
Z148 Perry Klein	.05	.15
Z149 Ryan Yarborough	.08	.25
Z150 Tydus Winans	.05	.15

1995 Zenith Rookie Roll Call

This 18 card standard-size set was randomly inserted into packs at a rate of one in 72. These cards, limited to not more than 1,200 of each, feature leading 1994 rookies. The cards are numbered with a "RC" prefix.

COMPLETE SET (18)	40.00	100.00
STATED ODDS 1:72		
RC1 Marshall Faulk	12.00	30.00
RC2 Charlie Garner	3.00	8.00
RC3 Derrick Alexander WR	3.00	8.00
RC4 Heath Shuler	3.00	8.00
RC5 Glenn Foley	2.00	5.00
RC6 Trent Dilfer	5.00	12.00
RC7 David Palmer	2.50	6.00
RC8 Gus Frerotte	2.50	6.00
RC9 Byron Bam Morris	2.50	6.00
RC10 Mario Bates	2.50	6.00
RC11 Greg Hill	2.50	6.00
RC12 Errict Rhett	3.00	8.00
RC13 Darnay Scott	3.00	8.00
RC14 Lake Dawson	2.00	5.00
RC15 Bert Emanuel	2.50	6.00
RC16 LeShon Johnson	2.50	6.00
RC17 William Floyd	3.00	8.00
RC18 Charles Johnson	2.50	6.00

1995 Zenith Second Season

This 25 card standard-size set was randomly inserted into packs at a rate of one in six. The set is sequenced in playoff game order.

COMPLETE SET (25)	12.50	30.00
STATED ODDS 1:6		
SS1 Brett Favre	1.50	4.00
SS2 Dan Marino	1.50	4.00
SS3 Marcus Allen	.25	.60
SS4 Joe Montana	1.50	4.00
SS5 Vinny Testaverde	.15	.40
SS6 Emmitt Smith	1.25	3.00
SS7 Troy Aikman	.75	2.00
SS8 Steve Young	.60	1.50
SS9 William Floyd	.15	.40
SS10 Yancey Thigpen	.25	.60
SS11 Barry Foster	.15	.40
SS12 Natrone Means	.15	.40
SS13 Mark Seay	.15	.40
SS14 Stan Humphries	.15	.40
SS15 Tony Martin	.25	.60
SS16 Jerry Rice	.75	2.00
SS17 Deion Sanders	.50	1.25
SS18 Steve Young	.60	1.50
SS19 Steve Young	.60	1.50
SS20 Emmitt Smith	1.25	3.00
SS21 Troy Aikman	.75	2.00
SS22 Jerry Rice	.75	2.00
SS23 Ricky Watters	.15	.40
SS24 Steve Young	.60	1.50
SS25 Jerry Rice S.Young	.75	2.00

1995 Zenith Z-Team

This 18 card standard-size set was randomly inserted into packs at a rate of one in 24 and features star offensive players. Cards are numbered with a "ZT" prefix.

COMPLETE SET (18)	50.00	100.00
STATED ODDS 1:24		
ZT1 Dan Marino	8.00	20.00
ZT2 Troy Aikman	4.00	10.00
ZT3 Emmitt Smith	6.00	15.00
ZT4 Barry Sanders	6.00	15.00
ZT5 Joe Montana	8.00	20.00
ZT6 Jerry Rice	5.00	12.00
ZT7 John Elway	8.00	20.00
ZT8 Marshall Faulk	4.00	10.00
ZT9 Brett Favre	8.00	20.00
ZT10 Steve Young	3.00	8.00
ZT11 Sterling Sharpe	3.00	8.00
ZT12 Drew Bledsoe	2.00	5.00
ZT13 Ricky Watters	1.25	3.00
ZT14 Cris Carter	2.00	5.00
ZT15 Warren Moon	1.25	3.00
ZT16 Natrone Means	1.00	2.50
ZT17 Michael Irvin	2.00	5.00
ZT18 Chris Warren	1.00	2.50

1996 Zenith Promos

This four-card set was issued by Pinnacle to preview its 1996 Zenith release. The cards are identical to their regular issue and Z-Team issue counterparts, except for the word "Promo" printed on the back of the card.

COMPLETE SET (4)	15.00	30.00
4 Emmitt Smith Z-Team	6.00	15.00
32 Jerry Rice	3.00	8.00
36 John Elway	4.00	10.00
NNO Title Card	.10	.30

1996 Zenith

The 1996 Zenith set was issued in one series totaling 150 standard-size cards. This was the second year Pinnacle Brands used the Zenith line to produce a high end football set during the off-season. The six card packs had a suggested retail price of $2.59 each. They were issued in 16 box cases with 24 packs in each box. Topical subsets in the set include 1995 Rookies (97-131), Proof Positive (132-146) and Checklist Cards (148-150). The Dallas Cowboy Triplets: Troy Aikman, Michael Irvin and Emmitt Smith are featured on card #147. There are no key Rookie Cards in this set.

COMPLETE SET (150)	10.00	25.00
1 Dan Marino	1.25	3.00
2 Yancey Thigpen	.08	.25
3 Marcus Allen	.20	.50
4 Curtis Conway	.20	.50
5 Troy Aikman	.60	1.50
6 William Floyd	.08	.25
7 Ricky Watters	.08	.25
8 Herman Moore	.08	.25
9 Jim Harbaugh	.08	.25
10 Isaac Bruce	.20	.50
11 Drew Bledsoe	.40	1.00
12 Jeff Blake	.20	.50
13 Tim Brown	.20	.50
14 Deion Sanders	.40	1.00
15 Greg Hill	.08	.25
16 Ben Coates	.08	.25
17 Errict Rhett	.08	.25
18 Barry Sanders	1.00	2.50
19 Erik Kramer	.02	.10
20 Emmitt Smith	1.00	2.50
21 Brett Favre	1.25	3.00
22 Jerome Bettis	.20	.50
23 Garrison Hearst	.08	.25
24 Michael Irvin	.20	.50
25 Chris Warren	.08	.25
26 Steve Young	.50	1.25
27 Cris Carter	.20	.50
28 Carl Pickens	.08	.25
29 Lake Dawson	.02	.10
30 Marshall Faulk	.25	.60
31 Vincent Brisby	.02	.10
32 Jerry Rice	.60	1.50
33 Eric Metcalf	.02	.10
34 Natrone Means	.08	.25
35 Steve Bono	.02	.10
36 John Elway	1.25	3.00
37 Jeff Hostetler	.02	.10
38 Scott Mitchell	.08	.25
39 Andre Rison	.08	.25
40 Daryl Johnston	.08	.25
41 Mark Brunell	.40	1.00
42 Jeff George	.08	.25
43 Mario Bates	.08	.25
44 Erric Pegram	.02	.10
45 Brent Jones	.02	.10
46 Trent Dilfer	.20	.50
47 Larry Centers	.08	.25
48 Anthony Miller	.08	.25
49 Reggie White	.20	.50
50 Bill Brooks	.02	.10
51 Chris Zorich	.02	.10
52 Jim Kelly	.20	.50
53 Junior Seau	.20	.50
54 Chris Miller	.02	.10
55 Gus Frerotte	.08	.25
56 Andre Reed	.08	.25
57 Darnay Scott	.08	.25
58 Brett Perriman	.02	.10
59 Edgar Bennett	.08	.25
60 Warren Moon	.08	.25
61 Neil O'Donnell	.08	.25
62 Jay Novacek	.02	.10
63 Byron Bam Morris	.02	.10
64 Jim Everett	.02	.10
65 Ken Norton, Jr.	.02	.10
66 Tony Martin	.08	.25
67 Steve Atwater	.02	.10
68 Henry Ellard	.02	.10
69 Rodney Hampton	.08	.25
70 Derrick Thomas	.20	.50
71 Stan Humphries	.08	.25
72 Harvey Williams	.02	.10
73 Greg Lloyd	.08	.25
74 Jake Reed	.08	.25
75 Charles Haley	.08	.25
76 Quinn Early	.02	.10
77 Rodney Peete	.02	.10
78 Brian Blades	.02	.10
79 Robert Brooks	.20	.50
80 Terry Allen	.08	.25
81 Dave Brown	.02	.10
82 Derrick Alexander WR	.08	.25
83 Terance Mathis	.02	.10
84 Rick Mirer	.08	.25
85 Herschel Walker	.08	.25
86 Charlie Garner	.08	.25
87 Jeff Graham	.02	.10
88 Bruce Smith	.08	.25
89 Terry Kirby	.08	.25
90 Craig Heyward	.02	.10
91 Bernie Parmalee	.02	.10
92 Adrian Murrell	.08	.25
93 Derek Loville	.02	.10
94 Heath Shuler	.08	.25
95 Shannon Sharpe	.08	.25
96 Bert Emanuel	.08	.25
97 Hugh Douglas	.08	.25
98 Lovell Pinkney	.02	.10
99 Sherman Williams	.02	.10
100 Tony Boselli	.02	.10
101 Wayne Chrebet	.20	.50
102 Orlando Thomas	.02	.10
103 Darick Holmes	.02	.10
104 Tyrone Wheatley	.08	.25
105 Christian Fauria	.02	.10
106 Frank Sanders	.08	.25
107 Chad May	.02	.10
108 James O. Stewart	.08	.25
109 Ken Dilger	.08	.25
110 Kyle Brady	.02	.10
111 Todd Collins	.08	.25
112 Terrell Fletcher	.02	.10
113 Eric Bjornson	.02	.10
114 Justin Armour	.02	.10
115 Rob Johnson	.20	.50
116 Terrell Davis	.40	1.00
117 J.J. Stokes	.20	.50
118 Rashaan Salaam	.08	.25
119 Chris Sanders	.08	.25
120 Kerry Collins	.20	.50
121 Michael Westbrook	.20	.50
122 Eric Zeier	.02	.10
123 Curtis Martin	.40	1.00
124 Rodney Thomas	.02	.10
125 Kordell Stewart	.20	.50
126 Joey Galloway	.20	.50
127 Steve McNair	.40	1.00
128 Napoleon Kaufman	.20	.50
129 Tamarick Vanover	.08	.25
130 Stoney Case	.02	.10
131 James A. Stewart	.02	.10
132 Carl Pickens PP	.08	.25
133 Jim Harbaugh PP	.08	.25
134 Yancey Thigpen PP	.08	.25
135 Ricky Watters PP	.08	.25
136 Isaac Bruce PP	.20	.50
137 Kordell Stewart PP	.20	.50
138 Jeff Blake PP	.08	.25
139 Terrell Davis PP	.20	.50
140 Scott Mitchell PP	.02	.10
141 Rodney Thomas PP	.02	.10
142 Robert Brooks PP	.20	.50
143 Joey Galloway PP	.20	.50
144 Brett Favre PP	.60	1.50
145 Kerry Collins PP	.20	.50
146 Herman Moore PP	.08	.25
147 E.Smith Aikman Irvin	.60	1.50
148 Dan Marino CL	.20	.50
149 Jerry Rice CL	.20	.50
150 Emmitt Smith CL	.20	.50

1996 Zenith Artist's Proofs

COMPLETE SET (150)	200.00	400.00
*ARTIST PROOFS: 3X TO 8X BASIC CARDS		
STATED ODDS 1:23		

1996 Zenith Noteworthy '95

Randomly inserted in packs at a rate of one in 12, this 18-card set focuses on noteworthy accomplishments of players during the 1995 season. The fronts have two player photos on a foil background as well as the identification of the feat. The cards are numbered "X" of 18.

COMPLETE SET (18)	15.00	40.00
STATED ODDS: 1:12		
1 Dan Marino	3.00	8.00
2 Jerry Rice	1.50	4.00
3 Michael Irvin	.50	1.25
4 Emmitt Smith	2.50	6.00
5 Emmitt Smith Irvin	2.50	6.00
6 Herman Moore	.25	.60
7 Brett Favre	3.00	8.00
8 Barry Sanders	2.50	6.00
9 Marcus Allen	.50	1.25
10 Steve Young	1.25	3.00
11 John Elway	3.00	8.00
12 Warren Moon	.25	.60
13 Jim Kelly	.50	1.25
14 Jim Everett	.08	.25
15 Charles Haley	.25	.60
16 Emmitt Smith	2.50	6.00
17 Troy Aikman	1.50	4.00
18 Larry Brown	.08	.25

1996 Zenith Rookie Rising

Randomly inserted in packs at a rate of one in 24, this 18-card set focuses on the top rookies of the 1995 season. The cards feature 3D printing with each side utilizing the dufex technology. The horizontal backs are numbered as "X" of 18.

COMPLETE SET (18)	20.00	40.00
STATED ODDS: 1:24		
1 Sherman Williams	.30	.75
2 Curtis Martin	3.00	8.00
3 Michael Westbrook	1.50	4.00
4 Darick Holmes	.30	.75
5 James O.Stewart	.75	2.00
6 Eric Zeier	.30	.75
7 Tamarick Vanover	.75	2.00
8 J.J. Stokes	1.50	4.00
9 Kordell Stewart	1.50	4.00
10 Rodney Thomas	.30	.75
11 Kerry Collins	1.50	4.00
12 Terrell Davis	3.00	8.00
13 Steve McNair	3.00	8.00
14 Rashaan Salaam	.75	2.00
15 Joey Galloway	1.50	4.00
16 Wayne Chrebet	1.50	4.00
17 Chris Sanders	.75	2.00
18 Frank Sanders	.75	2.00

1996 Zenith Z-Team

Randomly inserted in packs at a rate of one in 72, this 18-card set consists of the best players in the NFL during the 1995 season. The printing technology used for these sets was gold-foil stamped SpectroView printing. The cards are numbered as "X" of 18.

COMPLETE SET (18)	50.00	120.00
STATED ODDS: 1:72		
1 Troy Aikman	4.00	10.00
2 Drew Bledsoe	2.50	6.00
3 Errict Rhett	.60	1.50
4 Emmitt Smith	6.00	15.00
5 Jerry Rice	4.00	10.00
6 Cris Carter	1.25	3.00
7 Curtis Martin	2.50	6.00
8 Deion Sanders	2.50	6.00
9 Brett Favre	8.00	20.00
10 Michael Irvin	1.25	3.00
11 Chris Warren	.60	1.50
12 Dan Marino	8.00	20.00
13 Steve Young	3.00	8.00
14 Marshall Faulk	1.50	4.00
15 Barry Sanders	6.00	15.00
16 John Elway	8.00	20.00
17 Isaac Bruce	1.25	3.00
18 Carl Pickens	.60	1.50

1997 Zenith

The 1997 Zenith set was issued in one series totaling 150 cards and was distributed in six-card packs with a suggested retail of $3.99. The fronts feature color player photos printed on 24 point card stock. The backs carry player information.

COMPLETE SET (150)	8.00	20.00
1 Brett Favre	1.25	3.00
2 Jerry Rice	.60	1.50
3 Shannon Sharpe	.20	.50
4 Dan Marino	1.25	3.00
5 James O.Stewart	.20	.50
6 Warren Moon	.30	.75
7 Emmitt Smith	1.00	2.50
8 Kordell Stewart	.30	.75
9 Kerry Collins	.30	.75
10 Ricky Watters	.20	.50
11 Gus Frerotte	.10	.30
12 Barry Sanders	1.00	2.50
13 Joey Galloway	.20	.50
14 Marshall Faulk	.40	1.00
15 Todd Collins	.10	.30
16 Steve McNair	.40	1.00
17 Tyrone Wheatley	.20	.50
18 Isaac Bruce	.30	.75
19 Troy Aikman	.60	1.50
20 Larry Centers	.20	.50
21 Alvin Harper	.10	.30
22 Rashaan Salaam	.10	.30
23 Eric Metcalf	.20	.50
24 Jim Everett	.10	.30
25 Ken Dilger	.10	.30
26 Curtis Martin	.40	1.00
27 Neil O'Donnell	.20	.50
28 Thurman Thomas	.30	.75
29 Andre Rison	.20	.50
30 Steve Bono	.20	.50
31 Garrison Hearst	.20	.50
32 Junior Seau	.30	.75
33 Napoleon Kaufman	.30	.75
34 Jerome Bettis	.30	.75
35 Frank Wycheck	.10	.30
36 Lamar Smith	.30	.75
37 Derrick Alexander WR	.20	.50
38 Steve Young	.40	1.00
39 Cris Carter	.30	.75
40 O.J. McDuffie	.20	.50
41 Deion Sanders	.30	.75
42 Robert Brooks	.20	.50
43 Jeff Blake	.20	.50
44 Marcus Allen	.30	.75
45 Herman Moore	.20	.50
46 Ray Zellars	.10	.30
47 Tim Brown	.30	.75
48 John Elway	1.25	3.00
49 Charles Johnson	.20	.50
50 Rodney Peete	.10	.30
51 Curtis Conway	.20	.50
52 Kevin Greene	.20	.50
53 Andre Reed	.20	.50
54 Mark Brunell	.40	1.00
55 Tony Martin	.20	.50
56 Elvis Grbac	.20	.50
57 Wayne Chrebet	.30	.75
58 Vinny Testaverde	.20	.50
59 Terry Allen	.30	.75
60 Dave Brown	.10	.30
61 LeShon Johnson	.10	.30
62 Trent Dilfer	.30	.75
63 Chris Warren	.20	.50
64 Chris Sanders	.10	.30
65 Kevin Carter	.10	.30
66 Jim Harbaugh	.20	.50
67 Terance Mathis	.20	.50
68 Ben Coates	.20	.50
69 Robert Smith	.20	.50
70 Drew Bledsoe	.40	1.00
71 Henry Ellard	.10	.30
72 Scott Mitchell	.20	.50
73 Andre Hastings	.10	.30
74 Rodney Hampton	.20	.50
75 Michael Jackson	.20	.50
76 Jeff Hostetler	.10	.30
77 Reggie White	.30	.75
78 Desmond Howard	.20	.50
79 Adrian Murrell	.20	.50
80 Carl Pickens	.20	.50
81 Erik Kramer	.10	.30
82 Terrell Davis	.40	1.00
83 Sean Dawkins	.10	.30
84 Jamal Anderson	.30	.75
85 Stan Humphries	.20	.50
86 Chris T. Jones	.10	.30
87 Hardy Nickerson	.10	.30
88 Anthony Johnson	.10	.30
89 Michael Haynes	.10	.30
90 Irving Spikes	.10	.30
91 Bruce Smith	.20	.50
92 Keenan McCardell	.20	.50
93 Chris Chandler	.20	.50
94 Tamarick Vanover	.20	.50
95 Dorsey Levens	.30	.75
96 Roman Phifer	.10	.30
97 Michael Irvin	.30	.75
98 Tim Biakabutuka	.20	.50
99 Stepfret Williams	.10	.30
100 Eddie George	.30	.75
101 Karim Abdul-Jabbar	.30	.75
102 Amani Toomer	.20	.50
103 Tony Banks	.20	.50
104 Regan Upshaw	.10	.30
105 Leeland McElroy	.10	.30
106 Jason Dunn	.10	.30
107 Keyshawn Johnson	.30	.75
108 Winslow Oliver	.10	.30
109 Walt Harris	.10	.30
110 Stanley Pritchett	.10	.30
111 Eddie Kennison	.20	.50
112 Terrell Owens	.40	1.00
113 Duane Clemons	.10	.30
114 John Mobley	.10	.30
115 Simeon Rice	.20	.50
116 Tony Brackens	.10	.30
117 Eric Moulds	.30	.75
118 Marvin Harrison	.30	.75
119 Rickey Dudley	.20	.50
120 Mike Alstott	.30	.75
121 Terry Glenn	.30	.75
122 Brian Dawkins	.30	.75
123 Kevin Hardy	.10	.30
124 Bobby Engram	.20	.50
125 Alex Van Dyke	.10	.30
126 Zach Thomas	.30	.75
127 Bryan Still	.10	.30
128 Detron Smith	.10	.30
129 Jerome Woods	.10	.30
130 Muhsin Muhammad	.20	.50
131 Lawrence Phillips	.10	.30
132 Alex Molden	.10	.30
133 Steve Young SH	.10	.30
134 Troy Aikman SH	.30	.75
135 Junior Seau SH	.10	.30
136 John Elway SH	.60	1.50
137 Dan Marino SH	.60	1.50
138 Desmond Howard SH	.20	.50
139 Brett Favre SH	.60	1.50
140 Jerry Rice SH	.30	.75
141 Kerry Collins SH	.20	.50
142 Barry Sanders SH	.50	1.25
143 Mark Brunell SH	.30	.75
144 Drew Bledsoe SH	.30	.75
145 Eddie Kennison SH	.20	.50
146 Marvin Harrison SH	.30	.75
147 Emmitt Smith SH	.50	1.25
148 E.George Glenn Dudl Hoy.	.30	.75
149 Emmitt Smith CL	.30	.75
150 Dan Marino CL	.30	.75

1997 Zenith Artist's Proofs

COMPLETE SET (150)	75.00	200.00
*SINGLES: 2.5X TO 6X BASIC CARDS		
AP STATED ODDS 1:47		

1997 Zenith Rookie Rising

Randomly inserted in packs at a rate of one in 11, this 24-card set features color player photos of potential future young stars with all-foil Dufex printing.

COMPLETE SET (24)	20.00	50.00
STATED ODDS 1:11		
1 Eddie Kennison	1.00	2.50
2 Marvin Harrison	4.00	10.00
3 Keyshawn Johnson	3.00	8.00
4 Leeland McElroy	.60	1.50
5 Terrell Owens	4.00	10.00
6 Terry Glenn	2.50	6.00
7 Bobby Engram	.60	1.50
8 Karim Abdul-Jabbar	1.00	2.50
9 Lawrence Phillips	.60	1.50
10 Amani Toomer	1.50	4.00
11 Eric Moulds	3.00	8.00
12 Jason Dunn	.60	1.50
13 Stanley Pritchett	.60	1.50
14 Eddie George	2.50	6.00
15 Muhsin Muhammad	2.00	5.00
16 Rickey Dudley	1.50	4.00
17 Tony Banks	1.50	4.00
18 Bryan Still	.60	1.50
19 Tim Biakabutuka	1.50	4.00
20 Simeon Rice	1.00	2.50
21 Zach Thomas	2.00	5.00
22 Kevin Hardy	.60	1.50
23 Jerris McPhail	.60	1.50
24 Mike Alstott	2.50	6.00

1997 Zenith V2

Randomly inserted in packs at a rate of one in 23, this multi-phase animated set captures the achievements of 18 modern day legends in full motion lenticular technology with strip foil stamping. Each card delivers up to two seconds of actual game film footage.

COMPLETE SET (18)	100.00	200.00
STATED ODDS 1:18		
V1 Troy Aikman	5.00	12.00
V2 John Elway	10.00	25.00
V3 Jim Harbaugh	1.50	4.00
V4 Barry Sanders	8.00	20.00
V5 Deion Sanders	2.50	6.00
V6 Drew Bledsoe	3.00	8.00
V7 Dan Marino	10.00	25.00
V8 Terrell Davis	3.00	8.00
V9 Isaac Bruce	2.50	6.00
V10 Jerome Bettis	2.50	6.00
V11 Emmitt Smith	8.00	20.00
V12 Brett Favre	10.00	25.00
V13 Steve Young	3.00	8.00
V14 Mark Brunell	3.00	8.00
V15 Joey Galloway	1.50	4.00
V16 Kordell Stewart	2.50	6.00
V17 Jerry Rice	5.00	12.00
V18 Curtis Martin	3.00	8.00

1997 Zenith Z-Team Promos

This set of Promo cards was produced to promote the 1997 Zenith release. The cards are essentially parallels of the base insert set except for the word "Promo" clearly printed on the cardbacks. A Mirror Gold version of each Promo was also produced. We've added the "M" card number suffix below to the Mirrors to help with cataloging.

COMPLETE SET (6)	16.00	40.00
ZT2 Dan Marino	2.00	5.00
ZT2M Dan Marino	4.00	10.00
ZT11 Brett Favre	2.00	5.00
ZT11M Brett Favre	4.00	10.00
ZT14 Barry Sanders	2.00	5.00
ZT14M Barry Sanders	4.00	10.00

1997 Zenith Z-Team

Randomly inserted in packs at a rate of one in 71, this 18-card set features color player photos of some of the NFL's top stars printed with mirror mylar micro-etched technology. At least three promo cards with corresponding Mirror Gold versions were produced to promote this insert set.

COMPLETE SET (18)	125.00	250.00
STATED ODDS 1:71		
*MIRROR GOLDS: .6X TO 1.5X BASIC INS.		
MIRROR GOLD STATED ODDS 1:191		
ZT1 Emmitt Smith	10.00	25.00
ZT2 Dan Marino	12.50	30.00
ZT3 Jerry Rice	6.00	15.00
ZT4 John Elway	12.50	30.00
ZT5 Curtis Martin	4.00	10.00
ZT6 Deion Sanders	3.00	8.00
ZT7 Tony Banks	2.00	5.00
ZT8 Jim Harbaugh	2.00	5.00
ZT9 Joey Galloway	2.00	5.00
ZT10 Troy Aikman	6.00	15.00
ZT11 Brett Favre	12.50	30.00
ZT12 Keyshawn Johnson	3.00	8.00
ZT13 Eddie George	3.00	8.00
ZT14 Barry Sanders	10.00	25.00
ZT15 Kordell Stewart	3.00	8.00
ZT16 Steve Young	4.00	10.00
ZT17 Terrell Davis	4.00	10.00
ZT18 Drew Bledsoe	4.00	10.00

1998 Zenith Dare to Tear Promos

Z1 Brett Favre	3.00	8.00
Z2 John Elway	2.50	6.00
Z5 Kordell Stewart	.75	2.00
Z8 Mark Brunell	1.00	2.50
Z20 Barry Sanders	2.50	6.00
Z21 Dan Marino	3.00	8.00
Z22 Drew Bledsoe	1.00	2.50
Z35 Steve Young	1.25	3.00
Z45 Emmitt Smith	2.50	6.00

2005 Zenith

This 181-card set was released in November, 2005. The set was issued in five-card packs with an $5 SRP which came 18 packs to a box. Cards numbered 1-100 feature veterans in team alphabetical order while cards 101-181 are all rookies. There are two distinct groupings of rookies, both of which are basically sequenced in first name alphabetical order. Cards numbered 1-150 are unsigned while cards 151-181 are all autographed. Please note that the unsigned Rookie Cards are nearly identical to the Museum Collection parallel cards with the Museum cards also being serial numberied to 999. The Rookie Cards also have the word "Rookie" printed repeatedly in the background of the photo on the cardfronts.

COMP.SET w/o RCs (100)	10.00	25.00
ROOKIE/999 STATED ODDS 1:24 RETAIL		
150-181 AU PRINT RUN 99 SER.#'d SETS		
1 Larry Fitzgerald	.30	.75

2 Anquan Boldin .20 .50
3 Kurt Warner .25 .60
4 Alge Crumpler .25 .60
5 Michael Vick .25 .60
6 Warrick Dunn .20 .50
7 Jamal Lewis .25 .60
8 Kyle Boller .20 .50
9 Derrick Mason .20 .50
10 Ray Lewis .30 .75
11 Willis McGahee .20 .50
12 J.P. Losman .20 .50
13 Lee Evans .25 .60
14 Eric Moulds .20 .50
15 Jake Delhomme .20 .50
16 Steve Smith .30 .75
17 DeShaun Foster .25 .60
18 Rex Grossman .20 .50
19 Muhsin Muhammad .20 .50
20 Brian Urlacher .30 .75
21 Carson Palmer .25 .60
22 Chad Johnson .20 .50
23 Rudi Johnson .20 .50
24 Lee Suggs .20 .50
25 Reuben Droughns .20 .50
26 Trent Dilfer .20 .50
27 Drew Bledsoe .25 .60
28 Julius Jones .20 .50
29 Keyshawn Johnson .25 .60
30 Roy Williams S .20 .50
31 Ashley Lelie .20 .50
32 Jake Plummer .20 .50
33 Tatum Bell .20 .50
34 Joey Harrington .20 .50
35 Roy Williams WR .20 .50
36 Kevin Jones .20 .50
37 Ahman Green .25 .60
38 Brett Favre .60 1.50
39 Javon Walker .20 .50
40 David Carr .20 .50
41 Domanick Davis .20 .50
42 Andre Johnson .25 .60
43 Marvin Harrison .25 .60
44 Edgerrin James .25 .60
45 Peyton Manning .75 2.00
46 Fred Taylor .20 .50
47 Byron Leftwich .20 .50
48 Jimmy Smith .25 .60
49 Priest Holmes .20 .50
50 Trent Green .20 .50
51 Tony Gonzalez .25 .60
52 Chris Chambers .20 .50
53 A.J. Feeley .20 .50
54 Daunte Culpepper .25 .60
55 Michael Bennett .20 .50
56 Nate Burleson .20 .50
57 Tom Brady 1.25 3.00
58 Deion Branch .20 .50
59 Tedy Bruschi .25 .60
60 Corey Dillon .20 .50
61 Aaron Brooks .20 .50
62 Deuce McAllister .25 .60
63 Joe Horn .20 .50
64 Eli Manning .50 1.25
65 Tiki Barber .25 .60
66 Plaxico Burress .20 .50
67 Jeremy Shockey .20 .50
68 Chad Pennington .20 .50
69 Curtis Martin .25 .60
70 Laveranues Coles .20 .50
71 Kerry Collins .20 .50
72 LaMont Jordan .25 .60
73 Randy Moss .25 .60
74 Brian Westbrook .20 .50
75 Terrell Owens .25 .60
76 Donovan McNabb .25 .60
77 Ben Roethlisberger .50 1.25
78 Duce Staley .20 .50
79 Jerome Bettis .30 .75
80 Hines Ward .25 .60
81 Drew Brees .30 .75
82 Antonio Gates .30 .75
83 LaDainian Tomlinson .30 .75
84 Kevan Barlow .20 .50
85 Brandon Lloyd .20 .50
86 Matt Hasselbeck .20 .50
87 Shaun Alexander .20 .50
88 Darrell Jackson .20 .50
89 Torry Holt .25 .60
90 Marc Bulger .20 .50
91 Steven Jackson .20 .50
92 Brian Griese .20 .50
93 Michael Clayton .20 .50
94 Steve McNair .25 .60
95 Chris Brown .20 .50
96 Drew Bennett .25 .60
97 Patrick Ramsey .25 .60
98 Clinton Portis .20 .50
99 Santana Moss .25 .60
100 LaVar Arrington .20 .50
101 Adrian McPherson RC 1.00 2.50
102 Airese Currie RC 1.00 2.50
103 Alvin Pearman RC 1.00 2.50
104 Anthony Davis RC 1.00 2.50
105 Brandon Jacobs RC 1.25 3.00
106 Brandon Jones RC 1.25 3.00
107 Bryant McFadden RC 1.25 3.00
108 Cedric Houston RC 1.50 4.00
109 Chad Owens RC 1.00 2.50
110 Chris Henry RC 1.25 3.00
111 Craig Bragg RC 1.00 2.50
112 Craphonso Thorpe RC 1.00 2.50
113 Damien Nash RC 1.25 3.00
114 Dan Cody RC 1.00 2.50
115 Dan Orlovsky RC 1.00 2.50
116 Dante Ridgeway RC 1.00 2.50
117 Darren Sproles RC 1.50 4.00
118 David Greene RC 1.00 2.50
119 David Pollack RC 1.00 2.50
120 Deandra Cobb RC 1.00 2.50
121 DeMarcus Ware RC 3.00 8.00
122 Derek Anderson RC 1.25 3.00
123 Derrick Johnson RC 1.25 3.00
124 Erasmus James RC 1.00 2.50
125 Fabian Washington RC 1.00 2.50
126 Fred Gibson RC 1.00 2.50
127 Harry Williams RC 1.25 3.00
128 Heath Miller RC 2.00 5.00
129 J.R. Russell RC 1.00 2.50
130 James Kilian RC 1.00 2.50
131 Jerome Mathis RC 1.50 4.00
132 Larry Brackins RC 1.00 2.50
133 LeRon McCoy RC 1.00 2.50
134 Lionel Gates RC 1.00 2.50
135 Marcus Maxwell RC 1.00 2.50
136 Marcus Spears RC 1.00 2.50
137 Marion Barber RC 1.00 2.50
138 Marlin Jackson RC 1.00 2.50
139 Matt Cassel RC 1.00 2.50
140 Matt Roth RC 1.00 2.50
141 Mike Williams 1.25 3.00
142 Noah Herron RC 1.00 2.50
143 Paris Warren RC 1.25 3.00
144 Rasheed Marshall RC 1.25 3.00
145 Roydell Williams RC 1.25 3.00
146 Ryan Fitzpatrick RC 1.50 4.00
147 Shaun Cody RC 1.25 3.00
148 Shawne Merriman RC 1.50 4.00
149 Tab Perry RC 1.00 2.50
150 Thomas Davis RC 1.00 2.50
151 Adam Jones AU RC 8.00 20.00
152 Alex Smith QB AU RC 25.00 60.00
153 Antrel Rolle AU RC 12.00 30.00
154 Andrew Walter AU RC 8.00 20.00
155 Braylon Edwards AU RC 8.00 20.00
156 Cadillac Williams AU RC 8.00 20.00
157 Carlos Rogers AU RC 12.00 30.00
158 Charlie Frye AU RC 8.00 20.00
159 Ciatrick Fason AU RC 8.00 20.00
160 Courtney Roby AU RC 8.00 20.00
161 Eric Shelton AU RC 8.00 20.00
162 Frank Gore AU RC 25.00 60.00
163 J.J. Arrington AU RC 10.00 25.00
164 Kyle Orton AU RC 15.00 40.00
165 Jason Campbell AU RC 8.00 20.00
166 Mark Bradley AU RC 8.00 20.00
167 Mark Clayton AU RC 8.00 20.00
168 Matt Jones AU RC 8.00 20.00
169 Maurice Clarett AU 8.00 20.00
170 Reggie Brown AU RC 8.00 20.00
171 Ronnie Brown AU RC 10.00 25.00
172 Roddy White AU RC 12.00 30.00
173 Ryan Moats AU RC 8.00 20.00
174 Roscoe Parrish AU RC 8.00 20.00
175 Stefan LeFors AU RC 8.00 20.00
176 Terrence Murphy AU RC 8.00 20.00
177 Troy Williamson AU RC 8.00 20.00
178 Vernand Morency AU RC 8.00 20.00
179 Vincent Jackson AU RC 12.00 30.00
180 Aaron Rodgers AU RC 250.00 400.00
181 Cedric Benson AU RC 8.00 20.00

2005 Zenith Artist's Proofs

*VETERANS: 2X TO 5X BASIC CARDS
*ROOKIES: .5X TO 1.2X BASIC CARDS
STATED ODDS 1:18 HOB, 1:48 RET

2005 Zenith Artist's Proofs Gold

*VETERANS 1-100: 6X TO 15X BASIC CARDS
1-100 VET PRINT RUN 50 SER.#'d SETS
*ROOKIES 101-150: 1.5X TO 4X BASIC CARDS
101-150 ROOKIE PRINT RUN 25 SER.#'d SETS
OVERALL STATED ODDS 1:70 HOBBY

2005 Zenith Museum Collection

*VETERANS: 1.2X TO 3X BASIC CARDS
*ROOKIES: .4X TO 1X BASIC CARDS
STATED ODDS 1:4 HOB, 1:24 RET

2005 Zenith Z-Gold

*VETERANS: 2X TO 5X BASIC CARDS
STATED ODDS 1:12 RETAIL

2005 Zenith Z-Silver

*VETERANS: 1.2X TO 3X BASIC CARDS
STATED ODDS 1:3 RETAIL

2005 Zenith Z-Titanium

*VETERANS: 3X TO 8X BASIC CARDS
STATED PRINT RUN 99 SER.#'d SETS

2005 Zenith Aerial Assault Silver

STATED ODDS 1:18 HOB, 1:24 RET
*GOLD: 1.2X TO 3X BASIC INSERTS
GOLD PRINT RUN 100 SER.#'d SETS
AA1 Aaron Brooks .60 1.50
AA2 Ben Roethlisberger 1.50 4.00
AA3 Brett Favre 2.00 5.00
AA4 Byron Leftwich .60 1.50
AA5 Carson Palmer .75 2.00
AA6 Chad Pennington .60 1.50
AA7 David Carr .60 1.50
AA8 J.P. Losman .60 1.50
AA9 Jake Plummer .60 1.50
AA10 Kyle Boller .60 1.50
AA11 Michael Vick .75 2.00
AA12 Peyton Manning 2.50 6.00
AA13 Rex Grossman .60 1.50
AA14 Eli Manning 1.50 4.00
AA15 Drew Brees 1.00 2.50
AA16 Drew Bledsoe .75 2.00
AA17 Jake Delhomme .60 1.50
AA18 Joey Harrington .60 1.50
AA19 Daunte Culpepper .75 2.00
AA20 Donovan McNabb .75 2.00
AA21 Matt Hasselbeck .60 1.50
AA22 Marc Bulger .60 1.50
AA23 Steve McNair .75 2.00
AA24 Trent Green .60 1.50
AA25 Tom Brady 4.00 10.00

2005 Zenith Aerial Assault Jerseys

STATED PRINT RUN 250 SER.#'d SETS
*PRIME: .8X TO 2X BASIC JERSEYS
PRIME PRINT RUN 25 SER.#'d SETS
AA1 Aaron Brooks 3.00 8.00
AA2 Ben Roethlisberger 10.00 25.00
AA3 Brett Favre 10.00 25.00
AA4 Byron Leftwich 4.00 10.00
AA5 Carson Palmer 4.00 10.00
AA6 Chad Pennington 4.00 10.00
AA7 David Carr 4.00 10.00
AA8 J.P. Losman 4.00 10.00
AA9 Jake Plummer 3.00 8.00
AA10 Kyle Boller 3.00 8.00
AA11 Michael Vick 6.00 15.00
AA12 Peyton Manning 7.50 20.00
AA13 Rex Grossman 3.00 8.00
AA14 Eli Manning 10.00 25.00
AA15 Drew Brees 4.00 10.00
AA16 Drew Bledsoe 4.00 10.00
AA17 Jake Delhomme 4.00 10.00
AA18 Joey Harrington 4.00 10.00
AA19 Daunte Culpepper 4.00 10.00
AA20 Donovan McNabb 5.00 12.00
AA21 Matt Hasselbeck 3.00 8.00
AA22 Marc Bulger 4.00 10.00
AA23 Steve McNair 4.00 10.00
AA24 Trent Green 3.00 8.00
AA25 Tom Brady 7.50 20.00

2005 Zenith Autumn Warriors Silver

STATED ODDS 1:18 HOB, 1:24 RET
*GOLD: .8X TO 2X BASIC INSERTS
GOLD PRINT RUN 100 SER.#'d SETS
AW1 Roeth./Pennington 3.00 8.00
AW2 W.Payton/B.Sanders 5.00 12.00
AW3 M.Allen/B.Jackson 2.00 5.00
AW4 R.Lewis/B.Urlacher 1.25 3.00
AW5 B.Favre/D.Carr 3.00 8.00
AW6 C.Dillon/C.Portis 1.25 3.00
AW7 D.McNabb/D.Culpepper 1.25 3.00
AW8 D.Marino/P.Manning 5.00 12.00
AW9 J.Rice/M.Harrison 2.00 5.00
AW10 J.Montana/T.Brady 5.00 12.00
AW11 J.Namath/E.Manning 2.50 6.00
AW12 J.Jones/K.Jones 1.25 3.00
AW13 P.Holmes/L.Tomlinson 1.25 3.00
AW14 M.Vick/B.Leftwich 1.25 3.00
AW15 J.Walker/R.Williams WR 1.25 3.00
AW16 T.Owens/A.Johnson 1.25 3.00
AW17 H.Ward/C.Johnson 1.25 3.00
AW18 S.Alexander/D.McAllister 1.25 3.00
AW19 E.James/J.Lewis 1.25 3.00
AW20 M.Bulger/M.Hasselbeck 1.25 3.00

2005 Zenith Autumn Warriors Materials

STATED PRINT RUN 250 SER.#'d SETS
*PRIME: 1X TO 2.5X BASIC JERSEYS
PRIME PRINT RUN 25 SER.#'d SETS
AW1 Roethlis/Pennington 7.50 20.00
AW2 W.Payton/B.Sanders 15.00 40.00
AW3 M.Allen/B.Jackson 7.50 20.00
AW4 R.Lewis/B.Urlacher 7.50 20.00
AW5 B.Favre/D.Carr 10.00 25.00
AW6 C.Dillon/C.Portis 3.00 8.00
AW7 D.McNabb/D.Culpepper 4.00 10.00
AW8 D.Marino/P.Manning 15.00 40.00
AW9 J.Rice/M.Harrison 8.00 20.00
AW10 J.Montana/T.Brady 15.00 40.00
AW11 J.Namath/E.Manning 7.50 20.00
AW12 J.Jones/K.Jones 3.00 8.00
AW13 P.Holmes/L.Tomlinson 5.00 12.00
AW14 M.Vick/B.Leftwich 4.00 10.00
AW15 J.Walker/R.Williams WR 3.00 8.00
AW16 T.Owens/A.Johnson 4.00 10.00
AW17 H.Ward/C.Johnson 4.00 10.00
AW18 S.Alexander/D.McAllister 4.00 10.00
AW19 E.James/J.Lewis 4.00 10.00
AW20 M.Bulger/M.Hasselbeck 3.00 8.00

2005 Zenith Black 'N Blue Silver

*GOLD: .8X TO 2X BASIC INSERTS
GOLD PRINT RUN 100 SER.#'d SETS
BB1 Ben Roethlisberger 2.50 6.00
BB2 Brett Favre 3.00 8.00
BB3 Brian Urlacher 1.50 4.00
BB4 Clinton Portis 1.00 2.50
BB5 Corey Dillon 1.00 2.50
BB6 Daunte Culpepper 1.25 3.00
BB7 Domanick Davis 1.00 2.50
BB8 Donovan McNabb 1.25 3.00
BB9 Edgerrin James 1.25 3.00
BB10 Eli Manning 2.50 6.00
BB11 Hines Ward 1.25 3.00
BB12 Jake Delhomme 1.00 2.50
BB13 Jamal Lewis 1.25 3.00
BB14 Jerome Bettis 1.50 4.00
BB15 Kevin Jones 1.00 2.50
BB16 LaDainian Tomlinson 1.50 4.00
BB17 Michael Vick 1.25 3.00
BB18 Peyton Manning 4.00 10.00
BB19 Priest Holmes 1.00 2.50
BB20 Shaun Alexander 1.00 2.50
BB21 Steven Jackson 1.00 2.50
BB22 Tedy Bruschi 1.25 3.00
BB23 Terrell Owens 1.25 3.00
BB24 Tiki Barber 1.25 3.00
BB25 Willis McGahee 1.00 2.50

2005 Zenith Canton Bound Silver

*GOLD: 1X TO 2.5X BASIC INSERTS
GOLD PRINT RUN 100 SER.#'d SETS
CB1 Brett Favre 2.50 6.00
CB2 Daunte Culpepper 1.00 2.50
CB3 Peyton Manning 3.00 8.00
CB4 Jerry Rice 2.50 6.00
CB5 Dan Marino 3.00 8.00
CB6 Michael Vick 1.00 2.50
CB7 Randy Moss 1.00 2.50
CB8 Priest Holmes .75 2.00
CB9 Tom Brady 5.00 12.00
CB10 LaDainian Tomlinson 1.25 3.00
CB11 Walter Payton 4.00 10.00
CB12 Terrell Owens 1.00 2.50
CB13 Donovan McNabb 1.00 2.50
CB14 Larry Fitzgerald 1.25 3.00
CB15 Carson Palmer 1.00 2.50
CB16 Brian Urlacher 1.25 3.00
CB17 Ben Roethlisberger 2.00 5.00
CB18 Edgerrin James 1.00 2.50
CB19 Willis McGahee .75 2.00
CB20 Julius Jones .75 2.00
CB21 Kevin Jones .75 2.00
CB22 Joe Montana 5.00 12.00
CB23 Earl Campbell 1.50 4.00
CB24 Eli Manning 2.00 5.00
CB25 Steve Young 2.00 5.00

2005 Zenith Canton Bound Materials

STATED PRINT RUN 199 SER.#'d SETS
*PRIME: .8X TO 2X BASIC JERSEYS
PRIME PRINT RUN 25 SER.#'d SETS
CB1 Brett Favre 10.00 25.00
CB2 Daunte Culpepper 4.00 10.00
CB3 Peyton Manning 7.50 20.00
CB4 Jerry Rice 6.00 15.00
CB5 Dan Marino 12.50 30.00
CB6 Michael Vick 6.00 15.00
CB7 Randy Moss 4.00 10.00
CB8 Priest Holmes 4.00 10.00
CB9 Tom Brady 7.50 20.00
CB10 LaDainian Tomlinson 4.00 10.00
CB11 Walter Payton 15.00 40.00
CB12 Terrell Owens 4.00 10.00
CB13 Donovan McNabb 5.00 12.00
CB14 Larry Fitzgerald 4.00 10.00
CB15 Carson Palmer 4.00 10.00
CB16 Brian Urlacher 4.00 10.00
CB17 Ben Roethlisberger 10.00 25.00
CB18 Edgerrin James 4.00 10.00
CB19 Willis McGahee 4.00 10.00
CB20 Julius Jones 5.00 12.00
CB21 Kevin Jones 4.00 10.00
CB22 Joe Montana 12.50 30.00
CB23 Earl Campbell 6.00 15.00
CB24 Eli Manning 8.00 20.00
CB25 Steve Young 6.00 15.00

2005 Zenith Epix Black 1st Down

*BLACK 1st/100: 1X TO 2.5X ORANGE 1
BLACK 1 PRINT RUN 100 SER.#'d SETS
*BLACK 2nd/50: 1.2X TO 3X ORANGE 1
BLACK 2 PRINT RUN 50 SER.#'d SETS
*BLACK 3rd/25: 2X TO 5X ORANGE 1
BLACK 3 PRINT RUN 25 SER.#'d SETS
*BLACK 4th/10: 3X TO 8X ORANGE 1
UNPRICED BLACK 4 PRINT RUN 10 SETS

2005 Zenith Epix Blue 1st Down

*BLUE 1st/600: .4X TO 1X ORANGE 1
BLUE 1 PRINT RUN 600 SER.#'d SETS
*BLUE 2nd/400: .5X TO 1.2X ORANGE 1
BLUE 2 PRINT RUN 400 SER.#'d SETS
*BLUE 3rd/250: .6X TO 1.5X ORANGE 1
BLUE 3 PRINT RUN 250 SER.#'d SETS
*BLUE 4th/150: .8X TO 2X ORANGE 1
BLUE 4 PRINT RUN 150 SER.#'d SETS

2005 Zenith Epix Emerald 1st Down

*EMERALD 1st/150: .8X TO 2X ORANGE 1
EMERALD 1 PRINT RUN 150 SER.#'d SETS
*EMERALD 2nd/100: 1X TO 2.5X ORANGE 1
EMERALD 2 PRINT RUN 100 SER.#'d SETS
*EMERALD 3rd/50: 1.2X TO 3X ORANGE 1
EMERALD 3 PRINT RUN 50 SER.#'d SETS
*EMERALD 4th/25: 2X TO 5X ORANGE 1
EMERALD 4 PRINT RUN 25 SER.#'d SETS

2005 Zenith Epix Orange 1st Down

ORANGE 1 PRINT RUN 1000 SER.#'d SETS
*ORANGE 2nd/600: .4X TO 1X ORANGE 1
ORANGE 2 PRINT RUN 600 SER.#'d SETS
*ORANGE 3rd/400: .5X TO 1.2X ORANGE 1
ORANGE 3 PRINT RUN 400 SER.#'d SETS
*ORANGE 4th/250: .6X TO 1.5X ORANGE 1
ORANGE 4 PRINT RUN 250 SER.#'d SETS
1 Alex Smith QB 2.50 6.00
2 Ben Roethlisberger 1.50 4.00
3 Brett Favre 2.00 5.00
4 Brian Urlacher 1.00 2.50
5 Cadillac Williams .60 1.50
6 Carson Palmer .75 2.00
7 Troy Williamson .60 1.50
8 Chad Pennington .60 1.50
9 Michael Vick .75 2.00
10 David Carr .60 1.50
11 Donovan McNabb .75 2.00
12 Edgerrin James .75 2.00
13 Eli Manning 1.50 4.00
14 J.P. Losman .60 1.50
15 Steven Jackson .60 1.50
16 Daunte Culpepper .75 2.00
17 Julius Jones .60 1.50
18 Kevin Jones .60 1.50
19 LaDainian Tomlinson 1.00 2.50
20 Peyton Manning 2.50 6.00
21 Randy Moss .75 2.00
22 Ronnie Brown .75 2.00
23 Clinton Portis .60 1.50
24 Tom Brady 4.00 10.00
25 Willis McGahee .60 1.50

2005 Zenith Epix Purple 1st Down

*PURPLE 1st/500: .4X TO 1X ORANGE 1
PURPLE 1 PRINT RUN 500 SER.#'d SETS
*PURPLE 2nd/250: .6X TO 1.5X ORANGE 1
PURPLE 2 PRINT RUN 250 SER.#'d SETS
*PURPLE 3rd/150: .8X TO 2X ORANGE 1
PURPLE 3 PRINT RUN 150 SER.#'d SETS
*PURPLE 4th/100: 1X TO 2.5X ORANGE 1
PURPLE 4 PRINT RUN 100 SER.#'d SETS

2005 Zenith Epix Red 1st Down

*RED 1st/250: .6X TO 1.5X ORANGE 1
RED 1 PRINT RUN 250 SER.#'d SETS
*RED 2nd/150: .8X TO 2X ORANGE 1
RED 2 PRINT RUN 150 SER.#'d SETS
*RED 3rd/100: 1X TO 2.5X ORANGE 1
RED 3 PRINT RUN 100 SER.#'d SETS
*RED 4th/50: 1.2X TO 3X ORANGE 1
RED 4 PRINT RUN 50 SER.#'d SETS

2005 Zenith Mozaics Silver

*GOLD: 1X TO 2.5X BASIC INSERTS
GOLD PRINT RUN 100 SER.#'d SETS
M1 Vick/Dunn/Crumpler 1.00 2.50
M2 Boller/J.Lewis/Heap 1.00 2.50
M3 Losman/McGahee/Evans 1.00 2.50
M4 Palmer/Rudi/Chad 1.00 2.50
M5 Harrington/Jones/Will WR .75 2.00
M6 Favre/Green/Walker 2.50 6.00
M7 Carr/Davis/Johnson 1.00 2.50
M8 Peyton/James/Harrison 3.00 8.00
M9 Brady/Dillon/Branch 5.00 12.00
M10 Delhomme/Peppers/Foster 1.00 2.50
M11 McNabb/Westbrk/Owens 1.00 2.50
M12 Ben/Bettis/Ward 2.00 5.00
M13 Brees/L.T./Gates 1.25 3.00
M14 Bulger/Jackson/Holt 1.00 2.50
M15 McNair/Brown/Bennett 1.00 2.50

2005 Zenith Mozaics Materials

STATED PRINT RUN 100 SER.#'d SETS
M1 Vick/Dunn/Crumpler 5.00 12.00
M2 Boller/J.Lewis/Heap 5.00 12.00
M3 Losman/McGahee/Evans 5.00 12.00
M4 Palmer/Rudi/Chad 5.00 12.00
M5 Harrington/Jones/Will WR 4.00 10.00
M6 Favre/Green/Walker 12.00 30.00
M7 Carr/Davis/Johnson 5.00 12.00
M8 P.Mann/James/Harrison 15.00 40.00
M9 Brady/Dillon/Branch 25.00 60.00
M10 Delhomme/Peppers/Foster 5.00 12.00
M11 McNabb/Westbrk/Owens 8.00 20.00
M12 Roeth/Bettis/Ward 10.00 25.00
M13 Brees/L.T./Gates 6.00 15.00
M14 Bulger/Jackson/Holt 5.00 12.00
M15 McNair/Brown/Bennett 5.00 12.00

2005 Zenith Prime Signature Cuts Gold

UNPRICED PRIME SIGS GOLD #'d TO 5

2005 Zenith Prime Signature Cuts Platinum

UNPRICED PRIME SIGS PLATINUM #'d TO 1

2005 Zenith Rookie Roll Call Silver

STATED ODDS 1:18 HOB, 1:24 RET
*GOLD: .8X TO 2X BASIC INSERTS
GOLD PRINT RUN 100 SER.#'d SETS
RC1 Adam Jones .60 1.50
RC2 Alex Smith QB 2.50 6.00
RC3 Antrel Rolle 1.00 2.50
RC4 Andrew Walter .60 1.50
RC5 Braylon Edwards .60 1.50
RC6 Cadillac Williams .60 1.50
RC7 Carlos Rogers 1.00 2.50
RC8 Charlie Frye .60 1.50
RC9 Ciatrick Fason .60 1.50
RC10 Courtney Roby .60 1.50
RC11 Eric Shelton .60 1.50
RC12 Frank Gore 1.25 3.00
RC13 J.J. Arrington .75 2.00
RC14 Kyle Orton .60 1.50
RC15 Jason Campbell .60 1.50
RC16 Mark Bradley .60 1.50
RC17 Mark Clayton .60 1.50
RC18 Matt Jones .60 1.50
RC19 Maurice Clarett .60 1.50
RC20 Reggie Brown .60 1.50
RC21 Ronnie Brown .75 2.00
RC22 Roddy White 1.00 2.50
RC23 Ryan Moats .60 1.50
RC24 Roscoe Parrish .60 1.50
RC25 Stefan LeFors .60 1.50
RC26 Terrence Murphy .60 1.50
RC27 Troy Williamson .60 1.50
RC28 Vernand Morency .60 1.50
RC29 Vincent Jackson 1.00 2.50

2005 Zenith Rookie Roll Call Autographs

STATED PRINT RUN 25-300
RC1 Adam Jones/200 5.00 12.00
RC2 Alex Smith QB/25 30.00 80.00
RC3 Antrel Rolle/100 8.00 20.00
RC5 Braylon Edwards/50 25.00 60.00
RC6 Cadillac Williams/25 10.00 25.00
RC7 Carlos Rogers/250 8.00 20.00
RC8 Charlie Frye/200 5.00 12.00
RC9 Ciatrick Fason/150 5.00 12.00
RC10 Courtney Roby/150 5.00 12.00
RC11 Eric Shelton/250 5.00 12.00
RC12 Frank Gore/150 10.00 25.00
RC13 J.J. Arrington/25 12.00 30.00
RC14 Kyle Orton/150 5.00 12.00
RC15 Jason Campbell/25 10.00 25.00
RC16 Mark Bradley/100 5.00 12.00
RC17 Mark Clayton/25 10.00 25.00
RC18 Matt Jones/25 10.00 25.00
RC20 Reggie Brown/100 5.00 12.00
RC21 Ronnie Brown/25 12.00 30.00
RC22 Roddy White/25 15.00 40.00
RC23 Ryan Moats/300 5.00 12.00
RC24 Roscoe Parrish/25 10.00 25.00
RC25 Stefan LeFors/125 5.00 12.00
RC26 Terrence Murphy/250 5.00 12.00
RC27 Troy Williamson/25 10.00 25.00
RC28 Vernand Morency/50 6.00 15.00
RC29 Vincent Jackson/175 8.00 20.00

2005 Zenith Rookie Roll Call Jerseys

*PRIME: .8X TO 2X BASIC JERSEYS
PRIME PRINT RUN 25 SER.#'d SETS
RC1 Adam Jones 3.00 8.00
RC2 Alex Smith QB 7.50 20.00
RC3 Antrel Rolle 3.00 8.00
RC4 Andrew Walter 3.00 8.00
RC5 Braylon Edwards 4.00 10.00
RC6 Cadillac Williams 5.00 12.00
RC7 Carlos Rogers 3.00 8.00
RC8 Charlie Frye 3.00 8.00
RC9 Ciatrick Fason 3.00 8.00
RC10 Courtney Roby 3.00 8.00
RC11 Eric Shelton 3.00 8.00
RC12 Frank Gore 5.00 12.00
RC13 J.J. Arrington 3.00 8.00
RC14 Kyle Orton 3.00 8.00
RC15 Jason Campbell 4.00 10.00
RC16 Mark Bradley 3.00 8.00
RC17 Mark Clayton 3.00 8.00
RC18 Matt Jones 3.00 8.00
RC19 Maurice Clarett 3.00 8.00
RC20 Reggie Brown 3.00 8.00
RC21 Ronnie Brown 7.50 20.00
RC22 Roddy White 4.00 10.00
RC23 Ryan Moats 3.00 8.00
RC24 Roscoe Parrish 3.00 8.00
RC25 Stefan LeFors 3.00 8.00
RC26 Terrence Murphy 3.00 8.00
RC27 Troy Williamson 3.00 8.00
RC28 Vernand Morency 3.00 8.00
RC29 Vincent Jackson 4.00 10.00

2005 Zenith Spellbound Silver

*GOLD: .8X TO 2X BASIC INSERTS
GOLD PRINT RUN 100 SER.#'d SETS
S1 Tom Brady T 6.00 15.00
S2 Tom Brady O 6.00 15.00
S3 Tom Brady M 6.00 15.00
S4 Ben Roethlisberger B 2.50 6.00
S5 Ben Roethlisberger E 2.50 6.00
S6 Ben Roethlisberger N 2.50 6.00
S7 Dan Marino D 4.00 10.00
S8 Dan Marino A 4.00 10.00
S9 Dan Marino N 4.00 10.00
S10 Eli Manning E 2.50 6.00
S11 Eli Manning L 2.50 6.00
S12 Eli Manning I 2.50 6.00
S13 Joe Montana J 6.00 15.00
S14 Joe Montana O 6.00 15.00
S15 Joe Montana E 6.00 15.00
S16 Jerry Rice J 3.00 8.00
S17 Jerry Rice E 3.00 8.00
S18 Jerry Rice R 3.00 8.00
S19 Jerry Rice R 3.00 8.00
S20 Jerry Rice Y 3.00 8.00
S21 Steve Young S 2.50 6.00
S22 Steve Young T 2.50 6.00
S23 Steve Young E 2.50 6.00
S24 Steve Young V 2.50 6.00
S25 Steve Young E 2.50 6.00

2005 Zenith Spellbound Jerseys

STATED PRINT RUN 250 SER.#'d SETS
*PRIME: 1.2X TO 3X BASIC JERSEYS
PRIME PRINT RUN 25 SER.#'d SETS
S1 Tom Brady T 8.00 20.00
S2 Tom Brady O 8.00 20.00
S3 Tom Brady M 8.00 20.00
S4 Ben Roethlisberger B 10.00 25.00
S5 Ben Roethlisberger E 10.00 25.00
S6 Ben Roethlisberger N 10.00 25.00
S7 Dan Marino D 12.50 30.00
S8 Dan Marino A 12.50 30.00
S9 Dan Marino N 12.50 30.00
S10 Eli Manning E 10.00 25.00
S11 Eli Manning L 10.00 25.00
S12 Eli Manning I 10.00 25.00
S13 Joe Montana J 12.50 30.00
S14 Joe Montana O 12.50 30.00
S15 Joe Montana E 12.50 30.00
S16 Jerry Rice J 6.00 15.00
S17 Jerry Rice E 6.00 15.00
S18 Jerry Rice R 6.00 15.00
S19 Jerry Rice R 6.00 15.00
S20 Jerry Rice Y 6.00 15.00
S21 Steve Young S 6.00 15.00
S22 Steve Young T 6.00 15.00
S23 Steve Young E 6.00 15.00
S24 Steve Young V 6.00 15.00
S25 Steve Young E 6.00 15.00

2005 Zenith Team Zenith Silver

STATED ODDS 1:18 HOB, 1:24 RET
*GOLD: 1.2X TO 3X BASIC INSERTS
GOLD PRINT RUN 100 SER.#'d SETS
TZ1 Ben Roethlisberger 1.50 4.00
TZ2 Brett Favre 2.00 5.00
TZ3 Michael Vick .75 2.00
TZ4 Julius Jones .60 1.50
TZ5 Peyton Manning 2.50 6.00
TZ6 Tom Brady 4.00 10.00
TZ7 Kevin Jones .60 1.50
TZ8 Willis McGahee .60 1.50
TZ9 Daunte Culpepper .75 2.00
TZ10 Donovan McNabb .75 2.00

2005 Zenith Team Zenith Jerseys

STATED PRINT RUN 100 SER.#'d SETS
*PRIME: .6X TO 1.5X BASIC JERSEYS
PRIME PRINT RUN 25 SER.#'d SETS
TZ1 Ben Roethlisberger 12.50 30.00
TZ2 Brett Favre 12.50 30.00
TZ3 Michael Vick 7.50 20.00
TZ4 Julius Jones 6.00 15.00
TZ5 Peyton Manning 10.00 25.00
TZ6 Tom Brady 10.00 25.00
TZ7 Kevin Jones 5.00 12.00
TZ8 Willis McGahee 5.00 12.00
TZ9 Daunte Culpepper 5.00 12.00
TZ10 Donovan McNabb 6.00 15.00

2005 Zenith Z-Graphs

1 Anquan Boldin 6.00 15.00
5 Michael Vick 25.00 50.00
7 Jake Delhomme 6.00 15.00
10 Steve Smith 10.00 25.00
11 Brian Urlacher 10.00 25.00
12 Rex Grossman 10.00 25.00
14 Chad Johnson 6.00 15.00
15 Rudi Johnson 6.00 15.00
17 Drew Bledsoe 8.00 20.00
18 Julius Jones 10.00 25.00
19 Keyshawn Johnson 8.00 20.00
20 Roy Williams S 6.00 15.00
22 Ashley Lelie 6.00 15.00
26 Joey Harrington 6.00 15.00
28 Roy Williams WR 6.00 15.00
29 Ahman Green 8.00 20.00
32 Andre Johnson 8.00 20.00
33 David Carr 6.00 15.00
34 Domanick Davis 6.00 15.00
36 Marvin Harrison 15.00 40.00
39 Byron Leftwich 6.00 15.00
41 Jimmy Smith 8.00 20.00
43 Priest Holmes 6.00 15.00
56 Aaron Brooks 6.00 15.00
57 Deuce McAllister 8.00 20.00
58 Eli Manning 50.00 100.00
63 Chad Pennington 6.00 15.00
75 Donovan McNabb 15.00 40.00
80 Duce Staley 6.00 15.00
81 Hines Ward 20.00 40.00
89 Matt Hasselbeck 10.00 25.00
93 Michael Clayton 6.00 15.00
97 Clinton Portis 6.00 15.00
98 Patrick Ramsey 8.00 20.00

2005 Zenith Z-Jerseys

STATED ODDS 1:215 RET
*PRIME/75-100: .6X TO 1.5X BASIC JERSEYS
*PRIME/50-55: .6X TO 1.5X BASIC JERSEYS
*PRIME/25-30: .8X TO 2X BASIC JERSEYS
PRIME SER.#'d UNDER 25 NOT PRICED
1 Anquan Boldin 2.50 6.00
2 Bryant Johnson
3 Josh McCown 3.00 8.00
4 Larry Fitzgerald
5 Michael Vick 3.00 8.00
6 Warrick Dunn 2.50 6.00
7 Jake Delhomme 2.50 6.00
8 Julius Peppers 3.00 8.00
9 Stephen Davis 2.50 6.00
10 Steve Smith 4.00 10.00
11 Brian Urlacher 4.00 10.00
12 Rex Grossman 2.50 6.00
13 Carson Palmer 3.00 8.00
14 Chad Johnson 2.50 6.00
15 Rudi Johnson 2.50 6.00
16 Kellen Winslow Jr. 2.50 6.00
17 Drew Bledsoe 3.00 8.00
18 Julius Jones 2.50 6.00
19 Keyshawn Johnson 3.00 8.00
20 Roy Williams S 2.50 6.00
21 Troy Aikman 7.50 20.00
22 Ashley Lelie 2.50 6.00
23 Jake Plummer 2.50 6.00
24 Quentin Griffin 2.50 6.00
25 Tatum Bell 2.50 6.00
26 Joey Harrington
27 Kevin Jones 2.50 6.00
28 Roy Williams WR 2.50 6.00
29 Ahman Green 3.00 8.00
30 Brett Favre 8.00 20.00
31 Javon Walker 2.50 6.00
32 Andre Johnson 3.00 8.00
33 David Carr 2.50 6.00
34 Domanick Davis 2.50 6.00
35 Edgerrin James 3.00 8.00
36 Marvin Harrison 3.00 8.00
37 Peyton Manning 10.00 25.00
38 Reggie Wayne 3.00 8.00
39 Byron Leftwich 2.50 6.00
40 Fred Taylor 2.50 6.00
41 Jimmy Smith 3.00 8.00
42 Reggie Williams 2.50 6.00
43 Priest Holmes 2.50 6.00
44 Tony Gonzalez 3.00 8.00
45 Trent Green 2.50 6.00
46 Chris Chambers 2.50 6.00
47 Jason Taylor 3.00 8.00
48 Dan Marino 12.50 30.00
49 Junior Seau 3.00 8.00
50 Daunte Culpepper 3.00 8.00
51 Michael Bennett 2.50 6.00
52 Bethel Johnson 2.50 6.00
53 Corey Dillon 2.50 6.00
54 Tom Brady 15.00 40.00
55 Ty Law 4.00 10.00
56 Aaron Brooks 2.50 6.00
57 Deuce McAllister 3.00 8.00
58 Eli Manning 6.00 15.00
59 Jeremy Shockey 2.50 6.00
60 Michael Strahan 3.00 8.00
61 Aaron Glenn 2.50 6.00
62 Anthony Becht 2.50 6.00
63 Chad Pennington 2.50 6.00
64 Curtis Martin 3.00 8.00
65 Charles Woodson 4.00 10.00
66 Jerry Rice 6.00 15.00
67 Rich Gannon 3.00 8.00
68 Sebastian Janikowski 2.50 6.00
69 Tyrone Wheatley 2.50 6.00
70 Kerry Collins 2.50 6.00
71 A.J. Feeley 2.50 6.00
72 Brian Westbrook 2.50 6.00
73 Corey Simon 2.50 6.00
74 Correll Buckhalter 2.50 6.00
75 Donovan McNabb 3.00 8.00
76 Hugh Douglas 2.50 6.00
77 Terrell Owens 3.00 8.00
78 Todd Pinkston 2.50 6.00
79 Ben Roethlisberger 6.00 15.00
80 Duce Staley 2.50 6.00
81 Hines Ward 3.00 8.00
82 Jerome Bettis 6.00 15.00
83 Drew Brees 4.00 10.00
84 LaDainian Tomlinson 4.00 10.00
85 Bryant Young 2.50 6.00
86 Jerry Rice 6.00 15.00
87 Steve Young 6.00 15.00
88 Koren Robinson 2.50 6.00
89 Matt Hasselbeck 2.50 6.00
90 Shaun Alexander 2.50 6.00
91 Marc Bulger 2.50 6.00
92 Torry Holt 3.00 8.00
93 Michael Clayton 2.50 6.00
94 Mike Alstott 2.50 6.00
95 Chris Brown 2.50 6.00
96 Steve McNair 3.00 8.00
97 Clinton Portis 2.50 6.00
98 Patrick Ramsey 3.00 8.00
99 Sean Taylor 12.00 30.00
100 LaVar Arrington 2.50 6.00

2005 Zenith Z-Team Silver

*GOLD: 1.2X TO 3X BASIC INSERTS
GOLD PRINT RUN 100 SER.#'d SETS
ZT1 Larry Fitzgerald 1.00 2.50
ZT2 Michael Vick .75 2.00
ZT3 Willis McGahee .60 1.50
ZT4 Cedric Benson .60 1.50
ZT5 Brian Urlacher 1.00 2.50
ZT6 Carson Palmer .75 2.00
ZT7 Braylon Edwards .60 1.50
ZT8 Julius Jones .60 1.50
ZT9 Kevin Jones .60 1.50
ZT10 Brett Favre 2.00 5.00
ZT11 David Carr .60 1.50
ZT12 Peyton Manning 2.50 6.00
ZT13 Byron Leftwich .60 1.50
ZT14 Priest Holmes .60 1.50
ZT15 Ronnie Brown .75 2.00
ZT16 Daunte Culpepper .75 2.00
ZT17 Tom Brady 4.00 10.00
ZT18 Eli Manning 1.50 4.00
ZT19 Chad Pennington .60 1.50
ZT20 Randy Moss .75 2.00
ZT21 Donovan McNabb .75 2.00
ZT22 Ben Roethlisberger 1.50 4.00
ZT23 LaDainian Tomlinson 1.00 2.50
ZT24 Alex Smith QB 2.50 6.00
ZT25 Steven Jackson .60 1.50

2006 Aspire

This 36-card set was released in May, 2006. The set was issued into the hobby in four-card packs with an $4.99 SRP which came 24 packs to a box.
COMPLETE SET (36) 10.00 25.00
1 Reggie Bush .40 1.00
2 Matt Leinart .25 .60
3 Vince Young .25 .60
4 Mario Williams .40 1.00
5 Michael Huff .30 .75
6 Vernon Davis .30 .75
7 LenDale White .25 .60
8 Brodie Croyle .25 .60
9 Drew Olson .25 .60
10 Maurice Drew .40 1.00
11 Tye Hill .25 .60
12 Michael Robinson .25 .60
13 Joseph Addai .25 .60
14 Paul Pinegar .25 .60
15 Jimmy Williams .25 .60
16 D.J. Shockley .30 .75
17 Mike Hass .25 .60
18 Demetrius Williams .25 .60
19 Reggie McNeal .25 .60
20 Charlie Whitehurst .25 .60
21 Maurice Stovall .25 .60
22 Sinorice Moss .25 .60
23 Jason Avant .25 .60
24 Omar Jacobs .25 .60
25 Laurence Maroney .25 .60
26 Martin Nance .25 .60
27 Leonard Pope .40 1.00
28 Rodrique Wright .25 .60
29 David Thomas .25 .60
30 Will Blackmon .25 .60
31 Dominique Byrd .25 .60
32 D'Brickashaw Ferguson .25 .60
33 Reggie Bush .40 1.00
34 Matt Leinart .25 .60
35 Vince Young .25 .60
36 Jay Cutler .30 .75

2006 Aspire Autographs

OVERALL AUTO ODDS 1:8 H, 1:24 R
1A Reggie Bush 4.00 10.00
2A Matt Leinart 2.50 6.00
3A Vince Young 2.50 6.00
4A Mario Williams 4.00 10.00
5A Michael Huff 3.00 8.00
6A Vernon Davis 3.00 8.00
7A LenDale White 2.50 6.00
8A Brodie Croyle 2.50 6.00
9A Drew Olson 2.50 6.00
10A Maurice Drew 4.00 10.00
11A Tye Hill 2.50 6.00
12A Michael Robinson 2.50 6.00
13A Joseph Addai 2.50 6.00
14A Paul Pinegar 2.50 6.00
15A Jimmy Williams 2.50 6.00
16A D.J. Shockley 3.00 8.00
17A Mike Hass 2.50 6.00
18A Demetrius Williams 2.50 6.00
19A Reggie McNeal 2.50 6.00
20A Charlie Whitehurst 2.50 6.00
21A Maurice Stovall 2.50 6.00
22A Sinorice Moss 2.50 6.00
23A Jason Avant 2.50 6.00
24A Omar Jacobs 2.50 6.00
26A Martin Nance 2.50 6.00
27A Leonard Pope 4.00 10.00
28A Rodrique Wright 2.50 6.00
29A David Thomas 2.50 6.00
30A Will Blackmon 2.50 6.00
31A Dominique Byrd 2.50 6.00
32A D'Brickashaw Ferguson 2.50 6.00
36A Jay Cutler 3.00 8.00

2006 Aspire Century Club Autographs

CENT.CLUB/100 ODDS 1:69 H, 1:207 R
1A Reggie Bush 6.00 15.00
2A Matt Leinart 15.00 40.00
3A Vince Young 10.00 25.00
4A Mario Williams 6.00 15.00
5A Michael Huff 5.00 12.00
6A Vernon Davis 5.00 12.00
7A LenDale White 4.00 10.00
8A Brodie Croyle 4.00 10.00
9A Drew Olson 4.00 10.00
10A Maurice Drew 6.00 15.00
11A Tye Hill 4.00 10.00
12A Michael Robinson 4.00 10.00
13A Joseph Addai 12.00 30.00
14A Paul Pinegar 4.00 10.00
15A Jimmy Williams 4.00 10.00
16A D.J. Shockley 5.00 12.00
17A Mike Hass 4.00 10.00
18A Demetrius Williams 4.00 10.00
19A Reggie McNeal 4.00 10.00
20A Charlie Whitehurst 4.00 10.00
21A Maurice Stovall 4.00 10.00
22A Sinorice Moss 4.00 10.00
23A Jason Avant 4.00 10.00
24A Omar Jacobs 4.00 10.00
26A Martin Nance 4.00 10.00
27A Leonard Pope 6.00 15.00
28A Rodrique Wright 4.00 10.00
29A David Thomas 4.00 10.00
30A Will Blackmon 4.00 10.00
31A Dominique Byrd 4.00 10.00
32A D'Brickashaw Ferguson 4.00 10.00
36A Jay Cutler 5.00 12.00

2006 Aspire Combo Autographs

UNPRICED AU/5 ODDS 1:4800H,1:14,400R

2006 Aspire 5 Star

COMPLETE SET (25) 12.50 30.00
5 CARDS PER PLAYER OF EQUAL VALUE
STATED ODDS 1:6 HOB, 1:18 RET
FS1 Reggie Bush .30 .75
FS6 Jay Cutler .25 .60
FS11 Matt Leinart .20 .50
FS16 LenDale White .20 .50
FS21 Vince Young .20 .50

2006 Aspire 5 Star Autographs

AUTO/25 ODDS 1:384 H/R
5 CARDS PER PLAYER OF EQUAL VALUE
FS1 Reggie Bush 10.00 25.00
FS6 Jay Cutler 10.00 25.00
FS11 Matt Leinart 20.00 50.00
FS16 LenDale White 12.00 30.00
FS21 Vince Young 10.00 25.00

2006 Aspire Hype

COMPLETE SET (7) 10.00 25.00
1 Vernon Davis .40 1.00
2 Reggie Bush .50 1.25
3 Joseph Addai .30 .75
4 Matt Leinart .30 .75
5 Vince Young .30 .75
6 Jay Cutler .40 1.00
7 Laurence Maroney .30 .75

2006 Aspire School Pride

STATED ODDS 1:100 HOB, 1:300 RET
SPRB Reggie Bush 1 6.00 15.00
SPBC1 Bobby Carpenter 1 6.00 15.00
SPBC2 Bobby Carpenter 2 8.00 20.00
SPJC1 Jay Cutler 1 12.50 30.00
SPJC2 Jay Cutler 2 15.00 40.00
SPJC3 Jay Cutler 3 20.00 50.00
SPTH1 Tye Hill 1 5.00 12.00
SPTH2 Tye Hill 2 5.00 12.00
SPTH3 Tye Hill 3 8.00 20.00
SPOJ1 Omar Jacobs 1 8.00 20.00
SPOJ2 Omar Jacobs 2 10.00 25.00
SPOJ3 Omar Jacobs 3 10.00 25.00
SPLP1 Leonard Pope 1 6.00 15.00
SPLP2 Leonard Pope 2 8.00 20.00
SPLP3 Leonard Pope 3 8.00 20.00
SPDS1 D.J. Shockley 2 6.00 15.00
SPDS2 D.J. Shockley 3 5.00 12.00
SPCW1 Charlie Whitehurst 1 5.00 12.00
SPCW2 Charlie Whitehurst 2 6.00 15.00
SPCW3 Charlie Whitehurst 3
SPMW1 Mario Williams 1 12.50 25.00
SPMW2 Mario Williams 2 15.00 30.00
SPAY1 Ashton Youboty 1 8.00 20.00
SPAY2 Ashton Youboty 2 10.00 25.00

2006 Aspire Title Ticket

TITLE TICKET/50 ODDS 1:1920H, 1:5760R
UNPRICED AUTO/10 ODDS 1:4800
1 Vince Young 12.00 30.00
2 Michael Huff 12.00 30.00
3 David Thomas 12.00 30.00
4 Reggie Bush 6.00 15.00
5 Matt Leinart 20.00 50.00
6 LenDale White 15.00 40.00

2006 Aspire Title Ticket Autographs

UNPRICED AU/10 ODDS 1:4800H,1:14,400R

2006 Aspire National Promos

These cards were issued at the 2006 National Sports Collector Convention. Each card appears to be from the base Aspire set but for the addition of "/5" after the card number on the backs.
1 Matt Leinart .30 .75
2 Vince Young .30 .75
3 Jay Cutler .40 1.00
4 LenDale White .30 .75
5 Reggie Bush .50 1.25

2006 Aspire National VIP Promos
COMPLETE SET (3) 6.00 15.00
1 Reggie Bush .75 2.00
2 Matt Leinart .50 1.25
3 Vince Young .50 1.25

2007 Aspire
This 33-card set was released in May, 2007. The set was issued to the hobby in four-card packs, with an $4.99 SRP, which came 24 packs to a box.
COMPLETE SET (34) 8.00 20.00
1 JaMarcus Russell .25 .60
2 Brady Quinn .25 .60
3 Drew Stanton .25 .60
4 John Beck .25 .60
5 Trent Edwards .25 .60
6 Troy Smith .25 .60
7 Kevin Kolb .30 .75
8 Jared Zabransky .25 .60
9 Jordan Palmer .30 .75
10 Chris Leak .25 .60
11 Adrian Peterson .75 2.00
12 Marshawn Lynch .50 1.25
13 Brian Leonard .25 .60
14 Antonio Pittman .25 .60
15 Kenny Irons .25 .60
16 Michael Bush .25 .60
17 Darius Walker .25 .60
18 Calvin Johnson .75 2.00
19 Robert Meachem .30 .75
20 Dwayne Bowe .25 .60
21 Sidney Rice .30 .75
22 Craig Buster Davis .25 .60
23 Steve Smith USC .25 .60
24 Anthony Gonzalez .25 .60
25 Greg Olsen .40 1.00
26 Zach Miller .25 .60
27 Levi Brown .25 .60
28 Gaines Adams .30 .75
29 Leon Hall .25 .60
30 Ted Ginn Jr. .30 .75
31 Patrick Willis .40 1.00
32 Adam Carriker .25 .60
33 Aaron Ross .25 .60
34 Lein/Yng/Bush CL .20 .50

2007 Aspire 5 Star
STATED ODDS 1:6
5 CARDS PER PLAYER OF EQUAL VALUE
FS1 Calvin Johnson .60 1.50
FS2 Calvin Johnson .60 1.50
FS3 Calvin Johnson .60 1.50
FS4 Calvin Johnson .60 1.50
FS5 Calvin Johnson .60 1.50
FS6 Marshawn Lynch .40 1.00
FS7 Marshawn Lynch .40 1.00
FS8 Marshawn Lynch .40 1.00
FS9 Marshawn Lynch .40 1.00
FS10 Marshawn Lynch .40 1.00
FS11 Adrian Peterson .60 1.50
FS12 Adrian Peterson .60 1.50
FS13 Adrian Peterson .60 1.50
FS14 Adrian Peterson .60 1.50
FS15 Adrian Peterson .60 1.50
FS16 Brady Quinn .20 .50
FS17 Brady Quinn .20 .50
FS18 Brady Quinn .20 .50
FS19 Brady Quinn .20 .50
FS20 Brady Quinn .20 .50
FS21 JaMarcus Russell .20 .50
FS22 JaMarcus Russell .20 .50
FS23 JaMarcus Russell .20 .50
FS24 JaMarcus Russell .20 .50
FS25 JaMarcus Russell .20 .50

2007 Aspire 5 Star Autographs
AUTOGRAPH/25 ODDS 1:538
5 CARDS PER PLAYER OF EQUAL VALUE
FS6 Marshawn Lynch 15.00 40.00
FS7 Marshawn Lynch 15.00 40.00
FS8 Marshawn Lynch 15.00 40.00
FS9 Marshawn Lynch 15.00 40.00
FS10 Marshawn Lynch 15.00 40.00
FS11 Adrian Peterson 75.00 150.00
FS12 Adrian Peterson 75.00 150.00
FS13 Adrian Peterson 75.00 150.00
FS14 Adrian Peterson 75.00 150.00
FS15 Adrian Peterson 75.00 150.00
FS16 Brady Quinn 15.00 14.00
FS17 Brady Quinn 15.00 14.00
FS18 Brady Quinn 15.00 14.00
FS19 Brady Quinn 15.00 14.00
FS20 Brady Quinn 15.00 14.00
FS21 JaMarcus Russell 12.00 30.00
FS22 JaMarcus Russell 12.00 30.00
FS23 JaMarcus Russell 12.00 30.00
FS24 JaMarcus Russell 12.00 30.00
FS25 JaMarcus Russell 12.00 30.00

2007 Aspire Autographs
OVERALL AUTO ODDS 1:8
*CENTURY CLUB: .5X TO 1.2X BASIC AUTOS
CENTURY CLUB/100 ODDS 1:112
1 JaMarcus Russell 3.00 8.00
2 Brady Quinn 3.00 8.00
3 Drew Stanton 3.00 8.00
4 John Beck 3.00 8.00
5 Trent Edwards 3.00 8.00
6 Troy Smith SP 10.00 25.00
7 Kevin Kolb 4.00 10.00
8 Jared Zabransky 3.00 8.00
9 Jordan Palmer 4.00 10.00
10 Chris Leak SP 8.00 20.00
11 Adrian Peterson 50.00 100.00
12 Marshawn Lynch 6.00 15.00
13 Brian Leonard 3.00 8.00
14 Antonio Pittman 3.00 8.00
15 Kenny Irons 3.00 8.00
16 Michael Bush 3.00 8.00
17 Darius Walker 3.00 8.00
19 Robert Meachem 4.00 10.00
20 Dwayne Bowe 3.00 8.00
21 Sidney Rice 4.00 10.00
22 Craig Buster Davis 3.00 8.00
23 Steve Smith USC 3.00 8.00
24 Anthony Gonzalez 3.00 8.00
25 Greg Olsen 5.00 12.00
26 Zach Miller 3.00 8.00
27 Levi Brown 3.00 8.00
28 Gaines Adams 4.00 10.00
29 Leon Hall 3.00 8.00
31 Patrick Willis 5.00 12.00
32 Adam Carriker 3.00 8.00
33 Aaron Ross 3.00 8.00

2007 Aspire Autographs Dual
UNPRICED DUAL AUTO/5 ODDS 1:6720

2007 Aspire Century Club
COMPLETE SET (33) 12.50 30.00
STATED ODDS 1:2
C1 JaMarcus Russell .40 1.00
C2 Brady Quinn .40 1.00
C3 Drew Stanton .40 1.00
C4 John Beck .40 1.00
C5 Trent Edwards .40 1.00
C6 Troy Smith .40 1.00
C7 Kevin Kolb .50 1.25
C8 Jared Zabransky .40 1.00
C9 Jordan Palmer .50 1.25
C10 Chris Leak .40 1.00
C11 Adrian Peterson 1.25 3.00
C12 Marshawn Lynch .75 2.00
C13 Brian Leonard .40 1.00
C14 Antonio Pittman .40 1.00
C15 Kenny Irons .40 1.00
C16 Michael Bush .40 1.00
C17 Darius Walker .40 1.00
C18 Calvin Johnson 1.25 3.00
C19 Robert Meachem .50 1.25
C20 Dwayne Bowe .40 1.00
C21 Sidney Rice .50 1.25
C22 Craig Buster Davis .40 1.00
C23 Steve Smith USC .40 1.00
C24 Anthony Gonzalez .40 1.00
C25 Greg Olsen .60 1.50
C26 Zach Miller .40 1.00
C27 Levi Brown .40 1.00
C28 Gaines Adams .50 1.25
C29 Leon Hall .40 1.00
C30 Ted Ginn Jr. .50 1.25
C31 Patrick Willis .60 1.50
C32 Adam Carriker .40 1.00
C33 Aaron Ross .40 1.00

2007 Aspire Date and Place Ticket Swatches
TICKET PRINT RUN 50 SER.#'d SETS
*PROGRAM: .2X TO .5X TICKET
*PROGM/TICK/20: .5X TO 1.2X TICKET
PROGRAM/TICKET PRINT RUN 20
UNPRICED AUTO/10 ODDS 1:1244
DP1 Chris Leak 10.00 25.00
DP2 Dallas Baker 10.00 25.00
DP3 Jarvis Moss 12.00 30.00
DP4 Earl Everett 8.00 20.00
DP5 Troy Smith 12.00 30.00
DP6 Antonio Pittman 12.00 30.00
DP7 Anthony Gonzalez 15.00 40.00
DP8 Ted Ginn Jr. 12.00 30.00
DP9 Steve Smith USC 10.00 25.00
DP10 Leon Hall 10.00 25.00
DP11 LaMarr Woodley 10.00 25.00
DP12 Steve Breaston 8.00 20.00
DP13 JaMarcus Russell 20.00 50.00
DP14 Dwayne Bowe 10.00 25.00
DP15 Craig Buster Davis 12.00 30.00
DP16 Brady Quinn 15.00 40.00
DP17 Darius Walker 12.00 30.00
DP18 Adrian Peterson 30.00 80.00

2007 Aspire School Pride
STATED ODDS 1:40
SP1 Gaines Adams 5.00 12.00
SP2 Aundrae Allison SP 10.00 25.00
SP3 John Beck 5.00 12.00
SP4 Ted Ginn Jr. 6.00 15.00
SP5 Anthony Gonzalez 8.00 20.00
SP6 Antonio Pittman 8.00 20.00
SP7 Troy Smith 6.00 15.00
SP9A DeMarcus Tank Tyler 1 4.00 10.00
SP9B DeMarcus Tank Tyler 2 5.00 12.00

2007 Aspire Hype Orange
*BRONZE/550: .4X TO 1X ORANGE
*GOLD/220: .5X TO 1.2X ORANGE
*SILVER/480: .4X TO 1X ORANGE
1 JaMarcus Russell .20 .50
2 Adrian Peterson .60 1.50
3 Calvin Johnson .60 1.50
4 Brady Quinn .20 .50
5 Ted Ginn .25 .60
6 Marshawn Lynch .40 1.00
7 John Beck .20 .50

2008 Aspire
COMPLETE SET (33) 8.00 20.00
1 Matt Ryan .75 2.00
2 Brian Brohm .25 .60
3 Chad Henne .30 .75
4 Joe Flacco .50 1.25
5 John David Booty .25 .60
6 Josh Johnson .25 .60
7 Erik Ainge .25 .60
8 Dennis Dixon .25 .60
9 Darren McFadden .25 .60
10 Rashard Mendenhall .25 .60
11 Jonathan Stewart .40 1.00
12 Jamaal Charles .40 1.00
13 Felix Jones .25 .60
14 Ray Rice .25 .60
15 Kevin Smith .25 .60
16 Steve Slaton .25 .60
17 Mike Hart .25 .60
18 Malcolm Kelly .25 .60
19 DeSean Jackson .50 1.25
20 Limas Sweed .25 .60
21 Early Doucet .25 .60
22 Andre Caldwell .25 .60
23 Devin Thomas .25 .60
24 James Hardy .25 .60
25 Fred Davis .25 .60
26 Jake Long .40 1.00
27 Sedrick Ellis .25 .60
28 Vernon Gholston .25 .60
29 Keith Rivers .25 .60
30 Mike Jenkins .25 .60
31 Derrick Harvey .25 .60
32 Dan Connor .25 .60
33 Leodis McKelvin .30 .75

2008 Aspire 5 Star
STATED ODDS 1:6
5 CARDS PER PLAYER OF EQUAL VALUE
F1 Brian Brohm .25 .60
F6 Chad Henne .30 .75
F11 Darren McFadden .25 .60
F16 Rashard Mendenhall .25 .60
F21 Matt Ryan .75 2.00

2008 Aspire 5 Star Autographs
5 STAR AUTO/25 ODDS 1:307
5 CARDS PER PLAYER OF EQUAL VALUE
F1 Brian Brohm 6.00 15.00
F6 Chad Henne 8.00 20.00
F11 Darren McFadden 6.00 15.00
F16 Rashard Mendenhall 6.00 15.00
F21 Matt Ryan 40.00 80.00

2008 Aspire Autographs
OVERALL AUTO ODDS 1:4
UNPRICED COMBO AU/5 ODDS 1:6720
A1 Matt Ryan 20.00 50.00
A2 Brian Brohm 3.00 8.00
A3 Chad Henne 4.00 10.00
A4 Joe Flacco 6.00 15.00
A5 John David Booty 3.00 8.00
A6 Josh Johnson 3.00 8.00
A7 Erik Ainge 3.00 8.00
A8 Dennis Dixon 3.00 8.00
A9A Darren McFadden BLK 3.00 8.00
A9B Darren McFadden BLUE 6.00 15.00
A9C Darren McFadden RED 8.00 20.00
A10 Rashard Mendenhall 3.00 8.00
A11 Jonathan Stewart 5.00 12.00
A12 Jamaal Charles 5.00 12.00
A13 Felix Jones 3.00 8.00
A14 Ray Rice 3.00 8.00
A15 Kevin Smith 3.00 8.00
A16 Steve Slaton 3.00 8.00
A17 Mike Hart 3.00 8.00
A18 Malcolm Kelly 3.00 8.00
A20 Limas Sweed 3.00 8.00
A22 Andre Caldwell 3.00 8.00
A23 Devin Thomas 3.00 8.00
A24 James Hardy 3.00 8.00
A25 Fred Davis 3.00 8.00
A26 Jake Long 5.00 12.00
A27 Sedrick Ellis 3.00 8.00
A28 Vernon Gholston 3.00 8.00
A29 Keith Rivers 3.00 8.00
A30 Mike Jenkins 3.00 8.00
A31 Derrick Harvey 3.00 8.00
A32 Dan Connor 3.00 8.00
A33 Leodis McKelvin 4.00 10.00

2008 Aspire Century Club
COMPLETE SET (33) 12.00 30.00
*SINGLES: .6X TO 1.5X BASIC CARDS
STATED ODDS 1:2

2008 Aspire Century Club Autographs
*CENTURY CLUB: .5X TO 1.2X BASIC AUTOS
CENTURY CLUB/100 ODDS 1:64

2008 Aspire Autographs Dual
UNPRICED COMBO AU/5 ODDS 1:6720

2008 Aspire Date and Place Ticket Swatches
DATE AND PLACE/50 ODDS 1:210
UNPRICED AUTOS SER.#'d TO 10
DP1 Early Doucet BCS 5.00 12.00
DP2 Matt Flynn BCS 5.00 12.00
DP3 Jacob Hester BCS 5.00 12.00
DP4 Vernon Gholston BCS 5.00 12.00
DP5 John David Booty Rose Bowl 5.00 12.00
DP6 Fred Davis Rose Bowl 10.00 25.00
DP7 Sedrick Ellis Rose Bowl 10.00 25.00
DP8 L.Jackson Rose Bowl 8.00 20.00
DP9 Keith Rivers Rose Bowl 5.00 12.00
DP10 R.Mendenhall Rose Bowl 5.00 12.00
DP11 Darius Reynaud Fiesta Bowl 5.00 12.00
DP12 Owen Schmitt Fiesta Bowl 12.00 30.00
DP13 Steve Slaton Fiesta Bowl 5.00 12.00
DP14 Malcolm Kelly Fiesta Bowl 5.00 12.00
DP15 Marcus Howard Sugar Bowl 8.00 20.00
DP16 Jason Rivers Sugar Bowl 5.00 12.00
DP17 Xavier Adibi Orange Bowl 10.00 25.00
DP18 Brandon Flowers Orange Bowl 10.00 25.00

2008 Aspire Hula Bowl Autographs
*SILVER/250: .5X TO 1.2X BASIC AUTOS
SILVER PRINT RUN 250 SER.#'d SETS
*GOLD/50: .6X TO 1.5X BASIC AUTOS
GOLD PRINT RUN 50 SER.#'d SETS
OVERALL HULA BOWL AUTO ODDS 1:12
H1 Jabari Arthur 3.00 8.00
H2 Yvenson Bernard 4.00 10.00
H3 Alex Brink 3.00 8.00
H4 Andre Callender 4.00 10.00
H5 Jordon Dizon 2.50 6.00
H6 Marcus Fitzgerald 3.00 8.00
H7 Bruce Hocker 4.00 10.00
H8 Marcus Howard 4.00 10.00
H9 Tyrell Johnson 2.50 6.00
H10 Robert Jordan 3.00 8.00
H11 Keon Lattimore 3.00 8.00
H12 Gerard Lawson 3.00 8.00
H13 Justin McKinney 3.00 8.00
H14 Kalvin McRae 2.50 6.00
H15 Brent Miller 3.00 8.00
H16 Bernard Morris 3.00 8.00
H17 Kevin O'Connell 2.50 6.00
H18 T.C. Ostrander 3.00 8.00
H19 Maurice Purify 4.00 10.00
H20 Paul Raymond 3.00 8.00
H21 Jason Rivers 2.50 6.00
H22 Ricky Santos 4.00 10.00
H23 Paul Smith 2.50 6.00
H24 Darrell Strong 3.00 8.00
H25 Marcus Thomas 3.00 8.00
H26 Danny Woodhead 20.00 50.00

2008 Aspire School Pride
STATED ODDS 1:24
SP1 Marcus Howard 5.00 12.00
SP2 Keenan Burton 3.00 8.00
SP3 Bernard Morris 4.00 10.00
SP4 Devin Thomas 3.00 8.00
SP5 Vernon Gholston 3.00 8.00
SP6 Dustin Keller 4.00 10.00
SP7 Mike Jenkins 3.00 8.00

2009 Aspire Autographs
These cards were issued directly to dealers in May 2009 since SAGE suspended the Aspire brand for that year. No base cards were issued, just these ten autographed cards.
A1 Nick Reed 5.00 12.00
A2 Ryan Mouton 4.00 10.00
A3 Brandon Hughes 4.00 10.00
A4 Jerome Johnson 5.00 12.00
A5 Andy Kemp 4.00 10.00
A6 Jaimie Thomas 4.00 10.00
A7 Anthony Felder 5.00 12.00
A8 Ray Feinga 4.00 10.00
A9 John Faletoese 5.00 12.00
A10 Bret Lockett 5.00 12.00

2011 Aspire Autographs
UNPRICED AUTO PRINT RUN 5

2013 Aspire
*BLACK/25: 1X TO 2.5X BASIC CARDS/99
1 Matt Barkley .25 .60
2 Geno Smith .25 .60
3 EJ Manuel .25 .60
4 Mike Glennon .25 .60
5 Tyler Wilson .25 .60
6 Ryan Nassib .25 .60

1994-95 Assets
Produced by Classic, the 1994 Assets set features stars from basketball, hockey, football, baseball, and auto racing. The set was released in two series of 50 cards each. 1,994 cases were produced of each series. This standard-sized card set features a player photo with his name in silver letters on the lower left corner and the Assets logo on the upper right. The back has a color photo on the left side along with a biography on the right side of the card. A Sprint phone card is randomly inserted in each five-card pack.
COMPLETE SET (100) 6.00 15.00
3 Troy Aikman .20 .50
7 Marshall Faulk .40 1.00
9 Drew Bledsoe .20 .50
11 Steve Young .15 .40
12 Dan Wilkinson .05 .15
15 Charlie Garner .08 .25
16 Derrick Alexander .05 .15
23 Antonio Langham .05 .15
24 Greg Hill .05 .15
25 Marshall Faulk CL .20 .50
28 Troy Aikman .20 .50
32 Marshall Faulk .40 1.00
34 Drew Bledsoe .20 .50
36 Steve Young .15 .40
37 Dan Wilkinson .05 .15
40 Charlie Garner .08 .25
41 Derrick Alexander .05 .15
48 Antonio Langham .05 .15
49 Greg Hill .05 .15
52 Rashaan Salaam .05 .15
55 Emmitt Smith .40 1.00
59 Byron Bam Morris .05 .15
61 Errict Rhett .05 .15
63 Heath Shuler .05 .15
66 William Floyd .07 .20
67 Willie McGinest .08 .25
70 Steve McNair .30 .75
71 Ki-Jana Carter .05 .15
74 Drew Bledsoe .20 .50
77 Rashaan Salaam .05 .15
80 Emmitt Smith .40 1.00
84 Byron Bam Morris .05 .15
86 Errict Rhett .05 .15
88 Heath Shuler .05 .15
91 William Floyd .07 .20
92 Willie McGinest .08 .25
95 Steve McNair .30 .75
96 Ki-Jana Carter .05 .15
99 Drew Bledsoe .20 .50
100 Steve Young CL .07 .20

1994-95 Assets Silver Signature
This 48-card standard-size set was randomly inserted at a rate of four per box. The cards are identical to the first twenty-four cards in the each series, except that these show a silver facsimile autograph on their fronts. The first 24 cards correspond to cards 1-24 in the first series while the second 24 cards correspond to cards 51-74 in the second series.
*SILVER SIGS: 1.2X TO 3X BASIC CARDS

1994-95 Assets Die Cuts
This 25-card standard-size set was randomly inserted into packs. DC1-10 were included in series one while DC11-25 were included in series two packs. These cards feature the player on the card and the ability to separate the player's photo. The back contains information about the player on the section of the card that is separable.
COMPLETE SET (25) 30.00 80.00
DC3 Troy Aikman 2.50 6.00
DC7 Marshall Faulk 4.00 10.00
DC8 Steve Young 1.25 3.00
DC14 Heath Shuler .60 1.50
DC16 Byron Bam Morris .60 1.50
DC21 Steve McNair 2.50 6.00
DC23 Errict Rhett .60 1.50
DC25 Emmitt Smith 3.00 8.00

1994-95 Assets Phone Cards One Minute
Measuring 2" by 3 1/4", these cards have rounded corners and were inserted one per pack. Cards 1-24 were in first series packs while 25-48 were included with second series packs. The front features the player's photo and on the side is how long the card is good for. The Assets logo is in the bottom left corner. The back gives instructions on how to use the phone card. The first series cards expired on December 1, 1995 while the second series cards expired on March 31, 1996. The cards with a $2 logo are worth a mulitple of the regular cards. Please refer to the values below for these cards.
COMPLETE SET (48) 7.50 20.00
*PIN NUMB.REVEALED: .2X TO .5X BASIC INS.
*TWO DOLLAR: .5X TO 1.2X BASIC INSERTS
1 Troy Aikman .50 1.25
2 Derrick Alexander .15 .40
3 Drew Bledsoe .20 .50
6 Marshall Faulk .60 1.50
7 Charlie Garner .15 .40
9 Greg Hill .15 .40
12 Antonio Langham .15 .40
22 Dan Wilkinson .15 .40
24 Steve Young .40 1.00
25 Drew Bledsoe .40 1.00
27 Ki-Jana Carter .15 .40
29 William Floyd .15 .40
35 Willie McGinest .15 .40
36 Steve McNair .40 1.00
38 Byron Bam Morris .15 .40
43 Errict Rhett .15 .40
45 Rashaan Salaam .15 .40
46 Heath Shuler .15 .40
47 Emmitt Smith .60 1.50

1994-95 Assets Phone Cards $5
These cards measure 2" by 3 1/4", have rounded corners and were randomly inserted into packs. Cards 1-5 were inserted into first series packs while 6-15 were in second series packs. The front features the player's photo, with "Five Dollars" written in cursive script along the left edge. In the bottom left corner is the Assets logo. The back gives instructions on how to use the phone card. Series one cards expired on December 1, 1995 while second series cards expired on March 31, 1996.
COMPLETE SET (15) 8.00 20.00
*PIN NUMBER REVEALED: .2X TO .5X
1 Troy Aikman .75 2.00
2 Drew Bledsoe .50 1.25
6 Drew Bledsoe .50 1.25
8 Ki-Jana Carter .30 .75
11 Byron Bam Morris .30 .75
12 Rashaan Salaam .30 .75
13 Emmitt Smith 1.00 2.50

1994-95 Assets Phone Cards $100
These 2" by 3 1/4" rounded corner cards were randomly inserted into packs. These cards were placed into series one packs. The front features the player's photo, with "One Hundred Dollars" written in cursive script along the left edge. The Assets logo is in the bottom left corner. The back gives instructions on how to use the phone card. These cards are listed in alphabetical order. These cards expired on December 1, 1995.
COMPLETE SET (5) 15.00 40.00
*PIN NUMBER REVEALED: .2X TO .5X
1 Troy Aikman 5.00 12.00
2 Drew Bledsoe 4.00 10.00

1994-95 Assets Phone Cards $200
These rounded corner cards were randomly inserted into second series packs and measure 2" by 3 1/4". The front features the player's photo, with "Two Hundred Dollars" written in cursive script along the left edge. In the bottom left corner is the Assets logo. The back gives instructions on how to use the phone card. These cards are arranged in alphabetical order. These cards expired on March 31, 1996.
COMPLETE SET (5) 25.00 50.00
*PIN NUMBER REVEALED: .2X TO .5X
1 Drew Bledsoe 6.00 15.00
3 Ki-Jana Carter 4.00 10.00
5 Rashaan Salaam 4.00 10.00

1994-95 Assets Phone Cards $2000
These rounded-corner cards measuring 2" by 3 1/4" were randomly inserted into second series packs. Just four of each of these cards were produced. The front features the player's photo, with "Two Thousand Dollars" written in cursive script along the left edge. In the bottom left corner is the Assets logo. The back gives instructions on how to use the phone card. Two differnt Emmitt Smith promo cards were also issued to promote the product. The cards are unnumbered and checklisted below in alphabetical order. The cards expired on March 31, 1996.
HAW Emmitt Smith Hawaii X promo 5.00 12.00
SAM Emmitt Smith sample 4.00 10.00

1995 Assets Gold
This 50-card set measures the standard size. The fronts feature borderless player action photos with the player's name printed in gold at the bottom. The backs carry a portrait of the player with his name, career highlights, and statistics. The Dale Earnhardt card was pulled from circulation early in the product's release. It is considered a Short Print (SP) but is not included in the complete set price.
COMPLETE SET (49) 6.00 15.00
15 Rashaan Salaam .05 .15
16 Kyle Brady .05 .15
17 J.J. Stokes .10 .30
18 James O. Stewart .20 .50
19 Michael Westbrook .10 .30
20 Ki-Jana Carter .07 .20
21 Steve McNair .40 1.00
22 Kerry Collins .30 .75
23 Byron Bam Morris .05 .15
24 Errict Rhett .08 .25
25 William Floyd .07 .20
26 Drew Bledsoe .08 .25
27 Marshall Faulk .40 1.00
28 Troy Aikman .25 .60
29 Steve Young .15 .40
30 Trent Dilfer .08 .25
31 Emmitt Smith .40 1.00
50 Ki-Jana Carter CL .05 .15

1995 Assets Gold Die Cuts Silver
This 20-card set was randomly inserted in packs at a rate of one in 18. The fronts feature a borderless player color action photo with a diamond-shaped top and the player's action taking place in front of the card name. The backs carry the card name, player's name and career highlights. The cards are numbered on the backs. Gold versions were inserted at a rate of one in 72 packs.
COMPLETE SET (20) 10.00 25.00
*GOLDS: .8X TO 2X SILVERS
GOLD STATED ODDS 1:72
SDC3 Kyle Brady .40 1.00
SDC5 Marshall Faulk .75 2.00
SDC11 Ki-Jana Carter .50 1.25
SDC12 Rashaan Salaam .50 1.25
SDC15 Emmitt Smith 1.50 4.00
SDC16 Drew Bledsoe .75 2.00
SDC17 Kerry Collins 1.00 2.50
SDC19 Michael Westbrook .40 1.00
SDC20 Heath Shuler .50 1.25

1995 Assets Gold Printer's Proofs
*PRINT PROOF: 2X TO 5X BASIC CARDS

1995 Assets Gold Silver Signatures
COMP. SILVER SIG SET (50) 15.00 40.00
*SILVER SIGS: .8X TO 2X BASIC CARDS

1995 Assets Gold Phone Cards $2
This 47-card set was randomly inserted in packs and measures 2 1/8" by 3 3/8". The fronts feature color action player photos with the player's name below. The $2 calling value is printed vertically down the left. The backs carry the instructions on how to use the cards which expired on 7/31/96. The cards are unnumbered.
COMPLETE SET (47) 15.00 40.00
*PIN NUMBER REVEALED: HALF VALUE
15 Rashaan Salaam .30 .75
16 Kyle Brady .30 .75
17 J.J. Stokes .30 .75
18 James O. Stewart .30 .75
19 Michael Westbrook .30 .75
20 Ki-Jana Carter .30 .75
21 Steve McNair 1.50 4.00
22 Kerry Collins .75 2.00
23 Byron Bam Morris .30 .75
24 Errict Rhett .30 .75
25 William Floyd .30 .75
26 Drew Bledsoe .60 1.50
27 Marshall Faulk .60 1.50
28 Troy Aikman 1.00 2.50
29 Steve Young .75 2.00
30 Trent Dilfer .30 .75
31 Emmitt Smith 1.25 3.00

1995 Assets Gold Phone Cards $5
This 16-card set measures 2 1/8" by 3 3/8" and was randomly inserted in packs. The fronts feature color action player photos with the player's name below. The $5 calling value is printed vertically down the left. The backs carry the instructions on how to use the cards which expired on 7/31/96. The cards are unnumbered. The Microlined versions are inserted at a rate of one in 18 packs versus one in six packs for the basic $5 card.
COMPLETE SET (16) 25.00 60.00
*MICROLINED: .6X TO 1.5X BASIC INSERTS
STATED ODDS 1:18
*PIN NUMBER REVEALED: HALF VALUE
1 Drew Bledsoe .75 2.00
2 Marshall Faulk .75 2.00
5 Emmitt Smith 1.50 4.00
6 J.J. Stokes .50 1.25
8 Michael Westbrook .50 1.25
9 Troy Aikman 1.25 3.00
11 Ki-Jana Carter .50 1.25

1995 Assets Gold Phone Cards $25
This 5-card set measures 2 1/8" by 3 3/8" and was randomly inserted in packs. The fronts feature color action player photos of two different players with the player's name in gold below each photo. The $25 calling value is printed vertically in gold separating the two players. The backs carry the instructions on how to use the cards which expired on 7/31/96. The cards are unnumbered.
COMPLETE SET (5) 20.00 50.00
*PIN NUMBER REVEALED: HALF VALUE
1 Marshall Faulk 5.00 12.00
Ki-Jana Carter
2 Steve McNair3(Kerry Collins 5.00 12.00

1995 Assets Gold Phone Cards $100
This five-card set measures 2 1/8" by 3 3/8". The fronts feature color action player photos with the player's name below. The $100 calling value is printed on the left. The backs carry the instructions on how to use the cards which expired on 7/31/96. The cards are unnumbered and checklisted below in alphabetical order.
*PIN NUMBER REVEALED: HALF VALUE
1 Kerry Collins 6.00 15.00
3 Emmitt Smith 20.00 50.00
5 Steve Young 10.00 25.00

1996 Assets
The 1996 Classic Assets was issued in one set totalling 50 cards. This 50-card premium set has a tremendous selection of the top athletes in the world headlines. Each card features action photos, up-to-date statistics and is printed on high-quality, foil-stamped stock. Hot Print cards are parallel cards randomly inserted in Hot Packs and are valued at a multiple of the regular cards below.
COMPLETE SET (50) 5.00 10.00
1 Troy Aikman .25 .60
2 Drew Bledsoe .10 .30
5 Isaac Bruce .08 .25
6 Kerry Collins .08 .25
7 Trent Dilfer .05 .15
10 Marshall Faulk .20 .50
11 William Floyd .05 .15
12 Joey Galloway .05 .15
24 Steve McNair .20 .50
25 Byron Bam Morris .05 .15
35 Errict Rhett .05 .15
36 Curtis Martin .10 .30
40 Darnay Scott .05 .15
41 Emmitt Smith .40 1.00
49 Steve Young .20 .50
50 Eric Zeier .05 .15

1996 Assets Hot Prints
*HOT PRINTS: .8X TO 2X BASIC CARDS

1996 Assets A Cut Above
The even cards were randomly inserted in retail packs at a rate of one in eight, and the odd cards were inserted in clear asset packs at a rate of one in 20, this 20-card die-cut set is composed of 10 phone cards and 10 trading cards. The cards have rounded corners except for one which is cut in a straight corner design. The fronts feature a color action player cut-out superimposed over a gray background with the words "cut above" printed throughout and resembled to be cut so it displays a basketball game behind it. The backs carry a color action player photo with the player's name and a short career summary.
COMPLETE SET (20) 20.00 50.00
CA1 Keyshawn Johnson 1.25 3.00
CA2 Troy Aikman 1.50 4.00
CA7 Kevin Hardy .50 1.25
CA8 Emmitt Smith 2.00 5.00
CA11 Marshall Faulk 1.00 2.50
CA13 Drew Bledsoe 1.00 2.50
CA19 Kerry Collins .60 1.50
A96 Emmitt Smith Promo

1996 Assets A Cut Above Phone Cards
This 10-card set, which were inserted at a rate of one in eight, measures approximately 2 1/8" by 3 3/8" have rounded corners except for one corner which is cut out and made straight. The fronts feature a color action player cut-out superimposed over a gray background with the words "cut above" printed throughout and resembled to be cut so that it displays a game going on behind the background. The backs carry the instructions on how to use the card. The cards expired on 1/31/97.
COMPLETE SET (10) 12.50 30.00
*PIN NUMBER REVEALED: HALF VALUE
6 Marshall Faulk 1.25 3.00
7 Drew Bledsoe 1.25 3.00
10 Kerry Collins .60 1.50

1996 Assets Crystal Phone Cards
Randomly inserted in retail packs at a rate of one in 250, this high-tech, 10-card insert set contains clear holographic phone cards worth five minutes of long distance calling time. The cards measure approximately 2 1/8" by 3 3/8" with rounded corners. The fronts display a color action double-image player cut-out on a clear crystal background with the player's name printed vertically on the side. The backs carry instructions on how to use the card. The cards expired January 31, 1997. Twenty dollar phone cards of these athletes were issued, they are valued as a multiple of the cards below.
COMPLETE SET (10) 20.00 50.00
*PIN NUMBER REVEALED: HALF VALUE
1 Troy Aikman 1.50 4.00
2 Drew Bledsoe 1.00 2.50
4 Marshall Faulk 1.25 3.00

1996 Assets Crystal Phone Cards $20
1 Troy Aikman 4.00 10.00
2 Drew Bledsoe 2.50 6.00
4 Marshall Faulk 3.00 8.00

1996 Assets Phone Cards $2
COMPLETE SET (30) 12.50 30.00
*$2 CARDS: .6X TO 1.5X $1 CARDS
*PIN NUMBER REVEALED: HALF VALUE

1996 Assets Phone Cards $5
This 20-card set was randomly inserted in retail packs at a rate of 1 in 5. The cards measure approximately 2 1/8" by 3 3/8" with rounded corners. The fronts display color action player photos with the player's name in a red bar below. The backs carry the instructions on how to use the cards and the expiration date of 1/31/97.
COMPLETE SET (20) 30.00 80.00
*PIN NUMBER REVEALED: HALF VALUE
1 Troy Aikman 1.50 4.00
2 Drew Bledsoe 1.00 2.50
4 Isaac Bruce .60 1.50
5 Kerry Collins .60 1.50
7 Marshall Faulk 1.25 3.00
16 Emmitt Smith 2.00 5.00
20 Steve Young 1.25 3.00

1996 Assets Phone Cards $10
This 10-card set was randomly inserted in packs at a rate of 1 in 20. The cards measure approximately 2 1/8" by 3 3/8" with rounded corners. The fronts display color action player photos with the player's name in a red bar below. The backs carry the instructions on how to use the cards and the expiration date of 1/31/97.
COMPLETE SET (10) 25.00 60.00
*PIN NUMBER REVEALED: HALF VALUE
1 Troy Aikman 2.50 6.00
2 Drew Bledsoe 2.00 5.00
4 Marshall Faulk 2.00 5.00
8 Emmitt Smith 3.00 8.00

1996 Assets Phone Cards $20
This five card set measures approximately 2 1/8" by 3 3/8" with rounded corners and were randomly inserted in retail packs. The fronts display color action player photos with the player's name. The backs carry the instructions on how to use the cards and the expiration date of 1/31/97.
COMPLETE SET (5) 25.00 60.00
*PIN NUMBER REVEALED: HALF VALUE
3 Emmitt Smith 5.00 12.00

1996 Assets Phone Cards $100
This five card set, randomly inserted in packs, measures approximately 2 1/8" by 3 3/8" with rounded corners. The fronts display color action player photos with the player's name. The backs carry the instructions on how to use the cards and the expiration date of 1/31/97.
COMPLETE SET (5) 40.00 80.00
*PIN NUMBER REVEALED: HALF VALUE
2 Marshall Faulk 6.00 15.00

1996 Assets Phone Cards $2000
NOT PRICED DUE TO SCARCITY
1 Emmitt Smith

1996 Assets Silksations
Randomly inserted in retail packs at a rate of one in 100, this 10-card standard-size set features duplexed fabric-stock with top athletes. The fronts display a color action player cut-out with a two-tone background. The player's name is printed below. The backs carry a head photo of the player made to appear as if it is coming out of a square hole in gold cloth. The player's name and a short career summary are below. The cards are numbered with a "S" prefix and sequenced in alphabetical order.
COMPLETE SET (10) 40.00 80.00
2 Kerry Collins 3.00 8.00
4 Marshall Faulk 5.00 12.00
8 Emmitt Smith 8.00 20.00

1997 Best Heroes of the Gridiron Promos
This set was produced to promote a football figurines product by the Best Card Company. Each card in this series was printed with a different design on the front presumably to represent a basic issue card and two insert sets that were never produced. The players are all pictured in their college uniforms. The unnumbered cardbacks include the Players Inc. and Collegiate Licensing Company logos within a larger "Heroes of the Gridiron" logo.
COMPLETE SET (3) 2.50 6.00
1 Mike Alstott .75 2.00
2 Warrick Dunn 1.00 2.50
3 Curtis Martin .75 2.00

1991 Classic Promos
These 1991 Classic Football Draft Pick promos measure the standard size. The front features an action color photo on a two-toned spotted gray background of the player with his name below in aqua or black print. The borders are a white and gray spotty pattern, with "Premiere Classic Edition" in the upper left hand corner and "'91" in the upper right hand corner. The back states that these cards are for promotional purposes only. These five player cards (minus the "B" variations) were also issued as an unperforated promo sheet that measures approximately 7 1/2" by 7 1/8". The sheets were given away during the 1991 12th National Sports Collectors Convention in Anaheim (July 2nd-7th). The promo sheets bear a unique serial number("X of 10,000"). The backs have the warning "For Promotional Use Only" plastered over the Premier Classic Edition logo.
COMPLETE SET (7) 1.20 3.00
1 Antone Davis .20 .50
Black print on front
2A Rocket Ismail .40 1.00
Black print on front
2B Rocket Ismail .40 1.00
Blue print on front
3A Todd Lyght .20 .50
Black print on front
3B Todd Lyght .20 .50
Blue print on front
4 Russell Maryland .20 .50
Black print on front
5 Eric Turner .20 .50
Black print on front

1991 Classic
This 50-card set was distributed by Classic Games in factory set form. Top players from the 1991 NFL Draft are featured, including early cards of Brett Favre and Ricky Watters. Neither NFL team nor college team names are mentioned on the cards.
COMPLETE SET (50) 1.50 4.00
1 Rocket Ismail .15 .40
2 Russell Maryland .01 .05
3 Eric Turner .02 .10
4 Bruce Pickens .01 .05
5 Mike Croel .01 .05
6 Todd Lyght .01 .05
7 Eric Swann .02 .10
8 Antone Davis .01 .05
9 Stanley Richard .01 .05
10 Pat Harlow .01 .05
11 Alvin Harper .01 .05
12 Mike Pritchard .02 .10
13 Leonard Russell .02 .10
14 Dan McGwire .01 .05
15 Bobby Wilson .01 .05
16 Alfred Williams .01 .05
17 Vinnie Clark .01 .05
18 Kelvin Pritchett .01 .05
19 Harvey Williams .02 .10
20 Stan Thomas .01 .05
21 Randal Hill .02 .10
22 Todd Marinovich .01 .05
23 Henry Jones .01 .05
24 Jarrod Bunch .02 .10
25 Mike Dumas .01 .05
26 Ed King .01 .05
27 Reggie Johnson .01 .05
28 Roman Phifer .01 .05
29 Mike Jones .01 .05
30 Brett Favre 2.00 5.00
31 Browning Nagle .01 .05
32 Esera Tuaolo .01 .05
33 George Thornton .01 .05
34 Dixon Edwards .01 .05
35 Darryl Lewis .01 .05
36 Eric Bieniemy .01 .05
37 Shane Curry .01 .05
38 Jerome Henderson .01 .05
39 Wesley Carroll .02 .10
40 Nick Bell .01 .05
41 John Flannery .01 .05
42 Ricky Watters .25 .60
43 Jeff Graham .08 .25
44 Eric Moten .01 .05
45 Jesse Campbell .01 .05
46 Chris Zorich .02 .10
47 Doug Thomas .01 .05
48 Phil Hansen .02 .10
49 Kanavis McGhee .02 .10
50 Reggie Barrett .01 .05
P1 National Promo Sheet/10000 1.00 2.50
NNO Rocket Ismail AU/1500 10.00 20.00

1992 Classic Promos
This six-card standard-size set was issued by Classic to preview the forthcoming draft pick issue. As with the regular issue foil and blister pack cards, the fronts have glossy color player photos enclosed by thin black borders. However, the color player photos on these promo cards differ from those used in the regular issue set. The Classic logo in the lower left corner is superimposed over a blue bottom stripe that includes player information. For background, the backs display the same unfocused image of a ball carrier breaking through the line in the deep, rich purple and maroon of the blister-pack cards. The backs present biography, but only the headings of the college stat categories appear. Further, the color close-up photos are also different, and the career summary has been replaced by a "News Flash" in the form of an advertisement for the draft pick set. Finally, the disclaimer "For Promotional Purposes Only" is stamped where the statistics would have been listed.
COMPLETE SET (6) 1.25 3.00
1 Desmond Howard .30 .75
2 David Klingler .20 .50
3 Quentin Coryatt .20 .50
4 Carl Pickens .50 1.25
5 Derek Brown .20 .50
6 Casey Weldon .20 .50

1992 Classic
The 1992 Classic Draft Picks Foil set contains 100 standard-size cards featuring the highest rated football players eligible for the 1992 NFL draft. The production run of the foil was limited to 14,000 ten-box cases, and to 40,000 of each bonus card. The fronts have glossy color player photos enclosed by thin black borders. A Classic logo in the lower left corner is superimposed over a blue bottom stripe that includes player information. Against the background of an unfocused image of a ball carrier breaking through the line, the backs have biography, college statistics, and career summary, with a color head shot in the lower left corner. This 100-card set needs to be distinguished from the 60-card set sold in blister packs only, which essentially was a re-package of the first 60-cards in the set. Though both sets are identical in design, the photos displayed on the fronts are different, as are the head shots on the backs. On some of the cards, the career summary also differs. However, the most distinctive feature is that background on the backs of the foil-pack cards are ghosted, whereas the same background on the blister-pack cards exhibits a deep, rich purple and maroon. Cards #30 and #54 are different in both versions. Key cards include Edgar Bennett, Marco Coleman, Quentin Coryatt, Sean Gilbert, Desmond Howard, David Klingler, Johnny Mitchell and Carl Pickens.
COMP.BLISTER SET (60) 2.00 5.00
COMPLETE FOIL SET (100) 4.00 10.00
1 Desmond Howard .20 .50
2 David Klingler .02 .10
3 Quentin Coryatt .02 .10
4 Bill Johnson .01 .05
5 Eugene Chung .01 .05
6 Derek Brown TE .01 .05
7 Carl Pickens .30 .75
8 Chris Mims .01 .05
9 Charles Davenport .01 .05
10 Ray Roberts .01 .05
11 Chuck Smith .01 .05
12 Joe Bowden .01 .05
13 Mirko Jurkovic .01 .05
14 Tony Smith .01 .05
15 Ken Swilling .01 .05
16 Greg Skrepenak .01 .05
17 Phillippi Sparks .02 .10
18 Alonzo Spellman .02 .10
19 Bernard Dafney .01 .05
20 Edgar Bennett .15 .40
21 Shane Dronett .01 .05
22 Jeremy Lincoln .01 .05
23 Dion Lambert .01 .05
24 Siran Stacy .01 .05
25 Tony Sacca .01 .05
26 Sean Lumpkin .01 .05
27 Tommy Vardell .02 .10
28 Keith Hamilton .08 .25
29 Ashley Ambrose .02 .10
30 Sean Gilbert .08 .25
31 Casey Weldon .02 .10
32 Marc Boutte .01 .05
33 Santana Dotson .02 .10
34 Ronnie West .01 .05
35 Michael Bankston .01 .05
36 Mike Pawlawski .02 .10
37 Dale Carter .02 .10
38 Carlos Snow .01 .05
39 Corey Barlow .01 .05

40 Mark D'Onofrio .01 .05
41 Matt Blundin .01 .05
42 George Rooks .01 .05
43 Patrick Rowe .01 .05
44 Dwight Hollier .01 .05
45 Joel Steed .01 .05
46 Erick Anderson .01 .05
47 Rodney Culver .01 .05
48 Chris Hakel .01 .05
49 Luke Fisher .01 .05
50 Kevin Smith .02 .10
51 Robert Brooks .20 .50
52 Bucky Richardson .01 .05
53 Steve Israel .01 .05
54 Marco Coleman .08 .25
55 Johnny Mitchell .02 .10
56 Scottie Graham .02 .10
57 Keith Goganious .01 .05
58 Tommy Maddox .50 1.25
59 Terrell Buckley .02 .10
60 Dana Hall .01 .05
61 Ty Detmer .08 .25
62 Darryl Williams .01 .05
63 Jason Hanson .02 .10
64 Leon Searcy .01 .05
65 Gene McGuire .01 .05
66 Will Furrer .01 .05
67 Darren Woodson .08 .25
68 Tracy Scroggins .01 .05
69 Corey Widmer .01 .05
70 Robert Harris .01 .05
71 Larry Tharpe .01 .05
72 Lance Olberding .01 .05
73 Stacey Dillard .01 .05
74 Troy Auzenne .01 .05
75 Tommy Jeter .01 .05
76 Mike Evans .01 .05
77 Shane Collins .01 .05
78 Mark Thomas .01 .05
79 Chester McGlockton .02 .10
80 Robert Porcher .08 .25
81 Marquez Pope .02 .10
82 Rico Smith .01 .05
83 Tyrone Williams .02 .10
84 Rod Smith DB .02 .10
85 Tyrone Legette .01 .05
86 Wayne Hawkins .01 .05
87 Derrick Moore .01 .05
88 Tim Lester .01 .05
89 Calvin Holmes .01 .05
90 Reggie Dwight .01 .05
91 Eddie Robinson .01 .05
92 Robert Jones .01 .05
93 Ricardo McDonald .01 .05
94 Howard Dinkins .01 .05
95 Todd Collins LB .01 .05
96 Eddie Blake .01 .05
97 Classic Quarterbacks .02 .10
98 T.Detmer/D.Howard BB .08 .25
NNO Checklist Card 1 .01 .05
NNO Checklist Card 2 .01 .05

1992 Classic Gold

COMP.FACT.GOLD (101) 20.00 50.00
*GOLDS: 1.5X TO 4X BASIC CARDS
AU1 D.Howard/5000 AUTO 10.00 25.00

1992 Classic Blister

COMP.BLISTER SET (60) 2.50 6.00
*BLISTER CARDS: .4X TO 1X BASIC CARDS
30 John Ray UER .08 .25
54 Tyrone Ashley .08 .25

1992 Classic Autographs

These signed cards were issued by Classic as part of a factory set. Each features an authentic player autograph on the front that is identical to the player's corresponding card in the base set. A brief congratulatory message from Classic is included on the backs that serves to authenticate the signature.

1 Alonzo Spellman 5.00 12.00
2 Erick Anderson 4.00 10.00
3 Troy Auzenne 4.00 10.00
4 Michael Bankston 4.00 10.00
5 Corey Barlow 4.00 10.00
6 Matt Blundin 4.00 10.00
7 Robert Brooks 6.00 15.00
8 Derek Brown TE 4.00 10.00
9 Terrell Buckley 5.00 12.00
10 Eugene Chung 4.00 10.00
11 Marco Coleman 6.00 15.00
12 Shane Collins 4.00 10.00
13 Todd Collins LB 4.00 10.00
14 Quentin Coryatt 5.00 12.00
15 Rodney Culver 10.00 25.00
16 Stacey Dillard 4.00 10.00
17 Howard Dinkins 4.00 10.00
18 Shane Dronett 4.00 10.00
19 Reggie Dwight 4.00 10.00
20 Mike Evans 4.00 10.00
21 Luke Fisher 4.00 10.00
22 Keith Goganious 4.00 10.00
23 Chris Hakel 4.00 10.00
24 Dana Hall 4.00 10.00
25 Jason Hanson 5.00 12.00
26 Robert Harris 4.00 10.00
27 Wayne Hawkins 4.00 10.00
28 Calvin Holmes 4.00 10.00
29 Desmond Howard 10.00 25.00
30 Steve Israel 4.00 10.00
31 Tommy Jeter 4.00 10.00
32 Bill Johnson 4.00 10.00
33 Dion Lambert 4.00 10.00
34 David Klingler 5.00 12.00
35 Tyrone Legette 4.00 10.00
36 Jeremy Lincoln 4.00 10.00
37 Sean Lumpkin 4.00 10.00
38 Gene McGuire 4.00 10.00
39 Derrick Moore 4.00 10.00
40 Mike Pawlawski 5.00 12.00
41 Robert Porcher 6.00 15.00
42 Bucky Richardson 4.00 10.00
43 Eddie Robinson 4.00 10.00
44 Tony Sacca 4.00 10.00
45 Greg Skrepenak 4.00 10.00
46 Kevin Smith 5.00 12.00
47 Rod Smith DB 5.00 12.00
48 Tony Smith 4.00 10.00
49 Carlos Snow 4.00 10.00
50 Phillippi Sparks 5.00 12.00
51 Larry Tharpe 4.00 10.00
52 Mark Thomas 4.00 10.00
53 Tommy Vardell 5.00 12.00
54 Casey Weldon 5.00 12.00
55 Ronnie West 4.00 10.00
56 Darryl Williams 4.00 10.00
57 Tyrone Williams 5.00 12.00
98 T.Detmer/D.Howard/1500 12.00 30.00

1992 Classic LPs

The 1992 Classic Draft Picks Gold LP Insert set contains ten standard-size cards featuring the highest rated football players eligible for the 1992 NFL draft. These ten gold foil stamped bonus cards were randomly inserted in foil packs. The production run of the foil was limited to 14,000, ten-box cases, and to 40,000 of each bonus card.

COMPLETE SET (10) 1.50 4.00
STATED PRINT RUN 40,000 SETS
LP1 Desmond Howard 1.25 3.00
LP2 David Klingler .25 .60
LP3 Siran Stacy .10 .30
LP4 Casey Weldon .25 .60
LP5 Sean Gilbert .60 1.50
LP6 Matt Blundin .10 .30
LP7 Tommy Maddox 3.00 8.00
LP8 Derek Brown TE .10 .30
LP9 Tony Smith RB .10 .30
LP10 Tony Sacca .10 .30

1992-93 Classic C3

Limited to only 25,000 members, the Classic Collectors Club (also known as C3) featured two types of memberships: 1) the Presidential Charter membership (5,000), and 2) the Charter membership (20,000). As a bonus, the first 10,000 members received three packs of the bilingual edition of the 1991 Classic Draft Picks Collection. Exclusive to Presidential members were the following: a Brien Taylor autograph card (hand numbered "X/5,000"); an uncut sheet of either 1992 baseball, football, or hockey draft picks; and three special promo cards. In addition to other items (promo cards, T-shirt, newsletter, membership card, and posters), all members received a 30-card standard-size multi-sport set featuring tomorrow's future stars. Each set was accompanied by a certificate of limited edition, giving the set serial number and total production run (25,000). The sports represented are baseball (1-7, 25-27), basketball (8-13), football (14-20), hockey (21-24), track and field (28), and swimming (29).

COMP.FACT SET (30) 6.00 15.00
14 Desmond Howard .30 .75
15 David Klingler .20 .50
16 Quentin Coryatt .20 .50
17 Carl Pickens .20 .50
18 Tony Smith .20 .50
19 Rocket Ismail .30 .75
20 Terrell Buckley .20 .50

1993 Classic Gold Promos

These standard-size promo cards were sent to Classic Collectors Club members. The fronts feature color action player photos. The player's name, the word "Gold," and his position are gold foil stamped in a black stripe at the bottom. The production run "1 of 5,000" is gold foil stamped above this black stripe. The gold foil Classic logo at the upper left rounds out the front. On a blue-gray variegated background, the horizontal back has a narrowly cropped action photo, biography, and player profile. A tan pebble-grain panel designed for college statistics carries the disclaimer "For Promotional Purposes Only." The card is numbered on the back with a "PR" prefix.

COMPLETE SET (2) 1.60 4.00
PR1 Terry Kirby .60 1.50
PR2 Jerome Bettis 1.20 3.00

1993 Classic

The 1993 Classic Football Draft Picks set consists of 100 standard-size cards. Randomly inserted throughout the foil packs were ten limited-print foil stamped cards, 1993 Classic Basketball Draft Pick Preview cards, 1993 Classic NFL Pro Line Preview cards, and 1,000 autographed cards by Super Bowl MVP Troy Aikman. Cards of number one pick Drew Bledsoe and number two pick Rick Mirer were exclusive to Classic until these players signed their NFL contracts. The production figures were 15,000 ten-box sequentially numbered cases, with 36 ten-card packs per box. The fronts feature color action player photos with blue stone-textured borders. The player's name and position is printed in a mustard bar at the bottom of the picture. The Classic Draft Picks logo overlaps the bar and the photo slightly to the right of center. The horizontal backs carry a small action photo, biographical information, statistics, and a player profile. Key cards include Jerome Bettis, Drew Bledsoe, Terry Kirby and Rick Mirer. Classic also issued 5,000 Gold Factory sets which include autographed cards of Drew Bledsoe and Rick Mirer.

COMPLETE SET (100) 2.50 6.00
1 Drew Bledsoe .50 1.25
2 Rick Mirer .08 .25
3 Garrison Hearst .20 .50
4 Marvin Jones .01 .05
5 John Copeland .01 .05
6 Eric Curry .01 .05
7 Curtis Conway .08 .25
8 Willie Roaf .10 .30
9 Lincoln Kennedy .01 .05
10 Jerome Bettis .75 2.00
11 Mike Compton .01 .05
12 John Gerak .01 .05
13 Will Shields .02 .10
14 Ben Coleman .01 .05
15 Ernest Dye .01 .05
16 Lester Holmes .01 .05
17 Brad Hopkins .01 .05
18 Everett Lindsay .01 .05
19 Todd Rucci .01 .05
20 Lance Gunn .01 .05
21 Elvis Grbac .60 1.50
22 Shane Matthews .25 .60
23 Rudy Harris .01 .05
24 Richie Anderson .08 .25
25 Derek Brown RB .01 .05
26 Roger Harper .01 .05
27 Terry Kirby .08 .25
28 Natrone Means .08 .25
29 Glyn Milburn .02 .10
30 Adrian Murrell .08 .25
31 Lorenzo Neal .01 .05
32 Roosevelt Potts .01 .05
33 Kevin Williams RBK .01 .05
34 Russell Copeland .01 .05
35 Fred Baxter .01 .05
36 Troy Drayton .02 .10
37 Chris Gedney .01 .05
38 Irv Smith .01 .05
39 Olanda Truitt .01 .05
40 Victor Bailey .01 .05
41 Horace Copeland .01 .05
42 Ron Dickerson Jr. .01 .05
43 Willie Harris .01 .05
44 Tyrone Hughes .01 .05
45 Qadry Ismail .08 .25
46 Reggie Brooks .02 .10
47 Sean LaChapelle .01 .05
48 O.J.McDuffie UER .20 .50
49 Larry Ryans .01 .05
50 Kenny Shedd .02 .10
51 Brian Stablein .01 .05
52 Lamar Thomas .01 .05
53 Kevin Williams WR .02 .10
54 Othello Henderson .01 .05
55 Kevin Henry .01 .05
56 Todd Kelly .01 .05
57 Devon McDonald .01 .05
58 Michael Strahan .75 2.00
59 Dan Williams .01 .05
60 Gilbert Brown .08 .25
61 Mark Caesar .01 .05
62 Ronnie Dixon .01 .05
63 John Parrella .01 .05
64 Leonard Renfro .01 .05
65 Coleman Rudolph .01 .05
66 Ronnie Bradford .01 .05
67 Tom Carter .01 .05
68 Deon Figures .01 .05
69 Derrick Frazier .01 .05
70 Darrien Gordon .02 .10
71 Carlton Gray .01 .05
72 Adrian Hardy .01 .05
73 Mike Reid .01 .05
74 Thomas Smith .01 .05
75 Robert O'Neal .01 .05
76 Chad Brown .01 .05
77 Demetrius DuBose .01 .05
78 Reggie Givens .01 .05
79 Travis Hill .01 .05
80 Rich McKenzie .01 .05
81 Barry Minter .01 .05
82 Darrin Smith .01 .05
83 Steve Tovar .01 .05
84 Patrick Bates .01 .05
85 Dan Footman .01 .05
86 Ryan McNeil .08 .25
87 Danan Hughes .01 .05
88 Mark Brunell .75 2.00
89 Ron Moore .02 .10
90 Antonio London .01 .05
91 Steve Everitt .01 .05
92 Wayne Simmons .01 .05
93 Robert Smith .30 .75
94 Dana Stubblefield .02 .10
95 George Teague .02 .10
96 Carl Simpson .01 .05
97 Billy Joe Hobert .02 .10
98 Gino Torretta .02 .10
99 Checklist 1 .01 .05
100 Checklist 2 .01 .05
POY1 Troy Aikman POY/17,500 2.00 5.00
AU1 Troy Aikman AU/1000 20.00 50.00
AU2 Drew Bledsoe AU/5000 12.00 30.00
AU3 Rick Mirer AU/5000 8.00 20.00
PR1A Drew Bledsoe Promo 1.00 2.50
PR1B Drew Bledsoe Promo .75 2.00
PR2 Garrison Hearst
P2 Rick Mirer Promo .60 1.50

1993 Classic Gold

COMPLETE SET (100) 20.00 40.00
COMP.FACT.GOLD (102) 50.00 100.00
*GOLDS: 1.5X TO 4X BASIC CARDS
STATED PRINT RUN 5000 SETS

1993 Classic Autographs

13 Will Shields 3.00 8.00
70 Darrien Gordon 3.00 8.00

1993 Classic Draft Stars

These standard-size cards were issued one per 1993 Classic Football Draft Pick jumbo pack. This 20-card set features "Draft Stars". The cards have "1 of 20,000" printed at the top. There was approximately one Bledsoe/Mirer "jumbo card" in every other box.

COMPLETE SET (20) 7.50 20.00
ONE PER JUMBO PACK
STATED PRINT RUN 20,000 SETS
DS1 Drew Bledsoe 1.25 3.00
DS2 Rick Mirer .25 .60
DS3 Garrison Hearst .50 1.25
DS4 Marvin Jones .05 .15
DS5 John Copeland .05 .15
DS6 Eric Curry .05 .15
DS7 Curtis Conway .25 .60
DS8 Jerome Bettis 2.00 5.00
DS9 Patrick Bates .05 .15
DS10 Tom Carter .05 .15
DS11 Irv Smith .05 .15
DS12 Robert Smith .75 2.00
DS13 O.J.McDuffie .50 1.25
DS14 Roosevelt Potts .05 .15
DS15 Natrone Means .25 .60
DS16 Glyn Milburn .08 .25
DS17 Reggie Brooks .08 .25
DS18 Kevin Williams WR .08 .25
DS19 Qadry Ismail .25 .60
DS20 Billy Joe Hobert .08 .25
NNO Bledsoe 4.00 10.00
Mirer Jumbo

1993 Classic LPs

These limited print, foil-stamped cards were randomly inserted in 1993 Classic Football Draft Pick foil packs. The cards measure the standard size, and 45,000 of each card was produced. The fronts feature color action player photos with bluish-gray variegated borders. The player's name, position, and the Classic 1993 Draft emblem appear in the golden foil stripe that edges the bottom of the picture. In addition, "1 of 45,000" and "LP" are gold foil stamped just above the stripe. On a bluish-gray background, the horizontal back carries a second color action photo and player profile.

COMPLETE SET (10) 7.50 20.00
STATED PRINT RUN 45,000 SETS
LP1 Drew Bledsoe 3.00 8.00
LP2 Rick Mirer .60 1.50
LP3 Garrison Hearst 1.25 3.00
LP4 Marvin Jones .10 .30
LP5 John Copeland .10 .30
LP6 Eric Curry .10 .30
LP7 Curtis Conway .60 1.50
LP8 Jerome Bettis 5.00 12.00
LP9 Reggie Brooks .25 .60
LP10 Qadry Ismail .60 1.50

1993 Classic Superhero Comics

Illustrated by Neal Adams of Deathwatch 2,000 fame, these four standard-size cards were randomly inserted in 1993 Classic Football Draft Pick foil packs. 15,000 of each card were produced. The fronts feature full-bleed color comic-style action poses of the player. The player's name and position appear in a mustard stripe toward the bottom of the picture. Over a ghosted version of the front photo, the horizontal backs carry a small color action photo and a summary of the player's performance. The cards are numbered on the back with an "SH" prefix.

COMPLETE SET (4) 10.00 25.00
STATED PRINT RUN 15,000 SETS
SH1 Troy Aikman 10.00 12.00
SH2 Drew Bledsoe 4.00 10.00
SH3 Rick Mirer .75 2.00
SH4 Garrison Hearst 1.50 4.00

1994 Classic Previews

Randomly inserted in Images packs, this five-card standard-size set features color player action shots on the fronts. These photos are borderless, except for the blue triangle in a lower corner that carries the player's position in white lettering. The player's name appears in the other corner. The back carries a borderless color player action shot, which is ghosted, except for the area around the player's head. A congratulatory message at the bottom gives the number of sets produced: 1,950. The cards are numbered on the back with a "PR" prefix.

COMPLETE SET (5) 4.00 7.00
PR1 Heath Shuler .60 1.50
PR2 Trent Dilfer 1.25 3.00
PR3 Dan Wilkinson .40 1.00
PR4 David Palmer .40 1.00
PR5 Johnnie Morton .40 1.00

1994 Classic Promos

These standard-size cards were issued to preview the design of the 1994 Classic Football Draft Picks series. The fronts feature color action shots of the players in their college uniforms. The photos are borderless, except for a royal blue lower corner that carries the player's position. The player's name is printed in the other lower corner. The borderless back carries a player action shot that is ghosted, with the exception of the area around the player's head. Player biography, statistics, and career highlights round out the back. Along the bottom are the words, "For promotional purposes only." The cards are numbered on the back with a "PR" prefix.

COMPLETE SET (3) 2.00 5.00
PR1 Marshall Faulk 1.20 3.00
PR2 Heath Shuler .40 1.00
PR3 Heath Shuler .40 1.00

1994 Classic

This 105-card standard-size set features color player action shots on the fronts. These photos are borderless, except for the blue triangle in a lower corner that carries the player's position in white lettering. The draftee's name and his new NFL team helmet logo appear in the other corner. The back carries a borderless color player action shot, which is ghosted, except for the area around the player's head. The player's statistics, brief biography, and career highlights round out the back. A parallel gold set was issued one per pack. The cards are valued as a multiple of the regular cards. Key players in this set include Isaac Bruce, Marshall Faulk and Errict Rhett. Two special inserts (one signed) featuring Jerry Rice were randomly inserted into packs, both in honor of Rice becoming the all-time TD reception leader. Signed versions of the Jerry Rice were hand signed on card front in silver and hand numbered to 1994 of each.

COMPLETE SET (105) 2.50 6.00
1 Heath Shuler .02 .10
2 Trent Dilfer .30 .75
3 Marshall Faulk .75 2.00
4 Errict Rhett .08 .25
5 Charlie Garner .25 .60
6 Sam Adams .01 .05
7 Shante Carver .01 .05
8 Dwayne Chandler .01 .05
9 Andre Coleman .01 .05
10 Carlester Crumpler .01 .05
11 Charles Johnson .08 .25
12 David Palmer .02 .10
13 Dan Wilkinson .02 .10
14 LeShon Johnson .01 .05
15 Mario Bates .02 .10
16 Glenn Foley .01 .05
17 William Gaines .01 .05
18 Wayne Gandy .01 .05
19 Jason Gildon .02 .10
20 Eric Gant .01 .05
21 Tre Johnson .01 .05
22 Calvin Jones .01 .05
23 Jake Kelchner .01 .05
24 Perry Klein .01 .05
25 Chuck Levy .01 .05
26 Corey Louchiey .01 .05
27 Chris Maumalanga .01 .05
28 Jamir Miller .02 .10
29 Jim Miller .50 1.25
30 Johnnie Morton .25 .60
31 Doug Nussmeier .02 .10
32 Vaughn Parker .01 .05
33 Darnay Scott .15 .40
34 Fernando Smith .01 .05
35 Lamar Smith .40 1.00
36 Marcus Spears .01 .05
37 Irving Spikes .01 .05
38 Todd Steussie .01 .05
39 Aaron Taylor .01 .05
40 John Thierry .01 .05
41 Dewayne Washington .01 .05
42 Jason Winrow .01 .05
43 Ronnie Woolfork .01 .05
44 Bryant Young .15 .40
45 Arthur Bussie .01 .05
46 Derrick Alexander WR .08 .25
47 Larry Allen .25 .60
48 Aubrey Beavers .01 .05
49 James Bostic .01 .05
50 Jeff Burris .01 .05
51 Lindsey Chapman .01 .05
52 Isaac Davis .01 .05
53 Lake Dawson .02 .10
54 Tyronne Drakeford .01 .05
55 William Floyd .02 .10
56 Henry Ford .01 .05
57 Rob Fredrickson .02 .10
58 Aaron Glenn .08 .25
59 Shelby Hill .01 .05
60 Willie Jackson .08 .25
61 Joe Johnson .01 .05
62 Aaron Laing .01 .05
63 Kevin Lee .01 .05
64 Eric Mahlum .01 .05
65 Steve Matthews .01 .05
66 Willie McGinest .08 .25
67 Kevin Mitchell .01 .05
68 Byron Bam Morris .02 .10
69 Thomas Randolph .01 .05
70 Tony Richardson .01 .05
71 Corey Sawyer .02 .10
72 Jason Sehorn .08 .25
73 Rob Waldrop .01 .05
74 Jay Walker .01 .05
75 Bernard Williams .01 .05
76 Marvin Goodwin .01 .05
77 Romeo Bandison .01 .05
78 Bucky Brooks .01 .05
79 James Folston .01 .05
80 Donnell Bennett .02 .10
81 Charlie Ward .08 .25
82 Antonio Langham .01 .05
83 Greg Hill .02 .10
84 Anthony Phillips .01 .05
85 Winfred Tubbs .01 .05
86 Trev Alberts .01 .05
87 Tim Bowens .01 .05
88 Thomas Lewis .01 .05
89 Allen Aldridge .01 .05
90 Bert Emanuel .08 .25
91 Ryan Yarborough .01 .05
92 Lonnie Johnson .01 .05
93 Isaac Bruce .75 2.00
94 Checklist 1 .01 .05
95 Checklist 2 .01 .05
96 Troy Aikman FLB .30 .75
97 Steve Young FLB .08 .25
98 Rick Mirer FLB .02 .10
99 Drew Bledsoe FLB .20 .50
100 Jerry Rice FLB .30 .75
101 Heath Shuler COMIC SP .02 .10
102 Marshall Faulk COMIC SP .30 .75
103 Trent Dilfer COMIC SP .15 .40
104 Dan Wilkinson COMIC SP .02 .10
105 David Palmer COMIC SP .02 .10
JR1 Jerry Rice Special 6.00 15.00
NNO Marshall Faulk Promo .50 1.25
NNO Jerry Rice AU/1994 30.00 80.00

1994 Classic Gold

COMPLETE SET (105) 15.00 30.00
*GOLDS: 1.5X TO 4X BASIC CARDS
ONE PER PACK

1994 Classic Draft Stars

Inserted one per periodical pack, this 20-card standard-size set features some of the NFL's top draft picks. The full-bleed color action photos on the fronts have a metallic sheen to them. The player's name, position, and the helmet of the team which drafted him are printed toward the bottom. A second color photo appears on the back. A diagonal line divides the photo into two, and on the lower ghosted portion appears biographical information. The cards are numbered on the back "X of 20." The Rick Mirer card was a special insert randomly placed in periodical packs.

COMPLETE SET (20) 4.00 10.00
ONE DRAFT STARS PER MAGAZINE PACK
MIRER SPECIAL RANDOM INSERT IN MAG
1 Trev Alberts .05 .15
2 Jeff Burris .05 .15
3 Shante Carver .05 .15
4 Trent Dilfer .75 2.00
5 Marshall Faulk 2.00 5.00
6 William Floyd .08 .25
7 Aaron Glenn .25 .60
8 Greg Hill .08 .25
9 Charles Johnson .25 .60
10 Calvin Jones .05 .15
11 Antonio Langham .05 .15
12 Thomas Lewis .05 .15
13 Willie McGinest .25 .60
14 Jamir Miller .08 .25
15 Johnnie Morton .60 1.50
16 David Palmer .08 .25
17 Darnay Scott .40 1.00
18 Heath Shuler .08 .25
19 Dan Wilkinson .08 .25
20 Bryant Young .40 1.00
NNO Rick Mirer Special .40 1.00

1994 Classic Game Cards

Inserted one per jumbo pack, this ten-card set measures the standard size. The fronts feature borderless color action player photos on a computer-generated background resembling water. The player's name and the team name appear on the bottom, while the words "Game Card" are printed alongside the left. The backs carry a small sepia-toned player photo, along with biography, rules on how to play the game and a checklist. Unnumbered Drew Bledsoe cards were randomly inserted in jumbo packs. Winning cards were redeemable for a 1994 Classic NFL Draft Gold Uncut Sheet, or a 1994 NFL Draft Day Set. The cards were redeemable until February 28, 1995.

COMPLETE SET (10) 3.00 6.00
ONE PER JUMBO PACK
DB1 BLEDSOE INSERTED IN JUMBOS
*PRIZE BOX SCRATCHED: .2X TO .5X
GC1 Trent Dilfer .60 1.50
GC2 Marshall Faulk 1.50 4.00
GC3 Heath Shuler .07 .20
GC4 Dan Wilkinson .07 .20
GC5 Antonio Langham .02 .10
GC6 Willie McGinest .20 .50
GC7 Greg Hill .07 .20
GC8 Trev Alberts .02 .10
GC9 Charles Johnson .20 .50
GC10 Errict Rhett .20 .50
DB1 Drew Bledsoe Special 5.00 12.00

1994 Classic Picks

Randomly inserted in packs, these five standard-size cards have borderless fronts featuring color action player cutouts set on textured metallic backgrounds. The player's name appears in an upper corner in colored metallic lettering. The back carries a borderless ghosted color player action shot. A color headshot appears in a lower corner. Career highlights appear near the top and a brief player biography appears near the bottom. A message in blue lettering states that production was limited to 20,000 of each card. The cards are numbered on the back with an "LP" prefix.

COMPLETE SET (5) 6.00 15.00
STATED ODDS 1:36 HOBBY
1 Heath Shuler .20 .50
2 Trent Dilfer 1.50 4.00
3 Johnnie Morton 1.25 3.00
4 David Palmer .20 .50
5 Marshall Faulk 4.00 10.00

1994 Classic ROY Sweepstakes

Randomly inserted in packs, these 20 standard-size cards feature candidates for the '94 NFL offensive Rookie of the Year. The card of the player who won the award was redeemable for a football signed by the player. The white-bordered fronts feature color action player cutouts set on an image of a football. The player's name appears in red lettering within the margin above the photo. The question, "Rookie of the Year" appears in the margin below the picture. The production run of 2,500 appears in gold foil within an upper corner of the photo. The white horizontal back carries sweepstake rules and set checklist. The player's ghosted NFL team helmet also appears. The cards are numbered on the back with a "ROY" prefix. The prizes were redeemable until March 31, 1995.

COMPLETE SET (20) 20.00 50.00
STATED ODDS 1:73
ROY1 Trent Dilfer 3.00 8.00
ROY2 Mario Bates .40 1.00
ROY3 Darnay Scott 1.50 4.00
ROY4 Johnnie Morton 2.50 6.00
ROY5 William Floyd .40 1.00
ROY6 Errict Rhett 1.00 2.50
ROY7 Greg Hill .40 1.00
ROY8 Lake Dawson .40 1.00
ROY9 Charlie Garner 2.50 6.00
ROY10 Heath Shuler .40 1.00
ROY11 Derrick Alexander WR 1.00 2.50
ROY12 LeShon Johnson .20 .50
ROY13 Kevin Lee .20 .50
ROY14 David Palmer .40 1.00
ROY15 Charles Johnson 1.00 2.50
ROY16 Chuck Levy .20 .50
ROY17 Calvin Jones .20 .50
ROY18 Thomas Lewis .20 .50
ROY19 Marshall Faulk WIN 8.00 20.00
ROY20 Field Card .20 .50

1994 Classic Draft Day Autographs

FD1 Trent Dilfer 5.00 12.00
FD2 Marshall Faulk 10.00 25.00
FD4 Dan Wilkinson 4.00 10.00

1995 Classic Five Sport

The 1995 Classic Five Sport set was issued in one series of 200 standard-size cards. Cards were issued in 10-card regular packs (SRP $1.99). Boxes contained 36 packs. One autographed card was guaranteed in each pack and one certified autographed card (with an embossed logo) appeared in each box. There were also memorabilia redemption cards included in some packs and were guaranteed in at least one pack per box. The cards are numbered and divided into the five sports as follows: Basketball (1-42), Football (43-92), Baseball (93-122), Hockey (123-160), Racing (161-180), Alma Maters (181-190), Picture Perfect (191-200).

COMPLETE SET (200) 6.00 15.00
43 Ki-Jana Carter .08 .25
44 Tony Boselli .07 .20
45 Steve McNair .40 1.00
46 Michael Westbrook .08 .25
47 Kerry Collins .40 1.00
48 Kevin Carter .05 .15
49 Mike Mamula .05 .15
50 Joey Galloway .20 .50
51 Kyle Brady .07 .20
52 J.J. Stokes .08 .25
53 Derrick Alexander .07 .20
54 Warren Sapp .20 .50
55 Mark Fields .05 .15
56 Ruben Brown .05 .15
57 Ellis Johnson .05 .15
58 Hugh Douglas .08 .25
59 Tyrone Wheatley .08 .25
60 Napoleon Kaufman .15 .40
61 James O. Stewart .08 .25
62 Luther Elliss .05 .15
63 Rashaan Salaam .08 .25
64 Tyrone Poole .07 .20
65 Ty Law .08 .25
66 Korey Stringer .15 .40
67 Devin Bush .05 .15
68 Mark Bruener .05 .15
69 Derrick Brooks .20 .50
70 Craig Powell .05 .15
71 Craig Newsome .05 .15
72 Anthony Cook .05 .15
73 Ray Zellars .05 .15
74 Todd Collins .20 .50
75 Sherman Williams .05 .15
76 Frank Sanders .08 .25
77 Corey Fuller .05 .15
78 Kordell Stewart .20 .50
79 Curtis Martin .60 1.50
80 Lorenzo Styles .05 .15
81 Chris T. Jones .05 .15
82 Zack Crockett .05 .15
83 Stoney Case .05 .15
84 Eric Zeier .08 .25
85 Jimmy Hitchcock .05 .15
86 Rodney Thomas .07 .20
87 Rob Johnson .20 .50
88 Tyrone Davis .05 .15
89 Chad May .05 .15
90 Ed Hervey .05 .15
91 Terrell Davis .50 1.25
92 John Walsh .05 .15
181 Stackhouse .15 .40
Hitchcock
182 McDyess .10 .30
Williams
184 DeClercq .07 .20
K.J.Carter
185 Wheatley .10 .30
King
186 J.J. Stokes .10 .30
O'Bannon
187 Sapp .10 .30
Popa
188 Wilson .40 1.00
Brooks
190 Sura .05 .15
Alexander
191 Steve Young .25 .60
194 Marshall Faulk .20 .50
195 Troy Aikman .30 .75
196 Drew Bledsoe .20 .50
197 Emmitt Smith .40 1.00

1995 Classic Five Sport Printer's Proofs

*PRINTER PROOF/75: 4X TO 10X BASIC CARDS
STATED PRINT RUN 795 SETS

1995 Classic Five Sport Red Die Cuts

*RED DIE CUT: 1.2X TO 3X BASIC CARDS
RED DIE CUT STATED ODDS 1:8

1995 Classic Five Sport Silver Die Cuts

COMPLETE SET (200) 12.00 30.00
*SILVER DC: .8X TO 2X BASIC CARDS

1995 Classic Five Sport Autographs

This set was randomly inserted into packs and is a signed version of the basic issue cards. The backs carry a "Congratulations" message stating that it is an autographed 1995 Five Sport Autograph Edition Card with the sport's hall pictured at the bottom. The cards are unnumbered. Many of these autographed cards were later re-issued in 1995-96 Classic Five Sport Signings witha a slightly different cardback that reads "...Received a Limited-Edition Autographed Card." This message is the same one used on the Hot Box Autographs but these Five Sport Signings Autographs are not serial numbered on the back.

*SIGNINGS VERSION: .4X TO 1X
45 Steve McNair 12.00 30.00
47 Kerry Collins 6.00 15.00
49 Mike Mamula 2.00 5.00
50 Joey Galloway 5.00 12.00
51 Kyle Brady 2.50 6.00
55 Mark Fields 2.00 5.00
58 Hugh Douglas 2.00 5.00
60 Napoleon Kaufman SP 3.00 8.00
64 Tyrone Poole 2.00 5.00
77 Corey Fuller 2.00 5.00
84 Eric Zeier 2.50 6.00
87 Rob Johnson 3.00 8.00
89 Chad May 2.50 6.00
92 John Walsh 2.00 5.00

1995 Classic Five Sport Autographs Numbered

Cards in this set were issued primarily in 1995-96 Classic Five Sport Signings packs and are essentially a parallel verson of the basic 1995 Classic Five Sport Autographs insert. The only differences are in the hand serial numbering on the cardbacks (of 225 or 295) and the embossing crimp on the card's corner.

47 Kerry Collins/225 8.00 20.00
50 Joey Galloway/225 8.00 20.00
60 Napoleon Kaufman/225 6.00 15.00
191 Steve Young/225 25.00 60.00
196 Drew Bledsoe/225 15.00 40.00

1995 Classic Five Sport Classic Standouts

Randomly inserted in regular packs at a rate of one in 216, this 10-card standard-size set features both the hot new stars and the established elite of all five sports. Fronts have full-color action player cutouts set against a gold and black foil background. The player's name is printed in gold foil at the top. Backs contain a full-color action shot with the player's name printed in yellow and a career highlights box. The cards are numbered with a "CS" prefix.

COMPLETE SET (10) 15.00 40.00
CS4 Rashaan Salaam .75 2.00
CS7 Kerry Collins 1.50 4.00
CS9 Michael Westbrook 1.00 2.50
CS10 Emmitt Smith 3.00 8.00
NNO Kerry Collins Sample 1.00 2.50

1995 Classic Five Sport Fast Track

Randomly inserted in retail packs, this 20-card standard-size set spotlights the young stars of sports who are fast becoming major stars. Borderless fronts contain a player in full-color action while the rest of the shot is printed in colored foil. Backs have a color action shot in one box and two color separted boxes with the rest of the photo. A player profile appears underneath the photo. The cards are numbered with a "FT" prefix.

COMPLETE SET (20) 15.00 40.00
FT2 Michael Westbrook .50 1.25
FT4 Kyle Brady .40 1.00
FT8 Napoleon Kaufman .50 1.25
FT11 J.J. Stokes .40 1.00
FT15 Tyrone Wheatley .60 1.50
FT17 Rashaan Salaam .50 1.25
FT19 Steve McNair 1.50 4.00

1995 Classic Five Sport Hot Box Autographs

This set of six autographed standard-sized cards were randomly inserted in Hobby Hot boxes. The cards are nearly identical to the basic Five Sports Autographs with the exception of the hand written serial number on the backs and the slightly different congratulatory message on the back that reads "...Received a Limited-Edition Autographed Card."

2 Kerry Collins/625 10.00 25.00
5 Steve McNair/630 12.00 30.00

1995 Classic Five Sport NFL Experience Previews

Randomly inserted into 1995 Classic Five-Sport "hot packs", this five-card set features top NFL stars in full-color action shots. The cards were issued to preview the 1995 NFL Experience release.

COMPLETE SET (5) 12.00 30.00
EP1 Emmitt Smith 6.00 15.00
EP2 Drew Bledsoe 2.00 5.00
EP3 Steve Young 4.00 8.00
EP4 Rashaan Salaam 1.50 4.00
EP5 Marshall Faulk 2.50 6.00

1995 Classic Five Sport On Fire

Ten of the 20-cards in this set were released in Hobby Hot Packs while the other ten were released in retail Hot packs. Fronts have full-color player cutouts set against a flame background with the On Fire logo printed at the bottom. The player's name is printed vertically in white type on the left side. backs feature biography and players's statistics.

COMPLETE SET (20) 30.00 80.00
H1 Drew Bledsoe 2.50 6.00
H4 Ki-Jana Carter 1.50 4.00
H5 Michael Westbrook 1.50 4.00
H8 Tyrone Wheatley 2.00 5.00
R4 Steve McNair 2.50 6.00
R5 Rashaan Salaam 2.00 5.00
R7 J.J. Stokes 1.50 4.00
R8 Kyle Brady 1.50 4.00
R10 Napoleon Kaufman 2.00 5.00

1995 Classic Five Sport Phone Cards $3

The five-card set of $3 Foncards were found one per 72 retail packs. The credit-card size plastic pieces have a borderless front with a full-color action player photo and the $3 emblem printed on the upper right in blue. The player's name is printed in white type vertically on the lower left. The Sprint logo appears on the bottom also. White backs carry information of how to place calls using the card.

COMPLETE SET (5) 4.00 8.00
4 Rashaan Salaam .40 1.00

1995 Classic Five Sport Phone Cards $4

These cards were inserted randomly into packs at a rate of one in 72 and featured the five top prospects or performers of the individual sports. The borderless fronts feature full-color action photos with the athlete's name printed in white across the bottom. The Sprint logo and $4 are printed along the top. White backs contain information about placing calls using the card.

COMPLETE SET (5) 6.00 15.00
5 Michael Westbrook .50 1.25

1995 Classic Five Sport Previews

Randomly inserted in Classic hockey packs, this five-card standard-size set salutes the leaders and the up-and-coming rookies of the five sports. Borderless fronts have a full-color action shot with gold foil stamp of "preview" and the player's name, school and position printed vertically on the right side of the card. The player's sport's ball (or tire) is printed in a montage on the right. Backs have another full-color action shot and also a biography, statistics and profile. The cards are numbered with a "SP" prefix.

COMPLETE SET (5) 3.00 8.00
SP3 Michael Westbrook .40 1.00

1995 Classic Five Sport Record Setters

This 10-card standard-size set was inserted in retail packs and feature the stars and rookies of the five sports. The fronts display full-bleed color action photos; the set title "Record Setters" iin prismatic block lettering appears toward the bottom. On a sepia-tone photo, the backs carry a player profile. The cards are numbered on the back with an "RS" prefix and hand-numbered out of 1250.

COMPLETE SET (10) 12.00 30.00
RS1 Kerry Collins 1.25 3.00
RS8 Rashaan Salaam .60 1.50

1995 Classic Five Sport Strive For Five

This interactive game card set consists of 65 cards to be used like playing cards. Collector's gained a full suit of cards to redeem prizes. The odds of finding the card in packs were one in 10. Fronts are bordered in metallic silver foil and picture the player in full-color action. The cards are numbered on both top and bottom in silver foil and the player's name is printed vertically in silver foil. Backs have green backgrounds with the game rules printed in white type.

COMPLETE SET (65) 12.00 30.00
FB1 Ki-Jana Carter .20 .50
FB2 Rashaan Salaam .25 .60
FB3 Napoleon Kaufman .20 .50
FB4 Tyrone Wheatley .20 .50
FB5 J.J. Stokes .20 .50
FB6 Joey Galloway .40 .75
FB7 Kerry Collins .50 1.25
FB8 Michael Westbrook .20 .50
FB9 Steve McNair .75 2.00
FB10 Drew Bledsoe .40 1.00
FB11 Marshall Faulk .40 1.00
FB12 Troy Aikman .75 2.00
FB13 Steve Young .60 1.50
P1 Emmitt Smith Promo 1.25 3.00

1995-96 Classic Five Sport Signings

COMPLETE SET (100) 6.00 15.00
31 Ki-Jana Carter .10 .30
32 Tony Boselli .08 .25
33 Steve McNair .50 1.25
34 Michael Westbrook .10 .30
35 Kerry Collins .40 1.00
36 Kevin Carter .07 .20
37 Mike Mamula .07 .20
38 Joey Galloway .25 .60
39 Kyle Brady .08 .25
40 J.J. Stokes .10 .30
41 Derrick Alexander .08 .25
42 Warren Sapp .25 .60
43 Hugh Douglas .10 .30
44 Tyrone Wheatley .10 .30
45 Napoleon Kaufman .20 .50
46 James O. Stewart .10 .30
47 Rashaan Salaam .10 .30
48 Ty Law .10 .30
49 Mark Bruener .07 .20
50 Derrick Brooks .25 .60
51 Curtis Martin .75 2.00
52 Todd Collins .25 .60
53 Sherman Williams .07 .20
54 Frank Sanders .10 .30
55 Eric Zeier .10 .30
56 Rob Johnson .25 .60
57 Chad May .07 .20
58 Terrell Davis .60 1.50
59 Stoney Case .07 .20
91 Steve Young .30 .75
94 Marshall Faulk .25 .60
95 Troy Aikman .40 1.00
96 Drew Bledsoe .25 .60
97 Emmitt Smith .50 1.25

1995-96 Classic Five Sport Signings Blue Signature

*BLUE SIGN: 1.5X TO 4X BASIC CARDS

1995-96 Classic Five Sport Signings Die Cuts

*DIE CUT: .8X TO 2X BASIC CARDS
STATED ODDS 1:4

1995-96 Classic Five Sport Signings Red Signature

*RED SIGN: 1.5X TO 4X BASIC CARDS

1995-96 Classic Five Sport Signings Etched in Stone

This 10-card set, printed on 16-point foil board, was randomly inserted in Hot boxes only. Hot boxes were distributed at a rate of 1:5 cases.

5 Emmitt Smith 4.00 10.00
6 Troy Aikman 3.00 8.00
7 Steve Young 2.50 6.00

1995-96 Classic Five Sport Signings Freshly Inked

This 30-card set was randomly inserted in 1995 Classic Five Sport Signings packs. The fronts features borderless player color action photos with the player's name printed in gold foil across the bottom. The backs carry an artist's drawing of the player with the player's name at the top.

COMPLETE SET (30) 12.00 30.00
STATED ODDS 1:10
FS11 Hugh Douglas .60 1.50
FS12 Curtis Martin 2.50 6.00
FS13 Michael Westbrook .60 1.50
FS14 Kerry Collins 1.25 3.00
FS15 Kevin Carter .40 1.00
FS16 Joey Galloway 1.00 2.50
FS17 Eric Zeier .60 1.50
FS18 Terrell Davis 1.50 4.00
FS19 Napoleon Kaufman .75 2.00
FS20 Rashaan Salaam .60 1.50

1991 Classic Four Sport

This 230-card multi-sport standard-size set includes all 200 draft picks players from the four Classic Draft Picks sets (football, baseball, basketball, and hockey), plus an additional 30 draft picks not previously found in these other sets. A subset within the 230 cards consists of five cards highlighting the publicized one-on-one game between Billy Owens and Larry Johnson. As an additional incentive to collectors, Classic randomly inserted over 60,000 autographed cards into the 15-card foil packs; it is claimed that each case should contain two or more autographed cards. The autographed cards feature 61 different players, approximately two-thirds of whom were hockey players. The production run for the English version was 25,000 cases, and a bilingual (French) version of the set was also produced at 20 percent of the English production.

Card	Low	High
COMPLETE SET (230)	5.00	12.00
1 Future Superstars	.15	.40
102 Rocket Ismail	.20	.50
103 Russell Maryland	.05	.15
104 Eric Turner	.05	.15
105 Bruce Pickens	.05	.15
106 Mike Croel	.05	.15
107 Todd Lyght	.05	.15
108 Eric Swann	.05	.15
109 Antone Davis	.05	.15
110 Stanley Richard	.05	.15
111 Pat Harlow	.05	.15
112 Alvin Harper	.05	.15
113 Mike Pritchard	.05	.15
114 Leonard Russell	.05	.15
115 Dan McGwire	.05	.15
117 Vinnie Clark	.05	.15
118 Kelvin Pritchett	.05	.15
119 Harvey Williams	.05	.15
120 Stan Thomas	.05	.15
121 Randal Hill	.05	.15
122 Todd Marinovich	.05	.15
123 Henry Jones	.05	.15
124 Mike Dumas	.05	.15
125 Ed King	.05	.15
126 Reggie Johnson	.05	.15
127 Roman Phifer	.05	.15
128 Mike Jones	.05	.15
129 Brett Favre	1.25	3.00
130 Browning Nagle	.05	.15
131 Esera Tuaolo	.05	.15
132 George Thornton	.05	.15
133 Dixon Edwards	.05	.15
135 Eric Bieniemy	.05	.15
136 Shane Curry	.05	.15
137 Jerome Henderson	.05	.15
138 Wesley Carroll	.05	.15
139 Nick Bell	.05	.15
140 John Flannery	.05	.15
141 Ricky Watters	.20	.50
142 Jeff Graham	.05	.15
143 Eric Moten	.05	.15
144 Jesse Campbell	.05	.15
145 Chris Zorich	.05	.15
146 Doug Thomas	.05	.15
147 Phil Hansen	.05	.15
148 Reggie Barrett	.05	.15
203 Gary Brown	.05	.15
204 Rob Carpenter	.05	.15
205 Ricky Ervins	.05	.15
206 Donald Hollas	.05	.15
207 Greg Lewis	.05	.15
208 Darren Lewis	.05	.15
209 Anthony Morgan	.05	.15
211 Perry Carter	.05	.15
212 Melvin Cheatum	.05	.15
213 Jerome Harmon	.05	.15
217 Ed McCaffrey	.30	.75
220 Moe Gardner	.05	.15
221 Jon Vaughn	.05	.15
222 Lawrence Dawsey	.05	.15
223 Michael Stonebreaker	.05	.15
224 Shawn Moore	.05	.15

1991 Classic Four Sport French

Card	Low	High
COMPLETE SET (230)	6.00	15.00
*FRENCH VERSION: .4X TO 1X		

1991 Classic Four Sport Autographs

The 1991 Classic Draft Collection Autograph set consists of 61 standard-size cards. They were randomly inserted throughout the foil packs. Listed after the player's name is how many cards were autographed by that player. An "A" suffix after card number is used here for convenience.

Card	Low	High
102A Rocket Ismail/2000	8.00	20.00
103A Russell Maryland/1000	3.00	8.00

1991 Classic Four Sport LPs

This ten-card set was randomly inserted in 1991 Classic Draft Picks Collection foil packs. The cards are distinguished from the regular issue in that nine of them have a silver inner border while one has a gold inner border. A five-card Ismail subset is also to be found within the nine silver-bordered cards. The "1991 Classic Draft Picks" emblem appears as a wine-colored wax seal at the upper left corner. The horizontally oriented backs carry brief comments superimposed over a dusted version of Classic's wax seal emblem. There was also a French parallel set produced.

Card	Low	High
COMPLETE SET (10)	5.00	12.00
*FRENCH: SAME VALUE		
RANDOM INSERTS IN PACKS	.40	1.00
LP1 Rocket Lands In Canada	.60	1.50
LP2 Rocket Surveys The Future	.60	1.50
LP3 Rocket Ismail Launch	.60	1.50
LP4 Track Star (Rocket Ismail)	.60	1.50
LP5 Rocket Ismail Knows Classic	.60	1.50
LP10 Russell Maryland	.50	1.25

1992 Classic Four Sport

The 1992 Classic Draft Picks Collection consists of 325 standard-size cards, featuring the top picks from football, basketball, baseball, and hockey drafts. According to Classic, 40,000 12-box foil cases were produced. Randomly inserted in the 12-card packs were over 100,000 autograph cards from over 50 of the top draft picks from basketball, football, baseball, and hockey, including cards autographed by Shaquille O'Neal, Desmond Howard, Roman Hamrlik, and Phil Nevin. Also inserted in the packs were "Instant Win Giveway Cards" that entitled the collector to the 500,000.00 sports memorabilia giveway that Classic offered in this contest. There was also a factory set produced with gold parallel cards.

Card	Low	High
COMPLETE SET (326)	6.00	15.00
76 Desmond Howard	.15	.40
77 David Klingler	.05	.15
78 Quentin Coryatt	.05	.15
79 Bill Johnson	.05	.15
80 Eugene Chung	.05	.15
81 Derek Brown	.05	.15
82 Carl Pickens	.08	.25
83 Chris Mims	.05	.15
84 Charles Davenport	.05	.15
85 Ray Roberts	.05	.15
86 Chuck Smith	.05	.15
87 Tony Smith RB	.05	.15
88 Ken Swilling	.05	.15
89 Greg Skrepenak	.05	.15
90 Phillippi Sparks	.05	.15
91 Alonzo Spellman	.05	.15
92 Bernard Dafney	.05	.15
93 Edgar Bennett	.08	.25
94 Shane Dronett	.05	.15
95 Jeremy Lincoln	.05	.15
96 Dion Lambert	.05	.15
97 Siran Stacy	.05	.15
98 Tony Sacca	.05	.15
99 Sean Lumpkin	.05	.15
100 Tommy Vardell	.05	.15
101 Keith Hamilton	.05	.15
102 Sean Gilbert	.05	.15
103 Casey Weldon	.05	.15
104 Marc Boutte	.05	.15
105 Arthur Marshall	.05	.15
106 Santana Dotson	.05	.15
107 Ronnie West	.05	.15
108 Mike Pawlawski	.05	.15
109 Dale Carter	.05	.15
110 Carlos Snow	.05	.15
111 Mark D'Onofrio	.05	.15
112 Matt Blundin	.05	.15
113 Patrick Rowe	.05	.15
114 Joel Steed	.05	.15
115 Erick Anderson	.05	.15
116 Rodney Culver	.05	.15
117 Chris Hakel	.05	.15
118 Kevin Smith	.05	.15
119 Robert Brooks	.07	.20
120 Bucky Richardson	.05	.15
121 Steve Israel	.05	.15
122 Marco Coleman	.05	.15
123 Johnny Mitchell	.05	.15
124 Scottie Graham	.05	.15
125 Keith Goganious	.05	.15
126 Tommy Maddox	.05	.15
127 Terrell Buckley	.05	.15
128 Dana Hall	.05	.15
129 Ty Detmer	.15	.40
130 Darryl Williams	.05	.15
131 Jason Hanson	.15	.40
132 Leon Searcy	.05	.15
133 Will Furrer	.05	.15
134 Darren Woodson	.20	.50
135 Corey Widmer	.05	.15
136 Larry Tharpe	.05	.15
137 Lance Olberding	.05	.15
138 Stacey Dillard	.05	.15
139 Anthony Hamlet	.05	.15
140 Mike Evans	.05	.15
141 Chester McGlockton	.05	.15
142 Marquez Pope	.05	.15
143 Tyrone Legette	.05	.15
144 Derrick Moore	.05	.15
145 Calvin Holmes	.05	.15
146 Eddie Robinson Jr.	.05	.15
147 Robert Jones	.05	.15
148 Ricardo McDonald	.05	.15
149 Howard Dinkins	.05	.15
150 Todd Collins	.05	.15
310 Rocket Ismail FLB	.05	.15
313 Ty Detmer Desmond Howard	.15	.40

1992 Classic Four Sport Gold

Card	Low	High
COMP.FACT.SET (326)	60.00	120.00
*GOLD: 1.2X TO 3X BASIC CARDS		
AU Future Superstars AU	30.00	60.00

1992 Classic Four Sport Autographs

The 1992 Classic Four Sport Autograph set consists of base cards hand signed by the featured player with a congratulatory message on the backs. They were randomly inserted throughout the foil packs. Each card also included a hand written serial number on the front and the checklist below reflects the quantity of cards each player signed. We've assigned card number according to the player's base card. Jan Caloun and Jan Vopat were not included in the regular set and hence are listed as unnumbered.

Card	Low	High
76 Desmond Howard/975	4.00	10.00
77 David Klingler/1125	2.00	5.00
78A Quentin Coryatt/3500	2.50	6.00
82 Carl Pickens/1475	4.00	10.00
87 Tony Smith/3450	2.00	5.00
97 Siran Stacy/4325	2.00	5.00
98 Tony Sacca/1575	2.00	5.00
103 Casey Weldon/4350	2.00	5.00
108 Mike Pawlawski/1475	2.00	5.00
112 Matt Blundin/1575	2.00	5.00
126 Tommy Maddox/4575	6.00	15.00
127 Terrell Buckley/1475	2.00	5.00
129 Ty Detmer/1475	3.00	8.00
144 Derrick Moore/1575	2.00	5.00
301 Dave Brown/1575	2.00	5.00

1992 Classic Four Sport BCs

Inserted one per jumbo pack, these 20 bonus cards measure the standard size. The cards are numbered on the dark gray stripe and arranged according to sport as follows: basketball (1-6), hockey (7-12), football (13-17), and baseball (18-20). A randomly inserted Future Superstars card has a picture of all four players on its front, shot against a horizon with dark clouds and lightning; the back indicates that just 10,000 of these cards were produced.

Card	Low	High
COMPLETE SET (20)	3.00	8.00
BC13 Desmond Howard	.15	.40
BC14 David Klingler	.08	.25
BC15 Terrell Buckley	.08	.25
BC16 Quentin Coryatt	.08	.25
BC17 Carl Pickens	.08	.25

1992 Classic Four Sport LPs

Randomly inserted in foil packs, this 25-card standard-size insert set features full-bleed glossy color action player photos on the fronts. The sports represented are football (1-7, 16), basketball (8-14), baseball (17-21), and hockey (22-25). An 8 1/2" by 11" version of Shaquille O'Neal is known to exist.

Card	Low	High
LP1 Desmond Howard	.20	.50
LP2 David Klingler	.15	.40
LP3 Tommy Maddox	.20	.50
LP4 Casey Weldon	.15	.40
LP5 Tony Smith RB	.20	.50
LP6 Terrell Buckley	.15	.40
LP7 Carl Pickens	.20	.50
LP15 Future Superstars	1.50	4.00
LP16 Classic QBs	.20	.50
LP15P Phil Nevin Shaquille O'Neal Roman Hamrlik Desmond Howard (Super Bowl Show promo)	2.00	5.00

1992 Classic Four Sport Previews

These five preview standard-size cards were randomly inserted in baseball and hockey draft picks foil packs. According to the backs, just 10,000 of each card were produced. The fronts display the full-bleed glossy color player photos. At the upper right corner, the word "Preview" surmounts the Classic logo. This logo overlays a black stripe that runs down the left side and features the player's name and position. The gray backs have the word "Preview" in red lettering at the top and are accented by short purple diagonal stripes on each side. Between the stripes are a congratulations and an advertisement. The cards are numbered on the back with a "CC" prefix.

Card	Low	High
COMPLETE SET (5)	6.00	15.00
CC2 Desmond Howard	.60	1.50

1992 Classic Four Sport Promos

These five promo cards were packaged in a cello pack and distributed to dealers. The cards measure the standard size (2 1/2" by 3 1/2"). The fronts display the same full-bleed glossy color player photos as the above-mentioned preview cards. They differ in that the Classic logo at the upper left corner is not surmounted by the word Preview." The promo backs have a different design than the preview backs, displaying a second color player photo on the right side as well as biography and player profile in black print on a silver background. The cards are numbered on the back.

Card	Low	High
COMPLETE SET (5)	6.00	15.00
PR2 Desmond Howard	.60	1.50

1993 Classic Four Sport

The 1993 Classic Four-Sport Draft Pick Collection set consists of 325 standard-size cards of the top 1993 draft picks from football, basketball, baseball, and hockey. Just 49,500 sequentially numbered 12-box cases were produced. The set includes two topical subsets: John R. Wooden Award (310-314) and All-Rookie Basketball Team (315-319).

Card	Low	High
COMPLETE SET (325)	4.00	10.00
91 Drew Bledsoe	.50	1.25
92 Rick Mirer	.08	.25
93 Garrison Hearst	.20	.50
94 Marvin Jones	.05	.15
95 John Copeland	.05	.15
96 Eric Curry	.05	.15
97 Curtis Conway	.05	.15
98 Willie Roaf	.15	.40
99 Lincoln Kennedy	.05	.15
100 Jerome Bettis	.60	1.50
101 Mike Compton	.05	.15
102 John Gerak	.05	.15
103 Will Shields	.05	.15
104 Ben Coleman	.05	.15
105 Ernest Dye	.05	.15
106 Lester Holmes	.05	.15
107 Brad Hopkins	.05	.15
108 Everett Lindsay	.05	.15
109 Todd Rucci	.05	.15
110 Lance Gunn	.05	.15
111 Elvis Grbac	.07	.20
112 Shane Matthews	.05	.15
113 Rudy Harris	.05	.15
114 Richie Anderson	.05	.15
115 Derek Brown	.05	.15
116 Roger Harper	.05	.15
117 Terry Kirby	.07	.20
118 Natrone Means	.08	.25
119 Glyn Milburn	.05	.15
120 Adrian Murrell	.08	.25
121 Lorenzo Neal	.05	.15
122 Roosevelt Potts	.05	.15
123 Kevin Williams WR	.05	.15
124 Fred Baxter	.05	.15
125 Troy Drayton	.05	.15
126 Chris Gedney	.05	.15
127 Irv Smith	.05	.15
128 Olanda Truitt	.05	.15
129 Victor Bailey	.05	.15
130 Horace Copeland	.05	.15
131 Ron Dickerson Jr.	.05	.15
132 Willie Harris	.05	.15
133 Tyrone Hughes	.05	.15
134 Qadry Ismail	.08	.25
135 Reggie Brooks	.08	.25
136 Sean LaChapelle	.05	.15
137 O.J.McDuffie	.08	.25
138 Kenny Shedd	.05	.15
139 Brian Stablein	.05	.15
140 Lamar Thomas	.05	.15
141 Kevin Williams RB	.05	.15
142 Othello Henderson	.05	.15
143 Kevin Henry	.05	.15
144 Todd Kelly	.05	.15
145 Devon McDonald	.05	.15
146 Michael Strahan	.40	1.00
147 Dan Williams	.05	.15
148 Gilbert Brown	.05	.15
149 Mark Caesar	.05	.15
150 John Parrella	.05	.15
151 Leonard Renfro	.05	.15
152 Coleman Rudolph	.05	.15
153 Ronnie Bradford	.05	.15
154 Tom Carter	.05	.15
155 Deon Figures	.05	.15
156 Derrick Frazier	.05	.15
157 Darrien Gordon	.05	.15
158 Carlton Gray	.05	.15
159 Adrian Hardy	.05	.15
160 Mike Reid	.05	.15
161 Thomas Smith	.05	.15
162 Robert O'Neal	.05	.15
163 Chad Brown	.08	.25
164 Demetrius DuBose	.05	.15
165 Reggie Givens	.05	.15
166 Travis Hill	.05	.15
167 Rich McKenzie	.05	.15
168 Darrin Smith	.05	.15
169 Steve Tovar	.05	.15
170 Patrick Bates	.05	.15
171 Dan Footman	.05	.15
172 Ryan McNeil	.05	.15
173 Danan Hughes	.05	.15
174 Mark Brunell	.30	.75
175 Ron Moore	.05	.15
176 Antonio London	.05	.15
177 Steve Everitt	.05	.15
178 Wayne Simmons	.05	.15
179 Robert Smith	.20	.50
180 Dana Stubblefield	.08	.25
181 George Teague	.05	.15
182 Carl Simpson	.05	.15
183 Billy Joe Hobert	.05	.15
184 Gino Torretta	.05	.15
PR1 Drew Bledsoe Promo	1.25	3.00

1993 Classic Four Sport Gold

Card	Low	High
COMP.FACT.SET (332)	150.00	250.00
*GOLD: 1.5X TO 4X BASIC CARDS		
AU1 Jerome Bettis AU/3900	8.00	20.00

1993 Classic Four Sport Acetates

Randomly inserted throughout the 1993 Classic Four-Sport foil packs, this 12-card standard-size acetate set features on its fronts clear-bordered color player action cutouts set on basketball, football, baseball, or hockey stick backgrounds. The cards are unnumbered but carry letter designations. They are checklisted in the order that spells '93 Rookie Class.

Card	Low	High
COMPLETE SET (12)	6.00	15.00
6 Drew Bledsoe	1.25	3.00
7 Rick Mirer	.40	1.00
8 Garrison Hearst	.75	2.00

1993 Classic Four Sport Autographs

Randomly inserted in '93 Classic Four-Sport packs, these standard-size cards feature on their fronts borderless color player action shots. The back carries a congratulatory message. The cards are listed below by their corresponding regular card numbers, except for Jennings and Klippenstein, which are shown as unnumbered cards (NNO) at the end of the checklist since they are not in the regular set. The number of cards each player signed is shown. The Rider card may have been autopenned.

Card	Low	High
91A Drew Bledsoe/275	30.00	60.00
92A Rick Mirer/375	5.00	12.00
93A Garrison Hearst/650	8.00	20.00
94A Marvin Jones/3650	1.50	4.00
184A Gino Torretta/3200	3.00	8.00
NNO Garrison Hearst Promo	10.00	25.00

1993 Classic Four Sport Chromium Draft Stars

Inserted one per jumbo pack, these 20 standard-size cards feature color player action cutouts on their borderless metallic fronts. The player's name, along with the production number (1 of 80,000), appear vertically in gold foil at the lower left. The cards are numbered on the back with a "DS" prefix.

Card	Low	High
COMPLETE SET (20)	8.00	20.00
DS48 Drew Bledsoe	.75	2.00
DS49 Rick Mirer	.40	1.00
DS50 Garrison Hearst	.75	2.00
DS51 Jerome Bettis	.75	2.00
DS52 Terry Kirby	.30	.75
DS53 Glyn Milburn	.30	.75
DS54 Reggie Brooks	.30	.75

1993 Classic Four Sport LP Jumbos

Random inserts in hobby boxes, these five oversized cards measure approximately 3 1/2" by 5" and feature on their fronts borderless color player action shots. The player's name, statistics, biography, and career highlights, along with the card's production number out of 8,000 produced, appear on a gray lithic background to the left. The cards are numbered on the back as "X of 5."

Card	Low	High
COMPLETE SET (5)	12.00	30.00
1 Drew Bledsoe	2.50	6.00

1993 Classic Four Sport LPs

Randomly inserted throughout the 1993 Classic Four-Sport foil packs, this 25-card standard-size set features the hottest draft pick players in 1993. The borderless fronts feature color player action shots. The player's name appears vertically at the lower left. The production number (1 of 63,400) appears in gold foil at the lower right. The cards are numbered on the back with an "LP" prefix.

Card	Low	High
COMPLETE SET (25)	20.00	40.00
LP1 Four in One	1.50	4.00
LP10 Drew Bledsoe	1.50	4.00
LP11 Rick Mirer	.40	1.00
LP12 Garrison Hearst	.75	2.00
LP13 Jerome Bettis	1.50	4.00
LP14 Marvin Jones	.30	.75
LP15 Terry Kirby	.40	1.00
LP16 Glyn Milburn	.30	.75
LP17 Reggie Brooks	.40	1.00

1993 Classic Four Sport MBNA Promos

This two-card set uses Classic's designs from its Four-Sport LPs "Four in One" insert number LP1. Card number 1 reproduces the Chris Webber/Alex Rodriguez side of LP1, card number 2 reproduces the Drew Bledsoe/Alexandre Daigle side. This set was issued exclusively to cardholders of the MBNA/ScoreBoard VISA. The backs contain congratulatory messages, information about the players depicted, and a notation than 10,000 sets were issued. Although the design and copyright reads 1993, these cards probably were first issued in 1994.

Card	Low	High
2 D.Bledsoe A.Daigle	2.00	5.00

1993 Classic Four Sport Power Pick Bonus

Issued one per jumbo sheet, these 20 standard-size cards feature on their borderless fronts color player action shots, the backgrounds for which are faded to black-and-white. The player's name and the sets production number (1 of 80,000) appear in green-foil cursive lettering near the bottom. The cards are numbered on the back with a "PP" prefix.

Card	Low	High
COMPLETE SET (20)	10.00	25.00
PP8 Drew Bledsoe	.75	2.00
PP9 Rick Mirer	.40	1.00
PP10 Garrison Hearst	.75	2.00
PP11 Jerome Bettis	.75	2.00
PP12 Terry Kirby	.40	1.00
PP13 Glyn Milburn	.40	1.00
PP14 Reggie Brooks	.40	1.00
NNO Four in One/60,000	1.50	4.00

1993 Classic Four Sport Previews

Issued as unnumbered inserts in '93 Classic hockey packs, these five cards measure the standard size. The fronts are similar in design to regular 1993 Classic Four-Sport cards. The backs carry a congratulatory message.

Card	Low	High
COMPLETE SET (5)	2.50	6.00
CC3 Rick Mirer	.30	.75

1993 Classic Four Sport Tri-Cards

Randomly inserted throughout the 1993 Classic Four-Sport foil packs, this set features five standard-size cards with three players on each card separated by perforations. The cards are numbered on the back with a "TC" prefix.

Card	Low	High
COMPLETE SET (5)	10.00	25.00
TC2 Bleds/7 Mir/12 Hear	2.00	5.00
TC5 Bleds/10 Web/15 A-Rod	3.00	8.00

1993 Classic Four Sport McDonald's

Classic produced this 35-card four-sport standard-size set for a promotion at McDonald's restaurants in central and southeastern Pennsylvania, southern New Jersey, Delaware, and central Florida. The cards were distributed in five-card packs. A five-card "limited production" subset was randomly inserted throughout these packs. The promotion also featured instant win cards awarding 2,000 pieces of autographed Score Board memorabilia. An autographed Chris Webber card was also randomly inserted in the packs on a limited basis. The set is arranged according to sports as follows: football (1-10), baseball (11, 26, 31-35), hockey (12-20), and basketball (21-25, 27-30). The cards are numbered on the back in the upper left, and the McDonald's trademark is gold foil stamped toward the bottom.

Card	Low	High
COMPLETE SET (35)	4.00	10.00
1 Troy Aikman	.60	1.50
2 Drew Bledsoe	.40	1.00
3 Eric Curry	.05	.15
4 Garrison Hearst	.20	.50
5 Lester Holmes	.05	.15
6 Marvin Jones	.05	.15
7 O.J. McDuffie	.08	.25
8 Rick Mirer	.08	.25
9 Leonard Renfro	.05	.15
10 Jerry Rice	.60	1.50
35 Trench Warfare	.05	.15
AU1 Troy Aikman/5000	40.00	80.00

1993 Classic Four Sport McDonald's LPs

Measuring the standard size, these five limited production cards were randomly inserted in 1993 Classic McDonald's five-card packs. Chris Webber, the number one pick in the NBA draft, autographed 1,250 of his cards. Printed vertically, and parallel and next to the gold foil band, "1 of 16,750" appears in gold foil. The Classic Four Sport logo appears in the upper right. The cards are numbered on the back in gold foil with an "LP" prefix.

Card	Low	High
COMPLETE SET (5)	3.00	8.00
LP2 Trench Warfare	.20	.50
LP5 Steve Young	1.25	3.00

1994 Classic Four Sport

Featuring top rookies from basketball, baseball, football and hockey, the 1994 Classic Four-Sport set consists of 200 standard-size cards. No more than 25,000 cases were produced. Over 100 players signed 100,000 cards that were randomly inserted four per case. Collectors who found one of 100 Glenn Robinson Instant Winner Cards received a complete Classic Four-Sport autographed card set. Also inserted on an average of one in every five cases were 4,695 hand-numbered 4-in-1 cards featuring all four number 1 picks. Classic's wrapper redemption program offered four levels of participation: 1) bronze-collect 20 wrappers and receive a 4-card Classic Player of the Year set, featuring Grant Hill, Shaquille O'Neal, Emmitt Smith, and Steve Young; 2) silver-collect 30 wrappers and receive the Classic Player of the Year set and a random autograph card; 3) gold-collect 144 wrappers and receive the Classic Player of the Year set and an autograph card by Muhammad Ali; and 4) platinum-collect 216 wrappers and receive the Classic Player of the Year set plus an autograph card by Shaquille O'Neal. The cards are numbered on the back and checklisted below by sport.

Card	Low	High
COMPLETE SET (200)	6.00	15.00
51 Dan Wilkinson	.07	.20
52 Marshall Faulk	.75	2.00
53 Heath Shuler	.08	.25
54 Willie McGinest	.07	.20
55 Trev Alberts	.05	.15
56 Trent Dilfer	.20	.50
57 Bryant Young	.08	.25
58 Sam Adams	.07	.20
59 Antonio Langham	.05	.15
60 Jamir Miller	.05	.15
61 John Thierry	.05	.15
62 Aaron Glenn	.08	.25
63 Joe Johnson	.05	.15
64 Bernard Williams	.05	.15
65 Wayne Gandy	.05	.15
66 Aaron Taylor	.05	.15
67 Charles Johnson	.15	.40
68 Dewayne Washington	.05	.15
69 Todd Steussie	.08	.25
70 Tim Bowens	.05	.15
71 Johnnie Morton	.08	.25
72 Rob Fredrickson	.05	.15
73 Shante Carver	.05	.15
74 Thomas Lewis	.05	.15
75 Calvin Jones	.05	.15
76 Henry Ford	.05	.15
77 Jeff Burris	.05	.15
78 William Floyd	.15	.40
79 Derrick Alexander	.08	.25
80 Darnay Scott	.15	.40
81 Tre Johnson	.05	.15
82 Eric Mahlum	.05	.15
83 Errict Rhett	.10	.30
84 Kevin Lee	.05	.15
85 Andre Coleman	.05	.15
86 Corey Sawyer	.05	.15
87 Chuck Levy	.07	.20
88 Greg Hill	.05	.15
89 David Palmer	.05	.15
90 Ryan Yarborough	.05	.15
91 Charlie Garner	.20	.50
92 Mario Bates	.05	.15
93 Bert Emanuel	.08	.25
94 Thomas Randolph	.05	.15
95 Bucky Brooks	.05	.15
96 Rob Waldrop	.05	.15
97 Charlie Ward	.20	.50
98 Winfred Tubbs	.05	.15
99 James Folston	.05	.15
100 Kevin Mitchell	.05	.15
101 Aubrey Beavers	.05	.15
102 Fernando Smith	.05	.15
103 Jim Miller	.10	.30
104 Byron Bam Morris	.07	.20
105 Donnell Bennett	.05	.15
106 Jason Sehorn	.10	.30
107 Glenn Foley	.05	.15
108 Lonnie Johnson	.05	.15
109 Tyronne Drakeford	.05	.15
110 Vaughn Parker	.05	.15
111 Doug Nussmeier	.05	.15
112 Perry Klein	.05	.15
113 Jason Gildon	.10	.30
114 Lake Dawson	.05	.15
F01 4-in-1 Glenn Robinson Dan Wilkinson Paul Wilson Ed Jovanovski Number One Draft Picks	1.00	2.50

1994 Classic Four Sport Gold

Card	Low	High
COMPLETE SET (200)	12.00	30.00
*GOLD: .8X TO 2X BASIC CARDS		

1994 Classic Four Sport Printer's Proofs

*PRINT PROOFS: 2.5X TO 6X BASIC CARDS

1994 Classic Four Sport Autographs

Randomly inserted in packs at a rate of one in 103, this standard-size set features players from the 1994 Classic Four-Sport set who autographed cards within the set. The fronts feature full-bleed color action player photos. The player's name is gold-foil stamped across the bottom of the picture. The backs have a congratulatory message about receiving an autographed card. Though the cards are unnumbered, we have assigned them the same number as their four-sport regular issue counterpart.

Card	Low	High
53A Heath Shuler/1330	4.00	10.00
55A Trev Alberts/2520	2.00	5.00
56A Trent Dilfer/1495	6.00	15.00
81A Tre Johnson/1000	2.00	5.00
82A Eric Mahlum/1090	2.00	5.00
90A Ryan Yarborough/1020	2.00	5.00
93A Bert Emanuel/1100	2.50	6.00
96A Rob Waldrop/1095	2.00	5.00
97A Charlie Ward/1520	4.00	10.00
99A James Folston/1100	2.00	5.00
100A Kevin Mitchell/1090	2.00	5.00
103A Jim Miller/1030	4.00	10.00
108A Lonnie Johnson/1050	2.00	5.00
110A Vaughn Parker/750	2.00	5.00

1994 Classic Four Sport BCs

This 20-card bonus standard-size set was inserted one per '94 Classic Four-Sport jumbo packs. The fronts feature full color player photos. The backs carry biographical and statistical information about the player.

Card	Low	High
COMPLETE SET (20)	6.00	15.00
BC1 Marshall Faulk	1.00	2.50
BC2 Heath Shuler	.30	.75
BC3 Antonio Langham	.20	.50
BC4 Derrick Alexander	.30	.75
BC5 Byron Bam Morris	.20	.50

1994 Classic Four Sport C3 Collector's Club

The cards were issued to members of the 1995 Classic Collectors Club. Each is numbered 1 of 10,000 on the cardbacks and carries a 1995 copyright line. However, the cards are in the design of the 1994 Classic Four Sport set.

Card	Low	High
C1 Marshall Faulk	1.50	4.00
C3 Antonio Langham	.40	1.00

1994 Classic Four Sport Classic Picks

This 10-card standard-size set was randomly inserted in packs at rate of one in 72. The fronts feature full-color action player photos with the player's name and card title below. The backs carry a small player photo, the player's name, biographical information, and career highlights printed over a ghosted photo of the same player.

Card	Low	High
COMPLETE SET (10)	6.00	15.00
21 Dan Wilkinson	.40	1.00
22 Willie McGinest	.40	1.00

1994 Classic Four Sport High Voltage

This 20-card sequentially-numbered standard-size set features the top draft picks. The cards are printed on holographic foil board with a striking design. 2,995 of each even-numbered card and 5,495 of each odd-numbered cards were produced. The cards were inserted on an average of 3 per case and had stated odds of one in 144 hobby packs. The fronts feature the players against a background of lightning while the backs feature a biography on the left side of the card. The right side shows more lightning and the player's photo.

Card	Low	High
COMPLETE SET (20)	40.00	100.00
HV1 Dan Wilkinson	.75	2.00
HV5 Marshall Faulk	3.00	8.00
HV9 Heath Shuler	1.00	2.50
HV13 Trent Dilfer	1.50	4.00
HV17 Willie McGinest	.75	2.00

1994 Classic Four Sport Phone Cards $1

This set of eight phone cards was randomly inserted in Four-Sport packs. Printed on hard plastic, each card measures 2 1/8" by 3 3/8" and has rounded corners. The fronts display full-bleed color action photos, with the phone time value ($1, $2, $3, $4 or $5) and the player's name printed vertically in red along the right edge. The horizontal backs carry instructions for use of the cards. The cards are unnumbered and checklisted below in alphabetical order. The $3 and $5 cards were inserted into retail packs. The phone cards could be used until November 30, 1995.

Card	Low	High
COMPLETE SET (8)	3.00	8.00
*TWO DOLLAR: .5X TO 1.2X $1 CARDS		
*THREE DOLLAR: .6X TO 1.5X $1 CARDS		
*FOUR DOLLAR: .8X TO 2X $1 CARDS		
*FIVE DOLLAR: 1X TO 2.5X $1 CARDS		
*PIN NUMBER REVEALED: HALF VALUE		
1 Trent Dilfer	.40	1.00
2 Marshall Faulk	1.00	2.50

1994 Classic Four Sport Previews

Randomly inserted in 1994-95 Classic hockey foil packs at a rate of three per case, these five standard-size preview cards show the design of the 1994-95 Classic Four-Sport series. The full-bleed color action photos are gold-foil stamped with the "4-Sport Preview" emblem and the player's name. The backs feature another full-bleed closeup photo, with biography and statistics displayed on a ghosted panel.

Card	Low	High
COMPLETE SET (5)	6.00	15.00
P2 Marshall Faulk	2.00	5.00

1994 Classic Four Sport Tri-Cards

Inserted one in every three cases, this five-card standard-size set features three top running backs, linebackers, hockey centers, pitchers and basketball guards and compares their individual skills. Every card is sequentially-numbered out of 2,695. The horizontal fronts feature the three players equally while the backs gives a brief biography of why the three players are grouped together.

Card	Low	High
COMPLETE SET (5)	4.00	10.00
TC1 Faulk Jones Rhett	2.00	5.00
TC2 McGinest Alberts Miller	.75	2.00

1995 Classic NFL Rookies

This 110-card standard-size set features first-year NFL players. The cards were issued in 10-card packs, with 36 packs in a box and 12 boxes per case. For the card hobby, 2,950 sequentially numbered cases were produced. This set includes all 32 first round draft choices as well as many prominent later round picks. The set closes with an "Award Winner" subset at cards (101-105) as well as a flashback set of leading NFL players (106-110). Printed in 18-point stock, the full-bleed fronts feature color action photos. The player is identified in white lettering near the bottom. His position is in red lettering directly underneath his name. The backs contain biographical information, collegiate states and a player profile. The bottom right is dedicated to another player photo. All of this information is set against a white background. Key players in this set include Kerry Collins, Terrell Davis, Joey Galloway, Curtis Martin, Rashaan Salaam, Kordell Stewart, J.J. Stokes and Michael Westbrook.

Card	Low	High
COMPLETE SET (110)	5.00	12.00
1 Ki-Jana Carter	.08	.25
2 Tony Boselli	.02	.10
3 Steve McNair	.60	1.50
4 Michael Westbrook	.08	.25
5 Kerry Collins	.50	1.25
6 Kevin Carter	.08	.25
7 Mike Mamula	.01	.05
8 Joey Galloway	.30	.75
9 Kyle Brady	.01	.05
10 J.J. Stokes	.08	.25
11 Derrick Alexander	.01	.05
12 Warren Sapp	.02	.10
13 Mark Fields	.08	.25
14 Ruben Brown	.08	.25
15 Ellis Johnson	.01	.05
16 Hugh Douglas	.08	.25
17 Tyrone Wheatley	.30	.75
18 Napoleon Kaufman	.15	.40
19 James O. Stewart	.30	.75
20 Luther Elliss	.01	.05
21 Rashaan Salaam	.02	.10
22 Tyrone Poole	.08	.25
23 Ty Law	.30	.75
24 Korey Stringer	.07	.20
25 Billy Milner	.01	.05
26 Devin Bush	.01	.05
27 Mark Bruener	.01	.05
28 Derrick Brooks	.08	.25
29 Blake Brockermeyer	.01	.05
30 Craig Powell	.01	.05
31 Trezelle Jenkins	.01	.05
32 Craig Newsome	.01	.05
33 Thomas Bailey	.01	.05
34 Chad May	.01	.05
35 J.J. Smith	.01	.05
36 Lorenzo Styles	.01	.05
37 Brian Williams	.01	.05
38 Damien Covington	.01	.05
39 Steve Stenstrom	.01	.05
40 Darius Holland	.01	.05
41 Pete Mitchell	.01	.05
42 Todd Collins	.30	.75
43 Kordell Stewart	.50	1.25
44 Eric Zeier	.02	.10
45 Frank Sanders	.08	.25
46 Ben Talley	.01	.05
47 Billy Williams	.01	.05
48 Chris T. Jones	.01	.05
49 Tamarick Vanover	.02	.10
50 Jimmy Hitchcock	.01	.05
51 Chris Hudson	.01	.05
52 Terrell Fletcher	.02	.10
53 Brent Moss	.01	.05
54 Terrell Davis	.60	1.50
55 Rodney Thomas	.02	.10
56 Larry Jones	.01	.05
57 Ray Zellars	.02	.10
58 David Sloan	.01	.05
59 Brandon Bennett	.01	.05
60 Brian DeMarco	.01	.05
61 Bryan Schwartz	.01	.05
62 Jack Jackson	.01	.05
63 Bobby Taylor	.08	.25
64 Kevin Hickman	.01	.05
65 Matt O'Dwyer	.01	.05
66 Patrick Riley	.01	.05
67 Ki-Jana Carter	.08	.25
68 Kerry Collins	.50	1.25
69 Steve McNair	.60	1.50
70 Tyrone Wheatley	.30	.75
71 Antonio Freeman	.30	.75
72 Clifton Abraham	.01	.05
73 Kez McCorvey	.01	.05
74 Lovell Pinkney	.01	.05
75 Lee DeRamus	.01	.05
76 John Walsh	.01	.05
77 Cory Raymer	.01	.05
78 Corey Fuller	.01	.05
79 Tyrone Davis	.01	.05
80 David Dunn	.01	.05
81 Dana Howard	.01	.05
82 Melvin Johnson	.01	.05
83 Robert Baldwin	.01	.05
84 Curtis Martin	.60	1.50
85 Zack Crockett	.02	.10
86 Jay Barker	.01	.05
87 Christian Fauria	.01	.05
88 Zach Wiegert	.01	.05
89 Barrett Brooks	.01	.05
90 Ken Dilger	.02	.10
91 James A. Stewart	.01	.05
92 Ed Hervey RC	.01	.05
93 Torey Hunter	.01	.05
94 Sherman Williams	.01	.05
95 Shawn King	.01	.05
96 Dave Barr	.01	.05
97 Rob Johnson	.15	.40
98 Stoney Case	.02	.10
99 Ki-Jana Carter CL	.01	.05
100 Steve McNair CL	.08	.25
101 Rashaan Salaam AW	.01	.05
102 Kerry Collins AW	.15	.40
103 Rashaan Salaam AW	.01	.05
104 Kerry Collins AW	.15	.40
105 Jay Barker AW	.01	.05
106 Drew Bledsoe	.15	.40
107 Marshall Faulk	.30	.75
108 Steve Young	.08	.25
109 Troy Aikman	.20	.50
110 Emmitt Smith	.40	1.00
MF1 Marshall Faulk	5.00	12.00

1995 Classic NFL Rookies Printer's Proofs

Card	Low	High
COMPLETE SET (110)	60.00	120.00
*SINGLES: 3X TO 8X HI COLUMN		
STATED PRINT RUN 595 SETS		

1995 Classic NFL Rookies Printer's Proofs Silver

Card	Low	High
COMPLETE SET (110)	100.00	200.00
*SINGLES: 5X TO 12X HI COLUMN		
STATED PRINT RUN 297 SETS		

1995 Classic NFL Rookies Silver

Card	Low	High
COMPLETE SET (110)	16.00	40.00
*SINGLES: 1.2X TO 3X HI COLUMN		
ONE PER PACK		

1995 Classic NFL Rookies Die Cuts

Inserted on average of two cards per box, the 32 players selected in the first round of the 1995 NFL Draft are featured in this set. These retail-only cards display an action photo die cut in the shape of the number 1. They are sequentially numbered to 4,500.

Card	Low	High
COMPLETE SET (32)	15.00	40.00
STATED PRINT RUN 4500 SER.#'d SETS		
*PRINT PROOF: 4X TO 10X BASIC INSERTS		
PP STATED PRINT RUN 97 SETS		
PP STATED ODDS 1:432 HOBBY		
*SILVER SIG: 1X TO 2.5X BASIC INSERTS		
SS STATED ODDS 1:48 RETAIL		
SS STATED PRINT RUN 1750 SER.#'d SETS		
1 Ki-Jana Carter	.75	2.00
2 Tony Boselli	.30	.75
3 Steve McNair	5.00	12.00
4 Michael Westbrook	.75	2.00
5 Kerry Collins	4.00	10.00
6 Kevin Carter	.75	2.00
7 Mike Mamula	.15	.40
8 Joey Galloway	2.50	6.00
9 Kyle Brady	.15	.40
10 J.J. Stokes	.75	2.00
11 Derrick Alexander DE	.15	.40
12 Warren Sapp	.30	.75
13 Mark Fields	.75	2.00
14 Ruben Brown	.75	2.00
15 Ellis Johnson	.15	.40
16 Hugh Douglas	.75	2.00
17 Tyrone Wheatley	2.50	6.00
18 Napoleon Kaufman	1.25	3.00
19 James O. Stewart	2.50	6.00
20 Luther Elliss	.15	.40
21 Rashaan Salaam	.30	.75
22 Tyrone Poole	.75	2.00
23 Ty Law	2.50	6.00
24 Korey Stringer	.60	1.50
25 Billy Milner	.15	.40
26 Devin Bush	.15	.40
27 Mark Bruener	.15	.40
28 Derrick Brooks	.75	2.00
29 Blake Brockermeyer	.15	.40
30 Craig Powell	.15	.40
31 Trezelle Jenkins	.15	.40
32 Craig Newsome	.15	.40

1995 Classic NFL Rookies Draft Review

The first fourteen cards of this standard-size set was originally handed out to the media on NFL Draft Day (April 22) but were later reissued at a rate of one per three Classic NFL Rookies Retail rack packs. Eight additional cards that updated team selections where Issued in packs only to complete the 22-card set. The original 14-card set also came with a certificate numbered out of 19,995 sets. The fronts feature full-bleed color action photos except at the bottom, where a red foil stripe edges the picture and displays the team logo, player's name and position, and a 1995 NFL Draft emblem. Since a player could be drafted by several different teams, the players are pictured in different pro uniforms. The backs carry biography, complete collegiate statistics, player profile, and a color player cutout.

Card	Low	High
COMPLETE SET (23)	12.50	15.00
1 Steve McNair-Oilers	1.25	3.00
2 Steve McNair-Vikings	.40	2.00
3 Steve McNair-Jaguars	.40	2.00
4 Ki-Jana Carter-Panthers	.20	.50
5 Ki-Jana Carter-Jaguars	.20	.50
6 Kerry Collins-Bills	.40	1.00
7 Kerry Collins-Colts	.40	1.00
8 Kerry Collins-Cardinals	.40	1.00
9 John Walsh-Panthers	.08	.25
10 John Walsh-Vikings	.08	.25
11 John Walsh-Dolphins	.08	.25
12 J.J. Stokes-Seahawks	.20	.50
13 J.J. Stokes-Rams	.20	.50
14 Emmitt Smith	1.00	2.50
15 Steve Young	.60	1.25
16 Marshall Faulk	.60	1.50
17 Troy Aikman	.60	1.50
18 Ki-Jana Carter-Bengals	.20	.50
19 Kerry Collins-Panthers	.40	1.00
20 J.J. Stokes-49ers	.20	.50
21 M. Westbrook-Redskins	.20	.50
22 Kyle Brady-Jets	.08	.25
NNO Draft Cover Card	.08	.25
NNO Checklist John Walsh Steve McNair Kerry Collins	.20	.50

1995 Classic NFL Rookies Draft

Card	Low	High
D1 Ki-Jana Carter	.60	1.50
D2 Kerry Collins	.75	2.00
D2S Kerry Collins Sample	.75	2.00

1995 Classic NFL Rookies Instant Energy

This 20-card standard-size set was inserted one per rack pack. On a background streaked with lightning, the fronts feature a full-bleed color player photo with a metallic sheen. The player's name and team name appear in a silver and black stripe across the bottom. The back carries a color player cutout and a player profile, again on a lightning-streaked background.

Card	Low	High
COMPLETE SET (20)	6.00	15.00
ONE PER RETAIL RACK PACK		
IE1 Ki-Jana Carter	.25	.60
IE2 Steve McNair	1.50	4.00
IE3 Michael Westbrook	.25	.60
IE4 Joey Galloway	.75	2.00
IE5 Tyrone Wheatley	.75	2.00
IE6 Napoleon Kaufman	.40	1.00
IE7 Warren Sapp	.08	.25
IE8 Kevin Carter	.25	.60
IE9 Todd Collins	.40	1.00
IE10 Rob Johnson	.40	1.00
IE11 Chad May	.05	.15
IE12 Mike Mamula	.05	.15
IE13 Sherman Williams	.05	.15
IE14 Tony Boselli	.08	.25
IE15 Kerry Collins	1.25	3.00
IE16 J.J. Stokes	.25	.60
IE17 Rashaan Salaam	.08	.25
IE18 Kordell Stewart	1.25	3.00
IE19 Derrick Brooks	.25	.60
IE20 Frank Sanders	.25	.60

1995 Classic NFL Rookies ROY Redemption

Inserted on average of one card every three boxes, these 20 interactive, holographic cards feature 19 players and one field card. Cards featuring the 1995 Associated Press NFL Offensive Rookie of the Year were redeemable for a 50.00 phone card of the player. The fronts feature a large holographic area and an action photo. Each card is numbered one of 2,500.

Card	Low	High
COMPLETE SET (20)	25.00	60.00
STATED ODDS 1:108 HOBBY		
STATED PRINT RUN 2500 SETS		

1 Ki-Jana Carter 1.00 2.50
2 Tony Boselli .40 1.00
3 Steve McNair 6.00 15.00
4 Michael Westbrook 1.00 2.50
5 Kerry Collins 4.00 10.00
6 Joey Galloway 3.00 8.00
7 Kyle Brady .20 .50
8 J.J. Stokes 1.00 2.50
9 Tyrone Wheatley 3.00 8.00
10 Napoleon Kaufman 1.50 4.00
11 Rashaan Salaam .40 1.00
12 James O. Stewart 3.00 8.00
13 Kordell Stewart 5.00 12.00
14 Frank Sanders 1.00 2.50
15 Ray Zellars .40 1.00
16 Zack Crockett .40 1.00
17 Tamarick Vanover .40 1.00
18 Chad May .20 .50
19 Eric Zeier .40 1.00
20 Field Card-C.Martin .20 .50
HP1 Ki-Jana Carter Sample .50 1.25
ROY1 Curtis Martin $50 PC 7.50 20.00

1995 Classic NFL Rookies Rookie Spotlight

This 30-card standard-size set was inserted one per jumbo pack. The fronts feature a full-bleed color player photo with a metallic sheen. The player's name and position appear in silver foil lettering at the lower right corner. On a background consisting of a blue-tinted action photo, the back carries a player profile, "Spotlight" feature, and a color headshot.
COMPLETE SET (30) 6.00 15.00
ONE PER JUMBO
*HOLOFOILS: 2X TO 5X BASIC INSERTS
HOLOFOIL STATED ODDS 1:30 JUMBO
RS1 Ki-Jana Carter .20 .50
RS2 Steve McNair 1.25 3.00
RS3 Michael Westbrook .20 .50
RS4 Joey Galloway .60 1.50
RS5 Tyrone Wheatley .60 1.50
RS6 Napoleon Kaufman .30 .75
RS7 Kordell Stewart 1.00 2.50
RS8 Frank Sanders .20 .50
RS9 Zack Crockett .07 .20
RS10 Tamarick Vanover .07 .20
RS11 Chad May .02 .10
RS12 Eric Zeier .07 .20
RS13 Mike Mamula .02 .10
RS14 Warren Sapp .07 .20
RS15 Kevin Carter .20 .50
RS16 Derrick Brooks .20 .50
RS17 Todd Collins .40 1.00
RS18 Rob Johnson .30 .75
RS19 Chris T. Jones .02 .10
RS20 Terrell Fletcher .07 .20
RS21 Sherman Williams .02 .10
RS22 Tony Boselli .07 .20
RS23 Kerry Collins 1.00 2.50
RS24 J.J. Stokes .20 .50
RS25 Rashaan Salaam .07 .20
RS26 James O. Stewart .60 1.50
RS27 Rodney Thomas .07 .20
RS28 Jack Jackson .02 .10
RS29 Lovell Pinkney .02 .10
RS30 Ruben Brown .20 .50

1996 Classic NFL Rookies

The 1996 Classic NFL Rookies set was issued in one series totaling 100 standard-size cards. The set was issued in 10-card packs with 36 packs in a box and 12 boxes in a case. Among the topical subsets are: All-Americans (65-74), NFL Greats (75-79) and Checklists (99-100). There is also a gold parallel set that was issued one per special retail jumbo pack. The key players in this set are Terry Glenn, Keyshawn Johnson and Lawrence Phillips.
COMPLETE SET (100) 3.00 8.00
1 Keyshawn Johnson .40 1.00
2 Jonathan Ogden .40 1.00
3 Kevin Hardy .15 .40
4 Leeland McElroy .07 .20
5 Terry Glenn .30 .75
6 Tim Biakabutuka .15 .40
7 Tony Brackens .15 .40
8 Duane Clemons .01 .05
9 Willie Anderson .01 .05
10 Karim Abdul-Jabbar .15 .40
11 Daryl Gardener .01 .05
12 Simeon Rice .20 .50
13 Eddie George .60 1.50
14 Andre Johnson .01 .05
15 Jon Runyan .01 .05
16 Jevon Langford .01 .05
17 Derrick Mayes .15 .40
18 Stephen Davis .50 1.25
19 Ray Farmer .01 .05
20 Chris Doering .01 .05
21 Jimmy Herndon .01 .05
22 Jerome Woods .01 .05
23 Scott Greene .01 .05
24 Jamain Stephens .01 .05
25 Tommie Frazier .15 .40
26 Dusty Zeigler .01 .05
27 Alex Molden .01 .05
28 Dietrich Jells .01 .05
29 Brian Roche .01 .05
30 Danny Kanell .15 .40
31 Roman Oben .01 .05
32 Chris Darkins .01 .05
33 Christian Peter .01 .05
34 Jeff Hartings .15 .40
35 Bobby Hoying .15 .40
36 Steve Taneyhill .01 .05
37 Lance Johnstone .07 .20
38 Zach Thomas .30 .75
39 Donnie Edwards .15 .40
40 Eric Moulds .40 1.00
41 Amani Toomer .30 .75
42 Scott Slutzker .01 .05
43 Matt Stevens .01 .05
44 Randall Godfrey .01 .05
45 Orpheus Roye .01 .05
46 Jason Odom .01 .05
47 Je'Rod Cherry .01 .05
48 Jeff Lewis .07 .20
49 Mike Alstott .40 1.00
50 Tony Banks .15 .40
51 Stepfret Williams .07 .20
52 Michael Cheever .01 .05
53 Bryant Mix .01 .05
54 James Ritchey .01 .05
55 Marcus Coleman .01 .05
56 Sedric Clark .01 .05
57 Kyle Wachholtz RC .01 .05
58 Johnny McWilliams .01 .05
59 Lawyer Milloy .20 .50
60 Alex Van Dyke .07 .20
61 Stanley Pritchett .01 .05
62 Ray Mickens .01 .05
63 Toraino Singleton .01 .05
64 Richard Huntley .07 .20
65 Eddie George AA .40 1.00
66 Terry Glenn AA .15 .40
67 Keyshawn Johnson AA .15 .40
68 Jonathan Ogden AA .20 .50
69 Tommie Frazier AA .07 .20
70 Kevin Hardy AA .01 .05
71 Zach Thomas AA .20 .50
72 Tony Brackens AA .07 .20
73 Lawyer Milloy AA .15 .40
74 Leeland McElroy AA .01 .05
75 Emmitt Smith .40 1.00
76 Steve McNair .15 .40
77 Kerry Collins .15 .40
78 Drew Bledsoe .15 .40
79 Marshall Faulk .30 .75
80 Pete Kendall .01 .05
81 Regan Upshaw .01 .05
82 Mercury Hayes .01 .05
83 Dou Innocent .01 .05
84 DeRon Jenkins .01 .05
85 Marco Battaglia .01 .05
86 John Mobley .01 .05
87 Cedric Jones .01 .05
88 Marvin Harrison .75 2.00
89 Israel Ifeanyi .01 .05
90 Reggie Brown .01 .05
91 Jermane Mayberry .01 .05
92 Brian Dawkins .40 1.00
93 Tedy Bruschi 1.00 2.50
94 Terrell Owens .75 2.00
95 Jermaine Lewis .07 .20
96 Sean Boyd .01 .05
97 Phillip Daniels .15 .40
98 Lawrence Phillips .01 .05
99 Keyshawn Johnson CL .15 .40
100 Terry Glenn CL .15 .40
P1 Keyshawn Johnson Promo .50 1.25

1996 Classic NFL Rookies Gold

COMPLETE SET (90) 15.00 40.00
*GOLD CARDS: 1.5X TO 4X BASIC CARDS
ONE PER RETAIL JUMBO

1996 Classic NFL Rookies Autographs

These cards were inserted one per special retail box as a boxtopper. Each is essentially a signed Classic NFL Rookies base card with a Score Board embossed logo in the corner. There is no "congratulations" message on the backs. Any additions to the below list are appreciated. Several players have been reported as autographs missing the authentication embossing so are not listed below: Alex Molden, Eric Moulds, Amani Toomer.
ONE PER SPECIAL RETAIL BOX
2 Jonathan Ogden 12.00 30.00
6 Tim Biakabutuka 6.00 15.00
11 Daryl Gardener 5.00 12.00
17 Derrick Mayes 6.00 15.00
22 Jerome Woods 5.00 12.00
34 Jeff Hartings 4.00 10.00
37 Lance Johnstone 6.00 15.00
44 Randall Godfrey 4.00 10.00
48 Jeff Lewis 6.00 15.00
49 Mike Alstott 15.00 40.00
51 Stepfret Williams 4.00 10.00
57 Kyle Wachholtz 4.00 10.00
58 Johnny McWilliams 4.00 10.00
80 Pete Kendall 5.00 12.00
85 Marco Battaglia 5.00 12.00

1996 Classic NFL Rookies Die Cuts

Randomly inserted in retail packs at the rate of 1:100, these cards feature players drafted in the first round of the 1996 NFL draft and some current NFL players under license by Classic.
COMPLETE SET (30) 30.00 80.00
STATED ODDS 1:100 RETAIL
1 Keyshawn Johnson 4.00 10.00
2 Kevin Hardy .75 2.00
3 Simeon Rice 1.25 3.00
4 Jonathan Ogden 3.00 8.00
5 Cedric Jones .75 2.00
6 Lawrence Phillips .75 2.00
7 Terry Glenn 2.50 6.00
8 Tim Biakabutuka 1.25 3.00
9 Emmitt Smith 6.00 15.00
10 Willie Anderson .75 2.00
11 Alex Molden .75 2.00
12 Regan Upshaw .75 2.00
13 Kerry Collins 2.50 6.00
14 Eddie George 4.00 10.00
15 John Mobley .75 2.00
16 Duane Clemons .75 2.00
17 Reggie Brown .75 2.00
18 Marshall Faulk 3.00 8.00
19 Marvin Harrison 6.00 15.00
20 Daryl Gardener .75 2.00
21 Pete Kendall .75 2.00
22 Joey Galloway 2.00 5.00
23 Jeff Hartings 1.25 3.00
24 Eric Moulds 3.00 8.00
25 Jermane Mayberry .75 2.00
26 Steve McNair 2.00 5.00
27 Kyle Brady .75 2.00
28 Jerome Woods .75 2.00
29 Jamain Stephens .75 2.00
30 Andre Johnson .75 2.00

1996 Classic NFL Rookies Home Jersey Image

Randomly inserted in retail packs at a rate of one in 15, this 30-card horizontal insert set features leading 1996 NFL Rookies photographed in their home college jersey. The background on the fronts also include a mocked-up white NFL jersey with a "mesh" type embossing to give the feel and look of the drafted player's jersey. The Home version is essentially a parallel to the Road inserts, except that cards #14, 16, and 22 are different players than the Road Jersey inserts.
COMPLETE SET (30) 40.00 80.00
STATED ODDS 1:15 RETAIL PACKS
HJ1 Keyshawn Johnson 4.00 8.00
HJ2 Kevin Hardy 1.50 3.00
HJ3 Jonathan Ogden 2.50 6.00
HJ4 Terry Glenn 3.00 6.00
HJ5 Tim Biakabutuka 1.50 3.00
HJ6 Karim Abdul-Jabbar 1.50 3.00
HJ7 Simeon Rice 2.00 4.00
HJ8 Eric Moulds 4.00 8.00
HJ9 Mike Alstott 4.00 8.00
HJ10 Leeland McElroy .75 1.50
HJ11 Daryl Gardener .15 .40
HJ12 Eddie George 6.00 12.00
HJ13 Amani Toomer 3.00 6.00
HJ14 Johnny McWilliams .15 .40
HJ15 Derrick Mayes 1.50 3.00
HJ16 Duane Clemons .15 .40
HJ17 Chris Darkins .15 .40
HJ18 Ray Farmer .15 .40
HJ19 Danny Kanell 1.50 3.00
HJ20 Bobby Hoying 1.50 3.00
HJ21 Zach Thomas 3.00 6.00
HJ22 Tony Banks 1.50 3.00
HJ23 Alex Van Dyke .75 1.50
HJ24 Stepfret Williams .75 1.50
HJ25 Chris Doering .15 .40
HJ26 Lance Johnstone .75 1.50
HJ27 Stephen Davis 5.00 10.00
HJ28 Scott Greene .15 .40
HJ29 Tony Brackens 1.50 3.00
HJ30 Jevon Langford .15 .40

1996 Classic NFL Rookies Road Jersey Images

Randomly inserted in hobby packs at a rate of one in 15, this 30-card horizontal insert set features leading 1996 NFL Rookies photographed in their road college jersey. The background on the fronts also include a mocked-up black NFL jersey with a "mesh" type embossing to give the feel and look of the drafted player's jersey.
COMPLETE SET (30) 40.00 80.00
ROAD JERSEY STATED ODDS 1:15 HOBBY
RJ1 Keyshawn Johnson 4.00 8.00
RJ2 Kevin Hardy 1.50 3.00
RJ3 Jonathan Ogden 2.50 6.00
RJ4 Terry Glenn 3.00 0.00
RJ5 Tim Biakabutuka 1.50 3.00
RJ6 Karim Abdul-Jabbar 1.50 3.00
RJ7 Simeon Rice 2.00 4.00
RJ8 Eric Moulds 4.00 8.00
RJ9 Mike Alstott 4.00 8.00
RJ10 Leeland McElroy .75 1.50
RJ11 Daryl Gardener .15 .40
RJ12 Eddie George 6.00 12.00
RJ13 Amani Toomer 3.00 6.00
RJ14 Marvin Harrison 8.00 15.00
RJ15 Derrick Mayes 1.50 3.00
RJ16 Dietrich Jells .15 .40
RJ17 Chris Darkins .15 .40
RJ18 Ray Farmer .15 .40
RJ19 Danny Kanell 1.50 3.00
RJ20 Bobby Hoying 1.50 3.00
RJ21 Zach Thomas 3.00 6.00
RJ22 Kyle Wachholtz .15 .40
RJ23 Alex Van Dyke .75 1.50
RJ24 Stepfret Williams .75 1.50
RJ25 Chris Doering .15 .40
RJ26 Lance Johnstone .75 1.50
RJ27 Stephen Davis 5.00 10.00
RJ28 Scott Greene .15 .40
RJ29 Tony Brackens 1.50 3.00
RJ30 Jevon Langford .15 .40

1996 Classic NFL Rookies Rookie Lasers

Randomly inserted in hobby packs only at a rate of one in 100, this 10-card insert standard-size set features explosive first-year players. The cards feature a dual player image, the words "Rookie Lasers" in the lower right and the player's name on the right.
COMPLETE SET (10) 25.00 60.00
STATED ODDS 1:100 HOBBY
RL1 Keyshawn Johnson 8.00 20.00
RL2 Jonathan Ogden 5.00 12.00
RL3 Eddie George 12.50 30.00
RL4 Terry Glenn 6.00 15.00
RL5 Tommie Frazier 3.00 8.00
RL6 Karim Abdul-Jabbar 3.00 8.00
RL7 Duane Clemons .40 1.00
RL8 Leeland McElroy 1.50 4.00
RL9 Tim Biakabutuka 3.00 8.00
RL10 Kevin Hardy 3.00 8.00

1996 Classic NFL Rookies ROY Contenders

Randomly inserted in special retail packs at the rate of 1:20, these cards feature 10 players expected to be strong candidates for 1996 NFL Offensive Rookie of the Year honors.
COMPLETE SET (10) 15.00 40.00
STATED ODDS 1:20 SPECIAL RETAIL
C1 Keyshawn Johnson 3.00 8.00
C2 Jonathan Ogden 2.00 5.00
C3 Eddie George 5.00 12.00
C4 Terry Glenn 2.50 6.00
C5 Eric Moulds 3.00 8.00
C6 Karim Abdul-Jabbar 1.25 3.00
C7 Leeland McElroy .60 1.50
C8 Tim Biakabutuka 1.25 3.00
C9 Bobby Hoying 1.25 3.00
C10 Stephen Davis 4.00 10.00

1996 Classic NFL Rookies ROY Interactive

Randomly inserted in packs at a rate of one in 35, this 20-card insert standard-size set features the top candidates eligible to win the AP NFL Offensive Rookie of the Year award. If the player on the card won an award then the card could be redeemed for an autographed collectible. The winning cards were to be redeemed by March 31, 1997 and they were not returned to the collector after being redeemed.
COMPLETE SET (20) 40.00 80.00
STATED ODDS 1:35
RY1 Keyshawn Johnson 4.00 10.00
RY2 Jonathan Ogden 2.50 6.00
RY3 Steve Taneyhill .20 .50
RY4 Leeland McElroy .75 2.00
RY5 Terry Glenn 3.00 8.00
RY6 Tim Biakabutuka 1.50 4.00
RY7 Karim Abdul-Jabbar 1.50 4.00
RY8 Eddie George 6.00 15.00
RY9 Johnny McWilliams .20 .50
RY10 Eric Moulds 4.00 10.00
RY11 Bobby Hoying 1.50 4.00
RY12 Chris Darkins .20 .50
RY13 Derrick Mayes 1.50 4.00
RY14 Mike Alstott 4.00 10.00
RY15 Chris Doering .20 .50
RY16 Danny Kanell 1.50 4.00
RY17 Stephen Davis 5.00 12.00
RY18 Amani Toomer 3.00 8.00
RY19 Dietrich Jells .20 .50
RY20 Field Card .20 .50

1996 Clear Assets

The 1996 Clear Assets set was issued in one series totaling 70 cards. The set features 75 upscale acetate cards of the most collectible athletes from baseball, basketball, football, hockey and auto racing. Also included is the debut appearance by many of the top players entering the 1996 football draft. Release date was April 1996.
COMPLETE SET (70) 6.00 15.00
29 Emmitt Smith .60 1.50
30 Jeff Lewis .08 .25
31 Joey Galloway .15 .40
32 Steve McNair .25 .60
33 Eric Moulds .30 .75
34 Steve Young .30 .75
35 Mike Alstott .30 .75
36 Marshall Faulk .20 .50
37 Kerry Collins .15 .40
38 Kyle Brady .10 .30
39 Drew Bledsoe .20 .50
40 Troy Aikman .40 1.00
41 Duane Clemons .08 .25
42 Napoleon Kaufman .10 .30
43 Stanley Pritchett .08 .25
44 Marcus Coleman .08 .25
45 Amani Toomer .25 .60
46 Richard Huntley .08 .25
47 Tony Banks .10 .30
48 Keyshawn Johnson .40 1.00
49 Kevin Hardy .08 .25
50 Karim Abdul-Jabbar .10 .30

1996 Clear Assets 3X

Randomly inserted in packs at a rate of one in 100, this 10-card set is another first from Classic. The cards resemble triplexed cards with acetate in the middle and an opaque covering.
COMPLETE SET (10) 40.00 100.00
X5 Emmitt Smith 10.00 25.00
X8 Keyshawn Johnson 5.00 12.00
X10 Troy Aikman 6.00 15.00

1996 Clear Assets A Cut Above

CA1 Keyshawn Johnson
CA8 Emmitt Smith 2.00 5.00
CA11 Marshall Faulk .75 2.00
CA13 Drew Bledsoe
CA19 Kerry Collins

1996 Clear Assets Phone Cards $1

COMPLETE SET (30) 5.00 12.00
*PIN NUMBER REVEALED: HALF VALUE
$1 CARDS ONE PER RETAIL PACK
*$2 CARDS: .6X TO 1.5X $1 CARDS
ONE PER HOBBY PACK
CARDS EXPIRED 10/1/97
2 Marshall Faulk .25 .60
7 Troy Aikman .40 1.00
10 Jeff Lewis .10 .30
12 Drew Bledsoe .25 .60
14 Eric Moulds .25 .60
18 Joey Galloway .15 .40
21 Kerry Collins .20 .50
23 Mike Alstott .30 .75
24 Duane Clemons .10 .30
26 Stanley Pritchett .10 .30
27 Steve Young .30 .75

1996 Clear Assets Phone Cards $5

Inserted at a rate of 1:10 packs, this 20-card set of acetate phone cards features many of the biggest names in sports. The Sprint phone cards carry expiration dates of 10/1/97.
COMPLETE SET (20) 12.00 30.00
*PIN NUMBER REVEALED: HALF VALUE
2 Emmitt Smith 2.00 5.00
6 Troy Aikman 1.25 3.00
7 Keyshawn Johnson 1.00 2.50
10 Drew Bledsoe .75 2.00
15 Kerry Collins .50 1.25
17 Mike Alstott .75 2.00
19 Steve Young 1.00 2.50
20 Marshall Faulk .75 2.00

1996 Clear Assets Phone Cards $10

Inserted at a rate of 1:30 packs, this 10-card set of acetate phone cards features many of the biggest names in sports. The Sprint phone cards carry expiration dates of 10/1/97.
COMPLETE SET (10) 20.00 50.00
*PIN NUMBER REVEALED:HALF VALUE
2 Troy Aikman .50 6.00
4 Keyshawn Johnson 1.50 4.00
7 Napoleon Kaufman 1.00 2.50

1992 Courtside Promos

The 1992 Courtside Draft Pix Promos include cards released at different times through different channels. Many are sometimes found with red overprint stamps on the back commemorating the card show where they were available as give-aways. The style of these promo and sample cards is very similar to that of the 1992 Courtside regular issue cards on the fronts with many different variations of cardbacks. Most of these promos are marked on the back clearly with "Promotion Not For Sale" or "Sample" or other similar line of type. Most of the cards contain a card number, while a few have been assigned card numbers based on their position in the regular issue set.
COMPLETE SET (12) 2.00 5.00
20A Tony Brooks .08 .25
20B Amp Lee .08 .25
22 Terrell Buckley .20 .50
30 Tommy Vardell .20 .50
40 Carl Pickens .80 2.00
44 Quentin Coryatt .20 .50
50 Mike Gaddis .08 .25
60 Steve Emtman .20 .50
66 Bucky Richardson .08 .25
70A Dana Hall .08 .25
70B Dana Hall .08 .25
75 Johnny Mitchell Sample .08 .25
60S Steve Emtman .08 .25

1992 Courtside

The 1992 Courtside Draft Pix football set contains 140 player cards. Ten short printed insert cards (five Award Winner and five All-America) were randomly inserted in the foil packs. This set also includes a foilgram card featuring Steve Emtman. Fifty thousand foilgram cards were printed, and collectors could receive one by sending in ten foil pack wrappers. Moreover, one set of foilgram cards and 20 free promo cards were offered to dealers for each case order. It has been reported that the production run was limited to 7,500 numbered cases, and that no factory sets were issued. Gold, silver, and bronze foil versions of the regular cards were randomly inserted within the foil cases in quantities of 1,000, 2,000, and 3,000 respectively. Reportedly more than 70,000 autographed cards were also inserted. The standard-size cards feature on the fronts glossy color action photos bordered in white (some of the cards are oriented horizontally). The player's name and position appear in a gold stripe cutting across the bottom. On the backs, the upper half has a color close-up photo, with biography and collegiate statistics below. Key cards include Quentin Coryatt, Amp Lee, Johnny Mitchell, Carl Pickens and Tommy Vardell.
COMPLETE SET (140) 2.00 5.00
1 Steve Emtman .05 .15
2 Quentin Coryatt .05 .15
3 Ken Swilling .01 .05
4 Jay Leeuwenburg .01 .05
5 Mazio Royster .01 .05
6 Matt Veatch .01 .05
7A Scott Lockwood ERR .01 .05
7B Scott Lockwood COR .01 .05
8 Todd Collins .01 .05
9 Gene McGuire .01 .05
10 Dale Carter .05 .15
11 Michael Bankston .01 .05
12 Jeremy Lincoln .01 .05
13A Troy Auzenne ERR .01 .05
13B Troy Auzenne COR .01 .05
14 Rod Smith DB .01 .05
15 Andy Kelly .10 .30
16 Chris Holder .01 .05
17 Rico Smith .01 .05
18 Chris Pedersen .01 .05
19 Brian Treggs .01 .05
20 Eugene Chung .01 .05
21 Joel Steed .01 .05
22 Ricardo McDonald .01 .05
23 Nate Turner .01 .05
24 Sean Lumpkin .01 .05
25 Ty Detmer .10 .30
26 Matt Darby .01 .05
27 Michael Warfield .01 .05
28 Tracy Scroggins .01 .05
29 Carl Pickens .30 .75
30 Chris Mims .01 .05
31 Mark D'Onofrio .01 .05
32 Dwight Hollier .01 .05
33 Siupeli Malamala .01 .05
34A Mark Barsotti ERR .01 .05
34B Mark Barsotti COR .01 .05
35 Charles Davenport .01 .05
36 Brian Bollinger .01 .05
37 Willie McClendon .01 .05
38 Calvin Holmes .01 .05
39 Phillippi Sparks .05 .15
40 Darryl Williams .01 .05
41 Greg Skrepenak .01 .05
42 Larry Webster .01 .05
43 Dion Lambert .01 .05
44 Sam Gash .10 .30
45 Patrick Rowe .01 .05
46 Scottie Graham .05 .15
47 Darian Hagan .01 .05
48 Arthur Marshall .01 .05
49 Amp Lee .05 .15
50 Tommy Vardell .05 .15
51 Robert Porcher .10 .30
52 Reggie Dwight .01 .05
53 Torrance Small .01 .05
54 Ronnie West .01 .05
55 Tony Brooks .01 .05
56 Anthony McDowell .01 .05
57 Chris Hakel .01 .05
58 Ed Cunningham .01 .05
59 Ashley Ambrose .10 .30
60 Alonzo Spellman .05 .15
61 Harold Heath .01 .05
62 Ron Lopez .05 .15
63 Bill Johnson .01 .05
64 Kent Graham .05 .15
65 Aaron Pierce .01 .05
66 Bucky Richardson .01 .05
67A Todd Kinchen ERR .01 .05
67B Todd Kinchen COR .01 .05
68 Ken Ealy .01 .05
69 Carlos Snow .01 .05
70 Dana Hall .01 .05
71 Matt Rodgers .01 .05
72 Howard Dinkins .01 .05
73 Tim Lester .01 .05
74 Mark Chmura .10 .30
75 Johnny Mitchell .05 .15
76 Mirko Jurkovic .01 .05
77 Anthony Lynn .01 .05
78 Roosevelt Collins .01 .05
79 Tony Sands .01 .05
80 Kevin Smith .01 .05
81 Tony Brown .01 .05
82 Bobby Fuller .01 .05
83 Darryl Ashmore .01 .05
84 Tyrone Legette .01 .05
85 Mike Gaddis .01 .05
86A Cal Dixon ERR .01 .05
86B Gerald Dixon COR .01 .05
87 T.J. Rubley .01 .05
88 Mark Thomas .01 .05
89 Corey Widmer .01 .05
90 Robert Jones .01 .05
91 Eddie Robinson .01 .05
92 Rob Tomlinson .01 .05
93 Russ Campbell .01 .05
94 Keith Goganious .01 .05
95 Rod Moore .01 .05
96 Jerry Ostroski .01 .05
97 Tyji Armstrong .01 .05
98 Ronald Humphrey .01 .05
99 Corey Harris .01 .05
100 Terrell Buckley .05 .15
101 Cal Dixon .01 .05
102 Tyrone Williams .05 .15
103 Joe Bowden .01 .05
104 Santana Dotson .05 .15
105 Jeff Blake .60 1.50
106 Erick Anderson .01 .05
107 Steve Israel .01 .05
108 Chad Roghair .01 .05
109 Todd Harrison .01 .05
110 Chester McGlockton .01 .05
111 Marquez Pope .01 .05
112 George Rooks .01 .05
113 Dion Johnson .01 .05
114 Tim Simpson .01 .05
115 Chris Walsh .01 .05
116 Marc Boutte .01 .05
117 Jamie Gill .01 .05
118 Willie Clay .01 .05
119 Tim Paulk .01 .05
120 Ray Roberts .01 .05
121 Jeff Thomason .01 .05
122 Leodis Flowers .01 .05
123 Robert Brooks .30 .75
124 Jeff Ellis .01 .05
125 John Fina .01 .05
126A Michael Smith ERR .01 .05
126B Michael Smith COR .01 .05
127 Mike Saunders .20 .50
128 John Brown III .01 .05
129 Reggie Yarbrough .01 .05
130 Leon Searcy .01 .05
131 Marcus Woods .01 .05
132 Shane Collins .01 .05
133 Chuck Smith .01 .05
134 Keith Hamilton .05 .15
135 Rodney Blackshear .01 .05
136 Corey Barlow .01 .05
137 Robert Harris .01 .05
138 Tony Smith WR .01 .05
139 Checklist 1 UER .01 .05
140 Checklist 2 .01 .05

1992 Courtside Bronze

COMPLETE SET (140) 4.00 10.00
*BRONZES: .8X TO 2X BASIC CARDS

1992 Courtside Gold

COMPLETE SET (140) 4.00 10.00
*GOLDS: .8X TO 2X BASIC CARDS

1992 Courtside Silver

COMPLETE SET (140) 4.00 10.00
*SILVERS: .8X TO 2X BASIC CARDS

1992 Courtside Autographs

COMMON AUTOGRAPH 1.25 3.00
SEMISTARS 2.00 5.00
UNLISTED STARS 4.00 10.00
29 Carl Pickens 8.00 20.00
105 Jeff Blake 10.00 25.00
123 Robert Brooks 10.00 25.00
127 Mike Saunders 6.00 15.00

1992 Courtside Foilgrams

These five special foilgram standard-size cards were redeemable by mail via a wrapper offer. They feature some leading prospects of the 1992 draft.
COMPLETE SET (5) 1.60 4.00
1 Steve Emtman .30 .75
2 Tommy Vardell .30 .75
3 Terrell Buckley .30 .75
4 Ty Detmer .60 1.50
5 Amp Lee .30 .75

1992 Courtside Inserts

These ten cards were included as random inserts within foil cases of 1992 Courtside Draft Pix football. They consist of five Award Winners and five All-America cards. The fronts of these standard-size cards have glossy color action photos enclosed by white borders. The player's name and position appear in a stripe that cuts across the top of the picture; a football icon with the words "All-America" or the award won appears in the lower left corner. The backs have a close-up player photo, with player profile printed on a color box alongside the picture.
COMPLETE SET (10) 2.50 6.00
AA1 Carl Pickens 1.25 3.00
AA2 Dale Carter .25 .60
AA3 Tommy Vardell .25 .60
AA4 Amp Lee .25 .60
AA5 Leon Searcy .07 .20
AW1 Steve Emtman .25 .60
AW2 Ty Detmer Heisman .50 1.25
AW3 Steve Emtman .25 .60
AW4 Terrell Buckley .25 .60
AW5 Erick Anderson .07 .20

1993 Courtside Sean Dawkins

Sean Dawkins, who was drafted in the first round by the Indianapolis Colts, is showcased in this five-card, standard-size set. Only 20,000 sets of each player were produced, and Dawkins personally autographed 5,000 cards for random insertion within the sets. The fronts display full-bleed glossy action photos, with the backgrounds blurred to highlight the player. Each card has a color bar carrying a gold foil football icon, the words "Draft Pix," and the player's name in gold foil lettering. On a background reflecting the same color as the front bar, the backs have a second color action photo and either biography, statistics, player profile, or highlights. The complete set price below is a sealed price since it is not known if there is an autograph sealed inside. The cards were also issued as promos with the disclaimer "Promotional Not for Sale" stamped on the front in a circular format. The promos also included the words "Authentic Signature" printed in silver lettering toward the bottom of the front even though they were not signed.
COMPLETE SET (5) 2.00 5.00
COMMON CARD (1-5) .40 1.00
*PROMOS: .6X TO 1.5X BASIC CARDS
AU1 Sean Dawkins AU/5000 4.00 10.00

1993 Courtside Russell White

Russell White, who was drafted in the third round by the Los Angeles Rams, is showcased in this five-card, standard-size set. Just 20,000 sets of each player were produced, and White personally autographed 5,000 cards for random insertion within the sets. The fronts display full-bleed glossy action photos, with the backgrounds blurred to highlight the player. Each card has a color bar carrying a gold foil football icon, the words "Draft Pix," and the player's name in gold foil lettering. On a background reflecting the same color as the front bar, the backs have a second color action photo and either biography, statistics, player profile, or highlights. The complete set price below is a sealed price since it is not known if there is an autograph sealed inside. The cards were also issued as promos and those are identical to the regular issue except for "Promotional Not for Sale" stamped on the fronts in a circular format. These promos also include the words "Authentic Signature" printed in silver lettering toward the bottom of the front even though the cards were not signed.
COMPLETE SET (5) 1.00 2.50
COMMON CARD (1-5) .20 .50
*PROMOS: .6X TO 1.5X BASIC INSERTS
AU1 Russell White AU/5000 2.00 5.00

1993 Front Row Gold Collection Promos

Along with an 11" by 8 1/2" promo sheet (listed below), these five standard sized cards were issued in honor of Spectrum Holdings Group's purchase of the Front Row trademark. The set's title, "The Gold Collection" is stamped in gold foil and runs down the left edge of the cardfront. The cardbacks carry a disclaimer, "For Promotional Purposes Only." The unnumbered cards have been assigned numbers below alphabetically. The promo sheet features all five players and contains a gold foil seal bearing the sheet number (of 5000) produced
COMPLETE SET (5) 2.00 5.00
1 Eric Curry .30 .75
2 Andre Hastings .30 .75
3 Qadry Ismail .50 1.25
4 Lincoln Kennedy .30 .75
5 O.J.McDuffie .80 2.00
NNO ECurry AHast. QIsm L.Kenn. O.J.McD. .40 1.00

1993 Front Row Gold Collection

These ten cards were issued with the set title "The Gold Collection" printed in gold foil down the left side of the cardfront. On the back of the even-numbered cards appears player biographical and statistical information. The back of the odd-numbered cards features a player profile within a gray box. The cards were issued in factory set form with a certificate of authenticity numbered of 5000 sets produced.
COMPLETE SET (10) 2.40 6.00
1 Eric Curry .20 .50
2 Eric Curry .20 .50
3 Lincoln Kennedy .20 .50
4 Lincoln Kennedy .20 .50
5 O.J.McDuffie .50 1.25
6 O.J.McDuffie .50 1.25
7 Qadry Ismail .30 .75
8 Qadry Ismail .30 .75
9 Andre Hastings .20 .50
10 Andre Hastings .20 .50

1997 Genuine Article

The Genuine Article base set is divided into three series with either a B, an M or R prefix on the card numbers. The B prefix cards feature potential 1997 NFL Draft picks. The M prefix cards feature four different cards of 12-players while the R prefix cards include 6-players with four cards each. Genuine Article presumably had these 28-players under contract since no licensing notation is made on the cardbacks. The card photo quality varies from good to poor with very brief write-ups on the cardbacks. There also is a gold foil GA logo and/or Dream Picks set title on the cardfronts.
COMPLETE SET (82) 4.00 10.00
B1 Ronde Barber .40 1.00
B2 Steve Bush .01 .05
B3 William Carr .01 .05
B4 James Cunningham .01 .05
B5 Pat Fitzgerland .01 .05
B6 Mike Jenkins .01 .05
B7 Damon Jones .01 .05
B8 Nathan Perryman .01 .05
B9 Tarek Saleh .01 .05
B10 Damond Wilkins .01 .05
M1 James Allen .30 .75
M2 Terry Battle .01 .05
M3 Tiki Barber .40 1.00
M4 Michael Booker .01 .05
M5 Troy Davis .01 .05
M6 Jim Druckenmiller .02 .10
M7 Yatil Green .02 .10
M8 Derrick Mason .30 .75
M9 Chris Miller WR .01 .05
M10 Sedrick Shaw .01 .05
M11 Antowain Smith .20 .50
M12 Shawn Springs .01 .05
M13 James Allen .30 .75
M14 Terry Battle .01 .05
M15 Tiki Barber .40 1.00
M16 Michael Booker .01 .05
M17 Troy Davis .01 .05
M18 Jim Druckenmiller .02 .10
M19 Yatil Green .02 .10
M20 Derrick Mason .30 .75
M21 Chris Miller WR .01 .05
M22 Sedrick Shaw .01 .05
M23 Antowain Smith .20 .50
M24 Shawn Springs .01 .05
M25 James Allen .30 .75
M26 Terry Battle .01 .05
M27 Tiki Barber .40 1.00
M28 Michael Booker .01 .05
M29 Troy Davis .01 .05
M30 Jim Druckenmiller .02 .10
M31 Yatil Green .02 .10
M32 Derrick Mason .30 .75
M33 Chris Miller WR .01 .05
M34 Sedrick Shaw .01 .05
M35 Antowain Smith .20 .50
M36 Shawn Springs .01 .05
M37 James Allen .30 .75
M38 Terry Battle .01 .05
M39 Tiki Barber .40 1.00
M40 Michael Booker .01 .05
M41 Troy Davis .01 .05
M42 Jim Druckenmiller .02 .10
M43 Yatil Green .02 .10
M44 Derrick Mason .30 .75
M45 Chris Miller WR .01 .05
M46 Sedrick Shaw .01 .05
M47 Antowain Smith UER .20 .50
M48 Shawn Springs .01 .05
R1 Mike Alstott .30 .75
R2 Tony Banks .08 .25
R3 Tim Biakabutuka .08 .25
R4 Terry Glenn .15 .40
R5 Leeland McElroy .01 .05
R6 Sherman Williams .01 .05
R7 Mike Alstott .30 .75
R8 Tony Banks .08 .25
R9 Tim Biakabutuka UER .08 .25
R10 Terry Glenn .15 .40
R11 Leeland McElroy .01 .05
R12 Sherman Williams .01 .05
R13 Mike Alstott .30 .75
R14 Tony Banks .08 .25
R15 Tim Biakabutuka UER .08 .25
R16 Terry Glenn .15 .40
R17 Leeland McElroy .01 .05
R18 Sherman Williams .01 .05
R19 Mike Alstott .30 .75
R20 Tony Banks .08 .25
R21 Tim Biakabutuka .08 .25
R22 Terry Glenn .15 .40
R23 Leeland McElroy .01 .05
R24 Sherman Williams .01 .05

1997 Genuine Article Autographs

These signed cards are essentially parallels to the base card issue along with an additional serial numbering on the cardfronts. They were inserted on average at the rate of 3-cards per box. Each cardfront features a silver foil "Genuine Autograph" notation along with a hand-written serial number with a silver foil total print run notation. The B prefix cards were numbered of 7500, the M prefix cards of 5000-cards signed, while the R prefix cards were numbered of 1500-signed.
B1 Ronde Barber 5.00 12.00
B2 Steve Bush .75 2.00
B3 William Carr .75 2.00
B4 James Cunningham .75 2.00
B5 Pat Fitzgerland .75 2.00
B6 Mike Jenkins .75 2.00
B7 Damon Jones .75 2.00
B8 Nathan Perryman .75 2.00
B9 Tarek Saleh .75 2.00
B10 Damond Wilkins .75 2.00
M1 James Allen 2.00 5.00
M2 Terry Battle .75 2.00
M3 Tiki Barber 10.00 25.00
M4 Michael Booker .75 2.00
M5 Troy Davis 1.25 3.00
M6 Jim Druckenmiller 1.25 3.00
M7 Yatil Green 1.25 3.00
M8 Derrick Mason 4.00 10.00
M9 Chris Miller WR .75 2.00
M10 Sedrick Shaw .75 2.00
M11 Antowain Smith 3.00 8.00
M12 Shawn Springs 1.25 3.00
R1 Mike Alstott 3.00 8.00
R2 Tony Banks 2.00 5.00
R3 Tim Biakabutuka 1.25 3.00
R4 Terry Glenn 2.00 5.00
R5 Leeland McElroy 1.25 3.00
R6 Sherman Williams .75 2.00
GA3 Eddie George/100 .75 2.00

1997 Genuine Article Checklists

These checklist cards were randomly inserted in packs of Genuine Article football and feature a player photo on the fronts and checklist information on the backs.
COMPLETE SET (4) 2.00 5.00
CK1 Terrell Davis .60 1.50
CK2 Terrell Davis .60 1.50
CK3 Eddie George .40 1.00
CK4 Eddie George .40 1.00

1997 Genuine Article Duo-Sport Preview

This 5-card set was randomly inserted and highlights five different professional, young football players. The card fronts have the insert name in the top left corner and the player's name and pro team at the bottom below a photo of the player in his college uniform. The card backs are numbered with a "DS" prefix
COMPLETE SET (5) 2.50 6.00
DS1 Eddie George .75 2.00
DS2 Karim Abdul-Jabbar .50 1.25
DS3 Jim Druckenmiller .50 1.25
DS4 Orlando Pace .60 1.50
DS5 Yatil Green .40 1.00

1997 Genuine Article Grand Achievements

is 5-card insert set recognizes top running back season rushing achievements. Each card includes gold foil highlights on the fronts and a brief write-up about the achievement on the backs.
COMPLETE SET (5) 3.00 8.00
GA1 Terrell Davis 2.50 6.00
GA2 Troy Davis .40 1.00
GA3 Eddie George 1.25 3.00
GA4 Karim Abdul-Jabbar .60 1.50
GA5 Troy Davis .40 1.00

1997 Genuine Article Orlando Pace

These 4-cards feature 1996 top NFL Draft pick Orlando Pace. Each includes the player's name in gold foil on the front with Pace in his Ohio State uniform.
COMPLETE SET (4) .40 1.00
COMMON CARD (P1-P4) .10 .30

1993-94 Images Four Sport

These 150 standard-size cards feature on their borderless fronts color player action shots with backgrounds that have been thrown out of focus. On the white background to the left, career highlights, biography and statistics are displayed. Just 6,500 of each card were produced. The set closes with Classic Headlines (128-147) and checklists (148-150). A redemption card inserted one per case entitled the collector to one set of basketball draft preview cards. This offered expired 9/30/94.
COMPLETE SET (150) 6.00 15.00
1 Drew Bledsoe .40 1.00
5 Rick Mirer .15 .40
9 Robert Smith .20 .50
25 Lincoln Kennedy .08 .25
26 Jerome Bettis .40 1.00
29 Deon Figures .08 .25
33 George Teague .08 .25
39 Glyn Milburn .10 .30
44 Gino Torretta .15 .40
45 Roger Harper .08 .25
48 Victor Bailey .08 .25
53 Thomas Smith .08 .25
55 Andre King .08 .25
57 Reggie Brooks .10 .30
58 Ron Moore .08 .25
61 Dan Footman .08 .25
64 Tom Carter .08 .25
65 Qadry Ismail .15 .40
70 Marvin Jones .08 .25
71 Garrison Hearst .20 .50
72 John Copeland .08 .25
73 Darrien Gordon .08 .25
78 Chad Brown .08 .25
82 Irv Smith .08 .25
83 Troy Drayton .08 .25
87 Carlton Gray .08 .25
88 Billy Joe Hobert .08 .25
91 Carl Simpson .08 .25
95 Roosevelt Potts .08 .25
97 Derek Brown RB .08 .25
102 Curtis Conway .15 .40
103 Lamar Thomas .08 .25
104 Willie Roaf .50 1.25
107 Eric Curry .08 .25
108 Todd Kelly .08 .25
114 Horace Copeland .08 .25
116 Terry Kirby .15 .40
117 Demetrius DuBose .08 .25
118 Will Shields .08 .25
119 Natrone Means .15 .40
120 O.J. McDuffie .10 .30
126 Kevin Williams WR .08 .25
127 Lorenzo Neal .08 .25
129 Drew Bledsoe B/W .30 .75
133 Rick Mirer B/W .08 .25
137 Jerome Bettis B/W .25 .60

140 Terry Kirby B/W .10 .30
144 Derek Brown RB B/W .08 .25

1993-94 Images Four Sport Acetates

Randomly inserted in 1993-94 Classic Images packs (four per case; 6,500 of each), these four standard-size clear acetate cards feature color player action cutouts on their fronts.

COMPLETE SET (4) 12.00 30.00
2 Jerome Bettis 3.00 8.00
3 Steve Young 4.00 10.00

1993-94 Images Four Sport Chrome

Randomly inserted one in every fourteen 1994 Classic Images packs, these 20 limited print (9,750 of each) cards measure the standard size and feature color player action shots on their borderless metallic fronts. The cards are numbered on the back with a "CC" prefix. This set was also available in uncut sheet form as a redeemed prize for the Marshall Faulk M5 card.

COMPLETE SET (20) 15.00 40.00
CC7 Drew Bledsoe 1.50 4.00
CC8 Jerome Bettis 1.50 4.00
CC9 Terry Kirby .40 1.00
CC10 Dana Stubblefield .40 1.00
CC11 Rick Mirer .60 1.50
NNO Uncut Sheet 30.00 80.00

1993-94 Images Four Sport Marshall Faulk

Randomly inserted one in every 144 1993-94 Classic Images packs (three per case; 3,250 each), these six standard-size cards feature Marshall Faulk. The cards are numbered on the back with an "M" prefix and feature the 1994 Classic Draft logo on the front, not the Images Four Sport logo. These cards listed various teams Faulk might have been drafted by. The winning card turned out to be the Indianapolis Colts. That was card M5 which was redeemable for a Classic Images Chrome sheet until October 1, 1994.

COMPLETE SET (6) 20.00 40.00
COMMON FAULK (M1-M6) 2.50 6.00
M1 Marshall Faulk 2.50 6.00
Tampa Bay Buccaneers
M2 Marshall Faulk 2.50 6.00
Cincinnati Bengals
M3 Marshall Faulk 2.50 6.00
Chicago Bears
M4 Marshall Faulk 2.50 6.00
New England Patriots
M5 Marshall Faulk 6.00 15.00
Indianapolis Colts
M6 Marshall Faulk 2.50 6.00
Field Card

1993-94 Images Four Sport Sudden Impact

Inserted one per '94 Classic Images pack, these 20 gold foil-board cards measure the standard-size. The gold metallic fronts feature borderless color player action shots on backgrounds that have been thrown out of focus. The player's name and position appear in vertical lettering within a black strip across the card near the right edge. The back carries a color player action shot at the top, followed below by career highlights on a white panel. The player's name appears in vertical black lettering within a ghosted action strip at the left edge. The cards are numbered on the back with an "SI" prefix.

COMPLETE SET (20) 4.00 10.00
SI15 Drew Bledsoe .40 1.00
SI16 Rick Mirer .25 .60
SI17 Derek Brown RB .15 .40
SI18 Ron Moore .15 .40
SI19 Jerome Bettis .40 1.00

1995 Images Four Sport

Printed on 18-point micro-lined foil board, the 1995 Classic Images set consists of 120 standard-size cards, featuring the top draft picks from the four major sports. Classic produced 1,995 sequentially-numbered 16-box hobby cases. This series also features one "Hot Box" in every four cases; each pack in it included at least one card from five insert sets, plus the special Clear Excitement chase cards not found anywhere else, for a total of 24 inserts per Hot Box. There was a promotional card issued, not inserted into '94-95 Assets packs, for Grant Hill numbered HP1. The front is the same as the card in the set, but the back has an orange background and describes the product's features.

COMPLETE SET (120) 6.00 15.00
38 Dan Wilkinson .15 .40
39 Marshall Faulk .30 .75
40 Heath Shuler .20 .50
41 Willie McGinest .15 .40
42 Trev Alberts .10 .30
43 Trent Dilfer .20 .50
44 Bryant Young .15 .40
45 Sam Adams .10 .30
46 Antonio Langham .10 .30
47 Jamir Miller .10 .30
48 Aaron Glenn .15 .40
49 Bernard Williams .10 .30
50 Charles Johnson .10 .30
51 Dewayne Washington .10 .30
52 Tim Bowens .10 .30
53 Johnnie Morton .20 .50
54 Rob Fredrickson .10 .30
55 Shante Carver .10 .30
56 Henry Ford .10 .30
57 Jeff Burris .10 .30
58 William Floyd .15 .40
59 Derrick Alexander .15 .40
60 Darnay Scott .20 .50
61 Errict Rhett .20 .50
62 Greg Hill .10 .30
63 David Palmer .15 .40
64 Charlie Garner .15 .40
65 Mario Bates .10 .30
66 Bert Emanuel .10 .30
67 Thomas Randolph .10 .30
68 Aubrey Beavers .10 .30
69 Byron Bam Morris .10 .30
70 Lake Dawson .10 .30
71 Todd Steussie .15 .40
72 Aaron Taylor .10 .30
73 Corey Sawyer .10 .30
74 Kevin Mitchell .10 .30
75 Emmitt Smith .60 1.50

1995 Images Four Sport Classic Performances

Randomly inserted in hobby boxes at a rate of one in every 12 packs, this 20-card standard-size set relives great moments from the careers of 20 top athletes. Each card is numbered out of 4,495. The fronts feature the player against a gold background. The back contains on the left side a description of the great moment and on the right side a color player photo. The cards are numbered with a "CP" prefix.

COMPLETE SET (20) 20.00 50.00
CP8 Steve Young 1.50 4.00
CP9 Marshall Faulk 1.50 4.00
CP10 Derrick Alexander .40 1.00
CP11 William Floyd .40 1.00
CP12 Errict Rhett .60 1.50
CP13 Byron Bam Morris .40 1.00
CP14 Heath Shuler .60 1.50
CP15 Emmitt Smith 3.00 8.00

1995 Images Four Sport Clear Excitement

Randomly inserted at a rate of one in every 24 packs in hobby and retail hot boxes (1:1536 over the product run), these two five-card acetate sets each feature five notable athletes from different sports. Cards with the prefix "E" were inserted in hobby hot boxes, while cards with the prefix "C" were found in retail hot boxes. The cards are numbered out of 300.

COMPLETE SET (10) 60.00 150.00
C2 Emmitt Smith 12.50 30.00
C3 Troy Aikman 8.00 20.00
C4 Steve Young 6.00 15.00
E2 Marshall Faulk 6.00 15.00
E3 Drew Bledsoe 5.00 12.00

1995 Images Four Sport Draft Challenge

Randomly inserted in hobby and retail boxes at a rate of one in every 24 packs, this 25-card standard-size set previews the next generation of NFL superstars. Five players are featured in four different uniforms and a field card. Just 3,195 of each card were produced. Collectors who received a player in the uniform of the team that drafted him could redeem the card, along with 15 wrappers, for a five-card acetate set. Each incorrect card, along with 10 wrappers, could be redeemed for one corresponding correct acetate card. Finally, the first 200 collectors who submitted all five cards featuring the players in the uniform of the team that drafted them, plus 20 wrappers, received a five-card autographed set of these future gridiron greats. After 200 sets were redeemed, collectors received one acetate set for each correct card. The redemption program ran until October 31, 1995. In the listing below, each player's highest-price card features him in the uniform of the team that drafted him.

COMPLETE SET (25) 15.00 40.00
DC1 Rashaan Salaam .50 1.25
DC2 Rashaan Salaam .50 1.25
DC3 Rashaan Salaam-Bears 1.25 3.00
DC4 Rashaan Salaam .50 1.25
DC5 Rashaan Salaam .50 1.25
DC6 Ki-Jana Carter .50 1.25
DC7 Ki-Jana Carter .50 1.25
DC8 Ki-Jana Carter .50 1.25
DC9 Ki-Jana Carter-Bengals 1.25 3.00
DC10 Ki-Jana Carter .50 1.25
DC11 John Walsh .40 1.00
DC12 John Walsh .40 1.00
DC13 John Walsh .40 1.00
DC14 John Walsh .40 1.00
DC15 John Walsh-Field Card .40 1.00
DC16 Steve McNair 1.25 3.00
DC17 Steve McNair 1.25 3.00
DC18 Steve McNair-Oilers 3.00 8.00
DC19 Steve McNair 1.25 3.00
DC20 Steve McNair 1.25 3.00
DC21 Kerry Collins .75 2.00
DC22 Kerry Collins .75 2.00
DC23 Kerry Collins .75 2.00
DC24 Kerry Collins .75 2.00
DC25 Kerry Collins-Field Card 2.50 6.00

1995 Images Four Sport Draft Challenge Acetates

This five-card set features a color action player image on a clear and colored background. The clear portion of the background contains the player's name and several images of his helmet. The back carries a congratulations message. The set was obtained through a mail-in wrapper offer.

COMPLETE SET (5) 5.00 12.00
1 Rashaan Salaam 1.00 2.50
2 Ki-Jana Carter 1.00 2.50
3 John Walsh .75 2.00
4 Steve McNair 2.00 5.00
5 Kerry Collins 1.25 3.00

1995 Images Four Sport Draft Challenge Acetates Autographs

1 Rashaan Salaam 10.00 25.00
2 Ki-Jana Carter 10.00 25.00
3 John Walsh 8.00 20.00
4 Steve McNair 15.00 40.00
5 Kerry Collins 12.00 30.00

1995 Images Four Sport EP

Randomly inserted in Classic Images boxes these standard-size cards feature a print run of 8000 sets. The fronts feature the player against a silver foil background. The backs contain another player photo and a short bio on the player. The cards are numbered with an "EP" prefix.

EP1 Drew Bledsoe 1.00 2.50
EP4 Marshall Faulk 1.00 2.50

1995 Images Four Sport Player of the Year

This four-card standard-size set was obtained through a mail-in wrapper offer, or one set was also included per retail box. The borderless fronts feature a color action player image on a metalic, starburst-look background. The player's name is printed in a black strip at the bottom with the card logo. The backs carry a small color head photo with the player's name, position, and team name below it. A black-and-white player action photo along with the player's statistics round out the back. The cards are numbered with a "POY" prefix.

COMPLETE SET (4) 4.00 10.00
POY1 Steve Young .75 2.00
POY2 Emmitt Smith 1.50 4.00

1995 Images Four Sport Previews

Randomly inserted one per 24 packs in second-series '94-95 Assets packs, this five-card standard-size set was issued to promote the Classic Images series. Just 5,000 of each card were produced. The fronts display the player's photo showcased against a metallic background. The backs are devoted on the left side to the player's identification and a note saying you have received a limited edition preview card. The right side of the reverse has a full-color photo of the player and the card is numbered at the upper right corner. The cards are numbered with an "IP" prefix.

COMPLETE SET (5) 6.00 15.00
IP3 Marshall Faulk 1.00 2.50
IP5 Emmitt Smith 2.00 5.00

2015 Leaf Clear Draft

BAAA1 Ameer Abdullah 4.00 10.00
BAAC1 Amari Cooper 20.00 40.00
BAAD1 Alvin Dupree 3.00 8.00
BAAG1 Antwan Goodley 2.50 6.00
BAAH1 Austin Hill 2.50 6.00
BABB1 Brandon Bridge 2.50 6.00
BABH1 Brett Hundley 2.50 6.00
BABK1 Ben Koyack 4.00 10.00
BABM1 Benardrick McKinney 2.50 6.00
BABP1 Bryce Petty 2.50 6.00
BACAP Cameron Artis-Payne 2.50 6.00
BACF1 Cody Fajardo 3.00 8.00
BADC1 David Cobb 2.50 6.00
BADF1 Dante Fowler Jr. 4.00 10.00
BADF2 Devin Funchess 4.00 10.00
BADGB Dorial Green-Beckham 2.50 6.00
BADH1 Danielle Hunter 3.00 8.00
BADJ1 Duke Johnson 4.00 10.00
BADJ2 David Johnson 6.00 15.00
BADP1 Denzel Perryman 2.50 6.00
BADP2 DeVante Parker 4.00 10.00
BADS1 Danny Shelton 2.50 6.00
BAEG1 Eddie Goldman EXCH 2.50 6.00
BAEJB E.J. Bibbs 3.00 8.00
BAJA1 Jay Ajayi 4.00 10.00
BAJA2 Javorius Allen 3.00 8.00
BAJH1 Josh Harper 2.50 6.00
BAJH2 Jeff Heuerman 3.00 8.00
BAJH3 Justin Hardy 2.50 6.00
BAJJ1 Jesse James 3.00 8.00
BAJL1 Jeremy Langford 2.50 6.00
BAJS1 Jaelen Strong 3.00 8.00
BAJW1 Jameis Winston 6.00 15.00
BAKB1 Kenny Bell 4.00 10.00
BAKJ1 Kevin Johnson 2.50 6.00
BAKW1 Karlos Williams 2.50 6.00
BAKW2 Kevin White 3.00 8.00
BAKW3 Kasen Williams 4.00 10.00
BALC1 Landon Collins 3.00 8.00
BAMD1 Mike Davis 2.50 6.00
BAMG1 Melvin Gordon 12.00 30.00
BAMG2 Markus Golden 2.50 6.00
BAMJ1 Matt Jones 2.50 6.00
BAMM1 Marcus Mariota 30.00 60.00
BAMP1 Marcus Peters 4.00 10.00
BAMW1 Maxx Williams 2.50 6.00
BANA1 Nelson Agholor 3.00 8.00
BANM1 Nick Marshall 5.00 12.00
BANO1 Nick O'Leary 2.50 6.00
BAPD1 Phillip Dorsett 2.50 6.00
BAPJW P.J. Williams 3.00 8.00
BARG1 Randy Gregory 2.50 6.00
BARG2 Rashad Greene 2.50 6.00
BASC1 Sammie Coates 3.00 8.00
BASC2 Shane Carden 2.50 6.00
BASD1 Stefon Diggs 6.00 15.00
BASR1 Shane Ray 2.50 6.00
BAST1 Shaq Thompson 3.00 8.00
BATC1 Tevin Coleman 3.00 8.00
BATG1 Todd Gurley 20.00 40.00
BATJY T.J. Yeldon 2.50 6.00
BATK1 Tyler Kroft 3.00 8.00
BATL2 Tony Lippett 2.50 6.00
BATM1 Ty Montgomery 2.50 6.00
BATW1 Trae Waynes 8.00 20.00
BAVB1 Vic Beasley 3.00 8.00
BAVM1 Vince Mayle 3.00 8.00

2015 Leaf Clear Draft Silver

*SILVER/25: .6X TO 1.5X BASIC AU
*SILVER/15: .8X TO 2X BASIC AU
BAJW1 Jameis Winston/15 12.00 30.00
BAMM1 Marcus Mariota/15 90.00 150.00

2015 Leaf Clear Draft Clear Potential

*SILVER/25: .6X TO 1.5X BASIC AU
*SILVER/15: .8X TO 2X BASIC AU
CPDJ1 Duke Johnson 4.00 10.00
CPGG1 Garrett Grayson 2.50 6.00
CPJH1 Josh Harper 2.50 6.00
CPJL1 Jeremy Langford 2.50 6.00
CPJS1 Jaelen Strong 3.00 8.00
CPKW2 Kevin White 3.00 8.00
CPNA1 Nelson Agholor 3.00 8.00
CPRG2 Rashad Greene 2.50 6.00
CPSM1 Sean Mannion 2.50 6.00
CPTC1 Tevin Coleman 3.00 8.00

2015 Leaf Clear Draft Crystal Clear Die Cuts

CCBH1 Brett Hundley 3.00 8.00
CCBP1 Bryce Petty 3.00 8.00
CCCW1 Clive Walford 3.00 8.00
CCJW1 Jameis Winston 8.00 20.00
CCMG1 Melvin Gordon 15.00 40.00
CCRG1 Randy Gregory 3.00 8.00
CCSC1 Sammie Coates 4.00 10.00
CCSR1 Shane Ray 3.00 8.00
CCTG1 Todd Gurley 25.00 50.00

2015 Leaf Clear Draft Crystal Clear Die Cuts Silver

*SILVER/25: .6X TO 1.5X BASIC AU
*SILVER/15: .8X TO 2X BASIC AU
CCJW1 Jameis Winston/15 15.00 40.00
CCMM1 Marcus Mariota/15 60.00 125.00

2015 Leaf Clear Draft State Pride

*SILVER/25: .6X TO 1.5X BASIC AU
*SILVER/15: .8X TO 2X BASIC AU
SPAA1 Ameer Abdullah 4.00 10.00
SPAC1 Amari Cooper 15.00 40.00
SPBS1 Blake Sims 2.50 6.00
SPBW1 Bo Wallace 2.50 6.00
SPDF2 Devin Funchess 4.00 10.00
SPDG1 Devin Gardner 4.00 10.00
SPIEO Ifo Ekpre-Olomu 2.50 6.00
SPKW1 Karlos Williams 2.50 6.00
SPLC1 Landon Collins 3.00 8.00
SPMB1 Malcolm Brown 3.00 8.00
SPTJY T.J. Yeldon 2.50 6.00
SPVB1 Vic Beasley 3.00 8.00

2011 Leaf Draft Las Vegas Summit Promos

COMPLETE SET (3) 8.00 20.00
IS1 Cam Newton AA 3.00 8.00
IS2 Mark Ingram 2.00 5.00
IS3 A.J. Green Ultimate 2.00 5.00

2011 Leaf Draft Limited Edition

COMPLETE SET (20) 6.00 15.00
RELEASED DIRECTLY TO DEALERS
*BLACK: 2.5X TO 6X BASIC CARDS
1 A.J. Green .40 1.00
2 Andy Dalton .30 .75
3A Blaine Gabbert .15 .40
3A Blainc Cabbert .15 .40
4A Cam Newton .75 2.00
4B Cam Newton .75 2.00
5 Christian Ponder .15 .40
6 Colin Kaepernick .25 .60
7 Daniel Thomas .15 .40
8 DeMarco Murray .30 .75
9 Jake Locker .15 .40
10 Julio Jones .50 1.25
11 Kendall Hunter .15 .40
12 Mark Ingram .25 .60
13 Mikel Leshoure .15 .40
14 Pat Devlin .25 .60
15 Ricky Stanzi .15 .40
16 Ryan Mallett .15 .40
17 Ryan Williams .15 .40
18 Tyrod Taylor .30 .75

2012 Leaf Draft

COMPLETE SET (50) 6.00 15.00
COMP.FACT.SET (54) 15.00 40.00
*BLUE BORDER: .4X TO 1X RED
*GOLD BORDER: 2X TO 5X RED
1 A.J. Jenkins .12 .30
2 Alshon Jeffery .25 .60
3 Andre Branch .12 .30
4 B.J. Cunningham .12 .30
5 Bernard Pierce .12 .30
6 Brandon Weeden .12 .30
7 Brock Osweiler .12 .30
8 Chris Polk .12 .30
9 Courtney Upshaw .15 .40
10 Cyrus Gray .12 .30
11 Darron Thomas .30 .75
12 Devier Posey .12 .30
13 Devon Still .15 .40
14 Dont'a Hightower .20 .50
15 Dontari Poe .12 .30
16 Doug Martin .20 .50
17 Dre Kirkpatrick .12 .30
18 Dwayne Allen .12 .30
19 Dwight Jones .12 .30
20 Fletcher Cox .20 .50
21 Isaiah Pead .12 .30
22 Jacory Harris .15 .40
23 Jeff Fuller .12 .30
24 Joe Adams .12 .30
25 Justin Blackmon .12 .30
26 Kellen Moore .15 .40
27 Kirk Cousins .50 1.25
28 Lamar Miller .20 .50
29 Luke Kuechly .30 .75
30 Marc Tyler .12 .30
31 Mark Barron .12 .30
32 Marquis Maze .12 .30
33 Matt Kalil .12 .30
34 Melvin Ingram .12 .30
35 Michael Floyd .12 .30
36 Mohamed Sanu .20 .50
37 Nick Foles .30 .75
38 Nick Perry .15 .40
39 Nick Toon .12 .30
40 Robert Griffin III .15 .40
41 Robert Turbin .12 .30
42 Ryan Broyles .12 .30
43 Ryan Tannehill .20 .50
44 Stephen Hill .12 .30
45 Stephon Gilmore .15 .40
46 T.Y. Hilton .25 .60
47 Tauren Poole .12 .30
48 Terrance Ganaway .15 .40
49 Trent Richardson .12 .30
50 Whitney Mercilus .12 .30

2012 Leaf Draft Army All-American Bowl

AABAL1 Andrew Luck 1.50 4.00

2012 Leaf Draft Autographs Red

TWO RED BORDER AU PER RETAIL BOX
*BLUE BORDER: .5X TO 1.2X RED BRDR
ONE BLUE BORDER AU PER FACTORY SET
AB1 Andre Branch SP 2.50 6.00
AB2 Antwon Bailey 3.00 8.00
AC2 Audie Cole 2.50 6.00
AD1 Alfonzo Dennard 2.50 6.00
AJJ A.J. Jenkins SP 2.50 6.00
AS1 Amini Silatolu 2.50 6.00
AT1 Alameda Ta'amu 3.00 8.00
BJC B.J. Cunningham SP 2.50 6.00
BM1 Bobby Massie 2.50 6.00
BM2 Brandon Mosley 2.50 6.00
BO1 Brock Osweiler SP 2.50 6.00
BP1 Bernard Pierce SP 2.50 6.00
BQ1 Brian Quick 2.50 6.00
BR1 Bobby Rainey 2.50 6.00
BT1 Brandon Thompson 3.00 8.00
BW1 Brandon Weeden SP 8.00 20.00
BW2 Bobby Wagner 4.00 10.00
CG1 Chris Givens 2.50 6.00
CG2 Cyrus Gray SP 2.50 6.00
CG3 Chris Galippo 3.00 8.00
CH2 Casey Hayward 2.50 6.00
CH3 Cliff Harris 4.00 10.00
CJ1 Chandler Jones 2.50 6.00
CJ2 Coryell Judie 2.50 6.00
CP1 Chris Polk SP 2.50 6.00
CU1 Courtney Upshaw SP 3.00 8.00
DA1 Dwayne Allen SP 2.50 6.00
DAL D'Anton Lynn 4.00 10.00
DDC David DeCastro 2.50 6.00
DF1 Donnie Fletcher 2.50 6.00
DH1 Dan Herron 2.50 6.00
DH2 Dont'a Hightower SP
DI1 Duke Ihenacho 4.00 10.00
DK1 Dre Kirkpatrick 2.50 6.00
DM2 Doug Martin SP 4.00 10.00
DM3 Derek Moye 4.00 10.00
DP1 Dan Persa 3.00 8.00
DP2 DeVier Posey SP 2.50 6.00
DS1 Devon Still SP 3.00 8.00
DT1 Darron Thomas SP 6.00 15.00
DW1 Devon Wylie 2.50 6.00
FW1 Fozzy Whittaker 2.50 6.00
GC1 Greg Childs 2.50 6.00
GI1 George Iloka 2.50 6.00
GR1 Gerell Robinson 2.50 6.00
HS1 Harrison Smith 2.50 6.00
IP1 Isaiah Pead SP 2.50 6.00
JA1 Joe Adams SP 2.50 6.00
JB2 Justin Blackmon SP 2.50 6.00
JC1 Jared Crick 2.50 6.00
JF1 Jeff Fuller SP 2.50 6.00
JH1 Jacory Harris SP 3.00 8.00
JH2 Jerrell Harris 3.00 8.00
JJ1 Janoris Jenkins 3.00 8.00
JK1 Josh Kaddu 3.00 8.00
JM1 Jonathan Martin 2.50 6.00
JMJ James-Michael Johnson 3.00 8.00
JN1 Josh Norman 3.00 8.00
JW1 Jarius Wright 2.50 6.00
KC1 Kirk Cousins SP 10.00 25.00
KK1 Kevin Koger 4.00 10.00
KM1 Kellen Moore SP 3.00 8.00
KM2 Keshawn Martin 3.00 8.00
KR1 Keenan Robinson 3.00 8.00
KR2 Kendall Reyes 2.50 6.00
LD1 Lavonte David 4.00 10.00
LJ1 LaMichael James 2.50 6.00
LJ2 Leonard Johnson 3.00 8.00
LK1 Luke Kuechly SP 6.00 15.00
LN1 Lucas Nix 2.50 6.00
MB1 Mark Barron SP 2.50 6.00
ME1 Michael Egnew 2.50 6.00
MF1 Marcus Forston 2.50 6.00
MF1 Michael Floyd SP 12.00 30.00
MI1 Melvin Ingram SP 2.50 6.00
MJ1 Marvin Jones 2.50 6.00
MM1 Marquis Maze SP 2.50 6.00
MM2 Markelle Martin 3.00 8.00
MM3 Mike Martin 3.00 8.00
MS1 Mohamed Sanu SP 4.00 10.00
MT1 Marc Tyler SP 2.50 6.00
NB1 Nigel Bradham 3.00 8.00
NF1 Nick Foles SP 6.00 15.00
NP1 Nick Perry SP 3.00 8.00
NT1 Nick Toon SP 2.50 6.00
OC1 Orson Charles 2.50 6.00
PK1 Peter Konz 2.50 6.00
PW1 Patrick Witt 3.00 8.00
RB1 Ryan Broyles SP
RB2 Robert Blanton 3.00 8.00
RE1 Rhett Ellison 3.00 8.00
RG3 Robert Griffin III SP 3.00 8.00
RS1 Ryan Steed 2.50 6.00
RT1 Robert Turbin SP 2.50 6.00
RT2 Ryan Tannehill SP 4.00 10.00
SG1 Stephon Gilmore SP 3.00 8.00
SH1 Stephen Hill SP 2.50 6.00
SM1 Shea McClellin 3.00 8.00
SP1 Shaun Prater 4.00 10.00
SS1 Sean Spence 3.00 8.00
TB1 Tim Benford 2.50 6.00
TG1 Terrance Ganaway SP 3.00 8.00
TG2 Trevor Guyton 3.00 8.00
TH1 Tyler Hansen 2.50 6.00
TL1 Travis Lewis 3.00 8.00
TM1 Thomas Mayo 2.50 6.00
TP1 Tauren Poole SP 2.50 6.00
TP2 Tydreke Powell 2.50 6.00
TR1 Trent Richardson SP 12.00 30.00
TR2 Trenton Robinson 3.00 8.00
TYH T.Y. Hilton SP 5.00 12.00
WM1 Whitney Mercilus SP 2.50 6.00
ZB1 Zach Brown 2.50 6.00
ZS1 Zebrie Sanders 2.50 6.00

2012 Leaf Draft Garden State Promos

NJPR1 Robert Griffin III 6.00 15.00
NJPR3 Trent Richardson 3.00 8.00

2012 Leaf Draft Robert Griffin

COMPLETE SET (3) 3.00 8.00
COMMON GRIFFIN (1-3) 1.00 2.50
ONE SET PER FACTORY SET

2013 Leaf Draft

COMPLETE SET (100) 10.00 25.00
1 Aaron Mellette .12 .30
2 Alex Carder .15 .40
3 Alex Okafor .12 .30
4 Andre Ellington .12 .30
6 Bjoern Werner .12 .30
7 Brad Sorensen .12 .30
8 Cierre Wood .12 .30
9 Cobi Hamilton .12 .30
10 Collin Klein .15 .40
11 Conner Vernon .12 .30
12 Cordarrelle Patterson .12 .30
13 Da'Rick Rogers .12 .30
14 DaMontre Moore .12 .30
15 DeAndre Hopkins .30 .75
16 Dee Milliner .12 .30
17 Denard Robinson .12 .30
18 Dion Jordan .12 .30
19 Dion Sims .12 .30
20 EJ Manuel .12 .30
21 Eddie Lacy .12 .30
22 Eric Reid .15 .40
23 Geno Smith .12 .30
24 Giovani Bernard .12 .30
25 Jake Stoneburner .20 .50
26 Jarvis Jones .12 .30
27 Jawan Jamison .12 .30
28 Jesse Williams .20 .50
29 Johnathan Franklin .12 .30
30 Jordan Reed .20 .50
31 Jordan Rodgers .15 .40
32 Joseph Fauria .12 .30
33 Joseph Randle .12 .30
34 Josh Boyce .12 .30
35 Justin Hunter .12 .30
36 Kawann Short .12 .30
37 Keenan Allen .25 .60
38 Kenjon Barner .12 .30
39 Kenny Stills .12 .30
40 Landry Jones .12 .30
41 Le'Veon Bell .40 1.00
42 Levine Toilolo .15 .40
43 Lucas Reed .12 .30
44 Manti Te'o .15 .40
45 Marcus Davis .12 .30
46 Marcus Lattimore .12 .30
47 Markus Wheaton .12 .30
48 Marquise Goodwin .12 .30
49 Matt Barkley .12 .30
50 Michael Williams .15 .40
51 Miguel Maysonet .12 .30
52 Mike Gillislee .12 .30
53 Mike Glennon .12 .30
54 Montee Ball .12 .30
55 Nick Kasa .12 .30
56 Philip Lutzenkirchen .20 .50
57 Quinton Patton .12 .30
58 Ray Graham .12 .30
59 Rex Burkhead .15 .40
60 Robert Woods .20 .50
61 Rodney Smith .12 .30
62 Ryan Swope .12 .30
63 Sharrif Floyd .12 .30
64 Sheldon Richardson .12 .30
65 Star Lotulelei .15 .40
66 Stedman Bailey .12 .30
67 Steptan Taylor .12 .30
68 T.J. McDonald .12 .30
69 T.J. Moe .15 .40
70 Tavon Austin .15 .40
71 Terrance Williams .12 .30
72 Tony Jefferson .20 .50
73 Tyler Bray .12 .30
74 Tyler Eifert .12 .30
75 Tyler Wilson .12 .30
76 Vance McDonald .15 .40
77 Zac Dysert .12 .30
78 Zach Line .12 .30
79 Akeem Spence .12 .30
80 Alec Ogletree .12 .30
81 Bennie Logan .15 .40
82 Braden Wilson .15 .40
83 Brandon Jenkins .15 .40
84 Brandon McGee .12 .30
85 Chase Thomas .12 .30
86 D.J. Fluker .12 .30
87 Datone Jones .12 .30
88 Eric Fisher .12 .30
89 Hugh Thornton .12 .30
90 Jelani Jenkins .15 .40
91 John Simon .20 .50
92 Kenny Vaccaro .12 .30
93 Kevin Minter .12 .30
94 Khaseem Greene .12 .30
95 Lonnie Pryor .12 .30
96 Luke Joeckel .12 .30
97 Michael Mauti .20 .50
98 Sam Montgomery .12 .30
99 Sean Porter .12 .30
100 Sylvester Williams .12 .30

2013 Leaf Draft Autographs

TWO AUTOS PER RETAIL BOX
BABW Bjoern Werner SP 2.50 6.00
BAAB1 Alvin Bailey 2.50 6.00
RAAC1 Alex Carder 3.00 0.00
BAAM1 Anthony McCloud 3.00 8.00
BAAO1 Alec Ogletree 2.50 6.00
RAAS1 Akeem Spence 2.50 6.00
BABJ1 Brandon Jenkins 3.00 8.00
BABJ2 Barrett Jones 2.50 6.00
BABL1 Bennie Logan
BABM1 Brandon McGee 2.50 6.00
BABW1 Blidi Wreh-Wilson 3.00 8.00
BABW2 Braden Wilson 3.00 8.00
BACF1 Chris Faulk 4.00 10.00
BACH1 Cobi Hamilton 2.50 6.00
BACH2 Chris Harper 2.50 6.00
BACT1 Chase Thomas 2.50 6.00
BACV1 Conner Vernon 2.50 6.00
BADC1 Duron Carter 6.00 15.00
BADF1 D.J. Fluker 2.50 6.00
BADF2 D.J. Fluker Natl Champs 4.00 10.00
BADH1 DeAndre Hopkins
BADJ1 Datone Jones 2.50 6.00
BADJ2 Dion Jordan 2.50 6.00
BADM1 Damontre Moore 2.50 6.00
BADR1 Denard Robinson SP 2.50 6.00
BADS1 D.J. Swearinger 2.50 6.00
BADT1 Desmond Trufant 2.50 6.00
BADT2 Dallas Thomas 5.00 12.00
BADT3 Drew Terrell 3.00 8.00
BAED1 Everett Dawkins 2.50 6.00
BAEF1 Eric Fisher 2.50 6.00
BAEL1 Eddie Lacy SP 2.50 6.00
BAER1 Eric Reid 6.00 15.00
BAGE1 Gavin Escobar 6.00 15.00
BAGH1 Gerald Hodges 5.00 12.00
BAHT1 Hugh Thornton 2.50 6.00
BAJB1 Jon Bostic 8.00 29.00
BAJC1 Jonathan Cooper 2.50 6.00
BAJE1 Josh Evans 3.00 8.00
BAJF1 Joseph Fauria 2.50 6.00
BAJH1 Justin Hunter SP 10.00 25.00
BAJH2 Jordan Hill 4.00 10.00
BAJJ1 Jelani Jenkins 3.00 8.00
BAJJ2 Jawan Jamison 2.50 6.00
BAJP1 Jordan Poyer 2.50 6.00
BAJR1 Jordan Rodgers 3.00 8.00
BAJS1 Jake Stoneburner 4.00 10.00
BAJS2 John Simon 5.00 12.00
BAJW1 John Wetzel 3.00 8.00
BAKA1 Kiko Alonso 3.00 8.00
BAKG1 Khaseem Greene 2.50 6.00
BAKM1 Kevin Minter 4.00 10.00
BAKV1 Kenny Vaccaro 2.50 6.00
BALB1 Le'Veon Bell SP 15.00 30.00
BALJ1 Luke Joeckel 2.50 6.00
BALJ2 Lane Johnson 3.00 8.00
BALM1 Lerentee McCray 2.50 6.00
BALM2 Leon McFadden 3.00 8.00
BALR1 Lucas Reed 2.50 6.00
BALT1 Levine Toilolo 3.00 8.00
BAMA1 Marc Anthony 2.50 6.00
BAMG1 Mike Gillislee 2.50 6.00
BAMH1 Margus Hunt 2.50 6.00
BAML1 Marcus Lattimore 2.50 6.00
BAMM1 Michael Mauti 4.00 10.00
BAMR1 Mychal Rivera 2.50 6.00
BAMW1 Markus Wheaton 2.50 6.00
BAMW2 Michael Williams 3.00 8.00
BANK1 Nick Kasa 2.50 6.00
BAOA1 Oday Aboushi 2.50 6.00
BAPL1 Philip Lutzenkirchen 4.00 10.00
BAPT1 Phillip Thomas 6.00 15.00
BARA1 Robert Alford 2.50 6.00
BARG1 Ray Graham 2.50 6.00
BARO1 Ryan Otten 2.50 6.00
BARR1 Robbie Rouse 2.50 6.00
BARS1 Ryan Swope 2.50 6.00
BASB1 Stedman Bailey 6.00 15.00
BASC1 Sanders Commings 2.50 6.00
BASL1 Star Lotulelei 3.00 8.00
BASP1 Sean Porter 2.50 6.00
BASR1 Sean Renfree 3.00 8.00
BAST1 Stepfan Taylor 2.50 6.00
BASW1 Sylvester Williams 2.50 6.00
BATA1 Tavon Austin SP 3.00 8.00
BATB1 Tommy Bohanon 3.00 8.00
BATE1 Tyler Eifert SP 2.50 6.00
BATF1 Travis Frederick 6.00 15.00
BATJ1 Tony Jefferson 4.00 10.00
BATJM T.J. Moe 3.00 8.00
BATK1 Tavarres King 2.50 6.00
BATM1 T.J. McDonald 2.50 6.00
BATW1 Trevardo Williams 3.00 8.00
BATW2 Terrance Williams SP 6.00 15.00
BAVM1 Vance McDonald 3.00 8.00
BAWD1 Will Davis 2.50 6.00
BAZG1 Zaviar Gooden 3.00 8.00

2014 Leaf Draft

COMPLETE SET (100) 10.00 25.00
1 Aaron Colvin .12 .30
2 Aaron Donald .30 .75
3 Aaron Murray .12 .30
4 Adrian Hubbard .15 .40
5 Anthony Johnson .12 .30
6 Arthur Lynch .12 .30
7 Ben Malena .15 .40
8 Bishop Sankey .12 .30
9 Bradley Roby .12 .30
10 Brandin Cooks .20 .50
11 Calvin Pryor .12 .30
12 Case McCoy .15 .40
13 Chase Rettig .12 .30
14 Connor Shaw .12 .30
15 Daquan Jones .15 .40
16 Davante Adams .20 .50
17 Devin Street .12 .30
18 Dion Bailey .12 .30
19 Ed Stinson .20 .50
20 Ego Ferguson .12 .30
21 Ha Ha Clinton-Dix .15 .40
22 Henry Josey .12 .30
23 Jacob Pedersen .15 .40
24 Jake Matthews .12 .30
25 James Franklin .15 .40
26 Jason Verrett .12 .30
27 Jeff Janis .12 .30
28 Jeremiah Attaochu .12 .30
29 Jeremy Hill .15 .40
30 Jerick McKinnon .15 .40
31 Justin Gilbert .12 .30
32 Ka'Deem Carey .12 .30
33 Khalil Mack .50 1.25
34 Kony Ealy .15 .40
35 Kyle Van Noy .15 .40
36 Logan Thomas .12 .30
37 Loucheiz Purifoy .12 .30
38 Marcus Roberson .15 .40
39 Marion Grice .12 .30
40 Marqise Lee .15 .40
41 Mike Campanaro .12 .30
42 Mike Evans .30 .75
43 Morgan Moses .12 .30
44 Odell Beckham Jr. .30 .75
45 Paul Richardson .15 .40
46 Ra'Shede Hageman .12 .30
47 Rajion Neal .12 .30
48 Rob Blanchflower .12 .30
49 Rob Herron .12 .30
50 Ryan Shazier .20 .50
51 Scott Crichton .12 .30
52 Silas Redd .15 .40
53 Stephen Morris .12 .30
54 Stephon Tuitt .20 .50
55 Tevin Reese .12 .30
56 Timmy Jernigan .12 .30
57 Tommy Rees .15 .40
58 Travis Swanson .12 .30
59 Trent Murphy .12 .30
60 Trevor Reilly .12 .30
61 Trey Millard .15 .40
62 Troy Niklas .12 .30
63 Xavier Grimble .15 .40
64 Zach Mettenberger .12 .30
65 Zack Martin .15 .40
66 Devonta Freeman .20 .50
67 Donte Moncrief .12 .30
68 Jerome Smith .12 .30
69 Tajh Boyd .12 .30
70 Isaiah Crowell .15 .40
71 Antonio Andrews .12 .30
72 James Wilder Jr. .15 .40
73 Alfred Blue .12 .30
74 Terrance West .12 .30
75 Bryn Renner .12 .30
76 Shaquelle Evans .12 .30
77 Andre Williams .12 .30
78 Blake Bortles .15 .40
79 Charles Sims .12 .30
80 Jace Amaro .12 .30
81 Brett Smith .12 .30
82 David Fales .12 .30
83 Jarvis Landry .25 .60
84 C.J. Mosley .15 .40
85 Taylor Lewan .12 .30
86 Tyler Gaffney .12 .30
87 Jeoffrey Pagan .12 .30
88 Derek Carr .75 2.00
89 Lache Seastrunk .12 .30
90 Victor Hampton .15 .40
AJM A.J. McCarron .12 .30
AR1 Allen Robinson .20 .50
CH1 Carlos Hyde .15 .40
DAT De'Anthony Thomas .12 .30
JC1 Jadeveon Clowney .15 .40
JMI Johnny Manziel .20 .50
KB1 Kelvin Benjamin .20 .50
SW1 Sammy Watkins .20 .50
TB2 Teddy Bridgewater .20 .50
TM4 Tre Mason .12 .30

2014 Leaf Draft Gold

*GOLD: 1.2X TO 3X BASIC CARDS

2014 Leaf Draft Autographs

AAA1 Antonio Andrews 2.50 6.00
AAB1 Alfred Blue 2.50 6.00
AAC1 Aaron Colvin 2.50 6.00
AACL A.C. Leonard 2.50 6.00
AAD1 Aaron Donald 6.00 15.00
AAE1 Antone Exum 2.50 6.00
AAH1 Andre Hal 2.50 6.00
AAJ1 Anthony Johnson 2.50 6.00
AAJM A.J. McCarron
AAL1 Arthur Lynch 2.50 6.00
AAM1 Aaron Murray
AAR1 Allen Robinson
AAW1 Andre Williams
ABB1 Blake Bortles
ABC1 Brandin Cooks
ABE1 Bruce Ellington 2.50 6.00
ABJ1 Bennett Jackson 2.50 6.00
ABM1 Ben Malena 3.00 8.00
ABR1 Bradley Roby 2.50 6.00
ABR2 Bryn Renner 2.50 6.00
ABS1 Bishop Sankey
ABS2 Bryan Stork 2.50 6.00
ABS3 Brett Smith 2.50 6.00
ACB1 Carl Bradford 2.50 6.00
ACB2 Carrington Byndom 2.50 6.00
ACH1 Carlos Hyde
ACJM C.J. Mosley
ACK1 Christian Kirksey 2.50 6.00
ACK2 Cyrus Kouandjio 3.00 8.00
ACMC Case McCoy 3.00 8.00
ACP1 Calvin Pryor 2.50 6.00
ACR1 Chase Rettig 2.50 6.00
ACR2 Cyril Richardson 2.50 6.00
ACS1 Connor Shaw 2.50 6.00
ACS2 Chris Smith 3.00 8.00
ACS3 Charles Sims 2.50 6.00
ACW1 Chris Watt 2.50 6.00
ADA1 Davante Adams 4.00 10.00
ADA2 Denicos Allen 2.50 6.00
ADAT De'Anthony Thomas
ADB1 Dion Bailey 2.50 6.00
ADC1 Derek Carr 20.00 50.00
ADE1 Dominique Easley 2.50 6.00
ADF2 David Fales 2.50 6.00
ADJ1 Daquan Jones 3.00 8.00
ADK1 Devon Kennard 3.00 8.00
ADM1 Donte Moncrief
ADMC Daniel McCullers 3.00 8.00
ADS1 David Sims 2.50 6.00
ADS2 Devin Street 2.50 6.00
AEF1 Ego Ferguson 2.50 6.00
AES1 Ed Stinson 4.00 10.00
AGI1 Gabe Ikard 2.50 6.00
AHCD Ha Ha Clinton-Dix 3.00 8.00
AHJ1 Henry Josey 2.50 6.00
AIC1 Isaiah Crowell 3.00 8.00
AJA1 Jeremiah Attaochu 2.50 6.00
AJA2 Jace Amaro 2.50 6.00
AJC1 Jadeveon Clowney 3.00 8.00
AJF1 James Franklin 3.00 8.00
AJH1 Jeremy Hill
AJJ1 Jeff Janis 5.00 12.00
AJJ2 Jaâ€™Wuan James 2.50 6.00
AJL1 Jarvis Landry
AJM1 Jerick McKinnon 3.00 8.00
AJM2 Jake Matthews 2.50 6.00
AJM3 Jack Mewhort 2.50 6.00
AJM4 Johnny Manziel
AJM5 Jordan Matthews 4.00 10.00
AJP1 Jacob Pedersen 3.00 8.00
AJP2 Jeoffrey Pagan 2.50 6.00
AJS1 James Stone 2.50 6.00
AJS2 Jerome Smith 2.50 6.00
AJV1 Jason Verrett 2.50 6.00
AJW1 Jaylen Watkins 2.50 6.00
AJWJ James Wilder Jr. 3.00 8.00
AJZ1 Jordan Zumwalt 2.50 6.00
AKB1 Kelvin Benjamin
AKDC Ka'Deem Carey 2.50 6.00
AKE1 Kony Ealy 3.00 8.00
AKF1 Kyle Fuller 2.50 6.00
AKM1 Khalil Mack 6.00 15.00
AKM2 Kareem Martin 2.50 6.00
AKQ1 Kelcy Quarles 3.00 8.00
AKS1 Kenny Shaw 4.00 10.00
AKVN Kyle Van Noy 3.00 8.00
ALP1 Loucheiz Purifoy 2.50 6.00
ALS1 Lache Seastrunk 2.50 6.00
ALT1 Logan Thomas
AMB1 Max Bullough 4.00 10.00
AMC1 Mike Campanaro 2.50 6.00
AME1 Mike Evans
AMG1 Marion Grice 2.50 6.00
AMH1 Marqueston Huff 2.50 6.00
AML1 Marqise Lee
AMM1 Morgan Moses 2.50 6.00
AMR1 Marcus Roberson 3.00 8.00
AMS1 Marcus Smith II 2.50 6.00
AOBJ Odell Beckham Jr.
APR1 Paul Richardson 5.00 12.00
ARB1 Rob Blanchflower 2.50 6.00
ARH1 Rob Herron 2.50 6.00
ARN1 Rajion Neal 2.50 6.00
ARR1 Rashaad Reynolds 2.50 6.00
ARS1 Ryan Shazier
ARSH Ra'Shede Hageman 2.50 6.00
ASC1 Scott Crichton 2.50 6.00
ASE1 Shaquelle Evans 2.50 6.00
ASM1 Stephen Morris 2.50 6.00
ASR1 Silas Redd 3.00 8.00
ASS1 Shamar Stephen 2.50 6.00
AST1 Stephon Tuitt 4.00 10.00
ASW1 Sammy Watkins 8.00 20.00
ATB1 Tajh Boyd
ATB2 Teddy Bridgewater 15.00 40.00
ATG1 Tyler Gaffney 2.50 6.00
ATJ1 Timmy Jernigan 2.50 6.00
ATL1 Taylor Lewan 2.50 6.00
ATM1 Trey Millard 3.00 8.00
ATM2 Trent Murphy 2.50 6.00
ATM3 Terrance Mitchell 4.00 10.00
ATM4 Tre Mason
ATN1 Troy Niklas 2.50 6.00
ATR1 Trevor Reilly 2.50 6.00
ATR2 Tommy Rees
ATR3 Tevin Reese 2.50 6.00
ATS1 Travis Swanson 2.50 6.00
ATW1 Terrance West 8.00 20.00
AVH1 Victor Hampton 3.00 8.00
AXG1 Xavier Grimble 3.00 8.00
AYS1 Yawin Smallwood 2.50 6.00
AZM1 Zack Martin 5.00 12.00
AZM2 Zach Mettenberger

2014 Leaf Draft Edition Gold

COMPLETE SET (20) 8.00 20.00
DE1A•Johnny Manziel .30 .75
DE2 Teddy Bridgewater .30 .75
DE3 Tre Mason .20 .50
DE4 Blake Bortles .25 .60
DE5 Sammy Watkins .30 .75
DE6 Derek Carr 1.25 3.00
DE7 Aaron Murray .20 .50
DE8 A.J. McCarron .20 .50
DE9 Jeremy Hill .25 .60
DE10 Ka'Deem Carey .20 .50
DE11 Mike Evans .50 1.25
DE12 Kelvin Benjamin .30 .75
DE13 De'Anthony Thomas .20 .50
DE14 Anthony Barr .20 .50
DE15 Khalil Mack .75 2.00
DE16 Odell Beckham .50 1.25
DE17 Eric Ebron .25 .60
DE18 Jake Matthews .20 .50
DE19 Brandin Cooks .30 .75
DE20 Marqise Lee .25 .60

2011 Leaf Draft Draft Day Edition

COMPLETE SET (20) 6.00 15.00
RELEASED DIRECTLY TO DEALERS
*BLACK: 2.5X TO 6X BASIC CARDS
DD1 A.J. Green .40 1.00
DD2 Andy Dalton .30 .75
DD3A Blaine Gabbert .15 .40
DD3B Blaine Gabbert .15 .40
DD4A Cam Newton .75 2.00
DD4B Cam Newton .75 2.00
DD5 Christian Ponder .15 .40
DD6 Colin Kaepernick .25 .60
DD7 Daniel Thomas .15 .40
DD8 DeMarco Murray .30 .75
DD9 Jake Locker .15 .40
DD10 Julio Jones .50 1.25
DD11 Kendall Hunter .15 .40
DD12 Mark Ingram .25 .60
DD13 Mikel Leshoure .15 .40

DD14 Pat Devlin .25 .60
DD15 Ricky Stanzi .15 .40
DD16 Ryan Mallett .15 .40
DD17 Ryan Williams .15 .40
DD18 Tyrod Taylor .30 .75

2014 Leaf Draft Day Edition Gold

COMPLETE SET (12) 5.00 12.00
*BLUE: .5X TO 1.2X GOLD
*ORANGE: .4X TO 1X GOLD
1 Johnny Manziel .25 .60
2 Blake Bortles .20 .50
3 Teddy Bridgewater .25 .60
4 Derek Carr 1.00 2.50
5 Sammy Watkins .25 .60
6 Jimmy Garoppolo 1.25 3.00
7 Mike Evans .40 1.00
8 Allen Robinson .25 .60
9 Carlos Hyde .20 .50
10 Ka'Deem Carey .15 .40
11 Zach Mettenberger .15 .40
12 Bishop Sankey .15 .40

2014 Leaf Draft Limited Edition Gold

COMPLETE SET (12) 5.00 12.00
*BLUE: .5X TO 1.2X GOLD
*ORANGE: .6X TO 1.5X GOLD
1 Johnny Manziel .25 .60
2 Blake Bortles .20 .50
3 Teddy Bridgewater .25 .60
4 Derek Carr 1.00 2.50
5 Sammy Watkins .25 .60
6 Eric Ebron .20 .50
7 Jadeveon Clowney .20 .50
8 Kelvin Benjamin .25 .60
9 Tre Mason .15 .40
10 Jeremy Hill .20 .50
11 Aaron Murray .15 .40
12 A.J. McCarron .15 .40

2015 Leaf Draft

1 Alvin Dupree .15 .40
2 Ameer Abdullah DP .20 .50
3 Antwan Goodley .12 .30
4 Austin Hill .12 .30
5 Ben Koyack .20 .50
6 Benardrick McKinney .12 .30
7 Blake Sims .12 .30
8 Bo Wallace .12 .30
9 Brandon Bridge .12 .30
10 Brett Hundley DP .12 .30
11 Bryce Petty DP .12 .30
12 Cameron Artis-Payne .12 .30
13 Clive Walford .12 .30
14 Cody Fajardo .15 .40
15 Danielle Hunter .15 .40
16 Danny Shelton .12 .30
17 Dante Fowler Jr. .20 .50
18 David Cobb .12 .30
19 David Johnson .30 .75
20 Denzel Perryman .12 .30
21 Devin Funchess DP .20 .50
22 E.J. Bibbs .15 .40
23 Eddie Goldman .12 .30
24 Garrett Grayson .12 .30
25 Ifo Ekpre-Olomu .12 .30
26 Jaelen Strong DP .15 .40
27 Javorius Allen .15 .40
28 Jay Ajayi .20 .50
29 Jeff Heuerman .15 .40
30 Jesse James .15 .40
31 Josh Harper .12 .30
32 Karlos Williams .12 .30
33 Kasen Williams .20 .50
34 Kenny Bell .20 .50
35 Kevin White DP .15 .40
36 Landon Collins .15 .40
37 Malcolm Brown .15 .40
38 Marcus Peters .20 .50
39 Markus Golden .12 .30
40 Matt Jones .12 .30
41 Melvin Gordon DP .30 .75
42 Mike Davis .12 .30
43 Nelson Agholor .15 .40
44 P.J. Williams .15 .40
45 Phillip Dorsett .12 .30
46 Randy Gregory .12 .30
47 Rashad Greene DP .12 .30
48 Sammie Coates DP .15 .40
49 Sean Mannion DP .12 .30
50 Shane Carden .12 .30
51 Shane Ray .12 .30
52 Shaq Thompson .15 .40
53 Stefon Diggs .30 .75
54 Tevin Coleman .15 .40
55 Todd Gurley DP .50 1.25
56 Tony Lippett .12 .30
57 Trae Waynes .12 .30
58 Ty Montgomery DP .12 .30
59 Tyler Kroft .15 .40
60 Tyler Lockett .20 .50
61 Vic Beasley .15 .40
62 Vince Mayle .15 .40
63 Devin Gardner .20 .50
64 Maxx Williams .12 .30
65 Nick Marshall .20 .50
66 Cedric Ogbuehi .12 .30
67 DaVaris Daniels .12 .30
68 Devante Davis .15 .40
69 Dres Anderson .12 .30
70 Jake Ryan .20 .50
71 Jamison Crowder .15 .40
72 Jaxon Shipley .12 .30
73 Jordon James .15 .40
74 Josh Robinson .12 .30
75 Kevin Parks .12 .30
76 Taylor Kelly .15 .40
77 Terrance Magee .20 .50
78 Titus Davis .15 .40
79 Marcus Mariota .50 1.25
80 Marcus Mariota .50 1.25
81 Marcus Mariota .50 1.25
82 Marcus Mariota .50 1.25
83 Marcus Mariota .50 1.25
84 Jameis Winston .30 .75
85 Jameis Winston .30 .75
86 Jameis Winston .30 .75
87 Jameis Winston .30 .75
88 Amari Cooper .40 1.00

2015 Leaf Draft Gold

*GOLD: 1.2X TO 3X BASIC CARDS

2015 Leaf Draft Autographs

BAAA1 Ameer Abdullah SP 6.00 15.00
BAAC01 Amari Cooper SP 25.00 50.00
BAAC1 Anthony Chickillo 3.00 8.00
BAAD1 Alvin Dupree SP 5.00 12.00
BAAG1 Antwan Goodley SP EXCH 4.00 10.00
BAAH1 Austin Hill SP EXCH 4.00 10.00
BAAH2 Anthony Harris 3.00 8.00
BAAJC A.J. Cann 4.00 10.00
BAAJT A.J. Tarpley 3.00 8.00
BAAP1 Andrus Peat 3.00 8.00
BAAS1 Austin Shepherd 3.00 8.00
BABB1 Brandon Bridge SP 4.00 10.00
BABB2 Blake Bell 5.00 12.00
BABB3 Bernard Blake 4.00 10.00
BABH1 Brett Hundley SP 4.00 10.00
BABH2 Ben Heeney 3.00 8.00
BABK1 Ben Koyack SP EXCH 6.00 15.00
BADM1 Denardrick McKinney SP EXCH 4.00 10.00
BABP1 Bryce Petty SP EXCH 4.00 10.00
BABS1 Blake Sims SP 4.00 10.00
BABW1 Bo Wallace SP EXCH 4.00 10.00
BACAP Cameron Artis-Payne SP 4.00 10.00
BACC1 Christian Covington 3.00 8.00
BACD1 Carl Davis 4.00 10.00
BACF1 Cody Fajardo SP 5.00 12.00
BACO1 Cedric Ogbuehi 3.00 8.00
BACR1 Cedric Reed 3.00 8.00
BACT1 Cam Thomas 3.00 8.00
BACW1 Clive Walford SP 4.00 10.00
BADA1 Dres Anderson 3.00 8.00
BADB1 Deion Barnes 3.00 8.00
BADC1 David Cobb SP 4.00 10.00
BADD1 DaVaris Daniels 3.00 8.00
BADD2 Devante Davis 4.00 10.00
BADE1 Durell Eskridge 3.00 8.00
BADF1 Devin Funchess SP EXCH 6.00 15.00
BADF2 Dante Fowler Jr. SP EXCH 6.00 15.00
BADG1 Devin Gardner 5.00 12.00
BADG2 Doran Grant 5.00 12.00
BADH1 Danielle Hunter SP 5.00 12.00
BADJ2 David Johnson SP 10.00 25.00
BADJH D.J. Humphries 3.00 8.00
BADK1 Darius Kilgo 3.00 8.00
BADP3 Denzel Perryman SP EXCH 4.00 10.00
BADS1 Danny Shelton SP 4.00 10.00
BADS2 Donovan Smith 3.00 8.00
BADS3 Derron Smith 3.00 8.00
BADT1 Dylan Thompson 3.00 8.00
BADW1 Daryl Williams 5.00 12.00
BAEG1 Eddie Goldman SP EXCH 4.00 10.00
BAEH1 Eli Harold 3.00 8.00
BAEJB E.J. Bibbs SP EXCH 5.00 12.00
BAEK1 Eric Kendricks 3.00 8.00
BAER1 Eric Rowe 3.00 8.00
BAGC1 Gerald Christian 4.00 10.00
BAGG1 Garrett Grayson SP 4.00 10.00
BAGJ1 Grady Jarrett 4.00 10.00
BAHA1 Henry Anderson 4.00 10.00
BAHG1 Hroniss Grasu 4.00 10.00
BAHM1 Hutson Mason 3.00 8.00
BAIEO Ifo Ekpre-Olomu 3.00 8.00
BAJA1 Jay Ajayi SP 6.00 15.00
BAJA2 Javorius Allen SP EXCH 5.00 12.00
BAJC1 Jamison Crowder 4.00 10.00
BAJC2 John Crockett 5.00 12.00
BAJH1 Josh Harper SP 4.00 10.00
BAJH2 Jordan Hicks 5.00 12.00
BAJH3 Jeff Heuerman SP EXCH 5.00 12.00
BAJJ1 Jesse James SP 5.00 12.00
BAJJ2 Jordon James 4.00 10.00
BAJM1 John Miller 3.00 8.00
BAJP1 Jordan Phillips 3.00 8.00
BAJR1 Jake Ryan 5.00 12.00
BAJR2 Jermauria Rasco 3.00 8.00
BAJR3 Jordan Richards 3.00 8.00
BAJR4 Josh Robinson 3.00 8.00
BAJS1 Jaelen Strong SP EXCH 5.00 12.00
BAJS2 JaCorey Shepherd 3.00 8.00
BAJS3 Josh Shaw 5.00 12.00
BAJS4 Josue Matias 3.00 8.00
BAJS5 Jaxon Shipley 3.00 8.00
BAJT1 Jaquiski Tartt 3.00 8.00
BAJW01 Jameis Winston SP EXCH
BAJW02 Jameis Winston SP EXCH
BAJW03 Jameis Winston SP EXCH
BAJW04 Jameis Winston SP EXCH
BAKA1 Kwon Alexander 4.00 10.00
BAKB1 Kenny Bell SP 6.00 15.00
BAKD1 Kurtis Drummond 4.00 10.00
BAKP1 Kevin Parks 3.00 8.00
BAKW1 Kasen Williams SP 6.00 15.00
BAKW2 Kevin White EXCH 30.00 60.00
BAKW3 Karlos Williams SP EXCH 4.00 10.00
BALC1 Landon Collins SP 5.00 12.00
BALC2 La'el Collins 4.00 10.00
BALD1 Lorenzo Doss 3.00 8.00
BALM1 Lorenzo Mauldin 3.00 8.00
BALT1 Laken Tomlinson 3.00 8.00
BAMA1 Mario Alford 3.00 8.00
BAMB1 Malcolm Brown SP EXCH 5.00 12.00
BAMB2 Malcom Brown 3.00 8.00
BAMD1 Mike Davis SP 4.00 10.00
BAMG1 Melvin Gordon SP 25.00 50.00
BAMG2 Markus Golden SP 4.00 10.00
BAMH1 Mike Hull 5.00 12.00
BAMJ1 Matt Jones SP 4.00 10.00
BAMM01 Marcus Mariota SP 90.00 150.00
BAMM02 Marcus Mariota SP 90.00 150.00
BAMM03 Marcus Mariota SP 90.00 150.00
BAMM04 Marcus Mariota SP 90.00 150.00
BAMM05 Marcus Mariota SP 90.00 150.00
BAMM1 Marcus Murphy 3.00 8.00
BAMP1 Marcus Peters SP EXCH 6.00 15.00
BAMW1 Maxx Williams 3.00 8.00
BANA1 Nelson Agholor SP EXCH 5.00 12.00
BANB1 Nick Boyle 3.00 8.00
BANM1 Nick Marshall 5.00 12.00
BANO1 Nate Orchard 3.00 8.00
BAOO1 Owamagbe Odighizuwa 4.00 10.00
BAOP1 Olsen Pierre 3.00 8.00
BAPD1 Phillip Dorsett SP EXCH 4.00 10.00
BAPD2 Paul Dawson 4.00 10.00
BAPJW P.J. Williams SP 5.00 12.00
BAQD1 Quandre Diggs 3.00 8.00
BAQD2 Quinton Dunbar 4.00 10.00
BAQR1 Quinten Rollins 6.00 15.00
BARA1 Rory Anderson 3.00 8.00
BARD1 Ray Drew 3.00 8.00
BARG1 Rashad Greene SP 4.00 10.00
BARG2 Randy Gregory SP EXCH 4.00 10.00
BARM1 Ronald Martin 3.00 8.00
BASA1 Stephone Anthony 3.00 8.00
BASC1 Sammie Coates EXCH 4.00 10.00
BASC2 Shane Carden SP 4.00 10.00
BASD1 Stefon Diggs SP EXCH 10.00 25.00
BASH1 Sean Hickey 3.00 8.00
BASM1 Sean Mannion SP EXCH 4.00 10.00
BASR1 Shane Ray SP EXCH 4.00 10.00
BAST1 Shaq Thompson SP EXCH 5.00 12.00
BATC1 Tevin Coleman SP EXCH 5.00 12.00
BATD1 Titus Davis 4.00 10.00
BATG1 Todd Gurley SP 30.00 60.00
BATJ1 Tre Jackson EXCH
BATJC T.J. Clemmings 3.00 8.00
BATK1 Tyler Kroft SP 5.00 12.00
BATK2 Taylor Kelly 4.00 10.00
BATL1 Tyler Lockett SP EXCH 6.00 15.00
BATL2 Tony Lippett SP EXCH 4.00 10.00
BATM1 Ty Montgomery SP EXCH 4.00 10.00
BATM2 Tre McBride 3.00 8.00
BATM3 Terrance Magee 5.00 12.00
BATT1 Tyrus Thompson 3.00 8.00
BATW1 Tony Washington 4.00 10.00
BATW1 Trae Waynes SP 4.00 10.00
BAVB1 Vic Beasley SP 5.00 12.00
BAVM1 Vince Mayle EXCH 4.00 10.00
BAWS1 Wes Saxton 4.00 10.00
BAXC1 Xavier Cooper 3.00 8.00

2015 Leaf Draft Limited Edition

COMPLETE SET (11) 15.00 25.00
*SUPER BREAK: .5X TO 1.2X BASIC CARDS
1 Ameer Abdullah .40 1.00
2 Brett Hundley .25 .60
3 Bryce Petty .25 .60
4 Devin Funchess .40 1.00
5 Kevin White .30 .75
6 Melvin Gordon .60 1.50
7 Sean Mannion .25 .60
8 Todd Gurley 1.00 2.50
9 Amari Cooper .75 2.00
10 Jameis Winston .60 1.50
11 Marcus Mariota 1.00 2.50

2015 Leaf Draft Special Issue

COMPLETE SET (20) 15.00 25.00
*BLACK/50: 1.2X TO 3X BASIC CARDS
*BLUE/25: 2X TO 5X BASIC CARDS
*GOLD/100: .8X TO 2X BASIC CARDS
PINK/200: .6X TO 1.5X BASIC CARDS
*RED/10: 3X TO 8X BASIC CARDS
SILVER/500: .6X TO 1.5X BASIC CARDS
1 Marcus Mariota .50 1.25
2 Jameis Winston .30 .75
3 Marcus Mariota .50 1.25
4 Jameis Winston .30 .75
5 Dorial Green-Beckham .12 .30
6 Brett Hundley .12 .30
7 Bryce Petty .12 .30
8 DeVante Parker .20 .50
9 Amari Cooper .40 1.00
10 Kevin White .15 .40
11 Todd Gurley .50 1.25
12 Jaelen Strong .15 .40
13 Melvin Gordon .30 .75
14 Ameer Abdullah .20 .50
15 Tevin Coleman .15 .40
16 Sammie Coates .15 .40
17 Devin Funchess .20 .50
18 Duke Johnson .20 .50
19 Garrett Grayson .12 .30
20 Jay Ajayi .20 .50

2016 Leaf Draft

*GOLD: 1.2X TO 3X BASIC CARDS
1 A'Shawn Robinson .12 .30
2 Aaron Burbridge .12 .30
3 Aaron Green .12 .30
4 Alex Collins .15 .40
5 Bralon Addison .12 .30
6 Brandon Allen .12 .30
7 Brandon Doughty .12 .30
8 Braxton Miller .12 .30
9 Bryce Williams .15 .40
10 C.J. Prosise .12 .30
11 Cardale Jones .12 .30
12 Carson Wentz 1.25 3.00
13 Cayleb Jones .12 .30
14 Chris Brown .15 .40
15 Christian Hackenberg .12 .30
16 Cody Kessler .12 .30
17 Connor Cook .15 .40
18 Corey Coleman .20 .50
19 Dak Prescott .60 1.50
20 Daniel Braverman .12 .30
21 Daniel Lasco .12 .30
22 Darron Lee .12 .30
23 De'Runnya Wilson .12 .30
24 DeAndre Washington .12 .30
25 DeForest Buckner .12 .30
26 Demarcus Robinson .12 .30
27 Derrick Henry .30 .75
28 Devon Cajuste .12 .30
29 Devontae Booker .15 .40
30 Eli Apple .15 .40
31 Ezekiel Elliott .60 1.50
32 Glenn Gronkowski .12 .30
33 Hunter Henry .15 .40
34 Jacoby Brissett .15 .40
35 Jalen Ramsey .20 .50
36 Jared Goff .75 2.00
37 Jaylon Smith .12 .30
38 Jayron Kearse .12 .30
39 Jeff Driskel .12 .30
40 Jerell Adams .12 .30
41 Joey Bosa .25 .60
42 Jonathan Bullard .12 .30
43 Jonathan Williams .15 .40
44 Jordan Howard .30 .75
45 Jordan Payton .12 .30
46 Jordan Williams .12 .30
47 Josh Doctson .15 .40
48 Josh Ferguson .12 .30
49 Keenan Reynolds .15 .40
50 Keith Marshall .12 .30
51 Kelvin Taylor .12 .30
52 Kenny Clark .12 .30
53 Kenyan Drake .20 .50
54 Kevin Hogan .15 .40
55 Keyarris Garrett .12 .30
56 Kolby Listenbee .12 .30
57 Kyle Carter .12 .30
58 Laquon Treadwell .15 .40
59 Laremy Tunsil .12 .30
60 Leonard Floyd .15 .40
61 Leonte Carroo .12 .30
62 Malcolm Mitchell .12 .30
63 Marquez North .12 .30
64 Mekale McKay .12 .30
65 Michael Thomas .25 .60
66 Myles Jack .15 .40
67 Nate Sudfeld .12 .30
68 Nelson Spruce .12 .30
69 Nick Vannett .12 .30
70 Noah Spence .12 .30
71 Paul Perkins .12 .30
72 Paxton Lynch .12 .30
73 Pharoh Cooper .12 .30
74 Rashard Higgins .12 .30
75 Reggie Ragland .12 .30
76 Robert Nkemdiche .15 .40
77 Roger Lewis Jr. .12 .30
78 Scooby Wright .12 .30
79 Shaq Lawson .12 .30
80 Shilique Calhoun .12 .30
81 Sterling Shepard .15 .40
82 Tajae Sharpe .15 .40
83 Tra Carson .12 .30
84 Tre Madden .12 .30
85 Trevone Boykin .12 .30
86 Tyler Boyd .15 .40
87 Tyler Ervin .12 .30
88 Tyler Higbee .12 .30
89 Vernon Hargreaves III .20 .50
90 Will Fuller .20 .50

2016 Leaf Draft All American

*GOLD: .5X TO 1.2X BASIC INSERTS
1 Cardale Jones .25 .60
2 Carson Wentz 2.50 6.00
3 Connor Cook .30 .75
4 Corey Coleman .40 1.00
5 Derrick Henry .60 1.50
6 Ezekiel Elliott 1.25 3.00
7 Jared Goff 1.50 4.00
8 Joey Bosa .50 1.25
9 Laquon Treadwell .30 .75
10 Paxton Lynch .25 .60

2016 Leaf Draft Autographs

AAB1 Aaron Burbridge SP 4.00 10.00
AAC1 Alex Collins SP 5.00 12.00
AAG1 Adam Gotsis 3.00 8.00
AAG2 Aaron Green SP 4.00 10.00
AAJ1 Austin Johnson 3.00 8.00
AAM1 Alex McCalister 5.00 12.00
AAM2 Antonio Morrison 4.00 10.00
AASR A'Shawn Robinson SP 4.00 10.00
AAW1 Adolphus Washington 3.00 8.00
ABA1 Bralon Addison SP 4.00 10.00
ABA2 Brandon Allen SP 4.00 10.00
ABBC Briean Boddy-Calhoun 3.00 8.00
ABD1 Brandon Doughty SP 4.00 10.00
ABK1 Bronson Kaufusi 3.00 8.00
ABM1 Blake Martinez 4.00 10.00
ABM2 Braxton Miller SP
ABW1 Bryce Williams SP 5.00 12.00
ACB1 Chris Brown SP 5.00 12.00
ACC1 Cody Core 3.00 8.00
ACC2 Connor Cook SP
ACC3 Corey Coleman SP 6.00 15.00
ACH1 Christian Hackenberg SP
ACJ1 Cardale Jones SP
ACJ1 Chris Jones 3.00 8.00
ACJ2 Cayleb Jones 3.00 8.00
ACJP C.J. Prosise SP 4.00 10.00
ACK1 Cody Kessler SP 4.00 10.00
ACM1 Chris Moore 4.00 10.00
ACM2 Curt Maggitt 5.00 12.00
ACN1 Carl Nassib 3.00 8.00
ACT1 Charles Tapper 4.00 10.00
ACW1 Cody Whitehair 5.00 12.00
ACW2 Carson Wentz SP
ADA1 Dominique Alexander 3.00 8.00
ADA2 Demarcus Ayers 3.00 8.00
ADB1 Daniel Braverman 3.00 8.00
ADB2 Devontae Booker SP 5.00 12.00
ADC1 Devon Cajuste SP 4.00 10.00
ADFB DeForest Buckner SP 4.00 10.00
ADH1 Derrick Henry SP
ADJ1 Deion Jones 3.00 8.00
ADJW D.J. White 3.00 8.00
ADL1 Daniel Lasco 3.00 8.00
ADL2 Darron Lee SP 4.00 10.00
ADM1 David Morgan II 5.00 12.00
ADMR Demarcus Robinson SP 4.00 10.00
ADP1 Dak Prescott SP
ADRW De'Runnya Wilson SP 4.00 10.00
ADV1 Dan Vitale 3.00 8.00
ADW1 Dom Williams 3.00 8.00
ADW2 DeAndre Washington 3.00 8.00
ADW3 Derek Watt 5.00 12.00
AEA1 Eli Apple 4.00 10.00
AEE1 Ezekiel Elliott EXCH
AES1 Eric Striker 4.00 10.00
AGG1 Glenn Gronkowski 3.00 8.00
AHH1 Hunter Henry SP 5.00 12.00
AJA1 Jerell Adams SP 4.00 10.00
AJB1 Jonathan Bullard 3.00 8.00
AJB2 Jacoby Brissett SP 5.00 12.00
AJB3 Joey Bosa EXCH 8.00 20.00
AJC1 Jeremy Cash 4.00 10.00
AJD1 Jeff Driskel SP 4.00 10.00
AJD2 Josh Doctson SP 5.00 12.00
AJF1 Jason Fanaika 3.00 8.00
AJF2 Josh Ferguson SP 4.00 10.00
AJG1 Joshua Garnett 3.00 8.00
AJG2 Jared Goff SP 30.00 60.00
AJH1 Jordan Howard SP 10.00 25.00
AJK1 Jayron Kearse EXCH 3.00 8.00
AJL1 Jay Lee 3.00 8.00
AJM1 Jalin Marshall 5.00 12.00
AJM2 Jalen Mills 4.00 10.00
AJM3 Jake McGee 4.00 10.00
AJP1 Jordan Payton SP 4.00 10.00
AJR1 Jalen Ramsey SP 6.00 15.00
AJS1 Joe Schobert 4.00 10.00
AJS2 Jason Spriggs 3.00 8.00
AJS3 Jaylon Smith SP 4.00 10.00
AJW2 Jonathan Williams SP 5.00 12.00
AJW3 Jordan Williams SP 4.00 10.00
AKB1 Kentrell Brothers 3.00 8.00
AKC1 Kamalei Correa 3.00 8.00
AKC2 Kenny Clark 3.00 8.00
AKC3 Ken Crawley 4.00 10.00
AKC4 Kyle Carter SP 4.00 10.00
AKD1 Kenyan Drake EXCH 5.00 12.00
AKF1 Kyler Fackrell 4.00 10.00
AKF2 Kendall Fuller 4.00 10.00
AKG1 Keyarris Garrett 3.00 8.00
AKH1 Kevin Hogan SP 5.00 12.00
AKJ1 Karl Joseph 3.00 8.00
AKL1 Kolby Listenbee 3.00 8.00
AKM1 Kyle Murphy 4.00 10.00
AKM2 Keith Marshall SP 4.00 10.00
AKR1 KeiVarae Russell 3.00 8.00
AKR2 Keenan Reynolds 4.00 10.00
ALC1 Leonte Carroo SP 4.00 10.00
ALF1 Leonard Floyd SP 5.00 12.00
ALT1 Laquon Treadwell EXCH 4.00 10.00
ALT2 Laremy Tunsil SP 4.00 10.00
AMC1 Maurice Canady 3.00 8.00
AMC2 Michael Caputo 4.00 10.00
AMC3 Maliek Collins 3.00 8.00
AMJ1 Myles Jack SP 5.00 12.00
AMK1 Miles Killebrew 3.00 8.00
AMM1 Malcolm Mitchell 3.00 8.00
AMM2 Mekale McKay SP 4.00 10.00
AMN1 Marquez North SP 4.00 10.00
AMT1 Max Tuerk 3.00 8.00
AMT2 Michael Thomas SP 8.00 20.00
ANK1 Nick Kwiatkoski 5.00 12.00
ANM1 Nick Martin 3.00 8.00
ANS1 Noah Spence 3.00 8.00
ANS2 Nate Sudfeld SP 4.00 10.00
ANS3 Nelson Spruce SP 4.00 10.00
ANV1 Nick Vigil 3.00 8.00
ANV2 Nick Vannett SP 4.00 10.00
APC1 Pharoh Cooper SP 4.00 10.00
APJ1 Paul James 3.00 8.00
APL1 Paxton Lynch SP 4.00 10.00
APP1 Paul Perkins SP 4.00 10.00
AQD1 Quinshad Davis 5.00 12.00
ARH1 Rashard Higgins SP 4.00 10.00
ARK1 Ryan Kelly 5.00 12.00
ARL1 Roger Lewis Jr. 3.00 8.00
ARN1 Robert Nkemdiche SP 5.00 12.00
ARR1 Reggie Ragland EXCH 3.00 8.00
ASBW Storm Woods 3.00 8.00
ASC1 Shon Coleman 3.00 8.00
ASC2 Shilique Calhoun 3.00 8.00
ASD1 Spencer Drango 3.00 8.00
ASD2 Sheldon Day 3.00 8.00
ASL1 Shaq Lawson EXCH 3.00 8.00
ASS1 Steven Scheu 3.00 8.00
ASS2 Sterling Shepard SP 5.00 12.00
ASV1 Soma Vainuku 4.00 10.00
ASW1 Scooby Wright SP 4.00 10.00
ATB1 Trevone Boykin EXCH 3.00 8.00
ATC1 Tevin Carter 3.00 8.00
ATC2 Tra Carson SP 4.00 10.00
ATE1 Trae Elston 5.00 12.00
ATE2 Tyler Ervin 3.00 8.00
ATH1 Tyler Higbee SP 4.00 10.00
ATM1 Tre Madden EXCH 3.00 8.00
ATP1 Tyvis Powell 10.00 25.00
ATS1 Tajae Sharpe SP 5.00 12.00
AVA1 Vadal Alexander 3.00 8.00
AVH3 Vernon Hargreaves III SP 6.00 15.00
AWF1 Will Fuller SP 6.00 15.00
AXH1 Xavien Howard 4.00 10.00

2017 Leaf Draft

*GOLD: 1.2X TO 3X BASIC CARDS
1 Alvin Kamara .50 1.25
2 Amara Darboh .12 .30
3 Artavis Scott .12 .30
4 ArDarius Stewart .12 .30
5 Brad Kaaya .12 .30
6 Brian Hill .12 .30
7 Bucky Hodges .12 .30
8 C.J. Beathard .12 .30
9 Carlos Henderson .12 .30
10 Chad Kelly .12 .30
11 Chris Godwin .15 .40
12 Christian McCaffrey .30 .75
13 Cooper Kupp .20 .50
14 Cooper Rush .15 .40
15 Corey Clement .15 .40
16 Corey Davis .20 .50
17 Curtis Samuel .15 .40
18 D'Onta Foreman .15 .40
19 Dalvin Cook .30 .75
20 Damore'ea Stringfellow .15 .40
21 David Njoku .15 .40
22 Davis Webb .12 .30
23 De'Veon Smith .30 .75
24 Dede Westbrook .12 .30
25 Derek Barnett .15 .40
26 Deshaun Watson .75 2.00
27 DeShone Kizer .12 .30
28 Donnel Pumphrey .15 .40
29 Evan Engram .15 .40
30 Jake Butt .15 .40
31 Jamaal Williams .12 .30
32 James Conner .25 .60
33 James Quick .15 .40
34 Cam Robinson .12 .30
35 Jehu Chesson .15 .40
36 Jeremy McNichols .12 .30
37 Jerod Evans .15 .40
38 Joe Mixon .25 .60
39 John Ross .15 .40
40 Jonathan Allen .15 .40
41 Jordan Leggett .12 .30
42 Josh Reynolds .12 .30
43 Malik Hooker .12 .30
44 Joshua Dobbs .15 .40
45 JuJu Smith-Schuster .30 .75
46 Kareem Hunt .25 .60
47 KD Cannon .12 .30
48 Malachi Dupre .12 .30
49 Malik McDowell .12 .30
50 Ryan Ramczyk .12 .30
51 Mike Williams .20 .50
52 Mitch Trubisky .60 1.50
53 Nathan Peterman .15 .40
54 O.J. Howard .15 .40
55 Takkarist McKinley .12 .30
56 Pat Mahomes II 1.50 4.00
57 Reuben Foster .12 .30
58 Ryan Switzer .15 .40
59 Samaje Perine .12 .30
60 Sidney Jones .12 .30
61 Stacy Coley .12 .30
62 T.J. Watt .40 1.00
63 Taco Charlton .12 .30
64 Tarean Folston .20 .50
65 Teez Tabor .15 .40
66 Tim Williams .15 .40
67 Travin Dural .15 .40
68 Travis Rudolph .12 .30
69 Tyrone Swoopes .12 .30

2017 Leaf Draft All American

*GOLD: .5X TO 1.2X BASIC INSERTS
AA01 ArDarius Stewart .25 .60
AA02 Brad Kaaya .25 .60
AA03 Chad Kelly .25 .60
AA04 Christian McCaffrey .60 1.50
AA05 Corey Clement .30 .75
AA06 Curtis Samuel .30 .75
AA07 Dalvin Cook .60 1.50
AA08 Davis Webb .25 .60
AA09 Deshaun Watson 1.50 4.00
AA10 DeShone Kizer .25 .60
AA11 Jake Butt .30 .75
AA12 Jerod Evans .30 .75
AA13 Jonathan Allen .30 .75
AA14 JuJu Smith-Schuster .60 1.50
AA15 Mike Williams .40 1.00
AA16 Mitch Trubisky 1.25 3.00
AA17 O.J. Howard .30 .75

2017 Leaf Draft TD Machines

*GOLD: .5X TO 1.2X BASIC INSERTS
TD01 Chris Godwin .30 .75
TD02 Christian McCaffrey .60 1.50
TD03 Corey Davis .40 1.00
TD04 D'Onta Foreman .30 .75
TD05 Dalvin Cook .60 1.50
TD06 Dede Westbrook .25 .60
TD07 Deshaun Watson 1.50 4.00
TD08 DeShone Kizer .25 .60
TD09 Donnel Pumphrey .30 .75
TD10 Jeremy McNichols .25 .60
TD11 John Ross .30 .75
TD12 Mike Williams .40 1.00
TD13 Mitch Trubisky 1.25 3.00
TD14 Samaje Perine .25 .60

2018 Leaf Draft

*GOLD: 1.2X TO 3X BASIC CARDS
1 Akrum Wadley .12 .30
2 Allen Lazard .12 .30
3 Anthony Miller .20 .50
4 Antonio Callaway .15 .40
5 Arden Key .12 .30
6 Auden Tate .12 .30
7 Baker Mayfield 1.25 3.00
8 Bo Scarbrough .15 .40
9 Bradley Chubb .20 .50
10 Calvin Ridley .30 .75
11 Christian Kirk .20 .50
12 Courtland Sutton .20 .50
13 D.J. Chark .15 .40
14 D.J. Moore .25 .60
15 Dante Pettis .20 .50
16 Da'ron Payne .20 .50
17 Denzel Ward .30 .75
18 Deon Cain .15 .40
19 Deontay Burnett .15 .40
20 Derrius Guice .25 .60
21 Derwin James .25 .60
22 Durham Smythe .12 .30
23 Equanimeous St. Brown .20 .50
24 Hayden Hurst .15 .40
25 Ito Smith .15 .40
26 J.T. Barrett .20 .50
27 James Washington .25 .60
28 Javon Wims .12 .30
29 John Kelly .15 .40
30 Josh Adams .25 .60
31 Josh Allen .50 1.25
32 Josh Rosen .40 1.00
33 Kerryon Johnson .20 .50
34 Kurt Benkert .15 .40
35 Luke Falk .15 .40
36 Marcell Ateman .15 .40
37 Mark Andrews .20 .50
39 Mason Rudolph .30 .75
40 Maurice Hurst .15 .40
41 Michael Gallup .25 .60
42 Mike Gesicki .15 .40
43 Minkah Fitzpatrick .25 .60
44 Nick Chubb .40 1.00
45 Quinton Flowers .12 .30
46 Ralph Webb .15 .40
47 Rashaad Penny .20 .50
48 Rashaan Evans .20 .50
49 Riley Ferguson .20 .50
50 Ronald Jones II .12 .30
51 Ronnie Harrison .15 .40
52 Roquan Smith .40 1.00
53 Royce Freeman .15 .40
54 Sam Darnold .75 2.00
55 Sam Hubbard .15 .40
56 Simmie Cobbs Jr. .20 .50
57 Sony Michel .40 1.00
58 Trenton Thompson .12 .30
59 Troy Fumagalli .15 .40
60 Vita Vea .20 .50

2018 Leaf Draft All American

*GOLD: .5X TO 1.2X BASIC INSERTS
AA01 Anthony Miller .40 1.00
AA02 Baker Mayfield 2.50 6.00
AA03 Bradley Chubb .40 1.00
AA04 Dante Pettis .40 1.00
AA05 Denzel Ward .60 1.50
AA06 James Washington .50 1.25
AA07 Mark Andrews .40 1.00
AA08 Maurice Hurst .30 .75
AA09 Michael Gallup .50 1.25
AA10 Minkah Fitzpatrick .50 1.25
AA11 Rashaad Penny .40 1.00
AA12 Roquan Smith .75 2.00

2018 Leaf Draft Autographs

BAAA1 Anthony Averett 2.50 6.00
BAAC1 Antonio Callaway EXCH
BAAF1 Armanti Foreman 2.00 5.00
BAAG1 Austin Golson 2.00 5.00
BAAK1 Arden Key EXCH 2.00 5.00
BAAL1 Allen Lazard EXCH
BAAM1 Anthony Miller EXCH 3.00 8.00
BAAT1 Auden Tate EXCH
BAAW1 Akrum Wadley EXCH 2.00 5.00
BABB1 Braxton Berrios 2.00 5.00
BABB2 Bryce Bobo 2.00 5.00
BABC1 Bradley Chubb EXCH 3.00 8.00
BABF1 Brandon Facyson 2.00 5.00
BABJH B.J. Hill 2.50 6.00
BABM1 Baker Mayfield EXCH 25.00 60.00
BABS1 Breeland Speaks 2.50 6.00
BABS2 Bo Scarbrough EXCH
BACD1 Carlton Davis EXCH 2.50 6.00
BACJ1 Chris Jones 2.00 5.00
BACK1 Christian Kirk EXCH 3.00 8.00
BACL1 Chase Litton 2.50 6.00
BACLC Christian LaCouture 2.00 5.00
BACO1 Chukwuma Okorafor 2.00 5.00
BACOC Cody Oâ€™Connell 2.00 5.00
BACP1 Cam Phillips 2.00 5.00
BACR1 Calvin Ridley EXCH 5.00 12.00
BACS1 Conor Sheehy 2.50 6.00
BACS2 Cam Serigne 2.00 5.00
BACS3 Courtland Sutton EXCH 3.00 8.00
BACW1 Cedrick Wilson Jr. EXCH 2.00 5.00
BACW3 Chris Worley 2.00 5.00
BACW4 Chris Warren 3.00 8.00
BADB1 Deontay Burnett EXCH 2.50 6.00
BADB2 Davin Bellamy 2.00 5.00
BADB3 Devonte Boyd 2.00 5.00
BADC1 Deon Cain EXCH 2.50 6.00
BADC2 Darren Carrington II EXCH 2.50 6.00
BADC3 Dylan Cantrell 2.00 5.00
BADE1 Duke Ejiofor 2.00 5.00
BADF1 Dimitri Flowers 2.00 5.00
BADG1 Derrius Guice EXCH
BADG2 DeAndre Goolsby 2.00 5.00
BADG3 Dallas Goedert EXCH
BADJ1 Derwin James EXCH
BADJC D.J. Chark EXCH
BADJM D.J. Moore EXCH
BADN1 Derrick Nnadi 2.00 5.00
BADP1 Dante Pettis EXCH 3.00 8.00
BADP2 Darius Phillips 2.50 6.00
BADRP Da'ron Payne EXCH 3.00 8.00
BADS2 Durham Smythe 2.00 5.00
BADS3 Dalton Schultz EXCH 2.50 6.00
BADSE DeShon Elliott 2.50 6.00
BADSH DaeSean Hamilton 2.50 6.00
BADSJ Diocemy Saint Juste 2.00 5.00
BADW1 Denzel Ward EXCH
BADW2 David Wells 2.00 5.00
BADW3 Damon Webb 2.50 6.00
BADW4 Darrel Williams 2.50 6.00
BAESB Equanimeous St. Brown EXCH
BAEW1 Ethan Wolf 2.00 5.00
BAFF1 Folorunso Fatukasi 2.00 5.00
BAFR1 Frank Ragnow 2.50 6.00
BAFW1 Fred Warner 2.00 5.00
BAHH1 Hayden Hurst EXCH 2.50 6.00
BAHH2 Holton Hill 2.50 6.00
BAHH3 Heath Harding 2.00 5.00
BAHL1 Harold Landry 2.00 5.00
BAHM1 Hercules Mata'afa 2.00 5.00
BAHP1 Harrison Phillips 2.00 5.00
BAIS1 Ito Smith EXCH 2.50 6.00
BAIT1 Ian Thomas 2.00 5.00
BAIW1 Isaiah Wynn 2.00 5.00
BAJA1 Josh Allen EXCH 40.00 80.00
BAJA2 Josh Adams EXCH
BAJC1 Jason Cabinda 2.00 5.00
BAJC2 Justin Crawford 2.00 5.00
BAJCJ JC Jackson 2.00 5.00
BAJH1 Jalyn Holmes 3.00 8.00
BAJJ1 Justin Jackson EXCH
BAJK1 John Kelly EXCH 2.50 6.00
BAJL1 James Looney 2.00 5.00
BAJMM J'Mon Moore EXCH 2.00 5.00
BAJR1 Josh Rosen EXCH 30.00 60.00
BAJS1 Jaleel Scott 2.00 5.00
BAJS2 Jaylen Samuels 2.50 6.00
BAJTB J.T. Barrett EXCH 3.00 8.00
BAJW1 Jake Wieneke 2.50 6.00
BAJW2 James Washington EXCH 4.00 10.00
BAJW3 Javon Wims EXCH 2.00 5.00
BAJW3 Javon Wims 2.00 5.00
BAJW4 Jeffery Wilson 3.00 8.00
BAJW5 Jester Weah 2.00 5.00
BAJW6 John Wolford 2.00 5.00
BAKA1 Kyle Allen 2.50 6.00
BAKB1 Kurt Benkert EXCH 2.50 6.00
BAKC1 Keke Coutee 2.50 6.00
BAKJ1 Kerryon Johnson EXCH 3.00 8.00
BAKK1 Kameron Kelly 2.50 6.00
BAKL1 Kyle Lauletta 3.00 8.00
BAKRW Ka'Raun White 2.50 6.00
BAKW2 Kyzir White 3.00 8.00
BALC1 Lorenzo Carter 2.00 5.00
BALF1 Luke Falk EXCH 2.50 6.00
BALVE Leighton Vander Esch 6.00 15.00
BALW1 Logan Woodside 3.00 8.00
BAMA1 Mark Andrews EXCH 3.00 8.00
BAMA2 Marcell Ateman EXCH 2.50 6.00
BAMB1 Marcus Baugh EXCH 2.00 5.00
BAMB2 Max Browne 2.50 6.00
BAMC1 Martez Carter 2.00 5.00
BAMC2 Mason Cole 2.00 5.00
BAMD1 Marcus Davenport 4.00 10.00
BAMF1 Minkah Fitzpatrick EXCH 4.00 10.00
BAMG1 Michael Gallup 4.00 10.00
BAMG2 Mike Gesicki EXCH 2.50 6.00
BAMH1 Maurice Hurst EXCH 2.50 6.00
BAMH2 Marquis Haynes 2.00 5.00
BAMJS M.J. Stewart 2.00 5.00
BAMM1 Mike McCray 2.50 6.00
BAMM2 Mike McGlinchey 4.00 10.00
BAMR1 Martinas Rankin 2.00 5.00
BAMR2 Mason Rudolph EXCH 10.00 25.00
BAMW1 Mark Walton EXCH 2.50 6.00
BANC1 Nick Chubb EXCH 6.00 15.00
BANO1 Nick Orr 2.00 5.00
BANS1 Nic Shimonek 3.00 8.00
BANS2 Nick Stevens 2.50 6.00
BAOB1 Orlando Brown 2.00 5.00
BAPL1 Phillip Lindsay 8.00 20.00
BAPP1 Peter Pujals 2.50 6.00
BAQF1 Quinton Flowers EXCH
BARE1 Rashaan Evans EXCH
BARF1 Royce Freeman EXCH
BARF2 Riley Ferguson EXCH
BARF3 Robert Foster 2.00 5.00
BARG1 Russell Gage 2.50 6.00
BARH1 Ronnie Harrison EXCH 2.50 6.00
BARJ2 Ronald Jones II EXCH 2.00 5.00
BARP1 Rashaad Penny EXCH 3.00 8.00
BARRM Ray-Ray McCloud 2.00 5.00
BARS1 Roquan Smith EXCH 6.00 15.00
BARW1 Ralph Webb 2.50 6.00
BASC1 Simmie Cobbs Jr. EXCH 3.00 8.00
BASD1 Sam Darnold EXCH
BASH1 Sam Hubbard 2.50 6.00
BASH2 Shaun Dion Hamilton 2.50 6.00
BASI1 Steve Ishmael 2.00 5.00
BASM1 Sony Michel EXCH
BASM2 Steven Mitchell Jr. 2.50 6.00
BATC1 Tyler Conklin 2.00 5.00
BATE1 Terrell Edmunds 6.00 15.00
BATE2 Tremaine Edmunds 4.00 10.00
BATF1 Troy Fumagalli EXCH
BATF2 Tre Flowers 2.00 5.00
BATL1 Tyquan Lewis 2.50 6.00
BATQ1 Trey Quinn 2.00 5.00
BATS1 Tim Settle 2.00 5.00
BATT1 Trenton Thompson 2.00 5.00
BATW1 Tracy Walker 2.50 6.00
BAUN1 Uchenna Nwosu 3.00 8.00
BAVV1 Vita Vea EXCH
BAWH1 Will Hernandez 2.50 6.00

2018 Leaf Draft Field Generals

*GOLD: .5X TO 1.2X BASIC INSERTS
FG01 Baker Mayfield 2.50 6.00
FG02 J.T. Barrett .40 1.00
FG03 Josh Allen 1.00 2.50
FG04 Josh Rosen .75 2.00
FG05 Kurt Benkert .30 .75
FG06 Luke Falk .30 .75
FG07 Mason Rudolph .60 1.50
FG08 Riley Ferguson .40 1.00
FG09 Sam Darnold 1.50 4.00

2018 Leaf Draft TD Machines

*GOLD: .5X TO 1.2X BASIC INSERTS
TD01 Akrum Wadley .25 .60
TD02 Bo Scarbrough .30 .75
TD03 Calvin Ridley .60 1.50
TD04 Christian Kirk .40 1.00
TD05 Courtland Sutton .40 1.00
TD06 Derrius Guice .50 1.25
TD07 Equanimeous St. Brown .40 1.00
TD08 John Kelly .30 .75
TD09 Josh Adams .50 1.25
TD10 Justin Jackson .30 .75
TD11 Kerryon Johnson .40 1.00
TD12 Marcell Ateman .30 .75
TD13 Mark Walton .30 .75
TD14 Nick Chubb .75 2.00
TD15 Ralph Webb .30 .75
TD16 Ronald Jones II .25 .60
TD17 Royce Freeman .30 .75
TD18 Simmie Cobbs Jr. .40 1.00
TD19 Sony Michel .75 2.00

2019 Leaf Draft

*GOLD: 1.2X TO 3X BASIC CARDS
1 A.J. Brown .30 .75
2 Alex Barnes .15 .40
3 Anthony Johnson .15 .40
4 Anthony Ratliff-Williams .25 .60
5 Benny Snell Jr. .40 1.00
6 Brett Rypien .15 .40
7 Bryce Love .20 .50
8 Caleb Wilson .12 .30
9 Christian Wilkins .50 1.25
10 Clayton Thorson .20 .50
11 Clelin Ferrell .20 .50
12 D.K. Metcalf .40 1.00
13 DaMarkus Lodge .12 .30
14 Damien Harris .30 .75
15 Darrell Henderson .30 .75
16 David Montgomery .50 1.25
17 David Sills V .40 1.00
18 Deandre Baker .30 .75
19 Deebo Samuel .30 .75
20 Deionte Thompson .15 .40
21 Devin Bush II .50 1.25
22 Devin Singletary .15 .40
23 Devin White .40 1.00
24 Dexter Lawrence .20 .50
25 Dre'Mont Jones .15 .40
26 Drew Lock .60 1.50
27 Dwayne Haskins .60 1.50
28 Ed Oliver .20 .50
29 Elijah Holyfield .20 .50
30 Emanuel Hall .12 .30
31 Gary Jennings Jr. .20 .50
32 Greedy Williams .40 1.00
33 Hakeem Butler .25 .60
34 Irv Smith Jr. .25 .60
35 Jace Sternberger .15 .40
36 Jarrett Stidham .40 1.00
37 Jaylen Smith .12 .30
38 Jeffery Simmons .12 .30
39 JJ Arcega-Whiteside .20 .50
40 Johnnie Dixon .15 .40
41 Jordan Scarlett .12 .30
42 Josh Allen .20 .50
43 Josh Jacobs .60 1.50
44 Justice Hill .20 .50
45 Daniel Jones .60 1.50
46 Kelvin Harmon .20 .50
47 Kyle Kempt .20 .50
48 Kyle Shurmur .25 .60
49 Lil'Jordan Humphrey .15 .40
50 L.J. Scott .20 .50
51 Mack Wilson .15 .40
52 Marquise Brown .40 1.00
53 Mecole Hardman .30 .75
54 Mike Weber .20 .50
55 Miles Boykin .15 .40
56 Miles Sanders .30 .75
57 Myles Gaskin .25 .60
58 N'Keal Harry .40 1.00
59 Nick Bosa .40 1.00
60 Noah Fant .25 .60
61 Parris Campbell .30 .75
62 Riley Ridley .20 .50
63 Rodney Anderson .15 .40
64 Ryan Finley .25 .60
65 Will Grier .40 1.00
66 Trace McSorley .30 .75
67 Travis Homer .12 .30
68 Trayveon Williams .15 .40
69 Tyree Jackson .30 .75
70 Daniel Jones AA .60 1.50
71 Will Grier AA .40 1.00
72 Jarrett Stidham AA .40 1.00
73 Dwayne Haskins AA .60 1.50
74 Josh Jacobs AA .60 1.50
75 Drew Lock AA .60 1.50
76 A.J. Brown AA .30 .75
77 Damien Harris AA .30 .75
78 Marquise Brown AA .40 1.00
79 Nick Bosa AA .40 1.00
80 Parris Campbell AA .30 .75
81 Deebo Samuel TK .30 .75
82 Kelvin Harmon TK .20 .50
83 Riley Ridley TK .20 .50
84 Josh Jacobs TK .60 1.50
85 Parris Campbell TK .30 .75
86 D.K. Metcalf TK .40 1.00
87 A.J. Brown TK .30 .75
88 Damien Harris TK .30 .75
89 Marquise Brown TK .40 1.00
90 N'Keal Harry TK .40 1.00
91 Barry Sanders DF .30 .75
92 Bo Jackson DF .25 .60
93 Brett Favre DF .40 1.00
94 Dick Butkus DF .25 .60
95 Earl Campbell DF .20 .50
96 Emmitt Smith DF .30 .75
97 Jerry Rice DF .30 .75
98 John Elway DF .30 .75
99 Roger Staubach DF .25 .60
100 Troy Aikman DF .25 .60
SPKM1 Kyler Murray 1.25 3.00
SPKM2 Kyler Murray AA 1.25 3.00
SPKM3 Kyler Murray TK 1.25 3.00

2013 Leaf Draft Matrix
*GREEEN/50: 1.2X TO 3X BASIC CARDS
DMAE1 Andre Ellington .40 1.00
DMCG1 Cordarrelle Patterson .40 1.00
DMCK1 Collin Klein .50 1.25
DMDH1 DeAndre Hopkins 1.00 2.50
DMDR1 Denard Robinson .40 1.00
DMEJM EJ Manuel .40 1.00
DMEL1 Eddie Lacy .40 1.00
DMGB1 Giovani Bernard .40 1.00
DMGS1 Geno Smith .40 1.00
DMJF1 Jonathan Franklin .40 1.00
DMJH1 Justin Hunter .40 1.00
DMJR1 Joseph Randle .40 1.00
DMKA1 Keenan Allen .75 2.00
DMLJ1 Landry Jones .40 1.00
DMMB1 Matt Barkley .40 1.00
DMMB2 Montee Ball .40 1.00
DMMG1 Mike Glennon .40 1.00
DMML1 Marcus Lattimore .40 1.00
DMMT1 Manti Te'o .50 1.25
DMRN1 Ryan Nassib .40 1.00
DMTA1 Tavon Austin .50 1.25
DMTB1 Tyler Bray .40 1.00
DMTE1 Tyler Eifert .40 1.00
DMTW1 Tyler Wilson .40 1.00
DMZD1 Zac Dysert .40 1.00

2018 Leaf Flash Autographs
*BLUE/50: .5X TO 1.2X BASIC AU/99
*PURPLE/25: .6X TO 1.5X BASIC AU/99
*GREEN/15: .8X TO 2X BASIC AU/99
BAAK1 Arden Key 4.00 10.00
BAAL1 Allen Lazard 4.00 10.00
BAAM1 Anthony Miller 6.00 15.00
BAAT1 Auden Tate 4.00 10.00
BAAW1 Akrum Wadley 4.00 10.00
BABB1 Braxton Berrios 4.00 10.00
BABM1 Baker Mayfield 40.00 80.00
BABS1 Bo Scarbrough 5.00 12.00
BACD1 Carlton Davis 5.00 12.00
BACK1 Christian Kirk 6.00 15.00
BACR1 Calvin Ridley 10.00 25.00
BACS1 Courtland Sutton 6.00 15.00
BACS2 Cam Serigne 4.00 10.00
BACW1 Cedrick Wilson Jr. 4.00 10.00
BADB1 Deontay Burnett 5.00 12.00
BADC1 Deon Cain 5.00 12.00
BADG1 Derrius Guice 8.00 20.00
BADG2 DeAndre Goolsby 4.00 10.00
BADG3 Dallas Goedert 5.00 12.00
BADJC D.J. Chark 5.00 12.00
BADJM D.J. Moore EXCH 8.00 20.00
BADP1 Dante Pettis 6.00 15.00
BADRP Daron Payne 6.00 15.00
BADS2 Durham Smythe 4.00 10.00
BADS3 Dalton Schultz 5.00 12.00
BADW1 Denzel Ward 10.00 25.00
BAHH1 Hayden Hurst 5.00 12.00
BAIS1 Ito Smith 5.00 12.00
BAIT1 Ian Thomas EXCH 4.00 10.00
BAJA1 Josh Allen 15.00 40.00
BAJA2 Josh Adams 8.00 20.00
BAJJ1 Justin Jackson 5.00 12.00
BAJK1 John Kelly 5.00 12.00
BAJMM J'Mon Moore 4.00 10.00
BAJR1 Josh Rosen 12.00 30.00
BAJTB J.T. Barrett 6.00 15.00
BAJW1 Jake Wieneke 5.00 12.00
BAJW2 James Washington 8.00 20.00
BAJW3 Javon Wims 4.00 10.00
BAKR1 Kurt Benkert 5.00 12.00
BAKC1 Keke Coutee 5.00 12.00
BAKH1 Kenny Hill 5.00 12.00
BAKJ1 Kerryon Johnson 6.00 15.00
BALF1 Luke Falk 5.00 12.00
BALW1 Logan Woodside 6.00 15.00
BAMA2 Marcell Ateman 5.00 12.00
BAMB1 Marcus Baugh 4.00 10.00
BAMC1 Martez Carter 4.00 10.00
BAMF1 Minkah Fitzpatrick 8.00 20.00
BAMG1 Michael Gallup 8.00 20.00
BAMG2 Mike Gesicki 5.00 12.00
BAMH1 Maurice Hurst 5.00 12.00
BAMR1 Mason Rudolph 10.00 25.00
BAMW1 Mark Walton 5.00 12.00
BAMW2 Mike White 5.00 12.00
BANC1 Nick Chubb 12.00 30.00
BAQF1 Quinton Flowers 4.00 10.00
DARF1 Royce Freeman 5.00 12.00
BARF2 Riley Ferguson 6.00 15.00
BARH1 Ronnie Harrison 5.00 12.00
BARJ2 Ronald Jones II 4.00 10.00
BARP1 Rashaad Penny EXCH 6.00 15.00
BARS1 Roquan Smith 12.00 30.00
BARW1 Ralph Webb 5.00 12.00
BASC1 Simmie Cobbs Jr. 6.00 15.00
BASD1 Sam Darnold 25.00 60.00
BASH1 Sam Hubbard 5.00 12.00
BASM1 Sony Michel 12.00 30.00
BATF1 Troy Fumagalli 5.00 12.00
BATT1 Trenton Thompson 4.00 10.00
BAVV1 Vita Vea 6.00 15.00

2018 Leaf Flash Flash Photography Autographs
*BLUE/50: .5X TO 1.2X BASIC AU/99
*PURPLE/25: .6X TO 1.5X BASIC AU/99
*GREEN/15: .8X TO 2X BASIC AU/99
FPCK1 Christian Kirk 6.00 15.00
FPCR1 Calvin Ridley 10.00 25.00
FPDG1 Derrius Guice 8.00 20.00
FPDW1 Denzel Ward 10.00 25.00
FPMF1 Minkah Fitzpatrick 8.00 20.00
FPMR1 Mason Rudolph 10.00 25.00
FPNC1 Nick Chubb 12.00 30.00
FPRP1 Rashaad Penny EXCH 6.00 15.00
FPSD1 Sam Darnold 25.00 60.00
FPSM1 Sony Michel 12.00 30.00

2018 Leaf Flash Flashbacks Autographs
*BLUE/25: .5X TO 1.2X BASIC AU/49
FCE1 Carl Eller 5.00 12.00
FEC1 Earl Campbell 8.00 20.00
FGB1 Gary Beban 5.00 12.00
FJL1 Jim Langer 5.00 12.00
FJM1 Johnny Manziel 10.00 25.00
FJO1 Jim Otto 5.00 12.00
FJR1 Jerry Rice 30.00 60.00
FLM1 Lenny Moore 5.00 12.00
FTB1 Terry Bradshaw
FYAT Y.A. Tittle 8.00 20.00

2019 Leaf Flash Autographs
BAAB1 Alex Barnes 2.50 6.00
BAAI1 Andy Isabella 3.00 8.00
BAAJB A.J. Brown EXCH 5.00 12.00
BAAO1 Amani Oruwariye 2.50 6.00
BAARW Anthony Ratliff-Williams 4.00 10.00
BAAW1 Antoine Wesley 2.00 5.00
BAAW2 Aeris Williams 2.50 6.00
BABB3 Brian Burns 2.50 6.00
BABR1 Brett Rypien 2.50 6.00
BABSJ Benny Snell Jr. 10.00 25.00
BACF1 Clelin Ferrell 3.00 8.00
BACT1 Clayton Thorson 3.00 8.00
BACW1 Caleb Wilson 2.00 5.00
BACW3 Chase Winovich 6.00 15.00
BADB1 Deandre Baker 5.00 12.00
BADH1 Damien Harris 5.00 12.00
BADH2 Dwayne Haskins EXCH
BADH3 Darrell Henderson 5.00 12.00
BADJ1 Daniel Jones 15.00 40.00
BADKM D.K. Metcalf 6.00 15.00
BADL1 Drew Lock 10.00 25.00
BADL2 DaMarkus Lodge 2.00 5.00
BADL3 Dexter Lawrence 3.00 8.00
BADM1 David Montgomery EXCH 8.00 20.00
BADS1 Deebo Samuel 5.00 12.00
BADS2 Devin Singletary 2.50 6.00
BADSV David Sills V 6.00 15.00
BADT1 Deionte Thompson EXCH 2.50 6.00
BADW1 Devin White 6.00 15.00
BAEH1 Emanuel Hall 2.00 5.00
BAEH2 Elijah Holyfield 3.00 8.00
BAEO1 Ed Oliver EXCH 3.00 8.00
BAGJJ Gary Jennings Jr. 3.00 8.00
BAGW1 Greedy Williams 6.00 15.00
BAHB1 Hakeem Butler 4.00 10.00
BAIB1 Isaiah Buggs 5.00 12.00
BAISJ Irv Smith Jr. 4.00 10.00
BAJA1 Josh Allen 8.00 20.00
BAJD1 Johnnie Dixon 2.50 6.00
BAJH1 Justice Hill 3.00 8.00
BAJH3 Jalen Hurd 2.50 6.00
BAJJ1 Jalen Jelks 2.50 6.00
BAJJ3 Josh Jacobs 10.00 25.00
BAJJA JJ Arcega-Whiteside 3.00 8.00
BAJP1 Jachai Polite 2.50 6.00
BAJS1 Jarrett Stidham 6.00 15.00
BAJS2 Jeffery Simmons 2.00 5.00
BAJS3 Jace Sternberger 2.50 6.00
BAJS4 Jordan Scarlett 2.00 5.00
BAJS5 Jaylen Smith 2.00 5.00
BAJW1 Jamarius Way 2.50 6.00
BAKH1 Kelvin Harmon 3.00 8.00
BAKH2 Karan Higdon 2.50 6.00
BAKK1 Kyle Kempt 3.00 8.00
BAKM1 Kyler Murray 40.00 80.00
BAKS1 Kaden Smith 2.00 5.00
BAKS2 Kyle Shurmur 4.00 10.00
BAKSJ KeeSean Johnson 2.00 5.00
BALJH Lil'Jordan Humphrey 2.50 6.00
BALJS L.J. Scott 3.00 8.00
BAMB1 Marquise Brown EXCH 6.00 15.00
BAMG3 Myles Gaskin 4.00 10.00
BAMW1 Mike Weber 3.00 8.00
BAMW2 Mack Wilson 2.50 6.00
BANB1 Nick Bosa 6.00 15.00
BANF1 Noah Fant 4.00 10.00
BANKH N'Keal Harry EXCH 6.00 15.00
BAPC1 Parris Campbell EXCH 5.00 12.00
BAQW1 Quinnen Williams EXCH 2.00 5.00
BARA1 Rodney Anderson 2.50 6.00
BARF1 Ryan Finley 4.00 10.00
BARR1 Riley Ridley 3.00 8.00
BATB1 Tyre Brady 2.00 5.00
BATL1 Tre Lamar 3.00 8.00
BAWG1 Will Grier 6.00 15.00
BAZA1 Zach Allen 3.00 8.00

2019 Leaf Flash Autographs Blue
*BLUE/50: .6X TO 1.5X BASIC AU
BAKM1 Kyler Murray 60.00 125.00

2019 Leaf Flash Autographs Pink
*PINK/15: 1X TO 2.5X BASIC AU
BAKM1 Kyler Murray 100.00 200.00

2019 Leaf Flash Autographs Purple
*PURPLE/25: .8X TO 2X BASIC AU
BAKM1 Kyler Murray 90.00 150.00

2019 Leaf Flash Flash of Greatness Autographs
*BLUE/50: .6X TO 1.5X BASIC AU
*GREEN/20: 1X TO 2.5X BASIC AU
*PINK/15: 1X TO 2.5X BASIC AU
*PURPLE/25: .8X TO 2X BASIC AU
FGAJB A.J. Brown EXCH 5.00 12.00
FGDJ1 Daniel Jones 15.00 40.00
FGDL1 Drew Lock 10.00 25.00
FGJJ3 Josh Jacobs 10.00 25.00
FGMB2 Miles Boykin 2.50 6.00
FGMH1 Mecole Hardman 5.00 12.00
FGMS2 Miles Sanders 5.00 12.00
FGTH1 Travis Homer 2.00 5.00
FGTJ1 Tyree Jackson 5.00 12.00
FGTW1 Trayveon Williams 2.50 6.00

2019 Leaf Flash Flash Photography Autographs
FPAJ1 Anthony Johnson 2.50 6.00
FPBSJ Benny Snell Jr. 6.00 15.00
FPDH1 Damien Harris 5.00 12.00
FPDJ2 Diontae Johnson 2.50 6.00
FPDM1 David Montgomery EXCH 8.00 20.00
FPDMJ Dre'Mont Jones 2.50 6.00
FPKM1 Kyler Murray 40.00 80.00
FPSM1 Stanley Morgan Jr 3.00 8.00
FPTM1 Trace McSorley 5.00 12.00

2019 Leaf Flash Flash Photography Autographs Blue
*BLUE/50: .6X TO 1.5X BASIC AU
FPKM1 Kyler Murray 60.00 125.00

2019 Leaf Flash Flash Photography Autographs Green
*GREEN/20: 1X TO 2.5X BASIC AU
FPKM1 Kyler Murray 100.00 200.00

2019 Leaf Flash Flash Photography Autographs Pink
*PINK/15: 1X TO 2.5X BASIC AU
FPKM1 Kyler Murray 100.00 200.00

2019 Leaf Flash Flash Photography Autographs Purple
*PURPLE/25: .8X TO 2X BASIC AU
FPKM1 Kyler Murray 90.00 150.00

2011 Leaf Metal Draft
UNPRICED GOLD PRINT RUN 1
UNPRICED RED PRINT RUN 5
RCAA1 Anthony Allen 3.00 8.00
RCAB1 Armon Binns 4.00 10.00
RCAD1 Andy Dalton 12.00 30.00
RCAJG A.J. Green 20.00 50.00
RCAP1 Austin Pettis 3.00 8.00
RCAS1 Aldon Smith 3.00 8.00
RCAW1 Aaron Williams 3.00 8.00
RCBG1 Blaine Gabbert 3.00 8.00
RCBP1 Bilal Powell 4.00 10.00
RCCH1 Cameron Heyward 4.00 10.00
RCCK1 Colin Kaepernick 5.00 12.00
RCCM1 Casey Matthews 3.00 8.00
RCCN1 Cam Newton 15.00 40.00
RCCP1 Christian Ponder 3.00 8.00
RCDA1 Darvin Adams 3.00 8.00
RCDB1 Damien Berry 4.00 10.00
RCDC1 Delone Carter 3.00 8.00
RCDH1 Dwayne Harris 3.00 8.00
RCDJW D.J. Williams 3.00 8.00
RCDL1 Derrick Locke 4.00 10.00
RCDL2 Dion Lewis 4.00 10.00
RCDM1 DeMarco Murray 6.00 15.00
RCDQB Da'Quan Bowers 3.00 8.00
RCDT1 Daniel Thomas 3.00 8.00
RCER1 Evan Royster 3.00 8.00
RCGC1 Graig Cooper 4.00 10.00
RCGL1 Greg Little 4.00 10.00
RCGM1 Greg McElroy 5.00 12.00
RCGS1 Greg Salas 3.00 8.00
RCJB1 Jonathan Baldwin 3.00 8.00
RCJC1 John Clay 5.00 12.00
RCJH1 Jamie Harper 3.00 8.00
RCJH2 Justin Houston 4.00 10.00
RCJJ1 Jerrel Jernigan 3.00 8.00
RCJJ2 Julio Jones 25.00 50.00
RCJJW J.J. Watt 35.00 60.00
RCJL1 Jake Locker 3.00 8.00
RCJT1 Jordan Todman 3.00 8.00
RCKH1 Kendall Hunter 3.00 8.00
RCKR1 Kyle Rudolph 3.00 8.00
RCLH1 Leonard Hankerson 3.00 8.00
RCLS1 Luke Stocker 3.00 8.00
RCMD1 Marcell Dareus 3.00 8.00
RCMH1 Mark Herzlich 3.00 8.00
RCMI1 Mark Ingram 5.00 12.00
RCML1 Mikel Leshoure 3.00 8.00
RCNE1 Nathan Enderle 3.00 8.00
RCNF1 Nick Fairley 3.00 8.00
RCNP1 Niles Paul 3.00 8.00
RCPA1 Prince Amukamara 3.00 8.00
RCPD1 Pat Devlin 5.00 12.00
RCRC1 Randall Cobb 5.00 12.00
RCRH1 Roy Helu 3.00 8.00
RCRJ1 Ronald Johnson 3.00 8.00
RCRM1 Ryan Mallett SP 3.00 8.00
RCRQ1 Robert Quinn 8.00 20.00
RCRS1 Ricky Stanzi 3.00 8.00
RCRW1 Ryan Williams 10.00 25.00
RCSR1 Stevan Ridley 3.00 8.00
RCSV1 Shane Vereen 4.00 10.00
RCTD1 Tandon Doss 3.00 8.00
RCTJY T.J. Yates 3.00 8.00
RCTS1 Torrey Smith 3.00 8.00
RCTI1 Terrence Toliver 4.00 10.00
RCTT2 Tyrod Taylor 6.00 15.00
RCTY1 Titus Young 3.00 8.00
RCVB1 Vincent Brown 3.00 8.00
RCVM1 Von Miller 8.00 20.00
RCWB1 Wes Bynum 3.00 8.00

2011 Leaf Metal Draft Prismatic Blue
*BLUE/25: .6X TO 1.5X BASIC AUTO
BLUE STATED PRINT RUN 25

2011 Leaf Metal Draft Prismatic Silver
*SILVER/50: .5X TO 1.2X BASIC AUTO
SILVER STATED PRINT RUN 50

2011 Leaf Metal Draft All-Americans
ATED PRINT RUN 50 SER.#'d SETS
UNPRICED BLUE PRINT RUN 10
UNPRICED GOLD PRINT RUN 1
UNPRICED RED PRINT RUN 5
*SILVER/25: .5X TO 1.2X BASIC INSERTS
AAAJG A.J. Green 20.00 50.00
AADM1 DeMarco Murray 8.00 20.00
AADQB Da'Quan Bowers 4.00 10.00
AAJJ2 Julio Jones 20.00 50.00
AAJL1 Jake Locker 4.00 10.00
AAMD1 Marcell Dareus 4.00 10.00
AAMI1 Mark Ingram 6.00 15.00
AAML1 Mikel Leshoure 4.00 10.00
AANF1 Nick Fairley 4.00 10.00
AARM1 Ryan Mallett 4.00 10.00

2011 Leaf Metal Draft Touchdown Kings
ATED PRINT RUN 50 SER.#'d SETS
UNPRICED BLUE PRINT RUN 10
UNPRICED GOLD PRINT RUN 1
UNPRICED RED PRINT RUN 5
*SILVER/25: .5X TO 1.2X BASIC INSERTS
TKAJG A.J. Green 25.00 50.00
TKDM1 DeMarco Murray 8.00 20.00
TKJB1 Jonathan Baldwin 4.00 10.00
TKJC1 John Clay 6.00 15.00
TKJJ2 Julio Jones 25.00 50.00
TKJT1 Jordan Todman 4.00 10.00
TKLH1 Leonard Hankerson 4.00 10.00
TKMI1 Mark Ingram 6.00 15.00
TKML1 Mikel Leshoure 4.00 10.00
TKSV1 Shane Vereen 5.00 12.00
TKTS1 Torrey Smith 4.00 10.00

2011 Leaf Metal Draft Young Guns
STATED PRINT RUN 50 SER.#'d SETS
UNPRICED BLUE PRINT RUN 10
UNPRICED GOLD PRINT RUN 1
UNPRICED RED PRINT RUN 5
*SILVER/25: .5X TO 1.2X BASIC INSERTS
YGAD1 Andy Dalton 15.00 40.00
YGBG1 Blaine Gabbert 4.00 10.00
YGCK1 Colin Kaepernick 6.00 15.00
YGCN1 Cam Newton 20.00 50.00
YGCP1 Christian Ponder 4.00 10.00
YGJL1 Jake Locker 4.00 10.00
YGNE1 Nathan Enderle 4.00 10.00
YGPD1 Pat Devlin 6.00 15.00
YGRM1 Ryan Mallett 4.00 10.00

2012 Leaf Metal Draft
AB1 Andre Branch 3.00 8.00
AC1 Aaron Corp 3.00 8.00
AD1 Alfonzo Dennard 3.00 8.00
AJ1 Alshon Jeffery 6.00 15.00
AJJ A.J. Jenkins 3.00 8.00
BJC B.J. Cunningham 3.00 8.00
BO1 Brock Osweiler 3.00 8.00
BP1 Bernard Pierce 3.00 8.00
BQ1 Brian Quick 3.00 8.00
BT1 Brandon Thompson 4.00 10.00
BW1 Brandon Weeden 6.00 15.00
CF1 Coby Fleener 3.00 8.00
CG1 Chris Givens 3.00 8.00
CG2 Cyrus Gray 3.00 8.00
CH1 Chandler Harnish 3.00 8.00
CJ1 Chandler Jones 3.00 8.00
CK1 Case Keenum 6.00 15.00
CP1 Chris Polk 3.00 8.00
CU1 Courtney Upshaw 4.00 10.00
DA1 Dwayne Allen 3.00 8.00
DH1 Dan Herron 3.00 8.00
DH2 Dont'a Hightower 5.00 12.00
DK1 Dre Kirkpatrick 3.00 8.00
DM2 Doug Martin 5.00 12.00
DP1 Dan Persa 4.00 10.00
DP2 DeVier Posey 3.00 8.00
DS1 Devon Still 4.00 10.00
DT1 Darron Thomas 8.00 20.00
GR1 Gerell Robinson 3.00 8.00
IP1 Isaiah Pead 3.00 8.00
JA1 Joe Adams 3.00 8.00
JB2 Justin Blackmon 3.00 8.00
JC1 Jared Crick 3.00 8.00
JC2 Juron Criner 3.00 8.00
JF1 Jeff Fuller 3.00 8.00
JH1 Jacory Harris 4.00 10.00
JW1 Jarius Wright 3.00 8.00
KC1 Kirk Cousins 12.00 30.00
KM1 Kellen Moore 4.00 10.00
KM2 Keshawn Martin 4.00 10.00
KR1 Keenan Robinson 4.00 10.00
KW1 Kendall Wright 3.00 8.00
LD1 Lavonte David 5.00 12.00
LJ1 LaMichael James 3.00 8.00
LK1 Luke Kuechly 8.00 20.00
LM1 Lamar Miller 5.00 12.00
MB1 Mark Barron 3.00 8.00
ME1 Michael Egnew 3.00 8.00
MF1 Michael Floyd 3.00 8.00
MI1 Melvin Ingram 3.00 8.00
MJ1 Marvin Jones 3.00 8.00
MK1 Matt Kalil 3.00 8.00
MM1 Marquis Maze 3.00 8.00
MS1 Mohamed Sanu 5.00 12.00
MT1 Marc Tyler 3.00 8.00
NF1 Nick Foles 8.00 20.00
NP1 Nick Perry 4.00 10.00
NT1 Nick Toon 3.00 8.00
OC1 Orson Charles 3.00 8.00
QC1 Quinton Coples 3.00 8.00
RB1 Ryan Broyles 3.00 8.00
RG3 Robert Griffin III 4.00 10.00
RL2 Ryan Lindley 3.00 8.00
RR1 Rueben Randle 3.00 8.00
RT1 Robert Turbin 3.00 8.00
RT2 Ryan Tannehill 5.00 12.00
RW1 Russell Wilson 30.00 80.00
SG1 Stephon Gilmore 4.00 10.00
SH1 Stephen Hill 3.00 8.00
TG1 Terrance Ganaway 4.00 10.00
TL1 Travis Lewis 4.00 10.00
TP1 Tauren Poole 3.00 8.00
TR1 Trent Richardson 3.00 8.00
TS1 Tommy Streeter 3.00 8.00
TYH T.Y. Hilton 6.00 15.00
WM1 Whitney Mercilus 3.00 8.00
ZB1 Zach Brown 3.00 8.00

2012 Leaf Metal Draft Prismatic Blue
*PRISM BLUE/25: .6X TO 1.5X BASIC AU
RG3 Robert Griffin III 6.00 15.00
RW1 Russell Wilson 60.00 120.00

2012 Leaf Metal Draft Prismatic Purple
*PRISM PURPLE/25: .6X TO 1.5X BASIC AU
RG3 Robert Griffin III 6.00 15.00
RW1 Russell Wilson 75.00 150.00

2012 Leaf Metal Draft Prismatic Silver
RISM SILVER/99: .5X TO 1.2X BASIC AU

2012 Leaf Metal Draft Army All-American Bowl Prismatic Silver
AUTO STATED PRINT RUN 50
*BASE LUCK: .1X TO .3X SLVR/99
*PRISM PRPL LUCK/25: 1X TO 2.5X SLVR/99
*PRISM BLUE LUCK/25: 1X TO 2.5X SLVR/99
*PRISM GREEN AU/25: .5X TO 1.2X SLVR/50
ATAAA1 Anthony Alford AU 6.00 15.00
ATAAA2 Arik Armstead AU 10.00 25.00
ATABM1 Byron Marshall AU 8.00 20.00
ATABS1 Barry Sanders Jr. AU 50.00 100.00
ATACM1 Cyler Miles AU 10.00 25.00
ATADF1 Devin Fuller AU 6.00 15.00
ATADGB Dorial Green-Beckham AU 30.00 60.00
ATADN1 Durron Neal AU 10.00 25.00
ATADS1 Dwayne Stanford AU 8.00 20.00
ATADW2 Derrick Woods AU 8.00 20.00
ATAGH1 Germone Hopper AU 8.00 20.00
ATAGK1 Gunner Kiel AU 40.00 80.00
ATAJC1 Joel Caleb AU 10.00 25.00
ATAJP1 Jordan Payton AU 10.00 25.00
ATAKR1 Kei'Varae Russell AU 10.00 25.00
ATAKT1 Kent Taylor AU 10.00 25.00
ATASD1 Stefon Diggs AU 20.00 50.00
ATATJY T.J. Yeldon AU 20.00 50.00
ATATM1 Tyler Matthews AU 10.00 25.00
BAL1 Andrew Luck/99 40.00 80.00

2013 Leaf Metal Draft
BAAE1 Andre Ellington 6.00 15.00
BAAM2 Aaron Mellette 3.00 8.00
BAAO1 Alex Okafor 3.00 8.00
BABM1 Barkevious Mingo 3.00 8.00
RABS1 Brad Sorensen 3.00 8.00
BABW1 Bjoern Werner 3.00 8.00
BACH1 Cobi Hamilton 3.00 8.00
BACK1 Collin Klein SP 4.00 10.00
BACP2 Cordarrelle Patterson 3.00 8.00
BACV1 Conner Vernon 3.00 8.00
BACW2 Cierre Wood 3.00 8.00
BADA1 David Amerson 3.00 8.00
BADAH DeAndre Hopkins 8.00 20.00
BADM1 Dee Milliner 3.00 8.00
BADR1 Denard Robinson 3.00 8.00
BADRR Da'Rick Rogers 3.00 8.00
BADS1 Dion Sims 3.00 8.00
BAEJM EJ Manuel 3.00 8.00
BAEL1 Eddie Lacy SP 3.00 8.00
BAER1 Eric Reid 4.00 10.00
BAGB1 Giovani Bernard 3.00 8.00
BAGS1 Geno Smith 3.00 8.00
DAJB2 Josh Buyce 3.00 8.00
BAJF1 Joseph Fauria 3.00 8.00
BAJF2 Johnathan Franklin 3.00 8.00
BAJH1 Justin Hunter 3.00 8.00
BAJH2 Johnathan Hankins SP 3.00 8.00
BAJJ4 Jarvis Jones SP 3.00 8.00
BAJR1 Joseph Randle 3.00 8.00
BAJR2 Jordan Reed 5.00 12.00
BAJS1 Jake Stoneburner 5.00 12.00
BAJW2 Jesse Williams 5.00 12.00
BAKA1 Keenan Allen 6.00 15.00
BAKB1 Kenjon Barner 3.00 8.00
BAKS1 Kawann Short 3.00 8.00
BAKS2 Kenny Stills 3.00 8.00
BALJ1 Landry Jones SP 3.00 8.00
BALT2 Levine Toilolo 4.00 10.00
BALVB Le'Veon Bell 10.00 25.00
BAMB1 Matt Barkley SP 6.00 15.00
BAMB2 Montee Ball 3.00 8.00
BAMD1 Marcus Davis 3.00 8.00
BAMG1 Mike Gillislee 3.00 8.00
BAMG2 Mike Glennon 3.00 8.00
BAMG3 Marquise Goodwin 3.00 8.00
BAML1 Marcus Lattimore 3.00 8.00
BAMM1 Miguel Maysonet 3.00 8.00
BAMT1 Manti Te'o 4.00 10.00
BAMW2 Michael Williams 4.00 10.00
BAQP1 Quinton Patton 3.00 8.00
BARB1 Rex Burkhead 4.00 10.00
BARG1 Ray Graham 3.00 8.00
BARN1 Ryan Nassib 3.00 8.00
BARS2 Rodney Smith 3.00 8.00
BARS3 Ryan Swope 3.00 8.00
BARW1 Robert Woods SP 5.00 12.00
BASF1 Sharrif Floyd 3.00 8.00
BASL1 Star Lotulelei 4.00 10.00
BAST1 Steptan Taylor 3.00 8.00
BATA1 Tavon Austin 4.00 10.00
BATB1 Tyler Bray 15.00 30.00
BATE1 Tyler Eifert 3.00 8.00
BATJ1 Tony Jefferson 5.00 12.00
BATJM T.J. McDonald 3.00 8.00
BATM1 Tyrann Mathieu 5.00 12.00
BATW1 Tyler Wilson SP 3.00 8.00
BATW2 Terrance Williams 3.00 8.00
BAZD1 Zac Dysert 3.00 8.00
BAZL1 Zach Line 3.00 8.00
NNO Johnny Manziel Art AU 40.00 80.00

2013 Leaf Metal Draft Prismatic Silver
*PRISM SILVER/99: .5X TO 1.2X BASIC AU

2013 Leaf Metal Draft All-American
RISM BLUE/25: .6X TO 1.5X BASIC AA AU
*PRISM SLVR/50: .5X TO 1.2X BASIC AA AU
AABW1 Bjoern Werner 3.00 8.00
AAEL1 Eddie Lacy 3.00 8.00
AAGS1 Geno Smith 3.00 8.00
AAJH2 Johnathan Hankins 3.00 8.00
AAJJ4 Jarvis Jones 6.00 15.00
AAKA1 Keenan Allen 6.00 15.00
AALJ1 Landry Jones 3.00 8.00
AAMB1 Matt Barkley 6.00 15.00
AAML1 Marcus Lattimore 3.00 8.00
AARW1 Robert Woods 5.00 12.00
AASL1 Star Lotulelei 4.00 10.00
AATE1 Tyler Eifert 3.00 8.00
AATW2 Terrance Williams 3.00 8.00

2013 Leaf Metal Draft Army All-American Bowl
*PRISM BLUE/15: .5X TO 1.2X BASIC AU
*PRISM SILVER/25: .5X TO 1.2X BASIC AU
ATAAF1 Ahmad Fulwood 6.00 15.00
ATAASR A'Shawn Robinson 5.00 12.00
ATAAW1 Asiantii Woulard 6.00 15.00
ATADG1 Derrick Green 12.00 30.00
ATADG2 Derrick Griffin UER 8.00 20.00
ATADH1 Derrick Henry 20.00 50.00
ATADMR DeMarcus Robinson 5.00 12.00
ATAGB1 Greg Bryant 6.00 15.00
ATAHR1 Hayden Rettig 8.00 20.00
ATAJD1 Justin Davis 10.00 25.00
ATAJD2 John Diarse 6.00 15.00
ATAJHB1 Jake Butt 6.00 15.00
ATAJM1 Johnathon McCrary 6.00 15.00
ATAJO1 Jake Oliver 6.00 15.00
ATAJQ1 James Quick 8.00 20.00
ATAJR1 Jalen Ramsey 12.00 30.00
ATAJS1 Jaylon Smith 8.00 20.00
ATAMB1 Max Browne 12.00 30.00
ATAMN1 Marquez North 10.00 25.00
ATARSJ Ricky Seals-Jones 10.00 25.00
ATASC1 Su'a Cravens 5.00 12.00
ATASM1 Steven Mitchell 6.00 15.00
ATATH1 Torii Hunter 8.00 20.00
ATATJ1 Tyren Jones 8.00 20.00
ATATS1 Tyrone Swoopes 8.00 20.00
ATATT1 Thomas Tyner 12.00 30.00

2013 Leaf Metal Draft Future Stars
*PRISM BLUE/15: .6X TO 1.5X BASIC AA AU
*PRISM SLVR/25: .5X TO 1.2X BASIC AA AU
FSCK1 Collin Klein 5.00 12.00
FSDRR Da'Rick Rogers 4.00 10.00
FSGS1 Geno Smith 4.00 10.00
FSJH1 Justin Hunter 4.00 10.00
FSLJ1 Landry Jones 4.00 10.00
FSMB1 Matt Barkley 8.00 20.00
FSRW1 Robert Woods 6.00 15.00
FSTW1 Tyler Wilson 4.00 10.00
FSTW2 Terrance Williams 4.00 10.00

2013 Leaf Metal Draft State Pride
*PRISM BLUE/25: .6X TO 1.5X BASIC AA AU
*PRISM SLVR/50: .5X TO 1.2X BASIC AA AU
SPAE1 Andre Ellington 4.00 10.00
SPBM1 Barkevious Mingo 4.00 10.00
SPBW1 Bjoern Werner 4.00 10.00
SPCH1 Cobi Hamilton 4.00 10.00
SPCK1 Collin Klein SP 5.00 12.00
SPDR1 Denard Robinson 4.00 10.00
SPDRR Da'Rick Rogers 4.00 10.00
SPEJM EJ Manuel 4.00 10.00
SPEL1 Eddie Lacy 4.00 10.00
SPJF2 Johnathan Franklin 4.00 10.00
SPJH1 Justin Hunter 4.00 10.00
SPKB1 Kenjon Barner 4.00 10.00
SPMB2 Montee Ball 4.00 10.00
SPMG2 Mike Glennon 4.00 10.00
SPRG1 Ray Graham 4.00 10.00
SPTA1 Tavon Austin 5.00 12.00
SPTB1 Tyler Bray 4.00 10.00
SPTW1 Tyler Wilson SP 4.00 10.00

2014 Leaf Metal Draft
BAAB1 Anthony Barr 2.50 6.00
BAAJ1 Anthony Johnson 2.50 6.00
BAAJM A.J. McCarron SP 3.00 8.00
BAAM1 Aaron Murray SP 3.00 8.00
BAAR1 Allen Robinson SP 5.00 12.00
BAASJ Austin Seferian-Jenkins 2.50 6.00
BAAW1 Andre Williams 2.50 6.00
BABB1 Blake Bortles 25.00 50.00
BABC1 Brandin Cooks 4.00 10.00
BABC2 Brandon Coleman 2.50 6.00
BABR1 Bradley Roby 5.00 12.00
BABS1 Bishop Sankey SP 10.00 25.00
BABS2 Brett Smith 2.50 6.00
BACH1 Carlos Hyde 3.00 8.00
BACJM C.J. Mosley 3.00 8.00
BACK1 Cyrus Kouandjio 3.00 8.00
BACS1 Charles Sims 2.50 6.00
BADAT De'Anthony Thomas SP 3.00 8.00
BADC1 Derek Carr SP 20.00 50.00
BADF1 David Fales 2.50 6.00
BADM1 Donte Moncrief 2.50 6.00
BADS1 Devin Street 2.50 6.00
BADW1 Damien Williams 2.50 6.00
BAEE1 Eric Ebron SP 4.00 10.00
BAHCD Ha Ha Clinton-Dix SP 4.00 10.00
BAIC1 Isaiah Crowell 3.00 8.00
BAJA1 Jace Amaro 2.50 6.00
BAJA2 Jared Abbrederis 2.50 6.00
BAJC1 Jadeveon Clowney 3.00 8.00
BAJG1 Jimmy Garoppolo 40.00 80.00
BAJH1 Josh Huff 6.00 15.00
BAJL1 Jarvis Landry 5.00 12.00
BAJM1 Jake Matthews 5.00 12.00
BAJM2 Johnny Manziel SP 5.00 12.00
BAJM3 Jordan Matthews 4.00 10.00
BAJWJ James Wilder Jr. 3.00 8.00
BAKB1 Kelvin Benjamin 4.00 10.00
BAKDC Ka'Deem Carey SP 3.00 8.00
BALN3 Louis Nix III 2.50 6.00
BALS1 Lache Seastrunk 2.50 6.00
BALT1 Logan Thomas 2.50 6.00
BAMD1 Mike Davis 2.50 6.00
BAME1 Mike Evans SP 8.00 20.00
BAMG1 Marion Grice 4.00 10.00
BAML1 Marqise Lee SP 8.00 20.00
BAOBJ Odell Beckham Jr. 30.00 60.00
BAPR1 Paul Richardson 5.00 12.00
BASM1 Stephen Morris 2.50 6.00
BASR1 Silas Redd SP 4.00 10.00
BASW1 Sammy Watkins 4.00 10.00
BATB1 Tajh Boyd SP 3.00 8.00
BATB2 Teddy Bridgewater SP 30.00 60.00
BATJ1 Timmy Jernigan 2.50 6.00
BATL1 Taylor Lewan 2.50 6.00
BATM1 Tre Mason SP 12.00 30.00
BAZM1 Zach Mettenberger SP 3.00 8.00

2014 Leaf Metal Draft Prismatic Blue
*BLUE/50: .6X TO 1.5X BASIC AUTO
*BLUE/50: .5X TO 1.2X SP AUTO

2014 Leaf Metal Draft Prismatic Green
*GREEN/10: 1X TO 2.5X BASIC AUTO
*GREEN/10: .8X TO 2X SP AUTO
BABB1 Blake Bortles 8.00 20.00

2014 Leaf Metal Draft Prismatic Purple
*PURPLE/25: .8X TO 2X BASIC AUTO
*PURPLE/25: .6X TO 1.5X SP AUTO

2014 Leaf Metal Draft Army All-American Bowl
*BLUE/20: .5X TO 1.2X BASIC INSERTS
*GREEN/10: .6X TO 1.5X BASIC INSERTS
*PURPLE/15: .4X TO 1X BASIC INSERTS
ATAAL1 Allen Lazard 4.00 10.00
ATACH2 Caleb Henderson 4.00 10.00
ATADB1 Drew Barker 10.00 25.00
ATADJ1 Demetrius Johnson 4.00 10.00
ATADK1 Demarre Kitt 5.00 12.00
ATAEH1 Elijah Hood 10.00 25.00
ATAJB1 Jalen Brown 5.00 12.00
ATAJD1 Johnnie Dixon 6.00 15.00
ATAJH2 Jalen Hurd 15.00 40.00
ATAJH3 Jerrod Heard 6.00 15.00
ATAJK1 Jamil Kamara 4.00 10.00
ATAJM4 Josh Malone 6.00 15.00
ATAKA1 Kyle Allen 12.00 30.00
ATAKDC KD Cannon 5.00 12.00
ATANS1 Nathan Starks 5.00 12.00
ATASM2 Sony Michel 8.00 20.00
ATAWG1 Will Grier 10.00 25.00

2014 Leaf Metal Draft Award Winners
*SINGLES: .4X TO 1X BASIC AU

2014 Leaf Metal Draft State Pride
*SINGLES: .4X TO 1X BASIC AU
SPAR1 Allen Robinson 5.00 12.00
SPBS1 Bishop Sankey 3.00 8.00
SPDAT De'Anthony Thomas 3.00 8.00
SPEE1 Eric Ebron 4.00 10.00
SPJC1 Jadeveon Clowney 4.00 10.00
SPJM2 Johnny Manziel 5.00 12.00
SPKDC Ka'Deem Carey 3.00 8.00
SPME1 Mike Evans 8.00 20.00
SPML1 Marqise Lee 4.00 10.00
SPSW1 Sammy Watkins 5.00 12.00
SPTB2 Teddy Bridgewater 25.00 50.00

2014 Leaf Metal Draft '13 Leaf Metal
*SINGLES: .4X TO 1X BASIC METAL AU

2014 Leaf Metal Draft '13 Metal State Pride
*SINGLES: .4X TO 1X BASIC AU
SPAM1 Aaron Murray 3.00 8.00
SPTB2 Tajh Boyd

2014 Leaf Metal Draft '13 Valiant On Target
*SINGLES: .4X TO 1X BASIC AU

2014 Leaf Metal Draft '13 Valiant Stars
*SINGLES: .4X TO 1X BASIC AU

2015 Leaf Metal Draft
BAAA1 Ameer Abdullah 4.00 10.00
BAAC1 Amari Cooper 25.00 50.00
BAAD1 Alvin Dupree 3.00 8.00
BAAG1 Antwan Goodley 2.50 6.00
BAAH1 Austin Hill 2.50 6.00
BABB1 Brandon Bridge 2.50 6.00
BABH1 Brett Hundley SP 3.00 8.00
BABK1 Ben Koyack 4.00 10.00
BABM1 Benardrick McKinney 2.50 6.00
BABP1 Bryce Petty SP 3.00 8.00
BABS1 Blake Sims 2.50 6.00
BABW1 Bo Wallace 2.50 6.00
BACAP Cameron Artis-Payne 2.50 6.00
BACF1 Cody Fajardo 3.00 8.00
BACW1 Clive Walford 2.50 6.00
BADC1 David Cobb 2.50 6.00
BADF1 Devin Funchess 4.00 10.00
BADF2 Dante Fowler Jr. 4.00 10.00
BADGB Dorial Green-Beckham 2.50 6.00
BADH1 Danielle Hunter 3.00 8.00
BADJ1 Duke Johnson 4.00 10.00
BADJ2 David Johnson 6.00 15.00
BADP1 DeVante Parker 4.00 10.00
BADP3 Denzel Perryman 2.50 6.00
BADS1 Danny Shelton 2.50 6.00
BAEG1 Eddie Goldman 2.50 6.00
BAEJB E.J. Bibbs 3.00 8.00
BAGG1 Garrett Grayson 2.50 6.00
BAIEO Ifo Ekpre-Olomu 2.50 6.00
BAJA1 Jay Ajayi 4.00 10.00
BAJA2 Javorius Allen 3.00 8.00
BAJH1 Josh Harper 2.50 6.00
BAJH2 Justin Hardy 2.50 6.00
BAJH3 Jeff Heuerman 3.00 8.00
BAJJ1 Jesse James 3.00 8.00
BAJL1 Jeremy Langford 2.50 6.00
BAJS1 Jaelen Strong 3.00 8.00
BAJW1 Jameis Winston SP 75.00 125.00
BAKB1 Kenny Bell 4.00 10.00
BAKJ1 Kevin Johnson 2.50 6.00
BAKW1 Kasen Williams 4.00 10.00
BAKW2 Kevin White 12.00 30.00
BAKW3 Karlos Williams 2.50 6.00
BALC1 Landon Collins 3.00 8.00
BAMB1 Malcolm Brown 3.00 8.00
BAMD1 Mike Davis 2.50 6.00
BAMG1 Melvin Gordon SP 25.00 50.00
BAMG2 Markus Golden 2.50 6.00
BAMJ1 Matt Jones 2.50 6.00
BAMM1 Marcus Mariota SP 40.00 80.00
BAMP1 Marcus Peters 4.00 10.00
DANA1 Nelson Agholor 3.00 8.00
BANO1 Nick O'Leary 2.50 6.00
BAPD1 Phillip Dorsett 2.50 6.00
BAPJW P.J. Williams 3.00 8.00
BARG1 Rashad Greene 2.50 6.00
BARG2 Randy Gregory 2.50 6.00
BASC1 Sammie Coates 3.00 8.00
BASC2 Shane Carden 2.50 6.00
BASD1 Stefon Diggs 6.00 15.00
BASM1 Sean Mannion 2.50 6.00
BASR1 Shane Ray 2.50 6.00
BAST1 Shaq Thompson 3.00 8.00
BATC1 Tevin Coleman 3.00 8.00
BATG1 Todd Gurley SP 25.00 60.00
BATJY T.J. Yeldon SP 3.00 8.00
BATK1 Tyler Kroft 3.00 8.00
BATL1 Tyler Lockett 4.00 10.00
BATL2 Tony Lippett 2.50 6.00
BATM1 Ty Montgomery 2.50 6.00
BATW1 Trae Waynes 2.50 6.00
BAVB1 Vic Beasley 3.00 8.00
BAVM1 Vince Mayle 3.00 8.00

2015 Leaf Metal Draft Prismatic Blue
*BLUE/35-50: .5X TO 1.2X BASIC AU
*BLUE/25: .6X TO 1.5X BASIC AU
BAJW1 Jameis Winston/50 40.00 80.00
BAMG1 Melvin Gordon/25 30.00 80.00
BAMM1 Marcus Mariota/50 40.00 80.00

2015 Leaf Metal Draft Prismatic Purple
*PURPLE/25: .6X TO 1.5X BASIC AU
*PURPLE/25: .8X TO 2X BASIC AU
BAJW1 Jameis Winston/25 40.00 100.00
BAMG1 Melvin Gordon/15 30.00 80.00

2015 Leaf Metal Draft '14 Metal
BABH1 Brett Hundley 3.00 8.00
BABP1 Bryce Petty 3.00 8.00
BADG1 Devin Gardner 5.00 12.00
BADP1 DeVante Parker 5.00 12.00
BAIEO Ifo Ekpre-Olomu 3.00 8.00
BAKW1 Kasen Williams 5.00 12.00
BAMG2 Melvin Gordon 25.00 50.00
BAMM1 Marcus Mariota 40.00 80.00
BARG1 Rashad Greene 3.00 8.00
BAVB1 Vic Beasley 4.00 10.00

2015 Leaf Metal Draft '14 Metal Prismatic Blue
*BLUE/50: .5X TO 1.2X BASIC AU
*BLUE/25: .6X TO 1.5X BASIC AU
BAMM1 Marcus Mariota/25 60.00 125.00

2015 Leaf Metal Draft '14 Metal Prismatic Purple
BAMM1 Marcus Mariota/15 60.00 125.00

2015 Leaf Metal Draft Armed and Dangerous
ADBB1 Brandon Bridge 3.00 8.00
ADBH1 Brett Hundley 3.00 8.00
ADBP1 Bryce Petty 3.00 8.00
ADBS1 Blake Sims 3.00 8.00
ADBW1 Bo Wallace 3.00 8.00
ADCF1 Cody Fajardo 4.00 10.00
ADGG1 Garrett Grayson 3.00 8.00
ADJW1 Jameis Winston 75.00 125.00
ADMM1 Marcus Mariota 40.00 80.00
ADSC1 Shane Carden 3.00 8.00
ADSM1 Sean Mannion 3.00 8.00

2015 Leaf Metal Draft Armed and Dangerous Prismatic Blue
*BLUE/20: .6X TO 1.5X BASIC AU
ADJW1 Jameis Winston 60.00 125.00
ADMM1 Marcus Mariota 60.00 125.00

2015 Leaf Metal Draft Armed and Dangerous Prismatic Purple
*PURPLE/15: .6X TO 1.5X BASIC AU
ADJW1 Jameis Winston 60.00 125.00
ADMM1 Marcus Mariota 60.00 125.00

2015 Leaf Metal Draft Award Winners
AWBH1 Brett Hundley 3.00 8.00
AWBW1 Bo Wallace 3.00 8.00
AWJW1 Jameis Winston 40.00 80.00

2015 Leaf Metal Draft Award Winners Prismatic Blue
*BLUE/20: .6X TO 1.5X BASIC AU
AWJW1 Jameis Winston 60.00 125.00

2015 Leaf Metal Draft Award Winners Prismatic Purple
*PURPLE/15: .6X TO 1.5X BASIC AU
AWJW1 Jameis Winston 60.00 125.00

2015 Leaf Metal Draft State Pride
SPAA1 Ameer Abdullah 5.00 12.00
SPAC1 Amari Cooper 25.00 60.00
SPBH1 Brett Hundley 3.00 8.00
SPBP1 Bryce Petty 3.00 8.00
SPBW1 Bo Wallace 3.00 8.00
SPDGB Dorial Green-Beckham 3.00 8.00
SPJH3 Jeff Heuerman 4.00 10.00
SPJS1 Jaelen Strong 4.00 10.00
SPJW1 Jameis Winston 40.00 80.00
SPKW1 Kevin White 4.00 10.00
SPLC1 Landon Collins 4.00 10.00
SPMD1 Mike Davis 3.00 8.00
SPMG1 Melvin Gordon 15.00 40.00
SPMJ1 Matt Jones 3.00 8.00
SPMM1 Marcus Mariota 40.00 80.00
SPNO1 Nick O'Leary 3.00 8.00
SPRG1 Rashad Greene 3.00 8.00
SPSD1 Stefon Diggs 8.00 20.00
SPTC1 Tevin Coleman 4.00 10.00
SPTG1 Todd Gurley 25.00 50.00
SPTJY T.J. Yeldon 3.00 8.00
SPTM1 Ty Montgomery 3.00 8.00

2015 Leaf Metal Draft State Pride Prismatic Blue
*BLUE/20: .6X TO 1.5X BASIC AU
SPJW1 Jameis Winston 40.00 80.00
SPMM1 Marcus Mariota 50.00 125.00

2015 Leaf Metal Draft State Pride Prismatic Purple
*PURPLE/15: .6X TO 1.5X BASIC AU
SPJW1 Jameis Winston 40.00 80.00
SPMM1 Marcus Mariota 50.00 125.00

2015 Leaf Metal Draft State Pride '14 Metal
SPMG2 Melvin Gordon 15.00 40.00
SPMM1 Marcus Mariota 40.00 80.00

2015 Leaf Metal Draft State Pride '14 Metal Prismatic Blue
*BLUE/20-25: .6X TO 1.5X BASIC AU
SPMM1 Marcus Mariota/25 50.00 125.00

2015 Leaf Metal Draft State Pride '14 Metal Prismatic Purple
*PURPLE/15: .6X TO 1.5X BASIC AU
SPMM1 Marcus Mariota 50.00 125.00

2015 Leaf Metal Draft Touchdown Kings
TDKAA1 Ameer Abdullah 5.00 12.00
TDKAC1 Amari Cooper 25.00 50.00
TDKBH1 Brett Hundley 3.00 8.00
TDKBP1 Bryce Petty 3.00 8.00
TDKCAP Cameron Artis-Payne 3.00 8.00
TDKDC1 David Cobb 3.00 8.00
TDKDF1 Devin Funchess 5.00 12.00
TDKDJ1 Duke Johnson 5.00 12.00
TDKDJ2 David Johnson 8.00 20.00
TDKDP2 DeVante Parker 5.00 12.00
TDKJA1 Jay Ajayi 5.00 12.00
TDKJA2 Javorius Allen 4.00 10.00
TDKJL1 Jeremy Langford 3.00 8.00
TDKJS1 Jaelen Strong 4.00 10.00
TDKKW1 Kasen Williams 5.00 12.00
TDKKW2 Kevin White 4.00 10.00
TDKKW3 Karlos Williams 3.00 8.00
TDKMD1 Mike Davis 3.00 8.00
TDKMG1 Melvin Gordon 15.00 40.00
TDKMJ1 Matt Jones 3.00 8.00
TDKMM1 Marcus Mariota 30.00 60.00
TDKNA1 Nelson Agholor 4.00 10.00
TDKRG1 Rashad Greene 3.00 8.00
TDKSC1 Sammie Coates 4.00 10.00
TDKSD1 Stefon Diggs 8.00 20.00
TDKTC1 Tevin Coleman 4.00 10.00
TDKTG1 Todd Gurley 30.00 60.00
TDKTJY T.J. Yeldon 3.00 8.00
TDKTM1 Ty Montgomery 3.00 8.00

2015 Leaf Metal Draft Touchdown Kings Prismatic Blue
*BLUE/20: .6X TO 1.5X BASIC AU

2015 Leaf Metal Draft Touchdown Kings Prismatic Purple
*PURPLE/15: .6X TO 1.5X BASIC AU

2016 Leaf Metal Draft
BAAB1 Aaron Burbridge 2.50 6.00
BAAC1 Alex Collins 3.00 8.00
BAAG1 Aaron Green 2.50 6.00
BAASR A'Shawn Robinson 2.50 6.00
BABA1 Bralon Addison 2.50 6.00
BABA2 Brandon Allen 2.50 6.00
BABD1 Brandon Doughty 2.50 6.00
BABM2 Braxton Miller 2.50 6.00
BABW1 Bryce Williams 3.00 8.00
BACB1 Chris Brown 3.00 8.00
BACC1 Connor Cook 3.00 8.00
BACC3 Corey Coleman 4.00 10.00
BACH1 Christian Hackenberg 2.50 6.00
BACJ1 Cardale Jones 8.00 20.00
BACJP C.J. Prosise 2.50 6.00
BACK1 Cody Kessler 2.50 6.00
BACW1 Carson Wentz 25.00 60.00
BADB1 Devontae Booker 3.00 8.00
BADC1 Devon Cajuste 2.50 6.00
BADFB DeForest Buckner 2.50 6.00
BADH1 Derrick Henry 20.00 40.00
BADL1 Darron Lee 2.50 6.00
BADMR Demarcus Robinson 2.50 6.00
BADP1 Dak Prescott 40.00 80.00
BADRW De'Runnya Wilson 2.50 6.00
BAEE2 Ezekiel Elliott 40.00 80.00
BAHH1 Hunter Henry 3.00 8.00
BAJA1 Jerell Adams 2.50 6.00
BAJB1 Jacoby Brissett 3.00 8.00
BAJB3 Joey Bosa 25.00 50.00
BAJD1 Jeff Driskel 2.50 6.00
BAJD2 Josh Doctson 3.00 8.00
BAJF1 Josh Ferguson 2.50 6.00
BAJG1 Jared Goff 25.00 50.00
BAJH1 Jordan Howard 6.00 15.00
BAJK1 Jayron Kearse EXCH 2.50 6.00
BAJP1 Jordan Payton 2.50 6.00
BAJR1 Jalen Ramsey 4.00 10.00
BAJS1 Jaylon Smith 2.50 6.00
BAJW1 Jonathan Williams 3.00 8.00
BAJW2 Jordan Williams 2.50 6.00
BAKC1 Kyle Carter 2.50 6.00
BAKD1 Kenneth Dixon 2.50 6.00

BAKD2 Kenyan Drake EXCH 4.00 10.00
BAKH2 Kevin Hogan 3.00 8.00
BAKM1 Keith Marshall 2.50 6.00
BALC1 Leonte Carroo 2.50 6.00
BALF1 Lennard Floyd 3.00 8.00
BALT1 Laquon Treadwell 3.00 8.00
BALT2 Laremy Tunsil 2.50 6.00
BAMJ1 Myles Jack 3.00 8.00
BAMM2 Mekale McKay 2.50 6.00
BAMN1 Marquez North 2.50 6.00
BAMT1 Michael Thomas 5.00 12.00
BANS1 Nate Sudfeld 2.50 6.00
BANS2 Nelson Spruce 2.50 6.00
BANV1 Nick Vannett 2.50 6.00
BAPC1 Pharoh Cooper 2.50 6.00
BAPL1 Paxton Lynch 2.50 6.00
BAPP1 Paul Perkins 2.50 6.00
BARH1 Rashard Higgins 2.50 6.00
BARN1 Robert Nkemdiche 3.00 8.00
BARR1 Reggie Ragland 2.50 6.00
BASL1 Shaq Lawson 2.50 6.00
BASS1 Sterling Shepard 3.00 8.00
BASW1 Scooby Wright 2.50 6.00
BATB1 Tom Brady EXCH
BATB1 Trevone Boykin 2.50 6.00
BATC1 Tra Carson 2.50 6.00
BATH1 Tyler Higbee 2.50 6.00
BATM1 Tre Madden 2.50 6.00
BATS1 Tajae Sharpe 3.00 8.00
BAVH3 Vernon Hargreaves III 4.00 10.00
BAWF1 Will Fuller 4.00 10.00

2016 Leaf Metal Draft Prismatic Black
*BLACK/15: .8X TO 2X BASIC AU
BACW1 Carson Wentz/15 50.00 100.00
BADH1 Derrick Henry/15 50.00 100.00
BAEE2 Ezekiel Elliott/15 75.00 150.00

2016 Leaf Metal Draft Prismatic Blue
*BLUE/50: .5X TO 1.2X BASIC AU
*BLUE/25: .6X TO 1.5X BASIC AU
*BLUE/15: .8X TO 2X BASIC AU
BACW1 Carson Wentz/50 40.00 80.00
BADH1 Derrick Henry/50 25.00 50.00
BAEE2 Ezekiel Elliott/50 40.00 100.00

2016 Leaf Metal Draft Prismatic Pink
*PINK/20: .8X TO 2X BASIC AU
BACW1 Carson Wentz/20 60.00 125.00
BADH1 Derrick Henry/20 50.00 100.00
BAEE2 Ezekiel Elliott/20 75.00 150.00

2016 Leaf Metal Draft Prismatic Purple
*PURPLE/25: .6X TO 1.5X BASIC AU
*PURPLE/15: .8X TO 2X BASIC AU
BACW1 Carson Wentz/25 50.00 100.00
BADH1 Derrick Henry/25 30.00 60.00
BAEE2 Ezekiel Elliott/25 60.00 125.00

2016 Leaf Metal Draft '15 Metal
*BLUE/45-50: .5X TO 1.2X BASIC AU
*BLUE/25: .6X TO 1.5X BASIC AU
*PURPLE/25: .6X TO 1.5X BASIC AU
*PURPLE/15-20: .8X TO 2X BASIC AU
BACC1 Connor Cook 4.00 10.00
BACJ1 Cardale Jones 3.00 8.00
BADP2 Dak Prescott 40.00 100.00
BALF1 Leonard Floyd 4.00 10.00
BASC3 Shilique Calhoun 3.00 8.00
BASS1 Sterling Shepard 4.00 10.00

2016 Leaf Metal Draft Armed and Dangerous
ADBD1 Brandon Doughty 3.00 8.00
ADCH1 Christian Hackenberg 3.00 8.00
ADCJ1 Cardale Jones 3.00 8.00
ADCK1 Cody Kessler 3.00 8.00
ADJB1 Jacoby Brissett 4.00 10.00
ADJD1 Jeff Driskel 3.00 8.00
ADJG1 Jared Goff 30.00 60.00
ADKH2 Kevin Hogan 4.00 10.00
ADNS1 Nate Sudfeld 3.00 8.00
ADPL1 Paxton Lynch 3.00 8.00
ADTB1 Trevone Boykin 3.00 8.00
ADTB2 Tom Brady EXCH

2016 Leaf Metal Draft Armed and Dangerous Prismatic Blue
*BLUE/25: .6X TO 1.5X BASIC AU
*BLUE/18: .8X TO 2X BASIC AU
ADJG1 Jared Goff/25 50.00 100.00

2016 Leaf Metal Draft Armed and Dangerous Prismatic Purple
*PURPLE/15-20: .8X TO 2X BASIC AU

2016 Leaf Metal Draft State Pride
*'15 BLUE: .8X TO 2X BASIC AU
*'15 PURPLE/15: .8X TO 2X BASIC AU
SPBA1 Bralon Addison 3.00 8.00
SPBA2 Brandon Allen 3.00 8.00
SPBM2 Braxton Miller 3.00 8.00
SPCH1 Christian Hackenberg 3.00 8.00
SPCJ1 Cardale Jones 3.00 8.00
SPCW1 Carson Wentz 40.00 80.00
SPDB1 Devontae Booker 4.00 10.00
SPDH1 Derrick Henry 8.00 20.00
SPEE2 Ezekiel Elliott 40.00 80.00
SPJB3 Joey Bosa 25.00 50.00
SPJG1 Jared Goff 20.00 50.00
SPKD2 Kenyan Drake EXCH 5.00 12.00
SPMN1 Marquez North 3.00 8.00
SPMT1 Michael Thomas 6.00 15.00
SPPC1 Pharoh Cooper 3.00 8.00
SPSS1 Sterling Shepard 4.00 10.00

2016 Leaf Metal Draft State Pride Prismatic Blue
*BLUE/25: .6X TO 1.5X BASIC AU
SPCW1 Carson Wentz 60.00 125.00
SPEE2 Ezekiel Elliott 50.00 100.00
SPJG1 Jared Goff 30.00 80.00

2016 Leaf Metal Draft State Pride Prismatic Pink
*PINK/15: .8X TO 2X BASIC AU
SPCW1 Carson Wentz 75.00 150.00
SPEE2 Ezekiel Elliott 75.00 150.00
SPJG1 Jared Goff 75.00 150.00

2016 Leaf Metal Draft State Pride Prismatic Purple
*PURPLE/20: .8X TO 2X BASIC AU
SPCW1 Carson Wentz 75.00 150.00
SPEE2 Ezekiel Elliott 75.00 150.00
SPJG1 Jared Goff 60.00 120.00

2016 Leaf Metal Draft Touchdown Kings
*'15 BLUE/20: .8X TO 2X BASIC AU
*'15 PURPLE/15: .8X TO 2X BASIC AU
*BLUE/25: .6X TO 1.5X BASIC AU
*PINK/15: .8X TO 2X BASIC AU
*PURPLE/20: .8X TO 2X BASIC AU
TDKAC1 Alex Collins 4.00 10.00
TDKCC3 Corey Coleman 5.00 12.00
TDKCJP C.J. Prosise 3.00 8.00
TDKDMR Demarcus Robinson 3.00 8.00
TDKJD2 Josh Doctson 4.00 10.00
TDKLT1 Laquon Treadwell 4.00 10.00
TDKMT1 Michael Thomas 6.00 15.00
TDKWF1 Will Fuller 5.00 12.00

2017 Leaf Metal Draft
BAAD1 Amara Darboh 2.50 6.00
BAAK1 Alvin Kamara 10.00 25.00
BAAS1 Artavis Scott 2.50 6.00
BAAS2 ArDarius Stewart EXCH 2.50 6.00
BABH1 Bucky Hodges 2.50 6.00
BABH2 Brian Hill 2.50 6.00
BABK1 Brad Kaaya 2.50 6.00
[illegible] 2.00 8.00
BACD1 Corey Davis 4.00 10.00
BACG1 Chris Godwin 3.00 8.00
BACH1 Carlos Henderson 2.50 6.00
BACJB C.J. Beathard 2.50 6.00
BACK1 Chad Kelly 2.50 6.00
BACK2 Cooper Kupp 4.00 10.00
BACM1 Christian McCaffrey 6.00 15.00
BACR1 Cam Robinson 2.50 6.00
BACR2 Cooper Rush 3.00 8.00
BACS1 Curtis Samuel 3.00 8.00
BADB1 Derek Barnett 3.00 8.00
BADC1 Dalvin Cook EXCH 20.00 50.00
BADF1 D'Onta Foreman 3.00 8.00
BADK1 DeShone Kizer 2.50 6.00
BADN1 David Njoku 3.00 8.00
BADP1 Donnel Pumphrey 3.00 8.00
BADS1 Damore'ea Stringfellow 3.00 8.00
BADVS De'Veon Smith 6.00 15.00
BADW1 Dede Westbrook 2.50 6.00
BADW2 Deshaun Watson 50.00 100.00
BADW3 Davis Webb 2.50 6.00
BAEE1 Evan Engram 3.00 8.00
BAEH1 Elijah Hood 2.50 6.00
BAIF1 Isaiah Ford 2.50 6.00
BAJA1 Jonathan Allen 3.00 8.00
BAJB1 Jake Butt 3.00 8.00
BAJC1 James Conner 5.00 12.00
BAJC2 Jehu Chesson 3.00 8.00
BAJD1 Joshua Dobbs 3.00 8.00
BAJE1 Jerod Evans 3.00 8.00
BAJJS JuJu Smith-Schuster 6.00 15.00
BAJL1 Jordan Leggett 2.50 6.00
BAJM1 Jeremy McNichols 2.50 6.00
BAJM2 Joe Mixon 5.00 12.00
BAJP1 Jabrill Peppers 4.00 10.00
BAJQ1 James Quick 3.00 8.00
BAJR1 John Ross 3.00 8.00
BAJR2 Josh Reynolds 2.50 6.00
BAJW1 Jamaal Williams 2.50 6.00
BAKDC KD Cannon 2.50 6.00
BAKH1 Kareem Hunt 5.00 12.00
BAMD1 Malachi Dupre 2.50 6.00
BAMH1 Marlon Humphrey 2.50 6.00
BAMMD Malik McDowell 2.50 6.00
BAMT1 Mitch Trubisky 12.00 30.00
BAMW1 Mike Williams 4.00 10.00
BANP1 Nathan Peterman 3.00 8.00
BAOJH O.J. Howard 3.00 8.00
BAPM1 Pat Mahomes II 75.00 150.00
BARF1 Reuben Foster EXCH 2.50 6.00
BARS1 Ryan Switzer 3.00 8.00
BASC1 Stacy Coley EXCH 2.50 6.00
BASJ1 Sidney Jones 2.50 6.00
BASP1 Samaje Perine 2.50 6.00
BATC1 Taco Charlton 2.50 6.00
BATD1 Travin Dural 3.00 8.00
BATF1 Tarean Folston 4.00 10.00
BATJW T.J. Watt 8.00 20.00
BATR1 Travis Rudolph 2.50 6.00
BATS1 Tyrone Swoopes 2.50 6.00
BATT1 Teez Tabor EXCH 3.00 8.00
BATW1 Tim Williams 3.00 8.00
BAWG1 Wayne Gallman 3.00 8.00

2017 Leaf Metal Draft Prismatic Black
*BLACK/15: 1X TO 2.5X BASIC AU
BADW2 Deshaun Watson 100.00 200.00

2017 Leaf Metal Draft Prismatic Blue
*BLUE/50: .6X TO 1.5X BASIC AU
*BLUE/25: .8X TO 2X BASIC AU
BADW2 Deshaun Watson 75.00 150.00

2017 Leaf Metal Draft Prismatic Purple
*PURPLE/25: .8X TO 2X BASIC AU
*PURPLE/15: 1X TO 2.5X BASIC AU
BADW2 Deshaun Watson 75.00 150.00

2017 Leaf Metal Draft Prismatic Wave
*WAVE: .5X TO 1.2X BASIC AU
BADW2 Deshaun Watson 60.00 125.00

2017 Leaf Metal Draft '16 Metal
*BLACK/15: 1X TO 2.5X BASIC AU
*BLUE/50: .6X TO 1.5X BASIC AU
*PINK/20: 1X TO 2.5X BASIC AU
*PURPLE/25: .8X TO 2X BASIC AU
BACC2 Corey Clement 4.00 10.00
BACD1 Corey Davis 5.00 12.00
BACK2 Cooper Kupp 5.00 12.00
BAEE1 Evan Engram 4.00 10.00
BAJA2 Jonathan Allen 4.00 10.00
BAJB2 Jake Butt 4.00 10.00
BAJL1 Jordan Leggett 3.00 8.00
BAKH1 Kareem Hunt 6.00 15.00
BAOJH O.J. Howard 4.00 10.00
BASC1 Stacy Coley EXCH 3.00 8.00
BATD2 Travin Dural 4.00 10.00

2017 Leaf Metal Draft State Pride
*BLUE/35: .6X TO 1.5X BASIC AU
*PINK/15: 1X TO 2.5X BASIC AU
*PURPLE/25: .8X TO 2X BASIC AU
*WAVE: .5X TO 1.2X BASIC AU
SPAD1 Amara Darboh 3.00 8.00
SPAK1 Alvin Kamara 12.00 30.00
SPBH1 Brian Hill 3.00 8.00
SPBK1 Brad Kaaya 3.00 8.00
SPCC1 Corey Clement 4.00 10.00
SPCK1 Chad Kelly 3.00 8.00
SPCM1 Christian McCaffrey 8.00 20.00
SPCR1 Cam Robinson 3.00 8.00
SPCS1 Curtis Samuel 4.00 10.00
SPDB1 Derek Barnett 4.00 10.00
SPDC1 Dalvin Cook EXCH 25.00 60.00
SPDF1 D'Onta Foreman 4.00 10.00
SPDS1 Damore'ea Stringfellow 4.00 10.00
SPDVS De'Veon Smith 8.00 20.00
SPDW1 Dede Westbrook 3.00 8.00
SPDW2 Deshaun Watson 50.00 100.00
SPEE1 Evan Engram 4.00 10.00
SPJA2 Jonathan Allen 4.00 10.00
SPJB1 Jake Butt 4.00 10.00
SPJC1 Jehu Chesson 4.00 10.00
SPJD1 Joshua Dobbs 4.00 10.00
SPJJS JuJu Smith-Schuster 8.00 20.00
SPJP1 Jabrill Peppers 5.00 12.00
SPJR1 John Ross 4.00 10.00
SPMD1 Malachi Dupre 3.00 8.00
SPMH1 Marlon Humphrey EXCH 3.00 8.00
SPMT1 Mitch Trubisky 15.00 40.00
SPMW1 Mike Williams 5.00 12.00
SPOJH O.J. Howard 4.00 10.00
SPPM1 Pat Mahomes II 75.00 150.00
SPRF1 Reuben Foster EXCH 3.00 8.00
SPRS1 Ryan Switzer 4.00 10.00
SPSJ1 Sidney Jones 3.00 8.00
SPSP1 Samaje Perine 3.00 8.00
SPTD1 Travin Dural 4.00 10.00
SPTS1 Tyrone Swoopes 3.00 8.00
SPTT1 Teez Tabor EXCH 4.00 10.00

2017 Leaf Metal Draft State Pride '16 Metal
*BLUE/25: .8X TO 2X BASIC AU
*PINK/15: 1X TO 2.5X BASIC AU
*PURPLE/20: 1X TO 2.5X BASIC AU
SPCC2 Corey Clement 4.00 10.00
SPJB2 Jake Butt 4.00 10.00
SPTD2 Travin Dural 4.00 10.00

2017 Leaf Metal Draft Touchdown Kings
*BLUE/35: .6X TO 1.5X BASIC AU
*PINK/15: 1X TO 2.5X BASIC AU
*PURPLE/25: .8X TO 2X BASIC AU
*WAVE: .5X TO 1.2X BASIC AU
TKAK1 Alvin Kamara EXCH 12.00 30.00
TKAS1 Artavis Scott 3.00 8.00
TKBH1 Bucky Hodges 3.00 8.00
TKCD1 Corey Davis 5.00 12.00
TKCG1 Chris Godwin 4.00 10.00
TKCH1 Carlos Henderson 3.00 8.00
TKCK1 Cooper Kupp 5.00 12.00
TKCM1 Christian McCaffrey 8.00 20.00
TKCS1 Curtis Samuel 4.00 10.00
TKDC1 Dalvin Cook EXCH 25.00 60.00
TKDF1 D'Onta Foreman 4.00 10.00
TKDN1 David Njoku 4.00 10.00
TKDP1 Donnel Pumphrey 4.00 10.00
TKDW1 Dede Westbrook 3.00 8.00
TKIF1 Isaiah Ford 3.00 8.00
TKJC1 James Conner 6.00 15.00
TKJJS JuJu Smith-Schuster 8.00 20.00
TKJL1 Jordan Leggett 3.00 8.00
TKJM1 Jeremy McNichols 3.00 8.00
TKJQ1 James Quick 4.00 10.00
TKJR1 John Ross 4.00 10.00
TKJR2 Josh Reynolds 3.00 8.00
TKKH1 Kareem Hunt 6.00 15.00
TKMW1 Mike Williams 5.00 12.00
TKOJH O.J. Howard 4.00 10.00
TKSC1 Stacy Coley EXCH 3.00 8.00
TKSP1 Samaje Perine 3.00 8.00
TKTF1 Tarean Folston 5.00 12.00
TKTR1 Travis Rudolph 3.00 8.00
TKWG1 Wayne Gallman 4.00 10.00

2018 Leaf Metal Draft
BAAC1 Antonio Callaway 3.00 8.00
BAAK1 Arden Key 2.50 6.00
BAAL1 Allen Lazard 2.50 6.00
BAAM1 Anthony Miller 4.00 10.00
BAAT1 Auden Tate 2.50 6.00
BAAW1 Akrum Wadley EXCH 2.50 6.00
BABB1 Braxton Berrios 2.50 6.00
BABM1 Baker Mayfield 40.00 80.00
BABS1 Bo Scarbrough 3.00 8.00
BACD1 Carlton Davis 3.00 8.00
BACK1 Christian Kirk 4.00 10.00
BACR1 Calvin Ridley 6.00 15.00
BACS1 Courtland Sutton 4.00 10.00
BACS2 Cam Serigne 2.50 6.00
BACW1 Cedrick Wilson Jr. 2.50 6.00
BADB1 Deontay Burnett 3.00 8.00
BADC1 Deon Cain EXCH 3.00 8.00
BADC2 Darren Carrington II 3.00 8.00
BADG1 Derrius Guice 5.00 12.00
BADG2 DeAndre Goolsby 2.50 6.00
BADG3 Dallas Goedert 3.00 8.00
BADJC D.J. Chark EXCH 3.00 8.00
BADJM D.J. Moore 5.00 12.00
BADP1 Dante Pettis 4.00 10.00
BADRP Daron Payne EXCH 4.00 10.00
BADS2 Durham Smythe 2.50 6.00
BADS3 Dalton Schultz 3.00 8.00
BADW1 Denzel Ward 6.00 15.00
BAESB Equanimeous St. Brown 4.00 10.00
BAHH1 Hayden Hurst EXCH 3.00 8.00
BAIS1 Ito Smith 3.00 8.00
BAIT1 Ian Thomas 2.50 6.00
BAJA1 Josh Allen 20.00 40.00
BAJA2 Josh Adams 5.00 12.00
BAJJ1 Justin Jackson 3.00 8.00
BAJK1 John Kelly EXCH 3.00 8.00
BAJMM J'Mon Moore 2.50 6.00
BAJR1 Josh Rosen 25.00 60.00
BAJTB J.T. Barrett 4.00 10.00
BAJW1 Jake Wieneke 3.00 8.00
BAJW2 James Washington 5.00 12.00
BAJW3 Javon Wims 2.50 6.00
BAKB1 Kurt Benkert 3.00 8.00
BAKC1 Keke Coutee 3.00 8.00
BAKH1 Kenny Hill 3.00 8.00
BAKJ1 Kerryon Johnson EXCH 4.00 10.00
BALF1 Luke Falk 3.00 8.00
BALW1 Logan Woodside 4.00 10.00
BAMA1 Mark Andrews EXCH 4.00 10.00
BAMA2 Marcell Ateman 3.00 8.00
BAMB1 Marcus Baugh 2.50 6.00
BAMC1 Martez Carter EXCH 2.50 6.00
BAMF1 Minkah Fitzpatrick EXCH 5.00 12.00
BAMG1 Michael Gallup 5.00 12.00
BAMG2 Mike Gesicki 3.00 8.00
BAMH1 Maurice Hurst 3.00 8.00
BAMR1 Mason Rudolph 6.00 15.00
BAMW1 Mark Walton 3.00 8.00
BANC1 Nick Chubb 8.00 20.00
BAQF1 Quinton Flowers 2.50 6.00
BARE1 Rashaan Evans 4.00 10.00
BARF1 Royce Freeman 3.00 8.00
BARF2 Riley Ferguson 4.00 10.00
BARH1 Ronnie Harrison 3.00 8.00
BARJ2 Ronald Jones II 2.50 6.00
BARP1 Rashaad Penny 4.00 10.00
BARS1 Roquan Smith 8.00 20.00
BARW1 Ralph Webb 3.00 8.00
BASC1 Simmie Cobbs Jr. 4.00 10.00
BASD1 Sam Darnold 30.00 60.00
BASH1 Sam Hubbard 3.00 8.00
BASM1 Sony Michel 8.00 20.00
BATF1 Troy Fumagalli 3.00 8.00
BATT1 Trenton Thompson 2.50 6.00
BAVV1 Vita Vea 4.00 10.00

2018 Leaf Metal Draft Prismatic Black
*BLACK/15: 1X TO 2.5X BASIC AU
BABM1 Baker Mayfield/15 75.00 150.00
BAJA1 Josh Allen/15 75.00 150.00

2018 Leaf Metal Draft Prismatic Blue
*BLUE/35: .6X TO 1.5X BASIC AU
BABM1 Baker Mayfield 60.00 125.00
BAJA1 Josh Allen 60.00 125.00
BAJR1 Josh Rosen 60.00 125.00
BASD1 Sam Darnold 50.00 100.00

2018 Leaf Metal Draft Prismatic Pink
*PINK/20: 1X TO 2.5X BASIC AU
BABM1 Baker Mayfield/20 75.00 150.00
BAJA1 Josh Allen/20 75.00 150.00
BAJR1 Josh Rosen/10

2018 Leaf Metal Draft Prismatic Wave
*WAVE: .5X TO 1.2X BASIC AU
BABM1 Baker Mayfield 40.00 80.00
BAJA1 Josh Allen 50.00 100.00
BAJR1 Josh Rosen 50.00 100.00
BASD1 Sam Darnold 40.00 80.00

2018 Leaf Metal Draft Prismatic Wave Blue
*BLUE/20: 1X TO 2.5X BASIC AU
BABM1 Baker Mayfield 75.00 150.00
BAJA1 Josh Allen 75.00 150.00
BAJR1 Josh Rosen 75.00 150.00
BASD1 Sam Darnold 75.00 150.00

2018 Leaf Metal Draft Prismatic Wave Purple
*PURPLE/15: 1X TO 2.5X BASIC AU
BABM1 Baker Mayfield 75.00 150.00
BAJA1 Josh Allen 75.00 150.00
BAJR1 Josh Rosen 75.00 150.00
BASD1 Sam Darnold 75.00 150.00

2018 Leaf Metal Draft '17 Metal
BABM1 Baker Mayfield 40.00 80.00
BADC2 Darren Carrington II 4.00 10.00
BAJW2 James Washington EXCH 6.00 15.00

2018 Leaf Metal Draft Award Winners
AWBM1 Baker Mayfield 50.00 100.00
AWJW2 James Washington 6.00 15.00
AWMA1 Mark Andrews EXCH 5.00 12.00
AWMF1 Minkah Fitzpatrick 6.00 15.00
AWNC1 Nick Chubb 10.00 25.00
AWRS1 Roquan Smith 10.00 25.00

2018 Leaf Metal Draft State Pride
SPAC1 Antonio Callaway 4.00 10.00
SPAW1 Akrum Wadley EXCH 3.00 8.00
SPBS1 Bo Scarbrough 4.00 10.00
SPCR1 Calvin Ridley 8.00 20.00
SPDG1 Derrius Guice 6.00 15.00
SPDG2 DeAndre Goolsby 3.00 8.00
SPDG3 Dallas Goedert 4.00 10.00
SPDJC D.J. Chark EXCH 4.00 10.00
SPDJM D.J. Moore 6.00 15.00
SPDP1 Dante Pettis 5.00 12.00
SPHH1 Hayden Hurst EXCH 4.00 10.00
SPJK1 John Kelly EXCH 4.00 10.00
SPJMM J'Mon Moore 3.00 8.00
SPJTB J.T. Barrett 5.00 12.00
SPJW1 Jake Wieneke 4.00 10.00
SPJW3 Javon Wims 3.00 8.00
SPLF1 Luke Falk 4.00 10.00
SPMA1 Mark Andrews EXCH 5.00 12.00
SPMB1 Marcus Baugh 3.00 8.00
SPNC1 Nick Chubb 10.00 25.00
SPRF1 Royce Freeman 4.00 10.00
SPSC1 Simmie Cobbs Jr. 5.00 12.00
SPSM1 Sony Michel 10.00 25.00
SPTF1 Troy Fumagalli 4.00 10.00
SPTT1 Trenton Thompson EXCH 3.00 8.00

2018 Leaf Metal Draft State Pride '17 Metal
SPDC2 Darren Carrington II 4.00 10.00
SPJJ1 Justin Jackson 4.00 10.00

2018 Leaf Metal Draft Tenacious D
DFAK1 Arden Key 3.00 8.00
DFCD1 Carlton Davis 4.00 10.00
DFDRP Daron Payne EXCH 5.00 12.00
DFDW1 Denzel Ward 8.00 20.00
DFMF1 Minkah Fitzpatrick 6.00 15.00
DFMH1 Maurice Hurst 4.00 10.00
DFRE1 Rashaan Evans 5.00 12.00
DFRH1 Ronnie Harrison 4.00 10.00
DFRS1 Roquan Smith 10.00 25.00
DFSH1 Sam Hubbard 4.00 10.00
DFTT1 Trenton Thompson EXCH 3.00 8.00
DFVV1 Vita Vea 5.00 12.00

2018 Leaf Metal Draft Touchdown Kings
TKAC1 Antonio Callaway 4.00 10.00
TKAL1 Allen Lazard 3.00 8.00
TKAM1 Anthony Miller 5.00 12.00
TKAT1 Auden Tate 3.00 8.00
TKAW1 Akrum Wadley EXCH 3.00 8.00
TKBB1 Braxton Berrios 3.00 8.00
TKBS1 Bo Scarbrough 4.00 10.00
TKCK1 Christian Kirk 5.00 12.00
TKCR1 Calvin Ridley 8.00 20.00
TKCS1 Courtland Sutton 5.00 12.00
TKCS2 Cam Serigne 3.00 8.00
TKCW1 Cedrick Wilson Jr. 3.00 8.00
TKDB1 Deontay Burnett 4.00 10.00
TKDC1 Deon Cain EXCH 4.00 10.00
TKDC2 Darren Carrington II 4.00 10.00
TKDG1 Derrius Guice 6.00 15.00
TKDJC D.J. Chark EXCH 4.00 10.00
TKDS3 Dalton Schultz 4.00 10.00
TKESB Equanimeous St. Brown 5.00 12.00
TKIS1 Ito Smith 4.00 10.00
TKJA2 Josh Adams 6.00 15.00
TKJJ1 Justin Jackson 4.00 10.00
TKJK1 John Kelly EXCH 4.00 10.00
TKJW1 Jake Wieneke 4.00 10.00
TKJW2 James Washington 6.00 15.00
TKJW3 Javon Wims 3.00 8.00
TKKC1 Keke Coutee 4.00 10.00
TKKJ1 Kerryon Johnson EXCH 5.00 12.00
TKMA2 Marcell Ateman 4.00 10.00
TKMC1 Martez Carter EXCH 3.00 8.00
TKMG1 Michael Gallup 6.00 15.00
TKMG2 Mike Gesicki 4.00 10.00
TKMW1 Mark Walton 4.00 10.00
TKNC1 Nick Chubb 10.00 25.00
TKRF1 Royce Freeman 4.00 10.00
TKRJ2 Ronald Jones II 3.00 8.00
TKRP1 Rashaad Penny 5.00 12.00
TKRW1 Ralph Webb 4.00 10.00
TKSC1 Simmie Cobbs Jr. 5.00 12.00
TKSM1 Sony Michel 10.00 25.00

2018 Leaf Metal Draft Touchdown Kings '17 Metal
TKJW1 James Washington EXCH 6.00 15.00

2019 Leaf Metal Draft
BAAB1 Alex Barnes 3.00 8.00
BAAI1 Andy Isabella 4.00 10.00
BAAJ1 Anthony Johnson 3.00 8.00
BAAJB A.J. Brown 6.00 15.00
BAAO1 Amani Oruwariye 3.00 8.00
BAARW Anthony Ratliff-Williams 5.00 12.00
BAAW1 Antoine Wesley 2.50 6.00
BAAW2 Aeris Williams 3.00 8.00
BABL1 Bryce Love EXCH 4.00 10.00
BABR1 Brett Rypien 3.00 8.00
BABSJ Benny Snell Jr. 8.00 20.00
BACF1 Clelin Ferrell 4.00 10.00
BACT1 Clayton Thorson 4.00 10.00
BACW1 Caleb Wilson 2.50 6.00
BACW2 Christian Wilkins 10.00 25.00
BACW3 Chase Winovich 8.00 20.00
BADB1 Deandre Baker 6.00 15.00
BADBJ Devin Bush II 10.00 25.00
BADH1 Damien Harris 6.00 15.00
BADH2 Dwayne Haskins 12.00 30.00
BADH3 Darrell Henderson 6.00 15.00
BADJ1 Daniel Jones 12.00 30.00
BADJ2 Diontae Johnson 3.00 8.00
BADKM D.K. Metcalf 8.00 20.00
BADL1 Drew Lock 12.00 30.00
BADL2 DaMarkus Lodge 2.50 6.00
BADL3 Dexter Lawrence 4.00 10.00
BADM1 David Montgomery 10.00 25.00
BADMJ Dre'Mont Jones 3.00 8.00
BADS1 Deebo Samuel 6.00 15.00
BADS2 Devin Singletary 3.00 8.00
BADSV David Sills V 8.00 20.00
BADT1 Deionte Thompson 3.00 8.00
BADW1 Devin White 8.00 20.00
BAEH1 Emanuel Hall 2.50 6.00
BAEJ1 Elijah Holyfield 4.00 10.00
BAEO1 Ed Oliver 4.00 10.00
BAGW1 Greedy Williams 8.00 20.00
BAHB1 Hakeem Butler 5.00 12.00
BAIB1 Isaiah Buggs 6.00 15.00
BAISJ Irv Smith Jr. 5.00 12.00
BAJA1 Josh Allen EXCH 8.00 20.00
BAJD1 Johnnie Dixon 3.00 8.00
BAJH1 Justice Hill 4.00 10.00
BAJH3 Jalen Hurd 3.00 8.00
BAJJ1 Jalen Jelks 3.00 8.00
BAJJ3 Josh Jacobs 12.00 30.00
BAJJA JJ Arcega-Whiteside 4.00 10.00
BAJP1 Jachai Polite 3.00 8.00
BAJS1 Jarrett Stidham 8.00 20.00
BAJS2 Jaylen Smith 2.50 6.00
BAJS2 Jeffery Simmons 2.50 6.00
BAJS3 Jace Sternberger 3.00 8.00
BAJS4 Jordan Scarlett 2.50 6.00
BAJT1 Jerry Tillery 3.00 8.00
BAJW1 Jamarius Way 3.00 8.00
BAKH1 Kelvin Harmon 4.00 10.00
BAKK1 Kyle Kempt 4.00 10.00
BAKM1 Kyler Murray 75.00 150.00
BAKS1 Kaden Smith 2.50 6.00
BAKS2 Kyle Shurmur 5.00 12.00
BAKSJ KeeSean Johnson 2.50 6.00
BALJH Lil'Jordan Humphrey 3.00 8.00
BALJS L.J. Scott 4.00 10.00
BAMB1 Marquise Brown 8.00 20.00
BAMB2 Miles Boykin 3.00 8.00
BAMG3 Myles Gaskin 5.00 12.00
BAMH1 Mecole Hardman 6.00 15.00
BAMS1 Montez Sweat EXCH 8.00 20.00
BAMS2 Miles Sanders 6.00 15.00
BAMW1 Mike Weber 4.00 10.00
BAMW2 Mack Wilson 3.00 8.00
BANB1 Nick Bosa 8.00 20.00
BANF1 Noah Fant 5.00 12.00
BANKH N'Keal Harry 8.00 20.00
BAPC1 Parris Campbell 6.00 15.00
BARA1 Rodney Anderson 3.00 8.00
BARF1 Ryan Finley 5.00 12.00
BARR1 Riley Ridley 4.00 10.00
BASM1 Stanley Morgan Jr. 4.00 10.00
BATB1 Tyre Brady 2.50 6.00
BATH1 Travis Homer 2.50 6.00
BATJ1 Tyree Jackson 6.00 15.00
BATL1 Tre Lamar 4.00 10.00
BATW1 Trayveon Williams 3.00 8.00
BAWG1 Will Grier 8.00 20.00
BAZA1 Zach Allen 4.00 10.00

2019 Leaf Metal Draft Prismatic Black
*BLACK/15: 1.2X TO 2X BASIC AU
BAKM1 Kyler Murray 150.00 300.00

2019 Leaf Metal Draft Prismatic Blue
*BLUE/35: .8X TO 2X BASIC AU
BAKM1 Kyler Murray 125.00 250.00

2019 Leaf Metal Draft Prismatic Pink
*PINK/20: 1.2X TO 3X BASIC AU
BAKM1 Kyler Murray 150.00 300.00

2019 Leaf Metal Draft Prismatic Purple
*PURPLE/25: 1X TO 2.5X BASIC AU
BAKM1 Kyler Murray 125.00 250.00

2019 Leaf Metal Draft Prismatic Wave Blue
*WAV BLUE/20: 1.2X TO 3X BASIC AU
BAKM1 Kyler Murray 150.00 300.00

2019 Leaf Metal Draft Prismatic Wave Purple
*WAV PUR/15: 1.2X TO 3X BASIC AU
BAKM1 Kyler Murray 150.00 300.00

2019 Leaf Metal Draft Photo Variations
*PHOTO VAR: .5X TO 1.2X BASIC AU

2019 Leaf Metal Draft Photo Variations Prismatic Pink
*VAR PINK/20: 1.2X TO 3X BASIC AU

2019 Leaf Metal Draft Photo Variations Prismatic Purple
*VAR PURPLE/25: 1X TO 2.5X BASIC AU

2019 Leaf Metal Draft Photo Variations Prismatic Wave
*VAR WAVE: .6X TO 1.5X BASIC AU

2019 Leaf Metal Draft Photo Variations Prismatic Wave Blue
*VAR WAVE BL/20: 1.2X TO 3X BASIC AU

2019 Leaf Metal Draft Sepia Variations
*SEPIA: .6X TO 1.5X BASIC AU

2019 Leaf Metal Draft Sepia Variations Prismatic Black
*SEP BLACK/15: 1.2X TO 3X BASIC AU

2019 Leaf Metal Draft Sepia Variations Prismatic Blue
*SEP BLUE/35: .8X TO 2X BASIC AU

2019 Leaf Metal Draft Sepia Variations Prismatic Pink
*SEP PINK/20: 1.2X TO 3X BASIC AU

2019 Leaf Metal Draft Sepia Variations Prismatic Purple
*SEP PURPLE/25: 1X TO 2.5X BASIC AU

2019 Leaf Metal Draft Sepia Variations Prismatic Wave Blue
*SEP WAVE BLUE/20: 1.2X TO 3X BASIC AU

2019 Leaf Metal Draft Sepia Variations Prismatic Wave Purple
*SEP WAVE PUR/15: 1.2X TO 3X BASIC AU

2019 Leaf Metal Draft State Pride
SPDKM D.K. Metcalf 10.00 25.00
SPDL1 Drew Lock 15.00 40.00
SPDS1 Deebo Samuel 8.00 20.00
SPDW1 Devin White 10.00 25.00
SPISJ Irv Smith Jr. 6.00 15.00
SPKM1 Kyler Murray 100.00 200.00
SPLJH Lil'Jordan Humphrey 4.00 10.00
SPMG3 Myles Gaskin 6.00 15.00
SPMW1 Mike Weber 5.00 12.00

2019 Leaf Metal Draft State Pride Prismatic Black
*BLACK/15: 1X TO 2.5X BASIC AU
SPKM1 Kyler Murray 150.00 300.00

2019 Leaf Metal Draft State Pride Prismatic Blue
*BLUE/35: .6X TO 1.5X BASIC AU
SPKM1 Kyler Murray 125.00 250.00

2019 Leaf Metal Draft State Pride Prismatic Pink
*PINK/20: 1X TO 2.5X BASIC AU
SPKM1 Kyler Murray 150.00 300.00

2019 Leaf Metal Draft State Pride Prismatic Purple
*PURPLE/25: .8X TO 2X BASIC AU
SPKM1 Kyler Murray 125.00 250.00

2019 Leaf Metal Draft State Pride Prismatic Wave
*WAVE: .5X TO 1.2X BASIC AU
SPKM1 Kyler Murray 125.00 250.00

2019 Leaf Metal Draft State Pride Prismatic Wave Blue
*WAVE BLUE/20: 1X TO 2.5X BASIC AU
SPKM1 Kyler Murray 150.00 300.00

2019 Leaf Metal Draft State Pride Prismatic Wave Purple
*WAVE PUR/15: 1X TO 2.5X BASIC AU
SPKM1 Kyler Murray 150.00 300.00

2019 Leaf Metal Draft Tenacious D
*BLACK/15: 1X TO 2.5X BASIC AU
*BLUE/35: .6X TO 1.5X BASIC AU
*PINK/20: 1X TO 2.5X BASIC AU
*PURPLE/25: .8X TO 2X BASIC AU
*WAVE: .5X TO 1.2X BASIC AU
*WAVE BLUE/20: 1X TO 2.5X BASIC AU
*WAVE PUR/15: 1X TO 2.5X BASIC AU
TDCW2 Christian Wilkins 12.00 30.00
TDCF1 Clelin Ferrell 5.00 12.00
TDGW1 Greedy Williams 10.00 25.00

2014 Leaf Offensive ROY Predictor
BB Blake Bortles .30 .75
BC Brandin Cooks .40 1.00
BS Bishop Sankey .25 .60
FC Field Card .30 .75
JM Johnny Manziel .40 1.00
KB Kelvin Benjamin .40 1.00
ME Mike Evans .60 1.50
OD Odell Bookham Jr. 25.00 50.00
SW Sammy Watkins .40 1.00
TB Teddy Bridgewater .40 1.00
TM Tre Mason .25 .60
DC1 Derek Carr 1.50 4.00

2013 Leaf Rookie Retro Genetic Matrix
COMPLETE SET (25) 50.00 100.00
ONE CARD PER ROOKIE RETRO PACK
GMCP1 Cordarrelle Patterson 2.50 6.00
GMDAH Deandre Hopkins 1.50 4.00
GMDR1 Denard Robinson 2.00 5.00
GMEJM EJ Manuel 2.00 5.00
GMEL1 Eddie Lacy 4.00 10.00
GMGB1 Giovani Bernard 2.50 6.00
GMGS1 Geno Smith 4.00 10.00
GMLJ1 Landry Jones 1.50 4.00
GMMB1 Matt Barkley 2.50 6.00
GMMG1 Mike Glennon 2.00 5.00
GMML1 Marcus Lattimore 1.50 4.00
GMMT1 Manti Te'o 2.50 6.00
GMTA1 Tavon Austin 2.50 6.00
GMTW1 Tyler Wilson 1.50 4.00

2013 Leaf Rookie Retro Genetic Matrix Green
*GREEN/50: .6X TO 1.5X BASIC CARDS

2013 Leaf Trinity Inscriptions Bronze
STATED PRINT RUN 60 SER.#'d SETS
*SILVER/25: .5X TO 1.2X BRONZE/60
DIAE1 Andre Ellington 5.00 12.00
DIAM2 Aaron Mellette 5.00 12.00
DIAO1 Alex Okafor 5.00 12.00
DIBM1 Barkevious Mingo 5.00 12.00
DIBS1 Brad Sorensen 5.00 12.00
DIBW1 Bjoern Werner 5.00 12.00
DICH1 Cobi Hamilton 5.00 12.00
DICK1 Collin Klein 6.00 15.00
DICM1 Christine Michael 5.00 12.00
DICP2 Cordarrelle Patterson 5.00 12.00
DICV1 Conner Vernon 5.00 12.00
DICW2 Cierre Wood 5.00 12.00
DIDA1 David Amerson 5.00 12.00
DIDAH DeAndre Hopkins 12.00 30.00
DIDM1 Dee Milliner 5.00 12.00
DIDR1 Denard Robinson EXCH 5.00 12.00
DIDS1 Dion Sims 5.00 12.00
DIEJM EJ Manuel 5.00 12.00
DIEL1 Eddie Lacy 5.00 12.00
DIER1 Eric Reid 10.00 25.00
DIGB1 Giovani Bernard 5.00 12.00
DIGS1 Geno Smith 5.00 12.00
DIJB2 Josh Boyce 5.00 12.00
DIJF1 Joseph Fauria 5.00 12.00
DIJF2 Johnathan Franklin 5.00 12.00
DIJH1 Justin Hunter EXCH 5.00 12.00
DIJH2 Johnathan Hankins 5.00 12.00
DIJJ4 Jarvis Jones 5.00 12.00
DIJR1 Joseph Randle 5.00 12.00
DIJR2 Jordan Reed 12.00 30.00
DIJS1 Jake Stoneburner 8.00 20.00
DIJW2 Jesse Williams 10.00 25.00
DIKB1 Kenjon Barner 5.00 12.00
DIKS1 Kawann Short 5.00 12.00
DIKS2 Kenny Stills 5.00 12.00
DILJ1 Landry Jones 5.00 12.00
DILT2 Levine Toilolo 6.00 15.00
DIMB1 Matt Barkley 10.00 25.00
DIMB2 Montee Ball 5.00 12.00
DIMD1 Marcus Davis 5.00 12.00
DIMG1 Mike Gillislee 5.00 12.00
DIMG2 Mike Glennon 5.00 12.00
DIMG3 Marquise Goodwin 5.00 12.00
DIML1 Marcus Lattimore 5.00 12.00
DIMM1 Miguel Maysonet 5.00 12.00
DIMT1 Manti Te'o 6.00 15.00
DIMW2 Michael Williams 8.00 20.00
DIQP1 Quinton Patton 5.00 12.00
DIRB1 Rex Burkhead 20.00 50.00
DIRG1 Ray Graham 5.00 12.00
DIRN1 Ryan Nassib 5.00 12.00
DIRS2 Rodney Smith 5.00 12.00
DIRS3 Ryan Swope 5.00 12.00
DIRW1 Robert Woods 8.00 20.00
DISF1 Sharrif Floyd 5.00 12.00
DIST1 Stepfan Taylor 5.00 12.00
DITA1 Tavon Austin 6.00 15.00
DITB1 Tyler Bray 5.00 12.00
DITE1 Tyler Eifert 5.00 12.00
DITJ1 Tony Jefferson 8.00 20.00
DITW1 Tyler Wilson 5.00 12.00
DITW2 Terrance Williams 5.00 12.00
DIZD1 Zac Dysert 5.00 12.00
DIZL1 Zach Line 5.00 12.00

2013 Leaf Trinity Jumbo Patch Bronze
BRONZE STATED PRINT RUN 60
*SILVER/25: .5X TO 1.2X BRONZE/60
DPAE1 Andre Ellington 3.00 8.00
DPAM2 Aaron Mellette 3.00 8.00
DPAO1 Alex Okafor 3.00 8.00
DPBM1 Barkevious Mingo 5.00 12.00
DPCH1 Cobi Hamilton 5.00 12.00
DPCK1 Collin Klein 4.00 10.00
DPCM1 Christine Michael 3.00 8.00
DPCP2 Cordarrelle Patterson 3.00 8.00
DPCV1 Conner Vernon 6.00 15.00
DPCW2 Cierre Wood 6.00 15.00
DPDAH DeAndre Hopkins 8.00 20.00
DPDM1 Dee Milliner 3.00 8.00
DPDR1 Denard Robinson 3.00 8.00
DPDS1 Dion Sims 3.00 8.00
DPEJM EJ Manuel 10.00 25.00
DPEL1 Eddie Lacy 3.00 8.00
DPGB1 Giovani Bernard 3.00 8.00
DPJB2 Josh Boyce 3.00 8.00
DPJF1 Joseph Fauria 5.00 12.00
DPJF2 Johnathan Franklin 3.00 8.00
DPJH2 Johnathan Hankins 5.00 12.00
DPJJ4 Jarvis Jones 3.00 8.00
DPJR1 Joseph Randle 3.00 8.00
DPJS1 Jake Stoneburner 8.00 20.00
DPJW2 Jesse Williams 5.00 12.00
DPKA1 Keenan Allen 6.00 15.00
DPKS1 Kawann Short 3.00 8.00
DPKS2 Kenny Stills 3.00 8.00
DPLJ1 Landry Jones 3.00 8.00
DPLT2 Levine Toilolo 4.00 10.00
DPLVB Le'Veon Bell 8.00 20.00
DPMB2 Montee Ball 3.00 8.00
DPMD1 Marcus Davis 6.00 15.00
DPMG1 Mike Gillislee 8.00 20.00
DPMG2 Mike Glennon 3.00 8.00
DPMG3 Marquise Goodwin 3.00 8.00
DPML1 Marcus Lattimore 3.00 8.00
DPMW2 Michael Williams 4.00 10.00
DPQP1 Quinton Patton 3.00 8.00
DPRB1 Rex Burkhead 8.00 20.00
DPRN1 Ryan Nassib 3.00 8.00
DPRS2 Rodney Smith 3.00 8.00
DPRS3 Ryan Swope 3.00 8.00
DPRW1 Robert Woods 5.00 12.00
DPSF1 Sharrif Floyd 8.00 20.00
DPST1 Stepfan Taylor 3.00 8.00
DPTB1 Tyler Bray 3.00 8.00
DPTJ1 Tony Jefferson 6.00 15.00
DPTJM T.J. McDonald 3.00 8.00
DPZD1 Zac Dysert
DPZL1 Zach Line 3.00 8.00

2013 Leaf Trinity Pure Autographs Silver
*BLUE/17-25: .5X TO 1.2X SILVER/37-55
*BLUE/15-20: .4X TO 1X SILVER/25-28
PAE1 Andre Ellington/45 5.00 12.00
PAM2 Aaron Mellette/34 5.00 12.00
PAO1 Alex Okafor/47 5.00 12.00
PBM1 Barkevious Mingo/55 5.00 12.00
PBS1 Brad Sorensen/52 5.00 12.00
PBW1 Bjoern Werner/40 5.00 12.00
PCH1 Cobi Hamilton/15 6.00 15.00
PCK1 Collin Klein/18 8.00 20.00
PCP2 Cordarrelle Patterson/25 6.00 15.00
PCV1 Conner Vernon/39 5.00 12.00
PDM1 Dee Milliner/42 5.00 12.00
PDR1 Denard Robinson EXCH 6.00 15.00
PEL1 Eddie Lacy/27 6.00 15.00
PER1 Eric Reid/27 12.00 30.00
PGS1 Geno Smith/20 6.00 15.00
PJF1 Joseph Fauria/30 5.00 12.00
PJH1 Justin Hunter 12.00 30.00
PJJ4 Jarvis Jones/20 6.00 15.00
PJR1 Joseph Randle/18 6.00 15.00
PJR2 Jordan Reed/22 15.00 40.00
PKB1 Kenjon Barner/25 6.00 15.00
PLJ1 Landry Jones/28 6.00 15.00
PMB1 Matt Barkley/27 12.00 30.00
PMB2 Montee Ball EXCH 6.00 15.00
PMG2 Mike Glennon/22 6.00 15.00
PMG3 Marquise Goodwin/25 6.00 15.00
PML1 Marcus Lattimore/41 5.00 12.00
PMM1 Miguel Maysonet/15 6.00 15.00
PMT1 Manti Te'o/35 6.00 15.00
PRG1 Ray Graham/37 5.00 12.00
PRN1 Ryan Nassib/23 6.00 15.00
PRS3 Ryan Swope/25 6.00 15.00
PRW1 Robert Woods/39 8.00 20.00
PST1 Stepfan Taylor/19 6.00 15.00
PTA1 Tavon Austin/22 8.00 20.00

2014 Leaf Trinity Inscriptions Bronze
STATED PRINT RUN 35 SER.#'d SETS
DIAB1 Anthony Barr 6.00 15.00
DIAJ1 Anthony Johnson 6.00 15.00
DIAJM A.J. McCarron 6.00 15.00
DIAM1 Aaron Murray 6.00 15.00
DIAR1 Allen Robinson 10.00 25.00
DIASJ Austin Seferian-Jenkins 6.00 15.00
DIAW1 Andre Williams 6.00 15.00
DIBB1 Blake Bortles 8.00 20.00
DIBC1 Brandin Cooks 10.00 25.00
DIBE1 Bruce Ellington 6.00 15.00
DIBS1 Bishop Sankey 6.00 15.00
DIBS2 Brett Smith 6.00 15.00
DICH1 Carlos Hyde 8.00 20.00
DICJM C.J. Mosley 8.00 20.00
DICS1 Charles Sims 6.00 15.00
DIDA1 Davante Adams 10.00 25.00
DIDAT De'Anthony Thomas 6.00 15.00
DIDF1 David Fales 6.00 15.00
DIDF2 Devonta Freeman 10.00 25.00
DIDM1 Donte Moncrief 6.00 15.00
DIDS1 Devin Street 6.00 15.00
DIDW1 Damien Williams 6.00 15.00
DIEE1 Eric Ebron 8.00 20.00
DIHCD Ha Ha Clinton-Dix 8.00 20.00
DIJA1 Jace Amaro 12.00 30.00
DIJA2 Jared Abbrederis 6.00 15.00
DIJC1 Jadeveon Clowney 8.00 20.00
DIJG1 Jimmy Garoppolo 50.00 100.00
DIJH1 Josh Huff 15.00 40.00
DIJH2 Jeremy Hill 8.00 20.00
DIJL1 Jarvis Landry 12.00 30.00
DIJM1 Jake Matthews 6.00 15.00
DIJM2 Johnny Manziel 10.00 25.00
DIJM3 Jordan Matthews 10.00 25.00
DIJWJ James Wilder 8.00 20.00
DIKB1 Kelvin Benjamin 10.00 25.00
DILN3 Louis Nix III 6.00 15.00
DILS1 Lache Seastrunk 6.00 15.00
DILT1 Logan Thomas 6.00 15.00
DIMD1 Mike Davis 6.00 15.00
DIME1 Mike Evans 15.00 40.00
DIMG1 Marion Grice 6.00 15.00
DIML1 Marqise Lee 8.00 20.00
DIOBJ Odell Beckham Jr. 50.00 100.00
DIPR1 Paul Richardson 12.00 30.00
DIRS1 Ryan Shazier 10.00 25.00
DISM1 Stephen Morris 6.00 15.00
DISR1 Silas Redd 8.00 20.00
DIST1 Stephon Tuitt 10.00 25.00
DISW1 Sammy Watkins 10.00 25.00
DITB1 Tajh Boyd 6.00 15.00
DITB2 Teddy Bridgewater 30.00 60.00
DITJ1 Timmy Jernigan 6.00 15.00
DITL1 Taylor Lewan 12.00 30.00
DITM1 Trent Murphy 6.00 15.00
DITM2 Tre Mason 6.00 15.00
DIZM1 Zach Mettenberger 6.00 15.00
DIZM2 Zack Martin 15.00 30.00

2014 Leaf Trinity Inscriptions Gold
*GOLD/10: .5X TO 1.2X BRONZE AU/35

2014 Leaf Trinity Inscriptions Silver
*SILVER/15: .5X TO 1.2X BRONZE AU/35

2014 Leaf Trinity Jumbo Patch Bronze
*GOLD/10: .8X TO 2X BRONZE AU
*SILVER/25: .6X TO 1.5X BRONZE AU
DPAB1 Anthony Barr 5.00 12.00
DPAJ1 Anthony Johnson 5.00 12.00
DPAJM A.J. McCarron 5.00 12.00
DPAM1 Aaron Murray 5.00 12.00
DPAR1 Allen Robinson 8.00 20.00
DPASJ Austin Seferian-Jenkins 5.00 12.00
DPAW1 Andre Williams 8.00 20.00
DPBB1 Blake Bortles 6.00 15.00
DPBC1 Brandin Cooks 8.00 20.00
DPBC2 Brandon Coleman 5.00 12.00
DPBE1 Bruce Ellington 5.00 12.00
DPBS1 Bishop Sankey 5.00 12.00
DPBS2 Brett Smith 5.00 12.00
DPCH1 Carlos Hyde 6.00 15.00
DPCJM C.J. Mosley 6.00 15.00
DPCS1 Charles Sims 5.00 12.00
DPDA1 Davante Adams 8.00 20.00
DPDAT De'Anthony Thomas 5.00 12.00
DPDC1 Derek Carr 30.00 80.00
DPDF1 David Fales 5.00 12.00
DPDF2 Devonta Freeman 8.00 20.00
DPDM1 Donte Moncrief 5.00 12.00
DPDS1 Devin Street 5.00 12.00
DPDW1 Damien Williams 5.00 12.00
DPEE1 Eric Ebron 6.00 15.00
DPHCD Ha Ha Clinton-Dix 6.00 15.00
DPJA1 Jace Amaro 5.00 12.00
DPJA2 Jared Abbrederis 5.00 12.00
DPJC1 Jadeveon Clowney 6.00 15.00
DPJG1 Jimmy Garoppolo 50.00 100.00
DPJH1 Josh Huff 12.00 30.00
DPJH2 Jeremy Hill 6.00 15.00
DPJL1 Jarvis Landry 10.00 25.00
DPJM1 Jake Matthews 5.00 12.00
DPJM2 Johnny Manziel 8.00 20.00
DPJM3 Jordan Matthews 8.00 20.00
DPJWJ James Wilder 6.00 15.00
DPKB1 Kelvin Benjamin 8.00 20.00
DPKDC Ka'Deem Carey 5.00 12.00
DPLN3 Louis Nix III 5.00 12.00
DPLS1 Lache Seastrunk 5.00 12.00
DPLT1 Logan Thomas 5.00 12.00
DPMD1 Mike Davis 5.00 12.00
DPME1 Mike Evans 12.00 30.00
DPMG1 Marion Grice 5.00 12.00
DPML1 Marqise Lee 6.00 15.00
DPOBJ Odell Beckham Jr. 50.00 100.00
DPPR1 Paul Richardson 10.00 25.00
DPRS1 Ryan Shazier 8.00 20.00
DPSM1 Stephen Morris 5.00 12.00
DPSR1 Silas Redd 6.00 15.00
DPST1 Stephon Tuitt 8.00 20.00
DPSW1 Sammy Watkins 8.00 20.00
DPTB1 Tajh Boyd 5.00 12.00
DPTB2 Teddy Bridgewater 30.00 60.00
DPTG1 Tyler Gaffney 5.00 12.00
DPTJ1 Timmy Jernigan 5.00 12.00
DPTL1 Taylor Lewan 5.00 12.00

DPTM1 Trent Murphy 5.00 12.00
DPTM2 Tre Mason 5.00 12.00
DPZM1 Zach Mettenberger 5.00 12.00
DPZM2 Zack Martin 10.00 25.00

2014 Leaf Trinity Pure Autographs Charcoal

PAB1 Anthony Barr 4.00 10.00
PAD1 Aaron Donald 10.00 25.00
PAJM A.J. McCarron EXCH 4.00 10.00
PAM1 Aaron Murray 4.00 10.00
PAR1 Allen Robinson 6.00 15.00
PASJ Austin Seferian-Jenkins 4.00 10.00
PAW1 Andre Williams 4.00 10.00
PBB1 Blake Bortles 5.00 12.00
PBC1 Brandin Cooks 6.00 15.00
PBC2 Brandon Coleman 4.00 10.00
PBE1 Bruce Ellington 4.00 10.00
PBS1 Bishop Sankey 4.00 10.00
PBS2 Brett Smith 4.00 10.00
PCH1 Carlos Hyde 5.00 12.00
PCJM C.J. Mosley 5.00 12.00
PCS1 Charles Sims 4.00 10.00
PDA1 Davante Adams 6.00 15.00
PDAT De'Anthony Thomas 4.00 10.00
PDC1 Derek Carr 25.00 60.00
PDF1 David Fales 4.00 10.00
PDF2 Devonta Freeman 6.00 15.00
PDM1 Donte Moncrief 4.00 10.00
PDS1 Devin Street 4.00 10.00
PDW1 Damien Williams 4.00 10.00
PEE1 Eric Ebron 5.00 12.00
PHCD Ha Ha Clinton-Dix 5.00 12.00
PJA1 Jace Amaro 4.00 10.00
PJA2 Jared Abbrederis 4.00 10.00
PJC1 Jadeveon Clowney 5.00 12.00
PJG1 Jimmy Garoppolo 40.00 80.00
PJH1 Josh Huff 10.00 25.00
PJH2 Jeremy Hill 5.00 12.00
PJL1 Jarvis Landry 8.00 20.00
PJM1 Jake Matthews 4.00 10.00
PJM2 Johnny Manziel 6.00 15.00
PJM3 Jordan Matthews 6.00 15.00
PJWJ James Wilder 5.00 12.00
PKB1 Kelvin Benjamin 6.00 15.00
PKDC Ka'Deem Carey 4.00 10.00
PLN3 Louis Nix III 4.00 10.00
PLS1 Lache Seastrunk 4.00 10.00
PME1 Mike Evans 10.00 25.00
PMG1 Marion Grice 4.00 10.00
PML1 Marqise Lee 5.00 12.00
POBJ Odell Beckham Jr. 20.00 50.00
PPR1 Paul Richardson 8.00 20.00
PRS1 Ryan Shazier 6.00 15.00
PSE1 Shaquelle Evans 4.00 10.00
PSM1 Stephen Morris 4.00 10.00
PSR1 Silas Redd 5.00 12.00
PST1 Stephon Tuitt 6.00 15.00
PSW1 Sammy Watkins 6.00 15.00
PTB1 Tajh Boyd 4.00 10.00
PTB2 Teddy Bridgewater 25.00 50.00
PTG1 Tyler Gaffney 4.00 10.00
PTM1 Trent Murphy 4.00 10.00
PTM2 Tre Mason 4.00 10.00
PZM1 Zach Mettenberger 4.00 10.00
PZM2 Zack Martin 8.00 20.00

2014 Leaf Trinity Pure Autographs Blue

*BLUE/24-25: .6X TO 1.5X CHARCOAL AU
PJM2 Johnny Manziel/25 10.00 25.00

2014 Leaf Trinity Pure Autographs Green

*GREEN/9-10: .8X TO 2X CHARCOAL AU
PBB1 Blake Bortles/9 10.00 25.00
PJM2 Johnny Manziel/10 12.00 30.00

2015 Leaf Trinity Inscriptions Bronze

TSAA1 Ameer Abdullah 4.00 10.00
TSAC1 Amari Cooper 30.00 60.00
TSAD1 Alvin Dupree 3.00 8.00
TSAG1 Antwan Goodley 2.50 6.00
TSAH1 Austin Hill 2.50 6.00
TSBB1 Brandon Bridge 2.50 6.00
TSBH1 Brett Hundley 2.50 6.00
TSBK1 Ben Koyack 4.00 10.00
TSBP1 Bryce Petty 2.50 6.00
TSBS1 Blake Sims 2.50 6.00
TSBW1 Bo Wallace 2.50 6.00
TSCAP Cameron Artis-Payne 2.50 6.00
TSCF1 Cody Fajardo 3.00 8.00
TSCW1 Clive Walford 2.50 6.00
TSDC1 David Cobb 2.50 6.00
TSDF1 Devin Funchess 4.00 10.00
TSDG1 Devin Gardner 4.00 10.00
TSDGB Dorial Green-Beckham 6.00 15.00
TSDH1 Danielle Hunter 3.00 8.00
TSDJ1 David Johnson 6.00 15.00
TSDJ2 Duke Johnson 4.00 10.00
TSDP2 DeVante Parker 4.00 10.00
TSDS1 Danny Shelton 2.50 6.00
TSEJB E.J. Bibbs 3.00 8.00
TSGG1 Garrett Grayson 2.50 6.00
TSIEO Ifo Ekpre-Olomu 2.50 6.00
TSJA1 Javorius Allen 3.00 8.00
TSJA2 Jay Ajayi 4.00 10.00
TSJH1 Jeff Heuerman 3.00 8.00
TSJH2 Josh Harper 2.50 6.00
TSJH3 Justin Hardy 2.50 6.00
TSJJ1 Jesse James 3.00 8.00
TSJL1 Jeremy Langford 2.50 6.00
TSJS1 Jaelen Strong 3.00 8.00
TSJW1 Jameis Winston 25.00 50.00
TSKB1 Kenny Bell 4.00 10.00
TSKJ1 Kevin Johnson 2.50 6.00
TSKW2 Kevin White 10.00 25.00
TSKW3 Kasen Williams 4.00 10.00
TSLC1 Landon Collins 3.00 8.00
TSMB1 Malcolm Brown 3.00 8.00
TSMD1 Mike Davis 2.50 6.00
TSMG1 Markus Golden 2.50 6.00
TSMG2 Melvin Gordon 12.00 30.00
TSMM1 Marcus Mariota 30.00 60.00
TSMW1 Maxx Williams 2.50 6.00
TSNA1 Nelson Agholor 3.00 8.00
TSNO1 Nick O'Leary 2.50 6.00
TSPD1 Phillip Dorsett 2.50 6.00
TSPJW P.J. Williams 3.00 8.00
TSRG1 Randy Gregory 2.50 6.00
TSRG2 Rashad Greene 2.50 6.00
TSSC1 Sammie Coates 3.00 8.00
TSSC2 Shane Carden 2.50 6.00
TSSD1 Stefon Diggs 6.00 15.00
TSSM1 Sean Mannion 2.50 6.00
TSSR1 Shane Ray 6.00 15.00
TSST1 Shaq Thompson 3.00 8.00
TSTG1 Todd Gurley 30.00 60.00
TSTJY T.J. Yeldon 2.50 6.00
TSTK1 Tyler Kroft 3.00 8.00
TSTL1 Tony Lippett 2.50 6.00
TSTL2 Tyler Lockett 4.00 10.00
TSTW1 Trae Waynes 8.00 20.00
TSVB1 Vic Beasley 3.00 8.00

2015 Leaf Trinity Inscriptions Blue

TSJW1 Jameis Winston/25 30.00 60.00
TSMM1 Marcus Mariota/25 50.00 100.00

2015 Leaf Trinity Patch Autographs Bronze

PAAA1 Ameer Abdullah 5.00 12.00
PAAC1 Amari Cooper 30.00 60.00
PAAD1 Alvin Dupree 4.00 10.00
PAAG1 Antwan Goodley 3.00 8.00
PAAH1 Austin Hill 3.00 8.00
PABH1 Brett Hundley 3.00 8.00
PABK1 Ben Koyack 5.00 12.00
PABP1 Bryce Petty 3.00 8.00
PABS1 Blake Sims 3.00 8.00
PABW1 Bo Wallace 3.00 8.00
PACAP Cameron Artis-Payne 3.00 8.00
PACF1 Cody Fajardo 4.00 10.00
PACW1 Clive Walford 3.00 8.00
PADC1 David Cobb 3.00 8.00
PADF1 Devin Funchess 5.00 12.00
PADGB Dorial Green-Beckham 3.00 8.00
PADH1 Danielle Hunter 4.00 10.00
PADJ2 Duke Johnson 5.00 12.00
PADS1 Danny Shelton 3.00 8.00
PAEJB E.J. Bibbs 4.00 10.00
PAGG1 Garrett Grayson 3.00 8.00
PAIEO Ifo Ekpre-Olomu 3.00 8.00
PAJA1 Javorius Allen 4.00 10.00
PAJA2 Jay Ajayi 5.00 12.00
PAJH1 Jeff Heuerman 4.00 10.00
PAJH2 Josh Harper 3.00 8.00
PAJH3 Justin Hardy 3.00 8.00
PAJJ1 Jesse James 4.00 10.00
PAJL1 Jeremy Langford 3.00 8.00
PAJS1 Jaelen Strong 4.00 10.00
PAJW1 Jameis Winston 25.00 60.00
PAKB1 Kenny Bell 5.00 12.00
PAKJ1 Kevin Johnson 3.00 8.00
PAKW2 Kevin White 15.00 40.00
PAKW3 Kasen Williams 5.00 12.00
PALC1 Landon Collins 4.00 10.00
PAMB1 Malcolm Brown 4.00 10.00
PAMD1 Mike Davis 3.00 8.00
PAMG1 Markus Golden 3.00 8.00
PAMG2 Melvin Gordon 20.00 50.00
PAMM1 Marcus Mariota 40.00 80.00
PAMW1 Maxx Williams 3.00 8.00
PANA1 Nelson Agholor 4.00 10.00
PANO1 Nick O'Leary 3.00 8.00
PAPD1 Phillip Dorsett 3.00 8.00
PAPJW P.J. Williams 4.00 10.00
PARG1 Randy Gregory 3.00 8.00
PARG2 Rashad Greene 3.00 8.00
PASC1 Sammie Coates 4.00 10.00
PASC2 Shane Carden 3.00 8.00
PASD1 Stefon Diggs 8.00 20.00
PASM1 Sean Mannion 3.00 8.00
PASR1 Shane Ray 10.00 25.00
PAST1 Shaq Thompson 4.00 10.00
PATG1 Todd Gurley 25.00 50.00
PATJY T.J. Yeldon 3.00 8.00
PATK1 Tyler Kroft 4.00 10.00
PATL1 Tony Lippett 3.00 8.00
PATL2 Tyler Lockett 5.00 12.00
PATW1 Trae Waynes 3.00 8.00
PAVB1 Vic Beasley 4.00 10.00

2015 Leaf Trinity Patch Autographs Blue

*BLUE/25: .6X TO 1.5X BRONZE JSY AU
PAMM1 Marcus Mariota/25 50.00 125.00

2015 Leaf Trinity Pure Autographs Charcoal

PAAA1 Ameer Abdullah 3.00 8.00
PAAC1 Amari Cooper 20.00 40.00
PAAD1 Alvin Dupree 2.50 6.00
PAAG1 Antwan Goodley 2.00 5.00
PAAH1 Austin Hill 2.00 5.00
PABB1 Brandon Bridge 2.00 5.00
PABH1 Brett Hundley 2.00 5.00
PABK1 Ben Koyack 3.00 8.00
PABP1 Bryce Petty 2.00 5.00
PABS1 Blake Sims 2.00 5.00
PABW1 Bo Wallace 2.00 5.00
PACAP Cameron Artis-Payne 2.00 5.00
PACF1 Cody Fajardo 2.50 6.00
PACW1 Clive Walford 2.00 5.00
PADC1 David Cobb 2.00 5.00
PADF1 Devin Funchess 3.00 8.00
PADG1 Devin Gardner 3.00 8.00
PADGB Dorial Green-Beckham 2.00 5.00
PADH1 Danielle Hunter 2.50 6.00
PADJ1 David Johnson 5.00 12.00
PADJ2 Duke Johnson 3.00 8.00
PADP2 DeVante Parker 3.00 8.00
PADS1 Danny Shelton 2.00 5.00
PAEJB E.J. Bibbs 2.50 6.00
PAGG1 Garrett Grayson 2.00 5.00
PAIEO Ifo Ekpre-Olomu 2.00 5.00
PAJA1 Javorius Allen 2.50 6.00
PAJA2 Jay Ajayi 3.00 8.00
PAJH1 Jeff Heuerman 2.50 6.00
PAJH2 Josh Harper 2.00 5.00
PAJH3 Justin Hardy 2.00 5.00
PAJJ1 Jesse James 2.50 6.00
PAJL1 Jeremy Langford 2.00 5.00
PAJS1 Jaelen Strong 2.50 6.00
PAJW1 Jameis Winston 15.00 40.00
PAKB1 Kenny Bell 3.00 8.00
PAKJ1 Kevin Johnson 2.00 5.00
PAKW2 Kevin White 2.50 6.00
PAKW3 Kasen Williams 3.00 8.00
PALC1 Landon Collins 2.50 6.00
PAMB1 Malcolm Brown 2.50 6.00
PAMD1 Mike Davis 2.00 5.00
PAMG1 Markus Golden 2.00 5.00
PAMG2 Melvin Gordon 10.00 25.00
PAMM1 Marcus Mariota 25.00 50.00
PAMW1 Maxx Williams 2.00 5.00
PANA1 Nelson Agholor 2.50 6.00
PANM1 Nick Marshall 3.00 8.00
PANO1 Nick O'Leary 2.00 5.00
PAPD1 Phillip Dorsett 2.00 5.00
PAPJW P.J. Williams 2.50 6.00
PARG1 Randy Gregory 2.00 5.00
PARG2 Rashad Greene 2.00 5.00
PASC1 Sammie Coates 2.50 6.00
PASC2 Shane Carden 2.00 5.00
PASD1 Stefon Diggs 5.00 12.00
PASM1 Sean Mannion 2.00 5.00
PASR1 Shane Ray 2.00 5.00
PAST1 Shaq Thompson 2.50 6.00
PATG1 Todd Gurley 12.00 30.00
PATJY T.J. Yeldon 2.00 5.00
PATK1 Tyler Kroft 2.50 6.00
PATL1 Tony Lippett 2.00 5.00
PATL2 Tyler Lockett 3.00 8.00
PATW1 Trae Waynes 2.00 5.00
PAVB1 Vic Beasley 2.50 6.00

2016 Leaf Trinity

AAB1 Aaron Burbridge 3.00 8.00
AAC1 Alex Collins 4.00 10.00
AAG1 Aaron Green 3.00 8.00
AASR A'Shawn Robinson 3.00 8.00
ABA1 Bralon Addison 3.00 8.00
ABA2 Brandon Allen 3.00 8.00
ABD1 Brandon Doughty 3.00 8.00
ABM1 Braxton Miller 3.00 8.00
ABW1 Bryce Williams 4.00 10.00
ACB1 Chris Brown 4.00 10.00
ACC1 Connor Cook 4.00 10.00
ACC2 Corey Coleman 5.00 12.00
ACH1 Christian Hackenberg 12.00 30.00
ACJ1 Cardale Jones 10.00 25.00
ACJP C.J. Prosise 3.00 8.00
ACK1 Cody Kessler 3.00 8.00
ACW1 Carson Wentz 60.00 100.00
ADB1 Devontae Booker 4.00 10.00
ADC1 Devon Cajuste 3.00 8.00
ADFB DeForest Buckner 3.00 8.00
ADH1 Derrick Henry 25.00 60.00
ADMR Demarcus Robinson 3.00 8.00
ADP1 Dak Prescott 60.00 125.00
ADRW De'Runnya Wilson 3.00 8.00
AEE1 Ezekiel Elliott 60.00 100.00
AHH1 Hunter Henry 8.00 20.00
AJA1 Jerell Adams 3.00 8.00
AJB1 Jacoby Brissett 4.00 10.00
AJB2 Joey Bosa 6.00 15.00
AJD1 Jeff Driskel 3.00 8.00
AJD2 Josh Doctson 4.00 10.00
AJF1 Josh Ferguson 3.00 8.00
AJG1 Jared Goff 30.00 60.00
AJH1 Jordan Howard 8.00 20.00
AJP1 Jordan Payton 3.00 8.00
AJR1 Jalen Ramsey 5.00 12.00
AJS1 Jaylon Smith 15.00 30.00
AJW1 Jonathan Williams 4.00 10.00
AJW2 Jordan Williams 3.00 8.00
AKC1 Kyle Carter 3.00 8.00
AKD1 Kenyan Drake 15.00 30.00
AKD2 Kenneth Dixon 3.00 8.00
AKH1 Kevin Hogan 4.00 10.00
AKM1 Keith Marshall 3.00 8.00
ALC1 Leonte Carroo 3.00 8.00
ALT1 Laquon Treadwell 4.00 10.00
AMM1 Mekale McKay 3.00 8.00
AMN1 Marquez North 3.00 8.00
AMT1 Michael Thomas 6.00 15.00
ANS1 Nate Sudfeld 3.00 8.00
ANS2 Nelson Spruce 3.00 8.00
ANV1 Nick Vannett 3.00 8.00
APC1 Pharoh Cooper 3.00 8.00
APL1 Paxton Lynch 25.00 60.00
APP1 Paul Perkins 3.00 8.00
ARH1 Rashard Higgins 3.00 8.00
ARR1 Reggie Ragland 3.00 8.00
ASS1 Sterling Shepard 8.00 20.00
ASW1 Scooby Wright 3.00 8.00
ATB1 Trevone Boykin 3.00 8.00
ATC1 Tra Carson 3.00 8.00
ATH1 Tyler Higbee 3.00 8.00
ATM1 Tre Madden 3.00 8.00
ATS1 Tajae Sharpe 4.00 10.00
AVH3 Vernon Hargreaves III 5.00 12.00
AWF1 Will Fuller 5.00 12.00

2016 Leaf Trinity Red

*RED/25: .6X TO 1.5X BASIC AU
ACW1 Carson Wentz 75.00 150.00
AEE1 Ezekiel Elliott 75.00 150.00

2016 Leaf Trinity Clear Autographs

CAAB1 Aaron Burbridge 3.00 8.00
CAAC1 Alex Collins 4.00 10.00
CAAG1 Aaron Green 3.00 8.00
CAASR A'Shawn Robinson 3.00 8.00
CABA1 Bralon Addison 3.00 8.00
CABA2 Brandon Allen 3.00 8.00
CABD1 Brandon Doughty 3.00 8.00
CABM1 Braxton Miller 3.00 8.00
CABW1 Bryce Williams 4.00 10.00
CACB1 Chris Brown 4.00 10.00
CACC2 Corey Coleman EXCH 5.00 12.00
CACJP C.J. Prosise 3.00 8.00
CACK1 Cody Kessler 3.00 8.00
CACW1 Carson Wentz 60.00 100.00
CADB1 Devontae Booker 4.00 10.00
CADC1 Devon Cajuste 3.00 8.00
CADFB DeForest Buckner 3.00 8.00
CADH1 Derrick Henry 8.00 20.00
CADMR Demarcus Robinson 3.00 8.00
CADP1 Dak Prescott 60.00 125.00
CADRW De'Runnya Wilson 3.00 8.00
CAEE1 Ezekiel Elliott 60.00 100.00
CAHH1 Hunter Henry 6.00 15.00
CAJA1 Jerell Adams 3.00 8.00
CAJB1 Jacoby Brissett 4.00 10.00
CAJD1 Jeff Driskel 3.00 8.00
CAJD2 Josh Doctson 4.00 10.00
CAJF1 Josh Ferguson 3.00 8.00
CAJG1 Jared Goff 20.00 50.00
CAJH1 Jordan Howard 8.00 20.00
CAJP1 Jordan Payton 3.00 8.00
CAJR1 Jalen Ramsey 5.00 12.00
CAJS1 Jaylon Smith 3.00 8.00
CAJW1 Jonathan Williams 4.00 10.00
CAJW2 Jordan Williams 3.00 8.00
CAKC1 Kyle Carter 3.00 8.00
CAKD1 Kenyan Drake 6.00 15.00
CAKD2 Kenneth Dixon 3.00 8.00
CAKH1 Kevin Hogan 4.00 10.00
CAKM1 Keith Marshall 3.00 8.00
CALC1 Leonte Carroo 3.00 8.00
CALT1 Laquon Treadwell 4.00 10.00
CAMM1 Mekale McKay 3.00 8.00
CAMN1 Marquez North 3.00 8.00
CANS1 Nate Sudfeld 3.00 8.00
CANS2 Nelson Spruce 3.00 8.00
CANV1 Nick Vannett 3.00 8.00
CAPC1 Pharoh Cooper 3.00 8.00
CAPL1 Paxton Lynch 25.00 60.00
CAPP1 Paul Perkins 3.00 8.00
CARH1 Rashard Higgins 3.00 8.00
CARR1 Reggie Ragland 3.00 8.00
CASS1 Sterling Shepard 4.00 10.00
CASW1 Scooby Wright 3.00 8.00
CATB1 Trevone Boykin 3.00 8.00
CATC1 Tra Carson 3.00 8.00
CATH1 Tyler Higbee 3.00 8.00
CATM1 Tre Madden 3.00 8.00
CATS1 Tajae Sharpe 4.00 10.00
CAVH3 Vernon Hargreaves III 5.00 12.00
CAWF1 Will Fuller 5.00 12.00

2016 Leaf Trinity Clear Autographs Silver

*SILVER/25: .5X TO 1.5X BASIC AU
CACH1 Christian Hackenberg 5.00 12.00
CACW1 Carson Wentz 75.00 150.00
CAEE1 Ezekiel Elliott 75.00 150.00

2016 Leaf Trinity Patch Autographs Red

PACW1 Carson Wentz 100.00 200.00
PAEE1 Ezekiel Elliott 100.00 200.00

2016 Leaf Trinity Patch Autographs Gold

PAAB1 Aaron Burbridge 4.00 10.00
PAAC1 Alex Collins 5.00 12.00
PAAG1 Aaron Green 4.00 10.00
PAASR A'Shawn Robinson 4.00 10.00
PABA1 Bralon Addison 4.00 10.00
PABA2 Brandon Allen 4.00 10.00
PABD1 Brandon Doughty 4.00 10.00
PABM1 Braxton Miller 4.00 10.00
PABW1 Bryce Williams 5.00 12.00
PACB1 Chris Brown 5.00 12.00
PACC1 Connor Cook 5.00 12.00
PACC2 Corey Coleman 6.00 15.00
PACH1 Christian Hackenberg 4.00 10.00
PACJ1 Cardale Jones 4.00 10.00
PACJP C.J. Prosise 4.00 10.00
PACK1 Cody Kessler 4.00 10.00
PACW1 Carson Wentz 75.00 150.00
PADB1 Devontae Booker 5.00 12.00
PADC1 Devon Cajuste 4.00 10.00
PADFB DeForest Buckner 4.00 10.00
PADH1 Derrick Henry 25.00 60.00
PADMR Demarcus Robinson 8.00 20.00
PADP1 Dak Prescott 60.00 125.00
PADRW De'Runnya Wilson 4.00 10.00
PAEE1 Ezekiel Elliott 75.00 150.00
PAHH1 Hunter Henry 5.00 12.00
PAJA1 Jerell Adams 4.00 10.00
PAJB1 Jacoby Brissett 5.00 12.00
PAJB2 Joey Bosa 8.00 20.00
PAJD1 Jeff Driskel 4.00 10.00
PAJD2 Josh Doctson 5.00 12.00
PAJF1 Josh Ferguson 4.00 10.00
PAJG1 Jared Goff 50.00 100.00
PAJH1 Jordan Howard 10.00 25.00
PAJP1 Jordan Payton 4.00 10.00
PAJR1 Jalen Ramsey 6.00 15.00
PAJS1 Jaylon Smith 15.00 30.00
PAJW1 Jonathan Williams 5.00 12.00
PAJW2 Jordan Williams 4.00 10.00
PAKC1 Kyle Carter 4.00 10.00
PAKD1 Kenyan Drake 6.00 15.00
PAKD2 Kenneth Dixon 4.00 10.00
PAKH1 Kevin Hogan 5.00 12.00
PAKM1 Keith Marshall 4.00 10.00
PALC1 Leonte Carroo 4.00 10.00
PALT1 Laquon Treadwell 25.00 50.00
PAMM1 Mekale McKay 4.00 10.00
PAMN1 Marquez North 4.00 10.00
PAMT1 Michael Thomas 8.00 20.00
PANS1 Nate Sudfeld 4.00 10.00
PANS2 Nelson Spruce 4.00 10.00
PANV1 Nick Vannett 4.00 10.00
PAPC1 Pharoh Cooper 4.00 10.00
PAPP1 Paul Perkins 4.00 10.00
PARH1 Rashard Higgins 4.00 10.00
PARR1 Reggie Ragland 4.00 10.00
PASS1 Sterling Shepard 5.00 12.00
PASW1 Scooby Wright 4.00 10.00
PATB1 Trevone Boykin 4.00 10.00
PATC1 Tra Carson 4.00 10.00
PATH1 Tyler Higbee 4.00 10.00
PATM1 Tre Madden 4.00 10.00
PATS1 Tajae Sharpe 5.00 12.00
PAVH3 Vernon Hargreaves III 6.00 15.00
PAWF1 Will Fuller 6.00 15.00

2017 Leaf Trinity

AAD1 Amara Darboh 3.00 8.00
AAK1 Alvin Kamara 12.00 30.00
AAS2 Artavis Scott 3.00 8.00
ABH1 Brian Hill EXCH 3.00 8.00
ABK1 Brad Kaaya 3.00 8.00
ACC1 Corey Clement 4.00 10.00
ACD1 Corey Davis 5.00 12.00
ACG1 Chris Godwin 4.00 10.00
ACH1 Carlos Henderson 3.00 8.00
ACJB C.J. Beathard 3.00 8.00
ACK1 Chad Kelly 3.00 8.00
ACK2 Cooper Kupp 5.00 12.00
ACM1 Christian McCaffrey 25.00 60.00
ACR1 Cam Robinson 3.00 8.00
ACR2 Cooper Rush 4.00 10.00
ACS1 Curtis Samuel 4.00 10.00
ADB1 Derek Barnett 4.00 10.00
ADC1 Dalvin Cook 8.00 20.00
ADF1 D'Onta Foreman 4.00 10.00
ADK1 DeShone Kizer 3.00 8.00
ADN1 David Njoku 4.00 10.00
ADP1 Donnel Pumphrey 4.00 10.00
ADS1 Damore'ea Stringfellow EXCH 4.00 10.00
ADVS De'Veon Smith 8.00 20.00
ADW1 Davis Webb 3.00 8.00
ADW2 Dede Westbrook 3.00 8.00
ADW3 Deshaun Watson 20.00 50.00
AEE2 Evan Engram 4.00 10.00
AEH1 Elijah Hood 3.00 8.00
AIF1 Isaiah Ford 3.00 8.00
AJA1 Jonathan Allen 4.00 10.00
AJB1 Jake Butt 4.00 10.00
AJC1 James Conner 6.00 15.00
AJC2 Jehu Chesson 4.00 10.00
AJD1 Joshua Dobbs 4.00 10.00
AJE1 Jerod Evans 4.00 10.00
AJJS JuJu Smith-Schuster 8.00 20.00
AJL1 Jordan Leggett 3.00 8.00
AJM1 Jeremy McNichols 3.00 8.00
AJM2 Joe Mixon EXCH 6.00 15.00
AJP1 Jabrill Peppers 5.00 12.00
AJQ1 James Quick 4.00 10.00
AJR1 John Ross 4.00 10.00
AJR2 Josh Reynolds 3.00 8.00
AJW1 Jamaal Williams 3.00 8.00
AKDC KD Cannon 3.00 8.00
AKH1 Kareem Hunt 6.00 15.00
AMD1 Malachi Dupre 3.00 8.00
AMH1 Malik Hooker 3.00 8.00
AMH2 Marlon Humphrey 3.00 8.00
AMMD Malik McDowell EXCH 3.00 8.00
AMT1 Mitch Trubisky 30.00 60.00
AMW1 Mike Williams 5.00 12.00
ANP1 Nathan Peterman 4.00 10.00
AOJH O.J. Howard 4.00 10.00
APM1 Pat Mahomes II 100.00 200.00
ARF1 Reuben Foster 3.00 8.00
ARS1 Ryan Switzer 4.00 10.00
ASC1 Stacy Coley 3.00 8.00
ASJ1 Sidney Jones 3.00 8.00
ASP1 Samaje Perine 3.00 8.00
ATC1 Taco Charlton 3.00 8.00
ATD1 Travin Dural 4.00 10.00
ATF1 Tarean Folston 5.00 12.00
ATJW T.J. Watt 10.00 25.00
ATR1 Travis Rudolph 3.00 8.00
ATS1 Tyrone Swoopes 3.00 8.00
ATT1 Teez Tabor 4.00 10.00
ATW1 Tim Williams 4.00 10.00
AWG1 Wayne Gallman EXCH 4.00 10.00

2017 Leaf Trinity Platinum Spectrum

*PLATINUM/25: .6X TO 1.5X BASIC AU

2017 Leaf Trinity Clear Autographs

CAAD1 Amara Darboh 3.00 8.00
CAAK1 Alvin Kamara 12.00 30.00
CAAS2 Artavis Scott 3.00 8.00
CABH1 Brian Hill EXCH 3.00 8.00
CABK1 Brad Kaaya 3.00 8.00
CACC1 Corey Clement 4.00 10.00
CACD1 Corey Davis 5.00 12.00
CACG1 Chris Godwin 4.00 10.00
CACH1 Carlos Henderson 3.00 8.00
CACJB C.J. Beathard 3.00 8.00
CACK1 Chad Kelly 3.00 8.00
CACK2 Cooper Kupp 5.00 12.00
CACM1 Christian McCaffrey 25.00 60.00
CACR1 Cam Robinson 3.00 8.00
CACR2 Cooper Rush 4.00 10.00
CACS1 Curtis Samuel 4.00 10.00
CACT1 Cordrea Tankersley 4.00 10.00
CADB1 Derek Barnett 4.00 10.00
CADC1 Dalvin Cook 8.00 20.00
CADF1 D'Onta Foreman 4.00 10.00
CADK1 DeShone Kizer 3.00 8.00
CADN1 David Njoku 4.00 10.00
CADP1 Donnel Pumphrey 4.00 10.00
CADS1 Damore'ea Stringfellow EXCH 4.00 10.00
CADVS De'Veon Smith 8.00 20.00
CADW1 Davis Webb 3.00 8.00
CADW2 Dede Westbrook 3.00 8.00
CADW3 Deshaun Watson 20.00 50.00
CAEE2 Evan Engram 4.00 10.00
CAEH1 Elijah Hood 3.00 8.00
CAIF1 Isaiah Ford 3.00 8.00
CAJA1 Jonathan Allen 4.00 10.00
CAJB1 Jake Butt 4.00 10.00
CAJC1 James Conner 6.00 15.00
CAJC2 Jehu Chesson 4.00 10.00
CAJD1 Joshua Dobbs 4.00 10.00
CAJE1 Jerod Evans 4.00 10.00
CAJJS JuJu Smith-Schuster 8.00 20.00
CAJL1 Jordan Leggett 3.00 8.00
CAJM1 Jeremy McNichols 3.00 8.00
CAJM2 Joe Mixon EXCH 6.00 15.00
CAJP1 Jabrill Peppers 5.00 12.00
CAJQ1 James Quick 4.00 10.00
CAJR1 John Ross 4.00 10.00
CAJR2 Josh Reynolds 3.00 8.00
CAJW1 Jamaal Williams 3.00 8.00
CAKDC KD Cannon 3.00 8.00
CAKH1 Kareem Hunt 6.00 15.00
CAMD1 Malachi Dupre 3.00 8.00
CAMH1 Malik Hooker 3.00 8.00
CAMH2 Marlon Humphrey 3.00 8.00
CAMMD Malik McDowell EXCH 3.00 8.00
CAMT1 Mitch Trubisky 30.00 60.00
CAMW1 Mike Williams 5.00 12.00
CANP1 Nathan Peterman 4.00 10.00
CAOJH O.J. Howard 4.00 10.00
CAPM1 Pat Mahomes II 100.00 200.00
CAQW1 Quincy Wilson 3.00 8.00
CARF1 Reuben Foster 3.00 8.00
CARS1 Ryan Switzer 4.00 10.00
CASC1 Stacy Coley 3.00 8.00
CASJ1 Sidney Jones 3.00 8.00
CASP1 Samaje Perine 3.00 8.00
CAST1 Solomon Thomas 3.00 8.00
CATC1 Taco Charlton 3.00 8.00
CATD1 Travin Dural 4.00 10.00
CATF1 Tarean Folston 5.00 12.00
CATJW T.J. Watt 10.00 25.00
CATR1 Travis Rudolph 3.00 8.00
CATS1 Tyrone Swoopes 3.00 8.00
CATT1 Teez Tabor 4.00 10.00
CATW1 Tim Williams 4.00 10.00
CAWG1 Wayne Gallman EXCH 4.00 10.00

2017 Leaf Trinity Clear Autographs Platinum Spectrum

CAPM1 Pat Mahomes II 250.00 500.00

2017 Leaf Trinity Patch Autographs Bronze Spectrum

PAAD1 Amara Darboh 4.00 10.00
PAAK1 Alvin Kamara 15.00 40.00
PAAS2 Artavis Scott 4.00 10.00
PABK1 Brad Kaaya 4.00 10.00
PACC1 Corey Clement 5.00 12.00
PACD1 Corey Davis 6.00 15.00
PACG1 Chris Godwin 5.00 12.00
PACH1 Carlos Henderson 4.00 10.00
PACJB C.J. Beathard 4.00 10.00
PACK1 Chad Kelly 4.00 10.00
PACK2 Cooper Kupp 6.00 15.00
PACM1 Christian McCaffrey 10.00 25.00
PACR2 Cooper Rush 5.00 12.00
PACS1 Curtis Samuel 5.00 12.00
PADB1 Derek Barnett 5.00 12.00
PADC1 Dalvin Cook 10.00 25.00
PADF1 D'Onta Foreman 5.00 12.00
PADK1 DeShone Kizer 4.00 10.00
PADN1 David Njoku 5.00 12.00
PADP1 Donnel Pumphrey 5.00 12.00
PADS1 Damore'ea Stringfellow EXCH 5.00 12.00
PADVS De'Veon Smith 10.00 25.00
PADW1 Davis Webb 4.00 10.00
PADW2 Dede Westbrook 4.00 10.00
PADW3 Deshaun Watson 60.00 125.00
PAEE2 Evan Engram 5.00 12.00
PAEH1 Elijah Hood 4.00 10.00
PAIS1 Isaiah Ford 4.00 10.00
PAJA1 Jonathan Allen 5.00 12.00
PAJB1 Jake Butt 5.00 12.00
PAJC1 James Conner 8.00 20.00
PAJC2 Jehu Chesson 5.00 12.00
PAJD1 Joshua Dobbs 5.00 12.00
PAJE1 Jerod Evans 5.00 12.00
PAJJS JuJu Smith-Schuster 10.00 25.00
PAJL1 Jordan Leggett 4.00 10.00
PAJM1 Jeremy McNichols 4.00 10.00
PAJM2 Joe Mixon EXCH 20.00 40.00
PAJP1 Jabrill Peppers 20.00 40.00
PAJQ1 James Quick 5.00 12.00
PAJR1 John Ross 5.00 12.00
PAJR2 Josh Reynolds 4.00 10.00
PAJW1 Jamaal Williams 4.00 10.00
PAKDC KD Cannon 4.00 10.00
PAMD1 Malachi Dupre 4.00 10.00
PAMH1 Malik Hooker 4.00 10.00
PAMH2 Marlon Humphrey 4.00 10.00
PAMMD Malik McDowell EXCH 4.00 10.00
PAMT1 Mitch Trubisky 40.00 80.00
PAMW1 Mike Williams 6.00 15.00
PANP1 Nathan Peterman 5.00 12.00
PAOJH O.J. Howard 5.00 12.00
PAPM1 Pat Mahomes II 200.00 400.00
PARS1 Ryan Switzer 5.00 12.00
PASC1 Stacy Coley 4.00 10.00
PASJ1 Sidney Jones 4.00 10.00
PASP1 Samaje Perine 4.00 10.00
PATC1 Taco Charlton 4.00 10.00
PATD1 Travin Dural 5.00 12.00
PATF1 Tarean Folston 6.00 15.00
PATJW T.J. Watt 12.00 30.00
PATR1 Travis Rudolph 4.00 10.00
PATS1 Tyrone Swoopes 4.00 10.00
PATT1 Teez Tabor 5.00 12.00
PATW1 Tim Williams 5.00 12.00

2017 Leaf Trinity Patch Autographs Platinum Spectrum

*PLATINUM/25: .6X TO 1.5X BASIC JSY AU
PADW3 Deshaun Watson 75.00 150.00

2018 Leaf Trinity

*PLATINUM/25: .8X TO 2X BASIC AU
AAK1 Arden Key 2.50 6.00
AAL1 Allen Lazard 2.50 6.00
AAM1 Anthony Miller 4.00 10.00
AAT1 Auden Tate 2.50 6.00
AAW1 Akrum Wadley 2.50 6.00
ABB1 Braxton Berrios 2.50 6.00
ABC1 Bradley Chubb 4.00 10.00
ABM1 Baker Mayfield EXCH 50.00 100.00
ABS1 Bo Scarbrough 3.00 8.00
ACD1 Carlton Davis 3.00 8.00
ACK1 Christian Kirk 4.00 10.00
ACR1 Calvin Ridley EXCH 6.00 15.00
ACS1 Courtland Sutton 4.00 10.00
ACS2 Cam Serigne 2.50 6.00
ACW1 Cedrick Wilson Jr. 2.50 6.00
ADB1 Deontay Burnett 3.00 8.00
ADC1 Deon Cain EXCH 3.00 8.00
ADC2 Darren Carrington II 3.00 8.00
ADG1 Derrius Guice 5.00 12.00
ADG2 DeAndre Goolsby 2.50 6.00
ADG3 Dallas Goedert 3.00 8.00
ADJ1 Derwin James EXCH 5.00 12.00
ADJC D.J. Chark 3.00 8.00
ADJM D.J. Moore EXCH 5.00 12.00
ADP1 Dante Pettis 4.00 10.00
ADRP Daron Payne 4.00 10.00
ADS2 Durham Smythe 2.50 6.00
ADS3 Dalton Schultz 3.00 8.00
ADW1 Denzel Ward 6.00 15.00
AESB Equanimeous St. Brown 4.00 10.00
AHH1 Hayden Hurst 3.00 8.00
AIS1 Ito Smith 3.00 8.00
AIT1 Ian Thomas EXCH 2.50 6.00
AJA1 Josh Allen 15.00 40.00
AJA2 Josh Adams 5.00 12.00
AJJ1 Justin Jackson 3.00 8.00
AJK1 John Kelly 3.00 8.00
AJMM J'Mon Moore 2.50 6.00
AJR1 Josh Rosen 25.00 60.00
AJW1 Jake Wieneke 3.00 8.00
AJW2 James Washington 5.00 12.00
AJW3 Javon Wims 2.50 6.00
AKB1 Kurt Benkert 3.00 8.00
AKC1 Keke Coutee 3.00 8.00
AKH1 Kenny Hill 3.00 8.00
AKJ1 Kerryon Johnson 4.00 10.00
ALF1 Luke Falk 3.00 8.00
AMA1 Mark Andrews 4.00 10.00
AMA2 Marcell Ateman 3.00 8.00
AMB1 Marcus Baugh 2.50 6.00
AMF1 Minkah Fitzpatrick 5.00 12.00
AMG1 Michael Gallup 5.00 12.00
AMG2 Mike Gesicki 3.00 8.00
AMH1 Maurice Hurst 3.00 8.00
AMR1 Mason Rudolph 6.00 15.00
AMW1 Mark Walton 3.00 8.00
AMW2 Mike White 3.00 8.00
ANC1 Nick Chubb 8.00 20.00
AQF1 Quinton Flowers 2.50 6.00
ARE1 Rashaan Evans 4.00 10.00
ARF1 Royce Freeman 3.00 8.00
ARF2 Riley Ferguson 4.00 10.00
ARJ2 Ronald Jones II 2.50 6.00
ARP1 Rashaad Penny 4.00 10.00
ARS1 Roquan Smith 8.00 20.00
ARW1 Ralph Webb 3.00 8.00
ASC1 Simmie Cobbs Jr. 4.00 10.00
ASD1 Sam Darnold 25.00 60.00
ASM1 Sony Michel 8.00 20.00
ATF1 Troy Fumagalli EXCH 3.00 8.00
ATT1 Trenton Thompson 2.50 6.00

2018 Leaf Trinity Clear Autographs

*BLUE/25: .8X TO 2X BASIC AU
CAAK1 Arden Key 2.50 6.00
CAAL1 Allen Lazard 2.50 6.00
CAAM1 Anthony Miller 4.00 10.00
CAAT1 Auden Tate 2.50 6.00
CABB1 Braxton Berrios 2.50 6.00
CABC1 Bradley Chubb 4.00 10.00
CABM1 Baker Mayfield EXCH 50.00 100.00
CABS1 Bo Scarbrough 3.00 8.00
CACD1 Carlton Davis 3.00 8.00
CACK1 Christian Kirk 4.00 10.00
CACR1 Calvin Ridley EXCH 6.00 15.00
CACS1 Courtland Sutton 4.00 10.00
CACS2 Cam Serigne 2.50 6.00
CACW1 Cedrick Wilson Jr. 2.50 6.00
CADB1 Deontay Burnett 3.00 8.00
CADC1 Deon Cain EXCH 3.00 8.00
CADC2 Darren Carrington II 3.00 8.00
CADG1 Derrius Guice 5.00 12.00
CADG2 DeAndre Goolsby 2.50 6.00
CADG3 Dallas Goedert 3.00 8.00
CADJ1 Derwin James EXCH 5.00 12.00
CADJC D.J. Chark 3.00 8.00
CADJM D.J. Moore EXCH 5.00 12.00
CADP1 Dante Pettis 4.00 10.00
CADRP Daron Payne 4.00 10.00
CADS2 Durham Smythe 2.50 6.00
CADS3 Dalton Schultz 3.00 8.00
CADW1 Denzel Ward 6.00 15.00
CAESB Equanimeous St. Brown 4.00 10.00
CAHH1 Hayden Hurst 3.00 8.00
CAIS1 Ito Smith 3.00 8.00
CAIT1 Ian Thomas EXCH 2.50 6.00
CAJA1 Josh Allen 15.00 40.00
CAJA2 Josh Adams 5.00 12.00
CAJJ1 Justin Jackson 3.00 8.00
CAJK1 John Kelly 3.00 8.00
CAJMM J'Mon Moore 2.50 6.00
CAJR1 Josh Rosen 25.00 60.00
CAJW1 Jake Wieneke 3.00 8.00
CAJW2 James Washington 5.00 12.00
CAJW3 Javon Wims 2.50 6.00
CAKB1 Kurt Benkert 3.00 8.00
CAKC1 Keke Coutee 3.00 8.00
CAKH1 Kenny Hill 3.00 8.00
CAKJ1 Kerryon Johnson 4.00 10.00
CALF1 Luke Falk 3.00 8.00
CAMA1 Mark Andrews 4.00 10.00
CAMA2 Marcell Ateman 3.00 8.00
CAMB1 Marcus Baugh 2.50 6.00
CAMF1 Minkah Fitzpatrick 5.00 12.00
CAMG1 Michael Gallup 5.00 12.00
CAMG2 Mike Gesicki 3.00 8.00
CAMH1 Maurice Hurst 3.00 8.00
CAMR1 Mason Rudolph 6.00 15.00
CAMW1 Mark Walton 3.00 8.00
CAMW2 Mike White 3.00 8.00
CANC1 Nick Chubb 8.00 20.00
CAQF1 Quinton Flowers 2.50 6.00
CARE1 Rashaan Evans 4.00 10.00
CARF1 Royce Freeman 3.00 8.00
CARF2 Riley Ferguson 4.00 10.00
CARJ2 Ronald Jones II 2.50 6.00
CARP1 Rashaad Penny 4.00 10.00
CARS1 Roquan Smith 8.00 20.00
CARW1 Ralph Webb 3.00 8.00
CASC1 Simmie Cobbs Jr. 4.00 10.00
CASD1 Sam Darnold 25.00 60.00
CASM1 Sony Michel 8.00 20.00
CATF1 Troy Fumagalli EXCH 3.00 8.00
CATT1 Trenton Thompson 2.50 6.00

2018 Leaf Trinity Patch Autographs Bronze Spectrum

*PLATINUM/25: .6X TO 1.5X BRONZE JSY AU
PAAK1 Arden Key 5.00 12.00
PAAL1 Allen Lazard 5.00 12.00
PAAT1 Auden Tate 5.00 12.00
PAAW1 Akrum Wadley 5.00 12.00
PABB1 Braxton Berrios 5.00 12.00
PABC1 Bradley Chubb 8.00 20.00
PABM1 Baker Mayfield EXCH 90.00 150.00
PABS1 Bo Scarbrough 6.00 15.00
PACD1 Carlton Davis 6.00 15.00
PACK1 Christian Kirk 8.00 20.00
PACR1 Calvin Ridley 12.00 30.00
PACS1 Courtland Sutton 8.00 20.00
PACS2 Cam Serigne 5.00 12.00
PACW1 Cedrick Wilson Jr. 5.00 12.00
PADB1 Deontay Burnett 6.00 15.00
PADC1 Deon Cain EXCH 6.00 15.00
PADC2 Darren Carrington II 6.00 15.00
PADG1 Derrius Guice 10.00 25.00
PADG2 DeAndre Goolsby 5.00 12.00
PADJ1 Derwin James EXCH 10.00 25.00
PADJC D.J. Chark 6.00 15.00
PADJM D.J. Moore EXCH 10.00 25.00
PADP1 Dante Pettis 8.00 20.00
PADRP Daron Payne 8.00 20.00
PADS2 Durham Smythe 5.00 12.00
PADS3 Dalton Schultz 6.00 15.00
PADW1 Denzel Ward 12.00 30.00
PAESB Equanimeous St. Brown 8.00 20.00
PAHH1 Hayden Hurst 6.00 15.00
PAIS1 Ito Smith 6.00 15.00
PAIT1 Ian Thomas EXCH 5.00 12.00
PAJA1 Josh Allen 50.00 100.00
PAJA2 Josh Adams 10.00 25.00
PAJJ1 Justin Jackson 6.00 15.00
PAJK1 John Kelly 6.00 15.00
PAJMM J'Mon Moore 5.00 12.00
PAJR1 Josh Rosen 15.00 40.00
PAJW2 James Washington 10.00 25.00
PAJW3 Javon Wims 5.00 12.00
PAKB1 Kurt Benkert 6.00 15.00
PAKC1 Keke Coutee 6.00 15.00
PAKH1 Kenny Hill 6.00 15.00
PAKJ1 Kerryon Johnson 8.00 20.00
PALF1 Luke Falk 6.00 15.00
PAMA1 Mark Andrews 8.00 20.00
PAMA2 Marcell Ateman 6.00 15.00
PAMB1 Marcus Baugh 5.00 12.00
PAMF1 Minkah Fitzpatrick 10.00 25.00
PAMG1 Michael Gallup 10.00 25.00
PAMG2 Mike Gesicki 6.00 15.00
PAMR1 Mason Rudolph 12.00 30.00
PAMW1 Mark Walton 6.00 15.00
PANC1 Nick Chubb 15.00 40.00
PAQF1 Quinton Flowers 5.00 12.00
PARE1 Rashaan Evans 8.00 20.00
PARF1 Royce Freeman 6.00 15.00
PARJ2 Ronald Jones II 5.00 12.00
PARS1 Roquan Smith 15.00 40.00
PARW1 Ralph Webb 6.00 15.00
PASC1 Simmie Cobbs Jr. 8.00 20.00
PASD1 Sam Darnold 50.00 100.00
PASM1 Sony Michel 15.00 40.00
PATF1 Troy Fumagalli EXCH 6.00 15.00
PATT1 Trenton Thompson 5.00 12.00

2014 Leaf TRISTAR Promo

SPJM1 Johnny Manziel/1000 5.00 12.00

2011 Leaf Ultimate Draft

STATED PRINT RUN 49 SER.#'d SETS
*GOLD/20: .5X TO 1.2X BASIC CARDS
UNPRICED PURPLE PRINT RUN 5
UNPRICED RED PRINT RUN 1
UAA1 Anthony Allen 4.00 10.00
UAB1 Armon Binns 5.00 12.00
UAD1 Andy Dalton 15.00 40.00
UAJG A.J. Green 25.00 50.00
UAP1 Austin Pettis 4.00 10.00
UAS1 Aldon Smith 4.00 10.00
UAW1 Aaron Williams 4.00 10.00
UBG1 Blaine Gabbert 4.00 10.00
UBP1 Bilal Powell 5.00 12.00
UCH1 Cameron Heyward 5.00 12.00
UCK1 Colin Kaepernick 6.00 15.00
UCM1 Casey Matthews 4.00 10.00
UCN1 Cam Newton 20.00 50.00
UCP1 Christian Ponder 4.00 10.00
UDA1 Darvin Adams 4.00 10.00
UDB1 Damien Berry 5.00 12.00
UDC1 Delone Carter 4.00 10.00
UDH1 Dwayne Harris 4.00 10.00
UDJW D.J. Williams 4.00 10.00
UDL1 Derrick Locke 5.00 12.00
UDL2 Dion Lewis 8.00 20.00
UDM1 DeMarco Murray 8.00 20.00
UDQB Da'Quan Bowers 4.00 10.00
UER1 Evan Royster 4.00 10.00
UGC1 Graig Cooper 5.00 12.00
UGL1 Greg Little 5.00 12.00
UGM1 Greg McElroy 6.00 15.00
UGS1 Gregory Salas 4.00 10.00
UJB1 Jonathan Baldwin 4.00 10.00
UJC1 John Clay 6.00 15.00
UJH1 Jamie Harper 4.00 10.00
UJH2 Justin Houston 5.00 12.00
UJJ1 Jerrel Jernigan 4.00 10.00
UJJ2 Julio Jones 25.00 50.00
UJJW J.J. Watt 35.00 60.00
UJL1 Jake Locker 4.00 10.00
UJT1 Jordan Todman 4.00 10.00
UKH1 Kendall Hunter 8.00 20.00
UKR1 Kyle Rudolph 4.00 10.00
ULH1 Leonard Hankerson 4.00 10.00
ULS1 Luke Stocker 4.00 10.00
UMD1 Marcell Dareus 4.00 10.00
UMH1 Mark Herzlich 4.00 10.00
UMI1 Mark Ingram 6.00 15.00
UML1 Mikel Leshoure 4.00 10.00
UNE1 Nathan Enderle 4.00 10.00
UNF1 Nick Fairley 4.00 10.00
UNP1 Niles Paul 4.00 10.00
UPA1 Prince Amukamara 4.00 10.00
UPD1 Pat Devlin 6.00 15.00
UPP1 Patrick Peterson 8.00 20.00
URC1 Randall Cobb 6.00 15.00
URH1 Roy Helu 4.00 10.00
URJ1 Ronald Johnson 4.00 10.00
URM1 Ryan Mallett 4.00 10.00
URQ1 Robert Quinn 4.00 10.00
URS1 Ricky Stanzi 4.00 10.00
URW1 Ryan Williams 4.00 10.00
USR1 Stevan Ridley 4.00 10.00
USV1 Shane Vereen 5.00 12.00
UTD1 Tandon Doss 4.00 10.00
UTS1 Torrey Smith 4.00 10.00
UTT1 Terrence Toliver 5.00 12.00
UTT2 Tyrod Taylor 8.00 20.00
UTY1 Titus Young 4.00 10.00
UTYY T.J. Yates 4.00 10.00
UVB1 Vincent Brown 4.00 10.00
UVM1 Von Miller 10.00 25.00
UWB1 Wes Bynum 4.00 10.00

2011 Leaf Ultimate Draft Football Die Cuts

*FB DIE CUT/49: .4X TO 1X BASIC CARD/49
STATED PRINT RUN 49 SER.#'d SETS
*GOLD FB/20: .5X TO 1.2X BASIC CARD/49
UNPRICED PURPLE PRINT RUN 5
UNPRICED RED PRINT RUN 1

2011 Leaf Ultimate Draft Helmet Die Cuts

*HELMET DC/49: .4X TO 1X BASIC CARD/49
STATED PRINT RUN 49 SER.#'d SETS
*GOLD HEL/20: .5X TO 1.2X BASIC CARD/49
UNPRICED PURPLE PRINT RUN 5
UNPRICED RED PRINT RUN 1

2011 Leaf Ultimate Draft Metal

*METAL/49: .4X TO 1X BASIC CARD/49
STATED PRINT RUN 49 SER.#'d SETS
*BLUE/20: .5X TO 1.2X BASIC CARD/49
UNPRICED PRISM RED PRINT RUN 5
UNPRICED PRISM SLVR PRINT RUN 1

2012 Leaf Ultimate Draft

AJ1 Alshon Jeffery 6.00 15.00
BO1 Brock Osweiler 3.00 8.00
BP1 Bernard Pierce 3.00 8.00
BQ1 Brian Quick 3.00 8.00
BW1 Brandon Weeden 3.00 8.00
CF1 Coby Fleener 3.00 8.00
CG1 Chris Givens 3.00 8.00
CP1 Chris Polk 3.00 8.00
CU1 Courtney Upshaw 4.00 10.00
DA1 Dwayne Allen 3.00 8.00
DDC David DeCastro 3.00 8.00
DM2 Doug Martin 5.00 12.00
DP3 Dontari Poe 3.00 8.00
DS1 Devon Still 4.00 10.00
FC1 Fletcher Cox 5.00 12.00
IP1 Isaiah Pead 3.00 8.00
JA1 Joe Adams 3.00 8.00
JB2 Justin Blackmon 3.00 8.00
JC2 Juron Criner 3.00 8.00
JJ1 Janoris Jenkins 4.00 10.00
JM1 Jonathan Martin 3.00 8.00
KC1 Kirk Cousins 12.00 30.00
KW1 Kendall Wright 3.00 8.00
LJ1 LaMichael James 3.00 8.00
LK1 Luke Kuechly 8.00 20.00
LM1 Lamar Miller 5.00 12.00
MB1 Mark Barron EXCH 3.00 8.00
MF1 Michael Floyd 3.00 8.00
MI1 Melvin Ingram 3.00 8.00
MJ1 Marvin Jones 3.00 8.00
MS1 Mohamed Sanu 5.00 12.00
NF1 Nick Foles 8.00 20.00
NP1 Nick Perry 4.00 10.00
NT1 Nick Toon 3.00 8.00
OC1 Orson Charles 3.00 8.00
QC1 Quinton Coples 3.00 8.00

RG3 Robert Griffin III 4.00 10.00
RR1 Rueben Randle 3.00 8.00
RT1 Robert Turbin 3.00 8.00
RT2 Ryan Tannehill 5.00 12.00
RW1 Russell Wilson 50.00 100.00
SG1 Stephon Gilmore 4.00 10.00
SH1 Stephen Hill 3.00 8.00
TR1 Trent Richardson 3.00 8.00
WM1 Whitney Mercilus 3.00 8.00

2012 Leaf Ultimate Draft Silver

*SILVER/25: .6X TO 1.5X BASIC CARDS
STATED PRINT RUN 25 SER.#'d SETS
RG3 Robert Griffin III 6.00 15.00
RW1 Russell Wilson 100.00 175.00

2012 Leaf Ultimate Draft Inscriptions

*INSCRIPTION/25: .8X TO 2X BASIC CARDS
STATED PRINT RUN 25 SER.#'d SETS
RG3 Robert Griffin III 8.00 20.00
RW1 Russell Wilson 100.00 175.00

2012 Leaf Ultimate Draft Numeration

STATED PRINT RUN 6-41
NUBO1 Brock Osweiler/17 8.00 20.00
NURP1 Bernard Pierce/30 6.00 15.00
NUCU1 Courtney Upshaw/41 8.00 20.00
NUDM2 Doug Martin/22 12.00 30.00
NUIP1 Isaiah Pead/23 8.00 20.00
NULJ1 LaMichael James/21 8.00 20.00
NULK1 Luke Kuechly/40 15.00 40.00
NURT2 Ryan Tannehill/17 12.00 30.00
NURW1 Russell Wilson/16 100.00 175.00

2012 Leaf Ultimate Draft TD Countdown

STATED PRINT RUN 8-37
TDCBP1 Bernard Pierce/27 8.00 20.00
TDCBW1 Brandon Weeden/37 6.00 15.00
TDCDM2 Doug Martin/16 12.00 30.00
TDCIP1 Isaiah Pead/15 8.00 20.00
TDCJB2 Justin Blackmon/18 8.00 20.00
TDCKC1 Kirk Cousins/25 15.00 40.00
TDCLJ1 LaMichael James/18 8.00 20.00
TDCNF1 Nick Foles/28 20.00 50.00
TDCRT1 Robert Turbin/19 8.00 20.00
TDCRW1 Russell Wilson/33 75.00 150.00
TDCTR1 Trent Richardson/24 8.00 20.00

2015 Leaf Ultimate Draft

BAAA1 Ameer Abdullah/40 6.00 15.00
BAAC1 Amari Cooper/40 30.00 60.00
BAAD1 Alvin Dupree/99 EXCH 4.00 10.00
BAAG1 Antwan Goodley/99 3.00 8.00
BAAH1 Austin Hill/99 3.00 8.00
BABB1 Brandon Bridge/99 3.00 8.00
BABH1 Brett Hundley/40 4.00 10.00
BABK1 Ben Koyack/99 5.00 12.00
BABM1 Benardrick McKinney/99 3.00 8.00
BABP1 Bryce Petty/40 4.00 10.00
BABS1 Blake Sims/40 4.00 10.00
BABW1 Bo Wallace/99 3.00 8.00
BACAP Cameron Artis-Payne/40 4.00 10.00
BACF1 Cody Fajardo/99 4.00 10.00
BACW1 Clive Walford/99 3.00 8.00
BADC1 David Cobb/40 4.00 10.00
BADF1 Dante Fowler Jr./99 EXCH 5.00 12.00
BADF2 Devin Funchess/99 5.00 12.00
BADG1 Devin Gardner/99 5.00 12.00
BADGB Dorial Green-Beckham/99 3.00 8.00
BADH1 Danielle Hunter/99 4.00 10.00
BADJ1 Duke Johnson/40 6.00 15.00
BADJ2 David Johnson/99 8.00 20.00
BADP1 Denzel Perryman/99 3.00 8.00
BADP2 DeVante Parker/99 5.00 12.00
BADS1 Danny Shelton/99 3.00 8.00
BAEG1 Eddie Goldman/99 EXCH 3.00 8.00
BAEJB E.J. Bibbs/99 4.00 10.00
BAGG1 Garrett Grayson/40 4.00 10.00
BAIEO Ifo Ekpre-Olomu/99 3.00 8.00
BAJA1 Jay Ajayi/40 6.00 15.00
BAJA2 Javorius Allen/99 4.00 10.00
BAJH1 Josh Harper/99 3.00 8.00
BAJH2 Jeff Heuerman/99 4.00 10.00
BAJH3 Justin Hardy/99 3.00 8.00
BAJJ1 Jesse James/99 4.00 10.00
BAJL1 Jeremy Langford/40 4.00 10.00
BAJS1 Jaelen Strong/99 4.00 10.00
BAJW1 Jameis Winston/40 25.00 50.00
BAKB1 Kenny Bell/99 5.00 12.00
BAKJ1 Kevin Johnson/99 3.00 8.00
BAKW1 Karlos Williams/40 4.00 10.00
BAKW2 Kevin White/40 12.00 30.00
BAKW3 Kasen Williams/99 5.00 12.00
BALC1 Landon Collins/99 4.00 10.00
BAMB1 Malcolm Brown/99 4.00 10.00
BAMD1 Mike Davis/99 3.00 8.00
BAMG1 Melvin Gordon/40 15.00 40.00
BAMG2 Markus Golden/99 3.00 8.00
BAMJ1 Matt Jones/99 3.00 8.00
BAMM1 Marcus Mariota/40 40.00 100.00
BAMP1 Marcus Peters/99 5.00 12.00
BAMW1 Maxx Williams/99 3.00 8.00
BANA1 Nelson Agholor/99 4.00 10.00
BANM1 Nick Marshall/99 5.00 12.00
BANO1 Nick O'Leary/40 4.00 10.00
BAPD1 Phillip Dorsett/99 3.00 8.00
BAPJW P.J. Williams/99 4.00 10.00
BARG1 Randy Gregory/40 4.00 10.00
BARG2 Rashad Greene/40 4.00 10.00
BASC1 Sammie Coates/99 4.00 10.00
BASC2 Shane Carden/40 4.00 10.00
BASD1 Stefon Diggs/99 8.00 20.00
BASM1 Sean Mannion/99 3.00 8.00
BASR1 Shane Ray/40 10.00 25.00
BAST1 Shaq Thompson/99 4.00 10.00
BATC1 Tevin Coleman/40 5.00 12.00
BATG1 Todd Gurley/40 30.00 60.00
BATJY T.J. Yeldon/40 4.00 10.00
BATK1 Tyler Kroft/99 4.00 10.00
BATL1 Tyler Lockett/40 6.00 15.00
BATL2 Tony Lippett/99 3.00 8.00
BATM1 Ty Montgomery/99 3.00 8.00
BATW1 Trae Waynes/99 8.00 20.00
BAVB1 Vic Beasley/99 4.00 10.00
BAVM1 Vince Mayle/99 4.00 10.00

2015 Leaf Ultimate Draft Silver

*SILVER/25: .6X TO 1.5X BASIC AU/99
*SILVER/15: .5X TO 1.2X BASIC AU/40

2015 Leaf Ultimate Draft Helmet Die Cuts

*SILVER/15: .5X TO 1.2X BASIC INSERTS/40
UHAA1 Ameer Abdullah 6.00 15.00
UHBH1 Brett Hundley 4.00 10.00
UHDJ1 Duke Johnson 6.00 15.00
UHJW1 Jameis Winston 25.00 50.00
UHKW1 Karlos Williams 4.00 10.00
UHKW2 Kevin White 12.00 30.00
UHMG1 Melvin Gordon 15.00 40.00
UHNO1 Nick O'Leary 4.00 10.00
UHRG1 Randy Gregory 4.00 10.00
UHTG1 Todd Gurley 40.00 80.00

2015 Leaf Ultimate Draft Ultimate Numbers

*SILVER/15: .5X TO 1.2X BASIC INSERTS/40
UNAC1 Amari Cooper 30.00 60.00
UNBP1 Bryce Petty 4.00 10.00
UNBS1 Blake Sims 4.00 10.00
UNCAP Cameron Artis-Payne 4.00 10.00
UNDC1 David Cobb 4.00 10.00
UNGG1 Garrett Grayson 4.00 10.00
UNJA1 Jay Ajayi 6.00 15.00
UNJL1 Jeremy Langford 4.00 10.00
UNMM1 Marcus Mariota 40.00 100.00
UNRG2 Rashad Greene 4.00 10.00
UNSC2 Shane Carden 4.00 10.00
UNSR1 Shane Ray 4.00 10.00
UNTC1 Tevin Coleman 5.00 12.00

2016 Leaf Ultimate Draft

BAAB1 Aaron Burbridge 3.00 8.00
BAAC1 Alex Collins 4.00 10.00
BAAG1 Aaron Green 3.00 8.00
BAASR A'Shawn Robinson 3.00 8.00
BABA1 Bralon Addison 3.00 8.00
BABA2 Brandon Allen 3.00 8.00
BABD1 Brandon Doughty 3.00 8.00
BABM2 Braxton Miller EXCH 3.00 8.00
BABW1 Bryce Williams 4.00 10.00
BACB1 Chris Brown 4.00 10.00
BACC1 Connor Cook 4.00 10.00
BACC3 Corey Coleman 5.00 12.00
BACH1 Christian Hackenberg 3.00 8.00
BACJ1 Cardale Jones 3.00 8.00
BACJP C.J. Prosise 3.00 8.00
BACK1 Cody Kessler 3.00 8.00
BACW1 Carson Wentz 50.00 100.00
BADB1 Devontae Booker 4.00 10.00
BADC1 Devon Cajuste 3.00 8.00
BADFB DeForest Buckner 3.00 8.00
BADH1 Derrick Henry 8.00 20.00
BADL1 Darron Lee 3.00 8.00
BADMR Demarcus Robinson 3.00 8.00
BADP1 Dak Prescott 50.00 100.00
BADRW De'Runnya Wilson 3.00 8.00
BAEE2 Ezekiel Elliott 60.00 125.00
BAHH1 Hunter Henry 4.00 10.00
BAJA1 Jerell Adams 3.00 8.00
BAJB1 Jacoby Brissett 4.00 10.00
BAJB3 Joey Bosa 6.00 15.00
BAJD1 Jeff Driskel 3.00 8.00
BAJD2 Josh Doctson 4.00 10.00
BAJF1 Josh Ferguson 3.00 8.00
BAJG1 Jared Goff 20.00 50.00
BAJH1 Jordan Howard 8.00 20.00
BAJK1 Jayron Kearse EXCH 3.00 8.00
BAJP1 Jordan Payton 3.00 8.00
BAJR1 Jalen Ramsey 5.00 12.00
BAJS1 Jaylon Smith 3.00 8.00
BAJW1 Jonathan Williams 4.00 10.00
BAJW2 Jordan Williams 3.00 8.00
BAKC1 Kyle Carter 3.00 8.00
BAKD1 Kenneth Dixon 3.00 8.00
BAKD2 Kenyan Drake 5.00 12.00
BAKH2 Kevin Hogan 4.00 10.00
BAKM1 Keith Marshall 3.00 8.00
BALC1 Leonte Carroo 3.00 8.00
BALF1 Leonard Floyd 4.00 10.00
BALT1 Laquon Treadwell 4.00 10.00
BALT2 Laremy Tunsil 3.00 8.00
BAMJ1 Myles Jack 4.00 10.00
BAMM2 Mekale McKay 3.00 8.00
BAMN1 Marquez North 3.00 8.00
BAMT1 Michael Thomas 6.00 15.00
BANS1 Nate Sudfeld 3.00 8.00
BANS2 Nelson Spruce 3.00 8.00
BANV1 Nick Vannett 3.00 8.00
BAPC1 Pharoh Cooper 3.00 8.00
BAPL1 Paxton Lynch 3.00 8.00
BARH1 Rashard Higgins 3.00 8.00
BARN1 Robert Nkemdiche 4.00 10.00
BARR1 Reggie Ragland 3.00 8.00
BASL1 Shaq Lawson 3.00 8.00
BASS1 Sterling Shepard 4.00 10.00
BASW1 Scooby Wright 3.00 8.00
BATB1 Tom Brady SP 200.00 350.00
BATB2 Trevone Boykin 3.00 8.00
BATC1 Tra Carson 3.00 8.00
BATH1 Tyler Higbee 3.00 8.00
BATM1 Tre Madden 3.00 8.00
BATS1 Tajae Sharpe 4.00 10.00
BAVH3 Vernon Hargreaves III 5.00 12.00
BAWF1 Will Fuller 5.00 12.00

2016 Leaf Ultimate Draft Gold

*GOLD/50: .5X TO 1.2X BASIC AU
BACW1 Carson Wentz/50 60.00 120.00
BAEE2 Ezekiel Elliott/50 75.00 150.00

2016 Leaf Ultimate Draft Silver Spectrum

*SILVER/25: .6X TO 1.5X BASIC AU
BACW1 Carson Wentz/25 75.00 150.00
BAEE2 Ezekiel Elliott/25 100.00 200.00

2016 Leaf Ultimate Draft '91 Rookie Autographs

GLRAC1 Alex Collins 4.00 10.00
GLRASR A'Shawn Robinson
GLRBA1 Bralon Addison 3.00 8.00
GLRBD1 Brandon Doughty 3.00 8.00
GLRBM2 Braxton Miller EXCH 3.00 8.00
GLRCC1 Connor Cook 4.00 10.00
GLRCC3 Corey Coleman 5.00 12.00
GLRCH1 Christian Hackenberg 3.00 8.00
GLRCJ1 Cardale Jones
GLRCJP C.J. Prosise 3.00 8.00
GLRCK1 Cody Kessler 3.00 8.00
GLRCW1 Carson Wentz
GLRDB1 Devontae Booker 4.00 10.00
GLRDH1 Derrick Henry 8.00 20.00
GLRDP1 Dak Prescott 50.00 100.00
GLREE2 Ezekiel Elliott 60.00 125.00
GLRHH1 Hunter Henry 4.00 10.00
GLRJB1 Jacoby Brissett 4.00 10.00
GLRJB3 Joey Bosa 6.00 15.00
GLRJD2 Josh Doctson 4.00 10.00
GLRJG1 Jared Goff 20.00 50.00
GLRJP1 Jordan Payton 3.00 8.00
GLRJW1 Jonathan Williams 4.00 10.00
GLRKD1 Kenneth Dixon 3.00 8.00
GLRKD2 Kenyan Drake 5.00 12.00
GLRKH2 Kevin Hogan 4.00 10.00
GLRLC1 Leonte Carroo 3.00 8.00
GLRLT1 Laquon Treadwell 4.00 10.00
GLRMJ1 Myles Jack 4.00 10.00
GLRMN1 Marquez North 3.00 8.00
GLRMT1 Michael Thomas 6.00 15.00
GLRNS1 Nate Sudfeld 3.00 8.00
GLRNV1 Nick Vannett 3.00 8.00
GLRPC1 Pharoh Cooper 3.00 8.00
GLRPL1 Paxton Lynch 3.00 8.00
GLRPP1 Paul Perkins 3.00 8.00
GLRRH1 Rashard Higgins 3.00 8.00
GLRRN1 Robert Nkemdiche 4.00 10.00
GLRSS1 Sterling Shepard 4.00 10.00
GLRTB2 Trevone Boykin 3.00 8.00
GLRTM1 Tre Madden 3.00 8.00
GLRWF1 Will Fuller 5.00 12.00

2016 Leaf Ultimate Draft '91 Rookie Autographs Gold

*GOLD/20: .6X TO 1.5X BASIC AU
GLRCW1 Carson Wentz 75.00 150.00
GLREE2 Ezekiel Elliott 100.00 200.00

2016 Leaf Ultimate Draft '91 Rookie Autographs Silver Spectrum

*SILVER/15: .6X TO 1.5X BASIC AU
GLRCW1 Carson Wentz 75.00 150.00
GLREE2 Ezekiel Elliott 100.00 200.00

2016 Leaf Ultimate Draft '92 Rookie Autographs

BGAB1 Aaron Burbridge 3.00 8.00
DCAC1 Alox Collins 4.00 10.00
BGAG1 Aaron Green 3.00 8.00
BGBA1 Bralon Addison 3.00 8.00
BGBA2 Brandon Allen 3.00 8.00
BGBM2 Braxton Miller EXCH 3.00 8.00
BGCB1 Chris Brown 4.00 10.00
BGCC1 Connor Cook 4.00 10.00
BGCC3 Corey Coleman 5.00 12.00
BGCH1 Christian Hackenberg 3.00 8.00
BGCJ1 Cardale Jones
BGCJP C.J. Prosise 3.00 8.00
BGCK1 Cody Kessler 3.00 8.00
BGCW1 Carson Wentz
BGDB1 Devontae Booker
BGDC1 Devon Cajuste 3.00 8.00
BGDFB DeForest Buckner 3.00 8.00
BGDH1 Derrick Henry 8.00 20.00
BGDMR Demarcus Robinson 3.00 8.00
BGDRW De'Runnya Wilson 3.00 8.00
BGEE2 Ezekiel Elliott 60.00 125.00
BGJB3 Joey Bosa 6.00 15.00
BGJD1 Jeff Driskel 3.00 8.00
BGJF1 Josh Ferguson 3.00 8.00
BGJG1 Jared Goff 20.00 50.00
BGJR1 Jalen Ramsey 5.00 12.00
BGJS1 Jaylon Smith 3.00 8.00
BGJW2 Jordan Williams 3.00 8.00
BGKC1 Kyle Carter 3.00 8.00
BGKD1 Kenneth Dixon 3.00 8.00
BGKD2 Kenyan Drake 5.00 12.00
BGLT1 Laquon Treadwell 4.00 10.00
BGMT1 Michael Thomas 6.00 15.00
BGNS2 Nelson Spruce 3.00 8.00
BGNV1 Nick Vannett 3.00 8.00
BGPC1 Pharoh Cooper 3.00 8.00
BGPL1 Paxton Lynch 3.00 8.00
BGRN1 Robert Nkemdiche 4.00 10.00
BGRR1 Reggie Ragland 3.00 8.00
BGVH3 Vernon Hargreaves III 5.00 12.00

2016 Leaf Ultimate Draft '92 Rookie Autographs Gold

*GOLD/20: .6X TO 1.5X BASIC AU
BGCW1 Carson Wentz 75.00 150.00
BGEE2 Ezekiel Elliott 100.00 200.00

2016 Leaf Ultimate Draft '92 Rookie Autographs Silver Spectrum

*SILVER/15: .6X TO 1.5X BASIC AU
BGCW1 Carson Wentz 75.00 150.00
BGEE2 Ezekiel Elliott 100.00 200.00

2017 Leaf Ultimate Draft

*GOLD/25: .6X TO 1.5X BASIC AU
*SILVER/15: .8X TO 2X BASIC AU
UBAAD1 Amara Darboh 3.00 8.00
UBAAK1 Alvin Kamara 12.00 30.00
UBAAS1 ArDarius Stewart 3.00 8.00
UBAAS2 Artavis Scott 3.00 8.00
UBABH1 Brian Hill EXCH 3.00 8.00
UBABH2 Bucky Hodges EXCH 3.00 8.00
UBABK1 Brad Kaaya 3.00 8.00
UBACG1 Chris Godwin 4.00 10.00
UBACH1 Carlos Henderson 3.00 8.00
UBACJB C.J. Beathard 3.00 8.00
UBACK1 Chad Kelly 3.00 8.00
UBACM1 Christian McCaffrey 8.00 20.00
UBACR2 Cooper Rush 4.00 10.00
UBACS1 Curtis Samuel 4.00 10.00
UBACT1 Cordrea Tankersley 4.00 10.00
UBADB1 Derek Barnett 4.00 10.00
UBADC1 Dalvin Cook 20.00 50.00
UBADF1 D'Onta Foreman 4.00 10.00
UBADK1 DeShone Kizer 10.00 25.00
UBADN1 David Njoku 4.00 10.00
UBADP1 Donnel Pumphrey 4.00 10.00
UBADS1 Damore'ea Stringfellow 4.00 10.00
UBADVS De'Veon Smith 8.00 20.00
UBADW1 Davis Webb 3.00 8.00
UBADW2 Dede Westbrook 3.00 8.00
UBADW3 Deshaun Watson 20.00 50.00
UBAEH1 Elijah Hood 3.00 8.00
UBAIF1 Isaiah Ford 3.00 8.00
UBAJC1 James Conner 6.00 15.00
UBAJC2 Jehu Chesson 4.00 10.00
UBAJD1 Joshua Dobbs 4.00 10.00
UBAJE1 Jerod Evans 4.00 10.00
UBAJJS JuJu Smith-Schuster 8.00 20.00
UBAJM1 Jeremy McNichols 3.00 8.00
UBAJM2 Joe Mixon 6.00 15.00
UBAJP1 Jabrill Peppers 5.00 12.00
UBAJQ1 James Quick 4.00 10.00
UBAJR1 John Ross 4.00 10.00
UBAJR2 Josh Reynolds 3.00 8.00
UBAJW1 Jamaal Williams 3.00 8.00
UBAKDC KD Cannon 3.00 8.00
UBAMD1 Malachi Dupre 3.00 8.00
UBAMH1 Malik Hooker 3.00 8.00
UBAMH2 Marlon Humphrey 3.00 8.00
UBAMMD Malik McDowell 3.00 8.00
UBAMT1 Mitch Trubisky 30.00 60.00
UBAMW1 Mike Williams 5.00 12.00
UBANP1 Nathan Peterman 4.00 10.00
UBAPM1 Pat Mahomes II 100.00 200.00
UBAQW1 Quincy Wilson EXCH 3.00 8.00
UBARF1 Reuben Foster 3.00 8.00
UBARS1 Ryan Switzer 4.00 10.00
UBASJ1 Sidney Jones 3.00 8.00
UBASP1 Samaje Perine 3.00 8.00
UBAST1 Solomon Thomas 3.00 8.00
UBATC1 Taco Charlton 3.00 8.00
UBATF1 Tarean Folston 5.00 12.00
UBATJW T.J. Watt 10.00 25.00
UBATR1 Travis Rudolph 3.00 8.00
UBATS1 Tyrone Swoopes 3.00 8.00
UBATT1 Teez Tabor 4.00 10.00

2017 Leaf Ultimate Draft '91 Rookie Autographs

*GOLD/25: .6X TO 1.5X BASIC AU
*SILVER/15: .8X TO 2X BASIC AU
GLRAS1 ArDarius Stewart 3.00 8.00
GLRCD1 Corey Davis 5.00 12.00
GLRCG1 Chris Godwin 4.00 10.00
GLRCM1 Christian McCaffrey 8.00 20.00
GLRDB1 Derek Barnett 4.00 10.00
GLRDK1 DeShone Kizer 10.00 25.00
GLRDN1 David Njoku 4.00 10.00
GLRDW1 Deshaun Watson 20.00 50.00
GLRJD1 Joshua Dobbs 4.00 10.00
GLRJM1 Joe Mixon 6.00 15.00
GLRJP1 Jabrill Peppers 5.00 12.00
GLRJR1 John Ross 4.00 10.00
GLRMD1 Malachi Dupre 3.00 8.00
GLRMH1 Malik Hooker 3.00 8.00
GLRMT1 Mitch Trubisky 25.00 60.00
GLRST1 Solomon Thomas 3.00 8.00
GLRTC1 Taco Charlton 3.00 8.00
GLRTT1 Teez Tabor 4.00 10.00

2017 Leaf Ultimate Draft '92 Rookie Autographs

*GOLD/25: .6X TO 1.5X BASIC AU
*SILVER/15: .8X TO 2X BASIC AU
BGAD1 Amara Darboh 3.00 8.00
BGAS1 ArDarius Stewart 3.00 8.00
BGCJB C.J. Beathard 3.00 8.00
BGCK1 Chad Kelly 3.00 8.00
BGCT1 Cordrea Tankersley 4.00 10.00
BGDC1 Dalvin Cook 25.00 60.00
BGEH1 Elijah Hood 3.00 8.00
BGJM1 Joe Mixon 6.00 15.00
BGJW1 Jamaal Williams 3.00 8.00
BGKDC KD Cannon 3.00 8.00
BGMMD Malik McDowell 3.00 8.00
BGMW1 Mike Williams 5.00 12.00
BGQW1 Quincy Wilson EXCH 3.00 8.00
BGTJW T.J. Watt 10.00 25.00

2017 Leaf Ultimate Draft Flashback '90

*GOLD/50: .5X TO 1.2X BASIC AU
*SILVER/25: .6X TO 1.5X BASIC AU
BACC2 Corey Clement SP 4.00 10.00
BACD1 Corey Davis 5.00 12.00
BACK2 Cooper Kupp 5.00 12.00
BAEE1 Evan Engram 4.00 10.00
BAJA2 Jonathan Allen SP 4.00 10.00
BAJB2 Jake Butt SP 4.00 10.00
BAJL1 Jordan Leggett 3.00 8.00
BAKH1 Kareem Hunt 6.00 15.00
BAOJH O.J. Howard SP 4.00 10.00
BASC1 Stacy Coley SP 3.00 8.00
BATD2 Travin Dural SP 4.00 10.00

2017 Leaf Ultimate Draft Flashback '91 Rookie Autographs

*GOLD/20: .8X TO 2X BASIC AU
*SILVER/15: .8X TO 2X BASIC AU
GLRCC2 Corey Clement 4.00 10.00
GLREE1 Evan Engram 4.00 10.00
GLRJA2 Jonathan Allen 4.00 10.00
GLRJB2 Jake Butt 4.00 10.00
GLROJH O.J. Howard 4.00 10.00
GLRSC1 Stacy Coley 3.00 8.00
GLRTD2 Travin Dural 4.00 10.00

2017 Leaf Ultimate Draft Flashback '92 Rookie Autographs

*GOLD/20: .8X TO 2X BASIC AU
*SILVER/15: .8X TO 2X BASIC AU
BGCK2 Cooper Kupp 5.00 12.00
BGJL1 Jordan Leggett 3.00 8.00
BGKH1 Kareem Hunt 6.00 15.00
BGTD2 Travin Dural 4.00 10.00

2018 Leaf Ultimate Draft

*GOLD/25: .6X TO 1.5X BASIC AU
*SILVER/15: .8X TO 2X BASIC AU
BAAK1 Arden Key EXCH 3.00 8.00
BAAL1 Allen Lazard 3.00 8.00
BAAM1 Anthony Miller 5.00 12.00
BAAT1 Auden Tate 3.00 8.00
BABB1 Braxton Berrios 3.00 8.00
BABC1 Bradley Chubb EXCH 5.00 12.00
BABM1 Baker Mayfield 50.00 100.00
BABS1 Bo Scarbrough 4.00 10.00
BACD1 Carlton Davis 4.00 10.00
BACK1 Christian Kirk 5.00 12.00
BACR1 Calvin Ridley 8.00 20.00
BACS1 Courtland Sutton 5.00 12.00
BACS2 Cam Serigne 3.00 8.00
BACW1 Cedrick Wilson Jr. 3.00 8.00
BADB1 Deontay Burnett 4.00 10.00
BADC1 Deon Cain 4.00 10.00
BADC2 Darren Carrington II 4.00 10.00
BADG1 Derrius Guice 6.00 15.00
BADG2 DeAndre Goolsby 3.00 8.00
BADG3 Dallas Goedert 4.00 10.00
BADJ1 Derwin James EXCH 6.00 15.00
BADJC D.J. Chark 4.00 10.00
BADJM D.J. Moore 6.00 15.00
BADP1 Dante Pettis 5.00 12.00
BADRP Daron Payne 5.00 12.00
BADS2 Durham Smythe 3.00 8.00
BADS3 Dalton Schultz 4.00 10.00
BADW1 Denzel Ward 8.00 20.00
BAESB Equanimeous St. Brown 5.00 12.00
BAHH1 Hayden Hurst 4.00 10.00
BAIS1 Ito Smith 4.00 10.00
BAIT1 Ian Thomas 3.00 8.00
BAJA1 Josh Allen 12.00 30.00
BAJA2 Josh Adams 6.00 15.00
BAJJ1 Justin Jackson 4.00 10.00
BAJK1 John Kelly 4.00 10.00
BAJMM J'Mon Moore 3.00 8.00
BAJR1 Josh Rosen 10.00 25.00
BAJTB J.T. Barrett 5.00 12.00
BAJW1 Jake Wieneke 4.00 10.00
BAJW2 James Washington 6.00 15.00
BAKB1 Kurt Benkert 4.00 10.00
BAKC1 Keke Coutee 4.00 10.00
BAKH1 Kenny Hill 4.00 10.00
BAKJ1 Kerryon Johnson 5.00 12.00
BALF1 Luke Falk 4.00 10.00
BALW1 Logan Woodside EXCH 5.00 12.00
BAMA1 Mark Andrews 5.00 12.00
BAMA2 Marcell Ateman 4.00 10.00
BAMB1 Marcus Baugh 3.00 8.00
BAMC1 Martez Carter 3.00 8.00
BAMF1 Minkah Fitzpatrick 6.00 15.00
BAMG1 Michael Gallup 6.00 15.00
BAMG2 Mike Gesicki 4.00 10.00
BAMH1 Maurice Hurst 4.00 10.00
BAMR1 Mason Rudolph 8.00 20.00
BAMW1 Mark Walton 4.00 10.00
BAMW2 Mike White 4.00 10.00
BANC1 Nick Chubb 10.00 25.00
BAQF1 Quinton Flowers 3.00 8.00
BARE1 Rashaan Evans 5.00 12.00
BARF1 Royce Freeman 4.00 10.00
BARF2 Riley Ferguson 5.00 12.00
BARH1 Ronnie Harrison 4.00 10.00
BARJ2 Ronald Jones II 3.00 8.00
BARP1 Rashaad Penny 5.00 12.00
BARS1 Roquan Smith 10.00 25.00
BARW1 Ralph Webb 4.00 10.00
BASC1 Simmie Cobbs Jr. 5.00 12.00
BASD1 Sam Darnold 20.00 50.00
BASH1 Sam Hubbard 4.00 10.00
BASM1 Sony Michel 10.00 25.00
BATT1 Trenton Thompson 3.00 8.00
BAVV1 Vita Vea 5.00 12.00

2018 Leaf Ultimate Draft '92 Black Gold Autographs

*GOLD/25: .6X TO 1.5X BASIC AU
*SILVER/15: .8X TO 2X BASIC AU
BGAK1 Arden Key EXCH 3.00 8.00
BGBC1 Bradley Chubb EXCH 5.00 12.00
BGBM1 Baker Mayfield 50.00 100.00
BGBS1 Bo Scarbrough 4.00 10.00
BGCR1 Calvin Ridley 8.00 20.00
BGCS2 Cam Serigne 3.00 8.00
BGCW1 Cedrick Wilson Jr. 3.00 8.00
BGDC1 Deon Cain 4.00 10.00
BGDG1 Derrius Guice 6.00 15.00
BGDJ1 Derwin James EXCH 6.00 15.00
BGDJC D.J. Chark 4.00 10.00
BGDJM D.J. Moore 6.00 15.00
BGDP1 Dante Pettis 5.00 12.00
BGDS3 Dalton Schultz 4.00 10.00
BGHH1 Hayden Hurst 4.00 10.00
BGIS1 Ito Smith 4.00 10.00
BGJA2 Josh Adams 6.00 15.00
BGJMM J'Mon Moore 3.00 8.00
BGJR1 Josh Rosen 10.00 25.00
BGJW2 James Washington 6.00 15.00
BGKC1 Keke Coutee 4.00 10.00
BGKJ1 Kerryon Johnson 5.00 12.00
BGLW1 Logan Woodside EXCH 5.00 12.00
BGMA2 Marcell Ateman 4.00 10.00
BGMC1 Martez Carter 3.00 8.00
BGMF1 Minkah Fitzpatrick 6.00 15.00
BGMH1 Maurice Hurst 4.00 10.00
BGQF1 Quinton Flowers 3.00 8.00
BGRF1 Royce Freeman 4.00 10.00
BGRF2 Riley Ferguson 5.00 12.00
BGRH1 Ronnie Harrison 4.00 10.00
BGRP1 Rashaad Penny 5.00 12.00
BGSC1 Simmie Cobbs Jr. 5.00 12.00
BGSD1 Sam Darnold 20.00 50.00
BGTT1 Trenton Thompson 3.00 8.00
BGVV1 Vita Vea 5.00 12.00

2018 Leaf Ultimate Draft Flashback '90

*GOLD/50: .5X TO 1.2X BASIC AU
*SILVER/25: .6X TO 1.5X BASIC AU
BABM1 Baker Mayfield 50.00 100.00

2018 Leaf Ultimate Draft Flashback '91 Rookie Autographs

*GOLD/20: .8X TO 2X BASIC AU
*SILVER/15: .8X TO 2X BASIC AU
GLRBM1 Baker Mayfield 50.00 100.00

2012 Leaf Valiant Draft

AB1 Andre Branch 3.00 8.00
AC1 Aaron Corp 3.00 8.00
AD1 Alfonzo Dennard 3.00 8.00
AJ1 Alshon Jeffery 6.00 15.00
AJJ A.J. Jenkins 3.00 8.00
BJC B.J. Cunningham 3.00 8.00
BO1 Brock Osweiler 3.00 8.00
BP1 Bernard Pierce 3.00 8.00
BQ1 Brian Quick 3.00 8.00
BR1 Bobby Rainey 3.00 8.00
BT1 Brandon Thompson 4.00 10.00
BW1 Brandon Weeden 3.00 8.00
CF1 Coby Fleener 3.00 8.00
CG1 Chris Givens 3.00 8.00
CG2 Cyrus Gray 3.00 8.00
CH1 Chandler Harnish 3.00 8.00
CJ1 Chandler Jones 3.00 8.00
CK1 Case Keenum 6.00 15.00
CP1 Chris Polk 3.00 8.00
CU1 Courtney Upshaw 4.00 10.00
DA1 Dwayne Allen 3.00 8.00
DH1 Dan Herron 3.00 8.00
DH2 Dont'a Hightower 5.00 12.00
DJ1 Dwight Jones 3.00 8.00
DK1 Dre Kirkpatrick 3.00 8.00
DM2 Doug Martin 5.00 12.00
DP1 Dan Persa 4.00 10.00
DP2 DeVier Posey 3.00 8.00
DP3 Dontari Poe 3.00 8.00
DS1 Devon Still 4.00 10.00
DT1 Darron Thomas 8.00 20.00
FC1 Fletcher Cox 5.00 12.00
GC1 Greg Childs 3.00 8.00
GR1 Gerell Robinson 3.00 8.00
IP1 Isaiah Pead 3.00 8.00
JA1 Joe Adams 3.00 8.00
JB2 Justin Blackmon 3.00 8.00
JC2 Juron Criner 3.00 8.00
JF1 Jeff Fuller 3.00 8.00
JH1 Jacory Harris 4.00 10.00
JJ1 Janoris Jenkins 4.00 10.00
JW1 Jarius Wright 3.00 8.00
KC1 Kirk Cousins 12.00 30.00
KM1 Kellen Moore 4.00 10.00
KM2 Keshawn Martin 4.00 10.00
KR1 Keenan Robinson 4.00 10.00
KW1 Kendall Wright 3.00 8.00
LD1 Lavonte David 5.00 12.00
LJ1 LaMichael James 3.00 8.00
LK1 Luke Kuechly 8.00 20.00
LM1 Lamar Miller 5.00 12.00
MB1 Mark Barron 3.00 8.00
ME1 Michael Egnew 3.00 8.00
MF1 Michael Floyd 3.00 8.00
MI1 Melvin Ingram 3.00 8.00
MJ1 Marvin Jones 3.00 8.00
MM1 Marquis Maze 3.00 8.00
MS1 Mohamed Sanu 5.00 12.00
MT1 Marc Tyler 3.00 8.00
NF1 Nick Foles 8.00 20.00
NP1 Nick Perry 4.00 10.00
NT1 Nick Toon 3.00 8.00
OC1 Orson Charles 3.00 8.00
QC1 Quinton Coples 3.00 8.00
RB1 Ryan Broyles 3.00 8.00
RG3 Robert Griffin III 4.00 10.00
RL2 Ryan Lindley 3.00 8.00
RR1 Rueben Randle 3.00 8.00
RT1 Robert Turbin 3.00 8.00
RT2 Ryan Tannehill 5.00 12.00
RW1 Russell Wilson 50.00 100.00
SG1 Stephon Gilmore 4.00 10.00
SH1 Stephen Hill 3.00 8.00
TG1 Terrance Ganaway 4.00 10.00
TL1 Travis Lewis 4.00 10.00
TP1 Tauren Poole 3.00 8.00
TR1 Trent Richardson 3.00 8.00
TS1 Tommy Streeter 3.00 8.00
TYH T.Y. Hilton 6.00 15.00
WM1 Whitney Mercilus 3.00 8.00
ZB1 Zach Brown 3.00 8.00

2012 Leaf Valiant Draft Blue

*BLUE/99: .5X TO 1.2X BASIC CARDS
BLUE STATED PRINT RUN 99

2012 Leaf Valiant Draft Purple

*PURPLE/25: .6X TO 1.5X BASIC CARD
PURPLE STATED PRINT RUN 25

2012 Leaf Valiant Draft Army All-American Bowl Black

*BLACK/20-25: 1.5X TO 4X BASIC GREEN
AL1 Andrew Luck/25 50.00 100.00

2012 Leaf Valiant Draft Army All-American Bowl Green

RANDOM INSERTS IN PACKS
*BLUE: .5X TO 1.2X BASIC GREEN
*PURPLE/100-125: .8X TO 2X BASIC GREEN
*YELLOW/40-50: 1.2X TO 3X BASIC GREEN
AL1 Andrew Luck 10.00 25.00
BS1 Barry Sanders Jr. 3.00 8.00
GK1 Gunner Kiel 2.50 6.00

2013 Leaf Valiant Draft

BAAE1 Andre Ellington 3.00 8.00
BAAM2 Aaron Mellette 3.00 8.00
BAAO1 Alex Okafor 3.00 8.00
BABM1 Barkevious Mingo 3.00 8.00
BABS1 Brad Sorensen 3.00 8.00
BABW1 Bjoern Werner 3.00 8.00
BACH1 Cobi Hamilton 3.00 8.00
BACK1 Collin Klein SP 4.00 10.00
BACP2 Cordarrelle Patterson 3.00 8.00
BACV1 Conner Vernon 3.00 8.00
BACW2 Cierre Wood 3.00 8.00
BADA1 David Amerson 3.00 8.00
BADAH DeAndre Hopkins 8.00 20.00
BADM1 Dee Milliner 3.00 8.00
BADR1 Denard Robinson 3.00 8.00
BADRR Da'Rick Rogers SP 3.00 8.00
BADS1 Dion Sims 3.00 8.00
BAEJM EJ Manuel SP 3.00 8.00
BAEL1 Eddie Lacy SP 3.00 8.00
BAER1 Eric Reid 4.00 10.00
BAGB1 Giovani Bernard 3.00 8.00
BAGS1 Geno Smith SP 3.00 8.00
BAJB2 Josh Boyce 3.00 8.00
BAJF1 Joseph Fauria 3.00 8.00
BAJF2 Johnathan Franklin 3.00 8.00
BAJH1 Justin Hunter 3.00 8.00
BAJH2 Johnathan Hankins SP 3.00 8.00
BAJJ4 Jarvis Jones SP 3.00 8.00
BAJR1 Joseph Randle 3.00 8.00
BAJR2 Jordan Reed 5.00 12.00
BAJS1 Jake Stoneburner 5.00 12.00
BAJW2 Jesse Williams 5.00 12.00
BAKA1 Keenan Allen SP 6.00 15.00
BAKB1 Kenjon Barner SP 3.00 8.00
BAKS1 Kawann Short 3.00 8.00
BAKS2 Kenny Stills 3.00 8.00
BALJ1 Landry Jones SP 6.00 15.00
BALT2 Levine Toilolo 4.00 10.00
BALVB Le'Veon Bell 10.00 25.00
BAMB1 Matt Barkley SP 6.00 15.00
BAMB2 Montee Ball 3.00 8.00
BAMD1 Marcus Davis 3.00 8.00
BAMG1 Mike Gillislee 3.00 8.00
BAMG2 Mike Glennon SP 3.00 8.00
BAMG3 Marquise Goodwin 3.00 8.00
BAML1 Marcus Lattimore 3.00 8.00
BAMM1 Miguel Maysonet 3.00 8.00
BAMT1 Manti Te'o 4.00 10.00
BAMW2 Michael Williams 4.00 10.00
BAQP1 Quinton Patton 3.00 8.00
BARB1 Rex Burkhead 4.00 10.00
BARG1 Ray Graham 3.00 8.00
BARN1 Ryan Nassib 3.00 8.00
BARS2 Rodney Smith 3.00 8.00
BARS3 Ryan Swope 3.00 8.00
BARW1 Robert Woods SP 5.00 12.00
BASF1 Sharrif Floyd 3.00 8.00
BASL1 Star Lotulelei 4.00 10.00
BAST1 Stepfan Taylor 3.00 8.00
BATA1 Tavon Austin 4.00 10.00
BATB1 Tyler Bray SP 3.00 8.00
BATE1 Tyler Eifert 3.00 8.00
BATJ1 Tony Jefferson 5.00 12.00
BATJM T.J. McDonald 3.00 8.00
BATM1 Tyrann Mathieu 5.00 12.00
BATW1 Tyler Wilson SP 3.00 8.00
BATW2 Terrance Williams SP 6.00 15.00
BAZD1 Zac Dysert 3.00 8.00
BAZL1 Zach Line 3.00 8.00
NNO J.Manziel Art AU EXCH 150.00 300.00

2013 Leaf Valiant Draft Purple

*PURPLE/25: .6X TO 1.5X BASIC CARDS

2013 Leaf Valiant Draft Orange

*ORANGE/50: .5X TO 1.2X BASIC CARDS

2013 Leaf Valiant Draft Honor Guard Die Cut

*ORANGE/25: .5X TO 1.2X BASIC INSERTS
*PURPLE/15: .5X TO 1.2X BASIC INSERTS
HGBM1 Barkevious Mingo 4.00 10.00
HGCK1 Collin Klein 5.00 12.00
HGEL1 Eddie Lacy 4.00 10.00
HGGS1 Geno Smith 4.00 10.00
HGJH1 Justin Hunter 4.00 10.00
HGJJ4 Jarvis Jones 4.00 10.00
HGKA1 Keenan Allen 8.00 20.00
HGKB1 Kenjon Barner 4.00 10.00
HGLJ1 Landry Jones 8.00 20.00
HGMB1 Matt Barkley 8.00 20.00
HGMB2 Montee Ball 4.00 10.00
HGML1 Marcus Lattimore 4.00 10.00
HGRW1 Robert Woods 6.00 15.00
HGSL1 Star Lotulelei 5.00 12.00
HGTB1 Tyler Bray 4.00 10.00
HGTE1 Tyler Eifert 4.00 10.00
HGTW1 Tyler Wilson 4.00 10.00
HGTW2 Terrance Williams 4.00 10.00

2013 Leaf Valiant Draft On Target

*ORANGE/25: .5X TO 1.2X BASIC INSERTS
*PURPLE/15: .5X TO 1.2X BASIC INSERTS
OTBS1 Brad Sorensen 4.00 10.00
OTCK1 Collin Klein 5.00 12.00
OTEJM EJ Manuel 4.00 10.00
OTLJ1 Landry Jones SP 8.00 20.00
OTMB1 Matt Barkley 8.00 20.00
OTMG2 Mike Glennon 4.00 10.00
OTRN1 Ryan Nassib 4.00 10.00
OTTB1 Tyler Bray 4.00 10.00
OTTW1 Tyler Wilson 4.00 10.00
OTZD1 Zac Dysert 4.00 10.00

2013 Leaf Valiant Draft Stars

*ORANGE/25: .5X TO 1.2X BASIC INSERTS
*PURPLE/15-25: .5X TO 1.2X BASIC INSERTS
SAE1 Andre Ellington 4.00 10.00
SBW1 Bjoern Werner 4.00 10.00
SCH1 Cobi Hamilton 4.00 10.00
SDR1 Denard Robinson 4.00 10.00
SDRR Da'Rick Rogers 4.00 10.00
SEJM EJ Manuel 4.00 10.00
SJF2 Johnathan Franklin 4.00 10.00
SJH2 Johnathan Hankins SP 4.00 10.00
SJJ4 Jarvis Jones 4.00 10.00
SKA1 Keenan Allen 8.00 20.00
SKB1 Kenjon Barner 4.00 10.00
SMB2 Montee Ball 4.00 10.00
SMG2 Mike Glennon 4.00 10.00
SML1 Marcus Lattimore 4.00 10.00
SRG1 Ray Graham 4.00 10.00
SRW1 Robert Woods 6.00 15.00
STA1 Tavon Austin 5.00 12.00

2014 Leaf Valiant Draft

BAAB1 Anthony Barr 2.50 6.00
BAAD1 Aaron Donald 6.00 15.00
BAAJM A.J. McCarron 2.50 6.00
BAAM1 Aaron Murray 2.50 6.00
BAAR1 Allen Robinson 4.00 10.00
BAASJ Austin Seferian-Jenkins 2.50 6.00
BABB1 Blake Bortles 3.00 8.00
BABC1 Brandin Cooks 4.00 10.00
BABE1 Bruce Ellington 2.50 6.00
BABS1 Bishop Sankey 2.50 6.00
BACH1 Carlos Hyde 3.00 8.00
BACS1 Charles Sims 2.50 6.00
BACS2 Connor Shaw 2.50 6.00
BADAT De'Anthony Thomas 2.50 6.00
BADC1 Derek Carr 12.00 30.00
BADM1 Donte Moncrief 2.50 6.00
BAEE1 Eric Ebron 3.00 8.00
BAJA1 Jace Amaro 2.50 6.00
BAJA2 Jared Abbrederis 2.50 6.00
BAJC1 Jadeveon Clowney 3.00 8.00
BAJG1 Jimmy Garoppolo 40.00 80.00
BAJH1 Josh Huff 8.00 20.00
BAJL1 Jarvis Landry 5.00 12.00
BAJM1 Jake Matthews 2.50 6.00
BAJM2 J.Manziel EXCH 4.00 10.00
BAJM3 Jordan Matthews 4.00 10.00
BAJWJ James Wilder Jr. 3.00 8.00
BAKB1 K.Benjamin EXCH 4.00 10.00
BAKDC Ka'Deem Carey 2.50 6.00
BAKE1 Kony Ealy 3.00 8.00
BAKM1 Khalil Mack 10.00 25.00
BALS1 Lache Seastrunk 5.00 12.00
BALT1 Logan Thomas 2.50 6.00
BAME1 Mike Evans 6.00 15.00
BAML1 Marqise Lee 4.00 10.00
BAOBJ Odell Beckham Jr. 40.00 80.00
BAPR1 Paul Richardson 5.00 12.00
BARSH Ra'Shede Hageman 2.50 6.00
BASE1 Shaquelle Evans 2.50 6.00
BASM1 Stephen Morris 2.50 6.00
BASW1 Sammy Watkins 4.00 10.00
BATB1 Tajh Boyd 2.50 6.00
BATB2 Teddy Bridgewater 20.00 40.00
BATL1 Taylor Lewan 2.50 6.00
BATM1 T.Mason EXCH 2.50 6.00
BAZM1 Zach Mettenberger 2.50 6.00
BAZM2 Zack Martin 5.00 12.00

2014 Leaf Valiant Draft Orange

*ORANGE/50-99: .5X TO 1.2X TO BASIC CARDS

2014 Leaf Valiant Draft Purple

*PURPLE/25: .8X TO 2X BASIC CARDS

2014 Leaf Valiant Draft Honor Guard Die Cut

HGAJM A.J. McCarron 2.50 6.00
HGAM1 Aaron Murray 2.50 6.00
HGBC1 Brandin Cooks 4.00 10.00
HGDAT De'Anthony Thomas 2.50 6.00
HGJC1 Jadeveon Clowney 3.00 8.00
HGJG1 Jimmy Garoppolo 30.00 60.00
HGJM2 Johnny Manziel SP 4.00 10.00
HGME1 Mike Evans 6.00 15.00
HGOBJ Odell Beckham Jr. 30.00 60.00
HGTB2 Teddy Bridgewater 4.00 10.00

2014 Leaf Valiant Draft Honor Guard Die Cut Orange

*ORANGE/50: .6X TO 1.5X BASIC INSERTS
*ORANGE/25: .8X TO 2X BASIC INSERTS
HGJM2 Johnny Manziel/25 8.00 20.00
HGLT1 Logan Thomas/25 5.00 12.00

2014 Leaf Valiant Draft Honor Guard Die Cut Purple

*PURPLE/15-25: .8X TO 2X BASIC INSERTS
HGJM2 Johnny Manziel/15
HGLT1 Logan Thomas/15 5.00 12.00

2014 Leaf Valiant Draft In the Spotlight

*ORANGE/50: .6X TO 1.5X BASE INSERTS
*PURPLE/25: .8X TO 2X BASE INSERTS
SAB1 Anthony Barr 2.50 6.00
SAD1 Aaron Donald 6.00 15.00
SAR1 Allen Robinson 4.00 10.00
SCH1 Carlos Hyde 3.00 8.00
SEE1 Eric Ebron 3.00 8.00
SJC1 Jadeveon Clowney 3.00 8.00
SJM1 Jake Matthews 2.50 6.00
SJM2 Johnny Manziel 4.00 10.00
SKDC Ka'Deem Carey 2.50 6.00
SOBJ Odell Beckham Jr. 40.00 80.00
STB1 Tajh Boyd 2.50 6.00
STM1 T.Mason EXCH 8.00 20.00

2014 Leaf Valiant Draft Lightning Fast

*ORANGE/50: .6X TO 1.5X BASE INSERTS
*ORANGE/25: .8X TO 2X BASE INSERTS
*PURPLE/15-25: .8X TO 2X BASE INSERTS
LFBC1 Brandin Cooks 4.00 10.00
LFBE1 Bruce Ellington 2.50 6.00
LFDAT De'Anthony Thomas 2.50 6.00
LFDW1 Damien Williams 2.50 6.00
LFJC1 Jadeveon Clowney 3.00 8.00
LFMC1 Mike Campanaro 2.50 6.00
LFME1 Mike Evans 6.00 15.00
LFML1 Marqise Lee 3.00 8.00
LFOBJ Odell Beckham Jr. 40.00 80.00
LFPR1 Paul Richardson 5.00 12.00
LFSW1 Sammy Watkins 4.00 10.00
LFTG1 Tyler Gaffney 2.50 6.00

2014 Leaf Valiant Draft On Target

OTAJM A.McCarron EXCH 3.00 8.00
OTAM1 Aaron Murray 3.00 8.00
OTBB1 Blake Bortles SP 4.00 10.00
OTDC1 Derek Carr 20.00 50.00
OTJG1 Jimmy Garoppolo 40.00 100.00
OTJM2 J.Manziel EXCH 5.00 12.00
OTTB2 Teddy Bridgewater 5.00 12.00
OTZM1 Zach Mettenberger 3.00 8.00

2014 Leaf Valiant Draft On Target Orange

*ORANGE/50: .5X TO 1.2X BASE INSERTS
*ORANGE/25: .6X TO 1.5X BASE INSERTS
OTATB Tajh Boyd/25 5.00 12.00
OTJM2 Johnny Manziel/25 8.00 20.00

2014 Leaf Valiant Draft On Target Purple

*PURPLE/15-25: .6X TO 1.5X BASE INSERTS
OTATB Tajh Boyd/15 5.00 12.00

2014 Leaf Valiant Draft Rising Stock

*ORANGE/50: .5X TO 1.2X BASE INSERTS
*ORANGE/25: .6X TO 1.5X BASE INSERTS
*PURPLE/15-25: .6X TO 1.5X BASE INSERTS
RSBB1 Blake Bortles 4.00 10.00
RSBE1 Bruce Ellington 3.00 8.00
RSJA2 Jared Abbrederis 3.00 8.00
RSJM2 J.Manziel EXCH 5.00 12.00
RSJM3 Jordan Matthews 5.00 12.00
RSKM1 Khalil Mack 8.00 20.00
RSPR1 Paul Richardson 6.00 15.00
RSSW1 Sammy Watkins 5.00 12.00
RSTL1 Taylor Lewan 3.00 8.00
RSTM1 T.Mason EXCH 3.00 8.00

2012 Leaf Young Stars Draft

COMPLETE SET (100) 10.00 25.00
1 A.J. Jenkins .15 .40
2 Alameda Ta'amu .20 .50
3 Alfonzo Dennard .15 .40
4 Alshon Jeffery .30 .75
5 Amini Silatolu .15 .40
6 Andre Branch .15 .40
7 Audie Cole .15 .40
8 B.J. Cunningham .15 .40
9 Bernard Pierce .15 .40
10 Bobby Massie .15 .40
11 Bobby Wagner .25 .60
12 Brandon Mosley .15 .40
13 Brandon Thompson .20 .50
14 Brandon Weeden .15 .40
15 Brian Quick .15 .40
16 Casey Hayward .15 .40
17 Chandler Jones .15 .40
18 Chris Givens .15 .40
19 Chris Polk .15 .40
20 Cliff Harris .25 .60
21 Coby Fleener .15 .40
22 Coryell Judie .15 .40
23 Courtney Upshaw .20 .50
24 Cyrus Gray .15 .40
25 D'Anton Lynn .25 .60
26 Dan Herron .15 .40
27 David DeCastro .15 .40
28 DeVier Posey .15 .40
29 Devon Still .20 .50
30 Devon Wylie .15 .40
31 Dont'a Hightower .25 .60
32 Donnie Fletcher .15 .40
33 Dontari Poe .15 .40
34 Doug Martin .25 .60
35 Dre Kirkpatrick .15 .40
36 Duke Ihenacho .25 .60
37 Dwight Jones .15 .40
38 George Iloka .15 .40
39 Greg Childs .15 .40
40 Harrison Smith .15 .40
41 Janoris Jenkins .20 .50
42 Jared Crick .15 .40
43 Jarius Wright .15 .40
44 Jerrell Harris .20 .50
45 Joe Adams .15 .40
46 Jonathan Martin .15 .40
47 Juron Criner .15 .40
48 Justin Blackmon .15 .40
49 Keenan Robinson .20 .50
50 Kendall Wright .15 .40
51 Kirk Cousins .60 1.50
52 Lamar Miller .25 .60
53 LaMichael James .15 .40
54 Lavonte David .25 .60
55 Lucas Nix .15 .40
56 Luke Kuechly .40 1.00
57 Marcus Forston .15 .40
58 Mark Barron .15 .40
59 Markelle Martin .20 .50
60 Marvin Jones .15 .40
61 Matt Kalil .15 .40
62 Melvin Ingram .15 .40
63 Michael Egnew .15 .40
64 Michael Floyd .15 .40
65 Mike Martin .20 .50
66 Mohamed Sanu .25 .60
67 Nick Perry .20 .50
68 Nick Toon .15 .40
69 Nigel Bradham .20 .50
70 Orson Charles .15 .40
71 Peter Konz .15 .40
72 Quinton Coples .15 .40
73 Rhett Ellison .20 .50

74 Robert Blanton .20 .50
75 Robert Griffin III .20 .50
76 Rueben Randle .15 .40
77 Russell Wilson 1.25 3.00
78 Ryan Broyles .15 .40
79 Ryan Tannehill .25 .60
80 Sean Spence .20 .50
81 Shea McClellin .20 .50
82 Stephen Hill .12 .30
83 Thomas Mayo .15 .40
84 Tommy Streeter .15 .40
85 Travis Lewis .20 .50
86 Trent Richardson .15 .40
87 Trenton Robinson .20 .50
88 Tydreke Powell .15 .40
89 Whitney Mercilus .15 .40
90 Zach Brown .15 .40
91 Zebrie Sanders .15 .40
92 Antwon Bailey .20 .50
93 Bobby Rainey .15 .40
94 Chris Galippo .20 .50
95 Dwayne Allen .15 .40
96 Gerell Robinson .15 .40
97 Keshawn Martin .20 .50
98 Kevin Koger .25 .60
99 Tim Benford .15 .40
100 Tyler Hansen .15 .40

2012 Leaf Young Stars Draft Autographs

TWO AUTOS PER RETAIL BOX
AB1 Andre Branch 2.00 5.00
AC2 Audie Cole 2.00 5.00
AD1 Alfonzo Dennard 2.00 5.00
AJ1 Alshon Jeffery SP
AJJ A.J. Jenkins SP
AS1 Amini Silatolu 2.00 5.00
AT1 Alameda Ta'amu 2.50 6.00
BJC B.J. Cunningham SP
BM1 Bobby Massie 2.00 5.00
BM2 Brandon Mosley 2.00 5.00
BP1 Bernard Pierce SP
BQ1 Brian Quick SP
BR1 Bobby Rainey 2.00 5.00
BT1 Brandon Thompson 2.50 6.00
BW1 Brandon Weeden SP 2.50 6.00
BW2 Bobby Wagner 4.00 10.00
CF1 Coby Fleener SP
CG1 Chris Givens SP
CG2 Cyrus Gray SP
CH2 Casey Hayward 2.00 5.00
CH3 Cliff Harris 3.00 8.00
CJ1 Chandler Jones SP 2.50 6.00
CJ2 Coryell Judie 2.00 5.00
CP1 Chris Polk SP
DA1 Dwayne Allen 2.00 5.00
DAL D'Anton Lynn 3.00 8.00
DDC David DeCastro 2.00 5.00
DF1 Donnie Fletcher 2.00 5.00
DH1 Dan Herron 2.00 5.00
DH2 Dont'a Hightower SP
DI1 Duke Ihenacho 3.00 8.00
DJ1 Dwight Jones SP
DK1 Dre Kirkpatrick 2.00 5.00
DM2 Doug Martin SP 4.00 10.00
DP1 Dan Persa 2.50 6.00
DP2 DeVier Posey SP
DP3 Dontari Poe SP
DS1 Devon Still SP
DW1 Devon Wylie 2.00 5.00
FW1 Fozzy Whittaker 2.00 5.00
GC1 Greg Childs 2.00 5.00
GI1 George Iloka 2.00 5.00
GR1 Gerell Robinson 2.00 5.00
HS1 Harrison Smith 2.00 5.00
JA1 Joe Adams SP
JB2 Justin Blackmon SP
JC2 Juron Criner SP
JH1 Jerrell Harris 2.50 6.00
JJ1 Janoris Jenkins SP
JM1 Jonathan Martin 2.00 5.00
JW1 Jarius Wright 2.00 5.00
KC1 Kirk Cousins SP 8.00 20.00
KK1 Kevin Koger 3.00 8.00
KM2 Keshawn Martin 2.50 6.00
KR1 Keenan Robinson 2.50 6.00
KW1 Kendall Wright SP
LD1 Lavonte David 3.00 8.00
LJ1 LaMichael James 2.00 5.00
LK1 Luke Kuechly SP
LM1 Lamar Miller SP
LN1 Lucas Nix 2.00 5.00
ME1 Michael Egnew SP
MF2 Marcus Forston 2.00 5.00
MI1 Melvin Ingram SP
MJ1 Marvin Jones 2.00 5.00
MK1 Matt Kalil SP
MM2 Markelle Martin 2.50 6.00
MM3 Mike Martin 2.50 6.00
MS1 Mohamed Sanu SP
NB1 Nigel Bradham 2.50 6.00
NP1 Nick Perry SP
NT1 Nick Toon SP
OC1 Orson Charles 2.00 5.00
PK1 Peter Konz 2.00 5.00
QC1 Quinton Coples SP
RB1 Ryan Broyles SP
RB2 Robert Blanton 2.50 6.00
RE1 Rhett Ellison 2.50 6.00
RG3 Robert Griffin III SP 3.00 8.00
RR1 Rueben Randle SP
RT2 Ryan Tannehill SP 4.00 10.00
RW1 Russell Wilson SP 40.00 80.00
SG1 Stephon Gilmore SP
SH1 Stephen Hill SP
SM1 Shea McClellin 2.50 6.00
SS1 Sean Spence 2.50 6.00
TB1 Tim Benford 2.00 5.00
TH1 Tyler Hansen 2.00 5.00
TM1 Thomas Mayo 2.00 5.00
TP2 Tydreke Powell 2.00 5.00
TR2 Trenton Robinson 2.50 6.00
WM1 Whitney Mercilus SP 6.00 15.00
ZB1 Zach Brown 2.00 5.00
ZS1 Zebrie Sanders 2.00 5.00

1996 Press Pass

The Press Pass set was issued in one series totalling 55 standard-size cards. The set was issued in three card packs. The fronts have two photos as well as the player's name and position on the bottom. The "96 Press Pass Draft Pick" logo is in the upper left. The backs include vital statistics, statistical information and some career information.

COMPLETE SET (55) 7.50 20.00
1 Keyshawn Johnson .60 1.50
2 Jonathan Ogden .40 1.00
3 Duane Clemons .07 .20
4 Kevin Hardy .07 .20
5 Eddie George 1.00 2.50
6 Karim Abdul-Jabbar .25 .60
7 Terry Glenn .25 .60
8 Leeland McElroy .15 .40
9 Simeon Rice .30 .75
10 Roman Oben .07 .20
11 Daryl Gardener .07 .20
12 Marcus Coleman .07 .20
13 Christian Peter .07 .20
14 Tim Biakabutuka .25 .60
15 Eric Moulds .60 1.50
16 Chris Darkins .07 .20
17 Andre Johnson .07 .20
18 Lawyer Milloy .25 .60
19 Jon Runyan .07 .20
20 Mike Alstott .60 1.50
21 Jeff Hartings .25 .60
22 Amani Toomer .50 1.25
23 Danny Kanell .25 .60
24 Marco Battaglia .07 .20
25 Stephen Davis .60 1.50
26 Johnny McWilliams .07 .20
27 Israel Ifeanyi .07 .20
28 Scott Slutzker .07 .20
29 Bryant Mix .07 .20
30 Brian Roche .07 .20
31 Stanley Pritchett .07 .20
32 Jerome Woods .07 .20
33 Tommie Frazier .15 .40
34 Stepfret Williams .07 .20
35 Ray Mickens .07 .20
36 Alex Van Dyke .07 .20
37 Bobby Hoying .25 .60
38 Tony Brackens .25 .60
39 Dietrich Jells .07 .20
40 Jason Odom .07 .20
41 Randall Godfrey .07 .20
42 Willie Anderson .07 .20
43 Tony Banks .25 .60
44 Michael Cheever .07 .20
45 Je'Rod Cherry .07 .20
46 Chris Doering .07 .20
47 Steve Taneyhill .07 .20
48 Kyle Wachholtz .07 .20
49 Dusty Zeigler .07 .20
50 Derrick Mayes .15 .40
51 Orpheus Roye .07 .20
52 Sedric Clark .07 .20
53 Richard Huntley .15 .40
54 Donnie Edwards .25 .60
55 Zach Thomas CL .25 .60
RED Lawrence Phillips 2.50 6.00
P1 Tim Biakabutuka .40 1.00
Promo

1996 Press Pass Holofoil

COMPLETE SET (55) 20.00 50.00
*HOLOFOILS: 1.2X TO 3X BASIC CARDS
ONE PER PACK

1996 Press Pass Holofoil Emerald Proofs

*EMERALDS: 8X TO 20X BASIC CARDS
STATED ODDS 1:36

1996 Press Pass Autographs

These cards were inserted approximately one every 72 packs. The cards have a player autograph on the front. The backs of the card state that the collector has received an authentic, limited edition Press Pass autograph card. The cards are unnumbered and we have sequenced them in alphabetical order.

COMPLETE SET (12) 100.00 200.00
STATED ODDS 1:72
1 Karim Abdul-Jabbar 10.00 25.00
2 Tony Banks 10.00 25.00
3 Tim Biakabutuka 10.00 25.00
4 Duane Clemons 3.00 8.00
5 Stephen Davis 12.50 30.00
6 Chris Doering 3.00 8.00
7 Bobby Hoying 6.00 15.00
8 Keyshawn Johnson 15.00 40.00
9 Danny Kanell 6.00 15.00
10 Leeland McElroy 6.00 15.00
11 Jonathan Ogden 15.00 30.00
12 Steve Taneyhill 3.00 8.00

1996 Press Pass Crystal Ball

These cards were inserted one every 18 packs. The die cut cards feature a player's photo within a multi-colored crystal ball. The words "Crystal Ball" as well as the player's name are on the bottom. The cards are numbered with a "CB" prefix and are also numbered as "X" of 12.

COMPLETE SET (12) 20.00 40.00
STATED ODDS 1:18
CB1 Lawyer Milloy 1.50 3.00
CB2 Terry Glenn 1.50 3.00
CB3 Duane Clemons .40 1.00
CB4 Kevin Hardy .40 1.00
CB5 Eddie George 6.00 12.00
CB6 Jonathan Ogden 2.00 5.00
CB7 Karim Abdul-Jabbar 1.50 3.00
CB8 Tim Biakabutuka 1.50 3.00
CB9 Eric Moulds 4.00 8.00
CB10 Danny Kanell 1.50 3.00
CB11 Leeland McElroy 1.00 2.00
CB12 Keyshawn Johnson 4.00 8.00

1996 Press Pass Phone Cards $5

These cards were randomly inserted into packs. The checklists for all three sets are the same; however, they were inserted in different ratios. The $5 cards were inserted one every 36 packs, while the $10 were included one every 216 packs and the $20 phone cards were included one every 864 packs. There are also $1996 phone cards and those cards were inserted one every forty-four thousand packs. These $1996 cards are not valued at the present. The standard-size cards feature a player photo. The dollar amount of the card is located in the upper right with the player's name in the lower left. The back has user information, with the cards usable until April 30, 1997. The cards are numbered as "X" of nine.

COMPLETE SET (9) 6.00 15.00
STATED ODDS 1:36
*$10 CARDS: .6X TO 1.5X BASIC INSERTS
STATED ODDS 1:216
*$20 CARDS: 1.2X TO 3X BASIC INSERTS
STATED ODDS 1:864
1 Keyshawn Johnson 1.25 3.00
2 Jonathan Ogden .75 2.00
3 Tommie Frazier .30 .75
4 Eddie George 2.00 5.00
5 Karim Abdul-Jabbar .50 1.25
6 Terry Glenn .50 1.25
7 Leeland McElroy .30 .75
8 Tim Biakabutuka .50 1.25
9 Kevin Hardy .15 .40

1996 Press Pass Paydirt

These 75 standard-size cards were issued in five-card packs. This set is the retail version of Press Pass and also features various insert cards. This set features players projected to be among the leading rookies of the 1996 NFL season. The RED Lawrence Phillips card was the prize for an expired mail order pack redemption.

COMPLETE SET (75) 12.50 25.00
1 Keyshawn Johnson .75 2.00
2 Jonathan Ogden .50 1.25
3 Duane Clemons .02 .10
4 Kevin Hardy .10 .30
5 Eddie George 1.00 2.50
6 Karim Abdul-Jabbar .30 .75
7 Terry Glenn .60 1.50
8 Leeland McElroy .10 .30
9 Simeon Rice .40 1.00
10 Roman Oben .02 .10
11 Daryl Gardener .02 .10
12 Marcus Coleman .02 .10
13 Christian Peter UER .02 .10
Chris Doering stamp on front
14 Tim Biakabutuka .30 .75
15 Eric Moulds .30 .75
16 Chris Darkins .02 .10
17 Andre Johnson .02 .10
18 Lawyer Milloy .30 .75
19 Jon Runyan .02 .10
20 Mike Alstott .60 1.50
21 Jeff Hartings .30 .75
22 Amani Toomer .50 1.25
23 Danny Kanell .30 .75
24 Marco Battaglia .02 .10
25 Stephen Davis .60 1.50
26 Johnny McWilliams .02 .10
27 Israel Ifeanyi .02 .10
28 Scott Slutzker .02 .10
29 Bryant Mix .02 .10
30 Brian Roche .02 .10
31 Stanley Pritchett .02 .10
32 Jerome Woods .02 .10
33 Tommie Frazier .10 .30
34 Stepfret Williams .02 .10
35 Ray Mickens .02 .10
36 Alex Van Dyke .02 .10
37 Bobby Hoying .30 .75
38 Tony Brackens .30 .75
39 Dietrich Jells .02 .10
40 Jason Odom .02 .10
41 Randall Godfrey .02 .10
42 Willie Anderson .02 .10
43 Tony Banks .30 .75
44 Michael Cheever .02 .10
45 Je'Rod Cherry .02 .10
46 Chris Doering .02 .10
47 Steve Taneyhill .02 .10
48 Kyle Wachholtz .02 .10
49 Dusty Zeigler .02 .10
50 Derrick Mayes .10 .30
51 Orpheus Roye .02 .10
52 Sedric Clark .02 .10
53 Richard Huntley .10 .30
54 Donnie Edwards .30 .75
55 Zach Thomas .50 1.25
56 Alex Molden .02 .10
57 Jimmy Herndon .02 .10
58 Mike Alstott .60 1.50
59 Scott Greene .02 .10
60 Danny Kanell .30 .75
61 Jonathan Ogden .50 1.25
62 Simeon Rice .40 1.00
63 Kevin Hardy .10 .30
64 Jon Runyan .02 .10
65 Stephen Davis .60 1.50
66 Tim Biakabutuka .30 .75
67 Terry Glenn .60 1.50
68 Leeland McElroy .10 .30
69 Eric Moulds .75 2.00
70 Karim Abdul-Jabbar .30 .75
71 Lawyer Milloy .10 .30
72 Derrick Mayes .30 .75
73 Tommie Frazier .10 .30
74 Bobby Hoying .30 .75
75 Kyle Wachholtz CL .02 .10
RED Lawrence Phillips 2.50 6.00

1996 Press Pass Paydirt Holofoil

COMPLETE SET (75) 30.00 80.00
*HOLOFOILS: 1.5X TO 4X BASIC CARDS
STATED ODDS 1:4

1996 Press Pass Paydirt Red

COMPLETE SET (75) 20.00 50.00
*REDS: .8X TO 2X BASIC CARDS
ONE PER PACK

1996 Press Pass Paydirt Autographs

These cards are insetrted one every 72 packs. The cards are autographed on the front and have the words "You have received an authentic limited-edition Press Pass Paydirt card on the back. These cards are unnumbered and we have sequenced them in alphabetical order.

COMPLETE SET (16) 100.00 200.00
STATED ODDS 1:72
1 Karim Abdul-Jabbar 7.50 20.00
2 Tony Banks 7.50 20.00
3 Tim Biakabutuka 7.50 20.00
4 Duane Clemons 3.00 8.00
5 Stephen Davis 15.00 40.00
6 Chris Doering 3.00 8.00
7 Bobby Hoying 7.50 20.00
8 Keyshawn Johnson 15.00 40.00
9 Danny Kanell 6.00 15.00
10 Derrick Mayes 6.00 15.00
11 Leeland McElroy 3.00 8.00
12 Lawyer Milloy 7.50 20.00
13 Eric Moulds 15.00 40.00
14 Jonathan Ogden 15.00 30.00
15 Steve Taneyhill 3.00 8.00
16 Alex Van Dyke 3.00 8.00

1996 Press Pass Paydirt Game Breakers

This 12-card standard-size set features players who dominated games in college. The cards were inserted one every 18 packs. The set is numbered with a "GB" prefix.

COMPLETE SET (12) 20.00 40.00
STATED ODDS 1:18
GB1 Lawyer Milloy 2.00 4.00
GB2 Terry Glenn 4.00 8.00
GB3 Duane Clemons .20 .50
GB4 Kevin Hardy .75 1.50
GB5 Eddie George 6.00 12.00
GB6 Jonathan Ogden 2.50 6.00
GB7 Karim Abdul-Jabbar 2.00 4.00
GB8 Tim Biakabutuka 2.00 4.00
GB9 Eric Moulds 2.00 4.00
GB10 Danny Kanell 2.00 4.00
GB11 Leeland McElroy .75 1.50
GB12 Keyshawn Johnson 5.00 10.00

1996 Press Pass Paydirt Eddie George

1995 Heisman Trophy winner Eddie George is featured in this four-card standard-size set. The cards were inserted into packs at a staggered rate: Card #1 was one in 36, Card #2 was one in 72, Card #3 was one in 216, and Card #4 was one in 864 packs. The fronts feature a photo of George against a silver background of his name repeating while the backs contain four different action shots. The cards are numbered with an "EG" prefix.

COMPLETE SET (4) 75.00 125.00
EG1 Eddie George 2.50 6.00
EG2 Eddie George 5.00 10.00
EG3 Eddie George 15.00 30.00
EG4 Eddie George 45.00 90.00

1997 Press Pass

This 49-card set features some leading NFL prospects entering the 1997 season. The borderless full color shots feature an action photo on the front with the players name and position on the bottom. The backs feature biographical information, a brief blurb as well as collegiate stats for these players. Card #48, Joe Paterno, was pulled at the last minute due to licensing problems. However, a very small amount of cards did make it into packs. Card #48 is not considered part of the base set.

COMPLETE SET (49) 7.50 20.00
1 Orlando Pace .20 .50
2 Warrick Dunn .50 1.25
3 Danny Wuerffel .20 .50
4 Darnell Autry .07 .20
5 Troy Davis .07 .20
6 Jake Plummer .60 1.50
7 Corey Dillon .60 1.50
8 Reidel Anthony .20 .50
9 Byron Hanspard .10 .30
10 Tiki Barber 1.00 2.50
11 Ike Hilliard .20 .50
12 Rae Carruth .07 .20
13 Yatil Green .10 .30
14 Peter Boulware .20 .50
15 Jim Druckenmiller .10 .30
16 Pat Barnes .07 .20
17 Trevor Pryce .20 .50
18 Kevin Lockett .07 .20
19 Koy Detmer .20 .50
20 Bryant Westbrook .07 .20
21 Darrell Russell .07 .20
22 Tony Gonzalez .60 1.50
23 Shawn Springs .10 .30
24 Chris Canty .07 .20
25 David LaFleur .07 .20
26 Dwayne Rudd .07 .20
27 Bob Sapp .20 .50
28 Mike Vrabel .75 2.00
29 Antowain Smith .40 1.00
30 Keith Poole .07 .20
31 Sedrick Shaw .10 .30
32 Tremain Mack .07 .20
33 Matt Russell .07 .20
34 Reinard Wilson .10 .30
35 Marc Edwards .10 .30
36 Greg Jones .07 .20
37 Michael Booker .07 .20
38 James Farrior .20 .50
39 Danny Wuerffel HL .10 .30
40 Troy Davis HL .07 .20
41 Corey Dillon HL .40 1.00
42 Jake Plummer HL .30 .75
43 Peter Boulware HL .10 .30
44 Eddie Robinson CO .20 .50
45 Bobby Bowden CO .30 .75
46 Steve Spurrier CO .50 1.25
47 Gary Barnett CO .07 .20
48 Joe Paterno CO SP 30.00 50.00
49 Tom Osborne CO .50 1.25
50 Jarrett Irons CL .07 .20

1997 Press Pass Combine

COMPLETE SET (45) 10.00 25.00
*STARS: .6X TO 1.5X BASIC CARDS
ONE PER PACK
P1 Warrick Dunn Promo .60 1.50

1997 Press Pass Red Zone

COMPLETE SET (49) 10.00 25.00
*STARS: .6X to 1.5X BASIC CARDS
ONE PER HOBBY PACK
48 Joe Paterno CO SP 50.00 100.00

1997 Press Pass Torquers Blue

COMPLETE SET (49) 10.00 25.00
*STARS: .6X to 1.5X BASIC CARDS
ONE PER RETAIL PACK
48 Joe Paterno CO SP 30.00 80.00

1997 Press Pass Autographs

This 31 card set features signed cards of some of the people in the Press Pass set. The cards do not have the UV coating which are on the regular cards so the signing was easier. The backs mention that the collector is now an owner of a 1997 Press Pass Autographed Football card and encourages them to finish the rest of the set. These cards were inserted one every 72 packs.

COMPLETE SET (31) 200.00 400.00
STATED ODDS 1:72
1 Reidel Anthony 7.50 20.00
2 Michael Booker 3.00 8.00
3 Peter Boulware 7.50 20.00
4 Bobby Bowden CO 15.00 40.00
5 Chris Canty 3.00 8.00
6 Rae Carruth 5.00 12.00
7 Troy Davis 5.00 12.00
8 Koy Detmer 7.50 20.00
9 Corey Dillon 12.00 30.00
10 Jim Druckenmiller 5.00 12.00
11 Warrick Dunn 12.00 30.00
12 James Farrior 15.00 30.00
13 Tony Gonzalez 15.00 30.00
14 Yatil Green 5.00 12.00
15 Byron Hanspard 5.00 12.00
16 Ike Hilliard 10.00 25.00
17 Greg Jones 3.00 8.00
18 David LaFleur 3.00 8.00
19 Kevin Lockett 3.00 8.00
20 Tom Osborne CO 30.00 60.00
21 Orlando Pace 7.50 20.00
22 Keith Poole 3.00 8.00
23 Darrell Russell 3.00 8.00
24 Matt Russell 3.00 8.00
25 Bob Sapp 3.00 8.00
26 Steve Spurrier CO 12.50 30.00
27 Gene Stallings CO 10.00 25.00
28 Mike Vrabel 25.00 50.00
29 Bryant Westbrook 3.00 8.00
30 Reinard Wilson 3.00 8.00
31 Danny Wuerffel 7.50 20.00

1997 Press Pass Big 12

This set features not only players from the collegiate ranks but also 12 players who look as though they will have sucsessfull pro careers. These cards are inserted one every 12 packs and are numbered with a "B" prefix on the card backs.

COMPLETE SET (12) 10.00 20.00
STATED ODDS 1:12
B1 Orlando Pace 1.00 2.50
B2 Peter Boulware 1.00 2.50
B3 Shawn Springs .60 1.50
B4 Warrick Dunn 2.50 6.00
B5 Dwayne Rudd .40 1.00
B6 Rae Carruth .40 1.00
B7 Bryant Westbrook .40 1.00
B8 Darrell Russell .40 1.00
B9 Yatil Green .60 1.50
B10 David LaFleur .40 1.00
B11 Jim Druckenmiller .60 1.50
B12 Reidel Anthony 1.00 2.50

1997 Press Pass Can't Miss

This six card set features the players Press Pass believed would be the best players in their draft class. The cards are printed in ascending difficulty with card #1 being inserted one every 720 packs, card #2 one every 360, card #3 is one of 180; card #4 are one every 90; card #5 is one every 45 and card #6 is one every 36.

COMPLETE SET (6) 30.00 60.00
CM1 Warrick Dunn 12.00 30.00
CM2 Jim Druckenmiller 6.00 15.00
CM3 Yatil Green 3.00 8.00
CM4 Orlando Pace 3.00 8.00
CM5 Rae Carruth 2.50 6.00
CM6 Peter Boulware 3.00 8.00

1997 Press Pass Head Butt

These cards feature leading NFL prospects as of the beginning of the 1997 season. The cards are numbered with a "HB" parallel on the back and there is also a die-cut parallel version.

COMPLETE SET (9) 12.50 30.00
STATED ODDS 1:18
*DIE CUTS: .6X TO 1.5X BASIC INSERTS
DIE CUT STATED ODDS 1:36
HB1 Warrick Dunn 4.00 10.00
HB2 Orlando Pace 1.50 4.00
HB3 Troy Davis .60 1.50
HB4 Reidel Anthony 1.50 4.00
HB5 Rae Carruth .60 1.50
HB6 Yatil Green 1.00 2.50
HB7 Corey Dillon 5.00 12.00
HB8 Danny Wuerffel 1.50 4.00
HB9 Darnell Autry .60 1.50

1997 Press Pass Marquee Matchups

This nine card insert set was issued one every 18 packs. Each card pictures two players who are both looking to make an NFL impact at the same position.

COMPLETE SET (9) 15.00 30.00
STATED ODDS 1:18
MM1 J.Druckenmil 1.50 4.00
D.Wuerf
MM2 W.Dunn 4.00 10.00
C.Dillon
MM3 D.Autry .75 2.00
Troy Davis
MM4 B.Hanspard 3.00 8.00
T.Barber
MM5 R.Anthony 1.50 4.00
B.Westbrook
MM6 P.Boulware 2.00 5.00
O.Pace
MM7 R.Carruth 1.50 4.00
I.Hilliard
MM8 Y.Green .75 2.00
S.Springs
MM9 D.LaFleur 2.50 6.00
T.Gonzalez

1998 Press Pass

This 50-card set features some leading NFL prospects entering the 1998 season. The borderless full color shots feature an action photo on the front with the players name and position on the bottom. The backs feature biographical information, a brief blurb as well as collegiate stats for these players.

COMPLETE SET (50) 7.50 20.00
1 Peyton Manning 3.00 8.00
2 Ryan Leaf .20 .50
3 Charles Woodson .30 .75
4 Andre Wadsworth .10 .30
5 Randy Moss 2.00 5.00
6 Curtis Enis .08 .25
7 Tra Thomas .08 .25
8 Flozell Adams .08 .25
9 Jason Peter .08 .25
10 Brian Simmons .10 .30
11 Takeo Spikes .20 .50
12 Michael Myers .08 .25
13 Kevin Dyson .20 .50
14 Grant Wistrom .10 .30
15 Fred Taylor .50 1.25
16 Germane Crowell .10 .30
17 Sam Cowart .10 .30
18 Anthony Simmons LB .10 .30
19 Robert Edwards .10 .30
20 Shaun Williams .10 .30
21 Phil Savoy .08 .25
22 Leonard Little .20 .50
23 Saladin McCullough .08 .25
24 Duane Starks .08 .25
25 John Avery .10 .30
26 Vonnie Holliday .20 .50
27 Tim Dwight .20 .50
28 Donovin Darius .10 .30
29 Alonzo Mayes .08 .25
30 Jerome Pathon .20 .50
31 Brian Kelly .10 .30
32 Hines Ward 1.25 2.50
33 Jacquez Green .10 .30
34 Marcus Nash .08 .25
35 Ahman Green .60 1.50
36 Joe Jurevicius .20 .50
37 Tavian Banks .10 .30
38 Donald Hayes .10 .30
39 Robert Holcombe .10 .30
40 E.G. Green .10 .30
41 John Dutton .08 .25
42 Skip Hicks .10 .30
43 Pat Johnson .10 .30
44 Keith Brooking .20 .50
45 Alan Faneca 6.00 15.00
46 Steve Spurrier CO .40 1.00
47 Mike Price CO .08 .25
48 Bobby Bowden CO .10 .30
49 Tom Osborne CO .40 1.00
50 Peyton Manning CL .60 1.50
P1 Randy Moss Promo 1.50 4.00
1S Peyton Manning SportsFest 2.00 5.00

1998 Press Pass Paydirt Red

COMPLETE SET (50) 10.00 25.00
*PAYDIRT STARS: .6X TO 1.5X BASIC CARDS
ONE PER HOBBY PACK

1998 Press Pass Pick Offs Blue

COMPLETE SET (50) 10.00 25.00
*BLUE: .6X TO 1.5X BASIC CARDS
ONE PER RETAIL PACK

1998 Press Pass Reflectors

*REFLECTORS: 10X TO 25X BASIC CARDS
STATED ODDS 1:180 PACKS
R1 Peyton Manning 150.00 250.00

1998 Press Pass Autographs

This 38-card set is a quasi-parallel of the base set with 32 different players/coaches signing versions of their respective cards. Peyton Manning, Ryan Leaf, Germane Crowell, Shaun Williams, John Avery, Robert Holcombe were only made available through redemption cards. Andre Wadsworth, Donald Hayes, Jason Peter, Anthony Simmons, Skip Hicks, Ahman Green, Jacquez Green were available in packs and also as redemptions. Redemption cards have an expiration date of May 31, 1999. Autographs were inserted 1:18 hobby packs and 1:36 retail packs. There was also a limited edition Peyton Manning autograph card that was only made available to attendees of the SportsFest card show in Philadelphia via a redemption for opened wrappers at the Press Pass company booth.

STATED ODDS 1:18 HOB/1:36 RET
1 Peyton Manning 100.00 200.00
2 Ryan Leaf 6.00 15.00
4 Andre Wadsworth 4.00 10.00
5 Randy Moss 40.00 100.00
6 Curtis Enis 3.00 8.00
9 Jason Peter 3.00 8.00
10 Brian Simmons 4.00 10.00
11 Takeo Spikes 6.00 15.00
12 Michael Myers 3.00 8.00
13 Kevin Dyson 6.00 15.00
14 Grant Wistrom 6.00 15.00
15 Fred Taylor 12.00 30.00
16 Germane Crowell 4.00 10.00
18 Anthony Simmons LB 4.00 10.00
19 Robert Edwards 4.00 10.00
20 Shaun Williams 6.00 15.00
21 Phil Savoy 3.00 8.00
25 John Avery 4.00 10.00
26 Vonnie Holliday 6.00 15.00
27 Tim Dwight 6.00 15.00
28 Donovin Darius 4.00 10.00
29 Alonzo Mayes 3.00 8.00
31 Brian Kelly 4.00 10.00
32 Hines Ward 35.00 60.00
33 Jacquez Green 4.00 10.00
34 Marcus Nash 3.00 8.00
35 Ahman Green 10.00 25.00
36 Joe Jurevicius 6.00 15.00
37 Tavian Banks 6.00 15.00
38 Donald Hayes 4.00 10.00
39 Robert Holcombe 4.00 10.00
42 Skip Hicks 4.00 10.00
43 Pat Johnson 4.00 10.00
45 Alan Faneca 12.00 30.00
46 Steve Spurrier CO 12.00 30.00
47 Mike Price CO 3.00 8.00
48 Bobby Bowden CO 20.00 40.00
49 Tom Osborne CO 15.00 30.00
NNO P.Manning SportsFest 125.00 250.00

1998 Press Pass Fields of Fury

This 9-card set of some of the 1998 NFL draft's best players has a horizontal card front design with a refelctive action shot of a player in the middle. The backs contain another player photo and some biographical information. Cards were inserted 1:36 packs.

COMPLETE SET (9) 30.00 60.00
STATED ODDS 1:36
FF1 Peyton Manning 12.00 30.00
FF2 Marcus Nash .60 1.50
FF3 Ryan Leaf 1.25 3.00
FF4 Randy Moss 10.00 25.00
FF5 Robert Edwards .75 2.00
FF6 Curtis Enis .60 1.50
FF7 Kevin Dyson 1.25 3.00
FF8 Fred Taylor 3.00 8.00
FF9 Jacquez Green .75 2.00

1998 Press Pass Game Jerseys

These four cards, serial numbered out of 425 on the card backs, contain actual pieces of a game-used player jersey. Cards were inserted 1:720 packs. Peyton Manning and Ryan Leaf jersey cards were only made available through redemption cards that were seeded into packs.

COMPLETE SET (4) 125.00 250.00
STATED ODDS 1:720
STATED PRINT RUN 425 SERIAL #'d SETS
JC1 Peyton Manning 60.00 120.00
JC2 Ryan Leaf 10.00 25.00
JC3 Kevin Dyson 10.00 25.00
JC4 Tavian Banks 7.50 20.00
JCTB Tavian Banks Promo 4.00 10.00

1998 Press Pass Head Butt

These nine cards, inserted 1:18 packs, highlight nine high-profile rookies heading into the 1998 NFL season. The cards have an embossed helmet design from the players' respective college teams on the card fronts. There is also a die-cut parallel, inserted 1:36.

COMPLETE SET (9) 15.00 30.00
STATED ODDS 1:18
*DIE CUTS: .6X TO 1.5X BASIC INSERTS
DIE CUT STATED ODDS 1:36
HB1 Peyton Manning 8.00 20.00
HB2 Charles Woodson 1.00 2.50
HB3 Ryan Leaf .60 1.50
HB4 Curtis Enis .30 .75
HB5 Jacquez Green .40 1.00
HB6 Ahman Green 2.00 5.00
HB7 Randy Moss 5.00 12.00
HB8 Tavian Banks .40 1.00
HB9 Robert Edwards .40 1.00

1998 Press Pass Kick-Off

This 36-card set was inserted one per pack in 1988 Press Pass. These die-cut cards feature a metaphorical image of the players busting through a large football image. The card backs contain combine results from rookie training camps.

COMPLETE SET (36) 10.00 25.00
ONE PER PACK
KO1 Peyton Manning 4.00 10.00
KO2 Ryan Leaf .25 .60
KO3 Charles Woodson .40 1.00
KO4 Andre Wadsworth .15 .40
KO5 Randy Moss 2.00 5.00
KO6 Curtis Enis .10 .30
KO7 Donald Hayes .15 .40
KO8 Flozell Adams .10 .30
KO9 Jason Peter .10 .30
KO10 Brian Simmons .15 .40
KO11 Takeo Spikes .25 .60
KO12 Germane Crowell .15 .40
KO13 Donovin Darius .15 .40
KO14 Grant Wistrom .15 .40
KO15 Alonzo Mayes .10 .30
KO16 Kevin Dyson .25 .60
KO17 John Avery .15 .40
KO18 Anthony Simmons LB .15 .40
KO19 Robert Edwards .15 .40
KO20 Shaun Williams .15 .40
KO21 Leonard Little .25 .60
KO22 Skip Hicks .15 .40
KO23 Phil Savoy .10 .30
KO24 Tavian Banks .15 .40
KO25 Robert Holcombe .15 .40
KO26 E.G. Green .15 .40
KO27 Tim Dwight .25 .60
KO28 Saladin McCullough .10 .30
KO29 Fred Taylor .60 1.50
KO30 Jerome Pathon .25 .60
KO31 Brian Kelly .15 .40
KO32 Hines Ward 1.25 3.00
KO33 Jacquez Green .15 .40
KO34 Marcus Nash .10 .30
KO35 Ahman Green .75 2.00
KO36 Joe Jurevicius CL .25 .60

1998 Press Pass Triple Threat

This nine card set contains three cards of each highlighted player. When placed side by side these die-cut cards form a complete puzzles for each player. Cards were inserted 1:12 packs.

COMPLETE SET (9) 15.00 30.00
STATED ODDS 1:12
TT1 Peyton Manning 4.00 10.00
TT2 Peyton Manning 4.00 10.00
TT3 Peyton Manning 4.00 10.00
TT4 Ryan Leaf 2.00 5.00
TT5 Ryan Leaf 2.00 5.00
TT6 Ryan Leaf 2.00 5.00
TT7 Charles Woodson 1.00 2.50
TT8 Charles Woodson 1.00 2.50
TT9 Charles Woodson 1.00 2.50

1998 Press Pass Trophy Case

The cards in this 12-card set, inserted one in nine packs, highlight the nation's 12 top award honorees for the 1997 collegiate season. Cards are pictured with a silver foil, micro-etched card mantle. The card backs contain biographical information.

COMPLETE SET (12) 20.00 40.00
STATED ODDS 1:9
TC1 Peyton Manning 6.00 15.00
TC2 Ryan Leaf .50 1.25
TC3 Charles Woodson .75 2.00
TC4 Randy Moss 4.00 10.00
TC5 Curtis Enis .25 .60
TC6 Grant Wistrom .30 .75
TC7 Kevin Dyson .50 1.25
TC8 Fred Taylor 1.25 3.00
TC9 Tavian Banks .30 .75
TC10 Ahman Green 1.50 4.00
TC11 Skip Hicks .30 .75
TC12 Andre Wadsworth .30 .75

1999 Press Pass

The 1999 Press Pass set was issued in one series totalling 45 cards. The fronts feature color action photos of the newest rookies of the NFL. The backs carry player information.

COMPLETE SET (45) 6.00 15.00
1 Ricky Williams .30 .75
2 Tim Couch .25 .60
3 Champ Bailey .40 1.00
4 Chris Claiborne .20 .50
5 Donovan McNabb .60 1.50
6 Edgerrin James .30 .75
7 Akili Smith .20 .50
8 John Tait .20 .50
9 Jevon Kearse .25 .60
10 Torry Holt .40 1.00
11 Troy Edwards .20 .50
12 Chris McAlister .20 .50
13 Daunte Culpepper .30 .75
14 Andy Katzenmoyer .25 .60
15 David Boston .20 .50
16 Ebenezer Ekuban .20 .50
17 Peerless Price .20 .50
18 Shaun King .20 .50
19 Joe Germaine .25 .60
20 Brock Huard .20 .50
21 Michael Bishop .25 .60
22 Amos Zereoue .20 .50
23 Sedrick Irvin .20 .50
24 Autry Denson .20 .50
25 Kevin Faulk .20 .50
26 James Johnson .20 .50
27 D'Wayne Bates .20 .50
28 Kevin Johnson .25 .60
29 Tai Streets .25 .60
30 Craig Yeast .20 .50
31 Dre Bly .30 .75
32 Anthony Poindexter .20 .50
33 Jared DeVries .20 .50
34 Rob Konrad .20 .50
35 Dat Nguyen .30 .75
36 Cade McNown .20 .50
37 Scott Covington .20 .50
38 Jon Jansen .20 .50
39 Rufus French .20 .50
40 Mike Rucker .20 .50
41 Aaron Gibson .20 .50
42 Kris Farris .20 .50
43 Anthony McFarland .25 .60
44 Matt Stinchcomb .20 .50
45 Dee Miller CL .20 .50

1999 Press Pass Paydirt Silver

COMPLETE SET (45) 10.00 25.00
*PAYDIRTS: .5X TO 1.2X BASIC CARDS
STATED ODDS 1 PER HOBBY PACK

1999 Press Pass Reflectors

*REFLECTORS: 8X TO 20X BASIC CARDS
STATED ODDS 1:180

1999 Press Pass Reflectors Solos

STATED PRINT RUN 1 SET

1999 Press Pass Torquers Blue

COMPLETE SET (45) 12.50 30.00
*TORQUERS: .6X TO 1.5X BASIC CARDS
STATED ODDS 1 PER RETAIL PACK

1999 Press Pass Autographs

Randomly inserted in packs at the rate of one in 16, this set features color player photos with the player's autograph across the bottom. Some of the player's autographed cards could only be obtained by a redemption offer. Others could be found both in the packs and obtained through the redemption program.

COMPLETE SET (50) 300.00 600.00
STATED ODDS 1:16
1 Ricky Williams 7.50 20.00
2 Tim Couch 6.00 15.00
3 Champ Bailey 7.50 20.00
4 Chris Claiborne 4.00 10.00
5 Donovan McNabb 10.00 25.00
6 Edgerrin James 12.00 30.00
7 Akili Smith 6.00 15.00
8 John Tait 5.00 12.00
9 Jevon Kearse 7.50 20.00
10 Torry Holt 10.00 25.00
11 Troy Edwards 5.00 12.00
12 Chris McAlister 5.00 12.00
13 Daunte Culpepper 7.50 20.00
14 Andy Katzenmoyer 8.00 20.00
15 David Boston 5.00 12.00
16 Ebenezer Ekuban 4.00 10.00
17 Peerless Price 5.00 12.00
18 Shaun King 5.00 12.00
19 Joe Germaine 5.00 12.00
20 Brock Huard 6.00 15.00
21 Michael Bishop 5.00 12.00
22 Amos Zereoue 5.00 12.00
23 Sedrick Irvin 4.00 10.00
24 Autry Denson 4.00 10.00
25 Kevin Faulk 6.00 15.00
26 James Johnson 4.00 10.00
27 D'Wayne Bates 4.00 10.00
28 Kevin Johnson 5.00 12.00
29 Tai Streets 5.00 12.00
30 Craig Yeast 4.00 10.00
31 Dre Bly 5.00 12.00
32 Anthony Poindexter 4.00 10.00
33 Jared DeVries 4.00 10.00
34 Rob Konrad 5.00 12.00
35 Dat Nguyen 6.00 15.00
36 Cade McNown 5.00 12.00
37 Scott Covington 5.00 12.00
38 Jon Jansen 4.00 10.00
39 Rufus French 4.00 10.00
40 Mike Rucker 6.00 15.00
41 Aaron Gibson 4.00 10.00
42 Kris Farris 4.00 10.00
43 Anthony McFarland 6.00 15.00
44 Matt Stinchcomb 5.00 12.00
45 Dee Miller CL 4.00 10.00
46 Antuan Edwards 5.00 12.00
47 Mike Peterson 4.00 10.00
48 Mike Cloud 4.00 10.00
49 Darnell McDonald 4.00 10.00
50 Jerame Tuman 6.00 15.00

1999 Press Pass Big Numbers

Randomly inserted into packs at the rate of one in 16, this nine-card set features color action photos of top rookies who have the ability to put up big numbers during the season printed on embossed cards. There is also a Die-Cut version that were inserted at a rate of 1:32.

COMPLETE SET (9) 15.00 30.00
STATED ODDS 1:16
*DIE CUTS: .6X TO 1.5X BASIC INSERTS
DIE CUT STATED ODDS: 1:32
BN1 Tim Couch .50 1.25
BN2 Ricky Williams 1.00 2.50
BN3 Donovan McNabb 2.50 6.00
BN4 Edgerrin James 2.00 5.00
BN5 Peerless Price .50 1.25
BN6 Amos Zereoue .50 1.25
BN7 Daunte Culpepper 2.00 5.00
BN8 Tai Streets .50 1.25
BN9 Akili Smith .75 2.00

1999 Press Pass Game Jerseys

Randomly inserted in packs at the rate of one in 640, this six-card set features color photos of top NFL rookies along with a piece of a game-used jersey embedded in the cards.

COMPLETE SET (6) 125.00 250.00
STATED ODDS 1:640
JCAS Akili Smith 10.00 25.00
JCCM Cade McNown 10.00 25.00
JCDC Daunte Culpepper 40.00 80.00
JCPP Peerless Price 12.00 30.00
JCTC Tim Couch 12.00 30.00
JCTH Torry Holt 20.00 50.00

1999 Press Pass Goldenarm

Randomly inserted in packs at the rate of one in 10, this nine-card set features color action photos of top rookie quarterbacks printed on holofoil cards.

COMPLETE SET (9) 10.00 20.00
STATED ODDS 1:10
GA1 Tim Couch .50 1.25
GA2 Donovan McNabb 2.50 6.00
GA3 Akili Smith .75 2.00
GA4 Daunte Culpepper 2.00 5.00
GA5 Cade McNown .30 .75
GA6 Brock Huard .50 1.25
GA7 Joe Germaine .30 .75
GA8 Shaun King .30 .75
GA9 Michael Bishop .50 1.25

1999 Press Pass Gridiron

These 3-cards were inserted one per special retail box of 1999 Press Pass. Each features a top Draft Pick along with the word "Gridiron" on the cardfront.

COMPLETE SET (3) 2.00 5.00
ONE PER SPECIAL RETAIL BOX
1 Tim Couch .60 1.50
2 Akili Smith .60 1.50
3 Ricky Williams .75 2.00

1999 Press Pass Hardware
Randomly inserted into packs at the rate of one in eight, this 12-card set features color action photos of top award-winning rookies printed on all-foil Nitrokrome etched cards.
COMPLETE SET (12) 10.00 25.00
STATED ODDS 1:8
H1 Cade McNown .30 .75
H2 Ricky Williams 1.00 2.50
H3 Torry Holt 1.25 3.00
H4 Tim Couch .50 1.25
H5 David Boston .50 1.25
H6 Troy Edwards .30 .75
H7 Michael Bishop .50 1.25
H8 Champ Bailey .75 2.00
H9 Mike Cloud .30 .75
H10 Kevin Faulk .50 1.25
H11 Autry Denson .30 .75
H12 Donovan McNabb 2.50 6.00

1999 Press Pass X's and O's
Inserted one per pack, this 36-card set features action color photos of top rookies printed on interior die-cut, embossed cards.
COMPLETE SET (36) 7.50 20.00
ONE PER PACK
P1 Daunte Culpepper X's PROMO 1.00 2.50
XO1 Ricky Williams .60 1.50
XO2 Tim Couch .30 .75
XO3 Champ Bailey .50 1.25
XO4 Donovan McNabb 1.50 4.00
XO5 Edgerrin James 1.25 3.00
XO6 Akili Smith .50 1.25
XO7 Torry Holt .75 2.00
XO8 Troy Edwards .20 .50
XO9 Daunte Culpepper 1.25 3.00
XO10 Andy Katzenmoyer .20 .50
XO11 David Boston .30 .75
XO12 Peerless Price .30 .75
XO13 Shaun King .20 .50
XO14 Joe Germaine .20 .50
XO15 Brock Huard .30 .75
XO16 Michael Bishop .30 .75
XO17 Amos Zereoue .30 .75
XO18 Sedrick Irvin .15 .40
XO19 Autry Denson .20 .50
XO20 Kevin Faulk .30 .75
XO21 James Johnson .20 .50
XO22 D'Wayne Bates .20 .50
XO23 Kevin Johnson .50 1.25
XO24 Tai Streets .30 .75
XO25 Cade McNown .20 .50
XO26 Scott Covington .30 .75
XO27 Chris Claiborne .15 .40
XO28 Jevon Kearse .60 1.50
XO29 Rob Konrad .30 .75
XO30 Dat Nguyen .30 .75
XO31 Chris McAlister .20 .50
XO32 Craig Yeast .20 .50
XO33 Anthony Poindexter .15 .40
XO34 Dre Bly .30 .75
XO35 Mike Rucker .30 .75
XO36 Tim Couch CL .30 .75

2000 Press Pass
Press Pass was released as a 45-card set featuring top NCAA draft picks. Card backs carry college statistics and pertinent information highlighting each players most impressive skills. Press Pass was released in both Hobby and Retail form. Hobby was packaged in boxes of 24-packs containing five cards each and carried a suggested retail price of $3.59. Retail was packaged in boxes of 36-packs containing four cards each and carried a suggested retail price of $2.99.
COMPLETE SET (45) 10.00 25.00
1 Peter Warrick .12 .30
2 Travis Claridge .12 .30
3 Courtney Brown .15 .40
4 Plaxico Burress .15 .40
5 Chad Pennington .15 .40
6 Thomas Jones .15 .40
7 Ron Dayne .20 .50
8 Brian Urlacher .60 1.50
9 Corey Simon .15 .40
10 Chris Samuels .20 .50
11 Stockar McDougle .12 .30
12 Deon Grant .12 .30
13 Cosey Coleman .12 .30
14 Sylvester Morris .12 .30
15 Shyrone Stith .12 .30
16 Shaun Alexander .20 .50
17 Dez White .12 .30
18 John Engelberger .12 .30
19 Tim Rattay .15 .40
20 Todd Pinkston .12 .30
21 John Abraham .20 .50
22 R.Jay Soward .12 .30
23 Shaun Ellis .15 .40
24 Keith Bulluck .15 .40
25 Jerry Porter .20 .50
26 Darren Howard .12 .30
27 Joe Hamilton .12 .30
28 Deltha O'Neal .12 .30
29 Chris Redman .12 .30
30 Deon Dyer .12 .30
31 Jamal Lewis .20 .50
32 Chris Hovan .15 .40
33 Raynoch Thompson .12 .30
34 Travis Taylor .12 .30
35 Sebastian Janikowski .20 .50
36 Travis Prentice .12 .30
37 Tom Brady 25.00 50.00
38 Tee Martin .12 .30
39 J.R. Redmond .12 .30
40 Dennis Northcutt .12 .30
41 Laveranues Coles .15 .40
42 Danny Farmer .12 .30
43 Darrell Jackson .12 .30
44 Chris McIntosh .12 .30
45 Peter Warrick CL .10 .25
P1 Peter Warrick Promo .75 2.00

2000 Press Pass Gold Zone
COMPLETE SET (45) 10.00 25.00
*GOLD ZONE: .6X TO 1.5X BASIC CARDS
ONE GOLD PER HOBBY PACK

2000 Press Pass Reflectors
COMPLETE SET (45) 150.00 300.00
*REFLECTOR: 5X TO 12X BASIC CARDS
REFLECTOR/500 ODDS 1:72
UNPRICED REF.SOLO PRINT RUN 1
37 Tom Brady 100.00 200.00

2000 Press Pass Torquers
COMPLETE SET (45) 15.00 30.00
*TORQUERS: .6X TO 1.5X BASIC CARDS
ONE PER RETAIL PACK

2000 Press Pass Autographs
ndomly inserted in Hobby packs at the rate of one in eight and Retail packs at the rate of one in 36, this 51-card set features authentic autographs by the NFL's top prospects for 2000. Cards are not numbered so they appear in alphabetical order. Some were issued via mail redemption cards that carried an expiration date of 5/15/2001. A Peter Warrick card was released via redemption that was printed on clear plastic stock and serial numbered of 50. Finally, some players signed in both blue or black ink.
STATED ODDS 1:8 HOB, 1:36 RET
1 John Abraham 6.00 15.00
2 Shaun Alexander 5.00 12.00
3 Tom Brady 500.00 1000.00
4 Courtney Brown 4.00 10.00
5 Keith Bulluck 4.00 10.00
6 Plaxico Burress 4.00 10.00
7 Giovanni Carmazzi 3.00 8.00
9 Travis Claridge 3.00 8.00
10 Cosey Coleman 3.00 8.00
11 Laveranues Coles 4.00 10.00
12 Ron Dayne 5.00 12.00
13 Na'il Diggs 3.00 8.00
14 Ron Dugans 3.00 8.00
15 Deon Dyer 3.00 8.00
16 Shaun Ellis 4.00 10.00
17 John Engelberger 3.00 8.00
18 Danny Farmer 3.00 8.00
19 Deon Grant 3.00 8.00
20 Joe Hamilton 3.00 8.00
21 Darren Howard 3.00 8.00
22 Chris Hovan 4.00 10.00
23 Darrell Jackson 3.00 8.00
24 Sebastian Janikowski 6.00 15.00
25 Thomas Jones 4.00 10.00
26 Jamal Lewis 5.00 12.00
27 Tee Martin 3.00 8.00
28 Stockar McDougle 3.00 8.00
29 Chris McIntosh 3.00 8.00
30 Corey Moore 3.00 8.00
31 Rob Morris 4.00 10.00
32 Sylvester Morris 3.00 8.00
33 Dennis Northcutt 3.00 0.00
34 Deltha O'Neal 3.00 8.00
35 Chad Pennington 4.00 10.00
36 Todd Pinkston 3.00 8.00
37 Jerry Porter 5.00 12.00
38 Travis Prentice 3.00 8.00
39 Tim Rattay 4.00 10.00
40 Chris Redman 3.00 8.00
41 J.R. Redmond 3.00 8.00
42 Chris Samuels 5.00 12.00
43 Corey Simon 4.00 10.00
44 Marvel Smith 5.00 12.00
45 Shyrone Stith 3.00 8.00
46 Travis Taylor 3.00 8.00
47 Raynoch Thompson 3.00 8.00
48 Brian Urlacher 12.00 30.00
49 Todd Wade 3.00 8.00
50 Peter Warrick 3.00 8.00
50C Peter Warrick Clear/50 20.00 50.00
51 Dez White 3.00 8.00

2000 Press Pass Autographs Gold Standout Signatures
*GOLD STANDOUT/100: .6X TO 1.5X BASIC AU
*GOLD STANDOUT/50: 1X TO 2.5X BASIC AU
STATED PRINT RUN 100 SETS
3 Tom Brady 600.00 1200.00

2000 Press Pass Big Numbers
Randomly inserted in packs at one in 12, this 8-card set features eight top draft picks on an embossed card stock showcasing their top performances. Card backs carry a "BN" prefix.
COMPLETE SET (8) 4.00 10.00
STATED ODDS 1:12
*DIE CUTS: .6X TO 1.5X BASIC INSERTS
DIE CUT STATED ODDS 1:24
BN1 Peter Warrick .30 .75
BN2 Ron Dayne .50 1.25
BN3 Courtney Brown .40 1.00
BN4 Plaxico Burress .40 1.00
BN5 Shaun Alexander .50 1.25
BN6 Thomas Jones .40 1.00
BN7 Chad Pennington .40 1.00
BN8 Chris Redman .30 .75

2000 Press Pass Breakout
Randomly inserted in packs at the rate of one per pack, this 35-card set showcases top prospects on a die-cut card. Card fronts feature foil highlights and card backs carry a "BO" prefix.
COMPLETE SET (35) 6.00 15.00
ONE PER PACK
BO1 Peter Warrick .15 .40
BO2 Sebastian Janikowski .25 .60
BO3 Courtney Brown .20 .50
BO4 Plaxico Burress .20 .50
BO5 Chad Pennington .20 .50
BO6 Thomas Jones .20 .50
BO7 Ron Dayne .25 .60
BO8 Brian Urlacher .75 2.00
BO9 Deon Dyer .15 .40
BO10 Chris Samuels .25 .60
BO11 Stockar McDougle .15 .40
BO12 Deon Grant .15 .40
BO13 Cosey Coleman .15 .40
BO14 Shyrone Stith .15 .40
BO15 Tim Rattay .20 .50
BO16 Shaun Alexander .25 .60
BO17 Dez White .15 .40
BO18 John Engelberger .15 .40
BO19 Laveranues Coles .20 .50
BO20 J.R. Redmond .15 .40
BO21 R.Jay Soward .15 .40
BO22 Chris McIntosh .15 .40
BO23 Shaun Ellis .20 .50
BO24 Keith Bulluck .20 .50
BO25 Jerry Porter .25 .60
BO26 Darren Howard .15 .40
BO27 Tee Martin .15 .40
BO28 Deltha O'Neal .15 .40
BO29 Chris Redman .15 .40
BO30 Danny Farmer .15 .40
BO31 Jamal Lewis .25 .60
BO32 Chris Hovan .20 .50
BO33 Corey Simon .20 .50
BO34 Travis Taylor .15 .40
BO35 Ron Dayne CL .20 .50

2000 Press Pass Game Jerseys
Randomly inserted in hobby packs at one in 380 and retail packs at one in 720, this 6-card set features swatches of game-used jerseys from some of 2000's top prospects. Card backs carry a "JC" prefix and each is serial numbered to either 325 or 475 cards produced.
HOBBY STATED ODDS 1:380
RETAIL STATED ODDS 1:720
STATED PRINT RUN 325-475
JC1 Ron Dayne 6.00 15.00
JC2 Thomas Jones 5.00 12.00
JC3 Chad Pennington 5.00 12.00
JC4 Chris Redman 4.00 10.00
JC5 Corey Simon 5.00 12.00
JC6 Peter Warrick AU/325 10.00 25.00

2000 Press Pass Gridiron
These 3-cards were inserted one per special retail box of 1999 Press Pass. Each features a top Draft Pick along with the word "Gridiron" on the cardfront.
COMPLETE SET (3) 2.50 6.00
ONE PER SPECIAL RETAIL BOX
1 Peter Warrick .50 1.25
2 Chad Pennington .60 1.50
3 Ron Dayne .75 2.00

2000 Press Pass Paydirt
Randomly seeded in packs at one in 16, this 12-card set focuses on the most promising new TD men for the NFL. Card fronts utilize microetched holo-foil and card backs carry a "PD" prefix.
COMPLETE SET (12) 6.00 15.00
STATED ODDS 1:16
PD1 Peter Warrick .30 .75
PD2 Plaxico Burress .40 1.00
PD3 Chad Pennington .40 1.00
PD4 Thomas Jones .40 1.00
PD5 Ron Dayne .50 1.25
PD6 Shyrone Stith .30 .75
PD7 Shaun Alexander .50 1.25
PD8 Chris Redman .30 .75
PD10 Jamal Lewis .50 1.25
PD11 J.R. Redmond .30 .75
PD12 Travis Taylor .30 .75

2000 Press Pass Power Picks
Randomly inserted in packs at the rate of one in 12, this 10-card set features top draft choices in a partial parallel set that features the base card design and photograpy that has been enhanced with a Power Pick stamp and a textured finish. Card backs carry a "PP" prefix.
COMPLETE SET (10) 6.00 15.00
STATED ODDS 1:12
PP1 Peter Warrick .25 .60
PP2 Courtney Brown .30 .75
PP3 Plaxico Burress .30 .75
PP4 Chad Pennington .30 .75
PP5 Thomas Jones .30 .75
PP6 Ron Dayne .40 1.00
PP7 Corey Simon .30 .75
PP8 Shaun Alexander .40 1.00
PP9 Brian Urlacher 1.25 3.00
PP10 Chris Samuels .40 1.00

2000 Press Pass Showbound
Randomly inserted in packs at the rate of one in eight, this 8-card set showcases top rookies who are most likely to make an impact in the NFL. Card fronts feature rainbow holo-foil, and card backs carry an "SB" prefix.
COMPLETE SET (8) 3.00 8.00
STATED ODDS 1:8
SB1 Peter Warrick .25 .60
SB2 Dez White .25 .60
SB3 Courtney Brown .30 .75
SB4 Plaxico Burress .30 .75
SB5 Chad Pennington .30 .75
SB6 Thomas Jones .30 .75
SB7 Ron Dayne .40 1.00
SB8 Shaun Alexander .40 1.00

2001 Press Pass
Press Pass was released as a 50-card set featuring top NFL draft picks. The cardbacks carry college statistics and pertinent information highlighting each player's most impressive skills. The final four Power Picks subset cards were seeded at the rate of 1:16 packs. Press Pass was released in both hobby and retail pack form. Hobby was packaged in boxes of 24-packs containing five cards each and carried a suggested retail price of $3.49. Retail was packaged in boxes of 36-packs containing four cards each and carried a suggested retail price of $2.99.
COMPLETE SET (50) 10.00 25.00
COMP.FACT.SET (46) 10.00 25.00
COMP.SET w/o SP's (45) 7.50 20.00
UNPRICED SOLOS PRINT RUN 1/1
1 Michael Vick CL .30 .75
2 Drew Brees 1.25 3.00
3 Michael Vick .50 1.25
4 Chris Weinke .25 .60
5 Marques Tuiasosopo .25 .60
6 Josh Booty .25 .60
7 Josh Heupel .30 .75
8 Sage Rosenfels .25 .60
9 Mike McMahon .25 .60
10 Deuce McAllister .30 .75
11 LaDainian Tomlinson 1.00 2.50
12 LaMont Jordan .30 .75
13 James Jackson .20 .50
14 Travis Henry .25 .60
15 Anthony Thomas .30 .75
16 Travis Minor .25 .60
17 Michael Bennett .25 .60
18 Kevan Barlow .25 .60
19 Rudi Johnson .30 .75
20 Santana Moss .30 .75
21 Quincy Morgan .25 .60
22 Rod Gardner .25 .60
23 David Terrell .25 .60
24 Chris Chambers .20 .50
25 Reggie Wayne .40 1.00
26 Ken-Yon Rambo .20 .50
27 Chad Johnson .30 .75
28 Snoop Minnis .20 .50
29 Freddie Mitchell .20 .50
30 Koren Robinson .25 .60
31 Bobby Newcombe .25 .60
32 Robert Ferguson .30 .75
33 Todd Heap .25 .60
34 Steve Hutchinson .50 1.25
35 Leonard Davis .30 .75
36 Kenyatta Walker .20 .50
37 Justin Smith .40 1.00
38 Jamal Reynolds .20 .50
39 Richard Seymour .30 .75
40 Shaun Rogers .30 .75
41 Gerard Warren .25 .60
42 Jamar Fletcher .20 .50
43 Gary Baxter .20 .50
44 Nate Clements .25 .60
45 Derrick Gibson .20 .50
46 Drew Brees PP 2.50 6.00
47 Michael Vick PP 1.00 2.50
48 Deuce McAllister PP .60 1.50
49 LaDainian Tomlinson PP 2.00 5.00
50 David Terrell PP .50 1.25

2001 Press Pass Gold Zone
COMPLETE SET (45) 15.00 30.00
*GOLD ZONE 1-45: .65X TO 1.5X BASIC CARDS
*GOLD ZONE PP 46-50: .5X TO 1.2X BASIC PP
STATED ODDS 1:1 HOBBY

2001 Press Pass Reflectors
*REFLECTOR 1-45: 2.5X TO 6X BASIC CARDS
*REFLECTOR PP 46-50: 1.5X TO 4X BASIC PP
REFLECTOR/500 ODDS 1:60
STATED PRINT RUN 500 SERIAL #'d SETS

2001 Press Pass Torquers
COMPLETE SET (45) 20.00 40.00
*TORQUERS 1-45: .6X TO 1.5X BASIC CARDS
*TORQUER PP 46-50: .5X TO 1.2X BASIC PP
STATED ODDS 1:1 RETAIL

2001 Press Pass Autographs
Randomly inserted in Hobby packs at the rate of one in eight and retail packs at the rate of one in 36, this 49-card set features authentic autographs by the NFL's top prospects for 2001. The cards were not numbered so they appear in alphabetical order. Some cards were issued via redemption cards in packs, while others could be found in 2003 Press Pass packs as part of a "buy back" program in that product.
STATED ODDS 1:8 HOB, 1:36 RET
1 Dan Alexander 4.00 10.00
2 Brian Allen 3.00 8.00
3 Jeff Backus 3.00 8.00
4 Kevan Barlow 4.00 10.00
5 Michael Bennett 4.00 10.00
6 Drew Brees 40.00 80.00
7 Josh Booty 4.00 10.00
8 Chris Chambers 3.00 8.00
9 Nate Clements 4.00 10.00
10 Ennis Davis 3.00 8.00
11 Robert Ferguson 5.00 12.00
12 Jamar Fletcher 3.00 8.00
13 Rod Gardner 4.00 10.00
14 Casey Hampton 6.00 15.00
15 Todd Heap 4.00 10.00
16 Travis Henry 4.00 10.00
17 Jabari Holloway 3.00 8.00
19 Steve Hutchinson 6.00 15.00
20 James Jackson 3.00 8.00
21 Chad Johnson 8.00 20.00
22 Rudi Johnson 5.00 12.00
23 LaMont Jordan 5.00 12.00
24 Ben Leard 3.00 8.00
25 Torrance Marshall 3.00 8.00
26 Deuce McAllister 5.00 12.00
27 Mike McMahon 4.00 10.00
28 Snoop Minnis 3.00 8.00
29 Quincy Morgan 4.00 10.00
30 Santana Moss 5.00 12.00
31 Bobby Newcombe 4.00 10.00
32 Moran Norris 3.00 8.00
33 Jesse Palmer 4.00 10.00
34 Tommy Polley 3.00 8.00
35 Dominic Raiola 3.00 8.00
36 Ken-Yon Rambo 3.00 8.00
37 Jamal Reynolds 3.00 8.00
38 Koren Robinson 4.00 10.00
39 Sage Rosenfels 4.00 10.00
40 Justin Smith 6.00 15.00
41 David Terrell 4.00 10.00
42 Anthony Thomas 5.00 12.00
43 LaDainian Tomlinson 20.00 50.00
44 Marques Tuiasosopo 4.00 10.00
45 Michael Vick 15.00 40.00
46 Kenyatta Walker 3.00 8.00
47 Chad Ward 3.00 8.00
48 Gerard Warren 4.00 10.00
49 Reggie Wayne 10.00 25.00
50 Chris Weinke 4.00 10.00
18 Willie Howard 3.00 8.00

2001 Press Pass Big Numbers
Randomly inserted in packs at one in 12, this nine-card set features top draft picks on an embossed card stock showcasing their top performances. Card backs carry a "BN" prefix.
COMPLETE SET (9) 6.00 15.00
STATED ODDS 1:12
*DIE CUTS: .6X TO 1.5X BASIC INSERTS
DIE CUT STATED ODDS 1:24
BN1 Drew Brees 1.25 3.00
BN2 Michael Vick .50 1.25
BN3 Deuce McAllister .30 .75
BN4 LaDainian Tomlinson 1.00 2.50
BN5 Santana Moss .30 .75
BN6 David Terrell .25 .60
BN7 Freddie Mitchell .20 .50
BN8 Koren Robinson .25 .60
BN9 Chad Johnson .30 .75

2001 Press Pass Breakout
Randomly inserted in packs at the rate of one per pack, this 36-card set showcases top prospects on a die-cut card. Card fronts feature foil highlights and card backs carry a "B" prefix.
COMPLETE SET (36) 12.50 30.00
ONE PER PACK
B1 Drew Brees 1.25 3.00
B2 Michael Vick .50 1.25
B3 Chris Weinke .25 .60
B4 Marques Tuiasosopo .25 .60
B5 Josh Heupel .30 .75
B6 Sage Rosenfels .25 .60
B7 Mike McMahon .25 .60
B8 Deuce McAllister .30 .75
B9 LaDainian Tomlinson 1.00 2.50
B10 LaMont Jordan .30 .75
B11 James Jackson .20 .50
B12 Travis Henry .25 .60
B13 Anthony Thomas .30 .75
B14 Michael Bennett .25 .60
B15 Kevan Barlow .25 .60
B16 Rudi Johnson .30 .75
B17 Travis Minor .25 .60
B18 Ken-Yon Rambo .20 .50
B19 Santana Moss .30 .75
B20 Quincy Morgan .25 .60
B21 Rod Gardner .25 .60
B22 David Terrell .25 .60
B23 Chris Chambers .20 .50
B24 Reggie Wayne .40 1.00
B25 Chad Johnson .30 .75
B26 Snoop Minnis .20 .50
B27 Freddie Mitchell .20 .50
B28 Koren Robinson .25 .60
B29 Todd Heap .25 .60
B30 Leonard Davis .30 .75
B31 Kenyatta Walker .20 .50
B32 Jamal Reynolds .20 .50
B33 Richard Seymour .30 .75
B34 Justin Smith .40 1.00
B35 Jamar Fletcher .20 .50
B36 David Terrell CL .20 .50

2001 Press Pass Game Jerseys
Randomly inserted in hobby packs at one in 320 and retail packs at one in 720, this 6-card set features swatches of game-used jerseys from some of 2000's top prospects. Card backs carry a "JC" prefix and each is serial numbered of 400-sets produced. A dual jersey Vick/Brees card was issued later to holders of the 2000 Press Pass Game Jersey Peter Warrick redemption card as a bonus for the delay in mailing out that card. A smaller number of these dual jersey cards were randomly seeded in 2001 Press Pass SE packs.
STATED ODDS 1:320 HOB, 1:720 RET
STATED PRINT RUN 400 SER.#'d SETS
JCCW Chris Weinke 8.00 20.00
JCDB Drew Brees 12.50 30.00
JCJS Justin Smith 8.00 20.00
JCLT LaDainian Tomlinson 12.50 30.00
JCMB Michael Bennett 8.00 20.00
JCMV Michael Vick 12.50 30.00
JCMVDB M.Vick/D.Brees 10.00 25.00

2001 Press Pass Paydirt
Randomly seeded in packs at one in 24, this 6-card set focuses on the most promising new TD men for the NFL. Card fronts utilize microetched holo-foil and card backs carry a "PD" prefix.
COMPLETE SET (6) 7.50 20.00
STATED ODDS 1:24
PD1 Drew Brees 2.50 6.00
PD2 Michael Vick 1.00 2.50
PD3 Deuce McAllister .60 1.50
PD4 LaDainian Tomlinson 2.00 5.00
PD5 Santana Moss .60 1.50
PD6 David Terrell .50 1.25

2001 Press Pass Power Pick Autographs
Randomly inserted in hobby packs at the rate of one in 320, this 8-card unnumbered set features top draft choices in a partial parallel set that features the base card design and photography that has been enhanced with a Power Pick stamp, a textured finish, and a stripe across the bottom of the card for the signature. The sets were serial numbered to 250 for each player with the exception of Vick who had only 100 cards produced. Deuce McAllister did not sign the Power Pick version although he was included in the initial checklist.
STATED PRINT RUN 250 SERIAL #'d SETS
STATED ODDS 1:320 HOBBY
1 Michael Bennett 6.00 15.00
2 Drew Brees 50.00 100.00
3 Santana Moss 10.00 25.00
4 Koren Robinson 6.00 15.00
5 David Terrell 6.00 15.00
6 LaDainian Tomlinson 30.00 80.00
7 Michael Vick/100 50.00 100.00
8 Chris Weinke 6.00 15.00

2001 Press Pass Showbound
Inserted in packs at the rate of one in eight, this 12-card set showcases top rookies who are most likely to make an impact in the NFL. Card fronts feature holo-foil, and card backs carry an "SB" prefix.
COMPLETE SET (12) 8.00 20.00
STATED ODDS 1:8
SB1 Drew Brees 1.50 4.00
SB2 Michael Vick .60 1.60
SB3 Chris Weinke .30 .75
SB4 Koren Robinson .30 .75
SB5 Deuce McAllister .40 1.00
SB6 Michael Bennett .30 .75
SB7 LaDainian Tomlinson 1.25 3.00
SB8 Santana Moss .40 1.00
SB9 Rod Gardner .30 .75
SB10 David Terrell .30 .75
SB11 Chris Chambers .25 .60
SB12 Chad Johnson .40 1.00

2002 Press Pass
Press Pass was released as a 50-card set featuring the top 2002 NFL draft picks with each card printed with silver foil highlights. The cardbacks carry college statistics and pertinent information highlighting each player's most impressive skills. Press Pass was released in both Hobby and Retail form. Hobby boxes included 24-packs containing five cards each and carried a suggested retail price of $3.59. Retail was issued in boxes of 36-packs containing four cards each and carried a suggested retail price of $2.99. Five short-printed (1:14 packs overall) Power Picks cards were included at the end of the set.
COMPLETE SET (50) 15.00 40.00
COMP.SET w/o SP's (45) 10.00 25.00
1 David Carr .25 .60
2 Eric Crouch .40 1.00
3 Rohan Davey .40 1.00
4 David Garrard .30 .75
5 Joey Harrington .25 .60
6 Kurt Kittner .25 .60
7 David Neill .25 .60
8 Patrick Ramsey .30 .75
9 Antwaan Randle El .30 .75
10 Damien Anderson .25 .60
11 T.J. Duckett .25 .60
12 DeShaun Foster .40 1.00
13 Lamar Gordon .30 .75
14 William Green .30 .75
15 Leonard Henry .25 .60
16 Adrian Peterson .30 .75
17 Clinton Portis .40 1.00
18 Jonathan Wells .30 .75
19 Brian Westbrook .50 1.25
20 Antonio Bryant .40 1.00
21 Reche Caldwell .30 .75
22 Kelly Campbell .30 .75
23 Andre Davis .25 .60
24 Jabar Gaffney .25 .60
25 Ron Johnson .30 .75
26 Ashley Lelie .25 .60
27 Josh Reed .30 .75
28 Cliff Russell .25 .60
29 Donte Stallworth .40 1.00
30 Javon Walker .40 1.00
31 Marquise Walker .25 .60
32 Daniel Graham .30 .75
33 Jeremy Shockey .40 1.00
34 Bryant McKinnie .25 .60
35 Mike Pearson .25 .60
36 Mike Williams .25 .60
37 Phillip Buchanon .40 1.00
38 Quentin Jammer .40 1.00
39 Kalimba Edwards .30 .75
40 Julius Peppers .60 1.50
41 Wendell Bryant .25 .60
42 John Henderson .30 .75
43 Ryan Sims .40 1.00
44 Roy Williams .25 .60
45 David Carr CL .20 .50
46 David Carr PP .75 2.00
47 Joey Harrington PP .75 2.00
48 T.J. Duckett PP .75 2.00
49 Donte Stallworth PP 1.25 3.00
50 William Green PP 1.00 2.50

2002 Press Pass Gold Zone
*1-45 SINGLES: .5X TO 1.2X BASIC CARDS
*46-50 POWER PICK: .15X TO .4X BASIC PP
ONE PER HOBBY PACK

2002 Press Pass Reflectors
*SINGLES: 3X TO 8X BASIC CARDS
STATED PRINT RUN 500 SER.#'d SETS

2002 Press Pass Torquers
*1-45 SINGLES: .8X TO 2X BASIC CARDS
*46-50 POWER PICK: .25X TO .6X BASIC CARDS
ONE PER RETAIL PACK

2002 Press Pass Autographs
Randomly inserted at a rate of 1:8 hobby and 1:36 retail packs, this 44-card set features top NFL draft picks with hand-signed autographs on the card fronts. The cards also have a congratulatory statement from the managing director on the backs. Please note that the Javon Walker card was only available in packs of 2003 Press Pass.
STATED ODDS 1:8 HOB, 1:36 RET
1 Damien Anderson 3.00 8.00
2 Antonio Bryant 5.00 12.00
3 Phillip Buchanon 5.00 12.00
4 Reche Caldwell 4.00 10.00
5 Rocky Calmus 4.00 10.00
6 Kelly Campbell 4.00 10.00
7 David Carr 3.00 8.00
8 Eric Crouch 5.00 12.00
9 Rohan Davey 5.00 12.00
10 Andre Davis 3.00 8.00
11 T.J. Duckett 3.00 8.00
12 Kalimba Edwards 4.00 10.00
13 DeShaun Foster 5.00 12.00
14 Jabar Gaffney 3.00 8.00
15 David Garrard 6.00 15.00
16 Lamar Gordon 4.00 10.00
17 Daniel Graham 4.00 10.00
18 William Green 4.00 10.00
19 Joey Harrington 3.00 8.00
20 John Henderson 4.00 10.00
21 Leonard Henry 3.00 8.00
22 Kyle Johnson 3.00 8.00
23 Ron Johnson 4.00 10.00
24 Levi Jones 3.00 8.00
25 Kurt Kittner 3.00 8.00
26 Ashley Lelie 3.00 8.00
27 Josh McCown 5.00 12.00
28 Freddie Milons 3.00 8.00
29 Maurice Morris 4.00 10.00
30 David Neill 3.00 8.00
31 Mike Pearson 3.00 8.00
32 Adrian Peterson 6.00 15.00
33 Patrick Ramsey 4.00 10.00
34 Antwaan Randle El 4.00 10.00
35 Josh Reed 4.00 10.00
36 Cliff Russell 3.00 8.00
37 Ryan Sims 5.00 12.00
38 Luke Staley 3.00 8.00
39 Donte Stallworth 5.00 12.00
40 Javon Walker 5.00 12.00
41 Marquise Walker 3.00 8.00
42 Anthony Weaver 3.00 8.00
43 Jonathan Wells 4.00 10.00
44 Brian Westbrook 10.00 25.00
45 Roy Williams 6.00 15.00

2002 Press Pass Big Numbers
This 36-card insert set is Press Pass' unique "set-within-a-set." One Big Numbers card was included in every pack. The standard-size cards are die-cut and printed on holographic foil.
COMPLETE SET (36) 12.50 30.00
ONE PER PACK
BN1 David Carr .30 .75
BN2 Eric Crouch .50 1.25
BN3 Rohan Davey .50 1.25
BN4 Joey Harrington .30 .75
BN5 Kurt Kittner .30 .75
BN6 Patrick Ramsey .40 1.00
BN7 Antwaan Randle El .40 1.00
BN8 T.J. Duckett .30 .75
BN9 DeShaun Foster .50 1.25
BN10 Lamar Gordon .40 1.00
BN11 William Green .40 1.00
BN12 Adrian Peterson .40 1.00
BN13 Clinton Portis .50 1.25
BN14 Javon Walker .50 1.25
BN15 Brian Westbrook .60 1.50
BN16 Antonio Bryant .50 1.25
BN17 Reche Caldwell .40 1.00
BN18 Kelly Campbell .40 1.00
BN19 Andre Davis .30 .75
BN20 Jabar Gaffney .30 .75
BN21 Ashley Lelie .30 .75
BN22 Josh Reed .40 1.00
BN23 Donte Stallworth .50 1.25
BN24 Marquise Walker .30 .75
BN25 Daniel Graham .40 1.00
BN26 Jeremy Shockey .50 1.25
BN27 Bryant McKinnie .30 .75
BN28 Mike Pearson .30 .75
BN29 Phillip Buchanon .50 1.25
BN30 Quentin Jammer .50 1.25
BN31 Kalimba Edwards .40 1.00
BN32 Julius Peppers .75 2.00
BN33 Wendell Bryant .30 .75
BN34 John Henderson .40 1.00
BN35 Roy Williams .30 .75
BN36 Joey Harrington CL .25 .60

2002 Press Pass Game Used Jerseys
Randomly inserted in hobby packs at the rate of 1:160 and retail at 1:720, this 13-card insert set features top NFL draft picks with an actual swatch of game used jersey on the fronts. The cards are serial numbered to 225-sets.
JERSEY/225 ODDS 1:160H, 1:720R
STATED PRINT RUN 225 SER.#'d SETS
JCAP Adrian Peterson 5.00 12.00
JCDC David Carr 4.00 10.00
JCDF DeShaun Foster 6.00 15.00
JCDG David Garrard 5.00 12.00
JCEC Eric Crouch 6.00 15.00
JCJH Joey Harrington 4.00 10.00
JCJM Josh McCown 6.00 15.00
JCJR Josh Reed 5.00 12.00
JCKK Kurt Kittner 4.00 10.00
JCLH Leonard Henry 4.00 10.00
JCLS Luke Staley 4.00 10.00
JCRW Roy Williams 4.00 10.00
JCWG William Green 5.00 12.00

2002 Press Pass Paydirt
This standard-size 9-card insert set is printed on silver foil board with gold over-stamping. The card were inserted at the rate of 1:12 packs. A die-cut parallel version was also produced and inserted at the rate of 1:24 packs.
COMPLETE SET (9) 6.00 15.00
STATED ODDS 1:12
*DIE CUT: .6X TO 1.5X BASIC INSERTS
PD1 David Carr .40 1.00
PD2 Joey Harrington .40 1.00
PD3 Kurt Kittner .40 1.00
PD4 T.J. Duckett .40 1.00
PD5 William Green .50 1.25
PD6 Clinton Portis .60 1.50
PD7 Antonio Bryant .60 1.50
PD8 DeShaun Foster .60 1.50
PD9 Donte Stallworth .60 1.50

2002 Press Pass Power Pick Autographs
Randomly inserted in packs, this 12-card set features hand signed cards of some of the top players in the draft. Each card is signed on the front and serial numbered to 250.
STATED PRINT RUN 250 SER.#'d SETS
1 Antonio Bryant 8.00 20.00
2 David Carr 5.00 12.00
3 Eric Crouch 8.00 20.00
4 Andre Davis 5.00 12.00
5 T.J. Duckett 5.00 12.00
6 DeShaun Foster 8.00 20.00
7 William Green 6.00 15.00
8 Joey Harrington 5.00 12.00
9 Kurt Kittner 5.00 12.00
10 Ashley Lelie 5.00 12.00
11 Josh Reed 6.00 15.00
12 Marquise Walker 5.00 12.00

2002 Press Pass Primetime
This 12-card insert set showcases players on etched holofoil. The cards were inserted at the rate of 1:8 packs.
COMPLETE SET (12) 7.50 20.00
STATED ODDS 1:8
PT1 David Carr .40 1.00
PT2 Joey Harrington .40 1.00
PT3 T.J. Duckett .40 1.00
PT4 William Green .50 1.25
PT5 DeShaun Foster .60 1.50
PT6 Clinton Portis .60 1.50
PT7 Antonio Bryant .60 1.50
PT8 Jabar Gaffney .40 1.00
PT9 Ashley Lelie .40 1.00
PT10 Josh Reed .50 1.25
PT11 Donte Stallworth .60 1.50
PT12 Julius Peppers 1.00 2.50

2002 Press Pass Rookie Chase
This 12-card insert set was a new concept Press Pass developed for their products in 2002. Collectors could send in contest cards for a chance to win a complete set of autographed cards from every player in the Press Pass autograph program. Eleven different players plus a Wild Card are featured. If the collector mailed in a contest card of the eventual 2002 ROY, the collector may have won one of ten complete sets of autographs. The cards were inserted at the rate of 1:24 packs.
COMPLETE SET (12) 15.00 40.00
STATED ODDS 1:24
RC1 David Carr 1.00 2.50
RC2 Joey Harrington 1.00 2.50
RC3 William Green 1.25 3.00
RC4 T.J. Duckett 1.00 2.50
RC5 Jabar Gaffney 1.00 2.50
RC6 Donte Stallworth 1.50 4.00
RC7 Antonio Bryant 1.50 4.00
RC8 Jeremy Shockey 1.50 4.00
RC9 Julius Peppers WIN 3.00 8.00
RC10 Josh Reed 1.25 3.00
RC11 DeShaun Foster 1.50 4.00
RC12 Field Card WIN 1.50 4.00

2002 Press Pass Showbound
This 6-card insert set spotlights rookies who are bound to make an impact in the NFL. The standard-size cards are etched on a holofoil background. The cards were inserted at the rate of 1:24 packs.
COMPLETE SET (6) 4.00 10.00
STATED ODDS 1:24
SB1 David Carr .50 1.25
SB2 Joey Harrington .50 1.25
SB3 William Green .60 1.50
SB4 T.J. Duckett .50 1.25
SB5 Antonio Bryant .75 2.00
SB6 Julius Peppers 1.25 3.00

2003 Press Pass
Released in April 2003, this set features 45 draft pick players, and five power pick subset cards, which were inserted 1:14 packs. Boxes contained 28 packs of 5 cards. SRP was $3.99.
COMPLETE SET (50) 20.00 50.00
COMP.SET w/o SP's (45) 10.00 25.00
1 Brad Banks .30 .75
2 Kyle Boller .25 .60
3 Ken Dorsey .30 .75
4 Jason Gesser .30 .75
5 Rex Grossman .30 .75
6 Kliff Kingsbury .40 1.00
7 Byron Leftwich .30 .75
8 Carson Palmer .50 1.25
9 Dave Ragone .25 .60
10 Chris Simms .25 .60
11 Brian St.Pierre .25 .60
12 Chris Brown .25 .60
13 Avon Cobourne .25 .60
14 Dahrran Diedrick .25 .60
15 Justin Fargas .40 1.00
16 Earnest Graham .40 1.00
17 Larry Johnson .30 .75
18 Willis McGahee .30 .75
19 Musa Smith .25 .60
20 Onterrio Smith .25 .60
21 Lee Suggs .25 .60
22 Anquan Boldin .40 1.00
23 Talman Gardner .25 .60
24 Taylor Jacobs .25 .60
25 Andre Johnson .60 1.50
26 Bryant Johnson .40 1.00
27 Brandon Lloyd .40 1.00
28 Charles Rogers .30 .75
29 Kelley Washington .25 .60
30 Teyo Johnson .30 .75
31 Bennie Joppru .25 .60
32 Jason Witten 1.00 2.50
33 Andrew Pinnock .30 .75
34 Jordan Gross .25 .60
35 Kwame Harris .25 .60
36 Eric Steinbach .25 .60
37 Brett Williams .25 .60
38 Terence Newman .40 1.00
39 Marcus Trufant .30 .75
40 Andre Woolfolk .25 .60
41 Terrell Suggs .30 .75
42 Jimmy Kennedy .30 .75
43 Boss Bailey .30 .75
44 Mike Doss .40 1.00
45 Carson Palmer CL .20 .50
46 Carson Palmer PP 1.00 2.50
47 Byron Leftwich PP .60 1.50
48 Charles Rogers PP .60 1.50
49 Kyle Boller PP .50 1.25
50 Andre Johnson PP 1.25 3.00

2003 Press Pass Retail
*RETAIL: .4X TO 1X HOBBY
RETAIL PRINTED WITH SILVER FOIL

2003 Press Pass Gold Zone
COMPLETE SET (45) 15.00 40.00
*GOLD: .6X TO 1.5X BASIC CARDS
ONE GOLD PER PACK

2003 Press Pass Reflectors
*REFLEC/500: 2.5X TO 6X BASIC CARDS
STATED PRINT RUN 500 SER.#'d SETS

2003 Press Pass Reflectors Proofs
*PROOF/100: 5X TO 12X BASIC CARDS
STATED PRINT RUN 100 SER.#'d SETS

2003 Press Pass Torquers
ONE PER RETAIL PACK

2003 Press Pass Autographed Footballs
Issued one per hobby case, this set features three of the top 2003 NFL Draft quarterbacks. Each player signed a white panel football. A Press Pass certificate of authenticity also accompanied each football.
ONE PER HOBBY CASE
PRICES ARE FOR SIGNED BALL AND COA
1 Byron Leftwich 20.00 50.00
2 Carson Palmer 25.00 60.00
3 Dave Ragone 12.50 30.00

2003 Press Pass Autographs Bronze
Inserted at the rate of 1:7 packs, this set features authentic player signatures on each card. The Bronze cards are not serial numbered and feature their college team logo in the lower right hand corner of the cardfront as well as bronze colored highlights. The cards are unnumbered and listed below alphabetically. Dewayne White, Terrell Suggs, and Bryant Johnson signed only for the Bronze version set. Please note that Tyrone Calico, Dahrran Diedrick, Mike Doss, Chris Kelsay, Jimmy Kennedy, Jerome McDougle, Eric Steinbach, and Bobby Wade were only available in packs of Press Pass JE.
OVERALL AUTO ODDS 1:7 HOB, 1:56 RET
*GOLD/100: .6X TO 1.5X BRONZE AU
GOLD PRINT RUN 100 SER.#'d SETS
*SILVER/200: .5X TO 1.2X BRONZE AU
SILVER PRINT RUN 200 SER.#'d SETS
1 Boss Bailey 5.00 12.00
2 Brad Banks 5.00 12.00
3 Anquan Boldin 6.00 15.00
4 Kyle Boller 4.00 10.00
5 Chris Brown 4.00 10.00
6 Mike Bush 4.00 10.00
7 Tyrone Calico 4.00 10.00
8 Avon Cobourne 4.00 10.00
9 Angelo Crowell 5.00 12.00
10 Chris Davis 5.00 12.00
11 Domanick Davis 5.00 12.00
12 Dahrran Diedrick 4.00 10.00
13 Ken Dorsey 5.00 12.00
14 Mike Doss 6.00 15.00
15 Justin Fargas 6.00 15.00
16 Talman Gardner 4.00 10.00
17 Jason Gesser 5.00 12.00
18 Earnest Graham 6.00 15.00
19 Justin Griffith 5.00 12.00
20 DeJuan Groce 6.00 15.00
21 Jordan Gross 4.00 10.00
22 Kwame Harris 4.00 10.00
23 Michael Haynes 4.00 10.00
24 Wayne Hunter 4.00 10.00
25 Taylor Jacobs 4.00 10.00
26 Larry Johnson 5.00 12.00
27 Teyo Johnson 5.00 12.00
28 Ben Johnson 4.00 10.00
29 Bryant Johnson 6.00 15.00
30 Bennie Joppru 4.00 10.00
31 Kareem Kelly 4.00 10.00
32 Chris Kelsay 5.00 12.00
33 Jimmy Kennedy 5.00 12.00
34 Kliff Kingsbury 6.00 15.00
35 Byron Leftwich 5.00 12.00
36 Brandon Lloyd 6.00 15.00
37 Vincent Manuwai 4.00 10.00
38 Rashean Mathis 4.00 10.00
39 Sultan McCullough 4.00 10.00
40 Jerome McDougle 4.00 10.00
41 Willis McGahee 5.00 12.00
42 Terence Newman 6.00 15.00
43 Tony Pashos 4.00 10.00
44 Carson Palmer 8.00 20.00
45 Andrew Pinnock 5.00 12.00
46 Dave Ragone 4.00 10.00
47 DeWayne Robertson 5.00 12.00
48 Steve Sciullo 4.00 10.00
49 Musa Smith 4.00 10.00
50 Brian St.Pierre 4.00 10.00
51 Eric Steinbach 4.00 10.00
52 Jon Stinchcomb 5.00 12.00
53 Terrell Suggs 8.00 20.00
54 LaBrandon Toefield 4.00 10.00
55 Marcus Trufant 5.00 12.00
56 Bobby Wade 5.00 12.00
57 Seneca Wallace 5.00 12.00
58 Shane Walton 4.00 10.00
59 Kelley Washington 4.00 10.00
60 Dennis Weathersby 4.00 10.00
61 DeWayne White 4.00 10.00
62 Brett Williams 4.00 10.00
63 Juston Wood 4.00 10.00
64 Andre Woolfolk 4.00 10.00

2003 Press Pass Big Numbers
Inserted one per pack, this 36 card set features top draft players in a horizontal number design.
COMPLETE SET (36) 10.00 25.00

STATED ODDS ONE PER PACK
BN1 Brad Banks .40 1.00
BN2 Anquan Boldin .50 1.25
BN3 Kyle Boller
BN4 Chris Brown .30 .75
BN5 Avon Cobourne .30 .75
BN6 Ken Dorsey .40 1.00
BN7 Mike Doss .50 1.25
BN8 Justin Fargas .50 1.25
BN9 Talman Gardner .30 .75
BN10 Earnest Graham .50 1.25
BN11 Rex Grossman .40 1.00
BN12 Taylor Jacobs .30 .75
BN13 Andre Johnson .75 2.00
BN14 Bryant Johnson .50 1.25
BN15 Larry Johnson .40 1.00
BN16 Teyo Johnson .40 1.00
BN17 Dennie Joppru .30 .75
BN18 Jimmy Kennedy .40 1.00
BN19 Byron Leftwich .40 1.00
BN20 Brandon Lloyd .50 1.25
BN21 Jerome McDougle .30 .75
BN22 Willis McGahee .40 1.00
BN23 Terence Newman
BN24 Carson Palmer .60 1.50
BN25 Dave Ragone .30 .75
BN26 Charles Rogers .40 1.00
BN27 Chris Simms .30 .75
BN28 Musa Smith .30 .75
BN29 Onterrio Smith .30 .75
BN30 Brian St.Pierre .30 .75
BN31 Lee Suggs .30 .75
BN32 Terrell Suggs .40 1.00
BN33 Kelley Washington .30 .75
BN34 Jason Witten 1.25 3.00
BN35 Andre Woolfolk .30 .75
BN36 Byron Leftwich .40 1.00

2003 Press Pass Game Used Jerseys Gold

serted at an overall rate of 1:84 hobby and 1:280 retail, this set features cards with swatches of college worn game-used jerseys. The Gold version cards are serial numbered to 475. In addition Press Pass also inserted Holofoil parallels numbered of 150 and silver versions numbered to 225.
GOLD PRINT RUN 475 SER.#'d SETS
*HOLOFOIL/150: .6X TO 1.5X GOLD/475
HOLOFOIL PRINT RUN 150 SER.#'d SETS
*SILVER/225: .5X TO 1.2X GOLD/475
SILVER PRINT RUN 225 SER.#'d SETS
OVERALL JERSEY ODDS 1:84 HOB, 1:280 RET
JCBJ Bennie Joppru 2.00 5.00
JCBL Byron Leftwich 3.00 8.00
JCCP Carson Palmer 4.00 10.00
JCEG Earnest Graham 4.00 8.00
JCKD Ken Dorsey 3.00 8.00
JCKK Kareem Kelly 2.00 5.00
JCSW Seneca Wallace 3.00 8.00
JCTJ Teyo Johnson 3.00 8.00

2003 Press Pass Paydirt

Inserted at a rate of 1:14, this set highlights 7 of the top offensive draft players.
COMPLETE SET (7) 10.00 25.00
STATED ODDS 1:14
PD1 Kyle Boller .50 1.25
PD2 Andre Johnson 1.25 3.00
PD3 Larry Johnson .60 1.50
PD4 Byron Leftwich .60 1.50
PD5 Carson Palmer 1.00 2.50
PD6 Rex Grossman .60 1.50
PD7 Charles Rogers .60 1.50

2003 Press Pass Power Pick Autographs

This 9-card set is an autographed version of the Power Pick subset found in the base set cards #'d 46-50. The set is serially numbered to 250 and inserted 1:14 packs.
STATED PRINT RUN 250 SER.#'d SETS
1 Brad Banks 5.00 12.00
2 Anquan Boldin 6.00 15.00
3 Kyle Boller 4.00 10.00
4 Taylor Jacobs 4.00 10.00
5 Larry Johnson 5.00 12.00
6 Byron Leftwich 5.00 12.00
7 Brandon Lloyd 6.00 15.00
8 Carson Palmer 40.00 80.00
9 Dave Ragone 4.00 10.00

2003 Press Pass Primetime

Inserted at a rate of 1:9, this set showcases several 2003 draft players.
COMPLETE SET (10) 10.00 25.00
STATED ODDS 1:9
PT1 Kyle Boller .50 1.25
PT2 Rex Grossman .60 1.50
PT3 Larry Johnson .60 1.50
PT4 Andre Johnson 1.25 3.00
PT5 Byron Leftwich .60 1.50
PT6 Carson Palmer 1.00 2.50
PT7 Dave Ragone .50 1.25
PT8 Charles Rogers .60 1.50
PT9 Chris Simms .50 1.25
PT10 Onterrio Smith .50 1.25

2003 Press Pass Rookie Chase

Inserted at a rate of 1:28, this set comes with a scratch off area that reveals a draft round. If your player is drafted in the round shown on the card, you are eligible to enter a contest for various prizes.
STATED ODDS 1:28
RC1 Taylor Jacobs .75 2.00
RC2 Larry Johnson 1.00 2.50
RC3 Andre Johnson 2.00 5.00
RC4 Byron Leftwich 1.00 2.50
RC5 Carson Palmer 1.50 4.00
RC6 Dave Ragone .75 2.00
RC7 Charles Rogers 1.00 2.50
RC8 Onterrio Smith .75 2.00
RC9 Terrell Suggs 1.00 2.50

2003 Press Pass Showbound

Inserted at a rate of 1:28, this set features top draft picks set to excel in the NFL.
COMPLETE SET (7) 12.00 30.00
STATED ODDS 1:28
SB1 Byron Leftwich 1.00 2.50
SB2 Carson Palmer 1.50 4.00
SB3 Dave Ragone .75 2.00
SB4 Larry Johnson 1.00 2.50
SB5 Charles Rogers 1.00 2.50
SB6 Andre Johnson 2.00 5.00
SB7 Kyle Boller .75 2.00

2004 Press Pass

The basic Press Pass product released in late April 2004. The base set consists of 50-cards including 5-Power Pick short prints at the end of the set. Mike Williams made an appearance in this product although he was declared ineligible for the NFL Draft. Hobby boxes contained 24-packs of 5-cards. Four parallel sets and a variety of inserts can be found seeded in hobby and retail packs highlighted by the Game Used Jerseys and the Autograph Inserts.
COMPLETE SET (50) 15.00 40.00
COMP.SET w/o SP's (45) 12.50 30.00
1 Casey Clausen .30 .75
2 Craig Krenzel .25 .60
3 J.P. Losman .25 .60
4 Eli Manning 2.00 5.00
5 Luke McCown .25 .60
6 John Navarre .25 .60
7 Cody Pickett .25 .60
8 Philip Rivers .75 2.00
9 Ben Roethlisberger 2.00 5.00
10 Matt Schaub .25 .60
11 Cedric Cobbs .25 .60
12 Steven Jackson .40 1.00
13 Kevin Jones .30 .75
14 Greg Jones .25 .60
15 Julius Jones .25 .60
16 Jarrett Payton .30 .75
17 Chris Perry .25 .60
18 Michael Turner .25 .60
19 Quincy Wilson .25 .60
20 Jason Wright .25 .60
21 Bernard Berrian .25 .60
22 Michael Clayton .30 .75
23 Devard Darling .25 .60
24 Lee Evans .40 1.00
25 Larry Fitzgerald 1.00 2.50
26 Devery Henderson .25 .60
27 Michael Jenkins .25 .60
28 Darius Watts .25 .60
29 Mike Williams .30 .75
30 Roy Williams WR .25 .60
31 Rashaun Woods .25 .60
32 Ben Troupe .25 .60
33 Shawn Andrews .30 .75
34 Robert Gallery .30 .75
35 Tommie Harris .30 .75
36 Vince Wilfork .40 1.00
37 Will Smith .30 .75
38 Teddy Lehman .25 .60
39 Jonathan Vilma .30 .75
40 D.J. Williams .40 1.00
41 DeAngelo Hall .40 1.00
42 Dunta Robinson .25 .60
43 Derrick Strait .25 .60
44 Keith Smith .25 .60
45 Eli Manning CL 1.00 2.50
46 Eli Manning PP 3.00 8.00
47 Ben Roethlisberger PP 3.00 8.00
48 Larry Fitzgerald PP 1.50 4.00
49 Roy Williams PP .40 1.00
50 Philip Rivers PP 1.25 3.00

2004 Press Pass Blue

COMPLETE SET (45) 30.00 60.00
*BLUES: .8X TO 2X BASIC CARDS
ONE PER RETAIL PACK

2004 Press Pass Gold

COMPLETE SET (45) 20.00 50.00
*GOLDS: .6X TO 1.5X BASIC CARDS
ONE GOLD PER HOBBY PACK

2004 Press Pass Reflectors

*REFLECTOR: 2.5X TO 6X BASIC CARDS
STATED PRINT RUN 500 SER.#'d SETS

2004 Press Pass Reflectors Proof

*REF.PROOFS: 5X TO 12X BASE CARD HI
STATED PRINT RUN 100 SER.#'d SETS

2004 Press Pass Autographs Bronze

Each card in this set features an authentic player's autograph. Three different colored backgrounds were used to create different sets: Bronze, Gold, and Silver. Press Pass packs featured autograph cards seeded at the rate of 1:7 with 46-different players appearing in that product. The cards were released again in packs of Press Pass SE with a selection of new players and a new parallel set - Blue. The following players were released in Press Pass SE packs only: Bernard Berrian, Jermaine Green, Devery Henderson, Steven Jackson, P.K. Sam, Andrae Thurman, and Jonathan Vilma. Please note that Kevin Jones was also issued in Press Pass SE packs only, but did not have a Bronze version autograph, only the other three colors. The following players were issued in Bronze only: Bernard Berrian, Jermaine Green, Devery Henderson, P.K. Sam, Andrae Thurman, Mike Williams, and Kellen Winslow Jr. Lastly, some players signed some card in red ink as well as blue. Those are listed below as such. Any additions to this list are appreciated.
OVERALL AUTO ODDS 1:7 PP PACKS
ALL ALSO INSERTED IN PRESS PASS SE
1 Bernard Berrian 3.00 8.00
2 Casey Clausen 4.00 10.00
2R Casey Clausen Red 5.00 12.00
3 Michael Clayton 4.00 10.00
3R Michael Clayton Red 5.00 12.00
4 Cedric Cobbs 3.00 8.00
5 Ricardo Colclough 3.00 8.00
6 Devard Darling 3.00 8.00
6R Devard Darling Red 4.00 10.00
7 Dwan Edwards 3.00 8.00
7R Dwan Edwards Red 4.00 10.00
8 Lee Evans 5.00 12.00
8R Lee Evans Red 6.00 15.00
9 Larry Fitzgerald 25.00 60.00
10 Robert Gallery 4.00 10.00
10R Robert Gallery Red 5.00 12.00
11 Jermaine Green 3.00 8.00
12 DeAngelo Hall 5.00 12.00
13 Tommie Harris 4.00 10.00
14 Ben Hartsock 3.00 8.00
15 Devery Henderson 3.00 8.00
16 Steven Jackson SP 5.00 12.00
17 Michael Jenkins 3.00 8.00
17R Michael Jenkins Red 4.00 10.00
18 Greg Jones 3.00 8.00
18R Greg Jones Red 4.00 10.00
19 Julius Jones 6.00 15.00
21 Sean Jones 3.00 8.00
22 Nate Kaeding 4.00 10.00
22R Nate Kaeding Red 5.00 12.00
23 Robert Kent 3.00 8.00
23R Robert Kent Red 4.00 10.00
24 Teddy Lehman 3.00 8.00
24R Teddy Lehman Red 4.00 10.00
25 Jared Lorenzen 4.00 10.00
25R Jared Lorenzen Red 5.00 12.00
26 Eli Manning 30.00 60.00
27 Luke McCown 3.00 8.00
28 Mewelde Moore 4.00 10.00
29 John Navarre 3.00 8.00
29R John Navarre Red 4.00 10.00
30 James Newson 5.00 12.00
30R James Newson Red 6.00 15.00
31 Tony Pape
31R Tony Pape Red
32 Jarrett Payton 4.00 10.00
33 Chris Perry 3.00 8.00
34 Cody Pickett 3.00 8.00
35 Philip Rivers 15.00 40.00
35R Philip Rivers Red 20.00 50.00
36 Ben Roethlisberger SP 60.00 120.00
36R Ben Roethlisberger Red 60.00 120.00
37 P.K. Sam 3.00 8.00
38 Matt Schaub 3.00 8.00
38R Matt Schaub Red 3.00 8.00
39 Justin Smiley 4.00 10.00
40 Keith Smith 3.00 8.00
40R Keith Smith Red 4.00 10.00
41 Will Smith 4.00 10.00
41R Will Smith Red 5.00 12.00
42 Jeff Smoker 4.00 10.00
42R Jeff Smoker Red 5.00 12.00
43 Derrick Strait 3.00 8.00
44 Andrae Thurman 3.00 8.00
44R Andrae Thurman Red 4.00 10.00
45 Ben Troupe 3.00 8.00
45R Ben Troupe Red 4.00 10.00
46 Michael Turner 3.00 8.00
47 Jonathan Vilma 4.00 10.00
47R Jonathan Vilma Red 5.00 12.00
48 Ben Watson 4.00 10.00
49 Darius Watts 3.00 8.00
49R Darius Watts Red 4.00 10.00
50 Vince Wilfork 5.00 12.00
51 D.J. Williams 5.00 12.00
51R D.J. Williams Red 6.00 15.00
52 Mike Williams 4.00 10.00
53 Quincy Wilson 3.00 8.00
53R Quincy Wilson Red 4.00 10.00
54 Kellen Winslow 3.00 8.00
54R Kellen Winslow Red 3.00 8.00
55 Rashaun Woods 3.00 8.00
56 Jason Wright 3.00 8.00

2004 Press Pass Autographs Blue

*BLUE: .6X TO 1.5X BRONZE AU
BLUE STATED PRINT RUN 25-50
BLUES INSERTED IN PRESS PASS SE
9 Larry Fitzgerald/25 60.00 120.00
20 Kevin Jones 6.00 15.00
26 Eli Manning 60.00 125.00
35 Philip Rivers 30.00 80.00
36 Ben Roethlisberger 100.00 200.00
36R Ben Roethlisberger Red 125.00 250.00

2004 Press Pass Autographs Gold

*GOLD: .6X TO 1.5X BRONZE AU
STATED PRINT RUN 50-100
20 Kevin Jones 6.00 15.00
26 Eli Manning 50.00 100.00
26R Eli Manning Red 50.00 100.00
35 Philip Rivers 25.00 60.00
36 Ben Roethlisberger 100.00 200.00
36R Ben Roethlisberger Red 125.00 225.00

2004 Press Pass Autographs Silver

*SILVER: .5X TO 1.2X BRONZE AU
SILVER STATED PRINT RUN 75-200
20 Kevin Jones 15.00 40.00
26 Eli Manning 40.00 80.00
35 Philip Rivers 20.00 50.00
36 Ben Roethlisberger 50.00 120.00

2004 Press Pass Big Numbers

COMPLETE SET (33) 12.50 30.00
ONE PER PACK
*COLLECTOR SERIES: .3X TO .8X
BN1 Casey Clausen .40 1.00
BN2 Michael Clayton .40 1.00
BN3 Cedric Cobbs .30 .75
BN4 Devard Darling .30 .75
BN5 Lee Evans .50 1.25
BN6 Larry Fitzgerald 1.25 3.00
BN7 Robert Gallery .40 1.00
BN8 DeAngelo Hall .50 1.25
BN9 Steven Jackson .50 1.25
BN10 Michael Jenkins .30 .75
BN11 Greg Jones .30 .75
BN12 Kevin Jones .40 1.00
BN13 Craig Krenzel .30 .75
BN14 J.P. Losman .30 .75
BN15 Eli Manning 2.50 6.00
BN16 John Navarre .30 .75
BN17 Jarrett Payton .40 1.00
BN18 Chris Perry .30 .75
BN19 Cody Pickett .30 .75
BN20 Philip Rivers 1.00 2.50
BN21 Ben Roethlisberger 2.50 6.00
BN22 Matt Schaub .30 .75
BN23 Will Smith .40 1.00
BN24 Ben Troupe .30 .75
BN25 Michael Turner .30 .75
BN26 Jonathan Vilma .40 1.00
BN27 Vince Wilfork .50 1.25
BN28 Quincy Wilson .30 .75
BN29 D.J. Williams .50 1.25
BN30 Mike Williams .40 1.00
BN31 Roy Williams WR .30 .75
BN32 Rashaun Woods .30 .75
BN33 Eli Manning CL 2.50 6.00

2004 Press Pass Game Used Jerseys Silver

SILVER PRINT RUN 300 SER.#'d SETS
*GOLD/100: .6X TO 1.5X SILVER/300
GOLD PRINT RUN 100 SER.#'d SETS
*HOLOFOIL/50: .8X TO 2X SILVER/300
HOLOFOIL PRINT RUN 50 SER.#'d SETS
OVERALL JERSEY ODDS 1:72 H
JCBR Ben Roethlisberger 15.00 40.00
JCCP Cody Pickett 2.50 6.00
JCDD Devard Darling 2.50 6.00
JCDW Darius Watts 2.50 6.00
JCEM Eli Manning 10.00 25.00
JCJG Jermaine Green 2.50 6.00
JCJL Jared Lorenzen 3.00 8.00
JCJP Jarrett Payton 3.00 8.00
JCLM Luke McCown 2.50 6.00
JCMM Mewelde Moore 3.00 8.00
JCMS Matt Schaub 2.50 6.00
JCSJ Steven Jackson 4.00 10.00

2004 Press Pass Paydirt

COMPLETE SET (12) 12.50 30.00
STATED ODDS 1:6
PD1 Eli Manning 3.00 8.00
PD2 Roy Williams WR .40 1.00
PD3 Kevin Jones .50 1.25
PD4 Philip Rivers 1.25 3.00
PD5 Rashaun Woods .40 1.00
PD6 Ben Roethlisberger 3.00 8.00
PD7 Ben Troupe .40 1.00
PD8 Steven Jackson .60 1.50
PD9 Michael Clayton .50 1.25
PD10 Chris Perry .40 1.00
PD11 Larry Fitzgerald 1.50 4.00
PD12 Greg Jones .40 1.00

2004 Press Pass Showbound

COMPLETE SET (9) 12.50 30.00
STATED ODDS 1:12
SB1 Steven Jackson .75 2.00
SB2 Larry Fitzgerald 2.00 5.00
SB3 Eli Manning 4.00 10.00
SB4 Kevin Jones .60 1.50
SB5 Roy Williams WR .50 1.25
SB6 Ben Roethlisberger 4.00 10.00
SB7 Philip Rivers 1.50 4.00
SB8 Chris Perry .50 1.25
SB9 J.P. Losman .50 1.25

2005 Press Pass

Press Pass was initially released in late April 2005. The base set consists of 50-cards with 5-short printed Power Picks. Hobby boxes contained 24-packs of 5-cards and carried an S.R.P. of $3.99 per pack. Four parallel sets and a variety of inserts can be found seeded in packs highlighted by the popular multi-tiered Autograph inserts. Red ink versions of many autographed cards were also created adding another level of collectibility.
COMPLETE SET (50) 25.00 50.00
COMP.SET w/o PP'S (45) 12.50 30.00
POWER PICK STATED ODDS 1:14 H/R
UNPRICED HOBBY SOLO PRINT RUN 1 SET
1 Derek Anderson .30 .75
2 Brock Berlin .25 .60
3 Charlie Frye .25 .60
4 Gino Guidugli .25 .60
5 David Greene .25 .60
6 Stefan LeFors .25 .60
7 Dan Orlovsky .25 .60
8 Kyle Orton .25 .60
9 Aaron Rodgers 3.00 8.00
10 Alex Smith QB 1.00 2.50
11 Andrew Walter .25 .60
12 Jason White .40 1.00
13 J.J. Arrington .30 .75
14 Ronnie Brown .30 .75
15 Anthony Davis .25 .60
16 Kay-Jay Harris .25 .60
17 T.A. McLendon .25 .60
18 Ryan Moats .25 .60
19 Vernand Morency .25 .60
20 Cadillac Williams .25 .60
21 Mark Bradley .25 .60
22 Reggie Brown .25 .60
23 Mark Clayton .25 .60
24 Braylon Edwards .25 .60
25 Fred Gibson .25 .60
26 Terrence Murphy .25 .60
27 J.R. Russell .25 .60
28 Craphonso Thorpe .25 .60
29 Roddy White .40 1.00
30 Mike Williams .30 .75
31 Troy Williamson .25 .60
32 Heath Miller .50 1.25
33 Alex Smith TE .25 .60
34 Khalif Barnes .25 .60
35 Jammal Brown .40 1.00
36 Brandon Browner .40 1.00
37 Marlin Jackson .25 .60
38 Carlos Rogers .40 1.00
39 Antrel Rolle .40 1.00
40 Dan Cody .25 .60
41 Erasmus James .25 .60
42 David Pollack .25 .60
43 Anttaj Hawthorne .25 .60
44 Derrick Johnson .30 .75
45 Ronnie Brown CL .15 .40
46 Cadillac Williams PP .50 1.25
47 Aaron Rodgers PP 6.00 15.00
48 Alex Smith QB PP 2.00 5.00
49 Braylon Edwards PP .50 1.25
50 Mike Williams PP .60 1.50

2005 Press Pass Blue

COMPLETE SET (45) 25.00 60.00
*SINGLES: .8X TO 2X BASIC CARDS
ONE PER RETAIL PACK

2005 Press Pass Reflectors

*SINGLES: 2.5X TO 6X BASIC CARDS
STATED PRINT RUN 500 SER.#'d SETS

2005 Press Pass Reflectors Proof

*SINGLES: 4X TO 10X BASIC CARDS
REFLECTORS/100 INSERTS IN HOBBY ONLY

2005 Press Pass Autographs Bronze

Press Pass Autographs were randomly seeded in packs of 2005 Press Pass and Press Pass SE. There were four different background colors used to print the cards creating four parallel sets. Many players also signed a number of cards in both blue ink and red ink creating a large number of ink color variations. Lastly, even more variations were created by many players signing along with an added notation of their choosing. Although these notations often sell for slight premiums, we have not cataloged them since there are no other distinguishing characteristics of the cards save for the additional notation.
AUTO OVERALL ODDS 1:7H, 1:56R
1 Derek Anderson 5.00 12.00
2 J.J. Arrington 5.00 12.00
3 Marion Barber 4.00 10.00
4 Khalif Barnes 4.00 10.00
5 Brock Berlin 4.00 10.00
6 Mark Bradley 4.00 10.00
7 Elton Brown 4.00 10.00
8 Jammal Brown 6.00 15.00
9 Reggie Brown 4.00 10.00
10 Ronnie Brown SP 20.00 50.00
11 Brandon Browner 6.00 15.00
12 Luis Castillo 5.00 12.00
13 Mark Clayton 4.00 10.00
14 Dan Cody 4.00 10.00
15 Jerome Collins 5.00 12.00
16 Sean Considine 4.00 10.00
17 Anthony Davis 4.00 10.00
18 Thomas Davis 4.00 10.00
19 Braylon Edwards SP 12.00 30.00
20 Ciatrick Fason 4.00 10.00
21 Diamond Ferri 4.00 10.00
22 Charlie Frye SP 8.00 20.00
23 Fred Gibson 4.00 10.00
24 David Greene 4.00 10.00
25 Gino Guidugli 4.00 10.00
26 Kay-Jay Harris 4.00 10.00
27 Anttaj Hawthorne 4.00 10.00
28 Chris Henry 5.00 12.00
29 Keron Henry 4.00 10.00
30 Noah Herron 4.00 10.00
31 Marlin Jackson 4.00 10.00
32 Erasmus James 4.00 10.00
33 Derrick Johnson 5.00 12.00
34 Stefan LeFors 4.00 10.00
35 T.A. McLendon 4.00 10.00
36 Heath Miller 10.00 25.00
37 Ryan Moats 4.00 10.00
38 Vernand Morency 4.00 10.00
39 Terrence Murphy 4.00 10.00
40 Dan Orlovsky 4.00 10.00
41 Kyle Orton 4.00 10.00
42 David Pollack 4.00 10.00
43 Walter Reyes 4.00 10.00
44 Aaron Rodgers SP 125.00 250.00
45 Carlos Rogers 6.00 15.00
46 Antrel Rolle 6.00 15.00
47 J.R. Russell 4.00 10.00
48 Barrett Ruud 5.00 12.00
49 Eric Shelton 4.00 10.00
50 Alex Smith TE 4.00 10.00
51 Craphonso Thorpe 4.00 10.00
52 Andrew Walter 4.00 10.00
53 Jason White 6.00 15.00
54 Roddy White 6.00 15.00
55 Cadillac Williams SP 8.00 20.00
56 Mike Williams SP 8.00 20.00
57 Troy Williamson 4.00 10.00
58 Stanley Wilson 5.00 12.00

2005 Press Pass Autographs Bronze Red Ink

*UNLISTED RED INK: .6X TO 1.5X
CARDS W/PRINT RUNS UNDER 20 NOT PRICED
1 Derek Anderson/50* 8.00 20.00
3 Marion Barber/20* 6.00 15.00
5 Brock Berlin/50* 6.00 15.00
6 Mark Bradley/11*
7 Elton Brown/17*
8 Jammal Brown/43* 10.00 25.00
9 Reggie Brown/50* 6.00 15.00
10 Ronnie Brown/10*
11 Brandon Browner/25* 10.00 25.00
12 Luis Castillo/9*
13 Mark Clayton/50* 6.00 15.00
14 Dan Cody/55* 6.00 15.00
15 Jerome Collins/49* 8.00 20.00
16 Sean Considine/45* 6.00 15.00
17 Anthony Davis/7*
18 Thomas Davis/277* 6.00 15.00
20 Ciatrick Fason/12*
21 Diamond Ferri/65* 6.00 15.00
22 Charlie Frye/9*
23 Fred Gibson/50* 6.00 15.00
24 David Greene/50* 6.00 15.00
25 Gino Guidugli/199* 6.00 15.00
27 Anttaj Hawthorne/25* 6.00 15.00
28 Chris Henry/50* 8.00 20.00
29 Keron Henry/33* 6.00 15.00
30 Noah Herron/49* 6.00 15.00
31 Marlin Jackson/50* 6.00 15.00
32 Erasmus James/34* 6.00 15.00
33 Derrick Johnson/50* 8.00 20.00
34 Stefan LeFors/50* 6.00 15.00
35 T.A. McLendon/2*
36 Heath Miller/10*
37 Ryan Moats/194* 6.00 15.00
38 Vernand Morency/29* 6.00 15.00
39 Terrence Murphy/27* 6.00 15.00
40 Dan Orlovsky/130* 6.00 15.00
41 Kyle Orton/50* 6.00 15.00
42 David Pollack/25* 6.00 15.00
43 Walter Reyes/50* 6.00 15.00
45 Carlos Rogers/45* 10.00 25.00
46 Antrel Rolle/50* 10.00 25.00
47 J.R. Russell/34* 6.00 15.00
48 Barrett Ruud/290* 0.00 20.00
49 Eric Shelton/50* 6.00 15.00
50 Alex Smith TE/112* 6.00 15.00
51 Craphon.Thorpe/100* 6.00 15.00
52 Andrew Walter/10*
53 Jason White/266* 10.00 25.00
54 Roddy White/138* 10.00 25.00
55 Cadillac Williams/10*
57 Troy Williamson 6.00 15.00
58 Stanley Wilson/49* 8.00 20.00

2005 Press Pass Autographs Blue

*BLUE: .8X TO 2X BRONZE AUTOS
*BLUE: .6X TO 1.5X BRONZE SP AUTOS
BLUES WERE INSERTED IN PRESS PASS SE
BLUE PRINT RUN 25-50
ANNOUNCED PRINT RUNS FOR RED INKS
10 Ronnie Brown/25 40.00 100.00
19 Braylon Edwards/20* 15.00 40.00
44 Aaron Rodgers/50 175.00 300.00
55 Cadillac Williams/15* 20.00 50.00
56 Mike Williams/25 10.00 25.00

2005 Press Pass Autographs Blue Red Ink

*RED INK: .5X TO 1.2X BASIC BLUE AUTOS
CARDS W/PRINT RUNS UNDER 20 NOT PRICED
3 Marion Barber/25* 20.00 50.00
21 Diamond Ferri/36* 10.00 25.00
37 Ryan Moats/21* 10.00 25.00

2005 Press Pass Autographs Gold

*GOLD: .6X TO 1.5X BRONZE AUTOS
*GOLD: .5X TO 1.2X BRONZE SP AUTOS
GOLD HOBBY PRINT RUN 50-100
SOME PRINT RUNS ADJUSTED FOR RED INKS
10 Ronnie Brown/50 40.00 100.00
19 Braylon Edwards/40* 15.00 40.00
44 Aaron Rodgers/95* 125.00 250.00
55 Cadillac Williams/40* 25.00 60.00
56 Mike Williams/50 10.00 25.00

2005 Press Pass Autographs Gold Red Ink

*RED INK: .5X TO 1.2X BASE GOLD AUs
CARDS W/PRINT RUNS UNDER 20 NOT PRICED
2 J.J. Arrington/50* 10.00 25.00
17 Anthony Davis/50* 8.00 20.00
37 Ryan Moats/28* 8.00 20.00

2005 Press Pass Autographs Silver

*SILVER: .5X TO 1.2X BRONZE AUTOS
SILVER PRINT RUN 75-200
19 Braylon Edwards/81* 15.00 40.00
44 Aaron Rodgers/186* 125.00 250.00
55 Cadillac Williams/90* 15.00 40.00
56 Mike Williams/75 10.00 25.00

2005 Press Pass Autographs Silver Red Ink

*UNLISTED RED INK: .6X TO 1.5X SILVER AU
PRINT RUNS UNDER 20 NOT PRICED
4 Khalif Barnes/50* 8.00 20.00
21 Diamond Ferri/22* 8.00 20.00
37 Ryan Moats/22* 8.00 20.00

2005 Press Pass Big Numbers

COMPLETE SET (25) 12.50 30.00
ONE PER PACK
BN1 Reggie Brown .30 .75
BN2 Ronnie Brown .40 1.00
BN3 Mark Clayton .30 .75
BN4 Dan Cody .30 .75
BN5 Anthony Davis .30 .75
DNG Braylon Edwards .30 .75
BN7 Charlie Frye .30 .75
BN8 Fred Gibson .30 .75
BN9 David Greene .30 .75
BN10 Gino Guidugli .30 .75
BN11 Derrick Johnson .40 1.00
BN12 T.A. McLendon .30 .75
BN13 Heath Miller .60 1.50
BN14 Vernand Morency .30 .75
BN15 Dan Orlovsky .30 .75
BN16 Kyle Orton .30 .75
BN17 Aaron Rodgers 4.00 10.00
BN18 J.R. Russell .30 .75
BN19 Alex Smith QB 1.25 3.00
BN20 Andrew Walter .30 .75
BN21 Jason White .50 1.25
BN22 Cadillac Williams .30 .75
BN23 Mike Williams .40 1.00
BN24 Troy Williamson .30 .75
BN25 Aaron Rodgers CL 4.00 10.00

2005 Press Pass Game Used Jerseys Silver

OVERALL JERSEY ODDS 1:72H, 1:280R
SILVER PRINT RUN 300 SER.#'d SETS
*GOLD: .5X TO 1.2X SILVER JSYs
GOLD PRINT RUN 125 SER.#'d SETS
*HOLOFOIL: .8X TO 2X SILVER JSYs
HOLOFOIL PRINT RUN 50 SER.#'d SETS
JCAS Alex Smith TE 3.00 8.00
JCCT Craphonso Thorpe 3.00 8.00
JCDO Dan Orlovsky 3.00 8.00
JCJC Jerome Collins 4.00 10.00
JCJW Jason White 5.00 12.00
JCKO Kyle Orton 3.00 8.00
JCMB Mark Bradley 3.00 8.00
JCMJ Marlin Jackson 3.00 8.00
JCRW Roddy White 5.00 12.00
JCSL Stefan LeFors 3.00 8.00
JCTM Terrence Murphy 3.00 8.00

2005 Press Pass Paydirt

COMPLETE SET (12) 15.00 30.00
STATED ODDS 1:6 H/R
PD1 Cadillac Williams .50 1.25
PD2 Charlie Frye .50 1.25
PD3 Mike Williams .60 1.50
PD4 Braylon Edwards .50 1.25
PD5 Alex Smith QB 2.00 5.00
PD6 Dan Orlovsky .50 1.25
PD7 Andrew Walter .50 1.25
PD8 Ronnie Brown .60 1.50
PD9 Heath Miller 1.00 2.50
PD10 Troy Williamson .50 1.25
PD11 Aaron Rodgers 6.00 15.00
PD12 Mark Clayton .50 1.25

2005 Press Pass Power Pick Autographs

STATED PRINT RUN 50-250
1 Ronnie Brown/76* 30.00 80.00
1R Ronnie Brown/24* Red 40.00 100.00
2 Braylon Edwards/40* 25.00 60.00
3 Charlie Frye/240* 12.00 30.00
4 Heath Miller/40* 15.00 40.00
5 Aaron Rodgers/246* 125.00 250.00
6 Andrew Walter/240* 10.00 25.00
7 Mike Williams/59* 15.00 40.00
7R Mike Williams/41* Red 20.00 50.00
8 Troy Williamson/250 12.00 30.00

2005 Press Pass Showbound

COMPLETE SET (9) 15.00 30.00
STATED ODDS 1:12 H/R
SB1 Alex Smith QB 2.00 5.00
SB2 Ronnie Brown .60 1.50
SB3 Aaron Rodgers 6.00 15.00
SB4 Cadillac Williams .50 1.25
SB5 Heath Miller 1.00 2.50
SB6 Braylon Edwards .50 1.25
SB7 Mark Clayton .50 1.25
SB8 Mike Williams .60 1.50
SB9 Troy Williamson .50 1.25

2006 Press Pass

This 50-card set was released in April, 2006. The set was issued in four-card packs into both hobby and retail channels. The hobby packs had an $3.99 SRP and came 28 to a box while the retails packs had an $2.99 SRP and came 24 to a box. Cards numbered 46-50 were "power pick" cards and those cards were inserted into packs at a stated rate of one in 14.
COMPLETE SET (50) 20.00 50.00
COMP.SET w/o SP's (45) 10.00 25.00
POWER PICK ODDS 1:14
UNPRICED SOLO SER.#'d TO 1
1 Brodie Croyle .25 .60
2 Jay Cutler .30 .75
3 Omar Jacobs .25 .60
4 Matt Leinart .25 .60
5 Drew Olson .25 .60
6 Michael Robinson .25 .60
7 D.J. Shockley .30 .75
8 Brad Smith .30 .75
9 Marcus Vick .25 .60
10 Charlie Whitehurst .25 .60
11 Vince Young .25 .60
12 Joseph Addai .25 .60
13 Reggie Bush .40 1.00
14 Jerome Harrison .25 .60
15 Laurence Maroney .25 .60
16 Leon Washington .25 .60
17 LenDale White .25 .60
18 DeAngelo Williams .30 .75
19 Jason Avant .25 .60
20 Derek Hagan .30 .75
21 Chris Hannon .30 .75
22 Santonio Holmes .30 .75
23 Chad Jackson .25 .60
24 Greg Lee .25 .60
25 Sinorice Moss .25 .60
26 Martin Nance .25 .60
27 Maurice Stovall .25 .60
28 Travis Wilson .25 .60
29 Dominique Byrd .25 .60
30 Vernon Davis .30 .75
31 Marcedes Lewis .25 .60
32 Leonard Pope .40 1.00
33 Jimmy Williams .25 .60
34 Darnell Bing .30 .75
35 Michael Huff .30 .75
36 Mathias Kiwanuka .40 1.00
37 Mario Williams .40 1.00
38 Haloti Ngata .30 .75
39 Gabe Watson .25 .60
40 Rodrique Wright .25 .60
41 D'Brickashaw Ferguson .25 .60
42 Chad Greenway .40 1.00
43 A.J. Hawk .30 .75
44 DeMeco Ryans .30 .75
45 Reggie Bush CL .20 .50
46 Reggie Bush PP .75 2.00
47 Matt Leinart PP .50 1.25
48 Vince Young PP .50 1.25
49 A.J. Hawk PP .60 1.50
50 DeAngelo Williams PP .60 1.50

2006 Press Pass Blue

*BLUE: .8X TO 2X BASIC CARDS
STATED ODDS 1:1 RETAIL

2006 Press Pass Reflectors

*SINGLES: 2X TO 5X BASIC CARDS
STATED PRINT RUN 500 SER.#'d SETS

2006 Press Pass Reflectors Proof

*SINGLES: 3X TO 8X BASIC CARDS
STATED PRINT RUN 100 SER.#'d SETS

2006 Press Pass Autographed 8X10 Redemption

1 Reggie Bush 40.00 80.00
2 Matt Leinart 30.00 80.00
3 Vince Young 40.00 100.00

2006 Press Pass Autographs Blue

*BLUE: .8X TO 2X BRONZE AUTOs
BLUE PRINT RUN 40-50 SER.#'d SETS
7 Reggie Bush/50 12.00 30.00
41 Matt Leinart/50 20.00 50.00
76 Vince Young/22* 25.00 60.00

2006 Press Pass Autographs Blue Red Ink

*RED INK: .5X TO 1.2X BASE BLUE AU
ANNCD PRINT RUNS UNDER 20 NOT PRICED
12 Jay Cutler/50 25.00 60.00
30 A.J. Hawk/35* 40.00 100.00
76 Vince Young/28* 30.00 80.00

2006 Press Pass Autographs Bronze

OVERALL AUTO ODDS 1:7
1 Joseph Addai 4.00 10.00
2 Devin Aromashodu 4.00 10.00
3 Jason Avant 4.00 10.00
4 Brett Basanez 6.00 15.00
5 Darnell Bing 5.00 12.00
6 Will Blackmon 4.00 10.00
7 Reggie Bush SP 6.00 15.00
8 Dominique Byrd 4.00 10.00
9 Bobby Carpenter 4.00 10.00
10 Barry Cofield 6.00 15.00
11 Brodie Croyle 4.00 10.00
12 Jay Cutler 10.00 25.00
13 Vernon Davis 5.00 12.00
14 Mike DeGory 4.00 10.00
15 Maurice Drew 6.00 15.00
16 Ray Edwards 6.00 15.00
17 Anthony Fasano 4.00 10.00
18 D'Brickashaw Ferguson 4.00 10.00
19 Charles Gordon 4.00 10.00
20 Bruce Gradkowski 5.00 12.00
21 Skyler Green 4.00 10.00
22 Chad Greenway 6.00 15.00
23 Darrell Hackney 5.00 12.00
24 Derek Hagan 5.00 12.00
25 Tamba Hali 6.00 15.00
26 Chris Hannon 5.00 12.00
27 Orien Harris 5.00 12.00
28 Jerome Harrison 4.00 10.00
29 Mike Hass 4.00 10.00
30 A.J. Hawk 12.00 30.00
31 Devin Hester 8.00 20.00
32 Tye Hill 4.00 10.00
33 Michael Huff 5.00 12.00
34 Chad Jackson 4.00 10.00
35 Tarvaris Jackson 4.00 10.00
36 Omar Jacobs SP 4.00 10.00
37 Jeff King 5.00 12.00
38 Mathias Kiwanuka 6.00 15.00
39 Joe Klopfenstein 4.00 10.00
40 Greg Lee 4.00 10.00
41 Matt Leinart SP 20.00 50.00
42 J.R. Lemon 4.00 10.00
43 Marcedes Lewis 4.00 10.00
44 John Madsen 4.00 10.00
45 Laurence Maroney 4.00 10.00
46 Reggie McNeal 4.00 10.00
47 DonTrell Moore 5.00 12.00
48 Martin Nance 4.00 10.00
49 Haloti Ngata 5.00 12.00
50 Drew Olson 4.00 10.00
51 Jonathan Orr 5.00 12.00
52 Paul Pinegar 4.00 10.00
53 Leonard Pope 6.00 15.00
54 Gerald Riggs 5.00 12.00
55 Michael Robinson 4.00 10.00
56 Cory Rodgers 4.00 10.00
57 DeMeco Ryans 5.00 12.00
58 D.J. Shockley 5.00 12.00
59 Ernie Sims 4.00 10.00
60 Brad Smith 5.00 12.00
61 Maurice Stovall 4.00 10.00
62 Marcus Vick SP 4.00 10.00
63 Leon Washington 4.00 10.00
64 Gabe Watson 4.00 10.00
65 LenDale White 4.00 10.00
66 Charlie Whitehurst 4.00 10.00
67 Gerris Wilkinson 4.00 10.00
68 Demetrius Williams 4.00 10.00
69 Jimmy Williams 4.00 10.00
70 Mario Williams 6.00 15.00
71 Travis Wilson 4.00 10.00
72 Eric Winston 4.00 10.00
73 Rodrique Wright 4.00 10.00
74 Claude Wroten 4.00 10.00
75 Ashton Youboty 4.00 10.00
76 Vince Young SP 25.00 60.00

2006 Press Pass Autographs Bronze Red Ink

*RED INK: .6X TO 1.5X BRNZ BLU INK
12 Jay Cutler/82* 15.00 40.00
20 Bruce Gradkowski/25* 8.00 20.00
30 A.J. Hawk/36* 30.00 80.00
45 Laurence Maroney/49* 6.00 15.00
63 Leon Washington/49* 6.00 15.00
76 Vince Young/23* 25.00 60.00

2006 Press Pass Autographs Gold

*GOLD: .6X TO 1.5X BRONZE AUTOS
GOLD PRINT RUN 63-100 CARDS
7 Reggie Bush/100 10.00 25.00
30 A.J. Hawk/62* 30.00 80.00
41 Matt Leinart/100 20.00 50.00
76 Vince Young/43* 30.00 80.00

2006 Press Pass Autographs Gold Red Ink

*RED INK: .5X TO 1.2X GOLD BLU INK
12 Jay Cutler/100 20.00 50.00
30 A.J. Hawk/38* 30.00 80.00
62 Marcus Vick/100 15.00 40.00
76 Vince Young/57* 20.00 50.00

2006 Press Pass Autographs Silver

ILVER: .5X TO 1.2X BRONZE AUTOS
SILVER PRINT RUN 200 UNLESS NOTED
7 Reggie Bush 8.00 20.00
30 A.J. Hawk 15.00 40.00
41 Matt Leinart 15.00 40.00
76 Vince Young/104* 25.00 60.00

2006 Press Pass Autographs Silver Red Ink

*RED INK: .5X TO 1.2X SILVER BLU INK
12 Jay Cutler/200 20.00 50.00
62 Marcus Vick/200 12.00 30.00
76 Vince Young/96* 25.00 60.00

2006 Press Pass Big Numbers

MPLETE SET (33) 8.00 20.00
STATED ODDS 1:1
BN1 Brodie Croyle .30 .75
BN2 Mathias Kiwanuka .50 1.25
BN3 Omar Jacobs .30 .75
BN4 Charlie Whitehurst .30 .75
BN5 Chad Jackson .30 .75
BN6 D.J. Shockley .40 1.00
BN7 Leonard Pope .50 1.25
BN8 Vernon Davis .40 1.00
BN9 DeAngelo Williams .40 1.00
BN10 Sinorice Moss .30 .75
BN11 Jason Avant .30 .75
BN12 Laurence Maroney .30 .75
BN13 Brad Smith .40 1.00
BN14 Mario Williams .50 1.25
BN15 Maurice Stovall .30 .75
BN16 A.J. Hawk .40 1.00
BN17 Santonio Holmes .40 1.00
BN18 Travis Wilson .30 .75
BN19 Haloti Ngata .40 1.00
BN20 Michael Robinson .30 .75
BN21 Vince Young .30 .75
BN22 Michael Huff .40 1.00
BN23 Drew Olson .30 .75
BN24 Marcedes Lewis .30 .75
BN25 Matt Leinart .30 .75
BN26 Reggie Bush .50 1.25
BN27 LenDale White .30 .75
BN28 Jay Cutler .40 1.00
BN29 D'Brickashaw Ferguson .30 .75
BN30 Jimmy Williams .30 .75
BN31 Marcus Vick .30 .75
BN32 Jerome Harrison .30 .75
BN33 Matt Leinart CL .15 .40

2006 Press Pass Game Used Jerseys Blue

*BLUE/150: .5X TO 1.2X RED JSYs
BLUE INSERTED IN COLLECTOR TIN SETS
BLUE PRINT RUN 150 SER.#'d SETS
JCCH Chris Hannon 5.00 12.00

2006 Press Pass Game Used Jerseys Green

*GREEN/25: .8X TO 2X RED JSYs
GREEN INSERTED IN COLLECTOR TIN SETS
JCCH Chris Hannon 8.00 20.00

2006 Press Pass Game Used Jerseys Red

RED/BLUE/GREEN ISSUED IN COLLECTOR TINS
JCAF Anthony Fasano 5.00 12.00
JCAH A.J. Hawk 8.00 20.00
JCBB Brett Basanez 4.00 10.00
JCBC Brodie Croyle 6.00 15.00
JCBS Brad Smith 4.00 10.00
JCCR Cory Rodgers 4.00 10.00
JCDA Devin Aromashodu 4.00 10.00
JCDH Darrell Hackney 4.00 10.00
JCDO Drew Olson 4.00 10.00
JCDR DeMeco Ryans 5.00 12.00
JCDS D.J. Shockley 5.00 12.00
JCDW2 Demetrius Williams 5.00 12.00
JCDW1 DeAngelo Williams 6.00 15.00
JCGL Greg Lee 4.00 10.00
JCJH Jerome Harrison 4.00 10.00
JCJK Joe Klopfenstein 4.00 10.00
JCMD Maurice Drew 8.00 20.00
JCMH Mike Hass 5.00 12.00
JCML Marcedes Lewis 5.00 12.00
JCML Matt Leinart Shirt 5.00 12.00
JCMR Michael Robinson 5.00 12.00
JCOJ Omar Jacobs 5.00 12.00
JCPP Paul Pinegar 5.00 12.00
JCRB Reggie Bush Shirt 4.00 10.00
JCTJ Tarvaris Jackson 6.00 15.00
JCVD Vernon Davis 6.00 15.00

2006 Press Pass Game Used Jerseys Silver

SILVER RETAIL PRINT RUN 299 SETS
*GOLD: .5X TO 1.2X SILVER JERSEYS
GOLD HOBBY PRINT RUN 199 SETS
*HOLOFOIL: .8X TO 2X SILVER JERSEYS
HOLOFOIL PRINT RUN 50 SETS
JCAH A.J. Hawk 15.00 40.00

JCBB Brett Basanez 4.00 10.00
JCBS Brad Smith 4.00 10.00
JCCH Chris Hannon 4.00 10.00
JCCR Cory Rodgers 4.00 10.00
JCCW Charlie Whitehurst 5.00 12.00
JCDA Devin Aromashodu 4.00 10.00
JCDH Darrell Hackney 4.00 10.00
JCDO Drew Olson 4.00 10.00
JCDS D.J. Shockley 4.00 10.00
JCDW Demetrius Williams 5.00 12.00
JCGL Greg Lee 4.00 10.00
JCHN Haloti Ngata 5.00 12.00
JCJH Jerome Harrison 4.00 10.00
JCJK Joe Klopfenstein 4.00 10.00
JCMD Maurice Drew 8.00 20.00
JCMN Martin Nance 4.00 10.00
JCOJ Omar Jacobs 5.00 12.00

2006 Press Pass Paydirt

COMPLETE SET (12) 10.00 25.00
STATED ODDS 1:4
PD1 Vince Young .40 1.00
PD2 Matt Leinart .40 1.00
PD3 Omar Jacobs .40 1.00
PD4 LenDale White .40 1.00
PD5 Jay Cutler .50 1.25
PD6 Reggie Bush .60 1.50
PD7 DeAngelo Williams .50 1.25
PD8 Brodie Croyle .40 1.00
PD9 Santonio Holmes .50 1.25
PD10 Marcedes Lewis .40 1.00
PD11 Maurice Stovall .40 1.00
PD12 Sinorice Moss .40 1.00

2006 Press Pass Power Pick Autographs

1 A.J. Hawk/250 8.00 20.00
2 Brodie Croyle/161* 6.00 15.00
3 Omar Jacobs/244* 6.00 15.00
4 Matt Leinart/150 12.00 30.00
5 Brad Smith/243* 8.00 20.00
6 Vince Young/82* 15.00 40.00
7 Reggie Bush/150 10.00 25.00
8 LenDale White/250 6.00 15.00
9 Marcus Vick/100 6.00 15.00

2006 Press Pass Target Exclusive

UR PER TARGET RETAIL BOX
1B Reggie Bush .60 1.50
2B Brodie Croyle .40 1.00
3B A.J. Hawk .50 1.25
4B Santonio Holmes .50 1.25
5B Omar Jacobs .40 1.00
6B Matt Leinart .40 1.00
7B LenDale White .40 1.00
8B DeAngelo Williams .50 1.25
9B Vince Young .40 1.00

2006 Press Pass Target Exclusive Autographs

STATED PRINT RUN 50 SER.#'d SETS
1 Reggie Bush 12.00 30.00
2 Brodie Croyle 15.00 40.00
3 A.J. Hawk 20.00 50.00
4 Omar Jacobs/45* 12.00 30.00
5 Matt Leinart 30.00 80.00
6 Brad Smith 12.00 30.00
8 LenDale White 20.00 50.00
9 Vince Young/30* 30.00 80.00

2006 Press Pass Target Exclusive Autographs Red Ink

Marcus Vick/50 15.00 40.00
9 Vince Young/20* 25.00 60.00

2006 Press Pass Teammates Autographs

1 R.Bush/L.White 20.00 50.00
2 R.Bush/M.Leinart 15.00 40.00
3 Bush/LenDale/Leinart 20.00 50.00
4 L.White/M.Leinart 40.00 100.00

2006 Press Pass Wal-Mart Exclusive

FOUR PER WAL-MART RETAIL BOX
1A Reggie Bush UER .60 1.50
2A Brodie Croyle .40 1.00
3A A.J. Hawk .50 1.25
4A Matt Leinart .40 1.00
5A Sinorice Moss .40 1.00
6A LenDale White .40 1.00
7A DeAngelo Williams ERR .50 1.25
8A Marcus Vick .40 1.00
9A Vince Young .40 1.00

2006 Press Pass Wal-Mart Exclusive Autographs

STATED PRINT RUN 50 SER.#'d SETS
1 Reggie Bush 12.00 30.00
2 Brodie Croyle 15.00 40.00
3 A.J. Hawk 50.00 100.00
4 Omar Jacobs/45* 12.00 30.00
5 Matt Leinart 25.00 60.00
6 Brad Smith 12.00 30.00
8 LenDale White 20.00 50.00
9 Vince Young/26* 40.00 100.00

2006 Press Pass Wal-Mart Exclusive Autographs Red Ink

8 Marcus Vick/50 25.00 50.00
9 Vince Young/24* 50.00 120.00

2007 Press Pass

This 105-card set was released in April, 2007. The set was issued into the hobby in four-card packs, with an $3.99 SRP which came 28 packs to a box. The set has the following subsets: Leaders (57-67), Trophy Club (68-74), All-Americans (75-87), Teammates (88-97), Sophmore Sensations (98-100) and Power Picks (101-105). The Power Pick cards were inserted into packs at a stated rate of one in 14.

COMPLETE SET (105) 25.00 60.00
COMP.SET w/o SP's (100) 15.00 40.00
101-105 POWER PICK ODDS 1:14
UNPRICED SOLO SER.#'d TO 1
1 Chris Leak .20 .50
2 Brady Quinn .20 .50
3 JaMarcus Russell .20 .50
4 Troy Smith .20 .50
5 Drew Stanton .20 .50
6 Michael Bush .20 .50
7 Tony Hunt .20 .50
8 Kenny Irons .20 .50
9 Brandon Jackson .20 .50
10 Marshawn Lynch .40 1.00
11 Adrian Peterson .60 1.50
12 Antonio Pittman .20 .50
13 Brian Leonard .20 .50
14 Dwayne Bowe .20 .50
15 Ted Ginn Jr. .25 .60
16 Anthony Gonzalez .20 .50
17 Dwayne Jarrett .25 .60
18 Calvin Johnson .60 1.50
19 Robert Meachem .25 .60
20 Sidney Rice .25 .60
21 Garrett Wolfe .20 .50
22 Leon Hall .20 .50
23 Gaines Adams .25 .60
24 Jamaal Anderson .25 .60
25 Alan Branch .20 .50
26 Amobi Okoye .25 .60
27 Paul Posluszny .20 .50
28 Lawrence Timmons .30 .75
29 LaRon Landry .30 .75
30 Reggie Nelson .20 .50
31 John Beck .20 .50
32 Trent Edwards .20 .50
33 Kevin Kolb .25 .60
34 Jordan Palmer .25 .60
35 Lorenzo Booker .25 .60
36 Darius Walker .20 .50
37 Dwayne Wright .20 .50
38 DeShawn Wynn .20 .50
39 Zach Miller .20 .50
40 Greg Olsen .30 .75
41 Aundrae Allison .20 .50
42 Dallas Baker .20 .50
43 Jason Hill .20 .50
44 Steve Smith USC .20 .50
45 Darrelle Revis .25 .60
46 Aaron Ross .20 .50
47 Adam Carriker .20 .50
48 Charles Johnson .20 .50
49 Jarvis Moss .20 .50
50 Patrick Willis .30 .75
51 John Beck LDR .20 .50
52 JaMarcus Russell LDR .20 .50
53 Troy Smith LDR .20 .50
54 Jordan Palmer LDR .25 .60
55 Kevin Kolb LDR .25 .60
56 Brady Quinn LDR .20 .50
57 Garrett Wolfe LDR .20 .50
58 Dwayne Wright LDR .20 .50
59 Ahmad Bradshaw LDR .30 .75
60 Johnnie Lee Higgins LDR .20 .50
61 Robert Meachem LDR .25 .60
62 Rhema McKnight LDR .20 .50
63 Calvin Johnson LDR .60 1.50
64 Joel Filani LDR .20 .50
65 Dwayne Bowe LDR .20 .50
66 Daymeion Hughes LDR .20 .50
67 Reggie Nelson LDR .20 .50
68 LaMarr Woodley TC .40 1.00
69 Troy Smith TC .20 .50
70 Brady Quinn TC .20 .50
71 Calvin Johnson TC .60 1.50
72 Paul Posluszny TC .20 .50
73 Aaron Ross TC .20 .50
74 Patrick Willis TC .30 .75
75 Troy Smith AA .20 .50
76 Marshawn Lynch AA .40 1.00
77 Johnnie Lee Higgins AA .20 .50
78 Dwayne Jarrett AA .25 .60
79 Calvin Johnson AA .60 1.50
80 Robert Meachem AA .25 .60
81 Zach Miller AA .20 .50
82 Gaines Adams AA .25 .60
83 Paul Posluszny AA .20 .50
84 Leon Hall AA .20 .50
85 LaRon Landry AA .30 .75
86 Reggie Nelson AA .20 .50
87 Aaron Ross AA .20 .50
88 M.Lynch
D.Hughes TM .40 1.00
89 C.Leak
R.Nelson TM .20 .50
90 L.Booker
L.Thomas TM .30 .75
91 J.Russell
D.Bowe TM .20 .50
92 B.Jackson
A.Carriker TM .20 .50
93 B.Quinn
D.Walker TM .20 .50
94 T.Smith
A.Pittman TM .20 .50
95 T.Ginn Jr.
A.Gonzalez TM .25 .60
96 T.Hunt
P.Posluszny TM .20 .50
97 D.Jarrett
S.Smith TM .25 .60
98 Joseph Addai SS .40 1.00
99 Reggie Bush SS .40 1.00
100 Vince Young SS .40 1.00
101 Brady Quinn PP .50 1.25
102 JaMarcus Russell PP .50 1.25
103 Adrian Peterson PP 1.50 4.00
104 Calvin Johnson PP 1.50 4.00
105 Ted Ginn Jr. PP .60 1.50

2007 Press Pass Reflectors

*REFLECT.1-97: 2.5X TO 6X BASIC CARDS
*REFLECT. 98-100: 2X TO 5X BASIC CARDS
STATED PRINT RUN 500 SER.#'d SETS

2007 Press Pass Reflectors Blue

LUE 1-97: 1.5X TO 4X BASIC CARDS
*BLUE 98-100: 1.2X TO 3X BASIC CARDS
ONE BLUE PER RETAIL PACK

2007 Press Pass Reflectors Proof

*SINGLES 1-97: 4X TO 10X BASIC CARDS
*SINGLES 98-100: 3X TO 8X BASIC CARDS
STATED PRINT RUN 100 SER.#'d SETS

2007 Press Pass Autographs Blue

*BLUE/40-50: .8X TO 2X BRONZE AUs
BLUE/40-50 INSERTED IN PRESS PASS SE
BLUE PRINT RUN 50 UNLESS NOTED
20 Ted Ginn Jr. 20.00 50.00
24 Chris Henry/25 15.00 40.00
47 Adrian Peterson/25 175.00 300.00
50 Brady Quinn/25 8.00 20.00
55 JaMarcus Russell/25 15.00 40.00

2007 Press Pass Autographs Blue Red Ink

*RED INK: .5X TO 1.2X BASIC BLUE AU
21 Anthony Gonzalez/47* 8.00 20.00
26 Jason Hill/46* 8.00 20.00
29 Brandon Jackson/50 8.00 20.00
69 LaMarr Woodley/50 15.00 40.00

2007 Press Pass Autographs Bronze

OVERALL AUTO ODDS 1:7 PP
UNPRICED PRINTING PLATES #'d TO 1
1 Gaines Adams 5.00 12.00
2 Joseph Addai SP 12.00 30.00
3 Aundrae Allison 4.00 10.00
4 Jamaal Anderson 5.00 12.00
5 Dallas Baker 4.00 10.00
6 John Beck 4.00 10.00
7 Lorenzo Booker 5.00 12.00
8 Dwayne Bowe 4.00 10.00
9 Ahmad Bradshaw 6.00 15.00
10 Alan Branch 4.00 10.00
11 Michael Bush 4.00 10.00
12 Adam Carriker 4.00 10.00
13 Scott Chandler 6.00 15.00
14 David Clowney 4.00 10.00
15 Tim Crowder 5.00 12.00
16 Kenneth Darby 4.00 10.00
17 Buster Davis 5.00 12.00
18 Craig Buster Davis 4.00 10.00
19 Joel Filani 4.00 10.00
20 Ted Ginn Jr. SP 12.00 30.00
21 Anthony Gonzalez 4.00 10.00
22 Michael Griffin 4.00 10.00
23 Leon Hall 4.00 10.00
24 Chris Henry 4.00 10.00
25 Johnnie Lee Higgins 4.00 10.00
26 Jason Hill 4.00 10.00
27 Daymeion Hughes 4.00 10.00
28 Kenny Irons
29 Brandon Jackson 4.00 10.00
30 Tanard Jackson 4.00 10.00
31 Calvin Johnson SP 60.00 120.00
32 Charles Johnson 4.00 10.00
33 Kevin Kolb 5.00 12.00
34 LaRon Landry 6.00 15.00
35 Chris Leak 4.00 10.00
36 Brian Leonard 4.00 10.00
37 Marcus McCauley 4.00 10.00
38 Rhema McKnight 4.00 10.00
39 Robert Meachem
40 Zach Miller 4.00 10.00
41 Matt Moore 6.00 15.00
42 Quentin Moses 4.00 10.00
43 Reggie Nelson 4.00 10.00
44 Amobi Okoye 5.00 12.00
45 Greg Olsen 6.00 15.00
46 Jordan Palmer 5.00 12.00
47 Adrian Peterson SP 100.00 200.00
48 Antonio Pittman SP 12.00 30.00
49 Paul Posluszny 4.00 10.00
50 Brady Quinn SP 4.00 10.00
51 Darrelle Revis 8.00 20.00
52 Sidney Rice 5.00 12.00
53 Aaron Ross 4.00 10.00
54 Jeff Rowe 4.00 10.00
55 JaMarcus Russell SP 10.00 25.00
56 Kolby Smith 4.00 10.00
57 Steve Smith USC 4.00 10.00
58 Troy Smith SP 15.00 40.00
59 Drew Stanton 4.00 10.00
60 Chansi Stuckey 5.00 12.00
61 Courtney Taylor 4.00 10.00
62 Zac Taylor 5.00 12.00
63 Lawrence Timmons 6.00 15.00
64 DeMarcus Tank Tyler 4.00 10.00
65 Darius Walker 4.00 10.00
66 Paul Williams 4.00 10.00
67 Patrick Willis 6.00 15.00
68 Garrett Wolfe 4.00 10.00
69 LaMarr Woodley 8.00 20.00
70 Dwayne Wright 4.00 10.00
71 DeShawn Wynn 4.00 10.00
72 Selvin Young 4.00 10.00
73 Vince Young SP 20.00 50.00

2007 Press Pass Autographs Bronze Red Ink

*RED INK: .6X TO 1.5X BRONZE BLUE INK
PRESS PASS ANNOUNCED PRINT RUNS BELOW
28 Kenny Irons/73* 6.00 15.00

2007 Press Pass Autographs Gold

*GOLD: .6X TO 1.5X BRONZE AUTOS
GOLD PRINT RUN 100 UNLESS NOTED
20 Ted Ginn Jr. 20.00 50.00
28 Kenny Irons 6.00 15.00
47 Adrian Peterson/40 100.00 200.00
48 Antonio Pittman 6.00 15.00
50 Brady Quinn/45* 6.00 15.00
55 JaMarcus Russell/34* 10.00 25.00

2007 Press Pass Autographs Gold Red Ink

*RED INK: .6X TO 1.5X GOLD BLUE INK
55 JaMarcus Russell/16* 20.00 50.00

2007 Press Pass Autographs Green

EEN/RED PRINT RUN 25 SER.#'d SETS
21 Anthony Gonzalez 10.00 25.00
31 Calvin Johnson/18* 75.00 150.00
45 Greg Olsen 15.00 40.00
47 Adrian Peterson/10* 150.00 300.00
50 Brady Quinn 10.00 25.00
55 JaMarcus Russell 15.00 40.00
59 Drew Stanton/15* 10.00 25.00

2007 Press Pass Autographs Green Red Ink

Ted Ginn Jr./25 15.00 40.00
31 Calvin Johnson/7* 100.00 200.00
47 Adrian Peterson/15* 125.00 250.00

2007 Press Pass Autographs Silver

*SILVER: .5X TO 1.2X BRONZE AUTOS
SILVER PRINT RUN 200 UNLESS NOTED
20 Ted Ginn Jr. 15.00 40.00
28 Kenny Irons 5.00 12.00
47 Adrian Peterson/43 75.00 150.00
48 Antonio Pittman 5.00 12.00
50 Brady Quinn/76* 6.00 15.00
55 JaMarcus Russell/67* 10.00 25.00

2007 Press Pass Autographs Silver Red Ink

ED INK: .6X TO 1.5X SILVER BLUE INK
PRESS PASS ANNOUNCED PRINT RUNS BELOW
29 Brandon Jackson/200* 5.00 12.00
50 Brady Quinn/24* 10.00 25.00
55 JaMarcus Russell/33* 15.00 40.00

2007 Press Pass Gridiron Gamers Jerseys Red

RANDOM INSERTS IN RETAIL PACKS
GGBB Brett Basanez 3.00 8.00
GGCS Chansi Stuckey 4.00 10.00
GGDR DeMeco Ryans 4.00 10.00
GGJJ Brandon Jackson 3.00 8.00
GGJR JaMarcus Russell 3.00 8.00
GGLH Leon Hall 3.00 8.00
GGMH Mike Hass 3.00 8.00
GGMJD Maurice Jones-Drew 3.00 8.00
GGML Marshawn Lynch 6.00 15.00

2007 Press Pass Gridiron Gamers Jerseys Silver

LVER PRINT RUN 199-299
*GOLD/100: .5X TO 1.2X SILVER JSYs
GOLD PRINT RUN 100 SER.#'d SETS
*HOLOFOIL/50: .8X TO 2X SILVER JSYs
HOLOFOIL PRINT RUN 50 SER.#'d SETS
GGBL Brian Leonard/275 6.00 15.00
GGBQ Brady Quinn/250 5.00 12.00
GGCD Craig Buster Davis/275 5.00 12.00
GGCL Chris Leak/299 8.00 20.00
GGDJ Dwayne Jarrett/275 6.00 15.00
GGDS Drew Stanton/275 6.00 15.00
GGDW Darius Walker/299 5.00 12.00
GGGO Greg Olsen/275 8.00 20.00
GGGW Garrett Wolfe/299 6.00 15.00
GGKD Kenneth Darby/299 6.00 15.00
GGKI Kenny Irons/275 6.00 15.00
GGKK Kevin Kolb/275 3.00 8.00
GGLB Lorenzo Booker/275 5.00 12.00
GGLL LaRon Landry/299 6.00 15.00
GGML Marshawn Lynch/275 6.00 15.00
GGRB Reggie Bush/199 12.00 30.00
GGZM Zach Miller/299 6.00 15.00
GGDB2 Dwayne Bowe/250 6.00 15.00
GGJR1 JaMarcus Russell/199 6.00 15.00
GGJR2 Jeff Rowe/299 4.00 10.00

2007 Press Pass Power Pick Autographs

STATED PRINT RUN 25-250
AP Adrian Peterson/50 125.00 200.00
BJ Brandon Jackson/250 10.00 25.00
BQ Brady Quinn/99* 6.00 15.00
CJ Calvin Johnson/17* 100.00 200.00
DW Darius Walker/240* 8.00 20.00
JR JaMarcus Russell/90* 12.00 30.00
KI Kenny Irons/250 10.00 25.00
RM Robert Meachem/250 10.00 25.00
SR Sidney Rice/250 12.00 30.00
TG Ted Ginn Jr./101* 15.00 40.00
TS Troy Smith/20* 25.00 60.00

2007 Press Pass Power Pick Autographs Red Ink

TG Ted Ginn Jr./149* 20.00 50.00

2007 Press Pass Primetime Players

COMPLETE SET (15) 10.00 25.00
STATED ODDS 1:4
1 Brady Quinn .60 1.50
2 JaMarcus Russell .60 1.50
3 Troy Smith .60 1.50
4 Drew Stanton .60 1.50
5 Brandon Jackson .60 1.50
6 Marshawn Lynch 1.25 3.00
7 Adrian Peterson 2.00 5.00
8 Antonio Pittman .60 1.50
9 Dwayne Bowe .60 1.50
10 Dwayne Jarrett .75 2.00
11 Calvin Johnson 2.00 5.00
12 Ted Ginn Jr. .75 2.00
13 Robert Meachem .75 2.00
14 Sidney Rice .75 2.00
15 Darius Walker .60 1.50

2007 Press Pass Sophomore Sensations Autographs

SSJA Joseph Addai 15.00 40.00
SSVY Vince Young 60.00 120.00
SSVYR Vince Young Red Ink/30* 75.00 150.00

2007 Press Pass Target Exclusive

COMPLETE SET (10) 10.00 25.00
STATED ODDS 4:1 TARGET BOXES
TAR1 Brady Quinn .40 1.00
TAR2 JaMarcus Russell .40 1.00
TAR3 Troy Smith .40 1.00
TAR4 Marshawn Lynch .75 2.00
TAR5 Adrian Peterson 1.25 3.00
TAR6 Darius Walker .40 1.00
TAR7 Dwayne Jarrett .50 1.25
TAR8 Calvin Johnson 1.25 3.00
TAR9 Sidney Rice .50 1.25
TAR10 Ted Ginn Jr. .50 1.25

2007 Press Pass Target Exclusive Autographs

STATED PRINT RUN 25-50
RED INK TOO SCARCE TO PRICE
AP Adrian Peterson/50 100.00 200.00
BQ Brady Quinn/50 6.00 15.00
CJ Calvin Johnson/25 75.00 150.00
DW Darius Walker/25 12.00 30.00
JR JaMarcus Russell/50 25.00 60.00
SR Sidney Rice/25 25.00 50.00
TG Ted Ginn Jr./50 20.00 50.00
TS Troy Smith/25 25.00 60.00

2007 Press Pass Wal-Mart Exclusive

MPLETE SET (10) 10.00 25.00
WM1 Brady Quinn .40 1.00
WM2 JaMarcus Russell .40 1.00
WM3 Troy Smith .40 1.00
WM4 Kenny Irons .40 1.00
WM5 Marshawn Lynch .75 2.00
WM6 Adrian Peterson 1.25 3.00
WM7 Dwayne Jarrett .50 1.25
WM8 Calvin Johnson 1.25 3.00
WM9 Robert Meachem .50 1.25
WM10 Ted Ginn Jr. .50 1.25

2007 Press Pass Wal-Mart Exclusive Autographs

STATED PRINT RUN 25-50
RED INK TOO SCARCE TO PRICE
AP Adrian Peterson/49 100.00 200.00
BQ Brady Quinn/50 6.00 15.00
CJ Calvin Johnson/25 75.00 150.00
JR JaMarcus Russell/50 25.00 60.00
KI Kenny Irons/30
RM Robert Meachem/25 40.00 80.00
TG Ted Ginn Jr./49 20.00 50.00
TS Troy Smith/25 25.00 60.00

2008 Press Pass

COMPLETE SET (105) 20.00 50.00
COMP.SET w/o SP's (100) 12.00 30.00
101-105 POWER PICK ODDS 1:14
1 Glenn Dorsey .20 .50
2 Chris Long .25 .60
3 Dan Connor .20 .50
4 Aqib Talib .30 .75
5 Kenny Phillips .20 .50
6 Erik Ainge .20 .50
7 John David Booty .20 .50
8 Colt Brennan .25 .60
9 Brian Brohm .20 .50
10 Joe Flacco .40 1.00
11 Chad Henne .25 .60
12 Matt Ryan .60 1.50
13 Andre Woodson .20 .50
14 Jamaal Charles .30 .75
15 Matt Forte .30 .75
16 Mike Hart .20 .50
17 Jacob Hester .20 .50
18 Chris Johnson .25 .60
19 Felix Jones .20 .50
20 Darren McFadden .20 .50
21 Rashard Mendenhall .20 .50
22 Ray Rice .20 .50
23 Steve Slaton .20 .50
24 Kevin Smith .20 .50
25 Jonathan Stewart .30 .75
26 Fred Davis .20 .50
27 Adrian Arrington .20 .50
28 Earl Bennett .30 .75
29 Adarius Bowman .25 .60
30 Early Doucet .20 .50
31 James Hardy .20 .50
32 DJ Hall .20 .50
33 DeSean Jackson .40 1.00
34 Malcolm Kelly .20 .50
35 Mario Manningham .20 .50
36 Limas Sweed .20 .50
37 Devin Thomas .20 .50
38 Lavelle Hawkins .25 .60
39 Andre Caldwell .20 .50
40 Vernon Gholston .20 .50
41 Derrick Harvey .20 .50
42 Keith Rivers .20 .50
43 Mike Jenkins .20 .50
44 Leodis McKelvin .25 .60
45 Dennis Dixon .20 .50
46 Josh Johnson .20 .50
47 Tashard Choice .20 .50
48 Chauncey Washington .25 .60
49 John Carlson .20 .50
50 Donnie Avery .25 .60
51 Darren McFadden TC .15 .40
52 Matt Ryan TC .50 1.25
53 Glenn Dorsey TC .15 .40
54 Dan Connor TC .15 .40
55 Fred Davis TC .15 .40
56 Chris Long TC .20 .50
57 Dennis Dixon COL .15 .40
58 Colt Brennan COL .20 .50
59 Matt Ryan COL .50 1.25
60 Brian Brohm COL .15 .40
61 Andre Woodson COL .15 .40
62 Erik Ainge COL .15 .40
63 Kevin Smith COL .15 .40
64 Matt Forte COL .25 .60
65 Darren McFadden COL .15 .40
66 Jonathan Stewart COL .25 .60
67 Rashard Mendenhall COL .15 .40
68 Ray Rice COL .15 .40
69 Jamaal Charles COL .25 .60
70 Chris Johnson COL .20 .50
71 Jordy Nelson COL .50 1.25
72 Davone Bess COL .20 .50
73 Donnie Avery COL .20 .50
74 Devin Thomas COL .15 .40
75 Mario Manningham COL .15 .40
76 Dan Connor AA .15 .40
77 Glenn Dorsey AA .15 .40
78 Mike Jenkins AA .15 .40
79 J Leman AA .15 .40
80 Chris Long AA .20 .50
81 Darren McFadden AA .15 .40
82 Jordy Nelson AA .50 1.25
83 Martin Rucker AA .15 .40
84 Matt Ryan AA .50 1.25
85 Kevin Smith AA .15 .40
86 Aqib Talib AA .25 .60
87 Steve Slaton AA .15 .40
88 Jonathan Stewart AA .25 .60
89 DeSean Jackson AA .30 .75
90 Woodson/K.Burton TM .12 .30
91 G.Dorsey/J.Hester TM .12 .30
92 B.Brohm/H.Douglas TM .12 .30
93 Henne/Manningham TM .15 .40
94 J.Charles/L.Sweed TM .20 .50
95 J.Booty/Washington TM .12 .30
96 J.Forsett/D.Jackson TM .25 .60
97 M.Flynn/E.Doucet TM .12 .30
98 M.Hart/A.Arrington TM .12 .30
99 D.Dixon/J.Stewart TM .20 .50
100 McFadden/Jones TM .12 .30
101 Darren McFadden PP .40 1.00
102 Matt Ryan PP 1.25 3.00
103 Brian Brohm PP .40 1.00
104 Jonathan Stewart PP .60 1.50
105 Malcolm Kelly PP .40 1.00

2008 Press Pass Black and White

*B&W: 4X TO 10X BASIC CARDS
ANNOUNCED ODDS 1:144

2008 Press Pass Reflectors

*REFLECTORS: 2X TO 5X BASIC CARDS
STATED PRINT RUN 500 SER.#'d SETS

2008 Press Pass Reflectors Blue

*BLUE: 1.5X TO 4X BASIC CARDS
ONE BLUE PER RETAIL PACK

2008 Press Pass Reflectors Gold

EFL GOLD: 3X TO 8X BASIC CARDS
STATED PRINT RUN 100 SER.#'d SETS

2008 Press Pass Reflectors Solo

UNPRICED SOLO PRINT RUN 1

2008 Press Pass Autographs Blue

LUE/35-50: .8X TO 2X BRONZE AU
BLUE AUTO PRINT RUN 10-50
BLUES INSERTED IN PRESS PASS SE
ANNC'D PRINT RUN ON CARDS W/RED INK VERSION
PPSBB Brian Brohm/25 6.00 15.00
PPSDM Darren McFadden/35* 8.00 20.00
PPSFJ Felix Jones/25 8.00 20.00
PPSJF Joe Flacco/16* 12.00 30.00
PPSMR Matt Ryan/50 30.00 80.00

2008 Press Pass Autographs Blue Red Ink

*RED INK: .6X TO 1.5X BASE BLUE AU
RED INK ANNOUNCED PRINT RUN 1-50

2008 Press Pass Autographs Bronze

FIVE AUTOS PER HOBBY BOX
INSERTS IN SE: BOWMAN, PATRICK
MAR.SMITH, TALIB, TRAE WILLIAMS
UNPRICED PRINT PLATES PRINT RUN 1
PPSAA Adrian Arrington 3.00 8.00
PPSAB Adarius Bowman 4.00 10.00
PPSAC Andre Caldwell 3.00 8.00
PPSAC2 Antoine Cason 4.00 10.00
PPSAP Allen Patrick 3.00 8.00
PPSAT Aqib Talib 5.00 12.00
PPSAW Andre Woodson 3.00 8.00
PPSBB Brian Brohm 3.00 8.00
PPSCB Colt Brennan 4.00 10.00
PPSCC Calais Campbell 4.00 10.00
PPSCH Chad Henne 4.00 10.00
PPSCJ2 Chris Johnson 4.00 10.00
PPSCL Chris Long 4.00 10.00
PPSCW Chauncey Washington 4.00 10.00
PPSDA Donnie Avery 4.00 10.00
PPSDB Dorien Bryant 4.00 10.00
PPSDB2 Davone Bess 4.00 10.00
PPSDC Dan Connor 3.00 8.00
PPSDD Dennis Dixon 3.00 8.00
PPSDH DJ Hall 3.00 8.00
PPSDJ DeSean Jackson 6.00 15.00
PPSDM Darren McFadden SP 3.00 8.00
PPSDR Darius Reynaud 3.00 8.00
PPSDR2 Darrell Robertson 3.00 8.00
PPSDS Dantrell Savage 4.00 10.00
PPSDT Devin Thomas 3.00 8.00
PPSEA Erik Ainge 3.00 8.00
PPSEB Earl Bennett 5.00 12.00
PPSED Early Doucet 3.00 8.00
PPSER Eddie Royal 3.00 8.00
PPSFD Fred Davis 3.00 8.00
PPSFJ Felix Jones SP 3.00 8.00
PPSHD Harry Douglas 4.00 10.00
PPSJC Jamaal Charles 5.00 12.00
PPSJC2 John Carlson 3.00 8.00
PPSJDB John David Booty 3.00 8.00
PPSJF Joe Flacco 6.00 15.00
PPSJF2 Justin Forsett 4.00 10.00
PPSJH Jacob Hester 3.00 8.00
PPSJJ Josh Johnson 3.00 8.00
PPSJL J Leman 3.00 8.00
PPSJM Josh Morgan 3.00 8.00
PPSJN Jordy Nelson 8.00 20.00
PPSJS Jonathan Stewart 15.00 40.00
PPSJS2 Jamie Silva 4.00 10.00
PPSJT Jacob Tamme 4.00 10.00
PPSKB Keenan Burton 3.00 8.00
PPSKP Kenny Phillips 3.00 8.00
PPSKR Keith Rivers 3.00 8.00
PPSKS Kevin Smith 3.00 8.00
PPSLH Lavelle Hawkins 4.00 10.00
PPSLM Leodis McKelvin 4.00 10.00
PPSLS Limas Sweed 8.00 20.00
PPSMF Matt Flynn 3.00 8.00
PPSMF2 Matt Forte 5.00 12.00
PPSMG Marcus Griffin 3.00 8.00
PPSMH Mike Hart 8.00 20.00
PPSMH2 Marcus Henry 3.00 8.00
PPSMK Malcolm Kelly 3.00 8.00
PPSMM2 Mario Manningham 3.00 8.00
PPSMR Matt Ryan 50.00 100.00
PPSMR2 Martin Rucker 3.00 8.00
PPSMS Marcus Smith 4.00 10.00
PPSOS Owen Schmitt 3.00 8.00
PPSPS Paul Smith 3.00 8.00
PPSRL Rafael Little 4.00 10.00
PPSRM Rashard Mendenhall 4.00 10.00
PPSRR Ray Rice 3.00 8.00
PPSSS Steve Slaton 3.00 8.00
PPSTC Tashard Choice 3.00 8.00
PPSTW Trae Williams 3.00 8.00
PPSVG Vernon Gholston 3.00 8.00

2008 Press Pass Autographs Bronze Red Ink

*RED INK: .6X TO 1.5X BRONZE BLUE INK
*RED INK: .5X TO 1.2X BRONZE BLUE INK SPs

2008 Press Pass Autographs Green

*GREEN/25: 1X TO 2.5X BRONZE AUTO
GREEN AUTO PRINT RUN 25
GREENS INSERTED IN PRESS PASS SE
PPSAW Andre Woodson 8.00 20.00
PPSBB Brian Brohm 8.00 20.00
PPSCL Chris Long 10.00 25.00
PPSDJ DeSean Jackson 15.00 40.00
PPSDM Darren McFadden 8.00 20.00
PPSFJ Felix Jones 8.00 20.00
PPSJC Jamaal Charles 12.00 30.00
PPSJDB John David Booty 8.00 20.00
PPSJS Jonathan Stewart 12.00 30.00
PPSMK Malcolm Kelly 8.00 20.00

2008 Press Pass Autographs Gold

*GOLD: .6X TO 1.5X BRONZE AUs
*GOLD: .5X TO 1.2X BRONZE SP AUs
GOLD PRINT RUN 25-99
PPSBB Brian Brohm/50 6.00 15.00
PPSCB Colt Brennan/25 8.00 20.00
PPSDM Darren McFadden 5.00 12.00
PPSFJ Felix Jones/50 5.00 12.00
PPSMR Matt Ryan 50.00 100.00

2008 Press Pass Autographs Gold Red Ink

*RED INK: .6X TO 1.5X BASIC GOLD AU
PPSDM Darren McFadden/53* 8.00 20.00

2008 Press Pass Autographs Red

*RED/25: 1X TO 2.5X BRONZE AUTO
RED AUTO PRINT RUN 25 SETS
REDS INSERTED IN PRESS PASS SE
ANNC'D PRINT RUN ON CARDS W/RED INK VERSION
PPSAW Andre Woodson 8.00 20.00
PPSCL Chris Long 10.00 25.00
PPSDJ DeSean Jackson 15.00 40.00
PPSDM Darren McFadden 8.00 20.00
PPSJC Jamaal Charles 12.00 30.00
PPSJDB John David Booty
PPSJS Jonathan Stewart 12.00 30.00
PPSLS Limas Sweed 8.00 20.00
PPSMK Malcolm Kelly 8.00 20.00

2008 Press Pass Autographs Red Red Ink

RED INK ANNOUNCED PRINT RUN 10-20
PPSBB Brian Brohm/18* 8.00 20.00
PPSFJ Felix Jones/20* 8.00 20.00

2008 Press Pass Autographs Silver

*SILVER: .5X TO 1.2X BRONZE AUs
*SILVER: .4X TO 1X BRONZE SP AUs
SILVER PRINT RUN 50-199
PPSBB Brian Brohm/100 5.00 12.00
PPSCB Colt Brennan/50 6.00 15.00
PPSDM Darren McFadden 5.00 12.00
PPSMR Matt Ryan 50.00 100.00

2008 Press Pass Autographs Silver Red Ink

*RED INK: .6X TO 1.5X BASIC SILVER AU

2008 Press Pass Gridiron Gamers Jerseys Silver

SILVER PRINT RUN 150-299
*GOLD/100: .6X TO 1.5X SLVR JSY/299
*GOLD/100: .5X TO 1.2X SLVR JSY/150-199
GOLD PRINT RUN 100 SER.#'d SETS
*HOLO/50: .8X TO 2X SLVR JSY/299
*HOLO/50: .6X TO 1.5X SLVR JSY/150-199
HOLOFOIL PRINT RUN 50 SER.#'d SETS
GRID GAMERS OVERALL ODDS 1:72 HOB
GGBB Brian Brohm/150 4.00 10.00
GGCB Colt Brennan/199 4.00 10.00
GGDB Davone Bess/299 4.00 10.00
GGDD Dennis Dixon/199 6.00 15.00
GGDH DJ Hall/299 4.00 10.00
GGED Early Doucet/199 4.00 10.00
GGJDB John David Booty/199 5.00 12.00
GGJF Justin Forsett/299 3.00 8.00
GGJH Jacob Hester/299 4.00 10.00
GGJS Jonathan Stewart/150 8.00 20.00
GGLH Lavelle Hawkins/299 3.00 8.00
GGMF Matt Forte/299 3.00 8.00
GGMH Mike Hart/199 6.00 15.00
GGMK Malcolm Kelly/150 6.00 15.00
GGMR Matt Ryan/150 10.00 25.00
GGRR Ray Rice/199 4.00 10.00
GGTC Tashard Choice/299 4.00 10.00
GGVG Vernon Gholston/299 4.00 10.00

2008 Press Pass Power Pick Autographs

STATED PRINT RUN 100-250
M.KELLY INSERTED IN PP SE
ANNC'D PRINT RUN ON CARDS W/RED INK VERSION
PPAW Andre Woodson/208* 5.00 12.00
PPBB Brian Brohm/100 5.00 12.00
PPCL Chris Long/100 12.00 30.00
PPDJ DeSean Jackson/154* 10.00 25.00
PPDM Darren McFadden/100 5.00 12.00
PPJS Jonathan Stewart/243* 15.00 40.00
PPLS Limas Sweed/237 5.00 12.00
PPMH Mike Hart/245* 5.00 12.00
PPMK Malcolm Kelly/250 5.00 12.00
PPMR Matt Ryan/80* 40.00 80.00
PPRM Rashard Mendenhall/230* 5.00 12.00

2008 Press Pass Power Pick Autographs Red Ink

*RED INK/20-76: .6X TO 1.5X BASIC AUTOS
PPAW Andre Woodson/10*
PPDJ DeSean Jackson/76* 15.00 40.00
PPJS Jonathan Stewart/7*
PPMH Mike Hart/5*
PPMR Matt Ryan/20* 60.00 120.00
PPRM Rashard Mendenhall/20* 8.00 20.00

2008 Press Pass Primetime Players

MPLETE SET (15) 10.00 25.00
STATED ODDS 1:4
PP1 Glenn Dorsey .50 1.25
PP2 Chris Long .60 1.50
PP3 Matt Ryan 1.50 4.00
PP4 Darren McFadden .50 1.25
PP5 Brian Brohm .50 1.25
PP6 DeSean Jackson 1.00 2.50
PP7 Andre Woodson .50 1.25
PP8 Malcolm Kelly .50 1.25
PP9 Jonathan Stewart .75 2.00
PP10 Limas Sweed .50 1.25
PP11 Rashard Mendenhall .50 1.25
PP12 Early Doucet .50 1.25
PP13 Chad Henne .60 1.50
PP14 Mario Manningham .50 1.25
PP15 Felix Jones .50 1.25

2008 Press Pass Target Exclusive

RANDOM INSERTS IN TARGET STORE PACKS
TAR1 Glenn Dorsey .50 1.25
TAR2 Chris Long .60 1.50
TAR3 Matt Ryan 1.50 4.00
TAR4 Brian Brohm .50 1.25
TAR5 Andre Woodson .50 1.25
TAR6 Darren McFadden .50 1.25
TAR7 Jonathan Stewart .75 2.00
TAR8 DeSean Jackson 1.00 2.50
TAR9 Malcolm Kelly .50 1.25
TAR10 Limas Sweed .50 1.25

2008 Press Pass Target Exclusive Autographs

STATED PRINT RUN 25 SER.#'d SETS
MALCOLM KELLY INSERTED IN PP SE
TARAW Andre Woodson 15.00 40.00
TARCL Chris Long
TARDJ DeSean Jackson/16* 12.00 30.00
TARDM Darren McFadden
TARED Early Doucet 15.00 40.00
TARJS Jonathan Stewart/24* 30.00 60.00
TARMK Malcolm Kelly
TARMR Matt Ryan/24* 60.00 120.00

2008 Press Pass Target Exclusive Autographs Red Ink

TARBB Brian Brohm/22* 12.00 30.00
TARDJ DeSean Jackson/9*
TARJS Jonathan Stewart/1*
TARLS Limas Sweed/23*
TARMR Matt Ryan/1*

2008 Press Pass Wal-Mart Exclusive

RANDOM INSERTS IN WAL-MART PACKS
WM1 Glenn Dorsey .50 1.25
WM2 Chris Long .60 1.50
WM3 Matt Ryan 1.50 4.00
WM4 Brian Brohm .50 1.25
WM5 Andre Woodson .50 1.25
WM6 Darren McFadden .50 1.25
WM7 Jonathan Stewart .75 2.00
WM8 DeSean Jackson 1.00 2.50
WM9 Malcolm Kelly .50 1.25
WM10 Limas Sweed .50 1.25

2008 Press Pass Wal-Mart Exclusive Autographs

ATED PRINT RUN 21-25
MALCOLM KELLY INSERTED IN PP SE
WMBB Brian Brohm
WMCL Chris Long 20.00 50.00
WMDJ DeSean Jackson/21* 12.00 30.00
WMDM Darren McFadden 15.00 40.00
WMJS Jonathan Stewart 30.00 60.00
WMLS Limas Sweed 20.00 50.00
WMMH Mike Hart/23* 20.00 50.00
WMMK Malcolm Kelly
WMMR Matt Ryan/21* 60.00 120.00

2008 Press Pass Game Breakers

is product was released as a separate boxed set at major retail outlets. Each sealed set included either one previously issued 2008 Press Pass autographed card and memorabilia card.

COMP.FACT.SET (26) 10.00 20.00
COMPLETE SET (25) 6.00 15.00

2009 Press Pass

is set was released on April 10, 2009. The base set consists of 105 cards. This product was released with 4 cards per pack and 28 packs per hobby box.

COMPLETE SET (105) 20.00 50.00
COMP.SET w/o PP's (100) 12.00 30.00
101-105 POWER PICK ODDS 1:14 HOB
1 Rhett Bomar .20 .50
2 Chase Daniel .25 .60
3 Nate Davis .20 .50
4 Josh Freeman .20 .50
5 Graham Harrell .20 .50
6 Mark Sanchez .20 .50
7 Matthew Stafford 1.00 2.50
8 Pat White .25 .60
9 Andre Brown .25 .60
10 Donald Brown .20 .50
11 Glen Coffee .20 .50
12 James Davis .20 .50
13 Mike Goodson .25 .60
14 Shonn Greene .20 .50
15 P.J. Hill .20 .50
16 Ian Johnson .20 .50
17 Jeremiah Johnson .20 .50
18 LeSean McCoy .50 1.25
19 Knowshon Moreno .20 .50
20 Javon Ringer .20 .50
21 Chris Wells .20 .50
22 Ramses Barden .20 .50
23 Kenny Britt .30 .75
24 Michael Crabtree .30 .75
25 Percy Harvin .20 .50
26 Darrius Heyward-Bey .30 .75
27 Juaquin Iglesias .20 .50
28 Jeremy Maclin .25 .60
29 Mohamed Massaquoi .20 .50
30 Louis Murphy .20 .50
31 Hakeem Nicks .25 .60
32 Brian Robiskie .20 .50
33 Brandon Tate .25 .60
34 Derrick Williams .20 .50
35 Chase Coffman .20 .50
36 Brandon Pettigrew .20 .50
37 Everette Brown .20 .50
38 Tyson Jackson .20 .50
39 Kenny McKinley .20 .50
40 Aaron Maybin .25 .60
41 Brian Orakpo .25 .60
42 Aaron Curry .30 .75
43 Brian Cushing .20 .50
44 James Laurinaitis .20 .50
45 Rey Maualuga .30 .75
46 Vontae Davis .20 .50
47 Victor Harris .25 .60
48 Malcolm Jenkins .20 .50
49 D.J. Moore .25 .60
50 Alphonso Smith .20 .50
51 Chase Coffman TC .15 .40
52 Michael Crabtree TC .25 .60
53 Shonn Greene TC .15 .40
54 Graham Harrell TC .15 .40
55 Malcolm Jenkins TC .15 .40
56 James Laurinaitis TC .15 .40
57 Rey Maualuga TC .25 .60
58 Brian Orakpo TC .20 .50
59 Kenny Britt LL .25 .60
60 Donald Brown LL .15 .40
61 Glen Coffee LL .15 .40
62 Quan Cosby LL .15 .40
63 Michael Crabtree LL .25 .60
64 Chase Daniel LL .20 .50
65 Nate Davis LL .15 .40
66 Jarett Dillard LL .15 .40
67 Shonn Greene LL .15 .40
68 Graham Harrell LL .15 .40
69 Austin Collie LL .15 .40
70 Gartrell Johnson LL .15 .40
71 Jeremy Maclin LL .20 .50
72 LeSean McCoy LL .40 1.00
73 Knowshon Moreno LL .15 .40
74 Hakeem Nicks LL .20 .50
75 Javon Ringer LL .15 .40
76 Mark Sanchez LL .15 .40
77 Matthew Stafford LL .75 2.00
78 Donald Brown AA .15 .40
79 Chase Coffman AA .15 .40
80 Michael Crabtree AA .25 .60
81 Aaron Curry AA .25 .60
82 Jarett Dillard AA .15 .40
83 Shonn Greene AA .15 .40
84 Malcolm Jenkins AA .15 .40
85 James Laurinaitis AA .15 .40
86 Jeremy Maclin AA .20 .50
87 Rey Maualuga AA .25 .60
88 Brian Orakpo AA .20 .50
89 Javon Ringer AA .15 .40
90 Alphonso Smith AA .15 .40
91 M.Stafford/K.Moreno TM .60 1.50
92 M.Sanchez/R.Maualuga TM .20 .50
93 G.Harrell/M.Crabtree TM .20 .50
94 C.Daniel/J.Maclin TM .15 .40
95 C.Wells/B.Robiskie TM .12 .30
96 P.Harvin/L.Murphy TM .12 .30
97 H.Nicks/B.Tate TM .15 .40
98 A.Maybin/D.Williams TM .15 .40
99 M.Jenkins/J.Laurinaitis TM .12 .30
100 J.Ringer/B.Hoyer TM .20 .50
101 Matthew Stafford PP 2.00 5.00
102 Mark Sanchez PP .40 1.00
103 Michael Crabtree PP .60 1.50
104 Chris Wells PP .40 1.00
105 Jeremy Maclin PP .50 1.25

2009 Press Pass Black and White

*B&W: 4X TO 10X BASIC CARDS
ANNOUNCED ODDS 1:140

2009 Press Pass Blue

*BLUE: 1.2X TO 3X BASIC CARDS
ONE BLUE PER RETAIL PACK

2009 Press Pass Reflectors

EFLECT/500: 2X TO 5X BASIC CARDS
REFLECTORS PRINT RUN 500

2009 Press Pass Reflectors Gold
EFLECT.GOLD/100: 3X TO 8X BASIC CARDS
REFLECTORS GOLD PRINT RUN 100

2009 Press Pass Autographs Bronze
ILVER/199: .5X TO 1.2X BRONZE AU
*SILVER/54-199: .4X TO 1X BRONZE AU SP
SILVER PRINT RUN 54-199
*GOLD/99: .6X TO 1.5X BRONZE AU
*GOLD/75-99: .5X TO 1.2X BRONZE AU SP
GOLD PRINT RUN 75-99
OVERALL AUTO ODDS 1:6
*BLUE/40-50: .6X TO 1.5X BRONZE AU
*BLUE/50: .5X TO 1.2X BRONZE AU SP
BLUE PRINT RUN 50
*RED INK: .5X TO 1.2X BASIC AU
PRESS PASS ANNC'D RED INK PRINT RUNS
ANNC'D PRINT RUN UNDER 20 NOT PRICED
AB Andre Brown 4.00 10.00
AC Aaron Curry 5.00 12.00
AC2 Austin Collie 3.00 8.00
AF Arian Foster 8.00 20.00
BC Brian Cushing 3.00 8.00
BG Brandon Gibson 4.00 10.00
BH Brian Hoyer 5.00 12.00
BO Brian Orakpo 4.00 10.00
BP Brandon Pettigrew 3.00 8.00
BR Brian Robiskie 3.00 8.00
BR2 B.J. Raji 4.00 10.00
BT Brandon Tate 4.00 10.00
BU Brandon Underwood 3.00 8.00
CC Chase Coffman 3.00 8.00
CD Chase Daniel 4.00 10.00
CH Cullen Harper 3.00 8.00
CP Cedric Peerman 3.00 8.00
CW Chris Wells SP 4.00 10.00
DB Donald Brown 3.00 8.00
DB Darius Butler 4.00 10.00
DHB Darrius Heyward-Bey 5.00 12.00
DM D.J. Moore 4.00 10.00
DM2 Devin Moore 3.00 8.00
DW Derrick Williams 3.00 8.00
EB Everette Brown 3.00 8.00
GC Glen Coffee 3.00 8.00
GH Graham Harrell 8.00 20.00
GJ Gartrell Johnson 3.00 8.00
HC Hunter Cantwell 3.00 8.00
HN Hakeem Nicks 4.00 10.00
IJ Ian Johnson 3.00 8.00
JC Jared Cook 4.00 10.00
JC3 James Casey 4.00 10.00
JC2 Jeremy Childs 3.00 8.00
JD James Davis 3.00 8.00
JD2 Jarett Dillard 3.00 8.00
JF Josh Freeman 3.00 8.00
JI Juaquin Iglesias 3.00 8.00
JJ Jeremiah Johnson 3.00 8.00
JL James Laurinaitis 3.00 8.00
JM Jeremy Maclin SP 10.00 25.00
JR Javon Ringer 3.00 8.00
JW John Parker Wilson 3.00 8.00
KB Kenny Britt 5.00 12.00
KM Knowshon Moreno SP 3.00 8.00
KM2 Kenny McKinley 3.00 8.00
KO Kevin Ogletree 4.00 10.00
LM2 Louis Murphy 3.00 8.00
LM LeSean McCoy 8.00 20.00
MC Michael Crabtree 5.00 12.00
MG Mike Goodson 4.00 10.00
MJ Malcolm Jenkins 3.00 8.00
ML Marlon Lucky 3.00 8.00
MM Mohamed Massaquoi 3.00 8.00
MR Mike Reilly 3.00 8.00
MS Matthew Stafford SP 20.00 50.00
MS2 Mark Sanchez SP 12.00 30.00
MT Mike Thomas 3.00 8.00
ND Nate Davis 3.00 8.00
PH2 Percy Harvin 3.00 8.00
PH P.J. Hill 3.00 8.00
PW Pat White 4.00 10.00
QC Quan Cosby 3.00 8.00
RB Rhett Bomar 3.00 8.00
RB2 Ramses Barden 3.00 8.00
RJ Rashad Jennings 4.00 10.00
RM Rey Maualuga 5.00 12.00
SG Shonn Greene SP 4.00 10.00
SM Stephen McGee 3.00 8.00
TJ Tyson Jackson 3.00 8.00
VD Vontae Davis 3.00 8.00
VH Victor Harris 4.00 10.00
WM William Moore 3.00 0.00

2009 Press Pass Autographs Blue Red Ink
*RED INK: .5X TO 1.2X BASIC AU
PRESS PASS ANNC'D RED INK PRINT RUNS
ANNC'D PRINT RUN UNDER 20 NOT PRICED
BU Brandon Underwood/50* 5.00 12.00

2009 Press Pass Autographs Green
*GREEN AU/25: .6X TO 1.5X BRONZE AU
GREEN/25 INSERTS IN WAL-MART PACKS
MC Michael Crabtree 8.00 20.00
MS Matthew Stafford 30.00 80.00
MS2 Mark Sanchez
PH2 Percy Harvin 5.00 12.00

2009 Press Pass Autographs Red
ED/25: .6X TO 1.5X BRONZE AU
RED/25 INSERTS IN TARGET PACKS
MC Michael Crabtree 8.00 20.00
MS Matthew Stafford 30.00 80.00
MS2 Mark Sanchez Red Ink 20.00 50.00
PH2 Percy Harvin 5.00 12.00

2009 Press Pass Banner Season
COMPLETE SET (15) 8.00 20.00
STATED ODDS 1:4
BS1 Donald Brown .30 .75
BS2 Michael Crabtree .50 1.25
BS3 Nate Davis .30 .75
BS4 Josh Freeman .30 .75
BS5 Shonn Greene .30 .75
BS6 Graham Harrell .30 .75
BS7 Percy Harvin .30 .75
BS8 Darrius Heyward-Bey .50 1.25
BS9 Jeremy Maclin .40 1.00
BS10 LeSean McCoy .75 2.00
BS11 Knowshon Moreno .30 .75
BS12 Hakeem Nicks .40 1.00
BS13 Mark Sanchez .30 .75
BS14 Matthew Stafford 1.50 4.00
BS15 Chris Wells .30 .75

2009 Press Pass Gridiron Gamers Jerseys Silver
LVER PRINT RUN 199-299
*GOLD/100: .5X TO 1.2X SILVER JSY
GOLD PRINT RUN 100 SER.#'d SETS
*HOLOFOIL/50: .6X TO 1.5X SILVER JSY
HOLOFOIL PRINT RUN 50 SER.#'d SETS
OVERALL GAMERS ODDS 1:72
GGAF Arian Foster/299 6.00 15.00
GGBG Brandon Gibson/299 3.00 8.00
GGCD Chase Daniel/299 3.00 8.00
GGCH Cullen Harper/299 2.50 6.00
GGDHB Darrius Heyward-Bey/299 4.00 10.00
GGGJ Gartrell Johnson/299 2.50 6.00
GGJF Josh Freeman/299 2.50 6.00
GGJJ Jeremiah Johnson/299 2.50 6.00
GGJM Jeremy Maclin/199 5.00 12.00
GGJW John Parker Wilson/299 6.00 15.00
GGKB Kenny Britt/299 4.00 10.00
GGKM Kenny McKinley/299 2.50 6.00
GGLM LeSean McCoy/250 5.00 12.00
GGML Marlon Lucky/299 6.00 15.00
GGMS Mark Sanchez/299 2.50 6.00
GGRM Rey Maualuga/299 4.00 10.00

2009 Press Pass Gridiron Gamers Jerseys Green
GREEN/75-100 IN RETAIL BLASTER BOXES
*BRONZE RETAIL: .3X TO .8X GREEN RETAIL
*RED RETAIL/25: .6X TO 1.5X GREEN RETAIL
BB Brian Brohm/75 3.00 8.00
BG Brandon Gibson/99 4.00 10.00
CB Colt Brennan/99 4.00 10.00
CH Chad Henne/82 4.00 10.00
DA Donnie Avery/99 3.00 8.00
DB Davone Bess/75 3.00 8.00
DC Dan Connor/75 3.00 8.00
DD Dennis Dixon/75 3.00 8.00
DT Devin Thomas/99 3.00 8.00
DW Derrick Williams/82 3.00 8.00
EA Erik Ainge/75 4.00 10.00
ED Early Doucet/75 4.00 10.00
GJ Gartrell Johnson/99 3.00 8.00
IJ Ian Johnson/99 3.00 8.00
JC Jamaal Charles/75 4.00 10.00
KM Kenny McKinley/99 3.00 8.00
KP Kenny Phillips/75 3.00 8.00
LM Louis Murphy/99 3.00 8.00
LS Limas Sweed/99 4.00 10.00
MH Mike Hart/99 4.00 10.00
MK Malcolm Kelly/95 3.00 8.00
ND Nate Davis/75 3.00 8.00
QC Quan Cosby/75 3.00 8.00
SM Stephen McGee/99 3.00 8.00
TC Tashard Choice/75 3.00 8.00
VG Vernon Gholston/100 3.00 8.00
JDB John David Booty/75 4.00 10.00
JPW John Parker Wilson/99 3.00 8.00
RB1 Ramses Barden/75 3.00 8.00
RB2 Rhett Bomar/99 3.00 8.00

2009 Press Pass Power Pick Autographs
STATED PRINT RUN 150-250
*SHOWBOUND/25: .8X TO 2X BASIC AUTO
SHOWBOUND PRINT RUN 5-25
PPDB Donald Brown/250 4.00 10.00
PPDHB Darrius Heyward-Bey/250 6.00 15.00
PPDW Derrick Williams/250 4.00 10.00
PPJM Jeremy Maclin/197 5.00 12.00
PPKM Knowshon Moreno/238* 4.00 10.00
PPLM LeSean McCoy/250 10.00 25.00
PPMC Michael Crabtree/250 6.00 15.00
PPMS Matthew Stafford/140* 25.00 60.00
PPMS2 Mark Sanchez/140* 15.00 40.00
PPPH Percy Harvin/250 4.00 10.00
PPSG Shonn Greene/250 4.00 10.00

2009 Press Pass Power Pick Autographs Red Ink
PRESS PASS ANNC'D RED INK PRINT RUNS
ANNC'D PRINT RUN UNDER 20 NOT PRICED
PPCW Chris Wells/199 12.00 30.00

2009 Press Pass Target Exclusive Autographs
STATED PRINT RUN 25 SER.#'d SETS
TARCW Chris Wells 25.00 60.00
TARDB Donald Brown/15* 20.00 50.00
TARDW Derrick Williams
TARJM Jeremy Maclin/21*
TARKM Knowshon Moreno
TARLM LeSean McCoy
TARMC Michael Crabtree 20.00 50.00
TARMS Matthew Stafford 50.00 100.00
TARMS2 Mark Sanchez 40.00 100.00
TARPH Percy Harvin
TARSG Shonn Greene/20*

2009 Press Pass Wal-Mart Exclusive Autographs
STATED PRINT RUN 25 SER.#'d SETS
WMCW Chris Wells
WMDB Donald Brown
WMDW Derrick Williams 8.00 20.00
WMJM Jeremy Maclin 10.00 25.00
WMKM Knowshon Moreno
WMLM LeSean McCoy
WMMC Michael Crabtree 20.00 50.00
WMMS Matthew Stafford
WMMS2 Mark Sanchez 40.00 100.00
WMPH Percy Harvin
WMSG Shonn Greene

2009 Press Pass Game Breakers
This product was released as a separate boxed set at major rctail outlets. Each sealed set included either one previously issued 2009 Press Pass autographed card and memorabilia card.
COMPLETE SET (25) 5.00 12.00
COMP.FACT.SET (26) 10.00 20.00
GB1 Matthew Stafford .75 2.00
GB2 Tyson Jackson .15 .40
GB3 Aaron Curry .25 .60
GB4 Mark Sanchez .15 .40
GB5 Darrius Heyward-Bey .25 .60
GB6 B.J. Raji .20 .50
GB7 Michael Crabtree .25 .60
GB8 Knowshon Moreno .15 .40
GB9 Brian Orakpo .20 .50
GB10 Josh Freeman .15 .40
GB11 Jeremy Maclin .20 .50
GB12 Brandon Pettigrew .15 .40
GB13 Percy Harvin .15 .40
GB14 Donald Brown .15 .40
GB15 Hakeem Nicks .20 .50
GB16 Kenny Britt .25 .60
GB17 Chris Wells .15 .40
GB18 James Laurinaitis .15 .40
GB19 Brian Robiskie .15 .40
GB20 Pat White .20 .50
GB21 Mohamed Massaquoi .15 .40
GB22 LeSean McCoy .40 1.00
GB23 Shonn Greene .15 .40
GB24 Glen Coffee .15 .40
GB25 Juaquin Iglesias .15 .40

2010 Press Pass
COMPLETE SET (105) 20.00 50.00
COMP.SET w/o PP's (100) 12.00 30.00
101-105 POWER PICK ODDS 1:14
1 Rolando McClain .20 .50
2 James Starks .25 .60
3 Jahvid Best .20 .50
4 Dan LeFevour .20 .50
5 Mardy Gilyard .20 .50
6 Tony Pike .20 .50
7 C.J. Spiller .20 .50
8 Jacoby Ford .20 .50
9 Antonio Brown 1.50 4.00
10 Aaron Hernandez .20 .50
11 Andre Roberts .25 .60
12 Tim Tebow .60 1.50
13 Ryan Mathews .20 .50
14 Mike Kafka .25 .60
15 Jonathan Dwyer .20 .50
16 Derrick Morgan .20 .50
17 Demaryius Thomas .50 1.25
18 Arrelious Benn .20 .50
19 Dezmon Briscoe .20 .50
20 Brandon LaFell .30 .75
21 Charles Scott .20 .50
22 Donovan Warren .20 .50
23 Eric Decker .25 .60
24 Anthony Dixon .20 .50
25 Danario Alexander .20 .50
26 Ndamukong Suh .40 1.00
27 Jimmy Clausen .20 .50
28 Golden Tate .25 .60
29 Dez Bryant .50 1.25
30 Sam Bradford .25 .60
31 Jermaine Gresham .20 .50
32 Gerald McCoy .20 .50
33 Dexter McCluster .25 .60
34 Jevan Snead .20 .50
35 Sean Canfield .20 .50
36 NaVorro Bowman .40 1.00
37 Jason Pierre-Paul .30 .75
38 Toby Gerhart .20 .50
39 Mike Williams .20 .50
40 Zac Robinson .25 .60
41 Montario Hardesty .20 .50
42 Jerry Hughes .20 .50
43 Joe Haden .30 .75
44 Jordan Shipley .20 .50
45 Daryll Clark .30 .75
46 Anthony McCoy .20 .50
47 Joe McKnight .20 .50
48 Damian Williams .20 .50
49 Earl Thomas .50 1.25
50 Jarrett Brown .20 .50
51 Tim Tebow TC .40 1.00
52 Toby Gerhart TC .12 .30
53 Golden Tate TC .15 .40
54 Aaron Hernandez TC .12 .30
55 Rolando McClain TC .12 .30
56 Sam Bradford TC .15 .40
57 Jerry Hughes TC .12 .30
58 Tim Tebow TC .40 1.00
59 Sam Bradford TC .15 .40
60 Ndamukong Suh TC .25 .60
61 Tim Tebow CL .40 1.00
62 Jimmy Clausen CL .12 .30
63 Joe Webb CL .12 .30
64 Dan LeFevour CL .12 .30
65 Sean Canfield CL .12 .30
66 Ndamukong Suh CL .25 .60
67 Tony Pike CL .12 .30
68 Toby Gerhart CL .12 .30
69 Ryan Mathews CL .12 .30
70 Danario Alexander CL .12 .30
71 Dezmon Briscoe CL .12 .30
72 Mardy Gilyard CL .12 .30
73 Freddie Barnes CL .12 .30
74 Jordan Shipley CL .12 .30
75 Golden Tate CL .15 .40
76 Brandon LaFell CL .20 .50
77 Sean Canfield AC .12 .30
78 Toby Gerhart AC .12 .30
79 Damian Williams AC .12 .30
80 Dez Bryant AC .30 .75
81 Eric Decker AC .15 .40
82 Jonathan Dwyer AC .12 .30
83 Demaryius Thomas AC .30 .75
84 C.J. Spiller AC .12 .30
85 Tim Tebow AC .40 1.00
86 Anthony Dixon AC .12 .30
87 Tony Pike AC .12 .30
88 Mardy Gilyard AC .12 .30
89 Dorin Dickerson AC .12 .30
90 Danario Alexander AC .12 .30
91 Dezmon Briscoe AC .12 .30
92 Jordan Shipley AC .12 .30
93 D.Bryant/Z.Robinson TM .30 .75
94 T.Tebow/A.Hernandez TM .40 1.00
95 J.Clausen/G.Tate TM .15 .40
96 S.Bradford/G.McCoy TM .15 .40
97 J.Snead/D.McCluster TM .15 .40
98 M.Gilyard/T.Pike TM .12 .30
99 J.Dwyer/D.Morgan TM .12 .30
100 J.McKnight/D.Williams TM .12 .30
101 Tim Tebow PP 1.25 3.00
102 Jimmy Clausen PP .40 1.00
103 Dez Bryant PP 1.00 2.50
104 Sam Bradford PP .50 1.25
105 C.J. Spiller PP .40 1.00

2010 Press Pass Black and White
*SINGLES: 3X TO 8X BASIC CARDS
ANNOUNCED B&W ODDS 1:140 HOB

2010 Press Pass Blue
*BLUE: 1X TO 2.5X BASIC CARDS
ONE BLUE PER RETAIL PACK

2010 Press Pass Reflectors
*SINGLES: 1.5X TO 4X BASIC CARDS
STATED PRINT RUN 500 SER.#'d SETS

2010 Press Pass Reflectors Gold
*SINGLES: 2.5X TO 6X BASIC CARDS
STATED PRINT RUN 100 SER.#'d SETS

2010 Press Pass All American Autographs
RANDOM INSERTS IN SPECIAL BOXES
STATED PRINT RUN 50-397
*RED INK: .5X TO 1.2X BASIC AU
AH Aaron Hernandez/100 5.00 12.00
CS2 C.J. Spiller/97* 5.00 12.00
DD Dorin Dickerson/100 5.00 12.00
DM2 Derrick Morgan/100 5.00 12.00
FB Freddie Barnes/397 4.00 10.00
GM Gerald McCoy/50 6.00 15.00
GT Golden Tate/178* 5.00 12.00
JG Jermaine Gresham/245 4.00 10.00
JH1 Joe Haden/139* 8.00 20.00
JH2 Jerry Hughes/48* 6.00 15.00
JS1 Jordan Shipley/293* 4.00 10.00
MG Mardy Gilyard/297 4.00 10.00
NS Ndamukong Suh/99* 15.00 40.00
RM2 Rolando McClain/50 4.00 10.00
SB Sam Bradford/100 12.00 30.00
TG Toby Gerhart/194* 4.00 10.00
TT Tim Tebow/125* 30.00 60.00

2010 Press Pass All American Autographs Platinum
ANNOUNCED PLATINUM PRINT RUN 14-25
AH Aaron Hernandez/25 8.00 20.00
CS2 C.J. Spiller/25 8.00 20.00
DM2 Derrick Morgan/25 8.00 20.00
FB Freddie Barnes/25 8.00 20.00
GM Gerald McCoy/25 8.00 20.00
GT Golden Tate/14* 10.00 25.00
JG Jermaine Gresham/24 8.00 20.00
JH1 Joe Haden/25 12.00 30.00
JH2 Jerry Hughes/20* 8.00 20.00
JS1 Jordan Shipley/20* 8.00 20.00
MG Mardy Gilyard/21* 8.00 20.00
NS Ndamukong Suh/25 25.00 60.00
RM2 Rolando McClain/25 8.00 20.00
SB Sam Bradford/25 30.00 80.00
TG Toby Gerhart/23* 8.00 20.00
TT Tim Tebow/25 40.00 80.00

2010 Press Pass Autographs Bronze
OVERALL AUTO ODDS 1:5.6 HOB
*RED INK: .5X TO 1.2X BASIC AUTO
PPSAB Arrelious Benn 3.00 8.00
PPSAB2 Antonio Brown 12.00 30.00
PPSAD Anthony Dixon 3.00 8.00
PPSAH Aaron Hernandez 3.00 8.00
PPSAM Anthony McCoy 3.00 8.00
PPSAR Andre Roberts 4.00 10.00
PPSAV Alterraun Verner 4.00 10.00
PPSBG Brandon Ghee 3.00 8.00
PPSBL Brandon LaFell 5.00 12.00
PPSCM Chris McGaha 3.00 8.00
PPSCS C.J. Spiller SP 3.00 8.00
PPSCS2 Charles Scott 3.00 8.00
PPSCW Corey Wootton 3.00 8.00
PPSDA Danario Alexander 3.00 8.00
PPSDB Dezmon Briscoe 3.00 8.00
PPSDB2 Dez Bryant SP 30.00 60.00
PPSDC Daryll Clark 5.00 12.00
PPSDD Dorin Dickerson 3.00 8.00
PPSDL Dan LeFevour 3.00 8.00
PPSDM Dexter McCluster 4.00 10.00
PPSDM2 Derrick Morgan 3.00 8.00
PPSDT Demaryius Thomas 8.00 20.00
PPSDW Damian Williams 3.00 8.00
PPSDW2 Donovan Warren 3.00 8.00
PPSED Eric Decker 4.00 10.00
PPSET Earl Thomas 8.00 20.00
PPSFB Freddie Barnes 3.00 8.00
PPSGM Gerald McCoy 3.00 8.00
PPSGS George Selvie 5.00 12.00
PPSGT Golden Tate 4.00 10.00
PPSJB Jahvid Best 3.00 8.00
PPSJB2 Jarrett Brown 3.00 8.00
PPSJC Jimmy Clausen SP 3.00 8.00
PPSJD Jonathan Dwyer 3.00 8.00
PPSJF Jacoby Ford 3.00 8.00
PPSJG Jermaine Gresham 3.00 8.00
PPSJH Joe Haden 6.00 15.00
PPSJH2 Jerry Hughes 3.00 8.00
PPSJJ Javarris James 3.00 8.00
PPSJM Joe McKnight 3.00 8.00
PPSJPP Jason Pierre-Paul 5.00 12.00
PPSJS Jordan Shipley 3.00 8.00
PPSJS2 Jevan Snead 3.00 8.00
PPSJST James Starks 4.00 10.00
PPSJW Joe Webb 3.00 8.00
PPSJW2 Juice Williams 4.00 10.00
PPSMH Montario Hardesty 3.00 8.00
PPSMK Mike Kafka 4.00 10.00
PPSMW Mike Williams 3.00 8.00
PPSNB NaVorro Bowman 6.00 15.00
PPSNG Mardy Gilyard 3.00 8.00
PPSNS Ndamukong Suh 12.00 30.00
PPSRG Rob Gronkowski 15.00 30.00
PPSRM Ryan Mathews 3.00 8.00
PPSRM2 Rolando McClain 3.00 8.00
PPSSB Sam Bradford SP 10.00 25.00
PPSSC Sean Canfield 3.00 8.00
PPSSL Sean Lee 8.00 20.00
PPSTG Toby Gerhart 3.00 8.00
PPSTP Tony Pike 3.00 8.00
PPSTT Tim Tebow 25.00 60.00
PPSZR Zac Robinson 4.00 10.00

2010 Press Pass Autographs Blue
*BLUE/50: .6X TO 1.5X BRONZE AU
*BLUE/30: .6X TO 2X BRONZE AU
*BLUE/25-50: .5X TO 1.2X BRONZE AU SP
BLUE STATED PRINT RUN 25-50
PPSCS C.J. Spiller/23* 5.00 12.00
PPSJC Jimmy Clausen/25 5.00 12.00
PPSNS Ndamukong Suh/50 20.00 50.00
PPSSB Sam Bradford/45* 15.00 40.00
PPSTT Tim Tebow/50 40.00 80.00

2010 Press Pass Autographs Blue Red Ink
PRESS PASS ANNC'D RED INK PRINT RUNS
PPSAB Arrelious Benn/49* 5.00 12.00
PPSDM Dexter McCluster/50* 6.00 15.00
PPSJD Jonathan Dwyer/47* 5.00 12.00
PPSJF Jacoby Ford/50* 5.00 12.00
PPSJG Jermaine Gresham/21* 5.00 12.00
PPSRM Rolando McClain/50* 5.00 12.00

2010 Press Pass Autographs Gold
*GOLD/85-99: .6X TO 1.5X BRONZE AU
*GOLD/50-75: .5X TO 1.2X BRONZE AU SP
GOLD STATED PRINT RUN 50-99
*RED INK: .5X TO 1.2X BASIC AUTO
PPSNS Ndamukong Suh/99 20.00 50.00
PPSSB Sam Bradford/70* 15.00 40.00
PPSTT Tim Tebow/99 30.00 80.00

2010 Press Pass Autographs Green
RANDOM INSERTS IN WAL-MART BLASTERS
STATED PRINT RUN 25 SER.#'d SETS
PPSCS C.J. Spiller
PPSDB Dez Bryant EXCH
PPSGT Golden Tate 12.00 30.00
PPSJB Jahvid Best
PPSJC Jimmy Clausen 8.00 20.00
PPSNS Ndamukong Suh
PPSSB Sam Bradford 20.00 50.00
PPSTT Tim Tebow 60.00 120.00

2010 Press Pass Autographs Red
RANDOM INSERTS IN TARGET BLASTERS
STATED PRINT RUN 25 SER.#'d SETS
PPSCS C.J. Spiller
PPSDB Dez Bryant
PPSGT Golden Tate 12.00 30.00
PPSJB Jahvid Best
PPSJC Jimmy Clausen 8.00 20.00
PPSNS Ndamukong Suh
PPSSB Sam Bradford 20.00 50.00
PPSTT Tim Tebow 60.00 120.00

2010 Press Pass Autographs Silver
*SILVER/150-199: .5X TO 1.2X BRONZE AU
*SILVER/75-100: .4X TO 1X BRONZE AU SP
SILVER PRINT RUN 75-199
*RED INK: .5X TO 1.2X BASIC SLVR AU
PPSSB Sam Bradford/95* 12.00 30.00
PPSTT Tim Tebow/149* 40.00 80.00

2010 Press Pass Banner Season
COMPLETE SET (15) 8.00 20.00
STATED ODDS 1:4 HOB
BS1 Jahvid Best .30 .75
BS2 C.J. Spiller .30 .75
BS3 Tim Tebow 1.00 2.50
BS4 Ryan Mathews .30 .75
BS5 Jonathan Dwyer .30 .75
BS6 Arrelious Benn .30 .75
BS7 Brandon LaFell .50 1.25
BS8 Ndamukong Suh .60 1.50
BS9 Jimmy Clausen .30 .75
BS10 Golden Tate .40 1.00
BS11 Dez Bryant .75 2.00
BS12 Sam Bradford .40 1.00
BS13 Toby Gerhart .30 .75
BS14 Gerald McCoy .30 .75
BS15 Rolando McClain .30 .75

2010 Press Pass Gridiron Gamers Jerseys Silver
SILVER PRINT RUN 199-299
*GOLD/99: .5X TO 1.2X SILVER
GOLD PRINT RUN 99 SER.#'d SETS
*HOLOFOIL/50: .6X TO 1.5X SILVER
HOLOFOIL PRINT RUN 50 SER.#'d SETS
PPAB Arrelious Benn/299 4.00 10.00
PPBL Brandon LaFell/299 4.00 10.00
GGDA Danario Alexander/299 4.00 10.00
PPDW Damian Williams/299 4.00 10.00
PPGT Golden Tate/199 4.00 10.00
PPJB Jahvid Best/199 4.00 10.00
PPJC Jimmy Clausen/199 2.50 6.00
PPJM Joe McKnight/299 4.00 10.00
PPJS Jevan Snead/299 5.00 12.00
PPMH Montario Hardesty/275 4.00 10.00
PPMW Mike Williams/299 5.00 12.00
PPSB Sam Bradford/199 10.00 25.00
PPSC Sean Canfield/299 4.00 10.00
PPTG Toby Gerhart/199 5.00 12.00

2010 Press Pass Power Pick Autographs
STATED PRINT RUN 74-250
*SHOWBOUND/25: .6X TO 1.5X AUTO/150-250
*SHOWBOUND/25: .5X TO 1.2X AUTO/75
SHOWBOUND PRINT RUN 25 SER.#'d SETS
*RED INK: .5X TO 1.2X BASIC AUTO
PPAB Arrelious Benn/173* 3.00 8.00
PPBL Brandon LaFell/246* 5.00 12.00
PPCS C.J. Spiller/149* 3.00 8.00
PPDB Dez Bryant/150 25.00 50.00
PPGT Golden Tate/235* 4.00 10.00
PPJB Jahvid Best/249* 3.00 8.00
PPJC Jimmy Clausen/75 3.00 8.00
PPRM Ryan Mathews/250 3.00 8.00
PPSB Sam Bradford/175 12.00 30.00
PPTG Toby Gerhart/247* 8.00 20.00
PPTT Tim Tebow/250 30.00 60.00

2010 Press Pass Saturday Signatures
RANDOM INSERTS IN SPECIAL BOXES
*PLATINUM: .8X TO 2X BASIC AUTO
AB Arrelious Benn 2.50 6.00
AD Anthony Dixon 2.50 6.00
AH Aaron Hernandez 2.50 6.00
AM Anthony McCoy
AR Andre Roberts 3.00 8.00
BL Brandon LaFell 4.00 10.00
CM Chris McGaha 2.50 6.00
CS1 Charles Scott 2.50 6.00
CS2 C.J. Spiller 2.50 6.00
DA Danario Alexander 2.50 6.00
DB Dezmon Briscoe 2.50 6.00
DC Daryll Clark 4.00 10.00
DL Dan LeFevour 2.50 6.00
DM1 Dexter McCluster 3.00 8.00
DM2 Derrick Morgan 2.50 6.00
DT Demaryius Thomas 6.00 15.00
DW Damian Williams 2.50 6.00
ED Eric Decker 8.00 20.00
ET Earl Thomas 6.00 15.00
FB Freddie Barnes 2.50 6.00
GM Gerald McCoy 2.50 6.00
GT Golden Tate 3.00 8.00
JB1 Jahvid Best 2.50 6.00
JB2 Jarrett Brown 2.50 6.00
JC Jimmy Clausen 2.50 6.00
JD Jonathan Dwyer 2.50 6.00
JF Jacoby Ford 2.50 6.00
JG Jermaine Gresham 2.50 6.00
JH1 Joe Haden 4.00 10.00
JH2 Jerry Hughes
JJ Javarris James 2.50 6.00
JM Joe McKnight 2.50 6.00
JP Jason Pierre-Paul 4.00 10.00
JS1 Jordan Shipley 2.50 6.00
JS2 Jevan Snead 2.50 6.00
JS3 James Starks 3.00 8.00
MG Mardy Gilyard 2.50 6.00
MH Montario Hardesty 2.50 6.00
MK Mike Kafka 3.00 8.00
MW Mike Williams 2.50 6.00
NB NaVorro Bowman 5.00 12.00
NS Ndamukong Suh
RG Rob Gronkowski 30.00 60.00
RM1 Ryan Mathews 2.50 6.00
RM2 Rolando McClain
SB Sam Bradford 20.00 50.00
SC Sean Canfield 2.50 6.00
TG Toby Gerhart 2.50 6.00
TP Tony Pike 2.50 6.00
TT Tim Tebow 25.00 60.00
ZR Zac Robinson

2010 Press Pass Saturday Signatures Platinum
*PLATINUM/15-25: .8X TO 2X BASIC AU
ANNOUNCED PRINT RUN 8-25
SB Sam Bradford/24 30.00 80.00

2010 Press Pass Saturday Signatures Platinum Red Ink
*RED INK: X TO X BASIC PLAT.AU
RED INK ANNOUNCED PRINT RUN 1-25
JG Jermaine Gresham/25
JM Joe McKnight/17*
TT Tim Tebow/25 40.00 80.00

2010 Press Pass Saturday Signatures Red Ink
*RED INK: X TO X BASIC AUTO
RED INK ANNOUNCED PRINT RUN 2-65
DC Daryll Clark/24*
DL Dan LeFevour/39*
DM1 Dexter McCluster/50*
DT Demaryius Thomas/50* 10.00 25.00
ED Eric Decker/58*
GT Golden Tate/14*
JB1 Jahvid Best/20* 4.00 10.00
JC Jimmy Clausen/24*
JD Jonathan Dwyer/65*
JF Jacoby Ford/47*
JM Joe McKnight/23*
MH Montario Hardesty/14*

2010 Press Pass Target Exclusive
RANDOM INSERTS IN TARGET PACKS
TAR1 Tim Tebow 2.00 5.00
TAR2 Jimmy Clausen .60 1.50
TAR3 Sam Bradford .75 2.00
TAR4 Jahvid Best .60 1.50
TAR5 Dez Bryant 1.50 4.00
TAR6 C.J. Spiller .60 1.50

2010 Press Pass Target Exclusive Autographs
STATED PRINT RUN 25 SER.#'d SETS
TARAB Arrelious Benn/1*
TARCS C.J. Spiller/20* 6.00 15.00
TARDB Dez Bryant/25 50.00 100.00
TARGT Golden Tate/19* 8.00 20.00
TARJB Jahvid Best/25 6.00 15.00
TARJC Jimmy Clausen/25 6.00 15.00
TARSB Sam Bradford/25 75.00 150.00
TARTG Toby Gerhart/22*
TARTT Tim Tebow/25 50.00 120.00

2010 Press Pass Wal-Mart Exclusive
RANDOM INSERTS IN WAL-MART PACKS
WM1 Tim Tebow 2.00 5.00
WM2 Jimmy Clausen .60 1.50
WM3 Sam Bradford .75 2.00
WM4 Jahvid Best .60 1.50
WM5 Dez Bryant 1.50 4.00
WM6 C.J. Spiller .60 1.50

2010 Press Pass Wal-Mart Exclusive Autographs
STATED PRINT RUN 25 SER.#'d SETS
WMBL Brandon LaFell/21*
WMCS C.J. Spiller/24* 6.00 15.00
WMDB Dez Bryant/18 50.00 100.00
WMGT Golden Tate/19* 8.00 20.00
WMJB Jahvid Best/22*
WMJC Jimmy Clausen/25 6.00 15.00
WMSB Sam Bradford/25 75.00 150.00
WMTG Toby Gerhart/22*
WMTT Tim Tebow/25 60.00 120.00

2011 Press Pass
COMPLETE SET (105) 25.00 50.00
COMP.SET w/o PP's (100) 12.00 30.00
101-105 POWER PICK ODDS 1:14 HOB
UNPRICED SOLO PRINT RUN 1
1 Marcell Dareus .15 .40
2 Mark Ingram .25 .60
3 Julio Jones .50 1.25
4 Ryan Mallett .15 .40
5 Nick Fairley .15 .40
6 Cam Newton .75 2.00
7 Austin Pettis .15 .40
8 Darvin Adams .15 .40
9 Shane Vereen .20 .50
10 Da'Quan Bowers .15 .40
11 DeAndre McDaniel .15 .40
12 Jordan Todman .15 .40
13 Titus Young .15 .40
14 Christian Ponder .15 .40
15 A.J. Green .40 1.00
16 Stevan Ridley .15 .40
17 Daniel Thomas .15 .40
18 Mikel Leshoure .15 .40
19 Torrey Smith .15 .40
20 Blaine Gabbert .15 .40
21 Prince Amukamara .15 .40
22 Roy Helu .15 .40
23 Niles Paul .15 .40
24 Colin Kaepernick .25 .60
25 Greg Little .20 .50
26 Ryan Williams .15 .40
27 Delone Carter .15 .40
28 Kyle Rudolph .15 .40
29 Cameron Heyward .20 .50
30 Dane Sanzenbacher .15 .40
31 Dion Lewis .20 .50
32 Kendall Hunter .15 .40
33 DeMarco Murray .30 .75
34 Stephen Paea .15 .40
35 Evan Royster .15 .40
36 Jonathan Baldwin .15 .40
37 Ryan Kerrigan .20 .50
38 Andy Dalton .30 .75
39 Von Miller .25 .60
40 Akeem Ayers .15 .40
41 Tyrod Taylor .30 .75
42 Jake Locker .15 .40
43 John Clay .25 .60
44 Tandon Doss .15 .40
45 Derrick Locke .20 .50
46 Greg Salas .15 .40
47 Rahim Moore .15 .40
48 Randall Cobb .25 .60
49 Terrence Toliver .20 .50
50 Aldon Smith .15 .40
51 Aaron Williams .15 .40
52 J.J. Watt .75 2.00
53 Luke Stocker .15 .40
54 Cam Newton TC .75 2.00
55 Nick Fairley TC .15 .40
56 Da'Quan Bowers TC .15 .40
57 Cam Newton TC .75 2.00
58 Mark Ingram TC .25 .60
59 Von Miller TC .25 .60
60 Cam Newton NL .75 2.00
61 Andy Dalton NL .30 .75
62 Tyrod Taylor NL .30 .75
63 Dane Sanzenbacher NL .15 .40
64 Ryan Mallett NL .15 .40
65 Colin Kaepernick NL .25 .60
66 Daniel Thomas NL .15 .40
67 DeMarco Murray NL .30 .75
68 Jordan Todman NL .15 .40
69 Kendall Hunter NL .15 .40
70 Titus Young NL .15 .40
71 Julio Jones NL .50 1.25
72 Jerrel Jernigan NL .15 .40
73 Torrey Smith NL .15 .40
74 Da'Quan Bowers NL .15 .40
75 Ryan Kerrigan NL .20 .50
76 Nick Fairley NL .15 .40
77 Tandon Doss BS .15 .40
78 Randall Cobb BS .25 .60
79 Ryan Williams BS .15 .40
80 Torrey Smith BS .15 .40
81 Blaine Gabbert BS .15 .40
82 A.J. Green BS .40 1.00
83 Jonathan Baldwin BS .15 .40
84 Mark Ingram BS .25 .60
85 Julio Jones BS .50 1.25
86 Jake Locker BS .15 .40
87 Ryan Mallett BS .15 .40
88 Cam Newton BS .75 2.00
89 Daniel Thomas BS .15 .40
90 Mikel Leshoure BS .15 .40
91 Jordan Todman BS .15 .40
92 D.Bowers/N.Fairley GC .15 .40
93 B.Gabbert/R.Mallett GC .15 .40
94 A.Green/J.Jones GC .50 1.25
95 C.Newton/T.Taylor GC .75 2.00
96 M.Ingram/D.Thomas GC .25 .60
97 J.Locker/C.Ponder GC .15 .40
98 J.Baldwin/T.Smith GC .15 .40
99 M.Leshoure/R.Williams GC .15 .40
100 D.Murray/K.Hunter GC .30 .75
101 Blaine Gabbert PP .40 1.00
102 A.J. Green PP 1.00 2.50
103 Cam Newton PP 2.00 5.00
104 Mark Ingram PP .60 1.50
105 Nick Fairley PP .40 1.00

2011 Press Pass Black and White
*BLACK/WHITE: 3X TO 8X BASIC CARDS
ANNOUNCED B&W ODDS 1:140 HOB

2011 Press Pass Reflectors
*REFLECTOR/299: 2X TO 5X BASIC INSERTS
REFLECTOR STATED PRINT RUN 299

2011 Press Pass Reflectors Blue
*BLUE: 1.2X TO 3X BASIC CARDS
ONE REFLECTOR BLUE PER RETAIL PACK

2011 Press Pass Reflectors Gold
*GOLD/100: 2.5X TO 6X BASIC INSERTS
GOLD STATED PRINT RUN 100

2011 Press Pass Reflectors Purple
*PURPLE/25: 5X TO 12X BASIC INSERTS
PURPLE STATED PRINT RUN 25

2011 Press Pass Autographs Blue
*BLUE/50: .6X TO 1.5X BRONZE
*BLUE/50: .5X TO 1.2X BRONZE SP
*BLUE/25: .6X TO 1.5X BRONZE
BLUE STATED PRINT RUN 25-50
*RED INK/15-25: .5X TO 1.2X BASIC AU

2011 Press Pass Autographs Bronze
OVERALL AUTO ODDS 1:7 HOB
EXCH EXPIRATION: 3/31/2012
*RED INK/15-99: .5X TO 1.2X BASIC AU
PPSAA Akeem Ayers EXCH 2.50 6.00
PPSAB Armon Binns 3.00 8.00
PPSAB2 Ahmad Black 3.00 8.00
PPSAD Andy Dalton 10.00 25.00
PPSAG A.J. Green SP 12.00 30.00
PPSAP Austin Pettis 2.50 6.00
PPSAS Aldon Smith 2.50 6.00
PPSAW Aaron Williams 2.50 6.00
PPSBB Brandon Burton 3.00 8.00
PPSBG Blaine Gabbert SP 5.00 12.00
PPSCH Cameron Heyward 3.00 8.00
PPSCK Colin Kaepernick 4.00 10.00
PPSCN Cam Newton 12.00 30.00
PPSCP Christian Ponder 2.50 6.00
PPSDA Darvin Adams 2.50 6.00
PPSDB Da'Quan Bowers SP 10.00 25.00
PPSDC Delone Carter 2.50 6.00
PPSDL Dion Lewis 3.00 8.00
PPSDL2 Derrick Locke 3.00 8.00
PPSDM DeMarco Murray SP 5.00 12.00
PPSDM2 DeAndre McDaniel 2.50 6.00
PPSDN Drake Nevis 2.50 6.00
PPSDS Dane Sanzenbacher 2.50 0.00
PPSDT Daniel Thomas 2.50 6.00
PPSDW D.J. Williams 2.50 6.00
PPSER Evan Royster 2.50 6.00
PPSGL Greg Little 3.00 8.00
PPSGS Greg Salas 2.50 6.00
PPSJB Jonathan Baldwin SP 5.00 12.00
PPSJC John Clay 4.00 10.00
PPSJJ Julio Jones SP 12.00 30.00
PPSJJ2 Jerrel Jernigan 2.50 6.00
PPSJL Jake Locker SP 2.50 6.00
PPSJR Jacquizz Rodgers 2.50 6.00
PPSJT Jordan Todman 2.50 6.00
PPSJW J.J. Watt 20.00 40.00
PPSKH Kendall Hunter 2.50 6.00
PPSKR Kyle Rudolph 2.50 6.00
PPSLS Luke Stocker 2.50 6.00
PPSMD Marcell Dareus 2.50 6.00
PPSMH Mark Herzlich 2.50 6.00
PPSMI Mark Ingram 4.00 10.00
PPSML Mikel Leshoure SP 8.00 20.00
PPSNF Nick Fairley SP 2.50 6.00
PPSNP Niles Paul 2.50 6.00
PPSPA Prince Amukamara SP 8.00 20.00
PPSRC Randall Cobb 4.00 10.00
PPSRH Roy Helu 2.50 6.00
PPSRK Ryan Kerrigan 3.00 8.00
PPSRM Ryan Mallett SP 3.00 8.00
PPSRM2 Rahim Moore SP 4.00 10.00
PPSRW Ryan Williams 2.50 6.00
PPSSP Stephen Paea 2.50 6.00
PPSSR Stevan Ridley 2.50 6.00
PPSSV Shane Vereen 3.00 8.00
PPSTD Tandon Doss 2.50 6.00
PPSTS Torrey Smith 2.50 6.00
PPSTT Tyrod Taylor 5.00 12.00
PPSTT2 Terrence Toliver 3.00 8.00
PPSTY Titus Young 2.50 6.00
PPSVM Von Miller 6.00 15.00

2011 Press Pass Autographs Gold
*GOLD/99: .6X TO 1.5X BRONZE
*GOLD/75: .5X TO 1.2X BRONZE SP
*GOLD/35-50: .6X TO 1.5X BRONZE
GOLD STATED PRINT RUN 35-99
*RED INK/15-50: .5X TO 1.2X BASIC AU

2011 Press Pass Autographs Green
*GREEN/25: .8X TO 2X BRONZE AU
RANDOM INSERTS IN WAL-MART BLASTER

2011 Press Pass Autographs Red
*RED/25: .8X TO 2X BRONZE AU
RANDOM INSERTS IN TARGET BLASTER

2011 Press Pass Autographs Silver
*SILVER/69-199: .5X TO 1.2X BRONZE
*SILVER/50-199: .4X TO 1X BRONZE SP
SILVER STATED PRINT RUN 50-199
*RED INK/19-50: .5X TO 1.2X BASIC AU

2011 Press Pass Class of 2011
COMPLETE SET (10) 8.00 20.00
STATED ODDS 1:7
CL1 Blaine Gabbert .40 1.00
CL2 Jake Locker .40 1.00
CL3 Ryan Mallett .40 1.00
CL4 Cam Newton 2.00 5.00
CL5 Jonathan Baldwin .40 1.00
CL6 Da'Quan Bowers .40 1.00
CL7 Nick Fairley .40 1.00
CL8 A.J. Green 1.00 2.50
CL9 Julio Jones 1.25 3.00
CL10 Mark Ingram .60 1.50

2011 Press Pass Class of 2011 Autographs
STATED PRINT RUN 35-199
*HOC/25: .6X TO 1.5X BASIC AU/199
*HOC/25: .5X TO 1.2X BASIC AU/35-110
*RED INK/22-35: .5X TO 1.2X BASIC AU
CLAG A.J. Green/50 20.00 50.00
CLBG Blaine Gabbert/90* 6.00 15.00
CLCN Cam Newton/194* 15.00 40.00
CLDB Da'Quan Bowers/100 8.00 20.00
CLDM DeMarco Murray/100
CLDT Daniel Thomas/164* 6.00 15.00
CLJB Jonathan Baldwin/199 6.00 15.00
CLJJ Julio Jones/177* 20.00 40.00
CLJL Jake Locker/77 10.00 25.00
CLMI Mark Ingram/189* 12.00 30.00
CLML Mikel Leshoure/75* 10.00 25.00
CLNF Nick Fairley/35 3.00 8.00
CLPA Prince Amukamara/110 10.00 25.00
CLRM Ryan Mallett/65* 15.00 40.00

2011 Press Pass Face to Face
STATED ODDS 1:4
FF1 B.Gabbert/D.Murray .60 1.50
FF2 A.Green/J.Jones 1.00 2.50
FF3 C.Newton/R.Mallett 1.50 4.00
FF4 J.Todman/D.Lewis .40 1.00
FF5 J.Baldwin/K.Rudolph .30 .75
FF6 D.Bowers/N.Fairley .30 .75
FF7 J.Locker/S.Vereen .50 1.25
FF8 N.Paul/K.Hunter .30 .75
FF9 D.Thomas/D.Carter .30 .75
FF10 M.Leshoure/T.Doss .30 .75
FF11 M.Dareus/S.Ridley .30 .75
FF12 R.Williams/A.Pettis .30 .75
FF13 T.Smith/C.Ponder .30 .75
FF14 C.Kaepernick/T.Young .50 1.25
FF15 A.Dalton/J.Clay .60 1.50

2011 Press Pass Gridiron Gamers Jerseys Silver
SILVER STATED PRINT RUN 225
*GOLD/99: .5X TO 1.2X SILVER/225
*HOLOFOIL/50: .6X TO 1.5X SILVER/225
*PURPLE/60: .6X TO 1.5X SILVER/225
JSY OVERALL ODDS 1:84 HOB
GGAD Andy Dalton 4.00 10.00
GGAG A.J. Green 5.00 12.00
GGBG Blaine Gabbert 2.50 6.00
GGDB Da'Quan Bowers 4.00 10.00
GGJB Jonathan Baldwin 4.00 10.00
GGJJ Julio Jones 8.00 20.00
GGJL Jake Locker 4.00 10.00
GGJR Jacquizz Rodgers 5.00 12.00
GGKR Kyle Rudolph 5.00 12.00
GGNP Niles Paul 8.00 20.00
GGPA Prince Amukamara 6.00 15.00
GGRH Roy Helu 6.00 15.00
GGRM Ryan Mallett 6.00 15.00
GGSR Stevan Ridley 5.00 12.00
GGSV Shane Vereen 2.50 6.00
GGTS Torrey Smith 3.00 8.00
GGTT Terrence Toliver 4.00 10.00

2011 Press Pass Power Pick Autographs
STATED PRINT RUN 35-250
*RED INK/16-53: .5X TO 1.2X BASIC AU
*SHOWBOUND/25: .6X TO 1.5X AU/125-250
*SHOWBOUND/25: .5X TO 1.2X AU/35-105
PPAG A.J. Green/52 25.00 50.00

PPBG Blaine Gabbert/95* 8.00 20.00
PPCN Cam Newton/230* 30.00 80.00
PPDB Da'Quan Bowers/125 8.00 20.00
PPDM DeMarco Murray/100 6.00 15.00
PPDT Daniel Thomas/234* 6.00 15.00
PPJB Jonathan Baldwin/197* 6.00 15.00
PPJJ Julio Jones/228* 12.00 30.00
PPJL Jake Locker/68* 30.00 60.00
PPMI Mark Ingram/246* 6.00 15.00
PPML Mikel Leshoure/55* 10.00 25.00
PPNF Nick Fairley/35 3.00 8.00
PPPA Prince Amukamara/150 10.00 25.00
PPRM Ryan Mallett/65* 6.00 15.00

2011 Press Pass Target Exclusive

RANDOM INSERTS IN TARGET PACKS
TAR1 Blaine Gabbert .60 1.50
TAR2 Cam Newton 3.00 8.00
TAR3 Ryan Mallett .60 1.50
TAR4 Jake Locker .60 1.50
TAR5 A.J. Green 1.50 4.00
TAR6 Mark Ingram 1.00 2.50

2011 Press Pass Wal-Mart Exclusive

RANDOM INSERTS IN WAL-MART PACKS
WM1 Blaine Gabbert .60 1.50
WM2 Cam Newton 3.00 8.00
WM3 Ryan Mallett .60 1.50
WM4 Jake Locker .60 1.50
WM5 A.J. Green 1.50 4.00
WM6 Mark Ingram 1.00 2.50

2012 Press Pass

COMPLETE SET (50) 6.00 15.00
1 Dwayne Allen .15 .40
2 Mark Barron .15 .40
3 Justin Blackmon .15 .40
4 Andre Branch .15 .40
5 Ryan Broyles .15 .40
6 Orson Charles .15 .40
7 Quinton Coples .15 .40
8 Kirk Cousins .60 1.50
9 Jared Crick .15 .40
10 Alfonzo Dennard .15 .40
11 Jeremy Ebert .15 .40
12 Michael Egnew .15 .40
13 Michael Floyd .15 .40
14 Nick Foles .40 1.00
15 Jeff Fuller .15 .40
16 Stephon Gilmore .20 .50
17 Chris Givens .15 .40
18 T.J. Graham .15 .40
19 Cyrus Gray .15 .40
20 Robert Griffin III .20 .50
21 Dan Herron .15 .40
22 Stephen Hill .15 .40
23 LaMichael James .15 .40
24 Alshon Jeffery .30 .75
25 Marvin Jones .15 .40
26 Case Keenum .30 .75
27 Luke Kuechly .40 1.00
28 Travis Lewis .20 .50
29 Ryan Lindley .15 .40
30 Andrew Luck 1.50 4.00
31 Doug Martin .25 .60
32 Marquis Maze .15 .40
33 Whitney Mercilus .15 .40
34 Lamar Miller .25 .60
35 Kellen Moore .20 .50
36 Brock Osweiler .15 .40
37 Isaiah Pead .15 .40
38 Dan Persa .20 .50
39 Dontari Poe .15 .40
40 DeVier Posey .15 .40
41 Trent Richardson .15 .40
42 Gerell Robinson .15 .40
43 Mohamed Sanu .25 .60
44 Devon Still .20 .50
45 Tommy Streeter .15 .40
46 Ryan Tannehill .25 .60
47 Courtney Upshaw .20 .50
48 Brandon Weeden .15 .40
49 Jarius Wright .15 .40
50 Kendall Wright .15 .40

2012 Press Pass Blue

*BLUE: 1X TO 2.5X BASIC CARDS
BLUE STATED ODDS 1:1 RETAIL

2012 Press Pass Gold

*GOLD: 1X TO 2.5X BASIC CARDS
GOLD STATED ODDS 1:1 HOBBY

2012 Press Pass Reflectors

*REFLECTOR/299: 1.5X TO 4X BASIC CARDS
REFLECTOR STATED PRINT RUN 299
30 Andrew Luck 8.00 20.00

2012 Press Pass Reflectors Proof

*PROOF/100: 2.5X TO 6X BASIC CARDS
HOBBY ONLY PROOF PRINT RUN 100
30 Andrew Luck 12.00 30.00

2012 Press Pass All American Autographs Silver

SILVER PRINT RUN 99 SER.#'d SETS
*BLUE/50: .5X TO 1.2X SILVER/99
*RED/25: .6X TO 1.5X SILVER/99
AL Andrew Luck 75.00 150.00
CF Coby Fleener 3.00 8.00
CK Case Keenum 6.00 15.00
JB Justin Blackmon 3.00 8.00
KM Kellen Moore 4.00 10.00
LJ LaMichael James 3.00 8.00
MF Michael Floyd 3.00 8.00
RG Robert Griffin III 4.00 10.00
TR Trent Richardson 3.00 8.00

2012 Press Pass Autographs Blue

BLUE STATED PRINT RUN 50-99
PPSAB Andre Branch/50 3.00 8.00
PPSAC Audie Cole/47* 3.00 8.00
PPSAD Alfonzo Dennard/50 3.00 8.00
PPSAJ A.J. Jenkins/50 3.00 8.00
PPSAJ2 Alshon Jeffery/50 6.00 15.00
PPSAL Andrew Luck/50 75.00 150.00
PPSBO Brock Osweiler/47* 3.00 8.00
PPSBQ Brian Quick/99 3.00 8.00
PPSBT Brandon Thompson/34* 4.00 10.00
PPSBW Brandon Weeden/50 3.00 8.00
PPSBW2 Billy Winn/35* 5.00 12.00
PPSCF Coby Fleener/48* 3.00 8.00
PPSCG Cyrus Gray/30* 3.00 8.00
PPSCG2 Chris Givens/45* 3.00 8.00
PPSCH Casey Hayward/45* 3.00 8.00
PPSCJ Coryell Judie/45* 3.00 8.00
PPSCK Case Keenum/50 6.00 15.00
PPSCU Courtney Upshaw/50 4.00 10.00
PPSDA Dwayne Allen/50 3.00 8.00
PPSDH Dont'a Hightower/50 5.00 12.00
PPSDH2 Dan Herron/50 3.00 8.00
PPSDM Doug Martin/50 5.00 12.00
PPSDP Dan Persa/50 4.00 10.00
PPSDP2 Dontari Poe/50 3.00 8.00
PPSDP3 DeVier Posey/50 3.00 8.00
PPSDS Devon Still/50 4.00 10.00
PPSEA Emmanuel Acho/50 3.00 8.00
PPSFC Fletcher Cox/40* 5.00 12.00
PPSGR Gerell Robinson/50 3.00 8.00
PPSHS Harrison Smith/50 3.00 8.00
PPSIP Isaiah Pead/50 3.00 8.00
PPSJA Joe Adams/42* 3.00 8.00
PPSJB Justin Blackmon/50 3.00 8.00
PPSJC Jared Crick/50 3.00 8.00
PPSJE Jeremy Ebert/50 3.00 8.00
PPSJF Jeff Fuller/50 3.00 8.00
PPSJH Jayron Hosley/50 5.00 12.00
PPSJJ Janoris Jenkins/45* 4.00 10.00
PPSJW Jarius Wright/45* 3.00 8.00
PPSKC Kirk Cousins/50 12.00 30.00
PPSKK Kevin Koger/50 5.00 12.00
PPSKM Kellen Moore/50 12.00 30.00
PPSKR Kendall Reyes/50 3.00 8.00
PPSKW Kendall Wright/50 3.00 8.00
PPSLD Lavonte David/50 5.00 12.00
PPSLJ LaMichael James/50 3.00 8.00
PPSLK Luke Kuechly/50 8.00 20.00
PPSLM Lamar Miller/50 5.00 12.00
PPSMB Mark Barron/50 3.00 8.00
PPSME Michael Egnew/50 3.00 8.00
PPSMF Michael Floyd/50 8.00 20.00
PPSMI Melvin Ingram/40* 3.00 8.00
PPSMJ Marvin Jones/50 3.00 8.00
PPSMM Marquis Maze/50 3.00 8.00
PPSMS Mohamed Sanu/50 5.00 12.00
PPSNF Nick Foles/50 8.00 20.00
PPSNT Nick Toon/50 3.00 8.00
PPSOC Orson Charles/3*
PPSQC Quinton Coples/50 6.00 15.00
PPSRB Ryan Broyles/31* 8.00 20.00
PPSRG Robert Griffin III/49* 4.00 10.00
PPSRL Ryan Lindley/47* 3.00 8.00
PPSRT Ryan Tannehill/50 5.00 12.00
PPSRW Russell Wilson/50 40.00 80.00
PPSSG Stephon Gilmore/32* 4.00 10.00
PPSSH Stephen Hill/32* 3.00 8.00
PPSTG T.J. Graham/41* 3.00 8.00
PPSTH T.Y. Hilton/50 6.00 15.00
PPSTL Travis Lewis/46* 4.00 10.00
PPSTR Trent Richardson/41* 3.00 8.00
PPSTS Tommy Streeter/50
PPSVB Vick Ballard/50 4.00 10.00
PPSWM Whitney Mercilus/46* 3.00 8.00
PPSZB Zach Brown/50 3.00 8.00

2012 Press Pass Autographs Blue Red Ink

RED INK/15-20*: .5X TO 1.2X BLUE AUTO/50
ANNOUNCED RED INK PRINT RUN 1-47
PPSOC Orson Charles/47* 3.00 8.00

2012 Press Pass Autographs Bronze

*BRONZE AU/99-149: .3X TO .8X BLUE AU/50-99
BRONZE STATED PRINT RUN 25-149
PPSAL Andrew Luck/24* 125.00 250.00
PPSCK Case Keenum/25 8.00 20.00
PPSJB Justin Blackmon/23* 4.00 10.00
PPSKM Kellen Moore/25 15.00 40.00
PPSKW Kendall Wright/20* 4.00 10.00
PPSLJ LaMichael James/25 4.00 10.00
PPSLM Lamar Miller/24* 6.00 15.00
PPSMF Michael Floyd/25 10.00 25.00
PPSQC Quinton Coples/25 8.00 20.00
PPSTR Trent Richardson/25 4.00 10.00

2012 Press Pass Autographs Bronze Red Ink

RED INK/15-49*: .5X TO 1.2X GOLD AU
ANNOUNCED RED INK PRINT RUN 1-49

2012 Press Pass Autographs Gold

*GOLD AU/175-249: .25X TO .6X BLUE/50-99
GOLD STATED PRINT RUN 25-249
PPSAL Andrew Luck/24* 125.00 250.00
PPSCK Case Keenum/25 8.00 20.00
PPSJB Justin Blackmon/25 4.00 10.00
PPSKM Kellen Moore/24* 15.00 40.00
PPSKW Kendall Wright/20* 4.00 10.00
PPSLJ LaMichael James/25 4.00 10.00
PPSLM Lamar Miller/25 6.00 15.00
PPSMF Michael Floyd/25 10.00 25.00
PPSQC Quinton Coples/25 8.00 20.00
PPSTR Trent Richardson/19* 4.00 10.00

2012 Press Pass Autographs Gold Red Ink

RED INK/15-50*: .5X TO 1.2X GOLD AU
ANNOUNCED RED INK PRINT RUN 1-50

2012 Press Pass Autographs Silver

*SILVER AU: .25X TO .6X BLUE AU/50-99
OVERALL AUTO ODDS 1:5 HOB
PPSAJ2 Alshon Jeffery SP 8.00 20.00
PPSAL Andrew Luck 60.00 120.00
PPSBW Brandon Weeden SP 2.00 5.00
PPSCK Case Keenum SP 4.00 10.00
PPSJB Justin Blackmon SP 2.00 5.00
PPSKM Kellen Moore SP 8.00 20.00
PPSKW Kendall Wright SP 2.00 5.00
PPSLJ LaMichael James SP 2.00 5.00
PPSMF Michael Floyd SP 5.00 12.00
PPSQC Quinton Coples SP 6.00 15.00
PPSRG Robert Griffin III SP 2.50 6.00
PPSRW Russell Wilson SP 30.00 60.00
PPSTR Trent Richardson SP 2.00 5.00

2012 Press Pass Autographs Silver Red Ink

RED INK/15-218*: .5X TO 1.2X SLVR AU
ANNOUNCED RED INK PRINT RUN 1-218

2012 Press Pass Autographs Target Red

*RED/15: .6X TO 1.5X BLUE AU/50-99
RED/4-15 INSERTS IN TARGET PACKS
PPSRW Russell Wilson/15 50.00 100.00
PPSTR Trent Richardson/15 5.00 12.00

2012 Press Pass Autographs Target Red Red Ink

PPSRB Ryan Broyles/14* 20.00 40.00
PPSSH Stephen Hill/15* 5.00 12.00
PPSWM Whitney Mercilus/15*

2012 Press Pass Autographs Wal-Mart Green

*GREEN/15: .6X TO 1.5X BLUE AU/50-99
GREEN/3-15 INSERTS IN WAL-MART PACKS
PPSRW Russell Wilson/15 50.00 100.00
PPSTR Trent Richardson/15 5.00 12.00
PPSWM Whitney Mercilus/1*

2012 Press Pass Autographs Wal-Mart Green Red Ink

PPSRB Ryan Broyles/15 20.00 40.00
PPSSH Stephen Hill/15 6.00 15.00
PPSWM Whitney Mercilus/14* 5.00 12.00

2012 Press Pass Power Pick Autographs Blue

STATED PRINT RUN 50 SER.#'d SETS
*RED/25: .5X TO 1.2X BLUE/45-50
*SILVER/99: .3X TO .8X BLUE/45-50
AJ Alshon Jeffery 8.00 20.00
AL Andrew Luck 60.00 120.00
JB Justin Blackmon 4.00 10.00
KW Kendall Wright 4.00 10.00
LJ LaMichael James 4.00 10.00
LM Lamar Miller 6.00 15.00
MF Michael Floyd
NF Nick Foles 10.00 25.00
QC Quinton Coples
RG Robert Griffin III 5.00 12.00
RT Ryan Tannehill 6.00 15.00
TR Trent Richardson 4.00 10.00

2012 Press Pass Power Pick Autographs Blue Red Ink

MF Michael Floyd/47* 8.00 20.00
QC Quinton Coples/47* 4.00 10.00

2013 Press Pass

COMPLETE SET (50) 6.00 15.00
1 Keenan Allen .40 1.00
2 Tavon Austin .25 .60
3 Stedman Bailey .20 .50
4 Montee Ball .20 .50
5 Matt Barkley .20 .50
6 Kenjon Barner .20 .50
7 Le'Veon Bell .60 1.50
8 Giovani Bernard .20 .50
9 Tyler Bray .20 .50
10 Zac Dysert .20 .50
11 Tyler Eifert .20 .50
12 Andre Ellington .20 .50
13 Zach Ertz .40 1.00
14 Johnathan Franklin .20 .50
15 Mike Glennon .20 .50
16 Ray Graham .20 .50
17 Erik Highsmith .25 .60
18 DeAndre Hopkins .50 1.25
19 Justin Hunter .20 .50
20 Jawan Jamison .20 .50
21 Stepfhon Jefferson .25 .60
22 Jarvis Jones .20 .50
23 Landry Jones .20 .50
24 Tavarres King .20 .50
25 Collin Klein .25 .60
26 Eddie Lacy .20 .50
27 Marcus Lattimore .20 .50
28 Star Lotulelei .25 .60
29 EJ Manuel .20 .50
30 Dee Milliner .20 .50
31 Barkevious Mingo .20 .50
32 Damontre Moore .20 .50
33 Ryan Nassib .20 .50
34 Alec Ogletree .20 .50
35 Cordarrelle Patterson .20 .50
36 Joseph Randle .20 .50
37 Eric Reid .25 .60
38 Denard Robinson .20 .50
39 Dion Sims .20 .50
40 Geno Smith .20 .50
41 Kenny Stills .20 .50
42 Ryan Swope .20 .50
43 Stepfan Taylor .20 .50
44 Manti Te'o .25 .60
45 Kenny Vaccaro .20 .50
46 Bjoern Werner .20 .50
47 Markus Wheaton .20 .50
48 Terrance Williams .20 .50
49 Tyler Wilson .20 .50
50 Robert Woods .30 .75

2013 Press Pass Blue

*BLUE: 1X TO 2.5X BASIC CARDS

2013 Press Pass Gold

*GOLD: 1X TO 2.5X BASIC CARDS

2013 Press Pass Reflectors

*REFLECT/299: 1.5X TO 4X BASIC CARDS

2013 Press Pass Reflectors Proof

*PROOF/100: 2.5X TO 6X BASIC CARDS
STATED PRINT RUN 100 SER.#'d SETS

2013 Press Pass Autographs Blue

AD Aaron Dobson/50 3.00 8.00
AE Andre Ellington/50 3.00 8.00
AO Alec Ogletree/50 3.00 8.00
AOK Alex Okafor/50 3.00 8.00
BW Bjoern Werner/50 3.00 8.00
CH Cobi Hamilton/50 3.00 8.00
CK Collin Klein/50 4.00 10.00
CP Cordarrelle Patterson/50 3.00 8.00
DA David Amerson/50 3.00 8.00
DH DeAndre Hopkins/50 10.00 25.00
DJ Dion Jordan/35 3.00 8.00
DM Dee Milliner/50 3.00 8.00
DMO Damontre Moore/50 3.00 8.00
DR Denard Robinson/50 3.00 8.00
DRO Da'Rick Rogers/50 3.00 8.00
DS Dion Sims/50 3.00 8.00
DT Desmond Trufant/50 3.00 8.00
EA Ezekiel Ansah/17
EH Erik Highsmith/50 4.00 10.00
EL Eddie Lacy/50 3.00 8.00
EM EJ Manuel/50 3.00 8.00
ER Eric Reid/50 4.00 10.00
GB Giovani Bernard/50 3.00 8.00
GS Geno Smith/50 3.00 8.00
JF Johnathan Franklin/50 3.00 8.00
JH Justin Hunter/50 3.00 8.00
JJA Jawan Jamison/50 3.00 8.00
JJ Jarvis Jones/50 3.00 8.00
JP Jordan Poyer/50 3.00 8.00
JRA Joseph Randle/50 3.00 8.00
JR Jordan Rodgers/50 4.00 10.00
JW Jesse Williams/50 5.00 12.00
KA Keenan Allen/50 6.00 15.00
KB Kenjon Barner/50 3.00 8.00
KS Kawann Short/50 3.00 8.00
KST Kenny Stills/50 3.00 8.00
KV Kenny Vaccaro/50 3.00 8.00
LB Le'Veon Bell/50 10.00 25.00
LJ Landry Jones/50 3.00 8.00
MB Montee Ball/50 3.00 8.00
MBA Matt Barkley/50 20.00 50.00
MD Marcus Davis/50 3.00 8.00
MG Mike Glennon/50 3.00 8.00
ML Marcus Lattimore/50 3.00 8.00
MM Michael Mauti/50 5.00 12.00
MT Manti Te'o/50 4.00 10.00
MW Markus Wheaton/50 3.00 8.00
QP Quinton Patton/50 3.00 8.00
RB Rex Burkhead/50 4.00 10.00
RG Ray Graham/50 3.00 8.00
RN Ryan Nassib/50 3.00 8.00
RS Ryan Swope/50 3.00 8.00
RW Robert Woods/50 5.00 12.00
SB Stedman Bailey/50 3.00 8.00
SF Sharrif Floyd/50 3.00 8.00
SJ Stepfhon Jefferson/50 4.00 10.00
SR Sheldon Richardson/50 3.00 8.00
ST Stepfan Taylor/50 3.00 8.00
SW Sylvester Williams/50 3.00 8.00
TA Tavon Austin/50 4.00 10.00
TB Tyler Bray/50 3.00 8.00
TE Tyler Eifert/50 3.00 8.00
TK Tavarres King/50 3.00 8.00
TR Theo Riddick/50 3.00 8.00
TW Terrance Williams/50 3.00 8.00
TWI Tyler Wilson/50 3.00 8.00
ZD Zac Dysert/50 3.00 8.00
ZE Zach Ertz/50 6.00 15.00

2013 Press Pass Autographs Blue Red Ink

TA Tavon Austin/50 5.00 12.00

2013 Press Pass Autographs Bronze

*BRONZE/65-99: .3X TO .8X BLUE AU/35-50
*BRONZE/49: .4X TO 1X BLUE AU/50
*BRONZE/25: .5X TO 1.2X BLUE AU/50
STATED PRINT RUN 25-99
EA Ezekiel Ansah/99 2.50 6.00
GS Geno Smith/25 4.00 10.00
MBA Matt Barkley/25 25.00 50.00
MT Manti Te'o/25 5.00 12.00
TA Tavon Austin/99 3.00 8.00

2013 Press Pass Autographs Gold

*GOLD/149-199: .25X TO .6X BLUE
*GOLD/75-99: .3X TO .8X BLUE
GS Geno Smith/25 4.00 10.00
MBA Matt Barkley/25 25.00 60.00
MG Mike Glennon/50 3.00 8.00
MT Manti Te'o/25 20.00 40.00
TA Tavon Austin/199 3.00 8.00

2013 Press Pass Autographs Silver

*SILVER: .25X TO .6X BLUE AU/35-50
*SILVER SP: .3X TO .8X BLUE AU/35-50
RED INK/16-339: .5X TO 1.2X SLVR AU
EL Eddie Lacy SP 2.50 6.00
GS Geno Smith SP 2.50 6.00
MBA Matt Barkley SP 15.00 40.00
TA Tavon Austin SP 3.00 8.00

2013 Press Pass Playmakers Autographs Blue

*RED/25: .5X TO 1.2X BLUE AU/50
*SILVER/99: .3X TO .8X BLUE AU/50
AE Andre Ellington 4.00 10.00
CK Collin Klein 5.00 12.00
EM EJ Manuel 4.00 10.00
GB Giovani Bernard 4.00 10.00
GS Geno Smith 4.00 10.00
JH Justin Hunter 4.00 10.00
KA Keenan Allen 8.00 20.00
KB Kenjon Barner 4.00 10.00
LB Le'Veon Bell 12.00 30.00
MBA Matt Barkley/48* 30.00 60.00
MT Manti Te'o 5.00 12.00
RW Robert Woods 6.00 15.00
TW Terrance Williams 4.00 10.00

2013 Press Pass Power Pick Autographs Blue

*RED/25: .5X TO 1.2X BLUE AU/50
*SILVER/99: .3X TO .8X BLUE AU/50
EL Eddie Lacy 4.00 10.00
GS Geno Smith 4.00 10.00
JF Johnathan Franklin/40* 4.00 10.00
JH Justin Hunter 4.00 10.00
KA Keenan Allen 8.00 20.00
MB Montee Ball 4.00 10.00
MBA Matt Barkley/46* 30.00 60.00
ML Marcus Lattimore/41* 4.00 10.00
MT Manti Te'o 5.00 12.00
TA Tavon Austin 5.00 12.00
TWI Tyler Wilson 4.00 10.00

2014 Press Pass

COMPLETE SET (50) 6.00 15.00
1 Jared Abbrederis .20 .50
2 Davante Adams .30 .75
3 Jace Amaro .20 .50
4 Jadeveon Clowney .25 .60
5 Odell Beckham Jr. .50 1.25
6 Blake Bortles .25 .60
7 Tajh Boyd .20 .50
8 Teddy Bridgewater .30 .75
9 Ka'Deem Carey .20 .50
10 Derek Carr 1.25 3.00
11 Ha Ha Clinton-Dix .25 .60
12 Brandon Coleman .20 .50
13 Brandin Cooks .30 .75
14 Mike Davis .20 .50
15 Darqueze Dennard .25 .60
16 Eric Ebron .25 .60
17 Mike Evans .50 1.25
18 David Fales .20 .50
19 Tyler Gaffney .20 .50
20 Jimmy Garoppolo 1.50 4.00
21 Justin Gilbert .20 .50
22 Marion Grice .20 .50
23 Robert Herron .20 .50
24 Jeremy Hill .25 .60
25 Tre Mason .20 .50
26 Timmy Jernigan .20 .50
27 Jarvis Landry .40 1.00
28 Marqise Lee .25 .60
29 Khalil Mack .75 2.00
30 Johnny Manziel .30 .75
31 Jordan Matthews .30 .75
32 A.J. McCarron .20 .50
33 Zach Mettenberger .20 .50
34 Donte Moncrief .20 .50
35 Stephen Morris .20 .50
36 C.J. Mosley .25 .60
37 Aaron Murray .20 .50
38 Rajion Neal .20 .50
39 Louis Nix III .20 .50
40 Loucheiz Purifoy .20 .50
41 Paul Richardson .25 .60
42 Marcus Roberson .25 .60
43 Bishop Sankey .20 .50
44 Lache Seastrunk .20 .50
45 Austin Seferian-Jenkins .20 .50
46 Charles Sims .20 .50
47 Logan Thomas .20 .50
48 Stephon Tuitt .30 .75
49 James White .40 1.00
50 Andre Williams .20 .50

2014 Press Pass Blue

*BLUE: .8X TO 2X BASIC CARDS

2014 Press Pass Gold

*GOLD: .8X TO 2X BASIC CARDS

2014 Press Pass Reflectors

*REFLECTOR/199: 1.2X TO 3X BASIC CARDS

2014 Press Pass Reflectors Proof

*PROOF/99: 1.5X TO 4X BASIC CARDS

2014 Press Pass Autographs Blue

BLUE/31-50: .5X TO 1.2X GOLD/140-199
BLUE/15-27: .5X TO 1.2X GOLD AU/75-110

2014 Press Pass Autographs Bronze

*BRONZE/75-99: .5X TO 1.2X GOLD AU/140-199
*BRONZE/50: .4X TO 1X GOLD AU/75-99

2014 Press Pass Autographs Gold

AM A.J. McCarron/99 3.00 8.00
AMU Aaron Murray/199 2.50 6.00
AS Austin Seferian-Jenkins/199 2.50 6.00
AW Andre Williams/199 2.50 6.00
BB Blake Bortles/99 4.00 10.00
BC Brandin Cooks/199 4.00 10.00
BCL Brandon Coleman/199 2.50 6.00
BR Bradley Roby/199 2.50 6.00
BS Bishop Sankey/140 2.50 6.00
CH Cody Hoffman/199 2.50 6.00
CJ Christian Jones/199 3.00 8.00
CM C.J. Mosley/199 3.00 8.00
CS Charles Sims/184* 2.50 6.00
DA Davante Adams/199 4.00 10.00
DA2 Dri Archer/150* 2.50 6.00
DC Derek Carr/25 25.00 50.00
DD Darqueze Dennard/188* 3.00 8.00
DF David Fales/199 2.50 6.00
DM Donte Moncrief/199 2.50 6.00
DS Devin Street/199 2.50 6.00
EE Eric Ebron/185* 3.00 8.00
HC Ha Ha Clinton-Dix/199 3.00 8.00
IC Isaiah Crowell/199 3.00 8.00
JA Jared Abbrederis/199 2.50 6.00
JAM Jace Amaro/199 2.50 6.00
JC Jadeveon Clowney/199 3.00 8.00
JEM Jeff Mathews/199 3.00 8.00
JF James Franklin/199 3.00 8.00
JG Jimmy Garoppolo/199 20.00 50.00
JH Jeremy Hill/72* 4.00 10.00
JL Jarvis Landry/197* 5.00 12.00
JOM Jordan Matthews/199 4.00 10.00
JV Jason Verrett/199 2.50 6.00
JW James White/189* 5.00 12.00
KC Ka'Deem Carey/157* 2.50 6.00
KM Khalil Mack/149* 10.00 25.00
KS Kenny Shaw/199 4.00 10.00
KV Kyle Van Noy/199 3.00 8.00
LN Louis Nix III/197* 2.50 6.00
LP Loucheiz Purifoy/199 2.50 6.00
LS Lache Seastrunk/179* 2.50 6.00
LT Logan Thomas/150* 2.50 6.00
LW L'Damian Washington/149* 3.00 8.00
MC Michael Campanaro/199 2.50 6.00
MD Mike Davis/175 2.50 6.00
ME Mike Evans/99 8.00 20.00
MG Marion Grice/179* 2.50 6.00
ML Marqise Lee/89* 4.00 10.00
MR Marcus Roberson/189* 3.00 8.00
MS Michael Sam/175 2.50 6.00
OB Odell Beckham Jr./175 6.00 15.00
PR Paul Richardson/110 6.00 15.00
RH2 Robert Herron/193* 2.50 6.00
RHA Ra'Shede Hageman/99 3.00 8.00
RN Rajion Neal/151* 2.50 6.00
RS Ryan Shazier/199 4.00 10.00
SM Stephen Morris/189* 2.50 6.00
ST Stephon Tuitt/199 4.00 10.00
TB Teddy Bridgewater/99 5.00 12.00
TB2 Tajh Boyd/199 2.50 6.00
TG Tyler Gaffney/199 2.50 6.00
TIJ Timmy Jernigan/186* 2.50 6.00
TJ TJ Jones/190* 4.00 10.00
TM Trent Murphy/189* 2.50 6.00
TMA Tre Mason/199 EXCH 2.50 6.00
TR Tevin Reese/199 2.50 6.00
TS Telvin Smith/199 2.50 6.00
ZM Zach Mettenberger/174* 2.50 6.00

2014 Press Pass Autographs Silver

*SILVER: .4X TO .1X GOLD AU/140-199
*SILVER: .3X TO .8X GOLD AU/75-110
DC Derek Carr SP 20.00 40.00
JC Jadeveon Clowney 3.00 8.00
JM Johnny Manziel SP 4.00 10.00

2014 Press Pass Playmakers Autographs Gold

*BLUE/50: .4X TO 1X GOLD/75-99
*BLUE/15: .5X TO 1.2X GOLD/25
*RED/25: .5X TO 1.2X GOLD/75-99
BB Blake Bortles/22* 5.00 12.00
BS Bishop Sankey/69* 3.00 8.00
DC Derek Carr/25 25.00 60.00
JC Jadeveon Clowney/20* 5.00 12.00
JM Johnny Manziel/25 6.00 15.00
JMA Jordan Matthews/49* 5.00 12.00
KC Ka'Deem Carey/92 3.00 8.00
ME Mike Evans/75 8.00 20.00
ML Marqise Lee/25 5.00 12.00
TB Teddy Bridgewater/14* 6.00 15.00

2014 Press Pass Power Picks Autographs Gold

*BLUE/50: .4X TO 1X GOLD AU/75
*BLUE/15: .5X TO 1.2X GOLD AU/25
*RED/25: .5X TO 1.2X GOLD AU/75
AM A.J. McCarron/75 3.00 8.00
BB Blake Bortles/22* 5.00 12.00
BS Bishop Sankey/69* 3.00 8.00
DC Derek Carr/5*
JC Jadeveon Clowney/19* 5.00 12.00
JM Johnny Manziel/25 6.00 15.00
ME Mike Evans/75 8.00 20.00
ML Marqise Lee/25 5.00 12.00
TB Teddy Bridgewater/10*
TM Tre Mason/75 EXCH 3.00 8.00

2012 Press Pass Fanfare

*BASE AU: .3X TO .8X BRONZE/59-99
*BASE AU SP: .4X TO 1X BRONZE/59-99
RED INK/20-95: .5X TO 1.2X BASIC AU
FFAL Andrew Luck AU SP 75.00 125.00

2012 Press Pass Fanfare Blue

*BLUE/189-199: .4X TO 1X BRONZE/59-99
RED INK/25-50: .5X TO 1.2X BLUE/189-199

2012 Press Pass Fanfare Bronze

COMMON CARD/59-99 3.00 8.00
SEMISTARS/59-99 4.00 10.00
UNL.STARS/59-99 5.00 12.00
BRONZE STATED PRINT RUN 59-99
FFAB Andre Branch AU/69* 3.00 8.00
FFAC Audie Cole AU/99 3.00 8.00
FFAD Alfonzo Dennard AU/99 3.00 8.00
FFAJ1 Alshon Jeffery AU/99 8.00 20.00
FFAJ2 A.J. Jenkins AU/46* 3.00 8.00
FFAL Andrew Luck AU/98* 75.00 135.00
FFBO Brock Osweiler AU/99 3.00 8.00
FFBQ Brian Quick AU/99 3.00 8.00
FFBT Brandon Thompson AU/99 4.00 10.00
FFBW1 Brandon Weeden AU/99 3.00 8.00
FFBW2 Billy Winn AU/83* 5.00 12.00
FFCF Coby Fleener AU/94* 3.00 8.00
FFCG1 Chris Givens AU/90* 3.00 8.00
FFCG2 Cyrus Gray AU/99 3.00 8.00
FFCH Casey Hayward AU/87* 3.00 8.00
FFCJ Coryell Judie AU/99 3.00 8.00
FFCK Case Keenum AU/99 6.00 15.00
FFCU Courtney Upshaw AU/99 4.00 10.00
FFDA Dwayne Allen AU/97* 3.00 8.00
FFDH1 Dan Herron AU/99 3.00 8.00
FFDH2 Dont'a Hightower AU/99 5.00 12.00
FFDM Doug Martin AU/99 5.00 12.00
FFDP Dontari Poe AU/75* 3.00 8.00
FFDP1 Dan Persa AU/94*
FFDP2 DeVier Posey AU/88* 3.00 8.00
FFDS Devon Still AU/99 4.00 10.00
FFEA Emmanuel Acho AU/99 3.00 8.00
FFFC Fletcher Cox AU/82* 5.00 12.00
FFGR Gerell Robinson AU/75 3.00 8.00
FFHS Harrison Smith AU/99 3.00 8.00
FFIP Isaiah Pead AU/64* 3.00 8.00
FFJA Joe Adams AU/84* 3.00 8.00
FFJC Jared Crick AU/99 3.00 8.00
FFJE Jeremy Ebert AU/95* 3.00 8.00
FFJF Jeff Fuller AU/75* 3.00 8.00
FFJH Jayron Hosley AU/99 5.00 12.00
FFJJ Janoris Jenkins AU/88* 4.00 10.00
FFKC Kirk Cousins AU/99 12.00 30.00
FFKK Kevin Koger AU/97*
FFKM Kellen Moore AU/97* 4.00 10.00
FFKR Kendall Reyes AU/91* 3.00 8.00
FFKW Kendall Wright AU/97* 3.00 8.00
FFLD Lavonte David AU/99 5.00 12.00
FFLK Luke Kuechly AU/81* 8.00 20.00
FFLM Lamar Miller AU/97* 5.00 12.00
FFMB Mark Barron AU/49* 3.00 8.00
FFME Michael Egnew AU/99 3.00 8.00
FFMF Michael Floyd AU/99 3.00 8.00
FFMI Melvin Ingram AU/94* 3.00 8.00
FFMJ Marvin Jones AU/88* 3.00 8.00
FFMM Marquis Maze AU/99 3.00 8.00
FFMS Mohamed Sanu AU/88* 5.00 12.00
FFNF Nick Foles AU/85* 8.00 20.00
FFNT Nick Toon AU/99 3.00 8.00
FFOC Orson Charles AU/50* 3.00 8.00
FFQC Quinton Coples AU/99 3.00 8.00
FFRB Ryan Broyles AU/55* 3.00 8.00
FFRL Ryan Lindley AU/84* 3.00 8.00
FFRR Rueben Randle AU/75* 6.00 15.00
FFRT Ryan Tannehill AU/99 5.00 12.00
FFRW Russell Wilson AU/99 25.00 60.00
FFSG Stephon Gilmore AU/99 4.00 10.00
FFSH Stephen Hill AU/51* 3.00 8.00
FFTG T.J. Graham AU/99 3.00 8.00
FFTH T.Y. Hilton AU/59 6.00 15.00
FFTL Travis Lewis AU/78* 4.00 10.00
FFTS Tommy Streeter AU/99 3.00 8.00
FFVB Vick Ballard AU/98* 4.00 10.00
FFWM Whitney Mercilus AU/99 3.00 8.00
FFZB Zach Brown AU/93* 3.00 8.00

2012 Press Pass Fanfare Purple

*PURPLE/20-25: .8X TO 2X BRONZE/59-99
FFAL Andrew Luck AU* 125.00 200.00
FFJB Justin Blackmon AU/23* 6.00 15.00
FFJW Jarius Wright AU/25 UER 6.00 15.00
FFLJ LaMichael James AU/15* 6.00 15.00
FFRG Robert Griffin III AU/25 8.00 20.00
FFTR Trent Richardson AU/25 6.00 15.00

2012 Press Pass Fanfare Gridiron Graphs Blue

BLUE STATED PRINT RUN 50
*RED/25: .5X TO 1.2X BLUE/50
*SILVER/99: .3X TO .8X BLUE/50
AJ Alshon Jeffery 10.00 25.00
AL Andrew Luck 75.00 150.00
JB Justin Blackmon/48* 5.00 12.00
KW Kendall Wright/45* 5.00 12.00
LJ LaMichael James 5.00 12.00
LM Lamar Miller 8.00 20.00
MF Michael Floyd 5.00 12.00
NF Nick Foles 12.00 30.00
NT Nick Toon 5.00 12.00
QC Quinton Coples 5.00 12.00
RG Robert Griffin III 6.00 15.00
TR Trent Richardson/47* 5.00 12.00

2012 Press Pass Fanfare Next Level Ink Blue

BLUE STATED PRINT RUN 50
*RED/25: .5X TO 1.2X BLUE/50
*SILVER/99: .3X TO .8X BLUE/50
AJ Alshon Jeffery 10.00 25.00
AL Andrew Luck 75.00 150.00
JB Justin Blackmon/49* 5.00 12.00
LJ LaMichael James 5.00 12.00
LM Lamar Miller/47* 8.00 20.00
MF Michael Floyd 5.00 12.00
QC Quinton Coples 5.00 12.00
RG Robert Griffin III/48* 6.00 15.00
TR Trent Richardson/49* 5.00 12.00

2012 Press Pass Fanfare Paydirt Autographs Blue

BLUE STATED PRINT RUN 50
*RED/25: .5X TO 1.2X BLUE/50
*SILVER/99: .3X TO .8X BLUE/50
AL Andrew Luck 75.00 150.00
BW Brandon Weeden 5.00 12.00
CK Case Keenum 10.00 25.00
JB Justin Blackmon/49* 5.00 12.00
KM Kellen Moore/49* 6.00 15.00
KW Kendall Wright/46* 5.00 12.00
LJ LaMichael James 5.00 12.00
RG Robert Griffin III 6.00 15.00
RW Russell Wilson 50.00 100.00
TR Trent Richardson/47* 5.00 12.00

2013 Press Pass Fanfare

*BASE GOLD: .25X TO .6X PURPLE/20-25
*BASE GOLD SP: .3X TO .8X PURPLE/20-25
*RED INK: .5X TO 1.2X GOLD AU
FFEL Eddie Lacy AU SP 3.00 8.00

2013 Press Pass Fanfare Aqua

*AQUA/50-99: .8X TO .8X PURPLE/20-25
*RED INK: .5X TO 1.2X AQUA/50-99
FFDR1 Denard Robinson AU/99 3.00 8.00
FFLJ Landry Jones AU/99 3.00 8.00
FFMM Michael Mauti AU/96* 5.00 12.00
FFTB Tyler Bray AU/45* 3.00 8.00

2013 Press Pass Fanfare Blue

*BLUE/99-199: .3X TO .8X PURPLE/20-25
*RED INK: .5X TO 1.2X BLUE/99-199
FFDR1 Denard Robinson AU/149 3.00 8.00
FFLJ Landry Jones AU/149 3.00 8.00
FFTB Tyler Bray AU/69* 3.00 8.00

2013 Press Pass Fanfare Purple

FFAD Aaron Dobson AU/20* 4.00 10.00
FFAE Andre Ellington AU/25 4.00 10.00
FFAO1 Alec Ogletree/25 4.00 10.00
FFAO2 Alex Okafor AU/25 4.00 10.00
FFBW Bjoern Werner AU/25 4.00 10.00
FFCH Cobi Hamilton AU/25 4.00 10.00
FFCK Collin Klein AU/25 5.00 12.00
FFCP Cordarrelle Patterson AU/25 4.00 10.00
FFDH DeAndre Hopkins AU/25 10.00 25.00
FFDJ Dion Jordan AU/25 4.00 10.00
FFDM1 Dee Milliner AU/20* 4.00 10.00
FFDM2 Damontre Moore AU/25 4.00 10.00
FFDR1 Denard Robinson AU/25
FFDR2 Da'Rick Rogers AU/25 4.00 10.00
FFDS1 Dion Sims AU/25 4.00 10.00
FFDS2 D.J. Swearinger AU/20* 4.00 10.00
FFDT Desmond Trufant AU/25 4.00 10.00
FFEH Erik Highsmith AU/25 5.00 12.00
FFEL Eddie Lacy AU/25 4.00 10.00
FFER Eric Reid AU/25 5.00 12.00
FFGB Giovani Bernard AU/25 4.00 10.00
FFGS Geno Smith AU/25 4.00 10.00
FFJF Johnathan Franklin AU/25 4.00 10.00
FFJH Justin Hunter AU/20* 4.00 10.00
FFJJ1 Jawan Jamison AU/25 4.00 10.00
FFJJ2 Jarvis Jones AU/25 4.00 10.00
FFJP Jordan Poyer AU/25 4.00 10.00
FFJR1 Joseph Randle AU/25 4.00 10.00
FFJR2 Jordan Rodgers AU/20* 8.00 20.00
FFJW Jesse Williams AU/24* 6.00 15.00
FFKA Keenan Allen AU/25 8.00 20.00
FFKB Kenjon Barner AU/25 4.00 10.00
FFKS1 Kawann Short AU/25 4.00 10.00
FFKS2 Kenny Stills AU/25 4.00 10.00
FFKV Kenny Vaccaro AU/25 8.00 20.00
FFLB Le'Veon Bell AU/25 12.00 30.00
FFLJ Landry Jones AU/25
FFMB1 Montee Ball AU/25 4.00 10.00
FFMB2 Matt Barkley AU/24* 30.00 60.00
FFMD Marcus Davis AU/25 6.00 15.00
FFMG Mike Glennon AU/15* 4.00 10.00
FFML Marcus Lattimore AU/25 10.00 25.00
FFMM Michael Mauti AU/20*
FFMT Manti Te'o AU/2*
FFMW Markus Wheaton AU/23* 4.00 10.00
FFQP Quinton Patton AU/25 6.00 15.00
FFRB Rex Burkhead AU/25 5.00 12.00
FFRG Ray Graham AU/25 4.00 10.00
FFRN Ryan Nassib AU/25 4.00 10.00
FFRS Ryan Swope AU/25 4.00 10.00
FFRW Robert Woods AU/25 6.00 15.00
FFSB Stedman Bailey AU/25 12.00 30.00
FFSF Sharrif Floyd AU/25 4.00 10.00
FFSJ Stepfhon Jefferson AU/25 5.00 12.00
FFSR Sheldon Richardson AU/20 4.00 10.00
FFST Stepfan Taylor AU/23* 4.00 10.00
FFSW Sylvester Williams AU/25 4.00 10.00
FFTA Tavon Austin AU/25 5.00 12.00
FFTB Tyler Bray AU/20*
FFTE Tyler Eifert AU/25 10.00 25.00
FFTK Tavarres King AU/25 4.00 10.00
FFTW1 Terrance Williams AU/25 4.00 10.00
FFTW2 Tyler Wilson AU/25 4.00 10.00
FFZD Zac Dysert AU/25 4.00 10.00
FFZE Zach Ertz AU/25 8.00 20.00

2013 Press Pass Fanfare Purple Red Ink

ANNOUNCED PRINT RUN 1-25
FFDA David Amerson/25 6.00 15.00
FFMT Manti Te'o/23* 5.00 12.00

2013 Press Pass Fanfare Gridiron Graphs Red

*BLUE/50: .3X TO .8X RED/25
*SILVER/99-119: .3X TO .8X RED/25
GGAE Andre Ellington
GGGS Geno Smith/23 4.00 10.00
GGJH Justin Hunter 4.00 10.00
GGKA Keenan Allen 8.00 20.00
GGKB Kenjon Barner 4.00 10.00
GGMB2 Montee Ball 4.00 10.00
GGMB Matt Barkley/24* 30.00 60.00
GGMT Manti Te'o 5.00 12.00
GGST Stepfan Taylor 4.00 10.00
GGTW Terrance Williams 4.00 10.00

2013 Press Pass Fanfare Potent Passers Autographs Red

*BLUE/30-50: .3X TO .8X RED/25
*SILVER/69-99: .3X TO .8X RED/25
PPCK Collin Klein 6.00 12.00
PPDR Denard Robinson
PPEM EJ Manuel 4.00 10.00
PPGS Geno Smith 4.00 10.00
PPLJ Landry Jones 4.00 10.00
PPMB Matt Barkley/22* 30.00 60.00
PPMG Mike Glennon 4.00 10.00
PPRN Ryan Nassib 4.00 10.00
PPTB Tyler Bray 4.00 10.00
PPTW Tyler Wilson 4.00 10.00
PPZD Zac Dysert 4.00 10.00

2013 Press Pass Fanfare Saturday Starters Autographs Red

*BLUE/50: .3X TO .8X RED/25
*SILVER/89-99: .3X TO .8X RED/25
SSCK Collin Klein 5.00 12.00
SSEL Eddie Lacy 4.00 10.00
SSGB Giovani Bernard 4.00 10.00
SSGS Geno Smith 4.00 10.00
SSJH Justin Hunter
SSKA Keenan Allen 8.00 20.00
SSMB Matt Barkley 30.00 60.00
SSML Marcus Lattimore/18* 10.00 25.00
SSMLR Marcus Lattimore Red/7*
SSMT Manti Te'o/11* 5.00 12.00
SSMTR Manti Te'o Red/14* 5.00 12.00
SSRW Robert Woods/18* 6.00 15.00
SSRWR Robert Woods Red/7*
SSTA Tavon Austin 5.00 12.00
SSTW Terrance Williams 4.00 10.00

2009 Press Pass Fusion

COMPLETE SET (90) 15.00 40.00
37 Mike Alstott .15 .40
38 Kenny Britt .30 .75
39 Donald Brown .30 .75
40 Michael Crabtree .75 2.00
41 Matt Forte .30 .75
42 Josh Freeman .50 1.25
43 Frank Gifford .15 .40
44 Shonn Greene .30 .75
45 Darrius Heyward-Bey .25 .60
46 James Laurinaitis .30 .75
47 Jeremy Maclin .30 .75
48 LeSean McCoy .50 1.25
49 Darren McFadden .15 .40
50 Joe Montana .75 2.00
51 Matt Ryan .30 .75
52 Mark Sanchez 1.00 2.50
53 Deion Sanders .30 .75
54 Steve Slaton .15 .40
55 Kevin Smith .15 .40
56 Matthew Stafford 1.00 2.50
57 Jonathan Stewart .15 .40
58 Doug Williams .15 .40
59 Don Maynard .15 .40
61 Joe Flacco .30 .75
62 John Elway .75 2.00

2009 Press Pass Fusion Bronze

*BRONZE: 1X TO 2.5X BASE
STATED PRINT RUN 150 SER. #'d SETS

2009 Press Pass Fusion Gold

*GOLD: 2X TO 5X BASE
STATED PRINT RUN 50 SER. #'d SETS

2009 Press Pass Fusion Green

*GREEN: 3X TO 8X BASE
STATED PRINT RUN 25 SER. #'d SETS

2009 Press Pass Fusion Silver

*SILVER: 1.25X TO 3X BASE
STATED PRINT RUN 99 SER. #'d SETS

2009 Press Pass Fusion Autographs Gold

STATED PRINT RUN 10-199
EXCHANGE DEADLINE 12/1/10
SSDM Don Maynard/199 6.00 15.00
SSJE John Elway/49 75.00 125.00
SSJM Joe Montana/26 75.00 125.00

2009 Press Pass Fusion Autographs Green

STATED PRINT RUN 5-100
EXCHANGE DEADLINE 12/1/2010
SSDM Don Maynard/100 8.00 20.00
SSJE John Elway/25 100.00 150.00

2009 Press Pass Fusion Autographs Silver

RANDOM INSERT IN PACKS
EXCHANGE DEADLINE 12/1/2010
SSDM Don Maynard 6.00 15.00
SSDS2 Deion Sanders 25.00 50.00
SSFG Frank Gifford 25.00 50.00
SSJM Joe Montana 50.00 100.00

2009 Press Pass Fusion Classic Champions

COMPLETE SET (10) 6.00 15.00
STATED ODDS 1:10
CCH2 Doug Williams .60 1.50
CCH10 Deion Sanders 1.00 2.50

2009 Press Pass Fusion Collegiate Connections

COMPLETE SET (10) 6.00 15.00
STATED ODDS 1:10
CCN2 J.Montana/C.Yastrzemski 2.50 6.00
CCN4 F.Gifford/T.Seaver 1.00 2.50
CCN6 W.Reed/D.Williams .60 1.50
CCN7 D.Maynard/N.Archibald .60 1.50

2009 Press Pass Fusion Cross Training

COMPLETE SET (10) 6.00 15.00
STATED ODDS 1:10
CT3 D.Rose/D.Sanders 1.00 2.50
CT9 J.Elway/M.Stafford 2.50 6.00

2009 Press Pass Fusion Renowned Rivals

COMPLETE SET (10) 6.00 15.00
STATED ODDS 1:10
RR5 J.Montana/J.Elway 2.50 6.00

2009 Press Pass Fusion Revered Relics Gold

STATED PRINT RUN 5-50
*HOLOFOIL/25: .5X TO 1.2X BASIC RELIC
RRDB Donald Brown 4.00 10.00
RRJF Josh Freeman 6.00 15.00
RRLM LeSean McCoy 6.00 15.00
RRMC Michael Crabtree 6.00 15.00
RRMS Matthew Stafford 6.00 15.00
RRMS Mark Sanchez 8.00 20.00
RRSS Steve Slaton 6.00 15.00

2009 Press Pass Fusion Revered Relics Silver

STATED PRINT RUN 15-299
RRJF Josh Freeman/35 6.00 15.00
RRJL James Laurinaitis/99 4.00 10.00
RRLM LeSean McCoy/75 4.00 10.00
RRMA Mike Alstott/150 4.00 10.00
RRMC Michael Crabtree/65 6.00 15.00
RRMS Mark Sanchez/299 6.00 15.00
RRMS Matthew Stafford/199 6.00 15.00
RRSS Steve Slaton/55 4.00 10.00

2009 Press Pass Fusion Timeless Talent

COMPLETE SET (10) 6.00 15.00
STATED ODDS 1:10
TT3 Frank Gifford .60 1.50
TT9 Matt Ryan 1.00 2.50
TT10 Mark Sanchez 2.50 6.00

2009 Press Pass Fusion Timeless Talent Autographs Gold

STATED PRINT RUN 15-99

2009 Press Pass Fusion Timeless Talent Autographs Green

STATED PRINT RUN 10-50

2009 Press Pass Fusion Timeless Talent Autographs Silver

STATED PRINT RUN 26-193		
TTFG Frank Gifford/28	25.00	50.00

2013 Press Pass Gameday Gallery Gold

STATED PRINT RUN 20-99		
EXCH EXPIRATION: 12/31/2014		
GOLD RED INK/40-53*: .4X TO 1X GLD AU		
GOLD RED INK/15-35*: .5X TO 1.2X GLD AU		
AE Andre Ellington/91*	2.50	6.00
AO Alec Ogletree/87*	2.50	6.00
BM Barkevious Mingo/19*	3.00	8.00
BW Bjoern Werner/99	2.50	6.00
CH Cobi Hamilton/51*	2.50	6.00
CK Collin Klein/69*	3.00	8.00
CP Cordarrelle Patterson/56	2.50	6.00
DM Dee Milliner/55*	2.50	6.00
DR Denard Robinson EXCH	2.50	6.00
DT Desmond Trufant/51*	2.50	6.00
EL Eddie Lacy/71*	2.50	6.00
EM EJ Manuel/27*	3.00	8.00
ER Eric Reid/98*	3.00	8.00
GB Giovani Bernard/37	3.00	8.00
GS Geno Smith/25		
JF Johnathan Franklin/99	2.50	6.00
JH Justin Huntor/73*	2.50	6.00
JJ Jawan Jamison/26*	3.00	8.00
JJO Jarvis Jones EXCH	2.50	6.00
JR Joseph Randle/57	2.50	6.00
KA Keenan Allen/71*	5.00	12.00
KB Kenjon Barner/65*	2.50	6.00
KST Kenny Stills/68*	2.50	6.00
KV Kenny Vaccaro EXCH	2.50	6.00
LB Le'Veon Bell EXCH	8.00	20.00
LJ Landry Jones/52*	2.50	6.00
MB Matt Barkley/27*	3.00	8.00
MBA Montee Ball EXCH	2.50	6.00
ML Marcus Lattimore/20	3.00	8.00
MT Manti Te'o/28*	4.00	10.00
MW Markus Wheaton/81*	2.50	6.00
QP Quinton Patton/91*	2.50	6.00
RB Rex Burkhead/52*	10.00	25.00
RN Ryan Nassib/64*	2.50	6.00
RS Ryan Swope/99	2.50	6.00
RW Robert Woods/82*	4.00	10.00
SB Stedman Bailey/76*	2.50	6.00
SF Sharrif Floyd/99	2.50	6.00
SR Sheldon Richardson/91*	2.50	6.00
ST Stepfan Taylor/85*	2.50	6.00
SW Sylvester Williams/80*	2.50	6.00
TA Tavon Austin EXCH	4.00	10.00
TE Tyler Eifert/99	2.50	6.00
TK Tavarres King/96*	2.50	6.00
TR Theo Riddick/99	2.50	6.00
TW Terrance Williams/15*	3.00	8.00
TWI Tyler Wilson/89	2.50	6.00
ZD Zac Dysert/97*	2.50	6.00

2013 Press Pass Gameday Gallery Bronze

AD Aaron Dobson/199	4.00	10.00
BW Bjoern Werner/65	2.50	6.00
DT Desmond Trufant/25	3.00	8.00
JF Johnathan Franklin/19*	3.00	8.00
TR Theo Riddick/25	3.00	8.00
ZD Zac Dysert/65	2.50	6.00

2013 Press Pass Gameday Gallery Bronze Red Ink

ER Eric Reid/40	6.00	15.00
JF Johnathan Franklin/46*	2.50	6.00

2013 Press Pass Gameday Gallery Red

RED ANNC'd PRINT RUN 3-50		
AE Andre Ellington/50	2.50	6.00
AO Alec Ogletree/39*	2.50	6.00
BM Barkevious Mingo/50	2.50	6.00
CH Cobi Hamilton/50	2.50	6.00
CK Collin Klein/35*	3.00	8.00
DJ Dion Jordan/25*	3.00	8.00
DR Denard Robinson EXCH	2.50	6.00
EA Ezekiel Ansah/24*	2.50	6.00
ER Eric Reid/50	3.00	8.00
GB Giovani Bernard/25	3.00	8.00
GB2 Giovani Bernard NH/25	3.00	8.00
JF Johnathan Franklin/50	2.50	6.00
JH Justin Hunter/42*	2.50	6.00
JJ Jawan Jamison/50	2.50	6.00
JR Joseph Randle/26*	3.00	8.00
KA Keenan Allen/19*	6.00	15.00
KA2 Keenan Allen NH/18*	6.00	15.00
KB Kenjon Barner/40*	2.50	6.00
KST Kenny Stills/41*	2.50	6.00
KV Kenny Vaccaro EXCH	2.50	6.00
LB Le'Veon Bell	8.00	20.00
MB2 Matt Barkley NH/25	3.00	8.00
MBA Montee Ball EXCH	2.50	6.00
MG2 Mike Glennon NH/25	3.00	8.00
MT Manti Te'o/20*	4.00	10.00
MT2 Manti Te'o NH/20*	4.00	10.00
MW Markus Wheaton/27*	2.50	6.00
RB Rex Burkhead/50	10.00	25.00
RN Ryan Nassib/38*	2.50	6.00
RS Ryan Swope/16*	3.00	8.00
RW Robert Woods/31*	4.00	10.00
SB Stedman Bailey/28*	3.00	8.00
SF Sharrif Floyd/50	2.50	6.00
ST Stepfan Taylor/32*	2.50	6.00
SW Sylvester Williams/50	2.50	6.00
TE Tyler Eifert/50	2.50	6.00
TWI Tyler Wilson/50	2.50	6.00

2013 Press Pass Gameday Gallery Red Red Ink

RED INK/31-47*: .4X TO 1X RED AU
RED INK/15-26*: .5X TO 1.2X RED AU

2013 Press Pass Gameday Gallery Silver

AO Alec Ogletree/15	3.00	8.00
DT Desmond Trufant/40	2.50	6.00
EA Ezekiel Ansah/30*	3.00	8.00
JH Justin Hunter/119*	2.50	6.00
RB Rex Burkhead/90	3.00	8.00
RS Ryan Swope/75	2.50	6.00
SB Stedman Bailey/34	3.00	8.00
SF Sharrif Floyd/99*	2.50	6.00
TE Tyler Eifert/87	2.50	6.00
TK Tavarres King/149	2.50	6.00
TR Theo Riddick/41	2.50	6.00
ZE Zach Ertz/65*	5.00	12.00
TWI Tyler Wilson/92	2.50	6.00

2014 Press Pass Gameday Gallery Bronze

*BRONZE: .3X TO .8X GOLD AU		
GGJM2 Johnny Manziel SP	4.00	10.00

2014 Press Pass Gameday Gallery Blue

BLUE/15-25: .5X TO 1.2X GOLD AU		
GGMS Michael Sam/25	12.00	30.00

2014 Press Pass Gameday Gallery Gold

*RED INK: .5X TO 1.2X BASIC GOLD AU		
GGAJ Austin Seferian-Jenkins/76*	2.50	6.00
GGAM1 Aaron Murray/99	2.50	6.00
GGAM2 A.J. McCarron/25	20.00	40.00
GGAW Andre Williams/54*	2.50	6.00
GGBB Blake Bortles/25	4.00	10.00
GGBC Brandin Cooks/94*	4.00	10.00
GGBC Brandon Coleman/99	2.50	6.00
GGBR Bradley Roby/99	2.50	6.00
GGBS Bishop Sankey/50	2.50	6.00
GGCH Cody Hoffman/99	2.50	6.00
GGCJ Christian Jones/99	3.00	8.00
GGCM C.J. Mosley/99	3.00	8.00
GGCS Charles Sims/89*	2.50	6.00
GGDA1 Davante Adams/99	4.00	10.00
GGDA2 Dri Archer/84*	2.50	6.00
GGDC Derek Carr/15	15.00	40.00
GGDD Darqueze Dennard/99	3.00	8.00
GGDF David Fales/99	2.50	6.00
GGDM Donte Moncrief/99	2.50	6.00
GGDS Devin Street/91*	2.50	6.00
GGEE Eric Ebron/82*	3.00	8.00
GGHH Ha Ha Clinton-Dix/92*	3.00	8.00
GGIC Isaiah Crowell/99	3.00	8.00
GGJA1 Jace Amaro/99	2.50	6.00
GGJA2 Jared Abbrederis/98*	2.50	6.00
GGJC Jadeveon Clowney/25	4.00	10.00
GGJF James Franklin/76*	3.00	8.00
GGJG Jimmy Garoppolo/95*	10.00	25.00
GGJH Jeremy Hill/25	4.00	10.00
GGJL Jarvis Landry/99	5.00	12.00
GGJM1 Jeff Mathews/99	3.00	8.00
GGJM2 Johnny Manziel/25	5.00	12.00
GGJM3 Jordan Matthews/50	4.00	10.00
GGJV Jason Verrett/99	2.50	6.00
GGJW James White/99	5.00	12.00
GGKC Ka'Deem Carey/99	2.50	6.00
GGKM Khalil Mack/99	10.00	25.00
GGKN Kyle Van Noy/99	3.00	8.00
GGKS Kenny Shaw/99	4.00	10.00
GGLN Louis Nix III/99	2.50	6.00
GGLP Loucheiz Purifoy/99	2.50	6.00
GGLS Lache Seastrunk/99	2.50	6.00
GGLT Logan Thomas/94*	2.50	6.00
GGLW L'Damian Washington/44*	4.00	10.00
GGMC Michael Campanaro/99	2.50	6.00
GGMD Mike Davis/99	2.50	6.00
GGME Mike Evans/50	6.00	15.00
GGMG Marion Grice/99	2.50	6.00
GGML Marqise Lee/25	4.00	10.00
GGMR Marcus Roberson/99		
GGMS Michael Sam/50		
GGOB Odell Beckham Jr./99	6.00	15.00
GGPR Paul Richardson/99	5.00	12.00
GGRH1 Ra'Shede Hageman/99		
GGRH2 Robert Herron/99	2.50	6.00
GGRN Rajion Neal/96*	2.50	6.00
GGRS Ryan Shazier/99	4.00	10.00
GGSM Stephen Morris/99	2.50	6.00
GGST Stephon Tuitt/99	4.00	10.00
GGTB1 Tajh Boyd/99	2.50	6.00
GGTB2 Teddy Bridgewater/25	5.00	12.00
GGTG Tyler Gaffney/99	2.50	6.00
GGTJ1 Timmy Jernigan/90*	2.50	6.00
GGTJ2 TJ Jones/99	4.00	10.00
GGTM Trent Murphy/88*	2.50	6.00
GGTR Tevin Reese/99	2.50	6.00
GGTS Telvin Smith/20*		
GGZM Zach Mettenberger/95*	2.50	6.00

2014 Press Pass Gameday Gallery Silver

*SILVER/150: .3X TO .8X GOLD/99		
*SILVER/75-99: .4X TO 1X GOLD/50		
*SILVER/50: .3X TO .8X GOLD/25		
*SILVER/25: .4X TO 1X GOLD/15		
GGJC Jadeveon Clowney/50	3.00	8.00
GGJM2 Johnny Manziel/50	4.00	10.00
GGTB2 Teddy Bridgewater/50	4.00	10.00

2014 Press Pass Gameday Gallery Fantasy Team Gold

*BLUE/50: .4X TO 1X GOLD AU/75-99		
*BLUE/15: .4X TO 1X GOLD AU/25		
*RED/25: .5X TO 1.2X GOLD/75-99		
FTBB Blake Bortles/21*	4.00	10.00
FTBS Bishop Sankey/69*	2.50	6.00
FTJM1 Johnny Manziel/25	5.00	12.00
FTJM2 Jordan Matthews/99	4.00	10.00
FTKC Ka'Deem Carey/91	2.50	6.00
FTME Mike Evans/75	6.00	15.00
FTML Marqise Lee/25	4.00	10.00
FTTB Teddy Bridgewater/25	5.00	12.00

2014 Press Pass Gameday Gallery Primetime Players Gold

*BLUE/15-50: .4X TO 1X GOLD AU		
*GREEN/20: .5X TO 1.2X GOLD AU/75		
*RED/25: .5X TO 1.2X GOLD AU/75		
PTPAM A.J. McCarron/72*	2.50	6.00
PTPBB Blake Bortles/24*	4.00	10.00
PTPBS Bishop Sankey/69*	2.50	6.00
PTPJC Jadeveon Clowney/20*	4.00	10.00
PTPJM Johnny Manziel/25	5.00	12.00
PTPME Mike Evans/75	6.00	15.00
PTPML Marqise Lee/25	4.00	10.00
PTPTB Teddy Bridgewater/25	5.00	12.00

2012 Press Pass Industry Summit

*IS/15: .8X TO 2X BASIC CARD/50		
20 Robert Griffin III	.50	1.25
30 Andrew Luck	4.00	10.00
41 Trent Richardson	.40	1.00

2002 Press Pass JE

Press Pass JE was released as a 45-card set featuring top NFL draft picks. The standard sized cards were printed on premium 24 pt.stock. The card fronts feature a colored three-sided border with a full color action shot of the player. The Press Pass logo is in the upper left hand corner. The player's name and position is printed in silver lettering along the bottom half of the card. The card backs carry college statistics and pertinent information highlighting each players most impressive skills. Press Pass JE cards were released in both Hobby and Retail form.

COMPLETE SET (45)	10.00	25.00
1 David Carr	.25	.60
2 Julius Peppers	.60	1.50
3 Joey Harrington	.25	.60
4 Mike Williams	.25	.60
5 Quentin Jammer	.40	1.00
6 Ryan Sims	.40	1.00
7 Bryant McKinnie	.25	.60
8 Roy Williams	.25	.60
9 John Henderson	.30	.75
10 Wendell Bryant	.25	.60
11 Donte Stallworth	.40	1.00
12 Jeremy Shockey	.40	1.00
13 William Green	.30	.75
14 Phillip Buchanon	.40	1.00
15 T.J. Duckett	.25	.60
16 Ashley Lelie	.25	.60
17 Javon Walker	.40	1.00
18 Daniel Graham	.30	.75
19 Jerramy Stevens	.40	1.00
20 Patrick Ramsey	.30	.75
21 Jabar Gaffney	.25	.60
22 DeShaun Foster	.40	1.00
23 Kalimba Edwards	.30	.75
24 Josh Reed	.30	.75
25 Mike Pearson	.25	.60
26 Andre Davis	.25	.60
27 Reche Caldwell	.30	.75
28 Clinton Portis	.40	1.00
29 Maurice Morris	.30	.75
30 Ladell Betts	.40	1.00
31 Antwaan Randle El	.30	.75
32 Antonio Bryant	.40	1.00
33 Josh McCown	.40	1.00
34 Lamar Gordon	.30	.75
35 Marquise Walker	.25	.60
36 Cliff Russell	.25	.60
37 Brian Westbrook	.50	1.25
38 Eric Crouch	.40	1.00
39 Jonathan Wells	.30	.75
40 David Garrard	.30	.75
41 Rohan Davey	.40	1.00
42 Ron Johnson	.30	.75
43 Kurt Kittner	.25	.60
44 Adrian Peterson	.30	.75
45 David Carr CL	.20	.50

2002 Press Pass JE Autographs

Press Pass JE was released as a 43-card set featuring autographs of the top NFL draft picks. The standard-sized autographed cards were printed on premium 24 pt stock and were inserted in hobby packs only at a rate of 1:6. A few cards were issued via exchange cards with an expiration date of 6/1/2003. A silver parallel version was also produced with each silver card being serial numbered of 50.

STATED ODDS 1:6 HOBBY		
*SILVER AU/50: .8X TO 2X BASIC AUTO		
SILVER AUTO PRINT RUN 50		
1 Damien Anderson	2.50	6.00
2 Antonio Bryant	4.00	10.00
3 Phillip Buchanon	4.00	10.00
4 Reche Caldwell	3.00	8.00
5 Rocky Calmus	3.00	8.00
6 David Carr	2.50	6.00
7 Terry Charles	2.50	6.00
8 Eric Crouch	4.00	10.00
9 Najeh Davenport	2.50	6.00
10 Rohan Davey	4.00	10.00
11 Andre Davis	2.50	6.00
12 Kalimba Edwards	3.00	8.00
13 Jabar Gaffney	2.50	6.00
14 David Garrard	3.00	8.00
15 Lamar Gordon	3.00	8.00
16 Daniel Graham	3.00	8.00
17 William Green	3.00	8.00
18 Joey Harrington	2.50	6.00
19 John Henderson	3.00	8.00
20 Leonard Henry	2.50	6.00
21 Quentin Jammer	4.00	10.00
22 Ron Johnson	3.00	8.00
23 Kyle Johnson	2.50	6.00
24 Levi Jones	2.50	6.00
25 Kurt Kittner	2.50	6.00
26 Josh McCown	4.00	10.00
27 Freddie Milons	2.50	6.00
28 Maurice Morris	3.00	8.00
29 Mike Pearson	2.50	6.00
30 Adrian Peterson	3.00	8.00
31 Patrick Ramsey	3.00	8.00
32 Antwaan Randle El	3.00	8.00
33 Josh Reed	3.00	8.00
34 Cliff Russell	2.50	6.00
35 Josh Scobey	3.00	8.00
36 Ryan Sims	4.00	10.00
37 Luke Staley	2.50	6.00
38 Donte Stallworth	4.00	10.00
39 Marquise Walker	2.50	6.00
40 Anthony Weaver	2.50	6.00
41 Jonathan Wells	3.00	8.00
42 Brian Westbrook	12.00	30.00
43 Roy Williams	6.00	15.00

2002 Press Pass JE Class of 2002

is 9-card insert set was randomly inserted in packs at a rate of 1:8. The standard sized cards feature future stars of the NFL on microetched foil cards.

COMPLETE SET (9)	5.00	12.00
STATED ODDS 1:8		
CL1 David Carr	.40	1.00
CL2 T.J. Duckett	.40	1.00
CL3 Jabar Gaffney	.40	1.00
CL4 William Green	.50	1.25
CL5 Joey Harrington	.40	1.00
CL6 Ashley Lelie	.40	1.00
CL7 Julius Peppers	1.00	2.50
CL8 Jeremy Shockey	.60	1.50
CL9 Donte Stallworth	.60	1.50

2002 Press Pass JE Class of 2002 Autographs

This insert set is an autographed version of the Class 2002 set with at least one additional player. The standard sized cards feature future stars of the NFL on microetched foil cards. The cards are serial numbered to 200.

STATED PRINT RUN 200 SER.#'d SETS		
AB Antonio Bryant	5.00	12.00
AD Andre Davis	3.00	8.00
DC David Carr	3.00	8.00
DS Donte Stallworth	5.00	12.00
JH Joey Harrington	3.00	8.00
JR Josh Reed	4.00	10.00
KK Kurt Kittner	3.00	8.00
WG William Green	4.00	10.00
DRC Donald Reche Caldwell	3.00	8.00

2002 Press Pass JE Game Used Jerseys

This 19-card insert set was randomly inserted in hobby packs only at a rate of 1:24 and is serially numbered to 500. The standard sized cards feature game-used jersey cards from this year's best new rookies.

JERSEY/500 ODDS 1:24 HOBBY		
STATED PRINT RUN 500 SER.#'d SETS		
*NAMES/25: 1X TO 2.5X BASIC JSY		
NAMES PRINT RUN 25 SER.#'d SETS		
UNPRICED PATCH PRINT RUN 10		
JEAD Andre Davis	3.00	8.00
JEAL Ashley Lelie	3.00	8.00
JEAP Adrian Peterson	4.00	10.00
JEBW Brian Westbrook	6.00	15.00
JEDC David Carr	3.00	8.00
JEDF DeShaun Foster	5.00	12.00
JEDGA David Garrard	4.00	10.00
JEDN David Neill	3.00	8.00
JEEC Eric Crouch	5.00	12.00
JEJH Joey Harrington	3.00	8.00
JEJM Josh McCown	5.00	12.00
JEJR Josh Reed	4.00	10.00
JEKK Kurt Kittner	3.00	8.00
JELH Leonard Henry	3.00	8.00
JELS Luke Staley	3.00	8.00
JEMM Maurice Morris	4.00	10.00
JEPR Patrick Ramsey	4.00	10.00
JERW Roy Williams	3.00	8.00
JEWG William Green	4.00	10.00

2002 Press Pass JE Game Used Jersey Autographs

This 5-card insert set is serially numbered to 25. The standard sized cards feature autographed jerseys of this year's top NFL draft picks. The exchange expiration date was 6/1/2003.

STATED PRINT RUN 25 SER.#'d SETS		
AJEDC David Carr	15.00	40.00
AJEJM Josh McCown	25.00	60.00
AJEJR Josh Reed	20.00	50.00
AJERW Roy Williams	15.00	40.00
AJEWG William Green	20.00	50.00

2002 Press Pass JE Old School

ese inserts are randomly inserted in hobby packs at a rate of 1:1. The set contains 27-standard sized cards. The card fronts feature a retro design with a thick four-sided border. Inside the border is a color action shot of the player. The Press Pass logo is in the upper left hand corner. The player's name is divided with the first name in the top border and the last name in the bottom border. The card backs spotlight the player's college stats.

COMPLETE SET (27)	12.00	30.00
ONE PER PACK		
OS1 David Carr	.30	.75
OS2 Julius Peppers	.75	2.00
OS3 Joey Harrington	.30	.75
OS4 Mike Williams	.30	.75
OS5 Quentin Jammer	.50	1.25
OS6 Ryan Sims	.50	1.25
OS7 Bryant McKinnie	.30	.75
OS8 Roy Williams	.30	.75
OS9 Donte Stallworth	.50	1.25
OS10 Jeremy Shockey	.50	1.25
OS11 William Green	.40	1.00
OS12 T.J. Duckett	.30	.75
OS13 Ashley Lelie	.30	.75
OS14 Javon Walker	.50	1.25
OS15 Daniel Graham	.40	1.00
OS16 Patrick Ramsey	.40	1.00
OS17 Jabar Gaffney	.30	.75
OS18 DeShaun Foster	.50	1.25
OS19 Josh Reed	.40	1.00
OS20 Andre Davis	.30	.75
OS21 Reche Caldwell	.40	1.00
OS22 Clinton Portis	.50	1.25
OS23 Antwaan Randle El	.40	1.00
OS24 Antonio Bryant	.50	1.25
OS25 Marquise Walker	.30	.75
OS26 Eric Crouch	.50	1.25
OS27 Joey Harrington CL	.25	.60

2002 Press Pass JE Rookie Vision

Randomly inserted in packs at a rate of 1:4, this 12-card insert set carries a horizontal die-cut design. The player is featured twice on the card front - an action shot and a head shot. The head shot is found inside a circular design. The card backs include first-hand quotes by coaches about the featured player or quotes from the players themselves.

COMPLETE SET (12)	5.00	12.00
STATED ODDS 1:4		
RV1 David Carr	.30	.75
RV2 T.J. Duckett	.30	.75
RV3 DeShaun Foster	.50	1.25
RV4 Jabar Gaffney	.30	.75
RV5 William Green	.40	1.00
RV6 Joey Harrington	.30	.75
RV7 Ashley Lelie	.30	.75
RV8 Julius Peppers	.75	2.00
RV9 Patrick Ramsey	.40	1.00
RV10 Jeremy Shockey	.50	1.25
RV11 Donte Stallworth	.50	1.25
RV12 Javon Walker	.50	1.25

2002 Press Pass JE Up Close

Randomly inserted in packs at a rate of 1:12, this 6-card insert set is standard sized. The cardfronts are borderless and printed on silver metallic board. Each player is spotlighted with an "Up Close" head shot. His corresponding college logo is in the background.

COMPLETE SET (6)	3.00	8.00
STATED ODDS 1:12		
UC1 David Carr	.40	1.00
UC2 Jabar Gaffney	.40	1.00
UC3 William Green	.50	1.25
UC4 Joey Harrington	.40	1.00
UC5 Julius Peppers	1.00	2.50
UC6 T.J. Duckett	.40	1.00

2003 Press Pass JE

This 45-card set was released in May, 2003. The set was issued in four card packs which came 28 per box and 20 boxes per case. The hobby packs which included some exclusive inserts were available at $5.99 SRP and the retail packs were available at a $2.99 SRP.

COMPLETE SET (45)	10.00	25.00
1 Boss Bailey	.30	.75
2 Brad Banks	.30	.75
3 Anquan Boldin	.40	1.00
4 Kyle Boller	.25	.60
5 Chris Brown	.25	.60
6 Avon Cobourne	.25	.60
7 Ken Dorsey	.30	.75
8 Justin Fargas	.40	1.00
9 Talman Gardner	.25	.60
10 Jason Gesser	.30	.75
11 Earnest Graham	.40	1.00
12 Jordon Gross	.25	.60
13 Rex Grossman	.30	.75
14 Kwame Harris	.25	.60
15 Taylor Jacobs	.25	.60
16 Larry Johnson	.30	.75
17 Bryant Johnson	.40	1.00
18 Andre Johnson	.60	1.50
19 Teyo Johnson	.30	.75
20 William Joseph	.25	.60
21 Bennie Joppru	.25	.60
22 Jimmy Kennedy	.30	.75
23 Kliff Kingsbury	.40	1.00
24 Byron Leftwich	.30	.75
25 Brandon Lloyd	.40	1.00
26 Jerome McDougle	.25	.60
27 Willis McGahee	.30	.75
28 Terence Newman	.40	1.00
29 Carson Palmer	.50	1.25
30 Terry Pierce	.25	.60
31 Dave Ragone	.25	.60
32 DeWayne Robertson	.30	.75
33 Charles Rogers	.30	.75
34 Chris Simms	.25	.60
35 Musa Smith	.25	.60
36 Onterrio Smith	.25	.60
37 Brian St.Pierre	.25	.60
38 Lee Suggs	.25	.60
39 Terrell Suggs	.30	.75
40 Marcus Trufant	.30	.75
41 Seneca Wallace	.30	.75
42 Kelley Washington	.25	.60
43 Jason Witten	1.00	2.50
44 Andre Woolfolk	.25	.60
45 Byron Leftwich CL	.12	.30

2003 Press Pass JE Old School

Issued at a stated rate of one per pack, these twenty-seven cards feature a "set-within-a-set" with a retro design.

COMPLETE SET (27)	12.50	30.00
STATED ODDS ONE PER PACK		
OS1 Brad Banks	.40	1.00
OS2 Anquan Boldin	.50	1.25
OS3 Kyle Boller	.30	.75
OS4 Chris Brown	.30	.75
OS5 Avon Cobourne	.30	.75
OS6 Ken Dorsey	.40	1.00
OS7 Rex Grossman	.40	1.00
OS8 Taylor Jacobs	.30	.75
OS9 Andre Johnson	.75	2.00
OS10 Bryant Johnson	.50	1.25
OS11 Larry Johnson	.40	1.00
OS12 Jimmy Kennedy	.40	1.00
OS13 Byron Leftwich	.40	1.00
OS14 Brandon Lloyd	.50	1.25
OS15 Willis McGahee	.40	1.00
OS16 Terence Newman	.50	1.25
OS17 Carson Palmer	.60	1.50
OS18 Dave Ragone	.30	.75
OS19 Charles Rogers	.40	1.00
OS20 Chris Simms	.30	.75
OS21 Musa Smith	.30	.75
OS22 Onterrio Smith	.30	.75
OS23 Terrell Suggs	.40	1.00
OS24 Lee Suggs	.30	.75
OS25 Kelley Washington	.30	.75
OS26 Andre Woolfolk	.30	.75
OS27 Carson Palmer CL	.25	.60

2003 Press Pass JE Retail

*RETAIL: .4X TO 1X HOBBY

2003 Press Pass JE Tin

COMP.FACT.SET (46)	10.00	20.00
COMPLETE SET (45)	6.00	15.00
*SINGLES: .3X TO .8X BASIC JE		

2003 Press Pass JE Class of 2003

Inserted at a stated rate of one in nine, these nine holofoil embossed cards feature some of the top talent of the 2003 rookie class.

COMPLETE SET (9)	8.00	20.00
STATED ODDS 1:9		
CL1 Kyle Boller	.40	1.00
CL2 Rex Grossman	.50	1.25
CL3 Larry Johnson	.50	1.25
CL4 Andre Johnson	1.00	2.50
CL5 Byron Leftwich	.50	1.25
CL6 Carson Palmer	.75	2.00
CL7 Dave Ragone	.40	1.00
CL8 Charles Rogers	.50	1.25
CL9 Chris Simms	.40	1.00

2003 Press Pass JE Class of 2003 Autographs

Randomly inserted into packs, this is a parallel to the Class of 2003 insert set. These cards feature authentic autographs from the featured players.

STATED PRINT RUN 200 SER.#'d SETS		
1 Brad Banks	6.00	15.00
2 Anquan Boldin	8.00	20.00
3 Kyle Boller	5.00	12.00
4 Chris Brown	5.00	12.00
5 Justin Fargas	8.00	20.00
6 Taylor Jacobs	5.00	12.00
7 Byron Leftwich	6.00	15.00
8 Carson Palmer	10.00	25.00
9 Dave Ragone	5.00	12.00

2003 Press Pass JE Game Used Jerseys Autographs

Randomly inserted into packs, these cards feature authentic autographs of the featured players along with a jersey swatch. These cards were issued to a stated print run of 25 serial numbered sets.

STATED PRINT RUN 25 SER.#'d SETS		
AJCBL Byron Leftwich	30.00	80.00
AJCCP Carson Palmer	40.00	100.00

2003 Press Pass JE Game Used Jerseys Silver

ndomly inserted in packs, these cards feature jersey swatches along with a silver foil print. Please note that these cards were issued to varying amounts and we have notated that information in our checklist.

SILVER PRINT RUN 200-375		
*GOLD/450-575: .3X TO.8X SILVER		
GOLD/450-575 ODDS 1:28		
*HOLOFOIL/100-150: .6X TO 1.5X SILV		
HOLOFOIL PRINT RUN 100-150		
*NAMES/25: 1.2X TO 3X SILVER		
NAMES STATED PRINT RUN 25		
UNPRICED PATCH PRINT RUN 2-10		
JCAC Avon Cobourne/375	3.00	8.00
JCAW Andre Woolfolk/375	3.00	8.00
JCBJ Bennie Joppru/250	3.00	8.00
JCBL Byron Leftwich/250	4.00	10.00
JCBL1 Brandon Lloyd/375	5.00	12.00
JCCP Carson Palmer/200	6.00	15.00
JCDD Dahrran Diedrick/375	3.00	8.00
JCEG Earnest Graham/250	5.00	12.00
JCJM Jerome McDougle/375	3.00	8.00
JCJW Jason Witten/375	12.00	30.00
JCKD Ken Dorsey/250	4.00	10.00
JCKK Kareem Kelly/250	3.00	8.00
JCSW Seneca Wallace/250	4.00	10.00
JCTJ Teyo Johnson/250	4.00	10.00

2003 Press Pass JE Rookie Vision

Inserted at a stated rate of one in four, these 12 cards feature rookies with superstar potential discuss who they are preparing to achieve success in this foil insert.

COMPLETE SET (12)	8.00	20.00
STATED ODDS 1:4		
RV1 Kyle Boller	.30	.75
RV2 Justin Fargas	.50	1.25
RV3 Rex Grossman	.40	1.00
RV4 Taylor Jacobs	.30	.75
RV5 Larry Johnson	.40	1.00
RV6 Andre Johnson	.75	2.00
RV7 Byron Leftwich	.40	1.00
RV8 Carson Palmer	.60	1.50
RV9 Dave Ragone	.30	.75
RV10 Charles Rogers	.40	1.00
RV11 Chris Simms	.30	.75
RV12 Lee Suggs	.30	.75

2003 Press Pass JE Up Close

Inserted at a stated rate of one in 14, this six-card set features more in depth information on the featured 2003 rookies.

COMPLETE SET (6)	6.00	15.00
STATED ODDS 1:14		
UC1 Carson Palmer	.75	2.00
UC2 Byron Leftwich	.50	1.25
UC3 Chris Simms	.40	1.00
UC4 Charles Rogers	.50	1.25
UC5 Dave Ragone	.40	1.00
UC6 Larry Johnson	.50	1.25

2006 Press Pass Legends

This 92-card set was released in July, 2006. The set featured a mix of 2006 NFL rookies and retired greats (both players and coaches). The set was issued into the hobby in six-card mini boxes which came three boxes to a full box. Cards numbered 1-55 feature 2006 NFL rookies while cards numbered 57-92 feature the retired greats.

COMP.SET w/o SP's (90)	20.00	40.00
UNPRICED PLATINUM PRINT RUN 1		
UNPRICED PRINT PLATES SER.#'d TO 1		
1 Brodie Croyle	.30	.75
2 Tarvaris Jackson	.30	.75
3 Derek Hagan	.40	1.00
4 Devin Aromashodu	.30	.75
5 Mathias Kiwanuka	.50	1.25
6 Omar Jacobs	.30	.75
7 Tye Hill	.30	.75
8 Charlie Whitehurst	.30	.75
9 Joe Klopfenstein	.30	.75
10 Chad Jackson	.30	.75
11 Leon Washington	.30	.75
12 Ernie Sims	.30	.75
13 Leonard Pope	.50	1.25
14 D.J. Shockley	.40	1.00
15 Joseph Addai	.30	.75
16 Vernon Davis	.40	1.00
17 DeAngelo Williams	.40	1.00
18 Sinorice Moss	.30	.75
19 Martin Nance	.30	.75
20 Jason Avant	.30	.75
21 Laurence Maroney	.30	.75
22 Brad Smith	.40	1.00
23 Mario Williams	.50	1.25
24 Brett Basanez	.50	1.25
25 Anthony Fasano	.30	.75
26 Maurice Stovall	.30	.75
27 Bobby Carpenter	.30	.75
28 A.J. Hawk	.40	1.00
29 Santonio Holmes	.40	1.00
30 Ashton Youboty	.30	.75
31 Travis Wilson	.30	.75
32 Haloti Ngata	.40	1.00
33 Demetrius Williams	.30	.75
34 Mike Hass	.30	.75
35 Michael Robinson	.30	.75
36 Greg Lee	.30	.75
37 Cory Rodgers	.30	.75
38 Michael Huff	.40	1.00
39A Vince Young Clr	.30	.75
39B Vince Young B&W	.50	1.25
40 Reggie McNeal	.30	.75
41 Bruce Gradkowski	.40	1.00
42 Darrell Hackney	.40	1.00
43 Maurice Drew	.50	1.25
44 Marcedes Lewis	.30	.75
45 Drew Olson	.30	.75
46 Darnell Bing	.40	1.00
47A Reggie Bush Clr	.50	1.25
47B Reggie Bush B&W	.75	2.00
48 Dominique Byrd	.30	.75
49A Matt Leinart Clr	.30	.75
49B Matt Leinart B&W	.50	1.25
50 LenDale White	.30	.75
51A Jay Cutler Clr	.40	1.00
51B Jay Cutler B&W	.60	1.50
52 D'Brickashaw Ferguson	.30	.75
53 Marcus Vick	.30	.75
54 Jimmy Williams	.30	.75
55 Jerome Harrison	.30	.75
56 Ozzie Newsome	.50	1.25
57 Ken Stabler	.75	2.00
58A Bo Jackson B&W	.75	2.00
58B Bo Jackson Clr	1.25	3.00
59 Steve Spurrier	.75	2.00
60 Charlie Ward	.40	1.00
61 Fran Tarkenton	.60	1.50
62 Herschel Walker	.60	1.50
63 Billy Cannon	.50	1.25
64 Y.A. Tittle	.60	1.50
65 Roger Craig	.60	1.50
66 Tommie Frazier	.40	1.00
67 Rocky Bleier	.50	1.25
68A Tim Brown B&W	.60	1.50
68B Tim Brown Clr	1.00	2.50
69 Paul Hornung	.60	1.50
70 Joe Theismann	.60	1.50
71 Howard Cassady	.50	1.25
72 Archie Griffin	.40	1.00
73 Jack Tatum	.40	1.00
74 Paul Warfield	.50	1.25
75 Brian Bosworth	.60	1.50
76 Billy Sims	.50	1.25
77A Barry Sanders B&W	1.00	2.50
77B Barry Sanders Clr	1.50	4.00
78 Thurman Thomas	.50	1.25
79 Jack Ham	.50	1.25
80 Franco Harris	.60	1.50
81A Dan Marino B&W	1.25	3.00
81B Dan Marino Clr	2.00	5.00
82 Len Dawson	.60	1.50
83 Jim Plunkett	.50	1.25
84 Bob Lilly	.50	1.25
85 Steve Largent	.60	1.50
86 Ronnie Lott	.50	1.25
87 Bobby Bowden	.60	1.50
88 Bo Schembechler	.40	1.00
89 Darrell Royal	.50	1.25
90 Ara Parseghian	.50	1.25
91 Johnny Lattner SP	2.00	5.00
92 Desmond Howard SP	2.50	6.00

2006 Press Pass Legends Bronze

*BRONZE ROOKIE: .6X TO 1.5X BASIC CARDS		
*BRNZ ROOK.B VERSION: .4X TO 1X		
*BRONZE RETIRED: 1X TO 2.5X BASIC CARDS		
*BRNZ RETIRED B VERSION: .6X TO 1.5X		
BRONZE PRINT RUN 999 SER.#'d SETS		
B91 Johnny Lattner	1.00	2.50
B92 Desmond Howard	1.25	3.00

2006 Press Pass Legends Emerald

*EMER ROOKIE: 2.5X TO 6X BASIC CARDS		
*EMER.ROOKIE B VERSION: 1.5X TO 4X		
*EMER.RETIRED: 8X TO 20X BASIC CARDS		
*EMER.RETIRED B VERSION: 5X TO 12X		
EMERALD PRINT RUN 25 SER.#'d SETS		
E91 Johnny Lattner	6.00	15.00
E92 Desmond Howard	8.00	20.00

2006 Press Pass Legends Gold

*GOLD ROOKIE: 1.5X TO 4X BASIC CARDS		
*GOLD ROOKIE B VERSION: 1X TO 2.5X		
*GOLD RETIRED: 3X TO 8X BASIC CARDS		
*GOLD RETIRED B VERSION: 2X TO 5X		
GOLD PRINT RUN 99 SER.#'d SETS		
G91 Johnny Lattner	3.00	8.00
G92 Desmond Howard	4.00	10.00

2006 Press Pass Legends Silver

*SILVER ROOKIE: .8X TO 2X BASIC CARDS		
*SILVER ROOKIE B VERSION: .5X TO 1.2X		
*SILVER RETIRED: 1.5X TO 4X BASIC CARDS		
*SILVER RETIRED B VERSION: 1X TO 2.5X		
SILVER PRINT RUN 499 SER.#'d SETS		
S91 Johnny Lattner	1.50	4.00
S92 Desmond Howard	2.00	5.00

2006 Press Pass Legends All Conference

STATED ODDS 1:15		
AC1 Derek Hagan	.60	1.50
AC2 Mathias Kiwanuka	.75	2.00
AC3 D.J. Shockley	.60	1.50
AC4 Vernon Davis	.60	1.50
AC5 Jason Avant	.50	1.25
AC6 Laurence Maroney	.50	1.25
AC7 A.J. Hawk	.60	1.50
AC8 Marcedes Lewis	.50	1.25
AC9 Darnell Bing	.60	1.50
AC10 Michael Robinson	.50	1.25
AC11 Greg Lee	.50	1.25
AC12 Michael Huff	.60	1.50
AC13 Vince Young	.50	1.25
AC14 Darrell Hackney	.60	1.50
AC15 Reggie Bush	.75	2.00
AC16 Matt Leinart	.50	1.25
AC17 Jay Cutler	.60	1.50
AC18 D'Brickashaw Ferguson	.50	1.25
AC19 Mario Williams	.75	2.00
AC20 Jerome Harrison	.50	1.25

2006 Press Pass Legends All Conference Autographs Gold

LATINUM/25: .8X TO 2X GOLD/115-365		
*PLATINUM/25: .6X TO 1.5X GOLD/50		
*PLATINUM/25: .4X TO 1X GOLD/25		
1 Jason Avant/290		
2 Darnell Bing/255	4.00	10.00
3 Reggie Bush/25	10.00	25.00
4 Jay Cutler/25	15.00	40.00
5 Vernon Davis/50	10.00	25.00
6 D'Brickashaw Ferguson/340	3.00	8.00
7 Darrell Hackney/225	4.00	10.00
7R Darrell Hackney/225 Red	5.00	12.00
8 A.J. Hawk/260	10.00	25.00
9 Michael Huff/250	4.00	10.00
10 Mathias Kiwanuka/250	5.00	12.00
10R Mathias Kiwanuka/250 Red	6.00	15.00
11 Greg Lee/310	3.00	8.00
12 Matt Leinart/25	15.00	40.00
13 Marcedes Lewis/310	3.00	8.00
14 Laurence Maroney/122	3.00	8.00
15 Michael Robinson/350	3.00	8.00
16 D.J. Shockley/365	4.00	10.00
16R D.J. Shockley/365 Red	5.00	12.00
17 Mario Williams/260	10.00	25.00
17R Mario Williams/260 Red	12.00	30.00
18 Vince Young/25	15.00	40.00

2006 Press Pass Legends Alumni Association

ATED ODDS 1:30		
AA1 K.Stabler/B.Croyle	3.00	8.00
AA2 F.Tarkenton/H.Walker	1.50	4.00
AA3 L.White/R.Bush	4.00	10.00
AA4 J.Lattner/P.Hornung	2.00	5.00
AA5 P.Warfield/A.Hawk	2.00	5.00
AA6 B.Bosworth/B.Sims	2.50	6.00
AA7 T.Thomas/B.Sanders	3.00	8.00
AA8 D.Marino/G.Lee	4.00	10.00
AA9 R.Lott/M.Leinart	2.00	5.00

2006 Press Pass Legends Alumni Association Autographs

1C Stabler B/Croyle B/33*	100.00	175.00
2 Tarken/H.Walker/50 Red	40.00	100.00
3 L.White/Bush/35 Red	10.00	25.00
4 J.Lattner/P.Hornung/50	25.00	60.00
5 P.Warfield/A.Hawk/50	50.00	80.00
6 B.Bosworth/B.Sims/50	40.00	100.00
7 T.Thomas/B.Sanders/35	175.00	300.00
8 Marino/G.Lee/50	75.00	150.00
9 Lott/Leinart/35	40.00	100.00

2006 Press Pass Legends Autographs

STATED ODDS 1:5		
1 Joseph Addai	6.00	15.00
2 Devin Aromashodu	4.00	10.00
3 Jason Avant	5.00	12.00
4 Brett Basanez	4.00	10.00
4R Brett Basanez Red	8.00	20.00
5 Darnell Bing	5.00	12.00
6 Rocky Bleier	12.00	30.00
7 Brian Bosworth SP	25.00	50.00
7R Brian Bosworth SP Red	30.00	60.00
8 Bobby Bowden	15.00	30.00
8R Bobby Bowden Red	30.00	60.00
9 Tim Brown SP		
10 Reggie Bush SP	15.00	40.00
11 Dominique Byrd	4.00	10.00
12 Billy Cannon	10.00	25.00
13 Bobby Carpenter	5.00	12.00
13R Bobby Carpenter Red	10.00	25.00
14 Howard Cassady	8.00	20.00
15 Roger Craig Red	6.00	15.00
16 Brodie Croyle Red	8.00	20.00
17 Jay Cutler	10.00	25.00
17R Jay Cutler Red	10.00	25.00
18 Vernon Davis	6.00	15.00
19 Len Dawson SP	40.00	80.00
20 Maurice Drew	12.00	30.00
20R Maurice Drew Red	15.00	40.00
21 Anthony Fasano	5.00	12.00
21R Anthony Fasano Red	6.00	15.00
22 D'Brickashaw Ferguson	6.00	15.00
23 Tommie Frazier	6.00	15.00
23R Tommie Frazier Red	6.00	15.00
24 Bruce Gradkowski	6.00	15.00
25 Archie Griffin	8.00	20.00
25R Archie Griffin Red	8.00	20.00
26 Darrell Hackney	4.00	10.00
27 Jack Ham	15.00	30.00
28 Franco Harris SP	25.00	50.00
29 Mike Hass	4.00	10.00
29R Mike Hass Red	10.00	25.00
30 A.J. Hawk	12.00	30.00
31 Tye Hill	5.00	12.00
32 Paul Hornung	12.00	30.00
33 Desmond Howard SP		
34 Michael Huff	5.00	12.00
34R Michael Huff Red	6.00	15.00
35 Bo Jackson SP		
36 Chad Jackson	6.00	15.00
37 Tarvaris Jackson	6.00	15.00
37R Tarvaris Jackson Red	8.00	20.00
38 Omar Jacobs	5.00	12.00
39 Mathias Kiwanuka	6.00	15.00
40 Joe Klopfenstein	4.00	10.00
41 Steve Largent SP	15.00	30.00
42 Johnny Lattner	8.00	20.00
42R Johnny Lattner Red	10.00	25.00
43 Greg Lee	4.00	10.00
44 Matt Leinart SP	12.00	30.00
45 Marcedes Lewis	4.00	10.00
46 Bob Lilly	8.00	15.00
46R Bob Lilly Red	10.00	20.00
47 Ronnie Lott SP	40.00	80.00
48 Dan Marino SP	75.00	150.00
48R Dan Marino SP Red	100.00	200.00
49 Laurence Maroney	5.00	12.00
50 Reggie McNeal	5.00	12.00
51 Martin Nance	5.00	12.00
51R Martin Nance Red	10.00	20.00
52 Ozzie Newsome SP	15.00	30.00
53 Haloti Ngata	6.00	15.00
54 Drew Olson	4.00	10.00
55 Ara Parseghian	12.50	30.00
55R Ara Parseghian Red	15.00	40.00
56 Jim Plunkett	6.00	15.00
56R Jim Plunkett Red	8.00	20.00
57 Leonard Pope	5.00	12.00
58 Michael Robinson	6.00	15.00
59 Cory Rodgers	4.00	10.00
59R Cory Rodgers Red	5.00	12.00
60 Darrell Royal	8.00	25.00
60R Darrell Royal Red	10.00	30.00
61 Barry Sanders SP	100.00	200.00
62 Bo Schembechler	40.00	80.00
63 D.J. Shockley	5.00	12.00
64 Billy Sims	6.00	15.00
64R Billy Sims Red	10.00	25.00
65 Brad Smith	5.00	12.00
66 Steve Spurrier	15.00	40.00
67 Ken Stabler Red SP	75.00	150.00
68 Fran Tarkenton SP		
69 Jack Tatum SP	30.00	60.00
70 Joe Theismann	10.00	25.00
70R Joe Theismann Red	30.00	80.00
71 Thurman Thomas	10.00	25.00
72 Y.A. Tittle SP		
73 Herschel Walker SP	15.00	40.00
74 Charlie Ward	6.00	15.00
75 Paul Warfield	8.00	20.00
76 Leon Washington	6.00	20.00
77 LenDale White	6.00	15.00
78 Charlie Whitehurst	6.00	15.00
78R Charlie Whitehurst Red	10.00	25.00
79 Demetrius Williams	6.00	15.00
80 Mario Williams	8.00	20.00
80R Mario Williams Red	10.00	25.00
81 Vince Young SP	15.00	40.00

2006 Press Pass Legends Legendary Legacy

STATED ODDS 1:15		
1 Ken Stabler	3.00	8.00
2 Ozzie Newsome	2.00	5.00
3 Bo Jackson	3.00	8.00
4 Fran Tarkenton	2.50	6.00
5 Herschel Walker	2.50	6.00
6 Y.A. Tittle	2.50	6.00
7 Desmond Howard	2.00	5.00
8 Roger Craig	2.50	6.00
9 Tim Brown	2.50	6.00
10 Paul Hornung	2.50	6.00
11 Joe Theismann	2.50	6.00
12 Howard Cassady	2.00	5.00
13 Archie Griffin	1.50	4.00
14 Jack Tatum	1.50	4.00
15 Brian Bosworth	2.50	6.00
16 Steve Largent	2.50	6.00
17 Billy Sims	2.00	5.00
18 Franco Harris	2.50	6.00
19 Len Dawson	2.50	6.00
20 Ronnie Lott	2.00	5.00

2006 Press Pass Legends Legendary Legacy Autographs Gold

STATED PRINT RUN 100-400		
1 Brian Bosworth/275	25.00	50.00
1R Brian Bosworth/275 Red	25.00	60.00
2 Tim Brown/125	25.00	60.00
3 Howard Cassady/400	10.00	25.00
4 Roger Craig/400	8.00	20.00
5 Len Dawson/120	10.00	25.00

5R Len Dawson/130 Red 12.50 30.00
6R Archie Griffin/255 15.00 30.00
7R Franco Harris/105 25.00 50.00
8 Paul Hornung/310 15.00 40.00
9 Desmond Howard/320 12.00 30.00
9R Desmond Howard/320 Red 15.00 40.00
10 Bo Jackson/115 40.00 80.00
10R Bo Jackson/115 Red 40.00 100.00
11 Steve Largent/120 15.00 40.00
12 Ronnie Lott/100 20.00 40.00
13 Ozzie Newsome/258 12.50 30.00
14 Billy Sims/320 8.00 20.00
15 Ken Stabler/100 30.00 60.00
16 Fran Tarkenton/106 20.00 40.00
16R Fran Tarkenton/106 Red 25.00 50.00
17 Jack Tatum/175 15.00 40.00
18 Joe Theismann/130 15.00 40.00
19 Y.A. Tittle/155 15.00 40.00
20 Herschel Walker/300 25.00 50.00
20R Herschel Walker/300 Red 30.00 60.00

2006 Press Pass Legends Legendary Legacy Autographs Platinum

PLATINUM PRINT RUN 25 SER.#'d SETS
1 Ken Stabler 60.00 120.00
2 Ozzie Newsome 25.00 50.00
3 Bo Jackson 75.00 150.00
4 Fran Tarkenton 25.00 50.00
5 Herschel Walker
6 Y.A. Tittle 30.00 60.00
7 Desmond Howard 25.00 50.00
8 Roger Craig Red 20.00 40.00
9 Tim Brown 40.00 80.00
10 Paul Hornung 30.00 80.00
11 Joe Theismann 30.00 60.00
12 Howard Cassady 20.00 40.00
13 Archie Griffin 30.00 60.00
14 Jack Tatum 40.00 80.00
15 Brian Bosworth 30.00 80.00
16 Steve Largent 25.00 50.00
17 Billy Sims 20.00 40.00
18 Franco Harris 40.00 80.00
19 Len Dawson 30.00 60.00
20 Ronnie Lott 30.00 60.00

2006 Press Pass Legends Rookie Autographs 50

STATED PRINT RUN 50 SER.#'d SETS
1 Reggie Bush 15.00 40.00
2 Brodie Croyle 10.00 25.00
3 A.J. Hawk 12.00 30.00
4 Omar Jacobs 10.00 25.00
5 Matt Leinart 10.00 25.00
6 Brad Smith 12.00 30.00
6R Brad Smith Red 15.00 40.00
7 Marcus Vick 12.00 30.00
8 LenDale White 10.00 25.00
9 Vince Young 10.00 25.00
9R Vince Young Red 12.00 30.00

2006 Press Pass Legends Saturday Swatches

STATED ODDS 1:18
*PLATINUM: .8X TO 2X BASIC JSYs
PLATINUM PRINT RUN 50 SER.#'d SETS
AF Anthony Fasano SP 5.00 12.00
AH A.J. Hawk 10.00 25.00
BC Brodie Croyle 6.00 15.00
BS Brad Smith SP 3.00 8.00
CR Cory Rodgers SP 6.00 15.00
CW Charlie Whitehurst 2.50 6.00
DA Devin Aromashodu SP 2.50 6.00
DS D.J. Shockley SP 5.00 12.00
DW Demetrius Williams SP 2.50 6.00
JH Jerome Harrison 2.50 6.00
LW LenDale White 6.00 15.00
MD Maurice Drew SP 6.00 15.00
MH Mike Hass SP 6.00 15.00
ML Marcedes Lewis 2.50 6.00
MR Michael Robinson 2.50 6.00
OJ Omar Jacobs SP 5.00 12.00
TJ Tarvaris Jackson 2.50 6.00
VD Vernon Davis
DAW DeAngelo Williams 8.00 20.00
MHU Michael Huff 3.00 8.00

2007 Press Pass Legends

This 100-card set was released in July, 2007. The set was issued into the hobby in five card packs which came 18 to a box. Cards numbered 1-65 feature 2007 NFL rookies while cards numbered 66-100 feature retired greats.

COMPLETE SET (100) 20.00 40.00
UNPRICED PRINTING PLATES PRINT RUN 1
1 Kenneth Darby .30 .75
2 Chris Henry .30 .75
3 Zach Miller .30 .75
4 Jamaal Anderson .40 1.00
5 Kenny Irons .30 .75
6 Courtney Taylor .30 .75
7 John Beck .30 .75
8 Daymeion Hughes .30 .75
9 Marshawn Lynch .60 1.50
10 Gaines Adams .40 1.00
11 Chansi Stuckey .40 1.00
12 Aundrae Allison .30 .75
13 Dallas Baker .30 .75
14 Chris Leak .30 .75
15 Jarvis Moss .30 .75
16 Reggie Nelson .30 .75
17 DeShawn Wynn .30 .75
18 Paul Williams .30 .75
19 Dwayne Wright .30 .75
20 Lorenzo Booker .40 1.00
21 Buster Davis .40 1.00
22 Lawrence Timmons .50 1.25
23 Quentin Moses .30 .75
24 Calvin Johnson 1.00 2.50
25 Kevin Kolb .40 1.00
26 Michael Bush .30 .75
27 Amobi Okoye .40 1.00
28 Kolby Smith .30 .75
29 Joseph Addai .30 .75
30 Dwayne Bowe .30 .75
31 Craig Buster Davis .30 .75
32 LaRon Landry .50 1.25
33 JaMarcus Russell .30 .75
34 Greg Olsen .50 1.25
35 Alan Branch .30 .75
36 Leon Hall .30 .75
37 Drew Stanton .30 .75
38 Adam Carriker .30 .75
39 Brandon Jackson .30 .75
40 Jeff Rowe .30 .75
41 Garrett Wolfe .30 .75
42 Brady Quinn .30 .75
43 Ted Ginn Jr. .40 1.00
44 Anthony Gonzalez .30 .75
45 Antonio Pittman .30 .75
46 Troy Smith .30 .75
47 Adrian Peterson 1.00 2.50
48 Patrick Willis .50 1.25
49 Tony Hunt .30 .75
50 Paul Posluszny .30 .75
51 Darrelle Revis .40 1.00
52 Brian Leonard .30 .75
53 Sidney Rice .40 1.00
54 Trent Edwards .30 .75
55 Robert Meachem .40 1.00
56 Michael Griffin .30 .75
57 Aaron Ross .30 .75
58 Vince Young .30 .75
59 Joel Filani .30 .75
60 Dwayne Jarrett .40 1.00
61 Steve Smith USC .30 .75
62 Johnnie Lee Higgins .30 .75
63 Jordan Palmer .40 1.00
64 David Clowney .30 .75
65 Jason Hill .30 .75
66 Ozzie Newsome .50 1.25
67 Ken Stabler .75 2.00
68 Bart Starr 1.00 2.50
69 Pat Sullivan .40 1.00
70 Doug Flutie .60 1.50
71 Ty Detmer .40 1.00
72 Danny Wuerffel .40 1.00
73 Jack Youngblood .50 1.25
74 Fred Biletnikoff .60 1.50
75 Herschel Walker .60 1.50
76 Dick Butkus .75 2.00
77 Y.A. Tittle .60 1.50
78 Randy White .50 1.25
79 Jerry Rice 1.25 3.00
80 Joe Bellino .40 1.00
81 Tommie Frazier .40 1.00
82 Tom Osborne .50 1.25
83 Tom Rathman .40 1.00
84 Johnny Rodgers .40 1.00
85 Mike Rozier .40 1.00
86 Jerome Bettis .60 1.50
87 Paul Hornung .60 1.50
88 Alan Page .40 1.00
89 Rudy Ruettiger .60 1.50
90 Joe Theismann .60 1.50
91 Archie Griffin .40 1.00
92 Brian Bosworth .60 1.50
93 Steve Owens .40 1.00
94 Billy Sims .50 1.25
95 Archie Manning .50 1.25
96 Raymond Berry .50 1.25
97 James Lofton .40 1.00
98 Marcus Allen .60 1.50
99 John Hannah .40 1.00
100 Dick Butkus CL .50 1.25

2007 Press Pass Legends Bronze

*BRONZE ROOKIE: .8X TO 2X BASIC CARDS
*BRONZE RETIRED: 1X TO 2.5X BASIC CARDS
STATED PRINT RUN 999 SER.#'d SETS

2007 Press Pass Legends Emerald

*EMERALD ROOKIE: 3X TO 8X BASIC CARDS
*EMER.RETIRED: 4X TO 10X BASIC CARDS
STATED PRINT RUN 25 SER.#'d SETS

2007 Press Pass Legends Gold

*GOLD ROOKIE: 1.5X TO 4X BASIC CARDS
*GOLD RETIRED: 2X TO 5X BASIC CARDS
STATED PRINT RUN 99 SER.#'d SETS

2007 Press Pass Legends Platinum

UNPRICED PLATINUM PRINT RUN 1

2007 Press Pass Legends Red

UNPRICED RED PRINT RUN 10

2007 Press Pass Legends Silver

*SILVER ROOKIE: 1X TO 2.5X BASIC CARDS
*SILVER RETIRED: 1.2X TO 3X BASIC CARDS
STATED PRINT RUN 499 SER.#'d SETS

2007 Press Pass Legends All Conference

STATED ODDS 1:7
1 Jamaal Anderson .60 1.50
2 Kenny Irons .50 1.25
3 John Beck .50 1.25
4 Marshawn Lynch 1.00 2.50
5 Gaines Adams .60 1.50
6 Calvin Johnson 1.50 4.00
7 Kevin Kolb .60 1.50
8 Dwayne Bowe .50 1.25
9 LaRon Landry .75 2.00
10 JaMarcus Russell .50 1.25
11 Leon Hall .50 1.25
12 Adam Carriker .50 1.25
13 Ted Ginn Jr. .60 1.50
14 Anthony Gonzalez .50 1.25
15 Troy Smith .50 1.25
16 Adrian Peterson 1.50 4.00
17 Paul Posluszny .50 1.25
18 Robert Meachem .60 1.50
19 Dwayne Jarrett .60 1.50
20 Steve Smith USC .50 1.25

2007 Press Pass Legends All Conference Autographs Gold

STATED PRINT RUN 25-400
UNPRICED PRINTING PLATES PRINT RUN 1
ACAB Alan Branch/262* 5.00 12.00
ACABR Alan Branch Red Ink/50* 6.00 15.00
ACAC Adam Carriker/290 6.00 15.00
ACAG Anthony Gonzalez/285 4.00 10.00
ACAP Adrian Peterson/27* 100.00 200.00
ACAPR A.Peterson Red Ink/20* 100.00 200.00
ACAR Aaron Ross/235* 5.00 12.00
ACARR Aaron Ross Red Ink/50* 6.00 15.00
ACBD Buster Davis/160
ACCJ Calvin Johnson/17 75.00 150.00
ACCJR Calvin Johnson Red/8* 100.00 200.00
ACCS Chansi Stuckey/50 6.00 15.00
ACDB Dallas Baker/392 5.00 12.00
ACDB2 Dwayne Bowe/378* 8.00 20.00
ACDB2R Dwayne Bowe Red Ink/22* 8.00 20.00
ACDH Daymeion Hughes/267* 4.00 10.00
ACDHR D.Hughes Red/45* 5.00 12.00
ACGA Gaines Adams/303* 5.00 12.00
ACJA Jamaal Anderson/310 5.00 12.00
ACJB John Beck/349* 5.00 12.00
ACJBR John Beck Red Ink/51* 6.00 15.00
ACJH Johnnie Lee Higgins/235 5.00 12.00
ACJR JaMarcus Russell/75 15.00 40.00
ACKI Kenny Irons/400 4.00 10.00
ACKK Kevin Kolb/353* 6.00 15.00
ACKKR Kevin Kolb Red Ink/47* 8.00 20.00
ACLH Leon Hall/307 5.00 12.00
ACLL LaRon Landry/249* 5.00 12.00
ACLLR LaRon Landry Red Ink/50* 6.00 15.00
ACMG Michael Griffin/262 5.00 12.00
ACPP Paul Posluszny/240* 8.00 20.00
ACRM Robert Meachem/360* 8.00 20.00
ACRMR Robert Meachem Red/40* 10.00 25.00
ACSS Steve Smith USC/328* 6.00 15.00
ACSSR Steve Smith Red/72* 8.00 20.00
ACTGR Ted Ginn Red Ink/68* 15.00 40.00
ACTS Troy Smith/20* 30.00 60.00
ACZM Zach Miller/353* 6.00 15.00
ACZMR Zach Miller/47* 8.00 20.00

2007 Press Pass Legends All Conference Autographs Platinum

PLATINUM PRINT RUN 25 SER.#'d SETS
ACAB Alan Branch 10.00 25.00
ACAC Adam Carriker 12.00 30.00
ACAG Anthony Gonzalez 6.00 15.00
ACAR Aaron Ross 10.00 25.00
ACBD Buster Davis 8.00 20.00
ACCJ Calvin Johnson 75.00 150.00
ACCS Chansi Stuckey 8.00 20.00
ACDB Dwayne Bowe 15.00 40.00
ACDB Dallas Baker 10.00 25.00
ACDH Daymeion Hughes 6.00 15.00
ACGA Gaines Adams/15* 10.00 25.00
ACGAR G.Adams Red Ink/10* 12.00 30.00
ACJA Jamaal Anderson 10.00 25.00
ACJB John Beck 10.00 25.00
ACJH Johnnie Lee Higgins 8.00 20.00
ACJR JaMarcus Russell 25.00 60.00
ACKI Kenny Irons 10.00 25.00
ACKK Kevin Kolb/18* 10.00 25.00
ACLH Leon Hall 10.00 25.00
ACLL LaRon Landry 12.00 30.00
ACMG Michael Griffin 10.00 25.00
ACPP Paul Posluszny/23* 12.00 30.00
ACRMR Robert Meachem Red/24* 10.00 25.00
ACSS Steve Smith USC 10.00 25.00
ACTG Ted Ginn Jr./23* 12.00 30.00
ACTS Troy Smith/20* 15.00 40.00
ACZM Zach Miller/24* 8.00 20.00

2007 Press Pass Legends Alumni Association

STATED ODDS 1:14
1 D.Wuerffel/C.Leak 1.50 4.00
2 Y.Tittle/J.Russell 1.50 4.00
3 J.Theismann/B.Quinn 3.00 8.00
4 P.Hornung/J.Bettis 2.50 6.00
5 A.Griffin/T.Smith 2.00 5.00
6 B.Sims/A.Peterson 3.00 8.00
7 A.Manning/P.Willis 2.00 5.00
8 M.Allen/S.Smith USC 2.00 5.00
9 J.Rodgers/M.Rozier 2.50 6.00
10 T.Detmer/J.Beck 1.50 4.00

2007 Press Pass Legends Alumni Association Autographs

STATED PRINT RUN 50 SER.#'d SETS
AMPW A.Mann/P.Willis No Auto
AWKK A.Ware/K.Kolb 15.00 40.00
BSAPR1 Sims Red/Ptrsn Blue/44* 100.00 200.00
DWCL D.Wuerffel/C.Leak 25.00 60.00
JRMR J.Rodgers/M.Rozier 60.00 100.00
JTBQ Theismann/B.Quinn 10.00 25.00
MASS Allen Blu/Smith Blu/25* 20.00 50.00
MASSR Allen Blu/Smith Red/25* 40.00 80.00
PHJB P.Hornung/J.Bettis 50.00 100.00
RCTR R.Craig/T.Rathman 40.00 80.00
TDJB T.Detmer/J.Beck 15.00 40.00
TFBJ T.Frazier/B.Jackson 15.00 40.00
YTJR Tittle Blu/Russell Blu/10* 40.00 80.00
YTJRR1 Tittle Red/Russ Red/15* 40.00 80.00
YTJRR2 Tittl Blu/Russ Red JR/25* 40.00 80.00
YTJRR3 Tittle Blu/Russell Red/10* 40.00 80.00

2007 Press Pass Legends Autographs

*RED INK/19-181: .5X TO 1.2X BLUE INK
RED INK PRINT RUNS ANNCD BY PRESS PASS
UNPRICED PRINTING PLATES PRINT RUN 1
OVERALL AUTO ODDS 5:18
1 Gaines Adams
2 Joseph Addai 4.00 10.00
3 Marcus Allen 10.00 25.00
4 Aundrae Allison 4.00 10.00
5 Jamaal Anderson 6.00 15.00
6 Dallas Baker 4.00 10.00
7 John Beck 4.00 10.00
8 Joe Bellino 8.00 20.00
9 Raymond Berry 6.00 15.00
10 Jerome Bettis 40.00 80.00
11 Fred Biletnikoff 8.00 20.00
12 Lorenzo Booker 5.00 12.00
13 Brian Bosworth 15.00 40.00
14 Dwayne Bowe 4.00 10.00
15 Alan Branch 4.00 10.00
16 Michael Bush 4.00 10.00
17 Dick Butkus 20.00 50.00
18 Adam Carriker 4.00 10.00
19 David Clowney 4.00 10.00
20 Kenneth Darby 4.00 10.00
21 Buster Davis 5.00 12.00
22 Craig Buster Davis 4.00 10.00
23 Ty Detmer 5.00 12.00
24 Joel Filani 4.00 10.00
25 Doug Flutie 10.00 25.00
26 Tommie Frazier 10.00 25.00
27 Ted Ginn Jr. 5.00 12.00
28 Anthony Gonzalez 4.00 10.00
29 Archie Griffin 8.00 20.00
30 Michael Griffin 4.00 10.00
31 Leon Hall
32 John Hannah 6.00 15.00
33 Johnnie Lee Higgins 4.00 10.00
34 Jason Hill 4.00 10.00
35 Paul Hornung 12.50 30.00
36 Daymeion Hughes 4.00 10.00
37 Kenny Irons 4.00 10.00
38 Brandon Jackson 4.00 10.00
39 Calvin Johnson SP 50.00 100.00
40 Charles Johnson 4.00 10.00
41 Kevin Kolb 5.00 12.00
42 LaRon Landry 6.00 15.00
43 Chris Leak 4.00 10.00
44 Brian Leonard 4.00 10.00
45 James Lofton 8.00 20.00
46 Archie Manning 15.00 40.00
47 Rhema McKnight 4.00 10.00
48 Robert Meachem 6.00 15.00
49 Zach Miller 4.00 10.00
50 Matt Moore 6.00 15.00
51 Quentin Moses 4.00 10.00
52 Reggie Nelson 4.00 10.00
53 Ozzie Newsome 6.00 15.00
54 Amobi Okoye 5.00 12.00
55 Greg Olsen 6.00 15.00
56 Tom Osborne 15.00 30.00
57 Steve Owens 8.00 20.00
58 Alan Page 8.00 20.00
59 Jordan Palmer 5.00 12.00
60 William Perry 6.00 15.00
61 Adrian Peterson SP 75.00 150.00
62 Antonio Pittman 4.00 10.00
63 Paul Posluszny 4.00 10.00
64 Brady Quinn 4.00 10.00
65 Tom Rathman 8.00 20.00
66 Darrelle Revis 5.00 12.00
67 Jerry Rice
68 Sidney Rice 5.00 12.00
69 Johnny Rodgers 8.00 20.00
70 Aaron Ross 4.00 10.00
71 Mike Rozier 10.00 25.00
72 Rudy Ruettiger 25.00 50.00
73 JaMarcus Russell 4.00 10.00
74 Lee Roy Selmon 10.00 25.00
75 Billy Sims 8.00 20.00
76 Kolby Smith 4.00 10.00
77 Steve Smith USC 4.00 10.00
78 Troy Smith SP 8.00 20.00
79 Ken Stabler 35.00 60.00
80 Drew Stanton 4.00 10.00
81 Bart Starr 60.00 120.00
82 Chansi Stuckey 5.00 12.00
83 Pat Sullivan 6.00 15.00
84 Joe Theismann 10.00 25.00
85 Lawrence Timmons 6.00 15.00
86 Y.A. Tittle 15.00 30.00
87 Darius Walker 4.00 10.00
88 Herschel Walker 10.00 25.00
89 Andre Ware 10.00 25.00
90 Randy White 8.00 20.00
91 Paul Williams 4.00 10.00
92 Patrick Willis 12.50 30.00
93 Garrett Wolfe 4.00 10.00
94 Dwayne Wright 4.00 10.00
95 Danny Wuerffel 8.00 20.00
96 DeShawn Wynn 4.00 10.00
97 Selvin Young 4.00 10.00
98 Vince Young SP 20.00 50.00
99 Jack Youngblood 6.00 15.00

2007 Press Pass Legends Legendary Legacy

STATED ODDS 1:7
1 Ken Stabler 2.50 6.00
2 Doug Flutie 2.00 5.00
3 Herschel Walker 2.00 5.00
4 Dick Butkus 2.50 6.00
5 Y.A. Tittle 2.00 5.00
6 Jerry Rice 4.00 10.00
7 Joe Bellino 1.25 3.00
8 Tommie Frazier 1.25 3.00
9 Mike Rozier 1.25 3.00
10 Jerome Bettis 2.00 5.00
11 Paul Hornung 2.00 5.00
12 Alan Page 1.25 3.00
13 Joe Theismann 2.00 5.00
14 Archie Griffin 1.25 3.00
15 Brian Bosworth 2.00 5.00
16 Billy Sims 1.50 4.00
17 Archie Manning 1.50 4.00
18 Raymond Berry 1.50 4.00
19 James Lofton 1.25 3.00
20 Marcus Allen 2.00 5.00

2007 Press Pass Legends Legendary Legacy Autographs Gold

STATED PRINT RUN 50-400 SER.#'d SETS
AG Archie Griffin/175 12.50 30.00
AM Archie Manning/75 12.50 30.00
AP Alan Page/85 10.00 25.00
AW Andre Ware/400 6.00 15.00
BB Brian Bosworth/75* 25.00 50.00
BBR Brian Bosworth Red Ink/25* 30.00 60.00
BS Billy Sims/382* 6.00 15.00
DB Dick Butkus/33* 40.00 80.00
DBR Dick Butkus Red Ink/20* 50.00 100.00
DF Doug Flutie/125 12.00 30.00
DW Danny Wuerffel/400 6.00 15.00
HW Herschel Walker/100 10.00 25.00
JB1 Joe Bellino/396 6.00 15.00
JB2 Jerome Bettis/80 35.00 60.00
JL James Lofton/150 8.00 20.00
JR1 Jerry Rice/53 60.00 120.00
JR2 Johnny Rodgers/184* 12.50 30.00
JR2R J.Rodgers Red Ink/193* 12.50 30.00
JT Joe Theismann/100 15.00 40.00
MA Marcus Allen/55 15.00 40.00
MR Mike Rozier/400 6.00 15.00
PH Paul Hornung/153 15.00 40.00
PS Pat Sullivan/73* 8.00 20.00
RB Raymond Berry/345* 6.00 15.00
RBR Raymond Berry Red Ink/25* 10.00 25.00
TF Tommie Frazier/349* 6.00 15.00
TFR Tommie Frazier Red Ink/51* 8.00 20.00
YT Y.A. Tittle/40* 20.00 40.00

2007 Press Pass Legends Legendary Legacy Autographs Platinum

PLATINUM PRINT RUN 25 SER.#'d SETS
AG Archie Griffin 20.00 40.00
AM Archie Manning 25.00 50.00
AP Alan Page 12.50 30.00
AW Andre Ware 12.00 30.00
BS Billy Sims/22* 15.00 40.00
DB Dick Butkus/15* 25.00 60.00
DBR Dick Butkus Red Ink/10* 25.00 60.00
DF Doug Flutie 20.00 50.00
DW Danny Wuerffel 12.50 30.00
HW Herschel Walker 15.00 40.00
JB1 Joe Bellino 12.50 30.00
JB2 Jerome Bettis 40.00 80.00
JL James Lofton 12.50 30.00
JR1 Jerry Rice 90.00 150.00
JR2 Johnny Rodgers/22* 20.00 40.00
JT Joe Theismann 25.00 50.00
KS Ken Stabler 25.00 60.00
MA Marcus Allen 25.00 50.00
MR Mike Rozier 12.00 30.00
PH Paul Hornung 20.00 40.00
PSR Pat Sullivan Red Ink/23* 12.50 30.00
RB Raymond Berry 12.50 30.00
TF Tommie Frazier 25.00 50.00
YT Y.A. Tittle/15* 30.00 60.00
YTR Y.A. Tittle Red Ink/10* 30.00 60.00

2007 Press Pass Legends Saturday Swatches Silver

*PREMIUM/30-50: .8X TO 2X BASIC JSYs
PREMIUM PRINT RUN 10-50 SER.#'d SETS
UNPRICED PATCH PRINT RUN 5-10SETS
OVERALL SWATCH ODDS 1:18
SSAC Adam Carriker 3.00 8.00
SSAH A.J. Hawk 10.00 25.00
SSAP Adrian Peterson 10.00 25.00
SSBC Brodie Croyle 5.00 12.00
SSBJ Brandon Jackson 4.00 10.00
SSBQ Brady Quinn 5.00 12.00
SSCS Chansi Stuckey 3.00 8.00
SSDB2 Dwayne Bowe 4.00 10.00
SSDJ Dwayne Jarrett 3.00 8.00
SSDR DeMeco Ryans 4.00 10.00
SSDW Darius Walker 4.00 10.00
SSDW2 Dwayne Wright 3.00 8.00
SSDW3 DeShawn Wynn 3.00 8.00
SSGW Garrett Wolfe 3.00 8.00
SSJF Joel Filani 3.00 8.00
SSJP Jordan Palmer 3.00 8.00
SSJR JaMarcus Russell 3.00 8.00
SSKD Kenneth Darby 5.00 12.00
SSKI Kenny Irons 4.00 10.00
SSKK Kevin Kolb 4.00 10.00
SSKS Kolby Smith 4.00 10.00
SSLB Lorenzo Booker
SSMA Marcus Allen 6.00 15.00
SSMB Michael Bush 3.00 8.00
SSMJD Maurice Jones-Drew 4.00 10.00
SSML Marshawn Lynch 6.00 15.00
SSML2 Marcedes Lewis 3.00 8.00
SSSS Steve Smith USC 3.00 8.00
SSZM Zach Miller

2007 Press Pass Legends Student and Teacher Autographs

TOTF T.Osborne/T.Frazier 40.00 80.00

2008 Press Pass Legends

COMPLETE SET (100) 25.00 50.00
UNPRICED PRINT PLATE PRINT RUN 1
1 Felix Jones .30 .75
2 Darren McFadden .30 .75
3 Matt Ryan 1.00 2.50
4 Lavelle Hawkins .40 1.00
5 DeSean Jackson .60 1.50
6 Kevin Smith .30 .75
7 Joe Flacco .60 1.50
8 Chris Johnson .40 1.00
9 Andre Caldwell .30 .75
10 Derrick Harvey .30 .75
11 Tashard Choice .30 .75
12 Colt Brennan .40 1.00
13 Donnie Avery .40 1.00
14 Rashard Mendenhall .30 .75
15 Aqib Talib .50 1.25
16 Jordy Nelson 1.00 2.50
17 Andre Woodson .30 .75
18 Brian Brohm .30 .75
19 Harry Douglas .40 1.00
20 Glenn Dorsey .30 .75
21 Early Doucet .30 .75
22 Matt Flynn .30 .75
23 Jacob Hester .30 .75
24 Kenny Phillips .30 .75
25 Mike Hart .30 .75
26 Chad Henne .40 1.00
27 Mario Manningham .30 .75
28 Devin Thomas .30 .75
29 John Carlson .30 .75
30 Vernon Gholston .30 .75
31 Malcolm Kelly .30 .75
32 Dennis Dixon .30 .75
33 Jonathan Stewart .50 1.25
34 Dan Connor .30 .75
35 Ray Rice .30 .75
36 Josh Johnson .30 .75
37 Mike Jenkins .30 .75
38 Erik Ainge .30 .75
39 Jamaal Charles .50 1.25
40 Limas Sweed .30 .75
41 Leodis McKelvin .40 1.00
42 Matt Forte .50 1.25
43 John David Booty .30 .75
44 Fred Davis .30 .75
45 Sedrick Ellis .30 .75
46 Keith Rivers .30 .75
47 Eddie Royal .30 .75
48 Earl Bennett .50 1.25
49 Chris Long .40 1.00
50 Steve Slaton .30 .75
51 Ken Stabler .60 1.50
52 Gene Stallings .40 1.00
53 John Jefferson .40 1.00
54 Mike Singletary .60 1.50
55 Doug Flutie .50 1.25
56 Steve Young .75 2.00
57 Craig Morton .40 1.00
58 Cris Collinsworth .50 1.25
59 Steve Spurrier .60 1.50
60 Charlie Ward .40 1.00
61 Vince Dooley .40 1.00
62 Herschel Walker .60 1.50
63 Alex Karras .50 1.25
64A Gale Sayers dark jsy .60 1.50
64B Gale Sayers light jsy .60 1.50
65A Jack Lambert alone .60 1.50
65B Jack Lambert w/team .60 1.50
66 George Blanda .50 1.25
67 Leonard Marshall .40 1.00
68 Jimmy Johnson .50 1.25
69 Jim Kelly .60 1.50
70 Anthony Carter .40 1.00
71 Dan Dierdorf .40 1.00
72 Roger Craig .50 1.25
73 Tommie Frazier .40 1.00
74 Paul Hornung .60 1.50
75 Joe Montana running 2.00 5.00
75B Joe Montana pitching 2.00 5.00
76 Randy Gradishar .40 1.00
77 Chris Spielman .50 1.25
78 Brian Bosworth .60 1.50
79 Tommy McDonald .50 1.25
80 Barry Switzer .60 1.50
81 Eric Dickerson .50 1.25
82 Craig James .50 1.25
83 Brett Favre B&W 1.25 3.00
83B Brett Favre Clr 1.25 3.00
84 John Brodie .40 1.00
85 Floyd Little .40 1.00
86 Earl Campbell dark jsy .60 1.50
86B Earl Campbell light jsy .60 1.50
87 Tommy Nobis .40 1.00
88 Don Maynard .50 1.25
89 Troy Aikman .75 2.00
90 Billy Kilmer .50 1.25
91 Marcus Allen .60 1.50
92 Charles White .40 1.00
93 Hugh McElhenny .40 1.00
94 Warren Moon .60 1.50
95 Ollie Matson .50 1.25

2008 Press Pass Legends Bronze

*BRONZE ROOKIES: .6X TO 1.5X
*BRONZE RETIRED: 1X TO 2.5X
BRONZE PRINT RUN 999 SER.#'d SETS

2008 Press Pass Legends Emerald

*EMERALD ROOKIES: 3X TO 8X
*EMERALD RETIRED: 5X TO 12X
EMERALD PRINT RUN 25 SER.#'d SETS

2008 Press Pass Legends Gold

*GOLD ROOKIES: 1.2X TO 3X
*GOLD RETIRED: 2X TO 5X
GOLD PRINT RUN 99 SER.#'d SETS

2008 Press Pass Legends Silver Holofoil

*SILVER ROOKIES: .8X TO 2X
*SLVR RETIRED: 1.2X TO 3X
SILVER HOLO.PRINT RUN 499 SER.#'d SETS

2008 Press Pass Legends All Conference

COMPLETE SET (20) 10.00 25.00
STATED ODDS 1:7
AC1 Colt Brennan .50 1.25
AC2 Brian Brohm .40 1.00
AC3 Matt Ryan 1.25 3.00
AC4 Chris Long .50 1.25
AC5 Felix Jones .40 1.00
AC6 Darren McFadden .40 1.00
AC7 Jonathan Stewart .60 1.50
AC8 Rashard Mendenhall .40 1.00
AC9 Mike Hart .40 1.00
AC10 Chad Henne .50 1.25
AC11 DeSean Jackson .75 2.00
AC12 Mario Manningham .40 1.00
AC13 Limas Sweed .40 1.00
AC14 John David Booty .40 1.00
AC15 Ray Rice .40 1.00
AC16 Steve Slaton .40 1.00
AC17 Earl Bennett .60 1.50
AC18 Kevin Smith .40 1.00
AC19 Matt Forte .60 1.50
AC20 Jordy Nelson 1.25 3.00

2008 Press Pass Legends All Conference Autographs Gold

GOLD PRINT RUN 50-400
*PLAT/25: .6X TO 1.5X BASIC AU/100-400
*PLAT/25: .5X TO 1.2X BASIC AU/50
PLATINUM PRINT RUN 25 SER.#'d SETS
*RED INK/17-50: .5X TO 1.2X BASIC AUTO
ACAB Adarius Bowman/251 4.00 10.00
ACBB Brian Brohm/50 12.00 30.00
ACCB Colt Brennan/50 8.00 20.00
ACCH Chad Henne/150 4.00 10.00
ACCL Chris Long/99 8.00 20.00
ACDC Dan Connor/251 3.00 8.00
ACDD Dennis Dixon/245 3.00 8.00
ACDJ DeSean Jackson/150 6.00 15.00
ACDM Darren McFadden/100 4.00 10.00
ACEB Earl Bennett/250 5.00 12.00
ACFD Fred Davis/150 3.00 8.00
ACFJ Felix Jones/100 5.00 12.00
ACJDB John David Booty/200 3.00 8.00
ACJF Justin Forsett/400 4.00 10.00
ACJN Jordy Nelson/400 8.00 20.00
ACJS Jonathan Stewart/100 15.00 30.00
ACKS Kevin Smith/245 3.00 8.00
ACLS Limas Sweed/150 3.00 8.00
ACMF Matt Forte/399 12.00 30.00
ACMH Mike Hart/150 3.00 8.00
ACMM Mario Manningham/150 6.00 15.00
ACMR Matt Ryan/50 25.00 60.00
ACRM Rashard Mendenhall/147 4.00 10.00
ACRR Ray Rice/245 3.00 8.00
ACSS Steve Slaton/245 3.00 8.00
ACTC Tashard Choice/400 3.00 8.00

2008 Press Pass Legends Alumni Association

COMPLETE SET (10) 8.00 20.00
STATED ODDS 1:14
AA1 F.Jones/McFadden .40 1.00
AA2 D.Flutie/M.Ryan 1.25 3.00
AA3 R.Craig/T.Frazier 1.25 3.00
AA4 H.McElhenny/W.Moon 1.50 4.00
AA5 P.Hornung/J.Montana 5.00 12.00
AA6 Gradishar/C.Spielman 1.25 3.00
AA7 Collinsworth/S.Spurrier 1.50 4.00
AA8 McDonald/Bosworth 1.50 4.00
AA9 E.Campbell/T.Nobis 1.50 4.00
AA10 E.Dickerson/C.James 1.25 3.00

2008 Press Pass Legends Alumni Association Autographs

STATED PRINT RUN 25-50
TMBBR McDnld/Bswrth Red/28* 40.00 80.00
DFMR Flutie/M.Ryan/50 30.00 80.00
DMFJ McFadden/Jones/25 10.00 25.00
ECTN E.Camp/Nobis/50 EXCH 25.00 50.00
EDCJ Dickrsn/James/50 EXCH 20.00 40.00
HMWM McElhenny/W.Moon/50 20.00 40.00
PHJM Hornung/Mont/25 100.00 175.00
RCTF R.Craig/T.Frazier/50 20.00 40.00
RGCS Gradishar/Spielman/50 20.00 40.00
SSCC Spurr/Cllnswth Red/50 30.00 60.00
TMBB McDonald/Bosworth/50 40.00 80.00

2008 Press Pass Legends Legendary Legacy

COMPLETE SET (20) 12.00 30.00
STATED ODDS 1:7
LL1 Gale Sayers 1.50 4.00
LL2 Craig Morton 1.00 2.50
LL3 Charlie Ward 1.00 2.50
LL4 Warren Moon 1.50 4.00
LL5 Brett Favre 2.50 6.00
LL6 Joe Montana 5.00 12.00
LL7 Mike Singletary 1.50 4.00
LL8 Troy Aikman 2.00 5.00
LL9 Eric Dickerson 1.25 3.00
LL10 Steve Young 2.00 5.00
LL11 John Jefferson 1.00 2.50
LL12 Jack Lambert 1.50 4.00
LL13 Earl Campbell 1.50 4.00
LL14 Jim Kelly 1.50 4.00
LL15 Tommy McDonald 1.25 3.00
LL16 Craig James 1.25 3.00
LL17 Tommy Nobis 1.00 2.50
LL18 George Blanda 1.25 3.00
LL19 Chris Spielman 1.25 3.00
LL20 Cris Collinsworth 1.25 3.00

2008 Press Pass Legends Legendary Legacy Autographs Gold

GOLD PRINT RUN 25-392
*PLAT/21-25: .6X TO 1.5X GOLD AU/150-392
*PLAT/21-25: .5X TO 1.2X GOLD AU/50-130
*PLAT/21-25: .4X TO 1X GOLD AU/25
PLATINUM PRINT RUN 21-25
*RED INK: .5X TO 1.2X BASIC AUTO
LLBF Brett Favre/50 100.00 175.00
LLCJ Craig James/150 6.00 15.00
LLCM Craig Morton/392 5.00 12.00
LLCW Charlie Ward/311 5.00 12.00
LLEC Earl Campbell/100 EXCH
LLED Eric Dickerson/50 25.00 50.00
LLGB George Blanda/105 15.00 40.00
LLGS Gale Sayers/53 30.00 60.00
LLJJ John Jefferson/372 5.00 12.00
LLJK Jim Kelly/72 20.00 50.00
LLJL Jack Lambert/100 20.00 40.00
LLJM Joe Montana/25 75.00 150.00
LLMS Mike Singletary/130 10.00 25.00
LLSY Steve Young/75 25.00 60.00
LLTA Troy Aikman/50 40.00 80.00
LLTM Tommy McDonald/250 8.00 20.00
LLWM Warren Moon/100 10.00 25.00

2008 Press Pass Legends Saturday Signatures

*RED INK/20-82: .5X TO 1.2X BASIC AUTO
SSAA Adrian Arrington SP 8.00 20.00
SSAC Andre Caldwell 4.00 10.00
SSAC2 Antoine Cason SP
SSAC3 Anthony Carter 6.00 15.00
SSAD Adarius Bowman SP
SSAK Alex Karras 6.00 15.00
SSAP Allen Patrick 4.00 10.00
SSAT Aqib Talib SP
SSAW Andre Woodson 5.00 12.00
SSBB Brian Brohm 6.00 15.00
SSBB2 Brian Bosworth 12.00 30.00
SSBF Brett Favre 90.00 150.00
SSBK Billy Kilmer 5.00 12.00
SSBS Barry Switzer 30.00 60.00
SSCB Colt Brennan SP 10.00 25.00
SSCC Calais Campbell SP
SSCC2 Cris Collinsworth 5.00 12.00
SSCH Chad Henne
SSCJ Chris Johnson 4.00 10.00
SSCJ2 Craig James 5.00 12.00
SSCL Chris Long 4.00 10.00
SSCM Craig Morton 5.00 12.00
SSCS Chris Spielman 10.00 25.00
SSCW Chauncey Washington 5.00 12.00
SSCW2 Charlie Ward 8.00 20.00
SSCW3 Charles White 6.00 15.00
SSDA Donnie Avery 6.00 15.00
SSDB Dorien Bryant 4.00 10.00
SSDB2 Davone Bess 5.00 12.00
SSDC Dan Connor 5.00 12.00
SSDD Dennis Dixon 6.00 15.00
SSDD2 Dan Dierdorf 6.00 15.00
SSDF Doug Flutie 10.00 25.00
SSDH DJ Hall 5.00 12.00
SSDH2 Derrick Harvey 4.00 10.00
SSDJ DeSean Jackson 6.00 15.00
SSDM Darren McFadden 4.00 10.00
SSDM2 Don Maynard 5.00 12.00
SSDR Darius Reynaud 4.00 10.00
SSDS Dantrell Savage SP 4.00 10.00
SSDT Devin Thomas 5.00 12.00
SSEA Erik Ainge 6.00 15.00
SSEB Earl Bennett 5.00 12.00
SSEC Earl Campbell 20.00 40.00
SSED Early Doucet 5.00 12.00
SSED2 Eric Dickerson SP 25.00 50.00
SSER Eddie Royal 3.00 8.00
SSFD Fred Davis 5.00 12.00
SSFJ Felix Jones 4.00 10.00
SSFL Floyd Little 5.00 12.00
SSGB George Blanda 15.00 40.00
SSGS Gale Sayers SP 25.00 50.00
SSGS2 Gene Stallings 10.00 25.00
SSHM Hugh McElhenny 6.00 15.00
SSJB John Brodie 6.00 15.00
SSJC Jamaal Charles 8.00 25.00
SSJC2 John Carlson SP
SSJDB John David Booty 3.00 8.00
SSJF Joe Flacco 10.00 25.00
SSJF2 Justin Forsett 5.00 12.00
SSJH2 Jacob Hester 5.00 12.00
SSJJ Josh Johnson 4.00 10.00
SSJJ2 Jimmy Johnson 12.00 30.00
SSJJ3 John Jefferson 6.00 15.00
SSJK Jim Kelly 25.00 50.00
SSJL Jack Lambert SP 30.00 60.00
SSJM Joe Montana SP 50.00 100.00
SSJN Jordy Nelson 10.00 25.00
SSJS Jonathan Stewart 10.00 25.00
SSKB Keenan Burton SP 3.00 8.00
SSKP Kenny Phillips SP
SSKR Keith Rivers 5.00 12.00
SSKS Kevin Smith 6.00 15.00
SSKS2 Ken Stabler 20.00 40.00
SSLH Lavelle Hawkins 4.00 10.00
SSLM Leodis McKelvin SP 4.00 10.00
SSLM2 Leonard Marshall 4.00 10.00
SSLS Limas Sweed 3.00 8.00
SSMA Marcus Allen 20.00 40.00
SSMF Matt Forte 10.00 25.00
SSMH Mike Hart 6.00 15.00
SSMK Malcolm Kelly 6.00 15.00
SSMM Mario Manningham/162* 5.00 12.00
SSMR Matt Ryan 15.00 40.00
SSMS Mike Singletary SP 12.00 30.00
SSOS Owen Schmitt 5.00 12.00
SSPH Paul Hornung 10.00 25.00
SSRC Roger Craig 6.00 15.00
SSRG Randy Gradishar 5.00 12.00
SSRM Rashard Mendenhall 4.00 10.00
SSRR Ray Rice 4.00 10.00
SSSE Sedrick Ellis SP
SSSS Steve Slaton 6.00 15.00
SSSS2 Steve Spurrier 12.00 30.00
SSSY Steve Young 25.00 50.00
SSTA Troy Aikman SP 40.00 80.00
SSTC Tashard Choice 6.00 15.00
SSTF Tommie Frazier 6.00 15.00
SSTM Tommy McDonald 10.00 25.00
SSTN Tommy Nobis 5.00 12.00
SSVD Vince Dooley 6.00 15.00
SSVG Vernon Gholston 5.00 12.00
SSWM Warren Moon 10.00 25.00

2008 Press Pass Legends Saturday Swatches Silver

*PREMIUM/40-50: .8X TO 2X SLVR JSY
*PREMIUM/40-50: .5X TO 1.2X SLVR JSY SP
PREMIUM PRINT RUN 40-50
UNPRICED PATCH PRINT RUN 10
SSWAA Adrian Arrington 3.00 8.00
SSWBB Brian Brohm 2.50 6.00
SSWCB Colt Brennan 4.00 10.00
SSWCH Chad Henne 3.00 8.00
SSWDA Donnie Avery SP 3.00 8.00
SSWDC Dan Connor SP 6.00 15.00
SSWDM Darren McFadden 2.50 6.00
SSWDT Devin Thomas 4.00 10.00
SSWEA Erik Ainge SP 10.00 25.00
SSWED Early Doucet 4.00 10.00
SSWJC Jamaal Charles 4.00 10.00
SSWJH Jacob Hester 4.00 10.00
SSWJS Jonathan Stewart 6.00 15.00
SSWKS Kevin Smith 2.50 6.00
SSWLS Limas Sweed 2.50 6.00
SSWMA Marcus Allen 4.00 10.00
SSWMF Matt Forte 5.00 12.00
SSWMK Malcolm Kelly 5.00 12.00
SSWMR Matt Ryan 6.00 15.00
SSWSS Steve Slaton 2.50 6.00
SSWVG Vernon Gholston 4.00 10.00
SSWJDB John David Booty 2.50 6.00

2008 Press Pass Legends Student and Teacher Autographs

STATED PRINT RUN 25 SER.#'d SETS
BBBS Bosworth/Switzer 60.00 120.00
HWVD H.Walker/Dooley EXCH

2009 Press Pass Legends

COMPLETE SET (100) 25.00 50.00
1 Glen Coffee .30 .75
2 Mike Thomas .30 .75
3 Nate Davis .30 .75
4 Ian Johnson SP .50 1.25
5 B.J. Raji .40 1.00
6 Austin Collie .30 .75
7 Ramses Barden .30 .75
8 James Davis .30 .75
9 Gartrell Johnson .30 .75
10 Donald Brown .30 .75
11 Darius Butler .40 1.00
12 Percy Harvin .30 .75
13 Louis Murphy .30 .75
14 Everette Brown .30 .75
15 Mohamed Massaquoi .30 .75
16 Knowshon Moreno .30 .75
17 Matthew Stafford 1.50 4.00
18 Vontae Davis .30 .75
19 Shonn Greene .30 .75
20 Josh Freeman .30 .75
21 Rashad Jennings .40 1.00
22 Tyson Jackson .30 .75
23 Darrius Heyward-Bey .50 1.25
24 Javon Ringer .30 .75
25 Chase Coffman .30 .75
26 Jeremy Maclin .40 1.00
27 William Moore .30 .75
28 Andre Brown .40 1.00
29 Hakeem Nicks .40 1.00
30 Brandon Tate .40 1.00
31 Malcolm Jenkins .30 .75
32 James Laurinaitis .30 .75
33 Brian Robiskie .30 .75
34 Chris Wells .30 .75
35 Brandon Pettigrew .30 .75
36 Juaquin Iglesias SP .50 1.25
37 Aaron Maybin .40 1.00
38 Derrick Williams .30 .75
39 LeSean McCoy .75 2.00
40 James Casey .40 1.00
41 Jarett Dillard SP .50 1.25
42 Kenny Britt .50 1.25
43 Rhett Bomar .30 .75
44 Jared Cook .40 1.00
45 Kenny McKinley .30 .75
46 Brian Orakpo .40 1.00
47 Mike Goodson .40 1.00
48 Stephen McGee .30 .75
49 Graham Harrell SP .50 1.25
50 Michael Crabtree .50 1.25
51 Brian Cushing .30 .75
52 Rey Maualuga .50 1.25
53 Mark Sanchez .30 .75
54 D.J. Moore .40 1.00
55 Cedric Peerman .30 .75
56 Victor Harris .40 1.00
57 Aaron Curry .50 1.25
58 Alphonso Smith .30 .75
59 Brandon Gibson .40 1.00
60 Pat White .40 1.00
61 Ozzie Newsome .50 1.25
62 Dick Anderson .40 1.00
63 Cliff Branch .40 1.00
64 Bruce Smith SP .75 2.00
65 Deion Sanders .50 1.25
66 Fran Tarkenton .60 1.50
67 Doug Williams .50 1.25
68 Frank Gifford SP 1.00 2.50
69 Lee Corso .50 1.25
70 Tom Jackson .50 1.25
71 Boomer Esiason .50 1.25
72 Kellen Winslow .50 1.25
73 Bill Cowher .50 1.25
74 Tommie Frazier .40 1.00
75 Lawrence Taylor .60 1.50
76 Rocky Bleier .50 1.25
77 Dave Casper .40 1.00
78 Paul Hornung .60 1.50
79 Joe Theismann .60 1.50
80 Ricky Watters .40 1.00
81 Howard Cassady .40 1.00
82 Kirk Herbstreit .50 1.25
83 Paul Warfield SP .75 2.00
84 Billy Sims .50 1.25
85 Dan Fouts .50 1.25
86 Bruce Smith SP .75 2.00
87 Tony Dorsett .60 1.50
88 Mike Alstott .40 1.00
89 Rod Woodson .50 1.25
90 Bob Lilly .50 1.25
91 Gary Beban .40 1.00

92 Sam Huff .50 1.25
93 Jim Kiick .40 1.00
94 Charley Taylor .40 1.00
95 John Brodie .40 1.00
96 John Elway 1.00 2.50
97 Randall Cunningham .50 1.25
98 Bernie Kosar SP .75 2.00
99 Rod Woodson SP .75 2.00
100 John Elway CL .60 1.50

2009 Press Pass Legends Bronze

*ROOKIES 1-60: .6X TO 1.5X BASIC CARDS
*ROOKIE SP: .4X TO 1X BASIC CARDS
*LEGENDS 61-100: 1X TO 2.5X BASIC CARDS
*LEGEND SP: .6X TO 1.5X BASIC CARDS
BRONZE PRINT RUN 899 SER.#'d SETS

2009 Press Pass Legends Emerald

*ROOKIES 1-60: 3X TO 8X BASIC CARDS
*ROOKIE SP: 2X TO 5X BASIC CARDS
*LEGENDS 61-100: 5X TO 12X BASIC CARDS
*LEGEND SP: 3X TO 8X BASIC CARDS
EMERALD PRINT RUN 25 SER.#'d SETS

2009 Press Pass Legends Gold

*ROOKIES 1-60: 1.2X TO 3X BASIC CARDS
*ROOKIE SP: .8X TO 2X BASIC CARDS
*LEGENDS 61-100: 2X TO 5X BASIC CARDS
*LEGEND SP: 1.2X TO 3X BASIC CARDS
GOLD PRINT RUN 99 SER.#'d SETS

2009 Press Pass Legends Silver Holofoil

*ROOKIES 1-100: 1X TO 2.5X BASIC CARDS
*ROOKIE SP: .6X TO 1.5X BASIC CARDS
*LEGENDS 61-100: 1.5X TO 4X BASIC CARDS
*LEGEND SP: 1X TO 2.5X BASIC CARDS
SILVER HOLOFOIL PRINT RUN 299 SER.#'d SETS

2009 Press Pass Legends All Conference

STATED ODDS 1:7
AC1 Matthew Stafford 2.00 5.00
AC2 Glen Coffee .40 1.00
AC3 Knowshon Moreno .40 1.00
AC4 Percy Harvin .40 1.00
AC5 Mohamed Massaquoi .40 1.00
AC6 Hakeem Nicks .50 1.25
AC7 Darrius Heyward-Bey .60 1.50
AC8 Aaron Curry .60 1.50
AC9 Shonn Greene .40 1.00
AC10 Javon Ringer .40 1.00
AC11 Chris Wells .40 1.00
AC12 Derrick Williams .40 1.00
AC13 James Laurinaitis .40 1.00
AC14 Mark Sanchez .40 1.00
AC15 Pat White .50 1.25
AC16 Kenny Britt .60 1.50
AC17 LeSean McCoy 1.00 2.50
AC18 Donald Brown .40 1.00
AC19 Jeremy Maclin .50 1.25
AC20 Michael Crabtree .60 1.50

2009 Press Pass Legends All Conference Autographs

STATED PRINT RUN 99-299
*RED INK/49: .5X TO 1.2X BASIC AU
*PLATINUM/25: .6X TO 1.5X BASIC AUTO
PLAT.RED INK ANNC'D PRINT RUN 4-25
ACAC1 Aaron Curry/100 5.00 12.00
ACAC2 Austin Collie/299 3.00 8.00
ACBO Brian Orakpo/99 8.00 20.00
ACCW Chris Wells/141 3.00 8.00
ACDB Donald Brown/199 8.00 20.00
ACDHB Darrius Heyward-Bey/199 5.00 12.00
ACDM Mohamed Massaquoi/287 3.00 8.00
ACDW Derrick Williams/299 3.00 8.00
ACGC Glen Coffee/299 3.00 8.00
ACHN Hakeem Nicks/199 4.00 10.00
ACIJ Ian Johnson/299 3.00 8.00
ACJD Jarett Dillard/299 3.00 8.00
ACJL James Laurinaitis/150 8.00 20.00
ACJM Jeremy Maclin/199 4.00 10.00
ACJR Javon Ringer/299 3.00 8.00
ACKB Kenny Britt/299 5.00 12.00
ACKM Knowshon Moreno/150 3.00 8.00
ACLM LeSean McCoy/199 8.00 20.00
ACMC Michael Crabtree/150 5.00 12.00
ACMJ Malcolm Jenkins/150 3.00 8.00
ACMS1 Mark Sanchez/100 12.00 30.00
ACMS2 Matthew Stafford/150 25.00 60.00
ACND Nate Davis/138 3.00 8.00
ACPH Percy Harvin/199 3.00 8.00
ACPW Pat White/150 4.00 10.00
ACRB Rhett Bomar/299 3.00 8.00
ACRM Rey Maualuga/150 5.00 12.00
ACSG Shonn Greene/199 3.00 8.00

2009 Press Pass Legends Alumni Association

STATED ODDS 1:14
AA1 L.Taylor/H.Nicks .60 1.50
AA2 R.Woodson/M.Alstott 1.25 3.00
AA3 L.Corso/D.Sanders 1.25 3.00
AA4 F.Tarkenton/M.Stafford 2.50 6.00
AA5 T.Dorsett/L.McCoy 1.25 3.00
AA6 K.Winslow/J.Maclin .60 1.50
AA7 H.Cassady/C.Wells .50 1.25
AA8 J.Brodie/J.Elway 3.00 8.00
AA9 S.Huff/P.White .60 1.50
AA10 F.Gifford/M.Sanchez .50 1.25

2009 Press Pass Legends Alumni Association Autographs

STATED PRINT RUN 24-50
FTMS Tarkntn/Staffrd/50 EXCH 30.00 80.00
HCCW Cassady/Wells/50 20.00 50.00
JBJE Brodie/Elway/25 100.00 200.00
KWJM K.Winslow/J.Maclin/50 25.00 50.00
LCDS L.Corso/Deion/25 40.00 80.00
LTHN L.Tylr/Nicks/25 EXCH
RWMA R.Woodson/M.Alstott/49 30.00 60.00
TDLM T.Dorsett/L.McCoy/24 30.00 60.00
BEDHB Esisn/Hey-Bey/50 EXCH

2009 Press Pass Legends Legends of the Fall

STATED ODDS 1:7
LOF1 Mike Alstott 1.00 2.50
LOF2 Tony Dorsett 1.50 4.00
LOF3 Paul Hornung 1.50 4.00
LOF4 Ozzie Newsome 1.25 3.00
LOF5 Deion Sanders 1.25 3.00
LOF6 Billy Sims 1.25 3.00
LOF7 Lawrence Taylor 1.50 4.00
LOF8 Rod Woodson 1.25 3.00
LOF9 Howard Cassady 1.00 2.50
LOF10 Kellen Winslow 1.25 3.00
LOF11 Boomer Esiason 1.25 3.00
LOF12 Dan Fouts 1.25 3.00
LOF13 Sam Huff 1.25 3.00
LOF14 Dave Casper 1.00 2.50
LOF15 Bruce Smith 1.25 3.00
LOF16 Doug Williams 1.25 3.00
LOF17 John Elway 2.50 6.00
LOF18 Matt Ryan 1.25 3.00
LOF19 Frank Gifford 1.50 4.00
LOF20 Bernie Kosar 1.25 3.00

2009 Press Pass Legends Legends of the Fall Autographs

STATED PRINT RUN 25-355
*RED INK/20-35: .5X TO 1.2X BASIC AU
RED INK ANNC'D PRINT RUN 5-35
*PLAT/24-25: .5X TO 1.2X GOLD AU/71-355
*PLAT/25: .4X TO 1X GOLD AU/25-50
PLATINUM PRINT RUN 8-25
UNPRICED RED INK PLAT.ANNC'D PR 5-16
LOFBK Bernie Kosar/150 8.00 20.00
LOFDF Dan Fouts/50 25.00 50.00
LOFDS Deion Sanders/35 25.00 50.00
LOFDW Doug Williams/150 8.00 20.00
LOFHC Howard Cassady/280 10.00 25.00
LOFJE John Elway/25 75.00 150.00
LOFKW Kellen Winslow/150 8.00 20.00
LOFLT Lawrence Taylor/50 25.00 50.00
LOFMA Mike Alstott/150 10.00 25.00
LOFON Ozzie Newsome/199 6.00 15.00
LOFPH Paul Hornung/71 20.00 40.00
LOFSH Sam Huff/150 8.00 20.00
LOFTD Tony Dorsett/25 25.00 50.00
LOFBS1 Billy Sims/355 6.00 15.00
LOFBS2 Bruce Smith/50 20.00 40.00
LOFLBE Boomer Esiason/50 8.00 20.00

2009 Press Pass Legends Saturday Signatures

*RED INK/20-138: .5X TO 1.2X BASIC AU
ANNOUNCED RED INK PRINT RUN 3-138
*PLATINUM/18-25: .6X TO 1.5X BASIC AUTO
PLATINUM PRINT RUN 18-25
SIX AUTOS PER HOBBY BOX
SSAB Andre Brown 4.00 10.00
SSAC1 Aaron Curry 5.00 12.00
SSAC2 Austin Collie 3.00 8.00
SSAF Arian Foster 25.00 50.00
SSAS Alphonso Smith 3.00 8.00
SSBC1 Bill Cowher 15.00 40.00
SSBC2 Brian Cushing 3.00 8.00
SSBE Boomer Esiason 6.00 15.00
SSBG Brandon Gibson 4.00 10.00
SSBH Brian Hoyer 5.00 12.00
SSBK Bernie Kosar 8.00 20.00
SSBL Bob Lilly 8.00 20.00
SSBO Brian Orakpo 8.00 20.00
SSBP Brandon Pettigrew 3.00 8.00
SSBR Brian Robiskie 3.00 8.00
SSBS1 Billy Sims 6.00 15.00
SSBS2 Bruce Smith 20.00 40.00
SSBT Brandon Tate 4.00 10.00
SSCB Cliff Branch 5.00 12.00
SSCC Chase Coffman 3.00 8.00
SSCH Cullen Harper 3.00 8.00
SSCP Cedric Peerman 3.00 8.00
SSCT Charley Taylor 5.00 12.00
SSCW Chris Wells 3.00 8.00
SSDA Dick Anderson 5.00 12.00
SSDB Donald Brown 8.00 20.00
SSDC Dave Casper 5.00 12.00
SSDF Dan Fouts 20.00 40.00
SSDHB Darrius Heyward-Bey 5.00 12.00
SSDM Devin Moore 3.00 8.00
SSDW1 Derrick Williams 3.00 8.00
SSDW2 Doug Williams 10.00 25.00
SSEB Everette Brown 3.00 8.00
SSFG Frank Gifford 12.00 30.00
SSFT Fran Tarkenton 12.00 30.00
SSGB Gary Beban 5.00 12.00
SSGC Glen Coffee 3.00 8.00
SSGH Graham Harrell 3.00 8.00
SSGJ Gartrell Johnson 3.00 8.00
SSHC1 Hunter Cantwell 3.00 8.00
SSHC2 Howard Cassady SP 15.00 40.00
SSHN Hakeem Nicks 8.00 20.00
SSIJ Ian Johnson 3.00 8.00
SSJB John Brodie 6.00 15.00
SSJC Jared Cook 4.00 10.00
SSJD1 James Davis 3.00 8.00
SSJD2 Jarett Dillard 3.00 8.00
SSJE John Elway 60.00 100.00
SSJF Josh Freeman 3.00 8.00
SSJI Juaquin Iglesias 3.00 8.00
SSJJ Jeremiah Johnson 3.00 8.00
SSJK Jim Kiick 6.00 15.00
SSJL James Laurinaitis 3.00 8.00
SSJM Jeremy Maclin 4.00 10.00
SSJR Javon Ringer 3.00 8.00
SSJT Joe Theismann 10.00 25.00
SSJW John Parker Wilson 8.00 20.00
SSKB Kenny Britt 5.00 12.00
SSKH Kirk Herbstreit 8.00 20.00
SSKM Knowshon Moreno 3.00 8.00
SSKW Kellen Winslow 8.00 20.00
SSLC Lee Corso 8.00 20.00
SSLM1 LeSean McCoy 8.00 20.00
SSLM2 Louis Murphy 3.00 8.00
SSMA Mike Alstott 15.00 30.00
SSMC Michael Crabtree 5.00 12.00
SSMG Mike Goodson 4.00 10.00
SSMM Mohamed Massaquoi 3.00 8.00
SSMS1 Mark Sanchez 12.00 30.00
SSMS2 Matthew Stafford 20.00 50.00
SSMT Mike Thomas 3.00 8.00
SSND Nate Davis 3.00 8.00
SSON Ozzie Newsome 6.00 15.00
SSPH1 Percy Harvin 3.00 8.00
SSPH2 P.J. Hill 3.00 8.00
SSPH3 Paul Hornung 15.00 30.00
SSPW1 Paul Warfield 8.00 20.00
SSPW2 Pat White 4.00 10.00
SSQC Quan Cosby 3.00 8.00
SSRB Rocky Bleier 8.00 20.00
SSRB1 Ramses Barden 3.00 8.00
SSRB2 Rhett Bomar 3.00 8.00
SSRC Randall Cunningham 6.00 15.00
SSRJ Rashad Jennings 4.00 10.00
SSRW1 Ricky Watters 6.00 15.00
SSRW2 Rod Woodson 20.00 40.00
SSSG Shonn Greene 3.00 8.00
SSSH Sam Huff 8.00 20.00
SSTF Tommie Frazier 8.00 20.00
SSTJ1 Tom Jackson 6.00 15.00
SSTJ2 Tyson Jackson 3.00 8.00
SSVD Vontae Davis 3.00 8.00

2009 Press Pass Legends Saturday Swatches Premium

PREMIUM PRINT RUN 30-99
*PATCH/17-25: .8X TO 2X PREMIUM JSY
PATCHES PRINT RUN 2-25
*SILVER/125-199: .3X TO .8X PREMIUM/80-99
*SILVER/125-199: .25X TO .6X PREMIUM/50
*SILVER/125-199: .2X TO .5X PREMIUM/30
*SILVER/70-99: .4X TO 1X PREMIUM/70-99
*SILVER/70-99: .3X TO .8X PREMIUM/50
*SILVER/50: .5X TO 1.2X PREMIUM/99
*SILVER/50: .4X TO 1X PREMIUM/50
*SILVER/25: .6X TO 1.5X PREMIUM/99
SILVER PRINT RUN 25-199
SSWAF Arian Foster/99 8.00 20.00
SSWBG Brandon Gibson/99 4.00 10.00
SSWBR Brian Robiskie/75 3.00 8.00
SSWCD Chase Daniel/99 4.00 10.00
SSWCH Cullen Harper/99 3.00 8.00
SSWDB Donald Brown/99 3.00 8.00
SSWDM Darren McFadden/30 8.00 20.00
SSWDW Derrick Williams/99 3.00 8.00
SSWGJ Gartrell Johnson/50 4.00 10.00
SSWIJ Ian Johnson/99 3.00 8.00
SSWJF Josh Freeman/50 4.00 10.00
SSWJL James Laurinaitis/99 3.00 8.00
SSWJM Jeremy Maclin/35 6.00 15.00
SSWJS Jonathan Stewart/50 4.00 10.00
SSWJW John Parker Wilson/99 10.00 25.00
SSWKB Kenny Britt/99 5.00 12.00
SSWKM Kenny McKinley/99 3.00 8.00
SSWKS Kevin Smith/70 3.00 8.00
SSWLM LeSean McCoy/99 8.00 20.00
SSWMA Mike Alstott/99 10.00 25.00
SSWMC Michael Crabtree/99 5.00 12.00
SSWMF Matt Forte/50 4.00 10.00
SSWMG Mike Goodson/99 4.00 10.00
SSWMR Matt Ryan/80 6.00 15.00
SSWMS Mark Sanchez/99 3.00 8.00
SSWND Nate Davis/99 3.00 8.00
SSWQC Quan Cosby/99 3.00 8.00
SSWRB Ramses Barden/50 4.00 10.00
SSWRM Rey Maualuga/99 5.00 12.00
SSWSG Shonn Greene/99 3.00 8.00
SSWSM Stephen McGee/50 4.00 10.00
SSWSS Steve Slaton/99 4.00 8.00
SSWDHB Darrius Heyward-Bey/99 5.00 12.00
SSWLM2 Louis Murphy/99 3.00 8.00
SSWMS2 Matthew Stafford/50 12.00 30.00
SSWRB2 Rhett Bomar/50 4.00 10.00

2011 Press Pass Legends

COMP.SET w/o SPs (90) 15.00 30.00
91-100 SP ODDS 1:18 HOB
UNPRICED PLATINUM PRINT RUN 1
UNPRICED PRINT PLATE PRINT RUN 1
1 Blaine Gabbert .20 .50
2 Cam Newton 1.00 2.50
3 Ryan Mallett .20 .50
4 Jake Locker .20 .50
5 Andy Dalton .40 1.00
6 Christian Ponder .20 .50
7 Colin Kaepernick .30 .75
8 Tyrod Taylor .40 1.00
9 Mark Ingram .30 .75
10 Daniel Thomas .20 .50
11 Mikel Leshoure .20 .50
12 Jacquizz Rodgers .20 .50
13 Ryan Williams .20 .50
14 Shane Vereen .25 .60
15 Jordan Todman .20 .50
16 Dion Lewis .25 .60
17 DeMarco Murray .40 1.00
18 Stevan Ridley .20 .50
19 Evan Royster .20 .50
20 Kendall Hunter .20 .50
21 Delone Carter .20 .50
22 Derrick Locke .25 .60
23 Roy Helu .20 .50
24 John Clay .30 .75
25 Jonathan Baldwin .20 .50
26 A.J. Green .50 1.25
27 Julio Jones .60 1.50
28 Torrey Smith .20 .50
29 Greg Little .25 .60
30 Austin Pettis .20 .50
31 Tandon Doss .20 .50
32 Niles Paul .20 .50
33 Terrence Toliver .25 .60
34 Jerrel Jernigan .20 .50
35 Titus Young .20 .50
36 Armon Binns .25 .60
37 Greg Salas .20 .50
38 Dane Sanzenbacher .20 .50
39 Darvin Adams .20 .50
40 Randall Cobb .30 .75
41 Kyle Rudolph .20 .50
42 Luke Stocker .20 .50
43 D.J. Williams .20 .50
44 Da'Quan Bowers .20 .50
45 Aldon Smith .20 .50
46 J.J. Watt 1.00 2.50
47 Cameron Heyward .25 .60
48 Ryan Kerrigan .25 .60
49 Nick Fairley .20 .50
50 Marcell Dareus .20 .50
51 Drake Nevis .20 .50
52 Stephen Paea .20 .50
53 Akeem Ayers .20 .50
54 Mark Herzlich .20 .50
55 Von Miller .30 .75
56 Prince Amukamara .20 .50
57 Aaron Williams .20 .50
58 Brandon Burton .25 .60
59 DeAndre McDaniel .20 .50
60 Rahim Moore .20 .50
61 Ahmad Black .25 .60
62 Dan Hampton .30 .75
63 Karl Mecklenburg .30 .75
64 Ickey Woods .30 .75
65 Antonio Freeman .30 .75
66 Bo Jackson .60 1.50
67 Jim Plunkett .40 1.00
68 Steve Young .60 1.50
69 Hines Ward .40 1.00
70 Michael Irvin .50 1.25
71 Ed McCaffrey .30 .75
72 Emmitt Smith .75 2.00
73 Tommie Frazier .30 .75
74 Tony Rice .30 .75
75 Willie Brown .30 .75
76 Cris Carter .50 1.25
77 Paul Hornung .50 1.25
78 Tedy Bruschi .40 1.00
79 Gino Cappelletti .30 .75
80 Jim Otto .30 .75
81 Paul Krause .30 .75
82 Bob Griese .50 1.25
83 Dan Marino 1.00 2.50
84 Warren Sapp .40 1.00
85 Johnny Rodgers .30 .75
86 Willie Davis .30 .75
87 Mike Rozier .30 .75
88 Major Harris .30 .75
89 Dick LeBeau .30 .75
90 Franco Harris .50 1.25
91 Cam Newton SP 2.50 6.00
92 Mark Ingram SP .75 2.00
93 A.J. Green SP 1.25 3.00
94 Blaine Gabbert SP .50 1.25
95 Julio Jones SP 1.50 4.00
96 Emmitt Smith SP 1.50 4.00
97 Hines Ward SP .75 2.00
98 Michael Irvin SP 1.00 2.50
99 Steve Young SP 1.25 3.00
100 Bo Jackson SP 1.25 3.00

2011 Press Pass Legends Bronze

*1-61 ROOKIES: 1.5X TO 4X BASIC CARDS
*62-90 LEGENDS: 1.2X TO 3X BASIC CARDS
*91-95 ROOKIES: 1X TO 2.5X BASIC SP
*96-100 LEGENDS: .8X TO 2X BASIC SP
STATED PRINT RUN 250 SER.#'d SETS

2011 Press Pass Legends Emerald

*1-61 ROOKIES: 4X TO 10X BASIC CARDS
*62-90 LEGENDS: 3X TO 8X BASIC CARDS
*91-95 ROOKIES: 2.5X TO 6X BASIC SP
*96-100 LEGENDS: 2X TO 5X BASIC SP
STATED PRINT RUN 25 SER.#'d SETS

2011 Press Pass Legends Gold

*1-61 ROOKIES: 2.5X TO 6X BASIC CARDS
*62-90 LEGENDS: 2X TO 5X BASIC CARDS
*91-95 ROOKIES: 1.5X TO 4X BASIC SP
*96-100 LEGENDS: 1.2X TO 3X BASIC SP
STATED PRINT RUN 99 SER.#'d SETS

2011 Press Pass Legends Silver Holofoil

*1-61 ROOKIES: 2X TO 5X BASIC CARDS
*62-90 LEGENDS: 1.5X TO 4X BASIC CARDS
*91-95 ROOKIES: 1.2X TO 3X BASIC SP
*96-100 LEGENDS: 1X TO 2.5X BASIC SP
STATED PRINT RUN 175 SER.#'d SETS

2011 Press Pass Legends All Americans

COMPLETE SET (13) 6.00 15.00
STATED ODDS 1:10
AA1 Prince Amukamara .40 1.00
AA2 Da'Quan Bowers .40 1.00
AA3 Randall Cobb .60 1.50
AA4 Nick Fairley .40 1.00
AA5 Kendall Hunter .40 1.00
AA6 Mark Ingram .60 1.50
AA7 Ryan Kerrigan .50 1.25
AA8 Von Miller .60 1.50
AA9 Drake Nevis .40 1.00
AA10 Cam Newton 2.00 5.00
AA11 Stephen Paea .40 1.00
AA12 Jordan Todman .40 1.00
AA13 J.J. Watt 2.00 5.00

2011 Press Pass Legends All Americans Autographs

STATED PRINT RUN 75-305
*RED INK: .5X TO 1.2X BASIC AUTO
*PLATINUM/25: .6X TO 1.5X BASIC AUTO
EXCH EXPIRATION: 5/31/2012
AACN Cam Newton/230* 25.00 60.00
AADB Da'Quan Bowers/100* 3.00 8.00
AADN Drake Nevis/167* 3.00 8.00
AAJT Jordan Todman/305 3.00 8.00
AAJW J.J. Watt/195* 25.00 50.00
AAKH Kendall Hunter/305 3.00 8.00
AAMI Mark Ingram/245* 15.00 40.00
AANF Nick Fairley/58* 3.00 8.00
AAPA Prince Amukamara/124* 3.00 8.00
AARC Randall Cobb/195* 5.00 12.00
AARK Ryan Kerrigan/155* 4.00 10.00
AASP Stephen Paea/191* 3.00 8.00
AAVM Von Miller/199 8.00 20.00

2011 Press Pass Legends All-Americans Autographs Platinum Red Ink

ACDN Drake Nevis/25

2011 Press Pass Legends Legends of the Fall

COMPLETE SET (17) 8.00 20.00
STATED ODDS 1:7
UNPRICED PRINT PLATE PRINT RUN 1
LOF1 Bo Jackson 1.50 4.00
LOF2 Ickey Woods .75 2.00
LOF3 Antonio Freeman .75 2.00
LOF4 Jim Plunkett 1.00 2.50
LOF5 Tommie Frazier .75 2.00
LOF6 Michael Irvin 1.25 3.00
LOF7 Ed McCaffrey .75 2.00
LOF8 Emmitt Smith 2.00 5.00
LOF9 Steve Young 1.50 4.00
LOF10 Hines Ward 1.00 2.50
LOF11 Tony Rice .75 2.00
LOF12 Cris Carter 1.25 3.00
LOF13 Paul Hornung 1.25 3.00
LOF14 Tedy Bruschi 1.00 2.50
LOF15 Bob Griese 1.25 3.00
LOF16 Warren Sapp 1.00 2.50
LOF17 Franco Harris 1.25 3.00

2011 Press Pass Legends Legends of the Fall Autographs

STATED PRINT RUN 25-399
*PLAT15-25: .5X TO 1.2X BASIC AU/75-399
*PLAT/15-25: .4X TO 1X BASIC AU/25-50
LOFBG Bob Griese/65* 15.00 30.00
LOFBJ Bo Jackson/17* 30.00 60.00
LOFEM Ed McCaffrey/274* 6.00 15.00
LOFES Emmitt Smith/10* 100.00 175.00
LOFFH Franco Harris/25 20.00 40.00
LOFHW Hines Ward/75 25.00 50.00
LOFIW Ickey Woods/375 5.00 12.00
LOFJP Jim Plunkett/135* 8.00 20.00
LOFLAF Antonio Freeman/369* 5.00 12.00
LOFMI Michael Irvin/49 20.00 40.00
LOFPH Paul Hornung/75* 12.00 30.00
LOFSY Steve Young/25 30.00 60.00
LOFTB Tedy Bruschi/13* 20.00 40.00
LOFTF Tommie Frazier/299 6.00 15.00
LOFTR Tony Rice/399 5.00 12.00
LOFWS Warren Sapp/150 8.00 20.00

2011 Press Pass Legends Legends of the Fall Autographs Red Ink

*RED INK: .5X TO 1.2X BASIC AU
RED INK ANNOUNCED PRINT RUN 8-87
LOFCC Cris Carter/25 20.00 40.00
LOFTB Tedy Bruschi/37* 15.00 40.00

2011 Press Pass Legends Past and Present

COMPLETE SET (10) 8.00 20.00
STATED ODDS 1:14
PP1 B.Jackson/C.Newton 2.50 6.00
PP2 H.Ward/A.Green 1.25 3.00
PP3 E.Smith/M.Ingram 1.25 3.00
PP4 S.Young/J.Locker 1.00 2.50
PP5 M.Irvin/J.Jones 1.50 4.00
PP6 C.Carter/J.Baldwin .75 2.00
PP7 D.Marino/R.Mallett 1.50 4.00
PP8 B.Griese/B.Gabbert .75 2.00
PP9 W.Sapp/N.Fairley .60 1.50
PP10 F.Harris/E.Royster .75 2.00

2011 Press Pass Legends Past and Present Autographs

STATED PRINT RUN 25-50
BGBG B.Griese/B.Gabbert/50 20.00 50.00
BJCN B.Jackson/C.Newton/30* 100.00 200.00
BJCNR Jackson/Newton Red/14* 100.00 200.00
CCJB C.Carter/J.Baldwin/50 20.00 40.00
DMRM D.Marino/R.Mallett/50 40.00 100.00
ESMI E.Smith/M.Ingram/50 40.00 100.00
FHER F.Harris/E.Royster/50 25.00 50.00
HWAG H.Ward/A.Green/25 25.00 60.00
MIJJ M.Irvin/J.Jones/26* 30.00 60.00
MIJJR Irvin Red/J.Jones Red/24* 30.00 80.00
SYJL S.Young/J.Locker/50 40.00 80.00
WSNF W.Sapp/N.Fairley/25 20.00 50.00

2011 Press Pass Legends Saturday Signatures

RANDOM INSERTS IN PACKS
*EMERALD/39-99: .5X TO 1.2X BASIC AU
*EMERALD/20-25: .6X TO 1.5X BASIC AU
*PLATINUM/20-25: .6X TO 1.5X BASIC AU
*RED INK: .5X TO 1.2X BASIC AU
UNPRICED PRINT PLATE PRINT RUN 1
SSAA Akeem Ayers
SSAB Ahmad Black 4.00 10.00
SSAB2 Armon Binns 4.00 10.00
SSAD Andy Dalton 6.00 15.00
SSAF Antonio Freeman 5.00 12.00
SSAG A.J. Green 10.00 25.00
SSAP Austin Pettis 3.00 8.00
SSAS Aldon Smith 3.00 8.00
SSAW Aaron Williams 3.00 8.00
SSBB Brandon Burton 4.00 10.00
SSBG Blaine Gabbert 3.00 8.00
SSBJ Bo Jackson SP
SSCC Cris Carter SP 12.50 25.00
SSCH Cameron Heyward 4.00 10.00
SSCK Colin Kaepernick 5.00 12.00
SSCN Cam Newton 20.00 40.00
SSCP Christian Ponder 3.00 8.00
SSDA Darvin Adams 3.00 8.00
SSDB Da'Quan Bowers 3.00 8.00
SSDC Delone Carter 3.00 8.00
SSDH Dan Hampton 6.00 15.00
SSDL Dick LeBeau 15.00 30.00
SSDL2 Dion Lewis 4.00 10.00
SSDL3 Derrick Locke 4.00 10.00
SSDM Dan Marino SP 60.00 120.00
SSDM2 DeMarco Murray 6.00 15.00
SSDM3 DeAndre McDaniel 3.00 8.00
SSDN Drake Nevis 3.00 8.00
SSDS Dane Sanzenbacher 3.00 8.00
SSDT Daniel Thomas 3.00 8.00
SSDW D.J. Williams 3.00 8.00
SSEM Ed McCaffrey
SSER Evan Royster 3.00 8.00
SSES Emmitt Smith SP
SSFH Franco Harris SP 20.00 40.00
SSGC Gino Cappelletti 5.00 12.00
SSGL Greg Little 4.00 10.00
SSGS Greg Salas 3.00 8.00
SSHW Hines Ward SP 20.00 40.00
SSIW Ickey Woods 5.00 12.00
SSJB Jonathan Baldwin 3.00 8.00
SSJC John Clay 5.00 12.00
SSJJ Julio Jones 10.00 25.00
SSJJ2 Jerrel Jernigan 3.00 8.00
SSJL Jake Locker 20.00 40.00
SSJO Jim Otto 8.00 20.00
SSJP Jim Plunkett SP 8.00 20.00
SSJR Johnny Rodgers 5.00 12.00
SSJR2 Jacquizz Rodgers 6.00 15.00
SSJT Jordan Todman 3.00 8.00
SSJW J.J. Watt 25.00 50.00
SSKH Kendall Hunter 3.00 8.00
SSKM Karl Mecklenburg 5.00 12.00
SSKR Kyle Rudolph 3.00 8.00
SSLS Luke Stocker 3.00 8.00
SSMD Marcell Dareus 3.00 8.00
SSMH Major Harris 6.00 15.00
SSMH2 Mark Herzlich 3.00 8.00
SSMI Michael Irvin SP 20.00 40.00
SSMI2 Mark Ingram 5.00 12.00
SSML Mikel Leshoure 3.00 8.00
SSMR Mike Rozier 5.00 12.00
SSNF Nick Fairley 3.00 8.00
SSNP Niles Paul 3.00 8.00
SSPA Prince Amukamara 3.00 8.00
SSPH Paul Hornung SP 10.00 25.00
SSPK Paul Krause 6.00 15.00
SSRC Randall Cobb 5.00 12.00
SSRH Roy Helu 6.00 15.00
SSRK Ryan Kerrigan 6.00 15.00
SSRM Ryan Mallett 3.00 8.00
SSRM2 Rahim Moore 3.00 8.00
SSRW Ryan Williams 3.00 8.00
SSSP Stephen Paea 3.00 8.00
SSSR Stevan Ridley 3.00 8.00
SSSV Shane Vereen 5.00 12.00
SSSY Steve Young SP 25.00 50.00
SSTB Tedy Bruschi SP 20.00 40.00
SSTD Tandon Doss 3.00 8.00
SSTF Tommie Frazier 5.00 12.00
SSTR Tony Rice 5.00 12.00
SSTS Torrey Smith 3.00 8.00
SSTT Tyrod Taylor 6.00 15.00
SSTT2 Terrence Toliver 4.00 10.00
SSTY Titus Young 5.00 12.00
SSVM Von Miller 8.00 20.00
SSWB Willie Brown 5.00 12.00
SSWD Warrick Dunn 8.00 20.00
SSWD2 Willie Davis 6.00 15.00
SSWS Warren Sapp SP 15.00 30.00

2011 Press Pass Legends Saturday Swatches Silver

OVERALL JSY STATED ODDS 1:18
*PREMIUM/99: .6X TO 1.5X SILVER JSY
UNPRICED PATCH PRINT RUN 5-10
SSWAD Andy Dalton 5.00 12.00
SSWAG A.J. Green 5.00 12.00
SSWBG Blaine Gabbert 2.50 6.00
SSWDB Da'Quan Bowers 4.00 10.00
SSWDL Derrick Locke 3.00 8.00
SSWJB Jonathan Baldwin 4.00 10.00
SSWJJ Julio Jones 6.00 15.00
SSWJL Jake Locker 8.00 20.00
SSWJR Jacquizz Rodgers 5.00 12.00
SSWKR Kyle Rudolph 5.00 12.00
SSWNP Niles Paul 5.00 12.00
SSWPA Prince Amukamara 5.00 12.00
SSWRH Roy Helu 5.00 12.00
SSWRM Ryan Mallett 5.00 12.00
SSWSR Stevan Ridley 2.50 6.00
SSWSV Shane Vereen 3.00 8.00
SSWTS Torrey Smith 4.00 10.00
SSWTT Terrence Toliver 3.00 8.00

2008 Press Pass Legends Bowl Edition

This set was released on December 26, 2008. The base set consists of 100 cards.
STATED PRINT RUN 299 SER.#'d SETS
UNPRICED PRINT PLATE PRINT RUN 1
1 Troy Aikman 2.50 6.00
2 Tedy Bruschi 1.25 3.00
3 Earl Campbell 2.00 5.00
4 Cris Collinsworth 1.50 4.00
5 Bill Cowher 2.00 5.00
6 Eric Dickerson 1.50 4.00
7 Glenn Dorsey .60 1.50
8 Brett Favre 3.00 8.00
9 Joe Flacco 1.25 3.00
10 Matt Forte 1.00 2.50
11 Tommie Frazier 1.25 3.00
12 DeSean Jackson 1.25 3.00
13 Chris Johnson .75 2.00
14 Jimmy Johnson 1.50 4.00
15 Felix Jones .60 1.50
16 Lee Roy Jordan 1.50 4.00
17 Jim Kelly 2.00 5.00
18 Jack Lambert 2.00 5.00
19 Chris Long .75 2.00
20 Darren McFadden .60 1.50
21 Rashard Mendenhall .60 1.50
22 Joe Montana 5.00 12.00
23 Warren Moon 2.50 6.00
24 Ray Rice .60 1.50
25 Eddie Royal .60 1.50
26 Matt Ryan 2.00 5.00
27 Gale Sayers 2.00 5.00
28 Mike Singletary 2.00 5.00
29 Steve Slaton .60 1.50
30 Kevin Smith .60 1.50
31 Chris Spielman 1.50 4.00
32 Ken Stabler 2.00 5.00
33 Jonathan Stewart 1.00 2.50
34 Barry Switzer 2.00 5.00
35 Herschel Walker 2.00 5.00
36 Steve Young 2.50 6.00
37 Derrick Brooks 1.00 2.50
38 Joey Galloway 1.25 3.00
39 Frank Gore 1.25 3.00
40 Paul Hornung 2.00 5.00
41 Sonny Jurgensen 1.50 4.00
42 Ray Lewis 1.50 4.00
43 George Rogers 1.25 3.00
44 Dick Butkus 2.50 6.00
45 Cris Carter 2.00 5.00
46 Bob Griese 2.00 5.00
47 Bo Jackson 2.50 6.00
48 Billy Kilmer 1.50 4.00
49 Floyd Little 1.25 3.00
50 Tommy McDonald 1.50 4.00
51 Tom Rathman 1.50 4.00
52 Billy Sims 1.50 4.00
53 Steve Spurrier 2.00 5.00
54 Aaron Kampman 1.25 3.00
55 Mike Rozier 1.25 3.00
56 Y.A. Tittle 2.00 5.00
57 Craig Morton 1.25 3.00
58 Hugh McElhenny 1.25 3.00
59 Roger Craig 1.50 4.00
60 Ty Detmer 1.25 3.00
61 Craig James 1.50 4.00
62 Tommy Nobis 1.25 3.00
63 Pat Sullivan 1.25 3.00
64 Joe Theismann 2.00 5.00
65 Zach Thomas 1.25 3.00
66 Danny Wuerffel 1.25 3.00
67 Raymond Berry 1.50 4.00
68 Rocky Bleier 1.50 4.00
69 Billy Cannon 1.25 3.00
70 Anthony Carter 1.25 3.00
71 John Jefferson 1.25 3.00
72 Johnny Rodgers 1.25 3.00
73 Charles White 1.25 3.00
74 Sam Huff 1.50 4.00
75 Paul Warfield 1.50 4.00
76 Donnie Avery .75 2.00
77 Davone Bess .75 2.00
78 John David Booty .60 1.50
79 Colt Brennan .75 2.00
80 Jamaal Charles 1.00 2.50
81 Harry Douglas .75 2.00
82 Chad Henne .75 2.00
83 Malcolm Kelly .60 1.50
84 Josh Morgan .60 1.50
85 Jordy Nelson 2.00 5.00
86 Limas Sweed .60 1.50
87 Devin Thomas .60 1.50
88 James Lofton 1.25 3.00
89 Donnie Avery .75 2.00
90 Joe Flacco 1.25 3.00
91 Matt Forte 1.00 2.50
92 DeSean Jackson 1.25 3.00
93 Chris Johnson .75 2.00
94 Felix Jones .60 1.50
95 Darren McFadden .60 1.50
96 Eddie Royal .60 1.50
97 Matt Ryan 2.00 5.00
98 Steve Slaton .60 1.50
99 Kevin Smith .60 1.50
100 Jonathan Stewart 1.00 2.50

2008 Press Pass Legends Bowl Edition 20 Yard Line Red

*VETS: .5X TO 1.2X BASIC CARDS
*ROOKIES: .4X TO 1X BASIC CARDS
*RETIRED: .5X TO 1.2X BASIC CARDS
STATED PRINT RUN 150 SER.#'d SETS

2008 Press Pass Legends Bowl Edition 15 Yard Line Blue

*ACTIVE: .6X TO 1.5X BASIC CARDS
*ROOKIES: .5X TO 1.2X BASIC CARDS
*RETIRED: .6X TO 1.5X BASIC CARDS
STATED PRINT RUN 99 SER.#'d SETS

2008 Press Pass Legends Bowl Edition 10 Yard Line Holofoil

*ACTIVE: .6X TO 1.5X BASIC CARDS
*ROOKIES: .5X TO 1.2X BASIC CARDS
*RETIRED: .6X TO 1.5X BASIC CARDS
STATED PRINT RUN 75 SER.#'d SETS

2008 Press Pass Legends Bowl Edition 5 Yard Line Gold

*ACTIVE: .8X TO 2X BASIC CARDS
*ROOKIES: .6X TO 1.5X BASIC CARDS
*RETIRED: .8X TO 2X BASIC CARDS
STATED PRINT RUN 50 SER.#'d SETS

2008 Press Pass Legends Bowl Edition Goal Line Emerald

*ACTIVE: 1X TO 2.5X BASIC CARDS
*ROOKIES: .8X TO 2X BASIC CARDS
*RETIRED: 1X TO 2.5X BASIC CARDS
STATED PRINT RUN 25 SER.#'d SETS

2008 Press Pass Legends Bowl Edition Touchdown Platinum

UNPRICED PLATINUM PRINT RUN 1

2008 Press Pass Legends Bowl Edition Autographs

ATED PRINT RUN 15-296
UNPRICED PRINT PLATE PRINT RUN 1
SERIAL #'d UNDER 19 NOT PRICED
AC Anthony Carter/100 6.00 15.00
AK Aaron Kampman/150 15.00 40.00
BC Bill Cowher/50 15.00 30.00
BC2 Billy Cannon/185 12.00 30.00
BF Brett Favre/19 100.00 200.00
BG Bob Griese/35 12.00 30.00
BK Billy Kilmer/199 5.00 12.00
BS Billy Sims/48 10.00 25.00
BS2 Barry Switzer/75 25.00 50.00
CC2 Cris Collinsworth/50 8.00 20.00
CJ Craig James/160 5.00 12.00
CM Craig Morton/244 6.00 15.00
CS Chris Spielman/125 10.00 25.00
CW Charles White/100 6.00 15.00
DB Derrick Brooks/235 6.00 15.00
DB2 Dick Butkus/25 30.00 60.00
DM Darren McFadden/225 3.00 8.00
DW Danny Wuerffel/68 12.00 30.00
EC Earl Campbell/175 EXCH
ED Eric Dickerson/71 20.00 40.00
FG Frank Gore/100 8.00 20.00
FL Floyd Little/85 6.00 15.00
GR George Rogers/100 8.00 20.00
HM Hugh McElhenny/150 8.00 20.00
JG Joey Galloway/296 5.00 12.00
JJ John Jefferson/145 5.00 12.00
JJ Jimmy Johnson/100 8.00 20.00
JK Jack Lambert/46 25.00 50.00
JL James Lofton/55 6.00 15.00
JM Joe Montana/40 60.00 120.00
JP Jim Plunkett/125 8.00 20.00
JR Johnny Rodgers/29 8.00 20.00
JT Joe Theismann/65 10.00 25.00
LJ Lee Roy Jordan/150 8.00 20.00
MR Mike Rozier/91 10.00 25.00
MS Mike Singletary/25 12.00 30.00
PH Paul Hornung/60 10.00 25.00
PS Pat Sullivan/30 8.00 20.00
PW Paul Warfield/150 8.00 20.00
RB Raymond Berry/95 6.00 15.00
RB2 Rocky Bleier/150 8.00 20.00
RC Roger Craig/98 8.00 20.00
RL Ray Lewis/110 50.00 100.00
SH Sam Huff/100 10.00 25.00
TB Tedy Bruschi/25 10.00 25.00
TD Ty Detmer/148 5.00 12.00
TF Tommie Frazier/100 10.00 25.00
TM Tommy McDonald/50 10.00 25.00
TN Tommy Nobis/99 6.00 15.00
TR Tom Rathman/150 10.00 25.00
WM Warren Moon/25 15.00 40.00
ZT Zach Thomas/97 10.00 25.00

2008 Press Pass Legends Bowl Edition Autographs Emerald

*EMERALD: .5X TO 1.2X BASIC AUTOS
EMERALD PRINT RUN 4-99
SERIAL #'d UNDER 20 NOT PRICED
JP Jim Plunkett/25 15.00 30.00
RL Ray Lewis/25 75.00 150.00

2008 Press Pass Legends Bowl Edition Autographs Onyx

*ONYX: .6X TO 1.5X BASIC AUTOS
ONYX PRINT RUN 1-25
SERIAL #'d UNDER 10 NOT PRICED

2008 Press Pass Legends Bowl Edition Autographs Sapphire

*SAPPHIRE: .5X TO 1.2X BASIC AUTOS
SAPPHIRE PRINT RUN 10-170
SERIAL #'d UNDER 20 NOT PRICED
DB2 Dick Butkus/25 30.00 60.00
JM Joe Montana/20 60.00 120.00
RL Ray Lewis/50 60.00 120.00

2008 Press Pass Legends Bowl Edition Bowl Busters

STATED PRINT RUN 250 SER.#'d SETS
UNPRICED PRINT PLATE PRINT RUN 1
BB1 Tommie Frazier 1.50 4.00
BB2 John Jefferson 1.50 4.00
BB4 Herschel Walker 2.50 6.00
BB5 Bob Griese 2.50 6.00
BB6 Cris Carter 2.50 6.00
BB7 Bo Jackson 3.00 8.00
BB8 Billy Sims 2.00 5.00
BB9 Steve Spurrier 2.50 6.00
BB10 Joe Theismann 2.50 6.00
BB11 Anthony Carter 1.50 4.00
BB12 Johnny Rodgers 1.50 4.00

2008 Press Pass Legends Bowl Edition Bowl Busters Autographs

ATED PRINT RUN 15-150
*SAPPHIRE: .5X TO 1.2X BASIC AUTOS
SAPPHIRE PRINT RUN 25-75
*EMERALD: .5X TO 1.2X BASIC AUTOS
EMERALD PRINT RUN 5-50
*ONYX: .6X TO 1.5X BASIC AUTOS
ONYX PRINT RUN 1-25
SERIAL #'d UNDER 20 NOT PRICED
AC Anthony Carter/150 6.00 15.00
BG Bob Griese/50 12.00 30.00
BS Billy Sims/100 8.00 20.00
CC Cris Carter/75 35.00 60.00
EC Earl Campbell/50 20.00 40.00
JJ John Jefferson/100 5.00 12.00
JR Johnny Rodgers/100 8.00 20.00
JT Joe Theismann/124 8.00 20.00
SS Steve Spurrier/50 25.00 50.00

2008 Press Pass Legends Bowl Edition Bringing Down the Goal Posts

STATED PRINT RUN 250 SER.#'d SETS
UNPRICED PRINT PLATE PRINT RUN 1
BDGP1 Jim Kelly 2.50 6.00
BDGP2 Lee Roy Jordan 2.00 5.00
BDGP3 Bill Cowher 2.00 5.00
BDGP4 Tom Rathman 2.00 5.00
BDGP5 Tommy McDonald 2.00 5.00
BDGP6 Tommy Nobis 1.50 4.00
BDGP7 Roger Craig 2.00 5.00
BDGP8 Charles White 1.50 4.00
BDGP9 Troy Aikman 3.00 8.00

2008 Press Pass Legends Bowl Edition Bringing Down the Goal Posts Autographs

STATED PRINT RUN 10-299
*SAPPHIRE/20-199: .5X TO 1.2X BASIC AUTOS
SAPPHIRE PRINT RUN 8-199
*EMERALD/20-99: .5X TO 1.2X BASIC AUTOS
EMERALD PRINT RUN 5-99
*ONYX/25: .6X TO 1.5X BASIC AUTOS
ONYX PRINT RUN 1-25
SERIAL #'d UNDER 20 NOT PRICED
BC Bill Cowher/50 15.00 30.00
CW Charles White/150 6.00 15.00
JL James Lofton/120 5.00 12.00
LJ Lee Roy Jordan/299 8.00 20.00
RC Roger Craig/120 8.00 20.00
TM Tommy McDonald/90 6.00 15.00
TN Tommy Nobis/125 6.00 15.00
TR Tom Rathman/175 10.00 25.00

2008 Press Pass Legends Bowl Edition Dream Matchup

STATED PRINT RUN 250 SER.#'d SETS
UNPRICED PRINT PLATE PRINT RUN 1
DM1 J.Montana/B.Favre 8.00 20.00
DM2 S.Young/T.Aikman 3.00 8.00
DM3 B.Switzer/J.Johnson 3.00 8.00
DM4 W.Moon/J.Kelly 3.00 8.00
DM5 J.Lambert/B.Cowher 2.50 6.00
DM6 G.Sayers/D.McFadden 1.25 3.00
DM7 C.Spielman/T.Bruschi 1.50 4.00
DM8 Dickerson/Bo Jackson 3.00 8.00
DM9 E.Campbell/B.Sims 2.50 6.00
DM10 D.Butkus/M.Singletary 3.00 8.00
DM11 Y.Tittle/K.Stabler 2.50 6.00

2008 Press Pass Legends Bowl Edition Dream Matchup Autographs

STATED PRINT RUN 12-50
*ONYX/25: .5X TO 1.2X BASIC DUAL AU
ONYX PRINT RUN 10-25
SERIAL #'d UNDER 20 NOT PRICED
BSJJ Switzer Red/J.Johnson/24 60.00 100.00
ECBS Campbell Red/Sims Red/25 40.00 80.00
JLBC Lambert/Cowher/25
YTKS Tittle/Stabler Red/50 25.00 50.00

2008 Press Pass Legends Bowl Edition Institutional Icons

STATED PRINT RUN 250 SER.#'d SETS
UNPRICED PRINT PLATE PRINT RUN 1
II1 J.Johnson/J.Kelly 2.50 6.00
II2 L.Jordan/K.Stabler 2.50 6.00
II3 Craig/Frzier/Rzier/Rdgrs 2.50 6.00
II4 McDnld/Sims/Switzer 2.50 6.00
II5 Bo Jcksn/Sullivan 3.00 8.00
II6 S.Spurrier/D.Wuerffel 2.50 6.00
II7 S.Young/T.Detmer 3.00 8.00
II8 Y.Tittle/B.Cannon 2.50 6.00
II9 B.Kilmer/T.Aikman 3.00 8.00

2008 Press Pass Legends Bowl Edition Institutional Icons Autographs

STATED PRINT RUN 10-50
*ONYX/25: .5X TO 1.2X BASIC DUAL AU
ONYX PRINT RUN 10-25
SERIAL #'d UNDER 20 NOT PRICED
BJPS Bo Jcksn/Sullivan/15 60.00 120.00
BKTA Kilmer/Aikman/15 40.00 80.00
CFRR Crg Rd/Frzr/Rzr Rd/Rdgrs/48 50.00 100.00
LJKS Jordan/Stabler/50 25.00 60.00
MSS McDnld/Sims/Switzer/50 40.00 80.00
SSDW Spurrier/Wrffel/50 40.00 80.00
SYTD Young/Detmer/25 30.00 60.00
YTBC Y.Tittle/Cannon/50 40.00 80.00
YTBCR Tittle Red/Cannon Red/50 50.00 100.00

2008 Press Pass Legends Bowl Edition MVP

STATED PRINT RUN 250 SER.#'d SETS
UNPRICED PRINT PLATE PRINT RUN 1
MVP1 Chris Spielman 2.00 5.00
MVP2 Tedy Bruschi 1.50 4.00
MVP3 Steve Young 3.00 8.00
MVP4 Tommie Frazier 1.50 4.00
MVP5 Jim Kelly 2.50 6.00
MVP6 Warren Moon 2.50 6.00
MVP7 Ken Stabler 2.50 6.00
MVP8 Cris Collinsworth 2.00 5.00
MVP9 Bo Jackson 3.00 8.00
MVP10 Steve Spurrier 2.50 6.00
MVP11 Y.A. Tittle 2.50 6.00
MVP12 Pat Sullivan 1.50 4.00
MVP13 Danny Wuerffel 1.50 4.00
MVP14 Charles White 1.50 4.00
MVP15 John Jefferson 1.50 4.00

2008 Press Pass Legends Bowl Edition MVP Autographs

STATED PRINT RUN 15-150
*SAPPHIRE/15-100: .5X TO 1.2X BASIC AUTO
SAPPHIRE PRINT RUN 10-100
*EMERALD/20-60: .5X TO 1.2X BASIC AUTOS
EMERALD PRINT RUN 5-60
*ONYX/26: .6X TO 1.6X BASIC AUTOS

ONYX PRINT RUN 1-25
SERIAL #'d UNDER 20 NOT PRICED
BJ Bo Jackson/15 40.00 80.00
CC Cris Collinsworth/75 6.00 15.00
CS Chris Spielman/150 10.00 25.00
CW Charles White/148 5.00 12.00
DW Danny Wuerffel/150 10.00 25.00
JJ John Jefferson/100 6.00 15.00
KS Ken Stabler/24 20.00 40.00
PS Pat Sullivan/150 5.00 12.00
SS Steve Spurrier/50 25.00 60.00
SY Steve Young/50 35.00 60.00
TB Tedy Bruschi/25 30.00 50.00
TF Tommie Frazier/115 10.00 25.00
WM Warren Moon/25 20.00 50.00
YT Y.A. Tittle/20 20.00 40.00

2008 Press Pass Legends Bowl Edition Top 25

STATED PRINT RUN 250 SER.#'d SETS
UNPRICED PRINT PLATE PRINT RUN 1
TT1 Brett Favre 5.00 12.00
TT2 Herschel Walker 2.50 6.00
TT3 Steve Young 3.00 8.00
TT4 Jim Kelly 2.50 6.00
TT5 Warren Moon 3.00 8.00
TT6 George Rogers 1.50 4.00
TT7 Paul Hornung 2.50 6.00
TT8 Bo Jackson 3.00 8.00
TT9 Billy Sims 2.00 5.00
TT10 Dick Butkus 3.00 8.00
TT11 Floyd Little 1.50 4.00
TT12 Mike Rozier 1.50 4.00
TT13 Ty Detmer 1.50 4.00
TT14 Anthony Carter 1.50 4.00
TT15 Johnny Rodgers 1.50 4.00
TT16 Darren McFadden .75 2.00
TT17 Matt Ryan 2.00 5.00
TT18 Felix Jones .75 2.00
TT19 Mike Singletary 1.25 3.00
TT20 Troy Aikman 3.00 8.00
TT23 Gale Sayers 2.50 6.00

2008 Press Pass Legends Bowl Edition Top 25 Autographs

STATED PRINT RUN 15-174
*SAPPHIRE/20-84: .5X TO 1.2X BASIC AUTO
SAPPHIRE PRINT RUN 8-84
*EMERALD/20-52: .5X TO 1.2X BASIC AUTOS
EMERALD PRINT RUN 1-52
*ONYX/25: .6X TO 1.5X BASIC AUTOS
ONYX PRINT RUN 1-25
SERIAL #'d UNDER 18 NOT PRICED
AC Anthony Carter/155 5.00 12.00
BF Brett Favre/18 100.00 200.00
BS Billy Sims/100 8.00 20.00
DB Dick Butkus/25 30.00 60.00
EC Earl Campbell/75 15.00 30.00
FL Floyd Little/174 6.00 15.00
GR George Rogers/115 8.00 20.00
GS Gale Sayers/25 25.00 50.00
JK Jim Kelly/15 25.00 50.00
JR Johnny Rodgers/100 6.00 15.00
MR Mike Rozier/145 8.00 20.00
MS Mike Singletary/68 10.00 25.00
PH Paul Hornung/100 10.00 25.00
SY Steve Young/46 35.00 60.00
TD Ty Detmer/150 5.00 12.00
WM Warren Moon/35 15.00 40.00

2012 Press Pass Legends Hall of Fame Blue

LGAC Anthony Carter/35 6.00 15.00
LGAS Art Shell/35 8.00 20.00
LGBG Bud Grant/28* 15.00 40.00
LGBJ Bo Jackson/30* 30.00 60.00
LGCE Carl Eller/3*
LGCN Chuck Noll/35 12.00 30.00
LGDD Dermontti Dawson/31* 15.00 40.00
LGDF Doug Flutie/25* 12.00 30.00
LGDH Dan Hampton/35 8.00 20.00
LGDL Dick LeBeau/35 10.00 25.00
LGDW Dave Wilcox/30* 6.00 15.00
LGEB Elvin Bethea/35 10.00 25.00
LGGM Gino Marchetti/30 10.00 25.00
LGJB Joe Bellino/35 6.00 15.00
LGJGR Joe Greene/31* 12.00 30.00
LGJO Jim Otto/25* 8.00 20.00
LGJP Jim Plunkett/35 8.00 20.00
LGLK Leroy Kelly/35 8.00 20.00
LGLM Lenny Moore/35 10.00 25.00
LGLRJ Lee Roy Jordan/35 8.00 20.00
LGNB Nick Buoniconti/35 25.00 50.00
LGPH Paul Hornung/35 8.00 20.00
LGRG Roman Gabriel/35 8.00 20.00
LGRL Ronnie Lott/25* 25.00 50.00
LGRW Rod Woodson/22* 25.00 50.00
LGWD Willie Davis/30 8.00 20.00

2012 Press Pass Legends Hall of Fame Blue Red Ink

STATED PRINT RUN 2-35
LGBG Bud Grant/7*
LGBJ Bo Jackson/5*
LGCE Carl Eller/32* 8.00 20.00
LGDD Dermontti Dawson/4*
LGDF Doug Flutie/10*
LGDW Dave Wilcox/5*
LGJGR Joe Greene/4*
LGJO Jim Otto/10*
LGJR Johnny Rodgers/30 6.00 15.00
LGRL Ronnie Lott/10*
LGRW Rod Woodson/13*
LGWB Willie Brown/35 6.00 15.00

2012 Press Pass Legends Hall of Fame Bronze

*BRONZE/95-99: .3X TO .8X RED/50
*BRONZE/50: .4X TO 1X RED/50
*BRONZE/30: .5X TO 1.2X RED/50
PRINT RUN 19-99
LGAC Anthony Carter/99 5.00 12.00
LGDD Dermontti Dawson/19* 25.00 50.00
LGEB Elvin Bethea/99 8.00 20.00
LGJB Joe Bellino/49* 5.00 12.00
LGLM Lenny Moore/30 10.00 25.00
LGWB Willie Brown/99 5.00 12.00
LGWD Willie Davis/99 6.00 15.00

2012 Press Pass Legends Hall of Fame Bronze Red Ink

STATED PRINT RUN 11-50
LGJB Joe Bellino/50* 5.00 12.00
LGJP Jim Plunkett/40 6.00 15.00

2012 Press Pass Legends Hall of Fame Gold

LGAC Anthony Carter/75 5.00 12.00
LGAD Art Donovan EXCH
LGAS Art Shell/70 6.00 15.00
LGBG Bud Grant/57* 12.00 30.00
LGBJ Bo Jackson/32 [illegible]
LGCE Carl Eller/65 6.00 15.00
LGDD Dermontti Dawson/57* 12.00 30.00
LGDF Doug Flutie/49* 10.00 25.00
LGDH Dan Hampton/35* 8.00 20.00
LGDL Dick LeBeau/63* 8.00 20.00
LGDW Dave Wilcox/28* 6.00 15.00
LGEB Elvin Bethea/75 8.00 20.00
LGGM Gino Marchetti/40* 8.00 20.00
LGJB Joe Bellino/65 5.00 12.00
LGJGR Joe Greene/27* 12.00 30.00
LGJO Jim Otto/35 6.00 15.00
LGJP Jim Plunkett/65 6.00 15.00
LGJR Johnny Rodgers/65 5.00 12.00
LGLK Leroy Kelly/65 6.00 15.00
LGLM Lenny Moore/64* 8.00 20.00
LGLRJ Lee Roy Jordan/18*
LGPH Paul Hornung/10*
LGRG Roman Gabriel/65 6.00 15.00
LGRL Ronnie Lott/26* 25.00 50.00
LGWB Willie Brown/75 5.00 12.00
LGWD Willie Davis/62* 6.00 15.00
LGWW Willie Wood EXCH

2012 Press Pass Legends Hall of Fame Gold Red Ink

STATED PRINT RUN 1-65
LGBG Bud Grant/8*
LGBJ Bo Jackson/13*
LGDD Dermontti Dawson/8*
LGDF Doug Flutie/16* 15.00 40.00
LGDL Dick LeBeau/2*
LGDW Dave Wilcox/7*
LGGM Gino Marchetti/25* 10.00 25.00
LGJGR Joe Greene/8*
LGLM Lenny Moore/1*
LGLRJ Lee Roy Jordan/47* 6.00 15.00
LGNB Nick Buoniconti/65 15.00 40.00
LGPH Paul Hornung/8*
LGRL Ronnie Lott/4*
LGWD Willie Davis/13*

2012 Press Pass Legends Hall of Fame Red

STATED PRINT RUN 1-50
EXCH DEADLINE 12/31/2013
LGAS Art Shell/50 8.00 20.00
LGBG Bud Grant/39* 12.00 30.00
LGBJ Bo Jackson/37* 30.00 60.00
LGCE Carl Eller/50 6.00 15.00
LGCN Chuck Noll/17* 15.00 40.00
LGDD Dermontti Dawson/42* 15.00 40.00
LGDF Doug Flutie/46* 10.00 25.00
LGDL Dick LeBeau/50 8.00 20.00
LGDW Dave Wilcox/37* 6.00 15.00
LGGM Gino Marchetti/50 8.00 20.00
LGJB Joe Bellino/50 5.00 12.00
LGJGR Joe Greene/38* 12.00 30.00
LGJO Jim Otto/30* 6.00 15.00
LGJP Jim Plunkett/50 6.00 15.00
LGJR Johnny Rodgers/50 5.00 12.00
LGLK Leroy Kelly/50 6.00 15.00
LGNB Nick Buoniconti/26* 25.00 50.00
LGPH Paul Hornung/30* 8.00 20.00
LGRG Roman Gabriel/50 6.00 15.00
LGRL Ronnie Lott/42* 15.00 40.00
LGWB Willie Brown/50 5.00 12.00
LGWD Willie Davis/41* 6.00 15.00
LGLRJ Lee Roy Jordan/50 6.00 15.00

2012 Press Pass Legends Hall of Fame Red Red Ink

STATED PRINT RUN 3-50
LGAC Anthony Carter/50 6.00 15.00
LGCN Chuck Noll/18* 15.00 40.00
LGEB Elvin Bethea/47* 10.00 25.00
LGJO Jim Otto/20* 8.00 20.00
LGLM Lenny Moore/46* 8.00 20.00
LGNB Nick Buoniconti/24* 25.00 50.00
LGPH Paul Hornung/20* 10.00 25.00

2012 Press Pass Legends Hall of Fame Silver

STATED PRINT RUN 3-89
LGAC Anthony Carter/89 5.00 12.00
LGAS Art Shell/54* 8.00 20.00
LGBJ Bo Jackson/62* 30.00 60.00
LGCE Carl Eller/75 6.00 15.00
LGDD Dermontti Dawson/65* 12.00 30.00
LGDL Dick LeBeau/7*
LGEB Elvin Bethea/89 8.00 20.00
LGGM Gino Marchetti/50* 8.00 20.00
LGJB Joe Bellino/75 5.00 12.00
LGJP Jim Plunkett/8*
LGJR Johnny Rodgers/89 5.00 12.00
LGLK Leroy Kelly/28* 8.00 20.00
LGLM Lenny Moore/75 8.00 20.00
LGLRJ Lee Roy Jordan/75 6.00 15.00
LGPH Paul Hornung/29* 8.00 20.00
LGRG Roman Gabriel/27* 8.00 20.00
LGWB Willie Brown/89 5.00 12.00
LGWD Willie Davis/65* 6.00 15.00

2012 Press Pass Legends Hall of Fame Silver Red Ink

STATED PRINT RUN 1-48
LGAS Art Shell/1*
LGBJ Bo Jackson/13*
LGDD Dermontti Dawson/10*
LGDL Dick LeBeau/23* 10.00 25.00
LGGM Gino Marchetti/25* 10.00 25.00
LGJP Jim Plunkett/7*
LGLK Leroy Kelly/47* 6.00 15.00
LGPH Paul Hornung/1*
LGRG Roman Gabriel/48* 6.00 15.00
LGWD Willie Davis/24* 8.00 20.00

2012 Press Pass Legends Hall of Fame Champions Blue

STATED PRINT RUN 19-35
CHAS Art Shell/30 10.00 25.00
CHCN Chuck Noll/19* 15.00 40.00
CHGM Gino Marchetti/35 10.00 25.00

2012 Press Pass Legends Hall of Fame Champions Blue Red Ink

CHCN Chuck Noll/16* 15.00 40.00

2012 Press Pass Legends Hall of Fame Champions Purple

STATED PRINT RUN 8-25
CHAS Art Shell/25 10.00 25.00
CHCN Chuck Noll/25 12.00 30.00
CHGM Gino Marchetti/25 10.00 25.00
CHPH Paul Hornung/25 8.00 20.00

2012 Press Pass Legends Hall of Fame Champions Red

CHGM Gino Marchetti/40 8.00 20.00

2012 Press Pass Legends Hall of Fame Champions Red Red Ink

CHAS Art Shell/46* 8.00 20.00

2012 Press Pass Legends Hall of Fame Fan Favorites Blue

STATED PRINT RUN 12-35
FFCE Carl Eller/35 8.00 20.00
FFDH Dan Hampton/35 8.00 20.00
FFDK Dick LeBeau/35 10.00 25.00
FFDW Dave Wilcox/23* 8.00 20.00
FFJG Joe Greene/35 12.00 30.00
FFJO Jim Otto/25* 8.00 20.00
FFRW Rod Woodson/35 20.00 50.00

2012 Press Pass Legends Hall of Fame Fan Favorites Blue Red Ink

[illegible]

2012 Press Pass Legends Hall of Fame Fan Favorites Gold

STATED PRINT RUN 40-60
FFCE Carl Eller/60 6.00 15.00
FFDK Dick LeBeau/40* 8.00 20.00

2012 Press Pass Legends Hall of Fame Fan Favorites Gold Red Ink

FFDK Dick LeBeau/25* 10.00 25.00

2012 Press Pass Legends Hall of Fame Fan Favorites Purple

STATED PRINT RUN 10-25
FFCE Carl Eller/25 8.00 20.00
FFDH Dan Hampton/25 8.00 20.00
FFDK Dick LeBeau/25 10.00 25.00
FFDW Dave Wilcox/19* 8.00 20.00
FFJG Joe Greene/25 12.00 30.00
FFJO Jim Otto/25 8.00 20.00
FFRW Rod Woodson/25 20.00 50.00

2012 Press Pass Legends Hall of Fame Fan Favorites Red

*RED/43-50: .3X TO .8X PURPLE
STATED PRINT RUN 12-50

2012 Press Pass Legends Hall of Fame Fan Favorites Red Red Ink

STATED PRINT RUN 5-36
NO PRICING ON PRINT RUNS UNDER 20
FFDW Dave Wilcox/5*
FFJG Joe Greene/7*

2010 Press Pass Legends National Convention Silver

SILVER PRINT RUN 99 SER.#'d SETS
*GOLD/25: .6X TO 1.5X SILVER/99
NE1 Tim Tebow 8.00 20.00
NE2 Sam Bradford 3.00 8.00
NE3 C.J. Spiller 2.50 6.00
NE4 Jimmy Clausen 2.50 6.00

2010 Press Pass PE

COMPLETE SET (50) 7.50 20.00
1 Danario Alexander .20 .50
2 Arrelious Benn .20 .50
3 Jahvid Best .20 .50
4 NaVorro Bowman .40 1.00
5 Sam Bradford .25 .60
6 Dezmon Briscoe .20 .50
7 Antonio Brown 1.50 4.00
8 Jarrett Brown .20 .50
9 Dez Bryant .50 1.25
10 Sean Canfield .20 .50
11 Daryll Clark .30 .75
12 Jimmy Clausen .20 .50
13 Eric Decker .25 .60
14 Dorin Dickerson .20 .50
15 Anthony Dixon .20 .50
16 Jonathan Dwyer .20 .50
17 Jacoby Ford .20 .50
18 Toby Gerhart .20 .50
19 Mardy Gilyard .20 .50
20 Jermaine Gresham .20 .50
21 Rob Gronkowski .60 1.50
22 Joe Haden .30 .75
23 Montario Hardesty .20 .50
24 Aaron Hernandez .20 .50
25 Mike Kafka .25 .60
26 Brandon LaFell .30 .75
27 Dan LeFevour .20 .50
28 Ryan Mathews .20 .50
29 Rolando McClain .20 .50
30 Dexter McCluster .25 .60
31 Anthony McCoy .20 .50
32 Gerald McCoy .20 .50
33 Joe McKnight .20 .50
34 Derrick Morgan .20 .50
35 Jason Pierre-Paul .30 .75
36 Tony Pike .20 .50
37 Andre Roberts .25 .60
38 Zac Robinson .25 .60
39 Charles Scott .20 .50
40 Jordan Shipley .20 .50
41 Jevan Snead .20 .50
42 C.J. Spiller .20 .50
43 Ndamukong Suh .40 1.00
44 Golden Tate .25 .60
45 Tim Tebow .60 1.50
46 Demaryius Thomas .50 1.25
47 Earl Thomas .50 1.25
48 Donovan Warren .20 .50
49 Damian Williams .20 .50
50 Mike Williams .20 .50

2010 Press Pass PE Blue

*BLUE: 1X TO 2.5X BASIC CARDS
ONE BLUE PER RETAIL PACK

2010 Press Pass PE Gold

*GOLD: 1.2X TO 3X BASIC CARDS
STATED ODDS 1:4 HOBBY

2010 Press Pass PE Class of 2010

COMPLETE SET (10) 6.00 15.00
STATED ODDS 1:4 HOB
CL1 Jahvid Best .40 1.00
CL2 C.J. Spiller .40 1.00
CL3 Tim Tebow 1.25 3.00
CL4 Ryan Mathews .40 1.00
CL5 Arrelious Benn .40 1.00
CL6 Jimmy Clausen .40 1.00
CL7 Golden Tate .50 1.25
CL8 Dez Bryant 1.00 2.50
CL9 Sam Bradford .50 1.25
CL10 Toby Gerhart .40 1.00

2010 Press Pass PE Class of 2010 Autographs

STATED PRINT RUN 49-199
*HOC RED/25: .6X TO 1.5X BASIC AU/100-199
*HOC RED/25: .5X TO 1.2X BASIC AU/49
HOC PRINT RUN 25 SER.#'d SETS
CLAB Arrelious Benn/150 3.00 8.00
CLBL Brandon LaFell/199 5.00 12.00
CLCS C.J. Spiller/100 3.00 8.00
CLDB Dez Bryant/100 25.00 50.00
CLGT Golden Tate/199 4.00 10.00
CLJC Jimmy Clausen/49 3.00 8.00
CLRM Ryan Mathews/199 3.00 8.00
CLSB Sam Bradford/150 15.00 40.00
CLTG Toby Gerhart/199 10.00 25.00
CLTT Tim Tebow/199 30.00 60.00

2010 Press Pass PE Face To Face

COMPLETE SET (20) 8.00 20.00
STATED ODDS 1:2 HOB
FF1 J.Best/J.McKnight .30 .75
FF2 G.Tate/D.Williams .40 1.00
FF3 J.Clausen/T.Gerhart .30 .75
FF4 C.Spiller/A.Roberts .40 1.00
FF5 T.Pike/R.Mathews .30 .75
FF6 M.Gilyard/A.Benn .30 .75
FF7 D.Briscoe/D.Alexander .30 .75
FF8 B.LaFell/A.Hernandez .50 1.25
FF9 T.Tebow/J.Snead 1.00 2.50
FF10 F.Barnes/A.Brown 2.50 6.00
FF11 Z.Robinson/S.Bradford .40 1.00
FF12 J.Dwyer/J.James .30 .75
FF13 D.Thomas/J.Ford .75 2.00
FF14 A.Dixon/D.McCluster .40 1.00
FF15 D.Bryant/J.Shipley .75 2.00
FF16 S.Canfield/C.McGaha .30 .75
FF17 R.McClain/M.Hardesty .30 .75
FF18 E.Decker/M.Williams .40 1.00
FF19 J.Starks/D.LeFevour .40 1.00
FF20 N.Suh/G.McCoy .60 1.50

2010 Press Pass PE Game Day Gear Jerseys Silver

OVERALL JSY ODDS 1:6.7 HOB
*GOLD/199: .5X TO 1.2X SILVER JSY
GOLD PRINT RUN 199 SER.#'d SETS
*PREMIUM/25: 1X TO 2.5X SILVER JSY
PREMIUM PRINT RUN 25 SER.#'d SETS
*SILVER HOLO/99: .6X TO 1.5X SILVER JSY
SILVER HOLOFOIL PRINT RUN 99
GDGAB Arrelious Benn 4.00 10.00
GDGBL Brandon LaFell 4.00 10.00
GDGDA Danario Alexander 4.00 10.00
GDGDB Dezmon Briscoe 4.00 10.00
GDGDM Dexter McCluster 4.00 10.00
GDGDW Damian Williams 3.00 8.00
GDGED Eric Decker 4.00 10.00
GDGGT Golden Tate 4.00 10.00
GDGJB Jahvid Best 4.00 10.00
GDGJC Jimmy Clausen 5.00 12.00
GDGJF Jacoby Ford
GDGJJ Javarris James 3.00 8.00
GDGJM Joe McKnight 4.00 10.00
GDGJS Jevan Snead 4.00 10.00
GDGMH Montario Hardesty 2.50 6.00
GDGMK Mike Kafka 3.00 8.00
GDGMW Mike Williams 3.00 8.00
GDGNB NaVorro Bowman 5.00 12.00
GDGNS Ndamukong Suh 6.00 15.00
GDGSB Sam Bradford 6.00 15.00
GDGSC Sean Canfield 3.00 8.00
GDGSJ Stafon Johnson 4.00 10.00
GDGTG Toby Gerhart 4.00 10.00
GDGTT Tim Tebow 6.00 15.00
GDGZR Zac Robinson 4.00 10.00

2010 Press Pass PE Game Day Gear Jerseys Autographs

STATED PRINT RUN 25 SER.#'d SETS
GDGAB Arrelious Benn 15.00 40.00
GDGBL Brandon LaFell 15.00 40.00
GDGGT Golden Tate 30.00 80.00
GDGJB Jahvid Best 25.00 60.00
GDGJJ Javarris James 25.00 50.00
GDGJS Jevan Snead 25.00 50.00
GDGMH Montario Hardesty 15.00 40.00
GDGSB Sam Bradford 75.00 150.00
GDGSC Sean Canfield 20.00 40.00
GDGTG Toby Gerhart 30.00 60.00
GDGTT Tim Tebow 75.00 200.00

2010 Press Pass PE Graduating Class Autographs

STATED PRINT RUN 25 SER.#'d SETS
CSJB C.Spiller/J.Best 25.00 60.00
DBAB D.Bryant/A.Benn 50.00 100.00
DTBL D.Thomas/B.LaFell/20* 15.00 40.00
JCGT J.Clausen/G.Tate 20.00 50.00
TTRM T.Tebow/R.Mathews 75.00 150.00
DTBL2 D.Thomas/B.LaFell Red/5*

2010 Press Pass PE Headliners

COMPLETE SET (34) 10.00 25.00
ONE PER HOBBY PACK
HL1 Rolando McClain .30 .75
HL2 Jahvid Best .30 .75
HL3 Dan LeFevour .30 .75
HL4 Mardy Gilyard .30 .75
HL5 Tony Pike .30 .75
HL6 C.J. Spiller .30 .75
HL7 Joe Haden .50 1.25
HL8 Tim Tebow 1.00 2.50
HL9 Ryan Mathews .30 .75
HL10 Jonathan Dwyer .30 .75
HL11 Derrick Morgan .30 .75
HL12 Demaryius Thomas .75 2.00
HL13 Arrelious Benn .30 .75
HL14 Dezmon Briscoe .30 .75
HL15 Brandon LaFell .50 1.25
HL16 Eric Decker .40 1.00
HL17 Anthony Dixon .30 .75
HL18 Ndamukong Suh .60 1.50
HL19 Jimmy Clausen .30 .75
HL20 Golden Tate .40 1.00
HL21 Dez Bryant .75 2.00
HL22 Sam Bradford .40 1.00
HL23 Jermaine Gresham .30 .75
HL24 Gerald McCoy .30 .75
HL25 Dexter McCluster .40 1.00
HL26 Jason Pierre-Paul .50 1.25
HL27 Toby Gerhart .30 .75
HL28 Mike Williams .30 .75
HL29 Montario Hardesty .30 .75
HL30 Jordan Shipley .30 .75
HL31 Joe McKnight .30 .75
HL32 Damian Williams .30 .75
HL33 Jarrett Brown .30 .75
HL34 Tim Tebow CL .75 2.00

2010 Press Pass PE Sideline Signatures Gold

OVERALL AUTO ODDS 1:2.9 HOB
*GOLD RED INK/20-346: .5X TO 1.2X GOLD AU
GOLD RED INK ANNC'D PRINT RUN 2-346
*EMERALD/20-25: .8X TO 2X GOLD AUTO
EMERALD PRINT RUN 9-25
*EMER.RED INK/19--25: .5X TO 1.2X EMER.AU
EMERALD RED INK ANNC'D PRINT RUN 1-25
SSAB Arrelious Benn 2.50 6.00
SSAB2 Antonio Brown 20.00 50.00
SSAD Anthony Dixon 2.50 6.00
SSAH Aaron Hernandez 2.50 6.00
SSAM Anthony McCoy 2.50 6.00
SSAR Andre Roberts 3.00 8.00
SSAV Alterraun Verner 3.00 8.00
SSBG Brandon Ghee 2.50 6.00
SSBL Brandon LaFell 4.00 10.00
SSBS Bill Stull 2.50 6.00
SSCM Chris McGaha 2.50 6.00
SSCS C.J. Spiller 2.50 6.00
SSCS2 Charles Scott 2.50 6.00
SSCW Corey Wootton 2.50 6.00
SSDA Danario Alexander 2.50 6.00
SSDB2 Dezmon Briscoe 2.50 6.00
SSDC Daryll Clark 4.00 10.00
SSDD Dorin Dickerson 2.50 6.00
SSDL Dan LeFevour 2.50 6.00
SSDM Dexter McCluster 3.00 8.00
SSDM2 Derrick Morgan 2.50 6.00
SSDT Demaryius Thomas 6.00 15.00
SSDW Damian Williams 2.50 6.00
SSDW2 Donovan Warren 2.50 6.00
SSED Eric Decker 3.00 8.00
SSED2 Ed Dickson 2.50 6.00
SSET Earl Thomas 6.00 15.00
SSFB Freddie Barnes 2.50 6.00
SSGH Greg Hardy 6.00 15.00
SSGM Gerald McCoy 2.50 6.00
SSGS George Selvie 4.00 10.00
SSGT Golden Tate 3.00 8.00
SSJB Jahvid Best 10.00 25.00
SSJB2 Jarrett Brown 2.50 6.00
SSJC Jimmy Clausen
SSJD Jonathan Dwyer 2.50 6.00
SSJF Jacoby Ford 2.50 6.00
SSJG Jermaine Gresham 2.50 6.00
SSJH Joe Haden 4.00 10.00
SSJH2 Jerry Hughes 2.50 6.00
SSJJ Javarris James 2.50 6.00
SSJM Joe McKnight 2.50 6.00
SSJPP Jason Pierre-Paul 4.00 10.00
SSJS Jordan Shipley 2.50 6.00
SSJC2 James Clarke 3.00 8.00
SSJS3 Jevan Snead 2.50 6.00
SSJW Joe Webb 2.50 6.00
SSJW2 Jeremy Williams 2.50 6.00
SSJW3 Juice Williams 3.00 8.00
SSLB LeGarrette Blount 5.00 12.00
SSMG Mardy Gilyard 2.50 6.00
SSMH Montario Hardesty 2.50 6.00
SSMK Mike Kafka 3.00 8.00
SSMW Mike Williams 2.50 6.00
SSNB NaVorro Bowman 5.00 12.00
SSNR Naaman Roosevelt 4.00 10.00
SSNS Ndamukong Suh 15.00 40.00
SSRG Rob Gronkowski 12.00 30.00
SSRM Ryan Mathews 2.50 6.00
SSRM2 Rolando McClain 2.50 6.00
SSRS Rusty Smith 4.00 10.00
SSSB Sam Bradford 10.00 25.00
SSSC Sean Canfield 2.50 6.00
SSSH Shay Hodge 2.50 6.00
SSSJ Stafon Johnson 2.50 6.00
SSSL Sean Lee 5.00 12.00
SSSW Sean Weatherspoon 2.50 6.00
SSTG Toby Gerhart 2.50 6.00
SSTL Thaddeus Lewis 3.00 8.00
SSTP Tony Pike 2.50 6.00
SSTT Tim Tebow 15.00 40.00
SSZR Zac Robinson 3.00 8.00

2010 Press Pass PE Sideline Signatures Ruby

*RUBY/120-150: .5X TO 1.2X GOLD AU
RUBY PRINT RUN 25-150
*RUBY RED INK/20-92: .5X TO 1.2X RUBY AU
RUBY RED INK ANNC'D PRINT RUN 1-92
SSCS C.J. Spiller/50 4.00 10.00
SSJC Jimmy Clausen/25 5.00 12.00
SSSB Sam Bradford/50 5.00 12.00
SSTT Tim Tebow/150 15.00 40.00

2001 Press Pass SE

This 45-card set featured some of the top draft picks from the 2001 NFL Draft. The base set design had an action photo of the player with white borders on the sides and it was highlighted with silver foil markings on its borders. The card backs had their college statistics along with a summary of their abilities that will guide them in the NFL.

COMPLETE SET (45) 20.00 40.00
1 Michael Vick .50 1.25
2 Drew Brees 1.25 3.00
3 Quincy Carter .25 .60
4 Marques Tuiasosopo .25 .60
5 Chris Weinke .25 .60
6 Sage Rosenfels .25 .60
7 Jesse Palmer .25 .60
8 Mike McMahon .25 .60
9 Josh Booty .25 .60
10 Josh Heupel .30 .75
11 LaDainian Tomlinson 1.00 2.50
12 Deuce McAllister .30 .75
13 Michael Bennett .25 .60
14 Anthony Thomas .30 .75
15 LaMont Jordan .30 .75
16 Travis Henry .25 .60
17 James Jackson .20 .50
18 Kevan Barlow .25 .60
19 Travis Minor .25 .60
20 Rudi Johnson .30 .75
21 David Terrell .25 .60
22 Koren Robinson .25 .60
23 Rod Gardner .25 .60
24 Santana Moss .30 .75
25 Freddie Mitchell .20 .50
26 Reggie Wayne .40 1.00
27 Quincy Morgan .25 .60
28 Chris Chambers .20 .50
29 Robert Ferguson .30 .75
30 Chad Johnson .30 .75
31 Snoop Minnis .20 .50
32 Todd Heap .25 .60
33 Steve Hutchinson .50 1.25
34 Leonard Davis .30 .75
35 Kenyatta Walker .20 .50
36 Justin Smith .40 1.00
37 Andre Carter .25 .60
38 Jamal Reynolds .20 .50
39 Gerard Warren .25 .60
40 Richard Seymour .30 .75
41 Damione Lewis .25 .60
42 Jamar Fletcher .20 .50
43 Nate Clements .25 .60
44 Derrick Gibson .20 .50
45 David Terrell CL .20 .50

2001 Press Pass SE Gold

COMPLETE SET (45) 50.00 100.00
*GOLDS: .8X TO 2X BASIC CARDS
ONE PER RETAIL PACK

2001 Press Pass SE Autographs Bronze

Randomly inserted in hobby packs at a rate of one in one, and in retail packs at a rate of one in 28. It featured the top draft picks from the 2001 NFL Draft printed with bronze highlights on the front. These cards were not numbered on the back and are listed alphabetically. Nate Clements, Casey Hampton, and Shaun Rogers were not included in packs but appeared on the secondary market some time after the product went live. Michael Vick signed only for the Gold and Silver sets and Quincy Morgan signed only for the Bronze and Silver sets.

STATED ODDS 1:1 HOBBY, 1:28 RETAIL
1 Dan Alexander 3.00 8.00
2 Brian Allen 2.00 5.00
3 Jeff Backus 2.50 6.00
4 Kevan Barlow 3.00 8.00
5 Michael Bennett 3.00 8.00
6 Josh Booty 3.00 8.00
7 Drew Brees 50.00 80.00
8 Chris Chambers 2.50 6.00
9 Nate Clements 3.00 8.00
10 Ennis Davis 2.00 5.00
11 Jamar Fletcher 2.50 6.00
12 Rod Gardner 3.00 8.00
13 Casey Hampton 6.00 15.00
14 Todd Heap 3.00 8.00
15 Travis Henry 3.00 8.00
16 Josh Heupel 4.00 10.00
17 Jabari Holloway 2.50 6.00
18 Willie Howard 2.50 6.00
19 Steve Hutchinson 5.00 12.00
20 James Jackson 2.50 6.00
21 Chad Johnson 4.00 10.00
22 Rudi Johnson 4.00 10.00
23 LaMont Jordan 4.00 10.00
24 Ben Leard 2.50 6.00
25 Deuce McAllister 4.00 10.00
26 Mike McMahon 3.00 8.00
27 Snoop Minnis 2.50 6.00
28 Travis Minor 3.00 8.00
29 Freddie Mitchell 2.50 6.00
30 Quincy Morgan 3.00 8.00
31 Santana Moss 4.00 10.00
32 Bobby Newcombe 3.00 8.00
33 Moran Norris 2.00 5.00
34 Jesse Palmer 3.00 8.00
35 Tommy Polley 2.50 6.00
36 Dominic Raiola 2.50 6.00
37 Ken-Yon Rambo 2.50 6.00
38 Jamal Reynolds 2.50 6.00
39 Koren Robinson 3.00 8.00
40 Shaun Rogers 4.00 10.00
41 Sage Rosenfels 3.00 8.00
42 Richard Seymour 4.00 10.00
43 Justin Smith 5.00 12.00
44 David Terrell 3.00 8.00
45 Anthony Thomas 4.00 10.00
46 LaDainian Tomlinson 20.00 50.00
47 Marques Tuiasosopo 3.00 8.00
48 Kenyatta Walker 2.50 6.00
49 Chad Ward 2.50 6.00
50 Gerard Warren 3.00 8.00
51 Reggie Wayne 10.00 25.00
52 Chris Weinke 3.00 8.00
53 Maurice Williams 2.50 6.00
54 Jamie Winborn 3.00 8.00

2001 Press Pass SE Autographs Blue

*BLUES: .8X TO 2X SILVER AUTOS

2001 Press Pass SE Autographs Silver

*SILVER/250: .5X TO 1.2X BRONZE AU
*BLUE/25: .8X TO 2X SILVER AU/250
7 Drew Brees 60.00 120.00

2001 Press Pass SE Class of 2001

Randomly inserted in packs at a rate of one in six, this 9-card set featured top players from the class of 2001. The set design had foil-etched backgrounds on the front of the card in the main color from his alma mater, and the card backs had a photo along with a scouting report for the player.

COMPLETE SET (9) 6.00 15.00
STATED ODDS 1:6 HOBBY, 1:12 RETAIL
CL1 Michael Vick .60 1.50
CL2 LaDainian Tomlinson 1.25 3.00
CL3 David Terrell .30 .75
CL4 Koren Robinson .30 .75
CL5 Santana Moss .40 1.00
CL6 Deuce McAllister .40 1.00
CL7 Freddie Mitchell .25 .60
CL8 Drew Brees 1.50 4.00
CL9 Chris Weinke .30 .75

2001 Press Pass SE Class of 2001 Autographs

Randomly inserted in packs, this 9-card set featured top players from the class of 2001. The set design had foil-etched backgrounds on the front of the card in the main color from his alma mater, and the card backs had a photo along with a scouting report for the player. The fronts also featured a signature and they were hand numbered to 100.

STATED PRINT RUN 100 SER.#'d SETS
1 Michael Bennett 5.00 12.00
2 Drew Brees 60.00 120.00
3 Chris Chambers 8.00 20.00
4 Chad Johnson 8.00 20.00
6 Freddie Mitchell 4.00 10.00
7 Santana Moss 8.00 20.00
8 Koren Robinson 5.00 12.00
9 Justin Smith 8.00 20.00
10 David Terrell 5.00 12.00
11 LaDainian Tomlinson 50.00 100.00
12 Michael Vick 60.00 120.00
13 Chris Weinke 5.00 12.00

2001 Press Pass SE Game Jersey

Randomly inserted at a rate of one in 96 hobby packs and one in 560 retail packs this 6-card set featured the top players from the 2001 NFL Draft with a swatch of their game jersey. These cards were serial numbered to 250. A Patch version of each card was also inserted with each card being serial numbered of just 10.

STATED ODDS 1:96 HOB,1:560 RET
STATED PRINT RUN 250 SER.#'d SETS
*UNIF.NUM/25: 1X TO 2.5X BASIC JSY
UNIFORM NUMBER PRINT RUN 25
UNPRICED PATCH VERSION #'d OF 10
JCCW Chris Weinke 6.00 15.00
JCDB Drew Brees 12.00 30.00
JCJS Justin Smith 6.00 15.00
JCKYR Ken-Yon Rambo 6.00 15.00
JCLT LaDainian Tomlinson 15.00 40.00
JCMB Michael Bennett 6.00 15.00
JCMV Michael Vick 15.00 40.00

2001 Press Pass SE Game Jersey Autographs

Randomly inserted packs, this set featured the top players from the 2001 NFL Draft with a swatch of their game jersey. These cards were hand numbered to 25, and also featured a signature.

STATED PRINT RUN 25 SERIAL #'d SETS
AJCW Chris Weinke 20.00 50.00
AJDB Drew Brees 125.00 225.00
AJJS Justin Smith 30.00 60.00
AJLT LaDainian Tomlinson 75.00 150.00
AJMB Michael Bennett 20.00 50.00

2001 Press Pass SE Old School

Inserted in packs at a rate of one in two, this 27-card set had a vintage look, and feature some of the top draft picks form the 2001 NFL Draft. The card fronts feature an action photo of the player with pennant design on the bottom of the card with their name and 'Old School' printed on it.

COMPLETE SET (27) 12.00 30.00
STATED ODDS 1:2
OS1 Michael Vick .60 1.50
OS2 Drew Brees 1.50 4.00
OS3 Chris Weinke .30 .75
OS4 LaDainian Tomlinson 1.25 3.00
OS5 Deuce McAllister .40 1.00
OS6 Michael Bennett .30 .75
OS7 Anthony Thomas .40 1.00
OS8 LaMont Jordan .40 1.00
OS9 Travis Henry .30 .75
OS10 James Jackson .25 .60
OS11 Kevan Barlow .30 .75
OS12 David Terrell .30 .75
OS13 Koren Robinson .30 .75
OS14 Rod Gardner .30 .75
OS15 Santana Moss .40 1.00
OS16 Freddie Mitchell .25 .60
OS17 Reggie Wayne .50 1.25
OS18 Quincy Morgan .30 .75
OS19 Chad Johnson .40 1.00
OS20 Chris Chambers .25 .60
OS21 Todd Heap .30 .75
OS22 Justin Smith .50 1.25
OS23 Andre Carter .30 .75
OS24 Leonard Davis .40 1.00
OS25 Kenyatta Walker .25 .60
OS26 Richard Seymour .40 1.00
OS27 Michael Vick CL .40 1.00

2001 Press Pass SE Rookievision

Inserted in packs at a rate of one in three hobby and one in six retail, this 12-card set features a die-cut refracted card of one of the top picks from the 2001 NFL Draft.

COMPLETE SET (12) 8.00 20.00
STATED ODDS 1:3 HOBBY, 1:6 RETAIL
RV1 Michael Vick .60 1.50
RV2 LaDainian Tomlinson 1.25 3.00
RV3 David Terrell .30 .75
RV4 Koren Robinson .30 .75
RV5 Rod Gardner .30 .75
RV6 Deuce McAllister .40 1.00
RV7 Santana Moss .40 1.00
RV8 Michael Bennett .30 .75
RV9 Freddie Mitchell .25 .60
RV10 Todd Heap .30 .75
RV11 Drew Brees 1.50 4.00
RV12 Chad Johnson .40 1.00

2001 Press Pass SE Up Close

Inserted in packs at a rate of one in nine hobby and one in 18 retail, this 6-card set features the top players from the 2001 NFL Draft. The card design had a photo f the player and a metallic-etched background with the team logo highlighted to the side. The card backs feature highlights about the player that are not necessarily from his football career.

COMPLETE SET (6) 6.00 15.00
STATED ODDS 1:9 HOBBY, 1:18 RETAIL
UC1 Michael Vick .60 1.50
UC2 Drew Brees 1.50 4.00
UC3 LaDainian Tomlinson 1.25 3.00
UC4 David Terrell .30 .75
UC5 Deuce McAllister .40 1.00
UC6 Santana Moss .40 1.00

2004 Press Pass SE

The Press Pass SE (Signature Edition) product was released in early May 2004. The base set consists of 40-cards. Mike Williams made an apearance in this product although he was declared ineligible for the NFL Draft. Hobby boxes contained 12-packs of 5-cards and carried an S.R.P. of $12.99. Each hobby pack also included one autograph or game used jersey card. Retail boxes included 24-packs with 4-cards per packs. The autographs and jersey cards were randomly seeded in retail. One parallel set and a variety of inserts can be found seeded in hobby and retail packs highlighted by the Blue autographs parallel set, Game Used Jerseys Autographs and the Class of 2004 Autographs.

COMPLETE SET (40) 15.00 30.00
1 Shawn Andrews .30 .75
2 Casey Clausen .30 .75
3 Michael Clayton .30 .75
4 Cedric Cobbs .25 .60
5 Devard Darling .25 .60
6 Lee Evans .40 1.00
7 Larry Fitzgerald 1.00 2.50
8 Robert Gallery .30 .75
9 DeAngelo Hall .40 1.00
10 Tommie Harris .30 .75
11 Ben Hartsock .25 .60
12 Devery Henderson .25 .60
13 Steven Jackson .40 1.00
14 Michael Jenkins .25 .60
15 Greg Jones .25 .60
16 Kevin Jones .30 .75
17 Teddy Lehman .25 .60
18 J.P. Losman .25 .60
19 Eli Manning 2.00 5.00
20 Mewelde Moore .30 .75
21 John Navarre .25 .60
22 Jarrett Payton .30 .75
23 Chris Perry .25 .60
24 Cody Pickett .25 .60
25 Philip Rivers .75 2.00
26 Ben Roethlisberger 2.00 5.00
27 Matt Schaub .25 .60
28 Will Smith .30 .75
29 Ben Troupe .25 .60
30 Michael Turner .25 .60
31 Ben Watson .30 .75
32 Darius Watts .25 .60
33 Vince Wilfork .40 1.00
34 Mike Williams .30 .75
35 Reggie Williams .25 .60
36 Roy Williams WR .25 .60
37 Quincy Wilson .25 .60
38 Rashaun Woods .25 .60
39 Jason Wright .25 .60
40 Eli Manning CL 1.00 2.50
NNO Eli Manning Mini Helmet 60.00 120.00

2004 Press Pass SE First Down Gold

COMPLETE SET (40) 25.00 60.00
*GOLD: .8X TO 2X BASIC CARDS
ONE PER RETAIL PACK

2004 Press Pass SE Class of 2004

COMPLETE SET (9) 10.00 25.00
STATED ODDS 1:3 H, 1:6 R
CL1 Eli Manning 3.00 8.00
CL2 Ben Roethlisberger 3.00 8.00
CL3 Philip Rivers 1.25 3.00
CL4 Mike Williams .50 1.25
CL5 Kevin Jones .50 1.25
CL6 Rashaun Woods .40 1.00
CL7 Steven Jackson .60 1.50
CL8 Larry Fitzgerald 1.50 4.00
CL9 Roy Williams WR .40 1.00

2004 Press Pass SE Class of 2004 Autographs

OVERALL SE AUTOGRAPH ODDS 2:3
1 Steven Jackson/50 12.00 30.00
2 Kevin Jones/50 12.00 30.00
3 Eli Manning/200 60.00 150.00
4 Chris Perry/200 10.00 25.00
5 Philip Rivers/200 30.00 60.00
6 Ben Roethlisberger/25 125.00 250.00
7 Ben Troupe/200 7.50 20.00
8 Mike Williams/200 7.50 20.00
9 Rashaun Woods/200 7.50 20.00

2004 Press Pass SE Game Used Jerseys Autographs

STATED PRINT RUN 25 SER.#'d SETS
1 Eli Manning 175.00 300.00
2 Ben Roethlisberger 150.00 300.00
3 Matt Schaub 10.00 25.00

2004 Press Pass SE Game Used Jerseys Bronze

BRONZE STATED PRINT RUN 625-700
*GOLD/100: .6X TO 1.5X BRONZE JSY
GOLD STATED PRINT RUN 100
*NUMBER/25: 1.2X TO 3X BRONZE JSY
NUMBERS STATED PRINT RUN 25
UNPRICED PATCH PRINT RUN 10
*SILVER/330-400: .5X TO 1.2X BRONZE JSY
SILVER PRINT RUN 330-400
OVERALL JERSEY ODDS 1:3H, 1:280R
JCBB Bernard Berrian/700 2.50 6.00
JCBH Ben Hartsock/700 2.50 6.00
JCBR Ben Roethlisberger/700 15.00 40.00
JCCC Casey Clausen/700 3.00 8.00
JCCP Cody Pickett/700 2.50 6.00
JCDD Devard Darling/700 2.50 6.00
JCDW Darius Watts/675 2.50 6.00
JCEM Eli Manning/700 15.00 40.00
JCJG Jermaine Green/700 2.50 6.00
JCJL Jared Lorenzen/700 3.00 8.00
JCJP Jarrett Payton/625 3.00 8.00
JCLM Luke McCown/700 2.50 6.00
JCMM Mewelde Moore/700 3.00 8.00
JCMS Matt Schaub/700 2.50 6.00
JCPR Philip Rivers/700 8.00 20.00
JCSJ Steven Jackson/700 4.00 10.00

2004 Press Pass SE Old School

COMPLETE SET (27) 10.00 25.00
STATED ODDS 1:1 H, 1:2 R
OS1 Casey Clausen .40 1.00
OS2 J.P. Losman .30 .75
OS3 Eli Manning 2.50 6.00
OS4 John Navarre .30 .75
OS5 Cody Pickett .30 .75
OS6 Philip Rivers 1.00 2.50
OS7 Ben Roethlisberger 2.50 6.00
OS8 Matt Schaub .30 .75
OS9 Steven Jackson .50 1.25
OS10 Greg Jones .30 .75
OS11 Kevin Jones .40 1.00
OS12 Chris Perry .30 .75
OS13 Michael Clayton .40 1.00
OS14 Lee Evans .50 1.25
OS15 Larry Fitzgerald 1.25 3.00
OS16 Michael Jenkins .30 .75
OS17 Mike Williams .40 1.00
OS18 Roy Williams WR .30 .75
OS19 Rashaun Woods .30 .75
OS20 Ben Troupe .30 .75
OS21 Ben Watson .40 1.00
OS22 Kellen Winslow .30 .75
OS23 Robert Gallery .40 1.00
OS24 Tommie Harris .40 1.00
OS25 Will Smith .40 1.00
OS26 Vince Wilfork .50 1.25
OS27 Eli Manning CL 1.25 3.00

2004 Press Pass SE Up Close

COMPLETE SET (6) 7.50 20.00
STATED ODDS 1:4 H, 1:12 R
UC1 Eli Manning 2.50 6.00

UC2 Larry Fitzgerald 1.25 3.00
UC3 Roy Williams WR .30 .75
UC4 Ben Roethlisberger 2.50 6.00
UC5 Philip Rivers 1.00 2.50
UC6 Kevin Jones .40 1.00

2005 Press Pass SE

Press Pass SE was initially released in mid-May 2005. The base set consists of 40-cards. Hobby boxes contained 12-packs of 5-cards and carried an S.R.P. of $12.99 per pack with one jersey or autographed card inserted per pack. One parallel set and a variety of inserts can be found seeded in packs highlighted by the multi-tiered Game Used Jersey inserts.

COMPLETE SET (40) 10.00 25.00
1 Charlie Frye .25 .60
2 David Greene .25 .60
3 Gino Guidugli .25 .60
4 Stefan LeFors .25 .60
5 Dan Orlovsky .25 .60
6 Kyle Orton .25 .60
7 Aaron Rodgers 3.00 8.00
8 Alex Smith QB 1.00 2.50
9 Andrew Walter .25 .60
10 Jason White .40 1.00
11 J.J. Arrington .30 .75
12 Marion Barber .25 .60
13 Ronnie Brown .30 .75
14 Anthony Davis .25 .60
15 Ciatrick Fason .25 .60
16 T.A. McLendon .25 .60
17 Vernand Morency .30 .75
18 Walter Reyes .25 .60
19 Cadillac Williams .25 .60
20 Mark Bradley .25 .60
21 Reggie Brown .25 .60
22 Mark Clayton .25 .60
23 Braylon Edwards .25 .60
24 Fred Gibson .25 .60
25 Chris Henry .30 .75
26 Terrence Murphy .25 .60
27 J.R. Russell .25 .60
28 Craphonso Thorpe .25 .60
29 Roddy White .40 1.00
30 Mike Williams .30 .75
31 Troy Williamson .25 .60
32 Heath Miller .50 1.25
33 Alex Smith TE .25 .60
34 Jammal Brown .40 1.00
35 Marlin Jackson .25 .60
36 Antrel Rolle .40 1.00
37 Dan Cody .25 .60
38 Derrick Johnson .30 .75
39 Thomas Davis .25 .60
40 Aaron Rodgers CL 1.50 4.00

2005 Press Pass SE Gold

COMPLETE SET (40) 40.00 80.00
*GOLD: .8X TO 2X BASIC CARDS
ONE PER RETAIL PACK

2005 Press Pass SE Class of 2005

COMPLETE SET (9) 10.00 25.00
STATED ODDS 1:3 HOB, 1:6 RET
CL1 Aaron Rodgers 5.00 12.00
CL2 Braylon Edwards .40 1.00
CL3 Charlie Frye .40 1.00
CL4 Heath Miller .75 2.00
CL5 Troy Williamson .40 1.00
CL6 Alex Smith QB 1.50 4.00
CL7 Ronnie Brown .50 1.25
CL8 Andrew Walter .40 1.00
CL9 Cadillac Williams .40 1.00

2005 Press Pass SE Class of 2005 Autographs

AR1 Aaron Rodgers/190* 125.00 200.00
BE1 Braylon Edwards/45* 12.00 30.00
CW Cadillac Williams/200 25.00 60.00
DO Dan Orlovsky/200 10.00 25.00
HM Heath Miller/191* 12.00 30.00
RB2 Ronnie Brown/20* Red 40.00 100.00
TW Troy Williamson/200 10.00 25.00

2006 Press Pass SE Class of 2006 Autographs Red Ink

6 Brad Smith/45* 12.00 30.00
9 Vince Young/39* 30.00 80.00

2005 Press Pass SE Game Used Jerseys Silver

SILVER PRINT RUN 450-700 SER.#'d SETS
*GOLD: .5X TO 1.2X SILVER JERSEYS
GOLD PRINT RUN 450-550 SER.#'d SETS
*HOLOFOIL: .6X TO 1.5X SILVER JERSEYS
HOLOFOIL PRINT RUN 100 SER.#'d SETS
*NAMES: 1.2X TO 3X SILVER JERSEYS
NAMES PRINT RUN 25 SER.#'d SETS
UNPRICED PATCH PRINT RUN 1-10 SETS
OVERALL RETAIL ODDS 1:280
JCAS1 Alex Smith TE/700 2.50 6.00
JCAS2 Alex Smith TE/300 2.50 6.00
JCAW Andrew Walter/700 2.50 6.00
JCBB Brock Berlin/700 2.50 6.00
JCCT Craphonso Thorpe/700 2.50 6.00
JCDA Derek Anderson/700 3.00 8.00
JCDG David Greene/700 2.50 6.00
JCDO Dan Orlovsky/700 2.50 6.00
JCJC Jerome Collins/700 3.00 8.00
JCJW Jason White/700 4.00 10.00
JCKO Kyle Orton/700 2.50 6.00
JCMB Mark Bradley/700 2.50 6.00
JCMJ Marlin Jackson/700 2.50 6.00
JCRB Reggie Brown/700 2.50 6.00
JCRW Roddy White/700 4.00 10.00
JCSL Stefan LeFors/700 2.50 6.00
JCTM Terrence Murphy/450 2.50 6.00
JCVM Vernand Morency/700 3.00 8.00

2005 Press Pass SE Game Used Jerseys Autographs

STATED PRINT RUN 25 SER.#'d SETS
JCAW Andrew Walter 25.00 60.00
JCDG David Greene 25.00 60.00
JCDO Dan Orlovsky 25.00 60.00
JCJW Jason White 30.00 80.00
JCKO Kyle Orton 25.00 60.00
JCRB Reggie Brown 25.00 60.00

2005 Press Pass SE Old School

COMPLETE SET (27) 15.00 40.00
STATED ODDS 1:1 HOB, 1:2 RET
COLL.SERIES FACT.SET (28) 12.00 20.00
*COLLECTOR SERIES: .2X TO .5X BASIC INSERTS
COLL.SERIES ISSUED IN FACTORY SET FORM
OS1 Marion Barber .40 1.00
OS2 Reggie Brown .40 1.00
OS3 Ronnie Brown .50 1.25
OS4 Mark Clayton .40 1.00
OS5 Dan Cody .40 1.00
OS6 Anthony Davis .40 1.00
OS7 Braylon Edwards .40 1.00
OS8 Ciatrick Fason .40 1.00
OS9 Charlie Frye .40 1.00
OS10 David Greene .40 1.00
OS11 Gino Guidugli .40 1.00
OS12 Derrick Johnson .50 1.25
OS13 Heath Miller .75 2.00
OS14 Vernand Morency .50 1.25
OS15 Dan Orlovsky .40 1.00
OS16 Kyle Orton .40 1.00
OS17 Aaron Rodgers 5.00 12.00
OS18 Antrel Rolle .60 1.50
OS19 Eric Shelton .40 1.00
OS20 Alex Smith QB 1.50 4.00
OS21 Andrew Walter .40 1.00
OS22 Jason White .60 1.50
OS23 Roddy White .60 1.50
OS24 Cadillac Williams .40 1.00
OS25 Mike Williams .50 1.25
OS26 Troy Williamson .40 1.00
OS27 Braylon Edwards CL .20 .50

2005 Press Pass SE Up Close

COMPLETE SET (6) 7.50 20.00
STATED ODDS 1:4 HOB, 1:12 RET
UC1 Cadillac Williams .40 1.00
UC2 Aaron Rodgers 5.00 12.00
UC3 Mike Williams .50 1.25
UC4 Ronnie Brown .50 1.25
UC5 Braylon Edwards .40 1.00
UC6 Dan Orlovsky .40 1.00

2006 Press Pass SE

This 40-card set was released in May, 2006. The set was issued into the hobby in five-card packs with an $12.99 which came 12 packs to a box.

COMPLETE SET (40) 12.50 30.00
1 Joseph Addai .25 .60
2 Jason Avant .25 .60
3 Reggie Bush .40 1.00
4 Dominique Byrd .25 .60
5 Brodie Croyle .25 .60
6 Jay Cutler .30 .75
7 Vernon Davis .30 .75
8 Maurice Drew .40 1.00
9 Anthony Fasano .25 .60
10 D'Brickashaw Ferguson .25 .60
11 Bruce Gradkowski .30 .75
12 Darrell Hackney .30 .75
13 Derek Hagan .30 .75
14 Jerome Harrison .25 .60
15 A.J. Hawk .30 .75
16 Santonio Holmes .30 .75
17 Michael Huff .30 .75
18 Chad Jackson .25 .60
19 Omar Jacobs .25 .60
20 Matt Leinart .25 .60
21 Marcedes Lewis .25 .60
22 Laurence Maroney .25 .60
23 Reggie McNeal .25 .60
24 Sinorice Moss .25 .60
25 Martin Nance .25 .60
26 Haloti Ngata .30 .75
27 Leonard Pope .40 1.00
28 Michael Robinson .25 .60
29 D.J. Shockley .30 .75
30 Maurice Stovall .25 .60
31 Marcus Vick .25 .60
32 Leon Washington .25 .60
33 LenDale White .25 .60
34 Charlie Whitehurst .25 .60
35 Jimmy Williams .25 .60
36 Mario Williams .40 1.00
37 DeAngelo Williams .30 .75
38 Demetrius Williams .25 .60
39 Vince Young .25 .60
40 Vince Young CL .12 .30

2006 Press Pass SE Gold

*GOLD: .8X TO 2X BASIC CARDS
GOLD STATED ODDS 1:1 RETAIL

2006 Press Pass SE Class of 2006

COMPLETE SET (9) 12.50 30.00
STATED ODDS 1:3 HOB, 1:6 RET
CL1 Reggie Bush .60 1.50
CL2 Brodie Croyle .40 1.00
CL3 A.J. Hawk .50 1.25
CL4 Santonio Holmes .50 1.25
CL5 Matt Leinart .40 1.00
CL6 Sinorice Moss .40 1.00
CL7 LenDale White .40 1.00
CL8 DeAngelo Williams .50 1.25
CL9 Vince Young .40 1.00

2006 Press Pass SE Class of 2006 Autographs

1 Reggie Bush/100 8.00 20.00
2 Brodie Croyle/200 10.00 25.00
3 A.J. Hawk/200 20.00 50.00
4 Omar Jacobs/194* 8.00 20.00
5 Matt Leinart/100 15.00 40.00
6 Brad Smith/155* 10.00 25.00
7 Marcus Vick/50 15.00 40.00
8 LenDale White/190 20.00 50.00
9 Vince Young/61* 25.00 60.00

2006 Press Pass SE Game Used Jerseys Silver

OVERALL JERSEY ODDS 1:3 H, 1:280 R
*GOLD: .5X TO 1.2X SILVER JSY
*HOLOFOIL/99: .6X TO 1.5X SILVER JSY
HOLOFOIL PRINT RUN 99 SER.#'d SETS
*PREMIUM/25: 1X TO 2.5X SILVER JSY
PREMIUM PRINT RUN 25 SER.#'d SETS
JCAF Anthony Fasano 3.00 8.00
JCAH A.J. Hawk 4.00 10.00
JCBB Brett Basanez 5.00 12.00
JCBC Brodie Croyle 3.00 8.00
JCBS Brad Smith 4.00 10.00
JCCH Chris Hannon 4.00 10.00
JCCR Cory Rodgers 3.00 8.00
JCCW Charlie Whitehurst 3.00 8.00
JCDA Devin Aromashodu 3.00 8.00
JCDH Darrell Hackney 4.00 10.00
JCDO Drew Olson 3.00 8.00
JCDS D.J. Shockley 4.00 10.00
JCGL Greg Lee 3.00 8.00
JCHN Haloti Ngata 4.00 10.00
JCJH Jerome Harrison 3.00 8.00
JCJK Joe Klopfenstein 3.00 8.00
JCLW LenDale White 3.00 8.00
JCMD Maurice Drew 5.00 12.00
JCMN Martin Nance 3.00 8.00
JCMR Michael Robinson 3.00 8.00
JCOJ Omar Jacobs 3.00 8.00
JCPP Paul Pinegar 3.00 8.00
JCRB Reggie Bush Shirt 5.00 12.00
JCTJ Tarvaris Jackson 3.00 8.00
JCVD Vernon Davis 4.00 10.00
JCMH1 Mike Hass 3.00 8.00
JCMH2 Michael Huff 4.00 10.00
JCML1 Matt Leinart Shirt 3.00 8.00
JCML2 Marcedes Lewis 3.00 8.00
JCDW 1 DeAngelo Williams 4.00 10.00
JCDW 2 Demetrius Williams 3.00 8.00

2006 Press Pass SE Game Used Jerseys Autographs

STATED PRINT RUN 25 SER.#'d SETS
JCAF Anthony Fasano 25.00 50.00
JCAH A.J. Hawk 25.00 60.00
JCBB Brett Basanez 20.00 40.00
JCBS Brad Smith 25.00 60.00
JCCR Cory Rodgers 20.00 40.00
JCCW Charlie Whitehurst 20.00 50.00
JCDA Devin Aromashodu 25.00 50.00
JCDH Darrell Hackney 20.00 40.00
JCDO Drew Olson 25.00 50.00
JCDS D.J. Shockley 25.00 50.00
JCDW Demetrius Williams 25.00 50.00
JCGL Greg Lee 20.00 40.00
JCJH Jerome Harrison 25.00 50.00
JCLW LenDale White 25.00 60.00
JCMD Maurice Drew 40.00 80.00
JCML Marcedes Lewis 25.00 50.00
JCMN Martin Nance 20.00 40.00
JCOJ Omar Jacobs 25.00 50.00

2006 Press Pass SE Old School

COMPLETE SET (27) 15.00 40.00
STATED ODDS 1:1 HOB, 1:2 RET
*COLLECTORS SERIES: .25X TO .6X
COLL.SERIES ISSUED AS FACTORY SET
OS1 Brodie Croyle .40 1.00
OS2 Omar Jacobs .40 1.00
OS3 Charlie Whitehurst .40 1.00
OS4 Chad Jackson .40 1.00
OS5 Ernie Sims .40 1.00
OS6 Leonard Pope .60 1.50
OS7 Chad Greenway .60 1.50
OS8 Joseph Addai .40 1.00
OS9 Vernon Davis .50 1.25
OS10 DeAngelo Williams .50 1.25
OS11 Sinorice Moss .40 1.00
OS12 Laurence Maroney .40 1.00
OS13 Mario Williams .60 1.50
OS14 Anthony Fasano .40 1.00
OS15 Maurice Stovall .40 1.00
OS16 A.J. Hawk .50 1.25
OS17 Santonio Holmes .50 1.25
OS18 Haloti Ngata .50 1.25
OS19 Tamba Hali .60 1.50
OS20 Michael Huff .50 1.25
OS21 Vince Young .40 1.00
OS22 Reggie Bush .60 1.50
OS23 Matt Leinart .40 1.00
OS24 LenDale White .40 1.00
OS25 Jay Cutler .50 1.25
OS26 Jimmy Williams .40 1.00
OS27 Reggie Bush CL .30 .75

2007 Press Pass SE

This 50-card set was released in May, 2007. The set was issued into the hobby in five-card packs, with a $12.99 SRP, which came 12 packs to a box.

COMPLETE SET (50) 15.00 40.00
1 Reggie Nelson .25 .60
2 Patrick Willis .40 1.00
3 Brian Leonard .25 .60
4 Sidney Rice .30 .75
5 Robert Meachem .30 .75
6 Chris Leak .25 .60
7 Calvin Johnson .75 2.00
8 Charles Johnson .25 .60
9 Kevin Kolb .30 .75
10 Drew Stanton .25 .60
11 Antonio Pittman .25 .60
12 Troy Smith .25 .60
13 Steve Smith USC .25 .60
14 Leon Hall .25 .60
15 Brandon Jackson .25 .60
16 Ted Ginn Jr. .30 .75
17 Aundrae Allison .50 1.25
18 DeShawn Wynn .25 .60
19 Dwayne Wright .25 .60
20 Michael Bush .25 .60
21 Dwayne Bowe .25 .60
22 Adam Carriker .25 .60
23 Paul Posluszny .25 .60
24 Aaron Ross .25 .60
25 Lorenzo Booker .30 .75
26 Jamaal Anderson .40 1.00
27 Zach Miller .25 .60
28 Dallas Baker .30 .75
29 Adrian Peterson .75 2.00
30 Dwayne Jarrett .40 1.00
31 Greg Olsen .40 1.00
32 Darius Walker .30 .75
33 Alan Branch .25 .60
34 Marshawn Lynch .50 1.25
35 JaMarcus Russell .60 1.50
36 Anthony Gonzalez .25 .60
37 Gaines Adams .30 .75
38 Craig Buster Davis .25 .60
39 Jason Hill .25 .60
40 Kenny Irons .25 .60
41 John Beck .25 .60
42 Lawrence Timmons .40 1.00
43 Trent Edwards .25 .60
44 Tony Hunt .60 1.50
45 Darrelle Revis .30 .75
46 Jarvis Moss .25 .60
47 LaRon Landry .40 1.00
48 Brady Quinn .25 .60
49 Jordan Palmer .75 2.00
50 Rhema McKnight .25 .60

2007 Press Pass SE Gold

*GOLD: .8X TO 2X BASIC CARDS
ONE PER RETAIL PACK

2007 Press Pass SE Class of 2007

COMPLETE SET (10) 15.00 40.00
STATED ODDS 1:6 HOB/RET
1 Brady Quinn .50 1.25
2 JaMarcus Russell .50 1.25
3 Troy Smith .50 1.25
4 Marshawn Lynch 1.00 2.50
5 Adrian Peterson 1.50 4.00
6 Dwayne Jarrett .60 1.50
7 Calvin Johnson 1.50 4.00
8 Ted Ginn Jr. .60 1.50
9 Robert Meachem .60 1.50
10 Tony Hunt .50 1.25

2007 Press Pass SE Class of 2007 Autographs

STATED PRINT RUN 199 UNLESS NOTED
CLAP Adrian Peterson/75* 75.00 150.00
CLBJ Brandon Jackson/199 8.00 20.00
CLBQ Brady Quinn/198* 6.00 15.00
CLCJ Calvin Johnson/18* 75.00 150.00
CLDW Darius Walker/192* 6.00 15.00
CLJR JaMarcus Russell/188* 10.00 25.00
CLKI Kenny Irons/199 8.00 20.00
CLRM Robert Meachem/199 8.00 20.00
CLSR Sidney Rice/199 10.00 25.00
CLTG Ted Ginn Jr. /199 10.00 25.00
CLTS Troy Smith/20* 20.00 50.00

2007 Press Pass SE Class of 2007 Autographs Red Ink

CLAP Adrian Peterson/25* 75.00 150.00

2007 Press Pass SE Game Day Gear Jerseys Autographs

STATED PRINT RUN 25 SER.#'d SETS
AP Adrian Peterson 200.00 350.00
BL Brian Leonard 20.00 50.00
BQ Brady Quinn 10.00 25.00
GW Garrett Wolfe 25.00 60.00
KD Kenneth Darby 30.00 60.00
KK Kevin Kolb 20.00 50.00
LB Lorenzo Booker 25.00 50.00
MB Michael Bush 20.00 50.00
DB2 Dwayne Bowe 30.00 60.00
DW3 DeShawn Wynn 30.00 60.00
JR2 Jeff Rowe 25.00 50.00

2007 Press Pass SE Game Day Gear Jerseys Silver

*GOLD/299: .5X TO 1.2X SILVER JSYs
GOLD PRINT RUN 299 SER.#'d SETS
*HOLOFOIL/99: .6X TO 1.5X SILVER JSYs
HOLOFOIL PRINT RUN 99 SER.#'d SETS
*HOLO.PLATINUM/25: 1.5X TO 4X SILVER
HOLOFOIL PLATINUM PRINT RUN 25 SER.#'d SETS
OVERALL GD GEAR ODDS 1:3H, 1:280R
AP Adrian Peterson 20.00 50.00
BJ Brandon Jackson 4.00 10.00
BL Brian Leonard 4.00 10.00
BQ Brady Quinn 3.00 8.00
CD Craig Buster Davis 4.00 10.00
CL Chris Leak 5.00 12.00
CS Chansi Stuckey 3.00 8.00
DB2 Dwayne Bowe 5.00 12.00
DJ Dwayne Jarrett 4.00 10.00
DS Drew Stanton 4.00 10.00
DW Darius Walker 4.00 10.00
DW2 Dwayne Wright 3.00 8.00
DW3 DeShawn Wynn 4.00 10.00
GO Greg Olsen 5.00 12.00
GW Garrett Wolfe 4.00 10.00
JF Joel Filani 4.00 10.00
JP Jordan Palmer 4.00 10.00
JR1 JaMarcus Russell 5.00 12.00
JR2 Jeff Rowe 3.00 8.00
KD Kenneth Darby 5.00 12.00
KI Kenny Irons 5.00 12.00
KK Kevin Kolb 4.00 10.00
KS Kolby Smith 4.00 10.00
LB Lorenzo Booker 4.00 10.00
LL LaRon Landry 5.00 12.00
MB Michael Bush 4.00 10.00
ML Marshawn Lynch 6.00 15.00
RB Reggie Bush 10.00 25.00
SS Steve Smith USC 4.00 10.00
ZM Zach Miller 4.00 10.00

2007 Press Pass SE Gridiron Graphs Gold

OVERALL SE AUTO ODDS 2:3
UNPRICED PRINTING PLATES #'d TO 1
*RED INK: .6X TO 1.5X BASIC AUTOS
GGAA Aundrae Allison 4.00 10.00
GGAB Alan Branch 4.00 10.00
GGAG Anthony Gonzalez 4.00 10.00
GGAP Adrian Peterson SP 75.00 150.00
GGAPI Antonio Pittman 4.00 10.00
GGBJ Brandon Jackson 4.00 10.00
GGBL Brian Leonard 4.00 10.00
GGBQ Brady Quinn SP 4.00 10.00
GGCJ Calvin Johnson SP 75.00 150.00
GGCL Chris Leak 4.00 10.00
GGDB1 Dallas Baker 4.00 10.00
GGDB2 Dwayne Bowe 4.00 10.00
GGDS Drew Stanton 4.00 10.00
GGDW1 Darius Walker 4.00 10.00
GGDW2 Dwayne Wright 4.00 10.00
GGGA Gaines Adams 5.00 12.00
GGGO Greg Olsen 6.00 15.00
GGJA Jamaal Anderson 5.00 12.00
GGJB John Beck 4.00 10.00
GGJR JaMarcus Russell SP 12.00 30.00
GGKD Kenneth Darby 4.00 10.00
GGKI Kenny Irons 4.00 10.00
GGKK Kevin Kolb 5.00 12.00
GGLH Leon Hall 4.00 10.00
GGLL LaRon Landry 6.00 15.00
GGLT Lawrence Timmons 6.00 15.00
GGMB Michael Bush 4.00 10.00
GGMM Matt Moore 6.00 15.00
GGRM Robert Meachem 5.00 12.00
GGRN Reggie Nelson 4.00 10.00
GGSR Sidney Rice 5.00 12.00
GGSS Steve Smith USC 4.00 10.00
GGSY Selvin Young 4.00 10.00
GGTG Ted Ginn Jr. SP 15.00 40.00
GGTS Troy Smith SP 15.00 40.00

2007 Press Pass SE Gridiron Graphs Green

*GREEN/25: 1X TO 2.5X GOLD AUTOs
GREEN PRINT RUN 25 SER.#'d SETS
GGAP Adrian Peterson 150.00 300.00
GGBQ Brady Quinn/24* 8.00 20.00
GGCJ Calvin Johnson/19* 125.00 250.00
GGTG Ted Ginn Jr. 30.00 80.00
GGTS Troy Smith/20* 30.00 80.00

2007 Press Pass SE Gridiron Graphs Green Red Ink

RED INK ANNOUNCED PRINT RUN 1-25
GGJA Jamaal Anderson/25 12.00 30.00
GGMB Michael Bush/25 12.00 30.00
GGSY Selvin Young/25 12.00 30.00

2007 Press Pass SE Insider Insight

COMPLETE SET (34) 15.00 40.00
STATED ODDS 1:1 HOB, 1:2 RET
COLL.SERIES ISSUED AS FACTORY SET
1 Gaines Adams .60 1.50
2 Jamaal Anderson .60 1.50
3 Dwayne Bowe .50 1.25
4 Alan Branch .50 1.25
5 Michael Bush .50 1.25
6 Adam Carriker .50 1.25
7 Trent Edwards .50 1.25
8 Ted Ginn Jr. .60 1.50
9 Anthony Gonzalez .50 1.25
10 Leon Hall .50 1.25
11 Tony Hunt .50 1.25
12 Kenny Irons .50 1.25
13 Brandon Jackson .50 1.25
14 Dwayne Jarrett .60 1.50
15 Calvin Johnson 1.50 4.00
16 LaRon Landry .75 2.00
17 Brian Leonard .50 1.25
18 Marshawn Lynch 1.00 2.50
19 Robert Meachem .60 1.50
20 Reggie Nelson .50 1.25
21 Adrian Peterson 1.50 4.00
22 Antonio Pittman .50 1.25
23 Paul Posluszny .50 1.25
24 Brady Quinn .50 1.25
25 Sidney Rice .60 1.50
26 Aaron Ross .50 1.25
27 JaMarcus Russell .50 1.25
28 Steve Smith USC .50 1.25
29 Troy Smith .50 1.25
30 Drew Stanton .50 1.25
31 Kevin Kolb .60 1.50
32 Lawrence Timmons .75 2.00
33 Darius Walker .50 1.25
34 Brady Quinn CL .25 .60

2007 Press Pass SE Insider Insight Collectors Series

COMP.FACT.SET (26) 15.00 30.00
COMPLETE SET (25) 10.00 25.00
ISSUED IN FACTORY SET FORM
II1 Gaines Adams .40 1.00
II2 Dwayne Bowe .30 .75
II3 Michael Bush .30 .75
II4 Adam Carriker .30 .75
II5 Trent Edwards .30 .75
II6 Ted Ginn Jr. .40 1.00
II7 Anthony Gonzalez .30 .75
II8 Leon Hall .30 .75
II9 Tony Hunt .30 .75
II10 Brandon Jackson .30 .75
II11 Dwayne Jarrett .40 1.00
II12 Calvin Johnson 1.00 2.50
II13 LaRon Landry .50 1.25
II14 Brian Leonard .30 .75
II15 Marshawn Lynch .60 1.50
II16 Robert Meachem .40 1.00
II17 Adrian Peterson 1.00 2.50
II18 Paul Posluszny .30 .75
II19 Brady Quinn .30 .75
II20 Sidney Rice .40 1.00
II21 JaMarcus Russell .30 .75
II22 Steve Smith USC .30 .75
II23 Troy Smith .30 .75
II24 Drew Stanton .30 .75
II25 Kevin Kolb .40 1.00

2007 Press Pass SE Marquee Matchups

COMPLETE SET (20) 15.00 40.00
STATED ODDS 1:3 HOB/RET
1 J.Russell/B.Quinn .60 1.50
2 A.Peterson/S.Young 2.00 5.00
3 C.Johnson/D.Clowney 2.00 5.00
4 T.Ginn Jr./L.Hall .75 2.00
5 D.Jarrett/D.Walker .75 2.00
6 M.Lynch/Z.Miller 1.25 3.00
7 R.Meachem/D.Bowe .75 2.00
8 S.Rice/R.Nelson .75 2.00
9 T.Hunt/A.Branch .60 1.50
10 C.Leak/L.Landry 1.00 2.50
11 A.Gonzalez/A.Ross .60 1.50
12 G.Olsen/L.Booker 1.00 2.50
13 A.Pittman/P.Posluszny .60 1.50
14 B.Leonard/M.Bush .60 1.50
15 T.Smith/D.Stanton .60 1.50
16 K.Irons/K.Darby .60 1.50
17 M.Moore/S.Smith USC 1.00 2.50
18 B.Jackson/M.Griffin .60 1.50
19 T.Edwards/D.Hughes .60 1.50
20 R.Bush/V.Young .60 1.50

2007 Press Pass SE Teammates Autographs

DW B.Quinn/D.Walker 10.00 25.00
CLRN C.Leak/R.Nelson 20.00 50.00
JRDB J.Russell/D.Bowe 30.00 80.00

2007 Press Pass SE Teammates Autographs Red Ink

TSTG T.Smith/T.Ginn Jr. 30.00 80.00

2008 Press Pass SE

COMPLETE SET (50) 15.00 30.00
1 Glenn Dorsey .25 .60
2 Chris Long .30 .75
3 Dan Connor .25 .60
4 Aqib Talib .40 1.00
5 Kenny Phillips .25 .60
6 Erik Ainge .25 .60
7 John David Booty .25 .60
8 Colt Brennan .30 .75
9 Brian Brohm .25 .60
10 Joe Flacco .50 1.25
11 Chad Henne .30 .75
12 Matt Ryan .75 2.00
13 Andre Woodson .25 .60
14 Jamaal Charles .40 1.00
15 Matt Forte .40 1.00
16 Mike Hart .25 .60
17 Jacob Hester .25 .60
18 Chris Johnson .30 .75
19 Felix Jones .25 .60
20 Darren McFadden .25 .60
21 Rashard Mendenhall .25 .60
22 Ray Rice .25 .60
23 Steve Slaton .25 .60
24 Kevin Smith .25 .60
25 Jonathan Stewart .40 1.00
26 Fred Davis .25 .60
27 Adrian Arrington .25 .60
28 Earl Bennett .40 1.00
29 Adarius Bowman .30 .75
30 Early Doucet .25 .60
31 James Hardy .25 .60
32 DJ Hall .25 .60
33 DeSean Jackson .50 1.25
34 Malcolm Kelly .25 .60
35 Mario Manningham .25 .60
36 Limas Sweed .25 .60
37 Devin Thomas .25 .60
38 Lavelle Hawkins .30 .75
39 Andre Caldwell .25 .60
40 Vernon Gholston .25 .60
41 Derrick Harvey .25 .60
42 Keith Rivers .25 .60
43 Mike Jenkins .25 .60
44 Leodis McKelvin .30 .75
45 Dennis Dixon .25 .60
46 Josh Johnson .25 .60
47 Tashard Choice .25 .60
48 Chauncey Washington .30 .75
49 John Carlson .25 .60
50 Donnie Avery .30 .75

2008 Press Pass SE Gold

COMPLETE SET (50) 40.00 80.00
*GOLD: .8X TO 2X BASIC CARDS
ONE GOLD PER RETAIL PACK

2008 Press Pass SE Class of 2008

STATED ODDS 1:6 HOB/RET
CL1 Matt Ryan 1.50 4.00
CL2 Brian Brohm .50 1.25
CL3 Darren McFadden .50 1.25
CL4 Jonathan Stewart .75 2.00
CL5 DeSean Jackson 1.00 2.50
CL6 Malcolm Kelly .50 1.25
CL7 Limas Sweed .50 1.25
CL8 Glenn Dorsey .50 1.25
CL9 Chris Long .60 1.50
CL10 Rashard Mendenhall .50 1.25

2008 Press Pass SE Class of 2008 Autographs

STATED PRINT RUN 142-199
CLAW Andre Woodson/188* 4.00 10.00
CLBB Brian Brohm/199 4.00 10.00
CLCL Chris Long/185* 5.00 12.00
CLDJ DeSean Jackson/172* 8.00 20.00
CLDM Darren McFadden/199 4.00 10.00
CLJS Jonathan Stewart/199 6.00 15.00
CLLS Limas Sweed/142 4.00 10.00
CLMH Mike Hart/196* 4.00 10.00
CLMK Malcolm Kelly/170 4.00 10.00
CLMR Matt Ryan/169* 30.00 80.00
CLRM Rashard Mendenhall/174* 4.00 10.00

2008 Press Pass SE Class of 2008 Autographs Red Ink

*RED INK/14-30: .5X TO 1.2X BASE AU
RED INK ANNOUNCED PRINT RUN 3-30

2008 Press Pass SE Game Day Gear Jerseys Autographs

STATED PRINT RUN 25 SER.#'d SETS
GDGAA Adrian Arrington 10.00 25.00
GDGBB Brian Brohm 10.00 25.00
GDGCB Colt Brennan 12.00 30.00
GDGCH Chad Henne 12.00 30.00
GDGDA Donnie Avery 12.00 30.00
GDGDD Dennis Dixon 10.00 25.00
GDGDH DJ Hall 10.00 25.00
GDGDM Darren McFadden 10.00 25.00
GDGDT Devin Thomas 10.00 25.00
GDGEA Erik Ainge 20.00 50.00
GDGED Early Doucet 10.00 25.00
GDGJC Jamaal Charles 15.00 40.00
GDGJS Jonathan Stewart 25.00 60.00
GDGLS Limas Sweed 10.00 25.00
GDGMH Mike Hart 10.00 25.00
GDGMK Malcolm Kelly 10.00 25.00
GDGMR Matt Ryan 75.00 150.00
GDGRR Ray Rice 10.00 25.00
GDGSS Steve Slaton 10.00 25.00

2008 Press Pass SE Game Day Gear Jerseys Silver

*GOLD/199-299: .5X TO 1.2X BASIC INSERTS
GOLD PRINT RUN 199-299 SER.#'d SETS
*HOLOFOIL/99: .6X TO 1.5X BASIC INSERTS
HOLOFOIL PRINT RUN 99 SER.#'d SETS
*HOLOFOIL PLATINUM/25: 1.5X TO 4X
HOLOFOIL PLATINUM PRINT RUN 25
OVERALL ODDS 1:4 HOB, 1:280 RET
GDGAA Adrian Arrington 3.00 8.00
GDGBB Brian Brohm 4.00 10.00
GDGCB Colt Brennan 2.50 6.00
GDGCH Chad Henne 2.50 6.00
GDGCW Chauncey Washington 2.50 6.00
GDGDA Donnie Avery 2.50 6.00
GDGDB Davone Bess 2.50 6.00
GDGDB Dorien Bryant 3.00 8.00
GDGDC Dan Connor 3.00 8.00
GDGDD Dennis Dixon 2.00 5.00
GDGDH DJ Hall 3.00 8.00
GDGDM Darren McFadden 2.00 5.00
GDGDR Darius Reynaud 3.00 8.00
GDGDS Dantrell Savage 2.50 6.00
GDGDT Devin Thomas 2.00 5.00
GDGEA Erik Ainge 4.00 10.00
GDGED Early Doucet 2.00 5.00
GDGJC Jamaal Charles 3.00 8.00
GDGJDB John David Booty 4.00 10.00
GDGJF Justin Forsett 2.50 6.00
GDGJH Jacob Hester 3.00 8.00
GDGJS Jonathan Stewart 6.00 15.00
GDGJT Jacob Tamme 2.50 6.00
GDGKP Kenny Phillips 3.00 8.00
GDGKS Kevin Smith 2.00 5.00
GDGLH Lavelle Hawkins 2.50 6.00
GDGLS Limas Sweed 2.00 5.00
GDGMF Matt Forte 5.00 12.00
GDGMH Mike Hart 6.00 15.00
GDGMK Malcolm Kelly 4.00 10.00
GDGMR Matt Ryan 8.00 20.00
GDGRL Rafael Little 2.50 6.00
GDGRR Ray Rice 2.00 5.00
GDGSS Steve Slaton 2.00 5.00
GDGTC Tashard Choice 3.00 8.00
GDGVG Vernon Gholston 3.00 8.00

2008 Press Pass SE Gridiron Graphs Gold

UNPRICED PRINT PLATES PRINT RUN 1
GGAA Adrian Arrington 3.00 8.00
GGAB Adarius Bowman 4.00 10.00
GGAC Andre Caldwell 3.00 8.00
GGAC2 Antoine Cason 4.00 10.00
GGAP Allen Patrick 3.00 8.00
GGAW Andre Woodson 3.00 8.00
GGBB Brian Brohm 3.00 8.00
GGCB Colt Brennan 4.00 10.00
GGCC Calais Campbell 4.00 10.00
GGCH Chad Henne 4.00 10.00
GGCJ2 Chris Johnson 4.00 10.00
GGCL Chris Long 4.00 10.00
GGCW Chauncey Washington 4.00 10.00
GGDA Donnie Avery 4.00 10.00
GGDB Dorien Bryant 4.00 10.00
GGDB2 Davone Bess 4.00 10.00
GGDC Dan Connor 3.00 8.00
GGDD Dennis Dixon 3.00 8.00
GGDH DJ Hall 3.00 8.00
GGDJ DeSean Jackson 6.00 15.00
GGDM Darren McFadden 3.00 8.00
GGDR Darius Reynaud 3.00 8.00
GGDS Dantrell Savage 4.00 10.00
GGDT Devin Thomas 3.00 8.00
GGEA Erik Ainge 3.00 8.00
GGEB Earl Bennett 5.00 12.00
GGED Early Doucet 3.00 8.00
GGER Eddie Royal 3.00 8.00
GGFD Fred Davis 3.00 8.00
GGFJ Felix Jones 3.00 8.00
GGHD Harry Douglas 4.00 10.00
GGJC Jamaal Charles 5.00 12.00
GGJC2 John Carlson 3.00 8.00
GGJDB John David Booty 3.00 8.00
GGJF Joe Flacco 6.00 15.00
GGJF2 Justin Forsett 4.00 10.00
GGJH Jacob Hester 3.00 8.00
GGJJ Josh Johnson 3.00 8.00
GGJL J Leman 3.00 8.00
GGJM Josh Morgan 3.00 8.00
GGJN Jordy Nelson 8.00 20.00
GGJS Jonathan Stewart 5.00 12.00
GGJT Jacob Tamme 4.00 10.00
GGKB Keenan Burton 3.00 8.00
GGKP Kenny Phillips 3.00 8.00
GGKR Keith Rivers 3.00 8.00
GGKS Kevin Smith 3.00 8.00
GGLH Lavelle Hawkins 4.00 10.00
GGLM Leodis McKelvin 4.00 10.00
GGLS Limas Sweed 3.00 8.00
GGMF Matt Flynn 3.00 8.00
GGMF2 Matt Forte 5.00 12.00
GGMH Mike Hart 3.00 8.00
GGMH2 Marcus Henry 3.00 8.00
GGMK Malcolm Kelly 3.00 8.00
GGMM2 Mario Manningham 3.00 8.00
GGMR Matt Ryan 30.00 60.00
GGMR2 Martin Rucker 3.00 8.00
GGMS Marcus Smith 4.00 10.00
GGOS Owen Schmitt 3.00 8.00
GGPS Paul Smith 3.00 8.00
GGRL Rafael Little 4.00 10.00
GGRM Rashard Mendenhall 3.00 8.00
GGRR Ray Rice 3.00 8.00
GGSS Steve Slaton 3.00 8.00
GGTC Tashard Choice 3.00 8.00
GGTW Trae Williams 3.00 8.00
GGVG Vernon Gholston 3.00 8.00

2008 Press Pass SE Gridiron Graphs Gold Red Ink

*RED INK/15-149: .6X TO 1.5X BASE GOLD AU
RED INK ANNOUNCED PRINT RUN 1-149

2008 Press Pass SE Gridiron Graphs Green

*GREEN/25: 1X TO 2.5X GOLD AUTO
GREEN PRINT RUN 25 SER.#'d SETS
ANNC'D PRINT RUN ON CARDS W/RED INK VERSION
GGDM Darren McFadden 6.00 15.00
GGJF Joe Flacco 12.00 30.00
GGMR Matt Ryan/24* 60.00 120.00

2008 Press Pass SE Gridiron Graphs Green Red Ink

RED INK ANNOUNCED PRINT RUN 1-50
GGBB Brian Brohm/20* 10.00 25.00
GGCB Colt Brennan/24* 12.00 30.00
GGCW Chauncey Washington/25* 12.00 30.00
GGDT Devin Thomas/22* 10.00 25.00
GGJC Jamaal Charles/21* 15.00 40.00
GGRM Rashard Mendenhall/17* 10.00 25.00
GGSS Steve Slaton/14* 10.00 25.00

2008 Press Pass SE Insider Insight

COMPLETE SET (34) 15.00 40.00
STATED ODDS 1:1 HOB, 1:2 RET
1 Erik Ainge .40 1.00
2 Adrian Arrington .40 1.00
3 Earl Bennett .60 1.50
4 John David Booty .40 1.00
5 Adarius Bowman .50 1.25
6 Colt Brennan .50 1.25
7 Brian Brohm .40 1.00
8 Jamaal Charles .60 1.50
9 Fred Davis .40 1.00
10 Glenn Dorsey .40 1.00
11 Early Doucet .40 1.00
12 Joe Flacco .75 2.00
13 Matt Forte .60 1.50
14 DJ Hall .40 1.00
15 Mike Hart .40 1.00
16 Chad Henne .50 1.25
17 Jacob Hester .40 1.00
18 DeSean Jackson .75 2.00
19 Chris Johnson .50 1.25
20 Felix Jones .40 1.00
21 Malcolm Kelly .40 1.00
22 Chris Long .50 1.25
23 Mario Manningham .40 1.00
24 Darren McFadden .40 1.00
25 Rashard Mendenhall .40 1.00
26 Ray Rice .40 1.00
27 Matt Ryan 1.25 3.00
28 Steve Slaton .40 1.00
29 Kevin Smith .40 1.00
30 Jonathan Stewart .60 1.50
31 Limas Sweed .40 1.00
32 Aqib Talib .60 1.50
33 Andre Woodson .40 1.00
34 Darren McFadden CL .40 1.00

2008 Press Pass SE Marquee Matchups

STATED ODDS 1:3 HOB/RET
MM1 M.Ryan/K.Phillips 1.50 4.00
MM2 C.Johnson/M.Forte .75 2.00
MM3 J.Stewart/M.Hart .75 2.00
MM4 D.Jackson/E.Ainge 1.00 2.50
MM5 Arrington/Caldwell .50 1.25
MM6 Booty/Mendenhall .50 1.25
MM7 Dixon/Manningham .50 1.25
MM8 A.Woodson/B.Brohm .50 1.25
MM9 E.Doucet/D.Hall .50 1.25
MM10 McFadden/J.Hester .50 1.25
MM11 Dorsey/V.Gholston .50 1.25
MM12 J.Charles/K.Smith .75 2.00
MM13 M.Kelly/L.Sweed .50 1.25
MM14 A.Bowman/J.Nelson 1.50 4.00
MM15 S.Slaton/R.Rice .50 1.25
MM16 C.Henne/D.Harvey .60 1.50
MM17 K.Burton/F.Jones .50 1.25
MM18 Reynaud/H.Douglas .60 1.50
MM19 D.Thomas/J.Hardy .50 1.25
MM20 O.Schmitt/A.Patrick .50 1.25

2008 Press Pass SE Teammates Autographs

STATED PRINT RUN 25 SER.#'d SETS
AWKB Woodson/Burton 15.00 40.00
CHMH C.Henne/M.Hart 40.00 100.00
CHMHR Henne Red/Hart Red 40.00 100.00
DDJS D.Dixon/J.Stewart 30.00 80.00
DJJF D.Jackson/J.Forsett 12.00 30.00
JCLS J.Charles/L.Sweed 25.00 60.00

2009 Press Pass SE

COMPLETE SET (50) 12.50 30.00
1 Nate Davis .25 .60
2 Josh Freeman .25 .60
3 Graham Harrell .25 .60
4 Mark Sanchez .25 .60
5 Matthew Stafford 1.25 3.00
6 Pat White .30 .75
7 Andre Brown .30 .75
8 Donald Brown .25 .60
9 Glen Coffee .25 .60
10 Mike Goodson .30 .75
11 Shonn Greene .25 .60
12 Jeremiah Johnson .25 .60
13 LeSean McCoy .60 1.50
14 Knowshon Moreno .25 .60
15 Javon Ringer .25 .60
16 Chris Wells .25 .60
17 Ramses Barden .25 .60
18 Kenny Britt .40 1.00
19 Michael Crabtree .40 1.00
20 Percy Harvin .25 .60
21 Darrius Heyward-Bey .40 1.00
22 Juaquin Iglesias .25 .60
23 Jeremy Maclin .30 .75
24 Hakeem Nicks .30 .75
25 Brian Robiskie .25 .60
26 Brandon Tate .30 .75
27 Derrick Williams .25 .60
28 Brandon Pettigrew .25 .60
29 Everette Brown .25 .60
30 Tyson Jackson .25 .60
31 Aaron Maybin .30 .75
32 Brian Orakpo .30 .75
33 Aaron Curry .40 1.00
34 Brian Cushing .25 .60
35 James Laurinaitis .25 .60
36 Rey Maualuga .40 1.00
37 Vontae Davis .25 .60
38 Malcolm Jenkins .25 .60
39 D.J. Moore .30 .75
40 Victor Harris .30 .75
41 Alphonso Smith .25 .60
42 B.J. Raji .30 .75
43 Rhett Bomar .25 .60
44 Ian Johnson .25 .60
45 James Davis .25 .60
46 Cedric Peerman .25 .60
47 Jarett Dillard .25 .60
48 Louis Murphy .25 .60
49 Mike Thomas .25 .60
50 Jared Cook .30 .75

2009 Press Pass SE Gold

OLD: .8X TO 2X BASIC CARDS
ONE GOLD PER RETAIL PACK

2009 Press Pass SE Retail Holofoil

COMPLETE SET (8) 10.00 25.00
RANDOM INSERTS IN RETAIL PACKS
RE1 Mark Sanchez .40 1.00
RE2 Matthew Stafford 2.00 5.00
RE3 LeSean McCoy 1.00 2.50
RE4 Knowshon Moreno .40 1.00
RE5 Chris Wells .40 1.00
RE6 Michael Crabtree .60 1.50
RE7 Percy Harvin .40 1.00
RE8 Jeremy Maclin .50 1.25
RE9 Derrick Williams .40 1.00
RE10 Donald Brown .40 1.00

2009 Press Pass SE Class of 2009

STATED ODDS 1:6
CL1 Mark Sanchez .50 1.25
CL2 Matthew Stafford 2.50 6.00
CL3 LeSean McCoy 1.25 3.00
CL4 Knowshon Moreno .50 1.25
CL5 Chris Wells .50 1.25
CL6 Michael Crabtree .75 2.00
CL7 Percy Harvin .50 1.25
CL8 Darrius Heyward-Bey .75 2.00
CL9 Jeremy Maclin .60 1.50
CL10 Donald Brown .50 1.25

2009 Press Pass SE Class of 2009 Autographs

STATED PRINT RUN 141-199
*HEAD OF CLASS/25: .8X TO 2X BASE AU
HEAD OF CLASS PRINT RUN 1-25
CLDB Donald Brown/199 4.00 10.00
CLJM Jeremy Maclin/141 5.00 12.00
CLJR Javon Ringer/199 4.00 10.00
CLKM Knowshon Moreno/199 4.00 10.00
CLLM LeSean McCoy/191 10.00 25.00
CLMC Michael Crabtree/199 6.00 15.00
CLMS Matthew Stafford/150 30.00 80.00
CLPH Percy Harvin/199 4.00 10.00
CLSG Shonn Greene/199 4.00 10.00
CLDHB Darrius Heyward-Bey/199 6.00 15.00
CLMS2 Mark Sanchez/150 12.00 30.00

2009 Press Pass SE Class of 2009 Autographs Red Ink

CLCW Chris Wells 12.00 30.00
CLKM Knowshon Moreno

2009 Press Pass SE Double Feature

STATED ODDS 1:3
DF1 M.Stafford/P.Harvin 2.50 6.00

DF2 M.Sanchez/J.Johnson .50 1.25
DF3 M.Crabtree/J.Maclin .75 2.00
DF4 K.Moreno/G.Coffee .50 1.25
DF5 C.Wells/A.Maybin .60 1.50
DF6 H.Nicks/Heyward-Bey .75 2.00
DF7 L.McCoy/D.Brown 1.25 3.00
DF8 J.Freeman/G.Harrell .50 1.25
DF9 S.Greene/J.Ringer .50 1.25
DF10 K.Britt/B.Tate .75 2.00
DF11 Maualuga/Laurinaitis .75 2.00
DF12 M.Jenkins/D.Williams .50 1.25
DF13 A.Curry/J.Davis .75 2.00
DF14 A.Foster/K.McKinley 1.25 3.00
DF15 P.White/H.Cantwell .60 1.50
DF16 B.Orakpo/S.McGee .60 1.50
DF17 J.Iglesias/Q.Cosby .50 1.25
DF18 M.Massaquoi/L.Murphy .50 1.25
DF19 V.Davis/B.Robiskie .50 1.25
DF20 B.Pettigrew/M.Goodson .60 1.50

2009 Press Pass SE Game Day Gear Jerseys Silver

OVERALL GD GEAR ODDS 1:4H, 1:72R
*GOLD/100 299: .5X TO 1.2X SILVER JSY
GOLD JSY PRINT RUN 199-299
*HOLOFOIL/99: .6X TO 1.5X SILVER JSY
HOLOFOIL PRINT RUN 99
*HOLOFOIL PLAT/25: 1.2X TO 3X SLVR JSY
HOLOFOIL PLATINUM PRINT RUN 25
GDGAF Arian Foster 5.00 12.00
GDGBG Brandon Gibson 2.50 6.00
GDGBR Brian Robiskie 2.00 5.00
GDGCD Chase Daniel 2.50 6.00
GDGCH Cullen Harper 2.00 5.00
GDGDB Donald Brown 2.00 5.00
GDGDW Derrick Williams 2.00 5.00
GDGGJ Gartrell Johnson 2.00 5.00
GDGHC Hunter Cantwell 2.00 5.00
GDGIJ Ian Johnson 2.00 5.00
GDGJC James Casey 2.50 6.00
GDGJF Josh Freeman 2.00 5.00
GDGJJ Jeremiah Johnson 2.00 5.00
GDGJL James Laurinaitis 2.00 5.00
GDGJM Jeremy Maclin 2.50 6.00
GDGJR Javon Ringer 2.00 5.00
GDGJW John Parker Wilson 5.00 12.00
GDGKB Kenny Britt 3.00 8.00
GDGKM Kenny McKinley 2.00 5.00
GDGLM LeSean McCoy 6.00 15.00
GDGMC Michael Crabtree 3.00 8.00
GDGMG Mike Goodson 2.50 6.00
GDGML Marlon Lucky 5.00 12.00
GDGMS Mark Sanchez 2.00 5.00
GDGND Nate Davis 2.00 5.00
GDGPH P.J. Hill 2.00 5.00
GDGQC Quan Cosby 2.00 5.00
GDGRB Ramses Barden 2.00 5.00
GDGRM Rey Maualuga 3.00 8.00
GDGSG Shonn Greene 2.00 5.00
GDGSM Stephen McGee 2.00 5.00
GDGDHB Darrius Heyward-Bey 3.00 8.00
GDGLM2 Louis Murphy 2.00 5.00
GDGMS2 Matthew Stafford 8.00 20.00
GDGRB2 Rhett Bomar 2.00 5.00

2009 Press Pass SE Game Day Gear Jerseys Autographs

STATED PRINT RUN 25 SER.#'d SETS
GDGAF Arian Foster 75.00 150.00
GDGBR Brian Robiskie 12.00 30.00
GDGDB Donald Brown 12.00 30.00
GDGIJ Ian Johnson
GDGJC James Casey 15.00 40.00
GDGJF Josh Freeman 12.00 30.00
GDGJJ Jeremiah Johnson 12.00 30.00
GDGJL James Laurinaitis 12.00 30.00
GDGJM Jeremy Maclin 15.00 40.00
GDGKB Kenny Britt 20.00 50.00
GDGMC Michael Crabtree 20.00 50.00
GDGMG Mike Goodson 15.00 40.00
GDGML Marlon Lucky 12.00 30.00
GDGMS Mark Sanchez 30.00 60.00
GDGPH P.J. Hill 12.00 30.00
GDGSG Shonn Greene 12.00 30.00

2009 Press Pass SE Gridiron Graphs Gold

OVERALL AU ODDS 1:1.5 HOB, 1:72 RET
*GREEN/25: .8X TO 2X GOLD AU
GREEN PRINT RUN 6-25
*RED/100-150: .5X TO 1.2X GOLD AU
RED PRINT RUN 100-150
GGAB Andre Brown 4.00 10.00
GGAC Austin Collie 3.00 8.00
GGAC2 Aaron Curry 5.00 12.00
GGAF Arian Foster 12.00 30.00
GGAS Alphonso Smith 3.00 8.00
GGBC Brian Cushing 3.00 8.00
GGBG Brandon Gibson 4.00 10.00
GGBH Brian Hoyer 5.00 12.00
GGBO Brian Orakpo 4.00 10.00
GGBP Brandon Pettigrew 3.00 8.00
GGBR Brian Robiskie 3.00 8.00
GGBR2 B.J. Raji 4.00 10.00
GGBT Brandon Tate 4.00 10.00
GGCC Chase Coffman 3.00 8.00
GGCD Chase Daniel 4.00 10.00
GGCH Cullen Harper 3.00 8.00
GGCP Cedric Peerman 3.00 8.00
GGCW Chris Wells 3.00 8.00
GGDB Donald Brown 3.00 8.00
GGDHB Darrius Heyward-Bey 5.00 12.00
GGDM D.J. Moore 4.00 10.00
GGDM2 Devin Moore 3.00 8.00
GGDW Derrick Williams 3.00 8.00
GGEB Everette Brown 3.00 8.00
GGGC Glen Coffee 3.00 8.00
GGGH Graham Harrell 8.00 20.00
GGGJ Gartrell Johnson 3.00 8.00
GGHC Hunter Cantwell 3.00 8.00
GGHN Hakeem Nicks 4.00 10.00
GGIJ Ian Johnson 3.00 8.00
GGJC Jared Cook 4.00 10.00
GGJC2 Jeremy Childs 3.00 8.00
GGJD James Davis 3.00 8.00
GGJD2 Jarett Dillard 3.00 8.00
GGJF Josh Freeman 3.00 8.00
GGJI Juaquin Iglesias 3.00 8.00
GGJJ Jeremiah Johnson 3.00 8.00
GGJL James Laurinaitis 3.00 8.00
GGJM Jeremy Maclin 4.00 10.00
GGJR Javon Ringer 3.00 8.00
GGJW John Parker Wilson 3.00 8.00
GGKB Kenny Britt 5.00 12.00
GGKM Knowshon Moreno 3.00 8.00
GGKM2 Kenny McKinley 3.00 8.00
GGKO Kevin Ogletree 4.00 10.00
GGLM LeSean McCoy 8.00 20.00
GGLM2 Louis Murphy 3.00 8.00
GGMC Michael Crabtree 5.00 12.00
GGMG Mike Goodson 4.00 10.00
GGMJ Malcolm Jenkins 3.00 8.00
GGMM Mohamed Massaquoi 3.00 8.00
GGMR Mike Reilly 3.00 8.00
GGMS Matthew Stafford 25.00 60.00
GGMS2 Mark Sanchez 15.00 40.00
GGMT Mike Thomas 3.00 8.00
GGND Nate Davis 3.00 8.00
GGPH Percy Harvin 3.00 8.00
GGPH2 P.J. Hill 3.00 8.00
GGPW Pat White 4.00 10.00
GGQC Quan Cosby 3.00 8.00
GGRB Ramses Barden 3.00 8.00
GGRB2 Rhett Bomar 3.00 8.00
GGRJ Rashad Jennings 4.00 10.00
GGRM Rey Maualuga 5.00 12.00
GGSG Shonn Greene 3.00 8.00
GGSM Stephen McGee 3.00 8.00
GGTJ Tyson Jackson 3.00 8.00
GGVD Vontae Davis 3.00 8.00
GGVH Victor Harris 4.00 10.00
GGWM William Moore 3.00 8.00

2009 Press Pass SE Headliners

STATED ODDS 1:2
HL1 Nate Davis .40 1.00
HL2 Josh Freeman .40 1.00
HL3 Graham Harrell .40 1.00
HL4 Mark Sanchez .40 1.00
HL5 Matthew Stafford 2.00 5.00
HL6 Pat White .50 1.25
HL7 Andre Brown .50 1.25
HL8 Donald Brown .40 1.00
HL9 Glen Coffee .40 1.00
HL10 Shonn Greene .40 1.00
HL11 Mike Goodson .50 1.25
HL12 Knowshon Moreno .40 1.00
HL13 LeSean McCoy 1.00 2.50
HL14 Javon Ringer .40 1.00
HL15 Chris Wells .40 1.00
HL16 Kenny Britt .60 1.50
HL17 Michael Crabtree .60 1.50
HL18 Percy Harvin .40 1.00
HL19 Darrius Heyward-Bey .60 1.50
HL20 Juaquin Iglesias .40 1.00
HL21 Jeremy Maclin .50 1.25
HL22 Hakeem Nicks .50 1.25
HL23 Brandon Tate .50 1.25
HL24 Derrick Williams .40 1.00
HL25 Brandon Pettigrew .40 1.00
HL26 Everette Brown .40 1.00
HL27 Tyson Jackson .40 1.00
HL28 Aaron Maybin .50 1.25
HL29 Brian Orakpo .50 1.25
HL30 Aaron Curry .60 1.50
HL31 James Laurinaitis .40 1.00
HL32 Rey Maualuga .60 1.50
HL33 Malcolm Jenkins .40 1.00
HL34 Matthew Stafford CL 1.50 4.00

2009 Press Pass SE Teammates Autographs

STATED PRINT RUN 25 SER.#'d SETS
CWJL C.Wells/J.Laurinaitis 25.00 60.00
HNBT H.Nicks/B.Tate 12.00 30.00
JMCD J.Maclin/C.Daniel 40.00 80.00
MCGH M.Crabtree/G.Harrell 20.00 50.00
MSKS M.Stafford/K.Moreno 25.00 60.00
MSRM M.Sanchez/R.Maualuga 40.00 100.00
PHLM P.Harvin/L.Murphy 15.00 40.00

2014 Press Pass Showbound Gold

SIX AUTOs PER BOX OVERALL
*BLUE/50-99: .5X TO 1.2X GOLD AU
*BLUE/50-99: .4X TO 1X GOLD AU SP
*RED/15-25: .6X TO 1.5X GOLD AU
*RED/15-25: .5X TO 1.2X GOLD AU SP
PURPLE/36-50: .5X TO 1.2X GOLD AU
PURPLE/36-50: .4X TO 1X GOLD AU SP
PURPLE/15-25: .6X TO 1.5X GOLD AU
SBAM1 A.J. McCarron SP 2.50 6.00
SBAM2 Aaron Murray 2.50 6.00
SBASJ Austin Seferian-Jenkins 2.50 6.00
SBAW Andre Williams 2.50 6.00
SBBB Blake Bortles 3.00 8.00
SBBC1 Brandon Coleman 2.50 6.00
SBBC2 Brandin Cooks 4.00 10.00
SBBR Bradley Roby 2.50 6.00
SBBS Bishop Sankey 2.50 6.00
SBCH Cody Hoffman 2.50 6.00
SBCM C.J. Mosley 3.00 8.00
SBCS Charles Sims 2.50 6.00
SBDA Davante Adams 4.00 10.00
SBDC Derek Carr 15.00 40.00
SBDD Darqueze Dennard 3.00 8.00
SBDF David Fales 5.00 12.00
SBDM Donte Moncrief 2.50 6.00
SBEE Eric Ebron 3.00 8.00
SBHCD Ha Ha Clinton-Dix 3.00 8.00
SBIC Isaiah Crowell 3.00 8.00
SBJA Jace Amaro 5.00 12.00
SBJC Jadeveon Clowney SP 3.00 8.00
SBJH Jeremy Hill 3.00 8.00
SBJL Jarvis Landry 6.00 15.00
SBJM1 Johnny Manziel SP 4.00 10.00
SBJM2 Jordan Matthews 4.00 10.00
SBJV Jason Verrett 2.50 6.00
SBKC Ka'Deem Carey 2.50 6.00
SBKM Khalil Mack 10.00 25.00
SBKVN Kyle Van Noy 3.00 8.00
SBLN Louis Nix III 2.50 6.00
SBLP Loucheiz Purifoy 2.50 6.00
SBLS Lache Seastrunk 2.50 6.00
SBLW L'Damian Washington 3.00 8.00
SBME Mike Evans 6.00 15.00
SBMG Marion Grice 2.50 6.00
SBML Marqise Lee 6.00 15.00
SBMR Marcus Roberson 3.00 8.00
SBMS Michael Sam 8.00 20.00
SBOB Odell Beckham Jr. 6.00 15.00
SBPR Paul Richardson 5.00 12.00
SBRH Ra'Shede Hageman 2.50 6.00
SBST Stephon Tuitt 4.00 10.00
SBTB1 Tajh Boyd 2.50 6.00
SBTB2 Teddy Bridgewater SP
SBTG Tyler Gaffney 2.50 6.00
SBTJ1 Timmy Jernigan 2.50 6.00
SBTJ2 TJ Jones 4.00 10.00
SBTR Tevin Reese 2.50 6.00
SBZM Zach Mettenberger 2.50 6.00

2014 Press Pass Showbound Class of 2014 Gold

*BLUE/50: .4X TO 1X GOLD AU/75
*BLUE/15-25: .5X TO 1.2X GOLD AU/50
*BLUE/15-25: .5X TO 1.2X GOLD AU/25
*RED/15-25: .5X TO 1.2X GOLD AU/50-75
C14AM A.J. McCarron/75 3.00 8.00
C14BB Blake Bortles/21* 5.00 12.00
C14BS Bishop Sankey/44* 3.00 8.00
C14JC Jadeveon Clowney/20* 5.00 12.00
C14JM Johnny Manziel/25 6.00 15.00
C14ME Mike Evans/50 8.00 20.00
C14ML Marqise Lee/19* 10.00 25.00
C14TB Teddy Bridgewater/25 6.00 15.00

2014 Press Pass Showbound Paydirt Gold

*BLUE/50: .4X TO 1X GOLD AU/75
*BLUE/15: .4X TO 1X GOLD AU/25
*RED/25: .5X TO 1.2X GOLD AU/75
PDBB Blake Bortles/20* 5.00 12.00
PDKC Ka'Deem Carey/75 3.00 8.00
PDME Mike Evans/50 8.00 20.00
PDML Marqise Lee/11*
PDTB Teddy Bridgewater/25 6.00 15.00
PDJM1 Johnny Manziel/25 6.00 15.00
PDJM2 Jordan Matthews/75 5.00 12.00

2012 Press Pass Showcase

STATED PRINT RUN 1-299
RED INK/20-53: .6X TO 1.5X BASIC AU/299
SCAD Alfonzo Dennard/298* 2.50 6.00
SCAJ Alshon Jeffery/299 5.00 12.00
SCAL Andrew Luck/201* 75.00 150.00
SCBO Brock Osweiler/292* 2.50 6.00
SCBW Brandon Weeden/249* 2.50 6.00
SCCG1 Chris Givens/299 2.50 6.00
SCCG2 Cyrus Gray/246* 2.50 6.00
SCCK Case Keenum/299 5.00 12.00
SCCV Courtney Upshaw/299 3.00 8.00
SCDA Dwayne Allen/299 2.50 6.00
SCDH Dan Herron/299 2.50 6.00
SCDM Doug Martin/274* 4.00 10.00
SCDP DeVier Posey/299 2.50 6.00
SCGR Gerell Robinson/299 2.50 6.00
SCIP Isaiah Pead/299 2.50 6.00
SCJF Jeff Fuller/299 2.50 6.00
SCKC Kirk Cousins/249* 10.00 25.00
SCKM Kellen Moore/293* 3.00 8.00
SCKW Kendall Wright/273* 2.50 6.00
SCLJ LaMichael James/289* 2.50 6.00
SCLK Luke Kuechly/272* 6.00 15.00
SCMB Mark Barron/299 2.50 6.00
SCME Michael Egnew/299 2.50 6.00
SCMF Michael Floyd/299 2.50 6.00
SCMI Melvin Ingram/299 2.50 6.00
SCMM Marquis Maze/249* 2.50 6.00
SCMS Mohamed Sanu/249* 4.00 10.00
SCNF Nick Foles/273* 6.00 15.00
SCNT Nick Toon/279* 2.50 6.00
SCOC Orson Charles/299 2.50 6.00
SCRB Ryan Broyles/299 2.50 6.00
SCRL Ryan Lindley/299 2.50 6.00
SCRR Rueben Randle/299 2.50 6.00
SCRW Russell Wilson/299 30.00 60.00
SCSG Stephon Gilmore/299 3.00 8.00
SCSH Stephen Hill/249* 2.50 6.00
SCTG T.J. Graham/299 2.50 6.00

2012 Press Pass Showcase Blue

*BLUE/50: .6X TO 1.5X BASIC AU/299
ANNOUNCED PRINT RUN 3-50
SCLM Lamar Miller 6.00 15.00
SCQC Quinton Coples 4.00 10.00
SCRG Robert Griffin III/24* 6.00 15.00
SCTR Trent Richardson/49* 4.00 10.00
SCTS Tommy Streeter 4.00 10.00

2012 Press Pass Showcase Blue Red Ink

RED INK STATED PRINT RUN 1-47
SCOC Orson Charles/47* 4.00 10.00
SCRG Robert Griffin III/26*
SCRR Rueben Randle/47* 4.00 10.00
SCRT Ryan Tannehill/47* 6.00 15.00

2012 Press Pass Showcase Gold

*GOLD/99-149: .5X TO 1.2X BASIC AU/299
GOLD ANNOUNCED PRINT RUN 99-149
GOLD RED INK/23-50: .5X TO 1.2X GLD AU
SCAL Andrew Luck* 75.00 150.00
SCQC Quinton Coples 3.00 8.00

2012 Press Pass Showcase End Zone Autographs Blue

BLUE ANNOUNCED PRINT RUN 18-25
*GOLD/99: .25X TO .6X BLUE AU/25
*SILVER/50: .3X TO .8X BLUE AU/25
EZAL Andrew Luck/21* 75.00 150.00
EZBW Brandon Weeden 4.00 10.00
EZJB Justin Blackmon 4.00 10.00
EZKC Case Keenum/18* 8.00 20.00
EZKM Kellen Moore/23* 5.00 12.00
EZKW Kendall Wright 4.00 10.00
EZLJ LaMichael James 4.00 10.00
EZRB Robert Griffin III 5.00 12.00
EZTR Trent Richardson/21* 4.00 10.00

2012 Press Pass Showcase Fantasy Team Autographs Blue

BLUE STATED PRINT RUN 18-25
*GOLD/99: .25X TO .6X BLUE AU/25
*SILVER/50: .3X TO .8X BLUE AU/25
FTAL Andrew Luck 75.00 150.00
FTBW Brandon Weeden 4.00 10.00
FTCK Case Keenum 8.00 20.00
FTGR Gerell Robinson 4.00 10.00
FTJB Justin Blackmon 4.00 10.00
FTKM Kellen Moore 5.00 12.00
FTKW Kendall Wright 4.00 10.00
FTLJ LaMichael James 4.00 10.00
FTLM Lamar Miller 6.00 15.00
FTRB Robert Griffin III 5.00 12.00
FTRW Russell Wilson 30.00 80.00
FTTR Trent Richardson/18* 4.00 10.00

2012 Press Pass Showcase GameDay Threads Silver

ONE JERSEY PER PACK OVERALL
*BLUE/99: .5X TO 1.2X BASIC JSY
*GOLD/199: .5X TO 1.2X BASIC JSY
*GREEN/50: .6X TO 1.5X BASIC JSY
GDTAL Andrew Luck 8.00 20.00
GDTLJ LaMichael James 1.50 4.00
GDTLM Lamar Miller 2.50 6.00
GDTMF Michael Floyd 1.50 4.00
GDTRG Robert Griffin III 2.00 5.00

2012 Press Pass Showcase Making The Cut Autographs Blue

BLUE STATED PRINT RUN 25
*GOLD/99: .25X TO .6X BLUE AU/25
*SILVER/50: .3X TO .8X BLUE AU/25
MCAL Andrew Luck/24* 75.00 150.00
MCAS Alshon Jeffery 8.00 20.00
MCJB Justin Blackmon/24* 4.00 10.00
MCKW Kendall Wright 4.00 10.00
MCMF Michael Floyd 4.00 10.00
MCQC Quinton Coples 4.00 10.00
MCRG Robert Griffin III 5.00 12.00
MCTR Trent Richardson 4.00 10.00

2013 Press Pass Showcase

*SILVER/144-299: .3X TO .8X GOLD/99-149
SLVR RED INK/15-77*: .6X TO 1.5X SILVER AU
GS Geno Smith/50 4.00 10.00

2013 Press Pass Showcase Blue

BLUE/32-50: .5X TO 1.2X BASIC GOLD/99-149
BLUE/22-24*: .6X TO 1.5X BASIC GOLD/99-149
GS Geno Smith/50 4.00 10.00
MBA Matt Barkley/49* 4.00 10.00

2013 Press Pass Showcase Blue Red Ink

RED INK/26-28*: .4X TO 1X BLUE/22*-24*
RED INK/15-18*: .5X TO 1.2X BLUE/50
JP Jordan Poyer/41* 4.00 10.00
MT Manti Te'o/47* 5.00 12.00
DMO Damontre Moore/50 4.00 10.00

2013 Press Pass Showcase Gold

GOLD STATED PRINT RUN 99-149
RED INK/3-75: .5X TO 1.2X GOLD AU
AD Aaron Dobson/99 3.00 8.00
AE Andre Ellington/49* 3.00 8.00
CH Cobi Hamilton/90* 3.00 8.00
CK Collin Klein/89* 4.00 10.00
CP Cordarrelle Patterson/99 3.00 8.00
DH DeAndre Hopkins/99 8.00 20.00
DM Dee Milliner/89* 3.00 8.00
DMO Damontre Moore/99 3.00 8.00
DR Denard Robinson/74* 3.00 8.00
DRO Da'Rick Rogers/99 3.00 8.00
DS Dion Sims/99 3.00 8.00
EA Ezekiel Ansah/149 3.00 8.00
EH Erik Highsmith/99 4.00 10.00
EL Eddie Lacy/97* 3.00 8.00
EM EJ Manuel/65* 3.00 8.00
GB Giovani Bernard/99 3.00 8.00
GS Geno Smith/50* 3.00 8.00
JF Johnathan Franklin/89* 3.00 8.00
JH Justin Hunter/84* 3.00 8.00
JJ Jawan Jamison/99 3.00 8.00
JJO Jarvis Jones/99 3.00 8.00
JP Jordan Poyer/99 3.00 8.00
JR Joseph Randle/49* 3.00 8.00
JRO Jordan Rodgers/94* 4.00 10.00
KA Keenan Allen/99 6.00 15.00
KB Kenjon Barner/84* 3.00 8.00
KS Kenny Stills/99 3.00 8.00
LB Le'Veon Bell/50* 10.00 25.00
LJ Landry Jones/99 3.00 8.00
MB Montee Ball/99 3.00 8.00
MD Marcus Davis/99 3.00 8.00
MG Mike Glennon/74* 3.00 8.00
ML Marcus Lattimore/99 3.00 8.00
MW Markus Wheaton/99 3.00 8.00
QP Quinton Patton/99 3.00 8.00
RB Rex Burkhead/99 12.00 30.00
RG Ray Graham/82* 3.00 8.00
RN Ryan Nassib/75* 3.00 8.00
RS Ryan Swope/99 3.00 8.00
RW Robert Woods/84* 5.00 12.00
SB Stedman Bailey/75* 3.00 8.00
SJ Stefphon Jefferson/99 4.00 10.00
ST Stepfan Taylor/99 3.00 8.00
TA Tavon Austin/24* 4.00 10.00
TB Tyler Bray/89* 3.00 8.00
TE Tyler Eifert/99 3.00 8.00
TK Tavarres King/99 3.00 8.00
TR Theo Riddick/99* 3.00 8.00
TW Tyler Wilson/99 3.00 8.00
TWI Terrance Williams/99 3.00 8.00
ZD Zac Dysert/99 3.00 8.00
ZE Zach Ertz/86* 6.00 15.00

2013 Press Pass Showcase Class of 2013 Autographs Blue

*BASE AU/40-50: .3X TO .8X BLUE/23-25
COCK Collin Klein 5.00 12.00
COEL Eddie Lacy 4.00 10.00
COGB Giovani Bernard 4.00 10.00
COGS Geno Smith 4.00 10.00
COJH Justin Hunter 4.00 10.00
COKA Keenan Allen 8.00 20.00
COMB Matt Barkley/23* 4.00 10.00
COML Marcus Lattimore 4.00 10.00
COMT Manti Te'o 5.00 12.00
COTW Terrance Williams 4.00 10.00

2013 Press Pass Showcase End Zone Autographs Blue

*BASE AU/46-50: .3X TO .8X BLUE AU
EZCK Collin Klein 5.00 12.00
EZEL Eddie Lacy 4.00 10.00
EZGS Geno Smith 4.00 10.00
EZJH Justin Hunter 4.00 10.00
EZKA Keenan Allen 8.00 20.00
EZKB Kenjon Barner 4.00 10.00
EZLB Le'Veon Bell 12.00 30.00
EZMB Matt Barkley/23* 4.00 10.00
EZMB2 Montee Ball 4.00 10.00
EZRW Robert Woods 6.00 15.00
EZST Stepfan Taylor/15* 4.00 10.00
EZTW Tyler Wilson 4.00 10.00

2013 Press Pass Showcase Fantasy Team Autographs Blue

BASE AU/40-50: .3X TO .8X BLUE AU/17-25
FTAE Andre Ellington/25 4.00 10.00
FTCK Collin Klein/25 5.00 12.00
FTGB Giovani Bernard/25 4.00 10.00
FTGS Geno Smith/23 4.00 10.00
FTJH Justin Hunter/25 4.00 10.00
FTKA Keenan Allen/25 8.00 20.00
FTMB Matt Barkley/24* 4.00 10.00
FTMB2 Montee Ball/25 4.00 10.00
FTMT Manti Te'o/24 5.00 12.00
FTRW Robert Woods/25 6.00 15.00
FTTA Tavon Austin/17 5.00 12.00
FTTW2 Tyler Wilson/25 4.00 10.00

2013 Press Pass Showcase GameDay Threads Silver

*BLUE/99: .5X TO 1.2X SILVER JSY
*GOLD/149: .5X TO 1.2X SILVER JSY
*GOLD/25: .5X TO 1.2X SILVER JSY
*GREEN/50: .6X TO 1.5X SILVER JSY
AL Andrew Luck SP 4.00 10.00
DH DeAndre Hopkins 3.00 8.00
MB Montee Ball 1.25 3.00
MG Mike Glennon 1.25 3.00
RG Robert Griffin III SP 1.50 4.00
TE Tyler Eifert 1.25 3.00
TW Tyler Wilson 4.00 10.00

2012 Press Pass SportsTown

ANNOUNCED PRINT RUN 65-189
EXCH EXPIRATION: 12/31/2013
RED INK/31-52: .5X TO 1.2X BASIC AU
RED INK/20-25: .6X TO 1.5X BASIC AU
*SILVER/80-149: .4X TO 1X BASE/75-199
RED/40-75: .5X TO 1.2X BASE/75-199
RED/16-35: .6X TO 1.5X BASE/75-199
STAB Andre Branch/149
STAD Alfonzo Dennard/149
STBO Brock Osweiler/184* 2.50 6.00
STBQ Brian Quick/149 2.50 6.00
STBT Brandon Thompson/134* 3.00 8.00
STBW1 Brandon Weeden/149 2.50 6.00
STBW2 Billy Winn/140*
STCF Coby Fleener/129* 2.50 6.00
STCG Cyrus Gray/125
STCH Casey Hayward/140* 2.50 6.00
STCJ Coryell Judie/139* 2.50 6.00
STCK Case Keenum/134* 5.00 12.00
STCU Courtney Upshaw/160 3.00 8.00
STDA Dwayne Allen/133*
STDH Dan Herron/149 2.50 6.00
STDH2 Dont'a Hightower/149 4.00 10.00
STDM Doug Martin/125 4.00 10.00
STDP2 Devier Posey/128* 2.50 6.00
STEA Emmanuel Acho/105* 2.50 6.00
STHS Harrison Smith/137* 2.50 6.00
STIP Isaiah Pead/149 2.50 6.00
STJA Joe Adams/139*
STJE Jeremy Ebert/105* 2.50 6.00
STJF Jeff Fuller/165 2.50 6.00
STJW Jarius Wright/99* 2.50 6.00
STKC Kirk Cousins/125 10.00 25.00
STKM Kellen Moore/97* 3.00 8.00
STKR Kendall Reyes/122*
STLD Lavonte David/149 4.00 10.00
STLK Luke Kuechly/189* 8.00 20.00
STLM Lamar Miller/135* 4.00 10.00
STME Michael Egnew/149
STMF Michael Floyd EXCH 2.50 6.00
STMI Melvin Ingram/125
STMJ Marvin Jones/118* 2.50 6.00
STMM Marquis Maze/149 2.50 6.00
STMS Mohamed Sanu/99* 4.00 10.00
STNF Nick Foles/184* 6.00 15.00
STNT Nick Toon/100* 2.50 6.00
STOC Orson Charles/149 2.50 6.00
STQC Quinton Coples/65* 2.50 6.00
STRB Ryan Broyles/75* 5.00 12.00
STRL Ryan Lindley/139* 2.50 6.00
STRR Rueben Randle/105* 2.50 6.00
STRW Russell Wilson/105* 30.00 80.00
STSG Stephon Gilmore/75 3.00 8.00
STTL Travis Lewis/134*
STVB Vick Ballard/149
STWM Whitney Mercilus/93* 2.50 6.00

2012 Press Pass SportsTown Blue

*BLUE/50: .5X TO 1.2X BASE/75-199
*BLUE/25: .6X TO 1.5X BASE/75-199
BLUE ANNOUNCED PRINT RUN 2-99
STDM Doug Martin/25 6.00 15.00
STNF Nick Foles/41* 8.00 20.00
STRT Ryan Tannehill/25 6.00 15.00
STTR Trent Richardson/23* 4.00 10.00

2012 Press Pass SportsTown Gold

*GOLD/50-99: .5X TO 1.2X BASE/75-199
GOLD ANNOUNCED PRINT RUN 7-99
STRT Ryan Tannehill/89 5.00 12.00

2012 Press Pass SportsTown Purple

*PURPLE/15-25: .6X TO 1.5X BASE/75-199
ANNOUNCED PRINT RUN 1-25
STDM Doug Martin/15 6.00 15.00
STRG Robert Griffin III/21* 5.00 12.00
STRT Ryan Tannehill/15 6.00 15.00
STTR Trent Richardson/12* 4.00 10.00

1999 SAGE

The 1999 Sage set was issued in one series totalling 50 cards. The fronts feature borderless color action player photos. The backs carry another player photo with player information, career statistics and a statement about the player's ability. Only 4,200 sets were produced.

COMPLETE SET (50) 12.00 30.00
1 Rahim Abdullah .25 .60
2 Jerry Azumah .25 .60
3 Champ Bailey .50 1.25
4 D'Wayne Bates .25 .60
5 Michael Bishop .30 .75
6 David Boston .25 .60
7 Fernando Bryant .25 .60
8 Tony Bryant .25 .60
9 Chris Claiborne .25 .60
10 Mike Cloud .25 .60
11 Cecil Collins .25 .60
12 Tim Couch .30 .75
13 Daunte Culpepper .40 1.00
14 Jared DeVries .25 .60
15 Adrian Dingle .25 .60
16 Antuan Edwards .25 .60
17 Troy Edwards .25 .60
18 Kevin Faulk .25 .60
19 Rufus French .25 .60
20 Martin Gramatica .25 .60
21 Torry Holt .50 1.25
22 Sedrick Irvin .25 .60
23 Edgerrin James .40 1.00
24 Jon Jansen .25 .60
25 Andy Katzenmoyer .30 .75
26 Jevon Kearse .30 .75
27 Patrick Kerney .25 .60
28 Lamar King .25 .60
29 Shaun King .25 .60
30 Jim Kleinsasser .40 1.00
31 Rob Konrad .25 .60
32 Brian Kuklick .25 .60
33 Chris McAlister .25 .60
34 Darnell McDonald .25 .60
35 Reggie McGrew .25 .60
36 Donovan McNabb 1.50 4.00
37 Cade McNown .25 .60
38 Dat Nguyen .40 1.00
39 Solomon Page .25 .60
40 Mike Peterson .25 .60
41 Anthony Poindexter .25 .60
42 Peerless Price .25 .60
43 Mike Rucker .25 .60
44 L.J. Shelton .25 .60
45 Akili Smith .25 .60
46 John Tait .25 .60
47 Fred Vinson .25 .60
48 Al Wilson .40 1.00
49 Antoine Winfield .25 .60
50 Damien Woody .25 .60

1999 SAGE Autographs Red

Randomly inserted into packs at the rate of one in two, this 50-card set is an autographed red foil stamped parallel version of the base set. The number of cards produced follows the player's name in the checklist below with the maximum number being 999.

*BRONZE/565-650: .4X TO 1X RED AU
*BRONZE/140-285: .5X TO 1.2X RED AU
RED AUTO/209-999 ODDS 1:2
*SILVER/348-400: .5X TO 1.2X RED AU
*SILVER/75-180: .6X TO 1.5X RED AU
*GOLD/174-200: .6X TO 1.5X RED AU
*GOLD/45-90: .8X TO 2X RED AU
*PLATINUM/13-50: 1X TO 2.5X RED AU
*PLATINUM/13-25: 1.2X TO 3X RED AU
UNPRICED MASTER EDIT/1 ODDS 1;2000
A1 Rahim Abdullah/999 2.50 6.00
A2 Jerry Azumah/999 2.50 6.00
A3 Champ Bailey/999 5.00 12.00
A4 D'Wayne Bates/999 2.50 6.00
A5 Michael Bishop/999 3.00 8.00
A6 David Boston/869 2.50 6.00
A7 Fernando Bryant/999 2.50 6.00
A8 Tony Bryant/999 2.50 6.00
A9 Chris Claiborne/999 2.50 6.00
A10 Mike Cloud/434 2.50 6.00
A11 Cecil Collins/999 2.50 6.00
A12 Tim Couch/999 3.00 8.00
A13 Daunte Culpepper/419 4.00 10.00
A14 Jared DeVries/887 2.50 6.00
A15 Adrian Dingle/999 2.50 6.00
A16 Antuan Edwards/999 2.50 6.00
A17 Troy Edwards/999 2.50 6.00
A18 Kevin Faulk/999 2.50 6.00
A19 Rufus French/999 2.50 6.00
A20 Martin Gramatica/999 2.50 6.00
A21 Torry Holt/999 5.00 12.00
A22 Sedrick Irvin/999 2.50 6.00
A23 Edgerrin James/859 4.00 10.00
A24 Jon Jansen/999 2.50 6.00
A25 Andy Katzenmoyer/209 4.00 10.00
A26 Jevon Kearse/999 3.00 8.00
A27 Patrick Kerney/879 2.50 6.00
A28 Lamar King/999 2.50 6.00
A29 Shaun King/999 2.50 6.00
A30 Jim Kleinsasser/999 4.00 10.00
A31 Rob Konrad/999 2.50 6.00
A32 Brian Kuklick/999 2.50 6.00
A33 Chris McAlister/999 2.50 6.00
A34 Darnell McDonald/999 2.50 6.00
A35 Reggie McGrew/999 2.50 6.00
A36 Donovan McNabb/999 8.00 20.00
A37 Cade McNown/209 3.00 8.00
A38 Dat Nguyen/999 4.00 10.00
A39 Solomon Page/999 2.50 6.00
A40 Mike Peterson/999 2.50 6.00
A41 Anthony Poindexter/999 2.50 6.00
A42 Peerless Price/232 3.00 8.00
A43 Mike Rucker/999 2.50 6.00
A44 L.J. Shelton/999 2.50 6.00
A45 Akili Smith/419 2.50 6.00
A46 John Tait/999 2.50 6.00
A47 Fred Vinson/999 2.50 6.00
A48 Al Wilson/999 4.00 10.00
A49 Antoine Winfield/999 2.50 6.00
A50 Damien Woody/999 2.50 6.00

1999 SAGE Tim Couch

This 9-card set was issued by Sage as a stand alone set; not inserted in packs. Each card features a highlight from the career of Tim Couch. The cards are serial numbered of 1999 on the fronts and include the career highlight below the serial number.

COMPLETE SET (9) 12.50 25.00
COMMON CARD (1-9) 1.25 3.00

2000 SAGE

Released as a 50-card set, Sage football showcases top draft picks from the 2000 NFL draft. Packaged in 12-pack boxes, each pack contained three cards, one of which was sequentially numbered and autographed. At the time of it's release, Sage had the only approved LaVar Arrington card.

COMPLETE SET (50) 6.00 15.00
1 John Abraham .30 .75
2 Shaun Alexander .30 .75
3 LaVar Arrington .40 1.00
4 Courtney Brown .25 .60
5 Keith Bulluck .25 .60
6 Plaxico Burress .25 .60
7 Giovanni Carmazzi .20 .50
8 Kwame Cavil .20 .50
9 Cosey Coleman .20 .50
10 Laveranues Coles .25 .60
11 Tim Couch .25 .60
12 Ron Dayne .30 .75
13 Reuben Droughns .20 .50
14 Shaun Ellis .25 .60
15 John Engelberger .20 .50
16 Danny Farmer .20 .50
17 Dwayne Goodrich .20 .50
18 Deon Grant .20 .50
19 Chris Hovan .25 .60
20 Darren Howard .20 .50
21 Todd Husak .20 .50
22 Thomas Jones .25 .60
23 Curtis Keaton .20 .50
24 Jamal Lewis .30 .75
25 Anthony Lucas .20 .50
26 Tee Martin .20 .50
27 Stockar McDougle .20 .50
28 Corey Moore .20 .50
29 Rob Morris .25 .60
30 Sammy Morris .20 .50
31 Sylvester Morris .20 .50
32 Chad Pennington .25 .60
33 Todd Pinkston .20 .50
34 Ahmed Plummer .20 .50
35 Jerry Porter .30 .75
36 Travis Prentice .20 .50
37 Tim Rattay .25 .60
38 Chris Redman .20 .50
39 J.R. Redmond .20 .50
40 Chris Samuels .30 .75
41 Brandon Short .20 .50
42 Corey Simon .25 .60
43 R.Jay Soward .20 .50
44 Shyrone Stith .20 .50
45 Raynoch Thompson .20 .50
46 Brian Urlacher 1.00 2.50
47 Todd Wade .20 .50
48 Troy Walters .20 .50
49 Dez White .20 .50
50 Michael Wiley .20 .50

2000 SAGE Autographs Red

Randomly inserted in packs at the rate of one in two, this 50-card set parallels the base set in autographed format. Each card features a red background and contains a silver foil oval with an authentic autograph on the front. Cards are sequentially numbered to a maximum of 999.

RED/334-999 STATED ODDS 1:2
RED STATED PRINT RUN 334-999
*BRONZE/225-650: .5X TO 1.2X RED/334-650
BRONZE STATED PRINT RUN 225-650
*GOLD/110-200: .8X TO 2X RED/334-650
GOLD STATED PRINT RUN 110-200
UNPRICED MASTERS PRINT RUN 1 SET
*PLATINUM/20-50: 1X TO 2.5X RED/334-999
PLATINUM STATED PRINT RUN 20-50
*SILVER/140-400: .6X TO 1.5X RED/334-999
SILVER STATED PRINT RUN 140-400
A1 John Abraham/999 3.00 8.00
A2 Shaun Alexander/999 3.00 8.00
A3 LaVar Arrington/534 4.00 10.00
A4 Courtney Brown/554 2.50 6.00
A5 Keith Bulluck/999 2.50 6.00
A6 Plaxico Burress/999 2.50 6.00
A7 Giovanni Carmazzi/999 2.00 5.00
A8 Kwame Cavil/999 2.00 5.00
A9 Cosey Coleman/999 2.00 5.00
A10 Laveranues Coles/999 2.50 6.00
A11 Tim Couch/354 2.50 6.00
A12 Ron Dayne/334 3.00 8.00
A13 Reuben Droughns/999 2.00 5.00
A14 Shaun Ellis/999 2.50 6.00
A15 John Engelberger/999 2.00 5.00
A16 Danny Farmer/999 2.00 5.00
A17 Dwayne Goodrich/999 2.00 5.00
A18 Deon Grant/999 2.00 5.00
A19 Chris Hovan/999 2.50 6.00
A20 Darren Howard/999 2.00 5.00
A21 Todd Husak/999 2.00 5.00
A22 Thomas Jones/999 2.50 6.00
A23 Curtis Keaton/999 2.00 5.00
A24 Jamal Lewis/999 3.00 8.00
A25 Anthony Lucas/999 2.00 5.00
A26 Tee Martin/999 2.00 5.00
A27 Stockar McDougle/999 2.00 5.00
A28 Corey Moore/999 2.00 5.00
A29 Rob Morris/999 2.50 6.00
A30 Sammy Morris/999 2.00 5.00
A31 Sylvester Morris/999 2.00 5.00
A32 Chad Pennington/749 2.50 6.00
A33 Todd Pinkston/999 2.00 5.00
A34 Ahmed Plummer/999 2.00 5.00
A35 Jerry Porter/999 3.00 8.00
A36 Travis Prentice/999 2.00 5.00
A37 Tim Rattay/999 2.50 6.00
A38 Chris Redman/999 2.00 5.00
A39 J.R. Redmond/999 2.00 5.00
A40 Chris Samuels/999 3.00 8.00
A41 Brandon Short/999 2.00 5.00
A42 Corey Simon/999 2.50 6.00
A43 R.Jay Soward/999 2.00 5.00
A44 Shyrone Stith/999 2.00 5.00
A45 Raynoch Thompson/999 2.00 5.00
A46 Brian Urlacher/999 10.00 25.00
A47 Todd Wade/999 2.00 5.00
A48 Troy Walters/999 2.00 5.00
A49 Dez White/999 2.00 5.00
A50 Michael Wiley/999 2.00 5.00

2001 SAGE

Released as a 50-card set, Sage football showcases top draft picks from the 2001 NFL Draft. Packaged in 12-pack boxes, each pack contained three cards, one of which was sequentially numbered and autographed. These cards were serial numbered to 4500 sets.

COMPLETE SET (50) 7.50 20.00
1 Will Allen .30 .75
2 Adam Archuleta .25 .60
3 Jeff Backus .20 .50
4 Alex Bannister .20 .50
5 Gary Baxter .20 .50
6 Michael Bennett .25 .60
7 Josh Booty .25 .60
8 Drew Brees 1.25 3.00
9 Correll Buckhalter .20 .50
10 Quincy Carter .25 .60
11 Chris Chambers .20 .50
12 Alge Crumpler .30 .75
13 Andre Dyson .20 .50
14 Robert Ferguson .30 .75
15 Jamar Fletcher .20 .50
16 Rod Gardner .25 .60
17 Reggie Germany .20 .50
18 Derrick Gibson .20 .50
19 Casey Hampton .30 .75
20 Tim Hasselbeck .25 .60
21 Todd Heap .25 .60
22 Travis Henry .25 .60
23 Josh Heupel .30 .75
24 Willie Howard .20 .50
25 Steve Hutchinson .50 1.25
26 James Jackson .20 .50
27 Rudi Johnson .30 .75
28 LaMont Jordan .30 .75
29 Torrance Marshall .20 .50
30 Deuce McAllister .30 .75
31 Willie Middlebrooks .25 .60
32 Quincy Morgan .25 .60
33 Santana Moss .30 .75
34 Jesse Palmer .25 .60
35 Carlos Polk .20 .50
36 Ken-Yon Rambo .20 .50
37 Jamal Reynolds .20 .50
38 Koren Robinson .25 .60
39 Richard Seymour .30 .75
40 Justin Smith .40 1.00
41 Fred Smoot .25 .60
42 Marcus Stroud .25 .60
43 David Terrell .25 .60
44 LaDainian Tomlinson 1.00 2.50
45 Ja'Mar Toombs .20 .50
46 Michael Vick .50 1.25
47 Kenyatta Walker .20 .50
48 Gerard Warren .25 .60
49 Reggie Wayne .40 1.00
50 Jamie Winborn .25 .60

2001 SAGE Autographs Red

Randomly inserted in packs at the rate of one in two, this 48-card set parallels the base set in autographed format. Each card contains a silver foil oval with an authentic autograph on the front. Cards are sequentially numbered to a maximum of 999. This was the 'red' version of the autographs. Note that cards A15 and A48 did not exist.

RED/499-999 ODDS 1:2
RED PRINT RUN 499-999
*BRONZE/325-650: .5X TO 1.2X RED
BRONZE/325-650 ODDS 1:4
BRONZE PRINT RUN 325-650
*GOLD/100-200: .8X TO 2X RED
GOLD/100-200 ODDS 1:12
GOLD PRINT RUN 100-200
UNPRICED MASTER EDIT.PRINT RUN 1
*PLATINUM/25-50: 1.2X TO 3X RED
PLATINUM/25-50 ODDS 1:46
PLATINUM PRINT RUN 25-50
*SILVER/200-400: .6X TO 1.5X RED
SILVER/200-400 ODDS 1:6
SILVER PRINT RUN 200-400
A1 Will Allen 3.00 8.00
A2 Adam Archuleta 2.50 6.00
A3 Jeff Backus/900 2.00 5.00
A4 Alex Bannister 2.00 5.00
A5 Gary Baxter 2.00 5.00
A6 Michael Bennett 2.50 6.00
A7 Josh Booty/900 2.50 6.00
A8 Drew Brees/749 75.00 150.00
A9 Correll Buckhalter 2.00 5.00
A10 Quincy Carter 2.50 6.00
A11 Chris Chambers 2.00 5.00
A12 Alge Crumpler 3.00 8.00
A13 Andre Dyson 2.00 5.00
A14 Robert Ferguson 3.00 8.00
A16 Rod Gardner 2.50 6.00
A17 Reggie Germany 2.00 5.00
A18 Derrick Gibson 2.00 5.00
A19 Casey Hampton 4.00 10.00
A20 Tim Hasselbeck/900 2.50 6.00
A21 Todd Heap 2.50 6.00
A22 Travis Henry/800 2.50 6.00
A23 Josh Heupel 3.00 8.00
A24 Willie Howard/900 2.00 5.00
A25 Steve Hutchinson 5.00 12.00
A26 James Jackson 2.00 5.00
A27 Rudi Johnson 3.00 8.00
A28 LaMont Jordan 3.00 8.00
A29 Torrance Marshall 2.00 5.00
A30 Deuce McAllister/749 3.00 8.00
A31 Willie Middlebrooks 2.50 6.00
A32 Quincy Morgan 2.50 6.00
A33 Santana Moss 3.00 8.00
A34 Jesse Palmer 2.50 6.00
A35 Carlos Polk 2.00 5.00
A36 Ken-Yon Rambo/749 2.00 5.00
A37 Jamal Reynolds 2.00 5.00
A38 Koren Robinson 2.50 6.00
A39 Richard Seymour 3.00 8.00
A40 Justin Smith 4.00 10.00
A41 Fred Smoot 2.50 6.00
A42 Marcus Stroud 2.50 6.00
A43 David Terrell/649 2.50 6.00
A44 LaDainian Tomlinson 10.00 25.00
A45 Ja'Mar Toombs 2.00 5.00
A46 Michael Vick/499 10.00 25.00
A47 Kenyatta Walker 2.00 5.00
A49 Reggie Wayne 4.00 10.00
A50 Jamie Winborn 2.50 6.00

2001 SAGE Jerseys

Randomly inserted in packs at a rate of one in 205, this 3-card set features a piece of game worn jersey. There were 175 serial numberd cards for each player.

COMPLETE SET (3) 75.00 150.00
STATED ODDS 1:205
STATED PRINT RUN 175 SER.#'d SETS
J1 Michael Vick 12.50 30.00
J2 Drew Brees 12.50 30.00
J3 David Terrell 6.00 15.00

2001 SAGE Michael Vick

This two-card set was inserted in Sage Autographs and distributed directly to the hobby through a major distributor. One card features Vick with a swatch of jersey and the other is personally signed by Vick. Each card was hand serial numbered to 650.

COMPLETE SET (2) 60.00 120.00
STATED PRINT RUN 650 SER. #'d SETS
MV1 Michael Vick JSY 10.00 20.00
MV2 Michael Vick AU 25.00 50.00

2002 SAGE

Released as a 45-card set, Sage football showcases top draft picks from the 2002 NFL Draft. Packaged in 12-pack boxes, each pack contained three cards, one of which was autographed. The base cards read "1 of 3500" cards produced. The SRP was $10.99 per pack.

COMPLETE SET (45) 15.00 40.00
1 Ladell Betts .60 1.50
2 Antonio Bryant .60 1.50
3 Reche Caldwell .50 1.25
4 Kelly Campbell .50 1.25
5 David Carr .40 1.00
6 Tim Carter .50 1.25
7 Eric Crouch .60 1.50
8 Ronald Curr .40 1.00
9 Rohan Davey .60 1.50
10 Andre Davis .40 1.00
11 T.J. Duckett .40 1.00
12 Randy Fasani .40 1.00
13 DeShaun Foster .60 1.50
14 Dwight Freeney .75 2.00
15 Jabar Gaffney .40 1.00
16 Lamar Gordon .50 1.25
17 Daniel Graham .50 1.25
18 Joey Harrington .40 1.00
19 Napoleon Harris .50 1.25
20 Albert Haynesworth .60 1.50
21 John Henderson .50 1.25
22 Chad Hutchinson .40 1.00
23 Quentin Jammer .60 1.50
24 Ron Johnson .50 1.25
25 Kurt Kittner .40 1.00
26 Ashley Lelie .40 1.00
27 Bryant McKinnie .40 1.00
28 Maurice Morris .50 1.25

29 David Neill .40 1.00
30 J.T. O'Sullivan .50 1.25
31 Brian Poli-Dixon .40 1.00
32 Clinton Portis .60 1.50
33 Patrick Ramsey .50 1.25
34 Josh Reed .50 1.25
35 Cliff Russell .40 1.00
36 Lito Sheppard .60 1.50
37 Jeremy Shockey .60 1.50
38 Luke Staley .40 1.00
39 Donte Stallworth .60 1.50
40 Travis Stephens .40 1.00
41 Chester Taylor .60 1.50
42 Larry Tripplett .40 1.00
43 Javon Walker .60 1.50
44 Marquise Walker .40 1.00
45 Jonathan Wells .50 1.25

2002 SAGE Autographs Red

Inserted at an overall rate of 1 per pack, this 46-card set features authentic autographs on the card fronts. Signed cards were issued in six levels, varying in total numbers autographed and differentiated by the background color. Levels included: base Red, Bronze, Silver, Gold, Platinum and a 1 of 1 Master Edition. The cards carry a congratulatory statement from the Sage President on the back.
RED UNL.STARS/110-220 5.00 12.00
RED AUTO/40-860 ODDS 1:2
*BRONZE AU: .5X TO 1.2X RED
BRONZE AU/30-650 ODDS 1:4
*GOLD AU: .8X TO 2X RED
GOLD AU/15-200 ODDS 1:12
*PLATINUM/15-50: 1X TO 2.5X RED
PLATINUM AU/5-50 ODDS 1:48
*SILVER AU: .6X TO 1.5X RED
SILVER AU/20-400 ODDS 1:6
UNPRICED MASTER EDITION PRINT RUN 1
A1 Ladell Betts/40
A2 Antonio Bryant/740 4.00 10.00
A3 Reche Caldwell/630 3.00 8.00
A4 Kelly Campbell/750 3.00 8.00
A5 David Carr/220 3.00 8.00
A6 Tim Carter/720 3.00 8.00
A7 Eric Crouch/220 5.00 12.00
A8 Ronald Curry/800 2.50 6.00
A9 Rohan Davey/650 4.00 10.00
A10 Andre Davis/650 2.50 6.00
A11 T.J. Duckett/860 2.50 6.00
A12 Randy Fasani/700 2.50 6.00
A13 DeShaun Foster/500 4.00 10.00
A14 Dwight Freeney/800 5.00 12.00
A15 Jabar Gaffney/700 2.50 6.00
A16 Lamar Gordon/700 3.00 8.00
A17 Daniel Graham/750 3.00 8.00
A18 Joey Harrington/220 3.00 8.00
A19 Napoleon Harris/770 3.00 8.00
A20 Albert Haynesworth/125 8.00 20.00
A21 John Henderson/625 3.00 8.00
A22 Chad Hutchinson/500 2.50 6.00
A23 Quentin Jammer/300 4.00 10.00
A24 Ron Johnson/720 3.00 8.00
A25 Kurt Kittner/500 2.50 6.00
A26 Ashley Lelie/700 2.50 6.00
A27 Bryant McKinnie/720 2.50 6.00
A28 Maurice Morris/720 3.00 8.00
A29 David Neill/770 2.50 6.00
A30 J.T. O'Sullivan/660 3.00 8.00
A31 Brian Poli-Dixon/700 2.50 6.00
A32 Clinton Portis/70 25.00 60.00
A33 Patrick Ramsey/720 3.00 8.00
A34 Josh Reed/720 3.00 8.00
A35 Cliff Russell/720 2.50 6.00
A36 Lito Sheppard/670 4.00 10.00
A37 Jeremy Shockey/700 4.00 10.00
A38 Luke Staley//50 2.50 6.00
A39 Donte Stallworth/800 4.00 10.00
A40 Travis Stephens/660 2.50 6.00
A41 Chester Taylor/700 4.00 10.00
A42 Larry Tripplett/650 2.50 6.00
A43 Javon Walker/650 4.00 10.00
A44 Marquise Walker/600 2.50 6.00
A45 Jonathan Wells/680 3.00 8.00
VS1 Michael Vick/110 20.00 40.00

2002 SAGE Jerseys Red

Inserted in packs at a rate of 1 in 88, this 10-card set features color action shots on the card fronts along with the words "red level." A piece of game-used jersey in a silver foil circle is also included on the card front. The red cards are hand serial numbered to 99.
RED PRINT RUN 99 SER.#'d SETS
*BRONZE/75: .5X TO 1.2X RED/99
BRONZE PRINT RUN 75 SER.#'d SETS
*SILVER:/50 .6X TO 1.5X RED/99
SILVER PRINT RUN 50 SER.#'d SETS
*GOLD/25: 1X TO 2.5X RED/99
GOLD PRINT RUN 25 SER #'d SETS
UNPRICED MASTER EDIT.PRINT RUN 1
UNPRICED COMBO PRINT RUN 10
1 David Carr 4.00 10.00
2 Eric Crouch 8.00 20.00
3 Rohan Davey 6.00 15.00
4 T.J. Duckett 4.00 10.00
5 DeShaun Foster 6.00 15.00
6 Joey Harrington 4.00 10.00
7 Kurt Kittner 4.00 10.00
8 Clinton Portis 6.00 15.00
9 Patrick Ramsey 5.00 12.00
10 Michael Vick 8.00 20.00

2002 SAGE Jersey Edition Promos

These cards were issued by SAGE direct to dealers one card at a time. Each features one or two top 2002 draft picks with a swatch of jersey on the front and/or back. Each card was also serial numbered as noted below. The cards are not numbered but listed below alphabetically.
STATED PRINT RUN 5-25
4 E.Crouch/R.Davey/50 4.00 10.00
5 E.Crouch/K.Kittner/25 4.00 10.00
6 E.Crouch/P.Ramsey/25 4.00 10.00
7 E.Crouch/C.Portis/25 4.00 10.00
10 R.Davey/K.Kittner/50 4.00 10.00
13 T.Duckett/C.Portis/50 4.00 10.00

2003 SAGE

Released as a 45-card set, SAGE football showcases top draft picks from the 2003 NFL Draft. Packaged in 12-pack boxes, each pack contained three cards, including one that was autographed. The base cards were printed in quantities of only 2750. SRP was $10.99 per pack.
COMPLETE SET (45) 10.00 25.00
1 Sam Aiken .40 1.00
2 Boss Bailey .40 1.00
3 Brad Banks .40 1.00
4 Tully Banta-Cain .50 1.25
5 Arnaz Battle .50 1.25
6 Ronald Bellamy .40 1.00
7 Kyle Boller .30 .75
8 Chris Brown .30 .75
9 Tyrone Calico .30 .75
10 Dallas Clark .50 1.25
11 Kevin Curtis .30 .75
12 Sammy Davis .40 1.00
13 Dahrran Diedrick .30 .75
14 Ken Dorsey .40 1.00
15 Justin Fargas .50 1.25
16 Justin Gage .40 1.00
17 Jason Gesser .40 1.00
18 Cie Grant .40 1.00
19 Rex Grossman .40 1.00
20 E.J. Henderson .40 1.00
21 Taylor Jacobs .30 .75
22 Bryant Johnson .50 1.25
23 Larry Johnson .40 1.00
24 Teyo Johnson .40 1.00
25 Kliff Kingsbury .50 1.25
26 Brandon Lloyd .50 1.25
27 Rashean Mathis .30 .75
28 Jerome McDougle .25 .60
29 Willis McGahee .40 1.00
30 Billy McMullen .30 .75
31 Terence Newman .50 1.25
32 Donnie Nickey .30 .75
33 Terry Pierce .30 .75
34 Dave Ragone .30 .75
35 Charles Rogers .40 1.00
36 Chris Simms .30 .75
37 Musa Smith .30 .75
38 Lee Suggs .30 .75
39 Terrell Suggs .40 1.00
40 Marcus Trufant .40 1.00
41 Seneca Wallace .40 1.00
42 Kelley Washington .30 .75
43 Matt Wilhelm .40 1.00
44 Jason Witten 1.25 3.00
45 George Wrighster .30 .75

2003 SAGE Autographs Red

Inserted at a rate of 1 per pack, this 44 card set features authentic autographs on card front. Signed cards were issued in six levels varying in total numbers signed, and are differentiated by background color. Levels included base Red, Bronze, Silver, Gold, Platinum, Players Proofs, and a 1 of 1 Master Edition. Each card carries a congratulatory statement from the SAGE President on the card back.
RED STATED ODDS 1:2
*BRONZE: .5X TO 1.2X RED AU
BRONZE STATED ODDS 1:4
*GOLD: .8X TO 2X RED AU
GOLD STATED ODDS 1:12
UNPRICED ME 1/1 ODDS 1:1050
*PLATINUM/30-50: 2X TO 5X RED AU
*PLATINUM/15-20: 2.5X TO 6X RED AU
PLATINUM STATED ODDS 1:45
*PLAY.PROOF/20: 2.5X TO 6X RED AU
PLAYER PROOF/20 ODDS 1:105
*SILVER: .6X TO 1.5X RED AU
SILVER STATED ODDS 1:6
A1 Sam Aiken/379 3.00 8.00
A2 Boss Bailey/370 3.00 8.00
A3 Brad Banks/540 3.00 8.00
A4 Tully Banta-Cain/620 4.00 10.00
A5 Arnaz Battle/910 4.00 10.00
A6 Ronald Bellamy/810 3.00 8.00
A7 Kyle Boller/750 2.50 6.00
A8 Chris Brown/920 2.50 6.00
A9 Tyrone Calico/670 2.50 6.00
A10 Dallas Clark/670 4.00 10.00
A11 Kevin Curtis/930 2.50 6.00
A12 Sammy Davis/799 3.00 8.00
A13 Dahrran Diedrick/250 2.50 6.00
A14 Ken Dorsey/335 3.00 8.00
A15 Justin Fargas/999 4.00 10.00
A16 Justin Gage/690 3.00 8.00
A17 Jason Gesser/799 3.00 8.00
A19 Rex Grossman/395 4.00 10.00
A20 E.J. Henderson/640 3.00 8.00
A21 Taylor Jacobs/700 2.50 6.00
A22 Bryant Johnson/360 4.00 10.00
A23 Larry Johnson/360 4.00 10.00
A24 Teyo Johnson/679 3.00 8.00
A25 Kliff Kingsbury/675 4.00 10.00
A26 Brandon Lloyd/779 4.00 10.00
A27 Rashean Mathis/500 2.50 6.00
A28 Jerome McDougle/930 2.50 6.00
A29 Willis McGahee/360 3.00 8.00
A30 Billy McMullen/690 2.50 6.00
A31 Terence Newman/640 4.00 10.00
A32 Donnie Nickey/290 2.50 6.00
A33 Terry Pierce/930 2.50 6.00
A34 Dave Ragone/210 2.50 6.00
A35 Charles Rogers/220 3.00 8.00
A36 Chris Simms/350 2.50 6.00
A37 Musa Smith/360 2.50 6.00
A38 Lee Suggs/355 2.50 6.00
A39 Terrell Suggs/350 3.00 8.00
A40 Marcus Trufant/930 3.00 8.00
A41 Seneca Wallace/799 3.00 8.00
A42 Kelley Washington/75 15.00 40.00
A43 Matt Wilhelm/650 3.00 8.00
A44 Jason Witten/950 8.00 20.00
A45 George Wrighster/670 2.50 6.00

2003 SAGE Jerseys Red

Inserted into packs at a rate of 1:40, this set features swatches of game used jersey. Each card is serial numbered to 99. This set was also released in several parallel versions, including bronze, gold, masterpiece, platinum, players proofs, and silver.
RED/99 STATED ODDS 1:40
*BRONZE/75: .5X TO 1.2 RED JSY/99
BRONZE/75 STATED ODDS 1:53
*GOLD/25: 1X TO 2.5X RED JSY/99
GOLD/25 STATED ODDS 1:160
*SILVER/50: .6X TO 1.5X RED JSY/99
SILVER/50 STATED ODDS 1:80
UNPRICED ME 1/1 ODDS 1:3950
UNPRICED PLATINUM/10 ODDS 1:395
*PLAY.PROOF/20: 1.2X TO 3X RED JSY/99
PLAYER PROOF/20 ODDS 1:395
SJ1 Brad Banks 4.00 10.00
SJ2 Arnaz Battle 5.00 12.00
SJ3 Kyle Boller 3.00 8.00
SJ4 Chris Brown 3.00 8.00
SJ5 David Carr 3.00 8.00
SJ6 Ken Dorsey 4.00 10.00
SJ7 Rex Grossman 4.00 10.00
SJ8 Taylor Jacobs 3.00 8.00
SJ9 Bryant Johnson 5.00 12.00
SJ10 Larry Johnson 4.00 10.00
SJ11 Willis McGahee 4.00 10.00
SJ12 Dave Ragone 3.00 8.00
SJ13 Charles Rogers 4.00 10.00
SJ14 Chris Simms 3.00 8.00
SJ15 Musa Smith 3.00 8.00
SJ16 Lee Suggs 3.00 8.00
SJ17 Seneca Wallace 4.00 10.00
SJ18 Kelley Washington 3.00 8.00

2003 SAGE First Card

Cards from this set were released directly from SAGE primarily through internet outlets. Each card carried an initial price of either $6.95 or $9.95 and was intended to preview an expected top 2003 NFL Draft pick. A limited number of complete sets were offered at $199.95. Orders for the cards were cut off at the time of the NFL Draft in late April 2003 and SAGE destroyed all unsold cards. The announced final print runs are noted below.
COMPLETE SET (24) 75.00 150.00
FC1 Larry Johnson 2.00 5.00
FC2 Rex Grossman 2.00 5.00
FC3 Kyle Boller 1.50 4.00
FC4 Chris Brown 1.50 4.00
FC5 Lee Suggs 1.50 4.00
FC6 Taylor Jacobs 1.50 4.00
FC7 Justin Fargas 2.50 6.00
FC8 Bryant Johnson 2.50 6.00
FC9 Kliff Kingsbury 2.50 6.00
FC10 Chris Simms 1.50 4.00
FC11 Terence Newman 2.50 6.00
FC12 Musa Smith 1.50 4.00
FC13 Teyo Johnson 2.00 5.00
FC14 Arnaz Battle 2.50 6.00
FC15 Brad Banks 2.00 5.00
FC16 Charles Rogers 2.00 5.00
FC17 Ken Dorsey 2.00 5.00
FC18 Dave Ragone 1.50 4.00
FC19 Seneca Wallace 2.00 5.00
FC20 Kelley Washington 1.50 4.00
FC21 Jason Witten 6.00 15.00
FC22 Terrell Suggs 3.00 8.00
FC23 Jason Gesser 2.00 5.00
FC24 Willis McGahee 2.00 5.00

2004 SAGE

The basic issue SAGE product was released in late May 2004. The base set consists of 46-cards. Maurice Clarett made an apearance in this product although he was declared ineligible for the NFL Draft. Hobby boxes contained 12-packs of 3-cards and carried an S.R.P. of $12.99. Each hobby pack also included one autograph or jersey card which was the primary draw for this product. No other inserts were included in the product.
COMPLETE SET (46) 12.50 30.00
STATED PRINT RUN 3200 SETS
1 Tatum Bell .25 .60
2 Bernard Berrian .25 .60
3 Michael Boulware .40 1.00
4 Drew Carter .30 .75
5 Maurice Clarett .30 .75
6 Casey Clausen .30 .75
7 Michael Clayton .30 .75
8 Chris Collins .25 .60
9 Karlos Dansby .30 .75
10 Devard Darling .25 .60
11 Lee Evans .40 1.00
12 Clarence Farmer .25 .60
13 Chris Gamble .25 .60
14 Jake Grove .25 .60
15 DeAngelo Hall .40 1.00
16 Josh Harris .25 .60
17 Tommie Harris .30 .75
18 Devery Henderson .25 .60
19 Steven Jackson .40 1.00
20 Michael Jenkins .25 .60
21 Greg Jones .25 .60
22 Kevin Jones .30 .75
23 Sean Jones .25 .60
24 Derrick Knight .25 .60
25 Craig Krenzel .25 .60
26 Jared Lorenzen .30 .75
27 Eli Manning 2.00 5.00
28 John Navarre .25 .60
29 Chris Perry .25 .60
30 Cody Pickett .25 .60
31 Will Poole .40 1.00
32 Philip Rivers .75 2.00
33 Ell Roberson .40 1.00
34 Dunta Robinson .25 .60
35 Ben Roethlisberger 2.00 5.00
36 Rod Rutherford .25 .60
37 P.K. Sam .25 .60
38 Matt Schaub .25 .60
39 Will Smith .30 .75
40 Jeff Smoker .30 .75
41 Ben Troupe .25 .60
42 Ernest Wilford .30 .75
43 Reggie Williams .25 .60
44 Roy Williams WR .25 .60
45 Quincy Wilson .25 .60
46 Rashaun Woods .25 .60

2004 SAGE Autographs Red

RED PRINT RUN 300-999
*BRONZE/200-650: .5X TO 1.2X RED
BRONZE PRINT RUN 200-650
*GOLD/60-200: .8X TO 2X RED
GOLD PRINT RUN 60-200
*PLATINUM/15-50: 1.5X TO 4X RED
PLATINUM PRINT RUN 15-50
*PLAY.PROOF/20: 2X TO 5X RED/400-999
*PLAY.PROOF/20: 1.5X TO 4X RED/300-350
PLAYER PROOF PRINT RUN 20
*SILVER/120-400: .6X TO 1.5X RED
SILVER PRINT RUN 120-400
UNPRICED MASTER EDIT.PRIN RUN 1
A1 Tatum Bell/500 2.50 6.00
A2 Bernard Berrian/850 2.50 6.00
A3 Michael Boulware/600 4.00 10.00
A4 Drew Carter/700 3.00 8.00
A5 Maurice Clarett/350 10.00 25.00
A6 Casey Clausen/999 3.00 8.00
A7 Michael Clayton/970 3.00 8.00
A8 Chris Collins/300 3.00 8.00
A9 Karlos Dansby/770 3.00 8.00
A10 Devard Darling/550 2.50 6.00
A11 Lee Evans/770 4.00 10.00
A13 Chris Gamble/750 2.50 6.00
A14 Jake Grove/650 2.50 6.00
A15 DeAngelo Hall/470 4.00 10.00
A16 Josh Harris/770 2.50 6.00
A17 Tommie Harris/500 3.00 8.00
A18 Devery Henderson/700 2.50 6.00
A20 Michael Jenkins/850 2.50 6.00
A21 Greg Jones/750 2.50 6.00
A22 Kevin Jones/750 3.00 8.00
A23 Sean Jones/999 2.50 6.00
A24 Derrick Knight/550 2.50 6.00
A26 Jared Lorenzen/800 3.00 8.00
A27 Eli Manning/400 12.00 30.00
A28 John Navarre/440 2.50 6.00
A29 Chris Perry/750 2.50 6.00
A30 Cody Pickett/600 2.50 6.00
A31 Will Poole/420 4.00 10.00
A32 Philip Rivers/500 25.00 50.00
A33 Ell Roberson/999 4.00 10.00
A34 Dunta Robinson/720 2.50 6.00
A35 Ben Roethlisberger/300 40.00 80.00
A36 Rod Rutherford/500 2.50 6.00
A37 P.K. Sam/850 2.50 6.00
A38 Matt Schaub/600 2.50 6.00
A39 Will Smith/770 3.00 8.00
A40 Jeff Smoker/500 3.00 8.00
A41 Ben Troupe/999 2.50 6.00
A42 Ernest Wilford/350 4.00 10.00
A43 Reggie Williams/600 2.50 6.00
A44 Roy Williams WR/350 3.00 8.00
A45 Quincy Wilson/850 2.50 6.00
A46 Rashaun Woods/777 2.50 6.00

2004 SAGE Jerseys Red

RED PRINT RUN 99 SER.#'d SETS
*BRONZE/75: .4X TO 1X RED/99
BRONZE STATED PRINT RUN 75
*GOLD/25: .8X TO 2X RED/99
GOLD STATED PRINT RUN 25
*PLATINUM/10: 1.2X TO 3X RED/99
PLATINUM PRINT RUN 10
*PLAYER PRF/20: 1X TO 2.5X RED/99
PLAYER PROOF PRINT RUN 20
*SILVER/50: .5X TO 1.2X RED/99
SILVER STATED PRINT RUN 50
UNPRICED MASTER EDITION #'d OF 1
UNPRICED AUTO PRINT RUN 10
J1 Tatum Bell 3.00 8.00
J2 Maurice Clarett 4.00 10.00
J3 Casey Clausen 4.00 10.00
J4 Lee Evans 5.00 12.00
J5 Josh Harris 3.00 8.00
J6 Devery Henderson 3.00 8.00
J7 Michael Jenkins 3.00 8.00
J8 Greg Jones 3.00 8.00
J9 Kevin Jones 4.00 10.00
J10 Jared Lorenzen 4.00 10.00
J11 Eli Manning 15.00 40.00
J12 John Navarre 3.00 8.00
J13 Chris Perry 3.00 8.00
J14 Cody Pickett 3.00 8.00
J15 Philip Rivers 12.00 30.00
J16 Ell Roberson 5.00 12.00
J17 Ben Roethlisberger 15.00 40.00
J18 Rod Rutherford 3.00 8.00
J19 Matt Schaub 3.00 8.00
J20 Jeff Smoker 4.00 10.00
J21 Reggie Williams 3.00 8.00
J22 Roy Williams WR 3.00 8.00
J23 Quincy Wilson 3.00 8.00
J24 Rashaun Woods 3.00 8.00

2004 SAGE Jerseys Combos

UNPRICED COMBOS PRINT RUN 10 SETS

2004 SAGE First Card

These cards represent the first football card releases for 2004 and were sold exclusively through internet channels for $9.99 per. Each card includes the SAGE First Card title as well as a hand serial number. Autographed cards for four of the players were also produced. They originally retailed for $99 each.
1 Maurice Clarett/250 6.00 12.00
2 Casey Clausen/99 6.00 12.00
3 Michael Clayton/99 6.00 12.00
4 Lee Evans/99 6.00 12.00
5 Tommie Harris/99 5.00 10.00
6 Steven Jackson/150 6.00 15.00
7 Michael Jenkins/99 5.00 10.00
8 Greg Jones/99 5.00 10.00
9 Kevin Jones/150 6.00 12.00
10 Eli Manning/250 12.50 25.00
11 John Navarre/99 5.00 10.00
12 Chris Perry/150 6.00 12.00
13 Philip Rivers/150 7.50 15.00
14 Ell Roberson/99 5.00 10.00
15 Ben Roethlisberger/250 12.50 25.00
16 Reggie Williams/99 6.00 12.00
17 Roy Williams WR/150 7.50 15.00
18 Rashaun Woods/99 6.00 12.00

2004 SAGE First Card Autographs

ABR Ben Roethlisberger/99 60.00 125.00
AEM Eli Manning/99 30.00 60.00
AMC Maurice Clarett/99 15.00 40.00
APR Philip Rivers/99 30.00 60.00

2005 SAGE

SAGE was initially released in early-June 2005. The base set consists of 54-cards. Hobby boxes contained 12-packs of 3-cards and carried an S.R.P. of $10.99 per pack with one jersey or autographed card inserted in every pack. A variety of inserts can be found seeded in packs highlighted by the multi-tiered Autograph and Jersey inserts.
COMPLETE SET (54) 12.50 30.00
1 Derek Anderson .40 1.00
2 J.J. Arrington .40 1.00
3 Marion Barber .30 .75
4 Brock Berlin .30 .75
5 Jammal Brown .50 1.25
6 Reggie Brown .30 .75
7 Ronnie Brown .40 1.00
8 Jason Campbell .30 .75
9 Mark Clayton .30 .75
10 Channing Crowder .40 1.00
11 Anthony Davis .30 .75
12 Josh Davis .30 .75
13 Thomas Davis .30 .75
14 Ciatrick Fason .30 .75
15 Ryan Fitzpatrick .50 1.25
16 Charlie Frye .30 .75
17 Fred Gibson .30 .75
18 Johnathan Goddard .40 1.00
19 Frank Gore .60 1.50
20 David Greene .30 .75
21 Kay-Jay Harris .30 .75
22 Marlin Jackson .30 .75
23 Brandon Jacobs .40 1.00
24 Derrick Johnson .40 1.00
25 Matt Jones .30 .75
26 T.A. McLendon .30 .75
27 Adrian McPherson .30 .75
28 Justin Miller .30 .75
29 Vernand Morency .40 1.00
30 Terrence Murphy .30 .75
31 Dan Orlovsky .30 .75
32 Kyle Orton .30 .75
33 Roscoe Parrish .30 .75
34 Brodney Pool .50 1.25
35 Dante Ridgeway .30 .75
36 Chris Rix .40 1.00
37 Aaron Rodgers 4.00 10.00
38 Carlos Rogers .50 1.25
39 J.R. Russell .30 .75
40 Alex Smith TE .30 .75
41 Alex Smith QB 1.25 3.00
42 Taylor Stubblefield .30 .75
43 Craphonso Thorpe .30 .75
44 Andrew Walter .30 .75
45 DeMarcus Ware 1.00 2.50
46 Fabian Washington .30 .75
47 Corey Webster .40 1.00
48 Jason White .50 1.25
49 Roddy White .50 1.25
50 Cadillac Williams .30 .75
51 Troy Williamson .30 .75
52 Maurice Clarett .40 1.00
53 Ben Roethlisberger .75 2.00
54 Antrel Rolle .50 1.25

2005 SAGE Autographs Red

RED/50-999 ODDS 1:2
RED PRINT RUN 50-999
*BRONZE: .5X TO 1.2X REDS
BRONZE/40-650 ODDS 1:4
BRONZE PRINT RUN 40-650
*GOLD/40-200: .8X TO 2X REDS
GOLD/15-200 ODDS 1:12
GOLD PRINT RUN 15-200
*PLATINUM/20-50: 1X TO 2.5X REDS
PLATINUM/5-50 ODDS 1:45
PLATINUM PRINT RUN 5-50
*PLAY.PROOF/20: 1.5X TO 4X RED/770-999
*PLAY.PROOF/20: 1.2X TO 3X RED/400-700
PLAYER PROOF PRINT RUN 20
*SILVER: .6X TO 1.5X REDS
SILVER/25-400 ODDS 1:6
SILVER PRINT RUN 25-400
UNPRICED MASTER EDITION #'d OF 1
A1 Derek Anderson/999 3.00 8.00
A2 J.J. Arrington/650 4.00 10.00
A3 Marion Barber/700 3.00 8.00
A4 Brock Berlin/400 3.00 8.00
A5 Jammal Brown/660 5.00 12.00
A6 Reggie Brown/900 2.50 6.00
A7 Ronnie Brown/999 3.00 8.00
A8 Jason Campbell/600 3.00 8.00
A9 Mark Clayton/600 3.00 8.00
A10 Channing Crowder/700 4.00 10.00
A11 Anthony Davis/900 2.50 6.00
A12 Josh Davis/600 3.00 8.00
A13 Thomas Davis/999 2.50 6.00
A14 Ciatrick Fason/650 3.00 8.00
A15 Ryan Fitzpatrick/799 4.00 10.00
A16 Charlie Frye/550 3.00 8.00
A17 Fred Gibson/900 2.50 6.00
A18 Johnathan Goddard/600 4.00 10.00
A19 Frank Gore/600 10.00 25.00
A20 David Greene/600 3.00 8.00
A21 Kay-Jay Harris/650 3.00 8.00
A22 Marlin Jackson/600 2.50 6.00
A23 Brandon Jacobs/999 3.00 8.00
A24 Derrick Johnson/700 4.00 10.00
A25 Matt Jones/999 2.50 6.00
A26 T.A. McLendon/650 3.00 8.00
A27 Adrian McPherson/770 2.50 6.00
A28 Justin Miller/660 3.00 8.00
A29 Vernand Morency/650 3.00 8.00
A30 Terrence Murphy/900 2.50 6.00
A31 Dan Orlovsky/999 2.50 6.00
A32 Kyle Orton/900 2.50 6.00
A33 Roscoe Parrish/600 3.00 8.00
A34 Brodney Pool/650 4.00 10.00
A35 Dante Ridgeway/600 3.00 8.00
A36 Chris Rix/400 4.00 10.00
A37 Aaron Rodgers/200 100.00 175.00
A38 Carlos Rogers/650 5.00 12.00
A39 J.R. Russell/900 2.50 6.00
A40 Alex Smith TE/900 2.50 6.00
A41 Alex Smith QB/200 12.00 30.00
A42 Taylor Stubblefield/900 2.50 6.00
A43 Craphonso Thorpe/700 3.00 8.00
A44 Andrew Walter/940 2.50 6.00
A45 DeMarcus Ware/910 8.00 20.00
A46 Fabian Washington/900 2.50 6.00
A47 Corey Webster/500 4.00 10.00
A48 Jason White/550 5.00 12.00
A49 Roddy White/50 10.00 25.00
A50 Cadillac Williams/600
A51 Troy Williamson/700 3.00 8.00

2005 SAGE Jerseys Red

RED STATED ODDS 1:40
RED PRINT RUN 99 SER.#'d SETS
*BRONZE: .5X TO 1.2X REDS
BRONZE STATED ODDS 1:53
BRONZE PRINT RUN 75 SER.#'d SETS
*GOLD: 1X TO 2.5X REDS
GOLD STATED ODDS 1:160
GOLD PRINT RUN 25 SER.#'d SETS
UNPRICED PLATINUM PRINT RUN 10
UNPRICED JSY AUTO PRINT RUN 10 SETS
*PLAYER PROOF: 1.2X TO 3X REDS
PLAYER PROOF PRINT RUN 20 SER.#'d SETS
*SILVER: .6X TO 1.5X REDS
SILVER STATED ODDS 1:80
SILVER PRINT RUN 50 SER.#'d SETS
UNPRICED MASTER EDITION #'d OF 1
OVERALL JERSEY STATED ODDS 1:15
J1 J.J. Arrington 3.00 8.00
J2 Ronnie Brown 3.00 8.00
J3 Jason Campbell 2.50 6.00
J4 Mark Clayton 2.50 6.00
J5 Anthony Davis 2.50 6.00
J6 Ciatrick Fason 2.50 6.00
J7 Charlie Frye 2.50 6.00
J8 Fred Gibson 2.50 6.00
J9 Frank Gore 8.00 20.00
J10 David Greene 2.50 6.00
J11 Kay-Jay Harris 2.50 6.00
J12 Adrian McPherson 2.50 6.00
J13 Vernand Morency 3.00 8.00
J14 Dan Orlovsky 2.50 6.00
J15 Kyle Orton 2.50 6.00
J16 Roscoe Parrish 2.50 6.00
J17 Chris Rix 3.00 8.00
J18 Aaron Rodgers 20.00 40.00
J19 Alex Smith QB 12.00 30.00
J20 Taylor Stubblefield 2.50 6.00
J21 Craphonso Thorpe 2.50 6.00
J22 Andrew Walter 2.50 6.00
J23 Jason White 4.00 10.00
J24 Cadillac Williams 10.00 25.00

2005 SAGE Jerseys Combos

STATED PRINT RUN 99 SER.#'d SETS
RARE STATED ODDS 1:265
UNPRICED RARE PRINT 10 SER.#'d SETS
JJ1 A.Smith QB/Ro.Brown 20.00 50.00
JJ2 A.Smith QB/A.Rodgers 20.00 50.00
JJ3 A.Smith QB/J.Campbell 15.00 40.00
JJ4 A.Rodgers/J.Campbell 20.00 50.00
JJ5 Ro.Brown/C.Williams 25.00 60.00
JJ6 Ro.Brown/J.Campbell 10.00 25.00
JJ7 C.Williams/J.Campbell 20.00 50.00
JJ8 A.Rodgers/J.Arrington 20.00 50.00
JJ9 C.Rix/C.Thorpe 10.00 25.00
JJ10 C.Rix/A.McPherson 7.50 20.00
JJ11 C.Thorpe/McPherson 7.50 20.00
JJ12 D.Greene/F.Gibson 7.50 20.00
JJ13 R.Parrish/F.Gore 12.00 30.00
JJ14 M.Clayton/J.White 10.00 25.00
JJ15 K.Orton/T.Stubblefield 10.00 25.00
JJ16 A.Smith QB/J.White 12.50 30.00
JJ17 D.Greene/T.Stubblefield 7.50 20.00
JJ18 A.Rodgers/A.Walter 20.00 50.00
JJ19 Roethlisberger/C.Frye 15.00 40.00
JJ20 E.Manning/A.Smith QB 12.50 30.00
JJ21 Ben Gordon/Orlovsky 12.50 30.00
JJ22 Em.Okafor/Orlovsky 7.50 20.00
JJ23 Dia.Taurasi/Orlovsky 7.50 20.00
JJ24 Dev.Harris/A.Davis 7.50 20.00
JJ25 L.Evans/R.Parrish 10.00 25.00
JJ26 M.Clarett/T.Bell 7.50 20.00
JJ27 Ro.Will.WR/Orlovsky 10.00 25.00
JJ28 K.Jones/D.Orlovsky 7.50 20.00
JJ29 D.Henderson/McPherson 7.50 20.00
JJ30 Roethlisberger/F.Gibson 15.00 40.00
JJ31 A.Smith QB/F.Gore 20.00 40.00
JJ32 R.Woods/A.Smith QB 12.50 30.00
JJ33 T.Bell/V.Morency 7.50 20.00
JJ34 L.Evans/A.Davis 7.50 20.00
JJ35 E.Manning/J.Campbell 10.00 25.00
JJ36 Roethlisberger/A.Smith QB 10.00 25.00

2005 SAGE Beckett Promos

COMPLETE SET (3) 6.00 15.00
NNO Ronnie Brown 2.00 5.00
NNO Matt Jones 1.25 3.00
NNO Ben Roethlisberger 2.50 6.00

2005 SAGE Beckett

These cards were produced by SAGE and released through Beckett.com in complete set form. Each card includes the SAGE and Beckett Media logos on the front along with a hand serial numbering of either 199 or 25. Three promo cards were inserted into copies of the Summer 2005 issue of Beckett Football Card Plus. Those cards do not include a card number but have a Beckett Football Card Plus logo on the backs. Finally, two autographed cards were sold with the complete set serial numbered to 25.
COMPLETE SET (12) 18.00 30.00
*SERIAL #'d TO 25: 1.2X TO 3X
1 Cadillac Williams .30 .75
2 Aaron Rodgers 4.00 10.00
3 Alex Smith QB 1.25 3.00
4 Jason Campbell .30 .75
5 Troy Williamson .30 .75
6 Mark Clayton .30 .75
7 Derrick Johnson .40 1.00
8 DeMarcus Ware 1.00 2.50
9 Charlie Frye .30 .75
10 Matt Jones .30 .75
11 Ronnie Brown .40 1.00
12 Ben Roethlisberger 2.50 6.00
A10 Matt Jones AU/25 20.00 50.00
A11 Ronnie Brown AU/25 40.00 80.00

2005 SAGE First Card

These cards represent the first football card releases for 2005. They were originally sold exclusively through internet channels for $9.99 per card. Each card includes the SAGE First Card title as well as a hand serial number. Autographed cards for Alex Smith were also produced and serial numbered of 50.
1 Derrick Johnson/99 5.00 10.00
2 Ronnie Brown/150 7.50 15.00
3 Anthony Davis/99 5.00 10.00
4 Frank Gore/99 6.00 12.00
5 Vernand Morency/99 5.00 10.00
6 Dan Orlovsky/150 5.00 10.00
7 Kyle Orton/150 5.00 10.00
8 Chris Rix/99 5.00 10.00
9 Derek Anderson/99 3.00 12.00
10 Jason White/150 6.00 12.00
11 David Greene/99 5.00 10.00
12 Fred Gibson/99 5.00 10.00
13 Andrew Walter/150 6.00 12.00
14 J.J. Arrington/99 4.00 10.00
15 Cadillac Williams/99 7.50 15.00
16 Ciatrick Fason/99 5.00 10.00
17 Jason Campbell/99 6.00 12.00
18 Mark Clayton/150 3.00 8.00
19 Troy Williamson/99 5.00 10.00
20 Alex Smith QB/250 6.00 12.00
21 Aaron Rodgers/250 10.00 20.00

2005 SAGE First Card Autographs

1 Alex Smith QB/50 50.00 80.00

2006 SAGE

This 60-card set, featuring leading 2006 NFL prospects, was released in July, 2006. The set was issued into the hobby in three-card packs, with an $11.99 SRP, which came 12 packs to a box. The set is sequenced in player alphabetical order.
COMPLETE SET (60) 15.00 30.00
1 Joseph Addai .30 .75
2 Devin Aromashodu .30 .75
3 Jason Avant .30 .75
4 Hank Baskett .30 .75
5 Mike Bell .30 .75
6 Will Blackmon .30 .75
7 Daniel Bullocks .30 .75
8 Reggie Bush .50 1.25
9 Dominique Byrd .30 .75
10 Brian Calhoun .30 .75
11 Bobby Carpenter .30 .75
12 Antonio Cromartie .40 1.00
13 Brodie Croyle .30 .75
14 Jay Cutler .40 1.00
15 Vernon Davis .40 1.00
16 Anthony Fasano .30 .75
17 D'Brickashaw Ferguson .30 .75
18 Charles Gordon .30 .75
19 Bruce Gradkowski .40 1.00
20 Skyler Green .30 .75
21 Jerome Harrison .30 .75
22 Mike Hass .30 .75
23 Taurean Henderson .30 .75
24 Devin Hester .60 1.50
25 Tye Hill .30 .75
26 Michael Huff .40 1.00
27 Tarvaris Jackson .30 .75
28 Omar Jacobs .30 .75
29 Maurice Drew .50 1.25
30 Winston Justice .40 1.00
31 Matt Leinart .30 .75
32 Laurence Maroney .30 .75
33 Reggie McNeal .30 .75
34 Marcus McNeill .30 .75
35 Erik Meyer .30 .75
36 Sinorice Moss .30 .75
37 Martin Nance .30 .75
38 Drew Olson .30 .75
39 Jonathan Orr .40 1.00
40 Paul Pinegar .30 .75
41 Leonard Pope .50 1.25
42 Gerald Riggs Jr. .40 1.00
43 Michael Robinson .30 .75
44 DeMeco Ryans .40 1.00
45 D.J. Shockley .40 1.00
46 Ernie Sims .30 .75
47 Dwayne Slay .30 .75
48 Maurice Stovall .30 .75
49 David Thomas .30 .75
50 Leon Washington .30 .75
51 Pat Watkins .40 1.00
52 LenDale White .30 .75
53 Charlie Whitehurst .30 .75
54 Demetrius Williams .30 .75
55 Jimmy Williams .30 .75
56 Mario Williams .50 1.25
57 Rodrique Wright .30 .75
58 Ashton Youboty .30 .75
59 Vince Young .30 .75
60 Alan Zemaitis .30 .75

2006 SAGE Autographs Red

RED/100-999 STATED ODDS 1:2
*BRONZE/50-650: .5X TO 1.2X RED AU
BRONZE/50-650 STATED ODDS 1:4
*GOLD/20-200: .8X TO 2X RED AU
GOLD/20-200 STATED ODDS 1:12
UNPRICED ME 1/1 ODDS 1:1050
*PLATINUM/15-50: 1X TO 2.5X RED AU
PLATINUM/5-50 STATED ODDS 1:45
*PLAY.PRF/20: 1.5X TO 4X RED/450-999
*PLAY.PRF/20: 1.2X TO 3X RED/100-300
PLAYER PROOF/20 ODDS 1:105
*SILVER/40-400: .6X TO 1.5X RED AU
SILVER/40-400 STATED ODDS 1:6
OVERALL AUTO/JSY ODDS 1:1
A1 Joseph Addai/999 2.50 6.00
A2 Devin Aromashodu/750 2.50 6.00
A3 Jason Avant/999 2.50 6.00
A4 Hank Baskett/999 2.50 6.00
A5 Mike Bell/999 2.50 6.00
A6 Will Blackmon/200 3.00 8.00
A7 Daniel Bullocks/999 2.50 6.00
A8 Reggie Bush/150 5.00 12.00
A9 Dominique Byrd/999 2.50 6.00
A10 Brian Calhoun/999 2.50 6.00
A11 Bobby Carpenter/999 2.50 6.00
A12 Antonio Cromartie/999 3.00 8.00
A13 Brodie Croyle/700 2.50 6.00
A14 Jay Cutler/200 4.00 10.00
A15 Vernon Davis/700 3.00 8.00
A16 Anthony Fasano/999 2.50 6.00
A17 D'Brickashaw Ferguson/300 3.00 8.00
A18 Charles Gordon/240 3.00 8.00
A19 Bruce Gradkowski/999 3.00 8.00
A20 Skyler Green/999 2.50 6.00
A21 Jerome Harrison/999 2.50 6.00
A22 Mike Hass/999 2.50 6.00
A23 Taurean Henderson/290 3.00 8.00
A25 Tye Hill/999 2.50 6.00
A26 Michael Huff/700 3.00 8.00
A27 Tarvaris Jackson/999 2.50 6.00
A28 Omar Jacobs/700 2.50 6.00
A29 Maurice Drew/999 4.00 10.00
A30 Winston Justice/700 3.00 8.00
A31 Matt Leinart/200 3.00 8.00
A32 Laurence Maroney/700 2.50 6.00
A33 Reggie McNeal/700 2.50 6.00
A34 Marcus McNeill/999 2.50 6.00
A35 Erik Meyer/999 2.50 6.00
A36 Sinorice Moss/999 2.50 6.00
A37 Martin Nance/450 2.50 6.00
A38 Drew Olson/999 2.50 6.00
A39 Jonathan Orr/999 3.00 8.00
A40 Paul Pinegar/999 2.50 6.00
A41 Leonard Pope/650 4.00 10.00
A43 Michael Robinson/600 2.50 6.00
A44 DeMeco Ryans/999 3.00 8.00
A45 D.J. Shockley/999 3.00 8.00
A46 Ernie Sims/150 3.00 8.00
A47 Dwayne Slay/999 2.50 6.00
A48 Maurice Stovall/500 2.50 6.00
A49 David Thomas/999 2.50 6.00
A50 Leon Washington/999 2.50 6.00
A51 Pat Watkins/999 3.00 8.00
A52 LenDale White/900 2.50 6.00
A53 Charlie Whitehurst/700 2.50 6.00
A54 Demetrius Williams/999 2.50 6.00
A55 Jimmy Williams/999 2.50 6.00
A56 Mario Williams/700 4.00 10.00
A57 Rodrique Wright/700 2.50 6.00
A58 Ashton Youboty/999 2.50 6.00
A59 Vince Young/100 15.00 40.00
A60 Alan Zemaitis/999 2.50 6.00

2006 SAGE Jerseys Red

RED PRINT RUN 99 SER.#'d SETS
*BRONZE/75: .4X TO 1X RED JSY/99
BRONZE PRINT RUN 75 SER.#'d SETS
*GOLD/25: .8X TO 2X RED JSY/99
GOLD/25 STATED ODDS 1:160
UNPRICED ME 1/1 ODDS 1:3950
UNPRICED PLATINUM PRINT RUN 10
*PLAYER PRF/20: 1X TO 2.5X RED JSY/99
PLAYER PROOFS PRINT RUN 20
*SILVER/50: .5X TO 1.2X RED JSY/99
SILVER/50 STATED ODDS 1:80
UNPRICED DUAL JSY/10 ODDS 1:265
J1 Joseph Addai 3.00 8.00
J2 Jason Avant 3.00 8.00
J3 Reggie Bush 5.00 12.00
J4 Bobby Carpenter 3.00 8.00
J5 Brodie Croyle 3.00 8.00
J6 Jay Cutler 4.00 10.00
J7 Vernon Davis 4.00 10.00
J8 Omar Jacobs 3.00 8.00
J9 Maurice Drew 5.00 12.00
J10 Matt Leinart 3.00 8.00
J11 Laurence Maroney 3.00 8.00
J12 Reggie McNeal 3.00 8.00
J13 Sinorice Moss 3.00 8.00
J14 Michael Robinson 3.00 8.00
J15 D.J. Shockley 4.00 10.00
J16 LenDale White 3.00 8.00
J17 Charlie Whitehurst 3.00 8.00
J18 Vince Young 3.00 8.00

2006 SAGE First Card

These cards represent the first football cards released in 2006. They were originally sold exclusively through internet channels for $9.99 per card. Each card includes the SAGE First Card title as well as a hand serial number.

2006 SAGE Game Exclusive National Draft Swatch Promos

These oversized (2 3/4" by 6 1/4") cards were issued at the 2006 National Sports Collectors Convention in Anaheim. Each promo card includes a swatch from a game jersey provided by Game Exclusives.
1 Reggie Bush 5.00 12.00
2 Matt Leinart 8.00 20.00
3 Vince Young 10.00 25.00
NCCC-1 Young/Bush/Leinart 6.00 15.00

2006 SAGE National 2500 Promos

1 Mario Williams SAGE .40 1.00
2 Reggie Bush SAGE .40 1.00
3 Vince Young Aspire .25 .60
4 Vernon Davis Aspire .30 .75
5 Matt Leinart HIT .25 .60
6 Jay Cutler HIT .30 .75
7 White/Leinart/Bush .40 1.00
8 Leinart/Cutler/Young .30 .75
9 Leinart/Bush/Young .40 1.00
10 Williams/Bush/Young .40 1.00

2006 SAGE National Promos Autographs

NA1 Reggie Bush/20 30.00 80.00
NA2 Matt Leinart/20 20.00 50.00
NA3 LenDale White/20 10.00 25.00

2006 SAGE National VIP Promos

COMPLETE SET (3) 6.00 15.00
1 Reggie Bush .75 2.00
2 Matt Leinart .50 1.25
3 Vince Young .50 1.25

2007 SAGE

This 62-card set was released in June, 2007. The set was issued into the hobby in three-card packs, with a $12.99 SRP which came 12 packs to a box. The set is sequenced in alphabetical order.
COMPLETE SET (62) 15.00 30.00
1 Gaines Adams .40 1.00
2 Aundrae Allison .30 .75
3 Dallas Baker .30 .75
4 David Ball .30 .75
5 John Beck .30 .75
6 Dwayne Bowe .30 .75
7 Alan Branch .30 .75
8 Steve Breaston .30 .75
9 Levi Brown .30 .75
10 Michael Bush .30 .75
11 Adam Carriker .30 .75
12 David Clowney .30 .75
13 Ken Darby .30 .75
14 Craig Buster Davis .30 .75
15 Trent Edwards .30 .75
16 Earl Everett .30 .75
17 Yamon Figurs .30 .75
18 Joel Filani .30 .75
19 Ted Ginn Jr. .40 1.00
20 Anthony Gonzalez .30 .75
21 Michael Griffin .30 .75
22 Leon Hall .30 .75
23 Chris Henry .30 .75
24 Johnnie Lee Higgins .30 .75
25 Jason Hill .30 .75
26 David Irons .30 .75
27 Kenny Irons .30 .75
28 Calvin Johnson 1.00 2.50
29 Ryan Kalil .30 .75
30 Kevin Kolb .40 1.00
31 Chris Leak .30 .75
32 Brian Leonard .30 .75
33 Marshawn Lynch .60 1.50
34 Robert Meachem .40 1.00
35 Brandon Meriweather .40 1.00
36 Zach Miller .30 .75
37 Jarvis Moss .30 .75
38 Greg Olsen .50 1.25
39 Tyler Palko .50 1.25
40 Jordan Palmer .40 1.00
41 Adrian Peterson 1.00 2.50
42 Antonio Pittman .30 .75
43 Brady Quinn .30 .75
44 Sidney Rice .40 1.00
45 Aaron Ross .30 .75
46 Jeff Rowe .30 .75
47 JaMarcus Russell .30 .75
48 Kolby Smith .30 .75
49 Steve Smith USC .30 .75
50 Troy Smith .30 .75
51 Jason Snelling .30 .75
52 Isaiah Stanback .30 .75
53 Drew Stanton .30 .75
54 Courtney Taylor .30 .75
55 Lawrence Timmons .50 1.25
56 DeMarcus Tank Tyler .30 .75
57 Darius Walker .30 .75
58 Paul Williams .30 .75
59 Patrick Willis .50 1.25
60 Garrett Wolfe .30 .75
61 LaMarr Woodley .60 1.50
62 Jared Zabransky .30 .75

2007 SAGE Autographs Red

*BRONZE: .4X TO 1X RED AUTOS
*SILVER/400: .5X TO 1.2X RED AUTOS
*SILVER/400: .4X TO 1X RED SP AUTOS
SILVER PRINT RUN 400 SER.#'d SETS
*GOLD/200: .6X TO 1.5X RED AUTOS
*GOLD/200: .5X TO 1.2X RED SP AUTOS
GOLD PRINT RUN 200 SER.#'d SETS
*PLATINUM/50: 1X TO 2.5X RED AUTOS
*PLATINUM/50: .6X TO 1.5X RED SP AUTOS

PLATINUM PRINT RUN 50 SER.#'d SETS
UNPRICED MASTER EDITION PRINT RUN 1
A1 Gaines Adams 3.00 8.00
A2 Aundrae Allison 2.50 6.00
A3 Dallas Baker 2.50 6.00
A4 David Ball 2.50 6.00
A5 John Beck 2.50 6.00
A6 Dwayne Bowe 2.50 6.00
A8 Steve Breaston 2.50 6.00
A9 Levi Brown 2.50 6.00
A10 Michael Bush 2.50 6.00
A11 Adam Carriker 2.50 6.00
A12 David Clowney 2.50 6.00
A13 Ken Darby 2.50 6.00
A14 Craig Buster Davis 2.50 6.00
A15 Trent Edwards 2.50 6.00
A16 Earl Everett 2.50 6.00
A17 Yamon Figurs 2.50 6.00
A18 Joel Filani 2.50 6.00
A20 Anthony Gonzalez 2.50 6.00
A21 Michael Griffin 2.50 6.00
A22 Leon Hall 2.50 6.00
A23 Chris Henry 2.50 6.00
A24 Johnnie Lee Higgins 2.50 6.00
A25 Jason Hill 2.50 6.00
A26 David Irons 2.50 6.00
A27 Kenny Irons 2.50 6.00
A29 Ryan Kalil 2.50 6.00
A30 Kevin Kolb 3.00 8.00
A31 Chris Leak SP 4.00 10.00
A32 Brian Leonard 2.50 6.00
A33 Marshawn Lynch SP 8.00 20.00
A34 Robert Meachem 3.00 8.00
A35 Brandon Meriweather 3.00 8.00
A36 Zach Miller 2.50 6.00
A37 Jarvis Moss 2.50 6.00
A38 Greg Olsen 4.00 10.00
A39 Tyler Palko 4.00 10.00
A40 Jordan Palmer 3.00 8.00
A41 Adrian Peterson SP 40.00 80.00
A42 Antonio Pittman 2.50 6.00
A43 Brady Quinn SP 2.50 6.00
A44 Sidney Rice 3.00 8.00
A45 Aaron Ross 2.50 6.00
A46 Jeff Rowe 2.50 6.00
A47 JaMarcus Russell SP 3.00 8.00
A48 Kolby Smith 2.50 6.00
A49 Steve Smith USC 2.50 6.00
A50 Troy Smith SP 12.00 30.00
A51 Jason Snelling 2.50 6.00
A52 Isaiah Stanback 2.50 6.00
A53 Drew Stanton SP 2.50 6.00
A55 Lawrence Timmons 4.00 10.00
A56 DeMarcus Tank Tyler 2.50 6.00
A57 Darius Walker 2.50 6.00
A58 Paul Williams 2.50 6.00
A59 Patrick Willis 4.00 10.00
A60 Garrett Wolfe 2.50 6.00
A61 LaMarr Woodley 5.00 12.00
A62 Jared Zabransky 2.50 6.00

2007 SAGE Jerseys Red

RED PRINT RUN 99 SER.#'d SETS
*BRONZE/75: .4X TO 1X RED JSYs
BRONZE PRINT RUN 75 SER.#'d SETS
*SILVER/50: .5X TO 1.2X RED JSYs
SILVER PRINT RUN 50 SER.#'d SETS
*GOLD/25: .8X TO 2X RED JSYs
GOLD PRINT RUN 25 SER.#'d SETS
*PLATINUM/10: 1X TO 2.5X RED JSYs
PLATINUM PRINT RUN 10 SER.#'d SETS
UNPRICED JSY AUTO PRINT RUN 10
UNPRICED MASTER EDITION PRINT RUN 1
J1 Michael Bush 5.00 12.00
J2 Ken Darby 5.00 12.00
J3 Trent Edwards 5.00 12.00
J4 Anthony Gonzalez 5.00 12.00
J5 Kenny Irons 5.00 12.00
J6 Marshawn Lynch 5.00 12.00
J7 Robert Meachem 8.00 20.00
J8 Brandon Meriweather 5.00 12.00
J9 Greg Olsen 5.00 12.00
J10 Adrian Peterson 15.00 40.00
J11 Antonio Pittman 4.00 10.00
J12 Brady Quinn 4.00 10.00
J13 Sidney Rice 6.00 15.00
J14 JaMarcus Russell 5.00 12.00
J15 Troy Smith 5.00 12.00
J16 Drew Stanton 5.00 12.00
J17 Darius Walker 5.00 12.00

2007 SAGE Jerseys Dual

UNPRICED DUAL AUTO PRINT RUN 10

2007 SAGE First Card

1 Calvin Johnson/99 4.00 10.00
2 Brady Quinn/99 1.25 3.00

2007 SAGE National Convention National Heroes Jerseys

NH1 JaMarcus Russell 1.00 2.50
NH2 Adrian Peterson 3.00 8.00
NH3 Brady Quinn 1.00 2.50
NH4 Troy Smith 1.00 2.50

2007 SAGE Old School Autographs

RANDOM INSERTS IN PACKS
AA Aundrae Allison 4.00 10.00
BL Brian Leonard 4.00 10.00
BQ Brady Quinn 6.00 15.00
CD Craig Buster Davis 4.00 10.00
EE Earl Everett 4.00 10.00
JB John Beck 4.00 10.00
KK Kevin Kolb 5.00 12.00
ML Matt Leinart 4.00 10.00
TS Troy Smith 4.00 10.00
ZM Zach Miller 4.00 10.00
OS1 JaMarcus Russell 4.00 10.00
OS2 Gaines Adams 5.00 12.00
OS5 Dwayne Bowe 4.00 10.00
OS8 Anthony Gonzalez 4.00 10.00
OS12 Chris Henry 4.00 10.00
OS16 Jason Hill 4.00 10.00
OS17 Paul Williams 4.00 10.00
OS19 Garrett Wolfe 4.00 10.00
OS24 Jordan Palmer 5.00 12.00
OS26 David Ball 4.00 10.00
OS28 Chris Leak 4.00 10.00
OS30 Reggie Bush 10.00 25.00

2008 SAGE

COMPLETE SET (60) 20.00 40.00
1 Erik Ainge .30 .75
2 Adrian Arrington .30 .75
3 Donnie Avery .40 1.00
4 Sam Baker .30 .75
5 John David Booty .30 .75
6 Adarius Bowman .40 1.00
7 Brian Brohm .30 .75
8 Keenan Burton .30 .75
9 Andre Caldwell .30 .75
10 John Carlson .30 .75
11 Antoine Cason .40 1.00
12 Jamaal Charles .50 1.25
13 Tashard Choice .30 .75
14 Ryan Clady .40 1.00
15 Dan Connor .30 .75
16 Fred Davis .30 .75
17 Dennis Dixon .30 .75
18 Early Doucet .30 .75
19 Sedrick Ellis .30 .75
20 Joe Flacco .60 1.50
21 Brandon Flowers .40 1.00
22 Matt Flynn .30 .75
23 Will Franklin .40 1.00
24 Vernon Gholston .30 .75
25 James Hardy .30 .75
26 Mike Hart .30 .75
27 Derrick Harvey .30 .75
28 Lavelle Hawkins .40 1.00
29 Chad Henne .40 1.00
30 Jacob Hester .30 .75
31 DeSean Jackson .60 1.50
32 Lawrence Jackson .30 .75
33 Mike Jenkins .30 .75
34 Josh Johnson .30 .75
35 Felix Jones .30 .75
36 Dustin Keller .40 1.00
37 Sam Keller .30 .75
38 Malcolm Kelly .30 .75
39 Jake Long .50 1.25
40 Darren McFadden .30 .75
41 Leodis McKelvin .40 1.00
42 Rashard Mendenhall .30 .75
43 Jordy Nelson 1.00 2.50
44 Kevin O'Connell .30 .75
45 Allen Patrick .30 .75
46 Kenny Phillips .30 .75
47 Darius Reynaud .30 .75
48 Ray Rice .30 .75
49 Jason Rivers .30 .75
50 Keith Rivers .30 .75
51 Martin Rucker .30 .75
52 Matt Ryan 1.00 2.50
53 Owen Schmitt .30 .75
54 Steve Slaton .30 .75
55 Kevin Smith .30 .75
56 Paul Smith .30 .75
57 Jonathan Stewart .50 1.25
58 Limas Sweed .30 .75
59 Devin Thomas .30 .75
60 Tom Zbikowski .40 1.00

2008 SAGE Autographs Red

*BRONZE: .4X TO 1X RED AUTO
*SILVER/400: .5X TO 1.2X RED AUTO
*SILVER/400: .4X TO 1X RED AUTO SPs
SILVER PRINT RUN 400 SER.#'d SETS
*GOLD/200: .6X TO 1.5X RED AUTO
*GOLD/200: .5X TO 1.2X RED AUTO SPs
GOLD PRINT RUN 200 SER.#'d SETS
*PLATINUM/50: .8X TO 2X RED AUTO
*PLATINUM/50: .6X TO 1.5X RED AUTO SPs
PLATINUM PRINT RUN 50 SER.#'d SETS
UNPRICED MASTER EDITION PRINT RUN 1
UNPRICED TRIPLE AUTO PRINT RUN 5
1 Erik Ainge 2.50 6.00
2 Adrian Arrington 2.50 6.00
3 Donnie Avery 3.00 8.00
4 Sam Baker 2.50 6.00
5 John David Booty 2.50 6.00
6 Adarius Bowman 3.00 8.00
7 Brian Brohm 2.50 6.00
8 Keenan Burton 2.50 6.00
9 Andre Caldwell 2.50 6.00
10 John Carlson 2.50 6.00
11 Antoine Cason 3.00 8.00
12 Jamaal Charles 4.00 10.00
13 Tashard Choice 2.50 6.00
14 Ryan Clady 3.00 8.00
15 Dan Connor 2.50 6.00
16 Fred Davis 2.50 6.00
17 Dennis Dixon 2.50 6.00
19 Sedrick Ellis 2.50 6.00
20 Joe Flacco 5.00 12.00
21 Brandon Flowers 3.00 8.00
22 Matt Flynn 2.50 6.00
23 Will Franklin 3.00 8.00
24 Vernon Gholston 2.50 6.00
25 James Hardy 2.50 6.00
26 Mike Hart 2.50 6.00
27 Derrick Harvey 2.50 6.00
28 Lavelle Hawkins 3.00 8.00
29 Chad Henne 3.00 8.00
30 Jacob Hester 2.50 6.00
32 Lawrence Jackson 2.50 6.00
33 Mike Jenkins 2.50 6.00
34 Josh Johnson 2.50 6.00
35 Felix Jones 2.50 6.00
36 Dustin Keller 3.00 8.00
37 Sam Keller 2.50 6.00
38 Malcolm Kelly 2.50 6.00
39 Jake Long 4.00 10.00
40 Darren McFadden SP Blue 6.00 15.00
40R Darren McFadden SP Red 6.00 15.00
41 Leodis McKelvin 3.00 8.00
42 Rashard Mendenhall 2.50 6.00
43 Jordy Nelson 6.00 15.00
44 Kevin O'Connell 2.50 6.00
45 Allen Patrick 2.50 6.00
46 Kenny Phillips 2.50 6.00
47 Darius Reynaud 2.50 6.00
48 Ray Rice 2.50 6.00
49 Jason Rivers 2.50 6.00
50 Keith Rivers 2.50 6.00
51 Martin Rucker 2.50 6.00
52 Matt Ryan 8.00 20.00
53 Owen Schmitt 2.50 6.00
54 Steve Slaton 2.50 6.00
55 Kevin Smith 2.50 6.00
56 Paul Smith 2.50 6.00
57 Jonathan Stewart 4.00 10.00
58 Limas Sweed 2.50 6.00
59 Devin Thomas 2.50 6.00
60 Tom Zbikowski 3.00 8.00

2008 SAGE Darren McFadden Road to the Draft

COMPLETE SET (9) 15.00 40.00
COMMON CARD 2.00 5.00

2008 SAGE Darren McFadden Road to the Draft Autographs

COMMON CARD (RD1-RD9) 40.00 100.00

2008 SAGE Jersey Bonus

COMPLETE SET (5) 25.00 60.00
COMMON CARD (MCJ1-MCJ5) 6.00 15.00
MCJ1 Darren McFadden 1.25 3.00
MCJ2 Darren McFadden 1.25 3.00
MCJ3 Darren McFadden 1.25 3.00
MCJ4 Darren McFadden 1.25 3.00
MCJ5 Darren McFadden 1.25 3.00

2009 SAGE

COMPLETE SET (55) 20.00 40.00
1 Tom Brandstater .40 1.00
2 Andre Brown .40 1.00
3 Donald Brown .30 .75
4 Nathan Brown .40 1.00
5 Darius Butler .40 1.00
6 Demetrius Byrd .40 1.00
7 Hunter Cantwell .30 .75
8 James Casey .40 1.00
9 Chase Coffman .30 .75
10 Jared Cook .40 1.00
11 Michael Crabtree .50 1.25
12 Brian Cushing .30 .75
13 Nate Davis .30 .75
14 Jarett Dillard .30 .75
15 Brooks Foster .30 .75
16 Josh Freeman .30 .75
17 Marcus Freeman .30 .75
18 Cullen Harper .30 .75
19 Graham Harrell .30 .75
20 Darrius Heyward-Bey .50 1.25
21 Brian Hoyer .50 1.25
22 Juaquin Iglesias .30 .76
23 Cornelius Ingram .30 .75
24 Malcolm Jenkins .30 .75
25 Rashad Jennings .40 1.00
26 Gartrell Johnson .30 .75
27 Jeremiah Johnson .30 .75
28 Aaron Kelly .30 .75
29 James Laurinaitis .30 .75
30 Jeremy Maclin .40 1.00
31 Clay Matthews 1.25 3.00
32 Rey Maualuga .50 1.25
33 LeSean McCoy .75 2.00
34 Stephen McGee .30 .75
35 Eugene Monroe .30 .75
36 Devin Moore .30 .75
37 Knowshon Moreno .30 .75
38 Louis Murphy .30 .75
39 Hakeem Nicks .40 1.00
40 Brian Orakpo .40 1.00
41 Curtis Painter .30 .75
42 B.J. Raji .40 1.00
43 Mike Reilly .30 .75
44 Javon Ringer .30 .75
45 Brian Robiskie .30 .75
46 Mark Sanchez .30 .75
47 Clint Sintim .30 .75
48 Alphonso Smith .30 .75
49 Jason Smith .30 .75
50 Matthew Stafford 1.50 4.00
51 Mike Thomas .30 .75
52 Patrick Turner .30 .75
53 Chris Wells .30 .75
54 Pat White .40 1.00
55 John Parker Wilson .30 .75

2009 SAGE Autographs Red

ONE AUTO PER PACK
*GOLD/200: .6X TO 1.5X RED AUTO
GOLD PRINT RUN 200 SER.#'d SETS
*PLATINUM/50: .8X TO 2X RED AUTO
PLATINUM PRINT RUN 50 SER.#'d SETS
*SILVER/400: .5X TO 1.2X RED AUTO
SILVER PRINT RUN 400 SER.#'d SETS
1 Tom Brandstater 3.00 8.00
2 Andre Brown 3.00 8.00
3 Donald Brown 2.50 6.00
4 Nathan Brown 3.00 8.00
5 Darius Butler 3.00 8.00
6 Demetrius Byrd 3.00 8.00
7 Hunter Cantwell 2.50 6.00
8 James Casey 3.00 8.00
9 Chase Coffman 2.50 6.00
10 Jared Cook 3.00 8.00
11 Michael Crabtree 4.00 10.00
12 Brian Cushing 2.50 6.00
13 Nate Davis 2.50 6.00
14 Jarett Dillard 2.50 6.00
15 Brooks Foster 2.50 6.00
16 Josh Freeman 2.50 6.00
17 Marcus Freeman 2.50 6.00
18 Cullen Harper 2.50 6.00
19 Graham Harrell 6.00 15.00
20 Darrius Heyward-Bey 4.00 10.00
21 Brian Hoyer 4.00 10.00
22 Juaquin Iglesias 2.50 6.00
23 Cornelius Ingram 2.50 6.00
24 Malcolm Jenkins 2.50 6.00
25 Rashad Jennings 3.00 8.00
26 Gartrell Johnson 2.50 6.00
27 Jeremiah Johnson 2.50 6.00
28 Aaron Kelly 2.50 6.00
29 James Laurinaitis 2.50 6.00
30 Jeremy Maclin 3.00 8.00
31 Clay Matthews 15.00 40.00
32 Rey Maualuga 4.00 10.00
33 LeSean McCoy 6.00 15.00
34 Stephen McGee 2.50 6.00
35 Eugene Monroe 2.50 6.00
36 Devin Moore 2.50 6.00
37 Knowshon Moreno 2.50 6.00
38 Louis Murphy 2.50 6.00
39 Hakeem Nicks 3.00 8.00
40 Brian Orakpo 3.00 8.00
41 Curtis Painter 2.50 6.00
42 B.J. Raji 3.00 8.00
43 Mike Reilly 2.50 6.00
44 Javon Ringer 2.50 6.00
45 Brian Robiskie 2.50 6.00
46 Mark Sanchez 12.00 30.00
47 Clint Sintim 2.50 6.00
48 Alphonso Smith 2.50 6.00
49 Jason Smith 2.50 6.00
50 Matthew Stafford 15.00 40.00
51 Mike Thomas 2.50 6.00
52 Patrick Turner 2.50 6.00
53 Chris Wells 12.00 30.00
54 Pat White 3.00 8.00
55 John Parker Wilson 2.50 6.00

2010 SAGE

1 Seyi Ajirotutu .30 .75
2 Danario Alexander .30 .75
3 Andre Anderson .30 .75
4 Joique Bell .30 .75
5 Arrelious Benn .30 .75
6 Jahvid Best .30 .75
7 Sam Bradford .40 1.00
8 Dezmon Briscoe .30 .75
9 Antonio Brown 2.50 6.00
10 Jarrett Brown .30 .75
11 Dez Bryant .75 2.00
12 Nate Byham .30 .75
13 Sean Canfield .30 .75
14 Jimmy Clausen .30 .75
15 Chris Cook .30 .75
16 Rennie Curran .30 .75
17 Anthony Dixon .30 .75
18 Jonathan Dwyer .30 .75
19 Toby Gerhart .30 .75
20 Mardy Gilyard .30 .75
21 Garrett Graham .30 .75
22 Jermaine Gresham .30 .75
23 Rob Gronkowski 1.00 2.50
24 Montario Hardesty .30 .75
25 Aaron Hernandez .30 .75
26 Javarris James .30 .75
27 Stafon Johnson .30 .75
28 Dan LeFevour .30 .75
29 Ryan Mathews .30 .75
30 Rolando McClain .30 .75
31 Colt McCoy .40 1.00
32 Gerald McCoy .30 .75
33 Carlton Mitchell .30 .75
34 Tony Moeaki .40 1.00
35 Derrick Morgan .30 .75
36 Colin Peek .30 .75
37 Jason Pierre-Paul .50 1.25
38 Tony Pike .30 .75
39 Dennis Pitta .30 .75
40 Taylor Price .30 .75
41 Zac Robinson .40 1.00
42 Jordan Shipley .30 .75
43 John Skelton .40 1.00
44 Jevan Snead .30 .75
45 Brandon Spikes .30 .75
46 C.J. Spiller .30 .75
47 Ndamukong Suh .60 1.50
48 Ben Tate .30 .75
49 Earl Thomas .75 2.00
50 Sean Weatherspoon .30 .75
51 Joe Webb .30 .75
52 Blair White .30 .75
53 Damian Williams .30 .75
54 Jeremy Williams .30 .75
55 Mike Williams .30 .75

2010 SAGE Autographs Red

RED STATED ODDS 1:2
*GOLD/200: .5X TO 1.2X RED AUTO
GOLD/200 ODDS 1:6
*PLATINUM/50: .8X TO 2X RED AUTO
PLATINUM/50 ODDS 1:25
*SILVER/400: .4X TO 1X RED AUTO
SILVER/400 ODDS 1:3
1 Seyi Ajirotutu 2.50 6.00
2 Danario Alexander 2.50 6.00
3 Andre Anderson 2.50 6.00
4 Joique Bell SP 2.50 6.00
5 Arrelious Benn SP 2.50 6.00
6 Jahvid Best SP 2.50 6.00
7 Sam Bradford SP 15.00 40.00
8 Dezmon Briscoe SP 2.50 6.00
9 Antonio Brown SP 20.00 50.00
10 Jarrett Brown SP 2.50 6.00
12 Nate Byham 2.50 6.00
13 Sean Canfield 2.50 6.00
14 Jimmy Clausen SP 2.50 6.00
15 Chris Cook 2.50 6.00
16 Rennie Curran 2.50 6.00
17 Anthony Dixon SP 2.50 6.00
18 Jonathan Dwyer SP 2.50 6.00
19 Toby Gerhart SP 6.00 15.00
20 Mardy Gilyard 2.50 6.00
21 Garrett Graham SP 2.50 6.00
22 Jermaine Gresham SP 2.50 6.00
23 Rob Gronkowski SP 8.00 20.00
24 Montario Hardesty 2.50 6.00
25 Aaron Hernandez 2.50 6.00
26 Javarris James 2.50 6.00
27 Stafon Johnson 2.50 6.00
28 Dan LeFevour 2.50 6.00
29 Ryan Mathews 2.50 6.00
30 Rolando McClain SP 2.50 6.00
31 Colt McCoy SP 3.00 8.00
32 Gerald McCoy SP 8.00 20.00
33 Carlton Mitchell SP 2.50 6.00
34 Tony Moeaki 3.00 8.00
35 Derrick Morgan SP 2.50 6.00
36 Colin Peek 2.50 6.00
37 Jason Pierre-Paul 4.00 10.00
38 Tony Pike SP 2.50 6.00
39 Dennis Pitta 2.50 6.00
40 Taylor Price 2.50 6.00
41 Zac Robinson SP 3.00 8.00
42 Jordan Shipley 2.50 6.00
43 John Skelton SP 3.00 8.00
44 Jevan Snead SP 2.50 6.00
45 Brandon Spikes SP 2.50 6.00
46 C.J. Spiller SP 2.50 6.00
47 Ndamukong Suh SP 20.00 40.00
48 Ben Tate 2.50 6.00
49 Earl Thomas SP 6.00 15.00
50 Sean Weatherspoon SP 2.50 6.00
51 Joe Webb 2.50 6.00
52 Blair White 2.50 6.00
53 Damian Williams SP 2.50 6.00
54 Jeremy Williams SP 2.50 6.00
55 Mike Williams 2.50 6.00

2011 SAGE

1 Sam Acho .30 .75
2 Da'Quan Bowers .30 .75
3 Allen Bradford .30 .75
4 Curtis Brown .30 .75
5 Delone Carter .30 .75
6 Anthony Castonzo .30 .75
7 Charles Clay .30 .75
8 Randall Cobb .50 1.25
9 Nick Fairley .30 .75
10 Blaine Gabbert .30 .75
11 Charlie Gantt .30 .75
12 Edmond Gates .30 .75
13 A.J. Green .75 2.00
14 Jamie Harper .30 .75
15 Mark Herzlich .30 .75
16 Cameron Heyward .40 1.00
17 Rob Housler .30 .75
18 Mark Ingram .50 1.25
19 Lestar Jean .30 .75
20 Jerrel Jernigan .30 .75
21 Julio Jones 1.00 2.50
22 Taiwan Jones .30 .75
23 Jeremy Kerley .50 1.25
24 Ryan Kerrigan .40 1.00
25 Mikel Leshoure .30 .75
26 Dion Lewis .40 1.00
27 Jake Locker .30 .75
28 Jeff Maehl .30 .75
29 Ryan Mallett .30 .75
30 Casey Matthews .30 .75
31 DeAndre McDaniel .30 .75
32 Von Miller .50 1.25
33 Denarius Moore .30 .75
34 Rahim Moore .30 .75
35 DeMarco Murray .60 1.50
36 Cam Newton 1.50 4.00
37 Stephen Paea .30 .75
38 Austin Pettis .30 .75
39 Christian Ponder .30 .75
40 Taylor Potts .30 .75
41 Stevan Ridley .30 .75
42 Jacquizz Rodgers .30 .75
43 Kyle Rudolph .30 .75
44 Dane Sanzenbacher .30 .75
45 Cecil Shorts .30 .75
46 Aldon Smith .30 .75
47 Courtney Smith .30 .75
48 Torrey Smith .30 .75
49 Nate Solder .30 .75
50 Ricky Stanzi .30 .75
51 Luke Stocker .30 .75
52 Daniel Thomas .30 .75
53 Jordan Todman .30 .75
54 Shane Vereen .40 1.00
55 J.J. Watt 1.50 4.00
56 Adam Weber .30 .75
57 Aaron Williams .30 .75
58 D.J. Williams .30 .75
59 Ryan Williams .30 .75
60 T.J. Yates .30 .75

2011 SAGE Autographs Red

RED AU STATED ODDS 1:2 HOB
*GOLD/200: .5X TO 1.2X RED AUTO
*PLATINUM/50: .6X TO 1.5X BASIC AU
*SILVER: .4X TO 1X RED AUTO
UNPRICED MAST.EDIT/1 ODDS 1:1255 H
1 Sam Acho 2.50 6.00
2 Da'Quan Bowers 2.50 6.00
3 Allen Bradford 2.50 6.00
4 Curtis Brown 2.50 6.00
5 Delone Carter 2.50 6.00
6 Anthony Castonzo 2.50 6.00
7 Charles Clay 2.50 6.00
8 Randall Cobb 4.00 10.00
9 Nick Fairley 2.50 6.00
10 Blaine Gabbert 2.50 6.00
11 Charlie Gantt 2.50 6.00
12 Edmond Gates 2.50 6.00
13 A.J. Green 6.00 15.00
14 Jamie Harper 2.50 6.00
15 Mark Herzlich 2.50 6.00
16 Cameron Heyward 3.00 8.00
17 Rob Housler 2.50 6.00
18 Mark Ingram 4.00 10.00
19 Lestar Jean 2.50 6.00
20 Jerrel Jernigan 2.50 6.00
21 Julio Jones 12.00 30.00
22 Taiwan Jones 2.50 6.00
23 Jeremy Kerley 4.00 10.00
24 Ryan Kerrigan 3.00 8.00
25 Mikel Leshoure 2.50 6.00
26 Dion Lewis 3.00 8.00
27 Jake Locker 2.50 6.00
28 Jeff Maehl 2.50 6.00
29 Ryan Mallett 2.50 6.00
30 Casey Matthews 2.50 6.00
31 DeAndre McDaniel 2.50 6.00
32 Von Miller 6.00 15.00
33 Denarius Moore 2.50 6.00
34 Rahim Moore 2.50 6.00
35 DeMarco Murray 5.00 12.00
36 Cam Newton 12.00 30.00
37 Stephen Paea 2.50 6.00
38 Austin Pettis 2.50 6.00
39 Christian Ponder 2.50 6.00
40 Taylor Potts 2.50 6.00
41 Stevan Ridley 2.50 6.00
42 Jacquizz Rodgers 2.50 6.00
43 Kyle Rudolph 2.50 6.00
44 Dane Sanzenbacher 2.50 6.00
45 Cecil Shorts 2.50 6.00
46 Aldon Smith 2.50 6.00
47 Courtney Smith 2.50 6.00
48 Torrey Smith 2.50 6.00
49 Nate Solder 2.50 6.00
50 Ricky Stanzi 2.50 6.00
51 Luke Stocker 2.50 6.00
52 Daniel Thomas 2.50 6.00
53 Jordan Todman 2.50 6.00
54 Shane Vereen 3.00 8.00
55 J.J. Watt 25.00 50.00
56 Adam Weber 2.50 6.00
57 Aaron Williams 2.50 6.00
58 D.J. Williams 2.50 6.00
59 Ryan Williams 2.50 6.00
60 T.J. Yates 2.50 6.00

2011 SAGE Through the Lens

RANDOM INSERTS IN PACKS
RF1 Jerrel Jernigan .50 1.25
RF2 Mikel Leshoure .50 1.25
RF3 DeMarco Murray 1.00 2.50
RF4 Jacquizz Rodgers .50 1.25
RF5 Torrey Smith .50 1.25
RF6 Ryan Williams .50 1.25

2012 SAGE

1 Joe Adams .30 .75
2 Dwayne Allen .30 .75
3 Justin Blackmon .30 .75
4 Brandon Bolden .30 .75
5 Ryan Broyles .30 .75
6 Vontaze Burfict .40 1.00
7 Orson Charles .30 .75
8 Quinton Coples .30 .75
9 Kirk Cousins 1.25 3.00
10 Jared Crick .30 .75
11 Juron Criner .30 .75
12 Alfonzo Dennard .30 .75
13 Michael Egnew .30 .75
14 Michael Floyd .30 .75
15 Nick Foles .75 2.00
16 Jeff Fuller .30 .75
17 Chris Givens .30 .75
18 Cyrus Gray .30 .75
19 Ladarius Green .30 .75
20 Robert Griffin III .40 1.00
21 Boom Herron .30 .75
22 Ronnie Hillman .30 .75
23 T.Y. Hilton .60 1.50
24 Melvin Ingram .30 .75
25 LaMichael James .30 .75
26 Alshon Jeffery .60 1.50
27 Janoris Jenkins .40 1.00
28 Matt Kalil .30 .75
29 Case Keenum .60 1.50
30 Luke Kuechly .75 2.00
31 Ryan Lindley .30 .75
32 Doug Martin .50 1.25
33 Marvin McNutt .30 .75
34 Davin Meggett .30 .75
35 Lamar Miller .50 1.25
36 Kellen Moore .40 1.00
37 Brock Osweiler .30 .75
38 Eric Page .40 1.00
39 Bernard Pierce .30 .75
40 Dontari Poe .30 .75
41 Chris Polk .30 .75
42 Tauren Poole .30 .75
43 DeVier Posey .30 .75
44 Brian Quick .30 .75
45 Trent Richardson .30 .75
46 Tommy Streeter .30 .75
47 Ryan Tannehill .50 1.25
48 Brandon Weeden .30 .75
49 Jarius Wright .30 .75
50 Kendall Wright .30 .75

2012 SAGE Autographs Red

RED AU STATED ODDS 1:2 HOB
*GOLD/100: .5X TO 1.2X RED AU
*PLATINUM/50: .6X TO 1.5X RED AU
*SILVER AU: .4X TO 1X RED AU
A1 Joe Adams 2.50 6.00
A2 Dwayne Allen 2.50 6.00
A3 Justin Blackmon 2.50 6.00
A4 Brandon Bolden 2.50 6.00
A5 Ryan Broyles 2.50 6.00
A6 Vontaze Burfict 3.00 8.00
A7 Orson Charles 2.50 6.00
A8 Quinton Coples 2.50 6.00
A9 Kirk Cousins 10.00 25.00
A10 Jared Crick 2.50 6.00
A11 Juron Criner 2.50 6.00
A12 Alfonzo Dennard 2.50 6.00
A13 Michael Egnew 2.50 6.00
A14 Michael Floyd 6.00 15.00
A15 Nick Foles 6.00 15.00
A16 Jeff Fuller 2.50 6.00
A17 Chris Givens 2.50 6.00
A18 Cyrus Gray 2.50 6.00
A19 Ladarius Green 2.50 6.00
A20 Robert Griffin III 8.00 20.00
A21 Boom Herron 2.50 6.00
A22 Ronnie Hillman 2.50 6.00
A23 T.Y. Hilton 5.00 12.00
A24 Melvin Ingram 2.50 6.00
A25 LaMichael James 2.50 6.00
A26 Alshon Jeffery 5.00 12.00
A27 Janoris Jenkins 3.00 8.00
A28 Matt Kalil 2.50 6.00
A29 Case Keenum 5.00 12.00
A30 Luke Kuechly 6.00 15.00
A31 Ryan Lindley 2.50 6.00
A32 Doug Martin 4.00 10.00
A33 Marvin McNutt 2.50 6.00
A34 Davin Meggett 2.50 6.00
A35 Lamar Miller 4.00 10.00
A36 Kellen Moore 3.00 8.00
A37 Brock Osweiler 2.50 6.00
A38 Eric Page 3.00 8.00
A39 Bernard Pierce 2.50 6.00
A40 Dontari Poe 2.50 6.00
A41 Chris Polk 2.50 6.00
A42 Tauren Poole 2.50 6.00
A43 DeVier Posey 2.50 6.00
A44 Brian Quick 2.50 6.00
A45 Trent Richardson 2.50 6.00
A46 Tommy Streeter 2.50 6.00
A47 Ryan Tannehill 4.00 10.00
A48 Brandon Weeden 2.50 6.00
A49 Jarius Wright 2.50 6.00
A50 Kendall Wright 2.50 6.00

2013 SAGE

SP1 Keenan Allen 1.25 3.00
SP2 Ryan Aplin .60 1.50
SP3 Montee Ball .60 1.50
SP4 Matt Barkley .60 1.50
SP5 LeVeon Bell 2.00 5.00
SP6 Giovani Bernard .60 1.50
SP7 Tyler Bray .60 1.50
SP8 Dan Buckner .60 1.50
SP9 Rex Burkhead .75 2.00
SP10 Aaron Dobson .60 1.50
SP11 Zac Dysert .60 1.50
SP12 Tyler Eifert .60 1.50
SP13 Andre Ellington .60 1.50
SP14 Joseph Fauria .60 1.50
SP15 Mike Gillislee .60 1.50
SP16 Mike Glennon .60 1.50
SP17 Tyrone Goard .60 1.50
SP18 Marquise Goodwin .60 1.50
SP19 Ryan Griffin .60 1.50
SP20 DeAndre Hopkins 1.50 4.00
SP21 Justin Hunter .60 1.50
SP22 Luke Joeckel .60 1.50
SP23 Barrett Jones .60 1.50
SP24 Datone Jones .60 1.50
SP25 Landry Jones .60 1.50
SP26 Nick Kasa .60 1.50
SP27 Collin Klein .75 2.00
SP28 Eddie Lacy .60 1.50
SP29 Marcus Lattimore .60 1.50
SP30 EJ Manuel .60 1.50
SP31 T.J. McDonald .60 1.50
SP32 Vance McDonald .75 2.00
SP33 Johnny McEntee .60 1.50
SP34 Aaron Mellette .60 1.50
SP35 Damontre Moore .60 1.50
SP36 Latavius Murray .75 2.00
SP37 Ryan Nassib .60 1.50
SP38 Alec Ogletree .60 1.50
SP39 Alex Okafor .60 1.50
SP40 Cordarrelle Patterson .60 1.50
SP41 Sean Porter .60 1.50
SP42 Joseph Randle .60 1.50
SP43 Jordan Reed 1.00 2.50
SP44 Xavier Rhodes .60 1.50
SP45 Sheldon Richardson .60 1.50
SP46 Theo Riddick .60 1.50
SP47 Denard Robinson .60 1.50
SP48 Jordan Rodgers .75 2.00
SP49 Da'Rick Rogers .60 1.50
SP50 Geno Smith .60 1.50
SP51 Rodney Smith .60 1.50
SP52 Brad Sorensen .60 1.50
SP53 Kenny Stills .60 1.50
SP54 Ryan Swope .60 1.50
SP55 Manti Te'o .75 2.00
SP56 Kenny Vaccaro .60 1.50
SP57 Conner Vernon .60 1.50
SP58 Bjoern Werner .60 1.50
SP59 Terrance Williams .60 1.50
SP60 Braden Wilson .75 2.00
SP61 Tyler Wilson .60 1.50
SP62 Cierre Wood .60 1.50
SP63 Robert Woods 1.00 2.50
SP64 Sam Montgomery .60 1.50

2013 SAGE Black

*BLACK/50: .6X TO 1.5X BASIC CARDS

2013 SAGE Autographs Red

*GOLD/100: .5X TO 1.2X RED AU
*GREEN/50: .6X TO 1.5X RED AU
*SILVER AU: .4X TO 1X RED AU
2 Ryan Aplin 2.50 6.00
3 Montee Ball 2.50 6.00
4 Matt Barkley 2.50 6.00
5 LeVeon Bell 8.00 20.00
6 Giovani Bernard 2.50 6.00
7 Tyler Bray
8 Dan Buckner 2.50 6.00
9 Rex Burkhead 3.00 8.00
10 Aaron Dobson 2.50 6.00
11 Zac Dysert 2.50 6.00
12 Tyler Eifert 2.50 6.00
13 Andre Ellington 2.50 6.00
14 Joseph Fauria 2.50 6.00
15 Mike Gillislee 2.50 6.00
16 Mike Glennon 2.50 6.00
17 Tyrone Goard 2.50 6.00
18 Marquise Goodwin 2.50 6.00
19 Ryan Griffin 2.50 6.00
20 DeAndre Hopkins 6.00 15.00
21 Justin Hunter 2.50 6.00
22 Luke Joeckel 2.50 6.00
23 Barrett Jones 2.50 6.00
24 Datone Jones 2.50 6.00
25 Landry Jones 2.50 6.00
26 Nick Kasa 2.50 6.00
27 Collin Klein 3.00 8.00
28 Eddie Lacy 2.50 6.00
29 Marcus Lattimore 2.50 6.00
30 EJ Manuel 2.50 6.00
31 T.J. McDonald 2.50 6.00
32 Vance McDonald 3.00 8.00
33 Johnny McEntee 2.50 6.00
34 Aaron Mellette 2.50 6.00
35 Damontre Moore 2.50 6.00
36 Latavius Murray 3.00 8.00
37 Ryan Nassib
38 Alec Ogletree 2.50 6.00
39 Alex Okafor 2.50 6.00
40 Cordarrelle Patterson 2.50 6.00
41 Sean Porter 2.50 6.00
42 Joseph Randle 2.50 6.00
43 Jordan Reed 4.00 10.00
44 Xavier Rhodes 2.50 6.00
45 Sheldon Richardson 2.50 6.00
46 Theo Riddick 2.50 6.00
48 Jordan Rodgers 3.00 8.00
49 Da'Rick Rogers 2.50 6.00
50 Geno Smith 2.50 6.00
51 Rodney Smith 2.50 6.00
52 Brad Sorensen 2.50 6.00
53 Kenny Stills 2.50 6.00
54 Ryan Swope 2.50 6.00
55 Manti Te'o 3.00 8.00
56 Kenny Vaccaro 2.50 6.00
57 Conner Vernon 2.50 6.00
58 Bjoern Werner 2.50 6.00
59 Terrance Williams 2.50 6.00
60 Braden Wilson 3.00 8.00
61 Tyler Wilson 2.50 6.00
62 Cierre Wood 2.50 6.00
63 Robert Woods 4.00 10.00
64 Sam Montgomery 2.50 6.00

2014 SAGE Autographs Silver

1 Jared Abbrederis 2.50 6.00
2 Davante Adams 4.00 10.00
3 Odell Beckham Jr. 20.00 40.00
4 Blake Bortles 3.00 8.00
5 Tajh Boyd 2.50 6.00
6 Carl Bradford 2.50 6.00
7 Teddy Bridgewater 4.00 10.00
8 Michael Campanaro 2.50 6.00
9 Ka'Deem Carey 2.50 6.00
10 Derek Carr
11 Ha Ha Clinton-Dix 3.00 8.00
12 Jadeveon Clowney 3.00 8.00
13 Brandin Cooks 4.00 10.00
14 Mike Davis 2.50 6.00
15 Joe Don Duncan 2.50 6.00
16 Kony Ealy 3.00 8.00
17 Dominique Easley 2.50 6.00
18 Eric Ebron 3.00 8.00
19 Bruce Ellington 2.50 6.00
20 Mike Evans 6.00 15.00
21 Shaquelle Evans 2.50 6.00
22 David Fales 2.50 6.00
23 Jimmy Garoppolo 25.00 60.00
24 Ra'Shede Hageman 3.00 8.00
25 Robert Herron 2.50 6.00
26 Carlos Hyde 3.00 8.00
27 Henry Josey 2.50 6.00
28 Marqise Lee 3.00 8.00
29 Kareem Martin 2.50 6.00
30 Tre Mason 2.50 6.00
31 Jake Matthews 2.50 6.00
32 Keith McGill 2.50 6.00
33 Zach Mettenberger 2.50 6.00
34 Stephen Morris 2.50 6.00
35 Aaron Murray 2.50 6.00
36 Rajion Neal 2.50 6.00
37 Troy Niklas 2.50 6.00
38 Kevin Norwood 2.50 6.00
39 Calvin Pryor 2.50 6.00
40 Trevor Reilly 2.50 6.00
41 Paul Richardson 4.00 10.00
42 Allen Robinson 4.00 10.00
43 Michael Sam 2.50 6.00
44 Tom Savage 6.00 15.00
45 Brett Smith 2.50 6.00
46 Chris Smith 2.50 6.00
47 Jerome Smith 2.50 6.00
48 Lorenzo Taliaferro 2.50 6.00
49 Logan Thomas 2.50 6.00
50 Kyle Van Noy 3.00 8.00
51 Sammy Watkins
52 Terrance West 2.50 6.00
53 James White 5.00 12.00
54 Jordan Zumwalt 2.50 6.00

2014 SAGE Autographs Gold

*GOLD/50: .5X TO 1.2X SILVER/99
10 Derek Carr 15.00 40.00

2014 SAGE Autographs Platinum

*PLATINUM/25: .6X TO 1.5X SILVER/99
10 Derek Carr 20.00 50.00

2014 SAGE Autographs Sophomore Autographs Silver

*GOLD/25: .5X TO 1.2X SILVER/50
S1 Montee Ball 3.00 8.00
S2 Matt Barkley 3.00 8.00
S3 Le'Veon Bell 4.00 10.00
S4 Giovani Bernard 3.00 8.00
S5 Tyler Eifert 4.00 10.00
S6 Andre Ellington 3.00 8.00
S7 Mike Glennon 4.00 10.00
S8 Marquise Goodwin 3.00 8.00
S9 DeAndre Hopkins 4.00 10.00
S10 Eddie Lacy 3.00 8.00
S11 Marcus Lattimore 5.00 12.00
S12 EJ Manuel 6.00 15.00
S13 Cordarrelle Patterson
S14 Jordan Reed 3.00 8.00
S15 Sheldon Richardson 3.00 8.00
S16 Geno Smith 8.00 20.00
S17 Kenny Stills 3.00 8.00
S18 Manti Te'o 4.00 10.00
S19 Kenny Vaccaro 3.00 8.00
S20 Terrance Williams 3.00 8.00
S21 Robert Woods 4.00 10.00

2015 SAGE Autographs

*SILVER/30: .4X TO 1X BASIC AU/40
*GOLD/20: .5X TO 1.2X BASIC AU/40
1 Dres Anderson 2.00 5.00
2 Cameron Artis-Payne 2.00 5.00
3 Vic Beasley 2.50 6.00
4 Bryan Bennett 2.00 5.00
5 Brandon Bridge 2.00 5.00
6 Dominique Brown 2.00 5.00
7 Malcolm Brown 2.50 6.00
9 Shane Carden 2.00 5.00
10 Sammie Coates 2.50 6.00
11 Tevin Coleman 2.50 6.00
12 Landon Collins 2.50 6.00
13 Amari Cooper 6.00 15.00
14 Xavier Cooper 2.00 5.00
15 John Crockett 3.00 8.00
16 Ifo Ekpre-Olomu 2.00 5.00
17 Dante Fowler Jr. 3.00 8.00
18 Devin Funchess 3.00 8.00
19 Markus Golden 2.00 5.00
20 Garrett Grayson 6.00 15.00
21 Dorial Green-Beckham 2.00 5.00
22 Randy Gregory 8.00 20.00
23 Geneo Grissom 2.00 5.00
24 Todd Gurley 12.00 30.00
25 Rannell Hall 2.00 5.00
26 Josh Harper 2.00 5.00
27 Anthony Harris 2.00 5.00
28 Dee Hart 2.00 5.00
29 Taylor Heinicke 3.00 8.00
30 Austin Hill 2.00 5.00
31 Mike Hull 3.00 8.00
32 Brett Hundley 8.00 20.00
33 Grady jarrett 2.50 6.00
34 Tony Lippett 2.00 5.00
35 Tyler Lockett 3.00 8.00
36 Sean Mannion 2.00 5.00
37 Lorenzo Mauldin 2.00 5.00
38 Marcus Murphy 2.00 5.00
39 Levi Norwood 2.00 5.00
40 Bryce Petty 2.00 5.00
41 MyCole Pruitt 2.00 5.00
42 Quinten Rollins 4.00 10.00
43 Derron Smith 2.00 5.00
44 Devin Smith 2.00 5.00
45 Shaq Thompson 2.50 6.00
46 Davis Tull 2.00 5.00
47 Clive Walford 2.00 5.00
48 Darren Waller 2.50 6.00
49 Trae Waynes 2.00 5.00
50 Kevin White 2.50 6.00
51 Leonard Williams 2.00 5.00
52 Maxx Williams 2.00 5.00
53 P.J. Williams 2.50 6.00
54 Jameis Winston 40.00 80.00
55 T.J. Yeldon 2.00 5.00

2016 SAGE Autographs

SA1 Brandon Allen 2.00 5.00
SA2 Mike Bercovici 2.00 5.00
SA3 Joey Bosa 8.00 20.00
SA4 Daniel Braverman 2.00 5.00
SA5 DeForest Buckner 2.00 5.00
SA6 Aaron Burbridge 2.00 5.00
SA7 Jeremy Cash 2.50 6.00
SA8 Corey Coleman 3.00 8.00
SA9 Alex Collins 2.50 6.00
SA10 Pharoh Cooper 2.00 5.00
SA11 Marshaun Coprich 2.00 5.00
SA12 Cody Core 2.00 5.00
SA13 Josh Doctson 2.50 6.00
SA14 Brandon Doughty 2.00 5.00
SA15 Jeff Driskel 2.00 5.00
SA16 Ezekiel Elliott 40.00 80.00
SA17 Tyler Ervin 2.00 5.00
SA18 Blake Frohnapfel 2.00 5.00
SA19 Will Fuller 3.00 8.00
SA20 Jared Goff 12.00 30.00
SA21 Aaron Green 2.00 5.00
SA22 Hunter Henry 2.50 6.00
SA23 Jordan Howard 5.00 12.00
SA24 Cardale Jones 2.00 5.00
SA25 Cayleb Jones 2.00 5.00
SA26 Chuckie Keeton 2.00 5.00
SA27 Cody Kessler 2.00 5.00
SA28 Miles Killebrew 2.00 5.00
SA29 Daniel Lasco 2.00 5.00
SA30 Darron Lee 2.00 5.00
SA31 Paxton Lynch
SA32 Tre Madden 2.00 5.00
SA33 Keith Marshall 2.00 5.00
SA34 Malcolm Mitchell 2.00 5.00
SA35 Liam Nadler 2.00 5.00
SA36 Ammon Olsen 2.00 5.00
SA37 Paul Perkins 2.00 5.00
SA38 Dak Prescott

SA39 Jalen Ramsey 3.00 8.00
SA40 Hunter Sharp 2.50 6.00
SA41 Tajae Sharpe 2.50 6.00
SA42 Nelson Spruce 2.00 5.00
SA43 Michael Thomas 4.00 10.00
SA44 Laremy Tunsil 2.00 5.00
SA45 Soma Vainuku 2.50 6.00
SA46 Nick Vannett 2.00 5.00
SA47 Dan Vitale 2.00 5.00
SA48 Jonathan Williams 2.50 6.00
SA49 Jordan Williams-Lanbert 2.00 5.00
SA50 De'Runnya Wilson 2.00 5.00

2007 SAGE DECADEnce

This 56-card set was released in December, 2007. The set was issued into the hobby in three-card packs which came eight to a box.

COMPLETE SET (56) 8.00 20.00
1 JaMarcus Russell .25 .60
2 Calvin Johnson .75 2.00
3 Gaines Adams .30 .75
4 Levi Brown .25 .60
5 Adrian Peterson .75 2.00
6 Ted Ginn Jr. .30 .75
7 Patrick Willis .40 1.00
8 Marshawn Lynch .50 1.25
9 Adam Carriker .25 .60
10 Lawrence Timmons .40 1.00
11 Jarvis Moss .25 .60
12 Leon Hall .25 .60
13 Michael Griffin .25 .60
14 Aaron Ross .25 .60
15 Brady Quinn .25 .60
16 Dwayne Bowe .25 .60
17 Brandon Meriweather .30 .75
18 Robert Meachem .30 .75
19 Craig Buster Davis .25 .60
20 Greg Olsen .40 1.00
21 Anthony Gonzalez .25 .60
22 Alan Branch .25 .60
23 Kevin Kolb .30 .75
24 Zach Miller .25 .60
25 John Beck .25 .60
26 Drew Stanton .25 .60
27 Sidney Rice .30 .75
28 LaMarr Woodley .50 1.25
29 Kenny Irons .25 .60
30 Chris Henry RB .25 .60
31 Steve Smith USC .25 .60
32 Brian Leonard .25 .60
33 Ryan Kalil .25 .60
34 Yamon Figurs .25 .60
35 Jason Hill .25 .60
36 Paul Williams .25 .60
37 Demarcus Tank Tyler .25 .60
38 Trent Edwards .25 .60
39 Garrett Wolfe .25 .60
40 Johnnie Lee Higgins .25 .60
41 Michael Bush .25 .60
42 Isaiah Stanback .25 .60
43 Antonio Pittman .25 .60
44 Steve Breaston .25 .60
45 Aundrae Allison .25 .60
46 Kolby Smith .25 .60
47 Jeff Rowe .25 .60
48 David Clowney .25 .60
49 Troy Smith .25 .60
50 Joel Filani .25 .60
51 David Irons .25 .60
52 Courtney Taylor .25 .60
53 Jordan Palmer .30 .75
54 Dallas Baker .25 .60
55 Jason Snelling .25 .60
56 Kenneth Darby .25 .60

2007 SAGE DECADEnce Autographs Bronze

*SILVER/50: .5X TO 1.2X BRONZE AUTO
SILVER PRINT RUN 50 SER.#'d SETS
*GOLD/25: .6X TO 1.5X BRONZE AUTO
GOLD PRINT RUN 25 SER.#'d SETS
UNPRICED EMERALD PRINT RUN 5
UNPRICED PRINT PLATE PRINT RUN 1
UNPRICED RETRO AUTO PRINT RUN 10
A1 JaMarcus Russell 2.50 6.00
A3 Gaines Adams 3.00 8.00
A4 Levi Brown 2.50 6.00
A5 Adrian Peterson 60.00 120.00
A7 Patrick Willis 4.00 10.00
A8 Marshawn Lynch 5.00 12.00
A9 Adam Carriker 2.50 6.00
A10 Lawrence Timmons 4.00 10.00
A11 Jarvis Moss 2.50 6.00
A12 Leon Hall 2.50 6.00
A13 Michael Griffin 2.50 6.00
A14 Aaron Ross 2.50 6.00
A15 Brady Quinn 2.50 6.00
A16 Dwayne Bowe 2.50 6.00
A17 Brandon Meriweather 3.00 8.00
A18 Robert Meachem 3.00 8.00
A19 Craig Buster Davis 2.50 6.00
A20 Greg Olsen 4.00 10.00
A21 Anthony Gonzalez 2.50 6.00
A23 Kevin Kolb 3.00 8.00
A24 Zach Miller 2.50 6.00
A25 John Beck 2.50 6.00
A26 Drew Stanton 2.50 6.00
A27 Sidney Rice 3.00 8.00
A28 LaMarr Woodley 5.00 12.00
A29 Kenny Irons 2.50 6.00
A30 Chris Henry RB 2.50 6.00
A31 Steve Smith USC 2.50 6.00
A32 Brian Leonard 2.50 6.00
A33 Ryan Kalil 2.50 6.00
A34 Yamon Figurs 2.50 6.00
A35 Jason Hill 2.50 6.00
A36 Paul Williams 2.50 6.00
A37 Demarcus Tank Tyler 2.50 6.00
A38 Trent Edwards 2.50 6.00
A39 Garrett Wolfe 2.50 6.00
A40 Johnnie Lee Higgins 2.50 6.00
A41 Michael Bush 2.50 6.00
A42 Isaiah Stanback 2.50 6.00
A43 Antonio Pittman 2.50 6.00
A44 Steve Breaston 2.50 6.00
A45 Aundrae Allison 2.50 6.00
A46 Kolby Smith 2.50 6.00
A47 Jeff Rowe 2.50 6.00
A48 David Clowney 2.50 6.00
A49 Troy Smith 2.50 6.00
A50 Joel Filani 2.50 6.00
A51 David Irons 2.50 6.00
A53 Jordan Palmer 3.00 8.00
A54 Dallas Baker 2.50 6.00
A55 Jason Snelling 2.50 6.00
A56 Kenneth Darby 2.50 6.00

2011 SAGE Five Star

STATED PRINT RUN 50 SER.#'d SETS
SA01 Cam Newton 20.00 50.00
SA02 Von Miller 12.00 30.00
SA03 A.J. Green 10.00 25.00
SA04 Julio Jones 12.00 30.00
SA05 Aldon Smith 4.00 10.00
SA06 Jake Locker 4.00 10.00
SA07 Blaine Gabbert 12.00 30.00
SA08 J.J. Watt 30.00 60.00
SA09 Christian Ponder 4.00 10.00
SA10 Nick Fairley 4.00 10.00
SA11 Ryan Kerrigan 5.00 12.00
SA12 Mark Ingram 6.00 15.00
SA13 Cameron Heyward 8.00 20.00
SA14 Ryan Williams 4.00 10.00
SA15 Shane Vereen 5.00 12.00
SA16 Mikel LeShoure 4.00 10.00
SA17 Daniel Thomas 4.00 10.00
SA18 Randall Cobb 6.00 15.00
SA19 DeMarco Murray 8.00 20.00
SA20 Ryan Mallett 4.00 10.00
SA21 Torrey Smith 4.00 10.00
SA22 Denarius Moore 4.00 10.00
SA23 Terrelle Pryor 6.00 15.00

2011 SAGE Five Star Dual Autographs

STATED PRINT RUN 1-200
A1 R.Williams/R.Housler/15 4.00 10.00
A3 R.Housler/S.Acho/200 2.00 5.00
A4 J.Jones/J.Rodgers/50 8.00 20.00
A5 D.Murray/S.Chapas/200 6.00 15.00
A6 V.Miller/R.Moore/200 8.00 20.00
A8 R.Cobb/D.Williams/200 3.00 8.00
A9 J.Watt/T.Yates/20 25.00 60.00
A12 D.Thomas/E.Gates/200 2.00 5.00
A13 D.Thomas/C.Clay/200 2.00 5.00
A14 E.Gates/C.Clay/200 2.00 5.00
A15 C.Ponder/K.Rudolph/200 20.00 40.00
A16 N.Solder/S.Vereen/200 2.50 6.00
A17 S.Ridley/R.Mallett/15 4.00 10.00
A18 S.Vereen/S.Ridley/200 2.50 6.00
A21 N.Solder/S.Ridley/200 2.00 5.00
A22 C.Chekwa/T.Jones/200 2.50 6.00
A23 C.Chekwa/D.Moore/200 6.00 15.00
A24 T.Jones/D.Moore/200 8.00 20.00
A25 C.Matthews/D.Lewis/200 2.50 6.00
A26 C.Heyward/C.Brown/25 5.00 12.00
A27 M.Gilchrist/J.Todman/25 5.00 12.00
A28 D.Bowers/L.Stocker/200 2.00 5.00
A29 D.Bowers/A.Bradford/200 2.00 5.00
A30 L.Stocker/A.Bradford/200 6.00 15.00
A31 J.Locker/J.Harper/20 4.00 10.00
A32 J.Casey/J.Harper/200 2.00 5.00
A33 M.Ingram/J.Jones/50 20.00 50.00
A34 C.Newton/N.Fairley/100 25.00 60.00
A38 Castonzo/M.Herzlich/200 2.00 5.00
A43 Housler/J.Van Camp/200 2.50 6.00
A44 J.Van Camp/L.Jean/200 2.50 6.00
A48 T.Pryor/C.Chekwa/25 6.00 15.00
A49 Pryor/Sanzenbchr/25 6.00 15.00
A50 Heyward/Sanzen/200 2.50 6.00
A51 C.Matthews/J.Maehl/200 2.00 5.00
A52 S.Paea/J.Rodgers/25 4.00 10.00
A53 L.Stocker/D.Moore/200 8.00 20.00
A55 S.Acho/A.Williams/200 2.00 5.00
A57 C.Brown/A.Williams/20 4.00 10.00
A59 A.Williams/G.Smith/200 2.50 6.00
A60 K.Forbath/R.Moore/200 2.00 5.00
A61 J.Casey/A.Bradford/200 2.00 5.00
A62 D.Sanzenbacher/S.Paea/200 8.00 20.00
A63 K.Forbath/D.Murray/200 4.00 10.00
A67 L.Jean/J.Maehl/200 2.00 5.00
A68 L.Jean/T.Yates/200 2.00 5.00
A69 J.Maehl/T.Yates/200 2.00 5.00
A72 C.Gantt/R.Stanzi/200 2.00 5.00
A74 M.Herzlich/J.Jernigan/200 2.00 5.00
A75 C.Smith/J.Kerley/200 3.00 8.00
A78 C.Newton/J.Locker/50 20.00 50.00
A79 C.Newton/B.Gabbert/50 30.00 80.00
A80 C.Newton/C.Ponder/50 30.00 80.00
A81 J.Locker/C.Ponder/50 4.00 10.00
A82 C.Newton/M.Ingram/100 50.00 100.00
A84 M.Ingram/C.Matthews/200 3.00 8.00
A85 C.Heyward/C.Matthews/200 2.50 6.00
A86 A.Green/J.Jones/50 15.00 40.00
A87 C.Newton/V.Miller/50 50.00 80.00
A88 T.Pryor/D.Moore/50 6.00 15.00
A89 T.Smith/C.Smith/200 2.00 5.00
A90 R.Kerrigan/A.Smith/200 8.00 20.00
A92 J.Kerley/C.Shorts/200 3.00 8.00
A95 J.Kerley/E.Gates/200 3.00 8.00
A98 C.Smith/C.Shorts/200 2.00 5.00
A100 R.Stanzi/T.Potts/200 2.00 5.00
A101 C.Ponder/T.Potts/200 12.00 30.00
A102 R.Stanzi/T.Yates/200 2.00 5.00
A105 J.Todman/D.Lewis/200 2.50 6.00
A106 D.Williams/C.Gantt/200 2.00 5.00
A108 K.Rudolph/C.Gantt/200 2.00 5.00
A109 L.Stocker/C.Gantt/200 2.00 5.00
A110 K.Rudolph/C.Clay/200 2.00 5.00
A111 D.Williams/C.Clay/200 2.00 5.00
A115 R.Cobb/J.Jernigan/200 3.00 8.00
A116 D.Carter/D.Lewis/200 2.50 6.00
A117 D.Carter/J.Todman/200 2.00 5.00
A119 T.Smith/R.Cobb/200 3.00 8.00
A120 T.Smith/J.Jernigan/200 2.00 5.00
A122 V.Miller/A.Smith/25 8.00 20.00
A123 R.Cobb/S.Paea/200 3.00 8.00
A125 C.Heyward/N.Solder/200 2.50 6.00
A126 R.Kerrigan/N.Solder/200 6.00 15.00
A127 R.Kerrigan/M.Herzlich/200 6.00 15.00
A132 J.Jernigan/D.Sanzenbacher/200 2.00 5.00
A133 D.Moore/D.Sanzenbacher/200 8.00 20.00
A135 D.Thomas/S.Vereen/200 2.50 6.00
A136 T.Jones/D.Carter/200 2.00 5.00
A147 C.Newton/R.Cobb/50 30.00 80.00

2011 SAGE Five Star Then and Now Autographs

STATED PRINT RUN 25 SER.#'d SETS
TN1 Da'Quan Bowers 10.00 25.00
TN2 Blaine Gabbert 5.00 12.00
TN3 A.J. Green 12.00 30.00
TN4 Julio Jones 25.00 50.00
TN5 Jake Locker 5.00 12.00
TN6 Ryan Mallett 5.00 12.00
TN7 Cam Newton 25.00 60.00
TN8 Austin Pettis 8.00 20.00
TN9 Terrelle Pryor 8.00 20.00
TN10 Kyle Rudolph 5.00 12.00
TN11 Daniel Thomas 5.00 12.00
TN12 Shane Vereen 6.00 15.00
TN13 Casey Matthews 5.00 12.00
TN14 Allen Bradford 5.00 12.00

2011 SAGE Five Star Triple Autographs

STATED PRINT RUN 1-25
TA1 Newton/Fairley/Fannin/25 60.00 120.00
TA2 Newton/Ingram/Ridley/15 75.00 150.00
TA4 Heywrd/Chkwa/Sanzn/25 15.00 40.00
TA5 Williams/Acho/Brown/25 5.00 12.00
TA6 Williams/Acho/Smith/15 6.00 15.00
TA7 Williams/Brown/Smith/15 8.00 20.00
TA18 Ingrm/LeShure/Thoms/25 8.00 20.00
TA22 Vereen/Ridley/Mallett/25 6.00 15.00
TA23 Chekwa/Jones/Moore/25 15.00 40.00
TA26 Newton/Locker/Gabbert/15 25.00 60.00
TA27 Newton/Locker/Ponder/15 25.00 60.00
TA28 Newton/Gabbert/Ponder/15 75.00 150.00
TA29 Locker/Gabbert/Ponder/15 5.00 12.00
TA30 Matthws/Heywrd/Ingrm/25 8.00 20.00
TA31 Thomas/Gates/Clay/25 5.00 12.00
TA38 Newton/Miller/Green/15 60.00 120.00
TA39 Newton/Ingram/Green/15 75.00 150.00
TA40 Miller/Smith/Watt/25 40.00 80.00
TA46 Miller/Smith/Kerrigan/25 12.00 30.00

2006 SAGE Game Exclusive

This 36-card set was released in July, 2006. This set was issued into the hobby in three-card packs, with an $30.99 SRP, which came six packs to a box. Only a few of the select 2006 rookies were featured in this set, with three base cards per player. All the cards of the player are priced the same.

COMPLETE SET (36) 20.00 40.00
1 Mario Williams .50 1.25
2 Mario Williams .50 1.25
3 Mario Williams .50 1.25
4 Reggie Bush .50 1.25
5 Reggie Bush .50 1.25
6 Reggie Bush .50 1.25
7 Vince Young .30 .75
8 Vince Young .30 .75
9 Vince Young .30 .75
10 D'Brickashaw Ferguson .30 .75
11 D'Brickashaw Ferguson .30 .75
12 D'Brickashaw Ferguson .30 .75
13 Vernon Davis .40 1.00
14 Vernon Davis .40 1.00
15 Vernon Davis .40 1.00
16 Michael Huff .40 1.00
17 Michael Huff .40 1.00
18 Michael Huff .40 1.00
19 Donte Whitner .40 1.00
20 Donte Whitner .40 1.00
21 Donte Whitner .40 1.00
22 Ernie Sims .30 .75
23 Ernie Sims .30 .75
24 Ernie Sims .30 .75
25 Matt Leinart .30 .75
26 Matt Leinart .30 .75
27 Matt Leinart .30 .75
28 Jay Cutler .40 1.00
29 Jay Cutler .40 1.00
30 Jay Cutler .40 1.00
31 R.Bush/M.Leinart .50 1.25
32 Vince Young Champ .30 .75
33 Bush/Leinart/Young .50 1.25
34 Mario Williams #1 .50 1.25
35 Matt Leinart Heisman .30 .75
36 Reggie Bush Heisman .50 1.25

2006 SAGE Game Exclusive Autographs Bronze

UNPRICED ELITE 11 SER.#'d TO 11
UNPRICED ELITE 11 MASTERS SER.#'d TO 1
*GOLD/25: .6X TO 1.5X BRONZE
*SILVER/50: .5X TO 1.2X BRONZE
A1 Mario Williams 5.00 12.00
A2 Reggie Bush 5.00 12.00
A4 D'Brickashaw Ferguson 3.00 8.00
A5 Vernon Davis 4.00 10.00
A6 Michael Huff 4.00 10.00
A7 Donte Whitner 4.00 10.00
A8 Ernie Sims 3.00 8.00
A9 Matt Leinart 3.00 8.00
A10 Jay Cutler 4.00 10.00

2006 SAGE Game Exclusive Jersey Combos Bronze

*GOLD/25: .6X TO 1.5X BRONZE
UNPRICED PLATINUM PRINT RUN 5
*SILVER/50: .5X TO 1.2X BRONZE
CG1 Bush/Leinart Coll 2.00 5.00
CG2 Bush/Young Coll 2.00 5.00
CG3 Leinart/Young Coll 4.00 10.00
CG4 Bush/Leinart NFL 2.00 5.00
CG5 Bush/Young NFL 2.50 6.00
CG6 Leinart/Young NFL 4.00 10.00
LBY1 Bush/Leinart/Young Coll 2.00 5.00
LBY2 Bush/Leinart/Young NFL 2.00 5.00

2006 SAGE Game Exclusive Oversized Jerseys Bronze

UNPRICED ELITE 11 SER.#'d TO 11
UNPRICED ELITE 11 MASTERS SER.#'d TO 1
*GOLD/25: .6X TO 1.5X BRONZE
UNPRICED PLATINUM SER.#'d TO 5
*SILVER/50: .5X TO 1.2X BRONZE
SJ1 Reggie Bush 4.00 10.00
SJ2 Matt Leinart 8.00 20.00
SJ3 Vince Young 10.00 25.00
SJ4 Jay Cutler 8.00 20.00
SJ5 Vernon Davis 5.00 12.00

2006 SAGE Game Exclusive Oversized Jersey Combos Bronze

*GOLD/25: .6X TO 1.5X BRONZE
*SILVER/50: .5X TO 1.2X BRONZF
UNPRICED ELITE 11 SER.#'d TO 11
UNPRICED ELITE 11 MASTERS #'d TO 1
UNPRICED PLATINUM SER.#'d TO 5
CS1 Bush/Leinart 5.00 12.00
CS2 Bush/Young 5.00 12.00
CS3 Bush/Cutler 5.00 12.00
CS4 Bush/Davis 5.00 12.00
CS5 Leinart/Young 8.00 20.00
CS6 Cutler/Leinart 8.00 20.00
CS7 Davis/Leinart 6.00 15.00
CS8 Cutler/Young 10.00 25.00
CS9 Davis/Young 8.00 20.00
CS10 Cutler/Davis 6.00 15.00

2006 SAGE Game Exclusive Matt Leinart Jerseys Bronze

COMMON CARD (1-10) 4.00 10.00
*GOLD/25: .8X TO 2X BRONZE
UNPRICED PLATINUM PRINT RUN 5 SETS
*SILVER/50: .5X TO 1.2X BRONZE
ML10 Matt Leinart Dual 6.00 15.00

2006 SAGE Game Exclusive Reggie Bush Jerseys Bronze

COMMON CARD (1-10) 6.00 15.00
*GOLD/25: .6X TO 1.5X BRONZE
*SILVER/50: .5X TO 1.2X BRONZE
UNPRICED PLATINUM PRINT RUN 5 SETS
RB10 Reggie Bush Dual 10.00 25.00

2006 SAGE Game Exclusive Vince Young Jerseys Bronze

COMMON CARD (1-10) 5.00 12.00
*GOLD/25: .6X TO 1.5X BRONZE
*SILVER/50: .5X TO 1.2X BRONZE
UNPRICED PLATINUM PRINT RUN 5 SETS
VY10 Vince Young Dual 8.00 20.00

2000 SAGE HIT

Released as a 50-card set, Sage HIT features full color player action photos with a green and black border along the bottom of the card only. The SAGE logo appears in the upper right hand corner of the card front. HIT was packaged in 24-pack boxes where packs contained five cards each.

COMPLETE SET (50) 10.00 25.00
1 Jerry Porter .30 .75
2 Tim Couch .25 .60
3 Chris Samuels .30 .75
4 Plaxico Burress .25 .60
5 Michael Wiley .20 .50
6 Thomas Jones .25 .60
7 Chris Redman .20 .50
8 Anthony Lucas .20 .50
9 Kwame Cavil .20 .50
10 Chad Pennington .25 .60
11 LaVar Arrington .40 1.00
12 Giovanni Carmazzi .20 .50
13 Tim Rattay .25 .60
14 Laveranues Coles .25 .60
15 Mario Edwards .20 .50
16 John Engelberger .20 .50
17 Tee Martin .20 .50
18 R.Jay Soward .20 .50
19 Ahmed Plummer .20 .50
20 Na'il Diggs .20 .50
21 J.R. Redmond .20 .50
22 Dez White .20 .50
23 Reuben Droughns .20 .50
24 Sylvester Morris .20 .50
25 Cosey Coleman .20 .50
26 Corey Moore .20 .50
27 Curtis Keaton .20 .50
28 Danny Farmer .20 .50
29 Travis Claridge .20 .50
30 Troy Walters .20 .50
31 Jamal Lewis .30 .75
32 Shaun King .20 .50
33 Ron Dayne .30 .75
34 Keith Bulluck .25 .60
35 Corey Simon .25 .60
36 Deon Dyer .20 .50
37 Shaun Alexander .30 .75
38 Shyrone Stith .20 .50
39 Shaun Ellis .25 .60
40 Todd Pinkston .20 .50
41 Travis Prentice .20 .50
42 Chris Hovan .25 .60
43 Brandon Short .20 .50
44 Brian Urlacher 1.00 2.50
45 Rob Morris .25 .60
46 Raynoch Thompson .20 .50
47 Deon Grant .20 .50
48 Stockar McDougle .20 .50
49 Darren Howard .20 .50
50 Courtney Brown .25 .60

2000 SAGE HIT NRG

COMPLETE SET (50) 20.00 40.00
*NRG: .6X TO 1.5X BASIC CARDS
NRG STATED ODDS 1:1.5

2000 SAGE HIT Autographs Emerald

Randomly inserted in packs at the rate of 1:12, this 49-card set features player action photography with a green section below the image. Within that green section is an authentic player autograph on a silver oval sticker. An Emerald Die-Cut version (1:40 packs) was produced of each card as well as Diamond (1:20 packs) and Diamond Die-Cut (1:100 packs) versions. The overall odds for finding any autographed insert card was 1:6 packs.

EMERALD STATED ODDS 1:12
*EMER.DIE CUT: .6X TO 1.5X EMERALD
EMERALD DIE CUT STATED ODDS 1:40
*DIAMOND: .5X TO 1.2X EMERALD
*DIAM.DIE CUT: .8X TO 2X EMERALD
OVERALL AUTOGRAPH ODDS 1:6
1 Jerry Porter 4.00 10.00
2 Tim Couch 3.00 8.00
3 Chris Samuels 4.00 10.00
4 Plaxico Burress 3.00 8.00
5 Michael Wiley 2.50 6.00
6 Thomas Jones 3.00 8.00
7 Chris Redman 2.50 6.00
8 Anthony Lucas 2.50 6.00
9 Kwame Cavil 2.50 6.00
10 Chad Pennington 3.00 8.00
11 LaVar Arrington 5.00 12.00
12 Giovanni Carmazzi 2.50 6.00
13 Tim Rattay 3.00 8.00
14 Laveranues Coles 3.00 8.00
15 Mario Edwards 2.50 6.00
16 John Engelberger 2.50 6.00
17 Tee Martin 2.50 6.00
18 R.Jay Soward 2.50 6.00
19 Ahmed Plummer 2.50 6.00
20 Na'il Diggs 2.50 6.00
21 J.R. Redmond 2.50 6.00
22 Dez White 2.50 6.00
23 Reuben Droughns 2.50 6.00
24 Sylvester Morris 2.50 6.00
25 Cosey Coleman 2.50 6.00
26 Corey Moore 2.50 6.00
27 Curtis Keaton 2.50 6.00
28 Danny Farmer 2.50 6.00
29 Travis Claridge 2.50 6.00
30 Troy Walters 2.50 6.00
31 Jamal Lewis 4.00 10.00
32 Shaun King 2.50 6.00
33 Ron Dayne 4.00 10.00
35 Corey Simon 3.00 8.00
36 Deon Dyer 2.50 6.00
37 Shaun Alexander 4.00 10.00
38 Shyrone Stith 2.50 6.00
39 Shaun Ellis 3.00 8.00
40 Todd Pinkston 2.50 6.00
41 Travis Prentice 2.50 6.00
42 Chris Hovan 3.00 8.00
43 Brandon Short 2.50 6.00
44 Brian Urlacher 12.00 30.00
45 Rob Morris 3.00 8.00
46 Raynoch Thompson UER 2.50 6.00
47 Deon Grant 2.50 6.00
48 Stockar McDougle 2.50 6.00
49 Darren Howard 2.50 6.00
50 Courtney Brown 3.00 8.00

2000 SAGE HIT Prospectors Emerald

Randomly inserted in packs at the rate of one in 24, this 20-card set features player action shots set against a split color background. The bottom of the background is black, while the top is green. A diamond shape appears centered behind the player on the top half of the card, and a holofoil stamp with the word "Prospector" on it is present along the right side of the card. Emerald versions are sequentially numbered to 999.

COMPLETE SET (20) 30.00 60.00
EMERALD/999 ODDS 1:24
EMERALD PRINT RUN 999
*EMER.DIE CUT/300: .6X TO 1.5X EMERALD
EMERALD DIE CUT/300 ODDS 1:80
EMERALD DIE CUT PRINT RUN 300
*DIAMOND/600: .5X TO 1.2X EMERALD
DIAMOND/600 ODDS 1:40
*DIAM.DIE CUT/100: 1.2X TO 3X EMERALD
DIAMOND DIE CUT/100 ODDS 1:240
UNPRICED SOLITAIRE 1/1 ODDS 1:320
OVERALL PROSPECTOR ODDS 1:12
P1 Shaun Alexander 1.00 2.50
P2 LaVar Arrington 1.25 3.00
P3 Courtney Brown .75 2.00
P4 Plaxico Burress .75 2.00
P5 Giovanni Carmazzi .60 1.50
P6 Tim Couch .75 2.00
P7 Ron Dayne 1.00 2.50
P8 Thomas Jones .75 2.00
P9 Shaun King .60 1.50
P10 Jamal Lewis 1.00 2.50
P11 Tee Martin .60 1.50
P12 Sylvester Morris .60 1.50
P13 Chad Pennington .75 2.00
P14 Jerry Porter 1.00 2.50
P15 Travis Prentice .60 1.50
P16 Tim Rattay .75 2.00
P17 Chris Redman .60 1.50
P18 R.Jay Soward .60 1.50
P19 Dez White .60 1.50
P20 Michael Wiley .60 1.50

2001 SAGE HIT

Released as a 50-card set, Sage HIT features full color player action photos with a white border. The SAGE logo appears in the upper left hand corner of the card front. HIT was packaged in 16-box cases with 24-pack boxes and packs contained five cards each.

COMPLETE SET (50) 10.00 25.00
1 David Terrell .25 .60
2 Jamar Fletcher .20 .50
3 Koren Robinson .25 .60
4 Ken-Yon Rambo .20 .50
5 LaDainian Tomlinson 1.00 2.50
6 Santana Moss .30 .75
7 Michael Vick .50 1.25
8 Steve Hutchinson .50 1.25
9 Robert Ferguson .30 .75
10 Torrance Marshall .20 .50
11 Scotty Anderson .20 .50
12 Derrick Gibson .20 .50
13 Marcus Stroud .25 .60
14 Josh Heupel .30 .75
15 Drew Brees 1.25 3.00
16 Gerard Warren .25 .60
17 Quincy Carter .25 .60
18 Gary Baxter .20 .50
19 Alex Bannister .20 .50
20 Travis Henry .25 .60
21 Andre Dyson .20 .50
22 Deuce McAllister .30 .75
23 Rod Gardner .25 .60
24 Jamie Winborn .25 .60
25 Will Allen .30 .75
26 Kenyatta Walker .20 .50
27 Tim Hasselbeck .25 .60
28 Alge Crumpler .30 .75
29 Michael Bennett .25 .60
30 LaMont Jordan .30 .75
31 Jeff Backus .20 .50
32 Rudi Johnson .30 .75
33 Willie Howard .20 .50
34 Josh Booty .25 .60
35 Todd Heap .25 .60
36 Correll Buckhalter .20 .50
37 Jesse Palmer .25 .60
38 Carlos Polk .20 .50
39 Richard Seymour .30 .75
40 Adam Archuleta .25 .60
41 James Jackson .20 .50
42 Willie Middlebrooks .25 .60
43 Ja'Mar Toombs .20 .50
44 Chris Chambers .20 .50
45 Reggie Germany .20 .50
46 Casey Hampton .30 .75
47 Reggie Wayne .40 1.00
48 Jamal Reynolds .20 .50
49 Justin Smith .40 1.00
50 Quincy Morgan .25 .60

2001 SAGE HIT A-Game

Randomly inserted into packs at a rate of one in 42, this 9-card set feature three different cards of three of the hottest players to come out for the 2001 NFL Draft. These cards were serial numbered to 600 sets.

COMPLETE SET (9) 20.00 50.00
STATED ODDS 1:42
STATED PRINT RUN 600 SER.#'d SETS
1 Drew Brees 2.50 6.00
2 Drew Brees 2.50 6.00
3 Drew Brees 2.50 6.00
4 David Terrell .50 1.25
5 David Terrell .50 1.25
6 David Terrell .50 1.25
7 Michael Vick 1.00 2.50
8 Michael Vick 1.00 2.50
9 Michael Vick 1.00 2.50

2001 SAGE HIT Autographs

Randomly inserted into packs at a rate of one in nine, this 49-card set includes card A51 Fred Smoot in place of A2 Scotty Anderson, it also did not include A16 Gerard Warren. Derrick Gibson, Casey Hampton, James Jackson, and Ja'Mar Toombs were not issued in packs.

STATED ODDS 1:9
*DIE CUT/250: .6X TO 1.5X BASIC AUTO
DIE CUT/250 STATED ODDS 1:26
*FOILBOARD: .5X TO 1.2X BASIC AUTO
FOILBOARD STATED ODDS 1:13
*FOILBOARD DC/100: .8X TO 2X BASIC AU
FOILBOARD DC PRINT RUN 100 #'d SETS
FOILBOARD DIE CUT/100 ODDS 1:64
OVERALL AUTOGRAPH STATED ODDS 1:4
A1 David Terrell 4.00 10.00
A3 Koren Robinson 4.00 10.00
A4 Ken-Yon Rambo 3.00 8.00
A5 LaDainian Tomlinson 12.00 30.00
A6 Santana Moss 5.00 12.00
A7 Michael Vick 8.00 20.00
A8 Steve Hutchinson 8.00 20.00
A9 Robert Ferguson 5.00 12.00
A10 Torrance Marshall 3.00 8.00
A11 Scotty Anderson 3.00 8.00
A12 Derrick Gibson 3.00 8.00
A13 Marcus Stroud 4.00 10.00
A14 Josh Heupel 5.00 12.00
A15 Drew Brees 100.00 200.00
A17 Quincy Carter 4.00 10.00
A18 Gary Baxter 3.00 8.00
A19 Alex Bannister 3.00 8.00
A20 Travis Henry 4.00 10.00
A21 Andre Dyson 3.00 8.00
A22 Deuce McAllister 5.00 12.00
A23 Rod Gardner 4.00 10.00
A24 Jamie Winborn 4.00 10.00
A25 Will Allen 5.00 12.00
A26 Kenyatta Walker 3.00 8.00
A27 Tim Hasselbeck 4.00 10.00
A28 Alge Crumpler 5.00 12.00
A29 Michael Bennett 4.00 10.00
A30 LaMont Jordan 5.00 12.00
A31 Jeff Backus 3.00 8.00
A32 Rudi Johnson 5.00 12.00
A33 Willie Howard 3.00 8.00
A34 Josh Booty 4.00 10.00
A35 Todd Heap 4.00 10.00
A36 Correll Buckhalter 3.00 8.00
A37 Jesse Palmer 4.00 10.00
A38 Carlos Polk 3.00 8.00
A39 Richard Seymour 5.00 12.00
A40 Adam Archuleta 4.00 10.00
A41 James Jackson 3.00 8.00
A42 Willie Middlebrooks 4.00 10.00
A43 Ja'Mar Toombs 3.00 8.00
A44 Chris Chambers 3.00 8.00
A45 Reggie Germany 3.00 8.00
A46 Casey Hampton 6.00 15.00
A47 Reggie Wayne 6.00 15.00
A48 Jamal Reynolds 3.00 8.00
A49 Justin Smith 6.00 15.00
A50 Quincy Morgan 4.00 10.00
A51 Fred Smoot 4.00 10.00

2001 SAGE HIT Jerseys

Randomly inserted at a rate of one in 205 packs, this 9-card set featured the jersey swatch of one of three players. Each player had 3 different cards and the were numbered with a "J" prefix.

STATED ODDS 1:205
STATED PRINT RUN 175 SER.#'d SETS
J1 Michael Vick 5.00 12.00
J2 Michael Vick 5.00 12.00
J3 Michael Vick 5.00 12.00
J4 Drew Brees 12.00 30.00
J5 Drew Brees 12.00 30.00
J6 Drew Brees 12.00 30.00
J7 David Terrell 4.00 10.00
J8 David Terrell 4.00 10.00
J9 David Terrell 4.00 10.00

2001 SAGE HIT Prospectors Emerald

Randomly inserted in packs at the rate of one in 19, this 15-card set features player action shots set against a split color background. The background is black and white , while the front is color. A holofoil stamp with the word Prospectors on it is present along the bottom of the card. Emerald versions are sequentially numbered to 999.

COMPLETE SET (15) 40.00 80.00
STATED ODDS 1:19
EMERALD PRINT RUN 999 SER.#'d SETS
*EMER.DIE CUT/299: .6X TO 1.5X EMERALD
EMERALD DIE CUT/299 ODDS 1:63
EMERALD DC PRINT RUN 299 #'d SETS
*DIAMOND/599: .5X TO 1.2X EMERALD
DIAMOND/599 ODDS 1:32
*DIAM.DIE CUT/99: 1.5X TO 4X EMERALD
DIAMOND DIE CUT/99 ODDS 1:190
P1 Michael Bennett .60 1.50
P2 Drew Brees 3.00 8.00
P3 Quincy Carter .60 1.50
P4 Chris Chambers .50 1.25
P5 Rod Gardner .60 1.50
P6 Josh Heupel .75 2.00
P7 LaMont Jordan .75 2.00
P8 Deuce McAllister .75 2.00
P9 Quincy Morgan .60 1.50
P10 Santana Moss .75 2.00
P11 Koren Robinson .60 1.50
P12 David Terrell .60 1.50
P13 LaDainian Tomlinson 2.50 6.00
P14 Michael Vick 1.25 3.00
P15 Reggie Wayne 1.00 2.50

2001 SAGE HIT Rarefied

RAREFIED BRONZE/2001 ODDS 1:3
BRONZE PRINT RUN 2001 SER.#'d SETS
*SILVER/999: 1.2X TO 3X BASIC CARDS
RAREFIED SILVER/999 ODDS 1:6
SILVER PRINT RUN 999 SERIAL #'d SETS
*GOLD/500: 2.5X TO 6X BASIC CARDS
RAREFIED GOLD/500 ODDS 1:11
GOLD PRINT RUN 500 SERIAL #'d SETS

2002 SAGE HIT

Released as a 50-card set, Sage HIT features full color player action photos with a white border. The SAGE logo appears in the bottom left hand corner of the card front. HIT was packaged in 16-box cases with 24-pack boxes where packs contained five cards each.

COMPLETE SET (47) 10.00 25.00
1 John Henderson .30 .75
2 Tim Carter .30 .75
3 Joey Harrington .25 .60
4 Marquise Walker .25 .60
5 Quentin Jammer .40 1.00
6 Rohan Davey .40 1.00
7A Eric Crouch QB .40 1.00
7B Eric Crouch RB .40 1.00
8 David Carr .25 .60
9 Maurice Morris .30 .75
10 Jabar Gaffney .25 .60
11 David Neill .25 .60
12 Randy Fasani .25 .60
13 Alex Brown .40 1.00
14 J.T. O'Sullivan .30 .75
15 Kurt Kittner .25 .60
16 Ashley Lelie .25 .60
17 Reche Caldwell .30 .75
18 T.J. Duckett .25 .60
19 Chester Taylor .40 1.00
20 Jonathan Wells .30 .75
21 Kelly Campbell .30 .75
22 Bryant McKinnie .25 .60
23 Lito Sheppard .40 1.00
24 Donte Stallworth .40 1.00
25 Josh Reed .30 .75
26 DeShaun Foster .40 1.00
27 Patrick Ramsey .30 .75
28 Clinton Portis .40 1.00
29 Albert Haynesworth .40 1.00
31 Cliff Russell .25 .60
32 Luke Staley .25 .60
33 Ron Johnson .30 .75
34 Travis Stephens .25 .60
35 Chad Hutchinson .25 .60
36 Lamar Gordon .30 .75
37 Larry Tripplett .25 .60
38 Napoleon Harris .30 .75
39 Daniel Graham .30 .75
40 Antonio Bryant .40 1.00
41 Javon Walker .40 1.00
42 Brian Poli-Dixon .25 .60
43 Jeremy Shockey .40 1.00
44 Andre Davis .25 .60
45 Ladell Betts .40 1.00
46 Michael Vick .30 .75
NNO David Carr CL .20 .50

2002 SAGE HIT Rarefied Emerald

COMPLETE SET (45) 25.00 50.00
*EMERALD: .6X TO 1.5X BASIC CARDS
EMERALD STATED ODDS 1:2
R30 Ronald Curry .40 1.00

2002 SAGE HIT Rarefied Silver

COMPLETE SET (45) 40.00 80.00
*SILVER: 1X TO 2.5X BASIC CARDS
SILVER STATED ODDS 1:5
R30 Ronald Curry .60 1.50

2002 SAGE HIT Autographs Emerald

Randomly inserted at a rate of 1 in 8 packs. This 44-card autograph set features hand signed cards of top 2002 NFL draft picks. The cards have a white background with an emerald green inside border. Note the following card numbers do not exist for this set: H13, H24, and H46.

EMERALD STATED ODDS 1:8
*SILVER AU: .5X TO 1.2X EMERALD AU
SILVER AUTO ODDS 1:16
*GOLD AU/250: .6X TO 1.5X EMERALD AU
*GOLD AU/120-130: 1X TO 2.5X EMER
GOLD AUTO/120-250 ODDS 1:22
GOLD AUTO PRINT RUN 120-250
*RAREFIED GOLD/100: 1X TO 2.5X EMERALD
RAREFIED GOLD/100 ODDS 1:55
H1 John Henderson 3.00 8.00
H2 Tim Carter 3.00 8.00
H3 Joey Harrington 2.50 6.00
H4 Marquise Walker 2.50 6.00
H5 Quentin Jammer 4.00 10.00
H6 Rohan Davey 4.00 10.00
H7A Eric Crouch QB 4.00 10.00
H7B Eric Crouch RB 4.00 10.00
H8 David Carr 2.50 6.00
H9 Maurice Morris 3.00 8.00
H10 Jabar Gaffney 2.50 6.00
H11 David Neill 2.50 6.00
H12 Randy Fasani 2.50 6.00
H14 J.T. O'Sullivan 3.00 8.00
H15 Kurt Kittner 2.50 6.00
H16 Ashley Lelie 2.50 6.00
H17 Reche Caldwell 3.00 8.00
H18 T.J. Duckett 2.50 6.00
H19 Chester Taylor 4.00 10.00
H20 Jonathan Wells 3.00 8.00
H21 Kelly Campbell 3.00 8.00
H22 Bryant McKinnie 2.50 6.00
H23 Lito Sheppard 4.00 10.00
H25 Josh Reed 3.00 8.00
H26 DeShaun Foster 4.00 10.00
H27 Patrick Ramsey 3.00 8.00
H28 Clinton Portis 4.00 10.00
H29 Albert Haynesworth 4.00 10.00
H30 Ronald Curry 2.50 6.00
H31 Cliff Russell 2.50 6.00
H32 Luke Staley 2.50 6.00
H33 Ron Johnson 3.00 8.00
H34 Travis Stephens 2.50 6.00
H35 Chad Hutchinson 2.50 6.00
H36 Lamar Gordon 3.00 8.00
H37 Larry Tripplett 2.50 6.00
H38 Napoleon Harris 3.00 8.00
H39 Daniel Graham 3.00 8.00
H40 Antonio Bryant 4.00 10.00
H41 Javon Walker 4.00 10.00
H42 Brian Poli-Dixon 2.50 6.00
H43 Jeremy Shockey 4.00 10.00
H44 Andre Davis 2.50 6.00
H45 Ladell Betts 4.00 10.00

2002 SAGE HIT Jerseys

Randomly inserted at a rate of 1 in 75 packs. This 9 card set features a color action photo on card front along with a game used piece of uniform swatch which is located on bottom right card front outlined in silver foil. Back of card carries a guarantee from Sage as to the uniform swatches authenticity.

STATED ODDS 1:80
*PATCH/25: .8X TO 2X BASIC JSY
PATCH/25 STATED ODDS 1:950
PATCHES PRINT RUN 25 SER.#'d SETS
1 David Carr 4.00 10.00
2 Eric Crouch 8.00 20.00
3 Rohan Davey 6.00 15.00
4 T.J. Duckett 4.00 10.00
5 DeShaun Foster 6.00 15.00
6 Joey Harrington 4.00 10.00
7 Kurt Kittner 4.00 10.00
8 Clinton Portis 6.00 15.00
9 Patrick Ramsey 5.00 12.00

2002 SAGE HIT Write Stuff

Randomly inserted in packs at a rate of one in 20 packs, This 15 card set features a light brown background with a small color action photo on card front with a larger black and with action silhouette in background. Card front also has the words "The Write Stuff" written in silver foil.

COMPLETE SET (15) 12.00 30.00
STATED ODDS 1:20
1 Antonio Bryant 1.00 2.50
2 David Carr .60 1.50
3 Eric Crouch 1.00 2.50
4 Rohan Davey 1.00 2.50
5 T.J. Duckett .60 1.50
6 DeShaun Foster 1.00 2.50
7 Jabar Gaffney .60 1.50
8 Joey Harrington .60 1.50
9 Chad Hutchinson .60 1.50
10 Kurt Kittner .60 1.50
11 Ashley Lelie .60 1.50
12 Clinton Portis 1.00 2.50
13 Patrick Ramsey .75 2.00
14 Josh Reed .75 2.00
15 Michael Vick .75 2.00

2003 SAGE HIT

Released in April 2003, this set consists of 48-cards. Each box contained 30 packs of 5 cards. On average, each box contained nine autographs and one jersey card.

COMPLETE SET (48) 10.00 25.00
1 Charles Rogers .30 .75
2 Willis McGahee .30 .75
3 Arnaz Battle .40 1.00
4 Terence Newman .40 1.00
5 Larry Johnson .30 .75
6 Taylor Jacobs .25 .60
7 Kyle Boller .25 .60
8 Rex Grossman .30 .75
9 Jerome McDougle .25 .60
10 Jason Witten 1.00 2.50
11 Ken Dorsey .30 .75
12 Justin Gage .30 .75
13 Andy Groom .25 .60
14 Seneca Wallace .30 .75
15 Dave Ragone .25 .60
16 Kliff Kingsbury .40 1.00
17 Jason Gesser .30 .75
18 George Wrighster .25 .60
19 Ronald Bellamy .30 .75
20 Donnie Nickey .25 .60
21 Billy McMullen .25 .60
22 Lee Suggs .25 .60
23 Chris Brown .25 .60
24 Bryant Johnson .40 1.00
25 Justin Fargas .40 1.00
26 Brandon Lloyd .40 1.00
27 Tyrone Calico .25 .60
28 Sam Aiken .30 .75
29 Cie Grant .30 .75
30 Dahrran Diedrick .25 .60
31 Kelley Washington .25 .60
32 Musa Smith .25 .60
33 Kevin Curtis .25 .60
34 Terry Pierce .25 .60
35 Matt Wilhelm .30 .75
36 Rashean Mathis .25 .60
37 Brad Banks .30 .75
38 Tully Banta-Cain .40 1.00
39 Sammy Davis .30 .75
40 Teyo Johnson .30 .75
41 Chris Simms .25 .60
42 E.J. Henderson .30 .75
43 Terrell Suggs .30 .75
44 Dallas Clark .40 1.00
45 Marcus Trufant .30 .75
46 Boss Bailey .30 .75
47 David Carr .25 .60
NNO Charles Rogers CL .25 .60

2003 SAGE HIT Autographs Emerald

Inserted at a stated rate of one in six, this 45-card set features authentic autographs of most of the players featured in the SAGE HIT set.

EMERALD STATED ODDS 1:6
*GOLD/250: .6X TO 1.5X EMERALD
GOLD AUTO/250 ODDS 1:25
*SILVER: .5X TO 1.2X EMERALD
SILVER AUTO ODDS 1:9
A1 Charles Rogers 3.00 8.00
A2 Willis McGahee 3.00 8.00
A3 Arnaz Battle 4.00 10.00
A4 Terence Newman 4.00 10.00
A5 Larry Johnson 3.00 8.00
A6 Taylor Jacobs 2.50 6.00
A7 Kyle Boller 2.50 6.00
A8 Rex Grossman 3.00 8.00
A9 Jerome McDougle 2.50 6.00
A10 Jason Witten 12.00 30.00
A11 Ken Dorsey 3.00 8.00
A12 Justin Gage 3.00 8.00
A13 Andy Groom 2.50 6.00
A14 Seneca Wallace 3.00 8.00
A15 Dave Ragone 2.50 6.00
A16 Kliff Kingsbury 4.00 10.00
A17 Jason Gesser 3.00 8.00
A18 George Wrighster 2.50 6.00
A19 Ronald Bellamy 3.00 8.00
A20 Donnie Nickey 2.50 6.00
A21 Billy McMullen 2.50 6.00
A22 Lee Suggs 2.50 6.00
A23 Chris Brown 2.50 6.00
A24 Bryant Johnson 4.00 10.00
A25 Justin Fargas 4.00 10.00
A26 Brandon Lloyd 4.00 10.00
A27 Tyrone Calico 2.50 6.00
A28 Sam Aiken 3.00 8.00
A29 Cie Grant 3.00 8.00
A30 Dahrran Diedrick 2.50 6.00
A32 Musa Smith 2.50 6.00
A33 Kevin Curtis 2.50 6.00
A34 Terry Pierce 2.50 6.00
A35 Matt Wilhelm 3.00 8.00
A36 Rashean Mathis 2.50 6.00
A37 Brad Banks 3.00 8.00
A38 Tully Banta-Cain 4.00 10.00
A39 Sammy Davis 3.00 8.00
A40 Teyo Johnson 3.00 8.00
A41 Chris Simms 2.50 6.00
A42 E.J. Henderson 3.00 8.00
A43 Terrell Suggs 3.00 8.00
A44 Dallas Clark 4.00 10.00
A45 Marcus Trufant 3.00 8.00
A46 Boss Bailey 3.00 8.00

2003 SAGE HIT Class of 2003 Autographs

*CLASS AU/100: .8X TO 2X EMERALD AU
A31 Kelley Washington 10.00 25.00
A47 David Carr

2003 SAGE HIT Class of 2003 Emerald

COMPLETE SET (46) 25.00 50.00
*EMERALD: .8X TO 2X BASIC CARDS
EMERALD STATED ODDS 1:3

2003 SAGE HIT Class of 2003 Silver

COMPLETE SET (46) 30.00 60.00
*SILVER: 1X TO 2.5X BASIC CARDS
SILVER STATED ODDS 1:5

2003 SAGE HIT Jerseys

Randomly inserted into packs, this 12-card set features not only leading NFL prospects but also include a game-used jersey swatch.
*PREMIUM SWATCH/50: .8X TO 2X
PREMIUM SWATCH/50 ODDS 1:460
HJ1 Brad Banks 4.00 10.00
HJ2 Kyle Boller 3.00 8.00
HJ3 Ken Dorsey 4.00 10.00
HJ4 Rex Grossman 4.00 10.00
HJ5 Taylor Jacobs 3.00 8.00
HJ6 Larry Johnson 4.00 10.00
HJ7 Willis McGahee 4.00 10.00
HJ8 Dave Ragone 3.00 8.00
HJ9 Charles Rogers 4.00 10.00
HJ10 Chris Simms 3.00 8.00
HJ11 Lee Suggs 3.00 8.00
HJ12 Kelley Washington 3.00 8.00

2003 SAGE HIT Write Stuff

Inserted at a stated rate of one in 15, this 15-card insert set features players who were offensive stars in College.
COMPLETE SET (15) 12.00 30.00
STATED ODDS 1:15
1 Charles Rogers .75 2.00
2 Willis McGahee .75 2.00
3 Justin Fargas 1.00 2.50
4 Lee Suggs .60 1.50
5 Larry Johnson .75 2.00
6 Kliff Kingsbury 1.00 2.50
7 Kyle Boller .60 1.50
8 Rex Grossman .75 2.00
9 Seneca Wallace .75 2.00
10 Chris Simms .60 1.50
11 Ken Dorsey .75 2.00
12 Chris Brown .60 1.50
13 Musa Smith .60 1.50
14 Brad Banks .75 2.00
15 Dave Ragone .60 1.50

2003 SAGE HIT Write Stuff Autographs

Inserted at a stated rate of one in 720, this is a parallel to the Write Stuff insert set. Each of these cards was sequentially serial to 25 and feature a holographic sticker featuring an authentic signature.
WRITE STUFF AU/25 ODDS 1:720
WSA1 Charles Rogers 12.00 30.00
WSA2 Willis McGahee 12.00 30.00
WSA3 Justin Fargas 15.00 40.00
WSA4 Lee Suggs 10.00 25.00
WSA5 Larry Johnson 12.00 30.00
WSA6 Kliff Kingsbury 15.00 40.00
WSA7 Kyle Boller 10.00 25.00
WSA8 Rex Grossman 12.00 30.00
WSA9 Seneca Wallace 12.00 30.00
WSA10 Chris Simms 10.00 25.00
WSA11 Ken Dorsey 12.00 30.00
WSA12 Chris Brown 10.00 25.00
WSA13 Musa Smith 10.00 25.00
WSA14 Brad Banks 12.00 30.00
WSA15 Dave Ragone 10.00 25.00
WSA16 David Carr 12.00 30.00

2004 SAGE HIT

The SAGE HIT product was the first 2004 football card set on the market. It released in mid to late April 2004. The base set consists of 46-cards including an unnumbered Eli Manning checklist card. Maurice Clarett made an appearance in this product although he was declared ineligible for the NFL Draft. Boxes contained 30-packs of 5-cards. A variety of inserts can be found seeded in packs highlighted by the Autographs parallel sets. Two different special retail boxes were produced for Ohio State and the SEC which featured insert sets exclusive to those packs. Note that Craig Krenzel and Rex Grossman appear in the Autograph sets only.
COMPLETE SET (46) 12.50 30.00
1 Reggie Williams .25 .60
2 Bernard Berrian .25 .60
3 Lee Evans .40 1.00
4 Roy Williams WR .25 .60
5 Josh Harris .25 .60
6 Greg Jones .25 .60
7 Ben Roethlisberger 2.00 5.00
8 Drew Carter .30 .75
9 Devery Henderson .25 .60
10 Eli Manning 2.00 5.00
11 Karlos Dansby .30 .75
12 Michael Jenkins .25 .60
13 Maurice Clarett .30 .75
14 Michael Clayton .30 .75
15 Casey Clausen .30 .75
16 John Navarre .25 .60
17 Philip Rivers .75 2.00
18 Jeff Smoker .30 .75
19 Ernest Wilford .30 .75
20 Derrick Knight .25 .60
21 Chris Gamble .25 .60
22 Jared Lorenzen .30 .75
23 Chris Perry .25 .60
24 Rod Rutherford .25 .60
25 Kevin Jones .30 .75
26 Michael Boulware .40 1.00
27 Tatum Bell .25 .60
28 Will Poole .40 1.00
29 Jake Grove .25 .60
30 Ell Roberson .40 1.00
31 Devard Darling .25 .60
32 Dunta Robinson .25 .60
33 Cody Pickett .25 .60
34 Steven Jackson .40 1.00
35 Matt Schaub .25 .60
36 Sean Jones .25 .60
37 Tommie Harris .30 .75
38 Chris Collins .25 .60
39 Will Smith .30 .75
40 DeAngelo Hall .40 1.00
41 Rashaun Woods .25 .60
42 Ben Troupe .25 .60
43 Quincy Wilson .25 .60
44 P.K. Sam .25 .60
45 Clarence Farmer .25 .60
NNO Eli Manning CL 1.00 2.50
EM Eli Manning SEC/30 20.00 50.00

2004 SAGE HIT Autographs Emerald

STATED ODDS 1:10
*SILVER: .5X TO 1.2X EMERALD AU
SILVER AUTO ODDS 1:18
A1 Reggie Williams 2.50 6.00
A2 Bernard Berrian 2.50 6.00
A3 Lee Evans 4.00 10.00
A4 Roy Williams WR SP 2.50 6.00
A5 Josh Harris 2.50 6.00
A6 Greg Jones 2.50 6.00
A7 Ben Roethlisberger 20.00 50.00
A8 Drew Carter 3.00 8.00
A9 Devery Henderson 2.50 6.00
A10 Eli Manning 30.00 60.00
A11 Karlos Dansby 3.00 8.00
A12 Michael Jenkins 2.50 6.00
A13 Maurice Clarett SP 12.50 30.00
A14 Michael Clayton 3.00 8.00
A15 Casey Clausen 3.00 8.00
A16 John Navarre 2.50 6.00
A17 Philip Rivers 10.00 25.00
A18 Jeff Smoker 3.00 8.00
A19 Ernest Wilford 3.00 8.00
A20 Derrick Knight 2.50 6.00
A21 Olvis Gamble 2.50 6.00
A22 Jared Lorenzen 3.00 8.00
A23 Chris Perry 2.50 6.00
A24 Rod Rutherford 2.50 6.00
A25 Kevin Jones 3.00 8.00
A26 Michael Boulware 4.00 10.00
A27 Tatum Bell 2.50 6.00
A28 Will Poole 4.00 10.00
A29 Jake Grove 2.50 6.00
A30 Ell Roberson SP
A31 Devard Darling 2.50 6.00
A32 Dunta Robinson 2.50 6.00
A33 Cody Pickett 2.50 6.00
A35 Matt Schaub 2.50 6.00
A36 Sean Jones 2.50 6.00
A37 Tommie Harris 3.00 8.00
A38 Chris Collins 2.50 6.00
A39 Will Smith 3.00 8.00
A40 DeAngelo Hall 4.00 10.00
A41 Rashaun Woods 2.50 6.00
A42 Ben Troupe 2.50 6.00
A43 Quincy Wilson 2.50 6.00
A44 P.K. Sam 2.50 6.00
A46 Craig Krenzel SP
A47 Rex Grossman 2.50 6.00

2004 SAGE HIT Autographs Gold

*GOLD: .6X TO 1.5X EMERALD AU
GOLD/250 ODDS 1:30
GOLD PRINT RUN 250 SER.#'d SETS
A30 Ell Roberson SP 10.00 25.00
A46 Craig Krenzel 10.00 25.00

2004 SAGE HIT Inside the Numbers Silver

*EMERALD: .4X TO 1X SILVERS
*GOLD: .4X TO 1X SILVERS
OVERALL STATED ODDS 1:14
1 Pittsburgh Wide Receiver 1.25 3.00
2 USC Wide Receiver .75 2.00
3 Mississippi Quarterback 2.50 6.00
4 USC Quarterback 1.00 2.50
5 Ohio St. Running Back .75 2.00
6 Oklahoma Quarterback 1.00 2.50
7 Auburn Running Back 1.00 2.50
8 Texas Running Back 1.00 2.50
9 Kansas St. Running Back 1.00 2.50

2004 SAGE HIT Jerseys

STATED ODDS 1:31
*PREM.SWATCH/50: .8X TO 2X
PREMUIM SWATCH PRINT RUN 50
JBR Ben Roethlisberger 12.00 30.00
JCC Casey Clausen 4.00 10.00
JCP Chris Perry 3.00 8.00
JEM Eli Manning 12.00 30.00
JER Ell Roberson 5.00 12.00
JGJ Greg Jones 3.00 8.00
JJL Jared Lorenzen 4.00 10.00
JJN John Navarre 3.00 8.00
JKJ Kevin Jones 4.00 10.00
JLE Lee Evans 5.00 12.00
JMC Maurice Clarett 4.00 10.00
JMJ Michael Jenkins 3.00 8.00
JPR Philip Rivers 10.00 25.00
JRE Reggie Williams 3.00 8.00
JRO Roy Williams WR 3.00 8.00
JRW Rashaun Woods 3.00 8.00
JTB Tatum Bell 3.00 8.00

2004 SAGE HIT Ohio State Autographs

INSERTS IN SPECIAL OHIO STATE BOXES
STATED PRINT RUN 50 SER.#'d SETS
OA1 Drew Carter 12.00 30.00
OA2 Maurice Clarett 15.00 40.00
OA3 Chris Gamble 10.00 25.00
OA4 Michael Jenkins 10.00 25.00
OA5 Craig Krenzel 10.00 25.00
OA6 Will Smith 12.00 30.00

2004 SAGE HIT Q&A Autographs

STATED ODDS 1:70
STATED PRINT RUN 100 SER.#'d SETS
QA1 Reggie Williams 5.00 12.00
QA2 Bernard Berrian 5.00 12.00
QA3 Lee Evans 8.00 20.00
QA4 Roy Williams WR 5.00 12.00
QA5 Josh Harris 5.00 12.00
QA6 Greg Jones 5.00 12.00
QA7 Ben Roethlisberger 50.00 100.00
QA8 Drew Carter 6.00 15.00
QA9 Devery Henderson 5.00 12.00
QA10 Eli Manning 50.00 100.00
QA11 Karlos Dansby 6.00 15.00
QA12 Michael Jenkins 5.00 12.00
QA13 Maurice Clarett 6.00 15.00
QA14 Michael Clayton 6.00 15.00
QA15 Casey Clausen 6.00 15.00
QA16 John Navarre 5.00 12.00
QA17 Philip Rivers 20.00 50.00
QA18 Jeff Smoker 6.00 15.00
QA19 Ernest Wilford 6.00 15.00
QA20 Derrick Knight 5.00 12.00
QA21 Chris Gamble 5.00 12.00
QA22 Jared Lorenzen 6.00 15.00
QA23 Chris Perry 5.00 12.00
QA24 Rod Rutherford 5.00 12.00
QA25 Kevin Jones 6.00 15.00
QA26 Michael Boulware 8.00 20.00
QA27 Tatum Bell 5.00 12.00
QA28 Will Poole 8.00 20.00
QA29 Jake Grove 5.00 12.00
QA30 Ell Roberson SP
QA31 Devard Darling 5.00 12.00
QA32 Dunta Robinson 5.00 12.00
QA33 Cody Pickett 5.00 12.00
QA35 Matt Schaub 12.00 30.00
QA36 Sean Jones 5.00 12.00
QA37 Tommie Harris 6.00 15.00
QA38 Chris Collins 5.00 12.00
QA39 Will Smith 6.00 15.00
QA40 DeAngelo Hall 8.00 20.00
QA41 Rashaun Woods 5.00 12.00
QA42 Ben Troupe 5.00 12.00
QA43 Quincy Wilson 5.00 12.00
QA44 P.K. Sam 5.00 12.00
QA46 Craig Krenzel 5.00 12.00

2004 SAGE HIT Q&A Emerald

COMPLETE SET (46) 20.00 50.00
STATED ODDS 1:2
*SILVER: .5X TO 1.2X EMERALD
SILVER STATED ODDS 1:5
Q1 Reggie Williams .30 .75
Q2 Bernard Berrian .30 .75
Q3 Lee Evans .50 1.25
Q4 Roy Williams WR .30 .75
Q5 Josh Harris .30 .75
Q6 Greg Jones .30 .75
Q7 Ben Roethlisberger 2.50 6.00
Q8 Drew Carter .40 1.00
Q9 Devery Henderson .30 .75
Q10 Eli Manning 2.50 6.00
Q11 Karlos Dansby .40 1.00
Q12 Michael Jenkins .30 .75
Q13 Maurice Clarett .40 1.00
Q14 Michael Clayton .40 1.00
Q15 Casey Clausen .40 1.00
Q16 John Navarre .30 .75
Q17 Philip Rivers 1.00 2.50
Q18 Jeff Smoker .40 1.00
Q19 Ernest Wilford .40 1.00
Q20 Derrick Knight .30 .75
Q21 Chris Gamble .30 .75
Q22 Jared Lorenzen .40 1.00
Q23 Chris Perry .30 .75
Q24 Rod Rutherford .30 .75
Q25 Kevin Jones .40 1.00
Q26 Michael Boulware .50 1.25
Q27 Tatum Bell .30 .75
Q28 Will Poole .50 1.25
Q29 Jake Grove .30 .75
Q30 Ell Roberson .50 1.25
Q31 Devard Darling .30 .75
Q32 Dunta Robinson .30 .75
Q33 Cody Pickett .30 .75
Q34 Steven Jackson .50 1.25
Q35 Matt Schaub .30 .75
Q36 Sean Jones .30 .75
Q37 Tommie Harris .40 1.00
Q38 Chris Collins .30 .75
Q39 Will Smith .40 1.00
Q40 DeAngelo Hall .50 1.25
Q41 Rashaun Woods .30 .75
Q42 Ben Troupe .30 .75
Q43 Quincy Wilson .30 .75
Q44 P.K. Sam .30 .75
Q45 Clarence Farmer .30 .75
Q46 Craig Krenzel .30 .75

2004 SAGE HIT SEC Autographs

INSERTS IN SPECIAL SEC BOXES
STATED PRINT RUN 50 SER.#'d SETS
S1 Karlos Dansby 12.00 30.00
S2 Ben Troupe 10.00 25.00
S3 Sean Jones 10.00 25.00
S4 Michael Clayton UER 12.00 30.00
S5 Devery Henderson 10.00 25.00
S6 Jared Lorenzen 12.00 30.00
S7 Chris Collins 10.00 25.00
S8 Eli Manning 100.00 175.00
S9 Dunta Robinson 10.00 25.00
S10 Casey Clausen 12.00 30.00

2004 SAGE HIT Write Stuff

COMPLETE SET (15) 15.00 40.00
STATED ODDS 1:15
1 Eli Manning 4.00 10.00
2 Ben Roethlisberger 4.00 10.00
3 Philip Rivers 1.50 4.00
4 Matt Schaub .50 1.25
5 John Navarre .50 1.25
6 Cody Pickett .50 1.25
7 Roy Williams WR .50 1.25
8 Reggie Williams .50 1.25
9 Lee Evans .75 2.00
10 Rashaun Woods .50 1.25
11 Michael Clayton .60 1.50
12 Greg Jones .50 1.25
13 Maurice Clarett .60 1.50
14 Chris Perry .50 1.25
15 Kevin Jones .60 1.50

2004 SAGE HIT Write Stuff Autographs

STATED ODDS 1:845
STATED PRINT RUN 25 SER.#'d SETS
WSA1 Eli Manning 100.00 175.00
WSA2 Ben Roethlisberger 75.00 150.00
WSA3 Philip Rivers 40.00 100.00
WSA4 Matt Schaub 25.00 60.00
WSA5 John Navarre 12.00 30.00
WSA6 Cody Pickett 12.00 30.00
WSA7 Roy Williams WR 12.00 30.00
WSA8 Reggie Williams 12.00 30.00
WSA9 Lee Evans 20.00 50.00
WSA10 Rashaun Woods 12.00 30.00
WSA11 Michael Clayton 15.00 40.00
WSA12 Greg Jones 12.00 30.00
WSA13 Maurice Clarett 15.00 40.00
WSA14 Chris Perry 12.00 30.00
WSA15 Kevin Jones 15.00 40.00

2005 SAGE HIT

SAGE HIT was initially released in mid-April 2005 as the first football card release of the year. The base set consists of 50-cards including 11-short printed cards. Hobby boxes contained 30-packs of 5-cards and carried an S.R.P. of $3.99 per pack. A variety of inserts can be found seeded in packs highlighted by the multi-tiered Autograph and Reflect Gold Autograph inserts.
COMPLETE SET (50) 10.00 25.00
1 Craphonso Thorpe .25 .60
2 Derrick Johnson .30 .75
3 Frank Gore SP .60 1.50
4 Ciatrick Fason .25 .60
5 Charlie Frye .25 .60
6 Antrel Rolle .40 1.00
7 Dan Orlovsky .25 .60
8 Aaron Rodgers 3.00 8.00
9 Mark Clayton .25 .60
10 Thomas Davis .25 .60
11 Alex Smith QB 1.00 2.50
12 Fred Gibson SP .30 .75
13 Maurice Clarett SP .40 1.00
14 David Greene .25 .60
15 Carlos Rogers .40 1.00
16 Andrew Walter .25 .60
17 Jason Campbell .25 .60
18 Jason White .40 1.00
19 Matt Jones .25 .60
20 Marion Barber SP .30 .75
21 Taylor Stubblefield .25 .60
22 Jammal Brown SP .50 1.25
23 Ronnie Brown .30 .75
24 Cadillac Williams .25 .60
25 Kay-Jay Harris .25 .60
26 Reggie Brown .25 .60
27 Troy Williamson .25 .60
28 Anthony Davis .25 .60
29 Josh Davis SP .30 .75
30 J.J. Arrington .30 .75
31 Alex Smith TE .25 .60
32 Corey Webster SP .40 1.00
33 Vernand Morency .30 .75
34 Derek Anderson .30 .75
35 DeMarcus Ware SP 1.00 2.50
36 Kyle Orton .25 .60
37 Brock Berlin .25 .60
38 Marlin Jackson .25 .60
39 Channing Crowder .30 .75
40 Roddy White .40 1.00
41 Roscoe Parrish .25 .60
42 Adrian McPherson .25 .60
43 Brodney Pool .40 1.00
44 T.A. McLendon .25 .60
45 Terrence Murphy .25 .60
46 Chris Rix .30 .75
47 Ben Roethlisberger SP .75 2.00
48 Dante Ridgeway SP .30 .75
49 Justin Miller .25 .60
50 Johnathan Goddard SP .40 1.00
ROY Roethlisberger ROY/100 7.50 20.00

2005 SAGE HIT ACC Autographs

STATED PRINT RUN 50 SER.#'d SETS
ACC2 T.A. McLendon 8.00 20.00
ACC3 Frank Gore 30.00 60.00
ACC4 Roscoe Parrish 10.00 25.00
ACC5 Brock Berlin 10.00 25.00
ACC6 Justin Miller 8.00 20.00
ACC7 Chris Rix 8.00 20.00
ACC8 Craphonso Thorpe 8.00 20.00
ACC9 Adrian McPherson 10.00 25.00

2005 SAGE HIT Autographs Blue

BLUE AUTO STATED ODDS 1:10
*GOLD: .6X TO 1.5X BLUE AUTO
*GOLD: .5X TO 1.2X BLUE SP AUTO
GOLD PRINT RUN 250 SER.#'d SETS
GOLD AUTO STATED ODDS 1:30
*SILVER: .5X TO 1.2X BLUE AUTO
*SILVER: .4X TO 1X BLUE SP AUTO
SILVER AUTO STATED ODDS 1:18
1 Craphonso Thorpe 3.00 8.00
2 Derrick Johnson 4.00 10.00
3 Frank Gore 6.00 15.00
4 Ciatrick Fason 3.00 8.00
5 Charlie Frye 3.00 8.00
7 Dan Orlovsky 3.00 8.00
8 Aaron Rodgers SP 50.00 120.00
9 Mark Clayton 3.00 8.00
10 Thomas Davis 3.00 8.00
11 Alex Smith QB SP 15.00 40.00
12 Fred Gibson 3.00 8.00
14 David Greene 3.00 8.00
15 Carlos Rogers 5.00 12.00
16 Andrew Walter 3.00 8.00
17 Jason Campbell 3.00 8.00
18 Jason White 5.00 12.00
19 Matt Jones 3.00 8.00
20 Marion Barber 3.00 8.00
21 Taylor Stubblefield 3.00 8.00
22 Jammal Brown 5.00 12.00
23 Ronnie Brown 4.00 10.00
24 Cadillac Williams 3.00 8.00
25 Kay-Jay Harris 3.00 8.00
26 Reggie Brown 3.00 8.00
27 Troy Williamson 3.00 8.00
28 Anthony Davis 3.00 8.00
29 Josh Davis 3.00 8.00
30 J.J. Arrington 4.00 10.00
31 Alex Smith TE 3.00 8.00
32 Corey Webster 4.00 10.00
33 Vernand Morency 4.00 10.00
34 Derek Anderson SP 5.00 12.00
35 Demarcus Ware 10.00 25.00
36 Kyle Orton 3.00 8.00
37 Brock Berlin SP 4.00 10.00
38 Marlin Jackson 3.00 8.00
39 Channing Crowder 4.00 10.00
41 Roscoe Parrish 3.00 8.00
42 Adrian McPherson 3.00 8.00
43 Brodney Pool 5.00 12.00
44 T.A. McLendon 3.00 8.00
45 Terrence Murphy 3.00 8.00
46 Chris Rix SP 5.00 12.00
48 Dante Ridgeway 3.00 8.00
49 Justin Miller 3.00 8.00
50 Johnathan Goddard 4.00 10.00

2005 SAGE HIT Ben Roethlisberger

COMPLETE SET (36) 20.00 50.00
COMMON CARD (1-36) 1.00 2.50
ONE PER MAC SPECIAL PACK

2005 SAGE HIT Jerseys

STATED ODDS 1:31
*PREMIUM SWATCH: 1X TO 2.5X BASIC JSY
*PREMIUM SWATCH: .5X TO 1.2X SP JSY
PREMIUM SWATCH STATED ODDS 1:540
PREMIUM SWATCH PRINT RUN 50 SETS
AD Anthony Davis 2.50 6.00
AM Adrian McPherson 2.50 6.00
AR Aaron Rodgers 15.00 40.00
AS Alex Smith QB 12.00 30.00
AW Andrew Walter 2.50 6.00
BR Ben Roethlisberger SP 10.00 25.00
CF Ciatrick Fason 2.50 6.00
CR Chris Rix 3.00 8.00
CW Cadillac Williams 8.00 20.00
DG David Greene 2.50 6.00
DO Dan Orlovsky 2.50 6.00
JA J.J. Arrington 3.00 8.00
JC Jason Campbell 2.50 6.00
JW Jason White 4.00 10.00
KO Kyle Orton 2.50 6.00
MC Mark Clayton 2.50 6.00
MO Maurice Clarett SP 2.50 6.00
RB Ronnie Brown 12.00 30.00
RP Roscoe Parrish 2.50 6.00
VM Vernand Morency 2.50 6.00

2005 SAGE HIT MAC Autographs

STATED PRINT RUN 50 SER.#'d SETS
MAC2 Charlie Frye 10.00 25.00
MAC3 Johnathan Goddard 8.00 20.00
MAC4 Josh Davis 8.00 20.00
MAC5 Dante Ridgeway 8.00 20.00

2005 SAGE HIT Reflect Blue

COMPLETE SET (55) 20.00 50.00
*REFLECT BLUE: .6X TO 1.5X BASIC CARDS
*REFLECT BLUE: .5X TO 1.2X BASIC SP's
*REFLECT BLUE SP's: .8X TO 2X BASIC CARDS
OVERALL REFLECT ODDS 1:1.5
R51 Michigan RB #20 SP 1.50 4.00
R52 Oklahoma RB #28 SP 2.50 6.00
R53 Texas QB #10 UER SP 2.50 6.00
R54 USC RB #5 SP 2.50 6.00
R55 USC QB #11 SP 2.50 6.00

2005 SAGE HIT Reflect Silver

COMPLETE SET (55) 20.00 50.00
*REFLECT SILVER: .6X TO 1.5X BASIC CARDS
*REFLECT SILVER: .5X TO 1.2X BASIC SP's
*REFLECT SILV.SP's: .8X TO 2X BASIC CARDS
OVERALL REFLECT ODDS 1:1.5
R51 Michigan RB #20 SP 1.50 4.00
R52 Oklahoma RB #28 SP 2.50 6.00
R53 Texas QB #10 SP 2.50 6.00
R54 USC RB #5 SP 2.50 6.00
R55 USC QB #11 SP 2.50 6.00

2005 SAGE HIT Reflect Gold Autographs

*REFLECT GOLD: .8X TO 2X BLUE AUTO
*REFLECT GOLD: .6X TO 1.5X BLUE SP AUTO
REFLECT GOLD/100 ODDS 1:70

2005 SAGE HIT SEC Autographs

STATED PRINT RUN 50 SER.#'d SETS
SEC2 Cadillac Williams 20.00 50.00
SEC3 Ronnie Brown 30.00 80.00
SEC4 Jason Campbell 15.00 40.00
SEC5 Carlos Rogers 10.00 25.00
SEC6 David Greene 8.00 20.00
SEC7 Reggie Brown 10.00 25.00
SEC8 Fred Gibson 8.00 20.00
SEC9 Thomas Davis 8.00 20.00
SEC10 Troy Williamson 10.00 25.00
SEC11 Matt Jones 12.00 30.00
SEC12 Corey Webster 10.00 25.00
SEC13 Ciatrick Fason 8.00 20.00
SEC14 Channing Crowder 8.00 20.00

2005 SAGE HIT Write Stuff

COMPLETE SET (15) 15.00 40.00
STATED ODDS 1:15
1 Ronnie Brown .60 1.50
2 Jason Campbell .50 1.25
3 Mark Clayton .50 1.25
4 Ciatrick Fason .50 1.25
5 Charlie Frye .50 1.25
6 David Greene .50 1.25
7 Derrick Johnson .60 1.50
8 Dan Orlovsky .50 1.25
9 Kyle Orton .50 1.25
10 Aaron Rodgers 6.00 15.00
11 Alex Smith QB 2.00 5.00
12 Andrew Walter .50 1.25
13 Jason White .75 2.00
14 Cadillac Williams .50 1.25
15 Troy Williamson .50 1.25

2005 SAGE HIT Write Stuff Autographs

WS AU/25 ODDS 1:845
WSA1 Ronnie Brown 15.00 40.00
WSA2 Jason Campbell 12.00 30.00
WSA3 Mark Clayton 12.00 30.00
WSA4 Ciatrick Fason 12.00 30.00
WSA5 Charlie Frye 12.00 30.00
WSA6 David Greene 12.00 30.00
WSA7 Derrick Johnson 15.00 40.00
WSA8 Dan Orlovsky 12.00 30.00
WSA9 Kyle Orton 12.00 30.00
WSA10 Aaron Rodgers 125.00 200.00
WSA11 Alex Smith QB 50.00 100.00
WSA12 Andrew Walter 12.00 30.00
WSA13 Jason White 20.00 50.00
WSA14 Cadillac Williams 12.00 30.00
WSA15 Troy Williamson 12.00 30.00

2006 SAGE HIT

This 55-card set was released in April, 2006. The set was issued into the hoby in five-card packs with an $3.99 SRP which came 30 packs to a box. A few cards were issued in shorter quantity and we have notated those cards with an SP in our checklist. In addition, card number 56, Jay Cutler, was issued at the 2006 Anaheim National Convention. That card is not considered part of the set.
COMPLETE SET (55) 10.00 25.00
#56 ISSUED AT 2006 ANAHEIM NATIONAL
1 Reggie McNeal .25 .60
2 Jimmy Williams SP .25 .60
3 D.J. Shockley SP .30 .75
4 Omar Jacobs .25 .60
5 Reggie Bush .40 1.00
6 Charlie Whitehurst .25 .60
7 Michael Huff .30 .75
8 Tye Hill .25 .60
9 Mario Williams .40 1.00
10 Vince Young .25 .60
11 Matt Leinart UER .25 .60
12 Brodie Croyle .25 .60
13 Paul Pinegar .25 .60
14 Drew Olson .25 .60
15 Martin Nance .25 .60
16 David Thomas .25 .60
17 Dwayne Slay SP .30 .75
18 Vernon Davis .30 .75
19 Taurean Henderson SP .25 .60
20 Maurice Drew .40 1.00
21 LenDale White .25 .60
22 Laurence Maroney .25 .60
23 Leon Washington .25 .60
24 Erik Meyer SP .25 .60
25 Maurice Stovall .25 .60
26 Ashton Youboty .25 .60
27 Devin Aromashodu .25 .60
28 Mike Hass .25 .60
29 Jonathan Orr .30 .75
30 Joseph Addai .25 .60
31 Leonard Pope .40 1.00
32 Michael Robinson .25 .60
33 Mike Bell .25 .60
34 Ernie Sims SP .25 .60
35 Skyler Green .25 .60
36 Demetrius Williams .25 .60
37 Winston Justice .30 .75
38 Sinorice Moss .25 .60
39 Charles Gordon SP .25 .60
40 Gerald Riggs .30 .75
41 Jerome Harrison .25 .60
42 Bobby Carpenter .25 .60
43 Dominique Byrd .25 .60
44 Bruce Gradkowski .30 .75
45 Rodrique Wright .25 .60
46 D'Brickashaw Ferguson .25 .60
47 Daniel Bullocks SP .25 .60
48 Jason Avant .25 .60
49 Will Blackmon .25 .60
50 Devin Hester SP .50 1.25
51 Alan Zemaitis SP .25 .60
52 Hank Baskett .25 .60
53 Cadillac Williams ROY SP 1.25 3.00
54 Bush/Leinart CL SP .30 .75
55 Vince Young CL SP .20 .50
56 Jay Cutler .30 .75

2006 SAGE HIT Autographs Blue

BLUE ODDS 1:10 HOB, 1:50 RET
1 Reggie McNeal 3.00 8.00
3 D.J. Shockley 4.00 10.00
4 Omar Jacobs 3.00 8.00
5 Reggie Bush SP 5.00 12.00
6 Charlie Whitehurst 3.00 8.00
7 Michael Huff 4.00 10.00
8 Tye Hill 3.00 8.00
9 Mario Williams 5.00 12.00
10 Vince Young SP 12.00 30.00
11 Matt Leinart SP 12.00 30.00
12 Brodie Croyle 3.00 8.00
13 Paul Pinegar 3.00 8.00
14 Drew Olson 3.00 8.00
15 Martin Nance 3.00 8.00
16 David Thomas 3.00 8.00
17 Dwayne Slay 4.00 10.00
18 Vernon Davis 4.00 10.00
19 Taurean Henderson 3.00 8.00
20 Maurice Drew 10.00 25.00
21 LenDale White SP 15.00 40.00
22 Laurence Maroney 3.00 8.00
24 Erik Meyer 3.00 8.00
25 Maurice Stovall 3.00 8.00
26 Ashton Youboty 3.00 8.00
27 Devin Aromashodu 3.00 8.00
28 Mike Hass 3.00 8.00
29 Jonathan Orr 4.00 10.00
30 Joseph Addai 8.00 20.00
31 Leonard Pope 5.00 12.00
32 Michael Robinson 3.00 8.00
33 Mike Bell 3.00 8.00
34 Ernie Sims 3.00 8.00
35 Skyler Green 3.00 8.00
36 Demetrius Williams 3.00 8.00
37 Winston Justice 4.00 10.00
38 Sinorice Moss 3.00 8.00
39 Charles Gordon 3.00 8.00
41 Jerome Harrison 3.00 8.00
42 Bobby Carpenter 3.00 8.00
43 Dominique Byrd 3.00 8.00
44 Bruce Gradkowski 4.00 10.00
45 Rodrique Wright 3.00 8.00
46 D'Brickashaw Ferguson 3.00 8.00
48 Jason Avant 3.00 8.00
49 Will Blackmon 3.00 8.00
51 Alan Zemaitis 3.00 8.00
52 Hank Baskett 3.00 8.00

2006 SAGE HIT Autographs Gold

*GOLD: .6X TO 1.5X BLUE AUTOS
*GOLD: .5X TO 1.2X BLUE SP AUTOS
GOLD/250 ODDS 1:30 HOB, 1:150 RET
5 Reggie Bush 6.00 15.00
10 Vince Young 12.00 30.00
11 Matt Leinart 10.00 25.00
53 Anthony Fasano 4.00 10.00

2006 SAGE HIT Autographs Silver

*SILVER: .5X TO 1.2X BLUE AUTOS
*CILVER: .4X TO 1X BLUE SP AUTOS
SILVER ODDS 1:18 HOB, 1:90 RET
5 Reggie Bush 6.00 15.00
10 Vince Young 25.00 60.00
11 Matt Leinart 12.00 30.00

2006 SAGE HIT BCS

COMPLETE SET (36) 15.00 40.00
ONE PER SPECIAL BCS PACK
BCS1 Vince Young .25 .60
BCS2 Michael Robinson .25 .60
BCS3 Bobby Carpenter .25 .60
BCS4 D.J. Shockley .30 .75
BCS5 Vince Young .25 .60
BCS6 David Thomas .25 .60
BCS7 Michael Huff .30 .75
BCS8 Rodrique Wright .25 .60
BCS9 Matt Leinart .25 .60
BCS10 Reggie Bush .40 1.00
BCS11 LenDale White .25 .60
BCS12 Dominique Byrd .25 .60
BCS13 Winston Justice .30 .75
BCS14 Michael Robinson .25 .60
BCS15 Alan Zemaitis .25 .60
BCS16 Leon Washington .25 .60
BCS17 Ernie Sims .25 .60
BCS18 Ashton Youboty .25 .60
BCS19 Maurice Stovall .25 .60
BCS20 Anthony Fasano .25 .60
BCS21 D.J. Shockley .30 .75
BCS22 Leonard Pope .40 1.00
BCS23 Vince Young .25 .60
BCS24 Vince Young .25 .60
BCS25 Vince Young .25 .60
BCS26 Vince Young .25 .60
BCS27 Vince Young .25 .60
BCS28 Vince Young .25 .60
BCS29 Vince Young .25 .60
BCS30 Vince Young .25 .60
BCS31 Matt Leinart .25 .60
BCS32 Matt Leinart .25 .60
BCS33 Matt Leinart .25 .60
BCS34 Reggie Bush .40 1.00
BCS35 Reggie Bush .40 1.00
BCS36 LenDale White .25 .60

2006 SAGE HIT BCS Autographs

TWO PER SPECIAL BCS BOX
STATED PRINT RUN 50 SER.#'d SETS
BCS1 Vince Young
BCS2 Michael Huff 10.00 25.00
BCS3 Rodrique Wright 8.00 20.00
BCS4 David Thomas 8.00 20.00
BCS5 Matt Leinart 8.00 20.00
BCS6 LenDale White 8.00 20.00
BCS7 Reggie Bush 12.00 30.00
BCS8 D.J. Shockley 10.00 25.00
BCS9 Dominique Byrd 8.00 20.00
BCS10 Michael Robinson 8.00 20.00
BCS11 Alan Zemaitis 8.00 20.00
BCS12 Bobby Carpenter 8.00 20.00
BCS13 Ashton Youboty 8.00 20.00
BCS14 Maurice Stovall 8.00 20.00
BCS15 Ernie Sims 8.00 20.00
BCS16 Leonard Pope 12.00 30.00
BCS17 Winston Justice 10.00 25.00
BCS19 Anthony Fasano 8.00 20.00

2006 SAGE HIT BIG-12 Autographs

TWO PER SPECIAL BIG 12 BOX
STATED PRINT RUN 50 SER.#'d SETS
BIG1 Vince Young 8.00 20.00
BIG9 Charles Gordon 8.00 20.00
BIG3 Rodrique Wright 8.00 20.00
BIG4 David Thomas 8.00 20.00
BIG5 Reggie McNeal 8.00 20.00
BIG6 Michael Huff 10.00 25.00
BIG7 Taurean Henderson 8.00 20.00
BIG8 Dwayne Slay 10.00 25.00

2006 SAGE HIT Design for Success Blue

BLUE STATED ODDS 1:2
*GREEN: .3X TO .8X BLUE
GREEN STATED ODDS 14:15 RETAIL
*SILVER: .5X TO 1.2X BLUE
SILVER STATED ODDS 1:5
D1 Reggie McNeal .30 .75
D2 Jimmy Williams .30 .75
D3 D.J. Shockley .40 1.00
D4 Omar Jacobs .30 .75
D5 Reggie Bush .50 1.25
D6 Charlie Whitehurst .30 .75
D7 Michael Huff .40 1.00
D8 Tye Hill .30 .75
D9 Mario Williams .50 1.25
D10 Vince Young .30 .75
D11 Matt Leinart .30 .75
D12 Brodie Croyle .30 .75
D13 Paul Pinegar .30 .75
D14 Drew Olson .30 .75
D15 Martin Nance .30 .75
D16 David Thomas .30 .75
D17 Dwayne Slay .40 1.00
D18 Vernon Davis .40 1.00
D19 Taurean Henderson .30 .75
D20 Maurice Drew .50 1.25
D21 LenDale White .30 .75
D22 Laurence Maroney .30 .75
D23 Leon Washington .30 .75
D24 Erik Meyer .30 .75
D25 Maurice Stovall .30 .75
D26 Ashton Youboty .30 .75
D27 Devin Aromashodu .30 .75
D28 Mike Hass .30 .75
D29 Jonathan Orr .40 1.00
D30 Joseph Addai .30 .75
D31 Leonard Pope .50 1.25
D32 Michael Robinson .30 .75
D33 Mike Bell .30 .75
D34 Ernie Sims .30 .75
D35 Skyler Green .30 .75
D36 Demetrius Williams .30 .75
D37 Winston Justice .40 1.00
D38 Sinorice Moss .30 .75
D39 Charles Gordon .30 .75
D40 Gerald Riggs .40 1.00
D41 Jerome Harrison .30 .75
D42 Bobby Carpenter .30 .75
D43 Dominique Byrd .30 .75
D44 Bruce Gradkowski .40 1.00
D45 Rodrique Wright .30 .75
D46 D'Brickashaw Ferguson .30 .75
D47 Daniel Bullocks .30 .75
D48 Jason Avant .30 .75
D49 Will Blackmon .30 .75
D50 Devin Hester .60 1.50
D51 Alan Zemaitis .30 .75
D52 Hank Baskett .30 .75
D53 Anthony Fasano .30 .75
D54 Jay Cutler .40 1.00
D55 DeMeco Ryans .40 1.00

2006 SAGE HIT Design for Success Gold Autographs

GOLD/100 STATED ODDS 1:70
DA1 Reggie McNeal 10.00 25.00
DA3 D.J. Shockley 10.00 25.00
DA4 Omar Jacobs 10.00 25.00
DA5 Reggie Bush 6.00 15.00
DA6 Charlie Whitehurst 10.00 25.00
DA7 Michael Huff 10.00 25.00
DA8 Tye Hill 10.00 25.00
DA9 Mario Williams 15.00 40.00
DA10 Vince Young 30.00 80.00
DA11 Matt Leinart 15.00 40.00
DA12 Brodie Croyle 12.00 30.00
DA13 Paul Pinegar 8.00 20.00
DA14 Drew Olson 10.00 25.00
DA15 Martin Nance 6.00 15.00
DA16 David Thomas 10.00 25.00
DA17 Dwayne Slay 8.00 20.00
DA18 Vernon Davis 12.00 30.00
DA19 Taurean Henderson 10.00 25.00
DA20 Maurice Drew 20.00 50.00
DA21 LenDale White 25.00 60.00
DA22 Laurence Maroney 8.00 20.00
DA24 Erik Meyer 8.00 20.00
DA25 Maurice Stovall 10.00 25.00
DA26 Ashton Youboty 10.00 25.00
DA27 Devin Aromashodu UER 8.00 20.00
DA28 Mike Hass 10.00 25.00
DA29 Jonathan Orr 8.00 20.00
DA30 Joseph Addai 20.00 50.00
DA31 Leonard Pope 12.50 30.00
DA32 Michael Robinson 10.00 25.00
DA33 Mike Bell 10.00 25.00
DA34 Ernie Sims 12.00 30.00
DA35 Skyler Green 10.00 25.00
DA36 Demetrius Williams 10.00 25.00
DA37 Winston Justice 10.00 25.00
DA38 Sinorice Moss 10.00 25.00
DA39 Charles Gordon 8.00 20.00
DA41 Jerome Harrison 10.00 25.00
DA42 Bobby Carpenter 10.00 25.00
DA43 Dominique Byrd 10.00 25.00
DA44 Bruce Gradkowski 12.00 30.00
DA45 Rodrique Wright 6.00 15.00
DA46 D'Brickashaw Ferguson 10.00 25.00
DA48 Jason Avant 10.00 25.00
DA49 Will Blackmon 8.00 20.00
DA51 Alan Zemaitis 10.00 25.00
DA52 Hank Baskett 10.00 25.00
DA53 Anthony Fasano 10.00 25.00
DA55 DeMeco Ryans 12.00 30.00

2006 SAGE HIT Hype

COMPLETE SET (7) 10.00 25.00
1 Jay Cutler .30 .75
2 Reggie Bush .40 1.00
3 Vince Young .25 .60
4 Matt Leinart .25 .60
5 Vernon Davis .30 .75
6 Joseph Addai .30 .75
7 Laurence Maroney .25 .60

2006 SAGE HIT Jerseys

STATED ODDS 1:31 HOB, 1:90 RET
AV Jason Avant 3.00 8.00
BC Bobby Carpenter 3.00 8.00
CW Charlie Whitehurst 3.00 8.00
DS D.J. Shockley 4.00 10.00
JA Joseph Addai 3.00 8.00
LW LenDale White 3.00 8.00
MD Maurice Drew 5.00 12.00
ML Matt Leinart 3.00 8.00
MR Michael Robinson 3.00 8.00
MS Maurice Stovall 3.00 8.00
OJ Omar Jacobs 3.00 8.00
RB Reggie Bush 5.00 12.00
RM Reggie McNeal 3.00 8.00
VD Vernon Davis 4.00 10.00
VY Vince Young 3.00 8.00

2006 SAGE HIT Jerseys Premium Swatches

*PREMIUM SWATCH: .8X TO 2X JSY
PREM.SWATCH/50 ODDS 1:540 H,1:2700 R
SM Sinorice Moss 6.00 15.00

2006 SAGE HIT PAC-10

RANDOM INSERTS IN SPECIAL RETAIL
P1 Matt Leinart .60 1.50
P2 Reggie Bush 1.00 2.50
P3 Matt Leinart .60 1.50
P4 Matt Leinart .60 1.50
P5 Reggie Bush 1.00 2.50
P6 Reggie Bush 1.00 2.50
P7 LenDale White .60 1.50
P8 LenDale White .60 1.50
P9 Matt Leinart .60 1.50
P10 Reggie Bush 1.00 2.50

2006 SAGE HIT PAC-10 Autographs

STATED PRINT RUN 50 SER.#'d SETS
PC1 Matt Leinart 8.00 20.00
PC2 Drew Olson 8.00 20.00
PC3 Reggie Bush 12.00 30.00
PC4 LenDale White 8.00 20.00
PC5 Dominique Byrd 8.00 20.00
PC6 Maurice Drew 12.00 30.00
PC7 Mike Hass 8.00 20.00
PC8 Demetrius Williams 8.00 20.00
PC9 Winston Justice 10.00 25.00
PC10 Mike Bell 8.00 20.00
PC11 Jerome Harrison 8.00 20.00

2006 SAGE HIT QB Autographs

STATED PRINT RUN 50 SER.#'d SETS
QB1 Matt Leinart 8.00 20.00
QB2 Erik Meyer 8.00 20.00
QB3 Vince Young 8.00 20.00
QB4 Omar Jacobs 8.00 20.00
QB5 Brodie Croyle 8.00 20.00
QB6 Michael Robinson 8.00 20.00
QB7 Charlie Whitehurst 8.00 20.00
QB8 D.J. Shockley 10.00 25.00
QB9 Drew Olson 8.00 20.00
QB10 Reggie McNeal 8.00 20.00
QB11 Paul Pinegar 8.00 20.00
QB12 Bruce Gradkowski 10.00 25.00

2006 SAGE HIT Write Stuff

STATED ODDS 1:15
1 Joseph Addai .50 1.25
2 Reggie Bush .75 2.00
3 Brodie Croyle .50 1.25
4 Vernon Davis .60 1.50
5 Maurice Drew .75 2.00
6 Michael Huff .60 1.50
7 Omar Jacobs .50 1.25
8 Matt Leinart .50 1.25
9 Laurence Maroney .50 1.25
10 Sinorice Moss .50 1.25
11 Michael Robinson .50 1.25
12 LenDale White .50 1.25
13 Charlie Whitehurst .50 1.25
14 Mario Williams .75 2.00
15 Vince Young .50 1.25

2006 SAGE HIT Write Stuff Autographs

AUTOS/25 ODDS 1:845 HOB, 1:4225 RET
WA1 Joseph Addai 12.00 30.00
WA2 Reggie Bush 20.00 50.00
WA3 Brodie Croyle 12.00 30.00
WA4 Vernon Davis 15.00 40.00
WA5 Maurice Drew 20.00 50.00
WA6 Michael Huff 15.00 40.00
WA7 Omar Jacobs 12.00 30.00
WA8 Matt Leinart 12.00 30.00
WA9 Laurence Maroney 12.00 30.00
WA10 Sinorice Moss 12.00 30.00
WA11 Michael Robinson 12.00 30.00
WA12 LenDale White 12.00 30.00
WA13 Charlie Whitehurst
WA14 Mario Williams 20.00 50.00
WA15 Vince Young 12.00 30.00

2006 SAGE HIT National Promos

These cards were issued at the 2006 National Sports Collector Convention. Each card appears to be from the base SAGE HIT set but for the addition of "/5" after the card number on the backs.
1 Matt Leinart .30 .75
2 Vince Young .30 .75
3 Jay Cutler .40 1.00
4 LenDale White .30 .75
5 Reggie Bush .50 1.25

2007 SAGE HIT

This 64-card set was released in April, 2007. The set was issued into the hobby in five-card packs with a $3.99 SRP which came 30 packs to a box. The three players listed at the end of this set were all stars of the 2006 NFL Draft.

COMPLETE SET (64) 10.00 25.00
1 Paul Williams .25 .60
2 JaMarcus Russell .25 .60
3 Robert Meachem .30 .75
4 Sidney Rice .30 .75
5 Drew Stanton .25 .60
6 Jeff Rowe .25 .60
7 Zach Miller .25 .60
8 Joel Filani .25 .60
9 Chris Henry .25 .60
10 Brady Quinn .25 .60
11 Anthony Gonzalez .25 .60
12 Chris Leak .25 .60
13 David Clowney .25 .60
14 Isaiah Stanback .25 .60
15 Steve Breaston .25 .60
16 Yamon Figurs .25 .60
17 Lawrence Timmons .40 1.00
18 Greg Olsen .40 1.00
19 Michael Bush .25 .60
20 Alan Branch .25 .60
21 Johnnie Lee Higgins .25 .60
22 Aundrae Allison .25 .60
23 Kenny Irons .25 .60
24 Marshawn Lynch .50 1.25
25 Earl Everett .25 .60
26 Courtney Taylor .25 .60
27 Michael Griffin .25 .60
28 Adrian Peterson .75 2.00
29 Leon Hall .25 .60
30 David Ball .25 .60
31 Aaron Ross .25 .60
32 John Beck .25 .60
33 Kolby Smith .25 .60
34 Kenneth Darby .25 .60
35 Trent Edwards .25 .60
36 Craig Buster Davis .25 .60
37 Ryan Kalil .25 .60
38 Jason Snelling .25 .60
39 Tyler Palko .40 1.00
40 Dwayne Bowe .25 .60
41 Dallas Baker .25 .60
42 Steve Smith USC .25 .60
43 Jason Hill .25 .60
44 Kevin Kolb .30 .75
45 Jared Zabransky .25 .60
46 Brian Leonard .25 .60
47 Darius Walker .25 .60
48 Adam Carriker .25 .60
49 Patrick Willis .40 1.00
50 Troy Smith .25 .60
51 Brandon Meriweather .30 .75
52 Jarvis Moss .25 .60
53 Levi Brown .25 .60
54 David Irons .25 .60
55 Garrett Wolfe .25 .60
56 LaMarr Woodley .50 1.25
57 DeMarcus Tank Tyler .25 .60
58 Jordan Palmer .30 .75
59 Antonio Pittman .25 .60
60 Gaines Adams .30 .75
61 Calvin Johnson .75 2.00
ML Matt Leinart .40 1.00
RB Reggie Bush .40 1.00
VY Vince Young .40 1.00

2007 SAGE HIT Playmakers Blue

COMPLETE SET (61) 15.00 40.00
*BLUES: .6X TO 1.5X BASIC CARDS
OVERALL PLAYMAKERS ODDS 1:2
*SILVER: .5X TO 1.2X BLUE
SILVER STATED ODDS 1:5

2007 SAGE HIT Playmakers Gold Autographs

*PLAY.GOLD/100: .6X TO 1.5X BASIC AUTOS
PLAYMAKERS GOLD/100 ODDS 1:70
PA10 Brady Quinn 5.00 12.00
PA28 Adrian Peterson 100.00 200.00
PA59 Antonio Pittman 5.00 12.00

2007 SAGE HIT Autographs

BASE AUTO ODDS 1:10
*SILVER: .4X TO 1X BASIC AUTO
SILVER AUTO ODDS 1:18
1 Paul Williams 3.00 8.00
2 JaMarcus Russell SP 10.00 25.00
3 Robert Meachem 3.00 8.00
4 Sidney Rice 3.00 8.00
5 Drew Stanton 2.50 6.00
6 Jeff Rowe 3.00 8.00
7 Zach Miller 3.00 8.00
8 Joel Filani 3.00 8.00
9 Chris Henry 3.00 8.00
10 Brady Quinn SP 3.00 8.00
11 Anthony Gonzalez 3.00 8.00
12 Chris Leak SP 3.00 8.00
13 David Clowney 3.00 8.00
14 Isaiah Stanback 3.00 8.00
15 Steve Breaston 2.50 6.00
16 Yamon Figurs 3.00 8.00
17 Lawrence Timmons 4.00 10.00
18 Greg Olsen 4.00 10.00
19 Michael Bush 2.50 6.00
21 Johnnie Lee Higgins SP 3.00 8.00
22 Aundrae Allison 3.00 8.00
23 Kenny Irons 3.00 8.00
24 Marshawn Lynch SP 6.00 15.00
25 Earl Everett 3.00 8.00
27 Michael Griffin 3.00 8.00
28 Adrian Peterson SP 75.00 150.00
29 Leon Hall 3.00 8.00
30 David Ball 3.00 8.00
31 Aaron Ross 3.00 8.00
32 John Beck 3.00 8.00
33 Kolby Smith 3.00 8.00
34 Kenneth Darby 3.00 8.00
35 Trent Edwards 3.00 8.00
36 Craig Buster Davis SP 3.00 8.00
37 Ryan Kalil 3.00 8.00
38 Jason Snelling SP 3.00 8.00
39 Tyler Palko 4.00 10.00
40 Dwayne Bowe 2.50 6.00
41 Dallas Baker 3.00 8.00
42 Steve Smith USC 3.00 8.00
43 Jason Hill 3.00 8.00
44 Kevin Kolb 4.00 10.00
45 Jared Zabransky 3.00 8.00
46 Brian Leonard 2.50 6.00
47 Darius Walker 3.00 8.00
48 Adam Carriker 3.00 8.00
49 Patrick Willis 4.00 10.00
50 Troy Smith SP 10.00 25.00
51 Brandon Meriweather SP 4.00 10.00
52 Jarvis Moss 3.00 8.00
53 Levi Brown 3.00 8.00
54 David Irons 3.00 8.00
55 Garrett Wolfe 2.50 6.00
56 LaMarr Woodley 5.00 12.00
57 DeMarcus Tank Tyler 3.00 8.00
58 Jordan Palmer 4.00 10.00
59 Antonio Pittman SP
60 Gaines Adams 3.00 8.00
61 Chris Vincent 2.50 6.00

2007 SAGE HIT Autographs Gold

*GOLD/250: .5X TO 1.2X BASIC AUTO
GOLD AUTO/250 ODDS 1:30
10 Brady Quinn 4.00 10.00
28 Adrian Peterson 75.00 150.00

2007 SAGE HIT Big-10

COMPLETE SET (35) 20.00 40.00
INSERTS IN SPECIAL BIG-10 BOXES
1 Troy Smith .40 1.00
2 Troy Smith .40 1.00
3 Troy Smith .40 1.00
4 Antonio Pittman .40 1.00
5 Antonio Pittman .40 1.00
6 Troy Smith .40 1.00
7 Antonio Pittman .40 1.00
8 Anthony Gonzalez .40 1.00
9 Anthony Gonzalez .40 1.00
10 Alan Branch .40 1.00
11 Alan Branch .40 1.00
12 Alan Branch .40 1.00
13 Steve Breaston .40 1.00
14 Steve Breaston .40 1.00
15 Anthony Gonzalez .40 1.00
16 Leon Hall .40 1.00
17 Steve Breaston .40 1.00
18 Steve Breaston .40 1.00
19 Leon Hall .40 1.00
20 Leon Hall .40 1.00
21 Leon Hall .40 1.00
22 LaMarr Woodley .75 2.00
23 LaMarr Woodley .75 2.00
24 LaMarr Woodley .75 2.00
25 LaMarr Woodley .75 2.00
26 Levi Brown .40 1.00
27 Levi Brown .40 1.00
28 Levi Brown .40 1.00
29 Levi Brown .40 1.00
30 Drew Stanton .40 1.00
31 Drew Stanton .40 1.00
32 Drew Stanton .40 1.00
33 Drew Stanton .40 1.00
34 Ted Ginn Jr. .50 1.25
35 Ted Ginn Jr. .50 1.25

2007 SAGE HIT Big-10 Autographs

STATED PRINT RUN 50 SER.#'d SETS
BTA1 Leon Hall 12.00 30.00
BTA3 Levi Brown 12.00 30.00
BTA5 Steve Breaston 10.00 25.00
BTA4 Anthony Gonzalez 15.00 40.00
BTA7 Troy Smith 20.00 50.00
BTA8 Drew Stanton 8.00 20.00
BTA9 LaMarr Woodley 15.00 40.00

2007 SAGE HIT Draft Diary

CARDS #1-2 INSERTED IN SAGE HIT 1:15
CARDS #3-4 INSERTED IN ASPIRE 1:20
CARDS #5-6 INSERTED IN SAGE
ALL CARDS FOR EACH PLAYER EQUAL PRICE
AP1 Adrian Peterson CR 1.00 2.50
AP2 Adrian Peterson WO 1.00 2.50
AP3 Adrian Peterson C 1.00 2.50
AP4 Adrian Peterson PD 1.00 2.50
AP5 Adrian Peterson TV 1.00 2.50
AP6 Adrian Peterson DD 1.00 2.50
BQ1 Brady Quinn CR .30 .75
BQ2 Brady Quinn WO .30 .75
BQ3 Brady Quinn C .30 .75
BQ4 Brady Quinn PD .30 .75
BQ5 Brady Quinn TV .30 .75
BQ6 Brady Quinn DD .30 .75
JR1 JaMarcus Russell CR .30 .75
JR2 JaMarcus Russell WO .30 .75
JR3 JaMarcus Russell C .30 .75
JR4 JaMarcus Russell PD .30 .75
JR5 JaMarcus Russell TV .30 .75
JR6 JaMarcus Russell DD .30 .75

2007 SAGE HIT Draft Diary Letter

1-2 LETTER/50 ODDS 1:3200 SAGE HIT
3-4 LETTER/100 ODDS 1:373 ASPIRE
AP1 Adrian Peterson CR 6.00 15.00
AP2 Adrian Peterson WO 6.00 15.00
AP3 Adrian Peterson C/100 4.00 10.00
AP4 Adrian Peterson PD/100 4.00 10.00
AP5 Adrian Peterson TV/100 4.00 10.00
AP6 Adrian Peterson DD/100 4.00 10.00
BQ1 Brady Quinn CR 2.00 5.00
BQ2 Brady Quinn WO 2.00 5.00
BQ3 Brady Quinn C/100 1.25 3.00
BQ4 Brady Quinn PD/100 1.25 3.00
BQ5 Brady Quinn TV/100 1.25 3.00
BQ6 Brady Quinn DD/100 1.25 3.00
JR1 JaMarcus Russell CR 2.00 5.00
JR2 JaMarcus Russell WO 2.00 5.00
JR3 JaMarcus Russell C/100 1.25 3.00
JR4 JaMarcus Russell PD/100 1.25 3.00
JR5 JaMarcus Russell TV/100 1.25 3.00
JR6 JaMarcus Russell DD/100 1.25 3.00

2007 SAGE HIT Jerseys

JERSEY STATED ODDS 1:30
*PREMIUM SWATCH/50: 1X TO 2.5X
PREMIUM SWATCH/50 ODDS 1:425
AD Adrian Peterson 12.00 30.00
AG Anthony Gonzalez 4.00 10.00
AP Antonio Pittman 4.00 10.00
BQ Brady Quinn 3.00 8.00
DS Drew Stanton 4.00 10.00
DW Darius Walker 4.00 10.00
JR JaMarcus Russell 5.00 12.00
KD Kenneth Darby 4.00 10.00
KI Kenny Irons 4.00 10.00
MB Michael Bush 4.00 10.00
ML Marshawn Lynch 6.00 15.00
RB Reggie Bush 6.00 15.00
RL Matt Leinart 5.00 12.00
RM Robert Meachem 5.00 12.00
RY Vince Young 6.00 15.00
SR Sidney Rice 6.00 15.00
TE Trent Edwards 4.00 10.00
TS Troy Smith 4.00 10.00

2007 SAGE HIT Jersey Bonus Red

*GOLD: .8X TO 2X RED
ONE PER RETAIL BOX BLASTER
MLC Matt Leinart College 3.00 8.00
MLP Matt Leinart Pro 3.00 8.00
RBC Reggie Bush College 5.00 12.00
RBP Reggie Bush Pro 5.00 12.00
VYC Vince Young College 4.00 10.00
VYP Vince Young Pro 4.00 10.00

2007 SAGE HIT Write Stuff

STATED ODDS 1:15
1 John Beck .50 1.25
2 Dwayne Bowe .50 1.25
3 Calvin Johnson 1.50 4.00
4 Kevin Kolb .60 1.50
5 Chris Leak .50 1.25
6 Brian Leonard .50 1.25
7 Marshawn Lynch 1.00 2.50
8 Robert Meachem .60 1.50
9 Greg Olsen .75 2.00
10 Adrian Peterson 1.50 4.00
11 Antonio Pittman .50 1.25
12 Brady Quinn .50 1.25
13 JaMarcus Russell .50 1.25
14 Troy Smith .50 1.25
15 Drew Stanton .50 1.25

2007 SAGE HIT Write Stuff Autographs

WRITE STUFF AUTO/25 ODDS 1:1000
1 John Beck 12.00 30.00
2 Dwayne Bowe 12.00 30.00
4 Kevin Kolb 15.00 40.00
5 Chris Leak 12.00 30.00
6 Brian Leonard 12.00 30.00
7 Marshawn Lynch 20.00 50.00
8 Robert Meachem 15.00 40.00
9 Greg Olsen 20.00 50.00
10 Adrian Peterson 100.00 200.00
11 Antonio Pittman 12.00 30.00
12 Brady Quinn 12.00 30.00
13 JaMarcus Russell 12.00 30.00
14 Troy Smith 12.00 30.00
15 Drew Stanton 12.00 30.00

2007 SAGE HIT Hype Orange

*BRONZE/550: .4X TO 1X ORANGE
*GOLD/220: .5X TO 1.2X ORANGE
*SILVER/480: .4X TO 1X ORANGE
1 Calvin Johnson .60 1.50
2 JaMarcus Russell .20 .50
3 Adrian Peterson .60 1.50
4 Brady Quinn .20 .50
5 Marshawn Lynch .40 1.00
6 JaMarcus Russell/Brady Quinn .20 .50
7 Adrian Peterson/Brady Quinn .60 1.50
8 JaMarcus Russell/Brady Quinn .20 .50
9 JaMarcus Russell/Drew Stanton .20 .50
10 Adrian Peterson/Calvin Johnson .60 1.50

2008 SAGE HIT

COMPLETE SET (100) 15.00 40.00
COMP.LOW SERIES (50) 7.50 20.00
COMP.HIGH SERIES (50) 7.50 20.00
1 John David Booty .25 .60
2 Will Franklin .30 .75
3 Danny Woodhead 1.25 3.00
4 Limas Sweed .25 .60
5 Joe Flacco .50 1.25
6 Brian Brohm .25 .60
7 Chad Henne .30 .75
8 Marcus Thomas .30 .75
9 Early Doucet .25 .60
10 Dennis Dixon .25 .60
11 Xavier Adibi .25 .60
12 Matt Ryan .75 2.00
13 T.C. Ostrander .30 .75
14 Bernard Morris .30 .75
15 Sam Baker .25 .60
16 Adrian Arrington .25 .60
17 Kevin O'Connell .25 .60
18 Jacob Hester .25 .60
19 Keenan Burton .25 .60
20 Darius Reynaud .25 .60
21 Keon Lattimore .30 .75
22 Tashard Choice .25 .60
23 Jake Long .40 1.00
24 Paul Smith .25 .60
25 Jamaal Charles .40 1.00
26 Yvenson Bernard .40 1.00
27 Alex Brink .30 .75
28 James Hardy .25 .60
29 Martin Rucker .25 .60
30 Steve Slaton .25 .60
31 Derrick Harvey .25 .60
32 Andre Callender .40 1.00
33 Jabari Arthur .30 .75
34 Bruce Hocker .40 1.00
35 Kalvin McRae .25 .60
36 Lawrence Jackson .25 .60
37 Tyrell Johnson .25 .60
38 Marcus Howard .40 1.00
39 Sam Keller .25 .60
40 Keith Rivers .25 .60
41 Brandon Flowers .30 .75
42 Adarius Bowman .30 .75
43 Ricky Santos .40 1.00
44 Jordon Dizon .25 .60
45 Robert Jordan .30 .75
46 Maurice Purify .40 1.00
47 Lavelle Hawkins .30 .75
48 Jason Rivers .25 .60
49 John Carlson .25 .60
50 Vernon Gholston .25 .60
51 D.McFadden/F.Jones .15 .40
52 M.Ryan/A.Callender .50 1.25
53 D.Jackson/M.Lynch .30 .75
54 M.Flynn/J.Russell .15 .40
55 B.Brohm/M.Bush .15 .40
56 C.Henne/M.Hart .20 .50
57 B.Quinn/J.Carlson .30 .75
58 J.Stewart/D.Dixon .25 .60
59 A.Peterson/M.Kelly .50 1.25
60 R.Rice/B.Leonard .15 .40
61 J.Booty/F.Davis .15 .40
62 J.Charles/L.Sweed .25 .60
63 M.Ryan/B.Brohm .50 1.25
64 D.McFadden/R.Mendenhall .15 .40
65 M.Kelly/D.Jackson .30 .75
66 J.Flacco/J.Johnson .30 .75
67 A.Peterson/P.Willis .50 1.25
68 Devin Thomas .25 .60
69 Beau Bell .30 .75
70 Owen Schmitt .25 .60
71 Paul Raymond .30 .75
72 Jordy Nelson .75 2.00
73 Ray Rice .25 .60
74 Darrell Strong .30 .75
75 Felix Jones .25 .60
76 Kevin Smith .25 .60
77 Justin Forsett .30 .75
78 Antoine Cason .30 .75
79 Ryan Clady .30 .75
80 Mike Hart .25 .60
81 Kenny Phillips .25 .60
82 Jonathan Stewart .40 1.00
83 Fred Davis .25 .60
84 Malcolm Kelly .25 .60
85 Matt Flynn .25 .60
86 Allen Patrick .25 .60
87 Brent Miller .30 .75
88 Andre Caldwell .25 .60
89 Josh Johnson .25 .60
90 Erik Ainge .25 .60
91 Tom Zbikowski .30 .75
92 Dan Connor .25 .60
93 Leodis McKelvin .30 .75
94 Sedrick Ellis .25 .60
95 Rashard Mendenhall .25 .60
96 Mike Jenkins .25 .60
97 Dustin Keller .30 .75
98 Donnie Avery .30 .75
99 DeSean Jackson .50 1.25
100 Darren McFadden .25 .60

2008 SAGE HIT Make Ready Black

*BLACK/50: 2.5X TO 6X BASIC CARDS
*CYAN/50: 2.5X TO 6X BASIC CARDS
*MAGENTA/50: 2.5X TO 6X BASIC CARDS
*YELLOW/50: 2.5X TO 6X BASIC CARDS
OVERALL MR/50 ODDS 1:30 LOW, 1:25 HI

2008 SAGE HIT Glossy

*GLOSSY: .6X TO 1.5X BASIC CARDS
ONE GLOSSY PER RETAIL PACK

2008 SAGE HIT Gold

*GOLD: 1X TO 2.5X BASIC CARDS
GOLD ODDS 1:10 LOW/HI

2008 SAGE HIT Silver

*SILVER: .6X TO 1.5X BASIC CARDS
SILVER ODDS 1:3 LOW/HI

2008 SAGE HIT Autographs

BLUE AUTO ODDS 1:10 LOW, 1:14 HI
UNPRICED PRINT PLATE PRINT RUN 1
A1 John David Booty 3.00 8.00
A2 Will Franklin 4.00 10.00
A3 Danny Woodhead 12.00 30.00
A4 Limas Sweed SP 8.00 20.00
A5 Joe Flacco 6.00 15.00
A6 Brian Brohm SP 4.00 10.00
A7 Chad Henne 4.00 10.00
A8 Marcus Thomas 4.00 10.00
A10 Dennis Dixon 3.00 8.00
A11 Xavier Adibi 3.00 8.00
A12 Matt Ryan 10.00 25.00
A13 T.C. Ostrander 4.00 10.00
A14 Bernard Morris 4.00 10.00
A15 Sam Baker 3.00 8.00
A16 Adrian Arrington 3.00 8.00
A17 Kevin O'Connell 3.00 8.00
A18 Jacob Hester 3.00 8.00
A19 Keenan Burton 3.00 8.00
A20 Darius Reynaud 3.00 8.00
A21 Keon Lattimore 4.00 10.00
A22 Tashard Choice 3.00 8.00
A23 Jake Long 5.00 12.00
A24 Paul Smith 3.00 8.00
A25 Jamaal Charles 5.00 12.00
A26 Yvenson Bernard 5.00 12.00
A27 Alex Brink 4.00 10.00
A28 James Hardy 3.00 8.00
A29 Martin Rucker 3.00 8.00
A30 Steve Slaton 3.00 8.00
A31 Derrick Harvey 3.00 8.00
A32 Andre Callender 5.00 12.00
A33 Jabari Arthur 4.00 10.00
A34 Bruce Hocker 5.00 12.00
A35 Kalvin McRae 3.00 8.00
A36 Lawrence Jackson 3.00 8.00
A37 Tyrell Johnson 3.00 8.00
A38 Marcus Howard 5.00 12.00
A39 Sam Keller 3.00 8.00
A40 Keith Rivers 3.00 8.00
A41 Brandon Flowers 4.00 10.00
A42 Adarius Bowman 4.00 10.00
A43 Ricky Santos 5.00 12.00
A44 Jordon Dizon 3.00 8.00
A45 Robert Jordan 4.00 10.00
A46 Maurice Purify 5.00 12.00
A47 Lavelle Hawkins 4.00 10.00
A48 Jason Rivers 3.00 8.00
A49 John Carlson 3.00 8.00
A50 Vernon Gholston 3.00 8.00
A68 Devin Thomas 3.00 8.00
A69 Beau Bell 4.00 10.00
A70 Owen Schmitt 3.00 8.00
A71 Paul Raymond 4.00 10.00
A72 Jordy Nelson 8.00 20.00
A73 Ray Rice 3.00 8.00
A74 Darrell Strong 4.00 10.00
A75 Felix Jones 3.00 8.00
A76 Kevin Smith SP 3.00 8.00
A77 Justin Forsett 4.00 10.00
A78 Antoine Cason 4.00 10.00
A79 Ryan Clady 4.00 10.00
A80 Mike Hart 3.00 8.00
A81 Kenny Phillips 3.00 8.00
A82 Jonathan Stewart SP 12.00 30.00
A83 Fred Davis 3.00 8.00
A84 Malcolm Kelly 3.00 8.00
A85 Matt Flynn 3.00 8.00
A86 Allen Patrick 3.00 8.00
A87 Brent Miller 4.00 10.00
A88 Andre Caldwell 3.00 8.00
A89 Josh Johnson 3.00 8.00
A90 Erik Ainge 3.00 8.00
A91 Tom Zbikowski 4.00 10.00
A92 Dan Connor 3.00 8.00
A93 Leodis McKelvin 4.00 10.00
A94 Sedrick Ellis 3.00 8.00
A95 Rashard Mendenhall SP 5.00 12.00
A96 Mike Jenkins 3.00 8.00
A97 Dustin Keller 4.00 10.00
A98 Donnie Avery 4.00 10.00
A100 Darren McFadden SP 3.00 8.00
A101 Justin McKinney 4.00 10.00
A102 Angelo Craig 3.00 8.00
A103 Larry Grant 3.00 8.00
A104 Nick Hayden 3.00 8.00
A105 Haruki Nakamura 3.00 8.00
A106 Darnell Terrell 3.00 8.00
A107 Nick Hill 3.00 8.00

2008 SAGE HIT Autographs Gold

*GOLD/250: .5X TO 1.2X BASIC AUTO
GOLD/250 ODDS 1:28 LOW, 1:26 HI
GOLD PRINT RUN 250 SER.#'d SETS
A4 Limas Sweed 5.00 12.00
A6 Brian Brohm 5.00 12.00
A7 Chad Henne 6.00 15.00
A82 Jonathan Stewart 8.00 20.00
A100 Darren McFadden 5.00 12.00

2008 SAGE HIT Autographs Silver

*SILVER: .4X TO 1X BASIC AUTO
SILVER ODDS 1:18 LOW, 1:21 HI
A4 Limas Sweed 8.00 20.00
A6 Brian Brohm 3.00 8.00
A7 Chad Henne 4.00 10.00
A100 Darren McFadden 3.00 8.00

2008 SAGE HIT Saturday Colors

COMPLETE SET (30) 10.00 25.00
STATED ODDS 1:5 LOW/HI
UNPRICED PRINT PLATE PRINT RUN 1
S1 Matt Ryan 1.50 4.00
S2 Brian Brohm .50 1.25
S3 Chad Henne .60 1.50
S4 Joe Flacco 1.00 2.50
S5 John David Booty .50 1.25
S6 Dennis Dixon .50 1.25
S7 Jamaal Charles .75 2.00
S8 Steve Slaton .50 1.25
S9 Early Doucet .50 1.25
S10 James Hardy .50 1.25
S11 Limas Sweed .50 1.25
S12 Vernon Gholston .50 1.25
S13 Derrick Harvey .50 1.25
S14 Keith Rivers .50 1.25
S15 Jake Long .75 2.00
S16 Josh Johnson .50 1.25
S17 Erik Ainge .50 1.25
S18 Darren McFadden .50 1.25
S19 Rashard Mendenhall .50 1.25
S20 Jonathan Stewart .75 2.00
S21 Felix Jones .50 1.25
S22 Ray Rice .50 1.25
S23 Kevin Smith .50 1.25
S24 Mike Hart .50 1.25
S25 DeSean Jackson 1.00 2.50
S26 Malcolm Kelly .50 1.25
S27 Devin Thomas .50 1.25
S28 Andre Caldwell .50 1.25
S29 Fred Davis .50 1.25
S30 Sedrick Ellis .50 1.25

2008 SAGE HIT Saturday Colors Autographs Gold

AUTO/100 ODDS 1:288 LOW, 1:192 HI
SA1 Matt Ryan 20.00 50.00
SA4 Joe Flacco 10.00 25.00
SA7 Jamaal Charles 8.00 20.00
SA18 Darren McFadden 5.00 12.00
SA19 Rashard Mendenhall 5.00 12.00
SA20 Jonathan Stewart 8.00 20.00
SA21 Felix Jones 5.00 12.00
SA22 Ray Rice 5.00 12.00

2008 SAGE HIT Write Stuff

COMPLETE SET (20) 10.00 25.00
STATED ODDS 1:10 LOW/HI
UNPRICED PRINT PLATE PRINT RUN 1
WS1 John David Booty .50 1.25
WS2 Brian Brohm .50 1.25
WS3 Jamaal Charles .75 2.00
WS4 Dennis Dixon .50 1.25
WS5 Early Doucet .50 1.25
WS6 Joe Flacco 1.00 2.50
WS7 James Hardy .50 1.25
WS8 Chad Henne .60 1.50
WS9 Matt Ryan 1.50 4.00
WS10 Steve Slaton .50 1.25
WS11 Erik Ainge .50 1.25
WS12 DeSean Jackson 1.00 2.50
WS13 Josh Johnson .50 1.25
WS14 Felix Jones .50 1.25
WS15 Malcolm Kelly .50 1.25
WS16 Darren McFadden .50 1.25
WS17 Rashard Mendenhall .50 1.25
WS18 Ray Rice .50 1.25
WS19 Kevin Smith .50 1.25
WS20 Jonathan Stewart .75 2.00

2008 SAGE HIT Write Stuff Autographs

WS AU/25 ODDS 1:1152 LOW, 1:770 HI
WSA1 John David Booty 8.00 20.00
WSA2 Brian Brohm 8.00 20.00
WSA3 Jamaal Charles 12.00 30.00
WSA4 Dennis Dixon 8.00 20.00
WSA6 Joe Flacco 15.00 40.00
WSA7 James Hardy 8.00 20.00
WSA8 Chad Henne 10.00 25.00
WSA9 Matt Ryan 25.00 60.00
WSA10 Steve Slaton 8.00 20.00
WSA11 Erik Ainge 8.00 20.00
WSA13 Josh Johnson 8.00 20.00
WSA14 Felix Jones 8.00 20.00
WSA15 Malcolm Kelly 8.00 20.00
WSA16 Darren McFadden 8.00 20.00
WSA17 Rashard Mendenhall 8.00 20.00
WSA18 Ray Rice 8.00 20.00
WSA19 Kevin Smith 8.00 20.00
WSA20 Jonathan Stewart 30.00 80.00

2009 SAGE HIT

SAGE HIT was issued in two series: low and high. The low series was released on March 18, 2009 and featured 50 cards (#1-50). High series went live on April 20 and featured cards #51-100 plus ten additional first series cards featuring different photos (listed as "B" card numbers below).

COMPLETE SET (110) 15.00 40.00
COMP.LOW SERIES (60) 7.50 20.00
COMP.HIGH SERIES (50) 10.00 25.00
1 Patrick Turner .25 .60
2 Malcolm Jenkins .25 .60
3 Eugene Monroe .25 .60
4 D.J. Boldin .25 .60
5A Michael Crabtree ball at chest .40 1.00
5B Michael Crabtree ball in air .40 1.00
6A Mark Sanchez facing left .25 .60
6B Mark Sanchez facing right .25 .60
7 Cornelius Ingram .25 .60
8A Darrius Heyward-Bey no ball .40 1.00
8B Darrius Heyward-Bey with ball .40 1.00
9A Jeremy Maclin no helmet visor .30 .75
9B Jeremy Maclin helmet visor .30 .75
10 Brian Cushing .25 .60
11A Josh Freeman hips hidden .25 .60
11B Josh Freeman hips in view .25 .60
12 Curtis Painter .25 .60
13A Nate Davis pointing .25 .60
13B Nate Davis holding ball .25 .60
14 Hunter Cantwell .25 .60
15A Pat White head shot .30 .75
15B Pat White running ball .30 .75
16 Mike Teel .25 .60
17 Tom Brandstater .30 .75
18 Jarett Dillard .25 .60
19 Sammie Stroughter .25 .60
20 Aaron Kelly .25 .60
21 Darius Passmore .25 .60
22 Alphonso Smith .25 .60
23A Javon Ringer one hand on ball .25 .60
23B Javon Ringer two hands on ball .25 .60
24 Jeremiah Johnson .25 .60
25A LeSean McCoy blu jsy .60 1.50
25B LeSean McCoy white jsy .60 1.50
26 Tim Jamison .30 .75
27 David Bruton .25 .60
28 Worrell Williams .25 .60
29 Matt Shaughnessy .30 .75
30 Nathan Brown .30 .75
31 Mike Reilly .25 .60
32 Darrell Mack .25 .60
33 James Laurinaitis .25 .60
34A Donald Brown two hands on ball .25 .60
34B Donald Brown one hand on ball .25 .60
35 Marlon Lucky .25 .60
36 Roy Miller .25 .60
37 Eric Wood .25 .60
38 Freddie Brown .25 .60
39 Taurus Johnson .25 .60
40 Ryan Purvis .25 .60
41 Darius Butler .30 .75
42 Ricky Jean-Francois .30 .75
43 Kaluka Maiava .25 .60
44 Brandon Underwood .25 .60
45 Chase Coffman .25 .60
46 Jamon Meredith .25 .60
47 Clay Matthews 1.00 2.50
48 Brian Orakpo .30 .75
49 Jeremy Childs .25 .60
50 Devin Moore .25 .60
51 M.Ryan/J.Flacco SO .40 1.00
52 M.Stafford/M.Sanchez SO .75 2.00
53 K.Moreno/C.Wells SO .15 .40
54 M.Crabtree/J.Maclin SO .25 .60
55 M.Crabtree/G.Harrell TM .25 .60
56 M.Stafford/K.Moreno TM .75 2.00
57 Sanchez/Maualuga TM .25 .60
58 C.Wells/J.Laurinaitis TM .15 .40
59 Matthew Stafford 1.25 3.00
60 Jason Boltus .25 .60
61 Chase Clement .40 1.00
62 Aaron Brown .30 .75
63 Kevin Ogletree .30 .75
64 Scott McKillop .25 .60
65 Clint Sintim .25 .60
66 Andre Brown .30 .75
67 John Parker Wilson .25 .60
68 Brian Hoyer .40 1.00
69 B.J. Raji .30 .75
70 Stephen McGee .25 .60
71 Louis Murphy .25 .60
72 Jason Smith .25 .60
73 Cullen Harper .25 .60
74 Johnny Knox .30 .75
75 Alex Boone .40 1.00
76 Tyrell Fenroy .30 .75
77 Eben Britton .30 .75
78 Chris Wells .25 .60
79 Mike Mickens .25 .60
80 Brian Robiskie .25 .60
81 Brooks Foster .25 .60
82 Jamarko Simmons .25 .60
83 Brian Mandeville [illegible] [illegible]
84 Jared Cook .30 .75
85 Brandon Williams .30 .75
86 Rashad Jennings .30 .75
87 James Casey .30 .75
88 Hakeem Nicks .30 .75
89 Juaquin Iglesias .25 .60
90 Mike Thomas .25 .60
91 Jared Bronson .25 .60
92 C.J. Spillman .30 .75
93 Marcus Freeman .25 .60
94 David Veikune .30 .75
95 Gartrell Johnson .25 .60
96 Graham Harrell .25 .60
97 Ryan Palmer .30 .75
98 Demetrius Byrd .30 .75
99 Rey Maualuga .40 1.00
100 Knowshon Moreno .25 .60
ROY Matt Ryan ROY SP

2009 SAGE HIT Glossy

*GLOSSY: .6X TO 1.5X BASIC CARDS
ONE GLOSSY PER RETAIL PACK

2009 SAGE HIT Gold

COMPLETE SET (110) 50.00 125.00
COMP.LOW SERIES (60) 25.00 60.00
COMP.HIGH SERIES (50) 30.00 80.00
*GOLD 1-100: 1X TO 2.5X BASIC CARDS
1-50 ODDS 1:10 LOW, 51-100 1:27 HIGH

2009 SAGE HIT Make Ready Black

*1-50 BLACK/50: 2.5X TO 6X BASIC CARDS
*1-50 CYAN/50: 2.5X TO 6X BASIC CARDS
*1-50 MAGENTA/50: 2.5X TO 6X BASIC CARDS
*1-50 YELLOW/50: 2.5X TO 6X BASIC CARDS
MAKE READY/50 ODDS 1:30 LOW, 1:13.5 HI

2009 SAGE HIT Silver

COMPLETE SET (110) 40.00 80.00
COMP.LOW SERIES (60) 15.00 40.00
COMP.HIGH SERIES (50) 20.00 50.00
*SILVER 1-100: .6X TO 1.5X BASIC CARDS
1-50 ODDS 1:3 LOW, 51-100 1:4.5 HIGH

2009 SAGE HIT Autographs

BLACK AU ODDS 1:10 LOW, 1:7.2 HIGH
*SILVER: .4X TO 1X BASIC AUTOS
SILVER AU ODDS 1:18 LOW, 1:11 HIGH
*GOLD/250: .5X TO 1.2X BASIC AU
GOLD/250 AU ODDS 1:28 LOW, 1:12 HIGH
OVERALL AUTO ODDS 1:5 LOW, 1:3 HIGH
1 Patrick Turner 3.00 8.00
2 Malcolm Jenkins 3.00 8.00
3 Eugene Monroe 3.00 8.00
4 D.J. Boldin 3.00 8.00
5 Michael Crabtree 5.00 12.00
6 Mark Sanchez 20.00 40.00
7 Cornelius Ingram 3.00 8.00
8 Darrius Heyward-Bey 5.00 12.00
9 Jeremy Maclin 4.00 10.00
10 Brian Cushing 3.00 8.00
11 Josh Freeman 3.00 8.00
12 Curtis Painter 3.00 8.00
13 Nate Davis 3.00 8.00
14 Hunter Cantwell 3.00 8.00
15 Pat White 4.00 10.00
16 Mike Teel 3.00 8.00
17 Tom Brandstater 4.00 10.00
18 Jarett Dillard 3.00 8.00
19 Sammie Stroughter 3.00 8.00
20 Aaron Kelly 3.00 8.00
22 Alphonso Smith 3.00 8.00
23 Javon Ringer 3.00 8.00
24 Jeremiah Johnson 3.00 8.00
25 LeSean McCoy 8.00 20.00
26 Tim Jamison 4.00 10.00
27 David Bruton 3.00 8.00
28 Worrell Williams 3.00 8.00
29 Matt Shaughnessy 4.00 10.00
30 Nathan Brown 4.00 10.00
31 Mike Reilly 3.00 8.00
32 Darrell Mack 3.00 8.00
33 James Laurinaitis 3.00 8.00
34 Donald Brown 3.00 8.00
35 Marlon Lucky 3.00 8.00
36 Roy Miller 3.00 8.00
37 Eric Wood 3.00 8.00
38 Freddie Brown 3.00 8.00
40 Ryan Purvis 3.00 8.00
41 Darius Butler 4.00 10.00
42 Ricky Jean-Francois 4.00 10.00
43 Kaluka Maiava 3.00 8.00
44 Brandon Underwood 3.00 8.00
45 Chase Coffman 3.00 8.00
46 Jamon Meredith 3.00 8.00
47 Clay Matthews 12.00 30.00
48 Brian Orakpo 4.00 10.00
49 Jeremy Childs 3.00 8.00
50 Devin Moore 3.00 8.00
59 Matthew Stafford 20.00 50.00
60 Jason Boltus 3.00 8.00
61 Chase Clement 5.00 12.00
62 Aaron Brown 4.00 10.00
63 Kevin Ogletree 4.00 10.00
64 Scott McKillop 3.00 8.00
65 Clint Sintim 3.00 8.00
66 Andre Brown 4.00 10.00
67 John Parker Wilson 3.00 8.00
68 Brian Hoyer 5.00 12.00
69 B.J. Raji 4.00 10.00
70 Stephen McGee 3.00 8.00
71 Louis Murphy 3.00 8.00
72 Jason Smith 3.00 8.00
73 Cullen Harper 3.00 8.00
74 Johnny Knox 4.00 10.00
75 Alex Boone 5.00 12.00
76 Tyrell Fenroy 4.00 10.00
77 Eben Britton 4.00 10.00
78 Chris Wells 3.00 8.00
79 Mike Mickens 3.00 8.00
80 Brian Robiskie 3.00 8.00
81 Brooks Foster 3.00 8.00
82 Jamarko Simmons 3.00 8.00
83 Brian Mandeville 3.00 8.00
84 Jared Cook 4.00 10.00
85 Brandon Williams 4.00 10.00
86 Rashad Jennings 4.00 10.00
87 James Casey 4.00 10.00
88 Hakeem Nicks 4.00 10.00
89 Juaquin Iglesias 3.00 8.00
90 Mike Thomas 3.00 8.00
91 Jared Bronson 3.00 8.00
92 C.J. Spillman 4.00 10.00
93 Marcus Freeman 3.00 8.00
94 David Veikune 4.00 10.00
95 Gartrell Johnson 3.00 8.00
96 Graham Harrell 8.00 20.00
97 Ryan Palmer 4.00 10.00
98 Demetrius Byrd 4.00 10.00
99 Rey Maualuga 5.00 12.00
100 Knowshon Moreno 3.00 8.00
101 Jason Williams 4.00 10.00
102 Jahi Word-Daniels 4.00 10.00
103 DeAndre Levy 4.00 10.00
104 Kyle Moore 4.00 10.00
105 Kory Sperry 3.00 8.00
106 Jarron Gilbert 4.00 10.00
107 Darcel McBath 3.00 8.00
108 Walt Mendenhall 4.00 10.00
109 Pannel Egboh 3.00 8.00
110 Will Johnson 4.00 10.00

2009 SAGE HIT Game Changers

MPLETE SET (30) 15.00 40.00
COMP.LOW SERIES (15) 8.00 20.00
COMP.HIGH SERIES (15) 8.00 20.00
STATED ODDS 1:5 LOW/HIGH
G1 Michael Crabtree .75 2.00
G2 Brian Cushing .50 1.25
G3 Nate Davis .50 1.25
G4 Graham Harrell .50 1.25
G5 Juaquin Iglesias .50 1.25
G6 Malcolm Jenkins .50 1.25
G7 James Laurinaitis .50 1.25
G8 Jeremy Maclin .60 1.50
G9 LeSean McCoy 1.25 3.00
G10 Devin Moore .50 1.25
G11 Hakeem Nicks .60 1.50
G12 Brian Orakpo .60 1.50
G13 Javon Ringer .50 1.25
G14 Mark Sanchez .50 1.25
G15 Pat White .60 1.50
G16 Donald Brown .50 1.25
G17 Chase Coffman .50 1.25
G18 Jared Cook .60 1.50
G19 Josh Freeman .50 1.25
G20 Cullen Harper .50 1.25
G21 Darrius Heyward-Bey .75 2.00
G22 Rashad Jennings .60 1.50
G23 Rey Maualuga .75 2.00
G24 Knowshon Moreno .50 1.25
G25 Louis Murphy .50 1.25
G26 B.J. Raji .60 1.50
G27 Brian Robiskie .50 1.25
G28 Matthew Stafford 2.50 6.00
G29 Chris Wells .50 1.25
G30 John Parker Wilson .50 1.25

2009 SAGE HIT Game Changers Autographs

AUTO/100 ODDS 1:288 LOW, 1:86 HIGH
G1 Michael Crabtree 8.00 20.00
G2 Brian Cushing 5.00 12.00
G3 Nate Davis 5.00 12.00
G4 Graham Harrell 12.00 30.00
G5 Juaquin Iglesias 5.00 12.00
G6 Malcolm Jenkins 5.00 12.00
G7 James Laurinaitis 5.00 12.00
G8 Jeremy Maclin 6.00 15.00
G9 LeSean McCoy 12.00 30.00
G10 Devin Moore 5.00 12.00
G11 Hakeem Nicks 6.00 15.00
G12 Brian Orakpo 6.00 15.00
G13 Javon Ringer 5.00 12.00
G14 Mark Sanchez 25.00 60.00
G15 Pat White 6.00 15.00
G16 Donald Brown 5.00 12.00
G17 Chase Coffman 5.00 12.00
G18 Jared Cook 6.00 15.00
G19 Josh Freeman 5.00 12.00
G20 Cullen Harper 5.00 12.00
G21 Darrius Heyward-Bey 8.00 20.00
G22 Rashad Jennings 6.00 15.00
G23 Rey Maualuga 8.00 20.00
G24 Knowshon Moreno 5.00 12.00
G25 Louis Murphy 5.00 12.00
G26 B.J. Raji 6.00 15.00
G27 Brian Robiskie 5.00 12.00
G28 Matthew Stafford 30.00 80.00
G29 Chris Wells 5.00 12.00
G30 John Parker Wilson 5.00 12.00

2009 SAGE HIT Write Stuff

COMPLETE SET (20) 15.00 40.00
COMP.LOW SERIES (10) 8.00 20.00
COMP.HIGH SERIES (10) 8.00 20.00
STATED ODDS 1:10 LOW, 1:9 HIGH
WS1 Michael Crabtree .75 2.00
WS2 Nate Davis .50 1.25
WS3 Graham Harrell .50 1.25
WS4 Juaquin Iglesias .50 1.25
WS5 Jeremy Maclin .60 1.50
WS6 LeSean McCoy 1.25 3.00
WS7 Hakeem Nicks UER .60 1.50
WS8 Javon Ringer .50 1.25
WS9 Mark Sanchez .50 1.25
WS10 Pat White .60 1.50
WS11 Donald Brown .50 1.25
WS12 Josh Freeman .50 1.25
WS13 Darrius Heyward-Bey .75 2.00
WS14 Rashad Jennings .60 1.50
WS15 James Laurinaitis .50 1.25
WS16 Rey Maualuga .75 2.00
WS17 Knowshon Moreno .50 1.25
WS18 Brian Robiskie .50 1.25
WS19 Matthew Stafford 2.50 6.00
WS20 Chris Wells .50 1.25

2009 SAGE HIT Write Stuff Autographs

AUTO/25 ODDS 1:1152 LOW, 1:518 HIGH
WS1 Michael Crabtree 10.00 25.00
WS2 Nate Davis 6.00 15.00
WS3 Graham Harrell 12.00 30.00
WS4 Juaquin Iglesias 6.00 15.00
WS5 Jeremy Maclin 10.00 25.00
WS6 LeSean McCoy 15.00 40.00
WS7 Hakeem Nicks 8.00 20.00
WS8 Javon Ringer 6.00 15.00
WS9 Mark Sanchez 30.00 80.00
WS10 Pat White 8.00 20.00
WS11 Donald Brown 6.00 15.00
WS12 Josh Freeman 6.00 15.00
WS13 Darrius Heyward-Bey 10.00 25.00
WS14 Rashad Jennings 8.00 20.00
WS15 James Laurinaitis 6.00 15.00
WS16 Rey Maualuga 10.00 25.00
WS17 Knowshon Moreno 6.00 15.00
WS18 Brian Robiskie 6.00 15.00
WS19 Matthew Stafford 50.00 120.00
WS20 Chris Wells 6.00 15.00

2010 SAGE HIT

COMP.LOW SERIES (50) 8.00 20.00
COMP.HIGH SERIES (50) 10.00 25.00
1 Mardy Gilyard .20 .50
2 Carlton Mitchell .20 .50
3 Gerald McCoy .20 .50
4 Joe McKnight .20 .50
5 Sean Canfield .20 .50
6 Donovan Warren .20 .50
7 Toby Gerhart DP .20 .50
8 Jordan Shipley .20 .50
9 Thaddeus Lewis .25 .60
10 Blair White .20 .50
11 Zac Robinson .25 .60
12 Colt McCoy DP .25 .60
13 Stafon Johnson .20 .50
14 Sam Bradford DP .25 .60
15 Brandon Spikes .20 .50
16 Jarrett Brown .20 .50
17 Sean Weatherspoon .20 .50
18 Damian Williams .20 .50
19 Jermaine Gresham .20 .50
20 Jeremy Williams .20 .50
21 Ryan Mathews .20 .50
22 Aaron Hernandez .20 .50
23 Greg Mathews .20 .50
24 Tony Moeaki .25 .60
25 Rolando McClain .20 .50
26 Joey Elliott .25 .60
27 Antonio Brown 1.50 4.00
28 C.J. Spiller DP .20 .50
29 Seyi Ajirotutu .20 .50
30 Javarris James .20 .50
31 Dan LeFevour .20 .50
32 Dennis Pitta .20 .50
33 Andre Anderson .20 .50
34 Colin Peek .20 .50
35 Rennie Curran .20 .50
36 Alabama Program .60 1.00
37 Florida Program .75 2.00

38 Florida State Program .40 1.00
39 Georgia Program .40 1.00
40 LSU Program .40 1.00
41 Miami Program .40 1.00
42 Michigan Program .40 1.00
43 Nebraska Program .75 2.00
44 Notre Dame Program .50 1.25
45 Ohio State Program .50 1.25
46 Oklahoma Program .60 1.50
47 Penn State Program .40 1.00
48 USC Program .50 1.25
49 Tennessee Program .40 1.00
50 Texas Program .40 1.00
51 Jimmy Clausen .20 .50
52 Mike Williams .20 .50
53 Martell Mallett .25 .60
54 Jevan Snead .20 .50
55 Joe Webb .20 .50
56 Bruce Campbell .25 .60
57 Derrick Morgan .20 .50
58 Montario Hardesty .20 .50
59 NaVorro Bowman .40 1.00
60 Earl Thomas .50 1.25
61 Jahvid Best IT .15 .40
62 Dan LeFevour IT .15 .40
63 Tony Pike IT .15 .40
64 C.J. Spiller IT .15 .40
65 Aaron Hernandez IT .15 .40
66 Ryan Mathews IT .15 .40
67 Jonathan Dwyer IT .15 .40
68 Ndamukong Suh IT .75 2.00
69 Jimmy Clausen IT .15 .40
70 Sam Bradford IT .20 .50
71 Zac Robinson IT .20 .50
72 Dez Bryant IT .40 1.00
73 Sean Canfield IT .15 .40
74 Damian Williams IT .15 .40
75 Toby Gerhart IT .15 .40
76 Colt McCoy IT .20 .50
77 Ndamukong Suh .75 2.00
78 Anthony Dixon .20 .50
79 Joique Bell .20 .50
80 Jahvid Best .20 .50
81 Danario Alexander .20 .50
82 Jonathan Dwyer .20 .50
83 Roddrick Muckelroy .20 .50
84 Rob Gronkowski .60 1.50
85 Tony Pike .20 .50
86 Kerry Meier .25 .60
87 Taylor Price .20 .50
88 Nate Byham .20 .50
89 Garrett Graham .20 .50
90 Jason Pierre-Paul .30 .75
91 John Skelton .25 .60
92 Brandon Lang .20 .50
93 Pat Simonds .20 .50
94 Cameron Sheffield .20 .50
95 C.J. Wilson .25 .60
96 Dezmon Briscoe .20 .50
97 Bryan Bulaga .20 .50
98 Jerry Hughes .20 .50
99 Arrelious Benn .20 .50
100 Dez Bryant .50 1.25
CL1 C.McC/Splr/Brdf CL/100

2010 SAGE HIT Gold

*GOLD: 1.2X TO 3X BASIC CARDS
1-50 GOLD ODDS 1:10 LOW SERIES
51-100 GOLD ODDS 1:10 HIGH SERIES

2010 SAGE HIT Make Ready Black

*MR BLACK: 2X TO 5X BASIC CARDS
*MR CYAN: 2X TO 5X BASIC CARDS
*MR MAGENTA: 2X TO 5 BASIC CARDS
*MR YELLOW: 2X TO 5X BASIC CARDS
MAKE READY/50 ODDS 1:30 LOW
MAKE READY/50 ODDS 1:13 HIGH

2010 SAGE HIT Silver

*SILVER: .8X TO 2X BASIC CARDS
1-50 SILVER ODDS 1:3 LOW SERIES
51-100 SILVER ODDS 1:4 HIGH SERIES

2010 SAGE HIT Autographs

A1-A43 ODDS 1:10 LOW SERIES
A51-A99 ODDS 1:7 HIGH SERIES
*GOLD/250: .5X TO 1.2X BASIC AUTO
*GOLD/250: .4X TO 1X BASIC AU SP
A1-A43 GOLD/250 ODDS 1:28 LOW
A51-A99 GOLD/250 ODDS 1:15 HIGH
*SILVER: .4X TO 1X BASIC AUTO
A1-A43 SILVER ODDS 1:18 LOW SERIES
A51-A99 SILVER ODDS 1:10 HIGH SER.
A1 Mardy Gilyard 3.00 8.00
A2 Carlton Mitchell 3.00 8.00
A3 Gerald McCoy 3.00 8.00
A4 Joe McKnight SP 8.00 20.00
A5 Sean Canfield 3.00 8.00
A6 Donovan Warren 3.00 8.00
A7 Toby Gerhart 3.00 8.00
A8 Jordan Shipley 3.00 8.00
A9 Thaddeus Lewis 6.00 15.00
A10 Blair White 3.00 8.00
A11 Zac Robinson 4.00 10.00
A12 Colt McCoy 4.00 10.00
A13 Stafon Johnson 3.00 8.00
A14 Sam Bradford SP 15.00 40.00
A15 Brandon Spikes 3.00 8.00
A16 Jarrett Brown 3.00 8.00
A17 Sean Weatherspoon 3.00 8.00
A18 Damian Williams 3.00 8.00
A19 Jermaine Gresham 3.00 8.00
A20 Jeremy Williams 3.00 8.00
A21 Ryan Mathews 3.00 8.00
A22 Aaron Hernandez 3.00 8.00
A23 Greg Mathews 3.00 8.00
A24 Tony Moeaki 4.00 10.00
A25 Rolando McClain 3.00 8.00
A26 Joey Elliott 4.00 10.00
A27 Antonio Brown 25.00 60.00
A28 C.J. Spiller SP 3.00 8.00
A29 Seyi Ajirotutu 3.00 8.00
A30 Javarris James 3.00 8.00
A31 Dan LeFevour 3.00 8.00
A32 Dennis Pitta 3.00 8.00
A33 Andre Anderson 3.00 8.00
A34 Colin Peek 3.00 8.00
A35 Rennie Curran 3.00 8.00
A36 Shawn Lauvao 3.00 8.00
A37 Eric Olsen 4.00 10.00
A38 Sam Young 4.00 10.00
A39 Matt Tennant 3.00 8.00
A40 Cam Thomas 4.00 10.00
A41 Chris Cook 3.00 8.00
A42 Kyle McCarthy 5.00 12.00
A43 Shamar Graves 3.00 8.00
A51 Jimmy Clausen 3.00 8.00
A52 Mike Williams 3.00 8.00
A53 Martell Mallett 4.00 10.00
A54 Jevan Snead 3.00 8.00
A55 Joe Webb 3.00 8.00
A56 Bruce Campbell 4.00 10.00
A57 Derrick Morgan 3.00 8.00
A58 Montario Hardesty 3.00 8.00
A59 NaVorro Bowman 6.00 15.00
A60 Earl Thomas 8.00 20.00
A77 Ndamukong Suh SP 15.00 40.00
A78 Anthony Dixon 3.00 8.00
A79 Joique Bell 3.00 8.00
A80 Jahvid Best 3.00 8.00
A81 Danario Alexander 3.00 8.00
A82 Jonathan Dwyer 3.00 8.00
A83 Roddrick Muckelroy 3.00 8.00
A84 Rob Gronkowski 15.00 30.00
A85 Tony Pike 3.00 8.00
A86 Kerry Meier 4.00 10.00
A87 Taylor Price 3.00 8.00
A88 Nate Byham 3.00 8.00
A89 Garrett Graham 3.00 8.00
A90 Jason Pierre-Paul 5.00 12.00
A91 John Skelton 4.00 10.00
A92 Brandon Lang 3.00 8.00
A93 Pat Simonds 3.00 8.00
A94 Cameron Sheffield 3.00 8.00
A95 C.J. Wilson 4.00 10.00
A96 Dezmon Briscoe 3.00 8.00
A97 Bryan Bulaga 3.00 8.00
A98 Jerry Hughes 3.00 8.00
A99 Arrelious Benn 3.00 8.00

2010 SAGE HIT Prospectus

COMPLETE SET (30) 12.00 30.00
COMP.LOW SERIES (15) 6.00 15.00
COMP.HIGH SERIES (15) 6.00 15.00
P1-P15 ODDS 1:5 LOW SERIES
P16-P30 ODDS 1:5 HIGH SERIES
P1 Arrelious Benn .40 1.00
P2 Dez Bryant 1.00 2.50
P3 Sean Canfield .40 1.00
P4 Jimmy Clausen .40 1.00
P5 Jonathan Dwyer .40 1.00
P6 Mardy Gilyard .40 1.00
P7 Jermaine Gresham .40 1.00
P8 Montario Hardesty .40 1.00
P9 Aaron Hernandez .40 1.00
P10 Dan LeFevour .40 1.00
P11 Ryan Mathews .40 1.00
P12 Colt McCoy .50 1.25
P13 Joe McKnight .40 1.00
P14 Jevan Snead .40 1.00
P15 Damian Williams .40 1.00
P16 Jahvid Best .40 1.00
P17 Sam Bradford .50 1.25
P18 Dezmon Briscoe .40 1.00
P19 Jarrett Brown .40 1.00
P20 Anthony Dixon .40 1.00
P21 Toby Gerhart .40 1.00
P22 Rob Gronkowski 1.25 3.00
P23 Carlton Mitchell .40 1.00
P24 Tony Pike .40 1.00
P25 Taylor Price .40 1.00
P26 Zac Robinson .50 1.25
P27 Jordan Shipley .40 1.00
P28 C.J. Spiller .40 1.00
P29 Ndamukong Suh 3.00 8.00
P30 Mike Williams .40 1.00

2010 SAGE HIT Prospectus Autographs

P1-P15 AU/100 ODDS 1:288 LOW
P16-P20 AU/100 ODDS 1:87 HIGH
P1 Arrelious Benn 5.00 12.00
P3 Sean Canfield 5.00 12.00
P4 Jimmy Clausen 5.00 12.00
P5 Jonathan Dwyer 5.00 12.00
P6 Mardy Gilyard 5.00 12.00
P7 Jermaine Gresham 5.00 12.00
P8 Montario Hardesty 5.00 12.00
P9 Aaron Hernandez 5.00 12.00
P10 Dan LeFevour 5.00 12.00
P11 Ryan Mathews 5.00 12.00
P12 Colt McCoy 6.00 15.00
P13 Joe McKnight 5.00 12.00
P14 Jevan Snead 5.00 12.00
P15 Damian Williams 5.00 12.00
P16 Jahvid Best 5.00 12.00
P17 Sam Bradford 30.00 80.00
P18 Dezmon Briscoe 5.00 12.00
P19 Jarrett Brown 5.00 12.00
P20 Anthony Dixon 5.00 12.00
P21 Toby Gerhart 5.00 12.00
P22 Rob Gronkowski 15.00 40.00
P23 Carlton Mitchell 5.00 12.00
P24 Tony Pike 5.00 12.00
P25 Taylor Price 5.00 12.00
P26 Zac Robinson 6.00 15.00
P27 Jordan Shipley 5.00 12.00
P28 C.J. Spiller 5.00 12.00
P29 Ndamukong Suh 25.00 60.00
P30 Mike Williams 5.00 12.00

2010 SAGE HIT Write Stuff

COMPLETE SET (20) 12.00 30.00
COMP.LOW SERIES (10) 6.00 15.00
COMP.HIGH SERIES (10) 6.00 15.00
WS1-WS10 ODDS 1:10 LOW SERIES
WS11-WS20 ODDS 1:10 HIGH SERIES
WS1 Arrelious Benn .40 1.00
WS2 Dez Bryant 1.00 2.50
WS3 Jimmy Clausen .40 1.00
WS4 Jonathan Dwyer .40 1.00
WS5 Mardy Gilyard .40 1.00
WS6 Montario Hardesty .40 1.00
WS7 Colt McCoy .50 1.25
WS8 Joe McKnight .40 1.00
WS9 Jevan Snead .40 1.00
WS10 Damian Williams .40 1.00
WS11 Jahvid Best .40 1.00
WS12 Sam Bradford .50 1.25
WS13 Anthony Dixon .40 1.00
WS14 Toby Gerhart .40 1.00
WS15 Dan LeFevour .40 1.00
WS16 Ryan Mathews .40 1.00
WS17 Tony Pike .40 1.00
WS18 Jordan Shipley .40 1.00
WS19 C.J. Spiller .40 1.00
WS20 Ndamukong Suh 3.00 8.00

2010 SAGE HIT Write Stuff Autographs

WS1-WS10 AU/25 ODDS 1:1152 LOW
WS11-WS20 AU/25 ODDS 1:208 LOW
WS1 Arrelious Benn 6.00 15.00
WS3 Jimmy Clausen 6.00 15.00
WS4 Jonathan Dwyer 6.00 15.00
WS5 Mardy Gilyard 6.00 15.00
WS6 Montario Hardesty 6.00 15.00
WS7 Colt McCoy 8.00 20.00
WS8 Joe McKnight 6.00 15.00
WS9 Jevan Snead 6.00 15.00
WS10 Damian Williams 6.00 15.00
WS11 Jahvid Best 6.00 15.00
WS12 Sam Bradford 40.00 100.00
WS13 Anthony Dixon 6.00 15.00
WS14 Toby Gerhart 6.00 15.00
WS15 Dan LeFevour 6.00 15.00
WS16 Ryan Mathews 6.00 15.00
WS17 Tony Pike 6.00 15.00
WS18 Jordan Shipley 6.00 15.00
WS19 C.J. Spiller 6.00 15.00
WS20 Ndamukong Suh 12.00 30.00

2011 SAGE HIT

MPLETE SET (100) 12.00 30.00
COMP.LOW SERIES (50) 6.00 15.00
COMP.HIGH SERIES (50) 6.00 15.00
1 DeMarco Sampson .15 .40
2 Delone Carter .15 .40
3 Jerrel Jernigan .15 .40
4 Aaron Williams .15 .40
5 Chimdi Chekwa .20 .50
6 Jeremy Kerley .25 .60
7 Christian Ponder .15 .40
8 Julio Jones .50 1.25
9 Kyle Rudolph .15 .40
10 Jake Locker .15 .40
11 Scotty McKnight .15 .40
12 Dane Sanzenbacher .15 .40
13 Jeff Van Camp .20 .50
14 Anthony Castonzo .15 .40
15 Ryan Mallett .15 .40
16 Greg Smith .20 .50
17 DeMarco Murray .30 .75
18 Anthony Allen .15 .40
19 Edmond Gates .15 .40
20 Stephen Skelton .15 .40
21 Allen Bradford .15 .40
22 Mark Ingram .25 .60
23 Jeff Maehl .15 .40
24 Stephen Paea .15 .40
25 Kai Forbath .15 .40
26 Taylor Potts .15 .40
27 Mario Fannin .20 .50
28 Dion Lewis .20 .50
29 Shaun Chapas .15 .40
30 Sam Acho .15 .40
31 Jurrell Casey .15 .40
32 Torrey Smith .15 .40
33 Rahim Moore .15 .40
34 Rob Housler .15 .40
35 Casey Matthews .15 .40
36 Courtney Smith .15 .40
37 Cameron Heyward .20 .50
38 Daniel Thomas .15 .40
39 Nick Fairley .15 .40
40 Von Miller .25 .60
41 Da'Quan Bowers Art .15 .40
42 Mark Ingram Art .25 .60
43 Julio Jones Art .50 1.25
44 Jake Locker Art .15 .40
45 Ryan Mallett Art .15 .40
46 DeMarco Murray Art .30 .75
47 Christian Ponder Art .15 .40
48 Kyle Rudolph Art .15 .40
49 Torrey Smith Art .15 .40
50 Jordan Todman Art .15 .40
51 Randall Cobb Art .25 .60
52 Nick Fairley Art .15 .40
53 Blaine Gabbert Art .15 .40
54 A.J. Green Art .40 1.00
55 Jerrel Jernigan Art .15 .40
56 Mikel Leshoure Art .15 .40
57 Cam Newton Art .75 2.00
58 Daniel Thomas Art .15 .40
59 Shane Vereen Art .20 .50
60 Ryan Williams Art .15 .40
61 Blaine Gabbert .15 .40
62 Ricky Stanzi .15 .40
63 T.J. Yates .15 .40
64 Stevan Ridley .15 .40
65 Kyle Adams .15 .40
66 Chase Reynolds .15 .40
67 Robert Sands .15 .40
68 Adam Weber .15 .40
69 Cecil Shorts .15 .40
70 James Cleveland .15 .40
71 Jacquizz Rodgers .15 .40
72 Taiwan Jones .15 .40
73 Curtis Brown .15 .40
74 Vai Taua .15 .40
75 D.J. Williams .15 .40
76 Marcus Gilchrist .15 .40
77 Jordan Todman .15 .40
78 Nate Solder .15 .40
79 Armand Robinson .20 .50
80 A.J. Green .40 1.00
81 Randall Cobb .25 .60
82 Austin Pettis .15 .40
83 Charlie Gantt .15 .40
84 Ryan Williams .15 .40
85 Aldon Smith .15 .40
86 Shane Vereen .20 .50
87 Denarius Moore .15 .40
88 Luke Stocker .15 .40
89 Charles Clay .15 .40
90 Mark Herzlich .15 .40
91 Mikel Leshoure .15 .40
92 Drake Nevis .15 .40
93 Da'Quan Bowers .15 .40
94 Ryan Kerrigan .20 .50
95 Jarvis Williams .15 .40
96 DeAndre McDaniel .15 .40
97 Lestar Jean .15 .40
98 Jamie Harper .15 .40
99 J.J. Watt .75 2.00
100A Cam Newton Blue .75 2.00
100B Cam Newton Blu Org .75 2.00

2011 SAGE HIT Gold

*GOLD: 1.2X TO 3X BASIC CARDS
1-50 GOLD ODDS 1:10 LOW SERIES
51-100 GOLD ODDS 1:10 HIGH SERIES

2011 SAGE HIT Make Ready Black

*MR BLACK: 2X TO 5X BASIC CARDS
*MR CYAN: 2X TO 5X BASIC CARDS
*MR MAGENTA: 2X TO 5X BASIC CARDS
*MR YELLOW: 2X TO 5X BASIC CARDS
1-50 MAKE READY/50 ODDS 1:30 LOW
51-100 MAKE READY/50 ODDS 1:30 HIGH

2011 SAGE HIT Silver

*SILVER: .8X TO 2X BASIC CARDS
1-50 SILVER ODDS 1:3 LOW SERIES
51-100 SILVER ODDS 1:3 HIGH SERIES

2011 SAGE HIT Autographs

1-41 AU ODDS 1:10 LOW SERIES
61-100 AU ODDS 1:5 HIGH SERIES
*GOLD/250: .5X TO 1.2X BASIC AUTO
*GOLD/250: .4X TO 1X BASIC AU SP
*SILVER: .4X TO 1X BASIC AUTO
OVERALL AU ODDS 1:5 LOW SERIES
1 DeMarco Sampson 2.50 6.00
2 Delone Carter 2.50 6.00
3 Jerrel Jernigan 2.50 6.00
4 Aaron Williams 2.50 6.00
5 Chimdi Chekwa 3.00 8.00
6 Jeremy Kerley 4.00 10.00
7 Christian Ponder 2.50 6.00
8 Julio Jones 15.00 30.00
9 Kyle Rudolph 2.50 6.00
10 Jake Locker SP 2.50 6.00
11 Scotty McKnight 2.50 6.00
12 Dane Sanzenbacher 2.50 6.00
13 Jeff Van Camp 3.00 8.00
14 Anthony Castonzo 2.50 6.00
15 Ryan Mallett SP 2.50 6.00
16 Greg Smith 3.00 8.00
17 DeMarco Murray 5.00 12.00
18 Anthony Allen 2.50 6.00
19 Edmond Gates 2.50 6.00
20 Stephen Skelton 2.50 6.00
21 Allen Bradford 2.50 6.00
22 Mark Ingram 4.00 10.00
23 Jeff Maehl 2.50 6.00
24 Stephen Paea 2.50 6.00
25 Kai Forbath 2.50 6.00
26 Taylor Potts 2.50 6.00
27 Mario Fannin 3.00 8.00
28 Dion Lewis 3.00 8.00
29 Shaun Chapas 2.50 6.00
30 Sam Acho 2.50 6.00
31 Jurrell Casey 2.50 6.00
32 Torrey Smith 2.50 6.00
33 Rahim Moore 2.50 6.00
34 Rob Housler 2.50 6.00
35 Casey Matthews 2.50 6.00
36 Courtney Smith 2.50 6.00
37 Cameron Heyward 3.00 8.00
38 Daniel Thomas 2.50 6.00
39 Nick Fairley 2.50 6.00
40 Von Miller 10.00 25.00
41 Marcus Cannon 2.50 6.00
61 Blaine Gabbert SP 10.00 25.00
62 Ricky Stanzi 2.50 6.00
63 T.J. Yates 2.50 6.00
64 Stevan Ridley 2.50 6.00
65 Kyle Adams 2.50 6.00
66 Chase Reynolds 2.50 6.00
67 Robert Sands 2.50 6.00
68 Adam Weber 2.50 6.00
69 Cecil Shorts 2.50 6.00
70 James Cleveland 2.50 6.00
71 Jacquizz Rodgers 2.50 6.00
72 Taiwan Jones 2.50 6.00
73 Curtis Brown 2.50 6.00
74 Vai Taua 2.50 6.00
75 D.J. Williams 2.50 6.00
76 Marcus Gilchrist 2.50 6.00
77 Jordan Todman 2.50 6.00
78 Nate Solder 2.50 6.00
79 Armand Robinson 3.00 8.00
80 A.J. Green SP 12.00 30.00
81 Randall Cobb 4.00 10.00
82 Austin Pettis 2.50 6.00
83 Charlie Gantt 2.50 6.00
84 Ryan Williams 2.50 6.00
85 Aldon Smith 2.50 6.00
86 Shane Vereen 3.00 8.00
87 Denarius Moore 2.50 6.00
88 Luke Stocker 2.50 6.00
89 Charles Clay 2.50 6.00
90 Mark Herzlich 2.50 6.00
91 Mikel Leshoure 2.50 6.00
92 Drake Nevis 2.50 6.00
93 Da'Quan Bowers 2.50 6.00
94 Ryan Kerrigan 3.00 8.00
95 Jarvis Williams 2.50 6.00
96 DeAndre McDaniel 2.50 6.00
97 Lestar Jean 2.50 6.00
98 Jamie Harper 2.50 6.00
99 J.J. Watt 20.00 40.00
100 Cam Newton SP 12.00 30.00

2011 SAGE HIT Big Time

COMPLETE SET (30) 12.00 30.00
COMP.LOW SERIES (15) 6.00 15.00
COMP.HIGH SERIES (15) 6.00 15.00
BA1-BA15 ODDS 1:5 LOW SERIES
BA16-BA30 ODDS 1:5 HIGH SERIES
B1 Da'Quan Bowers .30 .75
B2 Delone Carter .30 .75
B3 Mark Ingram .50 1.25
B4 Jerrel Jernigan .30 .75
B5 Julio Jones 1.00 2.50
B6 Dion Lewis .40 1.00
B7 Jake Locker .30 .75
B8 Ryan Mallett .30 .75
B9 DeMarco Murray .60 1.50
B10 Christian Ponder .30 .75
B11 Kyle Rudolph .30 .75
B12 Torrey Smith .30 .75
B13 Ricky Stanzi .30 .75
B14 Daniel Thomas .30 .75
B15 Shane Vereen .40 1.00
B16 Randall Cobb .50 1.25
B17 Nick Fairley .30 .75
B18 Blaine Gabbert .30 .75
B19 A.J. Green .75 2.00
B20 Jamie Harper .30 .75
B21 Mikel Leshoure .30 .75
B22 Von Miller .50 1.25
B23 Cam Newton 1.50 4.00
B24 Stevan Ridley .30 .75
B25 Jacquizz Rodgers .30 .75
B26 Cecil Shorts .30 .75
B27 Luke Stocker .30 .75
B28 Jordan Todman .30 .75
B29 Ryan Williams .30 .75
B30 T.J. Yates .30 .75

2011 SAGE HIT Big Time Autographs

BA1-BA15 BIG TIME AU/100 ODDS 1:288 LOW
BA16-BA30 BIG TIME AU/100 ODDS 1:288 HIGH
BA1 Da'Quan Bowers 5.00 12.00
BA2 Delone Carter 5.00 12.00
BA3 Mark Ingram 8.00 20.00
BA4 Jerrel Jernigan 5.00 12.00
BA5 Julio Jones 25.00 50.00
BA6 Dion Lewis 6.00 15.00
BA7 Jake Locker 5.00 12.00
BA8 Ryan Mallett 5.00 12.00
BA9 DeMarco Murray 10.00 25.00
BA10 Christian Ponder 5.00 12.00
BA11 Kyle Rudolph 5.00 12.00
BA12 Torrey Smith 5.00 12.00
BA13 Ricky Stanzi 5.00 12.00
BA14 Daniel Thomas 5.00 12.00
BA15 Shane Vereen 6.00 15.00
BA16 Randall Cobb 8.00 20.00
BA17 Nick Fairley 5.00 12.00
BA18 Blaine Gabbert 5.00 12.00
BA19 A.J. Green 12.00 30.00
BA20 Jamie Harper 5.00 12.00
BA21 Mikel Leshoure 5.00 12.00
BA22 Von Miller 12.00 30.00
BA23 Cam Newton 30.00 80.00
BA24 Stevan Ridley 5.00 12.00
BA25 Jacquizz Rodgers 5.00 12.00
BA26 Cecil Shorts 5.00 12.00
BA27 Luke Stocker 5.00 12.00
BA28 Jordan Todman 5.00 12.00
BA29 Ryan Williams 5.00 12.00
BA30 T.J. Yates 5.00 12.00

2011 SAGE HIT Pre-Rookie

COMP.LOW SERIES (5) 2.50 6.00
COMP.HIGH SERIES (5) 2.50 6.00
PR1-PR5 INSERTED IN LOW SERIES
PR6-PR10 INSERTED IN HIGH SERIES
*GOLD: 1.2X TO 3X BASIC INSERTS
*SILVER: .8X TO 2X BASIC INSERTS
PR1 Cam Newton 1.25 3.00
PR2 Blaine Gabbert .25 .60
PR3 Kyle Rudolph .25 .60
PR4 Julio Jones .75 2.00
PR5 Shane Vereen .30 .75
PR6 Ryan Mallett .25 .60
PR7 A.J. Green .60 1.50
PR8 Austin Pettis .25 .60
PR9 Daniel Thomas .25 .60
PR10 Da'Quan Bowers .25 .60

2011 SAGE HIT Write Stuff

COMPLETE SET (20) 10.00 25.00
COMP.LOW SERIES (10) 5.00 12.00
COMP.HIGH SERIES (10) 5.00 12.00
WS1-WS10 ODDS 1:10 LOW SERIES
WS11-WS20 ODDS 1:10 HIGH SERIES
WS1 Da'Quan Bowers .40 1.00
WS2 Randall Cobb .60 1.50
WS3 Blaine Gabbert .40 1.00
WS4 A.J. Green 1.00 2.50
WS5 Mikel Leshoure .40 1.00
WS6 Cam Newton 2.00 5.00
WS7 Kyle Rudolph .40 1.00
WS8 Jordan Todman .40 1.00
WS9 Shane Vereen .50 1.25
WS10 Ryan Williams .40 1.00
WS11 Nick Fairley .40 1.00
WS12 Mark Ingram .60 1.50
WS13 Jerrel Jernigan .40 1.00
WS14 Julio Jones 1.25 3.00
WS15 Jake Locker .40 1.00
WS16 Ryan Mallett .40 1.00
WS17 DeMarco Murray .75 2.00
WS18 Christian Ponder .40 1.00
WS19 Torrey Smith .40 1.00
WS20 Daniel Thomas .40 1.00

2011 SAGE HIT Write Stuff Autographs

WSA1-WS10 AU/25 ODDS 1:1152 LOW SER.
WSA11-WS20 AU/25 ODDS 1:1152 HIGH SER.
WSA1 Da'Quan Bowers 6.00 15.00
WSA2 Randall Cobb 10.00 25.00
WSA3 Blaine Gabbert 6.00 15.00
WSA4 A.J. Green 30.00 60.00
WSA5 Mikel Leshoure 6.00 15.00
WSA6 Cam Newton 75.00 150.00
WSA7 Kyle Rudolph 6.00 15.00
WSA8 Jordan Todman 6.00 15.00
WSA9 Shane Vereen 8.00 20.00
WSA10 Ryan Williams 20.00 40.00
WSA11 Nick Fairley 6.00 15.00
WSA12 Mark Ingram 10.00 25.00
WSA13 Jerrel Jernigan 6.00 15.00
WSA14 Julio Jones 30.00 60.00
WSA15 Jake Locker 6.00 15.00
WSA16 Ryan Mallett 6.00 15.00
WSA17 DeMarco Murray 12.00 30.00
WSA18 Christian Ponder
WSA19 Torrey Smith 6.00 15.00
WSA20 Daniel Thomas 6.00 15.00

2012 SAGE HIT

COMPLETE SET (150) 15.00 40.00
COMP.LOW SERIES (75) 8.00 20.00
COMP.HIGH SERIES (75) 8.00 20.00
12R SUBSET CARDS: SAME PRICE
1 Alshon Jeffery .30 .75
2 Chris Givens .15 .40
3 Michael Floyd .15 .40
4 T.Y. Hilton .30 .75
5 Stephen Garcia .25 .60
6 Lamar Miller .25 .60
7 Orson Charles .15 .40
8 Nick Foles .40 1.00
9 Jeff Fuller .15 .40
10 Robert Griffin III .20 .50
10A R.Griffin III WAS 1-2 .15 .40
11 Kellen Moore .20 .50
12 Jacory Harris .20 .50
13 Davin Meggett .15 .40
14 Ryan Lindley .15 .40
15 Alfonzo Dennard .15 .40
16 Melvin Ingram .15 .40
17 Ryan Tannehill .25 .60
17A Ryan Tannehill MIA 1-8 .20 .50
18 Tommy Streeter .15 .40
19 Thomas Mayo .15 .40
20 Jayron Hosley .25 .60
21 LaMichael James .15 .40
22 Doug Martin .25 .60
23 Joe Adams .15 .40
24 Dominique Davis .20 .50
25 Ryan Broyles .15 .40
26 Chaz Powell .30 .75
27 Tony Jerod-Eddie .15 .40
28 Michael Egnew .15 .40
29 Jake Bequette .25 .60
30 Michael Smith .20 .50
31 Sean Spence .20 .50
32 Cyrus Gray .15 .40
33 Derrick Coleman .15 .40
34 Chris Galippo .20 .50
35 Chris Owusu .20 .50
36 Jared Crick .15 .40
37 Jason Ford .15 .40
38 Harrison Smith .15 .40
39 Devon Still .20 .50
40 Luke Kuechly .40 1.00
41 Rhett Ellison .20 .50
42 Keenan Robinson .20 .50
43 Quinton Coples .15 .40
44 David DeCastro 12R .15 .40
45 Matt Kalil 12R .15 .40
46 T.Y. Hilton 12R .30 .75
47 R.Griffin III 12R red jer. .20 .50
47A R.Griffin III 12R blk jer. .15 .40
48 Case Keenum 12R .30 .75
49 Jeff Fuller 12R .15 .40
50 LaMichael James 12R .15 .40
51 Jared Crick 12R .15 .40
52 Davin Meggett 12R .15 .40
53 Michael Floyd 12R .15 .40
54 Devon Still 12R .20 .50
55 Tommy Streeter 12R .15 .40
56 Nick Foles 12R .40 1.00
57 Michael Egnew 12R .15 .40
58 Jacory Harris 12R .20 .50
59 Lamar Miller 12R .25 .60
60 Alfonzo Dennard 12R .15 .40
61 Joe Adams 12R .15 .40
62 Ryan Lindley 12R .15 .40
63 Luke Kuechly 12R .40 1.00
64 Chris Givens 12R .15 .40
65 Doug Martin 12R .25 .60
66 Melvin Ingram 12R .15 .40
67 Ryan Broyles 12R .15 .40
68 Kellen Moore 12R .20 .50
69 Quinton Coples 12R .15 .40
70 Cyrus Gray 12R .15 .40
71 Dwayne Allen 12R .15 .40
72 Marvin McNutt 12R .15 .40
73 Chris Polk 12R .15 .40
74 Darron Thomas 12R .40 1.00
75 Brandon Weeden 12R .15 .40
76 Trent Richardson .15 .40
77 Marvin McNutt .15 .40
78 Brian Quick .15 .40
79 Dontari Poe .15 .40
80 Travis Lewis .20 .50
81 Justin Blackmon .15 .40
81A J.Blackmon JAX 1-5 .12 .30
82 Juron Criner .15 .40
83 Dwayne Allen .15 .40
84 Travis Benjamin .15 .40
85 Coryell Judie .15 .40
86 Damaris Johnson .15 .40
87 Cory Harkey .20 .50
88 DeVier Posey .15 .40
89 Ladarius Green .15 .40
90 Dont'a Hightower .25 .60
91 Boom Herron .15 .40
92 Broderick Green .20 .50
93 B.J. Cunningham .15 .40
94 Jonathan Massaquoi .15 .40
95 Donnie Fletcher .15 .40
96 Tauren Poole .15 .40
97 Vontaze Burfict .20 .50
98 Brandon Bolden .15 .40
99 Chris Polk .15 .40
100 Tim Fugger .15 .40
101 Kendall Wright .15 .40
102 Janoris Jenkins .20 .50
103 Brandon Weeden .15 .40
104 Jarius Wright .15 .40
105 Darron Thomas .40 1.00
106 Cam Johnson .25 .60
107 Case Keenum .30 .75
108 Kirk Cousins .60 1.50
109 Tyler Hansen .15 .40
110 Markelle Martin .20 .50
111 Alex Tanney .25 .60
112 Eric Page .20 .50
113 Ronnie Hillman .15 .40
114 G.J. Kinne .25 .60
115 Bernard Pierce .15 .40
116 George Iloka .15 .40
117 Brock Osweiler .15 .40
118 Emmanuel Acho .15 .40
119 Mike Willie .25 .60
120 Peter Konz 12R .15 .40
121 Orson Charles 12R .15 .40
122 Dominique Davis 12R .20 .50
123 Rhett Ellison 12R .20 .50
124 Stephen Garcia 12R .25 .60
125 Alshon Jeffery 12R .30 .75
126 R.Tannehill 12R VER .25 .60
126A R.Tannehill 12R HOR .20 .50
127 Alex Tanney 12R .25 .60
128 Ronnie Hillman 12R .15 .40
129 Ladarius Green 12R .15 .40
130 Brian Quick 12R .15 .40
131 Boom Herron 12R .15 .40
132 Janoris Jenkins 12R .20 .50
133 DeVier Posey 12R .15 .40
134 Bernard Pierce 12R .15 .40
135 Dont'a Hightower 12R .25 .60
136 Jarius Wright 12R .15 .40
137 Kirk Cousins 12R .60 1.50
138 Dontari Poe 12R .15 .40
139 Tauren Poole 12R .15 .40
140 Kendall Wright 12R .15 .40
141 Vontaze Burfict 12R .20 .50
142 Eric Page 12R .20 .50
143 Brock Osweiler 12R .15 .40
144 Brandon Bolden 12R .15 .40
145 G.J. Kinne 12R .25 .60
146 J.Blackmon 12R VER .15 .40
146A J.Blackmon 12R HOR .12 .30
147 Tyler Hansen 12R .15 .40
148 Travis Benjamin 12R .15 .40
149 Juron Criner 12R .15 .40
150 T.Richardson 12R VER .15 .40
150A T.Richardson 12R HOR .12 .30

2012 SAGE HIT Gold

*GOLD: 1.5X TO 4X BASIC CARDS
1-75 STATED ODDS 1:10 HOB LOW
76-150 STATED ODDS 1:10 HOB HIGH

2012 SAGE HIT Red

*RED: 1X TO 2.5X BASIC CARDS
SIX RED PER RETAIL FAT PACK

2012 SAGE HIT Silver

COMPLETE SET (150) 30.00 80.00
COMP. LOW SERIES (75) 15.00 40.00
COMP. HIGH SERIES (75) 15.00 40.00
*SILVER: 1X TO 2.5X BASIC CARDS
1-75 STATED ODDS 1:2.5 HOB LOW
76-150 STATED ODDS 1:3 HOB HIGH

2012 SAGE HIT Artistry

ART1-ART16 SILVER ODDS 1:6 HOB LOW
ART17-ART32 SILVER ODDS 1:6 HOB HIGH
*GOLD: .6X TO 1.5X BASIC INSERTS
ART1 Joe Adams .40 1.00
ART2 Ryan Broyles .40 1.00
ART3 Michael Floyd .40 1.00
ART4 Nick Foles 1.00 2.50
ART5 Cyrus Gray .40 1.00
ART6 Robert Griffin III .50 1.25
ART7 Jacory Harris .50 1.25
ART8 LaMichael James .40 1.00
ART9 Alshon Jeffery .75 2.00
ART10 Ryan Lindley .40 1.00
ART11 Doug Martin .60 1.50
ART12 Davin Meggett .40 1.00
ART13 Lamar Miller .60 1.50
ART14 Kellen Moore .50 1.25
ART15 Cam Newton .60 1.50
ART16 Ryan Tannehill .60 1.50
ART17 Dwayne Allen .40 1.00
ART18 Justin Blackmon .40 1.00
ART19 Kirk Cousins 1.50 4.00
ART20 Chris Givens .40 1.00
ART21 Boom Herron .40 1.00
ART22 Ronnie Hillman .40 1.00
ART23 Case Keenum .75 2.00
ART24 Marvin McNutt .40 1.00
ART25 Brock Osweiler .40 1.00
ART26 Bernard Pierce .40 1.00
ART27 Chris Polk .40 1.00
ART28 Brian Quick .40 1.00
ART29 Trent Richardson .40 1.00
ART30 Darron Thomas 1.00 2.50
ART31 Brandon Weeden .40 1.00
ART32 Kendall Wright .40 1.00

2012 SAGE HIT Artistry Autographs

AA1-AA16 AU/100 ODDS 1:288 HOB LOW
AA17-AA32 AU/100 ODDS 1:87 HOB HIGH
AA1 Joe Adams 5.00 12.00
AA2 Ryan Broyles 5.00 12.00
AA3 Michael Floyd 5.00 12.00
AA4 Nick Foles 12.00 30.00
AA5 Cyrus Gray 5.00 12.00
AA6 Robert Griffin III 10.00 25.00
AA7 Jacory Harris 6.00 15.00
AA8 LaMichael James 5.00 12.00
AA9 Alshon Jeffery 10.00 25.00
AA10 Ryan Lindley 5.00 12.00
AA11 Doug Martin 8.00 20.00
AA12 Davin Meggett 5.00 12.00
AA13 Lamar Miller 8.00 20.00
AA14 Kellen Moore 6.00 15.00
AA15 Cam Newton 25.00 60.00
AA16 Ryan Tannehill 8.00 20.00
AA17 Dwayne Allen 5.00 12.00
AA18 Justin Blackmon 5.00 12.00
AA19 Kirk Cousins 20.00 50.00
AA20 Chris Givens 5.00 12.00
AA21 Boom Herron 5.00 12.00
AA22 Ronnie Hillman 5.00 12.00
AA23 Case Keenum 10.00 25.00
AA24 Marvin McNutt 5.00 12.00
AA25 Brock Osweiler 5.00 12.00
AA26 Bernard Pierce 5.00 12.00
AA27 Chris Polk 5.00 12.00
AA28 Brian Quick 5.00 12.00
AA29 Trent Richardson 5.00 12.00
AA30 Darron Thomas 12.00 30.00
AA31 Brandon Weeden 5.00 12.00
AA32 Kendall Wright 5.00 12.00

2012 SAGE HIT Autographs

BASIC AU STATED ODDS 1:10 HOB
A1 Alshon Jeffery 5.00 12.00
A2 Chris Givens 2.50 6.00
A3 Michael Floyd 2.50 6.00
A4 T.Y. Hilton 5.00 12.00
A5 Stephen Garcia 4.00 10.00
A6 Lamar Miller 4.00 10.00
A7 Orson Charles 2.50 6.00
A8 Nick Foles 6.00 15.00
A9 Jeff Fuller 2.50 6.00
A10 Robert Griffin III 3.00 8.00
A11 Kellen Moore 3.00 8.00
A12 Jacory Harris 3.00 8.00
A13 Davin Meggett 2.50 6.00
A14 Ryan Lindley 2.50 6.00
A15 Alfonzo Dennard 2.50 6.00
A16 Melvin Ingram 2.50 6.00
A17 Ryan Tannehill 4.00 10.00
A18 Tommy Streeter 2.50 6.00
A19 Thomas Mayo 2.50 6.00
A20 Jayron Hosley 4.00 10.00
A21 LaMichael James 2.50 6.00
A22 Doug Martin 4.00 10.00
A23 Joe Adams 2.50 6.00
A24 Dominique Davis 3.00 8.00
A25 Ryan Broyles 2.50 6.00
A26 Chaz Powell 5.00 12.00
A27 Tony Jerod-Eddie 2.50 6.00
A28 Michael Egnew 2.50 6.00
A29 Jake Bequette 4.00 10.00
A30 Michael Smith 3.00 8.00
A31 Sean Spence 3.00 8.00
A32 Cyrus Gray 2.50 6.00
A33 Derrick Coleman 2.50 6.00
A34 Chris Galippo 3.00 8.00
A35 Chris Owusu 3.00 8.00
A36 Jared Crick 2.50 6.00
A37 Jason Ford 2.50 6.00
A38 Harrison Smith 2.50 6.00
A39 Devon Still 3.00 8.00
A40 Luke Kuechly 6.00 15.00
A41 Rhett Ellison 3.00 8.00
A42 Keenan Robinson 3.00 8.00
A43 Quinton Coples 2.50 6.00
A44 David DeCastro 2.50 6.00
A45 Matt Kalil 2.50 6.00
A46 Garth Gerhart 3.00 8.00
A47 Yoshi Hardrick 3.00 8.00
A48 Joe Long 3.00 8.00
A49 Ryan Miller 3.00 8.00
A50 Kelechi Osemele 2.50 6.00
A51 Moe Petrus 2.50 6.00
A76 Trent Richardson 2.50 6.00
A77 Marvin McNutt 2.50 6.00
A78 Brian Quick 2.50 6.00
A79 Dontari Poe 2.50 6.00
A80 Travis Lewis 3.00 8.00
A81 Justin Blackmon 2.50 6.00
A82 Juron Criner 2.50 6.00
A83 Dwayne Allen 2.50 6.00
A84 Travis Benjamin 2.50 6.00
A85 Coryell Judie 2.50 6.00
A86 Damaris Johnson 2.50 6.00
A87 Cory Harkey 3.00 8.00
A88 DeVier Posey 2.50 6.00
A89 Ladarius Green 2.50 6.00
A90 Dont'a Hightower 4.00 10.00
A91 Boom Herron 2.50 6.00
A92 Broderick Green 3.00 8.00
A93 B.J. Cunningham 2.50 6.00
A94 Jonathan Massaquoi 2.50 6.00
A95 Donnie Fletcher 2.50 6.00
A96 Tauren Poole 2.50 6.00
A97 Vontaze Burfict 3.00 8.00
A98 Brandon Bolden 2.50 6.00
A99 Chris Polk 2.50 6.00
A100 Tim Fugger 2.50 6.00
A101 Kendall Wright 2.50 6.00
A102 Janoris Jenkins 3.00 8.00
A103 Brandon Weeden 2.50 6.00
A104 Jarius Wright 2.50 6.00
A105 Darron Thomas 6.00 15.00
A106 Cam Johnson 4.00 10.00
A107 Case Keenum 5.00 12.00
A108 Kirk Cousins 10.00 25.00
A109 Tyler Hansen 2.50 6.00
A110 Markelle Martin 3.00 8.00
A111 Alex Tanney 4.00 10.00
A112 Eric Page 3.00 8.00
A113 Ronnie Hillman 2.50 6.00
A114 G.J. Kinne 4.00 10.00
A115 Bernard Pierce 2.50 6.00
A116 George Iloka 2.50 6.00
A117 Brock Osweiler 2.50 6.00
A118 Emmanuel Acho 2.50 6.00
A119 Mike Willie 4.00 10.00
A120 Peter Konz 2.50 6.00

2012 SAGE HIT Autographs Gold

*GOLD AU/250: .5X TO 1.2X BASIC AU
GOLD/250 STATED ODDS 1:28 HOB
A10 Robert Griffin III 4.00 10.00

2012 SAGE HIT Autographs Silver

*SILVER AU: .5X TO 1.2X BASIC AU
SILVER AUTO STATED ODDS 1:18 HOB
A10 Robert Griffin III 4.00 10.00

2012 SAGE HIT Sophomore Autographs

RANDOM INSERTS IN PACKS
A1 Da'Quan Bowers 3.00 8.00
A2 Randall Cobb 5.00 12.00
A3 Nick Fairley 5.00 12.00
A4 Blaine Gabbert 6.00 15.00
A5 A.J. Green 8.00 20.00
A6 Cameron Heyward 4.00 10.00
A7 Mark Ingram 8.00 20.00
A8 Jerrel Jernigan 3.00 8.00
A9 Julio Jones 8.00 20.00
A10 Taiwan Jones 4.00 10.00
A11 Jeremy Kerley 4.00 10.00
A12 Ryan Kerrigan 5.00 12.00
A13 Mikel Leshoure 5.00 12.00
A14 Dion Lewis 3.00 8.00
A15 Jake Locker 12.00 30.00
A16 Ryan Mallett 6.00 15.00
A17 Von Miller 5.00 12.00
A18 Denarius Moore 3.00 8.00
A19 DeMarco Murray 15.00 30.00
A20 Cam Newton 25.00 50.00
A21 Jake Locker 12.00 30.00
A22 Christian Ponder 3.00 8.00
A23 Stevan Ridley 4.00 10.00
A24 Jacquizz Rodgers 4.00 10.00
A25 Kyle Rudolph 4.00 10.00
A26 Dean Sanzenbacher 4.00 10.00
A27 Aldon Smith 5.00 12.00
A28 Torrey Smith 6.00 15.00
A29 Ricky Stanzi 3.00 8.00
A30 Daniel Thomas 5.00 12.00
A31 Shane Vereen 4.00 10.00
A32 J.J. Watt 25.00 50.00
A33 D.J. Williams 3.00 8.00
A34 Ryan Williams 5.00 12.00

2012 SAGE HIT Write Stuff

COMPLETE SET (20) 12.00 30.00
COMP.LOW SERIES (10) 6.00 15.00
COMP.HIGH SERIES (10) 6.00 15.00
WS1-WS10 SILVER ODDS 1:11 HOB LOW
WS11-WS20 SILVER ODDS 1:11 HOB HIGH
*GOLD: .6X TO 1.5X BASIC INSERTS

WS1 Kirk Cousins 1.50 4.00
WS2 Michael Floyd .40 1.00
WS3 Robert Griffin III .50 1.25
WS4 Ronnie Hillman .40 1.00
WS5 Alshon Jeffery .75 2.00
WS6 Doug Martin .60 1.50
WS7 Kellen Moore .50 1.25
WS8 Brock Osweiler .40 1.00
WS9 Chris Polk .40 1.00
WS10 Brandon Weeden .40 1.00
WS11 Justin Blackmon .40 1.00
WS12 Nick Foles 1.00 2.50
WS13 LaMichael James .40 1.00
WS14 Case Keenum .75 2.00
WS15 Ryan Lindley .40 1.00
WS16 Lamar Miller .60 1.50
WS17 Bernard Pierce .40 1.00
WS18 Trent Richardson .40 1.00
WS19 Ryan Tannehill .60 1.50
WS20 Kendall Wright .40 1.00

2012 SAGE HIT Write Stuff Autographs

WS1-WS10 AUTO/25 ODDS 1:1152 HOB LOW
WS11-WS20 AUTO/25 ODDS 1:208 HOB HIGH
WS1 Kirk Cousins 25.00 50.00
WS2 Michael Floyd 6.00 15.00
WS3 Robert Griffin III 8.00 20.00
WS4 Ronnie Hillman 6.00 15.00
WS5 Alshon Jeffery 12.00 30.00
WS6 Doug Martin 10.00 25.00
WS7 Kellen Moore 8.00 20.00
WS8 Brock Osweiler 6.00 15.00
WS9 Chris Polk 6.00 15.00
WS10 Brandon Weeden 6.00 15.00
WS11 Justin Blackmon 6.00 15.00
WS12 Nick Foles 15.00 40.00
WS13 LaMichael James 6.00 15.00
WS14 Case Keenum 12.00 30.00
WS15 Ryan Lindley 6.00 15.00
WS16 Lamar Miller 10.00 25.00
WS17 Bernard Pierce 6.00 15.00
WS18 Trent Richardson 6.00 15.00
WS19 Ryan Tannehill 10.00 25.00
WS20 Kendall Wright 6.00 15.00

2012 SAGE HIT Complete Exclusive

D1 Robert Griffin III .12 .30
D2 Trent Richardson .10 .25
D3 Matt Kalil .10 .25
D4 Justin Blackmon .10 .25
D5 Ryan Tannehill .15 .40

2013 SAGE HIT

COMP.LOW SERIES (75) 8.00 20.00
COMP.HIGH SERIES (75) 8.00 20.00
*SUBSETS: .4X TO 1X BASE CARD
1 Eric Reid .20 .50
2 Conner Vernon .15 .40
3 Collin Klein .20 .50
4 Brad Sorensen .15 .40
5 Manti Te'o .20 .50
6 DeAndre Hopkins .40 1.00
7 Matt Barkley .15 .40
8 Tyler Wilson .15 .40
9 Damontre Moore .15 .40
10 Sean Porter .15 .40
11 Justin Hunter .15 .40
12 Landry Jones .15 .40
13 Onterio McCalebb .20 .50
14 Cordarrelle Patterson .15 .40
15 Rex Burkhead .20 .50
16 Tyrone Goard .15 .40
17 Braxston Cave .25 .60
18 Jeff Locke .15 .40
19 Ryan Griffin .15 .40
20 Cierre Wood .15 .40
21 Da'Rick Rogers .15 .40
22 Matt Elam .15 .40
23 Andre Ellington .15 .40
24 Le'Veon Bell .50 1.25
25 Ryan Swope .15 .40
26 Luke Joeckel .15 .40
27 Travis Frederick .15 .40
28 Montee Ball .15 .40
29 Logan Ryan .20 .50
30 Alex Okafor .15 .40
31 Jordan Rodgers .20 .50
32 Mike Gillislee .15 .40
33 Dennis Johnson .15 .40
34 Datone Jones .15 .40
35 Bjoern Werner .15 .40
36 Joseph Fauria .15 .40
37 Ricky Wagner .15 .40
38 Tyler Bray .15 .40
39 Montori Hughes .15 .40
40 Tyler Eifert .15 .40
41 Zac Dysert NL .15 .40
42 Mike Glennon NL .15 .40
43 Conner Vernon NL .15 .40
44 Brad Sorensen NL .15 .40
45 Landry Jones NL .15 .40
46 Mike Gillislee NL .15 .40
47 Collin Klein NL .20 .50
48 Tyler Wilson NL .15 .40
49 Sean Porter NL .15 .40
50 Montee Ball NL .15 .40
51 Logan Ryan NL .20 .50
52 Ryan Swope NL .15 .40
53 Onterio McCalebb NL .20 .50
54 Tyrone Goard NL .15 .40
55 Justin Hunter NL .15 .40
56 Datone Jones NL .15 .40
57 Cierre Wood NL .15 .40
58 Joseph Fauria NL .15 .40
59 Bjoern Werner NL .15 .40
60 Alex Okafor NL .15 .40
61 Eric Reid NL .20 .50
62 Rex Burkhead NL .20 .50
63 Ryan Griffin NL .15 .40
64 Matt Elam NL .15 .40
65 Tyler Eifert NL .15 .40
66 Dennis Johnson NL .15 .40
67 Luke Joeckel NL .15 .40
68 Tyler Bray NL .15 .40
69 Manti Te'o NL .20 .50
70 Matt Barkley NL .15 .40
71 Montee Ball SL .15 .40
72 Matt Barkley SL .15 .40
73 Landry Jones SL .15 .40
74 Manti Te'o SL .20 .50
75 Tyler Wilson SL .15 .40
76 Mike Glennon SL .15 .40
77 Eddie Lacy SL .15 .40
78 EJ Manuel SL .15 .40
79 Ryan Nassib SL .15 .40
80 Geno Smith SL .15 .40
81 Xavier Rhodes NL .15 .40
82 Terrance Williams NL .15 .40
83 Marquise Goodwin NL .15 .40
84 Cordarrelle Patterson NL .15 .40
85 Keenan Allen NL .30 .75
86 Denard Robinson NL .15 .40
87 Le'Veon Bell NL .50 1.25
88 Vance McDonald NL .20 .50
89 Jordan Reed NL .25 .60
90 Kenny Stills NL .15 .40
91 Da'Rick Rogers NL .15 .40
92 Eddie Lacy NL .15 .40
93 Andre Ellington NL .15 .40
94 Damontre Moore NL .15 .40
95 Sheldon Richardson NL .15 .40
96 Theo Riddick NL .15 .40
97 Aaron Dobson NL .15 .40
98 Ryan Nassib NL .15 .40
99 Giovani Bernard NL .15 .40
100 Geno Smith NL .15 .40
101 Joseph Randle NL .15 .40
102 Robert Woods NL .25 .60
103 EJ Manuel NL .15 .40
104 Kenny Vaccaro NL .15 .40
105 Nick Kasa NL .15 .40
106 DeAndre Hopkins NL .40 1.00
107 Jordan Rodgers NL .20 .50
108 Aaron Mellette NL .15 .40
109 Alec Ogletree NL .15 .40
110 Marcus Lattimore NL .15 .40
111 Jordan Reed .25 .60
112 Ryan Nassib .15 .40
113 Aaron Mellette .15 .40
114 Dan Buckner .15 .40
115 Zach Maynard .20 .50
116 Ryan Aplin .15 .40
117 Denard Robinson .15 .40
118 Mike Glennon .15 .40
119 Seth Thomas .15 .40
120 Keenan Allen .30 .75
121 Marcus Lattimore .15 .40
122 Terrance Williams .15 .40
123 Aaron Dobson .15 .40
124 Alec Ogletree .15 .40
125 Barrett Jones .15 .40
126 Giovani Bernard .15 .40
127 Xavier Rhodes .15 .40
128 Latavius Murray .20 .50
129 Khaled Holmes .15 .40
130 Jelani Jenkins .20 .50
131 Joseph Randle .15 .40
132 Robert Woods .25 .60
133 EJ Manuel .15 .40
134 Sheldon Richardson .15 .40
135 Brandon Jenkins .20 .50
136 Theo Riddick .15 .40
137 John Wetzel .20 .50
138 Vance McDonald .20 .50
139 David Bakhtiari .15 .40
140 Kenny Vaccaro .15 .40
141 Kenny Stills .15 .40
142 Eddie Lacy .15 .40
143 Philip Lutzenkirchen .25 .60
144 Nick Kasa .15 .40
145 Dave Kruger .15 .40
146 Zac Dysert .15 .40
147 T.J. McDonald .15 .40
148 Marquise Goodwin .15 .40
149 Joe Kruger .20 .50
150 Geno Smith .15 .40

2013 SAGE HIT Gold

*GOLD: 1.5X TO 4X BASIC CARDS
GOLD STATED ODDS 1:10

2013 SAGE HIT Red

*RED: .6X TO 1.5X BASIC CARDS
SIX RED PER FAT PACK

2013 SAGE HIT Silver

*SILVER: .8X TO 2X BASIC CARDS
SILVER STATED ODDS 1:2.5

2013 SAGE HIT Artistry

COMPLETE SET (24) 15.00 40.00
STATED ODDS 1:6
*GOLD: .6X TO 1.5X BASIC INSERTS
ART1 Montee Ball .40 1.00
ART2 Matt Barkley .40 1.00
ART3 Le'Veon Bell 1.25 3.00
ART4 Tyler Bray .40 1.00
ART5 Zac Dysert .40 1.00
ART6 Andre Ellington .40 1.00
ART7 Landry Jones .40 1.00
ART8 Collin Klein .50 1.25
ART9 Cordarrelle Patterson .40 1.00
ART10 Manti Te'o .50 1.25
ART11 Tyler Wilson .40 1.00
ART12 Robert Woods .60 1.50
ART13 Keenan Allen .75 2.00
ART14 Giovani Bernard .40 1.00
ART15 Mike Glennon .40 1.00
ART16 DeAndre Hopkins 1.00 2.50
ART17 Eddie Lacy .40 1.00
ART18 Marcus Lattimore .40 1.00
ART19 EJ Manuel .40 1.00
ART20 Ryan Nassib .40 1.00
ART21 Joseph Randle .40 1.00
ART22 Denard Robinson .40 1.00
ART23 Geno Smith .40 1.00
ART24 Terrance Williams .40 1.00

2013 SAGE HIT Artistry Autographs

STATED PRINT RUN 100 SER.#'d SETS
AA1 Montee Ball 4.00 10.00
ART2 Matt Barkley 12.00 30.00
AA4 Tyler Bray 4.00 10.00
AA5 Zac Dysert 4.00 10.00
AA6 Andre Ellington 4.00 10.00
AA7 Landry Jones 4.00 10.00
AA8 Collin Klein 5.00 12.00
AA9 Cordarrelle Patterson 4.00 10.00
AA10 Manti Te'o 5.00 12.00
AA11 Tyler Wilson 4.00 10.00
AA12 Robert Woods 6.00 15.00
AA14 Giovani Bernard 4.00 10.00
AA15 Mike Glennon 4.00 10.00
AA16 DeAndre Hopkins 10.00 25.00
AA17 Eddie Lacy 4.00 10.00
AA18 Marcus Lattimore 4.00 10.00
AA19 EJ Manuel 4.00 10.00
AA20 Ryan Nassib 4.00 10.00
AA21 Joseph Randle 4.00 10.00
AA23 Geno Smith 4.00 10.00
AA24 Terrance Williams 4.00 10.00

2013 SAGE HIT Autographs Gold

GOLD AU/250 ODDS 1:28
*BASE RED: .3X TO .8X GOLD AU/250
*SILVER: .4X TO 1X GOLD AU/250
A1 Eric Reid 4.00 10.00
A2 Conner Vernon 3.00 8.00
A3 Collin Klein 4.00 10.00
A4 Brad Sorensen 3.00 8.00
A5 Manti Te'o 4.00 10.00
A6 DeAndre Hopkins 8.00 20.00
A7 Matt Barkley 6.00 15.00
A8 Tyler Wilson 3.00 8.00
A9 Damontre Moore 3.00 8.00
A10 Sean Porter 3.00 8.00
A11 Justin Hunter 3.00 8.00
A12 Landry Jones 3.00 8.00
A14 Cordarrelle Patterson 3.00 8.00
A15 Rex Burkhead 4.00 10.00
A16 Tyrone Goard 3.00 8.00
A17 Braxston Cave 5.00 12.00
A18 Jeff Locke 3.00 8.00
A19 Ryan Griffin 3.00 8.00
A20 Cierre Wood 3.00 8.00
A21 Da'Rick Rogers 3.00 8.00
A22 Matt Elam 3.00 8.00
A23 Andre Ellington 3.00 8.00
A25 Ryan Swope 3.00 8.00
A26 Luke Joeckel 3.00 8.00
A27 Travis Frederick 6.00 15.00
A28 Montee Ball 3.00 8.00
A29 Logan Ryan 4.00 10.00
A30 Alex Okafor 3.00 8.00
A31 Jordan Rodgers 4.00 10.00
A32 Mike Gillislee 3.00 8.00
A33 Dennis Johnson 3.00 8.00
A34 Datone Jones 3.00 8.00
A35 Bjoern Werner 3.00 8.00
A36 Joseph Fauria 3.00 8.00
A37 Ricky Wagner 3.00 8.00
A38 Tyler Bray 3.00 8.00
A39 Montori Hughes 3.00 8.00
A40 Tyler Eifert 3.00 8.00
A107 Johnny McEntee 3.00 8.00
A108 Braden Wilson 4.00 10.00
A109 Rodney Smith 3.00 8.00
A111 Jordan Reed 5.00 12.00
A112 Ryan Nassib 3.00 8.00
A113 Aaron Mellette 3.00 8.00
A114 Dan Buckner 3.00 8.00
A116 Ryan Aplin 3.00 8.00
A118 Mike Glennon 3.00 8.00
A119 Seth Thomas 3.00 8.00
A121 Marcus Lattimore 3.00 8.00
A122 Terrance Williams 3.00 8.00
A123 Aaron Dobson 3.00 8.00
A124 Alec Ogletree 3.00 8.00
A125 Barrett Jones 3.00 8.00
A126 Giovani Bernard 3.00 8.00
A127 Xavier Rhodes 3.00 8.00
A128 Latavius Murray 4.00 10.00
A129 Khaled Holmes 3.00 8.00
A130 Jelani Jenkins 4.00 10.00
A131 Joseph Randle 3.00 8.00
A132 Robert Woods 5.00 12.00
A133 EJ Manuel 3.00 8.00
A134 Sheldon Richardson 3.00 8.00
A135 Brandon Jenkins 4.00 10.00
A136 Theo Riddick 3.00 8.00
A138 Vance McDonald 4.00 10.00
A139 David Bakhtiari 3.00 8.00
A140 Kenny Vaccaro 3.00 8.00
A141 Kenny Stills 3.00 8.00
A142 Eddie Lacy 3.00 8.00
A143 Philip Lutzenkirchen 5.00 12.00
A144 Nick Kasa 3.00 8.00
A145 Dave Kruger 3.00 8.00
A146 Zac Dysert 3.00 8.00
A147 T.J. McDonald 3.00 8.00
A148 Marquise Goodwin 3.00 8.00
A149 Joe Kruger 4.00 10.00
A150 Geno Smith 3.00 8.00

2013 SAGE HIT Write Stuff

STATED ODDS 1:11
*GOLD: .6X TO 1.5X BASIC INSERTS
WS1 Montee Ball .40 1.00
WS2 Matt Barkley .40 1.00
WS3 Tyler Bray .40 1.00
WS4 Landry Jones .40 1.00
WS5 Manti Te'o .50 1.25
WS6 Tyler Wilson .40 1.00
WS7 Giovani Bernard .40 1.00
WS8 Mike Glennon .40 1.00
WS9 Eddie Lacy .40 1.00
WS10 EJ Manuel .40 1.00
WS11 Ryan Nassib .40 1.00
WS12 Geno Smith .40 1.00

2013 SAGE HIT Write Stuff Autographs

AUTO/25 STATED ODDS 1:1152
WS1 Montee Ball 5.00 12.00
WS2 Matt Barkley 50.00 100.00
WS3 Tyler Bray 20.00 40.00
WS4 Landry Jones 5.00 12.00
WS5 Manti Te'o 6.00 15.00
WS6 Tyler Wilson 5.00 12.00
WS7 Giovani Bernard 5.00 12.00
WS8 Mike Glennon 5.00 12.00
WS9 Eddie Lacy 5.00 12.00
WS10 EJ Manuel 5.00 12.00
WS11 Ryan Nassib 5.00 12.00
WS12 Geno Smith 5.00 12.00

2014 SAGE HIT

COMP.LOW SERIES (75) 8.00 20.00
COMP.HIGH SERIES (75) 8.00 20.00
*SUBSETS: .4X TO 1X BASE CARD
1 Mike Davis .15 .40
2 Sammy Watkins .25 .60
3 Logan Thomas .15 .40
4 Jared Abbrederis .15 .40
5 Teddy Bridgewater .25 .60
6 De'Anthony Thomas .15 .40
7 Jadeveon Clowney .20 .50
8 Trey Burton .15 .40
9 Marqise Lee .20 .50
10 Jimmy Garoppolo 1.25 3.00
11 Tommy Rees .20 .50
12 David Fales .15 .40
13 Michael Campanaro .15 .40
14 Jaylen Watkins .15 .40
15 Lorenzo Taliaferro .15 .40
16 Brett Smith .15 .40
17 Stephen Morris .15 .40
18 Dion Bailey .15 .40
19 Trevor Reilly .15 .40
20 Henry Josey .15 .40
21 Bene Benwikjere .15 .40
22 Trey Watts .15 .40
23 Bruce Ellington .15 .40
24 Colin Lockett .15 .40
25 Ka'Deem Carey .15 .40
26 Jeremy Butler .15 .40
27 Carl Bradford .15 .40
28 Jet Jones .15 .40
29 Ross Cockrell .15 .40
30 Kyle Van Noy .20 .50
31 Allen Hurns .20 .50
32 Dominique Easley .15 .40
33 John Hubert .15 .40
34 Carlos Hyde .20 .50
35 Jordan Zumwalt .15 .40
36 Kiero Small .15 .40
37 Charlie Moore .15 .40
38 Kevin Norwood .15 .40
39 Joe Don Duncan .15 .40
40 Max Bullough .25 .60
41 Isaiah Crowell .20 .50
42 Kareem Martin .15 .40
43 Xavier Grimble .20 .50
44 Austin Franklin .20 .50
45 Jerome Smith .15 .40
46 Alfred Blue .15 .40
47 James Franklin .20 .50
48 Quincy Enunwa .25 .60
49 RaShede Hageman .15 .40
50 Shaquelle Evans .15 .40
51 Blake Bortles NL .20 .50
52 Bryn Renner NL .15 .40
53 Tajh Boyd NL .15 .40
54 Jerome Smith NL .15 .40
55 Logan Thomas NL .15 .40
56 Brett Smith NL .15 .40
57 Stephen Morris NL .15 .40
58 Kevin Norwood NL .15 .40
59 Derek Carr NL 1.00 2.50
60 Jimmy Garoppolo NL 1.25 3.00
61 Mike Davis NL .15 .40
62 Allen Hurns NL .20 .50
63 Kyle Van Noy NL .20 .50
64 Jared Abbrederis NL .15 .40
65 Ka'Deem Carey NL .15 .40
66 De'Anthony Thomas NL .15 .40
67 Tre Mason NL .15 .40
68 Jordan Zumwalt NL .15 .40
69 Ha Ha Clinton-Dix NL .20 .50
70 Henry Josey NL .15 .40
71 Shaquelle Evans NL .15 .40
72 David Fales NL .15 .40
73 Michael Campanaro NL .15 .40
74 Jaylen Watkins NL .15 .40
75 Teddy Bridgewater NL .25 .60
76 Marqise Lee NL .20 .50
77 JaDeveon Clowney NL .20 .50
78 Paul Richardson NL .20 .50
79 Terrance West NL .15 .40
80 James White NL .30 .75
81 Martavis Bryant NL .20 .50
82 Michael Sam NL .15 .40
83 Odell Beckham Jr. NL .40 1.00
84 Carlos Hyde NL .20 .50
85 Eric Ebron NL .20 .50
86 Troy Niklas NL .15 .40
87 Brandin Cooks NL .25 .60
88 Allen Robinson NL .25 .60
89 Rajion Neal NL .15 .40
90 Dee Ford NL .15 .40
91 Aaron Murray NL .15 .40
92 Calvin Pryor NL .15 .40
93 Mike Evans NL .40 1.00
94 Bruce Ellington NL .15 .40
95 Davante Adams NL .25 .60
96 Robert Herron NL .15 .40
97 Kony Ealy NL .20 .50
98 Zach Mettenberger NL .15 .40
99 Trevor Reilly NL .15 .40
100 Sammy Watkins NL .25 .60
101 Terrance West .15 .40
102 Bryn Renner .15 .40
103 Odell Beckham Jr. .40 1.00
104 Alden Darby .20 .50
105 Blake Bortles .20 .50
106 Derek Carr 1.00 2.50
107 Brandin Cooks .25 .60
108 Allen Robinson .25 .60
109 Brandon Wimberly .20 .50
110 Rajion Neal .15 .40
111 Aaron Murray .15 .40
112 Dede Lattimore .20 .50
113 Mike Evans .40 1.00
114 Robert Herron .15 .40
115 Davante Adams .25 .60
116 Tajh Boyd .15 .40
117 Tom Savage .15 .40
118 Zach Mettenberger .15 .40
119 Keith McGill .15 .40
120 James White .30 .75
121 Tre Mason .15 .40
122 Telvin Smith .15 .40
123 Timothy Flanders .15 .40
124 Chris Smith .15 .40
125 Calvin Pryor .15 .40
126 Ha Ha Clinton-Dix .20 .50
127 Jake Matthews .15 .40
128 Paul Richardson .20 .50
129 Ed Stinson .25 .60
130 Dee Ford .15 .40
131 Kenny Shaw .25 .60
132 Michael Sam .15 .40
133 Pierre Desir .15 .40
134 Martavis Bryant .20 .50
135 Eric Ebron .20 .50
136 Troy Niklas .15 .40
137 Kony Ealy .20 .50
138 Marcus Lucas .20 .50
139 Reggie Jordan .20 .50
140 Will Sutton .20 .50
141 Blake Bortles SL .20 .50
142 Teddy Bridgewater SL .25 .60
143 Ka'Deem Carey SL .15 .40
144 Derek Carr SL 1.00 2.50
145 JaDeveon Clowney SL .20 .50
146 Mike Evans SL .40 1.00
147 Carlos Hyde SL .20 .50
148 Marqise Lee SL .20 .50
149 Tre Mason SL .15 .40
150 Sammy Watkins SL .25 .60

2014 SAGE HIT Gold

*GOLD: 1.5X TO 4X BASIC CARDS

2014 SAGE HIT Red

*RED: .8X TO 2X BASIC CARDS
RANDOM INSERTS IN PACKS

2014 SAGE HIT Silver

*SILVER: .8X TO 2X BASIC CARDS

2014 SAGE HIT Artistry

*GOLD: .8X TO 2X BASIC INSERTS
ART1 Teddy Bridgewater .50 1.25
ART2 Ka'Deem Carey .30 .75
ART3 Jadeveon Clowney .40 1.00
ART4 David Fales .30 .75
ART5 Jimmy Garoppolo 2.50 6.00
ART6 Carlos Hyde .40 1.00
ART7 Marqise Lee .40 1.00
ART8 Michael Sam .30 .75
ART9 De'Anthony Thomas .30 .75
ART10 Sammy Watkins .50 1.25
ART11 Odell Beckham Jr. .75 2.00
ART12 Blake Bortles .40 1.00
ART13 Tajh Boyd .30 .75
ART14 Derek Carr 2.00 5.00
ART15 Brandin Cooks .50 1.25
ART16 Eric Ebron .40 1.00
ART17 Mike Evans .75 2.00
ART18 Tre Mason .30 .75
ART19 Zach Mettenberger .30 .75
ART20 Allen Robinson .50 1.25

2014 SAGE HIT Artistry Autographs

AA1 Teddy Bridgewater 5.00 12.00
AA2 Ka'Deem Carey 3.00 8.00
AA3 Jadeveon Clowney 4.00 10.00
AA4 David Fales 3.00 8.00
AA5 Jimmy Garoppolo 25.00 60.00
AA6 Carlos Hyde 4.00 10.00
AA7 Marqise Lee 4.00 10.00
AA8 Michael Sam 10.00 25.00
AA10 Sammy Watkins 5.00 12.00
AA11 Odell Beckham Jr. 30.00 60.00
AA12 Blake Bortles 4.00 10.00
AA13 Tajh Boyd 3.00 8.00
AA14 Derek Carr 20.00 50.00
AA15 Brandin Cooks 5.00 12.00
AA16 Eric Ebron 4.00 10.00
AA17 Mike Evans 8.00 20.00
AA18 Tre Mason 3.00 8.00
AA19 Zach Mettenberger 3.00 8.00
AA20 Allen Robinson 5.00 12.00

2014 SAGE HIT Autographs Gold

*BASE RED: .3X TO .8X GOLD/250
*BASE RED SP: .4X TO 1X GOLD/250
*BLACK: .4X TO 1X GOLD/250
*BLACK SP: .5X TO 1.2X GOLD/250
A1 Mike Davis 2.50 6.00
A2 Sammy Watkins 4.00 10.00
A3 Logan Thomas 2.50 6.00
A4 Jared Abbrederis 2.50 6.00
A5 Teddy Bridgewater 4.00 10.00
A7 Jadeveon Clowney 3.00 8.00
A8 Trey Burton 2.50 6.00
A9 Marqise Lee 3.00 8.00
A10 Jimmy Garoppolo 20.00 50.00
A11 Tommy Rees 3.00 8.00
A12 David Fales 2.50 6.00
A13 Michael Campanaro 2.50 6.00
A15 Lorenzo Taliaferro 2.50 6.00
A16 Brett Smith 2.50 6.00
A17 Stephen Morris 2.50 6.00
A18 Dion Bailey 2.50 6.00
A19 Trevor Reilly 2.50 6.00
A20 Henry Josey 2.50 6.00
A21 Bene Benwikjere 2.50 6.00
A22 Trey Watts 2.50 6.00
A23 Bruce Ellington 2.50 6.00
A24 Colin Lockett 2.50 6.00
A25 Ka'Deem Carey 2.50 6.00
A26 Jeremy Butler 2.50 6.00
A27 Carl Bradford 2.50 6.00
A28 Jet Jones 2.50 6.00
A29 Ross Cockrell 2.50 6.00
A30 Kyle Van Noy 3.00 8.00
A31 Allen Hurns 3.00 8.00
A32 Dominique Easley 2.50 6.00
A33 John Hubert 2.50 6.00
A34 Carlos Hyde 3.00 8.00
A35 Jordan Zumwalt 2.50 6.00
A36 Kiero Small 2.50 6.00
A37 Charlie Moore 2.50 6.00
A38 Kevin Norwood 2.50 6.00
A39 Joe Don Duncan 2.50 6.00
A40 Max Bullough 4.00 10.00
A41 Isaiah Crowell 3.00 8.00
A42 Kareem Martin 2.50 6.00
A43 Xavier Grimble 3.00 8.00
A44 Austin Franklin 3.00 8.00
A45 Jerome Smith 2.50 6.00
A46 Alfred Blue 2.50 6.00
A47 James Franklin 3.00 8.00
A48 Quincy Enunwa 4.00 10.00
A49 RaShede Hageman 2.50 6.00
A50 Shaquelle Evans 2.50 6.00
A51 Shaquil Barrett 2.50 6.00
A52 Kadeem Edwards 2.50 6.00
A53 Ryan Groy 2.50 6.00
A54 Toney Hurd Jr. 2.50 6.00
A55 Marcus Martin 2.50 6.00
A56 Keith Reaser 2.50 6.00
A57 Chaz Sutton 2.50 6.00
A58 Travis Swanson 2.50 6.00
A59 Brock Vereen 2.50 6.00
A60 Asa Watson 2.50 6.00
A101 Terrance West 2.50 6.00
A102 Bryn Renner 2.50 6.00
A103 Odell Beckham Jr. 25.00 50.00
A104 Alden Darby 3.00 8.00
A105 Blake Bortles 3.00 8.00
A106 Derek Carr 15.00 30.00
A107 Brandin Cooks 4.00 10.00
A108 Allen Robinson 4.00 10.00
A109 Brandon Wimberly 3.00 8.00
A110 Rajion Neal 2.50 6.00
A111 Aaron Murray 2.50 6.00
A112 De De Lattimore 3.00 8.00
A113 Mike Evans 6.00 15.00
A114 Robert Herron 2.50 6.00
A115 Davante Adams 4.00 10.00
A116 Tajh Boyd 2.50 6.00
A117 Tom Savage 2.50 6.00
A118 Zach Mettenberger 2.50 6.00
A119 Keith McGill 2.50 6.00
A120 James White 5.00 12.00
A121 Tre Mason 2.50 6.00
A123 Timothy Flanders 2.50 6.00
A124 Chris Smith 3.00 8.00
A125 Calvin Pryor 2.50 6.00
A126 Ha Ha Clinton-Dix 3.00 8.00
A127 Jake Matthews 2.50 6.00
A128 Paul Richardson 5.00 12.00
A131 Kenny Shaw 4.00 10.00
A132 Michael Sam 6.00 15.00
A133 Pierre Desir 2.50 6.00
A135 Eric Ebron 3.00 8.00
A136 Troy Niklas 2.50 6.00
A137 Kony Ealy 3.00 8.00
A138 Marcus Lucas 3.00 8.00
A139 Reggie Jordan 3.00 8.00
A141 Quandon Christian 3.00 8.00
A142 Tyler Starr 2.50 6.00
A143 Chris Young 3.00 8.00
A144 Lee Doss 3.00 8.00

2014 SAGE HIT Versus

*BRONZE: .4X TO 1X BASIC INSERTS
*GOLD: .6X TO 1.5X BASIC INSERTS
VS1 B.Bortles/T.Bridgewater .60 1.50
VS2 S.Watkins/M.Evans 1.00 2.50
VS3 M.Sam/J.Clowney .50 1.25
VS4 T.Mason/C.Hyde .50 1.25
VS5 D.Carr/J.Garoppolo 3.00 8.00

2014 SAGE HIT Virtuosity

*GOLD: .8X TO 2 BASIC INSERTS
V1 Teddy Bridgewater .60 1.50
V2 Jadeveon Clowney .50 1.25
V3 Eddie Lacy .75 2.00
V4 Blake Bortles .50 1.25
V5 Tre Mason .40 1.00
V6 Sammy Watkins .60 1.50

2014 SAGE HIT Write Stuff

*GOLD: .8X TO 2X BASIC INSERTS
WS1 Teddy Bridgewater .50 1.25
WS2 Ka'Deem Carey .30 .75
WS3 Jadeveon Clowney .40 1.00
WS4 Carlos Hyde .40 1.00
WS5 Sammy Watkins .50 1.25
WS6 Blake Bortles .40 1.00
WS7 Derek Carr 2.00 5.00
WS8 Mike Evans .75 2.00
WS9 Marqise Lee .40 1.00
WS10 Tre Mason .30 .75

2014 SAGE HIT Write Stuff Autographs

WSA1 Teddy Bridgewater 6.00 15.00
WSA2 Ka'Deem Carey 8.00 20.00
WSA3 Jadeveon Clowney 5.00 12.00
WSA4 Carlos Hyde 5.00 12.00
WSA5 Sammy Watkins 6.00 15.00
WSA6 Blake Bortles 5.00 12.00
WSA7 Derek Carr 25.00 60.00
WSA8 Mike Evans 10.00 25.00
WSA9 Marqise Lee 5.00 12.00
WSA10 Tre Mason 4.00 10.00

2015 SAGE HIT

COMPLETE SET (150) 15.00 40.00
COMP.LOW SERIES (75) 8.00 20.00
COMP.HIGH SERIES (75) 8.00 20.00
*SUBSETS: .4X TO 1X BASE CARD
1 Devin Funchess .25 .60
2 Quinten Rollins .30 .75
3 Josh Harper .15 .40
4 Randy Gregory .15 .40
5 Jameis Winston .40 1.00
6 Tevin Coleman .20 .50
7 Brandon Bridge .15 .40
8 Nate Orchard .15 .40
9 Zack Hodges .15 .40
10 DaVaris Daniels .15 .40
11 Dorial Green-Beckham .15 .40
12 Dres Anderson .15 .40
13 Josh Robinson .15 .40
14 Ifo Ekpre-Olomu .15 .40
15 Trae Waynes .15 .40
16 Tyler Lockett .25 .60
17 Dylan Thompson .15 .40
18 Sammie Coates .20 .50
19 Hutson Mason .15 .40
20 Gary Nova .15 .40
21 Akeem Hunt .15 .40
22 Andre Davis .15 .40
23 Brandon Wegher .30 .75
24 Sean Mannion .15 .40
25 Kevin Parks .15 .40
26 Landon Collins .20 .50
27 P.J. Williams .20 .50
28 Malcolm Brown .20 .50
29 Malcom Brown .15 .40
30 Synjyn Days .15 .40
31 Rory Anderson .15 .40
32 John Crockett .25 .60
33 Markus Golden .15 .40
34 Taylor Heinicke .25 .60
35 Shane Carden .15 .40
36 Dante Fowler Jr. .25 .60
37 Tony Lippett .15 .40
38 Maxx Williams .15 .40
39 Charles Gaines .25 .60
40 T.J. Yeldon .15 .40
41 Bo Wallace .15 .40
42 Jaxon Shipley .15 .40
43 Mike Hull .25 .60
44 Cameron Artis-Payne .15 .40
45 Levi Norwood .15 .40
46 Clive Walford .15 .40
47 Jake Ryan .25 .60
48 Anthony Harris .15 .40
49 Lorenzo Mauldin .15 .40
50 Grady Jarrett .20 .50
51 Jake Waters .20 .50
52 Duke Johnson .25 .60
53 Gabe Holmes .15 .40
54 MyCole Pruitt .15 .40
55 Cedric Reed .15 .40
56 Quandre Diggs .15 .40
57 Bryan Bennett .15 .40
58 Geneo Grissom .15 .40
59 Marcus Murphy .15 .40
60 Dominique Brown .15 .40
61 Lorenzo Doss .15 .40
62 Darren Waller .20 .50
63 Donatella Luckett .20 .50
64 Josh Shirley .15 .40
65 Todd Gurley .60 1.50
66 Sammie Coates NL .20 .50
67 Tevin Coleman NL .20 .50
68 Amari Cooper NL .50 1.25
69 Todd Gurley NL .60 1.50
70 Dorial Green-Beckham NL .15 .40
71 Randy Gregory NL .15 .40
72 Devin Funchess NL .25 .60
73 Brett Hundley NL .15 .40
74 Maxx Williams NL .15 .40
75 Jameis Winston NL .40 1.00
76 Cameron Artis-Payne NL .15 .40
77 Vic Beasley NL .20 .50
78 Landon Collins NL .20 .50
79 Dante Fowler Jr. NL .25 .60
80 Garrett Grayson NL .15 .40
81 Duke Johnson NL .25 .60
82 Tyler Lockett NL .25 .60
83 Sean Mannion NL .15 .40
84 Bryce Petty NL .15 .40
85 Devin Smith NL .15 .40
86 Clive Walford NL .15 .40
87 Trae Waynes NL .15 .40
88 Kevin White NL .20 .50
89 Leonard Williams NL .15 .40
90 T.J. Yeldon NL .15 .40
91 Sammie Coates SL .20 .50
92 Amari Cooper SL .50 1.25
93 Garrett Grayson SL .15 .40
94 Todd Gurley SL .60 1.50
95 Brett Hundley SL .15 .40
96 Bryce Petty SL .15 .40
97 Devin Smith SL .15 .40
98 Kevin White SL .20 .50
99 Maxx Williams SL .15 .40
100 Jameis Winston SL .40 1.00
101 Quinton Dunbar .20 .50
102 Matt Miller .15 .40
103 Vic Beasley .20 .50
104 Adrian Amos .20 .50
105 Amari Cooper .50 1.25
106 Gus Johnson .25 .60
107 Shaq Thompson LB .20 .50
107RB Shaq Thompson RBK .20 .50
108 Jordan Richards .15 .40
109 Devin Smith .15 .40
110 Dee Hart .15 .40
111 Kevin White .20 .50
112 Steven Nelson .15 .40
113 Derron Smith .15 .40
114 Pete Thomas .20 .50
115 DeAndre Smelter .15 .40
116 Jordon James .20 .50
117 Brett Hundley .15 .40
118 Garrett Grayson .15 .40
119 Kenny Cook .15 .40
120 Chris Hackett .15 .40
121 Marcus Hardison .15 .40
122 Christion Jones .15 .40
123 Prince-Tyson Gulley .15 .40
124 Bryce Petty .15 .40
125 Amarlo Herrera .15 .40
126 Xavier Cooper .15 .40
127 Rannell Hall .15 .40
128 Deshazor Everett .15 .40
129 Austin Hill .15 .40
130 Davis Tull .15 .40
131 Trey DePriest .15 .40
132 Randall Telfer .15 .40
133 Justin Coleman .15 .40
134 Kenny Williams .15 .40
135 Tavaris Barnes .15 .40
136 Michael Bennett .15 .40
137 Lynden Trail .15 .40
138 Kaelin Clay .15 .40
139 Grant Hedrick .15 .40
140 Eddie Goldman .15 .40
141 Cam Worthy .15 .40
142 Detrick Bonner .15 .40
143 Ryan Delaire .15 .40
144 Darious Cummings .15 .40
145 Leonard Williams .15 .40
146 Jameis Winston 5S .25 .60
147 Jameis Winston 5S .25 .60
148 Jameis Winston 5S .25 .60
149 Jameis Winston 5S .25 .60
150 Jameis Winston 5S .25 .60
ROY Odell Beckham ROY .40 1.00

2015 SAGE HIT Artistry

1-12 RANDOM INSERTS IN LOW SERIES
1-12 RANDOM INSERTS IN HIGH SERIES
ART1 Cameron Artis-Payne .30 .75
ART2 Sammie Coates .40 1.00
ART3 Tevin Coleman .40 1.00
ART4 Devin Funchess .50 1.25
ART5 Dorial Green-Beckham .30 .75
ART6 Randy Gregory .30 .75
ART7 Todd Gurley 1.25 3.00
ART8 Josh Harper .30 .75
ART9 Duke Johnson .50 1.25
ART10 Maxx Williams .30 .75
ART11 Jameis Winston .75 2.00
ART12 T.J. Yeldon .30 .75
ART13 Shane Carden .30 .75
ART14 Amari Cooper 1.00 2.50
ART15 Dante Fowler Jr. .50 1.25
ART16 Garrett Grayson .30 .75
ART17 Brett Hundley .30 .75
ART18 Sean Mannion .30 .75
ART19 Bryce Petty .30 .75
ART20 Devin Smith .30 .75
ART21 Clive Walford .30 .75
ART22 Kevin White .40 1.00
ART23 Leonard Williams .30 .75
ART24 Odell Beckham Jr. .50 1.25

2015 SAGE HIT Artistry Autographs

ART1 Cameron Artis-Payne 3.00 8.00
ART2 Sammie Coates 4.00 10.00
ART3 Tevin Coleman 4.00 10.00
ART4 Devin Funchess 5.00 12.00
ART5 Dorial Green-Beckham 3.00 8.00
ART6 Randy Gregory 3.00 8.00
ART7 Todd Gurley 20.00 50.00
ART8 Josh Harper 3.00 8.00
ART10 Maxx Williams 3.00 8.00
ART11 Jameis Winston 50.00 100.00
ART12 T.J. Yeldon 3.00 8.00
ART13 Shane Carden 3.00 8.00
ART14 Amari Cooper 10.00 25.00
ART15 Dante Fowler Jr. 5.00 12.00
ART16 Garrett Grayson 3.00 8.00
ART17 Brett Hundley 3.00 8.00
ART18 Sean Mannion 3.00 8.00
ART19 Bryce Petty 3.00 8.00
ART20 Devin Smith 3.00 8.00
ART21 Clive Walford 3.00 8.00
ART22 Kevin White 4.00 10.00
ART23 Leonard Williams
ART24 Odell Beckham Jr. 25.00 50.00

2015 SAGE HIT Autographs Gold

*BASE RED: .3X TO .8X GOLD AU/250
*BASE RED SP: .4X TO 1X GOLD AU/250
*BLACK: .4X TO 1X GOLD AU/250
A1 Devin Funchess 4.00 10.00
A2 Quinten Rollins 5.00 12.00
A3 Josh Harper 2.50 6.00
A4 Randy Gregory 2.50 6.00
A5 Jameis Winston 20.00 50.00
A6 Tevin Coleman 3.00 8.00
A7 Brandon Bridge 2.50 6.00
A10 DaVaris Daniels 2.50 6.00
A11 Dorial Green-Beckham 2.50 6.00
A12 Dres Anderson 2.50 6.00
A14 Ifo Ekpre-Olomu 2.50 6.00
A15 Trae Waynes 2.50 6.00
A16 Tyler Lockett 4.00 10.00
A17 Dylan Thompson 2.50 6.00
A18 Sammie Coates 3.00 8.00
A19 Hutson Mason 2.50 6.00
A20 Gary Nova 2.50 6.00
A22 Andre Davis 2.50 6.00
A23 Brandon Wegher 5.00 12.00
A24 Sean Mannion 2.50 6.00
A25 Kevin Parks 2.50 6.00
A26 Landon Collins 3.00 8.00
A27 P.J. Williams 3.00 8.00
A28 Malcolm Brown 3.00 8.00
A29 Malcom Brown 2.50 6.00
A30 Synjyn Days 2.50 6.00
A32 John Crockett 4.00 10.00
A33 Markus Golden 2.50 6.00
A34 Taylor Heinicke 4.00 10.00
A35 Shane Carden 2.50 6.00
A36 Dante Fowler Jr. 4.00 10.00
A37 Tony Lippett 2.50 6.00
A38 Maxx Williams 2.50 6.00
A39 Charles Gaines 4.00 10.00
A40 T.J. Yeldon 2.50 6.00
A41 Bo Wallace 2.50 6.00
A42 Jaxon Shipley 2.50 6.00
A43 Mike Hull 4.00 10.00
A44 Cameron Artis-Payne 2.50 6.00
A45 Levi Norwood 2.50 6.00
A46 Clive Walford 2.50 6.00
A47 Jake Ryan 4.00 10.00
A48 Anthony Harris 2.50 6.00
A49 Lorenzo Mauldin 2.50 6.00
A50 Grady Jarrett 3.00 8.00
A51 Jake Waters 3.00 8.00
A53 Gabe Holmes 2.50 6.00
A54 MyCole Pruitt 2.50 6.00
A55 Cedric Reed 2.50 6.00
A56 Quandre Diggs 2.50 6.00
A57 Bryan Bennett 2.50 6.00
A58 Geneo Grissom 2.50 6.00
A59 Marcus Murphy 2.50 6.00
A60 Dominique Brown 2.50 6.00
A61 Lorenzo Doss 2.50 6.00
A62 Darren Waller 3.00 8.00
A63 Donatella Luckett 3.00 8.00
A64 Josh Shirley 2.50 6.00
A65 Todd Gurley 15.00 40.00
A66 Cameron Erving 3.00 8.00
A67 Rob Havenstein 3.00 8.00
A68 Akeem King 2.50 6.00
A69 Cole Manhart 2.50 6.00
A70 Cedric Ogbuehi 2.50 6.00
A71 Laken Tomlinson 2.50 6.00
A95 Geoff Swaim 3.00 8.00
A96 Bronson Hill
A97 David Mayo
A98 Joshua McCain
A99 Isiah Myers 3.00 8.00
A100 Garry Peters 2.50 6.00
A101 Quinton Dunbar 3.00 8.00
A102 Matt Miller 2.50 6.00
A103 Vic Beasley
A104 Adrian Amos 3.00 8.00
A105A Amari Cooper 8.00 20.00
A105B Zack Hodges 2.50 6.00
A106 Gus Johnson 4.00 10.00
A107 Shaq Thompson LB 3.00 8.00
A108 Jordan Richards 2.50 6.00
A109 Devin Smith 2.50 6.00
A110 Dee Hart 2.50 6.00
A111 Kevin White 3.00 8.00
A112 Steven Nelson 2.50 6.00
A113 Derron Smith 2.50 6.00
A114 Pete Thomas 3.00 8.00
A115 DeAndre Smelter
A116 Jordon James 3.00 8.00
A117 Brett Hundley 2.50 6.00
A118 Garrett Grayson 2.50 6.00
A119 Kenny Cook 2.50 6.00
A120 Chris Hackett 2.50 6.00
A121 Marcus Hardison 2.50 6.00
A122 Christion Jones 2.50 6.00
A123 Prince-Tyson Gulley 2.50 6.00
A124 Bryce Petty 2.50 6.00
A125 Amarlo Herrera 2.50 6.00
A126 Xavier Cooper 2.50 6.00
A127 Rannell Hall 2.50 6.00
A128 Deshazor Everett 2.50 6.00
A129 Austin Hill 2.50 6.00
A130 Davis Tull 2.50 6.00
A131 Trey DePriest
A132 Randall Telfer 2.50 6.00
A133 Justin Coleman 2.50 6.00
A134 Kenny Williams 2.50 6.00
A135 Tavaris Barnes 2.50 6.00
A136 Michael Bennett
A137 Lynden Trail 2.50 6.00
A138 Kaelin Clay 2.50 6.00
A139 Grant Hedrick 2.50 6.00
A140 Eddie Goldman
A141 Cam Worthy 2.50 6.00
A142 Detrick Bonner 2.50 6.00
A143 Ryan Delaire 2.50 6.00
A144 Darious Cummings 2.50 6.00
A145 Leonard Williams

2015 SAGE HIT Write Stuff

COMPLETE SET (12) 6.00 15.00
COMP.LOW SERIES (6) 3.00 8.00
COMP.HIGH SERIES (6) 3.00 8.00
1-6 RANDOM INSERTS IN LOW SERIES
7-12 RANDOM INSERTS IN HIGH SERIES

WS1 Sammie Coates .40 1.00
WS2 Devin Funchess .50 1.25
WS3 Dorial Green-Beckham .30 .75
WS4 Todd Gurley 1.25 3.00
WS5 Maxx Williams .30 .75
WS6 Jameis Winston .75 2.00
WS7 Amari Cooper 1.00 2.50
WS8 Garrett Grayson .30 .75
WS9 Brett Hundley .30 .75
WS10 Bryce Petty .30 .75
WS11 Devin Smith .30 .75
WS12 Kevin White .40 1.00

2015 SAGE HIT Write Stuff Autographs

WS1 Sammie Coates 5.00 12.00
WS2 Devin Funchess 6.00 15.00
WS3 Dorial Green-Beckham 4.00 10.00
WS4 Todd Gurley 20.00 50.00
WS5 Maxx Williams 4.00 10.00
WS6 Jameis Winston 60.00 120.00
WS7 Amari Cooper
WS8 Garrett Grayson 12.00 30.00
WS9 Brett Hundley 4.00 10.00
WS10 Bryce Pelly 4.00 10.00
WS11 Devin Smith 4.00 10.00
WS12 Kevin White 5.00 12.00

2016 SAGE HIT

*SILVER: .8X TO 2X BASIC CARDS
1 Derrick Alexander .15 .40
2 Liam Nadler .15 .40
3 Pharoh Cooper .15 .40
4 Max Tuerk .15 .40
5 Ezekiel Elliott .75 2.00
6 Leonard Floyd .20 .50
7 Nelson Spruce .15 .40
8 Laremy Tunsil .15 .40
9 Derek Watt .25 .60
10 Marshaun Coprich .15 .40
11 Bronson Kaufusi .15 .40
12 De'Runnya Wilson .15 .40
13 Austin Johnson .15 .40
14 Hunter Henry .20 .50
15 Sebastian Tretola .15 .40
16 Roberto Aguayo .15 .40
17 Cody Kessler .15 .40
18 Nick Martin .15 .40
19 Briean Brody-Calhoun .15 .40
20 Dominique Alexander .15 .40
21 Keivarae Russell .15 .40
22 Paul Perkins .15 .40
23 Cayleb Jones .15 .40
24 Jalen Ramsey .25 .60
25 Aaron Burbridge .15 .40
26 Joey Bosa .30 .75
27 Michael Thomas .30 .75
28 Xavien Howard .20 .50
29 Sheldon Day .15 .40
30 Maliek Collins .15 .40
31 Kenny Clark .15 .40
32 Will Fuller .25 .60
33 Charles Tapper .20 .50
34 Tre Madden .15 .40
35 Blake Frohnapfel .15 .40
36 Joshua Garnett .15 .40
37 Keith Marshall .15 .40
38 Shon Coleman .15 .40
39 Sean Price .15 .40
40 Mike Bercovici .15 .40
41 Darion Griswold .20 .50
42 Terenn Houk .15 .40
43 Cardale Jones .15 .40
44 Trae Elston .25 .60
45 Kyler Fackrell .20 .50
46 Joe Schobert .20 .50
47 Jeremy Cash .20 .50
48 Geronimo Allison .15 .40
49 Jakeem Grant .15 .40
50 Devon Johnson .20 .50
51 Jalen Ramsey AR .25 .60
52 Hunter Henry AR .20 .50
53 Shon Coleman AR .15 .40
54 Joshua Garnett AR .15 .40
55 Michael Thomas AR .30 .75
56 Joey Bosa AR .30 .75
57 Will Fuller AR .25 .60
58 Keith Marshall AR .15 .40
59 Ezekiel Elliott AR .75 2.00
60 Jeremy Cash AR .20 .50
61 Jalen Ramsey NL .25 .60
62 Charles Tapper NL
63 Blake Frohnapfel NL .15 .40
64 Joey Bosa NL .30 .75
65 Paul Perkins NL
66 Will Fuller NL .25 .60
67 Hunter Henry NL .20 .50
68 Ezekiel Elliott NL .75 2.00
69 De'Runnya wilson NL .15 .40
70 Cayleb Jones NL .15 .40
71 Keivarae Russell NL .15 .40
72 Michael Thomas NL .30 .75
73 Alex Collins NL .20 .50
74 Aaron Burbridge NL .15 .40
75 Pharoh Cooper NL .15 .40
76 Alex Collins .20 .50
77 Macolm Mitchell .15 .40
78 Jack Allen .20 .50
79 Devon Blackmon .15 .40
80 Soma Vainuku .20 .50
81 Hunter Sharp .20 .50
82 Tre Roberson .20 .50
83 Chuckie Keeton .15 .40
84 Antwaun Woods .25 .60
85 Leviticus Payne .15 .40
86 Matt Weiser .20 .50
87 Brandon Allen .15 .40
88 Cody Core .15 .40
89 Nick Vannett .15 .40
90 Corey Coleman .25 .60
91 Aaron Green .15 .40
92 Luke Rhodes .15 .40
93 Darron Lee .15 .40
94 Brandon Doughty .15 .40
95 Michael Jordan .20 .50
96 Kyle Peko .20 .50
97 Daniel Braverman .15 .40
98 Miles Killebrew .15 .40
99 Daniel Lasco .15 .40
100 Jordan Howard .40 1.00
101 Steven Scheu .15 .40
102 Conner McGovern .15 .40
103 Jeff Driskel .15 .40
104 Ugonna Awuruonye .15 .40
105 Jordan Williams .15 .40
106 DeForest Buckner .15 .40
107 Ka'imi Fairbairn .20 .50
108 Evan Boehm .15 .40
109 Carl Nassib .15 .40
110 Jared Goff 1.00 2.50
111 Kendall Fuller .20 .50
112 Tajae Sharpe .20 .50
113 Vadal Alexander .15 .40
114 Dan Vitale .15 .40
115 Maurice Harris .20 .50
116 Josh Doctson .20 .50
117 Jonathan Williams .20 .50
118 Kavon Frazier .15 .40
119 Ammon Olsen .15 .40
120 Dak Prescott .75 2.00
121 Paxton Lynch .15 .40
122 Tyler Ervin .15 .40
123 Jimmy Pruitt .15 .40
124 Ezekiel Elliott 5S .75 2.00
125 Ezekiel Elliott 5S .75 2.00
126 Ezekiel Elliott 5S .75 2.00
127 Ezekiel Elliott 5S .75 2.00
128 Ezekiel Elliott 5S .75 2.00
129 Jared Goff AR 1.00 2.50
130 Dak Prescott AR .75 2.00
131 Corey Coleman AR .25 .60
132 Josh Doctson AR .20 .50
133 Alex Collins AR .20 .50
134 Paxton Lynch AR .15 .40
135 DeForest Buckner AR .15 .40
136 Tajae Sharpe NL .20 .50
137 Jared Goff NL 1.00 2.50
138 Jordan Howard NL .40 1.00
139 Jeff Driskel NL .15 .40
140 Josh Doctson NL .20 .50
141 Daniel Braverman NL .15 .40
142 Brandon Allen NL .15 .40
143 Brandon Doughty NL .15 .40
144 Corey Coleman NL .25 .60
145 Tyler Ervin NL .15 .40
146 Hunter Sharp NL .20 .50
147 Aaron Green NL .15 .40
148 Nick Vannett NL .15 .40
149 Paxton Lynch NL .15 .40
150 Dak Prescott NL .75 2.00

2016 SAGE HIT Artistry

COMMON CARD .30 .75
UNLISTED STARS .40 1.00
ART1 Nelson Spruce .25 .60
ART2 Hunter Henry .30 .75
ART3 Ezekiel Elliott 1.25 3.00
ART4 De'Runnya Wilson .25 .60
ART5 Pharoh Cooper .25 .60
ART6 Joey Bosa .50 1.25
ART7 Paul Perkins .25 .60
ART8 Cody Kessler .25 .60
ART9 Jalen Ramsey .40 1.00
ART10 Brandon Allen .25 .60
ART11 Jeff Driskel .25 .60
ART12 Maurice Harris .30 .75
ART13 Jonathan Williams .30 .75
ART14 Jared Goff 1.50 4.00
ART15 Paxton Lynch .25 .60

2016 SAGE HIT Artistry Autographs

ART1 Nelson Spruce 3.00 8.00
ART2 Hunter Henry 4.00 10.00
ART3 Ezekiel Elliott 15.00 40.00
ART4 De'Runnya Wilson 3.00 8.00
ART5 Pharoh Cooper 3.00 8.00
ART6 Joey Bosa 6.00 15.00
ART7 Paul Perkins 3.00 8.00
ART8 Cody Kessler 3.00 8.00
ART9 Jalen Ramsey 5.00 12.00
ART10 Brandon Allen 3.00 8.00
ART11 Jeff Driskel 3.00 8.00
ART12 Maurice Harris 4.00 10.00
ART13 Jonathan Williams 4.00 10.00
ART14 Jared Goff 20.00 50.00
ART15 Paxton Lynch 3.00 8.00

2016 SAGE HIT Autographs

*RED: .5X TO 1.2X BASIC AU
*GOLD/250: .5X TO 1.2X BASIC AU
A1 Ezekiel Elliott 10.00 25.00
A2 Trae Elston 3.00 8.00
A3 Darion Griswold 2.50 6.00
A4 Will Fuller 3.00 8.00
A5 Laremy Tunsil 2.00 5.00
A6 Blake Frohnapfel 2.00 5.00
A7 Sheldon Day 2.00 5.00
A8 Joe Schobert 2.50 6.00
A9 Dominique Alexander 2.00 5.00
A10 Roberto Aguayo 2.00 5.00
A11 Max Tuerk 2.00 5.00
A12 De'Runnya Wilson 2.00 5.00
A13 Shon Coleman 2.00 5.00
A14 Keith Marshall 2.00 5.00
A15 Xavien Howard 2.50 6.00
A16 Michael Thomas
A17 Liam Nadler 2.00 5.00
A18 Sebastian Tretola 2.00 5.00
A19 Sean Price 2.00 5.00
A20 Aaron Burbridge 2.00 5.00
A21 Kenny Clark 2.00 5.00
A22 Joey Bosa 4.00 10.00
A23 Pharoh Cooper 2.00 5.00
A24 Maliek Collins 2.00 5.00
A25 Keivarae Russell 2.00 5.00
A26 Terenn Houk 2.00 5.00
A27 Cody Kessler 2.00 5.00
A28 Kyler Fackrell 2.50 6.00
A29 Derek Watt 3.00 8.00
A30 Jalen Ramsey 3.00 8.00
A31 Marshaun Coprich 2.00 5.00
A32 Derrick Alexander 2.00 5.00
A33 Nelson Spruce 2.00 5.00
A34 Joshua Garnett 2.00 5.00
A35 Briean Brody-Calhoun 2.00 5.00
A36 Tre Madden 2.00 5.00
A37 Cardale Jones 2.00 5.00
A38 Jeremy Cash 2.50 6.00
A39 Bronson Kaufusi 2.00 5.00
A40 Hunter Henry 2.50 6.00
A41 Austin Johnson 2.00 5.00
A42 Paul Perkins 2.00 5.00
A43 Geronimo Allison 2.00 5.00
A44 Nick Martin 2.00 5.00
A45 Mike Bercovici 2.00 5.00
A46 Joe Schobert 2.50 6.00
A47 Jakeem Grant 2.00 5.00
A48 Cayleb Jones 2.00 5.00
A49 TBD
A50 Devon Johnson 2.50 6.00
A51 Aaron Green 2.00 5.00
A52 DeForest Buckner 2.00 5.00
A53 Josh Doctson 2.50 6.00
A54 Jordan Howard 5.00 12.00
A55 Brandon Allen 2.00 5.00
A56 Connor McGovern 2.00 5.00
A57 Jared Goff 25.00 50.00
A58 Nick Vannett 2.00 5.00
A59 Jack Allen 2.50 6.00
A60 Daniel Lasco 2.00 5.00
A61 Matt Weiser 2.50 6.00
A62 Corey Coleman 3.00 8.00
A63 Luke Rhodes 2.00 5.00
A64 Ka'imi Fairbairn 2.50 6.00
A65 Dan Vitale 2.00 5.00
A66 Alex Collins 2.50 6.00
A67 Dak Prescott 25.00 50.00
A68 Ugonna Awuruonye 2.00 5.00
A69 Soma Vainuku 2.50 6.00
A70 Steven Scheu 2.00 5.00
A71 Malcolm Mitchell 2.00 5.00
A72 Miles Killebrew 2.00 5.00
A73 Vadal Alexander 2.00 5.00
A74 Tre Roberson 2.50 6.00
A75 Jonathan Williams 2.50 6.00
A76 Evan Boehm 2.00 5.00
A77 Tajae Sharpe 2.50 6.00
A78 Mike Matthews 2.00 5.00
A79 Daneil Braverman 2.00 5.00
A80 Jeff Driskel 2.00 5.00
A81 Jordan Williams 2.00 5.00
A82 Devon Blackmon 2.00 5.00
A83 Darron Lee 2.00 5.00
A84 Kendall Fuller 2.50 6.00
A85 Cody Core 2.00 5.00
A86 Carl Nassib 2.00 5.00
A87 Hunter Sharp 2.50 6.00
A88 Brandon Doughty 2.00 5.00
A89 TDD
A90 Kyle Peko 2.50 6.00
A91 Michael Jordan 2.50 6.00
A92 Maurice Harris 2.50 6.00
A93 Kavon Frazier 2.00 5.00
A94 Ammon Olsen 2.00 5.00
A95 Paxton Lynch 2.00 5.00
A96 Leviticus Payne 2.00 5.00
A97 Jimmy Pruitt 2.00 5.00
A98 Tyler Ervin 2.00 5.00
A99 Chuckie Keeton 2.00 5.00

2016 SAGE HIT Premium Portraits

*GOLD: .5X TO 1.2X BASIC INSERTS
PP1 Alex Collins .40 1.00
PP2 Jared Goff 2.00 5.00
PP3 Corey Coleman .50 1.25
PP4 Paul Perkins .30 .75
PP5 Hunter Henry .40 1.00
PP6 Joey Bosa .60 1.50
PP7 Pharoh Cooper .30 .75
PP8 Jeremy Cash .40 1.00
PP9 Cardale Jones .30 .75
PP10 Jalen Ramsey .50 1.25
PP11 Laremy Tunsil .30 .75
PP12 Ezekiel Elliott 1.50 4.00
PP13 Will Fuller .50 1.25
PP14 Paxton Lynch .30 .75
PP15 Josh Doctson .40 1.00
PP16 Chuckie Keeton .30 .75
PP17 Jordan Howard .75 2.00
PP18 Dak Prescott 1.50 4.00
PP19 DeForest Buckner .30 .75
PP20 Brandon Allen .30 .75
PP21 Brandon Doughty .30 .75

2017 SAGE HIT Premier Draft

*GOLD: .5X TO 1.2 X BASIC CARDS
*RED: .6X TO 1.5X BASIC CARDS
*SILVER: .8X TO 2X BASIC CARDS
1 Corey Clement .20 .50
2 Keon Hatcher .15 .40
3 Gehrig Dieter .15 .40
4 Zane Gonzalez .15 .40
5 Patrick Mahomes II 2.00 5.00
6 Solomon Thomas .15 .40
7 Adrian Colbert .15 .40
8 Dane Evans .15 .40
9 Dorian Johnson .15 .40
10 Cooper Rush .20 .50
11 Dede Westbrook .15 .40
12 Jamaal Williams .15 .40
13 Damien Mama .15 .40
14 DeShone Kizer .15 .40
15 Garrettt Fugate .15 .40
16 Josh Magee .15 .40
17 Ishmael Zamora .15 .40
18 Tyler O'Connor .25 .60
19 Jerome Lane .20 .50
20 Mike Fafaul .15 .40
21 DeAngelo Yancey .15 .40
22 Zack Ryan .15 .40
23 Dante Barnett .15 .40
24 Sidney Jones IV .15 .40
25 Alvin Kamara .60 1.50
26 Dakota Prukop .15 .40
27 Chris Wormley .15 .40
28 Trent Taylor .20 .50
29 Greg Ward Jr. .15 .40
30 Jadar Johnson .15 .40
31 Dontre Wilson .15 .40
32 Samaje Perine .15 .40
33 Amara Darboh .15 .40
34 Zach Banner .15 .40
35 Takkarist McKinley .15 .40
36 Darreus Rogers .30 .75
37 Budda Baker .15 .40
38 Evan Engram .20 .50
39 Ryan Ramczyk .15 .40
40 Juju Smith-Schuster .40 1.00
41 Corey Clement IF .20 .50
42 Amara Darboh IF .15 .40
43 Patrick Mahomes II IF 2.00 5.00
44 Corey Davis IF .25 .60
45 Samaje Perine IF .15 .40
46 Juju Smith-Schuster IF .40 1.00
47 Dane Evans IF .15 .40
48 Evan Engram IF .20 .50
49 Sidney Jones IV IF .15 .40
50 Cooper Rush IF .20 .50
51 Alvin Kamara IF .60 1.50
52 Dede Westbrook IF .15 .40
53 DeShone Kizer IF .15 .40
54 Jamaal Williams IF .15 .40
55 Ezekiel Elliott II .30 .75
56 Corey Coleman II .15 .40
57 Jared Goff II .25 .60
58 Michael Thomas II .25 .60
59 Jalen Ramsey II .15 .40
60 Dak Prescott II .25 .60
61 Jordan Howard II .25 .60
62 Paxton Lynch II .15 .40
63 Tajae Sharpe II .15 .40
64 Malcolm Mitchell II .20 .50
65 Cody Kessler II .15 .40
66 Wes Lunt .20 .50
67 Chad Kelly .15 .40
68 Montravius Adams .20 .50
69 I'Tavius Mathers .15 .40
70 James Onwualu .20 .50
71 Donell Pumphrey Jr. .20 .50
72 Justin Davis .25 .60
73 Adam Bisnowaty .15 .40
74 Dalvin Cook .40 1.00
75 Montae Nicholson .20 .50
76 Joshua Dobbs .20 .50
77 Josh Atkinson .25 .60
78 Zach Cunningham .20 .50
79 Corey Davis .25 .60
80 Jake Elliott .30 .75
81 Taywan Taylor .15 .40
82 Cole Hikutini .15 .40
83 Malik Hooker .15 .40
84 Brad Kaaya .15 .40
85 John Ross III .20 .50
86 Trevor Knight .20 .50
87 C.J. Beathard .15 .40
88 Davis Webb .15 .40
89 Ardarius Stewart .15 .40
90 Sefo Liufau .20 .50
91 Charles Harris .15 .40
92 Jeremy McNichols .15 .40
93 Tim Patrick .20 .50
94 Joshua Reynolds .20 .50
95 Tim Williams .20 .50
96 Ryan Higgins .30 .75
97 Tarean Folston .25 .60
98 Aaron Bailey .20 .50
99 Paul Magloire Jr. .20 .50
100 Michael Roberts .25 .60
101 Shelton Gibson .15 .40
102 Carlos Henderson .15 .40
103 James Conner .30 .75
104 Marcus Williams .15 .40
105 River Cracraft .20 .50
106 Garrett Bolles .30 .75
107 Chad Hansen .15 .40
108 Garry Brown .30 .75
109 Austin Appleby .20 .50
110 Patrick Towles .30 .75
111 Seth Russell .20 .50
112 Christian McCaffrey .40 1.00
113 Riley Bullough .15 .40
114 Drew Morgan .25 .60
115 T.J. Logan .25 .60
116 Robert Davis .15 .40
117 Issac Rochell .15 .40
118 Fabian Moreau .15 .40
119 James Conner IF .30 .75
120 Dalvin Cook IF .40 1.00
121 Joshua Dobbs IF .20 .50
122 Carlos Henderson IF .15 .40
123 Ryan Higgins IF .30 .75
124 Seth Russell IF .20 .50
125 Brad Kaaya IF .15 .40
126 Chad Kelly IF .15 .40
127 Christian McCaffrey IF .40 1.00
128 Donell Pumphrey Jr. IF .20 .50
129 John Ross III IF .20 .50
130 Tim Williams IF .20 .50
131 Davis Webb IF .15 .40
132 Geronimo Allison II .20 .50
133 John Ross III RB .20 .50
134 Ezekiel Elliott LL .30 .75
135 Dak Prescott ROY .25 .60

2017 SAGE HIT Premier Draft Autographs

A1 Corey Clement 2.50 6.00
A2 Takkarist McKinley 2.00 5.00
A3 Samaje Perine 2.00 5.00
A4 Zane Gonzalez 2.00 5.00
A5 DeAngelo Yancey 2.00 5.00
A6 Jamaal Williams 2.00 5.00
A7 Amara Darboh 2.00 5.00
A8 Alvin Kamara 8.00 20.00
A8 Jeremy McNichols 2.00 5.00
A9 Josh Magee 2.00 5.00
A10 Cooper Rush 2.50 6.00
A11 Dede Westbrook 2.00 5.00
A12 Damien Mama 2.00 5.00
A13 Dane Evans 2.00 5.00
A14 DeShone Kizer 15.00 40.00
A15 Gehrig Dieter 2.00 5.00
A16 Mike Fafaul 2.00 5.00
A17 Charles Harris 2.00 5.00
A18 Jadar Johnson 2.00 5.00
A19 Tyler O'Connor 3.00 8.00
A20 Adrian Colbert 2.00 5.00
A21 Sidney Jones IV 2.00 5.00
A22 Zack Ryan 2.00 5.00
A23 Patrick Mahomes II 125.00 250.00
A24 Solomon Thomas 2.00 5.00
A25 Chris Wormley 2.00 5.00
A26 Dakota Prukop 2.00 5.00
A27 Darreus Rogers 4.00 10.00
A28 Zach Banner 2.00 5.00
A29 Garrett Fugate 2.00 5.00
A30 Keon Hatcher 2.00 5.00
A31 Ryan Ramczyk 2.00 5.00
A32 Budda Baker 2.00 5.00
A33 Jerome Lane 2.50 6.00
A34 Juju Smith-Schuster 5.00 12.00
A35 Dontre Wilson 2.00 5.00
A36 Dante Barnett 2.00 5.00
A37 Evan Engram 2.50 6.00
A38 Dorian Johnson 2.00 5.00
A39 Ishmael Zamora 2.00 5.00
A40 Greg Ward Jr. 2.00 5.00
A41 James Onwualu 2.50 6.00
A42 Trent Taylor
A43 Chad Kelly 2.00 5.00
A44 Jake Elliott 4.00 10.00
A45 I'Tavius Mathers 2.00 5.00
A47 Ardarius Stewart 2.00 5.00
A49 Josh Atkinson 3.00 8.00
A50 Wes Lunt 2.50 6.00
A51 Donel Pumphrey Jr. 2.50 6.00
A52 Carlos Henderson 2.00 5.00
A53 Tarean Folston 3.00 8.00
A54 Shelton Gibson 2.00 5.00
A55 Michael Roberts 3.00 8.00
A56 Malik Hooker 2.00 5.00
A57 Davis Webb 2.00 5.00
A60 Joshua Reynolds 2.50 6.00
A61 Montravius Adams 2.50 6.00
A62 Tim Williams 2.50 6.00
A63 Taywan Taylor 2.00 5.00
A64 Justin Davis 3.00 8.00
A65 Corey Davis 8.00 20.00
A66 Tim Patrick 2.50 6.00
A67 Aaron Bailey 2.50 6.00
A68 Trevor Knight 2.50 6.00
A69 Montae Nicholson 2.50 6.00
A70 Sefo Liufau 2.50 6.00
A71 Ryan Higgins 4.00 10.00
A72 Cole Hikutini 2.00 5.00
A73 Riley Bullough 2.00 5.00
A74 Dalvin Cook 20.00 50.00
A74 Brad Kaaya 2.00 5.00
A76 Joshua Dobbs 2.50 6.00
A76 Marcus Williams 2.00 5.00
A78 Zach Cunningham 2.50 6.00
A78 Adam Bisnowaty 2.00 5.00
A80 River Cracraft 2.50 6.00
A81 Chad Hansen 2.00 5.00
A82 Issac Rochell 2.00 5.00
A83 Garry Brown 4.00 10.00
A84 Austin Appleby 2.50 6.00
A85 Seth Russell 2.50 6.00
A85 John Ross III 2.50 6.00
A86 Patrick Towles 4.00 10.00
A87 Paul Magloire Jr. 2.50 6.00
A88 James Conner 4.00 10.00
A89 C.J. Beathard 2.00 5.00
A90 Drew Morgan 3.00 8.00
A91 Robert Davis 2.00 5.00
A91 Charles Harris 2.00 5.00
A93 Christian McCaffrey 5.00 12.00
A106 Garrett Bolles 4.00 10.00
A115 T.J. Logan 3.00 8.00
A118 James Conner IF 4.00 10.00
A119 Dalvin Cook IF 20.00 50.00
A120 Joshua Dobbs IF 2.50 6.00
A121 Carlos Henderson IF 2.00 5.00
A122 Ryan Higgins IF 4.00 10.00
A123 Seth Russell IF 2.50 6.00
A124 Brad Kaaya IF 2.00 5.00
A125 Chad Kelly IF 2.00 5.00
A126 I'Tavius Mathers IF 2.00 5.00
A127 Christian McCaffrey IF 5.00 12.00
A128 Donell Pumphrey Jr. IF 2.50 6.00
A129 John Ross III IF 2.50 6.00
A130 Tim Williams IF 2.50 6.00
A131 Davis Webb IF 2.00 5.00
A132 Geronimo Allison II 2.50 6.00
A133 John Ross III RB 2.50 6.00
A134 Ezekiel Elliott LL 30.00 80.00
A135 Dak Prescott ROY 25.00 60.00

2017 SAGE HIT Premier Draft Instant Impact Autographs Blue

55 Ezekiel Elliott 30.00 80.00
56 Corey Coleman 3.00 8.00
57 Jared Goff 5.00 12.00
58 Michael Thomas 5.00 12.00
59 Jalen Ramsey 3.00 8.00
60 Dak Prescott 25.00 60.00
61 Jordan Howard 5.00 12.00
62 Paxton Lynch 3.00 8.00
63 Tajae Sharpe 3.00 8.00
64 Malcolm Mitchell 4.00 10.00
65 Cody Kessler II 3.00 8.00

2017 SAGE HIT Premier Draft Peak Performance

PKAD Amara Darboh .30 .75
PKAK Alvin Kamara 1.25 3.00
PKAS Ardarius Stewart .30 .75
PKBK Brad Kaaya .30 .75
PKCC Corey Clement .40 1.00
PKCD Corey Davis .50 1.25
PKCH Chad Hansen .30 .75
PKCH Charles Harris .30 .75
PKCK Chad Kelly .30 .75
PKCM Christian McCaffrey .75 2.00
PKCR Cooper Rush .40 1.00
PKDC Dalvin Cook .75 2.00
PKDE Dane Evans .30 .75
PKDF Garrett Fugate .30 .75
PKDP Dak Prescott .50 1.25
PKDR Darreus Rogers .60 1.50
PKDW Dede Westbrook .30 .75
PKDY DeAngelo Yancey .30 .75
PKEE Ezekiel Elliott .60 1.50
PKGB Garry Brown .60 1.50
PKGD Gehrig Dieter .30 .75
PKGW Greg Ward Jr. .30 .75
PKIM I'Tavius Mathers .30 .75
PKJA Josh Atkinson .50 1.25
PKJC James Conner .60 1.50
PKJD Justin Davis
PKJD Joshua Dobbs .40 1.00
PKJH Jordan Howard .50 1.25
PKJL Jerome Lane .40 1.00
PKJM Josh Magee .30 .75
PKJR Josh Reynolds .30 .75
PKJS Juju Smith-Schuste .75 2.00
PKJW Jamaal Williams .30 .75
PKKH Keon Hatcher .30 .75
PKMR Michael Roberts .50 1.25
PKMT Michael Thomas .50 1.25
PKPM Patrick Mahomes II 4.00 10.00
PKPM Paul Magloire Jr. .40 1.00
PKRC River Cracraft .40 1.00
PKRD Robert Davis .30 .75
PKRH Ryan Higgins .60 1.50
PKSG Shelton Gibson .30 .75
PKSJ Sidney Jones IV .30 .75
PKSL Sefo Liufau .40 1.00
PKSP Samaje Perine .30 .75
PKSR Seth Russell .40 1.00
PKST Solomon Thomas .30 .75
PKTF Tarean Folston .50 1.25
PKTK Trevor Knight .40 1.00
PKTM Takkarist McKinley .30 .75
PKTO Tyler O'Connor .50 1.25
PKTT Taywan Taylor .30 .75
PKTW Tim Williams .40 1.00
PKWL Wes Lunt .40 1.00
PKZC Zach Cunningham .40 1.00
PKZG Zane Gonzalez .30 .75
PDEVE Evan Engram .40 1.00
PK-PT Patrick Towles
PKCaH Carlos Henderson .30 .75
PKCJB C.J. Beathard .30 .75
PKDaW Davis Webb .30 .75
PKDK1 DeShone Kizer .30 .75
PKDK2 Dakota Prukop .30 .75
PKDoP Donnel Pumphrey .40 1.00
PKDOW Dontre Wilson .30 .75
PKDrW Drew Morgan .50 1.25
PKTJL T.J. Logan .50 1.25
PKTRT Trent Taylor .40 1.00

2017 SAGE HIT Premier Draft Peak Performance Autographs

PKAD Amara Darboh 2.50 6.00
PKAK Alvin Kamara 10.00 25.00
PKAS Ardarius Stewart 2.50 6.00
PKBK Brad Kaaya 2.50 6.00
PKCC Corey Clement 3.00 8.00
PKCD Corey Davis 4.00 10.00
PKCH Chad Hansen 2.50 6.00
PKCH Charles Harris 2.50 6.00
PKCK Chad Kelly 2.50 6.00
PKCM Christian McCaffrey 6.00 15.00
PKCR Cooper Rush 3.00 8.00
PKDC Dalvin Cook 6.00 15.00
PKDE Dane Evans 2.50 6.00
PKDF Garrett Fugate 2.50 6.00
PKDP Dak Prescott 25.00 60.00
PKDR Darreus Rogers 5.00 12.00
PKDW Dede Westbrook 2.50 6.00
PKDY DeAngelo Yancey 2.50 6.00
PKEE Ezekiel Elliott 30.00 80.00
PKGB Garry Brown 5.00 12.00
PKGD Gehrig Dieter 2.50 6.00
PKGW Greg Ward Jr. 2.50 6.00
PKIM I'Tavious Mathers 2.50 6.00
PKJA Josh Atkinson 4.00 10.00
PKJC James Conner 5.00 12.00
PKJD Joshua Dobbs 3.00 8.00
PKJH Jordan Howard 4.00 10.00
PKJL Jerome Lane 3.00 8.00
PKJM Josh Magee 2.50 6.00
PKJR Josh Reynolds 2.50 6.00
PKJS Juju Smith-Schuste 6.00 15.00
PKJW Jamaal Williams 2.50 6.00
PKKH Keon Hatcher 2.50 6.00
PKMR Michael Roberts 4.00 10.00
PKMT Michael Thomas 4.00 10.00
PKPM Patrick Mahomes II 30.00 80.00
PKPM Paul Magloire Jr. 3.00 8.00
PKRC River Cracraft 3.00 8.00
PKRD Robert Davis 2.50 6.00
PKRH Ryan Higgins 5.00 12.00
PKSG Shelton Gibson 2.50 6.00
PKSJ Sidney Jones IV 2.50 6.00
PKSL Sefo Liufau 3.00 8.00
PKSP Samaje Perine 2.50 6.00
PKSR Seth Russell 3.00 8.00
PKST Solomon Thomas 2.50 6.00
PKTF Tarean Folston 4.00 10.00
PKTK Trevor Knight 3.00 8.00
PKTM Takkarist McKinley 2.50 6.00
PKTO Tyler O'Connor 4.00 10.00
PKTT Taywan Taylor 2.50 6.00
PKTW Tim Williams 3.00 8.00
PKWL Wes Lunt 3.00 8.00
PKZC Zach Cunningham 3.00 8.00
PKZG Zane Gonzalez 2.50 6.00
PDEVE Evan Engram 3.00 8.00
PKCaH Carlos Henderson 2.50 6.00
PKCJB C.J. Beathard 2.50 6.00
PKDaW Davis Webb 2.50 6.00
PKDK1 DeShone Kizer 2.50 6.00
PKDK2 Dakota Prukop 2.50 6.00
PKDoP Donnel Pumphrey 3.00 8.00
PKDOW Dontre Wilson 2.50 6.00
PKDrW Drew Morgan 4.00 10.00
PKTJL T.J. Logan 4.00 10.00
PKTRT Trent Taylor 3.00 8.00

2017 SAGE HIT Premier Draft Premium Portraits

PPAD Amara Darboh .30 .75
PPBB Budda Baker .30 .75
PPBK Brad Kaaya .30 .75
PPCB C.J. Beathard .30 .75
PPCC Corey Clement .40 1.00
PPCD Corey Davis .50 1.25
PPCH Carlos Henderson .30 .75
PPCM Christian McCaffrey .75 2.00
PPCR Cooper Rush .40 1.00
PPDC Dalvin Cook .75 2.00
PPDK Deshone Kizer .30 .75
PPDP Donnel Pumphrey .40 1.00
PPDW Davis Webb .30 .75
PPEE Evan Engram .40 1.00
PPGW Greg Ward Jr. .30 .75
PPIM I'Tavius Mathers .30 .75
PPJC John Conner .60 1.50
PPJD Justin Davis .50 1.25
PPJL Jerome Lane .40 1.00
PPJM Jeremy McNichols .30 .75
PPJR John Ross III .40 1.00
PPPM Patrick Mahomes II 4.00 10.00
PPRR Ryan Ramszyk .30 .75
PPSL Sefo Liufau .40 1.00
PPSP Samaje Perine .30 .75
PPSR Seth Russell .40 1.00
PPTF Tarean Folston .50 1.25
PPTS Tyrone Swoopes .30 .75
PPTT Trent Taylor .40 1.00
PPWL Wes Lunt .40 1.00
PPDEW Dane Evans .30 .75
PPDEW Dede Westbrook .30 .75
PPRJD Joshua Dobbs .40 1.00
PPTaT Taywan Taylor .30 .75

2017 SAGE HIT Premier Draft Premium Portraits Blue

*BLUE: .5X TO 1.2X BASIC INSERTS

2017 SAGE HIT Premier Draft Premium Portraits Autographs

PPAD Amara Darboh 2.50 6.00
PPBB Budda Baker 2.50 6.00
PPBK Brad Kaaya 2.50 6.00
PPCB C.J. Beathard 2.50 6.00
PPCC Corey Clement 3.00 8.00
PPCD Corey Davis 4.00 10.00
PPCH Carlos Henderson 2.50 6.00
PPCM Christian McCaffrey 6.00 15.00
PPCR Cooper Rush 3.00 8.00
PPDC Dalvin Cook 6.00 15.00
PPDK Deshone Kizer 2.50 6.00
PPDP Donnel Pumphrey 3.00 8.00
PPDW Davis Webb 2.50 6.00
PPEE Evan Engram 3.00 8.00
PPGW Greg Ward Jr. 2.50 6.00
PPIM I'Tavius Mathers 2.50 6.00
PPJC John Conner 5.00 12.00
PPJD Justin Davis 4.00 10.00
PPJL Jerome Lane 3.00 8.00
PPJM Jeremy McNichols 2.50 6.00
PPJR John Ross III 3.00 8.00
PPPM Patrick Mahomes II 30.00 80.00
PPRR Ryan Ramszyk 2.50 6.00
PPSL Sefo Liufau 3.00 8.00
PPSP Samaje Perine 2.50 6.00
PPSR Seth Russell 3.00 8.00
PPTF Tarean Folston 4.00 10.00
PPTS Tyrone Swoopes 2.50 6.00
PPTT Trent Taylor 3.00 8.00
PPWL Wes Lunt 3.00 8.00
PPDEW Dane Evans 2.50 6.00
PPDEW Dede Westbrook 2.50 6.00
PPRJD Joshua Dobbs 3.00 8.00
PPTaT Taywan Taylor 2.50 6.00

2018 SAGE HIT

1 Daurice Fountain .20 .50
2 Jake Wieneke .20 .50
3 Josh Rosen .50 1.25
4 Derwin James .30 .75
5 Steven Mitchell Jr. .20 .50
6 Chris Hawkins .15 .40
7 Fred Warner .15 .40
8 Cedrick Wilson Jr. .15 .40
9 Orlando Brown Jr. .25 .60
10 Anthony Miller .25 .60
11 Riley Ferguson .25 .60
12 Nic Shimonek .25 .60
13 Logan Woodside .25 .60
14 John Wolford .15 .40
15 Leighton Vander Esch .50 1.25
16 Marcell Ateman .20 .50
17 Terry Swanson Jr. .25 .60
18 Chase Litton .20 .50
19 Jeffery Wilson .25 .60
20 Michael Dickson .15 .40
21 Adam Breneman .20 .50
22 Jeremiah Briscoe .20 .50
23 Poona Ford .15 .40
24 Akrum Wadley .15 .40
25 Bo Scarbrough .20 .50
26 Saeed Blacknall .40 1.00
27 John Franklin .20 .50
28 Jack Cichy .20 .50
29 Auden Tate .15 .40
30 Mark Andrews .25 .60
31 Will Hernandez .20 .50
32 Cody O'Connell .15 .40
33 Frank Ragnow .20 .50
34 Conor Sheehy .20 .50
35 Kyzir White .25 .60
36 Walter Payton Aspire 1 1.25 3.00
37 Walter Payton Aspire 2 1.25 3.00
38 Walter Payton Aspire 3 1.25 3.00
39 Walter Payton Aspire 4 1.25 3.00
40 Walter Payton Aspire 5 1.25 3.00
41 Roquan Smith IF .50 1.25
42 Mike Gesicki IF .20 .50
43 Josh Allen IF .60 1.50
44 Harold Landry IF .15 .40
45 Simmie Cobbs Jr. IF .25 .60
46 Bo Scarbrough IF .20 .50
47 Dante Pettis IF .25 .60
48 Auden Tate IF .15 .40
49 Equanimeous St. Brown IF .25 .60
50 Akrum Wadley IF .15 .40
51 Riley Ferguson IF .25 .60
52 Ryan Nall IF .30 .75
53 Sony Michel IF .50 1.25
54 C.J. Beathard II .15 .40
55 Jake Elliott II .20 .50
56 Zay Jones II .15 .40
57 Deshone Kizer II .20 .50
58 Christian McCaffrey II .25 .60
59 Patrick Mahomes II II .60 1.50
60 Samaje Perine II .15 .40
61 JuJu Smith-Schuster II .25 .60
62 Taywan Taylor II .15 .40
63 Trent Taylor II .15 .40
64 Dede Westbrook II .15 .40
65 Jamaal Williams II .15 .40
66 Josh Allen .60 1.50
67 Duke Williams .15 .40
68 Malik Williams .15 .40
69 Ryan Nall .30 .75
70 Davin Bellamy .15 .40
71 Chris Warren III .25 .60
72 Equanimeous St. Brown .25 .60
73 Sony Michel .50 1.25
74 Dante Pettis .25 .60
75 Simmie Cobbs Jr. .25 .60
76 Roquan Smith .50 1.25
77 Harold Landry .15 .40
78 Mike McGlinchey .30 .75
79 Maurice Hurst .20 .50
80 Mike Gesicki .20 .50
81 Tremaine Edmunds .30 .75
82 Terrell Edmunds .50 1.25
83 Troy Fumagalli .20 .50
84 Kurt Benkert .20 .50
85 Deon Cain .20 .50
86 Ka'Raun White .20 .50
87 Denzel Ward .40 1.00
88 Arden Key .15 .40
89 Mason Rudolph .40 1.00
90 Marcus Davenport .30 .75
91 Isaiah Wynn .15 .40
92 Trey Quinn .15 .40
93 Jaylen Samuels .20 .50
94 Keke Coutee .20 .50
95 Malik Jefferson .20 .50
96 Richie James .15 .40
97 Durham Smythe .15 .40
98 Armanti Foreman .15 .40
99 Tremon Smith .15 .40
100 Bradley Chubb .25 .60
101 Amari Coleman .15 .40
102 Diocemy Saint Juste .15 .40
103 Jake Roh .15 .40
104 Ronald Jones II .15 .40
105 Kerryon Johnson .25 .60
106 Geron Christian .15 .40
107 Bryce Bobo .15 .40
108 Josh Rosen ASP .50 1.25
109 Mason Rudolph ASP .40 1.00
110 Sony Michel ASP .50 1.25
111 Josh Allen ASP .60 1.50
112 Ronald Jones II ASP .15 .40
113 Jaylen Samuels IF .20 .50
114 Josh Rosen IF .50 1.25
115 Troy Fumagalli IF .20 .50
116 Deon Cain IF .20 .50
117 Marcus Davenport IF .30 .75
118 Daurice Fountain IF .20 .50
119 Chris Warren III IF .25 .60
120 Chase Litton IF .20 .50
121 Keke Coutee IF .20 .50
122 Mark Andrews IF .25 .60
123 Durham Smythe IF .15 .40
124 Bradley Chubb IF .25 .60
125 Mike Gesicki ART .20 .50
126 Josh Rosen ART .50 1.25
127 Sony Michel ART .50 1.25
128 Derwin James ART .30 .75
129 Josh Allen ART .60 1.50
130 Bradley Chubb ART .25 .60
131 Ronald Jones II ART .15 .40
132 Anthony Miller ART .25 .60
133 Mason Rudolph ART .40 1.00
134 Dante Pettis ART .25 .60

2018 SAGE HIT Blue

*BLUE: 1X TO 2.5X BASIC CARDS

2018 SAGE HIT Gold

*GOLD: .8X TO 2X BASIC CARDS

2018 SAGE HIT Red

*RED: .6X TO 1.5X BASIC CARDS

2018 SAGE HIT Autographs Black

*RED: .5X TO 1.2X BLACK AU
*GOLD/250: .6X TO 1.5X BLACK AU
A1 Adam Breneman 2.50 6.00
A2 Akrum Wadley 2.00 5.00
A3 Anthony Miller 3.00 8.00
A4 Auden Tate 2.00 5.00
A5 Cedrick Wilson Jr. 2.00 5.00
A6 Chase Litton 2.50 6.00
A7 Chris Hawkins 2.00 5.00
A8 Cody O'Connell 2.00 5.00
A9 Conor Sheehy 2.50 6.00
A10 Daurice Fountain 2.50 6.00
A11 Derwin James 4.00 10.00
A12 Frank Ragnow 2.50 6.00
A13 Fred Warner 2.00 5.00
A14 Jack Cichy 2.50 6.00
A15 Jake Wieneke 2.50 6.00
A16 Jeffery Wilson 3.00 8.00
A17 Jeremiah Briscoe 2.50 6.00
A18 John Franklin 2.50 6.00
A19 John Wolford 2.00 5.00
A20 Josh Rosen 30.00 60.00
A21 Kyzir White 3.00 8.00
A22 Leighton Vander Esch 6.00 15.00
A23 Logan Woodside 3.00 8.00
A24 Marcell Ateman 2.50 6.00
A25 Mark Andrews 3.00 8.00
A26 Michael Dickson 2.00 5.00
A27 Nic Shimonek 3.00 8.00
A28 Orlando Brown Jr. 3.00 8.00
A29 Poona Ford 2.00 5.00
A30 Riley Ferguson 3.00 8.00
A31 Bo Scarbrough 2.50 6.00
A32 Steven Mitchell Jr. 2.50 6.00
A33 Terry Swanson Jr. 3.00 8.00
A34 Will Hernandez 2.50 6.00
A35 Ryan Nall 4.00 10.00
A36 Duke Williams 2.00 5.00
A37 Dante Pettis 3.00 8.00
A38 Josh Allen
A39 Arden Key 2.00 5.00
A40 Malik Williams 2.00 5.00
A42 Kurt Benkert 2.50 6.00
A43 Roquan Smith 6.00 15.00
A44 Saeed Blacknal 5.00 12.00
A45 Terrell Edmunds 6.00 15.00
A46 Troy Fumagalli 2.50 6.00
A47 Simmie Cobbs Jr. 3.00 8.00
A48 Harold Landry 2.00 5.00
A49 Tremaine Edmunds 4.00 10.00
A50 Sony Michel 6.00 15.00
A52 Mike Gesicki 2.50 6.00
A53 Chris Warren III 3.00 8.00
A54 Trey Quinn 2.00 5.00
A55 Jaylen Samuels 2.50 6.00
A57 Bryce Bobo 2.00 5.00
A58 Isaiah Wynn 2.00 5.00
A59 Mason Rudolph 10.00 25.00
A60 Equanimeous St. Brown 3.00 8.00
A61 Marcus Davenport 4.00 10.00
A62 Keke Coutee 2.50 6.00
A63 Richie James 2.00 5.00
A64 Ka'Raun White 2.50 6.00
A65 Maurice Hurst 2.50 6.00
A66 Armanti Foreman 2.00 5.00
A67 Mike McGlinchey 4.00 10.00
A68 Durham Smythe 2.00 5.00
A69 Kerryon Johnson 3.00 8.00
A70 Ronald Jones II 2.00 5.00
A71 Geron Christian 2.00 5.00
A72 Jake Roh 2.00 5.00
A73 Tremon Smith 2.00 5.00
A74 Diocemy Saint Juste 2.00 5.00
A75 Amari Coleman 2.00 5.00
A76 Malik Jefferson 2.50 6.00

2018 SAGE HIT Instant Impact Autographs

IIACB C.J. Beathard 3.00 8.00
IIACM Christian McCaffrey 6.00 15.00
IIADK Deshone Kizer 4.00 10.00
IIADW Dede Westbrook 3.00 8.00
IIAJE Jake Elliott 4.00 10.00
IIAJSS JuJu Smith-Schuster 8.00 20.00
IIAJW Jamaal Williams 3.00 8.00
IIAPM Patrick Mahomes 12.00 30.00
IIASP Samaje Perine 3.00 8.00
IIATT1 Taywan Taylor 3.00 8.00
IIATT2 Trent Taylor 3.00 8.00
IIAZJ Zay Jones 3.00 8.00

2018 SAGE HIT Peak Performance Autographs Silver

*RED/25: .8X TO 2X SILVER AU
PKAAB Adam Breneman 3.00 8.00
PKAAF Armanti Foreman
PKAAM Anthony Miller 4.00 10.00
PKAAT Auden Tate 2.50 6.00
PKAAW Akrum Wadley 2.50 6.00
PKABB Bryce Bobo
PKABS Bo Scarbrough 3.00 8.00
PKACL Chase Litton 3.00 8.00
PKACW Cedrick Wilson Jr. 2.50 6.00
PKADC Deon Cain
PKADF Daurice Fountain 3.00 8.00
PKADJ Derwin James 5.00 12.00
PKADP Dante Pettis
PKADS Durham Smythe
PKAJB Jeremiah Briscoe 3.00 8.00
PKAJR Josh Rosen 40.00 80.00
PKAJS Jaylen Samuels
PKAJW Jake Wieneke 3.00 8.00
PKAKB Kurt Benkert
PKAKC Keke Coutee
PKAKJ Kerryon Johnson
PKAKW Kyzir White 4.00 10.00
PKALW Logan Woodside
PKAMA Mark Andrews 4.00 10.00
PKAMD Michael Dickson 2.50 6.00
PKAMG Mike Gesicki
PKAMJ Malik Jefferson
PKAMR Mason Rudolph
PKAMW Malik Williams
PKANS Nic Shimonek 4.00 10.00
PKARF Riley Ferguson 4.00 10.00
PKARJ Ronald Jones II
PKARS Roquan Smith
PKASB Saeed Blacknall 6.00 15.00
PKASM Steven Mitchell Jr. 3.00 8.00
PKASM Sony Michel
PKATF Troy Fumagalli
PKATQ Trey Quinn
PKATS Terry Swanson Jr. 4.00 10.00
PKACWa Chris Warren III
PKADSB Diocemy Saint Juste
PKAESB Simmie Cobbs Jr.
PKAESB Equanimeous St. Brown
PKAJaR Jake Roh
PKAJWI Jeffery Wilson 4.00 10.00
PKAJWO John Wolford 2.50 6.00
PKAKaW Ka'raun White
PKALVE Leighton Vander Esch 8.00 20.00
PKAMAT Marcell Ateman 3.00 8.00
PKARJa Richie James

2018 SAGE HIT Premium Portrait Autographs Copper

*RED/25: .8X TO 2X COPPER AU
PPA1 Nic Shimonek 4.00 10.00
PPA2 Cedrick Wilson Jr. 2.50 6.00
PPA3 Akrum Wadley 2.50 6.00
PPA4 Auden Tate 2.50 6.00
PPA5 Anthony Miller 4.00 10.00
PPA6 Bo Scarbrough 3.00 8.00
PPA7 Ryan Nall 5.00 12.00
PPA8 Mark Andrews 4.00 10.00
PPA9 Cedrick Wilson Jr. 2.50 6.00
PPA10 Jack Cichy 3.00 8.00
PPA11 Marcell Ateman 3.00 8.00
PPA12 Riley Ferguson 4.00 10.00
PPA13 Derwin James 5.00 12.00
PPA14 Adam Breneman 3.00 8.00
PPA15 Terry Swanson Jr. 4.00 10.00
PPA16 Jeremiah Briscoe 3.00 8.00
PPA17 Orlando Brown Jr. 4.00 10.00
PPA18 Josh Rosen 8.00 20.00
PPA19 Mason Rudolph 15.00 40.00
PPA20 Josh Allen 15.00 40.00
PPA21 Ronald Jones II 2.50 6.00
PPA22 Kerryon Johnson 4.00 10.00
PPA23 Mike Gesicki 3.00 8.00
PPA24 Arden Key 2.50 6.00
PPA25 Sony Michel 12.00 30.00
PPA26 Chase Litton 3.00 8.00
PPA27 Dante Pettis 4.00 10.00
PPA28 Jaylen Samuels 3.00 8.00
PPA29 Bradley Chubb 4.00 10.00
PPA30 Trey Quinn 2.50 6.00
PPA31 Keke Coutee 3.00 8.00
PPA32 Simmie Cobbs, Jr. 4.00 10.00
PPA33 Harold Landry 2.50 6.00
PPA34 Tremaine Edmunds 5.00 12.00

2019 SAGE HIT

*SILVER: .8X TO 2X BASIC CARDS
*GOLD: .8X TO 2X BASIC GOLD
1 Nick Bosa .50 1.25
2 Noah Fant .30 .75
3 Iman Marshall .20 .50
4 David Edwards .15 .40
5 Mike Weber Jr. .25 .60
6 Hjalte Froholdt .15 .40
7 John Santiago .15 .40
8 Drew Lock .75 2.00
9 Deebo Samuel .40 1.00
10 Dre'Mont Jones .25 .60
11 T.J. Edwards .15 .40
12 Devin Singletary .20 .50
13 Terry Mclaurin .20 .50
14 Blace Brown .15 .40
15 Deionte Thompson .20 .50
16 Gary Johnson .20 .50
17 Jakobi Meyers .15 .40
18 Michael Walker .15 .40
19 Dakota Allen .25 .60
20 Justice Hansen .20 .50
21 Keesean Johnson .15 .40
22 Caleb Wilson .15 .40
23 Mecole Hardman .40 1.00
24 Trenton Irwin .20 .50
25 Christian Wilkins .60 1.50
26 Kerrith Whyte .15 .40
27 David Long Jr. .30 .75
28 Nate Herbig .15 .40
29 Charles Omenihu .15 .40
30 Tre Watson .20 .50
31 Rob Rolle IV .15 .40
32 Brad Mayes .20 .50
33 Michael Deiter .20 .50
34 A.J. Brown .40 1.00
35 Alex Barnes .20 .50
36 Cameron Smith .20 .50
37 Rodney Anderson .20 .50
38 Diontae Johnson .20 .50
39 Beau Benzschawel .15 .40
40 Winston Dimel .15 .40
41 Chase Winovich .50 1.25
42 Dre Greenlaw .15 .40
43 Marquis Young .15 .40
44 Will Grier .50 1.25
45 Gerri Green .15 .40
46 Stephen Louis .20 .50
47 Jarrett Stidham .50 1.25
48 Jerome Washington .15 .40
49 Trey Quinn II .15 .40
50 Mark Andrews II .15 .40
51 Leighton Vander Esch II .20 .50
52 Kerryon Johnson II .20 .50
53 Bradley Chubb II .20 .50
54 Josh Rosen II .25 .60
55 Tremaine Edmunds II .20 .50
56 Dante Pettis II .20 .50
57 Terrell Edmunds II .25 .60
58 Josh Allen II .60 1.50
59 Roquan Smith II .25 .60
60 Anthony Miller II .20 .50
61 Anthony Miller II .20 .50
62 Dwayne Haskins NL .75 2.00
63 D.K. Metcalf NL .50 1.25
64 Damien Harris NL .40 1.00
65 Zach Allen NL .25 .60
66 Devin White NL .50 1.25
67 Kyle Shurmur NL .30 .75
68 Drew Lock NL .75 2.00
69 Marquise Brown NL .50 1.25
70 Brett Rypien NL .20 .50
71 Isaiah Matthews .20 .50
72 Drew Sample .15 .40
73 David Long Jr. .20 .50
74 Brett Rypien .20 .50
75 Josh Oliver .15 .40
76 Terrill Hanks .15 .40
77 Khalen Saunders .15 .40
78 Keelan Doss .20 .50
79 Marcus Epps .20 .50
80 Jake Dolegala .15 .40
81 Jeffery Simmons .15 .40
82 Aca'cedric Ware .20 .50
83 Ryan Connelly .20 .50
84 Kendall Joseph .30 .75
85 Blake Cashman .15 .40
86 Daniel Jones .75 2.00
87 Damien Harris .40 1.00
88 D.K. Metcalf .50 1.25
89 Zach Allen .25 .60
90 Carl Granderson .25 .60
91 Justice Hill .25 .60
92 Dwayne Haskins .75 2.00
93 Marquise Brown .50 1.25
94 Kyle Shurmur .30 .75
95 Emanuel Hall .15 .40
96 Tyler Wilkins .15 .40
97 Devin White .50 1.25
98 Jonathan Ledbetter .20 .50
99 Khari Willis .15 .40
100 Ryan Finley .30 .75
101 Amani Oruwariye .20 .50
102 Brian Burns .20 .50
103 Deonte Harris .15 .40
104 Clayton Thorson .25 .60
105 Davis Koppenhaver .15 .40
106 Johnathan Lloyd .20 .50
107 Damion Willis .20 .50
108 Alexander Hollins .15 .40
109 Papi White .20 .50
110 A.J. Bush Jr. .20 .50
111 Jah'shawn Johnson .15 .40
112 Tevin Mccaster .15 .40
113 James Madison .15 .40
114 Nick Watkins .20 .50
115 Jamie Gillan .15 .40
116 Mike Weber Jr. NL .25 .60
117 Terry Mclaurin NL .20 .50
118 Alex Barnes NL .20 .50
119 Rodney Anderson NL .20 .50
120 Jarrett Stidham NL .50 1.25
121 Ryan Finley NL .30 .75
122 Deebo Samuel NL .40 1.00
123 Caleb Wilson NL .15 .40
124 Christian Wilkins NL .60 1.50
125 Clayton Thorson NL .25 .60
126 Keelan Doss NL .20 .50
127 Chase Winovich NL .50 1.25
128 Josh Oliver NL .15 .40
129 Mecole Hardman NL .40 1.00
130 Dwayne Haskins ART .75 2.00
131 Drew Lock ART .75 2.00
132 D.K. Metcalf ART .50 1.25
133 Noah Fant ART .30 .75
134 A.J. Brown ART .40 1.00
135 Daniel Jones ART .75 2.00
136 Marquise Brown ART .50 1.25
137 Damien Harris ART .40 1.00
138 Nick Bosa ART .50 1.25
139 Justice Hill ART .25 .60
140 Christian Wilkins ART .60 1.50

2019 SAGE HIT Aspire

ASP1 Patrick Mahomes 1.25 3.00
ASP2 Patrick Mahomes 1.25 3.00
ASP3 Patrick Mahomes 1.25 3.00
ASP4 Patrick Mahomes 1.25 3.00
ASP5 Patrick Mahomes 1.25 3.00

2019 SAGE HIT Autographs Black

*RED: .5X TO 1.2X BASIC AU
*GOLD/100: .8X TO 2X BASIC AU
A1 Nick Bosa 6.00 15.00
A2 John Santiago 2.00 5.00
A3 Rodney Anderson 2.50 6.00
A4 Iman Marshall 2.50 6.00
A5 Mike Weber Jr. 3.00 8.00
A6 Noah Fant 4.00 10.00
A7 Terry Mclaurin 2.50 6.00
A8 Brad Mayes 2.50 6.00
A9 Deebo Samuel 5.00 12.00
A10 Tre Watson 2.50 6.00
A11 Rob Rolle IV 2.00 5.00
A12 Devin Singletary 2.50 6.00
A13 T.J. Edwards 2.00 5.00
A14 Caleb Wilson 2.00 5.00
A15 Alex Barnes 2.50 6.00
A16 Dre'Mont Jones 3.00 8.00
A17 Christian Wilkins 8.00 20.00
A18 Charles Omenihu 2.00 5.00
A19 Chase Winovich 6.00 15.00
A20 Michael Deiter 2.50 6.00
A21 Nate Herbig 2.00 5.00
A22 Beau Benzschawel 2.00 5.00
A23 David Long Jr. 4.00 10.00
A24 Kerrith Whyte 2.00 5.00
A25 Hjalte Froholdt 2.00 5.00
A26 Dre Greenlaw 2.00 5.00
A27 Winston Dimel 2.00 5.00
A28 Drew Lock 10.00 25.00
A29 David Edwards 2.00 5.00
A31 Will Grier 6.00 15.00
A32 Mecole Hardman 5.00 12.00
A33 Jakobi Meyers 2.00 5.00
A34 Gary Johnson 2.50 6.00
A35 Diontae Johnson 2.50 6.00
A36 Cameron Smith 2.50 6.00
A37 Trenton Irwin 2.50 6.00
A38 Michael Walker 2.00 5.00
A39 Keesean Johnson 2.00 5.00
A40 Justice Hansen 2.50 6.00
A41 Blace Brown 2.00 5.00
A42 Deionte Thompson 2.50 6.00
A43 Jarrett Stidham 6.00 15.00
A44 Marquis Young 2.00 5.00
A45 A.J. Brown 5.00 12.00
A46 David Long Jr. 2.50 6.00
A47 Josh Oliver 2.00 5.00
A48 D.K. Metcalf 6.00 15.00
A49 Emanuel Hall 2.00 5.00
A50 Damien Harris 5.00 12.00
A51 Terrill Hanks 2.00 5.00
A52 Brett Rypien 2.50 6.00
A53 Dakota Allen 3.00 8.00
A54 Khalen Saunders 2.00 5.00
A55 Drew Sample 2.00 5.00
A56 Dwayne Haskins 40.00 80.00
A57 Aca'cedric Ware 2.50 6.00
A58 Jeffery Simmons 2.00 5.00
A59 Marcus Epps 2.50 6.00
A60 Jake Dolegala 2.00 5.00
A61 Ryan Connelly 2.50 6.00
A62 Kendall Joseph 4.00 10.00
A63 Carl Granderson 3.00 8.00
A64 Zach Allen 3.00 8.00
A66 Khari Willis 2.00 5.00
A67 Gerri Green 2.00 5.00
A68 Marquise Brown 6.00 15.00
A69 Kyle Shurmur 4.00 10.00
A70 Devin White 6.00 15.00
A71 Jonathan Ledbetter 2.50 6.00
A72 Blake Cashman 2.00 5.00
A73 Daniel Jones 12.00 30.00
A74 Ryan Finley 4.00 10.00
A75 Clayton Thorson 3.00 8.00
A76 Deonte Harris 2.00 5.00
A77 Johnathan Lloyd 2.50 6.00
A78 Stephen Louis 2.50 6.00
A79 Tyler Wilkins 2.00 5.00
A80 Davis Koppenhaver 2.00 5.00
A81 Alexander Hollins 2.00 5.00
A82 Damion Willis 2.50 6.00
A83 Eurndraus Bryant 2.00 5.00
A84 Dexter Wright 2.00 5.00
A85 Ryan Pope 2.00 5.00
A86 Braxton Hoyett 2.00 5.00
A87 Juwan Foggie 2.00 5.00
A88 Amani Oruwariye 2.50 6.00
A89 Malik Henry 2.00 5.00
A90 Demetrius Knox 2.00 5.00
A91 Nick Watkins 2.50 6.00
A92 Papi White 2.50 6.00
A93 Jerome Washington 2.00 5.00
A94 Tevin Mccaster 2.00 5.00
A95 James Madison 2.00 5.00
A96 Justice Hill 3.00 8.00
A97 A.J. Bush Jr. 2.50 6.00
A98 Jah'shawn Johnson 2.00 5.00
A99 Brian Burns 2.50 6.00
A100 Jahlani Tavai 2.50 6.00
A101 Jaime Gillan 2.00 5.00
A102 Izzy Matthews 2.50 6.00
A103 Alex Bars 2.50 6.00
A104 Keelan Doss 2.50 6.00

2019 SAGE HIT Next Level Autographs Red

*SILVER/25: .8X TO 2X BASIC AU
NLAB Alex Barnes 3.00 8.00
NLAO Amani Oruwariye 3.00 8.00
NLAW Aca'Cedric Ware 3.00 8.00
NLBB Brian Burns 3.00 8.00
NLBR Brett Rypien 3.00 8.00
NLCB Caleb Wilson 2.50 6.00
NLCG Carl Granderson 4.00 10.00
NLCS Cameron Smith 3.00 8.00
NLCT Clayton Thorson 4.00 10.00
NLDA Dakota Allen 4.00 10.00
NLDJ Dre'Mont Jones 4.00 10.00
NLDK Davis Koppenhaver 2.50 6.00
NLDL Drew Lock 12.00 30.00
NLDS Deebo Samuel 6.00 15.00
NLDT Deionte Thompson 3.00 8.00
NLDW Devin White 8.00 20.00
NLEH Emanuel Hall 2.50 6.00
NLIM Iman Marshall 3.00 8.00
NLJD Jake Dolegala 2.50 6.00
NLJH Justice Hansen 3.00 8.00
NLJL Johnathan Lloyd 3.00 8.00
NLJO Josh Oliver 2.50 6.00
NLJS Jarrett Stidham 8.00 20.00
NLJS Jeffery Simmons 2.50 6.00
NLKD Keelan Doss 3.00 8.00
NLKS Kyle Shurmur 5.00 12.00
NLMB Marquise Brown 8.00 20.00
NLMH Mecole Hardman 6.00 15.00
NLMW Mike Weber Jr. 4.00 10.00
NLMY Marquis Young 2.50 6.00
NLNB Nick Bosa 8.00 20.00
NLNF Noah Fant 5.00 12.00
NLRA Rodney Anderson 3.00 8.00
NLRF Ryan Finley 5.00 12.00
NLTM Terry Mclaurin 3.00 8.00
NLWD Winston Dimel 2.50 6.00
NLWG Will Grier 8.00 20.00
NLZA Zach Allen 4.00 10.00
NLAJB A.J. Brown 6.00 15.00
NLCW1 Christian Wilkins 10.00 25.00
NLCW2 Chase Winovich 8.00 20.00
NLDH1 Damien Harris 6.00 15.00
NLDH2 Dwayne Haskins 12.00 30.00
NLDJ2 Daniel Jones 12.00 30.00
NLDKM D.K. Metcalf 8.00 20.00
NLDS2 Devin Singletary 3.00 8.00
NLTJE T.J. Edwards 2.50 6.00

2019 SAGE HIT Premium Portraits Autographs Red

*SILVER/25: .8X TO 2X BASIC AU
PPA01 Drew Lock 12.00 30.00
PPA02 Alex Barnes 3.00 8.00
PPA03 Jarrett Stidham 8.00 20.00
PPA04 Devin White 8.00 20.00
PPA05 Devin Singletary 3.00 8.00
PPA06 Mike Weber Jr. 4.00 10.00
PPA07 Marquise Brown 8.00 20.00
PPA08 Jakobi Meyers 2.50 6.00
PPA09 Emanuel Hall 2.50 6.00
PPA10 Charles Omenihu 2.50 6.00
PPA11 Justice Hansen 3.00 8.00
PPA12 Rodney Anderson 3.00 8.00
PPA13 Terry Mclaurin 3.00 8.00
PPA14 Will Grier 8.00 20.00
PPA15 Carl Granderson 4.00 10.00
PPA16 Dre'mont Jones
PPA17 Keesean Johnson
PPA18 Noah Fant
PPA19 A.J. Brown
PPA20 Deionte Thompson
PPA21 Mecole Hardman
PPA22 Deebo Samuel
PPA23 Caleb Wilson
PPA24 Josh Oliver
PPA25 Brett Rypien
PPA26 Diontae Johnson

2004 SAGE Jersey Update

This product was released in late 2004 with 6-packs per box and one jersey card per pack. Each card in the set features a game used jersey swatch. A Premium Swatch parallel serial numbered to 10 was also produced as well as signed jersey cards numbered to only 5.

*PREM.SWATCH/10: 1.2X TO 3X
PREMIUM SWATCH PRINT RUN 10
UNPRICED AUTO PRINT RUN 5
1 Tatum Bell 2.50 6.00
2 Maurice Clarett 3.00 8.00
3 Casey Clausen 3.00 8.00
4 Lee Evans 4.00 10.00
5 Josh Harris 2.50 6.00
6 Devery Henderson 2.50 6.00
7 Michael Jenkins 2.50 6.00
8 Greg Jones 2.50 6.00
9 Kevin Jones 3.00 8.00
10 Jared Lorenzen 3.00 8.00
11 Eli Manning 12.00 30.00
12 John Navarre 2.50 6.00
13 Chris Perry 2.50 6.00
14 Cody Pickett 2.50 6.00
15 Philip Rivers 10.00 25.00
16 Ell Roberson 4.00 10.00
17 Ben Roethlisberger 12.00 30.00
18 Rod Rutherford 2.50 6.00
19 Matt Schaub 2.50 6.00
20 Jeff Smoker 3.00 8.00
21 Reggie Williams 2.50 6.00
22 Roy Williams WR 2.50 6.00
23 Quincy Wilson 2.50 6.00
24 Rashaun Woods 2.50 6.00

2004 SAGE Jersey Update Roethlisberger

1B Ben Roethlisberger/70 40.00 80.00
1W Ben Roethlisberger/140 30.00 60.00
BR1 Ben Roethlisberger/210 15.00 40.00

2012 SAGE Next

STATED PRINT RUN 50 SER.#'d SETS
*DIE CUT/40: .4X TO 1X BASIC AU/50
*GOLD/20: .5X TO 1.2X BASIC AU/50
*SILVER/30: .5X TO 1.2X BASIC AU/50
1 Joe Adams 4.00 10.00
2 Dwayne Allen 4.00 10.00
3 Justin Blackmon 4.00 10.00
4 Ryan Broyles 4.00 10.00
5 Vontaze Burfict 5.00 12.00
6 Orson Charles 4.00 10.00
7 Quinton Coples 4.00 10.00
8 Kirk Cousins 15.00 40.00
9 Jared Crick 4.00 10.00
10 Juron Criner 4.00 10.00
11 B.J. Cunningham 4.00 10.00
12 Alfonzo Dennard 4.00 10.00
13 Rhett Ellison 5.00 12.00
14 Michael Floyd 4.00 10.00
15 Nick Foles 10.00 25.00
16 Jeff Fuller 4.00 10.00
17 Chris Givens 4.00 10.00
18 Cyrus Gray 4.00 10.00
19 Ladarius Green 4.00 10.00
20 Robert Griffin III 5.00 12.00
21 Boom Herron 4.00 10.00
22 Ronnie Hillman 4.00 10.00
23 T.Y. Hilton 8.00 20.00
24 Melvin Ingram 4.00 10.00
25 LaMichael James 4.00 10.00
26 Alshon Jeffery 8.00 20.00
27 Janoris Jenkins 5.00 12.00
28 Matt Kalil 4.00 10.00
29 Case Keenum 8.00 20.00
30 Luke Kuechly 10.00 25.00
31 Ryan Lindley 4.00 10.00
32 Doug Martin 6.00 15.00
33 Marvin McNutt 4.00 10.00
34 Davin Meggett 4.00 10.00
35 Lamar Miller 6.00 15.00
36 Kellen Moore 5.00 12.00
37 Brock Osweiler 4.00 10.00
38 Bernard Pierce 4.00 10.00
39 Dontari Poe 4.00 10.00
40 Chris Polk 4.00 10.00
41 Tauren Poole 4.00 10.00
42 DeVier Posey 4.00 10.00
43 Brian Quick 4.00 10.00
44 Trent Richardson 4.00 10.00
45 Tommy Streeter 4.00 10.00
46 Ryan Tannehill 6.00 15.00
47 Brandon Weeden 4.00 10.00
48 Jarius Wright 4.00 10.00
49 Kendall Wright 4.00 10.00

2013 SAGE Next Acetate Die Cut

STATED PRINT RUN 20 SER.#'d SETS
1 Geno Smith 5.00 12.00
2 EJ Manuel 5.00 12.00
3 Cordarrelle Patterson 5.00 12.00
4 Matt Barkley 5.00 12.00
5 Ryan Nassib 5.00 12.00
6 Ryan Tannehill 6.00 15.00
7 Landry Jones 5.00 12.00
8 Brad Sorensen 5.00 12.00
9 Zac Dysert 5.00 12.00
10 Tyler Bray 5.00 12.00
11 Jordan Rodgers 6.00 15.00
12 Mike Glennon 5.00 12.00
13 Robert Griffin III 5.00 12.00
14 Tyler Wilson 5.00 12.00
15 Eddie Lacy 5.00 12.00
16 Marcus Lattimore 5.00 12.00
17 Da'Rick Rogers 5.00 12.00
18 Mike Gillislee 5.00 12.00
19 Andre Ellington 5.00 12.00
20 Robert Woods 8.00 20.00
21 Rex Burkhead 6.00 15.00
22 Montee Ball 5.00 12.00
23 Justin Hunter 5.00 12.00
24 Doug Martin 6.00 15.00
25 Giovani Bernard 5.00 12.00
26 Vance McDonald 6.00 15.00
27 DeAndre Hopkins 12.00 30.00
28 Terrance Williams 5.00 12.00
29 Marquise Goodwin 5.00 12.00
30 Jordan Reed 8.00 20.00
31 Kenny Stills 5.00 12.00
32 Ryan Swope 5.00 12.00
33 Joseph Randle 5.00 12.00
34 Rodney Smith 5.00 12.00
35 Conner Vernon 5.00 12.00
36 Le'Veon Bell 15.00 40.00
37 Sheldon Richardson 5.00 12.00
38 Tyler Eifert 5.00 12.00
39 Bjoern Werner 5.00 12.00
40 Aaron Dobson 5.00 12.00
41 Datone Jones 5.00 12.00
42 Alec Ogletree 5.00 12.00
43 Xavier Rhodes 5.00 12.00
44 Damontre Moore 5.00 12.00
45 Sam Montgomery 5.00 12.00
46 Alex Okafor 5.00 12.00
47 Luke Joeckel 5.00 12.00
48 Manti Te'o 6.00 15.00
49 Trent Richardson 5.00 12.00
50 Kenny Vaccaro 5.00 12.00

2013 SAGE Next Dual Autographs

DA1 Manuel/G.Smith/40 4.00 10.00
DA2 G.Bernard/L.Bell 15.00 40.00
DA3 D.Hopkins/C.Patterson/10 10.00 25.00
DA5 G.Smith/M.Glennon/40 4.00 10.00
DA6 A.Okafor/R.Swope/40 4.00 10.00
DA7 A.Okafor/A.Ellington/40 4.00 10.00
DA8 T.Wilson/C.Vernon/40 4.00 10.00
DA9 M.Elam/A.Mellette/20 4.00 10.00
DA10 R.Woods/M.Goodwin/40 6.00 15.00
DA11 R.Woods/D.Rogers/40 6.00 15.00
DA12 M.Goodwin/D.Rogers/40 4.00 10.00
DA13 Manuel/R.Woods/40 6.00 15.00
DA14 X.Rhodes/R.Smith/40 4.00 10.00
DA15 Manuel/D.Rogers 4.00 10.00
DA16 R.Swope/A.Ellington/40 4.00 10.00
DA17 T.Eifert/R.Burkhead/40 5.00 12.00
DA18 G.Bernard/R.Burkhead/40 5.00 12.00
DA19A T.Williams/J.Randle/40 4.00 10.00
DA21 T.Riddick/J.Fauria 4.00 10.00
DA22 D.Jones/E.Lacy/40 4.00 10.00
DA23 D.Hopkins/S.Montgomery 10.00 25.00
DA24 L.Joeckel/J.Rodgers/40 5.00 12.00
DA25 B.Wilson/T.Bray/40 5.00 12.00
DA26 M.Gillislee/J.Jenkins/25 5.00 12.00
DA28 T.Eifert/G.Bernard 4.00 10.00
DA29 C.Patterson/R.Smith/40 4.00 10.00
DA30 A.Dobson/L.Ryan/20 5.00 12.00
DA31A K.Vaccaro/K.Stills/40 4.00 10.00
DA33 S.Richardson/G.Smith/40 4.00 10.00
DA35 M.Barkley/J.Kruger 5.00 12.00
DA37A M.Te'o/B.Sorensen/40 5.00 12.00
DA38A V.McDonald/M.Lattimore/40 5.00 12.00
DA46 M.Te'o/D.Klein/40 3.00 12.00
DA56 T.Bray/C.Patterson/40 4.00 10.00
DA57 T.Bray/J.Hunter/40 4.00 10.00
DA58 C.Patterson/J.Hunter/40 4.00 10.00

2005 SAGE Premium Action Autographs Gold

GOLD PRINT RUN 50 SER.#'d SETS
*BLACK PORTRAIT: .5X TO 1.2X GOLD ACT.
BLACK PORTRAIT PRINT RUN 25 SETS
A1 Aaron Rodgers 100.00 200.00
A2 Adrian McPherson 6.00 15.00
A3 Alex Smith QB 25.00 60.00
A4 Alex Smith TE 6.00 15.00
A5 Andrew Walter 6.00 15.00
A6 Anthony Davis 5.00 12.00
A7 Brandon Jacobs 10.00 25.00
A8 Brock Berlin 5.00 12.00
A9 Brodney Pool 5.00 12.00
A10 Cadillac Williams 15.00 40.00
A11 Carlos Rogers 6.00 15.00
A12 Channing Crowder 6.00 15.00
A13 Charlie Frye 6.00 15.00
A14 Chris Rix 5.00 12.00
A15 Ciatrick Fason 6.00 15.00
A16 Corey Webster 5.00 12.00
A17 Craphonso Thorpe 5.00 12.00
A18 Dan Orlovsky 6.00 15.00
A19 Dante Ridgeway 5.00 12.00
A20 David Greene 6.00 15.00
A21 DeMarcus Ware 10.00 25.00
A22 Derek Anderson 6.00 15.00
A23 Derrick Johnson 6.00 15.00
A24 Fabian Washington 8.00 20.00
A25 Frank Gore 15.00 40.00
A26 Fred Gibson 5.00 12.00
A27 J.J. Arrington 6.00 15.00
A28 J.R. Russell 5.00 12.00
A29 Jammal Brown 6.00 15.00
A30 Jason Campbell 12.50 30.00
A31 Jason White 6.00 15.00
A32 Johnathan Goddard 5.00 12.00
A33 Josh Davis 5.00 12.00
A34 Justin Miller 5.00 12.00
A35 Kay-Jay Harris 5.00 12.00
A36 Kyle Orton 6.00 15.00
A37 Mark Clayton 6.00 15.00
A38 Marlin Jackson 6.00 15.00
A39 Matt Jones 8.00 20.00
A40 Reggie Brown 6.00 15.00
A41 Roddy White 6.00 15.00
A42 Ronnie Brown 10.00 25.00
A43 Roscoe Parrish 6.00 15.00
A44 Ryan Fitzpatrick 10.00 25.00
A45 T.A. McLendon 3.00 8.00
A46 Taylor Stubblefield 3.00 8.00
A47 Terrence Murphy 6.00 15.00
A48 Thomas Davis 5.00 12.00
A49 Troy Williamson 6.00 15.00
A50 Vernand Morency 6.00 15.00

2005 SAGE Premium Jerseys Black

BLACK PRINT RUN 25 SER.#'d SETS
SJ1 Aaron Rodgers 40.00 100.00
SJ2 Adrian McPherson 6.00 15.00
SJ3 Alex Smith QB 30.00 80.00
SJ4 Andrew Walter 6.00 15.00
SJ5 Cadillac Williams 15.00 40.00
SJ6 Charlie Frye 6.00 15.00
SJ7 Ciatrick Fason 6.00 15.00
SJ8 Dan Orlovsky 6.00 15.00
SJ9 David Greene 6.00 15.00
SJ10 Frank Gore 20.00 50.00
SJ11 J.J. Arrington 8.00 20.00
SJ12 Jason Campbell 6.00 15.00
SJ13 Jason White 10.00 25.00
SJ14 Kyle Orton 6.00 15.00
SJ15 Mark Clayton 6.00 15.00
SJ16 Ronnie Brown 30.00 80.00
SJ17 Roscoe Parrish 6.00 15.00
SJ18 Vernand Morency 6.00 15.00

2008 SAGE Squared

This set was released on August 15, 2008. The base set consists of 87 cards, each of which feature two rookies.

1 Matt Ryan / Darren McFadden .60 1.50
2 Matt Ryan / Joe Flacco .60 1.50
3 D.McFadden/J.Stewart .30 .75
4 Darren McFadden / Felix Jones .20 .50
5 D.McFadden/R.Mendenhall .20 .50
6 Darren McFadden / Kevin Smith .20 .50
7 Darren McFadden / Ryan Clady .25 .60
8 Matt Ryan / Brian Brohm .60 1.50
9 Matt Ryan / Sam Baker .60 1.50
10 Tashard Choice / Matt Ryan .60 1.50
11 Matt Ryan / Kevin O'Connell .60 1.50
12 Joe Flacco / Ray Rice .40 1.00
13 Joe Flacco / Josh Johnson .40 1.00
14 Tom Zbikowski / Joe Flacco .40 1.00
15 Joe Flacco / Allen Patrick .40 1.00
16 Jonathan Stewart / Dennis Dixon .30 .75
17 Felix Jones / Jonathan Stewart .30 .75
18 Jonathan Stewart / Dan Connor .30 .75
19 R.Mendenhall/L.Sweed .20 .50
20 Tashard Choice / Felix Jones .20 .50
21 Josh Johnson / Sam Keller .20 .50
22 Dustin Keller / Sam Keller .25 .60
23 Tom Zbikowski / John Carlson .25 .60
24 Tom Zbikowski / Ray Rice .25 .60
25 Steve Slaton / Owen Schmitt .20 .50
26 Will Franklin / Martin Rucker .25 .60
27 Tashard Choice / Mike Jenkins .20 .50
28 Jordy Nelson / Brian Brohm .60 1.50
29 Matt Flynn / Brian Brohm .20 .50
30 B.Flowers/J.Charles .30 .75
31 Will Franklin / Jamaal Charles .30 .75
32 Brandon Flowers / Will Franklin .25 .60
33 Kevin O'Connell / Josh Johnson .20 .50
34 Erik Ainge / Dustin Keller .25 .60
35 Erik Ainge / Vernon Gholston .20 .50
36 Donnie Avery / Keenan Burton .25 .60
37 Paul Smith / Derrick Harvey .20 .50
38 Lawrence Jackson / John Carlson .20 .50
39 Lavelle Hawkins / Jason Rivers .25 .60
40 Darius Reynaud / John David Booty .20 .50
41 Adarius Bowman / Malcolm Kelly .25 .60
42 Ray Rice / Steve Slaton .20 .50
43 Darius Reynaud / Steve Slaton .20 .50
44 Dustin Keller / John Carlson .20 .50
45 Paul Smith / Kevin O'Connell .20 .50
46 Paul Smith / Kevin Smith .20 .50
47 Adarius Bowman / James Hardy .25 .60
48 Matt Flynn / Erik Ainge .20 .50
49 Keenan Burton / Andre Caldwell .20 .50
50 Martin Rucker / Malcolm Kelly .20 .50
51 Sam Baker / John David Booty .20 .50
52 Ryan Clady / Jake Long .30 .75
53 Fred Davis / John David Booty .20 .50
54 Devin Thomas / Fred Davis .20 .50
55 Kenny Phillips / Leodis McKelvin .25 .60
56 Kenny Phillips / Mike Jenkins .20 .50
57 Keith Rivers / Andre Caldwell .20 .50
58 Derrick Harvey / Andre Caldwell .20 .50
59 Felix Jones / Mike Jenkins .20 .50
60 Derrick Harvey / Jacob Hester .20 .50
61 Antoine Cason / Jacob Hester .20 .50
62 Jacob Hester / Matt Flynn .20 .50
63 Devin Thomas / Malcolm Kelly .20 .50
64 Donnie Avery / Devin Thomas .25 .60
65 Sedrick Ellis / Adrian Arrington .20 .50
66 Adrian Arrington / Chad Henne .25 .60
67 Adrian Arrington / Jake Long .30 .75
68 Limas Sweed / Jamaal Charles .30 .75
69 Limas Sweed / Dennis Dixon .20 .50
70 Antoine Cason / Dan Connor .25 .60
71 Vernon Gholston / Dan Connor .20 .50
72 Sedrick Ellis / Keith Rivers .20 .50
73 Donnie Avery / Jordy Nelson .60 1.50
74 Leodis McKelvin / James Hardy .25 .60
75 Jordy Nelson / James Hardy .60 1.50
76 Ray Rice / Allen Patrick .20 .50
77 Malcolm Kelly / Allen Patrick .20 .50
78 Sedrick Ellis / Lawrence Jackson .20 .50
79 R.Mendenhall/D.Dixon .20 .50
80 Mike Hart / Chad Henne .25 .60
81 M.Hart/R.Mendenhall .20 .50
82 Jake Long / Mike Hart .30 .75
83 Jake Long / Chad Henne .30 .75
84 Vernon Gholston / Dustin Keller .25 .60
85 Leodis McKelvin / Mike Jenkins .25 .60
86 Martin Rucker / Darnell Terrell .20 .50
87 Will Franklin / Darnell Terrell .25 .60

2008 SAGE Squared Autographs

ONE SINGLE AUTO PER PACK
A1A M.Ryan AU/D.McFadden 12.00 30.00
A1B D.McFadden AU/M.Ryan 12.00 30.00
A2A M.Ryan AU/J.Flacco 10.00 25.00
A2B Joe Flacco AU / Matt Ryan 12.00 30.00
A3A D.McFadden AU/J.Stewart 8.00 20.00
A3B J.Stewart AU/D.McFadden 6.00 15.00
A4A D.McFadden AU/F.Jones 6.00 15.00
A4B F.Jones AU/D.McFadden 6.00 15.00
A5A D.McFadden AU/Mendenhall 6.00 15.00
A5B R.Mendenhall AU/McFadden 6.00 15.00
A6A D.McFadden AU/K.Smith 12.00 30.00
A6B K.Smith AU/D.McFadden 4.00 10.00
A7A D.McFadden AU/R.Clady 12.00 30.00
A7B Ryan Clady AU / Darren McFadden 3.00 8.00
A8A M.Ryan AU/B.Brohm 25.00 60.00
A8B B.Brohm AU/M.Ryan 5.00 12.00
A9A M.Ryan AU/S.Baker 25.00 60.00
A9B Sam Baker AU / Matt Ryan 3.00 8.00
A10A T.Choice AU/M.Ryan 5.00 12.00
A10B M.Ryan AU/T.Choice 25.00 60.00
A11A M.Ryan AU/K.O'Connell 25.00 60.00
A11B Kevin O'Connell AU / Matt Ryan 4.00 10.00
A12A Joe Flacco AU / Ray Rice 12.00 30.00
A12B Ray Rice AU / Joe Flacco 6.00 15.00
A13A J.Flacco AU/J.Johnson 12.00 30.00
A13B Josh Johnson AU / Joe Flacco 4.00 10.00
A14A Tom Zbikowski AU / Joe Flacco 4.00 10.00
A14B J.Flacco AU/Zbikowski 10.00 25.00
A15A J.Flacco AU/A.Patrick 12.00 30.00
A15B A.Patrick AU/J.Flacco 5.00 12.00
A16A J.Stewart AU/D.Dixon 6.00 15.00
A16B D.Dixon AU/J.Stewart 6.00 15.00
A17A F.Jones AU/J.Stewart 6.00 15.00
A17B J.Stewart AU/F.Jones 6.00 15.00
A18A J.Stewart AU/D.Connor 6.00 15.00
A18B D.Connor AU/J.Stewart 5.00 12.00
A19A R.Mendenhall AU/Sweed 8.00 20.00
A19B L.Sweed AU/Mendenhall 4.00 10.00
A20A T.Choice AU/F.Jones 6.00 15.00
A20B F.Jones AU/T.Choice 6.00 15.00
A21A Josh Johnson AU / Sam Keller 4.00 10.00
A21B Sam Keller AU / Josh Johnson 4.00 10.00
A22A D.Keller AU/S.Keller 4.00 10.00
A22B Sam Keller AU / Dustin Keller 4.00 10.00
A23A Tom Zbikowski AU / John Carlson 4.00 10.00
A23B J.Carlson AU/Zbikowski 4.00 10.00
A24A Tom Zbikowski AU / Ray Rice 4.00 10.00
A24B R.Rice AU/Zbikowksi 8.00 20.00
A25A S.Slaton AU/O.Schmitt 4.00 10.00
A25B Owen Schmitt AU / Steve Slaton 4.00 10.00
A26A Will Franklin AU / Martin Rucker 3.00 8.00
A26B Martin Rucker AU / Will Franklin 3.00 8.00
A27A T.Choice AU/M.Jenkins 5.00 12.00
A27B Mike Jenkins AU / Tashard Choice 4.00 10.00
A28A J.Nelson AU/B.Brohm 8.00 20.00
A28B B.Brohm AU/Jordy Nelson 8.00 20.00
A29A M.Flynn AU/Brian Brohm 6.00 15.00
A29B B.Brohm AU/Matt Flynn 6.00 15.00
A30A Brandon Flowers AU / Jamaal Charles 4.00 10.00
A30B J.Charles AU/B.Flowers 6.00 15.00
A31A Will Franklin AU / Jamaal Charles 3.00 8.00
A31B J.Charles AU/Will Franklin 6.00 15.00
A32A Brandon Flowers AU / Will Franklin 4.00 10.00
A32B Will Franklin AU / Brandon Flowers 3.00 8.00
A33A Kevin O'Connell AU / Josh Johnson 4.00 10.00
A33B Josh Johnson AU / Kevin O'Connell 4.00 10.00
A34A E.Ainge AU/Dustin Keller 4.00 10.00
A34B D.Keller AU/Erik Ainge 4.00 10.00
A35A E.Ainge AU/VGholston 4.00 10.00
A35B Vernon Gholston AU / Erik Ainge 4.00 10.00
A36A D.Avery AU/K.Burton 4.00 10.00
A36B Keenan Burton AU / Donnie Avery 3.00 8.00
A37A Paul Smith AU / Derrick Harvey 3.00 8.00
A37B D.Harvey AU/Paul Smith 4.00 10.00
A38A Lawrence Jackson AU / John Carlson 4.00 10.00
A38B J.Carlson AU/L.Jackson 4.00 10.00
A39A Lavelle Hawkins AU / Jason Rivers 3.00 8.00
A39B Jason Rivers AU / Lavelle Hawkins 4.00 10.00
A40A Darius Reynaud AU / John David Booty 4.00 10.00
A40B J.Booty AU/D.Reynaud 4.00 10.00
A41A A.Bowman AU/M.Kelly 4.00 10.00
A41B Malcolm Kelly AU / Adarius Bowman 4.00 10.00
A42A R.Rice AU/Steve Slaton 8.00 20.00
A42B S.Slaton AU/Ray Rice 4.00 10.00
A43A Darius Reynaud AU / Steve Slaton 4.00 10.00
A43B S.Slaton AU/D.Reynard 4.00 10.00
A44A D.Keller AU/John Carlson 4.00 10.00
A44B J.Carlson AU/D.Keller 4.00 10.00
A45A Paul Smith AU / Kevin O'Connell 3.00 8.00
A45B Kevin O'Connell AU / Paul Smith 4.00 10.00
A46A Paul Smith AU / Kevin Smith 3.00 8.00
A46B K.Smith AU/Paul Smith 4.00 10.00
A47A A.Bowman AU/J.Hardy 4.00 10.00
A47B J.Hardy AU/A.Bowman 4.00 10.00
A48A M.Flynn AU/Erik Ainge 6.00 15.00
A48B E.Ainge AU/Matt Flynn 4.00 10.00
A49A Keenan Burton AU / Andre Caldwell 3.00 8.00
A49B Andre Caldwell AU / Keenan Burton 4.00 10.00
A50A Martin Rucker AU / Malcolm Kelly 3.00 8.00
A50B Malcolm Kelly AU / Martin Rucker 4.00 10.00
A51A Sam Baker AU / John David Booty 3.00 8.00
A51B J.Booty AU/Sam Baker 4.00 10.00
A52A Ryan Clady AU / Jake Long 3.00 8.00
A52B J.Long AU/Ryan Clady 4.00 10.00
A53A Fred Davis AU / John David Booty 4.00 10.00
A53B J.Booty AU/Fred Davis 4.00 10.00
A54A D.Thomas AU/Fred Davis 4.00 10.00
A54B Fred Davis AU / Devin Thomas 4.00 10.00
A55A Kenny Phillips AU / Leodis McKelvin 3.00 8.00
A55B Leodis McKelvin AU / Kenny Phillips 4.00 10.00
A56A Kenny Phillips AU / Mike Jenkins 3.00 8.00
A56B Mike Jenkins AU / Kenny Phillips 4.00 10.00
A57A Keith Rivers AU / Andre Caldwell 4.00 10.00
A57B Andre Caldwell AU / Keith Rivers 4.00 10.00
A58A D.Harvey AU/A.Caldwell 4.00 10.00
A58B Andre Caldwell AU / Derrick Harvey 4.00 10.00
A59A F.Jones AU/Mike Jenkins 6.00 15.00
A59B Mike Jenkins AU / Felix Jones 4.00 10.00
A60A D.Harvey AU/J.Hester 4.00 10.00
A60B Jacob Hester AU / Derrick Harvey 4.00 10.00

A61A Antoine Cason AU 4.00 10.00
Jacob Hester
A61B Jacob Hester AU 4.00 10.00
Antoine Cason
A62A Jacob Hester AU 4.00 10.00
Matt Flynn
A62B M.Flynn AU/Jacob Hester 6.00 16.00
A63A D.Thomas AU/M.Kelly 4.00 10.00
A63B Malcolm Kelly AU 4.00 10.00
Devin Thomas
A64A D.Avery AU/Devin Thomas 5.00 12.00
A64B D.Thomas AU/D.Avery 4.00 10.00
A65A Sedrick Ellis AU 4.00 10.00
Adrian Arrington
A65B A.Arrington AU/S.Ellis 4.00 10.00
A66A A.Arrington AU/C.Henne 4.00 10.00
A66B C.Henne AU/A.Arrington 8.00 20.00
A67A A.Arrington AU/Jake Long 4.00 10.00
A67B J.Long AU/A.Arrington 4.00 10.00
A68A L.Sweed AU/J.Charles 4.00 10.00
A68B J.Charles AU/Limas Sweed 6.00 15.00
A69A L.Sweed AU/Dennis Dixon 4.00 10.00
A69B D.Dixon AU/Limas Sweed 5.00 12.00
A70A Antoine Cason AU 4.00 10.00
Dan Connor
A70B D.Connor AU/A.Cason 4.00 10.00
A71A Vernon Gholston AU 4.00 10.00
Dan Connor
A71B D.Connor AU/V.Gholston 4.00 10.00
A72A Sedrick Ellis AU 4.00 10.00
Keith Rivers
A72B Keith Rivers AU 4.00 10.00
Sedrick Ellis
A73A D.Avery AU/Jordy Nelson 6.00 15.00
A73B J.Nelson AU/Donnie Avery 8.00 20.00
A74A Leodis McKelvin AU 4.00 10.00
James Hardy
A74B J.Hardy AU/L.McKelvin 5.00 12.00
A75A J.Nelson AU/James Hardy 8.00 20.00
A75B J.Hardy AU/Jordy Nelson 6.00 15.00
A76A R.Rice AU/Allen Patrick 8.00 20.00
A76B A.Patrick AU/Ray Rice 4.00 10.00
A77A Malcolm Kelly AU 4.00 10.00
Allen Patrick
A77B A.Patrick AU/Malcolm Kelly 4.00 10.00
A78A Sedrick Ellis AU 4.00 10.00
Lawrence Jackson
A78B Lawrence Jackson AU 4.00 10.00
Sedrick Ellis
A79A R.Mendenhall AU/Dixon 8.00 20.00
A79B D.Dixon AU/Mendenhall 5.00 12.00
A80A M.Hart AU/Chad Henne 5.00 12.00
A80B C.Henne AU/Mike Hart 8.00 20.00
A81A M.Hart AU/Mendenhall 5.00 12.00
A81B R.Mendenhall AU/M.Hart 8.00 20.00
A82A J.Long AU/Mike Hart 4.00 10.00
A82B M.Hart AU/Jake Long 4.00 10.00
A83A J.Long AU/Chad Henne 4.00 10.00
A83B C.Henne AU/Jake Long 6.00 15.00
A84A Vernon Gholston AU 4.00 10.00
Dustin Keller
A84B D.Keller AU/Vernon Gholston 4.00 10.00
A85A Leodis McKelvin AU 4.00 10.00
Mike Jenkins
A85B Mike Jenkins AU 4.00 10.00
Leodis McKelvin
A86A Martin Rucker AU 3.00 8.00
Darnell Terrell
A86B Darnell Terrell AU 4.00 10.00
Martin Rucker
A87A Will Franklin AU 3.00 8.00
Darnell Terrell
A87B Darnell Terrell AU 4.00 10.00
Will Franklin

2008 SAGE Squared Dual Autographs

ONE DUAL AUTO PER PACK
A1 Matt Ryan/D.McFadden 25.00 60.00
A2 Matt Ryan 25.00 60.00
Joe Flacco
A3 D.McFadden/J.Stewart 5.00 12.00
A4 D.McFadden/F.Jones 3.00 8.00
A5 McFadden/Mendenhall 3.00 8.00
A6 D.McFadden/K.Smith 3.00 8.00
A7 D.McFadden/R.Clady 4.00 10.00
A8 Matt Ryan 40.00 80.00
Brian Brohm
A9 Matt Ryan 25.00 60.00
Sam Baker
A10 T.Choice/Matt Ryan 40.00 80.00
A11 Matt Ryan/K.O'Connell 40.00 80.00
A12 Joe Flacco 20.00 50.00
Ray Rice
A13 Joe Flacco 15.00 40.00
Josh Johnson
A14 Zbikowski/Joe Flacco 12.00 30.00
A15 Joe Flacco 12.00 30.00
Allen Patrick
A16 J.Stewart/D.Dixon 5.00 12.00
A17 F.Jones/J.Stewart 5.00 12.00
A18 J.Stewart/D.Connor 5.00 12.00
A19 R.Mendenhall/L.Sweed 3.00 8.00
A20 T.Choice/Felix Jones 3.00 8.00
A21 Josh Johnson 3.00 8.00
Sam Keller
A22 Dustin Keller 4.00 10.00
Sam Keller
A23 Zbikowski/John Carlson 4.00 10.00
A24 Tom Zbikowski 4.00 10.00
Ray Rice
A25 Steve Slaton 3.00 8.00
Owen Schmitt
A26 Will Franklin 4.00 10.00
Martin Rucker
A27 Tashard Choice 3.00 8.00
Mike Jenkins
A28 Jordy Nelson 10.00 25.00
Brian Brohm
A29 Matt Flynn 8.00 20.00
Brian Brohm
A30 B.Flowers/J.Charles 5.00 12.00
A31 Will Franklin 5.00 12.00
Jamaal Charles
A32 Brandon Flowers 4.00 10.00
Will Franklin
A33 K.O'Connell/J.Johnson 3.00 8.00
A34 Erik Ainge 4.00 10.00
Dustin Keller
A35 Erik Ainge 3.00 8.00
Vernon Gholston
A36 D.Avery/K.Burton 4.00 10.00
A37 Paul Smith 3.00 8.00
Derrick Harvey
A38 Lawrence Jackson 3.00 8.00
John Carlson
A39 Lavelle Hawkins 4.00 10.00
Jason Rivers
A40 D.Reynaud/J.David Booty 3.00 8.00
A41 Adarius Bowman 4.00 10.00
Malcolm Kelly
A42 Ray Rice 3.00 8.00
Steve Slaton
A43 D.Reynaud/S.Slaton 3.00 8.00
A44 Dustin Keller 3.00 8.00
John Carlson
A45 Paul Smith/K.O'Connell 3.00 8.00
A46 Paul Smith 3.00 8.00
Kevin Smith
A47 Adarius Bowman 4.00 10.00
James Hardy
A48 Matt Flynn 8.00 20.00
Erik Ainge
A49 Keenan Burton 3.00 8.00
Andre Caldwell
A50 Martin Rucker 3.00 8.00
Malcolm Kelly
A51 S.Baker/J.David Booty 3.00 8.00
A52 Ryan Clady 5.00 12.00
Jake Long
A53 F.Davis/J.David Booty 3.00 8.00
A54 Devin Thomas 3.00 8.00
Fred Davis
A55 Kenny Phillips 4.00 10.00
Leodis McKelvin
A56 Kenny Phillips 3.00 8.00
Mike Jenkins
A57 Keith Rivers 3.00 8.00
Andre Caldwell
A58 Derrick Harvey 3.00 8.00
Andre Caldwell
A59 Felix Jones 3.00 8.00
Mike Jenkins
A60 Derrick Harvey 3.00 8.00
Jacob Hester
A61 Antoine Cason 3.00 8.00
Jacob Hester
A62 Jacob Hester 8.00 20.00
Matt Flynn
A63 Devin Thomas 3.00 8.00
Malcolm Kelly
A64 D.Avery/D.Thomas 4.00 10.00
A65 Sedrick Ellis 3.00 8.00
Adrian Arrington
A66 A.Arrington/C.Henne 4.00 10.00
A67 A.Arrington/J.Long 5.00 12.00
A68 L.Sweed/J.Charles 5.00 12.00
A69 L.Sweed/D.Dixon 3.00 8.00
A70 Antoine Cason 4.00 10.00
Dan Connor
A71 Vernon Gholston 3.00 8.00
Dan Connor
A72 Sedrick Ellis 3.00 8.00
Keith Rivers
A73 D.Avery/J.Nelson 8.00 20.00
A74 Leodis McKelvin 4.00 10.00
James Hardy
A75 J.Nelson/J.Hardy 8.00 20.00
A76 Ray Rice 3.00 8.00
Allen Patrick
A77 Malcolm Kelly 3.00 8.00
Allen Patrick
A78 Sedrick Ellis 3.00 8.00
Lawrence Jackson
A79 R.Mendenhall/D.Dixon 3.00 8.00
A80 Mike Hart 4.00 10.00
Chad Henne
A81 M.Hart/R.Mendenhall 3.00 8.00
A82 Jake Long 5.00 12.00
Mike Hart
A83 Jake Long 5.00 12.00
Chad Henne
A84 Vernon Gholston 4.00 10.00
Dustin Keller
A85 Leodis McKelvin 4.00 10.00
Mike Jenkins
A86 Martin Rucker 3.00 8.00
Darnell Terrell
A87 Will Franklin 4.00 10.00
Darnell Terrell

2009 SAGE Squared

1 L.Murphy/C.Ingram .20 .50
2 B.Raji/M.Ryan .25 .60
3 M.Stafford/K.Moreno 1.00 2.50
4 J.Ringer/D.Thomas .20 .50
5 J.Maclin/C.Coffman .25 .60
6 C.Wells/B.Robiskie .20 .50
7 C.Wells/M.Jenkins .20 .50
8 J.Iglesias/M.Kelly .20 .50
9 J.Casey/J.Dillard .25 .60
10 B.Orakpo/R.Miller .25 .60
11 M.Crabtree/G.Harrell .30 .75
12 D.Brown/D.Butler .25 .60
13 B.Cushing/C.Matthews .75 2.00
14 M.Sanchez/P.Turner .20 .50
15 P.White/S.Slaton .25 .60
16 M.Stafford/J.Long 1.00 2.50
17 M.Stafford/M.Ryan 1.00 2.50
18 K.Moreno/D.McFadden .20 .50
19 M.Stafford/J.Smith 1.00 2.50
20 M.Stafford/M.Sanchez 1.00 2.50
21 M.Stafford/J.Freeman 1.00 2.50
22 M.Sanchez/J.Freeman .20 .50
23 K.Moreno/D.Brown .20 .50
24 K.Moreno/C.Wells .20 .50
25 D.Brown/C.Wells .20 .50
26 D.Heyward-Bey/M.Crabtree .30 .75
27 D.Heyward-Bey/J.Maclin .30 .75
28 D.Heyward-Bey/H.Nicks .30 .75
29 M.Crabtree/J.Maclin .30 .75
30 M.Crabtree/H.Nicks .30 .75
31 J.Maclin/H.Nicks .25 .60
32 R.Maualuga/J.Laurinaitis .30 .75
33 R.Maualuga/C.Coffman .30 .75
34 K.Moreno/A.Smith .20 .50
35 M.Stafford/K.Smith 1.00 2.50
36 B.Raji/C.Matthews .25 .60
37 D.Brown/C.Painter .20 .50
38 P.White/C.Henne .25 .60
39 H.Nicks/A.Brown .25 .60
40 M.Sanchez/V.Gholston .20 .50
41 D.Heyward-Bey/L.Murphy .30 .75
42 D.Heyward-Bey/D.McFadden .30 .75
43 J.Maclin/L.McCoy .50 1.25
44 M.Crabtree/N.Davis .30 .75
45 J.Smith/J.Laurinaitis .20 .50

2009 SAGE Squared Dual Autographs

ONE AUTO PER PACK
1 L.Murphy/C.Ingram 2.50 6.00
2 M.Crabtree/G.Harrell 4.00 10.00
3 M.Stafford/K.Moreno 40.00 80.00
4 R.Maualuga/B.Cushing 2.50 6.00
5 J.Maclin/C.Coffman 3.00 8.00
6 C.Wells/B.Robiskie 12.00 30.00
7 P.Turner/P.White 3.00 8.00
8 J.Knox/D.Heyward-Bey 4.00 10.00
9 J.Casey/J.Dillard 3.00 8.00
10 J.Smith/E.Monroe 2.50 6.00
11 L.McCoy/S.McKillop 10.00 25.00
12 D.Brown/D.Butler 6.00 15.00
13 B.Cushing/C.Matthews 20.00 50.00
14 M.Sanchez/P.Turner 20.00 50.00
15 K.Moreno/T.Brandstater 3.00 8.00
16 C.Harper/A.Kelly 5.00 12.00
17 B.Orakpo/R.Miller 5.00 12.00
18 B.Orakpo/R.Palmer 5.00 12.00
19 R.Miller/R.Palmer 3.00 8.00
20 M.Stafford/M.Sanchez 60.00 120.00
21 M.Stafford/J.Freeman 40.00 80.00
22 M.Crabtree/J.Maclin
23 K.Moreno/D.Brown 2.50 6.00
24 C.Wells/K.Moreno 2.50 6.00
25 C.Wells/D.Brown 12.00 30.00
26 D.Heyward-Bey/M.Crabtree 4.00 10.00
27 D.Heyward-Bey/J.Maclin 4.00 10.00
28 J.Bronson/M.Reilly 2.50 6.00
29 M.Sanchez/J.Freeman 30.00 60.00
30 S.McGee/B.Williams 3.00 8.00
31 H.Mouton/D.Velkune 5.00 12.00
32 D.Byrd/R.J-Francois 3.00 8.00
33 R.Maualuga/C.Coffman 4.00 10.00
34 M.Teel/N.Reed 3.00 8.00
35 F.Brown/D.Mack 2.50 6.00
36 B.Raji/C.Matthews 25.00 50.00
37 D.Brown/C.Painter 8.00 20.00
38 D.Bolden/A.Smith 2.50 6.00
39 H.Nicks/A.Brown 3.00 8.00
40 J.Iglesias/J.Knox 3.00 8.00
41 D.Heyward-Bey/L.Murphy 4.00 10.00
42 B.Robiskie/D.Veikune 2.50 6.00
43 J.Maclin/L.McCoy 6.00 15.00
44 M.Crabtree/N.Davis 4.00 10.00
45 J.Smith/J.Laurinaitis 2.50 6.00
46 C.Sintim/A.Brown 3.00 8.00
47 S.Stroughter/B.Hughes 2.50 6.00
48 J.Ringer/B.Hoyer 4.00 10.00
49 J.Casey/C.Clement 3.00 8.00
50 M.Teel/P.White 3.00 8.00
51 J.Dillard/C.Clement 2.50 6.00
52 R.Maualuga/K.Maiava 8.00 20.00
53 E.Britton/M.Thomas 2.50 6.00
54 D.McBath/A.Smith 2.50 6.00
55 B.Robiskie/K.Maiava 2.50 6.00
56 E.Monroe/E.Britton 3.00 8.00
57 H.Cantwell/E.Wood 2.50 6.00
58 G.Johnson/K.Sperry 2.50 6.00
59 J.Cook/J.Ringer 3.00 8.00
60 J.Maclin/C.Ingram 3.00 8.00
61 L.McCoy/C.Ingram 6.00 15.00
62 H.Nicks/C.Sintim 3.00 8.00
63 M.Jenkins/M.Freeman 5.00 12.00
64 B.Cushing/J.Casey 2.50 6.00
65 M.Freeman/J.Laurinaitis 2.50 6.00
66 A.Smith/D.Bruton 2.50 6.00
67 J.Gilbert/J.Iglesias 3.00 8.00
68 M.Thomas/J.Dillard 2.50 6.00
69 E.Monroe/C.Sintim 2.50 6.00
70 B.Raji/R.Purvis 2.50 6.00
71 H.Nicks/B.Foster 3.00 8.00
72 M.Stafford/D.Levy 25.00 60.00
73 M.Jenkins/J.Laurinaitis 8.00 20.00

2010 SAGE Squared

1 S.Bradford/N.Suh .40 1.00
2 C.Spiller/R.Mathews .20 .50
3 C.McCoy/J.Clausen .25 .60
4 R.McClain/C.Peek .20 .50
5 M.Sanchez/J.Best .30 .75
6 D.LeFevour/A.Brown 1.50 4.00
7 S.Bradford/C.Spiller .25 .60
8 T.Pike/M.Gilyard .20 .50
9 J.Freeman/A.Benn .25 .60
10 M.Crabtree/D.Bryant .50 1.25
11 M.Sanchez/D.Williams .75 2.00
12 S.Bradford/M.Gilyard .25 .60
13 D.Heyward-Bey/R.McClain .25 .60
14 K.Moreno/C.Spiller .20 .50
15 C.McCoy/J.Shipley .25 .60
16 J.Freeman/M.Williams .25 .60
17 C.Spiller/J.Dwyer .20 .50
18 S.Bradford/G.McCoy .25 .60
19 R.Mathews/S.Ajirotutu .20 .50
20 M.Sanchez/J.McKnight .60 1.50
21 J.Clausen/T.Pike .20 .50
22 T.Gerhart/J.Best .20 .50
23 C.McCoy/E.Thomas .50 1.25
24 S.Bradford/J.Gresham .25 .60
25 B.Spikes/A.Hernandez .20 .50
26 M.Sanchez/S.Bradford .25 .60
27 J.Freeman/G.McCoy .25 .60
28 C.Spiller/J.Best .20 .50
29 A.Benn/M.Williams .20 .50
30 S.Bradford/C.McCoy .25 .60
31 T.Gerhart/C.Cook .20 .50
32 M.Sanchez/J.Clausen .20 .50
33 D.Morgan/J.Dwyer .20 .50
34 C.McCoy/N.Suh .40 1.00
35 J.Pierre-Paul/C.Mitchell .30 .75
36 K.Moreno/R.Curran .30 .75
37 M.Sanchez/J.Pierre-Paul .50 1.25
38 M.Crabtree/A.Dixon .30 .75
39 D.Heyward-Bey/D.Bryant .50 1.25
40 R.Mathews/J.Best .20 .50
41 J.Freeman/J.Snead .25 .60
42 C.McCoy/M.Hardesty .25 .60
43 M.Sanchez/T.Gerhart .75 2.50
44 N.Suh/G.McCoy .40 1.00
45 S.Bradford/J.Clausen .25 .60

2010 SAGE Squared Dual Autographs

ONE DUAL AUTO PER PACK
A1 S.Bradford/M.Stafford 50.00 100.00
A2 C.Spiller/R.Mathews 4.00 10.00
A3 C.Spiller/M.Sanchez 4.00 10.00
A4 R.McClain/C.Peek 12.00 30.00
A5 P.White/J.Webb 10.00 25.00
A6 D.LeFevour/A.Brown 30.00 80.00
A7 S.Bradford/C.Spiller 5.00 12.00
A8 T.Pike/M.Gilyard 4.00 10.00
A9 B.Tate/B.Cushing 4.00 10.00
A10 D.Heyward-Bey/L.Murphy 6.00 15.00
A11 J.Skelton/Z.Robinson 5.00 12.00
A12 S.Bradford/M.Gilyard 30.00 60.00
A13 R.McClain/D.Heyward-Bey 5.00 12.00
A14 C.Spiller/K.Moreno 4.00 10.00
A15 C.McCoy/J.Shipley 15.00 40.00
A16 J.Freeman/M.Williams 8.00 20.00
A17 C.Wilson/C.Matthews 10.00 25.00
A18 B.Cushing/G.Graham 4.00 10.00
A19 R.Mathews/S.Ajirotutu 4.00 10.00
A20 D.Williams/P.Turner 4.00 10.00
A21 J.Clausen/T.Pike 12.00 30.00
A22 D.Pitta/S.Ajirotutu 4.00 10.00
A23 C.McCoy/E.Thomas 10.00 25.00
A24 D.Brown/M.Jenkins 6.00 15.00
A25 A.Hernandez/B.Spikes 4.00 10.00
A26 D.LeFevour/Z.Robinson 5.00 12.00
A27 J.Freeman/G.McCoy 5.00 12.00
A28 S.Canfield/S.Stroughter 4.00 10.00
A29 A.Benn/M.Williams 4.00 10.00
A30 S.Young/K.McCarthy 6.00 15.00
A31 T.Gerhart/C.Cook 4.00 10.00
A32 A.Anderson/J.Williams 3.00 8.00
A33 J.Dwyer/D.Morgan 4.00 10.00
A34 E.Wilson/E.Thomas 10.00 25.00
A35 B.White/D.Brown 6.00 15.00
A36 R.Mathews/C.Thomas 5.00 12.00
A37 J.Skelton/C.Wells 5.00 12.00
A38 A.Dixon/M.Crabtree 8.00 20.00
A39 J.Maclin/S.Weatherspoon 4.00 10.00
A40 B.Orakpo/J.Shipley 4.00 10.00
A41 C.Sheffield/B.Lang 4.00 10.00
A42 M.Hardesty/C.McCoy 5.00 12.00
A43 R.Gronkowski/A.Hernandez 30.00 60.00
A44 T.Price/Z.Robinson 5.00 12.00
A45 S.Bradford/J.Clausen 25.00 60.00
A46 N.Suh/J.Best 15.00 40.00
A47 M.Stafford/R.Curran 15.00 40.00
A48 M.Hardesty/C.Mitchell 4.00 10.00
A49 S.Johnson/P.Turner 4.00 10.00
A50 A.Anderson/D.Heyward-Bey 5.00 12.00
A51 C.Wilson/C.Sheffield 5.00 12.00
A52 L.McCoy/N.Byham 6.00 15.00
A53 S.Ajirotutu/C.Thomas 5.00 12.00
A54 S.Weatherspoon/C.Peek 4.00 10.00
A55 G.McCoy/M.Williams 4.00 10.00
A56 B.White/M.Jenkins 4.00 10.00
A57 D.Briscoe/J.Shipley 4.00 10.00
A58 R.Maualuga/J.Gresham 4.00 10.00
A59 B.Tate/R.Curran 4.00 10.00
A60 S.Bradford/J.Smith 25.00 60.00
A61 A.Dixon/R.Curran 4.00 10.00
A62 J.Snead/M.Williams 4.00 10.00
A63 C.McCoy/C.Mitchell 10.00 25.00
A64 T.Gerhart/J.Webb 4.00 10.00
A65 M.Sanchez/Z.Robinson 20.00 40.00
A66 C.Matthews/B.Orakpo 12.00 30.00
A67 J.Dwyer/A.Brown 30.00 80.00
A68 M.Gilyard/J.Smith 4.00 10.00
A69 L.Murphy/R.Spikes 4.00 10.00
A70 C.Spiller/J.Bell 4.00 10.00
A71 J.Gresham/J.Shipley 4.00 10.00
A72 H.Nicks/C.Thomas 5.00 12.00
A73 T.Moeaki/C.Sheffield 5.00 12.00
A74 J.Skelton/J.Bell 5.00 12.00
A75 D.Pitta/R.Mathews 4.00 10.00
A76 D.Morgan/R.Curran 4.00 10.00
A77 M.Sanchez/C.Matthews 20.00 40.00
A78 P.White/J.Brown 8.00 20.00
A79 S.Johnson/C.Matthews
A80 D.LeFevour/J.Knox 4.00 10.00
A81 B.White/J.Shipley 4.00 10.00
A82 E.Wilson/C.Thomas 5.00 12.00
A83 B.Orakpo/E.Thomas 10.00 25.00
A84 H.Nicks/E.Wilson 4.00 10.00
A85 B.Tate/G.Graham 4.00 10.00
A86 A.Dixon/N.Byham 4.00 10.00
A87 C.Cook/J.Webb 4.00 10.00
A88 J.Best/M.Stafford 15.00 40.00
A89 N.Suh/M.Stafford 30.00 60.00
A90 J.Dwyer/C.McCoy 12.00 30.00
A91 B.White/A.Benn 4.00 10.00
A92 M.Tennant/E.Olsen 5.00 12.00
A93 T.Moeaki/D.Pitta 5.00 12.00
A94 J.McKnight/S.Lauvao 4.00 10.00
A95 T.Gerhart/C.Wells 4.00 10.00
A96 M.Sanchez/J.Clausen

2014 SAGE Squared

1 Blake Bortles
Teddy Bridgewater/25•
2 Kony Ealy
Michael Sam/25
3 Alec Ogletree
Aaron Murray/40
4 Odell Beckham Jr.
Zach Mettenberger/40
5 Carlos Hyde
Marcus Lattimore/40
6 Eric Ebron
Joseph Fauria/14
7 Datone Jones
Jordan Zumwalt/25
8 Eddie Lacy
Geno Smith 6/8
9 James White
Montee Ball/30
10 Sheldon Richardson
Bjoern Werner/44
13 Ha Ha Clinton-Dix
Datone Jones/50
14 Mike Evans
Mike Glennon/40•
15 Terrance West
Jordan Zumwalt/25
16 Tre Mason
Henry Josey/50
17 Zach Mettenberger
David Fales/50
18 Robert Woods
Marqise Lee/50
19 Odell Beckham Jr.
Kevin Norwood/50
20 Jadeveon Clowney
Sam Montgomery/40
22 Brandin Cooks
Ryan Griffin/14
23 Ka'Deem Carey
Brock Vereen/14
26 Ra'Shede Hageman
Jerome Smith/50
29 Shaq Evans
Jordan Zumwalt/50
32 Aaron Dobson
Jimmy Garappolo/40
35 Mike Evans
Robert Herron/50
36 Jimmy Garoppolo
Joe Don Duncan/50
37 Ka'Deem Carey
David Fales/50
38 Ka'Deem Carey
Lorenzo Taliaferro/50
39 Landry Jones
Jordan Zumwalt/50
40 Logan Thomas
David Fales/50
41 Marqise Lee
Chris Smith/50
42 Michael Sam
Henry Josey/50
43 Mike Evans
Brett Smith/50
44 Odell Beckham Jr.
Brandin Cooks/50
45 Ryan Nassib
Jerome Smith/50
53 Kareem Martin
Troy Niklas/50
54 Terrance West
Michael Campanaro/50
57 Lorenzo Taliaferro
Michael Campanaro/50
58 Blake Bortles
Chris Smith/50
73 Trevor Reilly
Keith McGill/50
75 Shaq Evans
Tajh Boyd/50
94 Ka'Deem Carey
Jerome Smith/25
97 Paul Richardson
Ka'Deem Carey/50
100 Jadeveon Clowney
Keith McGill/50
102 Chris Smith
Zach Mettenberger/25
103 James White
Joe Don Duncan/50
104 Jared Abbrederis
Rajion Neal/50
105 Jake Matthews
Troy Niklas/50
106 Eric Ebron
Kyle Van Noy/50
107 Eric Ebron
Kareem Martin/50
108 Dominique Easley
James White/50
109 Dominique Easley
Joe Don Duncan/50
110 Davante Adams
Carl Bradford/50
111 Jadeveon Clowney
Kyle Van Noy/50
112 Carl Bradford
Rajion Neal/50
113 Calvin Pryor
Trevor Reilly/50
114 Calvin Pryor
Ha Ha Clinton-Dix/50
115 Brandin Cooks
Marqise Lee/50
116 Michael Campanaro
Mike Davis/50
117 Blake Bortles
Chris Smith/50
119 Aaron Murray
Brett Smith/25

1997 Score Board NFL Rookies

The 1997 Score Board NFL Rookies set was issued in one series totaling 100 standard-size cards. The set was issued in 8-card packs with 36 packs in a box and 12 boxes in a case. Among the topical subsets are: All-Americans (94-98) and Checklists (99-100). The key players in this set are Duce Staley, Tony Gonzalez, Jake Plummer, Warrick Dunn and Corey Dillon.

COMPLETE SET (100) 4.00 10.00
1 Jake Plummer .50 1.25
2 Tony Gonzalez .50 1.25
3 Trevor Pryce .07 .20
4 Greg Jones .01 .05
5 Koy Detmer .07 .20
6 Rae Carruth .01 .05
7 Peter Boulware .07 .20
8 Warrick Dunn .40 1.00
9 Antowain Smith .30 .75
10 Troy Davis .01 .05
11 David LaFleur .01 .05
12 Yatil Green .07 .20
13 Michael Booker .01 .05
14 Shawn Springs .02 .10
15 Bryant Westbrook .02 .10
16 Byron Hanspard .02 .10
17 Darrell Russell .01 .05
18 Corey Dillon .50 1.25
19 Tyrus McCloud .01 .05
20 Reinard Wilson .02 .10
21 Adam Meadows .01 .05
22 Tremain Mack .01 .05
23 Ricky Parker .01 .05
24 George Jones .01 .05
25 Terry Battle .01 .05
26 Will Blackwell .02 .10
27 Jerald Sowell .01 .05
28 Isaac Byrd .07 .20
29 Chris Naeole .01 .05
30 Kevin Lockett .02 .10
31 Freddie Jones .01 .05
32 Pat Barnes .02 .10
33 Torrian Gray .01 .05
34 Brian Manning .01 .05
35 Dedric Ward .02 .10
36 Pete Monty .01 .05
37 Sam Madison .07 .20
38 Sedrick Shaw .02 .10
39 Mike Logan .01 .05
40 Albert Connell .07 .20
41 Canute Curtis .01 .05
42 Ronde Barber .30 .75
43 Orlando Pace .07 .20
44 Ed Perry .07 .20
45 Tiki Barber .75 2.00
46 Kevin Jackson .01 .05
47 Jerry Wunsch .01 .05
48 Michael Hamilton .01 .05
49 Darnell Autry .02 .10
50 Jim Druckenmiller .02 .10
51 James Farrior .07 .20
52 Derrick Mason .25 .60
53 Ty Howard .01 .05
54 Jason Taylor .07 .20
55 Reidel Anthony .07 .20
56 Bertrand Berry .30 .75
57 Marc Edwards .02 .10
58 James Hamilton .01 .05
59 Ike Hilliard .15 .40
60 Tommy Knight .01 .05
61 Walter Jones .12 .30
62 Chad Levitt .01 .05
63 Pratt Lyons .01 .05
64 Greg Clark .01 .05
65 Ryan Phillips .01 .05
66 Jason Martin .01 .05
67 Scott Sanderson .01 .05
68 Al Singleton .07 .20
69 Duce Staley .40 1.00
70 Jared Tomich .01 .05
71 Ross Verba .01 .05
72 Derrick Rodgers .01 .05
73 Mike Vrabel .75 2.00
74 John Allred .01 .05
75 Bob Sapp .07 .20
76 Brad Otton RC .01 .05
77 Tarik Glenn .07 .20
78 Chad Scott .02 .10
79 Nathan Davis .01 .05
80 Henri Crockett .01 .05
81 Tarek Saleh .01 .05
82 Seth Payne .01 .05
83 Pete Chryplewicz .01 .05
84 Reidel Anthony AA .01 .05
85 Reinard Wilson AA .01 .05
86 Byron Hanspard AA .02 .10
87 Shawn Springs AA .01 .05
88 David LaFleur AA .01 .05
89 Troy Davis AA .01 .05
90 Warrick Dunn AA .20 .50
91 Peter Boulware AA .02 .10
92 Rae Carruth AA .01 .05
93 Tony Gonzalez AA .20 .50
94 Jake Plummer AA .25 .60
95 Orlando Pace AA .02 .10
96 Ike Hilliard AA .07 .20
97 Kevin Jackson AA .01 .05
98 Jim Druckenmiller AA .02 .10
99 Shawn Springs CL .01 .05
100 Warrick Dunn CL .20 .50

1997 Score Board NFL Rookies Dean's List

COMP.DEAN'S LIST (100) 15.00 40.00
*DEAN'S LIST: 1.5X TO 4X BASIC CARDS
DEAN'S LIST STATED ODDS 1:5

1997 Score Board NFL Rookies Varsity Club

This 30-card horizontal insert set features some of the leading 1997 NFL Rookies with their school pennant. The cards are numbered with an "V" prefix and are randomly inserted in packs at a rate of one in 36.

COMPLETE SET (30) 30.00 80.00
STATED ODDS 1:36
V1 Tiki Barber 8.00 20.00
V2 Sedrick Shaw .40 1.00
V3 Kevin Lockett .40 1.00
V4 Byron Hanspard .40 1.00
V5 David LaFleur .20 .50
V6 Warrick Dunn 4.00 10.00
V7 Yatil Green .75 2.00
V8 Corey Dillon 5.00 12.00
V9 Orlando Pace .75 2.00
V10 Tony Gonzalez 5.00 12.00
V11 Darrell Russell .20 .50
V12 Jake Plummer 5.00 12.00
V13 Peter Boulware .75 2.00
V14 Shawn Springs .40 1.00
V15 Bryant Westbrook .40 1.00
V16 Rae Carruth .20 .50
V17 Antowain Smith 3.00 8.00
V18 Reidel Anthony .75 2.00
V19 Michael Booker .20 .50
V20 Freddie Jones .20 .50
V21 Pat Barnes .40 1.00
V22 Troy Davis .20 .50
V23 Walter Jones 1.25 3.00
V24 Reinard Wilson .40 1.00
V25 George Jones .20 .50
V26 Terry Battle .20 .50
V27 Tommy Knight .20 .50
V28 Tremain Mack .20 .50
V29 Jim Druckenmiller .40 1.00
V30 Ike Hilliard 1.50 4.00

1997 Score Board NFL Rookies War Room

This 20-card insert set features some of the leading 1997 NFL Rookies. The cards are numbered with an "W" prefix and are randomly inserted in packs at a rate of one in 100.

COMPLETE SET (20) 60.00 150.00
STATED ODDS 1:100
W1 Yatil Green 1.50 4.00
W2 Antowain Smith 6.00 15.00
W3 Tony Gonzalez 10.00 25.00
W4 Corey Dillon 10.00 25.00
W5 Jake Plummer 10.00 25.00
W6 Peter Boulware 1.50 4.00
W7 Orlando Pace 1.50 4.00
W8 Darrell Russell .40 1.00
W9 Reinard Wilson .75 2.00
W10 Shawn Springs .75 2.00
W11 Bryant Westbrook .75 2.00
W12 Rae Carruth .40 1.00
W13 Warrick Dunn 8.00 20.00
W14 David LaFleur .40 1.00
W15 Byron Hanspard .75 2.00
W16 Michael Booker .40 1.00
W17 Reidel Anthony 1.50 4.00
W18 Troy Davis .40 1.00
W19 Chris Naeole .40 1.00
W20 Jim Druckenmiller .75 2.00

1994 Signature Rookies Promos

1 Trev Alberts/5000* .30 .75
2 Sam Adams/5000* .30 .75
3 John Thierry/5000* .30 .75
4 Errict Rhett/7500* .40 1.00

1994 Signature Rookies Autograph Promos

These signed cards were released to promote the 1994 Signature Rookies football set. Each card was signed by the featured player and serial numbered with some player's cards hand numbered on the fronts as well.

C1 Perry Klein/5000 2.50 6.00
C2 Marvin Goodwin/5000 2.50 6.00
C3 Toddrick McIntosh/5000 2.50 6.00
C4 Bruce Walker/5000 2.50 6.00
PR1 Byron Bam Morris/1000 3.00 8.00

1994 Signature Rookies

These 60 standard-size cards feature borderless color action shots of top NFL prospects in their college uniforms. A wide gold-foil stripe adorns the left side and carries the words "1 of 45,000" or, for the autographed card included in every six-card pack, "Authentic Signature." The player's name and position appear at the bottom. Production was limited to 12,500 numbered boxes. Special subsets include the five-card Charlie Ward set, 2,500 cards of which were hand signed by the Heisman Trophy winner; the five-card "Hottest Prospect" set, 2,000 of which were hand signed by each of the five players; and also sets of Gale Sayers and Tony Dorsett, of which 2,000 and 1,000 cards, respectively, were autographed.

COMPLETE SET (60) 2.00 5.00
1 Sam Adams .01 .05
2 Trev Alberts .01 .05
3 Derrick Alexander WR .15 .40
4 Larry Allen .30 .75
5 Aubrey Beavers .01 .05
6 Lou Benfatti .01 .05
7 James Bostic .01 .05
8 Tim Bowens .01 .05
9 Rich Braham .01 .05
10 Isaac Bruce 1.00 2.50
11 Vaughn Bryant .01 .05
12 Brentson Buckner .01 .05
13 Jeff Burris .01 .05
14 Carlester Crumpler .01 .05
15 Lake Dawson .05 .15
16 Tyronne Drakeford .01 .05
17 Dan Eichloff .01 .05
18 Rob Fredrickson .01 .05
19 Gus Frerotte .50 1.25
20 William Gaines .01 .05
21 Wayne Gandy .01 .05
22 Jason Gildon .05 .15
23 Lemanski Hall .01 .05
24 Shelby Hill .01 .05
25 Willie Jackson .15 .40
26 LeShon Johnson .01 .05
27 Tre Johnson .01 .05
28 Alan Kline .01 .05
29 Darren Krein .01 .05
30 Antonio Langham .01 .05
31 Corey Louchiey .01 .05
32 Keith Lyle .01 .05
33 Eric Mahlum .01 .05
34 Van Malone .01 .05
35 Chris Maumalanga .01 .05
36 Jamir Miller .05 .15
37 Jim Miller .75 2.00
38 Byron Bam Morris .05 .15
39 Aaron Mundy .01 .05
40 Jeremy Nunley .01 .05
41 Turhon O'Bannon .01 .05
42 Brad Ottis .01 .05
43 David Palmer .05 .15
44 Joe Panos .01 .05
45 Jim Pyne .01 .05
46 John Reece .01 .05
47 Errict Rhett .15 .40
48 Tony Richardson .05 .15
49 Sam Rogers .01 .05
50 Tim Ruddy .01 .05
51 Corey Sawyer .05 .15
52 Malcolm Seabron .01 .05
53 Jason Sehorn .15 .40
54 John Thierry .01 .05
55 Jason Winrow .01 .05
56 Ronnie Woolfork .01 .05
57 Toby Wright .01 .05
58 Ryan Yarborough .01 .05
59 Eric Zomalt .01 .05
60 Checklist .01 .05

1994 Signature Rookies Autographs

These standard-size cards were produced in autographed form with one seeded in every six-card pack of 1994 Signature Rookies. Production was limited to 12,500 numbered boxes. Each signed card was numbered out of 7750 and featured the Signature Rookies gold foil authentication sticker on the back. Seven hundred Errict Rhett signatures are not authentic. If these cards were sent in, Signature Rookies then did a verification check and made a replacement if needed. A second #5 (Trent Pollard) card was released at some point after the product was fully issued, presumably after Signature Rookies stopped producing cards.

COMPLETE SET (60) 75.00 200.00
STATED PRINT RUN 7750 SETS
ONE CARD OR COUPON PER PACK
1 Sam Adams 1.50 4.00
2 Trev Alberts 1.50 4.00
3 Derrick Alexander WR 4.00 10.00
4 Larry Allen 8.00 20.00
5A Aubrey Beavers 1.50 4.00
5B Trent Pollard 1.50 4.00
6 Lou Benfatti 1.50 4.00
7 James Bostic 1.50 4.00
8 Tim Bowens 1.50 4.00
9 Rich Braham 1.50 4.00
10 Isaac Bruce 7.50 15.00
11 Vaughn Bryant 1.50 4.00
12 Brentson Buckner 1.50 4.00
13 Jeff Burris 1.50 4.00
14 Carlester Crumpler 1.50 4.00
15 Lake Dawson 2.50 6.00
16 Tyronne Drakeford 1.50 4.00
17 Dan Eichloff 1.50 4.00
18 Rob Fredrickson 1.50 4.00
19 Gus Frerotte 8.00 20.00
20 William Gaines 1.50 4.00
21 Wayne Gandy 1.50 4.00
22 Jason Gildon 5.00 12.00
23 Lemanski Hall 1.50 4.00
24 Shelby Hill 1.50 4.00
25 Willie Jackson 4.00 10.00
26 LeShon Johnson 1.50 4.00
27 Tre Johnson 1.50 4.00
28 Alan Kline 1.50 4.00
29 Darren Krein 1.50 4.00
30 Antonio Langham 1.50 4.00
31 Corey Louchiey 1.50 4.00
32 Keith Lyle 1.50 4.00
33 Eric Mahlum 1.50 4.00
34 Van Malone 1.50 4.00
35 Chris Maumalanga 1.50 4.00
36 Jamir Miller 2.50 6.00
37 Jim Miller 6.00 15.00
38 Byron Bam Morris 2.50 6.00
39 Aaron Mundy 1.50 4.00
40 Jeremy Nunley 1.50 4.00
41 Turhon O'Bannon 1.50 4.00
42 Brad Ottis 1.50 4.00
43 David Palmer 2.50 6.00
44 Joe Panos 1.50 4.00
45 Jim Pyne 1.50 4.00
46 John Reece 1.50 4.00
47 Errict Rhett 4.00 10.00
48 Tony Richardson 2.50 6.00
49 Sam Rogers 1.50 4.00
50 Tim Ruddy 1.50 4.00
51 Corey Sawyer 2.50 6.00
52 Malcolm Seabron 1.50 4.00
53 Jason Sehorn 5.00 12.00
54 John Thierry 1.50 4.00
55 Jason Winrow 1.50 4.00
56 Ronnie Woolfork 1.50 4.00
57 Toby Wright 1.50 4.00
58 Ryan Yarborough 1.50 4.00
59 Eric Zomalt 1.50 4.00

1994 Signature Rookies Bonus Autographs

Randomly inserted in 1994 Tetrad packs, each card in this standard-size set was serial numbered out of 7750 with some being hand serial numbered to fewer quantities. The fronts display color action player photos, with a gold foil stripe accenting the left side. The player's signature appears across the bottom. The back carries biography, player profile, and a Signature Rookies Bonus Signature gold foil seal. The cards are unnumbered and checklisted below in alphabetical order.

COMPLETE SET (16) 15.00 40.00
STATED PRINT RUN 7750 SETS
1 Jamal Anderson 7.50 20.00
7 Myron Bell 1.25 3.00
3 Mitch Berger 1.25 3.00
4 Jocelyn Borgella 1.25 3.00
5 Brant Boyer 1.25 3.00
6 Chris Brantley 1.25 3.00
2 Ron Edwards 1.25 3.00
8 Rob Holmberg 1.25 3.00
9 Fred Lester 1.25 3.00
10 Joseph Patton 1.25 3.00
11 Trent Pollard/5000 1.25 3.00
12 Eric Ravotti 1.25 3.00
13 Jim Reid 1.25 3.00
14 Jerry Reynolds 1.25 3.00
15 Bracy Walker 1.25 3.00
16 Gabe Wilkins 1.25 3.00
18 Lloyd Hill 1.25 3.00

1994 Signature Rookies Tony Dorsett

Randomly inserted in packs, these two standard-size cards feature borderless color action shots. A wide gold-foil stripe adorns the left side and carries the words "1 of 5,000". The player's name and position appear at the bottom. The backs carry player biography and profile. Dorsett autographed 1,000 of his cards.

COMPLETE SET (2) 1.50 4.00
D1 Tony Dorsett .75 2.00
D1A Tony Dorsett Auto/1000 20.00 40.00
D2 Tony Dorsett .75 2.00
D2A Tony Dorsett Auto/1000 20.00 40.00

1994 Signature Rookies Hottest Prospects

Randomly inserted in packs, these five standard-size cards feature borderless color action shots of top NFL prospects in their college uniforms. A gold-foil stripe adorns the left side and carries the words "1 of 15,000." The player's name and position are gold-foil stamped across the bottom. The backs carry player biography and profile. A "Special Offer" parallel set was later released with the cards numbered with an "M" prefix.

COMPLETE SET (5) 2.50 6.00
STATED PRINT RUN 150,000
*SPECIAL OFFER: .4X TO 1X BASIC INSERTS
A1 Willie McGinest
A2 Bryant Young .75 2.00
A3 Dewayne Washington .40 1.00
A4 Aaron Taylor .40 1.00
A5 Charles Johnson .75 2.00

1994 Signature Rookies Hottest Prospects Autographs

A1 Willie McGinest 3.00 6.00
A2 Bryant Young 8.00 20.00
A3 Dewayne Washington 3.00 6.00
A4 Aaron Taylor 3.00 6.00
A5 Charles Johnson 6.00 12.00

1994 Signature Rookies Gale Sayers

Randomly inserted in packs, these two standard-size cards feature borderless color action shots. A wide gold-foil stripe adorns the left side and carries the words "1 of 5,000". The player's name and position appear at the bottom. The backs carry player biography and profile. Sayers autographed 1,000 of his cards.

COMPLETE SET (2) 4.00 4.00
COMMON SAYERS (S1-S2) 2.00 2.00
GALE SAYERS AU/1000 12.50 30.00

1994 Signature Rookies Charlie Ward

Randomly inserted in packs, this 5-card standard-size set spotlights Charlie Ward, the 1993 Heisman Trophy Winner. On the front, the left side features in gold the words Future Great, the 5,000 of each card production number and the identification of Ward as a 2 sport star. The remainder of the card is used for a full-color photo which bleeds to the corner. The backs are numbered on the top of the card. Underneath the top, information about Ward is placed

between two goal posts. Each card includes information pertaining to Ward's career at Florida State. Ward autographed 525 of each of his cards as inserts.
COMPLETE SET (5) 2.00 4.00
COMMON WARD (C1-C5) .40 1.00
CHARLIE WARD AU/525 7.50 20.00
*PROMOS: 4X TO 1X BASIC INSERTS

1995 Signature Rookies Promos 7500

This set of promos was distributed to announce the release of the 1995 Signature Rookies Draft Preview set. Each card includes a gold foil "Promo 1 of 7500" designation on the cardfront.

COMPLETE SET (3) .80 2.00
FB1 Ki-Jana Carter .40 1.00
FB2 Rashaan Salaam .20 .50
FB3 Kevin Carter .30 .75

1995 Signature Rookies

These standard-size six-card packs retailed for $5 and included an autographed card. Each player autographed 7,750 of his own cards, and 39,000 of each card were produced. The fronts display a color action player photo. At the lower left corner, a black marblized stripe outlined in gold foil carries the player's name. The lower right corner has a triangular-shaped green football field design. Edged at the upper right and lower left corners with green grass, the backs show a closeup photo, with a ghosted panel carrying bio and player profile. The cards are numbered in the top right corner. An international version of this set was also issued; in which; players signed 2,750 of their own cards, and 13,500 of each card produced. These cards are similiar to the original set except they are stamped in silver foil with the words international appearing on the card fronts.

COMPLETE SET (80) 5.00 12.00
1 Derrick Alexander DE .02 .10
2 Kelvin Anderson .05 .15
3 Antonio Armstrong .02 .10
4 Jamie Asher .05 .15
5 Joe Aska .02 .10
6 Dave Barr .02 .10
7 Brandon Bennett .02 .10
8 Tony Berti .02 .10
9 Mark Birchmeier .02 .10
10 Tony Boselli .05 .15
11 Derrick Brooks .08 .25
12 Anthony Brown .02 .10
13 Ruben Brown .08 .25
14 Mark Bruener .02 .10
15 Ontiwaun Carter .02 .10
16 Stoney Case .05 .15
17 Byron Chamberlain .20 .50
18 Shannon Clavelle .02 .10
19 Jamal Cox .02 .10
20 Zack Crockett .05 .15
21 Terrell Davis .75 2.00
22 Tyrone Davis .02 .10
23 Lee DeRamus .02 .10
24 Ken Dilger .05 .15
25 Hugh Douglas .08 .25
26 David Dunn .02 .10
27 Chad Eaton .02 .10
28 Hicham El-Mashtoub .02 .10
29 Christian Fauria .02 .10
30 Terrell Fletcher .02 .10
31 Antonio Freeman .30 .75
32 Eddie Goines .02 .10
33 Roger Graham .02 .10
34 Carl Greenwood .02 .10
35 Ed Hervey .02 .10
36 Jimmy Hitchcock .02 .10
37 Darius Holland .02 .10
38 Torey Hunter .02 .10
39 Steve Ingram .02 .10
40 Jack Jackson .02 .10
41 Trezelle Jenkins .02 .10
42 Ellis Johnson .02 .10
43 Eric Johnson RBK .02 .10
44 Rob Johnson .15 .40
45 Chris T. Jones .05 .15
46 Larry Jones .02 .10
47 Shawn King .02 .10
48 Scotty Lewis .02 .10
49 Curtis Martin .75 2.00
50 Oscar McBride .02 .10
51 Kez McCorvey .02 .10
52 Bronzell Miller .02 .10
53 Pete Mitchell .02 .10
54 Brent Moss .02 .10
55 Craig Newsome .02 .10
56 Herman O'Berry .02 .10
57 Matt O'Dwyer .02 .10
58 Tyrone Poole .08 .25
59 Brian Pruitt .02 .10
60 Cory Raymer .02 .10
61 John Sacca .02 .10
62 Frank Sanders .08 .25
63 J.J. Smith .02 .10
64 Brendan Stai .02 .10
65 Steve Stenstrom .02 .10
66 James O. Stewart .30 .75
67 Kordell Stewart .50 1.25
68 Ben Talley .02 .10
69 Bobby Taylor .08 .25
70 Johnny Thomas .02 .10
71 Orlando Thomas .02 .10
72 Rodney Thomas .05 .15
73 Zach Wiegert .02 .10
74 Jerrott Willard .02 .10
75 Billy Williams .02 .10
76 Sherman Williams .02 .10
77 Jamal Willis .02 .10
78 Dave Wohlabaugh .02 .10
79 Eric Zeier .08 .25
80 Checklist .02 .10

1995 Signature Rookies International

COMPLETE SET (80) 8.00 20.00
*INTERNATIONALS: .8X TO 2X BASIC CARDS
STATED PRINT RUN 13,500 SETS

1995 Signature Rookies Autographs

These 79 standard-size cards were also available in autographed form; an autograph card was included in each six-card pack. Each player autographed 7,750 of his own cards, and 39,000 of each regular card were produced. The design is identical to that of the regular issue, except for the autograph inscribed across the front. An international version of this set was also issued; in which; players signed 2,750 of their own cards, and 13,500 of each card produced. These cards are similiar to the original set except they are stamped in silver foil with the words international appearing on the card fronts.

COMPLETE SET (79) 125.00 250.00
STATED PRINT RUN 7750 SER.#'d SETS
*INTERNATIONAL: 1X TO 2X BASIC AUTOS
1 Derrick Alexander DE 1.50 4.00
2 Kelvin Anderson 1.50 4.00
3 Antonio Armstrong 1.50 4.00
4 Jamie Asher 1.50 4.00
5 Joe Aska 1.50 4.00
6 Dave Barr 1.50 4.00
7 Brandon Bennett 1.50 4.00
8 Tony Berti 1.50 4.00
9 Mark Birchmeier 1.50 4.00
10 Tony Boselli 2.00 5.00
11 Derrick Brooks 4.00 10.00
12 Anthony Brown 1.50 4.00
13 Ruben Brown 3.00 8.00
14 Mark Bruener 2.00 5.00
15 Ontiwaun Carter 1.50 4.00
16 Stoney Case 2.00 5.00
17 Byron Chamberlain 3.00 8.00
18 Shannon Clavelle 1.50 4.00
19 Jamal Cox 1.50 4.00
20 Zack Crockett 2.00 5.00
21 Terrell Davis 6.00 15.00
22 Tyrone Davis 1.50 4.00
23 Lee DeRamus 1.50 4.00
24 Ken Dilger 2.00 5.00
25 Hugh Douglas 2.00 5.00
26 David Dunn 1.50 4.00
27 Chad Eaton 1.50 4.00
28 Hicham El-Mashtoub 1.50 4.00
29 Christian Fauria 1.50 4.00
30 Terrell Fletcher 1.50 4.00
31 Antonio Freeman 6.00 15.00
32 Eddie Goines 1.50 4.00
33 Roger Graham 1.50 4.00
34 Carl Greenwood 1.50 4.00
35 Ed Hervey 1.50 4.00
36 Jimmy Hitchcock 1.50 4.00
37 Darius Holland 1.50 4.00
38 Torey Hunter 1.50 4.00
39 Steve Ingram 1.50 4.00
40 Jack Jackson 1.50 4.00
41 Trezelle Jenkins 1.50 4.00
42 Ellis Johnson 1.50 4.00
43 Eric Johnson RBK 1.50 4.00
44 Rob Johnson 5.00 12.00
45 Chris T. Jones 1.50 4.00
46 Larry Jones 1.50 4.00
47 Shawn King 1.50 4.00
48 Scotty Lewis 1.50 4.00
49 Curtis Martin 6.00 15.00
50 Oscar McBride 1.50 4.00
51 Kez McCorvey 1.50 4.00
52 Bronzell Miller 1.50 4.00
53 Pete Mitchell 1.50 4.00
54 Brent Moss 1.50 4.00
55 Craig Newsome 1.50 4.00
56 Herman O'Berry 1.50 4.00
57 Matt O'Dwyer 1.50 4.00
58 Tyrone Poole 3.00 8.00
59 Brian Pruitt 1.50 4.00
60 Cory Raymer 1.50 4.00
61 John Sacca 1.50 4.00
62 Frank Sanders 3.00 8.00
63 J.J. Smith 1.50 4.00
64 Brendan Stai 1.50 4.00
65 Steve Stenstrom 1.50 4.00
66 James O. Stewart 3.00 8.00
67 Kordell Stewart 5.00 12.00
68 Ben Talley 1.50 4.00
69 Bobby Taylor 3.00 8.00
70 Johnny Thomas 1.50 4.00
71 Orlando Thomas 1.50 4.00
72 Rodney Thomas 2.00 5.00
73 Zach Wiegert 1.50 4.00
74 Jerrott Willard 1.50 4.00
75 Billy Williams 1.50 4.00
76 Sherman Williams 1.50 4.00
77 Jamal Willis 1.50 4.00
78 Dave Wohlabaugh 1.50 4.00
79 Eric Zeier 2.00 5.00

1995 Signature Rookies Franchise Rookies

Randomly inserted at a ratio of one per every eight packs, this 10-card standard-size set captures some top draft picks. Each player autographed 2,575 of his own cards, and just 10,000 sets were produced. The fronts feature a player action photo with a small head shot at the bottom in a gold football frame on top a gold triangle. The player's first name runs along the left side with the last name on the right. The backs carry the player's name, position, school, college statistics, biographical information and career highlights on a background of a one hundred dollar bill. An international version of this set was also issued. These cards are similiar to the original set except they are stamped in silver foil with the word "International" appearing on the card fronts.

COMPLETE SET (R1-10) 1.50 4.00
OVERALL STATED ODDS 1:8
*INTERNATIONAL: .8X TO 2X BASIC INSERTS
*SAMPLES: .4X TO 1X BASIC INSERTS
R1 Kyle Brady .40 1.00
R2 Kevin Carter .40 1.00
R3 Ki-Jana Carter .40 1.00
R4 Luther Elliss .08 .25
R5 Rashaan Salaam .20 .50
R6 Warren Sapp .40 1.00
R7 James A. Stewart .08 .25
R8 J.J. Stokes .40 1.00
R9 Michael Westbrook .40 1.00
R10 Ray Zellars .08 .25

1995 Signature Rookies Franchise Rookies Autographs

R1 Kyle Brady/2575 2.50 6.00
R2 Kevin Carter/2575 2.50 6.00
R3 Ki-Jana Carter/2575 3.00 8.00
R4 Luther Elliss/2575 1.50 4.00
R5 Rashaan Salaam/2575 2.50 6.00
R6 Warren Sapp/1125 6.00 15.00
R7 James A. Stewart/2575 1.50 4.00
R8 J.J. Stokes/2575 2.50 6.00
R9 Michael Westbrook/2575 3.00 8.00
R10 Ray Zellars/2575 1.50 4.00

1995 Signature Rookies International Franchise Duo

Randomly inserted at a ratio of one per every eight packs, this 10-card standard-size set captures one top draft pick on each side of the card. Each player autographed a number of his own cards, The fronts feature a player action photo with a small head shot at the bottom in a silver football frame on top a silver triangle. The word international appears in the silver triangle. The player's first name runs along the left side with the last name on the right. The cards were not numbered.

COMPLETE SET (10) 6.00 15.00
STATED ODDS 1:8 INTERNATIONAL PACKS
1 D.Alexander DE .75 2.00
W.Sapp
2 K.Brady 1.25 3.00
K.Collins
3 Kev.Carter .75 2.00
Ki.Carter
4 Ki.Carter .50 1.25
R.Salaam
5 S.Case 1.00 2.50
R.Johnson
6 K.Collins 2.00 5.00
S.McNair
7 J.A.Stewart 1.25 3.00
J.O.Stewart
8 K.Stewart 1.25 3.00
E.Zeier
9 J.J.Stokes .75 2.00
M.Westbrook
10 S.Williams .30 .75
R.Zellars

1995 Signature Rookies International Franchise Duo Autographs

Randomly inserted into International packs, this 16-card standard-size set captures one top draft pick on each side of the card. Each player signed only one side of the card. The number of cards each player autographed appears below. James A. Stewart and Warren Sapp were the only players featured in this set that did not autograph any cards. The design is identical to that of the regular issue, except for the autograph inscribed across the front and the authentic signature sticker that appears on the opposite side. We've alphabetized the cards for ease in cataloging.

COMPLETE SET (16) 100.00 200.00
INSERTS IN INTERNATIONAL PACKS
1 Derrick Alexander AU/200 2.50 6.00
2 Kyle Brady AU/242 6.00 15.00
3 Kevin Carter AU/315 6.00 15.00
4 Ki-Jana Carter AU/400 4.00 10.00
5 Stoney Case AU/200 4.00 10.00
6 Kerry Collins AU/600 7.50 20.00
7 Rob Johnson AU/309 10.00 25.00
8 Steve McNair AU/300 15.00 40.00
9 Rashaan Salaam AU/299 4.00 10.00
10 Kordell Stewart AU/309 12.50 30.00
11 James O. Stewart AU/200 12.50 30.00
12 J.J. Stokes AU/284 6.00 15.00
13 M. Westbrook AU/282 6.00 15.00
14 Sherman Williams AU/312 2.50 6.00
15 Eric Zeier AU/314 4.00 10.00
16 Ray Zellars AU/310 2.50 6.00

1995 Signature Rookies Masters Of The Mic

Randomly inserted at a ratio of one card per every four packs, this 5-card standard-size set profiles some top sports announcers. Each announcer autographed 1,030 of his own cards, and just 30,000 sets were produced. The fronts feature a picture of the announcer on a photo background with a small head shot on a blue press pass in the right lower corner. The backs carry the same large photo with a short profile on a white background over the picture. The cards are numbered in the top right corner. An International version of this set was also issued. These cards are similiar to the original set except they are stamped in silver foil with the word "International" on the card fronts.

COMPLETE SET (5) 1.25 3.00
STATED ODDS 1:4
STATED PRINT RUN 30,000 SETS
*INTERNATIONALS: .8X TO 2X BASIC CARDS
M1 Todd Christensen .25 .60
M2 Jerry Glanville .25 .60
M3 Howie Long .30 .75
M4 Dick Stockton .25 .60
M5 Joe Theismann UER .30 .75

1995 Signature Rookies Masters Of The Mic Autographs

Randomly inserted at an overall ratio of 1:4 packs, this 5-card standard-size set is the signed parallel version of the basic inserts. Each announcer autographed 1030 of his own cards. The design is identical to that of the regular issue, except for the autograph inscribed across the front.

COMPLETE SET (5) 15.00 30.00
STATED PRINT RUN 1030 SETS
OVERALL STATED ODDS 1:4
M1 Todd Christensen 2.00 5.00
M2 Jerry Glanville 3.00 8.00
M3 Howie Long 12.00 30.00
M4 Dick Stockton 3.00 8.00
M5 Joe Theismann UER 8.00 20.00

1995 Signature Rookies Old Judge Previews

Randomly inserted at a ratio of one per every 24 packs, this 5-card set spotlights collegiate stars. Just 5000 sets were produced, with 515 autographs of each player. The cards measure 2" by 3". Inside white borders, the fronts display a color action cutout on a solid color background. The series name "Old Judge, T-95 Test Issue" is printed across the top, while the player's last name and school appear in the bottom white border. The backs carry biographical and statistical information.

COMPLETE SET (5) 4.00 10.00
OVERALL STATED ODDS 1:24
STATED PRINT RUN 5000 SETS
1 Blake Brockermeyer .50 1.25
2 Kerry Collins 1.50 4.00
3 Steve McNair 2.50 6.00
4 J.J. O'Laughlin .50 1.25
5 John Walsh .50 1.25

1995 Signature Rookies Old Judge Previews Autographs

Randomly inserted at a ratio of one per 24 packs, this 5-card standard-size set was also available in autographed form. Each player autographed 515 of his cards with the serial numbering being hand written on the front. The cardbacks feature a Signature Rookies authentication sticker. A second Steve McNair serial numberd to 500 was released at a later date.

COMPLETE SET (5) 50.00 100.00
STATED PRINT RUN 515 SETS
OVERALL STATED ODDS 1:24
1 Blake Brockermeyer 6.00 15.00
2 Kerry Collins 15.00 40.00
3A Steve McNair/515 25.00 60.00
3B Steve McNair 25.00 60.00
4 J.J. O'Laughlin 6.00 15.00
5 John Walsh 6.00 15.00

1996 Signature Rookies Autobilia

This 55 card standard-size set was issued by Signature Rookies The fronts feature a player photo as well as the words "Autobilia" on the front. The back has vital statistics, seasonal and career information as well as another player photo. Rookies from the 1995 season as well as those for the upcoming 1996 season are featured in this set.

COMPLETE SET (55) 6.00 15.00
1 Ruben Brown .02 .10
2 Kevin Carter .07 .20
3 Ki-Jana Carter .07 .20
4 Stoney Case .02 .10
5 Kerry Collins .25 .60
6 Terrell Davis .50 1.25
7 Antonio Freeman .25 .60
8 Joey Galloway .20 .50
9 Darick Holmes .02 .10
10 Jack Jackson .02 .10
11 Curtis Martin .30 .75
12 O.J. McDuffie .15 .40
13 Steve McNair .30 .75
14 Byron Bam Morris .02 .10
15 Craig Newsome .02 .10
16 Errict Rhett .07 .20
17 Rashaan Salaam .07 .20
18 Frank Sanders .15 .40
19 James O. Stewart .25 .60
20 Kordell Stewart .30 .75
21 J.J. Stokes .15 .40
22 Rodney Thomas .02 .10
23 Tamarick Vanover .07 .20
24 Michael Westbrook .15 .40
25 Sherman Williams .02 .10
26 Eric Zeier .15 .40
27 Karim Abdul-Jabbar .25 .60
28 Mike Alstott .60 1.50
29 Willie Anderson .02 .10
30 Tony Danko .16 .40
31 Marco Battaglia .02 .10
32 Tim Biakabutuka .15 .40
33 Stephen Davis .75 2.00
34 Chris Doering .02 .10
35 Daryl Gardener .02 .10
36 Eddie George 1.00 2.50
37 Terry Glenn .25 .60
38 Randall Godfrey .02 .10
39 Marvin Harrison 1.25 3.00
40 Aaron Hayden .02 .10
41 Mercury Hayes .02 .10
42 Dietrich Jells .07 .20
43 Cedric Jones .02 .10
44 Jeff Lewis .07 .20
45 Derrick Mayes .15 .40
46 Leeland McElroy .07 .20
47 Jerald Moore .02 .10
48 Eric Moulds .60 1.50
49 Kendrick Nord .02 .10
50 Stanley Pritchett .02 .10
51 Jon Stark .02 .10
52 Steve Taneyhill .02 .10
53 Amani Toomer .40 1.00
54 Stepfret Williams .02 .10
55 Checklist .02 .10
P1 Eddie George Promo .30 .75

1996 Signature Rookies Autobilia Club Set Autographs

These cards were released as promos and dealer incentives to carry the Autobilia product. The cards are essentially a parallel to the base set with only a few minor differences. Each is hand numbered of 500 and features the words "Club Set" printed in gold foil at the top of the cardfront.

COMPLETE SET (5) 30.00 80.00
ISSUED VIA MAIL PROMOTION
STATED PRINT RUN 500 SER.#'d SETS
6 Terrell Davis 12.50 30.00
12 O.J. McDuffie 5.00 12.00
32 Tim Biakabutuka 5.00 12.00
36 Eddie George 12.50 30.00
46 Leeland McElroy 5.00 12.00

1995 Signature Rookies Auto-Phonex Bonus Promos

These cards look very similar to the base Auto-Phonex phone cards except for the words "Bonus Promo" under the Signatures Rookies logo on the card fronts. Each was numbered with a BP prefix as well.

BP2 Derrick Alexander DE .30 .75
BP11 Ki-Jana Carter .40 1.00
BP13 Sherman Williams .30 .75
BP16 Rashaan Salaam .40 1.00

1995 Signature Rookies Auto-Phonex Phone Card Promos

There were a number of different promo/sample phone cards issued for the 1995 Signature Rookie Tetrad Auto-Phonex product. We've listed below all known versions, any additions to the list are appreciated.

2 Kevin Carter $25 .40 1.00
3 Ki-Jana Carter $5/1000 .75 2.00
4 Ki-Jana Carter $1000 .80 2.00
5 Rashaan Salaam Promo .40 1.00
6 J.J. Stokes $5 1.20 3.00

1995 Signature Rookies Auto-Phonex

These 40 standard-size cards feature 1995 NFL Draft picks. The fronts feature triple-exposure color action player photos. The player's name in gold-foil letters appears on a marbleized background above the photo, while "1 of 19,000" is printed on the bottom. The horizontal backs carry another color action player photo with biography and stats. Four hundred and ninety-nine 16-box cases of the product were produced. Each pack contained five regular base cards and one calling card worth either $2.00, $5.00, or $25.00 in phone time. Every case of Auto-Phonex contained randomly inserted Hot Packs, which included an autographed phone card and five additional autographed cards.

COMPLETE SET (40) 3.00 6.00
1 Warren Sapp .25 .60
2 Kevin Carter .08 .25
3 Ki-Jana Carter .08 .25
4 J.J.Stokes .08 .25
5 Derrick Alexander DE .01 .05
6 Rashaan Salaam .02 .10
7 Jamal Willis .01 .05
8 Frank Sanders .08 .25
9 Rob Johnson .20 .50
10 Derrick Brooks .08 .25
11 Sherman Williams .01 .05
12 Dave Barr .01 .05
13 Christian Fauria .01 .05
14 Stoney Case .02 .10
15 Rodney Thomas .02 .10
16 James A. Stewart .01 .05
17 Ray Zellars .02 .10
18 Jack Jackson .01 .05
19 Terrell Davis .50 1.25
20 Kyle Brady .08 .25
21 Ruben Brown .08 .25
22 Brent Moss .01 .05
23 John Sacca .01 .05
24 David Dunn .01 .05
25 Eddie Goines .01 .05
26 Curtis Martin .50 1.25
27 Billy Williams .01 .05
28 Steve Stenstrom .01 .05
29 Mark Bruener .01 .05
30 Kelvin Anderson .08 .25
31 Ellis Johnson .01 .05
32 Steve Ingram .01 .05
33 Larry Jones .01 .05
34 Bobby Taylor .08 .25
35 Joe Aska .01 .05
36 Jerrott Willard .01 .05
37 Chris T. Jones .01 .05
38 Mark Birchmeier .01 .05
39 Jimmy Hitchcock .01 .05
40 Tyrone Davis .01 .05
NNO Ki-Jana Carter CL .02 .10
NNO Rashaan Salaam CL .02 .10

1995 Signature Rookies Auto-Phonex Autographs

Every case of Auto-Phonex contained randomly inserted Hot Packs, which included an MCI autographed phone card and five additional autographed cards. By sending in a redemption insert, the collector received one of two 5-card hot packs. The cards are identical in design to their regular issue counterparts except for the signatures. Each card was serial numbered out of 300.

COMPLETE SET (10) 40.00 80.00
FIVE AUTOGRAPHS PER HOT PACK
STATED PRINT RUN 300 SER.#'d SETS
3A Ki-Jana Carter 6.00 15.00
6A Rashaan Salaam 3.00 8.00
8A Frank Sanders 6.00 15.00
11A Sherman Williams 2.50 6.00
12A Dave Barr 2.50 6.00
14A Stoney Case 3.00 8.00
16A James A.Stewart 2.50 6.00
17A Ray Zellars 3.00 8.00
20A Kyle Brady 3.00 8.00
23A John Sacca 2.50 6.00

1995 Signature Rookies Auto-Phonex Phone Cards

COMPLETE SET (40) 4.00 10.00
*SINGLES: .6X TO 1.5X BASE CARD HI
ONE PHONE CARD PER PACK
STATED PRINT RUN 3750 SER.#'d SETS
NNO J.J. Stokes/500 $5 PC 1.50 4.00
NNO Kevin Carter/100 $25 PC 4.00 10.00
NNO Warren Sapp $100
NNO Ki-Jana Carter $1000
NNO Rashaan Salaam $1000

1995 Signature Rookies Auto-Phonex Phone Card Autographs

This set is essentially a parallel to the basic Phone Cards inserts. Each includes an authentic player autograph along with a hand serial number of 3750. Every case of Auto-Phonex contained randomly-inserted Hot Packs, which included one of these Autographed Phone Cards and five additional autographed cards.

COMPLETE SET (40) 60.00 120.00
STATED PRINT RUN 3750 SER.#'d SETS
1 Warren Sapp 6.00 15.00
2 Kevin Carter 4.00 8.00
3 Ki-Jana Carter 4.00 8.00
4 J.J.Stokes 4.00 8.00
5 Derrick Alexander DE 1.25 3.00
6 Rashaan Salaam 2.00 5.00
7 Jamal Willis 1.25 3.00
8 Frank Sanders 4.00 8.00
9 Eric Zeier 2.00 5.00
10 Derrick Brooks 3.00 8.00
11 Sherman Williams 1.25 3.00
12 Dave Barr 1.25 3.00
13 Christian Fauria 1.25 3.00
14 Stoney Case 2.00 5.00
15 Rodney Thomas 2.00 5.00
16 James A. Stewart 1.25 3.00
17 Ray Zellars 2.00 5.00
18 Jack Jackson 1.25 3.00
19 Terrell Davis 10.00 25.00
20 Kyle Brady 4.00 8.00
21 Ruben Brown 4.00 8.00
22 Brent Moss 1.25 3.00
23 John Sacca 1.25 3.00
24 David Dunn 1.25 3.00
25 Eddie Goines 1.25 3.00
26 Curtis Martin 20.00 40.00
27 Billy Williams 1.25 3.00
28 Steve Stenstrom 1.25 3.00
29 Mark Bruener 1.25 3.00
30 Kelvin Anderson 1.25 3.00
31 Ellis Johnson 1.25 3.00
32 Steve Ingram 1.25 3.00
33 Larry Jones 1.25 3.00
34 Bobby Taylor 4.00 8.00
35 Joe Aska 1.25 3.00
36 Jerrott Willard 1.25 3.00
37 Chris T. Jones 1.25 3.00
38 Mark Birchmeier 1.25 3.00
39 Jimmy Hitchcock 1.25 3.00
40 Tyrone Davis 1.25 3.00

1994 Signature Rookies Gold Standard

This multi-sport set consists of 100 standard-size cards. The fronts feature color action players photos with a circular gold foil seal at the upper left corner. The player's name appears on a diagonal black stripe edged by yellow. The horizontal backs carry a narrowly-cropped closeup photo and, on a ghosted panel, biography and player profile. The set is subdivided according to sport as follows: basketball (1-25), football (26-50), baseball (51-75), and hockey (76-100). Each sport is sequenced in alphabetical order.

COMPLETE SET (100) 5.00 12.00
26 Sam Adams .07 .20
27 Trev Alberts .07 .20
28 Derrick Alexander .10 .30
29 Mitch Berger .07 .20
30 Tim Bowens .07 .20
31 Jeff Burris .07 .20
32 Shante Carver .07 .20
33 Lake Dawson .07 .20
34 Marshall Faulk .75 2.00
35 Glenn Foley .07 .20
36 Rob Fredrickson .07 .20
37 Wayne Gandy .07 .20
38 Charles Johnson FB .10 .30
39 Tre Johnson .07 .20
40 Perry Klein .07 .20
41 Antonio Langham .10 .30
42 Eric Mahlum .07 .20
43 Willie McGinest .20 .50
44 Jamir Miller .07 .20
45 Byron Bam Morris .07 .20
46 Errict Rhett .10 .30
47 John Thierry .07 .20
48 Dewayne Washington .08 .25
49 Dan Wilkinson .07 .20
50 Bernard Williams .07 .20

1994 Signature Rookies Gold Standard Facsimile

This 20-card standard-size set was inserted one per pack. The fronts display full-bleed color player photos. A facsimile autograph, the "Gold Standard" seal, and another emblem are gold-foil stamped on the fronts. Also a diagonal line carrying the player's name (also in gold foil) is edged by gold foil stripes. On the left side, the horizontal backs show a narrowly-cropped closeup of the front photo. The remainder of the backs carry biography, statistics, and player profile, all on a ghosted background. In addition to card number, each back carries a serial number.

COMPLETE SET (20) 5.00 12.00
GS1 Marshall Faulk 1.25 3.00
GS2 Josh Booty .20 .50
GS5 Sam Adams .30 .75
GS13 Willie McGinest .40 1.00
GS15 Perry Klein .30 .75
GS17 Dan Wilkinson .30 .75

1994 Signature Rookies Gold Standard HOF

COMPLETE SET (24) 8.00 20.00
STATED PRINT RUN 20,000 SETS
ISSUED VIA MAIL REDEMPTION
HOF9 Otto Graham 1.00 2.50
HOF10 Jack Ham .60 1.50
HOF13 Paul Hornung .75 2.00
HOF14 Sam Huff .60 1.50
HOF16 Bob Lilly .60 1.50
HOF17 Don Maynard .50 1.25
HOF18 Ray Nitschke .75 2.00
HOF21 Y.A.Tittle .75 2.00
HOF23 Paul Warfield .75 2.00
HOF24 Randy White .75 2.00

1994 Signature Rookies Gold Standard HOF Autographs

Inserted at a rate of one per box, this 24-card standard-sized set is identical to the regular set except for the signatures inscribed across the front and the expression "Hall of Fame" gold-foil stamped at the upper left. Each card is numbered out of 2500. The collector could obtain unsigned versions by mailing in a redemption card that was randomly inserted in packs. These redemption cards are valued at 1/10 the value of the signed cards. The cards are numbered with an "HOF" prefix.

9 Otto Graham 20.00 50.00
10 Jack Ham 15.00 30.00
13 Paul Hornung 15.00 40.00
14 Sam Huff 10.00 25.00
16 Bob Lilly 8.00 20.00
17 Don Maynard 6.00 15.00
18 Ray Nitschke 30.00 60.00
21 Y.A.Tittle 15.00 30.00
23 Paul Warfield 10.00 25.00
24 Randy White 10.00 25.00

1994 Signature Rookies Gold Standard Promos

COMPLETE SET (5) .75 2.00
ANNOUNCED PRINT RUN 10000
P3 Willie McGinest .20 .50

1995 Signature Rookies Fame and Fortune

The 1995 Fame and Fortune set was issued in one series totalling 100 cards and featured NBA and NFL draft picks. Cards were distributed in eight-card packs. Five insert card sets were produced with the set and include Collector's Pick, Top 5, Erstad, Star Squad and #1 Pick. The first 48 cards are basketball draft picks and the remaining 52 are football picks. Fronts have full-color action cutout photos with a black background with either a football or basketball. The player's first name is printed in gold foil horizontally while his last name is printed twice vertically in both gold foil and a larger green type on the left side. Backs have another action shot that is seprated with a color screen process. Backs include college statistics, a short biography and a player profile.

COMPLETE SET (100) 5.00 12.00
49 Derrick Alexander DE .07 .20
50 Joe Aska .07 .20
51 Dave Barr .07 .20
52 Tony Boselli .08 .25
53 Kyle Brady .07 .20
54 Derrick Brooks .25 .60
55 Ruben Brown .07 .20
56 Mark Bruener .07 .20
57 Kevin Carter .08 .25
58 Ki-Jana Carter .08 .25
59 Stoney Case .07 .20
60 Kerry Collins .50 1.25
61 Terrell Davis 1.00 2.50
62 Tyrone Davis .07 .20
63 Hugh Douglas .08 .25
64 David Dunn .07 .20
65 Luther Elliss .07 .20
66 Christian Fauria .07 .20
67 Mark Fields .07 .20
68 Joey Galloway .15 .40
69 Eddie Goines .07 .20
70 Jimmy Hitchcock .07 .20
71 Stephen Ingram .07 .20
72 Jack Jackson .07 .20
73 Ellis Johnson .07 .20
74 Chris T. Jones .07 .20
75 Larry Jones .07 .20
76 Mike Mamula .07 .20
77 Curtis Martin .60 1.50
78 Steve McNair .60 1.50
79 Brent Moss .07 .20
80 Craig Newsome .07 .20
81 Tyrone Poole .07 .20
82 Rashaan Salaam .08 .25
83 Frank Sanders .08 .25
84 Warren Sapp .20 .50
85 J.J. Smith .07 .20
86 Steve Stenstrom .07 .20
87 James A. Stewart .07 .20
88 James O. Stewart .20 .50
89 J.J. Stokes .08 .25
90 Bobby Taylor .15 .40
91 Rodney Thomas .08 .25
92 John Walsh .07 .20
93 Michael Westbrook .10 .30
94 Zach Wiegert .07 .20
95 Jerrott Willard .07 .20
96 Billy Williams .07 .20
97 Sherman Williams .07 .20
98 Jamal Willis .07 .20
99 Eric Zeier .08 .25
100 Ray Zellars .08 .25

1995 Signature Rookies Fame and Fortune #1 Pick

Randomly inserted in packs at a rate of three in 16, this five-card set features the No. 1 pick in the NHL, the NFL, The NBA and Major leagues. The No. 5 card pictures all four of the picks. Fronts have a psychedelic background and feature the player in a full-color action cutout. "#1 Pick" appears in a sky blue and green type at the top and the bottom has a gold foil strip that contains the player's name, or names in the case of the #5 card, in raised white letters. Backs continue with the psychedelic background and picture the player or players in action. Player stats and biographies also appear on the back

COMPLETE SET (5) 1.00 2.50
P2 Ki-Jana Carter .20 .50
P5 Borard .30 .75
Carter
Erstad
J.Smith

1995 Signature Rookies Fame and Fortune Collectors Pick

Randomly inserted in packs at a rate of one in 16, this 10-card set highlights the first five NBA picks and the first five NFL picks. Fronts are borderless with white backgrounds with "Collectors" on the top third and "Pick" in a vertically stretched type on the rest of the front. The player is pictured in a full-color action cutout in the foreground. His name is printed vertically in gold foil on the lower left. Backs have a small player head shot, and a faded screen action shot for a background. Player biography, statistics and profile appear on the back.

COMPLETE SET (100) 4.00 10.00
B1 Kerry Collins 1.00 2.50
B5 Rashaan Salaam .30 .75
B6 Warren Sapp .60 1.50
B9 J.J. Stokes .30 .75

1995 Signature Rookies Fame and Fortune Darin Erstad

Randomly inserted in packs at a rate of one in 4, this 5-card set highlights the college career of baseball's #1 draft pick. Borderless fronts have a full-color action shot of Erstad in his Nebraska uniform with "Erstad" printed in varying type sizes in the background. Erstad is also printed in gold foil vertically on the left side. The backs have a cropped action photo of Erstad at an angle with a white background for the rest of the back. Stats and biography appear on the back along with a short profile.

COMMON CARD .75 2.00

1995 Signature Rookies Fame and Fortune Red Hot Rookies

This 10-card set randomly inserted in packs of 1995 Signature Rookies Fame and Fortune. Each card was printed on red foil stock and include a photo of one football or basketball draft pick from 1995.

COMPLTE SET (10) 5.00 12.00
R1 Curtis Martin 1.25 3.00
R3 Terrell Davis 1.50 4.00
R5 Joey Galloway .40 1.00
R7 Rashaan Salaam .20 .50
R9 Kerry Collins .60 1.50

1995 Signature Rookies Fame and Fortune Star Squad

Randomly inserted in packs at a rate of one in four, this five-card set salutes the star picks of the major sports. Fronts have blue backgrounds and full-folor action player cutouts. "Star Squad is printed vertically in light blue with a pink shadow on the left side. The player's name is printed in gold foil at the bottom. Backs have a blue-screened color action photo that serves as a background for a biography, stats and college statistics. A small full-color vertical player photo appears on the lower left of the back.

COMPLETE SET (5) 1.50 4.00
S1 Ki-Jana Carter .20 .50
S2 Kerry Collins .40 1.00
S3 Steve McNair 1.00 2.50
S4 J.J. Stokes .20 .50
S5 Eric Zeier .20 .50

1995 Signature Rookies Peripheral Vision

Randomly inserted at a ratio of one per every 24 packs, this 5-card standard-size set spotlights two outstanding running backs. Each card was numbered of 5000 cards made. Each player signed 100 of his own cards. The set consists of two Salaam cards, two Carter cards, and a Head-to-Head card featuring both players. One hundred Head-to-Head cards bear signatures by both players. An International version of this set was also issued. These cards are similiar to the original set except they are stamped in silver foil with the word "International" appearing on the card fronts.

COMPLETE SET (5) 1.50 3.00
STATED PRINT RUN 5000 SETS
OVERALL STATED ODDS 1:24
*INTERNATIONAL: .8X TO 2X BASIC INSERTS
*SAMPLES: .4X TO 1X BASIC INSERTS
V1 Rashaan Salaam .30 .75
V2 Rashaan Salaam .30 .75
V3 Ki-Jana Carter .30 .75
V4 Ki-Jana Carter .30 .75
V5 K.Carter .30 .75
R.Salaam

1995 Signature Rookies Peripheral Vision Autographs

Randomly inserted at a ratio of one per every 24 packs, this 5-card standard-size set was available in autographed form. The design is identical to that of the regular issue, except for the autograph inscribed across the front. Approximately 105 of each autograph exist.

COMPLETE SET (5) 100.00 200.00
OVERALL STATED ODDS 1:24
STATED PRINT RUN 105 SETS
V1 Rashaan Salaam 15.00 40.00
V2 Rashaan Salaam 15.00 40.00
V3 Ki-Jana Carter 15.00 40.00
V4 Ki-Jana Carter 15.00 40.00
V5 K.Carter 25.00 60.00
R.Salaam

1995 Signature Rookies Signature Prime Previews

Randomly inserted in Basketball Autobilia packs, this five-card standard-size set features color player action shots on the fronts. These photos are borderless and carries the player's name in gold lettering in a red stripe that appears on the left side of the card. The red stripe starts with the Signature Prime logo and ends with the Signature Rookies logo. The back carries an additional photograph of the player, his position and college stats.

COMPLETE SET (5) 5.00 8.00
1 Ki-Jana Carter .50 1.25
2 Kyle Brady .30 .75
3 J.J. Stokes .75 2.00
4 Rashaan Salaam .50 1.25
5 Steve McNair 1.25 5.00

1995 Signature Rookies Signature Prime

This 50-card standard-size set features color player action shots on the fronts. Each player autographed 3,000 of his own cards. These photos are borderless and carries the player's name in gold lettering in a red stripe that appears on the left side of the card. The red stripe starts with the Signature Prime logo and ends with the Signature Rookies logo. The back carries an additional photograph of the player, his position and college stats.

COMPLETE SET (50) 5.00 12.00
1 Justin Armour .05 .15
2 Joe Aska .05 .15
3 Henry Bailey .05 .15
4 Jay Barker .05 .15
5 Dave Barr .05 .15
6 Kevin Bouie .05 .15
7 Mark Bruener .08 .25
8 Stoney Case .08 .25
9 Curtis Ceaser .05 .15
10 Todd Collins QB .60 1.50
11 Jerry Colquitt .05 .15
12 Terrell Davis 1.00 2.50
13 David Dunn .05 .15
14 Omar Ellison .05 .15
15 Christian Fauria .05 .15
16 Antonio Freeman .50 1.25
17 Eddie Goines .05 .15
18 Aaron Hayden .05 .15
19 William Henderson .15 .40
20 Kevin Hickman .05 .15
21 Jack Jackson .05 .15
22 Travis Jervey .05 .15
23 Rob Johnson .40 1.00
24 Chris T. Jones .08 .25
25 Larry Jones .05 .15
26 Curtis Marsh .05 .15
27 Curtis Martin 1.00 2.50
28 Fred McCrary .05 .15
29 Mike Miller .05 .15
30 Shannon Myers .05 .15
31 Jimmy Oliver .05 .15
32 Dino Philyaw .05 .15
33 Lovell Pinkney .05 .15
34 Michael Roan .05 .15
35 Chris Sanders .15 .40
36 Frank Sanders .15 .40
37 Cory Schlesinger .08 .25
38 Charlie Simmons .05 .15
39 David Sloan .05 .15
40 Steve Stenstrom .05 .15
41 James A. Stewart .05 .15
42 Rodney Thomas .08 .25
43 A.C. Tellison .05 .15
44 Tamarick Vanover .08 .25
45 John Walsh .05 .15
46 Kendell Watkins .05 .15
47 Charles Way .08 .25
48 Craig Whelihan .08 .25
49 Eric Zeier .15 .40
50 Ray Zellars .08 .25
NNO Checklist Card .05 .15
P1 J.J. Stokes Promo .20 .50

1995 Signature Rookies Signature Prime Autographs

This 50-card standard-size set features color player action shots on the fronts. Each player autographed 3,000 of his own cards. These autographed cards were inserted at a rate of one per pack and were sealed in a protective holder. The design is identical to that of the regular issue, except for the autograph, the words authentic signature and the numbering appearing in an outlined gold foil football in the bottom right hand corner on the front of the card.

STATED PRINT RUN 3000 SER.#'d SETS
ONE AUTOGRAPH PER PACK
1 Justin Armour 2.50 6.00
2 Joe Aska 1.50 4.00
3 Henry Bailey 1.50 4.00
4 Jay Barker 1.50 4.00
5 Dave Barr 1.50 4.00
6 Kevin Bouie 1.50 4.00

7 Mark Bruener 2.50 6.00
8 Stoney Case 2.50 6.00
9 Curtis Ceaser 1.50 4.00
10 Todd Collins QB 5.00 12.00
11 Jerry Colquitt 1.50 4.00
12 Terrell Davis 10.00 25.00
13 David Dunn 1.50 4.00
14 Omar Ellison 1.50 4.00
15 Christian Fauria 4.00 10.00
16 Antonio Freeman 6.00 15.00
17 Eddie Goines 1.50 4.00
18 Aaron Hayden 2.50 6.00
19 William Henderson 7.50 20.00
20 Kevin Hickman 1.50 4.00
21 Jack Jackson 1.50 4.00
22 Travis Jervey 1.50 4.00
23 Rob Johnson 5.00 12.00
24 Chris T. Jones 1.50 4.00
25 Larry Jones 1.50 4.00
26 Curtis Marsh 1.50 4.00
27 Curtis Martin 6.00 15.00
28 Fred McCrary 1.50 4.00
29 Mike Miller 1.50 4.00
30 Shannon Myers 1.50 4.00
31 Jimmy Oliver 1.50 4.00
32 Dino Philyaw 1.50 4.00
33 Lovell Pinkney 1.50 4.00
34 Michael Roan 1.50 4.00
35 Chris Sanders 2.50 6.00
36 Frank Sanders 4.00 10.00
37 Cory Schlesinger 4.00 10.00
38 Charlie Simmons 1.50 4.00
39 David Sloan 1.50 4.00
40 Steve Stenstrom 2.50 6.00
41 James A. Stewart 1.50 4.00
42 Rodney Thomas 2.50 6.00
43 A.C. Tellison 1.50 4.00
44 Tamarick Vanover 2.50 6.00
45 John Walsh 1.50 4.00
46 Kendell Watkins 1.50 4.00
47 Charles Way 2.50 6.00
48 Craig Whelihan 2.50 6.00
49 Eric Zeier 4.00 10.00
50 Ray Zellars 1.50 4.00

1995 Signature Rookies Signature Prime TD Club

This 10-card set was inserted at a rate of one per pack. Each player autographed 1000 cards of the 15,000 cards produced. A photo of the player appears on the right side of the card front with a silver foil background. The player's name appears on the left side of the card with a green/blue background with the Signature Prime and TD Club logos.

COMPLETE SET (10) 3.00 8.00
ONE PER PACK
OVERALL PRINT RUN 15,000 SETS
*PREVIEWS: .4X TO 1X BASIC INSERTS
T1 Kyle Brady .20 .50
T2 Ki-Jana Carter .20 .50
T3 Kerry Collins .60 1.50
T4 Joey Galloway .50 1.25
T5 Steve McNair 1.00 2.50
T6 Rashaan Salaam .05 .15
T7 James O. Stewart .60 1.50
T8 J.J. Stokes .20 .50
T9 Michael Westbrook .20 .50
T10 Sherman Williams .05 .15

1995 Signature Rookies Signature Prime TD Club Autographs

This 10-card signature set was randomly inserted in packs. Each player autographed 1,000 of his own cards of the 15,000 cards produced. Each autograph came sealed in a protective holder. The design is identical to that of the regular issue, except for the autograph and numbering on the front.

COMPLETE SET (10) 60.00 120.00
STATED PRINT RUN 1050
T1 Kyle Brady 4.00 10.00
T2 Ki-Jana Carter 5.00 12.00
T3 Kerry Collins 8.00 20.00
T4 Joey Galloway 6.00 15.00
T5 Steve McNair 10.00 25.00
T6 Rashaan Salaam 4.00 10.00
T7 James O. Stewart 5.00 12.00
T8 J.J. Stokes 4.00 10.00
T9 Michael Westbrook 5.00 12.00
T10 Sherman Williams 3.00 8.00

1995 Signature Rookies Club Promos

S1 Josh Booty .40 1.00
S2 Ki-Jana Carter .50 1.25

1995 Signature Rookies Sports Slammers Stackers

Printed on 18-point card stock, this set of 40 stackers and 5 slammers POGs combines football and basketball stars in a game. Each pack contained five sports stackers as well as one rule card.

1 Dave Barr FB .15 .40
2 Charlie Garner FB .20 .50
4 James A. Stewart FB .15 .40
5 Gus Frerotte FB .30 .75
6 Michael Westbrook FB .20 .50
7 Ki-Jana Carter FB .20 .50
10 Tim Bowens FB .15 .40
11 Kevin Carter FB .15 .40
13 Rashaan Salaam FB .30 .75
14 Byron Bam Morris FB .15 .40
15 Sherman Williams FB .15 .40
16 Warren Sapp FB .60 1.50
17 Kyle Brady FB .20 .50
18 William Floyd FB .20 .50
19 Rodney Thomas FB .20 .50
21 Tim Bowens FB .15 .40
22 Sherman Williams FB .15 .40
23 Gus Frerotte FB .30 .75
25 Kyle Brady FB .20 .50
26 James A. Stewart FB .15 .40
29 William Floyd FB .20 .50
30 Michael Westbrook FB .20 .50
32 Dave Barr FB .15 .40
33 Byron Bam Morris FB .15 .40
34 Charlie Garner FB .20 .50
35 Kevin Carter FB .15 .40
37 Rodney Thomas FB .20 .50
38 Ki-Jana Carter FB .30 .75
39 Warren Sapp FB .60 1.50
40 Rashaan Salaam FB .30 .75
S1 Warren Sapp FB .75 2.00
Squasher
S2 Kyle Brady FB .30 .75
Bruiser
S4 Byron Bam Morris FB .30 .75
Bammer

1996 Signature Rookies Super Stars

COMPLETE SET (6) 3.00 8.00
SS2 Ki-Jana Carter FB .75 2.00

1994 Signature Rookies Tetrad

These 120 standard-size cards feature borderless color player action shots on their fronts. The player's name appears in gold-foil lettering near the bottom. The words "1 of 45,000" appear in vertical gold-foil lettering within a simulated marble column near the left edge. The cards of this four-sport set are numbered on the back in Roman numerals and organized as follows: Football (1-40), Basketball (41-83), Baseball (84-103), and Hockey (104-118).

COMPLETE SET (120) 3.00 8.00
1 Jay Walker .07 .20
2 Ricky Brady .07 .20
3 Paul Duckworth .07 .20
4 Jim Flanigan .07 .20
5 Brice Abrams .07 .20
6 William Floyd .10 .30
7 Charlie Garner .20 .50
8 Pete Bercich .07 .20
9 Frank Harvey .07 .20
10 Willie Clark .07 .20
11 Bernard Williams .07 .20
12 Kurt Haws .07 .20
13 Dennis Collier .07 .20
14 Filmel Johnson .07 .20
15 Zane Beehn .07 .20
16 Johnnie Morton .20 .50
17 Lonnie Johnson .07 .20
18 Jay Kearney .07 .20
19 Steve Shine .07 .20
20 Dexter Nottage .07 .20
21 Ervin Collier .07 .20
22 Dorsey Levens .20 .50
23 Kevin Knox .07 .20
24 Doug Nussmeier .07 .20
25 Bill Schroeder .20 .50
26 Winfred Tubbs .07 .20
27 Rodney Harrison .07 .20
28 Rob Waldrop .07 .20
29 Mike Davis .07 .20
30 John Burke .07 .20
31 Allen Aldridge .07 .20
32 Kevin Mitchell .07 .20
33 Greg Hill .10 .30
34 Ernest Jones .07 .20
35 Kevin Mawae .10 .30
36 John Covington .07 .20
37 Mike Wells .07 .20
38 Thomas Lewis .07 .20
39 Chad Bratzke .07 .20
40 Darren Studstill .07 .20

1994 Signature Rookies Tetrad Autographs

Inserted one card (or trade coupon) per pack, these 117 standard-size autographed cards comprise a parallel set to the regular '94 Tetrad set. Aside from the autographs and each card's numbering out of 7,750 produced, they are identical in design to their regular issue counterparts. The cards of this four-sport set are numbered on the back in Roman numerals and organized as follows: Football (1-40), Basketball (41-83), Baseball (84-103), and Hockey (104-118). Bernard Williams (card number 11) did not sign his cards.

1 Jay Walker 1.50 4.00
2 Ricky Brady 1.50 4.00
3 Paul Duckworth 1.50 4.00
4 Jim Flanigan 1.50 4.00
5 Brice Abrams 1.50 4.00
6 William Floyd 2.50 6.00
7 Charlie Garner 3.00 8.00
8 Pete Bercich 1.50 4.00
9 Frank Harvey 1.50 4.00
10 Willie Clark 1.50 4.00
12 Kurt Haws 1.50 4.00
13 Dennis Collier 1.50 4.00
14 Filmel Johnson 1.50 4.00
15 Zane Beehn 1.50 4.00
16 Johnnie Morton 3.00 8.00
17 Lonnie Johnson 1.50 4.00
18 Jay Kearney 1.50 4.00
19 Steve Shine 1.50 4.00
20 Dexter Nottage 1.50 4.00
21 Ervin Collier 1.50 4.00
22 Dorsey Levens 3.00 8.00
23 Kevin Knox 1.50 4.00
24 Doug Nussmeier 1.50 4.00
25 Bill Schroeder 4.00 10.00
26 Winfred Tubbs 1.50 4.00
27 Rodney Harrison 6.00 15.00
28 Rob Waldrop 1.50 4.00
29 Mike Davis 1.50 4.00
30 John Burke 1.50 4.00
31 Allen Aldridge 2.00 5.00
32 Kevin Mitchell 1.50 4.00
33 Greg Hill 2.50 6.00
34 Ernest Jones 1.50 4.00
35 Kevin Mawae 2.50 6.00
36 John Covington 1.50 4.00
37 Mike Wells 1.50 4.00
38 Thomas Lewis 1.50 4.00
39 Chad Bratzke 1.50 4.00
40 Darren Studstill 1.50 4.00

1994 Signature Rookies Tetrad Flip Cards

Randomly inserted in packs, these five standard-size two-player cards feature a borderless color action shot of one player per side. The player's name appears in gold-foil lettering near the bottom. The words "1 of 7,500" appear in vertical gold-foil lettering within a simulated marble column near the left edge. The cards are numbered on both sides.

COMPLETE SET (5) 10.00 25.00
1 Charles Johnson BB 1.25 3.00
Charles Johnson FB
2 Tony Dorsett 3.00 8.00
Gale Sayers
3 Charlie Ward BK 2.00 5.00
Charlie Ward FB

1994 Signature Rookies Tetrad Flip Cards Autographs

Randomly inserted in packs, this three-card set features two-player cards with a borderless color action shot of one player per side. The player's name appears in gold-foil lettering near the bottom. Each card is autographed. The cards are numbered on both sides.

AU1 Charles Johnson BB/275 2.00 5.00
AU3 Charlie Ward FB/BK/275 6.00 15.00

1994 Signature Rookies Tetrad Previews

Randomly inserted in Signature Rookies Football packs, these seven standard-size cards feature borderless color player action shots on their fronts. The player's name and position appear in gold-foil lettering near the bottom. The words "Promo, 1 of 10,000" appear in vertical gold-foil lettering within a simulated marble column near the left edge. On a ghosted background drawing of a Greek temple, the back carries the player's name, position, team, height and weight, and career highlights. The cards of this multisport set are numbered on the back with a "T" prefix.

COMPLETE SET (7) 1.25 3.00
T6 O.J. Simpson .60 1.50

1994 Signature Rookies Tetrad Titans

Randomly inserted in packs, these 12 standard-size cards feature borderless color player action shots on their fronts. The player's name appears in gold-foil lettering near the bottom. The words "1 of 10,000" appear in vertical gold-foil lettering within a simulated marble column near the left edge. On a ghosted background drawing of a Greek temple, the back carries the player's name, position, team, height and weight, and career highlights. The cards of this multisport set are numbered on the back in Roman numerals.

COMPLETE SET (12) 3.00 8.00
129 O.J.Simpson UER T6 .40 1.00

1994 Signature Rookies Tetrad Titans Autographs

Randomly inserted in packs, these 12 standard-size autographed cards comprise a parallel set to the regular 1994 Tetrad Titans set. Aside from the autographs (some cards issued as redemptions in packs) and each card's numbering out of 1,050 produced (except the 2,500 signed O.J. cards), they are identical in design to their regular issue counterparts. The cards of this multisport set are numbered on the back in Roman numerals.

COMPLETE SET (12) 125.00 250.00
129 O.J.Simpson/2500 20.00 50.00

1994 Signature Rookies Tetrad Top Prospects

Randomly inserted in packs, these four standard-size cards feature borderless color player action shots on their fronts. The player's name appears in gold-foil lettering near the bottom. The words "1 of 20,000" appear in vertical gold-foil lettering within a simulated marble column near the left edge. On a ghosted background drawing of a Greek temple, the back carries the player's name, biography, statistics, and career highlights. The cards of this multisport set are numbered on the back in Roman numerals.

COMPLETE SET (4) 1.00 2.50
132 Willie McGinest .30 .75
133 Shante Carver .20 .50

1994 Signature Rookies Tetrad Top Prospects Autographs

This four-card standard size set was randomly inserted in packs. The fronts feature borderless color player action shots with the player's name in gold-foil lettering near the bottom. The cards are autographed on the fronts. The backs carry the player's name, biography, statistics, and career highlights on a ghosted background drawing of a Greek temple. The cards are numbered on the back in Roman numerals. Other than Shante Carver, the cards are numbered out of 2,000.

132A Willie McGinest 4.00 10.00
133A Shante Carver/2025 2.00 5.00

1995 Signature Rookies Tetrad

This 76-card standard-size set features borderless fronts with color action player photos. The named player stands out on a faded background with his name printed in gold below. The backs carry an elongated color action player photo on one side while a head photo, biographical information, position, college, and career statistics round out the backs.

COMPLETE SET (76) 5.00 12.00
1 Kevin Carter .15 .40
2 Ruben Brown .08 .25
3 Kyle Brady .07 .20
4 Tony Boselli .08 .25
5 Derrick Alexander .05 .15
6 Mike Mamula .05 .15
7 Ellis Johnson .05 .15
8 Mark Fields .08 .25
9 Luther Elliss .05 .15
10 Hugh Douglas .05 .15
51 James O. Stewart .40 1.00
52 Rashaan Salaam .08 .25
53 Tyrone Poole .15 .40
54 Craig Newsome .05 .15
55 Devin Bush .05 .15
P3 Kyle Brady Promo .30 .75

1995 Signature Rookies Tetrad Autographs

SIGS NUMBERED OUT OF 5000
1 Kevin Carter 1.50 4.00
2 Ruben Brown 1.25 3.00
3 Kyle Brady 1.50 4.00
4 Tony Boselli 2.50 6.00
5 Derrick Alexander 1.50 4.00
6 Mike Mamula 1.25 3.00
7 Ellis Johnson 1.25 3.00
8 Mark Fields 1.25 3.00
9 Luther Ellis 1.25 3.00
10 Hugh Douglas 1.50 4.00
51 James O. Stewart 3.00 8.00
52 Rashaan Salaam 1.50 4.00
53 Tyrone Poole 2.00 5.00
54 Craig Newsome 1.25 3.00
55 Devin Bush 1.25 3.00

1995 Signature Rookies Tetrad Mail-In

This five-card standard size set was available through the mail from Signature Rookies. The set highlights the 1995 first overall draft picks in basketball, football, baseball and hockey. The fronts picture color action photos blended with a fractal-swirling design. In a gold foil stamp, the players name is found vertically on the right, "Mail In" and "#1 Pick" adorn the top and bottom respectively on the left. The back has another color action photo in the upper-right corner. The rest is devoted to a player biography and statistics set on top of the same fractal-swirling design. The cards are numbered with a "P" prefix (P1-P5).

COMPLETE SET (5) 1.50 4.00
P2 Ki-Jana Carter .40 1.00
P5 Joe Smith .60 1.50
Ki-Jana Carter
Darin Erstad
Bryan Berard

1995 Signature Rookies Tetrad Previews

This five-card standard-size set was randomly inserted in SR BK autobilia packs. The fronts display borderless color action player photos. The named player stands out on a faded background with his name printed in gold below. The backs carry an elongated color action player photo on one side while a head photo, biographical information, position, college, and career statistics round out the backs.

COMPLETE SET (5) 1.00 2.50
5 Ki-Jana Carter .20 .50

1995 Signature Rookies Tetrad SR Force

This 35-card standard-size set features color action player photos on the front on a white background. Pictures of one foot, the head, and one arm are set out as separate photos on the side of the main picture. The words, "SR Force," are printed in the white border at the top, while the player's name is in gold at the bottom of the picture. The backs carry the same photo as a faded background with photos of the head and parts of one leg. The player's name, position, team, biographical information, and statistics round out the back. The cards are numbered with an "F" prefix.

COMPLETE SET (35) 6.00 15.00
F26 Ki-Jana Carter .15 .40
F27 Joey Galloway .20 .50
F28 Michael Westbrook .15 .40
F29 J.J. Stokes .20 .50
F30 Eric Zeier .10 .30
F31 Errict Rhett .15 .40
F32 Steve McNair .75 2.00
F33 Kerry Collins .20 .50
F34 Stoney Case .10 .30
F35 Mark Bruener .10 .30

1995 Signature Rookies Tetrad SR Force Autographs

RANDOM INSERTS IN PACKS
F26 Ki-Jana Carter 1.50 4.00
F27 Joey Galloway 4.00 10.00
F28 Michael Westbrook 2.00 5.00
F29 J.J. Stokes 1.50 4.00
F30 Eric Zeier 1.25 3.00
F31 Errict Rhett 1.50 4.00
F32 Steve McNair 10.00 25.00
F33 Kerry Collins 6.00 15.00
F34 Stoney Case 1.25 3.00
F35 Mark Bruener 1.25 3.00

1995 Signature Rookies Tetrad Titans

This five card standard-size set features borderless fronts with color player action photos on a black background. The player's name is printed at the top with the card name in gold running vertically down the side. The horizontal backs carry another player action photo on a black background with the player's name and a short personal and career summary. The player's position and team round out the back. The cards are numbered with an "T" prefix.

COMPLETE SET (5) 2.00 6.00
T5 Bob Griese .60 1.60

1995 Signature Rookies Tetrad Titans Autographs

T5 Bob Griese 10.00 25.00

1995 Signature Rookies Tetrad Autobilia

The 1995 Signature Rookies Tetrad Autobilia set was issued in one series with a total of 100 cards. The fronts feature a color action player cut-out on a background of a repeated action player photo with the player's name printed in a gold bar at the bottom. The words" Club Set" are printed in gold foil on the fronts as well. The backs carry two player photos with the player's name, position, biographical information, career statistics, and a player fact.

COMPLETE SET (100) 10.00 25.00
*SILVER: .4X TO 1X GOLD
55 Dave Barr .08 .25
56 Brandon Bennett .08 .25
57 Kyle Brady .10 .30
58 Kevin Carter .30 .75
59 Terrell Davis 1.25 3.00
60 Luther Ellis .08 .25
61 Jack Jackson .08 .25
62 Frank Sanders .15 .40
63 Ki-Jana Carter .15 .40
64 Steve Stenstrom .08 .25
65 James A. Stewart .08 .25
66 James O. Stewart .40 1.00
67 Bobby Taylor .15 .40
68 Michael Westbrook .15 .40
69 Rashaan Salaam .15 .40
70 Ray Zellars .08 .25
75 J.J. Stokes .15 .40
76 Sherman Williams .08 .25
80 Kerry Collins .50 1.25
81 Joey Galloway .30 .75
82 Steve McNair .60 1.50
83 Errict Rhett .10 .30
84 Eric Zeier .10 .30

1995 Signature Rookies Tetrad Autobilia Auto-Phonex Test

This 3-card set was issued in packs of 1995 Signature Rookies Autobilia packs. Each card follows a similar design to the base cards except for the addition of the words 'Auto-Phonex Test Issue' on the left hand side of the cardfronts. The title 'Autobilia' at the top was also replaced with the word Tetrad.

COMPLETE SET (3) 1.25 3.00
T2 Ki-Jana Carter .40 1.00

1995 Signature Rookies Tetrad Autobilia Autographed Cards

55 Dave Barr 1.25 3.00
56 Brandon Bennett 1.25 3.00
57 Kyle Brady 1.50 4.00
58 Kevin Carter 2.50 6.00
59 Terrell Davis 12.00 30.00
60 Luther Ellis 1.25 3.00
61 Jack Jackson 1.25 3.00
62 Frank Sanders 1.25 3.00
63 Ki-Jana Carter 2.00 5.00
64 Steve Stenstrom 1.25 3.00
65 James A. Stewart 1.25 3.00
66 James O. Stewart 4.00 10.00
67 Bobby Taylor 2.50 6.00
68 Michael Westbrook 2.50 6.00
69 Rashaan Salaam 2.00 5.00
70 Ray Zellars 1.25 3.00
75 J.J. Stokes 1.50 4.00
76 Sherman Williams 1.50 4.00
80 Kerry Collins 6.00 15.00
81 Joey Galloway 4.00 10.00
82 Steve McNair 10.00 25.00
83 Errict Rhett 1.50 4.00
84 Eric Zeier 1.50 4.00

1995 Signature Rookies Tetrad Autobilia Autographed Photos

ANNOUNCED PRINT RUN 3000
55 Dave Barr 1.25 3.00
56 Brandon Bennett 1.25 3.00
57 Kyle Brady 1.50 4.00
58 Kevin Carter 2.50 6.00
59 Terrell Davis 12.00 30.00
60 Luther Ellis 1.25 3.00
61 Jack Jackson 1.25 3.00
62 Frank Sanders 1.25 3.00
63 Ki-Jana Carter 2.00 5.00
64 Steve Stenstrom 1.25 3.00
65 James A. Stewart 1.25 3.00
66 James O. Stewart 4.00 10.00
67 Bobby Taylor 2.50 6.00
68 Michael Westbrook 2.50 6.00
69 Rashaan Salaam 2.00 5.00
70 Ray Zellars 1.25 3.00
75 J.J. Stokes 1.50 4.00
76 Sherman Williams 1.50 4.00
80 Kerry Collins 6.00 15.00
81 Joey Galloway 4.00 10.00
82 Steve McNair 10.00 25.00
83 Errict Rhett 1.50 4.00
84 Eric Zeier 1.50 4.00

1991 Star Pics Promos

These promo cards measure the standard size and preview the 1991 Star Pics football set. The cards were distributed in two-card panels with Aaron Craver paired with Mark Carrier and Dan McGwire paired with Eric Turner. These promos were quite plentiful because they were also bound into the Pro Football Weekly annual football preview publication.

COMPLETE SET (4) .80 2.00
1 Mark Carrier DB .20 .50
2 Aaron Craver .20 .50
3 Dan McGwire .20 .50
4 Eric Turner .20 .50

1991 Star Pics

This 112-card standard-size set features on the front an action color photo enclosed by a thin white border against a background of footballs. The player's name appears in white print on a maroon-colored box below the picture. The back has a full-color posed photo in the upper left hand corner and the card number (enclosed in a red star) in the upper right hand corner. The biographical information, including accomplishments, strengths, and weaknesses, is printed on a pale green diagram of a football field with a diagrammed play. The set also includes player agents and flashback cards of top young players. Autographed cards were inserted in some of the sets on a random basis. The key players in this set are Brett Favre, Herman Moore, and Ricky Watters.

COMP.FACT.SET (113) 3.00 8.00
1 1991 NFL Draft Overview .01 .05
2 Barry Sanders FLB .40 1.00
3 Nick Bell .01 .05
4 Kelvin Pritchett .01 .05
5 Huey Richardson .01 .05
6 Mike Croel .01 .05
7 Paul Justin .02 .10
8 Ivory Lee Brown .01 .05
9 Herman Moore .08 .25
10 Derrick Thomas FLB .08 .25
11 Keith Traylor .01 .05
12 Joe Johnson .01 .05
13 Dan McGwire .01 .05
14 Harvey Williams .02 .10
15 Eric Moten .01 .05
16 Steve Zucker .01 .05
17 Randal Hill .01 .05
18 Browning Nagle .01 .05
19 Stan Thomas .01 .05
20 Emmitt Smith FLB .75 2.00
21 Ted Washington .01 .05
22 Lamar Rogers .01 .05
23 Kenny Walker .01 .05
24 Howard Griffith .01 .05
25 Reggie Johnson .01 .05
26 Lawrence Dawsey .01 .05
27 Joe Garten .01 .05
28 Moe Gardner .01 .05
29 Michael Stonebreaker RC .01 .05
30 Jeff George FLB .02 .10
31 Leigh Steinberg .01 .05
32 John Flannery .01 .05
33 Pat Harlow .01 .05
34 Kanavis McGhee .01 .05
35 Mike Dumas .01 .05
36 Godfrey Myles .01 .05
37 Shawn Moore .01 .05
38 Jeff Graham .02 .10
39 Ricky Watters .25 .60
40 Andre Ware .02 .10
41 Henry Jones .01 .05
42 Eric Turner .01 .05
43 Bob Woolf .01 .05
44 Randy Baldwin .01 .05
45 Mo Lewis .01 .05
46 Jerry Evans .01 .05
47 Derek Russell .01 .05
48 Merton Hanks .02 .10
49 Kevin Donnalley .01 .05
50 Troy Aikman FLB .30 .75
51 William Thomas .02 .10
52 Chris Thome .01 .05
53 Ricky Ervins .01 .05
54 Jake Reed .08 .25
55 Jerome Henderson .01 .05
56 Mark Vander Poel .01 .05
57 Bernard Ellison .01 .05
58 Jack Mills .01 .05
59 Jarrod Bunch .01 .05
60 Mark Carrier DB .01 .05
61 Rocen Keeton .01 .05
62 Louis Riddick .01 .05
63 Bobby Wilson .01 .05
64 Steve Jackson .01 .05
65 Brett Favre 1.25 3.00
66 Ernie Mills .02 .10
67 Joe Valerio .01 .05
68 Chris Smith .01 .05
69 Ralph Cindrich .01 .05
70 Christian Okoye .02 .10
71 Charles McRae .01 .05
72 Jon Vaughn .01 .05
73 Eric Swann .02 .10
74 Bill Musgrave .01 .05
75 Eric Bieniemy .01 .05
76 Pat Tyrance .01 .05
77 Vinnie Clark .01 .05
78 Eugene Williams .01 .05
79 Rob Carpenter .01 .05
80 Deion Sanders FLB .08 .25
81 Roman Phifer .01 .05
82 Greg Lewis .01 .05
83 John Johnson .01 .05
84 Richard Howell .01 .05
85 Jesse Campbell .01 .05
86 Stanley Richard .01 .05
87 Alfred Williams .01 .05
88 Mike Pritchard .02 .10
89 Mel Agee .01 .05
90 Aaron Craver .01 .05
91 Tim Barnett .01 .05
92 Wesley Carroll .02 .10
93 Kevin Scott .01 .05
94 Darren Lewis .01 .05
95 Tim Bruton .01 .05
96 Tim James .01 .05
97 Darryll Lewis .01 .05
98 Shawn Jefferson .08 .25
99 Mitch Donahue .01 .05
100 Marvin Demoff .01 .05
101 Adrian Cooper .01 .05
102 Bruce Pickens .01 .05
103 Scott Zolak .01 .05
104 Phil Hansen .01 .05
105 Ed King .01 .05
106 Mike Jones DE .01 .05
107 Alvin Harper .02 .10
108 Robert Young .01 .05
109 Favre/Bell/Harp/McRae .40 1.00
110 M.Croel/Swann/E.Turner .02 .10
111 Checklist 1 .01 .05
112 Checklist 2 .01 .05
NNO Salute Advertisement .01 .05

1991 Star Pics Autographs

Signed cards were randomly inserted in factory sets of 1991 Star Pics. Each card is essentially a parallel to the base card with an authentic signature (on the front or back), along with a Star Pics gold foil sticker of authenticity. Beware that some cards are known to have been forged with a sticker from a common card removed and added to one of the star players, such as Brett Favre.

RANDOM INSERTS IN FACTORY SETS
2 Barry Sanders FLB 50.00 120.00
3 Nick Bell 2.00 5.00
4 Kelvin Pritchett 2.00 5.00
5 Huey Richardson 2.00 5.00
6 Mike Croel 3.00 8.00
7 Paul Justin 3.00 8.00
8 Ivory Lee Brown 2.00 5.00
9 Herman Moore 6.00 15.00
11 Keith Traylor 2.00 5.00
12 Joe Johnson 2.00 5.00
13 Dan McGwire 3.00 8.00
14 Harvey Williams 3.00 8.00
15 Eric Moten 2.00 5.00
16 Steve Zucker 2.00 5.00
17 Randal Hill 3.00 8.00
18 Browning Nagle 2.00 5.00
19 Stan Thomas 2.00 5.00
20 Emmitt Smith FLB 60.00 150.00
21 Ted Washington 2.00 5.00
22 Lamar Rogers 2.00 5.00
23 Kenny Walker 2.00 5.00
24 Howard Griffith 3.00 8.00
25 Reggie Johnson 2.00 5.00
26 Lawrence Dawsey 2.00 5.00
27 Joe Garten 2.00 5.00
28 Moe Gardner 2.00 5.00
29 Michael Stonebreaker 2.00 5.00
30 Jeff George FLB 6.00 15.00
32 John Flannery 2.00 5.00
33 Pat Harlow 2.00 5.00
34 Kanavis McGhee 2.00 5.00
35 Mike Dumas 2.00 5.00
36 Godfrey Myles 2.00 5.00
37 Shawn Moore 2.00 5.00
38 Jeff Graham 3.00 8.00
39 Ricky Watters 10.00 25.00
40 Andre Ware 3.00 8.00
41 Henry Jones 3.00 8.00
42 Eric Turner 3.00 8.00
43 Bob Woolf 2.00 5.00
44 Randy Baldwin 2.00 5.00
45 Mo Lewis 2.00 5.00
46 Jerry Evans 2.00 5.00
47 Derek Russell 2.00 5.00
48 Merton Hanks 3.00 8.00
49 Kevin Donnalley 2.00 5.00
50 Troy Aikman FLB 50.00 120.00
51 William Thomas 3.00 8.00
52 Chris Thome 2.00 5.00
53 Ricky Ervins 3.00 8.00
54 Jake Reed 6.00 15.00
55 Jerome Henderson 2.00 5.00
56 Mark Vander Poel 2.00 5.00
57 Bernard Ellison 2.00 5.00
58 Jack Mills 2.00 5.00
59 Jarrod Bunch 2.00 5.00
60 Mark Carrier DB 2.00 5.00
61 Rocen Keeton 2.00 5.00
62 Louis Riddick 2.00 5.00
63 Bobby Wilson 2.00 5.00
64 Steve Jackson 2.00 5.00
65 Brett Favre 60.00 120.00
66 Ernie Mills 3.00 8.00
67 Joe Valerio 2.00 5.00
68 Chris Smith 2.00 5.00
69 Ralph Cindrich 2.00 5.00
70 Christian Okoye 3.00 8.00
71 Charles McRae 2.00 5.00
72 Jon Vaughn 2.00 5.00
73 Eric Swann 3.00 8.00
74 Bill Musgrave 2.00 5.00
75 Eric Bieniemy 3.00 8.00
76 Pat Tyrance 2.00 5.00
77 Vinnie Clark 2.00 5.00
78 Eugene Williams 2.00 5.00
79 Rob Carpenter 2.00 5.00
81 Roman Phifer 2.00 5.00
82 Greg Lewis 3.00 8.00
83 John Johnson 2.00 5.00
84 Richard Howell 2.00 5.00
85 Jesse Campbell 2.00 5.00
86 Stanley Richard 2.00 5.00
87 Alfred Williams 2.00 5.00
88 Mike Pritchard 3.00 8.00
89 Mel Agee 2.00 5.00
90 Aaron Craver 2.00 5.00
91 Tim Barnett 2.00 5.00
92 Wesley Carroll 3.00 8.00
93 Kevin Scott 2.00 5.00
94 Darren Lewis 2.00 5.00
95 Tim Bruton 2.00 5.00
96 Tim James 2.00 5.00
97 Darryll Lewis 2.00 5.00
98 Shawn Jefferson 6.00 15.00
99 Mitch Donahue 2.00 5.00
100 Marvin Demoff 2.00 5.00
101 Adrian Cooper 2.00 5.00
102 Bruce Pickens 2.00 5.00
103 Scott Zolak 2.00 5.00
104 Phil Hansen 3.00 8.00
105 Ed King 2.00 5.00
106 Mike Jones DE 2.00 5.00
107 Alvin Harper 3.00 8.00
108 Robert Young 2.00 5.00

1992 Star Pics

This 100-card standard-size set highlights more than 80 of the top college prospects in the country. The set was available in ten-card foil StarPaks and factory sets, with randomly inserted autograph cards in both. It was reported that the production run did not exceed 195,000 factory sets and 12,000 ten-box foil cases. The fronts feature glossy color action photos bordered in white. A color stripe runs the length of the card on the right side, and the player's position and name are printed vertically. The Star Pics logo is superimposed at the lower right corner. The backs present an in-depth scouting report (accomplishments, strengths, and weaknesses), biographical information, and a color head shot in a circular format at the lower right corner. The five-card Flashback subset (10, 20, 30, 50, 70) displays illustrations by sports artist Scott Medlock. The StarStat subset, ten cards in all, compares the top pro prospects' stats to the collegiate stats of NFL greats; two of these were included in each set and eight others were randomly inserted in the foil packs. Autographed cards were inserted in sets and wax on a random basis.

COMPLETE SET (100) 2.00 5.00
COMP.FACT SET (100) 2.00 5.00
1 Steve Emtman SS .02 .10
2 Chris Hakel .02 .10
3 Phillippi Sparks .02 .10
4 Howard Dinkins .02 .10
5 Robert Brooks .30 .75
6 Chris Pedersen .02 .10
7 Bucky Richardson .02 .10
8 Keith Goganious .02 .10
9 Robert Porcher .15 .40
10 Andre Rison FLB .08 .25
11 Jason Hanson .08 .25
12 Tommy Vardell .08 .25
13 Kurt Barber .02 .10
14 Bernard Dafney .02 .10
15 Levon Kirkland .02 .10
16 Corey Widmer .02 .10
17 Santana Dotson .08 .25
18 Chris Holder .02 .10
19 Elbert Turner .08 .25
20 Mike Croel .08 .25
21 Darren Perry .02 .10
22 Troy Vincent .08 .25
23 Quentin Coryatt .08 .25
24 John Brown III .02 .10
25 John Ray .02 .10
26 Vaughn Dunbar .02 .10
27 Stacey Dillard .02 .10
28 Alonzo Spellman .08 .25
29 Darren Woodson .15 .40
30 Pat Swilling FLB .02 .10
31 Eddie Robinson .02 .10
32 Tyji Armstrong .02 .10
33 Bill Johnson .02 .10
34 Eugene Chung .02 .10
35 Ricardo McDonald .02 .10
36 Sean Lumpkin .02 .10
37 Greg Skrepenak .02 .10
38 Ashley Ambrose .15 .40
39 Kevin Smith .02 .10
40 Todd Collins LB .02 .10
41 Shane Dronett .02 .10
42 Ronnie West .02 .10
43 Darryl Williams .02 .10
44 Rodney Blackshear .02 .10
45 Dion Lambert .02 .10
46 Mike Saunders .20 .50
47 Keo Coleman .02 .10
48 Dana Hall .02 .10
49 Arthur Marshall .02 .10
50 Leonard Russell .02 .10
51 Matt Rodgers .02 .10
52 Shane Collins .02 .10
53 Courtney Hawkins .08 .25
54 Chuck Smith .02 .10
55 Joe Bowden .02 .10
56 Gene McGuire .02 .10
57 Tracy Scroggins .02 .10
58 Mark D'Onofrio .02 .10
59 Jimmy Smith 1.00 2.50
60 Carl Pickens .20 .50
61 Robert Harris .02 .10
62 Erick Anderson .02 .10
63 Doug Rigby .02 .10
64 Keith Hamilton .08 .25
65 Vaughn Dunbar .02 .10
66 Willie Clay .02 .10
67 Robert Jones .02 .10
68 Leon Searcy .02 .10
69 Elliot Pifer .02 .10
70 Thurman Thomas FLB .15 .40
71 Mark Wheeler .02 .10
72 Jeremy Lincoln .02 .10
73 Tony McCoy .02 .10
74 Charles Davenport .02 .10
75 Patrick Rowe .02 .10
76 Tommy Jeter .02 .10
77 Rod Smith DB .02 .10
78 Johnny Mitchell .02 .10
79 Corey Barlow .02 .10
80 Scottie Graham .08 .25
81 Mark Bounds .02 .10
82 Chester McGlockton .02 .10
83 Ray Roberts .02 .10
84 Dale Carter .08 .25
85 James Patton .02 .10
86 Tyrone Legette .02 .10
87 Leodis Flowers .02 .10
88 Rico Smith .02 .10
89 Kevin Turner .02 .10
90 Steve Emtman .02 .10
91 Rodney Culver .02 .10
92 Chris Mims .02 .10
93 Carlos Snow .02 .10
94 Corey Harris .02 .10
95 Nate Williams .02 .10
96 Timothy Roberts .02 .10
97 Steve Israel .02 .10
98 Tony Smith WR .02 .10
99 Dwayne Sabb .02 .10
100 Checklist .02 .10
NNO Steve Emtman BC .15 .40

1992 Star Pics Autographs

Signed cards were randomly inserted in both foil packs and factory sets of 1992 Star Pics. Each card is essentially a parallel to the base card with an authentic signature, along with a Star Pics stamp of authenticity.

1992 Star Pics StarStats

This eight-card standard-size set highlights top college prospects. The cards were available as an insert in ten-card foil StarPaks. The StarStat concept compares top pro prospects' stats to the collegiate stats of NFL greats.

COMPLETE SET (8) 2.50 6.00
SS1 Dale Carter .20 .50
SS2 Carl Pickens .40 1.00
SS3 Alonzo Spellman .20 .50
SS4 Jimmy Smith 2.00 5.00
SS5 Quentin Coryatt .20 .50
SS6 Troy Vincent .20 .50
SS7 Darryl Williams .07 .20
SS8 Courtney Hawkins .20 .50

1994 Superior Rookies Side Line Promos

These two promo cards measure the standard size and feature white-bordered color action shots of the players in their college uniforms. The player's name, the set's title, and a football icon appear within a brownish marbleized bar near the bottom. Aside from the "Promotional Card" disclaimer printed diagonally within a ghosted gray football, the backs are blank. The cards are unnumbered and checklisted below in alphabetical order. The company was previously named Goal Line and Side Line. Both cards can be found with either company name on the cardfronts.

COMPLETE SET (4) 1.60 4.00
1A Rick Mirer .40 1.00
1B Rick Mirer .40 1.00
2A Charlie Ward .50 1.25
2B Charlie Ward .50 1.25

1994 Superior Rookies

These 80 standard-size cards were issued by Superior Rookies. The white-bordered fronts carry color action shots of NFL rookies in their college uniforms. The player's name, set name, and a football icon appear in a color marbleized bar near the bottom. Over a ghosted player photo, the white-bordered back carries the player's name, biography, career highlights, and statistics. The production figures are given as "1 of 26,730". Just 9,900 boxes were produced. Each case included 144 autographed cards and 144 gold foil-stamped cards. The first 300 two-case orders received an individually numbered autographed Jerome Bettis card.

COMPLETE SET (80) 2.50 6.00
1 Rick Mirer FLB .05 .15
2 Jerome Bettis .40 1.00
3 Reggie Brooks .05 .15
4 Trent Pollard .01 .05
5 Willie Clark .01 .05
6 Tim Ruddy .01 .05
7 Lindsey Chapman .01 .05
8 Van Malone .01 .05
9 Jeff Burris .01 .05
10 Charles Johnson .10 .30
11 Brice Abrams .01 .05
12 Steve Shine .01 .05
13 Brentson Buckner .01 .05
14 Marty Moore .10 .30
15 Ryan Yarborough .01 .05
16 Aaron Taylor .01 .05
17 Charlie Ward .30 .75
18 Aubrey Beavers .01 .05
19 Zane Beehn .01 .05
20 Johnnie Morton .40 1.00
21 Jeremy Nunley .01 .05
22 Bucky Brooks .01 .05
23 Dewayne Washington .01 .05
24 Mario Bates .05 .15
25 David Palmer .10 .30
26 Kevin Mawae .10 .30
27 Chris Brantley .01 .05
28 Bruce Walker .01 .05
29 Jamir Miller .05 .15
30 Thomas Lewis .01 .05
31 Chad Bratzke .01 .05
32 Anthony Phillips .01 .05
33 Errict Rhett .10 .30
34 Tre Johnson .01 .05
35 Perry Klein .01 .05
36 Tyronne Drakeford .01 .05
37 Bernard Williams .01 .05
38 Carlester Crumpler .01 .05
39 Myron Bell .01 .05
40 Greg Hill .10 .30
41 James Burton .01 .05
42 Lloyd Hill .01 .05
43 Antonio Langham .01 .05
44 Jim Flanigan .01 .05
45 Byron Bam Morris .05 .15
46 Brad Ottis .01 .05
47 Wayne Gandy .01 .05
48 Rob Holmberg .01 .05
49 Bryant Young .20 .50
50 William Floyd .05 .15
51 Kevin Mitchell .01 .05
52 Ervin Collier .01 .05
53 Winfred Tubbs .01 .05
54 Mark Montgomery .01 .05
55 Willie McGinest .10 .30
56 Jim Miller .50 1.25
57 Doug Nussmeier .01 .05
58 Joe Panos .01 .05
59 Sam Adams .01 .05
60 Derrick Alexander WR .10 .30
61 Pete Bercich .01 .05
62 Eric Ravotti .01 .05
63 Eric Mahlum .01 .05
64 Corey Louchiey .01 .05
65 Lake Dawson .05 .15
66 Rob Fredrickson .05 .15
67 Sam Rogers .01 .05
68 John Covington .01 .05
69 Larry Allen .30 .75
70 LeShon Johnson .01 .05
71 Jerry Reynolds .01 .05
72 Eric Zomalt .01 .05
73 Gus Frerotte .30 .75
74 Jason Winrow .01 .05
75 Corey Sawyer .05 .15
76 Malcolm Seabron .01 .05
77 Cory Fleming .01 .05
78 Chris Maumalanga .01 .05

79 Chris Penn .01 .05
80 Checklist .01 .05

1994 Superior Rookies Gold

COMP.GOLD SET (80) 10.00 25.00
*GOLD STARS: 1.5X TO 4X BASIC CARDS
ONE PER PACK

1994 Superior Rookies Autographs

These 79 standard-size autograph cards were issued one per pack by Superior Rookies. The white-bordered fronts carry color action shots of NFL rookies in their college uniforms. The player's autograph appears on the front. His name, the set name, and a football icon appear in a brown marbleized bar near the bottom. Over a ghosted player photo, the white-bordered back carries the player's name, biography, career highlights, and statistics. The cards are numbered on the back and listed below with the number of cards each player autographed.

COMPLETE SET (79) 75.00 150.00
ONE CARD OR COUPON PER PACK
1 Rick Mirer FLB/1000 4.00 10.00
2 Jerome Bettis FLB/1000 30.00 60.00
3 Reggie Brooks FLB/1000 1.25 3.00
4 Trent Pollard/6000 .75 2.00
5 Willie Clark/5000 .75 2.00
6 Tim Ruddy/5000 .75 2.00
7 Lindsey Chapman/6000 .75 2.00
8 Van Malone/5000 .75 2.00
9 Jeff Burris/4000 .75 2.00
10 Charles Johnson/5000 2.50 6.00
11 Brice Abrams/6000 .75 2.00
12 Steve Shine/6000 .75 2.00
13 Brenson Buckner/4000 .75 2.00
14 Marty Moore/6000 2.50 6.00
15 Ryan Yarborough/5000 .75 2.00
16 Aaron Taylor/4000 .75 2.00
17 Charlie Ward/4000 3.00 8.00
18 Aubrey Beavers/5000 .75 2.00
19 Zane Beehn/6000 .75 2.00
20 Johnnie Morton/4000 6.00 15.00
21 Jeremy Nunley/5000 .75 2.00
22 Bucky Brooks/5000 .75 2.00
23 Dewayne Washington/4000 .75 2.00
24 Mario Bates/5000 1.25 3.00
25 David Palmer/4000 1.25 3.00
26 Kevin Mawae/5000 2.50 6.00
27 Chris Brantley/5000 .75 2.00
28 Bruce Walker/5000 .75 2.00
29 Jamir Miller/4000 .75 2.00
30 Thomas Lewis/5000 .75 2.00
31 Chad Bratzke/6000 .75 2.00
32 Anthony Phillips/5000 .75 2.00
33 Errict Rhett/5000 2.50 6.00
34 Tre Johnson/4000 .75 2.00
35 Perry Klein/5000 .75 2.00
36 Tyronne Drakeford/5000 .75 2.00
37 Bernard Williams/4000 .75 2.00
38 Carlester Crumpler/6000 .75 2.00
39 Myron Bell/6000 .75 2.00
40 Greg Hill/5000 1.25 3.00
41 James Burton/6000 .75 2.00
42 Lloyd Hill/5000 .75 2.00
43 Antonio Langham/4000 .75 2.00
44 Jim Flanigan/5000 .75 2.00
45 Dyron Dem Morris/5000 1.25 3.00
46 Brad Ottis/5000 .75 2.00
47 Wayne Gandy/4000 .75 2.00
48 Rob Holmberg/6000 .75 2.00
49 Bryant Young/4000 6.00 15.00
50 William Floyd/5000 .75 2.00
51 Kevin Mitchell/5000 .75 2.00
52 Ervin Collier/5000 .75 2.00
53 Winfred Tubbs/5000 .75 2.00
54 Mark Montgomery/6000 .75 2.00
55 Willie McGinest/4000 4.00 10.00
56 Jim Miller/5000 5.00 12.00
57 Doug Nussmeier/6000 .75 2.00
58 Joe Panos/6000 .75 2.00
59 Sam Adams/5000 .75 2.00
60 Derrick Alexander WR/5000 2.50 6.00
61 Pete Bercich/6000 .75 2.00
62 Eric Ravotti/6000 .75 2.00
63 Eric Mahlum/4000 .75 2.00
64 Corey Louchiey/5000 .75 2.00
65 Lake Dawson/5000 1.25 3.00
66 Rob Fredrickson/4000 .75 2.00
67 Sam Rogers/5000 .75 2.00
68 John Covington/6000 .75 2.00
69 Larry Allen/5000 8.00 20.00
70 LeShon Johnson/5000 .75 2.00
71 Jerry Reynolds/6000 .75 2.00
72 Eric Zomalt/5000 .75 2.00
73 Gus Frerotte/5000 6.00 15.00
74 Jason Winrow/6000 .75 2.00
75 Corey Sawyer/6000 1.25 3.00
76 Malcolm Seabron/5000 .75 2.00
77 Cory Fleming/5000 .75 2.00
78 Chris Maumalanga/5000 .75 2.00
79 Chris Penn/6000 .75 2.00

1994 Superior Rookies Deep Threat

These five standard-size cards were issued by Superior Rookies. Collectors could receive one free card by sending in ten wrappers and a self-addressed stamped envelope. Thicker than the usual card stock, the laminated cards feature color player action shots on their metallic fronts. The player's name appears within a purplish oblique triangle at the lower right, which itself rests upon a black and gold stripe near the bottom. The borderless back carries the player's name in yellow cursive lettering at the upper left. A large football icon in the middle carries the set's name. The cards are individually numbered out of 1,000. Clearly marked "Sample" cards were produced for each card as well.

COMPLETE SET (5) 2.50 6.00
ONE CARD PER 10 WRAPPERS VIA MAIL
*SAMPLE CARDS: SAME PRICE
1 Charles Johnson .50 1.25
2 Johnnie Morton 1.50 4.00
3 Derrick Alexander WR .50 1.25
4 David Palmer .50 1.25
5 Thomas Lewis .07 .20

1994 Superior Rookies Instant Impact

Randomly inserted in packs, these 10 standard-size cards were issued by Superior Rookies. Thicker than the usual card stock, the laminated cards feature color player action shots on their metallic fronts. The player's name appears within a purplish oblique triangle at the lower right, which itself rests upon a black and gold stripe near the bottom. The borderless back carries the player's name in yellow cursive lettering at the upper left. A large football icon in the middle carries the set's name. The cards are individually numbered out of 2,970. Clearly marked "Sample" cards were produced as well and priced below.

COMPLETE SET (10) 5.00 12.00
STATED ODDS 1:12
1 Rick Mirer .30 .75
2 Jerome Bettis 2.00 5.00
3 Reggie Brooks .30 .75
4 Charlie Ward 1.25 3.00
5 Willie McGinest .60 1.50
6 Greg Hill .60 1.50
7 William Floyd .30 .75
8 Bryant Young 1.00 2.50
9 Errict Rhett .60 1.50
10 Sam Adams .08 .25

1995 Superior Pix Promos

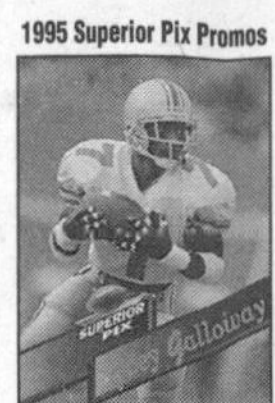

This 4-card set was issued to preview the 1995 Superior Pix Draft series. The set was mailed out as well as distributed at the National Sports Collectors Convention in St. Louis (July 24-30, 1995). The fronts display full-bleed color action photos, with the player's name in a red variegated diagonal bar across the bottom. A second diagonal bar carries the manufacturer's name. Two versions exist for each of the four-cards. The first release included a write-up about each player on the cardback, while the second version was released at The National and features The National logo. The backs carry a head shot and the National Convention logo.

COMPLETE SET (4) 1.60 4.00
*NATIONAL PROMOS: SAME PRICE
1 Steve McNair .50 1.25
2 Kerry Collins .40 1.00
3 Tyrone Wheatley .30 .75
4 Joey Galloway .40 1.00

1995 Superior Pix

These standard-size cards came in eight-card packs with an autographed card in each pack. Each player autographed a number of his own cards. The fronts display a color action player photo with the words '95 Draft in gold foil in either at the top right of left hand corner of the card. The players name and the Superior Pix logo appear on two stripes that appear at an angle across the bottom of the card. The backs includes a box with a head shot photo of the player at the top left hand corner followed by some facts and history on the player.

COMPLETE SET (110) 5.00 12.00
1 Ki-Jana Carter .08 .25
2 Tony Boselli .02 .10
3 Steve McNair .60 1.50
4 Michael Westbrook .08 .25
5 Kerry Collins .40 1.00
6 Terrell Davis .60 1.50
7 Kevin Bouie .01 .05
8 Brian Williams .01 .05
9 Kez McCorvey .01 .05
10 Kyle Brady .08 .25
11 Rob Johnson .25 .60
12 Carl Greenwood .01 .05
13 Mark Fields .08 .25
14 Andrew Greene .01 .05
15 Orlando Thomas .01 .05
16 Don Sasa .01 .05
17 Brent Moss .01 .05
18 Jamal Willis .01 .05
19 Michael Hendricks .01 .05
20 Rashaan Salaam .02 .10
21 John Sacca .01 .05
22 Cory Raymer .01 .05
23 Kirby Dar Dar .01 .05
24 Lee DeRamus .01 .05
25 Joey Galloway .30 .75
26 Mike Frederick .01 .05
27 Todd Collins QB .02 .10
28 Stoney Case .02 .10
29 Devin Bush .01 .05
30 Chad May .01 .05
31 Darick Holmes .02 .10
32 Johnny Thomas .01 .05
33 Luther Elliss .01 .05
34 Tyrone Wheatley .25 .60
35 Terry Connealy .01 .05
36 Ruben Brown .08 .25
37 Kelvin Anderson .01 .05
38 Tony Berti .01 .05
39 Steve Ingram .01 .05
40 Kevin Carter .08 .25
41 Dave Wohlabaugh .01 .05
42 Mike Morton .01 .05
43 Steve Stenstrom .01 .05
44 Zach Wiegert .01 .05
45 Rodney Thomas .02 .10
46 Eddie Goines .01 .05
47 Kenny Gales .01 .05
48 Jamal Ellis .01 .05
49 Demetrius Edwards .01 .05
50 Justin Armour .01 .05
51 Billy Williams .01 .05
52 Ed Hervey .01 .05
53 Antonio Armstrong .01 .05
54 Oliver Gibson .01 .05
55 David Dunn .01 .05
56 Tyrone Davis .01 .05
57 Craig Newsome .01 .05
58 William Strong .01 .05
59 Sherman Williams .01 .05
60 James O. Stewart .25 .60
61 Bryan Schwartz .01 .05
62 Frank Sanders .08 .25
63 Barrett Robbins .01 .05
64 Bronzell Miller .01 .05
65 Curtis Martin .60 1.50
66 Chris T. Jones .02 .10
67 Dave Barr .01 .05
68 Anthony Brown .01 .05
69 Ken Dilger .02 .10
70 Warren Sapp .25 .60
71 James A. Stewart .01 .05
72 Corey Fuller .01 .05
73 Christian Fauria .02 .10
74 Brian DeMarco .01 .05
75 J.J. Stokes .08 .25
76 Hicham El-Mashtoub .01 .05
77 Anthony Cook .01 .05
78 Mark Bruener .02 .10
79 Blake Brockermeyer .01 .05
80 Derrick Brooks .08 .25
81 Joe Aska .01 .05
82 Lance Brown .01 .05
83 Pete Mitchell .01 .05
84 Kordell Stewart .50 1.25
85 Bobby Taylor .08 .25
86 Jimmy Hitchcock .01 .05
87 Jack Jackson .01 .05
88 Ray Zellars .01 .05
89 Darius Holland .01 .05
90 Derrick Alexander DE .01 .05
91 Torey Hunter .01 .05
92 Scotty Lewis .01 .05
93 Carl Reeves .01 .05
94 Terrell Fletcher .01 .05
95 Ontiwaun Carter .01 .05
96 Trezelle Jenkins .01 .05
97 Mark Birchmeier .01 .05
98 Len Raney .01 .05
99 Ronald Cherry .01 .05
100 Tyrone Wheatley .25 .60
101 John Jones .01 .05
102 Zack Crockett .02 .10
103 Larry Jones .01 .05
104 Michael McCoy .01 .05
105 Ellis Johnson .01 .05
106 Jerrott Willard .01 .05
107 Jason James .01 .05
108 J.J. Smith .01 .05
109 Mike Mamula .01 .05
110 Checklist .01 .05

1995 Superior Pix Autographs

These standard-size cards came in eight-card packs with an autographed card in each pack. Each player autographed a different number of his own cards. The number of cards each player autographed appears below. The design is identical to that of the regular issue, except for the autograph, the words authentic signature and numbering on the front.

COMPLETE SET (109) 150.00 300.00
ONE CARD OR COUPON PER PACK
1 Ki-Jana Carter/1000 3.00 8.00
2 Tony Boselli/4000 2.00 5.00
3 Steve McNair/3000 10.00 25.00
4 Michael Westbrook/4000 2.00 5.00
5 Kerry Collins/3000 6.00 15.00
6 Terrell Davis/5000 7.50 20.00
7 Kevin Bouie/6500 1.50 4.00
8 Brian Williams/6500 1.50 4.00
9 Kez McCorvey/6500 1.50 4.00
10 Kyle Brady/3500 3.00 8.00
11 Rob Johnson/3000 5.00 12.00
12 Carl Greenwood/6500 1.50 4.00
13 Mark Fields/5000 3.00 8.00
14 Andrew Greene/5000 1.50 4.00
15 Orlando Thomas/6000 1.50 4.00
16 Don Sasa/6500 1.50 4.00
17 Brent Moss/4000 1.50 4.00
18 Jamal Willis/5000 1.50 4.00
19 Michael Hendricks/6500 1.50 4.00
20 Rashaan Salaam/3500 2.00 5.00
21 John Sacca/4000 1.50 4.00
22 Cory Raymer/6000 1.50 4.00
23 Kirby Dar Dar/6500 1.50 4.00
24 Lee DeRamus/6500 1.50 4.00
25 Joey Galloway/4000 4.00 10.00
26 Mike Frederick/6000 1.50 4.00
27 Todd Collins/5000 5.00 12.00
28 Stoney Case/4000 2.00 5.00
29 Devin Bush/5000 1.50 4.00
30 Chad May/4000 1.50 4.00
31 Darick Holmes/6500 1.50 4.00
32 Johnny Thomas/6500 1.50 4.00
33 Luther Elliss/5000 1.50 4.00
34 Tyrone Wheatley/5000 3.00 8.00
35 Terry Connealy/6500 1.50 4.00
36 Ruben Brown/3500 3.00 8.00
37 Kelvin Anderson/4000 2.00 5.00
38 Tony Berti/6500 1.50 4.00
39 Steve Ingram/3500 1.50 4.00
40 Kevin Carter/4000 3.00 8.00
41 Dave Wohlabaugh/6500 1.50 4.00
42 Mike Morton/6500 1.50 4.00
43 Steve Stenstrom/5000 1.50 4.00
44 Zach Wiegert/5000 1.50 4.00
45 Rodney Thomas/5000 1.50 4.00
46 Eddie Goines/4000 1.50 4.00
47 Kenny Gales/6500 1.50 4.00
48 Jamal Ellis/6500 1.50 4.00
49 Demetrius Edwards/6500 1.50 4.00
50 Justin Armour/5000 2.00 5.00
51 Billy Williams/5000 1.50 4.00
52 Ed Hervey/6500 1.50 4.00
53 Antonio Armstrong/6500 1.50 4.00
54 Oliver Gibson/6500 1.50 4.00
55 David Dunn/5000 1.50 4.00
56 Tyrone Davis 1.50 4.00
57 Craig Newsome/4000 1.50 4.00
58 William Strong/6500 1.50 4.00
59 Sherman Williams/3500 1.50 4.00
60 James O. Stewart/4000 3.00 8.00
61 Bryan Schwartz/6000 1.50 4.00
62 Frank Sanders/5000 2.00 5.00
63 Barrett Robbins/6000 1.50 4.00
64 Bronzell Miller/6500 1.50 4.00
65 Curtis Martin/4000 8.00 20.00
66 Chris T. Jones/4000 2.00 5.00
67 Dave Barr/5000 1.50 4.00
68 Anthony Brown/6500 1.50 4.00
69 Ken Dilger/6000 3.00 8.00
70 Warren Sapp/4000
71 James A. Stewart/4000 1.50 4.00
72 Corey Fuller/5000 1.50 4.00
73 Christian Fauria/5000 1.50 4.00
74 Brian DeMarco/6000 1.50 4.00
75 J.J. Stokes/1000 3.00 8.00
76 Hicham El-Mashtoub/6500 1.50 4.00
77 Anthony Cook/6000 1.50 4.00
78 Mark Bruener/4000 2.00 5.00
79 Blake Brockermeyer/4000 1.50 4.00
80 Derrick Brooks/4000 10.00 25.00
81 Joe Aska/4000 2.00 5.00
82 Lance Brown/6500 1.50 4.00
83 Pete Mitchell/6500 2.00 5.00
84 Kordell Stewart/6500 5.00 12.00
85 Bobby Taylor/4000 3.00 8.00
86 Jimmy Hitchcock/4000 1.50 4.00
87 Jack Jackson/5000 1.50 4.00
88 Ray Zellars/4000 1.50 4.00
89 Darius Holland/6000 1.50 4.00
90 Derrick Alexander DE/4000 1.50 4.00
91 Torey Hunter/6000 1.50 4.00
92 Scotty Lewis/6500 1.50 4.00
93 Carl Reeves/6500 1.50 4.00
94 Terrell Fletcher/6000 1.50 4.00
95 Ontiwaun Carter/6500 1.50 4.00
96 Trezelle Jenkins/5000 1.50 4.00
97 Mark Birchmeier/4000 1.50 4.00
98 Len Raney/6500 1.50 4.00
99 Ronald Cherry/6500 1.50 4.00
100 Tyrone Wheatley/6500 3.00 8.00
101 John Jones/6500 1.50 4.00
102 Zack Crockett/6000 2.00 5.00
103 Larry Jones/4000 1.50 4.00
104 Michael McCoy/6500 1.50 4.00
105 Ellis Johnson/3500 1.50 4.00
106 Jerrott Willard/5000 1.50 4.00
107 Jason James/6500 1.50 4.00
108 J.J. Smith/5000 1.50 4.00
109 Mike Mamula/4000 1.50 4.00

1995 Superior Pix Deep Threat

Randomly inserted at a rate of one in nine packs, these 5 standard-size cards display a color player photo in front of a football with a prism background of sorted colors with the players name appearing in silver in a stripe across the bottom of the card. The words 1995 Draft Pix Series appears at the top of the card with the Superior Pix logo appearing in the bottom right hand corner. This set features the top wide receiver prospects from the 1995 NFL draft. Each card was also produced in a "Promo" version.

COMPLETE SET (5) 2.50 6.00
STATED ODDS 1:9
*PROMO CARDS: .25X TO .5X BASIC INSERTS
1 Michael Westbrook .25 .60
2 Joey Galloway .75 2.00
3 J.J. Stokes .25 .60
4 Kyle Brady .25 .60
5 Frank Sanders .25 .60

1995 Superior Pix Instant Impact

Randomly inserted at a rate of one in 18 packs, these 5 standard-size cards display a color action player photo with a split blue/silver/green foil background. The player's name appears within a gold/purple strip across the lower right hand corner of the card. The Superior Pix logo appears across the upper left hand corner of the card. This set features those players expected to have the most immediate impact in the league. Each card was also produced in a "Promo" version.

COMPLETE SET (5) 3.00 8.00
STATED ODDS 1:18
*PROMO CARDS: .25X TO .5X BASIC CARDS
1 Steve McNair 2.00 5.00
2 Kerry Collins 1.25 3.00
3 Tyrone Wheatley .30 .75
4 Joey Galloway .60 1.50
5 Tony Boselli .30 .75

1995 Superior Pix Open Field

Randomly inserted at a rate of one in 18 packs, these 5 standard-size cards display a color action player photo with a split silver/purple prism like background. The player's name appears in black in the top left or right of the card with the Superior Pix logo appearing in the bottom left or right section of the card. This set features the top running back prospects from the draft. Each card was also produced in a "Promo" version.

COMPLETE SET (5) 2.00 5.00
STATED ODDS 1:18
*PROMO CARDS: .25X TO .5X BASIC CARDS
1 Ki-Jana Carter .25 .60
2 Tyrone Wheatley .60 1.50
3 James O. Stewart .60 1.50
4 Rashaan Salaam .08 .25
5 Ray Zellars .08 .25

1995 Superior Pix Top Defender

Randomly inserted at a rate of one in nine packs, these five standard-size cards display a color player photo in front of a split blue/gold wood grain background. The player's first and last name appear in two separate stripes to the immediate left of the player. This set features the top defensive lineman prospects from the draft. Each card was also produced in a "Promo" version.

COMPLETE SET (5) .75 2.00
*PROMO CARDS: .25X TO .5X BASIC CARDS
1 Kevin Carter .30 .75
2 Derrick Alexander DE .05 .15
3 Warren Sapp .75 2.00
4 Derrick Brooks .30 .75
5 Mike Mamula .05 .15

1996 Visions

The 1996 Classic Visions set consists of 150 standard-size cards. The fronts feature full-bleed color action player photos. The player's position and name are presented in blue foil, while the Classic logo and set title "96 Visions" are stamped in gold foil. The back carries a second color photo, college statistics, biography, and a player fact.

COMPLETE SET (150) 6.00 15.00
39 Troy Aikman .25 .60
40 Emmitt Smith .40 1.00
41 Marshall Faulk .15 .40
42 Kerry Collins .15 .40
43 Michael Westbrook .08 .25
44 Steve Young .15 .40
45 Mike Mamula .05 .15
46 Joey Galloway .15 .40
47 Kyle Brady .05 .15
48 J.J. Stokes .08 .25
49 Steve McNair .25 .60
50 Kordell Stewart .15 .40
51 Drew Bledsoe .15 .40
52 Hugh Douglas .08 .25
53 Curtis Martin .20 .50
54 Ki-Jana Carter .08 .25
55 Tyrone Wheatley .15 .40
56 Napoleon Kaufman .15 .40
57 James O. Stewart .08 .25
58 Rashaan Salaam .05 .15
59 Eric Zeier .08 .25
60 Bobby Taylor .08 .25
61 Ty Law .15 .40
62 Mark Bruener .05 .15
63 Devin Bush .05 .15
64 Frank Sanders .08 .25
65 Derrick Brooks .15 .40
66 Craig Powell .05 .15
67 Craig Newsome .05 .15
68 Trent Dilfer .15 .40
69 Sherman Williams .05 .15
70 Chris T. Jones .05 .15
71 Corey Fuller .05 .15
72 Luther Ellis .05 .15
73 Warren Sapp .15 .40
74 Isaac Bruce .15 .40
75 Tamarick Vanover .05 .15
76 Terrell Davis .40 1.00
77 Byron Bam Morris .08 .25
78 Rodney Thomas .05 .15
79 Errict Rhett .08 .25
80 Kevin Carter .05 .15
81 Darnay Scott .08 .25
122 Troy Aikman .25 .60
126 Emmitt Smith .40 1.00
129 Marshall Faulk .15 .40
141 Joey Galloway .15 .40
142 Kerry Collins .15 .40
143 Michael Westbrook .08 .25
144 Terrell Davis .40 1.00
145 Kyle Brady .05 .15
146 Kordell Stewart .15 .40
147 Curtis Martin .20 .50
148 Tyrone Wheatley .15 .40
149 Napoleon Kaufman .15 .40
150 Rashaan Salaam .05 .15

1996 Visions Action 21

1 Troy Aikman .40 1.00
4 Michael Westbrook .08 .25
10 Kerry Collins .20 .50

1996 Visions Signings

The 1996 Visions Signings set consists of 100 standard-size cards. The fronts feature full-bleed color action player photos. The player's position and name are stamped in prismatic foil along with the Classic logo and set title "96 Visions Signings." This set contains standouts from five sports grouped together in this order: basketball, football, hockey, baseball and racing. Cards were distributed in six-card packs. Release date was June 1996. The main allure to this product, in addition to the conventional inserts, were autographed memorabilia redemption cards inserted one per 10 packs.

COMPLETE SET (100) 6.00 15.00
29 Troy Aikman .30 .75
30 Emmitt Smith .60 1.50
31 Marshall Faulk .20 .50
32 Kerry Collins .15 .40
33 Steve Young .15 .40
34 Drew Bledsoe .15 .40
35 Kyle Brady .05 .15
36 Steve McNair .15 .40
37 Napoleon Kaufman .10 .30
38 Karim Abdul-Jabbar .08 .25
39 Mike Alstott .15 .40
40 Tim Biakabutuka .08 .25
41 Duane Clemons .05 .15
42 Daryl Gardener .05 .15
43 Joey Galloway .15 .40
44 Eddie George .60 1.50
45 Terry Glenn .08 .25
46 Kevin Hardy .05 .15
47 Bobby Hoying .08 .25
48 Keyshawn Johnson .50 1.25
49 Derrick Mayes .08 .25
50 Eric Moulds .30 .75
51 Jonathan Ogden .30 .75
52 Simeon Rice .08 .25
53 Orpheus Roye .05 .15
54 Amani Toomer .15 .40
55 Chris Doering .08 .25
56 Jevon Langford .05 .15
57 Jeff Lewis .08 .25
58 Jamain Stephens .08 .25
59 Steve Taneyhill .05 .15
60 Alex Van Dyke .05 .15

1996 Visions Signings Artistry

This 10-card insert set was printed on thick 24-point stock. Cards were inserted at a rate of 1:60 Vision Signings packs.

COMPLETE SET (10) 20.00 50.00
2 Emmitt Smith 4.00 10.00
5 Joey Galloway 2.00 5.00
8 Kordell Stewart 3.00 8.00
10 Rashaan Salaam 1.25 3.00

1996 Visions Signings Autographs Gold

Certified autographed cards were inserted in Visions Signings packs at an overall rate of 1:12. Some players signed only the silver version while others signed both gold and silver cards. The Gold foil cards were not individually serial numbered. The quantity signed is unknown but assumed to be significantly higher than the corresponding number signed for the silver foil cards. We've listed the unnumbered cards alphabetically.

1 Karim Abdul-Jabbar 4.00 10.00
5 Mike Alstott 5.00 12.00
7 Tim Biakabutuka 2.50 6.00
10 Jerod Cherry 1.50 4.00
12 Sedric Clark 1.50 4.00
13 Marcus Coleman 1.50 4.00
15 Chris Darkins 1.50 4.00
18 Chris Doering 1.50 4.00
20 Donnie Edwards 1.50 4.00
21 Ray Farmer 1.50 4.00
24 Randall Godfrey 1.50 4.00
25 Scott Greene 1.50 4.00
27 Jeff Hartings 1.50 4.00
28 Jimmy Herndon 1.50 4.00
30 Richard Huntley 1.50 4.00
32 Dietrich Jells 1.50 4.00
36 Jeff Lewis 1.50 4.00
38 Ray Mickens 1.50 4.00
39 Lawyer Milloy 2.50 6.00
40 Bryant Mix 1.50 4.00
41 Alex Molden 1.50 4.00
45 Jason Odom 1.50 4.00
49 Christian Peter 2.00 5.00
54 James Ritchey 1.50 4.00
55 Brian Roche 1.50 4.00
56 Orpheus Roye 1.50 4.00
57 Jon Runyan 1.50 4.00
58 Scott Slutzker 1.50 4.00
60 Jamain Stephens 1.50 4.00
61 Matt Stevens 1.50 4.00
64 Steve Taneyhill 1.50 4.00
65 Zach Thomas 8.00 20.00
66 Alex Van Dyke 1.50 4.00
68 Kyle Wacholtz 1.50 4.00
70 Stepfret Williams 1.50 4.00
71 Jerome Woods 1.50 4.00
72 Dusty Zeigler 1.50 4.00

1996 Visions Signings Autographs Silver

Certified autographed cards were inserted in Visions Signings packs at an overall rate of 1:12. Some players signed only silver cards while others signed gold and silver foil cards. The Silver cards were individually serial numbered as noted below. We've listed the unnumbered cards alphabetically.

1 Karim Abdul-Jabbar/365 6.00 15.00
2 Troy Aikman/190 20.00 50.00
6 Mike Alstott/345 8.00 20.00
8 Tim Biakabutuka/390 6.00 15.00
9 Drew Bledsoe/110 15.00 40.00
13 Jerod Cherry/355 2.00 5.00
15 Sedric Clark/410 2.00 5.00
16 Marcus Coleman/395 2.00 5.00
18 Chris Darkins/395 2.00 5.00
21 Chris Doering/390 2.00 5.00
23 Donnie Edwards/395 2.00 5.00
24 Ray Farmer/395 2.00 5.00
25 Marshall Faulk/185 12.50 30.00
28 Randall Godfrey/380 2.00 5.00
29 Scott Greene/395 2.00 5.00
31 Jeff Hartings/380 2.00 5.00
32 Jimmy Herndon/380 2.00 5.00
34 Richard Huntley/380 2.00 5.00
37 Dietrich Jells/350 2.00 5.00
41 Jeff Lewis/385 2.00 5.00
44 Ray Mickens/390 2.00 5.00
45 Lawyer Milloy/365 3.00 8.00
46 Bryant Mix/390 2.00 5.00
47 Alex Molden/365 2.00 5.00
51 Jason Odom/390 2.00 5.00
55 Christian Peter 2.00 5.00
60 James Ritchey/360 2.00 5.00
61 Brian Roche/395 2.00 5.00
62 Orpheus Roye/350 2.00 5.00
64 Jon Runyan/430 2.00 5.00
65 Scott Slutzker/385 2.00 5.00
66 Emmitt Smith/90 60.00 120.00
68 Jamain Stephens/380 2.00 5.00
69 Matt Stevens/390 2.00 5.00
72 Steve Taneyhill/420 2.00 5.00
73 Zach Thomas/390 10.00 25.00
75 Alex Van Dyke/385 2.00 5.00
77 Kyle Wacholtz/385 2.00 5.00
80 Stepfret Williams/385 2.00 5.00
81 Jerome Woods/430 2.00 5.00
82 Steve Young/95 50.00
83 Dusty Zeigler/395 2.00 5.00

1997 Visions Signings

Score Board's follow-up to the 1996 Visions Signings debut product was released in June 1997. The second-year product had more of a memorabilia emphasis. According to Score Board, 1,700 sequentially numbered cases were produced with five cards per pack, 16 packs per box and 10 boxes per case. Each pack contains either an autographed card or an insert card. The 50-card regular set includes stars and prospects from all four major team sports. Also, one in every two packs contained a gold parallel card to the base set.

COMPLETE SET (50) 5.00 10.00
4 Steve Young .30 .75
29 Eddie George .20 .50
30 Warrick Dunn .30 .75
31 Darrell Russell .05 .15
32 Peter Boulware .05 .15
33 Shawn Springs .05 .15
34 Yatil Green .05 .15
35 David LaFleur .05 .15
36 Bryant Westbrook .05 .15
37 Rae Carruth .05 .15
38 Brett Favre .50 1.25
39 Emmitt Smith .40 1.00
47 Leeland McElroy .05 .15
48 Troy Davis .05 .15
49 Tony Gonzalez .30 .75
50 Byron Hanspard .05 .15

1997 Visions Signings Gold

COMPLETE SET (50) 10.00 25.00
*GOLD: .8X TO 2X BASIC CARDS
GOLD STATED ODDS 1:2

1997 Visions Signings Artistry

The cards in this 20-card set feature Score Board's "exclusive printing technology" and were inserted at a rate of 1:6 Vision Signings packs.

COMPLETE SET (20) 20.00 40.00
A12 Eddie George 1.50 4.00
A13 Warrick Dunn 1.25 3.00
A14 Darrell Russell .40 1.00
A15 Peter Boulware .40 1.00
A16 Shawn Springs .40 1.00
A17 Yatil Green .40 1.00
A18 Brett Favre 3.00 8.00
A19 Emmitt Smith 2.50 6.00

1997 Visions Signings Artistry Autographs

These certified autographed cards feature Score Board's "exclusive printing technology" and were inserted at a rate of 1:18 packs. These 20 cards are autographed parallels of the Artistry insert set.

A12 Eddie George 10.00 25.00
A13 Warrick Dunn 12.50 30.00
A14 Darrell Russell 3.00 8.00
A15 Peter Boulware 3.00 8.00
A16 Shawn Springs 2.50 6.00
A17 Yatil Green 3.00 8.00
A18 Brett Favre 75.00 135.00
A19 Emmitt Smith 40.00 100.00

1997 Visions Signings Autographs

Each 1997 Visions Signings pack contained either an autographed card or an insert card. One in six packs contain a regular autograph card. Four cards, Troy Aikman, Brett Favre, Allen Iverson, and Emmitt Smith were never issued although they appeared on early checklists. One additional key card, Tony Gonzalez, surfaced long after the manufacturer ceased operations.

4 Tony Banks 2.50 6.00
5 Michael Booker 1.50 4.00
6 Peter Boulware 1.50 4.00
8 Rae Carruth 2.50 6.00
12 Koy Detmer 2.00 5.00
13 Corey Dillon 10.00 25.00
14 Warrick Dunn 15.00 30.00
18 Tony Gonzalez 12.00 30.00
(not issued in packs)
19 Yatil Green 1.50 4.00
23 Byron Hanspard 2.00 5.00
24 Kevin Hardy 2.00 5.00
30 DeRon Jenkins 1.50 4.00
31 Andre Johnson 1.50 4.00
32 Greg Jones 1.50 4.00
33 Danny Kanell 2.50 6.00
35 Pete Kendall 1.50 4.00
37 David LaFleur 1.50 4.00
38 Jeff Lewis 1.50 4.00
42 Leeland McElroy 1.50 4.00
43 Ray Mickens 1.50 4.00
46 Trevor Pryce 2.50 6.00
50 Darrell Russell 1.50 4.00
52 Antowain Smith 4.00 10.00
56 Amani Toomer 6.00 15.00
59 Bryant Westbrook 1.50 4.00
61 Stepfret Williams 1.50 4.00

1991 Wild Card Draft National Promos

These cards were given away at the 1991 12th Annual Sports Collectors Convention in Anaheim, California. The fronts of these standard-size cards have high gloss color player photos on a black card face with different colored numbers above and to the right of the picture. Striped versions of these cards with a football-shaped hologram in the upper left corner were also issued. The cards are numbered in the upper right corner of the cardback and begin with Prototype-2.

COMPLETE SET (3) .60 1.50
*5 STRIPES: SAME PRICE
*10 STRIPES: .5X TO 1.2X BASIC CARDS
*20 STRIPES: .6X TO 1.5X BASIC CARDS
*50 STRIPES: .8X TO 2X BASIC CARDS
*100 STRIPES: 1.2X TO 3X BASIC CARDS
*1000 STRIPES: 2X TO 5X BASIC CARDS
P2 Dan McGwire .20 .50
P3 Randal Hill .20 .50
P4 Todd Marinovich .20 .50

1991 Wild Card Draft

The Wild Card College Football Draft Picks set contains 160 cards measuring the standard size. Reportedly, production quantities were limited to 20,000 numbered cases (or 630,000 sets). The front design features glossy color action player photos on a black card face with an orange frame around the picture and different color numbers appearing in the top and right borders. The words "1st edition" in a circular emblem overlay the lower left corner of the picture. One of out every 100 cards is "wild," with a numbered stripe to indicate how many cards it can be redeemed for. There are 5, 10, 20, 50, 100, and 1000 denominations, with the highest numbers the scarcest. Whatever the "wild" number, the card could be redeemed for that number of regular cards of the same player (plus a redemption fee of $1.95). The set included three surprise wild cards (#1, #15, and #22). If these cards were redeemed before April 30, 1992, the collector received three cards to complete the set (listed below as B versions) and a bonus set of six 1992 collegiate football prototype cards. Collectors who redeemed their cards after April 30 did not receive the prototype cards. Also, Kenny Anderson and Larry Johnson promo cards, numbers P2 and P1 respectively, were randomly inserted, and they could be redeemed after January 2, 1992 for then-unknown player cards. Key cards in this set include Bryan Cox, Craig Erickson, Brett Favre, Alvin Harper, Randal Hill, Rocket Ismail (issued as a surprise card), Herman Moore, Mike Pritchard, Leonard Russell and Ricky Watters.

COMPLETE SET (160) 3.00 8.00
1A Wild Card 1 .01 .05
1B Todd Lyght .01 .05
2 Kelvin Pritchett .01 .05
3 Robert Young .01 .05
4 Reggie Johnson .01 .05
5 Eric Turner .02 .10
6 Pat Tyrance .01 .05
7 Curvin Richards .01 .05
8 Calvin Stephens .01 .05
9 Corey Miller .01 .05
10 Michael Jackson .02 .10
11 Simmie Carter .01 .05
12 Roland Smith .01 .05
13 Pat O'Hara .01 .05
14 Scott Conover .01 .05
15A Wild Card 2 .01 .05
15B Russell Maryland .01 .05
16 Greg Amsler .01 .05
17 Moe Gardner .01 .05
18 Howard Griffith .01 .05
19 David Daniels .01 .05
20 Henry Jones .01 .05
21 Don Davey .01 .05
22A Wild Card 3 .01 .05
22B Rocket Ismail .15 .40
23 Richie Andrews .01 .05
24 Shawn Moore .01 .05
25 Anthony Moss .01 .05
26 Vince Moore .01 .05
27 Leroy Thompson .01 .05
28 Darrick Brown .01 .05
29 Mel Agee .01 .05
30 Darryll Lewis .01 .05
31 Hyland Hickson .01 .05
32 Leonard Russell .01 .05
33 Floyd Fields .01 .05
34 Esera Tuaolo .01 .05
35 Todd Marinovich .01 .05
36 Gary Wellman .01 .05
37 Ricky Ervins .01 .05
38 Pat Harlow .01 .05
39 Mo Lewis .01 .05
40 John Kasay .01 .05
41 Phil Hansen .01 .05
42 Kevin Donnalley .01 .05
43 Dexter Davis .01 .05
44 Vance Hammond .01 .05
45 Chris Gardocki .08 .25
46 Bruce Pickens .01 .05
47 Godfrey Myles .01 .05
48 Ernie Mills .02 .10
49 Derek Russell .01 .05
50 Chris Zorich .01 .05
51 Alfred Williams .01 .05
52 Jon Vaughn .01 .05
53 Adrian Cooper .01 .05
54 Eric Bieniemy .01 .05
55 Robert Bailey .01 .05
56 Ricky Watters .25 .60
57 Mark Vander Poel .01 .05
58 James Joseph .01 .05
59 Darren Lewis .01 .05
60 Wesley Carroll .02 .10
61 Dave Key .01 .05
62 Mike Pritchard .02 .10
63 Craig Erickson .02 .10
64 Browning Nagle .01 .05
65 Mike Dumas .01 .05
66 Andre Jones .01 .05
67 Herman Moore .08 .25
68 Greg Lewis .01 .05
69 James Goode .01 .05
70 Stan Thomas .01 .05
71 Jerome Henderson .01 .05
72 Doug Thomas .01 .05
73 Tony Covington .01 .05
74 Charles Mincy .01 .05
75 Kanavis McGhee .01 .05
76 Tom Backes .01 .05
77 Fernandus Vinson .01 .05
78 Marcus Robertson .01 .05
79 Eric Harmon .01 .05
80 Rob Selby .01 .05
81 Ed King .01 .05
82 William Thomas .01 .05
83 Mike Jones DE .01 .05
84 Paul Justin .01 .05
85 Robert Wilson .01 .05
86 Jesse Campbell .01 .05
87 Hayward Haynes .01 .05
88 Mike Croel .01 .05
89 Jeff Graham .02 .10
90 Vinnie Clark .01 .05
91 Keith Cash .01 .05
92 Tim Ryan .01 .05
93 Jarrod Bunch .01 .05
94 Stanley Richard .01 .05
95 Alvin Harper .01 .05
96 Bob Dahl .01 .05
97 Mark Gunn .01 .05
98 Frank Blevins .01 .05
99 Harvey Williams .02 .10
100 Dixon Edwards .01 .05
101 Blake Miller .01 .05
102 Bobby Wilson .01 .05
103 Chuck Webb .01 .05
104 Randal Hill .02 .10
105 Shane Curry .01 .05
106 Barry Sanders .40 1.00
107 Richard Fain .01 .05
108 Joe Garten .01 .05
109 Dean Dingman .01 .05
110 Mark Tucker .01 .05
111 Dan McGwire .01 .05
112 Paul Glonek .01 .05
113 Tom Dohring .01 .05
114 Joe Sims .01 .05
115 Bryan Cox .01 .05
116 Bobby Olive .01 .05
117 Blaise Bryant .01 .05
118 Charles Johnson .01 .05
119 Brett Favre 3.00 6.00
120 Luis Cristobal .01 .05
121 Don Gibson .01 .05
122 Scott Ross .01 .05
123 Huey Richardson .01 .05
124 Chris Smith .01 .05
125 Duane Young .01 .05
126 Eric Swann .02 .10
127 Jeff Fite .01 .05
128 Eugene Williams .01 .05
129 Harlan Davis .01 .05
130 James Bradley .01 .05
131 Rob Carpenter .01 .05
132 Dennis Ransom .01 .05
133 Mike Arthur .01 .05
134 Chuck Weatherspoon .01 .05
135 Darrell Malone .01 .05
136 George Thornton .01 .05
137 Lamar McGriggs .01 .05
138 Alex Johnson .01 .05
139 Eric Moten .01 .05
140 Joe Valerio .01 .05
141 Jake Reed .08 .25
142 Ernie Thompson .01 .05
143 Roland Poles .01 .05
144 Randy Bethel .01 .05
145 Terry Bagsby .01 .05
146 Tim James .01 .05
147 Kenny Walker .01 .05
148 Nolan Harrison .01 .05
149 Keith Traylor .01 .05
150 Nick Subis .01 .05
151 Scott Zolak .01 .05
152 Pio Sagapolutele .01 .05
153 James Jones .01 .05
154 Mike Sullivan .01 .05
155 Joe Johnson .01 .05
156 Todd Scott .01 .05
157 Checklist 1 .01 .05
158 Checklist 2 .01 .05
159 Checklist 3 .01 .05
160 Checklist 4 .01 .05

1991 Wild Card Draft 5 Stripe

*5 STRIPES: 1.2X TO 3X BASIC CARDS
119 Brett Favre 20.00 40.00

1991 Wild Card Draft 10 Stripe

*10 STRIPES: 2X TO 5X BASIC CARDS
119 Brett Favre 30.00 80.00

1991 Wild Card Draft 20 Stripe

*20 STRIPES: 3X TO 8X BASIC CARDS
119 Brett Favre 60.00 120.00

1991 Wild Card Draft 50 Stripe

*50 STRIPES: 6X TO 15X BASIC CARDS
119 Brett Favre 75.00 200.00

1991 Wild Card Draft 100 Stripe

*100 STRIPES: 10X TO 25X BASIC CARDS
119 Brett Favre 150.00 300.00

1991 Wild Card Draft 1000 Stripe

*1000 STRIPES: 40X TO 100X BASIC CARDS
119 Brett Favre 750.00 1500.00

1991 Wild Card Draft 1000 Promos

P1 All Pro Sports Staff 2.00 5.00
P2 All Time Great Backs 5.00 12.00
P3 The Patricks (Dan) 3.00 8.00

1991 Wild Card Draft Redemption Prizes

Collectors who redeemed their three 1991 Wild Card Draft Surprise Cards before April 30, 1992 received as a bonus this six-card set of 1992 Wild Card Draft Prototypes. Note that a 1992 Draft set was never issued. These standard-size cards feature glossy color player photos bordered in white. The player's name and position appear in the bottom white border. The backs shade from purple to white and back to purple and carry a color head shot, biography, and statistics. The cards are numbered on the back with a "P" prefix.

COMPLETE SET (6) 1.00 2.50
P1 Edgar Bennett .20 .50
P2 Jimmy Smith .75 2.00
P3 Will Furrer .07 .20
P4 Terrell Buckley .10 .30
P5 Tommy Vardell .10 .30
P6 Amp Lee .07 .20